Table of Contents

VOLUME 1

VOLUME 2

VOLUME 3

Food & Beverage Market Place

Volume 1

2012

Eleventh Edition

Food & Beverage Market Place

Volume 1

Food & Beverage Manufacturers

Product Categories

Company Profiles

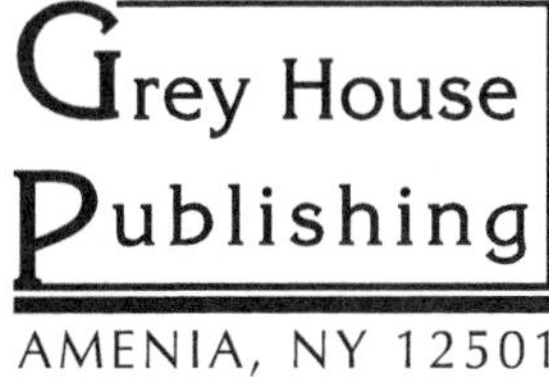

AMENIA, NY 12501

PUBLISHER: Leslie Mackenzie
EDITOR: Richard Gottlieb
EDITORIAL DIRECTOR: Laura Mars

PRODUCTION MANAGER: Kristen Thatcher
COMPOSITION: David Garoogian
PRODUCTION ASSISTANTS: Dennis Ciachin; Erica Schneider; Marko Udovicic

MARKETING DIRECTOR: Jessica Moody

Grey House Publishing, Inc.
4919 Route 22
Amenia, NY 12501
518.789.8700
FAX 845.373.6390
www.greyhouse.com
e-mail: books @greyhouse.com

First edition published 2001
Eleventh edition published 2012
Printed in Canada

Food & beverage market place. - 11th ed. (2012) -
3 v. ; 27.5 cm. Annual
Includes index.
ISSN: 1554-6334

1. Food industry and trade-United States-Directories. 2. Food industry and trade-Canada-Directories. 3. Beverage industry-United States-Directories. 4. Beverage industry-Canada-Directories. I. Grey House Publishing, Inc. II. Title: Food & beverage market place.

HD9003.T48
338-dc21

3-Volume Set ISBN: 978-1-59237-753-4
Volume 1 ISBN: 978-1-59237-754-1
Volume 2 ISBN: 978-1-59237-755-8
Volume 3 ISBN: 978-1-59237-756-5

Introduction

This eleventh edition of the 3-volume *Food & Beverage Market Place* represents the largest, most comprehensive resource of food and beverage manufacturers and service suppliers in the market today. Not only one of the fastest growing industries, food and beverage companies represent one of the most dynamic. This 2012 *Food & Beverage Market Place* addresses all aspects of the food and beverage industry, with detailed profiles of 38,691 listings that cover seven major food industry categories—finished goods and ingredient manufacturers, equipment and supply manufacturers, food transport, warehousing, wholesalers, food brokers, and importers and exporters.

According to the **Food Institute**, the consumer price index for all food in 2011 is expected to increase 3.5-4.5%, compared with the 0.8% CPI increase between 2009 and 2010 (the lowest inflation rate since 1962). For 2012, food inflation is expected to decrease from 2011 levels to 2.5-3.5%.

As people pay more for food, its health benefits are on the minds of more Americans than ever before. The 2011 **IFIC Functional Foods/Foods for Health Survey** shows that 90% of Americans can name at least one food and its associated health benefit, and 76% of those surveyed say that foods that promote health have a meaningful impact on their lives.

In addition to showing increased interest in the health benefits that foods can provide, consumers continue to create flavor trends. Sweet, exotic fruits and chocolate dominate dairy, especially yogurt, and coconut and ginger are gaining popularity in baked goods and cereals. Spicy snacks, especially potato chips, are Americans' preference, and man's best friend has discovered roast duck.

Data Statistics

Each of the seven chapters in *Food & Beverage Market Place* reflects year-long research. In addition to the hundreds of new company profiles in this new edition, you will find 83,787, key executives, 34,896 fax numbers, 26,155 web sites, 21,414 e-mails, and 26,633 unique brand names. In addition to these thousands of valuable data points, this 2012 edition includes 726 brand new company listings throughout the three volumes. The number of companies break down as follows:

Volume 1 Food, Beverage & Ingredient Manufacturers, 14,831

Volume 2 Equipment, Supply & Service Providers, 13,566

Volume 3 Third Party Logistics
Brokers, 1,428
Importers & Exporters, 9,638
Transportation Firms, 685
Warehouse Companies, 1,394
Wholesalers & Distributors, 6,263

Whatever slice of the market you cater to, you will find buyers, sellers, and users in *Food & Beverage Market Place*—a comprehensive reference tool, in 3 carefully arranged volumes, with the complete coverage our subscribers have come to expect. These volumes' extensive indexing—19 indexes in all—makes quick work of locating exactly the company, product or service you are looking for.

The product category sections for both food and beverage products in Volume 1 and equipment and supplies in Volume 2 begin with **Product Category Lists**. Here is where you will find 6,000 alphabetical terms for everything from Abalone to Zinc Citrate, from Adhesive Tapes to Zipper Application Systems. Use the detailed cross-references to find the full entry in the **Product Category** sections that immediately follow. Here you'll find layered categories, for example—**Fish & Seafood: Fish: Abalone** or **Ingredients, Flavors & Additives: Vitamins & Supplements: Zinc Citrate**—with the name, location, phone number and packaging format of companies who manufacturer/process the product you are looking for.

In addition to company profiles, this edition has 19 indexes, 17 chapter-specific, arranged by geographic region, product or company type, and two—**All Brands** and **All Companies**—that comprise all three volumes. See the Table of Contents for a complete list of specific indexes. Plus, chapters include **User Guides** that help you navigate chapter-specific data.

We are confident that this reference is the foremost research tool in the food and beverage industry. It will prove invaluable to manufacturers, buyers, specifiers, market researchers, consultants, and anyone working in food and beverage—one of the largest industries in the country.

Food & Beverage Market Place is also available for subscription on http://gold.greyhouse.com for even faster, easier access to this wealth of information. Subscribers can search by product category, state, sales volume, employee size, personnel name, title and much more. Plus, users can print out prospect sheets or download data into their own spreadsheet or database. This database is a must for anyone marketing a product or service to this vast industry. Visit the site, or call 800-562-2139 for a free trial.

MANUFACTURERS

Manufacturer User Guide

The **Food & Beverage Manufacturers Chapter** of *Food & Beverage Market Place* includes companies that manufacture food and beverage products, both finished goods and ingredients. The chapter begins with a **Product Category Listing** of food and beverage products that are manufactured by companies in this chapter. This category list is followed by a **Product Category Index**, organized by product. Each company listing includes packaging type, city and phone number.

Following the **Product Category Index** are the descriptive listings, which are organized alphabetically. Following the A – Z Food and Beverage Manufacturers listings are four indexes: **Brand Index**, which lists food and beverage brand names; **Ethnic Food Index**, which lists companies by ethnic type of food they manufacture; **Geographic Index**, which lists all companies by state, and **Parent Company Index**; which lists companies by their corporate parent. These Indexes refers to listing numbers, not page numbers.

Below is a sample listing illustrating the kind of information that is or might be included in a Food and Beverage Manufacturer listing. Each numbered item of information is described in the User Key on the following page.

---

1 → 100000

2 → **(HQ) AFF Specialties**

3 → 555 Maplewood Drive

Cordova, TN 38016

4 → 001-381-3222

5 → 001-381-3223

6 → 888-381-324

7 → info@AFF.com

8 → www.AFF.com

9 → Manufacturer of Italian cheese and dried pasta and cooking oils. Exporter of olive oil.

10 → President: Brian Miller
CFO: Philip George
COO: Blakeny Pinschell
Vice President: Kristin Rolls
Marketing: Melissa Backwith

11 → *Estimated Sales*: $65 Million

12 → *Number Employees*: 80

13 → *Sq. Footage*: 30000

14 → *Parent Co.*: Associated Foods

15 → *Type of Packaging:* Consumer, Food Service, Bulk

16 → *Company is also listed in the following section(s)*: Exporter

17 → *Other Locations*: AFF Specialties, Atlanta, GA

18 → *Brands:* Unique, Fiesta, Baking Rite, Carruso, Golden Dairy

Manufacturer User Key

1 → **Record Number:** Entries are listed alphabetically within each category and numbered sequentially. The entry number, rather than the page number, is used in the indexes to refer to listings.

2 → **Company Name:** Formal name of company. HQ indicates headquarter location. If names are completely capitalized, the listing will appear at the beginning of the alphabetized section.

3 → **Address:** Location or permanent address of the company. If the mailing address differs from the street address, it will appear second. Companies are indexed by state.

4 → **Phone Number:** The listed phone number is usually for the main office, but may also be for the sales, marketing, or public relations office as provided.

5 → **Fax Number:** This is listed when provided by the company.

6 → **Toll-Free Number:** This is listed when provided by the company.

7 → **E-Mail:** This is listed when provided, and is generally the main office e-mail.

8 → **Web Site:** This is listed when provided by the company and is also referred to as an URL address. These web sites are accessed through the Internet by typing http:// before the URL address.

9 → **Description**: This paragraph contains a brief description of the food and beverages manufactured by the company, as well as other services they provide. Companies are indexed by the ethnic food they manufacture.

10 → **Key Personnel:** Names and titles of company executives.

11 → **Estimated Sales:** This is listed when provided by the company.

12 → **Number of Employees:** Total number of employees within the company.

13 → **Sq. Footage:** Size of facility.

14 → **Parent Co.:** If the listing is a division of another company, the parent is listed here. Companies are indexed by the ethnic foods they manufacture.

15 → **Type of Packaging:** Indicates the market that the food or beverage products are packaged for.

16 → Indicates what other section in ***Food & Beverage Market Place*** this company is listed: Volume 1: Manufacturers. Volume 2: Equipment, Supplies & Services; Transportation; Warehouse; Wholesalers/Distributors. Volume 3: Brokers; Importers/Exporters.

17 → **Other locations:** Indicates other company locations.

18 → **Brands:** Listing of brand names that the company manufactures. Companies are indexed by brand names.

A

Abalone Fish *See Fish & Seafood: Fish: Abalone*
Aborio Rice *See Cereals, Grains, Rice & Flour: Rice: Aborio*
Acacia Gum *See Ingredients, Flavors & Additives: Gums: Acacia Gum*
Acetic Acidulants *See Ingredients, Flavors & Additives: Acidulants: Acetic*
Acidophilus Cultures *See Ingredients, Flavors & Additives: Cultures & Yeasts: Acidophilus Cultures*
Acids *See Ingredients, Flavors & Additives: Acids*
Acidulants *See Ingredients, Flavors & Additives: Acidulants*
Acorn Squash *See Fruits & Vegetables: Squash: Acorn*
Active Salt *See Spices, Seasonings & Seeds: Salt: Active*
Additives *See Ingredients, Flavors & Additives: Additives*
Additives Enzymes *See Ingredients, Flavors & Additives: Enzymes: Additives*
Ade Juices *See Beverages: Juices: Ade*
Adipic Acids *See Ingredients, Flavors & Additives: Acids: Adipic*
Adjuncts *See Ingredients, Flavors & Additives: Adjuncts*
Adobo Powders *See Ingredients, Flavors & Additives: Powders: Adobo*
Adzuki Beans *See Fruits & Vegetables: Beans: Adzuki*
Agar-Agar *See Ingredients, Flavors & Additives: Gums: Agar-Agar*
Agents *See Ingredients, Flavors & Additives: Agents*
Agnolotti *See Pasta & Noodles: Agnolotti*
Albacore Tuna Fish *See Fish & Seafood: Fish: Tuna: Albacore*
Albumen Solids *See Eggs & Egg Products: Solids: Albumen*
Alcoholic Beverages *See Beverages: Alcoholic Beverages*
Alcohols *See Ingredients, Flavors & Additives: Alcohols*
Alfalfa *See Cereals, Grains, Rice & Flour: Alfalfa*
Alfalfa Seeds *See Spices, Seasonings & Seeds: Seeds: Alfalfa*
Alfalfa Sprouts *See Fruits & Vegetables: Sprouts: Alfalfa*
Alfredo Sauces *See Sauces, Dips & Dressings: Sauces: Alfredo*
Algae *See Fruits & Vegetables: Algae*
Algin & Alginates *See Ingredients, Flavors & Additives: Gums: Algin & Alginates*
All Purpose Flour *See Cereals, Grains, Rice & Flour: Flour: All Purpose*
All Purpose Herbs Blends *See Ingredients, Flavors & Additives: Blends: Herbs: All Purpose*
Alligator Game *See Meats & Meat Products: Game: Alligator*
Allspice *See Spices, Seasonings & Seeds: Spices: Allspice*
Almond Biscotti *See Baked Goods: Cookies & Bars: Biscotti: Almond*
Almond Cookies *See Baked Goods: Cookies & Bars: Almond Cookies*
Almond Flavors *See Ingredients, Flavors & Additives: Flavors: Almond*
Almond Flour *See Cereals, Grains, Rice & Flour: Flour: Almond*
Almond Nut Butters *See Nuts & Nut Butters: Nut Butters: Almond*
Almond Nut Pastes *See Nuts & Nut Butters: Nut Pastes: Almond*
Almond Oils *See Oils, Shortening & Fats: Oils: Almond*
Almond Pastes *See Ingredients, Flavors & Additives: Pastes: Almond*
Almonds *See Nuts & Nut Butters: Nuts: Almonds*
Aloe Juices *See Beverages: Juices: Aloe*
Aloe Vera *See Fruits & Vegetables: Aloe Vera*
Amaranth *See Cereals, Grains, Rice & Flour: Grains: Amaranth*
Amaretto Cookies *See Baked Goods: Cookies & Bars: Amaretto Cookies*
Amaretto Flavors *See Ingredients, Flavors & Additives: Flavors: Amaretto*
Amaretto Liqueurs & Cordials *See Beverages: Spirits & Liqueurs: Liqueurs & Cordials: Amaretto*
Amber Ale *See Beverages: Beers: American & British Ale: Amber Ale*
Amber Jack *See Fish & Seafood: Fish: Amber Jack*
Amber Lager *See Beverages: Beers: Lager: Amber Lager*
American & British Ale *See Beverages: Beers: American & British Ale*
American Cheese *See Cheese & Cheese Products: Cheese: American*
American Cheese Imitations *See Cheese & Cheese Products: Imitation Cheeses & Substitutes: Imitation: American*
American Cheese Powders *See Ingredients, Flavors & Additives: Powders: Cheese: American*
American Cheese Substitutes *See Cheese & Cheese Products: Imitation Cheeses & Substitutes: Substitutes: American*
American/Skim Milk Cheese, Sliced Blend *See Cheese & Cheese Products: Cheese: Blend - American/Skim Milk: Sliced*
Aminoacetic Acids *See Ingredients, Flavors & Additives: Acids: Aminoacetic*
Ammonium Carbonate *See Ingredients, Flavors & Additives: Ammonium Carbonate*
Ammonium Phosphates *See Ingredients, Flavors & Additives: Phosphates: Ammonium Phosphates*
Analogs *See Ingredients, Flavors & Additives: Analogs*
Ancho Ground Chile Pepper *See Spices, Seasonings & Seeds: Spices: Chile Pepper: Ancho Ground*
Ancho Peppers *See Fruits & Vegetables: Peppers: Ancho*
Anchovies *See Fish & Seafood: Fish: Anchovies*
Anchovies Paste *See Fish & Seafood: Fish: Anchovies: Paste*
Andouille Sausage Seasonings *See Spices, Seasonings & Seeds: Seasonings: Sausage: Andouille*
Andouille Sausages *See Meats & Meat Products: Smoked, Cured & Deli Meats: Sausages: Andouille*
Angel Food Cake *See Baked Goods: Cakes & Pastries: Angel Food Cake*
Angel Hair *See Pasta & Noodles: Angel Hair*
Animal Crackers *See Baked Goods: Cookies & Bars: Animal Crackers*
Anise Flavors *See Ingredients, Flavors & Additives: Flavors: Anise; See also Spices/Anise Seed*
Anise Liqueur *See Beverages: Spirits & Liqueurs: Liqueurs & Cordials: Anise Liqueur*
Anise or Aniseed Oils *See Oils, Shortening & Fats: Oils: Anise or Aniseed*
Anise or Aniseed Seeds *See Spices, Seasonings & Seeds: Seeds: Anise or Aniseed*
Anise, Star *See Spices, Seasonings & Seeds: Spices: Anise - Star*
Annatto Colors *See Ingredients, Flavors & Additives: Colors: Annatto*
Annatto Natural Colors *See Ingredients, Flavors & Additives: Colors: Natural: Annatto*
Annatto Seeds *See Spices, Seasonings & Seeds: Seeds: Annatto*
Anthocyanins Grape Skin *See Ingredients, Flavors & Additives: Colors: Natural: Anthocyanins Grape Skin*
Anticaking Additives *See Ingredients, Flavors & Additives: Additives: Anticaking*
Anticaking Agents *See Ingredients, Flavors & Additives: Agents: Anticaking*
Antimicrobial Agents *See Ingredients, Flavors & Additives: Agents: Antimicrobial*
Antioxidants *See Specialty & Organic Foods: Organic Foods: Natural: Antioxidants; See also See Ingredients, Flavors & Additives: Antioxidants*
Antipasto *See Prepared Foods: Antipasto*
Antipasto Salads *See Prepared Foods: Prepared Salads: Antipasto*
Appaloosa Beans *See Fruits & Vegetables: Beans: Appaloosa*
Appetizers *See Prepared Foods: Appetizers; See also Prepared Foods: Appetizers: Fresh, Canned & Frozen*
Apple *See Fruits & Vegetables: Apple*
Apple Boysin Berry Juices *See Beverages: Juices: Apple Boysin Berry*
Apple Butter *See Jams, Jellies & Spreads: Spreads: Apple Butter*
Apple Cider Juices *See Beverages: Juices: Apple Cider*
Apple Cider Vinegar *See Sauces, Dips & Dressings: Vinegar: Apple Cider*
Apple Cobbler *See Baked Goods: Cakes & Pastries: Apple Cobbler*
Apple Cranberry Juices *See Beverages: Juices: Apple Cranberry*
Apple Flavors *See Ingredients, Flavors & Additives: Flavors: Apple*
Apple Grape Juices *See Beverages: Juices: Apple Grape*
Apple Juices *See Beverages: Juices: Apple*
Apple Pectins *See Ingredients, Flavors & Additives: Pectins: Apple*
Apple Pies *See Baked Goods: Pies: Apple*
Apple Rings *See Fruits & Vegetables: Apple: Rings*
Apple Sauces *See Fruits & Vegetables: Sauces: Apple*
Apple Sauces with Other Fruit or Spices *See Fruits & Vegetables: Sauces: Apple: with Other Fruit or Spices*
Apple Slices *See Fruits & Vegetables: Apple: Slices*
Apricot *See Fruits & Vegetables: Apricot*
Apricot Jams *See Jams, Jellies & Spreads: Jams: Apricot*
Apricot Juices *See Beverages: Juices: Apricot*
Apricot Kernals *See Fruits & Vegetables: Apricot: Kernals*
Aquaculture *See Specialty & Organic Foods: Aquaculture*
Arabic *See Ingredients, Flavors & Additives: Gums: Arabic*
Arctic Charr *See Fish & Seafood: Fish: Arctic Charr*
Ardouille Sausage *See Meats & Meat Products: Pork & Pork Products: Sausage: Ardouille*
Aroma Chemicals & Materials *See Ingredients, Flavors & Additives: Aroma Chemicals & Materials; See also See Ingredients, Flavors & Additives: Aroma Chemicals; See also See Ingredients, Flavors & Additives: Aroma Chemicals & Materials: Materials***Arrowroot Flour** *See Cereals, Grains, Rice & Flour: Flour: Arrowroot*
Arrowroot Starches *See Ingredients, Flavors & Additives: Starches: Arrowroot*
Arrowroot Thickening Agents *See Ingredients, Flavors & Additives: Agents: Thickening: Arrowroot*
Artichoke *See Fruits & Vegetables: Artichoke*
Artificial Flavors *See Ingredients, Flavors & Additives: Flavors: Artificial*
Artificial Sweeteners *See Sugars, Syrups & Sweeteners: Artificial*
Ascorbic Acid *See Ingredients, Flavors & Additives: Antioxidants: Ascorbic Acid; See also Flavors & Additives: Vitamins & Supplements: C: Ascorbic Acid*
Aseptic Packed Capsicums Peppers *See Fruits & Vegetables: Peppers: Capsicums: Aseptic Packed*
Asiago Cheese *See Cheese & Cheese Products: Cheese: Asiago*
Asian *See Ethnic Foods: Asian*
Asian Pear *See Fruits & Vegetables: Pear: Asian*
Asparagus *See Fruits & Vegetables: Asparagus*
Aspartame *See Sugars, Syrups & Sweeteners: Sugar Substitutes: Aspartame*
Au Gratin Potatoes *See Fruits & Vegetables: Potatoes: Au Gratin*
Autolysates Yeast *See Ingredients, Flavors & Additives: Cultures & Yeasts: Yeast: Autolysates*
Avocado *See Fruits & Vegetables: Avocado*
Avocado Oils *See Oils, Shortening & Fats: Oils: Avocado*
Avocado Products *See Fruits & Vegetables: Avocado: Avocado Products*

B

Babka *See Baked Goods: Cakes & Pastries: Babka*
Baby Carrot *See Fruits & Vegetables: Carrot: Baby*
Baby Spinach *See Fruits & Vegetables: Spinach: Baby*
Bacillus Cultures *See Ingredients, Flavors & Additives: Cultures & Yeasts: Bacillus*
Bacon *See Meats & Meat Products: Smoked, Cured & Deli Meats: Bacon*
Bacon Pork Rinds *See Snack Foods: Pork Rinds: Bacon*
Bacon Slices *See Meats & Meat Products: Smoked, Cured & Deli Meats: Bacon: Slices*
Bacteria *See Ingredients, Flavors & Additives: Cultures & Yeasts: Bacteria*
Bacterial Cultures, Starter Media & Culture Replacements *See Ingredients, Flavors & Additives: Cultures & Yeasts: Bacterial Cultures, Starter Media & Culture Replacements*
Bacteriological Cultures & Yeasts *See Ingredients, Flavors & Additives: Cultures & Yeasts: Bacteriological*
Bagel Chips *See Snack Foods: Chips: Bagel Chips*
Bagels *See Baked Goods: Breads: Bagels*
Bagged Parboiled Rice *See Cereals, Grains, Rice & Flour: Rice: Parboiled: Bagged*
Bagged Specialty-Packaged Candy *See Candy & Confectionery: Specialty-Packaged Candy: Bagged*
Bagged Wheat *See Cereals, Grains, Rice & Flour: Wheat: Bagged*
Baguettes *See Baked Goods: Breads: Baguettes*
Baita Fruli Cheese *See Cheese & Cheese Products: Cheese: Baita Fruli*
Baked & Stuffed Potatoes *See Fruits & Vegetables: Potatoes: Baked & Stuffed*

EXAMPLE: **Canadian Style Bacon** *See Meats & Meat Products: Smoked, Cured & Deli Meats: Bacon: Canadian Style*
(1 = Canadian Style Bacon; 2 = Meats & Meat Products; 3 = Smoked, Cured & Deli Meats; 4 = Bacon; 5 = Canadian Style)

1. Product or Service you are looking for
2. Main Category, in alphabetical order, located in the page headers starting on page 23
3. Category Description, located in black bars and in page headers
4. Product Category, located in gray bars
5. Product Type, located under gray bars, centered in bold

Baked Beans *See Prepared Foods: Baked Beans (see also Pork & Beans); See also Fruits & Vegetables: Beans: Baked*
Baked Chips *See Snack Foods: Chips: Baked*
Baked Goods *See Baked Goods*
Baked Potato Chips *See Snack Foods: Chips: Potato: Baked*
Bakers Active Yeast *See Ingredients, Flavors & Additives: Cultures & Yeasts: Yeast: Bakers Active*
Bakers Cheese Powders *See Ingredients, Flavors & Additives: Powders: Cheese: Bakers*
Bakers' & Confectioners' Supplies *See Ingredients, Flavors & Additives: Confectionery: Bakers' & Confectioners' Supplies*
Bakers' Yeast *See Ingredients, Flavors & Additives: Cultures & Yeasts: Yeast: Bakers'*
Bakery Ingredients *See Ingredients, Flavors & Additives: Ingredients: Bakery*
Bakery Mix Flour *See Cereals, Grains, Rice & Flour: Flour: Bakery Mix*
Baking Bits *See Ingredients, Flavors & Additives: Bits: Baking*
Baking Chocolate *See Candy & Confectionery: Chocolate Products: Baking Chocolate*
Baking Decorations *See Candy & Confectionery: Decorations & Icings: Decorations: Baking*
Baking Doughs *See Doughs, Mixes & Fillings: Doughs: Baking*
Baking Fillings *See Doughs, Mixes & Fillings: Fillings: Baking*
Baking Mixes *See Doughs, Mixes & Fillings: Mixes: Baking*
Baking Mixes Flour *See Cereals, Grains, Rice & Flour: Flour: Baking Mixes*
Baking Powders *See Ingredients, Flavors & Additives: Powders: Baking*
Baking Seasonings *See Spices, Seasonings & Seeds: Seasonings: Baking*
Baking Shells *See Baked Goods: Pies: Baking Shells*
Baking Soda *See Ingredients, Flavors & Additives: Leaveners: Baking Soda*
Baklava *See Baked Goods: Cakes & Pastries: Baklava*
Balsamic Vinegar *See Sauces, Dips & Dressings: Vinegar: Balsamic*
Balsamic Vinegar Salad Dressings *See Sauces, Dips & Dressings: Salad Dressings: Balsamic Vinegar*
Bamboo Shoots *See Fruits & Vegetables: Bamboo Shoots*
Banana *See Fruits & Vegetables: Banana*
Banana Chips *See Snack Foods: Chips: Banana*
Banana Flakes *See Ingredients, Flavors & Additives: Flakes: Banana*
Banana Flavors *See Ingredients, Flavors & Additives: Flavors: Banana*
Banana Peppers *See Fruits & Vegetables: Peppers: Banana*
Banana Products *See Fruits & Vegetables: Banana: Banana Products*
Bar Mixers *See Beverages: Mixers: Bar Mixers*
Bar Syrups *See Sugars, Syrups & Sweeteners: Syrups: Bar*
Barbecue Potato Chips *See Snack Foods: Chips: Potato: Barbecue*
Barbecue Products *See Specialty Processed Foods: Barbecue Products (See also Specific Foods)*
Barbecue Sauces *See Sauces, Dips & Dressings: Sauces: Barbecue*
Barbecue Seasonings *See Spices, Seasonings & Seeds: Seasonings: Barbecue*
Barbecued Beef *See Meats & Meat Products: Beef & Beef Products: Barbecued*
Barbecued Chicken *See Meats & Meat Products: Poultry: Chicken: Barbecued*
Barbecued Chicken, Frozen *See Meats & Meat Products: Poultry: Chicken: Barbecued Frozen*
Barbecued Pork *See Meats & Meat Products: Pork & Pork Products: Barbecued*
Barley *See Cereals, Grains, Rice & Flour: Barley*
Barley Bran Fiber *See Cereals, Grains, Rice & Flour: Fiber: Barley Bran*
Barley Flour *See Cereals, Grains, Rice & Flour: Flour: Barley*
Bars, Cereal *See Cereals, Grains, Rice & Flour: Cereal: Bars*
Bars, Cookies *See Baked Goods: Cookies & Bars: Bars*
Bartlett Pear *See Fruits & Vegetables: Pear: Bartlett*
Bases *See Ingredients, Flavors & Additives: Bases*
Bases, Ice Cream *See Dairy Products: Ice Cream: Bases*
Basil Leaf *See Spices, Seasonings & Seeds: Spices: Basil Leaf*
Basil Spices *See Spices, Seasonings & Seeds: Spices: Basil*
Basmati Rice *See Cereals, Grains, Rice & Flour: Rice: Basmati*
Bass *See Fish & Seafood: Fish: Bass*
Batters *See Doughs, Mixes & Fillings: Batters*
Bay Leaves *See Spices, Seasonings & Seeds: Spices: Bay Leaves*
Bean Dips *See Sauces, Dips & Dressings: Dips: Bean*
Bean Flour *See Cereals, Grains, Rice & Flour: Flour: Bean*
Bean Oils *See Oils, Shortening & Fats: Oils: Bean*
Bean Sprouts *See Fruits & Vegetables: Sprouts: Bean*
Beans *See Fruits & Vegetables: Beans*
Bearnaise Sauces *See Sauces, Dips & Dressings: Sauces: Bearnaise*
Bee Pollen & Propolis *See Sugars, Syrups & Sweeteners: Honey: Bee Pollen & Propolis*
Beech Mushrooms *See Fruits & Vegetables: Mushrooms: Beech*
Beef & Beef Products *See Meats & Meat Products: Beef & Beef Products*
Beef & Beef Products, Sliced *See Meats & Meat Products: Beef & Beef Products: Sliced*
Beef & Beef Products, Special Trim *See Meats & Meat Products: Beef & Beef Products: Special Trim*
Beef Bases *See Ingredients, Flavors & Additives: Bases: Beef*
Beef Bouillon *See Ingredients, Flavors & Additives: Bases: Bouillon: Beef*
Beef Casings *See Meats & Meat Products: Smoked, Cured & Deli Meats: Sausages: Casings: Sausage, Pork, Beef*
Beef Certified Organic *See Specialty & Organic Foods: Organic Foods: Certified: Beef*
Beef Dinners *See Meats & Meat Products: Beef & Beef Products: Dinners*
Beef Dinners, Prepared Meals *See Prepared Foods: Prepared Meals: Beef Dinner*
Beef Extracts *See Ingredients, Flavors & Additives: Extracts: Beef*
Beef Frankfurters *See Meats & Meat Products: Frankfurters: Beef*
Beef Jerky *See Meats & Meat Products: Smoked, Cured & Deli Meats: Beef Jerky*
Beef Marinades *See Sauces, Dips & Dressings: Marinades: Beef*
Beef Soup *See Prepared Foods: Soups & Stews: Beef Soup*
Beef Stew *See Meats & Meat Products: Beef & Beef Products: Stew; See also See Prepared Foods: Soups & Stews: Beef Stew*
Beef Stock Powders *See Ingredients, Flavors & Additives: Powders: Beef Stock*
Beef, Frozen Rolls *See Meats & Meat Products: Beef & Beef Products: Rolls - Frozen*
Beer Flavors *See Ingredients, Flavors & Additives: Flavors: Beer*
Beers *See Beverages: Beers*
Bees Wax *See Sugars, Syrups & Sweeteners: Honey: Bees Wax*
Beet Jellies *See Jams, Jellies & Spreads: Jellies: Beets*
Beet Juices *See Beverages: Juices: Beet*
Beet Powder *See Fruits & Vegetables: Dried & Dehydrated Vegetables: Beet Powder*
Beet Relishes *See Relishes & Pickled Products: Relishes: Beets*
Beets *See Fruits & Vegetables: Beets*
Belgian & French Ale *See Beverages: Beers: Belgian & French Ale*
Bell Peppers *See Fruits & Vegetables: Peppers: Bell*
Bell Peppers, Dehydrated *See Fruits & Vegetables: Dried & Dehydrated Vegetables: Bell Peppers*
Benzoate of Soda *See Ingredients, Flavors & Additives: Benzoate of Soda*
Benzoic Acids *See Ingredients, Flavors & Additives: Acids: Benzoic*
Berries *See Fruits & Vegetables: Berries*
Berries, Frozen *See Fruits & Vegetables: Frozen Fruit: Berries*
Beta Carotene *See Ingredients, Flavors & Additives: Vitamins & Supplements: Beta Carotene*
Betaine Beet *See Ingredients, Flavors & Additives: Colors: Natural: Betaine Beet*
Beverage Bases *See Ingredients, Flavors & Additives: Bases: Beverage*
Beverage Extracts *See Ingredients, Flavors & Additives: Extracts: Beverages*
Beverage Flavors *See Ingredients, Flavors & Additives: Flavors: Beverage*
Beverage Mixes *See Doughs, Mixes & Fillings: Mixes: Beverage*
Beverage Powders *See Ingredients, Flavors & Additives: Powders: Beverage*
Beverage Syrups *See Sugars, Syrups & Sweeteners: Syrups: Beverages*
Beverages *See Beverages*
Bialys *See Baked Goods: Breads: Bialys*
Binders *See Ingredients, Flavors & Additives: Binders*
Binders for Meat Products *See Ingredients, Flavors & Additives: Binders: for Meat Products*
Bing Cherries *See Fruits & Vegetables: Cherries: Bing*
Bioflavinoids *See Ingredients, Flavors & Additives: Bioflavinoids*
Biopolymers *See Ingredients, Flavors & Additives: Biopolymers*
Biotin *See Ingredients, Flavors & Additives: Vitamins & Supplements: Biotin*
Biscotti *See Baked Goods: Cookies & Bars: Biscotti*
Biscuit Mixes *See Doughs, Mixes & Fillings: Mixes: Biscuit*
Biscuits *See Baked Goods: Breads: Biscuits*
Bits *See Ingredients, Flavors & Additives: Bits*
Bits, Imitation Bacon *See Meats & Meat Products: Smoked, Cured & Deli Meats: Bacon: Bits Imitation*
Bits, Real Bacon *See Meats & Meat Products: Smoked, Cured & Deli Meats: Bacon: Bits Real*
Bitters *See Beverages: Bitters*
Black & Tan Ale *See Beverages: Beers: American & British Ale: Black & Tan*
Black Bean Sauces *See Sauces, Dips & Dressings: Sauces: Black Bean*
Black Beans *See Fruits & Vegetables: Beans: Black*
Black Cod Fish *See Fish & Seafood: Fish: Cod: Black*
Black Currant Tea *See Beverages: Coffee & Tea: Tea: Black Currant*
Black Forest Ham *See Meats & Meat Products: Smoked, Cured & Deli Meats: Ham: Black Forest*
Black Olives *See Fruits & Vegetables: Olives: Black*
Black Pepper *See Spices, Seasonings & Seeds: Spices: Pepper: Black - White - Red; See also See Spices, Seasonings & Seeds: Spices: Black Pepper - Ground*
Black Pepper Oils *See Oils, Shortening & Fats: Oils: Black Pepper*
Black Puinoa Rice *See Cereals, Grains, Rice & Flour: Rice: Black Puinoa*
Black Sesame Seeds *See Spices, Seasonings & Seeds: Seeds: Sesame: Black*
Black Sliced Truffles *See Fruits & Vegetables: Mushrooms: Truffles: Black Sliced*
Black Tea *See Beverages: Coffee & Tea: Tea: Black*
Black Thai Rice *See Cereals, Grains, Rice & Flour: Rice: Black Thai*
Black Tiger Shrimp *See Fish & Seafood: Shellfish: Shrimp: Black Tiger*
Black Trumpet Mushrooms *See Fruits & Vegetables: Mushrooms: Black Trumpet*
Black Trumpet Mushrooms, Dehydrated *See Fruits & Vegetables: Dried & Dehydrated Vegetables: Mushrooms: Black Trumpets*
Black Walnuts *See Nuts & Nut Butters: Nuts: Walnuts: Black*
Black Whole Truffles *See Fruits & Vegetables: Mushrooms: Truffles: Black Whole*
Black-eyed Peas *See Fruits & Vegetables: Peas: Black-eyed*
Blackberry *See Fruits & Vegetables: Berries: Blackberry*
Blackberry Flavors *See Ingredients, Flavors & Additives: Flavors: Blackberry*
Blackening Seasonings *See Spices, Seasonings & Seeds: Seasonings: Blackening*
Blackeye Beans *See Fruits & Vegetables: Beans: Blackeye (Cowpeas)*
Blended Scotch Whiskey *See Beverages: Spirits & Liqueurs: Scotch Whiskey: Blended*
Blends *See Ingredients, Flavors & Additives: Blends*
Blends, Butter *See Dairy Products: Butter: Blends*
Blends, Corn Syrups *See Sugars, Syrups & Sweeteners: Syrups: Corn: Blends*
Blintzes *See Baked Goods: Cakes & Pastries: Blintzes*
Blood Orange *See Fruits & Vegetables: Orange: Blood*
Blood Orange Juice *See Beverages: Juices: Orange: Blood*
Blood Sausages *See Meats & Meat Products: Smoked, Cured & Deli Meats: Sausages: Blood*
Blue Cheese *See Cheese & Cheese Products: Cheese: Blue*
Blue Cheese Salad Dressings *See Sauces, Dips & Dressings: Salad Dressings: Blue Cheese*
Blue Cheese Salad Dressings, Mixes *See Sauces, Dips & Dressings: Salad Dressings: Mixes: Blue Cheese*
Blue Crab *See Fish & Seafood: Shellfish: Crab: Blue*
Blue Lake Beans *See Fruits & Vegetables: Beans: Blue Lake*
Blueberry *See Fruits & Vegetables: Berries: Blueberry*
Blueberry Flavors *See Ingredients, Flavors & Additives: Flavors: Blueberry*
Blueberry Juices *See Beverages: Juices: Blueberry*
Blueberry Pies *See Baked Goods: Pies: Blueberry*
Bluefish *See Fish & Seafood: Fish: Bluefish*
Boar *See Meats & Meat Products: Game: Boar*
Bock Lager *See Beverages: Beers: Lager: Bock*

C

EXAMPLE: **Canadian Style Bacon** *See Meats & Meat Products: Smoked, Cured & Deli Meats: Bacon: Canadian Style* (1 = Canadian Style Bacon; 2 = Meats & Meat Products; 3 = Smoked, Cured & Deli Meats; 4 = Bacon; 5 = Canadian Style)

1. Product or Service you are looking for
2. Main Category, in alphabetical order, located in the page headers starting on page 23
3. Category Description, located in black bars and in page headers
4. Product Category, located in gray bars
5. Product Type, located under gray bars, centered in bold

Caramel Burnt Sugar Colors *See Ingredients, Flavors & Additives: Colors: Burnt Sugar: Caramel*
Caramel Candy *See Candy & Confectionery: Candy: Caramel*
Caramel Colors *See Ingredients, Flavors & Additives: Colors: Caramel*
Caramel Covered Apple *See Fruits & Vegetables: Apple: Covered: Caramel*
Caramel Flavors *See Ingredients, Flavors & Additives: Flavors: Caramel*
Caraway Oils *See Oils, Shortening & Fats: Oils: Caraway*
Caraway Seeds *See Spices, Seasonings & Seeds: Seeds: Caraway*
Carboxymethylcellulose *See Ingredients, Flavors & Additives: Gums: Carboxymethylcellulose*
Cardamom Oils *See Oils, Shortening & Fats: Oils: Cardamom*
Cardamom Seeds *See Spices, Seasonings & Seeds: Seeds: Cardamom*
Cardamom Spices *See Spices, Seasonings & Seeds: Spices: Cardamom*
Caribou *See Meats & Meat Products: Game: Caribou*
Carmine *See Ingredients, Flavors & Additives: Colors: Natural: Carmine*
Carob Candy *See Candy & Confectionery: Candy: Carob*
Carob Candy Coatings *See Candy & Confectionery: Candy Coatings: Carob*
Carob Ingredients *See Candy & Confectionery: Chocolate Products: Carob Ingredients*
Carob Powder Spices *See Spices, Seasonings & Seeds: Spices: Carob Powder*
Carob Powders *See Ingredients, Flavors & Additives: Powders: Carob*
Carotenoids *See Ingredients, Flavors & Additives: Colors: Natural: Carotenoids*
Carp *See Fish & Seafood: Fish: Carp*
Carrageenan *See Ingredients, Flavors & Additives: Gums: Carrageenan*
Carrot *See Fruits & Vegetables: Carrot*
Carrot Cake *See Baked Goods: Cakes & Pastries: Carrot Cake*
Carrot Juices *See Beverages: Juices: Carrot*
Cascabel Peppers *See Fruits & Vegetables: Peppers: Cascabel*
Casein *See Ingredients, Flavors & Additives: Casein & Caseinates; See also Ingredients, Flavors & Additives: Casein & Caseinates: Casein*
Cashews *See Nuts & Nut Butters: Nuts: Cashews*
Casings *See Meats & Meat Products: Smoked, Cured & Deli Meats: Sausages: Casings: Sausage, Pork, Beef*
Cassava Chips *See Snack Foods: Chips: Cassava*
Cassava Powders *See Ingredients, Flavors & Additives: Powders: Cassava*
Cassava Starches *See Ingredients, Flavors & Additives: Starches: Cassava*
Cassava Tapioca *See Cereals, Grains, Rice & Flour: Tapioca: Cassava*
Casseroles, Prepared Meals *See Prepared Foods: Prepared Meals: Casseroles*
Cassia *See Spices, Seasonings & Seeds: Spices: Cassia (Cinnamon); See also Spices, Seasonings & Seeds: Spices: Cinnamon: Cassia*
Cassia Oils *See Oils, Shortening & Fats: Oils: Cassia*
Castor Oils *See Oils, Shortening & Fats: Oils: Castor*
Catfish *See Fish & Seafood: Fish: Catfish*
Cauliflower *See Fruits & Vegetables: Cauliflower*
Cauliflower, Pickled *See Relishes & Pickled Products: Pickled Products: Cauliflower*
Cavatappi *See Pasta & Noodles: Cavatappi*
Cavatelli *See Pasta & Noodles: Cavatelli*
Caviar *See Fish & Seafood: Caviar (Roe)*
Cayenne Pepper *See Spices, Seasonings & Seeds: Spices: Cayenne Pepper*
Cayenne Spices *See Spices, Seasonings & Seeds: Spices: Cayenne*
Ceasar Salad Dressings *See Sauces, Dips & Dressings: Salad Dressings: Ceasar*
Ceasar Salad Dressings, Mixes *See Sauces, Dips & Dressings: Salad Dressings: Mixes: Ceasar*
Celery *See Fruits & Vegetables: Celery*
Celery Flakes *See Fruits & Vegetables: Dried & Dehydrated Vegetables: Celery Flakes; See also Spices, Seasonings & Seeds: Spices: Celery Flakes*
Celery Oils *See Oils, Shortening & Fats: Oils: Celery*
Celery Powders *See Ingredients, Flavors & Additives: Powders: Celery*
Celery Salt *See Spices, Seasonings & Seeds: Salt: Celery*
Celery Seeds *See Spices, Seasonings & Seeds: Seeds: Celery*
Celery Sticks *See Fruits & Vegetables: Celery: Sticks*
Cellulose Fiber *See Cereals, Grains, Rice & Flour: Fiber: Cellulose*
Cellulose Gel *See Ingredients, Flavors & Additives: Cellulose Gel*
Cereal *See Cereals, Grains, Rice & Flour: Cereal*
Cereal Bars *See Cereals, Grains, Rice & Flour: Cereal: Bars*
Cereal Binders *See Ingredients, Flavors & Additives: Binders: Cereal*
Cereal Crisps *See Cereals, Grains, Rice & Flour: Crisps: Cereal*
Cereal Solids Hydrolyzed Anticaking Agents *See Ingredients, Flavors & Additives: Agents: Anticaking: Cereal Solids Hydrolyzed*
Cereal Solids Hydrolyzed Products *See Ingredients, Flavors & Additives: Hydrolyzed Products: Cereal Solids*
Certified Dyes *See Ingredients, Flavors & Additives: Colors: Dyes: Certified*
Certified Organic Foods *See Specialty & Organic Foods: Organic Foods: Certified*
Chai Tea *See Beverages: Coffee & Tea: Tea: Chai*
Challah *See Baked Goods: Breads: Challah*
Chalupa Shells *See Ethnic Foods: Shells: Chalupa*
Chamomile Tea *See Beverages: Coffee & Tea: Tea: Chamomile*
Champagne *See Beverages: Wines: French: Champagne*
Champagne Vinegar *See Sauces, Dips & Dressings: Vinegar: Champagne*
Chanterelle *See Fruits & Vegetables: Mushrooms: Chanterelle*
Chardonnay *See Beverages: Wines: White Grape Varieties: Chardonnay*
Cheddar Cheese *See Cheese & Cheese Products: Cheese: Cheddar*
Cheddar Cheese, Imitation *See Cheese & Cheese Products: Imitation Cheeses & Substitutes: Imitation: Cheddar*
Cheddar Cheese, Powders *See Ingredients, Flavors & Additives: Powders: Cheese: Cheddar*
Cheddar Snack Seasonings *See Spices, Seasonings & Seeds: Seasonings: Snack: Cheddar*
Cheese *See Cheese & Cheese Products; See also Cheese & Cheese Products: Cheese*
Cheese Bacteria *See Ingredients, Flavors & Additives: Cultures & Yeasts: Bacteria: Cheese*
Cheese Blends *See Ingredients, Flavors & Additives: Blends: Cheese*
Cheese Cake *See Baked Goods: Cakes & Pastries: Cheese Cake*
Cheese Curls *See Snack Foods: Cheese Curls*
Cheese Dips *See Sauces, Dips & Dressings: Dips: Cheese*
Cheese Flavors *See Ingredients, Flavors & Additives: Flavors: Cheese*
Cheese Foods & Substitutes *See Cheese & Cheese Products: Imitation Cheeses & Substitutes: Cheese Foods & Substitutes*
Cheese Loaves, Yellow Process *See Cheese & Cheese Products: Cheese: Process Loaves: Yellow*
Cheese Pizza *See Prepared Foods: Pizza & Pizza Products: Pizza: Cheese*
Cheese Powders *See Ingredients, Flavors & Additives: Powders: Cheese*
Cheese Ravioli *See Pasta & Noodles: Ravioli: Cheese*
Cheese Sauces *See Sauces, Dips & Dressings: Sauces: Cheese*
Cheese Seasonings *See Spices, Seasonings & Seeds: Seasonings: Cheese*
Cheese Starter Media *See Ingredients, Flavors & Additives: Starter Media: Cheese*
Cheese Substitutes *See Cheese & Cheese Products: Imitation Cheeses & Substitutes: Substitutes*
Cheese Twists *See Snack Foods: Cheese Twists*
Cheese, Blend - American/Skim Milk *See Cheese & Cheese Products: Cheese: Blend - American/Skim Milk*
Cheese, No-Fat *See Cheese & Cheese Products: Cheese: No-Fat*
Cheese, White/Yellow Process Sliced *See Cheese & Cheese Products: Cheese: Process Sliced: White/Yellow*
Cheesecake Flavors *See Ingredients, Flavors & Additives: Flavors: Cheesecake*
Chelating Agents *See Ingredients, Flavors & Additives: Chelating Agents*
Chemicals *See Ingredients, Flavors & Additives: Chemicals*
Chemicals, Aroma *See Ingredients, Flavors & Additives: Aroma Chemicals & Materials: Chemicals*
Cherries *See Fruits & Vegetables: Cherries*
Cherry Flavors *See Ingredients, Flavors & Additives: Flavors: Cherry*
Cherry Juices *See Beverages: Juices: Cherry*
Cherry Peppers *See Fruits & Vegetables: Peppers: Cherry*
Cherry Pies *See Baked Goods: Pies: Cherry*
Cherry Tomato *See Fruits & Vegetables: Tomato: Cherry*
Chervil *See Spices, Seasonings & Seeds: Spices: Chervil*
Chestnut Flower Flour *See Cereals, Grains, Rice & Flour: Flour: Chestnut Flower*
Chestnuts *See Nuts & Nut Butters: Nuts: Chestnuts*
Chewing Gum *See Candy & Confectionery: Candy: Chewing Gum*
Chianti *See Beverages: Wines: Italian: Chianti*
Chick Beans *See Fruits & Vegetables: Beans: Chick*
Chicken *See Meats & Meat Products: Poultry: Chicken*
Chicken & Dumplings Soups & Stews *See Prepared Foods: Soups & Stews: Chicken & Dumplings*
Chicken & Noodles Soups & Stews *See Prepared Foods: Soups & Stews: Chicken & Noodles*
Chicken Bases *See Ingredients, Flavors & Additives: Bases: Chicken*
Chicken Broth *See Prepared Foods: Broth: Chicken*
Chicken Bulk *See Meats & Meat Products: Poultry: Chicken: Bulk (Leg Quarters, Legs, Thighs)*
Chicken Extenders *See Ingredients, Flavors & Additives: Extenders: Chicken*
Chicken Extracts *See Ingredients, Flavors & Additives: Extracts: Chicken*
Chicken Fats & Lard *See Oils, Shortening & Fats: Fats & Lard: Chicken*
Chicken Frankfurters *See Meats & Meat Products: Frankfurters: Chicken*
Chicken Marinades *See Sauces, Dips & Dressings: Marinades: Chicken*
Chicken Nuggets *See Meats & Meat Products: Poultry: Chicken: Nuggets*
Chicken Sausages *See Meats & Meat Products: Smoked, Cured & Deli Meats: Sausages: Chicken*
Chicken, Cut-Up Frozen *See Meats & Meat Products: Poultry: Chicken: Cut-Up Frozen*
Chicken, Cut-Up IQF *See Meats & Meat Products: Poultry: Chicken: Cut-Up IQF (Individually Quick Frozen)*
Chicken, Prepared Meals *See Prepared Foods: Prepared Meals: Chicken*
Chicken, Prepared Salads *See Prepared Foods: Prepared Salads: Chicken*
Chicks Hatcheries *See Eggs & Egg Products: Hatcheries: Chicks*
Chicory *See Fruits & Vegetables: Chicory*
Chile Pepper Spices *See Spices, Seasonings & Seeds: Spices: Chile Pepper*
Chile Peppers *See Fruits & Vegetables: Peppers: Chile*
Chili *See Prepared Foods: Chili*
Chili Beans *See Fruits & Vegetables: Beans: Chili*
Chili Crush *See Spices, Seasonings & Seeds: Spices: Chili Crush*
Chili Dips *See Sauces, Dips & Dressings: Dips: Chili*
Chili Mixes *See Doughs, Mixes & Fillings: Mixes: Chili*
Chili Pods *See Spices, Seasonings & Seeds: Spices: Chili Pods*
Chili Powder *See Spices, Seasonings & Seeds: Spices: Chili Powder; See also Ingredients, Flavors & Additives: Powders: Chili*
Chili Sauces *See Sauces, Dips & Dressings: Sauces: Chili*
Chili with Cheese *See Prepared Foods: Chili: with Cheese*
Chilled Apple Juices *See Beverages: Juices: Apple: Chilled*
Chilled Cherry Juices *See Beverages: Juices: Cherry: Chilled*
Chilled Grape Juices *See Beverages: Juices: Grape: Chilled*
Chimichangas *See Prepared Foods: Prepared Meals: Burritos: Chimichangas*
Chinese *See Ethnic Foods: Chinese*
Chinese Black Rice *See Cereals, Grains, Rice & Flour: Rice: Chinese Black*
Chinese Cabbage *See Fruits & Vegetables: Cabbage: Chinese*

1 2 3 4 5
EXAMPLE: **Canadian Style Bacon** *See Meats & Meat Products: Smoked, Cured & Deli Meats: Bacon: Canadian Style*

1. Product or Service you are looking for
2. Main Category, in alphabetical order, located in the page headers starting on page 23
3. Category Description, located in black bars and in page headers
4. Product Category, located in gray bars
5. Product Type, located under gray bars, centered in bold

Chinese Spices *See Spices, Seasonings & Seeds: Spices: Chinese*
Chinese Style Seasonings *See Spices, Seasonings & Seeds: Seasonings: Chinese Style*
Chip Dips *See Sauces, Dips & Dressings: Dips: Chip*
Chipotle Peppers *See Fruits & Vegetables: Peppers: Chipotle*
Chipped Beef *See Meats & Meat Products: Beef & Beef Products: Chipped*
Chips *See Snack Foods: Chips*
Chives *See Spices, Seasonings & Seeds: Spices: Chives; See also Fruits & Vegetables: Chives*
Chlorophyll *See Ingredients, Flavors & Additives: Chlorophyll*
Chocolate Almond Biscotti *See Baked Goods: Cookies & Bars: Biscotti: Chocolate Almond*
Chocolate Bars *See Candy & Confectionery: Chocolate Products: Chocolate Bars*
Chocolate Bases *See Ingredients, Flavors & Additives: Bases: Chocolate*
Chocolate Candy *See Candy & Confectionery: Chocolate Products: Chocolate Candy*
Chocolate Candy Coatings *See Candy & Confectionery: Candy Coatings: Chocolate*
Chocolate Cherries *See Candy & Confectionery: Chocolate Products: Chocolate Cherries*
Chocolate Chip Compound for Ice Cream *See Ingredients, Flavors & Additives: Chocolate Products: Chocolate Chip Compound for Ice Cream*
Chocolate Chip Cookies *See Baked Goods: Cookies & Bars: Chocolate Chip Cookies*
Chocolate Chips *See Candy & Confectionery: Chocolate Products: Chocolate Chips; See also Snack Foods: Chips: Chocolate*
Chocolate Chunks *See Candy & Confectionery: Chocolate Products: Chocolate Chunks*
Chocolate Coated Nuts *See Nuts & Nut Butters: Nuts: Coated: Chocolate*
Chocolate Coated Raisins *See Fruits & Vegetables: Raisins: Chocolate Coated*
Chocolate Covered Apple *See Fruits & Vegetables: Apple: Covered: Chocolate*
Chocolate Dessert Fillings *See Doughs, Mixes & Fillings: Fillings: Dessert: Chocolate*
Chocolate Dipped Biscotti *See Baked Goods: Cookies & Bars: Biscotti: Chocolate Dipped*
Chocolate Drinks *See Beverages: Cocoa & Chocolate Drinks: Chocolate Drinks*
Chocolate Fillings *See Doughs, Mixes & Fillings: Fillings: Chocolate*
Chocolate Flavors *See Ingredients, Flavors & Additives: Flavors: Chocolate*
Chocolate Liqueur *See Beverages: Spirits & Liqueurs: Liqueurs & Cordials: Chocolate Liqueur*
Chocolate Milk *See Dairy Products: Milk & Milk Products: Milk: Chocolate*
Chocolate Products *See Candy & Confectionery: Chocolate Products; See also Ingredients, Flavors & Additives: Chocolate Products*
Chocolate Pudding *See Dairy Products: Pudding: Chocolate*
Chop Suey *See Ethnic Foods: Chop Suey*
Chopped Broccoli *See Fruits & Vegetables: Broccoli: Chopped*
Chopped Broccoli, Dehydrated *See Fruits & Vegetables: Dried & Dehydrated Vegetables: Broccoli: Chopped*
Chopped Celery *See Fruits & Vegetables: Celery: Chopped*
Chopped Clam *See Fish & Seafood: Shellfish: Clam: Chopped*
Chopped Garlic *See Spices, Seasonings & Seeds: Spices: Garlic: Chopped*
Chopped Onion *See Spices, Seasonings & Seeds: Spices: Onion: Chopped*
Chopped Shellfish *See Fish & Seafood: Shellfish: Chopped*
Chorizo Sausages *See Meats & Meat Products: Smoked, Cured & Deli Meats: Sausages: Chorizo*
Chourico Sausages *See Meats & Meat Products: Smoked, Cured & Deli Meats: Sausages: Chourico*
Chow Chow *See Ethnic Foods: Chow Chow*
Chow Fun Noodles *See Pasta & Noodles: Noodles: Chow Fun*
Chow Mein *See Ethnic Foods: Chow Mein*
Chow Mein Noodles *See Pasta & Noodles: Noodles: Chow Mein*
Chowder *See Fish & Seafood: Fish: Chowder; See also Prepared Foods: Soups & Stews: Chowder; See also Prepared Foods: Chowder*
Christmas Specialty-Packaged Candy *See Candy & Confectionery: Specialty-Packaged Candy: Christmas*
Chub *See Fish & Seafood: Fish: Chub*
Chum Salmon *See Fish & Seafood: Fish: Salmon: Chum*
Chunky Salsa *See Sauces, Dips & Dressings: Salsa: Chunky*
Churros *See Baked Goods: Cakes & Pastries: Churros*
Chutney *See Prepared Foods: Chutney*
Cider & Vinegar Colors *See Ingredients, Flavors & Additives: Colors: Cider & Vinegar*
Cinnamon Flavors *See Ingredients, Flavors & Additives: Flavors: Cinnamon*
Cinnamon Leaf & Bark Oils *See Oils, Shortening & Fats: Oils: Cinnamon - Leaf & Bark*
Cinnamon Rolls *See Baked Goods: Breads: Rolls: Cinnamon*
Cinnamon Spices *See Spices, Seasonings & Seeds: Spices: Cinnamon*
Cinnamon Toast *See Baked Goods: Breads: Cinnamon Toast*
Cinnamon Toast, Snack Seasonings *See Spices, Seasonings & Seeds: Seasonings: Snack: Cinnamon Toast*
Citric Acidulants *See Ingredients, Flavors & Additives: Acidulants: Citric*
Citron *See Spices, Seasonings & Seeds: Spices: Citron*
Citrus Blends Juices *See Beverages: Juices: Citrus Blends*
Citrus Flavors *See Ingredients, Flavors & Additives: Flavors: Citrus*
Citrus Fruits *See Fruits & Vegetables: Citrus Fruits*
Citrus Oils *See Oils, Shortening & Fats: Oils: Citrus*
Citrus Pectins *See Ingredients, Flavors & Additives: Pectins: Citrus*
Citrus Peel Products *See Fruits & Vegetables: Citrus Peel Products*
Citrus Pulps & Purees *See Fruits & Vegetables: Pulps & Purees: Citrus*
Clam *See Fish & Seafood: Shellfish: Clam*
Clam & Fish Chowder *See Prepared Foods: Chowder: Clam & Fish*
Clam Juice *See Fish & Seafood: Shellfish: Clam: Juice*
Clam Sauces *See Sauces, Dips & Dressings: Sauces: Clam*
Clarifying Agents *See Ingredients, Flavors & Additives: Agents: Clarifying*
Cloudear Mushrooms *See Fruits & Vegetables: Mushrooms: Cloudear*
Clove Oils *See Oils, Shortening & Fats: Oils: Clove*
Cloves *See Spices, Seasonings & Seeds: Spices: Cloves*
Club Soda *See Beverages: Soft Drinks & Sodas: Club Soda*
Coagulants *See Ingredients, Flavors & Additives: Coagulants*
Coarse Frozen Ground Beef *See Meats & Meat Products: Beef & Beef Products: Ground: Coarse Frozen*
Coated Candy Bars *See Candy & Confectionery: Candy: Candy Bars: Coated*
Coated Nuts *See Nuts & Nut Butters: Nuts: Coated*
Coated Popcorn *See Snack Foods: Popcorn: Coated*
Coatings *See Ingredients, Flavors & Additives: Coatings*
Cocktail Fruit *See Fruits & Vegetables: Fruit: Cocktail*
Cocktail Mixes *See Doughs, Mixes & Fillings: Mixes: Cocktail*
Cocktail Onion *See Fruits & Vegetables: Onion: Cocktail*
Cocktail Sauces *See Sauces, Dips & Dressings: Sauces: Cocktail*
Cocktail Seafood *See Fish & Seafood: Seafood: Cocktail*
Cocktail Shrimp *See Fish & Seafood: Shellfish: Shrimp: Cocktail*
Cocktail Tomato *See Fruits & Vegetables: Tomato: Cocktail*
Cocktail Tomato Juices *See Beverages: Juices: Tomato: Cocktail*
Cocoa & Chocolate Drinks *See Beverages: Cocoa & Chocolate Drinks*
Cocoa & Cocoa Products *See Candy & Confectionery: Chocolate Products: Cocoa & Cocoa Products*
Cocoa & Rice Pellets *See Ingredients, Flavors & Additives: Half-Products: Cocoa & Rice Pellets*
Cocoa Butter *See Ingredients, Flavors & Additives: Cocoa Butter*
Cocoa Flavors *See Ingredients, Flavors & Additives: Flavors: Cocoa*
Cocoa Powders *See Ingredients, Flavors & Additives: Powders: Cocoa*
Cocoa Replacers *See Ingredients, Flavors & Additives: Replacers: Cocoa*
Cocoa Rice Crisps *See Cereals, Grains, Rice & Flour: Crisps: Cocoa Rice*
Cocoa Soy Crisps *See Cereals, Grains, Rice & Flour: Crisps: Cocoa Soy*
Coconut & Coconut Products *See Fruits & Vegetables: Coconut & Coconut Products*
Coconut Candy *See Candy & Confectionery: Candy: Coconut*
Coconut Flavors *See Ingredients, Flavors & Additives: Flavors: Coconut*
Coconut Juices *See Beverages: Juices: Coconut*
Coconut Oils *See Oils, Shortening & Fats: Oils: Coconut*
Cod *See Fish & Seafood: Fish: Cod*
Cod Liver Oils *See Oils, Shortening & Fats: Oils: Cod Liver*
Coffee *See Beverages: Coffee & Tea; See also Beverages: Coffee & Tea: Coffee*
Coffee Cake *See Baked Goods: Cakes & Pastries: Coffee Cake*
Coffee Creamers *See Dairy Products: Creamers: Coffee*
Coffee Extenders *See Ingredients, Flavors & Additives: Extenders: Coffee*
Coffee Extracts *See Ingredients, Flavors & Additives: Extracts: Coffee*
Coffee Flavors *See Ingredients, Flavors & Additives: Flavors: Coffee*
Coffee Liqueur *See Beverages: Spirits & Liqueurs: Liqueurs & Cordials: Coffee Liqueur*
Coho Salmon *See Fish & Seafood: Fish: Salmon: Coho*
Cola Soft Drinks *See Beverages: Soft Drinks & Sodas: Soft Drinks: Cola*
Colby *See Cheese & Cheese Products: Cheese: Colby*
Cold Smoked Seafood *See Fish & Seafood: Seafood: Smoked: Cold*
Cole Slaw *See Prepared Foods: Prepared Salads: Cole Slaw*
Collard Greens *See Fruits & Vegetables: Collard Greens*
Colloids Stabilizers *See Ingredients, Flavors & Additives: Stabilizers: Colloids*
Colored Crisps *See Cereals, Grains, Rice & Flour: Crisps: Colored*
Colored Pellets *See Ingredients, Flavors & Additives: Half-Products: Colored Pellets*
Colored Starch Bits *See Ingredients, Flavors & Additives: Toppings: Colored Starch Bits; See also Ingredients, Flavors & Additives: Bits: Colored Starch*
Colors *See Ingredients, Flavors & Additives: Colors*
Compacting Agents *See Ingredients, Flavors & Additives: Agents: Compacting*
Compound Coatings *See Ingredients, Flavors & Additives: Coatings: Compound*
Compounds *See Ingredients, Flavors & Additives: Compounds*
Concentrate Ade Juices *See Beverages: Juices: Ade: Concentrate*
Concentrate Apple Juices *See Beverages: Juices: Apple: Concentrate*
Concentrate Apricot Juices *See Beverages: Juices: Apricot: Concentrate*
Concentrate Cherry Juices *See Beverages: Juices: Cherry: Concentrate*
Concentrate Cranberry Juices *See Beverages: Juices: Cranberry: Concentrate*
Concentrate Drink Juices *See Beverages: Juices: Drink: Concentrate*
Concentrate Fruit & Vegetable Juices *See Beverages: Juices: Fruit & Vegetable: Concentrate*
Concentrate Fruit Juices *See Beverages: Juices: Fruit: Concentrate*
Concentrate Fruit Punch Juices *See Beverages: Juices: Fruit Punch: Concentrate*
Concentrate Fruit Puree Juices *See Beverages: Juices: Vegetable: Concentrates - Fruit Puree*
Concentrate Grape Juices *See Beverages: Juices: Grape: Concentrate*
Concentrate Grapefruit Juices *See Beverages: Juices: Grapefruit: Concentrate*
Concentrate Lemon Juices *See Beverages: Juices: Lemon: Concentrate*
Concentrate Lemonade Juices *See Beverages: Juices: Lemonade: Concentrate*
Concentrate Orange Juices *See Beverages: Juices: Orange: Concentrate*
Concentrate Orange Juices, Frozen *See Beverages: Juices: Orange: Concentrate - Frozen*
Concentrate Pineapple Juices *See Beverages: Juices: Pineapple: Concentrate*
Concentrate Soy Protein *See Fruits & Vegetables: Soy: Soy Protein: Concentrate*
Concentrates *See Ingredients, Flavors & Additives: Concentrates*
Conch Fish *See Fish & Seafood: Fish: Conch*
Conch Shellfish *See Fish & Seafood: Shellfish: Conch*
Conchigite Rigate *See Pasta & Noodles: Conchigite Rigate*
Condensed Buttermilk *See Dairy Products: Buttermilk & Buttermilk Products: Buttermilk Products: Condensed*
Condensed Milk *See Dairy Products: Milk & Milk Products: Milk: Condensed*
Condensed Milk, Bulk Only *See Dairy Products: Milk & Milk Products: Milk: Condensed - Bulk Only*
Condiments *See Sauces, Dips & Dressings: Condiments*
Cones *See Baked Goods: Cones*

Confectioners Crunch *See Candy & Confectionery: Confectionery: Confectioners Crunch*
Confectioners Dipping Fruit *See Fruits & Vegetables: Dipping Fruit: Confectioners'*
Confectionery *See Candy & Confectionery: Confectionery: Confectionery; See also Candy & Confectionery: Confectionery; See also Ingredients, Flavors & Additives: Confectionery*
Confectionery Candy Coatings *See Candy & Confectionery: Candy Coatings: Confectionery*
Confectionery Toppings *See Ingredients, Flavors & Additives: Toppings: Confectionery*
Convenience Food *See Prepared Foods: Convenience Food*
Convenience Prepared Meals *See Prepared Foods: Prepared Meals: Convenience*
Cooked *See Eggs & Egg Products: Cooked*
Cooked Chicken, Breaded - Frozen *See Meats & Meat Products: Poultry: Chicken: Cooked - Breaded - Frozen*
Cooked Corn-on-the-Cob *See Fruits & Vegetables: Corn: Corn-on-the-Cob: Cooked*
Cooked Crab *See Fish & Seafood: Shellfish: Crab: Cooked*
Cooked Frozen Hamburger *See Meats & Meat Products: Beef & Beef Products: Hamburger: Cooked Frozen*
Cooked Frozen Patties *See Meats & Meat Products: Beef & Beef Products: Patties: Cooked Frozen*
Cooked Ham, Water-added Chilled *See Meats & Meat Products: Smoked, Cured & Deli Meats: Ham: Cooked - Water-added Chilled*
Cooked Oysters *See Fish & Seafood: Shellfish: Oysters: Cooked*
Cooked Shrimp *See Fish & Seafood: Shellfish: Shrimp: Cooked*
Cookie Batters *See Doughs, Mixes & Fillings: Batters: Cookie*
Cookie Bits *See Ingredients, Flavors & Additives: Bits: Cookie*
Cookie Doughs *See Doughs, Mixes & Fillings: Doughs: Cookie*
Cookie Fillings *See Doughs, Mixes & Fillings: Fillings: Cookie*
Cookie Mixes *See Doughs, Mixes & Fillings: Mixes: Cookie*
Cookies *See Baked Goods: Cookies & Bars: Cookies*
Cookies & Bars *See Baked Goods: Cookies & Bars*
Cookies & Biscuits *See Baked Goods: Cookies & Bars: Cookies & Biscuits*
Cookies Bars *See Baked Goods: Cookies & Bars: Bars*
Cooking Compounds *See Ingredients, Flavors & Additives: Compounds: Cooking*
Cooking Compounds, Fats & Lard *See Oils, Shortening & Fats: Fats & Lard: Lard: Cooking Compounds*
Cooking Oils *See Oils, Shortening & Fats: Oils: Cooking*
Cooking Wines *See Beverages: Wines: Cooking*
Coriander *See Spices, Seasonings & Seeds: Spices: Coriander (Cilantro)*
Coriander Seed Oils *See Oils, Shortening & Fats: Oils: Coriander Seed*
Coriander Seeds *See Spices, Seasonings & Seeds: Seeds: Coriander*
Corn *See Fruits & Vegetables: Corn*
Corn Bran Fiber *See Cereals, Grains, Rice & Flour: Fiber: Corn Bran*
Corn Breads *See Baked Goods: Breads: Corn*
Corn Candy *See Candy & Confectionery: Candy: Corn*
Corn Chips *See Snack Foods: Chips: Corn*
Corn Dogs *See Meats & Meat Products: Frankfurters: Corn Dogs*
Corn Flour *See Cereals, Grains, Rice & Flour: Flour: Corn*
Corn Fritters *See Prepared Foods: Prepared Meals: Corn Fritters*
Corn Meal *See Cereals, Grains, Rice & Flour: Corn Meal*
Corn Nuts *See Snack Foods: Corn Nuts*
Corn Oils *See Oils, Shortening & Fats: Oils: Corn*
Corn Starches *See Ingredients, Flavors & Additives: Starches: Corn*
Corn Syrups *See Sugars, Syrups & Sweeteners: Syrups: Corn*
Corn-Based Cereal *See Cereals, Grains, Rice & Flour: Cereal: Corn-Based*
Corn-on-the-Cob *See Fruits & Vegetables: Corn: Corn-on-the-Cob*
Corned Beef *See Meats & Meat Products: Smoked, Cured & Deli Meats: Corned Beef*
Cornish Game Hens *See Meats & Meat Products: Poultry: Cornish Game Hens*
Corsignano *See Cheese & Cheese Products: Cheese: Corsignano*
Cottage Cheese *See Cheese & Cheese Products: Cheese: Cottage*
Cotton Candy *See Candy & Confectionery: Candy: Cotton*
Cottonseed Oils *See Oils, Shortening & Fats: Oils: Cottonseed*
Couscous *See Ethnic Foods: Couscous*
Covered Apple *See Fruits & Vegetables: Apple: Covered*
Crab *See Fish & Seafood: Shellfish: Crab; See also Prepared Foods: Prepared Meals: Crab*
Crab Extracts *See Ingredients, Flavors & Additives: Extracts: Crab*
Crab Meat *See Fish & Seafood: Shellfish: Crab: Meat*
Crackers *See Baked Goods: Crackers; See also Baked Goods: Crackers: Crackers*
Cranberry *See Fruits & Vegetables: Berries: Cranberry*
Cranberry Juices *See Beverages: Juices: Cranberry*
Cranberry Orange Biscotti *See Baked Goods: Cookies & Bars: Biscotti: Cranberry Orange*
Cranberry Sauces *See Fruits & Vegetables: Sauces: Cranberry*
Crayfish *See Fish & Seafood: Shellfish: Crayfish*
Cream *See Dairy Products: Cream*
Cream Ale *See Beverages: Beers: American & British Ale: Cream Ale*
Cream Cheese *See Cheese & Cheese Products: Cheese: Cream*
Cream Cheese Powders *See Ingredients, Flavors & Additives: Powders: Cheese: Cream*
Cream Dessert Fillings *See Doughs, Mixes & Fillings: Fillings: Dessert: Cream*
Cream from Milk *See Dairy Products: Cream: from Milk*
Cream of Broccoli Soups & Stews *See Prepared Foods: Soups & Stews: Cream of Broccoli*
Cream of Mushroom Soups & Stews *See Prepared Foods: Soups & Stews: Cream of Mushroom*
Cream of Potato Soups & Stews *See Prepared Foods: Soups & Stews: Cream of Potato*
Cream of Tartar *See Spices, Seasonings & Seeds: Spices: Tartar: Cream*
Cream Puff *See Baked Goods: Cakes & Pastries: Cream Puff*
Cream Soda *See Beverages: Soft Drinks & Sodas: Soft Drinks: Cream Soda - Vanilla; See also Beverages: Soft Drinks & Sodas: Soft Drinks: Cream Soda*
Creamers *See Dairy Products: Creamers*
Creamy Dijon Salad Dressings *See Sauces, Dips & Dressings: Salad Dressings: Mixes: Creamy Dijon; See also Sauces, Dips & Dressings: Salad Dressings: Creamy Dijon*
Creme Fillings *See Doughs, Mixes & Fillings: Fillings: Creme*
Cremes Candy *See Candy & Confectionery: Candy: Cremes*
Creole Chicken *See Prepared Foods: Prepared Meals: Chicken: Creole*
Crepes *See Prepared Foods: Crepes*
Criminis Mushrooms *See Fruits & Vegetables: Mushrooms: Criminis*
Crisp Rice Toppings *See Ingredients, Flavors & Additives: Toppings: Crisp Rice*
Crisped Bran Crisps *See Cereals, Grains, Rice & Flour: Crisps: Crisped Bran*
Crisped Corn Crisps *See Cereals, Grains, Rice & Flour: Crisps: Crisped Corn*
Crisped Oat Crisps *See Cereals, Grains, Rice & Flour: Crisps: Crisped Oat*
Crisped Rice Crisps *See Cereals, Grains, Rice & Flour: Crisps: Crisped Rice*
Crisped Soy Crisps *See Cereals, Grains, Rice & Flour: Crisps: Crisped Soy*
Crisped Wheat Crisps *See Cereals, Grains, Rice & Flour: Crisps: Crisped Wheat*
Crisps *See Cereals, Grains, Rice & Flour: Crisps*
Criterion Apple *See Fruits & Vegetables: Apple: Criterion*
Croaker *See Fish & Seafood: Fish: Croaker*
Croissant Sesame Crackers *See Baked Goods: Crackers: Croissant Sesame Crackers*
Croissants *See Baked Goods: Breads: Croissants*
Croquettes *See Prepared Foods: Croquettes*
Croutons *See Baked Goods: Bread Crumbs & Croutons: Croutons; See also Baked Goods: Bread Crumbs & Croutons: Crumbs*
Crumpets *See Baked Goods: Cakes & Pastries: Crumpets*
Crunch Toppings *See Ingredients, Flavors & Additives: Toppings: Crunch*
Crunches *See Baked Goods: Crunches*
Crunchy Peanut Butter *See Nuts & Nut Butters: Nut Butters: Peanut Butter: Crunchy*
Crushed Canned Tomato *See Fruits & Vegetables: Tomato: Canned: Crushed*
Crushed Fruits & Vegetables *See Fruits & Vegetables: Crushed*
Crushed Onion *See Fruits & Vegetables: Onion: Crushed*
Crushed Red Pepper *See Spices, Seasonings & Seeds: Spices: Red Pepper: Crushed*
Crysanthemums *See Fruits & Vegetables: Crysanthemums*
Crystalline Fructose *See Sugars, Syrups & Sweeteners: Fructose: Crystalline*
Crystallized Ginger *See Spices, Seasonings & Seeds: Spices: Ginger: Crystallized; See also Fruits & Vegetables: Ginger: Crystallized*
Crystallized, Glace Candied Fruits *See Fruits & Vegetables: Candied Fruits: Crystallized, Glace*
Cucumber *See Fruits & Vegetables: Cucumber*
Cucumber for Pickling *See Fruits & Vegetables: Cucumber: for Pickling*
Cultured Flavors *See Ingredients, Flavors & Additives: Flavors: Cultured*
Cultures *See Ingredients, Flavors & Additives: Cultures & Yeasts: Cultures*
Cultures & Yeasts *See Ingredients, Flavors & Additives: Cultures & Yeasts*
Cumin Seeds *See Spices, Seasonings & Seeds: Seeds: Cumin*
Cumin Spices *See Spices, Seasonings & Seeds: Spices: Cumin*
Cupcake *See Baked Goods: Cakes & Pastries: Cupcakes*
Curd Seasonings *See Spices, Seasonings & Seeds: Seasonings: Curd*
Cured Smoked Seafood *See Fish & Seafood: Seafood: Smoked: Cured*
Curing Preparations *See Ingredients, Flavors & Additives: Curing Preparations*
Currants Berries *See Fruits & Vegetables: Berries: Currants*
Curry Powder *See Spices, Seasonings & Seeds: Spices: Curry Powder; See also Ingredients, Flavors & Additives: Powders: Curry*
Curry Sauces *See Sauces, Dips & Dressings: Sauces: Curry*
Cusk *See Fish & Seafood: Fish: Cusk*
Custard *See Dairy Products: Custard*
Custard Dessert Fillings *See Doughs, Mixes & Fillings: Fillings: Dessert: Custard*
Custard Powders *See Ingredients, Flavors & Additives: Powders: Custard*
Custom Blends *See Ingredients, Flavors & Additives: Blends: Custom*
Custom Designed Colloid Stabilizers *See Ingredients, Flavors & Additives: Stabilizers: Colloids: Custom Designed*

D

D'Anjou/Bosc Pear *See Fruits & Vegetables: Pear: D'Anjou/Bosc*
Dairy Bases *See Ingredients, Flavors & Additives: Bases: Dairy*
Dairy Butter *See Dairy Products: Butter: Dairy*
Dairy Coagulants *See Ingredients, Flavors & Additives: Coagulants: Dairy*
Dairy Drinks *See Dairy Products: Dairy Drinks*
Dairy Flavors *See Ingredients, Flavors & Additives: Flavors: Dairy*
Dairy Ingredients *See Ingredients, Flavors & Additives: Ingredients: Dairy*
Dairy Products *See Dairy Products*
Dairy Seasonings *See Spices, Seasonings & Seeds: Seasonings: Dairy Products*
Dairy Whipped Toppings *See Ingredients, Flavors & Additives: Toppings: Whipped: Dairy*
Danish *See Baked Goods: Cakes & Pastries: Danish*
Darjeeling Tea *See Beverages: Coffee & Tea: Tea: Darjeeling*
Dark Green Zucchini *See Fruits & Vegetables: Zucchini: Dark Green*
Dark Red Kidney Beans *See Fruits & Vegetables: Beans: Kidney: Dark Red*
Dark Rum *See Beverages: Spirits & Liqueurs: Rum: Dark*

1 2 3 4 5

EXAMPLE: **Canadian Style Bacon** *See Meats & Meat Products: Smoked, Cured & Deli Meats: Bacon: Canadian Style*

1. Product or Service you are looking for
2. Main Category, in alphabetical order, located in the page headers starting on page 23
3. Category Description, located in black bars and in page headers
4. Product Category, located in gray bars
5. Product Type, located under gray bars, centered in bold

DarkLager/Dunkel Lager *See Beverages: Beers: Lager: DarkLager/Dunkel*
Dates *See Fruits & Vegetables: Dates*
De Arbol Peppers *See Fruits & Vegetables: Peppers: De Arbol*
Decaffeinated Coffee *See Beverages: Coffee & Tea: Coffee: Decaffeinated*
Decaffeinated Coffee, Naturally *See Beverages: Coffee & Tea: Coffee: Decaffeinated Naturally*
Decaffeinated Espresso *See Beverages: Coffee & Tea: Espresso: Decaffeinated*
Decaffeinated Tea *See Beverages: Coffee & Tea: Tea: Decaffeinated*
Decorations *See Candy & Confectionery: Decorations & Icings; See also Candy & Confectionery: Decorations & Icings: Decorations*
Decorative Items *See Ingredients, Flavors & Additives: Decorative Items*
Defatted Wheat Germ *See Cereals, Grains, Rice & Flour: Wheat: Germ: Defatted*
Defoamers *See Ingredients, Flavors & Additives: Defoamers*
Dehydrated Capsicums Peppers *See Fruits & Vegetables: Peppers: Capsicums: Dehydrated*
Dehydrated Carrot *See Fruits & Vegetables: Carrot: Dehydrated*
Dehydrated Celery *See Fruits & Vegetables: Celery: Dehydrated*
Dehydrated Egg *See Eggs & Egg Products: Dehydrated*
Dehydrated Food *See Specialty Processed Foods: Dehydrated Food (See also Specific Foods)*
Dehydrated Fruit *See Fruits & Vegetables: Dried & Dehydrated Fruits: Dehydrated Fruit; See also Fruits & Vegetables: Dehydrated*
Dehydrated Mushrooms *See Fruits & Vegetables: Mushrooms: Dehydrated*
Dehydrated Onion *See Fruits & Vegetables: Dried & Dehydrated Vegetables: Onion: Dehydrated*
Dehydrated Parsley *See Spices, Seasonings & Seeds: Spices: Parsley: Dehydrated*
Dehydrated Potatoes *See Fruits & Vegetables: Potatoes: Dehydrated*
Dehydrated Shellfish *See Fish & Seafood: Shellfish: Dehydrated*
Dehydrated Soup *See Prepared Foods: Soups & Stews: Dehydrated Soup*
Dehydrated Vegetables *See Fruits & Vegetables: Dried & Dehydrated Vegetables: Dehydrated Vegetables; See also Fruits & Vegetables: Dehydrated*
Deli Foods *See Meats & Meat Products: Smoked, Cured & Deli Meats: Deli Foods*
Deli Meats *See Meats & Meat Products: Smoked, Cured & Deli Meats: Deli Meats*
Deli Meats, Fresh Turkey Breast *See Meats & Meat Products: Smoked, Cured & Deli Meats: Turkey: Deli Breast - Fresh*
Deli Meats, Frozen Turkey Breast *See Meats & Meat Products: Smoked, Cured & Deli Meats: Turkey: Deli Breast - Frozen*
Deli Meats, Smoked Turkey Breast *See Meats & Meat Products: Smoked, Cured & Deli Meats: Turkey: Deli Breast - Smoked*
Desiccated & Shredded Coconut *See Fruits & Vegetables: Coconut & Coconut Products: Desiccated & Shredded*
Desiccated Egg *See Eggs & Egg Products: Dried: Desiccated*
Desiccated Fruit *See Fruits & Vegetables: Dried & Dehydrated Fruits: Desiccated Fruit*
Desiccated Vegetables *See Fruits & Vegetables: Dried & Dehydrated Vegetables: Desiccated Vegetables*
Dessert Fillings *See Doughs, Mixes & Fillings: Fillings: Dessert*
Dessert Mixes *See Doughs, Mixes & Fillings: Mixes: Dessert*
Dessert Mixes, Frozen *See Doughs, Mixes & Fillings: Mixes: Frozen: Dessert*
Dessert Sauces *See Sauces, Dips & Dressings: Sauces: Dessert*
Dessert Tarts *See Baked Goods: Cakes & Pastries: Dessert Tarts*
Dessert Toppings *See Ingredients, Flavors & Additives: Toppings: Dessert*
Desserts *See Baked Goods: Desserts*
Dextrin Starches *See Ingredients, Flavors & Additives: Starches: Dextrin*
Dextrose Corn Syrups *See Sugars, Syrups & Sweeteners: Syrups: Corn: Dextrose*
Dextrose Sweeteners *See Ingredients, Flavors & Additives: Sweeteners: Dextrose*
Diced & Cooked Chicken *See Meats & Meat Products: Poultry: Chicken: Diced & Cooked*
Diced Canned Pear *See Fruits & Vegetables: Pear: Canned: Diced*
Diced Frozen Chicken *See Meats & Meat Products: Poultry: Chicken: Diced Frozen*
Diced Tomato *See Fruits & Vegetables: Tomato: Diced*
Diet & Weight Loss Aids *See Specialty & Organic Foods: Dietary Products: Diet & Weight Loss Aids*
Dietary Products *See Specialty & Organic Foods: Dietary Products*
Dietary Supplements *See Specialty & Organic Foods: Dietary Products: Dietary Supplements*
Dietetic Candy *See Candy & Confectionery: Candy: Dietetic*
Dietetic Juices *See Beverages: Juices: Dietetic*
Digestive Aids *See Ingredients, Flavors & Additives: Digestive Aids*
Dijon Mixes *See Sauces, Dips & Dressings: Salad Dressings: Mixes: Dijon*
Dill Pickles *See Relishes & Pickled Products: Pickled Products: Pickles: Dill*
Dill Seeds *See Spices, Seasonings & Seeds: Seeds: Dill*
Dill Spices *See Spices, Seasonings & Seeds: Spices: Dill*
Dill Weed Spices *See Spices, Seasonings & Seeds: Spices: Dill Weed*
Dillweed Oils *See Oils, Shortening & Fats: Oils: Dillweed*
Dim Sum *See Ethnic Foods: Dim Sum*
Dip Mixes *See Doughs, Mixes & Fillings: Mixes: Dip*
Dipping Fruit *See Fruits & Vegetables: Dipping Fruit*
Dips *See Sauces, Dips & Dressings: Dips*
Distilled Water *See Beverages: Water: Distilled*
Divinity Candy *See Candy & Confectionery: Candy: Divinity*
Dogfish *See Fish & Seafood: Fish: Dogfish*
Dolcetto *See Beverages: Wines: Red Grape Wines: Dolcetto*
Dolphin *See Fish & Seafood: Fish: Dolphin*
Donut Mixes *See Doughs, Mixes & Fillings: Mixes: Donut*
Doughnut Doughs *See Doughs, Mixes & Fillings: Doughs: Doughnuts*
Doughnut Fillings *See Doughs, Mixes & Fillings: Fillings: Doughnuts*
Doughnuts *See Baked Goods: Cakes & Pastries: Doughnuts*
Doughs *See Doughs, Mixes & Fillings: Doughs*
Dressing Flavors *See Ingredients, Flavors & Additives: Flavors: Flavors: Dressing*
Dried & Dehydrated Fruits *See Fruits & Vegetables: Dried & Dehydrated Fruits*
Dried & Dehydrated Vegetables *See Fruits & Vegetables: Dried & Dehydrated Vegetables*
Dried Apple *See Fruits & Vegetables: Apple: Dried*
Dried Apricot *See Fruits & Vegetables: Apricot: Dried*
Dried Banana *See Fruits & Vegetables: Banana: Dried*
Dried Beans *See Fruits & Vegetables: Beans: Dried*
Dried Beet Pulp *See Fruits & Vegetables: Pulps & Purees: Pulp: Dried Beet*
Dried Blueberry *See Fruits & Vegetables: Berries: Blueberry: Dried*
Dried Cantaloupe *See Fruits & Vegetables: Melon: Cantaloupe: Dried*
Dried Cayenne Pepper *See Spices, Seasonings & Seeds: Spices: Cayenne Pepper: Dried*
Dried Cherries *See Fruits & Vegetables: Cherries: Dried*
Dried Chicken Fats *See Oils, Shortening & Fats: Fats & Lard: Chicken: Dried*
Dried Chile Peppers *See Fruits & Vegetables: Peppers: Chile: Dried Pods*
Dried Chives *See Fruits & Vegetables: Dried & Dehydrated Vegetables: Dried Chives*
Dried Coconut *See Fruits & Vegetables: Coconut & Coconut Products: Dried*
Dried Cranberry *See Fruits & Vegetables: Berries: Cranberry: Dried*
Dried Cream *See Dairy Products: Cream: Dried*
Dried Egg *See Eggs & Egg Products: Dried*
Dried Fruit *See Fruits & Vegetables: Dried & Dehydrated Fruits: Dried Fruit*
Dried Honey *See Sugars, Syrups & Sweeteners: Honey: Dried*
Dried Mango *See Fruits & Vegetables: Mango: Dried*
Dried Molasses *See Sugars, Syrups & Sweeteners: Molasses: Dried*
Dried Papaya *See Fruits & Vegetables: Papaya: Dried*
Dried Peach *See Fruits & Vegetables: Peach: Dried*
Dried Pear *See Fruits & Vegetables: Pear: Dried*
Dried Pineapple *See Fruits & Vegetables: Pineapple: Dried*
Dried Plums *See Fruits & Vegetables: Plums: Dried*
Dried Prunes *See Fruits & Vegetables: Prunes: Dried*
Dried Raisins *See Fruits & Vegetables: Raisins: Dried*
Dried Refried Beans *See Fruits & Vegetables: Beans: Refried: Dried*
Dried Sliced Beef *See Meats & Meat Products: Beef & Beef Products: Sliced: Dried*
Dried Spices *See Spices, Seasonings & Seeds: Spices: Dried*
Dried Strawberry *See Fruits & Vegetables: Berries: Strawberry: Dried*
Dried Tomato *See Fruits & Vegetables: Tomato: Dried*
Drink Mixes *See Doughs, Mixes & Fillings: Mixes: Drink*
Dry Beans *See Fruits & Vegetables: Beans: Dry*
Dry Buttermilk *See Dairy Products: Buttermilk & Buttermilk Products: Buttermilk Products: Dry*
Dry Malt *See Cereals, Grains, Rice & Flour: Malt: Dry*
Dry Pancake Batters *See Doughs, Mixes & Fillings: Batters: Pancake: Dry*
Dry Peas *See Fruits & Vegetables: Peas: Dry*
Dry Raisin Juice *See Ingredients, Flavors & Additives: Replacers: Raisin Juice: Dry*
Dry Sweetcream Buttermilk *See Dairy Products: Buttermilk & Buttermilk Products: Buttermilk Products: Dry Sweetcream*
Duck *See Meats & Meat Products: Poultry: Duck*
Duck Sauces *See Sauces, Dips & Dressings: Sauces: Duck*
Dumpling Mixes *See Doughs, Mixes & Fillings: Mixes: Dumplings*
Dumplings *See Baked Goods: Cakes & Pastries: Dumplings*
Dungeness Crab *See Fish & Seafood: Shellfish: Crab: Dungeness*
Dusting Starches *See Ingredients, Flavors & Additives: Starches: Dusting*
Dutch *See Ethnic Foods: Dutch*
Dyes *See Ingredients, Flavors & Additives: Colors: Dyes*

E

E - Tocopherol *See Ingredients, Flavors & Additives: Vitamins & Supplements: E - Tocopherol*
Earl Grey Tea *See Beverages: Coffee & Tea: Tea: Earl Grey*
Earl Grey Tea, Decaffeinated *See Beverages: Coffee & Tea: Tea: Earl Grey Decaffeinated*
Easter Specialty-Packaged Candy *See Candy & Confectionery: Specialty-Packaged Candy: Easter*
Eastern Oregon Dry Bulb Onion *See Fruits & Vegetables: Onion: Eastern Oregon Dry Bulb Onion*
Echinacea Purpurea Powders *See Ingredients, Flavors & Additives: Powders: Echinacea Purpurea*
Eclairs *See Baked Goods: Cakes & Pastries: Eclairs*
Edam *See Cheese & Cheese Products: Cheese: Edam*
Edible Coatings *See Ingredients, Flavors & Additives: Coatings: Edible*
Edible Dry Beans *See Fruits & Vegetables: Beans: Dry: Edible*
Edible Oils *See Oils, Shortening & Fats: Oils: Edible*
Edible Release, Grease Agents *See Ingredients, Flavors & Additives: Agents: Release,Grease: Edible*
Eel *See Fish & Seafood: Fish: Eel*
Egg Drop Soup *See Prepared Foods: Soups & Stews: Egg Drop Soup*
Egg Nog *See Dairy Products: Egg Nog*
Egg Noodles *See Pasta & Noodles: Noodles: Egg*
Egg Powders *See Ingredients, Flavors & Additives: Powders: Egg*
Egg Replacers *See Ingredients, Flavors & Additives: Replacers: Egg*
Egg Rolls *See Ethnic Foods: Egg Rolls*
Egg Substitutes *See Eggs & Egg Products: Substitutes*
Egg Tomato *See Fruits & Vegetables: Tomato: Roma (Egg)*
Eggplant *See Fruits & Vegetables: Eggplant*
Eggplant Parmigiana *See Prepared Foods: Prepared Meals: Eggplant Parmigiana*
Eggplant, Dried & Dehydrated *See Fruits & Vegetables: Dried & Dehydrated Vegetables: Eggplant*
Eggs & Egg Products *See Eggs & Egg Products*
Eggs, Pickled Products *See Relishes & Pickled Products: Pickled Products: Eggs*
Eggs, Prepared Meals *See Prepared Foods: Prepared Meals: Eggs*
Elbow Macaroni *See Pasta & Noodles: Elbow Macaroni*
Emu *See Meats & Meat Products: Game: Emu*
Emulsifiers *See Ingredients, Flavors & Additives: Emulsifiers*
Enchiladas *See Ethnic Foods: Enchiladas*
Endive *See Spices, Seasonings & Seeds: Spices: Endive*
Energy Bars *See Specialty & Organic Foods: Health & Dietary: Energy Bars*
English Breakfast Tea *See Beverages: Coffee & Tea: Tea: English Breakfast*
English Breakfast Tea, Decaffeinated *See Beverages: Coffee & Tea: Tea: English Breakfast Decaffeinated*
English Muffins *See Baked Goods: Breads: English Muffins*
English Style B Ale *See Beverages: Beers: American & British Ale: English Style B*
Enhancers *See Ingredients, Flavors & Additives: Enhancers*

Enokis Mushrooms *See Fruits & Vegetables: Mushrooms: Enokis*
Enrichment & Nutrient Additives *See Ingredients, Flavors & Additives: Additives: Enrichment & Nutrient*
Enrichment Blends *See Ingredients, Flavors & Additives: Blends: Enrichment*
Entrees Prepared Meals *See Prepared Foods: Prepared Meals: Entrees*
Enzymes *See Ingredients, Flavors & Additives: Enzymes*
Enzymes Additives *See Ingredients, Flavors & Additives: Additives: Enzymes*
Epazote Herb *See Spices, Seasonings & Seeds: Spices: Epazote Herb*
Escargot *See Prepared Foods: Prepared Meals: Escargot*
Escarole *See Spices, Seasonings & Seeds: Spices: Escarole*
Espresso *See Beverages: Coffee & Tea: Espresso*
Essential Fatty Acids *See Ingredients, Flavors & Additives: Fatty Acids: Essential*
Essential Oils *See Oils, Shortening & Fats: Oils: Essential*
Ethnic Foods *See Ethnic Foods*
Ethyleneamines *See Ingredients, Flavors & Additives: Ethyleneamines*
Etoufee *See Prepared Foods: Prepared Meals: Etoufee*
Evaporated Milk *See Dairy Products: Milk & Milk Products: Milk: Evaporated*
Extenders *See Ingredients, Flavors & Additives: Extenders*
Extra Virgin Olive Oils *See Oils, Shortening & Fats: Oils: Olive: Extra Virgin*
Extract Flavors *See Ingredients, Flavors & Additives: Flavors: Extract*
Extracts *See Ingredients, Flavors & Additives: Extracts*
Extracts, Spices *See Spices, Seasonings & Seeds: Spices: Extracts*
Extracts, Yeast *See Ingredients, Flavors & Additives: Cultures & Yeasts: Yeast: Extracts*

F

Fair-Trade Tea *See Beverages: Coffee & Tea: Tea: Fair-Trade*
Fajita Chicken Strips *See Meats & Meat Products: Poultry: Chicken: Fajita Strips*
Fajita Marinades *See Sauces, Dips & Dressings: Marinades: Fajita*
Fajita Seasonings *See Spices, Seasonings & Seeds: Seasonings: Fajita*
Farfalle *See Pasta & Noodles: Farfalle*
Farina Cereal *See Cereals, Grains, Rice & Flour: Cereal: Farina*
Farm-Raised Game *See Meats & Meat Products: Game: Farm-Raised*
Fat & Cholesterol Free *See Eggs & Egg Products: Fat & Cholesterol Free*
Fat Flavors *See Ingredients, Flavors & Additives: Flavors: Fat*
Fat Replacers *See Ingredients, Flavors & Additives: Replacers: Fat*
Fat-Free Ice Cream *See Dairy Products: Ice Cream: Fat-Free*
Fat-Free Milk *See Dairy Products: Milk & Milk Products: Milk: Fat-Free*
Fats *See Oils, Shortening & Fats*
Fats & Lard *See Oils, Shortening & Fats: Fats & Lard*
Fatty Acids *See Ingredients, Flavors & Additives: Fatty Acids*
Fava Beans *See Fruits & Vegetables: Beans: Fava*
Fennel Seeds *See Spices, Seasonings & Seeds: Seeds: Fennel*
Fennel Spices *See Spices, Seasonings & Seeds: Spices: Fennel*
Fenugreek Seeds *See Spices, Seasonings & Seeds: Seeds: Fenugreek*
Fenugreek Spices *See Spices, Seasonings & Seeds: Spices: Fenugreek*
Fermented Products *See Specialty Processed Foods: Fermented Products (See also Specific Foods)*
Feta Cheese *See Cheese & Cheese Products: Cheese: Feta*
Fettuccine *See Pasta & Noodles: Fettuccine*
Feverfew Powders *See Ingredients, Flavors & Additives: Powders: Feverfew*
Fiber *See Cereals, Grains, Rice & Flour: Fiber*
Fig Pastes *See Ingredients, Flavors & Additives: Pastes: Fig*
Fig, Dried *See Fruits & Vegetables: Dried & Dehydrated Fruits: Fig*
Figs *See Fruits & Vegetables: Figs*
Filberts *See Nuts & Nut Butters: Nuts: Filberts*
Filet Mignon *See Meats & Meat Products: Beef & Beef Products: Filet Mignon*
Filled Candy *See Candy & Confectionery: Candy: Filled*
Filled Doughnuts *See Baked Goods: Cakes & Pastries: Doughnuts: Filled*
Fillers *See Ingredients, Flavors & Additives: Fillers*
Fillets, Chicken *See Meats & Meat Products: Poultry: Chicken: Fillets*
Fillets, Fish *See Fish & Seafood: Fish: Fillets*
Fillets, Herring *See Fish & Seafood: Fish: Herring: Fillets*
Fillets, Turkey *See Meats & Meat Products: Poultry: Turkey: Fillets*
Fillings *See Doughs, Mixes & Fillings: Fillings*
Finfish *See Fish & Seafood: Fish: Finfish*
Fire Roasted Vegetables *See Fruits & Vegetables: Fire Roasted Vegetables*
Firming Agents *See Ingredients, Flavors & Additives: Agents: Firming*
Fish *See Fish & Seafood: Fish; See also Prepared Foods: Prepared Meals: Fish*
Fish & Chips *See Prepared Foods: Prepared Meals: Fish & Chips*
Fish Oils *See Oils, Shortening & Fats: Oils: Fish*
Fish Paste *See Fish & Seafood: Fish: Paste*
Fish Patties *See Prepared Foods: Prepared Meals: Fish Patties*
Fish Powders *See Ingredients, Flavors & Additives: Powders: Fish*
Fish Sauces *See Sauces, Dips & Dressings: Sauces: Fish*
Fish Steaks *See Fish & Seafood: Fish: Steaks*
Fish Sticks *See Prepared Foods: Prepared Meals: Fish Sticks; See also See Fish & Seafood: Fish: Sticks*
Flakes *See Ingredients, Flavors & Additives: Flakes*
Flat Breads *See Baked Goods: Breads: Flat*
Flavor Bases *See Ingredients, Flavors & Additives: Bases: Flavor*
Flavor Bits *See Ingredients, Flavors & Additives: Bits: Flavor*
Flavor Enhancers *See Ingredients, Flavors & Additives: Flavors: Flavors: Enhancers; See also See Ingredients, Flavors & Additives: Flavor Enhancers*
Flavored Cheese Cake *See Baked Goods: Cakes & Pastries: Cheese Cake: Flavored*
Flavored Coffee *See Beverages: Coffee & Tea: Coffee: Flavored*
Flavored Ice Cream *See Dairy Products: Ice Cream: Flavored*
Flavored Liquid Vinegar *See Sauces, Dips & Dressings: Vinegar: Liquid: Flavored*
Flavored Milk *See Dairy Products: Milk & Milk Products: Milk: Flavored*
Flavored Pellets *See Ingredients, Flavors & Additives: Half-Products: Flavored Pellets*
Flavored Popcorn *See Snack Foods: Popcorn: Flavored*
Flavored Pretzels *See Snack Foods: Pretzels: Flavored*
Flavored Stout *See Beverages: Beers: Stout & Porter: Flavored Stout*
Flavored Sugar Bits *See Ingredients, Flavors & Additives: Bits: Flavored Sugar*
Flavored Tea *See Beverages: Coffee & Tea: Tea: Flavored*
Flavored Water *See Beverages: Water: Flavored*
Flavored Wraps *See Baked Goods: Wraps: Flavored*
Flavoring Extracts *See Ingredients, Flavors & Additives: Extracts: Flavoring*
Flavors *See Ingredients, Flavors & Additives: Flavors; See also Ingredients, Flavors & Additives: Flavors: Flavors*
Flax Crisps *See Cereals, Grains, Rice & Flour: Crisps: Flax*
Flax Seeds *See Spices, Seasonings & Seeds: Seeds: Flax*
Flounder *See Fish & Seafood: Fish: Flounder*
Flour *See Cereals, Grains, Rice & Flour: Flour*
Flour, Rice Starch, Organic *See Specialty & Organic Foods: Organic Foods: Rice Starch: Flour*
Flowers, Edible *See Fruits & Vegetables: Flowers - Edible*
Fluid Shortening *See Oils, Shortening & Fats: Shortening: Fluid*
Fluke *See Fish & Seafood: Fish: Fluke*
Foaming & Whipping Agents *See Ingredients, Flavors & Additives: Agents: Foaming & Whipping*
Focaccia *See Baked Goods: Breads: Focaccia*
Foie Gras *See Meats & Meat Products: Pates & Fois Gras: Foie Gras*
Fondant *See Sugars, Syrups & Sweeteners: Sugar: Fondant*
Fondants *See Candy & Confectionery: Candy: Fondants*
Fontina Cheese *See Cheese & Cheese Products: Cheese: Fontina*
Food Bases *See Ingredients, Flavors & Additives: Bases: Food*
Food Ingredients *See Ingredients, Flavors & Additives: Ingredients: Food*
Food Preservatives *See Ingredients, Flavors & Additives: Preservatives: Food*
Food Releases *See Ingredients, Flavors & Additives: Releases: Food*
Foodservice, Individual Packets *See Prepared Foods: Individual Packets: Foodservice*
Formula *See Baby Foods: Formula*
Fortification Protein *See Ingredients, Flavors & Additives: Vitamins & Supplements: Protein Supplements: Fortification Protein*
Fortified Refined Vegetable Oils *See Oils, Shortening & Fats: Oils: Vegetable: Fortified Refined*
Fortune Cookies *See Baked Goods: Cookies & Bars: Fortune Cookies*
Fra Diavolo Sauces *See Sauces, Dips & Dressings: Sauces: Fra Diavolo*
Fragrances *See Ingredients, Flavors & Additives: Aroma Chemicals & Materials: Fragrances*
Frankfurters *See Meats & Meat Products: Frankfurters*
Frankfurters, Mini *See Meats & Meat Products: Frankfurters: Mini*
Free Flow Additives *See Ingredients, Flavors & Additives: Additives: Free Flow*
Freeze-Dried Food *See Specialty Processed Foods: Freeze Dried Food (See also Specific Foods)*
Freeze-Dried Fruits & Vegetables *See Fruits & Vegetables: Dehydrated: Freeze Dried; See also Fruits & Vegetables: Dried & Dehydrated Fruits: Freeze Dried; See also Fruits & Vegetables: Dried & Dehydrated Vegetables: Freeze Dried*
Freeze-Dried Mushrooms *See Fruits & Vegetables: Dried & Dehydrated Vegetables: Mushrooms: Freeze Dried*
Freeze-Dried Seafood *See Fish & Seafood: Seafood: Freeze-Dried*
French Breads *See Baked Goods: Breads: French*
French Fries *See Prepared Foods: French Fries*
French Salad Dressings *See Sauces, Dips & Dressings: Salad Dressings: French; See also See Sauces, Dips & Dressings: Salad Dressings: Mixes: French*
French Toast *See Prepared Foods: French Toast*
French Wines *See Beverages: Wines: French*
Fresh Apple *See Fruits & Vegetables: Apple: Fresh*
Fresh Bagels *See Baked Goods: Breads: Bagels: Fresh*
Fresh Bakes Goods *See Baked Goods: Fresh*
Fresh Beef *See Meats & Meat Products: Beef & Beef Products: Fresh*
Fresh Biscuits *See Baked Goods: Breads: Biscuits: Fresh*
Fresh Breads *See Baked Goods: Breads: Fresh*
Fresh Chicken *See Meats & Meat Products: Poultry: Chicken: Fresh*
Fresh Clam *See Fish & Seafood: Shellfish: Clam: Fresh*
Fresh Crab *See Fish & Seafood: Shellfish: Crab: Fresh*
Fresh Cream *See Dairy Products: Cream: Fresh*
Fresh Eggs *See Eggs & Egg Products: Fresh*
Fresh Fish *See Fish & Seafood: Fish: Fresh*
Fresh Fish Cakes *See Fish & Seafood: Fish: Cakes: Fresh*
Fresh Fruit *See Fruits & Vegetables: Fresh Fruit*
Fresh Ham *See Meats & Meat Products: Smoked, Cured & Deli Meats: Ham: Fresh*
Fresh Herring *See Fish & Seafood: Fish: Herring: Fresh*
Fresh Lamb *See Meats & Meat Products: Lamb: Fresh*
Fresh Lobster *See Fish & Seafood: Shellfish: Lobster: Fresh*
Fresh Milk *See Dairy Products: Milk & Milk Products: Milk: Fresh*
Fresh Mushrooms *See Fruits & Vegetables: Mushrooms: Fresh*
Fresh Oysters *See Fish & Seafood: Shellfish: Oysters: Fresh*
Fresh Peas *See Fruits & Vegetables: Peas: Fresh*
Fresh Pies *See Baked Goods: Pies: Fresh*
Fresh Pork *See Meats & Meat Products: Pork & Pork Products: Fresh*
Fresh Potatoes *See Fruits & Vegetables: Potatoes: Fresh*
Fresh Prepared Foods *See Prepared Foods: Fresh*
Fresh Rolls *See Baked Goods: Breads: Rolls: Fresh*
Fresh Sardines *See Fish & Seafood: Fish: Sardines: Fresh*
Fresh Seafood *See Fish & Seafood: Seafood: Fresh*
Fresh Shellfish *See Fish & Seafood: Shellfish: Fresh*
Fresh Shrimp *See Fish & Seafood: Shellfish: Shrimp: Fresh*
Fresh Soy *See Fruits & Vegetables: Soy: Fresh*

1 2 3 4 5

EXAMPLE: **Canadian Style Bacon** *See Meats & Meat Products: Smoked, Cured & Deli Meats: Bacon: Canadian Style*

1. Product or Service you are looking for
2. Main Category, in alphabetical order, located in the page headers starting on page 23
3. Category Description, located in black bars and in page headers
4. Product Category, located in gray bars
5. Product Type, located under gray bars, centered in bold

Fresh Stew *See Prepared Foods: Soups & Stews: Fresh Stew*
Fresh Succotash *See Fruits & Vegetables: Succotash: Fresh*
Fresh Tomato *See Fruits & Vegetables: Tomato: Fresh*
Fresh Turkey *See Meats & Meat Products: Poultry: Turkey: Fresh*
Fresh Veal *See Meats & Meat Products: Beef & Beef Products: Veal: Fresh*
Fresh Vegetables *See Fruits & Vegetables: Fresh Vegetables*
Fresh Yeast *See Ingredients, Flavors & Additives: Cultures & Yeasts: Yeast: Fresh*
Freshwater Fish *See Fish & Seafood: Fish: Freshwater*
Fried Chips *See Snack Foods: Chips: Fried*
Fried Oysters *See Fish & Seafood: Shellfish: Oysters: Fried*
Fried Porkskins *See Prepared Foods: Porkskins: Fried*
Fried Rice, Prepared Meals *See Prepared Foods: Prepared Meals: Fried Rice*
Fried Rice, Seasonings *See Spices, Seasonings & Seeds: Seasonings: Fried Rice*
Frozen Appetizers *See Prepared Foods: Appetizers: Frozen*
Frozen Apple *See Fruits & Vegetables: Apple: Frozen*
Frozen Apple Juices *See Beverages: Juices: Apple: Frozen*
Frozen Apricot *See Fruits & Vegetables: Apricot: Frozen*
Frozen Apricot Juices *See Beverages: Juices: Apricot: Frozen*
Frozen Artichoke *See Fruits & Vegetables: Artichoke: Frozen*
Frozen Asparagus *See Fruits & Vegetables: Asparagus: Frozen*
Frozen Au Gratin Potatoes *See Fruits & Vegetables: Potatoes: Au Gratin: Frozen*
Frozen Bagels *See Baked Goods: Breads: Bagels: Frozen*
Frozen Baked & Stuffed Potatoes *See Fruits & Vegetables: Potatoes: Baked & Stuffed: Frozen*
Frozen Baked Goods *See Baked Goods: Frozen*
Frozen Baking Doughs *See Doughs, Mixes & Fillings: Doughs: Baking: Frozen*
Frozen Barbecued Beef *See Meats & Meat Products: Beef & Beef Products: Barbecued: Frozen*
Frozen Barbecued Pork *See Meats & Meat Products: Pork & Pork Products: Barbecued: Frozen*
Frozen Beans *See Fruits & Vegetables: Beans: Frozen*
Frozen Beef & Beef Products *See Meats & Meat Products: Beef & Beef Products: Frozen*
Frozen Beef Stew *See Meats & Meat Products: Beef & Beef Products: Stew: Frozen*
Frozen Beets *See Fruits & Vegetables: Beets: Frozen*
Frozen Berries *See Fruits & Vegetables: Berries: Frozen*
Frozen Beverage Mixes *See Doughs, Mixes & Fillings: Mixes: Beverage: Frozen*
Frozen Biscuits *See Baked Goods: Breads: Biscuits: Frozen*
Frozen Black-eyed Peas *See Fruits & Vegetables: Peas: Black-eyed: Frozen*
Frozen Blackberry *See Fruits & Vegetables: Berries: Blackberry: Frozen*
Frozen Blintzes *See Baked Goods: Cakes & Pastries: Blintzes: Frozen*
Frozen Blue Lake Beans *See Fruits & Vegetables: Beans: Blue Lake: Frozen*
Frozen Blueberry *See Fruits & Vegetables: Berries: Blueberry: Frozen*
Frozen Boysenberry *See Fruits & Vegetables: Berries: Boysenberry: Frozen*
Frozen Breads *See Baked Goods: Breads: Frozen*
Frozen Broccoli *See Fruits & Vegetables: Broccoli: Frozen*
Frozen Broth *See Prepared Foods: Broth: Frozen*
Frozen Brussel Sprouts *See Fruits & Vegetables: Brussel Sprouts: Frozen*
Frozen Buns *See Baked Goods: Breads: Buns: Frozen*
Frozen Butter Beans *See Fruits & Vegetables: Beans: Butter: Frozen*
Frozen Cabbage *See Fruits & Vegetables: Cabbage: Frozen*
Frozen Cake Batters *See Doughs, Mixes & Fillings: Batters: Cake: Frozen*
Frozen Cakes *See Baked Goods: Cakes & Pastries: Frozen Cakes*
Frozen Cappuccino Mixes *See Doughs, Mixes & Fillings: Mixes: Cappuccino: Frozen*
Frozen Capsicums Peppers *See Fruits & Vegetables: Peppers: Capsicums: Frozen*
Frozen Carrot *See Fruits & Vegetables: Carrot: Frozen*
Frozen Cauliflower *See Fruits & Vegetables: Cauliflower: Frozen*
Frozen Celery *See Fruits & Vegetables: Celery: Frozen*
Frozen Cheese Cake *See Baked Goods: Cakes & Pastries: Cheese Cake: Frozen*
Frozen Cherries *See Fruits & Vegetables: Cherries: Frozen*
Frozen Cherry Juices *See Beverages: Juices: Cherry: Frozen*
Frozen Chicken *See Meats & Meat Products: Poultry: Chicken: Frozen*
Frozen Chicken Fats & Lard *See Oils, Shortening & Fats: Fats & Lard: Chicken: Frozen*
Frozen Chili *See Prepared Foods: Chili: Frozen*
Frozen Chop Suey *See Ethnic Foods: Chop Suey: Frozen*
Frozen Clam *See Fish & Seafood: Shellfish: Clam: Frozen*
Frozen Clam Strips *See Fish & Seafood: Shellfish: Clam: Frozen Strips*
Frozen Coconut & Coconut Products *See Fruits & Vegetables: Coconut & Coconut Products: Frozen*
Frozen Convenience Food *See Prepared Foods: Convenience Food: Frozen*
Frozen Cookies *See Baked Goods: Cookies & Bars: Frozen Cookies*
Frozen Corn *See Fruits & Vegetables: Corn: Frozen*
Frozen Corn-on-the-Cob *See Fruits & Vegetables: Corn: Corn-on-the-Cob: Frozen*
Frozen Crab *See Fish & Seafood: Shellfish: Crab: Frozen; See also See Prepared Foods: Prepared Meals: Crab: Frozen*
Frozen Crab Meat *See Fish & Seafood: Shellfish: Crab: Meat Frozen*
Frozen Cranberry *See Fruits & Vegetables: Berries: Cranberry: Frozen*
Frozen Cranberry Juices *See Beverages: Juices: Cranberry: Frozen*
Frozen Crayfish *See Fish & Seafood: Shellfish: Crayfish: Frozen*
Frozen Crepes *See Prepared Foods: Crepes: Frozen*
Frozen Dehydrated Potatoes *See Fruits & Vegetables: Potatoes: Dehydrated: Frozen*
Frozen Doughnuts *See Baked Goods: Cakes & Pastries: Doughnuts: Frozen*
Frozen Doughs *See Doughs, Mixes & Fillings: Doughs: Frozen*
Frozen Eggs *See Eggs & Egg Products: Frozen*
Frozen Enchiladas *See Ethnic Foods: Enchiladas: Frozen*
Frozen Entrees *See Prepared Foods: Prepared Meals: Entrees: Frozen*
Frozen Figs *See Fruits & Vegetables: Figs: Frozen*
Frozen Fish *See Fish & Seafood: Fish: Frozen*
Frozen Fish Cakes *See Fish & Seafood: Fish: Cakes: Frozen*
Frozen Fish Sticks *See Prepared Foods: Prepared Meals: Fish Sticks: Frozen*
Frozen Foods *See Specialty Processed Foods: Frozen Foods (See also Specific Foods)*
Frozen French Fries *See Prepared Foods: French Fries: Frozen*
Frozen French Toast *See Prepared Foods: French Toast: Frozen*
Frozen Fruit *See Fruits & Vegetables: Frozen Fruit*
Frozen Fruit & Vegetable Juices *See Beverages: Juices: Fruit & Vegetable: Frozen*
Frozen Fruit Juices *See Beverages: Juices: Fruit: Frozen*
Frozen Fruit Pies *See Baked Goods: Pies: Fruit: Frozen*
Frozen Garlic Breads *See Baked Goods: Breads: Garlic: Frozen*
Frozen Gnocchi *See Pasta & Noodles: Gnocchi: Frozen*
Frozen Grape Juices *See Beverages: Juices: Grape: Frozen*
Frozen Grapefruit Juices *See Beverages: Juices: Grapefruit: Frozen*
Frozen Green Beans *See Fruits & Vegetables: Beans: Green: Frozen*
Frozen Ground Beef & Beef Products *See Meats & Meat Products: Beef & Beef Products: Ground: Frozen*
Frozen Ham *See Meats & Meat Products: Smoked, Cured & Deli Meats: Ham: Frozen*
Frozen Herring *See Fish & Seafood: Fish: Herring: Frozen*
Frozen Kale *See Fruits & Vegetables: Kale: Frozen*
Frozen Kidney Beans *See Fruits & Vegetables: Beans: Kidney: Frozen*
Frozen Lamb *See Meats & Meat Products: Lamb: Frozen*
Frozen Lasagna *See Pasta & Noodles: Lasagna: Frozen*
Frozen Lemon Juices *See Beverages: Juices: Lemon: Frozen*
Frozen Lima Beans *See Fruits & Vegetables: Beans: Lima: Frozen*
Frozen Lobster *See Fish & Seafood: Shellfish: Lobster: Frozen*
Frozen Mashed Sweet Potatoes *See Fruits & Vegetables: Sweet Potatoes: Mashed: Frozen*
Frozen Meat Balls *See Prepared Foods: Meat Balls: Frozen*
Frozen Meat Pies *See Baked Goods: Pies: Meat: Frozen*
Frozen Melon Balls *See Fruits & Vegetables: Melon: Balls: Frozen*
Frozen Mixes *See Doughs, Mixes & Fillings: Mixes: Frozen*
Frozen Mozzarella Cheese, Lite Shredded *See Cheese & Cheese Products: Cheese: Mozzarella: Lite Shredded - Frozen*
Frozen Muffins *See Baked Goods: Cakes & Pastries: Muffins: Frozen*
Frozen Mushrooms *See Fruits & Vegetables: Mushrooms: Frozen*
Frozen Non-Dairy Desserts *See Baked Goods: Desserts: Non-Dairy: Frozen*
Frozen Non-Fruit Pies *See Baked Goods: Pies: Non-Fruit: Frozen*
Frozen Okra *See Fruits & Vegetables: Okra: Frozen*
Frozen Onion *See Fruits & Vegetables: Onion: Frozen*
Frozen Onion Rings *See Prepared Foods: Onion Rings: Frozen*
Frozen Oven Type Potatoes *See Fruits & Vegetables: Potatoes: Oven Type: Frozen*
Frozen Oysters *See Fish & Seafood: Shellfish: Oysters: Frozen*
Frozen Pancakes *See Prepared Foods: Pancakes: Frozen*
Frozen Pasta *See Pasta & Noodles: Pasta: Frozen*
Frozen Patties Beef & Beef Products *See Meats & Meat Products: Beef & Beef Products: Patties: Frozen*
Frozen Peach *See Fruits & Vegetables: Peach: Frozen*
Frozen Pear *See Fruits & Vegetables: Pear: Frozen*
Frozen Peas *See Fruits & Vegetables: Peas: Frozen*
Frozen Peas & Carrots *See Fruits & Vegetables: Vegetables Mixed: Peas & Carrots: Frozen*
Frozen Peppers *See Fruits & Vegetables: Peppers: Frozen*
Frozen Pineapple *See Fruits & Vegetables: Pineapple: Frozen*
Frozen Pineapple Juices *See Beverages: Juices: Pineapple: Frozen*
Frozen Pizza *See Prepared Foods: Pizza & Pizza Products: Pizza: Frozen*
Frozen Pizza Doughs *See Doughs, Mixes & Fillings: Doughs: Pizza: Frozen*
Frozen Pizza Shells *See Prepared Foods: Pizza & Pizza Products: Shells: Frozen*
Frozen Plums *See Fruits & Vegetables: Plums: Frozen*
Frozen Pork & Pork Products *See Meats & Meat Products: Pork & Pork Products: Frozen*
Frozen Potato Rounds *See Fruits & Vegetables: Potatoes: Frozen: Rounds*
Frozen Potatoes *See Fruits & Vegetables: Potatoes: Frozen*
Frozen Prepared Foods *See Prepared Foods: Frozen*
Frozen Prepared Meals *See Prepared Foods: Prepared Meals: Frozen*
Frozen Prepared Pork & Pork Products *See Meats & Meat Products: Pork & Pork Products: Prepared: Frozen*
Frozen Prunes *See Fruits & Vegetables: Prunes: Frozen*
Frozen Pumpkin *See Fruits & Vegetables: Pumpkin: Frozen*
Frozen Rabbit *See Meats & Meat Products: Game: Rabbit: Frozen*
Frozen Raspberries *See Fruits & Vegetables: Berries: Raspberries: Frozen*
Frozen Ravioli *See Pasta & Noodles: Ravioli: Frozen*
Frozen Rhubarb *See Fruits & Vegetables: Rhubarb: Frozen*
Frozen Rice *See Cereals, Grains, Rice & Flour: Rice: Frozen*
Frozen Rolls *See Baked Goods: Breads: Rolls: Frozen*
Frozen Rutabaga *See Fruits & Vegetables: Rutabaga: Frozen*
Frozen Sauces *See Sauces, Dips & Dressings: Sauces: Frozen*
Frozen Scampi *See Fish & Seafood: Shellfish: Scampi: Frozen*
Frozen Seafood *See Fish & Seafood: Seafood: Frozen*
Frozen Shellfish *See Fish & Seafood: Shellfish: Frozen*
Frozen Shrimp *See Fish & Seafood: Shellfish: Shrimp: Frozen*
Frozen Sliced Beef & Beef Products *See Meats & Meat Products: Beef & Beef Products: Sliced: Frozen*
Frozen Slices Apple *See Fruits & Vegetables: Apple: Slices: Frozen*
Frozen Soup *See Prepared Foods: Soups & Stews: Frozen Soup*
Frozen Spaghetti *See Pasta & Noodles: Spaghetti: Frozen*
Frozen Special Trim Beef & Beef Products *See Meats & Meat Products: Beef & Beef Products: Special Trim: Frozen*
Frozen Spinach *See Fruits & Vegetables: Spinach: Frozen*
Frozen Squash *See Fruits & Vegetables: Squash: Frozen*
Frozen Stew *See Prepared Foods: Soups & Stews: Frozen Stew*
Frozen Strawberry *See Fruits & Vegetables: Berries: Strawberry: Frozen*
Frozen Stuffed Cabbage *See Prepared Foods: Prepared Meals: Stuffed Cabbage: Frozen*
Frozen Substitutes *See Eggs & Egg Products: Substitutes: Frozen*
Frozen Succotash *See Fruits & Vegetables: Succotash: Frozen*

Frozen Sweet Potatoes *See Fruits & Vegetables: Sweet Potatoes: Frozen*
Frozen Tamales *See Ethnic Foods: Tamales: Frozen*
Frozen Tomato *See Fruits & Vegetables: Tomato: Frozen*
Frozen Tomato Juices *See Beverages: Juices: Tomato: Frozen*
Frozen Tomato Sauces *See Sauces, Dips & Dressings: Sauces: Tomato: Frozen*
Frozen Tuna *See Fish & Seafood: Fish: Tuna: Frozen*
Frozen Turkey *See Meats & Meat Products: Poultry: Turkey: Frozen*
Frozen Turnip *See Fruits & Vegetables: Turnip: Frozen*
Frozen Veal *See Meats & Meat Products: Beef & Beef Products: Veal: Frozen*
Frozen Vegetables *See Fruits & Vegetables: Frozen Vegetables*
Frozen Vegetables Mixed *See Fruits & Vegetables: Vegetables Mixed: Frozen*
Frozen Venison *See Meats & Meat Products: Game: Venison: Frozen*
Frozen Waffles *See Baked Goods: Waffles: Frozen*
Frozen Wax Beans *See Fruits & Vegetables: Beans: Wax: Frozen*
Frozen Yams *See Fruits & Vegetables: Yams: Frozen*
Frozen Yogurt *See Dairy Products: Yogurt: Frozen*
Frozen Yogurt Powders *See Ingredients, Flavors & Additives: Powders: Yogurt: Frozen*
Fructose *See Sugars, Syrups & Sweeteners: Fructose*
Fruit *See Fruits & Vegetables: Fruit*
Fruit & Vegetable Coating Waxes *See Ingredients, Flavors & Additives: Waxes: Fruit & Vegetable Coating*
Fruit & Vegetable Juices *See Beverages: Juices: Fruit & Vegetable*
Fruit & Vegetable Pulps & Purees *See Fruits & Vegetables: Pulps & Purees: Fruit & Vegetable*
Fruit & Vegetable Puree *See Fruits & Vegetables: Pulps & Purees: Puree: Fruit & Vegetable*
Fruit Bases *See Ingredients, Flavors & Additives: Bases: Fruit*
Fruit Butter Spreads *See Jams, Jellies & Spreads: Spreads: Fruit Butter*
Fruit Cake *See Baked Goods: Cakes & Pastries: Fruit Cake*
Fruit Cobbler *See Baked Goods: Cakes & Pastries: Fruit Cobbler*
Fruit Cocktail *See Fruits & Vegetables: Fruit Cocktail*
Fruit Concentrates *See Ingredients, Flavors & Additives: Concentrates: Fruit*
Fruit Extracts *See Ingredients, Flavors & Additives: Extracts: Fruit*
Fruit Fillings *See Doughs, Mixes & Fillings: Fillings: Fruit*
Fruit Flavors *See Ingredients, Flavors & Additives: Flavors: Fruit*
Fruit Juices *See Beverages: Juices: Fruit*
Fruit Oils *See Oils, Shortening & Fats: Oils: Fruit*
Fruit Pastes *See Ingredients, Flavors & Additives: Pastes: Fruit*
Fruit Pectins *See Ingredients, Flavors & Additives: Pectins: Fruit*
Fruit Pies *See Baked Goods: Pies: Fruit*
Fruit Powders *See Ingredients, Flavors & Additives: Powders: Fruit*
Fruit Pulp *See Fruits & Vegetables: Pulps & Purees: Pulp: Fruit*
Fruit Pulps & Purees *See Fruits & Vegetables: Pulps & Purees: Fruit*
Fruit Punch Juices *See Beverages: Juices: Fruit Punch*
Fruit Puree *See Fruits & Vegetables: Pulps & Purees: Puree: Fruit*
Fruit Puree Concentrates *See Ingredients, Flavors & Additives: Concentrates: Fruit Puree*
Fruit Salad *See Fruits & Vegetables: Fruit: Salad*
Fruit Syrups *See Sugars, Syrups & Sweeteners: Syrups: Fruit*
Fruit Toppings *See Ingredients, Flavors & Additives: Toppings: Fruit*
Fruit, Certified Organic *See Specialty & Organic Foods: Organic Foods: Certified: Fruit*
Fruits & Vegetables *See Fruits & Vegetables*
Fruits, Organic *See Specialty & Organic Foods: Organic Foods: Fruits*
Fryer Rabbit *See Meats & Meat Products: Game: Rabbit: Fryer*
Fudge Candy *See Candy & Confectionery: Candy: Fudge*
Fudge Chocolate Products *See Candy & Confectionery: Chocolate Products: Fudge*
Fudge Sauces *See Sauces, Dips & Dressings: Sauces: Fudge*
Fudgesicles *See Dairy Products: Ice Cream: Fudgesicles*
Fumaric Acidulants *See Ingredients, Flavors & Additives: Acidulants: Fumaric*
Fund Raising Specialty-Packaged Candy *See Candy & Confectionery: Specialty-Packaged Candy: Fund Raising*
Funnel Cake *See Baked Goods: Cakes & Pastries: Funnel Cake*

G

Galangal *See Fruits & Vegetables: Galangal*
Game Meat & Poultry *See Meats & Meat Products: Game: Meat & Poultry; See also See Meats & Meat Products: Game*
Garbanzo Beans *See Fruits & Vegetables: Beans: Garbanzo*
Garlic *See Fruits & Vegetables: Garlic*
Garlic Bread Sticks *See Baked Goods: Bread Sticks: Garlic*
Garlic Breads *See Baked Goods: Breads: Garlic*
Garlic Juices *See Beverages: Juices: Garlic*
Garlic Oils *See Oils, Shortening & Fats: Oils: Garlic*
Garlic Powders *See Ingredients, Flavors & Additives: Powders: Garlic (See also Spices/Garlic Powder)*
Garlic Salt *See Spices, Seasonings & Seeds: Salt: Garlic; See also See Spices, Seasonings & Seeds: Spices: Garlic Salt*
Garlic Sauces *See Sauces, Dips & Dressings: Sauces: Garlic*
Garlic Spices *See Spices, Seasonings & Seeds: Spices: Garlic*
Gefilte Fish *See Fish & Seafood: Fish: Gefilte*
Gelatin Thickeners *See Ingredients, Flavors & Additives: Thickeners: Gelatin*
Gelato *See Dairy Products: Ice Cream: Gelato*
Gellan *See Ingredients, Flavors & Additives: Gums: Gellan*
General Grocery *See General Grocery*
Geoduck Clams *See Fish & Seafood: Shellfish: Geoduck Clams*
Gewrurztraminer *See Beverages: Wines: White Grape Varieties: Gewrurztraminer*
Ghatti *See Ingredients, Flavors & Additives: Gums: Ghatti*
Gherkins Pickles *See Relishes & Pickled Products: Pickled Products: Pickles: Gherkins*
Giardiniera *See Prepared Foods: Giardiniera*
Gin *See Beverages: Spirits & Liqueurs: Gin*
Ginger *See Fruits & Vegetables: Ginger*
Ginger Ale *See Beverages: Soft Drinks & Sodas: Soft Drinks: Ginger Ale*
Ginger Oils *See Oils, Shortening & Fats: Oils: Ginger*
Ginger Pieces *See Spices, Seasonings & Seeds: Spices: Ginger: Pieces*
Ginger Sauces *See Sauces, Dips & Dressings: Sauces: Ginger*
Ginger Snaps *See Baked Goods: Cookies & Bars: Ginger Snaps*
Ginger Spices *See Spices, Seasonings & Seeds: Spices: Ginger*
Gingko Powders *See Ingredients, Flavors & Additives: Powders: Gingko*
Ginseng Powders *See Ingredients, Flavors & Additives: Powders: Ginseng*
Ginseng Spices *See Spices, Seasonings & Seeds: Spices: Ginseng*
Glace *See Fruits & Vegetables: Glace*
Glandulars *See Ingredients, Flavors & Additives: Glandulars*
Glass-Packed Apple Juices *See Beverages: Juices: Apple: Glass-Packed*
Glass-Packed Apricot Juices *See Beverages: Juices: Apricot: Glass-Packed*
Glass-Packed Cherry Juices *See Beverages: Juices: Cherry: Glass-Packed*
Glass-Packed Chilled Tomato Juices *See Beverages: Juices: Tomato: Glass-Packed Chilled*
Glass-Packed Cranberry Juices *See Beverages: Juices: Cranberry: Glass-Packed*
Glass-Packed Fish *See Fish & Seafood: Fish: Packed: Glass*
Glass-Packed Fruit & Vegetable Juices *See Beverages: Juices: Fruit & Vegetable: Glass-Packed*
Glass-Packed Fruit Juices *See Beverages: Juices: Fruit: Glass-Packed*
Glass-Packed Grape Juices *See Beverages: Juices: Grape: Glass-Packed*
Glass-Packed Grapefruit Juices *See Beverages: Juices: Grapefruit: Glass-Packed*
Glass-Packed Lemon Juices *See Beverages: Juices: Lemon: Glass-Packed*
Glass-Packed Pineapple Juices *See Beverages: Juices: Pineapple: Glass-Packed*
Glazed & Coated Nuts *See Nuts & Nut Butters: Nuts: Glazed & Coated*
Glazes *See Sauces, Dips & Dressings: Glazes*
Gluconates *See Ingredients, Flavors & Additives: Flavor Enhancers: Gluconates*
Gluconic Acids (Gluconolactone) *See Ingredients, Flavors & Additives: Acids: Gluconic (Gluconolactone)*
Glucose *See Sugars, Syrups & Sweeteners: Syrups: Corn: Glucose - Etc.*
Glutamic Acids *See Ingredients, Flavors & Additives: Acids: Glutamic*
Gluten Flour *See Cereals, Grains, Rice & Flour: Flour: Gluten*
Gluten Wheat *See Cereals, Grains, Rice & Flour: Wheat: Gluten*
Glycine *See Ingredients, Flavors & Additives: Glycine*
Gnocchi *See Pasta & Noodles: Gnocchi*
Goat *See Meats & Meat Products: Goat*
Goat Milk *See Dairy Products: Milk & Milk Products: Milk: Goat*
Goat's Cheese *See Cheese & Cheese Products: Cheese: Goat's*
Gold Kiwi *See Fruits & Vegetables: Kiwi: Gold*
Golden Delicious Apple *See Fruits & Vegetables: Apple: Golden Delicious*
Golden Scallopino Squash *See Fruits & Vegetables: Squash: Golden Scallopino*
Golden Trout *See Fish & Seafood: Fish: Trout: Golden*
Goose Berries *See Fruits & Vegetables: Berries: Goose*
Goose Poultry *See Meats & Meat Products: Poultry: Goose*
Gorgonzola Cheese *See Cheese & Cheese Products: Cheese: Gorgonzola*
Gotu Kola Powders *See Ingredients, Flavors & Additives: Powders: Gotu Kola*
Gouda Cheese *See Cheese & Cheese Products: Cheese: Gouda*
Gourmet & Specialty Foods *See Specialty & Organic Foods: Gourmet & Specialty Foods; See also Specialty & Organic Foods: Gourmet & Specialty Foods: Gourmet & Specialty Foods*
Gourmet Flavored Lollypops *See Candy & Confectionery: Candy: Lollypops: Gourmet Flavored*
Gourmet Potato Chips *See Snack Foods: Chips: Potato: Gourmet*
Gourmet Salad Dressings *See Sauces, Dips & Dressings: Salad Dressings: Gourmet*
Graham Toppings *See Ingredients, Flavors & Additives: Toppings: Graham*
Grain Flavors *See Ingredients, Flavors & Additives: Flavors: Grain*
Grain-Based Ingredients *See Ingredients, Flavors & Additives: Grain-Based*
Grains *See Cereals, Grains, Rice & Flour: Grains*
Granita Ice Cream *See Dairy Products: Ice Cream: Granita*
Granita Mixes *See Doughs, Mixes & Fillings: Mixes: Granita*
Granny Smith Apple *See Fruits & Vegetables: Apple: Granny Smith*
Granola *See Cereals, Grains, Rice & Flour: Granola*
Granola Toppings *See Ingredients, Flavors & Additives: Toppings: Granola*
Granulated Garlic *See Fruits & Vegetables: Garlic: Granulated; See also Spices, Seasonings & Seeds: Spices: Garlic: Granulated*
Granulated Onion *See Fruits & Vegetables: Dried & Dehydrated Vegetables: Onion: Granulated; See also Spices, Seasonings & Seeds: Spices: Onion: Granulated*
Granulated Peanuts *See Nuts & Nut Butters: Nuts: Peanuts: Granulated*
Granulated Starch Pearl Tapioca *See Cereals, Grains, Rice & Flour: Tapioca: Pearl: Granulated, Starch*
Granulated Sugar *See Sugars, Syrups & Sweeteners: Sugar: Granulated*
Granules Honey *See Sugars, Syrups & Sweeteners: Honey: Granules*
Grape *See Fruits & Vegetables: Grape*
Grape Ade Juices *See Beverages: Juices: Ade: Grape*
Grape Jams *See Jams, Jellies & Spreads: Jams: Grape*
Grape Juices *See Beverages: Juices: Grape*
Grape Leaves *See Fruits & Vegetables: Grape: Leaves*

EXAMPLE: **Canadian Style Bacon** *See Meats & Meat Products: Smoked, Cured & Deli Meats: Bacon: Canadian Style*
(1 = Canadian Style Bacon; 2 = See Meats & Meat Products; 3 = Smoked, Cured & Deli Meats; 4 = Bacon; 5 = Canadian Style)

1. Product or Service you are looking for
2. Main Category, in alphabetical order, located in the page headers starting on page 23
3. Category Description, located in black bars and in page headers
4. Product Category, located in gray bars
5. Product Type, located under gray bars, centered in bold

Grape Skin Extract Color *See Ingredients, Flavors & Additives: Colors: Grape Skin Extract Color*
Grapefruit *See Fruits & Vegetables: Grapefruit*
Grapefruit Juices *See Beverages: Juices: Grapefruit*
Grapefruit Oils *See Oils, Shortening & Fats: Oils: Grapefruit*
Grapeseed Oils *See Oils, Shortening & Fats: Oils: Grapeseed*
Grated Cheese *See Cheese & Cheese Products: Cheese: Grated*
Gravy *See Sauces, Dips & Dressings: Gravy*
Gravy Bases *See Ingredients, Flavors & Additives: Bases: Gravy*
Gravy Mixes *See Doughs, Mixes & Fillings: Mixes: Gravy*
Great Northern Beans *See Fruits & Vegetables: Beans: Great Northern*
Greek Beans *See Fruits & Vegetables: Beans: Greek*
Greek Olives *See Fruits & Vegetables: Olives: Greek*
Greek Oregano *See Spices, Seasonings & Seeds: Spices: Oregano: Greek*
Greek Style Seasonings *See Spices, Seasonings & Seeds: Seasonings: Greek Style*
Green & Yellow Split Peas, Dried *See Fruits & Vegetables: Peas: Green & Yellow Split - Dried*
Green Beans *See Fruits & Vegetables: Beans: Green*
Green Bell Peppers, Dried *See Fruits & Vegetables: Dried & Dehydrated Vegetables: Bell Peppers: Green*
Green Cabbage *See Fruits & Vegetables: Cabbage: Green*
Green Kiwi *See Fruits & Vegetables: Kiwi: Green*
Green Looseleaf Lettuce *See Fruits & Vegetables: Lettuce: Looseleaf: Green*
Green Mung Beans *See Fruits & Vegetables: Beans: Green Mung; See also Fruits & Vegetables: Beans: Mung: Green*
Green Olives *See Fruits & Vegetables: Olives: Green*
Green Olives with Pimiento *See Fruits & Vegetables: Olives: Green: with Pimiento*
Green Onion *See Fruits & Vegetables: Onion: Green*
Green Peas *See Fruits & Vegetables: Peas: Green*
Green Tea *See Beverages: Coffee & Tea: Tea: Green*
Greens Mustard *See Fruits & Vegetables: Mustard: Greens*
Grilled Patties Chicken *See Meats & Meat Products: Poultry: Chicken: Grilled Patties*
Grits *See Cereals, Grains, Rice & Flour: Grits; See also Cereals, Grains, Rice & Flour: Grits: Corn White & Yellow*
Groats *See Cereals, Grains, Rice & Flour: Oats & Oat Products: Groats*
Ground Allspice *See Spices, Seasonings & Seeds: Spices: Allspice: Ground*
Ground Bay Leaves *See Spices, Seasonings & Seeds: Spices: Bay Leaves: Ground*
Ground Beef & Beef Products *See Meats & Meat Products: Beef & Beef Products: Ground*
Ground Cardamom *See Spices, Seasonings & Seeds: Spices: Cardamom: Ground*
Ground Cayenne Pepper *See Spices, Seasonings & Seeds: Spices: Cayenne Pepper: Ground*
Ground Celery Seeds *See Spices, Seasonings & Seeds: Seeds: Celery: Ground*
Ground Cinnamon *See Spices, Seasonings & Seeds: Spices: Cinnamon: Ground*
Ground Cloves *See Spices, Seasonings & Seeds: Spices: Cloves: Ground*
Ground Coriander Seeds *See Spices, Seasonings & Seeds: Seeds: Coriander: Ground*
Ground Fennel Seeds *See Spices, Seasonings & Seeds: Seeds: Fennel: Ground*
Ground Ginger *See Spices, Seasonings & Seeds: Spices: Ginger: Ground*
Ground Mace *See Spices, Seasonings & Seeds: Spices: Mace (See also Nutmeg): Ground*
Ground Nutmeg *See Spices, Seasonings & Seeds: Spices: Nutmeg (See also Mace): Ground*
Ground Peppercorns *See Spices, Seasonings & Seeds: Spices: Peppercorns: Ground*
Ground Rosemary *See Spices, Seasonings & Seeds: Spices: Rosemary: Ground*
Ground Star Anise *See Spices, Seasonings & Seeds: Spices: Anise - Star: Ground*
Ground Thyme *See Spices, Seasonings & Seeds: Spices: Thyme: Ground*
Ground Turkey *See Meats & Meat Products: Poultry: Turkey: Ground*
Ground Turmeric *See Spices, Seasonings & Seeds: Spices: Turmeric: Ground*
Ground Veal *See Meats & Meat Products: Beef & Beef Products: Veal: Ground*
Ground White Pepper *See Spices, Seasonings & Seeds: Spices: White Pepper: Ground*
Grouper *See Fish & Seafood: Fish: Grouper*
Gruyere A1802 *See Cheese & Cheese Products: Cheese: Gruyere*
Guacamole *See Ethnic Foods: Guacamole*
Guacamole Dips *See Sauces, Dips & Dressings: Dips: Guacamole*
Guajillo Peppers *See Fruits & Vegetables: Peppers: Guajillo*
Guar Gum *See Ingredients, Flavors & Additives: Gums: Guar Gum*
Guava *See Fruits & Vegetables: Guava*
Guava Juices *See Beverages: Juices: Guava*
Guinea Hen *See Meats & Meat Products: Game: Guinea Hen*
Gumbo *See Prepared Foods: Soups & Stews: Gumbo*
Gums *See Ingredients, Flavors & Additives: Gums*
Gums & Jellies *See Candy & Confectionery: Candy: Gums & Jellies*
Gyros *See Prepared Foods: Prepared Meals: Gyros*

H

Habanero Peppers *See Fruits & Vegetables: Peppers: Habanero*
Habanero Sauces *See Sauces, Dips & Dressings: Sauces: Habanero*
Haddock *See Fish & Seafood: Fish: Haddock*
Hake *See Fish & Seafood: Fish: Hake*
Halal Foods *See Ethnic Foods: Halal Foods*
Half & Half *See Dairy Products: Milk & Milk Products: Milk: Half & Half*
Half & Half Flavors *See Ingredients, Flavors & Additives: Flavors: Half & Half*
Half-Products *See Ingredients, Flavors & Additives: Half-Products*
Half-Products, Calcium & Nutritionally Fortified Pellets *See Ingredients, Flavors & Additives: Half-Products: Calcium & Nutritionally Fortified Pellets*
Half-Products, Cocoa & Rice Pellets *See Ingredients, Flavors & Additives: Half-Products: Cocoa & Rice Pellets*
Half-Products, Colored Pellets *See Ingredients, Flavors & Additives: Half-Products: Colored Pellets*
Half-Products, Organic Pellets *See Ingredients, Flavors & Additives: Half-Products: Organic Pellets*
Half-Products, Veggie & Rice Pellets *See Ingredients, Flavors & Additives: Half-Products: Veggie & Rice Pellets*
Half_Products, Flavored Pellets *See Ingredients, Flavors & Additives: Half-Products: Flavored Pellets*
Halibut *See Fish & Seafood: Fish: Halibut*
Halloween Specialty-Packaged Candy *See Candy & Confectionery: Specialty-Packaged Candy: Halloween*
Ham *See Meats & Meat Products: Smoked, Cured & Deli Meats: Ham*
Ham Steak *See Meats & Meat Products: Smoked, Cured & Deli Meats: Ham: Steak*
Hamburger *See Meats & Meat Products: Beef & Beef Products: Hamburger*
Hard Candy *See Candy & Confectionery: Candy: Hard*
Hard-Boiled Eggs *See Eggs & Egg Products: Hard-Boiled*
Hash *See Prepared Foods: Hash*
Hash Browned Potatoes *See Prepared Foods: Potato Products: Hash Browned Potatoes*
Hatcheries *See Eggs & Egg Products: Hatcheries*
Hatcheries, Turkey Chicks *See Eggs & Egg Products: Hatcheries: Chicks: Turkey*
Havarti Cheese *See Cheese & Cheese Products: Cheese: Havarti*
Hazelnut Biscotti *See Baked Goods: Cookies & Bars: Biscotti: Hazelnut*
Hazelnut Flavors *See Ingredients, Flavors & Additives: Flavors: Hazelnut*
Hazelnut Flour *See Cereals, Grains, Rice & Flour: Flour: Hazelnut*
Hazelnut Nut Butters *See Nuts & Nut Butters: Nut Butters: Hazelnut*
Hazelnut Oils *See Oils, Shortening & Fats: Oils: Hazelnut*
Hazelnuts *See Nuts & Nut Butters: Nuts: Hazelnuts*
Head Cheese *See Meats & Meat Products: Smoked, Cured & Deli Meats: Head Cheese*
Health & Dietary *See Specialty & Organic Foods: Health & Dietary*
Health Products *See Specialty & Organic Foods: Dietary Products: Health Products*
Hearts Artichoke *See Fruits & Vegetables: Artichoke: Hearts*
Heat Stable Flavors *See Ingredients, Flavors & Additives: Flavors: Heat Stable*
Heather *See Spices, Seasonings & Seeds: Spices: Heather*
Hemp Nut Oils *See Oils, Shortening & Fats: Oils: Hemp Nut*
Herbal Supplements *See Spices, Seasonings & Seeds: Herbs: Herbal Supplements*
Herbal Tea *See Beverages: Coffee & Tea: Tea: Herbal*
Herbes de Provence *See Spices, Seasonings & Seeds: Spices: Herbes de Provence*
Herbs *See Spices, Seasonings & Seeds: Herbs*
Herbs & Spices Blends *See Ingredients, Flavors & Additives: Blends: Herbs & Spices*
Herbs Blends *See Ingredients, Flavors & Additives: Blends: Herbs*
Herbs for Beef *See Spices, Seasonings & Seeds: Herbs: for Beef*
Herbs for Pork *See Spices, Seasonings & Seeds: Herbs: for Pork*
Herbs for Poultry *See Spices, Seasonings & Seeds: Herbs: for Poultry*
Herbs for Seafood *See Spices, Seasonings & Seeds: Herbs: for Seafood*
Herring *See Fish & Seafood: Fish: Herring*
Herring Caviar *See Fish & Seafood: Caviar (Roe): Herring*
Hickory Smoke Oil Flavors *See Ingredients, Flavors & Additives: Flavors: Hickory Smoke Oil*
High Amylose Starches *See Ingredients, Flavors & Additives: Starches: High Amylose*
High Bush Blueberry *See Fruits & Vegetables: Berries: Blueberry: High Bush*
High Fructose Corn Syrups *See Sugars, Syrups & Sweeteners: Syrups: Corn: High Fructose*
Hoisin Sauces *See Sauces, Dips & Dressings: Sauces: Hoisin*
Hoki *See Fish & Seafood: Fish: Hoki*
Hollandaise *See Sauces, Dips & Dressings: Sauces: Hollandaise*
Hominy *See Cereals, Grains, Rice & Flour: Hominy*
Honey *See Sugars, Syrups & Sweeteners: Honey*
Honeydew *See Fruits & Vegetables: Melon: Honeydew*
Hops *See Cereals, Grains, Rice & Flour: Hops*
Horse *See Meats & Meat Products: Horse*
Horseradish *See Spices, Seasonings & Seeds: Spices: Horseradish; See also Sauces, Dips & Dressings: Sauces: Horseradish*
Hot Chili Powders *See Ingredients, Flavors & Additives: Powders: Chili: Hot*
Hot Chocolate *See Beverages: Cocoa & Chocolate Drinks: Hot Chocolate*
Hot Chocolate Mixes *See Doughs, Mixes & Fillings: Mixes: Hot Chocolate*
Hot Cocoa *See Beverages: Cocoa & Chocolate Drinks: Hot Cocoa*
Hot Cocoa with Marshmallows *See Beverages: Cocoa & Chocolate Drinks: Hot Cocoa: with Marshmallows*
Hot Cross Buns *See Baked Goods: Breads: Buns: Hot Cross*
Hot Curry Powders *See Ingredients, Flavors & Additives: Powders: Curry: Hot*
Hot Dogs *See Meats & Meat Products: Frankfurters: Hot Dogs*
Hot Italian Sausage Seasonings *See Spices, Seasonings & Seeds: Seasonings: Sausage: Hot Italian*
Hot Italian Sausages *See Meats & Meat Products: Smoked, Cured & Deli Meats: Sausages: Hot Italian*
Hot Pepper Sauces *See Sauces, Dips & Dressings: Sauces: Pepper: Hot*
Hot Salami *See Meats & Meat Products: Smoked, Cured & Deli Meats: Salami: Hot*
Hot Sauces *See Sauces, Dips & Dressings: Sauces: Hot*
Hot Sausages *See Meats & Meat Products: Smoked, Cured & Deli Meats: Sausages: Hot*
Hulled Sesame Seeds *See Spices, Seasonings & Seeds: Seeds: Sesame: Hulled*
Hulls Rice *See Cereals, Grains, Rice & Flour: Rice: Hulls*
Humectants *See Ingredients, Flavors & Additives: Humectants*
Hummus *See Cereals, Grains, Rice & Flour: Hummus*
Hush Puppies *See Prepared Foods: Hush Puppies*
Hush Puppies, Frozen & Mixes *See Prepared Foods: Hush Puppies: Frozen & Mixes*
Husks Corn *See Fruits & Vegetables: Corn: Husks*
Hydrocolloids *See Ingredients, Flavors & Additives: Hydrocolloids*
Hydrogenated Fats & Lard *See Oils, Shortening & Fats: Fats & Lard: Hydrogenated*
Hydrolyzed Products *See Ingredients, Flavors & Additives: Hydrolyzed Products*
Hydroxypropyl Methylcellulose *See Ingredients, Flavors & Additives: Gums: Hydroxypropyl Methylcellulose*

I

Ice Cream *See Dairy Products: Ice Cream*
Ice Cream Bases *See Dairy Products: Ice Cream: Bases*
Ice Cream Mixes *See Doughs, Mixes & Fillings: Mixes: Ice Cream*

Ice Cream Powders *See Ingredients, Flavors & Additives: Powders: Ice Cream*
Ice Cream, Ribbons *See Dairy Products: Ice Cream: Ribbons*
Ice Cream, Roll *See Dairy Products: Ice Cream: Roll*
Ice Milk *See Dairy Products: Ice Cream: Ice Milk*
Iceberg Lettuce Based Prepared Salads *See Prepared Foods: Prepared Salads: Iceberg Lettuce Based*
Iced Coffee *See Beverages: Coffee & Tea: Coffee: Iced*
Iced Tea *See Beverages: Coffee & Tea: Tea: Iced*
Ices *See Dairy Products: Ice Cream: Ices*
Icing Sugar *See Sugars, Syrups & Sweeteners: Sugar: Icing*
Icings *See Candy & Confectionery: Decorations & Icings: Icings*
Imitation Cheeses & Substitutes *See Cheese & Cheese Products: Imitation Cheeses & Substitutes; See also Cheese & Cheese Products: Imitation Cheeses & Substitutes: Imitation*
Imitation Crab *See Fish & Seafood: Shellfish: Crab: Imitation*
Imitation Fish *See Fish & Seafood: Fish: Imitation*
Improvers Doughs *See Doughs, Mixes & Fillings: Doughs: Improvers*
Inclusions *See Ingredients, Flavors & Additives: Inclusions*
India Pale Ale *See Beverages: Beers: American & British Ale: India Pale Ale*
Individual Packets *See Prepared Foods: Individual Packets*
Individual Quick Frozen Food *See Prepared Foods: Individual Quick Frozen Food*
Individually Packaged Cookies & Bars *See Baked Goods: Cookies & Bars: Individually Packaged*
Ingredients *See Ingredients, Flavors & Additives: Ingredients; See also Baked Goods: Ingredients*
Ingredients, Flavors & Additives *See Ingredients, Flavors & Additives*
Ingredients, Flavors & Additives, Almond Pastes *See Ingredients, Flavors & Additives: Pastes: Almond*
Ingredients, Organic Foods *See Specialty & Organic Foods: Organic Foods: Ingredients*
Ink Squid *See Fish & Seafood: Shellfish: Squid: Ink*
Inositol *See Ingredients, Flavors & Additives: Vitamins & Supplements: Inositol*
Instant Cereal *See Cereals, Grains, Rice & Flour: Cereal: Instant*
Instant Coffee *See Beverages: Coffee & Tea: Coffee: Instant*
Instant Coffee, Decaffeinated *See Beverages: Coffee & Tea: Coffee: Instant - Decaffeinated*
Instant Potatoes *See Fruits & Vegetables: Potatoes: Instant*
Instant Rice *See Cereals, Grains, Rice & Flour: Rice: Instant*
Instant Tea *See Beverages: Coffee & Tea: Tea: Instant*
Instantized Flour *See Cereals, Grains, Rice & Flour: Flour: Instantized*
Invert Sugar *See Sugars, Syrups & Sweeteners: Sugar: Invert*
IQF Frozen Cherries *See Fruits & Vegetables: Cherries: Frozen: IQF (Individually Quick Frozen)*
IQF Rice *See Cereals, Grains, Rice & Flour: Rice: IQF (Individual Quick Frozen)*
IQF Vegetables *See Fruits & Vegetables: Vegetables: IQF (Individual Quick Frozen)*
Irish Breakfast Tea *See Beverages: Coffee & Tea: Tea: Irish Breakfast*
Irish Creme Flavors *See Ingredients, Flavors & Additives: Flavors: Irish Creme*
Irish Whiskey *See Beverages: Spirits & Liqueurs: Irish Whiskey*
Isolate Soy Protein *See Fruits & Vegetables: Soy: Soy Protein: Isolate*
Italian *See Ethnic Foods: Italian*
Italian Beans *See Fruits & Vegetables: Beans: Italian*
Italian Beef & Beef Products *See Meats & Meat Products: Beef & Beef Products: Italian*
Italian Breads *See Baked Goods: Breads: Italian*
Italian Herbs Seasonings *See Spices, Seasonings & Seeds: Seasonings: Italian Herbs*
Italian Olives *See Fruits & Vegetables: Olives: Italian*
Italian Style Salad Dressings *See Sauces, Dips & Dressings: Salad Dressings: Italian Style*
Italian Style Salad Dressings, Mixes *See Sauces, Dips & Dressings: Salad Dressings: Mixes: Italian Style*
Italian Style Seasonings *See Spices, Seasonings & Seeds: Seasonings: Italian Style*
Italian Wines *See Beverages: Wines: Italian*

J

Jalapeno & Chiles Peppers *See Fruits & Vegetables: Peppers: Jalapeno & Chiles*
Jalapeno Peppers *See Fruits & Vegetables: Peppers: Jalapeno*
Jamacain Beef Patties *See Meats & Meat Products: Beef & Beef Products: Patties: Jamacain*
Jambalaya *See Ethnic Foods: Jambalaya*
Jambalaya Mixes *See Doughs, Mixes & Fillings: Mixes: Jambalaya*
Jams *See Jams, Jellies & Spreads: Jams*
Japanese *See Ethnic Foods: Japanese*
Japanese Wines *See Beverages: Wines: Japanese*
Japones Peppers *See Fruits & Vegetables: Peppers: Japones*
Jarred or Cupped Fruit *See Fruits & Vegetables: Fruit: Jarred or Cupped*
Jasmati Rice *See Cereals, Grains, Rice & Flour: Rice: Jasmati*
Jasmine Rice *See Cereals, Grains, Rice & Flour: Rice: Jasmine*
Jasmine Tea *See Beverages: Coffee & Tea: Tea: Jasmine*
Jellied Cranberry Sauces *See Fruits & Vegetables: Sauces: Cranberry: Jellied*
Jellies *See Jams, Jellies & Spreads: Jellies*
Jelly Beans *See Candy & Confectionery: Candy: Jelly Beans*
Jelly Powders *See Ingredients, Flavors & Additives: Powders: Jelly*
Jerk Sauces *See Sauces, Dips & Dressings: Sauces: Jerk*
Juice Bases *See Ingredients, Flavors & Additives: Bases: Juice*
Juice Concentrates *See Beverages: Juices: Concentrates*
Juice Drinks *See Beverages: Juices: Drink*
Juice, Tropical Fruit *See Beverages: Juices: Tropical Fruits*
Juices *See Beverages: Juices*
Juniper Berries *See Fruits & Vegetables: Berries: Juniper; See also Spices, Seasonings & Seeds: Spices: Juniper Berries*

K

Kale *See Fruits & Vegetables: Kale*
Karaya Gum *See Ingredients, Flavors & Additives: Gums: Karaya Gum*
Kasmati Rice *See Cereals, Grains, Rice & Flour: Rice: Kasmati*
Kefir *See Dairy Products: Milk & Milk Products: Kefir*
Kegged Beers *See Beverages: Beers: Kegged*
Kelp Products *See Fruits & Vegetables: Kelp Products*
Ketchup *See Sauces, Dips & Dressings: Ketchup*
Key Lime Juices *See Beverages: Juices: Key Lime*
Key Lime Pies *See Baked Goods: Pies: Key Lime*
Kidney Beans *See Fruits & Vegetables: Beans: Kidney*
Kielbasa Sausage Seasonings *See Spices, Seasonings & Seeds: Seasonings: Sausage: Kielbasa*
Kielbasa Sausages *See Meats & Meat Products: Smoked, Cured & Deli Meats: Sausages: Kielbasa*
Kiev Chicken *See Prepared Foods: Prepared Meals: Chicken: Kiev*
King Cod *See Fish & Seafood: Fish: King Cod*
King Crab *See Fish & Seafood: Shellfish: Crab: King*
King Salmon *See Fish & Seafood: Fish: Salmon: King*
Kingfish *See Fish & Seafood: Fish: Kingfish*
Kisses *See Candy & Confectionery: Candy: Kisses*
Kiwi *See Fruits & Vegetables: Kiwi*
Klingstone Peach *See Fruits & Vegetables: Peach: Klingstone*
Knishes *See Prepared Foods: Knishes*
Knockwurst *See Meats & Meat Products: Smoked, Cured & Deli Meats: Knockwurst*
Knockwurst Sausages *See Meats & Meat Products: Smoked, Cured & Deli Meats: Sausages: Knockwurst*
Kohlrabi *See Fruits & Vegetables: Kohlrabi*
Kolsch Belgian & French Ale *See Beverages: Beers: Belgian & French Ale: Kolsch*
Kosher Foods *See Ethnic Foods: Kosher Foods*
Kosher Frankfurters *See Meats & Meat Products: Frankfurters: Kosher*
Kosher Pickles *See Relishes & Pickled Products: Pickled Products: Pickles: Kosher*
Kumquat *See Fruits & Vegetables: Kumquat*

L

Lactic Acidulants *See Ingredients, Flavors & Additives: Acidulants: Lactic*
Lactobacillus Acidophilus *See Ingredients, Flavors & Additives: Cultures & Yeasts: Lactobacillus Acidophilus*
Lactoferrin *See Ingredients, Flavors & Additives: Lactoferrin*
Lactose Sweeteners *See Ingredients, Flavors & Additives: Sweeteners: Lactose*
Lactose-Free Milk *See Dairy Products: Milk & Milk Products: Milk: Lactose-Free*
Lady Fingers *See Baked Goods: Cookies & Bars: Lady Fingers; See also Baked Goods: Cakes & Pastries: Ladyfingers*
Lager Beers *See Beverages: Beers: Lager*
Lamb *See Meats & Meat Products: Lamb*
Lamb Marinades *See Sauces, Dips & Dressings: Marinades: Lamb*
Langostinos *See Fish & Seafood: Shellfish: Langostinos*
Lard *See Oils, Shortening & Fats: Fats & Lard: Lard*
Lasagna *See Pasta & Noodles: Lasagna; See also Prepared Foods: Prepared Meals: Lasagna*
Latte Coffee *See Beverages: Coffee & Tea: Coffee: Latte*
Lavender *See Spices, Seasonings & Seeds: Spices: Lavender*
Lavender Flowers *See Spices, Seasonings & Seeds: Spices: Lavender Flowers*
Leaveners *See Ingredients, Flavors & Additives: Leaveners*
Lecithin Emulsifiers *See Ingredients, Flavors & Additives: Emulsifiers: Lecithin*
Lecithinated Stabilizers *See Ingredients, Flavors & Additives: Stabilizers: Lecithinated*
Leek *See Fruits & Vegetables: Leek*
Leeks, Chopped Dried *See Fruits & Vegetables: Dried & Dehydrated Vegetables: Leeks - Chopped*
Leg of Lamb *See Meats & Meat Products: Lamb: Leg of*
Lemon *See Fruits & Vegetables: Lemon*
Lemon & Basil Seasonings *See Spices, Seasonings & Seeds: Seasonings: Lemon & Basil*
Lemon & Dill Seasonings *See Spices, Seasonings & Seeds: Seasonings: Lemon & Dill*
Lemon Ade Juices *See Beverages: Juices: Ade: Lemon*
Lemon Flavors *See Ingredients, Flavors & Additives: Flavors: Lemon*
Lemon Grass Oils *See Oils, Shortening & Fats: Oils: Lemon Grass*
Lemon Grass Spices *See Spices, Seasonings & Seeds: Spices: Lemon Grass*
Lemon Juices *See Beverages: Juices: Lemon*
Lemon Oils *See Oils, Shortening & Fats: Oils: Lemon*
Lemon Peel *See Spices, Seasonings & Seeds: Spices: Lemon Peel*
Lemon Pepper Seasonings *See Spices, Seasonings & Seeds: Seasonings: Lemon Pepper*
Lemon Sauces *See Sauces, Dips & Dressings: Sauces: Lemon*
Lemon Tea *See Beverages: Coffee & Tea: Tea: Lemon*
Lemon-Lime Soda *See Beverages: Soft Drinks & Sodas: Soft Drinks: Lemon-Lime Soda*
Lemon-Meringue Pies *See Baked Goods: Pies: Lemon-Meringue*
Lemonade Juices *See Beverages: Juices: Lemonade*
Lentil Beans *See Fruits & Vegetables: Beans: Lentil; See also Fruits & Vegetables: Beans: Dried: Lentil Blend*
Lentil Soup *See Prepared Foods: Soups & Stews: Lentil Soup*
Lettuce *See Fruits & Vegetables: Lettuce*
Licorice Candy *See Candy & Confectionery: Candy: Licorice*
Licorice Flavors *See Ingredients, Flavors & Additives: Flavors: Licorice*
Light Red Kidney Beans *See Fruits & Vegetables: Beans: Kidney: Light Red*
Lima Beans *See Fruits & Vegetables: Beans: Lima*
Limburger Cheese *See Cheese & Cheese Products: Cheese: Limburger*
Lime *See Fruits & Vegetables: Lime*
Lime Flavors *See Ingredients, Flavors & Additives: Flavors: Lime*
Lime Juices *See Beverages: Juices: Lime*
Lime Oils *See Oils, Shortening & Fats: Oils: Lime*
Lingonberries *See Fruits & Vegetables: Berries: Lingonberries*
Linguica Sausages *See Meats & Meat Products: Smoked, Cured & Deli Meats: Sausages: Linguica*

1 2 3 4 5

EXAMPLE: **Canadian Style Bacon** *See Meats & Meat Products: Smoked, Cured & Deli Meats: Bacon: Canadian Style*

1. Product or Service you are looking for
2. Main Category, in alphabetical order, located in the page headers starting on page 23
3. Category Description, located in black bars and in page headers
4. Product Category, located in gray bars
5. Product Type, located under gray bars, centered in bold

Link Sausages *See Meats & Meat Products: Smoked, Cured & Deli Meats: Sausages: Link*
Liqueur Cake *See Baked Goods: Cakes & Pastries: Liqueur Cake*
Liqueur Flavors *See Ingredients, Flavors & Additives: Flavors: Liqueur*
Liqueurs & Cordials *See Beverages: Spirits & Liqueurs: Liqueurs & Cordials*
Liquid *See Eggs & Egg Products: Liquid*
Liquid & Granulated Sugar *See Sugars, Syrups & Sweeteners: Sugar: Liquid & Granulated*
Liquid Beverage Mixes *See Doughs, Mixes & Fillings: Mixes: Beverage: Liquid*
Liquid Chicken Fats & Lard *See Oils, Shortening & Fats: Fats & Lard: Chicken: Liquid*
Liquid Egg Whites *See Eggs & Egg Products: Liquid: Whites*
Liquid Honey *See Sugars, Syrups & Sweeteners: Honey: Liquid*
Liquid Mixes *See Doughs, Mixes & Fillings: Mixes: Liquid*
Liquid Spices *See Spices, Seasonings & Seeds: Spices: Liquid*
Liquid Sugar *See Sugars, Syrups & Sweeteners: Sugar: Liquid*
Liquid Vegetable Shortening *See Oils, Shortening & Fats: Shortening: Vegetable: Liquid*
Liquid Vinegar *See Sauces, Dips & Dressings: Vinegar: Liquid*
Live Crab *See Fish & Seafood: Shellfish: Crab: Live*
Live Crayfish *See Fish & Seafood: Shellfish: Crayfish: Live*
Live Lobster *See Fish & Seafood: Shellfish: Lobster: Live*
Live Shellfish *See Fish & Seafood: Shellfish: Live*
Liver *See Meats & Meat Products: Beef & Beef Products: Liver*
Liver Extracts *See Ingredients, Flavors & Additives: Extracts: Liver*
Liverwurst *See Meats & Meat Products: Smoked, Cured & Deli Meats: Liverwurst*
Lobster *See Fish & Seafood: Shellfish: Lobster*
Lobster Meat *See Fish & Seafood: Shellfish: Lobster: Meat*
Lobster Mushrooms *See Fruits & Vegetables: Mushrooms: Lobster*
Lobster Tails *See Fish & Seafood: Shellfish: Lobster: Tails*
Locust Bean Gum *See Ingredients, Flavors & Additives: Gums: Locust Bean Gum*
Loganberries *See Fruits & Vegetables: Loganberries*
Loin Chop, Lamb *See Meats & Meat Products: Lamb: Loin Chop*
Loin Chop, Pork *See Meats & Meat Products: Pork & Pork Products: Loin Chop; See also Meats & Meat Products: Pork & Pork Products: Loins*
Loin Chop, Veal *See Meats & Meat Products: Beef & Beef Products: Veal: Loin Chop*
Lollypops *See Candy & Confectionery: Candy: Lollypops*
London Broil *See Meats & Meat Products: Beef & Beef Products: London Broil*
Loose Leaf Tea *See Beverages: Coffee & Tea: Tea: Loose Leaf*
Looseleaf Lettuce *See Fruits & Vegetables: Lettuce: Looseleaf*
Low Carb Bread Mixes *See Doughs, Mixes & Fillings: Mixes: Bread: Low Carb*
Low Carb Dessert Mixes *See Doughs, Mixes & Fillings: Mixes: Dessert: Low Carb*
Low Carb Desserts *See Baked Goods: Desserts: Low Carb*
Low Carb Ice Cream Mixes *See Doughs, Mixes & Fillings: Mixes: Ice Cream: Low Carb*
Low Fat Butter *See Dairy Products: Butter: Low Fat*
Low Moisture Part Skim Mozzarella Cheese *See Cheese & Cheese Products: Cheese: Mozzarella: Low Moisture Part Skim*
Low Moisture Part Skim Mozzarella Cheese, Shredded - Frozen *See Cheese & Cheese Products: Cheese: Mozzarella: Low Moisture Part Skim Shredded - Frozen*
Low-Calorie Desserts *See Specialty & Organic Foods: Dietary Products: Low-Calorie Desserts; See also See Baked Goods: Desserts: Low-Calorie*
Low-Calorie Non-Dairy Ice Cream *See Dairy Products: Ice Cream: Non-Dairy: Low-Calorie*
Low-Fat Cheese *See Cheese & Cheese Products: Cheese: Low-Fat*
Low-Fat Ice Cream *See Dairy Products: Ice Cream: Low-Fat*
Low-Fat Milk *See Dairy Products: Milk & Milk Products: Milk: Low-Fat*
Low-Fat Potato Chips *See Snack Foods: Chips: Potato: Low-Fat*
Low-Fat Yogurt *See Dairy Products: Yogurt: Low-Fat*
Lox Smoked Seafood *See Fish & Seafood: Seafood: Smoked: Lox*
Lozenges Candy *See Candy & Confectionery: Candy: Lozenges*
Lumpfish *See Fish & Seafood: Fish: Lumpfish*
Luncheon Meat *See Meats & Meat Products: Smoked, Cured & Deli Meats: Luncheon Meat*
Lupini Beans *See Fruits & Vegetables: Beans: Lupini*
Luxury Cognac Brandy *See Beverages: Spirits & Liqueurs: Brandy: Luxury Cognac*

M

Macadamia Flavors *See Ingredients, Flavors & Additives: Flavors: Macadamia*
Macadamia Nuts *See Nuts & Nut Butters: Nuts: Macadamia*
Macaroni, Prepared Meals *See Prepared Foods: Prepared Meals: Macaroni*
Macaroni, Prepared Salads *See Prepared Foods: Prepared Salads: Macaroni*
Macaroons *See Baked Goods: Cookies & Bars: Macaroons*
Mace Spices *See Spices, Seasonings & Seeds: Spices: Mace (See also Nutmeg)*
Mackerel *See Fish & Seafood: Fish: Mackerel*
Mahi-Mahi *See Fish & Seafood: Fish: Mahi-Mahi*
Maitakes *See Fruits & Vegetables: Mushrooms: Maitakes*
Malic Acidulants *See Ingredients, Flavors & Additives: Acidulants: Malic*
Malt *See Cereals, Grains, Rice & Flour: Malt*
Malt Extract Syrups *See Sugars, Syrups & Sweeteners: Syrups: Malt Extract*
Malt Liquor *See Beverages: Beers: Lager: Malt Liquor*
Malt Vinegar *See Sauces, Dips & Dressings: Vinegar: Malt*
Maltodextrin *See Ingredients, Flavors & Additives: Maltodextrin*
Mandarin Orange *See Fruits & Vegetables: Orange: Mandarin*
Mango *See Fruits & Vegetables: Mango*
Mango Juices *See Beverages: Juices: Mango*
Manhattan Chowder *See Prepared Foods: Soups & Stews: Chowder: Manhattan*
Maple Candy *See Candy & Confectionery: Candy: Maple*
Maple Flavors *See Ingredients, Flavors & Additives: Flavors: Maple*
Maple Sugar *See Sugars, Syrups & Sweeteners: Sugar: Maple*
Maple Syrups *See Sugars, Syrups & Sweeteners: Syrups: Maple*
Maraschino Cherries *See Fruits & Vegetables: Cherries: Maraschino*
Margarine *See Oils, Shortening & Fats: Margarine*
Marinades *See Sauces, Dips & Dressings: Marinades*
Marinara Sauces *See Sauces, Dips & Dressings: Sauces: Marinara*
Marinated Shellfish *See Fish & Seafood: Shellfish: Marinated*
Marinated Tomato *See Fruits & Vegetables: Tomato: Marinated*
Marjoram Spices *See Spices, Seasonings & Seeds: Spices: Marjoram*
Marlin *See Fish & Seafood: Fish: Marlin*
Marmalades & Preserves *See Jams, Jellies & Spreads: Marmalades & Preserves*
Marsala Cooking Wines *See Beverages: Wines: Cooking: Marsala*
Marshmallow Candy *See Candy & Confectionery: Candy: Marshmallow*
Marshmallow Creme Candy *See Candy & Confectionery: Candy: Marshmallow Creme*
Marshmallows *See Candy & Confectionery: Candy: Marshmallows*
Marzipan *See Candy & Confectionery: Candy: Marzipan*
Masa Flour *See Cereals, Grains, Rice & Flour: Flour: Masa*
Mascarpone Cheese *See Cheese & Cheese Products: Cheese: Mascarpone*
Mashed Sweet Potatoes *See Fruits & Vegetables: Sweet Potatoes: Mashed*
Masking Flavors *See Ingredients, Flavors & Additives: Flavors: Masking*
Mature Rabbit *See Meats & Meat Products: Game: Rabbit: Mature*
Matzo *See Ethnic Foods: Matzo*
Matzo Meal *See Ethnic Foods: Matzo: Meal*
Mayonaise *See Sauces, Dips & Dressings: Mayonaise*
Meal *See Fish & Seafood: Fish: Meal*
Meal Crackers *See Baked Goods: Crackers: Meal*
Meal Fillers *See Ingredients, Flavors & Additives: Fillers: Meal*
Meat Analogs *See Ingredients, Flavors & Additives: Analogs: Meat*
Meat Balls *See Prepared Foods: Meat Balls*
Meat Curing Preparations *See Ingredients, Flavors & Additives: Curing Preparations: Meat*
Meat Extenders *See Ingredients, Flavors & Additives: Extenders: Meat*
Meat Flavors *See Ingredients, Flavors & Additives: Flavors: Meat*
Meat Loaf *See Prepared Foods: Meat Loaf*
Meat Marinades *See Sauces, Dips & Dressings: Marinades: Meat*
Meat Meal *See Meats & Meat Products: Meat Meal*
Meat Pies *See Baked Goods: Pies: Meat*
Meat Powders *See Ingredients, Flavors & Additives: Powders: Meat*
Meat Products Seasonings *See Spices, Seasonings & Seeds: Seasonings: Meat Products*
Meat Ravioli *See Pasta & Noodles: Ravioli: Meat*
Meat Sauces *See Sauces, Dips & Dressings: Sauces: Meat*
Meat Spaghetti Sauces *See Sauces, Dips & Dressings: Sauces: Spaghetti: Meat*
Meat Stock Powders *See Ingredients, Flavors & Additives: Powders: Meat Stock*
Meat Stuffing *See Prepared Foods: Stuffing: Meat*
Meat Tenderizers *See Ingredients, Flavors & Additives: Tenderizers: Meat*
Meatless Spaghetti Sauces *See Sauces, Dips & Dressings: Sauces: Spaghetti: Meatless*
Meats & Meat Products *See Meats & Meat Products*
Medical Nutritionals *See Ingredients, Flavors & Additives: Vitamins & Supplements: Medical Nutritionals*
Mediterranean Sauces *See Sauces, Dips & Dressings: Sauces: Mediterranean*
Melba Toast *See Baked Goods: Breads: Melba Toast*
Melon *See Fruits & Vegetables: Melon*
Melon Balls *See Fruits & Vegetables: Melon: Balls*
Meringue Dessert Fillings *See Doughs, Mixes & Fillings: Fillings: Dessert: Meringue*
Meringue Powders *See Ingredients, Flavors & Additives: Powders: Meringue*
Meringue Toppings *See Ingredients, Flavors & Additives: Toppings: Meringue*
Merlot *See Beverages: Wines: Red Grape Wines: Merlot*
Mesquite BBQ Snack Seasonings *See Spices, Seasonings & Seeds: Seasonings: Snack: Mesquite BBQ*
Methoxypolyethylene Glycols *See Ingredients, Flavors & Additives: Methoxypolyethylene Glycols*
Methyl Salicylate *See Ingredients, Flavors & Additives: Aroma Chemicals & Materials: Chemicals: Methyl Salicylate*
Methylcellulose *See Ingredients, Flavors & Additives: Gums: Methylcellulose*
Mexican *See Ethnic Foods: Mexican*
Mexican Food Sauces *See Sauces, Dips & Dressings: Sauces: Mexican Food*
Mexican Oregano *See Spices, Seasonings & Seeds: Spices: Oregano: Mexican*
Mexican Style Seasonings *See Spices, Seasonings & Seeds: Seasonings: Mexican Style*
Microwavable Entrees *See Prepared Foods: Prepared Meals: Entrees: Microwavable*
Microwave Flavors *See Ingredients, Flavors & Additives: Flavors: Microwave*
Milano Salami *See Meats & Meat Products: Smoked, Cured & Deli Meats: Salami: Milano*
Mild Salsa *See Sauces, Dips & Dressings: Salsa: Mild*
Milk *See Dairy Products: Milk & Milk Products: Milk*
Milk & Milk Products *See Dairy Products: Milk & Milk Products*
Milk Calcium *See Ingredients, Flavors & Additives: Milk Calcium*
Milk Coconut *See Fruits & Vegetables: Coconut & Coconut Products: Milk*
Milk Enzyme *See Dairy Products: Milk & Milk Products: Milk Products: Milk & Milk Fat: Enzyme*
Milk Flavors *See Ingredients, Flavors & Additives: Flavors: Milk*
Milk Powders *See Ingredients, Flavors & Additives: Powders: Milk*
Milk Productss *See Dairy Products: Milk & Milk Products: Milk Products*
Milk Proteins *See Ingredients, Flavors & Additives: Hydrolyzed Products: Milk Proteins; See also Dairy Products: Milk & Milk Products: Milk Products: Milk Proteins*
Milk Rice Powders *See Ingredients, Flavors & Additives: Powders: Rice: Milk*
Milk Solids *See Dairy Products: Milk & Milk Products: Milk Solids*
Milk, Modified - Dry Blends *See Dairy Products: Milk & Milk Products: Milk Products: Modified - Dry Blends*
Milled Rice *See Cereals, Grains, Rice & Flour: Rice: Milled*

Millet *See Cereals, Grains, Rice & Flour: Millet*
Millet Flour *See Cereals, Grains, Rice & Flour: Flour: Millet*
Milo *See Beverages: Cocoa & Chocolate Drinks: Milo*
Minced Clam *See Fish & Seafood: Shellfish: Clam: Minced*
Minced Garlic *See Spices, Seasonings & Seeds: Spices: Garlic: Minced*
Minced Onion *See Fruits & Vegetables: Dried & Dehydrated Vegetables: Onion: Minced; See also Spices, Seasonings & Seeds: Spices: Onion: Minced; See also Fruits & Vegetables: Onion: Minced*
Mineral Blends *See Ingredients, Flavors & Additives: Vitamins & Supplements: Mineral Blends*
Mineral Supplements *See Ingredients, Flavors & Additives: Vitamins & Supplements: Supplements: Minerals; See also Ingredients, Flavors & Additives: Vitamins & Supplements: Minerals*
Mineral Water *See Beverages: Water: Mineral*
Miners Lettuce *See Fruits & Vegetables: Lettuce: Miners*
Mini Frankfurters *See Meats & Meat Products: Frankfurters: Mini*
Mint Herb Tea *See Beverages: Coffee & Tea: Tea: Mint Herb*
Mint Leaves *See Spices, Seasonings & Seeds: Spices: Mint Leaves*
Mint Sauces *See Sauces, Dips & Dressings: Sauces: Mint*
Mint Spices *See Spices, Seasonings & Seeds: Spices: Mint*
Mint Tea *See Beverages: Coffee & Tea: Tea: Mint*
Mints Candy *See Candy & Confectionery: Candy: Mints*
Miso *See Fruits & Vegetables: Miso*
Mix *See Eggs & Egg Products: Mix*
Mixed Nuts *See Nuts & Nut Butters: Nuts: Mixed Nuts*
Mixers *See Beverages: Mixers*
Mixes *See Doughs, Mixes & Fillings: Mixes*
Mixes, Salad Dressings *See Sauces, Dips & Dressings: Salad Dressings: Mixes*
Mixes, Sauces *See Sauces, Dips & Dressings: Sauces: Mixes*
Mocha Biscotti *See Baked Goods: Cookies & Bars: Biscotti: Mocha*
Mocha Coffee & Tea *See Beverages: Coffee & Tea: Mocha*
Modified Food Starches *See Ingredients, Flavors & Additives: Agents: Anticaking: Modified Food Starch*
Modified Rice Starches *See Ingredients, Flavors & Additives: Starches: Rice: Modified*
Modified Starches *See Ingredients, Flavors & Additives: Starches: Modified*
Modifiers Agents *See Ingredients, Flavors & Additives: Agents: Modifiers*
Molasses *See Sugars, Syrups & Sweeteners: Molasses*
Molasses Flakes *See Ingredients, Flavors & Additives: Flakes: Molasses*
Molasses Powders *See Ingredients, Flavors & Additives: Powders: Molasses*
Molding Starches *See Ingredients, Flavors & Additives: Starches: Molding*
Mole Sauces *See Sauces, Dips & Dressings: Sauces: Mole*
Monkfish *See Fish & Seafood: Fish: Monkfish*
Montasio *See Cheese & Cheese Products: Cheese: Montasio*
Monte Veronese *See Cheese & Cheese Products: Cheese: Monte Veronese*
Monterey Jack *See Cheese & Cheese Products: Cheese: Monterey Jack*
Morel Mushrooms *See Fruits & Vegetables: Mushrooms: Morel; See alsoFruits & Vegetables: Dried & Dehydrated Vegetables: Mushrooms: Morels Whole*
Mortadella Sausages *See Meats & Meat Products: Smoked, Cured & Deli Meats: Sausages: Mortadella*
Mousse Candy *See Candy & Confectionery: Candy: Mousse*
Mousseron *See Fruits & Vegetables: Mushrooms: Mousseron*
Mozzarella *See Cheese & Cheese Products: Cheese: Mozzarella*
Mozzarella Cheese, Low Moisture Part Skim *See Cheese & Cheese Products: Cheese: Mozzarella: Low Moisture Part Skim*
Mozzarella Cheese, Low Moisture Part Skim, Shredded - Frozen *See Cheese & Cheese Products: Cheese: Mozzarella: Low Moisture Part Skim Shredded - Frozen*
Mozzarella Sticks *See Prepared Foods: Prepared Meals: Mozzarella Sticks*
Mozzarella, Imitation *See Cheese & Cheese Products: Imitation Cheeses & Substitutes: Imitation: Mozzarella*
MSG & Salt Mixture *See Spices, Seasonings & Seeds: Salt: MSG & Salt Mixture*
Muenster *See Cheese & Cheese Products: Cheese: Muenster*
Muesli Cereal *See Cereals, Grains, Rice & Flour: Cereal: Muesli*
Muffin Batters *See Doughs, Mixes & Fillings: Batters: Muffin*
Muffin Loaves *See Baked Goods: Cakes & Pastries: Muffin Loaves*
Muffin Mixes *See Doughs, Mixes & Fillings: Mixes: Muffin*
Muffins *See Baked Goods: Cakes & Pastries: Muffins*
Mulato Peppers *See Fruits & Vegetables: Peppers: Mulato*
Mulberries *See Fruits & Vegetables: Berries: Mulberries*
Mulled Wine Spice *See Spices, Seasonings & Seeds: Spices: Mulled Wine Spice*
Mullet *See Fish & Seafood: Fish: Mullet*
Mulling *See Spices, Seasonings & Seeds: Spices: Mulling*
Multi-Grain Breads *See Baked Goods: Breads: Multi-Grain*
Multi-Packs Specialty-Packaged Candy *See Candy & Confectionery: Specialty-Packaged Candy: Multi-Packs*
Mung Bean Noodles *See Pasta & Noodles: Noodles: Mung Bean*
Mung Bean Sprouts *See Fruits & Vegetables: Sprouts: Mung Bean*
Mung Beans *See Fruits & Vegetables: Beans: Mung*
Muscovy Duck *See Meats & Meat Products: Game: Muscovy Duck*
Mushroom Sauces *See Sauces, Dips & Dressings: Sauces: Mushroom*
Mushrooms *See Fruits & Vegetables: Dried & Dehydrated Vegetables: Mushrooms; See also Fruits & Vegetables: Mushrooms*
Muskox *See Meats & Meat Products: Game: Muskox*
Mussels *See Fish & Seafood: Shellfish: Mussels*
Mustard *See Sauces, Dips & Dressings: Mustard; See also Fruits & Vegetables: Mustard*
Mustard Bran *See Cereals, Grains, Rice & Flour: Bran: Mustard*
Mustard Flour *See Cereals, Grains, Rice & Flour: Flour: Mustard*
Mustard Oils *See Oils, Shortening & Fats: Oils: Mustard*
Mustard Powder *See Spices, Seasonings & Seeds: Spices: Mustard Powder; See also Ingredients, Flavors & Additives: Powders: Mustard*
Mustard Seeds *See Spices, Seasonings & Seeds: Seeds: Mustard*
Mustard Spices *See Spices, Seasonings & Seeds: Spices: Mustards; See also Spices, Seasonings & Seeds: Spices: Mustard*
Mustard Spices, Dry - Prepared *See Spices, Seasonings & Seeds: Spices: Mustard: Dry - Prepared*
Mutton *See Meats & Meat Products: Mutton*

N

Nacho Cheese Sauces *See Sauces, Dips & Dressings: Sauces: Cheese: Nacho*
Nacho Cheese Snack Seasonings *See Spices, Seasonings & Seeds: Seasonings: Snack: Nacho Cheese*
Nacho Chips *See Snack Foods: Chips: Nacho*
Napoli Salami *See Meats & Meat Products: Smoked, Cured & Deli Meats: Salami: Napoli*
Natural Chemicals *See Ingredients, Flavors & Additives: Chemicals: Natural*
Natural Colors *See Ingredients, Flavors & Additives: Colors: Natural; See also See Ingredients, Flavors & Additives: Colors: Natural: Others*
Natural Flavorings Spices *See Spices, Seasonings & Seeds: Spices: Natural Flavorings*
Natural Granules Honey *See Sugars, Syrups & Sweeteners: Honey: Granules: Natural*
Natural Gums *See Ingredients, Flavors & Additives: Gums: Natural*
Natural Organic Foods *See Specialty & Organic Foods: Organic Foods: Natural*
Natural Sweeteners *See Sugars, Syrups & Sweeteners: Natural Sweeteners*
Naval Orange *See Fruits & Vegetables: Orange: Naval*
Navy Beans *See Fruits & Vegetables: Beans: Navy*
Nectar *See Fruits & Vegetables: Nectar*
Nectarines *See Fruits & Vegetables: Nectarines*
Neutral Spirits & Liqueurs *See Beverages: Spirits & Liqueurs: Neutral*
New England Chowder *See Prepared Foods: Soups & Stews: Chowder: New England*
New York Style Cheese Cake *See Baked Goods: Cakes & Pastries: Cheese Cake: New York Style*
Niacin *See Ingredients, Flavors & Additives: Vitamins & Supplements: Niacin*
No Salt Potato Chips *See Snack Foods: Chips: Potato: No Salt*
No-Fat Cheese *See Cheese & Cheese Products: Cheese: No-Fat*
No-Fat Yogurt *See Dairy Products: Yogurt: No-Fat*
Non-Alcoholic Beers *See Beverages: Beers: Non-Alcoholic*
Non-Alcoholic Beverages *See Beverages: Non-Alcoholic Beverages*
Non-Alcoholic Wines *See Beverages: Wines: Non-Alcoholic*
Non-Dairy & Imitation Dairy Bases *See Ingredients, Flavors & Additives: Bases: Dairy: Non-Dairy & Imitation*
Non-Dairy Coffee Creamers *See Dairy Products: Creamers: Coffee: Non-Dairy*
Non-Dairy Cream *See Dairy Products: Cream: Non-Dairy*
Non-Dairy Desserts *See Baked Goods: Desserts: Non-Dairy*
Non-Dairy Ice Cream *See Dairy Products: Ice Cream: Non-Dairy*
Non-Dairy Whipped Toppings *See Ingredients, Flavors & Additives: Toppings: Whipped: Non-Dairy*
Non-Fat Cheese Cake *See Baked Goods: Cakes & Pastries: Cheese Cake: Non-Fat*
Non-Fat Milk Solids *See Dairy Products: Milk & Milk Products: Milk Solids: Non-Fat*
Non-Fat Salad Dressings *See Sauces, Dips & Dressings: Salad Dressings: Non-Fat*
Non-Fruit Pies *See Baked Goods: Pies: Non-Fruit*
Non-Fruit Toppings *See Ingredients, Flavors & Additives: Toppings: Non-Fruit*
Non-Stick Coatings *See Ingredients, Flavors & Additives: Coatings: Non-Stick*
Nonpareils *See Candy & Confectionery: Candy: Nonpareils*
Noodles *See Pasta & Noodles: Noodles*
Nougats *See Candy & Confectionery: Candy: Nougats*
Novelties, Candy *See Candy & Confectionery: Candy: Novelties*
Novelties, Ice Cream *See Dairy Products: Ice Cream: Novelties*
Nut Breads *See Baked Goods: Breads: Nut*
Nut Butters *See Nuts & Nut Butters: Nut Butters*
Nut Flavors *See Ingredients, Flavors & Additives: Flavors: Nut*
Nut Flour *See Cereals, Grains, Rice & Flour: Flour: Nut*
Nut Meats *See Nuts & Nut Butters: Nuts: Nut Meats*
Nut Pastes *See Nuts & Nut Butters: Nut Pastes*
Nutmeg *See Spices, Seasonings & Seeds: Spices: Nutmeg (See also Mace)*
Nutmeg Oils *See Oils, Shortening & Fats: Oils: Nutmeg*
Nutraceuticals *See Ingredients, Flavors & Additives: Vitamins & Supplements: Nutraceuticals*
Nutritional Supplements *See Ingredients, Flavors & Additives: Vitamins & Supplements: Nutritional Supplements*
Nuts *See Nuts & Nut Butters: Nuts*
NY Strip Steak *See Meats & Meat Products: Beef & Beef Products: NY Strip Steak*

O

Oat Bran *See Cereals, Grains, Rice & Flour: Oats & Oat Products: Oat Bran*
Oat Bran Fiber *See Cereals, Grains, Rice & Flour: Fiber: Oat Bran*
Oat Fiber Crisps *See Cereals, Grains, Rice & Flour: Crisps: Oat Fiber*
Oat Flour *See Cereals, Grains, Rice & Flour: Flour: Oat*
Oatmeal *See Cereals, Grains, Rice & Flour: Oats & Oat Products: Oatmeal*
Oatmeal & Chocolate Chip Cookies *See Baked Goods: Cookies & Bars: Oatmeal & Chocolate Chip Cookies*
Oatmeal Cereal *See Cereals, Grains, Rice & Flour: Cereal: Oatmeal*
Oatmeal Cookies *See Baked Goods: Cookies & Bars: Oatmeal Cookies*
Oatmeal Raisin Cookies *See Baked Goods: Cookies & Bars: Oatmeal Raisin Cookies*
Oats & Oat Products *See Cereals, Grains, Rice & Flour: Oats & Oat Products*
Oats Fiber *See Cereals, Grains, Rice & Flour: Fiber: Oats*
Oats Flakes *See Ingredients, Flavors & Additives: Flakes: Oats*
Ocean Perch *See Fish & Seafood: Fish: Perch: Ocean*

1 2 3 4 5
EXAMPLE: **Canadian Style Bacon** *See Meats & Meat Products: Smoked, Cured & Deli Meats: Bacon: Canadian Style*

1. Product or Service you are looking for
2. Main Category, in alphabetical order, located in the page headers starting on page 23
3. Category Description, located in black bars and in page headers
4. Product Category, located in gray bars
5. Product Type, located under gray bars, centered in bold

Octopus *See Fish & Seafood: Shellfish: Octopus*
Oil & Vinegar Salad Dressings *See Sauces, Dips & Dressings: Salad Dressings: Oil & Vinegar*
Oil & Vinegar Salad Dressings, Mixes *See Sauces, Dips & Dressings: Salad Dressings: Mixes: Oil & Vinegar*
Oils *See Oils, Shortening & Fats; See also See Oils, Shortening & Fats: Oils*
Okra *See Fruits & Vegetables: Okra*
Olive Loaf *See Meats & Meat Products: Smoked, Cured & Deli Meats: Olive Loaf*
Olive Oil Anchovies *See Fish & Seafood: Fish: Anchovies: Olive Oil*
Olive Oil Bread Sticks *See Baked Goods: Bread Sticks: Olive Oil*
Olive Oils *See Oils, Shortening & Fats: Oils: Olive*
Olive Spreads *See Jams, Jellies & Spreads: Spreads: Olive*
Olives *See Fruits & Vegetables: Olives*
One Percent Milk *See Dairy Products: Milk & Milk Products: Milk: 1 Percent*
Onion *See Fruits & Vegetables: Onion*
Onion Bread Sticks *See Baked Goods: Bread Sticks: Onion*
Onion for Dehydration *See Fruits & Vegetables: Dried & Dehydrated Vegetables: Onion: for Dehydration*
Onion Juices *See Beverages: Juices: Onion*
Onion Oils *See Oils, Shortening & Fats: Oils: Onion*
Onion Powders *See Ingredients, Flavors & Additives: Powders: Onion (See also Spices/Onion Powder)*
Onion Rings *See Prepared Foods: Onion Rings*
Onion Salt *See Spices, Seasonings & Seeds: Salt: Onion*
Onion Spices *See Spices, Seasonings & Seeds: Spices: Onion*
Onion, Dried & Dehydrated *See Fruits & Vegetables: Dried & Dehydrated Vegetables: Onion*
Oolong Tea *See Beverages: Coffee & Tea: Tea: Oolong*
Orange *See Fruits & Vegetables: Orange*
Orange Ade Juices *See Beverages: Juices: Ade: Orange*
Orange Flavors *See Ingredients, Flavors & Additives: Flavors: Orange*
Orange Juices *See Beverages: Juices: Orange*
Orange Juices, Not Concentrated *See Beverages: Juices: Orange: Not Concentrated*
Orange Oils *See Oils, Shortening & Fats: Oils: Orange*
Orange Peel Pieces *See Fruits & Vegetables: Orange: Peels: Pieces*
Orange Pekoe Tea *See Beverages: Coffee & Tea: Tea: Orange Pekoe*
Orange Puree *See Fruits & Vegetables: Pulps & Purees: Puree: Orange*
Orange Roughy *See Fish & Seafood: Fish: Orange Roughy*
Orange Sauces *See Sauces, Dips & Dressings: Sauces: Orange*
Orange Sections *See Fruits & Vegetables: Orange: Sections*
Oregano Spices *See Spices, Seasonings & Seeds: Spices: Oregano*
Organic *See Baby Foods: Organic*
Organic Carrot *See Fruits & Vegetables: Carrot: Organic*
Organic Foods *See Specialty & Organic Foods: Organic Foods*
Organic Pellets *See Ingredients, Flavors & Additives: Half-Products: Organic Pellets*
Organic Rice *See Cereals, Grains, Rice & Flour: Rice: Organic*
Organic Sauces *See Sauces, Dips & Dressings: Sauces: Organic*
Oriental *See Ethnic Foods: Oriental*
Oriental Mustard *See Sauces, Dips & Dressings: Mustard: Oriental*
Oriental Noodles *See Pasta & Noodles: Noodles: Oriental*
Oriental Vegetables *See Fruits & Vegetables: Oriental Vegetables*
Orzo Pasta *See Pasta & Noodles: Pasta: Orzo*
Osaka Purple Mustard *See Fruits & Vegetables: Mustard: Osaka Purple*
Ostrich *See Meats & Meat Products: Game: Ostrich*
Oven Type Potatoes *See Fruits & Vegetables: Potatoes: Oven Type*
Oyster Mushrooms *See Fruits & Vegetables: Mushrooms: Oyster*
Oyster Mushrooms, Dried *See Fruits & Vegetables: Dried & Dehydrated Vegetables: Mushrooms: Oyster*
Oyster Sauces *See Sauces, Dips & Dressings: Sauces: Oyster*
Oysters *See Fish & Seafood: Shellfish: Oysters*

P

Packaged Meats *See Meats & Meat Products: Packaged*
Packed Fish *See Fish & Seafood: Fish: Packed*
Paella *See Ethnic Foods: Paella*
Pale Ale *See Beverages: Beers: American & British Ale: Pale Ale*
Palm Kernel Oils *See Oils, Shortening & Fats: Oils: Palm: Kernel*
Palm Oils *See Oils, Shortening & Fats: Oils: Palm*
Pan Coatings & Sprays *See Oils, Shortening & Fats: Pan Coatings & Sprays*
Pancake Batters *See Doughs, Mixes & Fillings: Batters: Pancake*
Pancake Flour *See Cereals, Grains, Rice & Flour: Flour: Pancake*
Pancake Mixes *See Doughs, Mixes & Fillings: Mixes: Pancake*
Pancake Syrups *See Sugars, Syrups & Sweeteners: Syrups: Pancake*
Pancakes *See Prepared Foods: Pancakes*
Pancakes with Fruit *See Prepared Foods: Pancakes: with Fruit*
Panettones *See Baked Goods: Cakes & Pastries: Panettones*
Pantothenic Acid *See Ingredients, Flavors & Additives: Vitamins & Supplements: Pantothenic Acid*
Papaya *See Fruits & Vegetables: Papaya*
Papaya Juices *See Beverages: Juices: Papaya*
Paprika *See Spices, Seasonings & Seeds: Spices: Paprika*
Paraffin Waxes *See Ingredients, Flavors & Additives: Waxes: Paraffin*
Parboiled Rice *See Cereals, Grains, Rice & Flour: Rice: Parboiled*
Parmesan Cheese *See Cheese & Cheese Products: Cheese: Parmesan*
Parmesan Cheese, Imitation *See Cheese & Cheese Products: Imitation Cheeses & Substitutes: Imitation: Parmesan*
Parmesan Salad Dressing Mixes *See Sauces, Dips & Dressings: Salad Dressings: Mixes: Parmesan*
Parsley Spices *See Spices, Seasonings & Seeds: Spices: Parsley*
Particulates *See Ingredients, Flavors & Additives: Particulates*
Partridge *See Meats & Meat Products: Game: Partridge*
Parve Foods *See Ethnic Foods: Parve Foods*
Passion Fruit Flavors *See Ingredients, Flavors & Additives: Flavors: Passion Fruit*
Passion Fruit Juices *See Beverages: Juices: Passion Fruit*
Pasta *See Pasta & Noodles: Pasta*
Pasta & Noodle Dishes *See Prepared Foods: Prepared Meals: Pasta & Noodle Dishes*
Pasta & Noodles *See Pasta & Noodles*
Pasta Prepared Salads *See Prepared Foods: Prepared Salads: Pasta*
Pasta Sauces *See Sauces, Dips & Dressings: Sauces: Pasta*
Pastes *See Ingredients, Flavors & Additives: Pastes*
Pastrami *See Meats & Meat Products: Smoked, Cured & Deli Meats: Pastrami*
Pastries *See Baked Goods: Cakes & Pastries: Pastries*
Pastry Flour *See Cereals, Grains, Rice & Flour: Flour: Pastry*
Pates *See Meats & Meat Products: Pates & Fois Gras: Pates*
Pates & Fois Gras *See Meats & Meat Products: Pates & Fois Gras*
Patti Sausages *See Meats & Meat Products: Smoked, Cured & Deli Meats: Sausages: Patti*
Patties, Beef *See Meats & Meat Products: Beef & Beef Products: Patties*
Patties, Breaded Chicken *See Meats & Meat Products: Poultry: Chicken: Patties Breaded*
Patties, Chicken *See Meats & Meat Products: Poultry: Chicken: Patties*
Patties, Fish *See Fish & Seafood: Fish: Patties*
Patties, Vegetarian *See Specialty & Organic Foods: Vegetarian Products: Patties*
Pau D'Arco Bark Powders *See Ingredients, Flavors & Additives: Powders: Pau D'Arco Bark*
Peach *See Fruits & Vegetables: Peach*
Peach Flavors *See Ingredients, Flavors & Additives: Flavors: Peach*
Peach Juices *See Beverages: Juices: Peach*
Peach Pies *See Baked Goods: Pies: Peach*
Peaches, Sliced *See Fruits & Vegetables: Peach: Sliced*
Peanut Brittle *See Candy & Confectionery: Candy: Peanut Brittle*
Peanut Butter *See Nuts & Nut Butters: Nut Butters: Peanut Butter*
Peanut Butter Chips *See Snack Foods: Chips: Peanut Butter*
Peanut Butter, No Additives *See Nuts & Nut Butters: Nut Butters: Peanut Butter: No Additives*
Peanut Butter, Smooth *See Nuts & Nut Butters: Nut Butters: Peanut Butter: Smooth*
Peanut Flour *See Cereals, Grains, Rice & Flour: Flour: Peanut*
Peanut Oils *See Oils, Shortening & Fats: Oils: Peanut*
Peanut Sauces *See Sauces, Dips & Dressings: Sauces: Peanut*
Peanut Seeds *See Spices, Seasonings & Seeds: Seeds: Peanut*
Peanuts *See Nuts & Nut Butters: Nuts: Peanuts*
Pear *See Fruits & Vegetables: Pear*
Pear Flavors *See Ingredients, Flavors & Additives: Flavors: Pear*
Pear Juices *See Beverages: Juices: Pear*
Pear, Canned Halves *See Fruits & Vegetables: Pear: Canned: Halves*
Pearl & Cocktail Onions *See Fruits & Vegetables: Onion: Pearl & Cocktail Onions*
Pearl Tapioca *See Cereals, Grains, Rice & Flour: Tapioca: Pearl*
Peas *See Fruits & Vegetables: Peas*
Peas & Carrots *See Fruits & Vegetables: Vegetables Mixed: Peas & Carrots*
Peas, Air-dried *See Fruits & Vegetables: Dried & Dehydrated Vegetables: Peas - Air-dried*
Pecan Butter Flavors *See Ingredients, Flavors & Additives: Flavors: Butter: Pecan*
Pecan Log *See Baked Goods: Cakes & Pastries: Pecan Log*
Pecan Nuts *See Nuts & Nut Butters: Nuts: Pecan*
Pecorino *See Cheese & Cheese Products: Cheese: Pecorino*
Pectin Gums *See Ingredients, Flavors & Additives: Gums: Pectin*
Pectins *See Ingredients, Flavors & Additives: Pectins*
Peeled Carrot *See Fruits & Vegetables: Carrot: Peeled*
Peeled Eggs *See Eggs & Egg Products: Peeled*
Peeled Shrimp *See Fish & Seafood: Shellfish: Shrimp: Peeled*
Peels, Citrus Fruits *See Fruits & Vegetables: Citrus Fruits: Peels*
Peels, Lemon *See Fruits & Vegetables: Lemon: Peels*
Peels, Orange *See Fruits & Vegetables: Orange: Peels*
Peking Duck *See Meats & Meat Products: Game: Peking Duck*
Penne *See Pasta & Noodles: Penne*
Pentanol *See Ingredients, Flavors & Additives: Alcohols: Pentanol*
Pepatello *See Cheese & Cheese Products: Cheese: Pepatello*
Pepper *See Spices, Seasonings & Seeds: Spices: Pepper*
Pepper Blends *See Ingredients, Flavors & Additives: Blends: Pepper*
Pepper Mash *See Spices, Seasonings & Seeds: Spices: Pepper Mash*
Pepper Oils *See Oils, Shortening & Fats: Oils: Pepper*
Pepper Sauces *See Sauces, Dips & Dressings: Sauces: Pepper*
Peppercorn Salad Dressing Mixes *See Sauces, Dips & Dressings: Salad Dressings: Mixes: Peppercorn*
Peppercorns *See Spices, Seasonings & Seeds: Spices: Peppercorns*
Peppermint *See Spices, Seasonings & Seeds: Spices: Peppermint*
Peppermint Flavors *See Ingredients, Flavors & Additives: Flavors: Peppermint*
Peppermint Leaf Tea *See Beverages: Coffee & Tea: Tea: Peppermint Leaf*
Peppermint Oils *See Oils, Shortening & Fats: Oils: Peppermint*
Pepperoncini Peppers *See Fruits & Vegetables: Peppers: Pepperoncini*
Pepperoni *See Meats & Meat Products: Smoked, Cured & Deli Meats: Pepperoni*
Pepperoni Salami *See Meats & Meat Products: Smoked, Cured & Deli Meats: Salami: Pepperoni*
Peppers *See Fruits & Vegetables: Peppers*
Peppers, Pickled *See Relishes & Pickled Products: Pickled Products: Peppers*
Perch *See Fish & Seafood: Fish: Perch*
Persimmons *See Fruits & Vegetables: Persimmons*
Pesto Sauces *See Sauces, Dips & Dressings: Sauces: Pesto*
Petit Fours *See Baked Goods: Cakes & Pastries: Petit Fours*
Pheasant *See Meats & Meat Products: Game: Pheasant*
Phosphates *See Ingredients, Flavors & Additives: Phosphates*
Phosphoric Acidulants *See Ingredients, Flavors & Additives: Acidulants: Phosphoric*
Picante Salsa *See Sauces, Dips & Dressings: Salsa: Picante*
Pickerel *See Fish & Seafood: Fish: Pickerel*
Pickled Ginger *See Fruits & Vegetables: Ginger: Pickled*
Pickled Meat Products *See Relishes & Pickled Products: Pickled Products: Meats*
Pickled Products *See Relishes & Pickled Products: Pickled Products*

Pickles *See Relishes & Pickled Products: Pickled Products: Pickles*
Pickling Spices *See Spices, Seasonings & Seeds: Spices: Pickling Spices*
Pie Crust Mixes *See Doughs, Mixes & Fillings: Mixes: Pie Crust*
Pie Fillings *See Doughs, Mixes & Fillings: Fillings: Pie*
Pierogies *See Prepared Foods: Pierogies*
Pies *See Baked Goods: Pies*
Pignolias Nuts *See Nuts & Nut Butters: Nuts: Pignolias*
Pigs' Feet *See Meats & Meat Products: Pork & Pork Products: Pigs' Feet*
Pike *See Fish & Seafood: Fish: Pike*
Pilsner Lager *See Beverages: Beers: Lager: Pilsner*
Pimiento Oils *See Oils, Shortening & Fats: Oils: Pimiento*
Pimientos *See Fruits & Vegetables: Pimientos*
Pine Nuts *See Nuts & Nut Butters: Nuts: Pine*
Pineapple *See Fruits & Vegetables: Pineapple*
Pineapple Flavors *See Ingredients, Flavors & Additives: Flavors: Pineapple*
Pineapple Juices *See Beverages: Juices: Pineapple*
Pink Beans *See Fruits & Vegetables: Beans: Pink*
Pink Grapefruit *See Fruits & Vegetables: Grapefruit: Pink*
Pink Salmon *See Fish & Seafood: Fish: Salmon: Pink*
Pinot Blanc *See Beverages: Wines: White Grape Varieties: Pinot Blanc*
Pinot Gris *See Beverages: Wines: White Grape Varieties: Pinot Gris*
Pinot Noir *See Beverages: Wines: Red Grape Wines: Pinot Noir*
Pinto Beans *See Fruits & Vegetables: Beans: Pinto*
Pistachio Nuts *See Nuts & Nut Butters: Nuts: Pistachio*
Pita Breads *See Baked Goods: Breads: Pita*
Pita Chips *See Snack Foods: Chips: Pita*
Pizelle *See Prepared Foods: Pizelle*
Pizza *See Prepared Foods: Pizza & Pizza Products: Pizza*
Pizza & Pizza Products *See Prepared Foods: Pizza & Pizza Products*
Pizza Bagels *See Prepared Foods: Pizza & Pizza Products: Pizza Bagels*
Pizza Crust *See Prepared Foods: Pizza & Pizza Products: Pizza: Crust*
Pizza Doughs *See Doughs, Mixes & Fillings: Doughs: Pizza*
Pizza Sauces *See Sauces, Dips & Dressings: Sauces: Pizza*
Pizza Seasonings *See Spices, Seasonings & Seeds: Seasonings: Pizza*
Pizza Shells *See Prepared Foods: Pizza & Pizza Products: Shells*
Pizza Toppings *See Prepared Foods: Pizza & Pizza Products: Pizza Toppings*
Plantain Chips *See Snack Foods: Chips: Plantain*
Plantains *See Fruits & Vegetables: Banana: Plantain*
Plum Pudding *See Dairy Products: Pudding: Plum*
Plum Sauces *See Sauces, Dips & Dressings: Sauces: Plum*
Plum Tomato *See Fruits & Vegetables: Tomato: Plum*
Plums *See Fruits & Vegetables: Plums*
Pocket Sandwiches *See Prepared Foods: Prepared Meals: Sandwiches: Pocket*
Poi *See Cereals, Grains, Rice & Flour: Poi*
Polenta *See Pasta & Noodles: Pasta: Polenta*
Polish Sausages *See Meats & Meat Products: Smoked, Cured & Deli Meats: Sausages: Polish*
Pollack *See Fish & Seafood: Fish: Pollack*
Polythylene Glycols *See Ingredients, Flavors & Additives: Polythylene Glycols*
Pomace Apple *See Fruits & Vegetables: Apple: Pomace*
Pomace Olive Oils *See Oils, Shortening & Fats: Oils: Olive: Pomace*
Pomegranate *See Fruits & Vegetables: Pomegranate*
Pompano *See Fish & Seafood: Fish: Pompano*
Popcorn *See Snack Foods: Popcorn*
Popcorn Specialties *See Candy & Confectionery: Candy: Popcorn Specialties*
Popping Corn Oils *See Oils, Shortening & Fats: Oils: Popping Corn*
Poppy & Sesame Crackers *See Baked Goods: Crackers: Poppy & Sesame Crackers*
Poppy Seed Oils *See Oils, Shortening & Fats: Oils: Poppy Seed*
Poppy Seeds *See Spices, Seasonings & Seeds: Seeds: Poppy*
Popsicles *See Dairy Products: Ice Cream: Popsicles*
Porcini Mushrooms *See Fruits & Vegetables: Mushrooms: Porcini*
Porcini Mushrooms, Dried *See Fruits & Vegetables: Dried & Dehydrated Vegetables: Mushrooms: Porcini*
Pork & Beans *See Prepared Foods: Pork & Beans (see also Baked Beans)*
Pork & Pork Products *See Meats & Meat Products: Pork & Pork Products*
Pork Casings *See Meats & Meat Products: Smoked, Cured & Deli Meats: Sausages: Casings: Sausage, Pork, Beef*
Pork Frankfurters *See Meats & Meat Products: Frankfurters: Pork*
Pork Rinds *See Snack Foods: Pork Rinds*
Pork Sausages *See Meats & Meat Products: Smoked, Cured & Deli Meats: Sausages: Pork*
Porkskins *See Prepared Foods: Porkskins*
Porter *See Beverages: Beers: Stout & Porter: Porter*
Porterhouse Beef *See Meats & Meat Products: Beef & Beef Products: Porterhouse*
Portion Contol & Packaged Foods *See Prepared Foods: Portion Contol & Packaged Foods*
Portioned Juices *See Beverages: Juices: Portioned*
Portobello Mushrooms *See Fruits & Vegetables: Mushrooms: Portobello*
Portuguese Port Wines *See Beverages: Wines: Portuguese: Port*
Portuguese Wines *See Beverages: Wines: Portuguese*
Pot Pies *See Prepared Foods: Pot Pies*
Pot Roast *See Meats & Meat Products: Beef & Beef Products: Pot Roast*
Pot Stickers *See Prepared Foods: Pot Stickers*
Potassium Bitartrate *See Ingredients, Flavors & Additives: Potassium Bitartrate (Cream of Tartar)*
Potassium Bromate *See Ingredients, Flavors & Additives: Potassium Bromate*
Potassium Citrate *See Ingredients, Flavors & Additives: Potassium Citrate*
Potassium Lactate *See Ingredients, Flavors & Additives: Potassium Lactate*
Potassium Sorbate *See Ingredients, Flavors & Additives: Potassium Sorbate*
Potato Chips *See Snack Foods: Chips: Potato*
Potato Chips, No Salt *See Snack Foods: Chips: Potato: No Salt*
Potato Flakes *See Ingredients, Flavors & Additives: Flakes: Potato*
Potato Flour *See Cereals, Grains, Rice & Flour: Flour: Potato*
Potato Products *See Prepared Foods: Potato Products*
Potato Puffs, Frozen Products *See Prepared Foods: Potato Products: Puffs - Frozen*
Potato Starches *See Ingredients, Flavors & Additives: Starches: Potato*
Potato Sticks *See Snack Foods: Potato Sticks*
Potato, Prepared Salads *See Prepared Foods: Prepared Salads: Potato*
Potatoes *See Fruits & Vegetables: Potatoes; See also See Fruits & Vegetables: Potatoes: Potatoes*
Potatoes, Frozen Wedges *See Fruits & Vegetables: Potatoes: Frozen: Wedges*
Pouch-Packed Fish *See Fish & Seafood: Fish: Packed: Pouch*
Pouch-Packed Tuna Fish *See Fish & Seafood: Fish: Tuna: Pouch-Packed*
Poultry *See Meats & Meat Products: Poultry*
Poultry & Game *See Meats & Meat Products: Smoked, Cured & Deli Meats: Smoked Meat: Poultry & Game*
Poultry Flavors *See Ingredients, Flavors & Additives: Flavors: Poultry*
Poultry, Certified Organic *See Specialty & Organic Foods: Organic Foods: Certified: Poultry*
Pound Cake *See Baked Goods: Cakes & Pastries: Pound Cake*
Powdered Broth *See Prepared Foods: Broth: Powdered*
Powdered Chicken Fats & Lard *See Oils, Shortening & Fats: Fats & Lard: Chicken: Powdered*
Powdered Fruit Juices *See Beverages: Juices: Powdered Fruit*
Powdered Garlic *See Spices, Seasonings & Seeds: Spices: Garlic: Powdered*
Powdered Mixes *See Doughs, Mixes & Fillings: Mixes: Powdered*
Powdered Sugar *See Sugars, Syrups & Sweeteners: Sugar: Powdered*
Powdered Vegetables *See Fruits & Vegetables: Powdered Vegetables*
Powders *See Ingredients, Flavors & Additives: Powders*
Powders Prepared for Further Processing *See Ingredients, Flavors & Additives: Powders: Prepared for Further Processing*
Pralines *See Nuts & Nut Butters: Nuts: Pralines (See also Confectionery)*
Prawns *See Fish & Seafood: Shellfish: Prawns*
Precooked Rice *See Cereals, Grains, Rice & Flour: Rice: Precooked*
Preformed Snack Pellets *See Snack Foods: Snack Pellets: Preformed*
Pregelatinized Powders *See Ingredients, Flavors & Additives: Powders: Pregelatinized*
Pregelatinized Starches *See Ingredients, Flavors & Additives: Starches: Pregelatinized*
Prepared Bases *See Ingredients, Flavors & Additives: Bases: Prepared*
Prepared Chicken *See Meats & Meat Products: Poultry: Chicken: Prepared*
Prepared Cocktail Mixes *See Beverages: Mixers: Prepared Cocktail Mixes*
Prepared Eggs *See Eggs & Egg Products: Prepared*
Prepared Foods *See Prepared Foods*
Prepared Frozen Chicken *See Meats & Meat Products: Poultry: Chicken: Prepared Frozen*
Prepared Gravy *See Sauces, Dips & Dressings: Gravy: Prepared*
Prepared Meals *See Prepared Foods: Prepared Meals*
Prepared Mustard *See Spices, Seasonings & Seeds: Spices: Mustard: Prepared*
Prepared Pork & Pork Products *See Meats & Meat Products: Pork & Pork Products: Prepared*
Prepared Salads *See Prepared Foods: Prepared Salads*
Prepared Yams *See Fruits & Vegetables: Yams: Prepared*
Preservatives *See Ingredients, Flavors & Additives: Preservatives*
Pressed Dextrose Candy *See Candy & Confectionery: Candy: Pressed Dextrose*
Pretzels *See Snack Foods: Pretzels*
Pretzels, Sticks or Rods *See Snack Foods: Pretzels: Sticks or Rods*
Primary Dried Yeast *See Ingredients, Flavors & Additives: Cultures & Yeasts: Yeast: Primary Dried*
Primavera Sauces *See Sauces, Dips & Dressings: Sauces: Primavera*
Process Cheese Loaves *See Cheese & Cheese Products: Cheese: Process Loaves*
Process Sliced Cheese *See Cheese & Cheese Products: Cheese: Process Sliced*
Processed American Cheese *See Cheese & Cheese Products: Cheese: Processed American*
Processed Beef & Beef Products *See Meats & Meat Products: Beef & Beef Products: Processed*
Processed Coconut & Coconut Products *See Fruits & Vegetables: Coconut & Coconut Products: Processed*
Processed Swiss Cheese *See Cheese & Cheese Products: Cheese: Processed Swiss*
Processed Tomato *See Fruits & Vegetables: Tomato: Processed*
Produce *See Fruits & Vegetables: Produce*
Produce, Certified Organic *See Specialty & Organic Foods: Organic Foods: Certified: Produce*
Products, Beef *See Meats & Meat Products: Beef & Beef Products: Products*
Products, Cranberry *See Fruits & Vegetables: Berries: Cranberry: Products*
Products, Tomato *See Fruits & Vegetables: Tomato: Products*
Propanol Alcohols *See Ingredients, Flavors & Additives: Alcohols: Propanol*
Propylene Glycols *See Ingredients, Flavors & Additives: Alcohols: Propylene Glycols*
Prosciutto *See Meats & Meat Products: Smoked, Cured & Deli Meats: Prosciutto*
Protein Clusters Toppings *See Ingredients, Flavors & Additives: Toppings: Protein Clusters*
Protein Powders *See Ingredients, Flavors & Additives: Powders: Protein*
Protein Supplements *See Ingredients, Flavors & Additives: Vitamins & Supplements: Protein Supplements*
Protein, Rice *See Cereals, Grains, Rice & Flour: Rice: Protein*
Protein, Soy *See Fruits & Vegetables: Soy: Protein*
Proteins *See Ingredients, Flavors & Additives: Proteins*
Provolone *See Cheese & Cheese Products: Cheese: Provolone*

1 2 3 4 5
EXAMPLE: **Canadian Style Bacon** *See Meats & Meat Products: Smoked, Cured & Deli Meats: Bacon: Canadian Style*

1. Product or Service you are looking for
2. Main Category, in alphabetical order, located in the page headers starting on page 23
3. Category Description, located in black bars and in page headers
4. Product Category, located in gray bars
5. Product Type, located under gray bars, centered in bold

Prune Juices *See Beverages: Juices: Prune*

Prunes *See Fruits & Vegetables: Prunes*

Pudding *See Dairy Products: Pudding*

Puff Pastry *See Baked Goods: Cakes & Pastries: Puff Pastry*

Puff Pastry Doughs *See Doughs, Mixes & Fillings: Doughs: Puff Pastry*

Pulp *See Fruits & Vegetables: Pulps & Purees: Pulp*

Pulps & Purees *See Fruits & Vegetables: Pulps & Purees*

Pumpernickel *See Baked Goods: Breads: Pumpernickel*

Pumpkin *See Fruits & Vegetables: Pumpkin*

Pumpkin Seed Oils *See Oils, Shortening & Fats: Oils: Pumpkin Seed*

Pumpkin Seeds *See Spices, Seasonings & Seeds: Seeds: Pumpkin*

Punch Mixes *See Doughs, Mixes & Fillings: Mixes: Punch*

Punch Powders *See Ingredients, Flavors & Additives: Powders: Punch*

Puree *See Fruits & Vegetables: Pulps & Purees: Puree*

Purple Sticky Rice *See Cereals, Grains, Rice & Flour: Rice: Purple Sticky*

Puttanesca Sauces *See Sauces, Dips & Dressings: Sauces: Puttanesca*

Q

Quail *See Meats & Meat Products: Game: Quail (See also Eggs: Quail)*

Quail Eggs *See Eggs & Egg Products: Quail*

Quiche *See Prepared Foods: Quiche*

Quince *See Fruits & Vegetables: Quince*

Quinoa *See Cereals, Grains, Rice & Flour: Quinoa*

R

Rabbit *See Meats & Meat Products: Game: Rabbit*

Radish *See Fruits & Vegetables: Radish*

Rainbow Trout *See Fish & Seafood: Fish: Trout: Rainbow*

Raisin Breads *See Baked Goods: Breads: Raisin*

Raisin Juice Replacers *See Ingredients, Flavors & Additives: Replacers: Raisin Juice*

Raisin Juices *See Beverages: Juices: Raisin*

Raisins *See Fruits & Vegetables: Raisins*

Ramen Noodles *See Pasta & Noodles: Noodles: Ramen*

Ranch Salad Dressing *See Sauces, Dips & Dressings: Salad Dressings: Ranch*

Ranch Salad Dressing Mixes *See Sauces, Dips & Dressings: Salad Dressings: Mixes: Ranch*

Ranch Snack Seasonings *See Spices, Seasonings & Seeds: Seasonings: Snack: Ranch*

Rape Seeds *See Spices, Seasonings & Seeds: Seeds: Rape*

Raschera *See Cheese & Cheese Products: Cheese: Raschera*

Raspberries *See Fruits & Vegetables: Berries: Raspberries*

Raspberry Flavors *See Ingredients, Flavors & Additives: Flavors: Raspberry*

Raspberry Juices *See Beverages: Juices: Raspberry*

Raspberry Vinegar *See Sauces, Dips & Dressings: Vinegar: Raspberry*

Raspberry Vinegrette Salad Dressing *See Sauces, Dips & Dressings: Salad Dressings: Raspberry Vinegrette*

Raspberry Vinegrette Salad Dressing Mixes *See Sauces, Dips & Dressings: Salad Dressings: Mixes: Raspberry Vinegrette*

Ravioli *See Pasta & Noodles: Ravioli*

Raw & Shelled Peanuts *See Nuts & Nut Butters: Nuts: Peanuts: Raw & Shelled*

Raw Beef & Beef Products *See Meats & Meat Products: Beef & Beef Products: Raw*

Raw Chicken *See Meats & Meat Products: Poultry: Chicken: Raw*

Raw Crayfish *See Fish & Seafood: Shellfish: Crayfish: Raw*

Raw Peanuts *See Nuts & Nut Butters: Nuts: Peanuts: Raw*

Raw Pork & Pork Products *See Meats & Meat Products: Pork & Pork Products: Raw*

Raw Turkey *See Meats & Meat Products: Poultry: Turkey: Raw*

Raw Veal *See Meats & Meat Products: Beef & Beef Products: Veal: Raw*

Ready to Use Icings *See Candy & Confectionery: Decorations & Icings: Icings: Ready to Use*

Red Bell Peppers, Dried *See Fruits & Vegetables: Dried & Dehydrated Vegetables: Bell Peppers: Red*

Red Bordeaux *See Beverages: Wines: French: Red Bordeaux*

Red Burgundy *See Beverages: Wines: French: Red Burgundy*

Red Cabbage *See Fruits & Vegetables: Cabbage: Red*

Red Currants *See Fruits & Vegetables: Berries: Currants: Red*

Red Delicious Apple *See Fruits & Vegetables: Apple: Red Delicious*

Red Grape Wines *See Beverages: Wines: Red Grape Wines; See also Beverages: Wines: Red Grapes*

Red Looseleaf Lettuce *See Fruits & Vegetables: Lettuce: Looseleaf: Red*

Red Meritage/Bordeaux *See Beverages: Wines: Red Grape Wines: Red Meritage/Bordeaux*

Red Onion *See Fruits & Vegetables: Onion: Red*

Red Pear *See Fruits & Vegetables: Pear: Red*

Red Pepper *See Spices, Seasonings & Seeds: Spices: Red Pepper; See also See Spices, Seasonings & Seeds: Spices: Pepper: Black - White - Red*

Red Potatoes *See Fruits & Vegetables: Potatoes: Red*

Reduced-Calorie Beer *See Beverages: Beers: Specialty &Cider: Reduced Calorie Beer*

Reduced-Calorie Salad Dressing Mixes *See Sauces, Dips & Dressings: Salad Dressings: Mixes: Reduced-Calorie*

Reduced-Fat Cheddar Cheese *See Cheese & Cheese Products: Cheese: Cheddar: Reduced Fat*

Reduced-Fat Milk *See Dairy Products: Milk & Milk Products: Milk: Reduced-Fat*

Reduced-Fat Shredded Cheddar Cheese *See Cheese & Cheese Products: Cheese: Cheddar: Reduced Fat - Shredded*

Refried Beans *See Fruits & Vegetables: Beans: Refried*

Refrigerated Appetizers *See Prepared Foods: Appetizers: Refrigerated*

Refrigerated Apple Juices *See Beverages: Juices: Apple: Refrigerated*

Refrigerated Apricot Juices *See Beverages: Juices: Apricot: Refrigerated*

Refrigerated Buns *See Baked Goods: Breads: Buns: Refrigerated*

Refrigerated Cherry Juices *See Beverages: Juices: Cherry: Refrigerated*

Refrigerated Cranberry Juices *See Beverages: Juices: Cranberry: Refrigerated*

Refrigerated Egg Substitutes *See Eggs & Egg Products: Substitutes: Refrigerated*

Refrigerated Fruit Juices *See Beverages: Juices: Fruit: Refrigerated*

Refrigerated Grape Juices *See Beverages: Juices: Grape: Refrigerated*

Refrigerated Grapefruit Juices *See Beverages: Juices: Grapefruit: Refrigerated*

Refrigerated Juices *See Beverages: Juices: Refrigerated*

Refrigerated Lemon Juices *See Beverages: Juices: Lemon: Refrigerated*

Refrigerated Pancakes *See Prepared Foods: Pancakes: Refrigerated*

Refrigerated Pineapple Juices *See Beverages: Juices: Pineapple: Refrigerated*

Regular & Lowfat Bakery Mix *See Cereals, Grains, Rice & Flour: Flour: Bakery Mix: Regular & Lowfat*

Regular Chili Powders *See Ingredients, Flavors & Additives: Powders: Chili: Regular*

Release, Grease Agents *See Ingredients, Flavors & Additives: Agents: Release, Grease*

Releases *See Ingredients, Flavors & Additives: Releases*

Relishes *See Relishes & Pickled Products: Relishes*

Relishes & Condiments *See Relishes & Pickled Products: Relishes: Relishes & Condiments*

Replacers *See Ingredients, Flavors & Additives: Replacers*

Replacers, Milk Solids *See Dairy Products: Milk & Milk Products: Milk Solids: Replacers*

Resistant Starch Fiber *See Cereals, Grains, Rice & Flour: Fiber: Resistant Starch*

Rhubarb *See Fruits & Vegetables: Rhubarb*

Rhubarb Pie *See Baked Goods: Pies: Rhubarb Pie*

Rib Center Cut Pork *See Meats & Meat Products: Pork & Pork Products: Rib Center Cut*

Rib Chop Lamb *See Meats & Meat Products: Lamb: Rib Chop*

Rib Chop Veal *See Meats & Meat Products: Beef & Beef Products: Veal: Rib Chop*

Rib Eye Roast Beef *See Meats & Meat Products: Beef & Beef Products: Rib Eye Roast*

Rib Eye Steak *See Meats & Meat Products: Beef & Beef Products: Rib Eye Steak*

Rib Rub Seasonings *See Spices, Seasonings & Seeds: Seasonings: Rib Rub*

Rib Steak *See Meats & Meat Products: Beef & Beef Products: Rib Steak*

Rice *See Cereals, Grains, Rice & Flour: Rice*

Rice Bran *See Cereals, Grains, Rice & Flour: Bran: Rice*

Rice Bran Oils *See Oils, Shortening & Fats: Oils: Rice Bran*

Rice Cakes *See Snack Foods: Rice Cakes*

Rice Crisps *See Cereals, Grains, Rice & Flour: Crisps: Rice*

Rice Flour *See Cereals, Grains, Rice & Flour: Flour: Rice*

Rice Mixes *See Doughs, Mixes & Fillings: Mixes: Rice*

Rice Pilaf *See Cereals, Grains, Rice & Flour: Rice: Pilaf*

Rice Powders *See Ingredients, Flavors & Additives: Powders: Rice*

Rice Pudding *See Dairy Products: Pudding: Rice*

Rice Starches *See Ingredients, Flavors & Additives: Starches: Rice*

Rice Starches, Organic *See Specialty & Organic Foods: Organic Foods: Rice Starch*

Rice, Bagged Parboiled *See Cereals, Grains, Rice & Flour: Rice: Parboiled: Bagged*

Rice, Parboiled, US #1 Long Grain *See Cereals, Grains, Rice & Flour: Rice: Parboiled: US #1 Long Grain*

Rice, Prepared Meals *See Prepared Foods: Prepared Meals: Rice*

Rice-Based Cereal *See Cereals, Grains, Rice & Flour: Cereal: Rice-Based*

Ricotta *See Cheese & Cheese Products: Cheese: Ricotta*

Riesling *See Beverages: Wines: White Grape Varieties: Riesling*

Rigatoni *See Pasta & Noodles: Rigatoni*

Riso *See Pasta & Noodles: Riso*

Risotto Rice *See Cereals, Grains, Rice & Flour: Rice: Risotto*

Roast Beef *See Meats & Meat Products: Beef & Beef Products: Roast Beef*

Roast Pork Tenderloin *See Meats & Meat Products: Pork & Pork Products: Tenderloin Roast*

Roasted Coffee *See Beverages: Coffee & Tea: Coffee: Roasted*

Roasted Garlic & Herb Crackers *See Baked Goods: Crackers: Roasted Garlic & Herb Crackers*

Roasted Nuts *See Nuts & Nut Butters: Nuts: Roasted*

Roasted Peanuts *See Nuts & Nut Butters: Nuts: Peanuts: Roasted*

Roasted Peppers *See Fruits & Vegetables: Peppers: Roasted*

Roasted Vegetables *See Fruits & Vegetables: Roasted Vegetables*

Rock Candy *See Candy & Confectionery: Candy: Rock*

Rock Fish *See Fish & Seafood: Fish: Rock Fish*

Rock Salt *See Spices, Seasonings & Seeds: Salt: Rock*

Rolled Oats *See Cereals, Grains, Rice & Flour: Oats & Oat Products: Rolled*

Rolls *See Baked Goods: Breads: Rolls*

Roma Tomato *See Fruits & Vegetables: Tomato: Roma (Egg)*

Romaine Lettuce *See Fruits & Vegetables: Lettuce: Romaine*

Romano *See Cheese & Cheese Products: Cheese: Romano*

Rome Beauty *See Fruits & Vegetables: Apple: Rome Beauty*

Root Beer Extracts *See Ingredients, Flavors & Additives: Extracts: Root Beer*

Root Beer Flavors *See Ingredients, Flavors & Additives: Flavors: Root Beer*

Roots & Tubers *See Fruits & Vegetables: Roots & Tubers*

Roquefort *See Cheese & Cheese Products: Cheese: Roquefort*

Rosellino *See Cheese & Cheese Products: Cheese: Rosellino*

Rosemary *See Spices, Seasonings & Seeds: Spices: Rosemary*

Rosemary Spices, Cut *See Spices, Seasonings & Seeds: Spices: Rosemary: Cut*

Rotelle *See Pasta & Noodles: Rotelle*

Rotini *See Pasta & Noodles: Rotini*

Royal Jellies *See Jams, Jellies & Spreads: Jellies: Royal*

Rubbed Sage *See Spices, Seasonings & Seeds: Spices: Sage: Rubbed*

Rugulach *See Baked Goods: Cakes & Pastries: Rugulach*

Rum *See Beverages: Spirits & Liqueurs: Rum*

Rum Cake *See Baked Goods: Cakes & Pastries: Rum Cake*

Rum Flavors *See Ingredients, Flavors & Additives: Flavors: Rum*

Rusk *See Baked Goods: Cakes & Pastries: Rusk*

Russet Potatoes, Fresh *See Fruits & Vegetables: Potatoes: Fresh: Russet*

Rutabaga *See Fruits & Vegetables: Rutabaga*

Rye *See Cereals, Grains, Rice & Flour: Rye*

Rye Breads *See Baked Goods: Breads: Rye*

Rye Flour *See Cereals, Grains, Rice & Flour: Flour: Rye*

S

Sablefish *See Fish & Seafood: Fish: Sablefish*

Saccharin *See Sugars, Syrups & Sweeteners: Sugar Substitutes: Saccharin*

Safflower Oils *See Oils, Shortening & Fats: Oils: Safflower*

Saffron *See Spices, Seasonings & Seeds: Spices: Saffron*

Sage *See Spices, Seasonings & Seeds: Spices: Sage*

Sage Leaves *See Spices, Seasonings & Seeds: Spices: Sage: Leaves*

Sage Oils *See Oils, Shortening & Fats: Oils: Sage*

EXAMPLE: **Canadian Style Bacon** *See Meats & Meat Products: Smoked, Cured & Deli Meats: Bacon: Canadian Style* (1 = Canadian Style Bacon; 2 = Meats & Meat Products; 3 = Smoked, Cured & Deli Meats; 4 = Bacon; 5 = Canadian Style)

1. Product or Service you are looking for
2. Main Category, in alphabetical order, located in the page headers starting on page 23
3. Category Description, located in black bars and in page headers
4. Product Category, located in gray bars
5. Product Type, located under gray bars, centered in bold

Soup Blend *See Fruits & Vegetables: Dried & Dehydrated Vegetables: Soup Blend*
Soup Mixes *See Doughs, Mixes & Fillings: Mixes: Soup*
Soups & Stews *See Prepared Foods: Soups & Stews*
Sour Cream *See Dairy Products: Sour Cream*
Sour Cream & Onion Potato Chips *See Snack Foods: Chips: Potato: Sour Cream & Onion*
Sour Cream & Onion Snack Seasonings *See Spices, Seasonings & Seeds: Seasonings: Snack: Sour Cream & Onion*
Sour Cream Flavors *See Ingredients, Flavors & Additives: Flavors: Sour: Cream*
Sour Flavors *See Ingredients, Flavors & Additives: Flavors: Sour*
Sourdough Breads *See Baked Goods: Breads: Sourdough*
Southern Peas *See Fruits & Vegetables: Peas: Southern*
Southwest Seasonings *See Spices, Seasonings & Seeds: Seasonings: Southwest*
Soy *See Fruits & Vegetables: Soy*
Soy Bean *See Fruits & Vegetables: Soy: Soy Bean*
Soy Bean Meal *See Cereals, Grains, Rice & Flour: Soy Bean Meal*
Soy Bran Fiber *See Cereals, Grains, Rice & Flour: Fiber: Soy Bran*
Soy Crisps *See Cereals, Grains, Rice & Flour: Crisps: Soy*
Soy Crumbs Toppings *See Ingredients, Flavors & Additives: Toppings: Soy Crumbs*
Soy Flakes *See Ingredients, Flavors & Additives: Flakes: Soy*
Soy Frankfurters *See Meats & Meat Products: Frankfurters: Soy*
Soy Milk *See Fruits & Vegetables: Soy: Soy Milk*
Soy Milk Powders *See Ingredients, Flavors & Additives: Powders: Soy Milk*
Soy Nuts *See Nuts & Nut Butters: Nuts: Soy*
Soy Powders *See Ingredients, Flavors & Additives: Powders: Soy*
Soy Protein *See Fruits & Vegetables: Soy: Soy Protein*
Soy Protein Flour *See Cereals, Grains, Rice & Flour: Flour: Soy Protein*
Soy Sauces *See Sauces, Dips & Dressings: Sauces: Soy*
Soybean Flour *See Cereals, Grains, Rice & Flour: Flour: Soybean*
Soybean Oils *See Oils, Shortening & Fats: Oils: Soybean*
Spaghetti *See Pasta & Noodles: Spaghetti*
Spaghetti Sauces *See Sauces, Dips & Dressings: Sauces: Spaghetti*
Spaghetti with Meatballs *See Prepared Foods: Prepared Meals: Spaghetti: with Meatballs*
Spaghetti, Prepared Meals *See Prepared Foods: Prepared Meals: Spaghetti*
Spanish Onion *See Fruits & Vegetables: Onion: Spanish*
Spanish Rice *See Cereals, Grains, Rice & Flour: Rice: Spanish*
Spanish Wines *See Beverages: Wines: Spanish*
Spareribs *See Meats & Meat Products: Pork & Pork Products: Spareribs*
Sparkling Apple Boysenberry Juices *See Beverages: Juices: Apple Boysenberry: Sparkling*
Sparkling Apple Cider Juices *See Beverages: Juices: Apple Cider: Sparkling*
Sparkling Apple Cranberry Juices *See Beverages: Juices: Apple Cranberry: Sparkling*
Sparkling Apple Grape Juices *See Beverages: Juices: Apple Grape: Sparkling*
Sparkling Apple Juices *See Beverages: Juices: Apple: Sparkling*
Sparkling Water *See Beverages: Soft Drinks & Sodas: Sparkling Water*
Sparkling Wines *See Beverages: Wines: Sparkling (See also French/Champagne)*
Spearmint *See Spices, Seasonings & Seeds: Spices: Spearmint*
Spearmint Flavors *See Ingredients, Flavors & Additives: Flavors: Spearmint*
Spearmint Leaves *See Spices, Seasonings & Seeds: Spices: Mint Leaves: Spearmint*
Specialty & Cider Beers *See Beverages: Beers: Specialty & Cider*
Specialty Bread Crumbs *See Ingredients, Flavors & Additives: Toppings: Specialty Bread Crumbs*
Specialty-Packaged Candy *See Candy & Confectionery: Specialty-Packaged Candy*
Specialty-Packaged Candy, Bagged *See Candy & Confectionery: Specialty-Packaged Candy: Bagged*
Specialty-Packaged Candy, Boxed *See Candy & Confectionery: Specialty-Packaged Candy: Boxed*
Specialty-Packaged Candy, Boxed Non-Chocolate *See Candy & Confectionery: Specialty-Packaged Candy: Non-Chocolate - Boxed*
Specialty-Packaged Candy, Christmas *See Candy & Confectionery: Specialty-Packaged Candy: Christmas*
Specialty-Packaged Candy, Easter *See Candy & Confectionery: Specialty-Packaged Candy: Easter*
Specialty-Packaged Candy, Fund-Raising *See Candy & Confectionery: Specialty-Packaged Candy: Fund Raising*
Specialty-Packaged Candy, Halloween *See Candy & Confectionery: Specialty-Packaged Candy: Halloween*
Specialty-Packaged Candy, Multi-Packs *See Candy & Confectionery: Specialty-Packaged Candy: Multi-Packs*
Specialty-Packaged Candy, Packaged for Racks *See Candy & Confectionery: Specialty-Packaged Candy: Packaged for Racks*
Specialty-Packaged Candy, Packaged for Theaters *See Candy & Confectionery: Specialty-Packaged Candy: Packaged for Theaters*
Specialty-Packaged Candy, Valentine *See Candy & Confectionery: Specialty-Packaged Candy: Valentine*
Specialty-Packaged Candy, Vending *See Candy & Confectionery: Specialty-Packaged Candy: Vending*
Spelt *See Pasta & Noodles: Spelt*
Spelt Flour *See Cereals, Grains, Rice & Flour: Flour: Spelt*
Spice Seeds *See Spices, Seasonings & Seeds: Seeds: Spice*
Spiced Herring *See Fish & Seafood: Fish: Herring: Spiced*
Spices *See Spices, Seasonings & Seeds: Spices*
Spinach *See Fruits & Vegetables: Spinach*
Spinach Pasta *See Pasta & Noodles: Spinach*
Spinach Powder *See Fruits & Vegetables: Dried & Dehydrated Vegetables: Spinach Powder*
Spirits & Liqueurs *See Beverages: Spirits & Liqueurs*
Spirulina *See Ingredients, Flavors & Additives: Spirulina*
Sponge Cake *See Baked Goods: Cakes & Pastries: Sponge Cake*
Sponge Gourd *See Fruits & Vegetables: Sponge Gourd*
Sports Drinks *See Beverages: Sports Drinks*
Spray Cooking Oils *See Oils, Shortening & Fats: Oils: Cooking: Spray*
Spreads *See Jams, Jellies & Spreads: Spreads*
Spring Rolls *See Ethnic Foods: Egg Rolls: Spring Rolls*
Spring Water *See Beverages: Water: Spring*
Spring Wheat *See Cereals, Grains, Rice & Flour: Wheat: Spring*
Sprinkles *See Ingredients, Flavors & Additives: Toppings: Sprinkles*
Sprouts *See Fruits & Vegetables: Sprouts*
Squab *See Meats & Meat Products: Game: Squab*
Squash *See Fruits & Vegetables: Squash*
Squid *See Fish & Seafood: Shellfish: Squid*
St. John's Wort *See Ingredients, Flavors & Additives: Powders: St. John's Wort*
Stabilizers *See Ingredients, Flavors & Additives: Stabilizers*
Star Anise *See Spices, Seasonings & Seeds: Spices: Star Anise; See also See Spices, Seasonings & Seeds: Spices: Anise - Star*
Star Fruit *See Fruits & Vegetables: Star Fruit*
Starches *See Ingredients, Flavors & Additives: Starches*
Starter Media *See Ingredients, Flavors & Additives: Starter Media*
Steak *See Meats & Meat Products: Beef & Beef Products: Steak*
Steak Sauces *See Sauces, Dips & Dressings: Sauces: Steak*
Steaks *See Meats & Meat Products: Steaks*
Stewed Tomato *See Fruits & Vegetables: Tomato: Stewed*
Sticky Buns *See Baked Goods: Breads: Buns: Sticky*
Stir-Fry Sauces *See Sauces, Dips & Dressings: Sauces: Stir-Fry*
Stone Crab *See Fish & Seafood: Shellfish: Crab: Stone*
Stone Crab Claws *See Fish & Seafood: Shellfish: Crab: Claws Stone*
Stored Corn *See Fruits & Vegetables: Corn: Stored*
Stout & Porter Beers *See Beverages: Beers: Stout & Porter*
Strawberry *See Fruits & Vegetables: Berries: Strawberry*
Strawberry Flavors *See Ingredients, Flavors & Additives: Flavors: Strawberry*
Strawberry Jams *See Jams, Jellies & Spreads: Jams: Strawberry*
Strawberry Juices *See Beverages: Juices: Strawberry*
Strawberry Milk *See Dairy Products: Milk & Milk Products: Milk: Strawberry*
Strawberry Shortcake *See Baked Goods: Cakes & Pastries: Strawberry Shortcake*
String Cheese *See Cheese & Cheese Products: Cheese: String*
Striped Bass *See Fish & Seafood: Fish: Bass: Striped*
Strudel *See Baked Goods: Cakes & Pastries: Strudel*
Stuffed Cabbage, Prepared Meals *See Prepared Foods: Prepared Meals: Stuffed Cabbage*
Stuffed Crab *See Fish & Seafood: Shellfish: Crab: Stuffed*
Stuffed Crab, Prepared Meals *See Prepared Foods: Prepared Meals: Crab: Stuffed*
Stuffed Fish, Prepared Meals *See Prepared Foods: Prepared Meals: Fish: Stuffed*
Stuffed Peppers, Prepared Meals *See Prepared Foods: Prepared Meals: Stuffed Peppers*
Stuffed Shells *See Pasta & Noodles: Stuffed Shells*
Stuffed Shells Prepared Meals *See Prepared Foods: Prepared Meals: Stuffed Shells*
Stuffing *See Baked Goods: Stuffing; See also Prepared Foods: Stuffing*
Stuffing for Meat *See Baked Goods: Stuffing: for Meat*
Stuffing for Poultry *See Baked Goods: Stuffing: for Poultry*
Sturgeon *See Fish & Seafood: Fish: Sturgeon*
Substitutes, Cheese *See Cheese & Cheese Products: Imitation Cheeses & Substitutes: Substitutes*
Substitutes, Egg *See Eggs & Egg Products: Substitutes*
Substitutes, Salt *See Spices, Seasonings & Seeds: Salt: Substitutes*
Succotash *See Fruits & Vegetables: Succotash*
Sucrose *See Sugars, Syrups & Sweeteners: Sucrose*
Sugar *See Sugars, Syrups & Sweeteners: Sugar*
Sugar Alternatives *See Sugars, Syrups & Sweeteners: Sugar Substitutes: Sugar Alternatives*
Sugar Beets *See Fruits & Vegetables: Beets: Sugar*
Sugar Cookies *See Baked Goods: Cookies & Bars: Sugar Cookies*
Sugar Substitutes *See Sugars, Syrups & Sweeteners: Sugar Substitutes*
Sugar Wafers *See Baked Goods: Cookies & Bars: Wafers: Sugar*
Sugar-Free Foods *See Specialty & Organic Foods: Dietary Products: Sugar-Free Foods*
Sugars, Syrups & Sweeteners *See Sugars, Syrups & Sweeteners*
Sumac Berries *See Spices, Seasonings & Seeds: Spices: Sumac Berries*
Sun Tea *See Beverages: Coffee & Tea: Tea: Sun*
Sun-Dried Fruit *See Fruits & Vegetables: Sun Dried Fruit*
Sun-Dried Tomato *See Fruits & Vegetables: Tomato: Sun-Dried*
Sundae Toppings *See Sugars, Syrups & Sweeteners: Syrups: Toppings: Sundae*
Sunflower *See Fruits & Vegetables: Sunflower*
Sunflower Oils *See Oils, Shortening & Fats: Oils: Sunflower*
Sunflower Seeds *See Spices, Seasonings & Seeds: Seeds: Sunflower*
Supplements *See Ingredients, Flavors & Additives: Vitamins & Supplements: Supplements*
Supplements, Fiber *See Cereals, Grains, Rice & Flour: Fiber: Supplements*
Surfactants & Solubilizers *See Ingredients, Flavors & Additives: Surfactants & Solubilizers*
Survival Foods *See Specialty & Organic Foods: Survival Foods*
Sushi *See Fish & Seafood: Sushi*
Swamp Cabbage *See Fruits & Vegetables: Cabbage: Swamp*
Swedish Meat Balls *See Prepared Foods: Meat Balls: Swedish*
Sweet & Sour Sauces *See Sauces, Dips & Dressings: Sauces: Sweet & Sour*
Sweet Cherries *See Fruits & Vegetables: Cherries: Sweet*
Sweet Corn *See Fruits & Vegetables: Corn: Sweet*
Sweet Italian Sausage Seasonings *See Spices, Seasonings & Seeds: Seasonings: Sausage: Sweet Italian*
Sweet Italian Sausages *See Meats & Meat Products: Smoked, Cured & Deli Meats: Sausages: Sweet Italian*
Sweet Peppers *See Fruits & Vegetables: Peppers: Sweet*
Sweet Pickles *See Relishes & Pickled Products: Pickled Products: Pickles: Sweet*
Sweet Potatoes *See Fruits & Vegetables: Sweet Potatoes*
Sweet Processed Corn *See Fruits & Vegetables: Corn: Sweet Processed*
Sweet Rolls *See Baked Goods: Breads: Rolls: Sweet*
Sweet Salami *See Meats & Meat Products: Smoked, Cured & Deli Meats: Salami: Sweet*
Sweet Sausages *See Meats & Meat Products: Smoked, Cured & Deli Meats: Sausages: Sweet*
Sweet Stout *See Beverages: Beers: Stout & Porter: Sweet Stout*
Sweetened & Condensed Milk *See Dairy Products: Milk & Milk Products: Milk: Sweetened & Condensed*
Sweetened Milk *See Dairy Products: Milk & Milk Products: Milk: Sweetened*
Sweeteners *See Ingredients, Flavors & Additives: Sweeteners*
Swiss Cheese *See Cheese & Cheese Products: Cheese: Swiss*
Swordfish *See Fish & Seafood: Fish: Swordfish*

T

U

V

EXAMPLE: **Canadian Style Bacon** *See Meats & Meat Products: Smoked, Cured & Deli Meats: Bacon: Canadian Style*
(1 = Canadian Style Bacon; 2 = Meats & Meat Products; 3 = Smoked, Cured & Deli Meats; 4 = Bacon; 5 = Canadian Style)

1. Product or Service you are looking for
2. Main Category, in alphabetical order, located in the page headers starting on page 23
3. Category Description, located in black bars and in page headers
4. Product Category, located in gray bars
5. Product Type, located under gray bars, centered in bold

Vegetable Pulp *See Fruits & Vegetables: Pulps & Purees: Pulp: Vegetable*

Vegetable Puree *See Fruits & Vegetables: Pulps & Purees: Puree: Vegetable*

Vegetable Ravioli *See Pasta & Noodles: Ravioli: Vegetable*

Vegetable Seeds *See Spices, Seasonings & Seeds: Seeds: Vegetable*

Vegetable Shortening *See Oils, Shortening & Fats: Shortening: Vegetable*

Vegetable Stuffing *See Prepared Foods: Stuffing: Vegetable*

Vegetables *See Fruits & Vegetables: Vegetables*

Vegetables, Mixed *See Fruits & Vegetables: Vegetables Mixed*

Vegetables, Organic *See Specialty & Organic Foods: Organic Foods: Vegetables*

Vegetables, Pickled *See Relishes & Pickled Products: Pickled Products: Vegetables*

Vegetarian Products *See Specialty & Organic Foods: Vegetarian Products*

Vegetarian, Prepared Meals *See Prepared Foods: Prepared Meals: Vegetarian*

Veggie & Rice Pellets *See Ingredients, Flavors & Additives: Half-Products: Veggie & Rice Pellets*

Vending Specialty-Packaged Candy *See Candy & Confectionery: Specialty-Packaged Candy: Vending*

Venison *See Meats & Meat Products: Game: Venison*

Venison Sausages *See Meats & Meat Products: Smoked, Cured & Deli Meats: Sausages: Venison*

Vermicelli *See Pasta & Noodles: Vermicelli*

Vinegar *See Sauces, Dips & Dressings: Vinegar*

Viognier *See Beverages: Wines: White Grape Varieties: Viognier*

Vitamin A *See Ingredients, Flavors & Additives: Vitamins & Supplements: A*

Vitamin C *See Ingredients, Flavors & Additives: Vitamins & Supplements: C*

Vitamin E *See Ingredients, Flavors & Additives: Vitamins & Supplements: E - Tocopherol*

Vitamin Oils *See Oils, Shortening & Fats: Oils: Vitamin*

Vitamins & Supplements *See Ingredients, Flavors & Additives: Vitamins & Supplements; See also Ingredients, Flavors & Additives: Vitamins & Supplements: Supplements: Vitamins; See also Ingredients, Flavors & Additives: Vitamins & Supplements: Vit*

Vodka *See Beverages: Spirits & Liqueurs: Vodka*

Volpino Salami *See Meats & Meat Products: Smoked, Cured & Deli Meats: Salami: Volpino*

W

Wafers *See Baked Goods: Cookies & Bars: Wafers*

Waffle Mixes *See Doughs, Mixes & Fillings: Mixes: Waffle*

Waffle Syrups *See Sugars, Syrups & Sweeteners: Syrups: Waffle*

Waffles *See Baked Goods: Waffles*

Walnut Oils *See Oils, Shortening & Fats: Oils: Walnut*

Walnuts Nuts *See Nuts & Nut Butters: Nuts: Walnuts*

Wasabi *See Spices, Seasonings & Seeds: Spices: Wasabi*

Water *See Beverages: Water*

Water Chestnuts *See Fruits & Vegetables: Water Chestnuts*

Water Pack Cherries *See Fruits & Vegetables: Cherries: Water Pack*

Watercress *See Fruits & Vegetables: Watercress*

Watermelon *See Fruits & Vegetables: Melon: Watermelon*

Watermelon, Seedless *See Fruits & Vegetables: Melon: Watermelon: Seedless*

Wax Beans *See Fruits & Vegetables: Beans: Wax*

Waxes *See Ingredients, Flavors & Additives: Waxes*

Waxy Maize Starches *See Ingredients, Flavors & Additives: Starches: Waxy Maize*

Waxy Starches *See Ingredients, Flavors & Additives: Starches: Waxy*

Wehani Rice *See Cereals, Grains, Rice & Flour: Rice: Wehani*

Wheat *See Cereals, Grains, Rice & Flour: Wheat*

Wheat Ale *See Beverages: Beers: Wheat: Wheat Ale*

Wheat Beers *See Beverages: Beers: Wheat*

Wheat Bran *See Cereals, Grains, Rice & Flour: Bran: Wheat*

Wheat Bran Fiber *See Cereals, Grains, Rice & Flour: Fiber: Wheat Bran*

Wheat Breads *See Baked Goods: Breads: Wheat*

Wheat Flakes *See Cereals, Grains, Rice & Flour: Wheat: Flakes*

Wheat Flour *See Cereals, Grains, Rice & Flour: Flour: Wheat*

Wheat Germ *See Cereals, Grains, Rice & Flour: Wheat: Germ*

Wheat Germ Oils *See Oils, Shortening & Fats: Oils: Wheat Germ*

Wheat Starches *See Ingredients, Flavors & Additives: Starches: Wheat*

Wheat, Bagged *See Cereals, Grains, Rice & Flour: Wheat: Bagged*

Wheat-Based Cereal *See Cereals, Grains, Rice & Flour: Cereal: Wheat-Based*

Whey & Whey Products *See Cereals, Grains, Rice & Flour: Whey & Whey Products*

Whey Crisps *See Cereals, Grains, Rice & Flour: Crisps: Whey*

Whey Protein Concentrates & Isolates *See Ingredients, Flavors & Additives: Concentrates: Whey Protein Concentrates & Isolates*

Whipped Cream *See Dairy Products: Cream: Whipped*

Whipped Toppings *See Ingredients, Flavors & Additives: Toppings: Whipped*

Whiskey, American *See Beverages: Spirits & Liqueurs: Whiskey, American*

Whiskey, Canadian *See Beverages: Spirits & Liqueurs: Whiskey, Canadian*

White Breads *See Baked Goods: Breads: White*

White Burgundy *See Beverages: Wines: French: White Burgundy*

White Chocolate Dipped Biscotti *See Baked Goods: Cookies & Bars: Biscotti: White Chocolate Dipped*

White Distilled Vinegar *See Sauces, Dips & Dressings: Vinegar: White Distilled*

White Fresh Potatoes *See Fruits & Vegetables: Potatoes: Fresh: White*

White Grape Wines *See Beverages: Wines: White Grape Varieties; See also See Beverages: Wines: White Grapes*

White Grapefruit *See Fruits & Vegetables: Grapefruit: White*

White Ground Pepper *See Spices, Seasonings & Seeds: Spices: Pepper: White Ground*

White Mushrooms *See Fruits & Vegetables: Mushrooms: White*

White Pepper *See Spices, Seasonings & Seeds: Spices: White Pepper; See also See Spices, Seasonings & Seeds: Spices: Pepper: Black - White - Red*

White Rice *See Cereals, Grains, Rice & Flour: Rice: White*

White Sesame Seeds *See Spices, Seasonings & Seeds: Seeds: Sesame: White*

White Silver Rum *See Beverages: Spirits & Liqueurs: Rum: White Silver*

White Unbleached Flour *See Cereals, Grains, Rice & Flour: Flour: White Unbleached*

White Whole Truffles *See Fruits & Vegetables: Mushrooms: Truffles: White Whole*

White/Yellow Process Sliced Cheese *See Cheese & Cheese Products: Cheese: Process Sliced: White/Yellow*

Whitefish *See Fish & Seafood: Fish: Whitefish*

Whiting *See Fish & Seafood: Fish: Whiting*

Whole & Dried Chili Pods *See Spices, Seasonings & Seeds: Spices: Chili Pods: Whole & Dried*

Whole Allspice *See Spices, Seasonings & Seeds: Spices: Allspice: Whole*

Whole Black Olives *See Fruits & Vegetables: Olives: Black: Whole*

Whole Broccoli *See Fruits & Vegetables: Broccoli: Whole*

Whole Cayenne Pepper *See Spices, Seasonings & Seeds: Spices: Cayenne Pepper: Whole*

Whole Cinnamon *See Spices, Seasonings & Seeds: Spices: Cinnamon: Whole*

Whole Clam *See Fish & Seafood: Shellfish: Clam: Whole*

Whole Coriander Seeds *See Spices, Seasonings & Seeds: Seeds: Coriander: Whole*

Whole Corn *See Fruits & Vegetables: Corn: Whole*

Whole Egg Solids *See Eggs & Egg Products: Solids: Whole Egg*

Whole Frozen Turkey *See Meats & Meat Products: Poultry: Turkey: Whole Frozen*

Whole Grain Muffins *See Baked Goods: Cakes & Pastries: Muffins: Whole Grain*

Whole Maraschino Cherries *See Fruits & Vegetables: Cherries: Maraschino: Whole*

Whole Milk *See Dairy Products: Milk & Milk Products: Milk: Whole*

Whole Milk Solids *See Dairy Products: Milk & Milk Products: Milk Solids: Whole*

Whole Nutmeg Spices *See Spices, Seasonings & Seeds: Spices: Nutmeg (See also Mace): Whole*

Whole Shiitake Mushrooms *See Fruits & Vegetables: Mushrooms: Shiitake: Whole*

Whole Threads Saffron *See Spices, Seasonings & Seeds: Spices: Saffron: Whole Threads*

Whole Wheat Bread Sticks *See Baked Goods: Bread Sticks: Whole Wheat*

Whole Wheat Flour *See Cereals, Grains, Rice & Flour: Flour: Whole wheat*

Whole wheat Pastry Flour *See Cereals, Grains, Rice & Flour: Flour: Whole wheat: Pastry*

Whole Yellow Mustard Seeds *See Spices, Seasonings & Seeds: Seeds: Mustard: Whole Yellow*

Wild Game *See Meats & Meat Products: Game: Wild*

Wild Mushrooms *See Fruits & Vegetables: Mushrooms: Wild*

Wild Rice *See Cereals, Grains, Rice & Flour: Rice: Wild*

Wild Turkey *See Meats & Meat Products: Game: Turkey: Wild*

Wine Flavors *See Ingredients, Flavors & Additives: Flavors: Wine*

Wine Grape *See Fruits & Vegetables: Grape: Wine*

Wine Vinegar *See Sauces, Dips & Dressings: Vinegar: Wine*

Wine Yeast *See Ingredients, Flavors & Additives: Cultures & Yeasts: Yeast: Wine*

Wines *See Beverages: Wines*

Winter Squash Pumpkin *See Fruits & Vegetables: Pumpkin: Winter Squash*

Winter Wheat *See Cereals, Grains, Rice & Flour: Wheat: Winter*

Wonton Chips *See Ethnic Foods: Wonton Chips*

Wonton Soup *See Prepared Foods: Soups & Stews: Wonton Soup*

Wontons *See Ethnic Foods: Wontons*

Wood Ear Mushrooms *See Fruits & Vegetables: Mushrooms: Wood Ear*

Wood Ear Mushrooms, Dried *See Fruits & Vegetables: Dried & Dehydrated Vegetables: Mushrooms: Wood Ears*

Wood Pigeon *See Meats & Meat Products: Game: Wood Pigeon*

Worcestershire Sauces *See Sauces, Dips & Dressings: Sauces: Worcestershire*

Wrappers, Egg Roll *See Ethnic Foods: Egg Rolls: Wrappers*

Wraps *See Baked Goods: Wraps*

X

X.O. Cognac Brandy *See Beverages: Spirits & Liqueurs: Brandy: X.O. Cognac*

Xanthan Gum *See Ingredients, Flavors & Additives: Gums: Xanthan Gum*

Y

Yams *See Fruits & Vegetables: Yams*

Yeast *See Ingredients, Flavors & Additives: Cultures & Yeasts: Yeast*

Yeast Extracts *See Ingredients, Flavors & Additives: Extracts: Yeast*

Yellow Cherry Tomato *See Fruits & Vegetables: Tomato: Yellow Cherry*

Yellow Mustard *See Sauces, Dips & Dressings: Mustard: Yellow*

Yellow Process Cheese Loaves *See Cheese & Cheese Products: Cheese: Process Loaves: Yellow*

Yellow Split Peas *See Fruits & Vegetables: Peas: Yellow Split*

Yellowfin Tuna *See Fish & Seafood: Fish: Tuna: Yellowfin*

Yogurt *See Dairy Products: Yogurt*

Yogurt Bacteria *See Ingredients, Flavors & Additives: Cultures & Yeasts: Bacteria: Yogurt*

Yogurt Bases *See Ingredients, Flavors & Additives: Bases: Yogurt*

Yogurt Bases, Flavors, Stabilizers *See Dairy Products: Yogurt: Bases, Flavors, Stabilizers*

Yogurt Coated Nuts *See Nuts & Nut Butters: Nuts: Coated: Yogurt*

Yogurt Coated Raisins *See Fruits & Vegetables: Raisins: Yogurt Coated*

Yogurt Cultures *See Ingredients, Flavors & Additives: Cultures & Yeasts: Yogurt*

Yogurt Flavors *See Ingredients, Flavors & Additives: Flavors: Yogurt*

Yogurt Powder Mixes *See Doughs, Mixes & Fillings: Mixes: Yogurt Powder*

Yogurt Powders *See Ingredients, Flavors & Additives: Powders: Yogurt*

Yogurt Stabilizers *See Ingredients, Flavors & Additives: Stabilizers: Yogurt*

Yogurt with Fruit *See Dairy Products: Yogurt: with Fruit*

Yogurt, No-Fat *See Dairy Products: Yogurt: No-Fat*

Yolk *See Eggs & Egg Products: Yolk*

Z

Zinc Citrate *See Ingredients, Flavors & Additives: Vitamins & Supplements: Zinc Citrate*

Zinfandel, Red *See Beverages: Wines: Red Grape Wines: Zinfandel*

Zucchini *See Fruits & Vegetables: Zucchini*

Baked Goods

General

A Southern Season
Chapel Hill, NC 877-929-7133
A Sprinkle and A Dash
Port Washington, NY 516-767-6431
A&M Cookie Company Canada
Kitchener, ON 800-265-6508
Adam Matthews, Inc.
Jeffersontown, KY 502-499-2253
Adams Foods
Dothan, AL 334-983-4233
Ak-Mak Bakeries
Sanger, CA 559-875-5511
Aladdin Bakers
Brooklyn, NY 718-499-1818
Alati-Caserta Desserts
Montreal, QC 514-271-3013
Albertson's Bakery
Palm Desert, CA 760-360-6322
Alfred & Sam Italian Bakery
Lancaster, PA 717-392-6311
Almondina®/YZ Enterprises, Inc.
Maumee, OH 800-736-8779
Alois J. Binder Bakery
New Orleans, LA 504-947-1111
Alpha Baking Company
La Porte, IN 219-324-7440
Alpha Baking Company
Chicago, IL 773-261-6000
Amalfitano's Italian Bakery
New Castle, DE 302-324-9005
Ambassador Foods
Van Nuys, CA 800-338-3369
Amberwave Foods
Oakmont, PA 412-828-3040
Amcan Industries
Elmsford, NY 914-347-4838
American Copak Corporation
Chatsworth, CA 818-576-1000
Ames International
Fife, WA 888-469-2637
Amoroso's Baking Company
Philadelphia, PA 800-377-6557
Andre French Bakery Retail
Fort Myers, FL 239-482-2011
Andre-Boudin Bakeries
San Francisco, CA 415-882-1849
Anthony & Sons Italian Bakery
Fairfield, NJ 973-244-9669
Antonio's Bakery
Jamaica, NY 718-322-1314
April Hill
Grand Rapids, MI 616-245-0595
Archway & Mother's Cookie Company
Oakland, CA 800-369-3997
Archway Cookies
Ashland, OH 888-427-2492
Arturo's Bakery
Waterbury, CT 203-754-3056
Artuso Pastry Foods Corp
Mt Vernon, NY 914-663-8806
Artuso Pastry Shop
Bronx, NY 718-367-2515
Athens Baking Company
Fresno, CA 559-485-3024
Athens Pastries & Frozen Foods
Cleveland, OH 800-837-5683
Atkinson Milling Company
Selma, NC 800-948-5707
Atlanta Bread Company
Smyrna, GA 800-398-3728
Atlas Biscuit Company
Verona, NJ 973-239-8300
August Food Limited
Lubbock, TX 806-744-1918
August Foods
Lubbock, TX 806-744-1918
Aunt Gussie Cookies & Crackers
Garfield, NJ 800-422-6654
Aunt Heddy's Bakery
Brooklyn, NY 718-782-0582
Aunt Millies Bakeries
Fort Wayne, IN 260-424-8245
Automatic Rolls of New Jersey
Edison, NJ 732-549-2243
Award Baking International
New Germany, MN 800-333-3523
Awrey Bakeries
Livonia, MI 800-950-2253
Azteca Foods
Summit Argo, IL 708-563-6600
B&A Bakery
Scarborough, ON 416-752-7436
B&M
Portland, ME 207-772-7043
Bagel Guys
Brooklyn, NY 718-222-4361
Bagels By Bell
Brooklyn, NY 718-272-2780
Bailey Street Bakery
Atlanta, GA 800-822-4634
Bake Crafters Food
Collegedale, TN 800-296-8935
Bake Rite Rolls
Bensalem, PA 215-638-2400
Bakehouse
Hallandale Beach, FL 954-458-1600
BakeMark USA
Schaumburg, IL 562-949-1054
Baker Boy Bake Shop
Dickinson, ND 800-437-2008
Baker Boys
Calgary, AB 877-246-6036

Baker's Dozen
Herkimer, NY 315-866-6770
Bakerhaus Veit Limited
Woodbridge, ON 800-387-8860
Bakers of Paris
Brisbane, CA 415-468-9100
Bakery Chef
Chicago, IL 773-384-1900
Bakery Corp
Miami, FL 800-521-4345
Bakery Europa
Honolulu, HI 808-845-5011
Bakery Management Corporation
Miami, FL 305-623-3838
Baldinger Bakery
Saint Paul, MN 651-224-5761
Balticshop.Com LLC
Glastonbury, CT
Baltimore Bakery
Norfolk, VA 757-855-4731
Banquet Schuster Bakery
Pueblo, CO 719-544-1062
Baptista's Bakery
Franklin, WI 877-261-3157
Barbara's Bakery
Petaluma, CA 707-765-2273
Barbero Bakery, Inc.
Trenton, NJ 609-394-5122
Barker System Bakery
Mt Carmel, PA 570-339-3380
Basque French Bakery
Fresno, CA 559-268-7088
Bay Star Baking Company
Alameda, CA 510-523-4202
BBU Bakeries
Denver, CO 303-691-6342
Beach Bagel Bakeries
Miami, FL 305-691-3514
Beatrice Bakery Company
Beatrice, NE 800-228-4030
Beatrice Bakery Company/Grandma's Bake Shoppe
Beatrice, NE 800-228-4030
Beck's Waffles of Oklahoma
Shawnee, OK 800-646-6254
Beckmann's Old World Bakery
Santa Cruz, CA 831-423-2566
Bella Napoli Italian Bakery
Troy, NY 888-800-0103
Bensons Bakery
Bogart, GA 800-888-6059
Berkshire Mountain Bakery
Housatonic, MA 866-274-6124
Berlin Natural Bakery
Berlin, OH 800-686-5334
Best Foods Baking Group
Frederick, MD 800-635-1700
Best Harvest Bakeries
Kansas City, KS 800-811-5715
Best Maid Cookie Company
River Falls, WI 888-444-0322
Beth's Fine Desserts
Mill Valley, CA 415-464-1891
Better Bagel Bakery
Sarasota, FL 941-924-0393
Betty Lou's Golden Smackers
McMinnville, OR 800-242-5205
Birkholm's Jr Danish Bakery
Solvang, CA 805-688-3872
Bishop Baking Company
Cleveland, TN 423-472-1561
Blackey's Bakery
Minneapolis, MN 612-789-5326
Blue Dog Bakery
Seattle, WA 888-749-7229
Blue Planet Foods
Collegedale, TN 877-396-3145
Bluepoint Bakery
Denver, CO 303-298-1100
Boboli Intl. Inc.
Stockton, CA 209-473-3507
Boca Foods Company
Madison, WI 608-285-3311
Bodacious Food Company
Jasper, GA 800-391-1979
Bonert's Slice of Pie
Santa Ana, CA 714-540-3535
Bonnie Baking Company
La Porte, IN 219-362-4561
Borden's Bread
Regina, SK 306-525-3341
Borinquen Biscuit Corporation
Yauco, PR 787-856-3030
Boudreaux's Foods
New Orleans, LA 504-733-8440
BP Gourmet
Hauppauge, NY 631-234-5200
Bread Alone Bakery
Boiceville, NY 800-769-3328
Bread Box
Virden, NB 204-748-1513
Breadsmith
Cincinnati, OH 513-791-8817
Breadworks Bakery & Deli
Charlottesville, VA 434-296-4663
Breakfast at Brennan's
New Orleans, LA 800-888-9932
Bremner Company
Poteau, OK 918-647-8630
Brenntag Pacific
Santa Fe Springs, CA 562-903-9626
Brooklyn Bagel Company
Staten Island, NY 800-349-3055
Brooklyn Baking Company
Waterbury, CT 203-574-9198
Brown's Bakery
Defiance, OH 419-784-3330
Brownie Products Company
Terre Haute, IN
Bruce Baking Company
New Rochelle, NY 914-636-0808
Bubbles Baking Company
Van Nuys, CA 800-777-4970
Bunge Foods
Tustin, CA 714-258-1223
Bunny Bread
Deridder, LA 337-463-7522

Bunny Bread Company
Cape Girardeau, MO. 573-332-7349
Buns & Roses Organic Wholegrain Bakery
Edmonton, AB 780-438-0098
Buns Master Bakery
Lethbridge, AB 403-320-2966
Buns Master Bakery
Richmond Hill, ON. 800-563-6688
Buon Italia Misono Food Ltd.
New York, NY 212-633-9090
Busken Bakery
Cincinnati, OH 513-871-5330
Butternut Breads
Kansas City, MO. 800-483-7253
Byrnes & Kiefer Company
Callery, PA 877-444-2240
Cains Foods LP/Olde CapeCod
Ayer, MA. 651-698-6832
Calgary Italian Bakery
Calgary, AB. 800-661-6868
California Pie Company
Livermore, CA 925-373-7700
California Smart Foods
San Francisco, CA 415-826-0449
Calise & Sons Bakery
Lincoln, RI 800-225-4737
Calmar Bakery
Calmar, AB 780-985-3583
Campagna-Turano Bakery
Berwyn, IL 708-788-9220
Campbell Soup Company
Camden, NJ. 800-257-8443
Canada Bread
Etobicoke, ON 416-926-2000
Canada Bread Atlantic
St. John's, NL 709-722-5410
Canada Bread Company
Edmonton, AB 780-435-2240
Canada Bread Company
Langley, BC 800-465-5515
Caravan Trading Company
Union City, CA. 510-487-2600
Caribbean Food Delights
Tappan, NY. 845-398-3000
Carmine's Bakery
Sanford, FL. 407-324-1200
Carole's Cheesecake Company
Toronto, ON 416-256-0000
Carolina Cupboard
Hillsborough, NC 800-400-3441
Carolina Foods
Charlotte, NC 800-234-0441
Cascade Cookie Company
St Louis, MO. 314-877-7000
Case Side Holdings Company
Kensington, PE 902-836-4214
Casino Bakery
Tampa, FL. 813-242-0311
Catania Bakery
Washington, DC 202-332-5135
Cateraid
Howell, MI 800-508-8217
CBC Foods
Little River, KS. 800-276-4770
Cedarlane Foods
Carson, CA 310-886-7720
Celebrity Cheesecake
Davie, FL 877-986-2253
Cellone Bakery
Pittsburgh, PA. 800-334-8438
Cemac Foods Corporation
Philadelphia, PA 800-724-0179
Central Bakery
Fall River, MA 508-675-7620
CGI Desserts
Sugar Land, TX. 281-240-1200
Charles Heitzman Bakery
Louisville, KY
Charles J. Ross
Reading, PA 610-685-5161
Charlie's Specialties
Hermitage, PA. 724-346-2350
Chattanooga Bakery
Chattanooga, TN. 800-251-3404
Cheesecake Aly
Glen Rock, NJ. 800-555-8862
Cheesecake Etc. Desserts
Miami Springs, FL 305-887-0258
Chella's Dutch Delicacies
Lake Oswego, OR. 800-458-3331
Chelsea Market Baskets
New York, NY 888-727-7887

Cheri's Desert Harvest
Tucson, AZ 800-743-1141
Chewys Rugulach
San Diego, CA 800-241-3456
Chex Finer Foods
Attleboro, MA. 800-322-2434
Chicago Baking Company
Chicago, IL 773-536-7700
Chisholm Bakery
Chisholm, MN 218-254-4006
Chloe Foods Corporation
Brooklyn, NY 718-827-9000
Chmuras Bakery
Indian Orchard, MA 413-543-2521
Chocolate Chix
Waxahachie, TX 214-744-2442
Chudleigh's
Milton, ON 905-878-8781
Cinderella Cheese Cake Company
Riverside, NJ. 856-461-6302
City Baker
Calgary, AB. 403-263-8578
City Cafe Bakery
Fayetteville, GA 770-461-6800
Clarkson Scottish Bakery
Mississauga, ON. 905-823-1500
Claudio Pastry Company
Elmwood Park, IL. 708-453-0598
Claxton Bakery
Claxton, GA 800-841-4211
Clear Lake Bakery
Saint Louis, MO 641-357-5264
Clements Pastry Shop
Hyattsville, MD 800-444-7428
Cloverhill Bakery-Vend Corporation
Chicago, IL 773-745-9800
Cloverland Sweets/Priester's Pecan Company
Fort Deposit, AL. 800-523-3505
Clydes Delicious Donuts
Addison, IL 630-628-6555
Coby's Cookies
Toronto, ON 416-633-1567
Cohen's Bakery
Buffalo, NY. 716-892-8149
Colchester Bakery
Colchester, CT 860-537-2415
Cold Spring Bakery
Cold Spring, MN 320-685-8681
Cole's Quality Foods
Grand Rapids, MI 616-975-0081
Collin Street Bakery
Corsicana, TX. 800-504-1896
Colombo Bakery
Sacramento, CA 916-648-1011
Colorado Baking Company
Lisle, IL. 630-799-8195
Colors Gourmet Pizza
Carlsbad, CA. 760-431-2203
Columbus Bakery
Columbus, OH 614-645-2275
Community Bakeries
Chicago, IL 773-384-1900
Community Orchard
Fort Dodge, IA 515-573-8212
Con Agra Foods
Holly Ridge, NC. 910-329-9061
ConAgra Foods
Boisbriand, QC. 450-433-1322
Confection Solutions
Sylmar, CA 800-284-2422
Consolidated Biscuit Company
Mc Comb, OH. 800-537-9544
Continental Food Products
Flushing, NY. 718-358-7894
Cookie Cupboard Baking Corporation
Fairfield, NJ 800-217-2938
Cookie Kingdom
Oglesby, IL 815-883-3331
Cookie Specialties
Wheeling, IL. 847-537-3888
Cookie Tree Bakeries
Salt Lake City, UT. 800-998-0111
Cookiezen, LLC
Falls Church, VA. 703-389-9274
Corfu Foods
Bensenville, IL 630-595-2510
Cottage Bakery
Lodi, CA 209-333-8044
Cotton Baking Company
Bossier City, LA 800-777-1832
Cougar Mountain Baking Company
Seattle, WA 206-467-5044

Country Club Bakery
Fairmont, WV 304-363-5690
Country Hearth Bread
Murfreesboro, TN 615-893-6041
Country Home Bakers
Torrance, CA. 800-989-9534
Creative Spices
Union City, CA 510-471-4956
Creme Curls Bakery
Hudsonville, MI 800-466-1219
Crispy Bagel Company
Baltimore, MD 800-522-7655
Crum Creek Mills
Springfield, PA 888-607-3500
Crusty Bakery, Inc.
New York, NY 646-356-0460
Culinar Canada
Baie-Comeau, QC. 418-296-4395
Culinary Masters Corporation
Alpharetta, GA 800-261-5261
Cupoladua Oven
Wexford, PA 412-592-5378
Cusano's Baking Company
Hollywood, FL 954-458-1010
Cutie Pie Corporation
Salt Lake City, UT 800-453-4575
Cw Resources
New Britain, CT 860-229-7700
Dairy State Foods
Milwaukee, WI. 800-435-4499
Dakota Brands Intl
Jamestown, ND. 800-844-5073
Dancing Deer Baking Company
Boston, MA. 888-699-3337
Daniel's Bagel & Baguette Corporation
Calgary, AB. 403-243-3207
Danish Baking Company
Van Nuys, CA 818-786-1700
Dare Foods
Kitchener, ON 800-265-8225
Dave's Bakery
Honesdale, PA. 570-253-1660
David's Cookies
Fairfield, NJ 800-500-2800
Davis Bakery & Delicatessen
Cleveland, OH 216-464-5599
Davis Bread & Desserts
Davis, CA 530-757-2700
Davis Cookie Company
Rimersburg, PA. 814-473-3125
Dawn Food Products
York, PA 800-405-6282
Dawn Food Products
Louisville, KY 800-626-2542
Day's Bakery
Honesdale, PA. 570-253-1660
De Bas Chocolatier
Fresno, CA 559-294-7638
De Beukelaer Corporation
Madison, MS. 601-856-7454
Dee Lite Bakery
Honolulu, HI. 808-847-5396
Dee's Cheesecake Factory/Dee's Foodservice
Albuquerque, NM. 505-884-1777
Deerfield Bakery
Buffalo Grove, IL 847-520-0068
Del Campo Baking Company
Wilmington, DE 302-656-6676
Del's Pastry
Etobicoke, ON 416-231-4383
Desserts by David Glass
South Windsor, CT. 860-462-7520
Desserts of Distinction
Milwaukie, OR 503-654-8370
Desserts On Us
Arcata, CA 707-822-0160
Dewey's Bakery
Winston-Salem, NC 800-274-2994
DF Stauffer Biscuit Company
York, PA 800-673-2473
Di Camillo Bakery
Niagara Falls, NY 800-634-4363
Di Paolo Baking Company
Rochester, NY. 585-232-3510
Diamond Bakery Company
Honolulu, HI. 808-847-3551
DiCarlo's Bakery
San Pedro, CA. 310-831-2524
Dimitria Delights
North Grafton, MA 800-763-1113
Dimpflmeier Bakery
Toronto, ON 800-268-2421

Dinkel's Bakery
Chicago, IL 800-822-8817
Divine Foods
Elizabethtown, NC 910-862-2576
Division Baking Corporation
New York, NY 800-934-9238
Dolly Madison Bakery Interstate Brands Corporation
Columbus, IN 812-376-7432
Dong Kee Company
Chicago, IL 312-225-6340
Doral International
Bayside, NY 718-224-7413
Dough Works Company
Horicon, WI 800-383-8808
Dough-To-Go
Santa Clara, CA 408-727-4094
Dpi Specialty Foods, Inc
Evanston, IL 503-692-0662
Drader Manufacturing Industries
Edmonton, AB 800-661-4122
Dufflet Pastries
Toronto, ON 416-536-9640
Dunford Bakers
Fayetteville, AR 479-521-3000
Dunford Bakers Company
West Jordan, UT 800-748-4335
Dutch Ann Foods Company
Natchez, MS 601-445-5566
Dutch Girl Donuts
Detroit, MI 313-368-3020
Dutchess Bakery
Charleston, WV 304-346-4237
Dynamic Foods
Lubbock, TX 806-747-2777
Earth Grains Baking Companies
Neenah, WI 800-323-7117
East Balt Bakery
Denver, CO 303-377-5533
East Balt Bakery
Kissimmee, FL 407-933-2222
East Balt Commissary
Chicago, IL 773-376-4444
Eddy's Bakery
Boise, ID 208-377-8100
Edelweiss Patisserie
Charlestown, MA 617-628-0225
Eden Vineyards Winery
Alva, FL 239-728-9463
Edner Corporation
Hayward, CA 510-441-8504
Edwards Baking Company
Atlanta, GA 800-241-0559
El Charro Mexican Food Industries
Roswell, NM 575-622-8590
El Peto Products
Cambridge, ON 800-387-4064
El Segundo Bakery
El Segundo, CA 310-322-3422
Elegant Desserts
Lyndhurst, NJ 201-933-0770
Eli's Cheesecake Company
Chicago, IL 800-999-8300
Ellison Bakery
Fort Wayne, IN 800-711-8091
Elmwood Pastry
West Hartford, CT 860-233-2029
Ener-G Foods
Seattle, WA 800-331-5222
Engel's Bakeries
Calgary, AB 403-250-9560
Entenmann's-Oroweat/BestFoods
South San Francisco, CA 650-583-5828
EPI Breads
Atlanta, GA 800-325-1014
Erba Food Products
Brooklyn, NY 718-272-7700
Esco Foods
San Francisco, CA 415-864-2147
EuroAm
Federal Way, WA 888-839-2702
European Bakers
Tucker, GA 770-723-6180
European Style Bakery
Beverly Hills, CA 818-368-6876
Evans Bakery
Cozad, NE 800-222-5641
F R LePage Bakeries
Auburn, ME 207-783-9161
Falcone's Cookieland
Brooklyn, NY 718-236-4200
Fancy Lebanese Bakery
Halifax, NS 902-429-0400
Fantasia
Sedalia, MO 660-827-1172
Fantasy Cookie Company
Sylmar, CA 800-354-4488
Fantini Baking Company
Haverhill, MA 800-343-2110
Fantis Foods
Carlstadt, NJ 201-933-6200
Farrell Baking Company
West Middlesex, PA 724-342-7906
Father Sam's Syrian Bread
Buffalo, NY 800-521-6719
Fayes Bakery Products
Dexter, MO 573-624-4920
Federal Pretzel Baking Company
Philadelphia, PA 215-467-0505
Felix Roma & Sons
Endicott, NY 607-748-3336
Ferrara Bakery & Cafe
New York, NY 212-226-6150
Field's
Pauls Valley, OK 800-286-7501
Fiera Foods
Toronto, ON 416-744-1010
Finkemeier Bakery
Kansas City, KS 913-831-3103
Fireside Kitchen
Halifax, NS 902-454-7387
Fisher Rex Sandwiches
Raleigh, NC 919-901-0739
Flamin' Red's Woodfired
Pawlet, VT 802-325-3641
Fleischer's Bagels
Macedon, NY 315-986-9999
Flowers Foods Bakeries
Thomasville, GA 229-226-9110
Food for Life Baking Company
Corona, CA 951-279-5090
Food Mill
Oakland, CA 510-482-3848
Food of Our Own Design
Maplewood, NJ 973-762-0985
Foodbrands America
Oklahoma City, OK 405-290-4000
Fortella Fortune Cookies
Chicago, IL 312-567-9000
Fortune Cookie Factory
Oakland, CA 510-832-5552
Forty Second Street Bagel Cafe
Upland, CA 909-949-7334
Foxtail Foods
Fairfield, OH 800-487-2253
France Croissant
New York, NY 212-888-1210
France Delices
Montreal, QC 800-663-1365
Franklin Baking Company
Kinston, NC 800-248-7494
Frankly Natural Bakers
San Diego, CA 800-727-7229
Franz Family Bakeries
Portland, OR 503-731-5670
Fred Meyer Bakery
Clackamas, OR 503-650-2000
Freedman's Bakery
Belmar, NJ 732-681-2334
French Baking
Stratford, CT 203-378-7381
Fresh Dairy Direct/Morningstar
Dallas, TX 800-395-7004
Fresh Start Bakeries
City of Industry, CA 626-961-2525
Fresh Start Bakeries
Brea, CA 714-256-8900
Freund Baking Company
Glendale, CA 818-502-1400
Frisco Baking Company
Los Angeles, CA 323-225-6111
Frito-Lay
Dallas, TX 800-352-4477
Frookie
Des Plaines, IL 847-699-3200
Frostbite
Toledo, OH 800-968-7711
Fujiya
Honolulu, HI 808-845-2921
Future Bakery & Cafe
Etobicoke, ON 416-231-1491
Gabilas Knishes
Brooklyn, NY
Gadoua Bakery
Napierville, QC 450-245-3326
Gai's Northwest Bakeries
Seattle, WA 206-322-0931
Galassos Bakery
Mira Loma, CA 951-360-1211
Gambino's
Kenner, LA 504-712-0809
Gardner Pie Company
Akron, OH 330-245-2030
Gartner Studios
Stillwater, MN 888-522-9722
Gemini Food Industries
Charlton, MA 508-248-2730
General Henry Biscuit Company
Du Quoin, IL 618-542-6222
General Mills
Federalsburg, MD 410-754-5000
General Taste Bakery
Commerce, CA 323-888-2170
George H Leidenheimer Baking
New Orleans, LA 800-259-9099
Georgia Fruit Cake Company
Claxton, GA 912-739-2683
Gerard's French Bakery
Longmont, CO 303-772-4710
German Bakery at Village Corner
Stone Mountain, GA 866-476-6443
GH Bent Company
Milton, MA 617-698-5945
GH Leidenheimer Baking Company
New Orleans, LA 800-259-9099
Giant Food
Lanham, MD 888-469-4426
Glencourt
Napa, CA 707-944-4444
Global Bakeries
Pacoima, CA 818-896-0525
Glutenus Minimus, LLC
Belmont, MA 617-484-3550
Glutino
Laval, QC 800-363-3438
Goglanian Bakeries
Santa Ana, CA 714-444-3500
Gold Coast Baking Company
Santa Ana, CA 714-545-2253
Gold Crust Baking Company, Inc.
Alexandria, VA 703-549-0420
Gold Medal Bakery
Fall River, MA 800-642-7568
Gold Medal Baking Company
Philadelphia, PA 215-627-4787
Gold Standard Baking
Chicago, IL 800-648-7904
Golden Boys Pies of San Diego
San Diego, CA 800-746-0280
Golden Brown Bakery
South Haven, MI 269-637-3418
Golden Edibles LLC
Davie, FL 866-779-7781
Golden Glow Cookie Company
Bronx, NY 718-379-6223
Goll's Bakery
Havre De Grace, MD 410-939-4321
Gonnella Frozen Products
Schaumburg, IL 847-884-8829
Good Old Days Foods
Little Rock, AR 501-565-1257
Gould's Maple Sugarhouse
Shelburne Falls, MA 413-625-6170
Gourmet Baker
Burnaby, BC 800-663-1972
Gourmet Croissant
Brooklyn, NY 718-499-4911
Grain Bin Bakers
Carmel, CA 831-624-3883
Grandma Beth's Cookies
Alliance, NE 308-762-8433
Granello Bakery
Las Vegas, NV 702-361-0311
Granny Roddy's LLC
Annandale, VA 703-503-3431
Great Cakes
Los Angeles, CA 310-287-0228
Grebe's Bakery & Delicatessen
Milwaukee, WI 800-356-9377
Grecian Delight Foods
Elk Grove Village, IL 800-621-4387
Greenhills Irish Bakery
Dorchester, MA 617-825-8187
Gregory's Foods
Eagan, MN 800-231-4734
Greyston Bakery
Yonkers, NY 800-289-2253

Grossinger's Home Bakery
New York, NY 800-479-6996
Grote Bakery
Hamilton, OH 513-874-7436
Guttenplan's Frozen Dough
Middletown, NJ 888-422-4357
GWB Foods Corporation
Brooklyn, NY 877-977-7610
H Cantin
Beauport, QC 800-463-5268
H&H Bagels
New York, NY 800-692-2435
H. & S Bakery
Baltimore, MD 800-959-7655
H.E. Butt Grocery Company
San Antonio, TX 800-432-3113
Haas Baking Company
St Louis, MO 800-325-3171
Haby's Alsatian Bakery
Castroville, TX 830-931-2118
Hafner USA
Stone Mountain, GA 888-725-4605
Hahn's Old Fashioned Cake Company
Farmingdale, NY 631-249-3456
Handy Pax
Randolph, MA 781-963-8300
Harbar Corporation
Canton, MA 800-881-7040
Hardin's Bakery
Tuscaloosa, AL 205-752-6431
Harlan Bakeries
Avon, IN 317-272-3600
Harold Food Company
Charlotte, NC 704-588-8061
Harris Baking Company
Rogers, AR 479-636-3313
Harting's Bakery
Bowmansville, PA 717-445-5644
Harvest Bakery
Bristol, CT 860-589-8800
Harvest Day Bakery
Buena Park, CA 714-739-6318
Harvest Valley Bakery
La Salle, IL 815-224-9030
Havi Food Services Worldwide
Oak Park, IL 708-445-1700
Hawaii Candy
Honolulu, HI 808-836-8955
Hawaii Star Bakery
Honolulu, HI 808-841-3602
Hawaiian Bagel
Honolulu, HI 808-596-0638
Hazelwood Farms Bakery
Rochester, NY 585-424-1240
Health Valley Company
Irwindale, CA 800-334-3204
Hedgehaven Specialty Foods
Ilwaco, WA 360-642-4700
Heidi's Gourmet Desserts
Tucker, GA 800-241-4166
Heinemann's Bakeries
Palatine, IL 847-358-3501
Heiner's Bakery
Huntington, WV 800-776-8411
Heino's German-Style Wholesale Bakery
Naples, FL 941-643-3911
Heinz Company of Canada
North York, ON 877-574-3469
Heisler Food Enterprises
Bronx, NY 718-543-0855
Heitzman Bakery
Louisville, KY 502-452-1891
Herman's Bakery Coffee Shop
Cambridge, MN 763-689-1515
Hershey International
Weston, FL 954-385-2600
Heyerly Bakery
Ossian, IN 260-622-4196
Highlandville Packing
Highlandville, MO 417-443-3365
Holsum Bakery
Toa Baja, PR 787-798-8282
Holsum Bakery
Phoenix, AZ 800-755-8167
Holsum Bread
Kenosha, WI 262-637-6544
Holt's Bakery
Douglas, GA 912-384-2202
Home Baked Group
Boca Raton, FL 561-995-0767
Home Bakery
Laramie, WY 307-742-2721
Home Baking Company
Birmingham, AL 205-252-1161
Home Maid Bakery
Wailuku, HI 808-244-4150
Home Style Bakery
Grand Junction, CO 970-243-1233
Homes Packaging Company
Millersburg, OH 800-401-2529
Homestead Baking Company
Rumford, RI 800-556-7216
Homestyle Bread
Phoenix, AZ 602-268-0677
Honey Rose Baking Company
Carlsbad, CA
Hostess Brands
Kansas City, MO 816-502-4000
Hostess Brands
Irving, TX 972-532-4500
Hunt Country Foods
Middleburg, VA 540-364-2622
Huval Baking Company
Lafayette, LA 337-232-1611
Hye Quality Bakery
Fresno, CA 877-445-1778
I & K Distributors
Delphos, OH 800-869-6337
IBC Holsum
Atlanta, GA 800-465-7861
Il Gelato
Astoria, NY 800-899-9299
Il Giardino Bakery
Chicago, IL 773-889-2388
Immaculate Consumption
Flat Rock, NC 888-826-6567
Independent Bakers Association
Washington, DC 202-333-8190
Innovative Health Products
Largo, FL 800-654-2347
Innovative Ingredients
Reisterstown, MD 888-403-2907
Interbake Foods Corporate Office
Richmond, VA 804-755-7107
International Baking Company
Vernon, CA 323-583-9841
International Brownie
East Weymouth, MA 800-230-1588
International Equipment International Equipment And Supplies
Arecibo, PR 787-879-3151
Irresistible Cookie Jar
Hayden Lake, ID 208-664-1261
Isabella's Healthy Bakery
Cuyahoga Falls, OH 800-476-6328
Italian Bakery
Virginia, MN 218-741-3464
Italian Baking Company
Youngstown, OH 330-782-1358
Italian Baking Company
Edmonton, AB 780-424-4830
Italian Peoples Bakery
Ewing, NJ 609-771-1369
Iversen Baking Company
Bedminster, PA 215-636-5904
J J Gandy's Pies
Palm Harbor, FL 727-938-7437
J W Allen Company
Wheeling, IL 847-459-5400
J&J Snack Foods Corporation
Vernon, CA 800-486-7622
J&J Snack Foods Corporation
Pennsauken, NJ 800-486-9533
J&J Wall Baking Company
Sacramento, CA 916-381-1410
J.P. Sunrise Bakery
Edmonton, AB 780-454-5797
Jacques' Bakery
San Juan Capistrano, CA 949-496-5322
Jaeger Bakery
Milwaukee, WI 414-263-1700
Jamae Natural Foods
Los Angeles, CA 800-343-0052
James Skinner Company
Omaha, NE 800-358-7428
JC'S Natural Bakery
El Cajon, CA 619-239-4043
Jerabek's New Bohemian Coffee House
Saint Paul, MN 651-228-1245
Jerusalem House
Eugene, OR 541-485-1012
Jewel Bakery
Melrose Park, IL 708-531-6000
Jim's Cheese Pantry
Waterloo, WI 800-345-3571
Jimmy's Cookies
Fair Lawn, NJ 201-797-8900
JM Swank Company
North Liberty, IA 800-593-6375
JMP Bakery Company
Brooklyn, NY 718-272-5400
Joe Fazio's Bakery
St Louis, MO 314-645-6239
Joey's Fine Foods
Newark, NJ 973-482-1400
John J. Nissen Baking Company
Brewer, ME 207-989-7654
John J. Nissen Baking Company
Wareham, MA 508-295-2337
John Wm. Macy's Cheesesticks
Elmwood Park, NJ 800-643-0573
Jon Donaire Pastry
Santa Fe Springs, CA 877-366-2473
Jonathan Lord Corporation
Bohemia, NY 800-814-7517
Jou Jou's Pita Bakery
Birmingham, AL 205-945-6001
Joyce Food Products
Elmwood Park, NJ 201-791-4300
Jubelt Variety Bakeries
Mount Olive, IL 217-999-5231
Jubilations
Columbus, MS 662-328-9210
Just Desserts
San Francisco, CA 415-602-9245
Just Off Melrose
Palm Springs, CA 800-743-4109
Just Off Melrose, Inc.
Palm Springs, CA 800-743-4103
K&S Bakery Products
Edmonton, AB 780-481-8155
Kahns Bakery Company
El Paso, TX 915-533-8433
Kammeh International Trade Co
Chicago, IL 800-252-6634
Kangaroo Brands
Milwaukee, WI 800-798-0857
Kapaa Bakery
Kapaa, HI 808-822-4541
Karam Elsaha Baking Company
Manlius, NY
Karp's
Georgetown, MA 800-373-5277
Karsh's Bakery
Phoenix, AZ 602-264-4874
Keebler Company
Battlecreek, MI 630-956-9742
Keebler Company
South River, NJ 732-613-4381
Keller's Bakery
Lafayette, LA 337-235-1568
Kellogg Canada Inc
Mississauga, ON 888-876-3750
Kemach Food Products Corporation
Brooklyn, NY 888-453-6224
Kerrobert Bakery
Kerrobert, SK 306-834-2461
Key Lime
Smyrna, GA 770-333-0840
Keystone Pretzel Bakery
Lititz, PA 888-572-4500
KHS-Bartelt
Sarasota, FL 800-829-9980
Kid's Kookie Company
San Clemente, CA 800-350-7577
Kim & Scott's Gourmet Pretzels
Chicago, IL 800-578-9478
King Soopers Bakery
Denver, CO 877-415-4647
King's Hawaiian
Torrance, CA 800-800-5461
Klosterman Baking Company
Springfield, OH 937-322-7658
Koepplinger Bakery
Detroit, MI 248-967-2020
Koffee Kup Bakery
Burlington, VT 802-863-2696
Kollar Cookies
Long Branch, NJ 732-229-3364
Korbs Baking Company
Pawtucket, RI 401-726-4422
Kosher French Baguettes
Brooklyn, NY 718-633-4994
Kossar's Bialystoker Kuchen Bakery
New York, NY 877-424-2597

Kotarides Baking Company of Virginia
Norfolk, VA. 757-625-0301
Kraft Foods
Atlanta, GA. 404-756-6000
Kraft Foods
East Hanover, NJ 973-503-2000
Kreamo Bakers
South Bend, IN .574-234-0188
Krispy Bakery
West Palm Beach, FL 561-585-5504
Krispy Kreme Doughnut Company
Winston Salem, NC. 800-457-4779
Kroger Anderson Bakery
Anderson, SC 864-226-9135
Kupris Home Bakery
Bolton, CT 860-649-4746
Kyger Bakery Products
Lafayette, IN. 765-447-1252
L&M Bakery
Lawrence, MA .978-687-7346
La Boulangerie
San Diego, CA .858-578-4040
La Buena Mexican Foods Products
Tucson, AZ 520-624-1796
La Cigale Bakery
Opa Locka, FL .800-333-8578
La Francaise Bakery
Melrose Park, IL. 800-654-7220
La Moderna
Col Centro, TL
La Parisienne Bakery
Manassas, VA 800-727-4790
La Patisserie
Phoenix, AZ 602-254-5868
La Piccolina
Decatur, GA 800-626-1624
La Tempesta
S San Francisco, CA. 800-762-8330
La Tortilla Factory
Santa Rosa, CA. 800-446-1516
Lady Walton's and Bronco Bob's Cowboy Brand
Specialty Foods
Dallas, TX. 800-552-8006
Lady Walton's Cookies
Dallas, TX. 800-552-8006
Laguna Cookie & Dessert Company
Santa Ana, CA .800-673-2473
Lake States Yeast
Rhinelander, WI 715-369-4949
Lakeview Bakery
Calgary, AB. 403-246-6127
Lamb-Weston
Kennewick, WA 800-766-7783
Lamonaca Bakery
Windber, PA 814-467-4909
Landolfi Food Products
Trenton, NJ 609-392-1830
Lanthier Bakery
Alexandria, ON. 613-525-4981
Lark Fine Foods
Essex, MA. 978-768-0012
Laronga Bakery
Somerville, MA 617-625-8600
LaRosa's Bakery
Shrewsbury, NJ. 800-527-6722
Latonia Bakery
Covington, KY .859-491-8855
Laura's French Baking Company
Los Angeles, CA. 888-353-5144
Lavash Corporation
Los Angeles, CA. 323-663-5249
Lawrences Delights
Doraville, GA 800-568-0021
Lax & Mandel Bakery
Cleveland, OH .216-382-8877
Le Chic French Bakery
Miami Beach, FL 305-673-5522
Ledonne Brothers Bakery
Roseto, PA. 610-588-0423
Lefse House
Camrose, AB. 780-672-7555
Leidenheimer Baking Company
New Orleans, LA 504-525-1575
Lenchner Bakery
Concord, ON. 905-738-8811
Lender's Bagel Bakery
Mattoon, IL. 217-235-3181
Leo's Bakery
Marshfield, MA 781-837-3300
LePage Bakeries
Auburn, ME 207-783-9161
Lepage Bakeries
Auburn, ME 207-783-9161
Lewis Bakeries
London, ON 519-434-5252
Lewis Brothers Bakeries
Murfreesboro, TN. 615-893-6041
Lewis Brothers Bakeries
Evansville, IN 812-425-4642
Lewis Brothers Bakeries
Vincennes, IN 812-886-6533
Lewis-Vincennes Bakery
Vincennes, IN 812-886-6533
Liberty Richter
Saddle Brook, NJ 201-291-8749
Linden Cookies
Congers, NY 800-660-5051
Little Angel Foods
Daytona Beach, FL. 904-257-3040
Little Dutch Boy Bakeries
Draper, UT 801-571-3800
Livermore Falls Baking Company
Livermore Falls, ME. 207-897-3442
Loafin' Around
Madison, AL. 301-570-4513
Log House Foods
Plymouth, MN. .763-546-8395
Lombardi's Bakery
Torrington, CT .860-489-4766
Lone Star Bakery
Round Rock, TX. 512-255-3629
Lone Star Consolidated Foods
Dallas, TX. 800-658-5637
Longo's Bakery
Hazleton, PA 570-454-5825
Lotus Bakery
Santa Rosa, CA. 800-875-6887
Louis Swiss Pastry
Aspen, CO. 970-925-8592
Love & Quiches Desserts
Freeport, NY 800-525-5251
Love's Bakery
Honolulu, HI 888-455-6837
Lucerne Foods
Calgary, AB. 403-790-3500
Lucy's Sweet Surrender
Cleveland, OH .216-752-0828
Ludwick's Frozen Donuts
Grand Rapids, MI 800-366-8816
Luna's Tortillas
Dallas, TX. 214-747-2661
Lupi Marchigiano Bakery
New Haven, CT 203-562-9491
Lusitania Bakery
Blandon, PA 610-926-1311
M.M. Bake Shop
Laurel, MS 601-428-5153
Mac's Donut Shop
Aliquippa, PA 724-375-6776
MacFarms of Hawaii
Captain Cook, HI 808-328-2435
Maggiora Baking Company
Richmond, CA .510-235-0274
Magna Foods Corporation
City of Industry, CA 800-995-4394
Main Street Custom Foods
Cuyahoga Falls, OH 800-533-6246
Main Street Gourmet
Cuyahoga Falls, OH 800-533-6246
Main Street Gourmet Fundraising
Cuyahoga Falls, OH 800-533-6246
Main Street Muffins
Cuyahoga Falls, OH 800-533-6246
Main Street's Cambritt Cookies
Cuyahoga Falls, OH 800-533-6246
Mancuso Cheese Company
Joliet, IL 815-722-2475
Manderfield Home Bakery
Menasha, WI. 920-725-7794
Maple Leaf Bakery
Montreal, Qu . . . . .ÿ1 -00 -68 3
Maplehurst Bakeries
Carrollton, GA .800-482-4810
Marika's Kitchen
Hancock, ME 800-694-9400
Marin Food Specialties
Byron, CA. 925-634-6126
Market Day Corporation
Itasca, IL 877-632-7753
Marshall Biscuits
Saraland, AL. 251-679-6226
Marshall's Biscuit Company
Saraland, AL. 800-368-9811
Martin Brothers Distributing Company
Cedar Falls, IA .319-266-1775
Martino's Bakery
Burbank, CA. 818-842-0715
Mary Ann's Baking Company
Sacramento, CA 916-681-7444
Mary of Puddin Hill
Greenville, TX .800-545-8889
Maui Bagel
Kahului, HI. 808-270-7561
Maurice Lenell Cooky Company
Chicago, IL. 800-323-1760
Mayer's Cider Mill
Webster, NY 800-543-0043
Mazelle's Cheesecakes Concoctions Creations
Dallas, TX. 214-328-9102
Mediterranean Gyros Products
Long Island City, NY 718-786-3399
Mehaffie Pies
Dayton, OH. 937-253-1163
Mememe Inc
Toronto, ON 416-972-0973
Mercado Latino
City of Industry, CA 626-333-6862
Merlino Italian Baking Company
Seattle, WA 800-207-2997
Metropolitan Baking Company
Hamtramck, MI. 313-875-7246
Metz Baking Company
Pekin, IL 309-347-7315
Meyer's Bakeries
Casa Grande, AZ. 800-528-5770
Meyer's Bakeries
Hope, AR 800-643-1542
Michael D's Cookies & Cakes
Aurora, IL 630-892-2525
Michel's Bakery
Philadelphia, PA 215-725-3900
Mikawaya Bakery
Vernon, CA
Milano Baking Company
Joliet, IL 815-727-4872
Millie's Pierogi
Chicopee Falls, MA 800-743-7641
Mississippi Bakery
Burlington, IA. .319-752-6315
Modern Italian Bakery of West Babylon
Oakdale, NY 631-589-7300
Molinaro's Fine Italian Foods
Mississauga, ON. 800-268-4959
Mom's Bakery
Atlanta, GA. 404-344-4189
Mom's Famous
Boca Raton, FL. 561-750-1903
Mom's Food Company
South El Monte, CA 800-969-6667
Monaco Baking Company
Santa Fe Springs, CA 800-569-4640
Monastery Bakery At HolyCross Abbey
Berryville, VA. .540-955-9440
Monk's Bread
Victor, NY. 585-243-0660
Monster Cone
Montreal, QC 800-542-9801
Montana Bakery
Stamford, CT. 203-969-7700
Montione's Biscotti & Baked Goods
Norton, MA. 800-559-1010
Morabito Baking Company
Norristown, PA .800-525-7747
Morrison Meat Pies
West Valley, UT 801-977-0181
Mothers Kitchen Inc
Burlington, NJ. .609-589-3026
Mozzicato De Pasquale Bakery Pastry
Hartford, CT 860-296-0426
Mozzicato Depasquale Bakery & Pastry Shop
Hartford, CT 860-296-0426
Mrs Baird's Bakery
Fort Worth, TX .817-864-2500
Mrs. Baird's Bakeries
Waco, TX 254-750-2500
Mrs. Baird's Bakeries
Abilene, TX. 325-692-3141
Mrs. Baird's Bakeries
Fort Worth, TX .817-293-6230
Mrs. Fly's Bakery
Collegeville, PA 610-489-7288
Mrs. Smith's Bakeries
Spartanburg, SC 800-756-4746
Mt View Bakery
Mountain View, HI 808-968-6353

Mt. Vikos, Inc.
Providence, RI 888-534-0246
Multi Marques
Montreal, QC 514-934-1866
Murray Biscuit Company
Atlanta, GA. 800-745-5582
My Bagel Chips
Long Beach, NY 516-889-0732
My Grandma's Coffee Cakee of New England
Boston, MA. 800-847-2636
Nabisco
Parsippany, NJ. 973-682-5000
Najla's
Louisville, KY 877-962-5527
Naleway Foods
Winnipeg, MB. 800-665-7448
Nancy's Specialty Foods
Newark, CA 510-494-1100
Nardi Bakery & Deli
East Hartford, CT 860-289-5458
National Bakers Services
Plantation, FL 954-920-7666
Natural Ovens Bakery
Manitowoc, WI. 800-558-3535
Naturally Delicious
Oakland Park, FL 954-485-6730
Nature's Hilights
Chico, CA 800-313-6454
Nature's Path Foods
Richmond, BC 604-248-8777
Ne-Mo's Bakery
Escondido, CA 800-325-2692
Nestle Prepared Foods Company
Englewood, CO. 800-225-2270
Neuman Bakery Specialties
Addison, IL. 800-253-5298
Nevada Baking Company
Las Vegas, NV 702-384-8950
New Bakery Company of Ohio
Zanesville, OH 800-848-9845
New England Country Bakers
Watertown, CT 800-225-3779
New England Muffin Company
Fall River, MA 508-675-2833
New Horizons Baking Company
Fremont, IN. 260-495-7055
New Salem Tea-Bread Company
New Salem, MA 800-897-5910
New York Bakeries
Hialeah, FL 305-882-1355
New York Bakery & Bagelry
Saint Louis, MO 314-731-0080
New York Frozen Foods
Cleveland, OH 216-292-5655
New York International Bread Company
Orlando, FL. 407-843-9744
Newly Weds Foods
Watertown, MA. 800-621-7521
Nickles Bakery of Indiana
Elkhart, IN. 574-293-0608
Nickles Bakery of Ohio
Lima, OH 419-224-7080
Nickles Bakery of Ohio
Martins Ferry, OH. 740-633-1711
Nickles Bakery of Ohio
Navarre, OH 800-362-9775
Nicole's Divine Crackers
Chicago, IL 312-640-8883
Nikki's Cookies
Milwaukee, WI 800-776-7107
Nonni's Food Company
Tulsa, OK 877-295-0289
North American Enterprises
Tucson, AZ 800-817-8666
North East Foods
Baltimore, MD 410-558-1050
North's Bakery Californi
North Hollywood, CA 818-761-2892
Norths Bakery California Inc
N Hollywood, CA. 818-761-2892
Northside Bakery
Richmond, VA. 804-968-7620
Northwest Candy Emporium
Everett, WA. 800-404-7266
Notre Dame Bakery
Conception Harbour, NL 709-535-2738
Novelty Kosher Pastry
Spring Valley, NY. 845-356-0428
Nustef Foods
Mississauga, ON. 905-896-3060
Nuthouse Company
Mobile, AL 800-633-1306
Nutrilicious Natural Bakery
Countryside, IL. 800-835-8097
Nylander's Vantage Products
Lakeport, CA 707-263-4220
Oak State Products
Wenona, IL 815-853-4348
Oakrun Farm Bakery
Ancaster, ON. 905-648-1818
Oh Boy! Corporation
San Fernando, CA. 818-361-1128
OH Chocolate
Calgary, AB. 800-887-3959
Ohta Wafer Factory
Honolulu, HI. 808-949-2775
Old Country Bakery
North Hollywood, CA 818-838-2302
Old Fashioned Kitchen
Lakewood, NJ. 732-364-4100
Olivia's Croutons
New Haven, VT 888-425-3080
Orange Bakery
Irvine, CA 949-863-1377
Original Ya-hoo! Baking Company
Sherman, TX. 800-575-9373
Oroweat Baking Company
Montebello, CA 323-721-5161
Orwasher's Bakery Handmade Bread
New York, NY 212-288-6569
Otis Spunkmeyer
San Leandro, CA. 800-938-1900
Ottenberg's Bakers
Hyattsville, MD 800-334-7264
Our Farms To You, LLC
Middletown, VA 703-507-7604
Our Thyme Garden
Cleburne, TX 800-482-4372
Oven Fresh Baking Company
Chicago, IL 773-638-1234
Ozery Bakery Inc
Vaughan, ON. 905-265-1143
Pacific Ocean Produce
Santa Cruz, CA. 831-423-2654
Palermo Bakery
Seaside, CA. 831-394-8212
Pan Pepin
Bayamon, PR 787-787-1717
Pan-O-Gold Baking Company
St Cloud, MN 800-444-7005
Pantry Shelf/Mixxm
Hutchinson, KS. 800-968-3346
Parco Foods
Blue Island, IL 708-371-9200
Paris Pastry
Van Nuys, CA 310-474-8888
Partners, A Tasteful Choice Company
Kent, WA. 800-632-7477
Pasco Corporation of America
Portland, OR 503-289-6500
Pasta Shoppe
Nashville, TN 800-247-0188
Pastry Chef
Pawtucket, RI 800-639-8606
Pati-Petite Cookies
Bridgeville, PA 800-253-5805
Patisserie Wawel
Montreal, QC 614-524-3348
PB&S Chemicals
Henderson, KY 800-950-7267
Pechters Baking
Harrison, NJ 800-525-5779
Peggy Lawton Kitchens
East Walpole, MA. 800-843-7325
Peking Noodle Company
Los Angeles, CA. 323-223-2023
Pellman Foods
New Holland, PA 717-354-8070
Pennant Foods Company
Northlake, IL. 800-877-1157
Pepperidge Farm
Norwalk, CT. 888-737-7374
Pete & Joy's Bakery
Little Falls, MN. 320-632-6388
Petri Baking Products Inc
Silver Creek, NY. 800-346-1981
Petrofsky's Bakery Products
Chesterfield, MO 636-519-1613
Phipps Desserts
Toronto, ON 416-481-9111
Piantedosi Baking Company
Malden, MA 800-339-0080
Pie Piper Products
Bensenville, IL 800-621-8183
Piemonte's Bakery
Rockford, IL 815-962-4833
Pierre Foods
Cincinnati, OH 513-874-8741
Pierre's French Bakery
Portland, OR 503-233-8871
Pinnacle Foods Group
Cherry Hill, NJ 877-852-7424
Pioneer French Baking
Venice, CA 310-392-4128
Pioneer Frozen Foods
Duncanville, TX 972-298-4281
Pita King Bakery
Everett, WA. 425-258-4040
Pittsfield Rye Bakery
Pittsfield, MA 413-443-9141
Plaidberry Company
Vista, CA. 760-727-5403
Plehn's Bakery
Louisville, KY 502-896-4438
Plumlife Company
Newbury, MA 978-462-8458
Pocono Cheesecake Factory
Swiftwater, PA 570-839-6844
Polka Dot Bake Shop Millchap Purveyors LLC
Charlotte, NC 704-527-0005
Pollman's Bake Shops
Mobile, AL 251-438-1511
Portuguese Baking Company
Newark, NJ 973-589-8875
Positively Third Street Bakery
Duluth, MN. 218-724-8619
Powers Baking Company
miami, FL 305-381-7000
Pratzel's Bakery
Saint Louis, MO
President's Choice International
Brampton, ON. 888-495-5111
Preuss Bake Shop
Waseca, MN 507-835-4320
Priester Pecan Company
Fort Deposit, AL. 800-277-3226
Prime Pastry
Brooklyn, NY 888-771-2464
Primos Northgate
Flowood, MS 601-936-3701
Prince of Peace Enterprises
Hayward, CA 800-732-2328
Productos Del Plata, Inc
Miami, FL. 786-357-8261
Productos La Tradicional, S.A. De C.V.
Apodaca, NL. 818-321-3702
Productos Tosti Gar
Col. Centro, CF. 818-371-2070
Protano's Bakery
Hollywood, FL 954-925-3474
Pure's Food Specialties
Broadview, IL 708-344-8884
Purity Factories
St.John's, NL. 800-563-3411
Quality Bakery
Invermere, BC. 888-681-9977
Quality Bakery Products
Fort Lauderdale, FL 800-590-3663
Quality Bakery/MM Deli
Port Colborne, ON 905-834-4911
Quality Croutons
Chicago, IL 800-334-2796
Quality Naturally! Foods
City of Industry, CA 888-498-6986
Quiche & Tell
Flushing, NY. 718-381-7562
Quinzani Bakery
Boston, MA. 800-999-1062
R&B Quality Foods
Scottsdale, AZ. 480-443-1415
R.M. Palmer Company
Reading, PA 610-372-8971
R.W. Frookies
Sag Harbor, NY. 800-913-3663
Ralph's Grocery Company
Los Angeles, CA. 888-437-3496
Ranaldi Bros Frozen Food Products Inc
Warwick, RI 401-738-3444
Randag & Associates Inc
Elmhurst, IL 630-530-2830
Real Food Marketing
Kansas City, MO. 816-221-4100
Real Torino
Morristown, NJ. 973-895-5420
Renaissance Baking Company
North Miami, FL. 305-893-2144

Reser's Fine Foods
Beaverton, OR 800-333-6431
Rhodes Bake-N-Serv
Salt Lake City, UT 800-695-0122
Rhodes International
Columbus, WI. . . . 800-876-7333
Rich Ice Cream Company
West Palm Beach, FL 561-833-7585
Rich Products Corporation
Winchester, VA. . . . 540-667-1955
Rich Products Corporation
Fresno, CA 559-486-7380
Rich Products Corporation
Hilliard, OH. . . . 614-771-1117
Rich Products Corporation
Buffalo, NY. . . . 800-356-7094
Rich Products Corporation
Buffalo, NY. . . . 800-828-2021
Rich Products of Canada
Buffalo, NY. . . . 800-457-4247
Richmond Baking Company
Richmond, IN 765-962-8535
Rising Dough Bakery
Sacramento, CA 916-387-9700
Robert's Bakery
Minnetonka, MN. . . . 612-473-9719
Rockland Bakery
Nanuet, NY. . . . 800-734-4376
Rolling Pin Bakery
Bow Island, AB. . . . 403-545-2434
Rolling Pin Bakery
Great Bend, KS. . . . 620-793-5381
Roma & Ray's Italian Bakery
Valley Stream, NY 516-825-7610
Roma Bakeries
Rockford, IL 815-964-6737
Roma Bakery
San Jose, CA. . . . 408-294-0123
Romero's Food Products
Santa Fe Springs, CA 562-802-1858
Rondo Specialty Foods LTD
Newcastle, DE. . . . 800-724-6636
Rosemark Bakery
Saint Paul, MN 651-698-3838
Roskam Baking Company
Grand Rapids, MI 616-574-5757
Rotella's Italian Bakery
La Vista, NE 402-592-6600
Rovira Biscuit Corporation
Ponce, PR 787-844-8585
Rowena's
Norfolk, VA. . . . 800-627-8699
Royal Home Bakery
Newmarket, ON 905-715-7044
Royal Wine Corp
Bayonne, NJ 718-384-2400
Rubschlager Baking Corporation
Chicago, IL 773-826-1245
Rudolph's Specialty Bakery
Toronto, ON 800-268-1589
Ruiz Mex. Foods
Ontario, CA. . . . 909-947-7811
Run-A-Ton Group
Chester, NJ 800-247-6580
Russell & Kohne
Newport Beach, CA 949-645-8441
Ruth Ashbrook Bakery
Portland, OR 503-240-7437
Ryals Bakery
Milledgeville, GA 478-452-0321
Ryke's Bakery
Muskegon, MI. . . . 231-722-3508
S&M Communion Bread Company
Nashville, TN 615-292-1969
Sacramento Baking Company
Sacramento, CA 916-361-2000
Safeway Dairy Products
Walnut Creek, CA. . . . 925-944-4000
Saint Amour/Powerline Foods
Costa Mesa, CA 714-754-1900
Saint Armands Baking Company
Bradenton, FL. . . . 941-753-7494
Salem Baking Company
Winston Salem, NC. . . . 800-274-2994
San Anselmo's Cookies & Biscotti
San Anselmo, CA 800-229-1249
San Francisco Bread Company
San Jose, CA. . . . 408-298-6914
San Francisco Fine Bakery
Redwood City, CA 650-369-8573
San Francisco French Bread
Oakland, CA 510-729-6232
San Luis Sourdough
San Luis Obispo, CA 800-266-7687
San-J International, Inc
Richmond, VA. . . . 800-446-5500
Sanborn Sourdough Bakery
Las Vegas, NV 702-795-1030
Sandors Bakeries
Miami, FL. . . . 305-642-8484
Sanitary Bakery
Little Falls, MN. . . . 320-632-6388
Santa Fe Bite-Size Bakery
Albuquerque, NM 505-342-1119
Sara Lee
Knoxville, TN. . . . 865-573-1941
Sara Lee Corporation
Downers Grove, IL. . . . 630-598-8100
Sarabeth's Bakery
Bronx, NY. . . . 800-773-7378
Sarsfield Foods
Kentville, NS 902-678-2241
SASIB Biscuits and Snacks Division
Hudson, OH 330-656-3317
Saxby Foods
Edmonton, AB 780-440-4179
Schadel's Bakery
Silver City, NM. . . . 505-538-3031
Schaller's Bakery Inc
Greensburg, PA. . . . 800-241-1777
Schat's Dutch Bakeries
Bishop, CA. . . . 760-873-7156
Schisa Brothers
Manlius, NY 315-463-0213
Schmidt Baking Company
Baltimore, MD 800-456-2253
Schott's Bakery
Houston, TX 713-869-5701
Schulze & Burch Biscuit Company
Chicago, IL 773-927-6622
Schwan Food Company
Marshall, MN 800-533-5290
Schwebel Baking Company
Youngstown, OH. . . . 330-783-2860
Schwebel Baking Company
Youngstown, OH. . . . 800-860-2867
Scialo Brothers
Providence, RI 877-421-0986
Scot Paris Fine Desserts
New York, NY 212-807-1802
Scotty Wotty's Creamy Cheesecake
Hillsborough, NJ. . . . 908-281-9720
Seavers Bakery
Johnson City, TN 423-928-8131
Shamrock Foods Company
Phoenix, AZ 800-289-3663
Shashy's Fine Foods
Montgomery, AL. . . . 334-263-7341
Shaw Baking Company
Thunder Bay, ON 807-345-7327
Sheila's Select Gourmet Recipe
Heber City, UT 800-516-7286
Sherwood Brands
Rockville, MD 401-434-7773
Sheryl's Chocolate Creations
Hicksville, NY 888-882-2462
Shipley Baking Company
Texarkana, AR 870-772-7146
Siljans Crispy Cup Company
Calgary, AB. . . . 403-275-0135
Silver Lake Cookie Company
Islip, NY 631-581-4000
Silver Tray Cookies
Fort Lauderdale, FL 305-883-0800
Simon Hubig Company
New Orleans, LA 504-945-2181
Sinbad Sweets
Fresno, CA 800-350-7933
SJR Foods
New Bedford, MA 781-821-3090
Smith's Bakery
Hattiesburg, MS 601-288-7000
Smoak's Bakery & Catering Service
Augusta, GA. . . . 706-738-1792
Solana Beach Baking Company
Carlsbad, CA. . . . 760-931-0148
Soloman Baking Company
Denver, CO 303-371-2777
Solvang Bakery
Solvang, CA 800-377-4253
South West Foods Tasty Bakery
Tyler, TX. . . . 903-877-3481
Southchem
Durham, NC 800-849-7000
Spanish Gardens Food Manufacturing
Kansas City, KS 913-831-4242
Specialty Bakers
Marysville, PA 800-233-0778
Spilke's Baking Company
Brooklyn, NY 718-384-2150
Spohrers Bakeries
Collingdale, PA. . . . 610-532-9959
Spot Bagel Bakery
Seattle, WA 206-623-0066
Spring Glen Fresh Foods
Ephrata, PA. . . . 800-641-2853
St. Cloud Bakery
Saint Cloud, MN. . . . 320-251-8055
St. Francis Pie Shop
Clayton, CA 510-655-0136
Stacy's Pita Chip Company
Randolph, MA 888-332-4477
Stagnos Bakery
East Liberty, PA 412-441-3485
Standard Bakery
Kealakekua, HI 808-322-3688
Stangl's Bakeries
Ambridge, PA 724-266-5080
Starbucks Coffee Company
Seattle, WA 800-782-7282
Stauffer's
Cuba, NY 585-968-2700
Stella D'Oro Biscuit Company
Valhalla, NY 800-995-2623
Sterling Foods
San Antonio, TX. . . . 210-490-1669
Steve's Mom
Bronx, NY. . . . 800-362-4545
Sticky Fingers Bakeries
Spokane, WA. . . . 800-458-5826
Strauss Bakeries
Elkhart, IN. . . . 574-293-9027

Stroehmann Bakeries
West Hazleton, PA 570-455-2066
Stroehmann Bakeries
Harrisburg, PA 800-220-2867
Stroehmann Bakeries
Horsham, PA 800-984-0989
Stroehmann Bakery
Horsham, PA 800-984-0989
Strossner's Bakery
Greenville, SC 864-233-3996
Sugar Bowl Bakery
Hayward, CA 510-782-2118
Sugar Kake Cookie
Tonawanda, NY 800-775-5180
Summerfield Foods
Santa Rosa, CA 707-579-3938
Sun Pac Foods
Brampton, ON 905-792-2700
Sunbeam
New Bedford, MA 800-458-8407
Sunbeam Baking Company
El Paso, TX 800-328-6111
Suncoast Foods Corporation
San Diego, CA 619-299-0475
Sunray Bakery Corporation
Salem, NH 603-898-3079
Sunset Specialty Foods
Sunset Beach, CA 562-592-4976
Superior Bakery
North Grosvenordale, CT 860-923-9555
Superior Cake Products
Southbridge, MA 508-764-3276
Supermoms
Saint Paul Park, MN 800-944-7276
Svenhard's Swedish Bakery
Oakland, CA 800-333-7836
Swatt Baking Company
Olean, NY 800-370-6656
Sweet Bakery Baltimore
Baltimore, MD 41- 7-8 22
Sweet Endings
West Palm Beach, FL 888-635-1177
Sweet Gallery Exclusive Pastry
Toronto, ON 416-766-0289
Sweet Life Enterprises
Santa Ana, CA 949-417-3205
Sweet Sam's Baking Company
Bronx, NY 718-822-0599
Sweetery
Anderson, SC 800-752-1188
T. Marzetti Company
Columbus, OH 614-846-2232
Table De France
Ontario, CA 909-923-5205
Table Pride
Atlanta, GA 770-455-7464
Table Talk Pie
Worcester, MA 508-798-8811
Tasty Baking Company
Philadelphia, PA 800-338-2789
Tasty Mix Quality Foods
Brooklyn, NY 866-TAS-TYMX
Tastykake
Philadelphia, PA 215-221-8500
Taystee Bakeries
Marquette, MI 906-226-7266
Teeny Foods Corporation
Portland, OR 503-252-3006
Tennessee Bun Company
Dickson, TN 888-486-2867
Terra Harvest Foods
Rockford, IL 815-636-9500
Terranetti's Italian Bakery
Mechanicsburg, PA 717-697-5434
Teti Bakery
Etobicoke, ON 800-465-0123
Texas Crumb & Food Products
Farmers Branch, TX 800-522-7862
The Bama Company
Tulsa, OK 800-756-2262
The Cheesecake Factory
Calabasas Hills, CA 818-871-3000
The Great San Saba RiverPecan Company
San Saba, TX 800-621-9121
The Pillsbury Company
Chelsea, MA 800-370-7834
Thornton Bakery
Memphis, TN 901-324-2118
Tina's
Anaheim, CA 714-630-4123
Titterington's Olde English Bake Shop
Woburn, MA 781-938-7600

Tom Cat Bakery
Long Island City, NY 718-786-4224
Tom Sturgis Pretzel Inc
Reading, PA 610-775-0335
Tomaro's Bakery
Clarksburg, WV 304-622-0691
Toufayan Bakeries
Orlando, FL 407-295-2257
Traditional Baking
Bloomington, CA 909-877-8471
Treasure Foods
West Valley, UT 801-974-0911
Tripoli Bakery
Lawrence, MA 978-682-7754
Tripp Bakers
Wheeling, IL 800-621-3702
Troppers
Santa Barbara, CA 805-969-4054
Turano Pastry Shops
Bloomingdale, IL 630-529-6161
Turnbull Bakeries of Lousiana
New Orleans, LA 504-581-5383
Tuscan Bakery
Portland, OR 800-887-2261
Twin City Bagels/National Choice Bakery
South St Paul, MN 651-554-0200
Twin Marquis
Brooklyn, NY 800-367-6868
Two Chefs on a Roll
Carson, CA 800-842-3025
ULDO USA
Lexington, MA 781-860-7800
Ultimate Biscotti
Eugene, OR 541-344-8220
Uncle Andy's Pic & Pay Bakery
South Portland, ME 207-799-7199
Uncle Ralph's Cookie Company
Frederick, MD 800-422-0626
Unified Western Grocers
Los Angeles, CA 323-232-6124
United Noodle Manufacturing Company
Salt Lake City, UT 801-485-0951
United Pies of Elkhart I
Elkhart, IN 574-294-3419
Upper Crust Bakery
Phoenix, AZ 602-255-0464
Upper Crust Baking Company
Pismo Beach, CA 800-676-1691
Upper Crust Biscotti
Pismo Beach, CA 866-972-6879
Uptown Bakers
Hyattsville, MD 301-864-1500
Valley Bakery
Rock Valley, IA 712-476-5386
Valley Lahvosh Baking Company
Fresno, CA 800-480-2704
Vallos Baking Company
Bethlehem, PA 610-866-1012
Van de Kamp's
Peoria, IL 800-798-3318
Vande Walle's Candies
Appleton, WI 920-738-7799
Venus Wafers
Hingham, MA 800-545-4538
Vermont Bread Company
Brattleboro, VT 877-293-0876
Vie de France Bakery
Bensenville, IL 630-595-9521
Vie de France Bakery
Vienna, VA 800-446-4404
Vie de France Bakery
Atlanta, GA 800-933-5486
Vie de France Yamazaki
Denver, CO 303-371-6280
Vie de France Yamazaki
Vernon, LA 323-582-1241
Vie de France Yamazaki
Vienna, VA 800-393-8926
Vie de France Yamazaki
Vienna, VA 800-446-4404
Vigneri Confections
Rochester, NY 877-843-6374
Vilotti & Marinelli Baking Company
Philadelphia, PA 215-627-5038
VIP Foodservice
Kahului, HI 808-877-5055
Vista Bakery
Burlington, IA 800-553-2343
Vocatura Bakery
Norwich, CT 860-887-2220
Voortman Cookies
Bloomington, CA 909-877-8471

Waldensian Bakeries
Valdese, NC 828-874-2136
Wally Biscotti
Denver, CO 866-659-2559
Way Baking Company
Jackson, MI 800-347-7373
Wedding Cake Studio
Williamsfield, OH 440-667-1765
Wedemeyer Bakery
South San Francisco, CA 650-873-1000
WendySue & Tobey's
Gardena, CA 310-516-9705
Wenger's Bakery
Reading, PA 610-372-6545
Wenner Bread Products
Bayport, NY 800-869-6262
Wenzel's Bakery
Tamaqua, PA 570-668-2360
Westco Bakemark
Pico Rivera, CA 800-695-5061
Weston Bakeries
Calgary, AB 403-259-1500
Weston Bakeries
Etobicoke, ON 416-252-7323
Weston Bakeries
Kingston, ON 800-267-0229
Weston Bakeries
Toronto, ON 800-590-6861
Wheat Montana Farms & Bakery
Three Forks, MT 800-535-2798
White Castle System
Columbus, OH 866-272-8372
Whole Earth Bakery
New York, NY 212-677-7597
Wick's Pies
Winchester, IN 800-642-5880
Widoffs Modern Bakery
Worcester, MA 508-752-7200
William Poll
New York, NY 800-993-7655
Williamsburg Chocolatier
Williamsburg, VA 757-253-1474
Willmar Cookie & Nut Company
Willmar, MN 320-235-0600
Willmark Sales Company
Brooklyn, NY 718-388-7141
Winder Dairy
West Valley, UT 800-946-3371
Wolferman's
Medford, OR
Wonder Bread
Provo, UT 800-483-7253
Wonton Food
Brooklyn, NY 800-776-8889
Woodie Pie Company
Artesia, NM 505-746-2132
World of Chantilly
Brooklyn, NY 718-859-1110
Wow! Factor Desserts
Sherwood Park, AB 800-604-2253
Wuollet Bakery
Minneapolis, MN 612-381-9400
Young's Bakery
Uniontown, PA 724-437-6361
Yrica's Rugelach & Baking Company
Brooklyn, NY 718-965-3657
YZ Enterprises
Maumee, OH 800-736-8779
Zeppys Bakery
Lawrence, MA 781-963-7022
Zoelsmanns Bakery & Deli
Pueblo, CO 719-543-0407

Bread Crumbs & Croutons

Biscotti Goddess
Charles City, VA 855-745-9490
General Mills
Federalsburg, MD 410-754-5000
Griffith Laboratories
Alsip, IL 800-346-9494
H&S Edible Products Corporation
Mount Vernon, NY 800-253-3364
Heinz Company of Canada
North York, ON 877-574-3469
Just Off Melrose
Palm Springs, CA 800-743-4109
Lecoq Cuisine Corp
Bridgeport, CT 203-334-1010
Lesley Stowe Fine Foods LTD.
Richmond, BC 604-731-3663
Mignardise
Chambly, QC 450-447-0777

Olivia's Croutons
New Haven, VT 888-425-3080
Quality Bakery Products
Fort Lauderdale, FL 800-590-3663
Quality Croutons
Chicago, IL 800-334-2796
Roskam Baking Company
Grand Rapids, MI 616-574-5757
Sugar Foods Corporation
New York, NY 212-753-6900
Sun Pac Foods
Brampton, ON 905-792-2700

Bread Crumbs

Colonna Brothers
North Bergen, NJ 201-864-1115
Duval Bakery Products
Jacksonville, FL 904-354-7878
Griffith Laboratories
Alsip, IL 800-346-9494
Lakeview Bakery
Calgary, AB 403-246-6127
Newly Weds Foods
Chicago, IL 800-621-7521
Quality Bakery Products
Fort Lauderdale, FL 800-590-3663
Richmond Baking Company
Richmond, IN 765-962-8535
Sun Pac Foods
Brampton, ON 905-792-2700
Texas Crumb & Food Products
Farmers Branch, TX 800-522-7862
Turnbull Bakeries of Lousiana
New Orleans, LA 504-581-5383
Vigo Importing Company
Tampa, FL 813-884-3491

Croutons

Aladdin Bakers
Brooklyn, NY 718-499-1818
Heaven Scent Natural Foods
Santa Monica, CA 310-829-9050
Icco Cheese Company
Orangeburg, NY 845-398-9800
Just Off Melrose
Palm Springs, CA 800-743-4109
Lakeview Bakery
Calgary, AB 403-246-6127
Live A Little Gourmet Foods
Newark, CA 888-744-2300
Olivia's Croutons
New Haven, VT 888-425-3080
Progresso Quality Foods
Vineland, NJ 800-200-9377
Quality Bakery Products
Fort Lauderdale, FL 800-590-3663
Quality Croutons
Chicago, IL 800-334-2796
Roskam Baking Company
Grand Rapids, MI 616-574-5757
San Francisco French Bread
Oakland, CA 510-729-6232
Sugar Foods
Sun Valley, CA 818-768-7900
Sun Pac Foods
Brampton, ON 905-792-2700

Crumbs

Aladdin Bakers
Brooklyn, NY 718-499-1818
Gonnella Frozen Products
Schaumburg, IL 847-884-8829
Griffith Laboratories
Alsip, IL 800-346-9494
Heaven Scent Natural Foods
Santa Monica, CA 310-829-9050
Icco Cheese Company
Orangeburg, NY 845-398-9800
Newly Weds Foods
Chicago, IL 800-621-7521
Progresso Quality Foods
Vineland, NJ 800-200-9377
Quality Bakery Products
Fort Lauderdale, FL 800-590-3663
Richmond Baking Company
Richmond, IN 765-962-8535
Sun Pac Foods
Brampton, ON 905-792-2700
Texas Crumb & Food Products
Farmers Branch, TX 800-522-7862

Vigo Importing Company
Tampa, FL 813-884-3491

Bread Sticks

Andre-Boudin Bakeries
San Francisco, CA 415-882-1849
Bake Crafters Food
Collegedale, TN 800-296-8935
Baker & Baker
Schaumburg, IL 800-593-5777
Baker & Baker, Inc.
Schaumburg, IL 800-593-5777
Clown-Gysin Brands
Northbrook, IL 800-323-5778
Colonna Brothers
North Bergen, NJ 201-864-1115
Dwayne Keith Brooks Company
Orangevale, CA 916-988-1030
Falcone's Cookieland
Brooklyn, NY 718-236-4200
Goglanian Bakeries
Santa Ana, CA 714-444-3500
John Wm. Macy's Cheesesticks
Elmwood Park, NJ 800-643-0573
Kemach Food Products Corporation
Brooklyn, NY 888-453-6224
La Piccolina
Decatur, GA 800-626-1624
Nature's Hilights
Chico, CA 800-313-6454
Real Food Marketing
Kansas City, MO 816-221-4100
Stella D'Oro Biscuit Company
Valhalla, NY 800-995-2623
Teeny Foods Corporation
Portland, OR 503-252-3006
Tomanetti Food Products
Oakmont, PA 800-875-3040
Toufayan Bakeries
Orlando, FL 407-295-2257
Tropical
Columbus, OH 800-538-3941
Turnbull Bakeries of Lousiana
New Orleans, LA 504-581-5383

Breads

1-2-3 Gluten Inc
Orange, OH 843-768-7231
Aunt Millies Bakeries
Fort Wayne, IN 260-424-8245
Bakemark Ingredients Canada
Richmond, BC 800-665-9441
Baker
Milford, NJ 800-995-3989
Baptista's Bakery
Franklin, WI 877-261-3157
Bella Chi-Cha Products
Santa Cruz, CA 831-423-1851
Berkshire Mountain Bakery
Housatonic, MA 866-274-6124
Bridgford Foods of North Carolina
Statesville, NC 704-878-2722
Buns Master Bakery
Richmond Hill, ON 800-563-6688
Butter Krust Baking Company
Sunbury, PA 800-282-8093
Chatila's Bakery
Salem, NH 603-898-5459
Chella's Dutch Delicacies
Lake Oswego, OR 800-458-3331
Clarmil Manufacturing Corporation
Hayward, CA 888-252-7645
Colchester Bakery
Colchester, CT 860-537-2415
Goglanian Bakeries
Santa Ana, CA 714-444-3500
Grandma's Recipe Ruglactch
New York, NY 212-627-2775
Haby's Alsatian Bakery
Castroville, TX 830-931-2118
Hela Spice Company
Uxbridge, ON 877-435-2649
Holsum Bakery
Phoenix, AZ 800-755-8167
Hostess Brands
Irving, TX 972-532-4500
Klosterman Baking Company
Cincinnati, OH 513-242-1004
Lakeview Bakery
Calgary, AB 403-246-6127

LePage Bakeries
Auburn, ME 207-783-9161
Martin's Famous Pastry Shoppe, Inc
Chambersburg, PA 800-548-1200
Metropolitan Bakery
Philadelphia, PA 877-412-7323
Morabito Baking Company
Norristown, PA 800-525-7747
Morse's Sauerkraut
Waldoboro, ME 866-832-5569
Mozzicato Depasquale Bakery & Pastry Shop
Hartford, CT 860-296-0426
Mrs Baird's Bakery
Fort Worth, TX 817-864-2500
Naturally Delicious
Oakland Park, FL 954-485-6730
Nature's Hilights
Chico, CA 800-313-6454
Neuman Bakery Specialties
Addison, IL 800-253-5298
New Horizon Foods
Union City, CA 510-489-8600
Oasis Breads
Escondido, CA 760-747-7390
Old World Bakery
Cincinatti, OH 513-931-1411
Orlando Baking Company
Cleveland, OH 800-362-5504
Orwasher's Bakery Handmade Bread
New York, NY 212-288-6569
Plehn's Bakery
Louisville, KY 502-896-4438
Ralph's Grocery Company
Los Angeles, CA 888-437-3496
Royal Caribbean Bakery
Mount Vernon, NY 888-818-0971
Safeway Inc
Pleasanton, CA 877-723-3929
Sandors Bakeries
Miami, FL 305-642-8484
Southeast Baking Corporation
Greer, SC 864-627-1380
Sterling Foods
San Antonio, TX 210-490-1669
Sunbeam Baking Company
El Paso, TX 800-328-6111
Superior Baking Company
Brockton, MA 800-696-2253

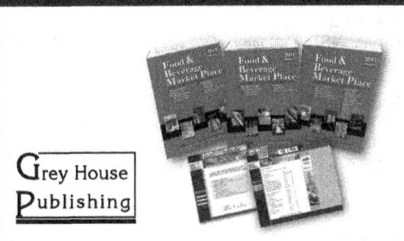

Taste Maker Foods
Memphis, TN 800-467-1407
Vantage USA
Chicago, IL 773-247-1086
Vermont Bread Company
Brattleboro, VT 802-254-4600
Wuollet Bakery
Minneapolis, MN 612-381-9400

Bagels

Aladdin Bakers
Brooklyn, NY 718-499-1818
Amoroso's Baking Company
Philadelphia, PA 800-377-6557
Andre-Boudin Bakeries
San Francisco, CA 415-882-1849
Awrey Bakeries
Livonia, MI 800-950-2253
Bagel Factory
Mountain Brk, AL 205-967-6931
Bagel Guys
Brooklyn, NY 718-222-4361
Bagel Works
Boca Raton, FL 561-852-8992
Bagelworks
New York, NY 212-744-6444
Bake Crafters Food
Collegedale, TN 800-296-8935
Baker Boy Bake Shop
Dickinson, ND 800-437-2008
BBU Bakeries
Denver, CO 303-691-6342
Beach Bagel Bakeries
Miami, FL 305-691-3514
Better Bagel Bakery
Sarasota, FL 941-924-0393
Bocconcino Food Products
Moonachie, NJ 201-933-7474
Brooklyn Bagel Company
Staten Island, NY 800-349-3055
Buckhead Gourmet
Atlanta, GA 800-673-6338
Chatila's Bakery
Salem, NH 603-898-5459
Crispy Bagel Company
Baltimore, MD 800-522-7655
Dakota Brands Intl. nal
Jamestown, ND 800-844-5073
Enjoy Life Foods
Schiller Park, IL 888-503-6569
Entenmann's-Oroweat/BestFoods
South San Francisco, CA 650-583-5828
Evans Bakery
Cozad, NE 800-222-5641
F R LePage Bakeries
Auburn, ME 207-783-9161
Felix Roma & Sons
Endicott, NY 607-748-3336
Fleischer's Bagels
Macedon, NY 315-986-9999
H&H Bagels
New York, NY 800-692-2435
Harlan Bakeries
Avon, IN 317-272-3600
Hostess Brands
Irving, TX 972-532-4500
JMP Bakery Company
Brooklyn, NY 718-272-5400
Kerrobert Bakery
Kerrobert, SK 306-834-2461
Kim and Scott's Gourmet Pretzels
Chicago, IL 800-578-9478
La Francaise Bakery
Melrose Park, IL 800-654-7220
Lakeview Bakery
Calgary, AB 403-246-6127
Lenchner Bakery
Concord, ON 905-738-8811
Lender's Bagel Bakery
Mattoon, IL 217-235-3181
Maui Bagel
Kahului, HI 808-270-7561
Meyer's Bakeries
Hope, AR 800-643-1542
Modern Baked Products
Oakdale, NY 877-727-2253
My Bagel Chips
Long Beach, NY 516-889-0732
New York Bakery & Bagelry
Saint Louis, MO 314-731-0080
Oroweat Baking Company
Montebello, CA 323-721-5161
Otis Spunkmeyer
San Leandro, CA 800-938-1900
Pechters Baking
Harrison, NJ 800-525-5779
Petrofsky's Bakery Products
Chesterfield, MO 636-519-1613
Pinnacle Foods Group
Cherry Hill, NJ 877-852-7424
Positively Third Street Bakery
Duluth, MN 218-724-8619
Prairie Malt
Biggar, SK 306-948-3500
Quality Naturally! Foods
City of Industry, CA 888-498-6986
Sara Lee Corporation
Downers Grove, IL 630-598-8100
SJR Foods
New Bedford, MA 781-821-3090
Spot Bagel Bakery
Seattle, WA 206-623-0066
Toufayan Bakeries
Orlando, FL 407-295-2257
Twin City Bagels/National Choice Bakery
South St Paul, MN 651-554-0200
Ultimate Bagel
Altoona, PA 814-944-4148
Upper Crust Baking Company
Pismo Beach, CA 800-676-1691
W&G Flavors
Hunt Valley, MD 410-771-6606
Wenner Bread Products
Bayport, NY 800-869-6262
Western Bagel Baking Corporation
Van Nuys, CA 818-786-5847
Zeppys Bakery
Lawrence, MA 781-963-7022

Fresh

Bagel Guys
Brooklyn, NY 718-222-4361
Canada Bread
North Bay, ON 800-461-6122
Felix Roma & Sons
Endicott, NY 607-748-3336
Fleischer's Bagels
Macedon, NY 315-986-9999
Harlan Bakeries
Avon, IN 317-272-3600
Pechters Baking
Harrison, NJ 800-525-5779
Russ & Daughters
New York, NY 800-787-7229
Western Bagel Baking Corporation
Van Nuys, CA 818-786-5847

Frozen

Aladdin Bakers
Brooklyn, NY 718-499-1818
Andre-Boudin Bakeries
San Francisco, CA 415-882-1849
Awrey Bakeries
Livonia, MI 800-950-2253
Bake Crafters Food
Collegedale, TN 800-296-8935
Bocconcino Food Products
Moonachie, NJ 201-933-7474
Brooklyn Bagel Company
Staten Island, NY 800-349-3055
Evans Bakery
Cozad, NE 800-222-5641
Fleischer's Bagels
Macedon, NY 315-986-9999
Guttenplan's Frozen Dough
Middletown, NJ 888-422-4357
Harlan Bakeries
Avon, IN 317-272-3600
Lender's Bagel Bakery
Mattoon, IL 217-235-3181
Ore-Ida Foods
Pittsburgh, PA 800-892-2401
Oroweat Baking Company
Montebello, CA 323-721-5161
Petrofsky's Bakery Products
Chesterfield, MO 636-519-1613
Quality Naturally! Foods
City of Industry, CA 888-498-6986
Sara Lee Corporation
Downers Grove, IL 630-598-8100
Wenner Bread Products
Bayport, NY 800-869-6262
Western Bagel Baking Corporation
Van Nuys, CA 818-786-5847

Baguettes

Kosher French Baguettes
Brooklyn, NY 718-633-4994
Tom Cat Bakery
Long Island City, NY 718-786-4224

Bialys

Harlan Bakeries
Avon, IN 317-272-3600
Russ & Daughters
New York, NY 800-787-7229

Biscuits

Almondina®/YZ Enterprises, Inc.
Maumee, OH 800-736-8779
American Vintage Wine Biscuits
Long Island City, NY 718-361-1003
Awrey Bakeries
Livonia, MI 800-950-2253
Bake Crafters Food
Collegedale, TN 800-296-8935
Baker Boy Bake Shop
Dickinson, ND 800-437-2008
Bakery Chef
Louisville, KY 800-594-0203
Blue Chip Group
Salt Lake City, UT 800-878-0099
Bob Evans Farms
Hillsdale, MI 517-437-3349
Borinquen Biscuit Corporation
Yauco, PR 787-856-3030
Bremner Biscuit Company
Denver, CO 800-722-1871
Bridgford Foods Corporation
Anaheim, CA 800-527-2105
Buon Italia Misono Food Ltd.
New York, NY 212-633-9090
Callie's Charleston Biscuits LLC
Charleston, SC 843-577-1198
Chelsea Market Baskets
New York, NY 888-727-7887
Chelsea Milling Company
Chelsea, MI 734-475-1361
Chex Finer Foods
Attleboro, MA 800-322-2434
Consolidated Biscuit Company
Mc Comb, OH 800-537-9544
Dare Foods
Kitchener, ON 800-265-8225
Del's Pastry
Etobicoke, ON 416-231-4383
Di Camillo Bakery
Niagara Falls, NY 800-634-4363
Dolly Madison Bakery Interstate Brands Corporation
Columbus, IN 812-376-7432
Ener-G Foods
Seattle, WA 800-331-5222
Falcone's Cookieland
Brooklyn, NY 718-236-4200
Franklin Baking Company
Goldsboro, NC 800-248-7494
Fresh Start Bakeries
Brea, CA 714-256-8900
General Henry Biscuit Company
Du Quoin, IL 618-542-6222
Godiva Chocolatier
New York, NY 800-946-3482
Grebe's Bakery & Delicatessen
Milwaukee, WI 800-356-9377
GWB Foods Corporation
Brooklyn, NY 877-977-7610
Heitzman Bakery
Louisville, KY 502-452-1891
Hershey International
Weston, FL 954-385-2600
Hostess Brands
Kansas City, MO 816-502-4000
Keebler Company
Battlecreek, MI 630-956-9742
Keebler Company
South River, NJ 732-613-4381
KHS-Bartelt
Sarasota, FL 800-829-9980
Lewis Brothers Bakeries
Evansville, IN 812-425-4642

Lewis Brothers Bakeries
Vincennes, IN 812-886-6533
Lone Star Bakery
Round Rock, TX. 512-255-3629
Marshall Biscuits
Saraland, AL 251-679-6226
Merlino Italian Baking Company
Seattle, WA 800-207-2997
Mom's Bakery
Atlanta, GA. 404-344-4189
Mom's Food Company
South El Monte, CA 800-969-6667
Native South Services
Fredericksburg, TX. 800-236-2848
Pacific Ocean Produce
Santa Cruz, CA. 831-423-2654
Pett Spice Products
Atlanta, GA. 404-691-5235
Pierre Foods
Cincinnati, OH 513-874-8741
Pioneer Frozen Foods
Duncanville, TX 972-298-4281
Purity Factories
St.John's, NL. 800-563-3411
Quality Naturally! Foods
City of Industry, CA 888-498-6986
Rovira Biscuit Corporation
Ponce, PR 787-844-8585
Royal Home Bakery
Newmarket, ON 905-715-7044
Royal Wine Corp
Bayonne, NJ 718-384-2400
Sara Lee
Knoxville, TN. 865-573-1941
Schulze & Burch Biscuit Company
Chicago, IL 773-927-6622
Southernfood Specialties
Atlanta, GA. 800-255-5323
Stella D'Oro Biscuit Company
Valhalla, NY 800-995-2623
Sterling Foods
San Antonio, TX. 210-490-1669
Superior Bakery
North Grosvenordale, CT 860-923-9555
The Bama Company
Tulsa, OK 800-756-2262
TIPIAK INC
Stamford, CT. 203-961-9117
Ultimate Biscotti
Eugene, OR. 541-344-8220
Wedemeyer Bakery
South San Francisco, CA 650-873-1000

Fresh

Automatic Rolls of New Jersey
Edison, NJ. 732-549-2243
Ener-G Foods
Seattle, WA 800-331-5222
Mrs. Kavanagh's English Muffins
Rumford, RI 800-556-7216
New Bakery Company of Ohio
Zanesville, OH 800-848-9845
Quinzani Bakery
Boston, MA. 800-999-1062

Frozen

Awrey Bakeries
Livonia, MI. 800-950-2253
Bake Crafters Food
Collegedale, TN 800-296-8935
Callie's Charleston Biscuits LLC
Charleston, SC 843-577-1198
Dynamic Foods
Lubbock, TX. 806-747-2777
Fresh Start Bakeries
Brea, CA 714-256-8900
Lone Star Bakery
Round Rock, TX. 512-255-3629
Pacific Ocean Produce
Santa Cruz, CA. 831-423-2654
The Bama Company
Tulsa, OK 800-756-2262

Brown

B&M
Portland, ME. 207-772-7043
Jou Jou's Pita Bakery
Birmingham, AL. 205-945-6001
Lewis Brothers Bakeries
Evansville, IN 812-425-4642
Schmidt Baking Company
Baltimore, MD 800-456-2253
Terranetti's Italian Bakery
Mechanicsburg, PA. 717-697-5434

Buns

Alois J. Binder Bakery
New Orleans, LA. 504-947-1111
Alpha Baking Company
La Porte, IN. 219-324-7440
Athens Baking Company
Fresno, CA 559-485-3024
Aunt Millies Bakeries
Fort Wayne, IN 260-424-8245
Baldinger Bakery
Saint Paul, MN 651-224-5761
Best Harvest Bakeries
Kansas City, KS 800-811-5715
Bread Box
Virden, NB 204-748-1513
Buns Master Bakery
Richmond Hill, ON. 800-563-6688
Calgary Italian Bakery
Calgary, AB. 800-661-6868
Caribbean Food Delights
Tappan, NY. 845-398-3000
Colombo Bakery
Sacramento, CA 916-648-1011
Columbus Bakery
Columbus, OH 614-645-2275
Country Club Bakery
Fairmont, WV. 304-363-5690
DiCarlo's Bakery
San Pedro, CA. 310-831-2524
Dimpflmeier Bakery
Toronto, ON 800-268-2421
East Balt Bakery
Denver, CO 303-377-5533
East Balt Bakery
Kissimmee, FL 407-933-2222
El Peto Products
Cambridge, ON. 800-387-4064
European Bakers
Tucker, GA 770-723-6180
Evans Bakery
Cozad, NE. 800-222-5641
F R LePage Bakeries
Auburn, ME 207-783-9161
Fancy Lebanese Bakery
Halifax, NS 902-429-0400
Fresh Start Bakeries
Stockton, CA. 209-462-3601
Fresh Start Bakeries
City of Industry, CA 626-961-2525
Gadoua Bakery
Napierville, QC. 450-245-3326
Gai's Northwest Bakeries
Seattle, WA 206-322-0931
Gourmet Baker
Burnaby, BC 800-663-1972
Hardin's Bakery
Tuscaloosa, AL. 205-752-6431
Harris Baking Company
Rogers, AR 479-636-3313
Harting's Bakery
Bowmansville, PA. 717-445-5644
Heiner's Bakery
Huntington, WV 800-776-8411
Holsum Bakery
Phoenix, AZ 800-755-8167
Home Baking Company
Birmingham, AL. 205-252-1161
Hostess Brands
Kansas City, MO. 816-502-4000
Hostess Brands
Irving, TX 972-532-4500
Huval Baking Company
Lafayette, LA 337-232-1611
J.P. Sunrise Bakery
Edmonton, AB 780-454-5797
Kerrobert Bakery
Kerrobert, SK 306-834-2461
Lakeview Bakery
Calgary, AB. 403-246-6127
Mrs Baird's Bakery
Fort Worth, TX 817-864-2500
Mrs. Baird's Bakeries
Waco, TX 254-750-2500
Mrs. Baird's Bakeries
Abilene, TX. 325-692-3141
Nardi Bakery & Deli
East Hartford, CT 860-289-5458
New Horizons Baking Company
Fremont, IN. 260-495-7055
Nickles Bakery of Ohio
Lima, OH 419-224-7080
Nickles Bakery of Ohio
Martins Ferry, OH. 740-633-1711
Ottenberg's Bakers
Hyattsville, MD 800-334-7264
Pan-O-Gold Baking Company
St Cloud, MN 800-444-7005
Pierre Foods
Cincinnati, OH 513-874-8741
Quality Bakery/MM Deli
Port Colborne, ON 905-834-4911
Roma Bakery
San Jose, CA. 408-294-0123
Rotella's Italian Bakery
La Vista, NE 402-592-6600
Royal Home Bakery
Newmarket, ON 905-715-7044
Rudi's Organic Bakery
Boulder, CO 877-293-0876
Schott's Bakery
Houston, TX 713-869-5701
Schwan Food Company
Marshall, MN 800-533-5290
Shipley Baking Company
Texarkana, AR 870-772-7146
Tennessee Bun Company
Dickson, TN 888-486-2867
Twin Marquis
Brooklyn, NY 800-367-6868
Wenger's Bakery
Reading, PA 610-372-6545

Sticky

Cinnamon Bakery
Braintree, MA. 800-886-2867

Challah

Atlanta Bread Company
Smyrna, GA 800-398-3728
Orwasher's Bakery Handmade Bread
New York, NY 212-288-6569

Cinnamon Toast

Log House Foods
Plymouth, MN. 763-546-8395

Corn

Bake Crafters Food
Collegedale, TN 800-296-8935
Dynamic Foods
Lubbock, TX. 806-747-2777
Main Street Gourmet
Cuyahoga Falls, OH 800-533-6246
Mom's Food Company
South El Monte, CA 800-969-6667
Pinahs Company
Waukesha, WI. 800-967-2447
Savannah Food Company
Savannah, TN 800-795-2550
Tova Industries
Louisville, KY 888-532-8682

Croissants

Andre-Boudin Bakeries
San Francisco, CA 415-882-1849
Bake Crafters Food
Collegedale, TN 800-296-8935
BakeMark Canada
Laval, QC 800-361-4998
Bakery Europa
Honolulu, HI. 808-845-5011
Edner Corporation
Hayward, CA 510-441-8504
France Croissant
New York, NY 212-888-1210
Norths Bakery California Inc
N Hollywood, CA. 818-761-2892
Overseas Food Trading
Fort Lee, NJ 201-585-8730
Vie de France Yamazaki
Vienna, VA 800-446-4404

English Muffins

Aunt Millies Bakeries
Fort Wayne, IN 260-424-8245
Canada Bread Company
Langley, BC 800-465-5515
Fresh Start Bakeries
City of Industry, CA 626-961-2525
Fresh Start Bakeries
Brea, CA 714-256-8900
Gourmet Baker
Burnaby, BC 800-663-1972
Homestead Baking Company
Rumford, RI 800-556-7216
LePage Bakeries
Auburn, ME 207-783-9161
Meyer's Bakeries
Casa Grande, AZ. 800-528-5770
Meyer's Bakeries
Hope, AR 800-643-1542
Mrs. Kavanagh's English Muffins
Rumford, RI 800-556-7216
New Horizons Baking Company
Fremont, IN. 260-495-7055
Norths Bakery California Inc
N Hollywood, CA. 818-761-2892
Oakrun Farm Bakery
Ancaster, ON. 905-648-1818
Sara Lee Corporation
Downers Grove, IL 630-598-8100
Weston Bakeries
Toronto, ON 800-590-6861
Wolferman's
Medford, OR

Flat

Aladdin Bakers
Brooklyn, NY 718-499-1818
American Flatbread
Waitsfield, VT. 802-496-8856
Baker & Baker
Schaumburg, IL. 800-593-5777
Baker & Baker, Inc.
Schaumburg, IL. 800-593-5777
Cosa de Rio Foods
Louisville, KY 502-772-2500
Di Camillo Bakery
Niagara Falls, NY 800-634-4363
Dr. Kracker
Plano, TX. 97- 63- 110
Falcone's Cookieland
Brooklyn, NY 718-236-4200
Goglanian Bakeries
Santa Ana, CA 714-444-3500
Good Wives, Inc.
Wilmington, MA. 800-521-8160
Goodwives Hors D'Oeuvres
Wilmington, MA. 800-521-8160
Harbar Corporation
Canton, MA 800-881-7040
Kemach Food Products Corporation
Brooklyn, NY 888-453-6224
Molinaro's Fine Italian Foods
Mississauga, ON. 800-268-4959
Nu-World Amaranth
Naperville, IL 630-369-6819
Real Food Marketing
Kansas City, MO. 816-221-4100
Rudolph's Specialty Bakery
Toronto, ON 800-268-1589
Teeny Foods Corporation
Portland, OR 503-252-3006
Teti Bakery
Etobicoke, ON 800-465-0123
Toufayan Bakeries
Orlando, FL. 407-295-2257
Valley Lahvosh Baking Company
Fresno, CA 800-480-2704

Focaccia

Amberwave Foods
Oakmont, PA. 412-828-3040
Atlanta Bread Company
Smyrna, GA 800-398-3728
Baker & Baker
Schaumburg, IL. 800-593-5777
Baker & Baker, Inc.
Schaumburg, IL. 800-593-5777
Clarmil Manufacturing Corporation
Hayward, CA 888-252-7645
Colors Gourmet Pizza
Carlsbad, CA. 760-431-2203
Goglanian Bakeries
Santa Ana, CA 714-444-3500
Molinaro's Fine Italian Foods
Mississauga, ON. 800-268-4959
Real Food Marketing
Kansas City, MO. 816-221-4100
Teeny Foods Corporation
Portland, OR 503-252-3006

French

Atlanta Bread Company
Smyrna, GA 800-398-3728
Galassos Bakery
Mira Loma, CA. 951-360-1211
Hawaii Star Bakery
Honolulu, HI. 808-841-3602
Ledonne Brothers Bakery
Roseto, PA. 610-588-0423
Leidenheimer Baking Company
New Orleans, LA 504-525-1575
Orlando Baking Company
Cleveland, OH 800-362-5504
Oroweat Baking Company
Montebello, CA 323-721-5161
Piemonte's Bakery
Rockford, IL 815-962-4833
Pioneer French Baking
Venice, CA 310-392-4128
Quinzani Bakery
Boston, MA. 800-999-1062
The Pillsbury Company
Chelsea, MA 800-370-7834
Tom Cat Bakery
Long Island City, NY 718-786-4224
Vantage USA
Chicago, IL 773-247-1086
Vermont Bread Company
Brattleboro, VT. 877-293-0876
Vie de France Yamazaki
Denver, CO 303-371-6280

Fresh

Alfred & Sam Italian Bakery
Lancaster, PA. 717-392-6311
Alois J. Binder Bakery
New Orleans, LA. 504-947-1111
Alpha Baking Company
La Porte, IN. 219-324-7440
Alpha Baking Company
Chicago, IL 773-261-6000
Amoroso's Baking Company
Philadelphia, PA 800-377-6557
Andre-Boudin Bakeries
San Francisco, CA 415-882-1849
Bakery Europa
Honolulu, HI. 808-845-5011
Baldinger Bakery
Saint Paul, MN 651-224-5761
Bensons Bakery
Bogart, GA 800-888-6059
Borden's Bread
Regina, SK 306-525-3341
Bread Alone Bakery
Boiceville, NY 800-769-3328
Brooklyn Baking Company
Waterbury, CT. 203-574-9198
Brown's Bakery
Defiance, OH 419-784-3330
Bunny Bread Company
Cape Girardeau, MO. 573-332-7349
Butternut Breads
Kansas City, MO. 800-483-7253
Canada Bread
North Bay, ON 800-461-6122
Canada Bread Atlantic
St. John's, NL 709-722-5410
Canada Bread Company
Edmonton, AB 780-435-2240
Canada Bread Company
Langley, BC 800-465-5515
Casino Bakery
Tampa, FL. 813-242-0311
Cole's Quality Foods
Grand Rapids, MI 616-975-0081
Colombo Bakery
Sacramento, CA 916-648-1011
Danish Baking Company
Van Nuys, CA. 818-786-1700
Dave's Bakery
Honesdale, PA. 570-253-1660
Del Campo Baking Company
Wilmington, DE 302-656-6676
Ener-G Foods
Seattle, WA 800-331-5222
Epi De France Bakery
Atlanta, GA. 800-325-1014
F R LePage Bakeries
Auburn, ME 207-783-9161
Father Sam's Syrian Bread
Buffalo, NY. 800-521-6719
Felix Roma & Sons
Endicott, NY 607-748-3336
Flowers Foods Bakeries
Thomasville, GA. 229-226-9110
Galassos Bakery
Mira Loma, CA. 951-360-1211
Glazier Packing Company
Potsdam, NY. 315-265-2500
Gold Standard Baking
Chicago, IL 800-648-7904
Harlan Bakeries
Avon, IN 317-272-3600
Highlandville Packing
Highlandville, MO 417-443-3365
Homestead Baking Company
Rumford, RI 800-556-7216
Huval Baking Company
Lafayette, LA 337-232-1611
International Baking Company
Vernon, CA 323-583-9841
JMP Bakery Company
Brooklyn, NY 718-272-5400
John J. Nissen Baking Company
Wareham, MA. 508-295-2337
Jou Jou's Pita Bakery
Birmingham, AL. 205-945-6001
Jubelt Variety Bakeries
Mount Olive, IL 217-999-5231
Karam Elsaha Baking Company
Manlius, NY
Klosterman Baking Company
Springfield, OH. 937-322-7658
Kosher French Baguettes
Brooklyn, NY 718-633-4994
L&M Bakery
Lawrence, MA 978-687-7346
Landolfi Food Products
Trenton, NJ 609-392-1830
Lanthier Bakery
Alexandria, ON. 613-525-4981
Leidenheimer Baking Company
New Orleans, LA 504-525-1575
Lewis Bakeries
London, ON 519-434-5252
Lewis Brothers Bakeries
Evansville, IN 812-425-4642
Lucerne Foods
Calgary, AB. 403-790-3500
Meyer's Bakeries
Hope, AR 800-643-1542
Mississippi Bakery
Burlington, IA. 319-752-6315
Mrs. Baird's Bakeries
Fort Worth, TX 817-293-6230
Multi Marques
Montreal, QC 514-934-1866
Natural Ovens Bakery
Manitowoc, WI 800-558-3535
Nevada Baking Company
Las Vegas, NV 702-384-8950
Norths Bakery California Inc
N Hollywood, CA. 818-761-2892
Oroweat Baking Company
Montebello, CA 323-721-5161
Ottenberg's Bakers
Hyattsville, MD 800-334-7264
Pechters Baking
Harrison, NJ 800-525-5779
Piemonte's Bakery
Rockford, IL 815-962-4833
Pioneer French Baking
Venice, CA 310-392-4128
Pittsfield Rye Bakery
Pittsfield, MA 413-443-9141
Positively Third Street Bakery
Duluth, MN. 218-724-8619
Quinzani Bakery
Boston, MA. 800-999-1062
Real Food Marketing
Kansas City, MO. 816-221-4100

Renaissance Baking Company
North Miami, FL 305-893-2144
Roma Bakery
San Jose, CA 408-294-0123
Saint Armands Baking Company
Bradenton, FL 941-753-7494
San Francisco French Bread
Oakland, CA 510-729-6232
Schmidt Baking Company
Baltimore, MD 800-456-2253
Schwebel Baking Company
Youngstown, OH 800-860-2867
Shaw Baking Company
Thunder Bay, ON 807-345-7327
Stroehmann Bakeries
Harrisburg, PA 800-220-2867
Stroehmann Bakeries
Horsham, PA 800-984-0989
Superior Bakery
North Grosvenordale, CT 860-923-9555
Swatt Baking Company
Olean, NY 800-370-6656
Teeny Foods Corporation
Portland, OR 503-252-3006
Terranetti's Italian Bakery
Mechanicsburg, PA 717-697-5434
Turano Pastry Shops
Bloomingdale, IL 630-529-6161
Vermont Bread Company
Brattleboro, VT 877-293-0876
Vie de France Bakery
Bensenville, IL 630-595-9521
Vie de France Bakery
Atlanta, GA 800-933-5486
Vie de France Yamazaki
Vienna, VA 800-393-8926
Weston Bakeries
Calgary, AB 403-259-1500
Weston Bakeries
Kingston, ON 800-267-0229
Weston Bakeries
Toronto, ON 800-590-6861
Wolferman's
Medford, OR

Frozen

American Flatbread
Waitsfield, VT 802-496-8856
Andre-Boudin Bakeries
San Francisco, CA 415-882-1849
Awrey Bakeries
Livonia, MI 800-950-2253
Bensons Bakery
Bogart, GA 800-888-6059
Caribbean Food Delights
Tappan, NY 845-398-3000
Cedarlane Foods
Carson, CA 310-886-7720
Cole's Quality Foods
Grand Rapids, MI 616-975-0081
Danish Baking Company
Van Nuys, CA 818-786-1700
Del Campo Baking Company
Wilmington, DE 302-656-6676
Epi De France Bakery
Atlanta, GA 800-325-1014
Evans Bakery
Cozad, NE 800-222-5641
Glazier Packing Company
Potsdam, NY 315-265-2500
Guttenplan's Frozen Dough
Middletown, NJ 888-422-4357
Harlan Bakeries
Avon, IN 317-272-3600
Hostess Brands
Irving, TX 972-532-4500
J&J Wall Baking Company
Sacramento, CA 916-381-1410
Leidenheimer Baking Company
New Orleans, LA 504-525-1575
Meyer's Bakeries
Hope, AR 800-643-1542
Mothers Kitchen Inc
Burlington, NJ 609-589-3026
New York Frozen Foods
Cleveland, OH 216-292-5655
Overseas Food Trading
Fort Lee, NJ 201-585-8730
Positively Third Street Bakery
Duluth, MN 218-724-8619
Real Food Marketing
Kansas City, MO 816-221-4100
Rich Products Corporation
Winchester, VA 540-667-1955
Rich Products Corporation
Fresno, CA 559-486-7380
Rich Products Corporation
Buffalo, NY 800-356-7094
Rich Products Corporation
Buffalo, NY 800-828-2021
Rudi's Organic Bakery
Boulder, CO 877-293-0876
Sara Lee Corporation
Downers Grove, IL 630-598-8100
The Pillsbury Company
Chelsea, MA 800-370-7834
Wenner Bread Products
Bayport, NY 800-869-6262
Winder Dairy
West Valley, UT 800-946-3371
Wolferman's
Medford, OR

Garlic

Cole's Quality Foods
Grand Rapids, MI 616-975-0081
Dabruzzi's Italian Foods
Hudson, WI 715-386-3653
Landolfi Food Products
Trenton, NJ 609-392-1830
Oh Boy! Corporation
San Fernando, CA 818-361-1128
Piemonte's Bakery
Rockford, IL 815-962-4833
Real Food Marketing
Kansas City, MO 816-221-4100
T. Marzetti Company
Columbus, OH 614-846-2232

Frozen

Better Baked Foods
North East, PA 814-725-8778

Italian

Armanino Foods of Distinction
Hayward, CA 510-441-9300
Butter Krust Baking Company
Sunbury, PA. 800-282-8093
Cusano's Baking Company
Hollywood, FL 954-458-1010
JMP Bakery Company
Brooklyn, NY 718-272-5400
Ledonne Brothers Bakery
Roseto, PA. 610-588-0423
Milano Baking Company
Joliet, IL 815-727-4872
Orlando Baking Company
Cleveland, OH 800-362-5504
Piemonte's Bakery
Rockford, IL 815-962-4833
Quinzani Bakery
Boston, MA. 800-999-1062
Scialo Brothers
Providence, RI 877-421-0986
Teeny Foods Corporation
Portland, OR 503-252-3006
Tom Cat Bakery
Long Island City, NY 718-786-4224
Vantage USA
Chicago, IL 773-247-1086
Wenner Bread Products
Bayport, NY 800-869-6262

Melba Toast

Turnbull Bakeries of Lousiana
New Orleans, LA 504-581-5383
Turnbull Cone Baking Company
Chattanooga, TN. 423-265-4551

Multi-Grain

Harvest Innovations
Indianola, IA 515-962-5063
Hostess Brands
Irving, TX 972-532-4500
Mother Nature's Goodies
Yucaipa, CA 909-795-6018

Nut

Hostess Brands
Irving, TX 972-532-4500
L&M Bakery
Lawrence, MA 978-687-7346

Pita

Athens Pastries & Frozen Foods
Cleveland, OH 800-837-5683
Bake Crafters Food
Collegedale, TN 800-296-8935
Byblos Bakery
Calgary, AB. 403-250-3711
Corfu Foods
Bensenville, IL 630-595-2510
Fancy Lebanese Bakery
Halifax, NS 902-429-0400
Father Sam's Syrian Bread
Buffalo, NY. 800-521-6719
Goglanian Bakeries
Santa Ana, CA 714-444-3500
Jou Jou's Pita Bakery
Birmingham, AL. 205-945-6001
Kangaroo Brands
Milwaukee, WI 800-798-0857
Karam Elsaha Baking Company
Manlius, NY
Konto's Foods
Paterson, NJ 973-278-2800
Mediterranean Gyros Products
Long Island City, NY 718-786-3399
Mediterranean Pita Bakery
Edmonton, AB 780-476-6666
Ozery's Pita Break
Toronto, ON 888-556-5560
Pechters Baking
Harrison, NJ 800-525-5779
Pita King Bakery
Everett, WA. 425-258-4040
Pita Products
Farmington Hills, MI 800-600-7482
Sara Lee Corporation
Downers Grove, IL 630-598-8100
Soloman Baking Company
Denver, CO 303-371-2777
Stacy's Pita Chip Company
Randolph, MA 888-332-4477
Teeny Foods Corporation
Portland, OR 503-252-3006
Toufayan Bakeries
Ridgefield, NJ. 201-941-2000
Toufayan Bakeries
Orlando, FL. 407-295-2257

Pumpernickel

Atlanta Bread Company
Smyrna, GA 800-398-3728
Colchester Bakery
Colchester, CT 860-537-2415
Dimpflmeier Bakery
Toronto, ON 800-268-2421
Orwasher's Bakery Handmade Bread
New York, NY 212-288-6569

Raisin

Clarmil Manufacturing Corporation
Hayward, CA 888-252-7645
Orwasher's Bakery Handmade Bread
New York, NY 212-288-6569

Rolls

Alois J. Binder Bakery
New Orleans, LA. 504-947-1111
Amoroso's Baking Company
Philadelphia, PA 800-377-6557
April Hill
Grand Rapids, MI 616-245-0595
Atlanta Bread Company
Smyrna, GA 800-398-3728
Aunt Millies Bakeries
Fort Wayne, IN 260-424-8245
Automatic Rolls of New Jersey
Edison, NJ. 732-549-2243
Awrey Bakeries
Livonia, MI 800-950-2253
B&A Bakery
Scarborough, ON 416-752-7436
Bake Rite Rolls
Bensalem, PA 215-638-2400
Baker
Milford, NJ 800-995-3989
Baker & Baker
Schaumburg, IL. 800-593-5777
Baker & Baker, Inc.
Schaumburg, IL. 800-593-5777
Baker Boy Bake Shop
Dickinson, ND 800-437-2008
Baker's Dozen
Herkimer, NY 315-866-6770
Bakers of Paris
Brisbane, CA. 415-468-9100
Bakery Chef
Louisville, KY 800-594-0203
Baldinger Bakery
Saint Paul, MN 651-224-5761
Basque French Bakery
Fresno, CA 559-268-7088
Bay Star Baking Company
Alameda, CA. 510-523-4202
Berlin Natural Bakery
Berlin, OH. 800-686-5334
Best Harvest Bakeries
Kansas City, KS 800-811-5715
Better Bagel Bakery
Sarasota, FL 941-924-0393
Birkholm's Jr Danish Bakery
Solvang, CA 805-688-3872
Bonnie Baking Company
La Porte, IN. 219-362-4561
Borden's Bread
Regina, SK 306-525-3341
Brown's Bakery
Defiance, OH 419-784-3330
Bunge Foods
Tustin, CA. 714-258-1223
Bunny Bread Company
Cape Girardeau, MO. 573-332-7349
Buns Master Bakery
Richmond Hill, ON. 800-563-6688
Busken Bakery
Cincinnati, OH 513-871-5330
Butter Krust Baking Company
Sunbury, PA. 800-282-8093
California Smart Foods
San Francisco, CA 415-826-0449
Canada Bread Atlantic
St. John's, NL 709-722-5410
Canada Bread Company
Edmonton, AB 780-435-2240
Canada Bread Company
Langley, BC 800-465-5515
Cellone Bakery
Pittsburgh, PA 800-334-8438
Chicago Baking Company
Chicago, IL 773-536-7700
Clarmil Manufacturing Corporation
Hayward, CA 888-252-7645
Clydes Delicious Donuts
Addison, IL. 630-628-6555
Cohen's Bakery
Buffalo, NY. 716-892-8149
Colombo Bakery
Sacramento, CA 916-648-1011
Country Club Bakery
Fairmont, WV. 304-363-5690
Dakota Brands Intl.   nal
Jamestown, ND. 800-844-5073
Dave's Bakery
Honesdale, PA. 570-253-1660
Davis Bread & Desserts
Davis, CA 530-757-2700
Dee Lite Bakery
Honolulu, HI. 808-847-5396
Dee's Cheesecake Factory/Dee's Foodservice
Albuquerque, NM. 505-884-1777
Del Campo Baking Company
Wilmington, DE 302-656-6676
Di Paolo Baking Company
Rochester, NY. 585-232-3510
Dimpflmeier Bakery
Toronto, ON 800-268-2421
Dolly Madison Bakery   Interstate Brands Corporation
Columbus, IN 812-376-7432
Earth Grains Baking Companies
Neenah, WI 800-323-7117
East Balt Bakery
Denver, CO 303-377-5533
Eden Vineyards Winery
Alva, FL 239-728-9463
Egypt Star Bakery
Whitehall, PA 610-434-3762
El Segundo Bakery
El Segundo, CA 310-322-3422
Ener-G Foods
Seattle, WA 800-331-5222
Evans Bakery
Cozad, NE. 800-222-5641
F R LePage Bakeries
Auburn, ME 207-783-9161
Felix Roma & Sons
Endicott, NY 607-748-3336
Flowers Foods Bakeries
Thomasville, GA. 229-226-9110
Forty Second Street Bagel Cafe
Upland, CA. 909-949-7334
Franklin Baking Company
Goldsboro, NC 800-248-7494
Fresh Start Bakeries
Brea, CA 714-256-8900
Gai's Northwest Bakeries
Seattle, WA 206-322-0931
Galassos Bakery
Mira Loma, CA. 951-360-1211
General Henry Biscuit Company
Du Quoin, IL. 618-542-6222
George H Leidenheimer Baking
New Orleans, LA 800-259-9099
German Bakery at Village Corner
Stone Mountain, GA. 866-476-6443
GH Leidenheimer Baking Company
New Orleans, LA 800-259-9099
Giant Food
Lanham, MD. 888-469-4426
Glazier Packing Company
Potsdam, NY. 315-265-2500
Global Bakeries
Pacoima, CA. 818-896-0525
Gold Medal Bakery
Fall River, MA 800-642-7568
Gold Medal Baking Company
Philadelphia, PA 215-627-4787
Golden Brown Bakery
South Haven, MI. 269-637-3418
Gonnella Frozen Products
Schaumburg, IL. 847-884-8829

Great Cakes
Los Angeles, CA 310-287-0228
Grebe's Bakery & Delicatessen
Milwaukee, WI 800-356-9377
Grote Bakery
Hamilton, OH 513-874-7436
Guttenplan's Frozen Dough
Middletown, NJ 888-422-4357
Hardin's Bakery
Tuscaloosa, AL 205-752-6431
Havi Food Services Worldwide
Oak Park, IL 708-445-1700
Hawaii Star Bakery
Honolulu, HI 808-841-3602
Heitzman Bakery
Louisville, KY 502-452-1891
Holsum Bakery
Phoenix, AZ 800-755-8167
Homestead Baking Company
Rumford, RI 800-556-7216
Hostess Brands
Kansas City, MO 816-502-4000
Hostess Brands
Irving, TX 972-532-4500
Huval Baking Company
Lafayette, LA 337-232-1611
IBC Holsum
Atlanta, GA 800-465-7861
International Baking Company
Vernon, CA 323-583-9841
International Equipment International Equipment And Supplies
Arecibo, PR 787-879-3151
J&J Wall Baking Company
Sacramento, CA 916-381-1410
James Skinner Company
Omaha, NE 800-358-7428
John J. Nissen Baking Company
Brewer, ME 207-989-7654
Koepplinger Bakery
Detroit, MI 248-967-2020
Kotarides Baking Company of Virginia
Norfolk, VA 757-625-0301
Kreamo Bakers
South Bend, IN 574-234-0188
Lake States Yeast
Rhinelander, WI 715-369-4949
Lanthier Bakery
Alexandria, ON 613-525-4981
Leidenheimer Baking Company
New Orleans, LA 504-525-1575
Lepage Bakeries
Auburn, ME 207-783-9161
Lewis Bakeries
London, ON 519-434-5252
Lewis Brothers Bakeries
Evansville, IN 812-425-4642
Livermore Falls Baking Company
Livermore Falls, ME 207-897-3442
Lone Star Consolidated Foods
Dallas, TX 800-658-5637
Longo's Bakery
Hazleton, PA 570-454-5825
Lucerne Foods
Calgary, AB 403-790-3500
M.M. Bake Shop
Laurel, MS 601-428-5153
Maggiora Baking Company
Richmond, CA 510-235-0274
Marshall's Biscuit Company
Saraland, AL 800-368-9811
Martin's Famous Pastry Shoppe, Inc
Chambersburg, PA 800-548-1200
Mary Ann's Baking Company
Sacramento, CA 916-681-7444
Maui Bagel
Kahului, HI 808-270-7561
Meyer's Bakeries
Hope, AR 800-643-1542
Milano Baking Company
Joliet, IL 815-727-4872
Mom's Food Company
South El Monte, CA 800-969-6667
Morabito Baking Company
Norristown, PA 800-525-7747
Mrs Baird's Bakery
Fort Worth, TX 817-864-2500
Mrs. Baird's Bakeries
Abilene, TX 325-692-3141
Mrs. Baird's Bakeries
Fort Worth, TX 817-293-6230
Mrs. Kavanagh's English Muffins
Rumford, RI 800-556-7216
Mt View Bakery
Mountain View, HI 808-968-6353
Multi Marques
Montreal, QC 514-934-1866
Nevada Baking Company
Las Vegas, NV 702-384-8950
New Bakery Company of Ohio
Zanesville, OH 800-848-9845
New York Bakeries
Hialeah, FL 305-882-1355
New York Frozen Foods
Cleveland, OH 216-292-5655
Nickles Bakery of Ohio
Lima, OH 419-224-7080
Novelty Kosher Pastry
Spring Valley, NY 845-356-0428
Orlando Baking Company
Cleveland, OH 800-362-5504
Oroweat Baking Company
Montebello, CA 323-721-5161
Orwasher's Bakery Handmade Bread
New York, NY 212-288-6569
Oven Ready Products
Guelph, ON 519-767-2415
Pechters Baking
Harrison, NJ 800-525-5779
Piantedosi Baking Company
Malden, MA 800-339-0080
Piemonte's Bakery
Rockford, IL 815-962-4833
Pittsfield Rye Bakery
Pittsfield, MA 413-443-9141
Portuguese Baking Company
Newark, NJ 973-589-8875
Powers Baking Company
miami, FL 305-381-7000
Quinzani Bakery
Boston, MA 800-999-1062
Renaissance Baking Company
North Miami, FL 305-893-2144
Rich Products Corporation
Winchester, VA 540-667-1955
Rich Products Corporation
Buffalo, NY 800-356-7094
Roma Bakeries
Rockford, IL 815-964-6737
Roma Bakery
San Jose, CA 408-294-0123
Rudi's Organic Bakery
Boulder, CO 877-293-0876
Ryals Bakery
Milledgeville, GA 478-452-0321
Saint Armands Baking Company
Bradenton, FL 941-753-7494
San Francisco French Bread
Oakland, CA 510-729-6232
Schmidt Baking Company
Baltimore, MD 800-456-2253
Schott's Bakery
Houston, TX 713-869-5701
Schwebel Baking Company
Youngstown, OH 330-783-2860
Schwebel Baking Company
Youngstown, OH 800-860-2867
Shaw Baking Company
Thunder Bay, ON 807-345-7327
Simon Hubig Company
New Orleans, LA 504-945-2181
Stagnos Bakery
East Liberty, PA 412-441-3485
Sterling Foods
San Antonio, TX 210-490-1669
Stroehmann Bakeries
Horsham, PA 800-984-0989
Stroehmann Bakery
Horsham, PA 800-984-0989
Sunbeam
New Bedford, MA 800-458-8407
Superior Bakery
North Grosvenordale, CT 860-923-9555
Swatt Baking Company
Olean, NY 800-370-6656
Table Pride
Atlanta, GA 770-455-7464
Terranetti's Italian Bakery
Mechanicsburg, PA 717-697-5434
Tom Cat Bakery
Long Island City, NY 718-786-4224
Tomaro's Bakery
Clarksburg, WV 304-622-0691
Tripoli Bakery
Lawrence, MA 978-682-7754
Turano Pasty Shops
Berwyn, IL 708-788-5320
Unified Western Grocers
Los Angeles, CA 323-232-6124
Upper Crust Baking Company
Pismo Beach, CA 800-676-1691
Valley Bakery
Rock Valley, IA 712-476-5386
Vallos Baking Company
Bethlehem, PA 610-866-1012
Vermont Bread Company
Brattleboro, VT 877-293-0876
Vie de France Bakery
Atlanta, GA 800-933-5486
Vie de France Yamazaki
Vienna, VA 800-393-8926
Vilotti & Marinelli Baking Company
Philadelphia, PA 215-627-5038
Wedemeyer Bakery
South San Francisco, CA 650-873-1000
Wenner Bread Products
Bayport, NY 800-869-6262
Weston Bakeries
Calgary, AB 403-259-1500
Weston Bakeries
Kingston, ON 800-267-0229
Weston Bakeries
Toronto, ON 800-590-6861
Zeppys Bakery
Lawrence, MA 781-963-7022
Zoelsmanns Bakery & Deli
Pueblo, CO 719-543-0407

Cinnamon

Baker & Baker
Schaumburg, IL 800-593-5777
Baker & Baker, Inc.
Schaumburg, IL 800-593-5777
Cinnamon Bakery
Braintree, MA 800-886-2867
Clarmil Manufacturing Corporation
Hayward, CA 888-252-7645
Honeybake Farms
Kansas City, KS 913-371-7777
James Skinner Company
Omaha, NE 800-358-7428
La Francaise Bakery
Melrose Park, IL 800-654-7220
Lone Star Bakery
Round Rock, TX 512-255-3629
Mrs Baird's Bakery
Fort Worth, TX 817-864-2500
Pacific Ocean Produce
Santa Cruz, CA 831-423-2654
Sara Lee Corporation
Downers Grove, IL 630-598-8100
Schwan Food Company
Marshall, MN 800-533-5290
Svenhard's Swedish Bakery
Oakland, CA 800-333-7836

Fresh

Best Harvest Bakeries
Kansas City, KS 800-811-5715
Borden's Bread
Regina, SK 306-525-3341
Brown's Bakery
Defiance, OH 419-784-3330
Canada Bread
North Bay, ON 800-461-6122
Canada Bread Atlantic
St. John's, NL 709-722-5410
Canada Bread Company
Edmonton, AB 780-435-2240
Canada Bread Company
Langley, BC 800-465-5515
East Balt Bakery
Denver, CO 303-377-5533
Felix Roma & Sons
Endicott, NY 607-748-3336
Flowers Foods Bakeries
Thomasville, GA 229-226-9110
Galassos Bakery
Mira Loma, CA 951-360-1211
Homestead Baking Company
Rumford, RI 800-556-7216
Lanthier Bakery
Alexandria, ON 613-525-4981

Leidenheimer Baking Company
New Orleans, LA 504-525-1575
Lewis Bakeries
London, ON 519-434-5252
Lucerne Foods
Calgary, AB....................... 403-790-3500
Mrs. Baird's Bakeries
Fort Worth, TX 817-293-6230
Multi Marques
Montreal, QC 514-934-1866
New York Frozen Foods
Cleveland, OH 216-292-5655
Ottenberg's Bakers
Hyattsville, MD 800-334-7264
Pechters Baking
Harrison, NJ 800-525-5779
Quinzani Bakery
Boston, MA....................... 800-999-1062
Roma Bakery
San Jose, CA...................... 408-294-0123
Schmidt Baking Company
Baltimore, MD 800-456-2253
Schwebel Baking Company
Youngstown, OH................... 800-860-2867
Shaw Baking Company
Thunder Bay, ON 807-345-7327
Terranetti's Italian Bakery
Mechanicsburg, PA................. 717-697-5434
Vie de France Yamazaki
Vienna, VA 800-393-8926
Weston Bakeries
Calgary, AB....................... 403-259-1500
Weston Bakeries
Kingston, ON 800-267-0229
Weston Bakeries
Toronto, ON 800-590-6861

Frozen

Awrey Bakeries
Livonia, MI....................... 800-950-2253
Bake Crafters Food
Collegedale, TN 800-296-8935
Del Campo Baking Company
Wilmington, DE 302-656-6676
Dwayne Keith Brooks Company
Orangevale, CA 916-988-1030
Dynamic Foods
Lubbock, TX...................... 806-747-2777
Evans Bakery
Cozad, NE........................ 800-222-5641
Flowers Foods Bakeries
Thomasville, GA................... 229-226-9110
Fresh Start Bakeries
Brea, CA......................... 714-256-8900
Guttenplan's Frozen Dough
Middletown, NJ 888-422-4357
J&J Wall Baking Company
Sacramento, CA 916-381-1410
James Skinner Company
Omaha, NE 800-358-7428
Leidenheimer Baking Company
New Orleans, LA 504-525-1575
Lone Star Bakery
Round Rock, TX................... 512-255-3629
Pacific Ocean Produce
Santa Cruz, CA.................... 831-423-2654
Rich Products Corporation
Winchester, VA.................... 540-667-1955
Rich Products Corporation
Buffalo, NY....................... 800-356-7094
Sara Lee Corporation
Downers Grove, IL................. 630-598-8100

Sweet

Awrey Bakeries
Livonia, MI....................... 800-950-2253
Baker Boy Bake Shop
Dickinson, ND 800-437-2008
Bunny Bread Company
Cape Girardeau, MO................ 573-332-7349
Clydes Delicious Donuts
Addison, IL....................... 630-628-6555
Earth Grains Baking Companies
Neenah, WI....................... 800-323-7117
International Baking Company
Vernon, CA....................... 323-583-9841
Saint Armands Baking Company
Bradenton, FL..................... 941-753-7494
Zoelsmanns Bakery & Deli
Pueblo, CO 719-543-0407

Rye

Alfred & Sam Italian Bakery
Lancaster, PA..................... 717-392-6311
Amoroso's Baking Company
Philadelphia, PA 800-377-6557
Atlanta Bread Company
Smyrna, GA 800-398-3728
Butternut Breads
Kansas City, MO.................. 800-483-7253
Chmuras Bakery
Indian Orchard, MA 413-543-2521
Colchester Bakery
Colchester, CT 860-537-2415
Cybros
Waukesha, WI..................... 800-876-2253
Dimpflmeier Bakery
Toronto, ON 800-268-2421
Hawaii Star Bakery
Honolulu, HI...................... 808-841-3602
Highlandville Packing
Highlandville, MO 417-443-3365
Holsum Bakery
Fort Wayne, IN 260-456-2130
Hostess Brands
Irving, TX........................ 972-532-4500
John J. Nissen Baking Company
Wareham, MA..................... 508-295-2337
Kreamo Bakers
South Bend, IN.................... 574-234-0188
Orlando Baking Company
Cleveland, OH 800-362-5504
Orwasher's Bakery Handmade Bread
New York, NY 212-288-6569
Patisserie Wawel
Montreal, QC 614-524-3348
Piemonte's Bakery
Rockford, IL 815-962-4833
Pyrenees French Bakery
Bakersfield, CA 888-898-7159
Quality Bakery
Invermere, BC..................... 888-681-9977
Rudolph's Specialty Bakery
Toronto, ON 800-268-1589
Terranetti's Italian Bakery
Mechanicsburg, PA................. 717-697-5434
Tribeca Oven
Carlstadt, NJ...................... 201-935-8800
Turano Pastry Shops
Bloomingdale, IL 630-529-6161
Waldensian Bakeries
Valdese, NC....................... 828-874-2136

Scones

Baker & Baker
Schaumburg, IL................... 800-593-5777
Baker & Baker, Inc.
Schaumburg, IL................... 800-593-5777
Bette's Diner Products
Berkeley, CA..................... 510-644-3230
Butter Baked Goods
Vancouver, BC 604-221-4333
Case Side Holdings Company
Kensington, PE.................... 902-836-4214
Immaculate Consumption
Flat Rock, NC..................... 888-826-6567
Main Street Gourmet
Cuyahoga Falls, OH 800-533-6246
Poppie's Dough
Chicago, IL 312-640-0404
Sticky Fingers Bakeries
San Francisco, CA 800-458-5826
Treasure Foods
West Valley, UT................... 801-974-0911
Uptown Bakers
Hyattsville, MD 301-864-1500

Short

Biscottea
Issaquah, WA 425-313-1993
Crookes & Hanson
Bedford, OH 800-999-0263
Golden West Specialty Foods
Brisbane, CA...................... 800-584-4481
Merlino Italian Baking Company
Seattle, WA 800-207-2997
R.M. Palmer Company
Reading, PA 610-372-8971
Sugar Kake Cookie
Tonawanda, NY 800-775-5180

Vermont Chocolatiers
Northfield, VT 877-485-4226
Walkers Shortbread
Hauppauge, NY 800-521-0141

Sourdough

Atlanta Bread Company
Smyrna, GA 800-398-3728
Berkshire Mountain Bakery
Housatonic, MA 866-274-6124
Hawaii Star Bakery
Honolulu, HI...................... 808-841-3602
Morabito Baking Company
Norristown, PA 800-525-7747
Orwasher's Bakery Handmade Bread
New York, NY 212-288-6569
Ottenberg's Bakers
Hyattsville, MD 800-334-7264
San Luis Sourdough
San Luis Obispo, CA 800-266-7687

Wheat

Atlanta Bread Company
Smyrna, GA 800-398-3728
Butter Krust Baking Company
Sunbury, PA....................... 800-282-8093
Butternut Breads
Kansas City, MO................... 800-483-7253
Entenmann's-Oroweat/BestFoods
South San Francisco, CA 650-583-5828
Highlandville Packing
Highlandville, MO 417-443-3365
Holsum Bakery
Fort Wayne, IN 260-456-2130
Hostess Brands
Irving, TX........................ 972-532-4500
John J. Nissen Baking Company
Wareham, MA..................... 508-295-2337
Jou Jou's Pita Bakery
Birmingham, AL................... 205-945-6001
Kreamo Bakers
South Bend, IN.................... 574-234-0188
Lewis Brothers Bakeries
Evansville, IN..................... 812-425-4642
Orlando Baking Company
Cleveland, OH 800-362-5504
Orwasher's Bakery Handmade Bread
New York, NY 212-288-6569
Pechters Baking
Harrison, NJ 800-525-5779
Pyrenees French Bakery
Bakersfield, CA 888-898-7159
Shaw Baking Company
Thunder Bay, ON 807-345-7327
Tribeca Oven
Carlstadt, NJ...................... 201-935-8800

White

Butternut Breads
Kansas City, MO................... 800-483-7253
Highlandville Packing
Highlandville, MO 417-443-3365
Holsum Bakery
Fort Wayne, IN 260-456-2130
Hostess Brands
Irving, TX........................ 972-532-4500
John J. Nissen Baking Company
Wareham, MA..................... 508-295-2337
Kreamo Bakers
South Bend, IN.................... 574-234-0188
Lewis Brothers Bakeries
Evansville, IN..................... 812-425-4642
Mrs. Baird's Bakeries
Waco, TX 254-750-2500
Orwasher's Bakery Handmade Bread
New York, NY 212-288-6569
Pan-O-Gold Baking Company
St Cloud, MN 800-444-7005
Pechters Baking
Harrison, NJ 800-525-5779
Pyrenees French Bakery
Bakersfield, CA 888-898-7159
Schmidt Baking Company
Baltimore, MD 800-456-2253
Shaw Baking Company
Thunder Bay, ON 807-345-7327
Terranetti's Italian Bakery
Mechanicsburg, PA................. 717-697-5434
Waldensian Bakeries
Valdese, NC....................... 828-874-2136

Cakes & Pastries

BakeMark Canada
Laval, QC . . . 800-361-4998

Angel Food Cake

Kyger Bakery Products
Lafayette, IN . . . 765-447-1252
Specialty Bakers
Marysville, PA . . . 800-233-0778

Apple Cobbler

Main Street Gourmet
Cuyahoga Falls, OH . . . 800-533-6246

Babka

Aunt Heddy's Bakery
Brooklyn, NY . . . 718-782-0582
Morse's Sauerkraut
Waldoboro, ME . . . 866-832-5569

Baklava

Athens Baking Company
Fresno, CA . . . 559-485-3024
Fillo Factory
Dumont, NJ . . . 800-653-4556
Lawrences Delights
Doraville, GA . . . 800-568-0021
Marika's Kitchen
Hancock, ME . . . 800-694-9400
Sinbad Sweets
Fresno, CA . . . 800-350-7933

Blintzes

Frozen

Echo Lake Farm Produce Company
Burlington, WI . . . 262-763-9551
Old Fashioned Kitchen
Lakewood, NJ . . . 732-364-4100

Brown Bettys

Euro Chocolate Fountain
San Diego, CA . . . 800-423-9303

Cakes

A Sprinkle and A Dash
Port Washington, NY . . . 516-767-6431
Adams Foods
Dothan, AL . . . 334-983-4233
Alati-Caserta Desserts
Montreal, QC . . . 514-271-3013
Amendt Corporation
Monroe, MI . . . 734-242-2411
Angel's Bakeries
Brooklyn, NY . . . 718-389-1400
Athena's Silverland®Desserts
Forest Park, IL . . . 800-737-3636
Atkins Elegant Desserts
Fishers, IN . . . 800-887-8808
Awrey Bakeries
Livonia, MI . . . 800-950-2253
Bake Crafters Food
Collegedale, TN . . . 800-296-8935
BakeMark Canada
Laval, QC . . . 800-361-4998
Baker Boy Bake Shop
Dickinson, ND . . . 800-437-2008
Bakery Chef
Chicago, IL . . . 773-384-1900
Bakery Corp
Miami, FL . . . 800-521-4345
Balboa Dessert Company
Santa Ana, CA . . . 800-974-9699
Banquet Schuster Bakery
Pueblo, CO . . . 719-544-1062
Bauducco Foods Inc.
Doral, FL . . . 305-477-9270
BBU Bakeries
Denver, CO . . . 303-691-6342
Beatrice Bakery Company
Beatrice, NE . . . 800-228-4030
Bensons Bakery
Bogart, GA . . . 800-888-6059
Berke-Blake Fancy Foods, Inc.
Longwood, FL . . . 888-386-2253
Big Fatty's Flaming Foods
Valley View, TX . . . 888-248-6332
Birkholm's Jr Danish Bakery
Solvang, CA . . . 805-688-3872
Bishop Baking Company
Cleveland, TN . . . 423-472-1561
Bittersweet Pastries
Norwood, NJ . . . 800-217-2938
Borden's Bread
Regina, SK . . . 306-525-3341
Breadworks Bakery & Deli
Charlottesville, VA . . . 434-296-4663
Brownie Baker
Fresno, CA . . . 800-598-6501
Busken Bakery
Cincinnati, OH . . . 513-871-5330
Cal Java International
Northridge, CA . . . 800-207-2750
Calmar Bakery
Calmar, AB . . . 780-985-3583
Caribbean Food Delights
Tappan, NY . . . 845-398-3000
Carole's Cheesecake Company
Toronto, ON . . . 416-256-0000
Carolina Foods
Charlotte, NC . . . 800-234-0441
Case Side Holdings Company
Kensington, PE . . . 902-836-4214
Cateraid
Howell, MI . . . 800-508-8217
Celebrity Cheesecake
Davie, FL . . . 877-986-2253
Cemac Foods Corporation
Philadelphia, PA . . . 800-724-0179
CGI Desserts
Sugar Land, TX . . . 281-240-1200
Chattanooga Bakery
Chattanooga, TN . . . 800-251-3404
Cheesecake Etc. Desserts
Miami Springs, FL . . . 305-887-0258
Cheesecake Factory
Calabasas Hills, CA . . . 818-871-3000
Cheryl & Company
Westerville, OH . . . 614-776-1500
Chocolate Chix
Waxahachie, TX . . . 214-744-2442
Cinderella Cheese Cake Company
Riverside, NJ . . . 856-461-6302
City Baker
Calgary, AB . . . 403-263-8578
City Bakery
New York, NY . . . 877-328-3687
Clarmil Manufacturing Corporation
Hayward, CA . . . 888-252-7645
Claudio Pastry Company
Elmwood Park, IL . . . 708-453-0598
Cloverhill Bakery-Vend Corporation
Chicago, IL . . . 773-745-9800
Clydes Delicious Donuts
Addison, IL . . . 630-628-6555
Collin Street Bakery
Corsicana, TX . . . 800-504-1896
Columbus Gourmet
Columbus, GA . . . 800-356-1858
Comanzo & Company Specialty Bakers
Smithfield, RI . . . 888-352-5455
Crane's Pie Pantry Restaurant
Fennville, MI . . . 269-561-2297
Creme Glacee Gelati
Montreal, QC . . . 888-322-0116
Culinar Canada
Baie-Comeau, QC . . . 418-296-4395
Dancing Deer Baking Company
Boston, MA . . . 888-699-3337
Danish Baking Company
Van Nuys, CA . . . 818-786-1700
Danvers Bakery
Danvers, MA . . . 978-774-9186
Dave's Bakery
Honesdale, PA . . . 570-253-1660
Davis Bakery & Delicatessen
Cleveland, OH . . . 216-464-5599
Dawn Food Products
York, PA . . . 800-405-6282
Decadent Desserts
Calgary, AB . . . 403-245-5535
Dee's Cheesecake Factory/Dee's Foodservice
Albuquerque, NM . . . 505-884-1777
Deerfield Bakery
Buffalo Grove, IL . . . 847-520-0068
Del's Pastry
Etobicoke, ON . . . 416-231-4383
Desserts by David Glass
South Windsor, CT . . . 860-462-7520
Di Camillo Bakery
Niagara Falls, NY . . . 800-634-4363
Dinkel's Bakery
Chicago, IL . . . 800-822-8817
Division Baking Corporation
New York, NY . . . 800-934-9238
Dolly Madison Bakery Interstate Brands Corporation
Columbus, IN . . . 812-376-7432
Dough Works Company
Horicon, WI . . . 800-383-8808
Dr. Cookie
Seattle, WA . . . 206-389-9321
Dufflet Pastries
Toronto, ON . . . 416-536-9640
Dunford Bakers
Fayetteville, AR . . . 479-521-3000
Dutch Kitchen Bakery
Fitchburg, MA . . . 978-345-1393
Dynamic Foods
Lubbock, TX . . . 806-747-2777
Eddy's Bakery
Boise, ID . . . 208-377-8100
Edelweiss Patisserie
Charlestown, MA . . . 617-628-0225
Eilenberger Bakery
Palestine, TX . . . 800-831-2544
El Peto Products
Cambridge, ON . . . 800-387-4064
El Segundo Bakery
El Segundo, CA . . . 310-322-3422
Elmwood Pastry
West Hartford, CT . . . 860-233-2029
European Style Bakery
Beverly Hills, CA . . . 818-368-6876
Evans Bakery
Cozad, NE . . . 800-222-5641
Fantasia
Sedalia, MO . . . 660-827-1172
Ferrara Bakery & Cafe
New York, NY . . . 212-226-6150
Fireside Kitchen
Halifax, NS . . . 902-454-7387
Food of Our Own Design
Maplewood, NJ . . . 973-762-0985
Foxtail Foods
Fairfield, OH . . . 800-487-2253
France Delices
Montreal, QC . . . 800-663-1365
Fresh Dairy Direct/Morningstar
Dallas, TX . . . 800-395-7004
Future Bakery & Cafe
Etobicoke, ON . . . 416-231-1491
Georgia Fruit Cake Company
Claxton, GA . . . 912-739-2683
Giant Food
Lanham, MD . . . 888-469-4426
Gold Medal Baking Company
Philadelphia, PA . . . 215-627-4787
Golden Brown Bakery
South Haven, MI . . . 269-637-3418
Golden Glow Cookie Company
Bronx, NY . . . 718-379-6223
Golden Walnut Specialty Foods
Zion, IL . . . 800-843-3645
Gourmet Baker
Burnaby, BC . . . 800-663-1972
Gourmet Treats
Torrance, CA . . . 800-444-9549
Grand Avenue Chocolates
Concord, CA . . . 877-934-1800
Great Cakes
Los Angeles, CA . . . 310-287-0228
Great Western Products Company
Assumption, IL . . . 217-226-3241
Great Western Products Company
Bismarck, MO . . . 573-734-2210
Grebe's Bakery & Delicatessen
Milwaukee, WI . . . 800-356-9377
Greyston Bakery
Yonkers, NY . . . 800-289-2253
Grossinger's Home Bakery
New York, NY . . . 800-479-6996
Grote Bakery
Hamilton, OH . . . 513-874-7436
GWB Foods Corporation
Brooklyn, NY . . . 877-977-7610
Haby's Alsatian Bakery
Castroville, TX . . . 830-931-2118
Hahn's Old Fashioned Cake Company
Farmingdale, NY . . . 631-249-3456

Harrington's In Vermont
Richmond, VT 802-434-7500
Hawaii Candy
Honolulu, HI 808-836-8955
Haydel's Bakery
Jefferson, LA 800-442-1342
Heidi's Gourmet Desserts
Tucker, GA 800-241-4166
Heinemann's Bakeries
Palatine, IL 847-358-3501
Heitzman Bakery
Louisville, KY 502-452-1891
Holton Food Products Company
La Grange, IL 708-352-5599
Hunt Country Foods
Middleburg, VA 540-364-2622
Italian Baking Company
Edmonton, AB 780-424-4830
Ivy Cottage Scone Mixes
S Pasadena, CA 626-441-2761
James Skinner Company
Omaha, NE 800-358-7428
Joey's Fine Foods
Newark, NJ 973-482-1400
John J. Nissen Baking Company
Brewer, ME 207-989-7654
Jon Donaire Pastry
Santa Fe Springs, CA 877-366-2473
Just Desserts
San Francisco, CA 415-602-9245
K&S Bakery Products
Edmonton, AB 780-481-8155
Kennedy Gourmet
Houston, TX 800-882-6253
King's Hawaiian
Torrance, CA 800-800-5461
Kyger Bakery Products
Lafayette, IN 765-447-1252
L&M Bakery
Lawrence, MA 978-687-7346
Laura's French Baking Company
Los Angeles, CA 888-353-5144
Lax & Mandel Bakery
Cleveland, OH 216-382-8877
Little Miss. Muffin
Chicago, IL 800-456-9328
Lone Star Bakery
Round Rock, TX 512-255-3629
Love & Quiches Desserts
Freeport, NY 800-525-5251
Love and Quiches Desserts
Freeport, NY 516-623-8800
M/S Smears
Chadbourn, NC 910-654-5163
Mac's Donut Shop
Aliquippa, PA 724-375-6776
Maplehurst Bakeries
Carrollton, GA 800-482-4810
Maridee's Country Kitchen Cakes
Lindsay, OK 800-798-7730
Market Fare Foods
Saint Louis, MO 888-669-6420
Martino's Bakery
Burbank, CA 818-842-0715
Mary of Puddin Hill
Greenville, TX 800-545-8889
Matthews 1812 House
Cornwall Bridge, CT 800-662-1812
Maurice French Pastries
Metairie, LA 888-285-8261
McKee Foods Corporation
Collegedale, TN 423-238-7111
Mehaffie Pies
Dayton, OH 937-253-1163
Michel's Bakery
Philadelphia, PA 215-725-3900
Mid-Atlantic Foods
Easton, MD 800-922-4688
Millers Ice Cream
Houston, TX 713-861-3138
Moravian Cookies Shop
Winston Salem, NC 800-274-2994
Mothers Kitchen Inc
Burlington, NJ 609-589-3026
Mozzicato De Pasquale Bakery Pastry
Hartford, CT 860-296-0426
Mrs. Fields' Original Cookies
Salt Lake City, UT 800-266-5437
Mrs. Smith's Bakeries
Spartanburg, SC 800-756-4746
Multi Marques
Montreal, QC 514-934-1866
My Daddy's Cheesecake
Cape Girardeau, MO 800-735-6765
My Grandma's Coffee Cakee of New England
Boston, MA 800-847-2636
Naturally Delicious
Oakland Park, FL 954-485-6730
New Glarus Bakery
New Glarus, WI 608-527-2916
New York Bakeries
Hialeah, FL 305-882-1355
Nickles Bakery of Ohio
Columbus, OH 800-335-9775
Northside Bakery
Richmond, VA 804-968-7620
O&H Danish Bakery
Racine, WI 262-554-1311
Ohta Wafer Factory
Honolulu, HI 808-949-2775
Old Country Bakery
North Hollywood, CA 818-838-2302
Original Ya-hoo! Baking Company
Sherman, TX 800-575-9373
Our Lady of Guadalupe Abbey
Lafayette, OR 503-852-0106
Pacific Ocean Produce
Santa Cruz, CA 831-423-2654
Parco Foods
Blue Island, IL 708-371-9200
Pastry Chef
Pawtucket, RI 800-639-8606
Patti's Plum Puddings
Lawndale, CA 310-376-1463
Pearl River Pastry & Chocolates
Pearl River, NY 800-632-2639
Pellman Foods
New Holland, PA 717-354-8070
Pie Piper Products
Bensenville, IL 800-621-8183
Plaza Sweets
Mamaroneck, NY 800-816-8416
Plehn's Bakery
Louisville, KY 502-896-4438
Plumlife Company
Newbury, MA 978-462-8458
Pocono Cheesecake Factory
Swiftwater, PA 570-839-6844
Quaker
Barrington, IL 800-333-8027
Quality Bakery/MM Deli
Port Colborne, ON 905-834-4911
Quiche & Tell
Flushing, NY 718-381-7562
Real Food Marketing
Kansas City, MO 816-221-4100
Red Mill Farms
Brooklyn, NY 800-344-2253
Rich Ice Cream Company
West Palm Beach, FL 561-833-7585
Rising Dough Bakery
Sacramento, CA 916-387-9700
Rolling Pin Bakery
Bow Island, AB 403-545-2434
Rowena's
Norfolk, VA 800-627-8699
Royal Caribbean Bakery
Mount Vernon, NY 888-818-0971
Royal Home Bakery
Newmarket, ON 905-715-7044
Rudolph's Specialty Bakery
Toronto, ON 800-268-1589
Ruth Ashbrook Bakery
Portland, OR 503-240-7437
Ryals Bakery
Milledgeville, GA 478-452-0321
Ryke's Bakery
Muskegon, MI 231-722-3508
Sacramento Baking Company
Sacramento, CA 916-361-2000
Samadi Sweets Cafe
Falls Church, VA 703-578-0606
Santa Fe Bite-Size Bakery
Moriarty, NM 800-342-1119
Sara Lee Corporation
Downers Grove, IL 630-598-8100
Sarabeth's Kitchen
Bronx, NY 718-589-2900
Saxby Foods
Edmonton, AB 780-440-4179
Schwan Food Company
Marshall, MN 800-533-5290
Scialo Brothers
Providence, RI 877-421-0986
Scot Paris Fine Desserts
New York, NY 212-807-1802
Sessions Company
Enterprise, AL 334-393-0200
Silver Tray Cookies
Fort Lauderdale, FL 305-883-0800
Smoak's Bakery & Catering Service
Augusta, GA 706-738-1792
Solvang Bakery
Solvang, CA 800-377-4253
Southeast Dairy Processors
Tampa, FL 813-621-3233
Specialty Bakers
Marysville, PA 800-233-0778
Spilke's Baking Company
Brooklyn, NY 718-384-2150
Standard Bakery
Kealakekua, HI 808-322-3688
Sterling Foods
San Antonio, TX 210-490-1669
Steve's Mom
Bronx, NY 800-362-4545
Stroehmann Bakeries
Norristown, PA 800-984-0989
Strossner's Bakery
Greenville, SC 864-233-3996
Sunbeam Baking Company
El Paso, TX 800-328-6111
Superior Cake Products
Southbridge, MA 508-764-3276
Swagger Foods Corporation
Vernon Hills, IL 847-913-1200
Sweet Bakery Baltimore
Baltimore, MD 41- 7-8 22
Sweet Endings
West Palm Beach, FL 888-635-1177
Sweet Gallery Exclusive Pastry
Toronto, ON 416-766-0289
Tasty Baking Company
Philadelphia, PA 800-338-2789
Tastykake
Philadelphia, PA 215-221-8500
Tate's Bake Shop
Southampton, NY 631-283-9830
The Cheesecake Factory
Calabasas Hills, CA 818-871-3000
The Great San Saba RiverPecan Company
San Saba, TX 800-621-9121
Thymly Products
Colora, MD 410-658-4820
Two Chicks and a Ladle
New York, NY 212-251-0025
Uncle Ralph's Cookie Company
Frederick, MD 800-422-0626
Uniquely Together
Chicago, IL 800-613-7276
Uptown Bakers
Hyattsville, MD 301-864-1500
Vickey's Vittles
North Hills, CA 818-841-1944
Vie de France Bakery
Bensenville, IL 630-595-9521
Vie de France Yamazaki
Denver, CO 303-371-6280
Vigneri Confections
Rochester, NY 877-843-6374
Waldensian Bakeries
Valdese, NC 828-874-2136
Warwick Ice Cream Company
Warwick, RI 401-821-8403
Wedding Cake Studio
Williamsfield, OH 440-667-1765
Weiss Homemade Kosher Bakery
Brooklyn, NY 800-498-3477
Wenger's Bakery
Reading, PA 610-372-6545
White Oak Farms
Sandown, NH 800-473-8869
Williamsburg Chocolatier
Williamsburg, VA 757-253-1474
Winder Dairy
West Valley, UT 800-946-3371
Wonder Bread
Provo, UT 800-483-7253
Wonder/Hostess
Jamaica, NY 201-837-8317
World of Chantilly
Brooklyn, NY 718-859-1110
Wow! Factor Desserts
Sherwood Park, AB 800-604-2253
Young's Bakery
Uniontown, PA 724-437-6361

Zeppys Bakery
Lawrence, MA 781-963-7022
Zoelsmanns Bakery & Deli
Pueblo, CO 719-543-0407

Cannoli

Artuso Pastry Foods Corp
Mt Vernon, NY 914-663-8806
Artuso Pastry Shop
Bronx, NY 718-367-2515

Carrot Cake

Clarmil Manufacturing Corporation
Hayward, CA 888-252-7645
Dee's Cheesecake Factory/Dee's Foodservice
Albuquerque, NM 505-884-1777
Eli's Cheesecake Company
Chicago, IL 800-999-8300
Main Street Gourmet
Cuyahoga Falls, OH 800-533-6246

Cheese Cake

Atkins Elegant Desserts
Fishers, IN 800-887-8808
Balboa Dessert Company
Santa Ana, CA 800-974-9699
Berke-Blake Fancy Foods, Inc.
Longwood, FL 888-386-2253
Brownie Baker
Fresno, CA 800-598-6501
Carberry's Home Made Ice Cream
Kissimmee, FL 407-933-7343
Carole's Cheesecake Company
Toronto, ON 416-256-0000
Cateraid
Howell, MI 800-508-8217
Celebrity Cheesecake
Davie, FL 877-986-2253
Cemac Foods Corporation
Philadelphia, PA 800-724-0179
CGI Desserts
Sugar Land, TX 281-240-1200
Chatila's Bakery
Salem, NH 603-898-5459
Cheesecake Aly
Glen Rock, NJ 800-555-8862
Cheesecake Etc. Desserts
Miami Springs, FL 305-887-0258
Cheesecake Momma
Ukiah, CA 707-462-2253
Cinderella Cheese Cake Company
Riverside, NJ 856-461-6302
Dee's Cheesecake Factory/Dee's Foodservice
Albuquerque, NM 505-884-1777
Desserts by David Glass
South Windsor, CT 860-462-7520
Division Baking Corporation
New York, NY 800-934-9238
Eli's Cheesecake Company
Chicago, IL 800-999-8300
Fresh Dairy Direct/Morningstar
Dallas, TX 800-395-7004
Future Bakery & Cafe
Etobicoke, ON 416-231-1491
Golden Walnut Specialty Foods
Zion, IL 800-843-3645
Gourmet Baker
Burnaby, BC 800-663-1972
Heidi's Gourmet Desserts
Tucker, GA 800-241-4166
Hoff's Bakery
Medford, MA 888-871-5100
Holey Moses Cheesecake
Westhampton Beach, NY 800-225-2253
Jon Donaire Pastry
Santa Fe Springs, CA 877-366-2473
Jubilations
Columbus, MS 662-328-9210
Little Angel Foods
Daytona Beach, FL 904-257-3040
Love & Quiches Desserts
Freeport, NY 800-525-5251
Love and Quiches Desserts
Freeport, NY 516-623-8800
Mazelle's Cheesecakes Concoctions Creations
Dallas, TX 214-328-9102
Mehaffie Pies
Dayton, OH 937-253-1163
New England Country Bakers
Watertown, CT 800-225-3779
Pellman Foods
New Holland, PA 717-354-8070
Pie Piper Products
Bensenville, IL 800-621-8183
Pocono Cheesecake Factory
Swiftwater, PA 570-839-6844
Sara Lee Corporation
Downers Grove, IL 630-598-8100
Scot Paris Fine Desserts
New York, NY 212-807-1802
Scotty Wotty's Creamy Cheesecake
Hillsborough, NJ 908-281-9720
Steve's Mom
Bronx, NY 800-362-4545
The Cheesecake Factory
Calabasas Hills, CA 818-871-3000
Two Chicks and a Ladle
New York, NY 212-251-0025
Wow! Factor Desserts
Sherwood Park, AB 800-604-2253

Flavored

Cemac Foods Corporation
Philadelphia, PA 800-724-0179
Jon Donaire Pastry
Santa Fe Springs, CA 877-366-2473
Junior's Cheesecake
Maspeth, NY 800-458-6467
Pellman Foods
New Holland, PA 717-354-8070

Frozen

Balboa Dessert Company
Santa Ana, CA 800-974-9699
Cateraid
Howell, MI 800-508-8217
Cemac Foods Corporation
Philadelphia, PA 800-724-0179
CGI Desserts
Sugar Land, TX 281-240-1200
Cinderella Cheese Cake Company
Riverside, NJ 856-461-6302
Dee's Cheesecake Factory/Dee's Foodservice
Albuquerque, NM 505-884-1777
Desserts of Distinction
Milwaukie, OR 503-654-8370
Division Baking Corporation
New York, NY 800-934-9238
Fresh Dairy Direct/Morningstar
Dallas, TX 800-395-7004
Galaxy Desserts
Richmond, CA 800-225-3523
Heidi's Gourmet Desserts
Tucker, GA 800-241-4166
Lawler Foods
Humble, TX 281-540-3321
Love & Quiches Desserts
Freeport, NY 800-525-5251
Mehaffie Pies
Dayton, OH 937-253-1163
Pellman Foods
New Holland, PA 717-354-8070
Sara Lee Corporation
Downers Grove, IL 630-598-8100

NewYork Style

Cannoli Factory
Wyandanch, NY 631-643-2700
Love and Quiches Desserts
Freeport, NY 516-623-8800

Non-Fat

Cemac Foods Corporation
Philadelphia, PA 800-724-0179
Two Chicks and a Ladle
New York, NY 212-251-0025

Churros

J&J Snack Foods Corporation
Pennsauken, NJ 800-486-9533

Coffee Cake

Awrey Bakeries
Livonia, MI 800-950-2253
Clydes Delicious Donuts
Addison, IL 630-628-6555
Dough Works Company
Horicon, WI 800-383-8808
James Skinner Company
Omaha, NE 800-358-7428
L&M Bakery
Lawrence, MA 978-687-7346
Main Street Gourmet
Cuyahoga Falls, OH 800-533-6246

Cream Puff

Creme Curls Bakery
Hudsonville, MI 800-466-1219
Hafner USA
Stone Mountain, GA 888-725-4605
Rich Ice Cream Company
West Palm Beach, FL 561-833-7585

Crumpets

Gourmet Baker
Burnaby, BC 800-663-1972
Norths Bakery California Inc
N Hollywood, CA 818-761-2892
Sara Lee Corporation
Downers Grove, IL 630-598-8100
Wolferman's
Medford, OR

Cupcakes

Butter Baked Goods
Vancouver, BC 604-221-4333
Crumbs Bake Shop
New York, NY 877-278-6270
Maplehurst Bakeries
Carrollton, GA 800-482-4810
Mrs Baird's Bakery
Fort Worth, TX 817-864-2500
Schwan Food Company
Marshall, MN 800-533-5290

Danish

Atlanta Bread Company
Smyrna, GA 800-398-3728
Awrey Bakeries
Livonia, MI 800-950-2253
BakeMark Canada
Laval, QC 800-361-4998
Baker & Baker
Schaumburg, IL 800-593-5777
Baker & Baker, Inc.
Schaumburg, IL 800-593-5777
Brownie Baker
Fresno, CA 800-598-6501
Bunny Bread Company
Cape Girardeau, MO 573-332-7349
Clydes Delicious Donuts
Addison, IL 630-628-6555
Del's Pastry
Etobicoke, ON 416-231-4383
Dimitria Delights
North Grafton, MA 800-763-1113
El Segundo Bakery
El Segundo, CA 310-322-3422
Fiera Foods
Toronto, ON 416-744-1010
France Croissant
New York, NY 212-888-1210
Gourmet Baker
Burnaby, BC 800-663-1972
Gourmet Croissant
Brooklyn, NY 718-499-4911
Heitzman Bakery
Louisville, KY 502-452-1891
James Skinner Company
Omaha, NE 800-358-7428
Joey's Fine Foods
Newark, NJ 973-482-1400
La Francaise Bakery
Melrose Park, IL 800-654-7220
Laura's French Baking Company
Los Angeles, CA 888-353-5144
Lusitania Bakery
Blandon, PA 610-926-1311
Mary Ann's Baking Company
Sacramento, CA 916-681-7444
Michel's Bakery
Philadelphia, PA 215-725-3900
Norths Bakery California Inc
N Hollywood, CA 818-761-2892
Roma Bakeries
Rockford, IL 815-964-6737

Sara Lee Corporation
Downers Grove, IL 630-598-8100
Schwan Food Company
Marshall, MN 800-533-5290
Shaw Baking Company
Thunder Bay, ON 807-345-7327
Strossner's Bakery
Greenville, SC 864-233-3996
Svenhard's Swedish Bakery
Oakland, CA 800-333-7836
Turano Pastry Shops
Bloomingdale, IL 630-529-6161
Uptown Bakers
Hyattsville, MD 301-864-1500
Vie de France Bakery
Bensenville, IL 630-595-9521
Vie de France Yamazaki
Vienna, VA 800-446-4404

Dessert Tarts

Solvang Bakery
Solvang, CA 800-377-4253

Doughnuts

All Round Foods
Westbury, NY 516-338-1888
Awrey Bakeries
Livonia, MI 800-950-2253
Bake Crafters Food
Collegedale, TN 800-296-8935
Baker Boy Bake Shop
Dickinson, ND 800-437-2008
Baker's Dozen
Herkimer, NY 315-866-6770
BBU Bakeries
Denver, CO 303-691-6342
Bunny Bread Company
Cape Girardeau, MO 573-332-7349
Busken Bakery
Cincinnati, OH 513-871-5330
Butter Krust Baking Company
Sunbury, PA 800-282-8093
Carolina Foods
Charlotte, NC 800-234-0441
Case Side Holdings Company
Kensington, PE 902-836-4214
Chatila's Bakery
Salem, NH 603-898-5459
Cloverhill Bakery-Vend Corporation
Chicago, IL 773-745-9800
Clydes Delicious Donuts
Addison, IL 630-628-6555
ConAgra Foods
Boisbriand, QC 450-433-1322
Davis Bakery & Delicatessen
Cleveland, OH 216-464-5599
Dunford Bakers
Fayetteville, AR 479-521-3000
Dunford Bakers Company
West Jordan, UT 800-748-4335
Dutch Girl Donuts
Detroit, MI 313-368-3020
Elmwood Pastry
West Hartford, CT 860-233-2029
Giant Food
Lanham, MD 888-469-4426
Glazier Packing Company
Potsdam, NY 315-265-2500
Granny's Kitchens
Frankfort, NY 315-735-5000
Grebe's Bakery & Delicatessen
Milwaukee, WI 800-356-9377
Haas Baking Company
St Louis, MO 800-325-3171
Harting's Bakery
Bowmansville, PA 717-445-5644
Heitzman Bakery
Louisville, KY 502-452-1891
Jubelt Variety Bakeries
Mount Olive, IL 217-999-5231
Kerrobert Bakery
Kerrobert, SK 306-834-2461
Koffee Kup Bakery
Burlington, VT 802-863-2696
Kristy Kremarie
Huntsville, AL 256-536-7475
LePage Bakeries
Auburn, ME 207-783-9161
Lepage Bakeries
Auburn, ME 207-783-9161
Lone Star Consolidated Foods
Dallas, TX 800-658-5637
Ludwick's Frozen Donuts
Grand Rapids, MI 800-366-8816
Mac's Donut Shop
Aliquippa, PA 724-375-6776
Maple Donuts
York, PA 800-627-5348
Maui Bagel
Kahului, HI 808-270-7561
Mrs. Willman's Baking
Burnaby, BC 604-434-0027
Mt View Bakery
Mountain View, HI 808-968-6353
Nutrilicious Natural Bakery
Countryside, IL 800-835-8097
Plehn's Bakery
Louisville, KY 502-896-4438
Quality Naturally! Foods
City of Industry, CA 888-498-6986
Rich Products Corporation
Hilliard, OH 614-771-1117
Rolling Pin Bakery
Bow Island, AB 403-545-2434
Ruth Ashbrook Bakery
Portland, OR 503-240-7437
Sara Lee Corporation
Downers Grove, IL 630-598-8100
Schwan Food Company
Marshall, MN 800-533-5290
Shaw Baking Company
Thunder Bay, ON 807-345-7327
Steve's Doughnut Shop
Somerset, MA 508-672-0865
Stroehmann Bakeries
Horsham, PA 800-984-0989
Tastykake
Philadelphia, PA 215-221-8500
Vallos Baking Company
Bethlehem, PA 610-866-1012

Filled

Ocean Spray Cranberries
Kenosha, WI 262-694-5200

Frozen

All Round Foods
Westbury, NY 516-338-1888
Awrey Bakeries
Livonia, MI 800-950-2253
Bake Crafters Food
Collegedale, TN 800-296-8935
Carolina Foods
Charlotte, NC 800-234-0441
Clydes Delicious Donuts
Addison, IL 630-628-6555
ConAgra Foods
Boisbriand, QC 450-433-1322
Glazier Packing Company
Potsdam, NY 315-265-2500
Granny's Kitchens
Frankfort, NY 315-735-5000
Haas Baking Company
St Louis, MO 800-325-3171
Lone Star Consolidated Foods
Dallas, TX 800-658-5637
Ludwick's Frozen Donuts
Grand Rapids, MI 800-366-8816
Mel-O-Cream Donuts International
Springfield, IL 217-483-7272
Overseas Food Trading
Fort Lee, NJ 201-585-8730
Rich Products Corporation
Hilliard, OH 614-771-1117
Sara Lee Corporation
Downers Grove, IL 630-598-8100

Dumplings

Atkinson Milling Company
Selma, NC 800-948-5707
Chang Food Company
Garden Grove, CA 714-265-9990
Chateau Food Products
Cicero, IL 708-863-4207
Chinese Spaghetti Factory
Boston, MA 617-445-7714
Community Orchard
Fort Dodge, IA 515-573-8212
Dimitria Delights
North Grafton, MA 800-763-1113
Harvest Food Products Company
Concord, CA 925-676-8208
Harvest Time Foods
Ayden, NC 252-746-6675
Jewel Date Company
Thermal, CA 760-399-4474
La Tang Cuisine Manufacturing
Houston, TX 713-780-4876
Mandoo
Englewood, NJ 201-568-9337
Marcetti Frozen Pasta
Altoona, IA 515-967-4254
Mayfield Farms
Caledon, ON 905-846-0506
Millie's Pierogi
Chicopee Falls, MA 800-743-7641
Naleway Foods
Winnipeg, MB 800-665-7448
On-Cor Foods Products
Northbrook, IL 847-205-1040
Pierre Foods
Cincinnati, OH 513-874-8741
Prime Food Processing Corporation
Brooklyn, NY 888-639-2323
Shine Foods Inc
Torrance, CA 310-533-6010
Sweet Sue Kitchens
Athens, AL 256-216-0500
Twin Marquis
Brooklyn, NY 800-367-6868
Wei-Chuan
Bell Gardens, CA 562-372-2020

Eclairs

Creme Curls Bakery
Hudsonville, MI 800-466-1219
Rich Ice Cream Company
West Palm Beach, FL 561-833-7585

Frozen Cakes

Alati-Caserta Desserts
Montreal, QC 514-271-3013
Awrey Bakeries
Livonia, MI 800-950-2253
Bensons Bakery
Bogart, GA 800-888-6059
Bodega Chocolates
Fountain Valley, CA 888-326-3342
Carolina Foods
Charlotte, NC 800-234-0441
Carousel Cakes
Nanuet, NY 800-659-2253
Cemac Foods Corporation
Philadelphia, PA 800-724-0179
CGI Desserts
Sugar Land, TX 281-240-1200
Cinderella Cheese Cake Company
Riverside, NJ 856-461-6302
Creme Glacee Gelati
Montreal, QC 888-322-0116
Danish Baking Company
Van Nuys, CA 818-786-1700
Division Baking Corporation
New York, NY 800-934-9238
Dynamic Foods
Lubbock, TX 806-747-2777
Evans Bakery
Cozad, NE 800-222-5641
Fantasia
Sedalia, MO 660-827-1172
French Patisserie
Pacifica, CA 800-300-2253
Fresh Dairy Direct/Morningstar
Dallas, TX 800-395-7004
Grossinger's Home Bakery
New York, NY 800-479-6996
Heidi's Gourmet Desserts
Tucker, GA 800-241-4166
James Skinner Company
Omaha, NE 800-358-7428
Kyger Bakery Products
Lafayette, IN 765-447-1252
Little Miss. Muffin
Chicago, IL 800-456-9328
Lone Star Bakery
Round Rock, TX 512-255-3629
Love & Quiches Desserts
Freeport, NY 800-525-5251
Main Street Gourmet
Cuyahoga Falls, OH 800-533-6246

Mehaffie Pies
Dayton, OH 937-253-1163
Mothers Kitchen Inc
Burlington, NJ. 609-589-3026
My Grandma's Coffee Cakee of New England
Boston, MA. 800-847-2636
Pacific Ocean Produce
Santa Cruz, CA 831-423-2654
Parco Foods
Blue Island, IL 708-371-9200
Pastry Chef
Pawtucket, RI 800-639-8606
Pellman Foods
New Holland, PA 717-354-8070
Real Food Marketing
Kansas City, MO. 816-221-4100
Rowena's
Norfolk, VA. 800-627-8699
Sara Lee Corporation
Downers Grove, IL 630-598-8100
Saxby Foods
Edmonton, AB 780-440-4179
The Daphne Baking Company, LLC
New York, NY 212-517-7626
Uncle Ralph's Cookie Company
Frederick, MD. 800-422-0626
Warwick Ice Cream Company
Warwick, RI 401-821-8403
Winder Dairy
West Valley, UT 800-946-3371

Fruit Cake

Beatrice Bakery Company
Beatrice, NE 800-228-4030
Caribbean Food Delights
Tappan, NY. 845-398-3000
Claxton Bakery
Claxton, GA 800-841-4211
Fireside Kitchen
Halifax, NS 902-454-7387
Multi Marques
Montreal, QC 514-934-1866
Neuman Bakery Specialties
Addison, IL 800-253-5298
Old Cavendish Products
Cavendish, VT 800-536-7899

Fruit Cobbler

Good Old Days Foods
Little Rock, AR. 501-565-1257
Harold Food Company
Charlotte, NC 704-588-8061
Lone Star Bakery
Round Rock, TX. 512-255-3629
Original Ya-hoo! Baking Company
Sherman, TX. 800-575-9373
Pacific Ocean Produce
Santa Cruz, CA 831-423-2654
Spring Glen Fresh Foods
Ephrata, PA 800-641-2853

Ladyfingers

Lawrences Delights
Doraville, GA 800-568-0021
Specialty Bakers
Marysville, PA 800-233-0778

Liqueur Cake

Beatrice Bakery Company
Beatrice, NE 800-228-4030
Dinkel's Bakery
Chicago, IL 800-822-8817

Muffin Loaves

Main Street Gourmet
Cuyahoga Falls, OH 800-533-6246

Muffins

Andre-Boudin Bakeries
San Francisco, CA 415-882-1849
Angel's Bakeries
Brooklyn, NY 718-389-1400
Atlanta Bread Company
Smyrna, GA 800-398-3728
Awrey Bakeries
Livonia, MI. 800-950-2253
Bake Crafters Food
Collegedale, TN 800-296-8935
Bake Rite Rolls
Bensalem, PA 215-638-2400
BakeMark Canada
Laval, QC 800-361-4998
Bakemark Ingredients Canada
Richmond, BC 800-665-9441
Baker & Baker
Schaumburg, IL. 800-593-5777
Baker & Baker, Inc.
Schaumburg, IL. 800-593-5777
Baker Boy Bake Shop
Dickinson, ND 800-437-2008
Bakery Chef
Chicago, IL 773-384-1900
BBU Bakeries
Denver, CO 303-691-6342
Breakfast at Brennan's
New Orleans, LA 800-888-9932
Brownie Baker
Fresno, CA 800-598-6501
Busken Bakery
Cincinnati, OH 513-871-5330
Calgary Italian Bakery
Calgary, AB. 800-661-6868
Canada Bread Company
Langley, BC 800-465-5515
Case Side Holdings Company
Kensington, PE 902-836-4214
Central Bakery
Fall River, MA 508-675-7620
Chatila's Bakery
Salem, NH. 603-898-5459
Cloverhill Bakery-Vend Corporation
Chicago, IL 773-745-9800
Community Bakeries
Chicago, IL 773-384-1900
Danish Baking Company
Van Nuys, CA 818-786-1700
Del's Pastry
Etobicoke, ON 416-231-4383
DiCarlo's Bakery
San Pedro, CA. 310-831-2524
Dolly Madison Bakery Interstate Brands Corporation
Columbus, IN 812-376-7432
Dough Works Company
Horicon, WI 800-383-8808
Dunford Bakers
Fayetteville, AR 479-521-3000
Edelweiss Patisserie
Charlestown, MA 617-628-0225
Edner Corporation
Hayward, CA 510-441-8504
El Peto Products
Cambridge, ON. 800-387-4064
Enterprises Pates et Croutes
Boucherville, QC 450-655-7790
Fireside Kitchen
Halifax, NS 902-454-7387
Foxtail Foods
Fairfield, OH. 800-487-2253
France Croissant
New York, NY 212-888-1210
Fresh Start Bakeries
City of Industry, CA 626-961-2525
Fresh Start Bakeries
Brea, CA 714-256-8900
Gold Medal Baking Company
Philadelphia, PA 215-627-4787
Gourmet Baker
Burnaby, BC 800-663-1972
Gourmet Croissant
Brooklyn, NY 718-499-4911
Greyston Bakery
Yonkers, NY 800-289-2253
Hawaii Star Bakery
Honolulu, HI. 808-841-3602
Heitzman Bakery
Louisville, KY 502-452-1891
Homestead Baking Company
Rumford, RI 800-556-7216
International Brownie
East Weymouth, MA. 800-230-1588
Irresistible Cookie Jar
Hayden Lake, ID. 208-664-1261
Isabella's Healthy Bakery
Cuyahoga Falls, OH 800-476-6328
J&J Snack Foods Corporation
Pennsauken, NJ. 800-486-9533
James Skinner Company
Omaha, NE 800-358-7428
Joey's Fine Foods
Newark, NJ 973-482-1400
Kerrobert Bakery
Kerrobert, SK 306-834-2461
Lone Star Bakery
Round Rock, TX. 512-255-3629
Lusitania Bakery
Blandon, PA 610-926-1311
Mac's Donut Shop
Aliquippa, PA 724-375-6776
Magnificent Muffin Corporation
Farmingdale, NY 631-454-8022
Main Street Gourmet
Cuyahoga Falls, OH 800-533-6246
Main Street Gourmet Fundraising
Cuyahoga Falls, OH 800-533-6246
Main Street Muffins
Cuyahoga Falls, OH 800-533-6246
Meyer's Bakeries
Casa Grande, AZ. 800-528-5770
Michel's Bakery
Philadelphia, PA 215-725-3900
Mt View Bakery
Mountain View, HI 808-968-6353
New England Muffin Company
Fall River, MA 508-675-2833
New Horizons Baking Company
Fremont, IN. 260-495-7055
Norths Bakery California Inc
N Hollywood, CA. 818-761-2892
Notre Dame Bakery
Conception Harbour, NL 709-535-2738
Oakrun Farm Bakery
Ancaster, ON. 905-648-1818
Oroweat Baking Company
Montebello, CA 323-721-5161
Otis Spunkmeyer
San Leandro, CA. 800-938-1900
Otis Spunkmeyer Company
Norcross, GA 800-438-9251
Oven Fresh Baking Company
Chicago, IL 773-638-1234
Pacific Ocean Produce
Santa Cruz, CA 831-423-2654
Plaidberry Company
Vista, CA. 760-727-5403
Rich Products Corporation
Buffalo, NY. 800-828-2021
Rising Dough Bakery
Sacramento, CA 916-387-9700
Sara Lee Corporation
Downers Grove, IL 630-598-8100
Shaw Baking Company
Thunder Bay, ON 807-345-7327
Sterling Foods
San Antonio, TX. 210-490-1669
Sweet Bakery Baltimore
Baltimore, MD 41- 7-8 22
Uptown Bakers
Hyattsville, MD 301-864-1500
Vie de France Bakery
Bensenville, IL 630-595-9521
Vitalicious
New York, NY 877-848-2877
Weston Bakeries
Toronto, ON 800-590-6861

Frozen

Dynamic Foods
Lubbock, TX. 806-747-2777
Isabella's Healthy Bakery
Cuyahoga Falls, OH 800-476-6328
Main Street Gourmet
Cuyahoga Falls, OH 800-533-6246
Main Street Gourmet Fundraising
Cuyahoga Falls, OH 800-533-6246
Main Street Muffins
Cuyahoga Falls, OH 800-533-6246

Whole Grain

Isabella's Healthy Bakery
Cuyahoga Falls, OH 800-476-6328
Main Street Gourmet
Cuyahoga Falls, OH 800-533-6246
Main Street Muffins
Cuyahoga Falls, OH 800-533-6246

Panettones

Vigneri Confections
Rochester, NY. 877-843-6374

Pastries

Alessi Bakery
Tampa, FL 813-879-4544
Artuso Pastry Foods Corp
Mt Vernon, NY 914-663-8806
Artuso Pastry Shop
Bronx, NY 718-367-2515
Athens Pastries & Frozen Foods
Cleveland, OH 800-837-5683
Atlanta Bread Company
Smyrna, GA 800-398-3728
Bakery Europa
Honolulu, HI 808-845-5011
Banquet Schuster Bakery
Pueblo, CO 719-544-1062
Big Fatty's Flaming Foods
Valley View, TX 888-248-6332
Birkholm's Jr Danish Bakery
Solvang, CA 805-688-3872
Bodega Chocolates
Fountain Valley, CA 888-326-3342
Borden's Bread
Regina, SK 306-525-3341
Calgary Italian Bakery
Calgary, AB 800-661-6868
Campbell Soup Company of Canada
Listowel, ON 800-575-7687
Caribbean Food Delights
Tappan, NY 845-398-3000
Case Side Holdings Company
Kensington, PE 902-836-4214
Castella Imports
Hauppauge, NY 866-227-8355
Chatila's Bakery
Salem, NH 603-898-5459
Chella's Dutch Delicacies
Lake Oswego, OR 800-458-3331
City Baker
Calgary, AB 403-263-8578
Clarkson Scottish Bakery
Mississauga, ON 905-823-1500
Claudio Pastry Company
Elmwood Park, IL 708-453-0598
Clements Pastry Shop
Hyattsville, MD 800-444-7428
Cohen's Bakery
Buffalo, NY 716-892-8149
Columbus Bakery
Columbus, OH 614-645-2275
Creme Curls Bakery
Hudsonville, MI 800-466-1219
Danish Baking Company
Van Nuys, CA 818-786-1700
Di Paolo Baking Company
Rochester, NY 585-232-3510
Dimitria Delights
North Grafton, MA 800-763-1113
Dufour Pastry Kitchens
Bronx, NY 800-439-1282
Edelweiss Patisserie
Charlestown, MA 617-628-0225
Elegant Desserts
Lyndhurst, NJ 201-933-0770
Ferrara Bakery & Cafe
New York, NY 212-226-6150
Fiera Foods
Toronto, ON 416-744-1010
Fillo Factory
Dumont, NJ 800-653-4556
Food of Our Own Design
Maplewood, NJ 973-762-0985
Foodbrands America
Oklahoma City, OK 405-290-4000
France Croissant
New York, NY 212-888-1210
Future Bakery & Cafe
Etobicoke, ON 416-231-1491
Golden Glow Cookie Company
Bronx, NY 718-379-6223
Gourmet Baker
Burnaby, BC 800-663-1972
Hafner USA
Stone Mountain, GA 888-725-4605
Heinemann's Bakeries
Palatine, IL 847-358-3501
Holt's Bakery
Douglas, GA 912-384-2202
International Equipment International Equipment And Supplies
Arecibo, PR 787-879-3151
James Skinner Company
Omaha, NE 800-358-7428
John J. Nissen Baking Company
Brewer, ME 207-989-7654
Just Desserts
San Francisco, CA 415-602-9245
Kerrobert Bakery
Kerrobert, SK 306-834-2461
King Soopers Bakery
Denver, CO 877-415-4647
Laura's French Baking Company
Los Angeles, CA 888-353-5144
Lax & Mandel Bakery
Cleveland, OH 216-382-8877
Lenchner Bakery
Concord, ON 905-738-8811
Let Them Eat Cake
Tampa, FL 813-837-6888
Lewis Bakeries
London, ON 519-434-5252
Little Miss. Muffin
Chicago, IL 800-456-9328
Lone Star Consolidated Foods
Dallas, TX 800-658-5637
Lucy's Sweet Surrender
Cleveland, OH 216-752-0828
Mac's Donut Shop
Aliquippa, PA 724-375-6776
Main Street Gourmet
Cuyahoga Falls, OH 800-533-6246
Main Street Gourmet Fundraising
Cuyahoga Falls, OH 800-533-6246
Mary Ann's Baking Company
Sacramento, CA 916-681-7444
Michel's Bakery
Philadelphia, PA 215-725-3900
Mikawaya Bakery
Vernon, CA
Moravian Cookies Shop
Winston Salem, NC 800-274-2994
Morse's Sauerkraut
Waldoboro, ME 866-832-5569
Mozzicato Depasquale Bakery & Pastry Shop
Hartford, CT 860-296-0426
Mrs. Willman's Baking
Burnaby, BC 604-434-0027
Nancy's Specialty Foods
Newark, CA 510-494-1100
Northside Bakery
Richmond, VA 804-968-7620
Oakrun Farm Bakery
Ancaster, ON 905-648-1818
Old Country Bakery
North Hollywood, CA 818-838-2302
Orange Bakery
Irvine, CA 949-863-1377
Pauline's Pastries
Vaughan, ON 877-292-6826
Prime Pastries
Concord, ON 905-669-5883
Quaker Bonnet
Buffalo, NY 800-283-2447
Quality Naturally! Foods
City of Industry, CA 888-498-6986
Ranaldi Bros Frozen Food Products Inc
Warwick, RI 401-738-3444
Rolling Pin Bakery
Bow Island, AB 403-545-2434
Royal Caribbean Bakery
Mount Vernon, NY 888-818-0971
Ryke's Bakery
Muskegon, MI 231-722-3508
Schulze & Burch Biscuit Company
Chicago, IL 773-927-6622
Scialo Brothers
Providence, RI 877-421-0986
Shaw Baking Company
Thunder Bay, ON 807-345-7327
Solana Beach Baking Company
Carlsbad, CA 760-931-0148
Spohrers Bakeries
Collingdale, PA 610-532-9959
St. Cloud Bakery
Saint Cloud, MN 320-251-8055
Standard Bakery
Kealakekua, HI 808-322-3688
Starbucks Coffee Company
Seattle, WA 800-782-7282
Strossner's Bakery
Greenville, SC 864-233-3996
Svenhard's Swedish Bakery
Oakland, CA 800-333-7836
Sweet Gallery Exclusive Pastry
Toronto, ON 416-766-0289
Taste It Presents
Kenilworth, NJ 908-241-9191
Teawolf Industries, Ltd
Pine Brook, NJ 973-575-4600
Turano Pastry Shops
Bloomingdale, IL 630-529-6161
Turano Pasty Shops
Berwyn, IL 708-788-5320
Uptown Bakers
Hyattsville, MD 301-864-1500
Valley Bakery
Rock Valley, IA 712-476-5386
Vie de France Yamazaki
Denver, CO 303-371-6280
Vie de France Yamazaki
Vienna, VA 800-393-8926
Vie de France Yamazaki
Vienna, VA 800-446-4404
Vienna Bakery
Edmonton, AB 780-489-4142
Vigneri Confections
Rochester, NY 877-843-6374
Weiss Homemade Kosher Bakery
Brooklyn, NY 800-498-3477
Wenger's Bakery
Reading, PA 610-372-6545
Zeppys Bakery
Lawrence, MA 781-963-7022

Pecan Log

Lawrences Delights
Doraville, GA 800-568-0021

Petit Fours

Ferrara Bakery & Cafe
New York, NY 212-226-6150
Mazelle's Cheesecakes Concoctions Creations
Dallas, TX 214-328-9102
Silver Lake Cookie Company
Islip, NY 631-581-4000

Pound Cake

Adams Foods
Dothan, AL 334-983-4233
Bakery Chef
Chicago, IL 773-384-1900
Brownie Baker
Fresno, CA 800-598-6501
Clarmil Manufacturing Corporation
Hayward, CA 888-252-7645
McDuffies Bakery
Clarence, NY 800-875-1598
New England Country Bakers
Watertown, CT 800-225-3779
Rowena's
Norfolk, VA 800-627-8699
Sara Lee Corporation
Downers Grove, IL 630-598-8100
Silver Tray Cookies
Fort Lauderdale, FL 305-883-0800
Waldensian Bakeries
Valdese, NC 828-874-2136

Puff Pastry

BakeMark USA
Schaumburg, IL 562-949-1054
Baker & Baker
Schaumburg, IL 800-593-5777
Baker & Baker, Inc.
Schaumburg, IL 800-593-5777
Dutchland Frozen Foods
Lester, IA 888-497-7243
France Croissant
New York, NY 212-888-1210
Gourmet Baker
Burnaby, BC 800-663-1972

Rugulach

Baker & Baker
Schaumburg, IL 800-593-5777
Baker & Baker, Inc.
Schaumburg, IL 800-593-5777
Chewys Rugulach
San Diego, CA 800-241-3456
Morse's Sauerkraut
Waldoboro, ME 866-832-5569
Neuman Bakery Specialties
Addison, IL 800-253-5298

Steve's Mom
Bronx, NY 800-362-4545
Suzanne's Sweets
Katonah, NY
Yrica's Rugelach & Baking Company
Brooklyn, NY 718-965-3657

Rusk

House-Autry Mills
Four Oaks, NC 800-849-0802

Sponge Cake

Clarmil Manufacturing Corporation
Hayward, CA 888-252-7645
Multi Marques
Montreal, QC 514-934-1866
Patisserie Wawel
Montreal, QC 614-524-3348
Specialty Bakers
Marysville, PA 800-233-0778
Sweet Gallery Exclusive Pastry
Toronto, ON 416-766-0289

Strawberry Shortcake

Penn Maid Crowley Foods
Philadelphia, PA 800-247-6269

Strudel

Athens Pastries & Frozen Foods
Cleveland, OH 800-837-5683
Creme Curls Bakery
Hudsonville, MI 800-466-1219
Dee's Cheesecake Factory/Dee's Foodservice
Albuquerque, NM 505-884-1777
Dimitria Delights
North Grafton, MA 800-763-1113
Fillo Factory
Dumont, NJ 800-653-4556
Gourmet Baker
Burnaby, BC 800-663-1972
Le Notre, Alain & Marie Baker
Houston, TX 800-536-6873
Rising Dough Bakery
Sacramento, CA 916-387-9700
Sinbad Sweets
Fresno, CA 800-350-7933
Svenhard's Swedish Bakery
Oakland, CA 800-333-7836

Tarts

CGI Desserts
Sugar Land, TX 281-240-1200
Clarmil Manufacturing Corporation
Hayward, CA 888-252-7645
Dufflet Pastries
Toronto, ON 416-536-9640
Dufour Pastry Kitchens
Bronx, NY 800-439-1282
Elegant Desserts
Lyndhurst, NJ 201-933-0770
Greyston Bakery
Yonkers, NY 800-289-2253
Health Valley Company
Irwindale, CA 800-334-3204
Honey Rose Baking Company
Carlsbad, CA
J.P. Sunrise Bakery
Edmonton, AB 780-454-5797
Joey's Fine Foods
Newark, NJ 973-482-1400
Kellogg Canada Inc
Mississauga, ON 888-876-3750
Love & Quiches Desserts
Freeport, NY 800-525-5251
Royal Home Bakery
Newmarket, ON 905-715-7044
Sinbad Sweets
Fresno, CA 800-350-7933
The Daphne Baking Company, LLC
New York, NY 212-517-7626

Tiramisu

Vantage USA
Chicago, IL 773-247-1086
Vigneri Confections
Rochester, NY 877-843-6374

Tortes

Alessi Bakery
Tampa, FL 813-879-4544
Balboa Dessert Company
Santa Ana, CA 800-974-9699
Danish Baking Company
Van Nuys, CA 818-786-1700
Dufflet Pastries
Toronto, ON 416-536-9640
Gourmet Baker
Burnaby, BC 800-663-1972
Heidi's Gourmet Desserts
Tucker, GA 800-241-4166
Hoff's Bakery
Medford, MA 888-871-5100
Scot Paris Fine Desserts
New York, NY 212-807-1802
Strossner's Bakery
Greenville, SC 864-233-3996
Sweet Endings
West Palm Beach, FL 888-635-1177
Sweet Gallery Exclusive Pastry
Toronto, ON 416-766-0289
Vigneri Confections
Rochester, NY 877-843-6374

Turnovers

BakeMark Canada
Laval, QC 800-361-4998
BakeMark USA
Schaumburg, IL 562-949-1054
Con Agra Foods
Holly Ridge, NC 910-329-9061
Creme Curls Bakery
Hudsonville, MI 800-466-1219
Del's Pastry
Etobicoke, ON 416-231-4383
Fiera Foods
Toronto, ON 416-744-1010
Oven Ready Products
Guelph, ON 519-767-2415

Cones

Ace Baking Company
Wadsworth, IL 800-879-2231
Edy's Dreyers Grand Ice Cream
Rockaway, NJ 800-362-7899
Foothills Creamery
Calgary, AB 800-661-4909
Great Western Products Company
Assumption, IL 217-226-3241
Great Western Products Company
Bismarck, MO 573-734-2210
Ice Cream Specialties
Lafayette, IN 765-474-2989
Interbake Foods
Green Bay, WI 804-576-3459
Joy Cone Company
Hermitage, PA 800-242-2663
Kemach Food Products Corporation
Brooklyn, NY 888-453-6224
Marshmallow Cone Company
Cincinnati, OH 800-641-8551
Monster Cone
Montreal, QC 800-542-9801
Norse Dairy Systems
Columbus, OH 614-294-4931
O'Boyle's Ice Cream Company
Bristol, PA 215-788-3882
Olde Tyme Food Corporation
East Longmeadow, MA 800-356-6533
Ono Cones of Hawaii
Pearl City, HI 808-487-8690
Sargeant's Army Marketing
Bowmanville, ON 905-623-2888
Table De France
Ontario, CA 909-923-5205
Turnbull Cone Baking Company
Chattanooga, TN 423-265-4551
Zimmer Custom Made Packaging
Columbus, OH 800-338-7465

Cookies & Bars

Almond Cookies

Andre-Boudin Bakeries
San Francisco, CA 415-882-1849
Balticshop.Com LLC
Glastonbury, CT
Dong Kee Company
Chicago, IL 312-225-6340
Erba Food Products
Brooklyn, NY 718-272-7700
Fortella Fortune Cookies
Chicago, IL 312-567-9000
Mamma Says
Butler, NJ 877-283-6282
YZ Enterprises
Maumee, OH 800-736-8779

Animal Crackers

Old Colony Baking Company
Spring Valley, IL 815- 44- 211

Bars

Agricore United
Winnipeg, MB 800-661-4844
Amt Labs
North Salt Lake, UT 801-299-1661
Bake Crafters Food
Collegedale, TN 800-296-8935
Barbara's Bakery
Petaluma, CA 707-765-2273
Betty Lou's Golden Smackers
McMinnville, OR 800-242-5205
Cambridge Food
Monterey, CA 800-433-2584
Carrie's Chocolates
Edmonton, AB 877-778-2462
Chase Candy Company
Saint Joseph, MO 800-786-1625
Cliff Bar
Emeryville, CA 800-884-5254
ConAgra Food Store Brands
Edina, MN 952-469-4981
Cream of the West
Harlowton, MT 800-477-2383
Edner Corporation
Hayward, CA 510-441-8504
Edy's Dreyers Grand Ice Cream
Rockaway, NJ 800-362-7899
Fieldbrook Farms
Dunkirk, NY 800-333-0805
Food of Our Own Design
Maplewood, NJ 973-762-0985
Frankly Natural Bakers
San Diego, CA 800-727-7229
Frozfruit Corporation
Gardena, CA 310-217-1034
GeniSoy
Tulsa, OK 800-228-4656
Global Health Laboratories
Amityville, NY 631-777-2134
Gourmet Baker
Burnaby, BC 800-663-1972
Govadinas Fitness Foods
San Diego, CA 800-900-0108
Health Valley Company
Irwindale, CA 800-334-3204
Hershey Chocolate & Confectionery Division
Pleasanton, CA 925-460-0359
Hi-Country Snack Food
Lincoln, MT 800-433-3916
Honey Acres
Ashippun, WI 800-558-7745
Increda-Meal
Cato, NY 315-626-2111
Jamae Natural Foods
Los Angeles, CA 800-343-0052
JSL Foods
Los Angeles, CA 800-745-3236
L&M Bakery
Lawrence, MA 978-687-7346
Lotus Bakery
Santa Rosa, CA 800-875-6887
Marin Food Specialties
Byron, CA 925-634-6126
Merlino Italian Baking Company
Seattle, WA 800-207-2997

MLO/GeniSoy Products Company
Tulas, OK 866-606-3829
Murray Biscuit Company
Atlanta, GA 800-745-5582
Nature's Plus
Long Beach, CA 562-494-2500
Nellson Candies
Irwindale, CA 626-334-4508
Oberweis Dairy
North Aurora, IL 888-645-5868
Prairie Sun Grains
Calgary, AB 800-556-6807
Premier Nutrition
Carlsbad, CA 888-836-8977
Quaker Oats Company
Danville, IL 217-443-4995
Randag & Associates Inc
Elmhurst, IL 630-530-2830
Schulze & Burch Biscuit Company
Chicago, IL 773-927-6622
Severn Peanut Company
Severn, NC 800-642-4064
Sturm Foods
Manawa, WI 800-347-8876
Sucesores de Pedro Cortes
San Juan, PR 787-754-7040
Sugar Kake Cookie
Tonawanda, NY 800-775-5180
Sweet Productions
Amityville, NY 631-842-0548
Sweety Novelty
Monterey Park, CA 626-282-4482
Ultimate Nutrition
Plainville, CT 860-409-7100
Weaver Nut Company
Ephrata, PA 717-738-3781
Your Bar Factory
LaSalle, QC 888-366-0258

Biscotti

All About Lollipops
Poway, CA 866-475-6554
Award Baking International
New Germany, MN 800-333-3523
Baker & Baker
Schaumburg, IL 800-593-5777
Baker & Baker, Inc.
Schaumburg, IL 800-593-5777
Be-Bop Biscotti
Bend, OR 888-545-7487
Bernadette Baking Company
Medford, MA 781-393-8700
Biscoti Di Suzy
Oakland, CA 800-211-5903
Biscotti Goddess
Richmond, VA 804-745-9490
Daniele Imports
Rochester, NY 800-298-9410
De Bas Chocolatier
Fresno, CA 559-294-7638
Di Camillo Bakery
Niagara Falls, NY 800-634-4363
Elliott Bay Baking Co.
Seattle, WA 206-762-7690
Ferrara Bakery & Cafe
New York, NY 212-226-6150
Godiva Chocolatier
New York, NY 800-946-3482
Grain-Free JK Gourmet
Toronto, ON 800-608-0465
Hansen's Juices
Azusa, CA 800-426-7367
Immaculate Consumption
Flat Rock, NC 888-826-6567
Just Off Melrose
Palm Springs, CA 800-743-4109
La Tempesta
S San Francisco, CA 800-762-8330
LaRosa's Bakery
Shrewsbury, NJ 800-527-6722
Mamma Says
Butler, NJ 877-283-6282
Merlino Italian Baking Company
Seattle, WA 800-207-2997
Montione's Biscotti & Baked Goods
Norton, MA 800-559-1010
Moosewood Hollow LLC
Morrisville, VT 800-828-2376
My Boy's Baking LLC
Allentown, 3A 610-759-4552
North American Enterprises
Tucson, AZ 800-817-8666
Our Thyme Garden
Cleburne, TX 800-482-4372
Poppie's Dough
Chicago, IL 312-640-0404
Royal Wine Corp
Bayonne, NJ 718-384-2400
Touche Bakery
London, ON 518-455-0044
Tuscan Bakery
Portland, OR 800-887-2261
Ultimate Biscotti
Eugene, OR 541-344-8220
Upper Crust Biscotti
Pismo Beach, CA 866-972-6879
Wally Biscotti
Denver, CO 866-659-2559

Almond

Main Street Gourmet
Cuyahoga Falls, OH 800-533-6246

Chocolate Almond

Main Street Gourmet
Cuyahoga Falls, OH 800-533-6246

Chocolate Dipped

Main Street Gourmet
Cuyahoga Falls, OH 800-533-6246

Hazelnut

Main Street Gourmet
Cuyahoga Falls, OH 800-533-6246

Mocha

Main Street Gourmet
Cuyahoga Falls, OH 800-533-6246

White Chocolate Dipped

Main Street Gourmet
Cuyahoga Falls, OH 800-533-6246

Brownies

Andre-Boudin Bakeries
San Francisco, CA 415-882-1849
Athena's Silverland®Desserts
Forest Park, IL 800-737-3636
Bake Crafters Food
Collegedale, TN 800-296-8935
BakeMark Canada
Laval, QC 800-361-4998
Baker & Baker
Schaumburg, IL 800-593-5777
Baker & Baker, Inc.
Schaumburg, IL 800-593-5777
Baker Boy Bake Shop
Dickinson, ND 800-437-2008
Bakers Breakfast Cookie
Bellingham, WA 877-889-1090
Boca Bons East,LLC.
Greenacres, FL 800-314-2835
Brownie Baker
Fresno, CA 800-598-6501
Browniepops LLC
Leawood, KS 816-797-0715
Cheryl & Company
Westerville, OH 614-776-1500
Christie Cookie Company
Nashville, TN 615-242-3817
Coby's Cookies
Toronto, ON 416-633-1567
Danish Baking Company
Van Nuys, CA 818-786-1700
Dee's Cheesecake Factory/Dee's Foodservice
Albuquerque, NM 505-884-1777
Dough Works Company
Horicon, WI 800-383-8808
Dufflet Pastries
Toronto, ON 416-536-9640
Dynamic Foods
Lubbock, TX 806-747-2777
Eilenberger Bakery
Palestine, TX 800-831-2544
Fairytale Brownies
Phoenix, AZ 800-324-7982
Food of Our Own Design
Maplewood, NJ 973-762-0985
Frankly Natural Bakers
San Diego, CA 800-727-7229
Handy Pax
Randolph, MA 781-963-8300
Harvest Valley Bakery
La Salle, IL 815-224-9030
Heavenscent Edibles
New York, NY 212-369-0310
Heidi's Gourmet Desserts
Tucker, GA 800-241-4166
Home Baked Group
Boca Raton, FL 561-995-0767
Lawler Foods
Humble, TX 281-540-3321
Lone Star Bakery
Round Rock, TX 512-255-3629
Mac's Donut Shop
Aliquippa, PA 724-375-6776
Main Street Gourmet
Cuyahoga Falls, OH 800-533-6246
Main Street Gourmet Fundraising
Cuyahoga Falls, OH 800-533-6246
Maplehurst Bakeries
Carrollton, GA 800-482-4810
Mari's New York
New York, NY
McDuffies Bakery
Clarence, NY 800-875-1598
Michel's Bakery
Philadelphia, PA 215-725-3900
Otis Spunkmeyer Company
Norcross, GA 800-438-9251
Pacific Ocean Produce
Santa Cruz, CA 831-423-2654
Parco Foods
Blue Island, IL 708-371-9200
Peggy Lawton Kitchens
East Walpole, MA 800-843-7325
Pie Piper Products
Bensenville, IL 800-621-8183
Selma's Cookies
Apopka, FL 800-922-6654
Sterling Foods
San Antonio, TX 210-490-1669
Sticky Fingers Bakeries
Spokane, WA 800-458-5826
Tate's Bake Shop
Southampton, NY 631-283-9830
Vitalicious
New York, NY 877-848-2877
William Poll
New York, NY 800-993-7655

with Nuts

Dinkel's Bakery
Chicago, IL 800-822-8817
Main Street Gourmet
Cuyahoga Falls, OH 800-533-6246

Chocolate Chip Cookies

Christie Cookie Company
Nashville, TN 615-242-3817
Confection Solutions
Sylmar, CA 800-284-2422
Country Choice Naturals
Eden Prairie, MN 952-829-8824
Dinkel's Bakery
Chicago, IL 800-822-8817
Erba Food Products
Brooklyn, NY 718-272-7700
Main Street Gourmet
Cuyahoga Falls, OH 800-533-6246
Main Street's Cambritt Cookies
Cuyahoga Falls, OH 800-533-6246
Mississippi Cheese StrawFactory
Yazoo City, MS 800-530-7496
Murray Biscuit Company
Atlanta, GA 800-745-5582
Peggy Lawton Kitchens
East Walpole, MA 800-843-7325
Sunset Specialty Foods
Sunset Beach, CA 562-592-4976

Cookies

A La Carte
Chicago, IL 800-722-2370
A&M Cookie Company Canada
Kitchener, ON 800-265-6508
Abraham's Natural Foods
Long Branch, NJ 800-327-9903

Alessi Bakery
Tampa, FL . . . 813-879-4544
All Wrapped Up
Plantation, FL . . . 800-891-2194
Almondina®/YZ Enterprises, Inc.
Maumee, OH. . . . 800-736-8779
Ambassador Foods
Van Nuys, CA . . . 800-338-3369
American Brittle
Sandusky, OH . . . 800-274-8853
Ames International
Fife, WA . . . 888-469-2637
Andre-Boudin Bakeries
San Francisco, CA . . . 415-882-1849
Angel's Bakeries
Brooklyn, NY . . . 718-389-1400
ARA Food Corporation
Miami, FL . . . 800-533-8831
Archway & Mother's Cookie Company
Oakland, CA . . . 800-369-3997
Archway Cookies
Ashland, OH . . . 888-427-2492
Arcor USA
Miami, FL . . . 800-572-7267
Arturo's Bakery
Waterbury, CT . . . 203-754-3056
Atlas Biscuit Company
Verona, NJ . . . 973-239-8300
Aunt Gussie Cookies & Crackers
Garfield, NJ . . . 800-422-6654
Austin Special Foods Company
Austin, TX . . . 866-372-8663
Authentic Marotti Biscotti
Lewisville, TX . . . 972-221-7295
Bake Crafters Food
Collegedale, TN . . . 800-296-8935
BakeMark Canada
Laval, QC . . . 800-361-4998
Bakemark Ingredients Canada
Richmond, BC . . . 800-665-9441
BakeMark USA
Schaumburg, IL . . . 562-949-1054
Baker & Baker
Schaumburg, IL . . . 800-593-5777
Baker & Baker, Inc.
Schaumburg, IL . . . 800-593-5777
Baker Boy Bake Shop
Dickinson, ND . . . 800-437-2008

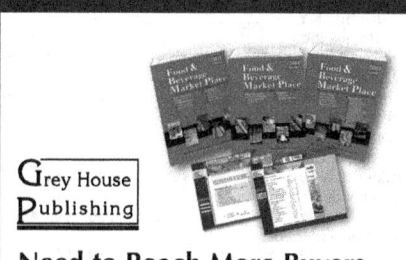

Bakers Breakfast Cookie
Bellingham, WA . . . 877-889-1090
Barbara's Bakery
Petaluma, CA . . . 707-765-2273
Berkshire Mountain Bakery
Housatonic, MA . . . 866-274-6124
Best Maid Cookie Company
River Falls, WI . . . 888-444-0322
Beth's Fine Desserts
Mill Valley, CA . . . 415-464-1891
Betty Lou's Golden Smackers
McMinnville, OR . . . 800-242-5205
Big Fatty's Flaming Foods
Valley View, TX . . . 888-248-6332
Big Island Candies
Hilo, HI . . . 800-935-5510
Big Shoulders Baking
Chicago, IL . . . 800-456-9328
Bloomfield Bakers
Los Alamitos, CA . . . 800-594-4111
Blue Chip Group
Salt Lake City, UT . . . 800-878-0099
Boca Foods Company
Madison, WI . . . 608-285-3311
Borden's Bread
Regina, SK . . . 306-525-3341
Borinquen Biscuit Corporation
Yauco, PR . . . 787-856-3030
Boston America Corporation
Woburn, MA . . . 617-923-1111
Botanical Bakery, LLC
Napa, CA . . . 707-344-8103
BP Gourmet
Hauppauge, NY . . . 631-234-5200
Breakfast at Brennan's
New Orleans, LA . . . 800-888-9932
Bremner Company
Poteau, OK . . . 918-647-8630
Brent & Sam's Cookies
N Little Rock, AR . . . 800-825-1613
Brooklyn Baking Company
Waterbury, CT . . . 203-574-9198
Brownie Baker
Fresno, CA . . . 800-598-6501
Buckeye Pretzel Company
Williamsport, PA . . . 800-257-6029
Buon Italia Misono Food Ltd.
New York, NY . . . 212-633-9090
Busken Bakery
Cincinnati, OH . . . 513-871-5330
Byrd Cookie Company
Savannah, GA . . . 800-291-2973
Carolina Cookie Company
Greensboro, NC . . . 800-447-5797
Carolina Cupboard
Hillsborough, NC . . . 800-400-3441
Cascade Cookie Company
St Louis, MO . . . 314-877-7000
Case Side Holdings Company
Kensington, PE . . . 902-836-4214
CGI Desserts
Sugar Land, TX . . . 281-240-1200
Charlie's Specialties
Hermitage, PA . . . 724-346-2350
Chatila's Bakery
Salem, NH . . . 603-898-5459
Chelsea Market Baskets
New York, NY . . . 888-727-7887
Chocoholics Divine Desserts
Linden, CA . . . 800-760-2462
Chocolate Chix
Waxahachie, TX . . . 214-744-2442
Chocolate Moon
Asheville, NC . . . 800-723-1236
Chocolates a La Carte
Valencia, CA . . . 800-818-2462
Christie Cookie Company
Nashville, TN . . . 615-242-3817
Clarmil Manufacturing Corporation
Hayward, CA . . . 888-252-7645
Columbus Bakery
Columbus, OH . . . 614-645-2275
Columbus Gourmet
Columbus, GA . . . 800-356-1858
Confection Solutions
Sylmar, CA . . . 800-284-2422
Consolidated Biscuit Company
Mc Comb, OH . . . 800-537-9544
Cookie Specialties
Wheeling, IL . . . 847-537-3888
Cookie Tree Bakeries
Salt Lake City, UT . . . 800-998-0111

Cookietree Bakeries
Salt Lake City, UT . . . 800-998-0111
Cooperstown Cookie Company
Cooperstown, NY . . . 888-269-7315
Country Choice Naturals
Eden Prairie, MN . . . 952-829-8824
Country Home Bakers
Torrance, CA . . . 800-989-9534
Cuisinary Fine Foods
Irving, TX . . . 888-283-5303
Cybros
Waukesha, WI . . . 800-876-2253
Dainty Confections
Windsor, ON . . . 800-268-0222
Dairy State Foods
Milwaukee, WI . . . 800-435-4499
Dancing Deer Baking Company
Boston, MA . . . 888-699-3337
Dangold
Flushing, NY . . . 718-591-5286
Dare Foods
Toronto, ON . . . 416-878-0253
Dare Foods
Kitchener, ON . . . 800-265-8225
Dare Foods
Spartanburg, NC . . . 800-668-3273
Dare Foods Incorporated
Kitchener, ON . . . 800-668-3273
Dave's Bakery
Honesdale, PA . . . 570-253-1660
Davis Cookie Company
Rimersburg, PA . . . 814-473-3125
Dayhoff
Clearwater, FL . . . 800-354-3372
De Beukelaer Corporation
Madison, MS . . . 601-856-7454
DF Stauffer Biscuit Company
York, PA . . . 800-673-2473
Di Camillo Bakery
Niagara Falls, NY . . . 800-634-4363
Diamond Bakery Company
Honolulu, HI . . . 808-847-3551
Dinkel's Bakery
Chicago, IL . . . 800-822-8817
Dong Kee Company
Chicago, IL . . . 312-225-6340
Donsuemor Madeleines
Alameda, CA . . . 888-420-4441
Dufflet Pastries
Toronto, ON . . . 416-536-9640
Dunford Bakers
Fayetteville, AR . . . 479-521-3000
Dutchess Bakery
Charleston, WV . . . 304-346-4237
Edelweiss Patisserie
Charlestown, MA . . . 617-628-0225
El Segundo Bakery
El Segundo, CA . . . 310-322-3422
Eleni's Cookies
New York, NY . . . 212-255-6804
Elite Bakery
Rochester, NY . . . 877-791-7376
Elliott Bay Baking Co.
Seattle, WA . . . 206-762-7690
Ellison Bakery
Fort Wayne, IN . . . 800-711-8091
Elmwood Pastry
West Hartford, CT . . . 860-233-2029
Ener-G Foods
Seattle, WA . . . 800-331-5222
Enjoy Life Foods
Schiller Park, IL . . . 888-503-6569
Erba Food Products
Brooklyn, NY . . . 718-272-7700
Ethnic Edibles
New York, NY . . . 718-320-0147
Evans Bakery
Cozad, NE . . . 800-222-5641
Falcone's Cookieland
Brooklyn, NY . . . 718-236-4200
Fantasy Cookie Company
Sylmar, CA . . . 800-354-4488
Fantis Foods
Carlstadt, NJ . . . 201-933-6200
Fauchon
New York, NY . . . 877-605-0130
Federal Pretzel Baking Company
Philadelphia, PA . . . 215-467-0505
Fernando C Pujals & Bros
Guaynabo, PR . . . 787-792-3080
Ferrara Bakery & Cafe
New York, NY . . . 212-226-6150

Firefly Fandango
Seattle, WA 206-760-3700
Fireside Kitchen
Halifax, NS 902-454-7387
Flathau's Fine Foods
Hattiesburg, MS 888-263-1299
FNI Group LLC
Sherborn, MA 508-655-4175
Food Mill
Oakland, CA 510-482-3848
Fortella Fortune Cookies
Chicago, IL 312-567-9000
Fortunate Cookie
Stowe, VT 866-266-5337
Fortune Cookie Factory
Oakland, CA 510-832-5552
Foxtail Foods
Fairfield, OH 800-487-2253
Frankly Natural Bakers
San Diego, CA 800-727-7229
Frookie
Des Plaines, IL 847-699-3200
Fujiya
Honolulu, HI 808-845-2921
GH Bent Company
Milton, MA 617-698-5945
Giant Food
Lanham, MD 888-469-4426
Gladder's Gourmet Cookies
Lockhart, TX 888-398-4523
Glazier Packing Company
Potsdam, NY 315-265-2500
Glennys
Freeport, NY 888-864-1243
Glutino
Laval, QC 800-363-3438
Golden Glow Cookie Company
Bronx, NY 718-379-6223
Golden Walnut Specialty Foods
Zion, IL 800-843-3645
Golden West Specialty Foods
Brisbane, CA 800-584-4481
Good Health Natural Foods
Northport, NY 631-261-2111
Gourmet Treats
Torrance, CA 800-444-9549
Grand Avenue Chocolates
Concord, CA 877-934-1800
Grandma Beth's Cookies
Alliance, NE 308-762-8433
Greyston Bakery
Yonkers, NY 800-289-2253
GWB Foods Corporation
Brooklyn, NY 877-977-7610
H.B. Trading
Totowa, NJ 973-812-1022
H.E. Butt Grocery Company
San Antonio, TX 800-432-3113
Haby's Alsatian Bakery
Castroville, TX 830-931-2118
Handy Pax
Randolph, MA 781-963-8300
Harvest Valley Bakery
La Salle, IL 815-224-9030
Hawaii Candy
Honolulu, HI 808-836-8955
Hawaiian King Candies
Honolulu, HI 800-570-1902
Health Valley Company
Irwindale, CA 800-334-3204
Heaven Scent Natural Foods
Santa Monica, CA 310-829-9050
Heavenscent Edibles
New York, NY 212-369-0310
Hedgehaven Specialty Foods
Ilwaco, WA 360-642-4700
Heinemann's Bakeries
Palatine, IL 847-358-3501
Heitzman Bakery
Louisville, KY 502-452-1891
HempNut
Henderson, NV 707-576-7050
Heritage Shortbread
Hilton Head Island, SC 843-342-7268
Hershey International
Weston, FL 954-385-2600
Heyerly Bakery
Ossian, IN 260-622-4196
Holt's Bakery
Douglas, GA 912-384-2202
Holton Food Products Company
La Grange, IL 708-352-5599

Honey Rose Baking Company
Carlsbad, CA
Hop Kee
Chicago, IL 312-791-9111
Hunt Country Foods
Middleburg, VA 540-364-2622
Immaculate Baking Company
Wakefield, MA 888-826-6567
Immaculate Consumption
Flat Rock, NC 888-826-6567
Indianola Pecan House, Inc./Wheeler's Gourmet Pecans
Indianola, MS 800-541-6252
Innovative Health Products
Largo, FL 800-654-2347
Interbake Foods Corporate Office
Richmond, VA 804-755-7107
Irresistible Cookie Jar
Hayden Lake, ID 208-664-1261
Iversen Baking Company
Bedminster, PA 215-636-5904
J&J Snack Foods Corporation
Vernon, CA 800-486-7622
J&J Snack Foods Corporation
Pennsauken, NJ 800-486-9533
Jaeger Bakery
Milwaukee, WI 414-263-1700
Jamae Natural Foods
Los Angeles, CA 800-343-0052
JFC International Inc.
Commerce, CA 323-721-6100
Jimmy's Cookies
Fair Lawn, NJ 201-797-8900
Joey's Fine Foods
Newark, NJ 973-482-1400
Joseph's Lite Cookies
Deming, NM 575-546-2839
JSL Foods
Los Angeles, CA 800-745-3236
Jubelt Variety Bakeries
Mount Olive, IL 217-999-5231
Just Desserts
San Francisco, CA 415-602-9245
K&F Select Fine Coffees
Portland, OR 800-558-7788
Karen's Fabulous Biscotti
White Plains, NY 914-682-2165
Kauai Kookie Kompany
Eleele, HI 800-361-1126
Keebler Company
Battlecreek, MI 630-956-9742
Keebler Company
South River, NJ 732-613-4381
Kellogg Food Away From Home
Elmhurst, IL 877-511-5777
Kelsen, Inc.
Melville, NY 888-253-5736
Kemach Food Products Corporation
Brooklyn, NY 888-453-6224
Kid's Kookie Company
San Clemente, CA 800-350-7577
Kollar Cookies
Long Branch, NJ 732-229-3364
Kraft Foods
East Hanover, NJ 973-503-2000
La Boulangerie
San Diego, CA 858-578-4040
Lady Walton's and Bronco Bob's Cowboy Brand Specialty Foods
Dallas, TX 800-552-8006
Lady Walton's Cookies
Dallas, TX 800-552-8006
Laguna Cookie & Dessert Company
Santa Ana, CA 800-673-2473
LaRosa's Bakery
Shrewsbury, NJ 800-527-6722
Lazzaroni USA
Saddle Brook, NJ 201-368-1240
Liberty Richter
Saddle Brook, NJ 201-291-8749
Linden Cookies
Congers, NY 800-660-5051
Little Dutch Boy Bakeries
Draper, UT 801-571-3800
Lotte USA
Battle Creek, MI 269-963-6664
Lotus Bakery
Santa Rosa, CA 800-875-6887
Lovin' Oven
Hertford, NC 888-775-0099
Ludwick's Frozen Donuts
Grand Rapids, MI 800-366-8816

Luv Yu Bakery
Louisville, KY 502-451-4511
LWC Brands Inc
Dallas, TX 800-552-8006
Mac's Donut Shop
Aliquippa, PA 724-375-6776
MacFarms of Hawaii
Captain Cook, HI 808-328-2435
Madrona Specialty Foods
Tukwila, WA 425-814-2500
Magna Foods Corporation
City of Industry, CA 800-995-4394
Main Street Gourmet
Cuyahoga Falls, OH 800-533-6246
Main Street's Cambritt Cookies
Cuyahoga Falls, OH 800-533-6246
Mamma Says
Butler, NJ 877-283-6282
Marin Food Specialties
Byron, CA 925-634-6126
Maurice Lenell Cooky Company
Chicago, IL 800-323-1760
Mayfair Sales
Buffalo, NY 800-248-2881
McDuffies Bakery
Clarence, NY 800-875-1598
McKee Foods Corporation
Collegedale, TN 423-238-7111
McTavish Company
Portland, OR 800-256-9844
Mercado Latino
City of Industry, CA 626-333-6862
Merlino Italian Baking Company
Seattle, WA 800-207-2997
Michael D's Cookies & Cakes
Aurora, IL 630-892-2525
Michael's Cookies
San Diego, CA 800-822-5384
Miss Meringue
San Marcos, CA 800-561-6516
Monaco Baking Company
Santa Fe Springs, CA 800-569-4640
Moravian Cookies Shop
Winston Salem, NC 800-274-2994
Mozzicato De Pasquale Bakery Pastry
Hartford, CT 860-296-0426
Mozzicato Depasquale Bakery & Pastry Shop
Hartford, CT 860-296-0426
Mrs. Denson's Cookie Company
Ukiah, CA 800-219-3199
Mt View Bakery
Mountain View, HI 808-968-6353
Murray Biscuit Company
Atlanta, GA 800-745-5582
My Boy's Baking LLC
Allentown, 3A 610-759-4552
Nabisco
Parsippany, NJ 973-682-5000
Natural Nectar
Huntington, NY 631-367-7280
Nikki's Cookies
Milwaukee, WI 800-776-7107
Northwest Candy Emporium
Everett, WA 800-404-7266
Notre Dame Bakery
Conception Harbour, NL 709-535-2738
Nustef Foods
Mississauga, ON 905-896-3060
Nutrilicious Natural Bakery
Countryside, IL 800-835-8097
Oak State Products
Wenona, IL 815-853-4348
Oh, Sugar! LLC
Roswell, GA 866-557-8427
Old Colony Baking Company
Spring Valley, IL 815- 44- 211
Olde Colony Bakery
Mt Pleasant, SC 800-722-9932
Original Ya-hoo! Baking Company
Sherman, TX 800-575-9373
Otis Spunkmeyer Company
Norcross, GA 800-438-9251
Our Cookie
Miami, FL 877-885-2715
Our Thyme Garden
Cleburne, TX 800-482-4372
Pamela's Products
Ukiah, CA 707-462-6605
Parco Foods
Blue Island, IL 708-371-9200
Paris Pastry
Van Nuys, CA 310-474-8888

Partners, A Tastful Cracker
Seattle, WA 800-632-7477
Pati-Petite Cookies
Bridgeville, PA 800-253-5805
Peggy Lawton Kitchens
East Walpole, MA 800-843-7325
Peking Noodle Company
Los Angeles, CA 323-223-2023
PepsiCo Chicago
Chicago, IL 312-821-1000
Petri Baking Products Inc
Silver Creek, NY 800-346-1981
Plehn's Bakery
Louisville, KY 502-896-4438
Poppie's Dough
Chicago, IL 888-767-7431
Positively Third Street Bakery
Duluth, MN 218-724-8619
Pure's Food Specialties
Broadview, IL 708-344-8884
Quaker Bonnet
Buffalo, NY 800-283-2447
Quality Naturally! Foods
City of Industry, CA 888-498-6986
R.W. Frookies
Sag Harbor, NY 800-913-3663
Ralcorp Holdings
St Louis, MO 800-772-6757
Real Cookies
Merrick, NY 800-822-5113
Redi-Froze
South Bend, IN 574-237-5111
Rene Rey Chocolates Ltd
North Vancouver, BC 888-985-0949
Rich Products Corporation
Buffalo, NY 800-356-7094
Rich Products Corporation
Buffalo, NY 800-828-2021
Richmond Baking Company
Richmond, IN 765-962-8535
Ryke's Bakery
Muskegon, MI 231-722-3508
Sacramento Cookie Factory
Sacramento, CA 877-877-2646
Saint Amour/Powerline Foods
Costa Mesa, CA 714-754-1900

Salem Baking Company
Winston Salem, NC 800-274-2994
San Anselmo's Cookies & Biscotti
San Anselmo, CA 800-229-1249
Sanitary Bakery
Little Falls, MN 320-632-6388
Santa Fe Bite-Size Bakery
Albuquerque, NM 505-342-1119
Sara Lee Corporation
Downers Grove, IL 630-598-8100
Sarabeth's Kitchen
Bronx, NY 718-589-2900
Sarabeth's Kitchen
Bronx, NY 800-773-7378
Schulze & Burch Biscuit Company
Chicago, IL 773-927-6622
Scialo Brothers
Providence, RI 877-421-0986
Selma's Cookies
Apopka, FL 800-922-6654
Shepherdsfield Bakery
Fulton, MO 573-642-1439
Sherwood Brands
Rockville, MD 301-309-6161
Sherwood Brands
Rockville, MD 401-434-7773
Sheryl's Chocolate Creations
Hicksville, NY 888-882-2462
Shur-Good Biscuit Co.
Cincinnati, OH 513-458-6200
Silver Lake Cookie Company
Islip, NY 631-581-4000
Silver Tray Cookies
Fort Lauderdale, FL 305-883-0800
Simply Gourmet Confections
Irvine, CA 714-505-3955
Sister's Gourmet
Dacula, GA 877-338-1388
Skipping Stone Productions
Paso Robles, CA 805-226-2998
Smoak's Bakery & Catering Service
Augusta, GA 706-738-1792
Snyder's-Lance Inc.
Charlotte, NC 800-438-1880
Somerset Industries
Spring House, PA 800-883-8728

Sorbee Intl.
Feasterville Trevose, PA 800-654-3997
Southernfood Specialties
Atlanta, GA 800-255-5323
Spilke's Baking Company
Brooklyn, NY 718-384-2150
Sporting Colors LLC
St. Louis, MO 888-394-2292
Spruce Foods
San Clemente, CA 800-326-3612
Sprucewood Handmade Cookie Company
Warkworth, ON 877-632-1300
St. Cloud Bakery
Saint Cloud, MN 320-251-8055
Stauffer Biscuit Company
York, PA 800-673-2473
Stauffer's
Cuba, NY 585-968-2700
Stella D'Oro Biscuit Company
Valhalla, NY 800-995-2623
Sterling Foods
San Antonio, TX 210-490-1669
Steve's Mom
Bronx, NY 800-362-4545
Stroehmann Bakeries
Norristown, PA 800-984-0989
Sugar Kake Cookie
Tonawanda, NY 800-775-5180
Sunset Specialty Foods
Sunset Beach, CA 562-592-4976
Table De France
Ontario, CA 909-923-5205
Taste of Nature
Beverly Hills, CA 310-396-4433
Tastykake
Philadelphia, PA 215-221-8500
Tate's Bake Shop
Southampton, NY 631-283-9830
Tea Aura
Toronto, ON 416-225-8868
The Bama Company
Tulsa, OK 800-756-2262
Todd's
Vernon, CA 800-938-6337
Torn Ranch
Novato, CA 415-506-3000

Touche Bakery
London, ON 518-455-0044
Traverse Bay Confections
Woodinville, WA
Turkey Hill Sugarbush
Waterloo, QC 450-539-4822
Turnbull Bakeries
Chattanooga, TN....................800-488-7628
Uncle Ralph's Cookie Company
Frederick, MD....................800-422-0626
United Noodle Manufacturing Company
Salt Lake City, UT 801-485-0951
Upper Crust Baking Company
Pismo Beach, CA 800-676-1691
Uptown Bakers
Hyattsville, MD 301-864-1500
V L Foods
White Plains, NY 914-697-4851
Valley Bakery
Rock Valley, IA....................712-476-5386
Vickey's Vittles
North Hills, CA....................818-841-1944
Vie de France Bakery
Bensenville, IL 630-595-9521
Vista Bakery
Burlington, IA....................800-553-2343
Voortman Cookies
Burlington, ON....................905-335-9500
Voortman Cookies
Bloomington, CA 909-877-8471
Walkers Shortbread
Hauppauge, NY 800-521-0141
Wenger's Bakery
Reading, PA 610-372-6545
Westbrae Natural Foods
Melville, NY....................800-434-4246
Wildlife Cookie Company
Saint Charles, IL....................630-377-6196
Willmar Cookie & Nut Company
Willmar, MN....................320-235-0600
Wonton Food
Brooklyn, NY 800-776-8889
Yohay Baking Company
Lindenhurst, NY....................631-225-0300
Young's Bakery
Uniontown, PA 724-437-6361
Yrica's Rugelach & Baking Company
Brooklyn, NY 718-965-3657
YZ Enterprises
Maumee, OH....................800-736-8779
Zazi Baking Company
Petaluma, CA 707-778-1635
Zeppys Bakery
Lawrence, MA 781-963-7022

Cookies & Biscuits

A&M Cookie Company Canada
Kitchener, ON....................800-265-6508
Almondina®/YZ Enterprises, Inc.
Maumee, OH....................800-736-8779
American Brittle
Sandusky, OH 800-274-8853
Ames International
Fife, WA 888-469-2637
ARA Food Corporation
Miami, FL....................800-533-8831
Archway & Mother's Cookie Company
Oakland, CA 800-369-3997
Archway Cookies
Ashland, OH 888-427-2492
Arcor USA
Miami, FL....................800-572-7267
Arturo's Bakery
Waterbury, CT....................203-754-3056
Atlas Biscuit Company
Verona, NJ....................973-239-8300
Aunt Gussie Cookies & Crackers
Garfield, NJ....................800-422-6654
Barbara's Bakery
Petaluma, CA 707-765-2273
Best Maid Cookie Company
River Falls, WI 888-444-0322
Betty Lou's Golden Smackers
McMinnville, OR 800-242-5205
Blue Chip Group
Salt Lake City, UT 800-878-0099
Blue Dog Bakery
Seattle, WA 888-749-7229
Boca Foods Company
Madison, WI 608-285-3311
Borden's Bread
Regina, SK 306-525-3341
Borinquen Biscuit Corporation
Yauco, PR 787-856-3030
Breakfast at Brennan's
New Orleans, LA 800-888-9932
Bremner Biscuit Company
Denver, CO 800-722-1871
Bremner Company
Poteau, OK 918-647-8630
Brooklyn Baking Company
Waterbury, CT....................203-574-9198
Buckeye Pretzel Company
Williamsport, PA....................800-257-6029
Buon Italia Misono Food Ltd.
New York, NY 212-633-9090
Busken Bakery
Cincinnati, OH 513-871-5330
Cains Foods LP/Olde CapeCod
Ayer, MA....................651-698-6832
Carolina Cupboard
Hillsborough, NC 800-400-3441
Cascade Cookie Company
St Louis, MO....................314-877-7000
Case Side Holdings Company
Kensington, PE 902-836-4214
CGI Desserts
Sugar Land, TX....................281-240-1200
Charlie's Specialties
Hermitage, PA....................724-346-2350
Chelsea Market Baskets
New York, NY 888-727-7887
Chocolate Chix
Waxahachie, TX 214-744-2442
Columbus Bakery
Columbus, OH 614-645-2275
Confection Solutions
Sylmar, CA 800-284-2422
Consolidated Biscuit Company
Mc Comb, OH....................800-537-9544
Cookie Specialties
Wheeling, IL....................847-537-3888
Cookie Tree Bakeries
Salt Lake City, UT....................800-998-0111
Country Home Bakers
Torrance, CA....................800-989-9534
Dairy State Foods
Milwaukee, WI 800-435-4499
Dancing Deer Baking Company
Boston, MA....................888-699-3337
Dare Foods
Toronto, ON 416-878-0253
Dare Foods
Kitchener, ON....................800-265-8225
Dave's Bakery
Honesdale, PA....................570-253-1660
Davis Cookie Company
Rimersburg, PA....................814-473-3125
De Bas Chocolatier
Fresno, CA 559-294-7638
De Beukelaer Corporation
Madison, MS....................601-856-7454
DF Stauffer Biscuit Company
York, PA 800-673-2473
Di Camillo Bakery
Niagara Falls, NY....................800-634-4363
Diamond Bakery Company
Honolulu, HI....................808-847-3551
Dinkel's Bakery
Chicago, IL 800-822-8817
Dong Kee Company
Chicago, IL 312-225-6340
Dough Works Company
Horicon, WI 800-383-8808
Dufflet Pastries
Toronto, ON 416-536-9640
Dunford Bakers
Fayetteville, AR 479-521-3000
Dutchess Bakery
Charleston, WV 304-346-4237
Edelweiss Patisserie
Charlestown, MA 617-628-0225
Edward & Sons Trading Company
Carpinteria, CA....................805-684-8500
El Segundo Bakery
El Segundo, CA 310-322-3422
Elmwood Pastry
West Hartford, CT....................860-233-2029
Erba Food Products
Brooklyn, NY 718-272-7700
Evans Bakery
Cozad, NE....................800-222-5641
Falcone's Cookieland
Brooklyn, NY 718-236-4200
Fantasy Cookie Company
Sylmar, CA 800-354-4488
Federal Pretzel Baking Company
Philadelphia, PA 215-467-0505
Fernando C Pujals & Bros
Guaynabo, PR....................787-792-3080
Ferrara Bakery & Cafe
New York, NY 212-226-6150
Fireside Kitchen
Halifax, NS 902-454-7387
Food Mill
Oakland, CA 510-482-3848
Fortella Fortune Cookies
Chicago, IL 312-567-9000
Fortune Cookie Factory
Oakland, CA 510-832-5552
Foxtail Foods
Fairfield, OH....................800-487-2253
Frankly Natural Bakers
San Diego, CA 800-727-7229
Fujiya
Honolulu, HI....................808-845-2921
GH Bent Company
Milton, MA 617-698-5945
Giant Food
Lanham, MD....................888-469-4426
Glazier Packing Company
Potsdam, NY 315-265-2500
Golden Glow Cookie Company
Bronx, NY....................718-379-6223
Grandma Beth's Cookies
Alliance, NE 308-762-8433
Granowska's
Toronto, ON 416-533-7755
Greyston Bakery
Yonkers, NY 800-289-2253
GWB Foods Corporation
Brooklyn, NY 877-977-7610
H.E. Butt Grocery Company
San Antonio, TX....................800-432-3113
Hain Celestial Group
Melville, NY....................800-434-4246
Handy Pax
Randolph, MA 781-963-8300
Harvest Valley Bakery
La Salle, IL 815-224-9030
Hawaii Candy
Honolulu, HI....................808-836-8955
Health Valley Company
Irwindale, CA 800-334-3204
Hedgehaven Specialty Foods
Ilwaco, WA 360-642-4700
Heinemann's Bakeries
Palatine, IL 847-358-3501
Hershey International
Weston, FL 954-385-2600
Heyerly Bakery
Ossian, IN 260-622-4196
Holt's Bakery
Douglas, GA 912-384-2202
Honey Rose Baking Company
Carlsbad, CA
Hunt Country Foods
Middleburg, VA 540-364-2622
Hye Quality Bakery
Fresno, CA 877-445-1778
Immaculate Consumption
Flat Rock, NC....................888-826-6567
Innovative Health Products
Largo, FL 800-654-2347
Interbake Foods Corporate Office
Richmond, VA....................804-755-7107
Irresistible Cookie Jar
Hayden Lake, ID....................208-664-1261
Iversen Baking Company
Bedminster, PA 215-636-5904
J&J Snack Foods Corporation
Vernon, CA 800-486-7622
J&J Snack Foods Corporation
Pennsauken, NJ....................800-486-9533
Jaeger Bakery
Milwaukee, WI 414-263-1700
Jamae Natural Foods
Los Angeles, CA....................800-343-0052
James Candy Company
Atlantic City, NJ 800-938-2339
JFC International Inc.
Commerce, CA 323-721-6100
Jim's Cheese Pantry
Waterloo, WI....................800-345-3571

Jimmy's Cookies
Fair Lawn, NJ 201-797-8900
Joey's Fine Foods
Newark, NJ 973-482-1400
Jubelt Variety Bakeries
Mount Olive, IL 217-999-5231
Just Desserts
San Francisco, CA 415-602-9245
Keebler Company
Battlecreek, MI 630-956-9742
Keebler Company
South River, NJ. 732-613-4381
Kemach Food Products Corporation
Brooklyn, NY 888-453-6224
KHS-Bartelt
Sarasota, FL 800-829-9980
Kid's Kookie Company
San Clemente, CA. 800-350-7577
Kinnikinnick Foods
Edmonton, AB 877-503-4466
Kollar Cookies
Long Branch, NJ. 732-229-3364
Koyo Foods
Richmond, CA 510-527-7066
Kraft Foods
Atlanta, GA. 404-756-6000
Kraft Foods
East Hanover, NJ 973-503-2000
La Boulangerie
San Diego, CA 858-578-4040
Lady Walton's and Bronco Bob's Cowboy Brand Specialty Foods
Dallas, TX. 800-552-8006
Lady Walton's Cookies
Dallas, TX. 800-552-8006
Laguna Cookie & Dessert Company
Santa Ana, CA 800-673-2473
LaRosa's Bakery
Shrewsbury, NJ. 800-527-6722
Liberty Richter
Saddle Brook, NJ 201-291-8749
Linden Cookies
Congers, NY 800-660-5051
Little Dutch Boy Bakeries
Draper, UT 801-571-3800
Log House Foods
Plymouth, MN. 763-546-8395
Lotus Bakery
Santa Rosa, CA. 800-875-6887
Ludwick's Frozen Donuts
Grand Rapids, MI 800-366-8816
Mac's Donut Shop
Aliquippa, PA 724-375-6776
MacFarms of Hawaii
Captain Cook, HI 808-328-2435
Magna Foods Corporation
City of Industry, CA 800-995-4394
Marin Food Specialties
Byron, CA. 925-634-6126
Marshall Biscuits
Saraland, AL. 251-679-6226
Maurice Lenell Cooky Company
Chicago, IL 800-323-1760
Mercado Latino
City of Industry, CA 626-333-6862
Merlino Italian Baking Company
Seattle, WA 800-207-2997
Michael D's Cookies & Cakes
Aurora, IL 630-892-2525
Mom's Food Company
South El Monte, CA 800-969-6667
Mozzicato De Pasquale Bakery Pastry
Hartford, CT 860-296-0426
Mozzicato Depasquale Bakery & Pastry Shop
Hartford, CT 860-296-0426
Mt View Bakery
Mountain View, HI 808-968-6353
Murray Biscuit Company
Atlanta, GA. 800-745-5582
Nabisco
Parsippany, NJ. 973-682-5000
Nicole's Divine Crackers
Chicago, IL 312-640-8883
Nikki's Cookies
Milwaukee, WI 800-776-7107
Northwest Candy Emporium
Everett, WA. 800-404-7266
Notre Dame Bakery
Conception Harbour, NL 709-535-2738
Nustef Foods
Mississauga, ON. 905-896-3060
Nutrilicious Natural Bakery
Countryside, IL 800-835-8097
Oak State Products
Wenona, IL 815-853-4348
Ohta Wafer Factory
Honolulu, HI. 808-949-2775
Original Ya-hoo! Baking Company
Sherman, TX. 800-575-9373
Our Thyme Garden
Cleburne, TX 800-482-4372
Parco Foods
Blue Island, IL 708-371-9200
Paris Pastry
Van Nuys, CA 310-474-8888
Pati-Petite Cookies
Bridgeville, PA 800-253-5805
Peggy Lawton Kitchens
East Walpole, MA. 800-843-7325
Peking Noodle Company
Los Angeles, CA. 323-223-2023
Petri Baking Products Inc
Silver Creek, NY. 800-346-1981
Pioneer Frozen Foods
Duncanville, TX 972-298-4281
Positively Third Street Bakery
Duluth, MN. 218-724-8619
Pure's Food Specialties
Broadview, IL 708-344-8884
Purity Factories
St.John's, NL. 800-563-3411
R.M. Palmer Company
Reading, PA 610-372-8971
R.W. Frookies
Sag Harbor, NY. 800-913-3663
Ralcorp Holdings
St Louis, MO. 800-772-6757
Rich Products Corporation
Buffalo, NY. 800-356-7094
Rich Products Corporation
Buffalo, NY. 800-828-2021
Richmond Baking Company
Richmond, IN 765-962-8535
Rovira Biscuit Corporation
Ponce, PR 787-844-8585
Royal Wine Corp
Bayonne, NJ 718-384-2400
Ryke's Bakery
Muskegon, MI. 231-722-3508
S&M Communion Bread Company
Nashville, TN 615-292-1969
Saint Amour/Powerline Foods
Costa Mesa, CA 714-754-1900
Salem Baking Company
Winston Salem, NC. 800-274-2994
San Anselmo's Cookies & Biscotti
San Anselmo, CA 800-229-1249
San-J International, Inc
Richmond, VA. 800-446-5500
Sanitary Bakery
Little Falls, MN. 320-632-6388
Santa Fe Bite-Size Bakery
Albuquerque, NM 505-342-1119
Sara Lee Corporation
Downers Grove, IL. 630-598-8100
Schulze & Burch Biscuit Company
Chicago, IL 773-927-6622
Scialo Brothers
Providence, RI 877-421-0986
Sherwood Brands
Rockville, MD 401-434-7773
Sheryl's Chocolate Creations
Hicksville, NY 888-882-2462
Silver Tray Cookies
Fort Lauderdale, FL 305-883-0800
Smoak's Bakery & Catering Service
Augusta, GA 706-738-1792
Snyder's-Lance Inc.
Charlotte, NC 800-438-1880
Spilke's Baking Company
Brooklyn, NY 718-384-2150
Sporting Colors LLC
St. Louis, MO 888-394-2292
St. Cloud Bakery
Saint Cloud, MN. 320-251-8055
Stauffer's
Cuba, NY 585-968-2700
Stella D'Oro Biscuit Company
Valhalla, NY 800-995-2623
Stroehmann Bakeries
Norristown, PA 800-984-0989
Sugar Kake Cookie
Tonawanda, NY 800-775-5180
Sunset Specialty Foods
Sunset Beach, CA 562-592-4976
Table De France
Ontario, CA. 909-923-5205
Tastykake
Philadelphia, PA 215-221-8500
Terra Harvest Foods
Rockford, IL 815-636-9500
The Bama Company
Tulsa, OK 800-756-2262
Treasure Foods
West Valley, UT. 801-974-0911
Triple-C
Hamilton, ON 800-263-9105
Turano Pastry Shops
Bloomingdale, IL 630-529-6161
Turnbull Cone Baking Company
Chattanooga, TN. 423-265-4551
Tuscan Bakery
Portland, OR 800-887-2261
Ultimate Biscotti
Eugene, OR. 541-344-8220
Uncle Ralph's Cookie Company
Frederick, MD. 800-422-0626
United Noodle Manufacturing Company
Salt Lake City, UT 801-485-0951
Upper Crust Baking Company
Pismo Beach, CA 800-676-1691
Uptown Bakers
Hyattsville, MD 301-864-1500
Utz Quality Foods
Hanover, PA 800-367-7629
V L Foods
White Plains, NY 914-697-4851
Venus Wafers
Hingham, MA. 800-545-4538
Vista Bakery
Burlington, IA. 800-553-2343
Voortman Cookies
Bloomington, CA 909-877-8471
Wenger's Bakery
Reading, PA 610-372-6545
Westbrae Natural Foods
Melville, NY. 800-434-4246
Willmar Cookie & Nut Company
Willmar, MN. 320-235-0600
Wise Foods
Kennesaw, GA 770-426-5821
Wonder Bread
Provo, UT 800-483-7253
Wonton Food
Brooklyn, NY 800-776-8889
Young's Bakery
Uniontown, PA 724-437-6361
Yrica's Rugelach & Baking Company
Brooklyn, NY 718-965-3657
YZ Enterprises
Maumee, OH. 800-736-8779
Zeppys Bakery
Lawrence, MA 781-963-7022

Fortune Cookies

Dong Kee Company
Chicago, IL 312-225-6340
Fortella Fortune Cookies
Chicago, IL 312-567-9000
Fortune Cookie Factory
Oakland, CA 510-832-5552
Hawaii Candy
Honolulu, HI. 808-836-8955
JFC International Inc.
Commerce, CA 323-721-6100
Ohta Wafer Factory
Honolulu, HI. 808-949-2775
Peking Noodle Company
Los Angeles, CA. 323-223-2023
United Noodle Manufacturing Company
Salt Lake City, UT 801-485-0951
Wings Foods of Alberta
Edmonton, AB 780-433-6406
Wonton Food
Brooklyn, NY 800-776-8889

Frozen Cookies

Baker & Baker, Inc.
Schaumburg, IL. 800-593-5777
Evans Bakery
Cozad, NE. 800-222-5641
Glazier Packing Company
Potsdam, NY. 315-265-2500

GWB Foods Corporation
Brooklyn, NY 877-977-7610
Parco Foods
Blue Island, IL 708-371-9200
Rich Products Corporation
Buffalo, NY. 800-356-7094
Rich Products Corporation
Buffalo, NY. 800-828-2021
Sara Lee Corporation
Downers Grove, IL 630-598-8100
Sunset Specialty Foods
Sunset Beach, CA 562-592-4976
The Bama Company
Tulsa, OK 800-756-2262

Ginger Snaps

Country Choice Naturals
Eden Prairie, MN 952-829-8824

Individually Packaged

Big Shoulders Baking
Chicago, IL 800-456-9328

Lady Fingers

Ambassador Foods
Van Nuys, CA 800-338-3369

Macaroons

Erba Food Products
Brooklyn, NY 718-272-7700
L&M Bakery
Lawrence, MA 978-687-7346
Red Mill Farms
Brooklyn, NY 800-344-2253
Steve's Mom
Bronx, NY. 800-362-4545

Mini Cookies

Bauducco Foods Inc.
Doral, FL. 305-477-9270

Oatmeal & Chocolate Chip Cookies

Main Street Gourmet
Cuyahoga Falls, OH 800-533-6246
Main Street's Cambritt Cookies
Cuyahoga Falls, OH 800-533-6246

Oatmeal Cookies

Country Choice Naturals
Eden Prairie, MN 952-829-8824
Main Street Gourmet
Cuyahoga Falls, OH 800-533-6246
Main Street's Cambritt Cookies
Cuyahoga Falls, OH 800-533-6246
Mississippi Cheese StrawFactory
Yazoo City, MS 800-530-7496
Murray Biscuit Company
Atlanta, GA 800-745-5582
Peggy Lawton Kitchens
East Walpole, MA 800-843-7325

Oatmeal Raisin Cookies

Main Street Gourmet
Cuyahoga Falls, OH 800-533-6246
Main Street's Cambritt Cookies
Cuyahoga Falls, OH 800-533-6246

Sandwich Creme Cookies

Country Choice Naturals
Eden Prairie, MN 952-829-8824
Sugar Kake Cookie
Tonawanda, NY 800-775-5180
Vista Bakery
Burlington, IA 800-553-2343

Soft Cookies

Oak State Products
Wenona, IL 815-853-4348

Sugar Cookies

Falcone's Cookieland
Brooklyn, NY 718-236-4200
Main Street Gourmet
Cuyahoga Falls, OH 800-533-6246
Main Street's Cambritt Cookies
Cuyahoga Falls, OH 800-533-6246
Murray Biscuit Company
Atlanta, GA 800-745-5582
Young's Bakery
Uniontown, PA 724-437-6361

Tea Cookies

Botanical Bakery, LLC
Napa, CA. 707-344-8103
Hawaii Candy
Honolulu, HI 808-836-8955
Ohta Wafer Factory
Honolulu, HI 808-949-2775

Wafers

Arcor USA
Miami, FL 800-572-7267
Castella Imports
Hauppauge, NY 866-227-8355
Ce De Candy
Union, NJ 800-631-7968
Dayhoff
Clearwater, FL 800-354-3372
Fernando C Pujals & Bros
Guaynabo, PR 787-792-3080
Functional Foods
Roseville, MI 877-372-0550
Gold Star Chocolate
Brooklyn, NY 718-330-0187
Honey Wafer Baking Company
Crestwood, IL 800-261-2984
Kitchen Table Bakers
Syosset, NY. 800-486-4582
Lady Walton's Cookies
Dallas, TX. 800-552-8006
Mayfair Sales
Buffalo, NY. 800-248-2881
PEZ Candy
Orange, CT 203-795-0531
Q Bell Foods
Nyack, NY 845-358-1475
Royal Wine Corp
Bayonne, NJ 718-384-2400
Sherwood Brands
Rockville, MD 301-309-6161
Snyder's-Lance Inc.
Charlotte, NC 800-438-1880
Table De France
Ontario, CA. 909-923-5205
Turnbull Bakeries
Chattanooga, TN. 800-488-7628
V L Foods
White Plains, NY 914-697-4851
Yohay Baking Company
Lindenhurst, NY 631-225-0300

Sugar

Abitec Corporation
Columbus, OH 800-555-1255
ADM Cocoa
Milwaukee, WI 800-558-9958
ADM Milling Company
Shawnee Mission, KS. 913-491-9400
Alfred L. Wolff, Inc.
Park Ridge, IL. 847-759-8888
American Culinary GardenNoble Communications Co
Springfield, MO 888-831-2433
Annie's Frozen Yogurt
Minneapolis, MN 800-969-9648
Aunt Aggie De's Pralines
Sinton, TX. 888-772-5463
BakeMark Canada
Laval, QC 800-361-4998
Bakery Crafts
West Chester, OH 800-543-1673
Barry Callebaut USA, Inc.
Pennsauken, NJ. 800-836-2626
Bouchard Family Farm
Fort Kent, ME. 800-239-3237
Brookside Foods
Abbotsford, BC. 877-793-3866
Calico Cottage
Amityville, NY 800-645-5345
California Cereal Products
Oakland, CA 510-452-4500
Canada Bread
Etobicoke, ON 416-926-2000
Cargill Flour Milling
Minneapolis, MN 800-227-4455
Chelsea Milling Company
Chelsea, MI. 734-475-1361
Country Choice Naturals
Eden Prairie, MN 952-829-8824
Crown Processing Company
Bellflower, CA 562-865-0293
Dutch Ann Foods Company
Natchez, MS 601-445-5566
Ellison Milling Company
Lethbridge, AB 403-328-6622
Embassy Flavours Ltd.
Brampton, ON. 800-334-3371
Flavormatic Industries
Wappingers Falls, NY
Flavtek Geneva Flavors Inc.
Beloit, WI 800-562-5880
Foley's Candies
Richmond, BC 888-236-5397
Georgia Nut Ingredients
Skokie, IL 877-674-2993
Ghirardelli Chocolate Company
San Leandro, CA. 800-877-9338
Gold Coast Ingredients
Commerce, CA 800-352-8673
Golden Foods
Commerce, CA 800-350-2462
Great Recipes Company
Beaverton, OR 800-273-2331
Gregory's Foods
Eagan, MN 800-231-4734
GWB Foods Corporation
Brooklyn, NY 877-977-7610
Ingredients, Inc.
Buffalo Grove, IL 847-419-9595
Karp's
Georgetown, MA 800-373-5277
Kerry Sweets Ingredients
Gridley, IL. 309-747-3534
La Cookie
Houston, TX 713-784-2722
Marie Callender's Gourmet Products/Goldrush Products
San Jose, CA. 800-729-5428
Martha Olson's Great Foods
Sutter Creek, CA. 800-973-3966
Mimac Glaze
Brampton, ON. 877-990-9975
Natrium Products
Cortland, NY. 800-962-4203
Ottens Flavors
Philadelphia, PA 800-523-0767
Paradise Island Foods
Nanaimo, BC. 800-889-3370
Petra International
Mississauga, ON. 800-261-7226
Pillsbury
Minneapolis, MN 800-775-4777
Produits Alimentaire
St Lambert De Lauzon, QC 800-463-1787
Purato's
Seattle, WA 206-762-5400
Riceland Foods Rice Milling Operations
Stuttgart, AR. 870-673-5500
Rich Products Corporation
Hilliard, OH. 614-771-1117
Rich Products Corporation
Cameron, WI. 715-458-4556
Royal Wine Corp
Bayonne, NJ 718-384-2400
Sanford Milling Company
Henderson, NC 252-438-4526
Southern Brown Rice
Weiner, AR 800-421-7423
Southern Style Nuts
Denison, TX 903-463-3161
Sugar Flowers Plus
Glendale, CA 800-972-2935
Tastee Fare
Buchanan, MI
Tasty Selections
Concord, ON. 905-760-2353
Teff Company
Caldwell, ID 888-822-2221
Vanco Products Company
Dorchester, MA. 617-265-3400
Westco-Bake Mark
Pico Rivera, CA 562-949-1054
Wilbur Chocolate
Lititz, PA. 800-233-0139
WILD Flavors
Cincinnati, OH 888-945-3352

Wilsonhill Farm
South Bend, IN 802-899-2154
Yorktown Baking Company
Yorktown Heights, NY 800-235-3961

Crackers

Crackers

American Vintage Wine Biscuits
Long Island City, NY 718-361-1003
Archway & Mother's Cookie Company
Oakland, CA 800-369-3997
Aunt Gussie Cookies & Crackers
Garfield, NJ 800-422-6654
Bake Crafters Food
Collegedale, TN 800-296-8935
Blue Dog Bakery
Seattle, WA 888-749-7229
Borinquen Biscuit Corporation
Yauco, PR 787-856-3030
Bremner Company
Poteau, OK 918-647-8630
Cains Foods
Ayer, MA 800-225-0601
Christie-Brown
East Hanover, NJ 973-503-4000
Columbus Bakery
Columbus, OH 614-645-2275
Confection Solutions
Sylmar, CA 800-284-2422
Dairyfood USA Inc
Blue Mounds, WI 800-236-3300
Dare Foods
Spartanburg, NC 800-668-3273
Dare Foods Incorporated
Kitchener, ON 800-668-3273
Dave's Bakery
Honesdale, PA 570-253-1660
DF Stauffer Biscuit Company
York, PA 800-673-2473
Diamond Bakery Company
Honolulu, HI 808-847-3551
Falcone's Cookieland
Brooklyn, NY 718-236-4200
Fortitude Brands LLC
Coral Gables, FL 305-661-8198
Frookie
Des Plaines, IL 847-699-3200
Glutino
Laval, QC 800-363-3438
Good Health Natural Foods
Northport, NY 631-261-2111
GWB Foods Corporation
Brooklyn, NY 877-977-7610
Handy Pax
Randolph, MA 781-963-8300
Health Valley Company
Irwindale, CA 800-334-3204
Herr Foods
Chillicothe, OH 800-523-8468
Hye Quality Bakery
Fresno, CA 877-445-1778
Interbake Foods Corporate Office
Richmond, VA 804-755-7107
Jim's Cheese Pantry
Waterloo, WI 800-345-3571
Keebler Company
Battlecreek, MI 630-956-9742
Keebler Company
South River, NJ 732-613-4381
Kemach Food Products Corporation
Brooklyn, NY 888-453-6224
KHS-Bartelt
Sarasota, FL 800-829-9980
Kraft Foods
East Hanover, NJ 973-503-2000
La Panzanella
Tukwila, WA 206-903-0500
La Piccolina
Decatur, GA 800-626-1624
Liberty Richter
Saddle Brook, NJ 201-291-8749
Linden Cookies
Congers, NY 800-660-5051
Magna Foods Corporation
City of Industry, CA 800-995-4394
Mary's Gone Crackers
Gridley, CA 888-258-1250
Murray Biscuit Company
Atlanta, GA 800-745-5582
Nabisco
Parsippany, NJ 973-682-5000
Nicole's Divine Crackers
Chicago, IL 312-640-8883
Oberweis Dairy
North Aurora, IL 888-645-5868
Partners, A Tastful Cracker
Seattle, WA 800-632-7477
Pinahs Company
Waukesha, WI 800-967-2447
R.A.B. Food Group LLC
Secaucus, NJ 201-553-1100
R.W. Garcia
San Jose, CA 408-287-4616
Ralcorp Holdings
St Louis, MO 800-772-6757
Richmond Baking Company
Richmond, IN 765-962-8535
Rovira Biscuit Corporation
Ponce, PR 787-844-8585
Royal Wine Corp
Bayonne, NJ 718-384-2400
Santa Fe Bite-Size Bakery
Albuquerque, NM 505-342-1119
Schulze & Burch Biscuit Company
Chicago, IL 773-927-6622
Snyder's-Lance Inc.
Charlotte, NC 800-438-1880
Stauffer Biscuit Company
York, PA 800-673-2473
Terra Harvest Foods
Rockford, IL 815-636-9500
The Bama Company
Tulsa, OK 800-756-2262
Urban Accents
Chicago, IL 877-872-7742
Urban Oven
Chandler, AZ 866-770-6836
Venus Wafers
Hingham, MA 800-545-4538
Vision Pack Brands
El Segundo, CA 877-477-8500
Vista Bakery
Burlington, IA 800-553-2343
Willmar Cookie & Nut Company
Willmar, MN 320-235-0600

Meal

Newly Weds Foods
Chicago, IL 800-621-7521
Richmond Baking Company
Richmond, IN 765-962-8535
Sugar Foods Corporation
New York, NY 212-753-6900

Crunches

Kerry Ingredients
Blue Earth, MN 507-526-7575

Desserts

Adams Foods
Dothan, AL 334-983-4233
AFP Advanced Food Products, LLC
Visalia, CA 559-627-2070
Aglamesis Brothers
Cincinnati, OH 513-531-5196
Agropur Cooperative Agro-Alimentaire
Granby, QC 800-363-5686
Al Gelato Bornay
Franklin Park, IL 847-455-5355
Alamance Foods/Triton Water Company
Burlington, NC 800-476-9111
Alati-Caserta Desserts
Montreal, QC 514-271-3013
Alpenrose Dairy Farms
Portland, OR 503-244-1133
AlpineAire Foods
Rocklin, CA 800-322-6325
Ambassador Foods
Van Nuys, CA 800-338-3369
Amboy Specialty Foods Company
Dixon, IL 800-892-0400
American Classic Ice Cream Company
Bay Shore, NY 631-666-1000
Andre-Boudin Bakeries
San Francisco, CA 415-882-1849
Anke Kruse Organics
Guelph, ON 519-824-6161
Ask Foods
Palmyra, PA 800-879-4275
Athens Pastries & Frozen Foods
Cleveland, OH 800-837-5683
Awrey Bakeries
Livonia, MI 800-950-2253
Baker & Baker
Schaumburg, IL 800-593-5777
Bakery Chef
Chicago, IL 773-384-1900
Bakery Corp
Miami, FL 800-521-4345
Bakery Europa
Honolulu, HI 808-845-5011
Balboa Dessert Company
Santa Ana, CA 800-974-9699
Banquet Schuster Bakery
Pueblo, CO 719-544-1062
Barnes Ice Cream Company
Manchester, ME
Baskin-Robbins Flavors
Burbank, CA 800-859-5339
BBU Bakeries
Denver, CO 303-691-6342
Beatrice Bakery Company
Beatrice, NE 800-228-4030
Bensons Bakery
Bogart, GA 800-888-6059
Bernie's Foods
Brooklyn, NY 718-417-6677
Best Maid Cookie Company
River Falls, WI 888-444-0322
Beth's Fine Desserts
Mill Valley, CA 415-464-1891
Bill Mack's Homemade Ice Cream
Dover, PA 717-292-1931
Birdsall Ice Cream Company
Mason City, IA 641-423-5365
Birkholm's Jr Danish Bakery
Solvang, CA 805-688-3872
Bittersweet Pastries
Norwood, NJ 800-217-2938
Black's Barbecue
Lockhart, TX 512-398-2712
Blue Bell Creameries
Brenham, TX 979-836-7977
Bonnie Doon Ice Cream Corporation
Elkhart, IN 574-264-3390
Borden's Bread
Regina, SK 306-525-3341
Bottineau Coop Creamery
Bottineau, ND 701-228-2216
Brighams
Arlington, MA 800-274-4426
Broughton Foods
Marietta, OH 800-283-2479
Brown's Ice Cream
Minneapolis, MN 612-378-1075
Browns Dairy
Valparaiso, IN 219-464-4141
Browns' Ice Cream Company
Bowling Green, KY 270-843-9882
Bubbies Homemade Ice Cream
Aiea, HI 808-487-7218
Buck's Spumoni Company
Milford, CT 203-874-2007
Bunny Bread Company
Cape Girardeau, MO 573-332-7349
Busken Bakery
Cincinnati, OH 513-871-5330
California Brands Flavors
Oakland, CA 800-348-0111
Calmar Bakery
Calmar, AB 780-985-3583
Cannoli Factory
Wyandanch, NY 631-643-2700
Caprine Estates
Bellbrook, OH 937-848-7406
Carbolite Foods
Evansville, IN 888-524-3314
Caribbean Food Delights
Tappan, NY 845-398-3000
Carole's Cheesecake Company
Toronto, ON 416-256-0000
Carolina Foods
Charlotte, NC 800-234-0441
Carousel Cakes
Nanuet, NY 800-659-2253
Cascadian Farm & MUIR Glen
Sedro Woolley, WA 360-855-0100
Case Side Holdings Company
Kensington, PE 902-836-4214
Cateraid
Howell, MI 800-508-8217

CBC Foods
Little River, KS 800-276-4770
Cedar Crest Specialties
Cedarburg, WI 800-877-8341
Cedarlane Natural Foods
Carson, CA 310-886-7720
Celebrity Cheesecake
Davie, FL 877-986-2253
Cemac Foods Corporation
Philadelphia, PA 800-724-0179
Centreside Dairy
Renfrew, ON 613-432-2914
CGI Desserts
Sugar Land, TX 281-240-1200
Chattanooga Bakery
Chattanooga, TN 800-251-3404
Cheesecake Aly
Glen Rock, NJ 800-555-8862
Cheesecake Etc. Desserts
Miami Springs, FL 305-887-0258
Chef Hans Gourmet Foods
Monroe, LA 800-890-4267
Chella's Dutch Delicacies
Lake Oswego, OR 800-458-3331
Chelsea Milling Company
Chelsea, MI 734-475-1361
Chewys Rugulach
San Diego, CA 800-241-3456
Chloe Foods Corporation
Brooklyn, NY 718-827-9000
Chocolaterie Bernard Callebaut
Calgary, AB 800-661-8367
Chudleigh's
Milton, ON 905-878-8781
Ciao Bella Gelato Company
Irvington, NJ 800-435-2863
Clarkson Scottish Bakery
Mississauga, ON 905-823-1500
Claudio Pastry Company
Elmwood Park, IL 708-453-0598
Claxton Bakery
Claxton, GA 800-841-4211
Clements Pastry Shop
Hyattsville, MD 800-444-7428
Cloverhill Bakery-Vend Corporation
Chicago, IL 773-745-9800
Cloverland Sweets/Priester's Pecan Company
Fort Deposit, AL 800-523-3505
Clydes Delicious Donuts
Addison, IL 630-628-6555
Coby's Cookies
Toronto, ON 416-633-1567
Cold Fusion Foods
West Hollywood, CA 310-287-3244
Collin Street Bakery
Corsicana, TX 800-504-1896
Columbus Bakery
Columbus, OH 614-645-2275
Community Orchard
Fort Dodge, IA 515-573-8212
Con Agra Foods
Holly Ridge, NC 910-329-9061
ConAgra Grocery Products
Irvine, CA 714-680-1000
ConAgra Grocery Products
Fullerton, CA 800-736-2212
Conifer Specialties Inc
Woodinville, WA 800-588-9160
Consun Food Industries
Elyria, OH 440-322-6301
Country Choice Naturals
Eden Prairie, MN 952-829-8824
Country Fresh
Grand Rapids, MI 800-748-0480
Country Home Bakers
Torrance, CA 800-989-9534
Cream O'Weaver Dairy
Salt Lake City, UT 801-973-9922
Creme Curls Bakery
Hudsonville, MI 800-466-1219
Creme Glacee Gelati
Montreal, QC 888-322-0116
Crystal Cream & Butter Company
Sacramento, CA 916-447-6455
Culinar Canada
Baie-Comeau, QC 418-296-4395
Cummings Studio Chocolates
Salt Lake City, UT 800-537-3957
Dairy Fresh Corporation
Greensboro, AL 800-239-5114
Dairy Land
Macon, GA 478-742-6461

Dairy Queen of Georgia
Decatur, GA 404-292-3553
Dancing Deer Baking Company
Boston, MA 888-699-3337
Danish Baking Company
Van Nuys, CA 818-786-1700
Dave's Bakery
Honesdale, PA 570-253-1660
Dave's Hawaiian Ice Cream
Pearl City, HI 808-453-0500
Davis Bakery & Delicatessen
Cleveland, OH 216-464-5599
Davis Bread & Desserts
Davis, CA 530-757-2700
Dee's Cheesecake Factory/Dee's Foodservice
Albuquerque, NM 505-884-1777
Deep Foods
Union, NJ 908-810-7500
Deerfield Bakery
Buffalo Grove, IL 847-520-0068
Del's Pastry
Etobicoke, ON 416-231-4383
Delicious Desserts
Brooklyn, NY 718-680-1156
Deluxe Ice Cream Company
Salem, OR 800-304-7172
Desserts by David Glass
South Windsor, CT 860-462-7520
Desserts of Distinction
Milwaukie, OR 503-654-8370
Di Camillo Bakery
Niagara Falls, NY 800-634-4363
Di Paolo Baking Company
Rochester, NY 585-232-3510
Dimitria Delights
North Grafton, MA 800-763-1113
Dinkel's Bakery
Chicago, IL 800-822-8817
Divine Delights
Petaluma, CA 800-443-2836
Division Baking Corporation
New York, NY 800-934-9238
Dolly Madison Bakery Interstate Brands Corporation
Columbus, IN 812-376-7432
Don's Food Products
Schwenksville, PA 888-321-3667
Dough Works Company
Horicon, WI 800-383-8808
Dreyer's Grand Ice Cream
Oakland, CA 877-437-3937
Dufflet Pastries
Toronto, ON 416-536-9640
Dunford Bakers
Fayetteville, AR 479-521-3000
Dunkin Brands Inc.
Canton, MA 800-458-7731
Dynamic Foods
Lubbock, TX 806-747-2777
Eddy's Bakery
Boise, ID 208-377-8100
Edelweiss Patisserie
Charlestown, MA 617-628-0225
Edwards Baking Company
Atlanta, GA 800-241-0559
Edy's Dreyers Grand Ice Cream
Rockaway, NJ 800-362-7899
Edy's Grand Ice Cream
Glendale Heights, IL 888-377-3397
El Segundo Bakery
El Segundo, CA 310-322-3422
Elegant Desserts
Lyndhurst, NJ 201-933-0770
Eli's Cheesecake Company
Chicago, IL 800-999-8300
Elmwood Pastry
West Hartford, CT 860-233-2029
European Style Bakery
Beverly Hills, CA 818-368-6876
Evans Bakery
Cozad, NE 800-222-5641
Faith Dairy
Tacoma, WA 253-531-3398
Famous Pacific Dessert Company
Seattle, WA 800-666-1950
Fantasia
Sedalia, MO 660-827-1172
Farr Candy Company
Idaho Falls, ID 208-522-8215
Fendall Ice Cream Company
Salt Lake City, UT 801-355-3583
Field's
Pauls Valley, OK 800-286-7501

Fieldbrook Farms
Dunkirk, NY 800-333-0805
Fiera Foods
Toronto, ON 416-744-1010
Fillo Factory
Dumont, NJ 800-653-4556
Fireside Kitchen
Halifax, NS 902-454-7387
Fisher Rex Sandwiches
Raleigh, NC 919-901-0739
Flagship Atlanta Dairy
Belleview, FL 800-224-0669
Flavor Right Foods Group
Columbus, OH 888-464-3734
Flavors from Florida
Bartow, FL 863-533-0408
FNI Group LLC
Sherborn, MA 508-655-4175
Food of Our Own Design
Maplewood, NJ 973-762-0985
Foodbrands America
Oklahoma City, OK 405-290-4000
Foothills Creamery
Calgary, AB 800-661-4909
Foxtail Foods
Fairfield, OH 800-487-2253
France Delices
Montreal, QC 800-663-1365
Frankly Natural Bakers
San Diego, CA 800-727-7229
French Patisserie
Pacifica, CA 800-300-2253
Fresh Dairy Direct/Morningstar
Dallas, TX 800-395-7004
Friendly Ice Cream Corporation
Wilbraham, MA 800-966-9970
Frostbite
Toledo, OH 800-968-7711
Frozfruit Corporation
Gardena, CA 310-217-1034
FrutStix Company
Santa Barbara, CA 805-965-1656
Future Bakery & Cafe
Etobicoke, ON 416-231-1491
Galliker Dairy
Johnstown, PA 800-477-6455
Garber Ice Cream Company
Winchester, VA 800-662-5422
Gardner Pie Company
Akron, OH 330-245-2030
Garelick Farms
Lynn, MA 800-487-8700
Gelato Fresco
Toronto, ON 416-785-5415
George L. Wells Meat Company
Philadelphia, PA 800-523-1730
Georgia Fruit Cake Company
Claxton, GA 912-739-2683
GH Bent Company
Milton, MA 617-698-5945
Giant Food
Lanham, MD 888-469-4426
Gifford's Dairy
Skowhegan, ME 207-474-9821
Gimbal's Fine Candies
S San Francisco, CA 800-344-6225
Gindi Gourmet
Boulder, CO 303-473-9177
Glover's Ice Cream
Frankfort, IN 800-686-5163
Golden Boys Pies of San Diego
San Diego, CA 800-746-0280
Golden Brown Bakery
South Haven, MI 269-637-3418
Golden Glow Cookie Company
Bronx, NY 718-379-6223
Good Humor Breyers Ice Cream Company
Green Bay, WI 920-499-5151
Good Old Days Foods
Little Rock, AR 501-565-1257
Gourmet Baker
Burnaby, BC 800-663-1972
Gourmet Croissant
Brooklyn, NY 718-499-4911
Govatos
Wilmington, DE 888-799-5252
Grainaissance
Emeryville, CA 800-472-4697
Granowska's
Toronto, ON 416-533-7755
Great American Dessert
Flushing, NY 718-894-3494

Great Cakes
Los Angeles, CA 310-287-0228
Great Northern Maple Products
Saint Honor, De Shenley, QC 418-485-7777
Grebe's Bakery & Delicatessen
Milwaukee, WI 800-356-9377
Grecian Delight Foods
Elk Grove Village, IL 800-621-4387
Greyston Bakery
Yonkers, NY 800-289-2253
Groezinger Provisions
Neptune, NJ 800-927-9473
Grossinger's Home Bakery
New York, NY 800-479-6996
Grote Bakery
Hamilton, OH 513-874-7436
Gumpert's Canada
Mississauga, ON 800-387-9324
H.E. Butt Grocery Company
San Antonio, TX 800-432-3113
Haby's Alsatian Bakery
Castroville, TX 830-931-2118
Hafner USA
Stone Mountain, GA 888-725-4605
Hahn's Old Fashioned Cake Company
Farmingdale, NY 631-249-3456
Handy Pax
Randolph, MA 781-963-8300
Hanover Foods Corporation
Hanover, PA 717-632-6000
Happy & Healthy Products
Boca Raton, FL 561-367-0739
Harold Food Company
Charlotte, NC 704-588-8061
Harry & David
Medford, OR 877-322-1200
Harvest Bakery
Bristol, CT 860-589-8800
Harvest Valley Bakery
La Salle, IL 815-224-9030
Hazelwood Farms Bakery
Rochester, NY 585-424-1240
Health Valley Company
Irwindale, CA 800-334-3204
Heidi's Gourmet Desserts
Tucker, GA 800-241-4166
Heinemann's Bakeries
Palatine, IL 847-358-3501
Heitzman Bakery
Louisville, KY 502-452-1891
Hershey Creamery Company
Harrisburg, PA 888-240-1905
HFI Foods
Redmond, WA 425-883-1320
Holt's Bakery
Douglas, GA 912-384-2202
Holton Food Products Company
La Grange, IL 708-352-5599
Home Made Brand Foods Company
Newburyport, MA 978-462-3663
Homer's Ice Cream
Wilmette, IL 847-251-0477
Honey Bar/Creme de la Creme
Kingston, NY 845-331-4643
Honey Rose Baking Company
Carlsbad, CA
Honeybake Farms
Kansas City, KS 913-371-7777
Hormel Foods Corporation
Cincinnati, OH 513-563-0211
Hormel Foods Corporation
Des Moines, IA 515-276-8872
Hormel Foods Corporation
Phoenix, AZ 602-230-2400
Hormel Foods Corporation
Austin, MN 800-523-4635
Hormel Foods Corporation
Lebanon, NJ 908-236-7009
Hostess Brands
Kansas City, MO 816-502-4000
Humble Cremery
Fortuna, CA 800-697-9925
Hunt Country Foods
Middleburg, VA 540-364-2622
Hunter Farms
High Point, NC 800-446-8035
Hygeia Dairy Company
McAllen, TX 956-686-0511
Ice Cream & Yogurt Club
Boynton Beach, FL 561-731-3331
Ice Cream Specialties
Saint Louis, MO 314-962-2550
Ice Cream Specialties
Lafayette, IN 765-474-2989
Icy Bird
Sparta, TN 931-738-3557
Il Gelato
Astoria, NY 800-899-9299
Il Tiramisu
Valley Stream, NY 516-599-1010
Incredible Cheesecake Company
San Diego, CA 619-563-9722
International Equipment International Equipment And Supplies
Arecibo, PR 787-879-3151
International Multifoods Corporation
Orrville, OH 800-664-2942
International Yogurt Company
Portland, OR 800-962-7326
It's It Ice Cream Company
Burlingame, CA 800-345-1928
Italian Bakery
Virginia, MN 218-741-3464
Italian Baking Company
Edmonton, AB 780-424-4830
J&J Snack Foods Corporation
Pennsauken, NJ 800-486-9533
J.A.M.B. Low Carb Distributor
Pompano Beach, FL 800-708-6738
J.P. Sunrise Bakery
Edmonton, AB 780-454-5797
J.W. Haywood & Sons Dairy
Louisville, KY 502-774-2311
Jack & Jill Ice Cream Company
Moorestown, NJ 856-813-2300
Jackson Ice Cream Company
Denver, CO 303-534-2454
Jackson Milk & Ice CreamCompany
Hutchinson, KS 620-663-1244
James Skinner Company
Omaha, NE 800-358-7428
Joey's Fine Foods
Newark, NJ 973-482-1400
John J. Nissen Baking Company
Brewer, ME 207-989-7654
Johnson's Real Ice Cream
Columbus, OH 614-231-0014
Jon Donaire Pastry
Santa Fe Springs, CA 877-366-2473
Josh & John's Ice Cream
Colorado Springs, CO 800-530-2855
Joyva Corporation
Brooklyn, NY 718-497-0170
Jubelt Variety Bakeries
Mount Olive, IL 217-999-5231
Just Desserts
San Francisco, CA 415-602-9245
Kan-Pac
Arkansas City, KS 620-442-6820
Kapaa Poi Factory
Kapaa, HI 808-822-5426
Karp's
Georgetown, MA 800-373-5277
Katrina's Tartufo
Port Jeffrsn Sta, NY 800-480-8836
Kerrobert Bakery
Kerrobert, SK 306-834-2461
King's Hawaiian
Torrance, CA 800-800-5461
Klinke Brothers Ice Cream Company
Memphis, TN 901-743-8250
Knouse Foods Coop
Peach Glen, PA 717-677-8181
Kohler Mix Specialties
White Bear Lake, MN 651-426-1633
Kohler Mix Specialties
Newington, CT 860-666-1511
Kokinos Purity Ice CreamCompany
Monroe, LA 318-322-2930
Kozy Shack
Hicksville, NY 516-870-3000
Kyger Bakery Products
Lafayette, IN 765-447-1252
L&M Bakery
Lawrence, MA 978-687-7346
La Francaise Bakery
Melrose Park, IL 800-654-7220
Laguna Cookie & Dessert Company
Santa Ana, CA 800-673-2473
Lamb-Weston
Weston, OR 800-766-7783
LaRosa's Bakery
Shrewsbury, NJ 800-527-6722
Lawrences Delights
Doraville, GA 800-568-0021
Lax & Mandel Bakery
Cleveland, OH 216-382-8877
Leader Candies
Brooklyn, NY 718-366-6900
Lenchner Bakery
Concord, ON 905-738-8811
Lewis Bakeries
London, ON 519-434-5252
Lewis Brothers Bakeries
Evansville, IN 812-425-4642
Little Angel Foods
Daytona Beach, FL 904-257-3040
Lone Star Bakery
Round Rock, TX 512-255-3629
Lone Star Consolidated Foods
Dallas, TX 800-658-5637
Louis Trauth Dairy
Newport, KY 800-544-6455
Love & Quiches Desserts
Freeport, NY 800-525-5251
Lucy's Sweet Surrender
Cleveland, OH 216-752-0828
Lusitania Bakery
Blandon, PA 610-926-1311
M&L Gourmet Ice Cream
Baltimore, MD 410-276-4880
Mac's Donut Shop
Aliquippa, PA 724-375-6776
Mack's Homemade Ice Cream
York, PA 717-741-2027
Mackie Intl.
Riverside, CA 800-733-9762
Main Street Custom Foods
Cuyahoga Falls, OH 800-533-6246
Main Street Gourmet
Cuyahoga Falls, OH 800-533-6246
Main Street Gourmet Fundraising
Cuyahoga Falls, OH 800-533-6246
Main Street's Cambritt Cookies
Cuyahoga Falls, OH 800-533-6246
Mama Lee's Gourmet Hot Chocolate
Nashville, TN . . . . . 1 8-8 m-male
Maola Milk & Ice Cream Company
New Bern, NC 252-514-2792
Maple Island
Saint Paul, MN 800-369-1022
Maplehurst Bakeries
Carrollton, GA 800-482-4810
Mar-Key Foods
Vidalia, GA 912-537-4204
Mario's Gelati
Vancouver, BC 604-879-9411
Martino's Bakery
Burbank, CA 818-842-0715
Mary Ann's Baking Company
Sacramento, CA 916-681-7444
Matador Processors
Blanchard, OK 800-847-0797
Mayer's Cider Mill
Webster, NY 800-543-0043
Mazelle's Cheesecakes Concoctions Creations
Dallas, TX 214-328-9102
McArthur Dairy
Miami, FL 877-803-6565
McConnell's Fine Ice Cream
Santa Barbara, CA 805-963-2958
Meadow Gold Dairies
Englewood, CO 800-525-3289
Meadows Country Products
Hollidaysburg, PA 888-499-1001
Mehaffie Pies
Dayton, OH 937-253-1163
Mia Products
Scranton, PA 570-457-7431
Michel's Bakery
Philadelphia, PA 215-725-3900
Michele's Family Bakery
York, PA 717-741-2027
Michelle Chocolatiers
Colorado Springs, CO 888-447-3654
Michigan Dairy
Livonia, MI 734-367-5390
Mid States Dairy
Hazelwood, MO 314-731-1150
Mikawaya Bakery
Vernon, CA
Millers Ice Cream
Houston, TX 713-861-3138
Millie's Pierogi
Chicopee Falls, MA 800-743-7641

Mississippi Bakery
Burlington, IA . . . 319-752-6315
Mississippi Cheese StrawFactory
Yazoo City, MS . . . 800-530-7496
Mister Cookie Face
Lakewood, NJ . . . 732-370-5533
Model Dairy
Reno, NV . . . 800-433-2030
Monaco Baking Company
Santa Fe Springs, CA . . . 800-569-4640
Mooresville Ice Cream Company
Mooresville, NC . . . 704-664-5456
Mothers Kitchen Inc
Burlington, NJ . . . 609-589-3026
Mozzicato De Pasquale Bakery Pastry
Hartford, CT . . . 860-296-0426
Mozzicato Depasquale Bakery & Pastry Shop
Hartford, CT . . . 860-296-0426
Mrs Baird's Bakery
Fort Worth, TX . . . 817-864-2500
Mrs. Baird's Bakeries
Abilene, TX . . . 325-692-3141
Mrs. Smith's Bakeries
Spartanburg, SC . . . 800-756-4746
Mrs. Sullivan's Pies
Jackson, TN . . . 731-427-2101
Mt View Bakery
Mountain View, HI . . . 808-968-6353
Multi Marques
Montreal, QC . . . 514-934-1866
Multiflex Company
Hawthorne, NJ . . . 973-636-9700
My Daddy's Cheesecake
Cape Girardeau, MO . . . 800-735-6765
My Grandma's Coffee Cakee of New England
Boston, MA . . . 800-847-2636
Najila's
Binghamton, NY . . . 607-722-4287
Nancy's Pies
Rock Island, IL . . . 800-480-0055
Natural Fruit Corporation
Hialeah, FL . . . 305-887-7525
Natural Quick Foods
Seattle, WA . . . 206-365-5757
Naturally Delicious
Oakland Park, FL . . . 954-485-6730
Nature's Hilights
Chico, CA . . . 800-313-6454
New York Bakeries
Hialeah, FL . . . 305-882-1355
Nickles Bakery of Ohio
Columbus, OH . . . 800-335-9775
Nikki's Cookies
Milwaukee, WI . . . 800-776-7107
Noh Foods of Hawaii
Gardena, CA . . . 310-324-6770
Northside Bakery
Richmond, VA . . . 804-968-7620
Notre Dame Bakery
Conception Harbour, NL . . . 709-535-2738
O'Boyle's Ice Cream Company
Bristol, PA . . . 215-788-3882
Oak Leaf Confections
Scarborough, ON . . . 877-261-7887
OH Chocolate
Calgary, AB . . . 800-887-3959
Old Country Bakery
North Hollywood, CA . . . 818-838-2302
Old Fashioned Kitchen
Lakewood, NJ . . . 732-364-4100
Orange Bakery
Irvine, CA . . . 949-863-1377
Original Ya-hoo! Baking Company
Sherman, TX . . . 800-575-9373
Orval Kent Food Company
Wheeling, IL . . . 847-459-9000
Out of a Flower
Lancaster, TX . . . 800-743-4696
Pacific Ocean Produce
Santa Cruz, CA . . . 831-423-2654
Parco Foods
Blue Island, IL . . . 708-371-9200
Parker Products
Fort Worth, TX . . . 800-433-5749
Pasta Factory
Melrose Park, IL . . . 800-615-6951
Pastry Chef
Pawtucket, RI . . . 800-639-8606
Patisserie Wawel
Montreal, QC . . . 614-524-3348
Pearl River Pastry & Chocolates
Pearl River, NY . . . 800-632-2639
Peggy Lawton Kitchens
East Walpole, MA . . . 800-843-7325
Pellman Foods
New Holland, PA . . . 717-354-8070
Perry's Ice Cream Company
Akron, NY . . . 800-873-7797
Pet Dairy
Portsmouth, VA . . . 757-397-2387
Pet Dairy
Spartanburg, SC . . . 864-576-6280
Petersen Ice Cream Company
Oak Park, IL . . . 708-386-6130
Pevely Dairy Company
Hazelwood, MO . . . 314-771-4400
Phipps Desserts
Toronto, ON . . . 416-481-9111
Pie Piper Products
Bensenville, IL . . . 800-621-8183
Piedmont Candy Corporation
Lexington, NC . . . 336-248-2477
Pinocchio Italian Ice Cream Company
Edmonton, AB . . . 780-455-1905
Plains Creamery
Amarillo, TX . . . 806-374-0385
Platte Valley Creamery
Scottsbluff, NE . . . 308-632-4225
Plehn's Bakery
Louisville, KY . . . 502-896-4438
Plumlife Company
Newbury, MA . . . 978-462-8458
Pocono Cheesecake Factory
Swiftwater, PA . . . 570-839-6844
Poudre Valley Creamery
Fort Collins, CO . . . 970-237-7000
Prairie Farms Dairy
Carlinville, IL . . . 217-854-2547
Precision Foods
Melrose Park, IL . . . 800-333-0003
Price Cold Storage & Packing Company
Yakima, WA . . . 509-966-4110
Price's Creameries
El Paso, TX . . . 915-565-2711
Puritan/ATZ Ice Cream
Kendallville, IN . . . 260-347-2700
Purity Dairies
Nashville, TN . . . 615-244-1900
Purity Ice Cream Company
Ithaca, NY . . . 607-272-1545
Quality Bakery/MM Deli
Port Colborne, ON . . . 905-834-4911
Quality Naturally! Foods
City of Industry, CA . . . 888-498-6986
Quiche & Tell
Flushing, NY . . . 718-381-7562
Real Food Marketing
Kansas City, MO . . . 816-221-4100
Refrigerated Foods Association
Chamblee, GA . . . 770-452-0660
Reinhold Ice Cream Company
Pittsburgh, PA . . . 412-321-7600
Reiter Dairy
Akron, OH . . . 800-362-0825
Reser's Fine Foods
Salt Lake City, UT . . . 801-972-5633
Rhino Foods
Burlington, VT . . . 800-639-3350
Rhodes Bake-N-Serv
Salt Lake City, UT . . . 800-695-0122
Rich Ice Cream Company
West Palm Beach, FL . . . 561-833-7585
Rich Products Corporation
Hilliard, OH . . . 614-771-1117
Rising Dough Bakery
Sacramento, CA . . . 916-387-9700
Roberts Dairy Foods
Omaha, NE . . . 402-371-3660
Roberts Dairy Foods
Kansas City, MO . . . 800-279-1692
Robinson Dairy
Denver, CO . . . 800-332-6355
Rolling Pin Bakery
Bow Island, AB . . . 403-545-2434
Roma Bakeries
Rockford, IL . . . 815-964-6737
Rosati Italian Water Ice
Clifton Heights, PA . . . 610-626-1818
Roselani Tropics Ice Cream
Wailuku, HI . . . 808-244-7951
Rowena's
Norfolk, VA . . . 800-627-8699
Royal Home Bakery
Newmarket, ON . . . 905-715-7044
RW Delights
Millington, NJ . . . 866-892-1096
Ryals Bakery
Milledgeville, GA . . . 478-452-0321
Ryke's Bakery
Muskegon, MI . . . 231-722-3508
Sacramento Baking Company
Sacramento, CA . . . 916-361-2000
Safeway Dairy Products
Capitol Heights, MD . . . 301-341-9555
Safeway Stores
Tempe, AZ . . . 480-966-0295
Sara Lee Corporation
Downers Grove, IL . . . 630-598-8100
Sarabeth's Bakery
Bronx, NY . . . 800-773-7378
Savino's Italian Ices
Deerfield Beach, FL . . . 954-426-4119
Saxby Foods
Edmonton, AB . . . 780-440-4179
Schneider Valley Farms Dairy
Williamsport, PA . . . 570-326-2021
Schneider's Dairy Holdings Inc
Pittsburgh, PA . . . 412-881-3525
Schoep's Ice Cream Company
Madison, WI . . . 800-236-0032
Schulze & Burch Biscuit Company
Chicago, IL . . . 773-927-6622
Schwan Food Company
Marshall, MN . . . 800-533-5290
Scialo Brothers
Providence, RI . . . 877-421-0986
Scot Paris Fine Desserts
New York, NY . . . 212-807-1802
Scotsburn Dairy Group
Scotsburn, NS . . . 902-485-8023
Scotty Wotty's Creamy Cheescake
Hillsborough, NJ . . . 908-281-9720
Seavers Bakery
Johnson City, TN . . . 423-928-8131
Serv-Agen Corporation
Cherry Hill, NJ . . . 856-663-6966
Sessions Company
Enterprise, AL . . . 334-393-0200
Shaw Baking Company
Thunder Bay, ON . . . 807-345-7327
Shef Products
Las Vegas, NV . . . 702-873-2275
Silver Tray Cookies
Fort Lauderdale, FL . . . 305-883-0800
Sinbad Sweets
Fresno, CA . . . 800-350-7933
Sisler's Ice & Ice Cream
Ohio, IL . . . 888-891-3856
Smart Ice
Fort Myers, FL . . . 239-334-3123
Smith Dairy Products Company
Orrville, OH . . . 800-776-7076
Smoak's Bakery & Catering Service
Augusta, GA . . . 706-738-1792
Snelgrove Ice Cream Company
Salt Lake City, UT . . . 800-569-0005
Solana Beach Baking Company
Carlsbad, CA . . . 760-931-0148
Solvang Bakery
Solvang, CA . . . 800-377-4253
Southern Ice Cream Specialties
Marietta, GA . . . 770-428-0452
Specialty Bakers
Marysville, PA . . . 800-233-0778
Spilke's Baking Company
Brooklyn, NY . . . 718-384-2150
Spohrers Bakeries
Collingdale, PA . . . 610-532-9959
Spring Glen Fresh Foods
Ephrata, PA . . . 800-641-2853
St. Cloud Bakery
Saint Cloud, MN . . . 320-251-8055
Standard Bakery
Kealakekua, HI . . . 808-322-3688
Starbucks Coffee Company
Seattle, WA . . . 800-782-7282
Stewart's Ice Cream
Saratoga Springs, NY . . . 518-581-1300
Sticky Fingers Bakeries
Spokane, WA . . . 800-458-5826
Stone's Home Made Candy Shop
Oswego, NY . . . 888-223-3928
Stroehmann Bakeries
Norristown, PA . . . 800-984-0989
Strossner's Bakery
Greenville, SC . . . 864-233-3996

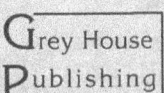

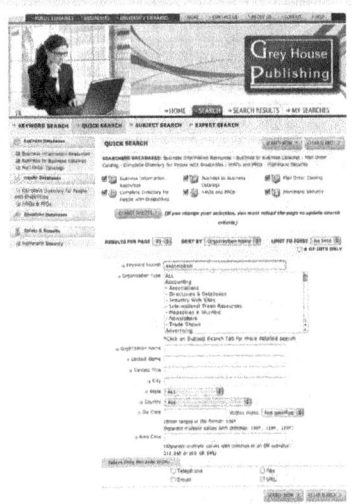

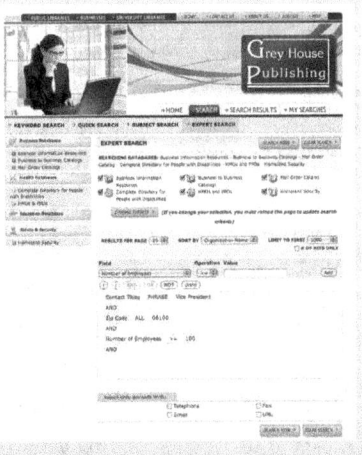

Sugar Creek/Eskimo Pie
Russellville, AR 800-445-2715
Sunbeam Baking Company
El Paso, TX 800-328-6111
SunMeadow Family of Products
Saint Petersburg, FL 727-573-2211
Sunshine Dairy Foods
Portland, OR 503-234-7526
Superior Cake Products
Southbridge, MA 508-764-3276
Superstore Industries
Fairfield, CA 707-864-0502
Svenhard's Swedish Bakery
Oakland, CA 800-333-7836
Sweenor Chocolate
Wakefield, RI 800-834-3123
Sweet Bakery Baltimore
Baltimore, MD 41- 7-8 22
Sweet Endings
West Palm Beach, FL 888-635-1177
Sweet Gallery Exclusive Pastry
Toronto, ON 416-766-0289
Sweet Shop
La Crosse, WI 608-784-7724
Sweet Street Desserts
Reading, PA 800-793-3897
Sweety Novelty
Monterey Park, CA 626-282-4482
Table De France
Ontario, CA 909-923-5205
Table Talk Pie
Worcester, MA 508-798-8811
Taste It Presents
Kenilworth, NJ 908-241-9191
Tastykake
Philadelphia, PA 215-221-8500
Teawolf Industries, Ltd
Pine Brook, NJ 973-575-4600
Tebay Dairy Company
Parkersburg, WV 304-422-1014
Terrapin Ridge Farms
Clearwater, FL 800-999-4052
The Bama Company
Tulsa, OK 800-756-2262
The Cheesecake Factory
Calabasas Hills, CA 818-871-3000
The Great San Saba RiverPecan Company
San Saba, TX 800-621-9121
Thrifty Ice Cream
El Monte, CA 626-571-0122
Tillamook County Creamery Association
Tillamook, OR 503-815-1300
Tipiak
Stamford, CT 203-961-9117
Toft Dairy
Sandusky, OH 800-521-4606
Tofutti Brands
Cranford, NJ 908-272-2400
Tom's Ice Cream Bowl
Zanesville, OH 740-452-5267
Tony's Ice Cream Company
Gastonia, NC 704-867-7085
Top Hat Company
Wilmette, IL 847-256-6565
Treat Ice Cream Company
San Jose, CA 408-292-9321
Tropical Treets
North York, ON 888-424-8229
Turano Pastry Shops
Bloomingdale, IL 630-529-6161
Turkey Hill Dairy
Conestoga, PA 800-693-2479
Turtle Mountain
Eugene, OR 541-338-9400
Two Chefs on a Roll
Carson, CA 800-842-3025
Two Chicks and a Ladle
New York, NY 212-251-0025
Umpqua Dairy Products Company
Roseburg, OR 541-672-2638
Uncle Ralph's Cookie Company
Frederick, MD 800-422-0626
United Dairy
Martins Ferry, OH 800-252-1542
United Dairy
Uniontown, PA 800-966-6455
United Pies of Elkhart I
Elkhart, IN 574-294-3419
Uptown Bakers
Hyattsville, MD 301-864-1500
Valley Dairy Fairview Dairy
Windber, PA 814-467-1384
Van de Kamp's
Peoria, IL 800-798-3318
Varda Chocolatier
Elizabeth, NJ 800-448-2732
Velda Farms
Winter Haven, FL 800-279-4166
Velda Farms
North Miami Beach, FL 800-795-4649
Velvet Ice Cream Company
Utica, OH 800-589-5000
Vickey's Vittles
North Hills, CA 818-841-1944
Vie de France Yamazaki
Denver, CO 303-371-6280
Vie de France Yamazaki
Vienna, VA 800-393-8926
Vie de France Yamazaki
Vienna, VA 800-446-4404
Vienna Sausage Company
Chicago, IL 800-366-3647
Vigneri Confections
Rochester, NY 877-843-6374
VIP Foods
Flushing, NY 718-821-5330
Vitamilk Dairy
Bellingham, WA 206-529-4128
Waldensian Bakeries
Valdese, NC 828-874-2136
Warwick Ice Cream Company
Warwick, RI 401-821-8403
Wayne Dairy Products
Richmond, IN 800-875-9294
Wedding Cake Studio
Williamsfield, OH 440-667-1765
Welch's Foods Inc
Concord, MA 800-340-6870
Weldon Ice Cream Company
Millersport, OH 740-467-2400
Wells' Dairy
Le Mars, IA 800-942-3800
Welsh Farms
Clifton, NJ 973-772-2388
Wenger's Bakery
Reading, PA 610-372-6545
White Coffee Corporation
Astoria, NY 800-221-0140
Whitey's Ice Cream Manufacturing
Moline, IL 888-594-4839
Wick's Pies
Winchester, IN 800-642-5880
Williamsburg Chocolatier
Williamsburg, VA 757-253-1474
Winder Dairy
West Valley, UT 800-946-3371
Winmix/Natural Care Products
Englewood, FL 941-475-7432
Wonder Bread
Provo, UT 800-483-7253
Woodie Pie Company
Artesia, NM 505-746-2132
Wright Ice Cream
Cayuga, IN 800-686-9561
Wuollet Bakery
Minneapolis, MN 612-381-9400
Yarnell Ice Cream Company
Searcy, AR 800-766-2414
Young's Bakery
Uniontown, PA 724-437-6361
Zeppys Bakery
Lawrence, MA 781-963-7022
Ziegenfelder Company
Wheeling, WV 304-232-6360
Zoelsmanns Bakery & Deli
Pueblo, CO 719-543-0407

Low Carb

Real Food Marketing
Kansas City, MO 816-221-4100

Low-Calorie

Cedar Crest Specialties
Cedarburg, WI 800-877-8341
ConAgra Grocery Products
Irvine, CA 714-680-1000
Fendall Ice Cream Company
Salt Lake City, UT 801-355-3583
Health Valley Company
Irwindale, CA 800-334-3204
J&J Snack Foods Corporation
Pennsauken, NJ 800-486-9533
Jackson Ice Cream Company
Denver, CO 303-534-2454
Master Mix
Placentia, CA 714-524-1698
O'Boyle's Ice Cream Company
Bristol, PA 215-788-3882
Price Cold Storage & Packing Company
Yakima, WA 509-966-4110
Real Food Marketing
Kansas City, MO 816-221-4100
SunMeadow Family of Products
Saint Petersburg, FL 727-573-2211
Tova Industries
Louisville, KY 888-532-8682
Wells' Dairy
Le Mars, IA 800-942-3800

Non-Dairy

Frozen

A&B Ingredients
Fairfield, NJ 973-227-1390

Fresh

Botanical Bakery, LLC
Napa, CA 707-344-8103
Fresh Start Bakeries
Brea, CA 714-256-8900

Frozen

Aladdin Bakers
Brooklyn, NY 718-499-1818
Alati-Caserta Desserts
Montreal, QC 514-271-3013
All Round Foods
Westbury, NY 516-338-1888
Andre-Boudin Bakeries
San Francisco, CA 415-882-1849
Athens Pastries & Frozen Foods
Cleveland, OH 800-837-5683
Atkins Elegant Desserts
Fishers, IN 800-887-8808
Awrey Bakeries
Livonia, MI 800-950-2253
Bake Crafters Food
Collegedale, TN 800-296-8935
Baker Boy Bake Shop
Dickinson, ND 800-437-2008
Beck's Waffles of Oklahoma
Shawnee, OK 800-646-6254
Bensons Bakery
Bogart, GA 800-888-6059
Best Maid Cookie Company
River Falls, WI 888-444-0322
Boboli Intl. Inc.
Stockton, CA 209-473-3507
Bodega Chocolates
Fountain Valley, CA 888-326-3342
Brooklyn Bagel Company
Staten Island, NY 800-349-3055
Brownie Products Company
Terre Haute, IN
Campbell Soup Company of Canada
Listowel, ON 800-575-7687
Caribbean Food Delights
Tappan, NY 845-398-3000
Carolina Foods
Charlotte, NC 800-234-0441
CBC Foods
Little River, KS 800-276-4770
Cedarlane Foods
Carson, CA 310-886-7720
Cemac Foods Corporation
Philadelphia, PA 800-724-0179
CGI Desserts
Sugar Land, TX 281-240-1200
Chewys Rugulach
San Diego, CA 800-241-3456
Chloe Foods Corporation
Brooklyn, NY 718-827-9000
Cinderella Cheese Cake Company
Riverside, NJ 856-461-6302
Cole's Quality Foods
Grand Rapids, MI 616-975-0081
Con Agra Foods
Holly Ridge, NC 910-329-9061
ConAgra Foods
Boisbriand, QC 450-433-1322
Concept 2 Bakers
Minneapolis, MN 800-266-2782

Continental Food Products
Flushing, NY. 718-358-7894
Cookie Tree Bakeries
Salt Lake City, UT. 800-998-0111
Danish Baking Company
Van Nuys, CA 818-786-1700
Dawn Food Products
Louisville, KY 800-626-2542
Dee's Cheesecake Factory/Dee's Foodservice
Albuquerque, NM. 505-884-1777
Del Campo Baking Company
Wilmington, DE 302-656-6676
Desserts of Distinction
Milwaukie, OR 503-654-8370
Dimitria Delights
North Grafton, MA 800-763-1113
Division Baking Corporation
New York, NY 800-934-9238
Dutch Ann Foods Company
Natchez, MS 601-445-5566
Dynamic Foods
Lubbock, TX. 806-747-2777
Edner Corporation
Hayward, CA 510-441-8504
Edwards Baking Company
Atlanta, GA. 800-241-0559
Eli's Cheesecake Company
Chicago, IL 800-999-8300
Engel's Bakeries
Calgary, AB. 403-250-9560
English Bay Batter
Columbus, OH 614-471-9994
Evans Bakery
Cozad, NE. 800-222-5641
Fantasia
Sedalia, MO 660-827-1172
Fantis Foods
Carlstadt, NJ 201-933-6200
Field's
Pauls Valley, OK. 800-286-7501
Fiera Foods
Toronto, ON 416-744-1010
Fleischer's Bagels
Macedon, NY 315-986-9999
France Croissant
New York, NY 212-888-1210
France Delices
Montreal, QC 800-663-1365
Fresh Dairy Direct/Morningstar
Dallas, TX. 800-395-7004
Fresh Start Bakeries
Brea, CA 714-256-8900
Gabilas Knishes
Brooklyn, NY
Gardner Pie Company
Akron, OH. 330-245-2030
Gemini Food Industries
Charlton, MA 508-248-2730
Good Old Days Foods
Little Rock, AR. 501-565-1257
Gourmet Croissant
Brooklyn, NY 718-499-4911
Grecian Delight Foods
Elk Grove Village, IL 800-621-4387
Gregory's Foods
Eagan, MN 800-231-4734
Grossinger's Home Bakery
New York, NY 800-479-6996
Guttenplan's Frozen Dough
Middletown, NJ 888-422-4357
GWB Foods Corporation
Brooklyn, NY 877-977-7610
H&H Bagels
New York, NY 800-692-2435
Haas Baking Company
St Louis, MO. 800-325-3171
Harlan Bakeries
Avon, IN 317-272-3600
Harold Food Company
Charlotte, NC 704-588-8061
Hazelwood Farms Bakery
Rochester, NY. 585-424-1240
Isabella's Healthy Bakery
Cuyahoga Falls, OH 800-476-6328
J&J Wall Baking Company
Sacramento, CA 916-381-1410
James Skinner Company
Omaha, NE 800-358-7428
Karp's
Georgetown, MA 800-373-5277
Kyger Bakery Products
Lafayette, IN. 765-447-1252

Lamb-Weston
Weston, OR. 800-766-7783
Le Notre, Alain & Marie Baker
Houston, TX 800-536-6873
Leidenheimer Baking Company
New Orleans, LA 504-525-1575
Lenchner Bakery
Concord, ON. 905-738-8811
Lender's Bagel Bakery
Mattoon, IL 217-235-3181
Lone Star Bakery
Round Rock, TX. 512-255-3629
Lone Star Consolidated Foods
Dallas, TX. 800-658-5637
Love & Quiches Desserts
Freeport, NY 800-525-5251
Ludwick's Frozen Donuts
Grand Rapids, MI 800-366-8816
Main Street Custom Foods
Cuyahoga Falls, OH 800-533-6246
Main Street Gourmet
Cuyahoga Falls, OH 800-533-6246
Main Street Gourmet Fundraising
Cuyahoga Falls, OH 800-533-6246
Main Street Muffins
Cuyahoga Falls, OH 800-533-6246
Main Street's Cambritt Cookies
Cuyahoga Falls, OH 800-533-6246
Mehaffie Pies
Dayton, OH. 937-253-1163
Merkel McDonald
Austin, TX. 800-356-0229
Meyer's Bakeries
Hope, AR 800-643-1542
Mother Nature's Goodies
Yucaipa, CA 909-795-6018
Mothers Kitchen Inc
Burlington, NJ. 609-589-3026
Mozzicato Depasquale Bakery & Pastry Shop
Hartford, CT 860-296-0426
Mrs. Kavanagh's English Muffins
Rumford, RI 800-556-7216
Mrs. Sullivan's Pies
Jackson, TN 731-427-2101
My Grandma's Coffee Cakee of New England
Boston, MA. 800-847-2636
Naleway Foods
Winnipeg, MB. 800-665-7448
Nancy's Specialty Foods
Newark, CA 510-494-1100
Nestle Prepared Foods Company
Englewood, CO. 800-225-2270
New England Muffin Company
Fall River, MA 508-675-2833
Old Fashioned Kitchen
Lakewood, NJ. 732-364-4100
Orange Bakery
Irvine, CA 949-863-1377
Ore-Ida Foods
Pittsburgh, PA. 800-892-2401
Oroweat Baking Company
Montebello, CA 323-721-5161
Pacific Ocean Produce
Santa Cruz, CA. 831-423-2654
Parco Foods
Blue Island, IL 708-371-9200
Pastry Chef
Pawtucket, RI 800-639-8606
Pellman Foods
New Holland, PA 717-354-8070
Petrofsky's Bakery Products
Chesterfield, MO 636-519-1613
Positively Third Street Bakery
Duluth, MN. 218-724-8619
Prairie City Bakery
Vernon Hills, IL 800-338-5122
Prime Pastry
Brooklyn, NY 888-771-2464
Ramona's Mex. Food Produoducts
Gardena, CA 310-323-1950
Ranaldi Bros Frozen Food Products Inc
Warwick, RI 401-738-3444
Randag & Associates Inc
Elmhurst, IL 630-530-2830
Ready Bake Foods
Mississauga, ON. 905-567-0660
Real Food Marketing
Kansas City, MO. 816-221-4100
Rhodes Bake-N-Serv
Salt Lake City, UT 800-695-0122
Rhodes International
Columbus, WI. 800-876-7333

Rich Products Corporation
Winchester, VA 540-667-1955
Rich Products Corporation
Fresno, CA 559-486-7380
Rich Products Corporation
Hilliard, OH. 614-771-1117
Rich Products Corporation
Buffalo, NY. 800-356-7094
Rich Products Corporation
Buffalo, NY. 800-828-2021
Rich Products of Canada
Buffalo, NY. 800-457-4247
Rowena's
Norfolk, VA. 800-627-8699
Rubschlager Baking Corporation
Chicago, IL 773-826-1245
Saxby Foods
Edmonton, AB 780-440-4179
Sunset Specialty Foods
Sunset Beach, CA 562-592-4976
Table De France
Ontario, CA. 909-923-5205
Tasty Mix Quality Foods
Brooklyn, NY. 866-TAS-TYMX
The Bama Company
Tulsa, OK 800-756-2262
The Pillsbury Company
Chelsea, MA 800-370-7834
Tripp Bakers
Wheeling, IL 800-621-3702
Two Chefs on a Roll
Carson, CA 800-842-3025
Uncle Ralph's Cookie Company
Frederick, MD. 800-422-0626
Wenner Bread Products
Bayport, NY 800-869-6262
Wick's Pies
Winchester, IN 800-642-5880
Winder Dairy
West Valley, UT 800-946-3371
Wolferman's
Medford, OR

Ingredients

ADM Food Ingredients
Olathe, KS. 800-255-6637
Al-Rite Fruits & Syrups
Miami, FL. 305-652-2540
AnaCon Foods Company
Atchison, KS. 800-328-0291
Bake Mark
Pico Rivera, CA 562-949-1054
Brolite Products
Streamwood, IL. 888-276-5483
Burnette Foods
Hartford, MI 616-621-3181
California Blending Corpany
El Monte, CA 626-448-1918
California Brands Flavors
Oakland, CA 800-348-0111
Caravan Products Company
Totowa, NJ 800-526-5261
Castella Imports
Hauppauge, NY 866-227-8355
Clofine Dairy & Food Products
Linwood, NJ 800-441-1001
Creme Curls Bakery
Hudsonville, MI 800-466-1219
Dawn Food Products
Louisville, KY 800-626-2542
Deer Creek Honey Farms
London, OH 740-852-0899
Dorothy Dawson Foods Products
Jackson, MI. 517-788-9830
Dufour Pastry Kitchens
Bronx, NY. 800-439-1282
Eden Processing
Poplar Grove, IL. 815-765-2000
Flavorchem
Downers Grove, IL. 800-435-8867
Fleischmann's Yeast
Chesterfield, MO 800-247-7473

Holton Food Products Company
La Grange, IL 708-352-5599
Hulman & Company
Terre Haute, IN 812-232-9446
Indiana Sugar
Burr Ridge, IL. 630-986-9150
Lake States Yeast
Rhinelander, WI 715-369-4949
Lucas Meyer
Decatur, IL 800-769-3660
Lyoferm & Vivolac Cultures
Indianapolis, IN 317-356-8460
Main Street Ingredients
La Crosse, WI. 800-359-2345
Nature's Hand
Burnsville, MN 952-890-6033
Pacific Westcoast Foods
Beaverton, OR 800-874-9333
Roland Industries
Saint Louis, MO 800-325-1183
Vrymeer Commodities
St Charles, IL 630-584-0069
Watson Inc
West Haven, CT 800-388-3481

Pies

Bake Crafters Food
Collegedale, TN 800-296-8935
Baker Boy Bake Shop
Dickinson, ND 800-437-2008
Bear Creek Smokehouse
Marshall, TX. 800-950-2327
Berke-Blake Fancy Foods, Inc.
Longwood, FL 888-386-2253
Bonert's Slice of Pie
Santa Ana, CA 714-540-3535
Chatila's Bakery
Salem, NH. 603-898-5459
Cheryl & Company
Westerville, OH. 614-776-1500
Clarmil Manufacturing Corporation
Hayward, CA 888-252-7645
Mrs Baird's Bakery
Fort Worth, TX 817-864-2500
Primos Northgate
Flowood, MS 601-936-3701
Shawnee Canning Company
Cross Junction, VA 800-713-1414

Apple

Cheryl & Company
Westerville, OH. 614-776-1500
Gould's Maple Sugarhouse
Shelburne Falls, MA. 413-625-6170
Mayer's Cider Mill
Webster, NY 800-543-0043
Mehaffie Pies
Dayton, OH. 937-253-1163
The Bama Company
Tulsa, OK 800-756-2262

Baking Shells

Calise & Sons Bakery
Lincoln, RI 800-225-4737
Canada Bread
Etobicoke, ON 416-926-2000
Dessert Innovations
Atlanta, GA. 800-359-7351
Dufour Pastry Kitchens
Bronx, NY. 800-439-1282
Dutch Ann Foods Company
Natchez, MS 601-445-5566
Father Sam's Syrian Bread
Buffalo, NY. 800-521-6719
Hafner USA
Stone Mountain, GA. 888-725-4605
Hong Kong Noodle Company
Chicago, IL 312-842-0480
Lamonaca Bakery
Windber, PA 814-467-4909
Livermore Falls Baking Company
Livermore Falls, ME. 207-897-3442
Lone Star Bakery
Round Rock, TX. 512-255-3629
Molinaro's Fine Italian Foods
Mississauga, ON. 800-268-4959
Pacific Ocean Produce
Santa Cruz, CA. 831-423-2654
Pasta Factory
Melrose Park, IL. 800-615-6951
Pidy Gourmet Pastry Shells
Inwood, NY. 516-239-6057
Pidy Gourmet Pastry Shells
Inwood, NY. 800-231-7439
Richmond Baking Company
Richmond, IN 765-962-8535
Specialty Bakers
Marysville, PA 800-233-0778
The Bama Company
Tulsa, OK 800-756-2262
Tomaro's Bakery
Clarksburg, WV 304-622-0691
Wick's Pies
Winchester, IN 800-642-5880

Blueberry

Mehaffie Pies
Dayton, OH. 937-253-1163

Brownie

The Bama Company
Tulsa, OK 800-756-2262

Cherry

Mehaffie Pies
Dayton, OH. 937-253-1163
The Bama Company
Tulsa, OK 800-756-2262

Fresh

August Food Limited
Lubbock, TX. 806-744-1918
August Foods
Lubbock, TX. 806-744-1918
Banquet Schuster Bakery
Pueblo, CO 719-544-1062
BBU Bakeries
Denver, CO. 303-691-6342
Borden's Bread
Regina, SK 306-525-3341
Busken Bakery
Cincinnati, OH 513-871-5330
California Pie Company
Livermore, CA 925-373-7700
Carole's Cheesecake Company
Toronto, ON 416-256-0000
Case Side Holdings Company
Kensington, PE. 902-836-4214
Celebrity Cheesecake
Davie, FL 877-986-2253
CGI Desserts
Sugar Land, TX. 281-240-1200
Clarkson Scottish Bakery
Mississauga, ON. 905-823-1500
Cloverland Sweets/Priester's Pecan Company
Fort Deposit, AL. 800-523-3505
Del's Pastry
Etobicoke, ON 416-231-4383
Dolly Madison Bakery Interstate Brands Corporation
Columbus, IN 812-376-7432
Dufflet Pastries
Toronto, ON 416-536-9640
El Peto Products
Cambridge, ON. 800-387-4064
Foxtail Foods
Fairfield, OH. 800-487-2253
Giant Food
Lanham, MD. 888-469-4426
Golden Boys Pies of San Diego
San Diego, CA 800-746-0280
Gourmet Baker
Burnaby, BC 800-663-1972
Greyston Bakery
Yonkers, NY 800-289-2253
Honey Rose Baking Company
Carlsbad, CA
Italian Bakery
Virginia, MN. 218-741-3464
L&M Bakery
Lawrence, MA 978-687-7346
Love & Quiches Desserts
Freeport, NY. 800-525-5251
Mehaffie Pies
Dayton, OH. 937-253-1163
Michel's Bakery
Philadelphia, PA 215-725-3900
Mrs. Baird's Bakeries
Abilene, TX. 325-692-3141
Mrs. Sullivan's Pies
Jackson, TN 731-427-2101
Mt View Bakery
Mountain View, HI 808-968-6353
New England Country Bakers
Watertown, CT 800-225-3779
Northside Bakery
Richmond, VA. 804-968-7620
Notre Dame Bakery
Conception Harbour, NL 709-535-2738
Plaidberry Company
Vista, CA. 760-727-5403
Rising Dough Bakery
Sacramento, CA 916-387-9700
Roma Bakeries
Rockford, IL 815-964-6737
Ryke's Bakery
Muskegon, MI. 231-722-3508
Sara Lee Corporation
Downers Grove, IL. 630-598-8100
Schwan Food Company
Marshall, MN 800-533-5290
Scialo Brothers
Providence, RI 877-421-0986
Scot Paris Fine Desserts
New York, NY 212-807-1802
Seavers Bakery
Johnson City, TN 423-928-8131
Sinbad Sweets
Fresno, CA 800-350-7933
Spring Glen Fresh Foods
Ephrata, PA. 800-641-2853
St. Cloud Bakery
Saint Cloud, MN. 320-251-8055
Standard Bakery
Kealakekua, HI 808-322-3688
Sweet Endings
West Palm Beach, FL 888-635-1177
Table Talk Pie
Worcester, MA 508-798-8811
Tastykake
Philadelphia, PA 215-221-8500
The Great San Saba RiverPecan Company
San Saba, TX 800-621-9121
United Pies of Elkhart I
Elkhart, IN. 574-294-3419
Van de Kamp's
Peoria, IL. 800-798-3318
Wenger's Bakery
Reading, PA 610-372-6545
Zoelsmanns Bakery & Deli
Pueblo, CO 719-543-0407

Fruit

Bonert's Slice of Pie
Santa Ana, CA 714-540-3535

Frozen

Cutie Pie Corporation
Salt Lake City, UT 800-453-4575
Dynamic Foods
Lubbock, TX. 806-747-2777
Edwards Baking Company
Atlanta, GA. 800-241-0559
Field's
Pauls Valley, OK. 800-286-7501
Gardner Pie Company
Akron, OH. 330-245-2030
Harold Food Company
Charlotte, NC 704-588-8061
Mehaffie Pies
Dayton, OH. 937-253-1163
Mothers Kitchen Inc
Burlington, NJ. 609-589-3026
Pastry Chef
Pawtucket, RI 800-639-8606
Sara Lee Corporation
Downers Grove, IL. 630-598-8100
The Bama Company
Tulsa, OK 800-756-2262

Key Lime

Cheesecake Etc. Desserts
Miami Springs, FL 305-887-0258

Lemon-Meringue

Kyger Bakery Products
Lafayette, IN. 765-447-1252

Mehaffie Pies
Dayton, OH 937-253-1163

Meat

Mexi-Frost Specialties Company
Brooklyn, NY 718-625-3324
Morrison Lamothe
Toronto, ON 877-677-6533
Mortimer's Fine Foods
Burlington, ON 905-336-0000

Frozen

Country Pies
Coombs, BC 250-248-6415
Mexi-Frost Specialties Company
Brooklyn, NY 718-625-3324

Non-Fruit

Ledonne Brothers Bakery
Roseto, PA. 610-588-0423
MacEwan's Meats
Calgary, AB. 403-228-9999
Snyder Foods
Port Perry, ON. 905-985-7373
T. Marzetti Company
Columbus, OH 614-846-2232

Frozen

CGI Desserts
Sugar Land, TX. 281-240-1200
Dimitria Delights
North Grafton, MA 800-763-1113
Dynamic Foods
Lubbock, TX. 806-747-2777
Edwards Baking Company
Atlanta, GA. 800-241-0559
Field's
Pauls Valley, OK. 800-286-7501
Gardner Pie Company
Akron, OH. 330-245-2030
Kyger Bakery Products
Lafayette, IN. 765-447-1252
Mothers Kitchen Inc
Burlington, NJ. 609-589-3026
Nancy's Specialty Foods
Newark, CA 510-494-1100
Pastry Chef
Pawtucket, RI 800-639-8606
Sara Lee Corporation
Downers Grove, IL. 630-598-8100
The Bama Company
Tulsa, OK 800-756-2262
Wick's Pies
Winchester, IN 800-642-5880

Peach

Mehaffie Pies
Dayton, OH. 937-253-1163
The Bama Company
Tulsa, OK 800-756-2262

Rhubarb Pie

Bear Stewart Corporation
Chicago, IL 800-697-2327

Stuffing

Amalgamated Produce
Bridgeport, CT 800-358-3808
Bodin Foods
New Iberia, LA. 337-367-1344
Coastal Seafoods
Ridgefield, CT 203-431-0453
Good Old Days Foods
Little Rock, AR. 501-565-1257
Griffith Laboratories
Alsip, IL 800-346-9494
Noodles By Leonardo
Devil's Lake, ND 701-662-8300
Pepperidge Farm
Norwalk, CT. 888-737-7374
Quality Bakery Products
Fort Lauderdale, FL 800-590-3663
Roskam Baking Company
Grand Rapids, MI 616-574-5757
Stroehmann Bakery
Horsham, PA. 800-984-0989
Sturm Foods
Manawa, WI 800-347-8876
Texas Crumb & Food Products
Farmers Branch, TX 800-522-7862
Weston Bakeries
Calgary, AB. 403-259-1500
Zatarain's
Gretna, LA 800-435-6639

Bread

Oroweat Baking Company
Montebello, CA 323-721-5161

for Meat

Blue Chip Group
Salt Lake City, UT 800-878-0099
Boekhout Farms
Ontario, NY. 315-524-4041
Leelanau Fruit Company
Suttons Bay, MI 231-271-3514
Savoie's Sausage & Food Products
Opelousas, LA. 337-948-4115
Scotsburn Dairy Group
Scotsburn, NS 902-485-8023
Texas Crumb & Food Products
Farmers Branch, TX 800-522-7862
Weston Bakeries
Calgary, AB. 403-259-1500
World Flavors
Warminster, PA 215-672-4400

for Poultry

Boekhout Farms
Ontario, NY. 315-524-4041
Leelanau Fruit Company
Suttons Bay, MI 231-271-3514
Savoie's Sausage & Food Products
Opelousas, LA. 337-948-4115
Scotsburn Dairy Group
Scotsburn, NS 902-485-8023
Weston Bakeries
Calgary, AB. 403-259-1500
World Flavors
Warminster, PA 215-672-4400

Waffles

Bake Crafters Food
Collegedale, TN 800-296-8935
ConAgra Store Brands, Inc.
Lakeville, MN. 800-328-6286
Continental Mills
Seattle, WA 253-872-8400
Kellogg Company
Hammonton, NJ 609-567-2300
Kloss Manufacturing Company
Allentown, PA. 800-445-7100
Meyer's Bakeries
Hope, AR 800-643-1542
Nature's Path Foods
Richmond, BC 604-248-8777
Nestle Prepared Foods Company
Englewood, CO. 800-225-2270
Shepherdsfield Bakery
Fulton, MO 573-642-1439
Van's International Foods
Torrance, CA. 310-320-8611

Frozen

Bake Crafters Food
Collegedale, TN 800-296-8935
Beck's Waffles of Oklahoma
Shawnee, OK 800-646-6254
ConAgra Store Brands, Inc.
Lakeville, MN. 800-328-6286
Continental Mills
Seattle, WA 253-872-8400
Echo Lake Farm Produce Company
Burlington, WI 262-763-9551
Kellogg Canada Inc
Mississauga, ON. 888-876-3750
Kellogg Company
Hammonton, NJ 609-567-2300
Meyer's Bakeries
Hope, AR 800-643-1542
Nestle Prepared Foods Company
Englewood, CO. 800-225-2270
Van's International Foods
Torrance, CA. 310-320-8611

Wraps

La Tortilla Factory
Santa Rosa, CA. 800-446-1516
Nanka Seimen Company
Vernon, CA 323-585-9967
Scott Adams Foods
Newton, NJ 973-300-2091
Toufayan Bakeries
Orlando, FL. 407-295-2257
Valley Lahvosh Baking Company
Fresno, CA 800-480-2704

Flavored

La Tortilla Factory
Santa Rosa, CA. 800-446-1516

Beverages

General

A. Duda & Sons
Labelle, FL ... 800-440-3265
A. Lassonde, Inc.
Rougemont, QC ... 888-477-6663
ABC Tea House
Baldwin Park, CA ... 888-220-3988
Abita Brewing Company
Abita Springs, LA ... 800-737-2311
Absopure Water Company
Champaign, IL ... 800-422-7678
Abunda Life Laboratories
Asbury Park, NJ ... 732-775-7575
Acacia Vineyard
Napa, CA ... 707-226-9991
Acqua Blox LLC
Santa Fe Springs, CA ... 562-693-9599
Adirondack Beverages
Scotia, NY ... 800-316-6096
Admiral Beverages
Worland, WY ... 307-347-4201
AFP Advanced Food Products, LLC
Visalia, CA ... 559-627-2070
Agri-Mark
Lawrence, MA ... 978-689-4442
Aimonetto and Sons
Renton, WA ... 866-823-2777
Ajiri Tea Company
Upper Black Eddy, PA ... 610-982-5075
Al-Rite Fruits & Syrups
Miami, FL ... 305-652-2540
Alacer Corporation
Foothill Ranch, CA ... 800-854-0249
Alamance Foods/Triton Water Company
Burlington, NC ... 800-476-9111
Alexander & Baldwin
Honolulu, HI ... 808-525-6611
Alfer Laboratories
Chatsworth, CA ... 818-709-0737
All American Foods, Inc.
Mankato, MN ... 800-833-2661
All Juice Food & Beverage
Hendersonville, NC ... 800-736-5674
Allegro Coffee Company
Thornton, CO ... 800-666-4869
Aloe Farms
Harlingen, TX ... 800-262-6771
Aloe Laboratories, Inc.
Harlingen, TX ... 800-258-5380
Aloha Distillers
Honolulu, HI ... 808-841-5787
Alpenglow Beverage Company
Linden, VA ... 540-635-2118
Alpine Valley Water
Harvey, IL ... 708-333-3910
Alternative Health & Herbs
Albany, OR ... 800-345-4152
Ambootia Tea Estate
Chicago, IL ... 312-661-1550
Amcan Industries
Elmsford, NY ... 914-347-4838
American Food Traders
Miami, FL ... 305-273-7090
American Fruit Processors
Pacoima, CA ... 818-899-9574
American Mercantile Corporation
Windermere, FL
American Purpac Technologies, LLC
Beloit, WI ... 877-787-7221
American Soy Products
Saline, MI ... 734-429-2310
Andalusia Distributing Company
Andalusia, AL ... 334-222-3671
Andrew Peller Limited
Grimsby, ON ... 905-643-4131
Anheuser-Busch
Columbus, OH ... 614-888-6644
Apple & Eve
Roslyn, NY ... 800-969-8018
Aqua Clara Bottling & Distribution
Clearwater, FL ... 727-446-2999
Arbuckle Coffee
Pittsburgh, PA ... 800-533-8278
Arcadian Estate Winery
Rock Stream, NY ... 800-298-1346
Ariel Vineyards
Napa, CA ... 800-456-9472
Arizona Beverage Company
Woodbury, NY ... 800-832-3775

asiamerica

Asiamerica Ingredients
Westwood, NJ ... 201-497-5531

Processor, importer, exporter and distributor of bulk vitamins, amino acids, nutraceuticals, aromatic chemicals, food additives, herbs, mineral nutrients and pharmaceuticals.

Atlanta Coffee Roasters
Atlanta, GA ... 800-252-8211
August Schell Brewing Company
New Ulm, MN ... 800-770-5020
Austrian Trade Commission
New York, NY ... 212-421-5250
Avalon Foodservice, Inc.
Canal Fulton, OH ... 800-362-0622
B.M. Lawrence & Company
San Francisco, CA ... 415-981-3650
Bacardi Canada, Inc.
Brampton, ON ... 905-451-6100
Banfi Vintners
Glen Head, NY ... 800-645-6511
Barrows Tea Company
New Bedford, MA ... 800-832-5024
Barton Brands
Louisville, KY ... 800-598-6352
Batavia Wine Cellars
Canandaigua, NY ... 585-396-7600
Baywood Cellars
Lodi, CA ... 800-214-0445
BCGA Concept Corporation
New York, NY ... 212-488-0661
Bean Forge
Coos Bay, OR ... 541-267-5191
Beckmen Vineyards
Los Olivos, CA ... 805-688-8664
Belton Foods
Dayton, OH ... 800-443-2266
Benmarl Wine Company
Marlboro, NY ... 845-236-4265
Berkeley Farms
Hayward, CA ... 510-265-8600
Bevco
Surrey, BC ... 800-663-0090
Beverage Capital Corporation
Baltimore, MD ... 410-242-7003
Bianchi Winery
Paso Robles, CA ... 805-226-9922
Big Red Bottling
Austin, TX ... 254-772-7791
Birdseye Dairy
Green Bay, WI ... 920-494-5388
Black Prince Distillery Inc.
Clifton, NJ ... 973-365-2050
Blue Sky Natural Beverage Company
Corona, CA ... 800-426-7367
Boisson Slow Cow Inc
, QC ... 418-266-0432
Bolthouse Farms
Bakersfield, CA ... 800-467-4683
Borgnine Beverage Company
Sherman Oaks, CA ... 818-501-5312
Boston's Best Coffee Roasters
South Easton, MA ... 800-898-8393
Bottineau Coop Creamery
Bottineau, ND ... 701-228-2216
Boulder Beer Company
Boulder, CO ... 303-444-8448
Brander Vineyard
Los Olivos, CA ... 800-970-9979
Brenntag Pacific
Santa Fe Springs, CA ... 562-903-9626
Briar's USA
North Brunswick, NJ ... 887-327-4277
Brick Brewery
Waterloo, ON ... 800-505-8971
Brimstone Hill Vineyard
Pine Bush, NY ... 845-744-2231
BRJ Coffee & Tea
Lincoln, CA ... 800-829-1300
Brooklyn Bottling Company
Milton, NY ... 845-795-2171
Broughton Foods
Marietta, OH ... 800-283-2479
Buckmaster Coffee
Hillsboro, OR ... 800-962-9148
Buena Vista Carneros Winery
Sonoma, CA ... 800-678-8504
Buffalo Trace Distillery
Frankfort, KY ... 800-654-8471
Bull Run Roasting Company
Hayward, WI ... 715-634-3646
Bully Hill Vineyards
Hammondsport, NY ... 607-868-3610
Burnette Foods
Hartford, MI ... 616-621-3181
C.F. Burger Creamery
Detroit, MI ... 800-229-2322
Cadillac Coffee Company
Madison Heights, MI ... 800-438-6900
Cafe Du Monde
New Orleans, LA ... 504-587-0835
Cafe Yaucono/Jimenez & Fernandez
Santurce, PR ... 787-721-3337
Cain's Coffee Company
Springfield, MO ... 800-641-4025
California Brands Flavors
Oakland, CA ... 800-348-0111
California Day Fresh
Asusa, CA ... 877-858-4237
California Natural Products
Lathrop, CA ... 209-858-2525
Callaway Vineyards & Winery
Temecula, CA ... 800-472-2377
Canada Dry Bottling Company
Flushing, NY ... 718-762-5967
Canadian Mist Distillers
Collingwood, ON ... 705-445-4690
Caracollillo Coffee Mills
Tampa, FL ... 800-682-0023
Caravan Company
Worcester, MA ... 508-752-3777
Cargill Juice Products
Frostproof, FL ... 800-227-4455
Carolina Products
Greer, SC ... 864-879-3084
Carolina Treet
Wilmington, NC ... 800-616-6344
Cascade Mountain Winery & Restaurant
Amenia, NY ... 845-373-9021
Cass Clay Creamery
Fargo, ND ... 701-293-6455
Castello Di Borghese
Cutchogue, NY ... 800-734-5158
Cawy Bottling Company
Miami, FL ... 877-917-2299
CB Beverage Corporation
Hopkins, MN ... 952-935-9905
Cecchetti Sebastiani Cellar
Sonoma, CA ... 707-996-8463
Cedar Creek Winery
Cedarburg, WI ... 800-827-8020
Cedar Lake Foods
Cedar Lake, MI ... 800-246-5039
Central Coca-Cola Bottling Company
Richmond, VA ... 800-359-3759
Central Dairies
St Johns, NL ... 800-563-6455
Chadler
Swedesboro, NJ ... 856-467-0099
Chase Brothers Dairy
Oxnard, CA ... 800-438-6455
Chateau des Charmes Wines
St. Davids, ON ... 800-263-2541
Chateau Julien Winery
Carmel, CA ... 831-624-2600
Chateau St. Jean Vineyards
Kenwood, CA ... 707-833-4134
Cheribundi
Geneva, NY ... 315-781-7308

Chestnut Mountain Winery
Hoschton, GA 770-867-6914
Chi Company/Tabor Hill Winery
Buchanan, MI 800-283-3363
Chicago Coffee Roastery
Huntley, IL 800-762-5402
Chicama Vineyards
West Tisbury, MA 888-244-2262
Chimere
Santa Maria, CA 805-922-9097
Chiquita Brands Intl. ional
Cincinnati, OH 800-438-0015
Chocolat
Bellevue, WA 800-808-2462
Chouinard Vineyards
Castro Valley, CA 510-582-9900
Christine Woods Winery
Philo, CA 707-895-2115
Christopher Creek Winery
Healdsburg, CA 707-431-8243
Chukar Cherries
Prosser, WA 800-624-9544
Chung's Gourmet Foods
Houston, TX 800-824-8647
Cienega Valley Winery/DeRose
Hollister, CA 831-636-9143
Cimarron Cellars
Caney, OK 580-889-5997
Cinnabar Vineyards & Winery
Saratoga, CA 408-741-5858
Citrus Citrosuco North America
Lake Wales, FL 800-356-4592
Citrus International
Winter Park, FL 407-629-8037
Citrus Service
Winter Garden, FL 407-656-4999
City Bean
Stevenson Ranch, CA 888-248-9232
City Brewery Latrobe
Latrobe, PA 724-537-5545
City Brewing Company
La Crosse, WI 608-785-4200
Claiborne & Churchill Vintners
San Luis Obispo, CA 805-544-4066
Claire's Grand River Winery
Madison, OH 440-298-9838
Classic Tea
Libertyville, IL 630-680-9934
Clayton's Coffee & Tea
Modesto, CA 209-522-7811
Clean Foods
Santa Paula, CA 800-526-8328
Clear Creek Distillery
Portland, OR 503-248-9470
Clear Mountain Coffee Company
Silver Spring, MD 301-587-2233
Clearwater Coffee Company
Lake Zurich, IL 847-540-7711
Cline Cellars
Sonoma, CA 800-543-2070
Clinton Milk Company
Newark, NJ 973-642-3000
Clinton Vineyards
Clinton Corners, NY 845-266-5372
Clos Du Bois
Geyserville, CA 800-222-3189
Clos du Lac Cellars
Ione, CA 209-274-2238
Clos Du Muriel
Temecula, CA 951-296-5400
Clos du Val Wine Company
Napa, CA 800-993-9463
Clos Pegase Winery
Calistoga, CA 800-866-8583
Cloudstone Vineyards
Los Altos Hills, CA 650-948-8621
Clover Hill Vineyards & Winery
Breinigsville, PA 800-256-8374
Coastal Goods
Barnstable, MA 508-375-1050
Coastlog Industries
Novi, MI 248-344-9556
Cobraz Brazilian Coffee
New York, NY 212-759-7700
Coburg Dairy
North Charleston, SC 843-554-4870
Coca-Cola Bottling Company
El Paso, TX 800-288-3228
Coca-Cola Bottling Company
Charlotte, NC 800-777-2653
Coca-Cola Bottling Company
Honolulu, HI 808-839-6711
Coca-Cola Bottling Company
West Memphis, AR 870-732-1460
Cocolalla Winery
Cocolalla, ID 208-263-3774
Coffee & Tea
Bloomington, MN 952-854-2883
Coffee Barrel
Okemos, MI 517-349-3888
Coffee Bean
Englewood, CO 303-922-1238
Coffee Bean International
Portland, OR 800-877-0474
Coffee Bean of Leesburg
Leesburg, VA 800-232-6872
Coffee Beanery
Flushing, MI 800-728-2326
Coffee Butler Service
Alexandria, VA 703-823-0028
Coffee Concepts
Dallas, TX 214-363-9331
Coffee Creations
Portland, OR 800-245-5856
Coffee Culture-A House
Lincoln, NE 402-438-8456
Coffee Holding Company
Staten Island, NY 800-458-2233
Coffee Masters
Spring Grove, IL 800-334-6485
Coffee Mill Roastery
Elon, NC 800-729-1727
Coffee Millers & Roasting
Cape Coral, FL 239-573-6800
Coffee People
Beaverton, OR 800-354-5282
Coffee Process Technology
Houston, TX 713-695-7530
Coffee Reserve
Phoenix, AZ 623-434-0939
Coffee Roasters
Oakland, NJ 201-337-8221
Coffee Roasters of New Orleans
New Orleans, LA 800-737-5464
Coffee Up
Chicago, IL 847-288-9330
Coffee Works
Sacramento, CA 800-275-3335
Cold Hollow Cider Mill
Waterbury Center, VT 800-327-7537
College Coffee Roasters
Mountville, PA 717-285-9561
Coloma Frozen Foods
Coloma, MI 800-642-2723
Colonial Coffee Roasters
Miami, FL 305-634-1843
Colorado Cellars Winery
Palisade, CO 970-464-7921
Colorado Spice
Boulder, CO 800-677-7423
Columbia Winery
Woodinville, WA 425-488-2776
Comfort Foods
North Andover, MA 800-514-3663
Comidas Y Bebidas Fermentadas
Col. San Jeronimo, MO
Commodities Marketing, Inc.
Edison, NJ 732-603-5077
Commonwealth Fish & Beer Company
Boston, MA 617-523-8383
Community Coffee Specialty
Baton Rouge, LA 800-525-5583
ConAgra Grocery Products
Irvine, CA 714-680-1000
Concannon Vineyard
Livermore, CA 800-258-9866
Condaxis Coffee Company
Jacksonville, FL 904-356-5330
Conn Creek Winery
Saint Helena, CA 800-793-7960
Conneaut Cellars Winery
Conneaut Lake, PA 877-229-9463
Conrotto A. Winery
Gilroy, CA 408-847-2233
Consolidated Distilled Products
Chicago, IL 773-927-4161
Consolidated Tea Company
Lynbrook, NY 516-887-1144
Consun Food Industries
Elyria, OH 440-322-6301
Contact International
Skokie, IL 847-324-4411
Continental Coffee Products Company
Houston, TX 800-323-6178
Cool
Richardson, TX 972-437-9352
Cooper Mountain Vineyards
Beaverton, OR 503-649-0027
Coors Brewing Company
Golden, CO 800-642-6116
Corim International Coff
Brick, NJ 800-942-4201
Corus Brands
Woodinville, WA 425-806-2600
Cosentino Winery Vintage Grapevine, Inc.
Yountville, CA 800-764-1220
Cotswold Cottage Foods
Arvada, CO 800-208-1977
Cott Concentrates/Royal Crown Cola International
Columbus, GA 800-652-5642
Cott Coporation
Tampa, FL 813-313-1800
Country Pure Foods
Akron, OH 330-753-2293
Country Pure Foods
Akron, OH 877-995-8423
Cow Palace Too
Granger, WA 509-829-5777
Cowie Wine Cellars
Paris, AR 479-963-3990
Crescini Wines
Soquel, CA 831-462-1466
Cristom Vineyards
Salem, OR 503-375-3068
Criveller Group
Niagara Falls, ON 888-849-2266
Cronin Vineyards
Woodside, CA 650-851-1452
Crown Regal Wine Cellars
Brooklyn, NY 718-604-1430
Cruse Vineyards
Chester, SC 803-377-3944
Crystal & Vigor Beverages
Kearny, NJ 201-991-2342
Crystal Geyser Roxanne LLC
Pensacola, FL 850-476-8844
Crystal Springs Water Company
Fort Lauderdale, FL 800-432-1321
Crystal Water Company
Orlando, FL 800-444-7873
CTL Foods
Colfax, WI 800-962-5227
Culligan Water Technologies
Rosemont, IL 1 8-6 7-5 02
Cuneo Cellars
Amity, OR 503-835-2782
Custom House Coffee RoasJodyana Corporation
Miami, FL 888-563-5282
Cutrale Citrus Juices
Leesburg, FL 352-728-7800
Cutrale Citrus Juices
Auburndale, FL 863-965-5000
Cuvaison Vineyard
Calistoga, CA 707-942-6266
Cygnet Cellars
Hollister, CA 831-637-7559
Dairy Fresh Corporation
Greensboro, AL 800-239-5114
Dairy Fresh Foods
Taylor, MI 313-295-6300
Dairy Land
Macon, GA 478-742-6461
Dairy Maid Dairy
Frederick, MD 301-695-0431
Dalla Valle Vineyards
Oakville, CA 707-944-2676
Dallis Brothers
Ozone Park, NY 800-424-4252
Damron Corporation
Chicago, IL 800-333-1860
Danone Waters
French Camp, CA 209-982-5412
Dark Mountain Winery and Brewery
Vail, AZ 520-762-5777
Daume Winery
Camarillo, CA 800-559-9922
David Bruce Winery
Los Gatos, CA 800-397-9972
David Rio
San Francisco, CA 800-454-9605
Davis Bynum Winery
Healdsburg, CA 800-826-1073
Daybreak Coffee Roasters
Glastonbury, CT 800-882-5282
Daymar Select Fine Coffees
El Cajon, CA 800-466-7590

Dazbog Coffee Company
Denver, CO 303-892-9999
De Coty Coffee Company
San Angelo, TX 800-588-8001
De Lima Company
Liverpool, NY 800-962-8864
De Loach Vineyards
Santa Rosa, CA 707-526-9111
De Lorimier Winery
Geyserville, CA 800-546-7718
Deaver Vineyards
Plymouth, CA 209-245-4099
Decoty Coffee Company
San Angelo, TX 800-588-8001
Deep Rock Fontenelle Water Company
Omaha, NE 800-433-1303
Deep Rock Water Company
Denver, CO 800-695-2020
Deep Rock Water Company
Minneapolis, MN 800-800-8986
Deer Meadow Vineyard
Winchester, VA 800-653-6632
Deer Park Winery
Elk Creek, MO 707-963-5411
Dehlinger Winery
Sebastopol, CA 707-823-2378
Del's Lemonade & Refreshments
Cranston, RI 401-463-6190
Delicato Vineyards
Napa, CA 877-824-3600
Denatale Vineyards
Healdsburg, CA 707-431-8460
Destileria Serralles Inc
Mercedita, PR 787-840-1000
Destileria Tlacolula
Tlacoulula De Matamoros, OA 951-562-1101
Devansoy
Carroll, IA 800-747-8605
Devine Foods
Media, PA 888-338-4631
Devlin Wine Cellars
Soquel, CA 831-476-7288
DG Yuengling & Son
Pottsville, PA 570-622-0153
Di Grazia Vineyards
Brookfield, CT 800-230-8853
Diageo Canada Inc.
Toronto, ON 416-626-2000
Diageo United Distillers
Norwalk, CT 203-229-2100
Diamond Creek Vineyards
Calistoga, CA 707-942-6926
Diamond Oaks Vineyard
Cloverdale, CA 707-894-3191
Diamond Water
Hot Springs, AR 501-623-1251
Diehl Food Ingredients
Defiance, OH 800-251-3033
Distant Lands Coffee Roaster
Tyler, TX 800-346-5459
Distillata Company
Cleveland, OH 800-999-2906
Divine Foods
Elizabethtown, NC 910-862-2576
Dixie Dairy Company
Gary, IN 219-885-6101
DMH Ingredients
Libertyville, IL 847-362-9977
Dole Food Company
Westlake Village, CA 818-879-6600
Domaine Chandon
Yountville, CA 800-242-6366
Domaine St. George Winery
Healdsburg, CA 707-433-5508
Don Francisco Coffee Traders
Los Angeles, CA 800-697-5282
Don Hilario Estate Coffee
Tampa, FL 800-799-1903
Don Jose Foods
Oceanside, CA 760-631-0243
Donatoni Winery
Inglewood, CA 310-645-5445
Door-Peninsula Winery
Sturgeon Bay, WI 800-551-5049
Douwe Egberts
Worthington, OH 800-582-6617
Downeast Coffee
Pawtucket, RI 800-345-2007
Dr. Frank's Vinifera Wine Cellar
Hammondsport, NY 800-320-0735
Dr. Konstantin Frank Vin
Hammondsport, NY 800-320-0735
Dr. Pepper/Seven-Up
Racine, WI 800-696-5891
Dream Foods International LLC
Santa Monica, CA 310-315-5739
Dreyer Sonoma
Woodside, CA 650-851-9448
Droubi's Imports
Houston, TX 713-988-7138
Dry Creek Vineyard
Healdsburg, CA 800-864-9463
DS Waters of America
Atlanta, GA 800-728-5508
Duck Pond Cellars
Dundee, OR 800-437-3213
Duckhorn Vineyards
St Helena, CA 888-354-8885
Duncan Peak Vineyards
Hopland, CA 707-744-1129
Dundee Wine Company
Dundee, OR 888-427-4953
Dunn Vineyards
Angwin, CA 707-965-3642
Duplin Wine Cellars
Rose Hill, NC 800-774-9634
Durney Vineyards
Carmel Valley, CA 800-625-8466
Dutch Henry Winery
Calistoga, CA 888-224-5879
E&J Gallo Winery
Modesto, CA 209-341-3111
E&J Gallo Winery
Livingston, CA 209-394-6219
E&J Gallo Winery
Fresno, CA 559-458-2480
Eagle Coffee Company
Baltimore, MD 800-545-4015
Eagle Crest Vineyards
Conesus, NY 585-346-2321
Easley Winery
Indianapolis, IN 317-636-4516
East India Coffee & Tea Company
Lincoln, CA 800-829-1300
East Side Winery/Oak Ridge Vineyards
Lodi, CA 209-369-4758
Eastern Tea Corporation
Monroe Township, NJ 800-221-0865
Eastrise Trading Corporation
Baldwin Park, CA
Eberle Winery
Paso Robles, CA 805-238-9607
Ed Oliveira Winery
Arcata, CA 707-822-3023
Eden Foods Inc.
Clinton, MI 800-248-0320
Edgewood Estate Winery
Napa, CA 800-755-2374
Edmunds St. John
Berkeley, CA 510-981-1510
Edna Valley Vineyard
San Luis Obispo, CA 805-544-5855
Eight O'Clock Coffee Company
Montvale, NJ 800-299-2739
El Dorado Coffee
Flushing, NY 800-635-2566
El Paso Winery
Ulster Park, NY 845-331-0491
Eldorado Artesian Springs
Eldorado Springs, CO 303-499-1316
Elk Cove Vineyards
Gaston, OR 877-355-2683
Elk Run Vineyards
Mount Airy, MD 800-414-2513
Ellis Coffee Company
Philadelphia, PA 800-822-3984
Elliston Vineyards
Sunol, CA 925-862-2377
Ellsworth Cooperative Creamery
Ellsworth, WI 715-273-4311
Emilio Guglielmo Winery
Morgan Hill, CA 408-779-2145
Empire Tea Services
Columbus, IN 800-790-0246
Empresas La Famosa/Coco Lopez
Toa Baja, PR 787-251-0060
Ener-G Foods
Seattle, WA 800-331-5222
Enz Vineyards
Hollister, CA 831-637-3956
Eola Hills Wine Cellars
Rickreall, OR 800-291-6730
EOS Estate Winery
Paso Robles, CA 800-349-9463
Erath Vineyards Winery
Dundee, OR 800-539-5463
Erba Food Products
Brooklyn, NY 718-272-7700
Espresso Vivace
Seattle, WA 206-860-2722
Essentia Water
Bothell, WA 425-402-9555
Eureka Water Company
Oklahoma City, OK 800-310-8474
Eurobubblies
Sherman Oaks, CA 800-273-0750
European Coffee
Cherry Hill, NJ 856-428-7202
European Roasterie
Le Center, MN 888-469-2233
Evans Properties
Dade City, FL 352-567-5662
Evco Wholesale Foods
Emporia, KS 620-343-7000
Evensen Vineyards
Oakville, CA 707-944-2396
Everfresh Beverages
Warren, MI 586-755-9500
Evesham Wood Vineyard & Winery
Salem, OR 503-371-8478
Ex Drinks
Henderson, NV 866-753-4929
Excellent Coffee Company
Pawtucket, RI 800-345-2007
Excelso Coffee Company
Norcross, GA 800-241-2138
Eyrie Vineyards
Mcminnville, OR 503-472-6315
F. Gavina & Sons
Vernon, CA 323-582-0671
F.X. Matt Brewing Company
Utica, NY 800-690-3181
Fall Creek Vineyards
Austin, TX 512-476-4477
Far Niente Winery
Oakville, CA 707-944-2861
Farella-Park Vineyards
Napa, CA 707-254-9489
Farfelu Vineyards
Flint Hill, VA 540-364-2930
Farmer Brothers Company
Torrance, CA 800-735-2878
Farmland Dairies
Wallington, NJ 888-727-6252
FCC Coffee Packers
Doral, FL 305-591-1128
Fee Brothers
Rochester, NY 800-961-3337
Fenestra Winery
Livermore, CA 800-789-9463
Fenn Valley Vineyards
Fennville, MI 800-432-6265
Ferolito Vultaggio & Sons
Woodbury, NY 800-832-3775
Ferrante Winery & Ristorante
Geneva, OH 440-466-6046
Ferrara Bakery & Cafe
New York, NY 212-226-6150
Ferrara Winery
Escondido, CA 760-745-7632
Ferrari-Carano Vineyards& Winery
Healdsburg, CA 800-831-0381
Ferrigno Vineyard & Winery
St James, MO 573-265-7742
Ferrigno Vineyards & Win
St James, MO 573-265-7742
Fess Parker Winery
Los Olivos, CA 800-446-2455
Ficklin Vineyards
Madera, CA 559-674-4598
Fidalgo Bay Coffee
Burlington, WA 800-310-5540
Field Stone Winery & Vineyard
Healdsburg, CA 800-544-7273
Fieldbrook Valley Winery
McKinleyville, CA 707-839-4140
Fife Vineyards
Redwood Valley, CA 707-485-0323

Fiji Water Company
Los Angeles, CA . . . 877-426-3454
Filsinger Vineyards & Winery
Temecula, CA . . . 951-302-6363
Fine Foods Northwest
Seattle, WA . . . 800-862-3965
Finlay Tea Solutions
Morristown, NJ . . . 973-539-8030
Fiore Winery
Pylesville, MD . . . 410-879-4007
Firelands Wine Company
Sandusky, OH . . . 800-548-9463
Firestone Vineyard
Los Olivos, CA . . . 805-688-3940
First Colony Coffee & Tea Company
Norfolk, VA . . . 800-446-8555
First Roasters of Central Florida
Longwood, FL . . . 407-699-6364
Fisher Ridge Wine Company
Charleston, WV . . . 304-342-8702
Fisher Vineyards
Santa Rosa, CA . . . 707-539-7511
Fitzpatrick Winery & Lodge
Somerset, CA . . . 800-245-9166
Fizz-O Water Company
Tulsa, OK . . . 918-834-3691
Flagship Atlanta Dairy
Belleview, FL . . . 800-224-0669
Flavouressence Products
Mississauga, ON . . . 866-209-7778
Flora Springs Wine Company
Saint Helena, CA . . . 707-963-5711
Florida Distillers Company
Lake Alfred, FL . . . 863-956-3477
Florida Food Products
Eustis, FL . . . 800-874-2331
Florida Fruit Juices
Chicago, IL . . . 773-586-6200
Florida Juice Products
Lakeland, FL . . . 863-802-4040
Florida Key West
Fort Myers, FL . . . 239-694-8787
Flynn Vineyards Winery
Rickreall, OR . . . 888-427-4953
Fmali Herb
Santa Cruz, CA . . . 831-423-7913
Foley Estates Vineyards & Winery
Lompoc, CA . . . 805-737-6222
Folgers Coffee Company
Orrville, OH . . . 877-693-6543
Folie a Deux Winery
Oakville, CA . . . 1 8-0 5-5 64
Folklore Foods
Toppenish, WA . . . 509-865-4772
Foltz Coffee Tea & Spice Company
New Orleans, LA . . . 504-486-1545
Foppiano Vineyard
Healdsburg, CA . . . 707-433-7272
Foremost Farms
Athens, WI . . . 715-257-7015
Foremost Farms
Clayton, WI . . . 715-948-2166
Foris Vineyards
Cave Junction, OR . . . 541-592-3752
Forman Vineyards
St Helena, CA . . . 707-963-3900
Fortino Winery
Gilroy, CA . . . 888-617-6606
Fortuna Cellars
Davis, CA . . . 530-756-6686
Fortunes International Teas
Mc Kees Rocks, PA . . . 800-551-8327
Fountainhead Water Company
Norcross, GA . . . 864-944-1993
Four Chimneys Farm Winery Trust
Himrod, NY . . . 607-243-7502
Four Sisters Winery
Belvidere, NJ . . . 908-475-3671
Fox Run Vineyards
Penn Yan, NY . . . 800-636-9786
Fox Vineyards Winery
Social Circle, GA . . . 770-787-5402
Foxen Vineyard
Santa Maria, CA . . . 805-937-4251
Franciscan Oakville Estates
Rutherford, CA . . . 800-529-9463
Franciscan Vineyards
St. Helena, CA . . . 800-529-9463
Franco's Cocktail Mixes
Pompano Beach, FL . . . 800-782-4508
Frank Family Vineyard
Calistoga, CA . . . 707-942-0859
Frank-Lin Distillers
San Jose, CA . . . 408-259-8900
Franklin Hill Vineyards
Bangor, PA . . . 888-887-2839
Franzia Winery
Ripon, CA . . . 209-599-4111
Fratelli Perata
Paso Robles, CA . . . 805-238-2809
Frederick Wildman & Sons
New York, NY . . . 800-733-9463
Freed, Teller & Freed
South San Francisco, CA . . . 800-370-7371
Freemark Abbey Winery
Helena, CA . . . 800-963-9698
Freixenet
Sonoma, CA . . . 707-996-4981
Fresh Roast Systems
Livermore, CA . . . 925-456-2270
Frey Vineyards
Redwood Valley, CA . . . 800-760-3739
Frick Winery
Geyserville, CA . . . 707-857-1980
Frisinger Cellars
Napa, CA . . . 707-255-3749
Frog's Leap Winery
Rutherford, CA . . . 800-959-4704
Frontenac Point Vineyard
Trumansburg, NY . . . 607-387-9619
Frontier Natural Co-op
Norway, IA . . . 303-449-8137
Fruit D'Or Inc
Notre-Dame De Lourdes, QC . . . 819-385-1126
Full Service Beverage Company
Wichita, KS . . . 800-540-0001
G&J Pepsi-Cola Bottlers
Cicinnati, OH . . . 513-785-6060
Gadsden Coffee/Caffe
Arivaca, AZ . . . 888-514-5282
Gainey Vineyard
Santa Ynez, CA . . . 805-688-0558
Galante Vineyards
Carmel Valley, CA . . . 800-425-2683
Galena Cellars Winery
Galena, IL . . . 800-397-9463
Galleano Winery
Mira Loma, CA . . . 951-685-5376
Galliker Dairy
Johnstown, PA . . . 800-477-6455
Galluccio Estate Vineyards
Cutchogue, NY . . . 631-734-7089
Garelick Farms
Lynn, MA . . . 800-487-8700
Gary Farrell Wines
Santa Rosa, CA . . . 707-433-6616
Gehl Foods, Inc.
Germantown, WI . . . 800-521-2873
Gehl Guernsey Farms
Germantown, WI . . . 800-434-5713
George A Dickel & Company
Tullahoma, TN . . . 888-342-5352
George H Hathaway Coffee Company
Summit Argo, IL . . . 708-458-7668
Georgia Sun
Newnan, GA . . . 770-251-2500
Georgia Winery
Ringgold, GA . . . 706-937-2177
Georis Winery
Carmel Valley, CA . . . 831-659-1050
Germanton Winery
Germanton, NC . . . 800-322-2894
Geyser Peak Winery
Geyserville, CA . . . 800-255-9463
Giacorelli Imports
Boca Raton, FL . . . 561-451-1415
Giasi Winery
Rock Stream, NY . . . 607-535-7785
Gibson Wine Company
Sanger, CA . . . 559-875-2505
Gilette Foods
Union, NJ . . . 908-688-0500
Ginseng Up Corporation
Rockleigh, NJ . . . 201-660-8081
Girard Spring Water
North Providence, RI . . . 800-477-9287
Girard Winery/Rudd Estates
Oakville, CA . . . 707-944-8577
Girardet Wine Cellars
Roseburg, OR . . . 541-679-7252
Giumarra Vineyards
Bakersfield, CA . . . 661-395-7000
Givaudan Flavors
Cincinnati, OH . . . 513-948-8000
Glen Summit Springs Water Company
Mountain Top, PA . . . 800-621-7596
Glencourt
Napa, CA . . . 707-944-4444
Glenora Wine Cellars
Dundee, NY . . . 800-243-5513
Global Beverage Company
Rochester, NY . . . 585-381-3560
Global Food Industries
Townville, SC . . . 800-225-4152
Global Health Laboratories
Amityville, NY . . . 631-777-2134
Global Marketing Associates
Schaumburg, IL . . . 847-397-2350
GlobeTrends
Morris Plains, NJ . . . 800-416-8327
Globus Coffee
Manhasset, NY . . . 631-390-2233
Gloria Ferrer Champagne
Sonoma, CA . . . 707-996-7256
Gloria Jean's Gourmet Coffees
Irvine, CA . . . 877-320-5282
Gloria Winery & Vineyard
Springfield, MO . . . 417-926-6263
Glunz Family Winery & Cellars
Grayslake, IL . . . 847-548-9463
Gold Star Coffee Company
Salem, MA . . . 888-505-5233
Golden Creek Vineyard
Santa Rosa, CA . . . 707-538-2350
Golden Moon Tea
Herndon, VA . . . 877-327-5473
Golden Town Apple Products
Rougemont, QC . . . 519-599-6300
Good Earth® Teas
Santa Cruz, CA . . . 888-625-8227
Good Harbor Vineyards
Lake Leelanau, MI . . . 231-256-7165
Good-O-Beverages Company
Bronx, NY . . . 718-328-6400
Goodson Brothers Coffee
Knoxville, TN . . . 865-531-8022
Goosecross Cellars
Yountville, CA . . . 800-276-9210
Gourmet Mondiale
Ste-Catherine, QC . . . 450-638-6380
Goya Foods
Secaucus, NJ . . . 201-348-4900
Grace Tea Company
Acton, MA . . . 978-635-9500
Grainaissance
Emeryville, CA . . . 800-472-4697
Grande River Vineyards
Palisade, CO . . . 800-264-7696
Granite Springs Winery
Somerset, CA . . . 800-638-6041
Great Eastern Sun
Asheville, NC . . . 800-334-5809
Great Western Juice Company
Maple Heights, OH . . . 800-321-9180
Green Mountain Chocolates
Franklin, MA . . . 508-520-7160
Green Mountain Cidery
Middlebury, VT . . . 802-388-0700
Green Spot Packaging
Claremont, CA . . . 800-456-3210
Greenfield Wine Company
Vallejo, CA . . . 707-552-5199
Greenwood Ridge Vineyards
Philo, CA . . . 707-895-2002
Gregory's Box'd Beverages
Newark, NJ . . . 973-465-1113
Groth Vineyards & Winery
Oakville, CA . . . 707-944-0290
Groupe Paul Masson
Longueuil, QC . . . 514-878-3050
Gruet Winery
Albuquerque, NM . . . 888-897-9463
Guilliams Winery
St Helena, CA . . . 707-963-9059
Guinness-Bass Import Company
Stamford, CT . . . 800-521-1591
Gundlach Bundschu Winery
Sonoma, CA . . . 707-938-5277
GWB Foods Corporation
Brooklyn, NY . . . 877-977-7610
H Coturri & Sons Winery
Glen Ellen, CA . . . 866-268-8774
H&H Products Company
Orlando, FL . . . 407-299-5410
H&K Products-Pappy's Sassafras Teas
Columbus Grove, OH . . . 877-659-5110

H. Meyer Dairy Company
Cincinnati, OH 800-347-6455
H.R. Nicholson Company
Baltimore, MD 800-638-3514
Haas Coffee Group
Miami, FL 305-371-7473
Habersham Winery
Helen, GA 770-983-1973
Hafner Vineyard
Healdsburg, CA 707-433-4606
Hahn Estates and Smith &Hook
Soledad, CA 866-925-7994
Haight-Brown Vineyard
Litchfield, CT 800-577-9463
Hains Celestial Group
Melville, NY 877-612-4246
Hallcrest Vineyards
Felton, CA 831-335-4441
Handley Cellars
Philo, CA 800-733-3151
Hank's Beverage Company
Feastervl Trvs, PA 800-289-4722
Hanover Foods Corporation
Hanover, PA 717-632-6000
Hansen Beverage
Corona, CA 800-426-7367
Hanzell Vineyards
Sonoma, CA 707-996-3860
Harbor Winery
West Sacramento, CA 916-371-6776
Harmony Cellars
Harmony, CA 800-432-9239
Harney & Sons Fine Teas
Millerton, NY 800-832-8463
Harold L. King & Company
Redwood City, CA 888-368-2233
Harpersfield Vineyard
Geneva, OH 440-466-4739
Harrisburg Dairies
Harrisburg, PA 800-692-7429
Hart Winery
Temecula, CA 877-638-8788
Hartford Family Winery
Forestville, CA 800-588-0234
Has Beans Coffee & Tea Company
Mount Shasta, CA 800-427-2326
Hastings Cooperative Creamery
Hastings, MN 651-437-9414
Hawaii Coffee Company
Honolulu, HI 800-338-8353
Hawaiian Isles Kona Coffee Co
Honolulu, HI 808-833-2244
Hawaiian Natural Water Company
Pearl City, HI 808-483-0520
Hawk Pacific Freight
Napa, CA 707-259-0266
Haydenergy Health
New York, NY 800-255-1660
Hazlitt's 1852 Vineyard
Hector, NY 888-750-0494
Heartland Vineyards
Cleveland, OH 440-871-0701
Heaven Hill Distilleries
Bardstown, KY 502-348-3921
Heck Cellars
Arvin, CA 661-854-6120
Hecker Pass Winery
Gilroy, CA 408-842-8755
Hegy's South Hills Vineyard & Winery
Twin Falls, ID 208-599-0074
Heineman's Winery
Put In Bay, OH 419-285-2811
Heitz Wine Cellar
Saint Helena, CA 707-963-3542
Helena View/Johnston Vineyard
Calistoga, CA 707-942-4956
Hells Canyon Winery
Caldwell, ID 800-318-7873
Hemisphere Associated
Huntington, NY 631-673-3840
Henry Estate Winery
Umpqua, OR 800-782-2686
Henry Hill & Company
Napa, CA 707-224-6565
Heritage Farms Dairy
Murfreesboro, TN 615-895-2790
Heritage Northwest
Juneau, AK 907-586-1088
Heritage Store
Virginia Beach, VA 800-862-2923
Heritage Wine Cellars
North East, PA 800-747-0083

Hermann J. Wiemer Vineyard
Dundee, NY 800-371-7971
Hermann Wiemer Vineyards
Dundee, NY 800-371-7971
Hermannhof Winery
Hermann, MO 800-393-0100
Heron Hill Winery
Hammondsport, NY 800-441-4241
Hershey
Mississauga, ON 800-468-1714
Hess Collection Winery
Napa, CA 877-707-4377
Hi-Country Corona
Selah, WA 951-272-2600
Hi-Country Foods Corporation
Selah, WA 509-697-7292
High Coffee Corporation
Houston, TX 713-465-2230
High Rise Coffee Roasters
Colorado Springs, CO 719-633-1833
Highland Manor Winery
Jamestown, TN 931-879-9519
Highwood Distillers
High River, AB 403-652-3202
Hiland Dairy Foods Company
Branson, MO 417-334-0090
Hiland Dairy Foods Company
Springfield, MO 417-862-9311
Hill of Beans Coffee Roasters
Los Angeles, CA 888-527-6278
Hillcrest Vineyard
Roseburg, OR 541-673-3709
Hiller Cranberries
Rochester, MA 508-763-5257
Hillsboro Coffee Company
Tampa, FL 813-877-2126
Hinckley Springs Water Company
Chicago, IL 773-586-8600
Hinzerling Winery
Prosser, WA 800-722-6702
Hiram Walker & Sons
Fort Smith, AR 479-646-6100
Home Roast Coffee
Lutz, FL 813-949-0807
Homewood Winery
Sonoma, CA 707-996-6353
Honest Tea
Bethesda, MD 800-865-4736
Honeywood Winery
Salem, OR 800-726-4101
Honig Vineyard and Winery
Rutherford, CA 800-929-2217
Hood River Coffee Company
Hood River, OR 800-336-2954
Hood River Distillers
Hood River, OR 541-386-1588
Hood River Vineyards and Winery
Hood River, OR 541-386-3772
Hoodsport Winery
Hoodsport, WA 800-580-9894
Hop Kiln Winery
Healdsburg, CA 707-433-6491
Hopkins Vineyard
Warren, CT 860-868-7954
Horizon Winery
Santa Rosa, CA 707-544-2961
House of Coffee Beans
Houston, TX 800-422-1799
Huber's Orchard Winery
Borden, IN 800-345-9463
Hudson Valley Fruit Juice
Highland, NY 845-691-8061
Hunter Farms
High Point, NC 800-446-8035
Husch Vineyards
Philo, CA 800-554-8724
Hygeia Dairy Company
Corpus Christi, TX 361-854-4561
Ideal Distributing Company
Bothell, WA 425-488-6121
IL HWA American Corporation
Worcester, MA 800-446-7364
Imperial Foods
Long Island City, NY 718-784-3400
Indian Hollow Farms
Richland Center, WI 800-236-3944
Indian River Foods
Fort Pierce, FL 772-462-2222
Indian Rock Vineyards
Murphys, CA 209-728-8514
Indian Springs Vineyards
Nevada City, CA 530-478-1068

Indigo Coffee Roasters
Florence, MA 800-447-5450
Ingleside Plantation Winery
Colonial Beach, VA 804-224-7111
Inland Northwest Dairies
Spokane, WA 509-489-8600
Inn Foods
Watsonville, CA 831-724-2026
Inniskillin Wines
Niagara-On-The-Lake, ON 888-466-4754
Innovative Food Solutions LLC
Columbus, OH 800-884-3314
Innovative Health Products
Largo, FL 800-654-2347
Innovative Ingredients
Reisterstown, MD 888-403-2907
Inter-American Products
Cincinnati, OH 800-645-2233
Inter-Continental Imports Company
Newington, CT 800-424-4422
Intercafe
Magdelena Apasco, OA 951-521-6011
International Coffee Corporation
New Orleans, LA 504-586-8700
International Trademarks
Darien, CT 203-656-4046
Irani & Company
Fairland, IN 317-862-1257
Iron Horse Ranch & Vineyard
Sebastopol, CA 707-887-1507
Ironstone Vineyards
Murphys, CA 209-728-1251
Island Sweetwater Beverage Company
Bryn Mawr, PA 610-525-7444
Italian Products USA Inc
Clark, NJ 201-770-9130
J Vineyards & Winery
Healdsburg, CA 800-885-9463
J&J Snack Foods Corporation
Pennsauken, NJ 800-486-9533
J. Filippi Winery
Etiwanda, CA 909-899-5755
J. Fritz Winery
Cloverdale, CA 707-894-3389
J. Stonestreet & Sons Vineyard
Healdsburg, CA 800-723-6336
J.B. Peel Coffee Roasters
Red Hook, NY 800-231-7372
J.G. British Imports
Bradenton, FL 888-965-1700
J.M. Smucker
Havre De Grace, MD 410-939-1403
Jack Daniel's Distillery
Lynchburg, TN 931-759-4221
Jackson Milk & Ice CreamCompany
Hutchinson, KS 620-663-1244
Jackson Valley Vineyards
Ione, CA 209-274-4721
Jamaica John
Franklin Park, IL 847-451-1730
Java Jungle
Visalia, CA 559-732-5282
Java Sun Coffee Roasters
Marblehead, MA 781-631-7788
Jayone Foods, Inc/G. East Co., LTD
Paramount, CA 562-633-7400
Jenny's Country Kitchen
Dover, MN 800-357-3497
Jeremiah's Pick Coffee Company
San Francisco, CA 800-537-3642
Jo Mints
Corona Del Mar, CA 877-566-4687
Jodar Vineyard & Winery
Placerville, CA 530-621-0324
Jogue Inc
Northville, MI 800-521-3888
Johlin Century Winery
Oregon, OH 419-693-6288
John A. Vassilaros & Son
Flushing, NY 718-886-4140
John C. Meier Juice Company
Cincinnati, OH 800-346-2941
John Conti Coffee Company
Louisville, KY 800-928-5282
Johnson Estate Wines
Westfield, NY 800-374-6569
Johnson's Alexander Valley Wines
Healdsburg, CA 800-888-5532
Johnston's Winery
Ballston Spa, NY 518-882-6310
Jones Brewing Company
Smithton, PA 800-237-2337

Joseph Filippi Winery
Rancho Cucamonga, CA 909-899-5755
Joseph Phelps Vineyards
Saint Helena, CA 707-967-9153
Josuma Coffee Corporation
Menlo Park, CA 650-366-5453
Joullian Vineyards
Carmel Valley, CA 877-659-2800
Juice Bowl Products
Lakeland, FL. 863-665-5515
Juice Guys
Cambridge, MA 800-896-8667
Juice Mart
West Hills, CA 877-888-1011
Juicy Whip
La Verne, CA 909-392-7500
Justin Lloyd Premium Tea Company
Carson, CA 310-834-4000
Justin Winery & Vineyard
Paso Robles, CA. 800-726-0049
Kaffe Magnum Opus
Millville, NJ 800-652-5282
Kagome
Los Banos, CA 209-826-8850
Kalin Cellars
Novato, CA. 415-883-3543
Kan-Pac
Arkansas City, KS. 620-442-6820
Kate's Vineyard
Napa, CA. 707-255-2644
Kathryn Kennedy Winery
Saratoga, CA. 408-867-4170
Kauai Coffee Company
Kalaheo, HI. 800-545-8605
Kava King
Ormond Beach, FL 888-670-5282
KDK Inc
Draper, UT 801-571-3506
Kelleys Island Wine Company
Kelleys Is, OH. 419-746-2678
Kemach Food Products Corporation
Brooklyn, NY 888-453-6224
Kemps
Cedarburg, WI. 262-377-5040
Kendall Citrus Corporation
Goulds, FL 305-258-1628
Kendall-Jackson Wine
Windsor, CA 800-544-4413
Kenlake Foods
Murray, KY. 800-632-6900
Kenwood Vineyards
Kenwood, CA 707-833-5891
Kicking Horse Coffee
Invermere, BC. 888-287-5282
King Brewing Company
Fairfield, CA. 707-428-4503
King Estate Winery
Eugene, OR. 800-884-4441
King Juice
Milwaukee, WI 414-482-0303
Kiona Vineyards Winery
Benton City, WA. 509-588-6716
Kirigin Cellars
Gilroy, CA. 408-847-8827
Kistler Vineyards
Sebastopol, CA 707-823-5603
Kittling Ridge Estate Wines & Spirits
Grimsby, ON. 905-945-9225
Kittridge & Fredrickson Fine Coffees
Portland, OR 800-558-7788
Klingshirn Winery
Avon Lake, OH 440-933-6666
Knapp Vineyards
Romulus, NY 800-869-9271
Knouse Foods Coop
Peach Glen, PA 717-677-8181
Knoxage Water Company
San Diego, CA 619-234-3333
Kobricks Coffee Company
Jersey City, NJ 800-562-3662
Kohler Mix Specialties
White Bear Lake, MN. 651-426-1633
Kona Coffee Council
Kealakekua, HI 808-323-2911
Kona Kava Coffee Company
Philo, CA. 707-985-3913
Koryo Winery Company
Gardena, CA 310-532-9616
Kraft Foods
Northfield, IL 800-323-0768
Kramer Vineyards
Gaston, OR 800-619-4637
Krier Foods
Random Lake, WI. 920-994-2469
Kunde Estate Winery
Kenwood, CA 707-833-5501
Kusmi Tea
New York, NY 646-346-1756
La Abra Farm & Winery
Lovingston, VA. 434-263-5392
La Buena Vida Vineyards
Grapevine, TX 817-481-9463
La Chiripada Winery
Dixon, NM 800-528-7801
La Costa Coffee Roasting
Carlsbad, CA. 760-438-8160
La Jota Vineyard Company
Angwin, CA 877-222-0292
La Rocca Vineyards
Forest Ranch, CA 800-808-9463
La Rochelle Winery
Livermore, CA 888-647-7768
La Vans Coffee Company
Bordentown, NJ 609-298-0688
La Vina Winery
Anthony, NM 575-882-7632
Labatt Breweries
Toronto, ON 800-268-2337
Lacas Coffee Company
Pennsauken, NJ. 800-220-1133
Laetitia Vineyard
Arroyo Grande, CA. 888-809-8463
Lafollette Vineyard & Winery
Belle Mead, NJ 908-359-5018
Laird & Company
North Garden, VA. 877-438-5247
Lake Arrowhead
Twin Peaks, CA 877-237-8528
Lake Sonoma Winery
Healdsburg, CA 877-850-9463
Lakeridge Winery & Vineyards
Clermont, FL. 800-768-9463
Lakeshore Winery
Romulus, NY 315-549-7075
Lakespring Winery
Yountville, CA 707-944-2475
Lakewood Juices
Miami, FL. 305-324-5932
Lakewood Vineyards
Watkins Glen, NY. 607-535-9252
Lambert Bridge Winery
Healdsburg, CA 800-975-0555
Lamoreaux Landing Wine Cellar
Lodi, NY 607-582-6011
Lancaster County Winery
Willow Street, PA 717-464-3555
Land O Lakes Milk
Sioux Falls, SD 605-330-9526
Land O'Lakes, Inc.
Arden Hills, MN 800-328-9680
Land-O-Sun Dairies
O Fallon, IL. 314-436-6820
Landmark Vineyards
Kenwood, CA 800- 45- 636
Landshire
Saint Louis, MO 800-468-3354
Lange Winery
Dundee, OR. 503-538-6476
Langer Juice Company
City of Industry, CA 626-336-1666
Langtry Estate & Vineyards
Middletown, CA 707-987-9127
Larry's Vineyards & Winery
Altamont, NY 518-355-7365
Latah Creek Wine Cellars
Spokane Valley, WA 509-926-0164
Latcham Vineyards
Mt Aukum, CA 800-750-5591
Laurel Glen Vineyard
Glen Ellen, CA 707-526-3914
Lava Cap Winery
Placerville, CA 530-621-0175
Lavazza Premium Coffee Corporation
New York, NY 800-466-3287
Lazy Creek Vineyard
Philo, CA. 888-529-9275
Le Bleu Corporation
Advance, NC. 800-854-4471
Le Boeuf & Associates
North Falmouth, MA 800-444-5666
Leaves Pure Teas
Scottsdale, AZ. 800-242-8807
Leelanau Wine Cellars
Omena, MI 800-782-8128
Leeward Winery
Oxnard, CA. 805-656-5054
Leidenfrost Vineyards
Hector, NY
Leisure Time Ice & Spring Water
Kiamesha Lake, NY 800-443-1412
Lemon Creek Winery
Berrien Springs, MI 269-471-1321
Lemon-X Corporation
Huntington Station, NY 800-220-1061
Lenox-Martell
Boston, MA. 617-442-7777
Leonetti Cellar
Walla Walla, WA. 509-525-1428
Leroy Hill Coffee Company
Mobile, AL 800-866-5282
Les Bourgeois Vineyards
Rocheport, MO 573-698-2300
Les Mouts De P.O.M.
Sain-Francois-Xavier, QC 819-845-5555
Level Valley Creamery
Antioch, TN 800-251-1292
Lewis Cellars
Napa, CA. 70- 2-5 34
Lexington Coffee & Tea Company
Lexington, KY 859-277-1102
Liberty Dairy
Evart, MI. 800-632-5552
Lifeway Foods Inc
Morton Grove, IL 877-281-3874
Light Rock Beverage Company
Danbury, CT 203-743-3410
Limur Winery
San Francisco, CA 415-781-8691
Lin Court Vineyards
Solvang, CA 805-688-8554
Linden Beverage Company
Linden, VA 540-635-2118
Lindsay's Tea
S San Francisco, CA. 800-624-7031
Lingle Brothers Coffee
Bell Gardens, CA 562-927-3317
Lion Brewery
Wilkes Barre, PA. 800-233-8327
Lipsey Mountain Spring Water
Norcross, GA 770-449-0001
Little Amana Winery
Amana, IA. 319-668-9664
Live Oaks Winery
Gilroy, CA. 408-842-2401
Lockcoffee
Larchmont, NY. 914-273-7838
Lola Savannah
Houston, TX 888-663-9166
Longo Coffee & Tea
New York, NY 212-477-5421
Lost Trail Root Beer Com
Louisburg, KS. 800-748-7765
Louis Dreyfus Citrus
Winter Garden, FL 800-549-4272
Louis Dreyfus Corporation - Coffee Division
Wilton, CT 203-761-2000
Louisburg Cider Mill
Louisburg, KS. 800-748-7765
Love Creek Orchards
Medina, TX. 800-449-0882
Lucas Vineyards
Interlaken, NY 800-682-9463
Lucas Winery
Lodi, CA 209-368-2006
Ludwigshof Winery
Eskridge, KS. 785-449-2498
LUXCO
St Louis, MO. 314-772-2626
Lynfred Winery
Roselle, IL. 888-298-9463
Lyons-Magnus
Fresno, CA 559-268-5966
M.E. Swing Company
Alexandria, VA 800-485-4019
M.S. Walker
Somerville, MA 617-776-6700
Mackie Intl.
Riverside, CA 800-733-9762
MacKinlay Teas
Ann Arbor, MI 734-846-0966
Madison Foods
Saint Paul, MN 651-265-8212
Madys Company
San Francisco, CA 415-822-2227
Magnetic Springs Water Company
Columbus, OH 800-572-2990

Magnum Coffee Roastery
Nunica, MI 888-937-5282
Majestic Coffee & Tea
San Carlos, CA 650-591-5678
Majestic Distilling Company
Baltimore, MD 410-242-0200
Makers Mark Distillery
Loretto, KY 270-865-2881
Mama Lee's Gourmet Hot Chocolate
Nashville, TN . . . . 1 8-8 m-male
Manhattan Coffee Company
Earth City, MO 800-926-3333
Manhattan Special Bottling Corporation
Brooklyn, NY 718-388-4144
Mar-Key Foods
Vidalia, GA 912-537-4204
Marie Brizard Wines & Spirits
St. Helena, CA 800-878-1123
Markham Vineyards
Saint Helena, CA 707-963-5292
Martini & Prati Wines
Santa Rosa, CA 707-823-2404
Marva Maid Dairy
Newport News, VA 800-544-4439
Maryland & Virginia Milk Producers Cooperative
Reston, VA 703-742-4250
Masala Chai Company
Santa Cruz, CA 831-475-8881
Master Brew
Northbrook, IL 847-564-3600
Matilija Water Company
Ventura, CA 805-643-4675
Maui Pineapple Company
Kahului, HI 808-877-3351
Maui Pineapple Company
Concord, CA 925-798-0240
Mayacamas Vineyards
Napa, CA 707-224-4030
Mayer Brothers
West Seneca, NY 800-696-2937
Mayer's Cider Mill
Webster, NY 800-543-0043
Mayfield Farms
Caledon, ON 905-846-0506
McArthur Dairy
Miami, FL 305-795-7700
McClancy Seasoning Company
Fort Mill, SC 800-843-1968
McCutcheon's Apple Products
Frederick, MD 800-888-7537
McGregor Vineyard Winery
Dundee, NY 800-272-0192
Meadow Brook Dairy
Erie, PA 800-352-4010
Melitta
Clearwater, FL 727-535-2111
Meramec Vineyards
Saint James, MO 877-216-9463
Merci Spring Water
Maryland Heights, MO 314-872-9323
Meridian Beverage Company
Atlanta, GA 800-728-1481
Merlinos
Canon City, CO 719-275-5558
Merritt Estate Wines
Forestville, NY 888-965-4800
Mh Zeigler & Sons
Lansdale, PA 215-855-5161
Michigan Dairy
Livonia, MI 734-367-5390
Mid States Dairy
Hazelwood, MO 314-731-1150
Miller Brewing Company
Milwaukee, WI 414-933-1846
Milsolv Corporation
Butler, WI 800-558-8501
Minnehaha Spring Water Company
Cleveland, OH 216-431-0243

Minute Maid Company
Sugar Land, TX 281-302-4317
Minute Maid Company
Dunedin, FL 800-237-0159
Mogen David Wine Corporation
Westfield, NY 716-326-3151
Mojave Foods Corporation
Commerce, CA 323-890-8900
Monarch Beverage Company
Atlanta, GA 800-241-3732
Mondial Foods Company
Los Angeles, CA 213-383-3531
Montebello Brands
Baltimore, MD 410-282-8800
Moran Coffee Company
Dublin, OH 614-889-2500
Mother Parker's Tea & Coffee
Mississauga, ON 800-387-9398
Mount Olympus Waters
Salt Lake City, UT 800-628-6056
Mountain Valley ProductsInc
Sunnyside, WA 509-837-8084
Mrs. Clark's Foods
Ankeny, IA 800-736-5674

Juices, salad dressings and sauces.

Murray Cider Company Inc
Roanoke, VA 540-977-9000
Music Mountain Water Company
Birmingham, AL 800-349-6555
Nagel's Beverages Company
East Nampa, ID 208-475-1250
Naterl
St. Bruno, QC 450-653-3655
Natural Spring Water Company
Johnson City, TN 423-926-7905
Nature's Plus
Long Beach, CA 562-494-2500
Navarro Vineyards & Winery
Philo, CA 800-537-9463
NC Mountain Water
Marion, NC 800-220-4718
Neenah Springs
Oxford, WI 608-586-5605
Nehalem Bay Winery
Nehalem, OR 888-368-9463
Nestle Professional Vitality
Solon, OH 800-288-8682
Newly Weds Foods
Chicago, IL 800-647-9314
Noh Foods of Hawaii
Gardena, CA 310-324-6770
North Country Natural Spring Water
Port Kent, NY 518-834-9400
North House Vineyards In
Jamesport, NY 631-722-5256
North Salem Vineyard
North Salem, NY 914-669-5518
Northland Cranberries
Jackson, WI 262-677-2221
Northwest Naturals Corporation
Bothell, WA 425-881-2200
Northwestern Coffee Mills
Washburn, WI 800-243-5283
Northwestern Foods
Saint Paul, MN 800-236-4937
NTC Marketing Inc
Williamsville, NY 800-333-1637
Nutritional Counselors of America
Spencer, TN 931-946-3600
O-At-Ka Milk Products Cooperative
Batavia, NY 800-828-8152
Ocean Spray Cranberries
Kenosha, WI 262-694-5200
Ocean Spray Cranberries
Bordentown, NJ 609-298-0905
Ocean Spray Cranberries
Vero Beach, FL 772-562-0800
Ocean Spray Cranberries
Lakeville-Middleboro, MA 800-662-3263
Octavia Tea LLC
Batavia, IL 866-505-6387
Odwalla
Denver, CO 303-282-0500
Office General des Eaux Minerales
Montreal, QC 514-482-7221
Old Dutch Mustard Company
Great Neck, NY 516-466-0522
Old Fashioned Natural Products
Santa Ana, CA 800-552-9045
Old Orchard Brands
Sparta, MI 616-887-1745

Omar Coffee Company
Newington, CT 800-394-6627
One World Enterprises
Los Angeles, CA 888-663-2626
Opa! Originals, Inc.
Rochester, NY 585-368-5623
Orange-Co of Florida
Arcadia, FL 863-494-4939
Orchid Island Juice Company
Fort Pierce, FL 800-373-7444
Orleans Coffee Exchange
Kenner, LA 800-737-5464
Ormand Peugeog Corporation
Miami, FL 305-624-6834
Pak Technologies
Milwaukee, WI 414-438-8600
Paramount Coffee Company
Lansing, MI 517-372-5500
Paramount Coffee Company
Lansing, MI 800-968-1222
Paramount Distillers
Cleveland, OH 800-821-2989
Parducci Wine Estates
Ukiah, CA 888-362-9463
Paris Foods Corporation
Trappe, MD 410-476-3185
Parmalat Canada
Toronto, ON 800-563-1515
Partners Coffee Company
Atlanta, GA 800-341-5282
Paul de Lima Company
Liverpool, NY 800-962-8864
PB&S Chemicals
Henderson, KY 800-950-7267
Pearl Coffee Company
Akron, OH 800-822-5282
Peerless Coffee Company
Oakland, CA 800-310-5662
PepsiCo Chicago
Chicago, IL 312-821-1000
Perfect Foods
Goshen, NY 800-933-3288
Pernod Ricard USA
Greendale, IN 812-537-0700
Pernod Ricard USA
Purchase, NY 914-848-4800
Perricone Juices
Beaumont, CA 951-769-7171
Perry Creek Winery
Fair Play, CA 800-880-4026
Personal Edge Nutrition
Ballwin, MO 877-982-3343
Pet Dairy
Spartanburg, SC 864-576-6280
Pet Milk
Florence, SC 800-735-3066
Pete's Brewing Company
San Antonio, TX 800-877-7383
Pevely Dairy Company
Hazelwood, MO 314-771-4400
Pfefferkorn's Coffee
Baltimore, MD 800-682-4665
Phamous Phloyd's Barbeque Sauce
Denver, CO 303-757-3285
Phillips Beverage Company
Minneapolis, MN 612-331-6230
Phillips Syrup Corporation
Westlake, OH 800-350-8443
Pleasant Valley Wine Company
Hammondsport, NY 607-569-6111
Pleasant View Dairy
Highland, IN 219-838-0155
Pod Pack International
Baton Rouge, LA 225-752-1110
Pokka Beverages
American Canyon, CA 800-972-5962
Poland Spring Water
Stamford, CT 800-955-4426
Polar Beverages
Worcester, MA 800-734-9800
Polar Water Company
Carnegie, PA 412-429-5550
Pontiac Coffee Break
Pontiac, MI 248-332-9403
Post Familie Vineyards
Altus, AR 800-275-8423
Powell & Mahoney LTD
Beverly, MA 978-922-4332
Prairie Farms Dairy
Carlinville, IL 217-854-2547
Premier Blending
Wichita, KS 316-267-5533

Premier Juices
Clearwater, FL 727-533-8200
Premium Water
Orange Springs, FL. 800-243-1163
Prince of Peace Enterprises
Hayward, CA 800-732-2328
Productos Del Plata, Inc
Miami, FL. 786-357-8261
Progenix Corporation
Wausau, WI. 800-233-3356
Purity Dairies
Nashville, TN 615-244-1900
Q.E. Tea
Bridgeville, PA 800-622-8327
Quaker Oats Company
Mountain Top, PA. 800-367-6287
Quality Brands
Deland, FL 888-676-2700
Quality Kitchen Corporation
Danbury, CT 203-744-2000
Quality Naturally! Foods
City of Industry, CA 888-498-6986
R. C. Bigelow
Fairfield, CT 888-244-3569
R.J. Corr Naturals
Posen, IL 708-389-4200
Rainbow Valley Orchards
Fallbrook, CA 760-728-2905
Ramar Foods International Inc
Pittsburg, CA 800-660-0962
Ray Brothers & Noble Canning Company
Hobbs, IN 765-675-7451
Rebound
Newburgh, NY 845-562-5400
Red Diamond
Birmingham, AL. 800-292-4651
Red Gold
Elwood, IN 877-748-9798
Redhook Ale Breweries
Newington, NH. 603-430-8600
Regency Coffee & VendingCompany
Olathe, KS. 913-829-1994
Regent Champagne Cellars
New York, NY
Reggie's Roast
Linden, NJ. 908-862-3700
Reily Foods/JFG Coffee Company
New Orleans, LA 800-535-1961
Reiter Dairy
Springfield, OH. 937-323-5777
Renault Winery
Egg Harbor City, NJ 609-965-2111
Rex Wine Vinegar Company
Newark, NJ 973-589-6911
Richland Beverage Associates
Carrollton, TX. 214-357-0248
Robert Keenan Winery
Saint Helena, CA 707-963-9177
Robert Mondavi Winery
Oakville, CA. 888-766-6328
Roberts Dairy Foods
Iowa City, IA
Roberts Dairy Foods
Kansas City, MO. 800-279-1692
Rodney Strong Vineyards
Healdsburg, CA. 707-433-6511
Rohtstein Corporation
Woburn, MA 781-935-8300
Rondo Specialty Foods LTD
Newcastle, DE. 800-724-6636
Ronnoco Coffee Company
Saint Louis, MO 800-428-2287
Ronzoni Foods Canada
Etobicoke, ON 800-387-5032
Roos Foods
Kenton, DE 800-343-3642
Roselani Tropics Ice Cream
Wailuku, HI. 808-244-7951
Rosenberger's Dairies
Hatfield, PA. 800-355-9074
Royal Coffee & Tea Company
Mississauga, ON. 800-667-6226
Royal Crown Bottling Company
Bowling Green, KY 270-842-8106
Royal Cup Coffee
Birmingham, AL. 800-366-5836
Royal Wine Corp
Bayonne, NJ 718-384-2400
Rubicon/Niebaum-Coppola Estate & Winery
Rutherford, CA 800-782-4266
Russo Farms
Vineland, NJ 856-692-5942
Rutherford Hill Winery
Rutherford, CA 707-963-1871
S&D Coffee, Inc
Concord, NC 704-782-3121
Safeway Beverage
Denver, CO 303-320-7960
Safeway Beverage
Bellevue, WA 425-455-6444
Safeway Dairy Products
Walnut Creek, CA. 925-944-4000
Safeway Milk Plant
Tempe, AZ 480-894-4391
Saint Arnold Brewing Company
Houston, TX 713-686-9494
San Antonio Winery
Los Angeles, CA. 800-626-7722
San-Ei Gen FFI
New York, NY 212-315-7850
Sandstone Winery
Amana, IA. 319-622-3081
Sara Lee Corporation
Downers Grove, IL 630-598-8100
Saratoga Beverage Group
Saratoga Springs, NY 888-426-8642
Schirf Brewing Company
Park City, UT 435-649-0900
Schneider's Dairy Holdings Inc
Pittsburgh, PA 412-881-3525
Schramsberg Vineyards
Calistoga, CA 800-877-3623
Scotian Gold Cooperative
Coldbrook, NS 902-679-2191
SECO & Golden 100
Deland, FL 386-734-3906
Seltzer & Rydholm
Auburn, ME 207-784-5791
Sesinco Foods
New York, NY 212-243-1306
Seven Up/RC Bottling Company
Paragould, AR. 870-236-8765
SEW Friel
Queenstown, MD 410-827-8811
Shasta Beverages
Lenexa, KS 913-888-6777
Silvan Ridge
Eugene, OR. 541-345-1945
Silver Oak Cellars
Oakville, CA. 800-273-8805
Silver Springs Citrus
Howey In the Hills, FL. 800-940-2277
Simpson & Vail
Brookfield, CT 800-282-8327
Sinton Dairy Foods Company
Colorado Springs, CO. 800-388-4970
Sinton Dairy Foods Company
Denver, CO 800-666-4808
Skjodt-Barrett Foods
Mississauga, ON. 877-600-1200
Smart Ice
Fort Myers, FL 239-334-3123
Smeltzer Orchard Company
Frankfort, MI 231-882-4421
Smith Dairy Products Company
Orrville, OH 800-776-7076
SnowBird Corporation
Bayonne, NJ 800-576-1616
Solana Gold Organics
Sebastopol, CA 800-459-1121
Somerset Syrup & Beverage
Edison, NJ. 800-526-8865
Sourthern Tea
Marietta, GA. 800-241-0896
Southchem
Durham, NC 800-849-7000
Southern Beverage Packers
Appling, GA 800-326-2469
Spangler Vineyards
Roseburg, OR 541-679-9654
Specialty Coffee Roasters
Delray Beach, FL 800-253-9363
Spoetzl Brewery
Shiner, TX. 361-594-3383
Spring Mountain Vineyards
Saint Helena, CA 877-769-4637
Spring Water Company
Chesapeake, VA 800-832-0271
St. Julian Wine Company
Paw Paw, MI. 800-732-6002
Starbucks Coffee Company
Seattle, WA 800-782-7282
Stash Tea Company
Portland, OR 800-547-1514
Ste Michelle Wine Estates
Woodinville, WA. 800-267-6793
Stevens Point Brewery
Stevens Point, WI 800-369-4911
Stevens Tropical Plantation
West Palm Beach, FL 561-683-4701
Stewart's Private Blend Foods
Chicago, IL 800-654-2862
Stockton Graham & Company
Raleigh, NC 800-835-5943
Stone Hill Wine Company
Hermann, MO. 573-486-2221
Stop & Shop Manufacturing
Readville, MA. 508-977-5132
Straub Brewery Industries
St Marys, PA 814-834-2875
Sturm Foods
Manawa, WI 800-347-8876
Suiza Dairy Corporation
San Juan, PR 787-792-7300
Summit Brewing Company
Saint Paul, MN 651-265-7800
Sun Orchard of Florida
Haines City, FL. 877-875-8423
Sun Pac Foods
Brampton, ON. 905-792-2700
Sunflower Restaurant Supply
Salina, KS 316-267-9881
SunkiStreet Growers
Ontario, CA. 800-225-3727
Sunlike Juice
Scarborough, ON 416-297-1140
Sunshine Farms
Portage, WI. 608-742-2016
Sunsweet Growers
Yuba City, CA. 800-417-2253
Suntory International
New York, NY 212-891-6600
Suntory Water Group
Atlanta, GA. 770-933-1400
Superbrand Dairies
Miami, FL. 305-769-6600
Superior Trading Company
San Francisco, CA 415-982-8722
Superstore Industries
Fairfield, CA. 707-864-0502
Sutter Home Winery
Saint Helena, CA 707-963-3104
Swan Joseph Vineyards
Forestville, CA 707-573-3747
Swire Coca-Cola
Draper, UT 800-497-2653
Swiss Valley Farms Company
Davenport, IA 563-468-6600
SYFO Beverage Company ofFlorida
Ponte Vedra Beach, FL 1 8-8 4-6 79
Talbott Farms
Palisade, CO 970-464-5943
Tamarack Farms Dairy
Newark, OH 866-221-4141
Tastee Apple Inc
Newcomerstown, OH 800-262-7753
Tatra Herb Company
Morrisville, PA 888-828-7248
Templar Food Products
New Providence, NJ 800-883-6752
Tequila XQ
Guadalajara Jalisco, ... 333-587-7799
Texas Coffee Company
Beaumont, TX. 800-259-3400
The Humphrey Co
Lockport, NY 716-597-1974
Thomas Canning/Maidstone
Maidstone, ON 519-737-1531
Thomas Kruse Winery
Gilroy, CA. 408-842-7016
Three Lakes Winery
Three Lakes, WI 800-944-5434
Todhunter Foods
Lake Alfred, FL. 863-956-1116
Toft Dairy
Sandusky, OH 800-521-4606
Torke Coffee Roasting Company
Sheboygan, WI 800-242-7671
Traditional Medicinals
Sebastopol, CA 800-543-4372
Tree Top
Selah, WA 800-367-6571
Tree Top
Selah, WA 800-542-4055
Trefethen Vineyards
Napa, CA. 800-556-4847

Trigo Corporation
Toa Baja, PR . . . 787-794-1300
Triple D Orchards
Empire, MI . . . 866-781-9410
Triple Springs Spring Water
Meriden, CT . . . 203-235-8374
Tropicana
Bradenton, FL . . . 800-237-7799
True Organic Products International
Miami, FL . . . 800-487-0379
Truesdale Packaging Company
Warrenton, MO . . . 636-456-6800
Turkey Hill Dairy
Conestoga, PA . . . 800-693-2479
Turkey Hill Sugarbush
Waterloo, QC . . . 450-539-4822
Turn on Beverages Inc
Spring Valley, NY . . . 845-354-7720
UDV Wines
San Francisco, CA . . . 415-835-7300
Unilever
Mont-Royal, QC . . . 514-735-1141
Unilever Bestfoods
Englewood Cliffs, NJ . . . 201-567-8000
United Dairy
Martins Ferry, OH . . . 800-252-1542
United Dairymen of Arizona
Tempe, AZ . . . 480-966-7211
Upstate Farms Cooperative
Rochester, NY . . . 585-458-1880
Upstate Farms Cooperative
Buffalo, NY . . . 866-874-6455
USA Sunrise Beverage
Spearfish, SD . . . 605-723-0690
V. Sattui Winery
Saint Helena, CA . . . 800-799-8888
Valley Fig Growers
Fresno, CA . . . 559-237-3893
Valley View Packing Company
San Jose, CA . . . 408-289-8300
Van Roy Coffee
Cleveland, OH . . . 877-826-7669
Vancouver Island Brewing Company
Victoria, BC . . . 800-663-6383
Varni Brothers/7-Up Bottling
Modesto, CA . . . 209-521-1777
Vegetable Juices
Chicago, IL . . . 888-776-9752
Velda Farms
Winter Haven, FL . . . 800-279-4166
Velda Farms
North Miami Beach, FL . . . 800-795-4649
Ventura Coastal Corporation
Ventura, CA . . . 805-653-7035
Venture Vineyards
Lodi, NY . . . 888-635-6277
Vie-Del Company
Fresno, CA . . . 559-834-2525
Viking Distillery
Albany, GA . . . 229-436-0181
Villa Mt. Eden Winery
Saint Helena, CA . . . 707-944-2414
Vincor International
Mississauga, ON . . . 800-265-9463
Vita Food Products
Chicago, IL . . . 312-738-4500
Vitamilk Dairy
Bellingham, WA . . . 206-529-4128
Von Stiehl Winery
Algoma, WI . . . 800-955-5208
W.J. Stearns & Sons/Mountain Dairy
Storrs Mansfield, CT . . . 860-423-9289
Wagner Vineyards
Lodi, NY . . . 866-924-6378
Wah Yet Group
Hayward, CA . . . 800-229-3392
Water Concepts
East Dundee, IL . . . 847-699-9797
Wayne Dairy Products
Richmond, IN . . . 800-875-9294
Weaver Nut Company
Ephrata, PA . . . 717-738-3781
Wechsler Coffee Corporation
Moonachie, NJ . . . 800-800-2633
Welch's Foods Inc
Kennewick, WA . . . 509-582-2131
Welch's Foods Inc
Concord, MA . . . 800-340-6870
Welch's Foods Inc.
North East, PA . . . 814-725-4577
Welsh Farms
Edison, NJ . . . 800-221-0663
Wengert's Dairy
Lebanon, PA . . . 800-222-2129
Westbrae Natural Foods
Melville, NY . . . 800-434-4246
Wheeling Coffee & SpicecCompany
Wheeling, WV . . . 800-500-0141
White Coffee Corporation
Astoria, NY . . . 800-221-0140
White Rock Products Corporation
Flushing, NY . . . 800-969-7625
White Wave
Broomfield, CO . . . 800-488-9283
Whittaker & Associates
Atlanta, GA . . . 404-266-1265
Whole Herb Company
Sonoma, CA . . . 707-935-1077
Widmer's Wine Cellars
Canandaigua, NY
Winchester Farms Dairy
Winchester, KY . . . 859-745-5500
Windmill Water
Edgewood, NM . . . 505-281-9287
Windsor Vineyards
Santa Rosa, CA . . . 800-289-9463
Windsor Vineyards
Windsor, CA . . . 800-333-9987
Winmix/Natural Care Products
Englewood, FL . . . 941-475-7432
Woodbury Vineyards
Fredonia, NY . . . 866-691-9463
World Citrus West
Lake Wales, FL . . . 863-676-1411
World of Coffee, World of Tea
Stirling, NJ . . . 908-647-1218
Yakima Craft Brewing Company
Yakima, WA . . . 509-654-7357
Yoder Dairies
Chesapeake, VA . . . 757-482-4068
Yoo-Hoo Chocolate Beverage Company
Carlstadt, NJ . . . 201-933-0070
York Mountain Winery
Templeton, CA . . . 805-237-7575
Young Winfield
Kleinburg, ON . . . 905-893-9682
Z.D. Wines
Napa, CA . . . 800-487-7757

Zephyr Hills
Tamarac, FL 954-597-7852

Alcoholic Beverages

A&G Food & Liquors
Chicago, IL 773-994-1541
A. Nonini Winery
Fresno, CA 559-275-1936
A. Rafanelli Winery
Healdsburg, CA 707-433-1385
Abita Brewing Company
Abita Springs, LA 800-737-2311
Acacia Vineyard
Napa, CA 707-226-9991
Ackerman Winery
Amana, IA 319-622-3379
Adair Vineyards
New Paltz, NY 845-255-1377
Adam Puchta Winery
Hermann, MO 573-486-5596
Adams County Winery
Orrtanna, PA
Adelaida Cellars
Paso Robles, CA 800-676-1232
Adelsheim Vineyard
Newberg, OR 503-538-3652
Adler Fels Vineyards & Winery
Santa Rosa, CA 707-569-1493
Admiral Wine Merchants
Irvington, NJ 800-582-9463
Aetna Springs Cellars
Pope Valley, CA 707-965-2675
Afton Mountain Vineyards
Afton, VA 540-456-8667
Ahlgren Vineyard
Boulder Creek, CA 800-338-6071
Airlie Winery
Monmouth, OR 503-838-6013
Alba Vineyard
Milford, NJ 908-995-7800
Alexander Johnson's Valley Wines
Healdsburg, CA 800-888-5532
Alexis Bailly Vineyard
Hastings, MN 651-437-1413
Allegro Vineyards
Brogue, PA 717-927-9148
Almarla Vineyards & Winery
Shubuta, MS 601-687-5548
Aloha Distillers
Honolulu, HI 808-841-5787
Alpen Cellars
Trinity Center, CA 530-266-9513
Alpine Vineyards
Monroe, OR 541-424-5851
Alta Vineyard Cellar
Calistoga, CA 707-942-6708
Altamura Vineyards & Winery
Napa, CA 707-253-2000
Alto Vineyards
Alto Pass, IL 618-893-4898
Amador Foothill Winery
Plymouth, CA 800-778-9463
Amalthea Cellars Farm Winery
Atco, NJ 856-767-8890
Amberg Wine Cellars
Clifton Springs, NY 585-526-6742
Americana Vineyards
Interlaken, NY 607-387-6801
Amity Vineyards
Amity, OR 888-264-8966
Amizetta Vineyards
Saint Helena, CA 707-963-1460
Amwell Valley Vineyard
Ringoes, NJ 908-788-5852
Anchor Brewing Company
San Francisco, CA 415-863-8350
Anderson Valley Brewing
Boonville, CA 707-895-2337
Anderson's Conn Valley Vineyards
Saint Helena, CA 800-946-3497
Andrew Peller Limited
Grimsby, ON 905-643-4131
Annapolis Winery
Annapolis, CA 707-886-5460
Antelope Valley Winery
Lancaster, CA 800-282-8332
Anthony Road Wine Company
Penn Yan, NY 800-559-2182
Arbor Crest Wine Cellars
Spokane, WA 509-927-9463
Arbor Hill Grapery
Naples, NY 800-554-7553
Argonaut Winery
Ione, CA 800-704-9463
Argyle Wines
Dundee, OR 888-427-4953
Arizona Vineyards
Nogales, AZ 520-287-7972
Arns Winery
Saint Helena, CA 707-963-3429
Arrowood Vineyards & Winery
Glen Ellen, CA 800-938-5170
Artesa Vineyards & Winery
Napa, CA 707-224-1668
Ashland Vineyards
Ashland, OR 541-488-0088
ASV Wines
Delano, CA 661-792-3159
Au Bon Climat Winery
Los Olivos, CA 805-937-9801
August Schell Brewing Company
New Ulm, MN 800-770-5020
Augusta Winery
Augusta, MO 888-667-9463
Autumn Wind Vineyard
Newberg, OR 503-538-6931
Babcock Winery & Vineyards
Lompoc, CA 805-736-1455
Bacardi Canada, Inc.
Brampton, ON 905-451-6100
Bacardi USA
Coral Gables, FL 800-222-2734
Baily Vineyard & Winery
Temecula, CA 951-676-9463
Balagna Winery Company
Los Alamos, NM 505-672-3678
Baldwin Vineyards
Pine Bush, NY 845-744-2226
Balic Winery
Mays Landing, NJ 609-625-1903
Bandiera Winery
Cloverdale, CA 707-894-4295
Banfi Vintners
Glen Head, NY 800-645-6511
Barca Wine Cellars
Roseville, CA 916-967-0770
Bargetto's Winery
Soquel, CA 800-422-7438
Baron Vineyards
Paso Robles, CA 805-239-3313
Barton Brands
Louisville, KY 800-598-6352
Basignani Winery
Sparks Glencoe, MD 410-472-0703
Baxter's Vineyard
Nauvoo, IL 800-854-1396
Baywood Cellars
Lodi, CA 800-214-0445
Beachaven Vineyards & Winery
Clarksville, TN 931-645-8867
Beam Global Spirits & Wine
Deerfield, IL 847-948-8888
Bear Creek Winery
Cave Junction, OR 877-273-4843
Beaucanon Estate Wines
Napa, CA 800-660-3520
Beckmen Vineyards
Los Olivos, CA 805-688-8664
Bedell North Fork, LLC
Cutchogue, NY 631-734-7537
Bell Mountain Vineyards
Fredericksburg, TX 830-685-3297
Bellerose Vineyard
Healdsburg, CA 707-433-1637
Belvedere Vineyards & Winery
Healdsburg, CA 800-433-8296
Benziger Family Winery
Glen Ellen, CA 888-490-2739
Bernardo Winery
San Diego, CA 858-487-1866
Bernardus Winery & Vineyards
Carmel Valley, CA 888-648-9463
Bernheim Distilling Company
Louisville, KY 800-303-0053
Bethel Heights Vineyard Inc.
Salem, OR 503-581-2262
Bianchi Winery
Paso Robles, CA 805-226-9922
Bias Vineyards & Winery
Berger, MO 573-834-5475
Bidwell Vineyard
Cutchogue, NY 631-734-5200
Biltmore Estate Wine Company
Asheville, NC 800-411-3812
Binns Vineyards & Winery
Las Cruces, NM 575-522-2211
Bishop Farms Winery
Cheshire, CT 203-272-8243
Black Mesa Winery
Velarde, NM 800-852-6372
Black Prince Distillery Inc.
Clifton, NJ 973-365-2050
Black Sheep Vintners
Murphys, CA 209-728-2157
Blumenhof Vineyards-Winery
Dutzow, MO 800-419-2245
Boeger Winery
Placerville, CA 800-655-2634
Bogle Vineyards
Clarksburg, CA 916-744-1139
Bohemian Brewery
Midvale, UT 801-566-5474
Boisset America
Sausalito, CA 800-878-1123
Bonny Doon Vineyard
Santa Cruz, CA 831-425-3625
Boordy Vineyards
Hydes, MD 410-592-5015
Bordoni Vineyards
Vallejo, CA 707-642-1504
Boskydel Vineyard
Lake Leelanau, MI 231-256-7272
Bouchaine Vineyards
Napa, CA 800-654-9463
Boulder Beer Company
Boulder, CO 303-444-8448
BR Cohn Winery
Glen Ellen, CA 707-938-4064
Brander Vineyard
Los Olivos, CA 800-970-9979
Braren Pauli Winery
Redwood Valley, CA 800-423-6519
Braswell's Winery
Dora, AL 205-648-8335
Bravard Vineyards & Winery
Hopkinsville, KY 270-269-2583
Breitenbach Wine Cellars
Dover, OH 330-343-3603
Briceland Vineyards
Redway, CA 707-923-2429
Brick Brewery
Waterloo, ON 800-505-8971
Brimstone Hill Vineyard
Pine Bush, NY 845-744-2231
Bristle Ridge Vineyard
Knob Noster, MO 800-994-9463
Broad Run Vineyards
Louisville, KY 502-231-0372
Broadley Vineyards
Monroe, OR 541-847-5934
Bronco Wine Company
Ceres, CA 800-692-5780
Brookmere Vineyards
Belleville, PA 717-935-5380
Brotherhood Winery
Washingtonville, NY 845-496-3661
Brown County Wine Company
Nashville, IN 888-298-2984
Brutocao Cellars
Hopland, CA 800-433-3689
Bryant Vineyard
Talladega, AL 256-268-2638
Buccia Vineyard
Conneaut, OH 440-593-5976
Buckingham Valley Vineyards
Buckingham, PA 215-794-7188
Buehler Vineyards
Saint Helena, CA 707-963-2155
Burnley Vineyards and Daniel Cellars
Barboursville, VA 540-832-2828
Butler Winery
Bloomington, IN 812-339-7233
Butterfly Creek Winery
Mariposa, CA 209-966-2097
Buttonwood Farm Winery
Solvang, CA 800-715-1404
Byington Winery & Vineyards
Los Gatos, CA 408-354-1111
Byron Vineyard & Winery
Santa Maria, CA 805-934-4770
Cache Cellars
Davis, CA 530-756-6068
Cain Vineyard & Winery
St Helena, CA 707-963-1616
Cakebread Cellars
Rutherford, CA 800-588-0298

Calafia Cellars
Saint Helena, CA 707-963-0114
Calera Wine Company
Hollister, CA...................... 831-637-9170
Callaway Vineyards & Winery
Temecula, CA 800-472-2377
Camas Prairie Winery
Moscow, ID....................... 800-616-0214
Cambria Winery & Vineyard
Santa Maria, CA 888-339-9463
Campari
New York, NY 212-891-3600
Canada Dry Bottling Company
Flushing, NY...................... 718-762-5967
Cantwell's Old Mill Winery
Geneva, OH....................... 440-466-5560
Cap Rock Winery
Lubbock, TX...................... 800-546-9463
Caparone Winery
Paso Robles, CA 805-467-3827
Caporale Winery
Napa, CA......................... 707-253-9230
Cardinale Winery
Oakville, CA 800-588-0279
Carlson Vineyards
Palisade, CO 888-464-5554
Carmela Vineyards
Glenns Ferry, ID 208-366-2313
Carneros Creek Winery
Napa, CA......................... 707-253-9464
Carrousel Cellars
Gilroy, CA........................ 408-847-2060
Casa Larga Vineyards
Fairport, NY 585-223-4210
Casa Nuestra
St Helena, CA 866-844-9463
Casco Bay Brewing
Portland, ME...................... 207-797-2020
Castello Di Borghese
Cutchogue, NY 800-734-5158
Catoctin Vineyards
Brookeville, MD 301-774-2310
Cavender Castle Winery
Atlanta, GA....................... 706-864-4759
Caymus Vineyards
Rutherford, CA 707-963-4204
Cayuga Ridge Estate Winery
Ovid, NY......................... 800-598-9463
Cedar Creek Winery
Cedarburg, WI..................... 800-827-8020
Cedar Mountain Winery
Livermore, CA 925-373-6636
Chaddsford Winery
Chadds Ford, PA 610-388-6221
Chadler
Swedesboro, NJ 856-467-0099
Chalet Debonne Vineyards
Madison, OH...................... 440-466-3485
Chalk Hill Estate Vineyards & Winery
Healdsburg, CA 707-838-4306
Champoeg Wine Cellars
Aurora, OR 503-678-2144
Channing Rudd Cellars
Middletown, CA 707-987-2209
Chappellet Winery
Saint Helena, CA 800-494-6379
Charles B. Mitchell Vineyards
Somerset, CA 800-704-9463
Charles Jacquin Et Cie
Philadelphia, PA 800-523-3811
Charles Spinetta Winery
Plymouth, CA 209-245-3384
Chateau Anne Marie
Carlton, OR....................... 503-864-2991
Chateau Boswell
St Helena, CA 707-963-5472
Chateau Chevre Winery
Napa, CA......................... 707-944-2184
Chateau des Charmes Wines
St. Davids, ON 800-263-2541
Chateau Diana Winery
Healdsburg, CA 707-433-6992
Chateau Grand Traverse
Traverse City, MI 231-223-7355
Chateau Julien Winery
Carmel, CA....................... 831-624-2600
Chateau Lafayette Reneau
Hector, NY 800-469-9463
Chateau Montelena Winery
Calistoga, CA 707-942-5105
Chateau Morisette Winery
Meadows of Dan, VA 540-593-2865

Chateau Potelle Winery
Napa, CA......................... 707-255-9440
Chateau Ra-Ha
Jerseyville, IL 866-639-4832
Chateau Souverain
Cloverdale, CA
Chateau St. Jean Vineyards
Kenwood, CA 707-833-4134
Chateau Thomas Winery
Plainfield, IN...................... 888-761-9463
Chatom Vineyards
Murphys, CA...................... 800-435-8852
Chestnut Mountain Winery
Hoschton, GA 770-867-6914
Chi Company/Tabor Hill Winery
Buchanan, MI 800-283-3363
Chicama Vineyards
West Tisbury, MA.................. 888-244-2262
Chimere
Santa Maria, CA 805-922-9097
Chouinard Vineyards
Castro Valley, CA 510-582-9900
Christine Woods Winery
Philo, CA......................... 707-895-2115
Christopher Creek Winery
Healdsburg, CA 707-431-8243
Cienega Valley Winery/DeRose
Hollister, CA...................... 831-636-9143
Cimarron Cellars
Caney, OK........................ 580-889-5997
Cinnabar Vineyards & Winery
Saratoga, CA...................... 408-741-5858
City Brewery Latrobe
Latrobe, PA....................... 724-537-5545
CK Mondavi Vineyards
St Helena, CA 707-967-2200
Claiborne & Churchill Vintners
San Luis Obispo, CA 805-544-4066
Claire's Grand River Winery
Madison, OH...................... 440-298-9838
Clear Creek Distillery
Portland, OR 503-248-9470
Cline Cellars
Sonoma, CA 800-543-2070
Clos Du Bois
Geyserville, CA 800-222-3189
Clos du Lac Cellars
Ione, CA 209-274-2238
Clos Du Muriel
Temecula, CA 951-296-5400
Clos du Val Wine Company
Napa, CA......................... 800-993-9463
Clos Pegase Winery
Calistoga, CA 800-866-8583
Cloudstone Vineyards
Los Altos Hills, CA 650-948-8621
Clover Hill Vineyards & Winery
Breinigsville, PA................... 800-256-8374
Cocolalla Winery
Cocolalla, ID...................... 208-263-3774
Colorado Cellars Winery
Palisade, CO 970-464-7921
Commonwealth Fish & Beer Company
Boston, MA....................... 617-523-8383
Concannon Vineyard
Livermore, CA 800-258-9866
Conn Creek Winery
Saint Helena, CA 800-793-7960
Conneaut Cellars Winery
Conneaut Lake, PA................. 877-229-9463
Conrotto A. Winery
Gilroy, CA........................ 408-847-2233
Consolidated Distilled Products
Chicago, IL 773-927-4161
Cooper Mountain Vineyards
Beaverton, OR 503-649-0027
Coors Brewing Company
Golden, CO 800-642-6116
Corby Distilleries
Toronto, ON 800-367-9079
Corus Brands
Woodinville, WA................... 425-806-2600
Cosentino Winery Vintage Grapevine, Inc.
Yountville, CA 800-764-1220
Cowie Wine Cellars
Paris, AR......................... 479-963-3990
Crescini Wines
Soquel, CA 831-462-1466

Cribari Vineyards
Fresno, CA 800-277-9095

Processor and exporter of high quality California bulk wine.

Cristom Vineyards
Salem, OR........................ 503-375-3068
Criveller Group
Niagara Falls, ON 888-849-2266
Cronin Vineyards
Woodside, CA..................... 650-851-1452
Crown Regal Wine Cellars
Brooklyn, NY 718-604-1430
Cruse Vineyards
Chester, SC 803-377-3944
Crystal Geyser Roxanne LLC
Pensacola, FL 850-476-8844
Cuneo Cellars
Amity, OR........................ 503-835-2782
Cuvaison Vineyard
Calistoga, CA 707-942-6266
Cygnet Cellars
Hollister, CA...................... 831-637-7559
Dalla Valle Vineyards
Oakville, CA 707-944-2676
Dark Mountain Winery and Brewery
Vail, AZ.......................... 520-762-5777
Daume Winery
Camarillo, CA..................... 800-559-9922
David Bruce Winery
Los Gatos, CA..................... 800-397-9972
Davis Bynum Winery
Healdsburg, CA 800-826-1073
De Loach Vineyards
Santa Rosa, CA.................... 707-526-9111
De Lorimier Winery
Geyserville, CA 800-546-7718
Deaver Vineyards
Plymouth, CA 209-245-4099
Deer Meadow Vineyard
Winchester, VA.................... 800-653-6632
Deer Park Winery
Elk Creek, MO 707-963-5411
Dehlinger Winery
Sebastopol, CA.................... 707-823-2378
Denatale Vineyards
Healdsburg, CA 707-431-8460
Devlin Wine Cellars
Soquel, CA 831-476-7288
DG Yuengling & Son
Pottsville, PA...................... 570-622-0153
Di Grazia Vineyards
Brookfield, CT 800-230-8853
Diageo Canada Inc.
Toronto, ON 416-626-2000
Diageo United Distillers
Norwalk, CT...................... 203-229-2100
Diamond Creek Vineyards
Calistoga, CA 707-942-6926
Diamond Oaks Vineyard
Cloverdale, CA.................... 707-894-3191
Diamond Water
Hot Springs, AR 501-623-1251
Domaine St. George Winery
Healdsburg, CA 707-433-5508
Donatoni Winery
Inglewood, CA 310-645-5445
Door-Peninsula Winery
Sturgeon Bay, WI 800-551-5049
Dr. Konstantin Frank Vin
Hammondsport, NY 800-320-0735
Dreyer Sonoma
Woodside, CA..................... 650-851-9448
Dry Creek Vineyard
Healdsburg, CA 800-864-9463
Duck Pond Cellars
Dundee, OR....................... 800-437-3213
Duckhorn Vineyards
St Helena, CA 888-354-8885
Duncan Peak Vineyards
Hopland, CA...................... 707-744-1129
Dundee Wine Company
Dundee, OR....................... 888-427-4953
Dunn Vineyards
Angwin, CA 707-965-3642
Duplin Wine Cellars
Rose Hill, NC 800-774-9634
Dutch Henry Winery
Calistoga, CA 888-224-5879
E&J Gallo Winery
Livingston, CA 209-394-6219

E&J Gallo Winery
Fresno, CA 559-458-2480
Eagle Crest Vineyards
Conesus, NY 585-346-2321
East Side Winery/Oak Ridge Vineyards
Lodi, CA 209-369-4758
Eberle Winery
Paso Robles, CA 805-238-9607
Ed Oliveira Winery
Arcata, CA 707-822-3023
Edgewood Estate Winery
Napa, CA. 800-755-2374
Edmunds St. John
Berkeley, CA. 510-981-1510
Edna Valley Vineyard
San Luis Obispo, CA 805-544-5855
El Molino Winery
Saint Helena, CA 707-963-3632
Elk Cove Vineyards
Gaston, OR 877-355-2683
Elk Run Vineyards
Mount Airy, MD 800-414-2513
Elliston Vineyards
Sunol, CA 925-862-2377
Emilio Guglielmo Winery
Morgan Hill, CA. 408-779-2145
Enz Vineyards
Hollister, CA. 831-637-3956
Eola Hills Wine Cellars
Rickreall, OR 800-291-6730
EOS Estate Winery
Paso Robles, CA. 800-349-9463
Erath Vineyards Winery
Dundee, OR. 800-539-5463
Esterlina Vineyard & Winery
Philo, CA. 707-895-2920
Evensen Vineyards
Oakville, CA. 707-944-2396
Evesham Wood Vineyard & Winery
Salem, OR. 503-371-8478
Eyrie Vineyards
Mcminnville, OR 503-472-6315
F.X. Matt Brewing Company
Utica, NY 800-690-3181
Fall Creek Vineyards
Austin, TX. 512-476-4477

Far Niente Winery
Oakville, CA. 707-944-2861
Farella-Park Vineyards
Napa, CA. 707-254-9489
Farfelu Vineyards
Flint Hill, VA 540-364-2930
Fenestra Winery
Livermore, CA .800-789-9463
Fenn Valley Vineyards
Fennville, MI 800-432-6265
Ferrante Winery & Ristorante
Geneva, OH. 440-466-6046
Ferrara Winery
Escondido, CA .760-745-7632
Ferrari-Carano Vineyards& Winery
Healdsburg, CA 800-831-0381
Ferrigno Vineyard & Winery
St James, MO 573-265-7742
Ferrigno Vineyards & Win
St James, MO 573-265-7742
Fess Parker Winery
Los Olivos, CA. 800-446-2455
Ficklin Vineyards
Madera, CA. 559-674-4598
Field Stone Winery & Vineyard
Healdsburg, CA 800-544-7273
Fieldbrook Valley Winery
McKinleyville, CA 707-839-4140
Fife Vineyards
Redwood Valley, CA. 707-485-0323
Filsinger Vineyards & Winery
Temecula, CA 951-302-6363
Fiore Winery
Pylesville, MD .410-879-4007
Firelands Wine Company
Sandusky, OH 800-548-9463
Firestone Vineyard
Los Olivos, CA. 805-688-3940
Fisher Ridge Wine Company
Charleston, WV 304-342-8702
Fisher Vineyards
Santa Rosa, CA. 707-539-7511
Fitzpatrick Winery & Lodge
Somerset, CA 800-245-9166
Flora Springs Wine Company
Saint Helena, CA 707-963-5711

Florida Distillers Company
Lake Alfred, FL 863-956-3477
Flynn Vineyards Winery
Rickreall, OR 888-427-4953
Foley Estates Vineyards & Winery
Lompoc, CA 805-737-6222
Folie a Deux Winery
Oakville, CA 1 8-0 5-5 64
Foris Vineyards
Cave Junction, OR 541-592-3752
Forman Vineyards
St Helena, CA 707-963-3900
Fortino Winery
Gilroy, CA. 888-617-6606
Fortuna Cellars
Davis, CA 530-756-6686
Four Sisters Winery
Belvidere, NJ 908-475-3671
Fox Run Vineyards
Penn Yan, NY 800-636-9786
Fox Vineyards Winery
Social Circle, GA 770-787-5402
Foxen Vineyard
Santa Maria, CA 805-937-4251
Franciscan Oakville Estates
Rutherford, CA .800-529-9463
Franciscan Vineyards
St. Helena, CA .800-529-9463
Frank Family Vineyard
Calistoga, CA 707-942-0859
Frank-Lin Distillers
San Jose, CA. 408-259-8900
Franklin Hill Vineyards
Bangor, PA 888-887-2839
Franzia Winery
Ripon, CA 209-599-4111
Fratelli Perata
Paso Robles, CA. 805-238-2809
Frederick Wildman & Sons
New York, NY .800-733-9463
Freemark Abbey Winery
Helena, CA 800-963-9698
Freixenet
Sonoma, CA 707-996-4981
Frey Vineyards
Redwood Valley, CA. 800-760-3739

Frick Winery
Geyserville, CA 707-857-1980
Frisinger Cellars
Napa, CA....... 707-255-3749
Frog's Leap Winery
Rutherford, CA....... 800-959-4704
Frontenac Point Vineyard
Trumansburg, NY....... 607-387-9619
Gainey Vineyard
Santa Ynez, CA....... 805-688-0558
Galante Vineyards
Carmel Valley, CA 800-425-2683
Galena Cellars Winery
Galena, IL 800-397-9463
Galluccio Estate Vineyards
Cutchogue, NY....... 631-734-7089
Gallup Sales Company
Gallup, NM....... 505-863-5241
Gary Farrell Wines
Santa Rosa, CA....... 707-433-6616
George A Dickel & Company
Tullahoma, TN 888-342-5352
Georgia Winery
Ringgold, GA 706-937-2177
Georis Winery
Carmel Valley, CA 831-659-1050
Germanton Winery
Germanton, NC....... 800-322-2894
Geyser Peak Winery
Geyserville, CA 800-255-9463
Giasi Winery
Rock Stream, NY 607-535-7785
Girard Winery/Rudd Estates
Oakville, CA....... 707-944-8577
Girardet Wine Cellars
Roseburg, OR 541-679-7252
Gloria Ferrer Champagne
Sonoma, CA 707-996-7256
Gloria Winery & Vineyard
Springfield, MO 417-926-6263
Glunz Family Winery & Cellars
Grayslake, IL....... 847-548-9463
Golden Creek Vineyard
Santa Rosa, CA....... 707-538-2350
Good Harbor Vineyards
Lake Leelanau, MI 231-256-7165
Goodson Brothers Coffee
Knoxville, TN....... 865-531-8022
Grand Teton Brewing
Victor, ID....... 888-899-1656
Grande River Vineyards
Palisade, CO 800-264-7696
Granite Springs Winery
Somerset, CA 800-638-6041
Great Divide Brewing Company
Denver, CO 303-296-9460
Greenfield Wine Company
Vallejo, CA 707-552-5199
Greenwood Ridge Vineyards
Philo, CA....... 707-895-2002
Groth Vineyards & Winery
Oakville, CA....... 707-944-0290
Groupe Paul Masson
Longueuil, QC 514-878-3050
Gruet Winery
Albuquerque, NM....... 888-897-9463
Guilliams Winery
St Helena, CA....... 707-963-9059
Gundlach Bundschu Winery
Sonoma, CA 707-938-5277
H Coturri & Sons Winery
Glen Ellen, CA 866-268-8774
Habersham Winery
Helen, GA....... 770-983-1973
Hafner Vineyard
Healdsburg, CA 707-433-4606
Hahn Estates and Smith &Hook
Soledad, CA 866-925-7994
Haight-Brown Vineyard
Litchfield, CT 800-577-9463
Hallcrest Vineyards
Felton, CA....... 831-335-4441
Handley Cellars
Philo, CA....... 800-733-3151
Hanzell Vineyards
Sonoma, CA 707-996-3860
Harbor Winery
West Sacramento, CA....... 916-371-6776
Harmony Cellars
Harmony, CA 800-432-9239
Harpersfield Vineyard
Geneva, OH....... 440-466-4739

Hart Winery
Temecula, CA 877-638-8788
Hartford Family Winery
Forestville, CA 800-588-0234
Hawk Pacific Freight
Napa, CA....... 707-259-0266
Hazlitt's 1852 Vineyard
Hector, NY 888-750-0494
Heartland Vineyards
Cleveland, OH 440-871-0701
Heck Cellars
Arvin, CA 661-854-6120
Hecker Pass Winery
Gilroy, CA....... 408-842-8755
Hegy's South Hills Vineyard & Winery
Twin Falls, ID 208-599-0074
Heineman's Winery
Put In Bay, OH 419-285-2811
Helena View/Johnston Vineyard
Calistoga, CA 707-942-4956
Hells Canyon Winery
Caldwell, ID 800-318-7873
Henry Estate Winery
Umpqua, OR....... 800-782-2686
Henry Hill & Company
Napa, CA....... 707-224-6565
Heritage Wine Cellars
North East, PA....... 800-747-0083
Hermann J. Wiemer Vineyard
Dundee, NY 800-371-7971
Hermannhof Winery
Hermann, MO....... 800-393-0100
Heron Hill Winery
Hammondsport, NY 800-441-4241
Hess Collection Winery
Napa, CA....... 877-707-4377
Hidden Mountain Ranch Winery
Paso Robles, CA....... 805-226-9907
Highland Manor Winery
Jamestown, TN....... 931-879-9519
Highwood Distillers
High River, AB....... 403-652-3202
Hillcrest Vineyard
Roseburg, OR 541-673-3709
Hinzerling Winery
Prosser, WA....... 800-722-6702
Hiram Walker & Sons
Fort Smith, AR 479-646-6100
Hiram Walker & Sons Limited
Windsor, ON....... 519-254-5171
Homewood Winery
Sonoma, CA 707-996-6353
Honeywood Winery
Salem, OR....... 800-726-4101
Honig Vineyard and Winery
Rutherford, CA....... 800-929-2217
Hood River Distillers
Hood River, OR 541-386-1588
Hood River Vineyards and Winery
Hood River, OR 541-386-3772
Hoodsport Winery
Hoodsport, WA....... 800-580-9894
Hop Kiln Winery
Healdsburg, CA 707-433-6491
Hopkins Vineyard
Warren, CT 860-868-7954
Horizon Winery
Santa Rosa, CA....... 707-544-2961
Huber's Orchard Winery
Borden, IN....... 800-345-9463
Hunt Country Vineyards
Branchport, NY....... 800-946-3289
Husch Vineyards
Philo, CA....... 800-554-8724
Ingleside Plantation Winery
Colonial Beach, VA....... 804-224-7111
Inniskillin Wines
Niagara-On-The-Lake, ON....... 888-466-4754
Iron Horse Ranch & Vineyard
Sebastopol, CA 707-887-1507
Ironstone Vineyards
Murphys, CA....... 209-728-1251
J Vineyards & Winery
Healdsburg, CA 800-885-9463
J. Filippi Winery
Etiwanda, CA 909-899-5755
J. Fritz Winery
Cloverdale, CA....... 707-894-3389
J. Stonestreet & Sons Vineyard
Healdsburg, CA 800-723-6336
Jack Daniel's Distillery
Lynchburg, TN 931-759-4221

Jackson Valley Vineyards
Ione, CA 209-274-4721
Jodar Vineyard & Winery
Placerville, CA 530-621-0324
Johlin Century Winery
Oregon, OH....... 419-693-6288
Johnson's Alexander Valley Wines
Healdsburg, CA 800-888-5532
Johnston's Winery
Ballston Spa, NY 518-882-6310
Jones Brewing Company
Smithton, PA....... 800-237-2337
Joseph Filippi Winery
Rancho Cucamonga, CA 909-899-5755
Joullian Vineyards
Carmel Valley, CA 877-659-2800
Justin Winery & Vineyard
Paso Robles, CA....... 800-726-0049
Kalin Cellars
Novato, CA....... 415-883-3543
Kate's Vineyard
Napa, CA....... 707-255-2644
Kathryn Kennedy Winery
Saratoga, CA....... 408-867-4170
Kelleys Island Wine Company
Kelleys Is, OH....... 419-746-2678
Kelson Creek Winery
Plymouth, CA 209-245-4700
Kendall-Jackson Wine
Windsor, CA 800-544-4413
King Brewing Company
Fairfield, CA....... 707-428-4503
King Estate Winery
Eugene, OR....... 800-884-4441
Kiona Vineyards Winery
Benton City, WA....... 509-588-6716
Kirigin Cellars
Gilroy, CA....... 408-847-8827
Kistler Vineyards
Sebastopol, CA....... 707-823-5603
Kittling Ridge Estate Wines & Spirits
Grimsby, ON....... 905-945-9225
Klingshirn Winery
Avon Lake, OH....... 440-933-6666
Knapp Vineyards
Romulus, NY 800-869-9271
Koryo Winery Company
Gardena, CA 310-532-9616
Kramer Vineyards
Gaston, OR 800-619-4637
Kunde Estate Winery
Kenwood, CA....... 707-833-5501
L. Mawby Vineyards
Suttons Bay, MI 231-271-3522
La Abra Farm & Winery
Lovingston, VA....... 434-263-5392
La Buena Vida Vineyards
Grapevine, TX 817-481-9463
La Chiripada Winery
Dixon, NM 800-528-7801
La Rocca Vineyards
Forest Ranch, CA 800-808-9463
La Vina Winery
Anthony, NM 575-882-7632
Labatt Breweries
Toronto, ON 800-268-2337
Laetitia Vineyard
Arroyo Grande, CA....... 888-809-8463
Lafollette Vineyard & Winery
Belle Mead, NJ 908-359-5018
Laird & Company
Scobeyville, NJ....... 877-438-5247
Lake Sonoma Winery
Healdsburg, CA 877-850-9463
Lakeridge Winery & Vineyards
Clermont, FL....... 800-768-9463
Lakeshore Winery
Romulus, NY 315-549-7075
Lakespring Winery
Yountville, CA 707-944-2475
Lakewood Vineyards
Watkins Glen, NY....... 607-535-9252
Lambert Bridge Winery
Healdsburg, CA 800-975-0555
Lamoreaux Landing Wine Cellar
Lodi, NY....... 607-582-6011
Lancaster County Winery
Willow Street, PA 717-464-3555
Landmark Vineyards
Kenwood, CA 800- 45- 636
Lange Winery
Dundee, OR....... 503-538-6476

Langtry Estate & Vineyards
Middletown, CA 707-987-9127
Larry's Vineyards & Winery
Altamont, NY 518-355-7365
Latah Creek Wine Cellars
Spokane Valley, WA 509-926-0164
Latcham Vineyards
Mt Aukum, CA 800-750-5591
Laurel Glen Vineyard
Glen Ellen, CA 707-526-3914
Lava Cap Winery
Placerville, CA 530-621-0175
Lazy Creek Vineyard
Philo, CA. 888-529-9275
Le Boeuf & Associates
North Falmouth, MA 800-444-5666
Leelanau Wine Cellars
Omena, MI 800-782-8128
Leidenfrost Vineyards
Hector, NY
Lemon Creek Winery
Berrien Springs, MI 269-471-1321
Leonetti Cellar
Walla Walla, WA. 509-525-1428
Les Bourgeois Vineyards
Rocheport, MO 573-698-2300
Lewis Cellars
Napa, CA. 70- 2-5 34
Limur Winery
San Francisco, CA 415-781-8691
Lin Court Vineyards
Solvang, CA 805-688-8554
Little Amana Winery
Amana, IA. 319-668-9664
Little Hills Winery
Saint Charles, MO 877-584-4557
Live Oaks Winery
Gilroy, CA. 408-842-2401
Livermore Valley Cellars
Livermore, CA 925-454-9463
Livingston Moffett Winery
Saint Helena, CA 800-788-0370
Llano Estacado Winery
Lubbock, TX. 800-634-3854
Lockwood Vineyards
Monterey, CA 831-642-9200
Loew Vineyards
Mount Airy, MD. 301-831-5464
Lohr Winery
San Jose, CA. 408-288-5057
Lolonis Winery
Walnut Creek, CA. 925-938-8066
Long Vineyards
St Helena, CA. 707-963-2496
Lonz Winery
Middle Bass, OH. 419-285-5411
Los Olivos Vintners
Los Olivos, CA. 800-824-8584
Lost Hills Winery
Acampo, CA. 209-369-2746
Lost Mountain Winery
Sequim, WA 888-683-5229
Louis M. Martini
St. Helena, CA 866-549-2582
Lucas Winery
Lodi, CA 209-368-2006
Ludwigshof Winery
Eskridge, KS. 785-449-2498
LUXCO
St Louis, MO. 314-772-2626
Lynfred Winery
Roselle, IL. 888-298-9463

M.S. Walker
Somerville, MA 617-776-6700
Madison Foods
Saint Paul, MN 651-265-8212
Madison Vineyard
Ribera, NM. 575-421-8028
Madonna Estate Mont St John
Napa, CA. 707-255-8864
Madrona Vineyards
Camino, CA 530-644-5948
Magnanini Winery
Wallkill, NY 845-895-2767
Magnotta Winery Corporation
Vaughan, ON. 800-461-9463
Maisons Marques & Domaines USA
Oakland, CA 510-286-2000
Mama Rap's & Winery
Gilroy, CA. 800-842-6262
Manfred Vierthaler Winery
Sumner, WA 360-863-633
Marie Brizard Wines & Spirits
St. Helena, CA 800-878-1123
Marietta Cellars
Geyserville, CA 707-433-2747
Marimar Torres Estate
Sebastopol, CA. 707-823-4365
Marin Brewing Company
Larkspur, CA. 415-461-4677
Mark West Vineyards
Forestville, CA 707-544-4813
Markham Vineyards
Saint Helena, CA 707-963-5292
Markko Vineyard
Conneaut, OH 800-252-3197
Marlow Wine Cellars
Monteagle, TN 931-924-2120
Martin & Weyrich Winery
Templeton, CA 805-239-1640
Mastantuono Winery
Templeton, CA 805-238-0676
Matanzas Creek Winery
Santa Rosa, CA. 800-500-6464
Matson Vineyards
Redding, CA. 530-222-2833
Maurice Carrie Winery
Temecula, CA 800-716-1711
Mayacamas Vineyards
Napa, CA. 707-224-4030
Mazzocco Vineyards
Healdsburg, CA 707-433-9035
McCormick Distilling Company
Weston, MO 888-640-3082
McDowell Valley Vineyards & Cellars
Hopland, CA. 707-744-1774
McHenry Vineyard
Davis, CA 530-756-3202
McIntosh's Ohio Valley Wines
Bethel, OH 937-379-1159
McKinlay Vineyards
Newberg, OR 503-625-2534
Meeker Vineyard
Healdsburg, CA 707-431-2148
Menghini Winery
Julian, CA 760-765-2072
Mercury Brewing Company
Ipswich, MA. 978-356-3329
Meredyth Vineyard
Middleburg, VA 540-687-6277
Meridian Vineyards
Paso Robles, CA. 805-237-6000
Merryvale Vineyards
Saint Helena, CA 800-326-6069
Messina Hof Wine Cellars & Vineyards
Bryan, TX 800-736-9463
Michel-Schlumberger
Healdsburg, CA 800-447-3060
Milano Winery
Hopland, CA. 800-564-2582
Milat Vineyards
St Helena, CA. 707-963-0758
Mill Creek Vineyards
Healdsburg, CA 877-349-2121
Millbrook Vineyard and Winery
Millbrook, NY 800-662-9463
Miller Brewing Company
Milwaukee, WI 414-933-1846
Milliaire Winery
Murphys, CA. 209-728-1658
Mission Mountain Winery
Dayton, MT. 406-849-5524
Missouri Winery Warehouse Outlet
Cuba, MO 573-885-2168

Mohawk Distilled Products
North Miami, FL. 305-892-3460
Molson Coors Brewing Company
Denver, CO 800-642-6116
Mon Ami Champagne Company
Port Clinton, OH. 800-777-4266
Montelle Winery
Augusta, MO. 888-595-9463
Monterey Vineyard
Gonzales, CA 831-675-4000
Montevina Winery
Plymouth, CA 209-245-6942
Montmorenci Vineyards
Aiken, SC 803-649-4870
Moonlight Brewing Company
Windsor, CA 707-528-2537
Moresco Vineyards
Stockton, CA. 209-467-3081
Mosby Winery
Buellton, CA 805-688-2415
Moss Creek Winery
Napa, CA. 707-252-1295
Mount Baker Vineyards
Everson, WA 360-592-2300
Mount Bethel Winery
Altus, AR 479-468-2444
Mount Eden Vineyards
Saratoga, CA. 408-867-5832
Mount Hope Estate Winery
Manheim, PA 717-665-7021
Mount Palomar Winery
Temecula, CA 800-854-5177
Mount Pleasant Winery
Augusta, MO. 800-467-9463
Mt. Nittany Vineyard
Centre Hall, PA. 814-466-6373
Murphy Goode Estate Winery
Healdsburg, CA 707-431-7644
Naked Mountain Vineyard & Winery
Markham, VA 540-364-1609
Nalle Winery
Healdsburg, CA 707-433-1040
Nantucket Vineyards
Nantucket, MA 508-228-9235
Napa Cellars
Oakville, CA. 800-848-9630
Napa Creek Winery
Saint Helena, CA 707- 25- 946
Napa Valley Port Cellars
Napa, CA. 707-257-7777
Napa Wine Company
Oakville, CA. 800-848-9630
Nashoba Valley Winery
Bolton, MA. 978-779-5521
National Wine & Spirits
Indianapolis, IN 800-562-7359
Navarro Vineyards & Winery
Philo, CA. 800-537-9463
Naylor Wine Cellars
Stewartstown, PA 800-292-3370
Nevada City Winery
Nevada City, CA. 800-203-9463
Nevada County Wine Guild
Nevada City, CA. 530-265-3662
New Belgium Brewing Company
Fort Collins, CO 888-622-4044
New Hope Winery
New Hope, PA. 800-592-9463
New Land Vineyard
Geneva, NY. 315-585-4432
Newport Vineyards & Winery
Middletown, RI. 401-848-5161
Newton Vineyard
Yountville, CA 707-963-9000
Nicasio Vineyards
Soquel, CA 831-423-1073
Nichelini Winery
Saint Helena, CA 707-963-0717
Niebaum-Coppola Estate Winery
Rutherford, CA 707-968-1100
Nissley Vineyards
Bainbridge, PA 800-522-2387
Nordman of California
Sanger, CA 559-638-9923
North House Vineyards In
Jamesport, NY. 631-722-5256
Northern Lights Brewing Company
Airway Heights, WA. 509-242-2739
Northern Vineyards Winery
Stillwater, MN. 651-430-1032
Northville Winery
Northville, MI. 248-349-3181

Nutmeg Vineyard
Andover, CT 860-742-8402
O'Vallon Winery
Washburn, MO 417-826-5830
Oak Grove Orchards Winery
Rickreall, OR 541-364-7052
Oak Hill Farm
Glen Ellen, CA 800-878-7808
Oak Knoll Winery
Hillsboro, OR 800-625-5665
Oak Ridge Winery
Lodi, CA 20- 3-9 47
Oak Ridge Winery
Lodi, CA 209-369-4758
Oak Spring Winery
Altoona, PA 814-946-3799
Oasis Winery
Hume, VA 800-304-7656
Obester Winery
Half Moon Bay, CA 650-726-9463
Oceania Cellars
Arroyo Grande, CA 805-481-5434
Ojai Vineyard
Oak View, CA 805-649-1674
Old Creek Ranch Winery
Ventura, CA 805-649-4132
Old Rip Van Winkle Distillery
Louisville, KY 502-897-9113
Old South Winery
Natchez, MS 601-445-9924
Old Wine Cellar
Amana, IA 319-622-3116
Olde Heurich Brewing Company
Washington, DC 202-333-2313
Oliver Wine Company
Bloomington, IN 800-258-2783
Olympic Cellars
Port Angeles, WA 360-452-0160
One Vineyard and Winery
Saint Helena, CA 707-963-1123
Optima Wine Cellars
Healdsburg, CA 707-431-8222
Opus One
Oakville, CA 800-292-6787
Orchard Heights Winery
Salem, OR 503-391-7308
Orfila Vineyards
Escondido, CA 760-738-6500
Organic Wine Company
San Francisco, CA 888-326-9463
Orleans Hill Vineyard Association
Woodland, CA 530-661-6538
Ormand Peugeog Corporation
Miami, FL 305-624-6834
Orr Mountain Winery
Madisonville, TN 423-442-5340
Ozeki Sake
Hollister, CA 831-637-9217
Pabst Brewing Company
San Antonio, TX 800-935-2337
Pacheco Ranch Winery
Novato, CA 415-883-5583
Pacific Echo Cellars
Philo, CA 707-895-2065
Pacific Hop Exchange Brewing Company
Novato, CA 415-884-2820
Page Mill Winery
Livermore, CA 925-456-3375
Pahlmeyer Winery
Saint Helena, CA
Pahrump Valley Vineyards
Pahrump, NV 800-368-9463
Palmer Vineyards
Riverhead, NY 800-901-8783
Panther Creek Cellars
McMinnville, OR 503-472-8080
Pantry Shelf/Mixxm
Hutchinson, KS 800-968-3346
Paper City Brewery
Holyoke, MA 413-535-1588
Paradise Valley Vineyards
Phoenix, AZ 602-233-8727
Paragon Vineyards
San Luis Obispo, CA 805-544-9080
Parasio Springs Vineyards
Soledad, CA 831-678-0300
Pastori Winery
Cloverdale, CA 707-857-3418
Paumanok Vineyards
Aquebogue, NY 631-722-8800
Peaceful Bend Vineyard
Steelville, MO 573-775-3000
Peconic Bay Winery
Cutchogue, NY 631-734-7361
Pedrizzetti Winery
Morgan Hill, CA 408-779-7389
Pedroncelli Winery
Geyserville, CA 800-836-3894
Peju Winery
Rutherford, CA 800-446-7358
Pellegrini Family Vineyards
Santa Rosa, CA 800-891-0244
Penn-Shore Vineyards
North East, PA 814-725-8688
Pernod Ricard USA
Purchase, NY 914-848-4800
Perry Creek Winery
Fair Play, CA 800-880-4026
Pete's Brewing Company
San Antonio, TX 800-877-7383
Peter Michael Winery
Calistoga, CA 800-354-4459
Peterson & Sons Winery
Kalamazoo, MI 269-626-9755
Pheasant Ridge Winery
Lubbock, TX 806-746-6033
Philip Togni Vineyard
Saint Helena, CA 707-963-3731
Phillips Beverage Company
Minneapolis, MN 612-331-6230
Phillips Farms & Michael David Vineyards
Lodi, CA 888-707-9463
Piedmont Vineyards & Winery
Middleburg, VA 540-687-5528
Piedra Creek Winery
San Luis Obispo, CA 805-541-1281
Pikes Peak Vineyards
Colorado Springs, CO 719-576-0075
Pindar Vineyards
Peconic, NY 631-734-6200
Pine Ridge Winery
Yountville, CA 800-575-9777
Plam Vineyards & Winery
La Quinta, CA 760-972-4465
Plum Creek Cellars
Palisade, CO 970-464-7586
Plymouth Colony Winery
Plymouth, MA 508-747-3334
Pommeraie Winery
Sebastopol, CA 707-823-9463
Ponderosa Valley Vineyard & Winery
Ponderosa, NM 575-834-7487
Ponzi Vineyards
Beaverton, OR 503-628-1227
Poplar Ridge Vineyards
Hector, NY 607-582-6421
Porter Creek Vineyards
Healdsburg, CA 707-433-6321
Prager Winery & Port Works
Saint Helena, CA 800-969-7678
Presque Isle Wine Cellar
North East, PA 800-488-7492
Preston Premium Wines
Pasco, WA 509-545-1990
Preston Vineyards
Healdsburg, CA 800-305-9707
Prince Michael Vineyards
Leon, VA 800-869-8242
Quady Winery
Madera, CA 800-733-8068
Quail Ridge Cellars & Vineyards
Saint Helena, CA 800-706-9463
Quilceda Creek Vintners
Snohomish, WA 360-568-2389
Quivira Vineyards
Healdsburg, CA 800-292-8339
R.H. Phillips
Esparto, CA 530-662-3504
Rabbit Ridge
Paso Robles, CA 80- 4-7 33
Radanovich Vineyards & Winery
Mariposa, CA 209-966-3187
Rainbow Hill Vineyards
Newcomerstown, OH 740-545-9305
Rancho De Philo
Alta Loma, CA 909-987-4208
Rancho Sisquoc Winery
Santa Maria, CA 805-934-4332
Rapazzini Winery
Gilroy, CA 800-842-6262
Ravenswood
Sonoma, CA 800-669-4679
Raymond Vineyard & Cellar
Saint Helena, CA 800-525-2659
Rebec Vineyards
Amherst, VA 434-946-5168
Redhawk Vineyard
Salem, OR 503-362-1596
Redhook Ale Breweries
Newington, NH 603-430-8600
Reeves Winery
Middletown, CA 707-987-9650
Regent Champagne Cellars
New York, NY
Renaissance Vineyard & Winery
Oregon House, CA 800-655-3277
Renault Winery
Egg Harbor City, NJ 609-965-2111
Renwood Winery
Plymouth, CA 800-348-8466
Retzlaff Vineyards
Livermore, CA 925-447-8941
Rex Wine Vinegar Company
Newark, NJ 973-589-6911
Richard L. Graeser Winery
Calistoga, CA 707-942-4437
Richardson Vineyards
Sonoma, CA 707-938-2610
Richland Beverage Associates
Carrollton, TX 214-357-0248
Ridge Vineyards
Cupertino, CA 408-867-3233
Ritchie Creek Vineyard
Saint Helena, CA 707-963-4661
Rivendell Winery
New Paltz, NY
River Road Vineyards
Sebastopol, CA 707-887-2243
River Run Vintners
Watsonville, CA 831-726-3112
Roberian Vineyards
Forestville, NY 716-679-1620
Robert F Pliska & Company Winery
Purgitsville, WV 877-747-2737
Robert Keenan Winery
Saint Helena, CA 707-963-9177
Robert Mondavi Winery
Oakville, CA 888-766-6238
Robert Mondavi Winery
Oakville, CA 888-766-6328
Robert Mueller Cellars
Windsor, CA 707-837-7399
Robert Pecota Winery
Calistoga, CA 707-942-6625
Robert Sinskey Vineyards
Napa, CA 800-869-2030
Robller Vineyard
New Haven, MO 573-237-3986
Roche Caneros Estate Winry
Sonoma, CA 800-825-9475
Rodney Strong Vineyards
Healdsburg, CA 707-433-6511
Rodney Strong Vineyards
Healdsburg, CA 800-474-9463
Rogue Ales
Newport, OR 541-867-3660
Rolling Hills Vineyards
Thousand Oaks, CA
Rombauer Vineyards
Saint Helena, CA 800- 62- 220
Rose Creek Vineyards
Hagerman, ID 208-837-4353
Rosenblum Cellars
Alameda, CA 510-865-7007
Ross Keller Winery
Nipomo, CA 805-929-3627
Roudon-Smith Vineyards
Scotts Valley, CA 831-438-1244
Round Hill Vineyards
St Helena, CA 800-778-0424
Royal Kedem Food & Wine Company
Bayonne, NJ 201-437-9131
Rudd Winery
Oakville, CA 707-944-8577
Rutherford Hill Winery
Rutherford, CA 707-963-1871
Saddleback Cellars
Oakville, CA 707-944-1305
Saint Arnold Brewing Company
Houston, TX 713-686-9494
Sainte Genevieve Winery
Ste Genevieve, MO 800-398-1298
Saintsbury
Napa, CA 707-252-0592
Sakeone Corporation
Forest Grove, OR 800-550-7253

Salamandre Wine Cellars
Aptos, CA 831-685-0321
Salishan Vineyards
La Center, WA 360-263-2713
San Dominique Winery
Camp Verde, AZ 480-945-8583
San Francisco Brewing Company
San Francisco, CA
Sand Castle Winery
Erwinna, PA 800-722-9463
Sandia Shadows Vineyard & Winery
Albuquerque, NM 505-856-1006
Sanford Winery
Lompoc, CA 800-426-9463
Santa Barbara Winery
Santa Barbara, CA 805-963-3633
Santa Cruz Mountain Vineyard
Felton, CA 831-426-6209
Santa Fe Vineyards
Espanola, NM 505-753-8100
Santa Margarita Vineyard & Winery
Temecula, CA 909-676-4431
Sarah's Vineyard
Gilroy, CA 408-842-4278
Satiety
Davis, CA 530-757-2699
Saucilito Canyon Vineyard
San Luis Obispo, CA 805-543-2111
Sausal Winery
Healdsburg, CA 800-500-2285
Savannah Chanelle Vineyards
Saratoga, CA 408-741-2934
Sawtooth Winery
Nampa, ID 208-467-1200
Sazerac Company
New Orleans, LA 800-899-9450
Scenic Valley Winery
Lanesboro, MN 507-259-4981
Schirf Brewing Company
Park City, UT 435-649-0900
Schloss Doepken Winery
Ripley, NY 716-326-3636
Schoppaul Hill Winery at Ivanhoe
Denton, TX 940-380-9463
Schramsberg Vineyards
Calistoga, CA 800-877-3623
Schug Carneros Estate Winery
Sonoma, CA 800-966-9365
Sea Ridge Winery
Occidental, CA 707-874-1707
Seavey Vineyard
Saint Helena, CA 707-963-8339
Secret House Vineyards
Veneta, OR 800-497-1574
Seghesio Family Vineyards
Healdsburg, CA 707-433-3579
Sellards Winery
Sebastopol, CA 707-823-8293
Sequoia Grove Vineyards
Rutherford, CA 800-851-7841
Serendipity Cellars
Monmouth, OR 503-838-4284
Serra Mission Winery
Saint Louis, MO 314-962-4600
Seven Hills Winery
Walla Walla, WA 877-777-7870
Seven Lakes Vineyards
Fenton, MI 810-629-5686
Shafer Vineyards
Napa, CA 707-944-2877
Shallon Winery
Astoria, OR 503-325-5978
Sharon Mill Winery
Manchester, MI 734-971-6337
Shenandoah Vineyards
Plymouth, CA 209-245-4455
Sierra Vista Winery
Placerville, CA 530-622-7221
Signore Winery
Brooktondale, NY 607-539-7935
Signorello Vineyards
Napa, CA 707-255-5990
Silvan Ridge
Eugene, OR 541-345-1945
Silver Creek Distillers
Rigby, ID 208-754-0042
Silver Fox Vineyard
Mariposa, CA 209-966-4800
Silver Mountain Vineyards
Santa Cruz, CA 408-353-2278
Silver Oak Cellars
Oakville, CA 800-273-8805

Silverado Hill Cellars
Napa, CA 707-253-9306
Silverado Vineyards
Napa, CA 707-257-1770
Simon Levi Cellars
Kenwood, CA 888-315-0040
Six Mile Creek Vineyard
Ithaca, NY 800-260-0612
Sky Vineyards
Glen Ellen, CA 707-935-1391
Slate Quarry Winery
Nazareth, PA 610-746-3900
Smart Ice
Fort Myers, FL 239-334-3123
Smith Vineyard & Winery
Grass Valley, CA 530-273-7032
Smith-Madrone Vineyards & Winery
Saint Helena, CA 707-963-2283
Smothers Winery/Remick Ridge
Glen Ellen, CA 800-795-9463
Sobon Estate
Plymouth, CA 209-333-6275
Sokol Blosser Winery
Dundee, OR 800-582-6668
Sonoita Vineyards
Elgin, AZ 520-455-5893
Sonoma Wine Services
Vineburg, CA 707-996-9773
Sonoma-Cutrer Vineyards
Fulton, CA 707-528-1181
Southern California Brewing Company
Torrance, CA 310-329-8881
Sow's Ear Winery
Brooksville, ME 207-326-4649
Spangler Vineyards
Roseburg, OR 541-679-9654
Spoetzl Brewery
Shiner, TX 361-594-3383
Spottswoode Winery
Saint Helena, CA 707-963-0134
Spring Mountain Vineyard
Saint Helena, CA 877-769-4637
Springhill Cellars
Albany, OR 541-928-1009
Spurgeon Vineyards & Winery
Highland, WI 800-236-5555
St. Francis Vineyards
Santa Rosa, CA 707-833-4668
St. Innocent Winery
Salem, OR 503-378-1526
St. James Winery
Saint James, MO 800-280-9463
St. Julian Wine Company
Paw Paw, MI 800-732-6002
Stags' Leap Winery
Napa, CA 800-640-5327
Star Hill Winery
Napa, CA 707-255-1957
Starr & Brown
Portland, OR 503-287-1775
Ste. Chapelle Winery
Caldwell, ID 877-783-2427
Stearns Wharf Vintners
Santa Barbara, CA 805-966-6624
Steltzner Vineyards
Napa, CA 707-252-7272
Steuk's Country Market &Winery
Sandusky, OH 419-625-8324
Stevenot Winery & Imports
Murphys, CA 20- 2-3 43
Stevens Point Brewery
Stevens Point, WI 800-369-4911
Stone Hill Wine Company
Hermann, MO 573-486-2221
Stonegate
St Helena, CA 707-603-2203
Stoneridge Winery
Sutter Creek, CA 209-223-1761
Stonington Vineyards
Stonington, CT 800-421-9463
Stony Hill Vineyard
Saint Helena, CA 707-963-2636
Stony Ridge Winery
Livermore, CA 925-449-0458
Storrs Winery
Santa Cruz, CA 831-458-5030
Story Winery
Plymouth, CA 800-712-6390
Storybook Mountain Winery
Calistoga, CA 707-942-5310
Straub Brewery Industries
St Marys, PA 814-834-2875

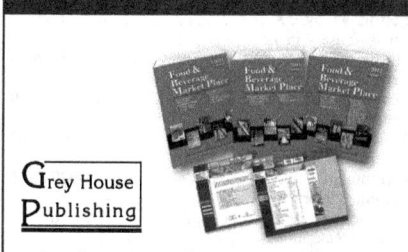

Streblow Vineyards
Saint Helena, CA 707-963-5892
Stryker Sonoma Winery Vineyards
Geyserville, CA 800-433-1944
Sudwerk Privatbrauerei Hubsch
Davis, CA 530-758-8700
Sugar Creek Winery
Defiance, MO 636-987-2400
Sullivan Vineyards Winery
Rutherford, CA 877-277-7337
Summit Brewing Company
Saint Paul, MN 651-265-7800
Summit Lake Vineyards & Winery
Angwin, CA 707-965-2488
Summum Winery
Salt Lake City, UT 801-355-0137
Sunrise Winery
San Jose, CA 408-741-1310
Sutter Home Winery
Saint Helena, CA 707-963-3104
Swan Joseph Vineyards
Forestville, CA 707-573-3747
Sweet Traders
Huntington Beach, CA 714-903-6800
Sycamore Vineyards
Saint Helena, CA 800-963-9698
Sylvester Winery
Paso Robles, CA 805-227-4000
Takara Sake
Berkeley, CA 510-540-8250
Talbott Vineyards
Gonzales, CA 831-675-3000
Talley Vineyards
Arroyo Grande, CA 805-489-2508
Tamuzza Vineyards
Hope, NJ 908-459-5878
Tarara Winery
Leesburg, VA 703-771-7100
Tartan Hill Winery
New Era, MI 231-861-4657
Tedeschi Vineyards
Kula, HI 808-878-1266
Tempest Vineyards
Amity, OR 503-835-2600
Tequila XQ
Guadalajara Jalisco, ... 333-587-7799
Thoma Vineyards
Dallas, OR 503-623-6420

Thomas Fogarty Winery
Portola Valley, CA 800-247-4163
Thomas Kruse Winery
Gilroy, CA. 408-842-7016
Thornton Winery
Temecula, CA 951-699-0099
Thorpe Vineyard
Wolcott, NY 315-594-2502
TKC Vineyards
Plymouth, CA 888-627-2356
Tomasello Winery
Hammonton, NJ 800-666-9463
Topolos at Russian River Vine
Forestville, CA 707-887-1575
Transamerica Wine Corporation
Brooklyn, NY 718-875-4017
Trefethen Vineyards
Napa, CA. 800-556-4847
Trentadue Winery
Geyserville, CA 888-332-3032
Triple Rock Brewing Company
Berkeley, CA. 510-843-2739
Troy Winery
Troy, OH 937-339-3655
Truchard Vineyards
Napa, CA. 707-253-7153
Truckee River Winery
Truckee, CA 530-587-4626
Tucker Cellars
Sunnyside, WA 509-837-8701
Tudal Winery
Saint Helena, CA 707-963-3947
Tularosa Vineyards
Tularosa, NM 800-687-4467
Tyee Wine Cellars
Corvallis, OR 541-753-8754
UDV Wines
San Francisco, CA 415-835-7300
Uinta Brewing
Salt Lake City, UT 801-467-0909
United Distillers & Vintners
Norwalk, CT 203-323-3311
US Distilled Products
Princeton, MN. 763-389-4903
UST
Danbury, CT 800-650-7411
Val Verde Winery
Del Rio, TX. 830-775-9714
Valley of the Moon Winery
Glen Ellen, CA 707-996-6941
Valley View Winery
Jacksonville, OR 800-781-9463
Van Der Heyden Vineyards
Napa, CA. 800-948-9463
Vancouver Island Brewing Company
Victoria, BC 800-663-6383
Varni Brothers/7-Up Bottling
Modesto, CA. 209-521-1777
Ventana Vineyards Winery
Monterey, CA 800-237-8846
Vetter Vineyards Winery
Westfield, NY 716-326-3100
Via Della Chiesa Vineyards
Raynham, MA. 508-822-7775
Viader Vineyards & Winery
Deer Park, CA. 707-963-3816
Viano Winery
Martinez, CA 925-228-6465
Viansa Winery
Sonoma, CA 800-995-4740
Vie-Del Company
Fresno, CA 559-834-2525
Villa Helena/Arger-Martucci Winery
St Helena, CA 707-963-4334
Villa Milan Vineyard
Milan, IN. 812-654-3419
Villa Mt. Eden Winery
Saint Helena, CA 707-944-2414
Villar Vintners of Valdese
Valdese, NC. 828-879-3202
Vina Vista Vineyard & Winery
Philo, CA 1 8-0 5-7 94
Vincent Arroyo Winery
Calistoga, CA 707-942-6995
Vincor International
Mississauga, ON. 800-265-9463
Vinoklet Winery & Vineyard
Cincinnati, OH 513-385-9309
Von Stiehl Winery
Algoma, WI. 800-955-5208
Von Strasser Winery
Calistoga, CA 888-359-9463

Vynecrest Vineyards and Winery
Breinigsville, PA. 800-361-0725
Wachusett Brewing Company
Westminster, MA 978-874-9965
Walker Valley Vineyards
Walker Valley, NY 845-744-3449
Warner Vineyards Winery
Paw Paw, MI. 800-756-5357
Wasson Brothers Winery
Sandy, OR 503-668-3124
Weibel Champagne Vineyards
Woodbridge, CA 80- 9-2 94
Wente Brothers Estate Winery
Livermore, CA 925-456-2300
Wermuth Winery
Calistoga, CA 707-942-5924
West Park Wine Cellars
West Park, NY. 845-384-6709
Westbend Vinyards
Lewisville, NC 866-901-5032
Westport Rivers Vineyard& Winery
Westport, MA 800-993-9695
Westwood Winery
Sonoma, CA 707-935-3246
Whaler Vineyard Winery
Ukiah, CA. 707-462-6355
What's Brewing
San Antonio, TX. 210-308-8883
Whitcraft Wines
Santa Barbara, CA 805-730-1680
White Oak Vineyards & Winery
Healdsburg, CA 707-433-8429
White Rock Distilleries
Lewiston, ME 207-783-1433
White Rock Vineyards
Napa, CA. 707-257-7922
Whitehall Lane Winery
Saint Helena, CA 707-963-9454
Whitford Cellars
Napa, CA. 707-942-0840
Wiederkehr Wine Cellars
Altus, AR 800-622-9463
Wild Hog Vineyard
Cazadero, CA 707-847-3687
Wild Horse Winery
Templeton, CA 805-434-2541
Wild Winds Farms
Naples, NY 800-836-5253
Wildhurst
Kelseyville, CA. 800-595-9463
William Grant & Sons
New York, NY 212-246-1760
William Harrison Vineyards & Winery LLC
Saint Helena, CA 707-963-8762
William Hill Winery
Napa, CA. 707-224-4477
Williams-Selym Winery
Healdsburg, CA 707-433-6425
Williamsburg Winery
Williamsburg, VA 757-258-0899
Willow Hill Vineyards
Johnstown, OH 740-587-4622
Wimberley Valley Winery
Driftwood, TX 512-847-2592
Windsor Vineyards
Santa Rosa, CA. 800-289-9463
Windwalker Vineyards
Somerset, CA 530-620-4054
Winters Winery
Winters, CA 530-795-3201
Witness Tree Vineyard
Salem, OR. 888-478-8766
Wolf Creek Vineyards
Norton, OH 800-436-0426
Wollersheim Winery
Prairie Du Sac, WI 800-847-9463
Wooden Valley Winery
Fairfield, CA 707-864-0730
Woodside Vineyards
Menlo Park, CA 650-851-3144
Woodward Canyon Winery
Touchet, WA 509-525-4129
Worden
Spokane, WA. 509-455-7835
Wyandotte Winery
Columbus, OH 614-476-3624
Yakima Craft Brewing Company
Yakima, WA 509-654-7357
Yakima River Winery
Prosser, WA. 509-786-2805
Yamhill Valley Vineyards
McMinnville, OR 800-825-4845

York Mountain Winery
Templeton, CA 805-237-7575
Z.D. Wines
Napa, CA. 800-487-7757
Zaca Mesa Winery
Los Olivos, CA 800-350-7972
Zayante Vineyards
Felton, CA. 831-335-7992
Ziem Vineyards
Fairplay, MD. 301-223-8352

Beers

Abita Brewing Company
Abita Springs, LA. 800-737-2311
Alaskan Brewing Company
Juneau, AK 907-780-5866
AleSmith Brewing Company
San Diego, CA 858-549-9888
Alley Kat Brewing Co, Lt
Edmonton, AB 780-436-8922
Amstell Holding
New Bedford, MA 508-995-6100
Amsterdam Brewing Company
Toronto, ON 416-504-1040
Anchor Brewing Company
San Francisco, CA 415-863-8350
Anderson Valley Brewing
Boonville, CA. 707-895-2337
Andrew's Brewing
Lincolnville, ME. 207-763-3305
Anheuser-Busch
Baldwinsville, NY 315-638-0365
Anheuser-Busch
Columbus, OH 614-888-6644
Anheuser-Busch
Fairfield, CA. 707-429-2000
Anheuser-Busch
Houston, TX 713-675-2311
Anheuser-Busch
Cartersville, GA 770-386-2000
Anheuser-Busch
Jacksonville, FL 800-342-5283
Anheuser-Busch
Van Nuys, CA 818-989-5300
Anheuser-Busch Inc.
Saint Louis, MO 800-342-5283
Anheuser-Busch North Brewery
Newark, NJ 973-645-7700
Apani Southwest
Abilene, TX. 325-690-1550
Arnold Foods Company
Greenwich, CT 203-531-4770
Assets Grille & Southwest Brewing Company
Albuquerque, NM. 505-889-6400
Atlanta Brewing Company
Bar Harbor, ME. 800-475-5417
Atwater Block Brewing Company
Detroit, MI 313-877-9205
August Schell Brewing Company
New Ulm, MN. 800-770-5020
Avery Brewing Company
Boulder, CO 877-844-5679
Bad Frog Brewing
Saint Augustine, FL 888-223-3764
Baltimore Brewing Company
Baltimore, MD 410-837-5000
Bar Harbor Brewing Company
Bar Harbor, ME. 207-288-4592
Bay Hawk Ales
Irvine, CA 949-442-7565
Beaver Street Brewery
Flagstaff, AZ. 928-779-0079
Belmont Brewing Company
Long Beach, CA 562-433-3891
Berkshire Brewing Company, Inc.
South Deerfield, MA 877-222-7468
Big Bucks Brewery & Steakhouse
Bloomfield Hills, MI
Big Rock Brewery
Calgary, AB. 800-242-3107
Big Sky Brewing Company
Missoula, MT 800-559-2774
Bison Brewing Company
Berkeley, CA. 510-697-1537
Black Mountain Brewing Company
Cave Creek, AZ 480-488-3553
Bloomington Brewing Company
Bloomington, IN 812-339-2256
Bluegrass Brewing Company
St Matthews, KY. 502-899-7070
Bohemian Brewery
Midvale, UT 801-566-5474

Boston Beer Company
Boston, MA........800-372-1131

Boston Stoker
Vandalia, OH........800-745-5282

Boulder Beer Company
Boulder, CO........303-444-8448

Boulder Creek Brewing Company
Boulder Creek, CA........831-338-7882

Boulder Street Coffee Roaster
Colorado Springs, CO........719-577-4291

Boulevard Brewing Company
Kansas City, MO........816-474-7095

Bow Valley Brewing Company
Canmore, AB........403-678-2739

Brasserie Brasel Brewery
Lasalle, QC........800-463-2728

Breckenridge Brewery
Denver, CO........303-573-0431

Brick Brewery
Waterloo, ON........800-505-8971

Bristol Brewing Company
Colorado Springs, CO........719-633-2555

Brooklyn Brewery
Brooklyn, NY........718-486-7422

Buffalo Bill Brewing Company
Hayward, CA........510-886-9823

Butterfields Brewing Company
Fresno, CA........559-264-5521

Canada Dry Bottling Company
Flushing, NY........718-762-5967

Capital Brewery
Middleton, WI........608-836-7100

Carolina Brewery
Chapel Hill, NC........919-942-1800

Carta Blanca
El Paso, TX........915-544-6367

Casco Bay Brewing
Portland, ME........207-797-2020

Champion Beverages
Darien, CT........203-655-9026

Chicago Pizza & Brewery
Huntington Beach, CA........714-500-2400

Christopher Joseph Brewing Company
Paradise Valley, AZ........480-948-7882

Cisco Brewers
Nantucket, MA........508-325-5929

City Brewery Latrobe
Latrobe, PA........724-537-5545

City Brewing Company
La Crosse, WI........608-785-4200

Clipper City Brewing
Baltimore, MD........410-247-7822

Cold Spring Brewing Company
Cold Spring, MN........320-685-8686

Columbus Brewing Company
Columbus, OH........614-464-2739

Commonwealth Brewing Company
Boston, MA........617-523-8383

Commonwealth Fish & Beer Company
Boston, MA........617-523-8383

Concord Brewery
Lowell, MA........978-937-1200

Coors Brewing Company
Golden, CO........800-642-6116

Copper Tank Brewing Company
Austin, TX........512-854-9380

Creemore Springs Brewery
Creemore, ON........800-267-2240

Criveller Group
Niagara Falls, ON........888-849-2266

Crooked River Brewing Company
Cleveland, OH........216-771-2337

Crowley Beverage Corporation
Wayland, MA........800-997-3337

Crown City Brewery
Compton, CA........626-577-5548

Crystal Geyser Roxanne LLC
Pensacola, FL........850-476-8844

D.L. Geary Brewing
Portland, ME........207-878-2337

Dark Mountain Winery and Brewery
Vail, AZ........520-762-5777

Dempseys Restaurant
Petaluma, CA........707-765-9694

Deschutes Brewery
Bend, OR........541-385-8606

DG Yuengling & Son
Pottsville, PA........570-622-0153

Dogfish Head Craft Brewery
Lewes, DE........888-834-3474

Dogwood Brewing Company
Atlanta, GA........404-367-0500

Drakes Brewing
San Leandro, CA........510-568-BREW

Durango Brewing
Durango, CO........970-247-3396

Eastern Brewing Corporation
Hammonton, NJ........609-561-2700

Etna Brewing Company
Etna, CA........530-467-5277

F&M Brewery 573054 Ontario Limited
Guelph, ON........877-316-2337

F.X. Matt Brewing Company
Utica, NY........800-690-3181

Falla Imports
Greenville, ME........609-476-4106

Flagstaff Brewing Company
Flagstaff, AZ........928-773-1442

Florida Brewery
Auburndale, FL........863-965-1825

Flying Dog Brewery
Frederick, MD........301-694-7899

Fort Garry Brewing Company
Winnipeg, NB........204-487-3678

Frederick Brewing Company
Frederick, MD........888-258-7434

French's Coffee
Walnut Creek, CA........925-978-6105

Full Sail Brewing Company
Hood River, OR........541-386-2281

Gambrinus Company
San Antonio, TX........210-490-9128

Gentle Ben's Brewing Company
Tucson, AZ........520-624-4177

Giumarra Vineyards
Bakersfield, CA........661-395-7000

Golden City Brewery
Golden, CO........303-279-8092

Goose Island Brewing
Chicago, IL........312-915-0071

Gordon Biersch Brewing Company
San Jose, CA........408-294-6785

Grand Rapids Brewing Company
Grand Rapids, MI........616-285-5970

Grand Teton Brewing
Victor, ID........888-899-1656

Gray Brewing Company
Janesville, WI........608-752-3552

Great Divide Brewing Company
Denver, CO........303-296-9460

Great Lakes Brewing
Etobicoke, ON........800-463-5435

Great Lakes Brewing Company
Cleveland, OH........216-771-4404

Great Northern Brewing Company
Whitefish, MT........406-863-1000

Great Western Brewing Company
Saskatoon, SK........800-764-4492

Guinness-Bass Import Company
Stamford, CT........800-521-1591

H.C. Berger Brewery
Fort Collins, CO........970-493-9044

Hair of the Dog Brewing Company
Portland, OR

Hale's Ales
Seattle, WA........206-706-1544

Harpoon Brewery
Boston, MA........800-427-7666

Heartland Brewery
New York, NY........212-645-3400

High Falls Brewing
Rochester, NY........585-546-1030

High Falls Brewing Company
Rochester, NY........800-729-4366

Hog Haus Brewing Company
Fayetteville, AR........479-521-2739

Hogtown Brewing Company
Mississauga, ON........905-855-9065

Hornell Brewing Company
New Hyde Park, NY........516-812-0300

Humbolt Brewing Company
Arcata, CA........707-826-1734

Il Vicino Pizzeria
Salida, CO........719-539-5219

Jones Brewing Company
Smithton, PA........800-237-2337

Kalamazoo Brewing Company
Galesburg, MI........269-382-2338

Kamloops Brewing Co
Kamloops, BC........250-851-2543

Karl Strauss Breweries
San Diego, CA........858-273-2739

Kevton Gourmet Tea
Streetman, TX........888-538-8668

Kona Brewing
Kailua Kona, HI........808-334-2739

Krinos Foods
Santa Barbara, CA........800-624-4896

La Brasserie McAuslan Brewing
Montreal, QC........514-939-3060

Labatt Breweries
London, ON........519-663-5050

Labatt Breweries
Toronto, ON........800-268-2337

Labatt Breweries
Edmonton, AB........800-268-2997

Labatt Brewing Company
Creston, BC........250-428-9344

Lafayette Brewing Company
Lafayette, IN........765-742-2591

Laguna Beach Brewing Company
Laguna Beach, CA........949-494-2739

Lake St. George Brewing
Liberty, ME........207-589-4690

Lake Titus Brewery
Malone, NY........518-483-2337

Lakefront Brewery
Milwaukee, WI........414-372-8800

Lakeport Brewing Corporation
Moncton, NB........800-268-2337

Lang Creek Brewery
Marion, MT........406-858-2200

Left Hand Brewing Company
Longmont, CO........303-772-0258

Legend Brewing Company
Richmond, VA........804-232-8871

Leininkugel Brewing Company
Chippewa Falls, WI........88- 53- 643

Les Brasseurs Du Nord
Blainville, QC........800-378-3733

Les Brasseurs GMT
Montreal, QC........888-253-8330

Lion Brewery
Wilkes Barre, PA........800-233-8327

Lone Wolf Brewing
Carbondale, CO........970-963-9757

Long Trail Brewing Company
Bridgewater Corners, VT........802-672-5011

Los Gatos Brewing Company
Los Gatos, CA........408-395-9929

Lost Coast Brewery
Eureka, CA........707-445-4480

Magnotta Winery Corporation
Vaughan, ON........800-461-9463

Main Street Brewery
Cincinnati, OH........513-665-4678

Manhattan Beach Brewing Company
Manhattan Beach, CA........310-798-2744

Marin Brewing Company
Larkspur, CA........415-461-4677

Maritime Pacific Brewing Company
Seattle, WA........206-782-6181

Mayer's Cider Mill
Webster, NY........800-543-0043

McNeill's Brewery
Brattleboro, VT........802-254-2553

Meier's Wine Cellars
Cincinnati, OH........800-346-2941

Mendocino Brewing Company
Ukiah, CA........707-463-2087

Mercury Brewing Company
Ipswich, MA........978-356-3329

Miller Brewing Company
Milwaukee, WI........414-933-1846

MillerCoors
Elkton, VA

MillerCoors
Eden, NC........336-627-2100

MillerCoors
Fort Worth, TX........800-645-5376

MillerCoors
Trenton, OH........800-944-5483

Millrose Brewing Company
South Barrington, IL........800-464-5576

Millstream Brewing
Amana, IA........319-622-3672

Mishawaka Brewing Company
Granger, IN........574-256-9993

MJ Barleyhoppers
Lewiston, ID........208-746-5300

Moet Hennessy USA
New York, NY........212-888-7575

Molson Coors Brewing Company
Denver, CO........800-642-6116

Moonlight Brewing Company
Windsor, CA........707-528-2537

Moosehead Breweries Ltd.
St. John, NB 877-888-2337
Mountain Crest Brewing SRL LLC
Monroe, WI. 608-325-3191
Mountain Sun Brewery
Boulder, CO 303-546-0886
Multnomah Brewing
Portland, OR 503-236-3106
Nevada City Brewing
Nevada City, CA. 530-265-2446
New Belgium Brewing Company
Fort Collins, CO 888-622-4044
New Glarus Brewing
New Glarus, WI 608-527-5850
New Holland Brewing
Holland, MI. 616-355-6422
Northampton Brewing Company
Northampton, MA. 413-584-9903
Northern Breweries
Marie, ON 514-908-7545
Northern Lights Brewing Company
Airway Heights, WA. 509-242-2739
Nutfield Brewing Company
Derry, NH 603-434-9678
Oak Creek Brewing Company
Sedona, AZ 928-204-1300
Odell Brewing Company
Fort Collins, CO 970-498-9070
Okanagan Spring Brewery
Vernon, BC 800-652-0755
Oland Breweries
Halifax, NS 800-268-2337
Old Credit Brewing Co LtOntario Craft Brewers
Toronto, ON 416-494-2766
Olde Heurich Brewing Company
Washington, DC 202-333-2313
Onalaska Brewing
Onalaska, WA 360-978-4253
Oregon Trader Brewing
Albany, OR 541-928-1931
Oskar Blues Brewery
Longmont, CO 303-776-1914
Pabst Brewing Company
San Antonio, TX. 800-935-2337
Pacific Coast Brewing Company
Oakland, CA 510-836-2739
Pacific Hop Exchange Brewing Company
Novato, CA 415-884-2820
Pacific Western Brewing Company
Prince George, BC 250-562-2424
Palmetto Brewing
Charleston, SC 843-937-0903
Paper City Brewery
Holyoke, MA 413-535-1588
Pennsylvania Brewing Company
Pittsburgh, PA 412-237-9400
Pete's Brewing Company
San Antonio, TX. 800-877-7383
Pike Place Brewery
Seattle, WA 206-622-6044
Pittsburgh Brewing Company
Pittsburgh, PA 412-682-7400
Prescott Brewing Company
Prescott, AZ 928-771-2795
Pyramid Brewing
Seattle, WA 206-682-3377
Red Bell Brewing
Philadelphia, PA 888-733-2355
Red White & Brew
Redding, CA 530-222-5891
Redhook Ale Breweries
Woodinville, WA. 425-483-3232
Redhook Ale Breweries
Newington, NH. 603-430-8600
Richland Beverage Associates
Carrollton, TX. 214-357-0248
River Market Brewing Company
Kansas City, MO. 816-471-6300
Rock Bottom Brewery
Denver, CO 303-534-7616
Rogue Ales
Newport, OR. 541-867-3660
Rohrbach Brewing Company
Rochester, NY. 585-594-9800
Russell Breweries, Inc.
Surrey, BC. 604-599-1190
S&P
Mill Valley, CA. 800-935-2337
Saint Arnold Brewing Company
Houston, TX 713-686-9494
San Andreas Brewing Company
Hollister, CA
San Francisco Brewing Company
San Francisco, CA
Santa Cruz Brewing Company
Santa Cruz, CA 831-425-1182
Santa Fe Brewing
Santa Fe, NM 505-424-3333
Sapporo
New York, NY 800-827-8234
Schafley Tap Room
St Louis, MO. 314-241-2337
Schirf Brewing Company
Park City, UT 435-649-0900
Sea Dog Brewing Company
Topsham, ME 207-725-0162
Seven Barrell Brewery
West Lebanon, NH 603-298-5566
Shipyard Brewing Company
Portland, ME. 800-789-0684
Short's Brewing Company
Bellaire, MI 231-828-2112
Sierra Nevada Brewing Company
Chico, CA 530-893-3520
Sleeman Brewereis, Ltd.
Guelph, ON. 800-268-8537
Sleeman Breweries, Ltd.
Delta, BC. 604-777-2537
Smuttynose Brewing
Portsmouth, NH 603-436-4026
Snake River Brewing Company
Jackson, WY 307-739-2337
Southern California Brewing Company
Torrance, CA. 310-329-8881
Spaten West
South San Francisco, CA 650-794-0800
Spoetzl Brewery
Shiner, TX. 361-594-3383
Sprecher Brewing
Milwaukee, WI 888-650-2739
St. Croix Beer Company
Saint Paul, MN 651-387-0708
St. Stan's Brewing Company
Modesto, CA. 209-527-7826
Star Creek Brewing Company
Dallas, TX. 214-999-0999
Star Union Brewing Company
Hennepin, IL 815-925-7400
Stevens Point Brewery
Stevens Point, WI 800-369-4911
Stone Brewing
Escondido, CA 760-471-4999
Stoudt Brewing Company
Adamstown, PA 717-484-4387
Straub Brewery Industries
St Marys, PA 814-834-2875
Sudwerk Privatbrauerei Hubsch
Davis, CA 530-758-8700
Summit Brewing Company
Saint Paul, MN 651-265-7800
Sweetwater Brewing Company
Atlanta, GA 404-691-2537
Tabernash Brewing Company
Longmont, CO 303-772-0258
Taos Trails Brewery
Ranchos De Taos, NM 505-758-0099
Thymly Products
Colora, MD 410-658-4820
Tin Whistle Brewing Co
Penticton, BC 250-770-1122
Toro Brewing
Morgan Hill, CA. 408-778-2739
Trafalgar Brewing Company
Oakville, ON. 905-337-0133
Triple Rock Brewing Company
Berkeley, CA. 510-843-2739
Triumph Brewing Company
Princeton, NJ. 609-924-7855
Troy Brewing Company
Troy, NY 518-273-2337
Tuscan Brewing
Red Bluff, CA. 530-520-0624
Uinta Brewing
Salt Lake City, UT 801-467-0909
Unibroue/Unibrew Sleeman Unibroue
Chambly, QC. 450-658-7658
Vancouver Island Brewing Company
Victoria, BC 800-663-6383
Vino's
Little Rock, AR. 501-375-8466
Wachusett Brewing Company
Westminster, MA 978-874-9965
Wagner Vineyards
Lodi, NY 866-924-6378
Wellington Brewing
Guelph, ON. 800-576-3853
What's Brewing
San Antonio, TX. 210-308-8883
Whistler Brewing Company
Burnaby, BC 604-438-2337
Whistler Brewing Company
Vancouver, BC 604-932-6185
Whitefish Brewing
Whitefish, MT. 406-862-2684
Widmer Brothers Brewing Company
Portland, OR 503-281-2437
William B. Reily & Company
Baltimore, MD 410-675-9550
Wilson Corn Products
Rochester, IN 574-223-3177
Yakima Craft Brewing Company
Yakima, WA 509-654-7357
Yellow Rose Brewing Company
San Antonio, TX. 210-496-6669
Yuengling Brewery
Pottsville, PA. 570-622-4141

American & British Ale

Amber Ale

Grand Teton Brewing
Victor, ID. 888-899-1656
Pete's Brewing Company
San Antonio, TX. 800-877-7383
Saint Arnold Brewing Company
Houston, TX 713-686-9494

Black & Tan

DG Yuengling & Son
Pottsville, PA. 570-622-0153

Cream Ale

Northern Lights Brewing Company
Airway Heights, WA. 509-242-2739

India Pale Ale

Saint Arnold Brewing Company
Houston, TX 713-686-9494

Pale Ale

DG Yuengling & Son
Pottsville, PA. 570-622-0153
Northern Lights Brewing Company
Airway Heights, WA. 509-242-2739
Pete's Brewing Company
San Antonio, TX. 800-877-7383

Belgian & French Ale

Kolsch

Saint Arnold Brewing Company
Houston, TX 713-686-9494

Bottled

Arizona Beverage Company
Woodbury, NY 800-832-3775
August Schell Brewing Company
New Ulm, MN. 800-770-5020
DG Yuengling & Son
Pottsville, PA. 570-622-0153
Jones Brewing Company
Smithton, PA 800-237-2337
Molson Coors Brewing Company
Denver, CO 800-642-6116
Spaten Beer
Little Neck, NY. 718-281-1912
Straub Brewery Industries
St Marys, PA 814-834-2875

Canned

Arizona Beverage Company
Woodbury, NY 800-832-3775
Jones Brewing Company
Smithton, PA 800-237-2337
Molson Coors Brewing Company
Denver, CO 800-642-6116

Kegged

Bohemian Brewery
Midvale, UT 801-566-5474

DG Yuengling & Son
Pottsville, PA....................570-622-0153
Jones Brewing Company
Smithton, PA....................800-237-2337

Lager

Amber Lager

DG Yuengling & Son
Pottsville, PA....................570-622-0153
Karl Strauss Breweries
San Diego, CA....................858-273-2739

Bock

Saint Arnold Brewing Company
Houston, TX....................713-686-9494

DarkLager/Dunkel

Brick Brewery
Waterloo, ON....................800-505-8971

Malt Liquor

Bad Frog Brewing
Saint Augustine, FL....................888-223-3764
Jones Brewing Company
Smithton, PA....................800-237-2337
Miller Brewing Company
Milwaukee, WI....................414-933-1846

Pilsner

Anderson Valley Brewing
Boonville, CA....................707-895-2337
Saint Arnold Brewing Company
Houston, TX....................713-686-9494

Non-Alcoholic

B.M. Lawrence & Company
San Francisco, CA....................415-981-3650
Coors Brewing Company
Golden, CO....................800-642-6116
Jones Brewing Company
Smithton, PA....................800-237-2337
Lion Brewery
Wilkes Barre, PA....................800-233-8327
Miller Brewing Company
Milwaukee, WI....................414-933-1846
Molson Coors Brewing Company
Denver, CO....................800-642-6116
Richland Beverage Associates
Carrollton, TX....................214-357-0248
Safeway Dairy Products
Walnut Creek, CA....................925-944-4000

Specialty &Cider

Reduced Calorie Beer

DG Yuengling & Son
Pottsville, PA....................570-622-0153

Stout & Porter

Flavored Stout

Saint Arnold Brewing Company
Houston, TX....................713-686-9494

Porter

DG Yuengling & Son
Pottsville, PA....................570-622-0153

Sweet Stout

Pete's Brewing Company
San Antonio, TX....................800-877-7383

Wheat

Wheat Ale

Alley Kat Brewing Co, Lt
Edmonton, AB....................780-436-8922
Grand Teton Brewing
Victor, ID....................888-899-1656

Bitters

Fee Brothers
Rochester, NY....................800-961-3337

Flora
Lynden, WA....................800-446-2110
Instantwhip: Florida
Tampa, FL....................813-621-3233
Kittling Ridge Estate Wines & Spirits
Grimsby, ON....................905-945-9225

Cocoa & Chocolate Drinks

Chocolate Drinks

Central Coca-Cola Bottling Company
Richmond, VA....................800-359-3759
North American Beverage Company
Ocean City, NJ....................609-399-1486
Richard's Gourmet Coffee
West Bridgewater, MA....................800-370-2633
Yoo-Hoo Chocolate Beverage Company
Carlstadt, NJ....................201-933-0070

Hot Chocolate

Gourmet Village
Morin Heights, QC....................800-668-2314
Madrona Specialty Foods
Tukwila, WA....................425-814-2500
S.J. McCullagh
Buffalo, NY....................800-753-3473

Hot Cocoa

Brewfresh Coffee Company
South Salt Lake, UT....................888-486-3334
Caffe D'Amore Gourmet Beverages
Monrovia, CA....................800-999-0171
Chatz Roasting Company
Ceres, CA....................800-792-6333
Chicago Coffee Roastery
Huntley, IL....................800-762-5402
Coffee Masters
Spring Grove, IL....................800-334-6485
Country Choice Naturals
Eden Prairie, MN....................952-829-8824
Gloria Jean's Gourmet Coffees
Irvine, CA....................877-320-5282
Jenny's Country Kitchen
Dover, MN....................800-357-3497
Keurig, Inc
Reading, MA....................781-928-0162
Mama Lee's Gourmet Hot Chocolate
Nashville, TN....................1 8-8 m-male
Nantucket Tea Traders
Nantucket, MA....................508-325-0203
Neighbors Coffee
Oklahoma City, OK....................800-299-9016
Nestle USA Inc
Glendale, CA....................800-225-2270
Northwestern Foods
Saint Paul, MN....................800-236-4937
Omanhene Cocoa Bean Company
Milwaukee, WI....................800-588-2462
Royal Coffee & Tea Company
Mississauga, ON....................800-667-6226
S&D Coffee, Inc
Concord, NC....................704-782-3121
S.J. McCullagh
Buffalo, NY....................800-753-3473
Sara Lee Corporation
Downers Grove, IL....................630-598-8100
Sara Lee Foodservice
Neenah, WI....................800-261-4754
Stephen's Gourmet Indulgent Foods
Farmington, UT....................800-845-2400
Subco Foods Inc.
West Chicago, IL....................630-231-0003
Swagger Foods Corporation
Vernon Hills, IL....................847-913-1200
White Coffee Corporation
Astoria, NY....................800-221-0140

with Marshmallows

Snapple Beverage Group
Ryebrook, NY....................800-762-7753
Todd's
Des Moines, IA....................800-247-5363

Coffee & Tea

A Southern Season
Chapel Hill, NC....................877-929-7133
Amelia Bay Beverage Systems
Alpharetta, GA....................800-650-8327

Aroma Coffee Company
Forest Park, IL....................708-488-8340
Atlanta Bread Company
Smyrna, GA....................800-398-3728
Borgnine Beverage Company
Sherman Oaks, CA....................818-501-5312
Burke Brands
Miami, FL....................877-436-6722
Fairwinds Gourmet Coffee
Lincoln, CA....................1 8-0 8-9 13
Kohana Coffee
Austin, TX....................512-904-1174
La Crema Coffee Company
West Chester, OH....................513-779-6278
Point Group
Satellite Beach, FL....................888-272-1249
Queen City Coffee Company
West Chester, OH....................800-487-7460
R. C. Bigelow
Fairfield, CT....................888-244-3569
Sara Lee Coffee & Tea
Suffolk, VA....................757-538-8083
Tetley Tea
Shelton, CT....................800-728-0084
Texas Spice Company
Cedar Park, TX....................800-880-8007
Zephyr Hills Bottled Watter Corporation
Tampa, FL....................800-950-9398

Cappuccino

Agropur Cooperative Agro-Alimentaire
Granby, QC....................800-363-5686
Alljuice
Hendersonville, NC....................800-736-5674
Aloe'Ha Drink Products
Houston, TX....................713-978-6359
American Instants
Flanders, NJ....................973-584-8811
Anheuser-Busch
Cartersville, GA....................770-386-2000
Aquafina
Purchase, NY....................914-253-2000
Arcadia Dairy Farms
Arden, NC....................828-684-3556
Arctic Beverages
Flin Flon, MB....................204-687-7517
Atlanta Coffee & Tea Company
Decatur, GA....................800-426-4781
Autocrat Coffee & Extracts
Lincoln, RI....................800-288-6272
Baltimore Brewing Company
Baltimore, MD....................410-837-5000
Barbe's Dairy
Westwego, LA....................504-347-6201
Beacon Drive In
Spartanburg, SC....................864-585-9387
Beaulieu Vineyard
Rutherford, CA....................800-264-6918
Beaver Street Brewery
Flagstaff, AZ....................928-779-0079
Beckman & Gast Company
Saint Henry, OH....................419-678-4195
Belmar Spring Water Company
Glen Rock, NJ....................201-444-1010
Better Beverages
Cerritos, CA....................562-924-8321
Bigelow Tea
Fairfield, CT....................888-244-3569
Blenheim Bottling Company
Hamer, SC....................800-270-9344
Blue Chip Group
Salt Lake City, UT....................800-878-0099
Boissons Miami Pomor
Longueuil, QC....................877-977-3744
Bottle Green Drinks Company
Mississauga, ON....................905-273-6137
Bow Valley Brewing Company
Canmore, AB....................403-678-2739
Brasserie Brasel Brewery
Lasalle, QC....................800-463-2728
Brenntag
Reading, PA....................888-926-4151
Caffe D'Oro
Chino, CA....................800-200-5005
Caffe D'Vita
Chino, CA....................800-200-5005
California Dairies
Visalia, CA....................559-625-2200
Campbell Soup Company
Camden, NJ....................800-257-8443

Celestial Seasonings Teas
Boulder, CO 800-434-4246
Chicago Coffee Roastery
Huntley, IL 800-762-5402
Christie Food Products
Randolph, MA 800-727-2523
Clark Spring Water Company
Pueblo, CO 719-543-1594
Clipper City Brewing
Baltimore, MD 410-247-7822
Coca-Cola Bottling Company
Atlanta, GA 800-438-2653
Cold Spring Brewing Company
Cold Spring, MN 320-685-8686
Coleman Dairy
Little Rock, AR 501-568-6237
Consolidated Mills
Houston, TX 713-896-4196
Cott Beverage West
Calgary, AB 403-279-6677
Cream O'Weaver Dairy
Salt Lake City, UT 801-973-9922
Creemore Springs Brewery
Creemore, ON 800-267-2240
Creme D'Lite
Irving, TX 972-255-7255
Crosby Molasses Company
St John, NB 506-634-7515
Crystal Foods
Brick, NJ 732-477-0073
Dean Dairy Products
Sharpsville, PA 800-942-8096
Dean Milk Company
Louisville, KY 800-451-3326
Decoty Coffee Company
San Angelo, TX 800-588-8001
Delta Distributors
Longview, TX 800-945-1858
Dogfish Head Craft Brewery
Lewes, DE 888-834-3474
Ensemble Beverages
Montgomery, AL 334-324-7719
Faygo Beverages
Detroit, MI 800-347-6591
Flora
Lynden, WA 800-446-2110
Florida Natural Flavors
Casselberry, FL 800-872-5979
Florida's Natural Growers
Lake Wales, FL 888-657-6600
Foster Farms Dairy
Fresno, CA 800-241-0008
Fresh Juice Company
Newark, NJ 973-465-7100
Fresh Samantha
Saco, ME 800-658-4635
Freshco
Stuart, FL 888-373-7426
Gerhart Coffee Company
Lancaster, PA 800-536-4310
GH Ford Tea Company
Shokangers Falls, NY 845-834-2068
Ghirardelli Chocolate Company
San Leandro, CA 800-877-9338
Golden Drop
Los Angeles, CA 323-225-9161
Great Lakes Brewing
Etobicoke, ON 800-463-5435
Great Northern Brewing Company
Whitefish, MT 406-863-1000
Great Western Brewing Company
Saskatoon, SK 800-764-4492
Gulf States Canners
Clinton, MS 601-924-0511
Halifax Group
Doraville, GA 770-452-8828
Hansen's Juices
Azusa, CA 800-426-7367
Healthmate Products
Highland Park, IL 800-584-8642
Hobarama Corporation
Miami, FL 880-439-2295
Hogtown Brewing Company
Mississauga, ON 905-855-9065
Honickman Affiliates
Pennsauken, NJ 800-573-7745
Humboldt Creamery Association
Fortuna, CA 707-725-6182
Hygeia Dairy Company
McAllen, TX 956-686-0511
Icy Bird
Sparta, TN 931-738-3557

Ideal American
Holland, IN 812-424-3351
Ideal Dairy
Richfield, UT 435-896-5061
IMS Food Service
Shelton, CT 800-235-7072
INCA Kola Golden Kola
New York, NY 212-688-1895
Jianlibao America
New York, NY 800-526-1688
Kamloops Brewing Co
Kamloops, BC 250-851-2543
Key Colony/Red Parrot Juices
Lyons, IL 800-424-0868
King's Cupboard
Red Lodge, MT 800-962-6555
Labatt Breweries
Edmonton, AB 800-268-2997
Labatt Brewing Company
Creston, BC 250-428-9344
Lacto Milk Products Corporation
Flemington, NJ 908-788-2200
Lake Country Foods
Oconomowoc, WI 262-567-5521
Lakefront Brewery
Milwaukee, WI 414-372-8800
LeHigh Valley Dairies
Lansdale, PA 215-855-8205
Louis Trauth Dairy
Newport, KY 800-544-6455
Lucerne Foods
Taber, AB 403-223-3546
M.A. Gedney
Chaska, MN 952-448-2612
Mafco Natural Products
Richmond, VA 804-222-1600
Magic Valley Quality Milk Producers
Jerome, ID 208-324-7519
Makers Mark Distillery
Loretto, KY 270-865-2881
Mama Lee's Gourmet Hot Chocolate
Nashville, TN .... 1 8-8 m-male
Maola Milk & Ice Cream Company
New Bern, NC 252-514-2792
Martin Coffee Company
Jacksonville, FL 904-355-9661
McArthur Dairy
Miami, FL 877-803-6565
Meadow Gold Dairies
Englewood, CO 800-525-3289
Mendocino Brewing Company
Ukiah, CA 707-463-2087
MEYENBERG Goat Milk Products
Turlock, CA 800-891-4628
MillerCoors
Elkton, VA
MillerCoors
Eden, NC 336-627-2100
MillerCoors
Fort Worth, TX 800-645-5376
MillerCoors
Trenton, OH 800-944-5483
Millstream Brewing
Amana, IA 319-622-3672
Minute Maid Company
Atlanta, GA 800-438-2653
Monticello Cellars
Napa, CA 707-253-2802
Moosehead Breweries Ltd.
St. John, NB 877-888-2337
Neighbors Coffee
Oklahoma City, OK 800-299-9016
Noel Corporation
Yakima, WA 509-248-4545
Nor-Cal Beverage Company
West Sacramento, CA 916-374-2621
Northumberland Cooperative
Miramichi, NB 800-332-3328
Northwestern Foods
Saint Paul, MN 800-236-4937
NSpired Natural Foods
Melville, NY 541-488-2747
Oak Farms
San Antonio, TX 800-292-2169
Oak Farms
El Paso, TX 800-395-7004
Ojai Cook
Los Angeles, CA 886-571-1551
Olympic Foods
Spokane, WA 509-455-8059
Our Thyme Garden
Cleburne, TX 800-482-4372

Peace River Citrus Products
Arcadia, FL 863-494-0440
Pennsylvania Brewing Company
Pittsburgh, PA 412-237-9400
Premier Blending
Wichita, KS 316-267-5533
Premium Waters
Minneapolis, MN 800-332-3332
Price's Creameries
El Paso, TX 915-565-2711
Quaker Oats Company
Dallas, TX 214-330-8681
Quality Naturally! Foods
City of Industry, CA 888-498-6986
Randag & Associates Inc
Elmhurst, IL 630-530-2830
Redco Foods
Windsor, CT 800-645-1190
Redwood Vintners
Novato, CA 415-892-6949
Richard's Gourmet Coffee
West Bridgewater, MA 800-370-2633
Royale International Beverage Co Inc
Davenport, IA 563-386-5222
Saint Albans Cooperative Creamery
Saint Albans, VT 800-559-0343
San Marco Coffee,Inc.
Charlotte, NC 800-715-9298
Santa Cruz Brewing Company
Santa Cruz, CA 831-425-1182
Sapporo
New York, NY 800-827-8234
Schepps Dairy
Dallas, TX 800-395-7004
Scotsburn Dairy Group
Scotsburn, NS 902-485-8023
Sebastiani Vineyards
Sonoma, CA 800-888-5532
Shipyard Brewing Company
Portland, ME 800-789-0684
Smucker Quality Beverages
Havre De Grace, MD 410-939-1403
Smucker Quality Beverages
Chico, CA 530-899-5000
Southeast Canners
Columbus, GA 706-324-0040
Southern Gardens Citrus Processing
Clewiston, FL 863-983-3030
Southern Heritage Coffee Company
Indianapolis, IN 800-486-1198
Steelback Brewery
Toronto, ON 416-679-0032
Stephen's Gourmet Indulgent Foods
Farmington, UT 800-845-2400
Stewart's Beverages
White Plains, NY 914-397-9200
Stremick's Heritage Foods
Santa Ana, CA 800-371-9010
SunMeadow Family of Products
Saint Petersburg, FL 727-573-2211
Swiss Dairy
Riverside, CA 951-898-9427
Swiss Valley Farms Company
Dubuque, IA 800-397-9156
Tabernash Brewing Company
Longmont, CO 303-772-0258
Taos Brewing Supply
Santa Fe, NM 505-983-0505
Tianfu China Cola
Katonah, NY 914-232-3102
Tonex
Wallington, NJ 973-773-5135
Tova Industries
Louisville, KY 888-532-8682
Triple H Food Processors
Riverside, CA 951-352-5700
True Beverages
O Fallon, MO 800-325-6152
Ultra Seal
New Paltz, NY 845-255-2490
Unibroue/Unibrew Sleeman Unibroue
Chambly, QC 450-658-7658
Unilever Canada
Saint John, NB 800-565-7273
United Dairy
Uniontown, PA 800-966-6455
Virgil's Root Beer
Los Angeles, CA 800-997-3337
Warren Laboratories
Abbott, TX 800-421-2563
Winder Dairy
West Valley, UT 800-946-3371

Yosemite Waters
Los Angeles, CA. 800-427-8420

Coffee

Alakef Coffee Roasters
Duluth, MN. 800-438-9228
Alaska Coffee Company
Anchorage, AK. 907-333-3626
Alexander & Baldwin
Honolulu, HI 808-525-6611
All Goode Organics
Santa Barbara, CA 805-683-3370
Allann Brothers Coffee Company
Albany, OR 800-926-6886
Allegro Coffee Company
Thornton, CO 800-666-4869
Alpen Sierra Coffee Company
Minden, NV 800-531-1405
Alpine Coffee Roasters
Leavenworth, WA. 800-246-2761
American Coffee Company
New Orleans, LA 800-554-7234
American Food & Equipment
Miami, FL. 305-377-8991
Ancora Coffee Roasters
Madison, WI 800-260-0217
Andresen Ryan Coffee Com
Superior, WI 715-395-3793
Anke Kruse Organics
Guelph, ON. 519-824-6161
Arbuckle Coffee
Pittsburgh, PA. 800-533-8278
Armenia Coffee Corporation
Purchase, NY 914-694-6100
Armeno Coffee Roasters
Northborough, MA 508-393-2821
Aroma Coffee Roasters
Hoboken, NJ 201-792-1730
Aroma Ridge
Marietta, GA 800-528-2123
Artist Coffee
Londonderry, NH 866-440-4511
Astor Products
Jacksonville, FL 904-783-5000
Atlanta Coffee Roasters
Atlanta, GA. 800-252-8211
Austin Chase Coffee
Seattle, WA 888-502-2333
Avalon Foodservice, Inc.
Canal Fulton, OH 800-362-0622
Avalon Organic Coffees
Albuquerque, NM. 800-662-2575
B.B. Bean Coffee
Monument, CO 719-481-1170
B.K. Coffee
Oneonta, NY. 800-432-1499
Baby's Coffee
Key West, FL 800-523-2326
Back Bay Trading
Alpharetta, GA 800-650-8327
Baltimore Coffee & Tea Company
Timonium, MD 800-823-1408
Barefoot Contessa Pantry
York, ME. 800-826-1752
Barnie's Coffee & Tea Company
Orlando, FL. 800-284-1416
Baronet Coffee
Hartford, CT 800-227-6638
Barrie House Gourmet Coffee
Yonkers, NY 800-876-2233
Barrington Coffee Roasting Company
Lee, MA 800-528-0998
Batdorf and Bronson Roasters
Olympia, WA 800-955-5282
Bay View Farm
Honaunau, HI 800-662-5880
Bean Forge
Coos Bay, OR 541-267-5191
Benbow's Coffee Roasters
Bar Harbor, ME. 207-288-5271
Berardi's Fresh Roast
Cleveland, OH 800-876-9109
Big Train Inc
Lake Forest, CA 800-244-8724
Blackbear Coffee Company
Hendersonville, NC 828-692-6333
Boston's Best Coffee Roasters
South Easton, MA. 800-898-8393
Bountiful Pantry
Nantucket, MA 888-832-6466
Boyd Coffee Company
Portland, OR 800-545-4077
Boyer Coffee Company
Denver, CO 800-452-5282
Breakfast at Brennan's
New Orleans, LA 800-888-9932
Brewfresh Coffee Company
South Salt Lake, UT 888-486-3334
Bridgetown Coffee
Portland, OR 800-726-0320
Brisk Coffee Company
Tampa, FL. 800-899-5282
BRJ Coffee & Tea
Lincoln, CA 800-829-1300
Broad Street Coffee Roasers
Durham, NC 800-733-9916
Brown & Jenkins Trading Company
Cambridge, VT 800-456-5282
Buckmaster Coffee
Hillsboro, OR 800-962-9148
Bucks County Coffee Company
Langhorne, PA 800-844-8790
Bull Run Roasting Company
Hayward, WI. 715-634-3646
Bustelo Coffee Roasting Company
Miami, FL. 305-592-7302
Buywell Coffee
Colorado Springs, CO. 719-598-7870
Cadillac Coffee Company
Madison Heights, MI 800-438-6900
Cafe Appassionato Coffee Company
Seattle, WA 888-522-2333
Cafe Bustelo
Miami, FL. 800-990-9039
Cafe Cartago
Denver, CO 800-443-8666
Cafe Del Mundo
Anchorage, AK. 907-562-2326
Cafe Descafeinado de Chiapas
Doral, FL. 305-499-9775
Cafe Du Monde
New Orleans, LA 504-587-0835
Cafe La Semeuse
Brooklyn, NY 800-242-6333
Cafe Moak
Rockford, MI 800-757-8776
Cafe Moto
San Diego, CA 800-818-3363
Cafe Society Coffee Company
Dallas, TX. 800-717-6000
Cafe Yaucono/Jimenez & Fernandez
Santurce, PR 787-721-3337
Caffe D'Oro
Chino, CA. 800-200-5005
Caffe Darte
Seattle, WA 800-999-5334
Caffe Luca
Tukwila, WA 800-728-9116
Caffe Trieste Superb Coffees
San Francisco, CA 415-550-1107
Cajun Creole Products
New Iberia, LA 800-946-8688
Cal Trading Company
Burlingame, CA 650-697-4615
Cape Cod Coffee Roasters
Mashpee, MA 508-477-2400
Capricorn Coffees
San Francisco, CA 800-541-0758
Captain Cook Coffee Company
Captain Cook, HI 808-488-1776
Caracollillo Coffee Mills
Tampa, FL. 800-682-0023
Caravan Company
Worcester, MA 508-752-3777
Caribbean Coffee Company
Goleta, CA 800-932-5282
Caribou Coffee Company
Brooklyn Ctr, MN. 888-227-4268
Carrabassett Coffee Roasters
Kingfield, ME. 888-292-2326
Cascade Coffee
Everett, WA. 425-347-3995
Cave Creek Coffee Company
Cave Creek, AZ 480-488-0603
Central Coast Coffee Roasting
Los Osos, CA 800-382-6837
Chatz Roasting Company
Ceres, CA 800-792-6333
Chauvin Coffee Corporation
Saint Louis, MO 800-455-5282
Chicago Coffee Roastery
Huntley, IL 800-762-5402
Chock Full O'Nuts
New York, NY 888-246-2598
City Bean
Stevenson Ranch, CA. 888-248-9232
Clayton's Coffee & Tea
Modesto, CA. 209-522-7811
Clean Foods
Santa Paula, CA 800-526-8328
Clear Mountain Coffee Company
Silver Spring, MD. 301-587-2233
Clearwater Coffee Company
Lake Zurich, IL. 847-540-7711
Cobraz Brazilian Coffee
New York, NY 212-759-7700
Coca-Cola Enterprises
Atlanta, GA. 800-233-7210
Coffee & Tea
Bloomington, MN. 952-854-2883
Coffee Associates
Edgewater, NJ. 201-945-1060
Coffee Barrel
Okemos, MI 517-349-3888
Coffee Bean
Englewood, CO. 303-922-1238
Coffee Bean & Tea Leaf
Los Angeles, CA. 800-832-5323
Coffee Bean International
Portland, OR 800-877-0474
Coffee Bean of Leesburg
Leesburg, VA 800-232-6872
Coffee Beanery
Flushing, MI 800-728-2326
Coffee Brothers
Colton, CA 888-443-5282
Coffee Butler Service
Alexandria, VA 703-823-0028
Coffee Concepts
Dallas, TX. 214-363-9331
Coffee Creations
Portland, OR 800-245-5856
Coffee Culture-A House
Lincoln, NE. 402-438-8456
Coffee Exchange
Providence, RI 800-263-3339
Coffee Express Company
Plymouth, MI 800-466-9000
Coffee Holding Company
Staten Island, NY 800-458-2233
Coffee Masters
Spring Grove, IL. 800-334-6485
Coffee Mill Roastery
Elon, NC 800-729-1727
Coffee Mill Roasting Company
Sudbury, ON 705-525-2700
Coffee Millers & Roasting
Cape Coral, FL 239-573-6800
Coffee People
Beaverton, OR 800-354-5282
Coffee Process Technology
Houston, TX 713-695-7530
Coffee Reserve
Phoenix, AZ 623-434-0939
Coffee Roasters
Oakland, NJ 201-337-8221
Coffee Roasters of New Orleans
New Orleans, LA 800-737-5464
Coffee Up
Chicago, IL 847-288-9330
Coffee Works
Sacramento, CA 800-275-3335
College Coffee Roasters
Mountville, PA 717-285-9561
Colonial Coffee Roasters
Miami, FL. 305-634-1843
Columbia Coffee & Tea Company
Weston, ON. 416-745-4235
Comfort Foods
North Andover, MA 800-514-3663
Community Coffee Specialty
Baton Rouge, LA 800-525-5583
Condaxis Coffee Company
Jacksonville, FL 904-356-5330
Continental Coffee Products Company
Houston, TX 800-323-6178
Corim International Coff
Brick, NJ. 800-942-4201
Country Pure Foods
Akron, OH. 877-995-8423
Cupper's Coffee Company
Lethbridge, AB 403-380-4555
Custom House Coffee RoasJodyana Corporation
Miami, FL. 888-563-5282

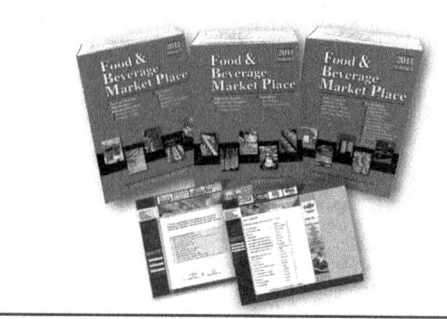

Dallis Brothers
Ozone Park, NY 800-424-4252
David Rio
San Francisco, CA 800-454-9605
Daybreak Coffee Roasters
Glastonbury, CT 800-882-5282
Daymar Select Fine Coffees
El Cajon, CA..................... 800-466-7590
Dazbog Coffee Company
Denver, CO....................... 303-892-9999
De Coty Coffee Company
San Angelo, TX 800-588-8001
De Lima Company
Liverpool, NY.................... 800-962-8864
Decoty Coffee Company
San Angelo, TX 800-588-8001
Diedrich Coffee
Irvine, CA....................... 800-354-5282
Dillanos Coffee Roasters
Sumner, WA 800-234-5282
Distant Lands Coffee Roaster
Tyler, TX........................ 800-346-5459
DMH Ingredients
Libertyville, IL 847-362-9977
Don Francisco Coffee Traders
Los Angeles, CA.................. 800-697-5282
Don Hilario Estate Coffee
Tampa, FL....................... 800-799-1903
Downeast Coffee
Pawtucket, RI 800-345-2007
Droubi's Imports
Houston, TX...................... 713-988-7138
Eagle Coffee Company
Baltimore, MD 800-545-4015
East India Coffee & Tea Company
Lincoln, CA 800-829-1300
East Indies Coffee & Tea Company
Lebanon, PA 800-220-2326
Eight O'Clock Coffee Company
Montvale, NJ..................... 800-299-2739
El Dorado Coffee
Flushing, NY..................... 800-635-2566
Ellis Coffee Company
Philadelphia, PA 800-822-3984
Equal Exchange
West Bridgewater, MA 774-776-7400
Erba Food Products
Brooklyn, NY 718-272-7700
Espresso Vivace
Seattle, WA...................... 206-860-2722
European Coffee
Cherry Hill, NJ 856-428-7202
European Roasterie
Le Center, MN 888-469-2233
Evco Wholesale Foods
Emporia, KS 620-343-7000
Excellent Coffee Company
Pawtucket, RI 800-345-2007
Excelso Coffee Company
Norcross, GA 800-241-2138
F Gavina & Sons Inc.
Vernon, CA 800-428-4627
F. Gavina & Sons
Vernon, CA 323-582-0671
Fama Sales
New York, NY 212-757-9433
Farmer Brothers Company
Torrance, CA..................... 800-735-2878
FCC Coffee Packers
Doral, FL........................ 305-591-1128
Ferrara Bakery & Cafe
New York, NY 212-226-6150
Fidalgo Bay Coffee
Burlington, WA................... 800-310-5540
Fine Foods Northwest
Seattle, WA...................... 800-862-3965
First Colony Coffee & Tea Company
Norfolk, VA...................... 800-446-8555
First Roasters of Central Florida
Longwood, FL 407-699-6364
Folgers Coffee Company
Orrville, OH 877-693-6543
Foltz Coffee Tea & Spice Company
New Orleans, LA 504-486-1545
Fratello Coffee Roasters
Calgary, AB...................... 800-465-7227
Freed, Teller & Freed
South San Francisco, CA 800-370-7371
Fresh Roast Systems
Livermore, CA 925-456-2270
Frontier Natural Co-op
Norway, IA 303-449-8137
Gadsden Coffee/Caffe
Arivaca, AZ...................... 888-514-5282
Gardner's Gourmet
Fremont, CA 800-676-8558
George H Hathaway Coffee Company
Summit Argo, IL.................. 708-458-7668
Gerhart Coffee Company
Lancaster, PA 800-536-4310
Global Food Industries
Townville, SC 800-225-4152
Globus Coffee
Manhasset, NY 631-390-2233
Gloria Jean's Gourmet Coffees
Irvine, CA....................... 877-320-5282
Godiva Chocolatier
New York, NY 800-946-3482
Gold Star Coffee Company
Salem, MA 888-505-5233
Gondwanaland
Corrales, NM 505-899-2843
Green Mountain Chocolates
Franklin, MA 508-520-7160
Green Mountain Coffee Roasters
Waterbury, VT.................... 800-545-2326
Greene Brothers Specialty Coffee Roaster
Hackettstown, NJ 908-979-0022
Greenwell Farms
Morganfield, KY.................. 270-389-3289
Haas Coffee Group
Miami, FL....................... 305-371-7473
Harold L. King & Company
Redwood City, CA 888-368-2233
Has Beans Coffee & Tea Company
Mount Shasta, CA................. 800-427-2326
Hawaii Coffee Company
Honolulu, HI..................... 800-338-8353
Hawaiian Isles Kona Coffee Co
Honolulu, HI..................... 808-833-2244
Hena Coffee
Brooklyn, NY 718-272-8237
Herbal Coffee International
Jacksonville Beach, FL............. 800-743-8774
Heritage Northwest
Juneau, AK 907-586-1088
High Coffee Corporation
Houston, TX 713-465-2230
High Rise Coffee Roasters
Colorado Springs, CO.............. 719-633-1833
Hill of Beans Coffee Roasters
Los Angeles, CA.................. 888-527-6278
Hillsboro Coffee Company
Tampa, FL....................... 813-877-2126
Home Roast Coffee
Lutz, FL......................... 813-949-0807
Hood River Coffee Company
Hood River, OR 800-336-2954
House of Coffee Beans
Houston, TX 800-422-1799
House of Tsang
San Francisco, CA 415-282-9952
Ideal Distributing Company
Bothell, WA...................... 425-488-6121
Indigo Coffee Roasters
Florence, MA 800-447-5450
Instant Products of America
Columbus, IN 812-372-9100
Inter-American Products
Cincinnati, OH 800-645-2233
Inter-Continental Imports Company
Newington, CT 800-424-4422
International Coffee Corporation
New Orleans, LA 504-586-8700
Itoen
Honolulu, HI..................... 808-847-4477
J.B. Peel Coffee Roasters
Red Hook, NY 800-231-7372
Jaguar Yerba Company
Ashland, OR 800-839-0775
Jamaica John
Franklin Park, IL.................. 847-451-1730
Jamaican Gourmet Coffee Company
Philadelphia, PA 800-261-2859
Jasper Products LLC
Joplin, MO 877-769-7367
Java Cabana
Miami, FL....................... 305-592-7302
Java Jungle
Visalia, CA 559-732-5282
Java Sun Coffee Roasters
Marblehead, MA.................. 781-631-7788
Java-Gourmet/Keuka Lake Coffee Roaster
Penn Yan, NY 888-478-2739
Jelks Coffee Roasters
Shreveport, LA 318-636-6391
Jenny's Country Kitchen
Dover, MN 800-357-3497
Jeremiah's Pick Coffee Company
San Francisco, CA 800-537-3642
JFG Coffee Co
Knoxville, TN 865-546-2120
John A. Vassilaros & Son
Flushing, NY..................... 718-886-4140
John Conti Coffee Company
Louisville, KY 800-928-5282
Josuma Coffee Corporation
Menlo Park, CA 650-366-5453
Kaffe Magnum Opus
Millville, NJ 800-652-5282
Kauai Coffee Company
Kalaheo, HI...................... 800-545-8605
Keurig, Inc
Reading, MA..................... 781-928-0162
Keystone Coffee Company
San Jose, CA..................... 408-998-2221
Kittridge & Fredrickson Fine Coffees
Portland, OR 800-558-7788
Kobricks Coffee Company
Jersey City, NJ 800-562-3662
Kohana Coffee
Austin, TX....................... 512-904-1174
Kona Coffee Council
Kealakekua, HI 808-323-2911
Kona Kava Coffee Company
Philo, CA........................ 707-985-3913
Kona Premium Coffee Company
Keauhou, HI 888-322-9550
Krinos Foods
Santa Barbara, CA 800-624-4896
La Costa Coffee Roasting
Carlsbad, CA..................... 760-438-8160

La Vans Coffee Company
Bordentown, NJ 609-298-0688
Lacas Coffee Company
Pennsauken, NJ 800-220-1133
Lake Arrowhead
Twin Peaks, CA 877-237-8528
Landshire
Saint Louis, MO 800-468-3354
Larry's Beans Inc
Raleigh, NC 919-828-1234
Lavazza Premium Coffee Corporation
New York, NY 800-466-3287
Leavenworth Coffee Roast
Leavenworth, WA 800-246-2761
Lenson Coffee & Tea Company
Pleasantville, NJ 609-646-3003
Leroy Hill Coffee Company
Mobile, AL 800-866-5282
Lexington Coffee & Tea Company
Lexington, KY 859-277-1102
Lindsay's Tea
S San Francisco, CA 800-624-7031
Lingle Brothers Coffee
Bell Gardens, CA 562-927-3317
Lockcoffee
Larchmont, NY 914-273-7838
Lola Savannah
Houston, TX 888-663-9166
Long Expected Coffee Co mpany
Yonkers, NY
Longbottom Coffee & Tea
Hillsboro, OR 800-288-1271
Longo Coffee & Tea
New York, NY 212-477-5421
Louis Dreyfus Corporation - Coffee Division
Wilton, CT 203-761-2000
Love Creek Orchards
Medina, TX 800-449-0882
Lowery's Premium Roast Coffee
Snohomish, WA 800-767-1783
M.E. Swing Company
Alexandria, VA 800-485-4019
Magnum Coffee Roastery
Nunica, MI 888-937-5282
Majestic Coffee & Tea
San Carlos, CA 650-591-5678
Manhattan Coffee Company
Earth City, MO 800-926-3333
Master Brew
Northbrook, IL 847-564-3600
Maui Coffee Roasters
Kahului, HI 800-645-2877
Mayorga Coffee
Rockville, MD 877-526-3322
Mazzoli Coffee
Brooklyn, NY 718-259-6194
Melitta
Clearwater, FL 727-535-2111
Mercon Coffee Corporation
Hoboken, NJ 201-418-9400
Mills Coffee Roasting Company
Providence, RI 888-781-5282
Milone Brothers Coffee
Modesto, CA 800-974-8500
Moka D'Oro Coffee
Farmingdale, NY 877-665-2367
Monarch Beverage Company
Atlanta, GA 800-241-3732
Montana Coffee Traders
Whitefish, MT 800-345-5282
Moran Coffee Company
Dublin, OH 614-889-2500
Morning Star Coffee
West Chester, PA 888-854-2233
Mother Parker's Tea & Coffee
Mississauga, ON 800-387-9398
Mountain City Coffee Roasters
Enka, NC 888-730-0869
Mountain Roastery Coffee Company
Port Huron, MI 416-256-2727
Moutanos Brothers Coffee Company
S San Francisco, CA 800-624-7031
Mr. Espresso
Oakland, CA 510-287-5200
Muqui Coffee Company
San Jose, CA 408-929-4405
Mystic Coffee Roasters
Mystic, CT 860-536-2999
Nantucket Tea Traders
Nantucket, MA 508-325-0203
Native American Tea & Cofee
Aberdeen, SD 605-226-2006

New Harmony Coffee Roasters
Philadelphia, PA 215-925-6770
New Jamaican Gold
Hayward, CA 800-672-9956
New York Coffee & Bagels
New York, NY 212-986-6116
Newly Weds Foods
Chicago, IL 800-647-9314
North American Coffees
Morriston, NJ 973-359-0300
Northwest Naturals Corporation
Bothell, WA 425-881-2200
Northwestern Coffee Mills
Washburn, WI 800-243-5283
O'Neill Coffee Company
West Middlesex, PA 724-528-9281
Oasis Coffee Company
Norwalk, CT 203-847-0554
Ocean Coffee Roasters
Pawtucket, RI 800-598-5282
Old Mansion Foods
Petersburg, VA 800-476-1877
Old Town Coffee & Tea Company
Baltimore, MD 410-752-1229
Olympic Coffee & Roasting
Bellevue, WA 888-244-8313
Omar Coffee Company
Newington, CT 800-394-6627
Orleans Coffee Exchange
Kenner, LA 800-737-5464
Oskri Organics
Lake Mills, WI 800-628-1110
Pan American Coffee Company
Hoboken, NJ 800-229-1883
Paramount Coffee Company
Lansing, MI 517-372-5500
Paramount Coffee Company
Lansing, MI 800-968-1222
Partners Coffee Company
Atlanta, GA 800-341-5282
Pascal Coffee
Yonkers, NY 914-969-7933
Paul de Lima Company
Liverpool, NY 800-962-8864
Peaberry's Coffee & Tea
Oakland, CA 510-653-0450
Pear's Coffee
Omaha, NE 800-317-1773
Pearl Coffee Company
Akron, OH 800-822-5282
Peerless Coffee Company
Oakland, CA 800-310-5662
Peet's Coffee & Tea
Emeryville, CA 800-999-2132
Pfefferkorn's Coffee
Baltimore, MD 800-682-4665
PJ's Coffee & Tea
New Orleans, LA 800-527-1055
Plantation Coffee
Elk Grove, CA 916-686-2633
Plaza House Coffee
Staten Island, NY 718-979-9555
Po'okela Enterprises
Kailua Kona, HI 866-328-9753
Pod Pack International
Baton Rouge, LA 225-752-1110
Pokka Beverages
American Canyon, CA 800-972-5962
Polly's Gourmet Coffee
Long Beach, CA 562-433-2996
Pontiac Coffee Break
Pontiac, MI 248-332-9403
Pontiac Foods
Columbia, SC 803-699-1600
Port Vue Coffee Company
Pottsville, PA 570-429-2690
Premier Roasters
Daly City, CA 415-337-4040
Puroast Coffee
Woodland, CA 877-569-2243
Q.E. Tea
Bridgeville, PA 800-622-8327
Queen Anne Coffee Roaster
Seattle, WA 206-284-2530
Randag & Associates Inc
Elmhurst, IL 630-530-2830
Reading Coffee Roasters
Birdsboro, PA 800-331-6713
Red Diamond
Birmingham, AL 800-292-4651
Regency Coffee & VendingCompany
Olathe, KS 913-829-1994

Reily Foods Company
New Orleans, LA 504-524-6131
Reily Foods/JFG Coffee Company
New Orleans, LA 800-535-1961
Rethemeyer Coffee Company
St Louis, MO 314-231-0990
Richard's Gourmet Coffee
West Bridgewater, MA 800-370-2633
Riffel's Coffee Company
Wichita, KS 888-399-4567
River Road Coffee
Lake Clear, NY 315-769-9941
Roasterie
Kansas City, MO 800-376-0245
Rocky Mountain Coffee Roasters
Jasper, Alberta T0E 1E0, ... 800-666-3465
Rodda Coffee Company
Yachats, OR 541-547-4132
Ronnoco Coffee Company
Saint Louis, MO 800-428-2287
Rostov's Coffee & Tea Company
Richmond, VA 800-637-6772
Royal Coffee
Emeryville, CA 510-652-4256
Royal Coffee & Tea Company
Mississauga, ON 800-667-6226
Royal Coffee New York
Edison, NJ 888-769-2569
Royal Cup Coffee
Birmingham, AL 800-366-5836
S A Piazza & Associates
Clackamas, OR 503-657-3123
S&D Coffee, Inc
Concord, NC 704-782-3121
S.J. McCullagh
Buffalo, NY 800-753-3473
Sahara Coffee
Reno, NV 775-825-5033
Sambets Cajun Deli
Austin, TX 800-472-6238
San Francisco Bay Coffee Company
Lincoln, CA 800-829-1300
San Jose Coffee Company
San Jose, CA 408-272-3311
San Juan Coffee RoastingCompany
Friday Harbor, WA 800-858-4276
San Marco Coffee,Inc.
Charlotte, NC 800-715-9298
SANGARIA USA
Torrance, CA 310-530-2202
Santa Barbara Roasting Company
Santa Barbara, CA 800-321-5282
Santa Elena Coffee Company
Hutto, TX 512-846-2908
Sara Lee Corporation
Downers Grove, IL 630-598-8100
Schuil Coffee Company
Kentwood, MI 616-956-1881
Seattle's Best Coffee
Seattle, WA 800-611-7793
Seven Hills Coffee Company
Cincinnati, OH 513-489-5220
Sierra Madre Organic Coffee
Denver, CO 303-446-0050
Simpson & Vail
Brookfield, CT 800-282-8327
Sivetz Coffee
Corvallis, OR 541-753-9713
Societe Cafe
Montreal-Nord, QC 514-325-9130
South Beach Coffee Company
Miami Beach, FL 305-576-9696
Southern Heritage Coffee Company
Indianapolis, IN 800-486-1198
Specialty Coffee Roasters
Delray Beach, FL 800-253-9363
Spices of Life Gourmet Coffee
Fort Myers, FL 239-334-8004
Spinelli Coffee Company
Seattle, WA 415-821-7100
Starbucks Coffee Company
Seattle, WA 800-782-7282
Stasero International
KENT, WA 888-929-2378
Steep & Brew Coffee Roasters
Monona, WI 800-876-1986
Stewart's Private Blend Foods
Chicago, IL 800-654-2862
Stockton Graham & Company
Raleigh, NC 800-835-5943
Subco Foods Inc.
West Chicago, IL 630-231-0003

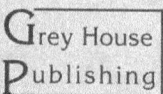

Sugai Kona Coffee
Kealakekua, HI 808-322-7717
Sundance Roasting Company
Sandpoint, ID 208-265-2445
Sunflower Restaurant Supply
Salina, KS 316-267-9881
Sweeney's Gourmet Coffee Roast
Henderson, NV 702-558-0505
Tadin Herb & Tea Company
Vernon, CA . . . . 180- TE-TADI
Texas Coffee Company
Beaumont, TX 800-259-3400
Thanksgiving Coffee Company
Fort Bragg, CA 800-462-1999
Toddy Products
Midland, TX 713-225-2066
Tom & Dave's Specialty Coffee
San Rafael, CA 800-249-5050
Torke Coffee Roasting Company
Sheboygan, WI 800-242-7671
Torrefazione Italia
Seattle, WA 800-827-2333
Torreo Coffee Company
Philadelphia, PA 888-286-7736
Tostino Coffee Roasters
Tucson, AZ 800-678-3519
Tradewinds Coffee Company
Raleigh, NC 800-457-0406
Tristao Trading
New York, NY 212-285-8120
Uncommon Grounds Coffee
Berkeley, CA 80- 5-7 91
United Intertrade
Houston, TX 800-969-2233
Valley Tea & Coffee
Alhambra, CA 626-281-5799
Van Roy Coffee
Cleveland, OH 877-826-7669
Vassilaros & Son
Flushing, NY 718-886-4140
Victor Allen Coffee Company
Albuquerque, NM 800-662-2575
Victor Allen's Coffee and Tea
Little Chute, WI 800-394-5282
Village Roaster
Lakewood, CO 800-237-3822
Wabash Coffee
Vincennes, IN 812-882-6066
Wallingford Coffee Company
Cleveland, OH 800-714-0944
Wallingford Coffee Mills
Cincinnati, OH 800-533-3690
Walsh's Coffee Roasters
San Mateo, CA 650-347-5112
Weaver Nut Company
Ephrata, PA 717-738-3781
Wechsler Coffee Corporation
Moonachie, NJ 800-800-2633
West Coast Specialty Coffee
Burlingame, CA 650-259-9308
Wheeling Coffee & SpicecCompany
Wheeling, WV 800-500-0141
White Cloud Coffee
Garden City, ID 800-627-0309
White Coffee Corporation
Astoria, NY 800-221-0140
William Turner
Frederick, MD 301-620-1135
Willoughby's Coffee & Tea
Branford, CT 800-388-8400
Winn-Dixie Stores
Jacksonville, FL 800-946-6349
World Cup Coffee & Tea
Portland, OR 503-228-5503
World of Coffee
Stirling, NJ 800-543-0062
World of Coffee, World of Tea
Stirling, NJ 908-647-1218
Young Winfield
Kleinburg, ON 905-893-9682

Cappuccino

American Purpac Technologies, LLC
Beloit, WI 877-787-7221
AREL Group
Atlanta, GA 800-737-3094
Caffe D'Amore
Monrovia, CA 800-999-0171
Caffe D'Amore Gourmet Beverages
Monrovia, CA 800-999-0171
Instant Products of America
Columbus, IN 812-372-9100

Decaffeinated

American Coffee Company
New Orleans, LA 800-554-7234
Arbuckle Coffee
Pittsburgh, PA 800-533-8278
Brewfresh Coffee Company
South Salt Lake, UT 888-486-3334
Caffe Luca
Tukwila, WA 800-728-9116
Chock Full O'Nuts
New York, NY 888-246-2598
Coffee Exchange
Providence, RI 800-263-3339
Folgers Coffee Company
Orrville, OH 877-693-6543
Heritage Northwest
Juneau, AK 907-586-1088
Jelks Coffee Roasters
Shreveport, LA 318-636-6391
Kaffe Magnum Opus
Millville, NJ 800-652-5282
Kohana Coffee
Austin, TX 512-904-1174
Leroy Hill Coffee Company
Mobile, AL 800-866-5282
Orleans Coffee Exchange
Kenner, LA 800-737-5464
Puroast Coffee
Woodland, CA 877-569-2243
San Francisco Bay Coffee Company
Lincoln, CA 800-829-1300
Sara Lee Corporation
Downers Grove, IL 630-598-8100
Stewart's Private Blend Foods
Chicago, IL 800-654-2862
Thanksgiving Coffee Company
Fort Bragg, CA 800-462-1999
Van Roy Coffee
Cleveland, OH 877-826-7669
Weaver Nut Company
Ephrata, PA 717-738-3781
Wechsler Coffee Corporation
Moonachie, NJ 800-800-2633

Flavored

American Coffee Company
New Orleans, LA 800-554-7234
Andresen Ryan Coffee Com
Superior, WI 715-395-3793
Arbuckle Coffee
Pittsburgh, PA 800-533-8278
Aroma Coffee Company
Forest Park, IL 708-488-8340
Brewfresh Coffee Company
South Salt Lake, UT 888-486-3334
Cafe Society Coffee Company
Dallas, TX 800-717-6000
Custom House Coffee RoasJodyana Corporation
Miami, FL 888-563-5282
Daymar Select Fine Coffees
El Cajon, CA 800-466-7590
Decoty Coffee Company
San Angelo, TX 800-588-8001
Distant Lands Coffee Roaster
Tyler, TX 800-346-5459
East Indies Coffee & Tea Company
Lebanon, PA 800-220-2326
Greene Brothers Specialty Coffee Roaster
Hackettstown, NJ 908-979-0022
Harold L. King & Company
Redwood City, CA 888-368-2233
Hawaii Coffee Company
Honolulu, HI 800-338-8353
Heritage Northwest
Juneau, AK 907-586-1088
Jelks Coffee Roasters
Shreveport, LA 318-636-6391
Kaffe Magnum Opus
Millville, NJ 800-652-5282
Kauai Coffee Company
Kalaheo, HI 800-545-8605
Longbottom Coffee & Tea
Hillsboro, OR 800-288-1271
Love Creek Orchards
Medina, TX 800-449-0882
Lowery's Premium Roast Coffee
Snohomish, WA 800-767-1783
Magnum Coffee Roastery
Nunica, MI 888-937-5282
Orleans Coffee Exchange
Kenner, LA 800-737-5464

Pearl Coffee Company
Akron, OH 800-822-5282
Puroast Coffee
Woodland, CA 877-569-2243
Riffel's Coffee Company
Wichita, KS 888-399-4567
San Francisco Bay Coffee Company
Lincoln, CA 800-829-1300
San Juan Coffee RoastingCompany
Friday Harbor, WA 800-858-4276
Sara Lee Corporation
Downers Grove, IL 630-598-8100
Starbucks Coffee Company
Seattle, WA 800-782-7282
Stewart's Private Blend Foods
Chicago, IL 800-654-2862
Thanksgiving Coffee Company
Fort Bragg, CA 800-462-1999
Weaver Nut Company
Ephrata, PA 717-738-3781
Wechsler Coffee Corporation
Moonachie, NJ 800-800-2633

Iced

Arizona Beverage Company
Woodbury, NY 800-832-3775
Kohana Coffee
Austin, TX 512-904-1174

Instant

Chock Full O'Nuts
New York, NY 888-246-2598
Coffee Holding Company
Staten Island, NY 800-458-2233
Daymar Select Fine Coffees
El Cajon, CA 800-466-7590
FCC Coffee Packers
Doral, FL 305-591-1128
Instant Products of America
Columbus, IN 812-372-9100
Tonex
Wallington, NJ 973-773-5135

Instant - Decaffeinated

Reily Foods Company
New Orleans, LA 504-524-6131
Swagger Foods Corporation
Vernon Hills, IL 847-913-1200

Roasted

Alakef Coffee Roasters
Duluth, MN 800-438-9228
Allegro Coffee Company
Thornton, CO 800-666-4869
Arbuckle Coffee
Pittsburgh, PA 800-533-8278
Boyd Coffee Company
Portland, OR 800-545-4077
Brewfresh Coffee Company
South Salt Lake, UT 888-486-3334
Brisk Coffee Company
Tampa, FL 800-899-5282
BRJ Coffee & Tea
Lincoln, CA 800-829-1300
Buckmaster Coffee
Hillsboro, OR 800-962-9148
Cafe Bustelo
Miami, FL 800-990-9039
Cafe Moto
San Diego, CA 800-818-3363
Cain's Coffee Company
Springfield, MO 800-641-4025
Clear Mountain Coffee Company
Silver Spring, MD 301-587-2233
Coffee Bean International
Portland, OR 800-877-0474
Coffee Reserve
Phoenix, AZ 623-434-0939
Colonial Coffee Roasters
Miami, FL 305-634-1843
Daymar Select Fine Coffees
El Cajon, CA 800-466-7590
Distant Lands Coffee Roaster
Tyler, TX 800-346-5459
El Dorado Coffee
Flushing, NY 800-635-2566
Finger Lakes Coffee Roasters
Farmington, NY 800-420-6154
Folgers Coffee Company
Orrville, OH 877-693-6543

Green Mountain Coffee Roasters
Waterbury, VT. 800-545-2326
Grounds for Thought
Bowling Green, OH 419-354-2326
Heritage Northwest
Juneau, AK 907-586-1088
House of Coffee Beans
Houston, TX 800-422-1799
Indigo Coffee Roasters
Florence, MA 800-447-5450
Jeremiah's Pick Coffee Company
San Francisco, CA 800-537-3642
Kauai Coffee Company
Kalaheo, HI. 800-545-8605
Kohana Coffee
Austin, TX. 512-904-1174
Lola Savannah
Houston, TX 888-663-9166
Lucile's Famous Creole Seasonings
Boulder, CO 800-727-3653
M.E. Swing Company
Alexandria, VA 800-485-4019
Magnum Coffee Roastery
Nunica, MI 888-937-5282
Maui Coffee Roasters
Kahului, HI 800-645-2877
Milone Brothers Coffee
Modesto, CA. 800-974-8500
Montana Coffee Traders
Whitefish, MT. 800-345-5282
Morning Star Coffee
West Chester, PA. 888-854-2233
New Harmony Coffee Roasters
Philadelphia, PA 215-925-6770
Oasis Coffee Company
Norwalk, CT 203-847-0554
Olympic Coffee & Roasting
Bellevue, WA 888-244-8313
Pan American Coffee Company
Hoboken, NJ 800-229-1883
Pfefferkorn's Coffee
Baltimore, MD 800-682-4665
Puroast Coffee
Woodland, CA. 877-569-2243
Royal Blend Coffee Company
Bend, OR. 541-388-8164
Royal Coffee & Tea Company
Mississauga, ON. 800-667-6226
San Juan Coffee RoastingCompany
Friday Harbor, WA 800-858-4276
Sara Lee Corporation
Downers Grove, IL. 630-598-8100
Southern Heritage Coffee Company
Indianapolis, IN 800-486-1198
Steep & Brew Coffee Roasters
Monona, WI 800-876-1986
Stewart's Private Blend Foods
Chicago, IL 800-654-2862
Sunflower Restaurant Supply
Salina, KS 316-267-9881
Texas Coffee Company
Beaumont, TX. 800-259-3400
Torke Coffee Roasting Company
Sheboygan, WI 800-242-7671
U Roast Em
Hayward, WI. 715-634-6255
Van Roy Coffee
Cleveland, OH 877-826-7669
Weaver Nut Company
Ephrata, PA 717-738-3781
Wheeling Coffee & SpicecCompany
Wheeling, WV 800-500-0141
White Cloud Coffee
Garden City, ID. 800-627-0309
Young Winfield
Kleinburg, ON. 905-893-9682

Espresso

AREL Group
Atlanta, GA. 800-737-3094
Aroma Coffee Company
Forest Park, IL 708-488-8340
Blue Chip Group
Salt Lake City, UT 800-878-0099
Caffe Darte
Seattle, WA. 800-999-5334
Caffe Luca
Tukwila, WA. 800-728-9116
Chock Full O'Nuts
New York, NY 888-246-2598
Coca-Cola Bottling Company
Atlanta, GA. 800-438-2653
Cream O'Weaver Dairy
Salt Lake City, UT 801-973-9922
Distant Lands Coffee Roaster
Tyler, TX. 800-346-5459
Fama Sales
New York, NY 212-757-9433
Folklore Foods
Toppenish, WA 509-865-4772
Heritage Northwest
Juneau, AK 907-586-1088
Hygeia Dairy Company
McAllen, TX. 956-686-0511
Ideal Dairy
Richfield, UT 435-896-5061
Kobricks Coffee Company
Jersey City, NJ 800-562-3662
Lacto Milk Products Corporation
Flemington, NJ 908-788-2200
Louis Trauth Dairy
Newport, KY. 800-544-6455
Maola Milk & Ice Cream Company
New Bern, NC. 252-514-2792
Martin Coffee Company
Jacksonville, FL 904-355-9661
Meadow Gold Dairies
Englewood, CO. 800-525-3289
Moka D'Oro Coffee
Farmingdale, NY 877-665-2367
Monticello Cellars
Napa, CA. 707-253-2802
Oak Farms
El Paso, TX. 800-395-7004
Price's Creameries
El Paso, TX. 915-565-2711
Puroast Coffee
Woodland, CA. 877-569-2243
S A Piazza & Associates
Clackamas, OR. 503-657-3123
Saint Albans Cooperative Creamery
Saint Albans, VT. 800-559-0343
San Marco Coffee,Inc.
Charlotte, NC 800-715-9298
Sebastiani Vineyards
Sonoma, CA 800-888-5532
Smucker Quality Beverages
Havre De Grace, MD 410-939-1403
Smucker Quality Beverages
Chico, CA 530-899-5000
Sopralco
Plantation, FL 954-584-2225
Southern Heritage Coffee Company
Indianapolis, IN 800-486-1198
Starbucks Coffee Company
Seattle, WA. 800-782-7282
Swiss Valley Farms Company
Dubuque, IA 800-397-9156
Ultra Seal
New Paltz, NY 845-255-2490
Unilever Canada
Saint John, NB 800-565-7273
Winder Dairy
West Valley, UT 800-946-3371

Mocha

Foremost Farms
Clayton, WI. 715-948-2166
Jones Brewing Company
Smithton, PA. 800-237-2337

Tea

Abunda Life Laboratories
Asbury Park, NJ 732-775-7575
Ahmad Tea London
Deer Park, TX. 800-637-7704
Al-Rite Fruits & Syrups
Miami, FL. 305-652-2540
Alaska Herb Tea Company
Anchorage, AK. 800-654-2764
Alexander Gourmet Imports
Caledon, ON 800-265-5081
Allen Flavors
Edison, NJ. 908-561-5995
Alpine Pure USA
Cambridge, MA 866-832-7997
Alternative Health & Herbs
Albany, OR 800-345-4152
American Instants
Flanders, NJ 973-584-8811
American Soy Products
Saline, MI 734-429-2310
Artist Coffee
Londonderry, NH 866-440-4511
Astor Products
Jacksonville, FL 904-783-5000
Atlanta Coffee & Tea Company
Decatur, GA 800-426-4781
Bagai Tea Company
San Marcos, CA 760-591-3084
Barnes & Watson Fine Teas
Seattle, WA. 800-447-8832
Barrows Tea Company
New Bedford, MA 800-832-5024
Beacon Drive In
Spartanburg, SC 864-585-9387
Bigelow Tea
Fairfield, CT 888-244-3569
Blue Willow Tea Company
Emeryville, CA. 800-328-0353
Boston Tea Company
Hackensack, NJ. 201-440-3004
Bountiful Pantry
Nantucket, MA 888-832-6466
Boyd Coffee Company
Portland, OR 800-545-4077
Bread & Chocolate
Wells River, VT 800-524-6715
Cadillac Coffee Company
Madison Heights, MI 800-438-6900
Carolina Treet
Wilmington, NC 800-616-6344
Celestial Seasonings Teas
Boulder, CO 800-434-4246
Central Coca-Cola Bottling Company
Richmond, VA. 800-359-3759
Charleston Tea Plantation
Wadmalaw Island, SC. 800-443-5987
Chicago Coffee Roastery
Huntley, IL 800-762-5402
China Mist Tea Company
Scottsdale, AZ. 800-242-8807
Choice Organic Teas
Seattle, WA 206-525-0051
City Bean
Stevenson Ranch, CA 888-248-9232
Clayton's Coffee & Tea
Modesto, CA. 209-522-7811
Clear Mountain Coffee Company
Silver Spring, MD. 301-587-2233
Coffee & Tea
Bloomington, MN. 952-854-2883
Coffee Bean International
Portland, OR 800-877-0474
Coffee Mill Roastery
Elon, NC 800-729-1727
Colorado Spice
Boulder, CO 800-677-7423
Community Coffee Specialty
Baton Rouge, LA 800-525-5583
Company of a Philadelphia Gentleman
Philadelphia, PA 215-427-2827
Consolidated Tea Company
Lynbrook, NY 516-887-1144
Contact International
Skokie, IL 847-324-4411
Continental Coffee Products Company
Houston, TX 800-323-6178
Cora Italian Specialties
La Grange, IL 800-969-2672
Cotswold Cottage Foods
Arvada, CO 800-208-1977
Crosby Molasses Company
St John, NB 506-634-7515
Crystal Geyser Water Company
Calistoga, CA 800-443-9737
Da Vinci Gourmet
Seattle, WA 800-640-6779
Dallis Brothers
Ozone Park, NY 800-424-4252
Damron Corporation
Chicago, IL 800-333-1860
David Rio
San Francisco, CA 800-454-9605
Davidson's Organic Tea
Reno, NV 800-882-5888
Davidsons
Reno, NV 800-882-5888
De Coty Coffee Company
San Angelo, TX 800-588-8001
Decoty Coffee Company
San Angelo, TX 800-588-8001

DMH Ingredients
Libertyville, IL 847-362-9977
Droubi's Imports
Houston, TX 713-988-7138
East India Coffee & Tea Company
Lincoln, CA 800-829-1300
East Indies Coffee & Tea Company
Lebanon, PA 800-220-2326
Eastern Tea Corporation
Monroe Township, NJ 800-221-0865
Eastrise Trading Corporation
Baldwin Park, CA
Eden Foods Inc.
Clinton, MI 800-248-0320
Empire Tea Services
Columbus, IN 800-790-0246
F Gavina & Sons Inc.
Vernon, CA 800-428-4627
Father's Country Hams
Bremen, KY 270-525-3554
Fauchon
New York, NY 877-605-0130
Fee Brothers
Rochester, NY 800-961-3337
Finlay Tea Solutions
Morristown, NJ 973-539-8030
Flagship Atlanta Dairy
Belleview, FL 800-224-0669
Flavor Specialties
Corona, CA 951-734-6620
Flora
Lynden, WA 800-446-2110
Fmali Herb
Santa Cruz, CA 831-423-7913
Foltz Coffee Tea & Spice Company
New Orleans, LA 504-486-1545
Fortunes International Teas
Mc Kees Rocks, PA 800-551-8327
G.L. Mezzetta Inc
American Canyon, CA 707-648-1050
Generation Tea
Spring Valley, NY 866-742-5668
GH Ford Tea Company
Shokangers Falls, NY 845-834-2068
GlobeTrends
Morris Plains, NJ 800-416-8327
Gloria Jean's Gourmet Coffees
Irvine, CA 877-320-5282
Golden Moon Tea
Herndon, VA 877-327-5473
Good Earth® Teas
Santa Cruz, CA 888-625-8227
Grace Tea Company
Acton, MA 978-635-9500
Great Eastern Sun
Asheville, NC 800-334-5809
H&H Products Company
Orlando, FL 407-299-5410
H&K Products-Pappy's Sassafras Teas
Columbus Grove, OH 877-659-5110
Hain Celestial Group
Melville, NY 800-434-4246
Harney & Sons Fine Teas
Millerton, NY 800-832-8463
Has Beans Coffee & Tea Company
Mount Shasta, CA 800-427-2326
Herbs, Etc.
Santa Fe, NM 888-694-3727
Heritage Store
Virginia Beach, VA 800-862-2923
House of Coffee Beans
Houston, TX 800-422-1799
Ideal Distributing Company
Bothell, WA 425-488-6121
IL HWA American Corporation
Worcester, MA 800-446-7364
IMS Food Service
Shelton, CT 800-235-7072
India Tree Gourmet Spices & Specialties
Seattle, WA 800-369-4848
Indochina Tea Company
Los Angeles, CA 323-650-8020
Ineeka Inc
Chicago, IL 312-733-8327
International Tea Importers
Pico Rivera, CA 562-801-9600
Irani & Company
Fairland, IN 317-862-1257
J.G. British Imports
Bradenton, FL 888-965-1700
John A. Vassilaros & Son
Flushing, NY 718-886-4140

Justin Lloyd Premium Tea Company
Carson, CA 310-834-4000
Keurig, Inc
Reading, MA 781-928-0162
Krinos Foods
Santa Barbara, CA 800-624-4896
LA Lifestyle NutritionalProducts
Santa Ana, CA 800-387-4786
Leaves Pure Teas
Scottsdale, AZ 800-242-8807
Leroy Hill Coffee Company
Mobile, AL 800-866-5282
Lyons-Magnus
Fresno, CA 559-268-5966
MacKinlay Teas
Ann Arbor, MI 734-846-0966
Madys Company
San Francisco, CA 415-822-2227
Mafco Natural Products
Richmond, VA 804-222-1600
Masala Chai Company
Santa Cruz, CA 831-475-8881
Master Brew
Northbrook, IL 847-564-3600
Metropolitan Tea Company
Toronto, ON 800-388-0351
Mighty Leaf Tea
San Rafael, CA 415-491-2650
Mojave Foods Corporation
Commerce, CA 323-890-8900
Mother Parker's Tea & Coffee
Mississauga, ON 800-387-9398
Newly Weds Foods
Chicago, IL 800-647-9314
Noh Foods of Hawaii
Gardena, CA 310-324-6770
Northwestern Foods
Saint Paul, MN 800-236-4937
NSpired Natural Foods
Melville, NY 541-488-2747
Numi Organic Tea
Oakland, CA 866-972-6879
O'Mona International Tea
Port chester, NY 914-937-4389
O'Neil's Distributors
Goodland, IN 219-297-4521
O'Neill Coffee Company
West Middlesex, PA 724-528-9281
Old Town Coffee & Tea Company
Baltimore, MD 410-752-1229
Orleans Coffee Exchange
Kenner, LA 800-737-5464
Our Thyme Garden
Cleburne, TX 800-482-4372
Pet Milk
Florence, SC 800-735-3066
Plantextrakt/Martin Bower
Sacaucus, NJ 201-659-3100
Pokka Beverages
American Canyon, CA 800-972-5962
Prince of Peace Enterprises
Hayward, CA 800-732-2328
Progenix Corporation
Wausau, WI 800-233-3356
Q.E. Tea
Bridgeville, PA 800-622-8327
R. C. Bigelow
Fairfield, CT 888-244-3569
Randag & Associates Inc
Elmhurst, IL 630-530-2830
Redco Foods
Windsor, CT 800-645-1190
Reily Foods Company
New Orleans, LA 504-524-6131
Republic of Tea
Novato, CA 80- 2-8 48
Richard's Gourmet Coffee
West Bridgewater, MA 800-370-2633
Royal Food Distributors
Scottsdale, AZ 602-971-4910
Royal Pacific Tea & Coffee
Scottsdale, AZ 480-951-8251
Sampac Enterprises
South San Francisco, CA 650-876-0808
Sara Lee Corporation
Downers Grove, IL 630-598-8100
Schneider's Dairy Holdings Inc
Pittsburgh, PA 412-881-3525
Secret Tea Garden
Vancouver, BC 604-261-3070
Serendipitea
Manhasset, NY 888-832-5433

Simpson & Vail
Brookfield, CT 800-282-8327
Sourthern Tea
Marietta, GA 800-241-0896
Southern Tea Company
Marietta, GA 770-428-5555
SpecialTeas
Norwalk, CT 888-365-6983
Stewart's Private Blend Foods
Chicago, IL 800-654-2862
Sturm Foods
Manawa, WI 800-347-8876
Sunlike Juice
Scarborough, ON 416-297-1140
Superior Trading Company
San Francisco, CA 415-982-8722
Tata Tea
Plant City, FL 813-754-2602
Tatra Herb Company
Morrisville, PA 888-828-7248
Tea Beyond
West Caldwell, NJ 973-226-0327
Tea Forte
Concord, MA 978-369-7777
Tea Needs Inc
Boca Raton, FL 877-832-8289
Templar Food Products
New Providence, NJ 800-883-6752
Ten Ren Tea & Ginseng Company
New York, NY 800-292-2049
Thirs-Tea Corporation
Miami, FL 305-651-4350
Traditional Medicinals
Sebastopol, CA 800-543-4372
Truesdale Packaging Company
Warrenton, MO 636-456-6800
Twining R & Company
Greensboro, NC 336-275-8634
Two Leaves and a Bud
Basalt, CO 866-631-7973
U Roast Em
Hayward, WI 715-634-6255
Ultra Seal
New Paltz, NY 845-255-2490
Uncle Bum's Gourmet Foods
Riverside, CA 800-486-2867
Uncle Lee's Tea
South El Monte, CA 800-732-8830
Unilever
Mont-Royal, QC 514-735-1141
Unilever Canada
Saint John, NB 800-565-7273
Unilever United States
Englewood Cliffs, NJ 201-894-4000
Universal Commodities
Bronxville, NY 914-779-5700
Van Roy Coffee
Cleveland, OH 877-826-7669
VIP Foods
Flushing, NY 718-821-5330
Vita Specialty Foods
Inwood, WV 800-974-4778
Weaver Nut Company
Ephrata, PA 717-738-3781
Wechsler Coffee Corporation
Moonachie, NJ 800-800-2633
White Coffee Corporation
Astoria, NY 800-221-0140
White Rock Products Corporation
Flushing, NY 800-969-7625
Whole Herb Company
Sonoma, CA 707-935-1077
World Ginseng Center
San Francisco, CA 800-747-8808
Yellow Emperor
Eugene, OR 877-485-6664

Zhena's Gypsy Tea
Commerce, CA 800-448-0803

Bags

ABC Tea House
Baldwin Park, CA 888-220-3988
Barrows Tea Company
New Bedford, MA 800-832-5024
Blue Ridge Tea & Herb Company
Brooklyn, NY 718-625-3100
Choice Organic Teas
Seattle, WA 206-525-0051
Eastern Shore Tea
Lutherville, MD 800-823-1408
Eastern Tea Corporation
Monroe Township, NJ 800-221-0865
Empire Tea Services
Columbus, IN 800-790-0246
Harris Freeman & Company
Anaheim, CA 800-275-2378
Modern Tea Packers
Brooklyn, NY 718-417-1060
Sourthern Tea
Marietta, GA 800-241-0896
Tetley Tea
Shelton, CT 800-728-0084
World of Coffee, World of Tea
Stirling, NJ 908-647-1218

Black

Alpine Pure USA
Cambridge, MA 866-832-7997
Chieftain Wild Rice Company
Spooner, WI 800-262-6368
Harney & Sons Fine Teas
Millerton, NY 800-832-8463
SpecialTeas
Norwalk, CT 888-365-6983
Stash Tea Company
Portland, OR 800-547-1514
Talbott Teas
Chicago, IL 888-809-6062
Universal Commodities
Bronxville, NY 914-779-5700

Chai

Alpine Pure USA
Cambridge, MA 866-832-7997
Choice Organic Teas
Seattle, WA 206-525-0051
Da Vinci Gourmet
Seattle, WA 800-640-6779
David Rio
San Francisco, CA 800-454-9605
Father's Country Hams
Bremen, KY 270-525-3554
Masala Chai Company
Santa Cruz, CA 831-475-8881
Oregon Chai
Portland, OR 888-874-2424
Sattwa Chai
Newberg, OR 503-538-4715
Stash Tea Company
Portland, OR 800-547-1514
Templar Food Products
New Providence, NJ 800-883-6752
Toddy Products
Midland, TX 713-225-2066

Chamomile

Castella Imports
Hauppauge, NY 866-227-8355
Choice Organic Teas
Seattle, WA 206-525-0051

Darjeeling

Choice Organic Teas
Seattle, WA 206-525-0051

Decaffeinated

Alexander Gourmet Imports
Caledon, ON 800-265-5081
Ancora Coffee Roasters
Madison, WI 800-260-0217
Boston Tea Company
Hackensack, NJ 201-440-3004
Castella Imports
Hauppauge, NY 866-227-8355
Choice Organic Teas
Seattle, WA 206-525-0051
Green Mountain Coffee Roasters
Waterbury, VT 800-545-2326
Harney & Sons Fine Teas
Millerton, NY 800-832-8463
Masala Chai Company
Santa Cruz, CA 831-475-8881
Mother Parker's Tea & Coffee
Mississauga, ON 800-387-9398
Plantextrakt/Martin Bower
Sacaucus, NJ 201-659-3100
SpecialTeas
Norwalk, CT 888-365-6983
Universal Commodities
Bronxville, NY 914-779-5700
Weaver Nut Company
Ephrata, PA 717-738-3781

Earl Grey

Alpine Pure USA
Cambridge, MA 866-832-7997
Blue Willow Tea Company
Emeryville, CA 800-328-0353
Choice Organic Teas
Seattle, WA 206-525-0051

Earl Grey Decaffeinated

Choice Organic Teas
Seattle, WA 206-525-0051

English Breakfast

Choice Organic Teas
Seattle, WA 206-525-0051

Fair-Trade

Chieftain Wild Rice Company
Spooner, WI 800-262-6368

Flavored

Alaska Herb Tea Company
Anchorage, AK 800-654-2764
Aqua Vie Beverage Corporation
Ketchum, ID 800-744-7500
Arbuckle Coffee
Pittsburgh, PA 800-533-8278
Belmar Spring Water Company
Glen Rock, NJ 201-444-1010
Boston Tea Company
Hackensack, NJ 201-440-3004
Cafe Society Coffee Company
Dallas, TX 800-717-6000
Central Coca-Cola Bottling Company
Richmond, VA 800-359-3759
Choice Organic Teas
Seattle, WA 206-525-0051
Cold Spring Brewing Company
Cold Spring, MN 320-685-8686
Daymar Select Fine Coffees
El Cajon, CA 800-466-7590
East Indies Coffee & Tea Company
Lebanon, PA 800-220-2326
Empire Tea Services
Columbus, IN 800-790-0246
Father's Country Hams
Bremen, KY 270-525-3554
First Colony Coffee & Tea Company
Norfolk, VA 800-446-8555
Fortunes International Teas
Mc Kees Rocks, PA 800-551-8327
Frair & Grimes
Kent, WA 206-935-0134
H&K Products-Pappy's Sassafras Teas
Columbus Grove, OH 877-659-5110
Harney & Sons Fine Teas
Millerton, NY 800-832-8463
Houston Tea & Beverage
Houston, TX 800-585-4549
Masala Chai Company
Santa Cruz, CA 831-475-8881
Mother Parker's Tea & Coffee
Mississauga, ON 800-387-9398
Noh Foods of Hawaii
Gardena, CA 310-324-6770
Plantextrakt/Martin Bower
Sacaucus, NJ 201-659-3100
Premium Waters
Minneapolis, MN 800-332-3332
R. C. Bigelow
Fairfield, CT 888-244-3569
Royal Coffee & Tea Company
Mississauga, ON 800-667-6226
San Francisco Bay Coffee Company
Lincoln, CA 800-829-1300
SpecialTeas
Norwalk, CT 888-365-6983
Starbucks Coffee Company
Seattle, WA 800-782-7282
Stewart's Private Blend Foods
Chicago, IL 800-654-2862
Unilever Bestfoods
Englewood Cliffs, NJ 201-567-8000
Universal Commodities
Bronxville, NY 914-779-5700
Weaver Nut Company
Ephrata, PA 717-738-3781
Yosemite Waters
Los Angeles, CA 800-427-8420

Green

AIYA
New York, NY 212-499-0610
Aiya America Inc.
Torrance, CA
Alexander Gourmet Imports
Caledon, ON 800-265-5081
Alpine Pure USA
Cambridge, MA 866-832-7997
Ancora Coffee Roasters
Madison, WI 800-260-0217
AOI Tea Company - North America Office
Huntington Beach, CA 877-264-0877
Baycliff Company
New York, NY 212-772-6078
Boston Tea Company
Hackensack, NJ 201-440-3004
China Mist Tea Company
Scottsdale, AZ 800-242-8807
Choice Organic Teas
Seattle, WA 206-525-0051
Da Vinci Gourmet
Seattle, WA 800-640-6779
Eden Foods Inc.
Clinton, MI 800-248-0320
Empire Tea Services
Columbus, IN 800-790-0246
Flavor Specialties
Corona, CA 951-734-6620
Fmali Herb
Santa Cruz, CA 831-423-7913
Fortunes International Teas
Mc Kees Rocks, PA 800-551-8327
Harney & Sons Fine Teas
Millerton, NY 800-832-8463
Healthy Beverage
Doylestown, PA 800-295-1388
NuNaturals
Eugene, OR 800-753-4372
Plantextrakt/Martin Bower
Sacaucus, NJ 201-659-3100
R. C. Bigelow
Fairfield, CT 888-244-3569
RFI Ingredients
Blauvelt, NY 800-962-7663
Sencha Naturals
Los Angeles, CA 888-473-6242
SpecialTeas
Norwalk, CT 888-365-6983
Stash Tea Company
Portland, OR 800-547-1514
Talbott Teas
Chicago, IL 888-809-6062
Templar Food Products
New Providence, NJ 800-883-6752
The Long Life Beverage Company
Mission Hills, CA 800-848-7331
Universal Commodities
Bronxville, NY 914-779-5700

Herbal

Abunda Life Laboratories
Asbury Park, NJ 732-775-7575
Agrinom LLC
Hakalau, HI 808-963-6771
Alternative Health & Herbs
Albany, OR 800-345-4152
Ancora Coffee Roasters
Madison, WI 800-260-0217
Berardi's Fresh Roast
Cleveland, OH 800-876-9109

Body Breakthrough
Deer Park, NY 800-874-6299
Boston Spice & Tea Company
Boston, VA 800-966-4372
Boston Tea Company
Hackensack, NJ. 201-440-3004
China Mist Tea Company
Scottsdale, AZ. 800-242-8807
Choice Organic Teas
Seattle, WA 206-525-0051
Coffee Bean International
Portland, OR 800-877-0474
Common Folk Farm
Naples, ME 207-787-2764
Empire Tea Services
Columbus, IN 800-790-0246
Fmali Herb
Santa Cruz, CA 831-423-7913
Fortunes International Teas
Mc Kees Rocks, PA 800-551-8327
Ginkgoton
Gardena, CA 310-538-8383
Hansen's Natural
Fullerton, CA 714-870-0310
Herb Tea Company
Oxnard, CA 805-486-6477
HerbaSway Laboratories
Wallingford, CT 800-672-7322
Heritage Store
Virginia Beach, VA 800-862-2923
Hobe Laboratories
Tempe, AZ 800-528-4482
IL HWA American Corporation
Worcester, MA 800-446-7364
Kandia's Fine Teas
Lewiston, ME 207-782-6300
Madys Company
San Francisco, CA 415-822-2227
Mafco Natural Products
Richmond, VA. 804-222-1600
Maharishi Ayurveda Products International
Fairfield, IA 800-255-8332
Montana Tea & Spice Trading
Missoula, MT 406-721-4882
Mother Parker's Tea & Coffee
Mississauga, ON 800-387-9398
Native Scents
Taos, NM. 800-645-3471
Now Foods
Bloomingdale, IL 888-669-3663
Nutritional Counselors of America
Spencer, TN 931-946-3600
Old Fashioned Natural Products
Santa Ana, CA 800-552-9045
Organic India USA
Boulder, CO 888-550-8332
P.C. Teas Company
Burlingame, CA 800-423-8728
PC Teas Company
Burlingame, CA 800-423-8728
Plantextrakt/Martin Bower
Sacaucus, NJ 201-659-3100
Progenix Corporation
Wausau, WI 800-233-3356
R. C. Bigelow
Fairfield, CT 888-244-3569
San Francisco Bay Coffee Company
Lincoln, CA 800-829-1300
San Francisco Herb & Natural Food Company
Fremont, CA 800-227-2830
Stash Tea Company
Portland, OR 800-547-1514
Sugai Kona Coffee
Kealakekua, HI 808-322-7717
Superior Trading Company
San Francisco, CA 415-982-8722
Tatra Herb Company
Morrisville, PA 888-828-7248
Templar Food Products
New Providence, NJ 800-883-6752
Traditional Medicinals
Sebastopol, CA 800-543-4372
Triple Leaf Tea
S San Francisco, CA 800-552-7448
Unilever Bestfoods
Englewood Cliffs, NJ 201-567-8000
Vermont Liberty Tea Company
Waterbury, VT 802-244-6102
Wah Yet Group
Hayward, CA 800-229-3392
Whole Herb Company
Sonoma, CA 707-935-1077

Iced

Al-Rite Fruits & Syrups
Miami, FL 305-652-2540
Arizona Beverage Company
Woodbury, NY 800-832-3775
Bay Pac Beverages
Walnut Creek, CA 925-279-0800
Bigelow Tea
Fairfield, CT 888-244-3569
Boyd Coffee Company
Portland, OR 800-545-4077
Brooklyn Bottling Company
Milton, NY 845-795-2171
Central Coca-Cola Bottling Company
Richmond, VA. 800-359-3759
China Mist Tea Company
Scottsdale, AZ. 800-242-8807
Clement Pappas & Company
Carneys Point, NJ 800-257-7019
Coca-Cola Enterprises
Atlanta, GA 800-233-7210
Droubi's Imports
Houston, TX 713-988-7138
Ensemble Beverages
Montgomery, AL. 334-324-7719
Farmland Dairies
Wallington, NJ 888-727-6252
Galliker Dairy
Johnstown, PA. 800-477-6455
Global Beverage Company
Rochester, NY 585-381-3560
Good-O-Beverages Company
Bronx, NY 718-328-6400
Harney & Sons Fine Teas
Millerton, NY 800-832-8463
Harris Freeman & Company
Anaheim, CA 800-275-2378
Healthy Beverage
Doylestown, PA 800-295-1388
Honest Tea
Bethesda, MD 800-865-4736
Inko's White Iced Tea
Englewood, NJ 866-747-4656
Itoen
Honolulu, HI 808-847-4477
Leroy Hill Coffee Company
Mobile, AL 800-866-5282
Northwestern Foods
Saint Paul, MN 800-236-4937
Pokka Beverages
American Canyon, CA 800-972-5962
PR Bar
Carlsbad, CA 800-397-5556
Prairie Farms Dairy
O Fallon, IL 618-632-3632
Quaker Oats Company
Dallas, TX 214-330-8681
Rosenberger's Dairies
Hatfield, PA 800-355-9074
Rupari Food Service
Deerfield Beach, FL 800-578-7274
Schneider Valley Farms Dairy
Williamsport, PA 570-326-2021
Schneider's Dairy Holdings Inc
Pittsburgh, PA 412-881-3525
Serengeti Tea
Gardena, CA 888-604-2040
Snapple Beverage Group
Ryebrook, NY 800-762-7753
Stash Tea Company
Portland, OR 800-547-1514
Sturm Foods
Manawa, WI 800-347-8876
Sunlike Juice
Scarborough, ON 416-297-1140
Sweet Leaf Tea Company
Austin, TX 512-328-7775
Templar Food Products
New Providence, NJ 800-883-6752
Tradewinds-Tea Company
Carlisle, OH . . . . . 855-DRI-K TW
Turkey Hill Dairy
Conestoga, PA 800-693-2479
Unilever Bestfoods
Englewood Cliffs, NJ 201-567-8000
Wengert's Dairy
Lebanon, PA 800-222-2129
White Rock Products Corporation
Flushing, NY 800-969-7625

Instant

American Instants
Flanders, NJ 973-584-8811
Castella Imports
Hauppauge, NY 866-227-8355
Crosby Molasses Company
St John, NB 506-634-7515
Daymar Select Fine Coffees
El Cajon, CA 800-466-7590
Finlay Tea Solutions
Morristown, NJ 973-539-8030
H&K Products-Pappy's Sassafras Teas
Columbus Grove, OH 877-659-5110
Northwestern Foods
Saint Paul, MN 800-236-4937
Plantextrakt/Martin Bower
Sacaucus, NJ 201-659-3100
Prince of Peace Enterprises
Hayward, CA 800-732-2328
Robertet Flavors
Piscataway, NJ 732-271-1804
Unilever Bestfoods
Englewood Cliffs, NJ 201-567-8000
Universal Commodities
Bronxville, NY 914-779-5700
VIP Foods
Flushing, NY 718-821-5330
Weaver Nut Company
Ephrata, PA 717-738-3781
Whole Herb Company
Sonoma, CA 707-935-1077

Irish Breakfast

Choice Organic Teas
Seattle, WA 206-525-0051

Jasmine

Alpine Pure USA
Cambridge, MA 866-832-7997
Blue Willow Tea Company
Emeryville, CA 800-328-0353
Choice Organic Teas
Seattle, WA 206-525-0051

Lemon

Da Vinci Gourmet
Seattle, WA 800-640-6779
Father's Country Hams
Bremen, KY 270-525-3554

Loose Leaf

Bigelow Tea
Fairfield, CT 888-244-3569
Choice Organic Teas
Seattle, WA 206-525-0051
David Rio
San Francisco, CA 800-454-9605
Great Lakes Tea & Spice Company
Glen Arbor, MI 877-645-9363
Rishi Tea
Milwaukee, WI 866-747-4483
Vermont Tea & Trading Company
Middlebury, VT 802-388-4005

Mint

Choice Organic Teas
Seattle, WA 206-525-0051
Father's Country Hams
Bremen, KY 270-525-3554

Mint Herb

Choice Organic Teas
Seattle, WA 206-525-0051

Oolong

Astral Extracts Ltd.
Syosset, NY 516-496-2505
Choice Organic Teas
Seattle, WA 206-525-0051
Harney & Sons Fine Teas
Millerton, NY 800-832-8463
Plantextrakt/Martin Bower
Sacaucus, NJ 201-659-3100
SpecialTeas
Norwalk, CT 888-365-6983
Stash Tea Company
Portland, OR 800-547-1514

Templar Food Products
New Providence, NJ 800-883-6752
Whole Herb Company
Sonoma, CA 707-935-1077

Orange Pekoe

Choice Organic Teas
Seattle, WA 206-525-0051

Peppermint Leaf

Choice Organic Teas
Seattle, WA 206-525-0051
Plantextrakt/Martin Bower
Sacaucus, NJ 201-659-3100
Whole Herb Company
Sonoma, CA 707-935-1077

Sun

American Instants
Flanders, NJ 973-584-8811
Atlanta Coffee & Tea Company
Decatur, GA 800-426-4781
Crosby Molasses Company
St John, NB 506-634-7515
Redco Foods
Windsor, CT 800-645-1190
Thirs-Tea Corporation
Miami, FL 305-651-4350
Unilever Canada
Saint John, NB 800-565-7273

Juices

A. Duda & Sons
Labelle, FL 800-440-3265
A. Duda Farm Fresh Foods
Belle Glade, FL 561-996-7621
AFP Advanced Food Products, LLC
Visalia, CA 559-627-2070
Alfer Laboratories
Chatsworth, CA 818-709-0737
All Juice Food & Beverage
Hendersonville, NC 800-736-5674
Aloe Farms
Harlingen, TX 800-262-6771
Aloe Laboratories, Inc.
Harlingen, TX 800-258-5380
Amcan Industries
Elmsford, NY 914-347-4838
American Food Traders
Miami, FL 305-273-7090
American Fruit Processors
Pacoima, CA 818-899-9574
American Soy Products
Saline, MI 734-429-2310
Ameripec
Buena Park, CA 714-994-2990
Aseltine Cider Company
Comstock Park, MI 616-784-7676
Avalon Foodservice, Inc.
Canal Fulton, OH 800-362-0622
Berkeley Farms
Hayward, CA 510-265-8600
Beverage Capital Corporation
Baltimore, MD 410-242-7003
Birdseye Dairy
Green Bay, WI 920-494-5388
Bowman Apple Products Company
Mount Jackson, VA 800-346-5382
Bully Hill Vineyards
Hammondsport, NY 607-868-3610
Burnette Foods
Hartford, MI 616-621-3181
Byesville Aseptics
Byesville, OH 740-685-2548
California Custom Fruits & Flavors
Irwindale, CA 877-558-0056
Cargill Juice Products
Frostproof, FL 800-227-4455
Carolina Products
Greer, SC 864-879-3084
Cascadian Farm & MUIR Glen
Sedro Woolley, WA 360-855-0100
Central Coca-Cola Bottling Company
Richmond, VA 800-359-3759
Chase Brothers Dairy
Oxnard, CA 800-438-6455
Chiquita Brands Intl. ional
Cincinnati, OH 800-438-0015
Chung's Gourmet Foods
Houston, TX 800-824-8647
Citrus Citrosuco North America
Lake Wales, FL 800-356-4592
Citrus International
Winter Park, FL 407-629-8037
Citrus Service
Winter Garden, FL 407-656-4999
Clinton Milk Company
Newark, NJ 973-642-3000
Coastlog Industries
Novi, MI 248-344-9556
Coca-Cola Bottling Company
Honolulu, HI 808-839-6711
Cold Hollow Cider Mill
Waterbury Center, VT 800-327-7537
Commodities Marketing, Inc.
Edison, NJ 732-603-5077
Consun Food Industries
Elyria, OH 440-322-6301
Cott Coporation
Tampa, FL 813-313-1800
Country Life
Hauppauge, NY 800-645-5768
Country Pure Foods
Akron, OH 330-753-2293
Crown Regal Wine Cellars
Brooklyn, NY 718-604-1430
Cumberland Dairy
Rosenhayn, NJ 856-451-1300
Cutrale Citrus Juices
Leesburg, FL 352-728-7800
Cyclone Enterprises
Houston, TX 281-872-0087
Dairy Land
Macon, GA 478-742-6461
Dairy Maid Dairy
Frederick, MD 301-695-0431
Damon Industries
Sparks, NV 775-331-3200
Del's Lemonade & Refreshments
Cranston, RI 401-463-6190
Dole Food Company
Westlake Village, CA 818-879-6600
Empresa La Famosa
Toa Baja, PR 787-251-0060
Empresas La Famosa/Coco Lopez
Toa Baja, PR 787-251-0060
Evans Properties
Dade City, FL 352-567-5662
Everfresh Beverages
Warren, MI 586-755-9500
Farmland Dairies
Wallington, NJ 888-727-6252
Flagship Atlanta Dairy
Belleview, FL 800-224-0669
Flavouressence Products
Mississauga, ON 866-209-7778
Florida Bottling
Miami, FL 305-324-5932
Florida Juice Products
Lakeland, FL 863-802-4040
Florida Key West
Fort Myers, FL 239-694-8787
Foremost Farms
Athens, WI 715-257-7015
Four Chimneys Farm Winery Trust
Himrod, NY 607-243-7502
Garelick Farms
Lynn, MA 800-487-8700
Giacorelli Imports
Boca Raton, FL 561-451-1415
Gilette Foods
Union, NJ 908-688-0500
Glcc Company
Paw Paw, MI 269-657-3167
Global Beverage Company
Rochester, NY 585-381-3560
Global Marketing Associates
Schaumburg, IL 847-397-2350
Good-O-Beverages Company
Bronx, NY 718-328-6400
Green Spot Packaging
Claremont, CA 800-456-3210
Hains Celestial Group
Melville, NY 877-612-4246
Hallcrest Vineyards
Felton, CA 831-335-4441
Hansen Beverage
Corona, CA 800-426-7367
Harrisburg Dairies
Harrisburg, PA 800-692-7429
Hawaii Coffee Company
Honolulu, HI 800-338-8353
Heck Cellars
Arvin, CA 661-854-6120
Heritage Farms Dairy
Murfreesboro, TN 615-895-2790
Hero of America
Amsterdam, NY 877-437-6526
Hi-Country Corona
Selah, WA 951-272-2600
Hi-Country Foods Corporation
Selah, WA 509-697-7292
Hiller Cranberries
Rochester, MA 508-763-5257
Howard Foods
Danvers, MA 978-774-6207
Hudson Valley Fruit Juice
Highland, NY 845-691-8061
Hygeia Dairy Company
Corpus Christi, TX 361-854-4561
Inn Foods
Watsonville, CA 831-724-2026
J.M. Smucker
Havre De Grace, MD 410-939-1403
Johanna Foods
Flemington, NJ 800-727-6700
John C. Meier Juice Company
Cincinnati, OH 800-346-2941
Juice Bowl Products
Lakeland, FL 863-665-5515
Juice Mart
West Hills, CA 877-888-1011
Juice Tyme
Chicago, IL 800-236-5823
Juicy Whip
La Verne, CA 909-392-7500
Kagome
Los Banos, CA 209-826-8850
Kan-Pac
Arkansas City, KS 620-442-6820
Kemach Food Products Corporation
Brooklyn, NY 888-453-6224
Kemps
Cedarburg, WI 262-377-5040
Kendall Citrus Corporation
Goulds, FL 305-258-1628
King Juice
Milwaukee, WI 414-482-0303
Knouse Foods Coop
Paw Paw, MI 269-657-5524
Knouse Foods Coop
Peach Glen, PA 717-677-8181
Krier Foods
Random Lake, WI 920-994-2469
Krinos Foods
Santa Barbara, CA 800-624-4896
Land O Lakes Milk
Sioux Falls, SD 605-330-9526
Langer Juice Company
City of Industry, CA 626-336-1666
Lemon-X Corporation
Huntington Station, NY 800-220-1061
Lenox-Martell
Boston, MA 617-442-7777
Liberty Dairy
Evart, MI 800-632-5552
Louis Dreyfus Citrus
Winter Garden, FL 800-549-4272
LPO/ LaDolc
Overland Park, KS 913-681-7757
Lyons-Magnus
Fresno, CA 559-268-5966
M. & B. Products
Tampa, FL 800-899-7255
Magnotta Winery Corporation
Vaughan, ON 800-461-9463
Manzanita Ranch
Julian, CA 760-765-0102
Marva Maid Dairy
Newport News, VA 800-544-4439
Matanuska Maid Dairy
Anchorage, AK 907-561-5223
Maui Pineapple Company
Kahului, HI 808-877-3351
Maui Pineapple Company
Concord, CA 925-798-0240
Mayer Brothers
West Seneca, NY 800-696-2937
Mayer's Cider Mill
Webster, NY 800-543-0043
Mayfield Dairy Farms
Athens, TN 800-362-9546
Mayfield Farms
Caledon, ON 905-846-0506

McArthur Dairy
Miami, FL 305-795-7700
McCutcheon's Apple Products
Frederick, MD. 800-888-7537
Meduri Farms Inc.
Dallas, OR. 503-623-0308
Meramec Vineyards
Saint James, MO. 877-216-9463
Minute Maid Company
Sugar Land, TX. 281-302-4317
Minute Maid Company
Dunedin, FL 800-237-0159
Mission San Juan Juices
Dana Point, CA. 949-495-7929
Mott's
Elmsford, NY
Mott's
Rye Brook, NY 800-426-4891
Mountain Sun Organic & Natural Juices
Boulder, CO. 1 8-0 4-4 42
Mountain Valley ProductsInc
Sunnyside, WA 509-837-8084
Mrs. Clark's Foods
Ankeny, IA 800-736-5674

Juices, salad dressings and sauces.

Nana Mae's Organics
Sebastopol, CA 707-829-7359
Nantucket Nectars
Elmsford, NY
Natalie's Orchard Island Juice
Fort Pierce, FL 772-465-1122
National Grape Cooperative
Westfield, NY. 716-326-5200
Nestle Professional Vitality
Solon, OH 800-288-8682
Northland Cranberries
Jackson, WI. 262-677-2221
Northland Cranberries
Wisconsin Rapids, WI 608-252-4714
Northwest Naturals Corporation
Bothell, WA. 425-881-2200
Oakhurst Dairy
Portland, ME. 800-482-0718
Oberweis Dairy
North Aurora, IL. 888-645-5868
Ocean Spray Cranberries
Bordentown, NJ 609-298-0905
Ocean Spray Cranberries
Vero Beach, FL. 772-562-0800
Odwalla
Denver, CO 303-282-0500
Orchard Island Juice Company
Fort Pierce, FL 888-373-7444
Parmalat Canada
Toronto, ON 800-563-1515
Peace Mountain Natural Beverages Corporation
Springfield, MA 413-567-4942
Perfect Foods
Goshen, NY. 800-933-3288
Pet Milk
Florence, SC 800-735-3066
Pilgrim Foods
Greenville, NH 603-878-2100
Pokka Beverages
American Canyon, CA 800-972-5962
Prairie Farms Dairy
Carlinville, IL 217-854-2547
Prairie Farms Dairy
O Fallon, IL. 618-632-3632
Premier Juices
Clearwater, FL 727-533-8200
Purity Dairies
Nashville, TN 615-244-1900
Pyramid Juice Company
Ashland, OR 541-482-2292
Quality Brands
Deland, FL 888-676-2700
R.J. Corr Naturals
Posen, IL. 708-389-4200
R.W. Knudsen
Chico, CA 530-899-5000
Rainbow Valley Orchards
Fallbrook, CA 760-728-2905
Rapunzel Pure Organics
Bloomfield, NJ 800-225-1449
Regent Champagne Cellars
New York, NY
Reiter Dairy
Akron, OH. 800-362-0825
Reiter Dairy
Springfield, OH. 937-323-5777
Roberts Dairy Foods
Iowa City, IA
Rohtstein Corporation
Woburn, MA 781-935-8300
Ronzoni Foods Canada
Etobicoke, ON 800-387-5032
Royal Kedem Food & Wine Company
Bayonne, NJ 201-437-9131
SANGARIA USA
Torrance, CA. 310-530-2202
Saratoga Beverage Group
Saratoga Springs, NY 888-426-8642
Schneider Valley Farms Dairy
Williamsport, PA. 570-326-2021
Schneider's Dairy Holdings Inc
Pittsburgh, PA. 412-881-3525
SEW Friel
Queenstown, MD 410-827-8811
Sherrill Orchards
Arvin, CA 661-858-2035
Shonan Usa
Grandview, WA. 509-882-5583
Silver Springs Citrus
Howey In the Hills, FL. 800-940-2277
Sinton Dairy Foods Company
Colorado Springs, CO. 800-388-4970
Sir Real Foods
White Plains, NY 914-948-9342
Smeltzer Orchard Company
Frankfort, MI 231-882-4421
Snapple Beverage Group
Ryebrook, NY. 800-762-7753
Solana Gold Organics
Sebastopol, CA 800-459-1121
St. James Winery
Saint James, MO. 800-280-9463
St. Julian Wine Company
Paw Paw, MI. 800-732-6002
Stevens Tropical Plantation
West Palm Beach, FL 561-683-4701
Stevens Tropical Plantation
West Palm Beach, FL 800-785-1355
Stop & Shop Manufacturing
Readville, MA. 508-977-5132
Suiza Dairy Corporation
San Juan, PR 787-792-7300

Sun Orchard
Tempe, AZ 800-505-8423
Sun Pac Foods
Brampton, ON 905-792-2700
Sundance Industries
Newburgh, NY 845-565-6065
SunkiStreet Growers
Ontario, CA 800-225-3727
Sunlike Juice
Scarborough, ON 416-297-1140
Sunny Avocado
Jamul, CA 800-999-2862
Superbrand Dairies
Miami, FL 305-769-6600
Superstore Industries
Fairfield, CA 707-864-0502
Swiss Valley Farms Company
Davenport, IA 563-468-6600
Switch Beverage
Darien, CT 203-202-7383
Tamarack Farms Dairy
Newark, OH 866-221-4141
Tastee Apple Inc
Newcomerstown, OH 800-262-7753
Tazo Tea
Portland, OR 800-299-9445
Thomas Canning/Maidstone
Maidstone, ON 519-737-1531
Titusville Dairy Products
Titusville, PA 800-352-0101
Todhunter Foods
Lake Alfred, FL 863-956-1116
Toft Dairy
Sandusky, OH 800-521-4606
Tradewinds-Tea Company
Carlisle, OH . . . . . 855-DRI-K TW
Trailblazer Food Products
Portland, OR 800-777-7179
Tree Top
Selah, WA 800-542-4055
Treesweet Products
Houston, TX 281-876-3759
Tri-Boro Fruit Company
Fresno, CA 559-486-4141
Triple D Orchards
Empire, MI 866-781-9410
True Organic Products International
Miami, FL 800-487-0379
Truesdale Packaging Company
Warrenton, MO 636-456-6800
Upstate Farms Cooperative
Buffalo, NY 866-874-6455
Valley Fig Growers
Fresno, CA 559-237-3893
Valley View Packing Company
San Jose, CA 408-289-8300
Vegetable Juices
Chicago, IL 888-776-9752
Velda Farms
North Miami Beach, FL 800-795-4649
Ventura Coastal Corporation
Ventura, CA 805-653-7035
Veryfine Products
Littleton, MA 800-837-9346
Washington State Juice
Pacoima, CA 818-899-1195
Welch's Foods Inc
Concord, MA 800-340-6870
Welsh Farms
Edison, NJ 800-221-0663
White House Foods
Winchester, VA 540-662-3401
White Rock Products Corporation
Flushing, NY 800-969-7625
Wholesome Sweeteners
Sugar Land, TX 800-680-1896
William Bolthouse Farms
Bakersfield, CA 661-366-7270
Winmix/Natural Care Products
Englewood, FL 941-475-7432
Winter Garden Citrus
Winter Garden, FL 407-656-4423
World Citrus
Winston Salem, NC 336-723-1863
Yoder Dairies
Chesapeake, VA 757-482-4068

Ade

Country Pure Foods
Akron, OH 877-995-8423
Optimal Nutrients
Foster City, CA 707-528-1800
S&D Coffee, Inc
Concord, NC 704-782-3121

Concentrate

American Purpac Technologies, LLC
Beloit, WI 877-787-7221
California Custom Fruits & Flavors
Irwindale, CA 877-558-0056

Grape

Arizona Beverage Company
Woodbury, NY 800-832-3775

Lemon

Arizona Beverage Company
Woodbury, NY 800-832-3775

Orange

Arizona Beverage Company
Woodbury, NY 800-832-3775

Aloe

Alfer Laboratories
Chatsworth, CA 818-709-0737
Aloe Farms
Harlingen, TX 800-262-6771
Aloe Laboratories, Inc.
Harlingen, TX 800-258-5380
Emerling International Foods
Buffalo, NY 716-833-7381

We supply food manufacturers and food service customers worldwide (since 1988) with bulk ingredients including: Fruits & Vegetables; Juice Concentrates; Herbs & Spices; Oils & Vinegars; Flavors & Colors; Honey & Molasses. We also produce PURE MAPLE SYRUP.

Superbrand Dairies
Miami, FL 305-769-6600

Apple

All Juice Food & Beverage
Hendersonville, NC 800-736-5674
Apple & Eve
Roslyn, NY 800-969-8018
Aseltine Cider Company
Comstock Park, MI 616-784-7676
Birdseye Dairy
Green Bay, WI 920-494-5388
Bowman Apple Products Company
Mount Jackson, VA 800-346-5382
Brooklyn Bottling Company
Milton, NY 845-795-2171
Burnette Foods
Elk Rapids, MI 231-264-8116
Burnette Foods
Hartford, MI 616-621-3181
Cal India Foods International
Chino, CA 909-613-1660
Carolina Products
Greer, SC 864-879-3084
Cherry Central Cooperative Inc
Traverse City, MI 231-946-1860
Citrus Citrosuco North America
Lake Wales, FL 800-356-4592
Clement Pappas & Company
Carneys Point, NJ 800-257-7019
Cold Hollow Cider Mill
Waterbury Center, VT 800-327-7537
Coloma Frozen Foods
Coloma, MI 800-642-2723
Cott Coporation
Tampa, FL 813-313-1800
Country Pure Foods
Akron, OH 330-753-2293
Country Pure Foods
Ellington, CT 860-872-8346
Country Pure Foods
Akron, OH 877-995-8423
Erba Food Products
Brooklyn, NY 718-272-7700
Florida Fruit Juices
Chicago, IL 773-586-6200
Golden Town Apple Products
Rougemont, QC 519-599-6300
Green Spot Packaging
Claremont, CA 800-456-3210
Gregory's Box'd Beverages
Newark, NJ 973-465-1113
Hazel Creek Orchards
Mt Airy, GA 706-754-4899
Heritage Farms Dairy
Murfreesboro, TN 615-895-2790
Hi-Country Foods Corporation
Selah, WA 509-697-7292
Knouse Foods Coop
Paw Paw, MI 269-657-5524
Knouse Foods Coop
Peach Glen, PA 717-677-8181
LPO/ LaDolc
Overland Park, KS 913-681-7757
M. & B. Products
Tampa, FL 800-899-7255
Madera Enterprises
Madera, CA 800-507-9555
Manzanita Ranch
Julian, CA 760-765-0102
Marva Maid Dairy
Newport News, VA 800-544-4439
Mayer Brothers
West Seneca, NY 800-696-2937
Mayfield Farms
Caledon, ON 905-846-0506
McCutcheon's Apple Products
Frederick, MD 800-888-7537
Merlinos
Canon City, CO 719-275-5558
Minute Maid Company
Sugar Land, TX 281-302-4317
Minute Maid Company
Dunedin, FL 800-237-0159
Mott's
Elmsford, NY
Mott's
Rye Brook, NY 800-426-4891
Mountain Valley ProductsInc
Sunnyside, WA 509-837-8084
Murray Cider Company Inc
Roanoke, VA 540-977-9000
Nana Mae's Organics
Sebastopol, CA 707-829-7359
Old Dutch Mustard Company
Great Neck, NY 516-466-0522
Old Orchard Brands
Sparta, MI 616-887-1745
Quality Brands
Deland, FL 888-676-2700
Rosenberger's Dairies
Hatfield, PA 800-355-9074
Royal Kedem Food & Wine Company
Bayonne, NJ 201-437-9131
SEW Friel
Queenstown, MD 410-827-8811
Sinton Dairy Foods Company
Colorado Springs, CO 800-388-4970
Smeltzer Orchard Company
Frankfort, MI 231-882-4421
Solana Gold Organics
Sebastopol, CA 800-459-1121
Sunlike Juice
Scarborough, ON 416-297-1140
Tastee Apple Inc
Newcomerstown, OH 800-262-7753
Tree Top
Selah, WA 800-367-6571
Tree Top
Selah, WA 800-542-4055
Triple D Orchards
Empire, MI 866-781-9410
True Organic Products International
Miami, FL 800-487-0379
Valley View Packing Company
San Jose, CA 408-289-8300
White House Foods
Winchester, VA 540-662-3401
Yoder Dairies
Chesapeake, VA 757-482-4068

Bottled

Apple & Eve
Roslyn, NY 800-969-8018
Aseltine Cider Company
Comstock Park, MI 616-784-7676
Carolina Products
Greer, SC 864-879-3084
Cott Coporation
Tampa, FL 813-313-1800

Northland Cranberries
Wisconsin Rapids, WI 608-252-4714

Boxed

Cloverland Green Spring Dairy
Baltimore, MD 800-876-6455
Emerling International Foods
Buffalo, NY.......................716-833-7381

Tree Top
Selah, WA 800-367-6571

Canned

Alljuice
Hendersonville, NC 800-736-5674
Bowman Apple Products Company
Mount Jackson, VA.................800-346-5382
Burnette Foods
Hartford, MI 616-621-3181
Cott Coporation
Tampa, FL.........................813-313-1800
Country Pure Foods
Akron, OH.........................877-995-8423
Emerling International Foods
Buffalo, NY.......................716-833-7381

Florida's Natural Growers
Lake Wales, FL....................888-657-6600
Greenwood Associates
Highland Park, IL..................847-579-5500
Hansen's Juices
Azusa, CA.........................800-426-7367
Langer Juice Company
City of Industry, CA 626-336-3100
Manzana Products Company
Sebastopol, CA....................707-823-5313
Mason County Fruit Packers Cooperative
Ludington, MI.....................231-845-6248
McCutcheon's Apple Products
Frederick, MD.....................800-888-7537
Noel Corporation
Yakima, WA 509-248-4545
Old Dutch Mustard Company
Great Neck, NY 516-466-0522
Quality Brands
Deland, FL 888-676-2700
San Benito Foods
Vancouver, WA....................800-453-7832
SEW Friel
Queenstown, MD 410-827-8811
Steelback Brewery
Toronto, ON 416-679-0032
Sunlike Juice
Scarborough, ON 416-297-1140
Tree Top
Selah, WA 800-367-6571
Triple D Orchards
Empire, MI 866-781-9410

Chilled

Emerling International Foods
Buffalo, NY.......................716-833-7381

Tree Top
Selah, WA 800-367-6571

Concentrate

A. Duda Farm Fresh Foods
Belle Glade, FL....................561-996-7621
Citrus Citrosuco North America
Lake Wales, FL....................800-356-4592
Cott Coporation
Tampa, FL.........................813-313-1800
Georgia Sun
Newnan, GA 770-251-2500
Glcc Company
Paw Paw, MI......................269-657-3167
Green Spot Packaging
Claremont, CA 800-456-3210
Hemisphere Associated
Huntington, NY 631-673-3840
Mountain Valley ProductsInc
Sunnyside, WA 509-837-8084
Pacific Coast Fruit Company
Portland, OR 503-234-6411
Sun Pac Foods
Brampton, ON.....................905-792-2700
Tree Top
Selah, WA 800-542-4055
Valley View Packing Company
San Jose, CA......................408-289-8300

Frozen

Bowman Apple Products Company
Mount Jackson, VA.................800-346-5382
Country Pure Foods
Akron, OH.........................330-753-2293
Country Pure Foods
Akron, OH.........................877-995-8423
Greenwood Associates
Highland Park, IL..................847-579-5500
Gregory's Box'd Beverages
Newark, NJ 973-465-1113
Old Dutch Mustard Company
Great Neck, NY 516-466-0522
Old Orchard Brands
Sparta, MI 616-887-1745
Quality Brands
Deland, FL 888-676-2700
Smeltzer Orchard Company
Frankfort, MI 231-882-4421
Tree Top
Selah, WA 800-367-6571
Triple D Orchards
Empire, MI 866-781-9410

Glass-Packed

Bowman Apple Products Company
Mount Jackson, VA.................800-346-5382
Country Pure Foods
Akron, OH.........................877-995-8423
Emerling International Foods
Buffalo, NY.......................716-833-7381

Tree Top
Selah, WA 800-367-6571

Refrigerated

Bowman Apple Products Company
Mount Jackson, VA.................800-346-5382
Country Pure Foods
Akron, OH.........................877-995-8423

Apple Cider

American Purpac Technologies, LLC
Beloit, WI 877-787-7221
Clement Pappas & Company
Carneys Point, NJ 800-257-7019
Lost Trail Root Beer Com
Louisburg, KS.....................800-748-7765
Shawnee Canning Company
Cross Junction, VA 800-713-1414
Spotted Tavern Winery & Dodd's Cider Mill
Hartwood, VA.....................540-752-4453
Tree Top
Selah, WA 800-367-6571

Sparkling

Lost Trail Root Beer Com
Louisburg, KS.....................800-748-7765

Apricot

Country Pure Foods
Akron, OH.........................877-995-8423
Valley View Packing Company
San Jose, CA......................408-289-8300

Canned

Country Pure Foods
Akron, OH.........................877-995-8423
Emerling International Foods
Buffalo, NY.......................716-833-7381

Greenwood Associates
Highland Park, IL..................847-579-5500

Concentrate

Valley View Packing Company
San Jose, CA......................408-289-8300

Frozen

Country Pure Foods
Akron, OH.........................877-995-8423
Greenwood Associates
Highland Park, IL..................847-579-5500

Glass-Packed

Country Pure Foods
Akron, OH.........................877-995-8423
Emerling International Foods
Buffalo, NY.......................716-833-7381

Greenwood Associates
Highland Park, IL..................847-579-5500

Refrigerated

Country Pure Foods
Akron, OH.........................877-995-8423

Beet

Emerling International Foods
Buffalo, NY.......................716-833-7381

Vegetable Juices
Chicago, IL 888-776-9752

Blueberry

Blueberry Store
Grand Junction, MI.................877-654-2400
Clement Pappas & Company
Carneys Point, NJ 800-257-7019
Hazel Creek Orchards
Mt Airy, GA 706-754-4899

Carrot

Emerling International Foods
Buffalo, NY.......................716-833-7381

Post Familie Vineyards
Altus, AR 800-275-8423

Vegetable Juices
Chicago, IL 888-776-9752
William Bolthouse Farms
Bakersfield, CA 661-366-7270

Cherry

Cott Coporation
Tampa, FL 813-313-1800
Erba Food Products
Brooklyn, NY 718-272-7700
Greenwood Associates
Highland Park, IL 847-579-5500
Hazel Creek Orchards
Mt Airy, GA 706-754-4899
Knouse Foods Coop
Paw Paw, MI 269-657-5524
Langer Juice Company
City of Industry, CA 626-336-3100
M&B Fruit Juice Company
Akron, OH 330-253-7465
Manzana Products Company
Sebastopol, CA 707-823-5313
Manzanita Ranch
Julian, CA 760-765-0102
Merlinos
Canon City, CO 719-275-5558
Sunlike Juice
Scarborough, ON 416-297-1140
Tree Top
Selah, WA 800-367-6571

Bottled

Cott Coporation
Tampa, FL 813-313-1800

Boxed

Tree Top
Selah, WA 800-367-6571

Canned

Cott Coporation
Tampa, FL 813-313-1800
Emerling International Foods
Buffalo, NY 716-833-7381

We supply food manufacturers and food service customers worldwide (since 1988) with bulk ingredients including: Fruits & Vegetables; Juice Concentrates; Herbs & Spices; Oils & Vinegars; Flavors & Colors; Honey & Molasses. We also produce PURE MAPLE SYRUP.

Tree Top
Selah, WA 800-367-6571

Chilled

Tree Top
Selah, WA 800-367-6571

Concentrate

Cott Coporation
Tampa, FL 813-313-1800
Glcc Company
Paw Paw, MI 269-657-3167
Hemisphere Associated
Huntington, NY 631-673-3840

Frozen

Emerling International Foods
Buffalo, NY 716-833-7381

We supply food manufacturers and food service customers worldwide (since 1988) with bulk ingredients including: Fruits & Vegetables; Juice Concentrates; Herbs & Spices; Oils & Vinegars; Flavors & Colors; Honey & Molasses. We also produce PURE MAPLE SYRUP.

Milne Fruit Products
Prosser, WA 509-786-2611
Tree Top
Selah, WA 800-367-6571

Glass-Packed

Emerling International Foods
Buffalo, NY 716-833-7381

We supply food manufacturers and food service customers worldwide (since 1988) with bulk ingredients including: Fruits & Vegetables; Juice Concentrates; Herbs & Spices; Oils & Vinegars; Flavors & Colors; Honey & Molasses. We also produce PURE MAPLE SYRUP.

Greenwood Associates
Highland Park, IL 847-579-5500
Minute Maid Company
Atlanta, GA 800-438-2653
Peace River Citrus Products
Arcadia, FL 863-494-0440
Tree Top
Selah, WA 800-367-6571

Refrigerated

Country Pure Foods
Akron, OH 877-995-8423

Citrus Blends

A. Duda & Sons
Labelle, FL 800-440-3265
American Mercantile Corporation
Windermere, FL
Apac Chemical Corporation
Arcadia, CA 866-849-2722
Apple & Eve
Roslyn, NY 800-969-8018
Byesville Aseptics
Byesville, OH 740-685-2548
Citrus International
Winter Park, FL 407-629-8037
Citrus Service
Winter Garden, FL 407-656-4999
Country Pure Foods
Akron, OH 877-995-8423
Dairy Land
Macon, GA 478-742-6461
Emerling International Foods
Buffalo, NY 716-833-7381

We supply food manufacturers and food service customers worldwide (since 1988) with bulk ingredients including: Fruits & Vegetables; Juice Concentrates; Herbs & Spices; Oils & Vinegars; Flavors & Colors; Honey & Molasses. We also produce PURE MAPLE SYRUP.

Evans Properties
Dade City, FL 352-567-5662
Flagship Atlanta Dairy
Belleview, FL 800-224-0669
Florida's Natural Growers
Lake Wales, FL 888-657-6600
Fresh Juice Company
Newark, NJ 973-465-7100
Galliker Dairy
Johnstown, PA 800-477-6455
Green Spot Packaging
Claremont, CA 800-456-3210
Hansen's Juices
Azusa, CA 800-426-7367
Hi-Country Corona
Selah, WA 951-272-2600
Icy Bird
Sparta, TN 931-738-3557
Johanna Foods
Flemington, NJ 800-727-6700
Kendall Citrus Corporation
Goulds, FL 305-258-1628
Kennesaw Fruit & Juice
Pompano Beach, FL 800-949-0371
Key Colony/Red Parrot Juices
Lyons, IL 800-424-0868
Minute Maid Company
Atlanta, GA 800-438-2653
Mrs. Clark's Foods
Ankeny, IA 800-736-5674

Juices, salad dressings and sauces.

Orange-Co of Florida
Arcadia, FL 863-494-4939
Sales USA
Salado, TX 800-766-7344
Saratoga Beverage Group
Saratoga Springs, NY 888-426-8642
Silver Springs Citrus
Howey In the Hills, FL 800-940-2277
Southern Gardens Citrus Processing
Clewiston, FL 863-983-3030
Sun Orchard of Florida
Haines City, FL 877-875-8423
SunkiStreet Growers
Ontario, CA 800-225-3727
Sunlike Juice
Scarborough, ON 416-297-1140
Superbrand Dairies
Miami, FL 305-769-6600
T.G. Lee Dairy
Orlando, FL 407-894-4941
Ventura Coastal Corporation
Ventura, CA 805-653-7035
Winter Garden Citrus
Winter Garden, FL 407-656-4423
World Citrus
Winston Salem, NC 336-723-1863
World Citrus West
Lake Wales, FL 863-676-1411

Coconut

Coco Lopez
Miramar, FL 800-341-2242
Commodities Marketing, Inc.
Edison, NJ 732-603-5077

Concentrates

Chase Brothers Dairy
Oxnard, CA 800-438-6455
Citrus Citrosuco North America
Lake Wales, FL 800-356-4592
Citrus Service
Winter Garden, FL 407-656-4999
Coca-Cola Enterprises
Atlanta, GA 800-233-7210
Cott Coporation
Tampa, FL 813-313-1800
Daily Juice Products
Verona, PA 800-245-2929
David Michael & Company
Philadelphia, PA 800-363-5286
Del's Lemonade & Refreshments
Cranston, RI 401-463-6190
Delano Growers Grape Products
Delano, CA 661-725-3255
Fee Brothers
Rochester, NY 800-961-3337
Georgia Sun
Newnan, GA 770-251-2500
Gilette Foods
Union, NJ 908-688-0500
Glcc Company
Paw Paw, MI 269-657-3167
Global Citrus Resources
Lakeland, FL 863-647-9020
Green Spot Packaging
Claremont, CA 800-456-3210
Hemisphere Associated
Huntington, NY 631-673-3840
Hi-Country Corona
Selah, WA 951-272-2600
Imperial Flavors Beverage Company
Milwaukee, WI 414-536-7788
Indian River Foods
Fort Pierce, FL 772-462-2222
Kerr Concentrates
Salem, OR 800-910-5377
Lion Raisins
Selma, CA 559-834-6677
Louis Dreyfus Citrus
Winter Garden, FL 800-549-4272
Main Squeeze
Columbia, MO 573-817-5616
Maui Pineapple Company
Kahului, HI 808-877-3351
Maui Pineapple Company
Concord, CA 925-798-0240
Merci Spring Water
Maryland Heights, MO 314-872-9323
Minute Maid Company
Atlanta, GA 800-438-2653
Mountain Valley ProductsInc
Sunnyside, WA 509-837-8084
Northwest Naturals Corporation
Bothell, WA 425-881-2200
NTC Marketing Inc
Williamsville, NY 800-333-1637

Ocean Spray Cranberries
Vero Beach, FL 772-562-0800
Orange Bang
Sylmar, CA 818-833-1000
Pacific Coast Fruit Company
Portland, OR 503-234-6411
RFI Ingredients
Blauvelt, NY 800-962-7663
Rocket Products Company
Fenton, MO 800-325-9567
S&D Coffee, Inc
Concord, NC 704-782-3121
Sea Breeze Fruit Flavors
Towaco, NJ 800-732-2733
Silver Springs Citrus
Howey In the Hills, FL 800-940-2277
Sun Pac Foods
Brampton, ON 905-792-2700
Sun-Maid Growers of California
Kingsburg, CA 800-272-4746
Sunsweet Growers
Yuba City, CA 800-417-2253
Tone Products Company
Melrose Park, IL 708-681-3660
Tova Industries
Louisville, KY 888-532-8682
Tree Top
Selah, WA 800-367-6571
Tropicana
Bradenton, FL 800-237-7799
Valley Fig Growers
Fresno, CA 559-237-3893
Valley View Packing Company
San Jose, CA 408-289-8300
Vegetable Juices
Chicago, IL 888-776-9752
Vie-Del Company
Fresno, CA 559-834-2525
Vita-Pakt Citrus Company
Covina, CA 626-332-1101
Welch's Foods Inc
Concord, MA 800-340-6870
Welch's Foods Inc.
North East, PA 814-725-4577

Cranberry

Apple & Eve
Roslyn, NY 800-969-8018
Atoka Cranberries, Inc.
Manseau, Quebec, CN 819-356-2001
Clement Pappas & Company
Carneys Point, NJ 800-257-7019
Cott Coporation
Tampa, FL 813-313-1800
Country Pure Foods
Akron, OH 330-753-2293
Country Pure Foods
Akron, OH 877-995-8423
Delectable Gourmet LLC
Lindenhurst, NY 800-696-1350
Erba Food Products
Brooklyn, NY 718-272-7700
Gregory's Box'd Beverages
Newark, NJ 973-465-1113
Key Colony/Red Parrot Juices
Lyons, IL 800-424-0868
Langer Juice Company
City of Industry, CA 626-336-3100
McCutcheon's Apple Products
Frederick, MD 800-888-7537
Northland Cranberries
Wisconsin Rapids, WI 608-252-4714
Ocean Spray Cranberries
Kenosha, WI 262-694-5200
Ocean Spray Cranberries
Bordentown, NJ 609-298-0905
Old Orchard Brands
Sparta, MI 616-887-1745
Royal Kedem Food & Wine Company
Bayonne, NJ 201-437-9131
Smucker Quality Beverages
Havre De Grace, MD 410-939-1403
Sunlike Juice
Scarborough, ON 416-297-1140
Welch's Foods Inc
Concord, MA 800-340-6870

Bottled

Apple & Eve
Roslyn, NY 800-969-8018
Cott Coporation
Tampa, FL 813-313-1800
Northland Cranberries
Wisconsin Rapids, WI 608-252-4714

Boxed

Emerling International Foods
Buffalo, NY 716-833-7381

We supply food manufacturers and food service customers worldwide (since 1988) with bulk ingredients including: Fruits & Vegetables; Juice Concentrates; Herbs & Spices; Oils & Vinegars; Flavors & Colors; Honey & Molasses. We also produce PURE MAPLE SYRUP.

Ocean Spray Cranberries
Kenosha, WI 262-694-5200

Canned

Cott Coporation
Tampa, FL 813-313-1800
Country Pure Foods
Akron, OH 877-995-8423
Emerling International Foods
Buffalo, NY 716-833-7381

We supply food manufacturers and food service customers worldwide (since 1988) with bulk ingredients including: Fruits & Vegetables; Juice Concentrates; Herbs & Spices; Oils & Vinegars; Flavors & Colors; Honey & Molasses. We also produce PURE MAPLE SYRUP.

McCutcheon's Apple Products
Frederick, MD 800-888-7537
Ocean Spray Cranberries
Kenosha, WI 262-694-5200

Concentrate

Cott Coporation
Tampa, FL 813-313-1800
Glcc Company
Paw Paw, MI 269-657-3167
Hemisphere Associated
Huntington, NY 631-673-3840
Pacific Coast Fruit Company
Portland, OR 503-234-6411
Sea Breeze Fruit Flavors
Towaco, NJ 800-732-2733

Frozen

Country Pure Foods
Akron, OH 330-753-2293
Country Pure Foods
Akron, OH 877-995-8423
Gregory's Box'd Beverages
Newark, NJ 973-465-1113
Milne Fruit Products
Prosser, WA 509-786-2611
Ocean Spray Cranberries
Kenosha, WI 262-694-5200
Old Orchard Brands
Sparta, MI 616-887-1745

Glass-Packed

Country Pure Foods
Akron, OH 877-995-8423
Emerling International Foods
Buffalo, NY 716-833-7381

We supply food manufacturers and food service customers worldwide (since 1988) with bulk ingredients including: Fruits & Vegetables; Juice Concentrates; Herbs & Spices; Oils & Vinegars; Flavors & Colors; Honey & Molasses. We also produce PURE MAPLE SYRUP.

Ocean Spray Cranberries
Kenosha, WI 262-694-5200

Refrigerated

Country Pure Foods
Akron, OH 877-995-8423
Ocean Spray Cranberries
Kenosha, WI 262-694-5200

Dietetic

Boissons Miami Pomor
Longueuil, QC 877-977-3744

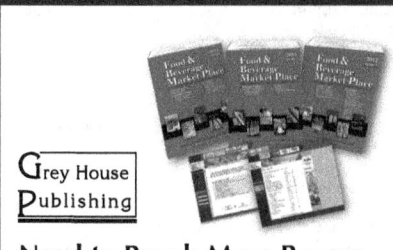

Florida Natural Flavors
Casselberry, FL 800-872-5979
H R Nicholson Company
Baltimore, MD 800-638-3514
Healthmate Products
Highland Park, IL 800-584-8642
Pride Beverages
Alpharetta, GA 770-663-0990
Southern Gardens Citrus Processing
Clewiston, FL 863-983-3030
Systems Bio-Industries
Langhorne, PA 215-702-1000

Drink

Concentrate

American Purpac Technologies, LLC
Beloit, WI 877-787-7221
Commodities Marketing, Inc.
Edison, NJ 732-603-5077

Fruit

A. Duda & Sons
Labelle, FL 800-440-3265
A. Lassonde, Inc.
Rougemont, QC 888-477-6663
Alca Trading Co.
Miami, FL 305-265-8331
All Juice Food & Beverage
Hendersonville, NC 800-736-5674
American Fruit Processors
Pacoima, CA 818-899-9574
American Mercantile Corporation
Windermere, FL
Apple & Eve
Roslyn, NY 800-969-8018
Aseltine Cider Company
Comstock Park, MI 616-784-7676
B.M. Lawrence & Company
San Francisco, CA 415-981-3650
Batavia Wine Cellars
Canandaigua, NY 585-396-7600
Birdseye Dairy
Green Bay, WI 920-494-5388
Brothers International Food Corporation
Rochester, NY 585-343-3007

Bully Hill Vineyards
Hammondsport, NY 607-868-3610
Burnette Foods
Hartford, MI 616-621-3181
Byesville Aseptics
Byesville, OH 740-685-2548
Cal India Foods International
Chino, CA 909-613-1660
California Day Fresh
Asusa, CA 877-858-4237
Carolina Products
Greer, SC 864-879-3084
Central Coca-Cola Bottling Company
Richmond, VA 800-359-3759
Century Foods International
Sparta, WI 800-269-1901
Ceres Fruit Juices
Markham, ON 800-905-1116
Chase Brothers Dairy
Oxnard, CA 800-438-6455
Chiquita Brands Intl. ional
Cincinnati, OH 800-438-0015
Citrus Citrosuco North America
Lake Wales, FL 800-356-4592
Coca-Cola Bottling Company
Honolulu, HI 808-839-6711
Cold Hollow Cider Mill
Waterbury Center, VT 800-327-7537
Consun Food Industries
Elyria, OH 440-322-6301
Cott Coporation
Tampa, FL 813-313-1800
Country Pure Foods
Akron, OH 330-753-2293
Crown Regal Wine Cellars
Brooklyn, NY 718-604-1430
Cutrale Citrus Juices
Leesburg, FL 352-728-7800
Cutrale Citrus Juices
Auburndale, FL 863-965-5000
Del's Lemonade & Refreshments
Cranston, RI 401-463-6190
Erba Food Products
Brooklyn, NY 718-272-7700
Everfresh Beverages
Warren, MI 586-755-9500
Fizzy Lizzy
New York, NY 800-203-9336
Flagship Atlanta Dairy
Belleview, FL 800-224-0669
Florida Fruit Juices
Chicago, IL 773-586-6200
Florida Juice Products
Lakeland, FL 863-802-4040
Florida Key West
Fort Myers, FL 239-694-8787
Four Chimneys Farm Winery Trust
Himrod, NY 607-243-7502
Galliker Dairy
Johnstown, PA 800-477-6455
Giacorelli Imports
Boca Raton, FL 561-451-1415
Global Beverage Company
Rochester, NY 585-381-3560
Global Marketing Associates
Schaumburg, IL 847-397-2350
Golden Town Apple Products
Rougemont, QC 519-599-6300
Great Western Juice Company
Maple Heights, OH 800-321-9180
Gregory's Box'd Beverages
Newark, NJ 973-465-1113
Hale Indian River Groves
Wabasso, FL 800-562-4502
Harrisburg Dairies
Harrisburg, PA 800-692-7429
Hawaii Coffee Company
Honolulu, HI 800-338-8353
Heck Cellars
Arvin, CA 661-854-6120
Heineman's Winery
Put In Bay, OH 419-285-2811
Heritage Farms Dairy
Murfreesboro, TN 615-895-2790
Hi-Country Corona
Selah, WA 951-272-2600
Hi-Country Foods Corporation
Selah, WA 509-697-7292
Hudson Valley Fruit Juice
Highland, NY 845-691-8061
Hygeia Dairy Company
Corpus Christi, TX 361-854-4561

Indian River Foods
Fort Pierce, FL 772-462-2222
Inn Foods
Watsonville, CA 831-724-2026
Jackson Milk & Ice CreamCompany
Hutchinson, KS 620-663-1244
Jersey Juice
Lebanon, NJ 609-406-0500
Kagome
Los Banos, CA 209-826-8850
Knouse Foods Coop
Paw Paw, MI 269-657-5524
Knouse Foods Coop
Peach Glen, PA 717-677-8181
Lakewood Juices
Miami, FL 305-324-5932
Langer Juice Company
City of Industry, CA 626-336-1666
Leeward Resources
Baltimore, MD 410-837-9003
Louis Dreyfus Citrus
Winter Garden, FL 800-549-4272
LPO/ LaDolc
Overland Park, KS 913-681-7757
Ludfords
Rancho Cucamonga, CA 909-948-0797
Madera Enterprises
Madera, CA 800-507-9555
Manzanita Ranch
Julian, CA 760-765-0102
Marva Maid Dairy
Newport News, VA 800-544-4439
Matanuska Maid Dairy
Anchorage, AK 907-561-5223
Maui Pineapple Company
Kahului, HI 808-877-3351
Maui Pineapple Company
Concord, CA 925-798-0240
Mayer Brothers
West Seneca, NY 800-696-2937
Mayer's Cider Mill
Webster, NY 800-543-0043
Mayfield Farms
Caledon, ON 905-846-0506
McArthur Dairy
Miami, FL 305-795-7700
McCutcheon's Apple Products
Frederick, MD 800-888-7537
Meduri Farms Inc.
Dallas, OR 503-623-0308
Meramec Vineyards
Saint James, MO 877-216-9463
Merlinos
Canon City, CO 719-275-5558
Minute Maid Company
Sugar Land, TX 281-302-4317
Minute Maid Company
Dunedin, FL 800-237-0159
Monarch Beverage Company
Atlanta, GA 800-241-3732
Mott's
Elmsford, NY
Mountain Valley ProductsInc
Sunnyside, WA 509-837-8084
Mrs. Denson's Cookie Company
Ukiah, CA 800-219-3199
Murray Cider Company Inc
Roanoke, VA 540-977-9000
Nana Mae's Organics
Sebastopol, CA 707-829-7359
Natalie's Orchard Island Juice
Fort Pierce, FL 772-465-1122
National Grape Cooperative
Westfield, NY 716-326-5200
Nestle Professional Vitality
Solon, OH 800-288-8682
Northland Cranberries
Jackson, WI 262-677-2221
Northland Cranberries
Wisconsin Rapids, WI 608-252-4714
Northwest Naturals Corporation
Bothell, WA 425-881-2200
NTC Marketing Inc
Williamsville, NY 800-333-1637
Ocean Spray Cranberries
Bordentown, NJ 609-298-0905
Ocean Spray Cranberries
Vero Beach, FL 772-562-0800
Oceana Foods
Shelby, MI 231-861-2141
Odwalla
Denver, CO 303-282-0500

Old Orchard Brands
Sparta, MI 616-887-1745
Paris Foods Corporation
Trappe, MD 410-476-3185
Point Group
Satellite Beach, FL 888-272-1249
Pokka Beverages
American Canyon, CA 800-972-5962
Prairie Farms Dairy
Carlinville, IL 217-854-2547
Prairie Farms Dairy Inc.
Carlinville, IL 217-854-2547
Premier Blending
Wichita, KS 316-267-5533
Premier Juices
Clearwater, FL 727-533-8200
Purity Dairies
Nashville, TN 615-244-1900
Quality Kitchen Corporation
Danbury, CT 203-744-2000
R.J. Corr Naturals
Posen, IL 708-389-4200
Rainbow Valley Orchards
Fallbrook, CA 760-728-2905
Ravifruit
Hackensack, NJ 201-939-5656
Reiter Dairy
Akron, OH 800-362-0825
Reiter Dairy
Springfield, OH 937-323-5777
Roberts Dairy Foods
Iowa City, IA
Rohtstein Corporation
Woburn, MA 781-935-8300
Rosenberger's Dairies
Hatfield, PA 800-355-9074
Royal Kedem Food & Wine Company
Bayonne, NJ 201-437-9131
Royal Wine Corp
Bayonne, NJ 718-384-2400
SANGARIA USA
Torrance, CA 310-530-2202
Saratoga Beverage Group
Saratoga Springs, NY 888-426-8642
Schneider Valley Farms Dairy
Williamsport, PA 570-326-2021
Schneider's Dairy Holdings Inc
Pittsburgh, PA 412-881-3525
Silver Springs Citrus
Howey In the Hills, FL 800-940-2277
Smart Juices
Bethlehem, PA 610-997-0500
Smeltzer Orchard Company
Frankfort, MI 231-882-4421
Smith Dairy Products Company
Orrville, OH 800-776-7076
Snapple Beverage Group
Ryebrook, NY 800-762-7753
Solana Gold Organics
Sebastopol, CA 800-459-1121
St. James Winery
Saint James, MO 800-280-9463
St. Julian Wine Company
Paw Paw, MI 800-732-6002
Stevens Tropical Plantation
West Palm Beach, FL 561-683-4701
Stevens Tropical Plantation
West Palm Beach, FL 800-785-1355
Stone Hill Wine Company
Hermann, MO 573-486-2221
Suiza Dairy Corporation
San Juan, PR 787-792-7300
Sun Pac Foods
Brampton, ON 905-792-2700
SunkiStreet Growers
Ontario, CA 800-225-3727
Sunlike Juice
Scarborough, ON 416-297-1140
Sunny Avocado
Jamul, CA 800-999-2862
Sunsweet Growers
Yuba City, CA 800-417-2253
Superbrand Dairies
Miami, FL 305-769-6600
Superstore Industries
Fairfield, CA 707-864-0502
Swiss Valley Farms Company
Davenport, IA 563-468-6600
Tamarack Farms Dairy
Newark, OH 866-221-4141
Tastee Apple Inc
Newcomerstown, OH 800-262-7753

Three Vee Food & Syrup Company
Brooklyn, NY 800-801-7330
Titusville Dairy Products
Titusville, PA 800-352-0101
Todhunter Foods
Lake Alfred, FL. . . . 863-956-1116
Toft Dairy
Sandusky, OH 800-521-4606
Tree Top
Selah, WA 800-542-4055
Treesweet Products
Houston, TX 281-876-3759
Tri-Boro Fruit Company
Fresno, CA 559-486-4141
Triple D Orchards
Empire, MI 866-781-9410
True Organic Products International
Miami, FL. . . . 800-487-0379
Valley Fig Growers
Fresno, CA 559-237-3893
Valley View Packing Company
San Jose, CA. . . . 408-289-8300
Velda Farms
North Miami Beach, FL 800-795-4649
Ventura Coastal Corporation
Ventura, CA. . . . 805-653-7035
Venture Vineyards
Lodi, NY. . . . 888-635-6277
Veryfine Products
Littleton, MA 800-837-9346
Welch's Foods Inc
Concord, MA 800-340-6870
Welch's Foods Inc.
North East, PA. . . . 814-725-4577
Wengert's Dairy
Lebanon, PA 800-222-2129
White Rock Products Corporation
Flushing, NY. . . . 800-969-7625
Widmer's Wine Cellars
Canandaigua, NY
Winmix/Natural Care Products
Englewood, FL 941-475-7432
World Citrus
Winston Salem, NC. . . . 336-723-1863
World Citrus West
Lake Wales, FL 863-676-1411
Yoder Dairies
Chesapeake, VA 757-482-4068

Bottled

Apple & Eve
Roslyn, NY 800-969-8018
Aseltine Cider Company
Comstock Park, MI. . . . 616-784-7676
Bully Hill Vineyards
Hammondsport, NY 607-868-3610
Carolina Products
Greer, SC. . . . 864-879-3084
Chiquita Brands Intl. ional
Cincinnati, OH 800-438-0015
Cott Coporation
Tampa, FL. . . . 813-313-1800
Langer Juice Company
City of Industry, CA 626-336-1666
Stevens Tropical Plantation
West Palm Beach, FL 800-785-1355

Canned

B.M. Lawrence & Company
San Francisco, CA 415-981-3650
Consun Food Industries
Elyria, OH. . . . 440-322-6301
Cott Coporation
Tampa, FL. . . . 813-313-1800
Hi-Country Corona
Selah, WA 951-272-2600
Langer Juice Company
City of Industry, CA 626-336-1666
McCutcheon's Apple Products
Frederick, MD. . . . 800-888-7537
Northland Cranberries
Jackson, WI. . . . 262-677-2221
Oceana Foods
Shelby, MI. . . . 231-861-2141
SANGARIA USA
Torrance, CA. . . . 310-530-2202
SEW Friel
Queenstown, MD 410-827-8811
Silver Springs Citrus
Howey In the Hills, FL. . . . 800-940-2277
Sun Pac Foods
Brampton, ON. . . . 905-792-2700
Triple D Orchards
Empire, MI 866-781-9410

Concentrate

Citrus Citrosuco North America
Lake Wales, FL. . . . 800-356-4592
Cutrale Citrus Juices
Leesburg, FL. . . . 352-728-7800
Glcc Company
Paw Paw, MI. . . . 269-657-3167
Green Spot Packaging
Claremont, CA 800-456-3210
Hemisphere Associated
Huntington, NY 631-673-3840
Hi-Country Corona
Selah, WA 951-272-2600
Louis Dreyfus Citrus
Winter Garden, FL 800-549-4272
Mountain Valley ProductsInc
Sunnyside, WA 509-837-8084
Ocean Spray Cranberries
Vero Beach, FL. . . . 772-562-0800
Pacific Coast Fruit Company
Portland, OR 503-234-6411
Sea Breeze Fruit Flavors
Towaco, NJ 800-732-2733
Tree Top
Selah, WA 800-542-4055
Valley Fig Growers
Fresno, CA 559-237-3893
Valley View Packing Company
San Jose, CA. . . . 408-289-8300

Frozen

California Day Fresh
Asusa, CA. . . . 877-858-4237
Citrus Citrosuco North America
Lake Wales, FL. . . . 800-356-4592
Country Pure Foods
Akron, OH. . . . 330-753-2293
Del's Lemonade & Refreshments
Cranston, RI 401-463-6190
Emerling International Foods
Buffalo, NY. . . . 716-833-7381

We supply food manufacturers and food service customers worldwide (since 1988) with bulk ingredients including: Fruits & Vegetables; Juice Concentrates; Herbs & Spices; Oils & Vinegars; Flavors & Colors; Honey & Molasses. We also produce PURE MAPLE SYRUP.

Florida Natural Flavors
Casselberry, FL. . . . 800-872-5979
Florida's Natural Growers
Lake Wales, FL. . . . 888-657-6600
Greenwood Associates
Highland Park, IL 847-579-5500
Gregory's Box'd Beverages
Newark, NJ 973-465-1113
Harrisburg Dairies
Harrisburg, PA 800-692-7429
Hi-Country Corona
Selah, WA 951-272-2600
Indian River Foods
Fort Pierce, FL 772-462-2222
Inn Foods
Watsonville, CA 831-724-2026
Jackson Milk & Ice CreamCompany
Hutchinson, KS. . . . 620-663-1244
Maui Pineapple Company
Concord, CA. . . . 925-798-0240
Minute Maid Company
Atlanta, GA. . . . 800-438-2653
Old Orchard Brands
Sparta, MI 616-887-1745
Paris Foods Corporation
Trappe, MD. . . . 410-476-3185
Saratoga Beverage Group
Saratoga Springs, NY 888-426-8642
Smeltzer Orchard Company
Frankfort, MI 231-882-4421
Tree Top
Selah, WA 800-367-6571
Triple D Orchards
Empire, MI 866-781-9410
Unique Ingredients
Naches, WA. . . . 509-653-1991
Wild Fruitz Beverages
Ambler, PA 888-688-7632

Glass-Packed

Northland Cranberries
Jackson, WI. . . . 262-677-2221

Refrigerated

Chiquita Brands Intl. ional
Cincinnati, OH 800-438-0015
Consun Food Industries
Elyria, OH. . . . 440-322-6301
Silver Springs Citrus
Howey In the Hills, FL. . . . 800-940-2277

Fruit & Vegetable

Aileen Quirk & Sons
Kansas City, MO. . . . 816-471-4580
Alamance Foods/Triton Water Company
Burlington, NC 800-476-9111
Alljuice
Hendersonville, NC 800-736-5674
Apple & Eve
Roslyn, NY 800-969-8018
Arcadia Dairy Farms
Arden, NC. . . . 828-684-3556
Astral Extracts Ltd.
Syosset, NY. . . . 516-496-2505
Barbe's Dairy
Westwego, LA. . . . 504-347-6201
Beckman & Gast Company
Saint Henry, OH 419-678-4195
Bevco
Surrey, BC. . . . 800-663-0090
Beverage Capital Corporation
Baltimore, MD 410-242-7003
Blue Moon Foods
White River Junction, VT. . . . 802-295-1165
Bowman Apple Products Company
Mount Jackson, VA. . . . 800-346-5382
Brooklyn Bottling Company
Milton, NY 845-795-2171
Burnette Foods
Hartford, MI 616-621-3181
Byesville Aseptics
Byesville, OH 740-685-2548
Cal-Tex Citrus Juice
Houston, TX 800-231-0133
California Day Fresh
Asusa, CA. . . . 877-858-4237
Campbell Soup Company
Camden, NJ. . . . 800-257-8443
Citrus Citrosuco North America
Lake Wales, FL. . . . 800-356-4592
Community Orchard
Fort Dodge, IA 515-573-8212
ConAgra Grocery Products
Irvine, CA 714-680-1000
Country Pure Foods
Akron, OH. . . . 330-753-2293
Country Pure Foods
Akron, OH. . . . 877-995-8423
Dean Dairy Products
Sharpsville, PA 800-942-8096
Florida Bottling
Miami, FL. . . . 305-324-5932
Florida's Natural Growers
Lake Wales, FL. . . . 888-657-6600
Fresh Juice Company
Newark, NJ 973-465-7100
Fresh Samantha
Saco, ME. . . . 800-658-4635
Freshco
Stuart, FL 888-373-7426
Golden State Vintners
Cutler, CA. . . . 559-528-3033
Great Western Juice Company
Maple Heights, OH. . . . 800-321-9180
Greenwood Associates
Highland Park, IL 847-579-5500
H.R. Nicholson Company
Baltimore, MD 800-638-3514
Hanover Foods Corporation
Hanover, PA 717-632-6000
Hansen's Juices
Azusa, CA. . . . 800-426-7367
Hudson Valley Fruit Juice
Highland, NY 845-691-8061
Icy Bird
Sparta, TN. . . . 931-738-3557
J.M. Smucker
Havre De Grace, MD 410-939-1403

Jackson Milk & Ice CreamCompany
Hutchinson, KS 620-663-1244
Jel-Sert Company
West Chicago, IL 800-323-2592
Key Colony/Red Parrot Juices
Lyons, IL 800-424-0868
Lane's Dairy
El Paso, TX 915-772-6700
Langer Juice Company
City of Industry, CA 626-336-3100
LeHigh Valley Dairies
Lansdale, PA 215-855-8205
Lenox-Martell
Boston, MA 617-442-7777
Leonard Fountain Specialties
Detroit, MI 313-891-4141
Louis Trauth Dairy
Newport, KY 800-544-6455
Lucerne Foods
Taber, AB 403-223-3546
M&B Fruit Juice Company
Akron, OH 330-253-7465
Manzana Products Company
Sebastopol, CA 707-823-5313
Marcus Dairy
Danbury, CT 800-243-2511
Mayfield Farms
Caledon, ON 905-846-0506
McArthur Dairy
Miami, FL 877-803-6565
Meier's Wine Cellars
Cincinnati, OH 800-346-2941
Minute Maid Company
Atlanta, GA 800-438-2653
Mrs. Clark's Foods
Ankeny, IA 800-736-5674

Juices, salad dressings and sauces.

Noel Corporation
Yakima, WA 509-248-4545
Ocean Spray Cranberries
Kenosha, WI 262-694-5200
Ocean Spray Cranberries
Lakeville-Middleboro, MA 800-662-3263
Odwalla
Denver, CO 303-282-0500
Old Dutch Mustard Company
Great Neck, NY 516-466-0522
Olympic Foods
Spokane, WA 509-455-8059
Pavich Family Farms
Bakersfield, CA 661-782-8700
Peace River Citrus Products
Arcadia, FL 863-494-0440
Plaidberry Company
Vista, CA 760-727-5403
Post Familie Vineyards
Altus, AR 800-275-8423
Quality Brands
Deland, FL 888-676-2700
Ray Brothers & Noble Canning Company
Hobbs, IN 765-675-7451
Red Gold
Elwood, IN 877-748-9798
RFI Ingredients
Blauvelt, NY 800-962-7663
Sales USA
Salado, TX 800-766-7344
Schepps Dairy
Dallas, TX 800-395-7004
SEW Friel
Queenstown, MD 410-827-8811
Smucker Quality Beverages
Havre De Grace, MD 410-939-1403
Smucker Quality Beverages
Chico, CA 530-899-5000
Southern Gardens Citrus Processing
Clewiston, FL 863-983-3030
SunkiStreet Growers
Ontario, CA 800-225-3727
Tamarack Farms Dairy
Newark, OH 866-221-4141
Tastee Apple Inc
Newcomerstown, OH 800-262-7753
Tree Top
Selah, WA 800-367-6571
Truesdale Packaging Company
Warrenton, MO 636-456-6800
Ultra Seal
New Paltz, NY 845-255-2490
Unique Ingredients
Naches, WA 509-653-1991
United Dairy
Uniontown, PA 800-966-6455
Vegetable Juices
Chicago, IL 888-776-9752
Welch's Foods Inc
Kennewick, WA 509-582-2131
Welch's Foods Inc
Westfield, NY 716-326-5252
Winder Dairy
West Valley, UT 800-946-3371

Bottled

Apple & Eve
Roslyn, NY 800-969-8018
Beverage Capital Corporation
Baltimore, MD 410-242-7003
Clement Pappas & Company
Carneys Point, NJ 800-257-7019
Odwalla
Denver, CO 303-282-0500
Polar Beverages
Worcester, MA 800-734-9800
Truesdale Packaging Company
Warrenton, MO 636-456-6800

Canned

B.M. Lawrence & Company
San Francisco, CA 415-981-3650
Beverage Capital Corporation
Baltimore, MD 410-242-7003
Burnette Foods
Hartford, MI 616-621-3181
Polar Beverages
Worcester, MA 800-734-9800
SEW Friel
Queenstown, MD 410-827-8811
Truesdale Packaging Company
Warrenton, MO 636-456-6800

Concentrate

American Purpac Technologies, LLC
Beloit, WI 877-787-7221
Astral Extracts Ltd.
Syosset, NY 516-496-2505
Citrus Citrosuco North America
Lake Wales, FL 800-356-4592
Emerling International Foods
Buffalo, NY 716-833-7381

We supply food manufacturers and food service customers worldwide (since 1988) with bulk ingredients including: Fruits & Vegetables; Juice Concentrates; Herbs & Spices; Oils & Vinegars; Flavors & Colors; Honey & Molasses. We also produce PURE MAPLE SYRUP.

Frozen

Citrus Citrosuco North America
Lake Wales, FL 800-356-4592
Country Pure Foods
Akron, OH 330-753-2293
Ludfords
Rancho Cucamonga, CA 909-948-0797

Glass-Packed

Burnette Foods
Hartford, MI 616-621-3181

Fruit Punch

Arizona Beverage Company
Woodbury, NY 800-832-3775
Barber's Dairy
Birmingham, AL 205-942-2351
Erba Food Products
Brooklyn, NY 718-272-7700
Minute Maid Company
Dunedin, FL 800-237-0159
Prairie Farms Dairy
O Fallon, IL 618-632-3632
Reilly Dairy & Food Company
Tampa, FL 813-839-8458
Reiter Dairy
Springfield, OH 937-323-5777
Rocket Products Company
Fenton, MO 800-325-9567
Sinton Dairy Foods Company
Colorado Springs, CO 800-388-4970
Sunlike Juice
Scarborough, ON 416-297-1140
Trailblazer Food Products
Portland, OR 800-777-7179

Concentrate

Mayer Brothers
West Seneca, NY 800-696-2937

Garlic

Emerling International Foods
Buffalo, NY 716-833-7381

We supply food manufacturers and food service customers worldwide (since 1988) with bulk ingredients including: Fruits & Vegetables; Juice Concentrates; Herbs & Spices; Oils & Vinegars; Flavors & Colors; Honey & Molasses. We also produce PURE MAPLE SYRUP.

Howard Foods
Danvers, MA 978-774-6207
Vegetable Juices
Chicago, IL 888-776-9752

Grape

A.W. Jantzi & Sons
Wellesley, ON 519-656-2400
Arcadia Dairy Farms
Arden, NC 828-684-3556
Bully Hill Vineyards
Hammondsport, NY 607-868-3610
Clement Pappas & Company
Carneys Point, NJ 800-257-7019
Cott Coporation
Tampa, FL 813-313-1800
Country Pure Foods
Ellington, CT 860-872-8346
Country Pure Foods
Akron, OH 877-995-8423
Crown Regal Wine Cellars
Brooklyn, NY 718-604-1430
Everfresh Beverages
Warren, MI 586-755-9500
Florida Fruit Juices
Chicago, IL 773-586-6200
Florida's Natural Growers
Lake Wales, FL 888-657-6600
Four Chimneys Farm Winery Trust
Himrod, NY 607-243-7502
Golden State Vintners
Cutler, CA 559-528-3033
Green Spot Packaging
Claremont, CA 800-456-3210
Greenwood Associates
Highland Park, IL 847-579-5500
Growers Cooperative Grape Juice Company
Westfield, NY 716-326-3161
Hillcrest Orchard
Lake Placid, FL 865-397-5273
Knouse Foods Coop
Peach Glen, PA 717-677-8181
Langer Juice Company
City of Industry, CA 626-336-3100
M&B Fruit Juice Company
Akron, OH 330-253-7465
Madera Enterprises
Madera, CA 800-507-9555
Manzana Products Company
Sebastopol, CA 707-823-5313
Manzanita Ranch
Julian, CA 760-765-0102
Mayer Brothers
West Seneca, NY 800-696-2937
Mayer's Cider Mill
Webster, NY 800-543-0043
McArthur Dairy
Miami, FL 305-795-7700
McCutcheon's Apple Products
Frederick, MD 800-888-7537
Meier's Wine Cellars
Cincinnati, OH 800-346-2941
Meramec Vineyards
Saint James, MO 877-216-9463
Merlinos
Canon City, CO 719-275-5558
Minute Maid Company
Atlanta, GA 800-438-2653
Paklab Products
Boucherville, QC 888-946-3233
Post Familie Vineyards
Altus, AR 800-275-8423

Prairie Farms Dairy
O Fallon, IL. 618-632-3632
Royal Kedem Food & Wine Company
Bayonne, NJ 201-437-9131
Royal Wine Corp
Bayonne, NJ 718-384-2400
SEW Friel
Queenstown, MD 410-827-8811
Smucker Quality Beverages
Havre De Grace, MD 410-939-1403
St. James Winery
Saint James, MO. 800-280-9463
St. Julian Wine Company
Paw Paw, MI. 800-732-6002
Sunlike Juice
Scarborough, ON 416-297-1140
Tree Top
Selah, WA 800-542-4055
True Organic Products International
Miami, FL. 800-487-0379
Venture Vineyards
Lodi, NY. 888-635-6277
Welch's Foods Inc
Kennewick, WA 509-582-2131
Welch's Foods Inc
Concord, MA 800-340-6870
Widmer's Wine Cellars
Canandaigua, NY

Bottled

Cott Coporation
Tampa, FL. 813-313-1800
Northland Cranberries
Wisconsin Rapids, WI 608-252-4714
R.A.B. Food Group LLC
Secaucus, NJ. 201-553-1100
Sunlike Juice
Scarborough, ON 416-297-1140
Welch's Foods Inc
Kennewick, WA 509-582-2131
Widmer's Wine Cellars
Canandaigua, NY

Boxed

American Purpac Technologies, LLC
Beloit, WI 877-787-7221
Cloverland Green Spring Dairy
Baltimore, MD 800-876-6455
Welch's Foods Inc
Kennewick, WA 509-582-2131

Canned

American Purpac Technologies, LLC
Beloit, WI 877-787-7221
Cott Coporation
Tampa, FL. 813-313-1800
Country Pure Foods
Akron, OH. 877-995-8423
Emerling International Foods
Buffalo, NY. 716-833-7381

We supply food manufacturers and food service customers worldwide (since 1988) with bulk ingredients including: Fruits & Vegetables; Juice Concentrates; Herbs & Spices; Oils & Vinegars; Flavors & Colors; Honey & Molasses. We also produce PURE MAPLE SYRUP.

Growers Cooperative Grape Juice Company
Westfield, NY 716-326-3161
McCutcheon's Apple Products
Frederick, MD. 800-888-7537
SEW Friel
Queenstown, MD 410-827-8811
Unique Ingredients
Naches, WA. 509-653-1991
Welch's Foods Inc
Kennewick, WA 509-582-2131

Chilled

American Purpac Technologies, LLC
Beloit, WI 877-787-7221
Emerling International Foods
Buffalo, NY. 716-833-7381

We supply food manufacturers and food service customers worldwide (since 1988) with bulk ingredients including: Fruits & Vegetables; Juice Concentrates; Herbs & Spices; Oils & Vinegars; Flavors & Colors; Honey & Molasses. We also produce PURE MAPLE SYRUP.

Welch's Foods Inc
Kennewick, WA 509-582-2131

Concentrate

Cott Coporation
Tampa, FL. 813-313-1800
Glcc Company
Paw Paw, MI. 269-657-3167
Green Spot Packaging
Claremont, CA 800-456-3210
Hemisphere Associated
Huntington, NY 631-673-3840
Louis Dreyfus Citrus
Winter Garden, FL 800-549-4272
Mayer Brothers
West Seneca, NY 800-696-2937
Mountain Valley ProductsInc
Sunnyside, WA 509-837-8084
Paklab Products
Boucherville, QC 888-946-3233
Sun Pac Foods
Brampton, ON. 905-792-2700
Tree Top
Selah, WA 800-542-4055

Frozen

American Purpac Technologies, LLC
Beloit, WI 877-787-7221
Country Pure Foods
Akron, OH. 877-995-8423
Emerling International Foods
Buffalo, NY. 716-833-7381

We supply food manufacturers and food service customers worldwide (since 1988) with bulk ingredients including: Fruits & Vegetables; Juice Concentrates; Herbs & Spices; Oils & Vinegars; Flavors & Colors; Honey & Molasses. We also produce PURE MAPLE SYRUP.

Growers Cooperative Grape Juice Company
Westfield, NY 716-326-3161
Louis Dreyfus Citrus
Winter Garden, FL 800-549-4272
Milne Fruit Products
Prosser, WA. 509-786-2611
Welch's Foods Inc
Kennewick, WA 509-582-2131

Glass-Packed

American Purpac Technologies, LLC
Beloit, WI 877-787-7221
Country Pure Foods
Akron, OH. 877-995-8423
Emerling International Foods
Buffalo, NY. 716-833-7381

We supply food manufacturers and food service customers worldwide (since 1988) with bulk ingredients including: Fruits & Vegetables; Juice Concentrates; Herbs & Spices; Oils & Vinegars; Flavors & Colors; Honey & Molasses. We also produce PURE MAPLE SYRUP.

Growers Cooperative Grape Juice Company
Westfield, NY 716-326-3161
Unique Ingredients
Naches, WA. 509-653-1991
Welch's Foods Inc
Kennewick, WA 509-582-2131

Refrigerated

Country Pure Foods
Akron, OH. 877-995-8423

Grapefruit

American Mercantile Corporation
Windermere, FL
Clement Pappas & Company
Carneys Point, NJ 800-257-7019
Cott Coporation
Tampa, FL. 813-313-1800
Country Pure Foods
Akron, OH. 330-753-2293
Country Pure Foods
Akron, OH. 877-995-8423
Cropp Cooperative-Organic Valley
La Farge, WI. 888-444-6455
Cutrale Citrus Juices
Auburndale, FL. 863-965-5000
Florida Fruit Juices
Chicago, IL 773-586-6200
Florida Juice Products
Lakeland, FL. 863-802-4040
Freshco
Stuart, FL 888-373-7426
Gene's Citrus Ranch
Sarasota, FL 888-723-2006
Great Western Juice Company
Maple Heights, OH. 800-321-9180
Greenwood Associates
Highland Park, IL 847-579-5500
Gregory's Box'd Beverages
Newark, NJ 973-465-1113
Hi-Country Corona
Selah, WA 951-272-2600
Indian River Foods
Fort Pierce, FL 772-462-2222
Kennesaw Fruit & Juice
Pompano Beach, FL 800-949-0371
Louis Dreyfus Citrus
Winter Garden, FL 800-549-4272
Marva Maid Dairy
Newport News, VA. 800-544-4439
Mayer Brothers
West Seneca, NY 800-696-2937
Minute Maid Company
Sugar Land, TX. 281-302-4317
Minute Maid Company
Dunedin, FL 800-237-0159
Minute Maid Company
Atlanta, GA. 800-438-2653
Natalie's Orchard Island Juice
Fort Pierce, FL 772-465-1122

Ocean Spray Cranberries
Vero Beach, FL 772-562-0800
Ocean Spray Cranberries
Lakeville-Middleboro, MA 800-662-3263
Perricone Juices
Beaumont, CA. . . . 951-769-7171
Quality Kitchen Corporation
Danbury, CT 203-744-2000
Rainbow Valley Orchards
Fallbrook, CA 760-728-2905
Reiter Dairy
Springfield, OH. . . . 937-323-5777
Saratoga Beverage Group
Saratoga Springs, NY 888-426-8642
Silver Springs Citrus
Howey In the Hills, FL. . . . 800-940-2277
Sun Orchard
Tempe, AZ 800-505-8423
Sunlike Juice
Scarborough, ON 416-297-1140
Superbrand Dairies
Miami, FL. . . . 305-769-6600
Tropicana
Bradenton, FL. . . . 800-237-7799
World Citrus West
Lake Wales, FL. . . . 863-676-1411
Yoder Dairies
Chesapeake, VA 757-482-4068

Bottled

Cott Coporation
Tampa, FL. . . . 813-313-1800
Northland Cranberries
Wisconsin Rapids, WI 608-252-4714

Boxed

American Purpac Technologies, LLC
Beloit, WI 877-787-7221
Emerling International Foods
Buffalo, NY. . . . 716-833-7381

We supply food manufacturers and food service customers worldwide (since 1988) with bulk ingredients including: Fruits & Vegetables; Juice Concentrates; Herbs & Spices; Oils & Vinegars; Flavors & Colors; Honey & Molasses. We also produce PURE MAPLE SYRUP.

Canned

American Purpac Technologies, LLC
Beloit, WI 877-787-7221
Country Pure Foods
Akron, OH. . . . 877-995-8423
Emerling International Foods
Buffalo, NY. . . . 716-833-7381

We supply food manufacturers and food service customers worldwide (since 1988) with bulk ingredients including: Fruits & Vegetables; Juice Concentrates; Herbs & Spices; Oils & Vinegars; Flavors & Colors; Honey & Molasses. We also produce PURE MAPLE SYRUP.

Hi-Country Corona
Selah, WA 951-272-2600
Ocean Spray Cranberries
Lakeville-Middleboro, MA 800-662-3263

Concentrate

Cott Coporation
Tampa, FL. . . . 813-313-1800
Georgia Sun
Newnan, GA 770-251-2500
Hi-Country Corona
Selah, WA 951-272-2600
Ocean Spray Cranberries
Vero Beach, FL. . . . 772-562-0800
Sea Breeze Fruit Flavors
Towaco, NJ 800-732-2733
Sun Pac Foods
Brampton, ON. . . . 905-792-2700

Frozen

A. Duda Farm Fresh Foods
Belle Glade, FL. . . . 561-996-7621
American Purpac Technologies, LLC
Beloit, WI 877-787-7221
Country Pure Foods
Akron, OH. . . . 330-753-2293
Country Pure Foods
Akron, OH. . . . 877-995-8423
Emerling International Foods
Buffalo, NY. . . . 716-833-7381

We supply food manufacturers and food service customers worldwide (since 1988) with bulk ingredients including: Fruits & Vegetables; Juice Concentrates; Herbs & Spices; Oils & Vinegars; Flavors & Colors; Honey & Molasses. We also produce PURE MAPLE SYRUP.

Hi-Country Corona
Selah, WA 951-272-2600
Ocean Spray Cranberries
Lakeville-Middleboro, MA 800-662-3263

Glass-Packed

American Purpac Technologies, LLC
Beloit, WI 877-787-7221
Country Pure Foods
Akron, OH. . . . 877-995-8423
Emerling International Foods
Buffalo, NY. . . . 716-833-7381

We supply food manufacturers and food service customers worldwide (since 1988) with bulk ingredients including: Fruits & Vegetables; Juice Concentrates; Herbs & Spices; Oils & Vinegars; Flavors & Colors; Honey & Molasses. We also produce PURE MAPLE SYRUP.

Ocean Spray Cranberries
Lakeville-Middleboro, MA 800-662-3263

Refrigerated

American Purpac Technologies, LLC
Beloit, WI 877-787-7221
Country Pure Foods
Akron, OH. . . . 877-995-8423
Ocean Spray Cranberries
Lakeville-Middleboro, MA 800-662-3263

Guava

Meadow Gold Dairies
Honolulu, HI. . . . 800-362-8531
Stevens Tropical Plantation
West Palm Beach, FL 561-683-4701

Key Lime

Florida Key West
Fort Myers, FL 239-694-8787

Lemon

Agrocan
Ville St Laurent, QC 877-247-6226
American Purpac Technologies, LLC
Beloit, WI 877-787-7221
Castella Imports
Hauppauge, NY 866-227-8355
Clement Pappas & Company
Carneys Point, NJ 800-257-7019
Erba Food Products
Brooklyn, NY 718-272-7700
Florida Key West
Fort Myers, FL 239-694-8787
Greenwood Associates
Highland Park, IL 847-579-5500
Hansen's Juices
Azusa, CA. . . . 800-426-7367
Hi-Country Corona
Selah, WA 951-272-2600
Jus-Made
Dallas, TX. . . . 800-969-3746
Louis Dreyfus Citrus
Winter Garden, FL 800-549-4272
Minute Maid Company
Atlanta, GA. . . . 800-438-2653
Natalie's Orchard Island Juice
Fort Pierce, FL 772-465-1122
Nielsen Citrus Products
Huntington Beach, CA 714-892-5586
Perricone Juices
Beaumont, CA. . . . 951-769-7171
Prairie Farms Dairy
O Fallon, IL. . . . 618-632-3632
Rainbow Valley Orchards
Fallbrook, CA 760-728-2905
Reiter Dairy
Springfield, OH. . . . 937-323-5777
Sun Orchard
Tempe, AZ 800-505-8423
Village Imports
Brisbane, CA. . . . 888-865-8714

Bottled

Cott Coporation
Tampa, FL. . . . 813-313-1800

Canned

American Purpac Technologies, LLC
Beloit, WI 877-787-7221
Cott Coporation
Tampa, FL. . . . 813-313-1800
Emerling International Foods
Buffalo, NY. . . . 716-833-7381

We supply food manufacturers and food service customers worldwide (since 1988) with bulk ingredients including: Fruits & Vegetables; Juice Concentrates; Herbs & Spices; Oils & Vinegars; Flavors & Colors; Honey & Molasses. We also produce PURE MAPLE SYRUP.

Hi-Country Corona
Selah, WA 951-272-2600

Concentrate

Citrico
Northbrook, IL 888-625-8516
Cott Coporation
Tampa, FL. . . . 813-313-1800
Hi-Country Corona
Selah, WA 951-272-2600
Louis Dreyfus Citrus
Winter Garden, FL 800-549-4272

Frozen

American Purpac Technologies, LLC
Beloit, WI 877-787-7221
Emerling International Foods
Buffalo, NY. . . . 716-833-7381

We supply food manufacturers and food service customers worldwide (since 1988) with bulk ingredients including: Fruits & Vegetables; Juice Concentrates; Herbs & Spices; Oils & Vinegars; Flavors & Colors; Honey & Molasses. We also produce PURE MAPLE SYRUP.

Hi-Country Corona
Selah, WA 951-272-2600
Louis Dreyfus Citrus
Winter Garden, FL 800-549-4272
Nielsen Citrus Products
Huntington Beach, CA 714-892-5586

Glass-Packed

American Purpac Technologies, LLC
Beloit, WI 877-787-7221
Emerling International Foods
Buffalo, NY. . . . 716-833-7381

We supply food manufacturers and food service customers worldwide (since 1988) with bulk ingredients including: Fruits & Vegetables; Juice Concentrates; Herbs & Spices; Oils & Vinegars; Flavors & Colors; Honey & Molasses. We also produce PURE MAPLE SYRUP.

Refrigerated

American Purpac Technologies, LLC
Beloit, WI 877-787-7221

Lemonade

Anderson Erickson Dairy
Des Moines, IA. . . . 515-265-2521
Calvert's
El Paso, TX. . . . 888-472-5727
Clement Pappas & Company
Carneys Point, NJ 800-257-7019
Del's Lemonade & Refreshments
Cranston, RI 401-463-6190
Jones Soda Company
Seattle, WA 800-656-6050
M&B Fruit Juice Company
Akron, OH. . . . 330-253-7465
Mh Zeigler & Sons
Lansdale, PA 215-855-5161

Naterl
St. Bruno, QC 450-653-3655
Newman's Own
Westport, CT. 203-222-0136
Prairie Farms Dairy
O Fallon, IL. 618-632-3632
Rocket Products Company
Fenton, MO. 800-325-9567
Sunlike Juice
Scarborough, ON 416-297-1140
Sweet Leaf Tea Company
Austin, TX. 512-328-7775

Concentrate

A. Duda Farm Fresh Foods
Belle Glade, FL. 561-996-7621
ADM Ethanol Sales
Decatur, IL 800-637-5843
Anheuser-Busch
Cartersville, GA 770-386-2000
Baltimore Brewing Company
Baltimore, MD 410-837-5000
Beaulieu Vineyard
Rutherford, CA 800-264-6918
Beaver Street Brewery
Flagstaff, AZ. 928-779-0079
Bow Valley Brewing Company
Canmore, AB 403-678-2739
Brasserie Brasel Brewery
Lasalle, QC 800-463-2728
Bravard Vineyards & Winery
Hopkinsville, KY 270-269-2583
Clipper City Brewing
Baltimore, MD 410-247-7822
Cold Spring Brewing Company
Cold Spring, MN 320-685-8686
Creemore Springs Brewery
Creemore, ON. 800-267-2240
Dogfish Head Craft Brewery
Lewes, DE. 888-834-3474
Golden State Vintners
Cutler, CA. 559-528-3033
Great Lakes Brewing
Etobicoke, ON 800-463-5435
Great Northern Brewing Company
Whitefish, MT. 406-863-1000
Great Western Brewing Company
Saskatoon, SK. 800-764-4492
Hogtown Brewing Company
Mississauga, ON. 905-855-9065
Kamloops Brewing Co
Kamloops, BC. 250-851-2543
Labatt Breweries
Edmonton, AB 800-268-2997
Labatt Brewing Company
Creston, BC. 250-428-9344
Lakefront Brewery
Milwaukee, WI. 414-372-8800
Makers Mark Distillery
Loretto, KY. 270-865-2881
Mayer Brothers
West Seneca, NY 800-696-2937
Mendocino Brewing Company
Ukiah, CA. 707-463-2087
MillerCoors
Irwindale, CA
MillerCoors
Eden, NC. 336-627-2100
MillerCoors
Fort Worth, TX 800-645-5376
MillerCoors
Trenton, OH 800-944-5483
Millstream Brewing
Amana, IA. 319-622-3672
Minute Maid Company
Atlanta, GA. 800-438-2653
Monticello Cellars
Napa, CA. 707-253-2802
Moosehead Breweries Ltd.
St. John, NB 877-888-2337
Natural Wonder Foods Inc
Brooklyn, NY
Pennsylvania Brewing Company
Pittsburgh, PA. 412-237-9400
Santa Cruz Brewing Company
Santa Cruz, CA 831-425-1182
Sapporo
New York, NY 800-827-8234
Sebastiani Vineyards
Sonoma, CA 800-888-5532
Shipyard Brewing Company
Portland, ME. 800-789-0684

Tabernash Brewing Company
Longmont, CO 303-772-0258
Unibroue/Unibrew Sleeman Unibroue
Chambly, QC. 450-658-7658

Lime

American Purpac Technologies, LLC
Beloit, WI 877-787-7221
Castella Imports
Hauppauge, NY 866-227-8355
Clement Pappas & Company
Carneys Point, NJ 800-257-7019
Emerling International Foods
Buffalo, NY. 716-833-7381

Florida's Natural Growers
Lake Wales, FL. 888-657-6600
Greenwood Associates
Highland Park, IL 847-579-5500
Hi-Country Corona
Selah, WA 951-272-2600
M&B Fruit Juice Company
Akron, OH. 330-253-7465
Mott's
Elmsford, NY
Natalie's Orchard Island Juice
Fort Pierce, FL 772-465-1122
Nielsen Citrus Products
Huntington Beach, CA 714-892-5586
Perricone Juices
Beaumont, CA. 951-769-7171
Reiter Dairy
Springfield, OH. 937-323-5777
Sun Orchard
Tempe, AZ 800-505-8423
True Organic Products International
Miami, FL. 800-487-0379

Mango

Stevens Tropical Plantation
West Palm Beach, FL 561-683-4701
Sunlike Juice
Scarborough, ON 416-297-1140

Onion

Emerling International Foods
Buffalo, NY. 716-833-7381

Howard Foods
Danvers, MA. 978-774-6207
Vegetable Juices
Chicago, IL 888-776-9752

Orange

A. Duda & Sons
Labelle, FL 800-440-3265
Alta Dena Certified Dairy
City of Industry, CA 800-535-1369
American Mercantile Corporation
Windermere, FL
American Purpac Technologies, LLC
Beloit, WI 877-787-7221
Anderson Erickson Dairy
Des Moines, IA. 515-265-2521
Arcadia Dairy Farms
Arden, NC. 828-684-3556
Barbe's Dairy
Westwego, LA. 504-347-6201
Barber's Dairy
Birmingham, AL. 205-942-2351
Birdseye Dairy
Green Bay, WI. 920-494-5388
Byrne Dairy
Syracuse, NY 800-899-1535
Cass Clay Creamery
Fargo, ND 701-293-6455

Chase Brothers Dairy
Oxnard, CA. 800-438-6455
Citrus Citrosuco North America
Lake Wales, FL. 800-356-4592
Clement Pappas & Company
Carneys Point, NJ. 800-257-7019
Cloverland Green Spring Dairy
Baltimore, MD 800-876-6455
Consun Food Industries
Elyria, OH. 440-322-6301
Cott Coporation
Tampa, FL. 813-313-1800
Country Pure Foods
Akron, OH. 330-753-2293
Country Pure Foods
Ellington, CT 860-872-8346
Country Pure Foods
Akron, OH. 877-995-8423
Cropp Cooperative-Organic Valley
La Farge, WI. 888-444-6455
Cutrale Citrus Juices
Leesburg, FL. 352-728-7800
Cutrale Citrus Juices
Auburndale, FL. 863-965-5000
Emerling International Foods
Buffalo, NY. 716-833-7381

Erba Food Products
Brooklyn, NY 718-272-7700
Everfresh Beverages
Warren, MI 586-755-9500
Flagship Atlanta Dairy
Belleview, FL 800-224-0669
Florida Fruit Juices
Chicago, IL 773-586-6200
Florida Juice Products
Lakeland, FL. 863-802-4040
Florida's Natural Growers
Lake Wales, FL. 888-657-6600
Freshco
Stuart, FL 888-373-7426
Galliker Dairy
Johnstown, PA. 800-477-6455
Gene's Citrus Ranch
Sarasota, FL 888-723-2006
Great Western Juice Company
Maple Heights, OH. 800-321-9180
Green Spot Packaging
Claremont, CA 800-456-3210
Greenwood Associates
Highland Park, IL 847-579-5500
Harrisburg Dairies
Harrisburg, PA 800-692-7429
Heritage Farms Dairy
Murfreesboro, TN. 615-895-2790
Hi-Country Corona
Selah, WA. 951-272-2600
Hygeia Dairy Company
Corpus Christi, TX 361-854-4561
Indian River Foods
Fort Pierce, FL 772-462-2222
Inn Foods
Watsonville, CA 831-724-2026
Jackson Milk & Ice CreamCompany
Hutchinson, KS. 620-663-1244
Jus-Made
Dallas, TX. 800-969-3746
Key Colony/Red Parrot Juices
Lyons, IL. 800-424-0868
Knouse Foods Coop
Peach Glen, PA 717-677-8181
Louis Dreyfus Citrus
Winter Garden, FL 800-549-4272
Louis Trauth Dairy
Newport, KY. 800-544-6455
M&B Fruit Juice Company
Akron, OH. 330-253-7465
M. & B. Products
Tampa, FL. 800-899-7255
Marcus Dairy
Danbury, CT 800-243-2511
Marva Maid Dairy
Newport News, VA. 800-544-4439
Matanuska Maid Dairy
Anchorage, AK. 907-561-5223

Mayer Brothers
West Seneca, NY 800-696-2937
McArthur Dairy
Miami, FL 877-803-6565
Meadow Gold Dairies
Honolulu, HI 800-362-8531
Minute Maid Company
Sugar Land, TX 281-302-4317
Minute Maid Company
Dunedin, FL 800-237-0159
Minute Maid Company
Atlanta, GA 800-438-2653
Natalie's Orchard Island Juice
Fort Pierce, FL 772-465-1122
Noel Corporation
Yakima, WA 509-248-4545
Northland Cranberries
Wisconsin Rapids, WI 608-252-4714
Peace River Citrus Products
Arcadia, FL 863-494-0440
Perricone Juices
Beaumont, CA 951-769-7171
Prairie Farms Dairy
Carlinville, IL 217-854-2547
Prairie Farms Dairy
Granite City, IL 618-451-5600
Prairie Farms Dairy
O Fallon, IL 618-632-3632
Prairie Farms Dairy Inc.
Carlinville, IL 217-854-2547
Quality Kitchen Corporation
Danbury, CT 203-744-2000
Rainbow Valley Orchards
Fallbrook, CA 760-728-2905
Reilly Dairy & Food Company
Tampa, FL 813-839-8458
Reiter Dairy
Akron, OH 800-362-0825
Reiter Dairy
Springfield, OH 937-323-5777
Roberts Dairy Foods
Iowa City, IA
Rocket Products Company
Fenton, MO 800-325-9567
Saratoga Beverage Group
Saratoga Springs, NY 888-426-8642
Sinton Dairy Foods Company
Colorado Springs, CO 800-388-4970
Sun Orchard
Tempe, AZ 800-505-8423
Sunlike Juice
Scarborough, ON 416-297-1140
Superbrand Dairies
Miami, FL 305-769-6600
Superstore Industries
Fairfield, CA 707-864-0502
Swiss Valley Farms Company
Davenport, IA 563-468-6600
Toft Dairy
Sandusky, OH 800-521-4606
Treesweet Products
Houston, TX 281-876-3759
Tropicana
Bradenton, FL 800-237-7799
True Organic Products International
Miami, FL 800-487-0379
Tuscan/Lehigh Valley Dais
Lansdale, PA 800-937-3233
Velda Farms
North Miami Beach, FL 800-795-4649
Wengert's Dairy
Lebanon, PA 800-222-2129
World Citrus West
Lake Wales, FL 863-676-1411
Yoder Dairies
Chesapeake, VA 757-482-4068

Blood

Gregory's Box'd Beverages
Newark, NJ 973-465-1113

Concentrate

CCPI/Valley Foods
Lindsay, CA 559-562-5169
Chase Brothers Dairy
Oxnard, CA 800-438-6455
Cott Coporation
Tampa, FL 813-313-1800
Country Pure Foods
Ellington, CT 860-872-8346
Cutrale Citrus Juices
Leesburg, FL 352-728-7800
Georgia Sun
Newnan, GA 770-251-2500
Green Spot Packaging
Claremont, CA 800-456-3210
Greenwood Associates
Highland Park, IL 847-579-5500
Hi-Country Corona
Selah, WA 951-272-2600
Indian River Foods
Fort Pierce, FL 772-462-2222
Louis Dreyfus Citrus
Winter Garden, FL 800-549-4272
Mayer Brothers
West Seneca, NY 800-696-2937
Minute Maid Company
Atlanta, GA 800-438-2653
Sea Breeze Fruit Flavors
Towaco, NJ 800-732-2733
Sun Pac Foods
Brampton, ON 905-792-2700

Concentrate - Frozen

A. Duda Farm Fresh Foods
Belle Glade, FL 561-996-7621
Indian River Foods
Fort Pierce, FL 772-462-2222
Louis Dreyfus Citrus
Winter Garden, FL 800-549-4272

Not Concentrated

Citrus Citrosuco North America
Lake Wales, FL 800-356-4592
Greenwood Associates
Highland Park, IL 847-579-5500
Minute Maid Company
Atlanta, GA 800-438-2653
Silver Springs Citrus
Howey In the Hills, FL 800-940-2277

Papaya

Stevens Tropical Plantation
West Palm Beach, FL 561-683-4701
Sunlike Juice
Scarborough, ON 416-297-1140

Passion Fruit

Meadow Gold Dairies
Honolulu, HI 800-362-8531

Peach

Green Spot Packaging
Claremont, CA 800-456-3210
Hazel Creek Orchards
Mt Airy, GA 706-754-4899
Sunlike Juice
Scarborough, ON 416-297-1140
Valley View Packing Company
San Jose, CA 408-289-8300

Pear

San Benito Foods
Vancouver, WA 800-453-7832
Valley View Packing Company
San Jose, CA 408-289-8300

Pineapple

American Purpac Technologies, LLC
Beloit, WI 877-787-7221
Cal India Foods International
Chino, CA 909-613-1660
Clement Pappas & Company
Carneys Point, NJ 800-257-7019
Commodities Marketing, Inc.
Edison, NJ 732-603-5077
Country Pure Foods
Ellington, CT 860-872-8346
Country Pure Foods
Akron, OH 877-995-8423
Emerling International Foods
Buffalo, NY 716-833-7381

We supply food manufacturers and food service customers worldwide (since 1988) with bulk ingredients including: Fruits & Vegetables; Juice Concentrates; Herbs & Spices; Oils & Vinegars; Flavors & Colors; Honey & Molasses. We also produce PURE MAPLE SYRUP.

Florida Fruit Juices
Chicago, IL 773-586-6200
Greenwood Associates
Highland Park, IL 847-579-5500
Langer Juice Company
City of Industry, CA 626-336-3100
M. & B. Products
Tampa, FL 800-899-7255
Maui Pineapple Company
Kahului, HI 808-877-3351
Maui Pineapple Company
Concord, CA 925-798-0240
Mondial Foods Company
Los Angeles, CA 213-383-3531
NTC Marketing Inc
Williamsville, NY 800-333-1637
Rohtstein Corporation
Woburn, MA 781-935-8300
SEW Friel
Queenstown, MD 410-827-8811
Smucker Quality Beverages
Havre De Grace, MD 410-939-1403
Sunlike Juice
Scarborough, ON 416-297-1140
True Organic Products International
Miami, FL 800-487-0379

Boxed

American Purpac Technologies, LLC
Beloit, WI 877-787-7221
Country Pure Foods
Akron, OH 877-995-8423

Canned

American Purpac Technologies, LLC
Beloit, WI 877-787-7221
Country Pure Foods
Akron, OH 877-995-8423
NTC Marketing Inc
Williamsville, NY 800-333-1637
SEW Friel
Queenstown, MD 410-827-8811

Concentrate

Georgia Sun
Newnan, GA 770-251-2500
Maui Pineapple Company
Kahului, HI 808-877-3351
Maui Pineapple Company
Concord, CA 925-798-0240
Pacific Coast Fruit Company
Portland, OR 503-234-6411
Sun Pac Foods
Brampton, ON 905-792-2700

Frozen

American Purpac Technologies, LLC
Beloit, WI 877-787-7221
Country Pure Foods
Akron, OH 877-995-8423
Maui Pineapple Company
Concord, CA 925-798-0240

Glass-Packed

American Purpac Technologies, LLC
Beloit, WI 877-787-7221
Country Pure Foods
Akron, OH. 877-995-8423

Refrigerated

American Purpac Technologies, LLC
Beloit, WI 877-787-7221
Country Pure Foods
Akron, OH. 877-995-8423

Portioned

Arcadia Dairy Farms
Arden, NC. 828-684-3556

Prune

American Purpac Technologies, LLC
Beloit, WI 877-787-7221
Clement Pappas & Company
Carneys Point, NJ 800-257-7019
Emerling International Foods
Buffalo, NY. 716-833-7381

Erba Food Products
Brooklyn, NY 718-272-7700
Knouse Foods Coop
Peach Glen, PA. 717-677-8181
Madera Enterprises
Madera, CA. 800-507-9555
McArthur Dairy
Miami, FL. 305-795-7700
SEW Friel
Queenstown, MD 410-827-8811
Sunsweet Growers
Yuba City, CA. 800-417-2253
Valley View Packing Company
San Jose, CA. 408-289-8300

Raisin

Victor Packing Company
Madera, CA. 559-673-5908

Raspberry

Hazel Creek Orchards
Mt Airy, GA 706-754-4899
Manzanita Ranch
Julian, CA 760-765-0102
Meduri Farms Inc.
Dallas, OR. 503-623-0308
Merlinos
Canon City, CO. 719-275-5558
Stone Hill Wine Company
Hermann, MO. 573-486-2221

Refrigerated

Apple & Eve
Roslyn, NY 800-969-8018
Foremost Farms
Athens, WI 715-257-7015
Perfect Foods
Goshen, NY. 800-933-3288
Wengert's Dairy
Lebanon, PA 800-222-2129
World Citrus West
Lake Wales, FL. 863-676-1411

Strawberry

Green Spot Packaging
Claremont, CA 800-456-3210
Madera Enterprises
Madera, CA. 800-507-9555
Merlinos
Canon City, CO. 719-275-5558

Tangerine

American Mercantile Corporation
Windermere, FL

American Purpac Technologies, LLC
Beloit, WI 877-787-7221
Emerling International Foods
Buffalo, NY. 716-833-7381

Greenwood Associates
Highland Park, IL 847-579-5500
Louis Dreyfus Citrus
Winter Garden, FL 800-549-4272
Minute Maid Company
Atlanta, GA. 800-438-2653
True Organic Products International
Miami, FL. 800-487-0379

Tomato

Alimentaire Whyte's Inc
Laval, QC 800-625-1979
American Purpac Technologies, LLC
Beloit, WI 877-787-7221
Beckman & Gast Company
Saint Henry, OH 419-678-4195
Burnette Foods
Hartford, MI 616-621-3181
Cal-Tex Citrus Juice
Houston, TX 800-231-0133
ConAgra Grocery Products
Irvine, CA 714-680-1000
Country Pure Foods
Akron, OH. 330-753-2293
Country Pure Foods
Akron, OH. 877-995-8423
Dei Fratelli
Toledo, OH 800-837-1631
Erba Food Products
Brooklyn, NY 718-272-7700
Ocean Spray Cranberries
Lakeville-Middleboro, MA 800-662-3263
Ray Brothers & Noble Canning Company
Hobbs, IN 765-675-7451
Red Gold
Elwood, IN 877-748-9798
SEW Friel
Queenstown, MD 410-827-8811
Sun Pac Foods
Brampton, ON. 905-792-2700
Thomas Canning/Maidstone
Maidstone, ON 519-737-1531
Welch's Foods Inc
Concord, MA 800-340-6870

Boxed

American Purpac Technologies, LLC
Beloit, WI 877-787-7221

Canned

Agrocan
Ville St Laurent, QC 877-247-6226
American Purpac Technologies, LLC
Beloit, WI 877-787-7221
Emerling International Foods
Buffalo, NY. 716-833-7381

Hirzel Canning Company &Farms
Northwood, OH 419-693-0531

Cocktail

Emerling International Foods
Buffalo, NY. 716-833-7381

Vegetable Juices
Chicago, IL 888-776-9752

Frozen

American Purpac Technologies, LLC
Beloit, WI 877-787-7221
Vegetable Juices
Chicago, IL 888-776-9752

Glass-Packed Chilled

American Purpac Technologies, LLC
Beloit, WI 877-787-7221
Emerling International Foods
Buffalo, NY. 716-833-7381

Tropical Fruits

American Purpac Technologies, LLC
Beloit, WI 877-787-7221
Clement Pappas & Company
Carneys Point, NJ 800-257-7019
Cott Coporation
Tampa, FL. 813-313-1800
Country Pure Foods
Akron, OH. 877-995-8423
Emerling International Foods
Buffalo, NY. 716-833-7381

Furmano Foods
Northumberland, PA. 877-877-6032
Green Spot Packaging
Claremont, CA 800-456-3210
Hawaiian Sun Products
Honolulu, HI. 808-845-3211
Healthmate Products
Highland Park, IL. 800-584-8642
International Trade Impa
Lawrenceville, NJ. 800-223-5484
Langer Juice Company
City of Industry, CA 626-336-3100
Mondial Foods Company
Los Angeles, CA. 213-383-3531
Sinton Dairy Foods Company
Colorado Springs, CO. 800-388-4970
Stevens Tropical Plantation
West Palm Beach, FL 561-683-4701
Sunlike Juice
Scarborough, ON 416-297-1140
True Organic Products International
Miami, FL. 800-487-0379

Vegetable

Apple & Eve
Roslyn, NY 800-969-8018
B.M. Lawrence & Company
San Francisco, CA 415-981-3650
Beckman & Gast Company
Saint Henry, OH 419-678-4195
Byesville Aseptics
Byesville, OH 740-685-2548
California Day Fresh
Asusa, CA. 877-858-4237
Campbell Soup Company
Camden, NJ. 800-257-8443
Carriage House Companies
Fredonia, NY 800-462-8125
Century Foods International
Sparta, WI. 800-269-1901
Florida Food Products
Eustis, FL 800-874-2331
Greenwood Associates
Highland Park, IL. 847-579-5500
Howard Foods
Danvers, MA. 978-774-6207
Hudson Valley Fruit Juice
Highland, NY 845-691-8061

Ludfords
Rancho Cucamonga, CA 909-948-0797
Rapunzel Pure Organics
Bloomfield, NJ 800-225-1449
RFI Ingredients
Blauvelt, NY 800-962-7663
SEW Friel
Queenstown, MD 410-827-8811
Tamarack Farms Dairy
Newark, OH 866-221-4141
Thomas Canning/Maidstone
Maidstone, ON 519-737-1531
Vegetable Juices
Chicago, IL 888-776-9752
William Bolthouse Farms
Bakersfield, CA 661-366-7270

Concentrates - Fruit Puree

Glcc Company
Paw Paw, MI 269-657-3167
Greenwood Associates
Highland Park, IL 847-579-5500
RFI Ingredients
Blauvelt, NY 800-962-7663

Mixers

Bar Mixers

Callie's Charleston Biscuits LLC
Charleston, SC 843-577-1198
Coastal Promotions
Destin, FL 561-626-6384
La Jota Vineyard Company
Angwin, CA 877-222-0292

Prepared Cocktail Mixes

A.C. Calderoni & Company
Brisbane, CA 866-468-1897
Al-Rite Fruits & Syrups
Miami, FL 305-652-2540
American Beverage Marketers
New Albany, IN 812-941-0072
American Beverage Marketers
Leawood, KS 913-451-8311
American Purpac Technologies, LLC
Beloit, WI 877-787-7221
Bacardi Canada, Inc.
Brampton, ON 905-451-6100
Bacardi USA
Coral Gables, FL 800-222-2734
Bartush-Schnitzius Foods Company
Lewisville, TX 972-219-1270
Beam Global Spirits & Wine
Deerfield, IL 847-948-8888
Beverage Specialties
Fredonia, NY 800-462-8125
Blue Crab Bay Company
Melfa, VA 800-221-2722
Brown-Forman Corporation
Louisville, KY 502-585-1100
Byesville Aseptics
Byesville, OH 740-685-2548
Callie's Charleston Biscuits LLC
Charleston, SC 843-577-1198
Carolina Treet
Wilmington, NC 800-616-6344
Commodities Marketing, Inc.
Edison, NJ 732-603-5077
Daily Juice Products
Verona, PA 800-245-2929
Demitri's Bloody Mary Seasonings
Seattle, WA 800-627-9649
Fee Brothers
Rochester, NY 800-961-3337
Flavouressence Products
Mississauga, ON 866-209-7778
Franciscan Oakville Estates
Rutherford, CA 800-529-9463
Franco's Cocktail Mixes
Pompano Beach, FL 800-782-4508
Frank & Dean's Cocktail Mixes
Pasadena, CA 626-351-4272
Giumarra Vineyards
Bakersfield, CA 661-395-7000
Great Western Juice Company
Maple Heights, OH 800-321-9180
Island Oasis Frozen Cocktail Company
Walpole, MA 800-777-4752
Jus-Made
Dallas, TX 800-969-3746
Key Colony/Red Parrot Juices
Lyons, IL 800-424-0868
Kittling Ridge Estate Wines & Spirits
Grimsby, ON 905-945-9225
La Paz Products
Brea, CA 714-990-0982
Lemate of New England
Foxboro, MA 508-543-9035
Lemon-X Corporation
Huntington Station, NY 800-220-1061
Main Squeeze
Columbia, MO 573-817-5616
Margarita Man
San Antonio, TX 800-950-8149
Mcllhenny Company
New Orleans, LA 504-523-7370
Mele-Koi Farms
Newport Beach, CA 949-660-9000
Miramar Fruit Trading Company
Doral, FL 305-883-4774
Misty
Lincoln, NE 402-466-8424
Mott's
Elmsford, NY
Nestle Professional Vitality
Solon, OH 800-288-8682
Prima Foods International
Silver Springs, FL 800-774-8751
Reser's Fine Foods
Beaverton, OR 800-333-6431
Royale International Beverage Co Inc
Davenport, IA 563-386-5222
Ruffner's
Wayne, PA 610-687-9800
S.J. McCullagh
Buffalo, NY 800-753-3473
Sea Breeze Fruit Flavors
Towaco, NJ 800-732-2733
Sirocco Enterprises
Jefferson, LA 504-834-1549
St. Julian Wine Company
Paw Paw, MI 800-732-6002
Toucan Enterprises
Marrero, LA 800-736-9289
Trader Vic's Food Products
Emeryville, CA 877-762-4824
Tree Ripe Products
East Hanover, NJ 800-873-3747
Tropical Illusions
Trenton, MO 660-359-5422
Vegetable Juices
Chicago, IL 888-776-9752
W&G Flavors
Hunt Valley, MD 410-771-6606
Wagner Excello Food Products
Broadview, IL 708-338-4488

Non-Alcoholic Beverages

American Instants
Flanders, NJ 973-584-8811
Anheuser-Busch Inc.
Saint Louis, MO 800-342-5283
Ariel Vineyards
Napa, CA 800-456-9472
Atlanta Coffee & Tea Company
Decatur, GA 800-426-4781
Autocrat Coffee & Extracts
Lincoln, RI 800-288-6272
B.M. Lawrence & Company
San Francisco, CA 415-981-3650
Coca-Cola Enterprises
Atlanta, GA 800-233-7210
Coors Brewing Company
Golden, CO 800-642-6116
Ex Drinks
Henderson, NV 866-753-4929
Fee Brothers
Rochester, NY 800-961-3337
Florida Distillers Company
Lake Alfred, FL 863-956-3477
Franco's Cocktail Mixes
Pompano Beach, FL 800-782-4508
Gerhart Coffee Company
Lancaster, PA 800-536-4310
Kristian Regale
Hudson, WI 715-386-8388
Lion Brewery
Wilkes Barre, PA 800-233-8327
Martin Coffee Company
Jacksonville, FL 904-355-9661
Meier's Wine Cellars
Cincinnati, OH 800-346-2941
Mercury Brewing Company
Ipswich, MA 978-356-3329
Miller Brewing Company
Milwaukee, WI 414-933-1846
Natural Group
Oxnard, CA 805-485-3420
Richland Beverage Associates
Carrollton, TX 214-357-0248
Safeway Dairy Products
Walnut Creek, CA 925-944-4000
Sweet Traders
Huntington Beach, CA 714-903-6800

Smoothies

Blue Chip Group
Salt Lake City, UT 800-878-0099
Caffe D'Amore Gourmet Beverages
Monrovia, CA 800-999-0171
California Dairies
Visalia, CA 559-625-2200
Cascade Fresh
Seattle, WA 800-511-0057
Coleman Dairy
Little Rock, AR 501-568-6237
Cream O'Weaver Dairy
Salt Lake City, UT 801-973-9922
Dairy Farmers of America
Knoxville, TN 865-218-8500
Dannon Company
Fort Worth, TX 800-211-6565
Gardner's Gourmet
Fremont, CA 800-676-8558
GPI USA LLC.
Athens, GA 706-850-7826
Hunter Farms
High Point, NC 800-446-8035
Ideal Dairy
Richfield, UT 435-896-5061
Jus-Made
Dallas, TX 800-969-3746
K&F Select Fine Coffees
Portland, OR 800-558-7788
Lane's Dairy
El Paso, TX 915-772-6700
Maola Milk & Ice Cream Company
New Bern, NC 252-514-2792
Marcus Dairy
Danbury, CT 800-243-2511
Meadow Gold Dairies
Englewood, CO 800-525-3289
MEYENBERG Goat Milk Products
Turlock, CA 800-891-4628
Mission San Juan Juices
Dana Point, CA 949-495-7929
Oak Farms
San Antonio, TX 800-292-2169
Oak Farms
El Paso, TX 800-395-7004
Plains Creamery
Amarillo, TX 806-374-0385
Price's Creameries
El Paso, TX 915-565-2711
Saint Albans Cooperative Creamery
Saint Albans, VT 800-559-0343
Saratoga Beverage Group
Saratoga Springs, NY 888-426-8642
Scotsburn Dairy Group
Scotsburn, NS 902-485-8023
Sheila's Select Gourmet Recipe
Heber City, UT 800-516-7286
Smucker Quality Beverages
Havre De Grace, MD 410-939-1403
Smucker Quality Beverages
Chico, CA 530-899-5000
Sunshine Dairy Foods
Portland, OR 503-234-7526
Swiss Valley Farms Company
Davenport, IA 563-468-6600
Swiss Valley Farms Company
Dubuque, IA 800-397-9156

Valley of the Rogue Dairy
Grants Pass, OR 541-476-2020
Victor Packing Company
Madera, CA. 559-673-5908
William Bolthouse Farms
Bakersfield, CA 661-366-7270
Winder Dairy
West Valley, UT 800-946-3371
YoCream International
Portland, OR 800-962-7326
Yoplait USA
Minneapolis, MN 800-248-7310

Soft Drinks & Sodas

Beverage Capital Corporation
Baltimore, MD 410-242-7003
Big Red Bottling
Austin, TX. 254-772-7791
BN Soda
Boston, MA. 617-782-7888
Briar's USA
North Brunswick, NJ 887-327-4277
Canada Dry Bottling Company
Flushing, NY. 718-762-5967
Cool
Richardson, TX. 972-437-9352
Fentimans North America
Burnaby, BC 877-326-3248
Grand Teton Brewing
Victor, ID. 888-899-1656
GuS Grown-up Soda
New York, NY 212-355-7454
Honest Tea
Bethesda, MD 800-865-4736
Jones Soda Company
Seattle, WA 800-656-6050
Jones Soda Vancouver
Vancouver, BC 800-656-6050
Krinos Foods
Santa Barbara, CA 800-624-4896
Mercury Brewing Company
Ipswich, MA 978-356-3329
Nagel's Beverages Company
East Nampa, ID. 208-475-1250
Snow Beverages
New York, NY 212-353-3270
Southwest Canners of Texas
Nacogdoches, TX 936-569-9737
Zevia
Culver City, CA 855-469-3842

Club Soda

Mercury Brewing Company
Ipswich, MA 978-356-3329

Soda Water

Central Coca-Cola Bottling Company
Richmond, VA. 800-359-3759

Soft Drinks

A-Treat Bottling Company
Allentown, PA. 800-220-1531
Abita Brewing Company
Abita Springs, LA. 800-737-2311
Admiral Beverages
Worland, WY 307-347-4201
American Food Traders
Miami, FL. 305-273-7090
B.M. Lawrence & Company
San Francisco, CA 415-981-3650
Beverage Capital Corporation
Baltimore, MD 410-242-7003
Blue Sky Natural Beverage Company
Corona, CA. 800-426-7367
BN Soda
Boston, MA. 617-782-7888
Brooklyn Bottling Company
Milton, NY 845-795-2171
Canada Dry Bottling Company
Flushing, NY. 718-762-5967
Cawy Bottling Company
Miami, FL. 877-917-2299
Central Coca-Cola Bottling Company
Richmond, VA. 800-359-3759
Coca-Cola Bottling Company
El Paso, TX. 800-288-3228
Coca-Cola Bottling Company
Charlotte, NC 800-777-2653
Coca-Cola Bottling Company
Honolulu, HI 808-839-6711
Coca-Cola Bottling Company
West Memphis, AR. 870-732-1460
Coca-Cola Bottling Company
Lenexa, KS 913-492-8100
Coca-Cola Enterprises
Atlanta, GA. 800-233-7210
Contact International
Skokie, IL 847-324-4411
Cool Mountain Beverages
Des Plaines, IL 847-759-9330
Cott Concentrates/Royal Crown Cola International
Columbus, GA 800-652-5642
Crystal & Vigor Beverages
Kearny, NJ. 201-991-2342
CTL Foods
Colfax, WI. 800-962-5227
Dr. Pepper/Seven-Up
Racine, WI 800-696-5891
Everfresh Beverages
Warren, MI 586-755-9500
F.X. Matt Brewing Company
Utica, NY 800-690-3181
Full Service Beverage Company
Wichita, KS. 800-540-0001
Functional Products LLC
Atlantic Beach, FL 800-628-5908
G&J Pepsi-Cola Bottlers
Cicinnati, OH 513-785-6060
Ginseng Up Corporation
Rockleigh, NJ 201-660-8081
Global Beverage Company
Rochester, NY. 585-381-3560
Good-O-Beverages Company
Bronx, NY. 718-328-6400
Hank's Beverage Company
Feastervl Trvs, PA. 800-289-4722
Haydenergy Health
New York, NY 800-255-1660
International Trademarks
Darien, CT. 203-656-4046
Iron Horse Products
Edina, MN. 952-920-7722
Island Sweetwater Beverage Company
Bryn Mawr, PA 610-525-7444
J&J Snack Foods Corporation
Pennsauken, NJ. 800-486-9533
Krier Foods
Random Lake, WI. 920-994-2469
Langer Juice Company
City of Industry, CA 626-336-1666
Lenox-Martell
Boston, MA. 617-442-7777
Lost Trail Root Beer Com
Louisburg, KS. 800-748-7765
Louisiana Coca-Cola Bottling Company
Harahan, LA 800-362-6996
Manhattan Special Bottling Corporation
Brooklyn, NY 718-388-4144
Mar-Key Foods
Vidalia, GA. 912-537-4204
Monarch Beverage Company
Atlanta, GA. 800-241-3732
Mount Claire Spring Water
Torrington, CT 888-525-2473
National Beverage Corporation
Fort Lauderdale, FL 877-622-3499
Nestle Professional Vitality
Solon, OH 800-288-8682
Original American Beverage Company
North Stonington, CT. 800-625-3767
Polar Beverages
Worcester, MA 800-734-9800
R.J. Corr Naturals
Posen, IL. 708-389-4200
R.W. Knudsen
Chico, CA 530-899-5000
Regent Champagne Cellars
New York, NY
Roselani Tropics Ice Cream
Wailuku, HI. 808-244-7951
Royal Crown Bottling Company
Bowling Green, KY 270-842-8106
Safeway Beverage
Denver, CO 303-320-7960
Safeway Beverage
Bellevue, WA 425-455-6444
SANGARIA USA
Torrance, CA. 310-530-2202
Seltzer & Rydholm
Auburn, ME 207-784-5791
Seven Up/RC Bottling Company
Paragould, AR. 870-236-8765
Shasta Beverages
Lenexa, KS 913-888-6777
Soho Beverages
Vienna, VA 703-689-2800
Southern Beverage Packers
Appling, GA 800-326-2469
Sparkling Water Distributors
Merrick, NY 800-277-2755
Spear Packing
New Brunswick, NJ 732-247-4212
Stop & Shop Manufacturing
Readville, MA. 508-977-5132
Swire Coca-Cola
Draper, UT 800-497-2653
Todhunter Foods
Lake Alfred, FL. 863-956-1116
Truesdale Packaging Company
Warrenton, MO 636-456-6800
USA Sunrise Beverage
Spearfish, SD 605-723-0690
Varni Brothers/7-Up Bottling
Modesto, CA. 209-521-1777
Vermont Sweetwater Bottling Company
Poultney, VT. 800-974-9877
Wet Planet Beverage
Monachie, NJ 201-288-1999
White Rock Products Corporation
Flushing, NY. 800-969-7625
Zevia
Culver City, CA 855-469-3842

Cola

A-Treat Bottling Company
Allentown, PA. 800-220-1531
Adirondack Beverages
Scotia, NY. 800-316-6096
Al's Beverage Company
East Windsor, CT 888-257-7632
Aloe'Ha Drink Products
Houston, TX 713-978-6359
American Bottling & Beverage
Walterboro, SC 843-538-7937
Bar Harbor Brewing Company
Bar Harbor, ME. 207-288-4592
Better Beverages
Cerritos, CA 562-924-8321
Beverage America
Holland, MI. 616-396-1281
Beverage House
Cartersville, GA 888-367-8327
Beverage Specialties
Fredonia, NY 800-462-8125
Boylan Bottling Company
Haledon, NJ 800-289-7978
Cable Car Beverage Corporation
Denver, CO 303-298-9038
Cadbury Schweppes
Plano, TX 800-696-5891
Castle Beverages
Ansonia, CT 203-734-0883
Catawissa Bottling Company
Catawissa, PA 800-892-4419
Central Coca-Cola Bottling Company
Richmond, VA. 800-359-3759
Champion Beverages
Darien, CT. 203-655-9026
Coca-Cola Bottling Company
Atlanta, GA. 800-438-2653
Coca-Cola Enterprises
Atlanta, GA. 800-233-7210
Cornell Beverages
Brooklyn, NY 718-381-3000
Crowley Beverage Corporation
Wayland, MA 800-997-3337
Double-Cola Company
Chattanooga, TN. 423-267-5691
Dr Pepper/Seven Up
Plano, TX 80- 6-6 58

Egg Cream America
Northbrook, IL ... 847-559-2703
Faygo Beverages
Detroit, MI ... 800-347-6591
Giumarra Vineyards
Bakersfield, CA ... 661-395-7000
Gulf States Canners
Clinton, MS ... 601-924-0511
Hampton Associates & Sons
Fairfax, VA ... 703-968-5847
Honickman Affiliates
Pennsauken, NJ ... 800-573-7745
Hosmer Mountain Bottling
Willimantic, CT ... 800-763-2445
INCA Kola Golden Kola
New York, NY ... 212-688-1895
Inca Kola/Golden Kola
New York, NY ... 973-688-0970
Jones Soda Company
Seattle, WA ... 800-656-6050
Kennebec Fruit Company
Lisbon Falls, ME ... 207-353-8173
Lenox-Martell
Boston, MA ... 617-442-7777
Millstream Brewing
Amana, IA ... 319-622-3672
Moceri South Western
San Diego, CA ... 619-297-7900
New Age Canadian Beverage
Hollywood, FL ... 954-438-1484
New York Bottling Company
Bronx, NY ... 718-378-2525
Noel Corporation
Yakima, WA ... 509-248-4545
North Shore Bottling Company
Brooklyn, NY ... 718-272-8900
Northern Neck Coca Cola ompany
Montross, VA ... 800-431-2693
Pennsylvania Dutch BirchBeer
Doylestown, PA ... 856-662-1869
Pocono Mountain Bottling Company
Wilkes Barre, PA ... 570-822-7695
Premier Beverages
Plano, TX ... 972-547-6295
Reed's Original Beverage Corporation
Los Angeles, CA ... 800-997-3337
Rivella USA
Boca Raton, FL ... 561-417-5810
Sarum Tea Company
Lakeville, CT ... 860-435-2086
Shasta Beverages
Lenexa, KS ... 913-888-6777
Smucker Quality Beverages
Chico, CA ... 530-899-5000
SoBe Beverages
Norwalk, CT ... 800-588-0548
Southeast Canners
Columbus, GA ... 706-324-0040
Stewart's Beverages
White Plains, NY ... 914-397-9200
Sun State Beverage
Atlanta, GA ... 770-451-3990
Taos Brewing Supply
Santa Fe, NM ... 505-983-0505
Thomas Kemper Soda Company
Seattle, WA ... 206-381-8712
Tianfu China Cola
Katonah, NY ... 914-232-3102
Triple XXX Root Beer Com
West Lafayette, IN ... ÿ76- 74- 537
USA Beverage
Warrenton, MO ... 636-456-5468
Virgil's Root Beer
Los Angeles, CA ... 800-997-3337

Cream Soda

Central Coca-Cola Bottling Company
Richmond, VA ... 800-359-3759
Cool Mountain Beverages
Des Plaines, IL ... 847-759-9330
Jones Soda Company
Seattle, WA ... 800-656-6050
Mercury Brewing Company
Ipswich, MA ... 978-356-3329
Sparkling Water Distributors
Merrick, NY ... 800-277-2755

Cream Soda - Vanilla

Thomas Kemper Soda Company
Seattle, WA ... 206-381-8712

Ginger Ale

Adirondack Beverages
Scotia, NY ... 800-316-6096
Central Coca-Cola Bottling Company
Richmond, VA ... 800-359-3759
Cool Mountain Beverages
Des Plaines, IL ... 847-759-9330
Grand Teton Brewing
Victor, ID ... 888-899-1656
Thomas Kemper Soda Company
Seattle, WA ... 206-381-8712

Lemon-Lime Soda

Cool Mountain Beverages
Des Plaines, IL ... 847-759-9330
Manhattan Special Bottling Corporation
Brooklyn, NY ... 718-388-4144
Mercury Brewing Company
Ipswich, MA ... 978-356-3329

Sarsaparilla

Manhattan Special Bottling Corporation
Brooklyn, NY ... 718-388-4144

Sparkling Water

Absopure Water Company
Champaign, IL ... 800-422-7678
Bevco
Surrey, BC ... 800-663-0090
Blue Sky Natural Beverage Company
Corona, CA ... 800-426-7367
Crystal Geyser Roxanne LLC
Pensacola, FL ... 850-476-8844
Crystal Geyser Water Company
San Francisco, CA ... 415-616-9590
Crystal Geyser Water Company
Calistoga, CA ... 800-443-9737
Crystal Rock Spring Water Company
Watertown, CT ... 860-443-5000
Giumarra Vineyards
Bakersfield, CA ... 661-395-7000
Hinckley Springs Water Company
Chicago, IL ... 773-586-8600
Jackson Milk & Ice CreamCompany
Hutchinson, KS ... 620-663-1244
Matilija Water Company
Ventura, CA ... 805-643-4675
Mount Olympus Waters
Salt Lake City, UT ... 800-628-6056
Poland Spring Water
Stamford, CT ... 800-955-4426
Polar Beverages
Worcester, MA ... 800-734-9800
Polar Water Company
Carnegie, PA ... 412-429-5550
R.J. Corr Naturals
Posen, IL ... 708-389-4200
Regent Champagne Cellars
New York, NY
Saratoga Beverage Group
Saratoga Springs, NY ... 888-426-8642
Southern Beverage Packers
Appling, GA ... 800-326-2469
Sparkling Water Distributors
Merrick, NY ... 800-277-2755
Sweet Earth Natural Foods
Pacific Grove, CA ... 800-737-3311
Universal Beverages
Ponte Vedra Bch, FL ... 904-280-7795
Yosemite Waters
Los Angeles, CA ... 800-427-8420

Spirits & Liqueurs

Miyasaka Brewery
Costa Mesa, CA ... 714-623-2163

Brandy

Corby Distilleries
Toronto, ON ... 800-367-9079
E&J Gallo Winery
Modesto, CA ... 209-341-3111
Germain-Robin
Ukiah, CA ... 800-782-8145
Golden State Vintners
Cutler, CA ... 559-528-3033
Heaven Hill Distilleries
Bardstown, KY ... 502-348-3921
Heck Cellars
Arvin, CA ... 661-854-6120
Hood River Distillers
Hood River, OR ... 541-386-1588
Ironstone Vineyards
Murphys, CA ... 209-728-1251
Kittling Ridge Estate Wines & Spirits
Grimsby, ON ... 905-945-9225
Laird & Company
North Garden, VA ... 877-438-5247
M.S. Walker
Somerville, MA ... 617-776-6700
Majestic Distilling Company
Baltimore, MD ... 410-242-0200
Marie Brizard Wines & Spirits
St. Helena, CA ... 800-878-1123
Oak Ridge Winery
Lodi, CA ... 20- 3-9 47
Pernod Ricard USA
Purchase, NY ... 914-848-4800
Todhunter Foods & Monarch Wine Company
West Palm Beach, FL ... 800-336-9463
Vie-Del Company
Fresno, CA ... 559-834-2525

Luxury Cognac

Heaven Hill Distilleries
Bardstown, KY ... 502-348-3921

V.S. Cognac Three Star

Corby Distilleries
Toronto, ON ... 800-367-9079

V.S.O.P. Cognac

Corby Distilleries
Toronto, ON ... 800-367-9079

X.O. Cognac

Corby Distilleries
Toronto, ON ... 800-367-9079

Gin

A. Smith Bowman Distillery
Fredericksburg, VA ... 540-373-4555
Beam Global Spirits & Wine
Deerfield, IL ... 847-948-8888
Brown-Forman Corporation
Louisville, KY ... 502-585-1100
Corby Distilleries
Toronto, ON ... 800-367-9079
Destileria Serralles Inc
Mercedita, PR ... 787-840-1000
Diageo Canada Inc.
Toronto, ON ... 416-626-2000
E&J Gallo Winery
Modesto, CA ... 209-341-3111
Heaven Hill Distilleries
Bardstown, KY ... 502-348-3921
Hiram Walker & Sons
Fort Smith, AR ... 479-646-6100
Hiram Walker & Sons Limited
Windsor, ON ... 519-254-5171
Hood River Distillers
Hood River, OR ... 541-386-1588
Laird & Company
Scobeyville, NJ ... 877-438-5247
Majestic Distilling Company
Baltimore, MD ... 410-242-0200
Marie Brizard Wines & Spirits
St. Helena, CA ... 800-878-1123
Pernod Ricard USA
Greendale, IN ... 812-537-0700
Pernod Ricard USA
Purchase, NY ... 914-848-4800
Viking Distillery
Albany, GA ... 229-436-0181
Vincor International
Mississauga, ON ... 800-265-9463

Irish Whiskey

Beam Global Spirits & Wine
Deerfield, IL ... 847-948-8888
Corby Distilleries
Toronto, ON ... 800-367-9079
Fortune Brands
Lincolnshire, IL ... 847-484-4529
George A Dickel & Company
Tullahoma, TN ... 888-342-5352

Heaven Hill Distilleries
Bardstown, KY 502-348-3921
Hiram Walker & Sons
Fort Smith, AR 479-646-6100
Hiram Walker & Sons Limited
Windsor, ON 519-254-5171
Jack Daniel's Distillery
Lynchburg, TN 931-759-4221
Kittling Ridge Estate Wines & Spirits
Grimsby, ON 905-945-9225
Laird & Company
Scobeyville, NJ 877-438-5247
Makers Mark Distillery
Loretto, KY 270-865-2881
Pernod Ricard USA
Greendale, IN 812-537-0700
Pernod Ricard USA
Purchase, NY 914-848-4800

Liqueurs & Cordials

Aloha Distillers
Honolulu, HI 808-841-5787
Bacardi Canada, Inc.
Brampton, ON 905-451-6100
Beam Global Spirits & Wine
Deerfield, IL 847-948-8888
Black Prince Distillery Inc.
Clifton, NJ 973-365-2050
Brown-Forman Corporation
Louisville, KY 502-585-1100
Charles Jacquin Et Cie
Philadelphia, PA 800-523-3811
Clear Creek Distillery
Portland, OR 503-248-9470
Consolidated Distilled Products
Chicago, IL 773-927-4161
Destileria Serralles Inc
Mercedita, PR 787-840-1000
Franciscan Oakville Estates
Rutherford, CA 800-529-9463
Hawk Pacific Freight
Napa, CA 707-259-0266
Heaven Hill Distilleries
Bardstown, KY 502-348-3921
Highwood Distillers
High River, AB 403-652-3202
Hiram Walker & Sons
Fort Smith, AR 479-646-6100
Hiram Walker & Sons Limited
Windsor, ON 519-254-5171
Kittling Ridge Estate Wines & Spirits
Grimsby, ON 905-945-9225
M.S. Walker
Somerville, MA 617-776-6700
Marie Brizard Wines & Spirits
St. Helena, CA 800-878-1123
Paramount Distillers
Cleveland, OH 800-821-2989
Pernod Ricard USA
Purchase, NY 914-848-4800
Phillips Beverage Company
Minneapolis, MN 612-331-6230
Renault Winery
Egg Harbor City, NJ 609-965-2111
Royal Wine Corp
Bayonne, NJ 718-384-2400
Sakeone Corporation
Forest Grove, OR 800-550-7253
Todhunter Foods & Monarch Wine Company
West Palm Beach, FL 800-336-9463
United Distillers & Vintners
Norwalk, CT 203-323-3311

Amaretto

Heaven Hill Distilleries
Bardstown, KY 502-348-3921

Anise Liqueur

Pernod Ricard USA
Purchase, NY 914-848-4800

Brandy Liqueur

Majestic Distilling Company
Baltimore, MD 410-242-0200

Chocolate Liqueur

Aloha Distillers
Honolulu, HI 808-841-5787

Coffee Liqueur

Aloha Distillers
Honolulu, HI 808-841-5787
Heaven Hill Distilleries
Bardstown, KY 502-348-3921

Schnapps Liqueuer

Marie Brizard Wines & Spirits
St. Helena, CA 800-878-1123

Neutral

Buffalo Trace Distillery
Frankfort, KY 800-654-8471
M.S. Walker
Somerville, MA 617-776-6700
Paramount Distillers
Cleveland, OH 800-821-2989

Rum

A. Smith Bowman Distillery
Fredericksburg, VA 540-373-4555
Bacardi Canada, Inc.
Brampton, ON 905-451-6100
Bacardi USA
Coral Gables, FL 800-222-2734
Beam Global Spirits & Wine
Deerfield, IL 847-948-8888
Buffalo Trace Distillery
Frankfort, KY 800-654-8471
Corby Distilleries
Toronto, ON 800-367-9079
Destileria Serralles Inc
Mercedita, PR 787-840-1000
Heaven Hill Distilleries
Bardstown, KY 502-348-3921
Highwood Distillers
High River, AB 403-652-3202
Hiram Walker & Sons Limited
Windsor, ON 519-254-5171
Hood River Distillers
Hood River, OR 541-386-1588
Kittling Ridge Estate Wines & Spirits
Grimsby, ON 905-945-9225
Majestic Distilling Company
Baltimore, MD 410-242-0200
Marie Brizard Wines & Spirits
St. Helena, CA 800-878-1123
Mohawk Distilled Products
North Miami, FL 305-892-3460
Terressentia Corporation
N Charleston, SC 843-225-3100
Trigo Corporation
Toa Baja, PR 787-794-1300

Dark

Bacardi Canada, Inc.
Brampton, ON 905-451-6100
Corby Distilleries
Toronto, ON 800-367-9079

White Silver

Corby Distilleries
Toronto, ON 800-367-9079

Scotch Whiskey

A. Smith Bowman Distillery
Fredericksburg, VA 540-373-4555
Bacardi Canada, Inc.
Brampton, ON 905-451-6100
Beam Global Spirits & Wine
Deerfield, IL 847-948-8888
Brown-Forman Corporation
Louisville, KY 502-585-1100
Canadian Mist Distillers
Collingwood, ON 705-445-4690
George A Dickel & Company
Tullahoma, TN 888-342-5352
Heaven Hill Distilleries
Bardstown, KY 502-348-3921
Hiram Walker & Sons Limited
Windsor, ON 519-254-5171
Hood River Distillers
Hood River, OR 541-386-1588
Jack Daniel's Distillery
Lynchburg, TN 931-759-4221
Kittling Ridge Estate Wines & Spirits
Grimsby, ON 905-945-9225
Laird & Company
Scobeyville, NJ 877-438-5247
Majestic Distilling Company
Baltimore, MD 410-242-0200
Makers Mark Distillery
Loretto, KY 270-865-2881
Marie Brizard Wines & Spirits
St. Helena, CA 800-878-1123
Montebello Brands
Baltimore, MD 410-282-8800
Pernod Ricard USA
Greendale, IN 812-537-0700
Pernod Ricard USA
Purchase, NY 914-848-4800

Blended

Hiram Walker & Sons
Fort Smith, AR 479-646-6100

Tequila and Mezcal

A. Smith Bowman Distillery
Fredericksburg, VA 540-373-4555
Beam Global Spirits & Wine
Deerfield, IL 847-948-8888
Corby Distilleries
Toronto, ON 800-367-9079
Heaven Hill Distilleries
Bardstown, KY 502-348-3921
Highwood Distillers
High River, AB 403-652-3202
Hiram Walker & Sons
Fort Smith, AR 479-646-6100
Hood River Distillers
Hood River, OR 541-386-1588
Majestic Distilling Company
Baltimore, MD 410-242-0200
Marie Brizard Wines & Spirits
St. Helena, CA 800-878-1123
Tequila XQ
Guadalajara Jalisco, ... 333-587-7799
Vincor International
Mississauga, ON 800-265-9463

Anejo Tequila

Tequila XQ
Guadalajara Jalisco, ... 333-587-7799

Reposado Tequila

Tequila XQ
Guadalajara Jalisco, ... 333-587-7799

Vodka

A. Smith Bowman Distillery
Fredericksburg, VA 540-373-4555
Bacardi Canada, Inc.
Brampton, ON 905-451-6100
Bacardi USA
Coral Gables, FL 800-222-2734
Beam Global Spirits & Wine
Deerfield, IL 847-948-8888
Brown-Forman Corporation
Louisville, KY 502-585-1100
Corby Distilleries
Toronto, ON 800-367-9079
Crillon Importers
Paramus, NJ 201-368-8878
Destileria Serralles Inc
Mercedita, PR 787-840-1000
Heaven Hill Distilleries
Bardstown, KY 502-348-3921
Highwood Distillers
High River, AB 403-652-3202
Hiram Walker & Sons
Fort Smith, AR 479-646-6100

Hiram Walker & Sons Limited
Windsor, ON ... 519-254-5171

Hood River Distillers
Hood River, OR ... 541-386-1588

Kittling Ridge Estate Wines & Spirits
Grimsby, ON ... 905-945-9225

Laird & Company
Scobeyville, NJ ... 877-438-5247

Majestic Distilling Company
Baltimore, MD ... 410-242-0200

Marie Brizard Wines & Spirits
St. Helena, CA ... 800-878-1123

Pernod Ricard USA
Purchase, NY ... 914-848-4800

R&A Imports
Pacific Palisades, CA ... 310-454-2247

Terressentia Corporation
N Charleston, SC ... 843-225-3100

Trigo Corporation
Toa Baja, PR ... 787-794-1300

Viking Distillery
Albany, GA ... 229-436-0181

Vincor International
Mississauga, ON ... 800-265-9463

Whiskey, American

Barton Brands
Louisville, KY ... 800-598-6352

Beam Global Spirits & Wine
Deerfield, IL ... 847-948-8888

Corby Distilleries
Toronto, ON ... 800-367-9079

George A Dickel & Company
Tullahoma, TN ... 888-342-5352

Heaven Hill Distilleries
Bardstown, KY ... 502-348-3921

Hiram Walker & Sons
Fort Smith, AR ... 479-646-6100

Hiram Walker & Sons Limited
Windsor, ON ... 519-254-5171

Jack Daniel's Distillery
Lynchburg, TN ... 931-759-4221

Kittling Ridge Estate Wines & Spirits
Grimsby, ON ... 905-945-9225

Laird & Company
Scobeyville, NJ ... 877-438-5247

Makers Mark Distillery
Loretto, KY ... 270-865-2881

Pernod Ricard USA
Greendale, IN ... 812-537-0700

Bourbon

A. Smith Bowman Distillery
Fredericksburg, VA ... 540-373-4555

Barton Brands
Louisville, KY ... 800-598-6352

Brown-Forman Corporation
Louisville, KY ... 502-585-1100

Buffalo Trace Distillery
Frankfort, KY ... 800-654-8471

Corby Distilleries
Toronto, ON ... 800-367-9079

Heaven Hill Distilleries
Bardstown, KY ... 502-348-3921

Laird & Company
Scobeyville, NJ ... 877-438-5247

Majestic Distilling Company
Baltimore, MD ... 410-242-0200

Marie Brizard Wines & Spirits
St. Helena, CA ... 800-878-1123

Old Rip Van Winkle Distillery
Louisville, KY ... 502-897-9113

Pernod Ricard USA
Purchase, NY ... 914-848-4800

Viking Distillery
Albany, GA ... 229-436-0181

Whiskey, Canadian

Beam Global Spirits & Wine
Deerfield, IL ... 847-948-8888

Corby Distilleries
Toronto, ON ... 800-367-9079

Sports Drinks

AC Gunter
Clear Brook, VA ... 540-662-5484

American Purpac Technologies, LLC
Beloit, WI ... 877-787-7221

Asiamerica Ingredients
Westwood, NJ ... 201-497-5531

Processor, importer, exporter and distributor of bulk vitamins, amino acids, nutraceuticals, aromatic chemicals, food additives, herbs, mineral nutrients and pharmaceuticals.

Captiva
Augusta, NJ ... 973-579-7883

Central Coca-Cola Bottling Company
Richmond, VA ... 800-359-3759

Century Foods International
Sparta, WI ... 800-269-1901

Choice Organic Teas
Seattle, WA ... 206-525-0051

Clement Pappas & Company
Carneys Point, NJ ... 800-257-7019

Cool
Richardson, TX ... 972-437-9352

Crystal Star Herbal Nutrition
Salinas, CA ... 831-422-7500

Eclipse Sports Supplements
Clarks Summit, PA ... 866-898-0885

I Rice & Company
Philadelphia, PA ... 800-232-6022

Innovative Food Solutions LLC
Columbus, OH ... 800-884-3314

Itoen
Honolulu, HI ... 808-847-4477

Jo Mints
Corona Del Mar, CA ... 877-566-4687

Masala Chai Company
Santa Cruz, CA ... 831-475-8881

Monarch Beverage Company
Atlanta, GA ... 800-241-3732

Natures Best
Hauppauge, NY ... 800-345-2378

Nutriwest
Douglas, WY ... 800-443-3333

Optimum Nutrition
Walterboro, SC ... 800-763-3444

Quaker Oats Company
Mountain Top, PA ... 800-367-6287

Randag & Associates Inc
Elmhurst, IL ... 630-530-2830

Tova Industries
Louisville, KY ... 888-532-8682

Uncle Bum's Gourmet Foods
Riverside, CA ... 800-486-2867

Water

Abita Springs Water Company
Metairie, LA ... 504-828-2500

Absopure Water Company
Plymouth, MI ... 800-422-7678

Acqua Blox LLC
Santa Fe Springs, CA ... 562-693-9599

Adobe Springs
Patterson, CA ... 408-897-3023

Alpine Valley Water
Harvey, IL ... 708-333-3910

Aqua Clara Bottling & Distribution
Clearwater, FL ... 727-446-2999

Arbor Springs Water Company
Ferndale, MI ... 800-343-7003

Blue Hills Spring Water Company
Norwell, MA

Blue Sky Natural Beverage Company
Corona, CA ... 800-426-7367

Camp Holly Springs
Richmond, VA ... 804-795-2096

Canada Dry Bottling Company
Flushing, NY ... 718-762-5967

Captiva
Augusta, NJ ... 973-579-7883

Cascade Clear Water
Burlington, WA ... 360-757-4441

Clearly Canadian Beverage Corporation
Vanghan, ON ... 800-735-7180

Coca-Cola Bottling Company
Honolulu, HI ... 808-839-6711

Coca-Cola Enterprises
Atlanta, GA ... 800-233-7210

Crystal Geyser Roxanne LLC
Pensacola, FL ... 850-476-8844

Crystal Springs
Mississauga, ON ... 800-822-5889

Crystal Springs Water Company
Fort Lauderdale, FL ... 800-432-1321

Crystal Water Company
Orlando, FL ... 800-444-7873

Culligan Water Technologies
Rosemont, IL ... 1 8-6 7-5 02

Danone Waters
French Camp, CA ... 209-982-5412

Deep Rock Fontenelle Water Company
Omaha, NE ... 800-433-1303

Deep Rock Water Company
Denver, CO ... 800-695-2020

Deep Rock Water Company
Minneapolis, MN ... 800-800-8986

Distillata Company
Cleveland, OH ... 800-999-2906

DS Waters of America
Atlanta, GA ... 800-728-5508

Eldorado Artesian Springs
Eldorado Springs, CO ... 303-499-1316

Essentia Water
Bothell, WA ... 425-402-9555

Eureka Water Company
Oklahoma City, OK ... 800-310-8474

Fantis Foods
Carlstadt, NJ ... 201-933-6200

Fiji Water Company
Los Angeles, CA ... 877-426-3454

Fizz-O Water Company
Tulsa, OK ... 918-834-3691

Fizzy Lizzy
New York, NY ... 800-203-9336

Fountainhead Water Company
Norcross, GA ... 864-944-1993

Full Service Beverage Company
Wichita, KS ... 800-540-0001

Girard Spring Water
North Providence, RI ... 800-477-9287

Glen Summit Springs Water Company
Mountain Top, PA ... 800-621-7596

Global Beverage Company
Rochester, NY ... 585-381-3560

GWB Foods Corporation
Brooklyn, NY ... 877-977-7610

Harrisburg Dairies
Harrisburg, PA ... 800-692-7429

Hawaiian Natural Water Company
Pearl City, HI ... 808-483-0520

Healing Light
Germantown, NY ... 877-307-4372

Heck Cellars
Arvin, CA ... 661-854-6120

Island Sweetwater Beverage Company
Bryn Mawr, PA ... 610-525-7444

Jackson Milk & Ice CreamCompany
Hutchinson, KS ... 620-663-1244

Knoxage Water Company
San Diego, CA ... 619-234-3333

Le Bleu Corporation
Advance, NC ... 800-854-4471

Leisure Time Ice & Spring Water
Kiamesha Lake, NY ... 800-443-1412

Light Rock Beverage Company
Danbury, CT ... 203-743-3410

Lipsey Mountain Spring Water
Norcross, GA ... 770-449-0001

Mayer Brothers
West Seneca, NY ... 800-696-2937

Metro Mint
San Francisco, CA ... 415-979-0781

Minnehaha Spring Water Company
Cleveland, OH ... 216-431-0243

Monarch Beverage Company
Atlanta, GA ... 800-241-3732

Mount Claire Spring Water
Torrington, CT ... 888-525-2473

Mountain Valley Spring Company
Hot Springs, AR ... 800-643-1501

Music Mountain Water Company
Birmingham, AL ... 800-349-6555

Nantze Springs
Dothan, AL ... 800-239-7873

Natural Group
Oxnard, CA ... 805-485-3420

Natural Spring Water Company
Johnson City, TN ... 423-926-7905

Naya
Montreal, QC ... 450-562-7911

NC Mountain Water
Marion, NC ... 800-220-4718

Neenah Springs
Oxford, WI 608-586-5605
North American Water Group
Overland Park, KS 913-469-1156
North Country Natural Spring Water
Port Kent, NY 518-834-9400
Northern Falls
Rockford, MI 616-915-0970
Oakhurst Dairy
Portland, ME. 800-482-0718
Office General des Eaux Minerales
Montreal, QC 514-482-7221
Peace Mountain Natural Beverages Corporation
Springfield, MA 413-567-4942
Pocono Spring Company
Mt Pocono, PA 800-634-4584
Poland Spring Water
Stamford, CT. 800-955-4426
Premium Water
Orange Springs, FL. 800-243-1163
Pure-Flo Water Company
Santee, CA 800-787-3356
Q Tonic
Brooklyn, NY
Quibell Spring Water Beverage
Martinsville, VA 540-632-0100
R.J. Corr Naturals
Posen, IL. 708-389-4200
Rebound
Newburgh, NY 845-562-5400
Regent Champagne Cellars
New York, NY
Reiter Dairy
Springfield, OH. 937-323-5777
Sand Springs Springwater
Williamstown, MA. 413-458-8281
Saratoga Beverage Group
Saratoga Springs, NY. 888-426-8642
Schneider's Dairy Holdings Inc
Pittsburgh, PA. 412-881-3525
Sinton Dairy Foods Company
Colorado Springs, CO. 800-388-4970
SnowBird Corporation
Bayonne, NJ 800-576-1616
Sparkling Spring Water Company
Vernon Hills, IL 800-772-7554
St. Clair Industries
Ft Lauderdale, FL. 954-491-0400
Suntory Water Group
Atlanta, GA. 770-933-1400
Talking Rain Beverage Company
Preston, WA 800-734-0748
Three Springs Water Company
Laurel Run, PA 800-332-7873
TRC Nutritional Laboratories
Tulsa, OK 800-421-7310
Triple Springs Spring Water
Meriden, CT 203-235-8374
Triton Water Company
Burlington, NC 800-476-9111
Universal Beverages
Leesburg, FL. 352-315-1010
USA Sunrise Beverage
Spearfish, SD 605-723-0690
Varni Brothers/7-Up Bottling
Modesto, CA. 209-521-1777
Vichy Springs Mineral Water Corporation
Ukiah, CA. 707-462-9515
Water Concepts
East Dundee, IL 847-699-9797
White Rock Products Corporation
Flushing, NY. 800-969-7625
Windmill Water
Edgewood, NM. 505-281-9287
Winterbrook Beverage Group
Greendale, IN 812-537-7348
Wissahickon Spring Water International
Philadelphia, PA 800-394-3733
Zephyr Hills
Tamarac, FL 954-597-7852

Bottled

Absopure Water Company
Plymouth, MI 800-422-7678
All Seasons International Distributors
New Albany, IN 812-949-1898
Alpine Valley Water
Harvey, IL. 708-333-3910
Aqua Clara Bottling & Distribution
Clearwater, FL 727-446-2999
Arbor Springs Water Company
Ferndale, MI 800-343-7003
Assouline & Ting
Huntingdon Valley, PA 800-521-4491
Bevco
Surrey, BC. 800-663-0090
Bio-Hydration Research Lab
Los Angeles, CA. 800-531-5088
Calcium Springs Water Company
Park City, UT 435-615-7600
Camp Holly Springs
Richmond, VA. 804-795-2096
Canada Dry Bottling Company
Flushing, NY. 718-762-5967
Captiva
Augusta, NJ. 973-579-7883
Central Coca-Cola Bottling Company
Richmond, VA. 800-359-3759
Coca-Cola Bottling Company
Honolulu, HI. 808-839-6711
Country Pure Foods
Ellington, CT 860-872-8346
Crystal Geyser Roxanne LLC
Pensacola, FL 850-476-8844
Crystal Rock Spring Water Company
Watertown, CT 860-443-5000
Crystal Springs
Mississauga, ON. 800-822-5889
Crystal Springs Water Company
Fort Lauderdale, FL 800-432-1321
Crystal Water Company
Orlando, FL. 800-444-7873
Danone Waters
French Camp, CA. 209-982-5412
Deep Rock Fontenelle Water Company
Omaha, NE 800-433-1303
Deep Rock Water Company
Minneapolis, MN 800-800-8986
Distillata Company
Cleveland, OH 800-999-2906
DS Waters of America
Atlanta, GA. 800-728-5508
Eldorado Artesian Springs
Eldorado Springs, CO. 303-499-1316
Eureka Water Company
Oklahoma City, OK 800-310-8474
Figuerola Laboratories
Santa Ynez, CA. 800-219-1147
Fiji Water Company
Los Angeles, CA. 877-426-3454
Fiji Water LLC
Los Angeles, CA. 888-426-3454
Fountainhead Water Company
Norcross, GA 864-944-1993
Full Service Beverage Company
Wichita, KS. 800-540-0001
Functional Products LLC
Atlantic Beach, FL 800-628-5908
Girard Spring Water
North Providence, RI 800-477-9287
Giumarra Vineyards
Bakersfield, CA 661-395-7000
Glen Summit Springs Water Company
Mountain Top, PA. 800-621-7596
Global Beverage Company
Rochester, NY. 585-381-3560
GWB Foods Corporation
Brooklyn, NY 877-977-7610
H3O
Beckley, WV. 888-436-9287
Hansen's Natural
Fullerton, CA 714-870-0310
Hawaiian Natural Water Company
Pearl City, HI 808-483-0520
Heck Cellars
Arvin, CA 661-854-6120
Hi-Country Foods Corporation
Selah, WA 509-697-7292
Hinckley Springs Water Company
Chicago, IL 773-586-8600
Island Sweetwater Beverage Company
Bryn Mawr, PA 610-525-7444
J. Weil & Company
Boise, ID. 800-755-3885
Jackson Milk & Ice CreamCompany
Hutchinson, KS. 620-663-1244
Le Bleu Corporation
Advance, NC. 800-854-4471
Leisure Time Ice & Spring Water
Kiamesha Lake, NY 800-443-1412
Light Rock Beverage Company
Danbury, CT 203-743-3410
Lipsey Mountain Spring Water
Norcross, GA 770-449-0001
Matilija Water Company
Ventura, CA. 805-643-4675
Merci Spring Water
Maryland Heights, MO. 314-872-9323
Mount Olympus Waters
Salt Lake City, UT 800-628-6056
Mountain Valley Spring Company
Hot Springs, AR 800-643-1501
Music Mountain Water Company
Birmingham, AL. 800-349-6555
Natural Spring Water Company
Johnson City, TN 423-926-7905
Naya
Montreal, QC 450-562-7911
NC Mountain Water
Marion, NC. 800-220-4718
North American Water Group
Overland Park, KS 913-469-1156
Peace Mountain Natural Beverages Corporation
Springfield, MA 413-567-4942
Pocono Mountain Bottling Company
Wilkes Barre, PA. 570-822-7695
Pocono Spring Company
Mt Pocono, PA 800-634-4584
Poland Spring Water
Stamford, CT. 800-955-4426
Polar Beverages
Worcester, MA 800-734-9800
Polar Water Company
Carnegie, PA. 412-429-5550
Premium Water
Orange Springs, FL. 800-243-1163
Pure-Flo Water Company
Santee, CA 800-787-3356
Quibell Spring Water Beverage
Martinsville, VA 540-632-0100
Regent Champagne Cellars
New York, NY
Reiter Dairy
Springfield, OH. 937-323-5777
Royal Crown Bottling Company
Bowling Green, KY 270-842-8106
SnowBird Corporation
Bayonne, NJ 800-576-1616
Southern Beverage Packers
Appling, GA 800-326-2469
Sparkling Spring Water Company
Vernon Hills, IL 800-772-7554
Spring Water Company
Chesapeake, VA 800-832-0271
Suntory Water Group
Atlanta, GA. 770-933-1400
Titusville Dairy Products
Titusville, PA 800-352-0101
Triton Water Company
Burlington, NC 800-476-9111
Universal Beverages
Leesburg, FL. 352-315-1010
Universal Beverages
Ponte Vedra Bch, FL. 904-280-7795
USA Sunrise Beverage
Spearfish, SD 605-723-0690
Vichy Springs Mineral Water Corporation
Ukiah, CA. 707-462-9515
Water Concepts
East Dundee, IL 847-699-9797
Windmill Water
Edgewood, NM. 505-281-9287

Winterbrook Beverage Group
Greendale, IN 812-537-7348
Wissahickon Spring Water International
Philadelphia, PA 800-394-3733
Yosemite Waters
Los Angeles, CA. 800-427-8420

Distilled

Absopure Water Company
Plymouth, MI 800-422-7678
Alacer Corporation
Foothill Ranch, CA. 800-854-0249
Alamance Foods/Triton Water Company
Burlington, NC 800-476-9111
Alpine Valley Water
Harvey, IL. 708-333-3910
Aquafina
Purchase, NY 914-253-2000
Arcadia Dairy Farms
Arden, NC. 828-684-3556
Belmar Spring Water Company
Glen Rock, NJ. 201-444-1010
Bevco
Surrey, BC. 800-663-0090
Clark Spring Water Company
Pueblo, CO 719-543-1594
Cold Spring Brewing Company
Cold Spring, MN 320-685-8686
Crystal Rock Spring Water Company
Watertown, CT 860-443-5000
Crystal Springs Water Company
Fort Lauderdale, FL 800-432-1321
Deep Rock Fontenelle Water Company
Omaha, NE 800-433-1303
Deep Rock Water Company
Denver, CO 800-695-2020
Distillata Company
Cleveland, OH 800-999-2906
Energy Brands/Haute Source
Flushing, NY. 800-746-0087
Fizz-O Water Company
Tulsa, OK 918-834-3691
Giumarra Vineyards
Bakersfield, CA 661-395-7000
Hinckley Springs Water Company
Chicago, IL 773-586-8600
Jackson Milk & Ice CreamCompany
Hutchinson, KS. 620-663-1244
Le Bleu Corporation
Advance, NC. 800-854-4471
Louis Trauth Dairy
Newport, KY. 800-544-6455
Matilija Water Company
Ventura, CA. 805-643-4675
Merci Spring Water
Maryland Heights, MO. 314-872-9323
Mount Olympus Waters
Salt Lake City, UT 800-628-6056
Mountain Valley Spring Company
Hot Springs, AR 800-643-1501
Poland Spring Water
Stamford, CT. 800-955-4426
Polar Beverages
Worcester, MA 800-734-9800
Polar Water Company
Carnegie, PA. 412-429-5550
Premium Water
Orange Springs, FL. 800-243-1163
Premium Waters
Minneapolis, MN 800-332-3332
SnowBird Corporation
Bayonne, NJ 800-576-1616
Southern Beverage Packers
Appling, GA 800-326-2469
Sparkling Spring Water Company
Vernon Hills, IL 800-772-7554
Spring Water Company
Chesapeake, VA 800-832-0271
Yosemite Waters
Los Angeles, CA. 800-427-8420
Zephyr Hills
Tamarac, FL 954-597-7852
Zephyr Hills Bottled Watter Corporation
Tampa, FL. 800-950-9398

Flavored

Captiva
Augusta, NJ. 973-579-7883
Clearly Canadian Beverage Corporation
Vanghan, ON. 800-735-7180
Ex Drinks
Henderson, NV 866-753-4929
Heritage Shortbread
Hilton Head Island, SC. 843-342-7268
Hi Ball Energy
San Francisco, CA 415-420-4801
Hint
San Francisco, CA 415-513-4050
Northern Falls
Rockford, MI 616-915-0970
Saratoga Beverage Group
Saratoga Springs, NY 888-426-8642
Watermark Innovation
Southampton, NY 631-259-2329

Mineral

Adobe Springs
Patterson, CA 408-897-3023
Beaulieu Vineyard
Rutherford, CA 800-264-6918
Canada Dry Bottling Company
Flushing, NY. 718-762-5967
Clearly Canadian Beverage Corporation
Vanghan, ON. 800-735-7180
Crystal Geyser Water Company
Calistoga, CA 800-443-9737
Deep Rock Fontenelle Water Company
Omaha, NE 800-433-1303
Golden State Vintners
Cutler, CA. 559-528-3033
Matilija Water Company
Ventura, CA. 805-643-4675
Moka D'Oro Coffee
Farmingdale, NY 877-665-2367
Monticello Cellars
Napa, CA. 707-253-2802
Office General des Eaux Minerales
Montreal, QC 514-482-7221
R.J. Corr Naturals
Posen, IL. 708-389-4200
Sebastiani Vineyards
Sonoma, CA 800-888-5532
Three Springs Water Company
Laurel Run, PA 800-332-7873
USA Sunrise Beverage
Spearfish, SD 605-723-0690

Spring

Abita Springs Water Company
Metairie, LA 504-828-2500
Absopure Water Company
Plymouth, MI 800-422-7678
Alamance Foods/Triton Water Company
Burlington, NC 800-476-9111
Amanda Hills Spring Water
Pataskala, OH 800-375-0885
Arizona Beverage Company
Woodbury, NY 800-832-3775
Bevco
Surrey, BC. 800-663-0090
Camp Holly Springs
Richmond, VA. 804-795-2096
Contact International
Skokie, IL 847-324-4411
Country Pure Foods
Ellington, CT 860-872-8346
Crystal Geyser Water Company
San Francisco, CA 415-616-9590
Crystal Geyser Water Company
Calistoga, CA 800-443-9737
Crystal Rock Spring Water Company
Watertown, CT 860-443-5000
Crystal Springs Water Company
Fort Lauderdale, FL 800-432-1321
Deep Rock Water Company
Denver, CO 800-695-2020
Fizz-O Water Company
Tulsa, OK 918-834-3691
Garelick Farms
Franklin, MA 800-343-4982
Girard Spring Water
North Providence, RI 800-477-9287
Glen Summit Springs Water Company
Mountain Top, PA. 800-621-7596
Harrisburg Dairies
Harrisburg, PA 800-692-7429
Hawaiian Natural Water Company
Pearl City, HI 808-483-0520
Hinckley Springs Water Company
Chicago, IL 773-586-8600
Jackson Milk & Ice CreamCompany
Hutchinson, KS. 620-663-1244
Matilija Water Company
Ventura, CA. 805-643-4675
Mayer Brothers
West Seneca, NY 800-696-2937
Merci Spring Water
Maryland Heights, MO. 314-872-9323
Meridian Beverage Company
Atlanta, GA. 800-728-1481
Minnehaha Spring Water Company
Cleveland, OH 216-431-0243
Miscoe Springs
Mendon, MA. 508-473-0550
Mount Olympus Waters
Salt Lake City, UT 800-628-6056
Mountain Valley Spring Company
Hot Springs, AR 800-643-1501
Music Mountain Water Company
Birmingham, AL. 800-349-6555
National Beverage Corporation
Fort Lauderdale, FL 877-622-3499
Natural Spring Water Company
Johnson City, TN 423-926-7905
Naya
Montreal, QC 450-562-7911
North Country Natural Spring Water
Port Kent, NY. 518-834-9400
Northern Falls
Rockford, MI 616-915-0970
Poland Spring Water
Stamford, CT. 800-955-4426
Polar Beverages
Worcester, MA 800-734-9800
Polar Water Company
Carnegie, PA. 412-429-5550
Premium Water
Orange Springs, FL. 800-243-1163
Regent Champagne Cellars
New York, NY
Sand Springs Springwater
Williamstown, MA 413-458-8281
Saratoga Beverage Group
Saratoga Springs, NY. 888-426-8642
SnowBird Corporation
Bayonne, NJ 800-576-1616
Southern Beverage Packers
Appling, GA 800-326-2469
Sparkling Spring Water Company
Vernon Hills, IL 800-772-7554
Sparkling Water Distributors
Merrick, NY 800-277-2755
Spring Water Company
Chesapeake, VA 800-832-0271
Triple Springs Spring Water
Meriden, CT 203-235-8374
Tumai Water
Martinsburg, WV 866-948-8624
USA Sunrise Beverage
Spearfish, SD 605-723-0690
White Rock Products Corporation
Flushing, NY. 800-969-7625
Windmill Water
Edgewood, NM. 505-281-9287
Yoder Dairies
Chesapeake, VA 757-482-4068
Zephyr Hills
Tamarac, FL 954-597-7852
Zephyr Hills Bottled Watter Corporation
Tampa, FL. 800-950-9398

Wines

A. Nonini Winery
Fresno, CA 559-275-1936
A. Rafanelli Winery
Healdsburg, CA 707-433-1385
Abingdon Vineyard & Winery
Abingdon, VA. 276-623-1255
Acacia Vineyard
Napa, CA. 707-226-9991
Ackerman Winery
Amana, IA. 319-622-3379
Adair Vineyards
New Paltz, NY 845-255-1377
Adam Puchta Winery
Hermann, MO. 573-486-5596
Adams County Winery
Orrtanna, PA
Adelaida Cellars
Paso Robles, CA. 800-676-1232
Adelsheim Vineyard
Newberg, OR 503-538-3652

Adler Fels Vineyards & Winery
Santa Rosa, CA . . . 707-569-1493
Admiral Wine Merchants
Irvington, NJ . . . 800-582-9463
Aetna Springs Cellars
Pope Valley, CA . . . 707-965-2675
Afton Mountain Vineyards
Afton, VA . . . 540-456-8667
Ahlgren Vineyard
Boulder Creek, CA . . . 800-338-6071
Airlie Winery
Monmouth, OR . . . 503-838-6013
Alba Vineyard
Milford, NJ . . . 908-995-7800
Alexander Johnson's Valley Wines
Healdsburg, CA . . . 800-888-5532
Alexis Bailly Vineyard
Hastings, MN . . . 651-437-1413
Allegro Vineyards
Brogue, PA . . . 717-927-9148
Allied Wine Corporation
Monticello, NY . . . 845-796-4160
Almarla Vineyards & Winery
Shubuta, MS . . . 601-687-5548
Alpen Cellars
Trinity Center, CA . . . 530-266-9513
Alpine Vineyards
Monroe, OR . . . 541-424-5851
Alta Vineyard Cellar
Calistoga, CA . . . 707-942-6708
Altamura Vineyards & Winery
Napa, CA . . . 707-253-2000
Alto Vineyards
Alto Pass, IL . . . 618-893-4898
Amador Foothill Winery
Plymouth, CA . . . 800-778-9463
Amalthea Cellars Farm Winery
Atco, NJ . . . 856-767-8890
Amberg Wine Cellars
Clifton Springs, NY . . . 585-526-6742
Americana Vineyards
Interlaken, NY . . . 607-387-6801
Amity Vineyards
Amity, OR . . . 888-264-8966
Amizetta Vineyards
Saint Helena, CA . . . 707-963-1460
AmRhein Wine Cellars
Bent Mountain, VA . . . 540-929-4632
Amwell Valley Vineyard
Ringoes, NJ . . . 908-788-5852
Anchor Brewing Company
San Francisco, CA . . . 415-863-8350
Anderson's Conn Valley Vineyards
Saint Helena, CA . . . 800-946-3497
Andrew Peller Limited
Grimsby, ON . . . 905-643-4131
Annapolis Winery
Annapolis, CA . . . 707-886-5460
Antelope Valley Winery
Lancaster, CA . . . 800-282-8332
Anthony Road Wine Company
Penn Yan, NY . . . 800-559-2182
Arbor Crest Wine Cellars
Spokane, WA . . . 509-927-9463
Arbor Hill Grapery
Naples, NY . . . 800-554-7553
Arbor Mist Winery
Canandaigua, NY . . . 866-396-7394
Arcadian Estate Winery
Rock Stream, NY . . . 800-298-1346
Argonaut Winery
Ione, CA . . . 800-704-9463
Argyle Wines
Dundee, OR . . . 888-427-4953
Ariel Vineyards
Napa, CA . . . 800-456-9472
Arizona Vineyards
Nogales, AZ . . . 520-287-7972
Arns Winery
Saint Helena, CA . . . 707-963-3429
Arrowood Vineyards & Winery
Glen Ellen, CA . . . 800-938-5170
Artesa Vineyards & Winery
Napa, CA . . . 707-224-1668
Ashland Vineyards
Ashland, OR . . . 541-488-0088
ASV Wines
Delano, CA . . . 661-792-3159
Atlas Peak Vineyards
Sonoma, CA . . . 866-522-9463
Atwater Block Brewing Company
Detroit, MI . . . 313-877-9205
Au Bon Climat Winery
Los Olivos, CA . . . 805-937-9801
Augusta Winery
Augusta, MO . . . 888-667-9463
Autumn Hill Vineyards/Blue Ridge Wine
Stanardsville, VA . . . 434-985-6100
Autumn Wind Vineyard
Newberg, OR . . . 503-538-6931
Avalon Organic Coffees
Albuquerque, NM . . . 800-662-2575
Babcock Winery & Vineyards
Lompoc, CA . . . 805-736-1455
Baily Vineyard & Winery
Temecula, CA . . . 951-676-9463
Balagna Winery Company
Los Alamos, NM . . . 505-672-3678
Baldwin Vineyards
Pine Bush, NY . . . 845-744-2226
Balic Winery
Mays Landing, NJ . . . 609-625-1903
Bandiera Winery
Cloverdale, CA . . . 707-894-4295
Banfi Vintners
Glen Head, NY . . . 800-645-6511
Barboursville Vineyards
Barboursville, VA . . . 540-832-3824
Barca Wine Cellars
Roseville, CA . . . 916-967-0770
Bargetto's Winery
Soquel, CA . . . 800-422-7438
Baron Vineyards
Paso Robles, CA . . . 805-239-3313
Basignani Winery
Sparks Glencoe, MD . . . 410-472-0703
Batavia Wine Cellars
Canandaigua, NY . . . 585-396-7600
Baxter's Vineyard
Nauvoo, IL . . . 800-854-1396
Baywood Cellars
Lodi, CA . . . 800-214-0445
Beachaven Vineyards & Winery
Clarksville, TN . . . 931-645-8867
Bear Creek Winery
Cave Junction, OR . . . 877-273-4843
Beaucanon Estate Wines
Napa, CA . . . 800-660-3520
Beaulieu Vineyard
Rutherford, CA . . . 800-264-6918
Beckmen Vineyards
Los Olivos, CA . . . 805-688-8664
Bedell North Fork, LLC
Cutchogue, NY . . . 631-734-7537
Bell Mountain Vineyards
Fredericksburg, TX . . . 830-685-3297
Bellerose Vineyard
Healdsburg, CA . . . 707-433-1637
Belvedere Vineyards & Winery
Healdsburg, CA . . . 800-433-8296
Benmarl Wine Company
Marlboro, NY . . . 845-236-4265
Benziger Family Winery
Glen Ellen, CA . . . 888-490-2739
Bernardo Winery
San Diego, CA . . . 858-487-1866
Bernardus Winery & Vineyards
Carmel Valley, CA . . . 888-648-9463
Bethel Heights Vineyard Inc.
Salem, OR . . . 503-581-2262
Bianchi Winery
Paso Robles, CA . . . 805-226-9922
Bias Vineyards & Winery
Berger, MO . . . 573-834-5475
Bidwell Vineyard
Cutchogue, NY . . . 631-734-5200
Biltmore Estate Wine Company
Asheville, NC . . . 800-411-3812
Binns Vineyards & Winery
Las Cruces, NM . . . 575-522-2211
Bishop Farms Winery
Cheshire, CT . . . 203-272-8243
Black Mesa Winery
Velarde, NM . . . 800-852-6372
Black Sheep Vintners
Murphys, CA . . . 209-728-2157
Blalock Seafood
Orange Beach, AL . . . 251-974-5811
Blue Hills Spring Water Company
Norwell, MA
Blue Mountain Vineyards
New Tripoli, PA . . . 610-298-3068
Blumenhof Vineyards-Winery
Dutzow, MO . . . 800-419-2245
Boeger Winery
Placerville, CA . . . 800-655-2634
Bogle Vineyards
Clarksburg, CA . . . 916-744-1139
Boisset America
Sausalito, CA . . . 800-878-1123
Bonny Doon Vineyard
Santa Cruz, CA . . . 831-425-3625
Bonterra Vineyard
Hopland, CA . . . 707-744-7575
Boordy Vineyards
Hydes, MD . . . 410-592-5015
Bordoni Vineyards
Vallejo, CA . . . 707-642-1504
Borra Vineyards
Lodi, CA . . . 209-368-2446
Boskydel Vineyard
Lake Leelanau, MI . . . 231-256-7272
Bouchaine Vineyards
Napa, CA . . . 800-654-9463
BR Cohn Winery
Glen Ellen, CA . . . 707-938-4064
Brandborg Cellars
Elkton, OR . . . 510-215-9553
Brander Vineyard
Los Olivos, CA . . . 800-970-9979
Braren Pauli Winery
Redwood Valley, CA . . . 800-423-6519
Braswell's Winery
Dora, AL . . . 205-648-8335
Bravard Vineyards & Winery
Hopkinsville, KY . . . 270-269-2583
Breaux Vineyards
Purcellville, VA . . . 800-492-9961
Breitenbach Wine Cellars
Dover, OH . . . 330-343-3603
Briceland Vineyards
Redway, CA . . . 707-923-2429
Bridgeview Winery
Cave Junction, OR . . . 877-273-4843
Brimstone Hill Vineyard
Pine Bush, NY . . . 845-744-2231
Bristle Ridge Vineyard
Knob Noster, MO . . . 800-994-9463
Broad Run Vineyards
Louisville, KY . . . 502-231-0372
Broadley Vineyards
Monroe, OR . . . 541-847-5934
Bronco Wine Company
Ceres, CA . . . 800-692-5780
Brookmere Vineyards
Belleville, PA . . . 717-935-5380
Brotherhood Winery
Washingtonville, NY . . . 845-496-3661
Brothers International Food Corporation
Rochester, NY . . . 585-343-3007
Brown County Wine Company
Nashville, IN . . . 888-298-2984
Brutocao Cellars
Hopland, CA . . . 800-433-3689
Bryant Vineyard
Talladega, AL . . . 256-268-2638
Buccia Vineyard
Conneaut, OH . . . 440-593-5976
Buckingham Valley Vineyards
Buckingham, PA . . . 215-794-7188
Buehler Vineyards
Saint Helena, CA . . . 707-963-2155
Buena Vista Carneros Winery
Sonoma, CA . . . 800-678-8504
Buffalo Trace Distillery
Frankfort, KY . . . 800-654-8471
Bully Hill Vineyards
Hammondsport, NY . . . 607-868-3610
Burnley Vineyards and Daniel Cellars
Barboursville, VA . . . 540-832-2828
Butler Winery
Bloomington, IN . . . 812-339-7233
Butterfly Creek Winery
Mariposa, CA . . . 209-966-2097
Buttonwood Farm Winery
Solvang, CA . . . 800-715-1404

Byington Winery & Vineyards
Los Gatos, CA 408-354-1111
Byron Vineyard & Winery
Santa Maria, CA 805-934-4770
Cache Cellars
Davis, CA 530-756-6068
Cain Vineyard & Winery
St Helena, CA 707-963-1616
Cakebread Cellars
Rutherford, CA 800-588-0298
Calafia Cellars
Saint Helena, CA 707-963-0114
Calera Wine Company
Hollister, CA 831-637-9170
California Olive Oil Corporation
Berkeley, CA 888-718-9830
Callaway Vineyards & Winery
Temecula, CA 800-472-2377
Camas Prairie Winery
Moscow, ID 800-616-0214
Cambria Winery & Vineyard
Santa Maria, CA 888-339-9463
Campagana Winery
Redwood Valley, CA 707-485-1221
Campari
New York, NY 212-891-3600
Cantwell's Old Mill Winery
Geneva, OH 440-466-5560
Cap Rock Winery
Lubbock, TX 800-546-9463
Caparone Winery
Paso Robles, CA 805-467-3827
Caporale Winery
Napa, CA 707-253-9230
Cardinale Winery
Oakville, CA 800-588-0279
Carlson Vineyards
Palisade, CO 888-464-5554
Carmela Vineyards
Glenns Ferry, ID 208-366-2313
Carneros Creek Winery
Napa, CA 707-253-9464
Carrousel Cellars
Gilroy, CA 408-847-2060
Casa Larga Vineyards
Fairport, NY 585-223-4210
Casa Nuestra
St Helena, CA 866-844-9463
Cascade Mountain Winery & Restaurant
Amenia, NY 845-373-9021
Castello Di Borghese
Cutchogue, NY 800-734-5158
Catoctin Vineyards
Brookeville, MD 301-774-2310
Cavender Castle Winery
Atlanta, GA 706-864-4759
Caymus Vineyards
Rutherford, CA 707-963-4204
Cayuga Ridge Estate Winery
Ovid, NY 800-598-9463
Cecchetti Sebastiani Cellar
Sonoma, CA 707-996-8463
Cedar Creek Winery
Cedarburg, WI 800-827-8020
Cedar Mountain Winery
Livermore, CA 925-373-6636
Chaddsford Winery
Chadds Ford, PA 610-388-6221
Chalet Debonne Vineyards
Madison, OH 440-466-3485
Chalk Hill Estate Vineyards & Winery
Healdsburg, CA 707-838-4306
Champoeg Wine Cellars
Aurora, OR 503-678-2144
Channing Rudd Cellars
Middletown, CA 707-987-2209
Chappellet Winery
Saint Helena, CA 800-494-6379
Charles B. Mitchell Vineyards
Somerset, CA 800-704-9463
Charles Jacquin Et Cie
Philadelphia, PA 800-523-3811
Charles Krug Winery
St Helena, CA 707-967-2200
Charles Spinetta Winery
Plymouth, CA 209-245-3384
Chateau Anne Marie
Carlton, OR 503-864-2991
Chateau Boswell
St Helena, CA 707-963-5472
Chateau Chevre Winery
Napa, CA 707-944-2184
Chateau des Charmes Wines
St. Davids, ON 800-263-2541
Chateau Diana Winery
Healdsburg, CA 707-433-6992
Chateau Grand Traverse
Traverse City, MI 231-223-7355
Chateau Julien Winery
Carmel, CA 831-624-2600
Chateau Lafayette Reneau
Hector, NY 800-469-9463
Chateau Montelena Winery
Calistoga, CA 707-942-5105
Chateau Morisette Winery
Meadows of Dan, VA 540-593-2865
Chateau Potelle Winery
Napa, CA 707-255-9440
Chateau Ra-Ha
Jerseyville, IL 866-639-4832
Chateau Souverain
Cloverdale, CA
Chateau St. Jean Vineyards
Kenwood, CA 707-833-4134
Chateau Thomas Winery
Plainfield, IN 888-761-9463
Chatom Vineyards
Murphys, CA 800-435-8852
Chestnut Mountain Winery
Hoschton, GA 770-867-6914
Chi Company/Tabor Hill Winery
Buchanan, MI 800-283-3363
Chicama Vineyards
West Tisbury, MA 888-244-2262
Chimere
Santa Maria, CA 805-922-9097
Chouinard Vineyards
Castro Valley, CA 510-582-9900
Christensen Ridge
Madison, VA 540-923-4800
Christine Woods Winery
Philo, CA 707-895-2115
Christopher Creek Winery
Healdsburg, CA 707-431-8243
Cienega Valley Winery/DeRose
Hollister, CA 831-636-9143
Cimarron Cellars
Caney, OK 580-889-5997
Cinnabar Vineyards & Winery
Saratoga, CA 408-741-5858
CK Mondavi Vineyards
St Helena, CA 707-967-2200
Claiborne & Churchill Vintners
San Luis Obispo, CA 805-544-4066
Claire's Grand River Winery
Madison, OH 440-298-9838
Clear Creek Distillery
Portland, OR 503-248-9470
Cline Cellars
Sonoma, CA 800-543-2070
Clinton Vineyards
Clinton Corners, NY 845-266-5372
Clos Du Bois
Geyserville, CA 800-222-3189
Clos du Lac Cellars
Ione, CA 209-274-2238
Clos Du Muriel
Temecula, CA 951-296-5400
Clos du Val Wine Company
Napa, CA 800-993-9463
Clos Pegase Winery
Calistoga, CA 800-866-8583
Cloudstone Vineyards
Los Altos Hills, CA 650-948-8621
Clover Hill Vineyards & Winery
Breinigsville, PA 800-256-8374
Cocolalla Winery
Cocolalla, ID 208-263-3774
Colorado Cellars Winery
Palisade, CO 970-464-7921
Columbia Winery
Woodinville, WA 425-488-2776
Concannon Vineyard
Livermore, CA 800-258-9866
Conn Creek Winery
Saint Helena, CA 800-793-7960
Conneaut Cellars Winery
Conneaut Lake, PA 877-229-9463
Conrotto A. Winery
Gilroy, CA 408-847-2233
Cooper Mountain Vineyards
Beaverton, OR 503-649-0027
Cooper Vineyards
Louisa, VA 540-894-5253
Corus Brands
Woodinville, WA 425-806-2600
Cosentino Winery Vintage Grapevine, Inc.
Yountville, CA 800-764-1220
Country Life
Hauppauge, NY 800-645-5768
Cowie Wine Cellars
Paris, AR 479-963-3990
Crescini Wines
Soquel, CA 831-462-1466
Cribari Vineyards
Fresno, CA 800-277-9095

Processor and exporter of high quality California bulk wine.

Cristom Vineyards
Salem, OR 503-375-3068
Cronin Vineyards
Woodside, CA 650-851-1452
Crown Regal Wine Cellars
Brooklyn, NY 718-604-1430
Cruse Vineyards
Chester, SC 803-377-3944
Cuneo Cellars
Amity, OR 503-835-2782
Cuvaison Vineyard
Calistoga, CA 707-942-6266
Cygnet Cellars
Hollister, CA 831-637-7559
Dalla Valle Vineyards
Oakville, CA 707-944-2676
Dark Mountain Winery and Brewery
Vail, AZ 520-762-5777
Daume Winery
Camarillo, CA 800-559-9922
David Bruce Winery
Los Gatos, CA 800-397-9972
Davis Bynum Winery
Healdsburg, CA 800-826-1073
De Loach Vineyards
Santa Rosa, CA 707-526-9111
De Lorimier Winery
Geyserville, CA 800-546-7718
Deaver Vineyards
Plymouth, CA 209-245-4099
Deer Meadow Vineyard
Winchester, VA 800-653-6632
Deer Park Winery
Elk Creek, MO 707-963-5411
Dehlinger Winery
Sebastopol, CA 707-823-2378
Delicato Vineyards
Napa, CA 877-824-3600
Denatale Vineyards
Healdsburg, CA 707-431-8460
Destileria Serralles Inc
Mercedita, PR 787-840-1000
Devlin Wine Cellars
Soquel, CA 831-476-7288
Di Grazia Vineyards
Brookfield, CT 800-230-8853
Diageo Canada Inc.
Toronto, ON 416-626-2000
Diamond Creek Vineyards
Calistoga, CA 707-942-6926
Diamond Oaks Vineyard
Cloverdale, CA 707-894-3191
Diamond Water
Hot Springs, AR 501-623-1251
Domaine Chandon
Yountville, CA 800-242-6366
Domaine St. George Winery
Healdsburg, CA 707-433-5508
Dominion Wine Cellars
Culpeper, VA 540-825-8772
Don Sebastiani & Sons
Sonoma, CA 707-933-1704
Donatoni Winery
Inglewood, CA 310-645-5445
Door-Peninsula Winery
Sturgeon Bay, WI 800-551-5049
Dr. Frank's Vinifera Wine Cellar
Hammondsport, NY 800-320-0735
Dr. Konstantin Frank Vin
Hammondsport, NY 800-320-0735
Dreyer Sonoma
Woodside, CA 650-851-9448
Dry Creek Vineyard
Healdsburg, CA 800-864-9463
Duck Pond Cellars
Dundee, OR 800-437-3213

Duckhorn Vineyards
St Helena, CA 888-354-8885
Duncan Peak Vineyards
Hopland, CA 707-744-1129
Dundee Wine Company
Dundee, OR. 888-427-4953
Dunn Vineyards
Angwin, CA 707-965-3642
Duplin Wine Cellars
Rose Hill, NC 800-774-9634
Durney Vineyards
Carmel Valley, CA 800-625-8466
Dutch Henry Winery
Calistoga, CA 888-224-5879
E&J Gallo Winery
Modesto, CA 209-341-3111
E&J Gallo Winery
Livingston, CA 209-394-6219
E&J Gallo Winery
Fresno, CA 559-458-2480
E&J Gallo Winery
Mississauga, ON. 905-819-9600
Eagle Crest Vineyards
Conesus, NY 585-346-2321
Easley Winery
Indianapolis, IN 317-636-4516
East Side Winery/Oak Ridge Vineyards
Lodi, CA 209-369-4758
Ed Oliveira Winery
Arcata, CA 707-822-3023
Edgewood Estate Winery
Napa, CA. 800-755-2374
Edmunds St. John
Berkeley, CA. 510-981-1510
Edna Valley Vineyard
San Luis Obispo, CA 805-544-5855
El Molino Winery
Saint Helena, CA 707-963-3632
El Paso Winery
Ulster Park, NY. 845-331-0491
Elk Cove Vineyards
Gaston, OR 877-355-2683
Elk Run Vineyards
Mount Airy, MD 800-414-2513
Elliston Vineyards
Sunol, CA 925-862-2377
Embassy Wine Company
Brooklyn, NY 718-272-0600
Emilio Guglielmo Winery
Morgan Hill, CA. 408-779-2145
Enz Vineyards
Hollister, CA. 831-637-3956
Eola Hills Wine Cellars
Rickreall, OR 800-291-6730
EOS Estate Winery
Paso Robles, CA 800-349-9463
Erath Vineyards Winery
Dundee, OR. 800-539-5463
Esterlina Vineyard & Winery
Philo, CA. 707-895-2920
Evensen Vineyards
Oakville, CA. 707-944-2396
Evergreen Juices
Toronto, CA 877-915-8423
Evesham Wood Vineyard & Winery
Salem, OR. 503-371-8478
Eyrie Vineyards
Mcminnville, OR 503-472-6315
Fall Creek Vineyards
Austin, TX. 512-476-4477
Fantis Foods
Carlstadt, NJ 201-933-6200
Far Niente Winery
Oakville, CA. 707-944-2861
Farella-Park Vineyards
Napa, CA. 707-254-9489
Farfelu Vineyards
Flint Hill, VA 540-364-2930
Fenestra Winery
Livermore, CA 800-789-9463
Fenn Valley Vineyards
Fennville, MI 800-432-6265
Ferrante Winery & Ristorante
Geneva, OH. 440-466-6046
Ferrara Winery
Escondido, CA 760-745-7632
Ferrari-Carano Vineyards& Winery
Healdsburg, CA 800-831-0381
Ferrigno Vineyard & Winery
St James, MO 573-265-7742
Ferrigno Vineyards & Win
St James, MO 573-265-7742
Fess Parker Winery
Los Olivos, CA 800-446-2455
Ficklin Vineyards
Madera, CA. 559-674-4598
Field Stone Winery & Vineyard
Healdsburg, CA 800-544-7273
Fieldbrook Valley Winery
McKinleyville, CA 707-839-4140
Fife Vineyards
Redwood Valley, CA. 707-485-0323
Filsinger Vineyards & Winery
Temecula, CA 951-302-6363
Fiore Winery
Pylesville, MD 410-879-4007
Firelands Wine Company
Sandusky, OH 800-548-9463
Firestone Vineyard
Los Olivos, CA 805-688-3940
First Colony Winery
Charlottesville, VA 877-979-7105
Fisher Ridge Wine Company
Charleston, WV 304-342-8702
Fisher Vineyards
Santa Rosa, CA 707-539-7511
Fitzpatrick Winery & Lodge
Somerset, CA 800-245-9166
Flora Springs Wine Company
Saint Helena, CA 707-963-5711
Flynn Vineyards Winery
Rickreall, OR 888-427-4953
Foley Estates Vineyards & Winery
Lompoc, CA 805-737-6222
Folie a Deux Winery
Oakville, CA 1 8-0 5-5 64
Foppiano Vineyard
Healdsburg, CA 707-433-7272
Foris Vineyards
Cave Junction, OR 541-592-3752
Forman Vineyards
St Helena, CA 707-963-3900
Fortino Winery
Gilroy, CA. 888-617-6606
Fortuna Cellars
Davis, CA 530-756-6686
Four Sisters Winery
Belvidere, NJ 908-475-3671
Fox Run Vineyards
Penn Yan, NY 800-636-9786
Fox Vineyards Winery
Social Circle, GA 770-787-5402
Foxen Vineyard
Santa Maria, CA 805-937-4251
Franciscan Oakville Estates
Rutherford, CA 800-529-9463
Franciscan Vineyards
St. Helena, CA 800-529-9463
Frank Family Vineyard
Calistoga, CA 707-942-0859
Franklin Hill Vineyards
Bangor, PA 888-887-2839
Franzia Winery
Ripon, CA 209-599-4111
Fratelli Perata
Paso Robles, CA 805-238-2809
Frederick Wildman & Sons
New York, NY 800-733-9463
Freemark Abbey Winery
Helena, CA 800-963-9698
Freixenet
Sonoma, CA 707-996-4981
Frey Vineyards
Redwood Valley, CA. 800-760-3739
Frick Winery
Geyserville, CA 707-857-1980
Frisinger Cellars
Napa, CA. 707-255-3749
Frog's Leap Winery
Rutherford, CA 800-959-4704
Frontenac Point Vineyard
Trumansburg, NY 607-387-9619
Gainey Vineyard
Santa Ynez, CA. 805-688-0558
Galante Vineyards
Carmel Valley, CA 800-425-2683
Galena Cellars Winery
Galena, IL 800-397-9463
Galleano Winery
Mira Loma, CA. 951-685-5376
Galluccio Estate Vineyards
Cutchogue, NY 631-734-7089
Gary Farrell Wines
Santa Rosa, CA. 707-433-6616
Georgia Winery
Ringgold, GA 706-937-2177
Georis Winery
Carmel Valley, CA 831-659-1050
Germanton Winery
Germanton, NC. 800-322-2894
Geyser Peak Winery
Geyserville, CA 800-255-9463
Giasi Winery
Rock Stream, NY 607-535-7785
Gibson Wine Company
Sanger, CA 559-875-2505
Girard Winery/Rudd Estates
Oakville, CA. 707-944-8577
Girardet Wine Cellars
Roseburg, OR 541-679-7252
Giumarra Vineyards
Bakersfield, CA 661-395-7000
Glenora Wine Cellars
Dundee, NY 800-243-5513
Gloria Ferrer Champagne
Sonoma, CA 707-996-7256
Gloria Winery & Vineyard
Springfield, MO 417-926-6263
Glunz Family Winery & Cellars
Grayslake, IL. 847-548-9463
Golden Creek Vineyard
Santa Rosa, CA. 707-538-2350
Golden State Vintners
Cutler, CA. 559-528-3033
Good Harbor Vineyards
Lake Leelanau, MI 231-256-7165
Goodson Brothers Coffee
Knoxville, TN. 865-531-8022
Goosecross Cellars
Yountville, CA 800-276-9210
Grand View Winery
East Calais, VT 802-456-7012
Grande River Vineyards
Palisade, CO 800-264-7696
Granite Springs Winery
Somerset, CA 800-638-6041
Greenfield Wine Company
Vallejo, CA 707-552-5199
Greenwood Ridge Vineyards
Philo, CA. 707-895-2002
Groth Vineyards & Winery
Oakville, CA. 707-944-0290
Groupe Paul Masson
Longueuil, QC 514-878-3050
Gruet Winery
Albuquerque, NM. 888-897-9463
Guilliams Winery
St Helena, CA 707-963-9059
Gundlach Bundschu Winery
Sonoma, CA 707-938-5277
H Coturri & Sons Winery
Glen Ellen, CA 866-268-8774
Habersham Winery
Helen, GA. 770-983-1973
Hafner Vineyard
Healdsburg, CA 707-433-4606
Hahn Estates and Smith &Hook
Soledad, CA 866-925-7994
Haight-Brown Vineyard
Litchfield, CT 800-577-9463
Hallcrest Vineyards
Felton, CA. 831-335-4441
Handley Cellars
Philo, CA. 800-733-3151
Hanzell Vineyards
Sonoma, CA 707-996-3860
Harbor Winery
West Sacramento, CA. 916-371-6776
Harmony Cellars
Harmony, CA 800-432-9239
Harpersfield Vineyard
Geneva, OH. 440-466-4739
Hart Winery
Temecula, CA 877-638-8788
Hartford Family Winery
Forestville, CA 800-588-0234
Hazlitt's 1852 Vineyard
Hector, NY 888-750-0494
Heartland Vineyards
Cleveland, OH 440-871-0701
Heaven Hill Distilleries
Bardstown, KY 502-348-3921
Heck Cellars
Arvin, CA 661-854-6120
Hecker Pass Winery
Gilroy, CA. 408-842-8755

Hegy's South Hills Vineyard & Winery
Twin Falls, ID 208-599-0074
Heineman's Winery
Put In Bay, OH 419-285-2811
Heitz Wine Cellar
Saint Helena, CA 707-963-3542
Helena View/Johnston Vineyard
Calistoga, CA 707-942-4956
Hells Canyon Winery
Caldwell, ID 800-318-7873
Henry Estate Winery
Umpqua, OR 800-782-2686
Henry Hill & Company
Napa, CA 707-224-6565
Heritage Wine Cellars
North East, PA 800-747-0083
Hermann J. Wiemer Vineyard
Dundee, NY 800-371-7971
Hermann Wiemer Vineyards
Dundee, NY 800-371-7971
Hermannhof Winery
Hermann, MO 800-393-0100
Heron Hill Winery
Hammondsport, NY 800-441-4241
Hess Collection Winery
Napa, CA 877-707-4377
Hidden Mountain Ranch Winery
Paso Robles, CA 805-226-9907
Highland Manor Winery
Jamestown, TN 931-879-9519
Hill Top Berry Farm & Winery
Nellysford, VA 434-361-1266
Hillcrest Vineyard
Roseburg, OR 541-673-3709
Hinzerling Winery
Prosser, WA 800-722-6702
Homewood Winery
Sonoma, CA 707-996-6353
Honeywood Winery
Salem, OR 800-726-4101
Honig Vineyard and Winery
Rutherford, CA 800-929-2217
Hood River Vineyards and Winery
Hood River, OR 541-386-3772
Hoodsport Winery
Hoodsport, WA 800-580-9894
Hop Kiln Winery
Healdsburg, CA 707-433-6491
Hopkins Vineyard
Warren, CT 860-868-7954
Horizon Winery
Santa Rosa, CA 707-544-2961
Horton Cellars Winery
Gordonsville, VA 800-829-4633
Houdini
Fullerton, CA 714-525-0325
Huber's Orchard Winery
Borden, IN 800-345-9463
Hunt Country Vineyards
Branchport, NY 800-946-3289
Husch Vineyards
Philo, CA 800-554-8724
Indian Rock Vineyards
Murphys, CA 209-728-8514
Indian Springs Vineyards
Nevada City, CA 530-478-1068
Ingleside Plantation Winery
Colonial Beach, VA 804-224-7111
Inniskillin Wines
Niagara-On-The-Lake, ON 888-466-4754
Iron Horse Ranch & Vineyard
Sebastopol, CA 707-887-1507
Ironstone Vineyards
Murphys, CA 209-728-1251
J Vineyards & Winery
Healdsburg, CA 800-885-9463
J. Filippi Winery
Etiwanda, CA 909-899-5755
J. Fritz Winery
Cloverdale, CA 707-894-3389
J. Stonestreet & Sons Vineyard
Healdsburg, CA 800-723-6336
Jackson Valley Vineyards
Ione, CA 209-274-4721
Jamaican Gourmet Coffee Company
Philadelphia, PA 800-261-2859
Jefferson Vineyards
Charlottesville, VA 800-272-3042
Jodar Vineyard & Winery
Placerville, CA 530-621-0324
Johlin Century Winery
Oregon, OH 419-693-6288

Johnson Estate Wines
Westfield, NY 800-374-6569
Johnson's Alexander Valley Wines
Healdsburg, CA 800-888-5532
Johnston's Winery
Ballston Spa, NY 518-882-6310
Joseph Filippi Winery
Rancho Cucamonga, CA 909-899-5755
Joseph Phelps Vineyards
Saint Helena, CA 707-967-9153
Joullian Vineyards
Carmel Valley, CA 877-659-2800
Justin Winery & Vineyard
Paso Robles, CA 800-726-0049
Kalin Cellars
Novato, CA 415-883-3543
Karly Wines
Plymouth, CA 209-245-3922
Kate's Vineyard
Napa, CA 707-255-2644
Kathryn Kennedy Winery
Saratoga, CA 408-867-4170
Kelleys Island Wine Company
Kelleys Is, OH 419-746-2678
Kelson Creek Winery
Plymouth, CA 209-245-4700
Kendall-Jackson Wine
Windsor, CA 800-544-4413
Kenwood Vineyards
Kenwood, CA 707-833-5891
King Brewing Company
Fairfield, CA 707-428-4503
King Estate Winery
Eugene, OR 800-884-4441
Kiona Vineyards Winery
Benton City, WA 509-588-6716
Kirigin Cellars
Gilroy, CA 408-847-8827
Kistler Vineyards
Sebastopol, CA 707-823-5603
Kittling Ridge Estate Wines & Spirits
Grimsby, ON 905-945-9225
Klingshirn Winery
Avon Lake, OH 440-933-6666
Kluge Estate Winery & Vineyard
Charlottesville, VA 434-977-3895
Knapp Vineyards
Romulus, NY 800-869-9271
Koryo Winery Company
Gardena, CA 310-532-9616
Kramer Vineyards
Gaston, OR 800-619-4637
Krinos Foods
Santa Barbara, CA 800-624-4896
Kristin Hill Winery
Amity, OR 503-835-4012
Kunde Estate Winery
Kenwood, CA 707-833-5501
L. Mawby Vineyards
Suttons Bay, MI 231-271-3522
La Abra Farm & Winery
Lovingston, VA 434-263-5392
La Buena Vida Vineyards
Grapevine, TX 817-481-9463
La Chiripada Winery
Dixon, NM 800-528-7801
La Jota Vineyard Company
Angwin, CA 877-222-0292
La Rocca Vineyards
Forest Ranch, CA 800-808-9463
La Rochelle Winery
Livermore, CA 888-647-7768
La Vina Winery
Anthony, NM 575-882-7632
Laetitia Vineyard
Arroyo Grande, CA 888-809-8463
Lafollette Vineyard & Winery
Belle Mead, NJ 908-359-5018
Laird & Company
North Garden, VA 877-438-5247

Lake Sonoma Winery
Healdsburg, CA 877-850-9463
Lakeridge Winery & Vineyards
Clermont, FL 800-768-9463
Lakeshore Winery
Romulus, NY 315-549-7075
Lakespring Winery
Yountville, CA 707-944-2475
Lakewood Vineyards
Watkins Glen, NY 607-535-9252
Lambert Bridge Winery
Healdsburg, CA 800-975-0555
Lamoreaux Landing Wine Cellar
Lodi, NY 607-582-6011
Lancaster County Winery
Willow Street, PA 717-464-3555
Landmark Vineyards
Kenwood, CA 800- 45- 636
Lange Winery
Dundee, OR 503-538-6476
Langtry Estate & Vineyards
Middletown, CA 707-987-9127
Larry's Vineyards & Winery
Altamont, NY 518-355-7365
Latah Creek Wine Cellars
Spokane Valley, WA 509-926-0164
Latcham Vineyards
Mt Aukum, CA 800-750-5591
Laurel Glen Vineyard
Glen Ellen, CA 707-526-3914
Lava Cap Winery
Placerville, CA 530-621-0175
Lazy Creek Vineyard
Philo, CA 888-529-9275
Le Boeuf & Associates
North Falmouth, MA 800-444-5666
Leelanau Wine Cellars
Omena, MI 800-782-8128
Leeward Winery
Oxnard, CA 805-656-5054
Leidenfrost Vineyards
Hector, NY
Lemon Creek Winery
Berrien Springs, MI 269-471-1321
Leonetti Cellar
Walla Walla, WA 509-525-1428
Les Bourgeois Vineyards
Rocheport, MO 573-698-2300
Lewis Cellars
Napa, CA 70- 2-5 34
Life Force Winery
Moscow, ID 208-882-9158
Limur Winery
San Francisco, CA 415-781-8691
Lin Court Vineyards
Solvang, CA 805-688-8554
Little Amana Winery
Amana, IA 319-668-9664
Little Hills Winery
Saint Charles, MO 877-584-4557
Live Oaks Winery
Gilroy, CA 408-842-2401
Livermore Valley Cellars
Livermore, CA 925-454-9463
Livingston Moffett Winery
Saint Helena, CA 800-788-0370
Llano Estacado Winery
Lubbock, TX 800-634-3854
Lockwood Vineyards
Monterey, CA 831-642-9200
Loew Vineyards
Mount Airy, MD 301-831-5464
Lohr Winery
San Jose, CA 408-288-5057
Lolonis Winery
Walnut Creek, CA 925-938-8066
Long Vineyards
St Helena, CA 707-963-2496
Lonz Winery
Middle Bass, OH 419-285-5411
Los Olivos Vintners
Los Olivos, CA 800-824-8584
Lost Hills Winery
Acampo, CA 209-369-2746
Lost Mountain Winery
Sequim, WA 888-683-5229
Louis M. Martini
St. Helena, CA 866-549-2582
Lucas Vineyards
Interlaken, NY 800-682-9463
Lucas Winery
Lodi, CA 209-368-2006

Ludwigshof Winery
Eskridge, KS . . . 785-449-2498
LUXCO
St Louis, MO. . . . 314-772-2626
Lynfred Winery
Roselle, IL. . . . 888-298-9463
M.S. Walker
Somerville, MA . . . 617-776-6700
Madison Foods
Saint Paul, MN . . . 651-265-8212
Madison Vineyard
Ribera, NM . . . 575-421-8028
Madonna Estate Mont St John
Napa, CA. . . . 707-255-8864
Madrona Vineyards
Camino, CA . . . 530-644-5948
Magnanini Winery
Wallkill, NY . . . 845-895-2767
Maisons Marques & Domaines USA
Oakland, CA. . . . 510-286-2000
Mama Rap's & Winery
Gilroy, CA. . . . 800-842-6262
Manfred Vierthaler Winery
Sumner, WA . . . 360-863-633
Marie Brizard Wines & Spirits
St. Helena, CA . . . 800-878-1123
Marietta Cellars
Geyservill, CA . . . 707-433-2747
Marimar Torres Estate
Sebastopol, CA. . . . 707-823-4365
Mark West Vineyards
Forestville, CA . . . 707-544-4813
Markham Vineyards
Saint Helena, CA . . . 707-963-5292
Markko Vineyard
Conneaut, OH. . . . 800-252-3197
Marlow Wine Cellars
Monteagle, TN . . . 931-924-2120
Martin & Weyrich Winery
Templeton, CA . . . 805-239-1640
Martini & Prati Wines
Santa Rosa, CA. . . . 707-823-2404
Mastantuono Winery
Templeton, CA . . . 805-238-0676
Matanzas Creek Winery
Santa Rosa, CA. . . . 800-500-6464
Matson Vineyards
Redding, CA. . . . 530-222-2833
Maurice Carrie Winery
Temecula, CA . . . 800-716-1711
Mayacamas Vineyards
Napa, CA. . . . 707-224-4030
Mazzocco Vineyards
Healdsburg, CA . . . 707-433-9035
McDowell Valley Vineyards & Cellars
Hopland, CA. . . . 707-744-1774
McGregor Vineyard Winery
Dundee, NY . . . 800-272-0192
McHenry Vineyard
Davis, CA . . . 530-756-3202
McIntosh's Ohio Valley Wines
Bethel, OH . . . 937-379-1159
McKinlay Vineyards
Newberg, OR . . . 503-625-2534
Meeker Vineyard
Healdsburg, CA . . . 707-431-2148
Meier's Wine Cellars
Cincinnati, OH . . . 800-346-2941
Menghini Winery
Julian, CA . . . 760-765-2072
Meredyth Vineyard
Middleburg, VA . . . 540-687-6277
Meridian Vineyards
Paso Robles, CA. . . . 805-237-6000
Merritt Estate Wines
Forestville, NY . . . 888-965-4800
Merryvale Vineyards
Saint Helena, CA . . . 800-326-6069
Messina Hof Wine Cellars & Vineyards
Bryan, TX . . . 800-736-9463
Michel-Schlumberger
Healdsburg, CA . . . 800-447-3060
Milano Winery
Hopland, CA. . . . 800-564-2582
Milat Vineyards
St Helena, CA. . . . 707-963-0758
Mill Creek Vineyards
Healdsburg, CA . . . 877-349-2121
Millbrook Vineyard and Winery
Millbrook, NY . . . 800-662-9463
Milliaire Winery
Murphys, CA. . . . 209-728-1658

Mission Mountain Winery
Dayton, MT. . . . 406-849-5524
Missouri Winery Warehouse Outlet
Cuba, MO . . . 573-885-2168
Mogen David Wine Corporation
Westfield, NY . . . 716-326-3151
Montelle Winery
Augusta, MO. . . . 888-595-9463
Monterey Vineyard
Gonzales, CA . . . 831-675-4000
Montevina Winery
Plymouth, CA. . . . 209-245-6942
Monticello Cellars
Napa, CA. . . . 707-253-2802
Montmorenci Vineyards
Aiken, SC . . . 803-649-4870
Moresco Vineyards
Stockton, CA. . . . 209-467-3081
Morgan Winery
Salinas, CA . . . 831-751-7777
Mosby Winery
Buellton, CA. . . . 805-688-2415
Moss Creek Winery
Napa, CA. . . . 707-252-1295
Mount Baker Vineyards
Everson, WA. . . . 360-592-2300
Mount Bethel Winery
Altus, AR . . . 479-468-2444
Mount Eden Vineyards
Saratoga, CA. . . . 408-867-5832
Mount Hope Estate Winery
Manheim, PA . . . 717-665-7021
Mount Palomar Winery
Temecula, CA . . . 800-854-5177
Mount Pleasant Winery
Augusta, MO. . . . 800-467-9463
Mountain Cove Vineyards & Winegarden
Lovingston, VA. . . . 434-263-5392
Mt. Nittany Vineyard
Centre Hall, PA. . . . 814-466-6373
Murphy Goode Estate Winery
Healdsburg, CA . . . 707-431-7644
Naked Mountain Vineyard & Winery
Markham, VA . . . 540-364-1609
Nalle Winery
Healdsburg, CA . . . 707-433-1040
Nantucket Vineyards
Nantucket, MA . . . 508-228-9235
Napa Cellars
Oakville, CA. . . . 800-848-9630
Napa Creek Winery
Saint Helena, CA . . . 707- 25- 946
Napa Valley Port Cellars
Napa, CA. . . . 707-257-7777
Napa Wine Company
Oakville, CA. . . . 800-848-9630
Nashoba Valley Winery
Bolton, MA. . . . 978-779-5521
Navarro Vineyards & Winery
Philo, CA. . . . 800-537-9463
Naylor Wine Cellars
Stewartstown, PA . . . 800-292-3370
Nevada City Winery
Nevada City, CA. . . . 800-203-9463
Nevada County Wine Guild
Nevada City, CA. . . . 530-265-3662
New Hope Winery
New Hope, PA. . . . 800-592-9463
New Land Vineyard
Geneva, NY. . . . 315-585-4432
Newman's Own
Westport, CT. . . . 203-222-0136
Newport Vineyards & Winery
Middletown, RI. . . . 401-848-5161
Newton Vineyard
Yountville, CA . . . 707-963-9000
Nicasio Vineyards
Soquel, CA . . . 831-423-1073
Nichelini Winery
Saint Helena, CA . . . 707-963-0717
Niebaum-Coppola Estate Winery
Rutherford, CA. . . . 707-968-1100
Nissley Vineyards
Bainbridge, PA . . . 800-522-2387
Nordman of California
Sanger, CA . . . 559-638-9923
North House Vineyards In
Jamesport, NY. . . . 631-722-5256
North Salem Vineyard
North Salem, NY . . . 914-669-5518
Northern Vineyards Winery
Stillwater, MN. . . . 651-430-1032

Northville Winery
Northville, MI. . . . 248-349-3181
Nutmeg Vineyard
Andover, CT . . . 860-742-8402
O'Vallon Winery
Washburn, MO . . . 417-826-5830
Oak Grove Orchards Winery
Rickreall, OR . . . 541-364-7052
Oak Knoll Winery
Hillsboro, OR . . . 800-625-5665
Oak Ridge Winery
Lodi, CA . . . 209-369-4758
Oak Spring Winery
Altoona, PA. . . . 814-946-3799
Oakencroft Vineyard & Winery
Charlottesville, VA . . . 434-296-4188
Oasis Winery
Hume, VA . . . 800-304-7656
Obester Winery
Half Moon Bay, CA . . . 650-726-9463
Oceania Cellars
Arroyo Grande, CA. . . . 805-481-5434
Ojai Vineyard
Oak View, CA. . . . 805-649-1674
Old Creek Ranch Winery
Ventura, CA. . . . 805-649-4132
Old Firehouse Winery
Geneva, OH. . . . 800-362-6751
Old House Vineyards
Culpeper, VA. . . . 540-423-1032
Old South Winery
Natchez, MS . . . 601-445-9924
Old Wine Cellar
Amana, IA. . . . 319-622-3116
Oliver Wine Company
Bloomington, IN. . . . 800-258-2783
Olympic Cellars
Port Angeles, WA . . . 360-452-0160
One Vineyard and Winery
Saint Helena, CA . . . 707-963-1123
Optima Wine Cellars
Healdsburg, CA . . . 707-431-8222
Opus One
Oakville, CA. . . . 800-292-6787
Orchard Heights Winery
Salem, OR. . . . 503-391-7308
Orfila Vineyards
Escondido, CA . . . 760-738-6500
Organic Wine Company
San Francisco, CA . . . 888-326-9463
Orleans Hill Vineyard Association
Woodland, CA. . . . 530-661-6538
Ormand Peugeog Corporation
Miami, FL. . . . 305-624-6834
Orr Mountain Winery
Madisonville, TN . . . 423-442-5340
Pacheco Ranch Winery
Novato, CA. . . . 415-883-5583
Pacific Echo Cellars
Philo, CA. . . . 707-895-2065
Page Mill Winery
Livermore, CA . . . 925-456-3375
Pahlmeyer Winery
Saint Helena, CA
Pahrump Valley Vineyards
Pahrump, NV . . . 800-368-9463
Palm Bay Imports
Boca Raton, FL. . . . 800-872-5622
Palmer Vineyards
Riverhead, NY . . . 800-901-8783
Panther Creek Cellars
McMinnville, OR . . . 503-472-8080
Paradise Valley Vineyards
Phoenix, AZ . . . 602-233-8727
Paragon Vineyards
San Luis Obispo, CA . . . 805-544-9080
Parasio Springs Vineyards
Soledad, CA . . . 831-678-0300
Parducci Wine Estates
Ukiah, CA. . . . 888-362-9463
Pastori Winery
Cloverdale, CA. . . . 707-857-3418
Paumanok Vineyards
Aquebogue, NY . . . 631-722-8800
Pazdar Winery
Scotchtown Branch, NY. . . . 845-695-1903
Peaceful Bend Vineyard
Steelville, MO. . . . 573-775-3000
Peconic Bay Winery
Cutchogue, NY . . . 631-734-7361
Pedrizzetti Winery
Morgan Hill, CA. . . . 408-779-7389

Pedroncelli Winery
Geyserville, CA 800-836-3894
Peju Winery
Rutherford, CA 800-446-7358
Pellegrini Family Vineyards
Santa Rosa, CA 800-891-0244
Penn-Shore Vineyards
North East, PA 814-725-8688
Pernod Ricard USA
Purchase, NY 914-848-4800
Perry Creek Winery
Fair Play, CA 800-880-4026
Peter Michael Winery
Calistoga, CA 800-354-4459
Peterson & Sons Winery
Kalamazoo, MI 269-626-9755
Pheasant Ridge Winery
Lubbock, TX 806-746-6033
Philip Togni Vineyard
Saint Helena, CA 707-963-3731
Phillips Farms & Michael David Vineyards
Lodi, CA 888-707-9463
Piedmont Vineyards & Winery
Middleburg, VA 540-687-5528
Piedra Creek Winery
San Luis Obispo, CA 805-541-1281
Pikes Peak Vineyards
Colorado Springs, CO 719-576-0075
Pindar Vineyards
Peconic, NY 631-734-6200
Pine Ridge Winery
Yountville, CA 800-575-9777
Plam Vineyards & Winery
La Quinta, CA 760-972-4465
Pleasant Valley Wine Company
Hammondsport, NY 607-569-6111
Plum Creek Cellars
Palisade, CO 970-464-7586
Plymouth Colony Winery
Plymouth, MA 508-747-3334
Pommeraie Winery
Sebastopol, CA 707-823-9463
Ponderosa Valley Vineyard & Winery
Ponderosa, NM 575-834-7487
Ponzi Vineyards
Beaverton, OR 503-628-1227
Poplar Ridge Vineyards
Hector, NY 607-582-6421
Porter Creek Vineyards
Healdsburg, CA 707-433-6321
Post Familie Vineyards
Altus, AR 800-275-8423
Prager Winery & Port Works
Saint Helena, CA 800-969-7678
Presque Isle Wine Cellar
North East, PA 800-488-7492
Preston Premium Wines
Pasco, WA 509-545-1990
Preston Vineyards
Healdsburg, CA 800-305-9707
Prince Michael Vineyards
Leon, VA 800-869-8242
Quady Winery
Madera, CA 800-733-8068
Quail Ridge Cellars & Vineyards
Saint Helena, CA 800-706-9463
Quilceda Creek Vintners
Snohomish, WA 360-568-2389
Quivira Vineyards
Healdsburg, CA 800-292-8339
R.A.B. Food Group LLC
Secaucus, NJ 201-553-1100
R.H. Phillips
Esparto, CA 530-662-3504
Rabbit Ridge
Paso Robles, CA 80- 4-7 33
Radanovich Vineyards & Winery
Mariposa, CA 209-966-3187
Rahco International
St Augustine, FL 800-851-7681
Rainbow Hill Vineyards
Newcomerstown, OH 740-545-9305
Rancho De Philo
Alta Loma, CA 909-987-4208
Rancho Sisquoc Winery
Santa Maria, CA 805-934-4332
Rapazzini Winery
Gilroy, CA 800-842-6262
Ravenswood
Sonoma, CA 800-669-4679
Raymond Vineyard & Cellar
Saint Helena, CA 800-525-2659

Rebec Vineyards
Amherst, VA 434-946-5168
Redhawk Vineyard
Salem, OR 503-362-1596
Reeves Winery
Middletown, CA 707-987-9650
Regent Champagne Cellars
New York, NY
Renaissance Vineyard & Winery
Oregon House, CA 800-655-3277
Renault Winery
Egg Harbor City, NJ 609-965-2111
Renwood Winery
Plymouth, CA 800-348-8466
Retzlaff Vineyards
Livermore, CA 925-447-8941
Rex Wine Vinegar Company
Newark, NJ 973-589-6911
Richard L. Graeser Winery
Calistoga, CA 707-942-4437
Richardson Vineyards
Sonoma, CA 707-938-2610
Ridge Vineyards
Cupertino, CA 408-867-3233
Ritchie Creek Vineyard
Saint Helena, CA 707-963-4661
Rivendell Winery
New Paltz, NY
River Road Vineyards
Sebastopol, CA 707-887-2243
River Run Vintners
Watsonville, CA 831-726-3112
Roberian Vineyards
Forestville, NY 716-679-1620
Robert F Pliska & Company Winery
Purgitsville, WV 877-747-2737
Robert Keenan Winery
Saint Helena, CA 707-963-9177
Robert Mondavi Winery
Oakville, CA 888-766-6238
Robert Mondavi Winery
Oakville, CA 888-766-6328
Robert Mueller Cellars
Windsor, CA 707-837-7399
Robert Pecota Winery
Calistoga, CA 707-942-6625
Robert Sinskey Vineyards
Napa, CA 800-869-2030
Robller Vineyard
New Haven, MO 573-237-3986
Roche Caneros Estate Winry
Sonoma, CA 800-825-9475
Rockbridge Vineyard
Raphine, VA 540-377-6204
Rodney Strong Vineyards
Healdsburg, CA 707-433-6511
Rodney Strong Vineyards
Healdsburg, CA 800-474-9463
Rogue Ales
Newport, OR 541-867-3660
Rolling Hills Vineyards
Thousand Oaks, CA
Rombauer Vineyards
Saint Helena, CA 800- 62- 220
Rose Creek Vineyards
Hagerman, ID 208-837-4353
Rosenblum Cellars
Alameda, CA 510-865-7007
Ross Keller Winery
Nipomo, CA 805-929-3627
Roudon-Smith Vineyards
Scotts Valley, CA 831-438-1244
Round Hill Vineyards
St Helena, CA 800-778-0424
Royal Kedem Food & Wine Company
Bayonne, NJ 201-437-9131
Royal Wine Corp
Bayonne, NJ 718-384-2400
Rubicon/Niebaum-Coppola Estate & Winery
Rutherford, CA 800-782-4266
Rudd Winery
Oakville, CA 707-944-8577
Rutherford Hill Winery
Rutherford, CA 707-963-1871
S. Anderson Vineyard
Yountville, CA 800-428-2259
Saddleback Cellars
Oakville, CA 707-944-1305
Sainte Genevieve Winery
Ste Genevieve, MO 800-398-1298
Saintsbury
Napa, CA 707-252-0592

Salamandre Wine Cellars
Aptos, CA 831-685-0321
Salishan Vineyards
La Center, WA 360-263-2713
San Antonio Winery
Los Angeles, CA 800-626-7722
San Dominique Winery
Camp Verde, AZ 480-945-8583
Sand Castle Winery
Erwinna, PA 800-722-9463
Sandia Shadows Vineyard & Winery
Albuquerque, NM 505-856-1006
Sandstone Winery
Amana, IA 319-622-3081
Sanford Winery
Lompoc, CA 800-426-9463
Santa Barbara Winery
Santa Barbara, CA 805-963-3633
Santa Cruz Mountain Vineyard
Felton, CA 831-426-6209
Santa Fe Vineyards
Espanola, NM 505-753-8100
Santa Margarita Vineyard & Winery
Temecula, CA 909-676-4431
Sarah's Vineyard
Gilroy, CA 408-842-4278
Satiety
Davis, CA 530-757-2699
Saucilito Canyon Vineyard
San Luis Obispo, CA 805-543-2111
Sausal Winery
Healdsburg, CA 800-500-2285
Savannah Chanelle Vineyards
Saratoga, CA 408-741-2934
Sawtooth Winery
Nampa, ID 208-467-1200
Scenic Valley Winery
Lanesboro, MN 507-259-4981
Schloss Doepken Winery
Ripley, NY 716-326-3636
Schoppaul Hill Winery at Ivanhoe
Denton, TX 940-380-9463
Schramsberg Vineyards
Calistoga, CA 800-877-3623
Schug Carneros Estate Winery
Sonoma, CA 800-966-9365
Sea Ridge Winery
Occidental, CA 707-874-1707
Seavey Vineyard
Saint Helena, CA 707-963-8339
Sebastiani Vineyards
Sonoma, CA 800-888-5532
Secret House Vineyards
Veneta, OR 800-497-1574
Seghesio Family Vineyards
Healdsburg, CA 707-433-3579
Sellards Winery
Sebastopol, CA 707-823-8293
Sequoia Grove Vineyards
Rutherford, CA 800-851-7841
Serendipity Cellars
Monmouth, OR 503-838-4284
Serra Mission Winery
Saint Louis, MO 314-962-4600
Seven Hills Winery
Walla Walla, WA 877-777-7870
Seven Lakes Vineyards
Fenton, MI 810-629-5686
Shafer Vineyards
Napa, CA 707-944-2877
Shallon Winery
Astoria, OR 503-325-5978
Sharon Mill Winery
Manchester, MI 734-971-6337
Sharp Rock Vineyards
Sperryville, VA 540-987-8020
Shenandoah Vineyards
Plymouth, CA 209-245-4455
Sierra Vista Winery
Placerville, CA 530-622-7221
Signore Winery
Brooktondale, NY 607-539-7935
Signorello Vineyards
Napa, CA 707-255-5990
Silvan Ridge
Eugene, OR 541-345-1945
Silver Fox Vineyard
Mariposa, CA 209-966-4800
Silver Mountain Vineyards
Santa Cruz, CA 408-353-2278
Silver Oak Cellars
Oakville, CA 800-273-8805

Silverado Hill Cellars
Napa, CA ... 707-253-9306
Silverado Vineyards
Napa, CA ... 707-257-1770
Simon Levi Cellars
Kenwood, CA ... 888-315-0040
Six Mile Creek Vineyard
Ithaca, NY ... 800-260-0612
Sky Vineyards
Glen Ellen, CA ... 707-935-1391
Slate Quarry Winery
Nazareth, PA ... 610-746-3900
Smith Vineyard & Winery
Grass Valley, CA ... 530-273-7032
Smith-Madrone Vineyards & Winery
Saint Helena, CA ... 707-963-2283
Smokehouse Winery
Sperryville, VA ... 540-987-3194
Smothers Winery/Remick Ridge
Glen Ellen, CA ... 800-795-9463
Sobon Estate
Plymouth, CA ... 209-333-6275
Sokol Blosser Winery
Dundee, OR ... 800-582-6668
Sonoita Vineyards
Elgin, AZ ... 520-455-5893
Sonoma Wine Services
Vineburg, CA ... 707-996-9773
Sonoma-Cutrer Vineyards
Fulton, CA ... 707-528-1181
Sow's Ear Winery
Brooksville, ME ... 207-326-4649
Spangler Vineyards
Roseburg, OR ... 541-679-9654
Spottswoode Winery
Saint Helena, CA ... 707-963-0134
Spring Mountain Vineyard
Saint Helena, CA ... 877-769-4637
Spring Mountain Vineyards
Saint Helena, CA ... 877-769-4637
Springhill Cellars
Albany, OR ... 541-928-1009
Spurgeon Vineyards & Winery
Highland, WI ... 800-236-5555
St. Francis Vineyards
Santa Rosa, CA ... 707-833-4668
St. Innocent Winery
Salem, OR ... 503-378-1526
St. James Winery
Saint James, MO ... 800-280-9463
St. Julian Wine Company
Paw Paw, MI ... 800-732-6002
Stags' Leap Winery
Napa, CA ... 800-640-5327
Star Hill Winery
Napa, CA ... 707-255-1957
Starr & Brown
Portland, OR ... 503-287-1775
Ste Michelle Wine Estates
Woodinville, WA ... 800-267-6793
Ste. Chapelle Winery
Caldwell, ID ... 877-783-2427
Stearns Wharf Vintners
Santa Barbara, CA ... 805-966-6624
Steltzner Vineyards
Napa, CA ... 707-252-7272
Steuk's Country Market &Winery
Sandusky, OH ... 419-625-8324
Stevenot Winery & Imports
Murphys, CA ... 20- 2-3 43
Stone Hill Wine Company
Hermann, MO ... 573-486-2221
Stonegate
St Helena, CA ... 707-603-2203
Stoneridge Winery
Sutter Creek, CA ... 209-223-1761
Stonington Vineyards
Stonington, CT ... 800-421-9463
Stony Hill Vineyard
Saint Helena, CA ... 707-963-2636
Stony Ridge Winery
Livermore, CA ... 925-449-0458
Storrs Winery
Santa Cruz, CA ... 831-458-5030
Story Winery
Plymouth, CA ... 800-712-6390
Storybook Mountain Winery
Calistoga, CA ... 707-942-5310
Streblow Vineyards
Saint Helena, CA ... 707-963-5892
Stryker Sonoma Winery Vineyards
Geyserville, CA ... 800-433-1944
Sugar Creek Winery
Defiance, MO ... 636-987-2400
Sullivan Vineyards Winery
Rutherford, CA ... 877-277-7337
Summit Lake Vineyards & Winery
Angwin, CA ... 707-965-2488
Summum Winery
Salt Lake City, UT ... 801-355-0137
Sunrise Winery
San Jose, CA ... 408-741-1310
Sunstone Vineyards & Winery
Santa Ynez, CA ... 800-313-9463
Susquehanna Valley Winery
Danville, PA ... 570-275-2364
Sutter Home Winery
Saint Helena, CA ... 707-963-3104
Swan Joseph Vineyards
Forestville, CA ... 707-573-3747
Swanson Vineyards & Winery
Rutherford, CA ... 800-942-0809
Swedish Hill Vineyard
Romulus, NY ... 888-549-9463
Sweet Traders
Huntington Beach, CA ... 714-903-6800
Sycamore Vineyards
Saint Helena, CA ... 800-963-9698
Sylvester Winery
Paso Robles, CA ... 805-227-4000
Sylvin Farms Winery
Egg Harbor City, NJ ... 609-965-1548
Talbott Vineyards
Gonzales, CA ... 831-675-3000
Talley Vineyards
Arroyo Grande, CA ... 805-489-2508
Tamuzza Vineyards
Hope, NJ ... 908-459-5878
Tarara Winery
Leesburg, VA ... 703-771-7100
Tartan Hill Winery
New Era, MI ... 231-861-4657
Tedeschi Vineyards
Kula, HI ... 808-878-1266
Tempest Vineyards
Amity, OR ... 503-835-2600
Thoma Vineyards
Dallas, OR ... 503-623-6420
Thomas Fogarty Winery
Portola Valley, CA ... 800-247-4163
Thomas Kruse Winery
Gilroy, CA ... 408-842-7016
Thornton Winery
Temecula, CA ... 951-699-0099
Thorpe Vineyard
Wolcott, NY ... 315-594-2502
Three Lakes Winery
Three Lakes, WI ... 800-944-5434
TKC Vineyards
Plymouth, CA ... 888-627-2356
Todhunter Foods
Lake Alfred, FL ... 863-956-1116
Todhunter Foods & Monarch Wine Company
West Palm Beach, FL ... 800-336-9463
Tomasello Winery
Hammonton, NJ ... 800-666-9463
Topolos at Russian River Vine
Forestville, CA ... 707-887-1575
Transamerica Wine Corporation
Brooklyn, NY ... 718-875-4017
Trefethen Vineyards
Napa, CA ... 800-556-4847
Trentadue Winery
Geyserville, CA ... 888-332-3032
Trigo Corporation
Toa Baja, PR ... 787-794-1300
Troy Winery
Troy, OH ... 937-339-3655
Truchard Vineyards
Napa, CA ... 707-253-7153
Truckee River Winery
Truckee, CA ... 530-587-4626
Tucker Cellars
Sunnyside, WA ... 509-837-8701
Tudal Winery
Saint Helena, CA ... 707-963-3947
Tularosa Vineyards
Tularosa, NM ... 800-687-4467
Tyee Wine Cellars
Corvallis, OR ... 541-753-8754
UDV Wines
San Francisco, CA ... 415-835-7300
United Distillers & Vintners
Norwalk, CT ... 203-323-3311
UST
Danbury, CT ... 800-650-7411
V. Sattui Winery
Saint Helena, CA ... 800-799-8888
Val Verde Winery
Del Rio, TX ... 830-775-9714
Valley of the Moon Winery
Glen Ellen, CA ... 707-996-6941
Valley View Winery
Jacksonville, OR ... 800-781-9463
Van Der Heyden Vineyards
Napa, CA ... 800-948-9463
Ventana Vineyards Winery
Monterey, CA ... 800-237-8846
Veramar Vineyard
Berryville, VA ... 540-955-5510
Vetter Vineyards Winery
Westfield, NY ... 716-326-3100
Via Della Chiesa Vineyards
Raynham, MA ... 508-822-7775
Viader Vineyards & Winery
Deer Park, CA ... 707-963-3816
Viano Winery
Martinez, CA ... 925-228-6465
Viansa Winery
Sonoma, CA ... 800-995-4740
Vie-Del Company
Fresno, CA ... 559-834-2525
Villa Helena/Arger-Martucci Winery
St Helena, CA ... 707-963-4334
Villa Milan Vineyard
Milan, IN ... 812-654-3419
Villa Mt. Eden Winery
Saint Helena, CA ... 707-944-2414
Village Imports
Brisbane, CA ... 888-865-8714
Villar Vintners of Valdese
Valdese, NC ... 828-879-3202
Vina Vista Vineyard & Winery
Philo, CA ... 1 8-0 5-7 94
Vincent Arroyo Winery
Calistoga, CA ... 707-942-6995
Vinoklet Winery & Vineyard
Cincinnati, OH ... 513-385-9309
Von Stiehl Winery
Algoma, WI ... 800-955-5208
Von Strasser Winery
Calistoga, CA ... 888-359-9463
Vynecrest Vineyards and Winery
Breinigsville, PA ... 800-361-0725
Wagner Vineyards
Lodi, NY ... 866-924-6378
Walker Valley Vineyards
Walker Valley, NY ... 845-744-3449
Warner Vineyards Winery
Paw Paw, MI ... 800-756-5357
Wasson Brothers Winery
Sandy, OR ... 503-668-3124
Weibel Champagne Vineyards
Woodbridge, CA ... 80- 9-2 94
Wente Brothers Estate Winery
Livermore, CA ... 925-456-2300
Wermuth Winery
Calistoga, CA ... 707-942-5924
West Park Wine Cellars
West Park, NY ... 845-384-6709
Westbend Vinyards
Lewisville, NC ... 866-901-5032
Westport Rivers Vineyard& Winery
Westport, MA ... 800-993-9695
Westwood Winery
Sonoma, CA ... 707-935-3246
Whaler Vineyard Winery
Ukiah, CA ... 707-462-6355
Whitcraft Wines
Santa Barbara, CA ... 805-730-1680

White Hall Vineyards
Crozet, VA....434-823-8615
White Oak Vineyards & Winery
Healdsburg, CA....707-433-8429
White Rock Vineyards
Napa, CA....707-257-7922
Whitehall Lane Winery
Saint Helena, CA....707-963-9454
Whitford Cellars
Napa, CA....707-942-0840
Widmer's Wine Cellars
Canandaigua, NY
Wiederkehr Wine Cellars
Altus, AR....800-622-9463
Wild Hog Vineyard
Cazadero, CA....707-847-3687
Wild Horse Winery
Templeton, CA....805-434-2541
Wild Winds Farms
Naples, NY....800-836-5253
Wildhurst
Kelseyville, CA....800-595-9463
William Grant & Sons
New York, NY....212-246-1760
William Harrison Vineyards & Winery LLC
Saint Helena, CA....707-963-8762
William Hill Winery
Napa, CA....707-224-4477
Williams-Selym Winery
Healdsburg, CA....707-433-6425
Williamsburg Winery
Williamsburg, VA....757-258-0899
Willow Hill Vineyards
Johnstown, OH....740-587-4622
Willowcroft Farm Vineyards
Leesburg, VA....703-777-8161
Wimberley Valley Winery
Driftwood, TX....512-847-2592
Windham Winery
Purcellville, VA....540-668-6464
Windsor Vineyards
Santa Rosa, CA....800-289-9463
Windsor Vineyards
Windsor, CA....800-333-9987
Windwalker Vineyards
Somerset, CA....530-620-4054
Wine Group
San Francisco, CA....415-986-8700
Wine-A-Rita
Texarkana, TX....903-832-0467
Wintergreen Winery
Nellysford, VA....434-361-2519
Winters Winery
Winters, CA....530-795-3201
Wishnev Wine Management
Walnut Creek, CA....925-930-6374
Witness Tree Vineyard
Salem, OR....888-478-8766
Wolf Creek Vineyards
Norton, OH....800-436-0426
Wollersheim Winery
Prairie Du Sac, WI....800-847-9463
Woodbury Vineyards
Fredonia, NY....866-691-9463
Wooden Valley Winery
Fairfield, CA....707-864-0730
Woodside Vineyards
Menlo Park, CA....650-851-3144
Woodward Canyon Winery
Touchet, WA....509-525-4129
Worden
Spokane, WA....509-455-7835
Wyandotte Winery
Columbus, OH....614-476-3624

Yakima River Winery
Prosser, WA....509-786-2805
Yamhill Valley Vineyards
McMinnville, OR....800-825-4845
York Mountain Winery
Templeton, CA....805-237-7575
Z.D. Wines
Napa, CA....800-487-7757
Zaca Mesa Winery
Los Olivos, CA....800-350-7972
Zayante Vineyards
Felton, CA....831-335-7992
Ziem Vineyards
Fairplay, MD....301-223-8352

Bulk

Brothers International Food Corporation
Rochester, NY....585-343-3007
Cribari Vineyards
Fresno, CA....800-277-9095

Processor and exporter of high quality California bulk wine.

Cooking

Batavia Wine Cellars
Canandaigua, NY....585-396-7600
California Olive Oil Corporation
Berkeley, CA....888-718-9830
Cribari Vineyards
Fresno, CA....800-277-9095

Processor and exporter of high quality California bulk wine.

Emerling International Foods
Buffalo, NY....716-833-7381

We supply food manufacturers and food service customers worldwide (since 1988) with bulk ingredients including: Fruits & Vegetables; Juice Concentrates; Herbs & Spices; Oils & Vinegars; Flavors & Colors; Honey & Molasses. We also produce PURE MAPLE SYRUP.

Fleischmanns Vinegar
Cerritos, CA....800-443-1067
Four Chimneys Farm Winery Trust
Himrod, NY....607-243-7502
Kari-Out Company
White Plains, NY....800-433-8799
Mizkan Americas
Mt Prospect, IL....800-323-4358
Rapazzini Winery
Gilroy, CA....800-842-6262
Rex Wine Vinegar Company
Newark, NJ....973-589-6911
Todhunter Foods
Lake Alfred, FL....863-956-1116
Todhunter Foods & Monarch Wine Company
West Palm Beach, FL....800-336-9463

Marsala

Cribari Vineyards
Fresno, CA....800-277-9095

Processor and exporter of high quality California bulk wine.

French

Brown-Forman Corporation
Louisville, KY....502-585-1100

Champagne

Briceland Vineyards
Redway, CA....707-923-2429
Brimstone Hill Vineyard
Pine Bush, NY....845-744-2231
Buena Vista Carneros Winery
Sonoma, CA....800-678-8504
Bully Hill Vineyards
Hammondsport, NY....607-868-3610
Chateau des Charmes Wines
St. Davids, ON....800-263-2541
Chi Company/Tabor Hill Winery
Buchanan, MI....800-283-3363
Chicama Vineyards
West Tisbury, MA....888-244-2262
Chouinard Vineyards
Castro Valley, CA....510-582-9900
Clinton Vineyards
Clinton Corners, NY....845-266-5372
Domaine Chandon
Yountville, CA....800-242-6366
Dr. Frank's Vinifera Wine Cellar
Hammondsport, NY....800-320-0735
Dr. Konstantin Frank Vin
Hammondsport, NY....800-320-0735
Fenn Valley Vineyards
Fennville, MI....800-432-6265
Glenora Wine Cellars
Dundee, NY....800-243-5513
Marie Brizard Wines & Spirits
St. Helena, CA....800-878-1123
Meier's Wine Cellars
Cincinnati, OH....800-346-2941
Mon Ami Champagne Company
Port Clinton, OH....800-777-4266
North Salem Vineyard
North Salem, NY....914-669-5518
Regent Champagne Cellars
New York, NY
Royal Wine Corp
Bayonne, NJ....718-384-2400
Schramsberg Vineyards
Calistoga, CA....800-877-3623
St. Julian Wine Company
Paw Paw, MI....800-732-6002
Stone Hill Wine Company
Hermann, MO....573-486-2221
Thornton Winery
Temecula, CA....951-699-0099
Westport Rivers Vineyard& Winery
Westport, MA....800-993-9695
Windsor Vineyards
Windsor, CA....800-333-9987
Woodbury Vineyards
Fredonia, NY....866-691-9463
York Mountain Winery
Templeton, CA....805-237-7575

Red Bordeaux

Babcock Winery & Vineyards
Lompoc, CA....805-736-1455

Red Burgundy

Cribari Vineyards
Fresno, CA....800-277-9095

Processor and exporter of high quality California bulk wine.

Heineman's Winery
Put In Bay, OH....419-285-2811

White Burgundy

Buena Vista Carneros Winery
Sonoma, CA 800-678-8504

Italian

Buena Vista Carneros Winery
Sonoma, CA 800-678-8504
E&J Gallo Winery
Modesto, CA. 209-341-3111
V. Sattui Winery
Saint Helena, CA 800-799-8888

Chianti

E&J Gallo Winery
Modesto, CA. 209-341-3111

Red

E&J Gallo Winery
Modesto, CA. 209-341-3111

Japanese

Sake

Ozeki Sake
Hollister, CA. 831-637-9217

Non-Alcoholic

Ariel Vineyards
Napa, CA. 800-456-9472
Cedar Creek Winery
Cedarburg, WI. 800-827-8020
Safeway Dairy Products
Walnut Creek, CA. 925-944-4000

Portuguese

Port

Alto Vineyards
Alto Pass, IL 618-893-4898
Chateau Grand Traverse
Traverse City, MI 231-223-7355
Chouinard Vineyards
Castro Valley, CA 510-582-9900
Cienega Valley Winery/DeRose
Hollister, CA. 831-636-9143
Fenestra Winery
Livermore, CA 800-789-9463
Fenn Valley Vineyards
Fennville, MI 800-432-6265
Ficklin Vineyards
Madera, CA. 559-674-4598

Red Grape Wines

Hazlitt's 1852 Vineyard
Hector, NY 888-750-0494
Hermann Wiemer Vineyards
Dundee, NY 800-371-7971
Hermannhof Winery
Hermann, MO 800-393-0100
Heron Hill Winery
Hammondsport, NY 800-441-4241

Cabernet Sauvignon

A. Rafanelli Winery
Healdsburg, CA 707-433-1385
AmRhein Wine Cellars
Bent Mountain, VA. 540-929-4632
Autumn Hill Vineyards/Blue Ridge Wine
Stanardsville, VA 434-985-6100
Babcock Winery & Vineyards
Lompoc, CA 805-736-1455
Barboursville Vineyards
Barboursville, VA 540-832-3824
Black Mesa Winery
Velarde, NM 800-852-6372
Breaux Vineyards
Purcellville, VA. 800-492-9961
Burnley Vineyards and Daniel Cellars
Barboursville, VA 540-832-2828
Catoctin Vineyards
Brookeville, MD. 301-774-2310
Cedar Creek Winery
Cedarburg, WI. 800-827-8020
Chateau Morisette Winery
Meadows of Dan, VA 540-593-2865
Chatom Vineyards
Murphys, CA. 800-435-8852
Chicama Vineyards
West Tisbury, MA. 888-244-2262
Chouinard Vineyards
Castro Valley, CA 510-582-9900
Cienega Valley Winery/DeRose
Hollister, CA. 831-636-9143
Cooper Vineyards
Louisa, VA 540-894-5253
Corus Brands
Woodinville, WA. 425-806-2600
Cosentino Winery Vintage Grapevine, Inc.
Yountville, CA 800-764-1220
Cribari Vineyards
Fresno, CA 800-277-9095

Processor and exporter of high quality California bulk wine.

Cuvaison Vineyard
Calistoga, CA 707-942-6266
Delicato Vineyards
Napa, CA. 877-824-3600
E&J Gallo Winery
Modesto, CA. 209-341-3111
Farfelu Vineyards
Flint Hill, VA 540-364-2930
Fenestra Winery
Livermore, CA 800-789-9463
Ficklin Vineyards
Madera, CA. 559-674-4598
First Colony Winery
Charlottesville, VA 877-979-7105
Foris Vineyards
Cave Junction, OR 541-592-3752
Freemark Abbey Winery
Helena, CA 800-963-9698
Greenwood Ridge Vineyards
Philo, CA. 707-895-2002
Groth Vineyards & Winery
Oakville, CA. 707-944-0290
Hazlitt's 1852 Vineyard
Hector, NY 888-750-0494
Heineman's Winery
Put In Bay, OH 419-285-2811
Honig Vineyard and Winery
Rutherford, CA 800-929-2217
Mayacamas Vineyards
Napa, CA. 707-224-4030
Oakencroft Vineyard & Winery
Charlottesville, VA 434-296-4188
Oasis Winery
Hume, VA 800-304-7656
Obester Winery
Half Moon Bay, CA 650-726-9463
Old House Vineyards
Culpeper, VA. 540-423-1032
Piedmont Vineyards & Winery
Middleburg, VA 540-687-5528
Plum Creek Cellars
Palisade, CO 970-464-7586
Retzlaff Vineyards
Livermore, CA 925-447-8941
Ritchie Creek Vineyard
Saint Helena, CA 707-963-4661
Robert Pecota Winery
Calistoga, CA 707-942-6625
Rodney Strong Vineyards
Healdsburg, CA 800-474-9463
Secret House Vineyards
Veneta, OR 800-497-1574
Seven Hills Winery
Walla Walla, WA. 877-777-7870
Shafer Vineyards
Napa, CA. 707-944-2877
Signorello Vineyards
Napa, CA. 707-255-5990
Silver Fox Vineyard
Mariposa, CA 209-966-4800
Silver Oak Cellars
Oakville, CA. 800-273-8805
Smith Vineyard & Winery
Grass Valley, CA. 530-273-7032
Smothers Winery/Remick Ridge
Glen Ellen, CA 800-795-9463
Sonoita Vineyards
Elgin, AZ. 520-455-5893
Spottswoode Winery
Saint Helena, CA 707-963-0134
Stone Mountain Vineyards
Dyke, VA. 434-990-9463
Sycamore Vineyards
Saint Helena, CA 800-963-9698
Sylvester Winery
Paso Robles, CA. 805-227-4000
Tularosa Vineyards
Tularosa, NM 800-687-4467
Veramar Vineyard
Berryville, VA. 540-955-5510
Veritas Vineyards & Winery
Afton, VA 540-456-8000
Vincent Arroyo Winery
Calistoga, CA 707-942-6995
Von Stiehl Winery
Algoma, WI. 800-955-5208
Westbend Vinyards
Lewisville, NC 866-901-5032
White Hall Vineyards
Crozet, VA. 434-823-8615
White Oak Vineyards & Winery
Healdsburg, CA 707-433-8429
Whitehall Lane Winery
Saint Helena, CA 707-963-9454
Willowcroft Farm Vineyards
Leesburg, VA 703-777-8161
Windham Winery
Purcellville, VA. 540-668-6464
Wintergreen Winery
Nellysford, VA 434-361-2519
Woodside Vineyards
Menlo Park, CA 650-851-3144
York Mountain Winery
Templeton, CA 805-237-7575
Z.D. Wines
Napa, CA. 800-487-7757

Dolcetto

Cosentino Winery Vintage Grapevine, Inc.
Yountville, CA 800-764-1220
Witness Tree Vineyard
Salem, OR. 888-478-8766

Malbec

E&J Gallo Winery
Modesto, CA. 209-341-3111

Merlot

A. Rafanelli Winery
Healdsburg, CA 707-433-1385
Autumn Hill Vineyards/Blue Ridge Wine
Stanardsville, VA 434-985-6100
Babcock Winery & Vineyards
Lompoc, CA 805-736-1455
Barboursville Vineyards
Barboursville, VA 540-832-3824
Breaux Vineyards
Purcellville, VA. 800-492-9961
Chateau Grand Traverse
Traverse City, MI 231-223-7355
Chateau Morisette Winery
Meadows of Dan, VA 540-593-2865
Chateau Souverain
Cloverdale, CA
Chicama Vineyards
West Tisbury, MA. 888-244-2262
Cienega Valley Winery/DeRose
Hollister, CA. 831-636-9143
Cooper Vineyards
Louisa, VA 540-894-5253
Corus Brands
Woodinville, WA. 425-806-2600
Cosentino Winery Vintage Grapevine, Inc.
Yountville, CA 800-764-1220
Cribari Vineyards
Fresno, CA 800-277-9095

Processor and exporter of high quality California bulk wine.

Cuvaison Vineyard
Calistoga, CA 707-942-6266
Delicato Vineyards
Napa, CA. 877-824-3600
E&J Gallo Winery
Modesto, CA. 209-341-3111
Fenestra Winery
Livermore, CA 800-789-9463
First Colony Winery
Charlottesville, VA 877-979-7105
Foris Vineyards
Cave Junction, OR 541-592-3752
Greenwood Ridge Vineyards
Philo, CA. 707-895-2002

Groth Vineyards & Winery
Oakville, CA 707-944-0290
Gundlach Bundschu Winery
Sonoma, CA 707-938-5277
Hazlitt's 1852 Vineyard
Hector, NY 888-750-0494
Heron Hill Winery
Hammondsport, NY 800-441-4241
Jefferson Vineyards
Charlottesville, VA 800-272-3042
Nevada City Winery
Nevada City, CA 800-203-9463
Oakencroft Vineyard & Winery
Charlottesville, VA 434-296-4188
Oasis Winery
Hume, VA 800-304-7656
Old House Vineyards
Culpeper, VA 540-423-1032
Plum Creek Cellars
Palisade, CO 970-464-7586
Retzlaff Vineyards
Livermore, CA 925-447-8941
Robert Pecota Winery
Calistoga, CA 707-942-6625
Rodney Strong Vineyards
Healdsburg, CA 800-474-9463
Seven Hills Winery
Walla Walla, WA 877-777-7870
Shafer Vineyards
Napa, CA 707-944-2877
Signorello Vineyards
Napa, CA 707-255-5990
Silver Fox Vineyard
Mariposa, CA 209-966-4800
Smith Vineyard & Winery
Grass Valley, CA 530-273-7032
Smothers Winery/Remick Ridge
Glen Ellen, CA 800-795-9463
Sycamore Vineyards
Saint Helena, CA 800-963-9698
Sylvester Winery
Paso Robles, CA 805-227-4000
Tularosa Vineyards
Tularosa, NM 800-687-4467
Veritas Vineyards & Winery
Afton, VA 540-456-8000
Vincent Arroyo Winery
Calistoga, CA 707-942-6995
Von Stiehl Winery
Algoma, WI 800-955-5208
Westbend Vinyards
Lewisville, NC 866-901-5032
White Hall Vineyards
Crozet, VA 434-823-8615
White Oak Vineyards & Winery
Healdsburg, CA 707-433-8429
Whitehall Lane Winery
Saint Helena, CA 707-963-9454
Windham Winery
Purcellville, VA 540-668-6464
York Mountain Winery
Templeton, CA 805-237-7575

Pinot Noir

Babcock Winery & Vineyards
Lompoc, CA 805-736-1455
Barboursville Vineyards
Barboursville, VA 540-832-3824
Buena Vista Carneros Winery
Sonoma, CA 800-678-8504
Byron Vineyard & Winery
Santa Maria, CA 805-934-4770
Chateau Grand Traverse
Traverse City, MI 231-223-7355
Corus Brands
Woodinville, WA 425-806-2600
Cosentino Winery   Vintage Grapevine, Inc.
Yountville, CA 800-764-1220
Cristom Vineyards
Salem, OR 503-375-3068
Cuvaison Vineyard
Calistoga, CA 707-942-6266
E&J Gallo Winery
Modesto, CA 209-341-3111
Edna Valley Vineyard
San Luis Obispo, CA 805-544-5855
Fenestra Winery
Livermore, CA 800-789-9463
Fess Parker Winery
Los Olivos, CA 800-446-2455
Foris Vineyards
Cave Junction, OR 541-592-3752
Greenwood Ridge Vineyards
Philo, CA 707-895-2002
Gundlach Bundschu Winery
Sonoma, CA 707-938-5277
Hermann Wiemer Vineyards
Dundee, NY 800-371-7971
Heron Hill Winery
Hammondsport, NY 800-441-4241
Mayacamas Vineyards
Napa, CA 707-224-4030
McGregor Vineyard Winery
Dundee, NY 800-272-0192
Nalle Winery
Healdsburg, CA 707-433-1040
Navarro Vineyards & Winery
Philo, CA 800-537-9463
Nehalem Bay Winery
Nehalem, OR 888-368-9463
Ritchie Creek Vineyard
Saint Helena, CA 707-963-4661
Rodney Strong Vineyards
Healdsburg, CA 800-474-9463
Secret House Vineyards
Veneta, OR 800-497-1574
Tualatin Estate Vineyards
Forest Grove, OR 503-357-5005
Westwood Winery
Sonoma, CA 707-935-3246
Whitford Cellars
Napa, CA 707-942-0840
Williams-Selym Winery
Healdsburg, CA 707-433-6425
Witness Tree Vineyard
Salem, OR 888-478-8766
Woodside Vineyards
Menlo Park, CA 650-851-3144
York Mountain Winery
Templeton, CA 805-237-7575
Z.D. Wines
Napa, CA 800-487-7757

Red Meritage/Bordeaux

Fenn Valley Vineyards
Fennville, MI 800-432-6265

Sangiovese

Babcock Winery & Vineyards
Lompoc, CA 805-736-1455
Corus Brands
Woodinville, WA 425-806-2600
Cosentino Winery   Vintage Grapevine, Inc.
Yountville, CA 800-764-1220
E&J Gallo Winery
Modesto, CA 209-341-3111
Fenestra Winery
Livermore, CA 800-789-9463
Nevada City Winery
Nevada City, CA 800-203-9463
Plum Creek Cellars
Palisade, CO 970-464-7586
Sylvester Winery
Paso Robles, CA 805-227-4000
Tularosa Vineyards
Tularosa, NM 800-687-4467
Vincent Arroyo Winery
Calistoga, CA 707-942-6995

Syrah

Babcock Winery & Vineyards
Lompoc, CA 805-736-1455
Black Mesa Winery
Velarde, NM 800-852-6372
Cedar Creek Winery
Cedarburg, WI 800-827-8020
Chouinard Vineyards
Castro Valley, CA 510-582-9900
Cooper Vineyards
Louisa, VA 540-894-5253
Corus Brands
Woodinville, WA 425-806-2600
Cosentino Winery   Vintage Grapevine, Inc.
Yountville, CA 800-764-1220
Cuvaison Vineyard
Calistoga, CA 707-942-6266
Fenestra Winery
Livermore, CA 800-789-9463
Fess Parker Winery
Los Olivos, CA 800-446-2455
Nevada City Winery
Nevada City, CA 800-203-9463
Plum Creek Cellars
Palisade, CO 970-464-7586
Signorello Vineyards
Napa, CA 707-255-5990
Sky Vineyards
Glen Ellen, CA 707-935-1391
Sylvester Winery
Paso Robles, CA 805-227-4000
Tularosa Vineyards
Tularosa, NM 800-687-4467
Westwood Winery
Sonoma, CA 707-935-3246
Whitford Cellars
Napa, CA 707-942-0840

Zinfandel

A. Nonini Winery
Fresno, CA 559-275-1936
A. Rafanelli Winery
Healdsburg, CA 707-433-1385
Burnley Vineyards and Daniel Cellars
Barboursville, VA 540-832-2828
Chateau Souverain
Cloverdale, CA
Chatom Vineyards
Murphys, CA 800-435-8852
Chouinard Vineyards
Castro Valley, CA 510-582-9900
Cienega Valley Winery/DeRose
Hollister, CA 831-636-9143
Corus Brands
Woodinville, WA 425-806-2600
Cosentino Winery   Vintage Grapevine, Inc.
Yountville, CA 800-764-1220
Cribari Vineyards
Fresno, CA 800-277-9095

Processor and exporter of high quality California bulk wine.

Cuvaison Vineyard
Calistoga, CA 707-942-6266
Delicato Vineyards
Napa, CA 877-824-3600
E&J Gallo Winery
Modesto, CA 209-341-3111
Fenestra Winery
Livermore, CA 800-789-9463
Fess Parker Winery
Los Olivos, CA 800-446-2455
Gundlach Bundschu Winery
Sonoma, CA 707-938-5277
Livermore Valley Cellars
Livermore, CA 925-454-9463
Nalle Winery
Healdsburg, CA 707-433-1040
Nevada City Winery
Nevada City, CA 800-203-9463
Old Wine Cellar
Amana, IA 319-622-3116
Rodney Strong Vineyards
Healdsburg, CA 800-474-9463
Silver Fox Vineyard
Mariposa, CA 209-966-4800
Sky Vineyards
Glen Ellen, CA 707-935-1391
Storybook Mountain Winery
Calistoga, CA 707-942-5310
Sylvester Winery
Paso Robles, CA 805-227-4000
Vincent Arroyo Winery
Calistoga, CA 707-942-6995
Von Stiehl Winery
Algoma, WI 800-955-5208
White Oak Vineyards & Winery
Healdsburg, CA 707-433-8429
Williams-Selym Winery
Healdsburg, CA 707-433-6425
Woodside Vineyards
Menlo Park, CA 650-851-3144
York Mountain Winery
Templeton, CA 805-237-7575

Red Grapes

Alto Vineyards
Alto Pass, IL 618-893-4898
Babcock Winery & Vineyards
Lompoc, CA 805-736-1455
Brown-Forman Corporation
Louisville, KY 502-585-1100
Chateau Grand Traverse
Traverse City, MI 231-223-7355

Chicama Vineyards
West Tisbury, MA 888-244-2262
Chouinard Vineyards
Castro Valley, CA 510-582-9900
Cienega Valley Winery/DeRose
Hollister, CA 831-636-9143
Corus Brands
Woodinville, WA 425-806-2600
Cosentino Winery Vintage Grapevine, Inc.
Yountville, CA 800-764-1220
Cribari Vineyards
Fresno, CA 800-277-9095

Processor and exporter of high quality California bulk wine.

E&J Gallo Winery
Modesto, CA 209-341-3111
Fess Parker Winery
Los Olivos, CA 800-446-2455
Galleano Winery
Mira Loma, CA 951-685-5376
Heineman's Winery
Put In Bay, OH 419-285-2811
Newport Vineyards & Winery
Middletown, RI 401-848-5161
Wildhurst
Kelseyville, CA 800-595-9463
Wooden Valley Winery
Fairfield, CA 707-864-0730

Spanish

Sherry

Cribari Vineyards
Fresno, CA 800-277-9095

Processor and exporter of high quality California bulk wine.

Pleasant Valley Wine Company
Hammondsport, NY 607-569-6111

Sparkling (See also French/Champagne)

Brimstone Hill Vineyard
Pine Bush, NY 845-744-2231
Brown-Forman Corporation
Louisville, KY 502-585-1100
Buena Vista Carneros Winery
Sonoma, CA 800-678-8504
Bully Hill Vineyards
Hammondsport, NY 607-868-3610
Clinton Vineyards
Clinton Corners, NY 845-266-5372
Diamond Water
Hot Springs, AR 501-623-1251
Domaine Chandon
Yountville, CA 800-242-6366
Dr. Frank's Vinifera Wine Cellar
Hammondsport, NY 800-320-0735
E&J Gallo Winery
Modesto, CA 209-341-3111
Glenora Wine Cellars
Dundee, NY 800-243-5513
Hazlitt's 1852 Vineyard
Hector, NY 888-750-0494
Hermann Wiemer Vineyards
Dundee, NY 800-371-7971
Hermannhof Winery
Hermann, MO 800-393-0100
Heron Hill Winery
Hammondsport, NY 800-441-4241
La Rochelle Winery
Livermore, CA 888-647-7768
Meier's Wine Cellars
Cincinnati, OH 800-346-2941
Mon Ami Champagne Company
Port Clinton, OH 800-777-4266
North Salem Vineyard
North Salem, NY 914-669-5518
Royal Wine Corp
Bayonne, NJ 718-384-2400
Schramsberg Vineyards
Calistoga, CA 800-877-3623
St. Innocent Winery
Salem, OR 503-378-1526
Tualatin Estate Vineyards
Forest Grove, OR 503-357-5005
V. Sattui Winery
Saint Helena, CA 800-799-8888
Windsor Vineyards
Windsor, CA 800-333-9987
Woodbury Vineyards
Fredonia, NY 866-691-9463

White Grape Varieties

Alto Vineyards
Alto Pass, IL 618-893-4898
Babcock Winery & Vineyards
Lompoc, CA 805-736-1455
Cienega Valley Winery/DeRose
Hollister, CA 831-636-9143
Hazlitt's 1852 Vineyard
Hector, NY 888-750-0494
Hermann Wiemer Vineyards
Dundee, NY 800-371-7971
Hermannhof Winery
Hermann, MO 800-393-0100
Heron Hill Winery
Hammondsport, NY 800-441-4241

Chardonnay

AmRhein Wine Cellars
Bent Mountain, VA 540-929-4632
Autumn Hill Vineyards/Blue Ridge Wine
Stanardsville, VA 434-985-6100
Babcock Winery & Vineyards
Lompoc, CA 805-736-1455
Barboursville Vineyards
Barboursville, VA 540-832-3824
Benmarl Wine Company
Marlboro, NY 845-236-4265
Breaux Vineyards
Purcellville, VA 800-492-9961
Buena Vista Carneros Winery
Sonoma, CA 800-678-8504
Burnley Vineyards and Daniel Cellars
Barboursville, VA 540-832-2828
Byron Vineyard & Winery
Santa Maria, CA 805-934-4770
Catoctin Vineyards
Brookeville, MD 301-774-2310
Cedar Creek Winery
Cedarburg, WI 800-827-8020
Chateau Grand Traverse
Traverse City, MI 231-223-7355
Chateau Morisette Winery
Meadows of Dan, VA 540-593-2865
Chateau Souverain
Cloverdale, CA
Chicama Vineyards
West Tisbury, MA 888-244-2262
Chouinard Vineyards
Castro Valley, CA 510-582-9900
Cienega Valley Winery/DeRose
Hollister, CA 831-636-9143
Cooper Vineyards
Louisa, VA 540-894-5253
Corus Brands
Woodinville, WA 425-806-2600
Cosentino Winery Vintage Grapevine, Inc.
Yountville, CA 800-764-1220
Cribari Vineyards
Fresno, CA 800-277-9095

Processor and exporter of high quality California bulk wine.

Cristom Vineyards
Salem, OR 503-375-3068
Cuvaison Vineyard
Calistoga, CA 707-942-6266
Delicato Vineyards
Napa, CA 877-824-3600
E&J Gallo Winery
Modesto, CA 209-341-3111
Edna Valley Vineyard
San Luis Obispo, CA 805-544-5855
Fenestra Winery
Livermore, CA 800-789-9463
Fenn Valley Vineyards
Fennville, MI 800-432-6265
Fess Parker Winery
Los Olivos, CA 800-446-2455
First Colony Winery
Charlottesville, VA 877-979-7105
Foris Vineyards
Cave Junction, OR 541-592-3752
Freemark Abbey Winery
Helena, CA 800-963-9698
Groth Vineyards & Winery
Oakville, CA 707-944-0290
Gundlach Bundschu Winery
Sonoma, CA 707-938-5277
Hazlitt's 1852 Vineyard
Hector, NY 888-750-0494
Heineman's Winery
Put In Bay, OH 419-285-2811
Hermann Wiemer Vineyards
Dundee, NY 800-371-7971
Heron Hill Winery
Hammondsport, NY 800-441-4241
Mayacamas Vineyards
Napa, CA 707-224-4030
McGregor Vineyard Winery
Dundee, NY 800-272-0192
Nalle Winery
Healdsburg, CA 707-433-1040
Nehalem Bay Winery
Nehalem, OR 888-368-9463
Nevada City Winery
Nevada City, CA 800-203-9463
Oakencroft Vineyard & Winery
Charlottesville, VA 434-296-4188
Oasis Winery
Hume, VA 800-304-7656
Obester Winery
Half Moon Bay, CA 650-726-9463
Old House Vineyards
Culpeper, VA 540-423-1032
Plum Creek Cellars
Palisade, CO 970-464-7586
Retzlaff Vineyards
Livermore, CA 925-447-8941
Rodney Strong Vineyards
Healdsburg, CA 800-474-9463
Secret House Vineyards
Veneta, OR 800-497-1574
Shafer Vineyards
Napa, CA 707-944-2877
Signorello Vineyards
Napa, CA 707-255-5990
Sky Vineyards
Glen Ellen, CA 707-935-1391
Smith Vineyard & Winery
Grass Valley, CA 530-273-7032
Stone Mountain Vineyards
Dyke, VA 434-990-9463
Stonington Vineyards
Stonington, CT 800-421-9463
Sylvester Winery
Paso Robles, CA 805-227-4000
Tularosa Vineyards
Tularosa, NM 800-687-4467
Veramar Vineyard
Berryville, VA 540-955-5510
Veritas Vineyards & Winery
Afton, VA 540-456-8000
Vincent Arroyo Winery
Calistoga, CA 707-942-6995
White Hall Vineyards
Crozet, VA 434-823-8615
White Oak Vineyards & Winery
Healdsburg, CA 707-433-8429
Whitehall Lane Winery
Saint Helena, CA 707-963-9454
Whitford Cellars
Napa, CA 707-942-0840
Williams-Selym Winery
Healdsburg, CA 707-433-6425
Willowcroft Farm Vineyards
Leesburg, VA 703-777-8161
Windham Winery
Purcellville, VA 540-668-6464
Wintergreen Winery
Nellysford, VA 434-361-2519
Witness Tree Vineyard
Salem, OR 888-478-8766
Woodside Vineyards
Menlo Park, CA 650-851-3144
Z.D. Wines
Napa, CA 800-487-7757

Gewrurztraminer

Babcock Winery & Vineyards
Lompoc, CA 805-736-1455
Chouinard Vineyards
Castro Valley, CA 510-582-9900
Corus Brands
Woodinville, WA 425-806-2600
Cosentino Winery Vintage Grapevine, Inc.
Yountville, CA 800-764-1220
Fenn Valley Vineyards
Fennville, MI 800-432-6265
Foris Vineyards
Cave Junction, OR 541-592-3752

Gundlach Bundschu Winery
Sonoma, CA 707-938-5277
Hazlitt's 1852 Vineyard
Hector, NY 888-750-0494
Hermann Wiemer Vineyards
Dundee, NY 800-371-7971
McGregor Vineyard Winery
Dundee, NY 800-272-0192
Nevada City Winery
Nevada City, CA 800-203-9463
Stonington Vineyards
Stonington, CT 800-421-9463
Tualatin Estate Vineyards
Forest Grove, OR 503-357-5005
White Hall Vineyards
Crozet, VA 434-823-8615

Pinot Blanc

Byron Vineyard & Winery
Santa Maria, CA 805-934-4770
Foris Vineyards
Cave Junction, OR 541-592-3752
Nehalem Bay Winery
Nehalem, OR 888-368-9463
Tualatin Estate Vineyards
Forest Grove, OR 503-357-5005
Witness Tree Vineyard
Salem, OR 888-478-8766

Pinot Gris

Babcock Winery & Vineyards
Lompoc, CA 805-736-1455
Byron Vineyard & Winery
Santa Maria, CA 805-934-4770
Corus Brands
Woodinville, WA 425-806-2600
Cosentino Winery Vintage Grapevine, Inc.
Yountville, CA 800-764-1220
Cristom Vineyards
Salem, OR 503-375-3068
Foris Vineyards
Cave Junction, OR 541-592-3752
Hazlitt's 1852 Vineyard
Hector, NY 888-750-0494
Heineman's Winery
Put In Bay, OH 419-285-2811
Jefferson Vineyards
Charlottesville, VA 800-272-3042
Secret House Vineyards
Veneta, OR 800-497-1574
Seven Hills Winery
Walla Walla, WA 877-777-7870
White Hall Vineyards
Crozet, VA 434-823-8615

Riesling

Abingdon Vineyard & Winery
Abingdon, VA 276-623-1255
Autumn Hill Vineyards/Blue Ridge Wine
Stanardsville, VA 434-985-6100
Barboursville Vineyards
Barboursville, VA 540-832-3824
Burnley Vineyards and Daniel Cellars
Barboursville, VA 540-832-2828
Catoctin Vineyards
Brookeville, MD 301-774-2310
Chateau Grand Traverse
Traverse City, MI 231-223-7355
Chouinard Vineyards
Castro Valley, CA 510-582-9900
Corus Brands
Woodinville, WA 425-806-2600
E&J Gallo Winery
Modesto, CA 209-341-3111
Fenestra Winery
Livermore, CA 800-789-9463
Fenn Valley Vineyards
Fennville, MI 800-432-6265
Fess Parker Winery
Los Olivos, CA 800-446-2455
Freemark Abbey Winery
Helena, CA 800-963-9698
Greenwood Ridge Vineyards
Philo, CA 707-895-2002
Gundlach Bundschu Winery
Sonoma, CA 707-938-5277
Hazlitt's 1852 Vineyard
Hector, NY 888-750-0494
Heineman's Winery
Put In Bay, OH 419-285-2811
Hermann Wiemer Vineyards
Dundee, NY 800-371-7971
Heron Hill Winery
Hammondsport, NY 800-441-4241
Jefferson Vineyards
Charlottesville, VA 800-272-3042
McGregor Vineyard Winery
Dundee, NY 800-272-0192
Oasis Winery
Hume, VA 800-304-7656
Obester Winery
Half Moon Bay, CA 650-726-9463
Plum Creek Cellars
Palisade, CO 970-464-7586
Secret House Vineyards
Veneta, OR 800-497-1574
Seven Hills Winery
Walla Walla, WA 877-777-7870
Tualatin Estate Vineyards
Forest Grove, OR 503-357-5005
Veramar Vineyard
Berryville, VA 540-955-5510
Westbend Vinyards
Lewisville, NC 866-901-5032
Willowcroft Farm Vineyards
Leesburg, VA 703-777-8161
Windham Winery
Purcellville, VA 540-668-6464
Wintergreen Winery
Nellysford, VA 434-361-2519

Sauvignon Blanc

Babcock Winery & Vineyards
Lompoc, CA 805-736-1455
Chateau Souverain
Cloverdale, CA
Chicama Vineyards
West Tisbury, MA 888-244-2262
Chouinard Vineyards
Castro Valley, CA 510-582-9900
Cosentino Winery Vintage Grapevine, Inc.
Yountville, CA 800-764-1220
Delicato Vineyards
Napa, CA 877-824-3600
E&J Gallo Winery
Modesto, CA 209-341-3111
Fenestra Winery
Livermore, CA 800-789-9463
Groth Vineyards & Winery
Oakville, CA 707-944-0290
Honig Vineyard and Winery
Rutherford, CA 800-929-2217
Mayacamas Vineyards
Napa, CA 707-224-4030
Nalle Winery
Healdsburg, CA 707-433-1040
Nevada City Winery
Nevada City, CA 800-203-9463
Plum Creek Cellars
Palisade, CO 970-464-7586
Retzlaff Vineyards
Livermore, CA 925-447-8941
Rodney Strong Vineyards
Healdsburg, CA 800-474-9463
Signorello Vineyards
Napa, CA 707-255-5990
Spottswoode Winery
Saint Helena, CA 707-963-0134
Westbend Vinyards
Lewisville, NC 866-901-5032
White Oak Vineyards & Winery
Healdsburg, CA 707-433-8429
Whitehall Lane Winery
Saint Helena, CA 707-963-9454

Viognier

AmRhein Wine Cellars
Bent Mountain, VA 540-929-4632
Breaux Vineyards
Purcellville, VA 800-492-9961
Chicama Vineyards
West Tisbury, MA 888-244-2262
Cienega Valley Winery/DeRose
Hollister, CA 831-636-9143
Corus Brands
Woodinville, WA 425-806-2600
Cosentino Winery Vintage Grapevine, Inc.
Yountville, CA 800-764-1220
Cristom Vineyards
Salem, OR 503-375-3068
Fenestra Winery
Livermore, CA 800-789-9463
Fess Parker Winery
Los Olivos, CA 800-446-2455
Seven Hills Winery
Walla Walla, WA 877-777-7870
Signorello Vineyards
Napa, CA 707-255-5990
Tularosa Vineyards
Tularosa, NM 800-687-4467
Witness Tree Vineyard
Salem, OR 888-478-8766

White Grapes

Brown-Forman Corporation
Louisville, KY 502-585-1100
Chateau Grand Traverse
Traverse City, MI 231-223-7355
Chicama Vineyards
West Tisbury, MA 888-244-2262
Chouinard Vineyards
Castro Valley, CA 510-582-9900
Corus Brands
Woodinville, WA 425-806-2600
Cribari Vineyards
Fresno, CA 800-277-9095

Processor and exporter of high quality California bulk wine.

Galleano Winery
Mira Loma, CA 951-685-5376
Heineman's Winery
Put In Bay, OH 419-285-2811
Newport Vineyards & Winery
Middletown, RI 401-848-5161
V. Sattui Winery
Saint Helena, CA 800-799-8888
Wildhurst
Kelseyville, CA 800-595-9463
Wooden Valley Winery
Fairfield, CA 707-864-0730

Candy & Confectionery

Candy

A La Carte
Chicago, IL 800-722-2370
A. Battaglia Processing Company
Chicago, IL 773-523-5900
Abbott's Candy Shop
Hagerstown, IN 877-801-1200
Acme Candy Company
Arlington, TX 254-634-2825
Across Foods, LLC
New Hope, PA 215-693-6274
Adirondack Maple Farms
Fonda, NY 518-853-4022
Aglamesis Brothers
Cincinnati, OH 513-531-5196
Alaska Jack's Trading Post
Anchorage, AK 888-660-2257
All Wrapped Up
Plantation, FL 800-891-2194
Alma-Leo
Buffalo Grove, IL 847-821-0411
Amano Artisan Chocolate
Orem, UT 801-655-1996
Ameri-Suisse Group
Plainfield, NJ 908-222-1001
American Food Products
Methuen, MA 978-682-1855
American Licorice Company
Union City, CA 866-442-2783
American Mint
New York, NY 800-401-6468
American Specialty Confections
Saint Paul, MN 800-776-2085
AmeriGift
Oxnard, CA 800-421-9039
Amour Chocolates
Albuquerque, NM 505-881-2803
Amros the Second, Inc.
Somerset, NJ 732-846-7755
Amster-Kirtz Company
Canton, OH 800-257-9338
Amurol Confections Company
Yorkville, IL 630-553-4800
Andalan Confections
Fort Oglethorpe, GA 877-263-2526
Andes Candy
Chicago, IL 773-838-3400
Andre Prost
Old Saybrook, CT 800-243-0897
Andre's Confiserie Suisse
Kansas City, MO 800-892-1234
Ann Hemyng Candy
Trumbauersville, PA 800-779-7004
Annabelle Candy Company
Hayward, CA 510-783-2900
Archibald Candy Corporation
Chicago, IL 800-333-3629
Arcor USA
Miami, FL 800-572-7267
Arizona Cowboy
Phoenix, AZ 602-956-4833
Art CoCo Chocolate Company
Denver, CO 800-779-8985
Arway Confections
Chicago, IL 773-267-5770
Asher's Chocolates
Souderton, PA 800-223-4420
Ashers Chocolates
Lewistown, PA 800-343-0520
Assouline & Ting
Huntingdon Valley, PA 800-521-4491
Asti Holdings Ltd
New Westminster, BC 604-523-6866
Athena's Silverland®Desserts
Forest Park, IL 800-737-3636
Atkinson Candy Company
Lufkin, TX 800-231-1203
Atlas Biscuit Company
Verona, NJ 973-239-8300
Aunt Aggie De's Pralines
Sinton, TX 888-772-5463
Aunt Sally's Praline Shops, Inc.
New Orleans, LA 800-642-7257
Aurora Products
Stratford, CT 800-398-1048
Azar Nut Company
El Paso, TX 800-592-8103
Bacci Chocolate Design
Swampscott, MA 888-725-2877
Baker Candy Company
Snohomish, WA 425-422-6331
Baker Maid Products, Inc.
New Orleans, LA 504-827-5500
Bakers Candy
Greenwood, NE 800-804-7330
Balticshop.Com LLC
Glastonbury, CT
Banner Candy Manufacturing Company
Brooklyn, NY 718-647-4747
Barcelona Nut Company
Baltimore, MD 800-292-6887
Bari & Gail
Walpole, MA 800-828-9318
Barricini Chocolate
Avoca, PA 570-457-6756
Bazaar
River Grove, IL 800-736-1888
Bee Int'l., Inc
Chula Vista, CA 800-421-6465
Beehive Botanicals, Inc.
Hayward, WI 800-233-4483
Ben Heggy's Candy Company
Canton, OH 330-455-7703
Bergen Marzipan & Chocolate
Bergenfield, NJ 201-385-8343
Betty Jane Homemade Candies
Dubuque, IA 800-642-1254
Betty Lou's Golden Smackers
McMinnville, OR 800-242-5205
Bidwell Candies
Mattoon, IL 217-234-3858
Birnn Chocolates
Highland Park, NJ 732-545-4400
Birnn Chocolates of Vermont
South Burlington, VT 800-338-3141
Biscomerica Corporation
Rialto, CA 909-877-5997
Black Hound New York
Brooklyn, NY 800-344-4417
Blanton's
Sweetwater, TN 423-337-3487
Blommer Chocolate Company
East Greenville, PA 800-825-8181
Bloomer Candy Company
Zanesville, OH 800-452-7501
Bluebird Restaurant
Logan, UT 435-752-3155
Bob's Candies
Albany, GA 800-841-3602
Boca Bons East,LLC.
Greenacres, FL 800-314-2835
Bogdon Candy Company
Canajoharie, NY 800-839-8938
Bohemian Biscuit Company
South San Francisco, CA 650-952-2226
Boston America Corporation
Woburn, MA 617-923-1111
Boston Fruit Slice & Confectionery Corporation
Lawrence, MA 978-686-2699
Bourbon Ball
Louisville, KY 800-280-0888
Brach's Confections
Halethorpe, MD 443-872-2094
Bread & Chocolate
Wells River, VT 800-524-6715
Brechet & Richter Company
Minneapolis, MN 763-545-0201
Brittle Kettle
Tigard, OR 800-447-2128
Brokay Products
Philadelphia, PA 215-676-4800
Buon Italia Misono Food Ltd.
New York, NY 212-633-9090
Burke Candy & Ingredient Corporation
Milwaukee, WI 888-287-5350
Butterfields/Sweet Concepts
Nashville, NC 800-945-5957
C. Howard Company
Bellport, NY 631-286-7940
Cadbury Trebor Allan
Granby, QC 800-387-3267
Cadbury Trebor Allan
Toronto, ON 800-565-6541
Caiazza Candy Company
New Castle, PA 800-651-1171
Callard & Bowser-Suchard
White Plains, NY 877-226-3900
Cambridge Brands
Cambridge, MA 617-491-2500
Cameo Confections
Bay Village, OH 440-871-5732
Cameron Birch Syrup & Confections
Wasilla, AK 800-962-4724
Campbell Soup Company
Camden, NJ 800-257-8443
Candy Bouquet of Elko
Elko, NV 888-855-3391
Candy Factory
Hayward, CA 800-736-6887
Canelake's
Virginia, MN 888-928-8889
Capco Enterprises
East Hanover, NJ 800-252-1011
Caprine Estates
Bellbrook, OH 937-848-7406
Caribbean Cookie Company
Virginia Beach, VA 800-326-5200
Carolina Cupboard
Hillsborough, NC 800-400-3441
Carolyn Candies
Clermont, FL 352-394-8555
Carolyn's Gourmet
Concord, MA 800-656-2940
Carrie's Chocolates
Edmonton, AB 877-778-2462
Catoris Candy
New Kensington, PA 724-335-4371
Cella's Confections
Chicago, IL 773-838-3400
Charles Faraud C/O Pramex
New York, NY
Charlotte's Confections
Millbrae, CA 800-798-2427
Chase Candy Company
Saint Joseph, MO 800-786-1625
Cheese Straws & More
Monroe, LA 800-997-1921
Cheri's Desert Harvest
Tucson, AZ 800-743-1141
Chevalier Chocolates
Enfield, CT 860-741-3330
Chex Finer Foods
Attleboro, MA 800-322-2434
Chocoholics Divine Desserts
Linden, CA 800-760-2462
Chocolat Belge Heyez
St-Lazare-De-Bellechasse, QC 450-653-5616
Chocolat Jean Talon
Montreal, QC 888-333-8540
Chocolate Moon
Asheville, NC 800-723-1236
Chocolate Soup
Steamboat Springs, CO 970-870-0224
Chocolate Street of Hartville
Hartville, OH 888-853-5904
Chocolate Studio
Norristown, PA 610-272-3872
Chocolaterie Stam
Des Moines, IA 877-782-6246
Chocolates by Mark
La Porte, TX 832-736-2626
Chocolates by Mr. Robert
Boca Raton, FL 561-392-3007
Chocolati Handmade Chocolates
Seattle, WA 206-784-5212
Chocolatier
Exeter, NH 888-246-5528
Chris A. Papas & Son Company
Covington, KY 859-431-0499
Chris Candies
Pittsburgh, PA 412-322-9400
Chupa Chups USA
Atlanta, GA 800-843-1858
Clarks Joe Fund Raising Candies & Novelties
Tarentum, PA 888-459-9520
Clasen Quality Coatings
Madison, WI 877-459-4500

Classic Confectionery
Fort Worth, TX 800-674-4435
Clear-Vu Industries
Ashland, MA. 508-881-9100
Cloud Nine
San Leandro, CA. 201-358-8588
Cloverland Sweets/Priester's Pecan Company
Fort Deposit, AL. 800-523-3505
CNS Confectionery Products
Bayonne, NJ 888-823-4330
Cocoline Chocolate Company
Brooklyn, NY 718-522-4500
Colts Chocolates
Nashville, TN 615-251-0100
Columbia Empire Farms
Sherwood, OR. 503-538-2156
Confection Solutions
Sylmar, CA 800-284-2422
Confectionately Yours
Buffalo Grove, IL 800-875-6978
Consolidated Simon Distributor
Union, NJ 973-674-2124
Consup North America
Lincoln Park, NJ 973-628-7330
Cowgirl Chocolates
Moscow, ID. 888-882-4098
Cranberry Sweets Company
Coos Bay, OR 541-888-9824
Creative Confections
Northbrook, IL 608-455-1448
Creme Curls Bakery
Hudsonville, MI 800-466-1219
Croft's Crackers
Monroe, WI. 608-325-1223
Crown Candy Corporation
Macon, GA 800-241-3529
CTC Manufacturing
Calgary, AB. 800-668-7677
Cummings Studio Chocolates
Salt Lake City, UT 800-537-3957
Cupid Candies
Chicago, IL 773-925-8191
Custom Confections & More
Algonquin, IL 888-457-4676
Cyclone Enterprises
Houston, TX 281-872-0087
Daprano & Company
Charlotte, NC 877-365-2337
Dare Foods
Toronto, ON 416-878-0253
Dare Foods
Kitchener, ON. 800-265-8225
Das Foods
Chicago, IL 312-224-8590
David Bradley Chocolatier
Windsor, NJ. 877-289-7933
Davidson of Dundee
Dundee, FL 800-294-2266
Day Spring Enterprises
Cheektowaga, NY. 800-879-7677
Dayhoff
Pocomoke City, MD 410-957-4301
Daymar Select Fine Coffees
El Cajon, CA. 800-466-7590
Dayton Nut Specialties
Dayton, OH. 800-548-1304
De Bas Chocolate
Fresno, CA 888-461-1276
De Bas Chocolatier
Fresno, CA 559-294-7638
DE Wolfgang Candy Company
York, PA 800-248-4273
Debrand Fine Chocolates
Fort Wayne, IN 260-969-8335
Decko Products
Sandusky, OH 800-537-6143
Delancey Dessert Company
New York, NY 800-254-5254
Dessert Innovations
Atlanta, GA. 800-359-7351
Dilettante Chocolates
Kent, WA. 888-600-2462
Dillon Candy Company
Boston, GA 800-382-8338
Dipasa
Brownsville, TX 956-831-5893
Divine Delights
Petaluma, CA 800-443-2836
Dno
Columbus, OH 800-686-2366
Donaldson's Finer Chocolates
Lebanon, IN 800-975-7236
Donells' Candies
Casper, WY. 877-461-2009
Donna & Company
Cranford, NJ 908-272-4380
Dorothy Timberlake Candies
Madison, NH. 603-447-2221
Doscher's Candies
Cincinnati, OH 513-381-8656
Doumak
Elk Grove Vlg, IL. 800-323-0318
Downeast Candies
Boothbay Harbor, ME. 207-633-5178
Dryden & Palmer Company
Canajoharie, NY
Dundee Brandied Fruit Company
Dundee, OR. 503-537-2500
Dundee Candy Shop
Louisville, KY 502-452-9266
Dynamic Confections
Salt Lake City, UT 800-288-8002
Eclat Chocolate
West Chester, PA. 610-672-5206
EcoNatural Solutions
Boulder, CO 877-684-5159
Ed & Don's Candies
Honolulu, HI 808-423-8200
Eda's Sugarfree Candies
Philadelphia, PA 215-324-3412
Edner Corporation
Hayward, CA 510-441-8504
Elaine's Toffee Co.
Clayton, CA 800-883-3050
Elegant Edibles
Houston, TX 800-227-3226
Elmer Candy Corporation
Ponchatoula, LA 800-843-9537
Emmy's Candy from Belgium
Charlotte, NC 704-588-5445
Energy Club
Pacoima, CA 800-688-6887
Enstrom Candies
Grand Junction, CO 800-367-8766
Esther Price Candies & Gifts
Dayton, OH. 800-782-0326
Euphoria Chocolate Company
Eugene, OR. 541-344-4914
Evans Creole Candy Company
New Orleans, LA 800-637-6675
Fabio Imports
Oceanside, CA 760-726-7040
Family Sweets Candy Company
Elk Grove Village, IL 800-334-1607
Fannie May Fine Chocolat
Melrose Park, IL. 800-999-3629
Farley's & Sathers Candy Company
Round Lake, MN 800-533-0330
Faroh Candies
Cleveland, OH 440-888-9866
Farr Candy Company
Idaho Falls, ID 208-522-8215
Fastachi
Watertown, MA. 800-466-3022
FB Washburn Candy Corporation
Brockton, MA 508-588-0820
Fernando C Pujals & Bros
Guaynabo, PR. 787-792-3080
Ferrara Bakery & Cafe
New York, NY 212-226-6150
Fieldbrook Farms
Dunkirk, NY. 800-333-0805
Fisher's Popcorn
Ocean City, MD 888-436-6388
Fitzkee's Candies
York, PA 717-741-1031
Flaherty
Skokie, IL 847-966-1005
Foley's Candies
Richmond, BC 888-236-5397
Forbes Candies
Virginia Beach, VA. 800-626-5898
Foreign Candy Company
Hull, IA. 800-831-8541
Fralinger's
Atlantic City, NJ 800-938-2339
Frankford Candy & Chocolate Company
Philadelphia, PA 800-523-9090
Freed, Teller & Freed
South San Francisco, CA 800-370-7371
Frolic Candy Company
Farmingdale, NY 516-756-2255
G Scaccianoce & Company
Bronx, NY. 718-991-4462
Galloway Company
Neenah, WI. 800-722-8903
Gardners Candies
Tyrone, PA. 800-242-2639
Gearharts Fine Chocolates, Inc.
Charlottesville, VA 434-972-9100
Gene & Boots Candies
Perryopolis, PA 800-864-4222
Genesee Farms
Oakfield, NY. 585-948-9418
Georgia Nut Company
Skokie, IL 800-621-1264
Georgia Nut Ingredients
Skokie, IL 877-674-2993
Germack Pistachio Company
Detroit, MI 800-872-4006
Ghirardelli Chocolate Company
San Leandro, CA. 800-877-9338
Gia Michael's Confections, Inc.
Elmont, NY. 516-354-3905
Gifford's Ice Cream & Candy Co
Silver Spring, MA. 800-708-1938
Gimbal's Fine Candies
S San Francisco, CA. 800-344-6225
Gingerhaus, LLC
Norfolk, VA. 757-348-4274
GKI Foods
Brighton, MI 248-486-0055
Gladstone Candies
Cleveland, OH 888-729-1960
Glee Gum
Providence, RI 401-351-6415
GNS Foods/Pacific Gold
Arlington, TX 817-795-4671
Godiva Chocolatier
New York, NY 800-946-3482
Goetze's Candy Company
Baltimore, MD 800-638-1456
Golden Apples Candy Company
Southport, CT 800-776-0393
Golden Edibles LLC
Davie, FL 866-779-7781
Golden Fluff Popcorn Company
Lakewood, NJ. 732-367-5448
Golf Mill Chocolate Factory
Niles, IL 847-635-1107
Goodart Candy
Lubbock, TX. 806-747-2600
Govadinas Fitness Foods
San Diego, CA 800-900-0108
Govatos
Wilmington, DE 888-799-5252
Grandpops Lollipops
Kansas City, MO. 800-255-7873
Gray & Company
Forest Grove, OR 503-357-3141
Great Expectations Confectionery Gourmet Foods
Chicago, IL 773-525-4865
Green County Foods
Monroe, WI. 800-233-3564
Green Mountain Chocolates
Franklin, MA 508-520-7160
Greenwell Farms
Morganfield, KY. 270-389-3289
Gregg Candy & Nut Company
Munhall, PA 412-461-0301
Gumtech International
Phoenix, AZ 602-252-7425
Gurley's Foods
Willmar, MN. 800-426-7845
GWB Foods Corporation
Brooklyn, NY 877-977-7610
H E Williams Candy Company
Chesapeake, VA 757-545-9311
H.B. Trading
Totowa, NJ 973-812-1022
Haby's Alsatian Bakery
Castroville, TX 830-931-2118
Hammer Corporation
Atlanta, GA. 800-621-1954
Happy Goat
Menlo Park, CA 650-922-8667
Hauser Chocolates
Westerly, RI. 800-289-8783
Haven's Candies
Westbrook, ME 800-639-6309
Hawaii Candy
Honolulu, HI. 808-836-8955
Hawaiian Candies & Nuts
Honolulu, HI 808-841-3344
Hawaiian Host
Honolulu, HI. 888-529-4678

Hawaiian Salrose Teas
Honolulu, HI . . . 808-848-0500
Hebert Candies
Shrewsbury, MA . . . 866-432-3781
Helms Candy Company
Bristol, VA . . . 276-669-2612
Hernan
Del Rio, TX . . . 646-263-3598
Hershey
Mississauga, ON . . . 800-468-1714
Hershey Canada Inc
Mississauga, ON . . . 800-468-1714
Hershey Chocolate & Confectionery Division
Pleasanton, CA . . . 925-460-0359
Hershey Company
Hershey, PA . . . 800-468-1714
Hershey Corporation
Hershey, PA . . . 800-468-1714
Hershey International
Weston, FL . . . 954-385-2600
Hialeah Products Company
Hollywood, FL . . . 800-923-3379
Hillside Candy
Hillside, NJ . . . 800-524-1304
Holistic Products Corporation
Englewood, NJ . . . 800-221-0308
Hospitality Mints
Boone, NC . . . 800-334-5181
Hospitality Mints LLC
Boone, NC . . . 800-334-5181
House of Spices India
Flushing, NY . . . 718-507-4900
Humphrey Company
Cleveland, OH . . . 800-486-3739
Hyde Candy Company
Seattle, WA . . . 206-322-5743
Image Development
San Rafael, CA . . . 415-626-0485
Imaginings 3
Niles, IL . . . 847-647-1370
Imperial Nougat Company
Santa Fe Springs, CA . . . 562-693-8423
Indianola Pecan House, Inc./Wheeler's Gourmet Pecans
Indianola, MS . . . 800-541-6252
Intergum North America
Winston Salem, NC . . . 336-760-5420
Internacional De Productos Y Semillas
Apodaca, NL . . . 811-160-0700
International Home Foods
Parsippany, NJ . . . 973-359-9920
International Leisure Activities
Springfield, OH . . . 800-782-7448
Issimo Food Group
La Jolla, CA . . . 619-260-1900
Italian Products USA Inc
Clark, NJ . . . 201-770-9130
Jakeman's Maple ProductsAuvergne Farms Limited
Beachville, ON . . . 800-382-9795
James Candy Company
Atlantic City, NJ . . . 800-938-2339
Jason & Son Specialty Foods
Rancho Cordova, CA . . . 800-810-9093
Jed's Maple Products
Westfield, VT . . . 866-478-7388
Jelly Belly Candy Company
Fairfield, CA . . . 800-522-3267
Jerbeau Chocolate
Camarillo, CA . . . 800-755-3723
Jerry's Nut House
Denver, CO . . . 888-214-0747
Jeryl's Jems
Tappan, NY . . . 201-236-8372
Jo Mints
Corona Del Mar, CA . . . 877-566-4687
Jo's Candies
Torrance, CA . . . 800-770-1946
Joray Candy
Brooklyn, NY . . . 718-871-6300
Joseph Schmidt Confections
Hershey, PA . . . 866-237-0152
Josh Early Candies
Allentown, PA . . . 610-395-4321
Joyva Corporation
Brooklyn, NY . . . 718-497-0170
Judy's Cream Caramels
Sherwood, OR . . . 503-625-7161
K&F Select Fine Coffees
Portland, OR . . . 800-558-7788
Kara Chocolates
Orem, UT . . . 800-284-5272
Karl Bissinger French Confections
St Louis, MO . . . 800-325-8881

Kastner's Pastry Shop & Grocery
Surfside, FL . . . 305-866-6993
Kate Latter Candy Company
New Orleans, LA . . . 800-825-5359
Kateri Foods
Hopkins, MN . . . 800-330-8351
Kehr's Kandy Kitchen
Milwaukee, WI . . . 414-344-4305
Kellbran Candies & Snacks
Akron, OH . . . 330-794-1448
Kemach Food Products Corporation
Brooklyn, NY . . . 888-453-6224
Kencraft
North Alpine, UT . . . 800-377-4368
Kerr Brothers
Toronto, ON . . . 416-252-7341
Key III Candies
Fort Wayne, IN . . . 800-752-2382
Kidsmania
Santa Fe Springs, CA . . . 562-946-8822
King Nut Company
Solon, OH . . . 800-860-5464
Kloss Manufacturing Company
Allentown, PA . . . 800-445-7100
Koeze Company
Wyoming, MI . . . 800-555-3909
Kopper's Chocolate
New York, NY . . . 800-325-0026
Krema Nut Company
Columbus, OH . . . 800-222-4132
L C Good Candy Company
Allentown, PA . . . 610-432-3290
L. Craven & Sons
Melrose Park, IL . . . 800-453-4303
Lagomarcino's
Moline, IL . . . 309-764-1814
Lake Champlain Chocolates
Burlington, VT . . . 800-465-5909
Lammes Candies Since 1885
Austin, TX . . . 800-252-1885
Lanco
Hauppauge, NY . . . 800-938-4500
Landies Candies Company
Buffalo, NY . . . 800-955-2634
LaRosa's Bakery
Shrewsbury, NJ . . . 800-527-6722
Laura Paige Candy Company
Newburgh, NY . . . 845-566-4209
Laymon Candy Company
San Bernardino, CA . . . 909-825-4408
Le Grand Confectionary, Inc.
Sacramento, CA . . . 888-361-2125
Leader Candies
Brooklyn, NY . . . 718-366-6900
Len Libby's Candy Shop
Scarborough, ME . . . 207-883-4897
Lerro Candy Company
Darby, PA . . . 610-461-8886
Lieber Chocolate & Food Products
Brooklyn, NY . . . 718-499-0888
Linette Quality Chocolates
Womelsdorf, PA . . . 610-589-4526
Log House Foods
Plymouth, MN . . . 763-546-8395
Long Grove ConfectioneryCompany
Buffalo Grove, IL . . . 800-373-3102
Longford-Hamilton Company
Beaverton, OR . . . 503-642-5661
Loretta's Authentic Pralines
New Orleans, LA . . . 504-529-6170
Lotte USA
Battle Creek, MI . . . 269-963-6664
Lou-Retta's Custom Chocolates
Buffalo, NY . . . 716-833-7111
Louis J. Rheb Candy Company
Baltimore, MD . . . 800-514-8293
Lowery's Home Made Candies
Muncie, IN . . . 800-541-3340
Lucille's Own Make Candies
Manahawkin, NJ . . . 800-426-9168
Lucky You
San Diego, CA . . . 619-450-6700
Ludo LLC
Solon, OH . . . 440-542-6000
Ludwick's Frozen Donuts
Grand Rapids, MI . . . 800-366-8816
Lukas Confections
York, PA . . . 717-843-0921
Lynard Company
Stamford, CT . . . 203-323-0231
MacFarms of Hawaii
Captain Cook, HI . . . 808-328-2435

Madrona Specialty Foods
Tukwila, WA . . . 425-814-2500
Mafco Worldwide Corporation
Camden, NJ . . . 856-964-8840
Magna Foods Corporation
City of Industry, CA . . . 800-995-4394
Manhattan Chocolates
Bayonne, NJ . . . 201-339-6886
Maple Grove Farms of Vermont
St Johnsbury, VT . . . 800-525-2540
Marich Confectionery Company
Hollister, CA . . . 800-624-7055
Marie's Candies
West Liberty, OH . . . 866-465-5781
Marin Food Specialties
Byron, CA . . . 925-634-6126
Maris Candy
Chicago, IL . . . 773-254-3351
Marlow Candy & Nut Company
Englewood, NJ . . . 201-569-7606
Mars, Inc.
Mc Lean, VA . . . 703-821-4900
Marshmallow Cone Company
Cincinnati, OH . . . 800-641-8551
Marshmallow Products
Cincinnati, OH . . . 800-641-8551
Marsyl
Cody, WY . . . 307-527-6277
Mary of Puddin Hill
Greenville, TX . . . 800-545-8889
Mary Sue Candies
Baltimore, MD . . . 410-467-9338
Marzipan Specialties
Nashville, TN . . . 615-226-4800
Masterfoods USA
Hackettstown, NJ . . . 908-852-1000
Masterson Company
Milwaukee, WI . . . 414-647-1132
Matangos Candies
Harrisburg, PA . . . 717-234-0882
Maxfield Candy
Salt Lake City, UT . . . 800-288-8002
Mayfair Sales
Buffalo, NY . . . 800-248-2881
MB Candies
Bridgeport, IL . . . 888-MBC-ANDY
Merbs Candies
Saint Louis, MO . . . 314-832-7117
Mercado Latino
City of Industry, CA . . . 626-333-6862
Merlin Candies
Harahan, LA . . . 800-899-1549
Michelle Chocolatiers
Colorado Springs, CO . . . 888-447-3654
Midwest/Northern
Minneapolis, MN . . . 800-328-5502
Miesse Candies
Lancaster, PA . . . 717-397-9415
Mille Lacs MP Company
Madison, WI . . . 800-843-1381
Minter Weisman Company
Minneapolis, MN . . . 800-742-5655
Miss Sophia's Old World Kits & Gingerbread
Dallas, TX . . . 877-446-4373
Mister Snacks
Amherst, NY . . . 800-333-6393
Mitch Chocolate
Melville, NY . . . 631-777-2400
Mojave Foods Corporation
Commerce, CA . . . 323-890-8900
Mom 'N Pops
New Windsor, NY . . . 866-368-6767
Monastery Bakery At HolyCross Abbey
Berryville, VA . . . 540-955-9440
Monogramme Confections
St Louis, MO . . . 888- 56- 409
Monterrey Products Company
San Antonio, TX . . . 210-435-2872
Moo Chocolate/Organic Children's Chocolate LLC
Cos Cob, CT . . . 203-561-8864
Moon Shine Trading Company
Woodland, CA . . . 800-678-1226
Moore's Candies
Baltimore, MD . . . 410-426-2705
Morris National
Azusa, CA . . . 626-385-2000
Mother Nature's Goodies
Yucaipa, CA . . . 909-795-6018
Mrs. Annie's Peanut Patch
Floresville, TX . . . 830-393-7845
Mrs. London's Confections
Swampscott, MA . . . 781-595-8140

Multiflex Company
Hawthorne, NJ 973-636-9700
Munson's Chocolates
Bolton, CT 888-686-7667
Muth Candies
Louisville, KY 502-585-2952
Mutiflex Company
Wyckoff, NJ 201-447-3888
My Sister's Caramels
Redlands, CA 909-792-6242
Naron Mary Sue Candy Company
Baltimore, MD 800-662-2639
Nassau Candy Company
Hicksville, NY 516-433-7100
National Importers
Richmond, BC 888-894-6464
Natural Foods
Toledo, OH 419-537-1713
Natural Rush
San Francisco, CA 415-863-2503
Nature's Candy
Fredericksburg, TX 800-729-0085
Naturex Inc.
South Hackensack, NJ 201-440-5000
Naylor Candies
Mount Wolf, PA 717-266-2706
Neal's Chocolates
Salt Lake City, UT 801-521-6500
Necco
Revere, MA 781-485-4500
Nestle Infant Nutrition
Florham Park, NJ
Nestle USA Inc
Glendale, CA 800-225-2270
New England Confectionery Company
Revere, MA 781-485-4500
New England Natural Baker
Greenfield, MA 800-910-2884
Newton Candy Company
Houston, TX 713-691-6969
Niagara Chocolates
Cheektowaga, NY 800-234-5750
Noble Ingredients
West Berlin, NJ
Nora's Candy Shop
Rome, NY 888-544-8224
Northwest Candy Emporium
Everett, WA 800-404-7266
Northwest Chocolate Factory
Salem, OR 503-362-1340
Novelty Specialties
Ontaria, CA 800-231-5309
NSpired Natural Foods
Boulder, CO 800-434-4246
Nutty Bavarian
Sanford, FL 800-382-4788
Oak Leaf Confections
Scarborough, ON 877-261-7887
OH Chocolate
Calgary, AB 800-887-3959
Oh, Sugar! LLC
Roswell, GA 866-557-8427
Old Dominion Peanut Corporation
Norfolk, VA 800-368-6887
Old Fashioned Candy
Berwyn, IL 708-788-6669
Old Monmouth Peanut Brittle
Freehold, NJ 732-462-1311
Olde Tyme Food Corporation
East Longmeadow, MA 800-356-6533
Olde Tyme Mercantile
Arroyo Grande, CA 805-489-7991
Ole Smoky Candy Kitchen
Gatlinburg, TN 865-436-6426
Olivier's Candies
Calgary, AB 403-266-6028
Ooh La La Candy
Mamaroneck, NY 914-381-8030
OraLabs
Parker, CO 800-290-0577
Pacific Gold Marketing
Fresno, CA
Palmer Candy Company
Sioux City, IA 800-831-0828
Pangburn Candy Company
Fort Worth, TX 817-332-8856
Pantry Shelf/Mixxm
Hutchinson, KS 800-968-3346
Parker Products
Fort Worth, TX 800-433-5749
Parkside Candy Company
Buffalo, NY 716-833-7540
Paron Chocolatier
New York, NY 800-326-5033
Patsy's Candies
Colorado Springs, CO 866-372-8797
Paul's Candy Factory
Salt Lake City, UT 800-825-9912
Paulaur Corporation
Cranbury, NJ 888-398-8844
Peanut Patch
Courtland, VA 866-732-6883
Pearl River Pastry & Chocolates
Pearl River, NY 800-632-2639
Pearson Candy Company
St Paul, MN 800-328-6507
Pease's Candy Shoppe
Springfield, IL 217-523-3721
Pecan Deluxe Candy Company
Dallas, TX 800-733-3589
Pecans De Chihuahua
Col. Sta. Rita, CH 614-420-1414
Pegi
Santa Ana, CA 800-292-3353
Penhurst Candy Company
Pittsburgh, PA 800-545-1336
Pennsylvania Dutch Candies
Camp Hill, PA 800-233-7082
Perfetti
Erlanger, KY 859-283-1234
PEZ Candy
Orange, CT 203-795-0531
Pfeil & Holing
Woodside, NY 800-247-7955
Pfizer
Parsippany, NJ 973-541-5900
Phillips Candies
Seaside, OR 503-738-5402
Phillips Candies of Seas
Seaside, OR 503-738-5402
Piedmont Candy Corporation
Lexington, NC 336-248-2477
Pine River Pre-Pack
Newton, WI 920-726-4216
Pippin Snack Pecans
Albany, GA 800-554-6887
Plantation Candies
Telford, PA 888-678-6468
Plyley's Candies
Lagrange, IN 260-463-3351
Popcorn Connection
North Hollywood, CA 800-852-2676
Poppers Supply Company
Allentown, PA 800-457-9810
Priester Pecan Company
Fort Deposit, AL 800-277-3226
Prifti Candy Company
Worcester, MA 800-447-7438
Primrose Candy Company
Chicago, IL 800-268-9522
Prince of Peace Enterprises
Hayward, CA 800-732-2328
Productos Medellin
Matehuala, SL 488-882-1491
Produits Alimentaire
St Lambert De Lauzon, QC 800-463-1787
Promotion in Motion Companies
Closter, NJ 800-369-7391
Pulakos
Erie, PA 814-452-4026
Pure Dark
Hackettstown, NJ 973-856-1899
Purity Candy Company
Lewisburg, PA 800-821-4748
Quality Candy Company
Walnut, CA 909-444-1025
Quality Candy Shoppes/Buddy Squirrel of Wisconsin
Saint Francis, WI 800-972-2658
Queen Bee Gardens
Lovell, WY 800-225-7553
Queensway Foods Company
Burlingame, CA 650-871-7770
Quick's Candy
Hummelstown, PA 800-443-9036
Quigley Manufacturing
Elizabethtown, PA 800-367-2441
Quintessential Chocolates Company
Fredericksburg, TX 830-990-9382
R.L. Albert & Son
Greenwich, CT 203-622-8655
R.M. Palmer Company
Reading, PA 610-372-8971
Ragold Confections
Wilton Manors, FL 954-566-9092
Ralphco
Worcester, MA 800-477-2574
Randag & Associates Inc
Elmhurst, IL 630-530-2830
Realsalt
Heber City, UT 800-367-7258
Rebecca Ruth Candy
Frankfort, KY 800-444-3866
Red Rocker Candy
Troy, VA 434-589-2011
Regent Confections
Orange, CA 714-348-8889
Republica Del Cacao LLC
Long Beach, CA 562-537-3656
Richard Donnelly Fine Chtes
Santa Cruz, CA 888-685-1871
Richards Maple Products
Chardon, OH 800-352-4052
Richardson Brands Company
Branford, CT 800-839-8938
Ricos Candy Snacks & Bakery
Hialeah, FL 305-885-7392
Riddles' Sweet Impressions
Edmonton, AB 780-465-8085
Rigoni Di Asiago
Miami, FL 305-470-7583
Rito Mints
Trois Rivieres, QC 819-379-1449
Rivard Popcorn Products
Lancaster, PA 717-393-1074
Riverdale Fine Foods
Dayton, OH 800-548-1304
Rosalind Candy Castle
New Brighton, PA 724-843-1144
Rosetti Fine Foods
Clovis, CA 559-323-6450
Ross Fine Candies
Waterford, MI 248-682-5640
Royal Wine Corp
Bayonne, NJ 718-384-2400
Russell Stover Candies
Kansas City, MO 800-477-8683
Ruth Hunt Candies
Mt Sterling, KY 800-927-0302
S. Zitner Company
Philadelphia, PA 215-229-4990
S.L. Kaye Company
New York, NY 212-683-5600
S.P. Enterprises
Las Vegas, NV 800-746-4774
Sahagian & Associates
Oak Park, IL 800-327-9273
Salem Old Fashioned Candies
Salem, MA 978-744-3242
Sally Lane's Candy Farm
Paris, TN 731-642-5801
Sambets Cajun Deli
Austin, TX 800-472-6238
Sanders Candy
Clinton Twp, MI 800-852-2253
Sayklly's Candies & Gifts
Escanaba, MI 906-786-3092
Scharffen Berger Chocolate Maker
San Francisco, CA 866- 60- 694
Sconza Candy Company
Oakdale, CA 877-568-8137
Scott's Candy
Glennville, GA 800-356-2100
Scott-Bathgate
Winnipeg, MB 800-216-2990
Scripture Candy
Adamsville, AL 888-317-7333
Seasons' Enterprises
Addison, IL 630-628-0211
Seattle Bar Company
Seattle, WA 206-601-4301
Seattle Gourmet Foods
Kent, WA 800-800-9490
See's Candies
Carson, CA 800-347-7337
Senor Murphy Candymaker
Santa Fe, NM 877-988-4311
Shade Foods
New Century, KS 800-225-6312
Shane Candy Company
Philadelphia, PA 215-922-1048
Shari Candies
Edina, MN 800-658-7059
Sherm Edwards Candies
Trafford, PA 800-436-5424
Sherwood Brands
Rockville, MD 301-309-6161

Sherwood Brands
Rockville, MD ... 401-434-7773
Sifers Valomilk Candy Company
Shawnee Mission, KS ... 913-722-0991
Silver Sweet Candies
Lawrence, MA ... 978-688-0474
Simply Lite Foods Corporation
Commack, NY ... 800-753-4282
Smith Enterprises
Rock Hill, SC ... 800-845-8311
Snackerz
Commerce, CA ... 888-576-2253
Sorbee Intl.
Feasterville Trevose, PA ... 800-654-3997
South Beach Novelties & Confectionery
Staten Island, NY ... 718-727-4500
Southern Style Nuts
Denison, TX ... 903-463-3161
Spangler Candy Company
Bryan, OH ... 888-636-4221
Spokandy Wedding Mints
Spokane, WA ... 509-624-1969
Squirrel Brand Company
McKinney, TX ... 800-624-8242
St. Laurent Brothers
Bay City, MI ... 800-289-7688
Standard Candy Company
Nashville, TN ... 800-226-4340
Star Kay White
Congers, NY ... 800-874-8518
Stark Candy Company
Revere, MA ... 800-621-1983
Startup's Candy Company
Provo, UT ... 801-373-8673
Stephany's Chocolates
Arvada, CO ... 800-888-1522
Sterling Candy
Hicksville, NY ... 516-932-8300
Stewart Candy Company
Waycross, GA ... 912-284-9320
Stichler Products
Reading, PA ... 610-921-0211
Stone's Home Made Candy Shop
Oswego, NY ... 888-223-3928
Storck
Chicago, IL ... 800-621-7772
Storck Canada
Mississauga, ON ... 800-305-7551
Stutz Candy Company
Hatboro, PA ... 888-692-2639
Sucesores de Pedro Cortes
San Juan, PR ... 787-754-7040
Sun Ridge Farms
Pajaro, CA ... 831-786-7000
Sweenor Chocolate
Wakefield, RI ... 800-834-3123
Sweet Candy Company
Salt Lake City, UT ... 800-669-8669
Sweet City Supply
Virginia Beach, VA ... 888-793-3824
Sweet Shop
La Crosse, WI ... 608-784-7724
Sweet Shop USA
Mt Pleasant, TX ... 800-222-2269
Sweet'N Low
Brooklyn, NY ... 718-858-4200
Sweetcraft Candies
Timonium, MD ... 410-252-0684
SweetWorks Inc
Buffalo, NY ... 716-634-0880
Swissart Candy Company
Wyckoff, NJ ... 201-447-0062
Tapper Candies
Cleveland, OH ... 216-825-1000
Tastee Apple Inc
Newcomerstown, OH ... 800-262-7753
Tell Chocolate Corporation
Barnegat, NJ
Temo's Candy
Akron, OH ... 330-376-7229
Terri Lynn
Elgin, IL ... 800-323-0775
Testamints
Randolph, NJ ... 888-879-0400
Texas Toffee
Odessa, TX ... 432-563-5373
The Great San Saba RiverPecan Company
San Saba, TX ... 800-621-9121
The Hampton Popcorn Company Inc.
Mineola, NY ... 888-947-6726
The Topps Company
Duryea, PA ... 570-457-6761
Thompson Candy Company
Meriden, CT ... 800-648-4058
Tim's Cascade Chips
Algona, WA ... 800-533-8467
Todd's
Vernon, CA ... 800-938-6337
Toffee Company
Houston, TX ... 713-840-9696
Tom & Sally's Handmade Chocolates
Brattleboro, VT ... 800-827-0800
Tootsie Roll Industries
Chicago, IL ... 800-877-7655
Torn & Glasser
Los Angeles, CA ... 800-282-6887
Totally Chocolate
Blaine, WA ... 800-255-5506
Toucan Chocolates
Waban, MA ... 617-964-8696
Trappistine Quality Candy
Wrentham, MA ... 86- 5-9 89
Traverse Bay Confections
Woodinville, WA
Tremblay's Sweet Shop
Hayward, WI ... 715-634-2785
Triple-C
Hamilton, ON ... 800-263-9105
Tropical
Charlotte, NC ... 800-220-1413
Tropical
Columbus, OH ... 800-538-3941
Tropical
Marietta, GA ... 800-544-3762
Tropical Nut & Fruit Company
Orlando, FL ... 800-749-8869
Truan's Candies
Detroit, MI ... 800-584-3004
Turkey Hill Sugarbush
Waterloo, QC ... 450-539-4822
Twenty First Century Snacks
Ronkonkoma, NY ... 800-975-2883
Twin City Wholesale
Opelika, AL ... 334-745-4564
Tyler Candy Company
Tyler, TX ... 903-561-3046
Ultimate Nut & Candy Company
Los Angeles, CA ... 800-767-5259
Valhrona
Los Angeles, CA ... 310-277-0401
Van Leer Chocolate Corporation
Hoboken, NJ ... 800-826-2462
Van Otis Chocolates
Manchester, NH ... 800-826-6847
Vande Walle's Candies
Appleton, WI ... 920-738-7799
Varda Chocolatier
Elizabeth, NJ ... 800-448-2732
Variety Foods
Warren, MI ... 586-268-4900
Vatore's Italian Caramel
Silver Spring, MD ... 88- 4-3 52
Vaughn-Russell Candy Kitchen
Greenville, SC ... 864-271-7786
Velvet Creme Popcorn Company
Westwood, KS ... 888-553-6708
Vigneri Confections
Rochester, NY ... 877-843-6374
Vitality Life Choice
Carson City, NV ... 800-423-8365
Vrymeer Commodities
St Charles, IL ... 630-584-0069
Warner-Lambert Confections
Cambridge, MA ... 617-491-2500
Warrell Corporation
Camp Hill, PA ... 800-233-7082
Washburn Candy Corporation
Brockton, MA ... 508-588-0820
Waymouth Farms
New Hope, MN ... 800-527-0094
Weaver Nut Company
Ephrata, PA ... 717-738-3781
Webbs Citrus Candy
Davenport, FL ... 863-422-1051
Wedding Cake Studio
Williamsfield, OH ... 440-667-1765
Westbrae Natural Foods
Melville, NY ... 800-434-4246
Westdale Foods Company
Orland Park, IL ... 708-458-7774
Whetstone Candy Company
St Augustine, FL ... 904-825-1710
White-Stokes Company
Chicago, IL ... 800-978-6537
Whitley's Peanut Factory
Hayes, VA ... 800-470-2244
Widmans Candy Shop
Crookston, MN ... 218-281-1487
Wilkinson-Spitz
Yonkers, NY ... 914-237-5000
Williams Candy Company
Somerville, MA ... 617-776-0814
Williamsburg Chocolatier
Williamsburg, VA ... 757-253-1474
Willy Wonka Candy
Itasca, IL ... 888-694-2656
Willy Wonka Candy Factory
Itasca, IL ... 630-773-0267
Wilson Candy Company
Jeannette, PA ... 724-523-3151
Wilson's Fantastic Candy
Memphis, TN ... 901-767-1900
Winans Chocolates & Coffees
Piqua, OH ... 937-773-1981
Windmill Candy
Lubbock, TX ... 806-785-4688
Windsor Confections
Oakland, CA ... 800-860-0021
Winfrey Fudge & Candy
Rowley, MA ... 888-946-3739
Wisconsin Cheese
Melrose Park, IL ... 708-450-0074
Wisconsin Dairyland Fudge Company
Wisconsin Dells, WI ... 608-254-4136
Wisteria Candy Cottage
Boulevard, CA ... 800-458-8246
World Confections
Brooklyn, NY ... 718-768-8100
Wright Ice Cream
Cayuga, IN ... 800-686-9561
Yost Candy Company
Dalton, OH ... 800-750-1976
Zitner Company
Philadelphia, PA ... 215-229-4990

Bon Bons

Candy Factory
Hayward, CA ... 800-736-6887
Ferrara Bakery & Cafe
New York, NY ... 212-226-6150

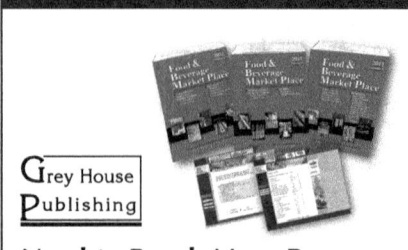

Mona Lisa® Chocolatier
Arlington, VA 866-662-5475

Breath Tablets

Ferrero Usa
Somerset, NJ 800-337-7376
Hospitality Mints
Boone, NC 800-334-5181
Jo Mints
Corona Del Mar, CA 877-566-4687
Liberty Natural Products
Oregon City, OR 800-289-8427
Mona Lisa® Chocolatier
Arlington, VA 866-662-5475
Pfizer
Parsippany, NJ 973-541-5900
Vitech America Corporation
Kent, WA 253-859-5985

Brittles

A.L. Bazzini Company
Bronx, NY 800-228-0172
Arway Confections
Chicago, IL 773-267-5770
B&B Pecan Processors of NC
Turkey, NC 866-328-7322
Brittle Bark Company
Mechanicsburg, PA 717-697-6950
Brittle Kettle
Tigard, OR 800-447-2128
Buddy Squirrel LLC
Milwaukee, WI 800-972-2658
Charlotte's Confections
Millbrae, CA 800-798-2427
Chase Candy Company
Saint Joseph, MO 800-786-1625
Cheese Straws & More
Monroe, LA 800-997-1921
Claeys Candy
South Bend, IN 800-348-2239
Confection Solutions
Sylmar, CA 800-284-2422
Crickle Company
Thomasville, GA 800-237-8689
Crown Candy Corporation
Macon, GA 800-241-3529
DE Wolfgang Candy Company
York, PA 800-248-4273
Dillon Candy Company
Boston, GA 800-382-8338
Elegant Edibles
Houston, TX 800-227-3226
Enstrom Candies
Grand Junction, CO 800-367-8766
Georgia Nut Ingredients
Skokie, IL 877-674-2993
Gilliam Candy Brands
Paducah, KY 800-445-3008
GKI Foods
Brighton, MI 248-486-0055
GNS Foods/Pacific Gold
Arlington, TX 817-795-4671
Gurley's Foods
Willmar, MN 800-426-7845
Hialeah Products Company
Hollywood, FL 800-923-3379
Idaho Candy Company
Boise, ID 800-898-6986
Kay Foods Company
Detroit, MI 313-393-1100
La Piccolina
Decatur, GA 800-626-1624
Laymon Candy Company
San Bernardino, CA 909-825-4408
Marie's Candies
West Liberty, OH 866-465-5781
Michele's Chocolate Truffles
Clackamas, OR 800-656-7112
Mrs. Annie's Peanut Patch
Floresville, TX 830-393-7845
Muth Candies
Louisville, KY 502-585-2952
Old Dominion Peanut Corporation
Norfolk, VA 800-368-6887
Olde Tyme Mercantile
Arroyo Grande, CA 805-489-7991
Olivier's Candies
Calgary, AB 403-266-6028
Palmer Candy Company
Sioux City, IA 800-831-0828
Patsy's Candies
Colorado Springs, CO 866-372-8797
Pennsylvania Dutch Candies
Camp Hill, PA 800-233-7082
Roger's Recipe
Glover, VT 802-525-3050
Sally Lane's Candy Farm
Paris, TN 731-642-5801
Sayklly's Candies & Gifts
Escanaba, MI 906-786-3092
Sconza Candy Company
Oakdale, CA 877-568-8137
Shari Candies
Edina, MN 800-658-7059
Snackerz
Commerce, CA 888-576-2253
Squirrel Brand Company
McKinney, TX 800-624-8242
St. Jacobs Candy Company Brittles 'n More
Waterloo, ON 519-884-3505
Susie's South 40 Confections
Midland, TX 800-221-4442
Trophy Nut
Tipp City, OH 800-219-9004
Vande Walle's Candies
Appleton, WI 920-738-7799

Butterscotch

Farley's & Sathers Candy Company
Round Lake, MN 800-533-0330
Regent Confections
Orange, CA 714-348-8889
Sayklly's Candies & Gifts
Escanaba, MI 906-786-3092
Weaver Nut Company
Ephrata, PA 717-738-3781

Candy Bars

AmeriCandy Company
Louisville, KY 502-583-1776
Ann Hemyng Candy
Trumbauersville, PA 800-779-7004
Bohemian Biscuit Company
South San Francisco, CA 650-952-2226
Cambridge Brands
Cambridge, MA 617-491-2500
Carrie's Chocolates
Edmonton, AB 877-778-2462
Chase Candy Company
Saint Joseph, MO 800-786-1625
Chocolate Street of Hartville
Hartville, OH 888-853-5904
Chris A. Papas & Son Company
Covington, KY 859-431-0499
Chris Candies
Pittsburgh, PA 412-322-9400
Cloud Nine
San Leandro, CA 201-358-8588
Cocoline Chocolate Company
Brooklyn, NY 718-522-4500
De Bas Chocolatier
Fresno, CA 559-294-7638
Doscher's Candies
Cincinnati, OH 513-381-8656
Eda's Sugarfree Candies
Philadelphia, PA 215-324-3412
Edner Corporation
Hayward, CA 510-441-8504
Ferrara Bakery & Cafe
New York, NY 212-226-6150
Gardners Candies
Tyrone, PA 800-242-2639
Ghirardelli Chocolate Company
San Leandro, CA 800-877-9338
Hershey
Mississauga, ON 800-468-1714
Hershey Chocolate & Confectionery Division
Pleasanton, CA 925-460-0359
Joyva Corporation
Brooklyn, NY 718-497-0170
Long Grove ConfectioneryCompany
Buffalo Grove, IL 800-373-3102
Lukas Confections
York, PA 717-843-0921
Mars, Inc.
Mc Lean, VA 703-821-4900
Mona Lisa® Chocolatier
Arlington, VA 866-662-5475
Mooresville Ice Cream Company
Mooresville, NC 704-664-5456
New England Confectionery Company
Revere, MA 781-485-4500
Niagara Chocolates
Cheektowaga, NY 800-234-5750
Randag & Associates Inc
Elmhurst, IL 630-530-2830
Ruth Hunt Candies
Mt Sterling, KY 800-927-0302
Sucesores de Pedro Cortes
San Juan, PR 787-754-7040
Sweet Productions
Amityville, NY 631-842-0548
Universal Laboratories
New Brunswick, NJ 800-872-0101
Vande Walle's Candies
Appleton, WI 920-738-7799
Weaver Nut Company
Ephrata, PA 717-738-3781
World Confections
Brooklyn, NY 718-768-8100

Coated

Mona Lisa® Chocolatier
Arlington, VA 866-662-5475

Canes

Asher Candy
Rockville, MD 301-309-6161

Caramel

Abdallah Candies
Burnsville, MN 800-348-7328
Bequet Confections
Bozeman, MT 877-423-7838
Bohemian Biscuit Company
South San Francisco, CA 650-952-2226
Cambridge Brands
Cambridge, MA 617-491-2500
Candy Factory
Hayward, CA 800-736-6887
Carousel Candies
Geneva, IL 888-656-1552
Charlotte's Confections
Millbrae, CA 800-798-2427
Cherrydale Farms
Allentown, PA 800-333-4525
Da Vinci Gourmet
Seattle, WA 800-640-6779
Das Foods
Chicago, IL 312-224-8590
Dno
Columbus, OH 800-686-2366
Farley's & Sathers Candy Company
Round Lake, MN 800-533-0330
Gene & Boots Candies
Perryopolis, PA 800-864-4222
GKI Foods
Brighton, MI 248-486-0055
Goetze's Candy Company
Baltimore, MD 800-638-1456
Jason & Son Specialty Foods
Rancho Cordova, CA 800-810-9093
Judy's Cream Caramels
Sherwood, OR 503-625-7161
Key III Candies
Fort Wayne, IN 800-752-2382
Leader Candies
Brooklyn, NY 718-366-6900
Lowery's Home Made Candies
Muncie, IN 800-541-3340
Lukas Confections
York, PA 717-843-0921
Matangos Candies
Harrisburg, PA 717-234-0882
Moore's Candies
Baltimore, MD 410-426-2705
Mrs. Prindable's Handmade Confections
Niles, IL 888-215-1100
Muth Candies
Louisville, KY 502-585-2952
My Sister's Caramels
Redlands, CA 909-792-6242
Necco
Revere, MA 781-485-4500
New England Confectionery Company
Revere, MA 781-485-4500
Nunes Farm Almonds
Newman, CA 209-862-3033
Randag & Associates Inc
Elmhurst, IL 630-530-2830

Saykily's Candies & Gifts
Escanaba, MI 906-786-3092
St. Jacobs Candy Company Brittles 'n More
Waterloo, ON 519-884-3505
Sweet Shop
Mount Pleasant, TX 800-222-2269
Tastee Apple Inc
Newcomerstown, OH 800-262-7753
Tropical
Columbus, OH 800-538-3941
Vande Walle's Candies
Appleton, WI 920-738-7799
Weaver Nut Company
Ephrata, PA 717-738-3781
White-Stokes Company
Chicago, IL 800-978-6537
World Confections
Brooklyn, NY 718-768-8100
Zitner Company
Philadelphia, PA 215-229-4990

Carob

Clasen Quality Coatings
Madison, WI 877-459-4500
Cocoline Chocolate Company
Brooklyn, NY 718-522-4500
Famarco
Virginia Beach, VA 757-460-3573
GKI Foods
Brighton, MI 248-486-0055
Naturex Inc.
South Hackensack, NJ 201-440-5000
NSpired Natural Foods
Boulder, CO 800-434-4246
Setton International Foods
Commack, NY 800-227-4397

Chewing Gum

Adams USA
New York, NY 212-733-2323
Amurol Confections Company
Yorkville, IL 630-553-4800
Arcor USA
Miami, FL 800-572-7267
Beehive Botanicals, Inc.
Hayward, WI 800-233-4483
C. Howard Company
Bellport, NY 631-286-7940
Candyrific
Louisville, KY 502-893-3626
Concord Confections
Chicago, IL 800-267-0037
Dayhoff
Clearwater, FL 800-354-3372
Fernando C Pujals & Bros
Guaynabo, PR 787-792-3080
Ford Gum & Machine Company
Akron, NY 800-225-5535
Foreign Candy Company
Hull, IA 800-831-8541
Glee Gum
Providence, RI 401-351-6415
Golden Fluff Popcorn Company
Lakewood, NJ 732-367-5448
Gumtech International
Phoenix, AZ 602-252-7425
Health-Tech
New York, NY 877-673-9777
Hershey Company
Hershey, PA 800-468-1714
Horriea 2000 Food Industries
Reynolds, GA 478-847-4186
Lotte USA
Battle Creek, MI 269-963-6664
Mayfair Sales
Buffalo, NY 800-248-2881
Mona Lisa® Chocolatier
Arlington, VA 866-662-5475
Oak Leaf Confections
Scarborough, ON 877-261-7887
Pfizer
Parsippany, NJ 973-541-5900
SP Enterprises
Las Vegas, NV 800-746-4774
Sweet Works
St Augustine, FL 877-261-7887
SweetWorks Inc
Buffalo, NY 716-634-0880
The Topps Company
Duryea, PA 570-457-6761

World Confections
Brooklyn, NY 718-768-8100
Wrigley Company
Chicago, IL 800-824-9681

Coconut

Chase Candy Company
Saint Joseph, MO 800-786-1625
Chris A. Papas & Son Company
Covington, KY 859-431-0499
Crown Candy Corporation
Macon, GA 800-241-3529
David Bradley Chocolatier
Windsor, NJ 877-289-7933
Davidson of Dundee
Dundee, FL 800-294-2266
GKI Foods
Brighton, MI 248-486-0055
Maris Candy
Chicago, IL 773-254-3351
Mona Lisa® Chocolatier
Arlington, VA 866-662-5475
New England Confectionery Company
Revere, MA 781-485-4500
Olde Tyme Mercantile
Arroyo Grande, CA 805-489-7991
Sally Lane's Candy Farm
Paris, TN 731-642-5801
Saykily's Candies & Gifts
Escanaba, MI 906-786-3092
Wisconsin Cheese
Melrose Park, IL 708-450-0074

Corn

American Food Products
Methuen, MA 978-682-1855
Blueberry Hill Foods
El Paso, TX 800-451-8664
El Brands
Ozark, AL 334-445-2828
Energy Club
Pacoima, CA 800-688-6887
Fernando C Pujals & Bros
Guaynabo, PR 787-792-3080
Frankford Candy & Chocolate Company
Philadelphia, PA 800-523-9090
Gurley's Foods
Willmar, MN 800-426-7845
Harmony Foods Corporation
Fishers, IN 800-837-2855
Hyde & Hyde
Corona, CA 951-817-2300
Jelly Belly Candy Company
Fairfield, CA 800-522-3267
Mayfair Sales
Buffalo, NY 800-248-2881
Rogers' Chocolates Ltd
Victoria, BC 800-663-2220
Seattle Bar Company
Seattle, WA 206-601-4301
Setton International Foods
Commack, NY 800-227-4397
Shari Candies
Edina, MN 800-658-7059
Snackerz
Commerce, CA 888-576-2253
Sweet Candy Company
Salt Lake City, UT 800-669-8669
Sweet City Supply
Virginia Beach, VA 888-793-3824
Todd's
Vernon, CA 800-938-6337
Triple-C
Hamilton, ON 800-263-9105
Trophy Nut
Tipp City, OH 800-219-9004

Cotton

Barcelona Nut Company
Baltimore, MD 800-292-6887
Brennan Snacks Manufacturing
Bogalusa, LA 800-290-7486
Bruno's Cajun Foods & Snacks
Slidell, LA 985-726-0544
Great Western Products Company
Assumption, IL 217-226-3241
Great Western Products Company
Bismarck, MO 573-734-2210
Kloss Manufacturing Company
Allentown, PA 800-445-7100

Olde Tyme Food Corporation
East Longmeadow, MA 800-356-6533
Porter's Food & Produce
Du Quoin, IL 618-542-2155
Taste of Nature
Beverly Hills, CA 310-396-4433

Cremes

Brown & Haley
Tacoma, WA 253-620-3000
Chocolates a La Carte
Valencia, CA 800-818-2462
Dayhoff
Clearwater, FL 800-354-3372
DeFluri's Fine Chocolates
Martinsburg, VA 304-264-3698
Energy Club
Pacoima, CA 800-688-6887
Fannie May/Fanny Farmer
Chicago, IL 800-333-3629
Fernando C Pujals & Bros
Guaynabo, PR 787-792-3080
Goetze's Candy Company
Baltimore, MD 800-638-1456
Lammes Candies Since 1885
Austin, TX 800-252-1885
Laymon Candy Company
San Bernardino, CA 909-825-4408
Lowery's Home Made Candies
Muncie, IN 800-541-3340
Maramor Chocolates
Columbus, OH 800-843-7722
Mona Lisa® Chocolatier
Arlington, VA 866-662-5475
Moon Shine Trading Company
Woodland, CA 800-678-1226
Moore's Candies
Baltimore, MD 410-426-2705
Palmer Candy Company
Sioux City, IA 800-831-0828
Patsy's Candies
Colorado Springs, CO 866-372-8797
Rene Rey Chocolates Ltd
North Vancouver, BC 888-985-0949
Sanders Candy
Clinton Twp, MI 800-852-2253
Shari Candies
Edina, MN 800-658-7059
Sweet City Supply
Virginia Beach, VA 888-793-3824
V L Foods
White Plains, NY 914-697-4851

Dietetic

Balanced Health Products
New York, NY 212-794-9878
Bidwell Candies
Mattoon, IL 217-234-3858
Bohemian Biscuit Company
South San Francisco, CA 650-952-2226
GKI Foods
Brighton, MI 248-486-0055
Go Lightly Candy
Hillside, NJ 800-524-1304
Lowery's Home Made Candies
Muncie, IN 800-541-3340
Lukas Confections
York, PA 717-843-0921
Olde Tyme Mercantile
Arroyo Grande, CA 805-489-7991
Peerless Confection Company
Lincolnwood, IL 773-281-6100
Sally Lane's Candy Farm
Paris, TN 731-642-5801
Setton International Foods
Commack, NY 800-227-4397
Wisconsin Cheese
Melrose Park, IL 708-450-0074

Divinity

Bohemian Biscuit Company
South San Francisco, CA 650-952-2226
Ludwick's Frozen Donuts
Grand Rapids, MI 800-366-8816

Filled

American Food Products
Methuen, MA 978-682-1855

Andre's Confiserie Suisse
Kansas City, MO. 800-892-1234
Arcor USA
Miami, FL. 800-572-7267
Atkinson Candy Company
Lufkin, TX 800-231-1203
Blueberry Hill Foods
El Paso, TX. 800-451-8664
Brockmann Chocolates
Delta, BC. 888-494-2270
Brown & Haley
Tacoma, WA 253-620-3000
Cadbury Trebor Allan
Granby, QC 800-387-3267
Cadbury Trebor Allan
Toronto, ON 800-565-6541
Candy Factory
Hayward, CA 800-736-6887
Chocolate By Design
Ronkonkoma, NY. 800-536-3618
Chocolate House
Milwaukee, WI 800-236-2022
Chocolates a La Carte
Valencia, CA. 800-818-2462
Chocolove
Boulder, CO 888-246-2656
Double Play Foods
New York, NY. 212-682-4611
El Brands
Ozark, AL 334-445-2828
Empress Chocolate Company
Brooklyn, NY 800-793-3809
Energy Club
Pacoima, CA. 800-688-6887
Fannie May/Fanny Farmer
Chicago, IL 800-333-3629
FB Washburn Candy Corporation
Brockton, MA. 508-588-0820
Fernando C Pujals & Bros
Guaynabo, PR. 787-792-3080
Ferrero Usa
Somerset, NJ. 800-337-7376
Frankford Candy & Chocolate Company
Philadelphia, PA 800-523-9090
Goetze's Candy Company
Baltimore, MD 800-638-1456
Gold Star Chocolate
Brooklyn, NY 718-330-0187
Hagensborg Chocolates LTD.
Burnaby, BC 877-554-7763
Harbor Sweets
Salem, MA 800-234-4887
Horriea 2000 Food Industries
Reynolds, GA 478-847-4186
Hospitality Mints
Boone, NC. 800-334-5181
Hyde & Hyde
Corona, CA. 951-817-2300
Idaho Candy Company
Boise, ID. 800-898-6986
Karl Bissinger French Confections
St Louis, MO. 800-325-8881
Leader Candies
Brooklyn, NY 718-366-6900
Lowery's Home Made Candies
Muncie, IN 800-541-3340
Mayfair Sales
Buffalo, NY. 800-248-2881
Mona Lisa® Chocolatier
Arlington, VA 866-662-5475
Morris National
Azusa, CA. 626-385-2000
Nature's Candy
Fredericksburg, TX. 800-729-0085
Peerless Confection Company
Lincolnwood, IL 773-281-6100
Plantation Candies
Telford, PA 888-678-6468
Primrose Candy Company
Chicago, IL 800-268-9522
Rebecca Ruth Candy
Frankfort, KY 800-444-3866
Richardson Brands Company
Branford, CT. 800-839-8938
Rucker's Makin' Batch Candies
Bridgeport, IL 618-945-7778
Setton International Foods
Commack, NY 800-227-4397
Shari Candies
Edina, MN. 800-658-7059
Sherwood Brands
Rockville, MD 301-309-6161
Snackerz
Commerce, CA 888-576-2253
Sweet Candy Company
Salt Lake City, UT 800-669-8669
Todd's
Vernon, CA 800-938-6337
V L Foods
White Plains, NY 914-697-4851
Warner Candy
El Paso, TX. 847-928-7200
Webbs Citrus Candy
Davenport, FL. 863-422-1051
Wisconsin Cheese
Melrose Park, IL 708-450-0074

Fondants

CHR Hansen
Gretna, LA 504-367-7727

Fudge

Amcan Industries
Elmsford, NY 914-347-4838
Bear Creek Smokehouse
Marshall, TX. 800-950-2327
Betty Lou's Golden Smackers
McMinnville, OR 800-242-5205
Bodega Chocolates
Fountain Valley, CA 888-326-3342
Bohemian Biscuit Company
South San Francisco, CA 650-952-2226
Cambridge Brands
Cambridge, MA 617-491-2500
Charlotte's Confections
Millbrae, CA. 800-798-2427
Country Fresh Food & Confections, Inc.
Oliver Springs, TN 800-545-8782
Crown Candy Corporation
Macon, GA 800-241-3529
Donells' Candies
Casper, WY. 877-461-2009
Downeast Candies
Boothbay Harbor, ME. 207-633-5178
Enstrom Candies
Grand Junction, CO 800-367-8766
Fieldbrook Farms
Dunkirk, NY 800-333-0805
Fudge Fatale
Studio City, CA. 800-809-8298
Gene & Boots Candies
Perryopolis, PA. 800-864-4222
Giambri's Quality Sweets
Clementon, NJ 866-238-0169
Golden Foods
Commerce, CA. 800-350-2462
Haven's Candies
Westbrook, ME. 800-639-6309
James Candy Company
Atlantic City, NJ 800-938-2339
Jody's Gourmet Popcorn
Virginia Beach, VA. 866-797-5639
Kelly's Candies
Pittsburgh, PA. 800-523-3051
Laymon Candy Company
San Bernardino, CA 909-825-4408
McJak Candy Company LLC
Medina, OH. 800-424-2942
Nancy's Candy
Meadows Of Dan, VA. 800-328-3834
Olde Tyme Mercantile
Arroyo Grande, CA. 805-489-7991
Phenomenal Fudge
Shoreham, VT. 800-430-5442
Phillips Candies
Seaside, OR. 503-738-5402
Rocky Top Country
Sevierville, TN 865-428-7311
St. Jacobs Candy Company Brittles 'n More
Waterloo, ON 519-884-3505
Stephany's Chocolates
Arvada, CO 800-888-1522
Sweenor Chocolate
Wakefield, RI 800-834-3123
Vande Walle's Candies
Appleton, WI 920-738-7799
Webbs Citrus Candy
Davenport, FL. 863-422-1051
Wisconsin Cheese
Melrose Park, IL 708-450-0074

Gums & Jellies

Albanese Confectionery Group
Merrillville, IN 800-536-0581
Amazing Candy Craft Company
Hollis, NY. 800-429-9368
American Food Products
Methuen, MA 978-682-1855
Arcor USA
Miami, FL. 800-572-7267
Au'some Candies
Monmouth Junction, NJ 732-951-8818
Beehive Botanicals, Inc.
Hayward, WI. 800-233-4483
Blueberry Hill Foods
El Paso, TX. 800-451-8664
Boston Fruit Slice & Confectionery Corporation
Lawrence, MA 978-686-2699
C. Howard Company
Bellport, NY 631-286-7940
Cadbury Trebor Allan
Granby, QC 800-387-3267
Cadbury Trebor Allan
Toronto, ON 800-565-6541
Cambridge Brands
Cambridge, MA 617-491-2500
Dare Foods
Kitchener, ON. 800-265-8225
Dayhoff
Clearwater, FL 800-354-3372
El Brands
Ozark, AL 334-445-2828
Energy Club
Pacoima, CA. 800-688-6887
Extreme Creations
El Dorado Hills, CA 916-941-0444
Fannie May Fine Chocolat
Melrose Park, IL 800-999-3629
Fannie May/Fanny Farmer
Chicago, IL 800-333-3629
Farley's & Sathers Candy Company
Round Lake, MN 800-533-0330
Fernando C Pujals & Bros
Guaynabo, PR. 787-792-3080
Ferrara Pan Candy Company
Forest Park, IL 800-323-1768
Foreign Candy Company
Hull, IA. 800-831-8541
Frankford Candy & Chocolate Company
Philadelphia, PA 800-523-9090
Ganong Bros Limited Corporate Office
St. Stephen, NB. 888-426-6647
Gene & Boots Candies
Perryopolis, PA. 800-864-4222
GNS Foods/Pacific Gold
Arlington, TX 817-795-4671
Golden Fluff Popcorn Company
Lakewood, NJ. 732-367-5448
Gumtech International
Phoenix, AZ 602-252-7425
Gurley's Foods
Willmar, MN. 800-426-7845
Haribo of America
Baltimore, MD 800-638-2327
Harmony Foods Corporation
Fishers, IN. 317-567-2700
Harmony Foods Corporation
Fishers, IN. 800-837-2855
Hershey Company
Hershey, PA. 800-468-1714
Hershey Corporation
Hershey, PA. 800-468-1714
Hyde & Hyde
Corona, CA. 951-817-2300
Jelly Belly Candy Company
Fairfield, CA. 800-522-3267
Joyva Corporation
Brooklyn, NY 718-497-0170
Judson-Atkinson Candies
San Antonio, TX. 800-962-3984
Kolatin Real Kosher Gelatin
Lakewood, NJ. 732-364-8700
Kopper's Chocolate
New York, NY 800-325-0026
Leader Candies
Brooklyn, NY 718-366-6900
Liberty Orchards Company
Cashmere, WA 800-888-5696
Little I
Blaine, WA 360-332-3258
Marketing & Sales Essentials
Blaine, WA 877-915-5191

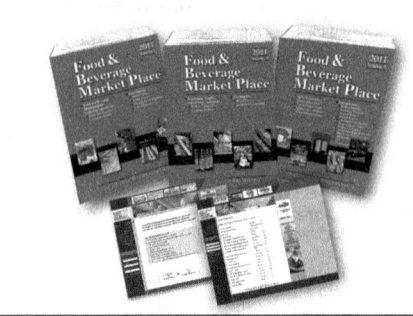

Mayfair Sales
Buffalo, NY....800-248-2881
Mona Lisa® Chocolatier
Arlington, VA....866-662-5475
Necco
Revere, MA....781-485-4500
New England Confectionery Company
Revere, MA....781-485-4500
Oak Leaf Confections
Scarborough, ON....877-261-7887
Original Foods, Quebec Division, Inc.
Vanier, QC....418-527-6277
Palmer Candy Company
Sioux City, IA....800-831-0828
Regent Confections
Orange, CA....714-348-8889
Richardson Brands Company
Branford, CT....800-839-8938
Roseville Corporation
Mountain View, CA....888-247-9338
Shari Candies
Edina, MN....800-658-7059
Sherwood Brands
Rockville, MD....301-309-6161
Snackerz
Commerce, CA....888-576-2253
Sorbee Intl.
Feasterville Trevose, PA....800-654-3997
Standard Candy Company
Nashville, TN....800-226-4340
Suity Confection Company
Miami, FL....305-639-3300
Sunrise Confections
El Paso, TX....800-685-1475
Sweet Blessings
Malibu, CA....310-317-1172
Sweet City Supply
Virginia Beach, VA....888-793-3824
SWELL Philadelphia Chewing Gum Corporation
Havertown, PA....610-449-1700
Taste of Nature
Beverly Hills, CA....310-396-4433
The Topps Company
Duryea, PA....570-457-6761
Toe-Food Chocolates and Candy
Berkeley, CA....888-863-3663
Triple-C
Hamilton, ON....800-263-9105
Trophy Nut
Tipp City, OH....800-219-9004
Warner Candy
El Paso, TX....847-928-7200
Weaver Nut Company
Ephrata, PA....717-738-3781
World Confections
Brooklyn, NY....718-768-8100
Wrigley Company
Chicago, IL....800-824-9681

Hard

A La Carte
Chicago, IL....800-722-2370
Adams & Brooks, Inc
Los Angeles, CA....800-999-9808
American Food Products
Methuen, MA....978-682-1855
Amurol Confections Company
Yorkville, IL....630-553-4800
Anastasia Confections Inc.
Orlando, FL....800-329-7100
Archibald Candy Corporation
Chicago, IL....800-333-3629
Arcor USA
Miami, FL....800-572-7267
Artek USA
Westlake Village, CA....866-278-3501
Atkinson Candy Company
Lufkin, TX....800-231-1203
Baker Candy Company
Snohomish, WA....425-422-6331
Barcelona Nut Company
Baltimore, MD....800-292-6887
Bidwell Candies
Mattoon, IL....217-234-3858
Blanton's
Sweetwater, TN....423-337-3487
Blueberry Hill Foods
El Paso, TX....800-451-8664
Bob's Candies
Albany, GA....800-841-3602
Butterfields/Sweet Concepts
Nashville, NC....800-945-5957
C. Howard Company
Bellport, NY....631-286-7940
Cadbury Trebor Allan
Granby, QC....800-387-3267
Cadbury Trebor Allan
Toronto, ON....800-565-6541
Cambridge Brands
Cambridge, MA....617-491-2500
Cap Candy
Napa, CA....707-251-9321
Ce De Candy
Union, NJ....800-631-7968
Claeys Candy
South Bend, IN....800-348-2239
Cloud Nine
San Leandro, CA....201-358-8588
Day Spring Enterprises
Cheektowaga, NY....800-879-7677
Dayhoff
Clearwater, FL....800-354-3372
Doscher's Candies
Cincinnati, OH....513-381-8656
Dryden & Palmer Company
Canajoharie, NY
Eda's Sugarfree Candies
Philadelphia, PA....215-324-3412
El Brands
Ozark, AL....334-445-2828
Energy Club
Pacoima, CA....800-688-6887
Enstrom Candies
Grand Junction, CO....800-367-8766
F & F Foods
Chicago, IL....800-621-0225
Fannie May Fine Chocolat
Melrose Park, IL....800-999-3629
Fannie May/Fanny Farmer
Chicago, IL....800-333-3629
Farley's & Sathers Candy Company
Round Lake, MN....800-533-0330
FB Washburn Candy Corporation
Brockton, MA....508-588-0820
Fernando C Pujals & Bros
Guaynabo, PR....787-792-3080
Ferrara Pan Candy Company
Forest Park, IL....800-323-1768
Foreign Candy Company
Hull, IA....800-831-8541
Frankford Candy & Chocolate Company
Philadelphia, PA....800-523-9090
Giambri's Quality Sweets
Clementon, NJ....866-238-0169
Gilliam Candy Brands
Paducah, KY....800-445-3008
Gimbal's Fine Candies
S San Francisco, CA....800-344-6225
Go Lightly Candy
Hillside, NJ....800-524-1304
Golden Apples Candy Company
Southport, CT....800-776-0393
Gurley's Foods
Willmar, MN....800-426-7845
H E Williams Candy Company
Chesapeake, VA....757-545-9311
Harmony Foods Corporation
Fishers, IN....800-837-2855
Hawaii Candy
Honolulu, HI....808-836-8955
Hershey Company
Hershey, PA....800-468-1714
Hillside Candy
Hillside, NJ....800-524-1304
Horriea 2000 Food Industries
Reynolds, GA....478-847-4186
Hyde & Hyde
Corona, CA....951-817-2300
Idaho Candy Company
Boise, ID....800-898-6986
Judson-Atkinson Candies
San Antonio, TX....800-962-3984
Kencraft
North Alpine, UT....800-377-4368
Leader Candies
Brooklyn, NY....718-366-6900
Lotte USA
Battle Creek, MI....269-963-6664
Masterfoods USA
Hackettstown, NJ....908-852-1000
Mayfair Sales
Buffalo, NY....800-248-2881
Mitch Chocolate
Melville, NY....631-777-2400
Mona Lisa® Chocolatier
Arlington, VA....866-662-5475
Moore's Candies
Baltimore, MD....410-426-2705
Morris National
Azusa, CA....626-385-2000
Nassau Candy Company
Hicksville, NY....516-433-7100
Necco
Revere, MA....781-485-4500
Nestle USA Inc
Glendale, CA....800-225-2270
New England Confectionery Company
Revere, MA....781-485-4500
Oak Leaf Confections
Scarborough, ON....877-261-7887
Old Dominion Peanut Corporation
Norfolk, VA....800-368-6887
Olivier's Candies
Calgary, AB....403-266-6028
Original Foods, Quebec Division, Inc.
Vanier, QC....418-527-6277
Palmer Candy Company
Sioux City, IA....800-831-0828
Peerless Confection Company
Lincolnwood, IL....773-281-6100
PEZ Candy
Orange, CT....203-795-0531
Piedmont Candy Corporation
Lexington, NC....336-248-2477
Plantation Candies
Telford, PA....888-678-6468

Primrose Candy Company
Chicago, IL 800-268-9522
Produits Alimentaire
St Lambert De Lauzon, QC 800-463-1787
Quigley Manufacturing
Elizabethtown, PA. . . . 800-367-2441
Rainbow Pops
Cheektowaga, NY. . . . 800-879-7677
Regent Confections
Orange, CA 714-348-8889
Richardson Brands Company
Branford, CT. . . . 800-839-8938
Ricos Candy Snacks & Bakery
Hialeah, FL 305-885-7392
Rucker's Makin' Batch Candies
Bridgeport, IL 618-945-7778
Salem Old Fashioned Candies
Salem, MA 978-744-3242
Sconza Candy Company
Oakdale, CA 877-568-8137
Scripture Candy
Adamsville, AL. . . . 888-317-7333
Setton International Foods
Commack, NY 800-227-4397
Shade Foods
New Century, KS 800-225-6312
Shari Candies
Edina, MN. . . . 800-658-7059
Sherwood Brands
Rockville, MD 301-309-6161
Sherwood Brands
Rockville, MD 401-434-7773
Snackerz
Commerce, CA 888-576-2253
SP Enterprises
Las Vegas, NV 800-746-4774
Spangler Candy Company
Bryan, OH. . . . 888-636-4221
St. Jacobs Candy Company Brittles 'n More
Waterloo, ON 519-884-3505
Storck
Chicago, IL 800-621-7772
Sunrise Confections
El Paso, TX. . . . 800-685-1475
Sweenor Chocolate
Wakefield, RI 800-834-3123
Sweet Candy Company
Salt Lake City, UT 800-669-8669
Sweet City Supply
Virginia Beach, VA. . . . 888-793-3824
Sweet'N Low
Brooklyn, NY 718-858-4200
SWELL Philadelphia Chewing Gum Corporation
Havertown, PA 610-449-1700
Todd's
Vernon, CA 800-938-6337
Tootsie Roll Industries
Chicago, IL. . . . 800-877-7655
Trophy Nut
Tipp City, OH 800-219-9004
Turkey Hill Sugarbush
Waterloo, QC 450-539-4822
V L Foods
White Plains, NY 914-697-4851
Warner Candy
El Paso, TX. . . . 847-928-7200
Weaver Nut Company
Ephrata, PA. . . . 717-738-3781
Webbs Citrus Candy
Davenport, FL. . . . 863-422-1051

Jelly Beans

American Food Products
Methuen, MA 978-682-1855
Arcor USA
Miami, FL. . . . 800-572-7267
Blueberry Hill Foods
El Paso, TX. . . . 800-451-8664
Cambridge Brands
Cambridge, MA 617-491-2500
Cap Candy
Napa, CA. . . . 707-251-9321
Dayhoff
Clearwater, FL 800-354-3372
El Brands
Ozark, AL 334-445-2828
Energy Club
Pacoima, CA 800-688-6887
Fannie May/Fanny Farmer
Chicago, IL 800-333-3629
Farley's & Sathers Candy Company
Round Lake, MN 800-533-0330
Fernando C Pujals & Bros
Guaynabo, PR. . . . 787-792-3080
Ganong Bros Limited Corporate Office
St. Stephen, NB. . . . 888-426-6647
Gimbal's Fine Candies
S San Francisco, CA 800-344-6225
GNS Foods/Pacific Gold
Arlington, TX 817-795-4671
Gurley's Foods
Willmar, MN. . . . 800-426-7845
Harmony Foods Corporation
Fishers, IN. . . . 800-837-2855
Jelly Belly Candy Company
Fairfield, CA 800-522-3267
Judson-Atkinson Candies
San Antonio, TX. . . . 800-962-3984
Just Born
Bethlehem, PA 800-445-5787
Leader Candies
Brooklyn, NY 718-366-6900
Masterfoods USA
Hackettstown, NJ 908-852-1000
Mayfair Sales
Buffalo, NY. . . . 800-248-2881
Palmer Candy Company
Sioux City, IA 800-831-0828
Setton International Foods
Commack, NY 800-227-4397
Shari Candies
Edina, MN. . . . 800-658-7059
Sherwood Brands
Rockville, MD 301-309-6161
Sherwood Brands
Rockville, MD 401-434-7773
Snackerz
Commerce, CA 888-576-2253
Sunrise Confections
El Paso, TX. . . . 800-685-1475
Sweet Candy Company
Salt Lake City, UT 800-669-8669
Sweet City Supply
Virginia Beach, VA. . . . 888-793-3824
Todd's
Vernon, CA 800-938-6337
Triple-C
Hamilton, ON 800-263-9105
Warner Candy
El Paso, TX. . . . 847-928-7200
Weaver Nut Company
Ephrata, PA. . . . 717-738-3781

Kisses

Cadbury Trebor Allan
Granby, QC. . . . 800-387-3267
Mona Lisa® Chocolatier
Arlington, VA 866-662-5475
Setton International Foods
Commack, NY 800-227-4397

Licorice

American Food Products
Methuen, MA 978-682-1855
American Licorice Company
Bend, OR. . . . 800-220-2399
American Licorice Company
Union City, CA 866-442-2783
Buddy Squirrel LLC
Milwaukee, WI 800-972-2658
Cadbury Trebor Allan
Granby, QC. . . . 800-387-3267
Cadbury Trebor Allan
Toronto, ON 800-565-6541
Cambridge Brands
Cambridge, MA 617-491-2500
Capco Enterprises
East Hanover, NJ. . . . 800-252-1011
El Brands
Ozark, AL 334-445-2828
Energy Club
Pacoima, CA 800-688-6887
Fannie May/Fanny Farmer
Chicago, IL 800-333-3629
Farley's & Sathers Candy Company
Round Lake, MN 800-533-0330
Fiesta Candy Company
Rochester, NH. . . . 800-285-9735
Foreign Candy Company
Hull, IA 800-831-8541
G Scaccianoce & Company
Bronx, NY. . . . 718-991-4462
Ganong Bros Limited Corporate Office
St. Stephen, NB. . . . 888-426-6647
Gimbal's Fine Candies
S San Francisco, CA 800-344-6225
Gladstone Candies
Cleveland, OH 888-729-1960
Gurley's Foods
Willmar, MN. . . . 800-426-7845
Haribo of America
Baltimore, MD 800-638-2327
Hershey Company
Hershey, PA. . . . 800-468-1714
Jelly Belly Candy Company
Fairfield, CA 800-522-3267
Kenny's Candy Company
Perham, MN 800-782-5152
Kookaburra Liquorice Co
Monroe, WA
Lucas World
Laredo, TX 888-675-8227
Mafco Worldwide Corporation
Camden, NJ. . . . 856-964-8840
Masterfoods USA
Hackettstown, NJ 908-852-1000
Mayfair Sales
Buffalo, NY. . . . 800-248-2881
Mona Lisa® Chocolatier
Arlington, VA 866-662-5475
Morre-Tec Industries
Union, NJ 908-688-9009
Naturex Inc.
South Hackensack, NJ 201-440-5000
Palmer Candy Company
Sioux City, IA 800-831-0828
Patsy's Candies
Colorado Springs, CO. . . . 866-372-8797
Sahagian & Associates
Oak Park, IL 800-327-9273
Shari Candies
Edina, MN. . . . 800-658-7059
Snackerz
Commerce, CA 888-576-2253
Sorbee Intl.
Feasterville Trevose, PA. . . . 800-654-3997
Sweet Candy Company
Salt Lake City, UT 800-669-8669
Sweet City Supply
Virginia Beach, VA. . . . 888-793-3824
Todd's
Vernon, CA 800-938-6337
Triple-C
Hamilton, ON 800-263-9105
Warner Candy
El Paso, TX. . . . 847-928-7200
Westbrae Natural Foods
Melville, NY. . . . 800-434-4246

Lollypops

Adams & Brooks, Inc
Los Angeles, CA. . . . 800-999-9808
All About Lollipops
Poway, CA 866-475-6554
Amazing Candy Craft Company
Hollis, NY. . . . 800-429-9368
American Food Products
Methuen, MA 978-682-1855
Amurol Confections Company
Yorkville, IL 630-553-4800
Ann Hemyng Candy
Trumbauersville, PA 800-779-7004
Arcor USA
Miami, FL. . . . 800-572-7267
Artek USA
Westlake Village, CA 866-278-3501
Au'some Candies
Monmouth Junction, NJ 732-951-8818
Baraboo Candy Company
Baraboo, WI 800-967-1690
Blueberry Hill Foods
El Paso, TX. . . . 800-451-8664
Bob's Candies
Albany, GA. . . . 800-841-3602
Browniepops LLC
Leawood, KS. . . . 816-797-0715
Cadbury Trebor Allan
Granby, QC. . . . 800-387-3267
Cadbury Trebor Allan
Toronto, ON 800-565-6541

Cap Candy
Napa, CA 707-251-9321
Carrie's Chocolates
Edmonton, AB 877-778-2462
Ce De Candy
Union, NJ 800-631-7968
CTC Manufacturing
Calgary, AB 800-668-7677
Das Foods
Chicago, IL 312-224-8590
David Bradley Chocolatier
Windsor, NJ 877-289-7933
Day Spring Enterprises
Cheektowaga, NY 800-879-7677
Dayhoff
Clearwater, FL 800-354-3372
El Brands
Ozark, AL 334-445-2828
Energy Club
Pacoima, CA 800-688-6887
Extreme Creations
El Dorado Hills, CA 916-941-0444
F & F Foods
Chicago, IL 800-621-0225
Farley's & Sathers Candy Company
Round Lake, MN 800-533-0330
Fernando C Pujals & Bros
Guaynabo, PR 787-792-3080
Foreign Candy Company
Hull, IA 800-831-8541
Frankford Candy & Chocolate Company
Philadelphia, PA 800-523-9090
Fun Factory
Milwaukee, WI 877-894-6767
Funkandy Corporation
Corona, CA 866-386-2263
Geeef America
Compton, CA 310-609-2940
Gladstone Candies
Cleveland, OH 888-729-1960
Glennys
Freeport, NY 888-864-1243
Golden Apples Candy Company
Southport, CT 800-776-0393
Gurley's Foods
Willmar, MN 800-426-7845
Harmony Foods Corporation
Fishers, IN 800-837-2855
Hershey Company
Hershey, PA 800-468-1714
Impact Confections
Littleton, CO 303-626-2222
James Candy Company
Atlantic City, NJ 800-938-2339
Jed's Maple Products
Westfield, VT 866-478-7388
Kencraft
North Alpine, UT 800-377-4368
Laura Paige Candy Company
Newburgh, NY 845-566-4209
Leader Candies
Brooklyn, NY 718-366-6900
Light Vision Confections
Cincinnati, OH 513-351-9444
Linda's Lollies Company
New York, NY 800-347-1545
Lucas World
Laredo, TX 888-675-8227
Masterfoods USA
Hackettstown, NJ 908-852-1000
Mayfair Sales
Buffalo, NY 800-248-2881
McIlhenny Company
Avery Island, LA 800-634-9599
McJak Candy Company LLC
Medina, OH 800-424-2942
Melville Candy Company
Weymouth, MA 781-331-2005
Mitch Chocolate
Melville, NY 631-777-2400
Mom 'N Pops
New Windsor, NY 866-368-6767
Mona Lisa® Chocolatier
Arlington, VA 866-662-5475
Multiflex Company
Hawthorne, NJ 973-636-9700
Original Foods, Quebec Division, Inc.
Vanier, QC 418-527-6277
Plymouth Lollipop Company
Carver, MA 800-777-0115
Primrose Candy Company
Chicago, IL 800-268-9522
Produits Alimentaire
St Lambert De Lauzon, QC 800-463-1787
Quick's Candy
Hummelstown, PA 800-443-9036
Rainbow Pops
Cheektowaga, NY 800-879-7677
Richardson Brands Company
Branford, CT 800-839-8938
Riddles' Sweet Impressions
Edmonton, AB 780-465-8085
Roseville Corporation
Mountain View, CA 888-247-9338
Salem Old Fashioned Candies
Salem, MA 978-744-3242
Scripture Candy
Adamsville, AL 888-317-7333
Setton International Foods
Commack, NY 800-227-4397
Shari Candies
Edina, MN 800-658-7059
Sherwood Brands
Rockville, MD 301-309-6161
Sherwood Brands
Rockville, MD 401-434-7773
Sorbee Intl.
Feasterville Trevose, PA 800-654-3997
SP Enterprises
Las Vegas, NV 800-746-4774
Spangler Candy Company
Bryan, OH 888-636-4221
Suity Confection Company
Miami, FL 305-639-3300
The Topps Company
Duryea, PA 570-457-6761
The Topps Company
New York, NY 800-489-9149
Tom & Sally's Handmade Chocolates
Brattleboro, VT 800-827-0800
Tootsie Roll Industries
Chicago, IL 800-877-7655
Triple-C
Hamilton, ON 800-263-9105
Turkey Hill Sugarbush
Waterloo, QC 450-539-4822
Williamsburg Chocolatier
Williamsburg, VA 757-253-1474
World Confections
Brooklyn, NY 718-768-8100
Yost Candy Company
Dalton, OH 800-750-1976

Gourmet Flavored

Bruno's Cajun Foods & Snacks
Slidell, LA 985-726-0544
Das Foods
Chicago, IL 312-224-8590

Lozenges

Adams USA
New York, NY 212-733-2323
BestSweet
Mooresville, NC 888-211-5530
Cadbury Trebor Allan
Granby, QC 800-387-3267
F & F Foods
Chicago, IL 800-621-0225
Ganong Bros Limited Corporate Office
St. Stephen, NB 888-426-6647
Hillside Candy
Hillside, NJ 800-524-1304
Holistic Products Corporation
Englewood, NJ 800-221-0308
Mona Lisa® Chocolatier
Arlington, VA 866-662-5475
MYNTZ!
Kent, WA 800-800-9490
Rito Mints
Trois Rivieres, QC 819-379-1449
Snackerz
Commerce, CA 888-576-2253
Sorbee Intl.
Feasterville Trevose, PA 800-654-3997

Maple

Butternut Mountain Farm
Morrisville, VT 800-828-2376
Jed's Maple Products
Westfield, VT 866-478-7388
Key III Candies
Fort Wayne, IN 800-752-2382
Maple Grove Farms of Vermont
St Johnsbury, VT 800-525-2540
Nature's Candy
Fredericksburg, TX 800-729-0085
Richards Maple Products
Chardon, OH 800-352-4052
Sugarwoods Farm
Glover, VT 800-245-3718
Swisser Sweet Maple
Castorland, NY 315-346-1034

Marshmallow

Charlotte's Confections
Millbrae, CA 800-798-2427
Clown-Gysin Brands
Northbrook, IL 800-323-5778
Doumak
Elk Grove Vlg, IL 800-323-0318
Durkee-Mower
Lynn, MA 781-593-8007
Georgia Nut Ingredients
Skokie, IL 877-674-2993
Gimbal's Fine Candies
S San Francisco, CA 800-344-6225
Glatech Productions
Lakewood, NJ 732-364-8700
Golden Fluff Popcorn Company
Lakewood, NJ 732-367-5448
Judson-Atkinson Candies
San Antonio, TX 800-962-3984
Kolatin Real Kosher Gelatin
Lakewood, NJ 732-364-8700
Philadelphia Candies
Hermitage, PA 724-981-6341
Sherwood Brands
Rockville, MD 401-434-7773
Sokol & Company
Countryside, IL 800-328-7656
White-Stokes Company
Chicago, IL 800-978-6537
Zitner Company
Philadelphia, PA 215-229-4990

Marshmallow Creme

Sokol & Company
Countryside, IL 800-328-7656

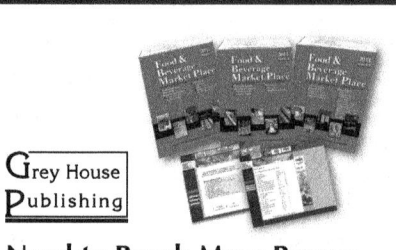

Marshmallows

Amros the Second, Inc.
Somerset, NJ 732-846-7755
Annabelle Candy Company
Hayward, CA 510-783-2900
Charlotte's Confections
Millbrae, CA 800-798-2427
Chris A. Papas & Son Company
Covington, KY 859-431-0499
David Bradley Chocolatier
Windsor, NJ 877-289-7933
Doumak
Elk Grove Vlg, IL 800-323-0318
Farley's & Sathers Candy Company
Round Lake, MN 800-533-0330
Frankford Candy & Chocolate Company
Philadelphia, PA 800-523-9090
Ganong Bros Limited Corporate Office
St. Stephen, NB 888-426-6647
Golden Fluff Popcorn Company
Lakewood, NJ 732-367-5448
Joyva Corporation
Brooklyn, NY 718-497-0170
Judson-Atkinson Candies
San Antonio, TX 800-962-3984
Just Born
Bethlehem, PA 800-445-5787
Marshmallow Cone Company
Cincinnati, OH 800-641-8551
Michele's Chocolate Truffles
Clackamas, OR 800-656-7112
Patsy's Candies
Colorado Springs, CO 866-372-8797
Pennsylvania Dutch Candies
Camp Hill, PA 800-233-7082
Richardson Brands Company
Branford, CT 800-839-8938
Roseville Corporation
Mountain View, CA 888-247-9338
Sherwood Brands
Rockville, MD 401-434-7773
Spangler Candy Company
Bryan, OH 888-636-4221
Suity Confection Company
Miami, FL 305-639-3300
Sweet City Supply
Virginia Beach, VA 888-793-3824
Zitner Company
Philadelphia, PA 215-229-4990

Marzipan

Ambassador Foods
Van Nuys, CA 800-338-3369
American Almond Products Company
Brooklyn, NY 800-825-6663
Amoretti
Oxnard, CA 800-266-7388
Mayfair Sales
Buffalo, NY 800-248-2881
Mona Lisa® Chocolatier
Arlington, VA 866-662-5475
Snackerz
Commerce, CA 888-576-2253
Sweet Swiss Confections
Spokane, WA 509-838-1334

Mints

Abdallah Candies
Burnsville, MN 800-348-7328
Adams USA
New York, NY 212-733-2323
American Mint
New York, NY 800-401-6468
AmeriCandy Company
Louisville, KY 502-583-1776
Amurol Confections Company
Yorkville, IL 630-553-4800
Andes Candy
Chicago, IL 773-838-3400
Art CoCo Chocolate Company
Denver, CO 800-779-8985
Atkinson Candy Company
Lufkin, TX 800-231-1203
Big Sky Brands
Mississauga, ON 888-624-4759
Blueberry Hill Foods
El Paso, TX 800-451-8664
Bob's Candies
Albany, GA 800-841-3602
Boston America Corporation
Woburn, MA 617-923-1111
Brown & Haley
Tacoma, WA 253-620-3000
Cadbury Trebor Allan
Granby, QC 800-387-3267
Caiazza Candy Company
New Castle, PA 800-651-1171
Chocolati Handmade Chocolates
Seattle, WA 206-784-5212
Clarks Joe Fund Raising Candies & Novelties
Tarentum, PA 888-459-9520
Cloud Nine
San Leandro, CA 201-358-8588
Energy Club
Pacoima, CA 800-688-6887
F & F Foods
Chicago, IL 800-621-0225
Farley's & Sathers Candy Company
Round Lake, MN 800-533-0330
Foley's Candies
Richmond, BC 888-236-5397
Ford Gum & Machine Company
Akron, NY 800-225-5535
Fun Factory
Milwaukee, WI 877-894-6767
G Scaccianoce & Company
Bronx, NY 718-991-4462
Go Lightly Candy
Hillside, NJ 800-524-1304
Health-Tech
New York, NY 877-673-9777
Hint Mint
Los Angeles, CA 800-991-6468
Horriea 2000 Food Industries
Reynolds, GA 478-847-4186
Hospitality Mints
Boone, NC 800-334-5181
Hospitality Mints LLC
Boone, NC 800-334-5181
IFive Brands
Seattle, WA 800-882-5615
Jelly Belly Candy Company
Fairfield, CA 800-522-3267
Jo Mints
Corona Del Mar, CA 877-566-4687
Judson-Atkinson Candies
San Antonio, TX 800-962-3984
Kopper's Chocolate
New York, NY 800-325-0026
Landies Candies Company
Buffalo, NY 800-955-2634
Little I
Blaine, WA 360-332-3258
Marich Confectionery Company
Hollister, CA 800-624-7055
Matangos Candies
Harrisburg, PA 717-234-0882
Maxfield Candy
Salt Lake City, UT 800-288-8002
Mayfair Sales
Buffalo, NY 800-248-2881
Mona Lisa® Chocolatier
Arlington, VA 866-662-5475
MYNTZ!
Kent, WA 800-800-9490
Naylor Candies
Mount Wolf, PA 717-266-2706
Necco
Revere, MA 781-485-4500
New England Confectionery Company
Revere, MA 781-485-4500
Palmer Candy Company
Sioux City, IA 800-831-0828
Perfetti
Erlanger, KY 859-283-1234
Pez Manufacturing Corporation
Orange, CT 800-243-6087
Pfizer
Parsippany, NJ 973-541-5900
Piedmont Candy Corporation
Lexington, NC 336-248-2477
Plantation Candies
Telford, PA 888-678-6468
Rebecca Ruth Candy
Frankfort, KY 800-444-3866
Reutter Candy & Chocolates
Baltimore, MD 800-392-0870
Rito Mints
Trois Rivieres, QC 819-379-1449
Salem Old Fashioned Candies
Salem, MA 978-744-3242
Schuster Marketing Corporation
Milwaukee, WI 888-254-8948
Scripture Candy
Adamsville, AL 888-317-7333
Sencha Naturals
Los Angeles, CA 888-473-6242
Setton International Foods
Commack, NY 800-227-4397
Shari Candies
Edina, MN 800-658-7059
SP Enterprises
Las Vegas, NV 800-746-4774
Sweenor Chocolate
Wakefield, RI 800-834-3123
Todd's
Vernon, CA 800-938-6337
Tootsie Roll Industries
Chicago, IL 800-877-7655
Unica
Glen Ellyn, IL 630-790-8107
Vermints
Burlington, VT 800-367-4442
Weaver Nut Company
Ephrata, PA 717-738-3781
Webbs Citrus Candy
Davenport, FL 863-422-1051

Mousse

Abel & Schafer
Ronkonkoma, NY 800-443-1260
Alati-Caserta Desserts
Montreal, QC 514-271-3013
Alexian Pates/GroezingerProvisions
Neptune, NJ 800-927-9473
Dave's Gourmet Albacore
Kirkland, WA 800-454-8862
Desserts by David Glass
South Windsor, CT 860-462-7520
Fresh Dairy Direct/Morningstar
Dallas, TX 800-395-7004
Granowska's
Toronto, ON 416-533-7755
Groezinger Provisions
Neptune, NJ 800-927-9473
HFI Foods
Redmond, WA 425-883-1320
Hormel Foods Corporation
Austin, MN 800-523-4635
Jon Donaire Pastry
Santa Fe Springs, CA 877-366-2473
Les Trois Petits Cochons
Brooklyn, NY 800-537-7283
Love & Quiches Desserts
Freeport, NY 800-525-5251
Paris Pastry
Van Nuys, CA 310-474-8888
Tova Industries
Louisville, KY 888-532-8682
W&G Flavors
Hunt Valley, MD 410-771-6606
World of Chantilly
Brooklyn, NY 718-859-1110

Nougats

Clarks Joe Fund Raising Candies & Novelties
Tarentum, PA 888-459-9520
Farley's & Sathers Candy Company
Round Lake, MN 800-533-0330
Ferrara Bakery & Cafe
New York, NY 212-226-6150
Lukas Confections
York, PA 717-843-0921
Mona Lisa® Chocolatier
Arlington, VA 866-662-5475
New England Confectionery Company
Revere, MA 781-485-4500
Webbs Citrus Candy
Davenport, FL 863-422-1051
White-Stokes Company
Chicago, IL 800-978-6537

Novelties

Ann Hemyng Candy
Trumbauersville, PA 800-779-7004
Bohemian Biscuit Company
South San Francisco, CA 650-952-2226
Carrie's Chocolates
Edmonton, AB 877-778-2462
Cella's Confections
Chicago, IL 773-838-3400

Chocolate Street of Hartville
Hartville, OH 888-853-5904
Chocolates by Mark
La Porte, TX 832-736-2626
Chris A. Papas & Son Company
Covington, KY 859-431-0499
Chris Candies
Pittsburgh, PA 412-322-9400
David Bradley Chocolatier
Windsor, NJ 877-289-7933
Doscher's Candies
Cincinnati, OH 513-381-8656
Ferrara Bakery & Cafe
New York, NY 212-226-6150
Hershey Corporation
Hershey, PA 800-468-1714
Jo Mints
Corona Del Mar, CA 877-566-4687
Laura Paige Candy Company
Newburgh, NY 845-566-4209
Leader Candies
Brooklyn, NY 718-366-6900
Long Grove ConfectioneryCompany
Buffalo Grove, IL 800-373-3102
Lucas World
Laredo, TX 888-675-8227
Maxfield Candy
Salt Lake City, UT 800-288-8002
Merbs Candies
Saint Louis, MO 314-832-7117
Merlin Candies
Harahan, LA 800-899-1549
Mona Lisa® Chocolatier
Arlington, VA 866-662-5475
Necco
Revere, MA 781-485-4500
New England Confectionery Company
Revere, MA 781-485-4500
Niagara Chocolates
Cheektowaga, NY 800-234-5750
Stichler Products
Reading, PA 610-921-0211
Weaver Nut Company
Ephrata, PA 717-738-3781
World Confections
Brooklyn, NY 718-768-8100
Yost Candy Company
Dalton, OH 800-750-1976

Peanut Brittle

Atkinson Candy Company
Lufkin, TX 800-231-1203
B&B Pecan Processors of NC
Turkey, NC 866-328-7322
Confection Solutions
Sylmar, CA 800-284-2422
DE Wolfgang Candy Company
York, PA 800-248-4273
Jer's Handmade Chocolates
Solana Beach, CA 800-540-7265
Maxwell's Gourmet Food
Raleigh, NC 800-952-6887
Moore's Candies
Baltimore, MD 410-426-2705
Muth Candies
Louisville, KY 502-585-2952
Peanut Shop of Williamsburg
Portsmouth, VA 800-637-3268
Sally Lane's Candy Farm
Paris, TN 731-642-5801
Severn Peanut Company
Severn, NC 800-642-4064

Popcorn Specialties

Cloud Nine
San Leandro, CA 201-358-8588
Eda's Sugarfree Candies
Philadelphia, PA 215-324-3412
Faroh Candies
Cleveland, OH 440-888-9866
Fun City Popcorn
Las Vegas, NV 800-423-1710
GKI Foods
Brighton, MI 248-486-0055
Heartland Gourmet Popcorn
Lake Geneva, WI 866-489-4676
Humphrey Company
Cleveland, OH 800-486-3739
Koeze Company
Wyoming, MI 800-555-3909
McCleary
South Beloit, IL 800-523-8644
Midwest/Northern
Minneapolis, MN 800-328-5502
Popcorn Connection
North Hollywood, CA 800-852-2676
Poppers Supply Company
Allentown, PA 800-457-9810
Randag & Associates Inc
Elmhurst, IL 630-530-2830
Rygmyr Foods
South Saint Paul, MN 800-545-3903
The Hampton Popcorn Company Inc.
Mineola, NY 888-947-6726
Vande Walle's Candies
Appleton, WI 920-738-7799
Weaver Popcorn Company
Noblesville, IN 800-634-8161

Rock

Salem Old Fashioned Candies
Salem, MA 978-744-3242
Setton International Foods
Commack, NY 800-227-4397

Taffy

Adams & Brooks, Inc
Los Angeles, CA 800-999-9808
Alaska Jack's Trading Post
Anchorage, AK 888-660-2257
Anastasia Confections Inc.
Orlando, FL 800-329-7100
Annabelle Candy Company
Hayward, CA 510-783-2900
Bidwell Candies
Mattoon, IL 217-234-3858
Cadbury Trebor Allan
Granby, QC 800-387-3267
Charlotte's Confections
Millbrae, CA 800-798-2427
Downeast Candies
Boothbay Harbor, ME 207-633-5178
El Brands
Ozark, AL 334-445-2828
Energy Club
Pacoima, CA 800-688-6887
Farley's & Sathers Candy Company
Round Lake, MN 800-533-0330
Forbes Candies
Virginia Beach, VA 800-626-5898
Foreign Candy Company
Hull, IA 800-831-8541
Gilliam Candy Brands
Paducah, KY 800-445-3008
Gurley's Foods
Willmar, MN 800-426-7845
Haven's Candies
Westbrook, ME 800-639-6309
Horriea 2000 Food Industries
Reynolds, GA 478-847-4186
Humphrey Company
Cleveland, OH 800-486-3739
James Candy Company
Atlantic City, NJ 800-938-2339
Jelly Belly Candy Company
Fairfield, CA 800-522-3267
Judson-Atkinson Candies
San Antonio, TX 800-962-3984
Kencraft
North Alpine, UT 800-377-4368
Lammes Candies Since 1885
Austin, TX 800-252-1885
Laymon Candy Company
San Bernardino, CA 909-825-4408
Lowery's Home Made Candies
Muncie, IN 800-541-3340
Lukas Confections
York, PA 717-843-0921
Masterfoods USA
Hackettstown, NJ 908-852-1000
Maxfield Candy
Salt Lake City, UT 800-288-8002
Mayfair Sales
Buffalo, NY 800-248-2881
Merbs Candies
Saint Louis, MO 314-832-7117
Metropolis Sambeve Specialty Foods
Lawrence, MA 978-683-2873
Necco
Revere, MA 781-485-4500
New England Confectionery Company
Revere, MA 781-485-4500
Original Foods, Quebec Division, Inc.
Vanier, QC 418-527-6277
Patsy's Candies
Colorado Springs, CO 866-372-8797
Pennsylvania Dutch Candies
Camp Hill, PA 800-233-7082
Phillips Candies
Seaside, OR 503-738-5402
Primrose Candy Company
Chicago, IL 800-268-9522
Queen Bee Gardens
Lovell, WY 800-225-7553
Sahagian & Associates
Oak Park, IL 800-327-9273
Salem Old Fashioned Candies
Salem, MA 978-744-3242
Sayklly's Candies & Gifts
Escanaba, MI 906-786-3092
Seattle Gourmet Foods
Kent, WA 800-800-9490
Setton International Foods
Commack, NY 800-227-4397
Shari Candies
Edina, MN 800-658-7059
Snackerz
Commerce, CA 888-576-2253
Squirrel Brand Company
McKinney, TX 800-624-8242
St. Jacobs Candy Company Brittles 'n More
Waterloo, ON 519-884-3505
Sweet Candy Company
Salt Lake City, UT 800-669-8669
Sweet City Supply
Virginia Beach, VA 888-793-3824
Taffy Town
Salt Lake City, UT 800-765-4770
Todd's
Vernon, CA 800-938-6337
Webbs Citrus Candy
Davenport, FL 863-422-1051

Toffee

Bohemian Biscuit Company
South San Francisco, CA 650-952-2226
Bt. McElrath Chocolatier
Minneapolis, MN 612-331-8800
Cadbury Trebor Allan
Granby, QC 800-387-3267
Cary's of Oregon
Grants Pass, OR 888-822-9300
Confectionately Yours
Buffalo Grove, IL 800-875-6978
Creative Confections
Northbrook, IL 608-455-1448
Elegant Edibles
Houston, TX 800-227-3226
Enstrom Candies
Grand Junction, CO 800-367-8766
Fancy's Candy's
Rougemont, NC 888-403-2629
Farley's & Sathers Candy Company
Round Lake, MN 800-533-0330
Georgia Nut Ingredients
Skokie, IL 877-674-2993
Jo's Candies
Torrance, CA 800-770-1946
Landies Candies Company
Buffalo, NY 800-955-2634
Leader Candies
Brooklyn, NY 718-366-6900
Lukas Confections
York, PA 717-843-0921
Madrona Specialty Foods
Tukwila, WA 425-814-2500
Marich Confectionery Company
Hollister, CA 800-624-7055
Marie's Candies
West Liberty, OH 866-465-5781
Mona Lisa® Chocolatier
Arlington, VA 866-662-5475
Mrs. Weinstein's Toffee
Mount Pleasant, TX 805-965-0422
Northern Flair Foods
Mound, MN 888-530-4453
NSpired Natural Foods
Boulder, CO 800-434-4246
Nunes Farm Almonds
Newman, CA 209-862-3033

Old Dominion Peanut Corporation
Norfolk, VA. 800-368-6887
Pecan Deluxe Candy Company
Dallas, TX. 800-733-3589
Quigley Manufacturing
Elizabethtown, PA. 800-367-2441
Regent Confections
Orange, CA 714-348-8889
Seasons' Enterprises
Addison, IL. 630-628-0211
Sherwood Brands
Rockville, MD 401-434-7773
Southernfood Specialties
Atlanta, GA. 800-255-5323
Stephany's Chocolates
Arvada, CO 800-888-1522
Sweet Productions
Amityville, NY. 631-842-0548
Sweet Shop USA
Mt Pleasant, TX 800-222-2269
Tall Grass Toffee
Shawnee Mission, KS. 877-344-0442
Texas Toffee
Odessa, TX 432-563-5373
Toffee Company
Houston, TX. 713-840-9696
Vande Walle's Candies
Appleton, WI 920-738-7799
Weaver Nut Company
Ephrata, PA 717-738-3781
Webbs Citrus Candy
Davenport, FL. 863-422-1051
Wisconsin Cheese
Melrose Park, IL. 708-450-0074

Truffles

Anette's Chocolate Factory
Napa, CA. 707-252-4228
Birnn Chocolates of Vermont
South Burlington, VT 800-338-3141
Boca Bons East,LLC.
Greenacres, FL 800-314-2835
Bodega Chocolates
Fountain Valley, CA 888-326-3342
Bt. McElrath Chocolatier
Minneapolis, MN 612-331-8800
Chocoholics Divine Desserts
Linden, CA 800-760-2462
Chocolati Handmade Chocolates
Seattle, WA 206-784-5212
De Bas Chocolatier
Fresno, CA 559-294-7638
DeFluri's Fine Chocolates
Martinsburg, VA 304-264-3698
GKI Foods
Brighton, MI 248-486-0055
Mona Lisa® Chocolatier
Arlington, VA 866-662-5475
Moore's Candies
Baltimore, MD 410-426-2705
Sabatino Truffles USA
Bronx, NY. 888-444-9971
Sweet Shop
Mount Pleasant, TX 800-222-2269
Tea Room
San Leandro, CA. 866-515-8866
Urbani Truffles
Culver City, CA 310-842-8850
Veritas Chocolatier
Glenview, IL 800-555-8331
Vosges Haut-Chocolat
Chicago, IL 888-309-866

Candy Coatings

Carob

Clasen Quality Coatings
Madison, WI 877-459-4500

Chocolate

ADM Cocoa
Milwaukee, WI 800-558-9958
Ambassador Foods
Van Nuys, CA 800-338-3369
Anette's Chocolate Factory
Napa, CA. 707-252-4228
Clasen Quality Coatings
Madison, WI 877-459-4500
Cocoline Chocolate Company
Brooklyn, NY 718-522-4500
Mona Lisa® Chocolatier
Arlington, VA 866-662-5475
Mootz Candy
Pottsville, PA
Pacific Gold Marketing
Fresno, CA
Sucesores de Pedro Cortes
San Juan, PR 787-754-7040
US Chocolate Corporation
Brooklyn, NY 718-788-8555

Confectionery

ADM Cocoa
Milwaukee, WI 800-558-9958
Cache Creek Foods
Woodland, CA. 530-662-1764

Chocolate Products

A La Carte
Chicago, IL 800-722-2370
A Southern Season
Chapel Hill, NC 877-929-7133
Abdallah Candies
Burnsville, MN 800-348-7328
Adams & Brooks, Inc
Los Angeles, CA. 800-999-9808
Aglamesis Brothers
Cincinnati, OH 513-531-5196
Al Richards Chocolates
Bayonne, NJ 888-777-6964
Al-Rite Fruits & Syrups
Miami, FL. 305-652-2540
Alaska Jack's Trading Post
Anchorage, AK 888-660-2257
American Nut & Chocolate Company
Boston, MA. 800-797-6887
AmeriCandy Company
Louisville, KY 502-583-1776
Ames International
Fife, WA 888-469-2637
Andes Candy
Chicago, IL 773-838-3400
Andre-Boudin Bakeries
San Francisco, CA 415-882-1849
Archibald Candy Corporation
Chicago, IL 800-333-3629
Ashers Chocolates
Lewistown, PA 800-343-0520
Baker Candy Company
Snohomish, WA 425-422-6331
Barry Callebaut USA LLC
Eddystone, PA. 610-872-4528
Betty Lou's Golden Smackers
McMinnville, OR 800-242-5205
Big Island Candies
Hilo, HI 800-935-5510
Blackberry Patch
Thomasville, GA. 800-853-5598
Blanton's
Sweetwater, TN. 423-337-3487
Blommer Chocolate Company
East Greenville, PA. 800-825-8181
Bloomsberry & Co
Salem, MA 800-745-5154
Bridge Brand Chocolate
San Francisco, CA 888-732-4626
Brighams
Arlington, MA 800-274-4426
Brix Chocolates
Youngstown, OH. 866-613-2749
Campbell Soup Company
Camden, NJ. 800-257-8443
Candy Cottage Company
Huntingdon Valley, PA 215-953-8288
Candy Factory
Hayward, CA 800-736-6887
Canelake's
Virginia, MN. 888-928-8889
Cape Cod Provisions
Pocasset, MA 508-564-5840
Cella's Confections
Chicago, IL 773-838-3400
Central Coca-Cola Bottling Company
Richmond, VA. 800-359-3759
Chase Candy Company
Saint Joseph, MO 800-786-1625
Chelsea Milling Company
Chelsea, MI. 734-475-1361
Chocolate Fantasies
Burr Ridge, IL. 630-572-0045
Chocolatique
Los Angeles, CA. 310-479-3849
Chris Candies
Pittsburgh, PA 412-322-9400
Chuao Chocolatier
Carlsbad, CA. 888-635-1444
Chukar Cherries
Prosser, WA. 800-624-9544
Clarks Joe Fund Raising Candies & Novelties
Tarentum, PA. 888-459-9520
Clasen Quality Coatings
Madison, WI 877-459-4500
Claudio Corallo Chocolate
Seattle, WA
Clear Mountain Coffee Company
Silver Spring, MD. 301-587-2233
Cloverland Sweets/Priester's Pecan Company
Fort Deposit, AL. 800-523-3505
Cocoline Chocolate Company
Brooklyn, NY 718-522-4500
Cocomira Confections
Toronto, ON 866-413-9049
Confection Solutions
Sylmar, CA 800-284-2422
Crown Candy Corporation
Macon, GA 800-241-3529
Cummings Studio Chocolates
Salt Lake City, UT 800-537-3957
D'Artagnan
Newark, NJ 800-327-8246
Da Vinci Gourmet
Seattle, WA 800-640-6779
Dare Foods
Kitchener, ON. 800-265-8225
Daymar Select Fine Coffees
El Cajon, CA. 800-466-7590
DE Wolfgang Candy Company
York, PA 800-248-4273
Dessert Innovations
Atlanta, GA. 800-359-7351
Desserts by David Glass
South Windsor, CT 860-462-7520
Dipasa
Brownsville, TX 956-831-5893
Donaldson's Finer Chocolates
Lebanon, IN 800-975-7236
East Shore Specialty Foods
Hartland, WI 800-236-1069

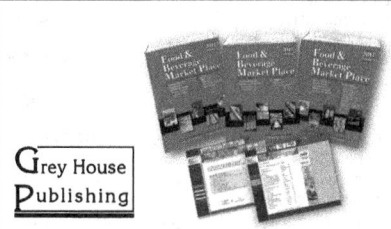

Eda's Sugarfree Candies
Philadelphia, PA 215-324-3412
Elmer Candy Corporation
Ponchatoula, LA 800-843-9537
Enstrom Candies
Grand Junction, CO 800-367-8766
Euro Chocolate Fountain
San Diego, CA 800-423-9303
Fabio Imports
Oceanside, CA 760-726-7040
Faroh Candies
Cleveland, OH 440-888-9866
Fastachi
Watertown, MA 800-466-3022
Figamajigs
Petaluma, CA 707-992-0023
Fine Foods Northwest
Seattle, WA 800-862-3965
Fitzkee's Candies
York, PA 717-741-1031
Fran's Chocolates
Seattle, WA 800-422-3726
Gardners Candies
Tyrone, PA 800-242-2639
GEM Berry Products
Sandpoint, ID 800-426-0498
Gene & Boots Candies
Perryopolis, PA 800-864-4222
Gertrude Hawk Chocolates
Dunmore, PA 800-706-6275
GH Bent Company
Milton, MA 617-698-5945
Ghirardelli Chocolate Company
San Leandro, CA 800-877-9338
Gloria Jean's Gourmet Coffees
Irvine, CA 877-320-5282
Golden Moon Tea
Herndon, VA 877-327-5473
Gorant Candies
Warren, OH 800-572-4139
Gourmedas Inc
Quebec, QC 418-210-3703
Govadinas Fitness Foods
San Diego, CA 800-900-0108
Gray & Company
Forest Grove, OR 503-357-3141
Green Mountain Chocolates
Franklin, MA 508-520-7160
H B Taylor Company
Chicago, IL 773-254-4805
H. Fox & Company
Brooklyn, NY 718-385-4600
Haven's Candies
Westbrook, ME 800-639-6309
Hawaiian Salrose Teas
Honolulu, HI 808-848-0500
Hialeah Products Company
Hollywood, FL 800-923-3379
Home Bakery
Laramie, WY 307-742-2721
Hospitality Mints
Boone, NC 800-334-5181
Hunt Country Foods
Middleburg, VA 540-364-2622
Island Princess
Honolulu, HI 866-872-8601
Ivydaro
Putney, VT 802-387-5597
Jason & Son Specialty Foods
Rancho Cordova, CA 800-810-9093
Jer's Handmade Chocolates
Solana Beach, CA 800-540-7265
John Kelly Chocolates
Los Angeles, CA 800-609-4243
Kamish Food Products
Chicago, IL 773-725-6959
Karl Bissinger French Confections
St Louis, MO 800-325-8881
Kemach Food Products Corporation
Brooklyn, NY 888-453-6224
Key III Candies
Fort Wayne, IN 800-752-2382
Knipschildt Chocolatier LLC
Norwalk, CT 203-838-3131
Koeze Company
Wyoming, MI 800-555-3909
Kopper's Chocolate
New York, NY 800-325-0026
Kozy Shack
Hicksville, NY 516-870-3000
Kraft Canada Headquarters
Don Mills, ON 888-572-3806

Landies Candies Company
Buffalo, NY 800-955-2634
Laymon Candy Company
San Bernardino, CA 909-825-4408
Lerro Candy Company
Darby, PA 610-461-8886
Liberty Richter
Saddle Brook, NJ 201-291-8749
Little Dutch Boy Bakeries
Draper, UT 801-571-3800
Log House Foods
Plymouth, MN 763-546-8395
Long Grove ConfectioneryCompany
Buffalo Grove, IL 800-373-3102
Lou-Retta's Custom Chocolates
Buffalo, NY 716-833-7111
Louis J. Rheb Candy Company
Baltimore, MD 800-514-8293
Lowery's Home Made Candies
Muncie, IN 800-541-3340
Lukas Confections
York, PA 717-843-0921
Lynch Foods
North York, ON 416-449-5464
Lyons-Magnus
Fresno, CA 559-268-5966
Mama Lee's Gourmet Hot Chocolate
Nashville, TN . . . . . 1 8-8 m-male
Masterson Company
Milwaukee, WI 414-647-1132
Matangos Candies
Harrisburg, PA 717-234-0882
Maxfield Candy
Salt Lake City, UT 800-288-8002
Merbs Candies
Saint Louis, MO 314-832-7117
Mille Lacs MP Company
Madison, WI 800-843-1381
Mona Lisa® Chocolatier
Arlington, VA 866-662-5475
Mont Blanc Gourmet
Denver, CO 800-877-3811
Moon Shine Trading Company
Woodland, CA 800-678-1226
Mooresville Ice Cream Company
Mooresville, NC 704-664-5456
Morse's Sauerkraut
Waldoboro, ME 866-832-5569
Munson's Chocolates
Bolton, CT 888-686-7667
Naron Mary Sue Candy Company
Baltimore, MD 800-662-2639
New England Confectionery Company
Revere, MA 781-485-4500
New England Natural Baker
Greenfield, MA 800-910-2884
Noble Ingredients
West Berlin, NJ
Northwest Chocolate Factory
Salem, OR 503-362-1340
Northwestern Foods
Saint Paul, MN 800-236-4937
Oak Leaf Confections
Scarborough, ON 877-261-7887
Old Fashioned Candy
Berwyn, IL 708-788-6669
Olde Tyme Mercantile
Arroyo Grande, CA 805-489-7991
Pacari Organic Chocolate
Miami, FL 561-214-4726
Paulaur Corporation
Cranbury, NJ 888-398-8844
Pecan Deluxe Candy Company
Dallas, TX 800-733-3589
PEZ Candy
Orange, CT 203-795-0531
Philadelphia Candies
Hermitage, PA 724-981-6341
Phillips Candies
Seaside, OR 503-738-5402
Phillips Syrup Corporation
Westlake, OH 800-350-8443
Pied-Mont/Dora
Ste Anne Des Plaines, QC 800-363-8003
Plantation Candies
Telford, PA 888-678-6468
Prince of Peace Enterprises
Hayward, CA 800-732-2328
Pulakos
Erie, PA 814-452-4026
Puratos Canada
Mississauga, ON 905-362-3668

Q Bell Foods
Nyack, NY 845-358-1475
Randag & Associates Inc
Elmhurst, IL 630-530-2830
Rapunzel Pure Organics
Bloomfield, NJ 800-225-1449
Rich Ice Cream Company
West Palm Beach, FL 561-833-7585
Roland Industries
Saint Louis, MO 800-325-1183
Rosalind Candy Castle
New Brighton, PA 724-843-1144
Royal Wine Corp
Bayonne, NJ 718-384-2400
Sara Lee Corporation
Downers Grove, IL 630-598-8100
Saxon Chocolates
Toronto, ON 416-675-6363
Sayklly's Candies & Gifts
Escanaba, MI 906-786-3092
Scharffen Berger Choclate Maker
San Francisco, CA 866-972-6879
Schratter Foods Inc
Fairfield, NJ 800-592-4337
Scott's Candy
Glennville, GA 800-356-2100
Sea Breeze Fruit Flavors
Towaco, NJ 800-732-2733
See's Candies
Carson, CA 800-347-7337
Seth Ellis Chocolatier
Boulder, CO 720-565-2462
Shade Foods
New Century, KS 800-225-6312
Shakespeare's
Davenport, IA 800-664-4114
Shane Candy Company
Philadelphia, PA 215-922-1048
Sherwood Brands
Rockville, MD 401-434-7773
Shoreline Chocolates
Alburg, VT 800-310-3730
Snack Works/Metrovox Snacks
Orange, CA 800-783-9870
Spice Rack Chocolates
Fredericksburg, VA 540-847-2063
Stutz Candy Company
Hatboro, PA 888-692-2639
Sucesores de Pedro Cortes
San Juan, PR 787-754-7040
Sweet Shop
La Crosse, WI 608-784-7724
Sweet Traders
Huntington Beach, CA 714-903-6800
Sweetbliss by Ilene C Shane
New York, NY
TCHO Ventures
San Francisco, CA 415-981-0189
Terri Lynn
Elgin, IL 800-323-0775
Theo Chocolate
Seattle, WA 206-632-5100
Tonex
Wallington, NJ 973-773-5135
Tropical Nut & Fruit Company
Orlando, FL 800-749-8869
US Chocolate Corporation
Brooklyn, NY 718-788-8555
V Chocolates
Salt Lake City, UT 801-269-8444
Valley View Blueberries
Vancouver, WA 360-892-2839
Vermont Confectionery
Bennington, VT 800-545-9243
Vigneri Confections
Rochester, NY 877-843-6374
Vintage Chocolate Imports
Newark, NJ 800-207-7058
Vrymeer Commodities
St Charles, IL 630-584-0069
Weaver Nut Company
Ephrata, PA 717-738-3781
Webbs Citrus Candy
Davenport, FL 863-422-1051
Western Syrup Company
Santa Fe Springs, CA 562-921-4485
William Bounds
Torrance, CA 800-473-0504
Wilson Candy Company
Jeannette, PA 724-523-3151
Wisconsin Cheese
Melrose Park, IL 708-450-0074

World Confections
Brooklyn, NY 718-768-8100
World's Finest Chocolate
Chicago, IL 888-821-8452
Yoo-Hoo Chocolate Beverage Company
Carlstadt, NJ 201-933-0070
Zitner Company
Philadelphia, PA 215-229-4990

Baking Chocolate

Ghirardelli Chocolate Company
San Leandro, CA 800-877-9338

Boxed Chocolate

Abdallah Candies
Burnsville, MN 800-348-7328
AmeriCandy Company
Louisville, KY 502-583-1776
Andes Candy
Chicago, IL 773-838-3400
Ann Hemyng Candy
Trumbauersville, PA 800-779-7004
Astor Chocolate
Lakewood, NJ 732-901-1000
Bissinger's Handcrafted Chocolatier
St Louis, MO 800-325-8881
Boca Bons East,LLC.
Greenacres, FL 800-314-2835
Bohemian Biscuit Company
South San Francisco, CA 650-952-2226
Brockmann Chocolates
Delta, BC 888-494-2270
Brown & Haley
Tacoma, WA 253-620-3000
Buddy Squirrel LLC
Milwaukee, WI 800-972-2658
Cella's Confections
Chicago, IL 773-838-3400
Charlotte's Confections
Millbrae, CA 800-798-2427
Chocolates a La Carte
Valencia, CA 800-818-2462
Chocolates by Mark
La Porte, TX 832-736-2626
Chocolates Turin
Plano, TX 972-731-6771
Chris A. Papas & Son Company
Covington, KY 859-431-0499
Clarks Joe Fund Raising Candies & Novelties
Tarentum, PA 888-459-9520
Claudia B Chocolates
San Antonio, TX 210-366-0319
Cocoline Chocolate Company
Brooklyn, NY 718-522-4500
Da Vinci Gourmet
Seattle, WA 800-640-6779
David Bradley Chocolatier
Windsor, NJ 877-289-7933
Elmer Candy Corporation
Ponchatoula, LA 800-843-9537
Empress Chocolate Company
Brooklyn, NY 800-793-3809
Fannie May/Fanny Farmer
Chicago, IL 800-333-3629
Faroh Candies
Cleveland, OH 440-888-9866
Fenton & Lee Chocolatiers
Eugene, OR 800-336-8661
Frankford Candy & Chocolate Company
Philadelphia, PA 800-523-9090
Functional Foods
Roseville, MI 877-372-0550
Ganong Bros Limited Corporate Office
St. Stephen, NB 888-426-6647
Gertrude Hawk Chocolates
Dunmore, PA 800-822-2032
Godiva Chocolatier
New York, NY 800-946-3482
Gold Star Chocolate
Brooklyn, NY 718-330-0187
Gorant Candies
Warren, OH 800-572-4139
Gray & Company
Forest Grove, OR 800-551-6009
Hagensborg Chocolates LTD.
Burnaby, BC 877-554-7763
Harbor Sweets
Salem, MA 800-234-4887
Harry London Candies Inc
North Canton, OH 800-321-0444
Hauser Chocolate
Westerly, RI 888-599-8231
Hawaiian King Candies
Honolulu, HI 800-570-1902
Hershey Company
Hershey, PA 800-468-1714
Hibiscus Aloha Corporation
Honolulu, HI 808-591-8826
Hillside Candy
Hillside, NJ 800-524-1304
Horriea 2000 Food Industries
Reynolds, GA 478-847-4186
Joyva Corporation
Brooklyn, NY 718-497-0170
Koeze Company
Wyoming, MI 800-555-3909
Lammes Candies Since 1885
Austin, TX 800-252-1885
Liberty Orchards Company
Cashmere, WA 800-888-5696
Lindt & Sprungli
Stratham, NH 800-338-0839
Long Grove ConfectioneryCompany
Buffalo Grove, IL 800-373-3102
Maggie Lyon Chocolatiers
Norcross, GA 800-969-3500
Maramor Chocolates
Columbus, OH 800-843-7722
Marshmallow Cone Company
Cincinnati, OH 800-641-8551
Maxfield Candy
Salt Lake City, UT 800-288-8002
Michele's Chocolate Truffles
Clackamas, OR 800-656-7112
Mona Lisa® Chocolatier
Arlington, VA 866-662-5475
Munson's Chocolates
Bolton, CT 888-686-7667
Naron Mary Sue Candy Company
Baltimore, MD 800-662-2639
Nestle USA Inc
Glendale, CA 800-225-2270
Niagara Chocolates
Cheektowaga, NY 800-234-5750
Olympia Candies
Cleveland, OH 800-574-7747
Over The Moon Chocolate Company Ltd
Vancouver, BC 800-933-2462
Patsy's Candies
Colorado Springs, CO 866-372-8797
Peanut Patch
Yuma, AZ 800-872-7688
Piedmont Candy Corporation
Lexington, NC 336-248-2477
Queen Bee Gardens
Lovell, WY 800-225-7553
R.M. Palmer Company
Reading, PA 610-372-8971
Rene Rey Chocolates Ltd
North Vancouver, BC 888-985-0949
Reutter Candy & Chocolates
Baltimore, MD 800-392-0870
RM Palmer Company
Reading, PA 610-372-8971
Rogers' Chocolates Ltd
Victoria, BC 800-663-2220
Russell Stover Candies
Kansas City, MO 800-477-8683
Sanders Candy
Clinton Twp, MI 800-852-2253
Scott's Candy
Glennville, GA 800-356-2100
Seattle Chocolate Company
Tukwila, WA 800-334-3600
Stutz Candy Company
Hatboro, PA 888-692-2639
Susie's South 40 Confections
Midland, TX 800-221-4442
Sweet Blessings
Malibu, CA 310-317-1172
Sweet Works
St Augustine, FL 877-261-7887
Tootsie Roll Industries
Chicago, IL 800-877-7655
Trophy Nut
Tipp City, OH 800-219-9004
Vande Walle's Candies
Appleton, WI 920-738-7799
Vrymeer Commodities
St Charles, IL 630-584-0069
Wilson Candy Company
Jeannette, PA 724-523-3151
Wisconsin Cheese
Melrose Park, IL 708-450-0074
World Confections
Brooklyn, NY 718-768-8100
Zachary Confections
Frankfort, IN 800-445-4222
Zitner Company
Philadelphia, PA 215-229-4990

Carob Ingredients

Naturex Inc.
South Hackensack, NJ 201-440-5000

Chocolate Bars

Chris Candies
Pittsburgh, PA 412-322-9400
Dina's Organic Chocolate
Mt Kisco, NY 888-625-2008
Divine Chocolate
Washington, DC 202-332-8913
Eda's Sugarfree Candies
Philadelphia, PA 215-324-3412
Funkychunky Inc.
Edina, MN 888-473-8659
Greenwell Farms
Morganfield, KY 270-389-3289
Malie Kai Hawaiian Chocolates
Honolulu, HI 808-599-8600
Munson's Chocolates
Bolton, CT 888-686-7667
New England Confectionery Company
Revere, MA 781-485-4500
Travel Chocolate
New York, NY 718-841-7030

Chocolate Candy

Abbott's Candy Shop
Hagerstown, IN 877-801-1200
Acme Candy Company
Arlington, TX 254-634-2825
Aglamesis Brothers
Cincinnati, OH 513-531-5196
Alexandra & Nicolay
Brooklyn, NY 718-253-9400
All American Snacks
Midland, TX 800-840-2455
All Wrapped Up
Plantation, FL 800-891-2194
Alma-Leo
Buffalo Grove, IL 847-821-0411
Ambassador Foods
Van Nuys, CA 800-338-3369
Ameri-Suisse Group
Plainfield, NJ 908-222-1001
American Nut & Chocolate Company
Boston, MA 800-797-6887
AmeriGift
Oxnard, CA 800-421-9039
Amour Chocolates
Albuquerque, NM 505-881-2803
Amros the Second, Inc.
Somerset, NJ 732-846-7755
Amster-Kirtz Company
Canton, OH 800-257-9338
Andes Candy
Chicago, IL 773-838-3400
Andre Prost
Old Saybrook, CT 800-243-0897
Andre's Confiserie Suisse
Kansas City, MO 800-892-1234
Ann Hemyng Candy
Trumbauersville, PA 800-779-7004
Anthony-Thomas Candy Company
Columbus, OH 877-226-3921
Archibald Candy Corporation
Chicago, IL 800-333-3629
Art CoCo Chocolate Company
Denver, CO 800-779-8985
Ashers Chocolates
Lewistown, PA 800-343-0520
Assouline & Ting
Huntingdon Valley, PA 800-521-4491
Athena's Silverland®Desserts
Forest Park, IL 800-737-3636
Aunt Sally's Praline Shops, Inc.
New Orleans, LA 800-642-7257
B&B Pecan Processors of NC
Turkey, NC 866-328-7322
Baker Candy Company
Snohomish, WA 425-422-6331

Baker Maid Products, Inc.
New Orleans, LA 504-827-5500
Bakers Candy
Greenwood, NE 800-804-7330
Banner Candy Manufacturing Company
Brooklyn, NY 718-647-4747
Baraboo Candy Company
Baraboo, WI 800-967-1690
Bari & Gail
Walpole, MA 800-828-9318
Barricini Chocolate
Avoca, PA 570-457-6756
Barry Callebaut USA LLC
Saint Albans, VT 800-556-8845
Barry Callebaut USA LLC
Chicago, IL 866-443-0460
Bee Int'l., Inc
Chula Vista, CA 800-421-6465
Ben Heggy's Candy Company
Canton, OH 330-455-7703
Bergen Marzipan & Chocolate
Bergenfield, NJ 201-385-8343
Best Chocolate In Town
Indianapolis, IN 888-294-2378
Bidwell Candies
Mattoon, IL 217-234-3858
Birnn Chocolates
Highland Park, NJ 732-545-4400
Birnn Chocolates of Vermont
South Burlington, VT 800-338-3141
Biscomerica Corporation
Rialto, CA 909-877-5997
Black Hound New York
Brooklyn, NY 800-344-4417
Blanton's
Sweetwater, TN 423-337-3487
Blommer Chocolate Company
East Greenville, PA 800-825-8181
Bloomer Candy Company
Zanesville, OH 800-452-7501
Bluebird Restaurant
Logan, UT 435-752-3155
Boca Bons East,LLC.
Greenacres, FL 800-314-2835
Bogdon Candy Company
Canajoharie, NY 800-839-8938

Bohemian Biscuit Company
South San Francisco, CA 650-952-2226
Bourbon Ball
Louisville, KY 800-280-0888
Boyer Candy Company
Altoona, PA 814-944-9401
Bread & Chocolate
Wells River, VT 800-524-6715
Brechet & Richter Company
Minneapolis, MN 763-545-0201
Brockmann Chocolates
Delta, BC 888-494-2270
Bt. McElrath Chocolatier
Minneapolis, MN 612-331-8800
Buddy Squirrel LLC
Milwaukee, WI 800-972-2658
Byrne & Carlson
Portsmouth, NH 888-559-9778
Caiazza Candy Company
New Castle, PA 800-651-1171
Callard & Bowser-Suchard
White Plains, NY 877-226-3900
Cambridge Brands
Cambridge, MA 617-491-2500
Cameo Confections
Bay Village, OH 440-871-5732
Campbell Soup Company
Camden, NJ 800-257-8443
Candy Factory
Hayward, CA 800-736-6887
Candy Flowers
Mentor, OH 888-476-6467
Canelake's
Virginia, MN 888-928-8889
Caribbean Cookie Company
Virginia Beach, VA 800-326-5200
Carolyn Candies
Clermont, FL 352-394-8555
Carousel Candies
Geneva, IL 888-656-1552
Carrie's Chocolates
Edmonton, AB 877-778-2462
Cella's Confections
Chicago, IL 773-838-3400
Charlotte's Confections
Millbrae, CA 800-798-2427

Chase Candy Company
Saint Joseph, MO 800-786-1625
Chevalier Chocolates
Enfield, CT 860-741-3330
Chocoholics Divine Desserts
Linden, CA 800-760-2462
Chocolat Belge Heyez
St-Lazare-De-Bellechasse, QC 450-653-5616
Chocolat Jean Talon
Montreal, QC 888-333-8540
Chocolate Creations
Glendale, CA 800-229-4140
Chocolate House
Milwaukee, WI 800-236-2022
Chocolate Moon
Asheville, NC 800-723-1236
Chocolate Street of Hartville
Hartville, OH 888-853-5904
Chocolate Studio
Norristown, PA 610-272-3872
Chocolaterie Bernard Callebaut
Calgary, AB 800-661-8367
Chocolaterie Stam
Des Moines, IA 877-782-6246
Chocolates a La Carte
Valencia, CA 800-818-2462
Chocolates by Mark
La Porte, TX 832-736-2626
Chocolates by Mr. Robert
Boca Raton, FL 561-392-3007
Chocolates El Rey
Fredericksburg, TX 830-997-2200
Chocolati Handmade Chocolates
Seattle, WA 206-784-5212
Chocolatier
Exeter, NH 888-246-5528
Chocolove
Boulder, CO 888-246-2656
Chris A. Papas & Son Company
Covington, KY 859-431-0499
Chris Candies
Pittsburgh, PA 412-322-9400
Christopher Norman Chocolates
New York, NY 212-402-1243
Clarks Joe Fund Raising Candies & Novelties
Tarentum, PA 888-459-9520

Clasen Quality Coatings
Madison, WI 877-459-4500
Classic Confectionery
Fort Worth, TX 800-674-4435
Clear-Vu Industries
Ashland, MA. 508-881-9100
Cloud Nine
San Leandro, CA. 201-358-8588
CNS Confectionery Products
Bayonne, NJ 888-823-4330
Colts Chocolates
Nashville, TN 615-251-0100
Confection Solutions
Sylmar, CA 800-284-2422
Consolidated Brands
Altoona, PA. 814-941-2200
Consolidated Simon Distributor
Union, NJ 973-674-2124
Consup North America
Lincoln Park, NJ. 973-628-7330
Cora Italian Specialties
La Grange, IL 800-969-2672
Cowgirl Chocolates
Moscow, ID. 888-882-4098
Creative Confections
Northbrook, IL 608-455-1448
Criterion Chocolates
Eatontown, NJ. 800-804-6060
Croft's Crackers
Monroe, WI. 608-325-1223
Crown Candy Corporation
Macon, GA 800-241-3529
Cummings Studio Chocolates
Salt Lake City, UT 800-537-3957
Dairy Management
Rosemont, IL. 800-248-8829
Daniele Imports
Rochester, NY. 800-298-9410
Daprano & Company
Charlotte, NC 877-365-2337
Dare Foods
Kitchener, ON. 800-265-8225
David Bradley Chocolatier
Windsor, NJ. 877-289-7933
Davidson of Dundee
Dundee, FL 800-294-2266
Daymar Select Fine Coffees
El Cajon, CA. 800-466-7590
Dayton Nut Specialties
Dayton, OH. 800-548-1304
De Bas Chocolate
Fresno, CA 888-461-1276
De Bas Chocolatier
Fresno, CA 559-294-7638
DE Wolfgang Candy Company
York, PA 800-248-4273
Delancey Dessert Company
New York, NY 800-254-5254
Dessert Innovations
Atlanta, GA. 800-359-7351
DGZ Chocolates
Houston, TX 877-949-9444
Dilettante Chocolates
Kent, WA. 888-600-2462
Dipasa
Brownsville, TX 956-831-5893
Divine Delights
Petaluma, CA 800-443-2836
Dolphin Natural Chocolates
Cambria, CA. 800-236-5744
Donaldson's Finer Chocolates
Lebanon, IN 800-975-7236
Donells' Candies
Casper, WY. 877-461-2009
Doscher's Candies
Cincinnati, OH 513-381-8656

Double Play Foods
New York, NY. 212-682-4611
Dundee Brandied Fruit Company
Dundee, OR. 503-537-2500
Dundee Candy Shop
Louisville, KY 502-452-9266
Ed & Don's Candies
Honolulu, HI 808-423-8200
Eda's Sugarfree Candies
Philadelphia, PA 215-324-3412
Emmy's Candy from Belgium
Charlotte, NC 704-588-5445
Endangered Species Chocolate
Indianapolis, IN 800-293-0160
Esther Price Candies & Gifts
Dayton, OH. 800-782-0326
Euphoria Chocolate Company
Eugene, OR. 541-344-4914
Evans Creole Candy Company
New Orleans, LA 800-637-6675
Fairytale Brownies
Phoenix, AZ 800-324-7982
Fancy's Candy's
Rougemont, NC 888-403-2629
Fannie May Fine Chocolat
Melrose Park, IL. 800-999-3629
Fantasy Chocolates
Delray Beach, FL 800-804-4962
Farb's
San Luis Obispo, CA 805-543-1412
Farley's & Sathers Candy Company
Round Lake, MN 800-533-0330
Faroh Candies
Cleveland, OH 440-888-9866
Fauchon
New York, NY 877-605-0130
Fenton & Lee Chocolatiers
Eugene, OR. 800-336-8661
Ferrero Usa
Somerset, NJ. 800-337-7376
Fitzkee's Candies
York, PA 717-741-1031
Flaherty
Skokie, IL 847-966-1005
Foley's Candies
Richmond, BC 888-236-5397
Forbes Chocolate
Broadview Hgts, OH 800-433-1090
Fralinger's
Atlantic City, NJ 800-938-2339
Frankford Candy & Chocolate Company
Philadelphia, PA 800-523-9090
Frolic Candy Company
Farmingdale, NY 516-756-2255
Functional Foods
Roseville, MI 877-372-0550
Ganong Bros Limited Corporate Office
St. Stephen, NB. 888-426-6647
Gardners Candies
Tyrone, PA. 800-242-2639
Garry Packing
Del Rey, CA 800-248-2126
Gene & Boots Candies
Perryopolis, PA. 800-864-4222
Genesee Farms
Oakfield, NY. 585-948-9418
Georgia Nut Ingredients
Skokie, IL 877-674-2993
Germack Pistachio Company
Detroit, MI 800-872-4006
Gertrude Hawk Chocolates
Dunmore, PA. 800-822-2032
Ghirardelli Chocolate Company
San Leandro, CA. 800-877-9338
Ghyslain Chocolatier
Union City, IN. 866-449-7524
GKI Foods
Brighton, MI 248-486-0055
Godiva Chocolatier
New York, NY 800-946-3482
Gold Star Chocolate
Brooklyn, NY 718-330-0187
Goldenberg Candy Company
Philadelphia, PA 800-727-2439
Golf Mill Chocolate Factory
Niles, IL 847-635-1107
Gorant Candies
Warren, OH. 800-572-4139
Govatos
Wilmington, DE 888-799-5252
Gray & Company
Forest Grove, OR 800-551-6009

Great Expectations Confectionery Gourmet Foods
Chicago, IL 773-525-4865
Green County Foods
Monroe, WI. 800-233-3564
Green Mountain Chocolates
Franklin, MA 508-520-7160
Greenwell Farms
Morganfield, KY. 270-389-3289
Gregg Candy & Nut Company
Munhall, PA 412-461-0301
Gurley's Foods
Willmar, MN 800-426-7845
H E Williams Candy Company
Chesapeake, VA 757-545-9311
Hagensborg Chocolates LTD.
Burnaby, BC 877-554-7763
Harbor Sweets
Salem, MA 800-234-4887
Hauser Chocolate
Westerly, RI. 888-599-8231
Hauser Chocolates
Westerly, RI. 800-289-8783
Haven's Candies
Westbrook, ME. 800-639-6309
Hawaiian Candies & Nuts
Honolulu, HI 808-841-3344
Hawaiian Host
Honolulu, HI. 888-529-4678
Hawaiian King Candies
Honolulu, HI. 800-570-1902
Hawaiian Salrose Teas
Honolulu, HI. 808-848-0500
Hebert Candies
Shrewsbury, MA. 866-432-3781
Helen Grace Chocolates
Lynwood, CA 800-367-4240
Helms Candy Company
Bristol, VA 276-669-2612
Hershey Canada Inc
Mississauga, ON. 800-468-1714
Hershey Chocolate & Confectionery Division
Pleasanton, CA 925-460-0359
Hershey Company
Hershey, PA. 800-468-1714
Hershey International
Weston, FL 954-385-2600
Hialeah Products Company
Hollywood, FL 800-923-3379
Hibiscus Aloha Corporation
Honolulu, HI. 808-591-8826
Hillside Candy
Hillside, NJ. 800-524-1304
Horriea 2000 Food Industries
Reynolds, GA 478-847-4186
Hospitality Mints
Boone, NC. 800-334-5181
Huppen Bakery
Los Angeles, CA. 323-656-7501
Hyde Candy Company
Seattle, WA 206-322-5743
Idaho Candy Company
Boise, ID. 800-898-6986
Image Development
San Rafael, CA 415-626-0485
Imperial Nougat Company
Santa Fe Springs, CA 562-693-8423
Intergum North America
Winston Salem, NC. 336-760-5420
International Leisure Activities
Springfield, OH. 800-782-7448
Issimo Food Group
La Jolla, CA 619-260-1900
Jason & Son Specialty Foods
Rancho Cordova, CA 800-810-9093
Jerbeau Chocolate
Camarillo, CA. 800-755-3723
Jeryl's Jems
Tappan, NY. 201-236-8372
Jo's Candies
Torrance, CA. 800-770-1946
Joseph Schmidt Confections
Hershey, PA. 866-237-0152
Josh Early Candies
Allentown, PA. 610-395-4321
Kara Chocolates
Orem, UT 800-284-5272
Karl Bissinger French Confections
St Louis, MO. 800-325-8881
Kastner's Pastry Shop & Grocery
Surfside, FL 305-866-6993
Kate Latter Candy Company
New Orleans, LA 800-825-5359

Kellbran Candies & Snacks
Akron, OH 330-794-1448
Kelly's Candies
Pittsburgh, PA 800-523-3051
Kemach Food Products Corporation
Brooklyn, NY 888-453-6224
Kennedy Gourmet
Houston, TX 800-882-6253
Key III Candies
Fort Wayne, IN 800-752-2382
Koeze Company
Wyoming, MI 800-555-3909
Kopper's Chocolate
New York, NY 800-325-0026
L C Good Candy Company
Allentown, PA 610-432-3290
Lake Champlain Chocolates
Burlington, VT 800-465-5909
Lanco
Hauppauge, NY 800-938-4500
Landies Candies Company
Buffalo, NY 800-955-2634
Laymon Candy Company
San Bernardino, CA 909-825-4408
Lazzaroni USA
Saddle Brook, NJ 201-368-1240
Len Libby's Candy Shop
Scarborough, ME 207-883-4897
Les Chocolats Vadeboncoeur
Montreal, QC 800-276-8504
Lieber Chocolate & Food Products
Brooklyn, NY 718-499-0888
Lindt & Sprungli
Stratham, NH 800-338-0839
Linette Quality Chocolates
Womelsdorf, PA 610-589-4526
Long Grove ConfectioneryCompany
Buffalo Grove, IL 800-373-3102
Longford-Hamilton Company
Beaverton, OR 503-642-5661
Loretta's Authentic Pralines
New Orleans, LA 504-529-6170
Lou-Retta's Custom Chocolates
Buffalo, NY 716-833-7111
Louis J. Rheb Candy Company
Baltimore, MD 800-514-8293
Lowery's Home Made Candies
Muncie, IN 800-541-3340
Lucille's Own Make Candies
Manahawkin, NJ 800-426-9168
Lukas Confections
York, PA 717-843-0921
Lynard Company
Stamford, CT 203-323-0231
Madrona Specialty Foods
Tukwila, WA 425-814-2500
Maggie Lyon Chocolatiers
Norcross, GA 800-969-3500
Manhattan Chocolates
Bayonne, NJ 201-339-6886
Mantrose-Haeuser Company
Westport, CT 800-344-4229
Maramor Chocolates
Columbus, OH 800-843-7722
Marich Confectionery Company
Hollister, CA 800-624-7055
Marlow Candy & Nut Company
Englewood, NJ 201-569-7606
Marshmallow Products
Cincinnati, OH 800-641-8551
Marsyl
Cody, WY 307-527-6277
Mary of Puddin Hill
Greenville, TX 800-545-8889
Mary Sue Candies
Baltimore, MD 410-467-9338
Masterfoods USA
Hackettstown, NJ 908-852-1000
Masterson Company
Milwaukee, WI 414-647-1132
Maxfield Candy
Salt Lake City, UT 800-288-8002
Mayfair Sales
Buffalo, NY 800-248-2881
Merbs Candies
Saint Louis, MO 314-832-7117
Merlin Candies
Harahan, LA 800-899-1549
Michele's Chocolate Truffles
Clackamas, OR 800-656-7112
Michelle Chocolatiers
Colorado Springs, CO 888-447-3654

Miesse Candies
Lancaster, PA 717-397-9415
Mille Lacs MP Company
Madison, WI 800-843-1381
Minter Weisman Company
Minneapolis, MN 800-742-5655
Mom 'N Pops
New Windsor, NY 866-368-6767
Mona Lisa Food Products
Hendersonville, NC 800-982-2546
Monogramme Confections
St Louis, MO 888- 56- 409
Moon Shine Trading Company
Woodland, CA 800-678-1226
Moore's Candies
Baltimore, MD 410-426-2705
Mooresville Ice Cream Company
Mooresville, NC 704-664-5456
Morris National
Azusa, CA 626-385-2000
Mrs. London's Confections
Swampscott, MA 781-595-8140
Munson's Chocolates
Bolton, CT 888-686-7667
Muth Candies
Louisville, KY 502-585-2952
Mutiflex Company
Wyckoff, NJ 201-447-3888
Nancy's Candy
Meadows Of Dan, VA 800-328-3834
Naron Mary Sue Candy Company
Baltimore, MD 800-662-2639
Nassau Candy Company
Hicksville, NY 516-433-7100
Natural Rush
San Francisco, CA 415-863-2503
Neal's Chocolates
Salt Lake City, UT 801-521-6500
Nestle Infant Nutrition
Florham Park, NJ
Nestle USA Inc
Glendale, CA 800-225-2270
Neuchatel Chocolates
Oxford, PA 800-597-0759
New England Confectionery Company
Revere, MA 781-485-4500
New England Natural Baker
Greenfield, MA 800-910-2884
Newton Candy Company
Houston, TX 713-691-6969
Niagara Chocolates
Cheektowaga, NY 800-234-5750
Nora's Candy Shop
Rome, NY 888-544-8224
Northern Flair Foods
Mound, MN 888-530-4453
Northwest Chocolate Factory
Salem, OR 503-362-1340
Novelty Specialties
Ontaria, CA 800-231-5309
NSpired Natural Foods
Boulder, CO 800-434-4246
Nunes Farm Almonds
Newman, CA 209-862-3033
Oak Leaf Confections
Scarborough, ON 877-261-7887
OH Chocolate
Calgary, AB 800-887-3959
Old Dominion Peanut Corporation
Norfolk, VA 800-368-6887
Old Fashioned Candy
Berwyn, IL 708-788-6669
Old Monmouth Peanut Brittle
Freehold, NJ 732-462-1311
Olde Tyme Mercantile
Arroyo Grande, CA 805-489-7991
Olivier's Candies
Calgary, AB 403-266-6028
Omanhene Cocoa Bean Company
Milwaukee, WI 800-588-2462
OraLabs
Parker, CO 800-290-0577
Over The Moon Chocolate Company Ltd
Vancouver, BC 800-933-2462
Pacific Gold Marketing
Fresno, CA
Palmer Candy Company
Sioux City, IA 800-831-0828
Pangburn Candy Company
Fort Worth, TX 817-332-8856
Paron Chocolatier
New York, NY 800-326-5033

Patsy's Candies
Colorado Springs, CO 866-372-8797
Paul's Candy Factory
Salt Lake City, UT 800-825-9912
Paulaur Corporation
Cranbury, NJ 888-398-8844
Peanut Patch
Yuma, AZ 800-872-7688
Pearl River Pastry & Chocolates
Pearl River, NY 800-632-2639
Pease's Candy Shoppe
Springfield, IL 217-523-3721
Pecan Deluxe Candy Company
Dallas, TX 800-733-3589
Pegi
Santa Ana, CA 800-292-3353
Penhurst Candy Company
Pittsburgh, PA 800-545-1336
Pennsylvania Dutch Candies
Camp Hill, PA 800-233-7082
Pfeil & Holing
Woodside, NY 800-247-7955
Phillips Candies
Seaside, OR 503-738-5402
Pine River Pre-Pack
Newton, WI 920-726-4216
Pippin Snack Pecans
Albany, GA 800-554-6887
Pittsburgh Snax & Nut Company
Pittsburgh, PA 800-404-6887
Plantation Candies
Telford, PA 888-678-6468
Plyley's Candies
Lagrange, IN 260-463-3351
Prifti Candy Company
Worcester, MA 800-447-7438
Prince of Peace Enterprises
Hayward, CA 800-732-2328
Pulakos
Erie, PA 814-452-4026
Purity Candy Company
Lewisburg, PA 800-821-4748
Queen Bee Gardens
Lovell, WY 800-225-7553
Quintessential Chocolates Company
Fredericksburg, TX 830-990-9382
Qzina Specialty Foods
Las Vegas, NV 702-451-3916
R.L. Albert & Son
Greenwich, CT 203-622-8655
Ragold Confections
Wilton Manors, FL 954-566-9092
Randag & Associates Inc
Elmhurst, IL 630-530-2830
Rebecca Ruth Candy
Frankfort, KY 800-444-3866
Rene Rey Chocolates Ltd
North Vancouver, BC 888-985-0949
Reutter Candy & Chocolates
Baltimore, MD 800-392-0870
Richard Donnelly Fine Chtes
Santa Cruz, CA 888-685-1871
Riddles' Sweet Impressions
Edmonton, AB 780-465-8085
Riverdale Fine Foods
Dayton, OH 800-548-1304
RM Palmer Company
Reading, PA 610-372-8971
Rogers' Chocolates Ltd
Victoria, BC 800-663-2220
Rosalind Candy Castle
New Brighton, PA 724-843-1144
Rosetti Fine Foods
Clovis, CA 559-323-6450
Roseville Corporation
Mountain View, CA 888-247-9338
Royal Baltic
Brooklyn, NY 718-385-8300
Royal Wine Corp
Bayonne, NJ 718-384-2400
S. Zitner Company
Philadelphia, PA 215-229-4990
S.L. Kaye Company
New York, NY 212-683-5600
S.P. Enterprises
Las Vegas, NV 800-746-4774
Sahagian & Associates
Oak Park, IL 800-327-9273
Sanders Candy
Clinton Twp, MI 800-852-2253
Sayklly's Candies & Gifts
Escanaba, MI 906-786-3092

Scharffen Berger Chocolate Maker
San Francisco, CA 866- 60- 694
Scott's Candy
Glennville, GA 800-356-2100
Seattle Bar Company
Seattle, WA 206-601-4301
Seattle Chocolate Company
Tukwila, WA 800-334-3600
Seattle Gourmet Foods
Kent, WA 800-800-9490
Setton International Foods
Commack, NY 800-227-4397
Shakespeare's
Davenport, IA 800-664-4114
Shane Candy Company
Philadelphia, PA 215-922-1048
Sherm Edwards Candies
Trafford, PA 800-436-5424
Sherwood Brands
Rockville, MD 301-309-6161
Sherwood Brands
Rockville, MD 401-434-7773
Sifers Valomilk Candy Company
Shawnee Mission, KS 913-722-0991
Silver Sweet Candies
Lawrence, MA 978-688-0474
Simply Lite Foods Corporation
Commack, NY 800-753-4282
Smith Enterprises
Rock Hill, SC 800-845-8311
Sorbee Intl.
Feasterville Trevose, PA 800-654-3997
South Beach Novelties & Confectionery
Staten Island, NY 718-727-4500
South Bend Chocolate
South Bend, IN 800-301-4961
SP Enterprises
Las Vegas, NV 800-746-4774
Spangler Candy Company
Bryan, OH 888-636-4221
Spokandy Wedding Mints
Spokane, WA 509-624-1969
Sporting Colors LLC
St. Louis, MO 888-394-2292
Squirrel Brand Company
McKinney, TX 800-624-8242
St. Jacobs Candy Company Brittles 'n More
Waterloo, ON 519-884-3505
Stanchfield Farms
Milo, ME 207-732-5173
Standard Candy Company
Nashville, TN 800-226-4340
Stephany's Chocolates
Arvada, CO 800-888-1522
Sterling Candy
Hicksville, NY 516-932-8300
Stewart Candy Company
Waycross, GA 912-284-9320
Storck
Chicago, IL 800-621-7772
Stutz Candy Company
Hatboro, PA 888-692-2639
Sucesores de Pedro Cortes
San Juan, PR 787-754-7040
Suity Confection Company
Miami, FL 305-639-3300
Sun Empire Foods
Kerman, CA 800-252-4786
Supreme Chocolatier
Staten Island, NY 718-761-9600
Susie's South 40 Confections
Midland, TX 800-221-4442
Sweenor Chocolate
Wakefield, RI 800-834-3123
Sweet Blessings
Malibu, CA 310-317-1172
Sweet Candy Company
Salt Lake City, UT 800-669-8669
Sweet Shop
La Crosse, WI 608-784-7724
Sweet Shop
Mount Pleasant, TX 800-222-2269
Sweet Shop USA
Mt Pleasant, TX 800-222-2269
Sweet Shop USA
Mt Pleasant, TX 903-575-0033
Sweet Works
St Augustine, FL 877-261-7887
Sweet'N Low
Brooklyn, NY 718-858-4200
Tapper Candies
Cleveland, OH 216-825-1000
Tell Chocolate Corporation
Barnegat, NJ
Testamints
Randolph, NJ 888-879-0400
The Madelaine Chocolate Company
Rockaway Beach, NY 800-322-1505
Thompson Candy Company
Meriden, CT 800-648-4058
Toe-Food Chocolates and Candy
Berkeley, CA 888-863-3663
Tom & Sally's Handmade Chocolates
Brattleboro, VT 800-827-0800
Tootsie Roll Industries
Chicago, IL 800-877-7655
Totally Chocolate
Blaine, WA 800-255-5506
Toucan Chocolates
Waban, MA 617-964-8696
Trappistine Quality Candy
Wrentham, MA 86- 5-9 89
Tremblay's Sweet Shop
Hayward, WI 715-634-2785
Triple-C
Hamilton, ON 800-263-9105
Trophy Nut
Tipp City, OH 800-219-9004
Tropical Nut & Fruit Company
Orlando, FL 800-749-8869
Truan's Candies
Detroit, MI 800-584-3004
Turnbull Bakeries
Chattanooga, TN 800-488-7628
Ultimate Nut & Candy Company
Los Angeles, CA 800-767-5259
US Chocolate Corporation
Brooklyn, NY 718-788-8555
V L Foods
White Plains, NY 914-697-4851
Valhrona
Los Angeles, CA 310-277-0401
Van Leer Chocolate Corporation
Hoboken, NJ 800-826-2462
Van Otis Chocolates
Manchester, NH 800-826-6847
Vande Walle's Candies
Appleton, WI 920-738-7799
Varda Chocolatier
Elizabeth, NJ 800-448-2732
Vaughn-Russell Candy Kitchen
Greenville, SC 864-271-7786
Vermont Nut Free Chocolates
Grand Isle, VT 888-468-8373
Vigneri Confections
Rochester, NY 877-843-6374
Vitality Life Choice
Carson City, NV 800-423-8365
Vrymeer Commodities
St Charles, IL 630-584-0069
Warner-Lambert Confections
Cambridge, MA 617-491-2500
Washburn Candy Corporation
Brockton, MA 508-588-0820
Waymouth Farms
New Hope, MN 800-527-0094
Weaver Nut Company
Ephrata, PA 717-738-3781
Webbs Citrus Candy
Davenport, FL 863-422-1051
Westdale Foods Company
Orland Park, IL 708-458-7774
Whetstone Candy Company
St Augustine, FL 904-825-1710
Widmans Candy Shop
Crookston, MN 218-281-1487
Wilbur Chocolate Company
Lititz, PA 800-448-1063
Wilkinson-Spitz
Yonkers, NY 914-237-5000
Williams Candy Company
Somerville, MA 617-776-0814
Williamsburg Chocolatier
Williamsburg, VA 757-253-1474
Willy Wonka Candy
Itasca, IL 888-694-2656
Wilson Candy Company
Jeannette, PA 724-523-3151
Windmill Candy
Lubbock, TX 806-785-4688
Windsor Confections
Oakland, CA 800-860-0021
Winfrey Fudge & Candy
Rowley, MA 888-946-3739
Wisconsin Cheese
Melrose Park, IL 708-450-0074
Wisconsin Dairyland Fudge Company
Wisconsin Dells, WI 608-254-4136
Wisteria Candy Cottage
Boulevard, CA 800-458-8246
Wm. Wrigley Jr. Company
Yorkville, IL 630-553-4800
World Confections
Brooklyn, NY 718-768-8100
Yamate Chocolatier
Highland Park, NJ 800-433-2462
Zachary Confections
Frankfort, IN 800-445-4222
Zenobia Company
Bronx, NY 866-936-6242
Zitner Company
Philadelphia, PA 215-229-4990

Chocolate Cherries

Cambridge Brands
Cambridge, MA 617-491-2500
Cella's Confections
Chicago, IL 773-838-3400
Chris A. Papas & Son Company
Covington, KY 859-431-0499
Faroh Candies
Cleveland, OH 440-888-9866
Farr Candy Company
Idaho Falls, ID 208-522-8215
GKI Foods
Brighton, MI 248-486-0055
Godiva Chocolatier
New York, NY 800-946-3482
Gray & Company
Forest Grove, OR 503-357-3141
Hialeah Products Company
Hollywood, FL 800-923-3379
Karl Bissinger French Confections
St Louis, MO 800-325-8881
Lerro Candy Company
Darby, PA 610-461-8886
Lowery's Home Made Candies
Muncie, IN 800-541-3340
Marich Confectionery Company
Hollister, CA 800-624-7055
Maxfield Candy
Salt Lake City, UT 800-288-8002
Moore's Candies
Baltimore, MD 410-426-2705
New England Confectionery Company
Revere, MA 781-485-4500
Terri Lynn
Elgin, IL 800-323-0775
Truan's Candies
Detroit, MI 800-584-3004

Chocolate Chips

ADM Cocoa
Milwaukee, WI 800-558-9958
Cocoline Chocolate Company
Brooklyn, NY 718-522-4500
Log House Foods
Plymouth, MN 763-546-8395
Masterson Company
Milwaukee, WI 414-647-1132
Setton International Foods
Commack, NY 800-227-4397

Chocolate Chunks

ADM Cocoa
Milwaukee, WI 800-558-9958
Mootz Candy
Pottsville, PA

Cocoa & Cocoa Products

ADM Cocoa
Milwaukee, WI 800-558-9958
ADM Cocoa
Mansfield, MA 800-637-2536
ADM Cocoa
Glassboro, NJ 856-881-4000
Al-Rite Fruits & Syrups
Miami, FL 305-652-2540
Alaska Herb Tea Company
Anchorage, AK 800-654-2764
Alexander Gourmet Imports
Caledon, ON 800-265-5081

American Health & Nutrition
Ann Arbor, MI . . . 734-677-5570
American Key Food Products
Closter, NJ . . . 800-767-0237
American Nut & Chocolate Company
Boston, MA . . . 800-797-6887
American Yeast/Lallemand
Pembroke, NH . . . 866-920-9885
Amros the Second, Inc.
Somerset, NJ . . . 732-846-7755
Andre's Confiserie Suisse
Kansas City, MO . . . 800-892-1234
Andre-Boudin Bakeries
San Francisco, CA . . . 415-882-1849
Ann Hemyng Candy
Trumbauersville, PA . . . 800-779-7004
Associated Brands Inc.
Medina, NY . . . 800-265-0050
Assouline & Ting
Huntingdon Valley, PA . . . 800-521-4491
Aunt Aggie De's Pralines
Sinton, TX . . . 888-772-5463
BakeMark Canada
Laval, QC . . . 800-361-4998
Barry Callebaut USA, Inc.
Pennsauken, NJ . . . 800-836-2626
Blommer Chocolate Company
East Greenville, PA . . . 800-825-8181
Bourbon Ball
Louisville, KY . . . 800-280-0888
Boyd Coffee Company
Portland, OR . . . 800-545-4077
Bread & Chocolate
Wells River, VT . . . 800-524-6715
Brookema Company
West Chicago, IL . . . 630-562-2290
Calico Cottage
Amityville, NY . . . 800-645-5345
Cambridge Brands
Cambridge, MA . . . 617-491-2500
Campbell Soup Company
Camden, NJ . . . 800-257-8443
Caprine Estates
Bellbrook, OH . . . 937-848-7406
Carrie's Chocolates
Edmonton, AB . . . 877-778-2462
Cella's Confections
Chicago, IL . . . 773-838-3400
Chadler
Swedesboro, NJ . . . 856-467-0099
Chatz Roasting Company
Ceres, CA . . . 800-792-6333
Chocolat Belge Heyez
St-Lazare-De-Bellechasse, QC . . . 450-653-5616
Chocolat Jean Talon
Montreal, QC . . . 888-333-8540
Chocolate Street of Hartville
Hartville, OH . . . 888-853-5904
Chocolaterie Bernard Callebaut
Calgary, AB . . . 800-661-8367
Chocolates by Mark
La Porte, TX . . . 832-736-2626
Cloud Nine
San Leandro, CA . . . 201-358-8588
Cocoline Chocolate Company
Brooklyn, NY . . . 718-522-4500
Coffee Bean International
Portland, OR . . . 800-877-0474
ConAgra Grocery Products
Irvine, CA . . . 714-680-1000
Consolidated Mills
Houston, TX . . . 713-896-4196
Creative Confections
Northbrook, IL . . . 608-455-1448
Crown Candy Corporation
Macon, GA . . . 800-241-3529
Cuisinary Fine Foods
Irving, TX . . . 888-283-5303
Dare Foods
Kitchener, ON . . . 800-265-8225
Davidsons
Reno, NV . . . 800-882-5888
De Bas Chocolatier
Fresno, CA . . . 559-294-7638
Donells' Candies
Casper, WY . . . 877-461-2009
Doscher's Candies
Cincinnati, OH . . . 513-381-8656
Erba Food Products
Brooklyn, NY . . . 718-272-7700
Foley's Candies
Richmond, BC . . . 888-236-5397
Forbes Chocolates
Broadview Heights, OH . . . 800-433-1090
Gel Spice Company, Inc
Bayonne, NJ . . . 800-922-0230
Georgia Nut Ingredients
Skokie, IL . . . 877-674-2993
Germack Pistachio Company
Detroit, MI . . . 800-872-4006
Ghirardelli Chocolate Company
San Leandro, CA . . . 800-877-9338
Givaudan Flavors
Cincinnati, OH . . . 513-948-8000
GKI Foods
Brighton, MI . . . 248-486-0055
Godiva Chocolatier
New York, NY . . . 800-946-3482
Golden Foods
Commerce, CA . . . 800-350-2462
Govatos
Wilmington, DE . . . 888-799-5252
Hauser Chocolates
Westerly, RI . . . 800-289-8783
Hebert Candies
Shrewsbury, MA . . . 866-432-3781
Herb Patch of Vermont
Bellows Falls, VT . . . 800-282-4372
Hershey
Mississauga, ON . . . 800-468-1714
Hershey Chocolate & Confectionery Division
Pleasanton, CA . . . 925-460-0359
Hershey Company
Hershey, PA . . . 800-468-1714
Hershey International
Weston, FL . . . 954-385-2600
Hialeah Products Company
Hollywood, FL . . . 800-923-3379
Home Bakery
Laramie, WY . . . 307-742-2721
Jason & Son Specialty Foods
Rancho Cordova, CA . . . 800-810-9093
Jenny's Country Kitchen
Dover, MN . . . 800-357-3497
King's Cupboard
Red Lodge, MT . . . 800-962-6555
Koeze Company
Wyoming, MI . . . 800-555-3909
Log House Foods
Plymouth, MN . . . 763-546-8395
Magna Foods Corporation
City of Industry, CA . . . 800-995-4394
Marich Confectionery Company
Hollister, CA . . . 800-624-7055
Martha Olson's Great Foods
Sutter Creek, CA . . . 800-973-3966
McSteven's, Inc
Vancouver, WA . . . 800-547-2803
Merlin Candies
Harahan, LA . . . 800-899-1549
Michelle Chocolatiers
Colorado Springs, CO . . . 888-447-3654
Mona Lisa® Chocolatier
Arlington, VA . . . 866-662-5475
Monster Cone
Montreal, QC . . . 800-542-9801
Nantucket Tea Traders
Nantucket, MA . . . 508-325-0203
Natra US
Chula Vista, CA . . . 800-262-6216
Nestle Infant Nutrition
Florham Park, NJ
New England Confectionery Company
Revere, MA . . . 781-485-4500
New England Natural Baker
Greenfield, MA . . . 800-910-2884
Niagara Chocolates
Cheektowaga, NY . . . 800-234-5750
Nora's Candy Shop
Rome, NY . . . 888-544-8224
NSpired Natural Foods
Melville, NY . . . 541-488-2747
NSpired Natural Foods
Boulder, CO . . . 800-434-4246
OH Chocolate
Calgary, AB . . . 800-887-3959
Olivier's Candies
Calgary, AB . . . 403-266-6028
Paulaur Corporation
Cranbury, NJ . . . 888-398-8844
Phillips Syrup Corporation
Westlake, OH . . . 800-350-8443
Pine River Pre-Pack
Newton, WI . . . 920-726-4216
Plantation Candies
Telford, PA . . . 888-678-6468
Quality Naturally! Foods
City of Industry, CA . . . 888-498-6986
R.M. Palmer Company
Reading, PA . . . 610-372-8971
Rapunzel Pure Organics
Bloomfield, NJ . . . 800-225-1449
Riddles' Sweet Impressions
Edmonton, AB . . . 780-465-8085
Schokinag North America
Milwaukee, WI
Service Packing Company
Vancouver, BC . . . 604-681-0264
Setton International Foods
Commack, NY . . . 800-227-4397
Shade Foods
New Century, KS . . . 800-225-6312
St. Charles Trading
Lake Saint Louis, MO . . . 800-336-1333
Sturm Foods
Manawa, WI . . . 800-347-8876
Sucesores de Pedro Cortes
San Juan, PR . . . 787-754-7040
Sweenor Chocolate
Wakefield, RI . . . 800-834-3123
Terri Lynn
Elgin, IL . . . 800-323-0775
Timber Peaks Gourmet
Parker, CO . . . 800-982-7687
Tom & Sally's Handmade Chocolates
Brattleboro, VT . . . 800-827-0800
Top Hat Company
Wilmette, IL . . . 847-256-6565
Tova Industries
Louisville, KY . . . 888-532-8682
Vande Walle's Candies
Appleton, WI . . . 920-738-7799
Varda Chocolatier
Elizabeth, NJ . . . 800-448-2732
Vigneri Confections
Rochester, NY . . . 877-843-6374
Vrymeer Commodities
St Charles, IL . . . 630-584-0069
Weber Flavors
Wheeling, IL . . . 800-558-9078
White Coffee Corporation
Astoria, NY . . . 800-221-0140
Wilbur Chocolate
Lititz, PA . . . 800-233-0139
Wilbur Chocolate Company
Lititz, PA . . . 800-448-1063
Williamsburg Chocolatier
Williamsburg, VA . . . 757-253-1474
Wisconsin Cheese
Melrose Park, IL . . . 708-450-0074
Wisconsin Cheeseman
Madison, WI . . . 608-837-5166

Fudge

Bakemark Ingredients Canada
Richmond, BC . . . 800-665-9441
Herkimer Foods
Herkimer, NY . . . 315-895-7832
Sokol & Company
Countryside, IL . . . 800-328-7656

Confectionery

Confectioners Crunch

Cocomira Confections
Toronto, ON . . . 866-413-9049
Island Princess
Honolulu, HI . . . 866-872-8601

Confectionery

A. Battaglia Processing Company
Chicago, IL . . . 773-523-5900
A.L. Bazzini Company
Bronx, NY . . . 800-228-0172
Aglamesis Brothers
Cincinnati, OH . . . 513-531-5196
Amcan Industries
Elmsford, NY . . . 914-347-4838
American Almond Products Company
Brooklyn, NY . . . 800-825-6663
American Food Products
Methuen, MA . . . 978-682-1855
American Key Food Products
Closter, NJ . . . 800-767-0237

American Licorice Company
Union City, CA 866-442-2783
Ames International
Fife, WA 888-469-2637
Amros the Second, Inc.
Somerset, NJ 732-846-7755
Amurol Confections Company
Yorkville, IL 630-553-4800
Andre's Confiserie Suisse
Kansas City, MO 800-892-1234
Andrews Caramel Apples
Chicago, IL 800-305-3004
Ann Hemyng Candy
Trumbauersville, PA 800-779-7004
Archibald Candy Corporation
Chicago, IL 800-333-3629
Arway Confections
Chicago, IL 773-267-5770
Ashers Chocolates
Lewistown, PA 800-343-0520
Assouline & Ting
Huntingdon Valley, PA 800-521-4491
Aunt Aggie De's Pralines
Sinton, TX 888-772-5463
Baker Candy Company
Snohomish, WA 425-422-6331
Barry Callebaut USA, Inc.
Pennsauken, NJ 800-836-2626
Beehive Botanicals, Inc.
Hayward, WI 800-233-4483
BestSweet
Mooresville, NC 888-211-5530
Betty Jane Homemade Candies
Dubuque, IA 800-642-1254
Betty Lou's Golden Smackers
McMinnville, OR 800-242-5205
Blanton's
Sweetwater, TN 423-337-3487
Blommer Chocolate Company
East Greenville, PA 800-825-8181
Boca Bons East,LLC.
Greenacres, FL 800-314-2835
Bodega Chocolates
Fountain Valley, CA 888-326-3342
Bogdon Candy Company
Canajoharie, NY 800-839-8938
Bourbon Ball
Louisville, KY 800-280-0888
Brach's Confections
Halethorpe, MD 443-872-2094
Brennan Snacks Manufacturing
Bogalusa, LA 800-290-7486
Brenntag
Reading, PA 888-926-4151
Brenntag Pacific
Santa Fe Springs, CA 562-903-9626
Brittle Kettle
Tigard, OR 800-447-2128
Brokay Products
Philadelphia, PA 215-676-4800
Brookside Foods
Abbotsford, BC 877-793-3866
Burke Candy & Ingredient Corporation
Milwaukee, WI 888-287-5350
Byrne & Carlson
Portsmouth, NH 888-559-9778
C. Howard Company
Bellport, NY 631-286-7940
Cambridge Brands
Cambridge, MA 617-491-2500
Campbell Soup Company
Camden, NJ 800-257-8443
Candy Factory
Hayward, CA 800-736-6887
Canelake's
Virginia, MN 888-928-8889
Caprine Estates
Bellbrook, OH 937-848-7406
Carrie's Chocolates
Edmonton, AB 877-778-2462
Casani Candy Company
Philadelphia, PA 215-535-0110
Catoris Candy
New Kensington, PA 724-335-4371
Ce De Candy
Union, NJ 800-631-7968
Cedarlane Natural Foods
Carson, CA 310-886-7720
Cella's Confections
Chicago, IL 773-838-3400
Charlotte's Confections
Millbrae, CA 800-798-2427

Chase Candy Company
Saint Joseph, MO 800-786-1625
Cheese Straws & More
Monroe, LA 800-997-1921
Chefmaster
Garden Grove, CA 800-333-7443
Cherrydale Farms
Allentown, PA 800-333-4525
Chex Finer Foods
Attleboro, MA 800-322-2434
Chocolat Belge Heyez
St-Lazare-De-Bellechasse, QC 450-653-5616
Chocolat Jean Talon
Montreal, QC 888-333-8540
Chocolate Street of Hartville
Hartville, OH 888-853-5904
Chocolates by Mark
La Porte, TX 832-736-2626
Chocolati Handmade Chocolates
Seattle, WA 206-784-5212
Chris Candies
Pittsburgh, PA 412-322-9400
Christopher Norman Chocolates
New York, NY 212-402-1243
Clarks Joe Fund Raising Candies & Novelties
Tarentum, PA 888-459-9520
Clasen Quality Coatings
Madison, WI 877-459-4500
Cloud Nine
San Leandro, CA 201-358-8588
Cloverland Sweets/Priester's Pecan Company
Fort Deposit, AL 800-523-3505
Cocoline Chocolate Company
Brooklyn, NY 718-522-4500
Coffee Bean International
Portland, OR 800-877-0474
Concord Confections
Chicago, IL 800-267-0037
Concord Foods
Brockton, MA 508-580-1700
Confection Solutions
Sylmar, CA 800-284-2422
Confectionately Yours
Buffalo Grove, IL 800-875-6978
Creative Confections
Northbrook, IL 608-455-1448
Creme Curls Bakery
Hudsonville, MI 800-466-1219
Creole Delicacies Pralines
New Orleans, LA 504-523-6425
Crown Candy Corporation
Macon, GA 800-241-3529
CTC Manufacturing
Calgary, AB 800-668-7677
Cuisinary Fine Foods
Irving, TX 888-283-5303
Cummings Studio Chocolates
Salt Lake City, UT 800-537-3957
Cupid Candies
Chicago, IL 773-925-8191
Custom Industries
St Louis, MO 314-787-2828
Dangold
Flushing, NY 718-591-5286
Dare Foods
Kitchener, ON 800-265-8225
David Bradley Chocolatier
Windsor, NJ 877-289-7933
Day Spring Enterprises
Cheektowaga, NY 800-879-7677
Daymar Select Fine Coffees
El Cajon, CA 800-466-7590
De Bas Chocolatier
Fresno, CA 559-294-7638
DE Wolfgang Candy Company
York, PA 800-248-4273
Decko Products
Sandusky, OH 800-537-6143
Delta Distributors
Longview, TX 800-945-1858
Dessert Innovations
Atlanta, GA 800-359-7351
Dillon Candy Company
Boston, GA 800-382-8338
Dipasa
Brownsville, TX 956-831-5893
DMH Ingredients
Libertyville, IL 847-362-9977
Dno
Columbus, OH 800-686-2366
Dolphin Natural Chocolates
Cambria, CA 800-236-5744

Donaldson's Finer Chocolates
Lebanon, IN 800-975-7236
Donells' Candies
Casper, WY 877-461-2009
Doscher's Candies
Cincinnati, OH 513-381-8656
Doumak
Elk Grove Vlg, IL 800-323-0318
Downeast Candies
Boothbay Harbor, ME 207-633-5178
Duo Delights
Sun Prairie, WI 800-843-1381
Dynatabs
Brooklyn, NY 718-376-4508
EcoNatural Solutions
Boulder, CO 877-684-5159
Eda's Sugarfree Candies
Philadelphia, PA 215-324-3412
Edward & Sons Trading Company
Carpinteria, CA 805-684-8500
El Brands
Ozark, AL 334-445-2828
Elite Industries
Syosset, NY 888-488-3458
Elmer Candy Corporation
Ponchatoula, LA 800-843-9537
Energy Club
Pacoima, CA 800-688-6887
Enstrom Candies
Grand Junction, CO 800-367-8766
F & F Foods
Chicago, IL 800-621-0225
Fannie May Fine Chocolat
Melrose Park, IL 800-999-3629
Fantazzmo Fun Stuff
Schaumburg, IL 847-413-1700
Farley's & Sathers Candy Company
Round Lake, MN 800-533-0330
Faroh Candies
Cleveland, OH 440-888-9866
Farr Candy Company
Idaho Falls, ID 208-522-8215
Fernando C Pujals & Bros
Guaynabo, PR 787-792-3080
Ferrara Bakery & Cafe
New York, NY 212-226-6150
Fitzkee's Candies
York, PA 717-741-1031
FNI Group LLC
Sherborn, MA 508-655-4175
Forbes Candies
Virginia Beach, VA 800-626-5898
Frankford Candy & Chocolate Company
Philadelphia, PA 800-523-9090
FrutStix Company
Santa Barbara, CA 805-965-1656
Fudge Farms
Buchanan, MI 800-874-0261
G Scaccianoce & Company
Bronx, NY 718-991-4462
Gardners Candies
Tyrone, PA 800-242-2639
Gene & Boots Candies
Perryopolis, PA 800-864-4222
Georgia Nut Ingredients
Skokie, IL 877-674-2993
Germack Pistachio Company
Detroit, MI 800-872-4006
Gertrude Hawk Ingredients
Dunmore, PA 800-822-2032
Ghirardelli Chocolate Company
San Leandro, CA 800-877-9338
Gimbal's Fine Candies
S San Francisco, CA 800-344-6225
Gindi Gourmet
Boulder, CO 303-473-9177
GKI Foods
Brighton, MI 248-486-0055
Gladstone Candies
Cleveland, OH 888-729-1960
Go Lightly Candy
Hillside, NJ 800-524-1304
Godiva Chocolatier
New York, NY 800-946-3482
Gold Cup Farms
Clayton, NY 800-752-1341
Golden Apples Candy Company
Southport, CT 800-776-0393
Golden Fluff Popcorn Company
Lakewood, NJ 732-367-5448
Golden Foods
Commerce, CA 800-350-2462

Golden Temple
Springfield, OR....................800-964-4832
Golf Mill Chocolate Factory
Niles, IL.........................847-635-1107
Goodart Candy
Lubbock, TX......................806-747-2600
Govatos
Wilmington, DE...................888-799-5252
Gray & Company
Forest Grove, OR.................503-357-3141
Green Mountain Chocolates
Franklin, MA.....................508-520-7160
Greenwell Farms
Morganfield, KY..................270-389-3289
Gumtech International
Phoenix, AZ......................602-252-7425
Gurley's Foods
Willmar, MN......................800-426-7845
GWB Foods Corporation
Brooklyn, NY.....................877-977-7610
H.B. Trading
Totowa, NJ.......................973-812-1022
Haby's Alsatian Bakery
Castroville, TX..................830-931-2118
Happy Hive
Dearborn Heights, MI.............313-562-3707
Harlow House Company
Atlanta, GA......................404-325-1270
Harold M. Lincoln Company
Toledo, OH.......................800-345-4911
Hauser Chocolates
Westerly, RI.....................800-289-8783
Haven's Candies
Westbrook, ME....................800-639-6309
Hawaii Candy
Honolulu, HI.....................808-836-8955
Hawaiian Salrose Teas
Honolulu, HI.....................808-848-0500
Hebert Candies
Shrewsbury, MA...................866-432-3781
Hershey
Mississauga, ON..................800-468-1714
Hershey Canada Inc
Mississauga, ON..................800-468-1714
Hershey Chocolate & Confectionery Division
Pleasanton, CA...................925-460-0359
Hershey Corporation
Hershey, PA......................800-468-1714
Hershey International
Weston, FL.......................954-385-2600
Hialeah Products Company
Hollywood, FL....................800-923-3379
Holistic Products Corporation
Englewood, NJ....................800-221-0308
Honey Bar/Creme de la Creme
Kingston, NY.....................845-331-4643
Horriea 2000 Food Industries
Reynolds, GA.....................478-847-4186
Hospitality Mints
Boone, NC........................800-334-5181
Hospitality Mints LLC
Boone, NC........................800-334-5181
J.A.M.B. Low Carb Distributor
Pompano Beach, FL................800-708-6738
James Candy Company
Atlantic City, NJ................800-938-2339
Jason & Son Specialty Foods
Rancho Cordova, CA...............800-810-9093
Jelly Belly Candy Company
Fairfield, CA....................800-522-3267
Joyva Corporation
Brooklyn, NY.....................718-497-0170
Judson-Atkinson Candies
San Antonio, TX..................800-962-3984
Judy's Cream Caramels
Sherwood, OR.....................503-625-7161
Karl Bissinger French Confections
St Louis, MO.....................800-325-8881
Kay Foods Company
Detroit, MI......................313-393-1100
Kemach Food Products Corporation
Brooklyn, NY.....................888-453-6224
Kerr Brothers
Toronto, ON......................416-252-7341
Key III Candies
Fort Wayne, IN...................800-752-2382
KHS-Bartelt
Sarasota, FL.....................800-829-9980
Kloss Manufacturing Company
Allentown, PA....................800-445-7100
Koeze Company
Wyoming, MI......................800-555-3909

Kolatin Real Kosher Gelatin
Lakewood, NJ.....................732-364-8700
Kopper's Chocolate
New York, NY.....................800-325-0026
Krinos Foods
Santa Barbara, CA................800-624-4896
Lanco
Hauppauge, NY....................800-938-4500
Landies Candies Company
Buffalo, NY......................800-955-2634
Landrin USA
Sunny Isles Beach, FL
Laura Paige Candy Company
Newburgh, NY.....................845-566-4209
Laymon Candy Company
San Bernardino, CA...............909-825-4408
Leader Candies
Brooklyn, NY.....................718-366-6900
Lerro Candy Company
Darby, PA........................610-461-8886
Log House Foods
Plymouth, MN.....................763-546-8395
Long Grove ConfectioneryCompany
Buffalo Grove, IL................800-373-3102
Lou-Retta's Custom Chocolates
Buffalo, NY......................716-833-7111
Louis J. Rheb Candy Company
Baltimore, MD....................800-514-8293
Lowery's Home Made Candies
Muncie, IN.......................800-541-3340
Lukas Confections
York, PA.........................717-843-0921
MacFarms of Hawaii
Captain Cook, HI.................808-328-2435
Magna Foods Corporation
City of Industry, CA.............800-995-4394
Maple Grove Farms of Vermont
St Johnsbury, VT.................800-525-2540
Marich Confectionery Company
Hollister, CA....................800-624-7055
Marie's Candies
West Liberty, OH.................866-465-5781
Maris Candy
Chicago, IL......................773-254-3351
Mary of Puddin Hill
Greenville, TX...................800-545-8889
Marzipan Specialties
Nashville, TN....................615-226-4800
Masterson Company
Milwaukee, WI....................414-647-1132
Matangos Candies
Harrisburg, PA...................717-234-0882
Maxfield Candy
Salt Lake City, UT...............800-288-8002
Mayfair Sales
Buffalo, NY......................800-248-2881
Merbs Candies
Saint Louis, MO..................314-832-7117
Mercado Latino
City of Industry, CA.............626-333-6862
Merlin Candies
Harahan, LA......................800-899-1549
Michelle Chocolatiers
Colorado Springs, CO.............888-447-3654
Midwest/Northern
Minneapolis, MN..................800-328-5502
Mille Lacs MP Company
Madison, WI......................800-843-1381
Milsolv Corporation
Butler, WI.......................800-558-8501
Milton A. Klein Company
New York, NY.....................800-221-0248
Mitch Chocolate
Melville, NY.....................631-777-2400
Mitsubishi Chemical America
White Plains, NY.................914-286-3600
Moon Shine Trading Company
Woodland, CA.....................800-678-1226
Moore's Candies
Baltimore, MD....................410-426-2705
Mootz Candy
Pottsville, PA
Morris National
Azusa, CA........................626-385-2000
Mrs. Annie's Peanut Patch
Floresville, TX..................830-393-7845
Mrs. Prindable's Handmade Confections
Niles, IL........................888-215-1100
Multiflex Company
Hawthorne, NJ....................973-636-9700
Munson's Chocolates
Bolton, CT.......................888-686-7667

Muth Candies
Louisville, KY...................502-585-2952
My Daddy's Cheesecake
Cape Girardeau, MO...............800-735-6765
My Sister's Caramels
Redlands, CA.....................909-792-6242
MYNTZ!
Kent, WA.........................800-800-9490
Naron Mary Sue Candy Company
Baltimore, MD....................800-662-2639
Natural Quick Foods
Seattle, WA......................206-365-5757
Nature's Candy
Fredericksburg, TX...............800-729-0085
Naylor Candies
Mount Wolf, PA...................717-266-2706
Necco
Revere, MA.......................781-485-4500
Nestle Infant Nutrition
Florham Park, NJ
Nestle USA Inc
Glendale, CA.....................800-225-2270
New England Confectionery Company
Revere, MA.......................781-485-4500
New England Natural Baker
Greenfield, MA...................800-910-2884
Niagara Chocolates
Cheektowaga, NY..................800-234-5750
Nora's Candy Shop
Rome, NY.........................888-544-8224
Northwest Candy Emporium
Everett, WA......................800-404-7266
Northwest Chocolate Factory
Salem, OR........................503-362-1340
NSpired Natural Foods
Boulder, CO......................800-434-4246
Nunes Farm Almonds
Newman, CA.......................209-862-3033
Oak Leaf Confections
Scarborough, ON..................877-261-7887
OCG Cacao
Whitinsville, MA.................888-482-2226
OH Chocolate
Calgary, AB......................800-887-3959
Old Fashioned Candy
Berwyn, IL.......................708-788-6669
Olde Tyme Food Corporation
East Longmeadow, MA..............800-356-6533
Olde Tyme Mercantile
Arroyo Grande, CA................805-489-7991
Ole Smoky Candy Kitchen
Gatlinburg, TN...................865-436-6426
Olivier's Candies
Calgary, AB......................403-266-6028
Palmer Candy Company
Sioux City, IA...................800-831-0828
Parker Products
Fort Worth, TX...................800-433-5749
Parkside Candy Company
Buffalo, NY......................716-833-7540
Paulaur Corporation
Cranbury, NJ.....................888-398-8844
PB&S Chemicals
Henderson, KY....................800-950-7267
Peanut Patch
Courtland, VA....................866-732-6883
Pecan Deluxe Candy Company
Dallas, TX.......................800-733-3589
PEZ Candy
Orange, CT.......................203-795-0531
Pez Manufacturing Corporation
Orange, CT.......................800-243-6087
Pfizer
Parsippany, NJ...................973-541-5900
Philadelphia Candies
Hermitage, PA....................724-981-6341
Phillips Candies
Seaside, OR......................503-738-5402
Pine River Pre-Pack
Newton, WI.......................920-726-4216
Pioneer Marketing International
Los Gatos, CA....................408-356-4990
Pittsburgh Snax & Nut Company
Pittsburgh, PA...................800-404-6887
Plaidberry Company
Vista, CA........................760-727-5403
Plantation Candies
Telford, PA......................888-678-6468
Popcorn Connection
North Hollywood, CA..............800-852-2676
Poppers Supply Company
Allentown, PA....................800-457-9810

Priester Pecan Company
Fort Deposit, AL 800-277-3226
Prince of Peace Enterprises
Hayward, CA 800-732-2328
Produits Alimentaire
St Lambert De Lauzon, QC 800-463-1787
Pulakos
Erie, PA 814-452-4026
Quigley Manufacturing
Elizabethtown, PA 800-367-2441
R.M. Palmer Company
Reading, PA 610-372-8971
Randag & Associates Inc
Elmhurst, IL 630-530-2830
Rebecca Ruth Candy
Frankfort, KY 800-444-3866
Richards Maple Products
Chardon, OH 800-352-4052
Ricos Candy Snacks & Bakery
Hialeah, FL 305-885-7392
Riddles' Sweet Impressions
Edmonton, AB 780-465-8085
Rito Mints
Trois Rivieres, QC 819-379-1449
Rivard Popcorn Products
Lancaster, PA 717-393-1074
Rosalind Candy Castle
New Brighton, PA 724-843-1144
Ross Fine Candies
Waterford, MI 248-682-5640
Royal Wine Corp
Bayonne, NJ 718-384-2400
Ruth Hunt Candies
Mt Sterling, KY 800-927-0302
Salem Old Fashioned Candies
Salem, MA 978-744-3242
Sally Lane's Candy Farm
Paris, TN 731-642-5801
Sayklly's Candies & Gifts
Escanaba, MI 906-786-3092
Scott's Candy
Glennville, GA 800-356-2100
Seasons' Enterprises
Addison, IL 630-628-0211
See's Candies
Carson, CA 800-347-7337
Senor Murphy Candymaker
Santa Fe, NM 877-988-4311
Sensational Sweets
Lewisburg, PA 570-524-4361
Shade Foods
New Century, KS 800-225-6312
Shane Candy Company
Philadelphia, PA 215-922-1048
Shari Candies
Edina, MN 800-658-7059
Sherm Edwards Candies
Trafford, PA 800-436-5424
Sherwood Brands
Rockville, MD 401-434-7773
Signature Brands
Ocala, FL 800-456-9573
Simply Gourmet Confections
Irvine, CA 714-505-3955
Snackerz
Commerce, CA 888-576-2253
Somerset Syrup & Beverage
Edison, NJ 800-526-8865
Southchem
Durham, NC 800-849-7000
Southern Style Nuts
Denison, TX 903-463-3161
Splendid Specialties
Novato, CA 415-506-3000
Star Kay White
Congers, NY 800-874-8518
Starbucks Coffee Company
Seattle, WA 800-782-7282
Stark Candy Company
Revere, MA 800-621-1983
Startup's Candy Company
Provo, UT 801-373-8673
Stichler Products
Reading, PA 610-921-0211
Stone's Home Made Candy Shop
Oswego, NY 888-223-3928
Stutz Candy Company
Hatboro, PA 888-692-2639
Sucesores de Pedro Cortes
San Juan, PR 787-754-7040
Sugar Plum Farm
Plumtree, NC 888-257-0019

Sweenor Chocolate
Wakefield, RI 800-834-3123
Sweet City Supply
Virginia Beach, VA 888-793-3824
Sweet Productions
Amityville, NY 631-842-0548
Sweet Shop
La Crosse, WI 608-784-7724
Sweet Shop
Mount Pleasant, TX 800-222-2269
Sweet Works
St Augustine, FL 877-261-7887
Taste of Nature
Beverly Hills, CA 310-396-4433
Taste Teasers
Dallas, TX 800-526-1840
Temo's Candy
Akron, OH 330-376-7229
Texas Toffee
Odessa, TX 432-563-5373
The Topps Company
Duryea, PA 570-457-6761
Tim's Cascade Chips
Algona, WA 800-533-8467
Todd's
Vernon, CA 800-938-6337
Tom & Sally's Handmade Chocolates
Brattleboro, VT 800-827-0800
Torn & Glasser
Los Angeles, CA 800-282-6887
Torn Ranch
Novato, CA 415-506-3000
Tropical
Charlotte, NC 800-220-1413
Tropical
Columbus, OH 800-538-3941
Tropical
Marietta, GA 800-544-3762
Tropical Nut & Fruit Company
Orlando, FL 800-749-8869
Vande Walle's Candies
Appleton, WI 920-738-7799
Varda Chocolatier
Elizabeth, NJ 800-448-2732
Variety Foods
Warren, MI 586-268-4900
Vigneri Confections
Rochester, NY 877-843-6374
Vrymeer Commodities
St Charles, IL 630-584-0069
Warner Candy
El Paso, TX 847-928-7200
Warrell Corporation
Camp Hill, PA 800-233-7082
Waymouth Farms
New Hope, MN 800-527-0094
Weaver Nut Company
Ephrata, PA 717-738-3781
Weaver Popcorn Company
Noblesville, IN 800-634-8161
Webbs Citrus Candy
Davenport, FL 863-422-1051
Wedding Cake Studio
Williamsfield, OH 440-667-1765
Westbrae Natural Foods
Melville, NY 800-434-4246
White-Stokes Company
Chicago, IL 800-978-6537
Wilbur Chocolate Company
Lititz, PA 800-448-1063
Williamsburg Chocolatier
Williamsburg, VA 757-253-1474
Willy Wonka Candy Factory
Itasca, IL 630-773-0267
Wilson Candy Company
Jeannette, PA 724-523-3151
Wilson's Fantastic Candy
Memphis, TN 901-767-1900
Winans Chocolates & Coffees
Piqua, OH 937-773-1981
Wisconsin Cheese
Melrose Park, IL 708-450-0074
Wisconsin Cheeseman
Madison, WI 608-837-5166
World Confections
Brooklyn, NY 718-768-8100
Wright Ice Cream
Cayuga, IN 800-686-9561
Xcell International Corporation
Lemont, IL 800-722-7751
Yamate Chocolatier
Highland Park, NJ 800-433-2462

Yost Candy Company
Dalton, OH 800-750-1976
Zitner Company
Philadelphia, PA 215-229-4990

Decorations & Icings

Decorations

Baking

Chefmaster
Garden Grove, CA 800-333-7443
Kerry Ingredients
Blue Earth, MN 507-526-7575
Signature Brands
Ocala, FL 800-456-9573

Cake

Adams Foods
Dothan, AL 334-983-4233
American Key Food Products
Closter, NJ 800-767-0237
BakeMark Canada
Laval, QC 800-361-4998
Bakery Crafts
West Chester, OH 800-543-1673
Chefmaster
Garden Grove, CA 800-333-7443
Decko Products
Sandusky, OH 800-537-6143
El Segundo Bakery
El Segundo, CA 310-322-3422
Erba Food Products
Brooklyn, NY 718-272-7700
Lucks Food Decorating Company
Tacoma, WA 800-426-9778
Multiflex Company
Hawthorne, NJ 973-636-9700
Paulaur Corporation
Cranbury, NJ 888-398-8844
Petra International
Mississauga, ON 800-261-7226
Signature Brands
Ocala, FL 800-456-9573
Sugar Flowers Plus
Glendale, CA 800-972-2935

Icings

BakeMark Canada
Laval, QC 800-361-4998
Bakemark Ingredients Canada
Richmond, BC 800-665-9441
Baker & Baker, Inc.
Schaumburg, IL 800-593-5777
Chefmaster
Garden Grove, CA 800-333-7443
Chelsea Milling Company
Chelsea, MI 734-475-1361
Cremes Unlimited
Matteson, IL 800-227-3637
Dawn Food Products
Louisville, KY 800-626-2542
Erba Food Products
Brooklyn, NY 718-272-7700
Fresh Dairy Direct/Morningstar
Dallas, TX 800-395-7004
Frostbite
Toledo, OH 800-968-7711
H.C. Brill Company
Tucker, GA 800-241-8526
Lawrence Foods
Elk Grove Village, IL 800-323-7848
Louisiana Gourmet Enterprises
La Place, LA 985-783-2446
Millers Ice Cream
Houston, TX 713-861-3138
Mimac Glaze
Brampton, ON 877-990-9975
Newport Flavours & Fragrances
Orange, CA 714-744-3700
Parrish's Cake Decorating Supplies
Gardena, CA 800-736-8443
Price's Creameries
El Paso, TX 915-565-2711
Quality Naturally! Foods
City of Industry, CA 888-498-6986
RIBUS
Saint Louis, MO 314-727-4287
Snelgrove Ice Cream Company
Salt Lake City, UT 800-569-0005

Sokol & Company
Countryside, IL 800-328-7656
Warwick Ice Cream Company
Warwick, RI 401-821-8403
Westco-Bake Mark
Pico Rivera, CA 562-949-1054

Ready to Use

Allen Canning Company
Siloam Springs, AR 800-234-2553
H.C. Brill Company
Tucker, GA 800-241-8526
Presto Avoset Group
Claremont, CA 909-399-0062

Specialty-Packaged Candy

Bagged

American Licorice Company
Union City, CA 866-442-2783
Ann Hemyng Candy
Trumbauersville, PA 800-779-7004
Bloomer Candy Company
Zanesville, OH 800-452-7501
Bohemian Biscuit Company
South San Francisco, CA 650-952-2226
Brach's Confections
Halethorpe, MD 443-872-2094
Cambridge Brands
Cambridge, MA 617-491-2500
Chase Candy Company
Saint Joseph, MO 800-786-1625
Chris A. Papas & Son Company
Covington, KY 859-431-0499
Cocoline Chocolate Company
Brooklyn, NY 718-522-4500
Crown Candy Corporation
Macon, GA 800-241-3529
David Bradley Chocolatier
Windsor, NJ 877-289-7933
Eda's Sugarfree Candies
Philadelphia, PA 215-324-3412
GKI Foods
Brighton, MI 248-486-0055
Go Lightly Candy
Hillside, NJ 800-524-1304
Golden Apples Candy Company
Southport, CT 800-776-0393
Hialeah Products Company
Hollywood, FL 800-923-3379
Jelly Belly Candy Company
Fairfield, CA 800-522-3267
Joyva Corporation
Brooklyn, NY 718-497-0170
Judson-Atkinson Candies
San Antonio, TX 800-962-3984
Leader Candies
Brooklyn, NY 718-366-6900
Ludwick's Frozen Donuts
Grand Rapids, MI 800-366-8816
Lukas Confections
York, PA 717-843-0921
Necco
Revere, MA 781-485-4500
New England Confectionery Company
Revere, MA 781-485-4500
Olde Tyme Mercantile
Arroyo Grande, CA 805-489-7991
Piedmont Candy Corporation
Lexington, NC 336-248-2477
Quigley Manufacturing
Elizabethtown, PA 800-367-2441
Randag & Associates Inc
Elmhurst, IL 630-530-2830
Salem Old Fashioned Candies
Salem, MA 978-744-3242
Sherwood Brands
Rockville, MD 401-434-7773
Weaver Nut Company
Ephrata, PA 717-738-3781
Webbs Citrus Candy
Davenport, FL 863-422-1051
World Confections
Brooklyn, NY 718-768-8100
Yost Candy Company
Dalton, OH 800-750-1976

Boxed

Anastasia Confections Inc.
Orlando, FL 800-329-7100
Anthony-Thomas Candy Company
Columbus, OH 877-226-3921
Arcor USA
Miami, FL 800-572-7267
Astor Chocolate
Lakewood, NJ 732-901-1000
Baraboo Candy Company
Baraboo, WI 800-967-1690
Best Chocolate In Town
Indianapolis, IN 888-294-2378
Blanton's
Sweetwater, TN 423-337-3487
Blommer Chocolate Company
East Greenville, PA 800-825-8181
Boyer Candy Company
Altoona, PA 814-944-9401
Chocolate House
Milwaukee, WI 800-236-2022
Ghirardelli Chocolate Company
San Leandro, CA 800-877-9338
GKI Foods
Brighton, MI 248-486-0055
Mona Lisa® Chocolatier
Arlington, VA 866-662-5475
Naron Mary Sue Candy Company
Baltimore, MD 800-662-2639
Ruth Hunt Candies
Mt Sterling, KY 800-927-0302
Scott's Candy
Glennville, GA 800-356-2100
Terri Lynn
Elgin, IL 800-323-0775

Christmas

Bee Int'l., Inc
Chula Vista, CA 800-421-6465
Blanton's
Sweetwater, TN 423-337-3487
Bohemian Biscuit Company
South San Francisco, CA 650-952-2226
Brach's Confections
Halethorpe, MD 443-872-2094
Charlotte's Confections
Millbrae, CA 800-798-2427
Chase Candy Company
Saint Joseph, MO 800-786-1625
Chocolat Jean Talon
Montreal, QC 888-333-8540
Chris A. Papas & Son Company
Covington, KY 859-431-0499
David Bradley Chocolatier
Windsor, NJ 877-289-7933
Day Spring Enterprises
Cheektowaga, NY 800-879-7677
Doscher's Candies
Cincinnati, OH 513-381-8656
Ferrara Bakery & Cafe
New York, NY 212-226-6150
Garry Packing
Del Rey, CA 800-248-2126
Gimbal's Fine Candies
S San Francisco, CA 800-344-6225
GKI Foods
Brighton, MI 248-486-0055
Gladstone Candies
Cleveland, OH 888-729-1960
Haven's Candies
Westbrook, ME 800-639-6309
Jelly Belly Candy Company
Fairfield, CA 800-522-3267
Judson-Atkinson Candies
San Antonio, TX 800-962-3984
Landies Candies Company
Buffalo, NY 800-955-2634
Leader Candies
Brooklyn, NY 718-366-6900
Lukas Confections
York, PA 717-843-0921
Madrona Specialty Foods
Tukwila, WA 425-814-2500
Mona Lisa® Chocolatier
Arlington, VA 866-662-5475
Necco
Revere, MA 781-485-4500
New England Confectionery Company
Revere, MA 781-485-4500
Old Dominion Peanut Corporation
Norfolk, VA 800-368-6887
Peerless Confection Company
Lincolnwood, IL 773-281-6100
Piedmont Candy Corporation
Lexington, NC 336-248-2477
R.M. Palmer Company
Reading, PA 610-372-8971
Randag & Associates Inc
Elmhurst, IL 630-530-2830
Setton International Foods
Commack, NY 800-227-4397
Shane Candy Company
Philadelphia, PA 215-922-1048
Sherwood Brands
Rockville, MD 401-434-7773
Wisconsin Cheese
Melrose Park, IL 708-450-0074
World Confections
Brooklyn, NY 718-768-8100

Easter

Bee Int'l., Inc
Chula Vista, CA 800-421-6465
Blanton's
Sweetwater, TN 423-337-3487
Bohemian Biscuit Company
South San Francisco, CA 650-952-2226
Charlotte's Confections
Millbrae, CA 800-798-2427
Chase Candy Company
Saint Joseph, MO 800-786-1625
Chocolat Jean Talon
Montreal, QC 888-333-8540
Chris A. Papas & Son Company
Covington, KY 859-431-0499
David Bradley Chocolatier
Windsor, NJ 877-289-7933
Day Spring Enterprises
Cheektowaga, NY 800-879-7677

Doscher's Candies
Cincinnati, OH 513-381-8656
Ferrara Bakery & Cafe
New York, NY 212-226-6150
Gimbal's Fine Candies
S San Francisco, CA. . . . 800-344-6225
GKI Foods
Brighton, MI 248-486-0055
Gladstone Candies
Cleveland, OH 888-729-1960
Golden Fluff Popcorn Company
Lakewood, NJ 732-367-5448
Jelly Belly Candy Company
Fairfield, CA 800-522-3267
Judson-Atkinson Candies
San Antonio, TX 800-962-3984
Leader Candies
Brooklyn, NY 718-366-6900
Madrona Specialty Foods
Tukwila, WA 425-814-2500
Mona Lisa® Chocolatier
Arlington, VA 866-662-5475
Multiflex Company
Hawthorne, NJ 973-636-9700
Necco
Revere, MA 781-485-4500
New England Confectionery Company
Revere, MA 781-485-4500
Piedmont Candy Corporation
Lexington, NC 336-248-2477
R.M. Palmer Company
Reading, PA 610-372-8971
Sayklly's Candies & Gifts
Escanaba, MI 906-786-3092
Sherwood Brands
Rockville, MD 401-434-7773
Vande Walle's Candies
Appleton, WI 920-738-7799
Variety Foods
Warren, MI 586-268-4900
Vigneri Confections
Rochester, NY 877-843-6374
Wisconsin Cheese
Melrose Park, IL 708-450-0074
World Confections
Brooklyn, NY 718-768-8100
Zitner Company
Philadelphia, PA 215-229-4990

Fund Raising

Chase Candy Company
Saint Joseph, MO 800-786-1625
Chris A. Papas & Son Company
Covington, KY 859-431-0499
Clarks Joe Fund Raising Candies & Novelties
Tarentum, PA 888-459-9520
David Bradley Chocolatier
Windsor, NJ 877-289-7933
Go Lightly Candy
Hillside, NJ 800-524-1304
Joyva Corporation
Brooklyn, NY 718-497-0170
Koeze Company
Wyoming, MI 800-555-3909
Leader Candies
Brooklyn, NY 718-366-6900
Lukas Confections
York, PA 717-843-0921
New England Confectionery Company
Revere, MA 781-485-4500
Old Dominion Peanut Corporation
Norfolk, VA 800-368-6887
Quigley Manufacturing
Elizabethtown, PA 800-367-2441
Randag & Associates Inc
Elmhurst, IL 630-530-2830
Sherwood Brands
Rockville, MD 401-434-7773
Sweet Productions
Amityville, NY 631-842-0548
Terri Lynn
Elgin, IL 800-323-0775
Vande Walle's Candies
Appleton, WI 920-738-7799
Wisconsin Cheese
Melrose Park, IL 708-450-0074

Halloween

Astor Chocolate
Lakewood, NJ 732-901-1000
Atkinson Candy Company
Lufkin, TX 800-231-1203
Bee Int'l., Inc
Chula Vista, CA 800-421-6465
Blanton's
Sweetwater, TN 423-337-3487
Bohemian Biscuit Company
South San Francisco, CA 650-952-2226
Brach's Confections
Halethorpe, MD 443-872-2094
Charlotte's Confections
Millbrae, CA 800-798-2427
Chase Candy Company
Saint Joseph, MO 800-786-1625
Chocolat Jean Talon
Montreal, QC 888-333-8540
David Bradley Chocolatier
Windsor, NJ 877-289-7933
Day Spring Enterprises
Cheektowaga, NY 800-879-7677
Ferrara Bakery & Cafe
New York, NY 212-226-6150
Gimbal's Fine Candies
S San Francisco, CA 800-344-6225
GKI Foods
Brighton, MI 248-486-0055
Gladstone Candies
Cleveland, OH 888-729-1960
Jelly Belly Candy Company
Fairfield, CA 800-522-3267
Joyva Corporation
Brooklyn, NY 718-497-0170
Judson-Atkinson Candies
San Antonio, TX 800-962-3984
Leader Candies
Brooklyn, NY 718-366-6900
Lukas Confections
York, PA 717-843-0921
Madrona Specialty Foods
Tukwila, WA 425-814-2500
New England Confectionery Company
Revere, MA 781-485-4500
Piedmont Candy Corporation
Lexington, NC 336-248-2477
R.M. Palmer Company
Reading, PA 610-372-8971
Shane Candy Company
Philadelphia, PA 215-922-1048
Sherwood Brands
Rockville, MD 401-434-7773
World Confections
Brooklyn, NY 718-768-8100
Yost Candy Company
Dalton, OH 800-750-1976

Multi-Packs

Mona Lisa® Chocolatier
Arlington, VA 866-662-5475
New England Confectionery Company
Revere, MA 781-485-4500
Wisconsin Cheese
Melrose Park, IL 708-450-0074
World Confections
Brooklyn, NY 718-768-8100

Non-Chocolate - Boxed

Go Lightly Candy
Hillside, NJ 800-524-1304
Hershey International
Weston, FL 954-385-2600
Leader Candies
Brooklyn, NY 718-366-6900
Moore's Candies
Baltimore, MD 410-426-2705
Necco
Revere, MA 781-485-4500
Ozone Confectioners & Bakers Supplies
Elmwood Park, NJ 201-791-4444
Webbs Citrus Candy
Davenport, FL 863-422-1051
Willy Wonka Candy Factory
Itasca, IL 630-773-0267

Packaged for Racks

American Licorice Company
Union City, CA 866-442-2783
David Bradley Chocolatier
Windsor, NJ 877-289-7933
Golden Apples Candy Company
Southport, CT 800-776-0393
Jason & Son Specialty Foods
Rancho Cordova, CA 800-810-9093
Jelly Belly Candy Company
Fairfield, CA 800-522-3267
Jo Mints
Corona Del Mar, CA 877-566-4687
Joyva Corporation
Brooklyn, NY 718-497-0170
Mona Lisa® Chocolatier
Arlington, VA 866-662-5475
Necco
Revere, MA 781-485-4500
New England Confectionery Company
Revere, MA 781-485-4500
Setton International Foods
Commack, NY 800-227-4397
Weaver Nut Company
Ephrata, PA 717-738-3781

Packaged for Theaters

American Licorice Company
Union City, CA 866-442-2783
Bruno's Cajun Foods & Snacks
Slidell, LA 985-726-0544
Joyva Corporation
Brooklyn, NY 718-497-0170
Mona Lisa® Chocolatier
Arlington, VA 866-662-5475
Necco
Revere, MA 781-485-4500
New England Confectionery Company
Revere, MA 781-485-4500

Valentine

Arway Confections
Chicago, IL 773-267-5770
Astor Chocolate
Lakewood, NJ 732-901-1000
Bee Int'l., Inc
Chula Vista, CA 800-421-6465
Blanton's
Sweetwater, TN 423-337-3487
Bohemian Biscuit Company
South San Francisco, CA 650-952-2226
Brach's Confections
Halethorpe, MD 443-872-2094
Charlotte's Confections
Millbrae, CA 800-798-2427
Chase Candy Company
Saint Joseph, MO 800-786-1625
David Bradley Chocolatier
Windsor, NJ 877-289-7933
Day Spring Enterprises
Cheektowaga, NY 800-879-7677
Ferrara Bakery & Cafe
New York, NY 212-226-6150
Gimbal's Fine Candies
S San Francisco, CA 800-344-6225
Gladstone Candies
Cleveland, OH 888-729-1960
Jelly Belly Candy Company
Fairfield, CA 800-522-3267
Judson-Atkinson Candies
San Antonio, TX 800-962-3984
Leader Candies
Brooklyn, NY 718-366-6900
Mona Lisa® Chocolatier
Arlington, VA 866-662-5475
Necco
Revere, MA 781-485-4500
New England Confectionery Company
Revere, MA 781-485-4500
R.M. Palmer Company
Reading, PA 610-372-8971
Rito Mints
Trois Rivieres, QC 819-379-1449
Shane Candy Company
Philadelphia, PA 215-922-1048
Sherwood Brands
Rockville, MD 401-434-7773
Vande Walle's Candies
Appleton, WI 920-738-7799
Wisconsin Cheese
Melrose Park, IL 708-450-0074
World Confections
Brooklyn, NY 718-768-8100

Vending

Bruno's Cajun Foods & Snacks
Slidell, LA 985-726-0544

Chase Candy Company
Saint Joseph, MO 800-786-1625
Chris A. Papas & Son Company
Covington, KY 859-431-0499
GKI Foods
Brighton, MI 248-486-0055
Jo Mints
Corona Del Mar, CA. 877-566-4687
Joyva Corporation
Brooklyn, NY 718-497-0170
Lukas Confections
York, PA 717-843-0921
Mona Lisa® Chocolatier
Arlington, VA 866-662-5475
Necco
Revere, MA. 781-485-4500
New England Confectionery Company
Revere, MA. 781-485-4500

Cereals, Grains, Rice & Flour

Alfalfa

American Health & Nutrition
Ann Arbor, MI 734-677-5570
Enray, Inc
Livermore, CA 925-218-2205
Herb Connection
Springville, UT 801-489-4254
Julie Anne's
Las Vegas, NV 702-767-4765
Naturex Inc.
South Hackensack, NJ 201-440-5000
S&E Organic Farms
Bakersfield, CA 661-325-2644
Sungarden Sprouts
Cookeville, TN 931-526-1106
Verhoff Alfalfa Mills
Ottawa, OH 800-834-8563

Barley

ADM Milling Company
Shawnee Mission, KS 800-422-1688
Agricore United
Winnipeg, MB 800-661-4844
AgriCulver Seeds
Trumansburg, NY 800-836-3701
Chieftain Wild Rice Company
Spooner, WI 800-262-6368
ConAgra Mills
Omaha, NE 800-851-9618
Cooperative Elevator Company
Pigeon, MI 989-453-4500
Ferris Organic Farm
Eaton Rapids, MI 800-628-8736
Fizzle Flat Farm
Yale, IL 618-793-2060
Grain Millers
Eden Prairie, MN 800-232-6287
Grain Millers Eugene
Eugene, OR 800-443-8972
Graysmarsh Farm
Sequim, WA 800-683-4367
Green Foods Corporation
Oxnard, CA 800-777-4430
Herb Connection
Springville, UT 801-489-4254
Honeyville Grain
Rancho Cucamonga, CA 888-810-3212
Natural Way Mills
Middle River, MN 218-222-3677
Ottawa Valley Grain Products
Renfrew, ON 613-432-3614
Pines International
Lawrence, KS 800-697-4637
Prairie Malt
Biggar, SK 306-948-3500
Quaker Oats Company
Cedar Rapids, IA 319-362-0200
Rahr Malting Company
Shakopee, MN 952-445-1431
Raymond-Hadley Corporation
Spencer, NY 800-252-5220
T.S. Smith & Sons
Bridgeville, DE 302-337-8271
Wallace Grain & Pea Company
Palouse, WA 509-878-1561
Weetabix Company
Clinton, MA 800-343-0590
Western Pacific Commodities
Henderson, NV 702-382-8880

Bran

ADM Food Ingredients
Olathe, KS 800-255-6637
American Health & Nutrition
Ann Arbor, MI 734-677-5570
Blue Chip Group
Salt Lake City, UT 800-878-0099
Bunge Milling
Woodland, CA 800-747-4764
Canadian Harvest
Cambridge, MN 888-689-5800
Chef Hans Gourmet Foods
Monroe, LA 800-890-4267
Dakota Organic Products
Watertown, SD 800-243-7264
Farmers Rice Milling Company
Lake Charles, LA 337-433-5205
Glorybee Foods
Eugene, OR 800-456-7923
Great Grains Milling Company
Scobey, MT 406-783-5581
GS Dunn & Company
Hamilton, ON 905-522-0833
J.R. Short Canadian Mills
Toronto, ON 416-421-3463
Knappen Milling Company
Augusta, MI 800-562-7736
Ohta Wafer Factory
Honolulu, HI 808-949-2775
Raymond-Hadley Corporation
Spencer, NY 800-252-5220
Ricex Company
El Dorado Hills, CA 916-933-3000
Riviana Foods
Houston, TX 713-529-3251
Riviana Foods
Memphis, TN 901-942-0540
SJH Enterprises
Middleton, WI 888-745-3845
Southern Brown Rice
Weiner, AR 800-421-7423
Star of the West MillingCompany
Frankenmuth, MI 989-652-9971
Stearns & Lehman
Mansfield, OH 800-533-2722
Wall-Rogalsky Milling Company
Mc Pherson, KS 800-835-2067
Weetabix Company
Clinton, MA 800-343-0590

Mustard

GS Dunn & Company
Hamilton, ON 905-522-0833

Rice

Beaumont Rice Mills
Beaumont, TX 409-832-2521
Bunge Milling
Woodland, CA 800-747-4764
Farmers Rice Milling Company
Lake Charles, LA 337-433-5205
Janca's Jojoba Oil & Seed Company
Mesa, AZ 480-497-9494
Louis Dreyfus Corporation
Wilton, CT 203-761-2000
Ricex Company
El Dorado Hills, CA 916-933-3000
Riviana Foods
Houston, TX 713-529-3251
Sahara Natural Foods
San Leandro, CA 510-352-5111
Southern Brown Rice
Weiner, AR 800-421-7423
Suzanne's Specialties
New Brunswick, NJ 800-762-2135

Wheat

ADM Food Ingredients
Olathe, KS 800-255-6637
American Health & Nutrition
Ann Arbor, MI 734-677-5570
Blue Chip Group
Salt Lake City, UT 800-878-0099
Canadian Harvest
Cambridge, MN 888-689-5800
Wall-Rogalsky Milling Company
Mc Pherson, KS 800-835-2067

Cereal

Amcan Industries
Elmsford, NY 914-347-4838
American Health & Nutrition
Ann Arbor, MI 734-677-5572
Barbara's Bakery
Petaluma, CA 707-765-2273
Bob's Red Mill Natural Foods
Milwaukie, OR 800-553-2258
Cambridge Food
Monterey, CA 800-433-2584
Clara Foods
Clara City, MN 888-844-8518
Coach's Oats
Yorba Linda, CA 714-692-6885
Earth Song Whole Foods
Fair Oaks, CA 877-327-8476
Fiddlers Green Farm
Belfast, ME 800-729-7935
Food Ingredients
Elgin, IL 800-500-7676
Gilster Mary Lee/Jasper Foods
Jasper, MO 800-777-2168
Golden Temple
Los Angeles, CA 310-275-9891
Golden Temple
Springfield, OR 800-964-4832
Grain Place Foods
Marquette, NE 888-714-7246
Grain Process Enterprises Ltd.
Scarborough, ON 800-387-5292
Harvest Innovations
Indianola, IA 515-962-5063
InfraReady Products Ltd.
Saskatoon, SK 800-510-1828
Inn Maid Food
Lenox, MA 413-637-2732
Kashi Company
La Jolla, CA 858-274-8870
Kemach Food Products Corporation
Brooklyn, NY 888-453-6224
Kraft Canada Headquarters
Don Mills, ON 888-572-3806
Malt-O-Meal Company
Northfield, MN 507-645-6681
McKee Foods Corporation
Collegedale, TN 423-238-7111
Nature's Path Foods
Richmond, BC 604-248-8777
New England Natural Baker
Greenfield, MA 800-910-2884
Newman's Own
Westport, CT 203-222-0136
Nu-World Amaranth
Naperville, IL 630-369-6819
Paktec-100% Tunisian Olive Oil
Johnson City, TN 423-467-9864
Prairie Mills Company
Rochester, IN 574-223-3177
Quaker
Barrington, IL 800-333-8027
Quaker Oats Company
Cedar Rapids, IA 319-362-0200
Raymond-Hadley Corporation
Spencer, NY 800-252-5220
Rhone-Poulenc Food Ingredients
Cranbury, NJ 609-860-4000
Ryt Way Industries
Lakeville, MN 952-469-1417
SBK Preserves
Bronx, NY 800-773-7378
Sun Ridge Farms
Pajaro, CA 831-786-7000
Sunridge Farms
Salinas, CA 831-755-1430
US Foods
Lincoln, NE 402-470-2021
Watson Inc
West Haven, CT 800-388-3481
Wildtime Foods
Eugene, OR 800-356-4458

Breakfast

Agricore United
Winnipeg, MB 800-661-4844
AlpineAire Foods
Rocklin, CA 800-322-6325
Aventine Renewable Energy
Pekin, IL 309-347-9200
Bake Crafters Food
Collegedale, TN 800-296-8935

Barbara's Bakery
Petaluma, CA 707-765-2273
Bartlett Milling Company
Coffeyville, KS 620-251-4650
Bede Inc
Haledon, NJ 866-239-6565
Birkett Mills
Penn Yan, NY 315-536-4112
Black Ranch Organic Grains
Etna, CA 530-467-3387
Blue Chip Group
Salt Lake City, UT 800-878-0099
Blue Planet Foods
Collegedale, TN 877-396-3145
C.H. Guenther & Son
San Antonio, TX 800-531-7912
California Cereal Products
Oakland, CA 510-452-4500
Carlisle Cereal Company
Bismarck, ND 800-809-6018
Cereal Food Processors
Mission Woods, KS 913-890-6300
Christine & Rob's
Stayton, OR 503-769-2993
Colorado Cereal
Fort Collins, CO 970-282-9733
Cook Natural Products
Oakland, CA 800-537-7589
Cook-In-The-Kitchen
White River Junction, VT 802-333-4141
Country Choice Naturals
Eden Prairie, MN 952-829-8824
Cream of the West
Harlowton, MT 800-477-2383
Eagle Agricultural Products
Huntsville, AR 501-738-2203
Edwards Mill
Point Lookout, MO 800-222-0525
Efco Products
Poughkeepsie, NY 800-284-3326
Ener-G Foods
Seattle, WA 800-331-5222
Farmers Rice Milling Company
Lake Charles, LA 337-433-5205
Fearn Natural Foods
Thiensville, WI 800-877-8935
Fry Krisp Food Products
Jackson, MI 517-784-8531
General Mills
Minneapolis, MN 800-248-7310
GFA Brands
Paramus, NJ 201-568-9300
Gilster Mary Lee/Jasper Foods
Jasper, MO 800-777-2168
Gilster-Mary Lee Corporation
Chester, IL 800-851-5371
GKI Foods
Brighton, MI 248-486-0055
Golden Temple, Sunshine & Yogi Tea
Los Angeles, CA 800-225-3623
Grain Process Enterprises Ltd.
Scarborough, ON 800-387-5292
Health Valley Company
Irwindale, CA 800-334-3204
Hilltown Whole Food Company
Cummington, MA 413-634-5677
Hodgson Mill Inc.
Effingham, IL 800-525-0177
Homestead Mills
Cook, MN 800-652-5233
House Autry Mills
Four Oaks, NC 800-849-0802
Indiana Grain Company
Baltimore, MD 410-685-6410
International Home Foods
Parsippany, NJ 973-359-9920
Kellogg Canada Inc
Mississauga, ON 888-876-3750
Kellogg Company
Omaha, NE 402-331-7717
Kellogg Company
Memphis, TN 901-743-0052
Klemme Cooperative Grainery
Klemme, IA 641-444-4262
Knappen Milling Company
Augusta, MI 800-562-7736
Lassen Foods
Santa Barbara, CA 805-683-7696
Liberty Richter
Saddle Brook, NJ 201-291-8749
Lincoln Mills
Jersey City, NJ 201-433-0070
Little Crow Foods
Warsaw, IN 800-288-2769
Louisiana Rice Company
Welsh, LA 337-734-4362
Luban International
Doral, FL 305-629-8730
Lundberg Family Farm
Richvale, CA 530-882-4551
Malt-O-Meal Company
Northfield, MN 507-645-6681
Malt-O-Meal Company
Northfield, MN 800-743-3029
Mantrose-Haeuser Company
Westport, CT 800-344-4229
Martha Olson's Great Foods
Sutter Creek, CA 800-973-3966
Mills Brothers International
Tukwila, WA 206-575-3000
Milner Milling
Chattanooga, TN 423-265-2313
Mixes By Danielle
Warren, OH 800-537-6499
Morrison Milling Company
Denton, TX 800-580-5487
National Vinegar Company
Houston, TX 713-223-4214
Natural Way Mills
Middle River, MN 218-222-3677
Nature's Hand
Burnsville, MN 952-890-6033
New England Natural Baker
Greenfield, MA 800-910-2884
Nutri Base
Phoenix, AZ 877-223-5459
Organic Milling Company
San Dimas, CA 800-638-8686
PepsiCo Chicago
Chicago, IL 312-821-1000
Prairie Sun Grains
Calgary, AB 800-556-6807
Premier Cereals
Clyde Hill, WA 425-451-1451
Quaker
Barrington, IL 800-333-8027
Quaker Oats Company
Stockton, CA 209-982-5580
Quaker Oats Company
Danville, IL 217-443-4995
Quaker Oats Company
Cedar Rapids, IA 319-362-0200
Quaker Oats Company
Peterborough, ON 800-267-6287
Ralcorp Holdings
St Louis, MO 800-772-6757
Roman Meal Milling Company
Fargo, ND 877-282-9743
Sam Wylde Flour Company
Seattle, WA 206-762-5400
Senor Pinos de Santa Fe
Santa Fe, NM 505-473-3437
Silver Palate Kitchens
Cresskill, NJ 800-872-5283
Stafford County Flour Mills Company
Hudson, KS 800-530-5640
Star of the West MillingCompany
Frankenmuth, MI 989-652-9971
Sturm Foods
Manawa, WI 800-347-8876
Thymly Products
Colora, MD 410-658-4820
Trinidad Benham Company
Mineola, TX 903-569-2636
US Foods
Lincoln, NE 402-470-2021
US Mills
Bala Cynwyd, PA 800-422-1125
Wanda's Nature Farm
Lincoln, NE 800-735-6828
Washington Quality Food Products
Ellicott City, MD 800-735-3585
Weetabix of Canada
Cobourg, ON 800-343-0590

Corn-Based

Quaker Oats Company
Cedar Rapids, IA 319-362-0200

Farina

Sturm Foods
Manawa, WI 800-347-8876

Instant

Malt-O-Meal Company
Northfield, MN 507-645-6681
Purity Foods
Okemos, MI 800-997-7358

Muesli

Baker
Milford, NJ 800-995-3989

Oatmeal

American Health & Nutrition
Ann Arbor, MI 734-677-5570
Sturm Foods
Manawa, WI 800-347-8876

Rice-Based

Fantastic Foods
Napa, CA 800-288-1089
Lundberg Family Farm
Richvale, CA 530-882-4551
Quaker Oats Company
Cedar Rapids, IA 319-362-0200

Rolled Oats

American Health & Nutrition
Ann Arbor, MI 734-677-5570

Wheat-Based

H. Fox & Company
Brooklyn, NY 718-385-4600
Malt-O-Meal Company
Northfield, MN 507-645-6681
Quaker Oats Company
Cedar Rapids, IA 319-362-0200

Corn Germ

Aussie Crunch
Nashville, TN 800-401-6534

Corn Meal

Adluh Flour Mill
Columbia, SC 800-692-3584
ADM Milling Company
Jackson, TN 731-424-3535
ADM Milling Company
Shawnee Mission, KS 913-491-9400
Agricor
Marion, IN 765-662-0606
American Key Food Products
Closter, NJ 800-767-0237
Ashland Milling
Ashland, VA 804-798-8329
Atkinson Milling Company
Selma, NC 800-948-5707
Bob's Red Mill Natural Foods
Milwaukie, OR 800-553-2258
California Oils Corporation
Richmond, CA 800-225-6457
Chieftain Wild Rice Company
Spooner, WI 800-262-6368
Eagle Agricultural Products
Huntsville, AR 501-738-2203
Hodgson Mill Inc.
Effingham, IL 800-525-0177
Homestead Mills
Cook, MN 800-652-5233
Honeyville Grain
Rancho Cucamonga, CA 888-810-3212
Hoople Country Kitchens
Rockport, IN 812-649-2351
J.P. Green Milling Company
Mocksville, NC 336-751-2126
Lakeside Mills
Rutherfordton, NC 828-286-4866
Maysville Milling Company
Maysville, NC 910-743-3481
Midstate Mills
Newton, NC 800-222-1032
Mills Brothers International
Tukwila, WA 206-575-3000
Nustef Foods
Mississauga, ON 905-896-3060
Scott's Auburn Mills
Russellville, KY 270-726-2080

Shawnee Milling Company
Shawnee, OK 405-273-7000
Shenandoah Mills
Lebanon, TN 615-444-0841
SJH Enterprises
Middleton, WI. 888-745-3845
Southeastern Mills
Rome, GA. 800-334-4468
UNOI Grainmill
Seaford, DE. 302-629-4083
War Eagle Mill
Rogers, AR 479-789-5343
White Lily Foods Company
Memphis, TN 800-595-1380
Wilkins-Rogers
Ellicott City, MD. 410-465-5800

Crisps

Brown Rice

Kerry Ingredients
Blue Earth, MN. 507-526-7575

Cereal

Kerry Ingredients
Blue Earth, MN. 507-526-7575

Cocoa Rice

Kerry Ingredients
Blue Earth, MN. 507-526-7575

Cocoa Soy

Kerry Ingredients
Blue Earth, MN. 507-526-7575

Colored

Kerry Ingredients
Blue Earth, MN. 507-526-7575

Crisped Bran

Kerry Ingredients
Blue Earth, MN. 507-526-7575

Crisped Corn

Kerry Ingredients
Blue Earth, MN. 507-526-7575

Crisped Oat

Kerry Ingredients
Blue Earth, MN. 507-526-7575

Crisped Rice

Kerry Ingredients
Blue Earth, MN. 507-526-7575

Crisped Soy

Kerry Ingredients
Blue Earth, MN. 507-526-7575

Crisped Wheat

Kerry Ingredients
Blue Earth, MN. 507-526-7575

Flax

Harvest Innovations
Indianola, IA. 515-962-5063
Kerry Ingredients
Blue Earth, MN. 507-526-7575

Oat Fiber

Kerry Ingredients
Blue Earth, MN. 507-526-7575

Rice

Kerry Ingredients
Blue Earth, MN. 507-526-7575

Soy

Kerry Ingredients
Blue Earth, MN. 507-526-7575

Whey

Kerry Ingredients
Blue Earth, MN. 507-526-7575

Fiber

ADM Corn Processing
Decatur, IL 800-553-8411
ADM Food Ingredients
Olathe, KS. 800-255-6637
Alfred L. Wolff, Inc.
Park Ridge, IL. 847-759-8888
Canadian Harvest
Cambridge, MN 888-689-5800
Cereal Ingredients
Kansas City, MO. 816-891-1055
CreaFill Fibers Corporation
Chestertown, MD 800-832-4662
Dakota Organic Products
Watertown, SD 800-243-7264
Eckhart Corporation
Novato, CA. 415-892-3880
Functional Foods
Englishtown, NJ 800-442-9524
Garuda International
Lemon Cove, CA 559-594-4380
Grain Millers
Eden Prairie, MN 800-232-6287
Great Grains Milling Company
Scobey, MT. 406-783-5581
Gum Technology Corporation
Tucson, AZ. 800-369-4867
International Fiber Corporation
North Tonawanda, NY 888-698-1936
Loders Croklaan
Channahon, IL 800-621-4710
Mineral & Pigment Solutions
South Plainfield, NJ 800-732-0562
ND Labs Inc
Lynbrook, NY. 888-263-5227
Omni-Pak Industries
Anaheim, CA 714-765-8323
Organic Milling Company
San Dimas, CA 800-638-8686
Ricex Company
El Dorado Hills, CA 916-933-3000
San-Ei Gen FFI
New York, NY 212-315-7850
Southern Brown Rice
Weiner, AR 800-421-7423
Sun Opta Ingredients
Chelmsford, MA. 800-353-6782
Suzanne's Specialties
New Brunswick, NJ 800-762-2135
Tastee Apple Inc
Newcomerstown, OH 800-262-7753
Tic Gums
Belcamp, MD 800-221-3953
Unique Ingredients
Naches, WA. 509-653-1991
Vivion
San Carlos, CA 800-479-0997
Watson Inc
West Haven, CT 800-388-3481
World Flavors
Warminster, PA 215-672-4400
Yerba Prima
Ashland, OR 800-488-4339

Barley Bran

Roman Meal Milling Company
Tacoma, WA 253-475-0964

Cellulose

Gum Technology Corporation
Tucson, AZ 800-369-4867

Corn Bran

Canadian Harvest
Cambridge, MN 888-689-5800

Oat Bran

American Health & Nutrition
Ann Arbor, MI 734-677-5570
Canadian Harvest
Cambridge, MN 888-689-5800

Oats

American Health & Nutrition
Ann Arbor, MI 734-677-5570
Canadian Harvest
Cambridge, MN 888-689-5800
Organic Planet
San Francisco, CA 415-765-5590
Roman Meal Milling Company
Tacoma, WA 253-475-0964

Resistant Starch

Cargill Texturizing Solutions
Cedar Rapids, IA. 877-650-7080

Soy Bran

Fibred-Maryland
Cumberland, MD 800-598-8894

Supplements

Abunda Life Laboratories
Asbury Park, NJ 732-775-7575
ADM Food Ingredients
Olathe, KS. 800-255-6637
Innovative Health Products
Largo, FL 800-654-2347
Southern Brown Rice
Weiner, AR 800-421-7423
Suzanne's Specialties
New Brunswick, NJ 800-762-2135
Tastee Apple Inc
Newcomerstown, OH 800-262-7753

Wheat Bran

Canadian Harvest
Cambridge, MN 888-689-5800
Cereal Ingredients
Kansas City, MO. 816-891-1055

Flour

Acadian Seaplants
Dartmouth, NS 800-575-9100
Adluh Flour Mill
Columbia, SC 800-692-3584
ADM Food Ingredients
Olathe, KS. 800-255-6637
ADM Milling Company
Chicago, IL 312-666-2465
ADM Milling Company
Carthage, MO 417-358-2197
ADM Milling Company
Cleveland, TN. 423-476-7551
ADM Milling Company
Chattanooga, TN. 423-756-0503
ADM Milling Company
Spokane, WA. 509-534-2636
ADM Milling Company
Arkansas City, KS. 620-442-6200
ADM Milling Company
Charlotte, NC 704-332-3165
ADM Milling Company
Abilene, KS. 785-263-1631
ADM Milling Company
Mississauga, ON. 800-267-8492
ADM Milling Company
Minneapolis, MN 800-528-7877
ADM Milling Company
Shawnee Mission, KS. 913-491-9400
AG Processing, Inc.
Omaha, NE 800-247-1345
Agri-Dairy Products
Purchase, NY 914-697-9580
Agricor
Marion, IN. 765-662-0606
Agricore United
Winnipeg, MB. 800-661-4844
Amendt Corporation
Monroe, MI. 734-242-2411
American Almond Products Company
Brooklyn, NY 800-825-6663
American Health & Nutrition
Ann Arbor, MI 734-677-5570
Ashland Milling
Ashland, VA 804-798-8329
Atlantic Seasonings
Kinston, NC 800-433-5261
Attala Company
Kosciusko, MS 800-824-2691

Azteca Milling
Irving, TX 800-364-0040
Bay State Milling Company
Winona, MN 800-533-8098
Bay State Milling Company
Quincy, MA. 800-553-5687
Beta Pure Foods
Aptos, CA 831-685-6565
Big J. Milling & Elevato Company
Brigham City, UT 435-723-3459
Birkett Mills
Penn Yan, NY 315-536-4112
Blend Pak
Bloomfield, KY 502-252-8000
Blue Chip Group
Salt Lake City, UT 800-878-0099
Bob's Red Mill Natural Foods
Milwaukie, OR 800-553-2258
Bouchard Family Farm
Fort Kent, ME. 800-239-3237
Brandt Mills
Mifflinville, PA. 570-752-4271
Byrd Mill Company
Ashland, VA 888-897-3336
California Cereal Products
Oakland, CA 510-452-4500
Cargill Dry Corn Ingredients
Paris, IL. 800-637-6481
Cargill Flour Milling
Minneapolis, MN 800-227-4455
Centennial Mills
Cheney, WA 509-235-6216
Central Milling Company
Logan, UT. 435-752-6625
Cereal Food Processors
Cleveland, OH 216-621-3206
Cereal Food Processors
Salt Lake City, UT 801-355-2981
Cereal Food Processors
Mission Woods, KS 913-890-6300
Champlain Valley Milling Corporation
Westport, NY. 518-962-4711
CHR Hansen
Elyria, OH. 800-558-0802
CHS
Inver Grove Heights, MN. 800-232-3639
Clofine Dairy & Food Products
Linwood, NJ 800-441-1001
Community Mill & Bean
Savannah, NY. 800-755-0554
ConAgra Flour Milling
Commerce City, CO 303-289-6141
ConAgra Flour Milling
Fremont, NE 402-721-4200
ConAgra Flour Milling
Macon, GA 478-743-5424
ConAgra Flour Milling
Oakland, CA 510-536-9555
ConAgra Flour Milling
Martins Creek, PA. 610-253-9341
ConAgra Flour Milling
Chester, IL. 618-826-2371
ConAgra Flour Milling
Red Lion, PA. 717-244-4559
ConAgra Flour Milling
York, PA 717-846-7773
ConAgra Flour Milling
Sherman, TX. 903-893-8111
ConAgra Mills
Tampa, FL. 800-582-1483
ConAgra Mills
Omaha, NE 800-851-9618
Dakota Organic Products
Watertown, SD 800-243-7264
Dan's Feed Bin
Superior, WI 715-394-6639
Devansoy
Carroll, IA. 800-747-8605
Dillman Farm
Bloomington, IN. 800-359-1362
Dipasa
Brownsville, TX 956-831-5893
Eagle Agricultural Products
Huntsville, AR 501-738-2203
Eden Foods Inc.
Clinton, MI 800-248-0320
El Peto Products
Cambridge, ON. 800-387-4064
Ellison Milling Company
Lethbridge, AB 403-328-6622
Ener-G Foods
Seattle, WA 800-331-5222
Erba Food Products
Brooklyn, NY 718-272-7700
Fairhaven Cooperative Flour Mill
Burlington, WA
Fastachi
Watertown, MA. 800-466-3022
Fearn Natural Foods
Thiensville, WI 800-877-8935
Fresh Hemp Foods
Winnipeg, NB 800-665-4367
General Mills
Minneapolis, MN 800-248-7310
Gilt Edge Flour Mills
Richmond, UT. 435-258-2425
Goldilocks Bakeshop
South San Francisco, CA 925-681-1888
Grain Process Enterprises Ltd.
Scarborough, ON 800-387-5292
Great Grains Milling Company
Scobey, MT. 406-783-5581
Greenfield Mills
Howe, IN. 260-367-2394
GS Dunn & Company
Hamilton, ON 905-522-0833
Harbar Corporation
Canton, MA 800-881-7040
Heartland Mill
Marienthal, KS 800-232-8533
Hialeah Products Company
Hollywood, FL 800-923-3379
Hodgson Mill Inc.
Effingham, IL 800-525-0177
Homestead Mills
Cook, MN 800-652-5233
Honeyville Grain
Rancho Cucamonga, CA 888-810-3212
Idaho Pacific Corporation
Ririe, ID 800-238-5503
Idaho-Frank Associates
Pleasant Hill, CA 925-609-8458
J.P. Green Milling Company
Mocksville, NC. 336-751-2126
J.R. Short Canadian Mills
Toronto, ON 416-421-3463
J.R. Short Milling Company
Kankakee, IL. 800-544-8734
Kaufman Ingredients
Vernon Hills, IL 847-573-0844
Kemach Food Products Corporation
Brooklyn, NY 888-453-6224
King Arthur Flour
Norwich, VT 802-649-3881
King Milling Company
Lowell, MI 616-897-9264
Knappen Milling Company
Augusta, MI 800-562-7736
Lacey Milling Company
Hanford, CA 559-584-6634
Lehi Roller Mills
Lehi, UT 800-660-4346
Lucas Meyer
Decatur, IL 800-769-3660
Mennel Milling Company
Fostoria, OH 419-435-8151
Mennel Milling Company
Fostoria, OH 800-688-8151
MexAmerica Foods
St Marys, PA 814-781-1447
Midstate Mills
Newton, NC 800-222-1032
Mills Brothers International
Tukwila, WA 206-575-3000
Minn-Dak Growers Ltd.
Grand Forks, ND. 701-746-7453
Montana Flour & Grain
Fort Benton, MT. 406-622-5436
Morris J. Golombeck
Brooklyn, NY 718-284-3505
Mother Earth Enterprises
New York, NY 866-436-7688
Natural Products
Grinnell, IA. 641-236-0852
Natural Way Mills
Middle River, MN. 218-222-3677
Naturex Inc.
South Hackensack, NJ 201-440-5000
New Hope Mills
Auburn, NY. 315-252-2676
Newly Weds Foods
Chicago, IL 800-621-7521
North Dakota Mill
Grand Forks, ND. 800-538-7721
Northwestern Foods
Saint Paul, MN 800-236-4937
Nunn Milling Company
Evansville, IN 800-547-6866
Oak Creek Farms
Edgar, NE 402-224-3038
Okeene Milling
Shawnee, OK 405-273-7000
Old Dutch Mustard Company
Great Neck, NY 516-466-0522
Oregon Potato Company
Boardman, OR 800-336-6311
Orlinda Milling Company
Orlinda, TN. 615-654-3633
Particle Control
Albertville, MN. 763-497-3075
Pendleton Flour Mills
Pendleton, OR. 541-276-6511
Pillsbury
Minneapolis, MN 800-775-4777
Prairie Mills Company
Rochester, IN 574-223-3177
Prairie Sun Grains
Calgary, AB. 800-556-6807
Premier Blending
Wichita, KS. 316-267-5533
Produits Alimentaire
St Lambert De Lauzon, QC 800-463-1787
Purato's
Seattle, WA 206-762-5400
Purity Foods
Okemos, MI 800-997-7358
Quality Naturally! Foods
City of Industry, CA 888-498-6986
R&J Farms
West Salem, OH 419-846-3179
Raymond-Hadley Corporation
Spencer, NY 800-252-5220
Research Products Company
Salina, KS 800-234-7174
Roman Meal Milling Company
Fargo, ND 877-282-9743
Sanford Milling Company
Henderson, NC 252-438-4526
Scott's Auburn Mills
Russellville, KY 270-726-2080
SFP Food Products
Conway, AR 800-654-5329
Shawnee Milling Company
Shawnee, OK 405-273-7000
Shepherdsfield Bakery
Fulton, MO 573-642-1439
Siemer Milling Company
Teutopolis, IL 800-826-1065
SJH Enterprises
Middleton, WI. 888-745-3845
Solnuts
Hudson, IA 800-648-3503
Southeastern Mills
Rome, GA 800-334-4468
Southern Brown Rice
Weiner, AR 800-421-7423
Star of the West
Kent, OH. 330-673-2941
Star of the West MillingCompany
Frankenmuth, MI 989-652-9971
Streamline Foods
West Bloomfield, MI. 248-851-2611
Teff Company
Caldwell, ID 888-822-2221
Uhlmann Company
Kansas City, MO. 800-383-8201
Wall-Rogalsky Milling Company
Mc Pherson, KS 800-835-2067
War Eagle Mill
Rogers, AR 479-789-5343
Western Pacific Commodities
Henderson, NV 702-382-8880
Wheat Montana Farms & Bakery
Three Forks, MT. 800-535-2798
White Lily Foods Company
Memphis, TN 800-595-1380
Wilkins-Rogers
Ellicott City, MD. 410-465-5800

All Purpose

ConAgra Flour Milling
Oakland, CA 510-536-9555
Dan's Feed Bin
Superior, WI 715-394-6639

Glorybee Foods
Eugene, OR....800-456-7923
Orlinda Milling Company
Orlinda, TN....615-654-3633
Uhlmann Company
Kansas City, MO....800-383-8201
UNOI Grainmill
Seaford, DE....302-629-4083
Wall-Rogalsky Milling Company
Mc Pherson, KS....800-835-2067
White Lily Foods Company
Memphis, TN....800-595-1380

Almond

Chieftain Wild Rice Company
Spooner, WI....800-262-6368

Arrowroot

American Key Food Products
Closter, NJ....800-767-0237

Bakery Mix

Regular & Lowfat

General Mills
Minneapolis, MN....800-248-7310

Baking Mixes

Harvest Innovations
Indianola, IA....515-962-5063
Okeene Milling
Shawnee, OK....405-273-7000
Wall-Rogalsky Milling Company
Mc Pherson, KS....800-835-2067
White Lily Foods Company
Memphis, TN....800-595-1380

Barley

ADM Milling Company
Abilene, KS....785-263-1631
American Health & Nutrition
Ann Arbor, MI....734-677-5570
CHS
Inver Grove Heights, MN....800-232-3639
Eden Foods Inc.
Clinton, MI....800-248-0320
Ettlinger Corporation
Lincolnshire, IL....847-564-5020
Grain Millers
Eden Prairie, MN....800-232-6287
Heartland Mill
Marienthal, KS....800-232-8533
Homestead Mills
Cook, MN....800-652-5233
Honeyville Grain
Rancho Cucamonga, CA....888-810-3212
SJH Enterprises
Middleton, WI....888-745-3845

Bean

Bob's Red Mill Natural Foods
Milwaukie, OR....800-553-2258

Buckwheat

American Health & Nutrition
Ann Arbor, MI....734-677-5570
Bouchard Family Farm
Fort Kent, ME....800-239-3237
Byrd Mill Company
Ashland, VA....888-897-3336
Eden Foods Inc.
Clinton, MI....800-248-0320
Ener-G Foods
Seattle, WA....800-331-5222
Fairhaven Cooperative Flour Mill
Burlington, WA
Greenfield Mills
Howe, IN....260-367-2394
Homestead Mills
Cook, MN....800-652-5233
Minn-Dak Growers Ltd.
Grand Forks, ND....701-746-7453
New Hope Mills
Auburn, NY....315-252-2676
Purity Foods
Okemos, MI....800-997-7358

UNOI Grainmill
Seaford, DE....302-629-4083
Woodland Foods
Gurnee, IL....847-625-8600

Cake

ADM Milling Company
Chicago, IL....312-666-2465
Byrd Mill Company
Ashland, VA....888-897-3336
Cereal Food Processors
Mission Woods, KS....913-890-6300
H. Nagel & Son Company
Cincinnati, OH....513-665-4550
Mennel Milling Company
Fostoria, OH....419-435-8151
Pillsbury
Minneapolis, MN....800-775-4777
Reily Foods Company
New Orleans, LA....504-524-6131

Chestnut Flower

Chieftain Wild Rice Company
Spooner, WI....800-262-6368

Corn

Adluh Flour Mill
Columbia, SC....800-692-3584
ADM Food Ingredients
Olathe, KS....800-255-6637
Agricor
Marion, IN....765-662-0606
Attala Company
Kosciusko, MS....800-824-2691
Azteca Milling
Irving, TX....800-364-0040
Byrd Mill Company
Ashland, VA....888-897-3336
ConAgra Flour Milling
Oakland, CA....510-536-9555
Eagle Agricultural Products
Huntsville, AR....501-738-2203
Ener-G Foods
Seattle, WA....800-331-5222
Fairhaven Cooperative Flour Mill
Burlington, WA
Harbar Corporation
Canton, MA....800-881-7040
Honeyville Grain
Rancho Cucamonga, CA....888-810-3212
J.R. Short Milling Company
Kankakee, IL....800-544-8734
MexAmerica Foods
St Marys, PA....814-781-1447
Mills Brothers International
Tukwila, WA....206-575-3000
Randag & Associates Inc
Elmhurst, IL....630-530-2830
Shenandoah Mills
Lebanon, TN....615-444-0841
White Lily Foods Company
Memphis, TN....800-595-1380

Gluten

ADM Food Ingredients
Olathe, KS....800-255-6637
Blue Chip Group
Salt Lake City, UT....800-878-0099
Clofine Dairy & Food Products
Linwood, NJ....800-441-1001
North Dakota Mill
Grand Forks, ND....800-538-7721
Organic Planet
San Francisco, CA....415-765-5590
SJH Enterprises
Middleton, WI....888-745-3845

Hazelnut

Fastachi
Watertown, MA....800-466-3022

Instantized

AlpineAire Foods
Rocklin, CA....800-322-6325

Masa

Harbar Corporation
Canton, MA....800-881-7040

Millet

American Health & Nutrition
Ann Arbor, MI....734-677-5570
Heartland Mill
Marienthal, KS....800-232-8533
Ore-Ida Foods
Pittsburgh, PA....800-892-2401
Purity Foods
Okemos, MI....800-997-7358

Mustard

GS Dunn & Company
Hamilton, ON....905-522-0833
Harvest Innovations
Indianola, IA....515-962-5063
Minn-Dak Growers Ltd.
Grand Forks, ND....701-746-7453
Montana Specialty Mills
Great Falls, MT....406-761-2338
Tova Industries
Louisville, KY....888-532-8682

Nut

American Almond Products Company
Brooklyn, NY....800-825-6663
Amoretti
Oxnard, CA....800-266-7388
Chieftain Wild Rice Company
Spooner, WI....800-262-6368
Fastachi
Watertown, MA....800-466-3022
Harvest Innovations
Indianola, IA....515-962-5063
Hialeah Products Company
Hollywood, FL....800-923-3379
Mother Earth Enterprises
New York, NY....866-436-7688
Naturex Inc.
South Hackensack, NJ....201-440-5000

Oat

American Health & Nutrition
Ann Arbor, MI....734-677-5570
Can-Oat Milling
Portage la Prairie, MB....800-663-6287
ConAgra Flour Milling
Oakland, CA....510-536-9555
ConAgra Mills
Omaha, NE....800-851-9618
Dakota Organic Products
Watertown, SD....800-243-7264
Eden Foods Inc.
Clinton, MI....800-248-0320
Grain Millers
Eden Prairie, MN....800-232-6287
Heartland Mill
Marienthal, KS....800-232-8533
Particle Control
Albertville, MN....763-497-3075
SJH Enterprises
Middleton, WI....888-745-3845

Pancake

ADM Milling Company
Shawnee Mission, KS....913-491-9400
Bette's Diner Products
Berkeley, CA....510-644-3230
Bouchard Family Farm
Fort Kent, ME....800-239-3237
Byrd Mill Company
Ashland, VA....888-897-3336
Carbon's Golden Malted
South Bend, IN....800-686-6258
Champlain Valley Milling Corporation
Westport, NY....518-962-4711
Crosby Molasses Company
St John, NB....506-634-7515
Foxtail Foods
Fairfield, OH....800-487-2253
Heritage Tymes/Pancake House
Spearsville, LA....806-765-8566
Homestead Mills
Cook, MN....800-652-5233

John Gust Foods & Products Corporation
Batavia, IL. 800-756-5886
Little Crow Foods
Warsaw, IN 800-288-2769
Marie Callender's Gourmet Products/Goldrush Products
San Jose, CA. 800-729-5428
Martha Olson's Great Foods
Sutter Creek, CA. 800-973-3966
New Hope Mills
Auburn, NY. 315-252-2676
Northwestern Foods
Saint Paul, MN 800-236-4937
Quality Naturally! Foods
City of Industry, CA 888-498-6986
Randag & Associates Inc
Elmhurst, IL 630-530-2830
SFP Food Products
Conway, AR 800-654-5329
Shenandoah Mills
Lebanon, TN. 615-444-0841
Wanda's Nature Farm
Lincoln, NE. 800-735-6828
Wilsonhill Farm
South Bend, IN 802-899-2154

Pastry

ADM Milling Company
Chicago, IL 312-666-2465
American Health & Nutrition
Ann Arbor, MI 734-677-5570
Brandt Mills
Mifflinville, PA. 570-752-4271
Cereal Food Processors
Mission Woods, KS 913-890-6300
Champlain Valley Milling Corporation
Westport, NY. 518-962-4711
Eden Foods Inc.
Clinton, MI 800-248-0320
Ellison Milling Company
Lethbridge, AB 403-328-6622
H. Nagel & Son Company
Cincinnati, OH 513-665-4550
Mennel Milling Company
Fostoria, OH 419-435-8151
Natural Way Mills
Middle River, MN. 218-222-3677
Purato's
Seattle, WA 206-762-5400
SJH Enterprises
Middleton, WI. 888-745-3845
Star of the West MillingCompany
Frankenmuth, MI 989-652-9971

Peanut

Synergy Foods
West Bloomfield, MI 313-849-2900

Potato

AgraWest Foods
Prince Edward Island, NS. 877-687-1400
CHR Hansen
Elyria, OH. 800-558-0802
ConAgra Flour Milling
Oakland, CA 510-536-9555
Emerling International Foods
Buffalo, NY. 716-833-7381

We supply food manufacturers and food service customers worldwide (since 1988) with bulk ingredients including: Fruits & Vegetables; Juice Concentrates; Herbs & Spices; Oils & Vinegars; Flavors & Colors; Honey & Molasses. We also produce PURE MAPLE SYRUP.

Ener-G Foods
Seattle, WA 800-331-5222
Ettlinger Corporation
Lincolnshire, IL 847-564-5020
Idaho Pacific Corporation
Ririe, ID 800-238-5503
Nonpareil Corporation
Blackfoot, ID 800-522-2223
Oregon Potato Company
Boardman, OR 800-336-6311

Pancake

Linda's Gourmet Latkes
Los Angeles, CA. 888-452-8537

Rice

A&B Ingredients
Fairfield, NJ 973-227-1390
ADM Food Ingredients
Olathe, KS. 800-255-6637
Affiliated Rice Milling
Alvin, TX 281-331-6176
California Cereal Products
Oakland, CA 510-452-4500
CHR Hansen
Elyria, OH. 800-558-0802
ConAgra Flour Milling
Oakland, CA 510-536-9555
Domino Specialty Ingredients
West Palm Beach, FL 800-446-9763
Eagle Agricultural Products
Huntsville, AR 501-738-2203
Eden Foods Inc.
Clinton, MI 800-248-0320
Ener-G Foods
Seattle, WA 800-331-5222
Fearn Natural Foods
Thiensville, WI 800-877-8935
Harvest Innovations
Indianola, IA. 515-962-5063
Koda Farms
South Dos Palos, CA 209-392-2191
Lundberg Family Farm
Richvale, CA. 530-882-4551
Sage V Foods LLC
Los Angeles, CA. 310-820-4496

Rye

Bay State Milling Company
Winona, MN 800-533-8098
Champlain Valley Milling Corporation
Westport, NY. 518-962-4711
ConAgra Flour Milling
Oakland, CA 510-536-9555
Ellison Milling Company
Lethbridge, AB 403-328-6622
Fairhaven Cooperative Flour Mill
Burlington, WA
Heartland Mill
Marienthal, KS 800-232-8533
Homestead Mills
Cook, MN 800-652-5233
SJH Enterprises
Middleton, WI. 888-745-3845

Self-Rising

Nunn Milling Company
Evansville, IN 800-547-6866
Orlinda Milling Company
Orlinda, TN. 615-654-3633
Wall-Rogalsky Milling Company
Mc Pherson, KS 800-835-2067
White Lily Foods Company
Memphis, TN 800-595-1380

Semolina

CHS
Inver Grove Heights, MN. 800-232-3639
Heartland Mill
Marienthal, KS 800-232-8533
Howson & Howson Limited
Blyth, ON 800-663-3653
North Dakota Mill
Grand Forks, ND. 800-538-7721
Woodland Foods
Gurnee, IL. 847-625-8600

Soy Protein

Champlain Valley Milling Corporation
Westport, NY. 518-962-4711

Soybean

Acatris USA
Edina, MN. 952-920-7700
AG Processing, Inc.
Omaha, NE 800-247-1345
American Health & Nutrition
Ann Arbor, MI 734-677-5570
CHR Hansen
Elyria, OH. 800-558-0802
Clofine Dairy & Food Products
Linwood, NJ 800-441-1001

Dakota Organic Products
Watertown, SD 800-243-7264
Devansoy
Carroll, IA. 800-747-8605
Fearn Natural Foods
Thiensville, WI 800-877-8935
Harvest States Processing & Refining
Mankato, MN 800-525-6237
J.R. Short Milling Company
Kankakee, IL. 800-544-8734
Lucas Meyer
Decatur, IL 800-769-3660
Modern Macaroni Company
Honolulu, HI. 808-845-6841
Solnuts
Hudson, IA 800-648-3503

Spelt

Heartland Mill
Marienthal, KS 800-232-8533
Purity Foods
Okemos, MI 800-997-7358
Woodland Foods
Gurnee, IL. 847-625-8600

Tapioca

American Key Food Products
Closter, NJ. 800-767-0237
CHR Hansen
Elyria, OH. 800-558-0802
Ener-G Foods
Seattle, WA 800-331-5222
Kinnikinnick Foods
Edmonton, AB 877-503-4466
Tipiak
Stamford, CT. 203-961-9117

Wheat

American Health & Nutrition
Ann Arbor, MI 734-677-5570
ConAgra Flour Milling
Fremont, NE 402-721-4200
ConAgra Flour Milling
Martins Creek, PA. 610-253-9341
ConAgra Flour Milling
Chester, IL. 618-826-2371
ConAgra Flour Milling
Red Lion, PA. 717-244-4559
ConAgra Flour Milling
York, PA 717-846-7773
ConAgra Flour Milling
Sherman, TX. 903-893-8111
Mennel Milling Company
Fostoria, OH 419-435-8151
Okeene Milling
Shawnee, OK 405-273-7000

White Unbleached

Champlain Valley Milling Corporation
Westport, NY. 518-962-4711
Eagle Agricultural Products
Huntsville, AR 501-738-2203
Ener-G Foods
Seattle, WA 800-331-5222
Great Grains Milling Company
Scobey, MT. 406-783-5581
Heartland Mill
Marienthal, KS 800-232-8533
King Milling Company
Lowell, MI 616-897-9264
Lehi Roller Mills
Lehi, UT 800-660-4346
Natural Way Mills
Middle River, MN. 218-222-3677
Star of the West MillingCompany
Frankenmuth, MI 989-652-9971
Uhlmann Company
Kansas City, MO. 800-383-8201
White Lily Foods Company
Memphis, TN 800-595-1380

Whole wheat

American Health & Nutrition
Ann Arbor, MI 734-677-5570
Brandt Mills
Mifflinville, PA. 570-752-4271
Cereal Food Processors
Mission Woods, KS 913-890-6300

Eagle Agricultural Products
Huntsville, AR 501-738-2203
Great Grains Milling Company
Scobey, MT. 406-783-5581
Homestead Mills
Cook, MN 800-652-5233
Keynes Brothers
Logan, OH. 740-385-6824
Montana Specialty Mills
Great Falls, MT. 406-761-2338
SJH Enterprises
Middleton, WI. 888-745-3845
Terra Botanica Products
Nakusp, BC. 888-410-9977
Uhlmann Company
Kansas City, MO. 800-383-8201
War Eagle Mill
Rogers, AR 479-789-5343

Pastry

American Health & Nutrition
Ann Arbor, MI 734-677-5570
Brandt Mills
Mifflinville, PA. 570-752-4271
Nuthouse Company
Mobile, AL 800-633-1306
SJH Enterprises
Middleton, WI. 888-745-3845

Grains

Acharice Specialties
Greenville, MS 800-432-4901
ADM Milling Company
Chattanooga, TN. 423-756-0503
ADM Milling Company
Charlotte, NC 704-332-3165
ADM Milling Company
Abilene, KS. 785-263-1631
ADM Milling Company
Shawnee Mission, KS. 913-491-9400
Agland, Inc.
Eaton, CO 800-433-4688
Agricor
Marion, IN. 765-662-0606
Aliments Trigone
St-Francois-De-La-Rivier, QC 877-259-7491
AlpineAire Foods
Rocklin, CA 800-322-6325
American Health & Nutrition
Ann Arbor, MI 734-677-5570
Attala Company
Kosciusko, MS 800-824-2691
Azteca Milling
Irving, TX 800-364-0040
Beaumont Rice Mills
Beaumont, TX. 409-832-2521
Beta Pure Foods
Aptos, CA 831-685-6565
Big J. Milling & Elevato Company
Brigham City, UT 435-723-3459
Black Ranch Organic Grains
Etna, CA 530-467-3387
Blue Planet Foods
Collegedale, TN 877-396-3145
Briess Industries
Chilton, WI 920-849-7711
Bunge Milling
Woodland, CA. 800-747-4764
Bush Brothers & Co.
Dandridge, TN 865-509-2361
California Cereal Products
Oakland, CA 510-452-4500
Canadian Harvest
Cambridge, MN 888-689-5800
Canasoy Enterprises
Vancouver, BC 800-663-1222
Cargill Dry Corn Ingredients
Paris, IL. 800-637-6481
Caribbean Food Delights
Tappan, NY 845-398-3000
Cayuga Grain
Cayuga, IN 765-492-3324
Central Milling Company
Logan, UT. 435-752-6625
Champlain Valley Milling Corporation
Westport, NY. 518-962-4711
Chef Hans Gourmet Foods
Monroe, LA. 800-890-4267
Chieftain Wild Rice Company
Spooner, WI 800-262-6368

China Doll Company
Saraland, AL 251-457-7641
CHS
Inver Grove Heights, MN. 800-232-3639
CHS Sunflower
Grandin, ND 701-484-5313
Cinnabar Specialty Foods
Prescott, AZ 866-293-6433
Coach's Oats
Yorba Linda, CA. 714-692-6885
ConAgra Foods Inc
Omaha, NE 402-595-7300
ConAgra Mills
Omaha, NE 800-851-9618
Conrad Rice Mill
New Iberia, LA. 800-551-3245
Continental Grain/ContiGroup Companies
New York, NY 212-207-5200
Cooperative Elevator Company
Pigeon, MI 989-453-4500
Cormier Rice Milling Company
De Witt, AR 870-946-3561
Dakota Organic Products
Watertown, SD 800-243-7264
Deer River Wild Rice
Deer River, MN. 218-246-2713
Devansoy
Carroll, IA. 800-747-8605
DMH Ingredients
Libertyville, IL 847-362-9977
Ellison Milling Company
Lethbridge, AB 403-328-6622
Fairhaven Cooperative Flour Mill
Burlington, WA
Falcon Rice Mill Inc
Crowley, LA 800-738-7423
Fall River Wild Rice
Fall River Mills, CA 800-626-4366
Farmers Rice Milling Company
Lake Charles, LA 337-433-5205
Ferris Organic Farm
Eaton Rapids, MI 800-628-8736
Fizzle Flat Farm
Yale, IL 618-793-2060
Food for Life Baking Company
Corona, CA 951-279-5090
Freeland Bean & Grain
Freeland, MI 800-447-9131
Garber Farms
Iota, LA. 800-824-2284
Goldilocks Bakeshop
South San Francisco, CA 925-681-1888
Good Star Foods
Reno, NV 775-851-2442
Grain Bin Bakers
Carmel, CA. 831-624-3883
Grain Millers Eugene
Eugene, OR. 800-443-8972
Grain Place Foods
Marquette, NE. 888-714-7246
Grain Process Enterprises Ltd.
Scarborough, ON 800-387-5292
Great Western Malting Company
Vancouver, WA. 877-770-7055
Grey Owl Foods
Grand Rapids, MN 800-527-0172
Hall Grain Company
Akron, CO. 970-345-2206
Harvest Innovations
Indianola, IA. 515-962-5063
HealthBest
San Marcos, CA 760-752-5230
Heartland Gourmet LLC
Lincoln, NE. 800-222-3276
Heartland Mill
Marienthal, KS 800-232-8533
Homegrown Naturals
Napa, CA. 800-288-1089
Homestead Mills
Cook, MN 800-652-5233
Honeyville Grain
Salt Lake City, UT 801-972-2168
Indian Harvest
Colusa, CA 800-294-2433
Indian Harvest Specialitifoods
Bemidji, MN. 800-346-7032
Inn Maid Food
Lenox, MA 413-637-2732
J&L Grain Processing
Riceville, IA. 800-244-9211
J.R. Short Canadian Mills
Toronto, ON 416-421-3463

JLH European Trading
San Francisco, CA 415-626-3672
Kashi Company
La Jolla, CA 858-274-8870
Kaufman Ingredients
Vernon Hills, IL 847-573-0844
Knappen Milling Company
Augusta, MI 800-562-7736
LaCrosse Milling Company
Cochrane, WI 800-441-5411
Landreth Wild Rice
Norman, OK 800-333-3533
Lassen Foods
Santa Barbara, CA 805-683-7696
Leech Lake Reservation
Cass Lake, MN 218-335-8200
Lone Pine Enterprises
Carlisle, AR 870-552-3217
Lowell Farms
El Campo, TX. 888-484-9213
Luxor California ExportsCorporation
San Diego, CA 619-692-9330
Maple Leaf Foods International
North York, ON. 416-480-8900
McKnight Milling Company
Hickory Ridge, AR. 870-697-2504
Mid-Kansas Cooperative
Moundridge, KS 800-864-4428
Mille Lacs Wild Rice Corporation
Aitkin, MN 800-626-3809
Mills Brothers International
Tukwila, WA. 206-575-3000
Minn-Dak Growers Ltd.
Grand Forks, ND. 701-746-7453
Minnesota Specialty Crops
McGregor, MN 800-328-6731
Montana Flour & Grain
Fort Benton, MT 406-622-5436
Montana Specialty Mills
Great Falls, MT. 406-761-2338
Mosher Products
Cheyenne, WY 307-632-1492
Mustard Seed
Central, SC 877-621-2591
Natural Way Mills
Middle River, MN. 218-222-3677
Naturex Inc.
South Hackensack, NJ 201-440-5000
NorCal Wild Rice
Davis, CA 530-758-8550
Northwestern Extract Company
Germantown, WI. 800-466-3034
Oak Creek Farms
Edgar, NE 402-224-3038
Osowski Farms
Minto, ND. 701-248-3341
Ottawa Valley Grain Products
Renfrew, ON 613-432-3614
Pendleton Flour Mills
Pendleton, OR. 541-276-6511
Perfect Foods
Goshen, NY. 800-933-3288
Pines International
Lawrence, KS 800-697-4637
Pizzey's Milling & Baking Company
Angusville, NB 204-773-2575
Pleasant Grove Farms
Pleasant Grove, CA 916-655-3391
Purity Foods
Okemos, MI 800-997-7358
R&J Farms
West Salem, OH 419-846-3179
Raymond-Hadley Corporation
Spencer, NY 800-252-5220
Rice Hull Specialty Products
Stuttgart, AR. 870-673-8507
Riceland Foods Rice Milling Operations
Stuttgart, AR. 800-226-9522
Riceselect
Alvin, TX 800-993-7423
Riviana Foods
Houston, TX 713-529-3251
Riviana Foods
Edison, NJ. 732-225-7210
Riviana Foods
Houston, TX 800-226-9522
Riviana Foods
Memphis, TN 901-942-0540
Roberts Seed
Axtell, NE. 308-743-2565
Roman Meal Milling Company
Fargo, ND 877-282-9743

S&E Organic Farms
Bakersfield, CA . . . 661-325-2644
Sage V Foods
Los Angeles, CA. . . 310-820-4496
Scott's Auburn Mills
Russellville, KY . . . 270-726-2080
SJH Enterprises
Middleton, WI. . . 888-745-3845
Sorrenti Family Farms
Newman, CA. . . 888-435-9490
Southeastern Mills
Rome, GA . . . 800-334-4468
Southern Brown Rice
Weiner, AR . . . 800-421-7423
Specialty Rice Marketing
Brinkley, AR. . . 800-467-1233
Stan-Mark Food Products
Chicago, IL . . . 800-651-0994
Star of the West MillingCompany
Frankenmuth, MI . . . 989-652-9971
Stengel Seed & Grain Company
Milbank, SD . . . 605-432-6030
Sun Ridge Farms
Pajaro, CA. . . 831-786-7000
Sunnyland Mills
Fresno, CA . . . 800-501-8017
SunOpta Grains
Hope, MN . . . 800-297-5997
Sunwest Foods
Davis, CA . . . 530-758-8550
Supreme Rice Mill
Crowley, LA . . . 337-783-5222
Suzanne's Specialties
New Brunswick, NJ . . . 800-762-2135
Sycamore Creek Company
Stockbridge, MI . . . 517-851-0049
T.S. Smith & Sons
Bridgeville, DE. . . 302-337-8271
Teff Company
Caldwell, ID . . . 888-822-2221
Tradewinds International
Ellendale, TN . . . 800-385-8884
Trinidad Benham Company
Denver, CO . . . 303-220-1400
Tundra Wild Rice
Pine Falls, NB. . . 204-367-8651
Uhlmann Company
Kansas City, MO. . . 800-383-8201
US Foods
Lincoln, NE. . . 402-470-2021
Viobin USA
Monticello, IL. . . 217-762-2561
Vitamins
Chicago, IL . . . 312-861-0700
Wagner Gourmet Foods
Lenexa, KS . . . 913-469-5411
Weetabix Company
Clinton, MA . . . 800-343-0590
Weisenberger Mills
Midway, KY . . . 800-643-8678
WG Thompson & Sons
Blenheim, ON. . . 519-676-5411
Wheat Montana Farms & Bakery
Three Forks, MT. . . 800-535-2798
Wild Rice Exchange
Woodland, CA. . . 800-223-7423
Woodland Foods
Gurnee, IL. . . 847-625-8600
World Nutrition
Scottsdale, AZ. . . 800-548-2710
WSI
Caldwell, ID . . . 800-632-3005

Amaranth

Kashi Company
La Jolla, CA . . . 858-274-8870
Woodland Foods
Gurnee, IL. . . 847-625-8600

Granola

Alvarado Street Bakery
Petaluma, CA . . . 707-283-0300
Ambrosial Granola
Brooklyn, NY . . . 718-491-1335
Baker
Milford, NJ . . . 800-995-3989
Barbara's Bakery
Petaluma, CA . . . 707-765-2273
Blue Planet Foods
Collegedale, TN . . . 877-396-3145
Chappaqua Crunch
Marblehead, MA. . . 781-631-8118
Cream of the West
Harlowton, MT . . . 800-477-2383
Edner Corporation
Hayward, CA . . . 510-441-8504
Energy Club
Pacoima, CA. . . 800-688-6887
Enjoy Life Foods
Schiller Park, IL . . . 888-503-6569
GKI Foods
Brighton, MI . . . 248-486-0055
Grain Process Enterprises Ltd.
Scarborough, ON . . . 800-387-5292
Grain-Free JK Gourmet
Toronto, ON . . . 800-608-0465
Health Valley Company
Irwindale, CA . . . 800-334-3204
Hialeah Products Company
Hollywood, FL . . . 800-923-3379
Inn Maid Food
Lenox, MA . . . 413-637-2732
Isabella's Healthy Bakery
Cuyahoga Falls, OH . . . 800-476-6328
Lassen Foods
Santa Barbara, CA . . . 805-683-7696
Lehi Valley Trading Company
Mesa, AZ. . . 480-684-1402
Main Street Gourmet
Cuyahoga Falls, OH . . . 800-533-6246
Masterfoods USA
Hackettstown, NJ . . . 908-852-1000
McKee Foods Corporation
Collegedale, TN . . . 423-238-7111
Michaelene's Gourmet Granola
Clarkston, MI . . . 248-625-0156
Mother Nature's Goodies
Yucaipa, CA . . . 909-795-6018
National Vinegar Company
Houston, TX . . . 713-223-4214
Nature's Hand
Burnsville, MN. . . 952-890-6033
New England Natural Baker
Greenfield, MA. . . 800-910-2884
Organic Milling Company
San Dimas, CA . . . 800-638-8686
Partners, A Tastful Cracker
Seattle, WA . . . 800-632-7477
Poppa's Granola
Perkinsville, VT . . . 802-263-5342
Positively Third Street Bakery
Duluth, MN. . . 218-724-8619
Quaker Oats Company
Danville, IL. . . 217-443-4995
Quaker Oats Company
Chicago, IL . . . 800-367-6287
Red Rose Trading Company
Wrightsville, PA . . . 717-252-5500
SBK Preserves
Bronx, NY. . . 800-773-7378
Schulze & Burch Biscuit Company
Chicago, IL . . . 773-927-6622
Shade Foods
New Century, KS . . . 800-225-6312
Snackerz
Commerce, CA . . . 888-576-2253
Torn & Glasser
Los Angeles, CA. . . 800-282-6887
Udi's Granola
Denver, CO . . . 303-657-6366
US Mills
Bala Cynwyd, PA . . . 800-422-1125
Well Dressed Food Company
Tupper Lake, NY . . . 866-567-0845

Grits

ADM Milling Company
Jackson, TN . . . 731-424-3535
Agricor
Marion, IN. . . 765-662-0606
Allen Canning Company
Siloam Springs, AR . . . 800-234-2553
Callie's Charleston Biscuits LLC
Charleston, SC . . . 843-577-1198
Cargill Dry Corn Ingredients
Paris, IL. . . 800-637-6481
Dakota Organic Products
Watertown, SD . . . 800-243-7264
J.P. Green Milling Company
Mocksville, NC. . . 336-751-2126
Minn-Dak Growers Ltd.
Grand Forks, ND. . . 701-746-7453
Natural Products
Grinnell, IA. . . 641-236-0852
Natural Way Mills
Middle River, MN. . . 218-222-3677
Quaker Oats Company
Cedar Rapids, IA. . . 319-362-0200
Sturm Foods
Manawa, WI . . . 800-347-8876
White Lily Foods Company
Memphis, TN . . . 800-595-1380

Corn White & Yellow

Mills Brothers International
Tukwila, WA. . . 206-575-3000

Hominy

Allen Canning Company
Siloam Springs, AR . . . 800-234-2553
Bush Brothers & Co.
Dandridge, TN . . . 865-509-2361
Cateraid
Howell, MI . . . 800-508-8217
Juanita's Foods
Wilmington, CA . . . 310-834-5339
Mercado Latino
City of Industry, CA . . . 626-333-6862

Canned

Juanita's Foods
Wilmington, CA . . . 310-834-5339

Hops

Hop Growers of America
Moxee, WA. . . 509-248-7043
Hops Extract Corporation of America
Yakima, WA . . . 509-248-1530
Hopunion LLC
Yakima, WA . . . 800-952-4873
John I. Haas
Washington, DC . . . 202-777-4800
Naturex Inc.
South Hackensack, NJ . . . 201-440-5000
Northwestern Extract Company
Germantown, WI. . . 800-466-3034
Steiner, S.S.
New York, NY . . . 212-515-7200
Watson Nutritional Ingredients
West Haven, CT . . . 203-932-3000

Hummus

Quong Hop & Company
S San Francisco, CA. . . 650-553-9900
Tribe Mediterranean Foods Company LLC
Taunton, MA. . . 774-961-0000

Malt

Briess Industries
Chilton, WI . . . 920-849-7711
Domino Specialty Ingredients
West Palm Beach, FL . . . 800-446-9763
Great Western Malting Company
Vancouver, WA . . . 877-770-7055
International Malting Company
Milwaukee, WI . . . 414-671-1166
Jones Brewing Company
Smithton, PA. . . 800-237-2337
Ladish Malting
Jefferson, WI. . . 920-674-3730
Lake Country Foods
Oconomowoc, WI. . . 262-567-5521
Lion Brewery
Wilkes Barre, PA. . . 800-233-8327
Malt Products Corporation
Saddle Brook, NJ . . . 800-526-0180
Northwestern Extract Company
Germantown, WI. . . 800-466-3034
Prairie Malt
Biggar, SK. . . 306-948-3500
Premier Malt Products
Warren, MI . . . 586-443-3355
Quality Ingredients Corporation
Chester, NJ . . . 800-843-6314
Rahr Malting Company
Shakopee, MN . . . 952-445-1431
Schreier Malting Companypecialty Malt Division
Sheboygan, WI . . . 800-669-6258
Suzanne's Specialties
New Brunswick, NJ . . . 800-762-2135

United Canadian Malt
Peterborough, ON 800-461-6400
Watson Nutritional Ingredients
West Haven, CT 203-932-3000

Syrup

Briess Industries
Chilton, WI 920-849-7711
Malt-Diastase Company
Garfield, NJ 800-772-0416
Schiff Food Products
North Bergen, NJ 201-868-6800
United Canadian Malt
Peterborough, ON 800-461-6400

Millet

American Key Food Products
Closter, NJ 800-767-0237
CHS Sunflower
Grandin, ND 701-484-5313
Dakota Organic Products
Watertown, SD 800-243-7264
Hialeah Products Company
Hollywood, FL 800-923-3379
Mills Brothers International
Tukwila, WA 206-575-3000
Natural Way Mills
Middle River, MN 218-222-3677
Organic Planet
San Francisco, CA 415-765-5590
Red River Commodities
Fargo, ND 701-282-2600

Oats & Oat Products

ADM Milling Company
Shawnee Mission, KS 800-422-1688
Agricore United
Winnipeg, MB 800-661-4844
Anna's Oatcakes
Weston, VT 802-824-3535
Barbara's Bakery
Petaluma, CA 707-765-2273
Blue Planet Foods
Collegedale, TN 877-396-3145
Can-Oat Milling
Portage la Prairie, MB 800-663-6287
ConAgra Mills
Omaha, NE 800-851-9618
Cooperative Elevator Company
Pigeon, MI 989-453-4500
Dakota Organic Products
Watertown, SD 800-243-7264
Fizzle Flat Farm
Yale, IL 618-793-2060
Grain Millers
Eden Prairie, MN 800-232-6287
Heartland Mill
Marienthal, KS 800-232-8533
Honeyville Grain
Salt Lake City, UT 801-972-2168
Honeyville Grain
Rancho Cucamonga, CA 888-810-3212
J. Rettenmaier
Schoolcraft, MI 877-243-4661
Kerry Ingredients
Blue Earth, MN 507-526-7575
Particle Control
Albertville, MN 763-497-3075
Roman Meal Milling Company
Tacoma, WA 253-475-0964
SJH Enterprises
Middleton, WI 888-745-3845
Weetabix Company
Clinton, MA 800-343-0590

Groats

Can-Oat Milling
Portage la Prairie, MB 800-663-6287

Oat Bran

Can-Oat Milling
Portage la Prairie, MB 800-663-6287
Foley's Candies
Richmond, BC 888-236-5397
Grain Millers
Eden Prairie, MN 800-232-6287
Natural Foods
Toledo, OH 419-537-1713
SJH Enterprises
Middleton, WI 888-745-3845

Oatmeal

Grain Millers
Eden Prairie, MN 800-232-6287
Honeyville Grain
Salt Lake City, UT 801-972-2168
Kenlake Foods
Murray, KY 800-632-6900
LaCrosse Milling Company
Cochrane, WI 800-441-5411
PepsiCo Chicago
Chicago, IL 312-821-1000
Quaker Oats Company
Stockton, CA 209-982-5580
Silver Palate Kitchens
Cresskill, NJ 800-872-5283

Rolled

Can-Oat Milling
Portage la Prairie, MB 800-663-6287
Grain Millers
Eden Prairie, MN 800-232-6287
Heartland Mill
Marienthal, KS 800-232-8533
Honeyville Grain
Salt Lake City, UT 801-972-2168
Honeyville Grain
Rancho Cucamonga, CA 888-810-3212

Poi

Aloha Poi Factory
Wailuku, HI 808-244-3536
Puueo Poi Factory
Hilo, HI 808-935-8435

Quinoa

Quinoa Corporation
Gardena, CA 310-217-8125
Woodland Foods
Gurnee, IL 847-625-8600

Rice

A&B Ingredients
Fairfield, NJ 973-227-1390
Acharice Specialties
Greenville, MS 800-432-4901
ADM Milling Company
Shawnee Mission, KS 800-422-1688
Affiliated Rice Milling
Alvin, TX 281-331-6176
Agrusa, Inc.
Leonia, NJ 201-592-5950
Ankeny Lakes Wild Rice
Salem, OR 800-555-5380
Baycliff Company
New York, NY 212-772-6078
Beaumont Rice Mills
Beaumont, TX 409-832-2521
Berberian Nut Company
Chico, CA 530-891-4900
Blue Chip Group
Salt Lake City, UT 800-878-0099
Bunge Milling
Woodland, CA 800-747-4764
Buon Italia Misono Food Ltd.
New York, NY 212-633-9090
California Cereal Products
Oakland, CA 510-452-4500
California Natural Products
Lathrop, CA 209-858-2525
Caribbean Food Delights
Tappan, NY 845-398-3000
Chef Hans Gourmet Foods
Monroe, LA 800-890-4267
Chef Merito
Encino, CA 800-637-4861
Chieftain Wild Rice Company
Spooner, WI 800-262-6368
China Doll Company
Saraland, AL 251-457-7641
Cinnabar Specialty Foods
Prescott, AZ 866-293-6433
Comet Rice
Houston, TX 281-272-8800
Commodities Marketing, Inc.
Edison, NJ 732-603-5077
Conrad Rice Mill
New Iberia, LA 800-551-3245
Cormier Rice Milling Company
De Witt, AR 870-946-3561
Country Cupboard
Virginia City, NV 775-847-7300
Deer River Wild Rice
Deer River, MN 218-246-2713
Dixie Rice
Gueydan, LA 337-536-9276
Domino Specialty Ingredients
West Palm Beach, FL 800-446-9763
Eagle Agricultural Products
Huntsville, AR 501-738-2203
Eden Foods Inc.
Clinton, MI 800-248-0320
Falcon Rice Mill Inc
Crowley, LA 800-738-7423
Fall River Wild Rice
Fall River Mills, CA 800-626-4366
Fantastic Foods
Napa, CA 800-288-1089
Farmers Rice Milling Company
Lake Charles, LA 337-433-5205
Farmers' Rice Cooperative
Sacramento, CA 800-326-2799
Florida Crystals
West Palm Beach, FL 877-835-2828
Garber Farms
Iota, LA 800-824-2284
Golden Gate Foods
Dallas, TX 214-747-2223
Golden Grain Company
Bridgeview, IL 708-458-7020
Gourmet House
Clearbrook, MN 218-776-2100
Goya Foods
Secaucus, NJ 201-348-4900
Goya Foods of Florida
Miami, FL 305-592-3150
Grey Owl Foods
Grand Rapids, MN 800-527-0172
Hershey Pasta Group
Louisville, KY 800-468-1714
Hung's Noodle House
Calgary, AB 403-250-1663
Indian Harvest
Colusa, CA 800-294-2433
Indian Harvest Specialitifoods
Bemidji, MN 800-346-7032
Kalustyan Corporation
Union, NJ 908-688-6111
Koda Farms
South Dos Palos, CA 209-392-2191
Kohinoor Foods
Edison, NJ 888-440-7423
Landreth Wild Rice
Norman, OK 800-333-3533
Leech Lake Reservation
Cass Lake, MN 218-335-8200
Liberty Richter
Saddle Brook, NJ 201-291-8749
Lone Pine Enterprises
Carlisle, AR 870-552-3217
Lotus Foods
Richmond, CA 510-525-3137
Louis Dreyfus Corporation
Wilton, CT 203-761-2000
Louisiana Gourmet Enterprises
La Place, LA 985-783-2446
Lowell Farms
El Campo, TX 888-484-9213
Lundberg Family Farm
Richvale, CA 530-882-4551
McKnight Milling Company
Hickory Ridge, AR 870-697-2504
Mercado Latino
City of Industry, CA 626-333-6862
Mermaid Spice Corporation
Fort Myers, FL 239-693-1986
Mille Lacs Wild Rice Corporation
Aitkin, MN 800-626-3809
Mills Brothers International
Tukwila, WA 206-575-3000
Minnesota Specialty Crops
McGregor, MN 800-328-6731
Natural Way Mills
Middle River, MN 218-222-3677
Near East Food Products
Chicago, IL 847-842-4654
North Bay Trading Company
Brule, WI 800-348-0164

Oak Grove Smokehouse
Prairieville, LA 225-673-6857
Pleasant Grove Farms
Pleasant Grove, CA 916-655-3391
Primo Foods
Toronto, ON 800-377-6945
Producers Rice Mill
Stuttgart, AR 870-673-4444
Raymond-Hadley Corporation
Spencer, NY 800-252-5220
Reggie Ball's Cajun Foods
Lake Charles, LA 337-436-0291
RIBUS
Saint Louis, MO 314-727-4287
Rice Company
Roseville, CA 916-784-7745
Rice Deerwood & Grain Processing
Deerwood, MN 218-534-3762
Rice Foods
Mount Vernon, IL 618-242-0026
Rice Hull Specialty Products
Stuttgart, AR 870-673-8507
Rice River Farms/Chieftan Wild Rice Company
Spooner, WI 800-262-6368
Rice Select
Alvin, TX 800-580-7423
Riceland Foods Rice Milling Operations
Stuttgart, AR 800-226-9522
Riceselect
Alvin, TX 800-993-7423
Riviana Foods
Abbeville, LA 337-893-2236
Riviana Foods
Houston, TX 713-529-3251
Riviana Foods
Edison, NJ 732-225-7210
Riviana Foods
Houston, TX 800-226-9522
Riviana Foods
Memphis, TN 901-942-0540
Royal Caribbean Bakery
Mount Vernon, NY 888-818-0971
Sage V Foods LLC
Los Angeles, CA 310-820-4496
Sara Lee Corporation
Downers Grove, IL 630-598-8100
Shah Trading Company
Toronto, ON 416-292-6927
Sorrenti Family Farms
Newman, CA 888-435-9490
Southern Brown Rice
Weiner, AR 800-421-7423
Specialty Rice Marketing
Brinkley, AR 800-467-1233
SPI Foods
Fremont, NE 866-266-1304
St Mary's & Ankeny Lakes Wild Rice Company
Salem, OR 503-363-3241
Sun West
Torrance, CA 310-320-4000
Sunwest Foods
Davis, CA 530-758-8550
SunWest Organics
Davis, CA 530-758-8550
Supreme Rice Mill
Crowley, LA 337-783-5222
Tipiak
Stamford, CT 203-961-9117
Torn & Glasser
Los Angeles, CA 800-282-6887
Tradewinds International
Ellendale, TN 800-385-8884
Trinidad Benham Company
Denver, CO 303-220-1400
Tropical
Marietta, GA 800-544-3762
Tundra Wild Rice
Pine Falls, NB 204-367-8651
Uncle Ben's
Houston, TX 713-674-9484
US Foods
Lincoln, NE 402-470-2021
Van Bennett Food Company
Reading, PA 800-423-8897
Vigo Importing Company
Tampa, FL 813-884-3491
Wagner Gourmet Foods
Lenexa, KS 913-469-5411
Weetabix Company
Clinton, MA 800-343-0590
Western Pacific Commodities
Henderson, NV 702-382-8880
Westlam Foods
Chino, CA 800-722-9519
Wild Rice Exchange
Woodland, CA 800-223-7423
Willow Foods
Beaverton, OR 800-338-3609
Woodland Foods
Gurnee, IL 847-625-8600
Wright Enrichment
Crowley, LA 800-201-3096
Wysong Corporation
Midland, MI 800-748-0188
Zatarain's
Gretna, LA 800-435-6639

Aborio

Chieftain Wild Rice Company
Spooner, WI 800-262-6368
Gourmet House
Clearbrook, MN 218-776-2100
Woodland Foods
Gurnee, IL 847-625-8600

Basmati

American Health & Nutrition
Ann Arbor, MI 734-677-5570
Asian Brands
Hayward, CA 510-523-7474
Chieftain Wild Rice Company
Spooner, WI 800-262-6368
Commodities Marketing, Inc.
Edison, NJ 732-603-5077
Eagle Agricultural Products
Huntsville, AR 501-738-2203
Gourmet House
Clearbrook, MN 218-776-2100
Kalustyan Corporation
Union, NJ 908-688-6111
Lone Pine Enterprises
Carlisle, AR 870-552-3217
McKnight Milling Company
Hickory Ridge, AR 870-697-2504
Rice Select
Alvin, TX 800-580-7423

Southern Brown Rice
Weiner, AR 800-421-7423
Specialty Rice Marketing
Brinkley, AR 800-467-1233
Wild Rice Exchange
Woodland, CA 800-223-7423
Woodland Foods
Gurnee, IL 847-625-8600

Black Puinoa

Chieftain Wild Rice Company
Spooner, WI 800-262-6368

Black Thai

Chieftain Wild Rice Company
Spooner, WI 800-262-6368

Brewers'

Beaumont Rice Mills
Beaumont, TX 409-832-2521
Commodities Marketing, Inc.
Edison, NJ 732-603-5077
Golden Gate Foods
Dallas, TX 214-747-2223
Riceland Foods Rice Milling Operations
Stuttgart, AR 870-673-5500

Brown

American Health & Nutrition
Ann Arbor, MI 734-677-5570
Bunge Milling
Woodland, CA 800-747-4764
California Natural Products
Lathrop, CA 209-858-2525
Chieftain Wild Rice Company
Spooner, WI 800-262-6368
Cormier Rice Milling Company
De Witt, AR 870-946-3561
Eagle Agricultural Products
Huntsville, AR 501-738-2203
Gourmet House
Clearbrook, MN 218-776-2100
Lone Pine Enterprises
Carlisle, AR 870-552-3217
McKnight Milling Company
Hickory Ridge, AR 870-697-2504
Rice Select
Alvin, TX 800-580-7423
Riceland Foods Rice Milling Operations
Stuttgart, AR 870-673-5500
Riviana Foods
Abbeville, LA 337-893-2236
Riviana Foods
Edison, NJ 732-225-7210
Sobaya
Cowansville, QC 800-319-8808
Southern Brown Rice
Weiner, AR 800-421-7423
Supreme Rice Mill
Crowley, LA 337-783-5222
Wild Rice Exchange
Woodland, CA 800-223-7423

Chinese Black

Woodland Foods
Gurnee, IL 847-625-8600

Frozen

Sage V Foods LLC
Los Angeles, CA 310-820-4496

Hulls

Rice Hull Specialty Products
Stuttgart, AR 870-673-8507

IQF (Individual Quick Frozen)

Emerling International Foods
Buffalo, NY 716-833-7381

We supply food manufacturers and food service customers worldwide (since 1988) with bulk ingredients including: Fruits & Vegetables; Juice Concentrates; Herbs & Spices; Oils & Vinegars; Flavors & Colors; Honey & Molasses. We also produce PURE MAPLE SYRUP.

Sage V Foods LLC
Los Angeles, CA 310-820-4496

Instant

Riceland Foods Rice Milling Operations
Stuttgart, AR 870-673-5500
Sage V Foods LLC
Los Angeles, CA 310-820-4496

Jasmine

American Health & Nutrition
Ann Arbor, MI 734-677-5570
Asian Brands
Hayward, CA 510-523-7474
Chieftain Wild Rice Company
Spooner, WI 800-262-6368
Commodities Marketing, Inc.
Edison, NJ 732-603-5077
Gourmet House
Clearbrook, MN 218-776-2100
KP USA Trading
Los Angeles, CA 323-881-9871
Lowell Farms
El Campo, TX 888-484-9213
Rice Select
Alvin, TX 800-580-7423
Woodland Foods
Gurnee, IL 847-625-8600

Milled

Cormier Rice Milling Company
De Witt, AR 870-946-3561
Riceland Foods Rice Milling Operations
Stuttgart, AR 870-673-5500

Organic

Domino Specialty Ingredients
West Palm Beach, FL 800-446-9763
Gourmet House
Clearbrook, MN 218-776-2100
Kashi Company
La Jolla, CA 858-274-8870
Sage V Foods LLC
Los Angeles, CA 310-820-4496

Parboiled

Riceland Foods Rice Milling Operations
Stuttgart, AR 870-673-5500

US #1 Long Grain

McKnight Milling Company
Hickory Ridge, AR 870-697-2504
Mercado Latino
City of Industry, CA 626-333-6862

Pilaf

Asian Brands
Hayward, CA 510-523-7474
Chef Hans Gourmet Foods
Monroe, LA 800-890-4267
Chieftain Wild Rice Company
Spooner, WI 800-262-6368
Country Cupboard
Virginia City, NV 775-847-7300
Geetha's Gourmet of India
Las Cruces, NM 800-274-0475
Riceland Foods Rice Milling Operations
Stuttgart, AR 870-673-5500
Wild Rice Exchange
Woodland, CA 800-223-7423

Precooked

Riviana Foods
Houston, TX 713-529-3251

Sage V Foods LLC
Los Angeles, CA 310-820-4496

Protein

A&B Ingredients
Fairfield, NJ 973-227-1390

Purple Sticky

Woodland Foods
Gurnee, IL 847-625-8600

Risotto

Agrusa, Inc.
Leonia, NJ 201-592-5950
Italian Foods Corporation
Raleigh, NC 888-516-7262

Spanish

Country Cupboard
Virginia City, NV 775-847-7300

Canned

Conrad Rice Mill
New Iberia, LA 800-551-3245

Wehani

Chieftain Wild Rice Company
Spooner, WI 800-262-6368

White

Gourmet House
Clearbrook, MN 218-776-2100

Wild

Ankeny Lakes Wild Rice
Salem, OR 800-555-5380
Chef Hans Gourmet Foods
Monroe, LA 800-890-4267
Chieftain Wild Rice Company
Spooner, WI 800-262-6368
Conrad Rice Mill
New Iberia, LA 800-551-3245
Country Cupboard
Virginia City, NV 775-847-7300
Deer River Wild Rice
Deer River, MN 218-246-2713
Fall River Wild Rice
Fall River Mills, CA 800-626-4366
Gourmet House
Clearbrook, MN 218-776-2100
Grey Owl Foods
Grand Rapids, MN 800-527-0172
Landreth Wild Rice
Norman, OK 800-333-3533
Leech Lake Reservation
Cass Lake, MN 218-335-8200
Mille Lacs Wild Rice Corporation
Aitkin, MN 800-626-3809
Minnesota Specialty Crops
McGregor, MN 800-328-6731
NorCal Wild Rice
Davis, CA 530-758-8550
North Bay Trading Company
Brule, WI 800-348-0164
Rice Deerwood & Grain Processing
Deerwood, MN 218-534-3762
Rice River Farms/Chieftan Wild Rice Company
Spooner, WI 800-262-6368
Riceland Foods Rice Milling Operations
Stuttgart, AR 870-673-5500
Riviana Foods
Abbeville, LA 337-893-2236
Riviana Foods
Houston, TX 800-226-9522
Secret Garden
Park Rapids, MN 800-950-4409
Sorrenti Family Farms
Newman, CA 888-435-9490
Southern Brown Rice
Weiner, AR 800-421-7423
St Mary's & Ankeny Lakes Wild Rice Company
Salem, OR 503-363-3241
Sunwest Foods
Davis, CA 530-758-8550
Tradewinds International
Ellendale, TN 800-385-8884

Tundra Wild Rice
Pine Falls, NB . . . 204-367-8651
US Foods
Lincoln, NE . . . 402-470-2021
Wild Rice Exchange
Woodland, CA . . . 800-223-7423
Woodland Foods
Gurnee, IL . . . 847-625-8600

Rye

Alfred & Sam Italian Bakery
Lancaster, PA . . . 717-392-6311
Dakota Organic Products
Watertown, SD . . . 800-243-7264
Fizzle Flat Farm
Yale, IL . . . 618-793-2060
Grain Millers Eugene
Eugene, OR . . . 800-443-8972
Honeyville Grain
Rancho Cucamonga, CA . . . 888-810-3212
Montana Specialty Mills
Great Falls, MT . . . 406-761-2338
Natural Way Mills
Middle River, MN . . . 218-222-3677
Naturex Inc.
South Hackensack, NJ . . . 201-440-5000

Sorghum

ADM Milling Company
Shawnee Mission, KS . . . 800-422-1688
Dakota Organic Products
Watertown, SD . . . 800-243-7264
Suzanne's Specialties
New Brunswick, NJ . . . 800-762-2135
Webbpak
Trussville, AL . . . 800-655-3500

Soy Bean Meal

Cargill Vegetable Oils
Minneapolis, MN . . . 612-378-0551
Clofine Dairy & Food Products
Linwood, NJ . . . 800-441-1001
International Service Group
Alpharetta, GA . . . 770-518-0988

Tapioca

American Key Food Products
Closter, NJ . . . 800-767-0237
Cargill Texturizing Solutions
Cedar Rapids, IA . . . 877-650-7080
Chloe Foods Corporation
Brooklyn, NY . . . 718-827-9000
Commodities Marketing, Inc.
Edison, NJ . . . 732-603-5077
ConAgra Grocery Products
Irvine, CA . . . 714-680-1000
Heartline Foods
Westport, CT . . . 203-222-0381
Organic Planet
San Francisco, CA . . . 415-765-5590
Primera Foods
Cameron, WI . . . 800-365-2409
Van Bennett Food Company
Reading, PA . . . 800-423-8897

Cassava

Cargill Texturizing Solutions
Cedar Rapids, IA . . . 877-650-7080

Pearl

Granulated, Starch

Cargill Texturizing Solutions
Cedar Rapids, IA . . . 877-650-7080

Wheat

ADM Milling Company
Carthage, MO . . . 417-358-2197
ADM Milling Company
Abilene, KS . . . 785-263-1631
ADM Milling Company
Shawnee Mission, KS . . . 800-422-1688
Agri-Dairy Products
Purchase, NY . . . 914-697-9580
Agricore United
Winnipeg, MB . . . 800-661-4844
AgriCulver Seeds
Trumansburg, NY . . . 800-836-3701
Aliments Trigone
St-Francois-De-La-Rivier, QC . . . 877-259-7491
American Health & Nutrition
Ann Arbor, MI . . . 734-677-5570
Blue Chip Group
Salt Lake City, UT . . . 800-878-0099
Briess Industries
Chilton, WI . . . 920-849-7711
Chieftain Wild Rice Company
Spooner, WI . . . 800-262-6368
ConAgra Flour Milling
Fremont, NE . . . 402-721-4200
ConAgra Flour Milling
Martins Creek, PA . . . 610-253-9341
ConAgra Flour Milling
Chester, IL . . . 618-826-2371
ConAgra Flour Milling
Red Lion, PA . . . 717-244-4559
ConAgra Flour Milling
York, PA . . . 717-846-7773
ConAgra Flour Milling
Sherman, TX . . . 903-893-8111
ConAgra Mills
Tampa, FL . . . 800-582-1483
ConAgra Mills
Omaha, NE . . . 800-851-9618
Cooperative Elevator Company
Pigeon, MI . . . 989-453-4500
Dakota Organic Products
Watertown, SD . . . 800-243-7264
El Peto Products
Cambridge, ON . . . 800-387-4064
Ferris Organic Farm
Eaton Rapids, MI . . . 800-628-8736
Fizzle Flat Farm
Yale, IL . . . 618-793-2060
Florence Macaroni Manufacturing
Chicago, IL . . . 800-647-2782
Gabriele Macaroni Company
City of Industry, CA . . . 626-964-2324
Grain Millers Eugene
Eugene, OR . . . 800-443-8972
Honeyville Grain
Rancho Cucamonga, CA . . . 888-810-3212
J. Rettenmaier
Schoolcraft, MI . . . 877-243-4661
Kaufman Ingredients
Vernon Hills, IL . . . 847-573-0844
Knappen Milling Company
Augusta, MI . . . 800-562-7736
Knight Seed Company
Burnsville, MN . . . 800-328-2999
Lone Pine Enterprises
Carlisle, AR . . . 870-552-3217
Louis Dreyfus Corporation
Wilton, CT . . . 203-761-2000
Manildra Milling Corporation
Fairway, KS . . . 800-323-8435
Montana Specialty Mills
Great Falls, MT . . . 406-761-2338
Natural Way Mills
Middle River, MN . . . 218-222-3677
Perfect Foods
Goshen, NY . . . 800-933-3288
Pines International
Lawrence, KS . . . 800-697-4637
Pleasant Grove Farms
Pleasant Grove, CA . . . 916-655-3391
Purity Foods
Okemos, MI . . . 800-997-7358
Roberts Seed
Axtell, NE . . . 308-743-2565
Roman Meal Milling Company
Tacoma, WA . . . 253-475-0964
SJH Enterprises
Middleton, WI . . . 888-745-3845
Sunnyland Mills
Fresno, CA . . . 800-501-8017
T.S. Smith & Sons
Bridgeville, DE . . . 302-337-8271
Weetabix Company
Clinton, MA . . . 800-343-0590
Western Pacific Commodities
Henderson, NV . . . 702-382-8880
Wysong Corporation
Midland, MI . . . 800-748-0188

Bread

Turano Pastry Shops
Bloomingdale, IL . . . 630-529-6161

Bulgar

ADM Milling Company
Mississauga, ON . . . 800-267-8492
Chieftain Wild Rice Company
Spooner, WI . . . 800-262-6368

Flakes

ADM Milling Company
Mississauga, ON . . . 800-267-8492
Attala Company
Kosciusko, MS . . . 800-824-2691

Germ

American Health & Nutrition
Ann Arbor, MI . . . 734-677-5570
Canadian Harvest
Cambridge, MN . . . 888-689-5800
Fearn Natural Foods
Thiensville, WI . . . 800-877-8935
Garuda International
Lemon Cove, CA . . . 559-594-4380
Green Foods Corporation
Oxnard, CA . . . 800-777-4430
Norac Technologies
Edmonton, AB . . . 780-414-9595
Star of the West MillingCompany
Frankenmuth, MI . . . 989-652-9971
VIOBIN
Monticello, IL . . . 888-473-9645
Viobin USA
Monticello, IL . . . 217-762-2561
Vitamins
Chicago, IL . . . 312-861-0700

Defatted

Vitamins
Chicago, IL . . . 312-861-0700

Gluten

ADM Food Ingredients
Olathe, KS . . . 800-255-6637
Blue Chip Group
Salt Lake City, UT . . . 800-878-0099
Clofine Dairy & Food Products
Linwood, NJ . . . 800-441-1001
El Peto Products
Cambridge, ON . . . 800-387-4064
Manildra Milling Corporation
Fairway, KS . . . 800-323-8435

Spring

ADM Milling Company
Abilene, KS . . . 785-263-1631

Winter

Natural Way Mills
Middle River, MN . . . 218-222-3677

Whey & Whey Products

Agri-Dairy Products
Purchase, NY . . . 914-697-9580
Alto Dairy Cooperative
Waupun, WI . . . 920-346-2215
Anderson Custom Processing
New Ulm, MN . . . 877-588-4950
Arla Foods Ingredients
Basking Ridge, NJ . . . 908-604-8551
Ault Foods
Toronto, ON . . . 416-626-1973
Berkshire Dairy & Food Products
Wyomissing, PA . . . 888-654-8008
Blossom Farm Products
Ridgewood, NJ . . . 800-729-1818
Bongard's Creameries
Perham, MN . . . 218-346-4680
Brewster Dairy
Brewster, OH . . . 800-874-8874
Calpro Ingredients
Corona, CA . . . 909-493-4890
Century Foods International
Sparta, WI . . . 800-269-1901

Clofine Dairy & Food Products
Linwood, NJ 800-441-1001
Con Yeager Spice Company
Zelienople, PA. 800-222-2460
CP Kelco
Atlanta, GA. 800-535-2687
Crest Foods Company
Ashton, IL. 800-435-6972
Crowley Foods
Binghamton, NY. 800-637-0019
Davisco Foods International
Eden Prairie, MN 800-757-7611
Davisco International
Le Sueur, MN 800-757-7611
Ellsworth Cooperative Creamery
Ellsworth, WI 715-273-4311
Empire Cheese
Cuba, NY 585-968-1552
First District Association
Litchfield, MN 320-693-3236
Foremost Farms
Preston, MN 507-765-3831
Foremost Farms
Sparta, WI. 608-269-3126
Foremost Farms
Reedsburg, WI 608-524-2351
Foremost Farms
Rothschild, WI 715-359-0534
Foremost Farms
Baraboo, WI 800-362-9196
Friendship Dairies
Friendship, NY 585-973-3031
Grande Custom Ingredients Group
Brownsville, WI 800-678-3122
Hilmar Cheese Company
Hilmar, CA 800-577-5772
Holmes Cheese Company
Millersburg, OH 330-674-6451
Honeyville Grain
Salt Lake City, UT 801-972-2168
Honeyville Grain
Rancho Cucamonga, CA 888-810-3212
Kantner Group
Wapakoneta, OH. 419-738-4060
Keebler Company
Battle Creek, MI 800-962-1413
Land O'Lakes, Inc.
Arden Hills, MN. 800-328-9680
Leprino Foods Company
Denver, CO. 800-537-7466
Main Street Ingredients
La Crosse, WI. 800-359-2345
Minerva Cheese Factory
Minerva, OH. 330-868-4196
Mount Capra Cheese
Chehalis, WA 800-574-1961
Particle Control
Albertville, MN. 763-497-3075
Plainview Milk Products Cooperative
Plainview, MN 507-534-3872
Quality Ingredients Corporation
Burnsville, MN 952-898-4002
San Fernando Creamery Farmdale Creamery
San Bernardino, CA 909-889-3002
Tillamook County Creamery Association
Tillamook, OR 503-815-1300
Valley Queen Cheese Factory
Milbank, SD 605-432-4563
Westin
Omaha, NE 800-228-6098

Cheese & Cheese Products

General

Agri-Mark
Lawrence, MA 978-689-4442
Agropur
Appleton, WI 608-441-3030
Alouette Cheese USA
New Holland, PA 717-355-8500
Arthur Schuman, Inc.
Fairfield, NJ 973-227-0630
Asiago PDO & Speck Alto Adige PGI
New York, NY 646-258-0689
Austrian Trade Commission
New York, NY 212-421-5250
Dairiconcepts
Springfield, MO 877-596-4374
Dairyfood USA Inc
Blue Mounds, WI 800-236-3300
Golden Valley Dairy Products
Tulare, CA. 559-687-1188
Hilmar Ingredients
Hilmar, CA 209-667-6076
Hormel Foods Corporation
Austin, MN. 800-523-4635
Italian Products USA Inc
Clark, NJ. 201-770-9130
J & M Foods
Little Rock, AR. 800-264-2278
Kantner Group
Wapakoneta, OH. 419-738-4060
Kraft Foods
Northfield, IL 800-323-0768
Krinos Foods
Santa Barbara, CA 800-624-4896
Lactalis USA Merrill Plant
Merrill, WI 888-766-3353
Maplebrook Farm
Bennington, VT 802-440-9950
Marathon Cheese
Marathon, WI 715-352-3391
Market Day Corporation
Itasca, IL 877-632-7753
Mozzarella Fresca Tipton Plant
Tipton, CA 559-752-4823
Mt. Vikos, Inc.
Providence, RI 888-534-0246
Old Tavern Food Products
Waukesha, WI. 888-425-1788
Parmalat Canada
Toronto, ON 800-563-1515
Point Reyes Farmstead Cheese Co.
Point Reyes Station, CA 800-591-6787
Pondini Imports, Inc
Somerset, NJ. 732-545-1255
Reilly Dairy & Food Company
Tampa, FL. 813-839-8458
Roaring Brook Dairy
Chappaqua, NY. 914-861-2666
Stanz Foodservice
South Bend, IN 800-342-5664
Swiss Heritage Cheese
Monticello, WI 608-938-4455
Twin County Dairy
Kalona, IA. 319-656-2776

Cheese

Aegean Cheese
Austin, MN. 507-433-1292
AFP Advanced Food Products, LLC
Visalia, CA 559-627-2070
Agri-Dairy Products
Purchase, NY 914-697-9580
Agri-Mark
Lawrence, MA 978-689-4442
Agropur
Appleton, WI 608-441-3030
Agropur Cooperative Agro-Alimentaire
Granby, QC. 800-363-5686
AgSource Milk Analysis Laboratory
Menomonie, WI 715-235-1128
Al Pete Meats
Muncie, IN 765-288-8817
Alberta Cheese Company
Calgary, AB. 403-279-4353
Alberto-Culver Company
Melrose Park, IL. 708-450-3000
Alouette Cheese USA
New Holland, PA 717-355-8500
Alpine Cheese Company
Winesburg, OH 330-359-6291
Alta Dena Certified Dairy
City of Industry, CA 800-535-1369
Alto Dairy Cooperative
Waupun, WI 920-346-2215
Alto Dairy Cooperative
Black Creek, WI 920-984-3331
Amberwave Foods
Oakmont, PA. 412-828-3040
Amboy Specialty Foods Company
Dixon, IL. 800-892-0400
American Cheesemen
Clear Lake, IA. 641-357-7176
Anchor Appetizer Group
Appleton, WI 920-997-2200
Anchor Food Products/ McCain Foods
Appleton, WI 920-734-0627
Anco Foods
Caldwell, NJ 800-526-2596
Annie's Homegrown
Napa, CA. 800-288-1089
Applegate Farms
Bridgewater, NJ 908-725-2768
Ardmore Cheese Company
Shelbyville, TN. 931-427-2191
Ariza Cheese Company
Paramount, CA 800-762-4736
Arla Foods Inc
Concord, ON. 905-669-9393
Associated Milk Producers
Duluth, MN. 218-624-4803
Associated Milk Producers
Paynesville, MN 320-243-3794
Associated Milk Producers
Dawson, MN. 320-769-2994
Associated Milk Producers
Rochester, MN 507-282-7401
Associated Milk Producers
Arlington, IA. 563-933-4521
Associated Milk Producers
Freeman, SD 605-925-4234
Associated Milk Producers
Hoven, SD. 605-948-2211
Associated Milk Producers
Portage, WI. 608-742-2114
Associated Milk Producers
Blair, WI 608-989-2535
Associated Milk Producers
Mason City, IA 641-424-6111
Associated Milk Producers
Fargo, ND 701-293-6455
Associated Milk Producers
Sanborn, IA. 712-729-3255
Associated Milk Producers
Jim Falls, WI. 715-382-4113
Associated Milk Producers
New Ulm, MN. 800-533-3580
Astro Dairy Products
Etobicoke, ON. 416-622-2811
Atwood Cheese Company
Atwood, ON 519-356-2271
Aunt Lizzie's
Memphis, TN 800-993-7788
Avanti Food Company
Walnut, IL 800-243-3739
B&D Foods
Boise, ID 208-344-1183
Baker Cheese Factory
Saint Cloud, WI 920-477-7871
Baker's Coconut
Memphis, TN 800-323-1092
Barnum-Goodfriend Farms
Jeffersonville, NY. 845-482-4123
Bass Lake Cheese Factory
Somerset, WI. 800-368-2437
Bel/Kaukauna USA
Kaukauna, WI. 800-558-3500
Belgioioso Cheese
Denmark, WI. 877-863-2123
Belle Plaine Cheese Factory
Shawano, WI. 866-245-5924
Bellwether Farms
Valley Ford, CA 707-763-0993
Berner Cheese Corporation
Dakota, IL. 800-819-8199
Berner Cheese Corporation
Rock City, IL. 815-865-5136
Berner Foods, Inc.
Roscoe, IL. 800-819-8199
Biazzo Dairy Products
Ridgefield, NJ. 201-941-6800
Bieri's Jackson Cheese
Jackson, WI. 262-677-3227
Biery Cheese Company
Louisville, OH 800-243-3731
Black Diamond Cheese
Toronto, ON 800-263-2858
Blakely Freezer Locker
Thomasville, GA. 229-723-3622
Blaser's USA, Inc.
Comstock, WI. 715-822-2437
Bletsoe's Cheese
Marathon, WI 715-443-2526
Blue Ribbon Meats
Cleveland, OH 216-631-8850
Bongard's Creameries
Perham, MN 218-346-4680
Bongards Creameries
Norwood, MN. 800-877-6417
Bongrain Cheese
New Holland, PA 717-355-8500
Bongrain North America
Mahwah, NJ 201-512-8825
Brenntag
Reading, PA 888-926-4151
Brenntag Pacific
Santa Fe Springs, CA 562-903-9626
Brewster Dairy
Brewster, OH 800-874-8874
Brier Run Farm
Birch River, WV. 304-649-2975
Broughton Foods
Marietta, OH. 800-283-2479
Brunkow Cheese Company
Darlington, WI 608-776-3716
Buon Italia Misono Food Ltd.
New York, NY 212-633-9090
Burnette Dairy Cooperative
Grantsburg, WI. 715-689-2468
Byrne Dairy
Syracuse, NY 800-899-1535
CA Fortune
Bloomingdale, IL
Cabot Creamery
Montpelier, VT. 888-792-2268
Cady Cheese Factory
Wilson, WI 715-772-4218
Calabro Cheese Corporation
East Haven, CT. 203-469-1311
Callie's Charleston Biscuits LLC
Charleston, SC 843-577-1198
Cantare Foods
San Diego, CA 619-690-7550
Cappiello Dairy Products
Schenectady, NY. 518-374-5064
Caprine Estates
Bellbrook, OH. 937-848-7406
Carr Cheese Factory/GileCheese Company
Cuba City, WI. 608-744-8455
Carr Valley Cheese Company
La Valle, WI 800-462-7258
Cascade Cheese Company
Cascade, WI 920-528-8221
Cass Clay
Fargo, ND 701-293-6455
Castle Cheese
Slippery Rock, PA. 800-252-4373
Caves Of Faribault/SwissValley
Faribault, MN 507-334-5260
Cedar Grove Cheese
Plain, WI. 800-200-6020
Cedar Valley Cheese
Belgium, WI 920-994-4415
Cemac Foods Corporation
Philadelphia, PA 800-724-0179
Chalet Cheese Coop e
Monroe, WI. 608-325-4343
Cheddar Box Cheese House
Shawano, WI. 715-526-5411

Cheese Factory
Borden, IN. 812-923-8861
CheeseLand
Seattle, WA 206-709-1220
Chianti Cheese Company
Wapakoneta, OH. 800-220-3503
Chicago 58 Food Products
Woodbridge, ON. 416-603-4244
Chicopee Provision Company
Chicopee, MA. 800-924-6328
Chloe Foods Corporation
Brooklyn, NY 718-827-9000
Chula Vista Cheese Company
Browntown, WI. 608-439-5211
Churny Company
Waupaca, WI. 715-258-4040
Clofine Dairy & Food Products
Linwood, NJ 800-441-1001
Clover Leaf Cheese
Calgary, AB. 888-835-0126
Cloverleaf Dairy
Stanley, WI 715-669-3145
Cobb Hill Chesse
Hartland, VT. 802-436-1612
Coburg Dairy
North Charleston, SC 843-554-4870
Colonna Brothers
North Bergen, NJ 201-864-1115
Commercial Creamery Company
Spokane, WA. 800-541-0850
ConAgra Grocery Products
Irvine, CA 714-680-1000
ConAgra Refrigerated Foods International
Omaha, NE 800-624-4724
Conlin Food Sales
Placentia, CA 800-429-1136
Consun Food Industries
Elyria, OH. 440-322-6301
Continental Culture Specialists
Los Angeles, CA. 818-240-7400
Corfu Foods
Bensenville, IL 630-595-2510
Country Fresh
Grand Rapids, MI 800-748-0480
Cow Girl Creamery
Point Reyes Sta, CA 415-663-8153
Cream O'Weaver Dairy
Salt Lake City, UT 801-973-9922
Creamland Dairies
Albuquerque, NM. 505-247-0721
Cropp Cooperative-Organic Valley
La Farge, WI. 888-444-6455
Crowley Cheese
Mount Holly, VT. 800-683-2606
Crowley Foods
Binghamton, NY. 800-637-0019
Cultured Specialties
Fullerton, CA 714-772-8861
Curran's Cheese Plant
Browntown, WI 608-966-3361
Cyclone Enterprises
Houston, TX 281-872-0087
D'Artagnan
Newark, NJ 800-327-8246
Dairy Concepts
Greenwood, WI. 888-680-5400
Dairy Farms of America
New Wilmington, PA 800-837-5214
Dairy Fresh Foods
Taylor, MI 313-295-6300
Dairy Group
Jericho, NY. 516-433-0080
Dakota Country Cheese
Mandan, ND 701-663-0246
Dan Carter
Richfield, WI 800-782-0741
Dave's Gourmet
San Francisco, CA 800-758-0372
DCI Cheese Company
Richfield, WI 262-677-3407
Dean Foods Company
Dallas, TX. 800-431-9214
Decatur Dairy
Brodhead, WI 608-897-8661
Delta Distributors
Longview, TX. 800-945-1858
Delta Valley Farms
Delta, UT. 435-864-2725
Deppeler Cheese Factory
Monroe, WI. 608-325-6311
Deutsch Kase Haus
Middlebury, IN 574-825-9511
Dimock Dairy Products
Dimock, SD. 605-928-3833
Dixie Dairy Company
Gary, IN. 219-885-6101
Dixon Associates
Mechanicsburg, PA. 717-691-0800
DPI Dairy Fresh Products Company
Ontario, CA. 909-605-7300
Drangle Foods
Gilman, WI 715-447-8241
Dulce de Leche Delcampo Products
Hialeah, FL 877-472-9408
Dupont Cheese
Marion, WI 800-895-2873
Durrett Cheese Sales
Manchester, TN. 800-209-6792
Eatem Foods Company
Vineland, NJ 800-683-2836
Eau Galle Cheese Factory Shop
Durand, WI 800-283-1085
Ellsworth Cooperative Creamery
Ellsworth, WI 715-273-4311
Elm City Cheese Company
Hamden, CT 203-865-5768
Emkay Trading Corporation
Elmsford, NY 914-592-9000
Empire Cheese
Cuba, NY 585-968-1552
Empire Foods
Bellmore, NY 516-679-1414
Enon Valley Cheese Compay
Enon Valley, PA 724-336-5207
Equinox Enterprises
Sherwood Park, AB 888-378-7364
Excelpro Manufacturing Corporation
Los Angeles, CA. 323-268-1918
Excelsior Dairy
Hilo, HI. 808-961-3608
F&A Dairy Products
Dresser, WI. 715-755-3485
F. Soderlund Company
Bonita Springs, FL 239-498-0600
Fairmont Products
Belleville, PA 717-935-2121
Fairview Swiss Cheese
Fredonia, PA 724-475-4154
Fanny Mason Farmstead Cheese
Walpole, NH 603-756-3300
Fantis Foods
Carlstadt, NJ 201-933-6200
Farmers Cooperative Dairy
Halifax, NS 800-565-1945
Father's Country Hams
Bremen, KY 270-525-3554
Fennimore Cheese
Fennimore, WI 888-499-3778
Finlandia Cheese
Parsippany, NJ. 973-316-6699
First District Association
Litchfield, MN 320-693-3236
Fleur De Lait Foods
New Holland, PA 717-355-8500
Floron Food Services
Edmonton, AB 780-438-9300
Foothills Creamery
Calgary, AB. 800-661-4909
Foremost Farms
Cochrane, WI 608-626-2121
Foremost Farms
Richland Center, WI. 608-647-2186
Foremost Farms
Lancaster, WI 608-723-7381
Foremost Farms
Marshfield, WI 715-384-5616
Foremost Farms
Alma Center, WI. 715-964-7411
Foremost Farms
Chilton, WI. 920-849-9339
Foster Farms Dairy
Modesto, CA. 209-576-2300
Frankfort Cheese
Edgar, WI 715-352-2345
Franklin Foods
Enosburg Falls, VT. 800-933-6114
Fried Provisions Company
Evans City, PA 724-538-3160
Friendship Dairies
Dallas, TX. 516-719-4000
Friendship Dairies
Friendship, NY 585-973-3031
Frog City Cheese
Plymouth Notch, VT. 802-672-3650
Froma-Dar
St. Boniface, QC 819-535-3946
Fry Foods
Tiffin, OH 800-626-2294
Gad Cheese Company
Medford, WI 715-748-4273
Galaxy Dairy Products, Incorporated
Ramsey, NJ 201-818-2030
Galaxy Nutritional Foods
North Kingstown, RI 800-441-9419
GFA Brands
Paramus, NJ 201-568-9300
Gibbsville Cheese Company
Sheboygan Falls, WI. 920-564-3242
Gile Cheese Company
Cuba City, WI 608-744-3456
Glanbia Foods
Twin Falls, ID. 208-733-7555
Glanbia Foods
Twin Falls, ID 800-427-9477
Gold Cup Farms
Clayton, NY 800-752-1341
Golden Cheese Company of California
Corona, CA 951-493-4700
Golden Cheese of California
Corona, CA 800-842-0264
Gossner Food
Logan, UT. 800-944-0454
GPI USA LLC.
Athens, GA 706-850-7826
Grafton Village Cheese
Grafton, VT. 800-472-3866
Graham Cheese Corporation
Elnoragton, IN 800-472-9178
Grande Cheese Company
Brownsville, WI 800-678-3122
Great American Appetizers
Nampa, ID. 800-282-4834
Great Lakes Cheese Company
Hiram, OH. 440-834-1002
Great Lakes Cheese of NY
Adams, NY 315-232-4511
Green Bay Cheese Company
Green Bay, WI. 920-434-3233
Green Valley Foods
Tranquility, NJ 800-853-8399
Greenberg Cheese Company
Le Canada, CA 800-301-4507
Guggisberg Cheese
Millersburg, OH 800-262-2505
H B Taylor Company
Chicago, IL 773-254-4805
H.E. Butt Grocery Company
San Antonio, TX. 800-432-3113
Hallman International
Louisville, KY 502-778-0459
Harrington's In Vermont
Richmond, VT. 802-434-7500
Heini's Cheese Company
Millersburg, OH 800-253-6636
Heluva Good Cheese
Sodus, NY. 315-483-6971
Henning's Cheese
Kiel, WI. 920-894-3032
Henningsen Foods
Purchase, NY 914-701-4020
Heritage Cheese House
Heuvelton, NY 315-344-2216
Heritage Farms Dairy
Murfreesboro, TN. 615-895-2790
Herkimer Foods
Herkimer, NY 315-895-7832
Hickory Farms
Maumee, OH. 419-893-7611
Hidden Villa Ranch
Fullerton, CA 800-326-3220
High Ridge Foods LLC
White Plains, NY 914-761-2900

Hiland Dairy Foods Company
Branson, MO ... 417-334-0090

Hiland Dairy Foods Company
Springfield, MO ... 417-862-9311

Hilmar Cheese Company
Hilmar, CA ... 800-577-5772

Hilmar Ingredients
Hilmar, CA ... 209-667-6076

Hitz Cheese Company
Linwood, MI ... 517-697-5932

Hollow Road Farms
Stuyvesant, NY ... 518-758-7214

Holmes Cheese Company
Millersburg, OH ... 330-674-6451

Hook's Cheese Company
Mineral Point, WI ... 608-987-3259

HP Hood
Lynnfield, MA ... 800-343-6592

Icco Cheese Company
Orangeburg, NY ... 845-398-9800

Idaho Milk Products
Jerome, ID ... 208-644-2882

IMAC
Oklahoma City, OK ... 888-878-7827

Imperia Foods
Fairfield, NJ ... 800-526-7333

Imperial Foods
Long Island City, NY ... 718-784-3400

Industria Lechera de Puerto Rico
San Juan, PR ... 787-753-0974

Inter-American Products
Cincinnati, OH ... 800-645-2233

International Cheese Company
Toronto, ON ... 416-769-3547

International Trading Company
Houston, TX ... 713-224-5901

Isaar Cheese
Seymour, WI ... 920-833-6190

Ito Cariani Sausage Company
Hayward, CA ... 510-887-0882

Ivanhoe Cheese Inc
Madoc, ON ... 613-473-4269

J&G Cheese Company
Columbus, OH ... 614-436-1070

J.B. Sons
Yonkers, NY ... 914-963-5192

Janes Family Foods
Mississauga, ON ... 800-565-2637

Jersey Pride
New Brunswick, NJ ... 732-214-2965

Jim's Cheese Pantry
Waterloo, WI ... 800-345-3571

John Koller & Sons
Fredonia, PA ... 724-475-4154

Jolina Foods
Hinesburg, VT ... 802-434-2185

Joseph Gallo Farms
Atwater, CA ... 209-394-7984

Kantner Group
Wapakoneta, OH ... 419-738-4060

Karoun Dairies
Sun Valley, CA ... 818-767-7000

Keebler Company
Battle Creek, MI ... 800-962-1413

Keller's Creamery
Harleysville, PA ... 800-535-5371

Key Ingredients
Harrisburg, PA ... 800-227-4448

Kirby & Holloway Provisions
Harrington, DE ... 800-995-4729

Klondike Cheese
Monroe, WI

Klondike Cheese Factory
Monroe, WI ... 608-325-3021

Kolb-Lena Cheese Company
Lena, IL ... 815-369-4577

Kraemer's Wisconsin Cheese
Watertown, WI ... 800-236-8033

Kraft Foods
Albany, MN ... 320-845-2131

Kraft Foods
Springfield, MO ... 417-881-2701

Kraft Foods
Walton, NY ... 607-865-7131

Kraft Foods
Allentown, PA ... 610-398-0311

Krohn Dairy Products
Luxemburg, WI ... 920-845-2901

Laack Brothers Cheese Company
Greenleaf, WI ... 800-589-5127

Lactalis Deli
New York, NY ... 888-766-3353

LaGrander Hillside Dairy
Stanley, WI ... 715-644-2275

Lake Erie Frozen Foods Company
Ashland, OH ... 800-766-8501

Lamagna Cheese Company
Verona, PA ... 412-828-6112

Lamex Foods
Bloomington, MN ... 952-844-0585

Land O'Lakes
Spencer, WI ... 715-659-2311

Land O'Lakes
Kiel, WI ... 920-894-2204

Land O'Lakes, Inc.
Arden Hills, MN ... 800-328-9680

Land-O-Sun Dairies
O Fallon, IL ... 314-436-6820

Laura Chenel's Chevre
Sonoma, CA ... 707-996-4477

Le Sueur Cheese
Le Sueur, MN ... 800-757-7611

Lebanon Cheese Company
Lebanon, NJ ... 908-236-2611

Lemke Cheese Company
Wausau, WI ... 715-842-3214

Lengacher's Cheese House
Kinzers, PA ... 717-355-6490

Leprino Foods Company
Denver, CO ... 800-537-7466

LeRaysville Cheese
Le Raysville, PA ... 800-595-5196

Level Valley Creamery
Antioch, TN ... 800-251-1292

LFI
Fairfield, NJ ... 973-882-0550

Liberty Enterprises
Stateline, NV ... 800-723-3690

Lifeline Food Company
Sand City, CA ... 831-899-5040

Lifeway Foods Inc
Morton Grove, IL ... 877-281-3874

Linden Cheese Factory
Linden, WI ... 800-660-5051

Lioni Latticini, Inc.
Union, NJ ... 908-686-6061

Lisanatti Foods
Oregon City, OR ... 866-864-3922

Lisanatti Foods P.J. Lisac & Associates, Inc
Oregon City, OR ... 866-864-3922

Lone Elm Sales
Van Dyne, WI ... 800-950-8275

Los Altos Food Products
City of Industry, CA ... 626-330-6555

Losurdo Creamery
Heuvelton, NY ... 315-344-2444

Lov-It Creamery
Green Bay, WI ... 800-344-0333

Lucille Farm Products
Montville, NJ ... 973-334-6030

Lynn Dairy
Granton, WI ... 715-238-7129

M.H. Greenebaum
Airmont, NY ... 973-538-9200

Mahoning Swiss Cheese Cooperative
Smicksburg, PA ... 814-257-8884

Mancuso Cheese Company
Joliet, IL ... 815-722-2475

Mann Packing
Salinas, CA ... 831-422-7405

Maple Leaf Cheesemakers
New Glarus, WI ... 608-527-2000

Marathon Cheese Corporation
Booneville, MS ... 662-728-6266

Marcus Dairy
Danbury, CT ... 800-243-2511

Marin French Cheese Company
Petaluma, CA ... 800-292-6001

Marrese Cheese Company
Lomira, WI ... 920-269-4288

Marshallville Packing Company
Marshallville, OH ... 330-855-2871

Marva Maid Dairy
Newport News, VA ... 800-544-4439

Masson Cheese Corporation
Vernon, CA ... 800-637-7262

Masters Gallery Foods
Plymouth, WI ... 800-236-8431

Matador Processors
Blanchard, OK ... 800-847-0797

McArthur Dairy
Miami, FL ... 877-803-6565

McCadam Cheese Company
Chateaugay, NY ... 518-497-6644

Meadow Gold Dairies
Englewood, CO ... 800-525-3289

Meister Cheese Company
Muscoda, WI ... 800-634-7837

Merkts Cheese Company
Bristol, WI ... 262-857-2316

Miceli Dairy Products Company
Cleveland, OH ... 800-551-7196

Michael Granese & Company
Norristown, PA ... 610-272-5099

Michigan Dairy
Livonia, MI ... 734-367-5390

Michigan Farm Cheese Dairy
Fountain, MI ... 231-462-3301

Mid States Dairy
Hazelwood, MO ... 314-731-1150

Middlefield Cheese House
Middlefield, OH ... 800-327-9477

Mille Lacs Gourmet Foods
Madison, WI ... 800-843-1381

Mille Lacs MP Company
Madison, WI ... 800-843-1381

Miller's Cheese Corp
Brooklyn, NY ... 718-965-1840

Milsolv Corporation
Butler, WI ... 800-558-8501

Minerva Cheese Factory
Minerva, OH ... 330-868-4196

Monroe Cheese Corporation
Monticello, WI ... 608-325-5161

Monterrey Provisions
San Diego, CA ... 800-201-1600

Morningland Dairy CheeseCompany
Mountain View, MO ... 417-469-3817

Morrisons Pastries/Turf Cheesecake
Harrison, NY ... ÿÿ -00 -21 8

Moscahlades Brothers
New York, NY ... 212-226-5410

Mossholder's Farm Cheese Factory
Appleton, WI 920-734-7575
Mozzarella Company
Dallas, TX. 800-798-2954
Mozzarella Fresca Corporate & Commercial Headquarters
Concord, CA. 800-572-6818
Murphy House
Louisburg, NC 919-496-6054
Nasonville Dairy
Marshfield, WI 715-676-2177
Nelson Cheese Factory
Nelson, WI 715-673-4725
Nelson Ricks Creamery
Salt Lake City, UT 801-364-3607
Nelson Ricks Creamery Company
Salt Lake City, UT 801-364-3607
Network Food Brokers
Haverford, PA. 610-649-7210
Newburg Corners Cheese Factory
Bangor, WI 608-452-3636
Nodine's Smokehouse
Torrington, CT 800-222-2059
Noon Hour Food Products
Chicago, IL. 800-621-6636
Nor-Tech Dairy Advisors
Sioux Falls, SD. 605-338-2404
Northern Utah Manufacturing
Wellsville, UT. 435-245-4542
Northern Wisconsin Cheese Company
Manitowoc, WI. 920-684-4461
Oak Grove Dairy
Clintonville, WI 715-823-6226
Old Chatham Sheepherding
Old Chatham, NY. 888-743-3760
Old Country Cheese
Cashton, WI 608-654-5411
Old Europe Cheese
Benton Harbor, MI 800-447-8182
Old Fashioned Foods Inc
Mayville, WI. 920-387-7920
Old Wisconsin Food Products
Homewood, IL 888-633-5684
Olde Tyme Food Corporation
East Longmeadow, MA 800-356-6533
Ore-Ida Foods
Pittsburgh, PA. 800-892-2401
Oshkosh Cold Storage Company
Oshkosh, WI. 800-580-4680
Owl's Nest Cheese
Kaukauna, WI. 608-825-6818
Pace Dairy Foods Company
Rochester, MN 507-288-6315
Pacific Cheese Company
Hayward, CA 510-784-8800
Park Cheese Company
Fond Du Lac, WI 800-752-7275
Parker Farm
Minneapolis, MN 800-869-6685
Parkers Farm
Coon Rapids, MN. 800-869-6685
Pastene Companies
Canton, MA 781-830-8200
Pastorelli Food Products
Chicago, IL. 800-767-2829
PB&S Chemicals
Henderson, KY 800-950-7267
Pearl Valley Cheese Company
Fresno, OH 740-545-6002
Pecoraro Dairy Products
Rome, NY. 315-339-0101
Peluso Cheese Company
Los Banos, CA 209-826-3744
Pend Oreille Cheese Company
Sandpoint, ID 208-263-2030
Penn Cheese Corporation
Winfield, PA 570-524-7700
Penn Maid Crowley Foods
Philadelphia, PA. 800-247-6269
Pine River Cheese & Butter Company
Ripley, ON. 800-265-1175
Pine River Pre-Pack
Newton, WI. 920-726-4216
Plumrose USA
East Brunswick, NJ. 800-526-4909
Plymouth Cheese Counter
Plymouth, WI 888-607-9477
Pollio Dairy Products
Campbell, NY. 607-527-4585
Polly-O Dairy Products
Mineola, NY 516-741-8000

Portion Pak
Stone Mountain, GA. 770-934-3200
Prairie Farms Dairy
Carlinville, IL 217-854-2547
Prairie Farms Dairy Inc.
Carlinville, IL 217-854-2547
Prima Kase
Monticello, WI 608-938-4227
Protein Palace
Hartford, WI 262-673-2698
Providence Cheese
Johnston, RI 401-421-5653
Purity Dairies
Nashville, TN 615-244-1900
Quality Ingredients Corporation
Burnsville, MN. 952-898-4002
Queensboro Farm Products
Canastota, NY. 315-697-2235
Queensboro Farm Products
Jamaica, NY 718-658-5000
Ragersville Swiss Cheese
Sugarcreek, OH. 330-897-3055
Rahco International
St Augustine, FL. 800-851-7681
Ranieri Fine Foods
Brooklyn, NY 718-599-0665
Raven Creamery Company
Portland, OR. 503-288-5101
Redi-Froze
South Bend, IN 574-237-5111
Redwood Hill Farm
Sebastopol, CA. 707-823-8250
Regez Cheese & Paper Supply
Monroe, WI. 608-325-3417
Renard's Cheese
Algoma, WI. 920-487-2825
Rey Food Company
Hoboken, NJ 201-792-1955
Rich-Seapak Corporation
St Simons Island, GA 800-654-9731
Roberto A Cheese Factory
East Canton, OH 330-488-1551
Rochester Cheese
Rochester, MN 888-288-6678
Roelli Cheese Company
Shullsburg, WI 800-575-4372
Rogue Creamery
Central Point, OR 541-665-1155
Ron's Wisconsin Cheese
Luxemburg, WI. 920-845-5330
Rondel, Specialty Foods
Merrill, WI 800-766-3353
Roos Foods
Kenton, DE 800-343-3642
Rosenberger's Dairies
Hatfield, PA. 800-355-9074
Roth Kase
Monroe, WI. 608-329-7666
Royal Baltic
Brooklyn, NY 718-385-8300
Rumiano Cheese Company
Crescent City, CA. 707-465-1535
Safeway Dairy Products
Walnut Creek, CA. 925-944-4000
Salemville Cheese Cooperative
Cambria, WI 920-394-3433
Salmans & Associates
Chicago, IL 312-226-1820
San Fernando Creamery Farmdale Creamery
San Bernardino, CA 909-889-3002
Saputo Foodservice USA
Lincolnshire, IL 800-824-3373
Sardinia Cheese
Seymour, CT. 203-735-3374
Sargento Foods Inc.
Plymouth, WI 800-243-3737
Sartori Food Corporation
Plymouth, WI 800-558-5888
Sartori Foods
Plymouth, WI 800-356-5655
Saxon Creamery
Cleveland, WI. 920-693-8500
Schepps Dairy
Dallas, TX. 800-395-7004
Schneider Cheese
Waldo, WI. 920-467-3351
Schneider's Dairy Holdings Inc
Pittsburgh, PA. 412-881-3525
Schobert's Cottage Cheese Corporation
Akron, OH. 216-733-6876
Schreiber Foods Plant
Logan, UT. 435-753-0504

Schreiber Foods Plant
Clinton, MO 660-885-6133
Schreiber Foods Plant
Shippensburg, PA 717-530-5000
Schreiber Foods Plant/Distribution Center
Wisconsin Rapids, WI 715-422-7500
Schreiber Foods Inc
Green Bay, WI. 800-344-0333
Schwartz Meat Company
Sophia, WV. 304-683-4595
Scotsburn Dairy Group
Scotsburn, NS 902-485-8023
Scott's of Wisconsin
Sun Prairie, WI 800-698-1721
Scray's Cheese Company
De Pere, WI. 920-336-8359
Sea Stars Goat Cheese
Santa Cruz, CA 831-423-7200
Sequoia Specialty Cheese Company
Visalia, CA 559-752-4106
Shelburne Farms
Shelburne, VT. 802-985-8686
Shenk's Foods
Lancaster, PA 717-393-4240
Sierra Cheese Manufacturing Company
Compton, CA 800-266-4270
Silani Sweet Cheese
Schomberg, ON. 905-939-2561
Simon's Specialty Cheese
Appleton, WI 800-444-0374
Sini Fulvi U.S.A.
Newark, NJ 973-274-0822
Sinton Dairy Foods Company
Colorado Springs, CO. 800-388-4970
Sinton Dairy Foods Company
Denver, CO 800-666-4808
Sisler's Ice & Ice Cream
Ohio, IL. 888-891-3856
Smith Dairy Products Company
Orrville, OH 800-776-7076
Smith, Weber & Swinton Company
Youngstown, OH. 800-860-2867
Sofo Foods
Toledo, OH 800-447-4211
Sommer Maid Creamery
Doylestown, PA 215-345-6160
Sorrento Lactalis
Buffalo, NY. 800-828-7031
Southchem
Durham, NC 800-849-7000
Southwestern Wisconsin Dairy Goat Products
Mt Sterling, WI. 608-734-3151
Sparboe Companies
Los Angeles, CA. 213-626-7538
Spaulding Sales
Brighton, MI 810-229-4166
Specialty Cheese Company
Reeseville, WI. 800-367-1711
Spring Grove Foods
Miamisburg, OH 937-866-4311
Springbank Cheese Company
Woodstock, ON. 800-265-1973
Springdale Cheese Factory
Richland Center, WI 608-538-3213
St. Charles Trading
Lake Saint Louis, MO. 800-336-1333
St. Maurice Laurent
St-Bruno-Lac-St-Jean, QC 418-343-3655
Stallings Headcheese Company
Houston, TX 713-523-1751
State of Maine Cheese Company
Rockport, ME 800-762-8895
Steiner Cheese
Baltic, OH. 888-897-5505
Stockton Cheese
Stockton, IL. 800-728-0111
Stremick's Heritage Foods
Santa Ana, CA 800-371-9010
Sugarbush Farm
Woodstock, VT. 800-281-1757
Sun States
Charlotte, NC 704-821-0615
Sun-Re Cheese
Sunbury, PA. 570-286-1511
Sunnyrose Cheese
Diamond City, AB 403-381-4024
Sunshine Farms
Portage, WI. 608-742-2016
Superstore Industries
Fairfield, CA. 707-864-0502
Suprema Specialties
Manteca, CA. 209-858-9696

Suprema Specialties
Paterson, NJ 800-543-2479
Supreme Dairy Farms Company
Warwick, RI 401-739-8180
Swiss Colony
Monroe, WI. . . . 608-328-8536
Swiss Valley Farms Company
Davenport, IA 563-468-6600
Swiss Way Cheese
Berne, IN. . . . 260-589-3531
Swiss-American
St Louis, MO. . . . 800-325-8150
T. Sterling Associates
Jamestown, NY. . . . 716-483-0769
Taftsville Country Store
Corinth, VT. . . . 800-854-0013
Tall Talk Dairy
Canby, OR. . . . 503-266-1644
Tate Cheese Company
Valley City, IL. . . . 217-833-2314
Taylor Cheese Corporation
Weyauwega, WI 920-867-2337
Thiel Cheese & Ingredients
Hilbert, WI 920-989-1440
Thiry Daems Cheese Factory
Luxemburg, WI. . . . 920-845-2117
Tholstrup Cheese
Muskegon, MI. . . . 800-426-0938
Thumann's
Carlstadt, NJ 201-935-3636
Tillamook County Creamery Association
Tillamook, OR 503-815-1300
Timber Lake Cheese Company
Timber Lake, SD. . . . 605-865-3605
Tony's Fine Foods
Broderick, CA. . . . 916-374-4000
Torkelson Cheese Company
Lena, IL. . . . 815-369-4265
Trega Foods
Weyauwega, WI 920-867-2137
Tropical Cheese Industries
Perth Amboy, NJ. . . . 800-487-7850
Twin County Dairy
Kalona, IA. . . . 319-656-2776
Ulfert Broockmann
Libertyville, IL 847-680-3771
Ultima Foods
Longueuil, ON 800-363-9496
Umpqua Dairy Products Company
Roseburg, OR 541-672-2638
V & V Supremo Foods
Chicago, IL 888-887-8773
Valley Grain Products
Madera, CA. . . . 559-675-3400
Valley Queen Cheese Factory
Milbank, SD 605-432-4563
Valley View Cheese Company
Conewango Vly, NY. . . . 716-296-5821
Vella Cheese
Sonoma, CA 800-848-0505
Vern's Cheese
Chilton, WI 920-849-7717
VOD Gourmet
Greenwich, CT 203-531-5172
Wapsie Valley Creamery
Independence, IA 319-334-7193
Warren Cheese Plant
Warren, IL. . . . 815-745-2627
Weaver Brothers
Berne, IN. . . . 219-589-2869
Welcome Dairy
Colby, WI 800-472-2315
Wells' Dairy
Le Mars, IA. . . . 800-942-3800
Wengers Springbrook Cheese
Davis, IL 815-865-5855
West Point Dairy Products
West Point, NE 402-372-5551
Western Dairy Products
Santa Rosa, CA. . . . 800-433-2479
Western Dairymen Corporation
Kansas City, MO. . . . 816-801-6455
Westfield Farm
Hubbardston, MA 877-777-3900
Weyauwega Star Dairy
Weyauwega, WI 920-867-2870
White Wave
Broomfield, CO 800-488-9283
Whitehall Specialties
Whitehall, WI 888-755-9900
Widmer's Cheese Cellars
Theresa, WI. . . . 888-878-1107
Williams Cheese Company
Linwood, MI. . . . 800-968-4462
Winder Dairy
West Valley, UT 800-946-3371
Winger Cheese
Towner, ND. . . . 701-537-5463
Wisconsin Cheese
Melrose Park, IL 708-450-0074
Wisconsin Cheese
Westwood, MA 781-320-0288
Wisconsin Cheese Group
Monroe, WI. . . . 800-332-6518
Wisconsin Dairy State Cheese
Rudolph, WI 715-435-3144
Wisconsin Farmers' Union Cheese Company
Montfort, WI. . . . 608-943-6753
Wohlt Cheese Corporation
New London, WI 920-982-9000
Woolwich Dairy
Orangeville, ON 877-438-3499
World Cheese Company
Brooklyn, NY 718-965-1700
Yerba Santa Goat Dairy
Lakeport, CA 707-263-8131
Zimmerman Cheese
South Wayne, WI 608-968-3414

American

Reilly Dairy & Food Company
Tampa, FL. . . . 813-839-8458
Sargento Foods Inc.
Plymouth, WI 800-243-3737
Schreiber Foods Plant
Monett, MO 417-235-6061
Schreiber Foods Plant
Green Bay, WI. . . . 800-344-0333

Asiago

Belgioioso Cheese
Denmark, WI. . . . 877-863-2123
Chianti Cheese Company
Wapakoneta, OH. . . . 800-220-3503
D'Artagnan
Newark, NJ 800-327-8246
Dairy Concepts
Greenwood, WI. . . . 888-680-5400
Kantner Group
Wapakoneta, OH. . . . 419-738-4060
Lactalis Deli
New York, NY 888-766-3353
Park Cheese Company
Fond Du Lac, WI 800-752-7275
Saputo Foodservice USA
Lincolnshire, IL 800-824-3373
Sargento Foods Inc.
Plymouth, WI 800-243-3737
Sorrento Lactalis
Buffalo, NY. . . . 800-828-7031
Vella Cheese
Sonoma, CA 800-848-0505

Blend - American/Skim Milk

Sliced

Kantner Group
Wapakoneta, OH. . . . 419-738-4060

Blue

Chianti Cheese Company
Wapakoneta, OH. . . . 800-220-3503
Clofine Dairy & Food Products
Linwood, NJ 800-441-1001
D'Artagnan
Newark, NJ 800-327-8246
Great Hill Dairy
Marion, MA 888-748-2208
Klondike Cheese Factory
Monroe, WI. . . . 608-325-3021
Marathon Cheese Corporation
Booneville, MS 662-728-6266
Reilly Dairy & Food Company
Tampa, FL. . . . 813-839-8458
Roth Kase
Monroe, WI. . . . 608-329-7666
Sargento Foods Inc.
Plymouth, WI 800-243-3737
Sorrento Lactalis
Buffalo, NY. . . . 800-828-7031

Brie

Foothills Creamery
Calgary, AB. . . . 800-661-4909
Kolb-Lena Cheese Company
Lena, IL. . . . 815-369-4577
Lactalis Deli
New York, NY 888-766-3353
Marin French Cheese Company
Petaluma, CA 800-292-6001
Reilly Dairy & Food Company
Tampa, FL. . . . 813-839-8458
Sorrento Lactalis
Buffalo, NY. . . . 800-828-7031
Wisconsin Cheese
Melrose Park, IL 708-450-0074
Woolwich Dairy
Orangeville, ON 877-438-3499

Camembert

Cheese Smokers
Brooklyn, NY
Foothills Creamery
Calgary, AB. . . . 800-661-4909
Glanbia Foods
Twin Falls, ID 800-427-9477
Kolb-Lena Cheese Company
Lena, IL. . . . 815-369-4577
Marin French Cheese Company
Petaluma, CA 800-292-6001
Nelson Ricks Creamery
Salt Lake City, UT 801-364-3607
Reilly Dairy & Food Company
Tampa, FL. . . . 813-839-8458
Swiss Valley Farms Company
Davenport, IA 563-468-6600
Wisconsin Cheese
Melrose Park, IL 708-450-0074

Cheddar

Alberta Cheese Company
Calgary, AB. . . . 403-279-4353
Alta Dena Certified Dairy
City of Industry, CA 800-535-1369
Alto Dairy Cooperative
Waupun, WI 920-346-2215
Ardmore Cheese Company
Shelbyville, TN. . . . 931-427-2191
Associated Milk Producers
Dawson, MN. . . . 320-769-2994
Associated Milk Producers
Rochester, MN 507-282-7401
Bass Lake Cheese Factory
Somerset, WI. . . . 800-368-2437
Cady Cheese Factory
Wilson, WI 715-772-4218
Cropp Cooperative-Organic Valley
La Farge, WI. . . . 888-444-6455
Father's Country Hams
Bremen, KY 270-525-3554
Golden Cheese of California
Corona, CA. . . . 800-842-0264
Golden Valley Dairy Products
Tulare, CA. . . . 559-687-1188
Guggisberg Cheese
Millersburg, OH 800-262-2505
Heritage Cheese House
Heuvelton, NY 315-344-2216
Hilmar Cheese Company
Hilmar, CA 800-577-5772
Kantner Group
Wapakoneta, OH. . . . 419-738-4060
Klondike Cheese Factory
Monroe, WI. . . . 608-325-3021
Nelson Cheese Factory
Nelson, WI 715-673-4725
Reilly Dairy & Food Company
Tampa, FL. . . . 813-839-8458
Sargento Foods Inc.
Plymouth, WI 800-243-3737
Trega Foods
Weyauwega, WI 920-867-2137
Twin County Dairy
Kalona, IA. . . . 319-656-2776
Welcome Dairy
Colby, WI 800-472-2315

Reduced Fat

Kantner Group
Wapakoneta, OH. . . . 419-738-4060

Reduced Fat - Shredded

Crowley Cheese
Mount Holly, VT. 800-683-2606
Kantner Group
Wapakoneta, OH. 419-738-4060

Shredded

Kantner Group
Wapakoneta, OH. 419-738-4060

Colby

Alto Dairy Cooperative
Waupun, WI 920-346-2215
Associated Milk Producers
Dawson, MN. 320-769-2994
Associated Milk Producers
Rochester, MN 507-282-7401
Bass Lake Cheese Factory
Somerset, WI. 800-368-2437
Belle Plaine Cheese Factory
Shawano, WI. 866-245-5924
Brunkow Cheese Company
Darlington, WI 608-776-3716
Burnette Dairy Cooperative
Grantsburg, WI 715-689-2468
Cady Cheese Factory
Wilson, WI 715-772-4218
Cream O'Weaver Dairy
Salt Lake City, UT 801-973-9922
Cropp Cooperative-Organic Valley
La Farge, WI. 888-444-6455
Crowley Foods
Binghamton, NY. 800-637-0019
Dupont Cheese
Marion, WI 800-895-2873
Foothills Creamery
Calgary, AB. 800-661-4909
Graham Cheese Corporation
Elnoragton, IN 800-472-9178
Guggisberg Cheese
Millersburg, OH 800-262-2505
Heluva Good Cheese
Sodus, NY. 315-483-6971
Henning's Cheese
Kiel, WI. 920-894-3032
Klondike Cheese Factory
Monroe, WI. 608-325-3021
Louis Trauth Dairy
Newport, KY. 800-544-6455
Marcus Dairy
Danbury, CT 800-243-2511
Nelson Cheese Factory
Nelson, WI 715-673-4725
Oak Grove Dairy
Clintonville, WI 715-823-6226
Pine River Cheese & Butter Company
Ripley, ON. 800-265-1175
Reilly Dairy & Food Company
Tampa, FL. 813-839-8458
Sargento Foods Inc.
Plymouth, WI 800-243-3737
Scotsburn Dairy Group
Scotsburn, NS 902-485-8023
Swiss Valley Farms Company
Davenport, IA 563-468-6600
Swiss-American
St Louis, MO. 800-325-8150
Wapsie Valley Creamery
Independence, IA 319-334-7193
Welcome Dairy
Colby, WI 800-472-2315
Wells' Dairy
Le Mars, IA. 800-942-3800
Widmer's Cheese Cellars
Theresa, WI. 888-878-1107
Winder Dairy
West Valley, UT 800-946-3371

Cottage

Aimonetto and Sons
Renton, WA. 866-823-2777
Alta Dena Certified Dairy
City of Industry, CA 800-535-1369
Anderson Erickson Dairy
Des Moines, IA. 515-265-2521
Astro Dairy Products
Etobicoke, ON. 416-622-2811
Berkeley Farms
Hayward, CA 510-265-8600
Broughton Foods
Marietta, OH. 800-283-2479
Byrne Dairy
Syracuse, NY 800-899-1535
Chloe Foods Corporation
Brooklyn, NY 718-827-9000
Clofine Dairy & Food Products
Linwood, NJ 800-441-1001
Cloverland Green Spring Dairy
Baltimore, MD 800-876-6455
Coburg Dairy
North Charleston, SC 843-554-4870
Consun Food Industries
Elyria, OH. 440-322-6301
Country Fresh
Grand Rapids, MI 800-748-0480
Cropp Cooperative-Organic Valley
La Farge, WI. 888-444-6455
Cultured Specialties
Fullerton, CA 714-772-8861
Dixie Dairy Company
Gary, IN. 219-885-6101
Fairmont Products
Belleville, PA 717-935-2121
Foster Farms Dairy
Modesto, CA. 209-576-2300
Friendship Dairies
Dallas, TX. 516-719-4000
Friendship Dairies
Friendship, NY 585-973-3031
Golden Cheese of California
Corona, CA 800-842-0264
H.E. Butt Grocery Company
San Antonio, TX. 800-432-3113
Heritage Farms Dairy
Murfreesboro, TN. 615-895-2790
Hiland Dairy Foods Company
Springfield, MO 417-862-9311
Kraft Foods
Walton, NY 607-865-7131
Land-O-Sun Dairies
O Fallon, IL. 314-436-6820
Marva Maid Dairy
Newport News, VA. 800-544-4439
Meadow Gold Dairies
Honolulu, HI 800-362-8531
Meadow Gold Dairies
Tulsa, OK 800-742-7349
Michigan Dairy
Livonia, MI. 734-367-5390
Mid States Dairy
Hazelwood, MO 314-731-1150
Oakhurst Dairy
Portland, ME. 800-482-0718
Old Home Foods
Saint Paul, MN 800-309-9035
Prairie Farms Dairy
Quincy, IL 217-223-5530
Prairie Farms Dairy
Carlinville, IL 217-854-2547
Prairie Farms Dairy
Granite City, IL. 618-451-5600
Prairie Farms Dairy
O Fallon, IL. 618-632-3632
Prairie Farms Dairy Inc.
Carlinville, IL 217-854-2547
Purity Dairies
Nashville, TN 615-244-1900
Queensboro Farm Products
Canastota, NY. 315-697-2235
Queensboro Farm Products
Jamaica, NY 718-658-5000
Reilly Dairy & Food Company
Tampa, FL. 813-839-8458
Sinton Dairy Foods Company
Colorado Springs, CO. 800-388-4970
Sinton Dairy Foods Company
Denver, CO 800-666-4808
Sisler's Ice & Ice Cream
Ohio, IL. 888-891-3856
Smith Dairy Products Company
Orrville, OH 800-776-7076
Springfield Creamery
Eugene, OR. 541-689-2911
Superstore Industries
Fairfield, CA. 707-864-0502
Swiss Valley Farms Company
Davenport, IA 563-468-6600
Umpqua Dairy Products Company
Roseburg, OR 541-672-2638

Cream

Astro Dairy Products
Etobicoke, ON. 416-622-2811
Clofine Dairy & Food Products
Linwood, NJ 800-441-1001
Don's Food Products
Schwenksville, PA 888-321-3667
Emkay Trading Corporation
Elmsford, NY 914-592-9000
Franklin Foods
Enosburg Falls, VT. 800-933-6114
Herkimer Foods
Herkimer, NY 315-895-7832
Kraft Foods
Springfield, MO 417-881-2701
Level Valley Creamery
Antioch, TN 800-251-1292
Level Valley Creamery
West Bend, WI 800-558-1707
Lov-It Creamery
Green Bay, WI. 800-344-0333
Mozzarella Company
Dallas, TX. 800-798-2954
National Food Corporation
Everett, WA. 425-349-4257
Penn Maid Crowley Foods
Philadelphia, PA 800-247-6269
Queensboro Farm Products
Jamaica, NY 718-658-5000
Reilly Dairy & Food Company
Tampa, FL. 813-839-8458
Schneider's Dairy Holdings Inc
Pittsburgh, PA. 412-881-3525
Schreiber Foods Plant
Shippensburg, PA 717-530-5000
Springfield Creamery
Eugene, OR. 541-689-2911
Springfield Smoked Fish Company
Springfield, MA 800-327-3412
Tofutti Brands
Cranford, NJ 908-272-2400
Woolwich Dairy
Orangeville, ON 877-438-3499

Edam

Alto Dairy Cooperative
Waupun, WI 920-346-2215
Lactalis Deli
New York, NY 888-766-3353

Feta

Alberta Cheese Company
Calgary, AB. 403-279-4353
Atwood Cheese Company
Atwood, ON 519-356-2271
Castella Imports
Hauppauge, NY 866-227-8355
Cropp Cooperative-Organic Valley
La Farge, WI. 888-444-6455
Fage USA
Johnsontown, NY 518-762-5912
Klondike Cheese Factory
Monroe, WI. 608-325-3021
Kolb-Lena Cheese Company
Lena, IL. 815-369-4577
Lactalis Deli
New York, NY 888-766-3353
Lucille Farm Products
Montville, NJ 973-334-6030
Michigan Farm Cheese Dairy
Fountain, MI 231-462-3301
Mount Capra Cheese
Chehalis, WA 800-574-1961
Mozzarella Company
Dallas, TX. 800-798-2954
Pecoraro Dairy Products
Rome, NY. 315-339-0101
Reilly Dairy & Food Company
Tampa, FL. 813-839-8458
Sierra Cheese Manufacturing Company
Compton, CA 800-266-4270
Sorrento Lactalis
Buffalo, NY. 800-828-7031
Southwestern Wisconsin Dairy Goat Products
Mt Sterling, WI. 608-734-3151
Trega Foods
Weyauwega, WI 920-867-2137
Woolwich Dairy
Orangeville, ON 877-438-3499

Fontina

Atwood Cheese Company
Atwood, ON 519-356-2271
Belgioioso Cheese
Denmark, WI. 877-863-2123
Lactalis Deli
New York, NY 888-766-3353
Park Cheese Company
Fond Du Lac, WI 800-752-7275
Prima Kase
Monticello, WI 608-938-4227
Sartori Food Corporation
Plymouth, WI 800-558-5888
Sorrento Lactalis
Buffalo, NY. 800-828-7031

Goat's

Alta Dena Certified Dairy
City of Industry, CA 800-535-1369
Bass Lake Cheese Factory
Somerset, WI. 800-368-2437
Brier Run Farm
Birch River, WV 304-649-2975
Cypress Grove Chevre
Arcata, CA 707-825-1100
Montchevre-Betin, Inc
Rolling Hills Estates, CA 310-541-3520
Mount Capra Cheese
Chehalis, WA 800-574-1961
Mozzarella Company
Dallas, TX. 800-798-2954
Quillisascut Cheese Company
Rice, WA. 509-738-2011
Rollingstone Chevre
Parma, ID 208-722-6460
Sorrento Lactalis
Buffalo, NY. 800-828-7031
Southwestern Wisconsin Dairy Goat Products
Mt Sterling, WI. 608-734-3151
Swiss-American
St Louis, MO. 800-325-8150
Vermont Butter & Cheese Company
Websterville, VT. 802-479-9371
West Field Farm
Hubbardston, MA 877-777-3900
Westfield Farm
Hubbardston, MA 877-777-3900

Gorgonzola

Belgioioso Cheese
Denmark, WI. 877-863-2123
Chianti Cheese Company
Wapakoneta, OH. 800-220-3503
Pastene Companies
Canton, MA 781-830-8200
Reilly Dairy & Food Company
Tampa, FL. 813-839-8458
Saputo Foodservice USA
Lincolnshire, IL 800-824-3373
Sorrento Lactalis
Buffalo, NY. 800-828-7031

Gouda

Bass Lake Cheese Factory
Somerset, WI. 800-368-2437
Bel/Kaukauna USA
Kaukauna, WI. 800-558-3500
Klondike Cheese Factory
Monroe, WI. 608-325-3021
Lactalis Deli
New York, NY 888-766-3353
Prima Kase
Monticello, WI 608-938-4227
Winchester Cheese Company
Winchester, CA. 951-926-4239
Woolwich Dairy
Orangeville, ON 877-438-3499

Grated

Calabro Cheese Corporation
East Haven, CT. 203-469-1311
Chianti Cheese Company
Wapakoneta, OH. 800-220-3503
Clofine Dairy & Food Products
Linwood, NJ 800-441-1001
Colonna Brothers
North Bergen, NJ 201-864-1115
Dairy Concepts
Greenwood, WI. 888-680-5400
Elm City Cheese Company
Hamden, CT 203-865-5768
Icco Cheese Company
Orangeburg, NY 845-398-9800
Kantner Group
Wapakoneta, OH. 419-738-4060
Lactalis Deli
New York, NY 888-766-3353
Mancuso Cheese Company
Joliet, IL 815-722-2475
Park Cheese Company
Fond Du Lac, WI 800-752-7275
Penn Maid Crowley Foods
Philadelphia, PA 800-247-6269
Sargento Foods Inc.
Plymouth, WI 800-243-3737
Sartori Food Corporation
Plymouth, WI 800-558-5888
Sun-Re Cheese
Sunbury, PA. 570-286-1511
Suprema Specialties
Paterson, NJ 800-543-2479

Gruyere

Castella Imports
Hauppauge, NY 866-227-8355

Havarti

Prima Kase
Monticello, WI 608-938-4227
Roth Kase
Monroe, WI. 608-329-7666

Limburger

Klondike Cheese Factory
Monroe, WI. 608-325-3021

Low-Fat

Cabot Creamery
Montpelier, VT 888-792-2268
Froma-Dar
St. Boniface, QC. 819-535-3946
Lactalis Deli
New York, NY 888-766-3353
Le Sueur Cheese
Le Sueur, MN 800-757-7611
Sorrento Lactalis
Buffalo, NY. 800-828-7031

Mascarpone

Belgioioso Cheese
Denmark, WI. 877-863-2123
Glanbia Foods
Twin Falls, ID 800-427-9477
Lactalis Deli
New York, NY 888-766-3353
Mozzarella Company
Dallas, TX. 800-798-2954
Mozzarella Fresca   Corporate & Commercial Headquarters
Concord, CA. 800-572-6818
Mozzarella Fresca   Tipton Plant
Tipton, CA 559-752-4823
Pecoraro Dairy Products
Rome, NY. 315-339-0101
Reilly Dairy & Food Company
Tampa, FL. 813-839-8458
Sorrento Lactalis
Buffalo, NY. 800-828-7031
Vermont Butter & Cheese Company
Websterville, VT. 802-479-9371

Monterey Jack

Alberta Cheese Company
Calgary, AB. 403-279-4353
Alta Dena Certified Dairy
City of Industry, CA 800-535-1369
Associated Milk Producers
Dawson, MN. 320-769-2994
Associated Milk Producers
Rochester, MN 507-282-7401
Avanti Food Company
Walnut, IL. 800-243-3739
Bass Lake Cheese Factory
Somerset, WI. 800-368-2437
Belle Plaine Cheese Factory
Shawano, WI. 866-245-5924
Brunkow Cheese Company
Darlington, WI 608-776-3716
Cabot Creamery
Montpelier, VT 888-792-2268
Cady Cheese Factory
Wilson, WI 715-772-4218
Cheese Smokers
Brooklyn, NY
Cropp Cooperative-Organic Valley
La Farge, WI. 888-444-6455
Foothills Creamery
Calgary, AB. 800-661-4909
Golden Cheese of California
Corona, CA. 800-842-0264
Henning's Cheese
Kiel, WI. 920-894-3032
Hilmar Cheese Company
Hilmar, CA 800-577-5772
Klondike Cheese Factory
Monroe, WI. 608-325-3021
Nelson Cheese Factory
Nelson, WI 715-673-4725
Nelson Ricks Creamery
Salt Lake City, UT 801-364-3607
Oak Grove Dairy
Clintonville, WI 715-823-6226
Pine River Cheese & Butter Company
Ripley, ON. 800-265-1175
Reilly Dairy & Food Company
Tampa, FL. 813-839-8458
Sargento Foods Inc.
Plymouth, WI 800-243-3737
Suprema Specialties
Manteca, CA. 209-858-9696
Swiss-American
St Louis, MO. 800-325-8150
Vella Cheese
Sonoma, CA 800-848-0505
Wapsie Valley Creamery
Independence, IA 319-334-7193
Welcome Dairy
Colby, WI 800-472-2315

Mozzarella

Antonio Mozzarella Factory
Newark, NJ 973-353-9411
Associated Milk Producers
Dawson, MN. 320-769-2994
Associated Milk Producers
Rochester, MN 507-282-7401
Atwood Cheese Company
Atwood, ON 519-356-2271
B&D Foods
Boise, ID 208-344-1183
Belgioioso Cheese
Denmark, WI. 877-863-2123
Biazzo Dairy Products
Ridgefield, NJ. 201-941-6800
Burnette Dairy Cooperative
Grantsburg, WI. 715-689-2468
Cacique
City of Industry, CA 626-961-3399
Cady Cheese Factory
Wilson, WI 715-772-4218
Calabro Cheese Corporation
East Haven, CT. 203-469-1311
Cappiello Dairy Products
Schenectady, NY. 518-374-5064
Chianti Cheese Company
Wapakoneta, OH. 800-220-3503
Clofine Dairy & Food Products
Linwood, NJ. 800-441-1001
Cropp Cooperative-Organic Valley
La Farge, WI. 888-444-6455
Crowley Foods
Binghamton, NY. 800-637-0019
Empire Cheese
Cuba, NY 585-968-1552
Floron Food Services
Edmonton, AB 780-438-9300
Foothills Creamery
Calgary, AB. 800-661-4909
Foremost Farms
Cochrane, WI 608-626-2121
Foremost Farms
Lancaster, WI 608-723-7381
Foremost Farms
Marshfield, WI 715-384-5616

Foremost Farms
Alma Center, WI 715-964-7411
Fry Foods
Tiffin, OH 800-626-2294
Golden Cheese of California
Corona, CA 800-842-0264
Golden Valley Dairy Products
Tulare, CA 559-687-1188
Henning's Cheese
Kiel, WI 920-894-3032
J.B. Sons
Yonkers, NY 914-963-5192
Kantner Group
Wapakoneta, OH 419-738-4060
Klondike Cheese Factory
Monroe, WI 608-325-3021
Laack Brothers Cheese Company
Greenleaf, WI 800-589-5127
Lactalis Deli
New York, NY 888-766-3353
Leprino Foods Company
Denver, CO 800-537-7466
Losurdo Creamery
Heuvelton, NY 315-344-2444
Lucille Farm Products
Montville, NJ 973-334-6030
Mancuso Cheese Company
Joliet, IL 815-722-2475
Marathon Cheese Corporation
Booneville, MS 662-728-6266
Michael Granese & Company
Norristown, PA 610-272-5099
Mozzarella Company
Dallas, TX 800-798-2954
Mozzarella Fresca Corporate & Commercial Headquarters
Concord, CA 800-572-6818
Mozzarella Fresca Tipton Plant
Tipton, CA 559-752-4823
Nelson Ricks Creamery
Salt Lake City, UT 801-364-3607
Pecoraro Dairy Products
Rome, NY 315-339-0101
Penn Maid Crowley Foods
Philadelphia, PA 800-247-6269
Pine River Cheese & Butter Company
Ripley, ON 800-265-1175
Pollio Dairy Products
Campbell, NY 607-527-4585
Reilly Dairy & Food Company
Tampa, FL 813-839-8458
Saputo Foodservice USA
Lincolnshire, IL 800-824-3373
Sargento Foods Inc.
Plymouth, WI 800-243-3737
Sartori Food Corporation
Plymouth, WI 800-558-5888
Sierra Cheese Manufacturing Company
Compton, CA 800-266-4270
Sorrento Lactalis
Buffalo, NY 800-828-7031
Sun-Re Cheese
Sunbury, PA 570-286-1511
Suprema Specialties
Manteca, CA 209-858-9696
Suprema Specialties
Paterson, NJ 800-543-2479
Supreme Dairy Farms Company
Warwick, RI 401-739-8180
Trega Foods
Weyauwega, WI 920-867-2137
Woolwich Dairy
Orangeville, ON 877-438-3499

Baby

Crowley Foods
Binghamton, NY 800-637-0019

Lite Shredded - Frozen

Kantner Group
Wapakoneta, OH 419-738-4060

Low Moisture Part Skim - U

Crowley Foods
Binghamton, NY 800-637-0019
Kantner Group
Wapakoneta, OH 419-738-4060

Low Moisture Part Skim Shredded - Frozen

Kantner Group
Wapakoneta, OH 419-738-4060

Muenster

Associated Milk Producers
Dawson, MN 320-769-2994
Associated Milk Producers
Rochester, MN 507-282-7401
Cady Cheese Factory
Wilson, WI 715-772-4218
Cropp Cooperative-Organic Valley
La Farge, WI 888-444-6455
Heluva Good Cheese
Sodus, NY 315-483-6971
Klondike Cheese Factory
Monroe, WI 608-325-3021
Reilly Dairy & Food Company
Tampa, FL 813-839-8458
Roth Kase
Monroe, WI 608-329-7666
Sargento Foods Inc.
Plymouth, WI 800-243-3737
Springdale Cheese Factory
Richland Center, WI 608-538-3213
Torkelson Cheese Company
Lena, IL 815-369-4265
Welcome Dairy
Colby, WI 800-472-2315
Wengers Springbrook Cheese
Davis, IL 815-865-5855

No-Fat

Le Sueur Cheese
Le Sueur, MN 800-757-7611
Shenk's Foods
Lancaster, PA 717-393-4240

Parmesan

Atwood Cheese Company
Atwood, ON 519-356-2271
Belgioioso Cheese
Denmark, WI 877-863-2123
Cass Clay
Fargo, ND 701-293-6455
Castella Imports
Hauppauge, NY 866-227-8355
Chianti Cheese Company
Wapakoneta, OH 800-220-3503
Clofine Dairy & Food Products
Linwood, NJ 800-441-1001
Colonna Brothers
North Bergen, NJ 201-864-1115
Cropp Cooperative-Organic Valley
La Farge, WI 888-444-6455
Dairy Concepts
Greenwood, WI 888-680-5400
Icco Cheese Company
Orangeburg, NY 845-398-9800
Kantner Group
Wapakoneta, OH 419-738-4060
Klondike Cheese Factory
Monroe, WI 608-325-3021
Lactalis Deli
New York, NY 888-766-3353
Mancuso Cheese Company
Joliet, IL 815-722-2475
Park Cheese Company
Fond Du Lac, WI 800-752-7275
Parmx
Calgary, AB 403-237-0707
Pastene Companies
Canton, MA 781-830-8200
Reilly Dairy & Food Company
Tampa, FL 813-839-8458
Saputo Foodservice USA
Lincolnshire, IL 800-824-3373
Sargento Foods Inc.
Plymouth, WI 800-243-3737
Sartori Food Corporation
Plymouth, WI 800-558-5888
Sorrento Lactalis
Buffalo, NY 800-828-7031
Suprema Specialties
Manteca, CA 209-858-9696
Suprema Specialties
Paterson, NJ 800-543-2479
Valley Grain Products
Madera, CA 559-675-3400

Wisconsin Cheese
Melrose Park, IL 708-450-0074

Pecorino

Chianti Cheese Company
Wapakoneta, OH 800-220-3503
Kantner Group
Wapakoneta, OH 419-738-4060
Pastene Companies
Canton, MA 781-830-8200

Process Loaves

Yellow

Kantner Group
Wapakoneta, OH 419-738-4060

Process Sliced

White/Yellow

Kantner Group
Wapakoneta, OH 419-738-4060

Processed American

Associated Milk Producers
Dawson, MN 320-769-2994
Associated Milk Producers
Rochester, MN 507-282-7401
Kantner Group
Wapakoneta, OH 419-738-4060
Welcome Dairy
Colby, WI 800-472-2315

Processed Swiss

Cheese Smokers
Brooklyn, NY

Provolone

Alberta Cheese Company
Calgary, AB 403-279-4353
Associated Milk Producers
Dawson, MN 320-769-2994
Associated Milk Producers
Rochester, MN 507-282-7401
Belgioioso Cheese
Denmark, WI 877-863-2123
Cady Cheese Factory
Wilson, WI 715-772-4218
Cropp Cooperative-Organic Valley
La Farge, WI 888-444-6455
Golden Valley Dairy Products
Tulare, CA 559-687-1188
Kantner Group
Wapakoneta, OH 419-738-4060
Klondike Cheese Factory
Monroe, WI 608-325-3021
Losurdo Creamery
Heuvelton, NY 315-344-2444
Lucille Farm Products
Montville, NJ 973-334-6030
Mancuso Cheese Company
Joliet, IL 815-722-2475
Park Cheese Company
Fond Du Lac, WI 800-752-7275
Pastene Companies
Canton, MA 781-830-8200
Penn Maid Crowley Foods
Philadelphia, PA 800-247-6269
Reilly Dairy & Food Company
Tampa, FL 813-839-8458
Saputo Foodservice USA
Lincolnshire, IL 800-824-3373
Sargento Foods Inc.
Plymouth, WI 800-243-3737
Sartori Food Corporation
Plymouth, WI 800-558-5888
Sorrento Lactalis
Buffalo, NY 800-828-7031
Trega Foods
Weyauwega, WI 920-867-2137

Ricotta

Alberta Cheese Company
Calgary, AB 403-279-4353
Belgioioso Cheese
Denmark, WI 877-863-2123

Biazzo Dairy Products
Ridgefield, NJ 201-941-6800
Calabro Cheese Corporation
East Haven, CT 203-469-1311
Cappiello Dairy Products
Schenectady, NY 518-374-5064
Castella Imports
Hauppauge, NY 866-227-8355
Chianti Cheese Company
Wapakoneta, OH 800-220-3503
Crowley Foods
Binghamton, NY 800-637-0019
J.B. Sons
Yonkers, NY 914-963-5192
Kantner Group
Wapakoneta, OH 419-738-4060
Lactalis Deli
New York, NY 888-766-3353
Losurdo Creamery
Heuvelton, NY 315-344-2444
Losurdo Creamery
Hackensack, NJ 800-245-6787
Mancuso Cheese Company
Joliet, IL 815-722-2475
Michael Granese & Company
Norristown, PA 610-272-5099
Mozzarella Company
Dallas, TX 800-798-2954
Mozzarella Fresca Corporate & Commercial Headquarters
Concord, CA 800-572-6818
Mozzarella Fresca Tipton Plant
Tipton, CA 559-752-4823
Pecoraro Dairy Products
Rome, NY 315-339-0101
Penn Maid Crowley Foods
Philadelphia, PA 800-247-6269
Pollio Dairy Products
Campbell, NY 607-527-4585
Reilly Dairy & Food Company
Tampa, FL 813-839-8458
Saputo Foodservice USA
Lincolnshire, IL 800-824-3373
Sargento Foods Inc.
Plymouth, WI 800-243-3737
Schneider's Dairy Holdings Inc
Pittsburgh, PA 412-881-3525
Sierra Cheese Manufacturing Company
Compton, CA 800-266-4270
Sorrento Lactalis
Buffalo, NY 800-828-7031
Sun-Re Cheese
Sunbury, PA 570-286-1511
Suprema Specialties
Paterson, NJ 800-543-2479
Supreme Dairy Farms Company
Warwick, RI 401-739-8180
Tofutti Brands
Cranford, NJ 908-272-2400

Romano

Belgioioso Cheese
Denmark, WI 877-863-2123
Castella Imports
Hauppauge, NY 866-227-8355
Chianti Cheese Company
Wapakoneta, OH 800-220-3503
Clofine Dairy & Food Products
Linwood, NJ 800-441-1001
Colonna Brothers
North Bergen, NJ 201-864-1115
Cropp Cooperative-Organic Valley
La Farge, WI 888-444-6455
Dairy Concepts
Greenwood, WI 888-680-5400
Kantner Group
Wapakoneta, OH 419-738-4060
Mancuso Cheese Company
Joliet, IL 815-722-2475
Park Cheese Company
Fond Du Lac, WI 800-752-7275
Pastene Companies
Canton, MA 781-830-8200
Reilly Dairy & Food Company
Tampa, FL 813-839-8458
Saputo Foodservice USA
Lincolnshire, IL 800-824-3373
Sargento Foods Inc.
Plymouth, WI 800-243-3737
Sartori Food Corporation
Plymouth, WI 800-558-5888

Suprema Specialties
Manteca, CA 209-858-9696
Suprema Specialties
Paterson, NJ 800-543-2479
Valley Grain Products
Madera, CA 559-675-3400
Wisconsin Cheese
Melrose Park, IL 708-450-0074

Roquefort

Lactalis Deli
New York, NY 888-766-3353

String

Baker Cheese Factory
Saint Cloud, WI 920-477-7871
Cropp Cooperative-Organic Valley
La Farge, WI 888-444-6455
Penn Maid Crowley Foods
Philadelphia, PA 800-247-6269

Swiss

Associated Milk Producers
Dawson, MN 320-769-2994
Associated Milk Producers
Rochester, MN 507-282-7401
Brewster Dairy
Brewster, OH 800-874-8874
Cady Cheese Factory
Wilson, WI 715-772-4218
Clofine Dairy & Food Products
Linwood, NJ 800-441-1001
Cropp Cooperative-Organic Valley
La Farge, WI 888-444-6455
Crowley Foods
Binghamton, NY 800-637-0019
Guggisberg Cheese
Millersburg, OH 800-262-2505
Heluva Good Cheese
Sodus, NY 315-483-6971
Holmes Cheese Company
Millersburg, OH 330-674-6451
Klondike Cheese Factory
Monroe, WI 608-325-3021
Kolb-Lena Cheese Company
Lena, IL 815-369-4577
Lactalis Deli
New York, NY 888-766-3353
Los Altos Food Products
City of Industry, CA 626-330-6555
Marathon Cheese Corporation
Booneville, MS 662-728-6266
Middlefield Cheese House
Middlefield, OH 800-327-9477
Penn Cheese Corporation
Winfield, PA 570-524-7700
Ragersville Swiss Cheese
Sugarcreek, OH 330-897-3055
Sargento Foods Inc.
Plymouth, WI 800-243-3737
Steiner Cheese
Baltic, OH 888-897-5505
Stockton Cheese
Stockton, IL 800-728-0111
Swiss Valley Farms Company
Davenport, IA 563-468-6600
Welcome Dairy
Colby, WI 800-472-2315
Wengers Springbrook Cheese
Davis, IL 815-865-5855

Imitation Cheeses & Substitutes

Cheese Foods & Substitutes

AFP Advanced Food Products, LLC
Visalia, CA 559-627-2070
Al Pete Meats
Muncie, IN 765-288-8817
Amberwave Foods
Oakmont, PA 412-828-3040
Anchor Food Products/ McCain Foods
Appleton, WI 920-734-0627
B&D Foods
Boise, ID 208-344-1183
Baker Cheese Factory
Saint Cloud, WI 920-477-7871
Bel/Kaukauna USA
Kaukauna, WI 800-558-3500

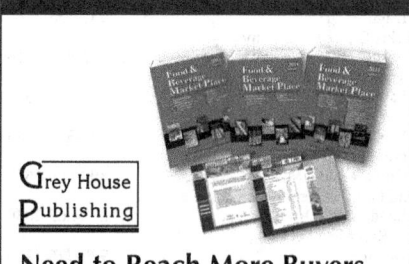

Bernardi Italian Foods Company
Bloomsburg, PA 570-389-5500
Birds Eye Foods
Berlin, PA 814-267-4641
Black Diamond Cheese
Toronto, ON 800-263-2858
Bongrain North America
Mahwah, NJ 201-512-8825
Brooks Food Group Corporate Office
Bedford, VA 800-873-4934
Carolina Cupboard
Hillsborough, NC 800-400-3441
Castle Cheese
Slippery Rock, PA 800-252-4373
Cemac Foods Corporation
Harrison, NY 800-724-0179
Century Foods International
Sparta, WI 800-269-1901
Cheese Straws & More
Monroe, LA 800-997-1921
Clofine Dairy & Food Products
Linwood, NJ 800-441-1001
Durrett Cheese Sales
Manchester, TN 800-209-6792
Earth Island Natural Foods
Canoga Park, CA 818-725-2820
Great American Appetizers
Nampa, ID 800-282-4834
Hormel Foods Corporation
Austin, MN 800-523-4635
Ingretec
Lebanon, PA 717-273-1360
John Wm. Macy's Cheesesticks
Elmwood Park, NJ 800-643-0573
Kantner Group
Wapakoneta, OH 419-738-4060
Laack Brothers Cheese Company
Greenleaf, WI 800-589-5127
Land O'Lakes
Spencer, WI 715-659-2311
Liono Latticini
Union, NJ 908-686-6061
Marcus Dairy
Danbury, CT 800-243-2511
Matador Processors
Blanchard, OK 800-847-0797
Medallion Foods
Newport, AR 870-523-3500

Mehaffie Pies
Dayton, OH....937-253-1163
Merkts Cheese Company
Bristol, WI....262-857-2316
Nelson Ricks Creamery Company
Salt Lake City, UT....801-364-3607
Omstead Foods Ltd
Wheatley, ON....905-315-8883
Parkers Farm
Coon Rapids, MN....800-869-6685
Pend Oreille Cheese Company
Sandpoint, ID....208-263-2030
Pine River Pre-Pack
Newton, WI....920-726-4216
Pocono Cheesecake Factory
Swiftwater, PA....570-839-6844
Schreiber Foods Inc
Green Bay, WI....800-344-0333
Sierra Cheese Manufacturing Company
Compton, CA....800-266-4270
Texas Heat
San Antonio, TX....800-656-5916
Trugman-Nash
New York, NY....212-869-6910
Tulkoff Food Products
Baltimore, MD....800-638-7343
Variety Foods
Warren, MI....586-268-4900
Wynn Starr Foods of Kentucky
Louisville, KY....800-996-7827

Imitation

American

Kantner Group
Wapakoneta, OH....419-738-4060

Cheddar

Kantner Group
Wapakoneta, OH....419-738-4060

Mozzarella

Kantner Group
Wapakoneta, OH....419-738-4060

Parmesan

Kantner Group
Wapakoneta, OH....419-738-4060

Substitutes

Alberto-Culver Company
Melrose Park, IL....708-450-3000
Black Diamond Cheese
Toronto, ON....800-263-2858
Earth Island Natural Foods
Canoga Park, CA....818-725-2820
Hormel Foods Corporation
Austin, MN....800-523-4635
Kantner Group
Wapakoneta, OH....419-738-4060

American

Kantner Group
Wapakoneta, OH....419-738-4060

Dairy Products

Butter

Agri-Mark
Lawrence, MA 978-689-4442
Alberto-Culver Company
Melrose Park, IL 708-450-3000
Allfresh Food Products
Evanston, IL 773-273-2343
American Almond Products Company
Brooklyn, NY 800-825-6663
Associated Milk Producers
Dawson, MN 320-769-2994
Associated Milk Producers
New Ulm, MN 800-533-3580
Ault Foods
Toronto, ON 416-626-1973
Beaver Meadow Creamery
Du Bois, PA 800-262-3711
Bongards Creameries
Norwood, MN 800-877-6417
Bottineau Coop Creamery
Bottineau, ND 701-228-2216
Butterball Farms
Grand Rapids, MI 616-243-0105
Byrne Dairy
Syracuse, NY 800-899-1535
California Dairies
Visalia, CA 559-625-2200
Cass Clay Creamery
Fargo, ND 701-293-6455
Challenge Dairy Products
Dublin, CA 800-733-2479
Cloverland Dairy
Saint Clairsville, OH 740-699-0509
Coburg Dairy
North Charleston, SC 843-554-4870
Cream O'Weaver Dairy
Salt Lake City, UT 801-973-9922
Cropp Cooperative-Organic Valley
La Farge, WI 888-444-6455
Dairy Farmers of America
East Syracuse, NY 315-431-1352
Dairy Farmers of America
Knoxville, TN 865-218-8500
Dixie Dairy Company
Gary, IN 219-885-6101
Ellsworth Cooperative Creamery
Ellsworth, WI 715-273-4311
Epicurean Butter
Federal Heights, CO 720-261-8175
George L. Wells Meat Company
Philadelphia, PA 800-523-1730
Graf Creamery
Bonduel, WI
Grassland Dairy Products
Greenwood, WI 800-428-8837
Green River Chocolates
Hinesburg, VT 802-482-6727
Grouse Hunt Farms
Tamaqua, PA 570-467-2850
H B Taylor Company
Chicago, IL 773-254-4805
Hope Creamery
Hope, MN 507-451-2029
Kozlowski Farms
Forestville, CA 800-473-2767
Land O'Lakes
Carlisle, PA 717-486-7000
Land O'Lakes
Kent, OH 800-328-9680
Land O'Lakes, Inc.
Arden Hills, MN 800-328-9680
Level Valley Creamery
Antioch, TN 800-251-1292
Level Valley Creamery
West Bend, WI 800-558-1707
Lost Trail Root Beer Com
Louisburg, KS 800-748-7765
Lov-It Creamery
Green Bay, WI 800-344-0333
Madison Dairy Produce Company
Madison, WI 608-256-5561
Marcus Dairy
Danbury, CT 800-243-2511
Meadow Gold Dairies
Englewood, CO 800-525-3289
Milnot Company
Neosho, MO 800-877-6455
Minerva Cheese Factory
Minerva, OH 330-868-4196
Naterl
St. Bruno, QC 450-653-3655
O-At-Ka Milk Products Cooperative
Batavia, NY 800-828-8152
Oakhurst Dairy
Portland, ME 800-482-0718
Oasis Foods Company
Hillside, NJ 908-964-0477
Once Again Nut Butter
Nunda, NY 888-800-8075
Penn Maid Crowley Foods
Philadelphia, PA 800-247-6269
Plainview Milk Products Cooperative
Plainview, MN 507-534-3872
Prairie Farms Dairy
O Fallon, IL 618-632-3632
Prairie Farms Dairy Inc.
Carlinville, IL 217-854-2547
Purity Farms
Sedalia, CO 800-568-4433
Queensboro Farm Products
Canastota, NY 315-697-2235
Reilly Dairy & Food Company
Tampa, FL 813-839-8458
Rogue Creamery
Central Point, OR 541-665-1155
San Fernando Creamery Farmdale Creamery
San Bernardino, CA 909-889-3002
Schneider's Dairy Holdings Inc
Pittsburgh, PA 412-881-3525
Scotsburn Dairy Group
Scotsburn, NS 902-485-8023
Shenk's Foods
Lancaster, PA 717-393-4240
Sinton Dairy Foods Company
Colorado Springs, CO 800-388-4970
Sisler's Ice & Ice Cream
Ohio, IL 888-891-3856
Sommer Maid Creamery
Doylestown, PA 215-345-6160
Sparboe Companies
Los Angeles, CA 213-626-7538
Turner & Pease Company
Seattle, WA 206-282-9535
Umpqua Dairy Products Company
Roseburg, OR 541-672-2638
United Dairymen of Arizona
Tempe, AZ 480-966-7211
Ventura Foods
Ontario, CA 323-262-9157
Vrymeer Commodities
St Charles, IL 630-584-0069
Westin
Omaha, NE 800-228-6098
Whitewave Foods Company
Broomfield, CO 303-635-4000

Blends

Schreiber Foods Inc
Green Bay, WI 800-344-0333

Dairy

Agropur Cooperative Agro-Alimentaire
Granby, QC 800-363-5686
Alberto-Culver Company
Melrose Park, IL 708-450-3000
Allfresh Food Products
Evanston, IL 773-273-2343
Alliston Creamery & Dairy
Alliston, ON 705-435-6751
Beaver Meadow Creamery
Du Bois, PA 800-262-3711
Century Foods International
Sparta, WI 800-269-1901
Clofine Dairy & Food Products
Linwood, NJ 800-441-1001
Crystal Cream & Butter Company
Sacramento, CA 916-447-6455
Danish Maid Butter Company
Chicago, IL 773-731-8787
Farmers Coop Creamery
McMinnville, OR 503-472-2157
Foothills Creamery
Calgary, AB 800-661-4909
Grassland Dairy Products
Greenwood, WI 800-428-8837
Keller's Creamery
Harleysville, PA 800-535-5371
LaRosa's Bakery
Shrewsbury, NJ 800-527-6722
Lov-It Creamery
Green Bay, WI 800-344-0333
Scotsburn Dairy Group
Scotsburn, NS 902-485-8023
Southwestern Wisconsin Dairy Goat Products
Mt Sterling, WI 608-734-3151
St. Maurice Laurent
St-Bruno-Lac-St-Jean, QC 418-343-3655
Swagger Foods Corporation
Vernon Hills, IL 847-913-1200
Tillamook County Creamery Association
Tillamook, OR 503-815-1300
United Dairymen of Arizona
Tempe, AZ 480-966-7211

Low Fat

Dixie Usa
Tomball, TX 800-233-3668

Salted

Associated Milk Producers
Dawson, MN 320-769-2994
Cropp Cooperative-Organic Valley
La Farge, WI 888-444-6455
Grassland Dairy Products
Greenwood, WI 800-428-8837
Reilly Dairy & Food Company
Tampa, FL 813-839-8458

Unsalted

Associated Milk Producers
Dawson, MN 320-769-2994
Cropp Cooperative-Organic Valley
La Farge, WI 888-444-6455
Grassland Dairy Products
Greenwood, WI 800-428-8837
Keller's Creamery
Harleysville, PA 800-535-5371
Reilly Dairy & Food Company
Tampa, FL 813-839-8458

Buttermilk & Buttermilk Products

Buttermilk

Agri-Dairy Products
Purchase, NY 914-697-9580
Alta Dena Certified Dairy
City of Industry, CA 800-535-1369
Barber's Dairy
Birmingham, AL 205-942-2351
Bell Dairy Products
Lubbock, TX 806-293-1367
California Dairies
Visalia, CA 559-625-2200
Century Foods International
Sparta, WI 800-269-1901
Chase Brothers Dairy
Oxnard, CA 800-438-6455
Clofine Dairy & Food Products
Linwood, NJ 800-441-1001
Cloverland Dairy
Saint Clairsville, OH 740-699-0509
Coburg Dairy
North Charleston, SC 843-554-4870
Consun Food Industries
Elyria, OH 440-322-6301
Cream O'Weaver Dairy
Salt Lake City, UT 801-973-9922
Crowley Foods
Binghamton, NY 800-637-0019
Dairy Maid Dairy
Frederick, MD 301-695-0431

Foremost Farms
Preston, MN 507-765-3831
Foremost Farms
Clayton, WI. . . . 715-948-2166
Friendship Dairies
Dallas, TX. . . . 516-719-4000
Graf Creamery
Bonduel, WI
Hygeia Dairy Company
McAllen, TX. . . . 956-686-0511
Inland Northwest Dairies
Spokane, WA. . . . 509-489-8600
Land O'Lakes
Carlisle, PA 717-486-7000
McArthur Dairy
Miami, FL. . . . 305-795-7700
Meadow Gold Dairies
Honolulu, HI 800-362-8531
Mid States Dairy
Hazelwood, MO 314-731-1150
Mom's Bakery
Atlanta, GA. . . . 404-344-4189
Plainview Milk Products Cooperative
Plainview, MN 507-534-3872
Pleasant View Dairy
Highland, IN 219-838-0155
Quality Ingredients Corporation
Burnsville, MN. . . . 952-898-4002
Queensboro Farm Products
Jamaica, NY 718-658-5000
Reilly Dairy & Food Company
Tampa, FL. . . . 813-839-8458
Schneider Valley Farms Dairy
Williamsport, PA. . . . 570-326-2021
Sinton Dairy Foods Company
Colorado Springs, CO. . . . 800-388-4970
Welsh Farms
Edison, NJ. . . . 800-221-0663
Winchester Farms Dairy
Winchester, KY. . . . 859-745-5500
Winder Dairy
West Valley, UT 800-946-3371
Yoder Dairies
Chesapeake, VA 757-482-4068

Buttermilk Products

Graf Creamery
Bonduel, WI

Condensed

Graf Creamery
Bonduel, WI

Dry

Foremost Farms
Preston, MN 507-765-3831
Kantner Group
Wapakoneta, OH. . . . 419-738-4060

Dry Sweetcream

Kantner Group
Wapakoneta, OH. . . . 419-738-4060

Cream

Alouette Cheese USA
New Holland, PA 717-355-8500
Alta Dena Certified Dairy
City of Industry, CA 800-535-1369
Anastasia Confections Inc.
Orlando, FL. . . . 800-329-7100
Arcor USA
Miami, FL. . . . 800-572-7267
Associated Milk Producers
New Ulm, MN. . . . 800-533-3580
Ault Foods
Toronto, ON 416-626-1973
Berkeley Farms
Hayward, CA 510-265-8600
Berkshire Dairy & Food Products
Wyomissing, PA 888-654-8008
Blue Chip Group
Salt Lake City, UT 800-878-0099
Byrne Dairy
Syracuse, NY 800-899-1535
Cass Clay Creamery
Fargo, ND 701-293-6455
Cropp Cooperative-Organic Valley
La Farge, WI. . . . 888-444-6455
Dairy Farmers of America
Knoxville, TN. . . . 865-218-8500
Dietrich's Milk Products
Reading, PA 800-526-6455
Dixie Dairy Company
Gary, IN. . . . 219-885-6101
Ellsworth Cooperative Creamery
Ellsworth, WI 715-273-4311
Fairmont Products
Belleville, PA 717-935-2121
First District Association
Litchfield, MN 320-693-3236
Flagship Atlanta Dairy
Belleview, FL 800-224-0669
GPI USA LLC.
Athens, GA. . . . 706-850-7826
H B Taylor Company
Chicago, IL. . . . 773-254-4805
Ideal Dairy
Richfield, UT 435-896-5061
Kemps
Cedarburg, WI. . . . 262-377-5040
Marcus Dairy
Danbury, CT 800-243-2511
Muller-Pinehurst Dairy C
Rockford, IL 815-968-0441
Oak Farms
El Paso, TX. . . . 800-395-7004
Oakhurst Dairy
Portland, ME. . . . 800-482-0718
Pioneer Dairy
Southwick, MA. . . . 413-569-6132
Plains Creamery
Amarillo, TX. . . . 806-374-0385
Prairie Farms Dairy
Carlinville, IL 217-854-2547
Prairie Farms Dairy
O Fallon, IL. . . . 618-632-3632
Price's Creameries
El Paso, TX. . . . 915-565-2711
Purity Dairies
Nashville, TN 615-244-1900
Queensboro Farm Products
Jamaica, NY 718-658-5000
Reilly Dairy & Food Company
Tampa, FL. . . . 813-839-8458
Reiter Dairy
Akron, OH. . . . 800-362-0825
Reiter Dairy
Springfield, OH. . . . 937-323-5777
Rosenberger's Dairies
Hatfield, PA. . . . 800-355-9074
Sabatino Truffles USA
Bronx, NY. . . . 888-444-9971
Saint Albans Cooperative Creamery
Saint Albans, VT. . . . 800-559-0343
San Fernando Creamery Farmdale Creamery
San Bernardino, CA 909-889-3002
Schneider's Dairy Holdings Inc
Pittsburgh, PA. . . . 412-881-3525
Sugarwoods Farm
Glover, VT 800-245-3718
Swiss Valley Farms Company
Davenport, IA 563-468-6600
Velda Farms
North Miami Beach, FL 800-795-4649
W.J. Stearns & Sons/Mountain Dairy
Storrs Mansfield, CT 860-423-9289
White Wave Foods
Jacksonville, FL 800-874-6765

Dried

Agri-Dairy Products
Purchase, NY 914-697-9580
Blossom Farm Products
Ridgewood, NJ 800-729-1818
Century Foods International
Sparta, WI. . . . 800-269-1901
Clofine Dairy & Food Products
Linwood, NJ 800-441-1001
Custom Food Processors International
New Hampton, IA. . . . 641-394-4802
Kantner Group
Wapakoneta, OH. . . . 419-738-4060
Quality Ingredients Corporation
Burnsville, MN. . . . 952-898-4002

Fresh

Agri-Dairy Products
Purchase, NY 914-697-9580
Agropur Cooperative Agro-Alimentaire
Granby, QC. . . . 800-363-5686
Auburn Dairy Products
Auburn, WA 800-950-9264
Barbe's Dairy
Westwego, LA. . . . 504-347-6201
Brum's Dairy
Pembroke, ON. . . . 613-735-2325
Clofine Dairy & Food Products
Linwood, NJ 800-441-1001
LaRosa's Bakery
Shrewsbury, NJ 800-527-6722
LeHigh Valley Dairies
Lansdale, PA 215-855-8205
Northumberland Cooperative
Miramichi, NB 800-332-3328
O-At-Ka Milk Products Cooperative
Batavia, NY. . . . 800-828-8152
Prairie Farms Dairy
Carlinville, IL 217-854-2547
Stremick's Heritage Foods
Santa Ana, CA 800-371-9010

Non-Dairy

ACH Food Companies
Cordova, TN 800-691-1106
Alamance Foods/Triton Water Company
Burlington, NC 800-476-9111
Bay Valley Foods
Platteville, WI 800-236-1119
Instantwhip Foods
San Antonio, TX. . . . 800-544-9447
Instantwhip: Arizona
Phoenix, AZ 800-454-7878
Sugar Foods
Sun Valley, CA 818-768-7900

Whipped

A.C. Petersen Farms
West Hartford, CT. . . . 860-233-8483
Alamance Foods/Triton Water Company
Burlington, NC 800-476-9111
Berkeley Farms
Hayward, CA 510-265-8600
Brighams
Arlington, MA 800-274-4426
Cass Clay Creamery
Fargo, ND 701-293-6455
Caughman's Meat Plant
Lexington, SC. . . . 803-356-0076
Clofine Dairy & Food Products
Linwood, NJ 800-441-1001
Consun Food Industries
Elyria, OH. . . . 440-322-6301
Crave Natural Foods
Northampton, MA. . . . 413-587-7999
Cropp Cooperative-Organic Valley
La Farge, WI. . . . 888-444-6455
Erba Food Products
Brooklyn, NY 718-272-7700
Instantwhip Foods
San Antonio, TX. . . . 800-544-9447
Marva Maid Dairy
Newport News, VA. . . . 800-544-4439
Mayfield Dairy Farms
Athens, TN 800-362-9546
Penn Maid Crowley Foods
Philadelphia, PA 800-247-6269
Prairie Farms Dairy Inc.
Carlinville, IL 217-854-2547
Rich Products Corporation
Claremont, CA 909-621-4711
Schneider's Dairy Holdings Inc
Pittsburgh, PA. . . . 412-881-3525
Tiller Foods Company
Dayton, OH. . . . 937-435-4601
Yoder Dairies
Chesapeake, VA 757-482-4068

from Milk

Auburn Dairy Products
Auburn, WA 800-950-9264

Creamers

Auburn Dairy Products
Auburn, WA 800-950-9264
Brewfresh Coffee Company
South Salt Lake, UT 888-486-3334

Broughton Foods
Marietta, OH 800-283-2479
Cropp Cooperative-Organic Valley
La Farge, WI 888-444-6455
Crowley Foods
Binghamton, NY 800-637-0019
Fresh Dairy Direct/Morningstar
Dallas, TX 800-395-7004
H B Taylor Company
Chicago, IL 773-254-4805
Instantwhip Foods
San Antonio, TX 800-544-9447
Kan-Pac
Arkansas City, KS 620-442-6820
Nulaid Foods
Ripon, CA 209-599-2121
Quality Ingredients Corporation
Burnsville, MN 952-898-4002
S.J. McCullagh
Buffalo, NY 800-753-3473
Schneider's Dairy Holdings Inc
Pittsburgh, PA 412-881-3525
Sinton Dairy Foods Company
Colorado Springs, CO 800-388-4970
Tiller Foods Company
Dayton, OH 937-435-4601
Tuscan/Lehigh Valley Dais
Lansdale, PA 800-937-3233
W.J. Stearns & Sons/Mountain Dairy
Storrs Mansfield, CT 860-423-9289

Coffee

Agri-Dairy Products
Purchase, NY 914-697-9580
Baldwin Richardson Foods
Frankfort, IL 866-644-2732

Liquid ingredient manufacturer specializing in signature sauces, dessert toppings, beverage/pancake syrups, specialty fruit fillings and condiments.

Boston's Best Coffee Roasters
South Easton, MA 800-898-8393
Byrne Dairy
Syracuse, NY 800-899-1535
Cropp Cooperative-Organic Valley
La Farge, WI 888-444-6455
Fresh Dairy Direct/Morningstar
Dallas, TX 800-395-7004
H B Taylor Company
Chicago, IL 773-254-4805
Hanan Products Company
Hicksville, NY 516-938-1000
Industrial Products
Defiance, OH 800-251-3033
Inland Northwest Dairies
Spokane, WA 509-489-8600
Innovative Food Solutions LLC
Columbus, OH 800-884-3314
Instantwhip Foods
San Antonio, TX 800-544-9447
Kemps
Cedarburg, WI 262-377-5040
Nestle Baking & Prepared Foods
Solon, OH
Rich Products Corporation
Claremont, CA 909-621-4711
Safeway Milk Plant
Tempe, AZ 480-894-4391
Tova Industries
Louisville, KY 888-532-8682

Non-Dairy

Bay Valley Foods
Platteville, WI 800-236-1119
Custom Food Processors International
New Hampton, IA 641-394-4802
Diehl Food Ingredients
Defiance, OH 800-251-3033
Erba Food Products
Brooklyn, NY 718-272-7700
Fresh Dairy Direct/Morningstar
Dallas, TX 800-395-7004
Lake City Foods
Mississauga, ON 905-625-8244
Ohio Processors Company
London, OH 740-852-9243
Quality Ingredients Corporation
Burnsville, MN 952-898-4002
S.J. McCullagh
Buffalo, NY 800-753-3473
Stickney & Poor Company
Peterborough, NH 603-924-2259
Tiller Foods Company
Dayton, OH 937-435-4601
Tonex
Wallington, NJ 973-773-5135

Custard

Artuso Pastry Shop
Bronx, NY 718-367-2515
Bakemark Ingredients Canada
Richmond, BC 800-665-9441

Dairy

Abbott Laboratories Nutritionals/Ross Products
Abbott Park, IL 847-937-6100
ADM Food Ingredients
Olathe, KS 800-255-6637
AFP Advanced Food Products, LLC
Visalia, CA 559-627-2070
Aglamesis Brothers
Cincinnati, OH 513-531-5196
Agri-Dairy Products
Purchase, NY 914-697-9580
Agri-Mark
Lawrence, MA 978-689-4442
Agropur Cooperative Agro-Alimentaire
Granby, QC 800-363-5686
Al Gelato Bornay
Franklin Park, IL 847-455-5355
Al Pete Meats
Muncie, IN 765-288-8817
Al's Beverage Company
East Windsor, CT 888-257-7632
Alamance Foods/Triton Water Company
Burlington, NC 800-476-9111
Alberto-Culver Company
Melrose Park, IL 708-450-3000
All American Foods, Inc.
Mankato, MN 800-833-2661
Allfresh Food Products
Evanston, IL 773-273-2343
Alliston Creamery & Dairy
Alliston, ON 705-435-6751
Alouette Cheese USA
New Holland, PA 717-355-8500
Alpenrose Dairy Farms
Portland, OR 503-244-1133
Alta-Dena Certified Dairy
City of Industry, CA 800-535-1369
Alto Dairy Cooperative
Waupun, WI 920-346-2215
Amberwave Foods
Oakmont, PA 412-828-3040
Amboy Specialty Foods Company
Dixon, IL 800-892-0400
American Classic Ice Cream Company
Bay Shore, NY 631-666-1000
American Lecithin Company
Oxford, CT 800-364-4416
Anchor Food Products/ McCain Foods
Appleton, WI 920-734-0627
Anderson Dairy
Las Vegas, NV 702-642-7507
Anderson Erickson Dairy
Des Moines, IA 515-265-2521
Ariza Cheese Company
Paramount, CA 800-762-4736
Arla Foods Inc
Concord, ON 905-669-9393
Arla Foods Ingredients
Basking Ridge, NJ 908-604-8551
Associated Bakers Products
Huntington, NY 631-673-3841
Associated Milk Producers
Rochester, MN 507-282-7401
Associated Milk Producers
New Ulm, MN 800-533-3580
Astro Dairy Products
Etobicoke, ON 416-622-2811
Atwood Cheese Company
Atwood, ON 519-356-2271
Auburn Dairy Products
Auburn, WA 800-950-9264
Avalon Foodservice, Inc.
Canal Fulton, OH 800-362-0622
Avanti Food Company
Walnut, IL 800-243-3739
Avent Luvel Dairy Products
Kosciusko, MS 800-281-1307
Avonmore Ingredients
Monroe, WI 800-336-2183
B&D Foods
Boise, ID 208-344-1183
Baird Dairies
Clarksville, IN 812-283-3345
Baker Cheese Factory
Saint Cloud, WI 920-477-7871
Ballas Egg Products Corporation
Zanesville, OH 740-453-0386
Barbe's Dairy
Westwego, LA 504-347-6201
Barber Pure Milk Ice Cream Company
Birmingham, AL 205-942-2351
Barber's Dairy
Birmingham, AL 205-942-2351
Barnes Ice Cream Company
Manchester, ME
Bartlett Dairy & Food Service
Jamaica, NY 718-658-2299
Beaver Meadow Creamery
Du Bois, PA 800-262-3711
Bel/Kaukauna USA
Kaukauna, WI 800-558-3500
Bell Dairy Products
Lubbock, TX 806-293-1367
Belle Plaine Cheese Factory
Shawano, WI 866-245-5924
Ben E. Keith DFW
Fort Worth, TX 877-317-6100
Bergey's Dairy Farm
Chesapeake, VA 757-482-4711
Berkeley Farms
Hayward, CA 510-265-8600
Bernardi Italian Foods Company
Bloomsburg, PA 570-389-5500
Berner Cheese Corporation
Dakota, IL 800-819-8199
Berner Cheese Corporation
Rock City, IL 815-865-5136
Bernie's Foods
Brooklyn, NY 718-417-6677
Biazzo Dairy Products
Ridgefield, NJ 201-941-6800
Biery Cheese Company
Louisville, OH 800-243-3731
Bill Mack's Homemade Ice Cream
Dover, PA 717-292-1931
Bio-K + International
Laval, QC 800-593-2465
Birdsall Ice Cream Company
Mason City, IA 641-423-5365
Black Diamond Cheese
Toronto, ON 800-263-2858
Blake's Creamery
Manchester, NH 603-623-7242
Bliss Brothers Dairy, Inc.
Attleboro, MA 800-622-8789
Bloomfield Bakers
Los Alamitos, CA 800-594-4111
Blossom Farm Products
Ridgewood, NJ 800-729-1818
Blue Bell Creameries
Brenham, TX 979-836-7977
Blue Chip Group
Salt Lake City, UT 800-878-0099
Blue Ribbon Dairy
Exeter, PA 570-655-5579
Bongard's Creameries
Perham, MN 218-346-4680
Bongrain North America
Mahwah, NJ 201-512-8825
Bonnie Doon Ice Cream Corporation
Elkhart, IN 574-264-3390
Borden
Tulsa, OK 800-733-2230

Boston's Best Coffee Roasters
South Easton, MA. 800-898-8393
Bottineau Coop Creamery
Bottineau, ND. 701-228-2216
Braum's Inc
Oklahoma City, OK 405-478-1656
Brenntag
Reading, PA 888-926-4151
Brenntag Pacific
Santa Fe Springs, CA 562-903-9626
Brewster Dairy
Brewster, OH 800-874-8874
Brier Run Farm
Birch River, WV. 304-649-2975
Brighams
Arlington, MA 800-274-4426
Brooks Food Group Corporate Office
Bedford, VA 800-873-4934
Brookside Foods
Abbotsford, BC. 877-793-3866
Broughton Foods
Marietta, OH. 800-283-2479
Brown Dairy
Coalville, UT 435-336-5952
Brown Produce Company
Farina, IL. 618-245-3301
Brown's Ice Cream
Minneapolis, MN 612-378-1075
Browns Dairy
Valparaiso, IN. 219-464-4141
Browns' Ice Cream Company
Bowling Green, KY 270-843-9882
Brum's Dairy
Pembroke, ON. 613-735-2325
Brunkow Cheese Company
Darlington, WI 608-776-3716
Bubbies Homemade Ice Cream
Aiea, HI. 808-487-7218
Buck's Spumoni Company
Milford, CT. 203-874-2007
Buon Italia Misono Food Ltd.
New York, NY 212-633-9090
Burger Dairy
Cleveland, OH 216-896-9100
Bush Boake Allen
New York, NY 212-765-5500
Bush Brothers Provision Company
West Palm Beach, FL. 800-327-1345
Butterball Farms
Grand Rapids, MI. 616-243-0105
Butterbuds Food Ingredients
Racine, WI. 800-426-1119
Byrne Dairy
Syracuse, NY 800-899-1535
C.F. Burger Creamery
Detroit, MI 800-229-2322
Cabot Creamery
Montpelier, VT. 888-792-2268
Cal-Maine Foods
Jackson, MS 601-948-6813
Calabro Cheese Corporation
East Haven, CT. 203-469-1311
California Dairies
Visalia, CA 559-625-2200
Calpro Ingredients
Corona, CA. 909-493-4890
Cappiello Dairy Products
Schenectady, NY. 518-374-5064
Caprine Estates
Bellbrook, OH. 937-848-7406
Carbolite Foods
Evansville, IN. 888-524-3314
Carl Colteryahn Dairy
Pittsburgh, PA. 412-881-1408
Cascade Fresh
Seattle, WA 800-511-0057
Casper's Ice Cream
Richmond, UT. 800-772-4182
Cass Clay
Fargo, ND 701-293-6455
Cass Clay Creamery
Fargo, ND 701-293-6455
Castle Cheese
Slippery Rock, PA. 800-252-4373
Cedar Crest Specialties
Cedarburg, WI. 800-877-8341
Cemac Foods Corporation
Harrison, NY. 800-724-0179
Central Dairies
St Johns, NL 800-563-6455
Central Dairy Company
Jefferson City, MO 573-635-6148
Central Valley Dairymen
Modesto, CA. 209-551-2667
Centreside Dairy
Renfrew, ON. 613-432-2914
Century Foods International
Sparta, WI. 800-269-1901
Challenge Dairy Products
Dublin, CA 800-733-2479
Chase Brothers Dairy
Oxnard, CA. 800-438-6455
Cheese Smokers
Brooklyn, NY
Cheese Straws & More
Monroe, LA. 800-997-1921
Cheezwhse.Com
Armonk, NY 800-922-4337
Chester Dairy Company
Chester, IL. 618-826-2394
Chicago 58 Food Products
Woodbridge, ON. 416-603-4244
Chloe Foods Corporation
Brooklyn, NY 718-827-9000
Chocolaterie Bernard Callebaut
Calgary, AB. 800-661-8367
Chozen Ice Cream
New York, NY 212-675-4191
Churny Company
Waupaca, WI. 715-258-4040
Ciao Bella Gelato Company
Irvington, NJ. 800-435-2863
Circus Man Ice Cream Corporation
Farmingdale, NY 516-249-4400
Clinton Milk Company
Newark, NJ 973-642-3000
Clofine Dairy & Food Products
Linwood, NJ 800-441-1001
Clover Farms Dairy Company
Reading, PA 800-323-0123
Clover Stornetta Farms
Petaluma, CA 800-237-3315
Cloverland Dairy
Saint Clairsville, OH. 740-699-0509
Cloverland Green Spring Dairy
Baltimore, MD 800-876-6455
Coastlog Industries
Novi, MI 248-344-9556
Coburg Dairy
North Charleston, SC 843-554-4870
Colchester Foods
Bozrah, CT 800-243-0469
Coleman Dairy
Little Rock, AR. 501-568-6237
Colonna Brothers
North Bergen, NJ 201-864-1115
Compton Dairy
Shelbyville, IN 317-398-8621
ConAgra Grocery Products
Irvine, CA. 714-680-1000
Conco Food Service
New Orleans, LA 800-488-3988
Consun Food Industries
Elyria, OH. 440-322-6301
Continental Culture Specialists
Los Angeles, CA. 818-240-7400
Cordon Bleu International
Anjou, QC. 514-352-3000
Corfu Foods
Bensenville, IL 630-595-2510
Country Delight Farms
Nashville, TN 615-320-1440
Country Fresh
Grand Rapids, MI 800-748-0480
Country Fresh Golden Valley
Livonia, MI. 734-261-7980
Cow Palace Too
Granger, WA. 509-829-5777
Cream O'Weaver Dairy
Salt Lake City, UT 801-973-9922
Creamland Dairies
Albuquerque, NM. 505-247-0721
Creighton Brothers
Atwood, IN. 574-267-3101
Creme Glacee Gelati
Montreal, QC 888-322-0116
Crescent Ridge Dairy
Sharon, MA. 800-660-2740
Crossroad Farms Dairy
Indianapolis, IN 317-229-7600
Crowley Cheese
Mount Holly, VT. 800-683-2606
Crowley Foods
Binghamton, NY. 800-637-0019
Crystal Cream & Butter Company
Sacramento, CA 916-447-6455
Crystal Farms
Chestnut Mtn, GA. 770-967-6152
Crystal Lake LLC
Warsaw, IN 574-858-2514
Culture Systems
Mishawaka, IN 574-258-0602
Cultured Specialties
Fullerton, CA 714-772-8861
Cumberland Dairy
Rosenhayn, NJ 856-451-1300
Cutler Egg Products
Abbeville, AL. 334-585-2268
Cyclone Enterprises
Houston, TX 281-872-0087
Czepiel Millers Dairy
Ludlow, MA 413-589-0828
Dairy Concepts
Greenwood, WI. 888-680-5400
Dairy Farmers of America
East Syracuse, NY 315-431-1352
Dairy Farmers of America
Medina, OH. 330-670-7800
Dairy Farmers of America
Salt Lake City, UT 801-977-3000
Dairy Farmers of America
Knoxville, TN. 865-218-8500
Dairy Farmers of America
Kansas City, MO. 888-332-6455
Dairy Fresh
Winston Salem, NC. 800-446-5577
Dairy Fresh Corporation
Greensboro, AL. 800-239-5114
Dairy Fresh Foods
Taylor, MI. 313-295-6300
Dairy King Milk Farms/Foodservice
Whitter, CA. 800-900-6455
Dairy Land
Macon, GA 478-742-6461
Dairy Maid Dairy
Frederick, MD. 301-695-0431
Dairy Queen of Georgia
Decatur, GA 404-292-3553
Dairy-Mix
St Petersburg, FL 727-525-6101
Dairytown Products Ltd
Sussex, NB 800-561-5598
Daisy Brand
Dallas, TX. 877-292-9830
Dakota Country Cheese
Mandan, ND 701-663-0246
Danish Creamery Association
Visalia, CA 559-625-2200
Danish Maid Butter Company
Chicago, IL. 773-731-8787
Dannon Company
Fort Worth, TX 800-211-6565
Darby Plains Dairy
Plain City, OH. 614-873-4574
Darifair Foods
Jacksonville, FL 904-268-8999
Dave's Gourmet
San Francisco, CA 800-758-0372
Dave's Hawaiian Ice Cream
Pearl City, HI 808-453-0500
Davisco International
Le Sueur, MN 800-757-7611
Daybreak Foods
Long Prairie, MN 320-732-2966
Dean Dairy Products
Sharpsville, PA 800-942-8096
Dean Foods Company
Dallas, TX. 800-431-9214
Dean Milk Company
Louisville, KY 800-451-3326

Deb-El Foods
Elizabeth, NJ 800-421-3447
Deep Foods
Union, NJ 908-810-7500
Delta Distributors
Longview, TX 800-945-1858
Deluxe Ice Cream Company
Salem, OR 800-304-7172
Deseret Dairy Products
Salt Lake City, UT 801-240-7350
Detroit City Dairy
Taylor, MI 313-295-6300
Dietrich's Milk Products
Reading, PA 800-526-6455
Dillon Dairy Company
Denver, CO 303-388-1645
Dimock Dairy Products
Dimock, SD 605-928-3833
Division Baking Corporation
New York, NY 800-934-9238
Dixie Dairy Company
Gary, IN 219-885-6101
Dixie Egg Company
Jacksonville, FL 800-394-3447
Double B Foods
Arlington, TX 800-679-0349
Dpi Specialty Foods, Inc
Evanston, IL 503-692-0662
Dreyer's Grand Ice Cream
Oakland, CA 877-437-3937
Driftwood Dairy
El Monte, CA 626-444-9591
Dunkin Brands Inc.
Canton, MA 800-458-7731
Dupont Cheese
Marion, WI 800-895-2873
Durrett Cheese Sales
Manchester, TN 800-209-6792
Eagle Family Foods
Orrville, OH 888-656-3245
Eatem Foods Company
Vineland, NJ 800-683-2836
Eberhard Creamery
Redmond, OR 541-548-5181
Echo Spring Dairy
Eugene, OR 541-342-1291

Edy's Dreyers Grand Ice Cream
Rockaway, NJ 800-362-7899
Edy's Grand Ice Cream
Glendale Heights, IL 888-377-3397
Edy's Grand Ice Cream
Weston, FL 954-384-7133
Eggland's Best Foods
King of Prussia, PA 888-922-3447
Ellsworth Cooperative Creamery
Ellsworth, WI 715-273-4311
Elm City Cheese Company
Hamden, CT 203-865-5768
Emkay Trading Corporation
Elmsford, NY 914-592-9000
Empire Cheese
Cuba, NY 585-968-1552
Erie Foods International
Erie, IL 800-447-1887
Erivan Dairy
Oreland, PA 215-887-2009
Everything Yogurt
Washington, DC 202-842-2990
F & A Dairy of California
Newman, CA 800-554-6455
Fairmont Products
Belleville, PA 717-935-2121
Fairview Swiss Cheese
Fredonia, PA 724-475-4154
Faith Dairy
Tacoma, WA 253-531-3398
Fanny Mason Farmstead Cheese
Walpole, NH 603-756-3300
Farbest-Tallman Foods Corporation
Montvale, NJ 201-573-4900
Farm Stores
Palmetto Bay, FL 800-726-3276
Farmdale Creamery
San Bernardino, CA 909-889-3002
Farmers Coop Creamery
McMinnville, OR 503-472-2157
Farmers Dairies
El Paso, TX 915-772-2736
Farmers Hen House
Kalona, IA 319-683-2206
Farmers Seafood Company
Shreveport, LA 800-874-0203

Farmland Dairies
Wallington, NJ 888-727-6252
Farr Candy Company
Idaho Falls, ID 208-522-8215
FDP
Santa Rosa, CA 707-547-1776
Feature Foods
Etobicoke, ON 416-675-7350
Fendall Ice Cream Company
Salt Lake City, UT 801-355-3583
Fieldbrook Farms
Dunkirk, NY 800-333-0805
First District Association
Litchfield, MN 320-693-3236
Flagship Atlanta Dairy
Belleview, FL 800-224-0669
Flavors from Florida
Bartow, FL 863-533-0408
Fleur De Lait Foods
New Holland, PA 717-355-8500
Food Ingredients
Elgin, IL 800-500-7676
Foodmark
Wellesley, MA 781-237-7088
Foothills Creamery
Calgary, AB 800-661-4909
Foremost Farms
Reedsburg, WI 608-524-2351
Foremost Farms
Wilson, WI 715-772-4211
Foremost Farms
Clayton, WI 715-948-2166
Foster Farms Dairy
Fresno, CA 800-241-0008
Freeman Industries
Tuckahoe, NY 800-666-6454
Freeze-Dry Products
Santa Rosa, CA 707-547-1776
Fresh Dairy Direct/Morningstar
Dallas, TX 800-395-7004
Fresh Farm
Arvada, CO 303-429-1536
Fried Provisions Company
Evans City, PA 724-538-3160
Friendly Ice Cream Corporation
Wilbraham, MA 800-966-9970

Friendship Dairies
Dallas, TX 516-719-4000
Friendship Dairies
Friendship, NY 585-973-3031
Frog City Cheese
Plymouth Notch, VT 802-672-3650
Froma-Dar
St. Boniface, QC 819-535-3946
Frostbite
Toledo, OH 800-968-7711
Frozfruit Corporation
Gardena, CA 310-217-1034
Gad Cheese Company
Medford, WI 715-748-4273
Gaf Seelig
Woodside, NY 718-899-5000
Galaxy Nutritional Foods
North Kingstown, RI 800-441-9419
Galliker Dairy
Johnstown, PA 800-477-6455
Gamay Flavors
New Berlin, WI 888-345-4560
Garber Ice Cream Company
Winchester, VA 800-662-5422
Garelick Farms
Lynn, MA 800-487-8700
Gelato Fresco
Toronto, ON 416-785-5415
George L. Wells Meat Company
Philadelphia, PA 800-523-1730
GFA Brands
Paramus, NJ 201-568-9300
Gibbsville Cheese Company
Sheboygan Falls, WI 920-564-3242
Gifford's Dairy
Skowhegan, ME 207-474-9821
Glanbia Foods
Twin Falls, ID 208-733-7555
Glanbia Foods
Twin Falls, ID 800-427-9477
Global Food Industries
Townville, SC 800-225-4152
Glover's Ice Cream
Frankfort, IN 800-686-5163
Gold Cup Farms
Clayton, NY 800-752-1341
Gold Star Dairy
Little Rock, AR 501-565-6125
Golden Valley Dairy Products
Tulare, CA 559-687-1188
Goldenrod Dairy Foods/ U C Milk Company
Madisonville, KY 800-462-2354
Good Humor Breyers Ice Cream Company
Green Bay, WI 920-499-5151
Goshen Dairy Company
New Philadelphia, OH 330-339-1959
Gossner Food
Logan, UT 800-944-0454
Grace Foods International
Astoria, NY 718-433-4789
Graf Creamery
Bonduel, WI
Graham Cheese Corporation
Elnoragton, IN 800-472-9178
Grande Cheese Company
Brownsville, WI 800-678-3122
Grassland Dairy Products
Greenwood, WI 800-428-8837
Great American Appetizers
Nampa, ID 800-282-4834
Great Valley Mills
Barto, PA 800-688-6455
Grossinger's Home Bakery
New York, NY 800-479-6996
Guers Dairy
Pottsville, PA 570-277-6611
Guida's Milk & Ice Cream
New Britain, CT 800-832-8929
Gustafsons Dairy
Green Cove Springs, FL 904-284-3750
H B Taylor Company
Chicago, IL 773-254-4805
H. Meyer Dairy Company
Cincinnati, OH 800-347-6455
H.E. Butt Grocery Company
San Antonio, TX 800-432-3113
Hanover Foods Corp
Hanover, PA 717-632-6000
Harold M. Lincoln Company
Toledo, OH 800-345-4911
Harrisburg Dairies
Harrisburg, PA 800-692-7429

Harvest Direct
Knoxville, TN 800-838-2727
Hastings Cooperative Creamery
Hastings, MN 651-437-9414
Heini's Cheese Company
Millersburg, OH 800-253-6636
Heluva Good Cheese
Sodus, NY 315-483-6971
HempNut
Henderson, NV 707-576-7050
Henning's Cheese
Kiel, WI 920-894-3032
Henningsen Foods
Omaha, NE 402-330-2500
Henningsen Foods
Purchase, NY 914-701-4020
Heritage Dairy Stores
Thorofare, NJ
Herkimer Foods
Herkimer, NY 315-895-7832
Hermany Farms
Bronx, NY 718-823-2989
Hershey Creamery Company
Harrisburg, PA 888-240-1905
Hershey International
Weston, FL 954-385-2600
High Road Craft Ice Cream, Inc.
Atlanta, GA 678-701-7623
High's Dairies
Jessup, MD 301-776-7727
Highland Dairies
Wichita, KS 800-336-0765
Hiland Dairy Foods Company
Branson, MO 417-334-0090
Hiland Dairy Foods Company
Joplin, MO 417-623-2272
Hiland Dairy Foods Company
Springfield, MO 417-862-9311
Hillandale Llc
Lake City, FL 386-397-1300
Hillside Dairy
Stanley, WI 715-644-2275
Holmes Cheese Company
Millersburg, OH 330-674-6451
Holton Food Products Company
La Grange, IL 708-352-5599
Homer's Ice Cream
Wilmette, IL 847-251-0477
Homestead Dairies
Massena, NY 315-769-2456
Honeyville Grain
Salt Lake City, UT 801-972-2168
Hope Creamery
Hope, MN 507-451-2029
Horizon Organic
Broomfield, CO 888-494-3020
Hormel Foods Corporation
Austin, MN 800-523-4635
Horstmann Mix & Cream
Long Island City, NY 718-932-4735
Houlton Farms Dairy
Houlton, ME 207-532-3170
Hudsonville Creamery & Ice Cream
Holland, MI 616-546-4005
Humble Cremery
Fortuna, CA 800-697-9925
Humboldt Creamery Association
Fortuna, CA 707-725-6182
Hunter Farms
High Point, NC 800-446-8035
Hygeia Dairy Company
Corpus Christi, TX 361-854-4561
Hygeia Dairy Company
McAllen, TX 956-686-0511
Icco Cheese Company
Orangeburg, NY 845-398-9800
Ice Cream & Yogurt Club
Boynton Beach, FL 561-731-3331
Ice Cream Specialties
Saint Louis, MO 314-962-2550
Ice Cream Specialties
Lafayette, IN 765-474-2989
Ideal American
Holland, IN 812-424-3351
Ideal Dairy
Richfield, UT 435-896-5061
IMAC
Oklahoma City, OK 888-878-7827
Imperial Foods
Long Island City, NY 718-784-3400
Independent Dairy
Monroe, MI 734-241-6016

Industrial Products
Defiance, OH 800-251-3033
Ingretec
Lebanon, PA 717-273-1360
Inland Northwest Dairies
Spokane, WA 509-489-8600
Innovative Ingredients
Reisterstown, MD 888-403-2907
Instantwhip Foods
San Antonio, TX 800-544-9447
Instantwhip: Arizona
Phoenix, AZ 800-454-7878
Instantwhip: Chicago
Chicago, IL 800-933-2500
Instantwhip: Florida
Tampa, FL 813-621-3233
International Cheese Company
Toronto, ON 416-769-3547
International Dairy Ingredients
Wapakoneta, OH 419-738-4060
International Farmers Market
Chamblee, GA 770-455-1777
International Yogurt Company
Portland, OR 800-962-7326
Inverness Dairy
Cheboygan, MI 231-627-4655
ISE America, Inc.
Galena, MD 410-755-6300
ISE Newberry
Newberry, SC 803-276-5803
Island Farms Dairies Cooperative Association
Victoria, BC 250-360-5200
It's It Ice Cream Company
Burlingame, CA 800-345-1928
Ito Cariani Sausage Company
Hayward, CA 510-887-0882
J&J Snack Foods Corporation
Pennsauken, NJ 800-486-9533
J.B. Sons
Yonkers, NY 914-963-5192
J.W. Haywood & Sons Dairy
Louisville, KY 502-774-2311
Jack & Jill Ice Cream Company
Moorestown, NJ 856-813-2300
Jackson Ice Cream Company
Denver, CO 303-534-2454
Jackson Milk & Ice CreamCompany
Hutchinson, KS 620-663-1244
James Cowan & Sons
Worcester, MA 508-753-3259
Janes Family Foods
Mississauga, ON 800-565-2637
Jim's Cheese Pantry
Waterloo, WI 800-345-3571
JM Swank Company
North Liberty, IA 800-593-6375
John Wm. Macy's Cheesesticks
Elmwood Park, NJ 800-643-0573
Johnson's Real Ice Cream
Columbus, OH 614-231-0014
Johnson, Nash, & Sons Farms
Rose Hill, NC 800-682-6843
Joseph Gallo Farms
Atwater, CA 209-394-7984
Josh & John's Ice Cream
Colorado Springs, CO 800-530-2855
Juniper Valley Farms
Jamaica, NY 718-291-3333
Kalamazoo Creamery
Kalamazoo, MI 616-343-2558
Kan-Pac
Arkansas City, KS 620-442-6820
Katrina's Tartufo
Port Jeffrsn Sta, NY 800-480-8836
Kauai Producers
Lihue, HI 808-245-4044
KDK Inc
Draper, UT 801-571-3506
Keebler Company
Battle Creek, MI 800-962-1413
Keller's Creamery
Harleysville, PA 800-535-5371
Kemps
Cedarburg, WI 262-377-5040
Kemps
Saint Paul, MN 800-322-9566
Kent Foods
Gonzales, TX 830-672-7993
Kentucky Beer Cheese
Nicholasville, KY 859-887-1645
Kerry Ingredients & Flavours
Beloit, WI 800-248-7310

Key Ingredients
Harrisburg, PA 800-227-4448
Kirby & Holloway Provisions
Harrington, DE 800-995-4729
Kleinpeter Farms Dairy
Baton Rouge, LA 225-753-2121
Klinke Brothers Ice Cream Company
Memphis, TN 901-743-8250
Klondike Cheese
Monroe, WI
Knouse Foods Coop
Peach Glen, PA 717-677-8181
Kohler Mix Specialties
White Bear Lake, MN. 651-426-1633
Kohler Mix Specialties
Newington, CT 860-666-1511
Kokinos Purity Ice CreamCompany
Monroe, LA. 318-322-2930
Kolb-Lena Cheese Company
Lena, IL. 815-369-4577
Kraft Foods
Albany, MN. 320-845-2131
Kraft Foods
Springfield, MO 417-881-2701
Kraft Foods
Walton, NY 607-865-7131
Kraft Foods
Allentown, PA. 610-398-0311
Kraft Foods
Northfield, IL 800-323-0768
Krohn Dairy Products
Luxemburg, WI. 920-845-2901
Laack Brothers Cheese Company
Greenleaf, WI 800-589-5127
Lactalis Deli
New York, NY 888-766-3353
Lacto Milk Products Corporation
Flemington, NJ 908-788-2200
LaGrander Hillside Dairy
Stanley, WI 715-644-2275
Lake Country Foods
Oconomowoc, WI. 262-567-5521
Lake Erie Frozen Foods Company
Ashland, OH 800-766-8501
Lakeview Farms
Delphos, OH 800-755-9925
Lancaster Packing Company
Lancaster, PA 717-397-9727
Land O Lakes Milk
Sioux Falls, SD. 605-330-9526
Land O'Lakes
Spencer, WI. 715-659-2311
Land O'Lakes
Carlisle, PA 717-486-7000
Land O'Lakes
Kent, OH. 800-328-9680
Land O'Lakes
Kiel, WI. 920-894-2204
Land O'Lakes Procurement
Sioux Falls, SD. 605-330-9526
Land O'Lakes, Inc.
Arden Hills, MN. 800-328-9680
Land-o-Sun
Johnson City, TN 800-283-5765
Land-O-Sun Dairies
O Fallon, IL. 314-436-6820
Lane's Dairy
El Paso, TX. 915-772-6700
Larkin
Long Island City, NY 718-937-2007
LaRosa's Bakery
Shrewsbury, NJ. 800-527-6722
Lee's Century Farms
Milton Freewater, OR. 541-938-6532
LeHigh Valley Dairies
Lansdale, PA. 215-855-8205
Leprino Foods Company
Denver, CO 800-537-7466
Level Valley Creamery
Antioch, TN 800-251-1292
Lewes Dairy
Lewes, DE. 302-645-6281
Liberty Dairy
Evart, MI. 800-632-5552
Lifeway Foods Inc
Morton Grove, IL 877-281-3874
Longacres Modern Dairy
Barto, PA. 610-845-7551
Losurdo Creamery
Heuvelton, NY 315-344-2444
Losurdo Foods
Hackensack, NJ. 888-567-8736
Louis Trauth Dairy
Newport, KY. 800-544-6455
Lov-It Creamery
Green Bay, WI. 800-344-0333
Lowell-Paul Dairy
Greeley, CO. 970-353-0278
Lubbers Dairy
Pella, IA 515-628-4284
Lucille Farm Products
Montville, NJ 973-334-6030
Ludwig Dairy
Dixon, IL. 815-284-7791
Lyoferm & Vivolac Cultures
Indianapolis, IN 317-356-8460
M-G
Weimar, TX. 800-460-8581
Mack's Homemade Ice Cream
York, PA 717-741-2027
Madison Dairy Produce Company
Madison, WI 608-256-5561
Magic Valley Quality Milk Producers
Jerome, ID. 208-324-7519
Main Street Ingredients
La Crosse, WI 800-359-2345
Mallorie's Dairy
Silverton, OR 503-873-5346
Mancuso Cheese Company
Joliet, IL 815-722-2475
Mann Packing
Salinas, CA 831-422-7405
Maola Milk & Ice Cream Company
New Bern, NC. 252-514-2792
Maola Milk & Ice Cream Company
Summerville, SC. 803-871-6311
Maple Hill Farms
Bloomfield, CT. 800-842-7304
Maple Leaf Foods International
North York, ON. 416-480-8900
Marantha Natural Foods
San Francisco, CA 866-972-6879
Marathon Cheese Corporation
Booneville, MS. 662-728-6266
Marburger Farm Dairy
Evans City, PA 800-331-1295
Marcus Dairy
Danbury, CT 800-243-2511
Marin French Cheese Company
Petaluma, CA 800-292-6001
Mario's Gelati
Vancouver, BC 604-879-9411
Marshall Egg Products
Seymour, IN 812-497-2557
Marshallville Packing Company
Marshallville, OH. 330-855-2871
Martin Brothers Distributing Company
Cedar Falls, IA 319-266-1775
Marva Maid Dairy
Newport News, VA. 800-544-4439
Marwood Sales
Mission, KS 913-722-1534
Maryland & Virginia Milk Cooperative Association
Reston, VA 703-742-6800
Maryland & Virginia Milk Producers Cooperative
Reston, VA 703-742-4250
Master Mix
Placentia, CA 714-524-1698
Matador Processors
Blanchard, OK 800-847-0797
Mayfield Dairy Farms
Athens, TN 800-362-9546
Maytag Dairy Farms
Newton, IA 800-247-2458
McAnally Enterprises
Lakeview, CA 800-726-2002
McArthur Dairy
Fort Myers, FL 239-334-1114
McArthur Dairy
Miami, FL. 305-795-7700
McArthur Dairy
Miami, FL. 877-803-6565
McCadam Cheese Company
Chateaugay, NY 518-497-6644
McConnell's Fine Ice Cream
Santa Barbara, CA 805-963-2958
ME Franks
Wayne, PA. 610-989-9688
Mead Johnson Nutritional
Zeeland, MI. 616-748-7100
Meadow Brook Dairy
Erie, PA. 800-352-4010
Meadow Gold Dairies
Honolulu, HI. 800-362-8531
Meadow Gold Dairies
Englewood, CO. 800-525-3289
Meadow Gold Dairies
Tulsa, OK 800-742-7349
Meadow Gold Dairies
Orem, UT 801-225-3660
Meadowbrook Farm
Bronx, NY. 718-828-6400
Medeiros Farms
Kalaheo, HI. 808-332-8211
Mercer's Dairy
Boonville, NY. 866-637-2377
Merkts Cheese Company
Bristol, WI. 262-857-2316
Meyer Brothers Dairy
Maple Plain, MN. 952-473-7343
Micalizzi Italian Ice
Bridgeport, CT 203-366-2353
Miceli Dairy Products Company
Cleveland, OH 800-551-7196
Michael Granese & Company
Norristown, PA 610-272-5099
Michele's Family Bakery
York, PA 717-741-2027
Michelle Chocolatiers
Colorado Springs, CO. 888-447-3654
Michigan Dairy
Livonia, MI. 734-367-5390
Michigan Farm Cheese Dairy
Fountain, MI 231-462-3301
Michigan Milk Producers Association
Ovid, MI 989-834-2221
Mid States Dairy
Hazelwood, MO 314-731-1150
Mid-States Dairy Company
St. Louis, MO 800-264-4400
Midstates Dairy
Hazelwood, MO 314-731-1150
Mikawaya Bakery
Vernon, CA
Milk Specialties Company
Carpentersville, IL 800-323-4274
Milk Specialties Global
Eden Praire, MN. 952-942-7310
Mille Lacs MP Company
Madison, WI 800-843-1381
Miller's Cheese Corp
Brooklyn, NY. 718-965-1840
Millers Ice Cream
Houston, TX 713-861-3138
Milnot Company
Neosho, MO 800-877-6455
Milnot Company
Saint Louis, MO 888-656-3245
Milsolv Corporation
Butler, WI 800-558-8501
Minerva Cheese Factory
Minerva, OH. 330-868-4196
Minerva Dairy
Minerva, OH. 330-868-4196
Mister Cookie Face
Lakewood, NJ. 732-370-5533
Mitchel Dairies
Bronx, NY. 718-324-6261
Model Dairy
Reno, NV 800-433-2030
Monument Dairy Farms
Weybridge, VT 802-545-2119
Monument Farms
Middlebury, VT. 802-545-2119
Mooresville Ice Cream Company
Mooresville, NC 704-664-5456
Morning Glory/Formost Farms
Baraboo, WI 800-362-9196
Morning Star Foods
Tempe, AZ 480-966-0080
Morning Star Foods
East Brunswick, NJ. 800-237-5320
Morningland Dairy CheeseCompany
Mountain View, MO. 417-469-3817
Moscahlades Brothers
New York, NY 212-226-5410
Mountain High Yogurt
Minneapolis, MN 303-761-2210
Mountainside Farms Dairy
Roxbury, NY. 607-326-3320
Muller-Pinehurst Dairy C
Rockford, IL 815-968-0441
Munroe Dairy
East Providence, RI 401-438-4450
Murdock Farm Dairy
Winchendon, MA 978-297-0143

Murphy House
Louisburg, NC ... 919-496-6054

Mystic Lake Dairy
Sammamish, WA ... 425-868-2029

Nash Finch Company
Statesboro, GA ... 912-681-4580

Naterl
St. Bruno, QC ... 450-653-3655

National Egg Products Company
Social Circle, GA ... 770-464-2652

Natural By Nature
West Grove, PA ... 610-268-6962

Natural Fruit Corporation
Hialeah, FL ... 305-887-7525

Nature's Dairy
Roswell, NM ... 575-623-9640

Nelson Ricks Creamery
Salt Lake City, UT ... 801-364-3607

Nelson Ricks Creamery Company
Salt Lake City, UT ... 801-364-3607

Newburgh Egg Processing
Woodridge, NY ... 888-434-8115

Niagara Milk Cooperative
Niagara Falls, NY ... 716-692-6543

Nodine's Smokehouse
Torrington, CT ... 800-222-2059

Noon Hour Food Products
Chicago, IL ... 800-621-6636

Nor-Tech Dairy Advisors
Sioux Falls, SD ... 605-338-2404

Norco Ranch
Fontana, CA ... 951-737-6735

Norpaco Gourmet Foods
Middletown, CT ... 800-252-0222

Northumberland Cooperative
Miramichi, NB ... 800-332-3328

Norwalk Dairy
Santa Fe Springs, CA ... 562-921-5712

O'Boyle's Ice Cream Company
Bristol, PA ... 215-788-3882

O-At-Ka Milk Products Cooperative
Batavia, NY ... 800-828-8152

Oak Farm's Dairy
Waco, TX ... 254-756-5421

Oak Farms
San Antonio, TX ... 800-292-2169

Oak Farms
El Paso, TX ... 800-395-7004

Oak Grove Dairy
Clintonville, WI ... 715-823-6226

Oak Grove Dairy
Saint Paul, MN ... 800-322-9566

Oakhurst Dairy
Portland, ME ... 800-482-0718

Oberweis Dairy
North Aurora, IL ... 888-645-5868

OCG Cacao
Whitinsville, MA ... 888-482-2226

Old Home Foods
Saint Paul, MN ... 800-309-9035

Olde Tyme Food Corporation
East Longmeadow, MA ... 800-356-6533

Omstead Foods Ltd
Wheatley, ON ... 905-315-8883

Ore-Ida Foods
Pittsburgh, PA ... 800-892-2401

Oregon Hill Farms
Saint Helens, OR ... 800-243-4541

Oskaloosa Food ProductscCorporation
Oskaloosa, IA ... 800-477-7239

Out of a Flower
Lancaster, TX ... 800-743-4696

P A Menard
New Orleans, LA ... 504-620-2022

Pak Technologies
Milwaukee, WI ... 414-438-8600

Papetti's Egg Products
Elizabeth, NJ ... 800-328-5474

Park Cheese Company
Fond Du Lac, WI ... 800-752-7275

Parkers Farm
Coon Rapids, MN ... 800-869-6685

Parmalat Canada
Toronto, ON ... 800-563-1515

Pascobel Inc
Longueuil, QC ... 450-677-2443

Pastene Companies
Canton, MA ... 781-830-8200

Pastorelli Food Products
Chicago, IL ... 800-767-2829

PB&S Chemicals
Henderson, KY ... 800-950-7267

Pearl Valley Cheese Company
Fresno, OH ... 740-545-6002

Pecoraro Dairy Products
Rome, NY ... 315-339-0101

Peeler's Jersey Farms
Gaffney, SC ... 864-487-9996

Pend Oreille Cheese Company
Sandpoint, ID ... 208-263-2030

Penn Cheese Corporation
Winfield, PA ... 570-524-7700

Penn Maid Crowley Foods
Philadelphia, PA ... 800-247-6269

Perham Cooperative Cream
Savannah, GA ... 800-551-0777

Perry's Ice Cream Company
Akron, NY ... 800-873-7797

Pet Dairy
Portsmouth, VA ... 757-397-2387

Pet Dairy
Winston Salem, NC ... 800-735-2050

Pet Dairy
Spartanburg, SC ... 864-576-6280

Pet Milk
Florence, SC ... 800-735-3066

Petersen Ice Cream Company
Oak Park, IL ... 708-386-6130

Pevely Dairy Company
Hazelwood, MO ... 314-771-4400

Philip R'S Frozen Desserts
Winchester, MA ... 781-721-6330

Pierz Cooperative Association
Pierz, MN ... 320-468-6655

Pine River Cheese & Butter Company
Ripley, ON ... 800-265-1175

Pine River Pre-Pack
Newton, WI ... 920-726-4216

Pioneer Dairy
Southwick, MA ... 413-569-6132

Plains Creamery
Amarillo, TX ... 806-374-0385

Plains Dairy Products
Amarillo, TX ... 800-365-5608

Plainview Milk Products Cooperative
Plainview, MN ... 507-534-3872

Platte Valley Creamery
Scottsbluff, NE ... 308-632-4225

Pleasant View Dairy
Highland, IN ... 219-838-0155

Plehn's Bakery
Louisville, KY ... 502-896-4438

Plumrose USA
East Brunswick, NJ ... 800-526-4909

Plymouth Cheese Counter
Plymouth, WI ... 888-607-9477

Pocono Cheesecake Factory
Swiftwater, PA ... 570-839-6844

Pollio Dairy Products
Campbell, NY ... 607-527-4585

Polly-O Dairy Products
Mineola, NY ... 516-741-8000

Pon Food Corporation
Ponchatoula, LA ... 985-386-6941

Potomac Farms
Cumberland, MD ... 301-722-4410

Potter Siding Creamery Company
Tripoli, IA ... 319-882-4444

Poudre Valley Creamery
Fort Collins, CO ... 970-237-7000

Powder Pak
Round Lake, IL ... 847-223-4683

Praire Farms Dairy
Anderson, IN ... 765-649-1261

Prairie Farms Dairy
Carlinville, IL ... 217-854-2547

Prairie Farms Dairy Inc.
Carlinville, IL ... 217-854-2547

Preferred Milks
Addison, IL ... 800-621-5046

Prestige Proteins
Boca Raton, FL ... 561-997-8770

Price's Creameries
El Paso, TX ... 915-565-2711

Primer Foods Corporation
Cameron, WI ... 80- 3-5 24

Producers Dairy Foods
Fresno, CA ... 559-264-6583

Protient (Land O Lakes)
St Paul, MN ... 800-328-9680

Pure Gourmet
Glenside, PA ... 215-609-4219

Puritan/ATZ Ice Cream
Kendallville, IN ... 260-347-2700

Purity Dairies
Nashville, TN ... 615-244-1900

Purity Farms
Sedalia, CO ... 800-568-4433

Purity Ice Cream Company
Ithaca, NY ... 607-272-1545

Quality Chekd Dairies
Naperville, IL ... 630-717-1110

Quality Dairy Company
East Lansing, MI ... 517-319-4114

Quality Ingredients Corporation
Burnsville, MN ... 952-898-4002

Queensboro Farm Products
Canastota, NY ... 315-697-2235

Queensboro Farm Products
Jamaica, NY ... 718-658-5000

R.D. Hemond Farms
Minot, ME ... 207-345-5611

Radlo Foods
Watertown, MA ... 800-370-1439

Radway's Dairy
New Britain, CT ... 800-472-3929

Ragersville Swiss Cheese
Sugarcreek, OH ... 330-897-3055

Ramar Foods International Inc
Pittsburg, CA ... 800-660-0962

Ramsen
Lakeville, MN ... 952-431-0400

Ratners Retail Foods
New York, NY ... 212-677-5588

Readington Farms
Whitehouse, NJ ... 908-534-2121

Regis Milk Company
Charleston, SC ... 843-723-3418

Reinhold Ice Cream Company
Pittsburgh, PA ... 412-321-7600

Reiter Dairy
Akron, OH ... 800-362-0825

Rich Ice Cream Company
West Palm Beach, FL ... 561-833-7585

Rich Products Corporation
Claremont, CA ... 909-621-4711

Rich-Seapak Corporation
St Simons Island, GA ... 800-654-9731

Richfood Dairy
Richmond, VA ... 804-746-6206

Riser Foods
Cleveland, OH ... 216-292-7000

Ritchey's Dairy
Martinsburg, PA ... 800-296-2157

Robertet Flavors
Piscataway, NJ ... 732-271-1804

Roberts Dairy Foods
Iowa City, IA

Roberts Dairy Foods
Omaha, NE ... 402-371-3660

Roberts Dairy Foods
Kansas City, MO ... 800-279-1692

Robinson Dairy
Denver, CO ... 800-332-6355

Rockview Farms
Downey, CA ... 800- 42- 247

Rocky Top Farms
Ellsworth, MI ... 800-862-9303

Rod's Food Products
City of Industry, CA ... 909-839-8925

Rogers Brothers
Galesburg, IL ... 309-342-2127

Rogue Creamery
Central Point, OR ... 541-665-1155

Ronnybrook Farm Dairy
Ancramdale, NY ... 800-772-6455

Ronzoni Foods Canada
Etobicoke, ON ... 800-387-5032

Roos Foods
Kenton, DE ... 800-343-3642

Rosebud Creamery
Plattsburgh, NY ... 518-561-5160

Roselani Tropics Ice Cream
Wailuku, HI ... 808-244-7951

Rosenberger's Dairies
Hatfield, PA ... 800-355-9074

Royal Crest Dairy Company
Denver, CO ... 303-777-2227

Rutter Brothers Dairy
York, PA ... 800-840-1664

S.B. Winsor Dairy
Johnston, RI ... 401-231-7832

S.T. Jerrell Company
Bessemer, AL ... 205-426-8930

Safeway Dairy Products
Capitol Heights, MD ... 301-341-9555

Safeway Dairy Products
Walnut Creek, CA 925-944-4000
Safeway Inc
Pleasanton, CA 877-723-3929
Safeway Milk Plant
Tempe, AZ 480-894-4391
Safeway Stores
Tempe, AZ 480-966-0295
Saint Albans Cooperative Creamery
Saint Albans, VT. 800-559-0343
San Fernando Creamery Farmdale Creamery
San Bernardino, CA 909-889-3002
Sani Dairy
Altoona, PA. 814-943-3077
Sani-Dairy
Punxsutawney, PA. 814-938-7200
Santee Dairies
City of Industry, CA 626-923-3000
Sara Lee Corporation
Downers Grove, IL 630-598-8100
Sargeant's Army Marketing
Bowmanville, ON 905-623-2888
Sartori Food Corporation
Plymouth, WI 800-558-5888
Schenkel's All Star Dairy
Huntington, IN 260-356-4225
Schepps Dairy
Dallas, TX. 800-395-7004
Schneider Valley Farms Dairy
Williamsport, PA. 570-326-2021
Schneider's Dairy Holdings Inc
Pittsburgh, PA 412-881-3525
Schoep's Ice Cream Company
Madison, WI 800-236-0032
Schreiber Foods Plant
Logan, UT. 435-753-0504
Schreiber Foods Plant
Clinton, MO 660-885-6133
Schreiber Foods Plant
Shippensburg, PA 717-530-5000
Schreiber Foods Plant
Gainesville, GA 770-534-2239
Schreiber Foods Plant/Distribution Center
Wisconsin Rapids, WI 715-422-7500
Schwartz Meat Company
Sophia, WV. 304-683-4595
Scotsburn Dairy Group
Scotsburn, NS 902-485-8023
Seger Egg Corporation
Farina, IL. 618-245-3301
Sequoia Specialty Cheese Company
Visalia, CA 559-752-4106
Sesinco Foods
New York, NY 212-243-1306
Shamrock Foods Company
Phoenix, AZ 800-289-3663
Shenandoah's Pride
Springfield, VA. 703-321-9500
Shenk's Foods
Lancaster, PA 717-393-4240
Siegel Egg Company
Cambridge, MA 800-593-3447
Sierra Cheese Manufacturing Company
Compton, CA 800-266-4270
Silani Sweet Cheese
Schomberg, ON. 905-939-2561
Sinton Dairy Foods Company
Colorado Springs, CO. 800-388-4970
Sinton Dairy Foods Company
Denver, CO 800-666-4808
Sisler's Ice & Ice Cream
Ohio, IL. 888-891-3856
Skim Delux Mendenhall Laboratories
Paris, TN. 800-642-9321
Skinners' Dairy
Ponte Vedra Beach, FL 904-733-5440
Smith Dairy Products Company
Orrville, OH 800-776-7076
Smith Packing Regional Meat
Utica, NY
Snelgrove Ice Cream Company
Salt Lake City, UT 800-569-0005
Snow Dairy
Springville, UT. 801-489-6081
Sommer Maid Creamery
Doylestown, PA 215-345-6160
Source Food Technology
Durham, NC 866-277-3849
Southchem
Durham, NC 800-849-7000
Southeast Dairy Processors
Tampa, FL. 813-621-3233

Southern Bell Dairy
Somerset, KY 800-468-4798
Southern Ice Cream Specialties
Marietta, GA. 770-428-0452
Southwestern Wisconsin Dairy Goat Products
Mt Sterling, WI. 608-734-3151
Sparboe Companies
Los Angeles, CA. 213-626-7538
Specialty Ingredients
Buffalo Grove, IL 847-419-9595
Spring Grove Foods
Miamisburg, OH 937-866-4311
Spring Hill Farm Dairy
Haverhill, MA. 978-373-3481
Springbank Cheese Company
Woodstock, ON. 800-265-1973
Springdale Cheese Factory
Richland Center, WI 608-538-3213
Springfield Creamery
Eugene, OR. 541-689-2911
Springfield Smoked Fish Company
Springfield, MA 800-327-3412
St. Maurice Laurent
St-Bruno-Lac-St-Jean, QC 418-343-3655
Starbucks Coffee Company
Seattle, WA 800-782-7282
Steiner Cheese
Baltic, OH. 888-897-5505
Stewart's Ice Cream
Saratoga Springs, NY 518-581-1300
Stockton Cheese
Stockton, IL. 800-728-0111
Stone's Home Made Candy Shop
Oswego, NY 888-223-3928
Stop & Shop Manufacturing
Readville, MA. 508-977-5132
Straus Family Creamery
Petaluma, CA 800-572-7783
Stremick's Heritage Foods
Santa Ana, CA 800-371-9010
Sturm Foods
Manawa, WI 800-347-8876
Sugar Creek/Eskimo Pie
Russellville, AR 800-445-2715
Suiza Dairy Corporation
San Juan, PR. 787-792-7300
Sunny Fresh Foods
Monticello, MN 800-872-3447
Sunnyslope Farms Egg Ranch
Cherry Valley, CA. 951-845-1131
Sunshine Dairy
Middletown, CT 860-346-6644
Sunshine Dairy Foods
Portland, OR 503-234-7526
Sunshine Farms
Portage, WI. 608-742-2016
Superbrand Dairies
Miami, FL. 305-769-6600
Superior Dairy
Canton, OH. 800-683-2479
Superstore Industries
Fairfield, CA. 707-864-0502
Suprema Specialties
Paterson, NJ 800-543-2479
Supreme Dairy Farms Company
Warwick, RI 401-739-8180
SW Red Smith
Davie, FL 954-581-1996
Swagger Foods Corporation
Vernon Hills, IL 847-913-1200
Sweet Shop
La Crosse, WI. 608-784-7724
Sweety Novelty
Monterey Park, CA. 626-282-4482
Swiss Dairy
Riverside, CA 951-898-9427
Swiss Valley Farms Company
Davenport, IA 563-468-6600
Swiss Valley Farms Company
Dubuque, IA 800-397-9156
Swiss-American
St Louis, MO. 800-325-8150
Tamarack Farms Dairy
Newark, OH 866-221-4141
Tanglewood Farms
Warsaw, VA. 804-394-4505
Taylor All Star Dairy Foods
Ambridge, PA 724-266-2370
Tebay Dairy Company
Parkersburg, WV. 304-422-1014
Texas Heat
San Antonio, TX. 800-656-5916

Thomas Dairy
Rutland, VT 802-773-6788
Thornton Foods Company
Eden Prairie, MN 952-944-1735
Thrifty Ice Cream
El Monte, CA 626-571-0122
Tillamook County Creamery Association
Tillamook, OR 503-815-1300
Tiller Foods Company
Dayton, OH. 937-435-4601
Titusville Dairy Products
Titusville, PA 800-352-0101
Toft Dairy
Sandusky, OH 800-521-4606
Tom Davis & Sons Dairy Company
Oak Park, MI. 800-399-6970
Tom's Ice Cream Bowl
Zanesville, OH 740-452-5267
Tony's Ice Cream Company
Gastonia, NC. 704-867-7085
Tropical Treets
North York, ON. 888-424-8229
Trugman-Nash
New York, NY 212-869-6910
Turner & Pease Company
Seattle, WA. 206-282-9535
Turner Dairy Farms
Penn Hills, PA. 800-892-1039
Tuscan/Lehigh Valley Dais
Lansdale, PA. 800-937-3233
Twin County Dairy
Kalona, IA. 319-656-2776
Ultima Foods
Longueuil, ON 800-363-9496
Umpqua Dairy Products Company
Roseburg, OR 541-672-2638
Unified Western Grocers
Los Angeles, CA. 323-731-8223
Union Dairy Fountain
Freeport, IL. 815-233-2233
United Dairy
Martins Ferry, OH. 800-252-1542
United Dairy
Uniontown, PA 800-966-6455
United Dairy Farmers
Cincinnati, OH 513-396-8700
United Dairymen of Arizona
Tempe, AZ. 480-966-7211
United Valley Bell Dairy
Charleston, WV. 304-344-2511
Upstate Farms Cooperative
Rochester, NY. 585-458-1880
Upstate Farms Cooperative
Buffalo, NY. 716-892-2121
Upstate Farms Cooperative
Buffalo, NY. 866-874-6455
US Food & Pharmaceuticals
Madison, WI. 608-278-1293
V & V Supremo Foods
Chicago, IL 888-887-8773
Valley Dairy Fairview Dairy
Windber, PA 814-467-1384
Valley Grain Products
Madera, CA. 559-675-3400
Valley Milk Products
Strasburg, VA 540-465-5113
Valley of the Rogue Dairy
Grants Pass, OR 541-476-2020
Valley Queen Cheese Factory
Milbank, SD 605-432-4563
Van Peenans Dairy
Wayne, NJ. 973-694-2551
Vance's Foods
Gilmer, TX 800-497-4834
Velda Farms
Winter Haven, FL 800-279-4166
Velda Farms
North Miami Beach, FL 800-795-4649
Vella Cheese
Sonoma, CA 800-848-0505
Velvet Freeze Ice Cream
Saint Louis, MO 800-589-5000
Velvet Ice Cream Company
Utica, OH 800-589-5000
Ventura Foods
City of Industry, CA 800-327-3906
Vita-Plus
Las Vegas, NV 702-733-8805
Vitamilk Dairy
Bellingham, WA 206-529-4128
Vitarich Ice Cream
Fortuna, CA 707-725-6182

W.J. Stearns & Sons/Mountain Dairy
Storrs Mansfield, CT 860-423-9289
Wabash Valley Produce
Dubois, IN. 812-678-3131
Wallaby Yogurt Company
American Canyon, CA 707-553-1233
Wapsie Valley Creamery
Independence, IA 319-334-7193
Warwick Ice Cream Company
Warwick, RI 401-821-8403
Waugh Foods
East Peoria, IL. 309-427-8000
Wawa Food Market
Media, PA 800-444-9292
Wayne Dairy Products
Richmond, IN 800-875-9294
Webco Foods
Miami, FL
Weldon Ice Cream Company
Millersport, OH. 740-467-2400
Wells' Dairy
Le Mars, IA. 800-942-3800
Welsh Farms
Edison, NJ. 800-221-0663
Welsh Farms
Newark, NJ 973-642-3000
Welsh Farms
Clifton, NJ. 973-772-2388
Wengers Springbrook Cheese
Davis, IL 815-865-5855
Wengert's Dairy
Lebanon, PA 800-222-2129
Wenk Foods Inc
Madison, SD 605-256-4569
Wessanan
Minneapolis, MN 612-331-3775
Westin
Omaha, NE 800-228-6098
Wetta Egg Farm
Andale, KS 316-445-2231
Whitewave Foods Company
Broomfield, CO 303-635-4000
Whitey's Ice Cream Manufacturing
Moline, IL. 888-594-4839
Whitney Foods
Jamaica, NY 718-291-3333
Widmer's Cheese Cellars
Theresa, WI. 888-878-1107
Winchester Farms Dairy
Winchester, KY. 859-745-5500
Winder Dairy
West Valley, UT 800-946-3371
Winmix/Natural Care Products
Englewood, FL 941-475-7432
Wisconsin Cheese
Melrose Park, IL. 708-450-0074
Wisconsin Cheeseman
Madison, WI 608-837-5166
Wolf Canyon Foods
Carmel, CA 831-626-1323
Woolwich Dairy
Orangeville, ON 877-438-3499
World Cheese Company
Brooklyn, NY 718-965-1700
Wright Ice Cream
Cayuga, IN 800-686-9561
Wurth Dairy
Caseyville, IL 217-271-7580
Yarnell Ice Cream Company
Searcy, AR 800-766-2414
Yoder Dairies
Chesapeake, VA 757-482-4068
Yoplait USA
Minneapolis, MN 800-248-7310
Young's Jersey Dairy
Yellow Springs, OH 937-325-0629
Ziegenfelder Company
Wheeling, WV 304-232-6360

Dehydrated

Cheeses, Buttermilk, Milk

Fleur De Lait Foods
New Holland, PA 717-355-8500
Florence Pasta & Cheese
Marshall, MN 800-533-5290

Dairy Drinks

Agri-Mark
Lawrence, MA 978-689-4442
Baskin-Robbins Flavors
Burbank, CA 800-859-5339
C.F. Burger Creamery
Detroit, MI 800-229-2322
Level Valley Creamery
Antioch, TN 800-251-1292
Maryland & Virginia Milk Producers Cooperative
Reston, VA 703-742-4250
Meadow Gold Dairies
Boise, ID 208-343-3671
Regis Milk Company
Charleston, SC 843-723-3418
Scotsburn Dairy Group
Scotsburn, NS 902-485-8023
SunMeadow Family of Products
Saint Petersburg, FL 727-573-2211

Egg Nog

Alta Dena Certified Dairy
City of Industry, CA 800-535-1369
Cass Clay Creamery
Fargo, ND 701-293-6455
Chase Brothers Dairy
Oxnard, CA. 800-438-6455
Crowley Foods
Binghamton, NY. 800-637-0019
Mid States Dairy
Hazelwood, MO 314-731-1150
Prairie Farms Dairy
O Fallon, IL. 618-632-3632
Sinton Dairy Foods Company
Colorado Springs, CO. 800-388-4970
Yoder Dairies
Chesapeake, VA 757-482-4068

Ice Cream

A.C. Petersen Farms
West Hartford, CT. 860-233-8483
Aglamesis Brothers
Cincinnati, OH 513-531-5196
Agropur Cooperative Agro-Alimentaire
Granby, QC 800-363-5686
Al Gelato Bornay
Franklin Park, IL. 847-455-5355
Al-Rite Fruits & Syrups
Miami, FL. 305-652-2540
Alpenrose Dairy Farms
Portland, OR 503-244-1133
American Classic Ice Cream Company
Bay Shore, NY 631-666-1000
Anderson Erickson Dairy
Des Moines, IA. 515-265-2521
Arctic Ice Cream Company
Ewing, NJ 609-393-4264
Artic Ice Cream Novelties
Seattle, WA. 206-324-0414
Asael Farr & Sons Company (Russells Ice Cream)
Salt Lake City, UT 801-484-8724
Associated Milk Producers
New Ulm, MN. 800-533-3580
Avalon Foodservice, Inc.
Canal Fulton, OH 800-362-0622
B&M Enterprises
Charlotte, NC 704-566-9332
Barnes Ice Cream Company
Manchester, ME
Bartolini Ice Cream
Bronx, NY. 718-589-5151
Baskin-Robbins Flavors
Burbank, CA 800-859-5339
Bassett's
Philadelphia, PA 888-999-6314
Beck's Ice Cream
York, PA 717-848-8400
Ben & Jerry's Homemade
South Burlington, VT 802-846-1500
Berkeley Farms
Hayward, CA 510-265-8600
Bernie's Foods
Brooklyn, NY 718-417-6677
Bill Mack's Homemade Ice Cream
Dover, PA 717-292-1931
Birdsall Ice Cream Company
Mason City, IA 641-423-5365
Blake's Creamery
Manchester, NH 603-623-7242
Blue Bell Creameries
Brenham, TX. 979-836-7977
Bonnie Doon Ice Cream Corporation
Elkhart, IN. 574-264-3390
Bonnie's Ice Cream
Paradise, PA 717-687-9301
Bottineau Coop Creamery
Bottineau, ND. 701-228-2216
Briggs Ice Cream
Hyattsville, MD 301-277-8787
Brighams
Arlington, MA 800-274-4426
Brookside Foods
Abbotsford, BC. 877-793-3866
Brothers International Desserts
Irvine, CA 949-655-0080
Broughton Foods
Marietta, OH 800-283-2479
Brown's Ice Cream
Minneapolis, MN 612-378-1075
Browns Dairy
Valparaiso, IN 219-464-4141
Browns' Ice Cream Company
Bowling Green, KY 270-843-9882
Bubbies Homemade Ice Cream
Aiea, HI. 808-487-7218
Buck's Spumoni Company
Milford, CT. 203-874-2007
Byrne Dairy
Syracuse, NY 800-899-1535
Carberry's Home Made Ice Cream
Kissimmee, FL 407-933-7343
Carbolite Foods
Evansville, IN 888-524-3314
Casper's Ice Cream
Richmond, UT. 800-772-4182
Cass Clay Creamery
Fargo, ND 701-293-6455
Cedar Crest Specialties
Cedarburg, WI. 800-877-8341
Celebration Foods
New Britain, CT 800-322-4848

Centreside Dairy
Renfrew, ON 613-432-2914
Chocolate Shoppe Ice Cream Company
Madison, WI 608-221-8640
Chocolaterie Bernard Callebaut
Calgary, AB 800-661-8367
Circus Man Ice Cream Corporation
Farmingdale, NY 516-249-4400
Clemmy's
Randcho Mirage, CA 877-253-6698
Consun Food Industries
Elyria, OH 440-322-6301
Cool Brands International
Ronkonkoma, NY 631-737-9700
Country Clubs Famous Desserts
Langhorne, PA 800-843-2253
Country Fresh
Grand Rapids, MI 800-748-0480
Country Fresh Golden Valley
Livonia, MI 734-261-7980
Crave Natural Foods
Northampton, MA 413-587-7999
Cream O'Weaver Dairy
Salt Lake City, UT 801-973-9922
Creamland Dairies
Albuquerque, NM 505-247-0721
Creme Glacee Gelati
Montreal, QC 888-322-0116
Crystal Cream & Butter Company
Sacramento, CA 916-447-6455
Dairy Fresh Corporation
Greensboro, AL 800-239-5114
Dairy Land
Macon, GA 478-742-6461
Dairy Queen of Georgia
Decatur, GA 404-292-3553
Dairyland Ice Cream Company
Irvington, NJ 973-923-7625
Dave's Hawaiian Ice Cream
Pearl City, HI 808-453-0500
De Ciantis Ice Cream Company
West Warwick, RI 401-821-2440
Deluxe Ice Cream Company
Salem, OR 800-304-7172
Dippin' Dots
Paducah, KY 270-443-8994
Dolci Gelati LLC
Washington, DC 202-257-5323
Double Rainbow Gourmet Ice Creams
San Francisco, CA 800-489-3580
Dreyer's Grand Ice Cream
Oakland, CA 877-437-3937
Dunkin Brands Inc.
Canton, MA 800-458-7731
Edy's Grand Ice Cream
Fort Wayne, IN 260-483-3102
Edy's Grand Ice Cream
Glendale Heights, IL 888-377-3397
Elgin Dairy Foods
Chicago, IL 800-786-9900
Faith Dairy
Tacoma, WA 253-531-3398
Farmers Cooperative Dairy
Halifax, NS 800-565-1945
Farmland Dairies
Wallington, NJ 888-727-6252
Farr Candy Company
Idaho Falls, ID 208-522-8215
Fendall Ice Cream Company
Salt Lake City, UT 801-355-3583
Fieldbrook Farms
Dunkirk, NY 800-333-0805
Flagship Atlanta Dairy
Belleview, FL 800-224-0669
Flavors from Florida
Bartow, FL 863-533-0408
Foothills Creamery
Calgary, AB 800-661-4909
Fosselman's Ice Cream Company
Alhambra, CA 626-282-6533
Fresh Dairy Direct/Morningstar
Dallas, TX 800-395-7004
Friendly Ice Cream Corporation
Wilbraham, MA 800-966-9970
Frostbite
Toledo, OH 800-968-7711
Frozfruit Corporation
Gardena, CA 310-217-1034
Galliker Dairy
Johnstown, PA 800-477-6455
Garber Ice Cream Company
Winchester, VA 800-662-5422
Garelick Farms
Lynn, MA 800-487-8700
Gelato Fresco
Toronto, ON 416-785-5415
Getchell Brothers
Brewer, ME 800-949-4423
Gifford's Dairy
Skowhegan, ME 207-474-9821
Gifford's Ice Cream & Candy Co
Silver Spring, MA 800-708-1938
Glover's Ice Cream
Frankfort, IN 800-686-5163
Good Humor Breyers Ice Cream Company
Green Bay, WI 920-499-5151
Grays Ice Cream
Tiverton, RI 401-624-4500
Green River Chocolates
Hinesburg, VT 802-482-6727
Greenwood Ice Cream Company
Atlanta, GA 770-455-6166
Herrell's Ice Cream
Northampton, MA 413-586-9700
Hershey Creamery Company
Harrisburg, PA 888-240-1905
Hey Brothers Ice Cream
Dixon, IL 815-288-4242
Hiland Dairy Foods Company
Branson, MO 417-334-0090
Homer's Ice Cream
Wilmette, IL 847-251-0477
Honey Hut Ice Cream
Cleveland, OH 216-749-7077
House of Flavors
Ludington, MI 800-930-7740
House of Spices India
Flushing, NY 718-507-4900
HP Hood
Lynnfield, MA 800-343-6592
Hudsonville Creamery & Ice Cream
Holland, MI 616-546-4005
Humble Cremery
Fortuna, CA 800-697-9925
Humboldt Creamery Association
Fortuna, CA 707-725-6182
Hunt-Wesson Foods
Minneapolis, MN 612-544-2761
Hunter Farms
High Point, NC 800-446-8035
Hygeia Dairy Company
McAllen, TX 956-686-0511
Ice Cream & Yogurt Club
Boynton Beach, FL 561-731-3331
Ice Cream Specialties
Saint Louis, MO 314-962-2550
Ice Cream Specialties
Lafayette, IN 765-474-2989
Ideal Dairy
Richfield, UT 435-896-5061
Il Gelato
Astoria, NY 800-899-9299
Imagine Foods
Melville, NY 800-333-6339
International Yogurt Company
Portland, OR 800-962-7326
It's It Ice Cream Company
Burlingame, CA 800-345-1928
J.W. Haywood & Sons Dairy
Louisville, KY 502-774-2311
Jack & Jill Ice Cream Company
Moorestown, NJ 856-813-2300
Jackson Ice Cream Company
Denver, CO 303-534-2454
Jackson Milk & Ice CreamCompany
Hutchinson, KS 620-663-1244
Jaxsons Ice Cream
Dania, FL 954-922-7650
Johnson's Real Ice Cream
Columbus, OH 614-231-0014
Josh & John's Ice Cream
Colorado Springs, CO 800-530-2855
K&B Company
Schulenburg, TX 979-743-4422
Kan-Pac
Arkansas City, KS 620-442-6820
Katie's Korner
Girard, OH 330-539-4140
Katrina's Tartufo
Port Jeffrsn Sta, NY 800-480-8836
Klinke Brothers Ice Cream Company
Memphis, TN 901-743-8250
Kohler Mix Specialties
Newington, CT 860-666-1511
Kokinos Purity Ice CreamCompany
Monroe, LA 318-322-2930
Leiby's Premium Ice Cream
Tamaqua, PA 877-453-4297
Living Harvest Foods
Portland, OR 888-690-3958
Lone Star Food Products
Dallas, TX 214-946-2185
Louis Sherry
Chicago, IL 773-486-8243
Louis Trauth Dairy
Newport, KY 800-544-6455
Lupi
Baltimore, MD 410-752-3370
M&L Gourmet Ice Cream
Baltimore, MD 410-276-4880
Mack's Homemade Ice Cream
York, PA 717-741-2027
MacKay's Cochrane Ice Cream
Cochrane, AB 403-932-2455
Mama Tish's Italian Specialties
Chicago, IL 708-929-2023
Maola Milk & Ice Cream Company
New Bern, NC 252-514-2792
Maple Island
Saint Paul, MN 800-369-1022
Mario's Gelati
Vancouver, BC 604-879-9411
Mattus Lowfat Ice Cream
Glen Cove, NY ÿ90- 56- 522
Mayfield Dairy Farms
Athens, TN 800-362-9546
McArthur Dairy
Miami, FL 877-803-6565
McConnell's Fine Ice Cream
Santa Barbara, CA 805-963-2958
Meadow Gold Dairies
Honolulu, HI 800-362-8531
Meadow Gold Dairies
Englewood, CO 800-525-3289
Micalizzi Italian Ice
Bridgeport, CT 203-366-2353
Michele's Family Bakery
York, PA 717-741-2027
Michelle Chocolatiers
Colorado Springs, CO 888-447-3654
Michigan Dairy
Livonia, MI 734-367-5390
Mid States Dairy
Hazelwood, MO 314-731-1150
Mikawaya Bakery
Vernon, CA
Millers Ice Cream
Houston, TX 713-861-3138
Mister Cookie Face
Lakewood, NJ 732-370-5533
Model Dairy
Reno, NV 800-433-2030
Mooresville Ice Cream Company
Mooresville, NC 704-664-5456
Mozzicato De Pasquale Bakery Pastry
Hartford, CT 860-296-0426
Muller-Pinehurst Dairy C
Rockford, IL 815-968-0441
Nafziger Ice Cream Company
Napoleon, OH 419-592-1112
Natural Fruit Corporation
Hialeah, FL 305-887-7525
Nelson's Ice Cream
Royersford, PA 610-948-3000
New Horizon Foods
Union City, CA 510-489-8600
North Star Distributing
St Louis, MO 314-631-8171
O'Boyle's Ice Cream Company
Bristol, PA 215-788-3882
O'Danny Boy Ice Cream
Dayton, OH 937-837-2100
Oberweis Dairy
North Aurora, IL 888-645-5868
Out of a Flower
Lancaster, TX 800-743-4696
Pal's Homemade Ice Cream
Toledo, OH 419-382-0615
Pecan Deluxe Candy Co.
Dallas, TX 800-733-3589
Perry's Ice Cream Company
Akron, NY 800-873-7797
Pet Dairy
Portsmouth, VA 757-397-2387
Pet Dairy
Spartanburg, SC 864-576-6280

Petersen Ice Cream Company
Oak Park, IL 708-386-6130
Pevely Dairy Company
Hazelwood, MO 314-771-4400
Pierre's French Ice Cream Company
Cleveland, OH 800-837-7342
Plains Creamery
Amarillo, TX. . . . 806-374-0385
Platte Valley Creamery
Scottsbluff, NE 308-632-4225
Plehn's Bakery
Louisville, KY 502-896-4438
Pony Boy Ice Cream
Acushnet, MA. . . . 508-994-4422
Poudre Valley Creamery
Fort Collins, CO 970-237-7000
Prairie Farms Dairy
Carlinville, IL 217-854-2547
Prairie Farms Dairy
O Fallon, IL. . . . 618-632-3632
Prairie Farms Dairy Inc.
Carlinville, IL 217-854-2547
Price's Creameries
El Paso, TX. . . . 915-565-2711
Puritan Ice Cream
Kendallville, IN 260-347-2700
Puritan/ATZ Ice Cream
Kendallville, IN 260-347-2700
Purity Dairies
Nashville, TN 615-244-1900
Purity Ice Cream Company
Ithaca, NY. . . . 607-272-1545
Reinhold Ice Cream Company
Pittsburgh, PA. . . . 412-321-7600
Reiter Dairy
Akron, OH. . . . 800-362-0825
Rhino Foods
Burlington, VT 800-639-3350
Rich Ice Cream Company
West Palm Beach, FL 561-833-7585
Richardson's Ice Cream
Middleton, MA. . . . 978-774-5450
Roberts Dairy Foods
Omaha, NE 402-371-3660
Roberts Dairy Foods
Kansas City, MO. . . . 800-279-1692
Robinson Dairy
Denver, CO 800-332-6355
Ronnybrook Farm Dairy
Ancramdale, NY. . . . 800-772-6455
Roselani Tropics Ice Cream
Wailuku, HI. . . . 808-244-7951
Safeway Dairy Products
Capitol Heights, MD. . . . 301-341-9555
Safeway Inc
Pleasanton, CA 877-723-3929
Safeway Stores
Tempe, AZ 480-966-0295
Sara Lee Corporation
Downers Grove, IL. . . . 630-598-8100
Schneider Valley Farms Dairy
Williamsport, PA. . . . 570-326-2021
Schneider's Dairy Holdings Inc
Pittsburgh, PA. . . . 412-881-3525
Schoep's Ice Cream Company
Madison, WI 800-236-0032
Seaside Ice Cream
Pelham, NY. . . . 914-636-2751
Shaner's Family Restaurant
South Paris, ME 207-743-6367
SheerBliss Ice Cream
Sunrise, FL
Sinton Dairy Foods Company
Colorado Springs, CO. . . . 800-388-4970
Sisler's Ice & Ice Cream
Ohio, IL. . . . 888-891-3856
Smith Dairy Products Company
Orrville, OH 800-776-7076
Snelgrove Ice Cream Company
Salt Lake City, UT 800-569-0005
Snow's Ice Cream Company
Greenfield, MA. . . . 413-774-7438
South County Creamery
Great Barrington, MA. . . . 413-528-8560
Southern Ice Cream Specialties
Marietta, GA. . . . 770-428-0452
Springdale Ice Cream & Beverages
Cincinnati, OH 513-671-2790
St. Clair Ice Cream Company
Norwalk, CT 203-853-4774
Starbucks Coffee Company
Seattle, WA 800-782-7282
Stewart's Ice Cream
Saratoga Springs, NY 518-581-1300
Stone's Home Made Candy Shop
Oswego, NY 888-223-3928
Sugar Creek/Eskimo Pie
Russellville, AR 800-445-2715
Superstore Industries
Fairfield, CA. . . . 707-864-0502
Sweet Mountain Magic
Chicago, IL 773-755-4539
Sweet Shop
La Crosse, WI. . . . 608-784-7724
Sweety Novelty
Monterey Park, CA. . . . 626-282-4482
Tebay Dairy Company
Parkersburg, WV. . . . 304-422-1014
Ted Drewes Frozen Custard
Saint Louis, MO 314-481-2652
Thrifty Ice Cream
El Monte, CA 626-571-0122
Tillamook County Creamery Association
Tillamook, OR 503-815-1300
Toft Dairy
Sandusky, OH 800-521-4606
Tom's Ice Cream Bowl
Zanesville, OH 740-452-5267
Tony's Ice Cream Company
Gastonia, NC. . . . 704-867-7085
Treat Ice Cream Company
San Jose, CA. . . . 408-292-9321
Tropical Treets
North York, ON. . . . 888-424-8229
Turkey Hill Dairy
Conestoga, PA. . . . 800-693-2479
Umpqua Dairy Products Company
Roseburg, OR 541-672-2638
United Dairy
Martins Ferry, OH. . . . 800-252-1542
United Dairy
Uniontown, PA 800-966-6455
Valley Dairy Fairview Dairy
Windber, PA 814-467-1384
Van Dyke Ice Cream
Ridgewood, NJ 201-444-1429
Velda Farms
Winter Haven, FL 800-279-4166
Velda Farms
North Miami Beach, FL 800-795-4649
Velvet Freeze Ice Cream
Saint Louis, MO 800-589-5000
Velvet Ice Cream Company
Utica, OH 800-589-5000
Velvet Milk
Owensboro, KY 207-684-9677
Vincent Giordano Corporation
Philadelphia, PA 215-467-6629
Vitamilk Dairy
Bellingham, WA 206-529-4128
Vitarich Ice Cream
Fortuna, CA 707-725-6182
Warwick Ice Cream Company
Warwick, RI 401-821-8403
Wayne Dairy Products
Richmond, IN 800-875-9294
Weldon Ice Cream Company
Millersport, OH. . . . 740-467-2400
Wells' Dairy
Le Mars, IA. . . . 800-942-3800
Welsh Farms
Edison, NJ. . . . 800-221-0663
Welsh Farms
Clifton, NJ. . . . 973-772-2388
Whitey's Ice Cream Manufacturing
Moline, IL. . . . 888-594-4839
Winmix/Natural Care Products
Englewood, FL 941-475-7432
World's Greatest Ice Cream
Miami Beach, FL 305-538-0207
Wright Ice Cream
Cayuga, IN 800-686-9561
WSU Creamery
Pullman, WA. . . . 800-457-5442
Yarnell Ice Cream Company
Searcy, AR 800-766-2414
YoCream International
Portland, OR 800-962-7326
Ziegenfelder Company
Wheeling, WV 304-232-6360

Bases

GPI USA LLC.
Athens, GA 706-850-7826
SensoryEffects Flavor Systems
Bridgeton, MO 314-291-5444
Sokol & Company
Countryside, IL. . . . 800-328-7656

Fat-Free

Cedar Crest Specialties
Cedarburg, WI. . . . 800-877-8341
Clay Center Locker Plant
Clay Center, KS 785-632-5550
Perry's Ice Cream Company
Akron, NY. . . . 800-873-7797

Flavored

Bill Mack's Homemade Ice Cream
Dover, PA 717-292-1931
Byrne Dairy
Syracuse, NY 800-899-1535
Petersen Ice Cream Company
Oak Park, IL 708-386-6130
Velvet Freeze Ice Cream
Saint Louis, MO 800-589-5000

Gelato

Casper's Ice Cream
Richmond, UT. . . . 800-772-4182
Ciao Bella Gelato Company
Irvington, NJ. . . . 800-435-2863
Ciao Bella Gellato Company
Florham Park, NJ
Creme Glacee Gelati
Montreal, QC 888-322-0116
Crowley Foods
Binghamton, NY. . . . 800-637-0019
Frostbite
Toledo, OH 800-968-7711
Gelato Giuliana LLC
New Haven, CT 203-772-0607
J&J Snack Foods Corporation
Pennsauken, NJ. . . . 800-486-9533
Millers Ice Cream
Houston, TX 713-861-3138
Mooresville Ice Cream Company
Mooresville, NC 704-664-5456
Snelgrove Ice Cream Company
Salt Lake City, UT 800-569-0005
Talenti
Dallas, TX. . . . 214-526-3600
Weldon Ice Cream Company
Millersport, OH. . . . 740-467-2400

Granita

Creme Glacee Gelati
Montreal, QC 888-322-0116
Folklore Foods
Toppenish, WA 509-865-4772

Ice Milk

Perry's Ice Cream Company
Akron, NY. . . . 800-873-7797
Safeway Dairy Products
Capitol Heights, MD. . . . 301-341-9555
Whitey's Ice Cream Manufacturing
Moline, IL. . . . 888-594-4839

Ices

Alamance Foods/Triton Water Company
Burlington, NC 800-476-9111
Cappola Foods
Toronto, ON 416-633-0389
Carbolite Foods
Evansville, IN 888-524-3314

Chill & Moore
Fort Worth, TX 800-676-3055
Edy's Dreyers Grand Ice Cream
Rockaway, NJ 800-362-7899
Gelato Fresco
Toronto, ON 416-785-5415
J&J Snack Foods Corporation
Pennsauken, NJ 800-486-9533
Kemach Food Products Corporation
Brooklyn, NY 888-453-6224
Mackie Intl.
Riverside, CA 800-733-9762
Mar-Key Foods
Vidalia, GA 912-537-4204
Rosati Italian Water Ice
Clifton Heights, PA 610-626-1818
Smart Ice
Fort Myers, FL 239-334-3123
Tova Industries
Louisville, KY 888-532-8682

Low-Fat

Friendly Ice Cream Corporation
Wilbraham, MA 800-966-9970
Hudsonville Creamery & Ice Cream
Holland, MI 616-546-4005
Mayfield Dairy Farms
Athens, TN 800-362-9546
Perry's Ice Cream Company
Akron, NY 800-873-7797
Stewart's Ice Cream
Saratoga Springs, NY 518-581-1300
Vitarich Ice Cream
Fortuna, CA 707-725-6182

Non-Dairy

Low-Calorie

Innovative Food Solutions LLC
Columbus, OH 800-884-3314

Novelties

Del's Lemonade & Refreshments
Cranston, RI 401-463-6190
Dreyer's Grand Ice Cream
Oakland, CA 877-437-3937
Edy's Dreyers Grand Ice Cream
Rockaway, NJ 800-362-7899
Fieldbrook Farms
Dunkirk, NY 800-333-0805
Flagship Atlanta Dairy
Belleview, FL 800-224-0669
Frozfruit Corporation
Gardena, CA 310-217-1034
Glover's Ice Cream
Frankfort, IN 800-686-5163
Good Humor Breyers Ice Cream Company
Green Bay, WI 920-499-5151
Grossinger's Home Bakery
New York, NY 800-479-6996
Ice Cream Specialties
Saint Louis, MO 314-962-2550
Ice Cream Specialties
Lafayette, IN 765-474-2989
It's It Ice Cream Company
Burlingame, CA 800-345-1928
Meadow Gold Dairies
Honolulu, HI 800-362-8531
Natural Fruit Corporation
Hialeah, FL 305-887-7525
Perry's Ice Cream Company
Akron, NY 800-873-7797
Roberts Dairy Foods
Omaha, NE 402-371-3660
Schneider's Dairy Holdings Inc
Pittsburgh, PA 412-881-3525
Schoep's Ice Cream Company
Madison, WI 800-236-0032
Southern Ice Cream Specialties
Marietta, GA 770-428-0452
Sweety Novelty
Monterey Park, CA 626-282-4482
Vitarich Ice Cream
Fortuna, CA 707-725-6182
Weldon Ice Cream Company
Millersport, OH 740-467-2400
Whitey's Ice Cream Manufacturing
Moline, IL 888-594-4839
Wright Ice Cream
Cayuga, IN 800-686-9561

Ziegenfelder Company
Wheeling, WV 304-232-6360

Popsicles

Hershey Corporation
Hershey, PA 800-468-1714
Ice Cream Specialties
Saint Louis, MO 314-962-2550
J&J Snack Foods Corporation
Pennsauken, NJ 800-486-9533
Leader Candies
Brooklyn, NY 718-366-6900
Mackie Intl.
Riverside, CA 800-733-9762
Mar-Key Foods
Vidalia, GA 912-537-4204
Oak Leaf Confections
Scarborough, ON 877-261-7887
Welch's Foods Inc
Concord, MA 800-340-6870

Ribbons

Sokol & Company
Countryside, IL 800-328-7656

Roll

Creme Glacee Gelati
Montreal, QC 888-322-0116
Dave's Hawaiian Ice Cream
Pearl City, HI 808-453-0500
Grossinger's Home Bakery
New York, NY 800-479-6996

Sherbet

A.C. Petersen Farms
West Hartford, CT 860-233-8483
Alamance Foods/Triton Water Company
Burlington, NC 800-476-9111
Browns Dairy
Valparaiso, IN 219-464-4141
Byrne Dairy
Syracuse, NY 800-899-1535
Cedar Crest Specialties
Cedarburg, WI 800-877-8341
Consun Food Industries
Elyria, OH 440-322-6301
Creme Glacee Gelati
Montreal, QC 888-322-0116
Dave's Hawaiian Ice Cream
Pearl City, HI 808-453-0500
Edy's Grand Ice Cream
Fort Wayne, IN 260-483-3102
Fieldbrook Farms
Dunkirk, NY 800-333-0805
Flavors from Florida
Bartow, FL 863-533-0408
Gelato Fresco
Toronto, ON 416-785-5415
Hudsonville Creamery & Ice Cream
Holland, MI 616-546-4005
Jel-Sert Company
West Chicago, IL 800-323-2592
Johnson's Real Ice Cream
Columbus, OH 614-231-0014
Mayfield Dairy Farms
Athens, TN 800-362-9546
Perry's Ice Cream Company
Akron, NY 800-873-7797
Prairie Farms Dairy
Carlinville, IL 217-854-2547
Prairie Farms Dairy
O Fallon, IL 618-632-3632
Schneider Valley Farms Dairy
Williamsport, PA 570-326-2021
Tova Industries
Louisville, KY 888-532-8682

Slushes

Al-Rite Fruits & Syrups
Miami, FL 305-652-2540
Fee Brothers
Rochester, NY 800-961-3337
Flavouressence Products
Mississauga, ON 866-209-7778
Royale International Beverage Co Inc
Davenport, IA 563-386-5222
Tropical Illusions
Trenton, MO 660-359-5422

Sorbet

Ben & Jerry's Homemade
South Burlington, VT 802-846-1500
Bernie's Foods
Brooklyn, NY 718-417-6677
Ciao Bella Gelato Company
Irvington, NJ 800-435-2863
Dunkin Brands Inc.
Canton, MA 800-458-7731
Fieldbrook Farms
Dunkirk, NY 800-333-0805
Gelati Celesti
Redondo Beach, CA 800-550-7550
Gelato Fresco
Toronto, ON 416-785-5415
Homer's Ice Cream
Wilmette, IL 847-251-0477
International Yogurt Company
Portland, OR 800-962-7326
MacKay's Cochrane Ice Cream
Cochrane, AB 403-932-2455
Royal Ice Cream Company
Manchester, CT 800-246-2958
Talenti
Dallas, TX 214-526-3600
Winmix/Natural Care Products
Englewood, FL 941-475-7432

Tortoni

Royal Ice Cream Company
Manchester, CT 800-246-2958

Milk & Milk Products

International Dairy Ingredients
Wapakoneta, OH 419-738-4060

Kefir

Continental Culture Specialists
Los Angeles, CA 818-240-7400
Emerling International Foods
Buffalo, NY 716-833-7381

We supply food manufacturers and food service customers worldwide (since 1988) with bulk ingredients including: Fruits & Vegetables; Juice Concentrates; Herbs & Spices; Oils & Vinegars; Flavors & Colors; Honey & Molasses. We also produce PURE MAPLE SYRUP.

Jamieson Laboratories
Windosr, ON 519-974-8482
Lifeway Foods Inc
Morton Grove, IL 877-281-3874

Milk

AFP Advanced Food Products, LLC
Visalia, CA 559-627-2070
Agri-Mark
Lawrence, MA 978-689-4442
Aimonetto and Sons
Renton, WA 866-823-2777
All American Foods, Inc.
Mankato, MN 800-833-2661
Alpenrose Dairy Farms
Portland, OR 503-244-1133
Alta Dena Certified Dairy
City of Industry, CA 800-535-1369
Anderson Erickson Dairy
Des Moines, IA 515-265-2521
Associated Milk Producers
New Ulm, MN 800-533-3580
Ault Foods
Toronto, ON 416-626-1973
Barber's Dairy
Birmingham, AL 205-942-2351
Bell Dairy Products
Lubbock, TX 806-293-1367
Berkeley Farms
Hayward, CA 510-265-8600
Bottineau Coop Creamery
Bottineau, ND 701-228-2216
Broughton Foods
Marietta, OH 800-283-2479
Byrne Dairy
Syracuse, NY 800-899-1535
C.F. Burger Creamery
Detroit, MI 800-229-2322
Cass Clay Creamery
Fargo, ND 701-293-6455

Cedar Lake Foods
Cedar Lake, MI 800-246-5039
Chase Brothers Dairy
Oxnard, CA 800-438-6455
Clinton Milk Company
Newark, NJ 973-642-3000
Coastlog Industries
Novi, MI 248-344-9556
Coburg Dairy
North Charleston, SC 843-554-4870
Consun Food Industries
Elyria, OH 440-322-6301
Country Fresh
Grand Rapids, MI 800-748-0480
Cow Palace Too
Granger, WA 509-829-5777
Cultured Specialties
Fullerton, CA 714-772-8861
Cumberland Dairy
Rosenhayn, NJ 856-451-1300
Dairy Fresh Corporation
Greensboro, AL 800-239-5114
Dairy Maid Dairy
Frederick, MD 301-695-0431
DairyAmerica
Fresno, CA 800-722-3110
Devansoy
Carroll, IA 800-747-8605
Dixie Dairy Company
Gary, IN 219-885-6101
Ellsworth Cooperative Creamery
Ellsworth, WI 715-273-4311
Farmland Dairies
Wallington, NJ 888-727-6252
Flagship Atlanta Dairy
Belleview, FL 800-224-0669
Fonterra USA
Chicago, IL 847-928-1872
Foster Farms Dairy
Modesto, CA 209-576-2300
Galliker Dairy
Johnstown, PA 800-477-6455
Garelick Farms
Franklin, MA 800-343-4982
Garelick Farms
Lynn, MA 800-487-8700
Golden Cheese of California
Corona, CA 800-842-0264
GPI USA LLC.
Athens, GA 706-850-7826
H. Meyer Dairy Company
Cincinnati, OH 800-347-6455
H.E. Butt Grocery Company
San Antonio, TX 800-432-3113
Harrisburg Dairies
Harrisburg, PA 800-692-7429
Hastings Cooperative Creamery
Hastings, MN 651-437-9414
Heritage Farms Dairy
Murfreesboro, TN 615-895-2790
Hiland Dairy Foods Company
Branson, MO 417-334-0090
Hiland Dairy Foods Company
Springfield, MO 417-862-9311
Hygeia Dairy Company
Corpus Christi, TX 361-854-4561
Inland Northwest Dairies
Spokane, WA 509-489-8600
International Dairy Ingredients
Wapakoneta, OH 419-738-4060
Jackson Milk & Ice CreamCompany
Hutchinson, KS 620-663-1244
KDK Inc
Draper, UT 801-571-3506
Keller's Creamery
Harleysville, PA 800-535-5371
Kemps
Cedarburg, WI 262-377-5040
Kohler Mix Specialties
White Bear Lake, MN 651-426-1633
Lafleur Dairy Products,
New Orleans, LA 504-729-3330
Land O Lakes Milk
Sioux Falls, SD 605-330-9526
Land O'Lakes, Inc.
Arden Hills, MN 800-328-9680
Land-O-Sun Dairies
O Fallon, IL 314-436-6820
Level Valley Creamery
Antioch, TN 800-251-1292
Liberty Dairy
Evart, MI 800-632-5552
Marva Maid Dairy
Newport News, VA 800-544-4439
Maryland & Virginia Milk Producers Cooperative
Reston, VA 703-742-4250
Matanuska Maid Dairy
Anchorage, AK 907-561-5223
Mayfield Dairy Farms
Athens, TN 800-362-9546
McArthur Dairy
Miami, FL 305-795-7700
Meadow Brook Dairy
Erie, PA 800-352-4010
Meadow Gold Dairies
Tulsa, OK 800-742-7349
Michigan Dairy
Livonia, MI 734-367-5390
Mid States Dairy
Hazelwood, MO 314-731-1150
Milk Specialties Global
Eden Praire, MN 952-942-7310
Muller-Pinehurst Dairy C
Rockford, IL 815-968-0441
Naterl
St. Bruno, QC 450-653-3655
Norwalk Dairy
Santa Fe Springs, CA 562-921-5712
Oakhurst Dairy
Portland, ME 800-482-0718
Parmalat Canada
Toronto, ON 800-563-1515
Pet Dairy
Portsmouth, VA 757-397-2387
Pet Dairy
Spartanburg, SC 864-576-6280
Pet Milk
Florence, SC 800-735-3066
Pevely Dairy Company
Hazelwood, MO 314-771-4400
Pleasant View Dairy
Highland, IN 219-838-0155
Prairie Farms Dairy
Carlinville, IL 217-854-2547
Prairie Farms Dairy
Granite City, IL 618-451-5600
Prairie Farms Dairy Inc.
Carlinville, IL 217-854-2547
Purity Dairies
Nashville, TN 615-244-1900
Queensboro Farm Products
Canastota, NY 315-697-2235
Queensboro Farm Products
Jamaica, NY 718-658-5000
Reilly Dairy & Food Company
Tampa, FL 813-839-8458
Reiter Dairy
Akron, OH 800-362-0825
Reiter Dairy
Springfield, OH 937-323-5777
Roberts Dairy Foods
Iowa City, IA
Roberts Dairy Foods
Kansas City, MO 800-279-1692
Robinson Dairy
Denver, CO 800-332-6355
Roland Industries
Saint Louis, MO 800-325-1183
Rosenberger's Dairies
Hatfield, PA 800-355-9074
Safeway Inc
Pleasanton, CA 877-723-3929
Safeway Milk Plant
Tempe, AZ 480-894-4391
Schneider Valley Farms Dairy
Williamsport, PA 570-326-2021
Schneider's Dairy Holdings Inc
Pittsburgh, PA 412-881-3525
Sinton Dairy Foods Company
Colorado Springs, CO 800-388-4970
Sinton Dairy Foods Company
Denver, CO 800-666-4808
Smith Dairy Products Company
Orrville, OH 800-776-7076
Stewart's Ice Cream
Saratoga Springs, NY 518-581-1300
Stop & Shop Manufacturing
Readville, MA 508-977-5132
SunMeadow Family of Products
Saint Petersburg, FL 727-573-2211
Sunshine Farms
Portage, WI 608-742-2016
Superbrand Dairies
Miami, FL 305-769-6600
Superstore Industries
Fairfield, CA 707-864-0502
Swiss Valley Farms Company
Davenport, IA 563-468-6600
Swissland Milk
Berne, IN 260-589-2761
Tamarack Farms Dairy
Newark, OH 866-221-4141
Toft Dairy
Sandusky, OH 800-521-4606
Turkey Hill Dairy
Conestoga, PA 800-693-2479
Tuscan/Lehigh Valley Dais
Lansdale, PA 800-937-3233
Umpqua Dairy Products Company
Roseburg, OR 541-672-2638
Unified Western Grocers
Los Angeles, CA 323-731-8223
United Dairy
Martins Ferry, OH 800-252-1542
United Dairymen of Arizona
Tempe, AZ 480-966-7211
Upstate Farms Cooperative
Rochester, NY 585-458-1880
Velda Farms
North Miami Beach, FL 800-795-4649
Vitamilk Dairy
Bellingham, WA 206-529-4128
W.J. Stearns & Sons/Mountain Dairy
Storrs Mansfield, CT 860-423-9289
Wayne Dairy Products
Richmond, IN 800-875-9294
Welsh Farms
Edison, NJ 800-221-0663
Wengert's Dairy
Lebanon, PA 800-222-2129
White Wave Foods
Jacksonville, FL 800-874-6765
Whitewave Foods Company
Broomfield, CO 303-635-4000
Winchester Farms Dairy
Winchester, KY 859-745-5500
Yoder Dairies
Chesapeake, VA 757-482-4068

1 Percent

Alta Dena Certified Dairy
City of Industry, CA 800-535-1369
Berkeley Farms
Hayward, CA 510-265-8600
Chase Brothers Dairy
Oxnard, CA 800-438-6455
Coburg Dairy
North Charleston, SC 843-554-4870
Cream O'Weaver Dairy
Salt Lake City, UT 801-973-9922
Cropp Cooperative-Organic Valley
La Farge, WI 888-444-6455
Crowley Foods
Binghamton, NY 800-637-0019
Cumberland Dairy
Rosenhayn, NJ 856-451-1300
Dairy Farmers of America
Knoxville, TN 865-218-8500
Dairy Maid Dairy
Frederick, MD 301-695-0431
KDK Inc
Draper, UT 801-571-3506
Meadow Brook Dairy
Erie, PA 800-352-4010
Mid States Dairy
Hazelwood, MO 314-731-1150
Pleasant View Dairy
Highland, IN 219-838-0155
Prairie Farms Dairy
O Fallon, IL 618-632-3632
Reiter Dairy
Springfield, OH 937-323-5777
Safeway Milk Plant
Tempe, AZ 480-894-4391
Schneider's Dairy Holdings Inc
Pittsburgh, PA 412-881-3525
Sinton Dairy Foods Company
Colorado Springs, CO 800-388-4970
Tuscan/Lehigh Valley Dais
Lansdale, PA 800-937-3233
Unified Western Grocers
Los Angeles, CA 323-731-8223
White Wave Foods
Jacksonville, FL 800-874-6765
Yoder Dairies
Chesapeake, VA 757-482-4068

2 Percent

Alta Dena Certified Dairy
City of Industry, CA 800-535-1369
Berkeley Farms
Hayward, CA 510-265-8600
Coburg Dairy
North Charleston, SC 843-554-4870
Cream O'Weaver Dairy
Salt Lake City, UT 801-973-9922
Cropp Cooperative-Organic Valley
La Farge, WI 888-444-6455
Crowley Foods
Binghamton, NY 800-637-0019
Cumberland Dairy
Rosenhayn, NJ 856-451-1300
Dairy Farmers of America
Knoxville, TN 865-218-8500
Dairy Maid Dairy
Frederick, MD 301-695-0431
KDK Inc
Draper, UT 801-571-3506
Meadow Brook Dairy
Erie, PA 800-352-4010
Mid States Dairy
Hazelwood, MO 314-731-1150
Oak Knoll Dairy
Windsor, VT 802-674-5426
Pleasant View Dairy
Highland, IN 219-838-0155
Prairie Farms Dairy
O Fallon, IL 618-632-3632
Reiter Dairy
Springfield, OH 937-323-5777
Safeway Milk Plant
Tempe, AZ 480-894-4391
Schneider's Dairy Holdings Inc
Pittsburgh, PA 412-881-3525
Sinton Dairy Foods Company
Colorado Springs, CO 800-388-4970
Stewart's Ice Cream
Saratoga Springs, NY 518-581-1300
T.G. Lee Dairy
Orlando, FL 407-894-4941
Unified Western Grocers
Los Angeles, CA 323-731-8223
Wengert's Dairy
Lebanon, PA 800-222-2129
White Wave Foods
Jacksonville, FL 800-874-6765
Winchester Farms Dairy
Winchester, KY 859-745-5500

Chocolate

Alta Dena Certified Dairy
City of Industry, CA 800-535-1369
Barbe's Dairy
Westwego, LA 504-347-6201
Berkeley Farms
Hayward, CA 510-265-8600
Chase Brothers Dairy
Oxnard, CA 800-438-6455
Cloverland Green Spring Dairy
Baltimore, MD 800-876-6455
Coburg Dairy
North Charleston, SC 843-554-4870
Crowley Foods
Binghamton, NY 800-637-0019
Harrisburg Dairies
Harrisburg, PA 800-692-7429
Hygeia Dairy Company
Corpus Christi, TX 361-854-4561
Hygeia Dairy Company
McAllen, TX 956-686-0511
Ideal American
Holland, IN 812-424-3351
Kemps
Cedarburg, WI 262-377-5040
McArthur Dairy
Miami, FL 305-795-7700
Naterl
St. Bruno, QC 450-653-3655
Norwalk Dairy
Santa Fe Springs, CA 562-921-5712
Oak Knoll Dairy
Windsor, VT 802-674-5426
Prairie Farms Dairy
O Fallon, IL 618-632-3632
Sinton Dairy Foods Company
Colorado Springs, CO 800-388-4970
Swiss Dairy
Riverside, CA 951-898-9427
Tuscan/Lehigh Valley Dais
Lansdale, PA 800-937-3233
Winchester Farms Dairy
Winchester, KY 859-745-5500
Yoder Dairies
Chesapeake, VA 757-482-4068
Yoo-Hoo Chocolate Beverage Company
Carlstadt, NJ 201-933-0070

Condensed

Abbott Laboratories Nutritionals/Ross Products
Abbott Park, IL 847-937-6100
Agri-Mark
Lawrence, MA 978-689-4442
All American Foods, Inc.
Mankato, MN 800-833-2661
Berkshire Dairy & Food Products
Wyomissing, PA 888-654-8008
Blossom Farm Products
Ridgewood, NJ 800-729-1818
Dairy Farmers of America
East Syracuse, NY 315-431-1352
Dietrich's Milk Products
Reading, PA 800-526-6455
Gehl Guernsey Farms
Germantown, WI 800-434-5713
Graf Creamery
Bonduel, WI
Land O'Lakes
Carlisle, PA 717-486-7000
Level Valley Creamery
Antioch, TN 800-251-1292
O-At-Ka Milk Products Cooperative
Batavia, NY 800-828-8152
Queensboro Farm Products
Jamaica, NY 718-658-5000
Ronzoni Foods Canada
Etobicoke, ON 800-387-5032
Saint Albans Cooperative Creamery
Saint Albans, VT 800-559-0343

Condensed - Bulk Only

Agri-Dairy Products
Purchase, NY 914-697-9580
Clofine Dairy & Food Products
Linwood, NJ 800-441-1001

Evaporated

Abbott Laboratories Nutritionals/Ross Products
Abbott Park, IL 847-937-6100
Agri-Dairy Products
Purchase, NY 914-697-9580
Associated Milk Producers
Dawson, MN 320-769-2994
Associated Milk Producers
Rochester, MN 507-282-7401
Clofine Dairy & Food Products
Linwood, NJ 800-441-1001
Cropp Cooperative-Organic Valley
La Farge, WI 888-444-6455
Industrial Products
Defiance, OH 800-251-3033
Mead Johnson Nutritional
Zeeland, MI 616-748-7100
MEYENBERG Goat Milk Products
Turlock, CA 800-891-4628
Milnot Company
Neosho, MO 800-877-6455

Fat-Free

Agri-Mark
Lawrence, MA 978-689-4442
Alta Dena Certified Dairy
City of Industry, CA 800-535-1369
Berkeley Farms
Hayward, CA 510-265-8600
California Dairies
Visalia, CA 559-625-2200
Chase Brothers Dairy
Oxnard, CA 800-438-6455
Clofine Dairy & Food Products
Linwood, NJ 800-441-1001
Darigold
Seattle, WA 800-333-6455
First District Association
Litchfield, MN 320-693-3236
Humboldt Creamery Association
Fortuna, CA 707-725-6182
Ideal American
Holland, IN 812-424-3351
IMAC
Oklahoma City, OK 888-878-7827
KDK Inc
Draper, UT 801-571-3506
Main Street Ingredients
La Crosse, WI 800-359-2345
Meadow Brook Dairy
Erie, PA 800-352-4010
Norwalk Dairy
Santa Fe Springs, CA 562-921-5712
Plainview Milk Products Cooperative
Plainview, MN 507-534-3872
Prairie Farms Dairy
O Fallon, IL 618-632-3632
Quality Ingredients Corporation
Burnsville, MN 952-898-4002
Ramsen
Lakeville, MN 952-431-0400
Reiter Dairy
Springfield, OH 937-323-5777
Safeway Inc
Pleasanton, CA 877-723-3929
Saint Albans Cooperative Creamery
Saint Albans, VT 800-559-0343
Schneider's Dairy Holdings Inc
Pittsburgh, PA 412-881-3525
Sinton Dairy Foods Company
Colorado Springs, CO 800-388-4970
Swiss Dairy
Riverside, CA 951-898-9427
Tuscan/Lehigh Valley Dais
Lansdale, PA 800-937-3233

Flavored

Berkeley Farms
Hayward, CA 510-265-8600
Chase Brothers Dairy
Oxnard, CA 800-438-6455
Coburg Dairy
North Charleston, SC 843-554-4870
Coco Lopez
Miramar, FL 800-341-2242
Kemps
Cedarburg, WI 262-377-5040
Norwalk Dairy
Santa Fe Springs, CA 562-921-5712
Prairie Farms Dairy
O Fallon, IL 618-632-3632
Schneider Valley Farms Dairy
Williamsport, PA 570-326-2021
Schneider's Dairy Holdings Inc
Pittsburgh, PA 412-881-3525
Tuscan/Lehigh Valley Dais
Lansdale, PA 800-937-3233
Winchester Farms Dairy
Winchester, KY 859-745-5500

Fresh

AFP Advanced Food Products, LLC
Visalia, CA 559-627-2070
Agropur Cooperative Agro-Alimentaire
Granby, QC 800-363-5686
Al's Beverage Company
East Windsor, CT 888-257-7632
Alpenrose Dairy Farms
Portland, OR 503-244-1133
Anderson Dairy
Las Vegas, NV 702-642-7507
Associated Milk Producers
Dawson, MN 320-769-2994
Associated Milk Producers
Rochester, MN 507-282-7401
Avent Luvel Dairy Products
Kosciusko, MS 800-281-1307
Barbe's Dairy
Westwego, LA 504-347-6201
Bartlett Dairy & Food Service
Jamaica, NY 718-658-2299
Bell Dairy Products
Lubbock, TX 806-293-1367
Bergey's Dairy Farm
Chesapeake, VA 757-482-4711
Berkeley Farms
Hayward, CA 510-265-8600
Bliss Brothers Dairy, Inc.
Attleboro, MA 800-622-8789
Blue Ribbon Dairy
Exeter, PA 570-655-5579
Braum's Inc
Oklahoma City, OK 405-478-1656

Broughton Foods
Marietta, OH 800-283-2479
Brown Dairy
Coalville, UT 435-336-5952
Brum's Dairy
Pembroke, ON. 613-735-2325
Burger Dairy
Cleveland, OH 216-896-9100
Caprine Estates
Bellbrook, OH. 937-848-7406
Carl Colteryahn Dairy
Pittsburgh, PA 412-881-1408
Central Dairy Company
Jefferson City, MO 573-635-6148
Chase Brothers Dairy
Oxnard, CA. 800-438-6455
Chester Dairy Company
Chester, IL. 618-826-2394
Clinton Milk Company
Newark, NJ 973-642-3000
Clover Farms Dairy Company
Reading, PA 800-323-0123
Clover Stornetta Farms
Petaluma, CA 800-237-3315
Cloverland Green Spring Dairy
Baltimore, MD 800-876-6455
Coastlog Industries
Novi, MI 248-344-9556
Coburg Dairy
North Charleston, SC 843-554-4870
Compton Dairy
Shelbyville, IN 317-398-8621
Consun Food Industries
Elyria, OH. 440-322-6301
Country Delight Farms
Nashville, TN 615-320-1440
Country Fresh
Grand Rapids, MI 800-748-0480
Cow Palace Too
Granger, WA 509-829-5777
Cream O'Weaver Dairy
Salt Lake City, UT 801-973-9922
Crescent Ridge Dairy
Sharon, MA. 800-660-2740
Crowley Foods
Binghamton, NY. 800-637-0019
Crystal Lake LLC
Warsaw, IN 574-858-2514
Cultured Specialties
Fullerton, CA 714-772-8861
Cypress Grove Chevre
Arcata, CA 707-825-1100
Czepiel Millers Dairy
Ludlow, MA 413-589-0828
Dairy Farmers of America
Kansas City, MO. 888-332-6455
Dairy Fresh
Winston Salem, NC. 800-446-5577
Dairy Fresh Corporation
Greensboro, AL. 800-239-5114
Dairy Management
Rosemont, IL. 800-248-8829
Dairymen's
Cleveland, OH 216-671-2300
Danish Creamery Association
Visalia, CA 559-625-2200
Dannon Company
Minster, OH 419-628-3861
Dannon Company
White Plains, NY 877-326-6668
Darby Plains Dairy
Plain City, OH. 614-873-4574
Darifair Foods
Jacksonville, FL 904-268-8999
Darigold
Seattle, WA 800-333-6455
Daybreak Foods
Long Prairie, MN 320-732-2966
Dean Dairy Products
Sharpsville, PA 800-942-8096
Dean Foods Company
Dallas, TX. 800-431-9214
Dean Milk Company
Louisville, KY 800-451-3326
Deseret Dairy Products
Salt Lake City, UT 801-240-7350
Detroit City Dairy
Taylor, MI. 313-295-6300
Dillon Dairy Company
Denver, CO. 303-388-1645
Eagle Family Foods
Orrville, OH 888-656-3245
Eggland's Best Foods
King of Prussia, PA. 888-922-3447
Everything Yogurt
Washington, DC 202-842-2990
F & A Dairy of California
Newman, CA. 800-554-6455
Fanny Mason Farmstead Cheese
Walpole, NH 603-756-3300
Farm Stores
Palmetto Bay, FL 800-726-3276
Farmdale Creamery
San Bernardino, CA 909-889-3002
Farmers Dairies
El Paso, TX. 915-772-2736
Farmland Dairies
Wallington, NJ 888-727-6252
Foster Farms Dairy
Fresno, CA 800-241-0008
Fresh Farm
Arvada, CO. 303-429-1536
Gaf Seelig
Woodside, NY. 718-899-5000
Garelick Farms
Rensselaer, NY 518-283-0820
Garelick Farms
Lynn, MA 800-487-8700
Gold Star Dairy
Little Rock, AR. 501-565-6125
Goldenrod Dairy Foods/ U C Milk Company
Madisonville, KY 800-462-2354
Goshen Dairy Company
New Philadelphia, OH 330-339-1959
Guers Dairy
Pottsville, PA. 570-277-6611
H. Meyer Dairy Company
Cincinnati, OH 800-347-6455
H.E. Butt Grocery Company
San Antonio, TX. 800-432-3113
Harrisburg Dairies
Harrisburg, PA 800-692-7429
Hastings Cooperative Creamery
Hastings, MN 651-437-9414
Heritage Dairy Stores
Thorofare, NJ
Heritage Farms Dairy
Murfreesboro, TN. 615-895-2790

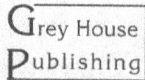

Herkimer Foods
Herkimer, NY 315-895-7832
High's Dairies
Jessup, MD 301-776-7727
Highland Dairies
Wichita, KS. . . . 800-336-0765
Hiland Dairy Foods Company
Joplin, MO 417-623-2272
Hillside Dairy
Stanley, WI 715-644-2275
Homestead Dairies
Massena, NY. . . . 315-769-2456
Horizon Organic
Broomfield, CO 888-494-3020
Horstmann Mix & Cream
Long Island City, NY 718-932-4735
Houlton Farms Dairy
Houlton, ME 207-532-3170
HP Hood
Lynnfield, MA 800-343-6592
Humboldt Creamery Association
Fortuna, CA 707-725-6182
Hygeia Dairy Company
Corpus Christi, TX 361-854-4561
Ideal American
Holland, IN 812-424-3351
Independent Dairy
Monroe, MI. . . . 734-241-6016
Inland Northwest Dairies
Spokane, WA. . . . 509-489-8600
Inverness Dairy
Cheboygan, MI 231-627-4655
Jackson Milk & Ice CreamCompany
Hutchinson, KS. . . . 620-663-1244
Juniper Valley Farms
Jamaica, NY 718-291-3333
Kalamazoo Creamery
Kalamazoo, MI 616-343-2558
KDK Inc
Draper, UT 801-571-3506
Kemps
Cedarburg, WI. . . . 262-377-5040
Kemps
Saint Paul, MN 800-322-9566
Kleinpeter Farms Dairy
Baton Rouge, LA 225-753-2121
Lakeview Farms
Delphos, OH 800-755-9925
Land O'Lakes Procurement
Sioux Falls, SD. . . . 605-330-9526
Land O'Lakes, Inc.
Arden Hills, MN 800-328-9680
Land-O-Sun Dairies
O Fallon, IL. . . . 314-436-6820
LeHigh Valley Dairies
Lansdale, PA 215-855-8205
Level Valley Creamery
Antioch, TN 800-251-1292
Liberty Dairy
Evart, MI. . . . 800-632-5552
Longacres Modern Dairy
Barto, PA. . . . 610-845-7551
Losurdo Foods
Hackensack, NJ. . . . 888-567-8736
Lowell-Paul Dairy
Greeley, CO. . . . 970-353-0278
Lubbers Dairy
Pella, IA 515-628-4284
Ludwig Dairy
Dixon, IL. . . . 815-284-7791
Magic Valley Quality Milk Producers
Jerome, ID. . . . 208-324-7519
Mallorie's Dairy
Silverton, OR 503-873-5346
Maola Milk & Ice Cream Company
Summerville, SC. . . . 803-871-6311
Maple Hill Farms
Bloomfield, CT. . . . 800-842-7304
Marburger Farm Dairy
Evans City, PA 800-331-1295
Maryland & Virginia Milk Cooperative Association
Reston, VA 703-742-6800
Maryland & Virginia Milk Producers Cooperative
Reston, VA 703-742-4250
Matanuska Maid Dairy
Anchorage, AK. . . . 907-561-5223
McArthur Dairy
Fort Myers, FL 239-334-1114
McArthur Dairy
Miami, FL. . . . 305-795-7700
McArthur Dairy
Miami, FL. . . . 877-803-6565

Meadow Brook Dairy
Erie, PA. . . . 800-352-4010
Meadow Gold Dairies
Honolulu, HI. . . . 800-362-8531
Meadow Gold Dairies
Orem, UT 801-225-3660
Meadowbrook Farm
Bronx, NY. . . . 718-828-6400
MEYENBERG Goat Milk Products
Turlock, CA 800-891-4628
Meyer Brothers Dairy
Maple Plain, MN. . . . 952-473-7343
Michigan Milk Producers Association
Ovid, MI 989-834-2221
Mid States Dairy
Hazelwood, MO 314-731-1150
Mid-States Dairy Company
St. Louis, MO 800-264-4400
Midstates Dairy
Hazelwood, MO 314-731-1150
Minerva Dairy
Minerva, OH. . . . 330-868-4196
Mitchel Dairies
Bronx, NY. . . . 718-324-6261
Monument Dairy Farms
Weybridge, VT 802-545-2119
Monument Farms
Middlebury, VT. . . . 802-545-2119
Morning Star Foods
Tempe, AZ 480-966-0080
Morning Star Foods
East Brunswick, NJ. . . . 800-237-5320
Mountainside Farms Dairy
Roxbury, NY. . . . 607-326-3320
Muller-Pinehurst Dairy C
Rockford, IL 815-968-0441
Munroe Dairy
East Providence, RI 401-438-4450
Murdock Farm Dairy
Winchendon, MA 978-297-0143
Mystic Lake Dairy
Sammamish, WA. . . . 425-868-2029
Natural By Nature
West Grove, PA. . . . 610-268-6962
Nature's Dairy
Roswell, NM. . . . 575-623-9640
Newburgh Egg Processing
Woodridge, NY. . . . 888-434-8115
Niagara Milk Cooperative
Niagara Falls, NY. . . . 716-692-6543
Norco Ranch
Fontana, CA 951-737-6735
Northumberland Cooperative
Miramichi, NB 800-332-3328
Norwalk Dairy
Santa Fe Springs, CA 562-921-5712
Oak Farm's Dairy
Waco, TX 254-756-5421
Oak Grove Dairy
Saint Paul, MN 800-322-9566
Oberweis Dairy
North Aurora, IL. . . . 888-645-5868
Peeler's Jersey Farms
Gaffney, SC. . . . 864-487-9996
Perham Cooperative Cream
Savannah, GA. . . . 800-551-0777
Pet Milk
Florence, SC 800-735-3066
Pierz Cooperative Association
Pierz, MN 320-468-6655
Pioneer Dairy
Southwick, MA. . . . 413-569-6132
Plains Dairy Products
Amarillo, TX. . . . 800-365-5608
Polly-O Dairy Products
Mineola, NY 516-741-8000
Potomac Farms
Cumberland, MD 301-722-4410
Potter Siding Creamery Company
Tripoli, IA. . . . 319-882-4444
Praire Farms Dairy
Anderson, IN. . . . 765-649-1261
Prairie Farms Dairy
Granite City, IL. . . . 618-451-5600
Primer Foods Corporation
Cameron, WI. . . . 80- 3-5 24
Producers Dairy Foods
Fresno, CA 559-264-6583
Purity Dairies
Nashville, TN 615-244-1900
Quality Chekd Dairies
Naperville, IL 630-717-1110

Quality Dairy Company
East Lansing, MI. . . . 517-319-4114
Queensboro Farm Products
Jamaica, NY 718-658-5000
R.D. Hemond Farms
Minot, ME. . . . 207-345-5611
Radway's Dairy
New Britain, CT 800-472-3929
Readington Farms
Whitehouse, NJ. . . . 908-534-2121
Reiter Dairy
Akron, OH. . . . 800-362-0825
Reiter Dairy
Springfield, OH. . . . 937-323-5777
Richardson's Ice Cream
Middleton, MA 978-774-5450
Richfood Dairy
Richmond, VA. . . . 804-746-6206
Riser Foods
Cleveland, OH 216-292-7000
Ritchey's Dairy
Martinsburg, PA 800-296-2157
Robinson Dairy
Denver, CO. . . . 800-332-6355
Rockview Farms
Downey, CA 800- 42- 247
Ronnybrook Farm Dairy
Ancramdale, NY. . . . 800-772-6455
Rosebud Creamery
Plattsburgh, NY 518-561-5160
Royal Crest Dairy Company
Denver, CO. . . . 303-777-2227
Rutter Brothers Dairy
York, PA 800-840-1664
S.B. Winsor Dairy
Johnston, RI 401-231-7832
S.T. Jerrell Company
Bessemer, AL 205-426-8930
Safeway Milk Plant
Tempe, AZ 480-894-4391
Saint Albans Cooperative Creamery
Saint Albans, VT. . . . 800-559-0343
Sani Dairy
Altoona, PA. . . . 814-943-3077
Sani-Dairy
Punxsutawney, PA. . . . 814-938-7200
Schneider's Dairy Holdings Inc
Pittsburgh, PA. . . . 412-881-3525
Schreiber Foods Plant
Gainesville, GA 770-534-2239
Seger Egg Corporation
Farina, IL. . . . 618-245-3301
Shenandoah's Pride
Springfield, VA. . . . 703-321-9500
Skinners' Dairy
Ponte Vedra Beach, FL. . . . 904-733-5440
Snow Dairy
Springville, UT. . . . 801-489-6081
Southeast Dairy Processors
Tampa, FL. . . . 813-621-3233
Southern Bell Dairy
Somerset, KY 800-468-4798
Spring Hill Farm Dairy
Haverhill, MA. . . . 978-373-3481
Stop & Shop Manufacturing
Readville, MA. . . . 508-977-5132
Stremick's Heritage Foods
Santa Ana, CA 800-371-9010
Sunshine Dairy
Middletown, CT 860-346-6644
Sunshine Dairy Foods
Portland, OR. . . . 503-234-7526
Superbrand Dairies
Miami, FL. . . . 305-769-6600
Superstore Industries
Fairfield, CA. . . . 707-864-0502
Swiss Dairy
Riverside, CA 951-898-9427
Swiss Valley Farms Company
Davenport, IA. . . . 563-468-6600
Tamarack Farms Dairy
Newark, OH 866-221-4141
Tanglewood Farms
Warsaw, VA. . . . 804-394-4505
Taylor All Star Dairy Foods
Ambridge, PA 724-266-2370
Thomas Dairy
Rutland, VT 802-773-6788
Toft Dairy
Sandusky, OH 800-521-4606
Tom Davis & Sons Dairy Company
Oak Park, MI. . . . 800-399-6970

Turner Dairy Farms
Penn Hills, PA 800-892-1039
Tuscan/Lehigh Valley Dais
Lansdale, PA 800-937-3233
Umpqua Dairy Products Company
Roseburg, OR 541-672-2638
Union Dairy Fountain
Freeport, IL 815-233-2233
United Dairy
Uniontown, PA 800-966-6455
United Dairy Farmers
Cincinnati, OH 513-396-8700
United Dairymen of Arizona
Tempe, AZ 480-966-7211
United Valley Bell Dairy
Charleston, WV 304-344-2511
Upstate Farms Cooperative
Rochester, NY 585-458-1880
Valley Milk Products
Strasburg, VA 540-465-5113
Van Peenans Dairy
Wayne, NJ 973-694-2551
Velvet Freeze Ice Cream
Saint Louis, MO 800-589-5000
Vitamilk Dairy
Bellingham, WA 206-529-4128
W.J. Stearns & Sons/Mountain Dairy
Storrs Mansfield, CT 860-423-9289
Wallaby Yogurt Company
American Canyon, CA 707-553-1233
Wawa Food Market
Media, PA 800-444-9292
Webco Foods
Miami, FL
Welsh Farms
Newark, NJ 973-642-3000
Wengert's Dairy
Lebanon, PA 800-222-2129
Wessanan
Minneapolis, MN 612-331-3775
Whitney Foods
Jamaica, NY 718-291-3333
Winchester Farms Dairy
Winchester, KY 859-745-5500
Wurth Dairy
Caseyville, IL 217-271-7580
Young's Jersey Dairy
Yellow Springs, OH 937-325-0629

Goat

Abunda Life Laboratories
Asbury Park, NJ 732-775-7575
C.F. Burger Creamery
Detroit, MI 800-229-2322
Coach Farm Enterprises
Pine Plains, NY 800-999-4628
Cypress Grove Chevre
Arcata, CA 707-825-1100
MEYENBERG Goat Milk Products
Turlock, CA 800-891-4628
Oak Knoll Dairy
Windsor, VT 802-674-5426
Sunshine Farms
Portage, WI 608-742-2016
Woolwich Dairy
Orangeville, ON 877-438-3499

Half & Half

Broughton Foods
Marietta, OH 800-283-2479
Cass Clay Creamery
Fargo, ND 701-293-6455
Chase Brothers Dairy
Oxnard, CA 800-438-6455
Cropp Cooperative-Organic Valley
La Farge, WI 888-444-6455
Flagship Atlanta Dairy
Belleview, FL 800-224-0669
Inland Northwest Dairies
Spokane, WA 509-489-8600
Instantwhip: Arizona
Phoenix, AZ 800-454-7878
Kemps
Cedarburg, WI 262-377-5040
Oak Knoll Dairy
Windsor, VT 802-674-5426
Prairie Farms Dairy Inc.
Carlinville, IL 217-854-2547
Safeway Milk Plant
Tempe, AZ 480-894-4391
Tiller Foods Company
Dayton, OH 937-435-4601
Whitewave Foods Company
Broomfield, CO 303-635-4000
Yoder Dairies
Chesapeake, VA 757-482-4068

Lactose-Free

Cropp Cooperative-Organic Valley
La Farge, WI 888-444-6455
Prairie Farms Dairy
O Fallon, IL 618-632-3632

Low-Fat

Anderson Erickson Dairy
Des Moines, IA 515-265-2521
Berkeley Farms
Hayward, CA 510-265-8600
Chase Brothers Dairy
Oxnard, CA 800-438-6455
Cloverland Green Spring Dairy
Baltimore, MD 800-876-6455
Coburg Dairy
North Charleston, SC 843-554-4870
Country Fresh Farms
Salt Lake City, UT 800-878-0099
Cream O'Weaver Dairy
Salt Lake City, UT 801-973-9922
Dairy Maid Dairy
Frederick, MD 301-695-0431
Darigold
Seattle, WA 800-333-6455
Humboldt Creamery Association
Fortuna, CA 707-725-6182
Ideal American
Holland, IN 812-424-3351
KDK Inc
Draper, UT 801-571-3506
Level Valley Creamery
Antioch, TN 800-251-1292
Marva Maid Dairy
Newport News, VA 800-544-4439
McArthur Dairy
Miami, FL 305-795-7700
Meadow Brook Dairy
Erie, PA 800-352-4010
Mid States Dairy
Hazelwood, MO 314-731-1150
Pleasant View Dairy
Highland, IN 219-838-0155
Reiter Dairy
Springfield, OH 937-323-5777
Safeway Milk Plant
Tempe, AZ 480-894-4391
Schneider Valley Farms Dairy
Williamsport, PA 570-326-2021
Schneider's Dairy Holdings Inc
Pittsburgh, PA 412-881-3525
Swiss Dairy
Riverside, CA 951-898-9427
T.G. Lee Dairy
Orlando, FL 407-894-4941
Tuscan/Lehigh Valley Dais
Lansdale, PA 800-937-3233
Wengert's Dairy
Lebanon, PA 800-222-2129
Winchester Farms Dairy
Winchester, KY 859-745-5500
Yoder Dairies
Chesapeake, VA 757-482-4068

Reduced-Fat

Berkeley Farms
Hayward, CA 510-265-8600
Coburg Dairy
North Charleston, SC 843-554-4870
Cream O'Weaver Dairy
Salt Lake City, UT 801-973-9922
Dairy Maid Dairy
Frederick, MD 301-695-0431
Darigold
Seattle, WA 800-333-6455
Humboldt Creamery Association
Fortuna, CA 707-725-6182
Ideal American
Holland, IN 812-424-3351
KDK Inc
Draper, UT 801-571-3506
Marva Maid Dairy
Newport News, VA 800-544-4439
McArthur Dairy
Miami, FL 305-795-7700
Meadow Brook Dairy
Erie, PA 800-352-4010
Mid States Dairy
Hazelwood, MO 314-731-1150
Norwalk Dairy
Santa Fe Springs, CA 562-921-5712
Pleasant View Dairy
Highland, IN 219-838-0155
Reiter Dairy
Springfield, OH 937-323-5777
Safeway Milk Plant
Tempe, AZ 480-894-4391
Schneider Valley Farms Dairy
Williamsport, PA 570-326-2021
Schneider's Dairy Holdings Inc
Pittsburgh, PA 412-881-3525
Swiss Dairy
Riverside, CA 951-898-9427
Tuscan/Lehigh Valley Dais
Lansdale, PA 800-937-3233
Wengert's Dairy
Lebanon, PA 800-222-2129
Winchester Farms Dairy
Winchester, KY 859-745-5500
Yoder Dairies
Chesapeake, VA 757-482-4068

Skim

Agri-Mark
Lawrence, MA 978-689-4442
Berkeley Farms
Hayward, CA 510-265-8600
Chase Brothers Dairy
Oxnard, CA 800-438-6455
Cloverland Green Spring Dairy
Baltimore, MD 800-876-6455
Coburg Dairy
North Charleston, SC 843-554-4870
Country Fresh Farms
Salt Lake City, UT 800-878-0099
Cream O'Weaver Dairy
Salt Lake City, UT 801-973-9922
Cropp Cooperative-Organic Valley
La Farge, WI 888-444-6455
Crowley Foods
Binghamton, NY 800-637-0019
Cumberland Dairy
Rosenhayn, NJ 856-451-1300
Dairy Farmers of America
Knoxville, TN 865-218-8500
Dairy Maid Dairy
Frederick, MD 301-695-0431
IMAC
Oklahoma City, OK 888-878-7827
KDK Inc
Draper, UT 801-571-3506
Marva Maid Dairy
Newport News, VA 800-544-4439
McArthur Dairy
Miami, FL 305-795-7700
Meadow Brook Dairy
Erie, PA 800-352-4010
Mid States Dairy
Hazelwood, MO 314-731-1150
Pleasant View Dairy
Highland, IN 219-838-0155
Prairie Farms Dairy
O Fallon, IL 618-632-3632
Reiter Dairy
Springfield, OH 937-323-5777
Safeway Milk Plant
Tempe, AZ 480-894-4391
Saint Albans Cooperative Creamery
Saint Albans, VT 800-559-0343
Schneider Valley Farms Dairy
Williamsport, PA 570-326-2021
Schneider's Dairy Holdings Inc
Pittsburgh, PA 412-881-3525
Stewart's Ice Cream
Saratoga Springs, NY 518-581-1300
Wengert's Dairy
Lebanon, PA 800-222-2129
White Wave Foods
Jacksonville, FL 800-874-6765
Winchester Farms Dairy
Winchester, KY 859-745-5500
Yoder Dairies
Chesapeake, VA 757-482-4068

Strawberry

Berkeley Farms
Hayward, CA 510-265-8600
Hygeia Dairy Company
Corpus Christi, TX 361-854-4561
Prairie Farms Dairy
O Fallon, IL. 618-632-3632
Tuscan/Lehigh Valley Dais
Lansdale, PA. 800-937-3233

Sweetened

All American Foods, Inc.
Mankato, MN 800-833-2661
Gateway Food Products Company
Dupo, IL 877-220-1963
Level Valley Creamery
Antioch, TN 800-251-1292

Sweetened & Condensed

Arnhem Group
Cranford, NJ 800-851-1052
Reilly Dairy & Food Company
Tampa, FL. 813-839-8458
Suprema Specialties
Manteca, CA. 209-858-9696

Vanilla Flavored

Prairie Farms Dairy
O Fallon, IL. 618-632-3632

Whole

Berkeley Farms
Hayward, CA 510-265-8600
Cloverland Green Spring Dairy
Baltimore, MD 800-876-6455
Coburg Dairy
North Charleston, SC 843-554-4870
Cream O'Weaver Dairy
Salt Lake City, UT 801-973-9922
Cropp Cooperative-Organic Valley
La Farge, WI. 888-444-6455
Crowley Foods
Binghamton, NY. 800-637-0019
Cumberland Dairy
Rosenhayn, NJ 856-451-1300
Dairy Farmers of America
Knoxville, TN. 865-218-8500
DairyAmerica
Fresno, CA 800-722-3110
Darigold
Seattle, WA. 800-333-6455
KDK Inc
Draper, UT 801-571-3506
Level Valley Creamery
Antioch, TN 800-251-1292
Marva Maid Dairy
Newport News, VA. 800-544-4439
McArthur Dairy
Miami, FL. 305-795-7700
Meadow Brook Dairy
Erie, PA. 800-352-4010
Plainview Milk Products Cooperative
Plainview, MN 507-534-3872
Pleasant View Dairy
Highland, IN. 219-838-0155
Prairie Farms Dairy
O Fallon, IL. 618-632-3632
Reiter Dairy
Springfield, OH. 937-323-5777
Safeway Milk Plant
Tempe, AZ 480-894-4391
Saint Albans Cooperative Creamery
Saint Albans, VT. 800-559-0343
Schneider Valley Farms Dairy
Williamsport, PA. 570-326-2021
Schneider's Dairy Holdings Inc
Pittsburgh, PA. 412-881-3525
Stewart's Ice Cream
Saratoga Springs, NY 518-581-1300
T.G. Lee Dairy
Orlando, FL. 407-894-4941
Tuscan/Lehigh Valley Dais
Lansdale, PA. 800-937-3233
Unified Western Grocers
Los Angeles, CA. 323-731-8223
Upstate Farms Cooperative
Buffalo, NY. 866-874-6455
Winchester Farms Dairy
Winchester, KY. 859-745-5500
Yoder Dairies
Chesapeake, VA 757-482-4068

Milk Products

Milk & Milk Fat: Enzyme

Brown's Dairy
New Orleans, LA 504-529-2221
Country Delite
Nashville, TN 615-320-1440
Country Fresh
Livonia, MI. 800-968-7980
Darigold
Seattle, WA. 800-333-6455
Farmers Cooperative Dairy
Halifax, NS. 800-565-1945
Garden Spot Distributors
New Holland, PA 800-829-5100
Idaho Milk Products
Jerome, ID. 208-644-2882
Maple Island
Saint Paul, MN 800-369-1022
Wilcox Farm
Roy, WA 360-458-7774

Milk Proteins

Arla Foods Ingredients
Basking Ridge, NJ 908-604-8551
Austrade Food Ingredients
Palm Beach Gdns, FL. 561-586-7145
Clofine Dairy & Food Products
Linwood, NJ 800-441-1001
Erie Foods International
Erie, IL 800-447-1887
Kantner Group
Wapakoneta, OH. 419-738-4060
Luxembourg Cheese Factory
Orangeville, IL 815-789-4227
Main Street Ingredients
La Crosse, WI. 800-359-2345

Modified - Dry Blends

Kantner Group
Wapakoneta, OH. 419-738-4060

Milk Solids

Non-Fat

California Dairies
Visalia, CA 559-625-2200
Kantner Group
Wapakoneta, OH. 419-738-4060
Main Street Ingredients
La Crosse, WI. 800-359-2345
Ramsen
Lakeville, MN. 952-431-0400

Replacers

Kantner Group
Wapakoneta, OH. 419-738-4060

Whole

Kantner Group
Wapakoneta, OH. 419-738-4060
MEYENBERG Goat Milk Products
Turlock, CA 800-891-4628
Preferred Milks
Addison, IL. 800-621-5046

Pudding

AFP Advanced Food Products, LLC
Visalia, CA 559-627-2070
Amboy Specialty Foods Company
Dixon, IL. 800-892-0400
Associated Milk Producers
Dawson, MN. 320-769-2994
Associated Milk Producers
Rochester, MN 507-282-7401
Associated Milk Producers
New Ulm, MN. 800-533-3580
Chloe Foods Corporation
Brooklyn, NY 718-827-9000
ConAgra Grocery Products
Irvine, CA 714-680-1000
Dufflet Pastries
Toronto, ON 416-536-9640
Echo Farms Puddings
Hinsdale, NH 866-488-3246
Gehl Foods, Inc.
Germantown, WI. 800-521-2873
Gehl Guernsey Farms
Germantown, WI. 800-434-5713
Good Old Days Foods
Little Rock, AR. 501-565-1257
Gourmet Baker
Burnaby, BC 800-663-1972
GPI USA LLC.
Athens, GA 706-850-7826
Grainaissance
Emeryville, CA. 800-472-4697
Hoffman Aseptic Packaging Company
Hoffman, MN 320-986-2084
Hormel Foods Corporation
Austin, MN 800-523-4635
Inter-American Products
Cincinnati, OH 800-645-2233
Kosto Food Products Company
Wauconda, IL 847-487-2600
Kozy Shack
Hicksville, NY 516-870-3000
Kraft Canada Headquarters
Don Mills, ON 888-572-3806
Michigan Dessert Corporation
Oak Park, MI. 800-328-8632
Noh Foods of Hawaii
Gardena, CA 310-324-6770
Reser's Fine Foods
Salt Lake City, UT 801-972-5633
Serv-Agen Corporation
Cherry Hill, NJ 856-663-6966
Spring Glen Fresh Foods
Ephrata, PA 800-641-2853
Terrapin Ridge Farms
Clearwater, FL 800-999-4052
Van Bennett Food Company
Reading, PA 800-423-8897

Chocolate

Associated Milk Producers
Dawson, MN. 320-769-2994
Associated Milk Producers
Rochester, MN 507-282-7401
Knouse Foods Coop
Peach Glen, PA. 717-677-8181
Kozy Shack
Hicksville, NY 516-870-3000

Plum

Patti's Plum Puddings
Lawndale, CA. 310-376-1463

Rice

Knouse Foods Coop
Peach Glen, PA. 717-677-8181
Kozy Shack
Hicksville, NY 516-870-3000
Penn Maid Crowley Foods
Philadelphia, PA 800-247-6269
Van Bennett Food Company
Reading, PA 800-423-8897

Tapioca

Associated Milk Producers
Dawson, MN. 320-769-2994
Associated Milk Producers
Rochester, MN 507-282-7401
Knouse Foods Coop
Peach Glen, PA. 717-677-8181
Kozy Shack
Hicksville, NY 516-870-3000
Van Bennett Food Company
Reading, PA 800-423-8897

Vanilla

Associated Milk Producers
Dawson, MN. 320-769-2994
Associated Milk Producers
Rochester, MN 507-282-7401
Knouse Foods Coop
Peach Glen, PA. 717-677-8181
Kozy Shack
Hicksville, NY 516-870-3000

Sour Cream

Aimonetto and Sons
Renton, WA. 866-823-2777
Alberto-Culver Company
Melrose Park, IL 708-450-3000
Alta Dena Certified Dairy
City of Industry, CA 800-535-1369
Anderson Erickson Dairy
Des Moines, IA. 515-265-2521
Astro Dairy Products
Etobicoke, ON. 416-622-2811
Auburn Dairy Products
Auburn, WA 800-950-9264
Berkeley Farms
Hayward, CA 510-265-8600
Byrne Dairy
Syracuse, NY 800-899-1535
Campbell Soup Company
Camden, NJ. 800-257-8443
Cascade Fresh
Seattle, WA 800-511-0057
Clofine Dairy & Food Products
Linwood, NJ 800-441-1001
Cloverland Green Spring Dairy
Baltimore, MD 800-876-6455
Coburg Dairy
North Charleston, SC 843-554-4870
ConAgra Grocery Products
Irvine, CA 714-680-1000
Consun Food Industries
Elyria, OH. 440-322-6301
Country Fresh
Grand Rapids, MI 800-748-0480
Creamland Dairies
Albuquerque, NM. 505-247-0721
Cropp Cooperative-Organic Valley
La Farge, WI. 888-444-6455
Crowley Foods
Binghamton, NY. 800-637-0019
Dairy Fresh Corporation
Greensboro, AL. 800-239-5114
Dairy Maid Dairy
Frederick, MD. 301-695-0431
Daisy Brand
Dallas, TX. 877-292-9830
Elgin Dairy Foods
Chicago, IL 800-786-9900
Fairmont Products
Belleville, PA 717-935-2121
Farmers Cooperative Dairy
Halifax, NS 800-565-1945
Friendship Dairies
Dallas, TX. 516-719-4000
Golden Cheese of California
Corona, CA. 800-842-0264
Hunter Farms
High Point, NC 800-446-8035
Inland Northwest Dairies
Spokane, WA. 509-489-8600
Instantwhip Foods
San Antonio, TX. 800-544-9447
Jackson Milk & Ice CreamCompany
Hutchinson, KS. 620-663-1244
Kraft Foods
Walton, NY. 607-865-7131
Marcus Dairy
Danbury, CT 800-243-2511
Marquez Brothers International
Hanford, CA 559-584-8000
Marva Maid Dairy
Newport News, VA. 800-544-4439
Mayfield Dairy Farms
Athens, TN 800-362-9546
Meadow Gold Dairies
Honolulu, HI 800-362-8531
Mid States Dairy
Hazelwood, MO 314-731-1150
Morning Glory/Formost Farms
Baraboo, WI 800-362-9196
Oakhurst Dairy
Portland, ME. 800-482-0718
Old Home Foods
Saint Paul, MN 800-309-9035
Pevely Dairy Company
Hazelwood, MO 314-771-4400
Pleasant View Dairy
Highland, IN 219-838-0155
Prairie Farms Dairy
Carlinville, IL 217-854-2547
Prairie Farms Dairy
Granite City, IL. 618-451-5600
Prairie Farms Dairy
O Fallon, IL. 618-632-3632
Prairie Farms Dairy Inc.
Carlinville, IL 217-854-2547
Purity Dairies
Nashville, TN 615-244-1900
Queensboro Farm Products
Canastota, NY. 315-697-2235
Queensboro Farm Products
Jamaica, NY 718-658-5000
Reilly Dairy & Food Company
Tampa, FL. 813-839-8458
Roberts Dairy Foods
Kansas City, MO. 800-279-1692
Robinson Dairy
Denver, CO 800-332-6355
Rod's Food Products
City of Industry, CA 909-839-8925
Roos Foods
Kenton, DE 800-343-3642
Rosenberger's Dairies
Hatfield, PA. 800-355-9074
Schepps Dairy
Dallas, TX. 800-395-7004
Schneider Valley Farms Dairy
Williamsport, PA. 570-326-2021
Schreiber Foods Plant
Shippensburg, PA 717-530-5000
Sinton Dairy Foods Company
Colorado Springs, CO. 800-388-4970
Sisler's Ice & Ice Cream
Ohio, IL. 888-891-3856
Springfield Creamery
Eugene, OR. 541-689-2911
Sterzing Food Company
Burlington, IA. 800-754-8467
Tiller Foods Company
Dayton, OH. 937-435-4601
Umpqua Dairy Products Company
Roseburg, OR 541-672-2638
Upstate Farms Cooperative
Buffalo, NY. 716-892-2121
V & V Supremo Foods
Chicago, IL 888-887-8773
Vitamilk Dairy
Bellingham, WA 206-529-4128
Wells' Dairy
Le Mars, IA. 800-942-3800
Winder Dairy
West Valley, UT 800-946-3371

Yogurt

Agro Farma Inc.
New Berlin, NY 877-847-6181
Aimonetto and Sons
Renton, WA. 866-823-2777
Alta Dena Certified Dairy
City of Industry, CA 800-535-1369
Anderson Erickson Dairy
Des Moines, IA. 515-265-2521
Associated Milk Producers
New Ulm, MN. 800-533-3580
Astro Dairy Products
Etobicoke, ON. 416-622-2811
Auburn Dairy Products
Auburn, WA 800-950-9264
Ben & Jerry's Homemade
South Burlington, VT 802-846-1500
Berkeley Farms
Hayward, CA 510-265-8600
Broughton Foods
Marietta, OH. 800-283-2479
Brown Cow Farm
Antioch, CA 888-429-5459
Browns Dairy
Valparaiso, IN 219-464-4141
Byrne Dairy
Syracuse, NY 800-899-1535
Cascade Fresh
Seattle, WA 800-511-0057
Cass Clay Creamery
Fargo, ND 701-293-6455
Cedar Crest Specialties
Cedarburg, WI. 800-877-8341
Clofine Dairy & Food Products
Linwood, NJ 800-441-1001
Cloverland Green Spring Dairy
Baltimore, MD 800-876-6455
Coach Farm Enterprises
Pine Plains, NY. 800-999-4628
Continental Yogurt
Glendale, CA 818-240-7400
Country Fresh
Grand Rapids, MI 800-748-0480
Dairy Maid Dairy
Frederick, MD. 301-695-0431
Dannon Company
Fort Worth, TX 800-211-6565
Dunkin Brands Inc.
Canton, MA 800-458-7731
Fage USA
Johnsontown, NY 518-762-5912
Farmers Cooperative Dairy
Halifax, NS 800-565-1945
Farmland Dairies
Wallington, NJ 888-727-6252
Fieldbrook Farms
Dunkirk, NY 800-333-0805
Flagship Atlanta Dairy
Belleview, FL 800-224-0669
Fresh Dairy Direct/Morningstar
Dallas, TX. 800-395-7004
Friendship Dairies
Dallas, TX. 516-719-4000
General Mills
Minneapolis, MN 800-248-7310
Glover's Ice Cream
Frankfort, IN. 800-686-5163
GPI USA LLC.
Athens, GA 706-850-7826
Heritage Farms Dairy
Murfreesboro, TN. 615-895-2790
Hiland Dairy Foods Company
Branson, MO. 417-334-0090
Icelandic Milk and Skyr Corporation
New York, NY 212-966-6950
Imperial Foods
Long Island City, NY 718-784-3400
Innovative Food Solutions LLC
Columbus, OH 800-884-3314
J&J Snack Foods Corporation
Pennsauken, NJ. 800-486-9533
Jackson Ice Cream Company
Denver, CO 303-534-2454
Jason & Son Specialty Foods
Rancho Cordova, CA 800-810-9093
Katie's Korner
Girard, OH 330-539-4140
Klinke Brothers Ice Cream Company
Memphis, TN 901-743-8250
Krinos Foods
Santa Barbara, CA 800-624-4896
Lifeway Foods Inc
Morton Grove, IL 877-281-3874
Lyo-San
Lachute, QC 450-562-8525
Master Mix
Placentia, CA 714-524-1698
Meadow Gold Dairies
Honolulu, HI. 800-362-8531
Michigan Dairy
Livonia, MI. 734-367-5390
Mid States Dairy
Hazelwood, MO 314-731-1150
Mister Snacks
Amherst, NY. 800-333-6393
Mountain High Yogurt
Minneapolis, MN 303-761-2210
Old Chatham Sheepherding
Old Chatham, NY. 888-743-3760
Old Home Foods
Saint Paul, MN 800-309-9035
Parmalat Canada
Toronto, ON 800-563-1515
Pecoraro Dairy Products
Rome, NY. 315-339-0101
Penn Maid Crowley Foods
Philadelphia, PA 800-247-6269
Pioneer Dairy
Southwick, MA. 413-569-6132
Prairie Farms Dairy
Carlinville, IL 217-854-2547
Prairie Farms Dairy
Granite City, IL. 618-451-5600
Prairie Farms Dairy
O Fallon, IL. 618-632-3632
Prairie Farms Dairy Inc.
Carlinville, IL 217-854-2547
Purity Dairies
Nashville, TN 615-244-1900
Quality Ingredients Corporation
Burnsville, MN. 952-898-4002
Queensboro Farm Products
Jamaica, NY 718-658-5000

Reilly Dairy & Food Company
Tampa, FL . . . 813-839-8458
Reiter Dairy
Springfield, OH . . . 937-323-5777
Restaurant Systems International
Staten Island, NY . . . 718-494-8888
Roberts Dairy Foods
Kansas City, MO . . . 800-279-1692
Robinson Dairy
Denver, CO . . . 800-332-6355
Safeway Inc
Pleasanton, CA . . . 877-723-3929
Safeway Stores
Tempe, AZ . . . 480-966-0295
Shade Foods
New Century, KS . . . 800-225-6312
Sinton Dairy Foods Company
Colorado Springs, CO . . . 800-388-4970
Springfield Creamery
Eugene, OR . . . 541-689-2911
Stonyfield Farm
Londonderry, NH . . . 603-437-4040
Superstore Industries
Fairfield, CA . . . 707-864-0502
Toft Dairy
Sandusky, OH . . . 800-521-4606
Tropical Illusions
Trenton, MO . . . 660-359-5422
Ultima Foods
Longueuil, ON . . . 800-363-9496
White Wave
Broomfield, CO . . . 800-488-9283
Yofarm Company
Naugatuck, CT . . . 203-720-0000
Yoplait USA
Minneapolis, MN . . . 800-248-7310

Bases, Flavors, Stabilizers

California Custom Fruits & Flavors
Irwindale, CA . . . 877-558-0056
Cargill Texturizing Solutions
Cedar Rapids, IA . . . 877-650-7080
Idaho Milk Products
Jerome, ID . . . 208-644-2882

Frozen

Blake's Creamery
Manchester, NH . . . 603-623-7242
Brighams
Arlington, MA . . . 800-274-4426
Browns Dairy
Valparaiso, IN . . . 219-464-4141
Byrne Dairy
Syracuse, NY . . . 800-899-1535
Cedar Crest Specialties
Cedarburg, WI . . . 800-877-8341
Dave's Hawaiian Ice Cream
Pearl City, HI . . . 808-453-0500
Edy's Dreyers Grand Ice Cream
Rockaway, NJ . . . 800-362-7899
Edy's Grand Ice Cream
Fort Wayne, IN . . . 260-483-3102
Edy's Grand Ice Cream
Glendale Heights, IL . . . 888-377-3397
Elgin Dairy Foods
Chicago, IL . . . 800-786-9900
Fieldbrook Farms
Dunkirk, NY . . . 800-333-0805
Foster Farms Dairy
Modesto, CA . . . 209-576-2300
Fresh Dairy Direct/Morningstar
Dallas, TX . . . 800-395-7004
Friendly Ice Cream Corporation
Wilbraham, MA . . . 800-966-9970
Glover's Ice Cream
Frankfort, IN . . . 800-686-5163
Hudsonville Creamery & Ice Cream
Holland, MI . . . 616-546-4005
International Yogurt Company
Portland, OR . . . 800-962-7326
J&J Snack Foods Corporation
Pennsauken, NJ . . . 800-486-9533
Jack & Jill Ice Cream Company
Moorestown, NJ . . . 856-813-2300
Jackson Ice Cream Company
Denver, CO . . . 303-534-2454
Klinke Brothers Ice Cream Company
Memphis, TN . . . 901-743-8250
Lafleur Dairy Products,
New Orleans, LA . . . 504-729-3330
MacKay's Cochrane Ice Cream
Cochrane, AB . . . 403-932-2455
Mayfield Dairy Farms
Athens, TN . . . 800-362-9546
O'Boyle's Ice Cream Company
Bristol, PA . . . 215-788-3882
Perry's Ice Cream Company
Akron, NY . . . 800-873-7797
Petersen Ice Cream Company
Oak Park, IL . . . 708-386-6130
Prairie Farms Dairy
O Fallon, IL . . . 618-632-3632
Rainbow Valley Frozen Yogurt
White Lake, MI . . . 800-979-8669
Reinhold Ice Cream Company
Pittsburgh, PA . . . 412-321-7600
Restaurant Systems International
Staten Island, NY . . . 718-494-8888
Sargeant's Army Marketing
Bowmanville, ON . . . 905-623-2888
Stonyfield Farm
Londonderry, NH . . . 603-437-4040
Toft Dairy
Sandusky, OH . . . 800-521-4606
Turkey Hill Dairy
Conestoga, PA . . . 800-693-2479
Vitarich Ice Cream
Fortuna, CA . . . 707-725-6182
Welsh Farms
Clifton, NJ . . . 973-772-2388
Whitey's Ice Cream Manufacturing
Moline, IL . . . 888-594-4839
YoCream International
Portland, OR . . . 800-962-7326

Low-Fat

Alta Dena Certified Dairy
City of Industry, CA . . . 800-535-1369
Auburn Dairy Products
Auburn, WA . . . 800-950-9264
Cascade Fresh
Seattle, WA . . . 800-511-0057
Continental Culture Specialists
Los Angeles, CA . . . 818-240-7400
Fage USA
Johnsontown, NY . . . 518-762-5912
Heini's Cheese Company
Millersburg, OH . . . 800-253-6636
Natren
Thousand Oaks, CA . . . 800-992-3323
Perry's Ice Cream Company
Akron, NY . . . 800-873-7797
Upstate Farms Cooperative
Buffalo, NY . . . 716-892-2121
Vitarich Ice Cream
Fortuna, CA . . . 707-725-6182

No-Fat

Agro Farma Inc.
New Berlin, NY . . . 877-847-6181
Cascade Fresh
Seattle, WA . . . 800-511-0057
Cedar Crest Specialties
Cedarburg, WI . . . 800-877-8341
Continental Culture Specialists
Los Angeles, CA . . . 818-240-7400
Fage USA
Johnsontown, NY . . . 518-762-5912
Gifford's Dairy
Skowhegan, ME . . . 207-474-9821
O'Boyle's Ice Cream Company
Bristol, PA . . . 215-788-3882
Perry's Ice Cream Company
Akron, NY . . . 800-873-7797
Vitarich Ice Cream
Fortuna, CA . . . 707-725-6182

with Fruit

Byrne Dairy
Syracuse, NY . . . 800-899-1535
Petersen Ice Cream Company
Oak Park, IL . . . 708-386-6130
Stonyfield Farm
Londonderry, NH . . . 603-437-4040
Yoplait USA
Minneapolis, MN . . . 800-248-7310

Doughs, Mixes & Fillings

Batters

Breading

ADM Food Ingredients
Olathe, KS. 800-255-6637
Blend Pak
Bloomfield, KY 502-252-8000
Chef Merito
Encino, CA 800-637-4861
Concord Foods
Brockton, MA 508-580-1700
Dorothy Dawson Foods Products
Jackson, MI. 517-788-9830
Drum Rock Specialty Company
Warwick, RI 401-737-5165
Fry Krisp Food Products
Jackson, MI. 517-784-8531
Griffith Laboratories
Alsip, IL 800-346-9494
Griffith Laboratories Worldwide
Alsip, IL 800-346-4743
Hydroblend
Nampa, ID. 208-467-7441
McCormick & Company
Sparks, MD 800-632-5847
Mojave Foods Corporation
Commerce, CA 323-890-8900
Newly Weds Foods
Decatur, AL. 800-521-6189
Old Mansion Foods
Petersburg, VA 800-476-1877
Premier Blending
Wichita, KS. 316-267-5533
Quality Naturally! Foods
City of Industry, CA 888-498-6986
Randag & Associates Inc
Elmhurst, IL 630-530-2830
Reggie Ball's Cajun Foods
Lake Charles, LA 337-436-0291
Richmond Baking Company
Richmond, IN 765-962-8535
Richmond Baking Company
Alma, GA 912-632-7213
Shenandoah Mills
Lebanon, TN. 615-444-0841
Specialty Products
Cleveland, OH 216-362-1050
Texas Crumb & Food Products
Farmers Branch, TX 800-522-7862
Tova Industries
Louisville, KY 888-532-8682
UFL Foods
Mississauga, ON. 905-670-7776
Wilkins-Rogers
Ellicott City, MD. 410-465-5800
World Flavors
Warminster, PA 215-672-4400
Yorktown Baking Company
Yorktown Heights, NY 800-235-3961

Cake

Frozen

BakeMark USA
Schaumburg, IL. 562-949-1054

Cookie

BakeMark USA
Schaumburg, IL. 562-949-1054
La Francaise Bakery
Melrose Park, IL. 800-654-7220

Muffin

Bagelworks
New York, NY 212-744-6444
BakeMark USA
Schaumburg, IL. 562-949-1054
Coby's Cookies
Toronto, ON 416-633-1567
France Croissant
New York, NY 212-888-1210

Pancake

Dry

Hansmann's Mills
Binghamton, NY. 607-722-1372

Breading

ADM Food Ingredients
Olathe, KS. 800-255-6637
Andy's Seasoning
St Louis, MO. 800-305-3004
Atkinson Milling Company
Selma, NC. 800-948-5707
Blend Pak
Bloomfield, KY 502-252-8000
Blendex Company
Jeffersontown, KY 800-626-6325
Care Ingredients
Melrose Park, IL. 708-450-3260
Chef Hans Gourmet Foods
Monroe, LA. 800-890-4267
Colonna Brothers
North Bergen, NJ 201-864-1115
Dorothy Dawson Foods Products
Jackson, MI. 517-788-9830
Drum Rock Specialty Company
Warwick, RI 401-737-5165
Drusilla Seafood Packing & Processing Company
Baton Rouge, LA 800-364-8844
Griffith Laboratories Worldwide
Alsip, IL 800-346-4743
House-Autry Mills
Four Oaks, NC 800-849-0802
Hydroblend
Nampa, ID. 208-467-7441
Kraft Canada Headquarters
Don Mills, ON 888-572-3806
Lakeside Mills
Rutherfordton, NC 828-286-4866
McClancy Seasoning Company
Fort Mill, SC. 800-843-1968
Newly Weds Foods
Chicago, IL 800-621-7521
Oak Grove Smokehouse
Prairieville, LA 225-673-6857
Old Mansion Foods
Petersburg, VA 800-476-1877
Praters Foods
Lubbock, TX. 806-745-2727
Premier Blending
Wichita, KS. 316-267-5533
Quality Bakery Products
Fort Lauderdale, FL 800-590-3663
Randag & Associates Inc
Elmhurst, IL 630-530-2830
Richmond Baking Company
Richmond, IN 765-962-8535
Roland Industries
Saint Louis, MO 800-325-1183
Shenandoah Mills
Lebanon, TN. 615-444-0841
Southeastern Mills
Rome, GA. 800-334-4468
Specialty Products
Cleveland, OH 216-362-1050
Taste Maker Foods
Memphis, TN 800-467-1407
Texas Crumb & Food Products
Farmers Branch, TX 800-522-7862
Tova Industries
Louisville, KY 888-532-8682
Wilkins-Rogers
Ellicott City, MD. 410-465-5800
World Flavors
Warminster, PA 215-672-4400

Doughs

Athens Baking Company
Fresno, CA 559-485-3024
Bridgford Foods Corporation
Anaheim, CA 800-527-2105
Carolina Foods
Charlotte, NC 800-234-0441
Cohen's Bakery
Buffalo, NY. 716-892-8149
Creme Curls Bakery
Hudsonville, MI 800-466-1219
Dimitria Delights
North Grafton, MA 800-763-1113
Dufour Pastry Kitchens
Bronx, NY. 800-439-1282
Entenmann's-Oroweat/BestFoods
South San Francisco, CA 650-583-5828
Gonnella Frozen Products
Schaumburg, IL. 847-884-8829
Leon's Bakery
North Haven, CT. 800-223-6844
Northwestern Foods
Saint Paul, MN 800-236-4937
Orange Bakery
Irvine, CA 949-863-1377
Ranaldi Bros Frozen Food Products Inc
Warwick, RI 401-738-3444
Rhodes International
Columbus, WI. 800-876-7333
Teeny Foods Corporation
Portland, OR 503-252-3006
TNT Crust
Green Bay, WI. 920-431-7240

Baking

Bridgford Foods Corporation
Anaheim, CA 800-527-2105
Clofine Dairy & Food Products
Linwood, NJ 800-441-1001
Creme Curls Bakery
Hudsonville, MI 800-466-1219
Dufour Pastry Kitchens
Bronx, NY. 800-439-1282
Mine & Mommy's Cookies
Abilene, TX. 325-721-1958
Northwestern Foods
Saint Paul, MN 800-236-4937

Frozen

Bakery Chef
Louisville, KY 800-594-0203
Best Brands Corporation
Minnetonka, MN. 800-866-3300
Callie's Charleston Biscuits LLC
Charleston, SC 843-577-1198
Creme Curls Bakery
Hudsonville, MI 800-466-1219
Dufour Pastry Kitchens
Bronx, NY. 800-439-1282

Bread

Baker Boy Bake Shop
Dickinson, ND 800-437-2008
Country Home Bakers
Atlanta, GA. 800-241-6445
Lone Star Bakery
Round Rock, TX. 512-255-3629
Lora Brody Products
Waltham, MA 617-928-1005
Pacific Ocean Produce
Santa Cruz, CA 831-423-2654
Pyrenees French Bakery
Bakersfield, CA 888-898-7159
Rhodes International
Columbus, WI. 800-876-7333
Senape's Bakery
Hazleton, PA. 570-454-0839

Cookie

Austin Special Foods Company
Austin, TX. 866-372-8663
Best Maid Cookie Company
River Falls, WI 888-444-0322
CBC Foods
Little River, KS. 800-276-4770
Coby's Cookies
Toronto, ON 416-633-1567
David's Cookies
Fairfield, NJ 800-500-2800

Fat Witch Bakery
New York, NY 888-419-4824
Gladder's Gourmet Cookies
Lockhart, TX......................888-398-4523
Lone Star Bakery
Round Rock, TX..................512-255-3629
Michael's Cookies
San Diego, CA 800-822-5384
Otis Spunkmeyer
San Leandro, CA..................800-938-1900
Pacific Ocean Produce
Santa Cruz, CA....................831-423-2654
Touche Bakery
London, ON 519-455-0044

Doughnuts

BakeMark Canada
Laval, QC 800-361-4998
Baker Boy Bake Shop
Dickinson, ND 800-437-2008
Country Home Bakers
Atlanta, GA.......................800-241-6445

Frozen

Annie's Frozen Yogurt
Minneapolis, MN 800-969-9648
Austin Special Foods Company
Austin, TX.......................866-372-8663
Baker & Baker, Inc.
Schaumburg, IL....................800-593-5777
Baker Boy Bake Shop
Dickinson, ND 800-437-2008
Bakery Chef
Louisville, KY 800-594-0203
Best Maid Cookie Company
River Falls, WI 888-444-0322
Bridgford Foods Corporation
Anaheim, CA 800-527-2105
Carolina Foods
Charlotte, NC 800-234-0441
City Baker
Calgary, AB.......................403-263-8578
Coby's Cookies
Toronto, ON 416-633-1567
Cookie Tree Bakeries
Salt Lake City, UT................800-998-0111
Country Home Bakers
Atlanta, GA.......................800-241-6445
Creme Curls Bakery
Hudsonville, MI 800-466-1219
Dakota Brands Intl. nal
Jamestown, ND.....................800-844-5073
De-Iorio's Frozen Dough
Utica, NY 800-649-7612
Dimitria Delights
North Grafton, MA 800-763-1113
Dough-To-Go
Santa Clara, CA 408-727-4094
Dufour Pastry Kitchens
Bronx, NY.........................800-439-1282
English Bay Batter
Columbus, OH 614-471-9994
Enterprises Pates et Croutes
Boucherville, QC 450-655-7790
Famous Specialties Company
Island Park, NY...................877-273-6999
France Croissant
New York, NY 212-888-1210
Gonnella Frozen Products
Schaumburg, IL....................847-884-8829
Guttenplan's Frozen Dough
Middletown, NJ 888-422-4357
H.C. Brill Company
Tucker, GA 800-241-8526
Harlan Bakeries
Avon, IN 317-272-3600
La Cookie
Houston, TX 713-784-2722
La Francaise Bakery
Melrose Park, IL..................800-654-7220
Leon's Bakery
North Haven, CT...................800-223-6844
Lone Star Bakery
Round Rock, TX....................512-255-3629
Main Street Custom Foods
Cuyahoga Falls, OH 800-533-6246
Main Street Gourmet
Cuyahoga Falls, OH 800-533-6246
Main Street Gourmet Fundraising
Cuyahoga Falls, OH 800-533-6246
Main Street Muffins
Cuyahoga Falls, OH 800-533-6246
Main Street's Cambritt Cookies
Cuyahoga Falls, OH 800-533-6246
Mel-O-Cream Donuts International
Springfield, IL...................217-483-7272
Michael's Cookies
San Diego, CA 800-822-5384
Morrison Meat Pies
West Valley, UT 801-977-0181
Orange Bakery
Huntersville, NC..................704-875-3003
Orange Bakery
Irvine, CA 949-863-1377
Original Ya-hoo! Baking Company
Sherman, TX.......................800-575-9373
Otis Spunkmeyer
San Leandro, CA...................800-938-1900
Parco Foods
Blue Island, IL 708-371-9200
Quality Naturally! Foods
City of Industry, CA 888-498-6986
Ranaldi Bros Frozen Food Products Inc
Warwick, RI 401-738-3444
Rhodes Bake-N-Serv
Salt Lake City, UT 800-695-0122
Rhodes International
Columbus, WI......................800-876-7333
Rich Products Corporation
Cameron, WI.......................715-458-4556
Rich Products Corporation
Buffalo, NY.......................800-356-7094
Rich Products of Canada
Buffalo, NY.......................800-457-4247
Sinbad Sweets
Fresno, CA 800-350-7933
Tasty Mix Quality Foods
Brooklyn, NY......................866-TAS-TYMX
TNT Crust
Green Bay, WI.....................920-431-7240
Vie de France Yamazaki
Vernon, LA 323-582-1241

Improvers

ADM Food Ingredients
Olathe, KS........................800-255-6637
California Blending Corpany
El Monte, CA 626-448-1918

Pizza

Baker Boy Bake Shop
Dickinson, ND 800-437-2008
BBU Bakeries
Denver, CO 303-691-6342
Cohen's Bakery
Buffalo, NY.......................716-892-8149
Entenmann's-Oroweat/BestFoods
South San Francisco, CA 650-583-5828
Northwestern Foods
Saint Paul, MN 800-236-4937
Oroweat Baking Company
Montebello, CA 323-721-5161
Senape's Bakery
Hazleton, PA......................570-454-0839
TNT Crust
Green Bay, WI.....................920-431-7240
Weisenberger Mills
Midway, KY 800-643-8678

Frozen

Oroweat Baking Company
Montebello, CA 323-721-5161
TNT Crust
Green Bay, WI.....................920-431-7240

Fillings

Abel & Schafer
Ronkonkoma, NY....................800-443-1260
Bake'n Joy Foods
North Andover, MA 800-666-4937
Best Brands Corporation
Minnetonka, MN....................800-866-3300
Frank Korinek & Company
Cicero, IL 773-242-1917
Lyons-Magnus
Fresno, CA 559-268-5966
Newport Flavours & Fragrances
Orange, CA........................714-744-3700
Oceana Foods
Shelby, MI........................231-861-2141
Original Ya-hoo! Baking Company
Sherman, TX.......................800-575-9373
Pacific Westcoast Foods
Beaverton, OR 800-874-9333
Patisserie Wawel
Montreal, QC 614-524-3348
Puratos Canada
Mississauga, ON...................905-362-3668
Skjodt-Barrett Foods
Mississauga, ON...................877-600-1200

Baking

Bear Stewart Corporation
Chicago, IL 800-697-2327
Burnette Foods
Elk Rapids, MI 231-264-8116
Burnette Foods
Hartford, MI 616-621-3181
Clements Foods Company
Oklahoma City, OK 800-654-8355
H.C. Brill Company
Tucker, GA 800-241-8526
W&G Flavors
Hunt Valley, MD...................410-771-6606

Cake

Abel & Schafer
Ronkonkoma, NY....................800-443-1260
American Key Food Products
Closter, NJ.......................800-767-0237
Bear Stewart Corporation
Chicago, IL 800-697-2327
Belcolade
Pennsauken, NJ....................856-661-9123
Brookside Foods
Abbotsford, BC....................877-793-3866
California Custom Fruits & Flavors
Irwindale, CA 877-558-0056
Erba Food Products
Brooklyn, NY 718-272-7700
Georgia Nut Ingredients
Skokie, IL 877-674-2993
Golden Foods
Commerce, CA 800-350-2462
Golden West Fruit Company
Commerce, CA 323-726-9419
H.C. Brill Company
Tucker, GA 800-241-8526
Lawrence Foods
Elk Grove Village, IL 800-323-7848
Original Ya-hoo! Baking Company
Sherman, TX.......................800-575-9373
Pacific Westcoast Foods
Beaverton, OR 800-874-9333
Plaidberry Company
Vista, CA.........................760-727-5403
Quality Naturally! Foods
City of Industry, CA 888-498-6986
Skjodt-Barrett Foods
Mississauga, ON...................877-600-1200
Sokol & Company
Countryside, IL...................800-328-7656
Westco-Bake Mark
Pico Rivera, CA 562-949-1054

Chocolate

Erba Food Products
Brooklyn, NY 718-272-7700

Creme

Baker & Baker
Schaumburg, IL....................800-593-5777

Dessert

Chocolate

W&G Flavors
Hunt Valley, MD...................410-771-6606

Cream

Dawn Food Products
Louisville, KY 800-626-2542
Flavor Right Foods Group
Columbus, OH 888-464-3734

Custard

Artuso Pastry Foods Corp
Mt Vernon, NY 914-663-8806

Meringue

Bear Stewart Corporation
Chicago, IL 800-697-2327

Doughnuts

BakeMark USA
Schaumburg, IL. 562-949-1054
James Cowan & Sons
Worcester, MA 508-753-3259
Pamlico Packing Company
Grantsboro, NC. 800-682-1113
Skjodt-Barrett Foods
Mississauga, ON. 877-600-1200

Fruit

Baker & Baker
Schaumburg, IL. 800-593-5777

Pie

Abel & Schafer
Ronkonkoma, NY. 800-443-1260
American Almond Products Company
Brooklyn, NY 800-825-6663
American Key Food Products
Closter, NJ. 800-767-0237
BakeMark Canada
Laval, QC 800-361-4998
Bakemark Ingredients Canada
Richmond, BC 800-665-9441
Baker & Baker, Inc.
Schaumburg, IL. 800-593-5777
Baldwin Richardson Foods
Frankfort, IL 866-644-2732

Liquid ingredient manufacturer specializing in signature sauces, dessert toppings, beverage/pancake syrups, specialty fruit fillings and condiments.

Bear Stewart Corporation
Chicago, IL 800-697-2327
Brookside Foods
Abbotsford, BC. 877-793-3866
Burnette Foods
Elk Rapids, MI 231-264-8116
Burnette Foods
Hartford, MI 616-621-3181
California Custom Fruits & Flavors
Irwindale, CA 877-558-0056
Carriere Foods Inc
Saint-Denis-Sur-Richelie, QC 450-787-3411
Cherry Hill Orchards Pelham
Fenwick, ON. 905-892-3782
Clements Foods Company
Oklahoma City, OK 800-654-8355
Country Cupboard
Virginia City, NV 775-847-7300
Eden Processing
Poplar Grove, IL 815-765-2000
Erba Food Products
Brooklyn, NY 718-272-7700
Frank Korinek & Company
Cicero, IL 773-242-1917
Fruit Fillings
Fresno, CA 559-237-4715
Golden Foods
Commerce, CA 800-350-2462
Golden West Fruit Company
Commerce, CA 323-726-9419
Grandma Hoerner's Foods
Alma, KS. 785-765-2300
H Cantin
Beauport, QC 800-463-5268
Indian Bay Frozen Foods
Centreville, NL 709-678-2844
Key Lime
Smyrna, GA 770-333-0840
Knouse Foods Coop
Paw Paw, MI. 269-657-5524
Knouse Foods Coop
Peach Glen, PA 717-677-8181
Lawrence Foods
Elk Grove Village, IL 800-323-7848
Leahy Orchards
Franklin Centre, QC 800-667-7380
Lynch Foods
North York, ON. 416-449-5464
Michigan Dessert Corporation
Oak Park, MI. 800-328-8632
Nationwide Canning
Cottam, ON. 519-839-4831
Oceana Foods
Shelby, MI. 231-861-2141
Original Ya-hoo! Baking Company
Sherman, TX. 800-575-9373
Pacific Westcoast Foods
Beaverton, OR 800-874-9333
Pearson's Berry Farm
Bowden, AB 403-224-3011
Pied-Mont/Dora
Ste Anne Des Plaines, QC 800-363-8003
Plaidberry Company
Vista, CA. 760-727-5403
Reinhart Foods
Markham, ON. 905-754-3500
Rohtstein Corporation
Woburn, MA 781-935-8300
Schmidt Brothers
Swanton, OH. 419-826-3671
Skjodt-Barrett Foods
Mississauga, ON. 877-600-1200
Steel's Gourmet Foods, Ltd.
Bridgeport, PA 800-678-3357
Valley View Blueberries
Vancouver, WA. 360-892-2839
White-Stokes Company
Chicago, IL 800-978-6537

Mixes

Bountiful Pantry
Nantucket, MA 888-832-6466
Boyd Coffee Company
Portland, OR 800-545-4077
Noh Foods of Hawaii
Honolulu, HI. 808-944-0655
Ontario Foods Exports
Mississauga, ON. 888-466-2372
Paradigm Food Works
Lake Oswego, OR. 503-595-4360
Shawnee Canning Company
Cross Junction, VA 800-713-1414
Terry Foods Inc
Idaho Falls, ID 208-604-8143

Baking

Abel & Schafer
Ronkonkoma, NY. 800-443-1260
ADM Food Ingredients
Olathe, KS. 800-255-6637
ADM Milling Company
Shawnee Mission, KS. 913-491-9400
Adventure Foods
Whittier, NC 828-497-4113
America's Classic Foods
Cambria, CA. 805-927-0745
Annie's Frozen Yogurt
Minneapolis, MN 800-969-9648
Bake'n Joy Foods
North Andover, MA 800-666-4937
Bakemark Ingredients Canada
Richmond, BC 800-665-9441
Baker & Baker
Schaumburg, IL. 800-593-5777
Baker & Baker, Inc.
Schaumburg, IL. 800-593-5777
Bakery Chef
Louisville, KY 800-594-0203
Bear Stewart Corporation
Chicago, IL 800-697-2327
Bernard Food Industries
Evanston, IL 800-323-3663
Beth's Fine Desserts
Mill Valley, CA. 415-464-1891
Bette's Diner Products
Berkeley, CA. 510-644-3230
Big Steer Enterprises
Beaumont, TX. 800-421-4951
Blend Pak
Bloomfield, KY 502-252-8000
Blue Chip Group
Salt Lake City, UT 800-878-0099
Brass Ladle Products
Concordville, PA. 800-955-2353
Brookema Company
West Chicago, IL 630-562-2290
Byrd Mill Company
Ashland, VA 888-897-3336
Cafe Du Monde
New Orleans, LA 504-587-0835
Calhoun Bend Mill
Alexandria, LA 800-519-6455
Calico Cottage
Amityville, NY 800-645-5345
Care Ingredients
Melrose Park, IL 708-450-3260
Carol Lee Products
Lawrence, KS 785-842-5489
Century Foods International
Sparta, WI 800-269-1901
Chefmaster
Garden Grove, CA 800-333-7443
Chelsea Milling Company
Chelsea, MI. 734-475-1361
CHR Hansen
Elyria, OH. 800-558-0802
Chukar Cherries
Prosser, WA. 800-624-9544
Cibolo Junction Food & Spice
Albuquerque, NM. 505-888-1987
Cinnabar Specialty Foods
Prescott, AZ 866-293-6433
Clabber Girl Corporation
Terre Haute, IN 812-232-9446
Commodities Marketing, Inc.
Edison, NJ. 732-603-5077
Continental Mills
Seattle, WA 253-872-8400
Cook-In-The-Kitchen
White River Junction, VT. 802-333-4141
Cotswold Cottage Foods
Arvada, CO 800-208-1977
Country Home Creations
Goodrich, MI 800-457-3477
Cowboy Foods
Bozeman, MT 800-759-5489
Cream of the West
Harlowton, MT 800-477-2383
Crum Creek Mills
Springfield, PA 888-607-3500
Cw Resources
New Britain, CT 860-229-7700
Dawn Food Products
Jackson, MI. 800-248-1144
Dawn Food Products
Louisville, KY 800-626-2542
De Coty Coffee Company
San Angelo, TX 800-588-8001
Dorothy Dawson Foods Products
Jackson, MI. 517-788-9830
Dowd & Rogers
Park City, UT 800-669-8877
Dr. Pete's
Savannah, GA. 912-233-3035
Drusilla Seafood Packing & Processing Company
Baton Rouge, LA 800-364-8844
El Peto Products
Cambridge, ON. 800-387-4064
Ellison Milling Company
Lethbridge, AB 403-328-6622
Embassy Flavours Ltd.
Brampton, ON. 800-334-3371
Ener-G Foods
Seattle, WA 800-331-5222
English Bay Batter
Columbus, OH 614-471-9994
Fearn Natural Foods
Thiensville, WI 800-877-8935
Fiera Foods
Toronto, ON 416-744-1010
Food Concentrate Corporation
Oklahoma City, OK 405-840-5633
Frank Korinek & Company
Cicero, IL 773-242-1917
Fresh Dairy Direct/Morningstar
Dallas, TX. 800-395-7004
Fry Krisp Food Products
Jackson, MI. 517-784-8531
Galloway Company
Neenah, WI. 800-722-8903
General Mills
Minneapolis, MN 800-248-7310
Gilster-Mary Lee Corporation
Chester, IL. 800-851-5371
Global Food Industries
Townville, SC 800-225-4152
Good Food
Honey Brook, PA 800-327-4406

Grain Millers
Eden Prairie, MN 800-232-6287
Grain Process Enterprises Ltd.
Scarborough, ON 800-387-5292
Great Grains Milling Company
Scobey, MT. 406-783-5581
Great Recipes Company
Beaverton, OR 800-273-2331
Gregory's Foods
Eagan, MN 800-231-4734
H. Nagel & Son Company
Cincinnati, OH 513-665-4550
H.C. Brill Company
Tucker, GA 800-241-8526
Hansmann's Mills
Binghamton, NY. 607-722-1372
HC Brill Company
Tucker, GA 800-241-8526
Heartland Food Products
Mission, KS 913-831-4446
Heidi's Gourmet Desserts
Tucker, GA 800-241-4166
Heritage Tymes/Pancake House
Spearsville, LA. 806-765-8566
Highland Sugarworks, Inc
Websterville, VT. 800-452-4012
Hodgson Mill Inc.
Effingham, IL 800-525-0177
Hollman Foods
Chicago, IL 888-926-2879
Homes Packaging Company
Millersburg, OH 800-401-2529
Homestead Mills
Cook, MN 800-652-5233
Honeyville Grain
Rancho Cucamonga, CA 888-810-3212
House-Autry Mills
Four Oaks, NC 800-849-0802
Ingredients, Inc.
Buffalo Grove, IL 847-419-9595
Inn Maid Food
Lenox, MA 413-637-2732
International Multifoods Corporation
Orrville, OH 800-664-2942
Iveta Gourmet
Santa Cruz, CA. 831-423-5149
John Gust Foods & Products Corporation
Batavia, IL. 800-756-5886
Johnson's Food Products
Dorchester, MA. 617-265-3400
Kamish Food Products
Chicago, IL 773-725-6959
Karp's
Georgetown, MA 800-373-5277
Little Crow Foods
Warsaw, IN 800-288-2769
Louisiana Gourmet Enterprises
La Place, LA. 985-783-2446
Lynch Foods
North York, ON. 416-449-5464
Maple Grove Farms of Vermont
St Johnsbury, VT. 800-525-2540
Marie Callender's Gourmet Products/Goldrush Products
San Jose, CA. 800-729-5428
Martha Olson's Great Foods
Sutter Creek, CA. 800-973-3966
Midstate Mills
Newton, NC 800-222-1032
Milani Gourmet
Melrose Park, IL. 800-333-0003
Mine & Mommy's Cookies
Abilene, TX. 325-721-1958
Minnesota Specialty Crops
McGregor, MN 800-328-6731
Modern Products/Fearn Natural Foods
Mequon, WI 800-877-8935
Mojave Foods Corporation
Commerce, CA. 323-890-8900
Nantucket Tea Traders
Nantucket, MA 508-325-0203
New Hope Mills
Auburn, NY. 315-252-2676
No Pudge! Foods
Wolfeboro Falls, NH. 888-667-8343
Northwestern Foods
Saint Paul, MN 800-236-4937
Old Country Farms
East Sandwich, MA 888-707-5558
Old Tyme Mill Company
Chicago, IL 773-521-9484
Pak Technologies
Milwaukee, WI. 414-438-8600
Paradise Island Foods
Nanaimo, BC. 800-889-3370
Pelican Bay
Dunedin, FL 800-826-8982
PepsiCo Chicago
Chicago, IL 312-821-1000
Pett Spice Products
Atlanta, GA. 404-691-5235
Pillsbury
Minneapolis, MN 800-775-4777
Premier Blending
Wichita, KS. 316-267-5533
Puratos Canada
Mississauga, ON. 905-362-3668
Purity Foods
Okemos, MI 800-997-7358
Quaker Oats Company
Stockton, CA. 209-982-5580
Quality Naturally! Foods
City of Industry, CA 888-498-6986
R.A.B. Food Group LLC
Secaucus, NJ 201-553-1100
Randag & Associates Inc
Elmhurst, IL 630-530-2830
Real Cookies
Merrick, NY 800-822-5113
Red Rose Trading Company
Wrightsville, PA 717-252-5500
Redco Foods
Windsor, CT 800-645-1190
Reggie Ball's Cajun Foods
Lake Charles, LA 337-436-0291
Reimann Food Classics
Palatine, IL 847-991-1366
Rich Products Corporation
Hilliard, OH. 614-771-1117
Rich Products Corporation
Cameron, WI. 715-458-4556
Richmond Baking Company
Alma, GA 912-632-7213
Roland Industries
Saint Louis, MO 800-325-1183
Roman Meal Milling Company
Fargo, ND 877-282-9743
Roskam Baking Company
Grand Rapids, MI 616-574-5757
S&N Food Company
Mesquite, TX 972-222-1184
Sells Best
Mishawaka, IN 800-837-8368
SFP Food Products
Conway, AR 800-654-5329
Shenandoah Mills
Lebanon, TN. 615-444-0841
SOUPerior Bean & Spice Company
Vancouver, WA 800-878-7687
Southeastern Mills
Rome, GA. 800-334-4468
Spice Advice
Ankeny, IA 800-247-5251
Sticky Fingers Bakeries
Spokane, WA. 800-458-5826
Strossner's Bakery
Greenville, SC. 864-233-3996
Subco Foods Inc
Sheboygan, WI 800-473-0757
Sundial Gardens
Higganum, CT. 860-345-4290
Swagger Foods Corporation
Vernon Hills, IL 847-913-1200
Tait Farm Foods
Centre Hall, PA. 800-787-2716
Tarazi Specialty Foods
Chino, CA. 909-628-3601
Taste Maker Foods
Memphis, TN 800-467-1407
Taste of Gourmet
Indianola, MS 800-833-7731
Tastee Fare
Buchanan, MI
Tasty Mix Quality Foods
Brooklyn, NY. 866-TAS-TYMX
Tasty Selections
Concord, ON. 905-760-2353
Texas Crumb & Food Products
Farmers Branch, TX 800-522-7862
The Lollipop Tree, Inc
Auburn, NY. 800-842-6691
Thorough Fare Gourmet
Marlboro, VT 802-257-5612
Timber Peaks Gourmet
Parker, CO. 800-982-7687
Tova Industries
Louisville, KY 888-532-8682
Valley View Blueberries
Vancouver, WA. 360-892-2839
VIP Foods
Flushing, NY. 718-821-5330
Wall-Rogalsky Milling Company
Mc Pherson, KS 800-835-2067
Wanda's Nature Farm
Lincoln, NE. 800-735-6828
War Eagle Mill
Rogers, AR 479-789-5343
Weisenberger Mills
Midway, KY 800-643-8678
West Pac
Idaho Falls, ID 800-973-7407
Westco-Bake Mark
Pico Rivera, CA 562-949-1054
White Lily Foods Company
Memphis, TN 800-595-1380
Wholesome Classics
Moraga, CA
Wilkins-Rogers
Ellicott City, MD. 410-465-5800
Wilsonhill Farm
South Bend, IN 802-899-2154
Wisconsin Wilderness Food Products
Milwaukee, WI. 800-359-3039
World Flavors
Warminster, PA 215-672-4400
Yorktown Baking Company
Yorktown Heights, NY 800-235-3961

Brownies

Blue Chip Group
Salt Lake City, UT 800-878-0099
Chelsea Milling Company
Chelsea, MI. 734-475-1361

Beverage

Abunda Life Laboratories
Asbury Park, NJ 732-775-7575
Al-Rite Fruits & Syrups
Miami, FL. 305-652-2540
Alexander International (USA)
Brightwaters, NY 866-965-0143
Alkinco
New York, NY. 800-424-7118
American Beverage Marketers
New Albany, IN 812-941-0072
American Beverage Marketers
Leawood, KS. 913-451-8311
Associated Brands Inc.
Medina, NY. 800-265-0050
Atlantic Seasonings
Kinston, NC 800-433-5261
Autocrat Coffee & Extracts
Lincoln, RI 800-288-6272
Bacardi Canada, Inc.
Brampton, ON. 905-451-6100
Bainbridge Festive Foods
Tunica, MS 800-545-9205
Baldwin Richardson Foods
Frankfort, IL 866-644-2732

Liquid ingredient manufacturer specializing in signature sauces, dessert toppings, beverage/pancake syrups, specialty fruit fillings and condiments.

Barber Pure Milk Ice Cream Company
Birmingham, AL. 205-942-2351
Bartush-Schnitzius Foods Company
Lewisville, TX 972-219-1270
Bede Inc
Haledon, NJ 866-239-6565
Beverage Specialties
Fredonia, NY 800-462-8125
Blue Crab Bay Company
Melfa, VA 800-221-2722
Boissons Miami Pomor
Longueuil, QC 877-977-3744
Boyd Coffee Company
Portland, OR 800-545-4077
Breakfast at Brennan's
New Orleans, LA 800-888-9932
Brookema Company
West Chicago, IL 630-562-2290
Cactus-Creek
Dallas, TX. 800-471-7723
Calico Cottage
Amityville, NY 800-645-5345

Cappuccine
Palm Springs, CA 800-511-3127
Carbolite Foods
Evansville, IN 888-524-3314
Carbonator Rental Service
Philadelphia, PA 800-220-3556
Carolina Treet
Wilmington, NC 800-616-6344
Century Foods International
Sparta, WI 800-269-1901
Chase Brothers Dairy
Oxnard, CA 800-438-6455
Christie Food Products
Randolph, MA 800-727-2523
Citrus Service
Winter Garden, FL 407-656-4999
Cocoline Chocolate Company
Brooklyn, NY 718-522-4500
ConAgra Grocery Products
Irvine, CA 714-680-1000
Consolidated Mills
Houston, TX 713-896-4196
Creative Foodworks
San Antonio, TX 210-212-4761
Crosby Molasses Company
St John, NB 506-634-7515
Crystal Foods
Brick, NJ 732-477-0073
Dairy-Mix
St Petersburg, FL 727-525-6101
Devansoy
Carroll, IA 800-747-8605
Diamond Crystal Brands
Savannah, GA 800-654-5115
Erba Food Products
Brooklyn, NY 718-272-7700
Fair Scones
Medina, WA 800-588-9160
Farmer Brothers Company
Torrance, CA 800-735-2878
Fine Foods International
St Louis, MO 314-842-4473
Flavor Systems Intl.
Cincinnati, OH 800-498-2783
Fountain Shakes/MS Foods
Minnetonka, MN 952-988-6940
Four Percent Company
Highland Park, MI 313-345-5880
Franco's Cocktail Mixes
Pompano Beach, FL 800-782-4508
Frank & Dean's Cocktail Mixes
Pasadena, CA 626-351-4272
Gerhart Coffee Company
Lancaster, PA 800-536-4310
Gilly's Hot Vanilla
Lenox, MA 413-637-1515
Gilster-Mary Lee Corporation
Chester, IL 800-851-5371
Glcc Company
Paw Paw, MI 269-657-3167
Global Marketing Associates
Schaumburg, IL 847-397-2350
Great Western Juice Company
Maple Heights, OH 800-321-9180
Green Foods Corporation
Oxnard, CA 800-777-4430
H. Fox & Company
Brooklyn, NY 718-385-4600
Halben Food Manufacturing Company
Saint Louis, MO 800-888-4855
Hena Coffee
Brooklyn, NY 718-272-8237
Highwood Distillers
High River, AB 403-652-3202
Hygeia Dairy Company
McAllen, TX 956-686-0511
Imagine Foods
Melville, NY 800-333-6339
Innovative Food Solutions LLC
Columbus, OH 800-884-3314
Instant Products of America
Columbus, IN 812-372-9100
J. Crow Company
New Ipswich, NH 800-878-1965
Jel-Sert Company
West Chicago, IL 800-323-2592
Jogue Inc
Northville, MI 800-521-3888
Jus-Made
Dallas, TX 800-969-3746
K&F Select Fine Coffees
Portland, OR 800-558-7788
Kemach Food Products Corporation
Brooklyn, NY 888-453-6224
Kittling Ridge Estate Wines & Spirits
Grimsby, ON 905-945-9225
Kohler Mix Specialties
Newington, CT 860-666-1511
La Paz Products
Brea, CA 714-990-0982
Lake City Foods
Mississauga, ON 905-625-8244
Lake Country Foods
Oconomowoc, WI 262-567-5521
Land O'Lakes
Carlisle, PA 717-486-7000
Land O'Lakes, Inc.
Arden Hills, MN 800-328-9680
Lemate of New England
Foxboro, MA 508-543-9035
Lynch Foods
North York, ON 416-449-5464
Main Street Ingredients
La Crosse, WI 800-359-2345
Mar-Key Foods
Vidalia, GA 912-537-4204
Margarita Man
San Antonio, TX 800-950-8149
McSteven's, Inc
Vancouver, WA 800-547-2803
Melchers Flavors of America
Indianapolis, IN 800-235-2867
Mele-Koi Farms
Newport Beach, CA 949-660-9000
Mingo Bay Beverages
Myrtle Beach, SC 843-448-5320
Minute Maid Company
Atlanta, GA 800-438-2653
MLO/GeniSoy Products Company
Tulas, OK 866-606-3829
Natural Formulas
Hayward, CA 510-372-1800
Naturally Fresh Foods
Atlanta, GA 800-765-1950
Nestle Professional Vitality
Solon, OH 800-288-8682
Northwestern Foods
Saint Paul, MN 800-236-4937
Paca Foods
Tampa, FL 800-388-7419
Phillips Syrup Corporation
Westlake, OH 800-350-8443
Pied-Mont/Dora
Ste Anne Des Plaines, QC 800-363-8003
Plainview Milk Products Cooperative
Plainview, MN 507-534-3872
PR Bar
Carlsbad, CA 800-397-5556
Premier Blending
Wichita, KS 316-267-5533
Price's Creameries
El Paso, TX 915-565-2711
Pro Form Labs
Orinda, CA 925-299-9000
Quality Instant Teas
Morristown, NJ 888-283-8327
Quality Naturally! Foods
City of Industry, CA 888-498-6986
Reser's Fine Foods
Beaverton, OR 800-333-6431
Robertet Flavors
Piscataway, NJ 732-271-1804
Roos Foods
Kenton, DE 800-343-3642
Ruffner's
Wayne, PA 610-687-9800
S.J. McCullagh
Buffalo, NY 800-753-3473
Sara Lee Corporation
Downers Grove, IL 630-598-8100
Schlotterbeck & Foss Company
Portland, ME 800-777-4666
Sea Breeze Fruit Flavors
Towaco, NJ 800-732-2733
Skim Delux Mendenhall Laboratories
Paris, TN 800-642-9321
Southern Gardens Citrus Processing
Clewiston, FL 863-983-3030
Steelback Brewery
Toronto, ON 416-679-0032
Sturm Foods
Manawa, WI 800-347-8876
Subco Foods Inc
Sheboygan, WI 800-473-0757
Sugar Creek/Eskimo Pie
Russellville, AR 800-445-2715
SunMeadow Family of Products
Saint Petersburg, FL 727-573-2211
Swagger Foods Corporation
Vernon Hills, IL 847-913-1200
Synergy Foods
West Bloomfield, MI 313-849-2900
Tex-Mex Gourmet
Brenham, TX 888-345-8467
The Peanut Butter Shop Of Williamsburg
Toano, VA 800-831-1828
Thirs-Tea Corporation
Miami, FL 305-651-4350
Toucan Enterprises
Marrero, LA 800-736-9289
Tova Industries
Louisville, KY 888-532-8682
Trader Vic's Food Products
Emeryville, CA 877-762-4824
Tree Ripe Products
East Hanover, NJ 800-873-3747
Ultra Seal
New Paltz, NY 845-255-2490
Unilever Bestfoods
Englewood Cliffs, NJ 201-567-8000
United Citrus Products
Norwood, MA 800-229-7300
VIP Foods
Flushing, NY 718-821-5330
Vita-Pakt Citrus Company
Covina, CA 626-332-1101
W&G Flavors
Hunt Valley, MD 410-771-6606
Wayne Dairy Products
Richmond, IN 800-875-9294
Webbpak
Trussville, AL 800-655-3500
Wechsler Coffee Corporation
Moonachie, NJ 800-800-2633
Welsh Farms
Edison, NJ 800-221-0663
World Flavors
Warminster, PA 215-672-4400

Frozen

Al-Rite Fruits & Syrups
Miami, FL 305-652-2540

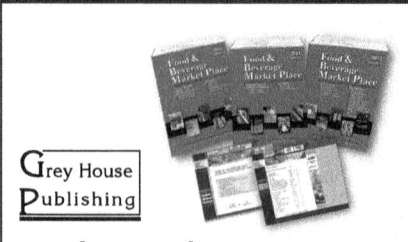

Associated Brands Inc.
Medina, NY. 800-265-0050
Baldwin Richardson Foods
Frankfort, IL 866-644-2732

Liquid ingredient manufacturer specializing in signature sauces, dessert toppings, beverage/pancake syrups, specialty fruit fillings and condiments.

J. Crow Company
New Ipswich, NH 800-878-1965
Jogue Inc
Northville, MI. 800-521-3888
Reser's Fine Foods
Beaverton, OR 800-333-6431

Liquid

Associated Brands Inc.
Medina, NY. 800-265-0050
Baldwin Richardson Foods
Frankfort, IL 866-644-2732

Liquid ingredient manufacturer specializing in signature sauces, dessert toppings, beverage/pancake syrups, specialty fruit fillings and condiments.

ConAgra Grocery Products
Irvine, CA 714-680-1000
Hummingbird Kitchens
Whitehouse, TX 800-921-9470
J. Crow Company
New Ipswich, NH 800-878-1965
Jogue Inc
Northville, MI. 800-521-3888
Reser's Fine Foods
Beaverton, OR 800-333-6431

Biscuit

Atkinson Milling Company
Selma, NC. 800-948-5707
Baker & Baker
Schaumburg, IL. 800-593-5777
Baker & Baker, Inc.
Schaumburg, IL. 800-593-5777
Bakery Chef
Louisville, KY 800-594-0203
Blackberry Patch
Thomasville, GA. 800-853-5598
Bountiful Pantry
Nantucket, MA 888-832-6466
Byrd Mill Company
Ashland, VA 888-897-3336
C.H. Guenther & Son, Inc
San Antonio, TX. 210-227-1401
Country Cupboard
Virginia City, NV 775-847-7300
Father's Country Hams
Bremen, KY 270-525-3554
Iveta Gourmet
Santa Cruz, CA 831-423-5149
Premier Blending
Wichita, KS. 316-267-5533
Weisenberger Mills
Midway, KY 800-643-8678
White Lily Foods Company
Memphis, TN 800-595-1380

Bread

Abel & Schafer
Ronkonkoma, NY. 800-443-1260
Ambassador Foods
Van Nuys, CA 800-338-3369
Aunt Millies Bakeries
Fort Wayne, IN 260-424-8245
BakeMark USA
Schaumburg, IL. 562-949-1054
Bountiful Pantry
Nantucket, MA 888-832-6466
Byrd Mill Company
Ashland, VA 888-897-3336
Chester Fried
Birmingham, AL. 800-288-1555
CHR Hansen
Elyria, OH. 800-558-0802
Cibolo Junction Food & Spice
Albuquerque, NM. 505-888-1987
Cotswold Cottage Foods
Arvada, CO. 800-208-1977
De Coty Coffee Company
San Angelo, TX 800-588-8001
Drusilla Seafood Packing & Processing Company
Baton Rouge, LA 800-364-8844
Grain Process Enterprises Ltd.
Scarborough, ON 800-387-5292
Hollman Foods
Chicago, IL. 888-926-2879
Kokopelli's Kitchen
Phoenix, AZ 888-943-9802
Old Tyme Mill Company
Chicago, IL. 773-521-9484
Pamela's Products
Ukiah, CA. 707-462-6605
Pett Spice Products
Atlanta, GA. 404-691-5235
Puratos Canada
Mississauga, ON. 905-362-3668
Purity Foods
Okemos, MI 800-997-7358
Rabbit Creek Products
Louisburg, KS. 800-837-3073
Sambets Cajun Deli
Austin, TX. 800-472-6238
Sassafras Enterprises
Chicago, IL. 800-537-4941
Sells Best
Mishawaka, IN 800-837-8368
SOUPerior Bean & Spice Company
Vancouver, WA 800-878-7687
Southeastern Mills
Rome, GA. 800-334-4468
Strossner's Bakery
Greenville, SC. 864-233-3996
The Lollipop Tree, Inc
Auburn, NY. 800-842-6691
Timber Peaks Gourmet
Parker, CO. 800-982-7687
Valley View Blueberries
Vancouver, WA 360-892-2839

Low Carb

Dixie Usa
Tomball, TX 800-233-3668

Breading

Blend Pak
Bloomfield, KY . . . 502-252-8000
Chef Hans Gourmet Foods
Monroe, LA. . . . 800-890-4267
CHR Hansen
Elyria, OH. . . . 800-558-0802
Dorothy Dawson Foods Products
Jackson, MI. . . . 517-788-9830
Griffith Laboratories Worldwide
Alsip, IL 800-346-4743
Newly Weds Foods
Chicago, IL 800-621-7521
Roland Industries
Saint Louis, MO 800-325-1183
Specialty Products
Cleveland, OH 216-362-1050
Texas Crumb & Food Products
Farmers Branch, TX 800-522-7862

Brownie

BakeMark USA
Schaumburg, IL. . . . 562-949-1054
Country Cupboard
Virginia City, NV 775-847-7300
Dawn Food Products
Jackson, MI. . . . 800-248-1144
No Pudge! Foods
Wolfeboro Falls, NH. . . . 888-667-8343
Pamela's Products
Ukiah, CA. . . . 707-462-6605
Rabbit Creek Products
Louisburg, KS. . . . 800-837-3073
Touche Bakery
London, ON 519-455-0044
White Lily Foods Company
Memphis, TN 800-595-1380

Cake

Abel & Schafer
Ronkonkoma, NY. . . . 800-443-1260
Atkinson Milling Company
Selma, NC. . . . 800-948-5707
Bakemark Ingredients Canada
Richmond, BC 800-665-9441
BakeMark USA
Schaumburg, IL. . . . 562-949-1054
Baker & Baker
Schaumburg, IL. . . . 800-593-5777
Baker & Baker, Inc.
Schaumburg, IL. . . . 800-593-5777
Bakery Chef
Louisville, KY 800-594-0203
Bear Stewart Corporation
Chicago, IL 800-697-2327
Beth's Fine Desserts
Mill Valley, CA. . . . 415-464-1891
Brass Ladle Products
Concordville, PA. . . . 800-955-2353
Brookema Company
West Chicago, IL 630-562-2290
Butternut Mountain Farm
Morrisville, VT. . . . 800-828-2376
Byrd Mill Company
Ashland, VA 888-897-3336
Chefmaster
Garden Grove, CA 800-333-7443
Chelsea Milling Company
Chelsea, MI. . . . 734-475-1361
Country Cupboard
Virginia City, NV 775-847-7300
Cuisinary Fine Foods
Irving, TX 888-283-5303
Dawn Food Products
Jackson, MI. . . . 800-248-1144
Embassy Flavours Ltd.
Brampton, ON. . . . 800-334-3371
Good Food
Honey Brook, PA 800-327-4406
Halladays Harvest Barn
Bellows Falls, VT. . . . 802-463-3331
Hansmann's Mills
Binghamton, NY. . . . 607-722-1372
Honeyville Grain
Rancho Cucamonga, CA 888-810-3212
Ingredients, Inc.
Buffalo Grove, IL 847-419-9595
Little Crow Foods
Warsaw, IN 800-288-2769
Louisiana Gourmet Enterprises
La Place, LA 985-783-2446
Martha Olson's Great Foods
Sutter Creek, CA. . . . 800-973-3966
Meadowvale
Yorkville, IL 800-953-0201
Northwestern Foods
Saint Paul, MN 800-236-4937
Oetker Limited
Mississauga, ON. . . . 800-387-6939
Pillsbury
Minneapolis, MN 800-775-4777
Premier Blending
Wichita, KS. . . . 316-267-5533
Quality Naturally! Foods
City of Industry, CA 888-498-6986
Rich Products Corporation
Cameron, WI. . . . 715-458-4556
Royal Resources
New Orleans, LA 800-888-9932
Sells Best
Mishawaka, IN 800-837-8368
Sundial Gardens
Higganum, CT. . . . 860-345-4290
Tasty Selections
Concord, ON. . . . 905-760-2353
Tova Industries
Louisville, KY 888-532-8682
VIP Foods
Flushing, NY. . . . 718-821-5330
Wanda's Nature Farm
Lincoln, NE. . . . 800-735-6828
West Pac
Idaho Falls, ID 800-973-7407

Cappuccino

Brewfresh Coffee Company
South Salt Lake, UT 888-486-3334
International Food Technologies
Evansville, IN 812-853-9432
McSteven's, Inc
Vancouver, WA. . . . 800-547-2803
Mont Blanc Gourmet
Denver, CO 800-877-3811

Frozen

International Food Technologies
Evansville, IN 812-853-9432

Chili

Chili Dude
Dallas, TX. . . . 214-354-9906
Fernandez Chili Company
Alamosa, CO. . . . 719-589-6043
Legumes Plus
Fairfield, WA. . . . 800-845-1349
Mojave Foods Corporation
Commerce, CA 800-995-8906
Monterrey Products Company
San Antonio, TX. . . . 210-435-2872
Red Lion Spicy Foods Company
Red Lion, PA. . . . 717-309-8303
Reily Foods Company
New Orleans, LA 504-524-6131
T. Marzetti Company
Columbus, OH 614-846-2232
Texas Heat
San Antonio, TX. . . . 800-656-5916
Tova Industries
Louisville, KY 888-532-8682
Westfield Foods
Greenville, RI 401-949-3558

Cocktail

Al-Rite Fruits & Syrups
Miami, FL. . . . 305-652-2540
Bacardi USA
Coral Gables, FL. . . . 800-222-2734
Byesville Aseptics
Byesville, OH 740-685-2548
Demitri's Bloody Mary Seasonings
Seattle, WA 800-627-9649
Franco's Cocktail Mixes
Pompano Beach, FL 800-782-4508
Frank & Dean's Cocktail Mixes
Pasadena, CA 626-351-4272
Great Western Juice Company
Maple Heights, OH. . . . 800-321-9180
La Paz Products
Brea, CA 714-990-0982
Lemon-X Corporation
Huntington Station, NY 800-220-1061
Main Squeeze
Columbia, MO 573-817-5616
Natural Fruit Corporation
Hialeah, FL 305-887-7525
Ruffner's
Wayne, PA. . . . 610-687-9800
Tree Ripe Products
East Hanover, NJ 800-873-3747
Wagner Excello Food Products
Broadview, IL 708-338-4488

Cookie

BakeMark USA
Schaumburg, IL. . . . 562-949-1054

Dessert

Abel & Schafer
Ronkonkoma, NY. . . . 800-443-1260
American Key Food Products
Closter, NJ. . . . 800-767-0237
Baird Dairies
Clarksville, IN. . . . 812-283-3345
Barber Pure Milk Ice Cream Company
Birmingham, AL. . . . 205-942-2351
Bear Stewart Corporation
Chicago, IL 800-697-2327
Blend Pak
Bloomfield, KY 502-252-8000
Brass Ladle Products
Concordville, PA. . . . 800-955-2353
Burnette Foods
Hartford, MI 616-621-3181
Byrd Mill Company
Ashland, VA 888-897-3336
C.H. Guenther & Son, Inc
San Antonio, TX. . . . 210-227-1401
California Custom Fruits & Flavors
Irwindale, CA 877-558-0056
Carolina Foods
Charlotte, NC 800-234-0441
Chefmaster
Garden Grove, CA 800-333-7443
Chelsea Milling Company
Chelsea, MI. . . . 734-475-1361
Cherry Hill Orchards Pelham
Fenwick, ON. . . . 905-892-3782
Clofine Dairy & Food Products
Linwood, NJ 800-441-1001
Consun Food Industries
Elyria, OH. . . . 440-322-6301
Creme Curls Bakery
Hudsonville, MI 800-466-1219
Cuisinary Fine Foods
Irving, TX 888-283-5303
Dairy-Mix
St Petersburg, FL 727-525-6101
Dawn Food Products
Louisville, KY 800-626-2542
Dutch Ann Foods Company
Natchez, MS 601-445-5566
Embassy Flavours Ltd.
Brampton, ON. . . . 800-334-3371
Famous Specialties Company
Island Park, NY. . . . 877-273-6999
First Foods Company
Dallas, TX. . . . 214-637-0214
Galliker Dairy
Johnstown, PA. . . . 800-477-6455
Galloway Company
Neenah, WI. . . . 800-722-8903
General Mills
Minneapolis, MN 800-248-7310
Golden Fluff Popcorn Company
Lakewood, NJ. . . . 732-367-5448
Great Recipes Company
Beaverton, OR 800-273-2331
Gumpert's Canada
Mississauga, ON. . . . 800-387-9324
Heidi's Gourmet Desserts
Tucker, GA 800-241-4166
Honeyville Grain
Rancho Cucamonga, CA 888-810-3212
Hygeia Dairy Company
McAllen, TX. . . . 956-686-0511
Ingredients, Inc.
Buffalo Grove, IL 847-419-9595

Kohler Mix Specialties
White Bear Lake, MN. 651-426-1633
Kohler Mix Specialties
Newington, CT 860-666-1511
Kosto Food Products Company
Wauconda, IL 847-487-2600
Kraft Canada Headquarters
Don Mills, ON 888-572-3806
Limpert Brothers
Vineland, NJ 800-691-1353
Lloyd's
Berwyn, PA. 610-293-0516
Louisiana Gourmet Enterprises
La Place, LA. 985-783-2446
Lynch Foods
North York, ON. 416-449-5464
Maple Island
Saint Paul, MN 800-369-1022
Master Mix
Placentia, CA 714-524-1698
Meadow Gold Dairies
Tulsa, OK 800-742-7349
Meadowvale
Yorkville, IL 800-953-0201
Michigan Dessert Corporation
Oak Park, MI. 800-328-8632
Milani Gourmet
Melrose Park, IL. 800-333-0003
Nanci's Frozen Yogurt
Mesa, AZ. 800-788-0808
Naterl
St. Bruno, QC 450-653-3655
Nog Incorporated
Dunkirk, NY 800-332-2664
Northwestern Foods
Saint Paul, MN 800-236-4937
Pasta Factory
Melrose Park, IL. 800-615-6951
Paulaur Corporation
Cranbury, NJ. 888-398-8844
Prairie Farms Dairy
Carlinville, IL 217-562-3956
Price's Creameries
El Paso, TX. 915-565-2711
Quality Naturally! Foods
City of Industry, CA 888-498-6986
Redco Foods
Windsor, CT 800-645-1190
Rich Products Corporation
Hilliard, OH. 614-771-1117
Rio Syrup Company
Saint Louis, MO 800-325-7666
Roberts Dairy Foods
Iowa City, IA
S&N Food Company
Mesquite, TX 972-222-1184
Schneider's Dairy Holdings Inc
Pittsburgh, PA. 412-881-3525
Sells Best
Mishawaka, IN 800-837-8368
Serv-Agen Corporation
Cherry Hill, NJ 856-663-6966
Sno-Shack
Rexburg, ID. 888-766-7425
Specialty Bakers
Marysville, PA 800-233-0778
Sugar Creek/Eskimo Pie
Russellville, AR 800-445-2715
Swagger Foods Corporation
Vernon Hills, IL 847-913-1200
Swiss Valley Farms Company
Davenport, IA 563-468-6600
Timber Peaks Gourmet
Parker, CO. 800-982-7687
Tova Industries
Louisville, KY 888-532-8682
Tropical Illusions
Trenton, MO 660-359-5422
VIP Foods
Flushing, NY. 718-821-5330
W&G Flavors
Hunt Valley, MD 410-771-6606
Welch's Foods Inc
Concord, MA 800-340-6870
Wisconsin Wilderness Food Products
Milwaukee, WI 800-359-3039

Low Carb

Dixie Usa
Tomball, TX 800-233-3668
International Food Technologies
Evansville, IN 812-853-9432

Dip

Amberland Foods
Harvey, ND 800-950-4558
Atlantic Quality Spice &Seasonings
New Brunswick, NJ 800-584-0422
Au Printemps Gourmet
Saint-Jerome, QC 800-663-0416
Big Steer Enterprises
Beaumont, TX. 800-421-4951
Chugwater Chili Corporation
Chugwater, WY 800-972-4454
Country Home Creations
Goodrich, MI 800-457-3477
Cw Resources
New Britain, CT 860-229-7700
Erba Food Products
Brooklyn, NY 718-272-7700
Fountain Valley Foods
Colorado Springs, CO. 719-573-6012
Gloria's Gourmet
New Britain, CT 860-225-9196
Heluva Good Cheese
Sodus, NY. 315-483-6971
Hollman Foods
Chicago, IL 888-926-2879
Jodie's Kitchen
Pinellas Park, FL
Jodie's Kitchen
Pinellas Park, FL. 800-728-3704
Just Delicious Gourmet Foods
Seal Beach, CA. 800-871-6085
Lesley Elizabeth
Lapeer, MI. 800-684-3300
Limited Edition
Midland, TX 432-686-2008
Look's Gourmet Food Company
East Machias, ME. 800-962-6258
Milani Gourmet
Melrose Park, IL. 800-333-0003
Olde Tyme Food Corporation
East Longmeadow, MA 800-356-6533
Rabbit Creek Products
Louisburg, KS. 800-837-3073
Reser's Fine Foods
Beaverton, OR 800-333-6431
Spice Hunter
San Luis Obispo, CA 800-444-3061
Swagger Foods Corporation
Vernon Hills, IL 847-913-1200

Donut

BakeMark USA
Schaumburg, IL. 562-949-1054

Drink

American Instants
Flanders, NJ 973-584-8811
Bread & Chocolate
Wells River, VT 800-524-6715
El Paso Chile Company
El Paso, TX. 888-472-5727
Frontera Foods
Chicago, IL 800-509-4441
Granny Blossom Specialty Foods
Wells, VT 802-645-0507

Dumplings

Tova Industries
Louisville, KY 888-532-8682

Frozen

Pro Form Labs
Orinda, CA 925-299-9000
Robertet Flavors
Piscataway, NJ 732-271-1804
Unilever Bestfoods
Englewood Cliffs, NJ 201-567-8000

Dessert

International Food Technologies
Evansville, IN 812-853-9432

Granita

International Food Technologies
Evansville, IN 812-853-9432
Nanci's Frozen Yogurt
Mesa, AZ. 800-788-0808

Gravy

Ailments E.D. Foods Inc.
Pointe Claire, QC 800-267-3333
C.H. Guenther & Son, Inc
San Antonio, TX. 210-227-1401
Campbell Soup Company of Canada
Listowel, ON. 800-575-7687
Dorothy Dawson Foods Products
Jackson, MI. 517-788-9830
Griffith Laboratories Worldwide
Alsip, IL 800-346-4743
Lawry's Foods
Monrovia, CA. 800-595-8917
Morgan Food
Austin, IN 888-430-1780
RC Fine Foods
Belle Mead, NJ 800-526-3953
Spice Advice
Ankeny, IA 800-247-5251
White Lily Foods Company
Memphis, TN 800-595-1380
Williams Foods, Inc
Lenexa, KS 800-255-6736
Williams-West & Witt Products
Michigan City, IN

Hot Chocolate

Brewfresh Coffee Company
South Salt Lake, UT 888-486-3334

Ice Cream

Agri-Dairy Products
Purchase, NY 914-697-9580
Al-Rite Fruits & Syrups
Miami, FL. 305-652-2540
America's Classic Foods
Cambria, CA. 805-927-0745
American Food & Equipment
Miami, FL. 305-377-8991
Baird Dairies
Clarksville, IN. 812-283-3345
Barber Pure Milk Ice Cream Company
Birmingham, AL. 205-942-2351
Blue Bell Creameries
Brenham, TX. 979-836-7977
Carbolite Foods
Evansville, IN 888-524-3314
Clofine Dairy & Food Products
Linwood, NJ 800-441-1001
Consun Food Industries
Elyria, OH. 440-322-6301
Crowley Foods
Binghamton, NY. 800-637-0019
Cumberland Dairy
Rosenhayn, NJ 856-451-1300
Dairy-Mix
St Petersburg, FL 727-525-6101
Fairmont Products
Belleville, PA 717-935-2121
Galliker Dairy
Johnstown, PA. 800-477-6455
Innovative Food Solutions LLC
Columbus, OH 800-884-3314
International Food Technologies
Evansville, IN 812-853-9432
Kalva Corporation
Gurnee, IL. 800-525-8220
Kohler Mix Specialties
White Bear Lake, MN. 651-426-1633
Kohler Mix Specialties
Newington, CT 860-666-1511
Kosto Food Products Company
Wauconda, IL 847-487-2600
Leiby's Premium Ice Cream
Tamaqua, PA. 877-453-4297
Master Mix
Placentia, CA 714-524-1698
Naterl
St. Bruno, QC 450-653-3655
Nog Incorporated
Dunkirk, NY 800-332-2664
Prairie Farms Dairy
Carlinville, IL 217-562-3956
Price's Creameries
El Paso, TX. 915-565-2711
Quality Naturally! Foods
City of Industry, CA 888-498-6986
Queensboro Farm Products
Canastota, NY. 315-697-2235

Queensboro Farm Products
Jamaica, NY 718-658-5000
Reiter Dairy
Akron, OH. 800-362-0825
Roberts Dairy Foods
Iowa City, IA
Schneider's Dairy Holdings Inc
Pittsburgh, PA 412-881-3525
Swiss Valley Farms Company
Davenport, IA 563-468-6600
Titusville Dairy Products
Titusville, PA 800-352-0101
Tova Industries
Louisville, KY 888-532-8682
Vitarich Ice Cream
Fortuna, CA 707-725-6182

Low Carb

International Food Technologies
Evansville, IN 812-853-9432

Jambalaya

Reggie Ball's Cajun Foods
Lake Charles, LA 337-436-0291

Liquid

National Fruit Flavor Company
New Orleans, LA 800-966-1123
Pro Form Labs
Orinda, CA 925-299-9000
Robertet Flavors
Piscataway, NJ 732-271-1804
Unilever Bestfoods
Englewood Cliffs, NJ 201-567-8000

Muffin

Abel & Schafer
Ronkonkoma, NY. 800-443-1260
ADM Milling Company
Jackson, TN 731-424-3535
Ambassador Foods
Van Nuys, CA 800-338-3369
Atkinson Milling Company
Selma, NC. 800-948-5707
Aunt Millies Bakeries
Fort Wayne, IN 260-424-8245
Bake'n Joy Foods
North Andover, MA 800-666-4937
C.H. Guenther & Son, Inc
San Antonio, TX. 210-227-1401
Fiera Foods
Toronto, ON 416-744-1010
Food Concentrate Corporation
Oklahoma City, OK 405-840-5633
Grain Process Enterprises Ltd.
Scarborough, ON 800-387-5292
Honeyville Grain
Rancho Cucamonga, CA 888-810-3212
Iveta Gourmet
Santa Cruz, CA 831-423-5149
John Gust Foods & Products Corporation
Batavia, IL. 800-756-5886
Kokopelli's Kitchen
Phoenix, AZ 888-943-9802
Oetker Limited
Mississauga, ON. 800-387-6939
Pemberton's Gourmet Foods
Gray, ME. 800-255-8401
Premier Blending
Wichita, KS. 316-267-5533
Purity Foods
Okemos, MI 800-997-7358
Sarabeth's Kitchen
Bronx, NY. 800-773-7378
Sells Best
Mishawaka, IN 800-837-8368
Shepherdsfield Bakery
Fulton, MO 573-642-1439
Sorrenti Family Farms
Newman, CA. 888-435-9490
White Lily Foods Company
Memphis, TN 800-595-1380

Pancake

Agricore United
Winnipeg, MB. 800-661-4844
Atkinson Milling Company
Selma, NC. 800-948-5707
Baker & Baker
Schaumburg, IL. 800-593-5777
Baker & Baker, Inc.
Schaumburg, IL. 800-593-5777
Bakery Chef
Louisville, KY 800-594-0203
Bette's Diner Products
Berkeley, CA. 510-644-3230
Blackberry Patch
Thomasville, GA. 800-853-5598
Brown Family Farm
Brattleboro, VT. 86- 2-4 87
Byrd Mill Company
Ashland, VA 888-897-3336
C.H. Guenther & Son, Inc
San Antonio, TX. 210-227-1401
Country Cupboard
Virginia City, NV 775-847-7300
Cream of the West
Harlowton, MT 800-477-2383
Fearn Natural Foods
Thiensville, WI 800-877-8935
Fresh Dairy Direct/Morningstar
Dallas, TX. 800-395-7004
Golden Malted
South Bend, IN 800-253-0590
Gormly's Orchard
South Burlington, VT 800-639-7604
Greenfield Mills
Howe, IN. 260-367-2394
Heartland Food Products
Mission, KS 913-831-4446
Highland Sugarworks, Inc
Websterville, VT. 800-452-4012
Homestead Mills
Cook, MN. 800-652-5233
Inn Maid Food
Lenox, MA 413-637-2732
John Gust Foods & Products Corporation
Batavia, IL. 800-756-5886
Kamish Food Products
Chicago, IL 773-725-6959
Kokopelli's Kitchen
Phoenix, AZ 888-943-9802
Little Crow Foods
Warsaw, IN 800-288-2769
Maple Grove Farms of Vermont
St Johnsbury, VT. 800-525-2540
Minnesota Specialty Crops
McGregor, MN 800-328-6731
Northwestern Foods
Saint Paul, MN 800-236-4937
Old Tyme Mill Company
Chicago, IL 773-521-9484
Pemberton's Gourmet Foods
Gray, ME. 800-255-8401
Prairie Sun Grains
Calgary, AB. 800-556-6807
Premier Blending
Wichita, KS. 316-267-5533
Purity Foods
Okemos, MI 800-997-7358
Reimann Food Classics
Palatine, IL 847-991-1366
SFP Food Products
Conway, AR 800-654-5329
Sugarwoods Farm
Glover, VT 800-245-3718
Tait Farm Foods
Centre Hall, PA. 800-787-2716
Turkey Hill Sugarbush
Waterloo, QC 450-539-4822
Valley View Blueberries
Vancouver, WA. 360-892-2839
Wall-Rogalsky Milling Company
Mc Pherson, KS 800-835-2067
Weisenberger Mills
Midway, KY 800-643-8678
White Lily Foods Company
Memphis, TN 800-595-1380

Pie Crust

Country Cupboard
Virginia City, NV 775-847-7300
Hansmann's Mills
Binghamton, NY. 607-722-1372

Powdered

Crystal Star Herbal Nutrition
Salinas, CA 831-422-7500
Northwestern Foods
Saint Paul, MN 800-236-4937
Pro Form Labs
Orinda, CA 925-299-9000
Robertet Flavors
Piscataway, NJ 732-271-1804
Schiff Nutrition International
Salt Lake City, UT 800-526-6251

Punch

Associated Brands Inc.
Medina, NY. 800-265-0050
Four Percent Company
Highland Park, MI 313-345-5880
Quality Naturally! Foods
City of Industry, CA 888-498-6986
Tova Industries
Louisville, KY 888-532-8682

Rice

R.A.B. Food Group LLC
Secaucus, NJ 201-553-1100
Riceland Foods Rice Milling Operations
Stuttgart, AR 870-673-5500

Shoofly

Good Food
Honey Brook, PA 800-327-4406

Smoothie Powder

International Food Technologies
Evansville, IN 812-853-9432
Nanci's Frozen Yogurt
Mesa, AZ. 800-788-0808

Soup

Ailments E.D. Foods Inc.
Pointe Claire, QC 800-267-3333
Amalgamated Produce
Bridgeport, CT 800-358-3808
Amberland Foods
Harvey, ND 800-950-4558
Associated Brands Inc.
Medina, NY. 800-265-0050
Atlantic Quality Spice &Seasonings
New Brunswick, NJ 800-584-0422
Bernard Food Industries
Evanston, IL 800-323-3663
Boston Spice & Tea Company
Boston, VA 800-966-4372
Bountiful Pantry
Nantucket, MA 888-832-6466
Brookema Company
West Chicago, IL 630-562-2290
Campbell Soup Company
Camden, NJ. 800-257-8443
Commodities Marketing, Inc.
Edison, NJ. 732-603-5077
Cook-In-The-Kitchen
White River Junction, VT. 802-333-4141
Country Home Creations
Goodrich, MI 800-457-3477
Crazy Jerry's
Roswell, GA 770-993-0651
Diamond Crystal Brands
Savannah, GA 800-654-5115
Dismat Corporation
Toledo, OH 419-531-8963
Dorothy Dawson Foods Products
Jackson, MI. 517-788-9830
Edward & Sons Trading Company
Carpinteria, CA. 805-684-8500
Fair Scones
Medina, WA 800-588-9160
Fearn Natural Foods
Thiensville, WI 800-877-8935
Flavor House
Adelanto, CA 760-246-9131
Gloria's Gourmet
New Britain, CT 860-225-9196
Halladays Harvest Barn
Bellows Falls, VT. 802-463-3331
High Country Gourmet
Orem, UT 801-426-4383
Hummingbird Kitchens
Whitehouse, TX 800-921-9470
Idaho Pacific Corporation
Ririe, ID 800-238-5503

Kemach Food Products Corporation
Brooklyn, NY 888-453-6224
Lake City Foods
Mississauga, ON 905-625-8244
Legumes Plus
Fairfield, WA 800-845-1349
Lynch Foods
North York, ON 416-449-5464
Magic Seasoning Blends
New Orleans, LA 800-457-2857
Milani Gourmet
Melrose Park, IL 800-333-0003
Nor-Cliff Farms
Port Colborne, ON 905-835-0808
North Bay Trading Company
Brule, WI 800-348-0164
Pasta Partners
Salt Lake City, UT 800-727-8284
Pasta USA
Spokane, WA 800-456-2084
Rabbit Creek Products
Louisburg, KS 800-837-3073
RC Fine Foods
Belle Mead, NJ 800-526-3953
Sheila's Select Gourmet Recipe
Heber City, UT 800-516-7286
Sorrenti Family Farms
Newman, CA 888-435-9490
Spice Hunter
San Luis Obispo, CA 800-444-3061
Swagger Foods Corporation
Vernon Hills, IL 847-913-1200
Tova Industries
Louisville, KY 888-532-8682
Tropical
Columbus, OH 800-538-3941
Unilever Bestfoods
Englewood Cliffs, NJ 201-567-8000
Vogue Cuisine
Sunnyvale, CA 888-236-4144
Westfield Foods
Greenville, RI 401-949-3558
White Coffee Corporation
Astoria, NY 800-221-0140
Williams-West & Witt Products
Michigan City, IN

Trail

A.L. Bazzini Company
Bronx, NY 800-228-0172
Aurora Products
Stratford, CT 800-398-1048
Chile Today
San Francisco, CA 800-758-0372
Chukar Cherries
Prosser, WA 800-624-9544
Durey-Libby Edible Nuts
Carlstadt, NJ 800-332-6887
Hialeah Products Company
Hollywood, FL 800-923-3379
Inn Maid Food
Lenox, MA 413-637-2732
Jason & Son Specialty Foods
Rancho Cordova, CA 800-810-9093
King Nut Company
Solon, OH 800-860-5464
Marantha Natural Foods
San Francisco, CA 866-972-6879
Midwest/Northern
Minneapolis, MN 800-328-5502
Nature Kist Snacks
Stockton, CA 209-944-7200
New England Natural Baker
Greenfield, MA 800-910-2884
Nspired Natural Foods
Boulder, CO 800-434-4246
Nut Factory
Spokane Valley, WA 888-239-5288
Randag & Associates Inc
Elmhurst, IL 630-530-2830
Sonne
Wahpeton, ND 800-727-6663
Sun Ridge Farms
Pajaro, CA 831-786-7000
Superior Nut & Candy Company
Chicago, IL 800-843-2238
Timber Peaks Gourmet
Parker, CO 800-982-7687
Tova Industries
Louisville, KY 888-532-8682
Tropical
Charlotte, NC 800-220-1413
Valley View Blueberries
Vancouver, WA 360-892-2839
Variety Foods
Warren, MI 586-268-4900
Waymouth Farms
New Hope, MN 800-527-0094
Weaver Nut Company
Ephrata, PA 717-738-3781
Wysong Corporation
Midland, MI 800-748-0188

Waffle

Baker & Baker
Schaumburg, IL 800-593-5777
Baker & Baker, Inc.
Schaumburg, IL 800-593-5777
Bountiful Pantry
Nantucket, MA 888-832-6466
Byrd Mill Company
Ashland, VA 888-897-3336
C.H. Guenther & Son, Inc
San Antonio, TX 210-227-1401
Country Cupboard
Virginia City, NV 775-847-7300
Cream of the West
Harlowton, MT 800-477-2383
Fresh Dairy Direct/Morningstar
Dallas, TX 800-395-7004
Golden Malted
South Bend, IN 800-253-0590
Great Grains Milling Company
Scobey, MT 406-783-5581
Hansmann's Mills
Binghamton, NY 607-722-1372
Heartland Food Products
Mission, KS 913-831-4446
Inn Maid Food
Lenox, MA 413-637-2732
John Gust Foods & Products Corporation
Batavia, IL 800-756-5886
Kamish Food Products
Chicago, IL 773-725-6959
Maple Grove Farms of Vermont
St Johnsbury, VT 800-525-2540
Old Tyme Mill Company
Chicago, IL 773-521-9484
Reimann Food Classics
Palatine, IL 847-991-1366
SFP Food Products
Conway, AR 800-654-5329
Wall-Rogalsky Milling Company
Mc Pherson, KS 800-835-2067

Yogurt Powder

International Food Technologies
Evansville, IN 812-853-9432
Kantner Group
Wapakoneta, OH 419-738-4060

Eggs & Egg Products

General

Almark Foods
Gainesville, GA 800-849-3447
Brown Produce Company
Farina, IL. 618-245-3301
Burn Brae Farms
Mississauga, ON. 519-245-1630
Cal-Maine Foods
Pine Grove, LA. 225-222-4148
Cal-Maine Foods
Jackson, MS 601-948-6813
Cordon Bleu International
Anjou, QC. 514-352-3000
Creighton Brothers
Atwood, IN 574-267-3101
Cropp Cooperative-Organic Valley
La Farge, WI 888-444-6455
Cutler Egg Products
Abbeville, AL 334-585-2268
Deb-El Foods
Elizabeth, NJ. 800-421-3447
Dixie Dairy Company
Gary, IN. 219-885-6101
Farbest-Tallman Foods Corporation
Montvale, NJ. 201-573-4900
Henningsen Foods
Omaha, NE 402-330-2500
Henningsen Foods
Purchase, NY 914-701-4020
Hillandale Llc
Lake City, FL 386-397-1300
Hormel Foods Corporation
Austin, MN 800-523-4635
ISE Newberry
Newberry, SC 803-276-5803
Marshall Egg Products
Seymour, IN 812-497-2557
Medeiros Farms
Kalaheo, HI. 808-332-8211
MFI Food Canada
Winnipeg, MB. 204-477-1830
National Egg Products Company
Social Circle, GA 770-464-2652
Nulaid Foods
Ripon, CA. 209-599-2121
Oliver Egg Products
Crewe, VA. 800-525-3447
Rembrandt Foods
Rembrandt, IA. 877-344-4055
Rosenberger's Dairies
Hatfield, PA. 800-355-9074
Smith Packing Regional Meat
Utica, NY
Wenk Foods Inc
Madison, SD 605-256-4569
Wetta Egg Farm
Andale, KS 316-445-2231
Yoder Dairies
Chesapeake, VA 757-482-4068

Boiled

Agri-Dairy Products
Purchase, NY 914-697-9580

Cooked

Egg Low Farms
Sherburne, NY 607-674-4653

Dehydrated

Associated Bakers Products
Huntington, NY 631-673-3841
Ballas Egg Products Corporation
Zanesville, OH 740-453-0386
Culinary Foods
Chicago, IL 800-621-4049
Oskaloosa Food ProductscCorporation
Oskaloosa, IA 800-477-7239

Dried

Associated Bakers Products
Huntington, NY 631-673-3841
Ballas Egg Products Corporation
Zanesville, OH 740-453-0386
Cutler Egg Products
Abbeville, AL 334-585-2268
Double B Foods
Arlington, TX 800-679-0349
Henningsen Foods
Omaha, NE 402-330-2500
Inovatech USA
Montreal, QC 800-367-3447
Kelly Flour Company
Addison, IL. 630-678-5300
MFI Food Canada
Winnipeg, MB. 204-477-1830
Oskaloosa Food ProductscCorporation
Oskaloosa, IA 800-477-7239
Papetti's Egg Products
Elizabeth, NJ. 800-328-5474
Sonstegard Foods Company
Sioux Falls, SD. 800-533-3184
W&G Flavors
Hunt Valley, MD. 410-771-6606
Wenk Foods Inc
Madison, SD 605-256-4569

Desiccated

Agri-Dairy Products
Purchase, NY 914-697-9580
American Health & Nutrition
Ann Arbor, MI 734-677-5570
Clofine Dairy & Food Products
Linwood, NJ 800-441-1001
Henningsen Foods
Purchase, NY 914-701-4020

Fat & Cholesterol Free

Hormel Foods Corporation
Austin, MN 800-523-4635
Tofutti Brands
Cranford, NJ 908-272-2400

Fresh

Agri-Dairy Products
Purchase, NY 914-697-9580
Creighton Brothers
Atwood, IN 574-267-3101
Dixie Egg Company
Jacksonville, FL 800-394-3447
Egg Low Farms
Sherburne, NY 607-674-4653
Feature Foods
Etobicoke, ON 416-675-7350
Great Valley Mills
Barto, PA. 800-688-6455
Happy Egg Dealers
Tampa, FL. 813-248-2362
Hi Point Industries
Vernon, CA 800-959-7292
ISE America, Inc.
Galena, MD. 410-755-6300
Oskaloosa Food ProductscCorporation
Oskaloosa, IA 800-477-7239
Rose Acre Farms
Seymour, IN 800-356-3447
Siegel Egg Company
Cambridge, MA 800-593-3447
Sinton Dairy Foods Company
Colorado Springs, CO. 800-388-4970
Sommer Maid Creamery
Doylestown, PA 215-345-6160
Sparboe Companies
Los Angeles, CA. 213-626-7538
Sunny Fresh Foods
Monticello, MN 800-872-3447
Sunnyslope Farms Egg Ranch
Cherry Valley, CA. 951-845-1131
Suter Company
Sycamore, IL. 800-435-6942
Wetta Egg Farm
Andale, KS 316-445-2231

Frozen

Agri-Dairy Products
Purchase, NY 914-697-9580
Almark Foods
Gainesville, GA 800-849-3447
Ballas Egg Products Corporation
Zanesville, OH 740-453-0386
Brown Produce Company
Farina, IL. 618-245-3301
Creighton Brothers
Atwood, IN 574-267-3101
Cutler Egg Products
Abbeville, AL 334-585-2268
Dixie Egg Company
Jacksonville, FL 800-394-3447
Global Egg Corporation
Etobicoke, ON 416-231-2309
Great Valley Mills
Barto, PA. 800-688-6455
Hi Point Industries
Vernon, CA 800-959-7292
ISE America, Inc.
Galena, MD. 410-755-6300
Kent Foods
Gonzales, TX 830-672-7993
Land O'Lakes, Inc.
Arden Hills, MN 800-328-9680
McAnally Enterprises
Lakeview, CA 800-726-2002
MFI Food Canada
Winnipeg, MB. 204-477-1830
Michael Foods, Inc.
Minnetonka, MN. 952-258-4000
Oliver Egg Products
Crewe, VA. 800-525-3447
Oskaloosa Food ProductscCorporation
Oskaloosa, IA 800-477-7239
Siegel Egg Company
Cambridge, MA 800-593-3447
Sonstegard Foods Company
Sioux Falls, SD. 800-533-3184
Sparboe Companies
Los Angeles, CA. 213-626-7538
Sunnyslope Farms Egg Ranch
Cherry Valley, CA. 951-845-1131
W&G Flavors
Hunt Valley, MD. 410-771-6606
Wenk Foods Inc
Madison, SD 605-256-4569

Hard-Boiled

Almark Foods
Gainesville, GA 800-849-3447
Creighton Brothers
Atwood, IN 574-267-3101
Dixie Egg Company
Jacksonville, FL 800-394-3447
Feature Foods
Etobicoke, ON 416-675-7350
ISE America, Inc.
Galena, MD. 410-755-6300
Newburgh Egg Corporation
Brooklyn, NY 718-692-4392
Sunny Fresh Foods
Monticello, MN 800-872-3447
Sunnyslope Farms Egg Ranch
Cherry Valley, CA. 951-845-1131
Suter Company
Sycamore, IL. 800-435-6942
Wetta Egg Farm
Andale, KS 316-445-2231

Hatcheries

Amick Farms, LLC
Leesville, SC. 800-926-4257
Hickory Baked Food
Castle Rock, CO 303-688-2633
Norfolk Hatchery
Norfolk, NE. 402-371-5710
Sanderson Farms
Laurel, MS 601-426-1454

Chicks

Turkey

Hickory Baked Food
Castle Rock, CO 303-688-2633

Liquid

Ballas Egg Products Corporation
Zanesville, OH 740-453-0386
Brown Produce Company
Farina, IL........................ 618-245-3301
Cutler Egg Products
Abbeville, AL..................... 334-585-2268
Eggology
Canoga Park, CA 818-610-2222
Global Egg Corporation
Etobicoke, ON 416-231-2309
Hi Point Industries
Vernon, CA....................... 800-959-7292
Kent Foods
Gonzales, TX 830-672-7993
McAnally Enterprises
Lakeview, CA..................... 800-726-2002
MFI Food Canada
Winnipeg, MB..................... 204-477-1830
Michael Foods, Inc.
Minnetonka, MN................... 952-258-4000
Nulaid Foods
Ripon, CA........................ 209-599-2121
Oskaloosa Food ProductscCorporation
Oskaloosa, IA..................... 800-477-7239
Sonstegard Foods Company
Sioux Falls, SD.................... 800-533-3184
Sunny Fresh Foods
Monticello, MN 800-872-3447

Whites

Eggology
Canoga Park, CA 818-610-2222
Michael Foods, Inc.
Minnetonka, MN................... 952-258-4000

Whole

Michael Foods, Inc.
Minnetonka, MN................... 952-258-4000

Yolk

Michael Foods, Inc.
Minnetonka, MN................... 952-258-4000

Mix

Oliver Egg Products
Crewe, VA........................ 800-525-3447
Sunny Fresh Foods
Monticello, MN 800-872-3447

Peeled

Agri-Dairy Products
Purchase, NY 914-697-9580
Dixie Egg Company
Jacksonville, FL 800-394-3447
Feature Foods
Etobicoke, ON 416-675-7350
Great Valley Mills
Barto, PA......................... 800-688-6455
ISE America, Inc.
Galena, MD....................... 410-755-6300
Newburgh Egg Corporation
Brooklyn, NY 718-692-4392
Sunnyslope Farms Egg Ranch
Cherry Valley, CA.................. 951-845-1131
Wetta Egg Farm
Andale, KS 316-445-2231

Prepared

Agri-Dairy Products
Purchase, NY 914-697-9580
Almark Foods
Gainesville, GA 800-849-3447
Clofine Dairy & Food Products
Linwood, NJ 800-441-1001

Quail

Squab Producers of California
Modesto, CA...................... 209-537-4744

Solids

Albumen

Brown Produce Company
Farina, IL........................ 618-245-3301
Holton Food Products Company
La Grange, IL 708-352-5599
National Egg Products Company
Social Circle, GA 770-464-2652
Newburgh Egg Corporation
Brooklyn, NY 718-692-4392
Papetti's Egg Products
Elizabeth, NJ...................... 800-328-5474
Wabash Valley Produce
Dubois, IN........................ 812-678-3131

Whole Egg

Oliver Egg Products
Crewe, VA........................ 800-525-3447

Substitutes

Bay Valley Foods
Platteville, WI..................... 800-236-1119
Cargill Texturizing Solutions
Cedar Rapids, IA................... 877-650-7080
Hi Point Industries
Vernon, CA....................... 800-959-7292
Michael Foods, Inc.
Minnetonka, MN................... 952-258-4000

Frozen

Clofine Dairy & Food Products
Linwood, NJ 800-441-1001

Refrigerated

Clofine Dairy & Food Products
Linwood, NJ 800-441-1001
Michael Foods, Inc.
Minnetonka, MN................... 952-258-4000

Yolk

Clofine Dairy & Food Products
Linwood, NJ 800-441-1001
Global Egg Corporation
Etobicoke, ON 416-231-2309
Henningsen Foods
Purchase, NY 914-701-4020
Hi Point Industries
Vernon, CA....................... 800-959-7292
Michael Foods, Inc.
Minnetonka, MN................... 952-258-4000
National Egg Products Company
Social Circle, GA 770-464-2652
Newburgh Egg Corporation
Brooklyn, NY 718-692-4392
Norac Technologies
Edmonton, AB 780-414-9595
Papetti's Egg Products
Elizabeth, NJ...................... 800-328-5474
Wabash Valley Produce
Dubois, IN........................ 812-678-3131

Ethnic Foods

General

Aina Hawaiian Tropical Products
Hilo, HI 877-961-4774
Amy's Kitchen
Petaluma, CA 707-568-4500
Bayou Cajun Foods
Monroe, LA. 318-388-2383
Bayou Crab
Grand Bay, AL 251-824-2076
Belleisle Foods Aliments Wong Wing Inc
Belleisle Creek, NB 506-485-2564
Blansh International
San Jose, CA. 408-997-2325
Blue Marble Brands
Providence, RI 401-528-8634
Bruce Foods Corporation
New Iberia, LA 800-299-9082
Burke Corporation
Nevada, IA 800-654-1152

Always make it your best® with Burke fully cooked meats. We specialize in Italian sausage, beef, and pork toppings, meatballs, taco meats, shredded meats, pepperoni, bacon, Canadian-style bacon, chicken and beef strips. Additionally, we offer a variety of specialty products: Hand-Pinched Style® brand toppings, chorizo, gyro topping, andouille sausage, and breakfast patties and links.

C&J Trading
San Francisco, CA 415-822-8910
C.N.L. Trading
Alhambra, CA. 626-282-1938
Calidad Foods
Grand Prairie, TX 972-933-4100
California Fresh Salsa
Woodland, CA. 530-662-0512
Canton Noodle
Chicago, IL 312-842-4900
Chi & Hing Food Service
Phoenix, AZ 623-939-8889
Chicago Oriental Wholesale
Chicago, IL. 312-842-9993
Chong Mei Trading
East Point, GA 404-768-3838
CJ Omni
South Gate, CA. 323-567-8171
Cocina de Mino
Yukon, OK 405-632-1036
Con Piacere Italian Specialty
Tulalip, WA. 800-204-3594
Corfu Tasty Gyros
Bensenville, IL 630-595-2510
DCL
Honolulu, HI. 808-845-3834
Discovery Foods
Hayward, CA 510-780-9238
Don Jose Foods
Oceanside, CA 760-631-0243
El Aguila Food Products
Salinas, CA 800-398-2929
El Perico Charro
Garden City, KS 620-275-6454
Elena's Food Specialties
S San Francisco, CA. 800-376-5368
Falafel Republic
Needham Heights, MA. 781-444-2790
Goya de Puerto Rico
Bayamon, PR 787-740-4900
H&W Foods
Kapolei, HI 808-682-8300
Hong Kong Supermarket
Atlanta, GA. 404-325-3999
Houston Calco
Houston, TX 713-236-8668
India's Rasoa
St Louis, MO. 314-361-6911
J.F.C. International
Norcross, GA 770-448-0070
Juanita's Foods
Wilmington, CA 310-834-5339
Just the Berries
Los Angeles, CA. 213-613-9807
Jyoti Cuisine India
Berwyn, PA. 610-296-4620
Kyong Hae Kim Company
Honolulu, HI. 808-926-8720
La Mexicana
Seattle, WA 206-763-1488
M&M Food Distributors/Oriental Pride
Virginia Beach, VA. 757-499-5676
Maria and Son Italian Products
Saint Louis, MO 866-481-9009
Marjie's Plantain Foods, Inc.
New York, NY 908-627-5627
Marukai Corporation
Gardena, CA 310-660-6300
Marukan Vinegar (U.S.A.) Inc.
Paramount, CA 562-630-6060
Marukome USA Inc.
Irvine, CA 949-863-0110
Maya Kaimal Fine Indian Foods
Rhinebeck, NY 845-876-8200
Mission Foods
Irving, TX 800-424-7862
My Own Meals, Inc.
Chicago, IL 773-378-6505
National Importers
Richmond, BC 888-894-6464
Natural Quick Foods
Seattle, WA 206-365-5757
Oriental Foods
Alhambra, CA. 626-293-1994
Portugalia Imports
Fall River, MA 508-679-9307
Power-Selles Imports
Lynnwood, WA. 425-398-9761
Preferred Brands International
Stamford, CT. 800-827-8900
R.A.B. Food Group LLC
Secaucus, NJ 201-553-1100
Raja Foods
Skokie, IL 800-800-7923
Refrigerated Foods Association
Chamblee, GA. 770-452-0660
Rico Foods
Paterson, NJ 973-278-0589
Rokeach Food Corporation
Newark, NJ 973-589-4900
Rothman's Foods
St Louis, MO. 314-367-5448
Sanchez Distributors
San Antonio, TX. 210-341-1682
Say Ying Leong Look Funn Factory
Honolulu, HI. 808-537-4304
Shell Ridge Jalapeno Project
Rockport, TX 512-790-8028
Snapdragon Foods
Oakland, CA 877-881-7627
Squair Food Company
Los Angeles, CA. 213-749-7041
Sukhi's Gourmet Indian Food
Hayward, CA 888-478-5447
Sun Sun Food Products
Edmonton, AB 780-454-4261
Taj Gourmet Foods
West Chester, PA. 610-692-2209
Tamashiro Market
Honolulu, HI. 808-841-8047
Taqueria El Milagro
Chicago, IL 312-433-7620
Tekita House Foods
El Paso, TX. 915-779-2181
Thai Kitchen
Berkeley, CA. 800-967-8424
Trappey's Fine Foods
New Iberia, LA. 337-365-8281
True World Foods of Boston
Boston, MA. 617-269-9988
True World Foods of Chicago
Elk Grove Vlg, IL. 847-718-0088
True World Foods of Hawaii
Honolulu, HI. 808-836-3222
VIP Sales Company
Hayward, CA 866-536-8008
Wing Seafood Company
Chicago, IL 312-942-9930
Wing Sing Chong Company
S San Francisco, CA. 415-552-1234
Yamasho
Elk Grove Village, IL 847-981-4004
Zippy's
Honolulu, HI. 808-973-0880

Asian

Asian Foods
Saint Paul, MN 651-558-2400
CJ Omni
South Gate, CA. 323-567-8171
House of Tsang
San Francisco, CA 415-282-9952
JMAC Trading, Inc.
Torrance, CA. 877-566-4569
Moody Dunbar
Johnson City, TN 800-251-8202
San-J International
Richmond, VA. 800-446-5500
San-J International, Inc
Richmond, VA. 800-446-5500
Snapdragon Foods
Oakland, CA 877-881-7627

Burritos

Baja Foods
Chicago, IL 773-376-9030
Camino Real Foods
Vernon, CA 800-421-6201
Cedarlane Foods
Carson, CA 310-886-7720
Don Miguel Mexican Foods
Orange, CA 714-634-8441
Elena's Food Specialties
S San Francisco, CA. 800-376-5368
Foodbrands America
Oklahoma City, OK 405-290-4000
Hacienda De Paco
Orlando, FL. 407-859-5417
La Tang Cuisine Manufacturing
Houston, TX 713-780-4876
McLane Foods
Phoenix, AZ 602-275-5509
Mexi-Frost Specialties Company
Brooklyn, NY 718-625-3324
O Chili Frozen Foods Inc
Northbrook, IL 847-562-1991
Odessa Tortilla & TamaleFactory
Odessa, TX 800-753-2445
Pepes Mexican Foods
Etobicoke, ON 416-674-0882
Queen International Foods
Monterey Park, CA. 800-423-4414
Ramona's Mex. Food Produoducts
Gardena, CA 310-323-1950
Reser's Fine Foods
Beaverton, OR 800-333-6431
Reser's Fine Foods
Salt Lake City, UT 801-972-5633
Ruiz Food Products
Dinuba, CA 800-477-6474
Specialty Brands
Ontario, CA. 800-782-1180
Supreme Frozen Products
Chicago, IL 773-622-3777
Sweet Earth Natural Foods
Pacific Grove, CA. 800-737-3311

Chinese

Belleisle Foods Aliments Wong Wing Inc
Belleisle Creek, NB 506-485-2564
First Oriental Market
Decatur, GA 404-377-6950
Grantstone Supermarket
Tucson, AZ 520-628-7445
Harvest 2000
Pomona, CA 909-622-8039
Hong Kong Supermarket
Atlanta, GA. 404-325-3999
Kahiki Foods
Gahanna, OH. 888-436-2500
National Importers
Richmond, BC 888-894-6464
P&S Food Trading
Chicago, IL 773-685-0088

Chop Suey

Canned

ConAgra Grocery Products
Archbold, OH 419-445-8015
Golden Gate Foods
Dallas, TX. 214-747-2223
Young's Noodle Factory
Honolulu, HI. 808-533-6478

Frozen

ConAgra Grocery Products
Archbold, OH 419-445-8015
Nanka Seimen Company
Vernon, CA 323-585-9967

Chow Chow

Golding Farms Foods
Winston Salem, NC. 336-766-6161
Lancaster Packing Company
Lancaster, PA 717-397-9727
Our Enterprises
Oklahoma City, OK 800-821-6375
United Pickle Products Corporation
Bronx, NY. 718-933-6060

Chow Mein

C&J Trading
San Francisco, CA 415-822-8910
Canton Noodle
Chicago, IL 312-842-4900
ConAgra Grocery Products
Archbold, OH 419-445-8015
Willow Foods
Beaverton, OR 800-338-3609

Couscous

Chieftain Wild Rice Company
Spooner, WI 800-262-6368
Organic Planet
San Francisco, CA 415-765-5590
Setton International Foods
Commack, NY 800-227-4397
TIPIAK INC
Stamford, CT. 203-961-9117

Dim Sum

Calco of Calgary
Calgary, AB. 403-295-3578
Fine Choice Foods
Richmond, BC. 604-522-3110
Golden Gate Foods
Dallas, TX. 214-747-2223
Shine Foods Inc
Torrance, CA. 310-533-6010

Dutch

Penn Dutch Food Center
Hollywood, FL 954-921-4635

Egg Rolls

Belleisle Foods Aliments Wong Wing Inc
Belleisle Creek, NB 506-485-2564
Cathay Foods Corporation
Boston, MA. 617-427-1507
Chang Food Company
Garden Grove, CA 714-265-9990
Chinese Spaghetti Factory
Boston, MA. 617-445-7714
Chungs Gourmet Foods
Houston, TX 713-741-2118
ConAgra Foods
Boisbriand, QC 450-433-1322
ConAgra Grocery Products
Archbold, OH 419-445-8015
Dong Kee Company
Chicago, IL 312-225-6340
Egg Roll Fantasy
Auburn, CA. 530-887-9197
Fine Choice Foods
Richmond, BC. 604-522-3110
Frozen Specialties
Archbold, OH 419-445-9015
Harvest Food Products Company
Concord, CA 925-676-8208
Health is Wealth Foods
Williamstown, NJ 856-728-1998
Kubla Khan Food Company
Portland, OR 503-234-7494
La Tang Cuisine Manufacturing
Houston, TX 713-780-4876
Mexi-Frost Specialties Company
Brooklyn, NY 718-625-3324
Nanka Seimen Company
Vernon, CA 323-585-9967
Peking Noodle Company
Los Angeles, CA. 323-223-2023
Prime Food Processing Corporation
Brooklyn, NY 888-639-2323
Shine Foods Inc
Torrance, CA. 310-533-6010
Valdez Food
Philadelphia, PA 215-634-6106
Wei-Chuan
Bell Gardens, CA 562-372-2020
Willow Foods
Beaverton, OR 800-338-3609
Wing Hing Noodle Company
Los Angeles, CA. 888-223-8899
Wong Wing Foods
Montreal, QC 800-361-4820
Wonton Food
Brooklyn, NY 800-776-8889

Spring Rolls

Calco of Calgary
Calgary, AB. 403-295-3578
Chang Food Company
Garden Grove, CA 714-265-9990
Clarmil Manufacturing Corporation
Hayward, CA 888-252-7645
Health is Wealth Foods
Williamstown, NJ 856-728-1998
Willow Foods
Beaverton, OR 800-338-3609

Wrappers

Delta Food Products
Edmonton, AB 780-424-3636
International Noodle Company
Madison Heights, MI 248-583-2479
Mandarin Noodle Manufacturing Company
Calgary, AB. 403-265-1383
Wing's Food Products
Etobicoke, ON 416-259-2662

Enchiladas

Canned & Frozen

Baja Foods
Chicago, IL 773-376-9030
New Mexico Food Distributors
Albuquerque, NM. 800-637-7084
O Chili Frozen Foods Inc
Northbrook, IL 847-562-1991
Queen International Foods
Monterey Park, CA. 800-423-4414
Reser's Fine Foods
Salt Lake City, UT 801-972-5633

Frozen

Cedarlane Foods
Carson, CA 310-886-7720
Don Miguel Mexican Foods
Orange, CA. 714-634-8441
Elena's Food Specialties
S San Francisco, CA. 800-376-5368
Ruiz Food Products
Dinuba, CA. 800-477-6474

Guacamole

Avo King Intl.
Orange, CA. 800-286-5464
Diversified Avocado Products
Mission Viejo, CA 800-879-2555
J.R. Simplot Company
Boise, ID 208-336-2110
Jalapeno Foods Company
The Woodlands, TX 800-896-2318
Sunny Avocado
Jamul, CA 800-999-2862

Halal Foods

Al Safa Halal
Niagara Falls, NY 800-268-8174
Burke Corporation
Nevada, IA 800-654-1152

Always make it your best® with Burke fully cooked meats. We specialize in Italian sausage, beef, and pork toppings, meatballs, taco meats, shredded meats, pepperoni, bacon, Canadian-style bacon, chicken and beef strips. Additionally, we offer a variety of specialty products: Hand-Pinched Style® brand toppings, chorizo, gyro topping, andouille sausage, and breakfast patties and links.

Butterball Farms
Grand Rapids, MI 616-243-0105
Global Food Industries
Townville, SC 800-225-4152
Henningsen Foods
Purchase, NY 914-701-4020
Midamar Corporation
Cedar Rapids, IA. 800-362-3711
Morning Glory/Formost Farms
Baraboo, WI 800-362-9196
My Own Meals, Inc.
Chicago, IL 773-378-6505
National Fruit Flavor Company
New Orleans, LA 800-966-1123
Northwestern Foods
Saint Paul, MN 800-236-4937
Somerset Industries
Spring House, PA 800-883-8728

Italian

Boscoli Foods
Kenner, LA 504-469-5500
Italian Connection
Dumont, NJ. 201-385-2226
Italian Foods
Holly Hill, FL 904-255-5200
Italian Specialty Foods
Seattle, WA 206-322-5790
Joe Fazio's Famous Italian
Charleston, WV 304-344-3071
Molto Italian Foods
Wildwood, NJ 609-522-5444
Moody Dunbar
Johnson City, TN 800-251-8202
Windsor Frozen Foods
Houston, TX 800-437-6936

Jambalaya

Chef Hans Gourmet Foods
Monroe, LA. 800-890-4267
Mama Amy's Quality Foods
Mississauga, ON. 905-456-0056
Reggie Ball's Cajun Foods
Lake Charles, LA 337-436-0291

Japanese

Marukai Corporation
Gardena, CA 310-660-6300
Marukome USA Inc.
Irvine, CA 949-863-0110
Miyasaka Brewery
Costa Mesa, CA 714-623-2163

Kosher Foods

A-1 Eastern Home Made Pickle Company
Los Angeles, CA. 323-223-1141
Abraham's Natural Foods
Long Branch, NJ. 800-327-9903
Adrienne's Gourmet Foods
Santa Barbara, CA 800-937-7010
Al-Rite Fruits & Syrups
Miami, FL. 305-652-2540
All American Foods, Inc.
Mankato, MN 800-833-2661
Alle Processing
Maspeth, NY. 718-894-2000
Alle Processing Corporation
Maspeth, NY. 800-245-5620
Allied Wine Corporation
Monticello, NY. 845-796-4160
Alta Dena Certified Dairy
City of Industry, CA 800-535-1369

Americana Marketing
Newbury Park, CA 800-742-7520
Anke Kruse Organics
Guelph, ON 519-824-6161
Annie Chun's
San Rafael, CA 415-479-8272
Arbre Farms Corporation
Walkerville, MI 231-873-3337
Aunt Gussie Cookies & Crackers
Garfield, NJ 800-422-6654
Avatar Corporation
University Park, IL 800-255-3181
Bake Crafters Food
Collegedale, TN 800-296-8935
Ballas Egg Products Corporation
Zanesville, OH 740-453-0386
Beatrice Bakery Company
Beatrice, NE 800-228-4030
Bella Viva Orchards
Denair, CA 800-552-8218
Benson's Gourmet Seasonings
Azusa, CA 800-325-5619
Biazzo Dairy Products
Ridgefield, NJ 201-941-6800
Blue Chip Group
Salt Lake City, UT 800-878-0099
Blue Planet Foods
Collegedale, TN 877-396-3145
Boca Bons East,LLC.
Greenacres, FL 800-314-2835
Bombay Breeze Specialty Foods
Mississauga, ON 416-410-2320
Briess Industries
Chilton, WI 920-849-7711
Bruno Specialty Foods
West Sayville, NY 631-589-1700
Butterball Farms
Grand Rapids, MI 616-243-0105
Cache Creek Foods
Woodland, CA 530-662-1764
Calhoun Bend Mill
Alexandria, LA 800-519-6455
California Custom Fruits & Flavors
Irwindale, CA 877-558-0056
Campbell Soup Company
Camden, NJ 800-257-8443
Carmi Flavor & Fragrance Company
City of Commerce, CA 800-421-9647
Casa Visco Finer Food Company
Schenectady, NY 888-607-2823
Caudill Seed Company
Louisville, KY 800-626-5357
Champlain Valley Milling Corporation
Westport, NY 518-962-4711
Cheese Smokers
Brooklyn, NY
Chewys Rugulach
San Diego, CA 800-241-3456
Chloe Foods Corporation
Brooklyn, NY 718-827-9000
Chris Candies
Pittsburgh, PA 412-322-9400
Claussen Pickle Company
Woodstock, IL 800-435-2817
Coach's Oats
Yorba Linda, CA 714-692-6885
Coffee Masters
Spring Grove, IL 800-334-6485
Columbus Foods Company
Des Plaines, IL 800-322-6457
Commissariat Imports
Los Angeles, CA 310-475-5628
Coombs Vermont Gourmet
Brattleboro, VT 888-266-6271
Country Choice Naturals
Eden Prairie, MN 952-829-8824
Creme Glacee Gelati
Montreal, QC 888-322-0116
Dakota Growers Pasta Company
New Hope, MN 763-531-5360
Deer Creek Honey Farms
London, OH 740-852-0899
Dr. Praeger's Sensible Foods
Elmwood Park, NJ 877-PRA-GER
Dreyer's Grand Ice Cream
Oakland, CA 877-437-3937
Dynamic Health Labs
Brooklyn, NY 800-396-2214
Eatem Foods Company
Vineland, NJ 800-683-2836
Eco-Cuisine
Boulder, CO 303-444-6634

Eggology
Canoga Park, CA 818-610-2222
Elan Chemical Company
Newark, NJ 973-344-8014
Embassy Wine Company
Brooklyn, NY 718-272-0600
Enrico's/Ventre Packing
Syracuse, NY 888-472-8237
Erba Food Products
Brooklyn, NY 718-272-7700
FNI Group LLC
Sherborn, MA 508-655-4175
Foodbrands America
Oklahoma City, OK 405-290-4000
Freeda Vitamins
Long Island City, NY 800-777-3737
Fresh Roasted Almond Company
Warren, MI 877-478-6887
Friendship Dairies
Dallas, TX 516-719-4000
Frookie
Des Plaines, IL 847-699-3200
Georgia Spice Company
Atlanta, GA 800-453-9997
Gerber Products Company
Parsippany, NJ 800-443-7237
Gimbal's Fine Candies
S San Francisco, CA 800-344-6225
GKI Foods
Brighton, MI 248-486-0055
GMI Products/Originates
Sunrise, FL 800-999-9373
Gold Pure Foods Products Company
Hempstead, NY 800-422-4681
Golden Fluff Popcorn Company
Lakewood, NJ 732-367-5448
Golden Temple
Los Angeles, CA 310-275-9891
Griffin Food Company
Muskogee, OK 800-580-6311
Hanan Products Company
Hicksville, NY 516-938-1000
Hansen's Natural
Fullerton, CA 714-870-0310
Happy & Healthy Products
Boca Raton, FL 561-367-0739
Harbar Corporation
Canton, MA 800-881-7040
Harvest Valley Bakery
La Salle, IL 815-224-9030
Hausbeck Pickle Company
Saginaw, MI 866-754-4721
Heisler Food Enterprises
Bronx, NY 718-543-0855
Herb Connection
Springville, UT 801-489-4254
Hermann Laue Spice Company
Uxbridge, ON 905-852-5100
Hermann Pickle Farm
Garrettsville, OH 800-245-2696
Hialeah Products Company
Hollywood, FL 800-923-3379
Honey Bar/Creme de la Creme
Kingston, NY 845-331-4643
HoneyRun Winery
Chico, CA 530-345-6405
Honeywood Winery
Salem, OR 800-726-4101
Hospitality Mints
Boone, NC 800-334-5181
House of Flavors
Ludington, MI 800-930-7740
I. Epstein & Sons
East Brunswick, NJ 800-237-5320
Ice Land Corporation
Pittsburgh, PA 412-441-9512
Imagine Foods
Melville, NY 800-333-6339
International Glatt Kosher
Brooklyn, NY 718-630-5555
Isabella's Healthy Bakery
Cuyahoga Falls, OH 800-476-6328
Joyva Corporation
Brooklyn, NY 718-497-0170
Jurgielewicz Duck Farm
Moriches, NY 800-543-8257
Kaplan & Zubrin
Camden, NJ 800-334-0002
Kemach Food Products Corporation
Brooklyn, NY 888-453-6224
Klein's Kosher Pickles
Phoenix, AZ 602-269-2072

L&S Packing Company
Farmingdale, NY 800-286-6487
Lee Kum Kee
City of Industry, CA 800-654-5082
Leiner Davis Gelatin
Jericho, NY 516-942-4940
Lenchner Bakery
Concord, ON 905-738-8811
Lifeway Foods Inc
Morton Grove, IL 877-281-3874
Loriva Culinary Oils Worldpantry.Com, Inc
San Francisco, CA 866-972-6879
Losurdo Creamery
Hackensack, NJ 800-245-6787
M&L Gourmet Ice Cream
Baltimore, MD 410-276-4880
Macabee Foods
West Nyack, NY 845-623-1300
Mada'n Kosher Foods
Dania, FL 954-925-0077
Magic Seasoning Blends
New Orleans, LA 800-457-2857
Main Street Custom Foods
Cuyahoga Falls, OH 800-533-6246
Main Street Gourmet
Cuyahoga Falls, OH 800-533-6246
Main Street Gourmet Fundraising
Cuyahoga Falls, OH 800-533-6246
Main Street Muffins
Cuyahoga Falls, OH 800-533-6246
Main Street's Cambritt Cookies
Cuyahoga Falls, OH 800-533-6246
Mancini Packing Company
Zolfo Springs, FL 863-735-2000
Maple Products
Sherbrooke, QC 819-569-5161
Maplehurst Bakeries
Carrollton, GA 800-482-4810
Marie Callender's Gourmet Products/Goldrush Products
San Jose, CA 800-729-5428
Martin Farms
Patterson, CA 877-838-7369
Marukan Vinegar (U.S.A.) Inc.
Paramount, CA 562-630-6060
Meal Mart
Maspeth, NY 800-245-5620
Mendocino Mustard
Fort Bragg, CA 800-964-2270
Mille Lacs Wild Rice Corporation
Aitkin, MN 800-626-3809
Miller's Cheese Corp
Brooklyn, NY 718-965-1840
Milligan & Higgins
Johnstown, NY 518-762-4638
Milmar Food Group
Goshen, NY 845-294-5400
Mogen David Wine Corporation
Westfield, NY 716-326-3151
Mon Cuisine
Flushing, NY 877-666-8348
Mona Lisa Food Products
Hendersonville, NC 800-982-2546
Morning Glory/Formost Farms
Baraboo, WI 800-362-9196
Mothers Kitchen Inc
Burlington, NJ 609-589-3026
Mozzicato Depasquale Bakery & Pastry Shop
Hartford, CT 860-296-0426
Mrs. Leeper's Pasta
Excelsior Springs, MO 800-848-5266
Mushroom Company
Cambridge, MD 410-221-8971
Musicon Deer Farm
Goshen, NY 845-294-6378
My Grandma's Coffee Cakee of New England
Boston, MA 800-847-2636
National Food Corporation
Everett, WA 425-349-4257
National Fruit Flavor Company
New Orleans, LA 800-966-1123
Navarro Pecan Company
Corsicana, TX 800-333-9507
Northwestern Foods
Saint Paul, MN 800-236-4937
Norwalk Dairy
Santa Fe Springs, CA 562-921-5712
Nu-World Amaranth
Naperville, IL 630-369-6819
Old Fashioned Kitchen
Lakewood, NJ 732-364-4100
Pac Moore Products
Hammond, IN 219-932-2666

Pacific Salmon Company
Edmonds, WA 425-774-1315
Pak Technologies
Milwaukee, WI 414-438-8600
Palmieri Food Products
New Haven, CT 800-845-5447
Preferred Brands International
Stamford, CT. 800-827-8900
Price Cold Storage & Packing Company
Yakima, WA 509-966-4110
Quality Naturally! Foods
City of Industry, CA 888-498-6986
R.A.B. Food Group LLC
Secaucus, NJ 201-553-1100
Ranaldi Bros Frozen Food Products Inc
Warwick, RI 401-738-3444
Real Kosher Sausage Company
Newark, NJ 973-690-5394
Redmond Minerals
Redmond, UT 800-367-7258
Rogers Sugar Inc
Vancouver, BC 800-661-5350
Roller Ed
Rochester, NY. 585-458-8020
Royal Palate Foods
Inglewood, CA 310-330-7701
Royal Wine Corp
Bayonne, NJ 718-384-2400
Russian Chef
New York, NY 212-249-1550
Sabroso Company
Medford, OR. 541-772-5653
Sandt's Honey Company
Easton, PA. 800-935-3960
Schwartz Pickle Company
Chicago, IL 773-927-7700
Seabrook Brothers & Sons
Seabrook, NJ. 856-455-8080
Setton International Foods
Commack, NY 800-227-4397
Shofar Kosher Foods
Linden, NJ. 888-874-6327
Sigma-Aldrich Corporation
St. Louis, MO 314-771-5765
Silver Lake Cookie Company
Islip, NY 631-581-4000
Silver Spring Gardens
Eau Claire, WI 800-826-7322
Simply Divine
New York, NY 212-541-7300
Solana Gold Organics
Sebastopol, CA 800-459-1121
Somerset Industries
Spring House, PA 800-883-8728
Spilke's Baking Company
Brooklyn, NY 718-384-2150
Springfield Smoked Fish Company
Springfield, MA 800-327-3412
Steve's Mom
Bronx, NY. 800-362-4545
Strub Pickles
Brantford, ON. 519-751-1717
Sun Harvest Foods
San Diego, CA 619-661-0909
Sunergia Soyfoods
Charlottesville, VA 800-693-5134
Sure Fresh Produce
Santa Maria, CA 888-423-5379
Thomas Canning/Maidstone
Maidstone, ON 519-737-1531
Todhunter Foods & Monarch Wine Company
West Palm Beach, FL 800-336-9463
Top Hat Company
Wilmette, IL 847-256-6565
Touche Bakery
London, ON 518-455-0044
Tova Industries
Louisville, KY 888-532-8682
Trebon European Specialties
South Hackensack, NJ 800-899-4332
Umanoff & Parsons
Bronx, NY. 800-248-9993
US Chocolate Corporation
Brooklyn, NY 718-788-8555
Vacaville Fruit Company
Vacaville, CA 707-448-5292
Ventura Foods
Portland, OR. 503-255-5512
Vermont Country Naturals
Charlotte, VT 800-528-7021
Vic Rossano Incorporated
Montreal, QC 514-766-5252
Vienna Sausage Company
Chicago, IL 800-366-3647
Weaver Nut Company
Ephrata, PA 717-738-3781
Weinberg Foods
Kirkland, WA 800-866-3447
Weiss Homemade Kosher Bakery
Brooklyn, NY 800-498-3477
Wenner Bread Products
Bayport, NY 800-869-6262
Widmer's Wine Cellars
Canandaigua, NY
World Cheese Company
Brooklyn, NY 718-965-1700
World Harbors
Auburn, ME 800-355-6221
World of Chantilly
Brooklyn, NY 718-859-1110
World's Finest Chocolate
Chicago, IL 888-821-8452
Your Bar Factory
LaSalle, QC. 888-366-0258
YZ Enterprises
Maumee, OH. 800-736-8779
Zapp's Potato Chips
Gramercy, LA 800-349-2447

Matzo

Aron Streit Inc.
New York, NY 212-475-7000
Erba Food Products
Brooklyn, NY 718-272-7700
R.A.B. Food Group LLC
Secaucus, NJ 201-553-1100

Meal

R.A.B. Food Group LLC
Secaucus, NJ 201-553-1100

Mexican

Alamo Tamale Corporation
Houston, TX 800-252-0586
Embassy of Spain Trades Commission
New York, NY 212-907-6481
Fiesta Mexican Foods
Brawley, CA 760-344-3577
Fresca Mex. Foods
Boise, ID 208-376-6922
Garcias Mexican Foods
Duluth, GA 770-638-0881
Gardunos Mexican Food
Pomona, CA 909-469-6611
Gladstone Food Products Company
Kansas City, MO. 816-436-1255
Intermex Products
Grand Prairie, TX 972-660-2071
JJ's Tamales & Barbacoa
San Antonio, TX. 210-737-1300
La Casita's Home Style Mexican Food
Holts Summit, MO 573-896-8306
La Chapalita
Los Angeles, CA
La Monita Mexican Food
Austin, TX. 512-524-4294
La Reina
Monterey, CA 831-372-4003
Los Pericos Food Products
Los Angeles, CA. 323-269-5816
LPI
Chicago, IL 773-254-7200
Mission Foodservice
Oldsmar, FL 800-443-7994
Moody Dunbar
Johnson City, TN 800-251-8202
National Importers
Richmond, BC 888-894-6464
Pancho's Mexican Foods
Memphis, TN 901-744-3900
T.W. Garner Food Company
Winston Salem, NC. 800-476-7383
Teasdale Quality Foods
Atwater, CA 209-358-5616
Windsor Frozen Foods
Houston, TX 800-437-6936

Oriental

Hanmi
Chicago, IL 773-271-0730
Hop Kee
Chicago, IL 312-791-9111
Koha Food
Honolulu, HI 808-845-4232
M&M Food Distributors/Oriental Pride
Virginia Beach, VA. 757-499-5676
Mah Chena Company
Chicago, IL 312-226-5100

Paella

Conrad Rice Mill
New Iberia, LA 800-551-3245
Cuizina Food Company
Woodinville, WA. 425-486-7000

Parve Foods

Anke Kruse Organics
Guelph, ON. 519-824-6161
Bombay Breeze Specialty Foods
Mississauga, ON. 416-410-2320
Bruno Specialty Foods
West Sayville, NY. 631-589-1700
Chloe Foods Corporation
Brooklyn, NY 718-827-9000
Coach's Oats
Yorba Linda, CA. 714-692-6885
Country Choice Naturals
Eden Prairie, MN 952-829-8824
Dr. Praeger's Sensible Foods
Elmwood Park, NJ. 877-PRA-GER
Dynamic Health Labs
Brooklyn, NY 800-396-2214
Eggology
Canoga Park, CA 818-610-2222
Enrico's/Ventre Packing
Syracuse, NY 888-472-8237
FNI Group LLC
Sherborn, MA 508-655-4175
Frookie
Des Plaines, IL 847-699-3200
Golden Temple
Los Angeles, CA. 310-275-9891
Hansen's Natural
Fullerton, CA 714-870-0310
Happy & Healthy Products
Boca Raton, FL. 561-367-0739
Honey Bar/Creme de la Creme
Kingston, NY 845-331-4643
HoneyRun Winery
Chico, CA 530-345-6405
Marukan Vinegar (U.S.A.) Inc.
Paramount, CA 562-630-6060
Mrs. Leeper's Pasta
Excelsior Springs, MO 800-848-5266
New World Pasta
Harrisburg, PA 717-526-2200
Northwestern Foods
Saint Paul, MN 800-236-4937
Touche Bakery
London, ON 518-455-0044
US Chocolate Corporation
Brooklyn, NY 718-788-8555
YZ Enterprises
Maumee, OH. 800-736-8779

Shells

Chalupa

B. Martinez & Sons Company
San Antonio, TX. 210-226-6772
Rudy's Tortillas
Dallas, TX. 800-878-2401

Taco

Abuelita Mexican Foods
Manassas Park, VA 703-369-0232
Amigos Canning Company
San Antonio, TX. 800-580-3477
Anita's Mexican Foods Corporation
San Bernardino, CA 909-890-4647
Azteca Foods
Summit Argo, IL. 708-563-6600
B. Martinez & Sons Company
San Antonio, TX. 210-226-6772
El Rancho Tortilla
San Antonio, TX. 210-922-8411
La Buena Mexican Foods Products
Tucson, AZ 520-624-1796

Las Cruces Foods
Mesilla Park, NM 575-526-2352
Li'l Guy Foods
Kansas City, MO. 800-886-8226
Luna's Tortillas
Dallas, TX. 214-747-2661
Mexisnax Corporation
El Paso, TX. 915-779-5709
Mission Foodservice
Oldsmar, FL 800-443-7994
Odessa Tortilla & TamaleFactory
Odessa, TX 800-753-2445
Perez Food Products
Kansas City, MO. 816-931-8761
Puebla Foods
Passaic, NJ 973-473-4494
Reser's Fine Foods
Beaverton, OR 800-333-6431
Rudy's Tortillas
Dallas, TX. 800-878-2401
Sams-Leon Mexican Supplies
Omaha, NE 402-733-3809
Spanish Gardens Food Manufacturing
Kansas City, KS 913-831-4242

Tabbouleh

Bishop Brothers
Bristow, OK 800-859-8304
Tarazi Specialty Foods
Chino, CA. 909-628-3601

Tacos

Amigos Canning Company
San Antonio, TX. 800-580-3477
Queen International Foods
Monterey Park, CA. 800-423-4414
R&S Mexican Food Products
Glendale, AZ. 602-272-2727
Ruiz Food Products
Dinuba, CA. 800-477-6474

Fillings

Burke Corporation
Nevada, IA 800-654-1152

Always make it your best® with Burke fully cooked meats. We specialize in Italian sausage, beef, and pork toppings, meatballs, taco meats, shredded meats, pepperoni, bacon, Canadian-style bacon, chicken and beef strips. Additionally, we offer a variety of specialty products: Hand-Pinched Style® brand toppings, chorizo, gyro topping, andouille sausage, and breakfast patties and links.

First Original Texas Chili Company
Fort Worth, TX 817-626-0983
Original Texas Chili Company
Fort Worth, TX 800-507-0009
Ready Foods
Denver, CO 720-889-1104

Tamales

Abuelita Mexican Foods
Manassas Park, VA. 703-369-0232
Alamo Tamale Corporation
Houston, TX 800-252-0586
Art's Tamales
Metamora, IL 309-367-2850
Baja Foods
Chicago, IL 773-376-9030
Comanche Tortilla Factory
Fort Stockton, TX. 432-336-3245
El-Rey Foods
Ferguson, MO 314-521-3113
Grande Tortilla Factory
Tucson, AZ 520-622-8338
Hacienda De Paco
Orlando, FL. 407-859-5417
Kelly Foods
Jackson, TN 731-424-2255
La Buena Mexican Foods Products
Tucson, AZ 520-624-1796
Leonas Foods
Chimayo, NM 505-351-4660
Luna's Tortillas
Dallas, TX. 214-747-2661
Mama Maria's Tortillas
Midvale, UT 801-566-5150
Mexi-Frost Specialties Company
Brooklyn, NY 718-625-3324
Mi Ranchito Foods
Bayard, NM. 575-537-3868
Mr Jay's Tamales & Chili
Lynwood, CA 310-537-3932
Odessa Tortilla & TamaleFactory
Odessa, TX 800-753-2445
R&S Mexican Food Products
Glendale, AZ. 602-272-2727
Ramona's Mex. Food Produoducts
Gardena, CA 310-323-1950
Reser's Fine Foods
Salt Lake City, UT 801-972-5633
Ruiz Food Products
Dinuba, CA. 800-477-6474
Specialty Brands
Ontario, CA. 800-782-1180
Supreme Frozen Products
Chicago, IL 773-622-3777
Supreme Frozen Products
Chicago, IL 888-643-0405
Tom Tom Tamale Manufacturing
Chicago, IL. 773-523-5675

Frozen

Art's Tamales
Metamora, IL 309-367-2850
Baja Foods
Chicago, IL 773-376-9030
Edmonds Chile Company
St Louis, MO. 314-772-1499
El-Rey Foods
Ferguson, MO 314-521-3113
Mexi-Frost Specialties Company
Brooklyn, NY 718-625-3324
Mi Ranchito Foods
Bayard, NM. 575-537-3868
Ramona's Mex. Food Produoducts
Gardena, CA 310-323-1950
Ruiz Food Products
Dinuba, CA. 800-477-6474
Tom Tom Tamale Manufacturing
Chicago, IL 773-523-5675

Taquitos

Queen International Foods
Monterey Park, CA. 800-423-4414
Ruiz Food Products
Dinuba, CA. 800-477-6474
Specialty Brands
Ontario, CA. 800-782-1180

Tempeh

Simple Soyman
Milwaukee, WI 414-444-8638
Twenty First Century Foods
Jamaica Plain, MA 617-522-7595
Twin Oaks Community Foods
Louisa, VA 540-894-4062
White Wave
Broomfield, CO 800-488-9283

Tortilla & Tortilla Products

Anita's Mexican Foods Corporation
San Bernardino, CA 909-890-4647
Calidad Foods
Grand Prairie, TX 972-933-4100
Comanche Tortilla Factory
Fort Stockton, TX. 432-336-3245
Cosa de Rio Foods
Louisville, KY 502-772-2500
Del-Rey Tortilleria
Chicago, IL 773-637-8900
El Matador Foods
Baytown, TX. 281-424-4555
Festida Food
Cedar Springs, MI. 616-696-0400
Fresca Mex. Foods
Boise, ID 208-376-6922
Good Wives, Inc.
Wilmington, MA. 800-521-8160
Harbar Corporation
Canton, MA 800-881-7040
La Casita's Home Style Mexican Food
Holts Summit, MO 573-896-8306
La Mexicana Tortilla Factory
Hayward, CA 510-889-8225
La Tolteca Foods
Pueblo, CO 719-543-5733
La Tortilla Factory
Santa Rosa, CA. 800-446-1516
Los Pericos Food Products
Los Angeles, CA. 323-269-5816
Mama Maria's Tortillas
Midvale, UT 801-566-5150
Rudolph's Specialty Bakery
Toronto, ON 800-268-1589

Tortillas

Abuelita Mexican Foods
Manassas Park, VA. 703-369-0232
Azteca Foods
Summit Argo, IL. 708-563-6600
Azteca Milling
Irving, TX 800-364-0040
B. Martinez & Sons Company
San Antonio, TX. 210-226-6772
Better Meat North
Bay City, MI 989-684-6271
Bien Padre Foods
Eureka, CA 707-442-4585
Bueno Food Products
Albuquerque, NM. 800-888-7336
Casa Valdez
Caldwell, ID 208-459-6461
Cedarlane Foods
Carson, CA 310-886-7720
Comanche Tortilla Factory
Fort Stockton, TX. 432-336-3245
Cosa de Rio Foods
Louisville, KY 502-772-2500
Custom Ingredients
New Braunfels, TX. 800-457-8935
Delicious Popcorn Company
Waupaca, WI. 715-258-7683
El Charro Mexican Food Industries
Roswell, NM. 575-622-8590
El Charro Mexican Foods
Roswell, NM. 575-622-8590
El Rancho Tortilla
San Antonio, TX. 210-922-8411
El-Milagro
Chicago, IL
Father Sam's Syrian Bread
Buffalo, NY. 800-521-6719
Fiesta Mexican Foods
Brawley, CA 760-344-3577
Food Products Corporation
Phoenix, AZ 602-273-7139
Grande Tortilla Factory
Tucson, AZ 520-622-8338
Great Western Tortilla
Denver, CO 303-298-0705
Hacienda De Paco
Orlando, FL. 407-859-5417
Harbar Corporation
Canton, MA 800-881-7040
La Buena Mexican Foods Products
Tucson, AZ 520-624-1796
La Canasta Mexican Food Products
Phoenix, AZ 855-269-7721
La Chapalita
Los Angeles, CA
La Chiquita Tortilla Manufacturing
Atlanta, GA. 800-486-3942
La Colonial/Robles Brothers
San Jose, CA. 408-436-5551
La Fronteriza
Toledo, OH 800-897-1772
La Mexicana Tortilla Factory
Duncanville, TX 214-943-7770
La Mexicana Tortilla Factory
Hayward, CA 510-889-8225
La Reina
Los Angeles, CA. 323-268-2791
La Tapatia Tortilleria
Fresno, CA 800-219-7329
La Tolteca Foods
Pueblo, CO 719-543-5733
La Tortilla Factory
Santa Rosa, CA. 800-446-1516
Lago Tortillas International
Austin, TX. 800-369-9017
Laredo Mexican Foods
Fort Wayne, IN 800-252-7336
Las Cruces Foods
Mesilla Park, NM 575-526-2352

Leonas Foods
Chimayo, NM 505-351-4660
Li'l Guy Foods
Kansas City, MO. 800-886-8226
Lone Star Bakery
Round Rock, TX. 512-255-3629
Los Amigos Tortilla Manufacturing
Atlanta, GA 800-969-8226
Los Arcos Tortillas
North Las Vegas, NV 702-399-3300
Luna's Tortillas
Dallas, TX. 214-747-2661
Manuel's Mexican-American Fine Foods
Salt Lake City, UT 800-748-5072
Manuel's Odessa Tortillaand Tamale Factory
Odessa, TX 432-332-6676
Metzger Popcorn Company
Delphos, OH 800-819-6072
Mex. Accent
New Berlin, WI. 262-784-4422
Mexi-Frost Specialties Company
Brooklyn, NY 718-625-3324
Mexisnax Corporation
El Paso, TX. 915-779-5709
Mi Mama's Tortilla Factory
Omaha, NE 402-345-2099
Mi Ranchito Foods
Bayard, NM. 575-537-3868
Mission Foodservice
Oldsmar, FL 800-443-7994
New Mexico Food Distributors
Albuquerque, NM 800-637-7084
O. Malley Grain
Fairmont, NE. 402-268-6001
Odessa Tortilla & TamaleFactory
Odessa, TX 800-753-2445
Ozuna Food Products Corporation
Sunnyvale, CA 408-400-0495
Pacific Ocean Produce
Santa Cruz, CA. 831-423-2654
Pepes Mexican Foods
Etobicoke, ON 416-674-0882
Perez Food Products
Kansas City, MO. 816-931-8761
Puebla Foods
Passaic, NJ 973-473-4494
R&S Mexican Food Products
Glendale, AZ. 602-272-2727
Ramona's Mex. Food Produoducts
Gardena, CA 310-323-1950
Ready Foods
Denver, CO 720-889-1104
Reser's Fine Foods
Beaverton, OR 800-333-6431
Reser's Fine Foods
Salt Lake City, UT 801-972-5633
Rudolph's Specialty Bakery
Toronto, ON 800-268-1589
Rudy's Tortillas
Dallas, TX. 800-878-2401
Ruiz Food Products
Dinuba, CA 800-477-6474
Ruiz Mex. Foods
Ontario, CA. 909-947-7811
Sams-Leon Mexican Supplies
Omaha, NE 402-733-3809
Sanitary Tortilla Manufacturing Company
San Antonio, TX. 210-226-9209
Selecto Sausage Company
Houston, TX 713-926-1626
Severance Foods
Hartford, CT 860-724-7063
Shirley Foods
Shirley, IN. 800-560-2908
Soloman Baking Company
Denver, CO 303-371-2777
Spanish Gardens Food Manufacturing
Kansas City, KS 913-831-4242
Specialty Brands
Ontario, CA. 800-782-1180
Sweet Corn Products Company
Bloomfield, NE. 877-628-6115
Tumaro's Gourmet Tortillas
Los Angeles, CA. 951-697-5950
Tumaro's Gourmet Tortillas & Snacks
Edison, NJ. 800-777-6317

Tostadas

Delicious Popcorn Company
Waupaca, WI. 715-258-7683
El Rancho Tortilla
San Antonio, TX. 210-922-8411
Happy's Potato Chip Company
Minneapolis, MN 612-781-3121
La Buena Mexican Foods Products
Tucson, AZ 520-624-1796
Luna's Tortillas
Dallas, TX. 214-747-2661
Manuel's Mexican-American Fine Foods
Salt Lake City, UT 800-748-5072
Mexisnax Corporation
El Paso, TX. 915-779-5709
Mission Foodservice
Oldsmar, FL 800-443-7994
Reser's Fine Foods
Beaverton, OR 800-333-6431
Rudy's Tortillas
Dallas, TX. 800-878-2401

Wonton Chips

Maebo Noodle Factory
Hilo, HI. 877-663-8667

Wontons

Chang Food Company
Garden Grove, CA 714-265-9990
Delta Food Products
Edmonton, AB 780-424-3636
Golden Gate Foods
Dallas, TX. 214-747-2223
Goodwives Hors D'Oeuvres
Wilmington, MA. 800-521-8160
Harvest Food Products Company
Concord, CA 925-676-8208
La Tang Cuisine Manufacturing
Houston, TX 713-780-4876
Mandarin Noodle Manufacturing Company
Calgary, AB. 403-265-1383
Montreal Chop Suey Company
Montreal, QC 514-522-3134
Nanka Seimen Company
Vernon, CA 323-585-9967
Peking Noodle Company
Los Angeles, CA. 323-223-2023
Roxy Trading
Pomona, CA
Wan Hua Foods
Seattle, WA 206-622-8417
Wing Hing Noodle Company
Los Angeles, CA. 888-223-8899
Wonton Food
Brooklyn, NY 800-776-8889

Fish & Seafood

Canned

Crusoe Seafood LLC
Sun Valley, CA 866-343-7629

General

Omega Pure
Irvine, CA 562-429-3335

Caviar (Roe)

Angy's Food Products Inc.
Westfield, MA 413-572-1010
Assouline & Ting
Huntingdon Valley, PA 800-521-4491
Bens Seafood Company
Crescent, GA 912-832-5121
Castella Imports
Hauppauge, NY 866-227-8355
D'Artagnan
Newark, NJ 800-327-8246
Ferroclad Fishery
Batchawana Bay, ON 705-882-2295
High Liner Foods Inc
Lunenburg, NS 902-634-9475
Kelley's Katch Caviar
Savannah, TN 888-681-8565
Liberty Richter
Saddle Brook, NJ 201-291-8749
Newell Lobsters
Yarmouth, NS 902-742-6272
Notre Dame Seafood
Comfort Cove, NL 709-244-5511
Paramount Caviar
Long Island City, NY 800-992-2842
Produits Belle Baie
Caraquet, NB 506-727-4414
Raffield Fisheries
Port St Joe, FL 850-229-8229
Royal Caviar
Glendale, CA 818-546-5858
Russ & Daughters
New York, NY 800-787-7229
Russian Chef
New York, NY 212-249-1550
T. Marzetti Company
Columbus, OH 614-846-2232
Tribe Mediterranean Foods Company LLC
Taunton, MA 774-961-0000

Herring

Cowart Seafood Corporation
Lottsburg, VA 804-529-6101
Icicle Seafoods
Seattle, WA 206-282-0988

Salmon

Assouline & Ting
Huntingdon Valley, PA 800-521-4491
Crown Prince
City of Industry, CA 800-255-5063
Icicle Seafoods
Seattle, WA 206-282-0988
Johns Cove Fisheries
Yarmouth, NS 902-742-8691
Pacific Alaska Seafoods
Seattle, WA 206-587-0002

Shad

Bailey Street Bakery
Atlanta, GA 800-822-4634
Calise & Sons Bakery
Lincoln, RI 800-225-4737
Carolina Foods
Charlotte, NC 800-234-0441
Dare Foods
Kitchener, ON 800-265-8225
Lewis Brothers Bakeries
Vincennes, IN 812-886-6533
Sara Lee
Knoxville, TN 865-573-1941
Stroehmann Bakeries
Harrisburg, PA 800-220-2867
Sunbeam Baking Company
El Paso, TX 800-328-6111
Weston Bakeries
Etobicoke, ON 416-252-7323
Winder Dairy
West Valley, UT 800-946-3371

Fish

A&C Quinlin Fisheries
McGray, NS 902-745-2742
Acme Smoked Fish Corporation
Brooklyn, NY 800-221-0795
Acme Steak & Seafood Company
Youngstown, OH 330-270-8000
Acushnet Fish Corporation
Fairhaven, MA 508-997-7482
Agger Fish
Brooklyn, NY 718-855-1717
Al Safa Halal
Niagara Falls, NY 800-268-8174
Alaska Sausage and Seafood Company
Anchorage, AK 800-798-3636
Alaska Seafood Company
Los Angeles, CA 213-626-1212
Alaskan Gourmet Seafoods
Anchorage, AK 800-288-3740
Alle Processing
Maspeth, NY 718-894-2000
Amano Fish Cake Factory
Hilo, HI 808-935-5555
Amcan Industries
Elmsford, NY 914-347-4838
American Seafoods International
New Bedford, MA 800-343-8046
Annabelle Lee
Cape Porpoise, ME 207-967-4611
Appert's Foodservice
St Cloud, MN 800-225-3883
Aquatec Seafoods Ltd.
Comox, BC 250-339-6412
Arcee Sales Company
Brooklyn, NY 718-383-0107
Arrowac Fisheries
Seattle, WA 206-282-5655
Art's Fisheries
Phoenix, AZ 602-252-9550
Atlantic Capes Fisheries
Cape May, NJ 609-884-3000
Atlantic Fish Specialties
Charlottetown, PE 902-894-7005
Atlantic Sea Pride
South Boston, MA 617-269-7700
B.M. Lawrence & Company
San Francisco, CA 415-981-3650
Baensch Food
Milwaukee, WI 800-562-8234
Bakalars Brothers Sausage Company
La Crosse, WI 608-784-0384
Baker's Point Fisheries
Oyster Pond Jeddore, NS 902-845-2347
Basin Crawfish Processors
Breaux Bridge, LA 337-332-6655
Bayou Foods
Kenner, LA 800-516-8283
Bayou Land Seafood
Breaux Bridge, LA 337-667-6118
Beaver Street Fisheries
Jacksonville, FL 800-874-6426
Becker Food Company
Milwaukee, WI 414-964-5353
Bell Buoy Crab Company
Seaside, OR 800-529-2722
Belle River Enterprises
Belle River, PE 902-962-2248
Billingsgate Fish Company
Calgary, AB 403-571-7700
Birch Street Seafoods
Digby, NS 902-245-6551
Blalock Seafood
Orange Beach, AL 251-974-5811
Blue Lakes Trout Farm
Jerome, ID 208-734-7151
Blue Wave Seafoods
Port Mouton, NS 902-683-2044
BlueWater Seafoods
Lachine, QC 888-560-2539
Bolner's Fiesta Products
San Antonio, TX 210-734-6404
Bornstein Seafoods
Bellingham, WA 360-734-7990
Bos Smoked Fish Inc
Woodstock, ON 519-537-5000
Boston Seafarms
Boston, MA 617-784-4777
Boutique Seafood
Atlanta, GA 404-752-8852
Breakwater Fisheries
St Josephs, NL 709-754-1999
Bumble Bee Foods
San Diego, CA 858-715-4000
Burleigh Brothers Seafoods
Ellerslie, PE 902-831-2349
Burris Mill & Feed
Franklinton, LA 800-928-2782
Caito Fisheries
Fort Bragg, CA 707-964-6368
California Shellfish Company
San Francisco, CA 415-923-7400
Canadian Fish Exporters
Watertown, MA 800-225-4215
Canus Fisheries
Clark's Harbour, NS 902-745-2888
Captain Alex Seafood
Niles, IL 847-803-8833
Captn's Pack Products
Columbia, MD 410-720-6668
Carrington Foods
Saraland, AL 251-675-9700
Certi-Fresh Foods
Bell Gardens, CA 562-806-1100
Charlton Deep Sea Charters
Warrenton, OR 503-338-0569
Cherokee Trout Farms
Cherokee, NC 800-732-0075
Cherry Point Products
Milbridge, ME 207-546-7056
Chicago Food Market
Chicago, IL 312-842-4361
Chicken of the Sea International
San Diego, CA 800-678-8862
Chuck's Seafoods
Charleston, OR 541-888-5525
Clear Springs Foods
Buhl, ID 800-635-8211
Completely Fresh Foods
Montebello, CA 323-722-9136
ConAgra Foods Inc
Omaha, NE 402-595-7300
Confish
Isola, MS 800-228-3474
Connors Aquaculture
Eastport, ME 207-853-6081
Consolidated Sea Products
Mobile, AL 251-433-3240
Cook Inlet Processing
Anchorage, AK 907-243-1166
Cook Inlet Processing
Nikiski, AK 907-776-8174
Cooke Aguaculture
Blacks Harbour, NB 506-456-6600
Cowart Seafood Corporation
Lottsburg, VA 804-529-6101
Crest International Corporation
San Diego, CA 800-548-1232
Crown Point
St John, IN 219-365-3200
Crown Prince
City of Industry, CA 800-255-5063
Cuizina Food Company
Woodinville, WA 425-486-7000
Culver's Fish Farm
Mc Pherson, KS 800-241-5205
Cushner Seafood
Baltimore, MD 410-358-5564
Dave's Gourmet Albacore
Kirkland, WA 800-454-8862
Deep Creek Custom Packing
Ninilchik, AK 800-764-0078
Delta Pride Catfish
Indianola, MS 800-421-1045
Depoe Bay Fish Company
Newport, OR 541-265-8833

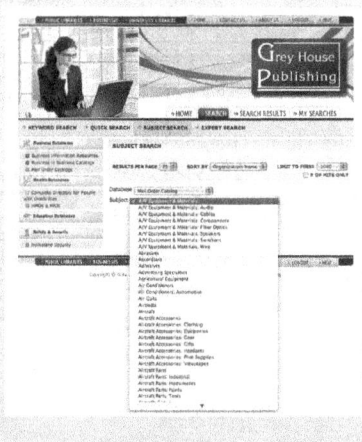

Dixon's Fisheries
East Peoria, IL....................309-694-1457
Dressel Collins Fish Company
Seattle, WA......................206-725-0121
Dynamic Foods
Lubbock, TX.....................806-747-2777
Ed Kasilof's Seafoods
Kasilof, AK......................800-982-2377
Edelman Meats
Antigo, WI......................715-623-7686
Emery Smith Fisheries Limited
Shag Harbour, NS.................902-723-2115
Erba Food Products
Brooklyn, NY....................718-272-7700
Farm Fresh Catfish Company
Hollandale, MS...................800-647-8264
Feature Foods
Etobicoke, ON...................416-675-7350
Ferroclad Fishery
Batchawana Bay, ON..............705-882-2295
Finestkind Fish Market
York, ME........................800-288-8154
First Oriental Market
Decatur, GA.....................404-377-6950
Fish Brothers
Blue Lake, CA...................800-244-0583
Fishermens Net
Portland, ME.....................207-772-3565
Fishery Products International
Danvers, MA.....................800-374-4700
Flavor House
Adelanto, CA....................760-246-9131
Fleet Fisheries
New Bedford, MA................508-996-3742
Fresh Island Fish Company
Kahului, HI......................808-871-1111
Freshwater Fish Market
Edmonton, AB...................800-345-3113
Garden & Valley Isle Seafood
Honolulu, HI.....................800-689-2733
George Robberecht Seafood
Montross, VA....................804-472-3556
Giovanni's Appetizing Food Products
Richmond, MI....................586-727-9355
Glenn Sales Company
Atlanta, GA......................770-952-9292
GMF Corporation
Gloucester, MA...................978-283-0479
Gold Star Smoked Fish
Brooklyn, NY....................718-522-1545
Gorton's Seafood
Gloucester, MA...................978-283-3000
Goya Foods of Florida
Miami, FL.......................305-592-3150
Great Glacier Salmon
Prince Rupert, BC.................250-627-4955
Great Northern Products
Warwick, RI.....................401-490-4590
Hallmark Fisheries
Charleston, OR...................541-888-3253
Hamilos Brothers Inspected Meats
Madison, IL......................618-451-7877
Handy International
Salisbury, MD....................800-426-3977
Harbor Fish Market
Portland, ME.....................207-775-0251
Harbor Lobster
Lower Wood Harbor, NS...........902-723-2500
Harbor Seafood
New Hyde Park, NY...............800-645-2211
Harry H. Park Company
Chicago, IL......................773-478-4424
Hawaii International Seafood
Honolulu, HI.....................808-839-5010
Heinz Company of Canada
North York, ON...................877-574-3469
HFI Foods
Redmond, WA....................425-883-1320
High Liner Foods Inc
Lunenburg, NS...................902-634-9475
Hilo Fish Company
Hilo, HI.........................808-961-0877
Homer's Wharf Seafood Company
New Bedford, MA................508-997-0766
Hygrade Ocean Products
New Bedford, MA................508-993-5700
Icelandic USA
Newport News, VA................757-820-4000
Icicle Seafoods
Seattle, WA......................206-282-0988
Idaho Trout Company
Buhl, ID.........................866-878-7688
Independent Packers Corporation
Seattle, WA......................206-285-6000
Indian Bay Frozen Foods
Centreville, NL...................709-678-2844
Indian Valley Meats
Indian, AK.......................907-653-7511
Inshore Fisheries
Middle West Pubnico, NS...........902-762-2522
International Seafoods of Alaska
Kodiak, AK......................907-486-4768
Island Marine Products
Clarks Harbour, NS................902-745-2222
J. Matassini & Sons Fish Company
Tampa, FL.......................813-229-0829
J. Moniz Company
Fall River, MA...................508-674-8451
J. Turner Seafoods
Gloucester, MA...................978-281-8535
J.S. McMillan Fisheries
Vancouver, BC...................604-255-5191
J.S. McMillan Fisheries
North Vancouver, BC..............604-981-4000
James Cowan & Sons
Worcester, MA...................508-753-3259
James L. Mood Fisheries
Lower Woods Harbour, NS..........902-723-2360
Jensen Seafood Packing Company
Dulac, LA
Jer-Mar Foods
Windsor, ON.....................519-256-3474
Jessie's Ilwaco Fish Company
Ilwaco, WA......................360-642-3773
John B. Wright Fish Company
Gloucester, MA...................978-283-4205
K&N Fisheries
Upper Port La Tour, NS............902-768-2478
Key Largo Fisheries
Key Largo, FL....................800-432-4358
Kodiak Salmon Packers
Larsen Bay, AK...................907-847-2250
Kwikpak Fisheries
Anchorage, AK...................800-509-3332
L&M Evans
Conyers, GA.....................770-918-8727
L. Isaacson
Chicago, IL......................312-421-2444
Lakeside Foods
Seymour, WI.....................920-833-2371
LEF McLean Brothers International
Wheatley, ON....................519-825-4656
Leo G. Atkinson Fisheries
Clarks Harbor, NS.................902-745-3047
Liberty Richter
Saddle Brook, NJ.................201-291-8749
LLJ's Sea Products
Round Pond, ME.................207-529-4224
Long Beach Seafoods
Long Beach, CA..................562-435-5357
Lougheed Fisheries
Owen Sound, ON.................519-376-1586
Lowland Seafood
Lowland, NC.....................252-745-3751
Lund's Fisheries
Cape May, NJ....................609-884-7600
Mada'n Kosher Foods
Dania, FL.......................954-925-0077
Marche Transatlantique
Montreal, QC....................514-287-3530
Mariner Seafoods
Montague, PE....................902-838-2481
Martin Brothers SeafoodcCompany
Westwego, LA....................504-341-2251
Mat Roland Seafood Company
Atlantic Beach, FL................904-246-9443
Maxim's Import Corporation
Miami, FL.......................800-331-6652
McDowell Fine Meats 2
Phoenix, AZ.....................602-254-6022
Menemsha Fish Market
Chilmark, MA....................508-645-2282
Mercado Latino
City of Industry, CA...............626-333-6862
Mersey Seafoods
Liverpool, NS....................902-354-3467
Mid-South Fish Company
Aubrey, AR......................870-295-5600
Milfico Foods
Elk Grove Vlg, IL.................847-427-0491
Mill Cove Lobster Pound
Boothbay Harbor, ME..............207-633-3340
Millen Fish
Millen, GA......................478-982-4988
Minor Fisheries
Port Colborne, ON................905-834-9232
Morey's Seafood Intl. ional
Motley, MN......................218-352-6345
Mutual Fish Company
Seattle, WA......................206-322-4368
National Fish and Seafood Limited
Brownsville, TX..................956-546-5525
Nelson Crab
Tokeland, WA....................800-262-0069
Neptune Foods
Vernon, CA......................323-232-8300
Nodine's Smokehouse
Torrington, CT...................800-222-2059
Noon Hour Food Products
Chicago, IL......................800-621-6636
Nordic Group
Boston, MA......................800-486-4002
North Atlantic
Portland, ME.....................207-774-6025
North Atlantic Fish Company
Gloucester, MA...................978-283-4121
North Atlantic Seafood
Stonington, ME...................207-367-5099
Northern Products Corporation
Seattle, WA......................206-448-6677
Notre Dame Seafood
Comfort Cove, NL................709-244-5511
Ocean Beauty Seafoods
Seattle, WA......................206-285-6800
Ocean Beauty Seafoods
Taunton, MA.....................774-961-0000
Ocean Fresh Seafoods
Seattle, WA......................206-285-2412
Okuhara Foods
Honolulu, HI.....................808-848-0581
Omstead Foods Ltd
Wheatley, ON....................905-315-8883
Pacific Alaska Seafoods
Seattle, WA......................206-587-0002
Pacific American Fish Co.,Inc.
Vernon, CA......................800-625-2525
Pacific Ocean Seafood
La Conner, WA...................360-466-4455
Pacific Salmon Company
Edmonds, WA....................425-774-1315
Pacific Seafoods International
Port Hardy, BC...................250-949-8781
Pacific Shrimp Company
Newport, OR.....................541-265-4215
Pacific Trade International
Hilo, HI.........................808-961-0877
Paramount Caviar
Long Island City, NY..............800-992-2842
Park 100 Foods
Tipton, IN.......................800-854-6504
Pastene Companies
Canton, MA......................781-830-8200
Paul Piazza & Sons
New Orleans, LA.................504-524-6011
Pelican Marine Supply
Belle Chasse, LA.................504-392-9062
Penguin Frozen Foods
Northbrook, IL...................847-291-9400
Peter Pan Seafoods
Seattle, WA......................206-728-6000
Pine Point Fisherman's Co-Op
Scarborough, ME.................207-883-3588
Point Adams Packing Company
Hammond, OR...................503-861-2226
Port Chatham Smoked Seafood
Everett, WA......................800-872-5666
Premier Smoked Fish Company
Bensalem, PA....................800-654-6682
Proacec USA
Santa Monica, CA.................310-996-7770
Produits Belle Baie
Caraquet, NB....................506-727-4414
Protein Products Inc
Whitehall, PA....................800-776-8422
Quinalt Pride Seafood
Taholah, WA.....................360-276-4431
R.A.B. Food Group LLC
Secaucus, NJ.....................201-553-1100
Raffield Fisheries
Port St Joe, FL...................850-229-8229
Red Lake Fisheries Associates
Redby, MN......................218-679-3513
Rego Smoked Fish Company
Flushing, NY.....................718-894-1400
Rivere's Seafood Processors
Paincourtville, LA.................985-369-2570

Roman Sausage Company
Santa Clara, CA 800-497-7462
Royal Seafood
Monterey, CA 831-655-8326
Russian Chef
New York, NY 212-249-1550
S.A.S. Foods
Norcross, GA
Sagaya Corporation
Anchorage, AK. 907-561-5173
Salmon River Smokehouse
Gustavus, AK 907-456-3885
Salt River Lobster
Boothbay, ME. 207-633-5357
Sau-Sea Foods
Tarrytown, NY 914-631-1717
SC Enterprises
Owen Sound, ON 519-371-0456
Scandia Seafood Company
Rockland, ME. 207-596-7102
Schafer Fisheries
Fulton, IL 815-589-3368
Sea Best Corporation
Ipswich, MA 978-768-7475
Sea Farm & Farmfresh Importing Company
Alhambra, CA. 323-265-7075
Sea Fresh Alaska
Kodiak, AK. 907-486-6226
Sea Fresh USA
Portland, ME. 207-773-6799
Sea Horse Wharf
Phippsburg, ME 207-389-2312
Sea K Fish Company
Blaine, WA 360-332-5121
Sea Level Seafoods
Wrangell, AK 907-874-2401
Sea Lyons
Spanish Fort, AL. 251-626-2841
Sea Safari
Belhaven, NC 800-688-6174
Sea-Fresh Seafood Market
Mobile, AL 251-478-3434
Seabear
Anacortes, WA 800-645-3474
Seabreeze Fish
Bakersfield, CA 661-323-7936
Seafood & Meat
Theodore, AL 251-653-4600
Seafood Connection
Honolulu, HI. 808-591-8550
Seafood Distributors
Savannah, GA. 912-233-6048
Seafood Express
Brunswick, ME. 207-729-0887
Seafood Hawaii
Honolulu, HI. 808-597-1971
Seafood International
Bayou La Batre, AL 251-824-4200
Seafood International Distributor, Inc
Henderson, LA 337-228-7568
Seafood Packaging
New Orleans, LA 504-522-6677
Seafood Plus Corporation
Berwyn, IL 708-795-4820
Seafood Producers Coop ative
Bellingham, WA 360-733-0120
Seafood Services
New Bedford, MA 508-999-6785
Seafood Specialty Sales
Ipswich, MA 978-356-2995
Seaway Company
Fairhaven, MA 508-992-1221
Service Marketing
Dunwoody, GA. 770-451-9183
Seven Seas Seafoods
Alhambra, CA. 626-570-9129
Sewell's Fish Market
Rogersville, AL. 256-247-1378
Seymour & Sons Seafood
Diberville, MS 228-392-4020
Sharkco Seafood International
Venice, LA 504-534-9577
Shore Trading Company
Alpharetta, GA 770-998-0566
Shuckman's Fish & Co. Smokery
Louisville, KY 502-775-6478
SIF
Shelburne, NS 902-875-2666
Silver Streak Bass Company
El Campo, TX. 979-543-6343
SOPAKCO Foods
Mullins, SC. 800-276-9678

Sorrento Lobster
Sorrento, ME. 207-422-9082
South Shores Seafood
Anaheim, CA 714-956-2722
Southern Fish & Oyster Company
Mobile, AL 251-438-2408
Southern Pride Catfish Company
Seattle, WA 800-343-8046
Spence & Company
Brockton, MA. 508-427-1627
Sportsmen's Cannery & Smokehouse
Winchester Bay, OR 800-457-8048
Sportsmen's Sea Foods
San Diego, CA 619-224-3551
Springfield Smoked Fish Company
Springfield, MA 800-327-3412
St. Simons Seafood
Brunswick, GA 912-265-5225
Star Fine Foods
Fresno, CA 559-498-2900
State Fish Company
San Pedro, CA. 310-832-2633
State Fish Distributors
Chicago, IL 773-451-0500
Stavis Seafoods
Boston, MA. 800-390-5103
Stinson Seafood Company
San Diego, CA
Stoller Fisheries
Spirit Lake, IA 712-336-1750
Stoller Fisheries
Spirit Lake, IA 800-831-5174
Stolt SeaFarm
Elverta, CA 800-525-0333
Strub Pickles
Brantford, ON. 519-751-1717
Sunshine Food Sales
Miami, FL. 305-696-2885
Sunshine Seafood
Stonington, ME. 207-367-2955
Super Snooty Sea Food Corporation
Boston, MA. 617-426-6390
Superior Seafoods
Tampa, FL. 813-248-2749
Sweet Water Seafood Corporation
Carlstadt, NJ 201-939-6622
Taku Smokehouse
Juneau, AK 800-582-5122
Tampa Maid Foods
Lakeland, FL. 800-237-7637
Tempest Fisheries Limited
New Bedford, MA 508-997-0720
Tenth & M. Seafoods
Anchorage, AK. 907-272-3474
Thompson Seafood
Darien, GA 912-437-4649
Three Rivers Fish Company
Simmesport, LA 318-941-2467
Tichon Seafood Corporation
New Bedford, MA 508-999-5607
Tri-Marine InternationalInc
San Pedro, CA. 310-732-6113
Tribe Mediterranean Foods Company LLC
Taunton, MA. 774-961-0000
Trident Seafoods Corporation
Salem, NH. 603-893-3368
Trident Seafoods Corporation
Seattle, WA 800-426-5490
Tropic Fish & Vegetable Center
Honolulu, HI. 808-591-2963
Trout of Paradise
Paradise, UT 435-245-3053
Ungars Food Products
Elmwood Park, NJ 201-703-1300
Union Fisheries Corporation
Chicago, IL 312-738-0448
United Fishing Agency Limited
Honolulu, HI. 808-536-2148
United Shellfish Company
Grasonville, MD 410-827-8171
Valdez Food
Philadelphia, PA 215-634-6106
Van De Kamp Frozen Foods
Mountain Lake, NJ 973-541-6620
Van de Kamp's
Peoria, IL. 800-798-3318
Van Dykes Chesapeake Seafood
Cambridge, MD 410-228-9000
Viking Seafoods Inc
Malden, MA 800-225-3020
Vinalhaven Fishermens Co-Op
Camden, ME. 207-236-0092

Virginia Trout Company
Monterey, VA 540-468-2280
Vita Food Products
Chicago, IL 312-738-4500
Wabash Seafood Company
Chicago, IL 312-733-5070
Wanchese Fish Company
Suffolk, VA 757-673-4500
Waterfield Farms
Amherst, MA 413-549-3558
West India Trading Company
Petit-Cap, NB 506-577-6214
Weyand Fisheries
Wyandotte, MI 800-521-9815
White Cap Fish Company
Islip, NY 631-581-0125
Wrangell Fisheries
Wrangell, AK 907-874-3346
Yamasa Fish Cake Company
Los Angeles, CA. 213-626-2211
York Beach Fish Market
York, ME. 207-363-2763

Abalone

Crown Prince
City of Industry, CA 800-255-5063
Sitka Sound Seafoods
Sitka, AK. 907-747-6662

Amber Jack

Griffin Seafood
Golden Meadow, LA. 985-396-2453

Anchovies

Chicken of the Sea International
San Diego, CA 800-678-8862
Crown Prince
City of Industry, CA 800-255-5063

Canned

Crown Prince Naturals
Petaluma, CA
Liberty Richter
Saddle Brook, NJ 201-291-8749
Ron-Son Foods
Swedesboro, NJ 856-241-7333

Olive Oil

Castella Imports
Hauppauge, NY 866-227-8355

Paste

Giovanni's Appetizing Food Products
Richmond, MI. 586-727-9355

Arctic Charr

Fumoir Grizzly
St-Augustin-De-Desmaures, QC 418-878-8941

Bass

Culver's Fish Farm
Mc Pherson, KS 800-241-5205
Louisiana Seafood Exchange
New Orleans, LA 504-283-9393
Minor Fisheries
Port Colborne, ON 905-834-9232
Wanchese Fish Company
Suffolk, VA 757-673-4500

Striped

Advanced Aquacultural Technologies
Syracuse, IN 574-457-5802

Bluefish

Menemsha Fish Market
Chilmark, MA. 508-645-2282
Raffield Fisheries
Port St Joe, FL. 850-229-8229

Bottomfish

Charlton Deep Sea Charters
Warrenton, OR 503-338-0569
Pacific Ocean Seafood
La Conner, WA 360-466-4455

Butterfish

Atlantic Capes Fisheries
Cape May, NJ 609-884-3000
Okuhara Foods
Honolulu, HI 808-848-0581
Raffield Fisheries
Port St Joe, FL. 850-229-8229

Cakes

Amano Fish Cake Factory
Hilo, HI 808-935-5555
Cherokee Trout Farms
Cherokee, NC 800-732-0075
Icelandic USA
Newport News, VA. 757-820-4000
LaMonica Fine Foods
Millville, NJ 856-825-8111
Valdez Food
Philadelphia, PA 215-634-6106
Viking Seafoods Inc
Malden, MA 800-225-3020
Yamasa Fish Cake Company
Los Angeles, CA. 213-626-2211

Canned

Cuizina Food Company
Woodinville, WA. 425-486-7000
LaMonica Fine Foods
Millville, NJ 856-825-8111

Fresh

Cuizina Food Company
Woodinville, WA. 425-486-7000
Ocean Delight Seafoods
Vancouver, BC 604-254-8351
Valdez Food
Philadelphia, PA 215-634-6106
Yamasa Fish Cake Company
Los Angeles, CA. 213-626-2211

Frozen

Amano Fish Cake Factory
Hilo, HI 808-935-5555
Cuizina Food Company
Woodinville, WA. 425-486-7000
Gorton's Seafood
Gloucester, MA. 978-283-3000
Icelandic USA
Newport News, VA. 757-820-4000
Viking Seafoods Inc
Malden, MA 800-225-3020
Yamasa Fish Cake Company
Los Angeles, CA. 213-626-2211

Canned

Alaskan Gourmet Seafoods
Anchorage, AK. 800-288-3740
Amano Fish Cake Factory
Hilo, HI 808-935-5555
B.M. Lawrence & Company
San Francisco, CA 415-981-3650
Bornstein Seafoods
Bellingham, WA 360-734-7990
Bumble Bee Foods
San Diego, CA 858-715-4000
Chicken of the Sea International
San Diego, CA 800-678-8862
Chuck's Seafoods
Charleston, OR 541-888-5525
Cowart Seafood Corporation
Lottsburg, VA 804-529-6101
Crown Point
St John, IN 219-365-3200
Deep Creek Custom Packing
Ninilchik, AK 800-764-0078
Dressel Collins Fish Company
Seattle, WA 206-725-0121
Fishhawk Fisheries
Astoria, OR. 503-325-5252
IMO Foods
Halifax, NS 902-450-5060
Indian Valley Meats
Indian, AK. 907-653-7511
J. Moniz Company
Fall River, MA 508-674-8451
J. Turner Seafoods
Gloucester, MA. 978-281-8535
J.S. McMillan Fisheries
Vancouver, BC 604-255-5191
J.S. McMillan Fisheries
North Vancouver, BC 604-981-4000
Kodiak Salmon Packers
Larsen Bay, AK. 907-847-2250
Liberty Richter
Saddle Brook, NJ 201-291-8749
LLJ's Sea Products
Round Pond, ME 207-529-4224
Mercado Latino
City of Industry, CA 626-333-6862
Monterey Fish Company
Salinas, CA 831-771-9221
Nelson Crab
Tokeland, WA 800-262-0069
Noon Hour Food Products
Chicago, IL 800-621-6636
Notre Dame Seafood
Comfort Cove, NL 709-244-5511
Ocean Fresh Seafoods
Seattle, WA 206-285-2412
Pacific Salmon Company
Edmonds, WA 425-774-1315
Pastene Companies
Canton, MA 781-830-8200
Petersburg Fisheries
Petersburg, AK 877-772-4294
Quinalt Pride Seafood
Taholah, WA 360-276-4431
Ron-Son Foods
Swedesboro, NJ 856-241-7333
S&D Bait Company
Morgan City, LA. 504-252-3500
Shafer-Haggart
Vancouver, BC 604-669-5512
Sportsmen's Cannery & Smokehouse
Winchester Bay, OR 800-457-8048
Sportsmen's Sea Foods
San Diego, CA 619-224-3551
Tri-Marine InternationalInc
San Pedro, CA. 310-732-6113
Trout of Paradise
Paradise, UT 435-245-3053
Ward Cove Packing Company
Seattle, WA 206-323-3200
Wrangell Fisheries
Wrangell, AK 907-874-3346

Carp

Culver's Fish Farm
Mc Pherson, KS 800-241-5205
Red Lake Fisheries Associates
Redby, MN 218-679-3513
Stoller Fisheries
Spirit Lake, IA 800-831-5174

Catfish

Alabama Catfish
Uniontown, AL. 334-628-3474
Americas Catch
Itta Bena, MS 800-242-0041
Bolner's Fiesta Products
San Antonio, TX. 210-734-6404
Carolina Classic Catfish
Ayden, NC. 252-746-2818
Catfish Wholesale
Abbeville, LA 800-334-7292
CJ's Seafood
Des Allemands, LA. 985-758-1237
Confish
Isola, MS. 800-228-3474

Culver's Fish Farm
Mc Pherson, KS 800-241-5205
Delta Catfish Products
Eudora, AR. 870-355-4192
Delta Pride Catfish
Indianola, MS 800-421-1045
Farm Fresh Catfish Company
Hollandale, MS. 800-647-8264
Guidry's Catfish
Breaux Bridge, LA 337-228-7546
Icelandic USA
Newport News, VA. 757-820-4000
Inshore Fisheries
Middle West Pubnico, NS. 902-762-2522
J. Matassini & Sons Fish Company
Tampa, FL. 813-229-0829
Milfico Foods
Elk Grove Vlg, IL. 847-427-0491
New Orleans Fish House
New Orleans, LA 800-839-3474
North Atlantic Fish Company
Gloucester, MA. 978-283-4121
Pickwick Catfish Farm
Counce, TN. 731-689-3805
Pond Pure Catfish
Moulton, AL. 256-974-6698
Rivere's Seafood Processors
Paincourtville, LA. 985-369-2570
Road Runner Seafood
Colquitt, GA 229-758-3485
Roy Dick Company
Griffin, GA 770-227-3916
Seymour & Sons Seafood
Diberville, MS 228-392-4020
Southern Farms Fish Processors
Kansas City, MO. 800-264-2594
Southern Pride Catfish Company
Seattle, WA 800-343-8046
Wisner Minnow Hatchery
Wisner, LA 318-724-6133

Chowder

LaMonica Fine Foods
Millville, NJ 856-825-8111

Chub

Raffield Fisheries
Port St Joe, FL. 850-229-8229
Russ & Daughters
New York, NY 800-787-7229

Cod

Angy's Food Products Inc.
Westfield, MA. 413-572-1010
Arctic Seas
Little Compton, RI 401-635-4000
Arrowac Fisheries
Seattle, WA 206-282-5655
BlueWater Seafoods
Lachine, QC 888-560-2539
Bolner's Fiesta Products
San Antonio, TX. 210-734-6404
Breakwater Fisheries
St Josephs, NL 709-754-1999
Buns & Things Bakery
Charlottetown, PE. 902-892-2600
C.L. Deveau & Son
Salmon River, NS 902-649-2812
Canadian Fish Exporters
Watertown, MA. 800-225-4215
Castella Imports
Hauppauge, NY 866-227-8355
Ceilidh Fisherman's Cooperative
Port Hood, NS. 902-787-2666
Certi-Fresh Foods
Bell Gardens, CA 562-806-1100
D Waybret & Sons Fisher ies
Shelburne, NS. 902-745-3477
Davis Strait Fisheries
Halifax, NS 902-450-5115
DB Kenney Fisheries
Westport, NS. 902-839-2023
Deep Creek Custom Packing
Ninilchik, AK 800-764-0078
Depoe Bay Fish Company
Newport, OR. 541-265-8833
Dorset Fisheries
St Josephs, NL 709-739-7147
Felix Custom Smoking
Monroe, WA 425-485-2439

Fishery Products International
Danvers, MA. 800-374-4700
Harbor Seafood
New Hyde Park, NY 800-645-2211
Helshiron Fisheries
Grand Manan, NB. 506-662-3111
High Liner Foods Inc
Lunenburg, NS .902-634-9475
Icelandic USA
Newport News, VA. 757-820-4000
Icicle Seafoods
Seattle, WA. 206-282-0988
Independent Packers Corporation
Seattle, WA. 206-285-6000
Inshore Fisheries
Middle West Pubnico, NS. 902-762-2522
K&N Fisheries
Upper Port La Tour, NS 902-768-2478
La Have Seafoods
La Have, NS 902-688-2773
Lund's Fisheries
Cape May, NJ 609-884-7600
M&M Fisheries
Shelburne, NS. .902-723-2390
Menemsha Fish Market
Chilmark, MA. .508-645-2282
Mersey Seafoods
Liverpool, NS 902-354-3467
MG Fisheries
Grand Manan, NB. 506-662-3471
Milfico Foods
Elk Grove Vlg, IL. 847-427-0491
Mutual Fish Company
Seattle, WA. 206-322-4368
Neptune Foods
Vernon, CA. 323-232-8300
Nordic Group
Boston, MA. 800-486-4002
Norquest Seafoods
Seattle, WA. 206-281-7022
North Atlantic Fish Company
Gloucester, MA. 978-283-4121
Northwest Fisheries
Hubbards, NS 902-228-2232
Notre Dame Seafood
Comfort Cove, NL 709-244-5511
Ocean Pride Fisheries
Lower Wedgeport, NS 902-663-4579
Omstead Foods Ltd
Wheatley, ON 905-315-8883
Pacific Ocean Seafood
La Conner, WA. 360-466-4455
Paul Piazza & Sons
New Orleans, LA 504-524-6011
Produits Belle Baie
Caraquet, NB 506-727-4414
Royal Seafood
Monterey, CA 831-655-8326
Seafood Producers Coop ative
Bellingham, WA 360-733-0120
Taku Smokehouse
Juneau, AK 800-582-5122
Tampa Bay Fisheries
Dover, FL 800-234-2561
Viking Seafoods Inc
Malden, MA 800-225-3020

Black

Dragnet Fisheries
Anchorage, AK. 907-276-4551
Fishhawk Fisheries
Astoria, OR. 503-325-5252
Pacific Ocean Seafood
La Conner, WA. 360-466-4455
Pacific Salmon Company
Edmonds, WA. .425-774-1315
Royal Seafood
Monterey, CA 831-655-8326
Seafood Producers Coop ative
Bellingham, WA 360-733-0120
Sitka Sound Seafoods
Sitka, AK. 907-747-6662

Conch

Anchor Frozen Foods
Westbury, NY 800-566-3474
Road Runner Seafood
Colquitt, GA 229-758-3485

Croaker

Glenn Sales Company
Atlanta, GA. 770-952-9292
Griffin Seafood
Golden Meadow, LA. 985-396-2453
Raffield Fisheries
Port St Joe, FL. .850-229-8229
Road Runner Seafood
Colquitt, GA 229-758-3485

Cusk

Canadian Fish Exporters
Watertown, MA. 800-225-4215

Dolphin

Wanchese Fish Company
Suffolk, VA 757-673-4500

Eel

George Robberecht Seafood
Montross, VA 804-472-3556
Ocean Union Company
Lawrenceville, GA 770-995-1957

Fillets

American Seafoods International
New Bedford, MA 800-343-8046
Arrowac Fisheries
Seattle, WA. 206-282-5655
Bayou Foods
Kenner, LA 800-516-8283
Cozy Harbor Seafood
Portland, ME. 800-225-2586
Ducktrap River Fish Farm
Belfast, ME 800-434-8727
Erba Food Products
Brooklyn, NY 718-272-7700
Good Harbor Fillet Company
Gloucester, MA. 978-675-9100
Icelandic USA
Newport News, VA. 757-820-4000
Jessie's Ilwaco Fish Company
Ilwaco, WA 360-642-3773
Neptune Foods
Vernon, CA. 323-232-8300
Nordic Group
Boston, MA. 800-486-4002
Ocean Beauty Seafoods
Seattle, WA. 206-285-6800
Pacific American Fish Co.,Inc.
Vernon, CA 800-625-2525
Pacific Seafoods International
Port Hardy, BC .250-949-8781
Penguin Frozen Foods
Northbrook, IL .847-291-9400
Roman Sausage Company
Santa Clara, CA 800-497-7462
Super Snooty Sea Food Corporation
Boston, MA. 617-426-6390
Taku Smokehouse
Juneau, AK 800-582-5122
Ungars Food Products
Elmwood Park, NJ 201-703-1300
Van De Kamp Frozen Foods
Mountain Lake, NJ 973-541-6620

Finfish

Arrowac Fisheries
Seattle, WA 206-282-5655
Depoe Bay Fish Company
Newport, OR. 541-265-8833
Highland Fisheries
Glace Bay, NS. .902-849-6016
James Cowan & Sons
Worcester, MA .508-753-3259

Flounder

Bolner's Fiesta Products
San Antonio, TX. 210-734-6404
Bon Secour Fisheries
Bon Secour, AL. 800-633-6854
Carrington Foods
Saraland, AL 251-675-9700
Catfish Wholesale
Abbeville, LA 800-334-7292
Depoe Bay Fish Company
Newport, OR. 541-265-8833
Fishery Products International
Danvers, MA. 800-374-4700
Glenn Sales Company
Atlanta, GA. 770-952-9292
Gorton's Seafood
Gloucester, MA. 978-283-3000
Griffin Seafood
Golden Meadow, LA. 985-396-2453
Gulf City Marine Supply
Bayou La Batre, AL 251-824-2516
Inshore Fisheries
Middle West Pubnico, NS. 902-762-2522
Lund's Fisheries
Cape May, NJ 609-884-7600
Menemsha Fish Market
Chilmark, MA. .508-645-2282
Mersey Seafoods
Liverpool, NS 902-354-3467
Milfico Foods
Elk Grove Vlg, IL. 847-427-0491
Mirasco
Atlanta, GA. 770-956-1945
N.A. Boullon
Cumming, GA. .770-889-2356
Pamlico Packing Company
Grantsboro, NC .800-682-1113
Road Runner Seafood
Colquitt, GA 229-758-3485
Royal Seafood
Monterey, CA 831-655-8326
Tampa Maid Foods
Lakeland, FL. 800-237-7637
Thompson Seafood
Darien, GA 912-437-4649
Wanchese Fish Company
Suffolk, VA. 757-673-4500
Ward Cove Packing Company
Seattle, WA 206-323-3200

Fluke

Agger Fish
Brooklyn, NY 718-855-1717

Fresh

Arrowac Fisheries
Seattle, WA 206-282-5655
Atlantic Salmon of Maine
Belfast, ME 800-508-7861
Baker's Point Fisheries
Oyster Pond Jeddore, NS 902-845-2347
Bama Fish Atlanta
East Point, GA .404-765-9896
Bayou Land Seafood
Breaux Bridge, LA 337-667-6118
Birch Street Seafoods
Digby, NS 902-245-6551
Blue Wave Seafoods
Port Mouton, NS. 902-683-2044
Bon Secour Fisheries
Bon Secour, AL. 800-633-6854
Cherokee Trout Farms
Cherokee, NC 800-732-0075
Crest International Corporation
San Diego, CA .800-548-1232
DCL
Honolulu, HI. 808-845-3834
Deep Creek Custom Packing
Ninilchik, AK 800-764-0078
Ferroclad Fishery
Batchawana Bay, ON 705-882-2295
Fish Breeders of Idaho
Boise, ID. 888-414-8818
Harbor Fish Market
Portland, ME. 207-775-0251
HFI Foods
Redmond, WA. .425-883-1320
High Liner Foods Inc
Lunenburg, NS .902-634-9475
Inshore Fisheries
Middle West Pubnico, NS. 902-762-2522
International Seafoods of Alaska
Kodiak, AK. 907-486-4768
Island Marine Products
Clarks Harbour, NS. 902-745-2222
J. Matassini & Sons Fish Company
Tampa, FL. 813-229-0829
Jessie's Ilwaco Fish Company
Ilwaco, WA 360-642-3773
Kyler Seafood
New Bedford, MA 888-859-5377

Lakeside Foods
Seymour, WI 920-833-2371
LaMonica Fine Foods
Millville, NJ 856-825-8111
Lougheed Fisheries
Owen Sound, ON 519-376-1586
MacKnight Smoked Foods
Miami, FL 305-655-0332
Marche Tramsatlantique
Montreal, QC 514-287-3530
Mariner Seafoods
Montague, PE 902-838-2481
Menemsha Fish Market
Chilmark, MA 508-645-2282
Mersey Seafoods
Liverpool, NS 902-354-3467
Minor Fisheries
Port Colborne, ON 905-834-9232
Morey's Seafood Intl. ional
Motley, MN 218-352-6345
Mutual Fish Company
Seattle, WA 206-322-4368
Ocean Beauty Seafoods
Seattle, WA 206-285-6800
Ocean Fresh Seafoods
Seattle, WA 206-285-2412
Pacific American Fish Co.,Inc.
Vernon, CA 800-625-2525
Pacific Seafoods International
Port Hardy, BC 250-949-8781
Pacific Shrimp Company
Newport, OR 541-265-4215
Paul Piazza & Sons
New Orleans, LA 504-524-6011
Royal Seafood
Monterey, CA 831-655-8326
Sunshine Food Sales
Miami, FL 305-696-2885
Tampa Bay Fisheries
Dover, FL 800-234-2561
Trout of Paradise
Paradise, UT 435-245-3053
Union Fisheries Corporation
Chicago, IL 312-738-0448
Virginia Trout Company
Monterey, VA 540-468-2280
Wanchese Fish Company
Suffolk, VA 757-673-4500
Weyand Fisheries
Wyandotte, MI 800-521-9815
Wrangell Fisheries
Wrangell, AK 907-874-3346
Yamasa Fish Cake Company
Los Angeles, CA 213-626-2211

Freshwater

Hamilos Brothers Inspected Meats
Madison, IL 618-451-7877

Frozen

Alaska Seafood Company
Los Angeles, CA 213-626-1212
Alaskan Gourmet Seafoods
Anchorage, AK 800-288-3740
Amano Fish Cake Factory
Hilo, HI 808-935-5555
American Seafoods International
New Bedford, MA 800-343-8046
Appert's Foodservice
St Cloud, MN 800-225-3883
Arctic Seas
Little Compton, RI 401-635-4000
Arrowac Fisheries
Seattle, WA 206-282-5655
Baker's Point Fisheries
Oyster Pond Jeddore, NS 902-845-2347
Bama Fish Atlanta
East Point, GA 404-765-9896

Barry Group
Corner Brook, NL 709-785-7387
Bayou Land Seafood
Breaux Bridge, LA 337-667-6118
Beaver Street Fisheries
Jacksonville, FL 800-874-6426
Big Al's Seafood
Bozman, MD 410-745-2637
Birch Street Seafoods
Digby, NS 902-245-6551
Birdie Pak Products
Chicago, IL 773-247-5293
Blue Wave Seafoods
Port Mouton, NS 902-683-2044
Bolner's Fiesta Products
San Antonio, TX 210-734-6404
Bon Secour Fisheries
Bon Secour, AL 800-633-6854
Breakwater Fisheries
St Josephs, NL 709-754-1999
Buedel Food Products
Bridgeview, IL 708-496-3500
Buns & Things Bakery
Charlottetown, PE 902-892-2600
Captn's Pack Products
Columbia, MD 410-720-6668
Carrington Foods
Saraland, AL 251-675-9700
Certi-Fresh Foods
Bell Gardens, CA 562-806-1100
Cherokee Trout Farms
Cherokee, NC 800-732-0075
Clear Springs Foods
Buhl, ID 800-635-8211
Cook Inlet Processing
Nikiski, AK 907-776-8174
Cozy Harbor Seafood
Portland, ME 800-225-2586
Crest International Corporation
San Diego, CA 800-548-1232
Crown Point
St John, IN 219-365-3200
Cuizina Food Company
Woodinville, WA 425-486-7000
DB Kenney Fisheries
Westport, NS 902-839-2023
Deep Creek Custom Packing
Ninilchik, AK 800-764-0078
Delta Pride Catfish
Indianola, MS 800-421-1045
Depoe Bay Fish Company
Newport, OR 541-265-8833
Farm Fresh Catfish Company
Hollandale, MS 800-647-8264
Ferroclad Fishery
Batchawana Bay, ON 705-882-2295
Fish Breeders of Idaho
Boise, ID 888-414-8818
Fishery Products International
Danvers, MA 800-374-4700
George Robberecht Seafood
Montross, VA 804-472-3556
Glacier Fish Company
Seattle, WA 206-298-1200
Great Glacier Salmon
Prince Rupert, BC 250-627-4955
Great Northern Products
Warwick, RI 401-490-4590
Hamilos Brothers Inspected Meats
Madison, IL 618-451-7877
Handy International
Salisbury, MD 800-426-3977
HFI Foods
Redmond, WA 425-883-1320
High Liner Foods Inc
Lunenburg, NS 902-634-9475
Icelandic USA
Newport News, VA 757-820-4000
Icicle Seafoods
Seattle, WA 206-282-0988
Independent Packers Corporation
Seattle, WA 206-285-6000
Inshore Fisheries
Middle West Pubnico, NS 902-762-2522
International Seafoods of Alaska
Kodiak, AK 907-486-4768
Island Marine Products
Clarks Harbour, NS 902-745-2222
J. Matassini & Sons Fish Company
Tampa, FL 813-229-0829
J.S. McMillan Fisheries
Vancouver, BC 604-255-5191

Jer-Mar Foods
Windsor, ON 519-256-3474
Jessie's Ilwaco Fish Company
Ilwaco, WA 360-642-3773
Key Largo Fisheries
Key Largo, FL 800-432-4358
Kodiak Salmon Packers
Larsen Bay, AK 907-847-2250
Kyler Seafood
New Bedford, MA 888-859-5377
Long Beach Seafoods
Long Beach, CA 562-435-5357
Lougheed Fisheries
Owen Sound, ON 519-376-1586
Lund's Fisheries
Cape May, NJ 609-884-7600
Mada'n Kosher Foods
Dania, FL 954-925-0077
Mariner Seafoods
Montague, PE 902-838-2481
Martin Brothers SeafoodcCompany
Westwego, LA 504-341-2251
Menemsha Fish Market
Chilmark, MA 508-645-2282
Mersey Seafoods
Liverpool, NS 902-354-3467
Milfico Foods
Elk Grove Vlg, IL 847-427-0491
Mill Cove Lobster Pound
Boothbay Harbor, ME 207-633-3340
Minor Fisheries
Port Colborne, ON 905-834-9232
Monterey Fish Company
Salinas, CA 831-771-9221
Morey's Seafood Intl. ional
Motley, MN 218-352-6345
Mutual Fish Company
Seattle, WA 206-322-4368
Nelson Crab
Tokeland, WA 800-262-0069
Nordic Group
Boston, MA 800-486-4002
North Atlantic Fish Company
Gloucester, MA 978-283-4121
Northwest Naturals
Olympia, WA 360-866-9661
Notre Dame Seafood
Comfort Cove, NL 709-244-5511
Ocean Beauty Seafoods
Seattle, WA 206-285-6800
Ocean Fresh Seafoods
Seattle, WA 206-285-2412
Okuhara Foods
Honolulu, HI 808-848-0581
Omstead Foods Ltd
Wheatley, ON 905-315-8883
Pacific American Fish Co.,Inc.
Vernon, CA 800-625-2525
Pacific Salmon Company
Edmonds, WA 425-774-1315
Pacific Seafoods International
Port Hardy, BC 250-949-8781
Pacific Shrimp Company
Newport, OR 541-265-4215
Pamlico Packing Company
Grantsboro, NC 800-682-1113
Paul Piazza & Sons
New Orleans, LA 504-524-6011
Penguin Frozen Foods
Northbrook, IL 847-291-9400
Peter Pan Seafoods
Seattle, WA 206-728-6000
Petersburg Fisheries
Petersburg, AK 877-772-4294
Quinalt Pride Seafood
Taholah, WA 360-276-4431
Royal Seafood
Monterey, CA 831-655-8326
Sea Safari
Belhaven, NC 800-688-6174
Seymour & Sons Seafood
Diberville, MS 228-392-4020
Stinson Seafood Company
San Diego, CA
Stolt SeaFarm
Elverta, CA 800-525-0333
Sunshine Food Sales
Miami, FL 305-696-2885
Super Snooty Sea Food Corporation
Boston, MA 617-426-6390
Taku Smokehouse
Juneau, AK 800-582-5122

Tampa Bay Fisheries
Dover, FL 800-234-2561
Tampa Maid Foods
Lakeland, FL...................... 800-237-7637
Tichon Seafood Corporation
New Bedford, MA 508-999-5607
Trident Seafoods Corporation
Salem, NH........................ 603-893-3368
Trident Seafoods Corporation
Seattle, WA....................... 800-426-5490
Union Fisheries Corporation
Chicago, IL....................... 312-738-0448
Van De Kamp Frozen Foods
Mountain Lake, NJ 973-541-6620
Viking Seafoods Inc
Malden, MA 800-225-3020
Virginia Trout Company
Monterey, VA 540-468-2280
Wanchese Fish Company
Suffolk, VA....................... 757-673-4500
Weyand Fisheries
Wyandotte, MI 800-521-9815
White Cap Fish Company
Islip, NY 631-581-0125
Wrangell Fisheries
Wrangell, AK 907-874-3346
Yamasa Fish Cake Company
Los Angeles, CA................... 213-626-2211

Gefilte

Erba Food Products
Brooklyn, NY 718-272-7700
R.A.B. Food Group LLC
Secaucus, NJ...................... 201-553-1100

Grouper

Bolner's Fiesta Products
San Antonio, TX................... 210-734-6404
Griffin Seafood
Golden Meadow, LA................ 985-396-2453
Milfico Foods
Elk Grove Vlg, IL.................. 847-427-0491
Mirasco
Atlanta, GA....................... 770-956-1945
N.A. Boullon
Cumming, GA..................... 770-889-2356
Ocean Union Company
Lawrenceville, GA 770-995-1957
Poseidon Enterprises
Atlanta, GA....................... 800-863-7886

Haddock

Adams Fisheries Ltd
Shag Harbour, NS.................. 902-723-2435
Arctic Seas
Little Compton, RI 401-635-4000
BlueWater Seafoods
Lachine, QC 888-560-2539
Canadian Fish Exporters
Watertown, MA.................... 800-225-4215
Davis Strait Fisheries
Halifax, NS 902-450-5115
DB Kenney Fisheries
Westport, NS...................... 902-839-2023
High Liner Foods Inc
Lunenburg, NS 902-634-9475
I. Deveau Fisheries
Barrington Passage, NS 902-769-0333
Icelandic USA
Newport News, VA................. 757-820-4000
Inshore Fisheries
Middle West Pubnico, NS............ 902-762-2522
Island Marine Products
Clarks Harbour, NS................. 902-745-2222
La Have Seafoods
La Have, NS 902-688-2773
Leo G. Atkinson Fisheries
Clarks Harbor, NS.................. 902-745-3047
M&M Fisheries
Shelburne, NS..................... 902-723-2390
Menemsha Fish Market
Chilmark, MA..................... 508-645-2282
Mersey Seafoods
Liverpool, NS 902-354-3467
MG Fisheries
Grand Manan, NB.................. 506-662-3471
Nordic Group
Boston, MA....................... 800-486-4002
Ocean Pride Fisheries
Lower Wedgeport, NS 902-663-4579
Omstead Foods Ltd
Wheatley, ON 905-315-8883

Hake

Canadian Fish Exporters
Watertown, MA.................... 800-225-4215
Helshiron Fisheries
Grand Manan, NB.................. 506-662-3111
Mirasco
Atlanta, GA....................... 770-956-1945

Halibut

Alaskan Gourmet Seafoods
Anchorage, AK.................... 800-288-3740
Angy's Food Products Inc.
Westfield, MA..................... 413-572-1010
Arrowac Fisheries
Seattle, WA 206-282-5655
Bell Buoy Crab Company
Seaside, OR....................... 800-529-2722
California Shellfish Company
San Francisco, CA 415-923-7400
Calkins & Burke
Vancouver, BC 604-669-3741
Certi-Fresh Foods
Bell Gardens, CA 562-806-1100
Charlton Deep Sea Charters
Warrenton, OR 503-338-0569
Chicago Steaks
Chicago, IL....................... 800-776-4174
Cook Inlet Processing
Nikiski, AK....................... 907-776-8174
D Waybret & Sons Fisher ies
Shelburne, NS..................... 902-745-3477
Deep Creek Custom Packing
Ninilchik, AK..................... 800-764-0078
Depoe Bay Fish Company
Newport, OR...................... 541-265-8833
Elwha Fish
Port Angeles, WA.................. 360-457-3344
Felix Custom Smoking
Monroe, WA 425-485-2439
Fishhawk Fisheries
Astoria, OR....................... 503-325-5252
Fjord Pacific Marine Industries
Richmond, BC 604-270-3393
High Liner Foods Inc
Lunenburg, NS 902-634-9475
His Catch Value Added Products
Homer, AK 800-215-7110
Icicle Seafoods
Seattle, WA....................... 206-282-0988
Independent Packers Corporation
Seattle, WA....................... 206-285-6000
Indian Valley Meats
Indian, AK........................ 907-653-7511
Island Marine Products
Clarks Harbour, NS................. 902-745-2222
J.S. McMillan Fisheries
Vancouver, BC 604-255-5191
Long Beach Seafoods
Long Beach, CA 562-435-5357
Menemsha Fish Market
Chilmark, MA..................... 508-645-2282
Mersey Seafoods
Liverpool, NS 902-354-3467
Milfico Foods
Elk Grove Vlg, IL.................. 847-427-0491
Neptune Foods
Vernon, CA....................... 323-232-8300
Norquest Seafoods
Seattle, WA....................... 206-281-7022
North Atlantic Fish Company
Gloucester, MA.................... 978-283-4121
Northwest Fisheries
Hubbards, NS 902-228-2232
Northwest Naturals
Olympia, WA 360-866-9661
Ocean Beauty Seafoods
Seattle, WA....................... 206-285-6800
Pacific Ocean Seafood
La Conner, WA.................... 360-466-4455
Pacific Salmon Company
Edmonds, WA..................... 425-774-1315
Pacific Shrimp Company
Newport, OR...................... 541-265-4215
Petersburg Fisheries
Petersburg, AK 877-772-4294
Sea K Fish Company
Blaine, WA 360-332-5121
Seafood Producers Coop ative
Bellingham, WA................... 360-733-0120
Sitka Sound Seafoods
Sitka, AK......................... 907-747-6662
Taku Smokehouse
Juneau, AK 800-582-5122
Tampa Bay Fisheries
Dover, FL 800-234-2561
Trident Seafoods Corporation
Seattle, WA....................... 800-426-5490
Viking Seafoods Inc
Malden, MA 800-225-3020
Wrangell Fisheries
Wrangell, AK 907-874-3346

Herring

Acme Smoked Fish Corporation
Brooklyn, NY 800-221-0795
Alimentaire Whyte's Inc
Laval, QC 800-625-1979
Angy's Food Products Inc.
Westfield, MA..................... 413-572-1010
Baensch Food
Milwaukee, WI.................... 800-562-8234
Bell Buoy Crab Company
Seaside, OR....................... 800-529-2722
Bos Smoked Fish Inc
Woodstock, ON.................... 519-537-5000
Breakwater Fisheries
St Josephs, NL 709-754-1999
Buns & Things Bakery
Charlottetown, PE.................. 902-892-2600
Canadian Fish Exporters
Watertown, MA.................... 800-225-4215
Canadian Silver Herring
Petit-Cap, NB 506-577-6426
Castella Imports
Hauppauge, NY 866-227-8355
Chicago 58 Food Products
Woodbridge, ON................... 416-603-4244
Comeau's Sea Foods
Saulnierville, NS................... 902-769-2101
Cowart Seafood Corporation
Lottsburg, VA 804-529-6101
Delta Pacific Seafoods
Delta, BC......................... 800-328-2547
Depoe Bay Fish Company
Newport, OR...................... 541-265-8833
Dragnet Fisheries
Anchorage, AK.................... 907-276-4551
Duguay Fish Packers
Cap-Pele, NB 506-577-2287
Feature Foods
Etobicoke, ON 416-675-7350
Ferroclad Fishery
Batchawana Bay, ON 705-882-2295
Fjord Pacific Marine Industries
Richmond, BC 604-270-3393
Flaum Appetizing
Brooklyn, NY 718-821-1970
Gaudet & Ouellette
Cap-Pele, NB 506-577-4016
GJ Shortall
Mount Pearl, NL................... 709-747-0655
Gorman Fisheries
Conception Bay, NL 709-229-6536
Great Northern Products
Warwick, RI 401-490-4590
High Sea Foods
Glovertown, NL 709-533-2626
Icicle Seafoods
Seattle, WA....................... 206-282-0988
Island Marine Products
Clarks Harbour, NS................. 902-745-2222
Leslie Leger & Sons
Trois-Ruisseaux, NB................ 506-577-4730
Lund's Fisheries
Cape May, NJ 609-884-7600
Menemsha Fish Market
Chilmark, MA..................... 508-645-2282
Mersey Seafoods
Liverpool, NS 902-354-3467
Newell Lobsters
Yarmouth, NS..................... 902-742-6272
Norquest Seafoods
Seattle, WA....................... 206-281-7022
Pacific Shrimp Company
Newport, OR...................... 541-265-4215
Petersburg Fisheries
Petersburg, AK 877-772-4294

Premier Smoked Fish Company
Bensalem, PA 800-654-6682
Produits Belle Baie
Caraquet, NB 506-727-4414
Raffield Fisheries
Port St Joe, FL.................... 850-229-8229
Royal Seafood
Monterey, CA 831-655-8326
Russ & Daughters
New York, NY 800-787-7229
Salmolux
Federal Way, WA 253-874-2026
Sitka Sound Seafoods
Sitka, AK........................ 907-747-6662
Springfield Smoked Fish Company
Springfield, MA 800-327-3412
Stinson Seafood Company
San Diego, CA
Strub Pickles
Brantford, ON.................... 519-751-1717
Tribe Mediterranean Foods Company LLC
Taunton, MA...................... 774-961-0000
Vita Food Products
Chicago, IL 312-738-4500
West India Trading Company
Petit-Cap, NB 506-577-6214
Wrangell Fisheries
Wrangell, AK 907-874-3346

Boned

Feature Foods
Etobicoke, ON 416-675-7350

Fillets

Angy's Food Products Inc.
Westfield, MA.................... 413-572-1010

Fresh

Angy's Food Products Inc.
Westfield, MA.................... 413-572-1010
Bella Coola Fisheries
Surrey, BC....................... 604-541-0339
Feature Foods
Etobicoke, ON 416-675-7350
Ferroclad Fishery
Batchawana Bay, ON 705-882-2295
Icicle Seafoods
Seattle, WA...................... 206-282-0988
Mersey Seafoods
Liverpool, NS 902-354-3467
Royal Seafood
Monterey, CA 831-655-8326
Wrangell Fisheries
Wrangell, AK 907-874-3346

Frozen

Angy's Food Products Inc.
Westfield, MA.................... 413-572-1010
Bella Coola Fisheries
Surrey, BC....................... 604-541-0339
Breakwater Fisheries
St Josephs, NL 709-754-1999
Depoe Bay Fish Company
Newport, OR...................... 541-265-8833
Ferroclad Fishery
Batchawana Bay, ON 705-882-2295
Great Northern Products
Warwick, RI 401-490-4590
Icicle Seafoods
Seattle, WA...................... 206-282-0988
Island Marine Products
Clarks Harbour, NS................ 902-745-2222
Lund's Fisheries
Cape May, NJ 609-884-7600

Menemsha Fish Market
Chilmark, MA..................... 508-645-2282
Mersey Seafoods
Liverpool, NS 902-354-3467
Pacific Shrimp Company
Newport, OR...................... 541-265-4215
Peter Pan Seafoods
Seattle, WA...................... 206-728-6000
Royal Seafood
Monterey, CA 831-655-8326
Stinson Seafood Company
San Diego, CA
Wrangell Fisheries
Wrangell, AK 907-874-3346

Salted & Marinated

Feature Foods
Etobicoke, ON 416-675-7350
High Liner Foods Inc
Lunenburg, NS 902-634-9475
Island Marine Products
Clarks Harbour, NS................ 902-745-2222

Spiced

Baensch Food
Milwaukee, WI.................... 800-562-8234
Feature Foods
Etobicoke, ON 416-675-7350

Hoki

Arctic Seas
Little Compton, RI 401-635-4000

Imitation

Flavor House
Adelanto, CA 760-246-9131
HFI Foods
Redmond, WA..................... 425-883-1320
National Fish and Seafood Limited
Brownsville, TX 956-546-5525
Ocean Food Company
Scarborough, ON 416-285-6487
Peter Pan Seafoods
Seattle, WA...................... 206-728-6000
Shining Ocean
Sumner, WA 253-826-3700
Trans-Ocean Products
Bellingham, WA 888-215-4815
Trident Seafoods Corporation
Seattle, WA...................... 800-426-5490

King Cod

Deep Creek Custom Packing
Ninilchik, AK 800-764-0078
Minor Fisheries
Port Colborne, ON 905-834-9232

Kingfish

Sunshine Food Sales
Miami, FL........................ 305-696-2885

Lumpfish

Notre Dame Seafood
Comfort Cove, NL 709-244-5511
Russian Chef
New York, NY 212-249-1550

Mackerel

Atlantic Capes Fisheries
Cape May, NJ 609-884-3000
Atlantic Fish Specialties
Charlottetown, PE................. 902-894-7005
Bos Smoked Fish Inc
Woodstock, ON.................... 519-537-5000
Breakwater Fisheries
St Josephs, NL 709-754-1999
Buns & Things Bakery
Charlottetown, PE................. 902-892-2600
Canadian Fish Exporters
Watertown, MA.................... 800-225-4215
Castella Imports
Hauppauge, NY 866-227-8355
Chicken of the Sea International
San Diego, CA 800-678-8862
Crown Point
St John, IN 219-365-3200

Crown Prince
City of Industry, CA 800-255-5063
Crown Prince Naturals
Petaluma, CA
Ducktrap River Fish Farm
Belfast, ME...................... 800-434-8727
Erba Food Products
Brooklyn, NY 718-272-7700
GJ Shortall
Mount Pearl, NL.................. 709-747-0655
Gorman Fisheries
Conception Bay, NL 709-229-6536
Griffin Seafood
Golden Meadow, LA............... 985-396-2453
Lund's Fisheries
Cape May, NJ 609-884-7600
Menemsha Fish Market
Chilmark, MA..................... 508-645-2282
Mersey Seafoods
Liverpool, NS 902-354-3467
Notre Dame Seafood
Comfort Cove, NL 709-244-5511
Ocean Union Company
Lawrenceville, GA 770-995-1957
Royal Seafood
Monterey, CA 831-655-8326
Russ & Daughters
New York, NY 800-787-7229
Sunshine Food Sales
Miami, FL........................ 305-696-2885
Tri-Marine InternationalInc
San Pedro, CA.................... 310-732-6113

Mahi-Mahi

Griffin Seafood
Golden Meadow, LA............... 985-396-2453
Milfico Foods
Elk Grove Vlg, IL................. 847-427-0491
N.A. Boullon
Cumming, GA..................... 770-889-2356
Ocean Beauty Seafoods
Seattle, WA...................... 206-285-6800
Omega Foods
Eugene, OR....................... 800-200-2356

Marlin

Mid-Pacific Hawaii Fishery
Hilo, HI......................... 808-935-6110
Sportsmen's Sea Foods
San Diego, CA 619-224-3551

Meal

Acatris USA
Edina, MN........................ 952-920-7700

Monkfish

Agger Fish
Brooklyn, NY 718-855-1717
Atlantic Capes Fisheries
Cape May, NJ 609-884-3000

Mullet

Griffin Seafood
Golden Meadow, LA............... 985-396-2453
Raffield Fisheries
Port St Joe, FL.................... 850-229-8229
Road Runner Seafood
Colquitt, GA 229-758-3485

Orange Roughy

Chicago Steaks
Chicago, IL 800-776-4174
Milfico Foods
Elk Grove Vlg, IL................. 847-427-0491
Neptune Foods
Vernon, CA 323-232-8300

Packed

Glass

Indian Valley Meats
Indian, AK....................... 907-653-7511
Noon Hour Food Products
Chicago, IL 800-621-6636
Petersburg Fisheries
Petersburg, AK 877-772-4294

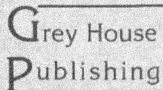

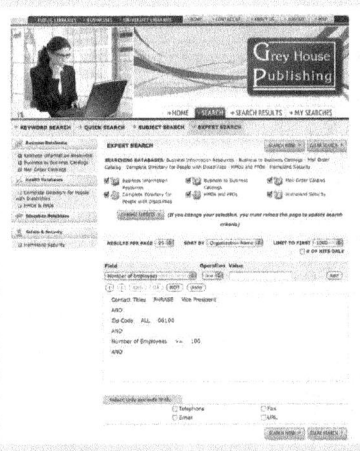

Pouch

Indian Valley Meats
Indian, AK. 907-653-7511
Noon Hour Food Products
Chicago, IL 800-621-6636
Petersburg Fisheries
Petersburg, AK 877-772-4294

Paste

Certified Savory
Countryside, IL. 800-328-7656
Giovanni's Appetizing Food Products
Richmond, MI. 586-727-9355

Patties

Roman Sausage Company
Santa Clara, CA 800-497-7462

Perch

A&A Marine & Drydock Company
Blenheim, ON. 519-676-2030
Depoe Bay Fish Company
Newport, OR. 541-265-8833
Fishery Products International
Danvers, MA. 800-374-4700
High Liner Foods Inc
Lunenburg, NS 902-634-9475
Inshore Fisheries
Middle West Pubnico, NS. 902-762-2522
Jer-Mar Foods
Windsor, ON 519-256-3474
Kingsville Fisherman's Company
Kingsville, ON 519-733-6534
Mersey Seafoods
Liverpool, NS 902-354-3467
Milfico Foods
Elk Grove Vlg, IL. 847-427-0491
Minor Fisheries
Port Colborne, ON 905-834-9232
Mutual Fish Company
Seattle, WA 206-322-4368
Omstead Foods Ltd
Wheatley, ON 905-315-8883
Paul Piazza & Sons
New Orleans, LA 504-524-6011
Red Lake Fisheries Associates
Redby, MN 218-679-3513
Royal Seafood
Monterey, CA 831-655-8326
Viking Seafoods Inc
Malden, MA 800-225-3020

Ocean

DB Kenney Fisheries
Westport, NS. 902-839-2023
Mill Cove Lobster Pound
Boothbay Harbor, ME. 207-633-3340

Pickerel

A&A Marine & Drydock Company
Blenheim, ON. 519-676-2030
Jer-Mar Foods
Windsor, ON 519-256-3474
Kingsville Fisherman's Company
Kingsville, ON 519-733-6534
Minor Fisheries
Port Colborne, ON 905-834-9232

Pike

Milfico Foods
Elk Grove Vlg, IL. 847-427-0491

Pollack

BlueWater Seafoods
Lachine, QC 888-560-2539
Bolner's Fiesta Products
San Antonio, TX. 210-734-6404
Glenn Sales Company
Atlanta, GA. 770-952-9292
Harbor Seafood
New Hyde Park, NY 800-645-2211
Icelandic USA
Newport News, VA. 757-820-4000
Inshore Fisheries
Middle West Pubnico, NS. 902-762-2522
K&N Fisheries
Upper Port La Tour, NS 902-768-2478
Milfico Foods
Elk Grove Vlg, IL. 847-427-0491
Neptune Foods
Vernon, CA 323-232-8300
Trident Seafoods Corporation
Seattle, WA 800-426-5490

Pompano

Griffin Seafood
Golden Meadow, LA. 985-396-2453

Rock Fish

Deep Creek Custom Packing
Ninilchik, AK 800-764-0078
Petersburg Fisheries
Petersburg, AK 877-772-4294
Seafood Producers Coop ative
Bellingham, WA 360-733-0120
Sitka Sound Seafoods
Sitka, AK. 907-747-6662

Sablefish

Petersburg Fisheries
Petersburg, AK 877-772-4294
Rego Smoked Fish Company
Flushing, NY. 718-894-1400
Russ & Daughters
New York, NY 800-787-7229

Salmon

Alaskan Gourmet Seafoods
Anchorage, AK. 800-288-3740
Alaskan Smoked Salmon International
Anchorage, AK. 907-349-8234
Alder Springs Smoked Salmon
Sequim, WA 360-683-2829
American Seafoods International
New Bedford, MA 800-343-8046
Angy's Food Products Inc.
Westfield, MA. 413-572-1010
Aquatec Seafoods Ltd.
Comox, BC 250-339-6412
Arrowac Fisheries
Seattle, WA. 206-282-5655
Atlantic Salmon of Maine
Belfast, ME. 800-508-7861
Bell Buoy Crab Company
Seaside, OR. 800-529-2722
Bella Coola Fisheries
Surrey, BC. 604-541-0339
Bering Sea Fisheries
Snohomish, WA 425-334-1498
Blundell Seafoods
Richmond, BC 604-270-3300
Bos Smoked Fish Inc
Woodstock, ON. 519-537-5000
Bumble Bee Foods
San Diego, CA 858-715-4000
California Shellfish Company
San Francisco, CA 415-923-7400
Calkins & Burke
Vancouver, BC 604-669-3741
Casey Fisheries
Digby, NS 902-245-5801
Certi-Fresh Foods
Bell Gardens, CA 562-806-1100
Charlton Deep Sea Charters
Warrenton, OR 503-338-0569
Chicago Steaks
Chicago, IL 800-776-4174
Chicken of the Sea International
San Diego, CA 800-678-8862
Chuck's Seafoods
Charleston, OR 541-888-5525
Cook Inlet Processing
Nikiski, AK. 907-776-8174
Crown Prince Naturals
Petaluma, CA
Dave's Gourmet Albacore
Kirkland, WA 800-454-8862
Deep Creek Custom Packing
Ninilchik, AK 800-764-0078
Delta Pacific Seafoods
Delta, BC. 800-328-2547
Depoe Bay Fish Company
Newport, OR. 541-265-8833
Dragnet Fisheries
Anchorage, AK. 907-276-4551
Dressel Collins Fish Company
Seattle, WA 206-725-0121
Ducktrap River Fish Farm
Belfast, ME. 800-434-8727
Elwha Fish
Port Angeles, WA 360-457-3344
Exclusive Smoked Fish
Toronto, ON 416-766-6007
Fiddlers Green Farm
Belfast, ME. 800-729-7935
Fishery Products International
Danvers, MA. 800-374-4700
Fishhawk Fisheries
Astoria, OR 503-325-5252
Fjord Pacific Marine Industries
Richmond, BC 604-270-3393
Freeze-Dry Ingredients
Berkeley, IL. 708-544-1880
Giovanni's Appetizing Food Products
Richmond, MI. 586-727-9355
Great Glacier Salmon
Prince Rupert, BC. 250-627-4955
Great Pacific Seafoods
Anchorage, AK. 907-248-7966
Handy International
Salisbury, MD 800-426-3977
Heritage Salmon Company
Richmond, BC 604-277-3093
High Liner Foods Inc
Lunenburg, NS 902-634-9475
High Sea Foods
Glovertown, NL 709-533-2626
High Tide Seafoods
Port Angeles, WA 360-452-8488
His Catch Value Added Products
Homer, AK 800-215-7110
Icelandic USA
Newport News, VA. 757-820-4000
Icicle Seafoods
Seattle, WA 206-282-0988
Independent Packers Corporation
Seattle, WA 206-285-6000
Indian Valley Meats
Indian, AK. 907-653-7511
J.S. McMillan Fisheries
Vancouver, BC 604-255-5191
J.S. McMillan Fisheries
North Vancouver, BC 604-981-4000
Jessie's Ilwaco Fish Company
Ilwaco, WA 360-642-3773
Kodiak Salmon Packers
Larsen Bay, AK. 907-847-2250
Long Beach Seafoods
Long Beach, CA 562-435-5357
Maine Coast Nordic
Mahiasport, ME 207-255-6714
Marche Tramsatlantique
Montreal, QC 514-287-3530
Menemsha Fish Market
Chilmark, MA. 508-645-2282
Mercado Latino
City of Industry, CA 626-333-6862
Milfico Foods
Elk Grove Vlg, IL. 847-427-0491
Morey's Seafood Intl. ional
Motley, MN. 218-352-6345
Mutual Fish Company
Seattle, WA 206-322-4368
Nelson Crab
Tokeland, WA 800-262-0069
Neptune Foods
Vernon, CA 323-232-8300
Nordic Group
Boston, MA. 800-486-4002
Norquest Seafoods
Seattle, WA. 206-281-7022
Northern Products Corporation
Seattle, WA 206-448-6677
Northwest Naturals
Olympia, WA 360-866-9661
Ocean Beauty Seafoods
Seattle, WA 206-285-6800
Ocean Beauty Seafoods
Taunton, MA. 774-961-0000
Ocean Food Company
Scarborough, ON 416-285-6487
Ocean Garden Products
San Diego, CA 858-571-5002
Okuhara Foods
Honolulu, HI 808-848-0581

Omega Foods
Eugene, OR 800-200-2356
Pacific Ocean Seafood
La Conner, WA 360-466-4455
Pacific Salmon Company
Edmonds, WA 425-774-1315
Pacific Seafoods International
Port Hardy, BC 250-949-8781
Pacific Shrimp Company
Newport, OR 541-265-4215
Paramount Caviar
Long Island City, NY 800-992-2842
Perona Farms Food Specialties
Andover, NJ 800-750-6190
Peter Pan Seafoods
Seattle, WA 206-728-6000
Petersburg Fisheries
Petersburg, AK 877-772-4294
Poseidon Enterprises
Atlanta, GA 800-863-7886
Premier Smoked Fish Company
Bensalem, PA 800-654-6682
Quinalt Pride Seafood
Taholah, WA 360-276-4431
Rego Smoked Fish Company
Flushing, NY 718-894-1400
Roman Sausage Company
Santa Clara, CA 800-497-7462
Royal Seafood
Monterey, CA 831-655-8326
Russian Chef
New York, NY 212-249-1550
Salmolux
Federal Way, WA 253-874-2026
SeaBear Smokehouse
Anacortes, WA 800-645-3474
Seafood Producers Coop ative
Bellingham, WA 360-733-0120
Shafer-Haggart
Vancouver, BC 604-669-5512
Sitka Sound Seafoods
Sitka, AK 907-747-6662
Splendid Spreads
Eagan, MN 877-773-2374
Sportsmen's Cannery & Smokehouse
Winchester Bay, OR 800-457-8048
Springfield Smoked Fish Company
Springfield, MA 800-327-3412
Stinson Seafood Company
San Diego, CA
Taku Smokehouse
Juneau, AK 800-582-5122
Tampa Bay Fisheries
Dover, FL 800-234-2561
Trident Seafoods Corporation
Seattle, WA 800-426-5490
Vita Food Products
Chicago, IL 312-738-4500
Walcan Seafood
Heroit Bay, BC 250-285-3361
Ward Cove Packing Company
Seattle, WA 206-323-3200
Woodsmoke Provisions
Atlanta, GA 404-355-5125
Wrangell Fisheries
Wrangell, AK 907-874-3346

Chum

Arctic Seas
Little Compton, RI 401-635-4000

Coho

Arctic Seas
Little Compton, RI 401-635-4000

King

Elwha Fish
Port Angeles, WA 360-457-3344

Pink

Arctic Seas
Little Compton, RI 401-635-4000
Chicken of the Sea International
San Diego, CA 800-678-8862
Crown Prince
City of Industry, CA 800-255-5063

Smoked

Alaska Bounty Seafoods & Smokery
Sitka, AK 907-966-2927
Alaska Jack's Trading Post
Anchorage, AK 888-660-2257
Alaska Seafood Company
Juneau, AK 800-451-1400
Alaska Smokehouse
Woodinville, WA 800-422-0852
Alaskan Gourmet Seafoods
Anchorage, AK 800-288-3740
Alaskan Smoked Salmon International
Anchorage, AK 907-349-8234
Alder Springs Smoked Salmon
Sequim, WA 360-683-2829
Assouline & Ting
Huntingdon Valley, PA 800-521-4491
California Shellfish Company
San Francisco, CA 415-923-7400
Charlie Trotter Foods
Chicago, IL 773-248-6228
Comeau's Sea Foods
Saulnierville, NS 902-769-2101
Dollar Food Manufacturing
Vancouver, BC 604-253-1422
Dressel Collins Fish Company
Seattle, WA 206-725-0121
E-Fish-Ent Fish Company
Sooke, BC 250-642-4007
Elwha Fish
Port Angeles, WA 360-457-3344
Felix Custom Smoking
Monroe, WA 425-485-2439
Fish Brothers
Blue Lake, CA 800-244-0583
Fish King Processors
Bellingham, WA 360-733-9090
Fjord Pacific Marine Industries
Richmond, BC 604-270-3393
Fumoir Grizzly
St-Augustin-De-Desmaures, QC 418-878-8941
Giovanni's Appetizing Food Products
Richmond, MI 586-727-9355
Homarus
Atlanta, GA 404-877-1988
Imperial Salmon House
Vancouver, BC 604-251-1114
Jensen's Old Fashioned Smokehouse
Seattle, WA 206-364-5569
Kasilof Fish Company
Everett, WA 800-322-7552
Katy's Smokehouse
Trinidad, CA 707-677-0151
Nordic Group
Boston, MA 800-486-4002
Ocean Beauty Seafoods
Taunton, MA 774-961-0000
Ocean Pride Fisheries
Lower Wedgeport, NS 902-663-4579
Oceanfood Sales
Vancouver, BC 877-255-1414
Oven Head Salmon Smokers
Bethel, NB 877-955-2507
Pacific Seafoods International
Port Hardy, BC 250-949-8781
Paramount Caviar
Long Island City, NY 800-992-2842
Pickwick Catfish Farm
Counce, TN 731-689-3805
Port Chatham Smoked Seafood
Everett, WA 800-872-5666
Portier Fine Foods
Mamaroneck, NY 800-272-9463
Premier Smoked Fish Company
Bensalem, PA 800-654-6682
Rego Smoked Fish Company
Flushing, NY 718-894-1400
Rier Smoked Salmon
Lubec, ME 888-733-0807
Russ & Daughters
New York, NY 800-787-7229
Russian Chef
New York, NY 212-249-1550
Southeast Alaska Smoked Salmon Company
Juneau, AK 907-463-4617
Sullivan Harbor Farm
Sullivan, ME 800-422-4014
Tribe Mediterranean Foods Company LLC
Taunton, MA 774-961-0000

Sockeye

Alaska Smokehouse
Woodinville, WA 800-422-0852
Arctic Seas
Little Compton, RI 401-635-4000
Elwha Fish
Port Angeles, WA 360-457-3344

Steak

Arrowac Fisheries
Seattle, WA 206-282-5655
Nelson Crab
Tokeland, WA 800-262-0069
Neptune Foods
Vernon, CA 323-232-8300

Salted

Canadian Fish Exporters
Watertown, MA 800-225-4215
DB Kenney Fisheries
Westport, NS 902-839-2023
Island Marine Products
Clarks Harbour, NS 902-745-2222
Taku Smokehouse
Juneau, AK 800-582-5122

Sardines

Castella Imports
Hauppauge, NY 866-227-8355
Continental Group
Huntington Beach, CA 858-391-5670
Crown Point
St John, IN 219-365-3200
Crown Prince
City of Industry, CA 800-255-5063
Erba Food Products
Brooklyn, NY 718-272-7700
Jessie's Ilwaco Fish Company
Ilwaco, WA 360-642-3773
Liberty Richter
Saddle Brook, NJ 201-291-8749
Mercado Latino
City of Industry, CA 626-333-6862
Pastene Companies
Canton, MA 781-830-8200
Raffield Fisheries
Port St Joe, FL 850-229-8229
Stinson Seafood Company
San Diego, CA

Canned

Chicken of the Sea International
San Diego, CA 800-678-8862
Crown Point
St John, IN 219-365-3200
Crown Prince
City of Industry, CA 800-255-5063
Crown Prince Naturals
Petaluma, CA
Liberty Richter
Saddle Brook, NJ 201-291-8749
Mercado Latino
City of Industry, CA 626-333-6862
Pastene Companies
Canton, MA 781-830-8200
Stinson Seafood Company
San Diego, CA
Tri-Marine InternationalInc
San Pedro, CA 310-732-6113

Fresh

Crown Point
St John, IN 219-365-3200
Jessie's Ilwaco Fish Company
Ilwaco, WA 360-642-3773

Sea Bass

Arrowac Fisheries
Seattle, WA 206-282-5655
Long Beach Seafoods
Long Beach, CA 562-435-5357
N.A. Boullon
Cumming, GA 770-889-2356
Ocean Beauty Seafoods
Seattle, WA 206-285-6800
Tampa Bay Fisheries
Dover, FL 800-234-2561

Sea Trout

Chicago Steaks
Chicago, IL 800-776-4174
Glenn Sales Company
Atlanta, GA 770-952-9292

Shad

Fishhawk Fisheries
Astoria, OR 503-325-5252
Lund's Fisheries
Cape May, NJ 609-884-7600
Nelson Crab
Tokeland, WA 800-262-0069

Shark

Agger Fish
Brooklyn, NY 718-855-1717
Arrowac Fisheries
Seattle, WA 206-282-5655
Bolner's Fiesta Products
San Antonio, TX 210-734-6404
Louisiana Seafood Exchange
New Orleans, LA 504-283-9393
Mid-Pacific Hawaii Fishery
Hilo, HI 808-935-6110
New Orleans Fish House
New Orleans, LA 800-839-3474
Ocean Beauty Seafoods
Seattle, WA 206-285-6800
Pacific Salmon Company
Edmonds, WA 425-774-1315
Scandinavian Laboratories
Mount Bethel, PA 570-897-7735

Sheephead

Griffin Seafood
Golden Meadow, LA 985-396-2453
Stoller Fisheries
Spirit Lake, IA 800-831-5174

Smelt

Bell Buoy Crab Company
Seaside, OR 800-529-2722
Burleigh Brothers Seafoods
Ellerslie, PE 902-831-2349
Certi-Fresh Foods
Bell Gardens, CA 562-806-1100
Fishhawk Fisheries
Astoria, OR 503-325-5252
Jessie's Ilwaco Fish Company
Ilwaco, WA 360-642-3773
Minor Fisheries
Port Colborne, ON 905-834-9232
North Atlantic Fish Company
Gloucester, MA 978-283-4121
Omstead Foods Ltd
Wheatley, ON 905-315-8883
Pacific Salmon Company
Edmonds, WA 425-774-1315

Smoked & Cured

Acme Smoked Fish Corporation
Brooklyn, NY 800-221-0795
Alaska Jack's Trading Post
Anchorage, AK 888-660-2257
Alaska Sausage and Seafood Company
Anchorage, AK 800-798-3636
Alaskan Gourmet Seafoods
Anchorage, AK 800-288-3740
Bos Smoked Fish Inc
Woodstock, ON 519-537-5000
Buedel Food Products
Bridgeview, IL 708-496-3500
California Shellfish Company
San Francisco, CA 415-923-7400
Cherokee Trout Farms
Cherokee, NC 800-732-0075
Chuck's Seafoods
Charleston, OR 541-888-5525
Deep Creek Custom Packing
Ninilchik, AK 800-764-0078
Dressel Collins Fish Company
Seattle, WA 206-725-0121
Ducktrap River Fish Farm
Belfast, ME 800-434-8727
Elwha Fish
Port Angeles, WA 360-457-3344
Fish Brothers
Blue Lake, CA 800-244-0583
Fjord Pacific Marine Industries
Richmond, BC 604-270-3393
Gold Star Smoked Fish
Brooklyn, NY 718-522-1545
High Liner Foods Inc
Lunenburg, NS 902-634-9475
Homarus
Atlanta, GA 404-877-1988
J. Moniz Company
Fall River, MA 508-674-8451
J. Turner Seafoods
Gloucester, MA 978-281-8535
MacKnight Smoked Foods
Miami, FL 305-655-0332
Menemsha Fish Market
Chilmark, MA 508-645-2282
Mersey Seafoods
Liverpool, NS 902-354-3467
Mutual Fish Company
Seattle, WA 206-322-4368
Nelson Crab
Tokeland, WA 800-262-0069
Nordic Group
Boston, MA 800-486-4002
Ocean Fresh Seafoods
Seattle, WA 206-285-2412
Paramount Caviar
Long Island City, NY 800-992-2842
Premier Smoked Fish Company
Bensalem, PA 800-654-6682
Quinalt Pride Seafood
Taholah, WA 360-276-4431
Rego Smoked Fish Company
Flushing, NY 718-894-1400
Russ & Daughters
New York, NY 800-787-7229
Russian Chef
New York, NY 212-249-1550
Seabear
Anacortes, WA 800-645-3474
Stolt SeaFarm
Elverta, CA 800-525-0333
Taku Smokehouse
Juneau, AK 800-582-5122
West India Trading Company
Petit-Cap, NB 506-577-6214

Snapper

Bolner's Fiesta Products
San Antonio, TX 210-734-6404
Bon Secour Fisheries
Bon Secour, AL 800-633-6854
California Shellfish Company
San Francisco, CA 415-923-7400
Griffin Seafood
Golden Meadow, LA 985-396-2453
Milfico Foods
Elk Grove Vlg, IL 847-427-0491
N.A. Boullon
Cumming, GA 770-889-2356
Ocean Union Company
Lawrenceville, GA 770-995-1957
Poseidon Enterprises
Atlanta, GA 800-863-7886

Sole

BlueWater Seafoods
Lachine, QC 888-560-2539
DB Kenney Fisheries
Westport, NS 902-839-2023
Gorton's Seafood
Gloucester, MA 978-283-3000
High Liner Foods Inc
Lunenburg, NS 902-634-9475
Milfico Foods
Elk Grove Vlg, IL 847-427-0491
Penguin Frozen Foods
Northbrook, IL 847-291-9400
Royal Seafood
Monterey, CA 831-655-8326

Steaks

Fjord Pacific Marine Industries
Richmond, BC 604-270-3393
Ocean Beauty Seafoods
Seattle, WA 206-285-6800

Sticks

High Liner Foods Inc
Lunenburg, NS 902-634-9475
Icelandic USA
Newport News, VA 757-820-4000
Van De Kamp Frozen Foods
Mountain Lake, NJ 973-541-6620
Viking Seafoods Inc
Malden, MA 800-225-3020

Sturgeon

Bell Buoy Crab Company
Seaside, OR 800-529-2722
Charlton Deep Sea Charters
Warrenton, OR 503-338-0569
Depoe Bay Fish Company
Newport, OR 541-265-8833
Fiddlers Green Farm
Belfast, ME 800-729-7935
Fish Brothers
Blue Lake, CA 800-244-0583
Fishhawk Fisheries
Astoria, OR 503-325-5252
Great Northern Products
Warwick, RI 401-490-4590
Homarus
Atlanta, GA 404-877-1988
Jessie's Ilwaco Fish Company
Ilwaco, WA 360-642-3773
Lund's Fisheries
Cape May, NJ 609-884-7600
Menemsha Fish Market
Chilmark, MA 508-645-2282
Port Chatham Smoked Seafood
Everett, WA 800-872-5666
Rego Smoked Fish Company
Flushing, NY 718-894-1400
Russ & Daughters
New York, NY 800-787-7229
Russian Chef
New York, NY 212-249-1550
Sportsmen's Cannery & Smokehouse
Winchester Bay, OR 800-457-8048
Stolt SeaFarm
Elverta, CA 800-525-0333

Swordfish

Arctic Seas
Little Compton, RI 401-635-4000
Arrowac Fisheries
Seattle, WA 206-282-5655
Caito Fisheries
Fort Bragg, CA 707-964-6368

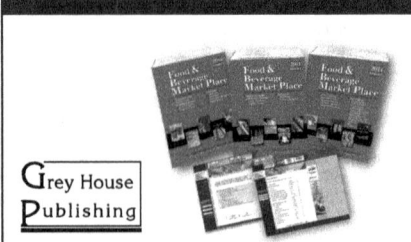

Chicago Steaks
Chicago, IL 800-776-4174
Griffin Seafood
Golden Meadow, LA. 985-396-2453
James L. Mood Fisheries
Lower Woods Harbour, NS. 902-723-2360
Long Beach Seafoods
Long Beach, CA 562-435-5357
Menemsha Fish Market
Chilmark, MA. 508-645-2282
Milfico Foods
Elk Grove Vlg, IL 847-427-0491
Ocean Beauty Seafoods
Seattle, WA 206-285-6800
Poseidon Enterprises
Atlanta, GA. 800-863-7886
Ralboray
New Orleans, LA 504-524-4800
Tampa Bay Fisheries
Dover, FL 800-234-2561

Tilapia

Bolner's Fiesta Products
San Antonio, TX. 210-734-6404
Fishery Products International
Danvers, MA. 800-374-4700
Icelandic USA
Newport News, VA. 757-820-4000
Milfico Foods
Elk Grove Vlg, IL 847-427-0491
Pots de Creme
Lexington, KY 859-299-2254
Vince's Seafoods
Gretna, LA 504-368-1544
Waterfield Farms
Amherst, MA 413-549-3558

Trout

Alleghany's Fish Farm
Saint Philemon, QC 418-469-2823
Atlantic Fish Specialties
Charlottetown, PE. 902-894-7005
Blue Lakes Trout Farm
Jerome, ID. 208-734-7151
Bos Smoked Fish Inc
Woodstock, ON. 519-537-5000
Burleigh Brothers Seafoods
Ellerslie, PE 902-831-2349
Catfish Wholesale
Abbeville, LA. 800-334-7292
Certi-Fresh Foods
Bell Gardens, CA 562-806-1100
Cherokee Trout Farms
Cherokee, NC 800-732-0075
Culver's Fish Farm
Mc Pherson, KS 800-241-5205
Dave's Gourmet Albacore
Kirkland, WA 800-454-8862
Ducktrap River Fish Farm
Belfast, ME. 800-434-8727
Ferroclad Fishery
Batchawana Bay, ON 705-882-2295
Fiddlers Green Farm
Belfast, ME. 800-729-7935
Fish Brothers
Blue Lake, CA 800-244-0583
Fumoir Grizzly
St-Augustin-De-Desmaures, QC 418-878-8941
Griffin Seafood
Golden Meadow, LA. 985-396-2453
Homarus
Atlanta, GA. 404-877-1988
Idaho Trout Company
Buhl, ID. 866-878-7688
J. Matassini & Sons Fish Company
Tampa, FL. 813-229-0829
Lenny's Bee Productions
Bearsville, NY 845-679-4514
Louisiana Seafood Exchange
New Orleans, LA 504-283-9393
Morey's Seafood Intl. ional
Motley, MN. 218-352-6345
Pamlico Packing Company
Grantsboro, NC. 800-682-1113
Portier Fine Foods
Mamaroneck, NY 800-272-9463
Pots de Creme
Lexington, KY 859-299-2254
Rego Smoked Fish Company
Flushing, NY. 718-894-1400
Russian Chef
New York, NY 212-249-1550
SC Enterprises
Owen Sound, ON 519-371-0456
Thompson Seafood
Darien, GA 912-437-4649
Vince's Seafoods
Gretna, LA 504-368-1544
Virginia Trout Company
Monterey, VA 540-468-2280
Wanchese Fish Company
Suffolk, VA. 757-673-4500
Woodsmoke Provisions
Atlanta, GA. 404-355-5125

Brook

Russ & Daughters
New York, NY 800-787-7229

Golden

Idaho Trout Company
Buhl, ID. 866-878-7688

Rainbow

Blue Lakes Trout Farm
Jerome, ID. 208-734-7151
Cherokee Trout Farms
Cherokee, NC 800-732-0075
Clear Springs Foods
Buhl, ID. 800-635-8211
Dave's Gourmet Albacore
Kirkland, WA 800-454-8862
Idaho Trout Company
Buhl, ID. 866-878-7688
Trout of Paradise
Paradise, UT 435-245-3053

Tuna

Bell Buoy Crab Company
Seaside, OR. 800-529-2722
Bolner's Fiesta Products
San Antonio, TX. 210-734-6404
Bumble Bee Foods
San Diego, CA 858-715-4000
Cape Ann Tuna
Gloucester, MA. 978-283-8188
Charlton Deep Sea Charters
Warrenton, OR 503-338-0569
Chicken of the Sea International
San Diego, CA 800-678-8862
Chuck's Seafoods
Charleston, OR 541-888-5525
Continental Group
Huntington Beach, CA 858-391-5670
Crown Prince
City of Industry, CA 800-255-5063
Dave's Gourmet Albacore
Kirkland, WA 800-454-8862
Depoe Bay Fish Company
Newport, OR. 541-265-8833
Elwha Fish
Port Angeles, WA 360-457-3344
Erba Food Products
Brooklyn, NY 718-272-7700
Great Northern Products
Warwick, RI 401-490-4590
Griffin Seafood
Golden Meadow, LA. 985-396-2453
Hallmark Fisheries
Charleston, OR 541-888-3253
Heinz Company of Canada
North York, ON. 877-574-3469
Homarus
Atlanta, GA. 404-877-1988
Independent Packers Corporation
Seattle, WA 206-285-6000
Island Marine Products
Clarks Harbour, NS. 902-745-2222
James L. Mood Fisheries
Lower Woods Harbour, NS. 902-723-2360
Jessie's Ilwaco Fish Company
Ilwaco, WA 360-642-3773
Lund's Fisheries
Cape May, NJ 609-884-7600
Menemsha Fish Market
Chilmark, MA. 508-645-2282
Mid-Pacific Hawaii Fishery
Hilo, HI 808-935-6110
Milfico Foods
Elk Grove Vlg, IL 847-427-0491
Neptune Foods
Vernon, CA 323-232-8300
New Orleans Fish House
New Orleans, LA 800-839-3474
Northwest Naturals
Olympia, WA 360-866-9661
Ocean Beauty Seafoods
Seattle, WA 206-285-6800
Ocean Union Company
Lawrenceville, GA 770-995-1957
Omega Foods
Eugene, OR. 800-200-2356
Pacific Shrimp Company
Newport, OR. 541-265-4215
Pastene Companies
Canton, MA 781-830-8200
Poseidon Enterprises
Atlanta, GA. 800-863-7886
Ralboray
New Orleans, LA 504-524-4800
Roman Sausage Company
Santa Clara, CA 800-497-7462
Royal Seafood
Monterey, CA 831-655-8326
Russ & Daughters
New York, NY 800-787-7229
Russian Chef
New York, NY 212-249-1550
Sportsmen's Cannery & Smokehouse
Winchester Bay, OR 800-457-8048
Sportsmen's Sea Foods
San Diego, CA 619-224-3551
Star-Kist Caribe
Mayaguez, PR. 787-834-2424
Stavis Seafoods
Boston, MA. 800-390-5103
Triangle Seafood
Louisville, KY 502-561-0055
Tuna Fresh
Gretna, LA 504-363-2744
Vince's Seafoods
Gretna, LA 504-368-1544
Wanchese Fish Company
Suffolk, VA. 757-673-4500
White Cap Fish Company
Islip, NY 631-581-0125

Albacore

Bumble Bee Foods
San Diego, CA 858-715-4000
Chicken of the Sea International
San Diego, CA 800-678-8862
Crown Prince
City of Industry, CA 800-255-5063
Dave's Gourmet Albacore
Kirkland, WA 800-454-8862
Elwha Fish
Port Angeles, WA 360-457-3344
Fish Brothers
Blue Lake, CA 800-244-0583
Pacific Shrimp Company
Newport, OR. 541-265-4215
Royal Seafood
Monterey, CA 831-655-8326
Sportsmen's Sea Foods
San Diego, CA 619-224-3551

Canned

Bumble Bee Foods
San Diego, CA 858-715-4000
Chicken of the Sea International
San Diego, CA 800-678-8862
Chuck's Seafoods
Charleston, OR 541-888-5525
Crown Prince
City of Industry, CA 800-255-5063
Crown Prince Naturals
Petaluma, CA
Elwha Fish
Port Angeles, WA 360-457-3344
Hallmark Fisheries
Charleston, OR 541-888-3253
Heinz Company of Canada
North York, ON. 877-574-3469
Scally's Imperial Importing Company Inc
Staten Island, NY 718-983-1938
Shafer-Haggart
Vancouver, BC 604-669-5512
Sportsmen's Cannery & Smokehouse
Winchester Bay, OR 800-457-8048

Sportsmen's Sea Foods
San Diego, CA 619-224-3551
Star-Kist
Pittsburgh, PA 412-323-7400
Tri-Marine InternationalInc
San Pedro, CA 310-732-6113

Canned - Chunk Light in Oil

Chicken of the Sea International
San Diego, CA 800-678-8862

Canned - Chunk Light in Water

Chicken of the Sea International
San Diego, CA 800-678-8862

Canned - Chunk Solid in Oil

Chicken of the Sea International
San Diego, CA 800-678-8862

Canned - Chunk Solid in Water

Chicken of the Sea International
San Diego, CA 800-678-8862

Frozen

Bell Buoy Crab Company
Seaside, OR 800-529-2722
Bolner's Fiesta Products
San Antonio, TX 210-734-6404
Cuizina Food Company
Woodinville, WA 425-486-7000
Depoe Bay Fish Company
Newport, OR 541-265-8833
Great Northern Products
Warwick, RI 401-490-4590
Hallmark Fisheries
Charleston, OR 541-888-3253
Independent Packers Corporation
Seattle, WA 206-285-6000
Jessie's Ilwaco Fish Company
Ilwaco, WA 360-642-3773
Lund's Fisheries
Cape May, NJ 609-884-7600
Menemsha Fish Market
Chilmark, MA 508-645-2282
Milfico Foods
Elk Grove Vlg, IL 847-427-0491
Pacific Shrimp Company
Newport, OR 541-265-4215
Royal Seafood
Monterey, CA 831-655-8326
Wanchese Fish Company
Suffolk, VA 757-673-4500
White Cap Fish Company
Islip, NY 631-581-0125

Pouch-Packed

Chicken of the Sea International
San Diego, CA 800-678-8862

Yellowfin

Russ & Daughters
New York, NY 800-787-7229

Turbot

Breakwater Fisheries
St Josephs, NL 709-754-1999
Buns & Things Bakery
Charlottetown, PE 902-892-2600
Norquest Seafoods
Seattle, WA 206-281-7022
Notre Dame Seafood
Comfort Cove, NL 709-244-5511
Penguin Frozen Foods
Northbrook, IL 847-291-9400
Stavis Seafoods
Boston, MA 800-390-5103

Whitefish

American Seafoods International
New Bedford, MA 800-343-8046
Bos Smoked Fish Inc
Woodstock, ON 519-537-5000
Ferroclad Fishery
Batchawana Bay, ON 705-882-2295
Flaum Appetizing
Brooklyn, NY 718-821-1970
Homarus
Atlanta, GA 404-877-1988
Minor Fisheries
Port Colborne, ON 905-834-9232
Rego Smoked Fish Company
Flushing, NY 718-894-1400
Russ & Daughters
New York, NY 800-787-7229
Russian Chef
New York, NY 212-249-1550
Springfield Smoked Fish Company
Springfield, MA 800-327-3412

Whiting

Arrowac Fisheries
Seattle, WA 206-282-5655
Bolner's Fiesta Products
San Antonio, TX 210-734-6404
Bon Secour Fisheries
Bon Secour, AL 800-633-6854
Certi-Fresh Foods
Bell Gardens, CA 562-806-1100
Depoe Bay Fish Company
Newport, OR 541-265-8833
Glenn Sales Company
Atlanta, GA 770-952-9292
Icelandic USA
Newport News, VA 757-820-4000
Jessie's Ilwaco Fish Company
Ilwaco, WA 360-642-3773
Milfico Foods
Elk Grove Vlg, IL 847-427-0491
Mirasco
Atlanta, GA 770-956-1945
Morey's Seafood Intl. ional
Motley, MN 218-352-6345
North Atlantic Fish Company
Gloucester, MA 978-283-4121
Pacific Shrimp Company
Newport, OR 541-265-4215
Pamlico Packing Company
Grantsboro, NC 800-682-1113
Stavis Seafoods
Boston, MA 800-390-5103

Seafood

A&C Quinlin Fisheries
McGray, NS 902-745-2742
Acadian Fine Foods
New Orleans, LA 504-581-2355
Acme Steak & Seafood Company
Youngstown, OH 330-270-8000
Agger Fish
Brooklyn, NY 718-855-1717
Agri-Best Foods
Chicago, IL 773-247-5060
Ah Dor Kosher Fish Corporation
Monsey, NY 845-425-7776
Alabama Seafood Producers
Bayou La Batre, AL 251-824-4396
Alaska Aquafarms
Moose Pass, AK 907-288-3667
Alaska Fresh Seafoods
Kodiak, AK 907-486-5749
Alaska General Seafood
Kenmore, WA 425-485-7755
Alaska Ocean Trading
Anchorage, AK 907-243-4399
Alaska Pacific Seafood
Kodiak, AK 907-486-3234
Alaska Sausage and Seafood Company
Anchorage, AK 800-798-3636
Alaska Sea Pack
Anchorage, AK 907-272-3474
Alaska Seafood Company
Los Angeles, CA 213-626-1212
Alaska Seafood International
Anchorage, AK 800-478-2903
Alaskan Glacier
Petersburg, AK 907-772-3333
Alaskan Gourmet Seafoods
Anchorage, AK 800-288-3740
Alaskan Leader Fisheries
Lynden, WA 360-318-1280
Aliotti Wholesale Fish Company
Monterey, CA 831-375-2881
Alphin Brothers
Dunn, NC 800-672-4502
Alyeska Seafoods
Seattle, WA 206-547-2100
Amcan Industries
Elmsford, NY 914-347-4838
American Canadian Fisheries
Bellingham, WA 800-344-7942
American Seafoods Group
Seattle, WA 800-275-2019
AmeriPure Processing Company
Franklin, LA 800-328-6729
Ameripure Processing Company
Franklin, LA 800-328-6729
Anchor Frozen Foods
Westbury, NY 800-566-3474
Annette Island Packing Company
Metlakatla, AK 907-886-4661
Appert's Foodservice
St Cloud, MN 800-225-3883
AquaCuisine
Eagle, ID 208-323-2782
Aquatec Seafoods Ltd.
Comox, BC 250-339-6412
Aquatech
Anchorage, AK 907-563-1387
Arcee Sales Company
Brooklyn, NY 718-383-0107
Arista Industries
Wilton, CT 800-255-6457
Arizona Sunland Foods
Tucson, AZ 520-624-7068
Arrowac Fisheries
Seattle, WA 206-282-5655
ASC Seafood
Largo, FL 800-876-3474
Atka Pride Seafoods
Juneau, AK 907-586-0161
Atlanta Fish Market
Atlanta, GA 404-262-3165
Atlantic Aqua Farms
Vernon Bridge, PE 902-651-2563
Atlantic Foods
Scotch Plains, NJ 908-322-9900
Atlantic Mussel Growers Corporation
Point Pleasant, PE 800-838-3106
Atlantic Queen Seafoods Limited
St Josephs, NL 709-739-6668
Atlantic Sea Pride
South Boston, MA 617-269-7700
Atlantic Seacove
Boston, MA 617-442-6206
Atlantic Seafood Direct
Rockland, ME 207-596-7152
Aurora Alaska Premium Smoked Salmon & Seafood
Anchorage, AK 800-653-3474
Axelsson & Johnson Fish Company
Cape May, NJ 609-884-8426
B&C Seafood Market
Vacherie, LA 225-265-8356
B&J Seafood Company
New Bern, NC 252-637-1552
B&M Fisheries
Georgetown, MA 978-352-6663
B.C. Fisheries
Hancock, ME 207-422-8205
B.M. Lawrence & Company
San Francisco, CA 415-981-3650
Baensch Food
Milwaukee, WI 800-562-8234
Bailey's Basin Seafood
Morgan City, LA 985-384-4926
Bakalars Brothers Sausage Company
La Crosse, WI 608-784-0384
Bandon Bay Fisheries
Bandon, OR 541-347-4454
Basin Crawfish Processors
Breaux Bridge, LA 337-332-6655
Bay Hundred Seafood
McDaniel, MD 410-745-9329
Bay Oceans Sea Foods
Garibaldi, OR 503-322-3316
Bayley Quality Seafoods
Scarborough, ME 207-883-4581
Bayley's Lobster Pound
Scarborough, ME 800-932-6456
Bayou Crab
Grand Bay, AL 251-824-2076
Bayou Foods
Kenner, LA 800-516-8283
Bayou Gourmet
Houma, LA 504-872-4825
Bayou Land Seafood
Breaux Bridge, LA 337-667-6118
Beaver Street Fisheries
Jacksonville, FL 800-874-6426

Becker Food Company
Milwaukee, WI 414-964-5353
Bell Buoy Crab Company
Seaside, OR 800-529-2722
Belle River Enterprises
Belle River, PE 902-962-2248
Benton's Seafood Center
Tifton, GA 229-382-4976
BG Smith Sons Oyster
Sharps, VA 877-483-8279
Big Island Seafood, LLC
Atlanta, GA 404-366-8667
Big River Seafood
Baton Rouge, LA 225-751-1116
Bill Lowden Seafood
Warren, ME 207-273-2162
Bill's Seafood
Baltimore, MD 410-256-9520
Billingsgate Fish Company
Calgary, AB 403-571-7700
Billy's Seafood
Bon Secour, AL 251-949-6288
Blakely Freezer Locker
Thomasville, GA 229-723-3622
Blalock Seafood
Orange Beach, AL 251-974-5811
Blau Oyster Company
Bow, WA 360-766-6171
Blount Fine Foods
Fall River, MA 774-888-1300
Blount Seafood Corporation
Fall River, MA 774-888-1300
Blue Crab Bay Company
Melfa, VA 800-221-2722
Blue Ribbon Meats
Cleveland, OH 216-631-8850
BlueWater Seafoods
Lachine, QC 888-560-2539
Bodin Foods
New Iberia, LA 337-367-1344
Bolner's Fiesta Products
San Antonio, TX 210-734-6404
Bon Secour Fisheries
Bon Secour, AL 800-633-6854
Bornstein Seafoods
Bellingham, WA 360-734-7990

Boston Seafarms
Boston, MA 617-784-4777
Boutique Seafood
Atlanta, GA 404-752-8852
Bradye P. Todd & Son
Cambridge, MD 410-228-8633
Braun Seafood Company
Cutchogue, NY 631-734-6700
Breakwater Fisheries
St Josephs, NL 709-754-1999
Breakwater Seafoods
Aberdeen, WA 360-532-5693
Brenntag
Reading, PA 888-926-4151
Brenntag Pacific
Santa Fe Springs, CA 562-903-9626
Bullock's Country Meats
Westminster, MD 410-848-6786
Bumble Bee Foods
San Diego, CA 858-715-4000
Burris Mill & Feed
Franklinton, LA 800-928-2782
Byrd's Seafood
Crisfield, MD 410-968-0990
C C Conway Seafoods
Wicomico, VA 804-642-2853
C. Gould Seafoods
Scottsdale, AZ 480-314-9250
C.E. Fish Company
Jonesboro, ME 207-434-2631
C.F. Gollott & Son Seafood
Biloxi, MS 866-846-3474
Cajun Crawfish Distributors
Mansura, LA 800-525-6813
Cajun Seafood Enterprises
Murrayville, GA 706-864-9688
Caleb Haley & Company
New York, NY 212-732-7474
California Shellfish Company
San Francisco, CA 415-923-7400
Callis Seafood
Lancaster, VA 804-462-7634
Cameron Seafood Processors
Cameron, LA 318-775-5510
Can Am Seafood
Lubec, ME 207-733-2267

Canadian Fish Exporters
Watertown, MA 800-225-4215
Cannery Row
Cordova, AK 907-424-5920
Cantrell's Seafood
Bath, ME 207-442-7261
Cape Ann Seafood
Gloucester, MA 978-283-0687
Captain Alex Seafood
Niles, IL 847-803-8833
Captain Collier Seafood
Coden, AL 251-824-4925
Captain's Choice
Federal Way, WA 253-941-1184
Captn's Pack Products
Columbia, MD 410-720-6668
Carolina Seafoods
Mc Clellanville, SC 843-887-3713
Carrington Foods
Saraland, AL 251-675-9700
Cathay Foods Corporation
Boston, MA 617-427-1507
Cedar Valley Fish Market
Waterloo, IA 319-236-2965
Centennial Food Corporation
Calgary, AB 403-214-0044
Central Coast Seafoods
Atascadero, CA 800-273-4741
Certi-Fresh Foods
Bell Gardens, CA 562-806-1100
Channel Fish ProcessingcCompany
Roxbury, MA 617-464-3366
Charles H. Parks & Company
Fishing Creek, MD 410-397-3400
Charlton Deep Sea Charters
Warrenton, OR 503-338-0569
Chases Lobster Pound
Port Howe, NS 902-243-2408
Chef Hans Gourmet Foods
Monroe, LA 800-890-4267
Cherbogue Fisheries
Yarmouth, NS 902-742-9157
Chester W. Howeth & Brother
Crisfield, MD 410-968-1398
Chicago Steaks
Chicago, IL 800-776-4174

Chris Hansen Seafood
Port Sulphur, LA....504-564-2888
Chuck's Seafoods
Charleston, OR....541-888-5525
City Market
Brunswick, GA....912-265-4430
City Seafood Company of Monroe
Monroe, LA....318-323-3281
Claytons Crab Company
Rockledge, FL....321-639-0161
Clearwater Fine Foods
Bedford, NS....902-443-0550
Clem's Seafood & Specialties
Buckner, KY....502-222-7571
Coast Seafoods Company
Bellevue, WA....800-423-2303
Coast to Coast Seafood
Seattle, WA....425-889-2862
Coastal Seafood Partners
Chicago, IL....773-989-7788
Coastal Seafood Processors
Harahan, LA....504-734-9444
Cobscook Bay Seafood
Perry, ME....207-853-2890
Cohen's Original Tasty Coddie
Baltimore, MD....410-539-0111
Coldwater Fish Farms
Lisco, NE....800-658-4450
Collier's Fisheries
Des Allemands, LA....985-758-7481
Collins Caviar Company
Michigan City, IN....219-809-8100
Comeaux's
Lafayette, LA....800-323-2492
ConAgra Foods Inc
Omaha, NE....402-595-7300
Conco Food Service
New Orleans, LA....800-488-3988
Confish
Isola, MS....662-962-3101
Conroy Foods
Pittsburgh, PA....412-781-1446
Consolidated Factors
Monterey, CA....831-375-5121
Consolidated Seafood Enterprises
Phoenix, AZ....480-348-9548
Cook Inlet Processing
Nikiski, AK....907-776-8174
Country Harbor Sea Farms
Larrys Riveror, NS....902-358-2002
Cowart Seafood Corporation
Lottsburg, VA....804-529-6101
Cozy Harbor Seafood
Portland, ME....800-225-2586
Craby's Fish Market
Blackwood, NJ....856-227-9743
Cranberry Isles Fisherman's Cooperative
Islesford, ME....207-244-5438
Craven Crab Company
New Bern, NC....252-637-3562
Crescent City Seafoods
Hilo, HI....808-961-0877
Crest International Corporation
San Diego, CA....800-548-1232
Crevettes Du Nord
Gaspe, QC....418-368-1414
Crustaces de la Malbaie
Gaspe, QC....418-368-1414
Cuizina Food Company
Woodinville, WA....425-486-7000
Cumberland Seafood Corporation
Cumberland, RI....401-728-6088
Cushner Seafood
Baltimore, MD....410-358-5564
Custom House Seafoods
Portland, ME....207-773-2778
D Seafood
Chicago, IL....312-808-1086
D&M Seafood
Honolulu, HI....808-531-0687
Daniels Seafood Company
Wanchese, NC....252-473-5779
Dave's Gourmet Albacore
Kirkland, WA....800-454-8862
David Gollott Seafood
Biloxi, MS....228-374-2555
David's Fish Market
Fall River, MA....508-676-1221
Davis Street Fish Market
Evanston, IL....847-869-3474
DB Kenney Fisheries
Westport, NS....902-839-2023
Deep Creek Custom Packing
Ninilchik, AK....800-764-0078
Deep Sea Foods
Bayou La Batre, AL....251-824-7000
Deepsouth Packing Company
New Orleans, LA....504-488-4413
Del's Seaway Shrimp & Oyster Company
Biloxi, MS....228-432-2604
Delta Distributors
Longview, TX....800-945-1858
Demaria Seafood
Newport News, VA....757-930-3474
Denzer's Food Products
Baltimore, MD....410-889-1500
Depoe Bay Fish Company
Newport, OR....541-265-8833
Diamond Seafood
Wood Dale, IL....630-787-1100
Dick & Casey's Gourmet Seafoods
Harbor, OR....800-662-9494
Dicola Seafood
Chicago, IL....773-238-7071
Dip Seafood
Mobile, AL....251-479-0123
Doc Miller's Fish & Seafood Company
Syracuse, IN....574-457-8469
Don's Dock Seafood
Des Plaines, IL....847-827-1817
Door County Fish Market
Northbrook, IL....847-559-9229
Dorchester Crab Company
Wingate, MD....410-397-8103
Doug Hardy Company
Deer Isle, ME....207-348-6604
Dow Distribution
Honolulu, HI....808-836-3511
Down East Specialty Products/Cape Bald Packers
Portland, ME....800-369-6327
Dressel Collins Fish Company
Seattle, WA....206-725-0121
Drusilla Seafood Packing & Processing Company
Baton Rouge, LA....800-364-8844
Dubois Seafood
Houma, LA....985-876-2514
Ducktrap River Fish Farm
Belfast, ME....800-434-8727
Duxbury Mussel & Seafood Corporation
Kingston, MA....781-585-5517
E. Gagnon & Fils
St Therese-De-Gaspe, QC....418-385-3011
E.J. Green & Company
Winterton, NL....709-583-2670
Eagle Seafood Producers
Brooklyn, NY....718-963-0939
East Coast Seafood of Phoenix
Phoenix, AZ....602-268-4591
East Point Seafood Company
South Bend, WA....888-317-8459
Eastern Fish Company
Teaneck, NJ....800-526-9066
Eastern Sea Products
Scoudouc, NB....800-565-6364
Eastern Seafood Company
Chicago, IL....312-243-2090
Eastern Shore Seafood Products
Mappsville, VA....800-466-8550
Eastside Seafood
Macon, GA....478-743-1888
Ed Kasilof's Seafoods
Kasilof, AK....800-982-2377
Edmonton Meat Packing Company
Edmonton, AB....800-361-6328
Eldorado Seafood Inc
Burlington, MA....800-416-5656
Elliott Seafood Company
Cushing, ME....207-354-2533
Elwha Fish
Port Angeles, WA....360-457-3344
Emery Smith Fisheries Limited
Shag Harbour, NS....902-723-2115
Errol Cajun Foods
Belle Rose, LA....225-746-1002
Eschete's Seafood
Houma, LA....985-872-4120
Eskimo Candy
Kihei, HI....808-879-5686
Europa Foods
Saddle Brook, NJ....201-368-8929
Facciola Meat
Fremont, CA....510-438-8600
Faidley Seafood
Baltimore, MD....410-727-4898
Fantis Foods
Carlstadt, NJ....201-933-6200
Farm 2 Market
Roscoe, NY....800-663-4326
Farm Fresh Catfish Company
Hollandale, MS....800-647-8264
Farmers Seafood Company
Shreveport, LA....800-874-0203
Feature Foods
Etobicoke, ON....416-675-7350
Ferme Ostreicole Dugas
Caraquet, NB....506-727-3226
Fine Line Seafood
Newtown, PA....215-860-1144
First Oriental Market
Decatur, GA....404-377-6950
Fish Brothers
Blue Lake, CA....800-244-0583
Fish Express
Lihue, HI....808-245-9918
Fish Market
Louisville, KY....502-587-7474
Fish Processors
Hagerman, ID....208-837-6114
Fishermens Net
Portland, ME....207-772-3565
Fishery Products International
Danvers, MA....800-374-4700
Fishhawk Fisheries
Astoria, OR....503-325-5252
FishKing
Glendale, CA....818-244-2161
Fishking
Bayou La Batre, AL....251-824-2118
Fishland Market
Honolulu, HI....808-523-6902
Fishmarket Seafoods
Louisville, KY....502-587-7474
Flannery Seafood Company
San Francisco, CA....415-346-1303
Flavor House
Adelanto, CA....760-246-9131
Fleet Fisheries
New Bedford, MA....508-996-3742
Flying Seafood Incorporated
Kailua Kona, HI....808-326-7708
Fortune Seas
Gloucester, MA....978-281-6666
Frank Mattes & Sons Reliable Seafood
Bel Air, MD....410-879-5444
Frank Pagano Company
Lockport, IL....815-838-0303
French Market Foods
Lake Charles, LA....337-477-9296
French Quarter Seafood
Chalmette, LA....504-277-1679
Fresh Fish
Birmingham, AL....205-252-0344
Fresh Island Fish Company
Kahului, HI....808-871-1111
Fresh Pack Seafood
Waldoboro, ME....207-832-7720
Fresh Seafood Distributors
Daphne, AL....251-626-1106
Freshwater Farms of Ohio
Urbana, OH....800-634-7434
Friendship International
Rockland, ME....207-273-4621
Frionor U.S.A.
New Bedford, MA....800-343-8046
Frozen Specialties
Archbold, OH....419-445-9015
Fulcher's Point Pride Seafood
Oriental, NC....252-249-0123
FW Thurston
Bernard, ME....207-244-3320
G&J Land and Marine Food Distributors
Morgan City, LA....800-256-9187
Galilean Seafoods
Bristol, RI....401-253-3030
Garden & Valley Isle Seafood
Honolulu, HI....800-689-2733
Gaskill Seafood
Bayboro, NC....252-745-4211
Gemini Food Industries
Charlton, MA....508-248-2730
George Braun Oyster Company
Cutchogue, NY....631-734-7770
George L. Wells Meat Company
Philadelphia, PA....800-523-1730
George Robberecht Seafood
Montross, VA....804-472-3556

Georgetown Fisherman's Co-Op
Georgetown, ME. 207-371-2950
Georgia Seafood Wholesale
Chamblee, GA. 770-936-0483
Gesco ENR
Gaspe, QC. 418-368-1414
Gilmore's Seafoods
Bath, ME. 800-849-9667
Giovanni's Appetizing Food Products
Richmond, MI. 586-727-9355
Glacier Bay Seafood & Meat Company
Lawrence, KS 785-832-2650
Glenn Sales Company
Atlanta, GA. 770-952-9292
Goedens Fish Market
Madison, WI 608-256-1991
Gold Star Seafood
Chicago, IL 773-376-8080
Golden Alaska Seafoods
Seattle, WA 206-441-1990
Golden Bounty Food Processors
Bell Gardens, CA 562-806-1100
Golden Eye Seafood
Piney Point, MD 301-994-2274
Golden Gulf Coast Packing Company
Biloxi, MS. 228-374-6121
Gollott Brothers Seafood Company
Biloxi, MS. 228-432-7865
Good Harbor Fillet Company
Gloucester, MA. 978-675-9100
Gorton's Seafood
Gloucester, MA. 978-283-3000
Graham & Rollins
Hampton, VA 800-272-2728
Graham Fisheries
Bayou La Batre, AL 251-824-2890
Great American Seafood Company
Los Angeles, CA. 323-262-8222
Great American Smokehouse & Seafood Company
Brookings, OR 800-828-3474
Great Glacier Salmon
Prince Rupert, BC. 250-627-4955
Great Northern Products
Warwick, RI 401-490-4590
Great Plains Seafood
Shawnee, KS. 913-262-6060
Great West of Hawaii
Honolulu, HI. 808-593-9981
Green Turtle Cannery & Seafood
Islamorada, FL 305-664-9595
Griffin Seafood
Golden Meadow, LA. 985-396-2453
Gulf Atlantic Freezers
Gretna, LA 504-392-3590
Gulf Central Seafood
Biloxi, MS. 228-436-6346
Gulf Crown Seafood
Delcambre, LA 337-685-4724
Gulf Food Products Company
New Orleans, LA 504-733-1516
Gulf Island Shrimp & Seafood
Lake Charles, LA 888-626-7264
Gulf Marine & Industrial Supplies
New Orleans, LA 800-886-6252
Gulf Pride Enterprises
Biloxi, MS. 888-689-0560
Gulf Shrimp, Inc.
Fort Myers Beach, FL. 239-463-8788
H&H Fisheries Limited
Eastern Passage, NS 902-465-6330
H. Gass Seafood
Hollywood, MD 301-373-6882
Hallmark Fisheries
Charleston, OR 541-888-3253
Hama Hama Oyster®Company
Lilliwaup, WA. 888-877-5844
Handy International
Salisbury, MD 800-426-3977
Hansen Caviar Company
Lake Katrine, NY 800-735-0441
Harbor Fish Market
Portland, ME. 207-775-0251
Harbor Food Sales & Services
Alameda, CA. 360-405-0677
Harbor Lobster
Lower Wood Harbor, NS 902-723-2500
Harbor Seafood
New Hyde Park, NY 800-645-2211
Haring's Pride Catfish
Wisner, LA 800-467-3474
Harlon's L.A. Fish, LLC
Kenner, LA 504-467-3809
Harper Seafood Company
Kinsale, VA. 804-472-3310
Harper's Seafood
Thomasville, GA. 229-226-7525
Harry H. Park Company
Chicago, IL 773-478-4424
Harvard Seafood Company
Grand Bay, AL 251-865-0558
Hawaii International Seafood
Honolulu, HI. 808-839-5010
Herb's Specialty Foods
Mount Holly, NJ 800-486-0276
Heritage Foods
Holicong, PA. 215-244-0900
Heritage Salmon
Eastport, ME. 207-853-6081
HFI Foods
Redmond, WA. 425-883-1320
Hickory Farms
Maumee, OH. 419-893-7611
Higgins Seafood
Lafitte, LA. 504-689-3577
High Liner Foods Inc
Lunenburg, NS 902-634-9475
High Liner Foods USA
Danvers, MA. 888-860-3664
Hillard Bloom Packing Co
Port Norris, NJ 856-785-0120
Hillman Shrimp & Oyster Company
Dickinson, TX. 800-582-4416
Homer's Wharf Seafood Company
New Bedford, MA 508-997-0766
Hong Kong Supermarket
Atlanta, GA. 404-325-3999
Honolulu Fish & Seafood Company
Honolulu, HI. 808-833-1123
Horst Alaskan Seafood
Juneau, AK 877-518-4300
Hosford & Wood Fresh Seafood Providers
Tucson, AZ 520-795-1920
Huck's Seafood
Easton, MD 410-770-9211
Hue's Seafood
Baton Rouge, LA 225-383-0809
Icelandic USA
Newport News, VA. 757-820-4000
Icicle Seafoods
Seattle, WA 206-282-0988
Idaho Trout Company
Buhl, ID. 866-878-7688
Imaex Trading
Norcross, GA 770-825-0848
Independent Packers Corporation
Seattle, WA 206-285-6000
Indian Bay Frozen Foods
Centreville, NL. 709-678-2844
Indian Ridge Shrimp Company
Chauvin, LA 985-594-3361
Indian Valley Meats
Indian, AK. 907-653-7511
Inland Fresh Seafood Corporation
Atlanta, GA. 404-350-5850
Inland Seafood
Milbridge, ME 207-546-7591
Inny's Wholesale
Honolulu, HI. 808-841-3172
Inshore Fisheries
Middle West Pubnico, NS. 902-762-2522
Inter-Ocean Seafood Traders
San Carlos, CA 650-508-0691
Interior Alaska Fish Processors
Fairbanks, AK. 800-478-3885
International Oceanic Enterprises of Alabama
Bayou La Batre, AL 800-816-1832
International Seafoods of Alaska
Kodiak, AK. 907-486-4768
International Seafoods of Chicago
Chicago, IL 312-243-2330
Ipswich Bay Seafoods
Ipswich, MA 978-356-9292
Ipswich Maritime Product Company
Ipswich, MA 978-356-9866
Ipswich Shellfish Company
Ipswich, MA 978-356-6800
ISF Trading
Portland, ME. 207-879-1575
Island Marine Products
Clarks Harbour, NS. 902-745-2222
Island Scallops
Qualicum Beach, BC 250-757-9811
Island Seafood
Eliot, ME. 207-439-8508
Island Seafoods
Kodiak, AK. 800-355-8575
Island Treasures Mussel Processing
Little Bay, NL 709-267-3146
J & B Seafood
Coden, AL. 251-824-4512
J Bernard Seafood & Processing
Cottonport, LA 318-876-3885
J M Clayton Company
Cambridge, MD 800-652-6931
J&L Seafood
Bayou La Batre, AL 251-824-2371
J&R Fisheries
Seward, AK. 907-224-5584
J&R Foods
Long Branch, NJ. 732-229-4020
J. Matassini & Sons Fish Company
Tampa, FL. 813-229-0829
J. Moniz Company
Fall River, MA 508-674-8451
J. Turner Seafoods
Gloucester, MA. 978-281-8535
J.P. Shellfish
Eliot, ME. 207-439-6018
J.R. Fish Company
Wrangell, AK 907-874-2399
J.R.'s Seafood
Oak Lawn, IL 708-422-4555
J.S. McMillan Fisheries
Vancouver, BC 604-255-5191
J.S. McMillan Fisheries
North Vancouver, BC 604-981-4000
Ja-Ca Seafood Products
Boston, MA. 978-281-8848
Jack's Lobsters
Musquodoboit Harbor, NS 902-889-2771
James L. Mood Fisheries
Lower Woods Harbour, NS. 902-723-2360
Janes Family Foods
Mississauga, ON. 800-565-2637
JBS Packing Company
Port Arthur, TX. 409-982-3216
Jcw Tawes & Son
Crisfield, MD 410-968-1288
Jenport International Distributors
Coquitlam, BC 604-464-9888
Jensen Seafood Packing Company
Dulac, LA
Jessie's Ilwaco Fish Company
Ilwaco, WA 360-642-3773
JF Clarke Corporation
Franklin Square, NY. 800-229-7474
Jim Foley Company
Marietta, GA. 770-427-0999
Joe Fazio's Famous Italian
Charleston, WV 304-344-3071
Joe Patti Seafood Company
Pensacola, FL 800-500-9929
Joel & Diane Laperyhouse Company
Chauvin, LA 504-594-9744
Joey Oysters
Amite, LA. 800-748-1525
John B. Wright Fish Company
Gloucester, MA. 978-283-4205
Johns Cove Fisheries
Yarmouth, NS 902-742-8691
Johnson Sea Products
Coden, AL. 251-824-2693
Jubilee Foods
Emmitsburg, MD 301-447-6688
K Horton Specialty Foods
Portland, ME. 207-228-2056
K.S.M. Seafood Corporation
Baton Rouge, LA 225-383-1517
Kachemak Bay Seafood
Homer, AK 907-235-2799
Kake Tribal Corporation
Kake, AK 907-785-3221
Kalamar Seafoods
Hialeah, FL. 305-822-5586
Kang's Seafood
Chicago, IL 800-269-8425
Karla's Smokehouse
Rockaway Beach, OR. 503-355-2362
Kenai Custom Seafoods
Kenai, AK. 907-283-9109
Kenai Packers
Seattle, WA 206-433-6917
Kent's Wharf
Swans Island, ME. 207-526-4186
Kettle Master
Hillsville, VA 276-728-7571

Key Largo Fisheries
Key Largo, FL 800-432-4358

Keyser Brothers
Lottsburg, VA 804-529-6837

Kibun Foods
Seattle, WA 206-467-6287

King & Prince Seafood Corporation
Brunswick, GA 800-841-0205

Kitchens Seafood
Plant City, FL 800-327-0132

Kodiak Salmon Packers
Larsen Bay, AK 907-847-2250

Kool Ice & Seafood Company
Cambridge, MD 410-228-2300

L&C Fisheries
Kensington, PE 902-886-2770

L&M Evans
Conyers, GA 770-918-8727

L&M Frosted Food Lockers
Belt, MT 406-277-3522

L.H. Rodriguez Wholesale Seafood
Tucson, AZ 520-623-1931

L.L. Curley Packing Company
Colonial Beach, VA 804-224-7544

La Font Shrimp Company
Golden Meadow, LA 504-475-5138

La Monegasque
Fort Lee, NJ 201-585-8834

Lady Gale Seafood
Baldwin, LA 337-923-2060

LaMonica Fine Foods
Millville, NJ 856-825-8111

Landlocked Seafoods
Carroll, IA 712-792-9599

Larry J. Williams Company
Jesup, GA 912-427-7729

Larry Towns Company
Wichita, KS 316-265-3474

Lartigue Seafood
Daphne, AL 251-625-6202

Leblanc Seafood
Lafitte, LA 504-689-2631

LEF McLean Brothers International
Wheatley, ON 519-825-4656

Lisbon Seafood Company
Fall River, MA 508-672-3617

Little River Seafood
Reedville, VA 804-453-3670

Livingston's Bull Bay Seafood
Mc Clellanville, SC 843-887-3519

LLJ's Sea Products
Round Pond, ME 207-529-4224

Lombardi's Seafood
Orlando, FL 800-879-8411

Long Beach Seafoods
Long Beach, CA 562-435-5357

Long Food Industries
Fripp Island, SC 843-838-3205

Los Angeles Smoking & Curing Company
Seattle, WA 213-628-1246

Louis Kemp Seafood Company
Downers Grove, IL 218-624-3636

Louis Kemp Seafood Company
Motley, MN 800-325-4732

Louisiana Oyster Processors
Baton Rouge, LA 225-291-6923

Louisiana Packing Company
Westwego, LA 800-666-1293

Louisiana Premium Seafoods
Palmetto, LA 800-222-4017

Louisiana Pride Seafood
New Orleans, LA 504-286-8736

Louisiana Royal Seafood
Henderson, LA 318-228-2988

Louisiana Royal Seafoods
Breaux Bridge, LA 318-228-7506

Lowland Seafood
Lowland, NC 252-745-3751

Lucky Seafood Corporation
Morrow, GA 770-960-9889

Lumar Lobster Corporatio
Lawrence, NY 516-371-0083

Lund's Fisheries
Cape May, NJ 609-884-7600

Lusty Lobster
Portland, ME 207-773-2829

Lyle's Seafoods
Ocean Park, WA 36- 6-5 41

M&M Shrimp Company
Biloxi, MS 228-435-4915

M-G
Weimar, TX 800-460-8581

MacGregors Meat & Seafood
Toronto, ON 888-383-3663

Machias Bay Seafood
Machias, ME 207-255-8671

Maloney Seafood Corporation
Quincy, MA 800-566-2837

Manchac Seafood Market
Ponchatoula, LA 985-370-7070

Maple Leaf Foods International
North York, ON 416-480-8900

Mar-Lees Seafood
New Bedford, MA 800-836-0975

Marine MacHines
Bar Harbor, ME 207-288-0107

Market Fisheries
Chicago, IL 773-483-3233

Marshall Smoked Fish Company
Miami, FL 305-625-5112

Martin Brothers Distributing Company
Cedar Falls, IA 319-266-1775

Martin Brothers SeafoodcCompany
Westwego, LA 504-341-2251

Martin Seafood Company
Jessup, MD 410-799-5822

Mat Roland Seafood Company
Atlantic Beach, FL 904-246-9443

Maxim's Import Corporation
Miami, FL 800-331-6652

Mazzetta Company
Highland Park, IL 847-433-1150

McCoy Matt Frontier International
Pismo Beach, CA 805-773-2994

McFarling Foods
Indianapolis, IN 317-635-2633

McLaughlin Seafood
Bangor, ME 800-222-9107

McNasby's Seafood Market
Annapolis, MD 410-295-9022

Meat & Fish Fellas
Glendale, AZ 623-931-6190

Menemsha Fish Market
Chilmark, MA 508-645-2282

Mercado Latino
City of Industry, CA 626-333-6862

Meredith & Meredith
Toddville, MD 410-397-8151

Merrill Seafood Center
Jacksonville, FL 904-744-3132

Mersey Seafoods
Liverpool, NS 902-354-3467

Metafoods, LLC
Atlanta, GA 404-843-2400

Metompkin Bay Oyster Company
Crisfield, MD 410-968-0662

Mid-Atlantic Foods
Easton, MD 800-922-4688

Midwest Seafood
Indianapolis, IN 317-466-1027

Miland Seafood
New Orleans, LA 888-821-1916

Miles J H & Company
Norfolk, VA 757-622-9264

Milfico Foods
Elk Grove Vlg, IL 847-427-0491

Mill Cove Lobster Pound
Boothbay Harbor, ME 207-633-3340

Miller Johnson Seafood
Coden, AL 251-873-4444

Mills Seafood ltd.
Bouctouche, NB 506-743-2444

Milsolv Corporation
Butler, WI 800-558-8501

Mino Corporation
Davenport, IA 563-388-4770

Mister Fish
Baltimore, MD 410-288-2722

Misty Islands Seafoods
Anchorage, AK 907-248-6678

Mitsubishi InternationalCorporation
Los Angeles, CA 213-620-8652

Mobile Bay Seafood
Coden, AL 251-973-0410

Mobile Processing
Mobile, AL 251-438-6944

Mohn's Fisheries
Harpers Ferry, IA 563-586-2269

Monarch Seafoods
Honolulu, HI 808-841-7877

Moon's Seafood Company
Melbourne, FL 800-526-5624

Morey's Seafood Intl. ional
Motley, MN 218-352-6345

Morgan Mill
Cherokee, NC 828-497-9227

Mortillaro Lobster Company
Gloucester, MA 978-282-4621

Motivatit Seafoods
Houma, LA 985-868-7191

Mutual Fish Company
Seattle, WA 206-322-4368

N.B.J. Enterprises
Mobile, AL 251-661-2122

N.Y.K. Line (North America)
Lombard, IL 888-695-7447

Nagasako Fish
Wailuku, HI 808-242-4073

Nan Sea Enterprises of Wisconsin
Waukesha, WI 262-542-8841

Nancy's Shellfish
Falmouth, ME 207-774-3411

National Fish & Seafood
Gloucester, MA 978-282-7880

National Fish and Seafood Limited
Brownsville, TX 956-546-5525

National Fisheries
Hialeah, FL 305-628-1231

National Fisheries - Marathon
Marathon, FL 305-743-5545

Nautilus Foods
Bellevue, WA 425-885-5900

Nelson Crab
Tokeland, WA 800-262-0069

Neptune Fisheries
Newport News, VA 800-545-7474

New Meadows Lobster
Portland, ME 800-668-1612

New Ocean
Atlanta, GA 770-458-5235

New Orleans Gulf Seafood
New Orleans, LA 504-733-1516

New York Fish House
Elizabeth, NJ 908-351-0045

Newfound Resources
St Josephs, NL 709-579-7676

Nisbet Oyster Company
Bay Center, WA 360-875-6629

Noon Hour Food Products
Chicago, IL 800-621-6636

Nordic Group
Boston, MA 800-486-4002

Norpac Fisheries
Honolulu, HI 808-528-3474

North Atlantic
Portland, ME 207-774-6025

North Atlantic Fish Company
Gloucester, MA 978-283-4121

North Atlantic Products
South Thomaston, ME 207-596-0331

North Atlantic Seafood
Stonington, ME 207-367-5099

North Pacific Processors
Seattle, WA 206-726-9900

Northern Discovery Seafoods
Grapeview, WA 800-843-6921

Northern Keta Caviar
Juneau, AK 907-586-6095

Northern Ocean Marine
Gloucester, MA 978-283-0222

Northern Products Corporation
Seattle, WA 206-448-6677

Northern Wind
New Bedford, MA 888-525-2525

Northwest Natural Foods
Olympia, WA 360-866-9661

Notre Dame Seafood
Comfort Cove, NL 709-244-5511

NTC Marketing Inc
Williamsville, NY 800-333-1637

O'Hara Corporation
Rockland, ME 207-594-0405

Oak Island Seafood Company
Portland, ME 207-594-9250

Ocean Beauty Seafoods
Seattle, WA 206-285-6800

Ocean Crest Seafoods
Gloucester, MA 978-281-0232

Ocean Diamond
Oakland, NJ 201-337-9515

Ocean Food Company
Scarborough, ON 416-285-6487

Ocean Foods of Astoria
Astoria, OR 503-325-2421

Ocean Fresh Seafoods
Seattle, WA 206-285-2412

Ocean King International
Alhambra, CA....................626-289-9399
Ocean Select Seafood
Delcambre, LA....................337-685-5315
Ocean Springs Seafood
Ocean Springs, MS....................228-875-0104
Ocean Union Company
Lawrenceville, GA....................770-995-1957
Oceanledge Seafoods
Rockland, ME....................207-594-4955
Oceans Prome Distributi ng
Glenview, IL....................847-998-5813
Off Shore Seafood Company
Point Lookout, NY....................516-432-0529
Offshore Systems
Dutch Harbor, AK....................907-581-1827
Ohana Seafood, LLC
Honolulu, HI....................808-843-1844
Okuhara Foods
Honolulu, HI....................808-848-0581
Old Salt Seafood Company
Narragansett, RI....................401-783-5770
Olsen Fish Company
Minneapolis, MN....................800-882-0212
Orca Bay Seafoods
Renton, WA....................800-932-6722
Oversea Fishery & Investment Company
Honolulu, HI....................808-847-2500
Oyster World
Kilmarnock, VA....................804-438-5470
P&E Foods
Honolulu, HI....................808-839-9094
P&J Oyster Company
New Orleans, LA....................504-523-2651
P&L Seafood of Venice
Gretna, LA....................504-363-2744
P. Janes & Sons
Hant's Harbor, NL....................709-586-2252
P.J. Markos Seafood Company
Ipswich, MA....................978-356-4347
P.J. Merrill Seafood
Portland, ME....................207-773-1321
P.M. Innis Lobster Company
Biddeford Pool, ME....................207-284-5000
P.T. Fish
Portland, ME....................207-772-0239
Pacific Alaska Seafoods
Seattle, WA....................206-587-0002
Pacific American Fish Co.,Inc.
Vernon, CA....................800-625-2525
Pacific Choice Seafood
Eureka, CA....................707-442-1113
Pacific Gourmet Seafood
Bakersfield, CA....................661-533-1260
Pacific Ocean Producers
Honolulu, HI....................808-537-2905
Pacific Ocean Seafood
La Conner, WA....................360-466-4455
Pacific Salmon Company
Edmonds, WA....................425-774-1315
Pacific Seafoods International
Port Hardy, BC....................250-949-8781
Pacific Shrimp Company
Newport, OR....................541-265-4215
Pacific Valley Foods
Bellevue, WA....................425-643-1805
Pacsea Corporation
Aiea, HI....................808-836-8888
Pamlico Packing Company
Grantsboro, NC....................800-682-1113
Parker Fish Company
Wrightsville, GA....................478-864-3406
Pastene Companies
Canton, MA....................781-830-8200
Paul Piazza & Sons
New Orleans, LA....................504-524-6011
PB&S Chemicals
Henderson, KY....................800-950-7267
PEI Mussel King
Morrell, PE....................800-673-2767
Pelican Marine Supply
Belle Chasse, LA....................504-392-9062
Pemaquid Fishermen's Co-Op
New Harbor, ME....................866-864-2897
Penguin Frozen Foods
Northbrook, IL....................847-291-9400
Perino's Seafood
Marrero, LA....................504-347-5410
Perona Farms Food Specialties
Andover, NJ....................800-750-6190
Peter Pan Seafoods
Seattle, WA....................206-728-6000

Petersburg Fisheries
Petersburg, AK....................877-772-4294
Phillips Foods
Baltimore, MD....................888-234-2722
Phillips Foods, Inc. & Seafood Restaurants
Baltimore, MD....................888-234-2722
Phillips Seafood
Townsend, GA....................912-832-4423
Piazza's Seafood World
St Rose, LA....................504-602-5050
Pilot Meat & Sea Food Company
Galena, IL....................319-556-0760
Pine Point Seafood
Scarborough, ME....................207-883-4701
Pioneer Live Shrimp
Oak Brook, IL....................630-789-1133
Plitt Company
Chicago, IL....................773-523-3876
Point Adolphus Seafoods
Gustavus, AK....................907-697-2246
Point Judith Fisherman'sCompany
Narragansett, RI....................401-782-1500
Point Saint George Fisheries
Santa Rosa, CA....................707-542-9490
Pon Food Corporation
Ponchatoula, LA....................985-386-6941
Pond Pure Catfish
Moulton, AL....................256-974-6698
Pontchartrain Blue Crab
Slidell, LA....................985-649-6645
Port Chatham Smoked Seafood
Everett, WA....................800-872-5666
Portland Shellfish Company
South Portland, ME....................207-799-9290
Portland Specialty Seafoods
Portland, ME....................207-775-5765
Portsmouth Chowder Company
Portsmouth, NH....................603-431-3132
Poseidon Enterprises
Atlanta, GA....................800-863-7886
Poteet Seafood Company
Brunswick, GA....................912-264-5340
Premiere Pacific Seafood
Seattle, WA....................206-286-8584
Premiere Seafood
Lexington, KY....................606-259-3474
Price Seafood
Chauvin, LA....................985-594-3067
Prime Cut Meat & Seafood Company
Phoenix, AZ....................602-455-8834
Produits Belle Baie
Caraquet, NB....................506-727-4414
Quality Alaska Seafood
Juneau, AK....................907-789-8495
Quality Crab Company
Elizabeth City, NC....................888-411-4410
Quality Fisheries
Niota, IL....................217-448-4241
Quality Foods From the Sea
Elizabeth City, NC....................252-338-5455
Quality Meats & Seafood
West Fargo, ND....................800-342-4250
Quality Seafood
Apalachicola, FL....................850-653-9696
R & R Seafood
Tybee Island, GA....................912-786-5504
R&J Seafoods
King Cove, AK....................907-497-3060
R.R. Fournier & Sons
Biloxi, MS....................228-392-4293
Raffield Fisheries
Port St Joe, FL....................850-229-8229
Rainbow Seafood Market
Baldwin Park, CA....................626-962-6888
Rainbow Seafoods
Topsfield, MA....................978-887-9121
Ralboray
New Orleans, LA....................504-524-4800
Randol
Lafayette, LA....................800-YO -AJUN
Red Chamber Company
Vernon, CA....................323-234-9000
Red Lake Fisheries Associates
Redby, MN....................218-679-3513
Registry Steaks & Seafood
Bridgeview, IL....................708-458-3100
Rego Smoked Fish Company
Flushing, NY....................718-894-1400
Reilly's Sea Products
South Bristol, ME....................207-644-1400
Resource Trading Company
Portland, ME....................207-772-2299

Rhone-Poulenc Food Ingredients
Cranbury, NJ....................609-860-4000
Rich-Seapak Corporation
St Simons Island, GA....................800-654-9731
Rich-Seapak Corporation
Brownsville, TX....................956-542-0001
Rippons Brothers Seafood
Fishing Creek, MD....................410-397-3200
Rivere's Seafood Processors
Paincourtville, LA....................985-369-2570
Road Runner Seafood
Colquitt, GA....................229-758-3485
Robin & Cohn Seafood Distributors
Chalmette, LA....................504-277-1679
Rock Point Oyster Company
Quilcene, WA....................360-765-3765
Rockland Boat
Rockland, ME....................207-594-8181
Rockport Lobster
Gloucester, MA....................978-281-0225
Rocky Point Shrimp Association
Phoenix, AZ....................602-254-8041
Rogers Brothers
Galesburg, IL....................309-342-2127
Rose Hill Seafood
Columbus, GA....................706-322-4410
Roy Dick Company
Griffin, GA....................770-227-3916
Royal Atlantic Seafood
Gloucester, MA....................978-281-6373
Royal Baltic
Brooklyn, NY....................718-385-8300
Royal Lagoon Seafood
Mobile, AL....................251-639-1103
Royal Pacific Fisheries
Kenai, AK....................907-283-9370
Royal Seafood
Monterey, CA....................831-373-7920
Royal Seafood
Monterey, CA....................831-655-8326
Ruark & Ashton
Woolford, MD....................800-725-5032
Rubino's Seafood Company
Chicago, IL....................312-258-0020
Ruggiero Seafood
Newark, NJ....................866-225-2627
Russo's Seafood
Savannah, GA....................912-341-8848
Rymer Seafood
Chicago, IL....................312-236-3266
Sahalee of Alaska
Anchorage, AK....................800-349-4151
Salamat of Seafoods
Kenai, AK....................907-283-7000
Salmolux
Federal Way, WA....................253-874-2026
Sanderson Farms
Bryan, TX....................979-778-5730
Sanwa Foods
San Lorenzo, CA....................510-317-8888
SC Enterprises
Owen Sound, ON....................519-371-0456
Sea Garden Seafoods
Meridian, GA....................912-832-4437
Sea K Fish Company
Blaine, WA....................360-332-5121
Sea Nik Food Company
Ninilchik, AK....................907-567-3980
Sea Pearl Seafood
Bayou La Batre, AL....................800-872-8804
Sea Products Company
Astoria, OR....................503-325-5023
Sea Safari
Belhaven, NC....................800-688-6174
Sea Safari Ltd.
Belhaven, NC....................800-688-6174
Sea Snack Foods
Los Angeles, CA....................213-622-2204
Sea View Fillet Company
New Bedford, MA....................508-984-1406
Sea Watch Intl.
Easton, MD....................410-822-7500
Seabear
Anacortes, WA....................800-645-3474
Seafare Market Wholesale
Moody, ME....................207-646-5160
Seafood Merchants
Vernon Hills, IL....................847-634-0900
Seafood Producers Coop ative
Bellingham, WA....................360-733-0120
Seafood Specialties
Coden, AL....................251-824-2693

Seafreeze Pizza
Seattle, WA 206-767-7350
Sealaska Corporation
Juneau, AK 800-848-5921
Seapac of Idaho
Filer, ID 208-326-3100
SeaPerfect Atlantic Farms
Charleston, SC 800-728-0099
SeaSpecialties
Miami, FL 800-654-6682
Seatech Corporation
Lynnwood, WA 425-487-3231
Seatrade Corporation
Hoboken, NJ 201-963-5700
Seaview Lobster Company
Kittery, ME 800-245-4997
Seymour & Sons Seafood
Diberville, MS 228-392-4020
Shamrock Foods Company
Phoenix, AZ 800-289-3663
Shawmut Fishing Company
Anchorage, AK 709-334-2559
Shemper Seafood Company
Biloxi, MS 228-435-2703
Shining Ocean
Sumner, WA 253-826-3700
Shore Seafood
Saxis, VA 757-824-5517
Sigma International
St Petersburg, FL 800-899-5717
Signature Seafoods
Seattle, WA 206-285-2815
Silver Lining Seafood
Ketchikan, AK 907-225-9865
Silverston Fisheries
Superior, WI 715-392-5551
Simeus Foods International
Mansfield, TX 888-772-3663
Sitka Sound Seafoods
Sitka, AK 907-747-6662
Sonoma Seafoods
Sonoma, CA 877-411-2123
Southchem
Durham, NC 800-849-7000
Southern Pride Catfish Company
Seattle, WA 800-343-8046
Southern Seafood Distributors
Franklinton, LA 985-839-6220
Southern Shell Fish Company
Harvey, LA 504-341-5631
Southern Shellfish
Savannah, GA 912-897-3650
Southside Seafood Company
Morrow, GA 404-366-6172
Southtowns Seafood & Meats
Blasdell, NY 716-824-4900
Spinney Creek Shellfish
Eliot, ME 877-778-6727
Sportsmen's Cannery
Winchester Bay, OR 800-457-8048
Sportsmen's Cannery & Smokehouse
Winchester Bay, OR 800-457-8048
Sportsmen's Sea Foods
San Diego, CA 619-224-3551
SS Lobster Limited
Fitchburg, MA 978-342-6135
St. Ours & Company
Norwell, MA 781-331-8520
St. Simons Seafood
Brunswick, GA 912-265-5225
Stacey's Famous Foods
Hayden, ID 800-782-2395
Stanley's Best Seafood
Coden, AL 251-824-2801
Star Seafood
Bayou La Batre, AL 251-824-3110
Starich
Daphne, AL 251-626-5037
State Fish Company
San Pedro, CA 310-832-2633
Steve Connolly Seafood Company
Roxbury, MA 800-225-5595
Stewarts Seafood
Coden, AL 251-824-7368
Stinson Seafood Company
San Diego, CA
Stone Crabs
Miami Beach, FL 800-260-2722
Straub's
Clayton, MO 888-725-2121
Sumida Fish Cake Factory
Hilo, HI 808-959-9857
Sunny's Seafood
Boston, MA 617-261-7123
Sunshine Food Sales
Miami, FL 305-696-2885
Sunshine Seafood
Stonington, ME 207-367-2955
Super Snooty Sea Food Corporation
Boston, MA 617-426-6390
Superior Ocean Produce
Chicago, IL 773-283-8400
Superior Seafood & Meat Company
South Bend, IN 574-289-0511
SYSCO Food Services of Northern New England
Portland, ME 800-632-4446
T&T Seafood
Baker, LA 225-261-5438
T. Cvitanovich
Metairie, LA 504-837-9586
T.B. Seafood
Portland, ME 207-871-2420
T.J. Kraft
Honolulu, HI 808-842-3474
Taku Smokehouse
Juneau, AK 800-582-5122
Tampa Maid Foods
Lakeland, FL 800-237-7637
Tempest Fisheries Limited
New Bedford, MA 508-997-0720
Terry Brothers
Willis Wharf, VA 757-824-3471
Tex-Mex Cold Storage
Brownsville, TX 956-831-9433
Tichon Seafood Corporation
New Bedford, MA 508-999-5607
Tideland Seafood Company
Dulac, LA 985-563-4516
TideWays
Peaks Island, ME 207-766-0062
Tony V'S Oyster House
Amite, LA 504-748-8110
Tony's Seafood
Baton Rouge, LA 225-357-9669
Trans-Ocean Products
Needham Heights, MA 508-626-0922
Tri-Cost Seafood
Baton Rouge, LA 225-757-8333
Tri-Marine InternationalInc
San Pedro, CA 310-732-6113
Triangle Seafood
Louisville, KY 502-561-0055
Tribe Mediterranean Foods Company LLC
Taunton, MA 774-961-0000
Trident Seafoods Corporation
Salem, NH 603-893-3368
Trident Seafoods Corporation
Seattle, WA 800-426-5490
Triton Seafood Company
Medley, FL 305-888-8999
Trosclair Canning Company
Bell City, LA 337-622-3698
Tsar Nicoulai Caviar
San Francisco, CA 800-952-2842
Turk Brothers Custom Meats
Ashland, OH 800-789-1051
U. Okada & Company
Honolulu, HI 808-597-1102
Union Fisheries Corporation
Chicago, IL 312-738-0448
Union Seafoods
Phoenix, AZ 602-254-4114
United Provision Meat Company
Columbus, OH 614-252-1126
United Shellfish Company
Grasonville, MD 410-827-8171
United Universal Enterprises Corporation
Phoenix, AZ 623-842-9691
Upcountry Fisheries
Makawao, HI 808-871-8484
Val's Seafood
Mobile, AL 251-639-2570
Valdez Food
Philadelphia, PA 215-634-6106
Van De Kamp Frozen Foods
Mountain Lake, NJ 973-541-6620
Van de Kamp's
Peoria, IL 800-798-3318
Van Dykes Chesapeake Seafood
Cambridge, MD 410-228-9000
Vantage USA
Chicago, IL 773-247-1086
Viking Seafoods Inc
Malden, MA 800-225-3020
Viking Trading
Atlanta, GA 770-455-8630
Vinalhaven Fishermens Co-Op
Camden, ME 207-236-0092
Vince's Seafoods
Gretna, LA 504-368-1544
Vincent Piazza Jr & Sons
Harahan, LA 800-259-5016
Virginia Trout Company
Monterey, VA 540-468-2280
Vision Seafood Partners
Kingston, MA 781-585-2000
W. Forrest Haywood Seafood Company
Poquoson, VA 757-868-6748
W. Roberts
Annapolis, MD 410-269-5380
W.O. Sasser
Savannah, GA 912-898-9504
W.T. Ruark & Company
Fishing Creek, MD 410-397-3133
Wabash Seafood Company
Chicago, IL 312-733-5070
Wabi Fishing Company
Marysville, WA 888-536-7696
Wagner Seafood
Oak Lawn, IL 708-636-2646
Wainani Kai Seafood
Honolulu, HI 808-847-7435
Walden Foods
Winchester, VA 800-648-7688
Walker Meats Corporation
Carrollton, GA 770-834-8171
Walker's Seafood
Jonesboro, AR 870-932-0375
Wallace Fisheries
Gulf Shores, AL 251-986-7211
Wallace Plant Company
Bath, ME 207-443-2640
Walsh's Seafood
Gouldsboro, ME 207-963-2578
Waltkoch
Decatur, GA 404-378-3666
Wanchese Fish Company
Suffolk, VA 757-673-4500
Waterfront Seafood
Bayou La Batre, AL 251-824-2185
Waterfront Seafood Market
West Des Moines, IA 515-223-5106
West Bay Fishing
Gouldsboro, ME 207-963-2392
Weyand Fisheries
Wyandotte, MI 800-521-9815
Wharton Seafood Sales
Paauilo, HI 800-352-8507
White Cap Fish Company
Islip, NY 631-581-0125
Wiegardt Brothers
Ocean Park, WA 360-665-4111
Wild Planet Foods
McKinleyville, CA 800-998-9945
William Atwood Lobster Company
Spruce Head, ME 80- 5-1 52
Winter Harbor Co-Op
Winter Harbor, ME 207-963-5857
WK Eckerd & Sons
Brunswick, GA 912-265-0332
Wolverton Seafood
Houlton, ME 506-276-4629
Woodfield Fish & Oyster Company
Galesville, MD 410-897-1093
World Flavors
Warminster, PA 215-672-4400
Wrangell Fisheries
Wrangell, AK 907-874-3346
Wright Brand Company
Bayou La Batre, AL 251-824-7880
Y&W Shellfish
Woodbine, GA 912-729-4814
Yarmer Boys Catfish International
Beaumont, TX 409-842-1962
Yeomen Seafoods
Gloucester, MA 978-283-7422
York Beach Fish Market
York, ME 207-363-2763
Young's Shellfish Company
Troy, ME

Canned

Charles H. Parks & Company
Fishing Creek, MD 410-397-3400

Chuck's Seafoods
Charleston, OR 541-888-5525
Cowart Seafood Corporation
Lottsburg, VA 804-529-6101
Crown Prince
City of Industry, CA 800-255-5063
Crown Prince Naturals
Petaluma, CA
Dressel Collins Fish Company
Seattle, WA 206-725-0121
Elwha Fish
Port Angeles, WA 360-457-3344
J. Moniz Company
Fall River, MA 508-674-8451
J. Turner Seafoods
Gloucester, MA 978-281-8535
J.S. McMillan Fisheries
Vancouver, BC 604-255-5191
Jenport International Distributors
Coquitlam, BC 604-464-9888
Kodiak Salmon Packers
Larsen Bay, AK 907-847-2250
LaMonica Fine Foods
Millville, NJ 856-825-8111
LLJ's Sea Products
Round Pond, ME 207-529-4224
Look's Gourmet Food Company
East Machias, ME 800-962-6258
Mercado Latino
City of Industry, CA 626-333-6862
Mid-Atlantic Foods
Easton, MD 800-922-4688
Noon Hour Food Products
Chicago, IL 800-621-6636
Notre Dame Seafood
Comfort Cove, NL 709-244-5511
Ocean Fresh Seafoods
Seattle, WA 206-285-2412
Sea Watch Intl.
Easton, MD 410-822-7500
Seatech Corporation
Lynnwood, WA 425-487-3231
Southern Shell Fish Company
Harvey, LA 504-341-5631
Sportsmen's Sea Foods
San Diego, CA 619-224-3551
Stinson Seafood Company
San Diego, CA
Tideland Seafood Company
Dulac, LA 985-563-4516
Wrangell Fisheries
Wrangell, AK 907-874-3346

Cocktail

Sea Snack Foods
Los Angeles, CA 213-622-2204

Freeze-Dried

Wolf Canyon Foods
Carmel, CA 831-626-1323

Fresh

Anderson Seafoods
Anaheim, CA 714-777-7100
Aquatec Seafoods Ltd.
Comox, BC 250-339-6412
Arrowac Fisheries
Seattle, WA 206-282-5655
Atlantic Capes Fisheries
Cape May, NJ 609-884-3000
Atlantic Sea Pride
South Boston, MA 617-269-7700
Bayou Land Seafood
Breaux Bridge, LA 337-667-6118
BG Smith Sons Oyster
Sharps, VA 877-483-8279
BlueWater Seafoods
Lachine, QC 888-560-2539
Bolner's Fiesta Products
San Antonio, TX 210-734-6404
Bornstein Seafoods
Bellingham, WA 360-734-7990
Briny Sea Delicacies
Tumwater, WA 888-772-5666
Buzzards Bay Trading Company
Fairhaven, MA 508-996-0242
Caraquet Ice Company
Caraquet, NB 506-727-7211
Charles H. Parks & Company
Fishing Creek, MD 410-397-3400
Coast Seafoods Company
Bellevue, WA 800-423-2303
Cowart Seafood Corporation
Lottsburg, VA 804-529-6101
Cozy Harbor Seafood
Portland, ME 800-225-2586
Crest International Corporation
San Diego, CA 800-548-1232
DB Kenney Fisheries
Westport, NS 902-839-2023
Depoe Bay Fish Company
Newport, OR 541-265-8833
Fishery Products International
Danvers, MA 800-374-4700
French Creek Seafood
Parksville, BC 250-248-7100
Granville Gates & Sons
Hubbards, NS 902-228-2559
Great Atlantic Trading Company
Ocean Isle Beach, NC 888-268-8780
Hallmark Fisheries
Charleston, OR 541-888-3253
Harbor Fish Market
Portland, ME 207-775-0251
Hillard Bloom Packing Co
Port Norris, NJ 856-785-0120
Hillman Shrimp & Oyster Company
Dickinson, TX 800-582-4416
Independent Packers Corporation
Seattle, WA 206-285-6000
International Seafoods of Alaska
Kodiak, AK 907-486-4768
Island Marine Products
Clarks Harbour, NS 902-745-2222
J. Matassini & Sons Fish Company
Tampa, FL 813-229-0829
Jessie's Ilwaco Fish Company
Ilwaco, WA 360-642-3773
Keyser Brothers
Lottsburg, VA 804-529-6837
LaMonica Fine Foods
Millville, NJ 856-825-8111
Little River Seafood
Reedville, VA 804-453-3670
Menemsha Fish Market
Chilmark, MA 508-645-2282
Mersey Seafoods
Liverpool, NS 902-354-3467
Minterbrook Oyster Company
Gig Harbor, WA 253-857-5251
Motivatit Seafoods
Houma, LA 985-868-7191
National Fish & Oysters Company
Olympia, WA 360-491-5550
Nordic Group
Boston, MA 800-486-4002
Norquest Seafoods
Seattle, WA 206-281-7022
Ocean Beauty Seafoods
Seattle, WA 206-285-6800
Ocean Fresh Seafoods
Seattle, WA 206-285-2412
Pacific American Fish Co.,Inc.
Vernon, CA 800-625-2525
Pacific Salmon Company
Edmonds, WA 425-774-1315
Pacific Seafoods International
Port Hardy, BC 250-949-8781
Pacific Shrimp Company
Newport, OR 541-265-4215
Pamlico Packing Company
Grantsboro, NC 800-682-1113
Paul Piazza & Sons
New Orleans, LA 504-524-6011
Plitt Company
Chicago, IL 773-523-3876
Portland Shellfish Company
South Portland, ME 207-799-9290
Quality Seafood
Apalachicola, FL 850-653-9696
Rippons Brothers Seafood
Fishing Creek, MD 410-397-3200
Royal Seafood
Monterey, CA 831-655-8326
Ruggiero Seafood
Newark, NJ 866-225-2627
Sea Garden Seafoods
Meridian, GA 912-832-4437
Sea K Fish Company
Blaine, WA 360-332-5121
Sitka Sound Seafoods
Sitka, AK 907-747-6662
Stone Crabs
Miami Beach, FL 800-260-2722
Sunshine Food Sales
Miami, FL 305-696-2885
Tampa Bay Fisheries
Dover, FL 800-234-2561
Taylor Shellfish Farms
Shelton, WA 360-426-6178
Terry Brothers
Willis Wharf, VA 757-824-3471
Union Fisheries Corporation
Chicago, IL 312-738-0448
United Shellfish Company
Grasonville, MD 410-827-8171
Wanchese Fish Company
Suffolk, VA 757-673-4500
Weyand Fisheries
Wyandotte, MI 800-521-9815
Wiegardt Brothers
Ocean Park, WA 360-665-4111
Wrangell Fisheries
Wrangell, AK 907-874-3346

Frozen

Acme Steak & Seafood Company
Youngstown, OH 330-270-8000
Ajinomoto Frozen Foods USA
Portland, OR 503-286-6548
Alaska Seafood Company
Los Angeles, CA 213-626-1212
Alaskan Gourmet Seafoods
Anchorage, AK 800-288-3740
Aliotti Wholesale Fish Company
Monterey, CA 831-375-2881
Alphin Brothers
Dunn, NC 800-672-4502
American Seafoods Group
Seattle, WA 800-275-2019
Anderson Seafoods
Anaheim, CA 714-777-7100
Appert's Foodservice
St Cloud, MN 800-225-3883
Aquatec Seafoods Ltd.
Comox, BC 250-339-6412
Arista Industries
Wilton, CT 800-255-6457
Arrowac Fisheries
Seattle, WA 206-282-5655
ASC Seafood
Largo, FL 800-876-3474
Atlantic Capes Fisheries
Cape May, NJ 609-884-3000
Atlantic Queen Seafoods Limited
St Josephs, NL 709-739-6668
Azuma Foods International
Hayward, CA
Bandon Bay Fisheries
Bandon, OR 541-347-4454
Bay Oceans Sea Foods
Garibaldi, OR 503-322-3316
Bayou Land Seafood
Breaux Bridge, LA 337-667-6118
Beaver Street Fisheries
Jacksonville, FL 800-874-6426
Bell Buoy Crab Company
Seaside, OR 800-529-2722
BG Smith Sons Oyster
Sharps, VA 877-483-8279
Blount Seafood Corporation
Fall River, MA 774-888-1300
BlueWater Seafoods
Lachine, QC 888-560-2539
Bolner's Fiesta Products
San Antonio, TX 210-734-6404
Bon Secour Fisheries
Bon Secour, AL 800-633-6854
Braun Seafood Company
Cutchogue, NY 631-734-6700
Bullock's Country Meats
Westminster, MD 410-848-6786
Buns & Things Bakery
Charlottetown, PE 902-892-2600
Buzzards Bay Trading Company
Fairhaven, MA 508-996-0242
C.F. Gollott & Son Seafood
Biloxi, MS 866-846-3474
Callis Seafood
Lancaster, VA 804-462-7634
Captn's Pack Products
Columbia, MD 410-720-6668

Caraquet Ice Company
Caraquet, NB. 506-727-7211
Carolina Atlantic Seafood Enterprises
Beaufort, NC. 252-504-2663
Carrington Foods
Saraland, AL. 251-675-9700
Cathay Foods Corporation
Boston, MA. 617-427-1507
Certi-Fresh Foods
Bell Gardens, CA 562-806-1100
Chases Lobster Pound
Port Howe, NS 902-243-2408
Cherbogue Fisheries
Yarmouth, NS 902-742-9157
Chester W. Howeth & Brother
Crisfield, MD 410-968-1398
Clearwater Fine Foods
Bedford, NS 902-443-0550
ConAgra Shrimp Companies
Tampa, FL. 813-241-1501
Cook Inlet Processing
Nikiski, AK. 907-776-8174
Cowart Seafood Corporation
Lottsburg, VA 804-529-6101
Cozy Harbor Seafood
Portland, ME. 800-225-2586
Crest International Corporation
San Diego, CA 800-548-1232
Crevettes Du Nord
Gaspe, QC. 418-368-1414
Cuizina Food Company
Woodinville, WA. 425-486-7000
Czimer's Game & Sea Foods
Homer Glen, IL. 708-301-0500
DB Kenney Fisheries
Westport, NS. 902-839-2023
Deep Creek Custom Packing
Ninilchik, AK 800-764-0078
Deep Sea Foods
Bayou La Batre, AL 251-824-7000
Del's Seaway Shrimp & Oyster Company
Biloxi, MS. 228-432-2604
Depoe Bay Fish Company
Newport, OR. 541-265-8833
Dick & Casey's Gourmet Seafoods
Harbor, OR 800-662-9494
E. Gagnon & Fils
St Therese-De-Gaspe, QC. 418-385-3011
Eastern Fish Company
Teaneck, NJ. 800-526-9066
Farm Fresh Catfish Company
Hollandale, MS. 800-647-8264
Fishery Products International
Danvers, MA. 800-374-4700
FishKing
Glendale, CA 818-244-2161
Fishmarket Seafoods
Louisville, KY 502-587-7474
French Creek Seafood
Parksville, BC. 250-248-7100
Frozen Specialties
Archbold, OH 419-445-9015
FW Bryce
Gloucester, MA. 978-283-7080
Gemini Food Industries
Charlton, MA 508-248-2730
George Robberecht Seafood
Montross, VA 804-472-3556
Gesco ENR
Gaspe, QC. 418-368-1414
Golden Gulf Coast Packing Company
Biloxi, MS. 228-374-6121
Good Harbor Fillet Company
Gloucester, MA. 978-675-9100
Gorton's Seafood
Gloucester, MA. 978-283-3000
Great Atlantic Trading Company
Ocean Isle Beach, NC. 888-268-8780
Great Glacier Salmon
Prince Rupert, BC. 250-627-4955
Great Northern Products
Warwick, RI 401-490-4590
Gulf Pride Enterprises
Biloxi, MS. 888-689-0560
H&H Fisheries Limited
Eastern Passage, NS 902-465-6330
Hallmark Fisheries
Charleston, OR 541-888-3253
Handy International
Salisbury, MD 800-426-3977
HFI Foods
Redmond, WA. 425-883-1320
Higgins Seafood
Lafitte, LA. 504-689-3577
High Liner Foods Inc
Lunenburg, NS 902-634-9475
Hillard Bloom Packing Co
Port Norris, NJ 856-785-0120
Hillman Shrimp & Oyster Company
Dickinson, TX. 800-582-4416
Icelandic USA
Newport News, VA. 757-820-4000
Icicle Seafoods
Seattle, WA. 206-282-0988
Independent Packers Corporation
Seattle, WA. 206-285-6000
Indian Ridge Shrimp Company
Chauvin, LA 985-594-3361
International Oceanic Enterprises of Alabama
Bayou La Batre, AL 800-816-1832
International Seafoods of Alaska
Kodiak, AK. 907-486-4768
Island Marine Products
Clarks Harbour, NS. 902-745-2222
Island Scallops
Qualicum Beach, BC 250-757-9811
J. Matassini & Sons Fish Company
Tampa, FL. 813-229-0829
J.S. McMillan Fisheries
Vancouver, BC 604-255-5191
Jack's Lobsters
Musquodoboit Harbor, NS 902-889-2771
Janes Family Foods
Mississauga, ON. 800-565-2637
JBS Packing Company
Port Arthur, TX. 409-982-3216
Jcw Tawes & Son
Crisfield, MD 410-968-1288
Jenport International Distributors
Coquitlam, BC 604-464-9888
Jessie's Ilwaco Fish Company
Ilwaco, WA 360-642-3773
Jubilee Foods
Emmitsburg, MD 301-447-6688
Key Largo Fisheries
Key Largo, FL. 800-432-4358
Keyser Brothers
Lottsburg, VA 804-529-6837
Kitchens Seafood
Plant City, FL 800-327-0132
Kodiak Salmon Packers
Larsen Bay, AK. 907-847-2250
L&C Fisheries
Kensington, PE. 902-886-2770
Lady Gale Seafood
Baldwin, LA 337-923-2060
LaMonica Fine Foods
Millville, NJ 856-825-8111
Lombardi's Seafood
Orlando, FL. 800-879-8411
Long Beach Seafoods
Long Beach, CA 562-435-5357
Louisiana Packing Company
Westwego, LA. 800-666-1293
Lund's Fisheries
Cape May, NJ 609-884-7600
M&M Shrimp Company
Biloxi, MS. 228-435-4915
Maple Leaf Foods International
North York, ON. 416-480-8900
Martin Seafood Company
Jessup, MD 410-799-5822
Maxim's Import Corporation
Miami, FL. 800-331-6652
Menemsha Fish Market
Chilmark, MA. 508-645-2282
Mid-Atlantic Foods
Easton, MD 800-922-4688
Miles J H & Company
Norfolk, VA. 757-622-9264
Milfico Foods
Elk Grove Vlg, IL. 847-427-0491
Minterbrook Oyster Company
Gig Harbor, WA 253-857-5251
Mobile Processing
Mobile, AL 251-438-6944
Morey's Seafood Intl. ional
Motley, MN. 218-352-6345
Motivatit Seafoods
Houma, LA 985-868-7191
Mutual Fish Company
Seattle, WA. 206-322-4368
Nan Sea Enterprises of Wisconsin
Waukesha, WI. 262-542-8841
National Fish & Oysters Company
Olympia, WA 360-491-5550
National Fish and Seafood Limited
Brownsville, TX 956-546-5525
Nelson Crab
Tokeland, WA 800-262-0069
Neptune Fisheries
Newport News, VA. 800-545-7474
Newfound Resources
St Josephs, NL 709-579-7676
Nordic Group
Boston, MA. 800-486-4002
Norquest Seafoods
Seattle, WA. 206-281-7022
North Atlantic Fish Company
Gloucester, MA. 978-283-4121
Northern Wind
New Bedford, MA 888-525-2525
Notre Dame Seafood
Comfort Cove, NL 709-244-5511
Ocean Beauty Seafoods
Seattle, WA. 206-285-6800
Ocean Food Company
Scarborough, ON 416-285-6487
Ocean Fresh Seafoods
Seattle, WA. 206-285-2412
Ocean Springs Seafood
Ocean Springs, MS. 228-875-0104
Okuhara Foods
Honolulu, HI. 808-848-0581
Omstead Foods Ltd
Wheatley, ON 905-315-8883
P&J Oyster Company
New Orleans, LA 504-523-2651
P. Janes & Sons
Hant's Harbor, NL. 709-586-2252
Pacific Alaska Seafoods
Seattle, WA. 206-587-0002
Pacific American Fish Co.,Inc.
Vernon, CA 800-625-2525
Pacific Seafoods International
Port Hardy, BC 250-949-8781
Pacific Shrimp Company
Newport, OR. 541-265-4215
Pacific Valley Foods
Bellevue, WA 425-643-1805
Pamlico Packing Company
Grantsboro, NC. 800-682-1113
Paul Piazza & Sons
New Orleans, LA 504-524-6011
PEI Mussel King
Morrell, PE 800-673-2767
Peter Pan Seafoods
Seattle, WA. 206-728-6000
Petersburg Fisheries
Petersburg, AK 877-772-4294
Plitt Company
Chicago, IL 773-523-3876
Port Chatham Smoked Seafood
Everett, WA. 800-872-5666
Portland Shellfish Company
South Portland, ME 207-799-9290
Prairie Cajun Whlse.
Eunice, LA 337-546-6195
Price Seafood
Chauvin, LA 985-594-3067
Quality Seafood
Apalachicola, FL. 850-653-9696
Resource Trading Company
Portland, ME. 207-772-2299
Rich-Seapak Corporation
Brownsville, TX 956-542-0001
Royal Seafood
Monterey, CA 831-655-8326
Ruggiero Seafood
Newark, NJ 866-225-2627
Sanderson Farms
Bryan, TX 979-778-5730
Sea K Fish Company
Blaine, WA 360-332-5121
Sea Pearl Seafood
Bayou La Batre, AL 800-872-8804
Sea Safari
Belhaven, NC 800-688-6174
Sea Safari Ltd.
Belhaven, NC 800-688-6174
Sea Snack Foods
Los Angeles, CA. 213-622-2204
Sea Watch Intl.
Easton, MD. 410-822-7500
Seafood Producers Coop ative
Bellingham, WA 360-733-0120

Seatech Corporation
Lynnwood, WA 425-487-3231
Seymour & Sons Seafood
Diberville, MS 228-392-4020
Shawmut Fishing Company
Anchorage, AK 709-334-2559
Silver Lining Seafood
Ketchikan, AK 907-225-9865
Sitka Sound Seafoods
Sitka, AK 907-747-6662
Southtowns Seafood & Meats
Blasdell, NY 716-824-4900
St. Ours & Company
Norwell, MA 781-331-8520
Stacey's Famous Foods
Hayden, ID 800-782-2395
Stinson Seafood Company
San Diego, CA
Stone Crabs
Miami Beach, FL 800-260-2722
Sunshine Food Sales
Miami, FL 305-696-2885
Super Snooty Sea Food Corporation
Boston, MA 617-426-6390
Sweet Water Seafood Corporation
Carlstadt, NJ 201-939-6622
Taku Smokehouse
Juneau, AK 800-582-5122
Tampa Bay Fisheries
Dover, FL 800-234-2561
Tampa Maid Foods
Lakeland, FL 800-237-7637
Taylor Shellfish Farms
Shelton, WA 360-426-6178
Tex-Mex Cold Storage
Brownsville, TX 956-831-9433
Tichon Seafood Corporation
New Bedford, MA 508-999-5607
Trident Seafoods Corporation
Salem, NH 603-893-3368
Trident Seafoods Corporation
Seattle, WA 800-426-5490
Triton Seafood Company
Medley, FL 305-888-8999
Union Fisheries Corporation
Chicago, IL 312-738-0448
Van De Kamp Frozen Foods
Mountain Lake, NJ 973-541-6620
Viking Seafoods Inc
Malden, MA 800-225-3020
Vince's Seafoods
Gretna, LA 504-368-1544
Vincent Piazza Jr & Sons
Harahan, LA 800-259-5016
Virginia Trout Company
Monterey, VA 540-468-2280
Wanchese Fish Company
Suffolk, VA 757-673-4500
Weyand Fisheries
Wyandotte, MI 800-521-9815
White Cap Fish Company
Islip, NY 631-581-0125
Wrangell Fisheries
Wrangell, AK 907-874-3346

Smoked

Bell Buoy Crab Company
Seaside, OR 800-529-2722
Blount Seafood Corporation
Fall River, MA 774-888-1300
Cooke Aguaculture
Blacks Harbour, NB 506-456-6600
Depoe Bay Fish Company
Newport, OR 541-265-8833
Dressel Collins Fish Company
Seattle, WA 206-725-0121
Indian Valley Meats
Indian, AK 907-653-7511
Norquest Seafoods
Seattle, WA 206-281-7022
Salmolux
Federal Way, WA 253-874-2026
Seabear
Anacortes, WA 800-645-3474

Cold

Tonex
Wallington, NJ 973-773-5135

Cured

J. Moniz Company
Fall River, MA 508-674-8451
J. Turner Seafoods
Gloucester, MA 978-281-8535
Ocean Fresh Seafoods
Seattle, WA 206-285-2412
Tideland Seafood Company
Dulac, LA 985-563-4516

Lox

Homarus
Atlanta, GA 404-877-1988
Vita Food Products
Chicago, IL 312-738-4500

Nova Style

Vita Food Products
Chicago, IL 312-738-4500

Turtle

Bayou Land Seafood
Breaux Bridge, LA 337-667-6118

Shellfish

Canned

Charles H. Parks & Company
Fishing Creek, MD 410-397-3400
Chicken of the Sea International
San Diego, CA 800-678-8862
Chuck's Seafoods
Charleston, OR 541-888-5525
Crown Prince
City of Industry, CA 800-255-5063
Cuizina Food Company
Woodinville, WA 425-486-7000
Eastern Shore Seafood Products
Mappsville, VA 800-466-8550
Elwha Fish
Port Angeles, WA 360-457-3344
Gulf City Marine Supply
Bayou La Batre, AL 251-824-2516
Hallmark Fisheries
Charleston, OR 541-888-3253
Mercado Latino
City of Industry, CA 626-333-6862
Mid-Atlantic Foods
Easton, MD 800-922-4688
Miles J H & Company
Norfolk, VA 757-622-9264
Nelson Crab
Tokeland, WA 800-262-0069
North Atlantic Fish Company
Gloucester, MA 978-283-4121
Notre Dame Seafood
Comfort Cove, NL 709-244-5511
NTC Marketing Inc
Williamsville, NY 800-333-1637
Omstead Foods Ltd
Wheatley, ON 905-315-8883
Pacific Salmon Company
Edmonds, WA 425-774-1315
Peter Pan Seafoods
Seattle, WA 206-728-6000
Petersburg Fisheries
Petersburg, AK 877-772-4294
Sea Safari
Belhaven, NC 800-688-6174
Southern Shell Fish Company
Harvey, LA 504-341-5631
Stinson Seafood Company
San Diego, CA
Sweet Water Seafood Corporation
Carlstadt, NJ 201-939-6622
Wrangell Fisheries
Wrangell, AK 907-874-3346

Chopped

S&M Fisheries
Kennebunkport, ME 207-985-3456

Clam

Atlantic Aqua Farms
Vernon Bridge, PE 902-651-2563
Atlantic Capes Fisheries
Cape May, NJ 609-884-3000
Bell Buoy Crab Company
Seaside, OR 800-529-2722
Big Al's Seafood
Bozman, MD 410-745-2637
Blount Fine Foods
Fall River, MA 774-888-1300
Blount Seafood Corporation
Fall River, MA 774-888-1300
Bon Secour Fisheries
Bon Secour, AL 800-633-6854
Braun Seafood Company
Cutchogue, NY 631-734-6700
Bumble Bee Foods
San Diego, CA 858-715-4000
C.E. Fish Company
Jonesboro, ME 207-434-2631
Cajun Crawfish Distributors
Mansura, LA 800-525-6813
Carolina Seafoods
Mc Clellanville, SC 843-887-3713
Certi-Fresh Foods
Bell Gardens, CA 562-806-1100
Chases Lobster Pound
Port Howe, NS 902-243-2408
Chester River Clam Co, Inc
Centreville, MD 410-758-3810
Chuck's Seafoods
Charleston, OR 541-888-5525
Clearwater Fine Foods
Bedford, NS 902-443-0550
Coast Seafoods Company
Bellevue, WA 800-423-2303
Comeaux's
Lafayette, LA 800-323-2492
Cook Inlet Processing
Nikiski, AK 907-776-8174
Crevettes Du Nord
Gaspe, QC 418-368-1414
Crown Prince
City of Industry, CA 800-255-5063
Cuizina Food Company
Woodinville, WA 425-486-7000
Del's Seaway Shrimp & Oyster Company
Biloxi, MS 228-432-2604
Dick & Casey's Gourmet Seafoods
Harbor, OR 800-662-9494
E. Gagnon & Fils
St Therese-De-Gaspe, QC 418-385-3011
Eastern Shore Seafood Products
Mappsville, VA 800-466-8550
Frozen Specialties
Archbold, OH 419-445-9015
Gesco ENR
Gaspe, QC 418-368-1414
Gulf Pride Enterprises
Biloxi, MS 888-689-0560
H&H Fisheries Limited
Eastern Passage, NS 902-465-6330
Hillard Bloom Packing Co
Port Norris, NJ 856-785-0120
Hillman Shrimp & Oyster Company
Dickinson, TX 800-582-4416
Huck's Seafood
Easton, MD 410-770-9211
Innovative Fishery Products
Belliveau Cove, NS 902-837-5163
International Enterprises
Herring Neck, NL 709-628-7406
Island Scallops
Qualicum Beach, BC 250-757-9811
Jack's Lobsters
Musquodoboit Harbor, NS 902-889-2771
JBS Packing Company
Port Arthur, TX 409-982-3216
Jubilee Foods
Emmitsburg, MD 301-447-6688
L&C Fisheries
Kensington, PE 902-886-2770
L&M Evans
Conyers, GA 770-918-8727
Lady Gale Seafood
Baldwin, LA 337-923-2060
LaMonica Fine Foods
Millville, NJ 856-825-8111
Louisiana Packing Company
Westwego, LA 800-666-1293
M&M Shrimp Company
Biloxi, MS 228-435-4915
Menemsha Fish Market
Chilmark, MA 508-645-2282
Mercado Latino
City of Industry, CA 626-333-6862

Mid-Atlantic Foods
Easton, MD 800-922-4688
Miles J H & Company
Norfolk, VA 757-622-9264
Mill Cove Lobster Pound
Boothbay Harbor, ME 207-633-3340
Mobile Processing
Mobile, AL 251-438-6944
Mutual Fish Company
Seattle, WA 206-322-4368
N.A. Boullon
Cumming, GA 770-889-2356
Nan Sea Enterprises of Wisconsin
Waukesha, WI 262-542-8841
Newfound Resources
St Josephs, NL 709-579-7676
Northern Wind
New Bedford, MA 888-525-2525
Ocean Springs Seafood
Ocean Springs, MS 228-875-0104
Pacific Alaska Seafoods
Seattle, WA 206-587-0002
PEI Mussel King
Morrell, PE 800-673-2767
Pine Point Seafood
Scarborough, ME 207-883-4701
Price Seafood
Chauvin, LA 985-594-3067
Resource Trading Company
Portland, ME 207-772-2299
SeaPerfect Atlantic Farms
Charleston, SC 800-728-0099
Shawmut Fishing Company
Anchorage, AK 709-334-2559
St. Ours & Company
Norwell, MA 781-331-8520
Stavis Seafoods
Boston, MA 800-390-5103
Tampa Bay Fisheries
Dover, FL 800-234-2561
Terry Brothers
Willis Wharf, VA 757-824-3471
United Shellfish Company
Grasonville, MD 410-827-8171
Vincent Piazza Jr & Sons
Harahan, LA 800-259-5016
Young's Lobster Pound
Belfast, ME 207-338-1160

Breaded Strips

LaMonica Fine Foods
Millville, NJ 856-825-8111

Canned

Blount Seafood Corporation
Fall River, MA 774-888-1300
Chicken of the Sea International
San Diego, CA 800-678-8862
Chuck's Seafoods
Charleston, OR 541-888-5525
Crown Prince Naturals
Petaluma, CA
Cuizina Food Company
Woodinville, WA 425-486-7000
Eastern Shore Seafood Products
Mappsville, VA 800-466-8550
Elwha Fish
Port Angeles, WA 360-457-3344
LaMonica Fine Foods
Millville, NJ 856-825-8111
Look's Gourmet Food Company
East Machias, ME 800-962-6258
Mercado Latino
City of Industry, CA 626-333-6862
Mid-Atlantic Foods
Easton, MD 800-922-4688
Mutual Fish Company
Seattle, WA 206-322-4368
Orleans Food Company
New Orleans, LA 800-628-4900
Seawatch International
Easton, MD 410-822-7500
Stavis Seafoods
Boston, MA 800-390-5103

Chopped

Eastern Shore Seafood Products
Mappsville, VA 800-466-8550
LaMonica Fine Foods
Millville, NJ 856-825-8111

Look's Gourmet Food Company
East Machias, ME 800-962-6258

Fresh

Coast Seafoods Company
Bellevue, WA 800-423-2303
Cuizina Food Company
Woodinville, WA 425-486-7000
LaMonica Fine Foods
Millville, NJ 856-825-8111
Menemsha Fish Market
Chilmark, MA 508-645-2282
Mutual Fish Company
Seattle, WA 206-322-4368
Sweet Water Seafood Corporation
Carlstadt, NJ 201-939-6622
Taylor Shellfish Farms
Shelton, WA 360-426-6178
Terry Brothers
Willis Wharf, VA 757-824-3471

Frozen

Cedar Key Aquaculture Farms
Mango, FL 888-252-6735
Certi-Fresh Foods
Bell Gardens, CA 562-806-1100
Clearwater Fine Foods
Bedford, NS 902-443-0550
ConAgra Shrimp Companies
Tampa, FL 813-241-1501
Cook Inlet Processing
Nikiski, AK 907-776-8174
Cuizina Food Company
Woodinville, WA 425-486-7000
Eastern Shore Seafood Products
Mappsville, VA 800-466-8550
Gorton's Seafood
Gloucester, MA 978-283-3000
Harbor Seafood
New Hyde Park, NY 800-645-2211
Hillard Bloom Packing Co
Port Norris, NJ 856-785-0120
LaMonica Fine Foods
Millville, NJ 856-825-8111
Menemsha Fish Market
Chilmark, MA 508-645-2282
Mid-Atlantic Foods
Easton, MD 800-922-4688
Minterbrook Oyster Company
Gig Harbor, WA 253-857-5251
Mutual Fish Company
Seattle, WA 206-322-4368
St. Ours & Company
Norwell, MA 781-331-8520
Taylor Shellfish Farms
Shelton, WA 360-426-6178

Frozen Strips

LaMonica Fine Foods
Millville, NJ 856-825-8111

Juice

Chincoteague Seafood Company
Parsonsburg, MD 443-260-4800
Crown Prince
City of Industry, CA 800-255-5063
Eastern Shore Seafood Products
Mappsville, VA 800-466-8550
Flavor House
Adelanto, CA 760-246-9131
Look's Gourmet Food Company
East Machias, ME 800-962-6258
Stinson Seafood Company
San Diego, CA

Minced

Eastern Shore Seafood Products
Mappsville, VA 800-466-8550
LaMonica Fine Foods
Millville, NJ 856-825-8111

Whole

Eastern Shore Seafood Products
Mappsville, VA 800-466-8550
LaMonica Fine Foods
Millville, NJ 856-825-8111

Conch

Denzer's Food Products
Baltimore, MD 410-889-1500
Harbor Seafood
New Hyde Park, NY 800-645-2211
LaMonica Fine Foods
Millville, NJ 856-825-8111
Sweet Water Seafood Corporation
Carlstadt, NJ 201-939-6622
Triton Seafood Company
Medley, FL 305-888-8999

Crab

Arrowac Fisheries
Seattle, WA 206-282-5655
Atlantic Queen Seafoods Limited
St Josephs, NL 709-739-6668
Bandon Bay Fisheries
Bandon, OR 541-347-4454
Bay Hundred Seafood
McDaniel, MD 410-745-9329
Bayou Foods
Kenner, LA 800-516-8283
Bayou Land Seafood
Breaux Bridge, LA 337-667-6118
Beaver Street Fisheries
Jacksonville, FL 800-874-6426
Bell Buoy Crab Company
Seaside, OR 800-529-2722
Big Al's Seafood
Bozman, MD 410-745-2637
Bolner's Fiesta Products
San Antonio, TX 210-734-6404
Bornstein Seafoods
Bellingham, WA 360-734-7990
Bradye P. Todd & Son
Cambridge, MD 410-228-8633
Bumble Bee Foods
San Diego, CA 858-715-4000
California Shellfish Company
San Francisco, CA 415-923-7400
Callis Seafood
Lancaster, VA 804-462-7634
Carrington Foods
Saraland, AL 251-675-9700
Catfish Wholesale
Abbeville, LA 800-334-7292
Cathay Foods Corporation
Boston, MA 617-427-1507
Ceilidh Fisherman's Cooperative
Port Hood, NS 902-787-2666
Certi-Fresh Foods
Bell Gardens, CA 562-806-1100
Charles H. Parks & Company
Fishing Creek, MD 410-397-3400
Clearwater Fine Foods
Bedford, NS 902-443-0550
Cook Inlet Processing
Nikiski, AK 907-776-8174
Crab Quarters
Baltimore, MD 410-686-2222
Crescent City Crab Corporation
New Orleans, LA 504-646-6645
Crown Prince
City of Industry, CA 800-255-5063
Cuizina Food Company
Woodinville, WA 425-486-7000
Dave's Gourmet Albacore
Kirkland, WA 800-454-8862
Day's Crabmeat & Lobster
Yarmouth, ME 207-846-5871
Depoe Bay Fish Company
Newport, OR 541-265-8833
Dorchester Crab Company
Wingate, MD 410-397-8103
Fisherman's Market International
Halifax, NS 902-445-3474
Fishery Products International
Danvers, MA 800-374-4700
Fishhawk Fisheries
Astoria, OR 503-325-5252
Goldcoast Salads
Naples, FL 239-304-0710
Great Northern Products
Warwick, RI 401-490-4590
Gulf Stream Crab Company
Bayou La Batre, AL 251-824-4717
H. Gass Seafood
Hollywood, MD 301-373-6882
Hallmark Fisheries
Charleston, OR 541-888-3253

Handy International
Salisbury, MD 800-426-3977
Huck's Seafood
Easton, MD 410-770-9211
Icicle Seafoods
Seattle, WA 206-282-0988
Independent Packers Corporation
Seattle, WA 206-285-6000
International Oceanic Enterprises of Alabama
Bayou La Batre, AL 800-816-1832
J. Matassini & Sons Fish Company
Tampa, FL 813-229-0829
Jcw Tawes & Son
Crisfield, MD 410-968-1288
Jessie's Ilwaco Fish Company
Ilwaco, WA 360-642-3773
Keyser Brothers
Lottsburg, VA 804-529-6837
Kitchens Seafood
Plant City, FL 800-327-0132
LaMonica Fine Foods
Millville, NJ 856-825-8111
Larry J. Williams Company
Jesup, GA 912-427-7729
Little River Seafood
Reedville, VA 804-453-3670
Look's Gourmet Food Company
East Machias, ME 800-962-6258
Lowland Seafood
Lowland, NC 252-745-3751
Martin Brothers SeafoodcCompany
Westwego, LA 504-341-2251
McGraw Seafood
Tracadie Sheila, NB 506-395-3374
Menemsha Fish Market
Chilmark, MA 508-645-2282
Mercado Latino
City of Industry, CA 626-333-6862
Mercer Processing
Modesto, CA 209-529-0150
Milfico Foods
Elk Grove Vlg, IL 847-427-0491
Moon Enterprises
Richmond, BC 604-270-0088
Mutual Fish Company
Seattle, WA 206-322-4368
Nelson Crab
Tokeland, WA 800-262-0069
Norquest Seafoods
Seattle, WA 206-281-7022
Notre Dame Seafood
Comfort Cove, NL 709-244-5511
Ocean Food Company
Scarborough, ON 416-285-6487
Ocean Union Company
Lawrenceville, GA 770-995-1957
Pacific Shrimp Company
Newport, OR 541-265-4215
Pamlico Packing Company
Grantsboro, NC 800-682-1113
Peter Pan Seafoods
Seattle, WA 206-728-6000
Petersburg Fisheries
Petersburg, AK 877-772-4294
Phillips Foods
Baltimore, MD 888-234-2722
Produits Belle Baie
Caraquet, NB 506-727-4414
Rippons Brothers Seafood
Fishing Creek, MD 410-397-3200
Sea Garden Seafoods
Meridian, GA 912-832-4437
Sea Safari
Belhaven, NC 252-943-3091
Sea Safari
Belhaven, NC 800-688-6174
Sea Safari Ltd.
Belhaven, NC 800-688-6174
Sea Watch Intl.
Easton, MD 410-822-7500
Silver Lining Seafood
Ketchikan, AK 907-225-9865
Southern Shell Fish Company
Harvey, LA 504-341-5631
St. Ours & Company
Norwell, MA 781-331-8520
Stinson Seafood Company
San Diego, CA
Stone Crabs
Miami Beach, FL 800-260-2722
Sunshine Food Sales
Miami, FL 305-696-2885

Taku Smokehouse
Juneau, AK 800-582-5122
Trident Seafoods Corporation
Seattle, WA 800-426-5490
Van Dykes Chesapeake Seafood
Cambridge, MD 410-228-9000
Vince's Seafoods
Gretna, LA 504-368-1544
W.H. Harris Seafood
North Grasonville, MD 410-827-9500
W.T. Ruark & Company
Fishing Creek, MD 410-397-3133
Ward Cove Packing Company
Seattle, WA 206-323-3200
Waverly Crabs
Baltimore, MD 410-243-1181
Wrangell Fisheries
Wrangell, AK 907-874-3346
Young's Lobster Pound
Belfast, ME 207-338-1160

Blue

Arctic Seas
Little Compton, RI 401-635-4000
Casey's Seafood
Newport News, VA 757-928-1979
J M Clayton Company
Cambridge, MD 800-652-6931
Jcw Tawes & Son
Crisfield, MD 410-968-1288
Little River Seafood
Reedville, VA 804-453-3670
Phillips Foods
Baltimore, MD 888-234-2722
Sea Safari
Belhaven, NC 800-688-6174

Cakes

Casey's Seafood
Newport News, VA 757-928-1979
Handy International
Salisbury, MD 800-426-3977
J. Matassini & Sons Fish Company
Tampa, FL 813-229-0829
LaMonica Fine Foods
Millville, NJ 856-825-8111
M&I Seafood Manufacturers
Essex, MD 410-780-0444
Tampa Bay Fisheries
Dover, FL 800-234-2561

Cakes Frozen

Chincoteague Seafood Company
Parsonsburg, MD 443-260-4800
Coastal Seafoods
Ridgefield, CT 203-431-0453
Cuizina Food Company
Woodinville, WA 425-486-7000
Handy International
Salisbury, MD 800-426-3977
J. Matassini & Sons Fish Company
Tampa, FL 813-229-0829
Phillips Foods
Baltimore, MD 888-234-2722

Canned

Cathay Foods Corporation
Boston, MA 617-427-1507
Charles H. Parks & Company
Fishing Creek, MD 410-397-3400
Chicken of the Sea International
San Diego, CA 800-678-8862
Crown Prince Naturals
Petaluma, CA
Cuizina Food Company
Woodinville, WA 425-486-7000
Elwha Fish
Port Angeles, WA 360-457-3344
Mercado Latino
City of Industry, CA 626-333-6862
Mutual Fish Company
Seattle, WA 206-322-4368
Scally's Imperial Importing Company Inc
Staten Island, NY 718-983-1938
Sea Safari
Belhaven, NC 800-688-6174
Southern Shell Fish Company
Harvey, LA 504-341-5631
Wrangell Fisheries
Wrangell, AK 907-874-3346

Claws Stone

Atlantic Queen Seafoods Limited
St Josephs, NL 709-739-6668

Cooked

Bayou Foods
Kenner, LA 800-516-8283

Dungeness

Arrowac Fisheries
Seattle, WA 206-282-5655
Bornstein Seafoods
Bellingham, WA 360-734-7990
Dave's Gourmet Albacore
Kirkland, WA 800-454-8862
Jessie's Ilwaco Fish Company
Ilwaco, WA 360-642-3773
Trident Seafoods Corporation
Seattle, WA 800-426-5490

Fresh

Arrowac Fisheries
Seattle, WA 206-282-5655
Bayou Land Seafood
Breaux Bridge, LA 337-667-6118
Bornstein Seafoods
Bellingham, WA 360-734-7990
Cathay Foods Corporation
Boston, MA 617-427-1507
Charles H. Parks & Company
Fishing Creek, MD 410-397-3400
Cuizina Food Company
Woodinville, WA 425-486-7000
Daley Brothers ltd.
St John's, NL 709-364-8844
Dave's Gourmet Albacore
Kirkland, WA 800-454-8862
Depoe Bay Fish Company
Newport, OR 541-265-8833
Fishery Products International
Danvers, MA 800-374-4700
Icicle Seafoods
Seattle, WA 206-282-0988
J. Matassini & Sons Fish Company
Tampa, FL 813-229-0829
Jcw Tawes & Son
Crisfield, MD 410-968-1288
Jessie's Ilwaco Fish Company
Ilwaco, WA 360-642-3773
Keyser Brothers
Lottsburg, VA 804-529-6837
Little River Seafood
Reedville, VA 804-453-3670
Lowland Seafood
Lowland, NC 252-745-3751
Menemsha Fish Market
Chilmark, MA 508-645-2282
Mutual Fish Company
Seattle, WA 206-322-4368
Nelson Crab
Tokeland, WA 800-262-0069
Phillips Foods
Baltimore, MD 888-234-2722
Portland Shellfish Company
South Portland, ME 207-799-9290
Rippons Brothers Seafood
Fishing Creek, MD 410-397-3200
Sea Garden Seafoods
Meridian, GA 912-832-4437
Sea Safari
Belhaven, NC 252-943-3091
Sea Watch Intl.
Easton, MD 410-822-7500
Stone Crabs
Miami Beach, FL 800-260-2722
Sunshine Food Sales
Miami, FL 305-696-2885
Taylor Shellfish Farms
Shelton, WA 360-426-6178
Wrangell Fisheries
Wrangell, AK 907-874-3346

Frozen

Arrowac Fisheries
Seattle, WA 206-282-5655
Atlantic Queen Seafoods Limited
St Josephs, NL 709-739-6668
Bandon Bay Fisheries
Bandon, OR 541-347-4454

Bayou Land Seafood
Breaux Bridge, LA 337-667-6118
Beaver Street Fisheries
Jacksonville, FL 800-874-6426
Bornstein Seafoods
Bellingham, WA 360-734-7990
Buns & Things Bakery
Charlottetown, PE. 902-892-2600
Callis Seafood
Lancaster, VA 804-462-7634
Carrington Foods
Saraland, AL. 251-675-9700
Cathay Foods Corporation
Boston, MA. 617-427-1507
Certi-Fresh Foods
Bell Gardens, CA 562-806-1100
Clearwater Fine Foods
Bedford, NS 902-443-0550
ConAgra Shrimp Companies
Tampa, FL. 813-241-1501
Cook Inlet Processing
Nikiski, AK. 907-776-8174
Cowart Seafood Corporation
Lottsburg, VA 804-529-6101
Cuizina Food Company
Woodinville, WA. 425-486-7000
Daley Brothers ltd.
St John's, NL. 709-364-8844
Dave's Gourmet Albacore
Kirkland, WA 800-454-8862
Depoe Bay Fish Company
Newport, OR. 541-265-8833
Fishery Products International
Danvers, MA. 800-374-4700
Fogo Island Cooperative Society
Seldom Come By, NL. 709-627-3452
Great Northern Products
Warwick, RI 401-490-4590
Higgins Seafood
Lafitte, LA. 504-689-3577
Icicle Seafoods
Seattle, WA 206-282-0988
Independent Packers Corporation
Seattle, WA 206-285-6000
International Oceanic Enterprises of Alabama
Bayou La Batre, AL 800-816-1832
J. Matassini & Sons Fish Company
Tampa, FL. 813-229-0829
Jessie's Ilwaco Fish Company
Ilwaco, WA 360-642-3773
Keyser Brothers
Lottsburg, VA 804-529-6837
Kitchens Seafood
Plant City, FL 800-327-0132
Menemsha Fish Market
Chilmark, MA. 508-645-2282
Milfico Foods
Elk Grove Vlg, IL. 847-427-0491
Mutual Fish Company
Seattle, WA 206-322-4368
Notre Dame Seafood
Comfort Cove, NL 709-244-5511
Pacific Shrimp Company
Newport, OR. 541-265-4215
Pamlico Packing Company
Grantsboro, NC. 800-682-1113
Portland Shellfish Company
South Portland, ME 207-799-9290
Sea Garden Seafoods
Meridian, GA 912-832-4437
Sea Safari
Belhaven, NC 800-688-6174
Sea Safari Ltd.
Belhaven, NC 800-688-6174
Sea Watch Intl.
Easton, MD. 410-822-7500
Silver Lining Seafood
Ketchikan, AK 907-225-9865
St. Ours & Company
Norwell, MA. 781-331-8520
Stone Crabs
Miami Beach, FL 800-260-2722
Sunshine Food Sales
Miami, FL. 305-696-2885
Taku Smokehouse
Juneau, AK 800-582-5122
Taylor Shellfish Farms
Shelton, WA 360-426-6178
Trident Seafoods Corporation
Seattle, WA 800-426-5490
Ward Cove Packing Company
Seattle, WA 206-323-3200
Wrangell Fisheries
Wrangell, AK 907-874-3346

Imitation

Harbor Seafood
New Hyde Park, NY 800-645-2211

King

Arctic Seas
Little Compton, RI 401-635-4000
Arrowac Fisheries
Seattle, WA 206-282-5655
Bolner's Fiesta Products
San Antonio, TX. 210-734-6404
Harbor Seafood
New Hyde Park, NY 800-645-2211
New Ocean
Atlanta, GA. 770-458-5235
Ocean Garden Products
San Diego, CA 858-571-5002
Sitka Sound Seafoods
Sitka, AK. 907-747-6662
Trident Seafoods Corporation
Seattle, WA 800-426-5490

Live

Dorchester Crab Company
Wingate, MD. 410-397-8103

Meat

Atlantic Queen Seafoods Limited
St Josephs, NL 709-739-6668
Bandon Bay Fisheries
Bandon, OR 541-347-4454
Bay Hundred Seafood
McDaniel, MD 410-745-9329
Bayou Foods
Kenner, LA 800-516-8283
Bayou Land Seafood
Breaux Bridge, LA 337-667-6118
Beaver Street Fisheries
Jacksonville, FL 800-874-6426
Blalock Seafood
Orange Beach, AL 251-974-5811
Blue Crab Bay Company
Melfa, VA 800-221-2722
Boja's Foods
Bayou La Batre, AL 251-824-4186
Certi-Fresh Foods
Bell Gardens, CA 562-806-1100
Charles H. Parks & Company
Fishing Creek, MD 410-397-3400
Dave's Gourmet Albacore
Kirkland, WA 800-454-8862
Day's Crabmeat & Lobster
Yarmouth, ME. 207-846-5871
Dorchester Crab Company
Wingate, MD. 410-397-8103
Hallmark Fisheries
Charleston, OR 541-888-3253
Harmon's Original Clam Cakes
Kennebunkport, ME 207-967-4100
Keyser Brothers
Lottsburg, VA 804-529-6837
Little River Seafood
Reedville, VA 804-453-3670
Martin Brothers SeafoodcCompany
Westwego, LA. 504-341-2251
Mercado Latino
City of Industry, CA 626-333-6862
Mutual Fish Company
Seattle, WA 206-322-4368
Nelson Crab
Tokeland, WA 800-262-0069
Pamlico Packing Company
Grantsboro, NC. 800-682-1113
Penguin Frozen Foods
Northbrook, IL 847-291-9400
Peter Pan Seafoods
Seattle, WA 206-728-6000
Petersburg Fisheries
Petersburg, AK 877-772-4294
Phillips Foods
Baltimore, MD 888-234-2722
Rippons Brothers Seafood
Fishing Creek, MD 410-397-3200
Sea Garden Seafoods
Meridian, GA 912-832-4437
Sea Safari
Belhaven, NC 252-943-3091
Sea Safari
Belhaven, NC 800-688-6174
Sea Safari Ltd.
Belhaven, NC 800-688-6174
Sea Watch Intl.
Easton, MD. 410-822-7500
Seafood Network
Brunswick, GA 912-267-0422
Southern Shell Fish Company
Harvey, LA 504-341-5631
Van Dykes Chesapeake Seafood
Cambridge, MD 410-228-9000
Victory Seafood
Abbeville, LA 337-893-9029
W.T. Ruark & Company
Fishing Creek, MD 410-397-3133

Meat Canned

Bayou Land Seafood
Breaux Bridge, LA 337-667-6118
Cathay Foods Corporation
Boston, MA. 617-427-1507
Charles H. Parks & Company
Fishing Creek, MD 410-397-3400
Day's Crabmeat & Lobster
Yarmouth, ME. 207-846-5871
Martin Brothers SeafoodcCompany
Westwego, LA. 504-341-2251
Mercado Latino
City of Industry, CA 626-333-6862
Miami Crab Corporation
Miami, FL. 800-269-8395
Orleans Food Company
New Orleans, LA 800-628-4900
Peter Pan Seafoods
Seattle, WA 206-728-6000
Petersburg Fisheries
Petersburg, AK 877-772-4294
Phillips Foods
Baltimore, MD 888-234-2722
Sea Safari
Belhaven, NC 800-688-6174
Southern Shell Fish Company
Harvey, LA 504-341-5631

Meat Frozen

Atlantic Queen Seafoods Limited
St Josephs, NL 709-739-6668
Bandon Bay Fisheries
Bandon, OR 541-347-4454
Bayou Land Seafood
Breaux Bridge, LA 337-667-6118
Beaver Street Fisheries
Jacksonville, FL 800-874-6426
Cathay Foods Corporation
Boston, MA. 617-427-1507
Certi-Fresh Foods
Bell Gardens, CA 562-806-1100
Day's Crabmeat & Lobster
Yarmouth, ME. 207-846-5871
International Oceanic Enterprises of Alabama
Bayou La Batre, AL 800-816-1832
Keyser Brothers
Lottsburg, VA 804-529-6837
Martin Brothers SeafoodcCompany
Westwego, LA. 504-341-2251
Miami Crab Corporation
Miami, FL. 800-269-8395
Nelson Crab
Tokeland, WA 800-262-0069
Penguin Frozen Foods
Northbrook, IL 847-291-9400
Peter Pan Seafoods
Seattle, WA 206-728-6000
Petersburg Fisheries
Petersburg, AK 877-772-4294
Phillips Foods
Baltimore, MD 888-234-2722
Sea Garden Seafoods
Meridian, GA 912-832-4437
Victory Seafood
Abbeville, LA 337-893-9029

Snow

Arctic Seas
Little Compton, RI 401-635-4000
Arrowac Fisheries
Seattle, WA 206-282-5655
Bolner's Fiesta Products
San Antonio, TX. 210-734-6404

Breakwater Fisheries
St Josephs, NL 709-754-1999
Buns & Things Bakery
Charlottetown, PE. 902-892-2600
Harbor Seafood
New Hyde Park, NY 800-645-2211
New Ocean
Atlanta, GA. 770-458-5235
Sea Safari Ltd.
Belhaven, NC 800-688-6174
Sitka Sound Seafoods
Sitka, AK. 907-747-6662
Taku Smokehouse
Juneau, AK 800-582-5122

Soft Shell

Bayou Foods
Kenner, LA 800-516-8283
Bolner's Fiesta Products
San Antonio, TX. 210-734-6404
Cowart Seafood Corporation
Lottsburg, VA 804-529-6101
Handy International
Salisbury, MD. 800-426-3977
Rippons Brothers Seafood
Fishing Creek, MD 410-397-3200
W.T. Ruark & Company
Fishing Creek, MD 410-397-3133

Stone

Stone Crabs
Miami Beach, FL 800-260-2722

Stuffed

Belle River Enterprises
Belle River, PE 902-962-2248
Bolner's Fiesta Products
San Antonio, TX. 210-734-6404
Bon Secour Fisheries
Bon Secour, AL. 800-633-6854
Claytons Crab Company
Rockledge, FL. 321-639-0161
Dave's Gourmet Albacore
Kirkland, WA 800-454-8862
Dick & Casey's Gourmet Seafoods
Harbor, OR 800-662-9494
E. Gagnon & Fils
St Therese-De-Gaspe, QC. 418-385-3011
Handy International
Salisbury, MD. 800-426-3977
International Oceanic Enterprises of Alabama
Bayou La Batre, AL 800-816-1832
Lowland Seafood
Lowland, NC. 252-745-3751
Menemsha Fish Market
Chilmark, MA. 508-645-2282
Nan Sea Enterprises of Wisconsin
Waukesha, WI. 262-542-8841
Pamlico Packing Company
Grantsboro, NC. 800-682-1113
Randol
Lafayette, LA. . . . . 800-YO -AJUN
Rippons Brothers Seafood
Fishing Creek, MD 410-397-3200
Shawmut Fishing Company
Anchorage, AK. 709-334-2559
Ward Cove Packing Company
Seattle, WA 206-323-3200

Crayfish

Bayou Land Seafood
Breaux Bridge, LA 337-667-6118
Catahoula Crawfish
Saint Martinville, LA 337-394-4223
Louisiana Crawfish Company
Natchitoches, LA 318-379-0539
Ocean Pride Seafood
Delcambre, LA 337-685-2336
Raffield Fisheries
Port St Joe, FL. 850-229-8229
Rivere's Seafood Processors
Paincourtville, LA. 985-369-2570
Vince's Seafoods
Gretna, LA 504-368-1544

Frozen

Bayou Land Seafood
Breaux Bridge, LA 337-667-6118

Live

Belle River Enterprises
Belle River, PE 902-962-2248
Depoe Bay Fish Company
Newport, OR. 541-265-8833

Raw

Bayou Land Seafood
Breaux Bridge, LA 337-667-6118

Dehydrated

Mercer Processing
Modesto, CA. 209-529-0150

Fresh

Acme Steak & Seafood Company
Youngstown, OH. 330-270-8000
Arrowac Fisheries
Seattle, WA 206-282-5655
Bay Oceans Sea Foods
Garibaldi, OR 503-322-3316
Bayou Land Seafood
Breaux Bridge, LA 337-667-6118
BG Smith Sons Oyster
Sharps, VA 877-483-8279
Blount Seafood Corporation
Fall River, MA 774-888-1300
BlueWater Seafoods
Lachine, QC 888-560-2539
Bolner's Fiesta Products
San Antonio, TX. 210-734-6404
Bon Secour Fisheries
Bon Secour, AL. 800-633-6854
Bornstein Seafoods
Bellingham, WA 360-734-7990
C.F. Gollott & Son Seafood
Biloxi, MS. 866-846-3474
Charles H. Parks & Company
Fishing Creek, MD 410-397-3400
Coast Seafoods Company
Bellevue, WA 800-423-2303
Cowart Seafood Corporation
Lottsburg, VA 804-529-6101

Cozy Harbor Seafood
Portland, ME....800-225-2586
Depoe Bay Fish Company
Newport, OR....541-265-8833
Eastern Shore Seafood Products
Mappsville, VA....800-466-8550
Fishery Products International
Danvers, MA....800-374-4700
Gulf City Marine Supply
Bayou La Batre, AL....251-824-2516
Gulf Pride Enterprises
Biloxi, MS....888-689-0560
Hallmark Fisheries
Charleston, OR....541-888-3253
Hillard Bloom Packing Co
Port Norris, NJ....856-785-0120
Hillman Shrimp & Oyster Company
Dickinson, TX....800-582-4416
Icicle Seafoods
Seattle, WA....206-282-0988
Independent Packers Corporation
Seattle, WA....206-285-6000
Intervest Trading Company Inc.
Halifax, NS....902-425-2018
IOE Atlanta
Galena, MD....410-755-6300
Island Marine Products
Clarks Harbour, NS....902-745-2222
J. Matassini & Sons Fish Company
Tampa, FL....813-229-0829
Jcw Tawes & Son
Crisfield, MD....410-968-1288
Jessie's Ilwaco Fish Company
Ilwaco, WA....360-642-3773
Keyser Brothers
Lottsburg, VA....804-529-6837
LaMonica Fine Foods
Millville, NJ....856-825-8111
Little River Seafood
Reedville, VA....804-453-3670
Mersey Seafoods
Liverpool, NS....902-354-3467
Miles J H & Company
Norfolk, VA....757-622-9264
Minterbrook Oyster Company
Gig Harbor, WA....253-857-5251
National Fish & Oysters Company
Olympia, WA....360-491-5550
Nelson Crab
Tokeland, WA....800-262-0069
North Atlantic Fish Company
Gloucester, MA....978-283-4121
Omstead Foods Ltd
Wheatley, ON....905-315-8883
P&J Oyster Company
New Orleans, LA....504-523-2651
Pacific Salmon Company
Edmonds, WA....425-774-1315
Pacific Shrimp Company
Newport, OR....541-265-4215
Paul Piazza & Sons
New Orleans, LA....504-524-6011
Peter Pan Seafoods
Seattle, WA....206-728-6000
Petersburg Fisheries
Petersburg, AK....877-772-4294
Portland Shellfish Company
South Portland, ME....207-799-9290
Quality Seafood
Apalachicola, FL....850-653-9696
Rippons Brothers Seafood
Fishing Creek, MD....410-397-3200
Royal Seafood
Monterey, CA....831-655-8326
Ruggiero Seafood
Newark, NJ....866-225-2627
Sea Garden Seafoods
Meridian, GA....912-832-4437
Seafood Producers Coop ative
Bellingham, WA....360-733-0120
Sportsmen's Cannery & Smokehouse
Winchester Bay, OR....800-457-8048
Stone Crabs
Miami Beach, FL....800-260-2722
Sweet Water Seafood Corporation
Carlstadt, NJ....201-939-6622
Taylor Shellfish Farms
Shelton, WA....360-426-6178
Terry Brothers
Willis Wharf, VA....757-824-3471
Tichon Seafood Corporation
New Bedford, MA....508-999-5607
Wanchese Fish Company
Suffolk, VA....757-673-4500
Ward Cove Packing Company
Seattle, WA....206-323-3200
Wiegardt Brothers
Ocean Park, WA....360-665-4111
Wrangell Fisheries
Wrangell, AK....907-874-3346
Young's Lobster Pound
Belfast, ME....207-338-1160

Frozen

Appert's Foodservice
St Cloud, MN....800-225-3883
Arctic Seas
Little Compton, RI....401-635-4000
Arista Industries
Wilton, CT....800-255-6457
Arrowac Fisheries
Seattle, WA....206-282-5655
Atlantic Queen Seafoods Limited
St Josephs, NL....709-739-6668
Bandon Bay Fisheries
Bandon, OR....541-347-4454
Bayou Land Seafood
Breaux Bridge, LA....337-667-6118
Beaver Street Fisheries
Jacksonville, FL....800-874-6426
BG Smith Sons Oyster
Sharps, VA....877-483-8279
Bon Secour Fisheries
Bon Secour, AL....800-633-6854
Bornstein Seafoods
Bellingham, WA....360-734-7990
Breakwater Fisheries
St Josephs, NL....709-754-1999
Buns & Things Bakery
Charlottetown, PE....902-892-2600
Callis Seafood
Lancaster, VA....804-462-7634
Carrington Foods
Saraland, AL....251-675-9700
Cathay Foods Corporation
Boston, MA....617-427-1507
Caver Shellfish
Beals, ME....207-497-2629
Certi-Fresh Foods
Bell Gardens, CA....562-806-1100
Clearwater Fine Foods
Bedford, NS....902-443-0550
ConAgra Foods
Tampa, FL....813-241-1500
Cook Inlet Processing
Nikiski, AK....907-776-8174
Cowart Seafood Corporation
Lottsburg, VA....804-529-6101
Cozy Harbor Seafood
Portland, ME....800-225-2586
Cuizina Food Company
Woodinville, WA....425-486-7000
Deep Sea Foods
Bayou La Batre, AL....251-824-7000
Eastern Fish Company
Teaneck, NJ....800-526-9066
Eastern Shore Seafood Products
Mappsville, VA....800-466-8550
Fishery Products International
Danvers, MA....800-374-4700
FishKing
Glendale, CA....818-244-2161
Florida Carib Fishery
Doral, FL....305-696-2896
Glacier Fish Company
Seattle, WA....206-298-1200
Golden Gulf Coast Packing Company
Biloxi, MS....228-374-6121
Great Northern Products
Warwick, RI....401-490-4590
Gulf City Marine Supply
Bayou La Batre, AL....251-824-2516
Hallmark Fisheries
Charleston, OR....541-888-3253
Handy International
Salisbury, MD....800-426-3977
Hillard Bloom Packing Co
Port Norris, NJ....856-785-0120
Hillman Shrimp & Oyster Company
Dickinson, TX....800-582-4416
Icelandic USA
Newport News, VA....757-820-4000
Icicle Seafoods
Seattle, WA....206-282-0988
Independent Packers Corporation
Seattle, WA....206-285-6000
Indian Ridge Shrimp Company
Chauvin, LA....985-594-3361
International Seafood Distributors
Hayes, VA....804-642-1417
Intervest Trading Company Inc.
Halifax, NS....902-425-2018
Island Marine Products
Clarks Harbour, NS....902-745-2222
J. Matassini & Sons Fish Company
Tampa, FL....813-229-0829
Janes Family Foods
Mississauga, ON....800-565-2637
Jessie's Ilwaco Fish Company
Ilwaco, WA....360-642-3773
Key Largo Fisheries
Key Largo, FL....800-432-4358
Keyser Brothers
Lottsburg, VA....804-529-6837
Lund's Fisheries
Cape May, NJ....609-884-7600
Maxim's Import Corporation
Miami, FL....800-331-6652
Menemsha Fish Market
Chilmark, MA....508-645-2282
Mersey Seafoods
Liverpool, NS....902-354-3467
Mid-Atlantic Foods
Easton, MD....800-922-4688
Miles J H & Company
Norfolk, VA....757-622-9264
Milfico Foods
Elk Grove Vlg, IL....847-427-0491
Minterbrook Oyster Company
Gig Harbor, WA....253-857-5251
National Fish & Oysters Company
Olympia, WA....360-491-5550
National Fish and Seafood Limited
Brownsville, TX....956-546-5525
Nelson Crab
Tokeland, WA....800-262-0069
Neptune Fisheries
Newport News, VA....800-545-7474
North Atlantic Fish Company
Gloucester, MA....978-283-4121
O'Hara Corporation
Rockland, ME....207-594-0405
Okuhara Foods
Honolulu, HI....808-848-0581
Omstead Foods Ltd
Wheatley, ON....905-315-8883
P&J Oyster Company
New Orleans, LA....504-523-2651
Pacific American Fish Co.,Inc.
Vernon, CA....800-625-2525
Pacific Salmon Company
Edmonds, WA....425-774-1315
Pacific Shrimp Company
Newport, OR....541-265-4215
Paul Piazza & Sons
New Orleans, LA....504-524-6011
Penguin Frozen Foods
Northbrook, IL....847-291-9400
Petersburg Fisheries
Petersburg, AK....877-772-4294
Pinnacle Foods Group
Cherry Hill, NJ....877-852-7424
Port Chatham Smoked Seafood
Everett, WA....800-872-5666
Portland Shellfish Company
South Portland, ME....207-799-9290
Quality Seafood
Apalachicola, FL....850-653-9696
Rich-Seapak Corporation
Brownsville, TX....956-542-0001
Royal Seafood
Monterey, CA....831-655-8326
Ruggiero Seafood
Newark, NJ....866-225-2627
Sea Garden Seafoods
Meridian, GA....912-832-4437
Sea Pearl Seafood
Bayou La Batre, AL....800-872-8804
Sea Safari Ltd.
Belhaven, NC....800-688-6174
Sea Snack Foods
Los Angeles, CA....213-622-2204
Seafood Producers Coop ative
Bellingham, WA....360-733-0120

Seymour & Sons Seafood
Diberville, MS 228-392-4020
Silver Lining Seafood
Ketchikan, AK 907-225-9865
St. Ours & Company
Norwell, MA...................... 781-331-8520
Stone Crabs
Miami Beach, FL 800-260-2722
Taku Smokehouse
Juneau, AK........................ 800-582-5122
Tampa Maid Foods
Lakeland, FL...................... 800-237-7637
Taylor Shellfish Farms
Shelton, WA 360-426-6178
Tichon Seafood Corporation
New Bedford, MA 508-999-5607
Trident Seafoods Corporation
Seattle, WA....................... 800-426-5490
Triton Seafood Company
Medley, FL 305-888-8999
Viking Seafoods Inc
Malden, MA 800-225-3020
Vince's Seafoods
Gretna, LA 504-368-1544
Wanchese Fish Company
Suffolk, VA....................... 757-673-4500
Wrangell Fisheries
Wrangell, AK 907-874-3346
Young's Lobster Pound
Belfast, ME....................... 207-338-1160

Geoduck Clams

Peter Pan Seafoods
Seattle, WA....................... 206-728-6000

Langostinos

Kitchens Seafood
Plant City, FL 800-327-0132

Live

Caver Shellfish
Beals, ME......................... 207-497-2629

Lobster

Acme Steak & Seafood Company
Youngstown, OH.................... 330-270-8000
Adams Fisheries Ltd
Shag Harbour, NS.................. 902-723-2435
Arista Industries
Wilton, CT 800-255-6457
Atlantic Queen Seafoods Limited
St Josephs, NL 709-739-6668
B.B.S. Lobster Company
Machiasport, ME 207-255-8888
Barry Group
Corner Brook, NL.................. 709-785-7387
Bauhaven Lobster
York, ME.......................... 207-363-5265
Beal's Lobster Pier
Southwest Harbor, ME 800-244-7178
Bickford Daniel Lobster Company
Vinalhaven, ME 207-863-4688
Black Duck Cove Lobster
Beals, ME......................... 207-497-2232
Blount Seafood Corporation
Fall River, MA 774-888-1300
Bolner's Fiesta Products
San Antonio, TX................... 210-734-6404
Bon Secour Fisheries
Bon Secour, AL.................... 800-633-6854
Boothbay Region Lobsterman
Boothbay Harbor, ME............... 207-633-4900
Boston Direct Lobster
New Orleans, LA 504-834-6404
C.B.S. Lobster Company
Portland, ME...................... 207-775-2917
Castle Hill Lobster
Ipswich, MA 978-356-3947
Ceilidh Fisherman's Cooperative
Port Hood, NS..................... 902-787-2666
Certi-Fresh Foods
Bell Gardens, CA 562-806-1100
Chases Lobster Pound
Port Howe, NS 902-243-2408
Clearwater Fine Foods
Bedford, NS 902-443-0550
Coastside Lobster Company
Stonington, ME.................... 207-367-2297
Corea Lobster Cooperative
Corea, ME......................... 207-963-7936
Cranberry Isles Fisherman's Cooperative
Islesford, ME 207-244-5438
Cummings Lobster Company
Kennebunk, ME 207-985-1677
D Waybret & Sons Fisher ies
Shelburne, NS..................... 902-745-3477
DB Kenney Fisheries
Westport, NS...................... 902-839-2023
Dick & Casey's Gourmet Seafoods
Harbor, OR 800-662-9494
Dorset Fisheries
St Josephs, NL 709-739-7147
Dunham's Lobster Pot
Avon, ME 207-639-2815
Fisherman's Market International
Halifax, NS 902-445-3474
Florida Carib Fishery
Doral, FL......................... 305-696-2896
FW Thurston
Bernard, ME 207-244-3320
Giovanni's Appetizing Food Products
Richmond, MI...................... 586-727-9355
Goldcoast Salads
Naples, FL........................ 239-304-0710
Gorman Fisheries
Conception Bay, NL 709-229-6536
Gouldsboro Enterprises
Gouldsboro, ME 207-963-2203
Graffam Brothers Lobster Company
Rockport, ME 800-535-5358
Great Northern Products
Warwick, RI 401-490-4590
Greg's Lobster Company
Harwich Port, MA.................. 508-432-8080
Grindle Point Lobster Company
Lincolnville, ME.................. 207-763-4142
H&H Fisheries Limited
Eastern Passage, NS 902-465-6330
Harbor Seafood
New Hyde Park, NY 800-645-2211
Howard Turner & Son
Marie Joseph, NS 902-347-2616
I. Deveau Fisheries
Barrington Passage, NS 902-769-0333
Innovative Fishery Products
Belliveau Cove, NS 902-837-5163
International Enterprises
Herring Neck, NL.................. 709-628-7406
Island Lobster
Matinicus, ME 207-366-3937
Island Marine Products
Clarks Harbour, NS................ 902-745-2222
J. Matassini & Sons Fish Company
Tampa, FL......................... 813-229-0829
Jack's Lobsters
Musquodoboit Harbor, NS 902-889-2771
Kitchens Seafood
Plant City, FL 800-327-0132
Kittery Lobster Company
Kittery, ME....................... 207-439-6035
Kona Cold Lobsters Ltd
Kailua Kona, HI 808-329-4332
L&C Fisheries
Kensington, PE.................... 902-886-2770
Little River Lobster Company
East Boothbay, ME................. 207-633-2648
Lobster Gram International
Chicago, IL 800-548-3562
Look Lobster
Jonesport, ME..................... 207-497-2353
Look's Gourmet Food Company
East Machias, ME.................. 800-962-6258
Lusty Lobster
Portland, ME...................... 207-773-2829
Maine Lobster Outlet
York, ME.......................... 207-363-9899
McGraw Seafood
Tracadie Sheila, NB 506-395-3374
Menemsha Fish Market
Chilmark, MA...................... 508-645-2282
Milfico Foods
Elk Grove Vlg, IL................. 847-427-0491
Mill Cove Lobster Pound
Boothbay Harbor, ME............... 207-633-3340
Moon Enterprises
Richmond, BC 604-270-0088
Nan Sea Enterprises of Wisconsin
Waukesha, WI...................... 262-542-8841
New England Marketers
Boston, MA........................ 800-688-9904
New Harbor Fisherman's Cooperative
New Harbor, ME.................... 866-883-2922
Newell Lobsters
Yarmouth, NS 902-742-6272
North Lake Fish Cooperative
Elmira, PE........................ 902-357-2572
Northern Wind
New Bedford, MA 888-525-2525
Notre Dame Seafood
Comfort Cove, NL 709-244-5511
P.M. Innis Lobster Company
Biddeford Pool, ME 207-284-5000
Paul Piazza & Sons
New Orleans, LA 504-524-6011
Paul Stevens Lobster
Hingham, MA....................... 781-740-8001
Penguin Frozen Foods
Northbrook, IL 847-291-9400
Pine Point Seafood
Scarborough, ME 207-883-4701
Port Lobster Company
Kennebunkport, ME................. 800-486-7029
Produits Belle Baie
Caraquet, NB 506-727-4414
Resource Trading Company
Portland, ME...................... 207-772-2299
Rockport Lobster
Gloucester, MA.................... 978-281-0225
Sealand Lobster Corporation
Tenants Harbor, ME 207-372-6247
Seymour & Sons Seafood
Diberville, MS 228-392-4020
St. Ours & Company
Norwell, MA....................... 781-331-8520
Stavis Seafoods
Boston, MA........................ 800-390-5103
Stone Crabs
Miami Beach, FL 800-260-2722
Stonington Lobster Cooperative
Stonington, ME.................... 207-367-5535
Straub's
Clayton, MO 888-725-2121
Sunshine Food Sales
Miami, FL......................... 305-696-2885
Thomas Lobster Company
Islesford, ME 207-244-5876
Three Rivers Fish Company
Simmesport, LA 318-941-2467
Trenton Bridge Lobster Pound
Trenton, ME 207-667-2977
United Shellfish Company
Grasonville, MD................... 410-827-8171
West Brothers Lobster
Steuben, ME 207-546-3622
Young's Lobster Pound
Belfast, ME....................... 207-338-1160

Fresh

Captain Joe & Sons
Gloucester, MA.................... 978-283-1454
CB Seafoods
Inverness, NS 902-895-8181
Clearwater Fine Foods
Bedford, NS 902-443-0550
High Sea Foods
Glovertown, NL 709-533-2626
J. Matassini & Sons Fish Company
Tampa, FL......................... 813-229-0829
Menemsha Fish Market
Chilmark, MA...................... 508-645-2282
Paul Piazza & Sons
New Orleans, LA 504-524-6011
Portland Shellfish Company
South Portland, ME 207-799-9290
Poseidon Enterprises
Atlanta, GA....................... 800-863-7886
St. Ours & Company
Norwell, MA....................... 781-331-8520
Stone Crabs
Miami Beach, FL 800-260-2722
Sunshine Food Sales
Miami, FL......................... 305-696-2885

Frozen

Acme Steak & Seafood Company
Youngstown, OH.................... 330-270-8000
Arista Industries
Wilton, CT 800-255-6457
Atlantic Queen Seafoods Limited
St Josephs, NL 709-739-6668

Bolner's Fiesta Products
San Antonio, TX 210-734-6404
CB Seafoods
Inverness, NS 902-895-8181
Certi-Fresh Foods
Bell Gardens, CA 562-806-1100
ConAgra Shrimp Companies
Tampa, FL 813-241-1501
Great Northern Products
Warwick, RI 401-490-4590
Island Marine Products
Clarks Harbour, NS 902-745-2222
J. Matassini & Sons Fish Company
Tampa, FL 813-229-0829
Kitchens Seafood
Plant City, FL 800-327-0132
Menemsha Fish Market
Chilmark, MA 508-645-2282
Milfico Foods
Elk Grove Vlg, IL 847-427-0491
North Bay Fisherman's Cooperative
Ballantyne's Cove, NS 902-863-4988
Notre Dame Seafood
Comfort Cove, NL 709-244-5511
Paul Piazza & Sons
New Orleans, LA 504-524-6011
Penguin Frozen Foods
Northbrook, IL 847-291-9400
Portland Shellfish Company
South Portland, ME 207-799-9290
Seymour & Sons Seafood
Diberville, MS 228-392-4020
Stone Crabs
Miami Beach, FL 800-260-2722
Sunshine Food Sales
Miami, FL 305-696-2885

Live

Canus Fisheries
Clark's Harbour, NS 902-745-2888
Chases Lobster Pound
Port Howe, NS 902-243-2408
Crustaces de la Malbaie
Gaspe, QC 418-368-1414
DB Kenney Fisheries
Westport, NS 902-839-2023
H&H Fisheries Limited
Eastern Passage, NS 902-465-6330
Harbor Lobster
Lower Wood Harbor, NS 902-723-2500
Island Marine Products
Clarks Harbour, NS 902-745-2222
James L. Mood Fisheries
Lower Woods Harbour, NS 902-723-2360
Johns Cove Fisheries
Yarmouth, NS 902-742-8691
Lumar Lobster Corporatio
Lawrence, NY 516-371-0083
Menemsha Fish Market
Chilmark, MA 508-645-2282
New England Marketers
Boston, MA 800-688-9904

Meat

Acme Steak & Seafood Company
Youngstown, OH 330-270-8000
Atlantic Queen Seafoods Limited
St Josephs, NL 709-739-6668
Island Marine Products
Clarks Harbour, NS 902-745-2222

Tails

Anchor Frozen Foods
Westbury, NY 800-566-3474
Arista Industries
Wilton, CT 800-255-6457
Florida Carib Fishery
Doral, FL 305-696-2896
Icelandic USA
Newport News, VA 757-820-4000
King & Prince Seafood Corporation
Brunswick, GA 800-841-0205
Milfico Foods
Elk Grove Vlg, IL 847-427-0491
Neptune Fisheries
Newport News, VA 800-545-7474
New Ocean
Atlanta, GA 770-458-5235
Ocean Garden Products
San Diego, CA 858-571-5002

Stone Crabs
Miami Beach, FL 800-260-2722
Tampa Bay Fisheries
Dover, FL 800-234-2561

Mussels

Atlantic Aqua Farms
Vernon Bridge, PE 902-651-2563
Atlantic Mussel Growers Corporation
Point Pleasant, PE 800-838-3106
Blount Seafood Corporation
Fall River, MA 774-888-1300
Country Harbor Sea Farms
Larrys Riveror, NS 902-358-2002
Harbor Seafood
New Hyde Park, NY 800-645-2211
Hillman Shrimp & Oyster Company
Dickinson, TX 800-582-4416
L&C Fisheries
Kensington, PE 902-886-2770
Look's Gourmet Food Company
East Machias, ME 800-962-6258
Milfico Foods
Elk Grove Vlg, IL 847-427-0491
Minterbrook Oyster Company
Gig Harbor, WA 253-857-5251
New England Marketers
Boston, MA 800-688-9904
PEI Mussel King
Morrell, PE 800-673-2767
Stavis Seafoods
Boston, MA 800-390-5103
Sweet Water Seafood Corporation
Carlstadt, NJ 201-939-6622
Tampa Bay Fisheries
Dover, FL 800-234-2561
Taylor Shellfish Farms
Shelton, WA 360-426-6178

Octopus

Anchor Frozen Foods
Westbury, NY 800-566-3474
Arista Industries
Wilton, CT 800-255-6457
FishKing
Glendale, CA 818-244-2161
Miles J H & Company
Norfolk, VA 757-622-9264

Oysters

AmeriPure Processing Company
Franklin, LA 800-328-6729
Ameripure Processing Company
Franklin, LA 800-328-6729
Aquatec Seafoods Ltd.
Comox, BC 250-339-6412
Atlantic Aqua Farms
Vernon Bridge, PE 902-651-2563
Atlantic Capes Fisheries
Cape May, NJ 609-884-3000
Bay Hundred Seafood
McDaniel, MD 410-745-9329
BG Smith Sons Oyster
Sharps, VA 877-483-8279
Blalock Seafood
Orange Beach, AL 251-974-5811
Blau Oyster Company
Bow, WA 360-766-6171
Bolner's Fiesta Products
San Antonio, TX 210-734-6404
Bon Secour Fisheries
Bon Secour, AL 800-633-6854
Braun Seafood Company
Cutchogue, NY 631-734-6700
Bumble Bee Foods
San Diego, CA 858-715-4000
Callis Seafood
Lancaster, VA 804-462-7634
Canoe Lagoon Oyster Company
Coffman Cove, AK 907-329-2253
Carolina Seafoods
Mc Clellanville, SC 843-887-3713
Coast Seafoods Company
Bellevue, WA 800-423-2303
Cowart Seafood Corporation
Lottsburg, VA 804-529-6101
Crown Prince
City of Industry, CA 800-255-5063
Dave's Gourmet Albacore
Kirkland, WA 800-454-8862

Elwha Fish
Port Angeles, WA 360-457-3344
Farm 2 Market
Roscoe, NY 800-663-4326
Ferme Ostreicole Dugas
Caraquet, NB 506-727-3226
Great Northern Products
Warwick, RI 401-490-4590
Gulf City Marine Supply
Bayou La Batre, AL 251-824-2516
H. Gass Seafood
Hollywood, MD 301-373-6882
Harper Seafood Company
Kinsale, VA 804-472-3310
Higgins Seafood
Lafitte, LA 504-689-3577
Hillard Bloom Packing Co
Port Norris, NJ 856-785-0120
Hillman Shrimp & Oyster Company
Dickinson, TX 800-582-4416
Huck's Seafood
Easton, MD 410-770-9211
J. Matassini & Sons Fish Company
Tampa, FL 813-229-0829
Joey Oysters
Amite, LA 800-748-1525
Louisiana Oyster Processors
Baton Rouge, LA 225-291-6923
McGraw Seafood
Tracadie Sheila, NB 506-395-3374
Mercado Latino
City of Industry, CA 626-333-6862
Milfico Foods
Elk Grove Vlg, IL 847-427-0491
Mill Cove Lobster Pound
Boothbay Harbor, ME 207-633-3340
Moon Enterprises
Richmond, BC 604-270-0088
Neptune Foods
Vernon, CA 323-232-8300
Nisbet Oyster Company
Bay Center, WA 360-875-6629
P&J Oyster Company
New Orleans, LA 504-523-2651
Pamlico Packing Company
Grantsboro, NC 800-682-1113
PEI Mussel King
Morrell, PE 800-673-2767
Port Chatham Smoked Seafood
Everett, WA 800-872-5666
Rich-Seapak Corporation
Brownsville, TX 956-542-0001
Rippons Brothers Seafood
Fishing Creek, MD 410-397-3200
Road Runner Seafood
Colquitt, GA 229-758-3485
Roy Dick Company
Griffin, GA 770-227-3916
Sea Pearl Seafood
Bayou La Batre, AL 800-872-8804
Southern Shell Fish Company
Harvey, LA 504-341-5631
Tampa Bay Fisheries
Dover, FL 800-234-2561
Tampa Maid Foods
Lakeland, FL 800-237-7637
Terry Brothers
Willis Wharf, VA 757-824-3471
W.H. Harris Seafood
North Grasonville, MD 410-827-9500
W.T. Ruark & Company
Fishing Creek, MD 410-397-3133
Wiegardt Brothers
Ocean Park, WA 360-665-4111
Wilson's Oysters
Houma, LA 985-857-8855

Canned

Chicken of the Sea International
San Diego, CA 800-678-8862
Crown Prince Naturals
Petaluma, CA
Mercado Latino
City of Industry, CA 626-333-6862
Olympia Oyster Company
Shelton, WA 360-426-3354
Orleans Food Company
New Orleans, LA 800-628-4900
Southern Shell Fish Company
Harvey, LA 504-341-5631

Cooked

Port Chatham Smoked Seafood
Everett, WA 800-872-5666

Fresh

BG Smith Sons Oyster
Sharps, VA 877-483-8279
Blau Oyster Company
Bow, WA 360-766-6171
Boquet's Oyster House
Chauvin, LA 504-594-5574
Coast Seafoods Company
Bellevue, WA 800-423-2303
Cowart Seafood Corporation
Lottsburg, VA 804-529-6101
Great Northern Products
Warwick, RI 401-490-4590
Hillman Shrimp & Oyster Company
Dickinson, TX 800-582-4416
J. Matassini & Sons Fish Company
Tampa, FL 813-229-0829
Mac's Oysters
Fanny Bay, BC 250-335-2233
Minterbrook Oyster Company
Gig Harbor, WA 253-857-5251
National Fish & Oysters Company
Olympia, WA 360-491-5550
P&J Oyster Company
New Orleans, LA 504-523-2651
Port Chatham Smoked Seafood
Everett, WA 800-872-5666
Rippons Brothers Seafood
Fishing Creek, MD 410-397-3200
Taylor Shellfish Farms
Shelton, WA 360-426-6178
Terry Brothers
Willis Wharf, VA 757-824-3471
Wiegardt Brothers
Ocean Park, WA 360-665-4111

Fried

J. Matassini & Sons Fish Company
Tampa, FL 813-229-0829

Frozen

BG Smith Sons Oyster
Sharps, VA 877-483-8279
Big Al's Seafood
Bozman, MD 410-745-2637
Bolner's Fiesta Products
San Antonio, TX 210-734-6404
Bon Secour Fisheries
Bon Secour, AL 800-633-6854
Boquet's Oyster House
Chauvin, LA 504-594-5574
Callis Seafood
Lancaster, VA 804-462-7634
ConAgra Shrimp Companies
Tampa, FL 813-241-1501
Cowart Seafood Corporation
Lottsburg, VA 804-529-6101
Dave's Gourmet Albacore
Kirkland, WA 800-454-8862
Great Northern Products
Warwick, RI 401-490-4590
Hillard Bloom Packing Co
Port Norris, NJ 856-785-0120
Hillman Shrimp & Oyster Company
Dickinson, TX 800-582-4416
Milfico Foods
Elk Grove Vlg, IL 847-427-0491
Minterbrook Oyster Company
Gig Harbor, WA 253-857-5251
National Fish & Oysters Company
Olympia, WA 360-491-5550
Olympia Oyster Company
Shelton, WA 360-426-3354
P&J Oyster Company
New Orleans, LA 504-523-2651
Pamlico Packing Company
Grantsboro, NC 800-682-1113
Rich-Seapak Corporation
Brownsville, TX 956-542-0001
Sea Pearl Seafood
Bayou La Batre, AL 800-872-8804
Tampa Maid Foods
Lakeland, FL 800-237-7637

Prawns

Norquest Seafoods
Seattle, WA 206-281-7022
Pots de Creme
Lexington, KY 859-299-2254

Scallops

American Seafoods International
New Bedford, MA 800-343-8046
Arctic Seas
Little Compton, RI 401-635-4000
Arista Industries
Wilton, CT 800-255-6457
Atlantic Capes Fisheries
Cape May, NJ 609-884-3000
BlueWater Seafoods
Lachine, QC 888-560-2539
Bolner's Fiesta Products
San Antonio, TX 210-734-6404
Bon Secour Fisheries
Bon Secour, AL 800-633-6854
Braun Seafood Company
Cutchogue, NY 631-734-6700
Casey Fisheries
Digby, NS 902-245-5801
Centennial Food Corporation
Calgary, AB 403-214-0044
Certi-Fresh Foods
Bell Gardens, CA 562-806-1100
Clearwater Fine Foods
Bedford, NS 902-443-0550
Contessa Food Products
San Pedro, CA 310-832-8000
DB Kenney Fisheries
Westport, NS 902-839-2023
Ducktrap River Fish Farm
Belfast, ME 800-434-8727
Exclusive Smoked Fish
Toronto, ON 416-766-6007
Farm 2 Market
Roscoe, NY 800-663-4326
FishKing
Glendale, CA 818-244-2161
Georgia Seafood Wholesale
Chamblee, GA 770-936-0483
Great Northern Products
Warwick, RI 401-490-4590
Hillman Shrimp & Oyster Company
Dickinson, TX 800-582-4416
Homarus
Atlanta, GA 404-877-1988
Hygrade Ocean Products
New Bedford, MA 508-993-5700
Innovative Fishery Products
Belliveau Cove, NS 902-837-5163
Island Scallops
Qualicum Beach, BC 250-757-9811
J. Matassini & Sons Fish Company
Tampa, FL 813-229-0829
LaMonica Fine Foods
Millville, NJ 856-825-8111
Lowland Seafood
Lowland, NC 252-745-3751
Menemsha Fish Market
Chilmark, MA 508-645-2282
Milfico Foods
Elk Grove Vlg, IL 847-427-0491
Mill Cove Lobster Pound
Boothbay Harbor, ME 207-633-3340
Mills Seafood ltd.
Bouctouche, NB 506-743-2444
Neptune Fisheries
Newport News, VA 800-545-7474
Neptune Foods
Vernon, CA 323-232-8300
New Ocean
Atlanta, GA 770-458-5235
North Bay Fisherman's Cooperative
Ballantyne's Cove, NS 902-863-4988
North Lake Fish Cooperative
Elmira, PE 902-357-2572
Northern Wind
New Bedford, MA 888-525-2525
O'Hara Corporation
Rockland, ME 207-594-0405
Pamlico Packing Company
Grantsboro, NC 800-682-1113
Portier Fine Foods
Mamaroneck, NY 800-272-9463
Resource Trading Company
Portland, ME 207-772-2299

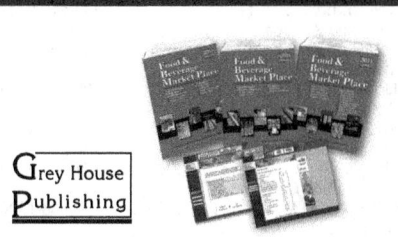

Tampa Bay Fisheries
Dover, FL 800-234-2561
Tampa Maid Foods
Lakeland, FL 800-237-7637
Taylor Shellfish Farms
Shelton, WA 360-426-6178
Tichon Seafood Corporation
New Bedford, MA 508-999-5607
United Shellfish Company
Grasonville, MD 410-827-8171
Viking Seafoods Inc
Malden, MA 800-225-3020
Wanchese Fish Company
Suffolk, VA 757-673-4500
Young's Lobster Pound
Belfast, ME 207-338-1160

Scampi

Frozen

Contessa Food Products
San Pedro, CA 310-832-8000

Shellfish

Acme Steak & Seafood Company
Youngstown, OH 330-270-8000
Anglo American Trading
Harvey, LA 504-341-5631
Appert's Foodservice
St Cloud, MN 800-225-3883
Aquatec Seafoods Ltd.
Comox, BC 250-339-6412
Arista Industries
Wilton, CT 800-255-6457
Arrowac Fisheries
Seattle, WA 206-282-5655
Atlantic Queen Seafoods Limited
St Josephs, NL 709-739-6668
Badger Island Shell-Fish & Lobster
Kittery, ME 207-439-3820
Bandon Bay Fisheries
Bandon, OR 541-347-4454
Bay Hundred Seafood
McDaniel, MD 410-745-9329
Bay Oceans Sea Foods
Garibaldi, OR 503-322-3316

Bayou Foods
Kenner, LA 800-516-8283
Bayou Land Seafood
Breaux Bridge, LA 337-667-6118
Beaver Street Fisheries
Jacksonville, FL 800-874-6426
Bell Buoy Crab Company
Seaside, OR. 800-529-2722
BG Smith Sons Oyster
Sharps, VA 877-483-8279
Blount Seafood Corporation
Fall River, MA 774-888-1300
BlueWater Seafoods
Lachine, QC 888-560-2539
Bolner's Fiesta Products
San Antonio, TX. 210-734-6404
Bornstein Seafoods
Bellingham, WA 360-734-7990
Boyton Shellfish
Ellsworth, ME. 207-667-8580
Bradye P. Todd & Son
Cambridge, MD 410-228-8633
Breakwater Fisheries
St Josephs, NL 709-754-1999
Burris Mill & Feed
Franklinton, LA 800-928-2782
C.F. Gollott & Son Seafood
Biloxi, MS. 866-846-3474
California Shellfish Company
San Francisco, CA 415-923-7400
Callis Seafood
Lancaster, VA 804-462-7634
Carolina Seafoods
Mc Clellanville, SC 843-887-3713
Carrington Foods
Saraland, AL. 251-675-9700
Cathay Foods Corporation
Boston, MA. 617-427-1507
Centennial Food Corporation
Calgary, AB. 403-214-0044
Certi-Fresh Foods
Bell Gardens, CA 562-806-1100
Charles H. Parks & Company
Fishing Creek, MD 410-397-3400
Chuck's Seafoods
Charleston, OR 541-888-5525
Clearwater Fine Foods
Bedford, NS 902-443-0550
Coast Seafoods Company
Bellevue, WA 800-423-2303
ConAgra Frozen Foods Company
Omaha, NE 402-595-6107
Contessa Food Products
San Pedro, CA. 310-832-8000
Cook Inlet Processing
Nikiski, AK. 907-776-8174
Cooke Aguaculture
Blacks Harbour, NB 506-456-6600
Cowart Seafood Corporation
Lottsburg, VA 804-529-6101
Cozy Harbor Seafood
Portland, ME. 800-225-2586
Crown Prince
City of Industry, CA 800-255-5063
Cuizina Food Company
Woodinville, WA. 425-486-7000
Dave's Gourmet Albacore
Kirkland, WA 800-454-8862
DB Kenney Fisheries
Westport, NS. 902-839-2023
Deep Sea Foods
Bayou La Batre, AL 251-824-7000
Denzer's Food Products
Baltimore, MD 410-889-1500
Depoe Bay Fish Company
Newport, OR. 541-265-8833
Dorchester Crab Company
Wingate, MD. 410-397-8103
Ducktrap River Fish Farm
Belfast, ME. 800-434-8727
Eastern Fish Company
Teaneck, NJ. 800-526-9066
Elwha Fish
Port Angeles, WA 360-457-3344
Fishery Products International
Danvers, MA. 800-374-4700
Fishhawk Fisheries
Astoria, OR 503-325-5252
FishKing
Glendale, CA 818-244-2161
French Market Foods
Lake Charles, LA 337-477-9296
Frozen Specialties
Archbold, OH 419-445-9015
Golden Gulf Coast Packing Company
Biloxi, MS. 228-374-6121
Gollott Brothers Seafood Company
Biloxi, MS. 228-432-7865
Gorton's Seafood
Gloucester, MA. 978-283-3000
Great Northern Products
Warwick, RI 401-490-4590
Gulf Pride Enterprises
Biloxi, MS. 888-689-0560
H. Gass Seafood
Hollywood, MD 301-373-6882
H.B. Dawe
Cupids, NL 709-528-4347
Handy International
Salisbury, MD. 800-426-3977
Henry H. Misner Ltd.
Simcoe, ON. 519-426-5546
Hillard Bloom Packing Co
Port Norris, NJ 856-785-0120
Hillman Shrimp & Oyster Company
Dickinson, TX. 800-582-4416
Hingham Shellfish
Hingham, MA. 781-749-1374
His Catch Value Added Products
Homer, AK 800-215-7110
Huck's Seafood
Easton, MD. 410-770-9211
Icelandic USA
Newport News, VA. 757-820-4000
Icicle Seafoods
Seattle, WA. 206-282-0988
Independent Packers Corporation
Seattle, WA 206-285-6000
Indian Ridge Shrimp Company
Chauvin, LA 985-594-3361
International Oceanic Enterprises of Alabama
Bayou La Batre, AL 800-816-1832
Island Marine Products
Clarks Harbour, NS. 902-745-2222
J M Clayton Company
Cambridge, MD 800-652-6931
J&R Foods
Long Branch, NJ. 732-229-4020
J. Matassini & Sons Fish Company
Tampa, FL. 813-229-0829
Jcw Tawes & Son
Crisfield, MD 410-968-1288
Jessie's Ilwaco Fish Company
Ilwaco, WA 360-642-3773
Joey Oysters
Amite, LA. 800-748-1525
Key Largo Fisheries
Key Largo, FL. 800-432-4358
Keyser Brothers
Lottsburg, VA 804-529-6837
King & Prince Seafood Corporation
Brunswick, GA 800-841-0205
Kitchens Seafood
Plant City, FL 800-327-0132
LaMonica Fine Foods
Millville, NJ 856-825-8111
Larry Matthews Company
Dennysville, ME. 207-726-0609
Little River Seafood
Reedville, VA 804-453-3670
Long Food Industries
Fripp Island, SC 843-838-3205
Lowland Seafood
Lowland, NC. 252-745-3751
Lund's Fisheries
Cape May, NJ 609-884-7600
Maine Mahogony Shellfish
Addison, ME. 207-483-2865
Martin Brothers SeafoodcCompany
Westwego, LA. 504-341-2251
Mat Roland Seafood Company
Atlantic Beach, FL 904-246-9443
Maxim's Import Corporation
Miami, FL. 800-331-6652
Menemsha Fish Market
Chilmark, MA. 508-645-2282
Mercado Latino
City of Industry, CA 626-333-6862
Mercer Processing
Modesto, CA. 209-529-0150
Mersey Seafoods
Liverpool, NS 902-354-3467
Mid-Atlantic Foods
Easton, MD. 800-922-4688
Milfico Foods
Elk Grove Vlg, IL. 847-427-0491
Nancy's Shellfish
Falmouth, ME. 207-774-3411
National Fish and Seafood Limited
Brownsville, TX 956-546-5525
Neptune Fisheries
Newport News, VA. 800-545-7474
Notre Dame Seafood
Comfort Cove, NL 709-244-5511
NTC Marketing Inc
Williamsville, NY. 800-333-1637
Okuhara Foods
Honolulu, HI. 808-848-0581
Pacific American Fish Co.,Inc.
Vernon, CA 800-625-2525
Pacific Ocean Seafood
La Conner, WA 360-466-4455
Pacific Salmon Company
Edmonds, WA. 425-774-1315
Pacific Shrimp Company
Newport, OR. 541-265-4215
Pamlico Packing Company
Grantsboro, NC. 800-682-1113
Paul Piazza & Sons
New Orleans, LA 504-524-6011
Penguin Frozen Foods
Northbrook, IL 847-291-9400
Phillips Foods
Baltimore, MD 888-234-2722
Produits Belle Baie
Caraquet, NB 506-727-4414
Quality Seafood
Apalachicola, FL. 850-653-9696
Raffield Fisheries
Port St Joe, FL. 850-229-8229
Rich-Seapak Corporation
Brownsville, TX 956-542-0001
Rippons Brothers Seafood
Fishing Creek, MD 410-397-3200
Rivere's Seafood Processors
Paincourtville, LA. 985-369-2570
Royal Seafood
Monterey, CA 831-655-8326
Ruggiero Seafood
Newark, NJ 866-225-2627
Sea Garden Seafoods
Meridian, GA 912-832-4437
Sea Pearl Seafood
Bayou La Batre, AL 800-872-8804
Sea Safari
Belhaven, NC 252-943-3091
Sea Safari
Belhaven, NC 800-688-6174
Sea Safari Ltd.
Belhaven, NC 800-688-6174
Sea Snack Foods
Los Angeles, CA. 213-622-2204
SeaPerfect Atlantic Farms
Charleston, SC 800-728-0099
Seymour & Sons Seafood
Diberville, MS 228-392-4020
Silver Lining Seafood
Ketchikan, AK 907-225-9865
Southern Shell Fish Company
Harvey, LA 504-341-5631
Sportsmen's Cannery & Smokehouse
Winchester Bay, OR 800-457-8048
St. Ours & Company
Norwell, MA. 781-331-8520
State Fish Company
San Pedro, CA. 310-832-2633
Stinson Seafood Company
San Diego, CA
Stone Crabs
Miami Beach, FL 800-260-2722
Sunshine Food Sales
Miami, FL. 305-696-2885
Sunshine Seafood
Stonington, ME. 207-367-2955
Taku Smokehouse
Juneau, AK 800-582-5122
Tampa Maid Foods
Lakeland, FL. 800-237-7637
Terry Brothers
Willis Wharf, VA 757-824-3471
Thompson Seafood
Darien, GA 912-437-4649
Trident Seafoods Corporation
Seattle, WA. 800-426-5490
Triton Seafood Company
Medley, FL 305-888-8999

Turner New Zealand
Aliso Viejo, CA....................949-622-6181
United Shellfish Company
Grasonville, MD...................410-827-8171
Valdez Food
Philadelphia, PA...................215-634-6106
Viking Seafoods Inc
Malden, MA......................800-225-3020
Vince's Seafoods
Gretna, LA.......................504-368-1544
W.T. Ruark & Company
Fishing Creek, MD.................410-397-3133
Wanchese Fish Company
Suffolk, VA.......................757-673-4500
Wiegardt Brothers
Ocean Park, WA..................360-665-4111
Wrangell Fisheries
Wrangell, AK.....................907-874-3346

Shrimp

Anchor Frozen Foods
Westbury, NY....................800-566-3474
Appert's Foodservice
St Cloud, MN....................800-225-3883
Arista Industries
Wilton, CT.......................800-255-6457
Atlantic Queen Seafoods Limited
St Josephs, NL...................709-739-6668
Bandon Bay Fisheries
Bandon, OR......................541-347-4454
Bay Oceans Sea Foods
Garibaldi, OR....................503-322-3316
Bayou Foods
Kenner, LA.......................800-516-8283
Bayou Land Seafood
Breaux Bridge, LA.................337-667-6118
Beaver Street Fisheries
Jacksonville, FL...................800-874-6426
Bell Buoy Crab Company
Seaside, OR.......................800-529-2722
Blalock Seafood
Orange Beach, AL.................251-974-5811
BlueWater Seafoods
Lachine, QC......................888-560-2539
Bolner's Fiesta Products
San Antonio, TX...................210-734-6404
Bon Secour Fisheries
Bon Secour, AL...................800-633-6854
Breakwater Fisheries
St Josephs, NL...................709-754-1999
Burris Mill & Feed
Franklinton, LA..................800-928-2782
C.F. Gollott & Son Seafood
Biloxi, MS.......................866-846-3474
Callis Seafood
Lancaster, VA....................804-462-7634
Carolina Seafoods
Mc Clellanville, SC...............843-887-3713
Carrington Foods
Saraland, AL.....................251-675-9700
Catfish Wholesale
Abbeville, LA....................800-334-7292
Certi-Fresh Foods
Bell Gardens, CA.................562-806-1100
Chuck's Seafoods
Charleston, OR...................541-888-5525
Clearwater Fine Foods
Bedford, NS.....................902-443-0550
Contessa Food Products
San Pedro, CA....................310-832-8000
Cozy Harbor Seafood
Portland, ME.....................800-225-2586
Crevettes Du Nord
Gaspe, QC........................418-368-1414
Crown Prince
City of Industry, CA...............800-255-5063
Dave's Gourmet Albacore
Kirkland, WA....................800-454-8862
Deep Sea Foods
Bayou La Batre, AL...............251-824-7000
Del's Seaway Shrimp & Oyster Company
Biloxi, MS.......................228-432-2604
Dick & Casey's Gourmet Seafoods
Harbor, OR......................800-662-9494
Ducktrap River Fish Farm
Belfast, ME......................800-434-8727
Eastern Fish Company
Teaneck, NJ......................800-526-9066
Eldorado Seafood Inc
Burlington, MA...................800-416-5656
Elwha Fish
Port Angeles, WA.................360-457-3344
Farm 2 Market
Roscoe, NY......................800-663-4326
Fishery Products International
Danvers, MA.....................800-374-4700
Fishhawk Fisheries
Astoria, OR......................503-325-5252
FishKing
Glendale, CA....................818-244-2161
French Market Foods
Lake Charles, LA.................337-477-9296
G&R Food Sales
Glendale, AZ.....................602-939-7337
Georgia Seafood Wholesale
Chamblee, GA....................770-936-0483
Gesco ENR
Gaspe, QC.......................418-368-1414
Golden Gulf Coast Packing Company
Biloxi, MS.......................228-374-6121
Gollott Brothers Seafood Company
Biloxi, MS.......................228-432-7865
Great Northern Products
Warwick, RI.....................401-490-4590
Gulf City Marine Supply
Bayou La Batre, AL...............251-824-2516
Gulf Island Shrimp & Seafood
Lake Charles, LA.................888-626-7264
Gulf Pride Enterprises
Biloxi, MS.......................888-689-0560
Hallmark Fisheries
Charleston, OR...................541-888-3253
Harbor Seafood
New Hyde Park, NY...............800-645-2211
Hi-Seas of Dulac
Dulac, LA.......................985-563-7155
Homarus
Atlanta, GA......................404-877-1988
Imaex Trading
Norcross, GA....................770-825-0848
Indian Ridge Shrimp Company
Chauvin, LA.....................985-594-3361
International Oceanic Enterprises of Alabama
Bayou La Batre, AL...............800-816-1832
J. Matassini & Sons Fish Company
Tampa, FL.......................813-229-0829
JBS Packing Company
Port Arthur, TX...................409-982-3216
Jessie's Ilwaco Fish Company
Ilwaco, WA......................360-642-3773
Jubilee Foods
Emmitsburg, MD.................301-447-6688
King & Prince Seafood Corporation
Brunswick, GA...................800-841-0205
Kitchens Seafood
Plant City, FL....................800-327-0132
Lady Gale Seafood
Baldwin, LA.....................337-923-2060
LaMonica Fine Foods
Millville, NJ.....................856-825-8111
Larry J. Williams Company
Jesup, GA.......................912-427-7729
Louisiana Packing Company
Westwego, LA....................800-666-1293
Louisiana Shrimp & Packing Company
New Orleans, LA.................504-286-8736
Lowland Seafood
Lowland, NC.....................252-745-3751
M&I Seafood Manufacturers
Essex, MD.......................410-780-0444
M&M Shrimp Company
Biloxi, MS.......................228-435-4915
Mat Roland Seafood Company
Atlantic Beach, FL................904-246-9443
Maxim's Import Corporation
Miami, FL.......................800-331-6652
Mercado Latino
City of Industry, CA...............626-333-6862
Mersey Seafoods
Liverpool, NS....................902-354-3467
Milfico Foods
Elk Grove Vlg, IL.................847-427-0491
Mill Cove Lobster Pound
Boothbay Harbor, ME..............207-633-3340
Mobile Processing
Mobile, AL......................251-438-6944
National Fish and Seafood Limited
Brownsville, TX..................956-546-5525
Nelson Crab
Tokeland, WA....................800-262-0069
Neptune Fisheries
Newport News, VA................800-545-7474
Neptune Foods
Vernon, CA......................323-232-8300
New Ocean
Atlanta, GA......................770-458-5235
Newfound Resources
St Josephs, NL...................709-579-7676
Norquest Seafoods
Seattle, WA......................206-281-7022
North Atlantic Fish Company
Gloucester, MA...................978-283-4121
NTC Marketing Inc
Williamsville, NY.................800-333-1637
Ocean Garden Products
San Diego, CA...................858-571-5002
Ocean Pride Seafood
Delcambre, LA...................337-685-2336
Ocean Springs Seafood
Ocean Springs, MS................228-875-0104
Omstead Foods Ltd
Wheatley, ON....................905-315-8883
Ore-Cal Corporation
Los Angeles, CA..................800-827-7474
Pacific American Fish Co.,Inc.
Vernon, CA......................800-625-2525
Pamlico Packing Company
Grantsboro, NC...................800-682-1113
Paul Piazza & Sons
New Orleans, LA.................504-524-6011
Penguin Frozen Foods
Northbrook, IL...................847-291-9400
Pioneer Live Shrimp
Oak Brook, IL....................630-789-1133
Price Seafood
Chauvin, LA.....................985-594-3067
Produits Belle Baie
Caraquet, NB....................506-727-4414
Quality Seafood
Apalachicola, FL..................850-653-9696
Randol
Lafayette, LA....................800-YO -AJUN
Resource Trading Company
Portland, ME.....................207-772-2299
Rich-Seapak Corporation
St Simons Island, GA..............800-654-9731
Rich-Seapak Corporation
Brownsville, TX..................956-542-0001
Rocky Point Shrimp Association
Phoenix, AZ.....................602-254-8041
Roy Dick Company
Griffin, GA......................770-227-3916
Sau-Sea Foods
Tarrytown, NY...................914-631-1717
Sea Pearl Seafood
Bayou La Batre, AL...............800-872-8804
Sea Snack Foods
Los Angeles, CA..................213-622-2204
Seafood Producers Coop ative
Bellingham, WA..................360-733-0120
Shrimp World
Gretna, LA......................504-368-1571
Singleton Seafood
Tampa, FL.......................800-553-3954
Smith & Son Seafood
Darien, GA......................912-437-6471
Southern Shell Fish Company
Harvey, LA......................504-341-5631
Stavis Seafoods
Boston, MA......................800-390-5103
Tampa Bay Fisheries
Dover, FL.......................800-234-2561
Tampa Maid Foods
Lakeland, FL.....................800-237-7637
Tex-Mex Cold Storage
Brownsville, TX..................956-831-9433
Thompson Seafood
Darien, GA......................912-437-4649
Tideland Seafood Company
Dulac, LA.......................985-563-4516
Triple T Enterprises
Chauvin, LA.....................985-594-5869
United Shellfish Company
Grasonville, MD..................410-827-8171
Valdez Food
Philadelphia, PA..................215-634-6106
Viking Seafoods Inc
Malden, MA.....................800-225-3020
Vincent Piazza Jr & Sons
Harahan, LA.....................800-259-5016
Wayne Estay Shrimp Company
Grand Isle, LA...................877-787-2166
Wrangell Fisheries
Wrangell, AK....................907-874-3346

Young's Lobster Pound
Belfast, ME 207-338-1160

Black Tiger

Arctic Seas
Little Compton, RI 401-635-4000
Bay Oceans Sea Foods
Garibaldi, OR 503-322-3316
Bell Buoy Crab Company
Seaside, OR. 800-529-2722
BlueWater Seafoods
Lachine, QC 888-560-2539
Bolner's Fiesta Products
San Antonio, TX. 210-734-6404
Crevettes Du Nord
Gaspe, QC. 418-368-1414
Del's Seaway Shrimp & Oyster Company
Biloxi, MS. 228-432-2604
Depoe Bay Fish Company
Newport, OR. 541-265-8833
Dick & Casey's Gourmet Seafoods
Harbor, OR 800-662-9494
Gesco ENR
Gaspe, QC. 418-368-1414
Gulf Pride Enterprises
Biloxi, MS. 888-689-0560
JBS Packing Company
Port Arthur, TX. 409-982-3216
Jubilee Foods
Emmitsburg, MD 301-447-6688
Lady Gale Seafood
Baldwin, LA 337-923-2060
Louisiana Packing Company
Westwego, LA. 800-666-1293
M&M Shrimp Company
Biloxi, MS. 228-435-4915
Mobile Processing
Mobile, AL 251-438-6944
Newfound Resources
St Josephs, NL 709-579-7676
Ocean Springs Seafood
Ocean Springs, MS. 228-875-0104
Price Seafood
Chauvin, LA 985-594-3067
Resource Trading Company
Portland, ME. 207-772-2299
Stavis Seafoods
Boston, MA. 800-390-5103
Vincent Piazza Jr & Sons
Harahan, LA 800-259-5016

Breaded

Appert's Foodservice
St Cloud, MN 800-225-3883
Depoe Bay Fish Company
Newport, OR. 541-265-8833
Eldorado Seafood Inc
Burlington, MA. 800-416-5656
Fishery Products International
Danvers, MA. 800-374-4700
FishKing
Glendale, CA 818-244-2161
Golden Gulf Coast Packing Company
Biloxi, MS. 228-374-6121
Icelandic USA
Newport News, VA. 757-820-4000
J. Matassini & Sons Fish Company
Tampa, FL. 813-229-0829
King & Prince Seafood Corporation
Brunswick, GA 800-841-0205
LaMonica Fine Foods
Millville, NJ 856-825-8111
M&I Seafood Manufacturers
Essex, MD. 410-780-0444
Milfico Foods
Elk Grove Vlg, IL. 847-427-0491
Neptune Foods
Vernon, CA 323-232-8300
Ocean Springs Seafood
Ocean Springs, MS. 228-875-0104
Pacific American Fish Co.,Inc.
Vernon, CA 800-625-2525
Penguin Frozen Foods
Northbrook, IL 847-291-9400
Rich-Seapak Corporation
Brownsville, TX 956-542-0001
Sea Pearl Seafood
Bayou La Batre, AL 800-872-8804
Tampa Bay Fisheries
Dover, FL 800-234-2561
Tampa Maid Foods
Lakeland, FL. 800-237-7637

Canned

Bayou Land Seafood
Breaux Bridge, LA 337-667-6118
Chicken of the Sea International
San Diego, CA 800-678-8862
Chuck's Seafoods
Charleston, OR 541-888-5525
Elwha Fish
Port Angeles, WA 360-457-3344
Mercado Latino
City of Industry, CA 626-333-6862
Nelson Crab
Tokeland, WA 800-262-0069
North Atlantic Fish Company
Gloucester, MA. 978-283-4121
NTC Marketing Inc
Williamsville, NY 800-333-1637
Ore-Cal Corporation
Los Angeles, CA. 800-827-7474
Orleans Food Company
New Orleans, LA 800-628-4900
Scally's Imperial Importing Company Inc
Staten Island, NY 718-983-1938
Seafood Producers Coop ative
Bellingham, WA 360-733-0120
Southern Shell Fish Company
Harvey, LA 504-341-5631
Wrangell Fisheries
Wrangell, AK 907-874-3346

Cocktail

Elwha Fish
Port Angeles, WA 360-457-3344

Cooked

Depoe Bay Fish Company
Newport, OR. 541-265-8833
King & Prince Seafood Corporation
Brunswick, GA 800-841-0205
Neptune Fisheries
Newport News, VA. 800-545-7474
Neptune Foods
Vernon, CA 323-232-8300
Pacific American Fish Co.,Inc.
Vernon, CA 800-625-2525
Tampa Bay Fisheries
Dover, FL 800-234-2561

Fresh

Cozy Harbor Seafood
Portland, ME. 800-225-2586
Great Northern Products
Warwick, RI 401-490-4590
J. Matassini & Sons Fish Company
Tampa, FL. 813-229-0829
Jessie's Ilwaco Fish Company
Ilwaco, WA 360-642-3773
Nelson Crab
Tokeland, WA. 800-262-0069
Paul Piazza & Sons
New Orleans, LA 504-524-6011
Quality Seafood
Apalachicola, FL. 850-653-9696
Wrangell Fisheries
Wrangell, AK 907-874-3346

Frozen

Appert's Foodservice
St Cloud, MN 800-225-3883
Arista Industries
Wilton, CT 800-255-6457
Atlantic Queen Seafoods Limited
St Josephs, NL 709-739-6668
Bandon Bay Fisheries
Bandon, OR 541-347-4454
Bayou Land Seafood
Breaux Bridge, LA 337-667-6118
Beaver Street Fisheries
Jacksonville, FL 800-874-6426
Bon Secour Fisheries
Bon Secour, AL. 800-633-6854
Breakwater Fisheries
St Josephs, NL 709-754-1999
Buns & Things Bakery
Charlottetown, PE. 902-892-2600
C.F. Gollott & Son Seafood
Biloxi, MS. 866-846-3474
Callis Seafood
Lancaster, VA 804-462-7634
Carrington Foods
Saraland, AL. 251-675-9700
Certi-Fresh Foods
Bell Gardens, CA 562-806-1100
Clearwater Fine Foods
Bedford, NS 902-443-0550
ConAgra Shrimp Companies
Tampa, FL. 813-241-1501
Cozy Harbor Seafood
Portland, ME. 800-225-2586
Deep Sea Foods
Bayou La Batre, AL 251-824-7000
Depoe Bay Fish Company
Newport, OR. 541-265-8833
Eastern Fish Company
Teaneck, NJ. 800-526-9066
Fisherman's Reef Shrimp Company
Beaumont, TX. 409-842-9528
Fishery Products International
Danvers, MA. 800-374-4700
Golden Gulf Coast Packing Company
Biloxi, MS. 228-374-6121
Great Northern Products
Warwick, RI 401-490-4590
Indian Ridge Shrimp Company
Chauvin, LA 985-594-3361
International Oceanic Enterprises of Alabama
Bayou La Batre, AL 800-816-1832
J. Matassini & Sons Fish Company
Tampa, FL. 813-229-0829
Jessie's Ilwaco Fish Company
Ilwaco, WA 360-642-3773
Kitchens Seafood
Plant City, FL 800-327-0132
Maxim's Import Corporation
Miami, FL. 800-331-6652
Mersey Seafoods
Liverpool, NS 902-354-3467
National Fish and Seafood Limited
Brownsville, TX 956-546-5525
Neptune Fisheries
Newport News, VA. 800-545-7474
North Atlantic Fish Company
Gloucester, MA. 978-283-4121
Pacific American Fish Co.,Inc.
Vernon, CA 800-625-2525
Paul Piazza & Sons
New Orleans, LA 504-524-6011
Penguin Frozen Foods
Northbrook, IL 847-291-9400
Portland Shellfish Company
South Portland, ME 207-799-9290
Quality Seafood
Apalachicola, FL. 850-653-9696
Rich-Seapak Corporation
Brownsville, TX 956-542-0001
Sea Pearl Seafood
Bayou La Batre, AL 800-872-8804
Sea Snack Foods
Los Angeles, CA. 213-622-2204
Seafood Producers Coop ative
Bellingham, WA 360-733-0120
Suram Trading Corporation
Miami, FL. 305-448-7165
Tampa Maid Foods
Lakeland, FL. 800-237-7637
Tex-Mex Cold Storage
Brownsville, TX 956-831-9433
Viking Seafoods Inc
Malden, MA 800-225-3020
Wrangell Fisheries
Wrangell, AK 907-874-3346

Peeled

Bayou Foods
Kenner, LA 800-516-8283
Depoe Bay Fish Company
Newport, OR. 541-265-8833
Fishery Products International
Danvers, MA. 800-374-4700
Neptune Fisheries
Newport News, VA. 800-545-7474
Tampa Bay Fisheries
Dover, FL 800-234-2561
Tampa Maid Foods
Lakeland, FL. 800-237-7637

Smoked

Menemsha Fish Market
Chilmark, MA. 508-645-2282
Port Chatham Smoked Seafood
Everett, WA. 800-872-5666

Squid

Aliotti Wholesale Fish Company
Monterey, CA 831-375-2881
Anchor Frozen Foods
Westbury, NY 800-566-3474
Arctic Seas
Little Compton, RI 401-635-4000
Atlantic Capes Fisheries
Cape May, NJ 609-884-3000
Blue Gold Mussels
Middletown, RI
Breakwater Fisheries
St Josephs, NL 709-754-1999
Buns & Things Bakery
Charlottetown, PE. 902-892-2600
GJ Shortall
Mount Pearl, NL 709-747-0655
Great Northern Products
Warwick, RI 401-490-4590
Harbor Seafood
New Hyde Park, NY 800-645-2211
International Seafood Distributors
Hayes, VA 804-642-1417
LaMonica Fine Foods
Millville, NJ 856-825-8111
Lund's Fisheries
Cape May, NJ 609-884-7600
Menemsha Fish Market
Chilmark, MA. 508-645-2282
Mutual Fish Company
Seattle, WA 206-322-4368
North Atlantic Fish Company
Gloucester, MA. 978-283-4121
Notre Dame Seafood
Comfort Cove, NL 709-244-5511
Pacific American Fish Co.,Inc.
Vernon, CA 800-625-2525
Pacific Salmon Company
Edmonds, WA 425-774-1315
Royal Seafood
Monterey, CA 831-655-8326
Ruggiero Seafood
Newark, NJ 866-225-2627
Sea Watch Intl.
Easton, MD 410-822-7500
Stavis Seafoods
Boston, MA. 800-390-5103
Sweet Water Seafood Corporation
Carlstadt, NJ 201-939-6622
Tampa Bay Fisheries
Dover, FL 800-234-2561
Tichon Seafood Corporation
New Bedford, MA 508-999-5607
Tri-Marine InternationalInc
San Pedro, CA. 310-732-6113

Ink

Chieftain Wild Rice Company
Spooner, WI 800-262-6368

Sushi

Azuma Foods International
Hayward, CA
IOE Atlanta
Galena, MD. 410-755-6300

Fruits & Vegetables

General

Alfred Louie
Bakersfield, CA 661-831-2520
Arbre Farms Corporation
Walkerville, MI. 231-873-3337
Black's Barbecue
Lockhart, TX. 512-398-2712
Coco Lopez
Miramar, FL 800-341-2242
Four Seasons Produce, Inc
Ephrata, PA 800-422-8384
Fruit D'Or Inc
Notre-Dame De Lourdes, QC. 819-385-1126
G Banis Company And Services, Inc.
Wilmington, DE 617-516-9092
Graceland Fruit Inc
Frankfort, MI 800-352-7181
Jain Ltd
Columbus, OH 614-850-9400
La Morena
Huamantla, TL 222-211-0515
Mercer Foods
Modesto, CA. 209-529-0150
NAR
Nashua, NH. 603-888-5420
Oberweis Dairy
North Aurora, IL. 888-645-5868
Patsy's
New York, NY 212-247-3491
Prairie Thyme
Santa Fe, NM 800-869-0009
Prodes
Col. El Porvenir, ZM 351-517-3400
Root Cellar Preserves
Wellesley, MA. 781-864-7440
Seneca Foods Corporation
Marion, NY. 315-926-8100
The Power Of Fruit
Lebanon, NJ 908-450-9806
Z&S Distributing
Fresno, CA 800-467-0788

Algae

Cell Tech International
Klamath Falls, OR 541-882-5406
Vitarich Laboratories
Naples, FL. 800-817-9999

Aloe Vera

Alfer Laboratories
Chatsworth, CA 818-709-0737
Aloe Commodities International
Carrollton, TX. 800-701-2563
Aloe Farms
Harlingen, TX. 800-262-6771
Aloe Laboratories, Inc.
Harlingen, TX. 800-258-5380
Emerling International Foods
Buffalo, NY. 716-833-7381

We supply food manufacturers and food service customers worldwide (since 1988) with bulk ingredients including: Fruits & Vegetables; Juice Concentrates; Herbs & Spices; Oils & Vinegars; Flavors & Colors; Honey & Molasses. We also produce PURE MAPLE SYRUP.

Florida Food Products
Eustis, FL 800-874-2331
Herb Connection
Springville, UT 801-489-4254
Naturex Inc.
South Hackensack, NJ 201-440-5000
Real Aloe Company
Carlsbad, CA. 800-541-7809
Russo Farms
Vineland, NJ 856-692-5942
Universal Preservachem Inc
Somerset, NJ. 732-568-1266
Warren Laboratories
Abbott, TX 800-421-2563
Winning Solutions
Dallas, TX. 800-899-2563

Apple

A. Gagliano Company
Milwaukee, WI. 800-272-1516
Agrinorthwest
Kennewick, WA 509-734-1195
AgroCepia
Miami, FL. 305-704-3488
Agvest
Cleveland, OH 216-464-3737
American Health & Nutrition
Ann Arbor, MI 734-677-5570
Apple Acres
La Fayette, NY 315-677-5144
Applewood Orchards
Deerfield, MI 800-447-3854
Baker Produce Company
Kennewick, WA 800-624-7553
Ballantine Produce Company
Reedley, CA 559-875-2583
Ben B. Schwartz & Sons
Detroit, MI 313-841-8300
Bennett's Apples & Cider
Ancaster, ON. 905-648-6878
Bluebird
Peshastin, WA. 509-548-1700
Boekhout Farms
Ontario, NY. 315-524-4041
Bridenbaughs Orchards
Martinsburg, PA 814-793-2364
Brothers International Food Corporation
Rochester, NY. 585-343-3007
Burnette Foods
Elk Rapids, MI 231-264-8116
Burnette Foods
Hartford, MI 616-621-3181
Cahoon Farms
Wolcott, NY 315-594-8081
Cal-Harvest Marketing
Hanford, CA 559-582-4000
Chazy Orchards
Chazy, NY. 518-846-7171
Chelan Fresh
Chelan, WA. 509-682-5133
Cherry Growers
Grawn, MI. 231-276-9241
Chief Wenatchee
Wenatchee, WA. 509-662-5197
Chiquita Brands Intl. ional
Cincinnati, OH 800-438-0015
Citrus Citrosuco North America
Lake Wales, FL. 800-356-4592
Clements Foods Company
Oklahoma City, OK 800-654-8355
Coloma Frozen Foods
Coloma, MI. 800-642-2723
Congdon Orchards
Yakima, WA 509-965-2886
Crane & Crane
Brewster, WA 509-689-3447
Del Mar Food Products Corporation
Watsonville, CA 831-722-3516
Diamond Fruit Growers
Odell, OR 541-354-5300
Dole Food Company
Westlake Village, CA 818-879-6600
Ever Fresh Fruit Company
Boring, OR 800-239-8026
Flippin-Seaman
Tyro, VA 434-277-5828
Fruit Growers Marketing Association
Newcomerstown, OH 800-466-5171
George W Saulpaugh & Sons
Germantown, NY 518-537-6500
Golden Town Apple Products
Rougemont, QC 519-599-6300
Green Valley Apples of California
Arvin, CA 661-854-4436
H H Dobbins
Lyndonville, NY 877-362-2467
H. Naraghi Farms
Escalon, CA 209-577-5777
Harner Farms
State College, PA 814-237-7919
Hazel Creek Orchards
Mt Airy, GA 706-754-4899
Henggeler Packing Company
Fruitland, ID 208-452-4212
Hillcrest Orchard
Lake Placid, FL. 865-397-5273
Indian Hollow Farms
Richland Center, WI. 800-236-3944
International Home Foods
Parsippany, NJ. 973-359-9920
J. Rettenmaier
Schoolcraft, MI. 877-243-4661
J.C. Watson Company
Parma, ID 208-722-5141
Kingsburg Apple Sale
Kingsburg, CA 559-897-5132
Knights Appleden Fruit
Colborne, ON 905-349-2521
Kozlowski Farms
Forestville, CA 800-473-2767
Leroux Creek Foods
Hotchkiss, CO. 877-970-5670
Love Creek Orchards
Medina, TX. 800-449-0882
Lucks Food Decorating Company
Tacoma, WA 253-383-4815
M&R Company
Lodi, CA 209-369-4760
Manzanita Ranch
Julian, CA. 760-765-0102
Mariani Packing Company
Vacaville, CA 800-672-8655
Marley Orchards Corporation
Yakima, WA 509-248-5231
Mason County Fruit Packers Cooperative
Ludington, MI. 231-845-6248
Matson Fruit Company
Selah, WA 509-697-7100
Mayer's Cider Mill
Webster, NY 800-543-0043
Mayfield Farms
Caledon, ON 905-846-0506
McCain Foods USA
Colton, CA 800-938-7799
Mrs. Prindable's Handmade Confections
Niles, IL 888-215-1100
Natural Foods
Toledo, OH 419-537-1713
Naumes
Medford, OR. 541-772-6268
New Era Canning Company
New Era, MI 231-861-2151
New York Apples Sales
Castletn on Hdsn, NY. 518-477-7200
Niagara Foods
Middleport, NY. 716-735-7722
North Bay Produce
Traverse City, MI 800-678-1941
Northern Fruit Company
Wenatchee, WA. 509-884-6651
Northern Michigan Fruit Company
Omena, MI 231-386-5142
Northern Orchard Company
Peru, NY 518-643-9718
Nuchief Sales
Wenatchee, WA. 888-269-4638
Oceana Foods
Shelby, MI. 231-861-2141
Oneonta Starr Ranch Growers
Wenatchee, WA. 509-663-2191
P-R Farms
Clovis, CA 559-299-0201
Pacific Coast Fruit Company
Portland, OR 503-234-6411
Pandol Brothers
Delano, CA 661-725-3755
Park 100 Foods
Tipton, IN 800-854-6504
Pastor Chuck Orchards
Portland, ME. 207-773-1314
Pavero Cold Storage Corporation
Highland, NY 800-435-2994
Per-Clin Orchards
Bear Lake, MI. 231-889-4289
Placerville Fruit Growers Association
Placerville, CA 530-622-2640
Premier Packing Company
Bakersfield, CA 661-393-3320

Reinhart Foods
Markham, ON....................905-754-3500
Rice Fruit Company
Gardners, PA....................800-627-3359
Scotian Gold Cooperative
Coldbrook, NS....................902-679-2191
Shafer Lake Fruit
Hartford, MI....................269-621-3194
Shawnee Canning Company
Cross Junction, VA....................800-713-1414
Smeltzer Orchard Company
Frankfort, MI....................231-882-4421
Snowcrest Packer
Abbotsford, BC....................800-265-5332
Solana Gold Organics
Sebastopol, CA....................800-459-1121
Stadelman Fruit
Zillah, WA....................509-829-5145
Sunmet
Del Rey, CA....................559-888-2702
Sunshine Farm & Gardens
Renick, WV....................304-497-2208
Symms Fruit Ranch
Caldwell, ID....................208-459-4821
T.S. Smith & Sons
Bridgeville, DE....................302-337-8271
Talbott Farms
Palisade, CO....................970-464-5943
Tastee Apple Inc
Newcomerstown, OH....................800-262-7753
Timber Crest Farms
Healdsburg, CA....................888-374-9325
Tom Ringhausen Orchards
Hardin, IL....................618-576-2311
Tony Vitrano Company
Jessup, MD....................800-481-3784
Trinity Fruit Sales
Fresno, CA....................559-433-3777
Triple D Orchards
Empire, MI....................866-781-9410
Trout-Blue Chelan
Chelan, WA....................509-682-2591
United Apple Sales
New Paltz, NY....................845-256-1500
United Fruits Corporation
Santa Monica, CA....................310-829-0261
White House Foods
Winchester, VA....................540-662-3401
Williams Creek Farms
Williams, OR....................541-846-6481
Yakima Fruit & Cold Storage Company
Wapato, WA....................509-877-2777
Zitner Company
Philadelphia, PA....................215-229-4990

Canned

American Health & Nutrition
Ann Arbor, MI....................734-677-5570
Burnette Foods
Elk Rapids, MI....................231-264-8116
Burnette Foods
Hartford, MI....................616-621-3181
Emerling International Foods
Buffalo, NY....................716-833-7381

Independent Food Processors
Sunnyside, WA....................509-837-3806
Knouse Foods Coop
Chambersburg, PA....................717-263-9177
Knouse Foods Coop
Orrtanna, PA....................717-642-8291
Lucks Food Decorating Company
Tacoma, WA....................253-383-4815
New Era Canning Company
New Era, MI....................231-861-2151
Setton International Foods
Commack, NY....................800-227-4397
Terri Lynn
Elgin, IL....................800-323-0775
Unique Ingredients
Naches, WA....................509-653-1991

Caramel

Andrews Caramel Apples
Chicago, IL....................800-305-3004
B&B Caramel Apple Company
Chicago, IL....................773-927-7559
Mrs. Prindable's Handmade Confections
Niles, IL....................888-215-1100
Tastee Apple Inc
Newcomerstown, OH....................800-262-7753
Zitner Company
Philadelphia, PA....................215-229-4990

Covered

Caramel

Carousel Candies
Geneva, IL....................888-656-1552
DGZ Chocolates
Houston, TX....................877-949-9444
Zitner Company
Philadelphia, PA....................215-229-4990

Chocolate

Ivydaro
Putney, VT....................802-387-5597

Criterion

Natural Foods
Toledo, OH....................419-537-1713
Weaver Nut Company
Ephrata, PA....................717-738-3781

Dried

AgroCepia
Miami, FL....................305-704-3488
American Health & Nutrition
Ann Arbor, MI....................734-677-5570
American Importing Company
Minneapolis, MN....................612-331-7000
Atwater Foods
Lyndonville, NY
Emerling International Foods
Buffalo, NY....................716-833-7381

Golden Town Apple Products
Rougemont, QC....................519-599-6300
Independent Food Processors Company
Yakima, WA....................800-476-5398
Just Tomatoes Company
Westley, CA....................800-537-1985
Kozlowski Farms
Forestville, CA....................800-473-2767
Leroux Creek Foods
Hotchkiss, CO....................877-970-5670
Mariani Packing Company
Vacaville, CA....................800-672-8655
Mayfield Farms
Caledon, ON....................905-846-0506
Niagara Foods
Middleport, NY....................716-735-7722
Quality Brands
Deland, FL....................888-676-2700
Seneca Foods Corporation
Marion, NY....................315-926-8100
Setton International Foods
Commack, NY....................800-227-4397
Solana Gold Organics
Sebastopol, CA....................800-459-1121
Tastee Apple Inc
Newcomerstown, OH....................800-262-7753
Terri Lynn
Elgin, IL....................800-323-0775
Timber Crest Farms
Healdsburg, CA....................888-374-9325
Unique Ingredients
Naches, WA....................509-653-1991

Fresh

Bridenbaughs Orchards
Martinsburg, PA....................814-793-2364
Ever Fresh Fruit Company
Boring, OR....................800-239-8026
Golden Town Apple Products
Rougemont, QC....................519-599-6300
H. Naraghi Farms
Escalon, CA....................209-577-5777
Price Cold Storage & Packing Company
Yakima, WA....................509-966-4110
Sunmet
Del Rey, CA....................559-888-2702
Unique Ingredients
Naches, WA....................509-653-1991

Frozen

Agvest
Cleveland, OH....................216-464-3737
American Health & Nutrition
Ann Arbor, MI....................734-677-5570
Cahoon Farms
Wolcott, NY....................315-594-8081
Citrus Citrosuco North America
Lake Wales, FL....................800-356-4592
Emerling International Foods
Buffalo, NY....................716-833-7381

Ever Fresh Fruit Company
Boring, OR....................800-239-8026
Mason County Fruit Packers Cooperative
Ludington, MI....................231-845-6248
Northern Michigan Fruit Company
Omena, MI....................231-386-5142
Oceana Foods
Shelby, MI....................231-861-2141
Pacific Coast Fruit Company
Portland, OR....................503-234-6411
Quality Brands
Deland, FL....................888-676-2700
Setton International Foods
Commack, NY....................800-227-4397
Sill Farms Market
Lawrence, MI....................269-674-3755
Smeltzer Orchard Company
Frankfort, MI....................231-882-4421
Snowcrest Packer
Abbotsford, BC....................800-265-5332
Terri Lynn
Elgin, IL....................800-323-0775
Triple D Orchards
Empire, MI....................866-781-9410
Unique Ingredients
Naches, WA....................509-653-1991

Granny Smith

Sunmet
Del Rey, CA....................559-888-2702

Pomace

Emerling International Foods
Buffalo, NY....................716-833-7381

Tree Top
Selah, WA....................800-367-6571
Unique Ingredients
Naches, WA....................509-653-1991

Rings

AgroCepia
Miami, FL....................305-704-3488
Timber Crest Farms
Healdsburg, CA....................888-374-9325
White House Foods
Winchester, VA....................540-662-3401

Slices

Bridenbaughs Orchards
Martinsburg, PA 814-793-2364
Ever Fresh Fruit Company
Boring, OR 800-239-8026
Golden Town Apple Products
Rougemont, QC 519-599-6300
Green Valley Apples of California
Arvin, CA 661-854-4436
H. Naraghi Farms
Escalon, CA 209-577-5777
Lucks Food Decorating Company
Tacoma, WA 253-383-4815
Mayfield Farms
Caledon, ON 905-846-0506
New Era Canning Company
New Era, MI 231-861-2151
Northern Michigan Fruit Company
Omena, MI 231-386-5142
White House Foods
Winchester, VA 540-662-3401

Canned

Lucks Food Decorating Company
Tacoma, WA 253-383-4815
Mayfield Farms
Caledon, ON 905-846-0506
New Era Canning Company
New Era, MI 231-861-2151

Frozen

Ever Fresh Fruit Company
Boring, OR 800-239-8026
Mayfield Farms
Caledon, ON 905-846-0506
Sill Farms Market
Lawrence, MI 269-674-3755

Apricot

Agrinorthwest
Kennewick, WA 509-734-1195
American Key Food Products
Closter, NJ. 800-767-0237
Ballantine Produce Company
Reedley, CA 559-875-2583
Brandt Farms
Reedley, CA 559-638-6961
California Fruit
Sanger, CA 559-266-7117
Copper Hills Fruit Sales
Fresno, CA 559-277-1970
Del Mar Food Products Corporation
Watsonville, CA 831-722-3516
Dole Food Company
Westlake Village, CA 818-879-6600
Fowler Packing Company
Fresno, CA 559-834-5911
Giumarra Companies
Reedley, CA 559-897-5060
HMC Marketing Group
Kingsburg, CA 559-897-1009
Janca's Jojoba Oil & Seed Company
Mesa, AZ. 480-497-9494
JR Wood/Big Valley
Atwater, CA 209-358-5643
Kalustyan Corporation
Union, NJ 908-688-6111
Kings Canyon Corrin
Reedley, CA 559-638-3571
Meridian Nut Growers
Clovis, CA 559-458-7272
Miss Scarlett's
Chandler, AZ. 800-345-6734
Muirhead Canning Company
The Dalles, OR 541-298-1660
Natural Foods
Toledo, OH 419-537-1713
P-R Farms
Clovis, CA 559-299-0201
Patterson Vegetable Company
Patterson, CA 209-892-2611
Stapleton-Spence PackingCompany
San Jose, CA. 800-297-8815
Sun-Maid Growers of California
Kingsburg, CA 800-272-4746
Sunsweet Growers
Yuba City, CA. 800-417-2253
Terri Lynn
Elgin, IL 800-323-0775
Trinity Fruit Sales
Fresno, CA 559-433-3777
Tufts Ranch
Winters, CA 530-795-4144
Unique Ingredients
Naches, WA. 509-653-1991
United Fruits Corporation
Santa Monica, CA. 310-829-0261
Vintage Produce Sales
Kingsburg, CA 559-897-1622
Wawona Packing Company
Cutler, CA. 559-528-9729
Z&S Distributing
Fresno, CA 800-467-0788

Canned

Emerling International Foods
Buffalo, NY. 716-833-7381

We supply food manufacturers and food service customers worldwide (since 1988) with bulk ingredients including: Fruits & Vegetables; Juice Concentrates; Herbs & Spices; Oils & Vinegars; Flavors & Colors; Honey & Molasses. We also produce PURE MAPLE SYRUP.

Pacific Coast Producers
Lodi, CA 209-367-8800
Stapleton-Spence PackingCompany
San Jose, CA. 800-297-8815

Dried

American Importing Company
Minneapolis, MN 612-331-7000
California Fruit
Sanger, CA 559-266-7117
Central California Raisin Packers
Del Rey, CA 559-888-2195
Chieftain Wild Rice Company
Spooner, WI 800-262-6368
Fastachi
Watertown, MA. 800-466-3022
Kalustyan Corporation
Union, NJ 908-688-6111
King Nut Company
Solon, OH. 800-860-5464
Mariani Packing Company
Vacaville, CA 800-672-8655
Natural Foods
Toledo, OH 419-537-1713
Purity Foods
Okemos, MI 800-997-7358
Setton International Foods
Commack, NY 800-227-4397
Stapleton-Spence PackingCompany
San Jose, CA. 800-297-8815
Sunsweet Growers
Yuba City, CA. 800-417-2253
Timber Crest Farms
Healdsburg, CA 888-374-9325
Weaver Nut Company
Ephrata, PA 717-738-3781

Frozen

Emerling International Foods
Buffalo, NY. 716-833-7381

We supply food manufacturers and food service customers worldwide (since 1988) with bulk ingredients including: Fruits & Vegetables; Juice Concentrates; Herbs & Spices; Oils & Vinegars; Flavors & Colors; Honey & Molasses. We also produce PURE MAPLE SYRUP.

JR Wood/Big Valley
Atwater, CA 209-358-5643
Pacific Coast Producers
Lodi, CA 209-367-8800

Kernals

Emerling International Foods
Buffalo, NY. 716-833-7381

We supply food manufacturers and food service customers worldwide (since 1988) with bulk ingredients including: Fruits & Vegetables; Juice Concentrates; Herbs & Spices; Oils & Vinegars; Flavors & Colors; Honey & Molasses. We also produce PURE MAPLE SYRUP.

Naturex Inc.
South Hackensack, NJ 201-440-5000

Artichoke

A.M. Braswell Jr. Food Company
Statesboro, GA 800-673-9388
Fayter Farms Produce
Bradley, CA. 831-385-8515
Ocean Mist
Castroville, CA 800-962-3738
Orleans Packing Company
Hyde Park, MA 617-361-6611
Scally's Imperial Importing Company Inc
Staten Island, NY 718-983-1938

SupHerb Farms
Turlock, CA 800-787-4372

Frozen culinary herb and specialty vegetable ingredients.

Vegetable Juices
Chicago, IL 888-776-9752

Canned

Agrocan
Ville St Laurent, QC 877-247-6226
Emerling International Foods
Buffalo, NY. 716-833-7381

We supply food manufacturers and food service customers worldwide (since 1988) with bulk ingredients including: Fruits & Vegetables; Juice Concentrates; Herbs & Spices; Oils & Vinegars; Flavors & Colors; Honey & Molasses. We also produce PURE MAPLE SYRUP.

Ron-Son Foods
Swedesboro, NJ 856-241-7333

Frozen

Emerling International Foods
Buffalo, NY. 716-833-7381

We supply food manufacturers and food service customers worldwide (since 1988) with bulk ingredients including: Fruits & Vegetables; Juice Concentrates; Herbs & Spices; Oils & Vinegars; Flavors & Colors; Honey & Molasses. We also produce PURE MAPLE SYRUP.

SupHerb Farms
Turlock, CA 800-787-4372

Frozen culinary herb and specialty vegetable ingredients.

Vegetable Juices
Chicago, IL 888-776-9752

Hearts

Castella Imports
Hauppauge, NY 866-227-8355
Colonna Brothers
North Bergen, NJ 201-864-1115

SupHerb Farms
Turlock, CA 800-787-4372

Frozen culinary herb and specialty vegetable ingredients.

Victoria Packing Corporation
Brooklyn, NY 718-927-3000

Asparagus

A. Duda Farm Fresh Foods
Belle Glade, FL. 561-996-7621
American Food & Equipment
Miami, FL. 305-377-8991
Arbre Farms Corporation
Walkerville, MI. 231-873-3337
Brock Seed Company
Finley, TN. 760-353-1632
Burnette Foods
Elk Rapids, MI 231-264-8116
Cal-Harvest Marketing
Hanford, CA 559-582-4000
Coloma Frozen Foods
Coloma, MI. 800-642-2723
Delta Packing Company of Lodi
Lodi, CA 209-334-0811
DiMare International Dmb Packing Corp
Indio, CA. 760-347-3336
Dole Food Company
Westlake Village, CA 818-879-6600
Foster Family Farm
South Windsor, CT 860-648-9366
George W Saulpaugh & Sons
Germantown, NY 518-537-6500
Indian Rock Produce
Perkasie, PA 800-882-0512
Lakeside Foods
Manitowoc, WI. 920-684-3356
M&R Company
Lodi, CA. 209-369-4760
Metzger Specialty Brands
New York, NY 212-957-0055
Michigan Freeze Pack
Hart, MI. 231-873-2175
Miss Scarlett's
Chandler, AZ. 800-345-6734
New Era Canning Company
New Era, MI 231-861-2151
Ocean Mist
Castroville, CA 800-962-3738
Pictsweet Frozen Foods
Bells, TN. 731-422-7600
Premier Packing Company
Bakersfield, CA 661-393-3320
Sedlock Farm
Lynn Center, IL. 309-521-8284
Shafer Lake Fruit
Hartford, MI 269-621-3194
Smeltzer Orchard Company
Frankfort, MI 231-882-4421
Snowcrest Packer
Abbotsford, BC. 800-265-5332
Superior Foods
Watsonville, CA 831-728-3691
Symms Fruit Ranch
Caldwell, ID 208-459-4821
T.S. Smith & Sons
Bridgeville, DE. 302-337-8271
Walla Walla Gardeners' Association
Walla Walla, WA. 800-553-5014
Weil's Food Processing
Wheatley, ON 519-825-4572

Canned

Carriere Foods Inc
Saint-Denis-Sur-Richelie, QC 450-787-3411
Emerling International Foods
Buffalo, NY. 716-833-7381

We supply food manufacturers and food service customers worldwide (since 1988) with bulk ingredients including: Fruits & Vegetables; Juice Concentrates; Herbs & Spices; Oils & Vinegars; Flavors & Colors; Honey & Molasses. We also produce PURE MAPLE SYRUP.

Fruit Belt Foods
Lawrence, MI 269-674-3939
Seneca Foods
Janesville, WI 608-757-6000
Seneca Foods Corporation
Marion, NY. 315-926-8100
Unique Ingredients
Naches, WA. 509-653-1991

Frozen

Emerling International Foods
Buffalo, NY. 716-833-7381

We supply food manufacturers and food service customers worldwide (since 1988) with bulk ingredients including: Fruits & Vegetables; Juice Concentrates; Herbs & Spices; Oils & Vinegars; Flavors & Colors; Honey & Molasses. We also produce PURE MAPLE SYRUP.

Fruit Belt Foods
Lawrence, MI 269-674-3939
Unique Ingredients
Naches, WA. 509-653-1991

Avocado

Brooks Tropicals
Homestead, FL 800-327-4833
Calavo Growers
Santa Paula, CA 800-422-5280
Chiquita Brands Intl. ional
Cincinnati, OH 800-438-0015
Del Monte Fresh Produce
Coral Gables, FL. 800-950-3683
Diversified Avocado Products
Mission Viejo, CA 800-879-2555
Emerling International Foods
Buffalo, NY. 716-833-7381

We supply food manufacturers and food service customers worldwide (since 1988) with bulk ingredients including: Fruits & Vegetables; Juice Concentrates; Herbs & Spices; Oils & Vinegars; Flavors & Colors; Honey & Molasses. We also produce PURE MAPLE SYRUP.

Giumarra Companies
Escondido, CA 760-480-8502
J.R. Simplot Company
Boise, ID 208-336-2110
Janca's Jojoba Oil & Seed Company
Mesa, AZ. 480-497-9494
McDaniel Fruit Company
Fallbrook, CA 760-728-8438
Prime Produce
Orange, CA. 714-771-0718
Reed Lang Farms
Rio Hondo, TX 956-748-2354
West Pak Avocado
Temecula, CA 800-266-4414

Bamboo Shoots

ConAgra Grocery Products
Archbold, OH 419-445-8015
Dong Kee Company
Chicago, IL 312-225-6340
Emerling International Foods
Buffalo, NY. 716-833-7381

We supply food manufacturers and food service customers worldwide (since 1988) with bulk ingredients including: Fruits & Vegetables; Juice Concentrates; Herbs & Spices; Oils & Vinegars; Flavors & Colors; Honey & Molasses. We also produce PURE MAPLE SYRUP.

Lee's Food Products
Toronto, ON 416-465-2407

SupHerb Farms
Turlock, CA 800-787-4372

Frozen culinary herb and specialty vegetable ingredients.

Banana

A. Gagliano Company
Milwaukee, WI. 800-272-1516
Chiquita Brands Intl. ional
Cincinnati, OH 800-438-0015
Del Monte Fresh Produce
Coral Gables, FL. 800-950-3683
Emerling International Foods
Buffalo, NY. 716-833-7381

We supply food manufacturers and food service customers worldwide (since 1988) with bulk ingredients including: Fruits & Vegetables; Juice Concentrates; Herbs & Spices; Oils & Vinegars; Flavors & Colors; Honey & Molasses. We also produce PURE MAPLE SYRUP.

Santanna Banana Company
Harrisburg, PA 717-238-8321
Surface Banana Company
Bluewell, WV 304-589-7202
Unique Ingredients
Naches, WA. 509-653-1991

Banana Products

Banana Distributing Company
San Antonio, TX. 210-227-8285
Chiquita Brands Intl. ional
Cincinnati, OH 800-438-0015
Kozy Shack
Hicksville, NY 516-870-3000
Spreda Group
Louisville, KY. 502-426-9411

Dried

Chieftain Wild Rice Company
Spooner, WI 800-262-6368
Fastachi
Watertown, MA. 800-466-3022
Mariani Packing Company
Vacaville, CA 800-672-8655
Setton International Foods
Commack, NY 800-227-4397

Plantain

MIC Foods
Miami, FL. 800-788-9335
Tantos Foods International
Markham, ON. 905-943-9993

Beans

A. Lassonde, Inc.
Rougemont, QC 888-477-6663
Agricore United
Winnipeg, MB. 800-661-4844
Allen Canning Company
Siloam Springs, AR 800-234-2553
Amigos Canning Company
San Antonio, TX. 800-580-3477
Atlantic Quality Spice &Seasonings
New Brunswick, NJ 800-584-0422
B&G Foods
Parsippany, NJ. 973-401-6500
B&M
Portland, ME. 207-772-7043
Beckman & Gast Company
Saint Henry, OH 419-678-4195
Buckhead Gourmet
Atlanta, GA. 800-673-6338
Burnette Foods
Elk Rapids, MI 231-264-8116
Bush Brothers & Co.
Dandridge, TN 865-509-2361
Bush Brothers & Company
Knoxville, TN. 865-588-7685

Buxton Foods
Buxton, ND 800-726-8057
Cajun Boy's Louisiana Products
Baton Rouge, LA 800-880-9575
California Fruit and Tomato Kitchens
Riverbank, CA 209-869-9300
Camellia Beans
Harahan, LA 504-733-8480
Campbell Soup Company
Camden, NJ 800-257-8443
Capco Enterprises
East Hanover, NJ 800-252-1011
Castella Imports
Hauppauge, NY 866-227-8355
Chef Merito
Encino, CA 800-637-4861
Chieftain Wild Rice Company
Spooner, WI 800-262-6368
China Doll Company
Saraland, AL 251-457-7641
Coffee Bean International
Portland, OR 800-877-0474
Colorado Bean Company/ Greeley Trading
Greeley, CO 888-595-2326
Cooperative Elevator
Pigeon, MI 989-453-4500
Cooperative Elevator Company
Pigeon, MI 989-453-4500
Country Cupboard
Virginia City, NV 775-847-7300
Crookston Bean
Crookston, MN 218-281-2567
Eckroat Seed Company
Oklahoma City, OK 405-427-2484
Eden Foods Inc.
Clinton, MI 800-248-0320
Faribault Foods
Minneapolis, MN 612-333-6461
Fine Foods Northwest
Seattle, WA 800-862-3965
Foster Family Farm
South Windsor, CT 860-648-9366
Furmano's Foods
Northumberland, PA 877-877-6032
Georgia Vegetable Company
Tifton, GA 229-386-2374
Goya Foods
Secaucus, NJ 201-348-4900
Goya Foods of Florida
Miami, FL 305-592-3150
Grandma Brown's Beans Inc
Mexico, NY 315-963-7221
Hanover Foods Corporation
Hanover, PA 717-632-6000
HealthBest
San Marcos, CA 760-752-5230
Heartline Foods
Westport, CT 203-222-0381
Heinz Company of Canada
North York, ON 877-574-3469
Hoopeston Foods
Burnsville, MN 952-854-0903
Hormel Foods Corporation
Austin, MN 800-523-4635
HP Schmid
San Francisco, CA 415-765-5925
Indian Harvest
Colusa, CA 800-294-2433
Inland Empire Foods
Riverside, CA 888-452-3267
Inter-American Products
Cincinnati, OH 800-645-2233
International Home Foods
Parsippany, NJ 973-359-9920
Kalustyan Corporation
Union, NJ 908-688-6111
Kelley Bean Company
Torrington, WY 307-532-2131
Kelley Bean Company
Scottsbluff, NE 308-635-6438
Knight Seed Company
Burnsville, MN 800-328-2999
Krinos Foods
Santa Barbara, CA 800-624-4896
L&S Packing Company
Farmingdale, NY 800-286-6487
Lakeside Foods
Plainview, MN 507-534-3141
Lakeside Foods
Seymour, WI 920-833-2371
Les Aliments Ramico Foods
St. Leonard, QC 514-329-1844
Louis Dreyfus Corporation
Wilton, CT 203-761-2000
Lucks Food Decorating Company
Tacoma, WA 253-383-4815
M&R Company
Lodi, CA 209-369-4760
McCain Foods Canada
Toronto, ON 866-622-2461
Mercado Latino
City of Industry, CA 626-333-6862
Midland Bean Company
Cahone, CO 970-562-4235
Mills Brothers International
Tukwila, WA 206-575-3000
Miramar Fruit Trading Company
Doral, FL 305-883-4774
Miyako Oriental Foods
Baldwin Park, CA 877-788-6476
Morgan Food
Austin, IN 888-430-1780
National Frozen Foods Corporation
Seattle, WA 206-322-8900
Nationwide Canning
Cottam, ON 519-839-4831
Natural Foods
Toledo, OH 419-537-1713
Naturex Inc.
South Hackensack, NJ 201-440-5000
New Era Canning Company
New Era, MI 231-861-2151
New Harvest Foods
Pulaski, WI 920-822-2578
New Meridian
Eaton, IN 765-396-3344
NORPAC Foods
Stayton, OR 503-769-2101
NORPAC Foods
Lake Oswego, OR 800-733-9311
North Bay Trading Company
Brule, WI 800-348-0164
Northern Feed & Bean Company
Lucerne, CO 800-316-2326
Old Ranchers Canning Company
Upland, CA 909-982-8895
Osowski Farms
Minto, ND 701-248-3341
Pacific Collier Fresh Company
Immokalee, FL 800-226-7274
Paisano Food Products
Elk Grove Village, IL 800-672-4726
Pastene Companies
Canton, MA 781-830-8200
Pictsweet Frozen Foods
Bells, TN 731-422-7600
Pleasant Grove Farms
Pleasant Grove, CA 916-655-3391
Producers Cooperative
Olathe, CO 970-874-9736
Produits Ronald
St. Damase, QC 800-465-0118
Quetzal Company
San Francisco, CA 888-673-8181
R&J Farms
West Salem, OH 419-846-3179
Randall Food Products
Cincinnati, OH 513-793-6525
Raymond-Hadley Corporation
Spencer, NY 800-252-5220
Red River Commodities
Fargo, ND 701-282-2600
Rice Company
Roseville, CA 916-784-7745
Roberts Seed
Axtell, NE 308-743-2565
Sambets Cajun Deli
Austin, TX 800-472-6238
Scally's Imperial Importing Company Inc
Staten Island, NY 718-983-1938
Seabrook Brothers & Sons
Seabrook, NJ 856-455-8080
Seapoint Farms
Huntington Beach, CA 888-722-7098
Seneca Foods
Marion, NY 315-926-8100
Seneca Foods
Cumberland, WI 715-822-2181
Smith Frozen Foods
Weston, OR 541-566-3515
Smith Frozen Foods
Weston, OR 800-547-0203
Snowcrest Packer
Abbotsford, BC 800-265-5332
Somerset Industries
Spring House, PA 800-883-8728
SOPAKCO Foods
Mullins, SC 800-276-9678
Spokane Seed Company
Spokane Valley, WA 509-535-3671
Sprague Foods
Belleville, ON 613-966-1200
Star of the West MillingCompany
Frankenmuth, MI 989-652-9971
Sugai Kona Coffee
Kealakekua, HI 808-322-7717
Talley Farms
Arroyo Grande, CA 805-489-5533
Tipiak
Stamford, CT 203-961-9117
Torn & Glasser
Los Angeles, CA 800-282-6887
Torrefazione Barzula & Import
Mississauga, ON 866-358-5488
Trappe Packing Corporation
Trappe, MD 410-476-3185
Trinidad Benham Company
Denver, CO 303-220-1400
Truitt Brothers Inc
Salem, OR 800-547-8712
Twin City Foods
Stanwood, WA 208-743-5568
United Intertrade Corporation
Houston, TX 800-969-2233
US Foods
Lincoln, NE 402-470-2021
Veronica Foods Company
Oakland, CA 800-370-5554
Vincent Formusa Company
Chicago, IL 312-421-0485
Weaver Nut Company
Ephrata, PA 717-738-3781
Webster Farms
Cambridge Station, NS 902-538-9492
Westlam Foods
Chino, CA 800-722-9519
WG Thompson & Sons
Blenheim, ON 519-676-5411
Wicklund Farms
Springfield, OR 541-747-5998
Wildcat Produce
McGrew, NE 308-783-2438
Woodland Foods
Gurnee, IL 847-625-8600
Z&S Distributing
Fresno, CA 800-467-0788
Zarda Bar-B-Q & Catering Company
Blue Springs, MO 800-776-7427

Adzuki

American Health & Nutrition
Ann Arbor, MI 734-677-5570
Chieftain Wild Rice Company
Spooner, WI 800-262-6368
Emerling International Foods
Buffalo, NY 716-833-7381

We supply food manufacturers and food service customers worldwide (since 1988) with bulk ingredients including: Fruits & Vegetables; Juice Concentrates; Herbs & Spices; Oils & Vinegars; Flavors & Colors; Honey & Molasses. We also produce PURE MAPLE SYRUP.

Organic Planet
San Francisco, CA 415-765-5590

Appaloosa

Chieftain Wild Rice Company
Spooner, WI 800-262-6368

Baked

A. Lassonde, Inc.
Rougemont, QC 888-477-6663
AlpineAire Foods
Rocklin, CA 800-322-6325
B&M
Portland, ME. 207-772-7043
Bush Brothers & Co.
Augusta, WI 715-286-2211
Capco Enterprises
East Hanover, NJ. 800-252-1011
Captain Ken's Foods
St Paul, MN. 651-298-0071
Grandma Brown's Beans Inc
Mexico, NY. 315-963-7221
Hanover Foods Corporation
Hanover, PA 717-632-6000
Mercado Latino
City of Industry, CA 626-333-6862
Produits Ronald
St. Damase, QC. 800-465-0118
Wornick Company
Cincinnati, OH 800-860-4555
Zarda Bar-B-Q & Catering Company
Blue Springs, MO. 800-776-7427

Beans: Snap Blue Lake

Arbre Farms Corporation
Walkerville, MI. 231-873-3337

Black

Agricore United
Winnipeg, MB. 800-661-4844
Buckhead Gourmet
Atlanta, GA. 800-673-6338
Bush Brothers & Co.
Augusta, WI 715-286-2211
Country Cupboard
Virginia City, NV 775-847-7300
Miyako Oriental Foods
Baldwin Park, CA. 877-788-6476

Blackeye (Cowpeas)

Bush Brothers & Co.
Augusta, WI 715-286-2211
Chieftain Wild Rice Company
Spooner, WI 800-262-6368
Hanover Foods Corporation
Hanover, PA 717-632-6000
Trinidad Benham Company
Denver, CO 303-220-1400

Blue Lake

Canned

Allen Canning Company
Siloam Springs, AR 800-234-2553
Emerling International Foods
Buffalo, NY. 716-833-7381

We supply food manufacturers and food service customers worldwide (since 1988) with bulk ingredients including: Fruits & Vegetables; Juice Concentrates; Herbs & Spices; Oils & Vinegars; Flavors & Colors; Honey & Molasses. We also produce PURE MAPLE SYRUP.

Faribault Foods
Minneapolis, MN 612-333-6461
Georgia Vegetable Company
Tifton, GA. 229-386-2374
Lakeside Foods
Seymour, WI. 920-833-2371
McCain Foods Canada
Toronto, ON 866-622-2461
New Era Canning Company
New Era, MI 231-861-2151
NORPAC Foods
Stayton, OR. 503-769-2101
Omstead Foods Ltd
Wheatley, ON 905-315-8883
Seneca Foods
Cumberland, WI 715-822-2181

Frozen

Allen Canning Company
Siloam Springs, AR 800-234-2553
Emerling International Foods
Buffalo, NY. 716-833-7381

We supply food manufacturers and food service customers worldwide (since 1988) with bulk ingredients including: Fruits & Vegetables; Juice Concentrates; Herbs & Spices; Oils & Vinegars; Flavors & Colors; Honey & Molasses. We also produce PURE MAPLE SYRUP.

Faribault Foods
Minneapolis, MN 612-333-6461
Georgia Vegetable Company
Tifton, GA. 229-386-2374
Lakeside Foods
Seymour, WI. 920-833-2371
McCain Foods Canada
Toronto, ON 866-622-2461
NORPAC Foods
Stayton, OR. 503-769-2101
Omstead Foods Ltd
Wheatley, ON 905-315-8883
Pictsweet Frozen Foods
Bells, TN. 731-422-7600
Seabrook Brothers & Sons
Seabrook, NJ. 856-455-8080
Seneca Foods
Marion, NY. 315-926-8100
Twin City Foods
Stanwood, WA 208-743-5568

Broad

Park 100 Foods
Tipton, IN 800-854-6504

Butter

Canned

Emerling International Foods
Buffalo, NY. 716-833-7381

We supply food manufacturers and food service customers worldwide (since 1988) with bulk ingredients including: Fruits & Vegetables; Juice Concentrates; Herbs & Spices; Oils & Vinegars; Flavors & Colors; Honey & Molasses. We also produce PURE MAPLE SYRUP.

Frozen

Emerling International Foods
Buffalo, NY. 716-833-7381

We supply food manufacturers and food service customers worldwide (since 1988) with bulk ingredients including: Fruits & Vegetables; Juice Concentrates; Herbs & Spices; Oils & Vinegars; Flavors & Colors; Honey & Molasses. We also produce PURE MAPLE SYRUP.

Canned

Carriere Foods Inc
Saint-Denis-Sur-Richelie, QC 450-787-3411
Goya of Great Lakes NewYYork
Angola, NY. 716-549-0076
Seneca Foods Corporation
Marion, NY. 315-926-8100

Cannellini

American Health & Nutrition
Ann Arbor, MI 734-677-5570
Bush Brothers & Co.
Augusta, WI 715-286-2211
Chieftain Wild Rice Company
Spooner, WI 800-262-6368
Emerling International Foods
Buffalo, NY. 716-833-7381

We supply food manufacturers and food service customers worldwide (since 1988) with bulk ingredients including: Fruits & Vegetables; Juice Concentrates; Herbs & Spices; Oils & Vinegars; Flavors & Colors; Honey & Molasses. We also produce PURE MAPLE SYRUP.

Organic Planet
San Francisco, CA 415-765-5590

Chick

Agrocan
Ville St Laurent, QC 877-247-6226
American Health & Nutrition
Ann Arbor, MI 734-677-5570
Emerling International Foods
Buffalo, NY. 716-833-7381

We supply food manufacturers and food service customers worldwide (since 1988) with bulk ingredients including: Fruits & Vegetables; Juice Concentrates; Herbs & Spices; Oils & Vinegars; Flavors & Colors; Honey & Molasses. We also produce PURE MAPLE SYRUP.

Organic Planet
San Francisco, CA 415-765-5590

Chili

Bush Brothers & Co.
Augusta, WI 715-286-2211
ConAgra Grocery Products
Irvine, CA 714-680-1000
Emerling International Foods
Buffalo, NY. 716-833-7381

We supply food manufacturers and food service customers worldwide (since 1988) with bulk ingredients including: Fruits & Vegetables; Juice Concentrates; Herbs & Spices; Oils & Vinegars; Flavors & Colors; Honey & Molasses. We also produce PURE MAPLE SYRUP.

Faribault Foods
Minneapolis, MN 612-333-6461
Hanover Foods Corporation
Hanover, PA 717-632-6000
Milnot Company
Litchfield, IL. 800-877-6455
Organic Planet
San Francisco, CA 415-765-5590
SOPAKCO Foods
Mullins, SC 800-276-9678

Dry

ADM Edible Bean Specialies
Kinde, MI 989-874-4720
Agland, Inc.
Eaton, CO 800-433-4688
American Health & Nutrition
Ann Arbor, MI 734-677-5570
Basic American Foods
Blackfoot, ID 800-227-4050
Basic American Foods
Walnut Creek, CA. 800-722-2084
Berberian Nut Company
Chico, CA 530-891-4900
Burnette Foods
Elk Rapids, MI 231-264-8116
Bush Brothers & Co.
Dandridge, TN 865-509-2361
C&F Foods
City of Industry, CA 626-723-1000
Camellia Beans
Harahan, LA 504-733-8480
Central Bean Company
Quincy, WA. 509-787-1544
Chieftain Wild Rice Company
Spooner, WI 800-262-6368
China Doll Company
Saraland, AL. 251-457-7641
Colorado Bean Company/ Greeley Trading
Greeley, CO. 888-595-2326
Commodities Marketing, Inc.
Edison, NJ. 732-603-5077
ConAgra Trading and Processing
Omaha, NE 402-595-5775
Continental Grain/ContiGroup Companies
New York, NY 212-207-5200
Cooperative Elevator
Pigeon, MI 989-453-4500
Cooperative Elevator Company
Pigeon, MI 989-453-4500
Crookston Bean
Crookston, MN. 218-281-2567
Eckhart Seed Company
Spreckels, CA 831-758-0925
Eckroat Seed Company
Oklahoma City, OK 405-427-2484

Emerling International Foods
Buffalo, NY. 716-833-7381

Faribault Foods
Minneapolis, MN 612-333-6461
Farmers Co-operative Grain Company
Kinde, MI 989-874-4200
Freeland Bean & Grain
Freeland, MI 800-447-9131
Greeley Elevator Company
Greeley, CO. 970-352-2575
H.K. Canning
Ventura, CA. 805-652-1392
High Country Elevators
Dove Creek, CO 970-677-2251
Hoopeston Foods
Burnsville, MN. 952-854-0903
HP Schmid
San Francisco, CA 415-765-5925
Jack's Bean Company
Holyoke, CO. 800-274-3702
Kalustyan Corporation
Union, NJ 908-688-6111
Kelley Bean Company
Torrington, WY. 307-532-2131
Kelley Bean Company
Scottsbluff, NE 308-635-6438
Knight Seed Company
Burnsville, MN. 800-328-2999
Lucks Food Decorating Company
Tacoma, WA 253-383-4815
Luxor California ExportsCorporation
San Diego, CA 619-692-9330
Michigan Ag Commodities
Breckenridge, MI 800-472-4629
Midland Bean Company
Cahone, CO. 970-562-4235
Mills Brothers International
Tukwila, WA. 206-575-3000
Morrison Farms
Clearwater, NE 402-887-5335
N.K. Hurst Company
Indianapolis, IN 317-634-6425
New Meridian
Eaton, IN. 765-396-3344
Northern Feed & Bean Company
Lucerne, CO 800-316-2326
Northwest Pea & Bean Company
Spokane Valley, WA 509-534-3821
Oakland Bean Cleaning & Storage
Knights Landing, CA 530-735-6203
Organic Planet
San Francisco, CA 415-765-5590
Osowski Farms
Minto, ND. 701-248-3341
Paisano Food Products
Elk Grove Village, IL 800-672-4726
Powell Bean
Powell, WY. 307-754-3121
Premier Packing Company
Bakersfield, CA 661-393-3320
Producers Cooperative
Olathe, CO 970-874-9736
Purity Foods
Okemos, MI 800-997-7358
R&J Farms
West Salem, OH 419-846-3179
Randag & Associates Inc
Elmhurst, IL 630-530-2830
Randall Food Products
Cincinnati, OH 513-793-6525
Red River Commodities
Fargo, ND 701-282-2600
Rhodes Bean & Supply Cooperative
Tracy, CA 209-835-1284
Roberts Seed
Axtell, NE. 308-743-2565
Russell E. Womack
Lubbock, TX. 877-787-3559
S&E Organic Farms
Bakersfield, CA 661-325-2644
Seed Enterprises
West Point, NE 888-440-7333
Smith Frozen Foods
Weston, OR. 541-566-3515
Somerset Industries
Spring House, PA 800-883-8728
Sprague Foods
Belleville, ON. 613-966-1200
Star of the West MillingCompany
Frankenmuth, MI 989-652-9971
Trinidad Bean & Elevator Company
Greeley, CO. 970-352-0346
Trinidad Benham Company
Denver, CO 303-220-1400
Trinidad Benham Company
Bridgeport, NE 308-262-1361
Trinidad/Benham Corporation
Patterson, CA 209-892-9051
Vege-Cool
Newman, CA. 209-862-2360
Webster Farms
Cambridge Station, NS. 902-538-9492
Westbrae Natural Foods
Melville, NY 800-434-4246
Westlam Foods
Chino, CA 800-722-9519
WG Thompson & Sons
Blenheim, ON 519-676-5411
WSI
Caldwell, ID 800-632-3005

Canned

Carriere Foods Inc
Saint-Denis-Sur-Richelie, QC 450-787-3411
Emerling International Foods
Buffalo, NY. 716-833-7381

We supply food manufacturers and food service customers worldwide (since 1988) with bulk ingredients including: Fruits & Vegetables; Juice Concentrates; Herbs & Spices; Oils & Vinegars; Flavors & Colors; Honey & Molasses. We also produce PURE MAPLE SYRUP.

Lucks Food Decorating Company
Tacoma, WA 253-383-4815

Edible

Agland, Inc.
Eaton, CO 800-433-4688
Russell E. Womack
Lubbock, TX. 877-787-3559
Star of the West MillingCompany
Frankenmuth, MI 989-652-9971

Fava

Chieftain Wild Rice Company
Spooner, WI 800-262-6368
Emerling International Foods
Buffalo, NY. 716-833-7381

We supply food manufacturers and food service customers worldwide (since 1988) with bulk ingredients including: Fruits & Vegetables; Juice Concentrates; Herbs & Spices; Oils & Vinegars; Flavors & Colors; Honey & Molasses. We also produce PURE MAPLE SYRUP.

Kalustyan Corporation
Union, NJ 908-688-6111
Organic Planet
San Francisco, CA 415-765-5590
Tarazi Specialty Foods
Chino, CA. 909-628-3601
Trappe Packing Corporation
Trappe, MD. 410-476-3185

Frozen

Agland, Inc.
Eaton, CO 800-433-4688
Allen Canning Company
Siloam Springs, AR 800-234-2553
Amigos Canning Company
San Antonio, TX. 800-580-3477
Buxton Foods
Buxton, ND. 800-726-8057
Campbell Soup Company
Camden, NJ. 800-257-8443
Canada Safeway Limited
Abbotsford, BC. 604-854-1191
Captain Ken's Foods
St Paul, MN. 651-298-0071
ConAgra Grocery Products
Irvine, CA 714-680-1000
Diversified Foods & Seasoning
Metairie, LA 504-846-5090
Emerling International Foods
Buffalo, NY. 716-833-7381

We supply food manufacturers and food service customers worldwide (since 1988) with bulk ingredients including: Fruits & Vegetables; Juice Concentrates; Herbs & Spices; Oils & Vinegars; Flavors & Colors; Honey & Molasses. We also produce PURE MAPLE SYRUP.

Faribault Foods
Minneapolis, MN 612-333-6461
Hanover Foods Corporation
Hanover, PA 717-632-6000
Lakeside Foods
Plainview, MN 507-534-3141
Lakeside Foods
Manitowoc, WI. 920-684-3356
Lakeside Foods
Seymour, WI 920-833-2371
National Frozen Foods Corporation
Seattle, WA 206-322-8900
New Meridian
Eaton, IN. 765-396-3344
NORPAC Foods
Stayton, OR. 503-769-2101
NORPAC Foods
Lake Oswego, OR. 800-733-9311
Omstead Foods Ltd
Wheatley, ON 905-315-8883
Pictsweet Frozen Foods
Bells, TN. 731-422-7600
Seabrook Brothers & Sons
Seabrook, NJ. 856-455-8080
Seneca Foods
Marion, NY. 315-926-8100
Smith Frozen Foods
Weston, OR. 541-566-3515
Smith Frozen Foods
Weston, OR. 800-547-0203
Snowcrest Packer
Abbotsford, BC. 800-265-5332
Trappe Packing Corporation
Trappe, MD. 410-476-3185
Twin City Foods
Stanwood, WA 208-743-5568

Garbanzo

Allen Canning Company
Siloam Springs, AR 800-234-2553
American Health & Nutrition
Ann Arbor, MI 734-677-5570
Buckhead Gourmet
Atlanta, GA. 800-673-6338
Bush Brothers & Co.
Augusta, WI 715-286-2211
California Fruit and Tomato Kitchens
Riverbank, CA 209-869-9300
Capco Enterprises
East Hanover, NJ. 800-252-1011
Chieftain Wild Rice Company
Spooner, WI 800-262-6368
Emerling International Foods
Buffalo, NY. 716-833-7381

We supply food manufacturers and food service customers worldwide (since 1988) with bulk ingredients including: Fruits & Vegetables; Juice Concentrates; Herbs & Spices; Oils & Vinegars; Flavors & Colors; Honey & Molasses. We also produce PURE MAPLE SYRUP.

Fastachi
Watertown, MA. 800-466-3022
Kalustyan Corporation
Union, NJ 908-688-6111
Northwest Pea & Bean Company
Spokane Valley, WA 509-534-3821
Organic Planet
San Francisco, CA 415-765-5590
Sprague Foods
Belleville, ON. 613-966-1200

Great Northern

Agricore United
Winnipeg, MB. 800-661-4844
American Health & Nutrition
Ann Arbor, MI 734-677-5570
Bush Brothers & Co.
Augusta, WI 715-286-2211

Callaway Packing Company
Delta, CO 800-332-6932
Chieftain Wild Rice Company
Spooner, WI 800-262-6368
Culinary Standards Corporation
Louisville, KY 800-778-3434
Emerling International Foods
Buffalo, NY. 716-833-7381

We supply food manufacturers and food service customers worldwide (since 1988) with bulk ingredients including: Fruits & Vegetables; Juice Concentrates; Herbs & Spices; Oils & Vinegars; Flavors & Colors; Honey & Molasses. We also produce PURE MAPLE SYRUP.

Hanover Foods Corporation
Hanover, PA 717-632-6000
Jack's Bean Company
Holyoke, CO. 800-274-3702
Kelley Bean Company
Scottsbluff, NE 308-635-6438
Lucks Food Decorating Company
Tacoma, WA 253-383-4815
Organic Planet
San Francisco, CA 415-765-5590
Randall Food Products
Cincinnati, OH 513-793-6525

Greek

Canned

Agrocan
Ville St Laurent, QC. 877-247-6226

Green

Allen Canning Company
Siloam Springs, AR 800-234-2553
Beckman & Gast Company
Saint Henry, OH 419-678-4195
Burnette Foods
Elk Rapids, MI 231-264-8116
Bush Brothers & Co.
Dandridge, TN 865-509-2361
Culinary Standards Corporation
Louisville, KY 800-778-3434
Faribault Foods
Minneapolis, MN 612-333-6461
Georgia Vegetable Company
Tifton, GA. 229-386-2374
Hanover Foods Corporation
Hanover, PA 717-632-6000
Lakeside Foods
Seymour, WI. 920-833-2371
Miss Scarlett's
Chandler, AZ. 800-345-6734
National Frozen Foods Corporation
Seattle, WA. 206-322-8900
New Era Canning Company
New Era, MI 231-861-2151
New Harvest Foods
Pulaski, WI 920-822-2578
NORPAC Foods
Stayton, OR. 503-769-2101
NORPAC Foods
Lake Oswego, OR. 800-733-9311
Patterson Frozen Foods
Patterson, CA 209-892-2611
Pictsweet Frozen Foods
Bells, TN. 731-422-7600
Princeville Canning Company
Princeville, IL 309-385-4301
Seabrook Brothers & Sons
Seabrook, NJ. 856-455-8080
Seneca Foods
Marion, NY. 315-926-8100
Sunrise Growers
Placentia, CA 714-630-6292
Trappe Packing Corporation
Trappe, MD. 410-476-3185
Twin City Foods
Stanwood, WA 208-743-5568
Veronica Foods Company
Oakland, CA 800-370-5554
Wicklund Farms
Springfield, OR. 541-747-5998
Wildcat Produce
McGrew, NE. 308-783-2438

Canned

Allen Canning Company
Siloam Springs, AR 800-234-2553
Beckman & Gast Company
Saint Henry, OH 419-678-4195
Burnette Foods
Elk Rapids, MI 231-264-8116
Carriere Foods Inc
Saint-Denis-Sur-Richelie, QC 450-787-3411
Commodities Marketing, Inc.
Edison, NJ. 732-603-5077
Emerling International Foods
Buffalo, NY. 716-833-7381

We supply food manufacturers and food service customers worldwide (since 1988) with bulk ingredients including: Fruits & Vegetables; Juice Concentrates; Herbs & Spices; Oils & Vinegars; Flavors & Colors; Honey & Molasses. We also produce PURE MAPLE SYRUP.

Faribault Foods
Minneapolis, MN 612-333-6461
Lakeside Foods
Mondovi, WI. 715-926-5075
Lakeside Foods
Seymour, WI. 920-833-2371
New Era Canning Company
New Era, MI 231-861-2151
New Harvest Foods
Pulaski, WI 920-822-2578
NORPAC Foods
Stayton, OR. 503-769-2101
NORPAC Foods
Lake Oswego, OR. 800-733-9311
Omstead Foods Ltd
Wheatley, ON 905-315-8883
Poynette Distribution Center
Poynette, WI 608-635-4396
Princeville Canning Company
Princeville, IL 309-385-4301
Seneca Foods
Cumberland, WI 715-822-2181
Truitt Brothers Inc
Salem, OR. 800-547-8712

Frozen

Lakeside Foods
Seymour, WI. 920-833-2371
National Frozen Foods Corporation
Seattle, WA. 206-322-8900
NORPAC Foods
Stayton, OR. 503-769-2101
NORPAC Foods
Lake Oswego, OR. 800-733-9311
Omstead Foods Ltd
Wheatley, ON 905-315-8883
Pictsweet Frozen Foods
Bells, TN. 731-422-7600
Seabrook Brothers & Sons
Seabrook, NJ. 856-455-8080
Seneca Foods
Marion, NY. 315-926-8100
Trappe Packing Corporation
Trappe, MD. 410-476-3185
Twin City Foods
Stanwood, WA 208-743-5568

Green Mung

American Health & Nutrition
Ann Arbor, MI 734-677-5570
Organic Planet
San Francisco, CA 415-765-5590

Italian

National Frozen Foods Corporation
Seattle, WA. 206-322-8900
Pictsweet Frozen Foods
Bells, TN. 731-422-7600

Kidney

Agland, Inc.
Eaton, CO 800-433-4688
Burnette Foods
Elk Rapids, MI 231-264-8116
ConAgra Grocery Products
Irvine, CA 714-680-1000
Cooperative Elevator Company
Pigeon, MI 989-453-4500
Cordon Bleu International
Anjou, QC. 514-352-3000
Hanover Foods Corporation
Hanover, PA 717-632-6000
International Home Foods
Parsippany, NJ. 973-359-9920
Jack's Bean Company
Holyoke, CO. 800-274-3702
Look's Gourmet Food Company
East Machias, ME. 800-962-6258
Lucks Food Decorating Company
Tacoma, WA 253-383-4815
Michigan Ag Commodities
Breckenridge, MI 800-472-4629
Nationwide Canning
Cottam, ON. 519-839-4831
New Era Canning Company
New Era, MI. 231-861-2151
Oakland Bean Cleaning & Storage
Knights Landing, CA 530-735-6203
Pleasant Grove Farms
Pleasant Grove, CA 916-655-3391
Red River Commodities
Fargo, ND 701-282-2600
Sprague Foods
Belleville, ON. 613-966-1200
WG Thompson & Sons
Blenheim, ON. 519-676-5411

Canned

Burnette Foods
Elk Rapids, MI 231-264-8116
Cordon Bleu International
Anjou, QC. 514-352-3000
Emerling International Foods
Buffalo, NY. 716-833-7381

We supply food manufacturers and food service customers worldwide (since 1988) with bulk ingredients including: Fruits & Vegetables; Juice Concentrates; Herbs & Spices; Oils & Vinegars; Flavors & Colors; Honey & Molasses. We also produce PURE MAPLE SYRUP.

International Home Foods
Parsippany, NJ. 973-359-9920
Lucks Food Decorating Company
Tacoma, WA 253-383-4815
Michigan Ag Commodities
Breckenridge, MI 800-472-4629
Nationwide Canning
Cottam, ON. 519-839-4831
New Era Canning Company
New Era, MI 231-861-2151
Red River Commodities
Fargo, ND 701-282-2600
Vegetable Juices
Chicago, IL 888-776-9752

Dark Red

Agrocan
Ville St Laurent, QC. 877-247-6226
Bush Brothers & Co.
Augusta, WI 715-286-2211
Cordon Bleu International
Anjou, QC. 514-352-3000
Red River Commodities
Fargo, ND 701-282-2600
Sprague Foods
Belleville, ON. 613-966-1200

Frozen

Emerling International Foods
Buffalo, NY. 716-833-7381

We supply food manufacturers and food service customers worldwide (since 1988) with bulk ingredients including: Fruits & Vegetables; Juice Concentrates; Herbs & Spices; Oils & Vinegars; Flavors & Colors; Honey & Molasses. We also produce PURE MAPLE SYRUP.

Michigan Ag Commodities
Breckenridge, MI 800-472-4629
Vegetable Juices
Chicago, IL 888-776-9752

Light Red

Jack's Bean Company
Holyoke, CO. 800-274-3702

Red River Commodities
Fargo, ND 701-282-2600

Lentil

Agricore United
Winnipeg, MB. 800-661-4844
Allen Canning Company
Siloam Springs, AR 800-234-2553
American Health & Nutrition
Ann Arbor, MI 734-677-5570
C&F Foods
City of Industry, CA 626-723-1000
Camellia Beans
Harahan, LA 504-733-8480
Chieftain Wild Rice Company
Spooner, WI 800-262-6368
China Doll Company
Saraland, AL. 251-457-7641
Emerling International Foods
Buffalo, NY. 716-833-7381

We supply food manufacturers and food service customers worldwide (since 1988) with bulk ingredients including: Fruits & Vegetables; Juice Concentrates; Herbs & Spices; Oils & Vinegars; Flavors & Colors; Honey & Molasses. We also produce PURE MAPLE SYRUP.

Garden Valley Foods
Sutherlin, OR 541-459-9565
HP Schmid
San Francisco, CA 415-765-5925
Inland Empire Foods
Riverside, CA 888-452-3267
Kalustyan Corporation
Union, NJ 908-688-6111
Mezza
Lake Forest, IL 888-206-6054
Mills Brothers International
Tukwila, WA. 206-575-3000
Northwest Pea & Bean Company
Spokane Valley, WA 509-534-3821
Primo Foods
Toronto, ON 800-377-6945
Sara Lee Corporation
Downers Grove, IL. 630-598-8100
Shah Trading Company
Toronto, ON 416-292-6927
Spokane Seed Company
Spokane Valley, WA. 509-535-3671
United Pulse Trading
Bismarck, ND 701-751-1623
Wallace Grain & Pea Company
Palouse, WA 509-878-1561
Woodland Foods
Gurnee, IL. 847-625-8600

Canned

Allen Canning Company
Siloam Springs, AR 800-234-2553
Organic Planet
San Francisco, CA 415-765-5590

Lima

Allen Canning Company
Siloam Springs, AR 800-234-2553
California Fruit and Tomato Kitchens
Riverbank, CA 209-869-9300
Chieftain Wild Rice Company
Spooner, WI 800-262-6368
Country Cupboard
Virginia City, NV 775-847-7300
Culinary Standards Corporation
Louisville, KY 800-778-3434
Hanover Foods Corporation
Hanover, PA 717-632-6000
Lakeside Foods
Plainview, MN 507-534-3141
Lucks Food Decorating Company
Tacoma, WA 253-383-4815
National Frozen Foods Corporation
Seattle, WA 206-322-8900
Patterson Frozen Foods
Patterson, CA 209-892-2611
Pictsweet Frozen Foods
Bells, TN. 731-422-7600
Seabrook Brothers & Sons
Seabrook, NJ. 856-455-8080
Smith Frozen Foods
Weston, OR. 541-566-3515
Smith Frozen Foods
Weston, OR. 800-547-0203
Trappe Packing Corporation
Trappe, MD. 410-476-3185
Trinidad Benham Company
Denver, CO 303-220-1400
Vege-Cool
Newman, CA. 209-862-2360

Canned

Allen Canning Company
Siloam Springs, AR 800-234-2553
Emerling International Foods
Buffalo, NY. 716-833-7381

We supply food manufacturers and food service customers worldwide (since 1988) with bulk ingredients including: Fruits & Vegetables; Juice Concentrates; Herbs & Spices; Oils & Vinegars; Flavors & Colors; Honey & Molasses. We also produce PURE MAPLE SYRUP.

Hanover Foods Corporation
Hanover, PA 717-632-6000
Lakeside Foods
Plainview, MN 507-534-3141
Lucks Food Decorating Company
Tacoma, WA 253-383-4815

Frozen

Allen Canning Company
Siloam Springs, AR 800-234-2553
Hanover Foods Corporation
Hanover, PA 717-632-6000
National Frozen Foods Corporation
Seattle, WA 206-322-8900
Pictsweet Frozen Foods
Bells, TN. 731-422-7600
Seabrook Brothers & Sons
Seabrook, NJ. 856-455-8080
Smith Frozen Foods
Weston, OR. 541-566-3515
Smith Frozen Foods
Weston, OR. 800-547-0203

Lupini

Castella Imports
Hauppauge, NY 866-227-8355
Chieftain Wild Rice Company
Spooner, WI 800-262-6368
Emerling International Foods
Buffalo, NY. 716-833-7381

We supply food manufacturers and food service customers worldwide (since 1988) with bulk ingredients including: Fruits & Vegetables; Juice Concentrates; Herbs & Spices; Oils & Vinegars; Flavors & Colors; Honey & Molasses. We also produce PURE MAPLE SYRUP.

L&S Packing Company
Farmingdale, NY 800-286-6487

Mung

Green

Chieftain Wild Rice Company
Spooner, WI 800-262-6368
Commodities Marketing, Inc.
Edison, NJ. 732-603-5077
Eckroat Seed Company
Oklahoma City, OK 405-427-2484
Emerling International Foods
Buffalo, NY. 716-833-7381

We supply food manufacturers and food service customers worldwide (since 1988) with bulk ingredients including: Fruits & Vegetables; Juice Concentrates; Herbs & Spices; Oils & Vinegars; Flavors & Colors; Honey & Molasses. We also produce PURE MAPLE SYRUP.

Jonathan's Sprouts
Rochester, MA 508-763-2577
Kalustyan Corporation
Union, NJ 908-688-6111

Navy

Central Bean Company
Quincy, WA. 509-787-1544
Chieftain Wild Rice Company
Spooner, WI 800-262-6368
Cooperative Elevator Company
Pigeon, MI 989-453-4500
Jack's Bean Company
Holyoke, CO. 800-274-3702
Lucks Food Decorating Company
Tacoma, WA 253-383-4815
New Era Canning Company
New Era, MI 231-861-2151
Sprague Foods
Belleville, ON. 613-966-1200

Canned

Emerling International Foods
Buffalo, NY. 716-833-7381

We supply food manufacturers and food service customers worldwide (since 1988) with bulk ingredients including: Fruits & Vegetables; Juice Concentrates; Herbs & Spices; Oils & Vinegars; Flavors & Colors; Honey & Molasses. We also produce PURE MAPLE SYRUP.

Lucks Food Decorating Company
Tacoma, WA 253-383-4815
New Era Canning Company
New Era, MI 231-861-2151

Pink

Central Bean Company
Quincy, WA. 509-787-1544
Oakland Bean Cleaning & Storage
Knights Landing, CA 530-735-6203

Pinto

ADM Edible Bean Specialies
Kinde, MI 989-874-4720
Agland, Inc.
Eaton, CO 800-433-4688
Agricore United
Winnipeg, MB. 800-661-4844
American Health & Nutrition
Ann Arbor, MI 734-677-5570
Bush Brothers & Co.
Augusta, WI 715-286-2211
Buxton Foods
Buxton, ND. 800-726-8057
Central Bean Company
Quincy, WA. 509-787-1544
Chieftain Wild Rice Company
Spooner, WI 800-262-6368
Crookston Bean
Crookston, MN 218-281-2567
Emerling International Foods
Buffalo, NY. 716-833-7381

We supply food manufacturers and food service customers worldwide (since 1988) with bulk ingredients including: Fruits & Vegetables; Juice Concentrates; Herbs & Spices; Oils & Vinegars; Flavors & Colors; Honey & Molasses. We also produce PURE MAPLE SYRUP.

Hanover Foods Corporation
Hanover, PA 717-632-6000
International Home Foods
Parsippany, NJ. 973-359-9920
Jack's Bean Company
Holyoke, CO. 800-274-3702
Kelley Bean Company
Scottsbluff, NE 308-635-6438
Lucks Food Decorating Company
Tacoma, WA 253-383-4815
Midland Bean Company
Cahone, CO. 970-562-4235
Northern Feed & Bean Company
Lucerne, CO 800-316-2326
Organic Planet
San Francisco, CA 415-765-5590
Powell Bean
Powell, WY. 307-754-3121

Premier Packing Company
Bakersfield, CA 661-393-3320
Producers Cooperative
Olathe, CO 970-874-9736
Randall Food Products
Cincinnati, OH 513-793-6525
Russell E. Womack
Lubbock, TX. 877-787-3559
Trinidad Benham Company
Denver, CO 303-220-1400
Vegetable Juices
Chicago, IL 888-776-9752
WSI
Caldwell, ID 800-632-3005

Refried

Allen Canning Company
Siloam Springs, AR 800-234-2553
Amigos Canning Company
San Antonio, TX. 800-580-3477
Colorado Bean Company/ Greeley Trading
Greeley, CO. 888-595-2326
Hormel Foods Corporation
Austin, MN 800-523-4635
Trappe Packing Corporation
Trappe, MD. 410-476-3185

Canned

Allen Canning Company
Siloam Springs, AR 800-234-2553
Amigos Canning Company
San Antonio, TX. 800-580-3477
Bush Brothers & Co.
Augusta, WI 715-286-2211
Morgan Food
Austin, IN 888-430-1780

Dried

Colorado Bean Company/ Greeley Trading
Greeley, CO. 888-595-2326

Small Red

Central Bean Company
Quincy, WA. 509-787-1544
ConAgra Grocery Products
Irvine, CA 714-680-1000

Snap Green

Arbre Farms Corporation
Walkerville, MI. 231-873-3337

Snap Wax

Arbre Farms Corporation
Walkerville, MI. 231-873-3337

Wax

Allen Canning Company
Siloam Springs, AR 800-234-2553
Hanover Foods Corporation
Hanover, PA 717-632-6000
Lakeside Foods
Seymour, WI. 920-833-2371
National Frozen Foods Corporation
Seattle, WA 206-322-8900
New Era Canning Company
New Era, MI 231-861-2151
NORPAC Foods
Stayton, OR. 503-769-2101
Pictsweet Frozen Foods
Bells, TN. 731-422-7600
Seabrook Brothers & Sons
Seabrook, NJ. 856-455-8080
Seneca Foods
Marion, NY. 315-926-8100
Trappe Packing Corporation
Trappe, MD. 410-476-3185
Twin City Foods
Stanwood, WA 208-743-5568

Canned

Allen Canning Company
Siloam Springs, AR 800-234-2553
Arbre Farms Corporation
Walkerville, MI. 231-873-3337
Carriere Foods Inc
Saint-Denis-Sur-Richelie, QC 450-787-3411
Emerling International Foods
Buffalo, NY. 716-833-7381

We supply food manufacturers and food service customers worldwide (since 1988) with bulk ingredients including: Fruits & Vegetables; Juice Concentrates; Herbs & Spices; Oils & Vinegars; Flavors & Colors; Honey & Molasses. We also produce PURE MAPLE SYRUP.

Lakeside Foods
Seymour, WI. 920-833-2371
New Era Canning Company
New Era, MI 231-861-2151
NORPAC Foods
Stayton, OR. 503-769-2101
Omstead Foods Ltd
Wheatley, ON 905-315-8883
Seneca Foods
Cumberland, WI 715-822-2181

Frozen

Allen Canning Company
Siloam Springs, AR 800-234-2553
Arbre Farms Corporation
Walkerville, MI. 231-873-3337
Emerling International Foods
Buffalo, NY. 716-833-7381

We supply food manufacturers and food service customers worldwide (since 1988) with bulk ingredients including: Fruits & Vegetables; Juice Concentrates; Herbs & Spices; Oils & Vinegars; Flavors & Colors; Honey & Molasses. We also produce PURE MAPLE SYRUP.

Lakeside Foods
Seymour, WI. 920-833-2371
National Frozen Foods Corporation
Seattle, WA 206-322-8900
NORPAC Foods
Stayton, OR. 503-769-2101
Omstead Foods Ltd
Wheatley, ON 905-315-8883
Pictsweet Frozen Foods
Bells, TN. 731-422-7600
Seabrook Brothers & Sons
Seabrook, NJ. 856-455-8080
Seneca Foods
Marion, NY. 315-926-8100
Trappe Packing Corporation
Trappe, MD. 410-476-3185
Twin City Foods
Stanwood, WA 208-743-5568

Beets

A. Duda Farm Fresh Foods
Belle Glade, FL. 561-996-7621
Dehydrates Inc.
Hewlett, NY 800-983-4443
Frank Capurro & Son
Moss Landing, CA 831-728-3904
Ghirardelli Ranch
Petaluma, CA 707-795-7616
Gouw Quality Onions
Taber, AB 403-223-1440
Indian Rock Produce
Perkasie, PA 800-882-0512
Lakeside Foods
Seymour, WI. 920-833-2371
NORPAC Foods
Lake Oswego, OR. 800-733-9311
Old Country Packers
Duryea, PA 570-655-9608
Osowski Farms
Minto, ND. 701-248-3341
S&G Products
Nicholasville, KY 800-826-7652
Schiff Food Products
North Bergen, NJ 201-868-6800
Seneca Foods
Marion, NY. 315-926-8100
Vegetable Juices
Chicago, IL 888-776-9752

Canned

Emerling International Foods
Buffalo, NY. 716-833-7381

We supply food manufacturers and food service customers worldwide (since 1988) with bulk ingredients including: Fruits & Vegetables; Juice Concentrates; Herbs & Spices; Oils & Vinegars; Flavors & Colors; Honey & Molasses. We also produce PURE MAPLE SYRUP.

Lakeside Foods
Seymour, WI. 920-833-2371
NORPAC Foods
Lake Oswego, OR. 800-733-9311
Seneca Foods
Marion, NY. 315-926-8100
Seneca Foods Corporation
Marion, NY. 315-926-8100

Frozen

Emerling International Foods
Buffalo, NY. 716-833-7381

We supply food manufacturers and food service customers worldwide (since 1988) with bulk ingredients including: Fruits & Vegetables; Juice Concentrates; Herbs & Spices; Oils & Vinegars; Flavors & Colors; Honey & Molasses. We also produce PURE MAPLE SYRUP.

NORPAC Foods
Lake Oswego, OR. 800-733-9311
Vegetable Juices
Chicago, IL 888-776-9752

Pickled

Seneca Foods Corporation
Marion, NY. 315-926-8100

Sugar

Agri-Dairy Products
Purchase, NY 914-697-9580
Imperial Sugar Company
Port Wentworth, GA 800-727-8427
Michigan Sugar Company
Bay City, MI 989-686-0161
Nyssa-Nampa Beet Growers
Nyssa, OR. 541-372-2904
Osowski Farms
Minto, ND. 701-248-3341
Western Sugar Cooperative
Denver, CO 303-830-3939

Berries

Abbotsford Growers Co-operative
Abbotsford, BC. 604-864-0022
Allen's Blueberry Freezer
Ellsworth, ME. 207-667-5561
Atlantic Blueberry Company
Hammonton, NJ 609-561-8600
Behm Blueberry Farms
Grand Haven, MI 616-846-1650
Blue Chip Group
Salt Lake City, UT 800-878-0099
Boekhout Farms
Ontario, NY. 315-524-4041
Brady Farms
West Olive, MI 616-842-3916
Cal-Sun Produce Company
Oxnard, CA. 805-985-2262
Carolina Blueberry Association
Garland, NC 910-588-4355
Cherry Central Cooperative Inc
Traverse City, MI 231-946-1860
Chieftain Wild Rice Company
Spooner, WI 800-262-6368
Coastal Classics
Duxbury, MA 508-746-6058
Columbia Empire Farms
Sherwood, OR. 503-538-2156
Decas Cranberry Products
Carver, MA 800-649-9811
Del Mar Food Products Corporation
Watsonville, CA 831-722-3516
E.W. Bowker Company
Pemberton, NJ. 609-894-9508
Europa Foods
Saddle Brook, NJ 201-368-8929

Firestone Packing Company
Vancouver, WA 360-695-9484
From Oregon
Springfield, OR 541-747-4222
Grove Fresh Distributors
Chicago, IL 773-288-2065
Grow-Pac
Cornelius, OR 503-357-9691
J.H. Verbridge & Son
Williamson, NY 315-589-2366
Jersey Fruit CooperativeAssociation
Glassboro, NJ 856-863-9100
JRL
Vineland, NJ 856-690-9000
K.B. Hall Ranch
Ojai, CA 805-646-4512
Kerr Concentrates
Salem, OR 800-910-5377
Krupka's Blueberries
Fennville, MI 269-857-4278
Leelanau Fruit Company
Suttons Bay, MI 231-271-3514
Macrie Brothers
Hammonton, NJ 609-561-6822
Meduri Farms Inc.
Dallas, OR 503-623-0308
Midwest Blueberry Farms
Holland, MI 616-399-2133
North American Blueberry Council
Folsom, CA 800-824-6395
Northern Michigan Fruit Company
Omena, MI 231-386-5142
Old Country Farms
East Sandwich, MA 888-707-5558
Overlake Blueberry Farm
Bellevue, WA 425-267-0501
Oxford Frozen Foods Limited
Oxford, NS 902-447-2100
Pacific Blueberries
Rochester, WA 360-273-5405
Pamlico Packing Company
Grantsboro, NC 800-682-1113
Pavich Family Farms
Bakersfield, CA 661-782-8700
Plaidberry Company
Vista, CA 760-727-5403
R M Lawton Cranberries
Middleboro, MA 508-947-7465
Ragold Confections
Wilton Manors, FL 954-566-9092
Richard Lanza
Hammonton, NJ 609-561-3984
Scenic Fruit Company
Gresham, OR 800-554-5578
Setton International Foods
Commack, NY 800-227-4397
Smeltzer Orchard Company
Frankfort, MI 231-882-4421
Snowcrest Packer
Abbotsford, BC 800-265-5332
Stanley Orchards
Modena, NY 845-883-7351
Stilwell Foods
Stilwell, OK 918-696-8325
Sun Groves
Safety Harbor, FL 800-672-6438
Terri Lynn
Elgin, IL 800-323-0775
Timber Crest Farms
Healdsburg, CA 888-374-9325
Tom Ringhausen Orchards
Hardin, IL 618-576-2311
Tru-Blu Cooperative Associates
New Lisbon, NJ 609-894-8717
Valley View Blueberries
Vancouver, WA 360-892-2839
Vintage Produce Sales
Kingsburg, CA 559-897-1622
Violore Foods Company
Laredo, TX 956-726-3633
Well Pict Berries
Watsonville, CA 831-722-3871
Wetherby Cranberry Company
Warrens, WI 608-378-4813
Wilhelm Foods
Newberg, OR 503-538-2929

Canned & Frozen

Abbotsford Growers Co-operative
Abbotsford, BC 604-864-0022
Allen's Blueberry Freezer
Ellsworth, ME 207-667-5561
Atlantic Blueberry Company
Hammonton, NJ 609-561-8600
Boekhout Farms
Ontario, NY 315-524-4041
Brady Farms
West Olive, MI 616-842-3916
Canada Safeway Limited
Abbotsford, BC 604-854-1191
Carolina Blueberry Association
Garland, NC 910-588-4355
Cherry Central Cooperative Inc
Traverse City, MI 231-946-1860
E.W. Bowker Company
Pemberton, NJ 609-894-9508
G. M. Allen & Son
Orland, ME 207-469-7060
Grow-Pac
Cornelius, OR 503-357-9691
J.H. Verbridge & Son
Williamson, NY 315-589-2366
JRL
Vineland, NJ 856-690-9000
Kerr Concentrates
Salem, OR 800-910-5377
Leelanau Fruit Company
Suttons Bay, MI 231-271-3514
Northern Michigan Fruit Company
Omena, MI 231-386-5142
Oxford Frozen Foods Limited
Oxford, NS 902-447-2100
Pacific Blueberries
Rochester, WA 360-273-5405
Plaidberry Company
Vista, CA 760-727-5403
Rainbow Farms
Upper Rawdon, NS 902-632-2548
Scenic Fruit Company
Gresham, OR 800-554-5578
Snowcrest Packer
Abbotsford, BC 800-265-5332
Stinson Seafood Company
San Diego, CA
Tru-Blu Cooperative Associates
New Lisbon, NJ 609-894-8717
Unique Ingredients
Naches, WA 509-653-1991
Wawona Frozen Foods
Clovis, CA 559-299-2901

Blackberry

Coloma Frozen Foods
Coloma, MI 800-642-2723
Driscoll Strawberry Associates
Watsonville, CA 831-763-5100
George Richter Farm
Fife, WA 253-922-5649
Grow-Pac
Cornelius, OR 503-357-9691
Kerr Concentrates
Salem, OR 800-910-5377
Oregon Fruit Products Company
Salem, OR 800-394-9333
Rain Sweet
Salem, OR 800-363-4293
Sand Hill Berries
Mt Pleasant, PA 724-547-4760
Symons Frozen Foods
Galvin, WA 360-736-1321
Tom Ringhausen Orchards
Hardin, IL 618-576-2311
Unique Ingredients
Naches, WA 509-653-1991
Venture Vineyards
Lodi, NY 888-635-6277

Frozen

Coloma Frozen Foods
Coloma, MI 800-642-2723
Emerling International Foods
Buffalo, NY 716-833-7381

We supply food manufacturers and food service customers worldwide (since 1988) with bulk ingredients including: Fruits & Vegetables; Juice Concentrates; Herbs & Spices; Oils & Vinegars; Flavors & Colors; Honey & Molasses. We also produce PURE MAPLE SYRUP.

George Richter Farm
Fife, WA 253-922-5649
Grow-Pac
Cornelius, OR 503-357-9691
Kerr Concentrates
Salem, OR 800-910-5377
Merrill's Blueberry Farms
Ellsworth, ME 800-711-6551
Oregon Fruit Products Company
Salem, OR 800-394-9333
Overlake Foods Corporation
Olympia, WA 800-683-1078
Rain Sweet
Salem, OR 800-363-4293
Symons Frozen Foods
Galvin, WA 360-736-1321
Townsend Farms
Fairview, OR 503-666-1780
Unique Ingredients
Naches, WA 509-653-1991

Blueberry

Agvest
Franklin, ME 207-565-3303
Agvest
Cleveland, OH 216-464-3737
Allen's Blueberry Freezer
Ellsworth, ME 207-667-5561
Blueberry Store
Grand Junction, MI 877-654-2400
Coloma Frozen Foods
Coloma, MI 800-642-2723
Diamond Blueberry
Hammonton, NJ 609-561-3661
Driscoll Strawberry Associates
Watsonville, CA 831-763-5100
E.W. Bowker Company
Pemberton, NJ 609-894-9508
Enfield Farms
Lynden, WA 360-354-3019
G. M. Allen & Son
Orland, ME 207-469-7060
Hawkins Farms
Pennfield, NB 506-755-6241
Hialeah Products Company
Hollywood, FL 800-923-3379
Indian Bay Frozen Foods
Centreville, NL 709-678-2844
International Food Trade
Amherst, NS 902-667-3013
Jasper Wyman & Son
Milbridge, ME 800-341-1758
JRL
Vineland, NJ 856-690-9000
Just Tomatoes Company
Westley, CA 800-537-1985
Krupka's Blueberries
Fennville, MI 269-857-4278
Macrie Brothers
Hammonton, NJ 609-561-6822
Maine Wild Blueberry Company
Cherryfield, ME 800-243-4005
Meduri Farms Inc.
Dallas, OR 503-623-0308
Memba
Lynden, WA 360-354-7708
Merrill's Blueberry Farms
Ellsworth, ME 800-711-6551
Midwest Blueberry Farms
Holland, MI 616-399-2133
New England Cranberry Company
Lynn, MA 800-410-2892
Niagara Foods
Middleport, NY 716-735-7722
North American Blueberry Council
Folsom, CA 800-824-6395
North Bay Produce
Traverse City, MI 800-678-1941
Northern Michigan Fruit Company
Omena, MI 231-386-5142
Oregon Fruit Products Company
Salem, OR 800-394-9333
Overlake Blueberry Farm
Bellevue, WA 425-267-0501
Pacific Blueberries
Rochester, WA 360-273-5405
Pacific Coast Fruit Company
Portland, OR 503-234-6411
Packers Canning Company
Lawton, MI 269-624-4681
Pandol Brothers
Delano, CA 661-725-3755

Producer Marketing Overlake
Olympia, WA 360-352-7989
Quality Brands
Deland, FL 888-676-2700
Rain Sweet
Salem, OR 800-363-4293
Richard Lanza
Hammonton, NJ 609-561-3984
Royal Ridge Fruits
Royal City, WA 509-346-1520
Royalmark Services
South Haven, MI 269-637-7450
Sill Farms Market
Lawrence, MI 269-674-3755
Smeltzer Orchard Company
Frankfort, MI 231-882-4421
Snowcrest Packer
Abbotsford, BC 800-265-5332
Symons Frozen Foods
Galvin, WA 360-736-1321
Terri Lynn
Elgin, IL 800-323-0775
Timber Crest Farms
Healdsburg, CA 888-374-9325
Townsend Farms
Fairview, OR 503-666-1780
Unique Ingredients
Naches, WA 509-653-1991
Valley View Blueberries
Vancouver, WA 360-892-2839
Venture Vineyards
Lodi, NY 888-635-6277
Vintage Produce Sales
Kingsburg, CA 559-897-1622
Wild Blueberry Companies
Old Town, ME 207-570-3535

Canned

Jasper Wyman & Son
Milbridge, ME 800-341-1758
Maine Wild Blueberry Company
Cherryfield, ME 800-243-4005
Merrill's Blueberry Farms
Ellsworth, ME 800-711-6551
Oregon Fruit Products Company
Salem, OR 800-394-9333
Packers Canning Company
Lawton, MI 269-624-4681

Dried

Atwater Foods
Lyndonville, NY
Chieftain Wild Rice Company
Spooner, WI 800-262-6368
Fastachi
Watertown, MA 800-466-3022
Setton International Foods
Commack, NY 800-227-4397

Frozen

Agvest
Cleveland, OH 216-464-3737
Allen's Blueberry Freezer
Ellsworth, ME 207-667-5561
Blueberry Store
Grand Junction, MI 877-654-2400
Canada Safeway Limited
Abbotsford, BC 604-854-1191
Diamond Blueberry
Hammonton, NJ 609-561-3661
E.W. Bowker Company
Pemberton, NJ 609-894-9508
Emerling International Foods
Buffalo, NY 716-833-7381

We supply food manufacturers and food service customers worldwide (since 1988) with bulk ingredients including: Fruits & Vegetables; Juice Concentrates; Herbs & Spices; Oils & Vinegars; Flavors & Colors; Honey & Molasses. We also produce PURE MAPLE SYRUP.

Enfield Farms
Lynden, WA 360-354-3019
G. M. Allen & Son
Orland, ME 207-469-7060
International Food Trade
Amherst, NS 902-667-3013
Jasper Wyman & Son
Milbridge, ME 800-341-1758
JRL
Vineland, NJ 856-690-9000
Maine Wild Blueberry Company
Cherryfield, ME 800-243-4005
Memba
Lynden, WA 360-354-7708
Northern Michigan Fruit Company
Omena, MI 231-386-5142
Oregon Fruit Products Company
Salem, OR 800-394-9333
Overlake Foods Corporation
Olympia, WA 800-683-1078
Pacific Blueberries
Rochester, WA 360-273-5405
Pacific Coast Fruit Company
Portland, OR 503-234-6411
Quality Brands
Deland, FL 888-676-2700
Rain Sweet
Salem, OR 800-363-4293
Rainbow Farms
Upper Rawdon, NS 902-632-2548
Sill Farms Market
Lawrence, MI 269-674-3755
Snowcrest Packer
Abbotsford, BC 800-265-5332
Townsend Farms
Fairview, OR 503-666-1780
Unique Ingredients
Naches, WA 509-653-1991

High Bush

Victor Packing Company
Madera, CA 559-673-5908

Boysenberry

Kerr Concentrates
Salem, OR 800-910-5377
Oregon Fruit Products Company
Salem, OR 800-394-9333
Rain Sweet
Salem, OR 800-363-4293

Canned

Oregon Fruit Products Company
Salem, OR 800-394-9333

Frozen

Emerling International Foods
Buffalo, NY 716-833-7381

We supply food manufacturers and food service customers worldwide (since 1988) with bulk ingredients including: Fruits & Vegetables; Juice Concentrates; Herbs & Spices; Oils & Vinegars; Flavors & Colors; Honey & Molasses. We also produce PURE MAPLE SYRUP.

Kerr Concentrates
Salem, OR 800-910-5377
Oregon Fruit Products Company
Salem, OR 800-394-9333
Rain Sweet
Salem, OR 800-363-4293
Townsend Farms
Fairview, OR 503-666-1780

Canned

Emerling International Foods
Buffalo, NY 716-833-7381

We supply food manufacturers and food service customers worldwide (since 1988) with bulk ingredients including: Fruits & Vegetables; Juice Concentrates; Herbs & Spices; Oils & Vinegars; Flavors & Colors; Honey & Molasses. We also produce PURE MAPLE SYRUP.

George Richter Farm
Fife, WA 253-922-5649
Jasper Wyman & Son
Milbridge, ME 800-341-1758
Maine Wild Blueberry Company
Cherryfield, ME 800-243-4005
Plaidberry Company
Vista, CA 760-727-5403

Cranberry

Agvest
Franklin, ME 207-565-3303
Agvest
Cleveland, OH 216-464-3737
Coastal Classics
Duxbury, MA 508-746-6058
Decas Cranberry Products
Carver, MA 800-649-9811
E.W. Bowker Company
Pemberton, NJ 609-894-9508
Fastachi
Watertown, MA 800-466-3022
Hialeah Products Company
Hollywood, FL 800-923-3379
Jasper Wyman & Son
Milbridge, ME 800-341-1758
Joseph J. White
Browns Mills, NJ 609-893-2332
New England Cranberry Company
Lynn, MA 800-410-2892
Niagara Foods
Middleport, NY 716-735-7722
Old Country Farms
East Sandwich, MA 888-707-5558
Pacific Coast Fruit Company
Portland, OR 503-234-6411
R M Lawton Cranberries
Middleboro, MA 508-947-7465
Savannah Food Company
Savannah, TN 800-795-2550
Setton International Foods
Commack, NY 800-227-4397
Smeltzer Orchard Company
Frankfort, MI 231-882-4421
Snowcrest Packer
Abbotsford, BC 800-265-5332
Terri Lynn
Elgin, IL 800-323-0775
Timber Crest Farms
Healdsburg, CA 888-374-9325
Unique Ingredients
Naches, WA 509-653-1991
Wetherby Cranberry Company
Warrens, WI 608-378-4813

Canned

Jasper Wyman & Son
Milbridge, ME 800-341-1758
Savannah Food Company
Savannah, TN 800-795-2550

Dried

American Importing Company
Minneapolis, MN 612-331-7000
Atwater Foods
Lyndonville, NY
Mariani Packing Company
Vacaville, CA 800-672-8655
Meridian Nut Growers
Clovis, CA 559-458-7272

Frozen

Agvest
Franklin, ME 207-565-3303
Agvest
Cleveland, OH 216-464-3737
Canada Safeway Limited
Abbotsford, BC 604-854-1191
E.W. Bowker Company
Pemberton, NJ 609-894-9508
Jasper Wyman & Son
Milbridge, ME 800-341-1758
Niagara Foods
Middleport, NY 716-735-7722
Pacific Coast Fruit Company
Portland, OR 503-234-6411
Snowcrest Packer
Abbotsford, BC 800-265-5332

Products

Emerling International Foods
Buffalo, NY....716-833-7381

We supply food manufacturers and food service customers worldwide (since 1988) with bulk ingredients including: Fruits & Vegetables; Juice Concentrates; Herbs & Spices; Oils & Vinegars; Flavors & Colors; Honey & Molasses. We also produce PURE MAPLE SYRUP.

Jasper Wyman & Son
Milbridge, ME....800-341-1758
Savannah Food Company
Savannah, TN....800-795-2550
Unique Ingredients
Naches, WA....509-653-1991

Currants

Chieftain Wild Rice Company
Spooner, WI....800-262-6368
Emerling International Foods
Buffalo, NY....716-833-7381

We supply food manufacturers and food service customers worldwide (since 1988) with bulk ingredients including: Fruits & Vegetables; Juice Concentrates; Herbs & Spices; Oils & Vinegars; Flavors & Colors; Honey & Molasses. We also produce PURE MAPLE SYRUP.

Fastachi
Watertown, MA....800-466-3022
George Richter Farm
Fife, WA....253-922-5649
Milne Fruit Products
Prosser, WA....509-786-2611
Pacific Coast Fruit Company
Portland, OR....503-234-6411
Setton International Foods
Commack, NY....800-227-4397

Red

George Richter Farm
Fife, WA....253-922-5649
Pacific Coast Fruit Company
Portland, OR....503-234-6411

Frozen

Abbotsford Growers Co-operative
Abbotsford, BC....604-864-0022
Agvest
Franklin, ME....207-565-3303
Agvest
Cleveland, OH....216-464-3737
Canada Safeway Limited
Abbotsford, BC....604-854-1191
Cleugh's Frozen Foods
Buena Park, CA....714-521-1002
Coloma Frozen Foods
Coloma, MI....800-642-2723
Diamond Blueberry
Hammonton, NJ....609-561-3661
E.W. Bowker Company
Pemberton, NJ....609-894-9508
Emerling International Foods
Buffalo, NY....716-833-7381

We supply food manufacturers and food service customers worldwide (since 1988) with bulk ingredients including: Fruits & Vegetables; Juice Concentrates; Herbs & Spices; Oils & Vinegars; Flavors & Colors; Honey & Molasses. We also produce PURE MAPLE SYRUP.

Enfield Farms
Lynden, WA....360-354-3019
Frozsun Foods
Placentia, CA....714-630-6292
G. M. Allen & Son
Orland, ME....207-469-7060
George Richter Farm
Fife, WA....253-922-5649
Grow-Pac
Cornelius, OR....503-357-9691
Hiscock Enterprises
Brigus, NL....709-528-4577
International Food Trade
Amherst, NS....902-667-3013
J.H. Verbridge & Son
Williamson, NY....315-589-2366
Jasper Wyman & Son
Milbridge, ME....800-341-1758
JRL
Vineland, NJ....856-690-9000
Maine Wild Blueberry Company
Cherryfield, ME....800-243-4005
Memba
Lynden, WA....360-354-7708
Niagara Foods
Middleport, NY....716-735-7722
Northern Michigan Fruit Company
Omena, MI....231-386-5142
Ocean Spray Cranberries
Lakeville-Middleboro, MA....800-662-3263
Oregon Fruit Products Company
Salem, OR....800-394-9333
Overlake Foods Corporation
Olympia, WA....800-683-1078
Pacific Blueberries
Rochester, WA....360-273-5405
Pacific Coast Fruit Company
Portland, OR....503-234-6411
Quality Brands
Deland, FL....888-676-2700
Rain Sweet
Salem, OR....800-363-4293
Rainbow Farms
Upper Rawdon, NS....902-632-2548
Sill Farms Market
Lawrence, MI....269-674-3755
Snowcrest Packer
Abbotsford, BC....800-265-5332
Symons Frozen Foods
Galvin, WA....360-736-1321
Webster Farms
Cambridge Station, NS....902-538-9492

Goose

Oregon Fruit Products Company
Salem, OR....800-394-9333

Juniper

Naturex Inc.
South Hackensack, NJ....201-440-5000
Schiff Food Products
North Bergen, NJ....201-868-6800

Lingonberries

Indian Bay Frozen Foods
Centreville, NL....709-678-2844

Mulberries

Kalustyan Corporation
Union, NJ....908-688-6111

Raspberries

Bridenbaughs Orchards
Martinsburg, PA....814-793-2364
Coloma Frozen Foods
Coloma, MI....800-642-2723
Decker Farms
Hillsboro, OR....503-628-1532
Driscoll Strawberry Associates
Watsonville, CA....831-763-5100
Enfield Farms
Lynden, WA....360-354-3019
George Richter Farm
Fife, WA....253-922-5649
Graysmarsh Farm
Sequim, WA....800-683-4367
Jasper Wyman & Son
Milbridge, ME....800-341-1758
Just Tomatoes Company
Westley, CA....800-537-1985
Kerr Concentrates
Salem, OR....800-910-5377
Oregon Fruit Products Company
Salem, OR....800-394-9333
Pacific Coast Fruit Company
Portland, OR....503-234-6411
Rain Sweet
Salem, OR....800-363-4293
Royal Ridge Fruits
Royal City, WA....509-346-1520
Sand Hill Berries
Mt Pleasant, PA....724-547-4760
Snowcrest Packer
Abbotsford, BC....800-265-5332
Strebin Farms
Troutdale, OR....503-665-8328
Symons Frozen Foods
Galvin, WA....360-736-1321
Terri Lynn
Elgin, IL....800-323-0775
Townsend Farms
Fairview, OR....503-666-1780
Unique Ingredients
Naches, WA....509-653-1991
Venture Vineyards
Lodi, NY....888-635-6277

Frozen

Abbotsford Growers Co-operative
Abbotsford, BC....604-864-0022
Coloma Frozen Foods
Coloma, MI....800-642-2723
Emerling International Foods
Buffalo, NY....716-833-7381

We supply food manufacturers and food service customers worldwide (since 1988) with bulk ingredients including: Fruits & Vegetables; Juice Concentrates; Herbs & Spices; Oils & Vinegars; Flavors & Colors; Honey & Molasses. We also produce PURE MAPLE SYRUP.

Enfield Farms
Lynden, WA....360-354-3019
Jasper Wyman & Son
Milbridge, ME....800-341-1758
Kerr Concentrates
Salem, OR....800-910-5377
Oregon Fruit Products Company
Salem, OR....800-394-9333
Overlake Foods Corporation
Olympia, WA....800-683-1078
Pacific Coast Fruit Company
Portland, OR....503-234-6411
Radar Farms
Lynden, WA....360-354-6574
Rain Sweet
Salem, OR....800-363-4293
Snowcrest Packer
Abbotsford, BC....800-265-5332
Strebin Farms
Troutdale, OR....503-665-8328
Symons Frozen Foods
Galvin, WA....360-736-1321
Townsend Farms
Fairview, OR....503-666-1780
Unique Ingredients
Naches, WA....509-653-1991

Strawberry

Blue Chip Group
Salt Lake City, UT....800-878-0099
Bridenbaughs Orchards
Martinsburg, PA....814-793-2364
CAL Sun Produce Company
Oxnard, CA....805-985-2262
Cal-Sun Produce Company
Oxnard, CA....805-985-2262
Chieftain Wild Rice Company
Spooner, WI....800-262-6368
Cleugh's Frozen Foods
Buena Park, CA....714-521-1002
Clofine Dairy & Food Products
Linwood, NJ....800-441-1001
Coloma Frozen Foods
Coloma, MI....800-642-2723
Decker Farms
Hillsboro, OR....503-628-1532
Del Mar Food Products Corporation
Watsonville, CA....831-722-3516
Driscoll Strawberry Associates
Watsonville, CA....831-763-5100
Fastachi
Watertown, MA....800-466-3022
Frozsun Foods
Placentia, CA....714-630-6292
Grow-Pac
Cornelius, OR....503-357-9691
Hialeah Products Company
Hollywood, FL....800-923-3379
J.H. Verbridge & Son
Williamson, NY....315-589-2366
Kerr Concentrates
Salem, OR....800-910-5377

Niagara Foods
Middleport, NY 716-735-7722
Northern Michigan Fruit Company
Omena, MI 231-386-5142
Oregon Fruit Products Company
Salem, OR 800-394-9333
Pacific Coast Fruit Company
Portland, OR 503-234-6411
Paradise
Plant City, FL 800-330-8952
Producer Marketing Overlake
Olympia, WA 360-352-7989
Rain Sweet
Salem, OR 800-363-4293
Sill Farms Market
Lawrence, MI 269-674-3755
Smeltzer Orchard Company
Frankfort, MI 231-882-4421
Snowcrest Packer
Abbotsford, BC 800-265-5332
Sunrise Growers
Placentia, CA 714-630-6292
T.S. Smith & Sons
Bridgeville, DE 302-337-8271
Terri Lynn
Elgin, IL 800-323-0775
Townsend Farms
Fairview, OR 503-666-1780
Unique Ingredients
Naches, WA 509-653-1991
Valley View Blueberries
Vancouver, WA 360-892-2839
Webster Farms
Cambridge Station, NS 902-538-9492
Well Pict Berries
Watsonville, CA 831-722-3871

Canned

Emerling International Foods
Buffalo, NY 716-833-7381

Oregon Fruit Products Company
Salem, OR 800-394-9333
Overlake Foods Corporation
Olympia, WA 800-683-1078
Unique Ingredients
Naches, WA 509-653-1991

Dried

Atwater Foods
Lyndonville, NY

Frozen

Cleugh's Frozen Foods
Buena Park, CA 714-521-1002
Coloma Frozen Foods
Coloma, MI 800-642-2723
Emerling International Foods
Buffalo, NY 716-833-7381

We supply food manufacturers and food service customers worldwide (since 1988) with bulk ingredients including: Fruits & Vegetables; Juice Concentrates; Herbs & Spices; Oils & Vinegars; Flavors & Colors; Honey & Molasses. We also produce PURE MAPLE SYRUP.

Frozsun Foods
Placentia, CA 714-630-6292
Fruit Belt Foods
Lawrence, MI 269-674-3939
Grow-Pac
Cornelius, OR 503-357-9691
J.H. Verbridge & Son
Williamson, NY 315-589-2366
J.R. Simplot Company
Boise, ID 208-336-2110
Kerr Concentrates
Salem, OR 800-910-5377
Niagara Foods
Middleport, NY 716-735-7722
Northern Michigan Fruit Company
Omena, MI 231-386-5142
Overlake Foods Corporation
Olympia, WA 800-683-1078

Pacific Coast Fruit Company
Portland, OR 503-234-6411
Rain Sweet
Salem, OR 800-363-4293
Sill Farms Market
Lawrence, MI 269-674-3755
Snowcrest Packer
Abbotsford, BC 800-265-5332
Townsend Farms
Fairview, OR 503-666-1780
Webster Farms
Cambridge Station, NS 902-538-9492

Brandied Fruits

Au Printemps Gourmet
Saint-Jerome, QC 800-663-0416
Dundee Brandied Fruit Company
Dundee, OR 503-537-2500
Hurd Orchards
Holley, NY 585-638-8838
Jubilee Gourmet Creations
Manchester, NH 603-625-0654
Silver Palate Kitchens
Cresskill, NJ 800-872-5283

Broccoli

A. Duda Farm Fresh Foods
Belle Glade, FL 561-996-7621
Cal-Harvest Marketing
Hanford, CA 559-582-4000
D'Arrigo Brothers Company of California
Salinas, CA 800-995-5939
Dehydrates Inc.
Hewlett, NY 800-983-4443
Dole Food Company
Westlake Village, CA 818-879-6600
Dole Fresh Vegetable Company
Soledad, CA 800-333-5454
Goebbert's Home Grown Vegetables
South Barrington, IL 847-428-6727
Great American Appetizers
Nampa, ID 800-282-4834
Hanover Foods Corporation
Hanover, PA 717-632-6000
Indian Rock Produce
Perkasie, PA 800-882-0512
JR Wood/Big Valley
Atwater, CA 209-358-5643
Kuhlmann's Market Gardens & Greenhouses
Edmonton, AB 780-475-7500
Mann Packing
Salinas, CA 831-422-7405
McCain Foods Canada
Toronto, ON 866-622-2461
Michigan Freeze Pack
Hart, MI 231-873-2175
Mills
Salinas, CA 831-757-1611
Omstead Foods Ltd
Wheatley, ON 905-315-8883
Paisley Farms
Willoughby, OH 800-676-8656
Patterson Frozen Foods
Patterson, CA 209-892-2611
Patterson Vegetable Company
Patterson, CA 209-892-2611
Pictsweet Frozen Foods
Bells, TN 731-422-7600
Snowcrest Packer
Abbotsford, BC 800-265-5332
Sunrise Growers
Placentia, CA 714-630-6292
Superior Foods
Watsonville, CA 831-728-3691
Talley Farms
Arroyo Grande, CA 805-489-5533
Tami Great Food
Monsey, NY 732-803-6366
Tanimura & Antle
Salinas, CA 831-455-2255
Teixeira Farms
Santa Maria, CA 805-928-3801
Trappe Packing Corporation
Trappe, MD 410-476-3185
Vegetable Juices
Chicago, IL 888-776-9752

Chopped

Pictsweet Frozen Foods
Bells, TN 731-422-7600

Frozen

Emerling International Foods
Buffalo, NY 716-833-7381

We supply food manufacturers and food service customers worldwide (since 1988) with bulk ingredients including: Fruits & Vegetables; Juice Concentrates; Herbs & Spices; Oils & Vinegars; Flavors & Colors; Honey & Molasses. We also produce PURE MAPLE SYRUP.

Great American Appetizers
Nampa, ID 800-282-4834
J.R. Simplot Company
Boise, ID 208-336-2110
JR Wood/Big Valley
Atwater, CA 209-358-5643
McCain Foods Canada
Toronto, ON 866-622-2461
Omstead Foods Ltd
Wheatley, ON 905-315-8883
Pictsweet Frozen Foods
Bells, TN 731-422-7600
Snowcrest Packer
Abbotsford, BC 800-265-5332
Sun Harvest Foods
San Diego, CA 619-661-0909
Superior Foods
Watsonville, CA 831-728-3691
Sure Fresh Produce
Santa Maria, CA 888-423-5379
Trappe Packing Corporation
Trappe, MD 410-476-3185
Unique Ingredients
Naches, WA 509-653-1991
Vegetable Juices
Chicago, IL 888-776-9752

Whole

Dole Fresh Vegetable Company
Soledad, CA 800-333-5454

Brussel Sprouts

Cara Mia Products
Fresno, CA 559-498-2900
Cleugh's Frozen Foods
Buena Park, CA 714-521-1002
Dole Food Company
Westlake Village, CA 818-879-6600
McCain Foods Canada
Toronto, ON 866-622-2461
Miss Scarlett's
Chandler, AZ 800-345-6734
Paisley Farms
Willoughby, OH 800-676-8656
Patterson Frozen Foods
Patterson, CA 209-892-2611
Pictsweet Frozen Foods
Bells, TN 731-422-7600
Snowcrest Packer
Abbotsford, BC 800-265-5332

Frozen

Canada Safeway Limited
Abbotsford, BC 604-854-1191
Cleugh's Frozen Foods
Buena Park, CA 714-521-1002
Emerling International Foods
Buffalo, NY 716-833-7381

We supply food manufacturers and food service customers worldwide (since 1988) with bulk ingredients including: Fruits & Vegetables; Juice Concentrates; Herbs & Spices; Oils & Vinegars; Flavors & Colors; Honey & Molasses. We also produce PURE MAPLE SYRUP.

McCain Foods Canada
Toronto, ON 866-622-2461
Pictsweet Frozen Foods
Bells, TN. 731-422-7600
Snowcrest Packer
Abbotsford, BC. 800-265-5332

Cabbage

A. Duda Farm Fresh Foods
Belle Glade, FL. 561-996-7621
Abbott & Cobb, Inc.
Langhorne, PA 800-345-7333
Carando Gourmet Frozen Foods
Agawam, MA 888-227-2636
Club Chef
Covington, KY 859-578-3100
Custom Cuts
Bay View, WI 414-483-0491
Dehydrates Inc.
Hewlett, NY 800-983-4443
Eckert Cold Storage
Escalon, CA 209-838-4040
Exeter Produce & Storage Company
Exeter, ON. 800-881-4861
F&S Produce Company
Rosenhayn, NJ 800-886-3316
Georgia Vegetable Company
Tifton, GA. 229-386-2374
Goebbert's Home Grown Vegetables
South Barrington, IL. 847-428-6727
H H Dobbins
Lyndonville, NY. 877-362-2467
Indian Rock Produce
Perkasie, PA 800-882-0512
Kuhlmann's Market Gardens & Greenhouses
Edmonton, AB 780-475-7500
Kurtz Produce
Ariss, ON 519-824-3279
Mills
Salinas, CA 831-757-1611
Pacific Collier Fresh Company
Immokalee, FL 800-226-7274
R.C. McEntire & Company
Columbia, SC 803-799-3388
Russo Farms
Vineland, NJ 856-692-5942
Sales USA
Salado, TX 800-766-7344
Sunrise Growers
Placentia, CA 714-630-6292
Sure Fresh Produce
Santa Maria, CA 888-423-5379
Teixeira Farms
Santa Maria, CA 805-928-3801
Vegetable Juices
Chicago, IL 888-776-9752
Vessey & Company
Holtville, CA. 760-356-0130

Bok Choy

Eckert Cold Storage
Escalon, CA 209-838-4040
Sure Fresh Produce
Santa Maria, CA 888-423-5379
Talley Farms
Arroyo Grande, CA. 805-489-5533
Vessey & Company
Holtville, CA. 760-356-0130

Canned

Emerling International Foods
Buffalo, NY. 716-833-7381

We supply food manufacturers and food service customers worldwide (since 1988) with bulk ingredients including: Fruits & Vegetables; Juice Concentrates; Herbs & Spices; Oils & Vinegars; Flavors & Colors; Honey & Molasses. We also produce PURE MAPLE SYRUP.

Sure Fresh Produce
Santa Maria, CA 888-423-5379

Chinese

Pioneer Growers Cooperative
Belle Glade, FL. 561-996-5211

Frozen

Carando Gourmet Frozen Foods
Agawam, MA 888-227-2636
Eckert Cold Storage
Escalon, CA 209-838-4040
Emerling International Foods
Buffalo, NY. 716-833-7381

We supply food manufacturers and food service customers worldwide (since 1988) with bulk ingredients including: Fruits & Vegetables; Juice Concentrates; Herbs & Spices; Oils & Vinegars; Flavors & Colors; Honey & Molasses. We also produce PURE MAPLE SYRUP.

Ripon Pickle Company
Ripon, WI 800-324-5493
Sure Fresh Produce
Santa Maria, CA 888-423-5379
Vegetable Juices
Chicago, IL 888-776-9752

Green

Baker Produce Company
Kennewick, WA 800-624-7553
Princeville Canning Company
Princeville, IL 309-385-4301
Vessey & Company
Holtville, CA. 760-356-0130

Red

F&S Produce Company
Rosenhayn, NJ 800-886-3316
Vessey & Company
Holtville, CA. 760-356-0130

Cactus

D'Arrigo Brothers Company of California
Salinas, CA 800-995-5939
Naturex Inc.
South Hackensack, NJ 201-440-5000

Candied Fruits

Crystallized, Glace

American Key Food Products
Closter, NJ........................800-767-0237
California Custom Fruits & Flavors
Irwindale, CA.....................877-558-0056
Emerling International Foods
Buffalo, NY.......................716-833-7381

We supply food manufacturers and food service customers worldwide (since 1988) with bulk ingredients including: Fruits & Vegetables; Juice Concentrates; Herbs & Spices; Oils & Vinegars; Flavors & Colors; Honey & Molasses. We also produce PURE MAPLE SYRUP.

Gray & Company
Forest Grove, OR..................503-357-3141
Hialeah Products Company
Hollywood, FL....................800-923-3379
Limpert Brothers
Vineland, NJ......................800-691-1353
Olde Tyme Food Corporation
East Longmeadow, MA.............800-356-6533
Paradise
Plant City, FL.....................800-330-8952
Reinhart Foods
Markham, ON.....................905-754-3500
Setton International Foods
Commack, NY....................800-227-4397
Unique Ingredients
Naches, WA.......................509-653-1991
Weaver Nut Company
Ephrata, PA.......................717-738-3781
White Swan Fruit Products
Plant City, FL.....................800-330-8952

Caneberries

Rain Sweet
Salem, OR........................800-363-4293

Canned Fruits

Agrocan
Ville St Laurent, QC................877-247-6226
B.M. Lawrence & Company
San Francisco, CA.................415-981-3650
Bob Gordon & Associates
Oak Park, IL......................708-524-9611
Bowman Apple Products Company
Mount Jackson, VA.................800-346-5382
Burnette Foods
Elk Rapids, MI....................231-264-8116
Cherry Growers
Grawn, MI........................231-276-9241
Coco Lopez
Miramar, FL......................800-341-2242
ConAgra Grocery Products
Irvine, CA........................714-680-1000
Curtice Burns Foods Glk Foods
Shortsville, NY....................585-289-4414
Derco Foods
Fresno, CA.......................559-435-2664
Emerling International Foods
Buffalo, NY.......................716-833-7381

We supply food manufacturers and food service customers worldwide (since 1988) with bulk ingredients including: Fruits & Vegetables; Juice Concentrates; Herbs & Spices; Oils & Vinegars; Flavors & Colors; Honey & Molasses. We also produce PURE MAPLE SYRUP.

Florida Citrus
Bartow, FL.......................863-537-3999
Hurd Orchards
Holley, NY.......................585-638-8838
Independent Food Processors
Sunnyside, WA....................509-837-3806
International Home Foods
Parsippany, NJ....................973-359-9920
Jasper Wyman & Son
Milbridge, ME....................800-341-1758
Jenport International Distributors
Coquitlam, BC....................604-464-9888
Kagome
Los Banos, CA....................209-826-8850
Knouse Foods Coop
Peach Glen, PA...................717-677-8181
L&S Packing Company
Farmingdale, NY..................800-286-6487
Lancaster Packing Company
Lancaster, PA.....................717-397-9727
Lucks Food Decorating Company
Tacoma, WA......................253-383-4815
Maine Wild Blueberry Company
Cherryfield, ME...................800-243-4005
Majestic Foods
Huntington, NY...................631-424-9444
Manzana Products Company
Sebastopol, CA....................707-823-5313
Maui Pineapple Company
Kahului, HI.......................808-877-3351
New Era Canning Company
New Era, MI......................231-861-2151
NTC Marketing Inc
Williamsville, NY..................800-333-1637
Oasis Foods
Planada, CA......................209-382-0263
Oregon Cherry Growers
Salem, OR........................800-367-2536
Oregon Fruit Products Company
Salem, OR........................800-394-9333
Pacific Coast Producers
Oroville, CA......................530-533-4311
Patterson Frozen Foods
Patterson, CA.....................209-892-2611
Plaidberry Company
Vista, CA.........................760-727-5403
San Benito Foods
Vancouver, WA....................800-453-7832
Seneca Foods
Marion, NY.......................315-926-0531
Snokist Growers
Yakima, WA......................800-377-2857
Stapleton-Spence PackingCompany
San Jose, CA......................800-297-8815
Triple D Orchards
Empire, MI.......................866-781-9410
Truitt Brothers Inc
Salem, OR........................800-547-8712
Tupman-Thurlow Company
Deerfield Beach, FL................954-596-9989
United Universal Enterprises Corporation
Phoenix, AZ......................623-842-9691
Zel R. Kahn & Sons
Corte Madera, CA.................415-924-9600

Canned Vegetables

A. Lassonde, Inc.
Rougemont, QC...................888-477-6663
Anchor Food Products/ McCain Foods
Appleton, WI.....................920-734-0627
Appleton Produce Company
Weiser, ID........................208-414-3352
B.M. Lawrence & Company
San Francisco, CA.................415-981-3650
Bob Gordon & Associates
Oak Park, IL......................708-524-9611
Border Foods Inc
Deming, NM......................888-737-7752
Burnette Foods
Elk Rapids, MI....................231-264-8116
Burnette Foods
Hartford, MI......................616-621-3181
Capitol Foods
Memphis, TN.....................662-781-9021
Carriere Foods Inc
Saint-Denis-Sur-Richelie, QC........450-787-3411
Chiquita Brands Intl. ional
Cincinnati, OH....................800-438-0015
Coco Lopez
Miramar, FL......................800-341-2242
ConAgra Grocery Products
Irvine, CA........................714-680-1000
Cordon Bleu International
Anjou, QC........................514-352-3000
Crown Point
St John, IN.......................219-365-3200
Curtice Burns Foods Glk Foods
Shortsville, NY....................585-289-4414
Deep Foods
Union, NJ........................908-810-7500
Dong Kee Company
Chicago, IL.......................312-225-6340
Ebro Foods
Chicago, IL.......................773-696-0150
Emerling International Foods
Buffalo, NY.......................716-833-7381

We supply food manufacturers and food service customers worldwide (since 1988) with bulk ingredients including: Fruits & Vegetables; Juice Concentrates; Herbs & Spices; Oils & Vinegars; Flavors & Colors; Honey & Molasses. We also produce PURE MAPLE SYRUP.

Escalon Premier Brand
Escalon, CA......................209-838-7341
Faribault Foods
Cokato, MN......................320-286-2166
Faribault Foods
Minneapolis, MN..................612-333-6461
Fiesta Canning Company
Mc Neal, AZ......................520-642-3376
Ful-Flav-R Foods
Alamo, CA.......................925-838-0300
G. L. Mezzetta
American Canyon, CA..............707-648-1050
GWB Foods Corporation
Brooklyn, NY.....................877-977-7610
Hanover Foods Corporation
Hanover, PA......................717-632-6000
Hartford City Foam Pack aging & Converting
Hartford City, IN...................765-348-2500
Hermann Pickle Farm
Garrettsville, OH...................800-245-2696
International Home Foods
Parsippany, NJ....................973-359-9920
John N Wright Jr
Federalsburg, MD..................410-754-9044
Juanita's Foods
Wilmington, CA...................310-834-5339
L&S Packing Company
Farmingdale, NY..................800-286-6487
Lakeside Foods
Plainview, MN....................507-534-3141
Lakeside Foods
Manitowoc, WI....................920-684-3356
Lakeside Foods
Seymour, WI......................920-833-2371
Lakeside Packing Company
Harrow, ON.......................519-738-2314
Lodi Canning Company
Lodi, WI.........................608-592-4236
Lucks Food Decorating Company
Tacoma, WA......................253-383-4815
Majestic Foods
Huntington, NY...................631-424-9444
McCall Farms
Effingham, SC.....................800-277-2012
Miami Purveyors
Miami, FL........................305-262-6170
Milroy Canning Company
Milroy, IN........................765-629-2221
Monterey Mushrooms
Watsonville, CA...................831-763-5300
Monticello Canning Company
Crossville, TN.....................931-484-3696
Moody Dunbar
Johnson City, TN..................800-251-8202
Musco Olive Products
Tracy, CA........................800-523-9828
Nationwide Canning
Cottam, ON.......................519-839-4831
New Era Canning Company
New Era, MI......................231-861-2151
New Harvest Foods
Pulaski, WI.......................920-822-2578
New Meridian
Eaton, IN.........................765-396-3344
Nickabood's Company
Los Angeles, CA...................213-746-1541
NORPAC Foods
Stayton, OR......................503-769-2101
NORPAC Foods
Lake Oswego, OR..................800-733-9311
Omstead Foods Ltd
Wheatley, ON.....................905-315-8883
Ore-Ida Foods
Pittsburgh, PA.....................800-892-2401
Paisley Farms
Willoughby, OH...................800-676-8656
Paradise Products Corporation
Boca Raton, FL....................800-826-1235
Pastene Companies
Canton, MA.......................781-830-8200
Patterson Frozen Foods
Patterson, CA.....................209-892-2611

Produits Ronald
St. Damase, QC 800-465-0118
Pure Food Ingredients
Verona, WI 800-355-9601
Ralph Sechler & Son Inc
St Joe, IN 800-332-5461
Ray Brothers & Noble Canning Company
Hobbs, IN 765-675-7451
Reckitt Benckiser
Parsippany, NJ 800-333-3899
Red Gold
Elwood, IN 877-748-9798
Red River Commodities
Fargo, ND 701-282-2600
Ron-Son Foods
Swedesboro, NJ 856-241-7333
San Benito Foods
Hollister, CA 831-637-4434
Saticoy Foods Corporation
Ventura, CA 805-647-5266
Seneca Foods
Marion, NY 315-926-0531
Seneca Foods
Marion, NY 315-926-8100
Seneca Foods
Janesville, WI 608-757-6000
Seneca Foods
Cumberland, WI 715-822-2181
SEW Friel
Queenstown, MD 410-827-8811
Simplot Food Group
Boise, ID 800-572-7783
Sopacko Packaging
Bennettsville, SC 843-479-3811
Sumida Pickle Products
Honolulu, HI 808-593-2487
Sun Harvest Foods
San Diego, CA 619-661-0909
Sun-Brite Canning
Kingsville, ON 519-326-9033
Tami Great Food
Monsey, NY 732-803-6366
Thomas Canning/Maidstone
Maidstone, ON 519-737-1531
Truitt Brothers Inc
Salem, OR 800-547-8712
Unilever Foods
Stockton, CA 209-467-2212
United Canning Corporation
North Lima, OH 330-549-9807
Van De Walle Farms
San Antonio, TX 210-436-5551
Van Drunen Farms
Momence, IL 815-472-3537
Weil's Food Processing
Wheatley, ON 519-825-4572
Western Pacific Commodities
Henderson, NV 702-382-8880
Wornick Company
Cincinnati, OH 800-860-4555

Carrot

A. Duda Farm Fresh Foods
Belle Glade, FL 561-996-7621
Atlantic Quality Spice &Seasonings
New Brunswick, NJ 800-584-0422
Beck Farms
Lethbridg, AB 403-227-1020
Cleugh's Frozen Foods
Buena Park, CA 714-521-1002
Columbia Foods
Quincy, WA 509-787-1585
Culinary Standards Corporation
Louisville, KY 800-778-3434
Dehydrates Inc.
Hewlett, NY 800-983-4443
Del Monte Fresh Produce
Kankakee, IL 815-936-7400
Exeter Produce & Storage Company
Exeter, ON 800-881-4861
F&S Produce Company
Rosenhayn, NJ 800-886-3316
Fresh Express
Salinas, CA 800-242-5472
Grimmway Farms
Bakersfield, CA 800-301-3101
Hanover Foods Corporation
Hanover, PA 717-632-6000
Indian Rock Produce
Perkasie, PA 800-882-0512
JES Foods
Cleveland, OH 216-883-8987
Just Tomatoes Company
Westley, CA 800-537-1985
Kern Ridge Growers
Arvin, CA 661-854-3141
Kuhlmann's Market Gardens & Greenhouses
Edmonton, AB 780-475-7500
Lakeside Foods
Seymour, WI 920-833-2371
Miss Scarlett's
Chandler, AZ 800-345-6734
National Frozen Foods Corporation
Seattle, WA 206-322-8900
New Harvest Foods
Pulaski, WI 920-822-2578
NORPAC Foods
Lake Oswego, OR 800-733-9311
Omstead Foods Ltd
Wheatley, ON 905-315-8883
Paisley Farms
Willoughby, OH 800-676-8656
Patterson Frozen Foods
Patterson, CA 209-892-2611
Pictsweet Frozen Foods
Bells, TN 731-422-7600
Pioneer Growers Cooperative
Belle Glade, FL 561-996-5211
R.C. McEntire & Company
Columbia, SC 803-799-3388
Ripon Pickle Company
Ripon, WI 800-324-5493
Rousseau Farming Company
Tolleson, AZ 623-936-1600
S. Kennedy Vegetable Lifestock Company
Clear Lake, IA 641-357-4227
Seneca Foods
Marion, NY 315-926-8100
Seneca Foods
Janesville, WI 608-757-6000
Smith Frozen Foods
Weston, OR 541-566-3515
Smith Frozen Foods
Weston, OR 800-547-0203
Strathroy Foods
Strathroy, ON 519-245-4600
Trappe Packing Corporation
Trappe, MD 410-476-3185
Twin City Foods
Stanwood, WA 208-743-5568
Vegetable Juices
Chicago, IL 888-776-9752
William Bolthouse Farms
Bakersfield, CA 661-366-7270

Baby

Sales USA
Salado, TX 800-766-7344

Canned

Arbre Farms Corporation
Walkerville, MI 231-873-3337
Emerling International Foods
Buffalo, NY 716-833-7381

We supply food manufacturers and food service customers worldwide (since 1988) with bulk ingredients including: Fruits & Vegetables; Juice Concentrates; Herbs & Spices; Oils & Vinegars; Flavors & Colors; Honey & Molasses. We also produce PURE MAPLE SYRUP.

Hanover Foods Corporation
Hanover, PA 717-632-6000
Lakeside Foods
Seymour, WI 920-833-2371
New Harvest Foods
Pulaski, WI 920-822-2578
NORPAC Foods
Lake Oswego, OR 800-733-9311
Omstead Foods Ltd
Wheatley, ON 905-315-8883
Seneca Foods
Marion, NY 315-926-8100

Dehydrated

Advanced Spice & Trading
Carrollton, TX 800-872-7811
Tova Industries
Louisville, KY 888-532-8682

Frozen

Arbre Farms Corporation
Walkerville, MI 231-873-3337
Cleugh's Frozen Foods
Buena Park, CA 714-521-1002
Columbia Foods
Quincy, WA 509-787-1585
Emerling International Foods
Buffalo, NY 716-833-7381

We supply food manufacturers and food service customers worldwide (since 1988) with bulk ingredients including: Fruits & Vegetables; Juice Concentrates; Herbs & Spices; Oils & Vinegars; Flavors & Colors; Honey & Molasses. We also produce PURE MAPLE SYRUP.

Hanover Foods Corporation
Hanover, PA 717-632-6000
J.R. Simplot Company
Boise, ID 208-336-2110
Lakeside Foods
Seymour, WI 920-833-2371
National Frozen Foods Corporation
Seattle, WA 206-322-8900
NORPAC Foods
Lake Oswego, OR 800-733-9311
Omstead Foods Ltd
Wheatley, ON 905-315-8883
Pictsweet Frozen Foods
Bells, TN 731-422-7600
Smith Frozen Foods
Weston, OR 541-566-3515
Smith Frozen Foods
Weston, OR 800-547-0203
Strathroy Foods
Strathroy, ON 519-245-4600
Trappe Packing Corporation
Trappe, MD 410-476-3185
Twin City Foods
Stanwood, WA 208-743-5568
Vegetable Juices
Chicago, IL 888-776-9752

Organic

Princeville Canning Company
Princeville, IL 309-385-4301

Peeled

Rousseau Farming Company
Tolleson, AZ 623-936-1600

Cauliflower

Al Pete Meats
Muncie, IN 765-288-8817
Anchor Food Products/ McCain Foods
Appleton, WI 920-734-0627
Crown Packing Company
Salinas, CA 831-424-2067
Exeter Produce & Storage Company
Exeter, ON 800-881-4861
F&S Produce Company
Rosenhayn, NJ 800-886-3316
Great American Appetizers
Nampa, ID 800-282-4834
Indian Rock Produce
Perkasie, PA 800-882-0512
L.I. Cauliflower Association
Riverhead, NY 631-727-2212
Lake Erie Frozen Foods Company
Ashland, OH 800-766-8501
McCain Foods Canada
Toronto, ON 866-622-2461
Mills
Salinas, CA 831-757-1611
Omstead Foods Ltd
Wheatley, ON 905-315-8883
Paradise Products Corporation
Boca Raton, FL 800-826-1235
Patterson Frozen Foods
Patterson, CA 209-892-2611
Pictsweet Frozen Foods
Bells, TN 731-422-7600
RES Food Products International
Green Bay, WI 800-255-3768
Ripon Pickle Company
Ripon, WI 800-324-5493
S&G Products
Nicholasville, KY 800-826-7652

Snowcrest Packer
Abbotsford, BC. . . . 800-265-5332
Sunrise Growers
Placentia, CA 714-630-6292
Tanimura & Antle
Salinas, CA. . . . 831-455-2255
Teixeira Farms
Santa Maria, CA. . . . 805-928-3801
Trappe Packing Corporation
Trappe, MD. . . . 410-476-3185
Vegetable Juices
Chicago, IL. . . . 888-776-9752

Canned

Anchor Food Products/ McCain Foods
Appleton, WI 920-734-0627
Emerling International Foods
Buffalo, NY. . . . 716-833-7381

We supply food manufacturers and food service customers worldwide (since 1988) with bulk ingredients including: Fruits & Vegetables; Juice Concentrates; Herbs & Spices; Oils & Vinegars; Flavors & Colors; Honey & Molasses. We also produce PURE MAPLE SYRUP.

McCain Foods Canada
Toronto, ON 866-622-2461
Omstead Foods Ltd
Wheatley, ON 905-315-8883
Paradise Products Corporation
Boca Raton, FL. . . . 800-826-1235
Seneca Foods
Clyman, WI. . . . 920-696-3331

Frozen

Al Pete Meats
Muncie, IN 765-288-8817
Anchor Food Products/ McCain Foods
Appleton, WI 920-734-0627
Emerling International Foods
Buffalo, NY. . . . 716-833-7381

We supply food manufacturers and food service customers worldwide (since 1988) with bulk ingredients including: Fruits & Vegetables; Juice Concentrates; Herbs & Spices; Oils & Vinegars; Flavors & Colors; Honey & Molasses. We also produce PURE MAPLE SYRUP.

Great American Appetizers
Nampa, ID. . . . 800-282-4834
J.R. Simplot Company
Boise, ID 208-336-2110
McCain Foods Canada
Toronto, ON 866-622-2461
Omstead Foods Ltd
Wheatley, ON 905-315-8883
Pictsweet Frozen Foods
Bells, TN. . . . 731-422-7600
Snowcrest Packer
Abbotsford, BC. . . . 800-265-5332
Trappe Packing Corporation
Trappe, MD. . . . 410-476-3185

Celery

A. Duda Farm Fresh Foods
Belle Glade, FL. . . . 561-996-7621
Crown Packing Company
Salinas, CA 831-424-2067
Dehydrates Inc.
Hewlett, NY 800-983-4443
F&S Produce Company
Rosenhayn, NJ 800-886-3316
JES Foods
Cleveland, OH 216-883-8987
Leach Farms Inc.
Berlin, WI 920-361-1880
Michigan Celery Promotion Cooperative
Hudsonville, MI 616-669-1250
Michigan Freeze Pack
Hart, MI. . . . 231-873-2175
Mills
Salinas, CA 831-757-1611
Nature Quality
San Martin, CA. . . . 408-683-2182
Pioneer Growers Cooperative
Belle Glade, FL. . . . 561-996-5211
R.C. McEntire & Company
Columbia, SC 803-799-3388
Sure Fresh Produce
Santa Maria, CA 888-423-5379
Tanimura & Antle
Salinas, CA 831-455-2255
Teixeira Farms
Santa Maria, CA 805-928-3801
Tri-Counties Packing Company
Salinas, CA 831-422-7841

Canned

A. Duda Farm Fresh Foods
Belle Glade, FL. . . . 561-996-7621
Duda Redifoods
Oviedo, FL 407-365-2111
Emerling International Foods
Buffalo, NY. . . . 716-833-7381

We supply food manufacturers and food service customers worldwide (since 1988) with bulk ingredients including: Fruits & Vegetables; Juice Concentrates; Herbs & Spices; Oils & Vinegars; Flavors & Colors; Honey & Molasses. We also produce PURE MAPLE SYRUP.

Sure Fresh Produce
Santa Maria, CA 888-423-5379

Dehydrated

Advanced Spice & Trading
Carrollton, TX. . . . 800-872-7811
Emerling International Foods
Buffalo, NY. . . . 716-833-7381

We supply food manufacturers and food service customers worldwide (since 1988) with bulk ingredients including: Fruits & Vegetables; Juice Concentrates; Herbs & Spices; Oils & Vinegars; Flavors & Colors; Honey & Molasses. We also produce PURE MAPLE SYRUP.

Tova Industries
Louisville, KY 888-532-8682
Unique Ingredients
Naches, WA. . . . 509-653-1991

Frozen

A. Duda Farm Fresh Foods
Belle Glade, FL. . . . 561-996-7621
Duda Redifoods
Oviedo, FL 407-365-2111
Emerling International Foods
Buffalo, NY. . . . 716-833-7381

We supply food manufacturers and food service customers worldwide (since 1988) with bulk ingredients including: Fruits & Vegetables; Juice Concentrates; Herbs & Spices; Oils & Vinegars; Flavors & Colors; Honey & Molasses. We also produce PURE MAPLE SYRUP.

Leach Farms
Berlin, WI 920-361-1880
Nature Quality
San Martin, CA. . . . 408-683-2182
Sure Fresh Produce
Santa Maria, CA 888-423-5379
Vegetable Juices
Chicago, IL 888-776-9752

Sticks

R.C. McEntire & Company
Columbia, SC 803-799-3388

Cherries

Agvest
Cleveland, OH 216-464-3737
Bob Gordon & Associates
Oak Park, IL 708-524-9611
Bridenbaughs Orchards
Martinsburg, PA 814-793-2364
Brothers International Food Corporation
Rochester, NY. . . . 585-343-3007
Burnette Foods
Elk Rapids, MI 231-264-8116
Cahoon Farms
Wolcott, NY 315-594-8081
Cal-Harvest Marketing
Hanford, CA 559-582-4000
California Fruit Processors
Stockton, CA. . . . 209-931-1760

Castella Imports
Hauppauge, NY 866-227-8355
Cherry Central Cooperative Inc
Traverse City, MI 231-946-1860
Cherry Growers
Grawn, MI. . . . 231-276-9241
Cherry Hut
Traverse City, MI 888-882-4431
Cherry Lane Frozen Fruits
Vineland Station, ON 877-243-7796
Chief Wenatchee
Wenatchee, WA. . . . 509-662-5197
Chieftain Wild Rice Company
Spooner, WI 800-262-6368
Chiquita Brands Intl. ional
Cincinnati, OH 800-438-0015
Christopher Ranch
Gilroy, CA. . . . 408-847-1100
Chukar Cherries
Prosser, WA. . . . 800-624-9544
Coloma Frozen Foods
Coloma, MI. . . . 800-642-2723
Delta Packing Company of Lodi
Lodi, CA 209-334-0811
Diamond Fruit Growers
Odell, OR 541-354-5300
Diana Fruit Company
Santa Clara, CA 408-727-9631
G. L. Mezzetta
American Canyon, CA 707-648-1050
Gray & Company
Forest Grove, OR 503-357-3141
Harner Farms
State College, PA 814-237-7919
J.H. Verbridge & Son
Williamson, NY 315-589-2366
Just Tomatoes Company
Westley, CA. . . . 800-537-1985
Kalustyan Corporation
Union, NJ 908-688-6111
L&S Packing Company
Farmingdale, NY 800-286-6487
Leroux Creek Foods
Hotchkiss, CO. . . . 877-970-5670
M&R Company
Lodi, CA 209-369-4760
Mason County Fruit Packers Cooperative
Ludington, MI. . . . 231-845-6248
Meduri Farms Inc.
Dallas, OR. . . . 503-623-0308
Miss Scarlett's
Chandler, AZ. . . . 800-345-6734
Natural Foods
Toledo, OH 419-537-1713
Niagara Foods
Middleport, NY. . . . 716-735-7722
North Bay Produce
Traverse City, MI 800-678-1941
Northern Fruit Company
Wenatchee, WA. . . . 509-884-6651
Northern Michigan Fruit Company
Omena, MI 231-386-5142
Oneonta Starr Ranch Growers
Wenatchee, WA. . . . 509-663-2191
Oregon Cherry Growers
Salem, OR. . . . 800-367-2536
Oregon Fruit Products Company
Salem, OR. . . . 800-394-9333
Packers Canning Company
Lawton, MI 269-624-4681
Pandol Brothers
Delano, CA 661-725-3755
Paradise
Plant City, FL 800-330-8952
Paradise Products Corporation
Boca Raton, FL. . . . 800-826-1235
Peninsula Fruit Exchange
Traverse City, MI 231-223-4282

Per-Clin Orchards
Bear Lake, MI 231-889-4289
Premier Packing Company
Bakersfield, CA 661-393-3320
Price Cold Storage & Packing Company
Yakima, WA 509-966-4110
Purity Products
Plainview, NY 888-769-7873
Quality Brands
Deland, FL 888-676-2700
Reinhart Foods
Markham, ON 905-754-3500
Shoreline Fruit
Traverse City, MI 800-836-3972
Sill Farms Market
Lawrence, MI 269-674-3755
Smeltzer Orchard Company
Frankfort, MI 231-882-4421
Snowcrest Packer
Abbotsford, BC 800-265-5332
Stadelman Fruit
Zillah, WA 509-829-5145
Symms Fruit Ranch
Caldwell, ID 208-459-4821
Terri Lynn
Elgin, IL 800-323-0775
Timber Crest Farms
Healdsburg, CA 888-374-9325
Trinity Fruit Sales
Fresno, CA 559-433-3777
Triple D Orchards
Empire, MI 866-781-9410
Unique Ingredients
Naches, WA 509-653-1991
United Fruits Corporation
Santa Monica, CA 310-829-0261
Wiard's Orchards
Ypsilanti, MI 734-482-7744
Yakima Fruit & Cold Storage Company
Wapato, WA 509-877-2777

Bing

Chieftain Wild Rice Company
Spooner, WI 800-262-6368

Canned

Arbre Farms Corporation
Walkerville, MI 231-873-3337
Bob Gordon & Associates
Oak Park, IL 708-524-9611
Burnette Foods
Elk Rapids, MI 231-264-8116
Cherry Growers
Grawn, MI 231-276-9241
Emerling International Foods
Buffalo, NY 716-833-7381

We supply food manufacturers and food service customers worldwide (since 1988) with bulk ingredients including: Fruits & Vegetables; Juice Concentrates; Herbs & Spices; Oils & Vinegars; Flavors & Colors; Honey & Molasses. We also produce PURE MAPLE SYRUP.

Independent Food Processors
Sunnyside, WA 509-837-3806
Independent Food Processors Company
Yakima, WA 800-476-5398
L&S Packing Company
Farmingdale, NY 800-286-6487
Northwest Packing Company
Vancouver, WA 800-543-4356
Oregon Cherry Growers
Salem, OR 800-367-2536
Oregon Fruit Products Company
Salem, OR 800-394-9333
Packers Canning Company
Lawton, MI 269-624-4681
Paradise Products Corporation
Boca Raton, FL 800-826-1235
Quality Brands
Deland, FL 888-676-2700
San Benito Foods
Vancouver, WA 800-453-7832
Triple D Orchards
Empire, MI 866-781-9410
Truitt Brothers Inc
Salem, OR 800-547-8712
Unique Ingredients
Naches, WA 509-653-1991

Dried

American Importing Company
Minneapolis, MN 612-331-7000
Atwater Foods
Lyndonville, NY
Chieftain Wild Rice Company
Spooner, WI 800-262-6368
Fastachi
Watertown, MA 800-466-3022
Royal Ridge Fruits
Royal City, WA 509-346-1520
Setton International Foods
Commack, NY 800-227-4397

Frozen

Agvest
Cleveland, OH 216-464-3737
Arbre Farms Corporation
Walkerville, MI 231-873-3337
Cahoon Farms
Wolcott, NY 315-594-8081
Cherry Growers
Grawn, MI 231-276-9241
Cherry Hill Orchards Pelham
Fenwick, ON 905-892-3782
Cherry Lane Frozen Fruits
Vineland Station, ON 877-243-7796
Coloma Frozen Foods
Coloma, MI 800-642-2723
Emerling International Foods
Buffalo, NY 716-833-7381

We supply food manufacturers and food service customers worldwide (since 1988) with bulk ingredients including: Fruits & Vegetables; Juice Concentrates; Herbs & Spices; Oils & Vinegars; Flavors & Colors; Honey & Molasses. We also produce PURE MAPLE SYRUP.

Fruithill
Yamhill, OR 503-662-3926
Great Lakes Packing Company
Kewadin, MI 231-264-5561
Independent Food Processors Company
Yakima, WA 800-476-5398
J.H. Verbridge & Son
Williamson, NY 315-589-2366
Leelanau Fruit Company
Suttons Bay, MI 231-271-3514
Mason County Fruit Packers Cooperative
Ludington, MI 231-845-6248
Muir-Roberts Company
Salt Lake City, UT 800-564-0949
Niagara Foods
Middleport, NY 716-735-7722
Norfood Cherry Growers
Simcoe, ON 519-426-5784
Northern Michigan Fruit Company
Omena, MI 231-386-5142
Oceana Foods
Shelby, MI 231-861-2141
Oregon Cherry Growers
Salem, OR 800-367-2536
Oregon Fruit Products Company
Salem, OR 800-394-9333
Packers Canning Company
Lawton, MI 269-624-4681
Peninsula Fruit Exchange
Traverse City, MI 231-223-4282
Quality Brands
Deland, FL 888-676-2700
Sill Farms Market
Lawrence, MI 269-674-3755
Smeltzer Orchard Company
Frankfort, MI 231-882-4421
Snowcrest Packer
Abbotsford, BC 800-265-5332
Townsend Farms
Fairview, OR 503-666-1780
Triple D Orchards
Empire, MI 866-781-9410
Unique Ingredients
Naches, WA 509-653-1991
Windatt Farms
Picton, ON 613-393-5289

IQF (Individually Quick Frozen)

Northern Michigan Fruit Company
Omena, MI 231-386-5142

Maraschino

A. Camacho
Plant City, FL 800-881-4534
Bob Gordon & Associates
Oak Park, IL 708-524-9611
Diana Fruit Company
Santa Clara, CA 408-727-9631
Eden Processing
Poplar Grove, IL 815-765-2000
Emerling International Foods
Buffalo, NY 716-833-7381

We supply food manufacturers and food service customers worldwide (since 1988) with bulk ingredients including: Fruits & Vegetables; Juice Concentrates; Herbs & Spices; Oils & Vinegars; Flavors & Colors; Honey & Molasses. We also produce PURE MAPLE SYRUP.

Eola Specialty Foods
Gervais, OR 503-390-1425
G. L. Mezzetta
American Canyon, CA 707-648-1050
Gray & Company
Forest Grove, OR 503-357-3141
Johnson Canning Company
Sunnyside, WA 509-837-4188
L&S Packing Company
Farmingdale, NY 800-286-6487
Metzger Specialty Brands
New York, NY 212-957-0055
Oregon Cherry Growers
Salem, OR 800-367-2536
Pacific Choice Brands
Fresno, CA 559-237-5583
Paradise Products Corporation
Boca Raton, FL 800-826-1235
Purity Products
Plainview, NY 888-769-7873
Reinhart Foods
Markham, ON 905-754-3500
Unique Ingredients
Naches, WA 509-653-1991

Sweet

Baker Produce Company
Kennewick, WA 800-624-7553
Northern Michigan Fruit Company
Omena, MI 231-386-5142

Tart

Baker Produce Company
Kennewick, WA 800-624-7553
Cherry Hill Orchards Pelham
Fenwick, ON 905-892-3782
Chieftain Wild Rice Company
Spooner, WI 800-262-6368
Fruit Belt Foods
Lawrence, MI 269-674-3939
Hygeia Dairy Company
McAllen, TX 956-686-0511
Northern Michigan Fruit Company
Omena, MI 231-386-5142

Chicory

Whole Herb Company
Sonoma, CA 707-935-1077

Chives

SupHerb Farms
Turlock, CA 800-787-4372

Frozen culinary herb and specialty vegetable ingredients.

Vegetable Juices
Chicago, IL 888-776-9752

Citrus Fruits

A. Duda & Sons
Oviedo, FL 407-365-2111
A. Duda Farm Fresh Foods
Belle Glade, FL. 561-996-7621
Armistead Citrus Company
Mesa, AZ. 480-830-2491
Ben Hill Griffin, Inc.
Frostproof, FL. 863-635-2251
Brooks Tropicals
Homestead, FL 800-327-4833
Brothers International Food Corporation
Rochester, NY. 585-343-3007
California Citrus Producer
Lindsay, CA 559-562-5169
Corona College Heights Orange & Lemon Associates
Riverside, CA 951-688-1811
Country Pure Foods
Akron, OH. 877-995-8423
Crown Processing Company
Bellflower, CA 562-865-0293
Davidson of Dundee
Dundee, FL 800-294-2266
DiMare International Dmb Packing Corp
Indio, CA. 760-347-3336
DNE World Fruit Sales
Fort Pierce, FL 800-327-6676
Dundee Citrus Growers
Dundee, FL 800-447-1574
Fillmore Piru Citrus Association
Piru, CA 800-524-8787
Golden River Fruit Company
Vero Beach, FL. 772-562-8610
Haines City Citrus Growers Association
Haines City, FL. 800-422-4245
Heller Brothers PackingcCorporation
Winter Garden, FL 407-656-2124
Hunt Brothers Cooperative
Lake Wales, FL. 863-676-9471
Leroy Smith & Sons Inc
Vero Beach, FL. 772-567-3421
Magnolia Citrus Association
Porterville, CA 559-784-4455
Mixon Fruit Farms
Bradenton, FL. 800-608-2525
Oneonta Starr Ranch Growers
Wenatchee, WA. 509-663-2191
Orange Cove Sanger Citrus Association
Orange Cove, CA 559-626-4453
P-R Farms
Clovis, CA 559-299-0201
Reed Lang Farms
Rio Hondo, TX. 956-748-2354
Shields Date Gardens
Indio, CA. 800-414-2555
Sun Orchard of Florida
Haines City, FL. 863-422-5062
Sunkist Growers
Stafford, TX 281-240-6446
Sunkist Growers
Detroit, MI 313-843-4160
Sunkist Growers
Pittsburgh, PA. 412-967-9801
Sunkist Growers
West Chester, OH 513-741-9494
Sunkist Growers
Visalia, CA 559-739-8392
Sunkist Growers
Chelsea, MA 617-884-9750
Sunkist Growers
Buffalo, NY. 716-895-3744
Sunkist Growers
Ontario, CA. 800-798-9005
Sunkist Growers
Cherry Hill, NJ 856-663-2343
Sunkist Growers
Cary, NC 919-859-7380
Tony Vitrano Company
Jessup, MD 800-481-3784
Wileman Bros & Elliott, Inc
Visalia, CA
Yokhol Valley Packing Company
Lindsay, CA 559-562-1327

Peels

Con Yeager Spice Company
Zelienople, PA. 800-222-2460
Crown Processing Company
Bellflower, CA 562-865-0293
Naturex Inc.
South Hackensack, NJ 201-440-5000
Paradise
Plant City, FL 800-330-8952
Vita-Pakt Citrus Company
Covina, CA 626-332-1101

Citrus Peel Products

Eden Processing
Poplar Grove, IL 815-765-2000
Fmali Herb
Santa Cruz, CA. 831-423-7913
Vita-Pakt Citrus Company
Covina, CA 626-332-1101

Coconut & Coconut Products

AFP Advanced Food Products, LLC
Visalia, CA 559-627-2070
American Key Food Products
Closter, NJ. 800-767-0237
Baker's Coconut
Memphis, TN 800-323-1092
C.F. Burger Creamery
Detroit, MI 800-229-2322
Catania-Spagna Corporation
Ayer, MA. 800-343-5522
Coco Rico
Montreal, QC 514-849-5554
Commodities Marketing, Inc.
Edison, NJ. 732-603-5077
Eden Processing
Poplar Grove, IL 815-765-2000
Emerling International Foods
Buffalo, NY. 716-833-7381

We supply food manufacturers and food service customers worldwide (since 1988) with bulk ingredients including: Fruits & Vegetables; Juice Concentrates; Herbs & Spices; Oils & Vinegars; Flavors & Colors; Honey & Molasses. We also produce PURE MAPLE SYRUP.

Far Eastern Coconut Company
Islandia, NY 631-851-8800
Hawaii Candy
Honolulu, HI 808-836-8955
Hialeah Products Company
Hollywood, FL 800-923-3379
L&M Bakery
Lawrence, MA 978-687-7346
Marx Brothers
Birmingham, AL. 800-633-6376
Mehaffie Pies
Dayton, OH. 937-253-1163
Mercado Latino
City of Industry, CA 626-333-6862
Miramar Fruit Trading Company
Doral, FL. 305-883-4774
New England Confectionery Company
Revere, MA. 781-485-4500
Olde Tyme Mercantile
Arroyo Grande, CA. 805-489-7991
Reinhart Foods
Markham, ON. 905-754-3500
Rv Industries
Buford, GA 770-729-8983
Sally Lane's Candy Farm
Paris, TN. 731-642-5801
Sayklly's Candies & Gifts
Escanaba, MI 906-786-3092
Sun Garden Growers
Bard, CA. 800-228-4690
White-Stokes Company
Chicago, IL 800-978-6537
Wisconsin Cheese
Melrose Park, IL. 708-450-0074

Desiccated & Shredded

Commodities Marketing, Inc.
Edison, NJ. 732-603-5077
Emerling International Foods
Buffalo, NY. 716-833-7381

We supply food manufacturers and food service customers worldwide (since 1988) with bulk ingredients including: Fruits & Vegetables; Juice Concentrates; Herbs & Spices; Oils & Vinegars; Flavors & Colors; Honey & Molasses. We also produce PURE MAPLE SYRUP.

Far Eastern Coconut Company
Islandia, NY 631-851-8800
International Coconut Corporation
Elizabeth, NJ. 908-289-1555
Log House Foods
Plymouth, MN. 763-546-8395
Organic Planet
San Francisco, CA 415-765-5590
Rv Industries
Buford, GA 770-729-8983
Service Packing Company
Vancouver, BC 604-681-0264
Setton International Foods
Commack, NY 800-227-4397

Dried

Far Eastern Coconut Company
Islandia, NY 631-851-8800
Hialeah Products Company
Hollywood, FL 800-923-3379

Frozen

Emerling International Foods
Buffalo, NY. 716-833-7381

We supply food manufacturers and food service customers worldwide (since 1988) with bulk ingredients including: Fruits & Vegetables; Juice Concentrates; Herbs & Spices; Oils & Vinegars; Flavors & Colors; Honey & Molasses. We also produce PURE MAPLE SYRUP.

Processed

Far Eastern Coconut Company
Islandia, NY 631-851-8800
Hialeah Products Company
Hollywood, FL 800-923-3379

Collard Greens

Abbott & Cobb, Inc.
Langhorne, PA 800-345-7333
Emerling International Foods
Buffalo, NY. 716-833-7381

We supply food manufacturers and food service customers worldwide (since 1988) with bulk ingredients including: Fruits & Vegetables; Juice Concentrates; Herbs & Spices; Oils & Vinegars; Flavors & Colors; Honey & Molasses. We also produce PURE MAPLE SYRUP.

Frank Capurro & Son
Moss Landing, CA 831-728-3904
Lucks Food Decorating Company
Tacoma, WA 253-383-4815
McCain Foods USA
Colton, CA 800-938-7799
Oxford Frozen Foods Limited
Oxford, NS 902-447-2100
Pictsweet Frozen Foods
Bells, TN. 731-422-7600
Seabrook Brothers & Sons
Seabrook, NJ. 856-455-8080

Canned & Frozen

Allen Canning Company
Siloam Springs, AR 800-234-2553
Lucks Food Decorating Company
Tacoma, WA 253-383-4815
Pictsweet Frozen Foods
Bells, TN. 731-422-7600
Seabrook Brothers & Sons
Seabrook, NJ. 856-455-8080
Walter P. Rawl & Sons
Pelion, SC 803-359-3645

Corn

A. Duda Farm Fresh Foods
Belle Glade, FL. 561-996-7621
A. Lassonde, Inc.
Rougemont, QC 888-477-6663
ADM Milling Company
Shawnee Mission, KS. 800-422-1688
Bush Brothers & Co.
Dandridge, TN .865-509-2361
Christopher Ranch
Gilroy, CA. 408-847-1100
Columbia Foods
Quincy, WA. 509-787-1585
Cooperative Elevator Company
Pigeon, MI 989-453-4500
Coutts Specialty Foods
Boxborough, MA 800-919-2952
Dehydrates Inc.
Hewlett, NY 800-983-4443
Didion Milling
Johnson Creek, WI 920-699-3633
F&S Produce Company
Rosenhayn, NJ 800-886-3316
Faribault Foods
Minneapolis, MN 612-333-6461
Furmano's Foods
Northumberland, PA 877-877-6032
Georgia Vegetable Company
Tifton, GA. 229-386-2374
Indian Rock Produce
Perkasie, PA 800-882-0512
John Copes Food Products
Manheim, PA. .800-745-8211
Just Tomatoes Company
Westley, CA. 800-537-1985
Lakeside Foods
Plainview, MN .507-534-3141
Lakeside Foods
Seymour, WI 920-833-2371
Lucks Food Decorating Company
Tacoma, WA 253-383-4815
McCain Foods Canada
Toronto, ON 866-622-2461
Miss Scarlett's
Chandler, AZ. .800-345-6734
National Frozen Foods Corporation
Seattle, WA 206-322-8900
Natural Way Mills
Middle River, MN. 218-222-3677
Nebraska Salt & Grain Company
Gothenburg, NE 308-537-7191
New Harvest Foods
Pulaski, WI 920-822-2578
Omstead Foods Ltd
Wheatley, ON .905-315-8883
Paisley Farms
Willoughby, OH 800-676-8656
Paradise Products Corporation
Boca Raton, FL. 800-826-1235
Pioneer Growers Cooperative
Belle Glade, FL. 561-996-5211
Produits Ronald
St. Damase, QC. 800-465-0118
Roberts Seed
Axtell, NE. 308-743-2565
Seneca Foods
Marion, NY. 315-926-8100
Seneca Foods
Arlington, MN .507-964-2204
SEW Friel
Queenstown, MD 410-827-8811
Smith Frozen Foods
Weston, OR. 541-566-3515
Sno Pac Foods
Caledonia, MN .800-533-2215
Snowcrest Packer
Abbotsford, BC. 800-265-5332
Sonne
Wahpeton, ND. .800-727-6663
Subco Foods Inc
Sheboygan, WI .800-473-0757
Symons Frozen Foods
Galvin, WA 360-736-1321
Trappe Packing Corporation
Trappe, MD. 410-476-3185
Twin City Foods
Stanwood, WA .208-743-5568
Unique Ingredients
Naches, WA. 509-653-1991
Vegetable Juices
Chicago, IL 888-776-9752
Veronica Foods Company
Oakland, CA 800-370-5554
Weetabix Company
Clinton, MA 800-343-0590
Western Pacific Commodities
Henderson, NV .702-382-8880
Woodland Foods
Gurnee, IL. 847-625-8600
Z&S Distributing
Fresno, CA 800-467-0788

Canned

A. Lassonde, Inc.
Rougemont, QC 888-477-6663
Carriere Foods Inc
Saint-Denis-Sur-Richelie, QC 450-787-3411
Chiquita Processed Foods
Markesan, WI 920-398-2386
Emerling International Foods
Buffalo, NY. 716-833-7381

We supply food manufacturers and food service customers worldwide (since 1988) with bulk ingredients including: Fruits & Vegetables; Juice Concentrates; Herbs & Spices; Oils & Vinegars; Flavors & Colors; Honey & Molasses. We also produce PURE MAPLE SYRUP.

Faribault Foods
Cokato, MN 320-286-2166
Faribault Foods
Minneapolis, MN 612-333-6461
Lakeside Foods
Plainview, MN .507-534-3141
Lakeside Foods
Manitowoc, WI. 920-684-3356
Lakeside Foods
Seymour, WI 920-833-2371
Lodi Canning Company
Lodi, WI 608-592-4236
Lucks Food Decorating Company
Tacoma, WA 253-383-4815
McCain Foods Canada
Toronto, ON 866-622-2461
New Harvest Foods
Pulaski, WI 920-822-2578
Omstead Foods Ltd
Wheatley, ON .905-315-8883
Paradise Products Corporation
Boca Raton, FL. 800-826-1235
Produits Ronald
St. Damase, QC. 800-465-0118
Seneca Foods
Buhl, ID. 208-543-4322
Seneca Foods
Marion, NY. 315-926-8100
Seneca Foods
Montgomery, MN 507-364-8231
Seneca Foods
Blue Earth, MN. 507-526-2131
Seneca Foods
Janesville, WI 608-757-6000
Seneca Foods
Oakfield, WI 920-583-3161
SEW Friel
Queenstown, MD 410-827-8811

Canned & Frozen

Princeville Canning Company
Princeville, IL 309-385-4301

Corn-on-the-Cob

A. Lassonde, Inc.
Rougemont, QC 888-477-6663
Emerling International Foods
Buffalo, NY. 716-833-7381

We supply food manufacturers and food service customers worldwide (since 1988) with bulk ingredients including: Fruits & Vegetables; Juice Concentrates; Herbs & Spices; Oils & Vinegars; Flavors & Colors; Honey & Molasses. We also produce PURE MAPLE SYRUP.

National Frozen Foods Corporation
Seattle, WA 206-322-8900
Pictsweet Frozen Foods
Bells, TN. 731-422-7600
Produits Ronald
St. Damase, QC. 800-465-0118
Smith Frozen Foods
Weston, OR. 541-566-3515
Smith Frozen Foods
Weston, OR. 800-547-0203
Twin City Foods
Stanwood, WA .208-743-5568

Frozen

Bennett's Apples & Cider
Ancaster, ON. 905-648-6878
National Frozen Foods Corporation
Seattle, WA 206-322-8900
Ore-Ida Foods
Pittsburgh, PA .800-892-2401
Pictsweet Frozen Foods
Bells, TN. 731-422-7600
Smith Frozen Foods
Weston, OR. 541-566-3515
Smith Frozen Foods
Weston, OR. 800-547-0203
Twin City Foods
Stanwood, WA .208-743-5568
Vessey & Company
Holtville, CA. 760-356-0130

Frozen

Columbia Foods
Quincy, WA. 509-787-1585
J.R. Simplot Company
Boise, ID 208-336-2110
Lakeside Foods
Plainview, MN .507-534-3141
Lakeside Foods
Manitowoc, WI. 920-684-3356
Lakeside Foods
Seymour, WI 920-833-2371
Lodi Canning Company
Lodi, WI 608-592-4236
Ocean Mist
Castroville, CA .800-962-3738
Omstead Foods Ltd
Wheatley, ON .905-315-8883
Seneca Foods
Marion, NY. 315-926-8100
Seneca Foods
Montgomery, MN 507-364-8231
Smith Frozen Foods
Weston, OR. 541-566-3515
Snowcrest Packer
Abbotsford, BC. 800-265-5332
Symons Frozen Foods
Galvin, WA 360-736-1321
Trappe Packing Corporation
Trappe, MD. 410-476-3185
Zuccaro's Fruit & Produce Company
Minneapolis, MN 612-333-1122

Husks

Woodland Foods
Gurnee, IL. 847-625-8600

Stored

Acme Steak & Seafood Company
Youngstown, OH. 330-270-8000
Seneca Foods
Clyman, WI. 920-696-3331

Sweet

Abbott & Cobb, Inc.
Langhorne, PA .800-345-7333
Christopher Ranch
Gilroy, CA. 408-847-1100
Goebbert's Home Grown Vegetables
South Barrington, IL. 847-428-6727
New Harvest Foods
Pulaski, WI 920-822-2578
T.S. Smith & Sons
Bridgeville, DE. 302-337-8271

Sweet Processed

Woodland Foods
Gurnee, IL. 847-625-8600

Whole

Abbott & Cobb, Inc.
Langhorne, PA .800-345-7333

Crushed

Baldwin Richardson Foods
Frankfort, IL 866-644-2732

Liquid ingredient manufacturer specializing in signature sauces, dessert toppings, beverage/pancake syrups, specialty fruit fillings and condiments.

Clofine Dairy & Food Products
Linwood, NJ 800-441-1001

Emerling International Foods
Buffalo, NY....................... 716-833-7381

We supply food manufacturers and food service customers worldwide (since 1988) with bulk ingredients including: Fruits & Vegetables; Juice Concentrates; Herbs & Spices; Oils & Vinegars; Flavors & Colors; Honey & Molasses. We also produce PURE MAPLE SYRUP.

Richardson Foods Corporation
Macedon, NY 315-986-2807

Crysanthemums

Heritage Farms Dairy
Murfreesboro, TN.................. 615-895-2790

Cucumber

Abbott & Cobb, Inc.
Langhorne, PA 800-345-7333

Ben B. Schwartz & Sons
Detroit, MI 313-841-8300

Carson City Pickle Company
Carson City, MI.................... 989-584-3148

Cates Addis Company
Parkton, NC 800-423-1883

F&S Produce Company
Rosenhayn, NJ 800-886-3316

Georgia Vegetable Company
Tifton, GA........................ 229-386-2374

Nash Produce Company
Nashville, NC 800-334-3032

Pacific Collier Fresh Company
Immokalee, FL 800-226-7274

Rene Produce Distributors
Nogales, AZ 520-281-9014

Russo Farms
Vineland, NJ 856-692-5942

Tony Vitrano Company
Jessup, MD 800-481-3784

United Pickle Products Corporation
Bronx, NY........................ 718-933-6060

Vegetable Juices
Chicago, IL....................... 888-776-9752

Wildcat Produce
McGrew, NE...................... 308-783-2438

Z&S Distributing
Fresno, CA 800-467-0788

for Pickling

Bissett Produce Company
Spring Hope, NC................... 800-849-5073

Dates

American Health & Nutrition
Ann Arbor, MI 734-677-5570

American Importing Company
Minneapolis, MN 612-331-7000

Amport Foods
Minneapolis, MN 800-989-5665

Bard Valley Medjool Date Growers
Yuma, AZ 928-726-0901

Bautista Organic Dates
Mecca, CA 760-396-2337

CalSungold
Indio, CA......................... 760-399-5646

Chieftain Wild Rice Company
Spooner, WI 800-262-6368

Emerling International Foods
Buffalo, NY....................... 716-833-7381

We supply food manufacturers and food service customers worldwide (since 1988) with bulk ingredients including: Fruits & Vegetables; Juice Concentrates; Herbs & Spices; Oils & Vinegars; Flavors & Colors; Honey & Molasses. We also produce PURE MAPLE SYRUP.

Fastachi
Watertown, MA.................... 800-466-3022

Hadley Date Gardens
Thermal, CA 760-399-5191

Kalustyan Corporation
Union, NJ 908-688-6111

Lee Andersons's Covalda Dates
Coachella, CA..................... 760-398-3441

Marin Food Specialties
Byron, CA........................ 925-634-6126

Nut Factory
Spokane Valley, WA 888-239-5288

Purity Foods
Okemos, MI 800-997-7358

Reinhart Foods
Markham, ON..................... 905-754-3500

Royal Medjool Date Gardens
Bard, CA......................... 760-572-0524

Service Packing Company
Vancouver, BC 604-681-0264

Setton International Foods
Commack, NY 800-227-4397

Shields Date Gardens
Indio, CA......................... 800-414-2555

Sun Garden Growers
Bard, CA......................... 800-228-4690

Terri Lynn
Elgin, IL 800-323-0775

Timber Crest Farms
Healdsburg, CA 888-374-9325

Dehydrated

Abbotsford Growers Co-operative
Abbotsford, BC.................... 604-864-0022

Advanced Spice & Trading
Carrollton, TX..................... 800-872-7811

Agvest
Cleveland, OH 216-464-3737

Amport Foods
Minneapolis, MN 800-989-5665

Associated Fruit Company
Phoenix, OR 541-535-1787

Atlantic Blueberry Company
Hammonton, NJ 609-561-8600

Atlantic Quality Spice &Seasonings
New Brunswick, NJ 800-584-0422

Baker Produce Company
Kennewick, WA 800-624-7553

Bay Cities Produce Company
San Leandro, CA................... 510-346-4943

Boekhout Farms
Ontario, NY....................... 315-524-4041

Brady Farms
West Olive, MI 616-842-3916

California Fruit and Tomato Kitchens
Riverbank, CA 209-869-9300

Caltex Foods
Canoga Park, CA 800-522-5839

Carolina Blueberry Association
Garland, NC 910-588-4355

Chazy Orchards
Chazy, NY........................ 518-846-7171

Cherry Central Cooperative Inc
Traverse City, MI 231-946-1860

Cherry Hill Orchards Pelham
Fenwick, ON...................... 905-892-3782

Chooljian Brothers Packing Company
Sanger, CA 559-875-5501

Chukar Cherries
Prosser, WA....................... 800-624-9544

Congdon Orchards
Yakima, WA 509-965-2886

Cooperative Elevator
Pigeon, MI 989-453-4500

Crane & Crane
Brewster, WA 509-689-3447

DeFrancesco & Sons
Firebaugh, CA..................... 209-364-7000

Del Rey Packing Company
Del Rey, CA 559-888-2031

Fig Garden Packing
Fresno, CA 559-275-2191

Fine Dried Foods International
Santa Cruz, CA.................... 831-426-1413

Gilroy Foods
Gilroy, CA........................ 800-921-7502

Henry Broch & Company/APK, Inc.
Libertyville, IL 847-816-6225

Hialeah Products Company
Hollywood, FL 800-923-3379

Jasper Wyman & Son
Milbridge, ME 800-341-1758

Larsen Farms
Hamer, ID 208-662-5501

Larsen of Idaho
Hamer, ID 800-767-6104

Made in Nature
Fresno, CA 800-906-7426

Maine Wild Blueberry Company
Cherryfield, ME 800-243-4005

Mayfield Farms
Caledon, ON 905-846-0506

McCain Foods USA
Colton, CA 800-938-7799

Mercer Processing
Modesto, CA...................... 209-529-0150

Oxford Frozen Foods Limited
Oxford, NS 902-447-2100

Pack Ryt, Inc.
La Quinta, CA..................... 770-771-8880

Paisano Food Products
Elk Grove Village, IL 800-672-4726

Quality Brands
Deland, FL 888-676-2700

Red River Foods
Richmond, VA..................... 800-443-6637

Reinhart Foods
Markham, ON..................... 905-754-3500

RFI Ingredients
Blauvelt, NY...................... 800-962-7663

Scotsburn Dairy Group
Scotsburn, NS..................... 902-485-8023

Seneca Foods
Marion, NY....................... 315-926-8100

Serv-Agen Corporation
Cherry Hill, NJ 856-663-6966

Shields Date Gardens
Indio, CA......................... 800-414-2555

Smeltzer Orchard Company
Frankfort, MI 231-882-4421

Solana Gold Organics
Sebastopol, CA 800-459-1121

Stapleton-Spence PackingCompany
San Jose, CA...................... 800-297-8815

Sterigenics International
Los Angeles, CA................... 800-472-4508

Tastee Apple Inc
Newcomerstown, OH 800-262-7753

Terri Lynn
Elgin, IL 800-323-0775

Timber Crest Farms
Healdsburg, CA 888-374-9325

Tova Industries
Louisville, KY 888-532-8682

Tree Top
Selah, WA 800-367-6571

Tru-Blu Cooperative Associates
New Lisbon, NJ 609-894-8717

Ursula's Island Farms
Seattle, WA 206-762-3113

Valley View Packing Company
San Jose, CA...................... 408-289-8300

Van Drunen Farms
Momence, IL...................... 815-472-3537

W&G Flavors
Hunt Valley, MD................... 410-771-6606

Washington Potato Company
Warden, WA 509-349-8803

Zuccaro's Fruit & Produce Company
Minneapolis, MN 612-333-1122

Freeze Dried

Advanced Spice & Trading
Carrollton, TX..................... 800-872-7811

RFI Ingredients
Blauvelt, NY...................... 800-962-7663

Setton International Foods
Commack, NY 800-227-4397

SupHerb Farms
Turlock, CA 800-787-4372

Frozen culinary herb and specialty vegetable ingredients.

Unique Ingredients
Naches, WA. 509-653-1991
Van Drunen Farms
Momence, IL. 815-472-3537

Dipping Fruit

Confectioners'

Baldwin Richardson Foods
Frankfort, IL 866-644-2732

Liquid ingredient manufacturer specializing in signature sauces, dessert toppings, beverage/pancake syrups, specialty fruit fillings and condiments.

Bella Viva Orchards
Denair, CA 800-552-8218
Terri Lynn
Elgin, IL 800-323-0775

Dried & Dehydrated Fruits

Dehydrated Fruit

Agvest
Cleveland, OH 216-464-3737
American Nut & Chocolate Company
Boston, MA. 800-797-6887
Amport Foods
Minneapolis, MN 800-989-5665
Atlantic Quality Spice &Seasonings
New Brunswick, NJ 800-584-0422
Basic American Foods
Walnut Creek, CA. 800-722-2084
Casados Farms
San Juan Pueblo, NM 505-852-2433
Cherry Central Cooperative Inc
Traverse City, MI 231-946-1860
Chia I Foods Company
South El Monte, CA 626-401-3038
Chukar Cherries
Prosser, WA. 800-624-9544
Desert Valley Date
Coachella, CA. 760-398-0999
Diamond Foods
Fishers, IN. 317-845-5534
Fig Garden Packing
Fresno, CA 559-275-2191
Fine Dried Foods International
Santa Cruz, CA. 831-426-1413
Freeman Industries
Tuckahoe, NY. 800-666-6454
Gilroy Foods
Gilroy, CA. 800-921-7502
Golden Town Apple Products
Rougemont, QC 519-599-6300
Hialeah Products Company
Hollywood, FL 800-923-3379
Hurd Orchards
Holley, NY 585-638-8838
Kamish Food Products
Chicago, IL 773-725-6959
Kozlowski Farms
Forestville, CA 800-473-2767
Leroux Creek Foods
Hotchkiss, CO. 877-970-5670
Made in Nature
Fresno, CA 800-906-7426
Maine Wild Blueberry Company
Cherryfield, ME 800-243-4005
Mariani Packing Company
Vacaville, CA 800-672-8655
Mercer Processing
Modesto, CA. 209-529-0150
Mojave Foods Corporation
Commerce, CA. 323-890-8900
New England Natural Baker
Greenfield, MA. 800-910-2884
Niagara Foods
Middleport, NY. 716-735-7722
Organic Planet
San Francisco, CA 415-765-5590
Ramos Orchards
Winters, CA 530-795-4748
Red River Foods
Richmond, VA. 800-443-6637
Seneca Foods
Marion, NY. 315-926-8100
Seneca Foods Corporation
Marion, NY. 315-926-8100
Shade Foods
New Century, KS 800-225-6312
Shields Date Gardens
Indio, CA. 800-414-2555
Silva International
Momence, IL. 815-472-3535
Specialty Commodities
Fargo, ND 701-282-8222
Specialty Ingredients
Buffalo Grove, IL 847-419-9595
Spice King Corporation
Beverly Hills, CA 310-836-7770
Spreda Group
Louisville, KY. 502-426-9411
Sun Garden Growers
Bard, CA. 800-228-4690
Timber Crest Farms
Healdsburg, CA 888-374-9325
Torn & Glasser
Los Angeles, CA. 800-282-6887
Torn Ranch
Novato, CA 415-506-3000
Ursula's Island Farms
Seattle, WA 206-762-3113
Valley View Packing Company
San Jose, CA. 408-289-8300
Van Drunen Farms
Momence, IL. 815-472-3537
W&G Flavors
Hunt Valley, MD. 410-771-6606
World Nutrition
Scottsdale, AZ. 800-548-2710

Desiccated Fruit

Fig Garden Packing
Fresno, CA 559-275-2191
Gilroy Foods
Gilroy, CA. 800-921-7502
Hialeah Products Company
Hollywood, FL 800-923-3379
Kozlowski Farms
Forestville, CA 800-473-2767
Leroux Creek Foods
Hotchkiss, CO. 877-970-5670
Maine Wild Blueberry Company
Cherryfield, ME 800-243-4005
New England Natural Baker
Greenfield, MA. 800-910-2884
Ramos Orchards
Winters, CA 530-795-4748
San Joaquin Figs
Fresno, 93 559-224-4963
Shade Foods
New Century, KS 800-225-6312
Spreda Group
Louisville, KY. 502-426-9411
Sun Garden Growers
Bard, CA. 800-228-4690

Dried Fruit

A.L. Bazzini Company
Bronx, NY. 800-228-0172
Agrexco USA
Jamaica, NY 718-481-8700
AlpineAire Foods
Rocklin, CA 800-322-6325
Amalgamated Produce
Bridgeport, CT 800-358-3808
American Food Ingredients
Oceanside, CA 760-929-9505
American Health & Nutrition
Ann Arbor, MI 734-677-5570
American Importing Company
Minneapolis, MN 612-331-7000
American Key Food Products
Closter, NJ. 800-767-0237
American Spoon Foods
Petoskey, MI 800-222-5886
Amport Foods
Minneapolis, MN 800-989-5665
Ann's House of Nuts, Inc.
Jessup, MD 301-498-4920
Atwater Foods
Lyndonville, NY
Aurora Products
Stratford, CT. 800-398-1048
Azar Nut Company
El Paso, TX. 800-592-8103
Bella Viva Orchards
Denair, CA 800-552-8218
Blueberry Store
Grand Junction, MI. 877-654-2400
Boghosian Raisin Packing Company
Fowler, CA 559-834-5348
Buchanan Hollow Nut Company
Le Grand, CA 800-532-1500
California Fruit
Sanger, CA 559-266-7117
California Fruit & Nut
Gustine, CA 888-747-8224
California Prune Packing Company
Live Oak, CA 530-671-4200
Casados Farms
San Juan Pueblo, NM 505-852-2433
Chia I Foods Company
South El Monte, CA 626-401-3038
Chieftain Wild Rice Company
Spooner, WI 800-262-6368
Chukar Cherries
Prosser, WA. 800-624-9544
Derco Foods
Fresno, CA 559-435-2664
Desert Valley Date
Coachella, CA. 760-398-0999
Diamond Foods
Fishers, IN. 317-845-5534
Energy Club
Pacoima, CA. 800-688-6887
Fannie May/Fanny Farmer
Chicago, IL 800-333-3629
Fine Dried Foods International
Santa Cruz, CA. 831-426-1413
Ganong Bros Limited Corporate Office
St. Stephen, NB. 888-426-6647
Garry Packing
Del Rey, CA 800-248-2126
Gilroy Foods
Gilroy, CA. 800-921-7502
GNS Foods/Pacific Gold
Arlington, TX 817-795-4671
Gold Pure Foods Products Company
Hempstead, NY. 800-422-4681
Golden Town Apple Products
Rougemont, QC 519-599-6300
Hadley Date Gardens
Thermal, CA 760-399-5191
Harmony Foods Corporation
Fishers, IN. 317-567-2700
Harmony Foods Corporation
Fishers, IN. 800-837-2855
HealthBest
San Marcos, CA 760-752-5230
Healthco Canada Enterprises
Victoria, BC 877-468-2875
Hialeah Products Company
Hollywood, FL 800-923-3379
Hickory Harvest Foods
Akron, OH. 330-644-6887
HP Schmid
San Francisco, CA 415-765-5925
International Food Trade
Amherst, NS 902-667-3013
International Harvest
Mt Vernon, NY 914-699-5600
JF Braun & Sons Inc.
Elizabeth, NJ. 800-997-7177
Just Tomatoes Company
Westley, CA. 800-537-1985
Kalustyan Corporation
Union, NJ 908-688-6111
Kamish Food Products
Chicago, IL 773-725-6959
King Nut Company
Solon, OH 800-860-5464
Kozlowski Farms
Forestville, CA 800-473-2767
Krispy Kernels
Sainte Foy, QC 877-791-9986
Leroux Creek Foods
Hotchkiss, CO. 877-970-5670

Liberty Richter
Saddle Brook, NJ 201-291-8749
Lion Raisins
Selma, CA 559-834-6677
Made in Nature
Fresno, CA 800-906-7426
Maine Wild Blueberry Company
Cherryfield, ME 800-243-4005
Majestic Foods
Huntington, NY 631-424-9444
Mariani Packing Company
Vacaville, CA 800-672-8655
Marx Brothers
Birmingham, AL 800-633-6376
Mayfair Sales
Buffalo, NY 800-248-2881
Meduri Farms Inc.
Dallas, OR 503-623-0308
Mezza
Lake Forest, IL 888-206-6054
Midwest/Northern
Minneapolis, MN 800-328-5502
Natural Foods
Toledo, OH 419-537-1713
New England Natural Baker
Greenfield, MA 800-910-2884
Newtown Foods
Langhorne, PA 215-579-2120
Niagara Foods
Middleport, NY 716-735-7722
Nspired Natural Foods
Boulder, CO 800-434-4246
Nut Factory
Spokane Valley, WA 888-239-5288
Oasis Foods
Planada, CA 209-382-0263
Old Country Farms
East Sandwich, MA 888-707-5558
Organically Grown Company
Eugene, OR 541-689-5320
Osage Pecan Company
Butler, MO 660-679-6137
Pacific Fruit Processors
South Gate, CA 562-531-1770
Pacific Gold Marketing
Fresno, CA
Patsy's Candies
Colorado Springs, CO 866-372-8797
Peloian Packing Company
Dinuba, CA 559-591-0101
Pittsburgh Snax & Nut Company
Pittsburgh, PA 800-404-6887
Primex International Trading Corporation
Los Angeles, CA 310-568-8855
Ramos Orchards
Winters, CA 530-795-4748
Raymond-Hadley Corporation
Spencer, NY 800-252-5220
Red River Foods
Richmond, VA 800-443-6637
Regal Health Foods International
Chicago, IL 773-252-1044
Reinhart Foods
Markham, ON 905-754-3500
Service Packing Company
Vancouver, BC 604-681-0264
Setton International Foods
Commack, NY 800-227-4397
Shade Foods
New Century, KS 800-225-6312
Shields Date Gardens
Indio, CA 800-414-2555
Shoreline Fruit
Traverse City, MI 800-836-3972
Smeltzer Orchard Company
Frankfort, MI 231-882-4421
Snackerz
Commerce, CA 888-576-2253
Society Hill Snacks
Philadelphia, PA 800-595-0050
Solana Gold Organics
Sebastopol, CA 800-459-1121
Spreda Group
Louisville, KY 502-426-9411
Stapleton-Spence PackingCompany
San Jose, CA 800-297-8815
Star Snacks Company
Jersey City, NJ 800-775-9909
Stretch Island Fruit
La Jolla, CA 800-700-9687
Sugar Plum Farm
Plumtree, NC 888-257-0019
Sun Empire Foods
Kerman, CA 800-252-4786
Sun Garden Growers
Bard, CA 800-228-4690
Sun Ridge Farms
Pajaro, CA 831-786-7000
Sunridge Farms
Salinas, CA 831-755-1430
SunRise Commodities
Englewood Cliffs, NJ 201-947-1000
Sunsweet Growers
Yuba City, CA 800-417-2253
Terri Lynn
Elgin, IL 800-323-0775
Timber Crest Farms
Healdsburg, CA 888-374-9325
Todd's
Vernon, CA 800-938-6337
Torn & Glasser
Los Angeles, CA 800-282-6887
TRAINA Foods
Patterson, CA 209-892-5472
Tree Top
Selah, WA 800-367-6571
Trophy Nut
Tipp City, OH 800-219-9004
Tropical
Charlotte, NC 800-220-1413
Tropical
Columbus, OH 800-538-3941
Tropical
Marietta, GA 800-544-3762
Twenty First Century Snacks
Ronkonkoma, NY 800-975-2883
Unique Ingredients
Naches, WA 509-653-1991
Unison
Hacienda Heights, CA 626-917-3668
Ursula's Island Farms
Seattle, WA 206-762-3113
Vacaville Fruit Company
Vacaville, CA 707-448-5292
Valley View Blueberries
Vancouver, WA 360-892-2839
Valley View Packing Company
San Jose, CA 408-289-8300
Van Drunen Farms
Momence, IL 815-472-3537
Vic Rossano Incorporated
Montreal, QC 514-766-5252
Waymouth Farms
New Hope, MN 800-527-0094
Weaver Nut Company
Ephrata, PA 717-738-3781
Woodland Foods
Gurnee, IL 847-625-8600
Z Foods Inc.
Madera, CA 888-400-1015

Fig

Chieftain Wild Rice Company
Spooner, WI 800-262-6368
Fig Garden Packing
Fresno, CA 559-275-2191
Kalustyan Corporation
Union, NJ 908-688-6111
Natural Foods
Toledo, OH 419-537-1713
Nut Factory
Spokane Valley, WA 888-239-5288
San Joaquin Figs
Fresno, 93 559-224-4963
Timber Crest Farms
Healdsburg, CA 888-374-9325
Unique Ingredients
Naches, WA 509-653-1991

Freeze Dried

Brothers International Food Corp
Rochester, NY 888-842-7477
Crispy Green Inc.
Fairfield, NJ 973-679-4515
FDP
Santa Rosa, CA 707-547-1776
Freeze-Dry Products
Santa Rosa, CA 707-547-1776
St. Charles Trading
Lake Saint Louis, MO 800-336-1333
Wolf Canyon Foods
Carmel, CA 831-626-1323

Dried & Dehydrated Vegetables

AgroCepia
Miami, FL 305-704-3488
DeFrancesco & Sons
Firebaugh, CA 209-364-7000
Emerling International Foods
Buffalo, NY 716-833-7381

We supply food manufacturers and food service customers worldwide (since 1988) with bulk ingredients including: Fruits & Vegetables; Juice Concentrates; Herbs & Spices; Oils & Vinegars; Flavors & Colors; Honey & Molasses. We also produce PURE MAPLE SYRUP.

Gilroy Foods
Gilroy, CA 800-921-7502
Healthco Canada Enterprises
Victoria, BC 877-468-2875
Hialeah Products Company
Hollywood, FL 800-923-3379
International Harvest
Mt Vernon, NY 914-699-5600
Jain Ltd
Columbus, OH 614-850-9400
Just the Berries
Los Angeles, CA 213-613-9807
Just Tomatoes Company
Westley, CA 800-537-1985
Made in Nature
Fresno, CA 800-906-7426
Mexnutri
San Luis Potosi, ... 444-841-5625
Mills Brothers International
Tukwila, WA 206-575-3000
Primera Foods
Cameron, WI 800-365-2409
Randag & Associates Inc
Elmhurst, IL 630-530-2830
RFI Ingredients
Blauvelt, NY 800-962-7663
Specialty Ingredients
Buffalo Grove, IL 847-419-9595
Sun Ray International
Davis, CA 530-758-0088

SupHerb Farms
Turlock, CA 800-787-4372

Frozen culinary herb and specialty vegetable ingredients.

Unison
Hacienda Heights, CA 626-917-3668
Van Eeghen International Inc
St Laurent, QC 514-332-6455

Beet Powder

RFI Ingredients
Blauvelt, NY 800-962-7663
Seneca Foods
Clyman, WI 920-696-3331

Bell Peppers

Green

RFI Ingredients
Blauvelt, NY 800-962-7663

Red

RFI Ingredients
Blauvelt, NY 800-962-7663

Broccoli

Chopped

RFI Ingredients
Blauvelt, NY ... 800-962-7663

Cabbage Flakes

RFI Ingredients
Blauvelt, NY ... 800-962-7663

Celery Flakes

RFI Ingredients
Blauvelt, NY ... 800-962-7663

Dehydrated Vegetables

AgroCepia
Miami, FL ... 305-704-3488
American Food Ingredients
Oceanside, CA ... 760-929-9505
Atlantic Quality Spice &Seasonings
New Brunswick, NJ ... 800-584-0422
Caltex Foods
Canoga Park, CA ... 800-522-5839
DeFrancesco & Sons
Firebaugh, CA ... 209-364-7000
Dehydrates Inc.
Hewlett, NY ... 800-983-4443
FDP
Santa Rosa, CA ... 707-547-1776
Freeman Industries
Tuckahoe, NY ... 800-666-6454
Garden Valley Foods
Sutherlin, OR ... 541-459-9565
Gilroy Foods
Gilroy, CA ... 800-921-7502
Henry Broch & Company/APK, Inc.
Libertyville, IL ... 847-816-6225
Idahoan
Lewisville, ID ... 800-635-6100
Inland Empire Foods
Riverside, CA ... 888-452-3267
Larsen Farms
Hamer, ID ... 208-662-5501
Larsen of Idaho
Hamer, ID ... 800-767-6104
Mercer Processing
Modesto, CA ... 209-529-0150
Minnesota Dehydrated Vegetables
Fosston, MN ... 218-435-1997
Mojave Foods Corporation
Commerce, CA ... 323-890-8900
New Season Foods
Forest Grove, OR ... 503-357-7124
Oregon Potato Company
Boardman, OR ... 800-336-6311
Paisano Food Products
Elk Grove Village, IL ... 800-672-4726
Sarant International Commodities
Centereach, NY ... 631-689-2845
Schiff Food Products
North Bergen, NJ ... 201-868-6800
Sensient Dehydrated Flavors
Turlock, CA ... 800-558-9892
Serv-Agen Corporation
Cherry Hill, NJ ... 856-663-6966
Silva International
Momence, IL ... 815-472-3535
South Mill Distribution
Kennett Square, PA ... 610-444-4800
Spice King Corporation
Beverly Hills, CA ... 310-836-7770
Sterigenics International
Los Angeles, CA ... 800-472-4508
Two Guys Spice Company
Jacksonville, FL ... 800-874-5656
Unified Foods
San Marcos, CA ... 760-744-7225
Vauxhall Foods
Vauxhall, AB ... 403-654-2771
Washington Potato Company
Warden, WA ... 509-349-8803
World Spice
Roselle, NJ ... 800-234-1060

Desiccated Vegetables

DeFrancesco & Sons
Firebaugh, CA ... 209-364-7000

Gilroy Foods
Gilroy, CA ... 800-921-7502

Dried Chives

SupHerb Farms
Turlock, CA ... 800-787-4372

Frozen culinary herb and specialty vegetable ingredients.

Eggplant

Setton International Foods
Commack, NY ... 800-227-4397

Freeze Dried

American Food Ingredients
Oceanside, CA ... 760-929-9505
Dno
Columbus, OH ... 800-686-2366
FDP
Santa Rosa, CA ... 707-547-1776
Freeze-Dry Products
Santa Rosa, CA ... 707-547-1776
Hanover Foods Corp
Hanover, PA ... 717-632-6000
Hanover Foods Corporation
Hanover, PA ... 717-632-6000
Ocean Mist
Castroville, CA ... 800-962-3738
RFI Ingredients
Blauvelt, NY ... 800-962-7663

SupHerb Farms
Turlock, CA ... 800-787-4372

Frozen culinary herb and specialty vegetable ingredients.

Wolf Canyon Foods
Carmel, CA ... 831-626-1323
Zuccaro's Fruit & Produce Company
Minneapolis, MN ... 612-333-1122

Leeks - Chopped

RFI Ingredients
Blauvelt, NY ... 800-962-7663

Mushrooms

Chieftain Wild Rice Company
Spooner, WI ... 800-262-6368
D'Artagnan
Newark, NJ ... 800-327-8246
North American Reishi/Nammex
Gibsons, BC ... 604-886-7799
South Mill Distribution
Kennett Square, PA ... 610-444-4800

Black Trumpets

D'Artagnan
Newark, NJ ... 800-327-8246

Freeze Dried

L.K. Bowman Company
Hanover, PA ... 800-853-1919

Morels Whole

D'Artagnan
Newark, NJ ... 800-327-8246

Porcini

D'Artagnan
Newark, NJ ... 800-327-8246

Onion

Dehydrated

Advanced Spice & Trading
Carrollton, TX ... 800-872-7811
American Key Food Products
Closter, NJ ... 800-767-0237
Atlantic Quality Spice &Seasonings
New Brunswick, NJ ... 800-584-0422
DeFrancesco & Sons
Firebaugh, CA ... 209-364-7000
Emerling International Foods
Buffalo, NY ... 716-833-7381

We supply food manufacturers and food service customers worldwide (since 1988) with bulk ingredients including: Fruits & Vegetables; Juice Concentrates; Herbs & Spices; Oils & Vinegars; Flavors & Colors; Honey & Molasses. We also produce PURE MAPLE SYRUP.

Gilroy Foods
Gilroy, CA ... 800-921-7502
Jain Ltd
Columbus, OH ... 614-850-9400
Schiff Food Products
North Bergen, NJ ... 201-868-6800
Swagger Foods Corporation
Vernon Hills, IL ... 847-913-1200

Granulated

Acme Steak & Seafood Company
Youngstown, OH ... 330-270-8000
Allen Canning Company
Siloam Springs, AR ... 800-234-2553
B&M
Portland, ME ... 207-772-7043
Basic American Foods
Blackfoot, ID ... 800-227-4050
Beckman & Gast Company
Saint Henry, OH ... 419-678-4195
Bottomline Foods
Davie, FL ... 954-843-0562
Bryant Preserving Company
Alma, AR ... 800-634-2413
Cut Above Foods
Carlsbad, CA ... 760-931-6777
H.K. Canning
Ventura, CA ... 805-652-1392
Heinz Company of Canada
North York, ON ... 877-574-3469
Hye Cuisine
Del Rey, CA ... 559-834-3000
Lakeside Foods
Mondovi, WI ... 715-926-5075
Les Aliments Livabec Foods
Sherrington, QC ... 450-454-7971
Lucerne Foods
Lethbridge, AB ... 403-328-5501
McCain Foods USA
Colton, CA ... 800-938-7799
Nor-Cliff Farms
Port Colborne, ON ... 905-835-0808
Oxford Frozen Foods Limited
Oxford, NS ... 902-447-2100
Pacific Valley Foods
Bellevue, WA ... 425-643-1805
Poynette Distribution Center
Poynette, WI ... 608-635-4396
Princeville Canning Company
Princeville, IL ... 309-385-4301
Seneca Foods
Clyman, WI ... 920-696-3331
Supreme Dairy Farms Company
Warwick, RI ... 401-739-8180

Minced

Chieftain Wild Rice Company
Spooner, WI ... 800-262-6368

for Dehydration

Ful-Flav-R Foods
Alamo, CA ... 925-838-0300

Peas - Air-dried

Allen Canning Company
Siloam Springs, AR ... 800-234-2553
Bryant Preserving Company
Alma, AR ... 800-634-2413

Oxford Frozen Foods Limited
Oxford, NS 902-447-2100

Shallots - Freeze Dried

Oxford Frozen Foods Limited
Oxford, NS 902-447-2100
RFI Ingredients
Blauvelt, NY 800-962-7663

SupHerb Farms
Turlock, CA 800-787-4372

Frozen culinary herb and specialty vegetable ingredients.

Soup Blend

Sentry Seasonings
Elmhurst, IL 630-530-5370

The product development experts of Sentry Seasonings are eager to offer the assistance and hands-on experience to food processors of all sizes. Sentry Seasonings will ensure the consistent high quality and repeat sales of your products, whether you choose one of our many off-the-shelf Bench Mark products or a modified version to meet your preferences. Sentry Seasonings can also duplicate and/or improve your present flavor profile; formulate, blend and package specifically for your requirements.

Spinach Powder

RFI Ingredients
Blauvelt, NY 800-962-7663

Tomatoes

Halves

Bryant Preserving Company
Alma, AR 800-634-2413
De Bruyn Produce Company
Zeeland, MI 800-733-9177
Dno
Columbus, OH 800-686-2366
Oxford Frozen Foods Limited
Oxford, NS 902-447-2100
Zuccaro's Fruit & Produce Company
Minneapolis, MN 612-333-1122

Tomato Powder

Bryant Preserving Company
Alma, AR 800-634-2413
De Bruyn Produce Company
Zeeland, MI 800-733-9177

Eggplant

Buona Vita
Bridgeton, NJ 856-453-7972
Castella Imports
Hauppauge, NY 866-227-8355
Dolce Nonna
Whitestone, NY 718-767-3501
Dominex
St Augustine, FL 904-810-2132
Georgia Vegetable Company
Tifton, GA 229-386-2374
Goebbert's Home Grown Vegetables
South Barrington, IL 847-428-6727
Indian Rock Produce
Perkasie, PA 800-882-0512
L&S Packing Company
Farmingdale, NY 800-286-6487
M&R Company
Lodi, CA 209-369-4760
McCain Foods USA
Colton, CA 800-938-7799
Michigan Freeze Pack
Hart, MI 231-873-2175
Miss Scarlett's
Chandler, AZ 800-345-6734
Ocean Mist
Castroville, CA 800-962-3738
Rene Produce Distributors
Nogales, AZ 520-281-9014
Russo Farms
Vineland, NJ 856-692-5942
Turris Italian Foods
Roseville, MI 586-773-6010
Vegetable Juices
Chicago, IL 888-776-9752
Z&S Distributing
Fresno, CA 800-467-0788

Figs

American Health & Nutrition
Ann Arbor, MI 734-677-5570
Chieftain Wild Rice Company
Spooner, WI 800-262-6368
DeBenedetto Farms
Fresno, CA 559-276-3447
Fig Garden Packing
Fresno, CA 559-275-2191
Figamajigs
Petaluma, CA 707-992-0023
Hadley Date Gardens
Thermal, CA 760-399-5191
Kalashian Packing Company
Fresno, CA 559-237-4287
Kalustyan Corporation
Union, NJ 908-688-6111
Meridian Nut Growers
Clovis, CA 559-458-7272
Natural Foods
Toledo, OH 419-537-1713
Oasis Foods
Planada, CA 209-382-0263
Purity Foods
Okemos, MI 800-997-7358
Service Packing Company
Vancouver, BC 604-681-0264
Setton International Foods
Commack, NY 800-227-4397
Terri Lynn
Elgin, IL 800-323-0775
Timber Crest Farms
Healdsburg, CA 888-374-9325
Valley Fig Growers
Fresno, CA 559-237-3893
Wawona Packing Company
Cutler, CA 559-528-9729

Canned

Oasis Foods
Planada, CA 209-382-0263

Frozen

Freeze-Dry Ingredients
Berkeley, IL 708-544-1880

Fire Roasted Vegetables

SupHerb Farms
Turlock, CA 800-787-4372

Frozen culinary herb and specialty vegetable ingredients.

Flowers - Edible

Fmali Herb
Santa Cruz, CA 831-423-7913
Generation Farms
Rice, TX 903-326-4263
Green House Fine Herbs
Encinitas, CA 760-942-5371

Fresh Fruit

Agrinorthwest
Kennewick, WA 509-734-1195
Bay Cities Produce Company
San Leandro, CA 510-346-4943
BelleHarvest Sales
Belding, MI 800-452-7753
Del Monte Fresh Produce
Coral Gables, FL 800-950-3683
Diamond Blueberry
Hammonton, NJ 609-561-3661
Dole Food Company
Westlake Village, CA 818-879-6600
Driscoll Strawberry Associates
Watsonville, CA 831-763-5100
Family Tree Farms
Reedley, CA 559-591-6280
Florida Citrus
Bartow, FL 863-537-3999
G&G Marketing
Naples, FL 239-593-4564
Glacier Foods
Sanger, CA 559-875-3354
Golden Town Apple Products
Rougemont, QC 519-599-6300
Maui Pineapple Company
Kahului, HI 808-877-3351
Modoc Orchard Company
Medford, OR 541-535-1437
Muir-Roberts Company
Salt Lake City, UT 800-564-0949
Nash Finch Company
Statesboro, GA 912-681-4580
Silver Creek Farms
Twin Falls, ID 208-736-0829
Snokist Growers
Yakima, WA 800-377-2857
Sun Rich Fresh Foods, Inc
Corona, CA 800-735-3801
Townsend Farms
Fairview, OR 503-666-1780
Verdelli Farms
Harrisburg, PA 800-422-8344
W.F. Cosart Packing Company
Exeter, CA 559-592-2821
Washington Fruit & Produce Company
Yakima, WA 509-457-6177

Fresh Vegetables

Bay Cities Produce Company
San Leandro, CA 510-346-4943
BelleHarvest Sales
Belding, MI 800-452-7753
Boskovich Farms
Oxnard, CA 805-487-2299
Dole Food Company
Westlake Village, CA 818-879-6600
G&G Marketing
Naples, FL 239-593-4564
Glacier Foods
Sanger, CA 559-875-3354
Hanover Foods Corporation
Hanover, PA 717-632-6000
Lakeside Foods
Seymour, WI 920-833-2371
Lennox Farm
Shelburne, ON 519-925-6444
Monterey Mushrooms
Watsonville, CA 800-333-6874
Monterey Mushrooms
Watsonville, CA 831-763-5300
Muir-Roberts Company
Salt Lake City, UT 800-564-0949
Musco Olive Products
Tracy, CA 800-523-9828
Nash Finch Company
Statesboro, GA 912-681-4580
Omstead Foods Ltd
Wheatley, ON 905-315-8883
R.C. McEntire & Company
Columbia, SC 803-799-3388
Silver Creek Farms
Twin Falls, ID 208-736-0829
Sungarden Sprouts
Cookeville, TN 931-526-1106
Verdelli Farms
Harrisburg, PA 800-422-8344
Western Pacific Commodities
Henderson, NV 702-382-8880

Frozen Fruit

Abbotsford Growers Co-operative
Abbotsford, BC 604-864-0022
Agvest
Franklin, ME 207-565-3303

Agvest
Cleveland, OH 216-464-3737
Assouline & Ting
Huntingdon Valley, PA 800-521-4491
Bay Cities Produce Company
San Leandro, CA. 510-346-4943
Beta Pure Foods
Aptos, CA 831-685-6565
Cahoon Farms
Wolcott, NY 315-594-8081
Canada Safeway Limited
Abbotsford, BC. 604-854-1191
Carriere Foods Inc
Saint-Denis-Sur-Richelie, QC 450-787-3411
Cherry Growers
Grawn, MI. 231-276-9241
Cherry Lane Frozen Fruits
Vineland Station, ON 877-243-7796
Chiquita Brands Intl. ional
Cincinnati, OH 800-438-0015
Clermont
Hillsboro, OR 503-648-8544
Cleugh's Frozen Foods
Buena Park, CA 714-521-1002
Clofine Dairy & Food Products
Linwood, NJ 800-441-1001
Coloma Frozen Foods
Coloma, MI. 800-642-2723
ConAgra Grocery Products
Irvine, CA 714-680-1000
Contessa Food Products
San Pedro, CA. 310-832-8000
Decker Farms
Hillsboro, OR 503-628-1532
Diamond Blueberry
Hammonton, NJ 609-561-3661
Dole Food Company
Westlake Village, CA 818-879-6600
E.W. Bowker Company
Pemberton, NJ. 609-894-9508
Eckert Cold Storage
Escalon, CA 209-838-4040
Emerling International Foods
Buffalo, NY. 716-833-7381

We supply food manufacturers and food service customers worldwide (since 1988) with bulk ingredients including: Fruits & Vegetables; Juice Concentrates; Herbs & Spices; Oils & Vinegars; Flavors & Colors; Honey & Molasses. We also produce PURE MAPLE SYRUP.

Enfield Farms
Lynden, WA 360-354-3019
Ever Fresh Fruit Company
Boring, OR 800-239-8026
Family Tradition Foods
Wheatley, ON 519-825-4673
Freeze-Dry Products
Santa Rosa, CA. 707-547-1776
Frozfruit Corporation
Gardena, CA. 310-217-1034
Frozsun Foods
Placentia, CA 714-630-6292
Fruit Belt Foods
Lawrence, MI 269-674-3939
Glacier Foods
Sanger, CA 559-875-3354
Global Trading
Buena Park, CA
Golden Town Apple Products
Rougemont, QC 519-599-6300
Grow-Pac
Cornelius, OR 503-357-9691
Hartog Rahal Foods
New York, NY 212-687-2000
Hiscock Enterprises
Brigus, NL. 709-528-4577
Inn Foods
Watsonville, CA 831-724-2026
Interfrost
East Rochester, NY. 585-381-0320
International Food Trade
Amherst, NS 902-667-3013
J.H. Verbridge & Son
Williamson, NY 315-589-2366
Jasper Wyman & Son
Milbridge, ME 800-341-1758
JR Wood/Big Valley
Atwater, CA 209-358-5643
JRL
Vineland, NJ 856-690-9000
Kerr Concentrates
Salem, OR. 800-910-5377
Maine Wild Blueberry Company
Cherryfield, ME 800-243-4005
Majestic Foods
Huntington, NY 631-424-9444
Mason County Fruit Packers Cooperative
Ludington, MI. 231-845-6248
Mercer Foods
Modesto, CA. 209-529-0150
Midwest Frozen Foods, Inc.
Hanover Park, IL. 866-784-0123
Milne Fruit Products
Prosser, WA. 509-786-2611
National Frozen Foods Corporation
Seattle, WA 206-322-8900
Niagara Foods
Middleport, NY. 716-735-7722
Northern Michigan Fruit Company
Omena, MI 231-386-5142
Oasis Foods
Planada, CA 209-382-0263
Ocean Spray Cranberries
Lakeville-Middleboro, MA 800-662-3263
Oceana Foods
Shelby, MI. 231-861-2141
Omstead Foods Ltd
Wheatley, ON 905-315-8883
Ore-Ida Foods
Pittsburgh, PA 800-892-2401
Oregon Cherry Growers
Salem, OR. 800-367-2536
Oregon Fruit Products Company
Salem, OR. 800-394-9333
Overlake Foods Corporation
Olympia, WA 800-683-1078
Pacific Blueberries
Rochester, WA 360-273-5405
Pacific Coast Fruit Company
Portland, OR 503-234-6411
Paris Foods Corporation
Trappe, MD. 410-476-3185
Patterson Frozen Foods
Patterson, CA 209-892-2611
Quality Brands
Deland, FL 888-676-2700
Rain Sweet
Salem, OR. 800-363-4293
Ravifruit
Hackensack, NJ. 201-939-5656
Seneca Foods Corporation
Marion, NY. 315-926-8100
Sill Farms Market
Lawrence, MI 269-674-3755
Smeltzer Orchard Company
Frankfort, MI 231-882-4421
Snowcrest Packer
Abbotsford, BC. 800-265-5332
Sparboe Companies
Los Angeles, CA. 213-626-7538
SunMeadow Family of Products
Saint Petersburg, FL 727-573-2211
Superior Foods
Watsonville, CA 831-728-3691
Symons Frozen Foods
Galvin, WA. 360-736-1321
Tatangelo's Wholesale Fruit & Vegetables
Woodbridge, ON. 877-328-8503
Townsend Farms
Fairview, OR. 503-666-1780
Tree Top
Selah, WA 800-367-6571
Triple D Orchards
Empire, MI 866-781-9410
Unique Ingredients
Naches, WA. 509-653-1991
VIP Sales Company
Hayward, CA 866-536-8008
Webster Farms
Cambridge Station, NS. 902-538-9492

Berries

Agvest
Franklin, ME. 207-565-3303
Cherry Central Cooperative Inc
Traverse City, MI 231-946-1860

Frozen Vegetables

Ajinomoto Frozen Foods USA
Portland, OR 503-286-6548
Al Pete Meats
Muncie, IN 765-288-8817
Anchor Food Products/ McCain Foods
Appleton, WI 920-734-0627
Appleton Produce Company
Weiser, ID 208-414-3352
Beta Pure Foods
Aptos, CA 831-685-6565
Boskovich Farms
Oxnard, CA. 805-487-2299
Bright Harvest Sweet Potato Company
Clarksville, AR 800-793-7440
Brooks Food Group Corporate Office
Bedford, VA 800-873-4934
Canada Safeway Limited
Abbotsford, BC. 604-854-1191
Carando Gourmet Frozen Foods
Agawam, MA 888-227-2636
Carriere Foods Inc
Saint-Denis-Sur-Richelie, QC 450-787-3411
Cavendish Farms
Jamestown, ND. 888-284-5687
Cavendish Farms
Dieppe, NB 888-883-7437
Cleugh's Frozen Foods
Buena Park, CA 714-521-1002
Coloma Frozen Foods
Coloma, MI. 800-642-2723
Columbia Foods
Snohomish, WA 360-568-0838
Columbia Foods
Quincy, WA. 509-787-1585
ConAgra Grocery Products
Archbold, OH 419-445-8015
ConAgra Grocery Products
Irvine, CA 714-680-1000
Contessa Food Products
San Pedro, CA. 310-832-8000
Crown Point
St John, IN 219-365-3200
Dairy King Milk Farms/Foodservice
Whitter, CA. 800-900-6455
Deep Foods
Union, NJ 908-810-7500
Dickinson Frozen Foods
Fruitland, ID 208-452-5200
Eckert Cold Storage
Escalon, CA 209-838-4040
Family Tradition Foods
Wheatley, ON 519-825-4673
Faribault Foods
Cokato, MN 320-286-2166
Faribault Foods
Minneapolis, MN 612-333-6461
Freeze-Dry Products
Santa Rosa, CA. 707-547-1776
Fresh Frozen Foods
Jefferson, GA 800-277-9851
Fruit Belt Foods
Lawrence, MI 269-674-3939
George L. Wells Meat Company
Philadelphia, PA 800-523-1730
Glacier Foods
Sanger, CA 559-875-3354
Great American Appetizers
Nampa, ID. 800-282-4834
Hanover Foods Corporation
Hanover, PA 717-632-6000
Hartford City Foam Pack aging & Converting
Hartford City, IN. 765-348-2500
Hermann Pickle Farm
Garrettsville, OH. 800-245-2696
Hunt-Wesson Food Service Company
Rochester, NY. 866-484-8676
Inn Foods
Watsonville, CA 831-724-2026
Interfrost
East Rochester, NY. 585-381-0320
J G Townsend Jr & Company
Georgetown, DE 302-856-2525
J.R. Simplot Company
Boise, ID 208-336-2110

John Copes Food Products
Manheim, PA. 800-745-8211
JR Wood/Big Valley
Atwater, CA 209-358-5643
Juanita's Foods
Wilmington, CA 310-834-5339
Lakeside Foods
Brooten, MN. 320-346-2900
Lakeside Foods
Plainview, MN 507-534-3141
Lakeside Foods
Manitowoc, WI. 920-684-3356
Lakeside Foods
Seymour, WI. 920-833-2371
Leach Farms
Berlin, WI 920-361-1880
Lennox Farm
Shelburne, ON 519-925-6444
Lodi Canning Company
Lodi, WI 608-592-4236
Mercer Foods
Modesto, CA. 209-529-0150
Miami Purveyors
Miami, FL. 305-262-6170
Midwest Frozen Foods, Inc.
Hanover Park, IL. 866-784-0123
Milroy Canning Company
Milroy, IN 765-629-2221
Monterey Mushrooms
Watsonville, CA 800-333-6874
Monticello Canning Company
Crossville, TN. 931-484-3696
National Frozen Foods Corporation
Seattle, WA. 206-322-8900
Nature Quality
San Martin, CA. 408-683-2182
New Meridian
Eaton, IN. 765-396-3344
Niagara Foods
Middleport, NY. 716-735-7722
NORPAC Foods
Stayton, OR. 503-769-2101
NORPAC Foods
Lake Oswego, OR. 800-733-9311
Oceana Foods
Shelby, MI. 231-861-2141
Ore-Ida Foods
Pittsburgh, PA. 800-892-2401
Oregon Potato Company
Boardman, OR 800-336-6311
Paisley Farms
Willoughby, OH 800-676-8656
Paris Foods Corporation
Trappe, MD. 410-476-3185
Patterson Frozen Foods
Patterson, CA 209-892-2611
Pictsweet Frozen Foods
Bells, TN. 731-422-7600
Rain Sweet
Salem, OR. 800-363-4293
Ray Brothers & Noble Canning Company
Hobbs, IN 765-675-7451
Red Gold
Elwood, IN 877-748-9798
Rich-Seapak Corporation
Brownsville, TX 956-542-0001
Roca Food Sales
Roswell, GA 770-993-0030
Seabrook Brothers & Sons
Seabrook, NJ. 856-455-8080
Seenergy Foods
Woodbridge, ON. 800-609-7674
Seneca Foods
Marion, NY. 315-926-8100
Seneca Foods Corporation
Marion, NY. 315-926-8100
Simplot Food Group
Boise, ID. 800-572-7783
Smeltzer Orchard Company
Frankfort, MI 231-882-4421
Smith Frozen Foods
Weston, OR. 541-566-3515
Smith Frozen Foods
Weston, OR. 800-547-0203
Snowcrest Packer
Abbotsford, BC. 800-265-5332
Strathroy Foods
Strathroy, ON 519-245-4600
Sungarden Sprouts
Cookeville, TN 931-526-1106
Superior Foods
Watsonville, CA 831-728-3691

SupHerb Farms
Turlock, CA 800-787-4372

Frozen culinary herb and specialty vegetable ingredients.

Symons Frozen Foods
Galvin, WA. 360-736-1321
Tatangelo's Wholesale Fruit & Vegetables
Woodbridge, ON. 877-328-8503
Trans Pecos Foods
San Antonio, TX. 210-228-0896
Trappe Packing Corporation
Trappe, MD. 410-476-3185
Twin City Foods
Stanwood, WA 208-743-5568
Unique Ingredients
Naches, WA. 509-653-1991
Van De Walle Farms
San Antonio, TX. 210-436-5551
Van Drunen Farms
Momence, IL. 815-472-3537
VIP Sales Company
Hayward, CA 866-536-8008
Washington Potato Company
Warden, WA 509-349-8803
Washington Rhubarb Growers Association
Sumner, WA 800-435-9911
Webster Farms
Cambridge Station, NS. 902-538-9492
Westin
Omaha, NE 800-228-6098
Wornick Company
Cincinnati, OH 800-860-4555

Fruit

A. Duda Farm Fresh Foods
Belle Glade, FL. 561-996-7621
A. Gagliano Company
Milwaukee, WI. 800-272-1516
Adobe Creek Packing
Kelseyville, CA. 707-279-4204
Agvest
Cleveland, OH 216-464-3737
Alamance Foods/Triton Water Company
Burlington, NC 800-476-9111
American Food Products
Methuen, MA 978-682-1855
American Yeast/Lallemand
Pembroke, NH. 866-920-9885
Amport Foods
Minneapolis, MN 800-989-5665
Anastasia Confections Inc.
Orlando, FL. 800-329-7100
Applewood Orchards
Deerfield, MI 800-447-3854
Arcor USA
Miami, FL. 800-572-7267
Ariel Natural Foods
Bellevue, WA 425-637-3345
Atlanta Bread Company
Smyrna, GA 800-398-3728
Ben B. Schwartz & Sons
Detroit, MI 313-841-8300
Bilgore's Groves
Clearwater, FL 727-442-2171
Bob Gordon & Associates
Oak Park, IL 708-524-9611
Bridenbaughs Orchards
Martinsburg, PA 814-793-2364
Burnette Foods
Elk Rapids, MI 231-264-8116
Burnette Foods
Hartford, MI 616-621-3181
Cahoon Farms
Wolcott, NY 315-594-8081
California Citrus Producer
Lindsay, CA 559-562-5169
Casados Farms
San Juan Pueblo, NM 505-852-2433
Cascadian Farm & MUIR Glen
Sedro Woolley, WA. 360-855-0100
Cherry Lane Frozen Fruits
Vineland Station, ON 877-243-7796

Chieftain Wild Rice Company
Spooner, WI 800-262-6368
Chiquita Brands Intl. ional
Cincinnati, OH 800-438-0015
Chudleigh's
Milton, ON 905-878-8781
Chukar Cherries
Prosser, WA. 800-624-9544
Cinnabar Specialty Foods
Prescott, AZ 866-293-6433
Citrus Citrosuco North America
Lake Wales, FL. 800-356-4592
Classic Commissary
Binghamton, NY. 800-929-3486
Clements Foods Company
Oklahoma City, OK 800-654-8355
Clermont
Hillsboro, OR 503-648-8544
Cleugh's Frozen Foods
Buena Park, CA 714-521-1002
Concannon Vineyard
Livermore, CA 800-258-9866
Concord Foods
Brockton, MA. 508-580-1700
Decas Cranberry Products
Carver, MA 800-649-9811
Del Mar Food Products Corporation
Watsonville, CA 831-722-3516
Del Monte Fresh Produce
Coral Gables, FL. 800-950-3683
Del Monte Fresh Produce
Kankakee, IL. 815-936-7400
Delta Packing Company of Lodi
Lodi, CA 209-334-0811
Desert Valley Date
Coachella, CA. 760-398-0999
Diamond Blueberry
Hammonton, NJ 609-561-3661
Diamond Foods
Fishers, IN. 317-845-5534
Diamond Fruit Growers
Odell, OR 541-354-5300
Diana Fruit Company
Santa Clara, CA 408-727-9631
DMH Ingredients
Libertyville, IL 847-362-9977
Dole Food Company
Westlake Village, CA 818-879-6600
Driscoll Strawberry Associates
Watsonville, CA 831-763-5100
E. Waldo Ward & Son Corporation
Sierra Madre, CA 800-355-9273
E.D. Smith Foods Ltd
Winona, ON 800-263-9246
E.W. Bowker Company
Pemberton, NJ. 609-894-9508
Eckert Cold Storage
Escalon, CA 209-838-4040
El Brands
Ozark, AL 334-445-2828
Energy Club
Pacoima, CA. 800-688-6887
Enfield Farms
Lynden, WA 360-354-3019
Ever Fresh Fruit Company
Boring, OR 800-239-8026
Family Tree Farms
Reedley, CA 559-591-6280
Fannie May/Fanny Farmer
Chicago, IL. 800-333-3629
Fernando C Pujals & Bros
Guaynabo, PR. 787-792-3080
Fillmore Piru Citrus Association
Piru, CA 800-524-8787
Fine Dried Foods International
Santa Cruz, CA. 831-426-1413
Fine Foods Northwest
Seattle, WA. 800-862-3965
Firestone Packing Company
Vancouver, WA. 360-695-9484
Flippin-Seaman
Tyro, VA 434-277-5828
Forakers Joy Orchard
Malaga, WA 509-663-6097
Freeze-Dry Products
Santa Rosa, CA. 707-547-1776
Frozfruit Corporation
Gardena, CA 310-217-1034
Frozsun Foods
Placentia, CA 714-630-6292
Fruit Fillings
Fresno, CA 559-237-4715

G&G Marketing
Naples, FL....239-593-4564
G. L. Mezzetta
American Canyon, CA....707-648-1050
Ganong Bros Limited Corporate Office
St. Stephen, NB....888-426-6647
Gene Belk Fruit Packers
Bloomington, CA....909-877-1819
Gilroy Foods
Gilroy, CA....800-921-7502
Glacier Foods
Sanger, CA....559-875-3354
Graceland Fruit
Frankfort, MI....800-352-7181
Gray & Company
Forest Grove, OR....503-357-3141
Graysmarsh Farm
Sequim, WA....800-683-4367
Green Valley Apples of California
Arvin, CA....661-854-4436
Grouse Hunt Farms
Tamaqua, PA....570-467-2850
Grove Fresh Distributors
Chicago, IL....773-288-2065
Grow-Pac
Cornelius, OR....503-357-9691
Gurley's Foods
Willmar, MN....800-426-7845
H H Dobbins
Lyndonville, NY....877-362-2467
H. Naraghi Farms
Escalon, CA....209-577-5777
Hallcrest Vineyards
Felton, CA....831-335-4441
Harmony Foods Corporation
Fishers, IN....800-837-2855
Harris Farms
Coalinga, CA....800-742-1955
Harry & David
Medford, OR....877-322-1200
Hartog Rahal Foods
New York, NY....212-687-2000
Heller Brothers PackingcCorporation
Winter Garden, FL....407-656-2124
Henggeler Packing Company
Fruitland, ID....208-452-4212
Hialeah Products Company
Hollywood, FL....800-923-3379
Hiscock Enterprises
Brigus, NL....709-528-4577
Indian Bay Frozen Foods
Centreville, NL....709-678-2844
Indian Hollow Farms
Richland Center, WI....800-236-3944
Indian Rock Produce
Perkasie, PA....800-882-0512
International Food Trade
Amherst, NS....902-667-3013
International Home Foods
Parsippany, NJ....973-359-9920
J.C. Watson Company
Parma, ID....208-722-5141
J.H. Verbridge & Son
Williamson, NY....315-589-2366
Jasper Wyman & Son
Milbridge, ME....800-341-1758
Jersey Fruit CooperativeAssociation
Glassboro, NJ....856-863-9100
JES Foods
Cleveland, OH....216-883-8987
JF Braun & Sons Inc.
Elizabeth, NJ....800-997-7177
Johnson Fruit Company
Sunnyside, WA....509-837-4600
Joseph J. White
Browns Mills, NJ....609-893-2332
JR Wood/Big Valley
Atwater, CA....209-358-5643
JRL
Vineland, NJ....856-690-9000
K.B. Hall Ranch
Ojai, CA....805-646-4512
Kagome
Los Banos, CA....209-826-8850
Kalashian Packing Company
Fresno, CA....559-237-4287
Kalustyan Corporation
Union, NJ....908-688-6111
Karl Bissinger French Confections
St Louis, MO....800-325-8881
Kettle Valley Fruits SunOpta Inc
Summerland, BC....888-297-6944
Kiona Vineyards Winery
Benton City, WA....509-588-6716
Knights Appleden Fruit
Colborne, ON....905-349-2521
Knouse Foods Coop
Peach Glen, PA....717-677-8181
Kozlowski Farms
Forestville, CA....800-473-2767
Krupka's Blueberries
Fennville, MI....269-857-4278
L&S Packing Company
Farmingdale, NY....800-286-6487
La Vigne Enterprises
Fallbrook, CA....760-723-9997
Lee Andersons's Covalda Dates
Coachella, CA....760-398-3441
Leroux Creek Foods
Hotchkiss, CO....877-970-5670
Leroy Smith & Sons Inc
Vero Beach, FL....772-567-3421
Liberty Orchards Company
Cashmere, WA....800-888-5696
Lucks Food Decorating Company
Tacoma, WA....253-383-4815
Macrie Brothers
Hammonton, NJ....609-561-6822
Made in Nature
Fresno, CA....800-906-7426
Maine Wild Blueberry Company
Cherryfield, ME....800-243-4005
Majestic Foods
Huntington, NY....631-424-9444
Manzanita Ranch
Julian, CA....760-765-0102
Mariani Packing Company
Vacaville, CA....800-672-8655
Mason County Fruit Packers Cooperative
Ludington, MI....231-845-6248
Maui Pineapple Company
Kahului, HI....808-877-3351
Maui Pineapple Company
Concord, CA....925-798-0240
Mayer's Cider Mill
Webster, NY....800-543-0043
Mayfair Sales
Buffalo, NY....800-248-2881
Mayfield Farms
Caledon, ON....905-846-0506
McCartney Produce Company
Paris, TN....800-522-2791
Melissa's
Los Angeles, CA....800-588-0151
Mercer Processing
Modesto, CA....209-529-0150
Midwest Blueberry Farms
Holland, MI....616-399-2133
Mira International Foods
East Brunswick, NJ....800-818-6472
Miramar Fruit Trading Company
Doral, FL....305-883-4774
Modoc Orchard Company
Medford, OR....541-535-1437
Nassau Candy Company
Hicksville, NY....516-433-7100
National Products Company
Kalamazoo, MI....269-344-3640
Natural Fruit Corporation
Hialeah, FL....305-887-7525
Naturex Inc.
South Hackensack, NJ....201-440-5000
Nekta
Lakeville, MN....952-898-8020
New England Natural Baker
Greenfield, MA....800-910-2884
New Era Canning Company
New Era, MI....231-861-2151
New York Apples Sales
Castletn on Hdsn, NY....518-477-7200
North American Blueberry Council
Folsom, CA....800-824-6395
Northern Michigan Fruit Company
Omena, MI....231-386-5142
Northern Orchard Company
Peru, NY....518-643-9718
Nutri-Fruit
Gresham, OR....866-343-7848
Orange Bang
Sylmar, CA....818-833-1000
Orange Cove Sanger Citrus Association
Orange Cove, CA....559-626-4453
Oregon Cherry Growers
Salem, OR....800-367-2536
Oregon Fruit Products Company
Salem, OR....800-394-9333
Organically Grown Company
Eugene, OR....541-689-5320
Overlake Blueberry Farm
Bellevue, WA....425-267-0501
Pacific Blueberries
Rochester, WA....360-273-5405
Pacific Coast Fruit Company
Portland, OR....503-234-6411
Pacific Coast Producers
Lodi, CA....209-367-8800
Pacific Coast Producers
Oroville, CA....530-533-4311
Pacific Trellis
Reedley, CA....559-638-5100
Pacific Westcoast Foods
Beaverton, OR....800-874-9333
Palmer Candy Company
Sioux City, IA....800-831-0828
Paradise Products Corporation
Boca Raton, FL....800-826-1235
Pavero Cold Storage Corporation
Highland, NY....800-435-2994
Peninsula Fruit Exchange
Traverse City, MI....231-223-4282
Plaidberry Company
Vista, CA....760-727-5403
Premium Waters
Minneapolis, MN....800-243-1163
Purity Products
Plainview, NY....888-769-7873
R M Lawton Cranberries
Middleboro, MA....508-947-7465
Rain Sweet
Salem, OR....800-363-4293
Ramos Orchards
Winters, CA....530-795-4748
Red River Foods
Richmond, VA....800-443-6637
Reed Lang Farms
Rio Hondo, TX....956-748-2354
Regal Health Foods International
Chicago, IL....773-252-1044
Reinhart Foods
Markham, ON....905-754-3500
Reter Fruit Company
Medford, OR....541-772-5256
Rice Fruit Company
Gardners, PA....800-627-3359
Richard Lanza
Hammonton, NJ....609-561-3984
Robert Rothschild Berry Farm
Urbana, OH....866-565-6790
Roche Fruit
Yakima, WA....509-248-7200
Royal Moonlight
Reedley, CA....559-637-7799
Russo Farms
Vineland, NJ....856-692-5942
SA Carlson
Yakima, WA....509-965-8333
Sand Hill Berries
Mt Pleasant, PA....724-547-4760
Santanna Banana Company
Harrisburg, PA....717-238-8321
Satiety
Davis, CA....530-757-2699
Schwan Food Company
Marshall, MN....800-533-5290
Scotian Gold Cooperative
Coldbrook, NS....902-679-2191
Shafer Lake Fruit
Hartford, MI....269-621-3194
Shari Candies
Edina, MN....800-658-7059
Shields Date Gardens
Indio, CA....800-414-2555
Signature Fruit
Bloomingdale, IL....630-980-2481
Sill Farms Market
Lawrence, MI....269-674-3755
Silver Palate Kitchens
Cresskill, NJ....800-872-5283
SKW Flavor & Fruit Preparation
Langhorne, PA....215-702-1000
Smeltzer Orchard Company
Frankfort, MI....231-882-4421
Snackerz
Commerce, CA....888-576-2253
Snowcrest Packer
Abbotsford, BC....800-265-5332

Solana Gold Organics
Sebastopol, CA 800-459-1121
SOPAKCO Foods
Mullins, SC 800-276-9678
Sparboe Companies
Los Angeles, CA 213-626-7538
Spreda Group
Louisville, KY 502-426-9411
Spring Ledge Farms
Dundee, NY 607-678-4038
Stanley Orchards
Modena, NY 845-883-7351
Stapleton-Spence PackingCompany
San Jose, CA 800-297-8815
Sugar Cane Industry Glades Correctional Institution
Belle Glade, FL 561-829-1400
Suity Confection Company
Miami, FL 305-639-3300
Sun Groves
Safety Harbor, FL 800-672-6438
Sundia
Oakland, CA 415-762-0600
SunMeadow Family of Products
Saint Petersburg, FL 727-573-2211
Sunsweet Growers
Yuba City, CA 800-417-2253
Superior Foods
Watsonville, CA 831-728-3691
Surface Banana Company
Bluewell, WV 304-589-7202
Sweet Candy Company
Salt Lake City, UT 800-669-8669
T.S. Smith & Sons
Bridgeville, DE 302-337-8271
Talbott Farms
Palisade, CO 970-464-5943
Tastee Apple Inc
Newcomerstown, OH 800-262-7753
Taylor Farms
Salinas, CA 831-754-0471
Tejon Ranch
Lebec, CA 661-248-5181
Tom Ringhausen Orchards
Hardin, IL 618-576-2311
Tony Vitrano Company
Jessup, MD 800-481-3784
Trailblazer Food Products
Portland, OR 800-777-7179
Trefethen Vineyards
Napa, CA 800-556-4847
Tri-Boro Fruit Company
Fresno, CA 559-486-4141
Triple D Orchards
Empire, MI 866-781-9410
Trophy Nut
Tipp City, OH 800-219-9004
Truitt Brothers Inc
Salem, OR 800-547-8712
Tuscarora Organic Growers Cooperative
Hustontown, PA 814-448-2173
Unimark Group Inc.
Bartonville, TX 972-518-1155
United Fruit Growers
Palisade, CO 970-464-7277
United Marketing Exchange
Delta, CO 970-874-3332
Ursula's Island Farms
Seattle, WA 206-762-3113
USA Fruit
Greenwich, CT 203-661-8280
Valley Fig Growers
Fresno, CA 559-237-3893
Valley View Blueberries
Vancouver, WA 360-892-2839
Valley View Packing Company
San Jose, CA 408-289-8300
Varet Street Market
Brooklyn, NY 718-302-0560
Verdelli Farms
Harrisburg, PA 800-422-8344
Violore Foods Company
Laredo, TX 956-726-3633
Visalia Produce Sales Inc
Kingsburg, CA 559-897-6652
Warner Candy
El Paso, TX 847-928-7200
Washington Fruit & Produce Company
Yakima, WA 509-457-6177
Webster Farms
Cambridge Station, NS 902-538-9492
Well Pict Berries
Watsonville, CA 831-722-3871
Wetherby Cranberry Company
Warrens, WI 608-378-4813
Wiard's Orchards
Ypsilanti, MI 734-482-7744
Woodland Foods
Gurnee, IL 847-625-8600
World Nutrition
Scottsdale, AZ 800-548-2710
Yakima Fruit & Cold Storage Company
Wapato, WA 509-877-2777
Yakima Valley Grape Producers
Grandview, WA 509-882-1223
Yokhol Valley Packing Company
Lindsay, CA 559-562-1327
Zitner Company
Philadelphia, PA 215-229-4990

Cocktail

Emerling International Foods
Buffalo, NY 716-833-7381

We supply food manufacturers and food service customers worldwide (since 1988) with bulk ingredients including: Fruits & Vegetables; Juice Concentrates; Herbs & Spices; Oils & Vinegars; Flavors & Colors; Honey & Molasses. We also produce PURE MAPLE SYRUP.

Orval Kent Food Company
Wheeling, IL 847-459-9000
Pacific Coast Producers
Lodi, CA 209-367-8800
Pacific Coast Producers
Oroville, CA 530-533-4311
Tupman-Thurlow Company
Deerfield Beach, FL 954-596-9989

Jarred or Cupped

Chiquita Brands Intl. ional
Cincinnati, OH 800-438-0015
Emerling International Foods
Buffalo, NY 716-833-7381

We supply food manufacturers and food service customers worldwide (since 1988) with bulk ingredients including: Fruits & Vegetables; Juice Concentrates; Herbs & Spices; Oils & Vinegars; Flavors & Colors; Honey & Molasses. We also produce PURE MAPLE SYRUP.

Orval Kent Food Company
Wheeling, IL 847-459-9000
Pacific Coast Producers
Oroville, CA 530-533-4311
Tupman-Thurlow Company
Deerfield Beach, FL 954-596-9989

Galangal

Nickabood's Company
Los Angeles, CA 213-746-1541

Garlic

Black Garlic Inc
Hayward, CA 888-811-9065
California Garlic Co
San Diego, CA 951-506-8883
Colonna Brothers
North Bergen, NJ 201-864-1115
Country Cupboard
Virginia City, NV 775-847-7300
Emerling International Foods
Buffalo, NY 716-833-7381

We supply food manufacturers and food service customers worldwide (since 1988) with bulk ingredients including: Fruits & Vegetables; Juice Concentrates; Herbs & Spices; Oils & Vinegars; Flavors & Colors; Honey & Molasses. We also produce PURE MAPLE SYRUP.

Miss Scarlett's
Chandler, AZ 800-345-6734

SupHerb Farms
Turlock, CA 800-787-4372

Frozen culinary herb and specialty vegetable ingredients.

Vegetable Juices
Chicago, IL 888-776-9752
Victoria Packing Corporation
Brooklyn, NY 718-927-3000

Granulated

American Key Food Products
Closter, NJ 800-767-0237
Emerling International Foods
Buffalo, NY 716-833-7381

We supply food manufacturers and food service customers worldwide (since 1988) with bulk ingredients including: Fruits & Vegetables; Juice Concentrates; Herbs & Spices; Oils & Vinegars; Flavors & Colors; Honey & Molasses. We also produce PURE MAPLE SYRUP.

Vegetable Juices
Chicago, IL 888-776-9752

Ginger

Atlantic Quality Spice &Seasonings
New Brunswick, NJ 800-584-0422
Christopher Ranch
Gilroy, CA 408-847-1100
Con Yeager Spice Company
Zelienople, PA 800-222-2460
Cut Above Foods
Carlsbad, CA 760-931-6777
Emerling International Foods
Buffalo, NY 716-833-7381

We supply food manufacturers and food service customers worldwide (since 1988) with bulk ingredients including: Fruits & Vegetables; Juice Concentrates; Herbs & Spices; Oils & Vinegars; Flavors & Colors; Honey & Molasses. We also produce PURE MAPLE SYRUP.

Fiji Ginger Company
Santa Monica, CA 310-452-0878
Ful-Flav-R Foods
Alamo, CA 925-838-0300
Ginger People®
Marina, CA 800-551-5284
Herb Connection
Springville, UT 801-489-4254
International Glace
Spokane, WA 800-884-5041
Morris J. Golombeck
Brooklyn, NY 718-284-3505
Paradise
Plant City, FL 800-330-8952
Schiff Food Products
North Bergen, NJ 201-868-6800

SupHerb Farms
Turlock, CA 800-787-4372

Frozen culinary herb and specialty vegetable ingredients.

Texas Coffee Company
Beaumont, TX 800-259-3400
Triple Leaf Tea
S San Francisco, CA 800-552-7448
Tulkoff Food Products
Baltimore, MD 800-638-7343

Ungerer & Company
Lincoln Park, NJ 973-628-0600
Vegetable Juices
Chicago, IL 888-776-9752

Crystallized

Emerling International Foods
Buffalo, NY. 716-833-7381

We supply food manufacturers and food service customers worldwide (since 1988) with bulk ingredients including: Fruits & Vegetables; Juice Concentrates; Herbs & Spices; Oils & Vinegars; Flavors & Colors; Honey & Molasses. We also produce PURE MAPLE SYRUP.

Fastachi
Watertown, MA. 800-466-3022
Organic Planet
San Francisco, CA 415-765-5590
Setton International Foods
Commack, NY 800-227-4397

Pickled

Paradise
Plant City, FL 800-330-8952

Glace

Dixie Dew Products
Erlanger, KY. 800-867-8548
Fruit Fillings
Fresno, CA 559-237-4715
International Glace
Spokane, WA. 800-884-5041

Grape

Ballantine Produce Company
Reedley, CA 559-875-2583
Brothers International Food Corporation
Rochester, NY. 585-343-3007
Cal-Harvest Marketing
Hanford, CA 559-582-4000
Concannon Vineyard
Livermore, CA 800-258-9866
Dan Tudor & Sons
Delano, CA 661-792-2933
Delta Packing Company of Lodi
Lodi, CA 209-334-0811
Fowler Packing Company
Fresno, CA 559-834-5911
George W Saulpaugh & Sons
Germantown, NY 518-537-6500
Gerawan Farming
Sanger, CA 559-787-8780
H. Naraghi Farms
Escalon, CA 209-577-5777
Hallcrest Vineyards
Felton, CA. 831-335-4441
Hillcrest Orchard
Lake Placid, FL. 865-397-5273
Janca's Jojoba Oil & Seed Company
Mesa, AZ. 480-497-9494
Jasmine Vineyards
Delano, CA 661-792-2141
M&R Company
Lodi, CA 209-369-4760
Oceana Foods
Shelby, MI. 231-861-2141
Oneonta Starr Ranch Growers
Wenatchee, WA. 509-663-2191
Pacific Trellis
Reedley, CA 559-638-5100
Pandol Brothers
Delano, CA 661-725-3755
Peter Rabbit Farms
Coachella, CA. 760-398-0151
Royal Moonlight
Reedley, CA 559-637-7799
Royal Vista Marketing
Visalia, CA 559-636-9198
Satiety
Davis, CA 530-757-2699
Spiech Farms
Paw Paw, MI. 269-657-1980
Spring Ledge Farms
Dundee, NY 607-678-4038
Sunmet
Del Rey, CA 559-888-2702
Tejon Ranch
Lebec, CA. 661-248-5181
Trefethen Vineyards
Napa, CA. 800-556-4847
United Fruits Corporation
Santa Monica, CA. 310-829-0261
Venture Vineyards
Lodi, NY 888-635-6277
Vintage Produce Sales
Kingsburg, CA 559-897-1622
Wawona Packing Company
Cutler, CA. 559-528-9729
Yakima Valley Grape Producers
Grandview, WA. 509-882-1223
Z&S Distributing
Fresno, CA 800-467-0788

Leaves

Castella Imports
Hauppauge, NY 866-227-8355
Corfu Foods
Bensenville, IL 630-595-2510
Grecian Delight Foods
Elk Grove Village, IL 800-621-4387
Hye Cuisine
Del Rey, CA 559-834-3000
Pacific Choice Brands
Fresno, CA 559-237-5583
Setton International Foods
Commack, NY 800-227-4397
Yergat Packing Co Inc
Fresno, CA 559-276-9180

Table

Anton Caratan & Son
Bakersfield, CA
Chiquita Brands Intl. ional
Cincinnati, OH 800-438-0015
Corrin Produce Sales
Dinuba, CA. 559-596-0517
Lindemann Produce
Los Banos, CA 209-826-2442
Lucich Farms
Delano, CA. 661-725-4550
Satiety
Davis, CA 530-757-2699
Sunmet
Del Rey, CA 559-888-2702
Vincent B. Zaninovich & Son
Richgrove, CA 661-725-2497
Z&S Distributing
Fresno, CA 800-467-0788

Wine

Galleano Winery
Mira Loma, CA. 951-685-5376
Kiona Vineyards Winery
Benton City, WA. 509-588-6716
Satiety
Davis, CA 530-757-2699
Symms Fruit Ranch
Caldwell, ID 208-459-4821
Tejon Ranch
Lebec, CA. 661-248-5181
Trefethen Vineyards
Napa, CA. 800-556-4847

Grapefruit

A. Duda Farm Fresh Foods
Belle Glade, FL. 561-996-7621
Agrexco USA
Jamaica, NY 718-481-8700
Bautista Organic Dates
Mecca, CA 760-396-2337
Ben Hill Griffin, Inc.
Frostproof, FL. 863-635-2251
Corona College Heights Orange & Lemon Associates
Riverside, CA 951-688-1811
Davidson of Dundee
Dundee, FL 800-294-2266
DNE World Fruit Sales
Fort Pierce, FL 800-327-6676
Dole Food Company
Westlake Village, CA 818-879-6600
Gene's Citrus Ranch
Sarasota, FL 888-723-2006
Golden River Fruit Company
Vero Beach, FL. 772-562-8610
Haines City Citrus Growers Association
Haines City, FL. 800-422-4245
Hale Indian River Groves
Wabasso, FL 800-562-4502
Heller Brothers PackingcCorporation
Winter Garden, FL 407-656-2124
Hunt Brothers Cooperative
Lake Wales, FL. 863-676-9471
Leroy Smith & Sons Inc
Vero Beach, FL. 772-567-3421
Reed Lang Farms
Rio Hondo, TX 956-748-2354
Seald Sweet Growers & Packers
Vero Beach, FL. 772-569-2244
Sugar Cane Industry Glades Correctional Institution
Belle Glade, FL. 561-829-1400
United Fruits Corporation
Santa Monica, CA. 310-829-0261

Pink

DNE World Fruit Sales
Fort Pierce, FL 800-327-6676

White

DNE World Fruit Sales
Fort Pierce, FL 800-327-6676

Guava

Brooks Tropicals
Homestead, FL 800-327-4833
Chieftain Wild Rice Company
Spooner, WI 800-262-6368
Unique Ingredients
Naches, WA. 509-653-1991

Canned & Frozen

Emerling International Foods
Buffalo, NY. 716-833-7381

We supply food manufacturers and food service customers worldwide (since 1988) with bulk ingredients including: Fruits & Vegetables; Juice Concentrates; Herbs & Spices; Oils & Vinegars; Flavors & Colors; Honey & Molasses. We also produce PURE MAPLE SYRUP.

Unique Ingredients
Naches, WA. 509-653-1991

Kale

Abbott & Cobb, Inc.
Langhorne, PA 800-345-7333
Emerling International Foods
Buffalo, NY. 716-833-7381

We supply food manufacturers and food service customers worldwide (since 1988) with bulk ingredients including: Fruits & Vegetables; Juice Concentrates; Herbs & Spices; Oils & Vinegars; Flavors & Colors; Honey & Molasses. We also produce PURE MAPLE SYRUP.

Frank Capurro & Son
Moss Landing, CA 831-728-3904
Seabrook Brothers & Sons
Seabrook, NJ. 856-455-8080

Frozen

Vegetable Juices
Chicago, IL 888-776-9752

Kelp Products

Acadian Seaplants
Dartmouth, NS 800-575-9100
Atlantic Laboratories
Waldoboro, ME. 207-832-5376
Gum Technology Corporation
Tucson, AZ 800-369-4867
Naturex Inc.
South Hackensack, NJ 201-440-5000
Silver Ferm Chemical
Seattle, WA 206-282-3376

Kiwi

Chiquita Brands Intl. ional
Cincinnati, OH 800-438-0015
Nekta
Lakeville, MN. 952-898-8020

Royal Vista Marketing
Visalia, CA 559-636-9198
Setton International Foods
Commack, NY 800-227-4397
Unique Ingredients
Naches, WA. 509-653-1991

Gold

Brandt Farms
Reedley, CA 559-638-6961

Kohlrabi

Abbott & Cobb, Inc.
Langhorne, PA 800-345-7333
Baker Produce Company
Kennewick, WA 800-624-7553
Princeville Canning Company
Princeville, IL 309-385-4301

Kumquat

Paradise Products Corporation
Boca Raton, FL. 800-826-1235
Setton International Foods
Commack, NY 800-227-4397
West Pak Avocado
Temecula, CA 800-266-4414

Leek

California Watercress
Fillmore, CA. 805-524-4808
Ghirardelli Ranch
Petaluma, CA 707-795-7616

SupHerb FARMS®

SupHerb Farms
Turlock, CA 800-787-4372

Frozen culinary herb and specialty vegetable ingredients.

Sure Fresh Produce
Santa Maria, CA 888-423-5379
Terry Foods Inc
Idaho Falls, ID 208-604-8143
Vegetable Juices
Chicago, IL 888-776-9752

Lemon

Corona College Heights Orange & Lemon Associates
Riverside, CA 951-688-1811
DiMare International Dmb Packing Corp
Indio, CA. 760-347-3336
DNE World Fruit Sales
Fort Pierce, FL 800-327-6676
Dole Food Company
Westlake Village, CA 818-879-6600
Paradise
Plant City, FL 800-330-8952
Seald Sweet Growers & Packers
Vero Beach, FL 772-569-2244
United Fruits Corporation
Santa Monica, CA. 310-829-0261
Z&S Distributing
Fresno, CA 800-467-0788

Peels

Fmali Herb
Santa Cruz, CA 831-423-7913

Lettuce

A. Duda Farm Fresh Foods
Belle Glade, FL. 561-996-7621
Baker Produce Company
Kennewick, WA 800-624-7553
Ben B. Schwartz & Sons
Detroit, MI 313-841-8300
Cal-Harvest Marketing
Hanford, CA 559-582-4000
Club Chef
Covington, KY 859-578-3100
Crown Packing Company
Salinas, CA 831-424-2067
Custom Cuts
Bay View, WI 414-483-0491
Del Monte Fresh Produce
Kankakee, IL. 815-936-7400
Dole Food Company
Westlake Village, CA 818-879-6600
Dole Fresh Vegetable Company
Soledad, CA 800-333-5454
F&S Produce Company
Rosenhayn, NJ 800-886-3316
Fresh Express
Salinas, CA 800-242-5472
Ghirardelli Ranch
Petaluma, CA 707-795-7616
Hari Om Farms
Eagleville, TN. 615-368-7778
Indian Rock Produce
Perkasie, PA 800-882-0512
Mills
Salinas, CA 831-757-1611
R.C. McEntire & Company
Columbia, SC 803-799-3388
Sales USA
Salado, TX 800-766-7344
Sunrise Growers
Placentia, CA 714-630-6292
Talley Farms
Arroyo Grande, CA. 805-489-5533
Tanimura & Antle
Salinas, CA 831-455-2255
Teixeira Farms
Santa Maria, CA 805-928-3801
Tony Vitrano Company
Jessup, MD 800-481-3784
Vegetable Juices
Chicago, IL 888-776-9752
Williams Creek Farms
Williams, OR. 541-846-6481

Butterhead

Boston

Tanimura & Antle
Salinas, CA 831-455-2255

Looseleaf

Green

Tanimura & Antle
Salinas, CA 831-455-2255

Red

Tanimura & Antle
Salinas, CA 831-455-2255

Romaine

Royce C. Bone Farms
Nashville, NC 252-443-3773
Talley Farms
Arroyo Grande, CA. 805-489-5533
Tanimura & Antle
Salinas, CA 831-455-2255

Lime

Agri-Dairy Products
Purchase, NY 914-697-9580
Brooks Tropicals
Homestead, FL 800-327-4833
DNE World Fruit Sales
Fort Pierce, FL 800-327-6676
Hunt Brothers Cooperative
Lake Wales, FL. 863-676-9471

Loganberries

Kerr Concentrates
Salem, OR. 800-910-5377

Mango

Brooks Tropicals
Homestead, FL 800-327-4833
Chieftain Wild Rice Company
Spooner, WI 800-262-6368
Clofine Dairy & Food Products
Linwood, NJ 800-441-1001
Commodities Marketing, Inc.
Edison, NJ. 732-603-5077
Couture Farms
Kettleman City, CA. 559-945-2226
Del Monte Fresh Produce
Coral Gables, FL. 800-950-3683
Dole Food Company
Westlake Village, CA 818-879-6600
Eckert Cold Storage
Escalon, CA 209-838-4040
Just Tomatoes Company
Westley, CA. 800-537-1985
Natural Foods
Toledo, OH 419-537-1713
Organic Planet
San Francisco, CA 415-765-5590
Setton International Foods
Commack, NY 800-227-4397
Townsend Farms
Fairview, OR. 503-666-1780
Unique Ingredients
Naches, WA. 509-653-1991

Dried

American Importing Company
Minneapolis, MN 612-331-7000
Mariani Packing Company
Vacaville, CA 800-672-8655

Melon

Chiquita Brands Intl. ional
Cincinnati, OH 800-438-0015
Custom Cuts
Bay View, WI 414-483-0491
Del Monte Fresh Produce
Coral Gables, FL. 800-950-3683
Emerling International Foods
Buffalo, NY. 716-833-7381

We supply food manufacturers and food service customers worldwide (since 1988) with bulk ingredients including: Fruits & Vegetables; Juice Concentrates; Herbs & Spices; Oils & Vinegars; Flavors & Colors; Honey & Molasses. We also produce PURE MAPLE SYRUP.

Balls

Frozen

Emerling International Foods
Buffalo, NY. 716-833-7381

We supply food manufacturers and food service customers worldwide (since 1988) with bulk ingredients including: Fruits & Vegetables; Juice Concentrates; Herbs & Spices; Oils & Vinegars; Flavors & Colors; Honey & Molasses. We also produce PURE MAPLE SYRUP.

Cantaloupe

Abbott & Cobb, Inc.
Langhorne, PA 800-345-7333
Couture Farms
Kettleman City, CA. 559-945-2226
F&S Produce Company
Rosenhayn, NJ 800-886-3316
Hialeah Products Company
Hollywood, FL 800-923-3379
Lindemann Produce
Los Banos, CA 209-826-2442
Vessey & Company
Holtville, CA. 760-356-0130
Zuccaro's Fruit & Produce Company
Minneapolis, MN 612-333-1122

Dried

Setton International Foods
Commack, NY 800-227-4397

Honeydew

Couture Farms
Kettleman City, CA. 559-945-2226
Lindemann Produce
Los Banos, CA 209-826-2442
Turlock Fruit Company
Turlock, CA 209-634-7207
United Fruits Corporation
Santa Monica, CA. 310-829-0261

Zuccaro's Fruit & Produce Company
Minneapolis, MN 612-333-1122

Watermelon

Bryant Preserving Company
Alma, AR 800-634-2413

Custom Cuts
Bay View, WI 414-483-0491

Del Monte Fresh Produce
Coral Gables, FL................... 800-950-3683

F&S Produce Company
Rosenhayn, NJ 800-886-3316

Zuccaro's Fruit & Produce Company
Minneapolis, MN 612-333-1122

Seedless

Bissett Produce Company
Spring Hope, NC................... 800-849-5073

Miso

Great Eastern Sun
Asheville, NC 800-334-5809

Miyako Oriental Foods
Baldwin Park, CA.................. 877-788-6476

Organic Gourmet
Sherman Oaks, CA 800-400-7772

Mushrooms

Al Pete Meats
Muncie, IN 765-288-8817

Alimentaire Whyte's Inc
Laval, QC 800-625-1979

Anchor Food Products/ McCain Foods
Appleton, WI 920-734-0627

Basciani Foods
Avondale, PA 610-268-3610

Bob Gordon & Associates
Oak Park, IL 708-524-9611

Buon Italia Misono Food Ltd.
New York, NY 212-633-9090

Cara Mia Products
Fresno, CA 559-498-2900

Chieftain Wild Rice Company
Spooner, WI 800-262-6368

Colonna Brothers
North Bergen, NJ 201-864-1115

Country Fresh Mushrooms
Avondale, PA 610-268-3033

Crazy Jerry's
Roswell, GA 770-993-0651

Creekside Mushrooms
Worthington, PA 724-297-5491

Cutone Specialty Foods
Chelsea, MA 617-889-1122

D'Artagnan
Newark, NJ 800-327-8246

Dong Kee Company
Chicago, IL 312-225-6340

Dove Mushrooms
Avondale, PA 610-268-3535

Emerling International Foods
Buffalo, NY....................... 716-833-7381

We supply food manufacturers and food service customers worldwide (since 1988) with bulk ingredients including: Fruits & Vegetables; Juice Concentrates; Herbs & Spices; Oils & Vinegars; Flavors & Colors; Honey & Molasses. We also produce PURE MAPLE SYRUP.

Flavor House
Adelanto, CA 760-246-9131

FungusAmongUs Inc
Snohomish, WA 360-568-3403

Giorgio Foods
Temple, PA 800-220-2139

Giovanni's Appetizing Food Products
Richmond, MI..................... 586-727-9355

Gourmet's Finest
Avondale, PA 610-268-6910

Great American Appetizers
Nampa, ID........................ 800-282-4834

Great Lakes Foods
Hamilton, ON 905-560-4223

H.K. Canning
Ventura, CA....................... 805-652-1392

Hanover Foods Corporation
Hanover, PA 717-632-6000

Health Concerns
Oakland, CA 800-233-9355

Kitchen Pride Mushroom Farms
Gonzales, TX 830-540-4517

L K Bowman & Company
Nottingham, PA.................... 800-853-1919

L&S Packing Company
Farmingdale, NY 800-286-6487

L.F. Lambert Spawn Company
Coatesville, PA 610-384-5031

L.K. Bowman Company
Hanover, PA 800-853-1919

Lake Erie Frozen Foods Company
Ashland, OH 800-766-8501

Lee's Food Products
Toronto, ON 416-465-2407

Les Aliments Livabec Foods
Sherrington, QC 450-454-7971

LK Bowman
Nottingham, PA.................... 800-853-1919

Matador Processors
Blanchard, OK 800-847-0797

Miss Scarlett's
Chandler, AZ...................... 800-345-6734

Modern Mushroom Farms
Avondale, PA 610-268-3535

Money's Mushrooms
Vancouver, BC 800-669-7992

Monterey Mushrooms
Watsonville, CA 800-333-6874

Monterey Mushrooms
Watsonville, CA 831-763-5300

Mushroom Company
Cambridge, MD 410-221-8971

Nationwide Canning
Cottam, ON....................... 519-839-4831

North American Reishi/Nammex
Gibsons, BC 604-886-7799

NTC Marketing Inc
Williamsville, NY.................. 800-333-1637

Omstead Foods Ltd
Wheatley, ON 905-315-8883

Ostrom Mushroom Farms
Lacey, WA........................ 206-628-9800

Paisley Farms
Willoughby, OH 800-676-8656

Paradise Products Corporation
Boca Raton, FL.................... 800-826-1235

Phillips Gourmet, Inc
Kennett Square, PA................. 610-925-0520

Prairie Mushrooms
Sherwood Park, AB 780-467-3555

Rain Sweet
Salem, OR........................ 800-363-4293

Ron-Son Foods
Swedesboro, NJ 856-241-7333

S.D. Mushrooms
Avondale, PA 610-268-8082

Sabatino Truffles USA
Bronx, NY........................ 888-444-9971

Scally's Imperial Importing Company Inc
Staten Island, NY 718-983-1938

Setton International Foods
Commack, NY 800-227-4397

South Mill Distribution
Kennett Square, PA................. 610-444-4800

Sunny Dell Foods
Oxford, PA 610-932-5164

Superior Mushroom Farms
Ardrossan, AB 866-687-2242

SupHerb FARMS

SupHerb Farms
Turlock, CA 800-787-4372

Frozen culinary herb and specialty vegetable ingredients.

Terry Foods Inc
Idaho Falls, ID 208-604-8143

Tiger Mushroom Farm
Nanton, AB 403-646-2578

Unique Foods
Raleigh, NC 919-779-5600

United Canning Corporation
North Lima, OH 330-549-9807

Vegetable Juices
Chicago, IL 888-776-9752

Victoria Packing Corporation
Brooklyn, NY 718-927-3000

Woodland Foods
Gurnee, IL........................ 847-625-8600

Beech

Modern Mushroom Farms
Avondale, PA 610-268-3535

Phillips Gourmet, Inc
Kennett Square, PA................. 610-925-0520

Black Trumpet

Chieftain Wild Rice Company
Spooner, WI 800-262-6368

D'Artagnan
Newark, NJ 800-327-8246

Woodland Foods
Gurnee, IL........................ 847-625-8600

Boletes

Chieftain Wild Rice Company
Spooner, WI 800-262-6368

Canned

Agrocan
Ville St Laurent, QC 877-247-6226

Bob Gordon & Associates
Oak Park, IL 708-524-9611

Dong Kee Company
Chicago, IL 312-225-6340

Giorgio Foods
Temple, PA 800-220-2139

Great Lakes Foods
Hamilton, ON 905-560-4223

L.K. Bowman Company
Hanover, PA 800-853-1919

Lee's Food Products
Toronto, ON 416-465-2407

Money's Mushrooms
Vancouver, BC 800-669-7992

Monterey Mushrooms
Bonne Terre, MO 800-333-6874

Mushroom Company
Cambridge, MD 410-221-8971

Nationwide Canning
Cottam, ON....................... 519-839-4831

NTC Marketing Inc
Williamsville, NY.................. 800-333-1637

Paradise Products Corporation
Boca Raton, FL.................... 800-826-1235

Ron-Son Foods
Swedesboro, NJ 856-241-7333

Shafer-Haggart
Vancouver, BC 604-669-5512

Sunny Dell Foods
Oxford, PA 610-932-5164

Unique Foods
Raleigh, NC 919-779-5600

United Canning Corporation
North Lima, OH 330-549-9807

Chanterelle

Chieftain Wild Rice Company
Spooner, WI 800-262-6368

D'Artagnan
Newark, NJ 800-327-8246

Emerling International Foods
Buffalo, NY....................... 716-833-7381

We supply food manufacturers and food service customers worldwide (since 1988) with bulk ingredients including: Fruits & Vegetables; Juice Concentrates; Herbs & Spices; Oils & Vinegars; Flavors & Colors; Honey & Molasses. We also produce PURE MAPLE SYRUP.

Modern Mushroom Farms
Avondale, PA 610-268-3535

Cloudear

Chieftain Wild Rice Company
Spooner, WI 800-262-6368

Criminis

Creekside Mushrooms
Worthington, PA 724-297-5491

Ostrom Mushroom Farms
Lacey, WA........................206-628-9800
Phillips Gourmet, Inc
Kennett Square, PA.................610-925-0520

Dehydrated

Emerling International Foods
Buffalo, NY.......................716-833-7381

We supply food manufacturers and food service customers worldwide (since 1988) with bulk ingredients including: Fruits & Vegetables; Juice Concentrates; Herbs & Spices; Oils & Vinegars; Flavors & Colors; Honey & Molasses. We also produce PURE MAPLE SYRUP.

Modern Mushroom Farms
Avondale, PA 610-268-3535
Nikken Foods Company
Saint Louis, MO 636-532-1019
South Mill Distribution
Kennett Square, PA.................610-444-4800
Unique Ingredients
Naches, WA.......................509-653-1991

Enokis

Creekside Mushrooms
Worthington, PA...................724-297-5491
Modern Mushroom Farms
Avondale, PA 610-268-3535
Monterey Mushrooms
Watsonville, CA 800-333-6874
Ostrom Mushroom Farms
Lacey, WA........................206-628-9800
Phillips Gourmet, Inc
Kennett Square, PA.................610-925-0520

Fresh

Country Fresh Mushrooms
Avondale, PA 610-268-3033
Creekside Mushrooms
Worthington, PA...................724-297-5491
L.K. Bowman Company
Hanover, PA 800-853-1919
Monterey Mushrooms
Watsonville, CA 800-333-6874

Frozen

Al Pete Meats
Muncie, IN 765-288-8817
Great American Appetizers
Nampa, ID........................800-282-4834
Hanover Foods Corporation
Hanover, PA 717-632-6000
L.K. Bowman Company
Hanover, PA 800-853-1919
Lake Erie Frozen Foods Company
Ashland, OH 800-766-8501
Matador Processors
Blanchard, OK 800-847-0797
Monterey Mushrooms
Watsonville, CA 800-333-6874
Monterey Mushrooms
Watsonville, CA 831-763-5300
Mushroom Company
Cambridge, MD 410-221-8971
Rain Sweet
Salem, OR........................800-363-4293

Lobster

Chieftain Wild Rice Company
Spooner, WI 800-262-6368
Modern Mushroom Farms
Avondale, PA 610-268-3535

Maitakes

D'Artagnan
Newark, NJ.......................800-327-8246
Hardscrabble Enterprises
Franklin, WV 304-358-2921
Modern Mushroom Farms
Avondale, PA 610-268-3535
Phillips Gourmet, Inc
Kennett Square, PA.................610-925-0520

Morel

Chieftain Wild Rice Company
Spooner, WI 800-262-6368
D'Artagnan
Newark, NJ.......................800-327-8246
Emerling International Foods
Buffalo, NY.......................716-833-7381

We supply food manufacturers and food service customers worldwide (since 1988) with bulk ingredients including: Fruits & Vegetables; Juice Concentrates; Herbs & Spices; Oils & Vinegars; Flavors & Colors; Honey & Molasses. We also produce PURE MAPLE SYRUP.

Modern Mushroom Farms
Avondale, PA 610-268-3535

Mousseron

Chieftain Wild Rice Company
Spooner, WI 800-262-6368

Oyster

Chieftain Wild Rice Company
Spooner, WI 800-262-6368
Concord Farms
Union City, CA....................510-429-8855
Creekside Mushrooms
Worthington, PA...................724-297-5491
Emerling International Foods
Buffalo, NY.......................716-833-7381

We supply food manufacturers and food service customers worldwide (since 1988) with bulk ingredients including: Fruits & Vegetables; Juice Concentrates; Herbs & Spices; Oils & Vinegars; Flavors & Colors; Honey & Molasses. We also produce PURE MAPLE SYRUP.

Modern Mushroom Farms
Avondale, PA 610-268-3535
Monterey Mushrooms
Watsonville, CA 800-333-6874
Ostrom Mushroom Farms
Lacey, WA........................206-628-9800
Phillips Gourmet, Inc
Kennett Square, PA.................610-925-0520

Porcini

Chieftain Wild Rice Company
Spooner, WI 800-262-6368
Emerling International Foods
Buffalo, NY.......................716-833-7381

We supply food manufacturers and food service customers worldwide (since 1988) with bulk ingredients including: Fruits & Vegetables; Juice Concentrates; Herbs & Spices; Oils & Vinegars; Flavors & Colors; Honey & Molasses. We also produce PURE MAPLE SYRUP.

Woodland Foods
Gurnee, IL........................847-625-8600

Portobello

Chieftain Wild Rice Company
Spooner, WI 800-262-6368
Creekside Mushrooms
Worthington, PA...................724-297-5491
Modern Mushroom Farms
Avondale, PA 610-268-3535
Ostrom Mushroom Farms
Lacey, WA........................206-628-9800
Phillips Gourmet, Inc
Kennett Square, PA.................610-925-0520
Woodland Foods
Gurnee, IL........................847-625-8600

Baby

Modern Mushroom Farms
Avondale, PA 610-268-3535

Shiitake

Baycliff Company
New York, NY 212-772-6078
Chieftain Wild Rice Company
Spooner, WI 800-262-6368
Concord Farms
Union City, CA....................510-429-8855
Creekside Mushrooms
Worthington, PA...................724-297-5491
Emerling International Foods
Buffalo, NY.......................716-833-7381

We supply food manufacturers and food service customers worldwide (since 1988) with bulk ingredients including: Fruits & Vegetables; Juice Concentrates; Herbs & Spices; Oils & Vinegars; Flavors & Colors; Honey & Molasses. We also produce PURE MAPLE SYRUP.

Hardscrabble Enterprises
Franklin, WV 304-358-2921
Modern Mushroom Farms
Avondale, PA 610-268-3535
Monterey Mushrooms
Watsonville, CA 800-333-6874
Ostrom Mushroom Farms
Lacey, WA........................206-628-9800
Phillips Gourmet, Inc
Kennett Square, PA.................610-925-0520

SupHerb Farms
Turlock, CA 800-787-4372

Frozen culinary herb and specialty vegetable ingredients.

Woodland Foods
Gurnee, IL........................847-625-8600

Truffles

Assouline & Ting
Huntingdon Valley, PA..............800-521-4491
Buon Italia Misono Food Ltd.
New York, NY 212-633-9090
Chieftain Wild Rice Company
Spooner, WI 800-262-6368
D'Artagnan
Newark, NJ.......................800-327-8246
Woodland Foods
Gurnee, IL........................847-625-8600

Black Whole

Assouline & Ting
Huntingdon Valley, PA..............800-521-4491

WhiteWhole

Assouline & Ting
Huntingdon Valley, PA..............800-521-4491

White

Creekside Mushrooms
Worthington, PA...................724-297-5491
Modern Mushroom Farms
Avondale, PA 610-268-3535
Ostrom Mushroom Farms
Lacey, WA........................206-628-9800
Phillips Gourmet, Inc
Kennett Square, PA.................610-925-0520

Wild

Grapevine Trading Company
Santa Rosa, CA....................800-469-6478

Wood Ear

Chieftain Wild Rice Company
Spooner, WI 800-262-6368

Modern Mushroom Farms
Avondale, PA 610-268-3535

Mustard

A. Bauer's Mustard
Flushing, NY. 718-821-3570
Arbor Hill Grapery
Naples, NY 800-554-7553
Ashman Manufacturing & Distributing Company
Virginia Beach, VA. 800-641-9924
Assouline & Ting
Huntingdon Valley, PA 800-521-4491
Baumer Foods
Metairie, LA 504-482-5761
Beaverton Foods
Beaverton, OR 800-223-8076
Boetje Foods
Rock Island, IL 877-726-3853
Booneway Farms
Knoxville, TN. 865-521-9500
Boston Spice & Tea Company
Boston, VA 800-966-4372
Brad's Taste of New York
Floral Park, NY. 516-354-9004
Bread & Chocolate
Wells River, VT 800-524-6715
Buon Italia Misono Food Ltd.
New York, NY 212-633-9090
Cains Foods LP/Olde CapeCod
Ayer, MA. 651-698-6832
California Style Gourmet Products
San Diego, CA 800-243-5226
Casa Visco Finer Food Company
Schenectady, NY. 888-607-2823
Cedarvale Food Products Lounsbury Food Ltd
Toronto, ON 416-656-3331
Cherchies
Malvern, PA 800-644-1980
Ciro Foods
Pittsburgh, PA. 412-771-9018
Clements Foods Company
Oklahoma City, OK 800-654-8355
Coastal Classics
Duxbury, MA 508-746-6058
Dean Distributing Inc
Green Bay, WI. 920-469-6500
Delicae Gourmet
Tarpon Springs, FL. 800-942-2502
Dorina/So-Good
Union, IL. 815-923-2144
East Shore Specialty Foods
Hartland, WI 800-236-1069
Erba Food Products
Brooklyn, NY 718-272-7700
Fauchon
New York, NY 877-605-0130
Fischer & Wieser Specialty Foods, Inc.
Fredericksburg, TX. 800-880-8526
Food Specialties
Indianapolis, IN 317-271-0862
Ford's Fancy Fruit
Raleigh, NC 800-446-0947
Fox Hollow Farm
Hanover, NH. 603-643-6002
French's Flavor Ingredients
Springfield, MO 800-437-3624
Garden Complements
Kansas City, MO. 800-966-1091
Garlic Festival Foods
Hollister, CA. 888-427-5423
GE Barbour
Sussex, NB 506-432-2300
Gold Pure Foods Products Company
Hempstead, NY. 800-422-4681
Golden State Foods
Irvine, CA. 949-252-2000
Gormly's Orchard
South Burlington, VT 800-639-7604
Grapevine Trading Company
Santa Rosa, CA. 800-469-6478
Groeb Farms
Onsted, MI 517-467-2065
Grouse Hunt Farms
Tamaqua, PA. 570-467-2850
GS Dunn & Company
Hamilton, ON 905-522-0833
Hawaiian Fruit Specialties
Kalaheo, HI. 808-332-9333
Heinz Company of Canada
North York, ON. 877-574-3469
Heinz Portion Control
Mason, OH 800-547-8924
Hot Licks Hot Sauces
Spring Valley, CA. 888-766-6468
International Home Foods
Parsippany, NJ. 973-359-9920
J.N. Bech
Elk Rapids, MI 800-232-4583
Kari-Out Company
White Plains, NY 800-433-8799
Kathy's Gourmet Specialties
Mendocino, CA. 707-937-1383
Kelchner's Horseradish
Dublin, PA. 215-249-3439
Knese Enterprise
Bellerose, NY 516-354-9004
Kozlowski Farms
Forestville, CA 800-473-2767
Kraft Foods
Garland, TX 972-272-7511
Liberty Richter
Saddle Brook, NJ 201-291-8749
Lounsbury Foods
Toronto, ON 416-656-6330
Mad Will's Food Company
Auburn, CA. 888-275-9455
McCutcheon's Apple Products
Frederick, MD. 800-888-7537
Mizkam Americas
Kansas City, MO. 816-483-1700
Morehouse Foods
City of Industry, CA 626-854-1655
Mothers Mountain Mustard
Falmouth, ME. 800-440-9891
Mountainbrook of Vermont
Jeffersonville, VT. 802-644-1988
Mucky Duck Mustard Company
Ferndale, MI 248-544-4610
Mutchler's Dakota Gold Mustard
Spearfish, SD 605-642-8166
New Canaan Farms
Dripping Springs, TX. 800-727-5267
Northeast Kingdom Mustard Company
Westfield, VT. 866-4PU-EVT
Old Cavendish Products
Cavendish, VT 800-536-7899
Olde Tyme Mercantile
Arroyo Grande, CA. 805-489-7991
Olds Products Company
Pleasant Prairie, WI 800-233-8064
Pemberton's Gourmet Foods
Gray, ME. 800-255-8401
Pictsweet Frozen Foods
Bells, TN. 731-422-7600
Piknik Products Company Inc
Montgomery, AL. 334-240-2218
Pilgrim Foods
Greenville, NH 603-878-2100
Plochman
Manteno, IL 815-468-3434
Purity Products
Plainview, NY. 888-769-7873
Quality Foods
San Pedro, CA. 877-833-7890
Rapazzini Winery
Gilroy, CA. 800-842-6262
Red Pelican Food Products
Detroit, MI 313-881-4095
Restaurant Lulu Gourmet Products
San Francisco, CA 888-693-5800
REX Pure Foods
New Orleans, LA 800-344-8314
Riba Foods
Houston, TX. 800-327-7422
Rising Sun Farms
Phoenix, OR 800-888-0795
Robert Rothschild Berry Farm
Urbana, OH. 866-565-6790
Robert Rothschild Farm
Urbana, OH. 866-565-6790
Schlotterbeck & Foss Company
Portland, ME. 800-777-4666
Scott-Bathgate
Winnipeg, MB. 800-216-2990
Select Food Products
Toronto, ON 800-699-8016
Silver Palate Kitchens
Cresskill, NJ 800-872-5283
Silver Spring Gardens
Eau Claire, WI 800-826-7322
Stello Foods
Punxsutawney, PA. 800-849-4599
Stonewall Kitchen
York, ME. 800-207-5267
T. Marzetti Company
Columbus, OH 614-846-2232
Terrapin Ridge
Clearwater, FL 800-999-4052
TexaFrance
Round Rock, TX. 800-776-8937
Tropical
Charlotte, NC 800-220-1413
UFL Foods
Mississauga, ON. 905-670-7776
Ultra Seal
New Paltz, NY 845-255-2490
Uncle Fred's Fine Foods
Rockport, TX 361-729-8320
Westport Rivers Vineyard& Winery
Westport, MA 800-993-9695
Wild Thymes Farm
Greenville, NY 800-724-2877
William Poll
New York, NY 800-993-7655
Wing Nien Company
Hayward, CA 510-487-8877
Wing's Food Products
Etobicoke, ON 416-259-2662
Wisconsin Spice
Berlin, WI. 920-361-3555
Woeber Mustard Manufacturing
Springfield, OH. 800-548-2929
Wood Brothers
West Columbia, SC. 803-796-5146

Cress

Koppert Cress USA
New Hyde Park, NY. 516-437-5700

Greens

Canned & Frozen

A. Bauer's Mustard
Flushing, NY. 718-821-3570
Allen Canning Company
Siloam Springs, AR 800-234-2553
Haus Barhyte
Pendleton, OR. 800-407-9241
Heintz & Weber Company
Buffalo, NY. 716-852-7171
Mendocino Mustard
Fort Bragg, CA 800-964-2270
Montana Specialty Mills
Great Falls, MT. 406-761-2338
Mrs. Dog's Products
Grand Rapids, MI 800-2Mr-Dog
Seabrook Brothers & Sons
Seabrook, NJ. 856-455-8080
Terrapin Ridge Farms
Clearwater, FL 800-999-4052
Wisconsin Wilderness Food Products
Milwaukee, WI 800-359-3039

Osaka Purple

Alfred L. Wolff, Inc.
Park Ridge, IL. 847-759-8888
Trade Farm
Oakland, CA 510-836-2938

Nectar

Mira International Foods
East Brunswick, NJ. 800-818-6472
Vilore Foods Company
Laredo, TX 956-726-3633
WCC Honey Marketing
City of Industry, CA 626-855-3086

Canned

Healthmate Products
Highland Park, IL 800-584-8642

Nectarines

Ballantine Produce Company
Reedley, CA 559-875-2583
Brandt Farms
Reedley, CA 559-638-6961
California Fruit
Sanger, CA 559-266-7117
Chiquita Brands Intl. ional
Cincinnati, OH 800-438-0015

Copper Hills Fruit Sales
Fresno, CA 559-277-1970
Corrin Produce Sales
Dinuba, CA. 559-596-0517
Dole Food Company
Westlake Village, CA 818-879-6600
Fastachi
Watertown, MA. 800-466-3022
Fowler Packing Company
Fresno, CA 559-834-5911
Giumarra Companies
Reedley, CA 559-897-5060
HMC Marketing Group
Kingsburg, CA 559-897-1009
Mountain View Fruit Sales
Reedley, CA 559-637-9933
P-R Farms
Clovis, CA 559-299-0201
Pandol Brothers
Delano, CA. 661-725-3755
Stadelman Fruit
Zillah, WA. 509-829-5145
Sun Valley
Reedley, CA 559-591-1515
Sunmet
Del Rey, CA 559-888-2702
Symms Fruit Ranch
Caldwell, ID 208-459-4821
T.S. Smith & Sons
Bridgeville, DE. 302-337-8271
Tom Ringhausen Orchards
Hardin, IL 618-576-2311
Trinity Fruit Sales
Fresno, CA 559-433-3777
Unique Ingredients
Naches, WA. 509-653-1991
United Fruits Corporation
Santa Monica, CA. 310-829-0261
Vintage Produce Sales
Kingsburg, CA 559-897-1622
Wawona Packing Company
Cutler, CA. 559-528-9729
Z&S Distributing
Fresno, CA 800-467-0788

Okra

Anchor Food Products/ McCain Foods
Appleton, WI 920-734-0627
Brooks Food Group Corporate Office
Bedford, VA 800-873-4934
Culinary Standards Corporation
Louisville, KY 800-778-3434
Miss Scarlett's
Chandler, AZ. 800-345-6734
Pictsweet Frozen Foods
Bells, TN. 731-422-7600
Talk O'Texas Brands
San Angelo, TX

Canned

Anchor Food Products/ McCain Foods
Appleton, WI 920-734-0627
Emerling International Foods
Buffalo, NY. 716-833-7381

We supply food manufacturers and food service customers worldwide (since 1988) with bulk ingredients including: Fruits & Vegetables; Juice Concentrates; Herbs & Spices; Oils & Vinegars; Flavors & Colors; Honey & Molasses. We also produce PURE MAPLE SYRUP.

Frozen

Anchor Food Products/ McCain Foods
Appleton, WI 920-734-0627
Brooks Food Group Corporate Office
Bedford, VA 800-873-4934
Emerling International Foods
Buffalo, NY. 716-833-7381

We supply food manufacturers and food service customers worldwide (since 1988) with bulk ingredients including: Fruits & Vegetables; Juice Concentrates; Herbs & Spices; Oils & Vinegars; Flavors & Colors; Honey & Molasses. We also produce PURE MAPLE SYRUP.

Pictsweet Frozen Foods
Bells, TN. 731-422-7600

Olives

A. Camacho
Plant City, FL 800-881-4534
ACH Food Companies
Cordova, TN 800-691-1106
Adams Olive Ranch
Lindsay, CA 888-216-5483
Agrocan
Ville St Laurent, QC 877-247-6226
Alimentaire Whyte's Inc
Laval, QC 800-625-1979
Bell-Carter Foods
Lafayette, CA 800-252-3557
Bob Gordon & Associates
Oak Park, IL 708-524-9611
Cains Foods LP/Olde CapeCod
Ayer, MA. 651-698-6832
California Olive Growers
Fresno, CA 888-965-4837
Caltex Foods
Canoga Park, CA 800-522-5839
Castella Imports
Hauppauge, NY 866-227-8355
Comet Rice
Houston, TX 281-272-8800
Consumers Vinegar & Spice Company
Chicago, IL 773-376-4100
Conway Import Company
Franklin Park, IL. 800-323-8801
Corfu Foods
Bensenville, IL 630-595-2510
Cormier Rice Milling Company
De Witt, AR 870-946-3561
Cosmo's Food Products
West Haven, CT 800-933-6766
Country Cupboard
Virginia City, NV 775-847-7300
Crazy Jerry's
Roswell, GA 770-993-0651
DeLallo Italian Foods
Jeannette, PA. 724-523-6577
DeLallo Italian Foods
Jeannette, PA. 800-433-9100
E. Waldo Ward & Son Corporation
Sierra Madre, CA 800-355-9273
Ehmann Olive Company
Oroville, CA 530-533-3303
Emerling International Foods
Buffalo, NY. 716-833-7381

We supply food manufacturers and food service customers worldwide (since 1988) with bulk ingredients including: Fruits & Vegetables; Juice Concentrates; Herbs & Spices; Oils & Vinegars; Flavors & Colors; Honey & Molasses. We also produce PURE MAPLE SYRUP.

Fantis Foods
Carlstadt, NJ 201-933-6200
FoodMatch Inc
New York, NY. 800-350-3411
G. L. Mezzetta
American Canyon, CA 707-648-1050
Goya Foods of Florida
Miami, FL. 305-592-3150
Grainaissance
Emeryville, CA. 800-472-4697
Greek Gourmet Limited
Mill Valley, CA. 415-480-8050
Heinz Company of Canada
North York, ON. 877-574-3469
HVJ International
Spring, TX. 877-730-3663
Kaiser Pickles
Cincinnati, OH 888-291-0608
Kerry Ingredients
Blue Earth, MN. 507-526-7575
Krinos Foods
Santa Barbara, CA 800-624-4896
L&S Packing Company
Farmingdale, NY 800-286-6487
Lakeside Packing Company
Harrow, ON. 519-738-2314
Liberty Richter
Saddle Brook, NJ 201-291-8749
M&CP Farms
Orland, CA 530-865-9810
Mancuso Cheese Company
Joliet, IL 815-722-2475
Moscahlades Brothers
New York, NY 212-226-5410
Musco Family Olive Company
Tracy, CA 800-523-9828
Musco Olive Products
Orland, CA 530-865-4111
Musco Olive Products
Tracy, CA 800-523-9828
Nature Quality
San Martin, CA. 408-683-2182
Northcenter Foodservice Corporation
Augusta, ME. 877-564-8081
NTC Marketing Inc
Williamsville, NY. 800-333-1637
Olde Tyme Mercantile
Arroyo Grande, CA. 805-489-7991
Olives & Foods Inc
Hialeah, FL 305-821-3444
Orleans Packing Company
Hyde Park, MA 617-361-6611
Pacific Choice Brands
Fresno, CA 559-237-5583
Paradise Products Corporation
Boca Raton, FL. 800-826-1235
Pastene Companies
Canton, MA 781-830-8200
Picklesmith
Taft, TX. 800-499-3401
Price Cold Storage & Packing Company
Yakima, WA 509-966-4110
Proacec USA
Santa Monica, CA. 310-996-7770
Pure Food Ingredients
Verona, WI 800-355-9601
Rahco International
St Augustine, FL. 800-851-7681
Ron-Son Foods
Swedesboro, NJ 856-241-7333
S&G Products
Nicholasville, KY 800-826-7652
San Marzano Foods
Nashville, TN 615-385-4398
Sandt's Honey Company
Easton, PA. 800-935-3960
Santa Barbara Olive Company
Santa Barbara, CA 800-624-4896
Scally's Imperial Importing Company Inc
Staten Island, NY 718-983-1938
Seasons' Enterprises
Addison, IL 630-628-0211
Sieco USA Corporation
Houston, TX 800-325-9443
SilverLeaf International
Stafford, TX 800-442-7542
Spruce Foods
San Clemente, CA. 800-326-3612
Star Fine Foods
Fresno, CA 559-498-2900
Tee Pee Olives
Rye, NY. 800-431-1529
Trotters Imports
Colrain, MA 800-863-8437
Vegetable Juices
Chicago, IL 888-776-9752
Ventura Foods
Philadelphia, PA 215-223-8700
Veronica Foods Company
Oakland, CA 800-370-5554
Victoria Packing Corporation
Brooklyn, NY 718-927-3000
Vincent Formusa Company
Chicago, IL 312-421-0485
West Coast Products Corporation
Orland, CA 800-382-3072
Woodlake Ranch
Woodlake, CA. 559-564-2161

Black

Agrocan
Ville St Laurent, QC 877-247-6226
Bell-Carter Foods
Lafayette, CA 800-252-3557
Bob Gordon & Associates
Oak Park, IL 708-524-9611

Whole

Adams Olive Ranch
Lindsay, CA 888-216-5483

Greek

A. Camacho
Plant City, FL 800-881-4534

Adams Olive Ranch
Lindsay, CA 888-216-5483
Castella Imports
Hauppauge, NY 866-227-8355

Green

Agrocan
Ville St Laurent, QC 877-247-6226
Bob Gordon & Associates
Oak Park, IL 708-524-9611
Ron-Son Foods
Swedesboro, NJ 856-241-7333
Woodlake Ranch
Woodlake, CA. 559-564-2161

with Pimiento

Bell-Carter Foods
Lafayette, CA 800-252-3557

Italian

Adams Olive Ranch
Lindsay, CA 888-216-5483
Castella Imports
Hauppauge, NY 866-227-8355

Onion

A. Duda Farm Fresh Foods
Belle Glade, FL. 561-996-7621
Agri-Pack
Pasco, WA. 509-545-6181
Alsum Produce
Friesland, WI 800-236-5127
Appleton Produce Company
Weiser, ID 208-414-3352
Atlantic Quality Spice &Seasonings
New Brunswick, NJ 800-584-0422
Boardman Foods
Boardman, OR 541-481-3000
Bob Gordon & Associates
Oak Park, IL 708-524-9611
Castella Imports
Hauppauge, NY 866-227-8355
Christopher Ranch
Gilroy, CA. 408-847-1100
Club Chef
Covington, KY 859-578-3100
Custom Cuts
Bay View, WI 414-483-0491
DeFrancesco & Sons
Firebaugh, CA. 209-364-7000
Del Monte Fresh Produce
Coral Gables, FL. 800-950-3683
Del Monte Fresh Produce
Kankakee, IL. 815-936-7400
Delta Packing Company of Lodi
Lodi, CA 209-334-0811
Dickinson Frozen Foods
Fruitland, ID 208-452-5200
Dole Food Company
Westlake Village, CA 818-879-6600
Exeter Produce & Storage Company
Exeter, ON. 800-881-4861
F&S Produce Company
Rosenhayn, NJ 800-886-3316
Fiesta Farms
Nyssa, OR. 541-372-2248
Fresh Express
Salinas, CA 800-242-5472
Ful-Flav-R Foods
Alamo, CA 925-838-0300
G. L. Mezzetta
American Canyon, CA 707-648-1050
Gill's Onions
Oxnard, CA. 800-348-2255
Gills Onions
Oxnard, CA. 800-348-2255
Gilroy Foods
Gilroy, CA. 800-921-7502
Gouw Quality Onions
Taber, AB 403-223-1440
Haliburton International Corporation
Ontario, CA. 877-980-4295
Harris Farms
Coalinga, CA 800-742-1955
Indian Rock Produce
Perkasie, PA 800-882-0512
Isadore A. Rapasadi & Son
Canastota, NY. 315-697-2216
J.C. Watson Company
Parma, ID 208-722-5141
JES Foods
Cleveland, OH 216-883-8987
Kurtz Produce
Ariss, ON 519-824-3279
L&S Packing Company
Farmingdale, NY 800-286-6487
Magic Valley Growers
Wendell, ID. 208-536-6693
Miss Scarlett's
Chandler, AZ. 800-345-6734
Muir-Roberts Company
Salt Lake City, UT 800-564-0949
Murakami Farms
Ontario, OR. 800-421-8814
National Frozen Foods Corporation
Seattle, WA 206-322-8900
Nature Quality
San Martin, CA. 408-683-2182
Ontario Produce Company
Ontario, OR. 541-889-6485
Pak-Wel Produce
Vauxhall, AB. 403-654-2116
Paradise Products Corporation
Boca Raton, FL. 800-826-1235
Peter Rabbit Farms
Coachella, CA. 760-398-0151
POG
Grand Bend, ON 519-238-5704
Premier Packing Company
Bakersfield, CA 661-393-3320
R.C. McEntire & Company
Columbia, SC 803-799-3388
Rain Sweet
Salem, OR. 800-363-4293
Reckitt Benckiser
Parsippany, NJ. 800-333-3899
S&G Products
Nicholasville, KY 800-826-7652
Schiff Food Products
North Bergen, NJ 201-868-6800
Seald Sweet Growers & Packers
Vero Beach, FL. 772-569-2244
Smith-Coulter Company
Chittenango, NY. 315-687-6510
Star Fine Foods
Fresno, CA 559-498-2900
Superior Nutrition Corporation
Wilmington, DE 302-655-5762

SupHerb Farms
Turlock, CA 800-787-4372
Frozen culinary herb and specialty vegetable ingredients.

Swagger Foods Corporation
Vernon Hills, IL 847-913-1200
Symms Fruit Ranch
Caldwell, ID 208-459-4821
Tanimura & Antle
Salinas, CA. 831-455-2255
Tony Vitrano Company
Jessup, MD 800-481-3784
Trappe Packing Corporation
Trappe, MD. 410-476-3185
United Marketing Exchange
Delta, CO 970-874-3332
Vegetable Juices
Chicago, IL 888-776-9752
Vessey & Company
Holtville, CA. 760-356-0130
Walla Walla Gardeners' Association
Walla Walla, WA. 800-553-5014
Wildcat Produce
McGrew, NE. 308-783-2438
William Bolthouse Farms
Bakersfield, CA 661-366-7270
William Karas & Sons
Churchville, NY 585-293-2109
Williams Creek Farms
Williams, OR. 541-846-6481
Z&S Distributing
Fresno, CA 800-467-0788

Canned

Appleton Produce Company
Weiser, ID 208-414-3352
Bob Gordon & Associates
Oak Park, IL 708-524-9611
Ful-Flav-R Foods
Alamo, CA 925-838-0300
G. L. Mezzetta
American Canyon, CA 707-648-1050
L&S Packing Company
Farmingdale, NY 800-286-6487
Paradise Products Corporation
Boca Raton, FL. 800-826-1235
Reckitt Benckiser
Parsippany, NJ. 800-333-3899

Cocktail

A. Camacho
Plant City, FL 800-881-4534
Castella Imports
Hauppauge, NY 866-227-8355

Crushed

Schiff Food Products
North Bergen, NJ 201-868-6800

Eastern Oregon dry bulb on

Tami Great Food
Monsey, NY 732-803-6366

Frozen

Appleton Produce Company
Weiser, ID 208-414-3352
Dickinson Frozen Foods
Fruitland, ID 208-452-5200
Gilroy Foods
Gilroy, CA. 800-921-7502
National Frozen Foods Corporation
Seattle, WA 206-322-8900
Nature Quality
San Martin, CA. 408-683-2182
POG
Grand Bend, ON 519-238-5704
Rain Sweet
Salem, OR. 800-363-4293

SupHerb Farms
Turlock, CA 800-787-4372
Frozen culinary herb and specialty vegetable ingredients.

Trappe Packing Corporation
Trappe, MD. 410-476-3185
Vegetable Juices
Chicago, IL 888-776-9752

Green

DiMare International Dmb Packing Corp
Indio, CA. 760-347-3336
Peter Rabbit Farms
Coachella, CA. 760-398-0151
Russo Farms
Vineland, NJ 856-692-5942

SupHerb Farms
Turlock, CA 800-787-4372

Frozen culinary herb and specialty vegetable ingredients.

Tanimura & Antle
Salinas, CA 831-455-2255
Walter P. Rawl & Sons
Pelion, SC 803-359-3645

Minced

Swagger Foods Corporation
Vernon Hills, IL 847-913-1200

Pearl & Cocktail Onions - O

Dave Kingston Produce
Idaho Falls, ID 800-888-7783
L&S Packing Company
Farmingdale, NY 800-286-6487
Les Trois Petits Cochons
Brooklyn, NY 800-537-7283
Magic Valley Growers
Wendell, ID 208-536-6693
National Frozen Foods Corporation
Seattle, WA 206-322-8900
POG
Grand Bend, ON 519-238-5704
Weiser River Packing
Weiser, ID 208-549-0200

Red

SupHerb Farms
Turlock, CA 800-787-4372

Frozen culinary herb and specialty vegetable ingredients.

Vessey & Company
Holtville, CA 760-356-0130

Spanish

SupHerb Farms
Turlock, CA 800-787-4372

Frozen culinary herb and specialty vegetable ingredients.

Orange

A. Duda Farm Fresh Foods
Belle Glade, FL 561-996-7621
A. Gagliano Company
Milwaukee, WI 800-272-1516
Agrexco USA
Jamaica, NY 718-481-8700
Ben Hill Griffin, Inc.
Frostproof, FL 863-635-2251
Cal-Harvest Marketing
Hanford, CA 559-582-4000
California Citrus Producer
Lindsay, CA 559-562-5169
Corona College Heights Orange & Lemon Associates
Riverside, CA 951-688-1811
Davidson of Dundee
Dundee, FL 800-294-2266
DiMare International Dmb Packing Corp
Indio, CA 760-347-3336
DNE World Fruit Sales
Fort Pierce, FL 800-327-6676
Dole Food Company
Westlake Village, CA 818-879-6600
Fillmore Piru Citrus Association
Piru, CA 800-524-8787
Gene's Citrus Ranch
Sarasota, FL 888-723-2006
Haines City Citrus Growers Association
Haines City, FL 800-422-4245
Hale Indian River Groves
Wabasso, FL 800-562-4502
Heller Brothers PackingcCorporation
Winter Garden, FL 407-656-2124
Hunt Brothers Cooperative
Lake Wales, FL 863-676-9471
J. Rettenmaier
Schoolcraft, MI 877-243-4661
Karl Bissinger French Confections
St Louis, MO 800-325-8881
Leroy Smith & Sons Inc
Vero Beach, FL 772-567-3421
Magnolia Citrus Association
Porterville, CA 559-784-4455
Orange Cove Sanger Citrus Association
Orange Cove, CA 559-626-4453
P-R Farms
Clovis, CA 559-299-0201
Paradise
Plant City, FL 800-330-8952
Premium Waters
Minneapolis, MN 800-243-1163
Reed Lang Farms
Rio Hondo, TX 956-748-2354
Seald Sweet Growers & Packers
Vero Beach, FL 772-569-2244
Sugar Cane Industry Glades Correctional Institution
Belle Glade, FL 561-829-1400
Tony Vitrano Company
Jessup, MD 800-481-3784
Unique Ingredients
Naches, WA 509-653-1991
United Fruits Corporation
Santa Monica, CA 310-829-0261
Yokhol Valley Packing Company
Lindsay, CA 559-562-1327
Z&S Distributing
Fresno, CA 800-467-0788

Blood

Z&S Distributing
Fresno, CA 800-467-0788

Mandarin

Agrocan
Ville St Laurent, QC 877-247-6226
Au Printemps Gourmet
Saint-Jerome, QC 800-663-0416
DNE World Fruit Sales
Fort Pierce, FL 800-327-6676
NTC Marketing Inc
Williamsville, NY 800-333-1637

Canned

NTC Marketing Inc
Williamsville, NY 800-333-1637

Naval

DNE World Fruit Sales
Fort Pierce, FL 800-327-6676
Johnston Farms
Edison, CA 661-366-3201
Kern Ridge Growers
Arvin, CA 661-854-3141
Magnolia Citrus Association
Porterville, CA 559-784-4455
Z&S Distributing
Fresno, CA 800-467-0788

Peels

California Citrus Pulp Company
Lindsay, CA 626-332-1101
Fmali Herb
Santa Cruz, CA 831-423-7913

Pieces

Citrico
Northbrook, IL 888-625-8516

Sections

Canned

Emerling International Foods
Buffalo, NY 716-833-7381

We supply food manufacturers and food service customers worldwide (since 1988) with bulk ingredients including: Fruits & Vegetables; Juice Concentrates; Herbs & Spices; Oils & Vinegars; Flavors & Colors; Honey & Molasses. We also produce PURE MAPLE SYRUP.

Valencia

Magnolia Citrus Association
Porterville, CA 559-784-4455
Z&S Distributing
Fresno, CA 800-467-0788

Oriental Vegetables

Canned

Lee's Food Products
Toronto, ON 416-465-2407
Nikken Foods Company
Saint Louis, MO 636-532-1019

Papaya

Brooks Tropicals
Homestead, FL 800-327-4833
Calavo Growers
Santa Paula, CA 800-422-5280
Chieftain Wild Rice Company
Spooner, WI 800-262-6368
Del Monte Fresh Produce
Coral Gables, FL 800-950-3683
Fastachi
Watertown, MA 800-466-3022
Natural Foods
Toledo, OH 419-537-1713
Organic Planet
San Francisco, CA 415-765-5590
Setton International Foods
Commack, NY 800-227-4397
Timber Crest Farms
Healdsburg, CA 888-374-9325
Unique Ingredients
Naches, WA 509-653-1991

Dried

American Importing Company
Minneapolis, MN 612-331-7000

Peach

Ballantine Produce Company
Reedley, CA 559-875-2583
Ben B. Schwartz & Sons
Detroit, MI 313-841-8300
Brandt Farms
Reedley, CA 559-638-6961
Bridenbaughs Orchards
Martinsburg, PA 814-793-2364
California Fruit
Sanger, CA 559-266-7117
Capitol Foods
Memphis, TN 662-781-9021
Central California Raisin Packers
Del Rey, CA 559-888-2195
Cherry Lane Frozen Fruits
Vineland Station, ON 877-243-7796
Chieftain Wild Rice Company
Spooner, WI 800-262-6368
Chiquita Brands Intl. ional
Cincinnati, OH 800-438-0015
Clofine Dairy & Food Products
Linwood, NJ 800-441-1001
Copper Hills Fruit Sales
Fresno, CA 559-277-1970
Corrin Produce Sales
Dinuba, CA 559-596-0517
Del Mar Food Products Corporation
Watsonville, CA 831-722-3516
Dole Food Company
Westlake Village, CA 818-879-6600
Giumarra Companies
Reedley, CA 559-897-5060

H. Naraghi Farms
Escalon, CA 209-577-5777
Hialeah Products Company
Hollywood, FL 800-923-3379
HMC Marketing Group
Kingsburg, CA 559-897-1009
JR Wood/Big Valley
Atwater, CA 209-358-5643
Kings Canyon Corrin
Reedley, CA 559-638-3571
Lane Packing Company
Fort Valley, GA 478-825-3362
Livingston Farmers Association
Livingston, CA 209-394-7941
Mason County Fruit Packers Cooperative
Ludington, MI 231-845-6248
Miss Scarlett's
Chandler, AZ 800-345-6734
Natural Foods
Toledo, OH 419-537-1713
North Bay Produce
Traverse City, MI 800-678-1941
Nut Factory
Spokane Valley, WA 888-239-5288
Oasis Foods
Planada, CA 209-382-0263
Omstead Foods Ltd
Wheatley, ON 905-315-8883
Organic Planet
San Francisco, CA 415-765-5590
Overlake Foods Corporation
Olympia, WA 800-683-1078
P-R Farms
Clovis, CA 559-299-0201
Pacific Coast Producers
Oroville, CA 530-533-4311
Pandol Brothers
Delano, CA 661-725-3755
Patterson Vegetable Company
Patterson, CA 209-892-2611
Rice Fruit Company
Gardners, PA 800-627-3359
Shafer Lake Fruit
Hartford, MI 269-621-3194
Shawnee Canning Company
Cross Junction, VA 800-713-1414
Stapleton-Spence PackingCompany
San Jose, CA 800-297-8815
Sun Valley
Reedley, CA 559-591-1515
Sun-Maid Growers of California
Kingsburg, CA 800-272-4746
Sunmet
Del Rey, CA 559-888-2702
Sunsweet Growers
Yuba City, CA 800-417-2253
Symms Fruit Ranch
Caldwell, ID 208-459-4821
T.S. Smith & Sons
Bridgeville, DE 302-337-8271
Talbott Farms
Palisade, CO 970-464-5943
Taylor Orchards
Reynolds, GA 478-847-4186
Terri Lynn
Elgin, IL 800-323-0775
Timber Crest Farms
Healdsburg, CA 888-374-9325
Tom Ringhausen Orchards
Hardin, IL 618-576-2311
Trinity Fruit Sales
Fresno, CA 559-433-3777
Unique Ingredients
Naches, WA 509-653-1991
United Fruit Growers
Palisade, CO 970-464-7277
Vintage Produce Sales
Kingsburg, CA 559-897-1622
Wawona Frozen Foods
Clovis, CA 559-299-2901
Wawona Packing Company
Cutler, CA 559-528-9729
Z&S Distributing
Fresno, CA 800-467-0788

Canned

Agrocan
Ville St Laurent, QC 877-247-6226
ConAgra Grocery Products
Irvine, CA 714-680-1000
Emerling International Foods
Buffalo, NY 716-833-7381

We supply food manufacturers and food service customers worldwide (since 1988) with bulk ingredients including: Fruits & Vegetables; Juice Concentrates; Herbs & Spices; Oils & Vinegars; Flavors & Colors; Honey & Molasses. We also produce PURE MAPLE SYRUP.

George Noroian
Arvin, CA 661-858-2457
Oasis Foods
Planada, CA 209-382-0263
Omstead Foods Ltd
Wheatley, ON 905-315-8883
Overlake Foods Corporation
Olympia, WA 800-683-1078
Pacific Coast Producers
Lodi, CA 209-367-8800
Pacific Coast Producers
Oroville, CA 530-533-4311
Shafer-Haggart
Vancouver, BC 604-669-5512
Shawnee Canning Company
Cross Junction, VA 800-713-1414
Stapleton-Spence PackingCompany
San Jose, CA 800-297-8815

Dried

Chieftain Wild Rice Company
Spooner, WI 800-262-6368
Fastachi
Watertown, MA 800-466-3022

Frozen

Cherry Lane Frozen Fruits
Vineland Station, ON 877-243-7796
ConAgra Grocery Products
Irvine, CA 714-680-1000
Emerling International Foods
Buffalo, NY 716-833-7381

We supply food manufacturers and food service customers worldwide (since 1988) with bulk ingredients including: Fruits & Vegetables; Juice Concentrates; Herbs & Spices; Oils & Vinegars; Flavors & Colors; Honey & Molasses. We also produce PURE MAPLE SYRUP.

George Noroian
Arvin, CA 661-858-2457
JR Wood/Big Valley
Atwater, CA 209-358-5643
Omstead Foods Ltd
Wheatley, ON 905-315-8883
Overlake Foods Corporation
Olympia, WA 800-683-1078
Pacific Coast Producers
Lodi, CA 209-367-8800

Klingstone

Canned - Sliced & Diced

Mountain View Fruit Sales
Reedley, CA 559-637-9933

Sliced

Producer Marketing Overlake
Olympia, WA 360-352-7989

Pear

A. Gagliano Company
Milwaukee, WI 800-272-1516
Adobe Creek Packing
Kelseyville, CA 707-279-4204
Ben B. Schwartz & Sons
Detroit, MI 313-841-8300
Bluebird
Peshastin, WA 509-548-1700
Brothers International Food Corporation
Rochester, NY 585-343-3007
California Fruit
Sanger, CA 559-266-7117
Chelan Fresh
Chelan, WA 509-682-5133
Chief Wenatchee
Wenatchee, WA 509-662-5197
Chieftain Wild Rice Company
Spooner, WI 800-262-6368
Chiquita Brands Intl. ional
Cincinnati, OH 800-438-0015
D'Arrigo Brothers Company of California
Salinas, CA 800-995-5939
Delta Packing Company of Lodi
Lodi, CA 209-334-0811
Diamond Fruit Growers
Odell, OR 541-354-5300
Dole Food Company
Westlake Village, CA 818-879-6600
George W Saulpaugh & Sons
Germantown, NY 518-537-6500
H H Dobbins
Lyndonville, NY 877-362-2467
Hialeah Products Company
Hollywood, FL 800-923-3379
M&R Company
Lodi, CA 209-369-4760
Matson Fruit Company
Selah, WA 509-697-7100
Miss Scarlett's
Chandler, AZ 800-345-6734
Mt. Konocti Growers
Kelseyville, CA 707-279-4213
Northern Fruit Company
Wenatchee, WA 509-884-6651
Nuchief Sales
Wenatchee, WA 888-269-4638
Oneonta Starr Ranch Growers
Wenatchee, WA 509-663-2191
Pavero Cold Storage Corporation
Highland, NY 800-435-2994
Placerville Fruit Growers Association
Placerville, CA 530-622-2640
Reter Fruit Company
Medford, OR 541-772-5256
Rice Fruit Company
Gardners, PA 800-627-3359
Scotian Gold Cooperative
Coldbrook, NS 902-679-2191
Stadelman Fruit
Zillah, WA 509-829-5145
Sun-Maid Growers of California
Kingsburg, CA 800-272-4746
Symms Fruit Ranch
Caldwell, ID 208-459-4821
Talbott Farms
Palisade, CO 970-464-5943
Terri Lynn
Elgin, IL 800-323-0775
Timber Crest Farms
Healdsburg, CA 888-374-9325
Trinity Fruit Sales
Fresno, CA 559-433-3777
Truitt Brothers Inc
Salem, OR 800-547-8712
Unique Ingredients
Naches, WA 509-653-1991
United Fruits Corporation
Santa Monica, CA 310-829-0261
Yakima Fruit & Cold Storage Company
Wapato, WA 509-877-2777

Asian

Ballantine Produce Company
Reedley, CA 559-875-2583
Fowler Packing Company
Fresno, CA 559-834-5911
Naumes
Medford, OR 541-772-6268

Price Cold Storage & Packing Company
Yakima, WA 509-966-4110

Bartlett

Adobe Creek Packing
Kelseyville, CA.................. 707-279-4204

Bosc

Adobe Creek Packing
Kelseyville, CA.................. 707-279-4204

Canned

Agrocan
Ville St Laurent, QC 877-247-6226
Arbre Farms Corporation
Walkerville, MI.................. 231-873-3337
ConAgra Grocery Products
Irvine, CA 714-680-1000
Emerling International Foods
Buffalo, NY...................... 716-833-7381

We supply food manufacturers and food service customers worldwide (since 1988) with bulk ingredients including: Fruits & Vegetables; Juice Concentrates; Herbs & Spices; Oils & Vinegars; Flavors & Colors; Honey & Molasses. We also produce PURE MAPLE SYRUP.

Northwest Packing Company
Vancouver, WA.................. 800-543-4356
Pacific Coast Producers
Lodi, CA 209-367-8800

D'Anjou/Bosc

Associated Fruit Company
Phoenix, OR 541-535-1787

Dried

Chieftain Wild Rice Company
Spooner, WI 800-262-6368
Fastachi
Watertown, MA.................. 800-466-3022

Frozen

Arbre Farms Corporation
Walkerville, MI.................. 231-873-3337
ConAgra Grocery Products
Irvine, CA 714-680-1000
Emerling International Foods
Buffalo, NY...................... 716-833-7381

We supply food manufacturers and food service customers worldwide (since 1988) with bulk ingredients including: Fruits & Vegetables; Juice Concentrates; Herbs & Spices; Oils & Vinegars; Flavors & Colors; Honey & Molasses. We also produce PURE MAPLE SYRUP.

Red

Adobe Creek Packing
Kelseyville, CA.................. 707-279-4204

Peas

Camellia Beans
Harahan, LA 504-733-8480
Caribbean Food Delights
Tappan, NY...................... 845-398-3000
Castella Imports
Hauppauge, NY 866-227-8355
Chieftain Wild Rice Company
Spooner, WI 800-262-6368
Columbia Foods
Quincy, WA...................... 509-787-1585
Culinary Standards Corporation
Louisville, KY 800-778-3434
Faribault Foods
Minneapolis, MN 612-333-6461
Garden Valley Foods
Sutherlin, OR 541-459-9565
Hanover Foods Corporation
Hanover, PA 717-632-6000
Hong Kong Market Company
Chicago, IL 312-791-9111
International Home Foods
Parsippany, NJ.................... 973-359-9920
Knight Seed Company
Burnsville, MN................... 800-328-2999
Lakeside Foods
Plainview, MN 507-534-3141
Lakeside Foods
Seymour, WI..................... 920-833-2371
Lucks Food Decorating Company
Tacoma, WA 253-383-4815
Mezza
Lake Forest, IL 888-206-6054
Mills Brothers International
Tukwila, WA..................... 206-575-3000
Miramar Fruit Trading Company
Doral, FL........................ 305-883-4774
National Frozen Foods Corporation
Seattle, WA 206-322-8900
New Harvest Foods
Pulaski, WI 920-822-2578
Norben Company
Willoughby, OH 888-466-7236
Omstead Foods Ltd
Wheatley, ON 905-315-8883
Pictsweet Frozen Foods
Bells, TN........................ 731-422-7600
Royal Caribbean Bakery
Mount Vernon, NY 888-818-0971
Seneca Foods
Arlington, MN 507-964-2204
Seneca Foods
Cumberland, WI 715-822-2181
Smith Frozen Foods
Weston, OR...................... 541-566-3515
Smith Frozen Foods
Weston, OR...................... 800-547-0203
Snowcrest Packer
Abbotsford, BC.................. 800-265-5332
Spokane Seed Company
Spokane Valley, WA 509-535-3671
Strathroy Foods
Strathroy, ON 519-245-4600
Superior Foods
Watsonville, CA 831-728-3691
Symons Frozen Foods
Galvin, WA 360-736-1321
Talley Farms
Arroyo Grande, CA................ 805-489-5533
Trappe Packing Corporation
Trappe, MD...................... 410-476-3185
Twin City Foods
Stanwood, WA 208-743-5568
Vege-Cool
Newman, CA..................... 209-862-2360
Veronica Foods Company
Oakland, CA 800-370-5554
Wallace Grain & Pea Company
Palouse, WA 509-878-1561
Woodland Foods
Gurnee, IL....................... 847-625-8600
Z&S Distributing
Fresno, CA 800-467-0788

Black-eyed

Lucks Food Decorating Company
Tacoma, WA 253-383-4815
Pictsweet Frozen Foods
Bells, TN........................ 731-422-7600

Canned

Emerling International Foods
Buffalo, NY...................... 716-833-7381

We supply food manufacturers and food service customers worldwide (since 1988) with bulk ingredients including: Fruits & Vegetables; Juice Concentrates; Herbs & Spices; Oils & Vinegars; Flavors & Colors; Honey & Molasses. We also produce PURE MAPLE SYRUP.

Lucks Food Decorating Company
Tacoma, WA 253-383-4815

Frozen

Emerling International Foods
Buffalo, NY...................... 716-833-7381

We supply food manufacturers and food service customers worldwide (since 1988) with bulk ingredients including: Fruits & Vegetables; Juice Concentrates; Herbs & Spices; Oils & Vinegars; Flavors & Colors; Honey & Molasses. We also produce PURE MAPLE SYRUP.

Pictsweet Frozen Foods
Bells, TN........................ 731-422-7600

Canned

Blue Runner Foods
Gonzales, LA 225-647-3016
Carriere Foods Inc
Saint-Denis-Sur-Richelie, QC 450-787-3411
Emerling International Foods
Buffalo, NY...................... 716-833-7381

We supply food manufacturers and food service customers worldwide (since 1988) with bulk ingredients including: Fruits & Vegetables; Juice Concentrates; Herbs & Spices; Oils & Vinegars; Flavors & Colors; Honey & Molasses. We also produce PURE MAPLE SYRUP.

Faribault Foods
Minneapolis, MN 612-333-6461
Hanover Foods Corporation
Hanover, PA 717-632-6000
International Home Foods
Parsippany, NJ.................... 973-359-9920
Lakeside Foods
Plainview, MN 507-534-3141
Lakeside Foods
Manitowoc, WI................... 920-684-3356
Lakeside Foods
Seymour, WI..................... 920-833-2371
Lodi Canning Company
Lodi, WI 608-592-4236
Lucks Food Decorating Company
Tacoma, WA 253-383-4815
New Harvest Foods
Pulaski, WI 920-822-2578
Seneca Foods
Buhl, ID......................... 208-543-4322
Seneca Foods
Marion, NY...................... 315-926-8100
Seneca Foods
Montgomery, MN 507-364-8231
Seneca Foods
Blue Earth, MN................... 507-526-2131
Seneca Foods
Janesville, WI 608-757-6000
Seneca Foods
Cumberland, WI 715-822-2181
Seneca Foods Corporation
Marion, NY...................... 315-926-8100

Dry

Camellia Beans
Harahan, LA 504-733-8480
Just Tomatoes Company
Westley, CA...................... 800-537-1985
Mills Brothers International
Tukwila, WA..................... 206-575-3000
Spokane Seed Company
Spokane Valley, WA 509-535-3671

Fresh

Lakeside Foods
Seymour, WI..................... 920-833-2371

Frozen

Canada Safeway Limited
Abbotsford, BC................... 604-854-1191
Cavendish Farms
Burlington, MA .... 888-88 -7437
Columbia Foods
Quincy, WA...................... 509-787-1585
Emerling International Foods
Buffalo, NY...................... 716-833-7381

We supply food manufacturers and food service customers worldwide (since 1988) with bulk ingredients including: Fruits & Vegetables; Juice Concentrates; Herbs & Spices; Oils & Vinegars; Flavors & Colors; Honey & Molasses. We also produce PURE MAPLE SYRUP.

Faribault Foods
Minneapolis, MN 612-333-6461
Hanover Foods Corporation
Hanover, PA 717-632-6000
J.R. Simplot Company
Boise, ID 208-336-2110
Lakeside Foods
Plainview, MN 507-534-3141

Lakeside Foods
Manitowoc, WI 920-684-3356
Lakeside Foods
Seymour, WI 920-833-2371
Lodi Canning Company
Lodi, WI 608-592-4236
National Frozen Foods Corporation
Seattle, WA 206-322-8900
Omstead Foods Ltd
Wheatley, ON 905-315-8883
Pictsweet Frozen Foods
Bells, TN 731-422-7600
Seneca Foods
Marion, NY 315-926-8100
Seneca Foods
Montgomery, MN 507-364-8231
Smith Frozen Foods
Weston, OR 541-566-3515
Smith Frozen Foods
Weston, OR 800-547-0203
Snowcrest Packer
Abbotsford, BC 800-265-5332
Strathroy Foods
Strathroy, ON 519-245-4600
Symons Frozen Foods
Galvin, WA 360-736-1321
Trappe Packing Corporation
Trappe, MD 410-476-3185
Twin City Foods
Stanwood, WA 208-743-5568

Green

Fastachi
Watertown, MA 800-466-3022
Knight Seed Company
Burnsville, MN 800-328-2999
Pictsweet Frozen Foods
Bells, TN 731-422-7600
Sno Pac Foods
Caledonia, MN 800-533-2215

Green & Yellow Split - Dried

American Health & Nutrition
Ann Arbor, MI 734-677-5570
Chieftain Wild Rice Company
Spooner, WI 800-262-6368
Country Cupboard
Virginia City, NV 775-847-7300
Emerling International Foods
Buffalo, NY 716-833-7381

We supply food manufacturers and food service customers worldwide (since 1988) with bulk ingredients including: Fruits & Vegetables; Juice Concentrates; Herbs & Spices; Oils & Vinegars; Flavors & Colors; Honey & Molasses. We also produce PURE MAPLE SYRUP.

Organic Planet
San Francisco, CA 415-765-5590
Spokane Seed Company
Spokane Valley, WA 509-535-3671
Unique Ingredients
Naches, WA 509-653-1991
Vege-Cool
Newman, CA 209-862-2360

Snap

Miss Scarlett's
Chandler, AZ 800-345-6734
National Frozen Foods Corporation
Seattle, WA 206-322-8900
Pictsweet Frozen Foods
Bells, TN 731-422-7600
Superior Foods
Watsonville, CA 831-728-3691

Southern

Naturex Inc.
South Hackensack, NJ 201-440-5000
Trinidad Benham Company
Denver, CO 303-220-1400

Yellow Split

Knight Seed Company
Burnsville, MN 800-328-2999
United Pulse Trading
Bismarck, ND 701-751-1623
Woodland Foods
Gurnee, IL 847-625-8600

Peppers

AgroCepia
Miami, FL 305-704-3488
Anchor Food Products/ McCain Foods
Appleton, WI 920-734-0627
Atlantic Quality Spice &Seasonings
New Brunswick, NJ 800-584-0422
B&G Foods
Parsippany, NJ 973-401-6500
Baumer Foods
Metairie, LA 504-482-5761
Bifulco Farms
Pittsgrove, NJ 856-692-0707
Big B Distributors
Evansville, IN 812-425-5235
Bloch & Guggenheimer
Hurlock, MD 800-541-2809
Bob Gordon & Associates
Oak Park, IL 708-524-9611
Border Foods Inc
Deming, NM 888-737-7752
Carando Gourmet Frozen Foods
Agawam, MA 888-227-2636
Cherchies
Malvern, PA 800-644-1980
Chieftain Wild Rice Company
Spooner, WI 800-262-6368
Christopher Ranch
Gilroy, CA 408-847-1100
Chugwater Chili Corporation
Chugwater, WY 800-972-4454
Cleugh's Frozen Foods
Buena Park, CA 714-521-1002
Comanche Tortilla Factory
Fort Stockton, TX 432-336-3245
Del Mar Food Products Corporation
Watsonville, CA 831-722-3516
Delta Packing Company of Lodi
Lodi, CA 209-334-0811
Dickinson Frozen Foods
Fruitland, ID 208-452-5200
Dolce Nonna
Whitestone, NY 718-767-3501
Dole Food Company
Westlake Village, CA 818-879-6600
Dunbar Foods
Dunn, NC 910-892-3175
Eckert Cold Storage
Escalon, CA 209-838-4040
Emerling International Foods
Buffalo, NY 716-833-7381

We supply food manufacturers and food service customers worldwide (since 1988) with bulk ingredients including: Fruits & Vegetables; Juice Concentrates; Herbs & Spices; Oils & Vinegars; Flavors & Colors; Honey & Molasses. We also produce PURE MAPLE SYRUP.

F&S Produce Company
Rosenhayn, NJ 800-886-3316
Fiesta Canning Company
Mc Neal, AZ 520-642-3376
Food City Pickle Company
Chicago, IL
Fountain Valley Foods
Colorado Springs, CO 719-573-6012
Frog Ranch Foods
Glouster, OH 800-742-2488
Ful-Flav-R Foods
Alamo, CA 925-838-0300
G. L. Mezzetta
American Canyon, CA 707-648-1050
Garon Industries
Mosinee, WI 715-693-0558
George Chiala Farms
Morgan Hill, CA 408-778-0562
Georgia Vegetable Company
Tifton, GA 229-386-2374
Gilroy Foods
Gilroy, CA 800-921-7502
Giulianos' Specialty Foods
Garden Grove, CA 714-895-9661
GNS Spices
Walnut, CA 909-594-9505
Goebbert's Home Grown Vegetables
South Barrington, IL 847-428-6727
Great American Appetizers
Nampa, ID 800-282-4834
Greek Gourmet Limited
Mill Valley, CA 415-480-8050
GWB Foods Corporation
Brooklyn, NY 877-977-7610
Haliburton International Corporation
Ontario, CA 877-980-4295
Harris Farms
Coalinga, CA 800-742-1955
Hermann Pickle Farm
Garrettsville, OH 800-245-2696
Indel Food Products
El Paso, TX 800-472-0159
Jalapeno Foods Company
The Woodlands, TX 800-896-2318
JES Foods
Cleveland, OH 216-883-8987
Johnston Farms
Edison, CA 661-366-3201
Kaiser Pickles
Cincinnati, OH 888-291-0608
Kaplan & Zubrin
Camden, NJ 800-334-0002
Krinos Foods
Santa Barbara, CA 800-624-4896
L&S Packing Company
Farmingdale, NY 800-286-6487
Lakeside Packing Company
Harrow, ON 519-738-2314
Landry's Pepper Company
Saint Martinville, LA 337-394-6097
Mama Lil's Peppers
Seattle, WA 206-322-8824
Matador Processors
Blanchard, OK 800-847-0797
Mercado Latino
City of Industry, CA 626-333-6862
Michigan Freeze Pack
Hart, MI 231-873-2175
Miguel's Stowe Away
Stowe, VT 800-448-6517
Mojave Foods Corporation
Commerce, CA 323-890-8900
Monticello Canning Company
Crossville, TN 931-484-3696
Moody Dunbar
Johnson City, TN 800-251-8202
Mount Olive Pickle Company
Mount Olive, NC 800-672-5041
Nature Quality
San Martin, CA 408-683-2182
Naturex Inc.
South Hackensack, NJ 201-440-5000
Norpaco
Middletown, CT 800-252-0222
Omstead Foods Ltd
Wheatley, ON 905-315-8883
Pacific Choice Brands
Fresno, CA 559-237-5583
Paisley Farms
Willoughby, OH 800-676-8656
Pastene Companies
Canton, MA 781-830-8200
Pastorelli Food Products
Chicago, IL 800-767-2829
Pepper Creek Farms
Lawton, OK 800-526-8132
Pure Food Ingredients
Verona, WI 800-355-9601
Ralph Sechler & Son Inc
St Joe, IN 800-332-5461
Rene Produce Distributors
Nogales, AZ 520-281-9014
RES Food Products International
Green Bay, WI 800-255-3768
Ripon Pickle Company
Ripon, WI 800-324-5493
Ron-Son Foods
Swedesboro, NJ 856-241-7333

S&G Products
Nicholasville, KY 800-826-7652
Saticoy Foods Corporation
Ventura, CA. 805-647-5266
Scally's Imperial Importing Company Inc
Staten Island, NY 718-983-1938
Schiff Food Products
North Bergen, NJ 201-868-6800
Sedlock Farm
Lynn Center, IL. 309-521-8284
Snowcrest Packer
Abbotsford, BC. 800-265-5332
South Mill Distribution
Kennett Square, PA. 610-444-4800
Star Fine Foods
Fresno, CA 559-498-2900
Strub Pickles
Brantford, ON. 519-751-1717

SupHerb Farms
Turlock, CA 800-787-4372

Frozen culinary herb and specialty vegetable ingredients.

Topor's Pickle Company
Detroit, MI 313-237-0288
Trappe Packing Corporation
Trappe, MD. 410-476-3185
Tropical
Charlotte, NC 800-220-1413
Van Drunen Farms
Momence, IL. 815-472-3537
Vega Food Industries
Cranston, RI 800-973-7737
Vegetable Juices
Chicago, IL. 888-776-9752
Victoria Packing Corporation
Brooklyn, NY 718-927-3000
Vincent Formusa Company
Chicago, IL 312-421-0485
Violet Packing
Williamstown, NJ 856-629-7428
Whyte's Food Corporation
Mississauga, ON. 905-624-5065
Woodland Foods
Gurnee, IL. 847-625-8600
Z&S Distributing
Fresno, CA 800-467-0788

Ancho

Chieftain Wild Rice Company
Spooner, WI 800-262-6368

Banana

A. Camacho
Plant City, FL 800-881-4534
Food City Pickle Company
Chicago, IL
G. L. Mezzetta
American Canyon, CA 707-648-1050
Indel Food Products
El Paso, TX. 800-472-0159
Kaplan & Zubrin
Camden, NJ. 800-334-0002
Topor's Pickle Company
Detroit, MI 313-237-0288

Bell

Chieftain Wild Rice Company
Spooner, WI 800-262-6368
Christopher Ranch
Gilroy, CA. 408-847-1100
Cleugh's Frozen Foods
Buena Park, CA 714-521-1002
Culinary Standards Corporation
Louisville, KY 800-778-3434
Dehydrates Inc.
Hewlett, NY 800-983-4443
Dickinson Frozen Foods
Fruitland, ID 208-452-5200
Eckert Cold Storage
Escalon, CA 209-838-4040
F&S Produce Company
Rosenhayn, NJ 800-886-3316
Ful-Flav-R Foods
Alamo, CA 925-838-0300
Gel Spice Company, Inc
Bayonne, NJ 800-922-0230
George Chiala Farms
Morgan Hill, CA. 408-778-0562
Grasso Foods
Swedesboro, NJ
Kern Ridge Growers
Arvin, CA 661-854-3141
M&R Company
Lodi, CA 209-369-4760
Moody Dunbar
Johnson City, TN 800-251-8202
Nature Quality
San Martin, CA. 408-683-2182
Oxford Frozen Foods Limited
Oxford, NS 902-447-2100
Rene Produce Distributors
Nogales, AZ 520-281-9014
Ripon Pickle Company
Ripon, WI 800-324-5493
Saticoy Foods Corporation
Ventura, CA. 805-647-5266
Schiff Food Products
North Bergen, NJ 201-868-6800

SupHerb Farms
Turlock, CA 800-787-4372

Frozen culinary herb and specialty vegetable ingredients.

Sure Fresh Produce
Santa Maria, CA. 888-423-5379
Talley Farms
Arroyo Grande, CA. 805-489-5533
Tropical
Charlotte, NC 800-220-1413
Vegetable Juices
Chicago, IL. 888-776-9752
Z&S Distributing
Fresno, CA 800-467-0788

Canned

Bob Gordon & Associates
Oak Park, IL 708-524-9611
Colonna Brothers
North Bergen, NJ 201-864-1115
Emerling International Foods
Buffalo, NY. 716-833-7381

We supply food manufacturers and food service customers worldwide (since 1988) with bulk ingredients including: Fruits & Vegetables; Juice Concentrates; Herbs & Spices; Oils & Vinegars; Flavors & Colors; Honey & Molasses. We also produce PURE MAPLE SYRUP.

Ful-Flav-R Foods
Alamo, CA 925-838-0300
L&S Packing Company
Farmingdale, NY 800-286-6487
Mancini Packing Company
Zolfo Springs, FL 863-735-2000
Moody Dunbar
Johnson City, TN 800-251-8202
Ron-Son Foods
Swedesboro, NJ 856-241-7333
Van Drunen Farms
Momence, IL. 815-472-3537
Violet Packing
Williamstown, NJ 856-629-7428

Capsicums

Advanced Spice & Trading
Carrollton, TX. 800-872-7811

Emerling International Foods
Buffalo, NY. 716-833-7381

We supply food manufacturers and food service customers worldwide (since 1988) with bulk ingredients including: Fruits & Vegetables; Juice Concentrates; Herbs & Spices; Oils & Vinegars; Flavors & Colors; Honey & Molasses. We also produce PURE MAPLE SYRUP.

Gilroy Foods
Gilroy, CA. 800-921-7502
Vegetable Juices
Chicago, IL 888-776-9752

Aseptic Packed

Allen Canning Company
Siloam Springs, AR 800-234-2553

Dehydrated

Gilroy Foods
Gilroy, CA. 800-921-7502
Naturex Inc.
South Hackensack, NJ 201-440-5000

Frozen

SupHerb Farms
Turlock, CA 800-787-4372

Frozen culinary herb and specialty vegetable ingredients.

Cascabel

Chieftain Wild Rice Company
Spooner, WI 800-262-6368

Cherry

A. Camacho
Plant City, FL 800-881-4534
B&G Foods
Parsippany, NJ. 973-401-6500
F&S Produce Company
Rosenhayn, NJ 800-886-3316
Kaplan & Zubrin
Camden, NJ. 800-334-0002
L&S Packing Company
Farmingdale, NY 800-286-6487
Norpaco
Middletown, CT 800-252-0222

Chile

American Key Food Products
Closter, NJ. 800-767-0237
Border Foods Inc
Deming, NM. 888-737-7752
Chieftain Wild Rice Company
Spooner, WI 800-262-6368
Chile Today
San Francisco, CA 800-758-0372
Chili Dude
Dallas, TX. 214-354-9906
Chugwater Chili Corporation
Chugwater, WY 800-972-4454
Emerling International Foods
Buffalo, NY. 716-833-7381

We supply food manufacturers and food service customers worldwide (since 1988) with bulk ingredients including: Fruits & Vegetables; Juice Concentrates; Herbs & Spices; Oils & Vinegars; Flavors & Colors; Honey & Molasses. We also produce PURE MAPLE SYRUP.

Fiesta Canning Company
Mc Neal, AZ. 520-642-3376
Ful-Flav-R Foods
Alamo, CA 925-838-0300
G. L. Mezzetta
American Canyon, CA 707-648-1050
George Chiala Farms
Morgan Hill, CA. 408-778-0562

Indel Food Products
El Paso, TX....................800-472-0159
Kern Ridge Growers
Arvin, CA....................661-854-3141
Magic Seasoning Blends
New Orleans, LA....................800-457-2857
Mancini Packing Company
Zolfo Springs, FL....................863-735-2000
Mercado Latino
City of Industry, CA....................626-333-6862
Pepperland Farms
Denham Springs, LA....................225-665-3555
Pure Food Ingredients
Verona, WI....................800-355-9601

SupHerb Farms
Turlock, CA....................800-787-4372

Frozen culinary herb and specialty vegetable ingredients.

Tropical Commodities
Miami, FL....................305-471-8120
Vega Food Industries
Cranston, RI....................800-973-7737
Vegetable Juices
Chicago, IL....................888-776-9752
Walker Foods
Los Angeles, CA....................800-966-5199
Z&S Distributing
Fresno, CA....................800-467-0788

Dried Pods

American Key Food Products
Closter, NJ....................800-767-0237
Emerling International Foods
Buffalo, NY....................716-833-7381

We supply food manufacturers and food service customers worldwide (since 1988) with bulk ingredients including: Fruits & Vegetables; Juice Concentrates; Herbs & Spices; Oils & Vinegars; Flavors & Colors; Honey & Molasses. We also produce PURE MAPLE SYRUP.

Gel Spice Company, Inc
Bayonne, NJ....................800-922-0230
Gilroy Foods
Gilroy, CA....................800-921-7502
Magic Seasoning Blends
New Orleans, LA....................800-457-2857
Mojave Foods Corporation
Commerce, CA....................323-890-8900

Chipotle

Chieftain Wild Rice Company
Spooner, WI....................800-262-6368
Emerling International Foods
Buffalo, NY....................716-833-7381

We supply food manufacturers and food service customers worldwide (since 1988) with bulk ingredients including: Fruits & Vegetables; Juice Concentrates; Herbs & Spices; Oils & Vinegars; Flavors & Colors; Honey & Molasses. We also produce PURE MAPLE SYRUP.

Jalapeno Foods Company
The Woodlands, TX....................800-896-2318
Magic Seasoning Blends
New Orleans, LA....................800-457-2857
Ripon Pickle Company
Ripon, WI....................800-324-5493
Vegetable Juices
Chicago, IL....................888-776-9752

Woodland Foods
Gurnee, IL....................847-625-8600

De Arbol

Chieftain Wild Rice Company
Spooner, WI....................800-262-6368

Frozen

Anchor Food Products/ McCain Foods
Appleton, WI....................920-734-0627
Carando Gourmet Frozen Foods
Agawam, MA....................888-227-2636
Cleugh's Frozen Foods
Buena Park, CA....................714-521-1002
Dickinson Frozen Foods
Fruitland, ID....................208-452-5200
Eckert Cold Storage
Escalon, CA....................209-838-4040
Emerling International Foods
Buffalo, NY....................716-833-7381

We supply food manufacturers and food service customers worldwide (since 1988) with bulk ingredients including: Fruits & Vegetables; Juice Concentrates; Herbs & Spices; Oils & Vinegars; Flavors & Colors; Honey & Molasses. We also produce PURE MAPLE SYRUP.

Great American Appetizers
Nampa, ID....................800-282-4834
Hermann Pickle Farm
Garrettsville, OH....................800-245-2696
Matador Processors
Blanchard, OK....................800-847-0797
Monticello Canning Company
Crossville, TN....................931-484-3696
Omstead Foods Ltd
Wheatley, ON....................905-315-8883
Rain Sweet
Salem, OR....................800-363-4293
Snowcrest Packer
Abbotsford, BC....................800-265-5332

SupHerb Farms
Turlock, CA....................800-787-4372

Frozen culinary herb and specialty vegetable ingredients.

Trappe Packing Corporation
Trappe, MD....................410-476-3185
Van De Walle Farms
San Antonio, TX....................210-436-5551
Van Drunen Farms
Momence, IL....................815-472-3537
Vegetable Juices
Chicago, IL....................888-776-9752

Guajillo

Chieftain Wild Rice Company
Spooner, WI....................800-262-6368

Habanero

Brooks Tropicals
Homestead, FL....................800-327-4833
Chieftain Wild Rice Company
Spooner, WI....................800-262-6368
Garon Industries
Mosinee, WI....................715-693-0558
George Chiala Farms
Morgan Hill, CA....................408-778-0562
Indel Food Products
El Paso, TX....................800-472-0159
Woodland Foods
Gurnee, IL....................847-625-8600

Jalapeno

A. Camacho
Plant City, FL....................800-881-4534
Advanced Spice & Trading
Carrollton, TX....................800-872-7811

AgroCepia
Miami, FL....................305-704-3488
Anchor Food Products/ McCain Foods
Appleton, WI....................920-734-0627
Arbre Farms Corporation
Walkerville, MI....................231-873-3337
Chieftain Wild Rice Company
Spooner, WI....................800-262-6368
Dehydrates Inc.
Hewlett, NY....................800-983-4443
Eckert Cold Storage
Escalon, CA....................209-838-4040
Emerling International Foods
Buffalo, NY....................716-833-7381

We supply food manufacturers and food service customers worldwide (since 1988) with bulk ingredients including: Fruits & Vegetables; Juice Concentrates; Herbs & Spices; Oils & Vinegars; Flavors & Colors; Honey & Molasses. We also produce PURE MAPLE SYRUP.

F&S Produce Company
Rosenhayn, NJ....................800-886-3316
Fountain Valley Foods
Colorado Springs, CO....................719-573-6012
Ful-Flav-R Foods
Alamo, CA....................925-838-0300
G. L. Mezzetta
American Canyon, CA....................707-648-1050
Garon Industries
Mosinee, WI....................715-693-0558
George Chiala Farms
Morgan Hill, CA....................408-778-0562
Gilroy Foods
Gilroy, CA....................800-921-7502
Great American Appetizers
Nampa, ID....................800-282-4834
Jalapeno Foods Company
The Woodlands, TX....................800-896-2318
L&S Packing Company
Farmingdale, NY....................800-286-6487
Leon's Texas Cuisine
Mc Kinney, TX....................972-529-5050
Limited Edition
Midland, TX....................432-686-2008
Matador Processors
Blanchard, OK....................800-847-0797
Miguel's Stowe Away
Stowe, VT....................800-448-6517
Nature Quality
San Martin, CA....................408-683-2182
Pepper Creek Farms
Lawton, OK....................800-526-8132
Pure Food Ingredients
Verona, WI....................800-355-9601
RES Food Products International
Green Bay, WI....................800-255-3768
Strub Pickles
Brantford, ON....................519-751-1717

SupHerb Farms
Turlock, CA....................800-787-4372

Frozen culinary herb and specialty vegetable ingredients.

Van De Walle Farms
San Antonio, TX....................210-436-5551
Van Drunen Farms
Momence, IL....................815-472-3537
Vegetable Juices
Chicago, IL....................888-776-9752
Vilore Foods Company
Laredo, TX....................956-726-3633
Walker Foods
Los Angeles, CA....................800-966-5199

Jalapeno & Chiles

Gilroy Foods
Gilroy, CA....................800-921-7502
La Victoria Foods
Rosemead, CA....................800-523-4635
Matador Processors
Blanchard, OK....................800-847-0797

Nature Quality
San Martin, CA 408-683-2182
Pure Food Ingredients
Verona, WI 800-355-9601

SupHerb Farms
Turlock, CA 800-787-4372

Frozen culinary herb and specialty vegetable ingredients.

Woodland Foods
Gurnee, IL 847-625-8600

Japones

Chieftain Wild Rice Company
Spooner, WI 800-262-6368

Mulato

Chieftain Wild Rice Company
Spooner, WI 800-262-6368

Pepperoncini

A. Camacho
Plant City, FL 800-881-4534
Agrocan
Ville St Laurent, QC 877-247-6226
Baumer Foods
Metairie, LA 504-482-5761
Big B Distributors
Evansville, IN 812-425-5235
Bob Gordon & Associates
Oak Park, IL 708-524-9611
Cains Foods LP/Olde CapeCod
Ayer, MA 651-698-6832
Castella Imports
Hauppauge, NY 866-227-8355
Emerling International Foods
Buffalo, NY 716-833-7381

We supply food manufacturers and food service customers worldwide (since 1988) with bulk ingredients including: Fruits & Vegetables; Juice Concentrates; Herbs & Spices; Oils & Vinegars; Flavors & Colors; Honey & Molasses. We also produce PURE MAPLE SYRUP.

Food City Pickle Company
Chicago, IL
G. L. Mezzetta
American Canyon, CA 707-648-1050
L&S Packing Company
Farmingdale, NY 800-286-6487
Ron-Son Foods
Swedesboro, NJ 856-241-7333
Vegetable Juices
Chicago, IL 888-776-9752

Roasted

Agrocan
Ville St Laurent, QC 877-247-6226
Bloch & Guggenheimer
Hurlock, MD 800-541-2809
Castella Imports
Hauppauge, NY 866-227-8355
Ful-Flav-R Foods
Alamo, CA 925-838-0300
Indel Food Products
El Paso, TX 800-472-0159
Mancini Packing Company
Zolfo Springs, FL 863-735-2000
Moody Dunbar
Johnson City, TN 800-251-8202
Ron-Son Foods
Swedesboro, NJ 856-241-7333

SupHerb Farms
Turlock, CA 800-787-4372

Frozen culinary herb and specialty vegetable ingredients.

Serrano

Chieftain Wild Rice Company
Spooner, WI 800-262-6368
Emerling International Foods
Buffalo, NY 716-833-7381

We supply food manufacturers and food service customers worldwide (since 1988) with bulk ingredients including: Fruits & Vegetables; Juice Concentrates; Herbs & Spices; Oils & Vinegars; Flavors & Colors; Honey & Molasses. We also produce PURE MAPLE SYRUP.

F&S Produce Company
Rosenhayn, NJ 800-886-3316
Jalapeno Foods Company
The Woodlands, TX 800-896-2318
RES Food Products International
Green Bay, WI 800-255-3768

SupHerb Farms
Turlock, CA 800-787-4372

Frozen culinary herb and specialty vegetable ingredients.

Van De Walle Farms
San Antonio, TX 210-436-5551

Sweet

Carando Gourmet Frozen Foods
Agawam, MA 888-227-2636
Coutts Specialty Foods
Boxborough, MA 800-919-2952
Georgia Vegetable Company
Tifton, GA 229-386-2374
Kaplan & Zubrin
Camden, NJ 800-334-0002
Mancini Packing Company
Zolfo Springs, FL 863-735-2000
Moody Dunbar
Johnson City, TN 800-251-8202
Ripon Pickle Company
Ripon, WI 800-324-5493

Persimmons

Ballantine Produce Company
Reedley, CA 559-875-2583
Copper Hills Fruit Sales
Fresno, CA 559-277-1970
Emerling International Foods
Buffalo, NY 716-833-7381

We supply food manufacturers and food service customers worldwide (since 1988) with bulk ingredients including: Fruits & Vegetables; Juice Concentrates; Herbs & Spices; Oils & Vinegars; Flavors & Colors; Honey & Molasses. We also produce PURE MAPLE SYRUP.

HMC Marketing Group
Kingsburg, CA 559-897-1009
Just Tomatoes Company
Westley, CA 800-537-1985
Naumes
Medford, OR 541-772-6268
Pandol Brothers
Delano, CA 661-725-3755
Tufts Ranch
Winters, CA 530-795-4144
West Pak Avocado
Temecula, CA 800-266-4414

Pimientos

Emerling International Foods
Buffalo, NY 716-833-7381

We supply food manufacturers and food service customers worldwide (since 1988) with bulk ingredients including: Fruits & Vegetables; Juice Concentrates; Herbs & Spices; Oils & Vinegars; Flavors & Colors; Honey & Molasses. We also produce PURE MAPLE SYRUP.

Indel Food Products
El Paso, TX 800-472-0159
Monticello Canning Company
Crossville, TN 931-484-3696
Moody Dunbar
Johnson City, TN 800-251-8202
Paradise Products Corporation
Boca Raton, FL 800-826-1235
Pastene Companies
Canton, MA 781-830-8200
Saticoy Foods Corporation
Ventura, CA 805-647-5266
Strub Pickles
Brantford, ON 519-751-1717
Victoria Packing Corporation
Brooklyn, NY 718-927-3000

Pineapple

Chieftain Wild Rice Company
Spooner, WI 800-262-6368
Chiquita Brands Intl. ional
Cincinnati, OH 800-438-0015
Custom Cuts
Bay View, WI 414-483-0491
Del Monte Fresh Produce
Coral Gables, FL 800-950-3683
F&S Produce Company
Rosenhayn, NJ 800-886-3316
Fastachi
Watertown, MA 800-466-3022
Hialeah Products Company
Hollywood, FL 800-923-3379
J.H. Verbridge & Son
Williamson, NY 315-589-2366
Maui Pineapple Company
Kahului, HI 808-877-3351
Maui Pineapple Company
Concord, CA 925-798-0240
NTC Marketing Inc
Williamsville, NY 800-333-1637
Nut Factory
Spokane Valley, WA 888-239-5288
Organic Planet
San Francisco, CA 415-765-5590
Pacific Coast Fruit Company
Portland, OR 503-234-6411
Paradise
Plant City, FL 800-330-8952
Setton International Foods
Commack, NY 800-227-4397
Terri Lynn
Elgin, IL 800-323-0775
Timber Crest Farms
Healdsburg, CA 888-374-9325
Unique Ingredients
Naches, WA 509-653-1991

Canned

Agrocan
Ville St Laurent, QC 877-247-6226
Emerling International Foods
Buffalo, NY 716-833-7381

We supply food manufacturers and food service customers worldwide (since 1988) with bulk ingredients including: Fruits & Vegetables; Juice Concentrates; Herbs & Spices; Oils & Vinegars; Flavors & Colors; Honey & Molasses. We also produce PURE MAPLE SYRUP.

Maui Pineapple Company
Kahului, HI 808-877-3351

Maui Pineapple Company
Concord, CA 925-798-0240
NTC Marketing Inc
Williamsville, NY 800-333-1637

Dried

American Importing Company
Minneapolis, MN 612-331-7000
Mariani Packing Company
Vacaville, CA 800-672-8655

Frozen

Emerling International Foods
Buffalo, NY 716-833-7381

J.H. Verbridge & Son
Williamson, NY 315-589-2366
Pacific Coast Fruit Company
Portland, OR 503-234-6411
Townsend Farms
Fairview, OR 503-666-1780

Plums

Ballantine Produce Company
Reedley, CA 559-875-2583
Brandt Farms
Reedley, CA 559-638-6961
Burnette Foods
Elk Rapids, MI 231-264-8116
Chiquita Brands Intl. ional
Cincinnati, OH 800-438-0015
Copper Hills Fruit Sales
Fresno, CA 559-277-1970
Corrin Produce Sales
Dinuba, CA 559-596-0517
Fowler Packing Company
Fresno, CA 559-834-5911
Giumarra Companies
Reedley, CA 559-897-5060
Henggeler Packing Company
Fruitland, ID 208-452-4212
J.C. Watson Company
Parma, ID 208-722-5141
Mountain View Fruit Sales
Reedley, CA 559-637-9933
North Bay Produce
Traverse City, MI 800-678-1941
Oregon Fruit Products Company
Salem, OR 800-394-9333
Organic Planet
San Francisco, CA 415-765-5590
P-R Farms
Clovis, CA 559-299-0201
Pandol Brothers
Delano, CA 661-725-3755
Shafer Lake Fruit
Hartford, MI 269-621-3194
Stadelman Fruit
Zillah, WA 509-829-5145
Sun Valley
Reedley, CA 559-591-1515
Sunmet
Del Rey, CA 559-888-2702

Symms Fruit Ranch
Caldwell, ID 208-459-4821
Terri Lynn
Elgin, IL 800-323-0775
Timber Crest Farms
Healdsburg, CA 888-374-9325
Trinity Fruit Sales
Fresno, CA 559-433-3777
Unique Ingredients
Naches, WA 509-653-1991
United Fruits Corporation
Santa Monica, CA 310-829-0261
Vintage Produce Sales
Kingsburg, CA 559-897-1622
Wawona Packing Company
Cutler, CA 559-528-9729
Z&S Distributing
Fresno, CA 800-467-0788

Canned

Burnette Foods
Elk Rapids, MI 231-264-8116
Emerling International Foods
Buffalo, NY 716-833-7381

Northwest Packing Company
Vancouver, WA 800-543-4356
Oregon Fruit Products Company
Salem, OR 800-394-9333
Packers Canning Company
Lawton, MI 269-624-4681
San Benito Foods
Vancouver, WA 800-453-7832
Truitt Brothers Inc
Salem, OR 800-547-8712

Dried

American Importing Company
Minneapolis, MN 612-331-7000
Fastachi
Watertown, MA 800-466-3022
Mariani Packing Company
Vacaville, CA 800-672-8655
Setton International Foods
Commack, NY 800-227-4397

Frozen

Coloma Frozen Foods
Coloma, MI 800-642-2723
Emerling International Foods
Buffalo, NY 716-833-7381

Fruithill
Yamhill, OR 503-662-3926
Oregon Fruit Products Company
Salem, OR 800-394-9333

Pomegranate

Ballantine Produce Company
Reedley, CA 559-875-2583
Copper Hills Fruit Sales
Fresno, CA 559-277-1970
Emerling International Foods
Buffalo, NY 716-833-7381

Fowler Packing Company
Fresno, CA 559-834-5911
HMC Marketing Group
Kingsburg, CA 559-897-1009

Naumes
Medford, OR 541-772-6268

Potatoes

Au Gratin

Captain Ken's Foods
St Paul, MN 651-298-0071
Idahoan Foods, LLC
Lewisville, ID 800-635-6100

Frozen

Captain Ken's Foods
St Paul, MN 651-298-0071

Baked & Stuffed

Oh Boy! Corporation
San Fernando, CA 818-361-1128
Sun-Glo of Idaho
Sugar City, ID 208-356-7346

Frozen

Penobscot McCrum
Belfast, ME 800-435-4456
Sun-Glo of Idaho
Sugar City, ID 208-356-7346

Canned

Burnette Foods
Elk Rapids, MI 231-264-8116
Burnette Foods
Hartford, MI 616-621-3181
ConAgra Grocery Products
Irvine, CA 714-680-1000
Emerling International Foods
Buffalo, NY 716-833-7381

Nationwide Canning
Cottam, ON 519-839-4831
New Harvest Foods
Pulaski, WI 920-822-2578
Nickabood's Company
Los Angeles, CA 213-746-1541
Omstead Foods Ltd
Wheatley, ON 905-315-8883
Ore-Ida Foods
Pittsburgh, PA 800-892-2401
Reckitt Benckiser
Parsippany, NJ 800-333-3899
Seneca Foods
Janesville, WI 608-757-6000
Weil's Food Processing
Wheatley, ON 519-825-4572

Dehydrated

Idahoan Foods, LLC
Lewisville, ID 800-635-6100
Specialty Ingredients
Buffalo Grove, IL 847-419-9595

Frozen

Agri-Dairy Products
Purchase, NY 914-697-9580
Emerling International Foods
Buffalo, NY 716-833-7381

Jones Produce
Quincy, WA 509-787-3537
Oregon Potato Company
Boardman, OR 800-336-6311
Unique Ingredients
Naches, WA 509-653-1991

Fresh

Beamon Brothers
Goldsboro, NC 919-734-4931
Del Monte Fresh Produce
Coral Gables, FL. 800-950-3683
Green Garden Food Products
Kent, WA. 800-304-1033
Hanover Potato Products
Hanover, PA 717-632-0700
McKenna Brothers
Cardigan, PE. 902-583-2951
Oregon Potato Company
Boardman, OR 800-336-6311
Pacific Collier Fresh Company
Immokalee, FL 800-226-7274
Pride of Sampson
Clinton, NC. 910-592-6188
Seald Sweet Growers & Packers
Vero Beach, FL. 772-569-2244
Symms Fruit Ranch
Caldwell, ID 208-459-4821

Russet

Bottomline Foods
Davie, FL 954-843-0562
Les Aliments Livabec Foods
Sherrington, QC 450-454-7971

Frozen

Burnette Foods
Hartford, MI 616-621-3181
Cavendish Farms
Jamestown, ND. 888-284-5687
Cavendish Farms
Burlington, MA . . . . 888-88 -7437
Cavendish Farms
Dieppe, NB 888-883-7437
Cleugh's Frozen Foods
Buena Park, CA 714-521-1002
ConAgra Grocery Products
Irvine, CA 714-680-1000
Emerling International Foods
Buffalo, NY. 716-833-7381

We supply food manufacturers and food service customers worldwide (since 1988) with bulk ingredients including: Fruits & Vegetables; Juice Concentrates; Herbs & Spices; Oils & Vinegars; Flavors & Colors; Honey & Molasses. We also produce PURE MAPLE SYRUP.

Endico Potatoes
Mount Vernon, NY 914-664-1151
Hot Potato Distributor
Chicago, IL 312-243-0640
J.R. Simplot Company
Boise, ID 208-336-2110
Lamb-Weston
Hermiston, OR 800-766-7783
McCain Foods USA
Easton, ME 800-938-7799
Michael Foods, Inc.
Minnetonka, MN. 952-258-4000
Mr. Dell Foods
Kearney, MO. 816-628-4644
Nickabood's Company
Los Angeles, CA. 213-746-1541
Omstead Foods Ltd
Wheatley, ON 905-315-8883
Ore-Ida Foods
Pittsburgh, PA 800-892-2401
Oregon Potato Company
Boardman, OR 800-336-6311
R.D. Offutt Company
Fargo, ND 701-237-6062
Sun-Glo of Idaho
Sugar City, ID 208-356-7346
Trappe Packing Corporation
Trappe, MD. 410-476-3185
Twin City Foods
Stanwood, WA 208-743-5568
Washington Potato Company
Warden, WA 509-349-8803

Rounds

Penobscot McCrum
Belfast, ME. 800-435-4456

Wedges

Penobscot McCrum
Belfast, ME. 800-435-4456

Instant

Barbara's Bakery
Petaluma, CA 707-765-2273
Gilster-Mary Lee Corporation
Chester, IL. 800-851-5371
Idahoan Foods, LLC
Lewisville, ID 800-635-6100

Oven Type

Frozen

Sun-Glo of Idaho
Sugar City, ID 208-356-7346

Potatoes

Aaland Potato Company
Hoople, ND. 701-894-6144
Alsum Produce
Friesland, WI 800-236-5127
Ben B. Schwartz & Sons
Detroit, MI 313-841-8300
Bjorneby Potato Company
Minto, ND. 701-248-3482
Burnette Foods
Elk Rapids, MI 231-264-8116
Burnette Foods
Hartford, MI 616-621-3181
Byrnes Packing
Hastings, FL 904-692-1643
Cavendish Farms
Jamestown, ND. 888-284-5687
Cavendish Farms
Dieppe, NB 888-883-7437
Chiquita Brands Intl. ional
Cincinnati, OH 800-438-0015
Cleugh's Frozen Foods
Buena Park, CA 714-521-1002
ConAgra Grocery Products
Irvine, CA. 714-680-1000
Crystal Seed Potato Company
Crystal, ND 701-657-2143
Custom Cuts
Bay View, WI 414-483-0491
Dave Kingston Produce
Idaho Falls, ID 800-888-7783
Edmonton Potato Growers
Edmonton, AB 780-447-1860
Green Garden Food Products
Kent, WA. 800-304-1033
Grower Shipper Potato Company
Monte Vista, CO 719-852-3569
Hanover Potato Products
Hanover, PA 717-632-0700
Idahoan
Lewisville, ID 800-635-6100
Idahoan Foods, LLC
Lewisville, ID 800-635-6100
Isadore A. Rapasadi & Son
Canastota, NY. 315-697-2216
J.C. Watson Company
Parma, ID 208-722-5141
Johnston Farms
Edison, CA 661-366-3201
Kiska Farms
Pasco, WA. 509-547-7765
Lamb-Weston
Hermiston, OR 800-766-7783
Larsen Farms
Hamer, ID 208-662-5501
Larsen of Idaho
Hamer, ID 800-767-6104
Larson Potato
Park River, ND 701-284-6437
Lehr Brothers
Edison, CA 661-366-3244
Livingston Farmers Association
Livingston, CA 209-394-7941
Maple Leaf Foods International
North York, ON. 416-480-8900
Marten's Country Kitchen
Port Byron, NY. 315-776-8821
McCain Foods USA
Lisle, IL. 800-938-7799
Michael Foods, Inc.
Minnetonka, MN. 952-258-4000
Mr. Dell Foods
Kearney, MO. 816-628-4644
Muir-Roberts Company
Salt Lake City, UT 800-564-0949
National Harvest
Kansas City, MO. 816-842-9600
Nationwide Canning
Cottam, ON. 519-839-4831
New Harvest Foods
Pulaski, WI 920-822-2578
Nonpareil Dehydrated Potatoes
Blackfoot, ID 800-522-2223
Northern Star Company
Chaska, MN 612-339-8981
Nu-Way Potato Products
North York, ON. 416-241-9151
OC Schulz & Sons
Crystal, ND 701-657-2152
Oetker Limited
Mississauga, ON 800-387-6939
Oh Boy! Corporation
San Fernando, CA. 818-361-1128
Oregon Potato Company
Boardman, OR 800-336-6311
Pak-Wel Produce
Vauxhall, AB. 403-654-2116
Penobscot McCrum
Belfast, ME. 800-435-4456
Premier Packing Company
Bakersfield, CA 661-393-3320
Reckitt Benckiser
Parsippany, NJ. 800-333-3899
Somerset Industries
Spring House, PA 800-883-8728
Sun-Glo of Idaho
Sugar City, ID 208-356-7346
Tami Great Food
Monsey, NY 732-803-6366
Trappe Packing Corporation
Trappe, MD. 410-476-3185
Twin City Foods
Stanwood, WA 208-743-5568
Vauxhall Foods
Vauxhall, AB. 403-654-2771
Vessey & Company
Holtville, CA. 760-356-0130
Washington Potato Company
Warden, WA 509-349-8803
Weil's Food Processing
Wheatley, ON 519-825-4572
Wildcat Produce
McGrew, NE. 308-783-2438
William Karas & Sons
Churchville, NY 585-293-2109

Red

Kiska Farms
Pasco, WA. 509-547-7765
Vessey & Company
Holtville, CA. 760-356-0130

Powdered Vegetables

Atlantic Quality Spice &Seasonings
New Brunswick, NJ 800-584-0422
Emerling International Foods
Buffalo, NY. 716-833-7381

We supply food manufacturers and food service customers worldwide (since 1988) with bulk ingredients including: Fruits & Vegetables; Juice Concentrates; Herbs & Spices; Oils & Vinegars; Flavors & Colors; Honey & Molasses. We also produce PURE MAPLE SYRUP.

Green Foods Corporation
Oxnard, CA. 800-777-4430
Idaho Supreme Potatoes
Firth, ID. 208-346-6841
Niagara Foods
Middleport, NY. 716-735-7722
Spreda Group
Louisville, KY. 502-426-9411
Vegetable Juices
Chicago, IL 888-776-9752
Weinberg Foods
Kirkland, WA 800-866-3447

Produce

A. Duda & Sons
Oviedo, FL 407-365-2111

Aaland Potato Company
Hoople, ND....................... 701-894-6144
Abbott & Cobb, Inc.
Langhorne, PA 800-345-7333
Adobe Creek Packing
Kelseyville, CA.................... 707-279-4204
Agrinorthwest
Kennewick, WA 509-734-1195
Alsum Produce
Friesland, WI 800-236-5127
Annapolis Produce & Restaurant Supply
Annapolis, MD 410-266-5211
Anton Caratan & Son
Bakersfield, CA
Apple Acres
La Fayette, NY 315-677-5144
Appleton Produce Company
Weiser, ID........................ 208-414-3352
Applewood Orchards
Deerfield, MI 800-447-3854
Argee Corporation
Santee, CA 800-449-3030
Associated Fruit Company
Phoenix, OR 541-535-1787
Atlantic Blueberry Company
Hammonton, NJ 609-561-8600
Avalon Foodservice, Inc.
Canal Fulton, OH 800-362-0622
Babe Farms
Santa Maria, CA................... 800-648-6772
Baker Produce Company
Kennewick, WA 800-624-7553
Ballantine Produce Company
Reedley, CA 559-875-2583
Banana Distributing Company
San Antonio, TX................... 210-227-8285
Bay Cities Produce Company
San Leandro, CA................... 510-346-4943
BelleHarvest Sales
Belding, MI....................... 800-452-7753
Ben B. Schwartz & Sons
Detroit, MI 313-841-8300
Ben E. Keith DFW
Fort Worth, TX.................... 877-317-6100
Ben Hill Griffin, Inc.
Frostproof, FL..................... 863-635-2251
Ben-Bud Growers Inc.
Boca Raton, FL.................... 561-347-3120
Bifulco Farms
Pittsgrove, NJ 856-692-0707
Bjorneby Potato Company
Minto, ND........................ 701-248-3482
Bluebird
Peshastin, WA..................... 509-548-1700
Bodek Kosher Produce
Brooklyn, NY 718-377-4163
Boekhout Farms
Ontario, NY....................... 315-524-4041
Boggiatto Produce
Salinas, CA....................... 831-424-4864
Brady Farms
West Olive, MI 616-842-3916
Brandt Farms
Reedley, CA 559-638-6961
Bridenbaughs Orchards
Martinsburg, PA 814-793-2364
Brooks Tropicals
Homestead, FL 800-327-4833
Bruce Church
Salinas, CA....................... 800-538-2861
Byrnes Packing
Hastings, FL 904-692-1643
CAL Sun Produce Company
Oxnard, CA....................... 805-985-2262
Cal-Harvest Marketing
Hanford, CA 559-582-4000
Calco of Calgary
Calgary, AB....................... 403-295-3578
California Citrus Producer
Lindsay, CA 559-562-5169
California Specialty Farms
Los Angeles, CA................... 800-437-2702
California Watercress
Fillmore, CA...................... 805-524-4808
CalSungold
Indio, CA......................... 760-399-5646
Capital Seaboard
Jessup, MD 443-755-1733
Caro Foods
Houma, LA....................... 985-858-2640
Carolina Blueberry Association
Garland, NC 910-588-4355

Carson City Pickle Company
Carson City, MI.................... 989-584-3148
Castellini Company
Newport, KY...................... 800-233-8560
Cates Addis Company
Parkton, NC 800-423-1883
Cattle Canada
Bentley, AB....................... 403-748-2474
Chazy Orchards
Chazy, NY........................ 518-846-7171
Chief Wenatchee
Wenatchee, WA.................... 509-662-5197
Chiquita Brands Intl. ional
Cincinnati, OH 800-438-0015
Chris' Farm Stand
Bradford, MA 978-994-4315
Christopher Ranch
Gilroy, CA........................ 408-847-1100
Circle Valley Produce
Idaho Falls, ID 208-524-2628
Claussen Pickle Company
Woodstock, IL..................... 800-435-2817
Clermont
Hillsboro, OR 503-648-8544
Cleugh's Frozen Foods
Buena Park, CA 714-521-1002
Columbia Empire Farms
Sherwood, OR..................... 503-538-2156
ConAgra Grocery Products
Irvine, CA........................ 714-680-1000
Concannon Vineyard
Livermore, CA 800-258-9866
Congdon Orchards
Yakima, WA 509-965-2886
Cooperative Elevator Company
Pigeon, MI 989-453-4500
Corona College Heights Orange & Lemon Associates
Riverside, CA 951-688-1811
Corrin Produce Sales
Dinuba, CA....................... 559-596-0517
Country Fresh Mushrooms
Avondale, PA 610-268-3033
Couture Farms
Kettleman City, CA................. 559-945-2226
Crane & Crane
Brewster, WA 509-689-3447
Creekside Mushrooms
Worthington, PA................... 724-297-5491
Crown Packing Company
Salinas, CA....................... 831-424-2067
Crystal Seed Potato Company
Crystal, ND....................... 701-657-2143
Custom Cuts
Bay View, WI 414-483-0491
Cut Above Foods
Carlsbad, CA...................... 760-931-6777
D'Arrigo Brothers Company of California
Salinas, CA....................... 800-995-5939
Dan Tudor & Sons
Delano, CA....................... 661-792-2933
Dave Kingston Produce
Idaho Falls, ID 800-888-7783
DCL
Honolulu, HI...................... 808-845-3834
De Bruyn Produce Company
Zeeland, MI....................... 800-733-9177
Delta Packing Company of Lodi
Lodi, CA 209-334-0811
Diamond Blueberry
Hammonton, NJ 609-561-3661
Diamond Fruit Growers
Odell, OR 541-354-5300
DiMare International Dmb Packing Corp
Indio, CA......................... 760-347-3336
Dimond Tager Company Products
Tampa, FL........................ 813-238-3111
DNE World Fruit Sales
Fort Pierce, FL 800-327-6676
Dno
Columbus, OH 800-686-2366
Dole Fresh Vegetable Company
Soledad, CA 800-333-5454
Driscoll Strawberry Associates
Watsonville, CA 831-763-5100
Dundee Citrus Growers
Dundee, FL....................... 800-447-1574
E.W. Bowker Company
Pemberton, NJ..................... 609-894-9508
Exeter Produce & Storage Company
Exeter, ON....................... 800-881-4861
F&S Produce Company
Rosenhayn, NJ 800-886-3316

Farm Pak Products
Spring Hope, NC................... 252-459-3101
Federation of Southern Cooperatives
East Point, GA 404-765-0991
Ferris Organic Farm
Eaton Rapids, MI 800-628-8736
Fiesta Farms
Nyssa, OR 541-372-2248
Fig Garden Packing
Fresno, CA 559-275-2191
Fillmore Piru Citrus Association
Piru, CA 800-524-8787
Finer Foods
Chicago, IL....................... 773-579-3870
Flippin-Seaman
Tyro, VA 434-277-5828
Florida Citrus
Bartow, FL 863-537-3999
Frank Capurro & Son
Moss Landing, CA 831-728-3904
Fresh Express
Salinas, CA....................... 800-242-5472
Fruit Acres
La Crescent, MN................... 507-895-4750
Ful-Flav-R Foods
Alamo, CA 925-838-0300
G Cefalu & Brothers
Jessup, MD....................... 410-799-3414
Garber Farms
Iota, LA.......................... 800-824-2284
Gentile Brothers Company
Cincinnati, OH 800-877-7954
George Chiala Farms
Morgan Hill, CA................... 408-778-0562
George Richter Farm
Fife, WA 253-922-5649
George W Saulpaugh & Sons
Germantown, NY 518-537-6500
Georgia Vegetable Company
Tifton, GA........................ 229-386-2374
Gerawan Farming
Sanger, CA 559-787-8780
Ghirardelli Ranch
Petaluma, CA 707-795-7616
Giumarra Companies
Escondido, CA 760-480-8502
Glacier Foods
Sanger, CA 559-875-3354
Godwin Produce Company
Dunn, NC 910-892-4171
Gold Seal Fruit Bouquet
Milwaukee, WI.................... 800-558-5558
Golden River Fruit Company
Vero Beach, FL.................... 772-562-8610
Golden Town Apple Products
Rougemont, QC 519-599-6300
Great Eastern Sun
Asheville, NC 800-334-5809
Grimmway Farms
Bakersfield, CA 800-301-3101
Grower Shipper Potato Company
Monte Vista, CO................... 719-852-3569
H H Dobbins
Lyndonville, NY................... 877-362-2467
H. Naraghi Farms
Escalon, CA 209-577-5777
Haines City Citrus Growers Association
Haines City, FL.................... 800-422-4245
Half Moon Fruit & Produce Company
Woodland, CA..................... 530-662-1727
Harlin Fruit Company
Monett, MO 417-235-7370
Harner Farms
State College, PA 814-237-7919
Harris Farms
Coalinga, CA 800-742-1955
Heller Brothers PackingcCorporation
Winter Garden, FL 407-656-2124
Henggeler Packing Company
Fruitland, ID 208-452-4212
Herold's Salad, Inc
Cleveland, OH 800-427-2523
Hong Kong Market Company
Chicago, IL....................... 312-791-9111
Hopkins Food Service
Cairo, GA 229-872-3214
Horton Fruit Company
Louisville, KY 800-626-2245
Hunt Brothers Cooperative
Lake Wales, FL.................... 863-676-9471
Indian Bay Frozen Foods
Centreville, NL.................... 709-678-2844

Indian Hollow Farms
Richland Center, WI 800-236-3944
International Specialty Supply
Cookeville, TN 931-526-1106
Isadore A. Rapasadi & Son
Canastota, NY. 315-697-2216
J&J Produce Company
Hattiesburg, MS 601-582-1512
J.C. Watson Company
Parma, ID 208-722-5141
Jack Brown Produce
Sparta, MI 800-348-0834
Jacobs, Malcolm, & Burtt
San Francisco, CA 415-285-0400
Jalapeno Foods Company
The Woodlands, TX 800-896-2318
Jasmine Vineyards
Delano, CA 661-792-2141
Jasper Wyman & Son
Milbridge, ME 800-341-1758
JES Foods
Cleveland, OH 216-883-8987
Jonathan's Sprouts
Rochester, MA 508-763-2577
Joseph J. White
Browns Mills, NJ 609-893-2332
JRL
Vineland, NJ 856-690-9000
Kaiser Pickles
Cincinnati, OH 888-291-0608
Kelley Bean Company
Torrington, WY. 307-532-2131
Kelley Bean Company
Scottsbluff, NE 308-635-6438
Kitchen Pride Mushroom Farms
Gonzales, TX 830-540-4517
Knight Seed Company
Burnsville, MN 800-328-2999
Knights Appleden Fruit
Colborne, ON 905-349-2521
Koch Foods
Chattanooga, TN. 423-266-0351
Krugers
St Paul, MN. 651-699-1356
Kurtz Produce
Ariss, ON 519-824-3279
L.F. Lambert Spawn Company
Coatesville, PA 610-384-5031
L.I. Cauliflower Association
Riverhead, NY 631-727-2212
Lagorio Enterprises
Manteca, CA. 209-982-5691
Lake Helen Sprout Farm
Lake Helen, FL. 386-228-2871
Lane Packing Company
Fort Valley, GA. 478-825-3362
Larson Potato
Park River, ND 701-284-6437
Lehr Brothers
Edison, CA 661-366-3244
Lennox Farm
Shelburne, ON 519-925-6444
Leroy Smith & Sons Inc
Vero Beach, FL. 772-567-3421
Lindemann Produce
Los Banos, CA 209-826-2442
Livingston Farmers Association
Livingston, CA 209-394-7941
Lou Pizzo Produce
Parkland, FL 954-941-8830
Lucich Farms
Delano, CA 661-725-4550
M&R Company
Lodi, CA. 209-369-4760
M&S Tomato Repacking Company
Springfield, MA 413-737-1308
M.A. Patout & Son
Jeanerette, LA 337-276-4592
Magnolia Citrus Association
Porterville, CA 559-784-4455
Mancuso Cheese Company
Joliet, IL 815-722-2475
Mann Packing
Salinas, CA 831-422-7405
Manzana Products Company
Sebastopol, CA 707-823-5313
Manzanita Ranch
Julian, CA 760-765-0102
Maple Leaf Foods International
North York, ON. 416-480-8900
Marley Orchards Corporation
Yakima, WA 509-248-5231

Marten's Country Kitchen
Port Byron, NY. 315-776-8821
Martin Brothers Distributing Company
Cedar Falls, IA 319-266-1775
Matson Fruit Company
Selah, WA 509-697-7100
Maui Pineapple Company
Kahului, HI. 808-877-3351
Maui Pineapple Company
Concord, CA. 925-798-0240
McDaniel Fruit Company
Fallbrook, CA 760-728-8438
McFarling Foods
Indianapolis, IN 317-635-2633
McKenna Brothers
Cardigan, PE. 902-583-2951
Merrill's Blueberry Farms
Ellsworth, ME. 800-711-6551
Michigan Celery Promotion Cooperative
Hudsonville, MI 616-669-1250
Mike & Jean's Berry Farm
Mount Vernon, WA. 360-424-7220
Mills
Salinas, CA 831-757-1611
Mister Spear
Stockton, CA. 800-677-7327
Mixon Fruit Farms
Bradenton, FL 800-608-2525
Modoc Orchard Company
Medford, OR. 541-535-1437
Monterey Mushrooms
Watsonville, CA 800-333-6874
Montreal Chop Suey Company
Montreal, QC 514-522-3134
Nathan Seagall Company
Montgomery, AL. 334-279-3174
National Raisin Company
Fowler, CA 559-834-5981
Nebraska Salt & Grain Company
Gothenburg, NE 308-537-7191
New York Apples Sales
Castletn on Hdsn, NY. 518-477-7200
Nonpareil Dehydrated Potatoes
Blackfoot, ID 800-522-2223
Nor-Cliff Farms
Port Colborne, ON 905-835-0808
North Bay Produce
Traverse City, MI 800-678-1941
Northern Feed & Bean Company
Lucerne, CO 800-316-2326
Northern Fruit Company
Wenatchee, WA. 509-884-6651
Northwest Pea & Bean Company
Spokane Valley, WA 509-534-3821
Nuchief Sales
Wenatchee, WA. 888-269-4638
Nunes Company
Salinas, CA 831-751-7500
Nut Factory
Spokane Valley, WA 888-239-5288
OC Schulz & Sons
Crystal, ND 701-657-2152
Ocean Mist
Castroville, CA 800-962-3738
Ocean Spray Cranberries
Lakeville-Middleboro, MA 800-662-3263
Ontario Produce Company
Ontario, OR. 541-889-6485
Orange Cove Sanger Citrus Association
Orange Cove, CA 559-626-4453
Oregon Potato Company
Boardman, OR 800-336-6311
Oxford Frozen Foods Limited
Oxford, NS 902-447-2100
P-R Farms
Clovis, CA 559-299-0201

Pacific Tomato Growers
Palmetto, FL 941-722-3291
Pandol Brothers
Delano, CA 661-725-3755
Pavero Cold Storage Corporation
Highland, NY 800-435-2994
Per-Clin Orchards
Bear Lake, MI. 231-889-4289
Peter Rabbit Farms
Coachella, CA. 760-398-0151
Pioneer Growers Cooperative
Belle Glade, FL. 561-996-5211
Placerville Fruit Growers Association
Placerville, CA 530-622-2640
Pleasant Grove Farms
Pleasant Grove, CA 916-655-3391
Pompeian
Baltimore, MD 800-638-1224
Post Familie Vineyards
Altus, AR 800-275-8423
Pots de Creme
Lexington, KY 859-299-2254
Prairie Mushrooms
Sherwood Park, AB 780-467-3555
Premier Packing Company
Bakersfield, CA 661-393-3320
Price Cold Storage & Packing Company
Yakima, WA 509-966-4110
Pride of Sampson
Clinton, NC. 910-592-6188
Prime Produce
Orange, CA. 714-771-0718
Produce Buyers Company
Detroit, MI 313-843-0132
Producers Cooperative
Olathe, CO 970-874-9736
Quality Brands
Deland, FL 888-676-2700
Quillin Produce Company
Huntsville, AL 256-883-7374
R&S Mexican Food Products
Glendale, AZ. 602-272-2727
R.C. McEntire & Company
Columbia, SC 803-799-3388
Red Hot Cooperative
Redcliff, AB 403-548-6453
Reed Lang Farms
Rio Hondo, TX. 956-748-2354
Reinhart Foods
Markham, ON. 905-754-3500
Rene Produce Distributors
Nogales, AZ 520-281-9014
Reter Fruit Company
Medford, OR. 541-772-5256
Rice Fruit Company
Gardners, PA. 800-627-3359
Rio Grande Valley Sugar Growers
Santa Rosa, TX. 956-636-1411
Rogers Brothers
Galesburg, IL 309-342-2127
Russo Farms
Vineland, NJ 856-692-5942
S&E Organic Farms
Bakersfield, CA 661-325-2644
S. Kennedy Vegetable Lifestock Company
Clear Lake, IA. 641-357-4227
Sales USA
Salado, TX 800-766-7344
Santanna Banana Company
Harrisburg, PA 717-238-8321
Schmidt Brothers
Swanton, OH. 419-826-3671
Scotian Gold Cooperative
Coldbrook, NS 902-679-2191
Seald Sweet Growers & Packers
Vero Beach, FL. 772-569-2244
Sedlock Farm
Lynn Center, IL. 309-521-8284
Shamrock Foods Company
Phoenix, AZ 800-289-3663
Shields Date Gardens
Indio, CA. 800-414-2555
SKW Biosystems
Philadelphia, PA 800-223-7073
Smith Frozen Foods
Weston, OR. 800-547-0203
Smith-Coulter Company
Chittenango, NY. 315-687-6510
Snokist Growers
Yakima, WA 800-377-2857
Solana Gold Organics
Sebastopol, CA 800-459-1121

South Mill Distribution
Kennett Square, PA 610-444-4800
Spring Ledge Farms
Dundee, NY 607-678-4038
Stadelman Fruit
Zillah, WA 509-829-5145
Star Route Farms
Bolinas, CA 415-868-1658
Strube Vegetable & Celery Company
Chicago, IL 773-446-4000
Sugar Cane Industry Glades Correctional Institution
Belle Glade, FL 561-829-1400
Sun Garden Growers
Bard, CA 800-228-4690
Sun Hing Foods
South San Francisco, CA 800-258-6669
Sun Orchard of Florida
Haines City, FL 863-422-5062
Sun Pacific Shippers
Exeter, CA 559-592-5168
Sungarden Sprouts
Cookeville, TN 931-526-1106
Sunkist Growers
Stafford, TX 281-240-6446
Sunkist Growers
Detroit, MI 313-843-4160
Sunkist Growers
Pittsburgh, PA 412-967-9801
Sunkist Growers
West Chester, OH 513-741-9494
Sunkist Growers
Visalia, CA 559-739-8392
Sunkist Growers
Chelsea, MA 617-884-9750
Sunkist Growers
Buffalo, NY 716-895-3744
Sunkist Growers
Ontario, CA 800-798-9005
Sunkist Growers
Cherry Hill, NJ 856-663-2343
Sunkist Growers
Cary, NC 919-859-7380
Sunmet
Del Rey, CA 559-888-2702
Sunrise Growers
Placentia, CA 714-630-6292
Superior Mushroom Farms
Ardrossan, AB 866-687-2242
Sure Fresh Produce
Santa Maria, CA 888-423-5379
Surface Banana Company
Bluewell, WV 304-589-7202
Talbott Farms
Palisade, CO 970-464-5943
Talley Farms
Arroyo Grande, CA 805-489-5533
Tanimura & Antle
Salinas, CA 831-455-2255
Taylor Farms
Salinas, CA 831-754-0471
Taylor Orchards
Reynolds, GA 478-847-4186
Teixeira Farms
Santa Maria, CA 805-928-3801
Tejon Ranch
Lebec, CA 661-248-5181
Thrifty Vegetable Company
Garden Grove, CA
Tiger Mushroom Farm
Nanton, AB 403-646-2578
Tony Vitrano Company
Jessup, MD 800-481-3784
Trefethen Vineyards
Napa, CA 800-556-4847
Trout-Blue Chelan
Chelan, WA 509-682-2591
Tru-Blu Cooperative Associates
New Lisbon, NJ 609-894-8717
Tucson Food Service
Tucson, AZ 520-622-4605
Tufts Ranch
Winters, CA 530-795-4144
Turlock Fruit Company
Turlock, CA 209-634-7207
United Apple Sales
New Paltz, NY 845-256-1500
United Fruit Growers
Palisade, CO 970-464-7277
United Fruits Corporation
Santa Monica, CA 310-829-0261
United Marketing Exchange
Delta, CO 970-874-3332
United Pickle Products Corporation
Bronx, NY 718-933-6060
Van de Kamp's
Peoria, IL 800-798-3318
Vaughn Rue Produce
Wilson, NC 800-388-8138
Venture Vineyards
Lodi, NY 888-635-6277
Verdelli Farms
Harrisburg, PA 800-422-8344
Veronica Foods Company
Oakland, CA 800-370-5554
Vidalia Sweets Brand
Lyons, GA 912-565-8881
Vincent B. Zaninovich & Son
Richgrove, CA 661-725-2497
Walla Walla Gardeners' Association
Walla Walla, WA 800-553-5014
Walter P. Rawl & Sons
Pelion, SC 803-359-3645
Washington Fruit & Produce Company
Yakima, WA 509-457-6177
Weiser River Packing
Weiser, ID 208-549-0200
West Pak Avocado
Temecula, CA 800-266-4414
Wetherby Cranberry Company
Warrens, WI 608-378-4813
Whitney & Son SeaFoods
Hudson, FL 727-868-4044
Wileman Bros & Elliott, Inc
Visalia, CA
William Bolthouse Farms
Bakersfield, CA 661-366-7270
William Karas & Sons
Churchville, NY 585-293-2109
Wisconsin Cheese
Melrose Park, IL 708-450-0074
Yakima Fruit & Cold Storage Company
Wapato, WA 509-877-2777
Yarbrough Produce Company
Birmingham, AL 205-324-4569
Yokhol Valley Packing Company
Lindsay, CA 559-562-1327
Zuccaro's Fruit & Produce Company
Minneapolis, MN 612-333-1122

Prunes

Central California Raisin Packers
Del Rey, CA 559-888-2195
Chieftain Wild Rice Company
Spooner, WI 800-262-6368
George W Saulpaugh & Sons
Germantown, NY 518-537-6500
H H Dobbins
Lyndonville, NY 877-362-2467
Henggeler Packing Company
Fruitland, ID 208-452-4212
Hialeah Products Company
Hollywood, FL 800-923-3379
Kalustyan Corporation
Union, NJ 908-688-6111
Meridian Nut Growers
Clovis, CA 559-458-7272
Organic Planet
San Francisco, CA 415-765-5590
Ramos Orchards
Winters, CA 530-795-4748
Service Packing Company
Vancouver, BC 604-681-0264
Shoei Foods USA
Olivehurst, CA 800-527-4712
Stadelman Fruit
Zillah, WA 509-829-5145
Stapleton-Spence PackingCompany
San Jose, CA 800-297-8815
Sunsweet Growers
Yuba City, CA 800-417-2253
Taylor Packing Company
Yuba City, CA 530-671-1505
Terri Lynn
Elgin, IL 800-323-0775
Timber Crest Farms
Healdsburg, CA 888-374-9325
Tufts Ranch
Winters, CA 530-795-4144
Unique Ingredients
Naches, WA 509-653-1991
Valley View Packing Company
San Jose, CA 408-289-8300
Wilbur Packing Company
Yuba City, CA 530-671-4911

Canned

Emerling International Foods
Buffalo, NY 716-833-7381

We supply food manufacturers and food service customers worldwide (since 1988) with bulk ingredients including: Fruits & Vegetables; Juice Concentrates; Herbs & Spices; Oils & Vinegars; Flavors & Colors; Honey & Molasses. We also produce PURE MAPLE SYRUP.

Oasis Foods
Planada, CA 209-382-0263
Stapleton-Spence PackingCompany
San Jose, CA 800-297-8815
Valley View Packing Company
San Jose, CA 408-289-8300

Dried

Chieftain Wild Rice Company
Spooner, WI 800-262-6368
Fastachi
Watertown, MA 800-466-3022
Setton International Foods
Commack, NY 800-227-4397

Frozen

Emerling International Foods
Buffalo, NY 716-833-7381

We supply food manufacturers and food service customers worldwide (since 1988) with bulk ingredients including: Fruits & Vegetables; Juice Concentrates; Herbs & Spices; Oils & Vinegars; Flavors & Colors; Honey & Molasses. We also produce PURE MAPLE SYRUP.

Packers Canning Company
Lawton, MI 269-624-4681

Pulps & Purees

Assouline & Ting
Huntingdon Valley, PA 800-521-4491
Frozsun Foods
Placentia, CA 714-630-6292
Pastorelli Food Products
Chicago, IL 800-767-2829
Rain Sweet
Salem, OR 800-363-4293
Rv Industries
Buford, GA 770-729-8983
SK Foods
Lemoore, CA 559-924-6527

SupHerb Farms
Turlock, CA 800-787-4372

Frozen culinary herb and specialty vegetable ingredients.

The Perfect Puree
Napa, CA 707-261-5100
Tulkoff Food Products
Baltimore, MD 800-638-7343

Citrus

Amboy Specialty Foods Company
Dixon, IL 800-892-0400
Chloe Foods Corporation
Brooklyn, NY 718-827-9000

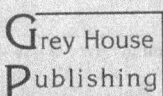

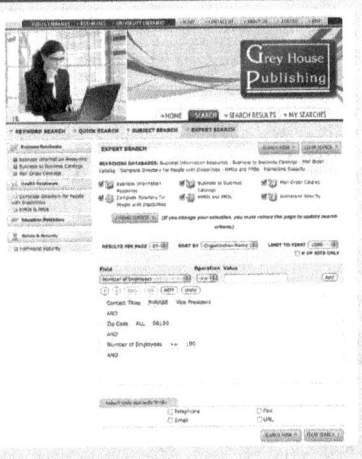

Fruit

Ravifruit
Hackensack, NJ 201-939-5656
Sabroso Company
Medford, OR 541-772-5653

Fruit & Vegetable

Assouline & Ting
Huntingdon Valley, PA 800-521-4491
Brady Farms
West Olive, MI 616-842-3916
California Custom Fruits & Flavors
Irwindale, CA 877-558-0056
ConAgra Grocery Products
Irvine, CA 714-680-1000
Emerling International Foods
Buffalo, NY 716-833-7381

Furmano Foods
Northumberland, PA 877-877-6032
Global Trading
Buena Park, CA
Golden Town Apple Products
Rougemont, QC 519-599-6300
Greenwood Associates
Highland Park, IL 847-579-5500
Hiller Cranberries
Rochester, MA 508-763-5257
Hirzel Canning Company &Farms
Northwood, OH 419-693-0531
Louis Dreyfus Citrus
Winter Garden, FL 800-549-4272
Pastorelli Food Products
Chicago, IL 800-767-2829
Peace River Citrus Products
Vero Beach, FL 772-467-1234
Prima Foods International
Silver Springs, FL 800-774-8751
Red Gold
Elwood, IN 877-748-9798
S&E Organic Farms
Bakersfield, CA 661-325-2644
Seneca Foods
Clyman, WI 920-696-3331
Vegetable Juices
Chicago, IL 888-776-9752
Vita-Pakt Citrus Company
Covina, CA 626-332-1101

Pulp

Dried Beet

Emerling International Foods
Buffalo, NY 716-833-7381

Fruit

Avo King Intl.
Orange, CA 800-286-5464
Calavo Growers
Santa Paula, CA 800-422-5280
Hiller Cranberries
Rochester, MA 508-763-5257
Miramar Fruit Trading Company
Doral, FL 305-883-4774
Sunny Avocado
Jamul, CA 800-999-2862
Tantos Foods International
Markham, ON 905-943-9993
Three Vee Food & Syrup Company
Brooklyn, NY 800-801-7330

Vegetable

Pastorelli Food Products
Chicago, IL 800-767-2829

Puree

Fruit

Assouline & Ting
Huntingdon Valley, PA 800-521-4491
Beta Pure Foods
Aptos, CA 831-685-6565
Calavo Growers
Santa Paula, CA 800-422-5280
Chiquita Brands Intl. ional
Cincinnati, OH 800-438-0015
Clermont
Hillsboro, OR 503-648-8544
Frozsun Foods
Placentia, CA 714-630-6292
Fruithill
Yamhill, OR 503-662-3926
Gerber Products Company
Parsippany, NJ 800-443-7237
Global Trading
Buena Park, CA
Golden Town Apple Products
Rougemont, QC 519-599-6300
Granny's Best Strawberry Products
Victoria, ON 519-426-0705
Greenwood Associates
Highland Park, IL 847-579-5500
Hartog Rahal Foods
New York, NY 212-687-2000
Hiller Cranberries
Rochester, MA 508-763-5257
Johnson Concentrates
Sunnyside, WA 509-837-4600
Johnson Fruit Company
Sunnyside, WA 509-837-4600
Milne Fruit Products
Prosser, WA 509-786-2611
National Frozen Foods Corporation
Seattle, WA 206-322-8900
Northern Michigan Fruit Company
Omena, MI 231-386-5142
Pacific Coast Fruit Company
Portland, OR 503-234-6411
Princeville Canning Company
Princeville, IL 309-385-4301
Radar Farms
Lynden, WA 360-354-6574
Rain Sweet
Salem, OR 800-363-4293
RFI Ingredients
Blauvelt, NY 800-962-7663
Rv Industries
Buford, GA 770-729-8983
Summerland Sweets
Summerland, DC 800-577-1277
Tupman-Thurlow Company
Deerfield Beach, FL 954-596-9989

Fruit & Vegetable

Ful-Flav-R Foods
Alamo, CA 925-838-0300
National Frozen Foods Corporation
Seattle, WA 206-322-8900
Pastorelli Food Products
Chicago, IL 800-767-2829

Orange

KMC Citrus Enterprises
Winter Haven, FL 352-821-3666

Tomato

ConAgra Grocery Products
Irvine, CA 714-680-1000
Emerling International Foods
Buffalo, NY 716-833-7381

Hirzel Canning Company &Farms
Northwood, OH 419-693-0531
Pastorelli Food Products
Chicago, IL 800-767-2829

Vegetable

Beta Pure Foods
Aptos, CA 831-685-6565
Furmano Foods
Northumberland, PA 877-877-6032
National Frozen Foods Corporation
Seattle, WA 206-322-8900
Pastorelli Food Products
Chicago, IL 800-767-2829

Tomato

Canned

Furmano Foods
Northumberland, PA 877-877-6032
Heinz Company of Canada
North York, ON 877-574-3469
Nationwide Canning
Cottam, ON 519-839-4831
Pastorelli Food Products
Chicago, IL 800-767-2829
Red Gold
Elwood, IN 877-748-9798
Seneca Foods
Clyman, WI 920-696-3331
Tip Top Canning Company
Tipp City, OH 800-352-2635
Vegetable Juices
Chicago, IL 888-776-9752
Violet Packing
Williamstown, NJ 856-629-7428

Pumpkin

Abbott & Cobb, Inc.
Langhorne, PA 800-345-7333
Bennett's Apples & Cider
Ancaster, ON 905-648-6878
Goebbert's Home Grown Vegetables
South Barrington, IL 847-428-6727
NORPAC Foods
Lake Oswego, OR 800-733-9311
Organic Planet
San Francisco, CA 415-765-5590
Schmidt Brothers
Swanton, OH 419-826-3671
Sunshine Farms The Nut House Inc
Roseboro, NC 910-564-2421
Tom Ringhausen Orchards
Hardin, IL 618-576-2311
Unique Ingredients
Naches, WA 509-653-1991
Wildcat Produce
McGrew, NE 308-783-2438

Canned

Agrocan
Ville St Laurent, QC 877-247-6226
Emerling International Foods
Buffalo, NY 716-833-7381

Harvest-Pac Products
Chatham, ON 519-436-0446
Lakeside Foods
Manitowoc, WI 920-684-3356
NORPAC Foods
Lake Oswego, OR 800-733-9311
Seneca Foods Corporation
Marion, NY 315-926-8100

Frozen

Emerling International Foods
Buffalo, NY 716-833-7381

Lakeside Foods
Manitowoc, WI 920-684-3356

NORPAC Foods
Lake Oswego, OR 800-733-9311

Winter Squash

NORPAC Foods
Lake Oswego, OR 800-733-9311

Quince

Hiller Cranberries
Rochester, MA 508-763-5257

Radish

A. Duda Farm Fresh Foods
Belle Glade, FL 561-996-7621
F&S Produce Company
Rosenhayn, NJ 800-886-3316
Frank Capurro & Son
Moss Landing, CA 831-728-3904
Gouw Quality Onions
Taber, AB 403-223-1440
Pioneer Growers Cooperative
Belle Glade, FL 561-996-5211
Vegetable Juices
Chicago, IL 888-776-9752
Walla Walla Gardeners' Association
Walla Walla, WA 800-553-5014

Raisins

American Health & Nutrition
Ann Arbor, MI 734-677-5570
American Key Food Products
Closter, NJ 800-767-0237
American Raisin Packers
Selma, CA 559-896-4760
Boghosian Raisin Packing Company
Fowler, CA 559-834-5348
Central California Raisin Packers
Del Rey, CA 559-888-2195
Chieftain Wild Rice Company
Spooner, WI 800-262-6368
Chooljian Brothers Packing Company
Sanger, CA 559-875-5501
Del Rey Packing Company
Del Rey, CA 559-888-2031
Dipasa
Brownsville, TX 956-831-5893
Emerling International Foods
Buffalo, NY 716-833-7381

We supply food manufacturers and food service customers worldwide (since 1988) with bulk ingredients including: Fruits & Vegetables; Juice Concentrates; Herbs & Spices; Oils & Vinegars; Flavors & Colors; Honey & Molasses. We also produce PURE MAPLE SYRUP.

Fig Garden Packing
Fresno, CA 559-275-2191
Foley's Candies
Richmond, BC 888-236-5397
Jason & Son Specialty Foods
Rancho Cordova, CA 800-810-9093
Jewel Date Company
Thermal, CA 760-399-4474
Just Tomatoes Company
Westley, CA 800-537-1985
Kalustyan Corporation
Union, NJ 908-688-6111
Lion Raisins
Selma, CA 559-834-6677
Mariani Packing Company
Vacaville, CA 800-672-8655
Meridian Nut Growers
Clovis, CA 559-458-7272
National Raisin Company
Fowler, CA 559-834-5981
NSpired Natural Foods
Boulder, CO 800-434-4246
Nut Factory
Spokane Valley, WA 888-239-5288
Organic Planet
San Francisco, CA 415-765-5590
Peloian Packing Company
Dinuba, CA 559-591-0101
Reinhart Foods
Markham, ON 905-754-3500
Setton International Foods
Commack, NY 800-227-4397
Shade Foods
New Century, KS 800-225-6312
Sun-Maid Growers of California
Kingsburg, CA 800-272-4746
Terri Lynn
Elgin, IL 800-323-0775
Timber Crest Farms
Healdsburg, CA 888-374-9325
Unique Ingredients
Naches, WA 509-653-1991
Victor Packing Company
Madera, CA 559-673-5908
Waymouth Farms
New Hope, MN 800-527-0094

Chocolate Coated

Shade Foods
New Century, KS 800-225-6312

Dried

Boghosian Raisin Packing Company
Fowler, CA 559-834-5348
Camara Raisin Packing Company
Fresno, CA 559-661-3780
Chieftain Wild Rice Company
Spooner, WI 800-262-6368
Fastachi
Watertown, MA 800-466-3022
Fig Garden Packing
Fresno, CA 559-275-2191
Jason & Son Specialty Foods
Rancho Cordova, CA 800-810-9093
Kalustyan Corporation
Union, NJ 908-688-6111
National Raisin Company
Fowler, CA 559-834-5981
Nut Factory
Spokane Valley, WA 888-239-5288
Shade Foods
New Century, KS 800-225-6312

Yogurt Coated

Foley's Candies
Richmond, BC 888-236-5397
GKI Foods
Brighton, MI 248-486-0055
Mariani Packing Company
Vacaville, CA 800-672-8655
Setton International Foods
Commack, NY 800-227-4397
Shade Foods
New Century, KS 800-225-6312
Terri Lynn
Elgin, IL 800-323-0775

Rhubarb

Allen Canning Company
Siloam Springs, AR 800-234-2553
Bryant Preserving Company
Alma, AR 800-634-2413
Cajun Chef Products
Saint Martinville, LA 337-394-7112
Cleugh's Frozen Foods
Buena Park, CA 714-521-1002
Coloma Frozen Foods
Coloma, MI 800-642-2723
Lennox Farm
Shelburne, ON 519-925-6444
McCain Foods USA
Colton, CA 800-938-7799
Snowcrest Packer
Abbotsford, BC 800-265-5332
Washington Rhubarb Growers Association
Sumner, WA 800-435-9911
Webster Farms
Cambridge Station, NS 902-538-9492

Canned

Emerling International Foods
Buffalo, NY 716-833-7381

We supply food manufacturers and food service customers worldwide (since 1988) with bulk ingredients including: Fruits & Vegetables; Juice Concentrates; Herbs & Spices; Oils & Vinegars; Flavors & Colors; Honey & Molasses. We also produce PURE MAPLE SYRUP.

Frozen

Cleugh's Frozen Foods
Buena Park, CA 714-521-1002
Coloma Frozen Foods
Coloma, MI 800-642-2723
Emerling International Foods
Buffalo, NY 716-833-7381

We supply food manufacturers and food service customers worldwide (since 1988) with bulk ingredients including: Fruits & Vegetables; Juice Concentrates; Herbs & Spices; Oils & Vinegars; Flavors & Colors; Honey & Molasses. We also produce PURE MAPLE SYRUP.

Lennox Farm
Shelburne, ON 519-925-6444
Radar Farms
Lynden, WA 360-354-6574
Snowcrest Packer
Abbotsford, BC 800-265-5332
Washington Rhubarb Growers Association
Sumner, WA 800-435-9911
Webster Farms
Cambridge Station, NS 902-538-9492
Windatt Farms
Picton, ON 613-393-5289

Roasted Vegetables

Moody Dunbar
Johnson City, TN 800-251-8202

SupHerb FARMS®

SupHerb Farms
Turlock, CA 800-787-4372

Frozen culinary herb and specialty vegetable ingredients.

Roots & Tubers

Allen Canning Company
Siloam Springs, AR 800-234-2553
American Botanicals
Eolia, MO 800-684-6070
Emerling International Foods
Buffalo, NY 716-833-7381

We supply food manufacturers and food service customers worldwide (since 1988) with bulk ingredients including: Fruits & Vegetables; Juice Concentrates; Herbs & Spices; Oils & Vinegars; Flavors & Colors; Honey & Molasses. We also produce PURE MAPLE SYRUP.

Penn Herb Company
Philadelphia, PA 800-523-9971
Pharmline
Florida, NY 845-651-4443
Winder Dairy
West Valley, UT 800-946-3371

Rutabaga

Arbre Farms Corporation
Walkerville, MI 231-873-3337
Exeter Produce & Storage Company
Exeter, ON 800-881-4861
Kurtz Produce
Ariss, ON 519-824-3279

Canned

Arbre Farms Corporation
Walkerville, MI 231-873-3337
Emerling International Foods
Buffalo, NY 716-833-7381

We supply food manufacturers and food service customers worldwide (since 1988) with bulk ingredients including: Fruits & Vegetables; Juice Concentrates; Herbs & Spices; Oils & Vinegars; Flavors & Colors; Honey & Molasses. We also produce PURE MAPLE SYRUP.

Frozen

Arbre Farms Corporation
Walkerville, MI....................231-873-3337
Emerling International Foods
Buffalo, NY......................716-833-7381

We supply food manufacturers and food service customers worldwide (since 1988) with bulk ingredients including: Fruits & Vegetables; Juice Concentrates; Herbs & Spices; Oils & Vinegars; Flavors & Colors; Honey & Molasses. We also produce PURE MAPLE SYRUP.

Salad Greens

Atlanta Bread Company
Smyrna, GA.....................800-398-3728
Del Monte Fresh Produce
Coral Gables, FL..................800-950-3683
Pasta USA
Spokane, WA.....................800-456-2084
Victoria Packing Corporation
Brooklyn, NY....................718-927-3000

Sauces

Apple

Blue Jay Orchards
Bethel, CT.......................203-748-0119
Bowman Apple Products Company
Mount Jackson, VA................800-346-5382
Burnette Foods
Elk Rapids, MI...................231-264-8116
Burnette Foods
Hartford, MI.....................616-621-3181
Cold Hollow Cider Mill
Waterbury Center, VT...............800-327-7537
Commodities Marketing, Inc.
Edison, NJ.......................732-603-5077
Coutts Specialty Foods
Boxborough, MA..................800-919-2952
Del Mar Food Products Corporation
Watsonville, CA..................831-722-3516
Emerling International Foods
Buffalo, NY......................716-833-7381

We supply food manufacturers and food service customers worldwide (since 1988) with bulk ingredients including: Fruits & Vegetables; Juice Concentrates; Herbs & Spices; Oils & Vinegars; Flavors & Colors; Honey & Molasses. We also produce PURE MAPLE SYRUP.

Graves Mountain Lodge Inc.
Syria, VA........................540-923-4747
Independent Food Processors Company
Yakima, WA.....................800-476-5398
Knouse Foods Coop
Paw Paw, MI.....................269-657-5524
Knouse Foods Coop
Chambersburg, PA................717-263-9177
Knouse Foods Coop
Orrtanna, PA.....................717-642-8291
Knouse Foods Coop
Peach Glen, PA...................717-677-8181
Leahy Orchards
Franklin Centre, QC...............800-667-7380
Leroux Creek Foods
Hotchkiss, CO....................877-970-5670
Let's Serve
Plattsburgh, NY
Love Creek Orchards
Medina, TX......................800-449-0882
Mott's
Elmsford, NY
Nana Mae's Organics
Sebastopol, CA...................707-829-7359
New Era Canning Company
New Era, MI.....................231-861-2151
Solana Gold Organics
Sebastopol, CA...................800-459-1121
Tree Top
Selah, WA.......................800-367-6571
Tree Top
Selah, WA.......................800-542-4055
Unique Ingredients
Naches, WA......................509-653-1991
White House Foods
Winchester, VA...................540-662-3401

Canned

Bowman Apple Products Company
Mount Jackson, VA................800-346-5382
Independent Food Processors Company
Yakima, WA.....................800-476-5398
Leahy Orchards
Franklin Centre, QC...............800-667-7380
New Era Canning Company
New Era, MI.....................231-861-2151

with Other Fruit or Spices

Leahy Orchards
Franklin Centre, QC...............800-667-7380

Cranberry

Chung's Gourmet Foods
Houston, TX.....................800-824-8647
Coastal Classics
Duxbury, MA....................508-746-6058
Columbia County Fruit Processors
Hanson, MA.....................508-763-5257
Delectable Gourmet LLC
Lindenhurst, NY..................800-696-1350
Fireside Kitchen
Halifax, NS......................902-454-7387
Golden Valley Foods
Abbotsford, BC...................888-299-8855
Johnston's Home Style Products
Charlottetown, PE.................902-629-1300
Ocean Spray Cranberries
Lakeville-Middleboro, MA..........800-662-3263
Savannah Food Company
Savannah, TN....................800-795-2550
Skjodt-Barrett Foods
Mississauga, ON..................877-600-1200
Steel's Gourmet Foods, Ltd.
Bridgeport, PA...................800-678-3357

Jellied

Ocean Spray Cranberries
Lakeville-Middleboro, MA..........800-662-3263

Scallions

Emerling International Foods
Buffalo, NY......................716-833-7381

We supply food manufacturers and food service customers worldwide (since 1988) with bulk ingredients including: Fruits & Vegetables; Juice Concentrates; Herbs & Spices; Oils & Vinegars; Flavors & Colors; Honey & Molasses. We also produce PURE MAPLE SYRUP.

Ferris Organic Farm
Eaton Rapids, MI.................800-628-8736
S&E Organic Farms
Bakersfield, CA..................661-325-2644

SupHerb Farms
Turlock, CA.....................800-787-4372

Frozen culinary herb and specialty vegetable ingredients.

Tanimura & Antle
Salinas, CA......................831-455-2255

Seaweeds & Sea Vegetables

Acadian Seaplants
Dartmouth, NS...................800-575-9100
Atlantic Laboratories
Waldoboro, ME...................207-832-5376
Chieftain Wild Rice Company
Spooner, WI.....................800-262-6368
Great Eastern Sun
Asheville, NC....................800-334-5809
Maine Coast Sea Vegetables
Franklin, ME.....................207-565-2907
Maine Seaweed Company
Steuben, ME.....................207-546-2875

Shallot

California Garlic Co
San Diego, CA...................951-506-8883
Chieftain Wild Rice Company
Spooner, WI.....................800-262-6368
Christopher Ranch
Gilroy, CA.......................408-847-1100
Haliburton International Corporation
Ontario, CA......................877-980-4295

SupHerb Farms
Turlock, CA.....................800-787-4372

Frozen culinary herb and specialty vegetable ingredients.

Tulkoff Food Products
Baltimore, MD...................800-638-7343
Van Drunen Farms
Momence, IL.....................815-472-3537
Vegetable Juices
Chicago, IL......................888-776-9752

Soy

Agri-Dairy Products
Purchase, NY....................914-697-9580
Ajinomoto Food Ingredients LLC
Chicago, IL......................773-714-1436
Avatar Corporation
University Park, IL................800-255-3181
Basic Food Flavors
North Las Vegas, NV..............702-643-0043
Blue Chip Group
Salt Lake City, UT................800-878-0099
California Natural Products
Lathrop, CA.....................209-858-2525
Cedar Lake Foods
Cedar Lake, MI...................800-246-5039
Central Soya Company
Saint Louis, MO..................800-325-7108
Clofine Dairy & Food Products
Linwood, NJ.....................800-441-1001
Columbus Foods Company
Des Plaines, IL...................800-322-6457
Cricklewood Soyfoods
Mertztown, PA...................610-682-4109
Dakota Organic Products
Watertown, SD...................800-243-7264
Ener-G Foods
Seattle, WA......................800-331-5222
Flavor House
Adelanto, CA....................760-246-9131
GeniSoy
Tulsa, OK.......................800-228-4656
Genisoy Food Company
Tulsa, OK.......................888-437-4769
Genisoy Products Company
Tulsa, OK.......................800-228-4656
Glennys
Freeport, NY.....................888-864-1243
Heartland Fields
West Des Moines, IA..............515-225-1166
Heartland Fields, Llc
West Des Moines, IA..............866-769-7200
Hialeah Products Company
Hollywood, FL...................800-923-3379
House Foods America Corporation
Garden Grove, CA................714-901-4350
Innovative Food Solutions LLC
Columbus, OH...................800-884-3314
International Service Group
Alpharetta, GA...................770-518-0988
Island Spring
Vashon, WA.....................206-463-9848
Lee's Food Products
Toronto, ON.....................416-465-2407
Lightlife Foods
Turners Falls, MA.................800-274-6001
Lisanatti Foods P.J. Lisac & Associates, Inc
Oregon City, OR..................866-864-3922
Mandarin Soy Sauce
Middletown, NY..................845-343-1505
Mei Shun Tofu Products Company
Chicago, IL......................312-842-7000

MicroSoy Corporation
Jefferson, IA 515-386-2100
Microsoy Corporation
Jefferson, IA 515-386-2100
Miyako Oriental Foods
Baldwin Park, CA. 877-788-6476
Modesto WholeSoy
Ceres, CA 209-523-5119
Nature Soy, Inc
Philadelphia, PA 215-765-8889
ND Labs Inc
Lynbrook, NY. 888-263-5227
New England Natural Baker
Greenfield, MA. 800-910-2884
Northern Soy
Rochester, NY. 585-235-8970
Pokonobe Industries
Santa Monica, CA. 310-392-1259
Pulmuone Wildwood
Fullerton, CA 641-236-5170
Purity Foods
Okemos, MI 800-997-7358
Red River Commodities
Fargo, ND 701-282-2600
San-Ei Gen FFI
New York, NY 212-315-7850
San-J International, Inc
Richmond, VA. 800-446-5500
Solnuts
Hudson, IA 800-648-3503
Soyfoods of America
Duarte, CA 626-358-3836
SoyLife Division
Edina, MN. 952-920-7700
Specialty Ingredients
Buffalo Grove, IL 847-419-9595
SunOpta Grains
Hope, MN 800-297-5997
Sunrich
Hope, MN 800-297-5997
Turtle Island Foods
Hood River, OR 800-508-8100
Vitasoy USA
Ayer, MA. 978-772-6880
White Wave
Broomfield, CO 800-488-9283

Fresh

Smoke & Fire Natural Food
Great Barrington, MA. 413-528-8008
Vitasoy USA
Ayer, MA. 978-772-6880

Protein

Texturized

Allen Canning Company
Siloam Springs, AR 800-234-2553
Princeville Canning Company
Princeville, IL. 309-385-4301

Soy Bean

Aarhus United USA, Inc.
Newark, NJ 800-776-1338
ADM Nutraceuticals
Decatur, IL 800-510-2178
AG Processing, Inc.
Omaha, NE 800-247-1345
American Culinary GardenNoble Communications Co
Springfield, MO 888-831-2433
Cargill Vegetable Oils
Minneapolis, MN 612-378-0551
Continental Grain/ContiGroup Companies
New York, NY 212-207-5200
Durey-Libby Edible Nuts
Carlstadt, NJ 800-332-6887
Felbro Food Products
Los Angeles, CA. 800-335-2761
Fizzle Flat Farm
Yale, IL 618-793-2060
Frontier Commodities
Byron, MN 507-775-2174
Gama Products
Medley, FL 305-883-1200
Hain Celestial Canada
Delta, BC. 866-983-7834
Heartland Fields, Llc
West Des Moines, IA 866-769-7200
IMAC
Oklahoma City, OK 888-878-7827
Ingredient Innovations
Kansas City, MO. 816-587-1426
Knight Seed Company
Burnsville, MN 800-328-2999
Lone Pine Enterprises
Carlisle, AR 870-552-3217
Louis Dreyfus Corporation
Wilton, CT 203-761-2000
Myron's Fine Foods
Millers Falls, MA 800-730-2820
Producers Rice Mill
Stuttgart, AR. 870-673-4444
Purity Foods
Okemos, MI 800-997-7358
R&J Farms
West Salem, OH 419-846-3179
Red River Commodities
Fargo, ND 701-282-2600
Roberts Seed
Axtell, NE. 308-743-2565
Seapoint Farms
Huntington Beach, CA 888-722-7098
Seed Enterprises
West Point, NE 888-440-7333
Shepherd Farms
Hillsboro, IL 800-383-2676
Sno Pac Foods
Caledonia, MN 800-533-2215
Sonne
Wahpeton, ND. 800-727-6663
Star of the West MillingCompany
Frankenmuth, MI 989-652-9971
T.S. Smith & Sons
Bridgeville, DE. 302-337-8271
The Solae Company
Saint Louis, MO 800-325-7108
Tofu Shop Specialty Foods
Arcata, CA 707-822-7401
Western Pacific Commodities
Henderson, NV 702-382-8880

Soy Milk

Agri-Dairy Products
Purchase, NY 914-697-9580
Chunco Foods Inc
Kansas City, MO. 816-283-0716
Clofine Dairy & Food Products
Linwood, NJ 800-441-1001
Commodities Marketing, Inc.
Edison, NJ. 732-603-5077
Devansoy
Carroll, IA. 800-747-8605
Eden Foods Inc.
Clinton, MI 800-248-0320
Ener-G Foods
Seattle, WA 800-331-5222
FarmSoy Company
Summertown, TN 931-964-2411
Local Tofu
Nyack, NY 845-727-6393
Mighty Soy, Inc
Los Angeles, CA. 323-266-6969
Nutrisoya Foods
Saint-Hyacinthe, QC. 450-796-4261
Pacific Foods of Oregon
Tualatin, OR 503-692-9666
San Diego Soy Dairy
El Cajon, CA. 619-447-8638
Soyfoods of America
Duarte, CA 626-358-3836
Sunrise Markets
Vancouver, BC 604-253-2326
Tofu Shop Specialty Foods
Arcata, CA 707-822-7401
Vance's Foods
Gilmer, TX 800-497-4834
White Wave
Broomfield, CO 800-488-9283

Soy Protein

Cemac Foods Corporation
Philadelphia, PA 800-724-0179
Farbest-Tallman Foods Corporation
Montvale, NJ. 201-573-4900
ND Labs Inc
Lynbrook, NY. 888-263-5227
SoyTex
West Orange, NJ 888-769-8391
The Solae Company
Saint Louis, MO 800-325-7108

Concentrate

The Solae Company
Saint Louis, MO 800-325-7108

Texturized

Kerry Ingredients
Blue Earth, MN. 507-526-7575

Spinach

Avon Heights Mushrooms
Avondale, PA 610-268-2092
F&S Produce Company
Rosenhayn, NJ 800-886-3316
Frank Capurro & Son
Moss Landing, CA 831-728-3904
J.R. Simplot Company
Boise, ID 208-336-2110
Leach Farms
Berlin, WI 920-361-1880
McCain Foods Canada
Toronto, ON 866-622-2461
Patterson Frozen Foods
Patterson, CA 209-892-2611
Patterson Vegetable Company
Patterson, CA 209-892-2611
Pictsweet Frozen Foods
Bells, TN. 731-422-7600
Seabrook Brothers & Sons
Seabrook, NJ. 856-455-8080
Snowcrest Packer
Abbotsford, BC. 800-265-5332
Tami Great Food
Monsey, NY 732-803-6366
Unique Ingredients
Naches, WA. 509-653-1991
Vegetable Juices
Chicago, IL 888-776-9752
Walla Walla Gardeners' Association
Walla Walla, WA. 800-553-5014

Canned

ConAgra Grocery Products
Irvine, CA 714-680-1000
Emerling International Foods
Buffalo, NY. 716-833-7381

We supply food manufacturers and food service customers worldwide (since 1988) with bulk ingredients including: Fruits & Vegetables; Juice Concentrates; Herbs & Spices; Oils & Vinegars; Flavors & Colors; Honey & Molasses. We also produce PURE MAPLE SYRUP.

McCain Foods Canada
Toronto, ON 866-622-2461

Frozen

Emerling International Foods
Buffalo, NY. 716-833-7381

We supply food manufacturers and food service customers worldwide (since 1988) with bulk ingredients including: Fruits & Vegetables; Juice Concentrates; Herbs & Spices; Oils & Vinegars; Flavors & Colors; Honey & Molasses. We also produce PURE MAPLE SYRUP.

Vegetable Juices
Chicago, IL 888-776-9752

Sponge Gourd

Acme Steak & Seafood Company
Youngstown, OH. 330-270-8000
Bifulco Farms
Pittsgrove, NJ 856-692-0707
Cajun Chef Products
Saint Martinville, LA 337-394-7112
McCain Foods USA
Colton, CA 800-938-7799

Sprouts

Amigos Canning Company
San Antonio, TX. 800-580-3477
Calco of Calgary
Calgary, AB. 403-295-3578
Chunco Foods Inc
Kansas City, MO. 816-283-0716

Jonathan's Sprouts
Rochester, MA 508-763-2577
Lake Helen Sprout Farm
Lake Helen, FL....................386-228-2871
Montreal Chop Suey Company
Montreal, QC 514-522-3134
Mung Dynasty
Pittsburgh, PA....................412-381-1350
Snowcrest Packer
Abbotsford, BC....................800-265-5332
Sungarden Sprouts
Cookeville, TN 931-526-1106

Alfalfa

Chunco Foods Inc
Kansas City, MO....................816-283-0716
International Specialty Supply
Cookeville, TN 931-526-1106
Jonathan's Sprouts
Rochester, MA 508-763-2577
Marjon Specialty Foods, Inc
Plant City, FL 813-752-3482
Sungarden Sprouts
Cookeville, TN 931-526-1106

Bean

ConAgra Grocery Products
Archbold, OH 419-445-8015
ConAgra Grocery Products
Irvine, CA....................714-680-1000
Emerling International Foods
Buffalo, NY....................716-833-7381

We supply food manufacturers and food service customers worldwide (since 1988) with bulk ingredients including: Fruits & Vegetables; Juice Concentrates; Herbs & Spices; Oils & Vinegars; Flavors & Colors; Honey & Molasses. We also produce PURE MAPLE SYRUP.

International Specialty Supply
Cookeville, TN 931-526-1106
Marjon Specialty Foods, Inc
Plant City, FL 813-752-3482
Sungarden Sprouts
Cookeville, TN 931-526-1106

Mung Bean

Chunco Foods Inc
Kansas City, MO....................816-283-0716
Hong Kong Market Company
Chicago, IL 312-791-9111

Squash

Anchor Food Products/ McCain Foods
Appleton, WI 920-734-0627
F&S Produce Company
Rosenhayn, NJ 800-886-3316
Frank Capurro & Son
Moss Landing, CA 831-728-3904
Georgia Vegetable Company
Tifton, GA....................229-386-2374
Goebbert's Home Grown Vegetables
South Barrington, IL....................847-428-6727
Haliburton International Corporation
Ontario, CA....................877-980-4295
Indian Rock Produce
Perkasie, PA 800-882-0512
McCain Foods Canada
Toronto, ON 866-622-2461
Michigan Freeze Pack
Hart, MI....................231-873-2175
National Frozen Foods Corporation
Seattle, WA....................206-322-8900
Organically Grown Company
Eugene, OR....................541-689-5320
Pacific Collier Fresh Company
Immokalee, FL 800-226-7274
Pictsweet Frozen Foods
Bells, TN....................731-422-7600
Rene Produce Distributors
Nogales, AZ 520-281-9014
Snowcrest Packer
Abbotsford, BC....................800-265-5332
Tom Ringhausen Orchards
Hardin, IL 618-576-2311
Tony Vitrano Company
Jessup, MD 800-481-3784
Vegetable Juices
Chicago, IL 888-776-9752
Walter P. Rawl & Sons
Pelion, SC 803-359-3645

Acorn

Georgia Vegetable Company
Tifton, GA....................229-386-2374

Canned

Emerling International Foods
Buffalo, NY....................716-833-7381

We supply food manufacturers and food service customers worldwide (since 1988) with bulk ingredients including: Fruits & Vegetables; Juice Concentrates; Herbs & Spices; Oils & Vinegars; Flavors & Colors; Honey & Molasses. We also produce PURE MAPLE SYRUP.

Sure Fresh Produce
Santa Maria, CA 888-423-5379

Frozen

Emerling International Foods
Buffalo, NY....................716-833-7381

We supply food manufacturers and food service customers worldwide (since 1988) with bulk ingredients including: Fruits & Vegetables; Juice Concentrates; Herbs & Spices; Oils & Vinegars; Flavors & Colors; Honey & Molasses. We also produce PURE MAPLE SYRUP.

Sure Fresh Produce
Santa Maria, CA 888-423-5379
Vegetable Juices
Chicago, IL 888-776-9752

Golden Scallopino

Agrinorthwest
Kennewick, WA 509-734-1195
Allen Canning Company
Siloam Springs, AR 800-234-2553
Baker Produce Company
Kennewick, WA 800-624-7553
Circle Valley Produce
Idaho Falls, ID 208-524-2628
Dno
Columbus, OH 800-686-2366
McCain Foods USA
Colton, CA 800-938-7799
Zuccaro's Fruit & Produce Company
Minneapolis, MN 612-333-1122

Star Fruit

Brooks Tropicals
Homestead, FL 800-327-4833

Succotash

Allen Canning Company
Siloam Springs, AR 800-234-2553
Emerling International Foods
Buffalo, NY....................716-833-7381

We supply food manufacturers and food service customers worldwide (since 1988) with bulk ingredients including: Fruits & Vegetables; Juice Concentrates; Herbs & Spices; Oils & Vinegars; Flavors & Colors; Honey & Molasses. We also produce PURE MAPLE SYRUP.

McCain Foods USA
Colton, CA 800-938-7799
Pictsweet Frozen Foods
Bells, TN....................731-422-7600
Symons Frozen Foods
Galvin, WA....................360-736-1321
Trappe Packing Corporation
Trappe, MD....................410-476-3185
Twin City Foods
Stanwood, WA 208-743-5568

Canned

Emerling International Foods
Buffalo, NY....................716-833-7381

We supply food manufacturers and food service customers worldwide (since 1988) with bulk ingredients including: Fruits & Vegetables; Juice Concentrates; Herbs & Spices; Oils & Vinegars; Flavors & Colors; Honey & Molasses. We also produce PURE MAPLE SYRUP.

Ore-Ida Foods
Pittsburgh, PA....................800-892-2401
Patterson Frozen Foods
Patterson, CA 209-892-2611

Frozen

Emerling International Foods
Buffalo, NY....................716-833-7381

We supply food manufacturers and food service customers worldwide (since 1988) with bulk ingredients including: Fruits & Vegetables; Juice Concentrates; Herbs & Spices; Oils & Vinegars; Flavors & Colors; Honey & Molasses. We also produce PURE MAPLE SYRUP.

Ore-Ida Foods
Pittsburgh, PA....................800-892-2401
Patterson Frozen Foods
Patterson, CA 209-892-2611
Pictsweet Frozen Foods
Bells, TN....................731-422-7600
Symons Frozen Foods
Galvin, WA....................360-736-1321
Trappe Packing Corporation
Trappe, MD....................410-476-3185

Sun Dried Fruit

Chooljian Brothers Packing Company
Sanger, CA 559-875-5501
Del Rey Packing Company
Del Rey, CA 559-888-2031
Sun-Maid Growers of California
Kingsburg, CA 800-272-4746

Sunflower

Sunopta Sunflower
Minnetonka, MN....................952-224-4764

Sweet Potatoes

B&B Produce
Benson, NC....................800-633-4902
Barnes Farming Corporation
Spring Hope, NC....................252-459-9380
Best Ever Bake Shop
Mount Vernon, NY....................914-665-7005
Bissett Produce Company
Spring Hope, NC....................800-849-5073
Bright Harvest Sweet Potato Company
Clarksville, AR....................800-793-7440
Burch Farms
Faison, NC 800-466-9668
Carolina Pride Products
Enfield, NC....................252-445-3154
Dunbar Foods
Dunn, NC 910-892-3175
Godwin Produce Company
Dunn, NC 910-892-4171
Johnson Brothers Produce Company
Whitakers, NC....................252-437-2111
Joseph D Teachey Produce
Wallace, NC 910-285-4502
Livingston Farmers Association
Livingston, CA 209-394-7941
Moody Dunbar
Johnson City, TN 800-251-8202
Nash Produce Company
Nashville, NC 800-334-3032
Royce C. Bone Farms
Nashville, NC 252-443-3773
Scott Farms
Lucama, NC 877-284-4030
Seneca Foods Corporation
Marion, NY....................315-926-8100
Spring Acres Sales Company
Spring Hope, NC....................800-849-5436
Tull Hill Farms
Kinston, NC 252-523-8503

Wayne E. Bailey Produce Company
Chadbourn, NC 800-845-6149

Frozen

Bright Harvest Sweet Potato Company
Clarksville, AR 800-793-7440
Emerling International Foods
Buffalo, NY 716-833-7381

We supply food manufacturers and food service customers worldwide (since 1988) with bulk ingredients including: Fruits & Vegetables; Juice Concentrates; Herbs & Spices; Oils & Vinegars; Flavors & Colors; Honey & Molasses. We also produce PURE MAPLE SYRUP.

Mashed

Bright Harvest Sweet Potato Company
Clarksville, AR 800-793-7440
Moody Dunbar
Johnson City, TN 800-251-8202

Frozen

Bright Harvest Sweet Potato Company
Clarksville, AR 800-793-7440

Tamarind

Cinnabar Specialty Foods
Prescott, AZ 866-293-6433

Tangelos

A. Duda Farm Fresh Foods
Belle Glade, FL 561-996-7621
Heller Brothers PackingcCorporation
Winter Garden, FL 407-656-2124

Tangerines

A. Duda Farm Fresh Foods
Belle Glade, FL 561-996-7621
DNE World Fruit Sales
Fort Pierce, FL 800-327-6676
Haines City Citrus Growers Association
Haines City, FL 800-422-4245
Hale Indian River Groves
Wabasso, FL 800-562-4502
Heller Brothers PackingcCorporation
Winter Garden, FL 407-656-2124
Hunt Brothers Cooperative
Lake Wales, FL 863-676-9471
Seald Sweet Growers & Packers
Vero Beach, FL 772-569-2244

Taro

Sweety Novelty
Monterey Park, CA 626-282-4482

Tartufo

Creme Glacee Gelati
Montreal, QC 888-322-0116
Gelato Fresco
Toronto, ON 416-785-5415
Vigneri Confections
Rochester, NY 877-843-6374

Textured Vegetable Protein

Advanced Spice & Trading
Carrollton, TX 800-872-7811
American Health & Nutrition
Ann Arbor, MI 734-677-5570
CHS, Inc.
Inner Grove Heights, MN 800-232-3639
Clofine Dairy & Food Products
Linwood, NJ 800-441-1001
First Spice Mixing Company
Long Island City, NY 800-221-1105
The Solae Company
Saint Louis, MO 800-325-7108
Westin
Omaha, NE 800-228-6098

Tomatillos

Emerling International Foods
Buffalo, NY 716-833-7381

We supply food manufacturers and food service customers worldwide (since 1988) with bulk ingredients including: Fruits & Vegetables; Juice Concentrates; Herbs & Spices; Oils & Vinegars; Flavors & Colors; Honey & Molasses. We also produce PURE MAPLE SYRUP.

George Chiala Farms
Morgan Hill, CA 408-778-0562
Haliburton International Corporation
Ontario, CA 877-980-4295

Tomato

AgroCepia
Miami, FL 305-704-3488
Agrusa, Inc.
Leonia, NJ 201-592-5950
Atlantic Quality Spice &Seasonings
New Brunswick, NJ 800-584-0422
Ballantine Produce Company
Reedley, CA 559-875-2583
BGS Jourdan & Sons
Darlington, MD 410-457-4904
Char-Wil Canning Company
Hurlock, MD 410-943-3580
Chieftain Wild Rice Company
Spooner, WI 800-262-6368
ConAgra Grocery Products
Irvine, CA 714-680-1000
Del Monte Fresh Produce
Coral Gables, FL 800-950-3683
Dixon Canning Company
Dixon, CA 707-678-4406
Eden Foods Inc.
Clinton, MI 800-248-0320
Escalon Premier Brand
Escalon, CA 209-838-7341
F&S Produce Company
Rosenhayn, NJ 800-886-3316
Fresh Express
Salinas, CA 800-242-5472
George Chiala Farms
Morgan Hill, CA 408-778-0562
Goebbert's Home Grown Vegetables
South Barrington, IL 847-428-6727
Haliburton International Corporation
Ontario, CA 877-980-4295
Harris Farms
Coalinga, CA 800-742-1955
Hermann Pickle Farm
Garrettsville, OH 800-245-2696
Indian Rock Produce
Perkasie, PA 800-882-0512
John N Wright Jr
Federalsburg, MD 410-754-9044
Kaplan & Zubrin
Camden, NJ 800-334-0002
Lagorio Enterprises
Manteca, CA 209-982-5691
M&S Tomato Repacking Company
Springfield, MA 413-737-1308
Mangia Inc.
Mission Viejo, CA 866-462-6442
Miramar Pickles & Food Products
Fort Lauderdale, FL 954-351-8030
Moscahlades Brothers
New York, NY 212-226-5410
Nationwide Canning
Cottam, ON 519-839-4831
Pacific Collier Fresh Company
Immokalee, FL 800-226-7274
Pacific Tomato Growers
Palmetto, FL 941-722-3291
Pastene Companies
Canton, MA 781-830-8200
Pastorelli Food Products
Chicago, IL 800-767-2829
Patterson Vegetable Company
Patterson, CA 209-892-2611
Pure Food Ingredients
Verona, WI 800-355-9601
Rene Produce Distributors
Nogales, AZ 520-281-9014
Royce C. Bone Farms
Nashville, NC 252-443-3773
San Benito Foods
Hollister, CA 831-637-4434
SEW Friel
Queenstown, MD 410-827-8811
Somerset Industries
Spring House, PA 800-883-8728
Spreda Group
Louisville, KY 502-426-9411
Stanislaus Food Products
Modesto, CA 800-327-7201
Sun-Brite Canning
Kingsville, ON 519-326-9033
Surface Banana Company
Bluewell, WV 304-589-7202
Talley Farms
Arroyo Grande, CA 805-489-5533
Thomas Canning/Maidstone
Maidstone, ON 519-737-1531
Timber Crest Farms
Healdsburg, CA 888-374-9325
Tip Top Canning Company
Tipp City, OH 800-352-2635
Topor's Pickle Company
Detroit, MI 313-237-0288
Topper Food Products
East Brunswick, NJ 800-377-2823
Transa
Libertyville, IL 847-281-9582
Unilever Foods
Stockton, CA 209-467-2212
Vegetable Juices
Chicago, IL 888-776-9752
Veronica Foods Company
Oakland, CA 800-370-5554
Vincent Formusa Company
Chicago, IL 312-421-0485
Violet Packing
Williamstown, NJ 856-629-7428
Waterfield Farms
Amherst, MA 413-549-3558
Weil's Food Processing
Wheatley, ON 519-825-4572
Wisconsin Cheese
Melrose Park, IL 708-450-0074
Woodland Foods
Gurnee, IL 847-625-8600
Z&S Distributing
Fresno, CA 800-467-0788

Canned

Agrocan
Ville St Laurent, QC 877-247-6226
Char-Wil Canning Company
Hurlock, MD 410-943-3580
ConAgra Grocery Products
Irvine, CA 714-680-1000
Dei Fratelli
Toledo, OH 800-837-1631
Eden Foods Inc.
Clinton, MI 800-248-0320
Escalon Premier Brand
Escalon, CA 209-838-7341
Hartford City Foam Pack aging & Converting
Hartford City, IN 765-348-2500
John N Wright Jr
Federalsburg, MD 410-754-9044
Milroy Canning Company
Milroy, IN 765-629-2221
Nationwide Canning
Cottam, ON 519-839-4831
Natural Value Products
Sacramento, CA 916-427-7242
Ottawa Foods
Ottawa, OH 800-837-1631
Pacific Coast Producers
Lodi, CA 209-367-8800
Pastene Companies
Canton, MA 781-830-8200
Pastorelli Food Products
Chicago, IL 800-767-2829
Pure Food Ingredients
Verona, WI 800-355-9601
Ray Brothers & Noble Canning Company
Hobbs, IN 765-675-7451
Red Gold
Elwood, IN 877-748-9798
Rio Valley Canning Company
Donna, TX 956-464-7843
San Benito Foods
Vancouver, WA 800-453-7832
San Benito Foods
Hollister, CA 831-637-4434

Shafer-Haggart
Vancouver, BC ... 604-669-5512
Stanislaus Food Products
Modesto, CA ... 800-327-7201
Sun-Brite Canning
Kingsville, ON ... 519-326-9033
Thomas Canning/Maidstone
Maidstone, ON ... 519-737-1531
Tip Top Canning Company
Tipp City, OH ... 800-352-2635
Violet Packing
Williamstown, NJ ... 856-629-7428
Weil's Food Processing
Wheatley, ON ... 519-825-4572

Crushed

Agrocan
Ville St Laurent, QC ... 877-247-6226
Colonna Brothers
North Bergen, NJ ... 201-864-1115
Furmano's Foods
Northumberland, PA ... 877-877-6032
Hirzel Canning Company &Farms
Northwood, OH ... 419-693-0531
Violet Packing
Williamstown, NJ ... 856-629-7428

Cherry

Exeter Produce & Storage Company
Exeter, ON ... 800-881-4861
Talley Farms
Arroyo Grande, CA ... 805-489-5533

Cocktail

Miss Scarlett's
Chandler, AZ ... 800-345-6734
Pacific Coast Producers
Lodi, CA ... 209-367-8800
Princeville Canning Company
Princeville, IL ... 309-385-4301

Diced

Furmano's Foods
Northumberland, PA ... 877-877-6032
Hirzel Canning Company &Farms
Northwood, OH ... 419-693-0531
Ingomar Packing Company
Los Banos, CA ... 209-826-9494
Tip Top Canning Company
Tipp City, OH ... 800-352-2635

Dried

Chieftain Wild Rice Company
Spooner, WI ... 800-262-6368
Emerling International Foods
Buffalo, NY ... 716-833-7381

We supply food manufacturers and food service customers worldwide (since 1988) with bulk ingredients including: Fruits & Vegetables; Juice Concentrates; Herbs & Spices; Oils & Vinegars; Flavors & Colors; Honey & Molasses. We also produce PURE MAPLE SYRUP.

Grapevine Trading Company
Santa Rosa, CA ... 800-469-6478
Just Tomatoes Company
Westley, CA ... 800-537-1985
Rising Sun Farms
Phoenix, OR ... 800-888-0795
Setton International Foods
Commack, NY ... 800-227-4397
Terri Lynn
Elgin, IL ... 800-323-0775
Timber Crest Farms
Healdsburg, CA ... 888-374-9325
Unique Ingredients
Naches, WA ... 509-653-1991
Woodland Foods
Gurnee, IL ... 847-625-8600

Fresh

F&S Produce Company
Rosenhayn, NJ ... 800-886-3316
Fresh Express
Salinas, CA ... 800-242-5472
G Cefalu & Brothers
Jessup, MD ... 410-799-3414
Harris Farms
Coalinga, CA ... 800-742-1955
Lagorio Enterprises
Manteca, CA ... 209-982-5691
Mixon Fruit Farms
Bradenton, FL ... 800-608-2525
Rene Produce Distributors
Nogales, AZ ... 520-281-9014
Talley Farms
Arroyo Grande, CA ... 805-489-5533

Frozen

Allen Canning Company
Siloam Springs, AR ... 800-234-2553
ConAgra Grocery Products
Irvine, CA ... 714-680-1000
Hartford City Foam Pack aging & Converting
Hartford City, IN ... 765-348-2500
Milroy Canning Company
Milroy, IN ... 765-629-2221
Ocean Mist
Castroville, CA ... 800-962-3738
Pacific Coast Producers
Lodi, CA ... 209-367-8800
Ray Brothers & Noble Canning Company
Hobbs, IN ... 765-675-7451
Red Gold
Elwood, IN ... 877-748-9798

SupHerb FARMS®

SupHerb Farms
Turlock, CA ... 800-787-4372

Frozen culinary herb and specialty vegetable ingredients.

Vegetable Juices
Chicago, IL ... 888-776-9752

Marinated

American Importing Company
Minneapolis, MN ... 612-331-7000

Plum

Kaplan & Zubrin
Camden, NJ ... 800-334-0002

Processed

Escalon Premier Brand
Escalon, CA ... 209-838-7341
Pastorelli Food Products
Chicago, IL ... 800-767-2829
Weil's Food Processing
Wheatley, ON ... 519-825-4572

Products

American Chalkis Intl. Foods Company
Walnut, CA ... 909-595-5358
Burnette Foods
Hartford, MI ... 616-621-3181
ConAgra Grocery Products
Irvine, CA ... 714-680-1000
Country Pure Foods
Akron, OH ... 330-753-2293
Emerling International Foods
Buffalo, NY ... 716-833-7381

We supply food manufacturers and food service customers worldwide (since 1988) with bulk ingredients including: Fruits & Vegetables; Juice Concentrates; Herbs & Spices; Oils & Vinegars; Flavors & Colors; Honey & Molasses. We also produce PURE MAPLE SYRUP.

Escalon Premier Brand
Escalon, CA ... 209-838-7341
F&S Produce Company
Rosenhayn, NJ ... 800-886-3316
Fresh Express
Salinas, CA ... 800-242-5472
George Chiala Farms
Morgan Hill, CA ... 408-778-0562
Golden Valley Foods
Abbotsford, BC ... 888-299-8855
Hermann Pickle Farm
Garrettsville, OH ... 800-245-2696
International Home Foods
Parsippany, NJ ... 973-359-9920
Lagorio Enterprises
Manteca, CA ... 209-982-5691
Lake Packing Company
Lottsburg, VA ... 804-529-6101
Los Gatos Tomato Products
Huron, CA ... 559-945-2700
Milroy Canning Company
Milroy, IN ... 765-629-2221
Nationwide Canning
Cottam, ON ... 519-839-4831
Pacific Coast Producers
Oroville, CA ... 530-533-4311
Paradise Tomato Kitchens
Louisville, KY ... 502-637-1700
Pasta Factory
Melrose Park, IL ... 800-615-6951
Pastene Companies
Canton, MA ... 781-830-8200
Pastorelli Food Products
Chicago, IL ... 800-767-2829
Precision Foods
Saint Louis, MO ... 800-647-8170
Progresso Quality Foods
Vineland, NJ ... 800-200-9377
Pure Food Ingredients
Verona, WI ... 800-355-9601
Ray Brothers & Noble Canning Company
Hobbs, IN ... 765-675-7451
Red Gold
Elwood, IN ... 877-748-9798
San Benito Foods
Hollister, CA ... 831-637-4434
SEW Friel
Queenstown, MD ... 410-827-8811
Somerset Industries
Spring House, PA ... 800-883-8728
Spreda Group
Louisville, KY ... 502-426-9411
Talley Farms
Arroyo Grande, CA ... 805-489-5533
Terry Foods Inc
Idaho Falls, ID ... 208-604-8143
Thomas Canning/Maidstone
Maidstone, ON ... 519-737-1531
Timber Crest Farms
Healdsburg, CA ... 888-374-9325
Tip Top Canning Company
Tipp City, OH ... 800-352-2635
Topper Food Products
East Brunswick, NJ ... 800-377-2823
Transa
Libertyville, IL ... 847-281-9582
Unilever Foods
Stockton, CA ... 209-467-2212
Unique Ingredients
Naches, WA ... 509-653-1991
Valley Tomato Products
Stockton, CA ... 209-982-4586
Vegetable Juices
Chicago, IL ... 888-776-9752
Veronica Foods Company
Oakland, CA ... 800-370-5554
Walker Foods
Los Angeles, CA ... 800-966-5199
Weil's Food Processing
Wheatley, ON ... 519-825-4572
Welch's Foods Inc
Concord, MA ... 800-340-6870
Wisconsin Cheese
Melrose Park, IL ... 708-450-0074

Roma (Egg)

Lagorio Enterprises
Manteca, CA ... 209-982-5691
McCain Foods USA
Colton, CA ... 800-938-7799

Stewed

Furmano's Foods
Northumberland, PA ... 877-877-6032
Nationwide Canning
Cottam, ON ... 519-839-4831
San Benito Foods
Hollister, CA ... 831-637-4434

Tip Top Canning Company
Tipp City, OH 800-352-2635

Sun-Dried

Agrocan
Ville St Laurent, QC 877-247-6226
American Importing Company
Minneapolis, MN 612-331-7000
Castella Imports
Hauppauge, NY 866-227-8355
Claussen Pickle Company
Woodstock, IL 800-435-2817
Martin Farms
Patterson, CA 877-838-7369
Mezza
Lake Forest, IL 888-206-6054
Mooney Farms
Chico, CA 530-899-2661
Pacific Choice Brands
Fresno, CA 559-237-5583
Quality Choice Foods
Toronto, ON 416-650-9595
Veronica Foods Company
Oakland, CA 800-370-5554
Victoria Packing Corporation
Brooklyn, NY 718-927-3000
Woodland Foods
Gurnee, IL 847-625-8600

Yellow Cherry

Beckman & Gast Company
Saint Henry, OH 419-678-4195
California Fruit and Tomato Kitchens
Riverbank, CA 209-869-9300
Supreme Dairy Farms Company
Warwick, RI 401-739-8180

Tropical & Exotic Fruit

Chieftain Wild Rice Company
Spooner, WI 800-262-6368
NTC Marketing Inc
Williamsville, NY 800-333-1637
Varet Street Market
Brooklyn, NY 718-302-0560

Turnip

Abbott & Cobb, Inc.
Langhorne, PA 800-345-7333
Lucks Food Decorating Company
Tacoma, WA 253-383-4815
Pictsweet Frozen Foods
Bells, TN 731-422-7600
Snowcrest Packer
Abbotsford, BC 800-265-5332
Tom Ringhausen Orchards
Hardin, IL 618-576-2311
Walter P. Rawl & Sons
Pelion, SC 803-359-3645

Canned

Emerling International Foods
Buffalo, NY 716-833-7381

We supply food manufacturers and food service customers worldwide (since 1988) with bulk ingredients including: Fruits & Vegetables; Juice Concentrates; Herbs & Spices; Oils & Vinegars; Flavors & Colors; Honey & Molasses. We also produce PURE MAPLE SYRUP.

Frozen

Emerling International Foods
Buffalo, NY 716-833-7381

We supply food manufacturers and food service customers worldwide (since 1988) with bulk ingredients including: Fruits & Vegetables; Juice Concentrates; Herbs & Spices; Oils & Vinegars; Flavors & Colors; Honey & Molasses. We also produce PURE MAPLE SYRUP.

Turnip Greens: Canned

Bush Brothers & Co.
Augusta, WI 715-286-2211

Vegetables

A. Duda Farm Fresh Foods
Belle Glade, FL 561-996-7621
A. Lassonde, Inc.
Rougemont, QC 888-477-6663
Aaland Potato Company
Hoople, ND 701-894-6144
Acme Steak & Seafood Company
Youngstown, OH 330-270-8000
Affiliated Rice Milling
Alvin, TX 281-331-6176
Agri-Northwest
Kennewick, WA 509-734-1195
Agro Foods, Inc.
Miami, FL 305-361-7200
Al Pete Meats
Muncie, IN 765-288-8817
ALDI
Cincinnati, OH 513-421-1671
Alimentaire Whyte's Inc
Laval, QC 800-625-1979
Allen Canning Company
Siloam Springs, AR 800-234-2553
Associated Potato Growers, Inc.
Grand Forks, ND 800-437-4685
B&G Foods
Parsippany, NJ 973-401-6500
B&M
Portland, ME 207-772-7043
B.M. Lawrence & Company
San Francisco, CA 415-981-3650
Baker Produce Company
Kennewick, WA 800-624-7553
Baumer Foods
Metairie, LA 504-482-5761
Bay Cities Produce Company
San Leandro, CA 510-346-4943
Bean Buddies
New Hyde Park, NY 516-775-3726
Ben B. Schwartz & Sons
Detroit, MI 313-841-8300
Big B Distributors
Evansville, IN 812-425-5235
Birds Eye Foods
Cherry Hill, NJ 800-999-5044
Bjorneby Potato Company
Minto, ND 701-248-3482
Bob Gordon & Associates
Oak Park, IL 708-524-9611
Border Foods Inc
Deming, NM 888-737-7752
Bornt Family Farms
Holtville, CA 760-356-2233
Bottomline Foods
Davie, FL 954-843-0562
Bright Harvest Sweet Potato Company
Clarksville, AR 800-793-7440
Brooks Food Group Corporate Office
Bedford, VA 800-873-4934
Brooks Tropicals
Homestead, FL 800-327-4833
Bruce Church
Salinas, CA 800-538-2861
Bruce Foods Corporation
New Iberia, LA 337-365-8101
Bryant Preserving Company
Alma, AR 800-634-2413
Bubbles of San Francisco
Stockton, CA 209-951-6071
Burnette Foods
Elk Rapids, MI 231-264-8116
Burnette Foods
Hartford, MI 616-621-3181
Bush Brothers & Co.
Dandridge, TN 865-509-2361
Byrnes Packing
Hastings, FL 904-692-1643
C.C. Graber Company
Ontario, CA 800-996-5483
Cagnon Foods Company
Brooklyn, NY 718-647-2244
Cajun Chef Products
Saint Martinville, LA 337-394-7112
California Fruit and Tomato Kitchens
Riverbank, CA 209-869-9300
Caltex Foods
Canoga Park, CA 800-522-5839
Cannon Potato Company
Center, CO 719-754-3445
Cara Mia Foods
Castroville, CA 831-633-2423
Carando Gourmet Frozen Foods
Agawam, MA 888-227-2636
Caribbean Food Delights
Tappan, NY 845-398-3000
Cascade Specialties
Boardman, OR 541-481-2522
Cascadian Farm & MUIR Glen
Sedro Woolley, WA 360-855-0100
Cates Addis Company
Parkton, NC 800-423-1883
Cebro Frozen Foods
Newman, CA 209-862-0150
Chiquita Brands Intl. ional
Cincinnati, OH 800-438-0015
Christopher Ranch
Gilroy, CA 408-847-1100
Chugwater Chili Corporation
Chugwater, WY 800-972-4454
Claussen Pickle Company
Woodstock, IL 800-435-2817
Cleugh's Frozen Foods
Buena Park, CA 714-521-1002
Club Chef
Covington, KY 859-578-3100
Coloma Frozen Foods
Coloma, MI 800-642-2723
Columbia Foods
Snohomish, WA 360-568-0838
Columbia Foods
Quincy, WA 509-787-1585
ConAgra Grocery Products
Archbold, OH 419-445-8015
Cooperative Elevator Company
Pigeon, MI 989-453-4500
Coutts Specialty Foods
Boxborough, MA 800-919-2952
Crown Point
St John, IN 219-365-3200
Crystal Seed Potato Company
Crystal, ND 701-657-2143
Culinary Standards Corporation
Louisville, KY 800-778-3434
Cut Above Foods
Carlsbad, CA 760-931-6777
D'Arrigo Brothers Company of California
Salinas, CA 800-995-5939
Dairy King Milk Farms/Foodservice
Whitter, CA 800-900-6455
Dairy Management
Rosemont, IL 800-248-8829
De Bruyn Produce Company
Zeeland, MI 800-733-9177
Deep Foods
Union, NJ 908-810-7500
DeFrancesco & Sons
Firebaugh, CA 209-364-7000
Del Mar Food Products Corporation
Watsonville, CA 831-722-3516
Del Monte Fresh Produce
Coral Gables, FL 800-950-3683
Delicious Valley Frozen Foods
McAllen, TX 956-631-7177
Delta Packing Company of Lodi
Lodi, CA 209-334-0811
Dickinson Frozen Foods
Fruitland, ID 208-452-5200
DMH Ingredients
Libertyville, IL 847-362-9977
Dno
Columbus, OH 800-686-2366
Dole Fresh Vegetable Company
Soledad, CA 800-333-5454
Dole Fresh Vegetables
Monterey, CA 831-422-8871
Dong Kee Company
Chicago, IL 312-225-6340
East Coast Fresh Cuts Company
Savage, MD 410-799-9900
Eckert Cold Storage
Escalon, CA 209-838-4040
Eden Foods Inc.
Clinton, MI 800-248-0320
Erba Food Products
Brooklyn, NY 718-272-7700
Escalon Premier Brand
Escalon, CA 209-838-7341
F&S Produce Company
Rosenhayn, NJ 800-886-3316
Faribault Foods
Minneapolis, MN 612-333-6461
Fearnow Brothers
Cape May, NJ 609-884-0440

Federation of Southern Cooperatives
East Point, GA 404-765-0991
Fiesta Canning Company
Mc Neal, AZ 520-642-3376
Florida Citrus
Bartow, FL 863-537-3999
Fort Boise Produce Company
Nyssa, OR 541-372-5174
Foster Family Farm
South Windsor, CT 860-648-9366
Fountain Valley Foods
Colorado Springs, CO 719-573-6012
Freeze-Dry Products
Santa Rosa, CA 707-547-1776
Fresh Frozen Foods
Jefferson, GA 800-277-9851
Frieda's
Los Alamitos, CA 800-421-9477
Ful-Flav-R Foods
Alamo, CA 925-838-0300
Furmano Foods
Northumberland, PA 877-877-6032
G&G Marketing
Naples, FL 239-593-4564
G. L. Mezzetta
American Canyon, CA 707-648-1050
Garber Farms
Iota, LA 800-824-2284
Garden Valley Foods
Sutherlin, OR 541-459-9565
Garon Industries
Mosinee, WI 715-693-0558
Gene Belk Fruit Packers
Bloomington, CA 909-877-1819
George Chiala Farms
Morgan Hill, CA 408-778-0562
George L. Wells Meat Company
Philadelphia, PA 800-523-1730
Ghirardelli Ranch
Petaluma, CA 707-795-7616
Gibsonburg Canning Company
Gibsonburg, OH 419-637-2221
Gilleshammer Thiele Farms
Saint Thomas, ND 701-257-6634
Gilroy Foods
Gilroy, CA 800-921-7502
Glacier Foods
Sanger, CA 559-875-3354
Glory Foods
Columbus, OH 614-252-2042
Godwin Produce Company
Dunn, NC 910-892-4171
Gotliebs Guacamole
Sharon, CT 860-364-0842
Grant & Janet Brians
Hollister, CA 831-637-8497
Great American Appetizers
Nampa, ID 800-282-4834
Great Lakes Kraut Company
Shortsville, NY 585-289-4414
Green Garden Food Products
Kent, WA 800-304-1033
Griffin Food Company
Muskogee, OK 800-580-6311
GS Dunn & Company
Hamilton, ON 905-522-0833
GWB Foods Corporation
Brooklyn, NY 877-977-7610
H H Dobbins
Lyndonville, NY 877-362-2467
H.K. Canning
Ventura, CA 805-652-1392
Haliburton International Corporation
Ontario, CA 877-980-4295
Hard-E Foods
Saint Louis, MO 314-533-2211
Harner Farms
State College, PA 814-237-7919
Harris Farms
Coalinga, CA 800-742-1955
Harvest-Pac Products
Chatham, ON 519-436-0446
Henderson's Gardens
Berwyn, AB 780-338-2128
Henry Broch & Company/APK, Inc.
Libertyville, IL 847-816-6225
Herold's Salad, Inc
Cleveland, OH 800-427-2523
Hetty Fair Foods Company
Buffalo, NY 716-876-4345
HMC Marketing Group
Kingsburg, CA 559-897-1009
Houston Calco
Houston, TX 713-236-8668
Hunt-Wesson Food Service Company
Rochester, NY 866-484-8676
Indian Rock Produce
Perkasie, PA 800-882-0512
Inland Empire Foods
Riverside, CA 888-452-3267
International Home Foods
Parsippany, NJ 973-359-9920
J.C. Watson Company
Parma, ID 208-722-5141
J.R. Simplot Company
Boise, ID 208-336-2110
Jalapeno Foods Company
The Woodlands, TX 800-896-2318
JES Foods
Cleveland, OH 216-883-8987
Jimmy's Chiles
Tinley Park, IL 708-532-2650
Joe's Vegetables
Hollister, CA 831-636-3224
John N Wright Jr
Federalsburg, MD 410-754-9044
JR Wood/Big Valley
Atwater, CA 209-358-5643
Jubilee-Sedgefield Salads
Greensboro, NC 336-288-6646
Jyoti Cruisine India Gourmail Inc
Berwyn, PA 610-296-4620
Kaplan & Zubrin
Camden, NJ 800-334-0002
Kings Processing
Middleton, NS 902-825-2188
Knight Seed Company
Burnsville, MN 800-328-2999
L&S Packing Company
Farmingdale, NY 800-286-6487
L.H. Hayward & Company
New Orleans, LA 504-733-8480
L.I. Cauliflower Association
Riverhead, NY 631-727-2212
Lagorio Enterprises
Manteca, CA 209-982-5691
Lake Helen Sprout Farm
Lake Helen, FL 386-228-2871
Lakeside Foods
Plainview, MN 507-534-3141
Lakeside Foods
Seymour, WI 920-833-2371
Lakeside Packing Company
Harrow, ON 519-738-2314
Lamb-Weston
Hermiston, OR 800-766-7783
Larson Potato
Park River, ND 701-284-6437
Lennox Farm
Shelburne, ON 519-925-6444
Limited Edition
Midland, TX 432-686-2008
Livingston Farmers Association
Livingston, CA 209-394-7941
Lodi Canning Company
Lodi, WI 608-592-4236
Louise Metafora Company
Watertown, MA 61- 39- 191
Lucks Food Decorating Company
Tacoma, WA 253-383-4815
Made in Nature
Fresno, CA 800-906-7426
Mancini Packing Company
Zolfo Springs, FL 863-735-2000
Maple Leaf Foods International
North York, ON 416-480-8900
Marten's Country Kitchen
Port Byron, NY 315-776-8821
Martha's Garden
Toronto, ON 866-773-2887
Maryland Fresh Tomato Company
Jessup, MD 410-799-5050
Matador Processors
Blanchard, OK 800-847-0797
McCain Foods USA
Colton, CA 800-938-7799
McCartney Produce Company
Paris, TN 800-522-2791
Melissa's
Los Angeles, CA 800-588-0151
Mercado Latino
City of Industry, CA 626-333-6862
Mercer Processing
Modesto, CA 209-529-0150
Miami Purveyors
Miami, FL 305-262-6170
Michael Foods, Inc.
Minnetonka, MN 952-258-4000
Michigan Celery Promotion Cooperative
Hudsonville, MI 616-669-1250
Miguel's Stowe Away
Stowe, VT 800-448-6517
Millie's Pierogi
Chicopee Falls, MA 800-743-7641
Mills Brothers International
Tukwila, WA 206-575-3000
Milos
New York, NY 212-245-7400
Minnesota Dehydrated Vegetables
Fosston, MN 218-435-1997
Miramar Fruit Trading Company
Doral, FL 305-883-4774
Mister Spear
Stockton, CA 800-677-7327
Mitake Trading International
La Verne, CA 909-596-1981
Mixon Fruit Farms
Bradenton, FL 800-608-2525
Monterey Mushrooms
Watsonville, CA 800-333-6874
Monterey Mushrooms Inc.
Temple, PA 800-763-0700
Monticello Canning Company
Crossville, TN 931-484-3696
Moody Dunbar
Johnson City, TN 800-251-8202
Moscahlades Brothers
New York, NY 212-226-5410
Mother Teresa's
Clute, TX 888-265-7429
Mount Olive Pickle Company
Mount Olive, NC 800-672-5041
Mrs. Mazzula's Food Products
Edison, NJ 732-248-0555
Muir Glen Organic Tomato
Sacramento, CA 916-557-0900
Musco Olive Products
Orland, CA 530-865-4111
National Frozen Foods Corporation
Seattle, WA 206-322-8900
Nationwide Canning
Cottam, ON 519-839-4831
Natural Choice Distribution
Oakland, CA 510-653-8212
Natural Quality Company
San Martin, CA 408-683-2182
Nature Quality
San Martin, CA 408-683-2182
Naturex Inc.
South Hackensack, NJ 201-440-5000
New Era Canning Company
New Era, MI 231-861-2151
New Harvest Foods
Pulaski, WI 920-822-2578
New Meridian
Eaton, IN 765-396-3344
Nicola International
Los Angeles, CA 818-545-1515
Nonpareil Dehydrated Potatoes
Blackfoot, ID 800-522-2223
NORPAC Foods
Stayton, OR 503-769-2101
NORPAC Foods
Lake Oswego, OR 800-733-9311
Northern Star Company
Chaska, MN 612-339-8981
Nunes Company
Salinas, CA 831-751-7500
OC Schulz & Sons
Crystal, ND 701-657-2152
Ocean Mist
Castroville, CA 800-962-3738
Oh Boy! Corporation
San Fernando, CA 818-361-1128
Ohio Mushroom Company
Lima, OH 419-221-1721
Omega Produce Company
Nogales, AZ 520-281-0410
Ontario Produce Company
Ontario, OR 541-889-6485
Oregon Potato Company
Boardman, OR 800-336-6311
Organically Grown Company
Eugene, OR 541-689-5320
Osowski Farms
Minto, ND 701-248-3341

Pacific Choice Brands
Fresno, CA 559-237-5583
Pacific Coast Producers
Lodi, CA 209-334-3352
Pacific Collier Fresh Company
Immokalee, FL 800-226-7274
Pacific Tomato Growers
Palmetto, FL 941-722-3291
Pacific Valley Foods
Bellevue, WA 425-643-1805
Paradise Products Corporation
Boca Raton, FL 800-826-1235
Paris Foods Corporation
Trappe, MD 410-476-3185
Pastene Companies
Canton, MA 781-830-8200
Pastorelli Food Products
Chicago, IL 800-767-2829
Pavich Family Farms
Bakersfield, CA 661-782-8700
Pictsweet Frozen Foods
Bells, TN 731-422-7600
Pompeian
Baltimore, MD 800-638-1224
Pride Enterprises Glades
Belle Glade, FL 561-996-1091
Princeville Canning Company
Princeville, IL 309-385-4301
Proacec USA
Santa Monica, CA 310-996-7770
Produits Ronald
St. Damase, QC 800-465-0118
Pure Food Ingredients
Verona, WI 800-355-9601
Queensway Foods Company
Burlingame, CA 650-871-7770
R&S Mexican Food Products
Glendale, AZ 602-272-2727
R.C. McEntire & Company
Columbia, SC 803-799-3388
Rain Sweet
Salem, OR 800-363-4293
Ralph Sechler & Son
St Joe, IN 800-332-5461
Ralph Sechler & Son Inc
St Joe, IN 800-332-5461
Raymond-Hadley Corporation
Spencer, NY 800-252-5220
Ready-Pac Produce
Irwindale, CA 800-800-7822
Reckitt Benckiser
Parsippany, NJ 800-333-3899
Red River Commodities
Fargo, ND 701-282-2600
Rene Produce Distributors
Nogales, AZ 520-281-9014
Rich-Seapak Corporation
Brownsville, TX 956-542-0001
Ripon Pickle Company
Ripon, WI 800-324-5493
Ron-Son Foods
Swedesboro, NJ 856-241-7333
S&G Products
Nicholasville, KY 800-826-7652
S. Kennedy Vegetable Lifestock Company
Clear Lake, IA 641-357-4227
Salad Depot
Moonachie, NJ 201-507-1980
San Benito Foods
Hollister, CA 831-637-4434
Santa Barbara Olive Company
Santa Barbara, CA 800-624-4896
Saticoy Foods Corporation
Ventura, CA 805-647-5266
Schiff Food Products
North Bergen, NJ 201-868-6800
Schmidt Brothers
Swanton, OH 419-826-3671
Scotsburn Dairy Group
Scotsburn, NS 902-485-8023
Seabrook Brothers & Sons
Seabrook, NJ 856-455-8080
Sedlock Farm
Lynn Center, IL 309-521-8284
Seneca Foods
Marion, NY 315-926-8100
Seneca Foods
Cumberland, WI 715-822-2181
Seneca Foods
Clyman, WI 920-696-3331
Serv-Agen Corporation
Cherry Hill, NJ 856-663-6966
Seville Olive Company
Los Angeles, CA 323-261-2218
SEW Friel
Queenstown, MD 410-827-8811
Shafer Lake Fruit
Hartford, MI 269-621-3194
Silva Farms
Gonzales, CA 831-675-2327
Smeltzer Orchard Company
Frankfort, MI 231-882-4421
Smith Frozen Foods
Weston, OR 541-566-3515
Smith Frozen Foods
Weston, OR 800-547-0203
Smith-Coulter Company
Chittenango, NY 315-687-6510
Snowcrest Packer
Abbotsford, BC 800-265-5332
Somerset Industries
Spring House, PA 800-883-8728
Sonne
Wahpeton, ND 800-727-6663
SOPAKCO Foods
Mullins, SC 800-276-9678
South Mill Distribution
Kennett Square, PA 610-444-4800
Spokane Seed Company
Spokane Valley, WA 509-535-3671
Spreda Group
Louisville, KY 502-426-9411
Stahlbush Island Farms
Corvallis, OR 541-757-1497
Star Fine Foods
Fresno, CA 559-498-2900
Sterigenics International
Los Angeles, CA 800-472-4508
Strathroy Foods
Strathroy, ON 519-245-4600
Strub Pickles
Brantford, ON 519-751-1717
Sumida Pickle Products
Honolulu, HI 808-593-2487
Sun-Brite Canning
Kingsville, ON 519-326-9033
Sun-Glo of Idaho
Sugar City, ID 208-356-7346
Sungarden Sprouts
Cookeville, TN 931-526-1106
Sunnyside Vegetable Packing
Millville, NJ 856-451-5077
Sunrise Growers
Placentia, CA 714-630-6292
Superior Bean & Spice Company
Brush Prairie, WA 360-694-0819
Superior Foods
Watsonville, CA 831-728-3691

SupHerb Farms
Turlock, CA 800-787-4372

Frozen culinary herb and specialty vegetable ingredients.

Surface Banana Company
Bluewell, WV 304-589-7202
Sysco Edmonton
Edmonton, AB 780-451-0742
T.S. Smith & Sons
Bridgeville, DE 302-337-8271
Talk O'Texas Brands
San Angelo, TX
Taylor Farms
Salinas, CA 831-754-0471
Teixeira Farms
Santa Maria, CA 805-928-3801
Thomas Canning/Maidstone
Maidstone, ON 519-737-1531
Timber Crest Farms
Healdsburg, CA 888-374-9325
Tom Ringhausen Orchards
Hardin, IL 618-576-2311
Tony Vitrano Company
Jessup, MD 800-481-3784
Topor's Pickle Company
Detroit, MI 313-237-0288
Trade Farm
Oakland, CA 510-836-2938
Trans Pecos Foods
San Antonio, TX 210-228-0896
Transa
Libertyville, IL 847-281-9582
Trappe Packing Corporation
Trappe, MD 410-476-3185
Tropic Fish & Vegetable Center
Honolulu, HI 808-591-2963
Tropical
Charlotte, NC 800-220-1413
Tuscarora Organic Growers Cooperative
Hustontown, PA 814-448-2173
Twin City Foods
Stanwood, WA 208-743-5568
Unilever Foods
Stockton, CA 209-467-2212
United Marketing Exchange
Delta, CO 970-874-3332
United Natural Foods
Dayville, CT 800-877-8898
Vegetable Juices
Chicago, IL 888-776-9752
Verdelli Farms
Harrisburg, PA 800-422-8344
Veronica Foods Company
Oakland, CA 800-370-5554
Violet Packing
Williamstown, NJ 856-629-7428
Visalia Produce Sales Inc
Kingsburg, CA 559-897-6652
W.F. Cosart Packing Company
Exeter, CA 559-592-2821
Wallace Grain & Pea Company
Palouse, WA 509-878-1561
Washington Potato Company
Warden, WA 509-349-8803
Washington Rhubarb Growers Association
Sumner, WA 800-435-9911
Webster Farms
Cambridge Station, NS 902-538-9492
Weil's Food Processing
Wheatley, ON 519-825-4572
Westin
Omaha, NE 800-228-6098
Wildcat Produce
McGrew, NE 308-783-2438
William Bolthouse Farms
Bakersfield, CA 661-366-7270
William Karas & Sons
Churchville, NY 585-293-2109
Winslow B. Whitley
Oakley, ID 208-862-3229
Wolter Farms
Carmel, CA 831-624-8807
Zuccaro's Fruit & Produce Company
Minneapolis, MN 612-333-1122

IQF (Individual Quick Frozen)

Eckert Cold Storage
Escalon, CA 209-838-4040
LaMonica Fine Foods
Millville, NJ 856-825-8111
Rain Sweet
Salem, OR 800-363-4293

SupHerb Farms
Turlock, CA 800-787-4372

Frozen culinary herb and specialty vegetable ingredients.

Washington Rhubarb Growers Association
Sumner, WA 800-435-9911

Vegetables Mixed

Agrocan
Ville St Laurent, QC 877-247-6226
Birds Eye Foods
Cherry Hill, NJ 800-999-5044
Deep Foods
Union, NJ 908-810-7500
DiMare International Dmb Packing Corp
Indio, CA 760-347-3336

JR Wood/Big Valley
Atwater, CA 209-358-5643
Just Tomatoes Company
Westley, CA........................ 800-537-1985
Lakeside Foods
Seymour, WI....................... 920-833-2371
Lucks Food Decorating Company
Tacoma, WA 253-383-4815
McCain Foods Canada
Toronto, ON 866-622-2461
Mills
Salinas, CA........................ 831-757-1611
Musco Olive Products
Orland, CA 530-865-4111
New Harvest Foods
Pulaski, WI 920-822-2578
Patterson Frozen Foods
Patterson, CA 209-892-2611
Seneca Foods
Marion, NY........................ 315-926-8100
Strathroy Foods
Strathroy, ON 519-245-4600
Trappe Packing Corporation
Trappe, MD........................ 410-476-3185

Broccoli, Peas & Carrots

Faribault Foods
Minneapolis, MN 612-333-6461

Canned

Bryant Preserving Company
Alma, AR 800-634-2413
Carriere Foods Inc
Saint-Denis-Sur-Richelie, QC 450-787-3411
Cates Addis Company
Parkton, NC 800-423-1883
Deep Foods
Union, NJ 908-810-7500
Emerling International Foods
Buffalo, NY........................ 716-833-7381

We supply food manufacturers and food service customers worldwide (since 1988) with bulk ingredients including: Fruits & Vegetables; Juice Concentrates; Herbs & Spices; Oils & Vinegars; Flavors & Colors; Honey & Molasses. We also produce PURE MAPLE SYRUP.

Lakeside Foods
Seymour, WI....................... 920-833-2371
Lucks Food Decorating Company
Tacoma, WA 253-383-4815
McCain Foods Canada
Toronto, ON 866-622-2461
New Harvest Foods
Pulaski, WI 920-822-2578
Seneca Foods
Marion, NY........................ 315-926-8100

Frozen

Birds Eye Foods
Cherry Hill, NJ 800-999-5044
Deep Foods
Union, NJ 908-810-7500
JR Wood/Big Valley
Atwater, CA 209-358-5643
Lakeside Foods
Seymour, WI....................... 920-833-2371
McCain Foods Canada
Toronto, ON 866-622-2461
Strathroy Foods
Strathroy, ON 519-245-4600
Symons Frozen Foods
Galvin, WA........................ 360-736-1321
Trappe Packing Corporation
Trappe, MD........................ 410-476-3185

Peas & Carrots

Cates Addis Company
Parkton, NC 800-423-1883

Lakeside Foods
Seymour, WI....................... 920-833-2371
Strathroy Foods
Strathroy, ON 519-245-4600
Symons Frozen Foods
Galvin, WA........................ 360-736-1321
Twin City Foods
Stanwood, WA 208-743-5568

Canned

Lakeside Foods
Seymour, WI....................... 920-833-2371

Frozen

Cates Addis Company
Parkton, NC 800-423-1883
Lakeside Foods
Seymour, WI....................... 920-833-2371
Strathroy Foods
Strathroy, ON 519-245-4600
Symons Frozen Foods
Galvin, WA........................ 360-736-1321
Twin City Foods
Stanwood, WA 208-743-5568

Water Chestnuts

Dong Kee Company
Chicago, IL........................ 312-225-6340
Emerling International Foods
Buffalo, NY........................ 716-833-7381

We supply food manufacturers and food service customers worldwide (since 1988) with bulk ingredients including: Fruits & Vegetables; Juice Concentrates; Herbs & Spices; Oils & Vinegars; Flavors & Colors; Honey & Molasses. We also produce PURE MAPLE SYRUP.

Lee's Food Products
Toronto, ON 416-465-2407

SupHerb FARMS®

SupHerb Farms
Turlock, CA 800-787-4372

Frozen culinary herb and specialty vegetable ingredients.

Watercress

California Watercress
Fillmore, CA....................... 805-524-4808

Yams

Agrinorthwest
Kennewick, WA 509-734-1195
Arbre Farms Corporation
Walkerville, MI.................... 231-873-3337
Baker Produce Company
Kennewick, WA 800-624-7553
Bright Harvest Sweet Potato Company
Clarksville, AR.................... 800-793-7440
Cut Above Foods
Carlsbad, CA...................... 760-931-6777
De Bruyn Produce Company
Zeeland, MI....................... 800-733-9177
Dno
Columbus, OH 800-686-2366
F&S Produce Company
Rosenhayn, NJ 800-886-3316
Garber Farms
Iota, LA........................... 800-824-2284
Godwin Produce Company
Dunn, NC 910-892-4171
Moody Dunbar
Johnson City, TN 800-251-8202
Ocean Mist
Castroville, CA 800-962-3738
Seneca Foods
Clyman, WI....................... 920-696-3331
Vaughn Rue Produce
Wilson, NC 800-388-8138
Zuccaro's Fruit & Produce Company
Minneapolis, MN 612-333-1122

Canned

Moody Dunbar
Johnson City, TN 800-251-8202

Frozen

Bright Harvest Sweet Potato Company
Clarksville, AR.................... 800-793-7440

Prepared

Moody Dunbar
Johnson City, TN 800-251-8202

Zucchini

Anchor Food Products/ McCain Foods
Appleton, WI 920-734-0627
Arbre Farms Corporation
Walkerville, MI.................... 231-873-3337
Bifulco Farms
Pittsgrove, NJ 856-692-0707
Emerling International Foods
Buffalo, NY........................ 716-833-7381

We supply food manufacturers and food service customers worldwide (since 1988) with bulk ingredients including: Fruits & Vegetables; Juice Concentrates; Herbs & Spices; Oils & Vinegars; Flavors & Colors; Honey & Molasses. We also produce PURE MAPLE SYRUP.

F&S Produce Company
Rosenhayn, NJ 800-886-3316
Ghirardelli Ranch
Petaluma, CA 707-795-7616
Great American Appetizers
Nampa, ID........................ 800-282-4834
Haliburton International Corporation
Ontario, CA....................... 877-980-4295
Miss Scarlett's
Chandler, AZ...................... 800-345-6734
Ore-Ida Foods
Pittsburgh, PA..................... 800-892-2401
Pictsweet Frozen Foods
Bells, TN......................... 731-422-7600
Sure Fresh Produce
Santa Maria, CA 888-423-5379
Talley Farms
Arroyo Grande, CA................. 805-489-5533
Tami Great Food
Monsey, NY 732-803-6366
Vegetable Juices
Chicago, IL 888-776-9752

Dark Green

Allen Canning Company
Siloam Springs, AR 800-234-2553

General Grocery

General

A Gift Basket by Carmela
Longmeadow, MA 413-746-1400
A.T. Gift Company
Harpers Ferry, WV 304-876-6680
Abitec Corporation
Columbus, OH 800-555-1255
Alamo Onions
Pharr, TX. 210-281-0962
Allied Food Products
Brooklyn, NY
Ameriqual Foods
Evansville, IN 812-867-1444
Arctic Glacier
Albany, NY 518-438-2082
Arctic Glacier
Utica, NY 800-792-5958
Arctic Glacier
Corning, NY 800-937-4423
Arctic Glacier
Winnipeg, MB. 888-573-9237
Ashley Food Company, Inc.
Sudbury, MA. 800-617-2823
Avenue Gourmet
Reistertown, MD. 410-902-5701
Baldwin Richardson Foods
Frankfort, IL 866-644-2732

Liquid ingredient manufacturer specializing in signature sauces, dessert toppings, beverage/pancake syrups, specialty fruit fillings and condiments.

Basic Grain Products
Coldwater, OH 419-678-2304
Ben E. Keith DFW
Fort Worth, TX 877-317-6100
Binding Brauerei USA
Norwalk, CT 203-229-0111
Boyajian, Inc.
Canton, MA 800-965-0665
Brazilian Home Collection
Passaic, NJ 973-365-5800
Brooks Food Group, Inc
Monroe, NC 800-873-4934
Bungalow Brand Foods
Santa Barbara, CA 800-899-5267
Canyon Specialty Foods
Dallas, TX. 877-815-3663
Capalbo's Gift Baskets
Clifton, NJ. 800-252-6262
Cargill Foods
Springdale, AR 479-750-6816
Central Grocers, Inc.
Joliet, IL 815-553-8800
Chicken of the Sea International
San Diego, CA 800-678-8862
Chong Mei Trading
East Point, GA 404-768-3838
Choyce Produce
Honolulu, HI. 808-839-1502
Christmas Point Wild Rice Company
Baxter, MN 218-828-0603
Classic Foods
San Francisco, CA 800-574-8122
Colony Foods
Lawrence, MA 978-682-9677
Con Agro Food
Peru, IN. 765-473-3086
ConAgra Food Store Brands
Edina, MN. 952-469-4981
ConAgra Grocery Products
Omaha, NE 402-595-4000
Conco Food Service
New Orleans, LA 800-488-3988
Consumer Packing Company
Lancaster, PA 717-397-6141
Cosgrove Distributors
Spring Valley, IL. 815-664-4121
Creative Foods
Osceola, AR 800-643-0006
Culinary Farms, Inc.
Woodland, CA. 888-383-2767
Dakota Organic Products
Watertown, SD 800-243-7264
Dalton's Best Maid Products
Fort Worth, TX 800-447-3581
Dick Garber Company
Davie, FL 954-236-0456
Dogswell LLC
Los Angeles, CA. 888-559-8833
Eat It Corporation
Brooklyn, NY 718-768-7950
Ellsworth Foods
Tifton, GA. 229-386-8448
Fabrique Delices
Hayward, CA 510-441-9500
Farallon Fisheries
South San Francisco, CA 650-583-3474
Fast Fixin Foods
Boaz, AL. 256-593-7221
Fehr Foods
Abilene, TX. 325-691-5425
Festive Foods
Virginia Beach, VA. 757-490-9186
Figueroa Brothers
Irving, TX 214-351-9060
Filippo Berio Brand
Lyndhurst, NJ 201-525-2900
Fontaine Sante Foods IncFountain Of Health
Montreal, QC 514-956-7730
Foodmark
Wellesley, MA. 781-237-7088
Formost Friedman Company
Merrick, NY 516-378-4919
Fountain Shakes/MS Foods
Minnetonka, MN. 952-988-6940
French and Brawn
Camden, ME. 207-236-3361
Fulgenzi Foods
Leland Grove, IL. 217-787-7495
G S Robins & Company
Saint Louis, MO 800-777-5155
Gallands Institutional Foodservice
Bakersfield, CA 661-631-5505
Giulia Specialty Food
Lodi, NJ. 973-478-3111
Gold Mine Natural Food Company
San Diego, CA 800-475-3663
Goya de Puerto Rico
Bayamon, PR 787-740-4900
Grantstone Supermarket
Tucson, AZ 520-628-7445
Great River Milling
Fountain City, WI 608-687-9580
Gregerson's Foods
Gadsden, AL. 256-549-0644
Gulf Marine & Industrial Supplies
New Orleans, LA 800-886-6252
H&W Foods
Kapolei, HI 808-682-8300
Haile Resources
Dallas, TX. 800-357-1471
Hand Made With Love Inc.
Boca Raton, FL. 561-400-7444
Hanmi
Chicago, IL 773-271-0730
Hans Kissle Company
Haverhill, MA. 978-372-2504
Harold M. Lincoln Company
Toledo, OH 800-345-4911
Hatch Chile Company
Brunswick, GA 972-459-2520
Hickey Foods
Sun Valley, ID. 208-788-9033
Holly's Oatmeal
Torrington, CT 860-618-0090
Hurd Orchards
Holley, NY 585-638-8838
I. Epstein & Sons
East Brunswick, NJ. 800-237-5320
Ice House
Big Pine Key, FL. 305-872-1215
Imperial Food Supply
Baton Rouge, LA 225-924-4222
Imsco Technology
North Andover, MA 978-689-2080
Inland Products
Carthage, MO 417-358-4048
International Delicacies
Emeryville, CA. 510-428-9364
Ira Higdon Grocery Company
Cairo, GA 229-377-1272
Island Treasures Gourmet
Manassas, VA 703-590-7900
Itella Foods
Los Angeles, CA. 213-765-0967
J. Frasinetti & Sons
Sacramento, CA 916-383-2444
James Cowan & Sons
Worcester, MA 508-753-3259
John Morrell & Company
Cincinnati, OH 800-445-2013
Johnston County Hams
Smithfield, NC 800-543-4267
Julian's Recipe, LLC
Montgomery, NY 888-640-8880
Kaladi Brothers
Anchorage, AK
Karabetian Import And Export, Inc.
Los Angeles, CA. 323-664-8956
Karlin Foods Corporation
Northfield, IL 847-441-8330
Kashi Company
La Jolla, CA 858-274-8870
Kaurina's, LLC
Dallas, TX. 972-888-9990
Kelley's Katch Caviar
Savannah, TN 888-681-8565
Khalsa International Trading
Los Angeles, CA. 310-275-9891
Kids Cooking Club
San Diego, CA 858-539-2620
Kilauea Agronomics
Kilauea, HI 808-828-1761
Kombucha King International
Phoenix, AZ 800-896-9676
Kraft Foods
Northfield, IL 800-323-0768
Kusha Inc.
Irvine, CA. 800-550-7423
L.P.B. LLC
Richmond, VA. 804-385-4700
La Pasta, Inc.
Silver Spring, MD. 301-588-1111
La Superior Food Products
Shawnee Mission, KS. 913-432-4933
Lahaha Tea Company
San Gabriel, CA 626-215-6960
Lamm Food Service
Lafayette, LA 800-223-7752
Lance Private Brands
Charlotte, NC 888-722-1163
Landry Armand Company
Cottonport, LA 318-876-2716
Latteria Soresina
Brooklyn, NY 347-725-4096
Lemke Wholesale
Rogers, AR 501-636-3288
Life International
Naples, FL. 239-592-9788
Linkmark International
Paxton, MA. 508-753-2797
Little Freddy's
Clearwater, FL. 727-791-1118
Loftshouse Foods
Ogden, UT. 800-877-7055
Lopez Foods
Oklahoma City, OK 405-789-7500
Lotus Manufacturing Company
San Antonio, TX. 210-223-1421
Lyman Jenkins
Jericho Center, VT 800-528-7021
M & M Label Company
Malden, MA 781-321-2737
M&L Ventures
Tucson, AZ 520-884-8232
M.J. Kellner Company
Springfield, IL. 217-483-1770
Magic Valley Fresh Frozen
McAllen, TX. 956-618-1251
Maher Marketing Services
Irving, TX 972-751-7700
Market Day Corporation
Itasca, IL 877-632-7753
Marshakk Smoked Fish Company
Flushing, NY. 718-326-2170

Martin Brothers Distributing Company
Cedar Falls, IA 319-266-1775
Marukan Vinegar (U.S.A.) Inc.
Paramount, CA 562-630-6060
Mary Of Pudding Hill
Greenville, TX 903-455-2651
Mathews Packing Company
Marysville, CA 530-743-1077
McCain Foods USA
Fort Atkinson, WI. 800-938-7799
McClure's Pickles LLC
Troy, MI 245-837-9323
McFarling Foods
Indianapolis, IN 317-635-2633
Meiji
York, PA
Mesa Cold Storage
Tolleson, AZ 623-478-9392
Mexbest/Apoyos Y Servicios A La Comercialization Agroprecuaria
Washington, DC 202-728-1729
Michael's Of Brooklyn
Brooklyn, NY 718-998-7851
Mid-Georgia Processing Company
Vienna, GA 229-268-6496
Milton A. Klein Company
New York, NY 800-221-0248
Minh Food Corporation Schwan's Food Company
Pasadena, TX 800-344-7655
Miss Jenny's Pickles
Kernersville, NC. 336-978-0041
Mission Foods
Goldsboro, NC 919-778-7889
Mission Valley Foods
Middlebury, CT. 203-573-0652
Mitsui Foods
Norwood, NJ. 800-777-2322
MKE Enterprises LTD
New York, NY 212-447-0051
Moledina Commodities
Flower Mound, TX. 817-490-1101
Monte Cristo Trading
Scarsdale, NY 914-725-8025
MoonLight Kitchen
Newark, DE. 302-266-0558
Morr-Ad Foodservice
Wailuku, HI. 808-877-2017
MPK Sonoma Company
Sonoma, CA 707-996-3931
My Brother's Salsa
Fayetteville, AR 479-271-9404
National Food Company
Honolulu, HI 808-839-1118
National Importers
Richmond, BC 888-894-6464
New City Packing Company
Aurora, IL 800-621-0397
Nikola's Biscotti & European Specialties
Bloomington, MN. 888-645-6527
O'Brines Pickling
Spokane, WA. 509-534-7255
Oasis Foods
Lake Charles, LA 337-439-5262
Oscar Mayer Foods
Northfield, IL 847-646-2000
Outerbridge Peppers
Wharton, NJ 800-989-7007
Pacific Resources International
Carpinteria, CA. 805-684-0624
Particle Control
Albertville, MN. 763-497-3075
Peanut Wonder Corporation
Water Mill, NY 631-726-4433
Pinnacle Food Products
Lake Zurich, IL. 847-438-1598
Pirate Brands
Roslyn Heights, NY 800-626-7557
Plantextrakt
Parsippany, NJ. 973-683-1411
PMC Specialties
Cincinnati, OH 800-543-2466
Pon Food Corporation
Ponchatoula, LA 985-386-6941
Pristine Foods
Baton Rouge, LA 225-926-4677
Pure Inventions
Red Bank, NJ 732-842-5777
Quality Foods Products
Chicago, IL 312-666-4559
Quantum Foods
Chicago, IL 630-679-2300
Quicklabel Systems
West Warwick, RI. 877-757-7978
R.H. Bauman & Company
Chatsworth, CA 818-709-1093
R.N.C. Industries, Inc
Lawrenceville, GA 770-368-8453
Ramsen
Lakeville, MN. 952-431-0400
Redi-Froze
South Bend, IN 574-237-5111
Richards Natural Foods
Eagle, MI. 517-627-7965
Roxy Trading
Pomona, CA
Salem Food Service
Salem, IN 812-883-2196
Sally Sherman Foods
Mt Vernon, NY 914-664-6262
Sapporo
New York, NY 800-827-8234
Select Origins
Mansfield, OH 419-924-5447
Seven Brothers Trading
La Habra, CA 562-697-8888
Severance Foods
Hartford, CT 860-724-7063
Solo Worldwide Enterprises
Falls Church, VA. 703-845-7072
Stassen North America
Louisville, CO. 303-527-1700
Stilwell Foods
Stilwell, OK 918-696-8325
Sun Garden Sprouts
Cookeville, TN 931-526-1106
Sun Opta Ingredients
Chelmsford, MA. 800-353-6782
Sun World International
Bakersfield, CA 661-631-4100
Sun-Rise
Alexandria, MN 320-846-5720
Sunny Delight Beverage Company
Atlanta, GA. 800-395-5849
Tase-Rite Company
Wakefield, RI 401-783-7300
The Revere Group
Seattle, WA 866-747-6871
Thermice Company
Old Greenwich, CT. 203-637-4500
Thymly Products
Colora, MD. 410-658-4820
Topco
Skokie, IL 847-676-3030
Trade Marcs Group
Brooklyn, NY 718-387-9696
Tradeshare Corporation
Brooklyn, NY 718-237-2295
Turnbull Bakeries
New Orleans, LA 504-581-5383
Ugo di Lullo & Sons
Westville, NJ. 856-456-3700
Unicof
Sterling, VA. 703-904-0777
Valley Sun Products of California
Newman, CA. 888-786-3743
Van Ekris & Company
New York, NY 212-898-9600
Venice Maid Foods
Vineland, NJ 800-257-7070
Volpi Italian Meats
St Louis, MO. 314-772-8550
Wallace Edwards & Sons
Surry, VA. 757-294-3121
Weathervane Foods
Woburn, MA 781-935-5458
Wendy's International
Dublin, OH 800-937-5449
Yamamotoyama of America
Pomona, CA 909-594-7356
Zausner Foods
New Holland, PA 717-355-8505

Ingredients, Flavors & Additives

Freeze Dried Ingredients

SupHerb Farms
Turlock, CA 800-787-4372

Frozen culinary herb and specialty vegetable ingredients.

Y Not Foods
Madison, WI 608-222-2860

General

Aloecorp
Keene, NH. 603-352-0650
American Specialty Foods
Lancaster, PA 800-335-6663
Ames Company
New Ringgold, PA 570-386-2131

Asiamerica Ingredients
Westwood, NJ 201-497-5531

Processor, importer, exporter and distributor of bulk vitamins, amino acids, nutraceuticals, aromatic chemicals, food additives, herbs, mineral nutrients and pharmaceuticals.

Atlantis Pak USA
Coral Gables, FL. 305-403-2603
Biothera
Saint Paul, MN 651-675-0300
Caremoli USA
Ames, IA. 515-233-1255
Chaucer Foods
Syosset, NY. 516-496-2500
Creative Flavors & Specialties LLP
Linden, NJ. 908-862-4678
Cremer North America
Laval, QC 450-629-2229
DEKO International
Earth City, MO 314-298-0910
Denomega Nutritional Oils
Boulder, CO 303-581-9000
Diversified Foods
Metairie, LA 504-831-6651
Dohler Milne Aseptics
Prosser, WA. 509-786-2611
Draco Natural Products
San Jose, CA. 408-287-7871
Dulcette Technologies
Lindenhurst, NY. 631-752-8700
Edlong Dairy Flavors
Elk Grove Village, IL 888-698-2783
Embria Health Science
Ankeny, IA 877-362-7421
Emerald Performance Materials
Cuyahoga Falls, OH 330-916-6700
Emerald Performance Materials
Cincinnati, OH 513-841-3859
Escalade
Huntington, NY 631-659-3374
Ethical Naturals
San Anselmo, CA 415-459-4454
Expro Manufacturing
Vernon, CA 323-415-8544

Fallwood Corp
White Plains, NY 914-304-4065
Fenchem Enterprises
Chino, CA. 909-627-5268
Fiberstar
River Falls, WI 715-425-7550
First Choice Ingredients
Germantown, WI. 262-251-4322
Fontana Flavors
Janesville, WI 608-754-9668
Fontana Flavors
Janesville, WI 608-754-9668
Fonterra USA
Chicago, IL 847-928-1872
Foreign Domestic Chemicals Corporation
Oakland, NJ 201-651-9700
Freeze-Dry Foods
Albion, NY 905-844-1471
FrieslandCampina Domo
, NJ 201-655-7786
Fuji Health Science
Burlington, NJ. 609-386-3030
Garuda International
Lemon Cove, CA 559-594-4380
Gelnex Gelatins
Manhasset, NY 516-869-1623
Glanbia Nutritionals
Monroe, WI. 608-329-2800
GLG Life Tech Corporation
Vancouver, BC 604-641-1368
Global Preservatives
Lake Charles, LA 800-256-2253
GMI Products/Originates
Sunrise, FL 800-999-9373
Graham Chemical Corporation
Barrington, IL 847-304-4400
Grain Processing Corporation
Muscatine, IA 563-264-4265
Great Earth Chemical
Portland, OR 608-752-7417
GTC Nutrition Company
Golden, CO 800-522-4682
H.B. Taylor
Chicago, IL 773-254-4805
Hangzhou Sanhe USA
Walnut, CA 909-869-6016
Hawkins Inc
Minneapolis, MN 800-328-5460
Heartland Flax
Valley City, ND. 866-599-3529
Heartland Mill
Marienthal, KS 620-379-4472
Hela Spice Company
Uxbridge, ON 877-435-2649
Helm New York
Piscataway, NJ 732-981-1160
Hilmar Ingredients
Hilmar, CA 209-667-6076
Horner International
Raleigh, NC. 919-787-3112
ICL Performance Products
St. Louis, MO 800-244-6169
Imperial Sensus
Sugar Land, TX. 281-490-9522
Ingredient Specialties
Exeter, CA. 559-594-4380
Ingredients Unlimited
Bell Gardens, CA 562-806-7560
Innophos
Cranbury, NJ 609-495-2495
Innova Flavors
Lombard, IL 630-928-4813
Interfood Ingredients
Waltham, MA 781-370-9983
International Dairy Ingredients
Wapakoneta, OH. 419-738-4060
International Flavors & Fragrances
New York, NY 212-765-5500
Jel-Sert Company
West Chicago, IL 800-323-2592
JM Swank Company
North Liberty, IA 800-593-6375
Jost Chemical
Saint Louis, MO 314-428-4300
Just the Berries
Los Angeles, CA. 213-613-9807

Kenko International
Los Angeles, CA. 323-721-8300
Konica Minolta Sensing Americas
Ramsey, NY 201-785-2413
Latitude
Huntington, NY 631-659-3374
Lionel Hitchen Essitional Oils
Sarasota, FL 941-379-1400
Lipid Nutrition
Channahan, IL. 815-730-5208
Log 5 Corporation
Phoenix, MD. 410-329-9580
Magrabar Chemical Corp
Morton Grove, IL 847-965-7550
Marroquin Organic International
Santa Cruz, CA. 831-423-3442
Marukan Vinegar (U.S.A.) Inc.
Paramount, CA 562-630-6060
McCormick Industrial Flavor Solutions
Sparks, MD 800-632-5847
Mexnutri
San Luis Potosi, ... 444-841-5625
Mgp Ingredients, Inc.
Atchison, KS. 800-255-0302
Morgan Specialties
Paris, IL. 217-465-8577
Muntons Ingredients
Bellevue, WA 425-372-3082
Nissin Foods USA Company
Gardena, CA 310-327-8478
NutraCea
Scottsdale, AZ. 877-723-1700
Old Cavendish Products
Cavendish, VT 800-536-7899
Phamous Phloyd's Barbeque Sauce
Denver, CO 303-757-3285
Pizzey's Nutritionals
Fitchburg, WI 800-336-2183
Primer Foods Corporation
Cameron, WI. 80- 3-5 24
R. Torre & Company
South San Francisco, CA 800-775-1925
Reheis
Berkeley Heights, NJ 908-464-1500
Ribus
Saint Louis, MO 314-727-4287
Savoury Systems
Branchburg, NJ. 908-526-2524
Sensus
Lawrenceville, NJ. 646-452-6147
Silliker, Inc
Chicago, IL 312-938-5151
Specialty Minerals
Bethlehem, PA 800-801-1031
Sunshine International Foods
Methuen, MA 978-837-3209
Vanilla Corporation of America, LLC
Hatfield, PA. 215-996-1978
Wiberg Corporation
Oakville, ON. 905-825-9900

Acids

ADM Food Ingredients
Olathe, KS. 800-255-6637
Amerol Corporation
Farmingdale, NY
Bartek Ingredients, Inc.
Stoney Creek, ON. 800-263-4165
BASF Corporation
Florham Park, NJ 800-526-1072
Cargill Corn Milling
Naperville, IL 800-344-1633
Cargill Worldwide Acidulants
Naperville, IL 800-344-1633
Gadot Biochemical Industries
Rolling Meadows, IL 888-424-1424
Henkel Corporation
Cincinnati, OH 800-543-7370
Jarchem Industries
Newark, NJ 973-578-4560
Jungbunzlauer
Newton, MA 800-828-0062
Particle Dynamics
Saint Louis, MO 800-452-4682
Pfanstiehl Laboratories
Waukegan, IL 847-623-0370

Phibro Animal Health
Ridgefield Park, NJ 888-403-0074
PMP Fermentation Products
Peoria, IL. 800-558-1031
Protein Research Associates
Livermore, CA 800-948-1991
Roquette America
Keokuk, IA 800-553-7035
Silver Ferm Chemical
Seattle, WA 206-282-3376
Symrise
Teterboro, NJ. 201-288-3200
Trumark
Linden, NJ. 800-752-7877
Wilke International
Shawnee Mission, KS. 800-779-5545

Adipic

Silver Ferm Chemical
Seattle, WA 206-282-3376
Universal Preservachem Inc
Somerset, NJ 732-568-1266

Aminoacetic

ADH Health Products
Congers, NY 845-268-0027
Ajinomoto Food Ingredients LLC
Chicago, IL 773-714-1436
Albion Laboratories
Clearfield, UT 866-243-5283
Amt Labs
North Salt Lake, UT 801-299-1661
Anabol Naturals
Santa Cruz, CA 800-426-2265

Asiamerica Ingredients
Westwood, NJ 201-497-5531

Processor, importer, exporter and distributor of bulk vitamins, amino acids, nutraceuticals, aromatic chemicals, food additives, herbs, mineral nutrients and pharmaceuticals.

Belmont Chemicals
Clifton, NJ. 800-722-5070
DMH Ingredients
Libertyville, IL 847-362-9977
Eckhart Corporation
Novato, CA 415-892-3880
Jo Mar Laboratories
Campbell, CA 800-538-4545
Kyowa Hakko
New York, NY 212-715-0572
Now Foods
Bloomingdale, IL 888-669-3663
NuNaturals
Eugene, OR 800-753-4372
Universal Preservachem Inc
Somerset, NJ 732-568-1266

Benzoic

Kalama Chemical
Kalama, WA 800-223-0035
Luyties Pharmacal Company
Saint Louis, MO 800-325-8080
Universal Preservachem Inc
Somerset, NJ 732-568-1266

Boric/Boracic

Universal Preservachem Inc
Somerset, NJ 732-568-1266

Gluconic (Gluconolactone)

Glucona America
Janesville, WI 608-752-0449
Jungbunzlauer
Newton, MA 800-828-0062
PMP Fermentation Products
Peoria, IL. 800-558-1031
Roquette America
Keokuk, IA 800-553-7035
Universal Preservachem Inc
Somerset, NJ 732-568-1266

Glutamic

Universal Preservachem Inc
Somerset, NJ 732-568-1266
Woodland Foods
Gurnee, IL. 847-625-8600

Acidulants

Asiamerica Ingredients
Westwood, NJ 201-497-5531

Processor, importer, exporter and distributor of bulk vitamins, amino acids, nutraceuticals, aromatic chemicals, food additives, herbs, mineral nutrients and pharmaceuticals.

Marukan Vinegar (U.S.A.) Inc.
Paramount, CA 562-630-6060

Acetic

Asiamerica Ingredients
Westwood, NJ 201-497-5531

Processor, importer, exporter and distributor of bulk vitamins, amino acids, nutraceuticals, aromatic chemicals, food additives, herbs, mineral nutrients and pharmaceuticals.

Jarchem Industries
Newark, NJ 973-578-4560
Universal Preservachem Inc
Somerset, NJ 732-568-1266

Citric

ADM Food Ingredients
Olathe, KS 800-255-6637
American Key Food Products
Closter, NJ. 800-767-0237
Archer Daniels Midland Company
Decatur, IL 800-637-5843

Asiamerica Ingredients
Westwood, NJ 201-497-5531

Processor, importer, exporter and distributor of bulk vitamins, amino acids, nutraceuticals, aromatic chemicals, food additives, herbs, mineral nutrients and pharmaceuticals.

Cargill Corn Milling
Naperville, IL 800-344-1633
Cargill Worldwide Acidulants
Naperville, IL 800-344-1633
Embassy Flavours Ltd.
Brampton, ON. 800-334-3371
FBC Industries
Schaumburg, IL. 888-322-4637
Gadot Biochemical Industries
Rolling Meadows, IL 888-424-1424
Hosemen & Roche Vitamins & Fine Chemicals
Nutley, NJ 800-526-6367
International Chemical
Milltown, NJ. 800-914-2436
Jungbunzlauer
Newton, MA 800-828-0062
Kimson Chemicals
Waltham, MA 781-893-6878
Luyties Pharmacal Company
Saint Louis, MO 800-325-8080
Nichem Company
Hillside, NJ 908-933-0770
Phibro Animal Health
Ridgefield Park, NJ. 888-403-0074
Shekou Chemicals
Waltham, MA 781-893-6878
Universal Preservachem Inc
Somerset, NJ 732-568-1266

Fumaric

Asiamerica Ingredients
Westwood, NJ 201-497-5531

Processor, importer, exporter and distributor of bulk vitamins, amino acids, nutraceuticals, aromatic chemicals, food additives, herbs, mineral nutrients and pharmaceuticals.

Bartek Ingredients, Inc.
Stoney Creek, ON. 800-263-4165
Gadot Biochemical Industries
Rolling Meadows, IL 888-424-1424
Jungbunzlauer
Newton, MA 800-828-0062
Silver Ferm Chemical
Seattle, WA 206-282-3376
Universal Preservachem Inc
Somerset, NJ 732-568-1266

Lactic

ADM Food Ingredients
Olathe, KS 800-255-6637
Archer Daniels Midland Company
Decatur, IL 800-637-5843

Asiamerica Ingredients
Westwood, NJ 201-497-5531

Processor, importer, exporter and distributor of bulk vitamins, amino acids, nutraceuticals, aromatic chemicals, food additives, herbs, mineral nutrients and pharmaceuticals.

Fleurchem
Middletown, NY. 845-341-2100
Jungbunzlauer
Newton, MA 800-828-0062
Pfanstiehl Laboratories
Waukegan, IL 847-623-0370
Trumark
Linden, NJ. 800-752-7877
Universal Preservachem Inc
Somerset, NJ 732-568-1266
Varied Industries Corporation
Mason City, IA 800-654-5617
Wilke International
Shawnee Mission, KS. 800-779-5545

Malic

asiamerica

Asiamerica Ingredients
Westwood, NJ 201-497-5531

Processor, importer, exporter and distributor of bulk vitamins, amino acids, nutraceuticals, aromatic chemicals, food additives, herbs, mineral nutrients and pharmaceuticals.

Bartek Ingredients, Inc.
Stoney Creek, ON. 800-263-4165
Jungbunzlauer
Newton, MA 800-828-0062
Universal Preservachem Inc
Somerset, NJ 732-568-1266

Phosphoric

Asiamerica Ingredients
Westwood, NJ 201-497-5531

Processor, importer, exporter and distributor of bulk vitamins, amino acids, nutraceuticals, aromatic chemicals, food additives, herbs, mineral nutrients and pharmaceuticals.

ICL Performance Products
St. Louis, MO 800-244-6169
Universal Preservachem Inc
Somerset, NJ 732-568-1266

Sorbic

Amerol Corporation
Farmingdale, NY

Asiamerica Ingredients
Westwood, NJ 201-497-5531

Processor, importer, exporter and distributor of bulk vitamins, amino acids, nutraceuticals, aromatic chemicals, food additives, herbs, mineral nutrients and pharmaceuticals.

Gadot Biochemical Industries
Rolling Meadows, IL 888-424-1424
International Chemical
Milltown, NJ 800-914-2436
Jungbunzlauer
Newton, MA 800-828-0062
Silver Ferm Chemical
Seattle, WA 206-282-3376
Universal Preservachem Inc
Somerset, NJ 732-568-1266

Tartaric

American Tartaric Products
Larchmont, NY 914-834-1881

Asiamerica Ingredients
Westwood, NJ 201-497-5531

Processor, importer, exporter and distributor of bulk vitamins, amino acids, nutraceuticals, aromatic chemicals, food additives, herbs, mineral nutrients and pharmaceuticals.

Bartek Ingredients, Inc.
Stoney Creek, ON 800-263-4165
H. Interdonati
Cold Spring Harbor, NY 800-367-6617
International Chemical
Milltown, NJ 800-914-2436
Jungbunzlauer
Newton, MA 800-828-0062
Universal Preservachem Inc
Somerset, NJ 732-568-1266

Additives

Foreign Domestic Chemicals Corporation
Oakland, NJ 201-651-9700
Great Earth Chemical
Portland, OR 608-752-7417
Hangzhou Sanhe USA
Walnut, CA 909-869-6016
ICL Performance Products
St. Louis, MO 800-244-6169
Jost Chemical
Saint Louis, MO 314-428-4300
Latitude
Huntington, NY 631-659-3374
Magrabar Chemical Corp
Morton Grove, IL 847-965-7550

Anticaking

Asiamerica Ingredients
Westwood, NJ 201-497-5531

Processor, importer, exporter and distributor of bulk vitamins, amino acids, nutraceuticals, aromatic chemicals, food additives, herbs, mineral nutrients and pharmaceuticals.

Bulking

Cargill Texturizing Solutions
Cedar Rapids, IA 877-650-7080

Enrichment & Nutrient

Single & Blended

Asiamerica Ingredients
Westwood, NJ 201-497-5531

Processor, importer, exporter and distributor of bulk vitamins, amino acids, nutraceuticals, aromatic chemicals, food additives, herbs, mineral nutrients and pharmaceuticals.

Cargill Texturizing Solutions
Cedar Rapids, IA 877-650-7080

Free Flow

Amerol Corporation
Farmingdale, NY

Asiamerica Ingredients
Westwood, NJ 201-497-5531

Processor, importer, exporter and distributor of bulk vitamins, amino acids, nutraceuticals, aromatic chemicals, food additives, herbs, mineral nutrients and pharmaceuticals.

Cargill Texturizing Solutions
Cedar Rapids, IA 877-650-7080
Crompton Corporation
Greenwich, CT 800-295-2392
Dmv Intl. Nutritional ional
Delhi, NY 607-746-0100
Garuda International
Lemon Cove, CA 559-594-4380
Hangzhou Sanhe Food Company
Walnut, CA 909-869-6016
Henkel Corporation
Countryside, IL 800-328-6199
Prolume Biolume
Lakeside, AZ 928-367-1200

Adjuncts

Brewing

Acadian Seaplants
Dartmouth, NS 800-575-9100
Boyd Coffee Company
Portland, OR 800-545-4077

Agents

Asiamerica Ingredients
Westwood, NJ 201-497-5531

Processor, importer, exporter and distributor of bulk vitamins, amino acids, nutraceuticals, aromatic chemicals, food additives, herbs, mineral nutrients and pharmaceuticals.

Crest Foods Company
Ashton, IL 800-435-6972
Gadot Biochemical Industries
Rolling Meadows, IL 888-424-1424
International Foodcraft Corporation
Linden, NJ 800-875-9393
Magrabar Chemical Corp
Morton Grove, IL 847-965-7550

Anticaking

Cereal Solids Hydrolyzed

Cargill Texturizing Solutions
Cedar Rapids, IA 877-650-7080

Modified Food Starch

Cargill Texturizing Solutions
Cedar Rapids, IA 877-650-7080

Tricalcium Phosphate

Gadot Biochemical Industries
Rolling Meadows, IL 888-424-1424

Antimicrobial

A&B Ingredients
Fairfield, NJ 973-227-1390
Inovatech USA
Montreal, QC 800-367-3447

Bulking

Cargill Texturizing Solutions
Cedar Rapids, IA 877-650-7080

Clarifying

American Laboratories
Omaha, NE 402-339-2494

Compacting

Tabletizing

Cargill Texturizing Solutions
Cedar Rapids, IA 877-650-7080

Firming

Cargill Texturizing Solutions
Cedar Rapids, IA 877-650-7080

Foaming & Whipping

Cargill Texturizing Solutions
Cedar Rapids, IA 877-650-7080

Modifiers

Texture

Domino Specialty Ingredients
West Palm Beach, FL 800-446-9763

Release,Grease

Edible

Shoei Foods USA
Olivehurst, CA 800-527-4712
Spray Dynamics
Saint Clair, MO 800-260-7366

Thickening

Cargill Texturizing Solutions
Cedar Rapids, IA 877-650-7080
P.L. Thomas
Morristown, NJ 973-984-0900
Sno-Shack
Rexburg, ID 888-766-7425

Arrowroot

Advanced Spice & Trading
Carrollton, TX 800-872-7811
Schiff Food Products
North Bergen, NJ 201-868-6800

Whipping

Kolatin Real Kosher Gelatin
Lakewood, NJ 732-364-8700
SensoryEffects Flavor Systems
Bridgeton, MO 314-291-5444

Ammonium Carbonate

ADM Food Ingredients
Olathe, KS 800-255-6637
Luyties Pharmacal Company
Saint Louis, MO 800-325-8080
Universal Preservachem Inc
Somerset, NJ 732-568-1266

Analogs

Meat

Alle Processing Corporation
Maspeth, NY 800-245-5620
Caribbean Food Delights
Tappan, NY 845-398-3000
Cedar Lake Foods
Cedar Lake, MI 800-246-5039
CHR Hansen
Elyria, OH 800-558-0802
CHS, Inc.
Inner Grove Heights, MN 800-232-3639
Earth Island Natural Foods
Canoga Park, CA 818-725-2820
Innovative Food Solutions LLC
Columbus, OH 800-884-3314
Ivy Foods
Phoenix, AZ 877-223-5459
Oogolow Enterprises
Chico, CA 800-816-6873
Tami Great Food
Monsey, NY 732-803-6366
Vitasoy USA
Ayer, MA 978-772-6880
Westin
Omaha, NE 800-228-6098
White Wave
Broomfield, CO 800-488-9283
Winmix/Natural Care Products
Englewood, FL 941-475-7432

Antioxidants

Action Labs
Park City, UT 800-669-8877
Amerol Corporation
Farmingdale, NY

Asiamerica Ingredients
Westwood, NJ 201-497-5531

Processor, importer, exporter and distributor of bulk vitamins, amino acids, nutraceuticals, aromatic chemicals, food additives, herbs, mineral nutrients and pharmaceuticals.

Avatar Corporation
University Park, IL 800-255-3181
Body Breakthrough
Deer Park, NY 800-874-6299
Dulcette Technologies
Lindenhurst, NY 631-752-8700
Escalade
Huntington, NY 631-659-3374
Escalade Ltd
Huntington, NY 631-659-3374
Ethical Naturals
San Anselmo, CA 415-459-4454
First Spice Mixing Company
Long Island City, NY 800-221-1105
Fuji Health Science
Burlington, NJ 609-386-3030
Henkel Corporation
Countryside, IL 800-328-6199
Herbal Products & Development
Aptos, CA 831-688-8706
IVC American Vitamin
Freehold, NJ 800-666-8482
Kenko International
Los Angeles, CA 323-721-8300
Latitude
Huntington, NY 631-659-3374
Now Foods
Bloomingdale, IL 888-669-3663
P.L. Thomas
Morristown, NJ 973-984-0900
QBI
South Plainfield, NJ 908-668-0088
RFI Ingredients
Blauvelt, NY 800-962-7663
RPM Total Vitality
Yorba Linda, CA 800-234-3092
Uas Laboratories
Eden Prairie, MN 800-422-3371

Ascorbic Acid

Asiamerica Ingredients
Westwood, NJ 201-497-5531

Processor, importer, exporter and distributor of bulk vitamins, amino acids, nutraceuticals, aromatic chemicals, food additives, herbs, mineral nutrients and pharmaceuticals.

China Pharmaceutical Enterprises
Baton Rougee, LA 800-345-1658
Gadot Biochemical Industries
Rolling Meadows, IL 888-424-1424
Hermann Laue Spice Company
Uxbridge, ON 905-852-5100
International Chemical
Milltown, NJ 800-914-2436
Kimson Chemicals
Waltham, MA 781-893-6878
Shekou Chemicals
Waltham, MA 781-893-6878
Universal Preservachem Inc
Somerset, NJ 732-568-1266

Aroma Chemicals

Asiamerica Ingredients
Westwood, NJ 201-497-5531

Processor, importer, exporter and distributor of bulk vitamins, amino acids, nutraceuticals, aromatic chemicals, food additives, herbs, mineral nutrients and pharmaceuticals.

Astral Extracts Ltd.
Syosset, NY 516-496-2505
Firmenich
Plainsboro, NJ 800-452-1090

Aroma Chemicals & Materials

Chemicals

Asiamerica Ingredients
Westwood, NJ 201-497-5531

Processor, importer, exporter and distributor of bulk vitamins, amino acids, nutraceuticals, aromatic chemicals, food additives, herbs, mineral nutrients and pharmaceuticals.

Native Scents
Taos, NM 800-645-3471

Methyl Salicylate

Asiamerica Ingredients
Westwood, NJ 201-497-5531

Processor, importer, exporter and distributor of bulk vitamins, amino acids, nutraceuticals, aromatic chemicals, food additives, herbs, mineral nutrients and pharmaceuticals.

Fragrances

A M Todd Company
Kalamazoo, MI 800-968-2603
AFF International
Marietta, GA 800-241-7764
Agilex Flavors & Fr agrances, Inc.
Piscataway, NJ 800-542-7662
Arizona Chemical Company
Jacksonville, FL 800-526-5294
Aroma Vera
Los Angeles, CA 800-669-9514
Aromachem
Brooklyn, NY 718-497-4664

Asiamerica Ingredients
Westwood, NJ 201-497-5531

Processor, importer, exporter and distributor of bulk vitamins, amino acids, nutraceuticals, aromatic chemicals, food additives, herbs, mineral nutrients and pharmaceuticals.

Avoca
Merry Hill, NC 252-482-2133
AVRI Companies
Richmond, CA 800-883-9574
Centflor Manufacturing Company
New York, NY 212-246-8307
Classic Flavors & Fragrances
New York, NY 212-777-0004
Dream Time
Santa Cruz, CA 877-464-6702
Elan Chemical Company
Newark, NJ 973-344-8014
Essential Products of America
Tampa, FL 800-822-9698
Firmenich
Plainsboro, NJ 800-452-1090
Flavor & Fragrance Specialties
Mahwah, NJ 800-998-4337
Flavormatic Industries
Wappingers Falls, NY
Fleurchem
Middletown, NY 845-341-2100
Flower Essence Services
Nevada City, CA 800-548-0075
Givaudan Flavors
Cincinnati, OH 513-948-3428
Green Spot Packaging
Claremont, CA 800-456-3210

H&R Florasynth
Teterboro, NJ. 201-288-3200
Haldin International
Closter, NJ. 201-784-0044
International Flavors & Fragrances
Dayton, NJ 732-329-4600
International Flavors & Fragrances
New York, NY 212-765-5500
Janca's Jojoba Oil & Seed Company
Mesa, AZ. 480-497-9494
Jogue Inc
Northville, MI 800-521-3888
Lebermuth Company
South Bend, IN 800-648-1123
Maryland & Virginia Milk Producers Cooperative
Reston, VA 703-742-4250
McCormick & Company
Sparks, MD. 800-632-5847
Millennium Specialty Chemicals
Jacksonville, FL 800-231-6728
Naturex Inc.
South Hackensack, NJ 201-440-5000
Newport Flavours & Fragrances
Orange, CA. 714-744-3700
Oxford Organics
Livingston, NJ. 908-351-0002
PMC Specialties Group
Cincinnati, OH 800-543-2466
Rcb Intl.
Albany, OR 541-967-3814
Sigma-Aldrich Corporation
St. Louis, MO 314-771-5765
SKW Nature Products
Langhorne, PA 215-702-1000
Symrise
Teterboro, NJ. 201-288-3200
T Hasegawa
Cerritos, CA 714-522-1900
Technology Flavors & Fragrances
Amityville, NY. 631-789-8228
Treatt USA
Lakeland, FL. 800-866-7704
Ungerer & Company
Lincoln Park, NJ. 973-628-0600
US Flavors & Fragrances
Wauconda, IL 847-487-1022

Materials

Uncompounded

Accurate Ingredients
Syosset, NY. 516-496-2500

Bases

Ailments E.D. Foods Inc.
Pointe Claire, QC 800-267-3333
Al-Rite Fruits & Syrups
Miami, FL. 305-652-2540
American Fruits and Flavors
Los Angeles, CA. 323-264-7790
American Saucery
Oak Park, MI. 877-728-2379
Atlantic Quality Spice &Seasonings
New Brunswick, NJ 800-584-0422
Autocrat Coffee & Extracts
Lincoln, RI 800-288-6272
BakeMark Canada
Laval, QC 800-361-4998
Bakemark Ingredients Canada
Richmond, BC 800-665-9441
Bartush-Schnitzius Foods Company
Lewisville, TX 972-219-1270
Beverage Technologies
East Brunswick, NJ. 888-204-4299
Blount Seafood Corporation
Fall River, MA 774-888-1300
Cagnon Foods Company
Brooklyn, NY 718-647-2244
California Brands Flavors
Oakland, CA 800-348-0111
California Dairies
Visalia, CA 559-625-2200
Chef Hans Gourmet Foods
Monroe, LA. 800-890-4267
Citrus Citrosuco North America
Lake Wales, FL. 800-356-4592
Classic Tea
Libertyville, IL 630-680-9934
Clofine Dairy & Food Products
Linwood, NJ 800-441-1001
ConAgra Food Ingredients
Omaha, NE 877-266-2472
Concord Foods
Brockton, MA. 508-580-1700
Consolidated Mills
Houston, TX 713-896-4196
Crest Foods Company
Ashton, IL. 800-435-6972
Crystal Foods
Brick, NJ. 732-477-0073
CTL Foods
Colfax, WI. 800-962-5227
Custom Culinary
Lombard, IL 800-621-8827
Dorothy Dawson Foods Products
Jackson, MI. 517-788-9830
Eatem Foods Company
Vineland, NJ 800-683-2836
Erba Food Products
Brooklyn, NY 718-272-7700
Flavor House
Adelanto, CA 760-246-9131
Folklore Foods
Toppenish, WA 509-865-4772
Fuji Foods
Browns Summit, NC. 336-375-3111
Givaudan Flavors
Cincinnati, OH 513-948-8000
Global Food Industries
Townville, SC 800-225-4152
GS-AFI
South Plainfield, NJ 800-345-4342
Gum Technology Corporation
Tucson, AZ 800-369-4867
Hormel Foods Corporation
Austin, MN. 800-523-4635
Illes Seasonings & Flavors
Carrollton, TX. 800-683-4553
JMH International
Delafield, WI. 888-741-4564
Johnson's Food Products
Dorchester, MA. 617-265-3400
Manildra Milling Corporation
Fairway, KS. 800-323-8435
Meat-O-Mat Corporation
Brooklyn, NY 718-965-7250
Merci Spring Water
Maryland Heights, MO. 314-872-9323
Microsoy Corporation
Jefferson, IA 515-386-2100
Olympia Oyster Company
Shelton, WA 360-426-3354
Pacific Harvest Products
Bellevue, WA 425-401-7990
Particle Dynamics
Saint Louis, MO 800-452-4682
Produits Ronald
St. Damase, QC. 800-465-0118
Roos Foods
Kenton, DE 800-343-3642
Serv-Agen Corporation
Cherry Hill, NJ 856-663-6966
Skjodt-Barrett Foods
Mississauga, ON. 877-600-1200
Spice Advice
Ankeny, IA 800-247-5251
Spice Hunter
San Luis Obispo, CA 800-444-3061
Stevens Tropical Plantation
West Palm Beach, FL 561-683-4701
Sweet Sue Kitchens
Athens, AL 256-216-0500
Swiss Food Products
Chicago, IL. 312-829-0100
Texas Spice Company
Cedar Park, TX. 800-880-8007
Tone Products Company
Melrose Park, IL. 708-681-3660
Unilever
Lisle, IL. 877-995-4483
United Citrus Products
Norwood, MA. 800-229-7300
V&E Kohnstamm
Brooklyn, NY 800-847-4500
Vita-Pakt Citrus Company
Covina, CA 626-332-1101
Welch's Foods Inc
Concord, MA 800-340-6870
Western Syrup Company
Santa Fe Springs, CA 562-921-4485
White Coffee Corporation
Astoria, NY. 800-221-0140
Williams-West & Witt Products
Michigan City, IN

Beef

Associated Brands Inc.
Medina, NY. 800-265-0050
Castella Imports
Hauppauge, NY 866-227-8355
Golden Specialty Foods
Norwalk, CA. 562-802-2537

Broth Cubes

Gel Spice Company, Inc
Bayonne, NJ 800-922-0230

Beverage

Allen Flavors
Edison, NJ. 908-561-5995
American Health & Nutrition
Ann Arbor, MI 734-677-5570
American Purpac Technologies, LLC
Beloit, WI 877-787-7221
Astral Extracts Ltd.
Syosset, NY. 516-496-2505
Autocrat Coffee & Extracts
Lincoln, RI 800-288-6272
Baldwin Richardson Foods
Frankfort, IL 866-644-2732

Liquid ingredient manufacturer specializing in signature sauces, dessert toppings, beverage/pancake syrups, specialty fruit fillings and condiments.

Bartush-Schnitzius Foods Company
Lewisville, TX 972-219-1270
California Brands Flavors
Oakland, CA 800-348-0111
California Custom Fruits & Flavors
Irwindale, CA 877-558-0056
Carmi Flavor & Fragrance Company
City of Commerce, CA. 800-421-9647
Century Foods International
Sparta, WI. 800-269-1901
Classic Tea
Libertyville, IL 630-680-9934
Consolidated Mills
Houston, TX 713-896-4196
Country Pure Foods
Akron, OH. 877-995-8423
Crystal Foods
Brick, NJ. 732-477-0073
CTL Foods
Colfax, WI. 800-962-5227
Delano Growers Grape Products
Delano, CA 661-725-3255
Essential Flavors & Fragrances, Inc
Corona, CA. 888-333-9935
Folklore Foods
Toppenish, WA 509-865-4772
Franco's Cocktail Mixes
Pompano Beach, FL 800-782-4508
Fruitcrown Products Corporation
Farmingdale, NY 800-441-3210
Georgia Sun
Newnan, GA 770-251-2500
Global Food Industries
Townville, SC. 800-225-4152
H R Nicholson Company
Baltimore, MD 800-638-3514
Hagelin & Company
Branchburg, NJ 800-229-2112
Hig-Country Corona
Selah, WA 509-697-7950
I Rice & Company
Philadelphia, PA 800-232-6022
Innovative Food Solutions LLC
Columbus, OH 800-884-3314
J.M. Smucker Company
Grandview, WA. 509-882-1530
Kalva Corporation
Gurnee, IL. 800-525-8220
Milne Fruit Products
Prosser, WA. 509-786-2611
Nedlog Company
Wheeling, IL. 800-323-6201
Plaidberry Company
Vista, CA. 760-727-5403
Precision Foods
Melrose Park, IL. 800-333-0003

Quality Naturally! Foods
City of Industry, CA 888-498-6986
Rio Syrup Company
Saint Louis, MO 800-325-7666
Roos Foods
Kenton, DE 800-343-3642
Schlotterbeck & Foss Company
Portland, ME. 800-777-4666
Singer Extract Laboratory
Livonia, MI 313-345-5880
Skjodt-Barrett Foods
Mississauga, ON. 877-600-1200
Stevens Tropical Plantation
West Palm Beach, FL 561-683-4701
SunPure
Lakeland, FL. 863-619-2222
Tampico Beverages
Chicago, IL 877-826-7426
Thirs-Tea Corporation
Miami, FL. 305-651-4350
Tova Industries
Louisville, KY 888-532-8682
Tupman-Thurlow Company
Deerfield Beach, FL 954-596-9989
Vance's Foods
Gilmer, TX 800-497-4834
Vegetable Juices
Chicago, IL 888-776-9752
Vita-Pakt Citrus Company
Covina, CA 626-332-1101
Wechsler Coffee Corporation
Moonachie, NJ 800-800-2633
Welch's Foods Inc
Concord, MA 800-340-6870
Western Syrup Company
Santa Fe Springs, CA 562-921-4485
Winmix/Natural Care Products
Englewood, FL 941-475-7432

Bouillon

Gel Spice Company, Inc
Bayonne, NJ 800-922-0230
Hormel Foods Corporation
Austin, MN 800-523-4635
Organic Gourmet
Sherman Oaks, CA 800-400-7772
Vilore Foods Company
Laredo, TX 956-726-3633

Beef

Hormel Foods Corporation
Austin, MN 800-523-4635
Supreme Dairy Farms Company
Warwick, RI 401-739-8180

Candy

Kolatin Real Kosher Gelatin
Lakewood, NJ. 732-364-8700

Chicken

Associated Brands Inc.
Medina, NY. 800-265-0050
Castella Imports
Hauppauge, NY 866-227-8355
Golden Specialty Foods
Norwalk, CA. 562-802-2537

Chocolate

US Chocolate Corporation
Brooklyn, NY 718-788-8555

Dairy

Givaudan Flavors
Cincinnati, OH 513-948-8000
Johnson's Food Products
Dorchester, MA. 617-265-3400
WILD Flavors (Canada)
Mississauga, ON. 800-263-5286

Non-Dairy & Imitation

Al-Rite Fruits & Syrups
Miami, FL. 305-652-2540
American Health & Nutrition
Ann Arbor, MI 734-677-5570
Bakemark Ingredients Canada
Richmond, BC 800-665-9441
California Custom Fruits & Flavors
Irwindale, CA 877-558-0056
Century Foods International
Sparta, WI. 800-269-1901
Clofine Dairy & Food Products
Linwood, NJ 800-441-1001
Forbes Chocolates
Broadview Heights, OH 800-433-1090
Freeman Industries
Tuckahoe, NY. 800-666-6454
Galloway Company
Neenah, WI. 800-722-8903
Givaudan Flavors
Cincinnati, OH 513-948-8000
Global Food Industries
Townville, SC. 800-225-4152
I Rice & Company
Philadelphia, PA 800-232-6022
Johnson's Food Products
Dorchester, MA. 617-265-3400
Land O'Lakes, Inc.
Arden Hills, MN. 800-328-9680
Limpert Brothers
Vineland, NJ 800-691-1353
Nog Incorporated
Dunkirk, NY 800-332-2664
Plaidberry Company
Vista, CA. 760-727-5403
Quality Naturally! Foods
City of Industry, CA 888-498-6986
Tova Industries
Louisville, KY 888-532-8682
Welsh Farms
Edison, NJ. 800-221-0663
Westin
Omaha, NE 800-228-6098

Flavor

Creative Flavors & Specialties LLP
Linden, NJ. 908-862-4678
GS-AFI
South Plainfield, NJ 800-345-4342
JMH International
Delafield, WI. 888-741-4564
Pecan Deluxe Candy Company
Dallas, TX. 800-733-3589
Proliant
Ankeny, IA 800-466-7317

Food

Abimco USA, Inc.
Mendham, NJ 973-543-7393
ADM Food Ingredients
Olathe, KS. 800-255-6637
American Purpac Technologies, LLC
Beloit, WI 877-787-7221
Atlantic Quality Spice &Seasonings
New Brunswick, NJ 800-584-0422
Clofine Dairy & Food Products
Linwood, NJ 800-441-1001
General Spice
South Plainfield, NJ 800-345-7742
GS-AFI
South Plainfield, NJ 800-345-4342
Henningsen Foods
Purchase, NY 914-701-4020
I Rice & Company
Philadelphia, PA 800-232-6022
Summit Hill Flavors
Middlesex, NJ. 732-805-0335
Tova Industries
Louisville, KY 888-532-8682
Vita-Pakt Citrus Company
Covina, CA 626-332-1101

Fruit

American Purpac Technologies, LLC
Beloit, WI 877-787-7221
California Custom Fruits & Flavors
Irwindale, CA 877-558-0056
Fee Brothers
Rochester, NY. 800-961-3337
Givaudan Flavors
Cincinnati, OH 513-948-8000
Ramsey/Sias
Cleveland, OH 800-477-3788
Tova Industries
Louisville, KY 888-532-8682

Gravy

Ailments E.D. Foods Inc.
Pointe Claire, QC 800-267-3333
Atlantic Quality Spice &Seasonings
New Brunswick, NJ 800-584-0422
Bernard Food Industries
Evanston, IL 800-323-3663
Con Yeager Spice Company
Zelienople, PA. 800-222-2460
Cordon Bleu International
Anjou, QC. 514-352-3000
Custom Culinary
Lombard, IL 800-621-8827
Dorothy Dawson Foods Products
Jackson, MI. 517-788-9830
Eatem Foods Company
Vineland, NJ 800-683-2836
Felbro Food Products
Los Angeles, CA. 800-335-2761
Fuji Foods
Browns Summit, NC. 336-375-3111
Gel Spice Company, Inc
Bayonne, NJ 800-922-0230
Geneva Ingredients
Waunakee, WI. 800-828-5924
Griffith Laboratories Worldwide
Alsip, IL 800-346-4743
Halben Food Manufacturing Company
Saint Louis, MO 800-888-4855
Henningsen Foods
Purchase, NY 914-701-4020
Hormel Foods Corporation
Austin, MN. 800-523-4635
Karlsburger Foods
Monticello, MN 800-383-6549
Lawry's Foods
Monrovia, CA. 800-595-8917
Magic Seasoning Blends
New Orleans, LA 800-457-2857
Meat-O-Mat Corporation
Brooklyn, NY 718-965-7250
More Than Gourmet
Akron, OH. 800-860-9385
Newly Weds Foods
Chicago, IL. 800-647-9314
Olympia Oyster Company
Shelton, WA 360-426-3354
Pacific Foods
Kent, WA. 800-347-9444
Premier Blending
Wichita, KS. 316-267-5533
Presco Food Seasonings
Flemington, NJ 800-526-1713
Produits Ronald
St. Damase, QC. 800-465-0118
Proliant Meat Ingredients
Harlan, IA 800-369-2672
RL Schreiber
Pompano Beach, FL 954-972-7102
Serv-Agen Corporation
Cherry Hill, NJ 856-663-6966
Shenandoah Mills
Lebanon, TN. 615-444-0841
Spice Advice
Ankeny, IA 800-247-5251
Sweet Sue Kitchens
Athens, AL 256-216-0500
Swiss Food Products
Chicago, IL 312-829-0100
Tova Industries
Louisville, KY 888-532-8682
Ventura Foods
Philadelphia, PA 215-223-8700
Ventura Foods
Salem, OR. 503-585-6423
Vogue Cuisine
Sunnyvale, CA 888-236-4144
Williams-West & Witt Products
Michigan City, IN
World Flavors
Warminster, PA 215-672-4400

Juice

Citrus Citrosuco North America
Lake Wales, FL. 800-356-4592
Delano Growers Grape Products
Delano, CA 661-725-3255
Merci Spring Water
Maryland Heights, MO. 314-872-9323
SensoryEffects Flavor Systems
Bridgeton, MO 314-291-5444

Sauce

Eatem Foods Company
Vineland, NJ 800-683-2836
Illes Seasonings & Flavors
Carrollton, TX...................... 800-683-4553
JMH International
Delafield, WI....................... 888-741-4564
Produits Ronald
St. Damase, QC...................... 800-465-0118
Summit Hill Flavors
Middlesex, NJ....................... 732-805-0335
UFL Foods
Mississauga, ON..................... 905-670-7776

Seafood

Blount Seafood Corporation
Fall River, MA 774-888-1300
Swiss Food Products
Chicago, IL 312-829-0100

Soup

Ailments E.D. Foods Inc.
Pointe Claire, QC 800-267-3333
Atlantic Quality Spice &Seasonings
New Brunswick, NJ 800-584-0422
Bernard Food Industries
Evanston, IL 800-323-3663
Blount Seafood Corporation
Fall River, MA 774-888-1300
Blue Chip Group
Salt Lake City, UT 800-878-0099
Chef Hans Gourmet Foods
Monroe, LA.......................... 800-890-4267
CHR Hansen
Elyria, OH.......................... 800-558-0802
Con Yeager Spice Company
Zelienople, PA...................... 800-222-2460
Custom Culinary
Lombard, IL 800-621-8827
Dean Distributors
Burlingame, CA 800-792-0816
Dismat Corporation
Toledo, OH 419-531-8963
Dorothy Dawson Foods Products
Jackson, MI......................... 517-788-9830
Erba Food Products
Brooklyn, NY 718-272-7700
Five Star Food Base Company
St Paul, MN......................... 800-505-7827
Flavor House
Adelanto, CA 760-246-9131
Fuji Foods
Browns Summit, NC................... 336-375-3111
Gel Spice Company, Inc
Bayonne, NJ 800-922-0230
Griffith Laboratories Worldwide
Alsip, IL 800-346-4743
Halben Food Manufacturing Company
Saint Louis, MO 800-888-4855
Henningsen Foods
Purchase, NY 914-701-4020
Hormel Foods Corporation
Austin, MN.......................... 800-523-4635
JMH International
Delafield, WI....................... 888-741-4564
Lake City Foods
Mississauga, ON..................... 905-625-8244
Magic Seasoning Blends
New Orleans, LA 800-457-2857
Meat-O-Mat Corporation
Brooklyn, NY 718-965-7250
Mermaid Spice Corporation
Fort Myers, FL 239-693-1986
Olympia Oyster Company
Shelton, WA 360-426-3354
Oskri Organics
Lake Mills, WI 800-628-1110
Pacific Foods
Kent, WA............................ 800-347-9444
Precision Foods
Melrose Park, IL.................... 800-333-0003
Presco Food Seasonings
Flemington, NJ 800-526-1713
Produits Alimentaires Berthelet
Laval, QC 450-665-6100
Produits Ronald
St. Damase, QC...................... 800-465-0118
Proliant Meat Ingredients
Harlan, IA 800-369-2672
R.L. Schreiber
Pompano Beach, FL 800-624-8777
R.L. Schreiber Company
Pompano Beach, FL 800-624-8777
RC Fine Foods
Belle Mead, NJ 800-526-3953
Sams Food Group
Chicago, IL 800-852-0283
Senba USA
Hayward, CA 888-922-5852
Serv-Agen Corporation
Cherry Hill, NJ 856-663-6966
Spice Hunter
San Luis Obispo, CA 800-444-3061
St. Ours & Company
Norwell, MA......................... 781-331-8520
Summit Hill Flavors
Middlesex, NJ....................... 732-805-0335
Superior Quality Foods
Ontario, CA......................... 800-300-4210
Sweet Sue Kitchens
Athens, AL 256-216-0500
Tone Products Company
Melrose Park, IL.................... 708-681-3660
Tova Industries
Louisville, KY 888-532-8682
UFL Foods
Mississauga, ON..................... 905-670-7776
Unilever
Lisle, IL........................... 877-995-4483
Ventura Foods
Philadelphia, PA 215-223-8700
Ventura Foods
Salem, OR........................... 503-585-6423
Vogue Cuisine
Sunnyvale, CA 888-236-4144
White Coffee Corporation
Astoria, NY......................... 800-221-0140
Williams-West & Witt Products
Michigan City, IN
World Flavors
Warminster, PA...................... 215-672-4400
Young Winfield
Kleinburg, ON....................... 905-893-9682

Seafood

Blount Seafood Corporation
Fall River, MA 774-888-1300

Vegetable

American Purpac Technologies, LLC
Beloit, WI 877-787-7221
Associated Brands Inc.
Medina, NY.......................... 800-265-0050
Cagnon Foods Company
Brooklyn, NY 718-647-2244
California Custom Fruits & Flavors
Irwindale, CA 877-558-0056

Yogurt

Givaudan Flavors
Cincinnati, OH 513-948-8000
Gum Technology Corporation
Tucson, AZ 800-369-4867
Honeyville Grain
Rancho Cucamonga, CA 888-810-3212
Johanna Foods
Flemington, NJ 800-727-6700
Maple Island
Saint Paul, MN 800-369-1022
Plaidberry Company
Vista, CA........................... 760-727-5403

Binders

Cereal

Griffith Laboratories
Alsip, IL 800-346-9494
Sentry Seasonings
Elmhurst, IL 630-530-5370

The product development experts of Sentry Seasonings are eager to offer the assistance and hands-on experience to food processors of all sizes. Sentry Seasonings will ensure the consistent high quality and repeat sales of your products, whether you choose one of our many off-the-shelf Bench Mark products or a modified version to meet your preferences. Sentry Seasonings can also duplicate and/or improve your present flavor profile; formulate, blend and package specifically for your requirements.

Sausage

Cargill Texturizing Solutions
Cedar Rapids, IA.................... 877-650-7080
Roland Industries
Saint Louis, MO 800-325-1183
Sentry Seasonings
Elmhurst, IL 630-530-5370

The product development experts of Sentry Seasonings are eager to offer the assistance and hands-on experience to food processors of all sizes. Sentry Seasonings will ensure the consistent high quality and repeat sales of your products, whether you choose one of our many off-the-shelf Bench Mark products or a modified version to meet your preferences. Sentry Seasonings can also duplicate and/or improve your present flavor profile; formulate, blend and package specifically for your requirements.

World Flavors
Warminster, PA...................... 215-672-4400
Yosemite Waters
Los Angeles, CA..................... 800-427-8420

for Meat Products

Cargill Texturizing Solutions
Cedar Rapids, IA.................... 877-650-7080
MGP
Atchinson, KS....................... 913-367-1480
Sentry Seasonings
Elmhurst, IL 630-530-5370

The product development experts of Sentry Seasonings are eager to offer the assistance and hands-on experience to food processors of all sizes. Sentry Seasonings will ensure the consistent high quality and repeat sales of your products, whether you choose one of our many off-the-shelf Bench Mark products or a modified version to meet your preferences. Sentry Seasonings can also duplicate and/or improve your present flavor profile; formulate, blend and package specifically for your requirements.

Bioflavinoids

Asiamerica Ingredients
Westwood, NJ........................ 201-497-5531

Processor, importer, exporter and distributor of bulk vitamins, amino acids, nutraceuticals, aromatic chemicals, food additives, herbs, mineral nutrients and pharmaceuticals.

Brewster Foods TestLab
Reseda, CA.......................... 818-881-4268
H. Interdonati
Cold Spring Harbor, NY.............. 800-367-6617
Naturex Inc.
South Hackensack, NJ 201-440-5000

P.L. Thomas
Morristown, NJ 973-984-0900
QBI
South Plainfield, NJ 908-668-0088

Biopolymers

Cargill Texturizing Solutions
Cedar Rapids, IA. 877-650-7080
CP Kelco
Atlanta, GA. 800-535-2687

Bits

Baking

Erba Food Products
Brooklyn, NY 718-272-7700
Kerry Ingredients
Blue Earth, MN. 507-526-7575

Colored Starch

Kerry Ingredients
Blue Earth, MN. 507-526-7575

Cookie

Kerry Ingredients
Blue Earth, MN. 507-526-7575

Flavor

Kerry Ingredients
Blue Earth, MN. 507-526-7575

Flavored Sugar

Kerry Ingredients
Blue Earth, MN. 507-526-7575
SensoryEffects Flavor Systems
Bridgeton, MO 314-291-5444

Ham

Imitation

Gel Spice Company, Inc
Bayonne, NJ 800-922-0230

Blends

Cheese

Cemac Foods Corporation
Harrison, NY. 800-724-0179
Classic Tea
Libertyville, IL 630-680-9934
Leprino Foods Company
Denver, CO 800-537-7466
Sentry Seasonings
Elmhurst, IL 630-530-5370

The product development experts of Sentry Seasonings are eager to offer the assistance and hands-on experience to food processors of all sizes. Sentry Seasonings will ensure the consistent high quality and repeat sales of your products, whether you choose one of our many off-the-shelf Bench Mark products or a modified version to meet your preferences. Sentry Seasonings can also duplicate and/or improve your present flavor profile; formulate, blend and package specifically for your requirements.

Custom

Cargill Texturizing Solutions
Cedar Rapids, IA. 877-650-7080
Maple Island
Saint Paul, MN 800-369-1022
Old Dominion Spice Company
Ashland, VA 804-550-2780
Sentry Seasonings
Elmhurst, IL 630-530-5370

The product development experts of Sentry Seasonings are eager to offer the assistance and hands-on experience to food processors of all sizes. Sentry Seasonings will ensure the consistent high quality and repeat sales of your products, whether you choose one of our many off-the-shelf Bench Mark products or a modified version to meet your preferences. Sentry Seasonings can also duplicate and/or improve your present flavor profile; formulate, blend and package specifically for your requirements.

World Flavors
Warminster, PA 215-672-4400

Enrichment

Nu-Tek Products, LLC
Minnetonka, MN. 952-936-3603
Sentry Seasonings
Elmhurst, IL 630-530-5370

The product development experts of Sentry Seasonings are eager to offer the assistance and hands-on experience to food processors of all sizes. Sentry Seasonings will ensure the consistent high quality and repeat sales of your products, whether you choose one of our many off-the-shelf Bench Mark products or a modified version to meet your preferences. Sentry Seasonings can also duplicate and/or improve your present flavor profile; formulate, blend and package specifically for your requirements.

Herbs

All Purpose

Sentry Seasonings
Elmhurst, IL 630-530-5370

The product development experts of Sentry Seasonings are eager to offer the assistance and hands-on experience to food processors of all sizes. Sentry Seasonings will ensure the consistent high quality and repeat sales of your products, whether you choose one of our many off-the-shelf Bench Mark products or a modified version to meet your preferences. Sentry Seasonings can also duplicate and/or improve your present flavor profile; formulate, blend and package specifically for your requirements.

SupHerb Farms
Turlock, CA 800-787-4372

Frozen culinary herb and specialty vegetable ingredients.

Herbs & Spices

Asiamerica Ingredients
Westwood, NJ. 201-497-5531

Processor, importer, exporter and distributor of bulk vitamins, amino acids, nutraceuticals, aromatic chemicals, food additives, herbs, mineral nutrients and pharmaceuticals.

CaJohns Fiery Foods
Westerville, OH. 888-703-3473
Colorado Spice
Boulder, CO 800-677-7423
Georgia Spice Company
Atlanta, GA. 800-453-9997
Jodie's Kitchen
Pinellas Park, FL. 800-728-3704
La Flor Spices
Hauppaugue, NY 631-885-9601
Marion-Kay Spices
Brownstown, IN 800-627-7423
Marnap Industries
Buffalo, NY. 716-897-1220
McCormick & Company
Sparks, MD 800-632-5847
North American Seasonings
Lake Oswego, OR. 503-636-7043
Pendery's
Dallas, TX. 800-533-1870
Premier Blending
Wichita, KS. 316-267-5533
Sentry Seasonings
Elmhurst, IL 630-530-5370

The product development experts of Sentry Seasonings are eager to offer the assistance and hands-on experience to food processors of all sizes. Sentry Seasonings will ensure the consistent high quality and repeat sales of your products, whether you choose one of our many off-the-shelf Bench Mark products or a modified version to meet your preferences. Sentry Seasonings can also duplicate and/or improve your present flavor profile; formulate, blend and package specifically for your requirements.

St. John's Botanicals
Bowie, MD 301-262-5302

SupHerb Farms
Turlock, CA 800-787-4372

Frozen culinary herb and specialty vegetable ingredients.

Wisconsin Spice
Berlin, WI 920-361-3555

Pepper

Sentry Seasonings
Elmhurst, IL 630-530-5370

The product development experts of Sentry Seasonings are eager to offer the assistance and hands-on experience to food processors of all sizes. Sentry Seasonings will ensure the consistent high quality and repeat sales of your products, whether you choose one of our many off-the-shelf Bench Mark products or a modified version to meet your preferences. Sentry Seasonings can also duplicate and/or improve your present flavor profile; formulate, blend and package specifically for your requirements.

Caffeine

Alcan Chemical
Stamford, CT. 800-736-7893

Asiamerica Ingredients
Westwood, NJ. 201-497-5531

Processor, importer, exporter and distributor of bulk vitamins, amino acids, nutraceuticals, aromatic chemicals, food additives, herbs, mineral nutrients and pharmaceuticals.

Certified Processing Corporation
Hillside, NJ 973-923-5200
Jungbunzlauer
Newton, MA 800-828-0062
Natra US
Chula Vista, CA 800-262-6216

Casein & Caseinates

Agri-Dairy Products
Purchase, NY 914-697-9580

American Casein Company
Burlington, NJ ... 609-387-3130
Arla Foods Ingredients
Basking Ridge, NJ ... 908-604-8551
Blossom Farm Products
Ridgewood, NJ ... 800-729-1818
Crest Foods Company
Ashton, IL ... 800-435-6972
Erie Foods International
Erie, IL ... 800-447-1887
Kantner Group
Wapakoneta, OH ... 419-738-4060

Casein

Austrade Food Ingredients
Palm Beach Gdns, FL ... 561-586-7145
Century Foods International
Sparta, WI ... 800-269-1901
Clofine Dairy & Food Products
Linwood, NJ ... 800-441-1001
Excelpro Manufacturing Corporation
Los Angeles, CA ... 323-268-1918
International Casein Corporation
Great Neck, NY ... 516-466-4363
Oxford Frozen Foods Limited
Oxford, NS ... 902-447-2100
Prestige Proteins
Boca Raton, FL ... 561-997-8770
Prestige Technology Corporation
Boca Raton, FL ... 888-697-4141
Silver Creek Specialty Meats
Oshkosh, WI ... 920-232-3581
St. Charles Trading
Lake Saint Louis, MO ... 800-336-1333

Cellulose Gel

asiamerica

Asiamerica Ingredients
Westwood, NJ ... 201-497-5531

Processor, importer, exporter and distributor of bulk vitamins, amino acids, nutraceuticals, aromatic chemicals, food additives, herbs, mineral nutrients and pharmaceuticals.

J. Rettenmaier
Schoolcraft, MI ... 877-243-4661
P.L. Thomas
Morristown, NJ ... 973-984-0900
Reed Corporation
Pompton Plains, NJ ... 800-820-REED

Chemicals

Natural

Arizona Chemical Company
Jacksonville, FL ... 800-526-5294

asiamerica

Asiamerica Ingredients
Westwood, NJ ... 201-497-5531

Processor, importer, exporter and distributor of bulk vitamins, amino acids, nutraceuticals, aromatic chemicals, food additives, herbs, mineral nutrients and pharmaceuticals.

BASF Corporation
Florham Park, NJ ... 800-526-1072
Cheese Smokers
Brooklyn, NY
Chempacific Corporation
Baltimore, MD ... 410-633-5771
Crompton Corporation
Greenwich, CT ... 800-295-2392
Flavorchem
Downers Grove, IL ... 800-435-8867
Graham Chemical Corporation
Barrington, IL ... 847-304-4400
Haldin International
Closter, NJ ... 201-784-0044
Specialty Industrial Products
Spartanburg, SC ... 800-747-9001
Symrise
Teterboro, NJ ... 201-288-3200
Van Waters & Roger
Summit, IL ... 708-728-6830
VANCO Trading
Darien, CT ... 203-656-2800

Chlorophyll

asiamerica

Asiamerica Ingredients
Westwood, NJ ... 201-497-5531

Processor, importer, exporter and distributor of bulk vitamins, amino acids, nutraceuticals, aromatic chemicals, food additives, herbs, mineral nutrients and pharmaceuticals.

DeSouza International
Beaumont, CA ... 800-373-5171
H. Interdonati
Cold Spring Harbor, NY ... 800-367-6617
Herb Connection
Springville, UT ... 801-489-4254
Naturex Inc.
South Hackensack, NJ ... 201-440-5000
World Organics Corporation
Huntington Beach, CA ... 714-893-0017

Chocolate Products

ADM Cocoa
Milwaukee, WI ... 800-558-9958
Chefmaster
Garden Grove, CA ... 800-333-7443
Qzina Specialty Foods
Las Vegas, NV ... 702-451-3916
SensoryEffects Flavor Systems
Bridgeton, MO ... 314-291-5444

Chocolate Chip Compound for Ice Cream

ADM Cocoa
Milwaukee, WI ... 800-558-9958

Chocolate Fudge Icing Base - Liquid Marble

Teawolf Industries, Ltd
Pine Brook, NJ ... 973-575-4600

Coagulants

Dairy

Cargill Texturizing Solutions
Cedar Rapids, IA ... 877-650-7080

Coatings

FrieslandCampina Domo
, NJ ... 201-655-7786
Garuda International
Exeter, CA ... 559-594-4380

Compound

BASF Corporation
Florham Park, NJ ... 800-526-1072
CHR Hansen
Stoughton, WI ... 608-877-8970

Edible

Garuda International
Exeter, CA ... 559-594-4380
Spray Dynamics
Saint Clair, MO ... 800-260-7366

Cocoa Butter

Aarhus United USA, Inc.
Newark, NJ ... 800-776-1338
ADM Cocoa
Milwaukee, WI ... 800-558-9958
Barry Callebaut USA LLC
Chicago, IL ... 866-443-0460
Chadler
Swedesboro, NJ ... 856-467-0099
Ecom Agroindustrial Corporation Ltd
New York, NY ... 212-248-1190
Natra US
Chula Vista, CA ... 800-262-6216
Vrymeer Commodities
St Charles, IL ... 630-584-0069
Wilbur Chocolate
Lititz, PA ... 800-233-0139

Colors

Ameri Color Corporation
Placentia, CA ... 800-556-0233
Emerald Performance Materials
Cuyahoga Falls, OH ... 330-916-6700
Erba Food Products
Brooklyn, NY ... 718-272-7700
Flavorchem
Downers Grove, IL ... 800-435-8867
H.B. Taylor
Chicago, IL ... 773-254-4805
LorAnn Oils Inc
Lansing, MI ... 888-456-7266
McCormick & Company
Sparks, MD ... 800-632-5847
Noveon
Cleveland, OH ... 216-447-5000
Particle Dynamics
Saint Louis, MO ... 800-452-4682
Sensient Food Colors
Milwaukee, WI ... 800-558-9892
Sensient Technologies
Milwaukee, WI ... 800-558-9892
Unette Corporation
Randolph, NJ ... 973-328-6800
Wild Flavors
Erlanger, KY ... 859-342-3600

Annatto

Burlington Bio-Medical Corporation
Farmingdale, NY ... 800-532-4808
Schiff Food Products
North Bergen, NJ ... 201-868-6800
SJH Enterprises
Middleton, WI ... 888-745-3845

Burnt Sugar

D.D. Williamson & Company
Louisville, KY ... 800-227-2635
DD Williamson & Company
Louisville, KY ... 800-227-2635
Four Percent Company
Highland Park, MI ... 313-345-5880
Produits Alimentaire
St Lambert De Lauzon, QC ... 800-463-1787
RFI Ingredients
Blauvelt, NY ... 800-962-7663
Sethness Products Company
Lincolnwood, IL ... 847-329-2080
Seydel International
Pendergrass, GA ... 706-693-2295

Caramel

Carmi Flavor & Fragrance Company
City of Commerce, CA ... 800-421-9647
Gel Spice Company, Inc
Bayonne, NJ ... 800-922-0230

Butter & Cheese

Agri-Dairy Products
Purchase, NY ... 914-697-9580
Carmi Flavor & Fragrance Company
City of Commerce, CA ... 800-421-9647
Prime Ingredients
Saddle Brook, NJ ... 888-791-6655
SJH Enterprises
Middleton, WI ... 888-745-3845

Caramel

D.D. Williamson & Company
Louisville, KY ... 800-227-2635
Sethness Products Company
Chicago, IL ... 888-772-1880

Cider & Vinegar

Asiamerica Ingredients
Westwood, NJ 201-497-5531

Processor, importer, exporter and distributor of bulk vitamins, amino acids, nutraceuticals, aromatic chemicals, food additives, herbs, mineral nutrients and pharmaceuticals.

Prime Ingredients
Saddle Brook, NJ 888-791-6655

Coloring Adjuncts

Roha USA LLC
Saint Louis, MO 314-531-0461

Dyes

Certified

Castella Imports
Hauppauge, NY 866-227-8355

Grape Skin Extract Color

Asiamerica Ingredients
Westwood, NJ 201-497-5531

Processor, importer, exporter and distributor of bulk vitamins, amino acids, nutraceuticals, aromatic chemicals, food additives, herbs, mineral nutrients and pharmaceuticals.

Natural

Asiamerica Ingredients
Westwood, NJ 201-497-5531

Processor, importer, exporter and distributor of bulk vitamins, amino acids, nutraceuticals, aromatic chemicals, food additives, herbs, mineral nutrients and pharmaceuticals.

LaMonde Wild Flavors
Placentia, CA 714-993-7700
P.L. Thomas
Morristown, NJ 973-984-0900

Annatto

SJH Enterprises
Middleton, WI. 888-745-3845

Anthocyanins Grape Skin

Asiamerica Ingredients
Westwood, NJ 201-497-5531

Processor, importer, exporter and distributor of bulk vitamins, amino acids, nutraceuticals, aromatic chemicals, food additives, herbs, mineral nutrients and pharmaceuticals.

RFI Ingredients
Blauvelt, NY 800-962-7663

Betaine Beet

RFI Ingredients
Blauvelt, NY 800-962-7663

Carmine

Asiamerica Ingredients
Westwood, NJ 201-497-5531

Processor, importer, exporter and distributor of bulk vitamins, amino acids, nutraceuticals, aromatic chemicals, food additives, herbs, mineral nutrients and pharmaceuticals.

RFI Ingredients
Blauvelt, NY 800-962-7663

Carotenoids

Asiamerica Ingredients
Westwood, NJ 201-497-5531

Processor, importer, exporter and distributor of bulk vitamins, amino acids, nutraceuticals, aromatic chemicals, food additives, herbs, mineral nutrients and pharmaceuticals.

RFI Ingredients
Blauvelt, NY 800-962-7663

Others

Asiamerica Ingredients
Westwood, NJ 201-497-5531

Processor, importer, exporter and distributor of bulk vitamins, amino acids, nutraceuticals, aromatic chemicals, food additives, herbs, mineral nutrients and pharmaceuticals.

Turmeric

Asiamerica Ingredients
Westwood, NJ 201-497-5531

Processor, importer, exporter and distributor of bulk vitamins, amino acids, nutraceuticals, aromatic chemicals, food additives, herbs, mineral nutrients and pharmaceuticals.

RFI Ingredients
Blauvelt, NY 800-962-7663

Vegetable

Moody Dunbar
Johnson City, TN 800-251-8202

Compounds

Cooking

Coast Packing Company
Vernon, CA 323-277-7700
Columbus Foods Company
Des Plaines, IL 800-322-6457
Mallet & Company
Carnegie, PA 800-245-2757
Prime Ingredients
Saddle Brook, NJ 888-791-6655

Tenderizing

Custom Culinary
Lombard, IL 800-621-8827
Tova Industries
Louisville, KY 888-532-8682
Turano Pastry Shops
Bloomingdale, IL 630-529-6161
World Flavors
Warminster, PA 215-672-4400

Concentrates

Fruit

Apple & Eve
Roslyn, NY 800-969-8018
Beta Pure Foods
Aptos, CA 831-685-6565
Citrus Citrosuco North America
Lake Wales, FL. 800-356-4592
Coloma Frozen Foods
Coloma, MI. 800-642-2723
Country Pure Foods
Akron, OH. 877-995-8423
Gerber Products Company
Parsippany, NJ. 800-443-7237
Greenwood Associates
Highland Park, IL 847-579-5500
Hiller Cranberries
Rochester, MA 508-763-5257
Johnson Concentrates
Sunnyside, WA 509-837-4600
Kerr Concentrates
Salem, OR. 800-910-5377
Miline Fruit Products
Prosser, WA. 509-786-2611
Minute Maid Company
Atlanta, GA. 800-438-2653
Sabroso Company
Medford, OR. 541-772-5653
Stiebs
Madera, CA. 559-661-0031
Three Vee Food & Syrup Company
Brooklyn, NY 800-801-7330
Tupman-Thurlow Company
Deerfield Beach, FL 954-596-9989

Fruit Puree

Greenwood Associates
Highland Park, IL 847-579-5500
Milne Fruit Products
Prosser, WA. 509-786-2611
RFI Ingredients
Blauvelt, NY 800-962-7663

Tomato

A&B Ingredients
Fairfield, NJ 973-227-1390

Vegetable

Beta Pure Foods
Aptos, CA 831-685-6565
Global Citrus Resources
Lakeland, FL. 863-647-9020
Greenwood Associates
Highland Park, IL 847-579-5500

Whey Protein Concentrates & Isolates

Arla Foods Ingredients
Basking Ridge, NJ 908-604-8551
Bongards Creameries
Norwood, MN. 800-877-6417
Calpro Ingredients
Corona, CA 909-493-4890
Glanbia Foods
Twin Falls, ID 800-427-9477
Glanbia Nutritionals
Monroe, WI. 608-329-2800
Glanbia Nutritionals
Monroe, WI. 800-336-2183
Hilmar Ingredients
Hilmar, CA 209-667-6076
Inovatech USA
Montreal, QC 800-367-3447
International Dairy Ingredients
Wapakoneta, OH 419-738-4060
Kantner Group
Wapakoneta, OH 419-738-4060

Main Street Ingredients
La Crosse, WI 800-359-2345
Milky Whey
Missoula, MT 800-379-6455
The Scoular Company
Omaha, NE 800-487-1474

Confectionery

Bakers' & Confectioners' Supplies

Abel & Schafer
Ronkonkoma, NY 800-443-1260
ADM Food Ingredients
Olathe, KS 800-255-6637
ADM Milling Company
Carthage, MO 417-358-2197
ADM Milling Company
Cleveland, TN 423-476-7551
ADM Milling Company
Chattanooga, TN 423-756-0503
ADM Milling Company
Minneapolis, MN 800-528-7877
ADM Milling Company
Shawnee Mission, KS 913-491-9400
Agricor
Marion, IN 765-662-0606
Al-Rite Fruits & Syrups
Miami, FL 305-652-2540
American Almond Products Company
Brooklyn, NY 800-825-6663
American Key Food Products
Closter, NJ 800-767-0237
AnaCon Foods Company
Atchison, KS 800-328-0291
Ann's House of Nuts, Inc.
Jessup, MD 301-498-4920
Arcor USA
Miami, FL 800-572-7267
Astor Chocolate
Lakewood, NJ 732-901-1000
Atlantic Quality Spice &Seasonings
New Brunswick, NJ 800-584-0422
Baker Boy Bake Shop
Dickinson, ND 800-437-2008
Barry Callebaut USA LLC
Saint Albans, VT 800-556-8845
Bay State Milling Company
Winona, MN 800-533-8098
Best Brands Corporation
Minnetonka, MN 800-866-3300
Best Maid Cookie Company
River Falls, WI 888-444-0322
Bette's Diner Products
Berkeley, CA 510-644-3230
Blend Pak
Bloomfield, KY 502-252-8000
Blommer Chocolate Company
Chicago, IL 800-621-1606
Blue Pacific Flavors & Fragrances
City of Industry, CA 800-248-7499
Blue Planet Foods
Collegedale, TN 877-396-3145
Bob's Red Mill Natural Foods
Milwaukie, OR 800-553-2258
Brass Ladle Products
Concordville, PA 800-955-2353
Brown & Haley
Tacoma, WA 253-620-3000
Byrd Mill Company
Ashland, VA 888-897-3336
Cadbury Trebor Allan
Toronto, ON 800-565-6541
California Brands Flavors
Oakland, CA 800-348-0111
California Independent Almond Growers
Merced, CA 209-667-4855
Cangel
Toronto, ON 800-267-4795
Carol Lee Products
Lawrence, KS 785-842-5489
Century Foods International
Sparta, WI 800-269-1901
Chadler
Swedesboro, NJ 856-467-0099
Charles H. Baldwin & Sons
West Stockbridge, MA 413-232-7785
Chase Brothers Dairy
Oxnard, CA 800-438-6455
Chefmaster
Garden Grove, CA 800-333-7443
CHS
Inver Grove Heights, MN 800-232-3639
Commodities Marketing, Inc.
Edison, NJ 732-603-5077
Cream of the West
Harlowton, MT 800-477-2383
Dakota Organic Products
Watertown, SD 800-243-7264
DD Williamson & Company
Louisville, KY 800-227-2635
De-Iorio's Frozen Dough
Utica, NY 800-649-7612
Dessert Innovations
Atlanta, GA 800-359-7351
Devansoy
Carroll, IA 800-747-8605
Dorothy Dawson Foods Products
Jackson, MI 517-788-9830
Eden Foods Inc.
Clinton, MI 800-248-0320
Eden Processing
Poplar Grove, IL 815-765-2000
EFCO Products
Poughkeepsie, NY 800-284-3326
Fizzle Flat Farm
Yale, IL 618-793-2060
Florida Shortening Corporation
Miami, FL 305-691-2992
Food Concentrate Corporation
Oklahoma City, OK 405-840-5633
France Croissant
New York, NY 212-888-1210
Frankford Candy & Chocolate Company
Philadelphia, PA 800-523-9090
Franklin Foods
Enosburg Falls, VT 800-933-6114
Fresh Dairy Direct/Morningstar
Dallas, TX 800-395-7004
Galloway Company
Neenah, WI 800-722-8903
General Mills
Minneapolis, MN 800-248-7310
Ghirardelli Chocolate Company
San Leandro, CA 800-877-9338
Golden Fluff Popcorn Company
Lakewood, NJ 732-367-5448
Gorant Candies
Warren, OH 800-572-4139
Greenfield Mills
Howe, IN 260-367-2394
Guittard Chocolate Company
Burlingame, CA 800-468-2462
Gurley's Foods
Willmar, MN 800-426-7845
H B Taylor Company
Chicago, IL 773-254-4805
Harlan Bakeries
Avon, IN 317-272-3600
Hauser Chocolate
Westerly, RI 888-599-8231
Heartland Food Products
Mission, KS 913-831-4446
Heidi's Gourmet Desserts
Tucker, GA 800-241-4166
Holton Food Products Company
La Grange, IL 708-352-5599
Homestead Mills
Cook, MN 800-652-5233
Honeyville Grain
Salt Lake City, UT 801-972-2168
Horriea 2000 Food Industries
Reynolds, GA 478-847-4186
I Rice & Company
Philadelphia, PA 800-232-6022
J.R. Short Canadian Mills
Toronto, ON 416-421-3463
J.R. Short Milling Company
Kankakee, IL 800-544-8734
John Gust Foods & Products Corporation
Batavia, IL 800-756-5886
Kalsec
Kalamazoo, MI 269-349-9711
Kargher Corporation
Hatfield, PA 800-355-1247
Kencraft
North Alpine, UT 800-377-4368
Kerry Ingredients
Blue Earth, MN 507-526-7575
Kimmie Candy Company
Reno, NV 888-532-1325
King Milling Company
Lowell, MI 616-897-9264
Knappen Milling Company
Augusta, MI 800-562-7736
Knouse Foods Coop
Peach Glen, PA 717-677-8181
L&S Packing Company
Farmingdale, NY 800-286-6487
Lacey Milling Company
Hanford, CA 559-584-6634
Lake States Yeast
Rhinelander, WI 715-369-4949
Lawrence Foods
Elk Grove Village, IL 800-323-7848
Leon's Bakery
North Haven, CT 800-223-6844
Little Crow Foods
Warsaw, IN 800-288-2769
Log House Foods
Plymouth, MN 763-546-8395
Louisiana Gourmet Enterprises
La Place, LA 985-783-2446
Lucas Meyer
Decatur, IL 800-769-3660
Lyoferm & Vivolac Cultures
Indianapolis, IN 317-356-8460
Main Street Ingredients
La Crosse, WI 800-359-2345
Malt Products Corporation
Saddle Brook, NJ 800-526-0180
Marx Brothers
Birmingham, AL 800-633-6376
Masterfoods USA
Hackettstown, NJ 908-852-1000
Mayfair Sales
Buffalo, NY 800-248-2881
Mennel Milling Company
Fostoria, OH 419-435-8151
Merlino Italian Baking Company
Seattle, WA 800-207-2997
Mills Brothers International
Tukwila, WA 206-575-3000
Minn-Dak Yeast Company
Wahpeton, ND 701-642-3300
Mississippi Blending Company
Keokuk, IA 800-758-4080
Moorhead & Company
Rocklin, CA 800-322-6325
Morris J. Golombeck
Brooklyn, NY 718-284-3505
Nature's Hand
Burnsville, MN 952-890-6033
Northwestern Foods
Saint Paul, MN 800-236-4937
Orange Bakery
Irvine, CA 949-863-1377
Orlinda Milling Company
Orlinda, TN 615-654-3633
Pacific Westcoast Foods
Beaverton, OR 800-874-9333
Palmer Candy Company
Sioux City, IA 800-831-0828
Pasta Factory
Melrose Park, IL 800-615-6951
Pelican Bay
Dunedin, FL 800-826-8982
Pied-Mont/Dora
Ste Anne Des Plaines, QC 800-363-8003
Plaidberry Company
Vista, CA 760-727-5403
Quali Tech
Chaska, MN 800-328-5870
Quality Ingredients Corporation
Chester, NJ 800-843-6314
Quality Naturally! Foods
City of Industry, CA 888-498-6986
R&J Farms
West Salem, OH 419-846-3179
Reinhart Foods
Markham, ON 905-754-3500
Rene Rey Chocolates Ltd
North Vancouver, BC 888-985-0949
Rhodes International
Columbus, WI 800-876-7333
Rich Products Corporation
Buffalo, NY 800-356-7094
Richmond Baking Company
Richmond, IN 765-962-8535
Roland Industries
Saint Louis, MO 800-325-1183
Roman Meal Milling Company
Fargo, ND 877-282-9743
Rucker's Makin' Batch Candies
Bridgeport, IL 618-945-7778

Rumford Baking Powder Company
Terre Haute, IN 812-232-9446
Rv Industries
Buford, GA 770-729-8983
Schlotterbeck & Foss Company
Portland, ME 800-777-4666
Scott's Auburn Mills
Russellville, KY 270-726-2080
Serv-Agen Corporation
Cherry Hill, NJ 856-663-6966
Service Packing Company
Vancouver, BC 604-681-0264
Setton Pistachio of Terra Bella
Terra Bella, CA 800-227-4397
Shawnee Milling Company
Shawnee, OK 405-273-7000
Signature Brands
Ocala, FL 800-456-9573
Skjodt-Barrett Foods
Mississauga, ON 877-600-1200
SOUPerior Bean & Spice Company
Vancouver, WA 800-878-7687
Southeastern Mills
Rome, GA 800-334-4468
Star of the West
Kent, OH 330-673-2941
Star of the West MillingCompany
Frankenmuth, MI 989-652-9971
Strossner's Bakery
Greenville, SC 864-233-3996
Sucesores de Pedro Cortes
San Juan, PR 787-754-7040
Swatt Baking Company
Olean, NY 800-370-6656
Tara Foods
Atlanta, GA 404-559-0605
Taste Maker Foods
Memphis, TN 800-467-1407
The Bama Company
Tulsa, OK 800-756-2262
The Lollipop Tree, Inc
Auburn, NY 800-842-6691
TNT Crust
Green Bay, WI 920-431-7240
Tova Industries
Louisville, KY 888-532-8682
Uhlmann Company
Kansas City, MO 800-383-8201
Valley View Blueberries
Vancouver, WA 360-892-2839
Vie de France Yamazaki
Vernon, LA 323-582-1241
VIP Foods
Flushing, NY 718-821-5330
Vrymeer Commodities
St Charles, IL 630-584-0069
Wall-Rogalsky Milling Company
Mc Pherson, KS 800-835-2067
Watson Inc
West Haven, CT 800-388-3481
Weaver Nut Company
Ephrata, PA 717-738-3781
West Pac
Idaho Falls, ID 800-973-7407
White Swan Fruit Products
Plant City, FL 800-330-8952
White-Stokes Company
Chicago, IL 800-978-6537
Whittaker & Associates
Atlanta, GA 404-266-1265
Willmark Sales Company
Brooklyn, NY 718-388-7141
Yohay Baking Company
Lindenhurst, NY 631-225-0300
Young Winfield
Kleinburg, ON 905-893-9682

Cultures & Yeasts

Acidophilus Cultures

Cargill Texturizing Solutions
Cedar Rapids, IA 877-650-7080

Bacillus

Cargill Texturizing Solutions
Cedar Rapids, IA 877-650-7080

Bacteria

Buttermilk

Cargill Texturizing Solutions
Cedar Rapids, IA 877-650-7080

Cheese

Cargill Texturizing Solutions
Cedar Rapids, IA 877-650-7080

Yogurt

Cargill Texturizing Solutions
Cedar Rapids, IA 877-650-7080

Bacterial Cultures, Starter Media & Culture Replac

Cargill Texturizing Solutions
Cedar Rapids, IA 877-650-7080
Kantner Group
Wapakoneta, OH 419-738-4060

Bacteriological

Cargill Texturizing Solutions
Cedar Rapids, IA 877-650-7080

Cultures

Alfer Laboratories
Chatsworth, CA 818-709-0737
Alternative Health & Herbs
Albany, OR 800-345-4152
Berkshire Dairy & Food Products
Wyomissing, PA 888-654-8008
Brewster Foods TestLab
Reseda, CA 818-881-4268
Cargill Texturizing Solutions
Cedar Rapids, IA 877-650-7080
Continental Culture Specialists
Los Angeles, CA 818-240-7400
Continental Custom Ingredients
Oakville, ON 905-815-8158
Crystal Cream & Butter Company
Sacramento, CA 916-447-6455
Fairmont Products
Belleville, PA 717-935-2121
GEM Cultures
Fort Bragg, CA 707-964-2922
IMAC
Oklahoma City, OK 888-878-7827
Ingredient Innovations
Kansas City, MO 816-587-1426
Lallemand Inc
Montreal, QC 514-522-2133
Lallemand/American Yeast
Addison, IL 630-932-1290
Lyoferm & Vivolac Cultures
Indianapolis, IN 317-356-8460
Maryland & Virginia Milk Producers Cooperative
Reston, VA 703-742-4250
Old Home Foods
Saint Paul, MN 800-309-9035
Quality Ingredients Corporation
Burnsville, MN 952-898-4002
Rhodia
Cranbury, NJ 800-343-8324
Sunshine Dairy Foods
Portland, OR 503-234-7526
Vivolac Cultures Corporation
Indianapolis, IN 317-356-8460

Lactobacillus Acidophilus

Cargill Texturizing Solutions
Cedar Rapids, IA 877-650-7080

Yeast

ADM Food Ingredients
Olathe, KS 800-255-6637
Bakon Yeast
Scottsdale, AZ 480-595-9370
Blue Chip Group
Salt Lake City, UT 800-878-0099
California Blending Corpany
El Monte, CA 626-448-1918
Cardi Foods
Fuquay Varina, NC 973-983-8818
Church & Dwight Company
Princeton, NJ 800-221-0453
DSM Food Specialties
Menomonee Falls, WI 800-423-7906
Fleischmann's Yeast
Chesterfield, MO 800-247-7473
Kyowa Hakko
New York, NY 212-715-0572
Lake States Yeast
Rhinelander, WI 715-369-4949
Lallemand/American Yeast
Addison, IL 630-932-1290
Lesaffre Yeast Corporation
Milwaukee, WI 414-271-6755
Luxor California ExportsCorporation
San Diego, CA 619-692-9330
Minn-Dak Yeast Company
Wahpeton, ND 701-642-3300
Mississippi Blending Company
Keokuk, IA 800-758-4080
Natural Foods
Toledo, OH 419-537-1713
Norcrest Consulting
Richland, WA
Organic Gourmet
Sherman Oaks, CA 800-400-7772
Pascobel Inc
Longueuil, QC 450-677-2443
RBW & Associates
Portland, OR 503-223-0843
Red Star Yeast
Milwaukee, WI 877-677-7000
SAS Bakers Yeast
Headland, AL 877-677-7000
Sensient Technologies
Milwaukee, WI 800-558-9892
Southeastern Wisconsin Products Company
Milwaukee, WI 414-482-1730
Vinquiry
Windsor, CA 707-838-6312

Autolysates

Lake States Yeast
Rhinelander, WI 715-369-4949

Bakers'

Lallemand/American Yeast
L.I.C., NY 773-267-2223
Minn-Dak Yeast Company
Wahpeton, ND 701-642-3300
SAS Bakers Yeast
Headland, AL 877-677-7000

Brewers'

Energen Products
Norwalk, CA 800-423-8837
NPC Dehydrators
Payette, ID 208-642-4471
Nutraceutical Corporation
Park City, UT 800-669-8877
Watson Nutritional Ingredients
West Haven, CT 203-932-3000

Extracts

Organic Gourmet
Sherman Oaks, CA 800-400-7772

Fresh

Lallemand/American Yeast
Addison, IL 630-932-1290

Primary Dried

Lallemand/American Yeast
Addison, IL 630-932-1290

Torula Dried

Lake States Yeast
Rhinelander, WI 715-369-4949

Whey

FrieslandCampina Domo
, NJ 201-655-7786
Hilmar Ingredients
Hilmar, CA 209-667-6076

Wine

Dave's Hawaiian Ice Cream
Pearl City, HI 808-453-0500
Lallemand
Petaluma, CA 800-423-6625

Yogurt

Cargill Texturizing Solutions
Cedar Rapids, IA . . . 877-650-7080
Lyo-San
Lachute, QC . . . 450-562-8525

Curing Preparations

Meat

Cargill Texturizing Solutions
Cedar Rapids, IA . . . 877-650-7080
First Spice Mixing Company
Long Island City, NY . . . 800-221-1105

Decorative Items

Petra International
Mississauga, ON . . . 800-261-7226
Sugar Flowers Plus
Glendale, CA . . . 800-972-2935

Digestive Aids

Arise & Shine Herbal Products
Medford, OR . . . 800-688-2444
Bio-K + International
Laval, QC . . . 800-593-2465
Bionutritional Research Group
Irvine, CA
Cargill Texturizing Solutions
Cedar Rapids, IA . . . 877-650-7080
Dancing Paws
Chatsworth, CA . . . 888-644-7297
Earth Products
Vista, CA . . . 760-494-2000
Enzymatic Therapy
Green Bay, WI . . . 800-783-2286
Enzyme Formulations
Madison, WI . . . 800-614-4400
National Enzyme Company
Forsyth, MO . . . 800-825-8545
Russo Farms
Vineland, NJ . . . 856-692-5942

Emulsifiers

ADM Food Ingredients
Olathe, KS . . . 800-255-6637
ADM Lecithin & Monoglycerides
Decatur, IL . . . 800-637-5843

Asiamerica Ingredients
Westwood, NJ . . . 201-497-5531

Processor, importer, exporter and distributor of bulk vitamins, amino acids, nutraceuticals, aromatic chemicals, food additives, herbs, mineral nutrients and pharmaceuticals.

Avatar Corporation
University Park, IL . . . 800-255-3181
Bunge Canada
Oakville, ON . . . 800-361-3043
Cargill Texturizing Solutions
Cedar Rapids, IA . . . 877-650-7080
Continental Custom Ingredients
Oakville, ON . . . 905-815-8158
Enterprise Foods
Atlanta, GA . . . 404-351-2251
Lambent Technologies
Skokie, IL . . . 800-432-7187
Mallet & Company
Carnegie, PA . . . 800-245-2757
Mitsubishi InternationalCorporation
New York, NY . . . 800-442-6266
Montello
Tulsa, OK . . . 800-331-4628
P.L. Thomas
Morristown, NJ . . . 973-984-0900
Quality Ingredients Corporation
Burnsville, MN . . . 952-898-4002
RIBUS
Saint Louis, MO . . . 314-727-4287
Specialty Industrial Products
Spartanburg, SC . . . 800-747-9001
Technical Oil
Easton, PA . . . 610-252-8350

Lecithin

Acatris USA
Edina, MN . . . 952-920-7700
ADM Food Ingredients
Olathe, KS . . . 800-255-6637
AG Processing, Inc.
Omaha, NE . . . 800-247-1345
American Lecithin Company
Oxford, CT . . . 800-364-4416

Asiamerica Ingredients
Westwood, NJ . . . 201-497-5531

Processor, importer, exporter and distributor of bulk vitamins, amino acids, nutraceuticals, aromatic chemicals, food additives, herbs, mineral nutrients and pharmaceuticals.

Avatar Corporation
University Park, IL . . . 800-255-3181
Blue Chip Group
Salt Lake City, UT . . . 800-878-0099
CanAmera Foods
Oakville, ON . . . 905-825-7900
Cargill Texturizing Solutions
Cedar Rapids, IA . . . 877-650-7080
Columbus Foods Company
Des Plaines, IL . . . 800-322-6457
Lucas Meyer
Decatur, IL . . . 800-769-3660
Mid Atlantic Vegetable Shortening Company
Kearny, NJ . . . 800-966-1645
Natural Foods
Toledo, OH . . . 419-537-1713
Riceland Foods Rice Milling Operations
Stuttgart, AR . . . 870-673-5500
Technical Oil Products
Newton, NJ

The Solae Company
Saint Louis, MO 800-325-7108
Trophic International
Salt Lake City, UT 800-878-0099
W.A. Cleary Products
Somerset, NJ..................... 800-238-7813
WA Cleary Products
Somerset, NJ..................... 800-238-7813
Westin
Omaha, NE 800-228-6098

Enhancers

Apple Flavor & FragranceUSA Corp.
Edison, NJ....................... 732-356-3800
Blue Chip Group
Salt Lake City, UT 800-878-0099
Cinnabar Specialty Foods
Prescott, AZ 866-293-6433
First Spice Mixing Company
Long Island City, NY 800-221-1105
Lora Brody Products
Waltham, MA 617-928-1005

Enzymes

ADM Food Ingredients
Olathe, KS....................... 800-255-6637
Ajinomoto Food Ingredients LLC
Chicago, IL...................... 773-714-1436
Amano Enzyme USA Company, Ltd
Elgin, IL 800-446-7652
American Laboratories
Omaha, NE 402-339-2494
American Yeast/Lallemand
Pembroke, NH.................... 866-920-9885

asiamerica

Asiamerica Ingredients
Westwood, NJ.................... 201-497-5531

Processor, importer, exporter and distributor of bulk vitamins, amino acids, nutraceuticals, aromatic chemicals, food additives, herbs, mineral nutrients and pharmaceuticals.

Bio-Nutritional Products
Northvale, NJ 201-784-8200
Brewster Foods TestLab
Reseda, CA 818-881-4268
Genencor International
Beloit, WI 608-365-1112
George A Jeffreys & Company
Salem, VA....................... 540-389-8220
Inovatech USA
Montreal, QC 800-367-3447
Malabar Formulas
Nuevo, CA 909-866-3678
Mitsubishi InternationalCorporation
New York, NY 800-442-6266
Novozymes North America
Franklinton, NC 800-879-6686
SKW Nature Products
Dubuque, IA 563-588-6244
Specialty Enzymes
Chino, CA....................... 909-613-1660
Universal Formulas
Kalamazoo, MI................... 800-342-6960
Valley Research
South Bend, IN 800-522-8110

Additives

Cargill Texturizing Solutions
Cedar Rapids, IA.................. 877-650-7080

Extenders

Arboris, Llc
Garden City, GA.................. 912-238-7537
Cargill Texturizing Solutions
Cedar Rapids, IA.................. 877-650-7080

Chicken

Valley Grain Products
Madera, CA...................... 559-675-3400

Coffee

I Rice & Company
Philadelphia, PA 800-232-6022

Meat

ADM Food Ingredients
Olathe, KS....................... 800-255-6637
Cargill Texturizing Solutions
Cedar Rapids, IA.................. 877-650-7080
Flavor House
Adelanto, CA 760-246-9131
Gum Technology Corporation
Tucson, AZ 800-369-4867
Proliant Meat Ingredients
Harlan, IA....................... 800-369-2672
Tova Industries
Louisville, KY 888-532-8682
World Flavors
Warminster, PA................... 215-672-4400

Extracts

A M Todd Company
Kalamazoo, MI................... 800-968-2603
Active Organics
Lewisville, TX 972-221-7500
Advanced Food Systems Inc.
Somerset, NJ..................... 732-873-6776
Al-Rite Fruits & Syrups
Miami, FL....................... 305-652-2540
American Instants
Flanders, NJ 973-584-8811
American Laboratories
Omaha, NE 402-339-2494
American Mercantile Corporation
Memphis, TN 901-454-1900
Aphrodisia Products
Brooklyn, NY 877-274-3677
Apotheca Naturale
Woodbine, IA 800-736-3130

asiamerica

Asiamerica Ingredients
Westwood, NJ.................... 201-497-5531

Processor, importer, exporter and distributor of bulk vitamins, amino acids, nutraceuticals, aromatic chemicals, food additives, herbs, mineral nutrients and pharmaceuticals.

Associated Bakers Products
Huntington, NY 631-673-3841
Autocrat Coffee & Extracts
Lincoln, RI 800-288-6272
Bartek Ingredients, Inc.
Stoney Creek, ON................. 800-263-4165
Bear Stewart Corporation
Chicago, IL 800-697-2327
Beck Flavors
Saint Louis, MO 800-851-8100
Berghausen Corporation
Cincinnati, OH 800-648-5887
Beta Pure Foods
Aptos, CA 831-685-6565
Bickford Flavors
Cleveland, OH 800-283-8322
Blessed Herbs
Oakham, MA..................... 800-489-4372
Blue California Company
Rcho Sta Marg, CA................ 949-635-1990
Blue Mountain Flavors
Kinston, NC 800-522-1544
Briess Industries
Chilton, WI...................... 920-849-7711
Brucia Plant Extracts
Shingle Springs, CA 530-676-2774
Burleson's Honey, Inc
Waxahachie, TX 972-937-4810
Cafe Du Monde
New Orleans, LA 504-587-0835
Cajun Chef Products
Saint Martinville, LA 337-394-7112
California Brands Flavors
Oakland, CA 800-348-0111
Cargill Corn Milling
Naperville, IL 800-344-1633
Castella Imports
Hauppauge, NY 866-227-8355
Cellu-Con
Strathmore, CA................... 559-568-0190
Charles Boggini
Coventry, CT..................... 860-742-2652
Chaucer Foods
Syosset, NY...................... 516-496-2500
Chefmaster
Garden Grove, CA 800-333-7443
Classic Flavors & Fragrances
New York, NY 212-777-0004
Clements Foods Company
Oklahoma City, OK 800-654-8355
Coco Rico
Montreal, QC 514-849-5554
Concord Foods
Brockton, MA.................... 508-580-1700
Consolidated Mills
Houston, TX 713-896-4196
Consumers Flavoring Extract Company
Brooklyn, NY 718-435-0201
Contact International
Skokie, IL 847-324-4411
Crestmont Enterprises
Camden, NJ...................... 856-966-0700
Crystal Foods
Brick, NJ........................ 732-477-0073
Dean Distributors
Burlingame, CA 800-792-0816
Draco Natural Products
San Jose, CA..................... 408-287-7871
Edgar A Weber & Company
Wheeling, IL..................... 800-558-9078
Erba Food Products
Brooklyn, NY 718-272-7700
Ethical Naturals
San Anselmo, CA 415-459-4454
Everfresh Food Corporation
Minneapolis, MN 612-331-6393
Fenchem Enterprises
Chino, CA....................... 909-627-5268
Flavor & Fragrance Specialties
Mahwah, NJ 800-998-4337
Flavor House
Adelanto, CA 760-246-9131
Flavor Sciences
Lenior, NC 800-535-2867
Flavorchem
Downers Grove, IL................ 800-435-8867
Florida Food Products
Eustis, FL 800-874-2331
FONA International Inc.
Geneva, IL....................... 630-578-8600
FoodScience of Vermont
Essex Junction, VT................ 800-874-9444
Garuda International
Exeter, CA....................... 559-594-4380
Genarom International
Cranbury, NJ..................... 609-409-6200
Green Foods Corporation
Oxnard, CA...................... 800-777-4430
H B Taylor Company
Chicago, IL 773-254-4805
H.B. Taylor
Chicago, IL 773-254-4805
Hagelin & Company
Branchburg, NJ................... 800-229-2112
Haldin International
Closter, NJ....................... 201-784-0044
Herb Connection
Springville, UT 801-489-4254
Herbs, Etc.
Santa Fe, NM 888-694-3727
Horner International
Raleigh, NC...................... 919-787-3112
Inter-American Products
Cincinnati, OH 800-645-2233
Just the Berries
Los Angeles, CA.................. 213-613-9807
Kalsec
Kalamazoo, MI................... 269-349-9711
Lochhead Manufacturing Company
Fenton, MO...................... 888-776-2088
Mafco Natural Products
Richmond, VA.................... 804-222-1600
MAFCO Worldwide Corporation
Camden, NJ...................... 856-964-8840
Malt-Diastase Company
Garfield, NJ...................... 800-772-0416
Maryland & Virginia Milk Producers Cooperative
Reston, VA 703-742-4250

McCormick & Company
Sparks, MD 800-632-5847
Metarom Corporation
Newport, VT 888-882-5555
Mother Murphy's Labs
Greensboro, NC 800-849-1277
Muntons Ingredients
Bellevue, WA 425-372-3082
Natra US
Chula Vista, CA 800-262-6216
Naturex Inc
South Hackensack, NJ 201-440-5000
Naturex Inc.
South Hackensack, NJ 201-440-5000
Newtown Foods
Langhorne, PA 215-579-2120
Now Foods
Bloomingdale, IL 888-669-3663
Nutricepts
Burnsville, MN 800-949-9060
Oregon Flavor Rack
Eugene, OR 541-342-2085
P.L. Thomas
Morristown, NJ 973-984-0900
Parker Flavors, Inc
Baltimore, MD 800-336-9113
Particle Control
Albertville, MN 763-497-3075
Particle Dynamics
Saint Louis, MO 800-452-4682
Perlarom Technology
Columbia, MD 410-997-5114
Phyto-Technologies
Woodbine, IA 877-809-3404
Phytotherapy Research Laboratory
Lobelville, TN 800-274-3727
PMC Specialties Group
Cincinnati, OH 800-543-2466
Pure World Botanicals
South Hackensack, NJ 201-270-2705
RC Fine Foods
Belle Mead, NJ 800-526-3953
RFI Ingredients
Blauvelt, NY 800-962-7663
Royal Foods & Flavors
Elk Grove Vlg, IL 847-595-9166
San-Ei Gen FFI
New York, NY 212-315-7850
Savoury Systems
Branchburg, NJ 908-526-2524
Scan American Food Compampany
Everett, WA 425-514-0500
Senba USA
Hayward, CA 888-922-5852
Simpson Spring Company
South Easton, MA 508-372-0914
Singer Extract Laboratory
Livonia, MI 313-345-5880
Sivetz Coffee
Corvallis, OR 541-753-9713
SJH Enterprises
Middleton, WI 888-745-3845
Sno-Shack
Rexburg, ID 888-766-7425
Star Kay White
Congers, NY 800-874-8518
Stearns & Lehman
Mansfield, OH 800-533-2722
Sterling Extract Company
Franklin Park, IL 847-451-9728
Stiebs
Madera, CA 559-661-0031
Target Flavors
Brookfield, CT 800-538-3350
Technology Flavors & Fragrances
Amityville, NY 631-789-8228
Texas Coffee Company
Beaumont, TX 800-259-3400
Texas Spice Company
Cedar Park, TX 800-880-8007
Triple K Manufacturing Company
Shenandoah, IA 888-987-2824
United Canadian Malt
Peterborough, ON 800-461-6400
V&E Kohnstamm
Brooklyn, NY 800-847-4500
Vanlaw Food Products
Fullerton, CA 714-870-9091
Virginia Dare
Brooklyn, NY 800-847-4500
W&G Flavors
Hunt Valley, MD 410-771-6606

Western Flavors & Fragrances
Livermore, CA 925-373-9433
Young Winfield
Kleinburg, ON 905-893-9682

Beef

Blue Mountain Flavors
Kinston, NC 800-522-1544
David Michael & Company
Philadelphia, PA 800-363-5286
Flavor House
Adelanto, CA 760-246-9131
Geneva Ingredients
Waunakee, WI 800-828-5924
Gold Coast Ingredients
Commerce, CA 800-352-8673
Henningsen Foods
Purchase, NY 914-701-4020
Prime Ingredients
Saddle Brook, NJ 888-791-6655
Proliant Meat Ingredients
Harlan, IA 800-369-2672
RFI Ingredients
Blauvelt, NY 800-962-7663
Superior Quality Foods
Ontario, CA 800-300-4210
Wynn Starr Foods of Kentucky
Louisville, KY 800-996-7827

Beverages

Mother Murphy's Labs
Greensboro, NC 800-849-1277
Muntons Ingredients
Bellevue, WA 425-372-3082
Virginia Dare
Brooklyn, NY 800-847-4500

Botanical

Abkit Camocare Nature Works
New York, NY 800-226-6227
Active Organics
Lewisville, TX 972-221-7500
Alta Health Products
Boise, ID 800-423-4155
AM Todd Company
Kalamazoo, MI 800-968-2603
American Biosciences
Blauvelt, NY 888-884-7770
American Fruit Processors
Pacoima, CA 818-899-9574
Apex Marketing Group
Las Vegas, NV 888-990-2739
Aphrodisia Products
Brooklyn, NY 877-274-3677
Apotheca Naturale
Woodbine, IA 800-736-3130

asiamerica

Asiamerica Ingredients
Westwood, NJ 201-497-5531

Processor, importer, exporter and distributor of bulk vitamins, amino acids, nutraceuticals, aromatic chemicals, food additives, herbs, mineral nutrients and pharmaceuticals.

Atlantic Quality Spice &Seasonings
New Brunswick, NJ 800-584-0422
Avoca
Merry Hill, NC 252-482-2133
Blue California Company
Rcho Sta Marg, CA 949-635-1990
Botanical Products
Springville, CA 559-539-3432
Brewster Foods TestLab
Reseda, CA 818-881-4268
Brucia Plant Extracts
Shingle Springs, CA 530-676-2774
Danisco-Cultor
Ardsley, NY 914-674-6300
Dolisos America
Henderson, NV 800-365-4767
Eclectic Institute
Sandy, OR 503-668-4120
Emerling International Foods
Buffalo, NY 716-833-7381

We supply food manufacturers and food service customers worldwide (since 1988) with bulk ingredients including: Fruits & Vegetables; Juice Concentrates; Herbs & Spices; Oils & Vinegars; Flavors & Colors; Honey & Molasses. We also produce PURE MAPLE SYRUP.

Energique
Woodbine, IA 800-869-8078
Extracts Plus
Vista, CA 760-597-0200
Frutarom Meer Corporation
North Bergen, NJ 800-526-7147
GCI Nutrients (USA)
Foster City, CA 650-697-4700
Geni
Noblesville, IN 888-656-4364
GMI Products/Originates
Sunrise, FL 800-999-9373
Graminex
Saginaw, MI 877-472-6469
Haldin International
Closter, NJ 201-784-0044
Health from the Sun/ArkoPharma
Maynard, MA 800-447-2229
Herb Connection
Springville, UT 801-489-4254
Herb Pharm
Williams, OR 800-348-4372
Herbalist & Alchemist
Washington, NJ 908-689-9020
Horner International
Raleigh, NC 919-787-3112
Kelatron Corporation
Ogden, UT 801-394-4558
Nature's Apothecary
Boulder, CO 800-999-7422
Naturex Inc
South Hackensack, NJ 201-440-5000
Naturex Inc.
South Hackensack, NJ 201-440-5000
P.L. Thomas
Morristown, NJ 973-984-0900
Pharmachem Laboratories
South Hackensack, NJ 201-343-3611
RFI Ingredients
Blauvelt, NY 800-962-7663
Sabinsa Corporation
East Windsor, NJ 732-777-1111
San Francisco Herb & Natural Food Company
Fremont, CA 800-227-2830
Shanks Extracts
Lancaster, PA 800-346-3135
Stevia LLC
Valley Forge, PA 888-878-3842
Terra Botanica Products
Nakusp, BC 888-410-9977
Universal Preservachem Inc
Somerset, NJ 732-568-1266
VitaTech International
Tustin, CA 714-832-9700
Whole Herb Company
Sonoma, CA 707-935-1077

Chicken

Blue Mountain Flavors
Kinston, NC 800-522-1544
Flavor House
Adelanto, CA 760-246-9131
Geneva Ingredients
Waunakee, WI 800-828-5924
Prime Ingredients
Saddle Brook, NJ 888-791-6655
Wynn Starr Foods of Kentucky
Louisville, KY 800-996-7827

Coffee

Advanced Food Technology
Littleton, CO 303-980-5221
Amelia Bay Beverage Systems
Alpharetta, GA 800-650-8327
American Instants
Flanders, NJ 973-584-8811
Autocrat Coffee & Extracts
Lincoln, RI 800-288-6272
Beck Flavors
Saint Louis, MO 800-851-8100
California Custom Fruits & Flavors
Irwindale, CA 877-558-0056
Coffee Enterprises
Burlington, VT 800-375-3398
Prime Ingredients
Saddle Brook, NJ 888-791-6655
Stearns & Lehman
Mansfield, OH 800-533-2722
Virginia Dare
Brooklyn, NY 800-847-4500
X Cafe
Princeton, MA. 877-492-2331

Crab

American Instants
Flanders, NJ 973-584-8811
Autocrat Coffee & Extracts
Lincoln, RI 800-288-6272
Barlean's
Ferndale, WA 360-384-0325
Blue Mountain Flavors
Kinston, NC 800-522-1544
Boyajian, Inc.
Canton, MA 800-965-0665
Brewster Foods TestLab
Reseda, CA 818-881-4268
Cajun Chef Products
Saint Martinville, LA 337-394-7112
Chefmaster
Garden Grove, CA 800-333-7443
CJ America
Downers Grove, IL 630-241-0112
Consolidated Mills
Houston, TX 713-896-4196
Consumers Flavoring Extract Company
Brooklyn, NY 718-435-0201
Danisco USA
Lakeland, FL. 863-646-0165
Delmonico's Winery
New York, NY. 212-509-1144
Dragoco
Teterboro, NJ. 973-256-3850
Elan Chemical Company
Newark, NJ 973-344-8014
Embassy Flavours Ltd.
Brampton, ON. 800-334-3371
Empire Spice Mills
Winnipeg, NB 204-786-1594
FBC Industries
Schaumburg, IL. 888-322-4637
Felbro Food Products
Los Angeles, CA. 800-335-2761
Flavor Sciences
Lenior, NC 800-535-2867
Flavor Systems Intl.
Cincinnati, OH 800-498-2783
Flavorganics
Newark, NJ 973-344-8014
Flavormatic Industries
Wappingers Falls, NY
Flavtek Geneva Flavors Inc.
Beloit, WI 800-562-5880
Flavurence Corporation
Commerce, CA 800-717-1957
Fleurchem
Middletown, NY. 845-341-2100
Four Percent Company
Highland Park, MI 313-345-5880
Geneva Ingredients
Waunakee, WI. 800-828-5924
Givaudan Flavors
Elgin, IL 847-608-6200
Glucona America
Janesville, WI 608-752-0449
Gold Coast Ingredients
Commerce, CA 800-352-8673
GSB & Associates
Kennesaw, GA 877-472-2776
Ingredient Innovations
Kansas City, MO. 816-587-1426
International Food Solutions
Germantown, WI. 262-251-9230
John I. Haas
Washington, DC 202-777-4800
Joseph Adams Corporation
Valley City, OH. 330-225-9135
Lochhead Manufacturing Company
Fenton, MO 888-776-2088
Magic Ice Products
Cincinnati, OH 800-776-7923
Medallion Intl.
Pompton Plains, NJ. 973-616-3401
Millennium Specialty Chemicals
Jacksonville, FL 800-231-6728
Mountain Lake Specialty Ingredients Company
Omaha, NE 402-595-7463
Naturex
South Hackensack, NJ 201-440-5000
Old 97 Manufacturing Company
Tampa, FL. 813-247-6677
Ottens Flavors
Philadelphia, PA 800-523-0767
Prime Ingredients
Saddle Brook, NJ 888-791-6655
Rcb Intl.
Albany, OR 541-967-3814
SKW Nature Products
Langhorne, PA 215-702-1000
Stirling Foods
Renton, WA. 800-332-1714
Takasago International Corporation
Rockleigh, NJ 201-767-9001
Torre Products Company
New York, NY 212-925-8989
Triple K Manufacturing Company
Shenandoah, IA. 888-987-2824
WILD Flavors
Cincinnati, OH 888-945-3352
Wynn Starr Foods of Kentucky
Louisville, KY 800-996-7827

Flavoring

Amoretti
Oxnard, CA. 800-266-7388
Dohler Milne Aseptics
Prosser, WA. 509-786-2611
I Rice & Company
Philadelphia, PA 800-232-6022
Kikkoman International
San Francisco, CA 415-956-7750
Paradigm Food Works
Lake Oswego, OR. 503-595-4360

Fruit

Brewster Foods TestLab
Reseda, CA 818-881-4268
Chefmaster
Garden Grove, CA 800-333-7443
Contact International
Skokie, IL 847-324-4411
Dohler Milne Aseptics
Prosser, WA. 509-786-2611
Horner International
Raleigh, NC. 919-787-3112
Ramsey/Sias
Cleveland, OH 800-477-3788

Root Beer

California Custom Fruits & Flavors
Irwindale, CA 877-558-0056
Flavtek Geneva Flavors Inc.
Beloit, WI 800-562-5880
Four Percent Company
Highland Park, MI 313-345-5880
Gold Coast Ingredients
Commerce, CA 800-352-8673
Prime Ingredients
Saddle Brook, NJ 888-791-6655
Rio Syrup Company
Saint Louis, MO 800-325-7666

Seafood

Ocean Cliff Corporation
New Bedford, MA 508-990-7900

Tea

California Custom Fruits & Flavors
Irwindale, CA 877-558-0056
Ethical Naturals
San Anselmo, CA 415-459-4454
Jogue Inc
Northville, MI. 800-521-3888
P.L. Thomas
Morristown, NJ. 973-984-0900
RFI Ingredients
Blauvelt, NY 800-962-7663
Stearns & Lehman
Mansfield, OH 800-533-2722
Virginia Dare
Brooklyn, NY 800-847-4500

Vanilla

Astral Extracts Ltd.
Syosset, NY. 516-496-2505
Beck Flavors
Saint Louis, MO 800-851-8100
Bickford Flavors
Cleveland, OH 800-283-8322
Bush Boake Allen
New York, NY 212-765-5500
California Custom Fruits & Flavors
Irwindale, CA 877-558-0056
Carmi Flavor & Fragrance Company
City of Commerce, CA. 800-421-9647
Castella Imports
Hauppauge, NY 866-227-8355
Clements Foods Company
Oklahoma City, OK 800-654-8355
David Michael & Company
Philadelphia, PA 800-363-5286
Elan Chemical Company
Newark, NJ. 973-344-8014
Embassy Flavours Ltd.
Brampton, ON. 800-334-3371
Emerling International Foods
Buffalo, NY. 716-833-7381

We supply food manufacturers and food service customers worldwide (since 1988) with bulk ingredients including: Fruits & Vegetables; Juice Concentrates; Herbs & Spices; Oils & Vinegars; Flavors & Colors; Honey & Molasses. We also produce PURE MAPLE SYRUP.

Everfresh Food Corporation
Minneapolis, MN 612-331-6393
Flavorchem
Downers Grove, IL. 800-435-8867
Flavorganics
Newark, NJ 973-344-8014
Flavtek Geneva Flavors Inc.
Beloit, WI 800-562-5880
Four Percent Company
Highland Park, MI 313-345-5880
Gel Spice Company, Inc
Bayonne, NJ 800-922-0230
Gold Coast Ingredients
Commerce, CA 800-352-8673
Goodman Manufacturing Company
Carthage, MO 417-358-3231
Grapevine Trading Company
Santa Rosa, CA. 800-469-6478
H B Taylor Company
Chicago, IL 773-254-4805
Hagelin & Company
Branchburg, NJ. 800-229-2112
Horner International
Raleigh, NC. 919-787-3112
I Rice & Company
Philadelphia, PA 800-232-6022
Jogue Inc
Northville, MI. 800-521-3888
Lochhead Manufacturing Company
Fenton, MO. 888-776-2088
LorAnn Oils Inc
Lansing, MI. 888-456-7266
Nielsen-Massey Vanillas
Waukegan, IL 800-525-7873
Parker Flavors, Inc
Baltimore, MD 800-336-9113
Prime Ingredients
Saddle Brook, NJ 888-791-6655
R.R. Lochhead Manufacturing
Paso Robles, CA 800-735-0545
Rio Syrup Company
Saint Louis, MO 800-325-7666
Rodelle Vanillas
Fort Collins, CO 800-898-5457
Shanks Extracts
Lancaster, PA 800-346-3135

Sterling Extract Company
Franklin Park, IL . . . 847-451-9728
Triple K Manufacturing Company
Shenandoah, IA . . . 888-987-2824
V&E Kohnstamm
Brooklyn, NY . . . 800-847-4500
Van Tone Creative Flavors Inc
Terrell, TX . . . 800-856-0802
Virginia Dare
Brooklyn, NY . . . 800-847-4500
Weber Flavors
Wheeling, IL . . . 800-558-9078

Vegetable

Basic American Foods
Blackfoot, ID . . . 800-227-4050
Cajun Chef Products
Saint Martinville, LA . . . 337-394-7112
Geneva Ingredients
Waunakee, WI . . . 800-828-5924
Gold Coast Ingredients
Commerce, CA . . . 800-352-8673
Kalsec
Kalamazoo, MI . . . 269-349-9711
Naturex Inc.
South Hackensack, NJ . . . 201-440-5000
Prime Ingredients
Saddle Brook, NJ . . . 888-791-6655
Ted Shear Associates
Larchmont, NY . . . 914-833-0017
Varied Industries Corporation
Mason City, IA . . . 800-654-5617
Vegetable Juices
Chicago, IL . . . 888-776-9752
Western Flavors & Fragrances
Livermore, CA . . . 925-373-9433

Yeast

Royal Foods & Flavors
Elk Grove Vlg, IL . . . 847-595-9166
Savoury Systems
Branchburg, NJ . . . 908-526-2524

Fatty Acids

Essential

ChildLife-Nutrition for Kids
Los Angeles, CA . . . 800-993-0332
RFI Ingredients
Blauvelt, NY . . . 800-962-7663

Fillers

Meal

Agri-Dairy Products
Purchase, NY . . . 914-697-9580

Flakes

Heartland Mill
Marienthal, KS . . . 620-379-4472

Banana

Agvest
Cleveland, OH . . . 216-464-3737
Emerling International Foods
Buffalo, NY . . . 716-833-7381

We supply food manufacturers and food service customers worldwide (since 1988) with bulk ingredients including: Fruits & Vegetables; Juice Concentrates; Herbs & Spices; Oils & Vinegars; Flavors & Colors; Honey & Molasses. We also produce PURE MAPLE SYRUP.

Gerber Products Company
Parsippany, NJ . . . 800-443-7237
Spreda Group
Louisville, KY . . . 502-426-9411
Unique Ingredients
Naches, WA . . . 509-653-1991

Oats

LaCrosse Milling Company
Cochrane, WI . . . 800-441-5411

Potato

AgraWest Foods
Prince Edward Island, NS . . . 877-687-1400
American Health & Nutrition
Ann Arbor, MI . . . 734-677-5570
Emerling International Foods
Buffalo, NY . . . 716-833-7381

We supply food manufacturers and food service customers worldwide (since 1988) with bulk ingredients including: Fruits & Vegetables; Juice Concentrates; Herbs & Spices; Oils & Vinegars; Flavors & Colors; Honey & Molasses. We also produce PURE MAPLE SYRUP.

Idaho Pacific Corporation
Ririe, ID . . . 800-238-5503
Idaho Supreme Potatoes
Firth, ID . . . 208-346-6841
McCain Foods Canada
Toronto, ON . . . 866-622-2461
Nonpareil Corporation
Blackfoot, ID . . . 800-522-2223
Oregon Potato Company
Boardman, OR . . . 800-336-6311
Terry Foods Inc
Idaho Falls, ID . . . 208-604-8143
Tova Industries
Louisville, KY . . . 888-532-8682
Unique Ingredients
Naches, WA . . . 509-653-1991

Soy

American Health & Nutrition
Ann Arbor, MI . . . 734-677-5570
Microsoy Corporation
Jefferson, IA . . . 515-386-2100

Flavor Enhancers

American Fruit Processors
Pacoima, CA . . . 818-899-9574

asiamerica

Asiamerica Ingredients
Westwood, NJ . . . 201-497-5531

Processor, importer, exporter and distributor of bulk vitamins, amino acids, nutraceuticals, aromatic chemicals, food additives, herbs, mineral nutrients and pharmaceuticals.

International Flavors & Fragrances
New York, NY . . . 212-765-5500
LifeSpice Ingredients
Palm Beach, FL . . . 561-844-6334
Mixerz All Natural Cocktail Mixers
Beverly, MA . . . 978-922-6497
Nutra Food Ingredients, LLC
Kentwood, MI . . . 616-656-9928
QST Ingredients, Inc.
Rancho Cucamonga, CA . . . 909-989-4343
Savoury Systems
Branchburg, NJ . . . 908-526-2524
SensoryEffects Flavor Systems
Bridgeton, MO . . . 314-291-5444
Summit Hill Flavors
Middlesex, NJ . . . 732-805-0335

Gluconates

asiamerica

Asiamerica Ingredients
Westwood, NJ . . . 201-497-5531

Processor, importer, exporter and distributor of bulk vitamins, amino acids, nutraceuticals, aromatic chemicals, food additives, herbs, mineral nutrients and pharmaceuticals.

Lifewise Ingredients
Lake Zurich, IL . . . 847-550-8270

Flavors

A M Todd Company
Kalamazoo, MI . . . 800-968-2603
ADM Food Ingredients
Olathe, KS . . . 800-255-6637
Advanced Food Systems Inc.
Somerset, NJ . . . 732-873-6776
AFF International
Marietta, GA . . . 800-241-7764
Ajinomoto Food Ingredients LLC
Chicago, IL . . . 773-714-1436
Al-Rite Fruits & Syrups
Miami, FL . . . 305-652-2540
Allen Flavors
Edison, NJ . . . 908-561-5995
American Instants
Flanders, NJ . . . 973-584-8811
American Laboratories
Omaha, NE . . . 402-339-2494
Armand's Coffee Flavors
Atlanta, GA . . . 404-696-4178
Aromor Flavors & Fragrances
Englewood Cliffs, NJ . . . 201-503-1662
Arylessence
Marietta, GA . . . 800-553-2440

asiamerica

Asiamerica Ingredients
Westwood, NJ . . . 201-497-5531

Processor, importer, exporter and distributor of bulk vitamins, amino acids, nutraceuticals, aromatic chemicals, food additives, herbs, mineral nutrients and pharmaceuticals.

Assets Health Foods
Hillsborough, NJ . . . 888-849-2048
Associated Bakers Products
Huntington, NY . . . 631-673-3841
Austin Special Foods Company
Austin, TX . . . 866-372-8663
Autocrat Coffee & Extracts
Lincoln, RI . . . 800-288-6272
AVRI Companies
Richmond, CA . . . 800-883-9574
Avron Resources
Richmond, CA . . . 800-883-9574
Baker's Coconut
Memphis, TN . . . 800-323-1092
Bartek Ingredients, Inc.
Stoney Creek, ON . . . 800-263-4165
Batko Flavors LLC
North Brunswick, NJ . . . 732-991-3462
Bear Stewart Corporation
Chicago, IL . . . 800-697-2327
Beck Flavors
Saint Louis, MO . . . 800-851-8100
Bedoukian Research, Inc.
Danbury, CT . . . 203-830-4000
Beta Pure Foods
Aptos, CA . . . 831-685-6565
Blendex Company
Jeffersontown, KY . . . 800-626-6325
Blue Pacific Flavors & Fragrances
City of Industry, CA . . . 800-248-7499
Borthwicks Flavors
Hauppauge, NY . . . 800-255-6837
Brewster Foods TestLab
Reseda, CA . . . 818-881-4268
Cajun Chef Products
Saint Martinville, LA . . . 337-394-7112
California Brands Flavors
Oakland, CA . . . 800-348-0111

Capriccio
Chatsworth, CA 818-718-7620
Cargill Corn Milling
Naperville, IL 800-344-1633
CHR Hansen
Milwaukee, WI 800-343-4680
Citrop
Tampa, FL 813-249-5955
Citrus and Allied Essences
New Hyde Park, NY 516-354-1200
Classic Flavors & Fragrances
New York, NY 212-777-0004
Clements Foods Company
Oklahoma City, OK 800-654-8355
Coca-Cola North America
Columbus, OH 614-492-6414
Comax Flavors
Melville, NY 800-992-0629
Commercial Creamery Company
Spokane, WA 800-541-0850
ConAgra Food Ingredients
Omaha, NE 877-266-2472
Consolidated Mills
Houston, TX 713-896-4196
Consumers Flavoring Extract Company
Brooklyn, NY 718-435-0201
Contact International
Skokie, IL 847-324-4411
Cosco International
Chicago, IL 800-621-4549
Creative Flavors
Chagrin Falls, OH 800-848-9043
Crestmont Enterprises
Camden, NJ 856-966-0700
Crystal Foods
Brick, NJ 732-477-0073
Danisco-Cultor
Ardsley, NY 914-674-6300
Dean Distributors
Burlingame, CA 800-792-0816
Dohler Milne Aseptics
Prosser, WA 509-786-2611
Ecom Manufacturing Corporation
Markham, ON 905-477-2441
Edlong Dairy Flavors
Elk Grove Village, IL 888-698-2783
Emerald Performance Materials
Cuyahoga Falls, OH 330-916-6700
Essential Flavors & Fragrances, Inc
Corona, CA 888-333-9935
Everfresh Food Corporation
Minneapolis, MN 612-331-6393
Fee Brothers
Rochester, NY 800-961-3337
First Choice Ingredients
Germantown, WI 262-251-4322
Flavor & Fragrance Specialties
Mahwah, NJ 800-998-4337
Flavor Dynamics
South Plainfield, NJ 888-271-8424
Flavor House
Adelanto, CA 760-246-9131
Flavorchem
Downers Grove, IL 800-435-8867
Flavors
Edwardsville, PA 570-287-8642
Flavors of North America
Geneva, IL 800-308-3662
Florida Food Products
Eustis, FL 800-874-2331
FONA International Inc.
Geneva, IL 630-578-8600
Fontana Flavors
Janesville, WI 608-754-9668
Food Ingredients Solutions
Blauvelt, NY 845-353-8501
Genarom International
Cranbury, NJ 609-409-6200
Givaudan Flavors
Cincinnati, OH 513-948-3428
Givaudan Flavors
Cincinnati, OH 513-948-8000
Givaudan Flavors
East Hanover, NJ 973-386-9800
GMI Products/Originates
Sunrise, FL 800-999-9373
Great Northern Maple Products
Saint Honor, De Shenley, QC 418-485-7777
Green Spot Packaging
Claremont, CA 800-456-3210
Griffith Laboratories
Alsip, IL 800-346-9494
Griffith Laboratories Worldwide
Alsip, IL 800-346-4743
Grow Company
Ridgefield, NJ 201-941-8777
Gum Technology Corporation
Tucson, AZ 800-369-4867
H B Taylor Company
Chicago, IL 773-254-4805
H.B. Taylor
Chicago, IL 773-254-4805
Hagelin & Company
Branchburg, NJ 800-229-2112
HB Taylor Company
Chicago, IL 773-254-4805
Horner International
Raleigh, NC 919-787-3112
I Rice & Company
Philadelphia, PA 800-232-6022
Illes Seasonings & Flavors
Carrollton, TX 800-683-4553
Innova Flavors
Lombard, IL 630-928-4813
International Flavors & Fragrances
Dayton, NJ 732-329-4600
International Flavors & Fragrances
New York, NY 212-765-5500
J&K Ingredients
Paterson, NJ 973-340-8700
JM Swank Company
North Liberty, IA 800-593-6375
Johnson's Food Products
Dorchester, MA 617-265-3400
Kalsec
Kalamazoo, MI 269-349-9711
Kerry Ingredients & Flavours
Beloit, WI 800-248-7310
Key Essentials
Rancho Santa Margarita, CA 949-635-1000
Latitude
Huntington, NY 631-659-3374
Lebermuth Company
South Bend, IN 800-648-1123
Liberty Natural Products
Oregon City, OR 800-289-8427
Lionel Hitchen Essitional Oils
Sarasota, FL 941-379-1400
Lochhead Manufacturing Company
Fenton, MO 888-776-2088
Lorann Oils
Lansing, MI 800-862-8620
Lucks Food Decorating Company
Tacoma, WA 800-426-9778
MAFCO Worldwide Corporation
Camden, NJ 856-964-8840
Mane Inc.
Milford, OH 513-248-9876
Marukome USA Inc.
Irvine, CA 949-863-0110
Maryland & Virginia Milk Producers Cooperative
Reston, VA 703-742-4250
McCormick & Company
Sparks, MD 800-632-5847
Metarom Corporation
Newport, VT 888-882-5555
Millers Blue Ribbon Beef
Hyrum, UT 800-873-0939
Mother Murphy's Labs
Greensboro, NC 800-849-1277
Mutual Flavors
South Jordan, UT 888-343-2922
Naturex Inc
South Hackensack, NJ 201-440-5000
Naturex Inc.
South Hackensack, NJ 201-440-5000
Newly Weds Foods
Chicago, IL 800-647-9314
Northeastern Products Company
S Plainfield, NJ 908-561-1660
Northwestern Extract Company
Germantown, WI 800-466-3034
Nutricepts
Burnsville, MN 800-949-9060
Ocean Cliff Corporation
New Bedford, MA 508-990-7900
Oregon Flavor Rack
Eugene, OR 541-342-2085
OSF Flavors
Windsor, CT 800-466-6015
Ottens Flavors
Philadelphia, PA 800-523-0767
Parker Flavors, Inc
Baltimore, MD 800-336-9113
Particle Control
Albertville, MN 763-497-3075
Particle Dynamics
Saint Louis, MO 800-452-4682
Perlarom Technology
Columbia, MD 410-997-5114
PMC Specialties Group
Cincinnati, OH 800-543-2466
Progressive Flavors
Hawley, PA 805-383-2640
Richard E. Colgin Company
Dallas, TX 888-226-5446
Rio Syrup Company
Saint Louis, MO 800-325-7666
Rose Brand Corporation
Brooklyn, NY 800-854-5356
Royal Foods & Flavors
Elk Grove Vlg, IL 847-595-9166
San-Ei Gen FFI
New York, NY 212-315-7850
Sartori Food Corporation
Plymouth, WI 800-558-5888
Savoury Systems
Branchburg, NJ 908-526-2524
Senomyx, Inc.
San Diego, CA 858-646-8300
Sensient Technologies
Milwaukee, WI 800-558-9892
Serv-Agen Corporation
Cherry Hill, NJ 856-663-6966
Sethness-Greenleaf
Chicago, IL 800-621-4549
Shanks Extracts
Lancaster, PA 800-346-3135
Silesia Flavors
Hoffman Estates, IL 847-645-0270
Singer Extract Laboratory
Livonia, MI 313-345-5880
SJH Enterprises
Middleton, WI 888-745-3845
SKW Nature Products
Dubuque, IA 563-588-6244
Sno-Shack
Rexburg, ID 888-766-7425
Southern Flavoring Company
Bedford, VA 800-765-8565
Star Kay White
Congers, NY 800-874-8518
Stearns & Lehman
Mansfield, OH 800-533-2722
Sterling Extract Company
Franklin Park, IL 847-451-9728
Sun Pure
Lakeland, FL 863-619-2222
Symrise
Teterboro, NJ 201-288-3200
T Hasegawa
Cerritos, CA 714-522-1900
Target Flavors
Brookfield, CT 800-538-3350
Technology Flavors & Fragrances
Amityville, NY 631-789-8228
Texas Spice Company
Cedar Park, TX 800-880-8007
Triple K Manufacturing Company
Shenandoah, IA 888-987-2824
Ungerer & Company
Lincoln Park, NJ 973-628-0600
US Chocolate Corporation
Brooklyn, NY 718-788-8555
US Ingredients
Naperville, IL 630-820-1711
V&E Kohnstamm
Brooklyn, NY 800-847-4500
Valley Grain Products
Madera, CA 559-675-3400
Vanlab Corporation
Rochester, NY 585-232-6647
Vanlaw Food Products
Fullerton, CA 714-870-9091
Virginia Dare
Brooklyn, NY 800-847-4500
W&G Flavors
Hunt Valley, MD 410-771-6606
Webbpak
Trussville, AL 800-655-3500
Western Flavors & Fragrances
Livermore, CA 925-373-9433
Western Syrup Company
Santa Fe Springs, CA 562-921-4485
Wild Flavors
Erlanger, KY 859-342-3600

WILD Flavors (Canada)
Mississauga, ON 800-263-5286
World Flavors
Warminster, PA 215-672-4400
Wynn Starr Flavors
Allendale, NJ 800-996-7827

Almond

Castella Imports
Hauppauge, NY 866-227-8355
Nielsen-Massey Vanillas
Waukegan, IL 800-525-7873
Shanks Extracts
Lancaster, PA 800-346-3135

Amaretto

Allen Flavors
Edison, NJ 908-561-5995

Anise (See also Spices/Anise Seed)

Castella Imports
Hauppauge, NY 866-227-8355

Apple

Allen Flavors
Edison, NJ 908-561-5995

Artificial

Citrus and Allied Essences
New Hyde Park, NY 516-354-1200
Clarendon Flavor Engineering
Louisville, KY 502-634-9215
Domino Specialty Ingredients
West Palm Beach, FL 800-446-9763

Banana

Allen Flavors
Edison, NJ 908-561-5995
Castella Imports
Hauppauge, NY 866-227-8355

Beverage

Allen Flavors
Edison, NJ 908-561-5995
Clarendon Flavor Engineering
Louisville, KY 502-634-9215
Flavor & Fragrance Specialties
Mahwah, NJ 800-998-4337
Flavors from Florida
Bartow, FL 863-533-0408
Mother Murphy's Labs
Greensboro, NC 800-849-1277
Sethness-Greenleaf
Chicago, IL 800-621-4549

Blackberry

Allen Flavors
Edison, NJ 908-561-5995

Blueberry

Allen Flavors
Edison, NJ 908-561-5995

Butter

DairyChem Inc
Fishers, IN 317-849-8400
Edlong Dairy Flavors
Elk Grove Village, IL 888-698-2783
First Choice Ingredients
Germantown, WI 262-251-4322

Pecan

Edlong Dairy Flavors
Elk Grove Village, IL 888-698-2783

Vanilla

Edlong Dairy Flavors
Elk Grove Village, IL 888-698-2783

Buttermilk

DairyChem Inc
Fishers, IN 317-849-8400

Edlong Dairy Flavors
Elk Grove Village, IL 888-698-2783

Butterscotch

Edlong Dairy Flavors
Elk Grove Village, IL 888-698-2783

Cajeta

Edlong Dairy Flavors
Elk Grove Village, IL 888-698-2783

Caramel

Edlong Dairy Flavors
Elk Grove Village, IL 888-698-2783
Mont Blanc Gourmet
Denver, CO 800-877-3811

Cheese

Dean Distributors
Burlingame, CA 800-792-0816
Edlong Dairy Flavors
Elk Grove Village, IL 888-698-2783
Flavor Dynamics
South Plainfield, NJ 888-271-8424
H B Taylor Company
Chicago, IL 773-254-4805
Ingretec
Lebanon, PA 717-273-1360
Sartori Food Corporation
Plymouth, WI 800-558-5888
Thiel Cheese & Ingredients
Hilbert, WI 920-989-1440

Cheesecake

Edlong Dairy Flavors
Elk Grove Village, IL 888-698-2783

Cherry

A M Todd Company
Kalamazoo, MI 800-968-2603
Allen Flavors
Edison, NJ 908-561-5995

Chocolate

Allen Flavors
Edison, NJ 908-561-5995
Big Shoulders Baking
Chicago, IL 800-456-9328
H B Taylor Company
Chicago, IL 773-254-4805
Mont Blanc Gourmet
Denver, CO 800-877-3811
US Chocolate Corporation
Brooklyn, NY 718-788-8555

Citrus

Allen Flavors
Edison, NJ 908-561-5995

Citrus and Allied Essences
New Hyde Park, NY 516-354-1200
H B Taylor Company
Chicago, IL 773-254-4805
Kendall Citrus Corporation
Goulds, FL 305-258-1628
Western Flavors & Fragrances
Livermore, CA 925-373-9433

Cocoa

Flavor Dynamics
South Plainfield, NJ 888-271-8424

Horner International
Raleigh, NC 919-787-3112

Coconut

Castella Imports
Hauppauge, NY 866-227-8355

Coffee

Acqua Blox LLC
Santa Fe Springs, CA 562-693-9599
American Instants
Flanders, NJ 973-584-8811
Autocrat Coffee & Extracts
Lincoln, RI 800-288-6272
Beck Flavors
Saint Louis, MO 800-851-8100
Coffee Grounds
St Paul, MN 651-644-9959
Flavor & Fragrance Specialties
Mahwah, NJ 800-998-4337
Flavor Dynamics
South Plainfield, NJ 888-271-8424
Tops Manufacturing Company
Darien, CT 203-655-9367
U Roast Em
Hayward, WI 715-634-6255

Cultured

DairyChem Inc
Fishers, IN 317-849-8400
Edlong Dairy Flavors
Elk Grove Village, IL 888-698-2783

Dairy

Blossom Farm Products
Ridgewood, NJ 800-729-1818
DairyChem Inc
Fishers, IN 317-849-8400
Edlong Dairy Flavors
Elk Grove Village, IL 888-698-2783
First Choice Ingredients
Germantown, WI 262-251-4322
GMI Products/Originates
Sunrise, FL 800-999-9373
H B Taylor Company
Chicago, IL 773-254-4805
Hilmar Ingredients
Hilmar, CA 209-667-6076
Ingretec
Lebanon, PA 717-273-1360
Southeastern Wisconsin Products Company
Milwaukee, WI 414-482-1730

Extract

Advanced Food Technology
Littleton, CO 303-980-5221
AM Todd Company
Kalamazoo, MI 800-968-2603
American Fruits and Flavors
Los Angeles, CA 323-264-7790

Bell Flavors & Fragrances
Northbrook, IL 800-323-4387
Bickford Flavors
Cleveland, OH 800-283-8322
California Custom Fruits & Flavors
Irwindale, CA 877-558-0056
Carmi Flavor & Fragrance Company
City of Commerce, CA 800-421-9647
Charles H. Baldwin & Sons
West Stockbridge, MA 413-232-7785
Citrus and Allied Essences
New Hyde Park, NY 516-354-1200
Crest Foods Company
Ashton, IL 800-435-6972

Crestmont Enterprises
Camden, NJ 856-966-0700
David Michael & Company
Philadelphia, PA 800-363-5286
Edlong Dairy Flavors
Elk Grove Village, IL 888-698-2783
Ervan Guttman Company
Cincinnati, OH 800-203-9213
FONA International Inc.
Geneva, IL. 630-578-8600
Freeman Industries
Tuckahoe, NY. 800-666-6454
Frutarom Meer Corporation
North Bergen, NJ 800-526-7147
Fuji Foods
Browns Summit, NC. 336-375-3111
Glcc Company
Paw Paw, MI. 269-657-3167
Goodman Manufacturing Company
Carthage, MO 417-358-3231
H.B. Taylor
Chicago, IL 773-254-4805
H.R. Nicholson Company
Baltimore, MD 800-638-3514
Hosemen & Roche Vitamins & Fine Chemicals
Nutley, NJ 800-526-6367
IMC-Agrico Company
Convent, LA 225-562-3501
International Bakers Services
South Bend, IN 800-345-7175
Jogue Inc
Northville, MI. 800-521-3888
Kloss Manufacturing Company
Allentown, PA. 800-445-7100
Marnap Industries
Buffalo, NY. 716-897-1220
Master Mix
Placentia, CA 714-524-1698
National Products Company
Kalamazoo, MI 269-344-3640
Newly Weds Foods
Chicago, IL 800-647-9314
Newport Flavours & Fragrances
Orange, CA 714-744-3700
Nielsen-Massey Vanillas
Waukegan, IL 800-525-7873
Pecan Deluxe Candy Company
Dallas, TX. 800-733-3589
Proliant
Ankeny, IA 800-466-7317
R.R. Lochhead Manufacturing
Paso Robles, CA 800-735-0545
Red Arrow Products Company LLC
Manitowoc, WI. 920-683-5500
Rhodia
Cranbury, NJ 800-343-8324
Robertet Flavors
Piscataway, NJ 732-271-1804
Senomyx, Inc.
San Diego, CA 858-646-8300
Simpson Spring Company
South Easton, MA. 508-372-0914
SnoWizard Extracts
New Orleans, LA 800-366-9766
Southeastern Wisconsin Products Company
Milwaukee, WI 414-482-1730
Southern Flavoring Company
Bedford, VA 800-765-8565
Southern Snow Manufacturing
Belle Chasse, LA 504-393-8967
Tara Foods
Atlanta, GA. 404-559-0605
Tops Manufacturing Company
Darien, CT. 203-655-9367
Van Tone Creative Flavors Inc
Terrell, TX. 800-856-0802
Vegetable Juices
Chicago, IL 888-776-9752
Virginia Dare
Brooklyn, NY 800-847-4500
Western Flavors & Fragrances
Livermore, CA 925-373-9433
Zatarain's
Gretna, LA 800-435-6639

Fat

Edlong Dairy Flavors
Elk Grove Village, IL 888-698-2783

Fish

Fontana Flavors
Janesville, WI 608-754-9668

Flavors

Dressing

Edlong Dairy Flavors
Elk Grove Village, IL 888-698-2783

Enhancers

Edlong Dairy Flavors
Elk Grove Village, IL 888-698-2783
Flavor & Fragrance Specialties
Mahwah, NJ 800-998-4337
H&A Canada, Inc.
Toronto, ON 416-412-9518
Proliant
Ankeny, IA 800-466-7317
Sensient Technologies
Milwaukee, WI 800-558-9892
Wti, Inc.
Jefferson, GA 800-827-1727

Fruit

Contact International
Skokie, IL 847-324-4411
Dohler Milne Aseptics
Prosser, WA. 509-786-2611
H B Taylor Company
Chicago, IL 773-254-4805
Ramsey/Sias
Cleveland, OH 800-477-3788

Grain

GKI Foods
Brighton, MI 248-486-0055

Half & Half

Edlong Dairy Flavors
Elk Grove Village, IL 888-698-2783

Hazelnut

Allen Flavors
Edison, NJ. 908-561-5995

Heat Stable

Edlong Dairy Flavors
Elk Grove Village, IL 888-698-2783

Hickory Smoke Oil

Talk O'Texas Brands
San Angelo, TX

Irish Creme

Edlong Dairy Flavors
Elk Grove Village, IL 888-698-2783

Lemon

Allen Flavors
Edison, NJ. 908-561-5995
Brewster Foods TestLab
Reseda, CA 818-881-4268
Castella Imports
Hauppauge, NY 866-227-8355
Charles H. Baldwin & Sons
West Stockbridge, MA 413-232-7785
Nielsen-Massey Vanillas
Waukegan, IL 800-525-7873
Serv-Agen Corporation
Cherry Hill, NJ 856-663-6966
Shanks Extracts
Lancaster, PA 800-346-3135
Ungerer & Company
Lincoln Park, NJ 973-628-0600

Licorice

A M Todd Company
Kalamazoo, MI 800-968-2603

Asiamerica Ingredients
Westwood, NJ 201-497-5531

Processor, importer, exporter and distributor of bulk vitamins, amino acids, nutraceuticals, aromatic chemicals, food additives, herbs, mineral nutrients and pharmaceuticals.

Horner International
Raleigh, NC. 919-787-3112

Lime

Allen Flavors
Edison, NJ. 908-561-5995
Ungerer & Company
Lincoln Park, NJ 973-628-0600

Liqueur

Edgar A Weber & Company
Wheeling, IL 800-558-9078

Macadamia

Allen Flavors
Edison, NJ. 908-561-5995
Buon Italia Misono Food Ltd.
New York, NY 212-633-9090

Maple

Allen Flavors
Edison, NJ. 908-561-5995
Castella Imports
Hauppauge, NY 866-227-8355

Butter

Edlong Dairy Flavors
Elk Grove Village, IL 888-698-2783

Masking

Edlong Dairy Flavors
Elk Grove Village, IL 888-698-2783

Meat

First Choice Ingredients
Germantown, WI. 262-251-4322
Flavor & Fragrance Specialties
Mahwah, NJ 800-998-4337
Flavor House
Adelanto, CA 760-246-9131
Fontana Flavors
Janesville, WI 608-754-9668
Genarom International
Cranbury, NJ. 609-409-6200
Griffith Laboratories
Alsip, IL 800-346-9494
Innova Flavors
Lombard, IL 630-928-4813

Microwave

Edlong Dairy Flavors
Elk Grove Village, IL 888-698-2783

Milk

DairyChem Inc
Fishers, IN. 317-849-8400
Edlong Dairy Flavors
Elk Grove Village, IL 888-698-2783
Fonterra USA
Chicago, IL 847-928-1872
FrieslandCampina Domo
, NJ 201-655-7786
International Dairy Ingredients
Wapakoneta, OH. 419-738-4060

Butter

Edlong Dairy Flavors
Elk Grove Village, IL 888-698-2783
Fonterra USA
Chicago, IL 847-928-1872
FrieslandCampina Domo
, NJ 201-655-7786

Nut

H B Taylor Company
Chicago, IL 773-254-4805

Orange

Allen Flavors
Edison, NJ 908-561-5995
Castella Imports
Hauppauge, NY 866-227-8355
Charles H. Baldwin & Sons
West Stockbridge, MA 413-232-7785
Nielsen-Massey Vanillas
Waukegan, IL 800-525-7873
Ungerer & Company
Lincoln Park, NJ 973-628-0600

Passion Fruit

Allen Flavors
Edison, NJ 908-561-5995

Peach

Allen Flavors
Edison, NJ 908-561-5995

Pear

Allen Flavors
Edison, NJ 908-561-5995

Peppermint

AM Todd Company
Kalamazoo, MI 800-968-2603
Castella Imports
Hauppauge, NY 866-227-8355
Ungerer & Company
Lincoln Park, NJ 973-628-0600

Pineapple

Allen Flavors
Edison, NJ 908-561-5995
Castella Imports
Hauppauge, NY 866-227-8355

Poultry

Flavor House
Adelanto, CA 760-246-9131

Raspberry

Allen Flavors
Edison, NJ 908-561-5995

Root Beer

Allen Flavors
Edison, NJ 908-561-5995

Rum

Butter Toffee

Edlong Dairy Flavors
Elk Grove Village, IL 888-698-2783

Seafood

Flavor House
Adelanto, CA 760-246-9131

Smoke

Dean Distributors
Burlingame, CA 800-792-0816
Red Arrow Products Company LLC
Manitowoc, WI 920-683-5500

Sour

Senomyx, Inc.
San Diego, CA 858-646-8300

Cream

DairyChem Inc
Fishers, IN 317-849-8400
Edlong Dairy Flavors
Elk Grove Village, IL 888-698-2783

Spearmint

AM Todd Company
Kalamazoo, MI 800-968-2603
Ungerer & Company
Lincoln Park, NJ 973-628-0600

Strawberry

Allen Flavors
Edison, NJ 908-561-5995
Castella Imports
Hauppauge, NY 866-227-8355

Tea

Acqua Blox LLC
Santa Fe Springs, CA 562-693-9599
Allen Flavors
Edison, NJ 908-561-5995
Flavor & Fragrance Specialties
Mahwah, NJ 800-998-4337
Flavor Dynamics
South Plainfield, NJ 888-271-8424

Vanilla

Agri-Dairy Products
Purchase, NY 914-697-9580
Allen Flavors
Edison, NJ 908-561-5995
American Health & Nutrition
Ann Arbor, MI 734-677-5570
Beck Flavors
Saint Louis, MO 800-851-8100
Carmi Flavor & Fragrance Company
City of Commerce, CA 800-421-9647
Charles H. Baldwin & Sons
West Stockbridge, MA 413-232-7785
Clements Foods Company
Oklahoma City, OK 800-654-8355
Everfresh Food Corporation
Minneapolis, MN 612-331-6393
Goodman Manufacturing Company
Carthage, MO 417-358-3231
Hagelin & Company
Branchburg, NJ 800-229-2112
Helm New York
Piscataway, NJ 732-981-1160
Jogue Inc
Northville, MI 800-521-3888
Serv-Agen Corporation
Cherry Hill, NJ 856-663-6966
Shanks Extracts
Lancaster, PA 800-346-3135
SnoWizard Extracts
New Orleans, LA 800-366-9766
Sterling Extract Company
Franklin Park, IL 847-451-9728
Teawolf Industries, Ltd
Pine Brook, NJ 973-575-4600
Triple K Manufacturing Company
Shenandoah, IA 888-987-2824
Webbpak
Trussville, AL 800-655-3500
Western Flavors & Fragrances
Livermore, CA 925-373-9433

Vanillin

A M Todd Company
Kalamazoo, MI 800-968-2603
Agri-Dairy Products
Purchase, NY 914-697-9580

asiamerica

Asiamerica Ingredients
Westwood, NJ 201-497-5531

Processor, importer, exporter and distributor of bulk vitamins, amino acids, nutraceuticals, aromatic chemicals, food additives, herbs, mineral nutrients and pharmaceuticals.

Astral Extracts Ltd.
Syosset, NY 516-496-2505
California Custom Fruits & Flavors
Irwindale, CA 877-558-0056

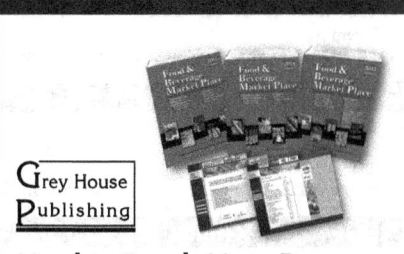

International Chemical
Milltown, NJ 800-914-2436
Naturex Inc.
South Hackensack, NJ 201-440-5000
Nichem Company
Hillside, NJ 908-933-0770
Rhodia
Cranbury, NJ 800-343-8324
Universal Preservachem Inc
Somerset, NJ 732-568-1266
Zink & Triest Company
Montgomeryville, PA 800-537-5070

Variegates

Triple K Manufacturing Company
Shenandoah, IA 888-987-2824

Vegetable

Kalsec
Kalamazoo, MI 269-349-9711
Summit Hill Flavors
Middlesex, NJ 732-805-0335
Western Flavors & Fragrances
Livermore, CA 925-373-9433

Wine

Edgar A Weber & Company
Wheeling, IL 800-558-9078

Yogurt

DairyChem Inc
Fishers, IN 317-849-8400
Edlong Dairy Flavors
Elk Grove Village, IL 888-698-2783
Givaudan Flavors
Cincinnati, OH 513-948-8000
Gum Technology Corporation
Tucson, AZ 800-369-4867
Johanna Foods
Flemington, NJ 800-727-6700
Plaidberry Company
Vista, CA 760-727-5403

Glandulars

Ultra Enterprises
Whittier, CA 800-543-0627

Grain-Based

Beaumont Rice Mills
Beaumont, TX. 409-832-2521
Kerry Ingredients
Blue Earth, MN. 507-526-7575

Gums

A M Todd Company
Kalamazoo, MI 800-968-2603
American Food Products
Methuen, MA 978-682-1855

Associated Bakers Products
Huntington, NY 631-673-3841
Au'some Candies
Monmouth Junction, NJ 732-951-8818
Beehive Botanicals, Inc.
Hayward, WI. 800-233-4483
Cap Candy
Napa, CA. 707-251-9321
Cargill Texturizing Solutions
Cedar Rapids, IA. 877-650-7080
Concord Confections
Chicago, IL 800-267-0037
DMH Ingredients
Libertyville, IL 847-362-9977
El Brands
Ozark, AL 334-445-2828
Food Ingredients Solutions
Blauvelt, NY 845-353-8501
Fun Factory
Milwaukee, WI 877-894-6767
Generation Foods Too
Woodland Hills, CA 818-887-5858
Gum Technology Corporation
Tucson, AZ 800-369-4867
Gurley's Foods
Willmar, MN 800-426-7845
H&A Canada, Inc.
Toronto, ON 416-412-9518
Jungbunzlauer
Newton, MA 800-828-0062
Kolatin Real Kosher Gelatin
Lakewood, NJ 732-364-8700
LA Dreyfus
Edison, NJ 732-549-1600
Lotte USA
Battle Creek, MI 269-963-6664
Magic Gumball International
Chatsworth, CA 800-576-2020
Main Street Ingredients
La Crosse, WI 800-359-2345
Maryland & Virginia Milk Producers Cooperative
Reston, VA 703-742-4250
Montello
Tulsa, OK 800-331-4628
Naturex Inc.
South Hackensack, NJ 201-440-5000
Oak Leaf Confections
Scarborough, ON 877-261-7887
P.L. Thomas
Morristown, NJ 973-984-0900
Polypro International
Minneapolis, MN 800-765-9776
Richardson Brands Company
Branford, CT 800-839-8938
Sahagian & Associates
Oak Park, IL 800-327-9273
Scripture Candy
Adamsville, AL 888-317-7333
Sherwood Brands
Rockville, MD 301-309-6161
Snackerz
Commerce, CA 888-576-2253
SP Enterprises
Las Vegas, NV 800-746-4774
Sweet Works
St Augustine, FL 877-261-7887
SWELL Philadelphia Chewing Gum Corporation
Havertown, PA 610-449-1700
The Topps Company
Duryea, PA 570-457-6761
The Topps Company
New York, NY 800-489-9149
Triple-C
Hamilton, ON 800-263-9105
World Confections
Brooklyn, NY 718-768-8100

Acacia Gum

Alfred L. Wolff, Inc.
Park Ridge, IL 847-759-8888
Gum Technology Corporation
Tucson, AZ 800-369-4867
Gumix International
Fort Lee, NJ 800-248-6492
Main Street Ingredients
La Crosse, WI 800-359-2345
Naturex Inc.
South Hackensack, NJ 201-440-5000
P.L. Thomas
Morristown, NJ 973-984-0900
Tic Gums
Belcamp, MD 800-221-3953

Agar-Agar

A M Todd Company
Kalamazoo, MI 800-968-2603
Cargill Texturizing Solutions
Cedar Rapids, IA 877-650-7080
Gum Technology Corporation
Tucson, AZ 800-369-4867
Naturex Inc.
South Hackensack, NJ 201-440-5000
P.L. Thomas
Morristown, NJ 973-984-0900
Tic Gums
Belcamp, MD 800-221-3953
Universal Preservachem Inc
Somerset, NJ 732-568-1266

Algin & Alginates

Associated Bakers Products
Huntington, NY 631-673-3841
Cargill Texturizing Solutions
Cedar Rapids, IA 877-650-7080
P.L. Thomas
Morristown, NJ 973-984-0900

Arabic

P.L. Thomas
Morristown, NJ 973-984-0900

Carboxymethylcellulose

P.L. Thomas
Morristown, NJ 973-984-0900

Carrageenan

Cargill Texturizing Solutions
Cedar Rapids, IA 877-650-7080
CP Kelco
Atlanta, GA 800-535-2687
GPI USA LLC.
Athens, GA 706-850-7826
Hermann Laue Spice Company
Uxbridge, ON 905-852-5100
P.L. Thomas
Morristown, NJ 973-984-0900

Gellan

CP Kelco
Atlanta, GA 800-535-2687
P.L. Thomas
Morristown, NJ 973-984-0900

Ghatti

P.L. Thomas
Morristown, NJ 973-984-0900

Guar Gum

Agri-Dairy Products
Purchase, NY 914-697-9580

Associated Bakers Products
Huntington, NY 631-673-3841
Cargill Texturizing Solutions
Cedar Rapids, IA 877-650-7080
Commodities Marketing, Inc.
Edison, NJ 732-603-5077
ConAgra Grocery Products
Irvine, CA 714-680-1000
Gum Technology Corporation
Tucson, AZ 800-369-4867
H. Fox & Company
Brooklyn, NY 718-385-4600
P.L. Thomas
Morristown, NJ 973-984-0900
Polypro International
Minneapolis, MN 800-765-9776
Tic Gums
Belcamp, MD 800-221-3953
Universal Preservachem Inc
Somerset, NJ 732-568-1266

Hydroxypropyl Methylcellulose

Karaya Gum

Gum Technology Corporation
Tucson, AZ 800-369-4867
Tic Gums
Belcamp, MD 800-221-3953
Universal Preservachem Inc
Somerset, NJ 732-568-1266

Locust Bean Gum

Cargill Texturizing Solutions
Cedar Rapids, IA 877-650-7080
CP Kelco
Atlanta, GA 800-535-2687
Gum Technology Corporation
Tucson, AZ 800-369-4867
Naturex Inc.
South Hackensack, NJ 201-440-5000
P.L. Thomas
Morristown, NJ 973-984-0900
Tic Gums
Belcamp, MD 800-221-3953

Methylcellulose

P.L. Thomas
Morristown, NJ 973-984-0900

Natural

Cargill Texturizing Solutions
Cedar Rapids, IA 877-650-7080
P.L. Thomas
Morristown, NJ 973-984-0900

Pectin

Cargill Texturizing Solutions
Cedar Rapids, IA..................877-650-7080
CP Kelco
Atlanta, GA......................800-535-2687

Tara

P.L. Thomas
Morristown, NJ...................973-984-0900

Tragacanth

Gum Technology Corporation
Tucson, AZ......................800-369-4867
Naturex Inc.
South Hackensack, NJ.............201-440-5000
Universal Preservachem Inc
Somerset, NJ.....................732-568-1266

Vegetable Gum

Functional Foods
Englishtown, NJ..................800-442-9524
Gum Technology Corporation
Tucson, AZ......................800-369-4867
Gumix International
Fort Lee, NJ.....................800-248-6492
Tic Gums
Belcamp, MD.....................800-221-3953

Xanthan Gum

A M Todd Company
Kalamazoo, MI...................800-968-2603
Archer Daniels Midland Company
Decatur, IL......................800-637-5843

asiamerica

Asiamerica Ingredients
Westwood, NJ....................201-497-5531

Processor, importer, exporter and distributor of bulk vitamins, amino acids, nutraceuticals, aromatic chemicals, food additives, herbs, mineral nutrients and pharmaceuticals.

Cargill Texturizing Solutions
Cedar Rapids, IA..................877-650-7080
CP Kelco
Atlanta, GA......................800-535-2687
Deosen USA Inc
Piscataway, NJ...................908-382-6518
Gum Technology Corporation
Tucson, AZ......................800-369-4867

Half-Products

Kerry Ingredients
Blue Earth, MN...................507-526-7575

Calcium & Nutritionally Fortified Pellets

Kerry Ingredients
Blue Earth, MN...................507-526-7575

Cocoa & Rice Pellets

Kerry Ingredients
Blue Earth, MN...................507-526-7575

Colored Pellets

Kerry Ingredients
Blue Earth, MN...................507-526-7575

Flavored Pellets

Kerry Ingredients
Blue Earth, MN...................507-526-7575

Organic Pellets

Kerry Ingredients
Blue Earth, MN...................507-526-7575

Veggie & Rice Pellets

Kerry Ingredients
Blue Earth, MN...................507-526-7575

Humectants

Cargill Texturizing Solutions
Cedar Rapids, IA..................877-650-7080
Crowley Foods
Binghamton, NY..................800-637-0019
Nutricepts
Burnsville, MN...................800-949-9060

Hydrocolloids

A&B Ingredients
Fairfield, NJ.....................973-227-1390
Cargill Texturizing Solutions
Cedar Rapids, IA..................877-650-7080
P.L. Thomas
Morristown, NJ...................973-984-0900
Tic Gums
Belcamp, MD.....................800-221-3953

Hydrolyzed Products

Cereal Solids

Cargill Texturizing Solutions
Cedar Rapids, IA..................877-650-7080

Milk Proteins

Arla Foods Ingredients
Basking Ridge, NJ................908-604-8551
First Spice Mixing Company
Long Island City, NY..............800-221-1105
Kantner Group
Wapakoneta, OH..................419-738-4060

Vegetable Proteins

Arla Foods Ingredients
Basking Ridge, NJ................908-604-8551
Flavor House
Adelanto, CA....................760-246-9131
Valley Meats
Coal Valley, IL...................309-799-7341

Inclusions

Kerry Ingredients
Blue Earth, MN...................507-526-7575

Ingredients

Blue California Company
Rcho Sta Marg, CA................949-635-1990
Carolina Ingredients
Rock Hill, SC....................803-323-6550
Century Foods International
Sparta, WI.......................800-269-1901
Diana Naturals
Valley Cottage, NY................845-268-5200
Fallwood Corp
White Plains, NY.................914-304-4065
Ful-Flav-R Foods
Alamo, CA......................925-838-0300
Garuda International
Exeter, CA.......................559-594-4380
Glanbia Nutritionals
Monroe, WI......................608-329-2800
Hayashibara Intl. Inc.
Broomfield, CO..................303-650-4590
Helm New York
Piscataway, NJ...................732-981-1160
Marukan Vinegar (U.S.A.) Inc.
Paramount, CA...................562-630-6060
Newtown Foods
Langhorne, PA...................215-579-2120
P.L. Thomas
Morristown, NJ...................973-984-0900
PGP International
Woodland, CA....................800-233-0110
Quali Tech
Chaska, MN.....................800-328-5870
Sabroso Company
Medford, OR.....................541-772-5653
Season Harvest Foods
Sunnyvale, CA...................408-749-8018
Sensus
Lawrenceville, NJ.................646-452-6147
Sentry Seasonings
Elmhurst, IL.....................630-530-5370

Sun Ray International
Davis, CA.......................530-758-0088
Taiyo
Minneapolis, MN.................763-398-3003
VAN HEES Inc
Cary, NC........................919-654-6862

Bakery

American Casein Company
Burlington, NJ....................609-387-3130
Amoretti
Oxnard, CA......................800-266-7388
Caremoli USA
Ames, IA........................515-233-1255
Chaucer Foods
Syosset, NY......................516-496-2500
New Horizon Foods
Union City, CA...................510-489-8600

Dairy

Cargill Texturizing Solutions
Cedar Rapids, IA..................877-650-7080
Century Foods International
Sparta, WI.......................800-269-1901
Kantner Group
Wapakoneta, OH..................419-738-4060
Trega Foods
Weyauwega, WI..................920-867-2137

Food

Acatris
Edina, MN.......................952-835-9590
AmTech Ingredients
Hudson, WI......................715-381-5746
Capriccio
Chatsworth, CA..................818-718-7620
Century Foods International
Sparta, WI.......................800-269-1901
Interfood Ingredients
Waltham, MA....................781-370-9983
Land O'Frost
Lansing, IL......................800-323-3308
Mallet & Company
Carnegie, PA.....................800-245-2757
P.L. Thomas
Morristown, NJ...................973-984-0900
Summit Hill Flavors
Middlesex, NJ....................732-805-0335

Lactoferrin

Glanbia Nutritionals
Monroe, WI......................800-336-2183

Leaveners

Baking Soda

Agri-Dairy Products
Purchase, NY....................914-697-9580
Bunny Bread
Deridder, LA.....................337-463-7522
Church & Dwight Company
Princeton, NJ.....................800-221-0453

Clabber Girl Corporation
Terre Haute, IN 812-232-9446
Natrium Products
Cortland, NY..................... 800-962-4203
Old Baldy Brewing Company
Upland, CA...................... 909-946-1750

Maltodextrin

ADM Corn Processing
Decatur, IL 800-553-8411
ADM Food Ingredients
Olathe, KS....................... 800-255-6637
Agri-Dairy Products
Purchase, NY 914-697-9580
American Health & Nutrition
Ann Arbor, MI 734-677-5570
California Natural Products
Lathrop, CA 209-858-2525
Cargill Texturizing Solutions
Cedar Rapids, IA.................. 877-650-7080
Clofine Dairy & Food Products
Linwood, NJ 800-441-1001
Corn Products International
Westchester, IL 800-443-2746
Grain Processing Corporation
Muscatine, IA 800-448-4472
Malt Products Corporation
Saddle Brook, NJ 800-526-0180
Roquette America
Keokuk, IA 800-553-7035

Milk Calcium

Garuda International
Exeter, CA....................... 559-594-4380
Glanbia Nutritionals
Monroe, WI...................... 800-336-2183
International Dairy Ingredients
Wapakoneta, OH.................. 419-738-4060
Kantner Group
Wapakoneta, OH.................. 419-738-4060

Particulates

Kerry Ingredients
Blue Earth, MN................... 507-526-7575

Pastes

Almond

Ingredients, Flavors & Additives:Pastes:Almond

Emerling International Foods
Buffalo, NY...................... 716-833-7381

We supply food manufacturers and food service customers worldwide (since 1988) with bulk ingredients including: Fruits & Vegetables; Juice Concentrates; Herbs & Spices; Oils & Vinegars; Flavors & Colors; Honey & Molasses. We also produce PURE MAPLE SYRUP.

Fig

Emerling International Foods
Buffalo, NY...................... 716-833-7381

We supply food manufacturers and food service customers worldwide (since 1988) with bulk ingredients including: Fruits & Vegetables; Juice Concentrates; Herbs & Spices; Oils & Vinegars; Flavors & Colors; Honey & Molasses. We also produce PURE MAPLE SYRUP.

Fig Garden Packing
Fresno, CA 559-275-2191
Kalashian Packing Company
Fresno, CA 559-237-4287
Unique Ingredients
Naches, WA...................... 509-653-1991

Fruit

Cinnabar Specialty Foods
Prescott, AZ 866-293-6433
Citadelle Maple Syrup Producers' Cooperative
Plessisville, QC................... 819-362-3241
Emerling International Foods
Buffalo, NY...................... 716-833-7381

We supply food manufacturers and food service customers worldwide (since 1988) with bulk ingredients including: Fruits & Vegetables; Juice Concentrates; Herbs & Spices; Oils & Vinegars; Flavors & Colors; Honey & Molasses. We also produce PURE MAPLE SYRUP.

Fig Garden Packing
Fresno, CA 559-275-2191
Kapaa Poi Factory
Kapaa, HI 808-822-5426
Lion Raisins
Selma, CA....................... 559-834-6677
Sun-Maid Growers of California
Kingsburg, CA 800-272-4746
Unique Ingredients
Naches, WA...................... 509-653-1991
Vacaville Fruit Company
Vacaville, CA 707-448-5292

Mushroom

Garuda International
Exeter, CA....................... 559-594-4380

Tomato

American Food & Equipment
Miami, FL....................... 305-377-8991
Dixon Canning Company
Dixon, CA....................... 707-678-4406
Emerling International Foods
Buffalo, NY...................... 716-833-7381

We supply food manufacturers and food service customers worldwide (since 1988) with bulk ingredients including: Fruits & Vegetables; Juice Concentrates; Herbs & Spices; Oils & Vinegars; Flavors & Colors; Honey & Molasses. We also produce PURE MAPLE SYRUP.

Hartford City Foam Pack aging & Converting
Hartford City, IN.................. 765-348-2500
Ingomar Packing Company
Los Banos, CA 209-826-9494
International Home Foods
Parsippany, NJ.................... 973-359-9920
Pacific Coast Producers
Oroville, CA 530-533-4311
Pastene Companies
Canton, MA 781-830-8200
San Benito Foods
Hollister, CA..................... 831-637-4434
Spreda Group
Louisville, KY.................... 502-426-9411
Stanislaus Food Products
Modesto, CA..................... 800-327-7201
Unilever Foods
Stockton, CA..................... 209-467-2212
Valley Tomato Products
Stockton, CA..................... 209-982-4586

Canned & Frozen

Crown Point
St John, IN 219-365-3200
Hartford City Foam Pack aging & Converting
Hartford City, IN.................. 765-348-2500
International Home Foods
Parsippany, NJ.................... 973-359-9920
Pastene Companies
Canton, MA 781-830-8200
Unilever Foods
Stockton, CA..................... 209-467-2212
Valley Tomato Products
Stockton, CA..................... 209-982-4586

Pectins

Apple

Asiamerica Ingredients
Westwood, NJ.................... 201-497-5531

Processor, importer, exporter and distributor of bulk vitamins, amino acids, nutraceuticals, aromatic chemicals, food additives, herbs, mineral nutrients and pharmaceuticals.

Cargill Texturizing Solutions
Cedar Rapids, IA.................. 877-650-7080
Gum Technology Corporation
Tucson, AZ 800-369-4867
Naturex Inc.
South Hackensack, NJ 201-440-5000
Spreda Group
Louisville, KY.................... 502-426-9411
Universal Preservachem Inc
Somerset, NJ..................... 732-568-1266
W&G Flavors
Hunt Valley, MD.................. 410-771-6606

Citrus

Asiamerica Ingredients
Westwood, NJ.................... 201-497-5531

Processor, importer, exporter and distributor of bulk vitamins, amino acids, nutraceuticals, aromatic chemicals, food additives, herbs, mineral nutrients and pharmaceuticals.

Cargill Texturizing Solutions
Cedar Rapids, IA.................. 877-650-7080
Citrico
Northbrook, IL 888-625-8516
Gum Technology Corporation
Tucson, AZ 800-369-4867
Naturex Inc.
South Hackensack, NJ 201-440-5000
Universal Preservachem Inc
Somerset, NJ..................... 732-568-1266
W&G Flavors
Hunt Valley, MD.................. 410-771-6606

Fruit

Cargill Texturizing Solutions
Cedar Rapids, IA.................. 877-650-7080
Naturex Inc.
South Hackensack, NJ 201-440-5000
Spreda Group
Louisville, KY.................... 502-426-9411
W&G Flavors
Hunt Valley, MD.................. 410-771-6606
Williams Foods, Inc
Lenexa, KS 800-255-6736

Phosphates

Asiamerica Ingredients
Westwood, NJ.................... 201-497-5531

Processor, importer, exporter and distributor of bulk vitamins, amino acids, nutraceuticals, aromatic chemicals, food additives, herbs, mineral nutrients and pharmaceuticals.

BK Giulini Corporation
Simi Valley, CA................... 800-526-2688
Escalade
Huntington, NY 631-659-3374

Fiberstar
River Falls, WI 715-425-7550
First Spice Mixing Company
Long Island City, NY 800-221-1105
Hawkins Inc
Minneapolis, MN 800-328-5460
ICL Performance Products
St. Louis, MO 800-244-6169
Innophos
Cranbury, NJ 609-495-2495
Wiberg Corporation
Oakville, ON 905-825-9900

Ammonium Phosphates

ADM Food Ingredients
Olathe, KS 800-255-6637
Luyties Pharmacal Company
Saint Louis, MO 800-325-8080
Universal Preservachem Inc
Somerset, NJ 732-568-1266

Calcium Phosphate

Asiamerica Ingredients
Westwood, NJ 201-497-5531

Processor, importer, exporter and distributor of bulk vitamins, amino acids, nutraceuticals, aromatic chemicals, food additives, herbs, mineral nutrients and pharmaceuticals.

Luyties Pharmacal Company
Saint Louis, MO 800-325-8080
Natural Enrichment Industries, LLC
Sesser, IL 618-625-2112

Potassium Bicarbonate

Innophos
Cranbury, NJ 609-495-2495

Sodium Phosphate

Agri-Dairy Products
Purchase, NY 914-697-9580

Asiamerica Ingredients
Westwood, NJ 201-497-5531

Processor, importer, exporter and distributor of bulk vitamins, amino acids, nutraceuticals, aromatic chemicals, food additives, herbs, mineral nutrients and pharmaceuticals.

Luyties Pharmacal Company
Saint Louis, MO 800-325-8080
Universal Preservachem Inc
Somerset, NJ 732-568-1266

Potassium Bitartrate (Cream of Tartar)

Advanced Spice & Trading
Carrollton, TX 800-872-7811
American Tartaric Products
Larchmont, NY 914-834-1881
Jungbunzlauer
Newton, MA 800-828-0062

Potassium Bromate

Morre-Tec Industries
Union, NJ 908-688-9009

Potassium Citrate

Agri-Dairy Products
Purchase, NY 914-697-9580

Asiamerica Ingredients
Westwood, NJ 201-497-5531

Processor, importer, exporter and distributor of bulk vitamins, amino acids, nutraceuticals, aromatic chemicals, food additives, herbs, mineral nutrients and pharmaceuticals.

Cargill Corn Milling
Naperville, IL 800-344-1633
Cargill Worldwide Acidulants
Naperville, IL 800-344-1633
Gadot Biochemical Industries
Rolling Meadows, IL 888-424-1424
Jungbunzlauer
Newton, MA 800-828-0062
Shekou Chemicals
Waltham, MA 781-893-6878
Universal Preservachem Inc
Somerset, NJ 732-568-1266

Potassium Lactate

Trumark
Linden, NJ 800-752-7877

Potassium Sorbate

Agri-Dairy Products
Purchase, NY 914-697-9580
Amerol Corporation
Farmingdale, NY

Asiamerica Ingredients
Westwood, NJ 201-497-5531

Processor, importer, exporter and distributor of bulk vitamins, amino acids, nutraceuticals, aromatic chemicals, food additives, herbs, mineral nutrients and pharmaceuticals.

Hermann Laue Spice Company
Uxbridge, ON 905-852-5100
Jungbunzlauer
Newton, MA 800-828-0062
Shekou Chemicals
Waltham, MA 781-893-6878
Silver Ferm Chemical
Seattle, WA 206-282-3376
Universal Preservachem Inc
Somerset, NJ 732-568-1266

Powders

Expro Manufacturing
Vernon, CA 323-415-8544
First Choice Ingredients
Germantown, WI 262-251-4322
Hayashibara Intl. Inc.
Broomfield, CO 303-650-4590
Just the Berries
Los Angeles, CA 213-613-9807
Marroquin Organic International
Santa Cruz, CA 831-423-3442

Adobo

American Key Food Products
Closter, NJ 800-767-0237
Gel Spice Company, Inc
Bayonne, NJ 800-922-0230
Magic Seasoning Blends
New Orleans, LA 800-457-2857

Baking

ADM Food Ingredients
Olathe, KS 800-255-6637
Agri-Dairy Products
Purchase, NY 914-697-9580
Allied Blending & Ingredients
Keokuk, IA 800-526-8102
American Tartaric Products
Larchmont, NY 914-834-1881
Church & Dwight Company
Princeton, NJ 800-221-0453
Erba Food Products
Brooklyn, NY 718-272-7700
Ghirardelli Chocolate Company
San Leandro, CA 800-877-9338
Groeb Farms
Onsted, MI 517-467-2065
Lallemand/American Yeast
Addison, IL 630-932-1290
Lynch Foods
North York, ON 416-449-5464
Mississippi Blending Company
Keokuk, IA 800-758-4080
Roland Industries
Saint Louis, MO 800-325-1183
Rumford Baking Powder Company
Terre Haute, IN 812-232-9446
Tasty Mix Quality Foods
Brooklyn, NY 866-TAS-TYMX
Young Winfield
Kleinburg, ON 905-893-9682

Beverage

Aromatech USA
Orlando, FL 407-277-5727
Associated Brands Inc.
Medina, NY 800-265-0050
Baldwin Richardson Foods
Frankfort, IL 866-644-2732

Liquid ingredient manufacturer specializing in signature sauces, dessert toppings, beverage/pancake syrups, specialty fruit fillings and condiments.

Cappuccine
Palm Springs, CA 800-511-3127
ConAgra Grocery Products
Irvine, CA 714-680-1000
First Choice Ingredients
Germantown, WI 262-251-4322
Instant Products of America
Columbus, IN 812-372-9100
J. Crow Company
New Ipswich, NH 800-878-1965
Lynch Foods
North York, ON 416-449-5464
Mele-Koi Farms
Newport Beach, CA 949-660-9000
Natural Formulas
Hayward, CA 510-372-1800
Northwestern Foods
Saint Paul, MN 800-236-4937
SensoryEffects Flavor Systems
Bridgeton, MO 314-291-5444
Unilever Bestfoods
Englewood Cliffs, NJ 201-567-8000
Unilever United States
Englewood Cliffs, NJ 201-894-4000
Wechsler Coffee Corporation
Moonachie, NJ 800-800-2633

Broth

International Dehydrated Foods
Springfield, MO 800-525-7435
Proliant
Ankeny, IA 800-466-7317

Buttermilk

Diehl Food Ingredients
Defiance, OH 800-251-3033
Kantner Group
Wapakoneta, OH 419-738-4060
St. Charles Trading
Lake Saint Louis, MO 800-336-1333

Cappuccino

International Food Technologies
Evansville, IN 812-853-9432

Carob

Universal Preservachem Inc
Somerset, NJ 732-568-1266

Cassava

Cargill Texturizing Solutions
Cedar Rapids, IA 877-650-7080

Celery

Advanced Spice & Trading
Carrollton, TX . . . 800-872-7811
American Key Food Products
Closter, NJ . . . 800-767-0237
Con Yeager Spice Company
Zelienople, PA . . . 800-222-2460
Emerling International Foods
Buffalo, NY . . . 716-833-7381

We supply food manufacturers and food service customers worldwide (since 1988) with bulk ingredients including: Fruits & Vegetables; Juice Concentrates; Herbs & Spices; Oils & Vinegars; Flavors & Colors; Honey & Molasses. We also produce PURE MAPLE SYRUP.

Gel Spice Company, Inc
Bayonne, NJ . . . 800-922-0230
Unique Ingredients
Naches, WA . . . 509-653-1991

Cheese

Anderson Custom Processing
New Ulm, MN . . . 877-588-4950
Baker's Coconut
Memphis, TN . . . 800-323-1092
DMH Ingredients
Libertyville, IL . . . 847-362-9977
First Choice Ingredients
Germantown, WI . . . 262-251-4322
Kantner Group
Wapakoneta, OH . . . 419-738-4060
Kraft Foods
Albany, MN . . . 320-845-2131

American

Kantner Group
Wapakoneta, OH . . . 419-738-4060

Bakers

Kantner Group
Wapakoneta, OH . . . 419-738-4060

Cheddar

Kantner Group
Wapakoneta, OH . . . 419-738-4060

Cream

Kantner Group
Wapakoneta, OH . . . 419-738-4060

Chicken Stock

Summit Hill Flavors
Middlesex, NJ . . . 732-805-0335

Chili

Advanced Spice & Trading
Carrollton, TX . . . 800-872-7811
American Key Food Products
Closter, NJ . . . 800-767-0237
Atlantic Quality Spice &Seasonings
New Brunswick, NJ . . . 800-584-0422
Bruce Foods Corporation
New Iberia, LA . . . 800-299-9082
Bueno Food Products
Albuquerque, NM . . . 800-888-7336
Chile Today
San Francisco, CA . . . 800-758-0372
Fernandez Chili Company
Alamosa, CO . . . 719-589-6043
Gel Spice Company, Inc
Bayonne, NJ . . . 800-922-0230
Gilroy Foods
Gilroy, CA . . . 800-921-7502
Mexnutri
San Luis Potosi, . . . 444-841-5625
Monterrey Products Company
San Antonio, TX . . . 210-435-2872
Morris J. Golombeck
Brooklyn, NY . . . 718-284-3505
New Mexico Food Distributors
Albuquerque, NM . . . 800-637-7084
Reily Foods Company
New Orleans, LA . . . 504-524-6131
Santa Cruz Chili & SpiceCompany
Tumacacori, AZ . . . 520-398-2591
Swagger Foods Corporation
Vernon Hills, IL . . . 847-913-1200
Texas Coffee Company
Beaumont, TX . . . 800-259-3400
Victoria Packing Corporation
Brooklyn, NY . . . 718-927-3000
Whole Herb Company
Sonoma, CA . . . 707-935-1077
Woodland Foods
Gurnee, IL . . . 847-625-8600

Hot

Atlantic Quality Spice &Seasonings
New Brunswick, NJ . . . 800-584-0422

Regular

Atlantic Quality Spice &Seasonings
New Brunswick, NJ . . . 800-584-0422

Salt-free

Atlantic Quality Spice &Seasonings
New Brunswick, NJ . . . 800-584-0422

Cocoa

Ambassador Foods
Van Nuys, CA . . . 800-338-3369
Chadler
Swedesboro, NJ . . . 856-467-0099
Cocoline Chocolate Company
Brooklyn, NY . . . 718-522-4500
Ecom Agroindustrial Corporation Ltd
New York, NY . . . 212-248-1190
Gilster-Mary Lee Corporation
Chester, IL . . . 800-851-5371
Mont Blanc Gourmet
Denver, CO . . . 800-877-3811
Natra US
Chula Vista, CA . . . 800-262-6216
Northwestern Foods
Saint Paul, MN . . . 800-236-4937
Sucesores de Pedro Cortes
San Juan, PR . . . 787-754-7040
Vrymeer Commodities
St Charles, IL . . . 630-584-0069
World's Finest Chocolate
Chicago, IL . . . 888-821-8452

Curry

American Key Food Products
Closter, NJ . . . 800-767-0237
Atlantic Quality Spice &Seasonings
New Brunswick, NJ . . . 800-584-0422
Bo-Ling's Products
Overland Park, KS . . . 913-888-8223
Commissariat Imports
Los Angeles, CA . . . 310-475-5628
Gel Spice Company, Inc
Bayonne, NJ . . . 800-922-0230
Victoria Packing Corporation
Brooklyn, NY . . . 718-927-3000

Hot

Atlantic Quality Spice &Seasonings
New Brunswick, NJ . . . 800-584-0422
Commissariat Imports
Los Angeles, CA . . . 310-475-5628

EchinaceaPurpurea

asiamerica

Asiamerica Ingredients
Westwood, NJ . . . 201-497-5531

Processor, importer, exporter and distributor of bulk vitamins, amino acids, nutraceuticals, aromatic chemicals, food additives, herbs, mineral nutrients and pharmaceuticals.

RFI Ingredients
Blauvelt, NY . . . 800-962-7663

Egg

Inovatech USA
Montreal, QC . . . 800-367-3447

Feverfew

asiamerica

Asiamerica Ingredients
Westwood, NJ . . . 201-497-5531

Processor, importer, exporter and distributor of bulk vitamins, amino acids, nutraceuticals, aromatic chemicals, food additives, herbs, mineral nutrients and pharmaceuticals.

RFI Ingredients
Blauvelt, NY . . . 800-962-7663

Fish

Certified Savory
Countryside, IL . . . 800-328-7656

Fruit

Agvest
Cleveland, OH . . . 216-464-3737
Blue California Company
Rcho Sta Marg, CA . . . 949-635-1990
Carmi Flavor & Fragrance Company
City of Commerce, CA . . . 800-421-9647
Emerling International Foods
Buffalo, NY . . . 716-833-7381

We supply food manufacturers and food service customers worldwide (since 1988) with bulk ingredients including: Fruits & Vegetables; Juice Concentrates; Herbs & Spices; Oils & Vinegars; Flavors & Colors; Honey & Molasses. We also produce PURE MAPLE SYRUP.

Mayfield Farms
Caledon, ON . . . 905-846-0506
Niagara Foods
Middleport, NY . . . 716-735-7722
Prime Ingredients
Saddle Brook, NJ . . . 888-791-6655
QBI
South Plainfield, NJ . . . 908-668-0088
RFI Ingredients
Blauvelt, NY . . . 800-962-7663
Spreda Group
Louisville, KY . . . 502-426-9411
Unique Ingredients
Naches, WA . . . 509-653-1991
United Citrus Products
Norwood, MA . . . 800-229-7300
Valley Fig Growers
Fresno, CA . . . 559-237-3893

Garlic (See also Spices/Garlic Powder)

Advanced Spice & Trading
Carrollton, TX . . . 800-872-7811
Alfred L. Wolff, Inc.
Park Ridge, IL . . . 847-759-8888
American Key Food Products
Closter, NJ . . . 800-767-0237

asiamerica

Asiamerica Ingredients
Westwood, NJ . . . 201-497-5531

Processor, importer, exporter and distributor of bulk vitamins, amino acids, nutraceuticals, aromatic chemicals, food additives, herbs, mineral nutrients and pharmaceuticals.

DeFrancesco & Sons
Firebaugh, CA . . . 209-364-7000

Emerling International Foods
Buffalo, NY 716-833-7381

We supply food manufacturers and food service customers worldwide (since 1988) with bulk ingredients including: Fruits & Vegetables; Juice Concentrates; Herbs & Spices; Oils & Vinegars; Flavors & Colors; Honey & Molasses. We also produce PURE MAPLE SYRUP.

Gel Spice Company, Inc
Bayonne, NJ 800-922-0230
Gilroy Foods
Gilroy, CA. 800-921-7502
Great Garlic Foods
Bradley Beach, NJ 732-775-3311
Italian Rose Garlic Products
West Palm Beach, FL 800-338-8899
RFI Ingredients
Blauvelt, NY. 800-962-7663
Texas Coffee Company
Beaumont, TX. 800-259-3400
Vegetable Juices
Chicago, IL 888-776-9752

Gingko

Asiamerica Ingredients
Westwood, NJ 201-497-5531

Processor, importer, exporter and distributor of bulk vitamins, amino acids, nutraceuticals, aromatic chemicals, food additives, herbs, mineral nutrients and pharmaceuticals.

RFI Ingredients
Blauvelt, NY. 800-962-7663

Ginseng

Asiamerica Ingredients
Westwood, NJ 201-497-5531

Processor, importer, exporter and distributor of bulk vitamins, amino acids, nutraceuticals, aromatic chemicals, food additives, herbs, mineral nutrients and pharmaceuticals.

RFI Ingredients
Blauvelt, NY. 800-962-7663

Gotu Kola

Asiamerica Ingredients
Westwood, NJ 201-497-5531

Processor, importer, exporter and distributor of bulk vitamins, amino acids, nutraceuticals, aromatic chemicals, food additives, herbs, mineral nutrients and pharmaceuticals.

RFI Ingredients
Blauvelt, NY. 800-962-7663

Ice Cream

Agri-Dairy Products
Purchase, NY 914-697-9580
America's Classic Foods
Cambria, CA. 805-927-0745
Clofine Dairy & Food Products
Linwood, NJ 800-441-1001
International Food Technologies
Evansville, IN 812-853-9432
Quality Naturally! Foods
City of Industry, CA 888-498-6986

Jelly

Lake City Foods
Mississauga, ON. 905-625-8244

Meat

American Key Food Products
Closter, NJ. 800-767-0237
Certified Savory
Countryside, IL. 800-328-7656
Flavor House
Adelanto, CA 760-246-9131
Henningsen Foods
Purchase, NY 914-701-4020
QST Ingredients, Inc.
Rancho Cucamonga, CA 909-989-4343
Summit Hill Flavors
Middlesex, NJ. 732-805-0335

Meat Stock

Aromont USA
Southlake, TX. 817-552-5544
Proliant Meat Ingredients
Harlan, IA 800-369-2672

Milk

Abunda Life Laboratories
Asbury Park, NJ 732-775-7575
Agri-Dairy Products
Purchase, NY 914-697-9580
All American Foods, Inc.
Mankato, MN 800-833-2661
Ault Foods
Toronto, ON 416-626-1973
Berkshire Dairy & Food Products
Wyomissing, PA 888-654-8008
Blossom Farm Products
Ridgewood, NJ 800-729-1818
California Dairies
Visalia, CA 559-625-2200
Century Foods International
Sparta, WI. 800-269-1901
Challenge Dairy Products
Dublin, CA 800-733-2479
Clofine Dairy & Food Products
Linwood, NJ 800-441-1001
Con Yeager Spice Company
Zelienople, PA. 800-222-2460
Country Fresh Farms
Salt Lake City, UT 800-878-0099
CTL Foods
Colfax, WI. 800-962-5227
Dairy Farmers of America
East Syracuse, NY 315-431-1352
Dairy Farmers of America
Medina, OH. 330-670-7800
Devansoy
Carroll, IA. 800-747-8605
Dietrich's Milk Products
Reading, PA 800-526-6455
Farmers Coop Creamery
McMinnville, OR 503-472-2157
Fearn Natural Foods
Thiensville, WI. 800-877-8935
First District Association
Litchfield, MN 320-693-3236
First Spice Mixing Company
Long Island City, NY 800-221-1105
Fonterra USA
Chicago, IL 847-928-1872
Graf Creamery
Bonduel, WI
Honeyville Grain
Rancho Cucamonga, CA 888-810-3212
Humboldt Creamery Association
Fortuna, CA 707-725-6182
IMAC
Oklahoma City, OK 888-878-7827
Kantner Group
Wapakoneta, OH. 419-738-4060
Kelly Flour Company
Addison, IL. 630-678-5300
Lake Country Foods
Oconomowoc, WI. 262-567-5521
Land O'Lakes
Carlisle, PA. 717-486-7000
Land O'Lakes, Inc.
Arden Hills, MN. 800-328-9680
Level Valley Creamery
Antioch, TN 800-251-1292
Main Street Ingredients
La Crosse, WI. 800-359-2345
Maple Island
Saint Paul, MN 800-369-1022
MEYENBERG Goat Milk Products
Turlock, CA 800-891-4628
Plainview Milk Products Cooperative
Plainview, MN 507-534-3872
Preferred Milks
Addison, IL. 800-621-5046
Protient (Land O Lakes)
St Paul, MN. 800-328-9680
Ramsen
Lakeville, MN. 952-431-0400
Rv Industries
Buford, GA. 770-729-8983
Safeway Inc
Pleasanton, CA 877-723-3929
Saint Albans Cooperative Creamery
Saint Albans, VT. 800-559-0343
SunMeadow Family of Products
Saint Petersburg, FL 727-573-2211
Swiss Valley Farms Company
Davenport, IA 563-468-6600
The Scoular Company
Omaha, NE 800-487-1474
United Dairymen of Arizona
Tempe, AZ. 480-966-7211
Vance's Foods
Gilmer, TX 800-497-4834
Weinberg Foods
Kirkland, WA 800-866-3447
Welsh Farms
Edison, NJ. 800-221-0663
Westin
Omaha, NE 800-228-6098

Molasses

Groeb Farms
Onsted, MI 517-467-2065
Rogers Sugar Inc
Vancouver, BC 800-661-5350
Smolich Brothers
Joliet, IL 815-727-2144

Mustard

Kathy's Gourmet Specialties
Mendocino, CA. 707-937-1383

Onion (See also Spices/Onion Powder)

Advanced Spice & Trading
Carrollton, TX. 800-872-7811
American Key Food Products
Closter, NJ. 800-767-0237
Atlantic Quality Spice &Seasonings
New Brunswick, NJ 800-584-0422
Con Yeager Spice Company
Zelienople, PA. 800-222-2460
DeFrancesco & Sons
Firebaugh, CA. 209-364-7000
Emerling International Foods
Buffalo, NY. 716-833-7381

We supply food manufacturers and food service customers worldwide (since 1988) with bulk ingredients including: Fruits & Vegetables; Juice Concentrates; Herbs & Spices; Oils & Vinegars; Flavors & Colors; Honey & Molasses. We also produce PURE MAPLE SYRUP.

Erba Food Products
Brooklyn, NY 718-272-7700
Gel Spice Company, Inc
Bayonne, NJ 800-922-0230
Gilroy Foods
Gilroy, CA. 800-921-7502

Texas Coffee Company
Beaumont, TX....................800-259-3400
Vegetable Juices
Chicago, IL......................888-776-9752

Pau D'Arco Bark

asiamerica

Asiamerica Ingredients
Westwood, NJ....................201-497-5531

Processor, importer, exporter and distributor of bulk vitamins, amino acids, nutraceuticals, aromatic chemicals, food additives, herbs, mineral nutrients and pharmaceuticals.

RFI Ingredients
Blauvelt, NY.....................800-962-7663

Pregelatinized

Cargill Texturizing Solutions
Cedar Rapids, IA..................877-650-7080

Prepared for Further Processing

Akay USA, LLC
Sayreville, NJ....................732-254-7177
Olcott Plastics
Saint Charles, IL..................888-313-5277

Protein

Fonterra USA
Chicago, IL......................847-928-1872
FrieslandCampina Domo
, NJ............................201-655-7786
International Food Technologies
Evansville, IN....................812-853-9432

Rice

Milk

A&B Ingredients
Fairfield, NJ.....................973-227-1390

Saw Palmetto Berry

asiamerica

Asiamerica Ingredients
Westwood, NJ....................201-497-5531

Processor, importer, exporter and distributor of bulk vitamins, amino acids, nutraceuticals, aromatic chemicals, food additives, herbs, mineral nutrients and pharmaceuticals.

RFI Ingredients
Blauvelt, NY.....................800-962-7663

Seafood

American Key Food Products
Closter, NJ.......................800-767-0237
Certified Savory
Countryside, IL...................800-328-7656
Flavor House
Adelanto, CA....................760-246-9131
Henningsen Foods
Purchase, NY....................914-701-4020

Seasoning

American Key Food Products
Closter, NJ.......................800-767-0237
Gel Spice Company, Inc
Bayonne, NJ.....................800-922-0230
Magic Seasoning Blends
New Orleans, LA.................800-457-2857
Summit Hill Flavors
Middlesex, NJ....................732-805-0335

Vegetable Juices
Chicago, IL......................888-776-9752
Victoria Packing Corporation
Brooklyn, NY....................718-927-3000

Smoothie

International Food Technologies
Evansville, IN....................812-853-9432
SensoryEffects Flavor Systems
Bridgeton, MO...................314-291-5444

Soy

Atlantis Pak USA
Coral Gables, FL..................305-403-2603
Cargill Texturizing Solutions
Cedar Rapids, IA..................877-650-7080

Soy Milk

Cedar Lake Foods
Cedar Lake, MI...................800-246-5039
Innovative Food Solutions LLC
Columbus, OH...................800-884-3314

St. John's Wort

RFI Ingredients
Blauvelt, NY.....................800-962-7663

Tofu

Clofine Dairy & Food Products
Linwood, NJ.....................800-441-1001
Dixie Usa
Tomball, TX.....................800-233-3668

Tomato

A&B Ingredients
Fairfield, NJ.....................973-227-1390
Transa
Libertyville, IL...................847-281-9582

Valerian Root

asiamerica

Asiamerica Ingredients
Westwood, NJ....................201-497-5531

Processor, importer, exporter and distributor of bulk vitamins, amino acids, nutraceuticals, aromatic chemicals, food additives, herbs, mineral nutrients and pharmaceuticals.

RFI Ingredients
Blauvelt, NY.....................800-962-7663

Vanilla

Agri-Dairy Products
Purchase, NY....................914-697-9580
Carmi Flavor & Fragrance Company
City of Commerce, CA.............800-421-9647
Emerling International Foods
Buffalo, NY......................716-833-7381

We supply food manufacturers and food service customers worldwide (since 1988) with bulk ingredients including: Fruits & Vegetables; Juice Concentrates; Herbs & Spices; Oils & Vinegars; Flavors & Colors; Honey & Molasses. We also produce PURE MAPLE SYRUP.

H B Taylor Company
Chicago, IL......................773-254-4805
Helm New York
Piscataway, NJ...................732-981-1160
Prime Ingredients
Saddle Brook, NJ.................888-791-6655
Sterling Extract Company
Franklin Park, IL..................847-451-9728
Whole Herb Company
Sonoma, CA.....................707-935-1077

Yogurt

Associated Bakers Products
Huntington, NY..................631-673-3841
Cargill Texturizing Solutions
Cedar Rapids, IA..................877-650-7080
Commercial Creamery Company
Spokane, WA.....................800-541-0850
Kantner Group
Wapakoneta, OH..................419-738-4060
Maple Island
Saint Paul, MN...................800-369-1022
Master Mix
Placentia, CA....................714-524-1698
Quality Ingredients Corporation
Burnsville, MN...................952-898-4002

Frozen

Cargill Texturizing Solutions
Cedar Rapids, IA..................877-650-7080
International Food Technologies
Evansville, IN....................812-853-9432

Preservatives

A&B Ingredients
Fairfield, NJ.....................973-227-1390
A. Camacho
Plant City, FL....................800-881-4534
Batko Flavors LLC
North Brunswick, NJ..............732-991-3462
Emerald Performance Materials
Cuyahoga Falls, OH...............330-916-6700
Escalade
Huntington, NY..................631-659-3374
Great Earth Chemical
Portland, OR.....................608-752-7417
Hangzhou Sanhe USA
Walnut, CA......................909-869-6016
Kenko International
Los Angeles, CA..................323-721-8300

Food

A.M. Braswell Jr. Food Company
Statesboro, GA...................800-673-9388
Cargill Corn Milling
Naperville, IL....................800-344-1633
FBC Industries
Schaumburg, IL...................888-322-4637
Hosemen & Roche Vitamins & Fine Chemicals
Nutley, NJ.......................800-526-6367
Hurd Orchards
Holley, NY......................585-638-8838
Jarchem Industries
Newark, NJ......................973-578-4560
Jungbunzlauer
Newton, MA.....................800-828-0062
Kalama Chemical
Kalama, WA.....................800-223-0035
Macco Organiques
Valleyfield, QC...................450-371-1066
Mineral & Pigment Solutions
South Plainfield, NJ...............800-732-0562
Nutricepts
Burnsville, MN...................800-949-9060
Parish Chemical Company
Orem, UT.......................801-226-2018
PMC Specialties Group
Cincinnati, OH...................800-543-2466
Shekou Chemicals
Waltham, MA....................781-893-6878
Silver Ferm Chemical
Seattle, WA......................206-282-3376
Tasty Mix Quality Foods
Brooklyn, NY..................866-TAS-TYMX
Universal Preservachem Inc
Somerset, NJ.....................732-568-1266
Wisconsin Wilderness Food Products
Milwaukee, WI...................800-359-3039

Proteins

American Casein Company
Burlington, NJ....................609-387-3130
Cargill Texturizing Solutions
Cedar Rapids, IA..................877-650-7080
Clofine Dairy & Food Products
Linwood, NJ.....................800-441-1001
Fonterra USA
Chicago, IL......................847-928-1872
FrieslandCampina Domo
, NJ............................201-655-7786

Glanbia Nutritionals
Monroe, WI 608-329-2800
International Dairy Ingredients
Wapakoneta, OH 419-738-4060
Kantner Group
Wapakoneta, OH 419-738-4060

Releases

Food

Barbara's Bakery
Petaluma, CA 707-765-2273
Barlean's
Ferndale, WA 360-384-0325
Black Diamond Cheese
Toronto, ON 800-263-2858
Capri Bagel & Pizza Corporation
Brooklyn, NY 718-497-4431
Cloud Nine
San Leandro, CA 201-358-8588
Corn Poppers
San Diego, CA 858-231-2617
Desert King International
Chula Vista, CA 800-982-2235
EcoNatural Solutions
Boulder, CO 877-684-5159
Ferris Organic Farm
Eaton Rapids, MI 800-628-8736
Flavorganics
Newark, NJ 973-344-8014
Glanbia Foods
Twin Falls, ID 800-427-9477
Ingredient Innovations
Kansas City, MO 816-587-1426
Jewel Date Company
Thermal, CA 760-399-4474
Leech Lake Reservation
Cass Lake, MN 218-335-8200
Lone Pine Enterprises
Carlisle, AR 870-552-3217
Lowell Farms
El Campo, TX 888-484-9213
Marantha Natural Foods
San Francisco, CA 866-972-6879
Martha Olson's Great Foods
Sutter Creek, CA 800-973-3966
Montana Specialty Mills
Great Falls, MT 406-761-2338
Nelson Ricks Creamery Company
Salt Lake City, UT 801-364-3607
Nicola Valley Apiaries
Merritt, BC 250-378-5208
NSpired Natural Foods
Melville, NY 541-488-2747
Pack Ryt, Inc.
La Quinta, CA 770-771-8880
S&E Organic Farms
Bakersfield, CA 661-325-2644
Schreiber Foods Plant/Distribution Center
Wisconsin Rapids, WI 715-422-7500
Southern Brown Rice
Weiner, AR 800-421-7423
Stengel Seed & Grain Company
Milbank, SD 605-432-6030
Sunnyland Mills
Fresno, CA 800-501-8017
Tianfu China Cola
Katonah, NY 914-232-3102
Top Hat Company
Wilmette, IL 847-256-6565
US Mills
Bala Cynwyd, PA 800-422-1125
Victor Packing Company
Madera, CA 559-673-5908

Replacers

Cocoa

Associated Bakers Products
Huntington, NY 631-673-3841

Egg

Associated Bakers Products
Huntington, NY 631-673-3841
Cargill Texturizing Solutions
Cedar Rapids, IA 877-650-7080
Inovatech USA
Montreal, QC 800-367-3447

Fat

Edlong Dairy Flavors
Elk Grove Village, IL 888-698-2783

Raisin Juice

Dry

Cajun Chef Products
Saint Martinville, LA 337-394-7112

Sodium

Asiamerica Ingredients
Westwood, NJ 201-497-5531

Processor, importer, exporter and distributor of bulk vitamins, amino acids, nutraceuticals, aromatic chemicals, food additives, herbs, mineral nutrients and pharmaceuticals.

Cargill Worldwide Acidulants
Naperville, IL 800-344-1633
Erie Foods International
Erie, IL 800-447-1887
Gadot Biochemical Industries
Rolling Meadows, IL 888-424-1424
Gum Technology Corporation
Tucson, AZ 800-369-4867
Jungbunzlauer
Newton, MA 800-828-0062
Luxembourg Cheese Factory
Orangeville, IL 815-789-4227
Nutricepts
Burnsville, MN 800-949-9060
PMP Fermentation Products
Peoria, IL 800-558-1031
Trumark
Linden, NJ 800-752-7877

Sodium Alginates

Asiamerica Ingredients
Westwood, NJ 201-497-5531

Processor, importer, exporter and distributor of bulk vitamins, amino acids, nutraceuticals, aromatic chemicals, food additives, herbs, mineral nutrients and pharmaceuticals.

Gum Technology Corporation
Tucson, AZ 800-369-4867
P.L. Thomas
Morristown, NJ 973-984-0900
Tic Gums
Belcamp, MD 800-221-3953

Sodium Benzoate

Agri-Dairy Products
Purchase, NY 914-697-9580

Asiamerica Ingredients
Westwood, NJ 201-497-5531

Processor, importer, exporter and distributor of bulk vitamins, amino acids, nutraceuticals, aromatic chemicals, food additives, herbs, mineral nutrients and pharmaceuticals.

Cargill Corn Milling
Naperville, IL 800-344-1633
Jarchem Industries
Newark, NJ 973-578-4560
Jungbunzlauer
Newton, MA 800-828-0062

Kalama Chemical
Kalama, WA 800-223-0035
Luyties Pharmacal Company
Saint Louis, MO 800-325-8080
Shekou Chemicals
Waltham, MA 781-893-6878
Silver Ferm Chemical
Seattle, WA 206-282-3376
Universal Preservachem Inc
Somerset, NJ 732-568-1266

Sodium Citrate

Asiamerica Ingredients
Westwood, NJ 201-497-5531

Processor, importer, exporter and distributor of bulk vitamins, amino acids, nutraceuticals, aromatic chemicals, food additives, herbs, mineral nutrients and pharmaceuticals.

Cargill Corn Milling
Naperville, IL 800-344-1633
Gadot Biochemical Industries
Rolling Meadows, IL 888-424-1424
International Chemical
Milltown, NJ 800-914-2436
Jungbunzlauer
Newton, MA 800-828-0062
Shekou Chemicals
Waltham, MA 781-893-6878
Universal Preservachem Inc
Somerset, NJ 732-568-1266

Sodium Lactate

Hawkins Inc
Minneapolis, MN 800-328-5460

Spirulina

Alternative Health & Herbs
Albany, OR 800-345-4152

Asiamerica Ingredients
Westwood, NJ 201-497-5531

Processor, importer, exporter and distributor of bulk vitamins, amino acids, nutraceuticals, aromatic chemicals, food additives, herbs, mineral nutrients and pharmaceuticals.

Cyanotech Corporation
Kailua Kona, HI 800-395-1353
Herb Connection
Springville, UT 801-489-4254

Stabilizers

Cargill Texturizing Solutions
Cedar Rapids, IA 877-650-7080
Mallet & Company
Carnegie, PA 800-245-2757
Marukan Vinegar (U.S.A.) Inc.
Paramount, CA 562-630-6060
P.L. Thomas
Morristown, NJ 973-984-0900

Colloids

Custom Designed

Cargill Texturizing Solutions
Cedar Rapids, IA. 877-650-7080

Lecithinated

Agri-Dairy Products
Purchase, NY 914-697-9580
American Health & Nutrition
Ann Arbor, MI 734-677-5570
Arnhem Group
Cranford, NJ 800-851-1052
McCain Foods USA
Colton, CA 800-938-7799
Universal Preservachem Inc
Somerset, NJ 732-568-1266

Yogurt

Cargill Texturizing Solutions
Cedar Rapids, IA. 877-650-7080
Johanna Foods
Flemington, NJ 800-727-6700
Maple Island
Saint Paul, MN 800-369-1022

Starches

ADM
Marshall, MN 800-328-4150
ADM Lecithin & Monoglycerides
Decatur, IL 800-637-5843
Anderson Custom Processing
New Ulm, MN. 877-588-4950
Cargill Corn Milling
Naperville, IL 800-344-1633
Cargill Texturizing Solutions
Cedar Rapids, IA. 877-650-7080
Domino Foods
West Palm Beach, FL 561-366-5150

EVERGREEN sweeteners
Your Total Sweetener Solution.

Evergreen Sweeteners, Inc
Hallandale Beach, FL 305-931-1321

Evergreen Sweeteners is a full service sweetener distributor serving the entire Southeastern United States. From bulk liquid sweeteners to bagged sweeteners, Evergreen provides its customers with industry-leading service and unsurpassed quality.

Marroquin Organic International
Santa Cruz, CA 831-423-3442
Marsan Foods
Toronto, ON 416-755-9262
Mississippi Blending Company
Keokuk, IA 800-758-4080
National Starch & Chemical Corporate Office
Bridgewater, NJ 908-685-5000
Norben Company
Willoughby, OH 888-466-7236
Raymond-Hadley Corporation
Spencer, NY 800-252-5220
Roquette America
Keokuk, IA 800-553-7035
Seydel International
Pendergrass, GA 706-693-2295
St. Lawrence Starch
Mississauga, ON. 905-271-8396
TIPIAK INC
Stamford, CT. 203-961-9117
Westin
Omaha, NE 800-228-6098

Arrowroot

American Key Food Products
Closter, NJ. 800-767-0237

Cassava

Cargill Texturizing Solutions
Cedar Rapids, IA. 877-650-7080

Corn

ADM
Marshall, MN 800-328-4150
American Health & Nutrition
Ann Arbor, MI 734-677-5570
American Key Food Products
Closter, NJ. 800-767-0237
Cargill Texturizing Solutions
Cedar Rapids, IA. 877-650-7080
Corn Products International
Westchester, IL 800-443-2746

EVERGREEN sweeteners
Your Total Sweetener Solution.

Evergreen Sweeteners, Inc
Hallandale Beach, FL 305-931-1321

Evergreen Sweeteners is a full service sweetener distributor serving the entire Southeastern United States. From bulk liquid sweeteners to bagged sweeteners, Evergreen provides its customers with industry-leading service and unsurpassed quality.

Grain Processing Corporation
Muscatine, IA 800-448-4472
Meelunie America
Farmington Hills, MI 248-473-2100
Mills Brothers International
Tukwila, WA 206-575-3000
Nacan Products
Brampton, ON. 905-454-4466
Westin
Omaha, NE 800-228-6098

Dextrin

ADM Corn Processing
Decatur, IL 800-553-8411
Cargill Texturizing Solutions
Cedar Rapids, IA. 877-650-7080
Penford Food Ingredients
Centennial, CO 303-649-1900
Seydel International
Pendergrass, GA 706-693-2295

Dusting

Cargill Texturizing Solutions
Cedar Rapids, IA. 877-650-7080
Mississippi Blending Company
Keokuk, IA 800-758-4080

High Amylose

Cargill Texturizing Solutions
Cedar Rapids, IA. 877-650-7080

Modified

Cargill Texturizing Solutions
Cedar Rapids, IA. 877-650-7080
Penford Food Ingredients
Centennial, CO 303-649-1900

Molding

Cargill Texturizing Solutions
Cedar Rapids, IA. 877-650-7080

Potato

Penford Food Ingredients
Centennial, CO 303-649-1900
Terry Foods Inc
Idaho Falls, ID 208-604-8143

Pregelatinized

A&B Ingredients
Fairfield, NJ 973-227-1390
Cargill Texturizing Solutions
Cedar Rapids, IA. 877-650-7080
Penford Food Ingredients
Centennial, CO 303-649-1900

Rice

A&B Ingredients
Fairfield, NJ 973-227-1390
American Key Food Products
Closter, NJ. 800-767-0237
AVEBE America, Inc.
Princeton, NJ

Modified

A&B Ingredients
Fairfield, NJ 973-227-1390

Tapioca

Cargill Texturizing Solutions
Cedar Rapids, IA. 877-650-7080
Penford Food Ingredients
Centennial, CO 303-649-1900

Thin Boiling

Cargill Texturizing Solutions
Cedar Rapids, IA. 877-650-7080

Waxy

Cargill Texturizing Solutions
Cedar Rapids, IA. 877-650-7080

Waxy Maize

Cargill Texturizing Solutions
Cedar Rapids, IA. 877-650-7080
Penford Food Ingredients
Centennial, CO 303-649-1900

Wheat

ADM Food Ingredients
Olathe, KS. 800-255-6637
Caremoli USA
Ames, IA. 515-233-1255

Starter Media

Cheese

Cargill Texturizing Solutions
Cedar Rapids, IA. 877-650-7080

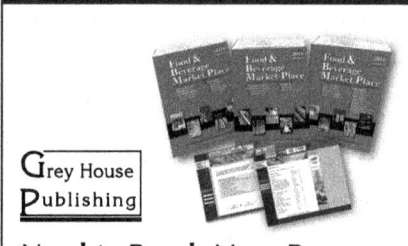

Hygeia Dairy Company
McAllen, TX 956-686-0511

Surfactants & Solubilizers

Solubilizers

P.L. Thomas
Morristown, NJ 973-984-0900

Sweeteners

Agri-Dairy Products
Purchase, NY 914-697-9580
Atlantic Chemicals Trading of North America, Inc.
Glendale, CA 818-246-0077
Dulcette Technologies
Lindenhurst, NY 631-752-8700
Escalade
Huntington, NY 631-659-3374

Evergreen Sweeteners, Inc
Hallandale Beach, FL 305-931-1321

Evergreen Sweeteners is a full service sweetener distributor serving the entire Southeastern United States. From bulk liquid sweeteners to bagged sweeteners, Evergreen provides its customers with industry-leading service and unsurpassed quality.

GLG Life Tech Corporation
Vancouver, BC 604-641-1368
GLG Life Tech Corporation
Vancouver, BC 604-669-2602
H&A Canada, Inc.
Toronto, ON 416-412-9518
Helm New York
Piscataway, NJ 732-981-1160
Ingredient Specialties
Exeter, CA 559-594-4380
Kenko International
Los Angeles, CA 323-721-8300
Marroquin Organic International
Santa Cruz, CA 831-423-3442
Natur Sweeteners, Inc.
Los Angeles, CA 310-445-0020
Rio Naturals
El Dorado Hills, CA 916-719-4514

Dextrose

ADM Corn Processing
Decatur, IL 800-553-8411
ADM Food Ingredients
Olathe, KS 800-255-6637
Agri-Dairy Products
Purchase, NY 914-697-9580
Cargill Corn Milling
Naperville, IL 800-344-1633
Corn Products International
Westchester, IL 800-443-2746
Domino Foods
West Palm Beach, FL 561-366-5150

Evergreen Sweeteners, Inc
Hallandale Beach, FL 305-931-1321

Evergreen Sweeteners is a full service sweetener distributor serving the entire Southeastern United States. From bulk liquid sweeteners to bagged sweeteners, Evergreen provides its customers with industry-leading service and unsurpassed quality.

Malt Products Corporation
Saddle Brook, NJ 800-526-0180
Roquette America
Keokuk, IA 800-553-7035
Westin
Omaha, NE 800-228-6098

Lactose

Agri-Dairy Products
Purchase, NY 914-697-9580

Asiamerica Ingredients
Westwood, NJ 201-497-5531

Processor, importer, exporter and distributor of bulk vitamins, amino acids, nutraceuticals, aromatic chemicals, food additives, herbs, mineral nutrients and pharmaceuticals.

Blossom Farm Products
Ridgewood, NJ 800-729-1818
Century Foods International
Sparta, WI 800-269-1901
Clofine Dairy & Food Products
Linwood, NJ 800-441-1001
Davisco International
Le Sueur, MN 800-757-7611
First District Association
Litchfield, MN 320-693-3236
Foremost Farms
Baraboo, WI 800-362-9196
Glanbia Foods
Twin Falls, ID 800-427-9477
Glanbia Nutritionals
Monroe, WI 800-336-2183
Grande Custom Ingredients Group
Brownsville, WI 800-678-3122
Hilmar Ingredients
Hilmar, CA 209-667-6076
Leprino Foods Company
Denver, CO 800-537-7466
Main Street Ingredients
La Crosse, WI 800-359-2345
Universal Preservachem Inc
Somerset, NJ 732-568-1266

Sorbitol

Agri-Dairy Products
Purchase, NY 914-697-9580
Archer Daniels Midland Company
Decatur, IL 800-637-5843

Asiamerica Ingredients
Westwood, NJ 201-497-5531

Processor, importer, exporter and distributor of bulk vitamins, amino acids, nutraceuticals, aromatic chemicals, food additives, herbs, mineral nutrients and pharmaceuticals.

EMD Chemicals
Gibbstown, NJ 800-364-4535
Roquette America
Keokuk, IA 800-553-7035
Universal Preservachem Inc
Somerset, NJ 732-568-1266

Tenderizers

A M Todd Company
Kalamazoo, MI 800-968-2603
ADM Food Ingredients
Olathe, KS 800-255-6637
Dean Distributors
Burlingame, CA 800-792-0816
Phamous Phloyd's Barbeque Sauce
Denver, CO 303-757-3285

Sentry Seasonings
Elmhurst, IL 630-530-5370

The product development experts of Sentry Seasonings are eager to offer the assistance and hands-on experience to food processors of all sizes. Sentry Seasonings will ensure the consistent high quality and repeat sales of your products, whether you choose one of our many off-the-shelf Bench Mark products or a modified version to meet your preferences. Sentry Seasonings can also duplicate and/or improve your present flavor profile; formulate, blend and package specifically for your requirements.

Three Vee Food & Syrup Company
Brooklyn, NY 800-801-7330
Wti, Inc.
Jefferson, GA 800-827-1727

Meat

A M Todd Company
Kalamazoo, MI 800-968-2603
ADM Food Ingredients
Olathe, KS 800-255-6637
Alltech Natural Food Division
Nicholasville, KY 859-885-9613
American Key Food Products
Closter, NJ 800-767-0237
Custom Culinary
Lombard, IL 800-621-8827
Enzyme Development Corporation
New York, NY 212-736-1580
Oregon Flavor Rack
Eugene, OR 541-342-2085
Sentry Seasonings
Elmhurst, IL 630-530-5370

The product development experts of Sentry Seasonings are eager to offer the assistance and hands-on experience to food processors of all sizes. Sentry Seasonings will ensure the consistent high quality and repeat sales of your products, whether you choose one of our many off-the-shelf Bench Mark products or a modified version to meet your preferences. Sentry Seasonings can also duplicate and/or improve your present flavor profile; formulate, blend and package specifically for your requirements.

Texas Coffee Company
Beaumont, TX 800-259-3400
Three Vee Food & Syrup Company
Brooklyn, NY 800-801-7330
Universal Concepts
Lauderhill, FL 918-367-0197
Valley Research
South Bend, IN 800-522-8110
World Flavors
Warminster, PA 215-672-4400

Thickeners

Cargill Texturizing Solutions
Cedar Rapids, IA 877-650-7080
Gelnex Gelatins
Manhasset, NY 516-869-1623

Gelatin

Asiamerica Ingredients
Westwood, NJ 201-497-5531

Processor, importer, exporter and distributor of bulk vitamins, amino acids, nutraceuticals, aromatic chemicals, food additives, herbs, mineral nutrients and pharmaceuticals.

Cangel
Toronto, ON 800-267-4795
Con Yeager Spice Company
Zelienople, PA 800-222-2460
Dynagel
Calumet City, IL 888-396-2435
Erba Food Products
Brooklyn, NY 718-272-7700

First Foods Company
Dallas, TX 214-637-0214
Gelita USA
Sergeant Bluff, IA 712-943-5516
Gelita/Kind & Knox Gelatine
Sergeant Bluff, IA 712-943-5516
Gelnex Gelatins
Manhasset, NY 516-869-1623
GMI Products
Plantation, FL 800-999-9373
GMI Products/Originates
Sunrise, FL 800-999-9373
Golden Fluff Popcorn Company
Lakewood, NJ 732-367-5448
Inter-American Products
Cincinnati, OH 800-645-2233
Kraft Canada Headquarters
Don Mills, ON 888-572-3806
Leiner Davis Gelatin
Jericho, NY 516-942-4940
Marquez Brothers International
Hanford, CA 559-584-8000
Maryland & Virginia Milk Producers Cooperative
Reston, VA 703-742-4250
Milligan & Higgins
Johnstown, NY 518-762-4638
Nitta Gelatin NA
Rochelle Park, NJ 800-278-7680
Protein Products Inc
Whitehall, PA 800-776-8422
Rousselot Gelatin
Mukwonago, WI 262-363-2789
Shionogi Qualicaps
Whitsett, NC 800-227-7853
SKW Nature Products
Langhorne, PA 215-702-1000
Spring Glen Fresh Foods
Ephrata, PA 800-641-2853
Synergy Foods
West Bloomfield, MI 313-849-2900
Tessenderlo Kerley
Phoenix, AZ 800-669-0559
Tova Industries
Louisville, KY 888-532-8682
Vyse Gelatin Company
Schiller Park, IL 800-533-2152
White Coffee Corporation
Astoria, NY 800-221-0140

Toppings

Al-Rite Fruits & Syrups
Miami, FL 305-652-2540
Bake'n Joy Foods
North Andover, MA 800-666-4937
Baker & Baker
Schaumburg, IL 800-593-5777
Baldwin Richardson Foods
Frankfort, IL 866-644-2732

Liquid ingredient manufacturer specializing in signature sauces, dessert toppings, beverage/pancake syrups, specialty fruit fillings and condiments.

Berner Foods, Inc.
Roscoe, IL 800-819-8199
C.F. Burger Creamery
Detroit, MI 800-229-2322
Consolidated Mills
Houston, TX 713-896-4196
Dark Tickle Company
St Lunaire-Griquet, NL 709-623-2354
Golden State Foods
Irvine, CA 949-252-2000
Gumpert's Canada
Mississauga, ON 800-387-9324
Instant Products of America
Columbus, IN 812-372-9100
Kerry Ingredients
Blue Earth, MN 507-526-7575
Mrs. Prindable's Handmade Confections
Niles, IL 888-215-1100
O Chili Frozen Foods Inc
Northbrook, IL 847-562-1991
Paulaur Corporation
Cranbury, NJ 888-398-8844
Phillips Syrup Corporation
Westlake, OH 800-350-8443
Presto Avoset Group
Claremont, CA 909-399-0062
Richardson Foods Corporation
Macedon, NY 315-986-2807
Shine Companies
Spring, TX 281-353-8392
Stearns & Lehman
Mansfield, OH 800-533-2722
World's Finest Chocolate
Chicago, IL 888-821-8452

Cakes & Donuts

Signature Brands
Ocala, FL 800-456-9573

Colored Starch Bits

Kerry Ingredients
Blue Earth, MN 507-526-7575

Confectionery

Kerry Ingredients
Blue Earth, MN 507-526-7575
Paulaur Corporation
Cranbury, NJ 888-398-8844
Ribble Production
Warminster, PA 215-674-1706

Crisp Rice

Kerry Ingredients
Blue Earth, MN 507-526-7575

Crunch

American Almond Products Company
Brooklyn, NY 800-825-6663
Kerry Ingredients
Blue Earth, MN 507-526-7575
Nature's Hand
Burnsville, MN 952-890-6033
Paulaur Corporation
Cranbury, NJ 888-398-8844

Dessert

Al-Rite Fruits & Syrups
Miami, FL 305-652-2540

Alamance Foods/Triton Water Company
Burlington, NC 800-476-9111
American Almond Products Company
Brooklyn, NY 800-825-6663
American Classic Ice Cream Company
Bay Shore, NY 631-666-1000
Aunt Aggie De's Pralines
Sinton, TX. 888-772-5463
Baldwin Richardson Foods
Frankfort, IL 866-644-2732

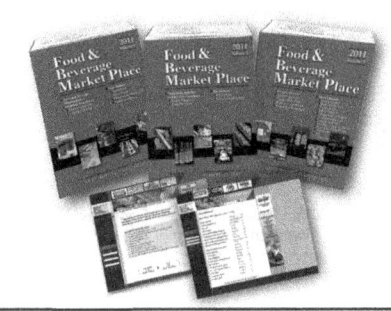

Liquid ingredient manufacturer specializing in signature sauces, dessert toppings, beverage/pancake syrups, specialty fruit fillings and condiments.

Brighams
Arlington, MA 800-274-4426
Broughton Foods
Marietta, OH. 800-283-2479
C.F. Burger Creamery
Detroit, MI 800-229-2322
Calhoun Bend Mill
Alexandria, LA 800-519-6455
California Custom Fruits & Flavors
Irwindale, CA 877-558-0056
Carole's Cheesecake Company
Toronto, ON 416-256-0000
Chocolaterie Bernard Callebaut
Calgary, AB. 800-661-8367
ConAgra Grocery Products
Irvine, CA 714-680-1000
ConAgra Refrigerated Foods International
Omaha, NE 800-624-4724
Consolidated Mills
Houston, TX 713-896-4196
Country Fresh Food & Confections, Inc.
Oliver Springs, TN 800-545-8782
Cremes Unlimited
Matteson, IL 800-227-3637
Cuisinary Fine Foods
Irving, TX. 888-283-5303
Durkee-Mower
Lynn, MA 781-593-8007
Felbro Food Products
Los Angeles, CA. 800-335-2761
Fresh Dairy Direct/Morningstar
Dallas, TX. 800-395-7004
Gold Coast Ingredients
Commerce, CA 800-352-8673
Golden Foods
Commerce, CA 800-350-2462
Golden West Fruit Company
Commerce, CA 323-726-9419
Gourmet Central
Romney, WV. 800-984-3722
H. Fox & Company
Brooklyn, NY 718-385-4600
H.C. Brill Company
Tucker, GA 800-241-8526
Hanan Products Company
Hicksville, NY 516-938-1000
Heinz Company of Canada
North York, ON. 877-574-3469
Homemade By Dorothy
Boise, ID 208-375-3720
I Rice & Company
Philadelphia, PA 800-232-6022
Industrial Products
Defiance, OH 800-251-3033
Instant Products of America
Columbus, IN 812-372-9100
Instantwhip Foods
San Antonio, TX. 800-544-9447
Instantwhip: Arizona
Phoenix, AZ 800-454-7878
Instantwhip: Chicago
Chicago, IL 800-933-2500
J.M. Smucker Company
Orrville, OH 888-550-9555
Jogue Inc
Northville, MI. 800-521-3888
Johnson's Food Products
Dorchester, MA. 617-265-3400
Kalva Corporation
Gurnee, IL. 800-525-8220
Kerry Ingredients
Blue Earth, MN. 507-526-7575
Kraus & Company
Commerce Township, MI 800-662-5871
Lyons-Magnus
Fresno, CA 559-268-5966
Masterson Company
Milwaukee, WI 414-647-1132
Michigan Dessert Corporation
Oak Park, MI. 800-328-8632
Newport Flavours & Fragrances
Orange, CA 714-744-3700
Oak State Products
Wenona, IL 815-853-4348
Ohio Processors Company
London, OH 740-852-9243
Oregon Hill Farms
Saint Helens, OR. 800-243-4541
Parker Products
Fort Worth, TX 800-433-5749
Paulaur Corporation
Cranbury, NJ 888-398-8844
Pearson's Berry Farm
Bowden, AB 403-224-3011
Pecan Deluxe Candy Company
Dallas, TX. 800-733-3589
Phillips Syrup Corporation
Westlake, OH 800-350-8443
Rich Products Corporation
Hilliard, OH. 614-771-1117
Rich Products Corporation
Claremont, CA 909-621-4711
Rich Products of Canada
Buffalo, NY. 800-457-4247
Rod's Food Products
City of Industry, CA 909-839-8925
Rose Brand Corporation
Brooklyn, NY 800-854-5356
Rowena's
Norfolk, VA. 800-627-8699
Sea Breeze Fruit Flavors
Towaco, NJ 800-732-2733
Spruce Mountain Blueberries
West Rockport, ME. 207-236-3538
Steel's Gourmet Foods, Ltd.
Bridgeport, PA 800-678-3357
Swatt Baking Company
Olean, NY. 800-370-6656
The Great San Saba RiverPecan Company
San Saba, TX 800-621-9121
Three Vee Food & Syrup Company
Brooklyn, NY 800-801-7330
Tiller Foods Company
Dayton, OH. 937-435-4601
Tom & Sally's Handmade Chocolates
Brattleboro, VT. 800-827-0800
Tone Products Company
Melrose Park, IL. 708-681-3660
Top Hat Company
Wilmette, IL 847-256-6565
Tres Classique
Ukiah, CA. 888-644-5127
Tropical
Marietta, GA. 800-544-3762
Valley Grain Products
Madera, CA. 559-675-3400
Vanlaw Food Products
Fullerton, CA 714-870-9091
Vermont BS
Hinesburg, VT. 802-482-2152
Wax Orchards
Seattle, WA 800-634-6132
Western Syrup Company
Santa Fe Springs, CA 562-921-4485
White-Stokes Company
Chicago, IL 800-978-6537
Williamsburg Chocolatier
Williamsburg, VA 757-253-1474

Fruit

E.D. Smith Foods Ltd
Winona, ON 800-263-9246
Kerry Ingredients
Blue Earth, MN. 507-526-7575

Graham

Kerry Ingredients
Blue Earth, MN. 507-526-7575

Granola

Kerry Ingredients
Blue Earth, MN. 507-526-7575

Meringue

Zuccaro's Fruit & Produce Company
Minneapolis, MN 612-333-1122

Non-Fruit

Kerry Ingredients
Blue Earth, MN. 507-526-7575
O Chili Frozen Foods Inc
Northbrook, IL 847-562-1991

Protein Clusters

Kerry Ingredients
Blue Earth, MN. 507-526-7575

Soy Crumbs

Kerry Ingredients
Blue Earth, MN. 507-526-7575

Specialty Bread Crumbs

Kerry Ingredients
Blue Earth, MN. 507-526-7575

Sprinkles

Erba Food Products
Brooklyn, NY 718-272-7700
Kerry Ingredients
Blue Earth, MN. 507-526-7575
Randag & Associates Inc
Elmhurst, IL 630-530-2830
Weaver Nut Company
Ephrata, PA 717-738-3781
Xcell International Corporation
Lemont, IL 800-722-7751

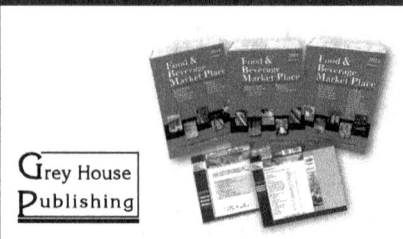

Whipped

Broughton Foods
Marietta, OH 800-283-2479
Bunge Canada
Oakville, ON. 800-361-3043
C.F. Burger Creamery
Detroit, MI 800-229-2322
CanAmera Foods
Oakville, ON. 905-825-7900
Consun Food Industries
Elyria, OH. 440-322-6301
Fieldbrook Farms
Dunkirk, NY 800-333-0805
Henkel Corporation
Countryside, IL. 800-328-6199
Johnson's Food Products
Dorchester, MA. 617-265-3400
Now & Zen
Mill Valley, CA. 800-335-1959
Ohio Processors Company
London, OH 740-852-9243
Rich Products of Canada
Buffalo, NY. 800-457-4247
Schneider's Dairy Holdings Inc
Pittsburgh, PA. 412-881-3525
Tiller Foods Company
Dayton, OH. 937-435-4601

Dairy

Brighams
Arlington, MA 800-274-4426
C.F. Burger Creamery
Detroit, MI 800-229-2322
Elgin Dairy Foods
Chicago, IL 800-786-9900
Instantwhip: Chicago
Chicago, IL 800-933-2500
Johnson's Food Products
Dorchester, MA. 617-265-3400

Non-Dairy

Broughton Foods
Marietta, OH 800-283-2479
ConAgra Grocery Products
Irvine, CA 714-680-1000
Elgin Dairy Foods
Chicago, IL 800-786-9900
Instantwhip: Chicago
Chicago, IL 800-933-2500
Johnson's Food Products
Dorchester, MA. 617-265-3400

Vitamins & Supplements

Aloecorp
Keene, NH. 603-352-0650
Embria Health Science
Ankeny, IA 877-362-7421
Fallwood Corp
White Plains, NY 914-304-4065
Fenchem Enterprises
Chino, CA. 909-627-5268
Great Earth Chemical
Portland, OR 608-752-7417
Latitude
Huntington, NY 631-659-3374

A

Asiamerica Ingredients
Westwood, NJ 201-497-5531

Processor, importer, exporter and distributor of bulk vitamins, amino acids, nutraceuticals, aromatic chemicals, food additives, herbs, mineral nutrients and pharmaceuticals.

Healthwave
Santa Barbara, CA 805-899-4240
Synergy Plus
Freehold, NJ 732-308-3000

Beta Carotene

Asiamerica Ingredients
Westwood, NJ 201-497-5531

Processor, importer, exporter and distributor of bulk vitamins, amino acids, nutraceuticals, aromatic chemicals, food additives, herbs, mineral nutrients and pharmaceuticals.

Biotin

Asiamerica Ingredients
Westwood, NJ 201-497-5531

Processor, importer, exporter and distributor of bulk vitamins, amino acids, nutraceuticals, aromatic chemicals, food additives, herbs, mineral nutrients and pharmaceuticals.

C

Asiamerica Ingredients
Westwood, NJ 201-497-5531

Processor, importer, exporter and distributor of bulk vitamins, amino acids, nutraceuticals, aromatic chemicals, food additives, herbs, mineral nutrients and pharmaceuticals.

ChildLife-Nutrition for Kids
Los Angeles, CA. 800-993-0332
Naturally Vitamin Supplements
Phoenix, AZ 800-899-4499
Vitech America Corporation
Kent, WA. 253-859-5985

Ascorbic Acid

World Ginseng Center
San Francisco, CA 800-747-8808

Calcium

Allied Custom Gypsum Company
Norman, OK 800-624-5963
American Micronutrients
Kansas City, MO. 816-254-6000

Asiamerica Ingredients
Westwood, NJ 201-497-5531

Processor, importer, exporter and distributor of bulk vitamins, amino acids, nutraceuticals, aromatic chemicals, food additives, herbs, mineral nutrients and pharmaceuticals.

Specialty Minerals
Bethlehem, PA 800-801-1031

E - Tocopherol

Asiamerica Ingredients
Westwood, NJ 201-497-5531

Processor, importer, exporter and distributor of bulk vitamins, amino acids, nutraceuticals, aromatic chemicals, food additives, herbs, mineral nutrients and pharmaceuticals.

JR Carlson Laboratories
Arlington Hts, IL 888-234-5656
World Ginseng Center
San Francisco, CA 800-747-8808

Inositol

Asiamerica Ingredients
Westwood, NJ 201-497-5531

Processor, importer, exporter and distributor of bulk vitamins, amino acids, nutraceuticals, aromatic chemicals, food additives, herbs, mineral nutrients and pharmaceuticals.

Tabco Enterprises
Pomona, CA 909-623-4565

Medical Nutritionals

Alternative Health & Herbs
Albany, OR 800-345-4152
Apotheca Naturale
Woodbine, IA 800-736-3130

Asiamerica Ingredients
Westwood, NJ 201-497-5531

Processor, importer, exporter and distributor of bulk vitamins, amino acids, nutraceuticals, aromatic chemicals, food additives, herbs, mineral nutrients and pharmaceuticals.

Atrium Biotech
Fairfield, NJ 866-628-2355
Champion Nutrition
Sunrise, FL 800-225-4831
Chattem Chemicals
Chattanooga, TN 423-822-5001
Eatem Foods Company
Vineland, NJ 800-683-2836
Green Turtle Bay Vitamin Company
Summit, NJ 800-887-8535
Mineral & Pigment Solutions
South Plainfield, NJ 800-732-0562
National Vinegar Company
Houston, TX 713-223-4214
Penta Manufacturing Company
Livingston, NJ 973-740-2300
Tova Industries
Louisville, KY 888-532-8682
Westar Nutrition Corporation
Costa Mesa, CA 800-645-1868

Mineral Blends

Asiamerica Ingredients
Westwood, NJ 201-497-5531

Processor, importer, exporter and distributor of bulk vitamins, amino acids, nutraceuticals, aromatic chemicals, food additives, herbs, mineral nutrients and pharmaceuticals.

M-CAP Technologies
Wilmington, DE 302-695-5329
World Nutrition
Scottsdale, AZ 800-548-2710

Minerals

Acta Health Products
Sunnyvale, CA 408-732-6830
ADH Health Products
Congers, NY 845-268-0027
Advanced Nutritional Research, Inc.
Ellicottville, NY 800-836-0644
Alacer Corporation
Foothill Ranch, CA 800-854-0249
Albion Laboratories
Clearfield, UT 866-243-5283
Alta Health Products
Idaho City, ID 800-423-4155
Ameri-Kal Inc
Wichita Falls, TX 940-322-5400
Anabol Naturals
Santa Cruz, CA 800-426-2265

Asiamerica Ingredients
Westwood, NJ 201-497-5531

Processor, importer, exporter and distributor of bulk vitamins, amino acids, nutraceuticals, aromatic chemicals, food additives, herbs, mineral nutrients and pharmaceuticals.

Beverly International Nutrition
Cold Spring, KY 800-888-3364
Bio-Tech Pharmacal
Fayetteville, AR 800-345-1199
Body Ammo Research Center
Byron, CA 925-513-8514
Champion Nutrition
Sunrise, FL 800-225-4831
ChildLife-Nutrition for Kids
Los Angeles, CA 800-993-0332
Coating Place
Verona, WI 608-845-9521
Connection Source
Alpharetta, GA 770-667-1051
Delavau LLC
Philadelphia, PA 215-671-1400
Designed Nutritional Products
Orem, UT 801-224-4518
Eidon Mineral Supplements
Poway, CA 800-700-1169
Foremost Farms
Baraboo, WI 800-362-9196
Fortitech
Schenectady, NY 800-950-5156
Grow Company
Ridgefield, NJ 201-941-8777
Healthy'N Fit Nutrition als
Croton on Hudson, NY 800-338-5200
Herbal Products & Development
Aptos, CA 831-688-8706
Jamieson Laboratories
Windosr, ON 519-974-8482
JR Carlson Laboratories
Arlington Hts, IL 888-234-5656
Jungbunzlauer
Newton, MA 800-828-0062
Michael's Naturopathic
San Antonio, TX 800-525-9643
Milwhite
Brownsville, TX 956-547-1970
Mineral & Pigment Solutions
South Plainfield, NJ 800-732-0562
Naturally Vitamin Supplements
Phoenix, AZ 800-899-4499
Nature's Sunshine Products Company
Provo, UT 800-223-8225
NatureMost Laboratories
Middletown, CT 800-234-2112
NBTY
Ronkonkoma, NY 800-920-6090
Now Foods
Bloomingdale, IL 888-669-3663
Nutricepts
Burnsville, MN 800-949-9060
Nutritech Corporation
Santa Barbara, CA 800-235-5727
Nutrition 21
Purchase, NY 914-701-4500
P.L. Thomas
Morristown, NJ 973-984-0900
Paragon Laboratories
Torrance, CA 800-231-3670
Particle Dynamics
Saint Louis, MO 800-452-4682
Performance Labs
Calabasas, CA 800-848-2537
PMP Fermentation Products
Peoria, IL 800-558-1031
Pro. Pac. Labs
Ogden, UT 888-277-6722
Protein Research Associates
Livermore, CA 800-948-1991
Randal Nutritional Products
Santa Rosa, CA 800-221-1697
Seppic
Newark, NJ 877-737-7421
Universal Formulas
Kalamazoo, MI 800-342-6960
US Food & Pharmaceuticals
Madison, WI 608-278-1293
USA Laboratories
Burns, TN 800-489-4872
Vitamin Power
Freeport, NY 800-645-6567
Watson Inc
West Haven, CT 800-388-3481

Niacin

Asiamerica Ingredients
Westwood, NJ 201-497-5531

Processor, importer, exporter and distributor of bulk vitamins, amino acids, nutraceuticals, aromatic chemicals, food additives, herbs, mineral nutrients and pharmaceuticals.

EMD Chemicals
Gibbstown, NJ 800-364-4535
NuNaturals
Eugene, OR 800-753-4372

Nutraceuticals

ADM Food Ingredients
Olathe, KS 800-255-6637
ADM Nutraceuticals
Decatur, IL 800-510-2178
AM Todd Company
Kalamazoo, MI 800-968-2603
Amcan Industries
Elmsford, NY 914-347-4838
American Supplement Technologies
Phoenix, AZ 888-469-0242
AquaTec Development
Sugar Land, TX 281-491-0808

Asiamerica Ingredients
Westwood, NJ 201-497-5531

Processor, importer, exporter and distributor of bulk vitamins, amino acids, nutraceuticals, aromatic chemicals, food additives, herbs, mineral nutrients and pharmaceuticals.

Assets Health Foods
Hillsborough, NJ 888-849-2048
Atlantic Quality Spice &Seasonings
New Brunswick, NJ 800-584-0422
BASF Corporation
Florham Park, NJ 800-526-1072
Basic American Foods
Blackfoot, ID 800-227-4050
Bio-Foods
Pine Brook, NJ 973-808-5856
Bio-Tech Pharmacal
Fayetteville, AR 800-345-1199
BioTech Corporation
Glastonbury, CT 800-880-7188
Century Foods International
Sparta, WI 800-269-1901

Cyanotech Corporation
Kailua Kona, HI 800-395-1353
Dulcette Technologies
Lindenhurst, NY 631-752-8700
Embria Health Science
Ankeny, IA 877-362-7421
Fallwood Corp
White Plains, NY 914-304-4065
Farbest-Tallman Foods Corporation
Montvale, NJ. 201-573-4900
Genesis Research Corporation
Lake Bluff, IL 888-225-2201
Innovative Food Solutions LLC
Columbus, OH 800-884-3314
Institut Rosell/Lallemand
Montreal, QC 800-452-4364
Jarrow Industries
Santa Fe Springs, CA 562-906-1919
Juice Guys
Cambridge, MA 800-896-8667
Kerry Ingredients
Blue Earth, MN. 507-526-7575
Mineral & Pigment Solutions
South Plainfield, NJ 800-732-0562
Natra US
Chula Vista, CA 800-262-6216
Naturex Inc
South Hackensack, NJ 201-440-5000
Naturex Inc.
South Hackensack, NJ 201-440-5000
Nutraceutics Corporation
Saint Louis, MO 314-664-6684
Nutranique Labs
Santa Rosa, CA. 707-545-9017
P.L. Thomas
Morristown, NJ. 973-984-0900
QBI
South Plainfield, NJ 908-668-0088
Soluble Products Company
Lakewood, NJ. 732-364-8855
SoyLife Division
Edina, MN. 952-920-7700
Trans-Packers Services Corporation
Brooklyn, NY 877-787-8837
Unique Ingredients
Naches, WA. 509-653-1991
Vitarich Laboratories
Naples, FL. 800-817-9999
Vivolac Cultures Corporation
Indianapolis, IN 317-356-8460
Westar Nutrition Corporation
Costa Mesa, CA 800-645-1868

Nutritional Supplements

ADH Health Products
Congers, NY 845-268-0027
Alfer Laboratories
Chatsworth, CA 818-709-0737
Alta Health Products
Boise, ID. 800-423-4155
Ameri-Kal Inc
Wichita Falls, TX 940-322-5400
American Health
Ronkonkoma, NY. 800-445-7137
American Supplement Technologies
Phoenix, AZ 888-469-0242
Amerifit Brands, Inc.
Cromwell, CT 800-722-3476
Amrion
Boulder, CO 800-627-7775
Anabol Naturals
Santa Cruz, CA. 800-426-2265
Arizona Natural Products
Phoenix, AZ 602-997-6098
Arizona Nutritional Supplements
Chandler, AZ. 888-742-7675

Atrium Biotech
Fairfield, NJ 866-628-2355
Belmont Chemicals
Clifton, NJ. 800-722-5070
Bio-Foods
Pine Brook, NJ 973-808-5856
BioSynergy
Boise, ID. 800-554-7145
Body Ammo Research Center
Byron, CA. 925-513-8514
Botanical Laboratories
Ferndale, WA 800-232-4005
Bricker Labs
Chandler, AZ. 800-274-2537
Bristol Myers-Squibb Company
New York, NY 212-546-2852
Broadmoor Labs
Ventura, CA. 800-822-3712
Century Foods International
Sparta, WI 800-269-1901
Champion Nutrition
Sunrise, FL 800-225-4831
CHR Hansen
Stoughton, WI. 608-877-8970
Cognis
Cincinnati, OH 513-641-4355
Cyanotech Corporation
Kailua Kona, HI 800-395-1353
Dean Distributors
Burlingame, CA 800-792-0816
Dr. Christopher's Original Foods
Spanish Fork, UT 800-453-1406
Eclipse Sports Supplements
Clarks Summit, PA 866-898-0885
Eco Foods
St Charles, IL 866-326-1646
Elan Nutrition
Grand Rapids, MI 616-940-6000
Embria Health Science
Ankeny, IA 877-362-7421
Esteem Products
Bellevue, WA 800-255-7631
Fallwood Corp
White Plains, NY 914-304-4065
Food Sciences Corporation
Mount Laurel, NJ 800-320-7928
FoodScience of Vermont
Essex Junction, VT. 800-874-9444
Gehl Guernsey Farms
Germantown, WI. 800-434-5713
Herbal Products & Development
Aptos, CA 831-688-8706
Impact Nutrition
Aurora, CO 720-374-7111
Integrated Therapeutics
Lake Oswego, OR. 800-648-4755
JSL Foods
Los Angeles, CA. 800-745-3236
Klaire Laboratories
Reno, NV 888-488-2488
Lewis Laboratories International
Westport, CT. 800-243-6020
Lifestar Millennium
Sedona, AZ 877-422-4739
Maitake Products
East Rutherford, NJ 800-747-7418
Matrix Health Products
Santee, CA 888-736-5609
Mead Johnson Pediatrics Nutritional Group
Evansville, IN. 812-429-5000
Mega Pro International
St George, UT. 800-541-9469
Metagenics, Inc.
San Clemente, CA. 800-621-6070
MLO/GeniSoy Products Company
Tulas, OK 866-606-3829
Natural Balance
Englewood, CO. 800-624-4260
Naturally Scientific
Leonia, NJ. 888-428-0700
Nature's Best Food Supplement
Hauppauge, NY 800-345-2378
Nature's Nutrition
Melbourne, FL 800-242-1115
ND Labs Inc
Lynbrook, NY. 888-263-5227
Nestle USA Inc
Glendale, CA 800-225-2270
New Horizon Foods
Union City, CA. 510-489-8600
Nurture
Devon, PA. 888-395-3300

Nutri-West
Douglas, WY. 800-443-3333
Nutritional Laboratories International
Missoula, MT 406-273-5493
Nutritional Life Support Systems
, OH. 800-533-4372
Nutritional Specialties
Orange, CA. 800-333-6168
Nutritional Supply Corporation
Carson City, NV 888-541-3997
O'Donnell Formula
San Marcos, CA 800-736-1991
Odwalla
Half Moon Bay, CA 800-639-2552
Orange Peel Enterprises
Vero Beach, FL. 800-643-1210
P-Bee Products
Oak Harbor, WA 800-322-5572
Pacific Nutritional
Vancouver, WA 360-253-3197
Pacific Standard Distributors
Sandy, OR. 503-668-0057
Paragon Laboratories
Torrance, CA. 800-231-3670
Performance Labs
Calabasas, CA. 800-848-2537
Phoenician Herbals
Scottsdale, AZ. 800-966-8144
Phyto-Technologies
Woodbine, IA 877-809-3404
Pioneer Nutritional Formulas
Shelburne Falls, MA. 800-458-8483
Premier Nutrition
Carlsbad, CA. 888-836-8977
Prosource
Alexandria, MN 320-763-2470
Protein Research Associates
Livermore, CA 800-948-1991
Quaker Oats Company
Chicago, IL 800-367-6287
Randal Nutritional Products
Santa Rosa, CA. 800-221-1697
Royal Body Care
Irving, TX 972-893-4000
Royal Products
Scottsdale, AZ. 480-948-2509
Shaklee Corporation
Pleasanton, CA 800-742-5533
Soft Gel Technologies
Commerce, CA 800-360-7484
Solgar Vitamin & Herb
Leonia, NJ. 201-944-2311
Source Food Technology
Burnsville, MN 612-890-6366
SportPharma USA
Concord, CA. 925-686-1451
St. John's Botanicals
Bowie, MD 301-262-5302
Stimo-O-Stam, Ltd.
Covington, LA 800-562-7514
Tabco Enterprises
Pomona, CA 909-623-4565
Twinlab
New York, NY 800-645-5626
Uas Laboratories
Eden Prairie, MN 800-422-3371
USA Laboratories
Burns, TN 800-489-4872
Valley Research
South Bend, IN 800-522-8110
Vita-Pure
Roselle, NJ 908-245-1212
Vitatech International
Tustin, CA. 714-832-9700
Vitech America Corporation
Kent, WA. 253-859-5985
Wakunaga of America
Mission Viejo, CA 800-421-2998
WCC Honey Marketing
City of Industry, CA 626-855-3086
Wilke International
Shawnee Mission, KS. 800-779-5545
World Ginseng Center
San Francisco, CA 800-747-8808
Zone Perfect Nutrition Company
Columbus, OH 800-390-6690

Pantothenic Acid

Asiamerica Ingredients
Westwood, NJ ... 201-497-5531

Processor, importer, exporter and distributor of bulk vitamins, amino acids, nutraceuticals, aromatic chemicals, food additives, herbs, mineral nutrients and pharmaceuticals.

Protein Supplements

Alkinco
New York, NY ... 800-424-7118

Asiamerica Ingredients
Westwood, NJ ... 201-497-5531

Processor, importer, exporter and distributor of bulk vitamins, amino acids, nutraceuticals, aromatic chemicals, food additives, herbs, mineral nutrients and pharmaceuticals.

Belmont Chemicals
Clifton, NJ ... 800-722-5070

Bio-Foods
Pine Brook, NJ ... 973-808-5856

Croda
Edison, NJ ... 732-417-0800

Energenetics International
Keokuk, IA ... 217-453-2340

Flavex Protein Ingredients
Cranford, NJ ... 800-851-1052

Hilmar Ingredients
Hilmar, CA ... 209-667-6076

Impact Nutrition
Aurora, CO ... 720-374-7111

Innovative Health Products
Largo, FL ... 800-654-2347

Mariner Neptune Fish & Seafood Company
Winnipeg, NB ... 800-668-8862

World Ginseng Center
San Francisco, CA ... 800-747-8808

Fortification Protein

Cargill Texturizing Solutions
Cedar Rapids, IA ... 877-650-7080

Supplements

Acta Health Products
Sunnyvale, CA ... 408-732-6830

Action Labs
Park City, UT ... 800-669-8877

ADH Health Products
Congers, NY ... 845-268-0027

Advanced Nutritional Research, Inc.
Ellicottville, NY ... 800-836-0644

Agger Fish
Brooklyn, NY ... 718-855-1717

Albion Laboratories
Clearfield, UT ... 866-243-5283

Alfer Laboratories
Chatsworth, CA ... 818-709-0737

Alkinco
New York, NY ... 800-424-7118

Aloe Farms
Harlingen, TX ... 800-262-6771

Amt Labs
North Salt Lake, UT ... 801-299-1661

Anabol Naturals
Santa Cruz, CA ... 800-426-2265

Archon Vitamin Corporation
Irvington, NJ ... 800-349-1700

Arizona Natural Products
Phoenix, AZ ... 602-997-6098

Asiamerica Ingredients
Westwood, NJ ... 201-497-5531

Processor, importer, exporter and distributor of bulk vitamins, amino acids, nutraceuticals, aromatic chemicals, food additives, herbs, mineral nutrients and pharmaceuticals.

Atlantic Laboratories
Waldoboro, ME ... 207-832-5376

Atrium Biotech
Fairfield, NJ ... 866-628-2355

Beehive Botanicals, Inc.
Hayward, WI ... 800-233-4483

Belmont Chemicals
Clifton, NJ ... 800-722-5070

BestSweet
Mooresville, NC ... 888-211-5530

Bio San Laboratories/MegaFood
Derry, NH ... 800-848-5022

Body Ammo Research Center
Byron, CA ... 925-513-8514

Brassica Protection Products
Baltimore, MD ... 877-747-1277

Cactu Life Inc
Corona Del Mar, CA ... 800-500-1713

Century Foods International
Sparta, WI ... 800-269-1901

Champion Nutrition
Sunrise, FL ... 800-225-4831

CVC Specialties
Vernon, CA ... 800-421-6175

Dean Distributors
Burlingame, CA ... 800-792-0816

Delavau LLC
Philadelphia, PA ... 215-671-1400

Doctors Best
San Clemente, CA ... 800-333-6977

Eckhart Corporation
Novato, CA ... 415-892-3880

En Garde Health Products
Reseda, CA

Food Reserves
Concordia, MO ... 800-944-1511

Gadot Biochemical Industries
Rolling Meadows, IL ... 888-424-1424

GCI Nutrients (USA)
Foster City, CA ... 650-697-4700

Global Health Laboratories
Amityville, NY ... 631-777-2134

Herb Connection
Springville, UT ... 801-489-4254

Herbal Products & Development
Aptos, CA ... 831-688-8706

Heritage Store
Virginia Beach, VA ... 800-862-2923

Hillestad Pharmaceuticals
Woodruff, WI ... 800-535-7742

Innovative Health Products
Largo, FL ... 800-654-2347

IVC American Vitamin
Freehold, NJ ... 800-666-8482

Jo Mar Laboratories
Campbell, CA ... 800-538-4545

JR Carlson Laboratories
Arlington Hts, IL ... 888-234-5656

National Enzyme Company
Forsyth, MO ... 800-825-8545

Natural Balance
Englewood, CO ... 800-624-4260

Nature's Herbs
Merritt, BC ... 800-437-2257

Nature's Plus
Long Beach, CA ... 562-494-2500

Nature's Provision Company
Olivebridge, NY ... 845-657-6020

NBTY
Ronkonkoma, NY ... 800-920-6090

Nutricepts
Burnsville, MN ... 800-949-9060

Nutritional Counselors of America
Spencer, TN ... 931-946-3600

Nutriwest
Douglas, WY ... 800-443-3333

O'Donnell Formula
San Marcos, CA ... 800-736-1991

Old Fashioned Natural Products
Santa Ana, CA ... 800-552-9045

Pharmavite Corporation
Mission Hills, CA ... 800-276-2878

Pro Form Labs
Orinda, CA ... 925-299-9000

Protein Research Associates
Livermore, CA ... 800-948-1991

Randal Nutritional Products
Santa Rosa, CA ... 800-221-1697

Royal Body Care
Irving, TX ... 972-893-4000

Source Naturals
Scotts Valley, CA ... 800-815-2333

Sweet Productions
Amityville, NY ... 631-842-0548

Tova Industries
Louisville, KY ... 888-532-8682

Twinlab
New York, NY ... 800-645-5626

Vita-Pure
Roselle, NJ ... 908-245-1212

Vitamer Laboratories
Irvine, CA ... 800-432-8355

Vitaminerals
Glendale, CA ... 818-500-8718

VitaTech International
Tustin, CA ... 714-832-9700

Wakunaga of America
Mission Viejo, CA ... 800-421-2998

Wilke International
Shawnee Mission, KS ... 800-779-5545

World Organics Corporation
Huntington Beach, CA ... 714-893-0017

Minerals

Action Labs
Park City, UT ... 800-669-8877

Advanced Nutritional Research, Inc.
Ellicottville, NY ... 800-836-0644

Albion Laboratories
Clearfield, UT ... 866-243-5283

Amt Labs
North Salt Lake, UT ... 801-299-1661

Asiamerica Ingredients
Westwood, NJ ... 201-497-5531

Processor, importer, exporter and distributor of bulk vitamins, amino acids, nutraceuticals, aromatic chemicals, food additives, herbs, mineral nutrients and pharmaceuticals.

Jamieson Laboratories
Windosr, ON ... 519-974-8482

Matrix Health Products
Santee, CA ... 888-736-5609

Nutricepts
Burnsville, MN ... 800-949-9060

Protein Research Associates
Livermore, CA ... 800-948-1991

Randal Nutritional Products
Santa Rosa, CA ... 800-221-1697

Watson Inc
West Haven, CT ... 800-388-3481

Vitamins

Advanced Nutritional Research, Inc.
Ellicottville, NY ... 800-836-0644

AHD International, LLC
Atlanta, GA ... 404-233-4022

Asiamerica Ingredients
Westwood, NJ ... 201-497-5531

Processor, importer, exporter and distributor of bulk vitamins, amino acids, nutraceuticals, aromatic chemicals, food additives, herbs, mineral nutrients and pharmaceuticals.

Bio San Laboratories/MegaFood
Derry, NH ... 800-848-5022

CVC Specialties
Vernon, CA 800-421-6175
FoodScience of Vermont
Essex Junction, VT 800-874-9444
Freeda Vitamins
Long Island City, NY 800-777-3737
Garcoa
Calabasas, CA 800-831-4247
Good 'N Natural
Ronkonkoma, NY 800-544-0095
Healthy'N Fit Nutrition als
Croton on Hudson, NY 800-338-5200
IVC American Vitamin
Freehold, NJ 800-666-8482
Jamieson Laboratories
Windosr, ON 519-974-8482
Nutribiotic
Lakeport, CA 800-225-4345
Nutrilabs
San Francisco, CA 877-468-8745
Nutritional International Enterprises Company
Irvine, CA 949-854-4855
Optimum Nutrition
Walterboro, SC 800-763-3444
Protein Research Associates
Livermore, CA 800-948-1991
Randal Nutritional Products
Santa Rosa, CA 800-221-1697
Sandco International
Northport, AL 800-382-2075
Scandinavian Formulas Inc
Sellersville, PA 800-288-2844
Solgar Vitamin & Herb
Leonia, NJ 201-944-2311
Tree of Life
St Augustine, FL 904-940-2100
Twinlab
New York, NY 800-645-5626
Vitatech International
Tustin, CA 714-832-9700
Watson Inc
West Haven, CT 800-388-3481
Wilke International
Shawnee Mission, KS 800-779-5545

Vitamins

21st Century Products
Fort Worth, TX 817-284-8299
Abunda Life Laboratories
Asbury Park, NJ 732-775-7575
Acatris
Edina, MN 952-835-9590
Accucaps Industries Limited
Windsor, ON 800-665-7210
Acta Health Products
Sunnyvale, CA 408-732-6830
Action Labs
Placentia, CA 800-400-5696
Action Labs
Park City, UT 800-669-8877
ADH Health Products
Congers, NY 845-268-0027
Advanced Nutritional Research, Inc.
Ellicottville, NY 800-836-0644
Agumm
Coral Springs, FL 954-344-0607
AHD International, LLC
Atlanta, GA 404-233-4022
Alacer Corporation
Foothill Ranch, CA 800-854-0249
Albion Laboratories
Clearfield, UT 866-243-5283
Alfer Laboratories
Chatsworth, CA 818-709-0737
Alternative Health & Herbs
Albany, OR 800-345-4152
Ameri-Kal Inc
Wichita Falls, TX 940-322-5400
American Biosciences
Blauvelt, NY 888-884-7770
Amerifit Brands, Inc.
Cromwell, CT 800-722-3476
Amerilab Technologies
Plymouth, MN 800-445-6468
Anabol Naturals
Santa Cruz, CA 800-426-2265
Anmar Nutrition
Bridgeport, CT 203-336-8330
Apotheca Naturale
Woodbine, IA 800-736-3130
Apple Valley Market
Berrien Springs, MI 800-237-7436
Archon Vitamin Corporation
Irvington, NJ 800-349-1700
Argee Corporation
Santee, CA 800-449-3030

At Last Naturals
Valhalla, NY 800-527-8123
Atkins Nutritionals
Melville, NY 800-628-5467
Banner Pharmacaps
High Point, NC 336-812-3442
BASF Corporation
Florham Park, NJ 800-526-1072
Belmont Chemicals
Clifton, NJ 800-722-5070
Beverly International Nutrition
Cold Spring, KY 800-888-3364
Bio San Laboratories/MegaFood
Derry, NH 800-848-5022
Bio-Tech Pharmacal
Fayetteville, AR 800-345-1199
Bioforce USA
Ghent, NY 800-641-7555
Botanical Products
Springville, CA 559-539-3432
Capsule Works
Bayport, NY 800-920-6090
Carlson Vitamins
Arlington Hts, IL 888-234-5656
Carob Tree
Arcadia, CA 626-445-0215
Champion Nutrition
Sunrise, FL 800-225-4831
ChildLife-Nutrition for Kids
Los Angeles, CA 800-993-0332
China Pharmaceutical Enterprises
Baton Rouge, LA 800-345-1658
Coating Place
Verona, WI 608-845-9521
Connection Source
Alpharetta, GA 770-667-1051
Continental Vitamin Company
Vernon, CA 800-421-6175
Country Life
Hauppauge, NY 800-645-5768
CVC Specialties
Vernon, CA 800-421-6175
Cyanotech Corporation
Kailua Kona, HI 800-395-1353
DeSouza International
Beaumont, CA 800-373-5171
DMH Ingredients
Libertyville, IL 847-362-9977
DynaPro International
Kaysville, UT 800-877-1413
Earth Science
Corona, CA 951-371-7565
Eastman Chemical Company
Kingsport, TN 800-327-8626
Eckhart Corporation
Novato, CA 415-892-3880
Eclectic Institute
Sandy, OR 503-668-4120
Edge Labs
Trenton, NJ 866-334-3522
Edom Laboratories
Deer Park, NY 800-723-3366
EMD Chemicals
Gibbstown, NJ 800-364-4535
Energen Products
Norwalk, CA 800-423-8837
Enzymatic Therapy
Green Bay, WI 800-783-2286
ERBL
Vista, CA 800-275-3725
Escalade Ltd
Huntington, NY 631-659-3374
Esteem Products
Bellevue, WA 800-255-7631
Europa Sports Products
Charlotte, NC 800-447-4795
Farbest-Tallman Foods Corporation
Montvale, NJ 201-573-4900
Figuerola Laboratories
Santa Ynez, CA 800-219-1147
Fortitech
Schenectady, NY 800-950-5156
Fortress Systems LLC
Omaha, NE 888-331-6601
Freeda Vitamins
Long Island City, NY 800-777-3737
Freeman Industries
Tuckahoe, NY 800-666-6454
Functional Products LLC
Atlantic Beach, FL 800-628-5908
Futurebiotics
Hauppauge, NY 800-645-1721
Garcoa
Calabasas, CA 800-831-4247
GCI Nutrients (USA)
Foster City, CA 650-697-4700
Geon Technologies
Whippany, NJ 800-467-3041
GINCO International
Simi Valley, CA 800-284-2598
Givaudan Flavors
Cincinnati, OH 513-948-8000
Global Nutrition Research Corporation
Tempe, AZ 602-454-2248
GMP Laboratories
Anaheim, CA 714-630-2467
Good 'N Natural
Ronkonkoma, NY 800-544-0095
Graminex
Saginaw, MI 877-472-6469
Green Foods Corporation
Oxnard, CA 800-777-4430
Green Turtle Bay Vitamin Company
Summit, NJ 800-887-8535
Greens Today®
Plainview, NY 800-473-3641
Grow Company
Ridgefield, NJ 201-941-8777
H. Reisman Corporation
Orange, NJ 973-677-9200
Hair Fitness
Long Beach, CA 888-348-4247
Health Products Corporation
Yonkers, NY 914-423-2900
Healthy'N Fit Nutrition als
Croton on Hudson, NY 800-338-5200
Helmuth Country Bakery
Hutchinson, KS 800-567-6360
Herbal Products & Development
Aptos, CA 831-688-8706
Heritage Store
Virginia Beach, VA 800-862-2923
Heterochemical Corporation
Valley Stream, NY 516-561-8225
Highland Laboratories
Mount Angel, OR 888-717-4917
Hillestad Pharmaceuticals
Woodruff, WI 800-535-7742
Hosemen & Roche Vitamins & Fine Chemicals
Nutley, NJ 800-526-6367
Indiana Botanic Gardens
Hobart, IN 219-947-4040
Innovative Health Products
Largo, FL 800-654-2347
Interhealth Nutraceuticals
Benicia, CA 800-783-4636
IVC American Vitamin
Freehold, NJ 800-666-8482
Jamieson Laboratories
Windosr, ON 519-974-8482
Jarrow Industries
Santa Fe Springs, CA 562-906-1919
JR Carlson Laboratories
Arlington Hts, IL 888-234-5656
K&K Laboratories
Carlsbad, CA 760-434-6044
Kabco
Amityville, NY 631-842-3600
Kemin Health
Des Moines, IA 888-248-5040
Leiner Health Products
Carson, CA 310-835-8400
Liberty Natural Products
Oregon City, OR 800-289-8427

Luyties Pharmacal Company
Saint Louis, MO 800-325-8080
Madys Company
San Francisco, CA 415-822-2227
Mead Johnson Pediatrics Nutritional Group
Evansville, IN 812-429-5000
Mega Pro International
St George, UT 800-541-9469
Metabolic Nutrition
Tamarac, FL 800-626-1022
Metagenics, Inc.
San Clemente, CA. 800-621-6070
Michael's Naturopathic
San Antonio, TX. 800-525-9643
Mineral & Pigment Solutions
South Plainfield, NJ 800-732-0562
Mission Pharmacal Company
San Antonio, TX. 800-292-7364
Motherland International Inc
Rancho Cucamonga, CA 800-590-5407
National Enzyme Company
Forsyth, MO 800-825-8545
Natural Food Supplements
Canoga Park, CA 818-341-3375
Naturally Vitamin Supplements
Phoenix, AZ 800-899-4499
Nature's Bounty
Ronkonkoma, NY. 800-433-2990
Nature's Sunshine Products Company
Provo, UT 800-223-8225
Nature's Way
Lehi, UT 800-962-8873
NatureMost Laboratories
Middletown, CT 800-234-2112
Naturex
South Hackensack, NJ 201-440-5000
NBTY
Ronkonkoma, NY. 800-920-6090
New Chapter
Brattleboro, VT. 800-543-7279
Northridge Laboratories
Chatsworth, CA 818-882-5622
NOW Foods
Bloomingdale, IL 888-669-3663
Now Foods
Bloomingdale, IL 888-669-3663
NuNaturals
Eugene, OR. 800-753-4372
Nutraceutical Solutions
Corpus Christi, TX 800-338-4788
Nutraceutics Corporation
Saint Louis, MO 314-664-6684
Nutri-Cell
Monterey Park, CA. 714-953-8307
Nutribiotic
Lakeport, CA 800-225-4345
Nutrilabs
San Francisco, CA 877-468-8745
Nutritech Corporation
Santa Barbara, CA 800-235-5727
Nutritional Counselors of America
Spencer, TN 931-946-3600
Nutritional Research Associates
South Whitley, IN. 800-456-4931
Nutro Laboratories
South Plainfield, NJ 800-446-8876
O C Lugo Company
Nyack, NY 845-708-7080
O'Donnell Formula
San Marcos, CA 800-736-1991
Old Fashioned Natural Products
Santa Ana, CA 800-552-9045
Optimal Nutrients
Foster City, CA. 707-528-1800
Ortho Molecular Products
Stevens Point, WI 800-332-2351
P.J. Noyes Company, Inc
Lancaster, NH 800-522-2469
Pacific Nutritional
Vancouver, WA 360-253-3197
Pak Technologies
Milwaukee, WI 414-438-8600
Paragon Laboratories
Torrance, CA. 800-231-3670
Parish Chemical Company
Orem, UT 801-226-2018
Particle Dynamics
Saint Louis, MO 800-452-4682
Pharmachem Laboratories
South Hackensack, NJ 201-343-3611
Phoenix Laboratories
Farmingdale, NY 800-236-6583
Pro. Pac. Labs
Ogden, UT. 888-277-6722
Proper-Chem
Dix Hills, NY 631-420-8000
Protein Research Associates
Livermore, CA 800-948-1991
Pure Source
Doral, FL. 800-324-6273
Randal Nutritional Products
Santa Rosa, CA. 800-221-1697
Sadkhin Complex
Brooklyn, NY 800-723-5446
Sandco International
Northport, AL. 800-382-2075
Scandinavian Formulas Inc
Sellersville, PA 800-288-2844
Select Supplements, Inc
Carlsbad, CA. 760-431-7509
Solgar Vitamin & Herb
Leonia, NJ. 201-944-2311
Source Naturals
Scotts Valley, CA 800-815-2333
Sportabs International
Los Angeles, CA. 888-814-7767
St. Charles Trading
Lake Saint Louis, MO. 800-336-1333
Super Nutrition Life Extension
Fort Lauderdale, FL 800-678-8989
Tabco Enterprises
Pomona, CA 909-623-4565
Terra Botanica Products
Nakusp, BC. 888-410-9977
Texas Coffee Company
Beaumont, TX. 800-259-3400
Thor Incorporated
Ogden, UT. 888-846-7462
Twinlab
New York, NY 800-645-5626
Unique Vitality Products
Agoura Hills, CA 818-889-7739
Universal Laboratories
New Brunswick, NJ 800-872-0101
USA Laboratories
Burns, TN 800-489-4872
Vita-Pure
Roselle, NJ 908-245-1212
Vitamer Laboratories
Irvine, CA. 800-432-8355
Vitamin Power
Freeport, NY. 800-645-6567
Vitaminerals
Glendale, CA 818-500-8718
Vitamins
Chicago, IL 312-861-0700
Vitarich Laboratories
Naples, FL. 800-817-9999
Vivion
San Carlos, CA 800-479-0997
Wakunaga of America
Mission Viejo, CA 800-421-2998
Watson Inc
West Haven, CT 800-388-3481
Westar Nutrition Corporation
Costa Mesa, CA 800-645-1868
Whole Life Nutritional Supplements
North Hollywood, CA 800-748-5841
Wilke International
Shawnee Mission, KS. 800-779-5545
World Ginseng Center
San Francisco, CA 800-747-8808
World Nutrition
Scottsdale, AZ. 800-548-2710
World Organics Corporation
Huntington Beach, CA 714-893-0017
World Softgel
Compton, CA 310-900-1199
Wright Enrichment
Crowley, LA 800-201-3096
Wright Group
Crowley, LA 800-201-3096
Wysong Corporation
Midland, MI 800-748-0188

Zinc Citrate

Gadot Biochemical Industries
Rolling Meadows, IL 888-424-1424

Waxes

Lanaetex Products Incorporated
Elizabeth, NJ. 908-351-9700

Paraffin

Stevenson-Cooper
Philadelphia, PA 215-223-2600

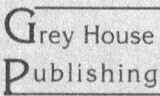

Jams, Jellies & Spreads

Jams

A Taste of the Kingdom
Kingdom City, MO 888-592-5080
Alaska Herb Tea Company
Anchorage, AK 800-654-2764
Algood Food Company
Louisville, KY 502-637-1401
Ambassador Foods
Van Nuys, CA 800-338-3369
Amberland Foods
Harvey, ND 800-950-4558
Au Printemps Gourmet
Saint-Jerome, QC 800-663-0416
Bakemark Ingredients Canada
Richmond, BC 800-665-9441
Bear Meadow Farm
Colrain, MA 800-653-9241
Bella Vista Farm
Lawton, OK 866-237-8526
Benbow's Coffee Roasters
Bar Harbor, ME 207-288-5271
Bonnie's Jams
Cambridge, MA 617-714-5380
Brad's Organic
Haverstraw, NY 845-429-9080
Bread & Chocolate
Wells River, VT 800-524-6715
Buckhead Gourmet
Atlanta, GA 800-673-6338
Buon Italia Misono Food Ltd.
New York, NY 212-633-9090
California Custom Fruits & Flavors
Irwindale, CA 877-558-0056
California Style Gourmet Products
San Diego, CA 800-243-5226
Carol Hall's Hot Pepper Jelly
Fort Bragg, CA 866-737-7379
Chelsea Market Baskets
New York, NY 888-727-7887
Choice of Vermont
Destin, FL 800-444-6261
Clements Foods Company
Oklahoma City, OK 800-654-8355
Coco Lopez
Miramar, FL 800-341-2242
Colorado Mountain Jams & Jellies
Palisade, CO 970-464-0745
Cornaby's LLC
Spanish Fork, UT 801-754-4968
Cotswold Cottage Foods
Arvada, CO 800-208-1977
Daregal Gourmet
Princeton, NJ 609-375-2312
Dark Tickle Company
St Lunaire-Griquet, NL 709-623-2354
Deborah's Kitchen Inc.
Littleton, MA 617-216-9908
Delicae Gourmet
Tarpon Springs, FL 800-942-2502
Doral International
Bayside, NY 718-224-7413
E.D. Smith Foods Ltd
Winona, ON 800-263-9246
Earth & Vine Provisions
Loomis, CA 888-723-8463
Erba Food Products
Brooklyn, NY 718-272-7700
Fruit Fillings
Fresno, CA 559-237-4715
Fruit of the Land Products
Thornhill, ON 877-311-5267
GEM Berry Products
Sandpoint, ID 800-426-0498
Granny Annie Jams
South Londonderry, VT 802-824-6625
Griffin Food Company
Muskogee, OK 800-580-6311
Heinz Portion Control
Mason, OH 800-547-8924
Herb Bee's Products
Colchester, VT 802-864-7387
Hilltop Herb Farm & Restaurant
Cleveland, TX 832-397-4020
Jim's Cheese Pantry
Waterloo, WI 800-345-3571
Kitchen Kettle Foods
Intercourse, PA 800-732-3538
Kozlowski Farms
Forestville, CA 800-473-2767
Mad River Farm
Arcata, CA 707-822-0248
Mardale Specialty Foods
Waukegan, IL 847-336-4777
Middlefield Cheese House
Middlefield, OH 800-327-9477
Mixon Fruit Farms
Bradenton, FL 800-608-2525
National Grape Cooperative
Westfield, NY 716-326-5200
New Canaan Farms
Dripping Springs, TX 800-727-5267
Oasis Foods Company
Hillside, NJ 908-964-0477
Old Country Cheese
Cashton, WI 608-654-5411
Pacific Westcoast Foods
Beaverton, OR 800-874-9333
Peanut Butter & Co
New York, NY 866-ILO-EPB
Pemberton's Gourmet Foods
Gray, ME 800-255-8401
Reid Foods
Gurnee, IL 888-295-8478
Rowena's
Norfolk, VA 800-627-8699
Sarabeth's Kitchen
Bronx, NY 800-773-7378
Sargent's Bear Necessities
North Troy, VT 802-988-2903
Scott Hams
Greenville, KY 800-318-1353
Shawnee Canning Company
Cross Junction, VA 800-713-1414
Side Hill Farm
Brattleboro, VT 802-254-2018
Spruce Mountain Blueberries
West Rockport, ME 207-236-3538
Stanchfield Farms
Milo, ME 207-732-5173
Steel's Gourmet Foods, Ltd.
Bridgeport, PA 800-678-3357
Sticky Fingers Bakeries
Spokane, WA 800-458-5826
Stonewall Kitchen
York, ME 800-207-5267
Summer In Vermont Jams
Hinesburg, VT 802-453-3793
Sunfresh Foods
Seattle, WA 800-669-9625
T.J. Blackburn Syrup Works
Jefferson, TX 800-527-8630
T.W. Garner Food Company
Winston Salem, NC 800-476-7383
Valley View Blueberries
Vancouver, WA 360-892-2839
Vermont Harvest Speciality Foods
Stowe, VT 800-338-5354
Welch's Foods Inc
Concord, MA 800-340-6870

Apricot

Allied Old English
Port Reading, NJ 732-636-2060
Erba Food Products
Brooklyn, NY 718-272-7700

Grape

Allied Old English
Port Reading, NJ 732-636-2060
T.W. Garner Food Company
Winston Salem, NC 800-476-7383

Strawberry

Allied Old English
Port Reading, NJ 732-636-2060
D'Artagnan
Newark, NJ 800-327-8246
Erba Food Products
Brooklyn, NY 718-272-7700
New Canaan Farms
Dripping Springs, TX 800-727-5267
T.W. Garner Food Company
Winston Salem, NC 800-476-7383

Jellies

Alaska Herb Tea Company
Anchorage, AK 800-654-2764
Aloha from Oregon
Eugene, OR 800-241-0300
B&B Pecan Processors of NC
Turkey, NC 866-328-7322
Bear Meadow Farm
Colrain, MA 800-653-9241
Beetroot Delights
Foothill, ON 888-842-3387
Coco Lopez
Miramar, FL 800-341-2242
Colorado Mountain Jams & Jellies
Palisade, CO 970-464-0745
Davidson of Dundee
Dundee, FL 800-294-2266
Deborah's Kitchen Inc.
Littleton, MA 617-216-9908
Kettle Master
Hillsville, VA 276-728-7571
Kitchen Kettle Foods
Intercourse, PA 800-732-3538
Low Country Produce
Lobeco, SC 800-935-2792
McIlhenny Company
Avery Island, LA 800-634-9599
Northeast Kingdom Mustard Company
Westfield, VT 866-4PU-EVT
Palmetto Canning Company
Palmetto, FL 941-722-1100
Shenk's Foods
Lancaster, PA 717-393-4240

Beets

Beetroot Delights
Foothill, ON 888-842-3387

Royal

Algood Food Company
Louisville, KY 502-637-1401
Bear Stewart Corporation
Chicago, IL 800-697-2327
Campagna
Lebanon, OR 800-959-4372
CC Pollen Company
Phoenix, AZ 800-875-0096
Dawes Hill Honey Company
Nunda, NY 888-800-8075
Delicae Gourmet
Tarpon Springs, FL 800-942-2502
Fiesta Gourmet of Tejas
Canyon Lake, TX 800-585-8250
Herb Bee's Products
Colchester, VT 802-864-7387
Moon Shine Trading Company
Woodland, CA 800-678-1226
Royal Resources
New Orleans, LA 800-888-9932
Sargent's Bear Necessities
North Troy, VT 802-988-2903
Stanchfield Farms
Milo, ME 207-732-5173
Summer In Vermont Jams
Hinesburg, VT 802-453-3793
Vermont Harvest Speciality Foods
Stowe, VT 800-338-5354
WCC Honey Marketing
City of Industry, CA 626-855-3086

Marmalades & Preserves

A Perfect Pear from NapaValley
Napa, CA 800-553-5753
A.M. Braswell Jr. Food Company
Statesboro, GA 800-673-9388
Alaska Jack's Trading Post
Anchorage, AK 888-660-2257

Algood Food Company
Louisville, KY . . . 502-637-1401
Allied Old English
Port Reading, NJ . . . 732-636-2060
Ambassador Foods
Van Nuys, CA . . . 800-338-3369
Amberland Foods
Harvey, ND . . . 800-950-4558
Amcan Industries
Elmsford, NY . . . 914-347-4838
American Spoon Foods
Petoskey, MI . . . 800-222-5886
Anna's Unlimited, Inc
Austin, TX . . . 800-849-7054
Arbor Hill Grapery
Naples, NY . . . 800-554-7553
Arizona Cowboy
Phoenix, AZ . . . 602-956-4833
Arome Fleurs & Fruits
St-Jean-Sur-Richelie, QC . . . 877-349-3282
Artichoke Kitchen
Hamilton, NC . . . 252-798-2471
Au Printemps Gourmet
Saint-Jerome, QC . . . 800-663-0416
Bainbridge Festive Foods
Tunica, MS . . . 800-545-9205
Bartons Fine Foods
Denniston, KY . . . 888-810-3750
Baumer Foods
Metairie, LA . . . 504-482-5761
Bear Meadow Farm
Colrain, MA . . . 800-653-9241
Bear Stewart Corporation
Chicago, IL . . . 800-697-2327
Blackberry Patch
Thomasville, GA . . . 800-853-5598
Blueberry Store
Grand Junction, MI . . . 877-654-2400
Booneway Farms
Knoxville, TN . . . 865-521-9500
Bowman Apple Products Company
Mount Jackson, VA . . . 800-346-5382
Breakfast at Brennan's
New Orleans, LA . . . 800-888-9932
California Custom Fruits & Flavors
Irwindale, CA . . . 877-558-0056
Carolina Cupboard
Hillsborough, NC . . . 800-400-3441
Carriage House Companies
Fredonia, NY . . . 800-462-8125
Castella Imports
Hauppauge, NY . . . 866-227-8355
Catamount Specialties ofVermont
Stowe, VT . . . 800-820-8096
Cherchies
Malvern, PA . . . 800-644-1980
Cheri's Desert Harvest
Tucson, AZ . . . 800-743-1141
Cherith Valley Gardens
Fort Worth, TX . . . 800-610-9813
Cherry Hut
Traverse City, MI . . . 888-882-4431
Chris' Farm Stand
Bradford, MA . . . 978-994-4315
Chugwater Chili Corporation
Chugwater, WY . . . 800-972-4454
Chukar Cherries
Prosser, WA . . . 800-624-9544
Cincinnati Preserves Company
Cincinnati, OH . . . 800-222-9966
Clements Foods Company
Oklahoma City, OK . . . 800-654-8355
Coco Lopez
Miramar, FL . . . 800-341-2242
Cold Hollow Cider Mill
Waterbury Center, VT . . . 800-327-7537
Country Cupboard
Virginia City, NV . . . 775-847-7300
Coutts Specialty Foods
Boxborough, MA . . . 800-919-2952
Cw Resources
New Britain, CT . . . 860-229-7700
D'Artagnan
Newark, NJ . . . 800-327-8246
Davidson of Dundee
Dundee, FL . . . 800-294-2266
Dawn's Foods
Portage, WI . . . 608-742-2494
Deep South Products
Fitzgerald, GA . . . 229-423-1121
Deer Mountain Berry Farms
Granite Falls, WA . . . 360-691-7586

Deneen Company
Belen, NM . . . 505-988-1515
Dennco
Chicago, IL . . . 708-862-0070
Dillman Farm
Bloomington, IN . . . 800-359-1362
E. Waldo Ward & Son Corporation
Sierra Madre, CA . . . 800-355-9273
EFCO Products
Poughkeepsie, NY . . . 800-284-3326
Erba Food Products
Brooklyn, NY . . . 718-272-7700
Esper Products DeLuxe
Kissimmee, FL . . . 800-268-0892
Eva Gates Homemade Preserves
Bigfork, MT . . . 800-682-4283
Eweberry Farms
Brownsville, OR . . . 541-466-3470
Fiesta Gourmet of Tejas
Canyon Lake, TX . . . 800-585-8250
Fireside Kitchen
Halifax, NS . . . 902-454-7387
Fischer & Wieser Specialty Foods, Inc.
Fredericksburg, TX . . . 800-880-8526
Forge Mountain Foods
Hendersonville, NC . . . 800-823-6743
Freed, Teller & Freed
South San Francisco, CA . . . 800-370-7371
From Oregon
Springfield, OR . . . 541-747-4222
Frostproof Sunkist Groves
Fort Meade, FL . . . 863-635-4873
Gem Berry Products
Sandpoint, ID . . . 800-426-0498
Glencourt
Napa, CA . . . 707-944-4444
Golden Valley Foods
Abbotsford, BC . . . 888-299-8855
Gormly's Orchard
South Burlington, VT . . . 800-639-7604
Gourmet Central
Romney, WV . . . 800-984-3722
Graves Mountain Lodge Inc.
Syria, VA . . . 540-923-4747
Graysmarsh Farm
Sequim, WA . . . 800-683-4367
Great Northern Maple Products
Saint Honor, De Shenley, QC . . . 418-485-7777
Greaves Jams & Marmalades
Niagara-on-the-Lake, ON . . . 800-515-9939
Green Grown Products Inc
Marina Del Ray, CA . . . 310-828-1686
Grey Eagle Distributors
Maryland Heights, MO . . . 314-429-9100
Grouse Hunt Farms
Tamaqua, PA . . . 570-467-2850
H Cantin
Beauport, QC . . . 800-463-5268
Hawaiian Fruit Specialties
Kalaheo, HI . . . 808-332-9333
Heinz Portion Control
Mason, OH . . . 800-547-8924
Hillcrest Orchard
Lake Placid, FL . . . 865-397-5273
Hilltop Herb Farm & Restaurant
Cleveland, TX . . . 832-397-4020
Hollman Foods
Chicago, IL . . . 888-926-2879
Homemade By Dorothy
Boise, ID . . . 208-375-3720
Honey Bear Fruit Basket
Denver, CO . . . 888-330-2327
House of Webster
Rogers, AR . . . 800-369-4641
Huckleberry Patch
Hungry Horse, MT . . . 800-527-7340
Hurd Orchards
Holley, NY . . . 585-638-8838
Indi-Bel
Indianola, MS . . . 662-887-1226
Indian Bay Frozen Foods
Centreville, NL . . . 709-678-2844
Inter-American Products
Cincinnati, OH . . . 800-645-2233
J.M. Smucker Company
Orrville, OH . . . 888-550-9555
Jim's Cheese Pantry
Waterloo, WI . . . 800-345-3571
JMS Specialty Foods
Ripon, WI . . . 800-535-5437
John C. Meier Juice Company
Cincinnati, OH . . . 800-346-2941

Kamish Food Products
Chicago, IL . . . 773-725-6959
Kerr Jellies
Dana, NC . . . 877-685-8381
King Kelly Marmalade Company
Bellflower, CA . . . 562-865-0291
Knott's Berry Farm Foods
Placentia, CA . . . 800-289-9927
Knouse Foods Coop
Peach Glen, PA . . . 717-677-8181
Kozlowski Farms
Forestville, CA . . . 800-473-2767
La Caboose Specialties
Sunset, LA . . . 337-662-5401
Lancaster Packing Company
Lancaster, PA . . . 717-397-9727
Lawrence Foods
Elk Grove Village, IL . . . 800-323-7848
Let's Serve
Plattsburgh, NY
Love Creek Orchards
Medina, TX . . . 800-449-0882
Lynch Foods
North York, ON . . . 416-449-5464
Lyons-Magnus
Fresno, CA . . . 559-268-5966
Mad River Farm
Arcata, CA . . . 707-822-0248
Minnesota Specialty Crops
McGregor, MN . . . 800-328-6731
Mixon Fruit Farms
Bradenton, FL . . . 800-608-2525
Moon Shine Trading Company
Woodland, CA . . . 800-678-1226
Mountainbrook of Vermont
Jeffersonville, VT . . . 802-644-1988
Mrs. Auld's Gourmet Foods
Reno, NV . . . 800-322-8537
New Canaan Farms
Dripping Springs, TX . . . 800-727-5267
New England Cranberry Company
Lynn, MA . . . 800-410-2892
Ocean Spray Cranberries
Kenosha, WI . . . 262-694-5200
Oregon Hill Farms
Saint Helens, OR . . . 800-243-4541
Our Enterprises
Oklahoma City, OK . . . 800-821-6375
Pacific Westcoast Foods
Beaverton, OR . . . 800-874-9333
Palmetto Canning Company
Palmetto, FL . . . 941-722-1100
Pearson's Berry Farm
Bowden, AB . . . 403-224-3011
Pepper Creek Farms
Lawton, OK . . . 800-526-8132
Pied-Mont/Dora
Ste Anne Des Plaines, QC . . . 800-363-8003
Plaidberry Company
Vista, CA . . . 760-727-5403
Poiret International
Tamarac, FL . . . 954-724-3261
Post Familie Vineyards
Altus, AR . . . 800-275-8423
Purity Factories
St.John's, NL . . . 800-563-3411
Purity Products
Plainview, NY . . . 888-769-7873
Quality Naturally! Foods
City of Industry, CA . . . 888-498-6986
R.E. Kimball & Company
Amesbury, MA . . . 978-388-1826
Rapazzini Winery
Gilroy, CA . . . 800-842-6262
Restaurant Lulu Gourmet Products
San Francisco, CA . . . 888-693-5800
Robert Rothschild Berry Farm
Urbana, OH . . . 866-565-6790
Robert Rothschild Farm
Urbana, OH . . . 866-565-6790
Rocky Top Farms
Ellsworth, MI . . . 800-862-9303
Rose City Pepperheads
Portland, OR . . . 503-226-0862
Roseland Manufacturing
Roseland, NJ . . . 973-228-2500
Rowena's
Norfolk, VA . . . 800-627-8699
Sambets Cajun Deli
Austin, TX . . . 800-472-6238
Sand Hill Berries
Mt Pleasant, PA . . . 724-547-4760

Sarabeth's Kitchen
Bronx, NY. 800-773-7378
SBK Preserves
Bronx, NY. 800-773-7378
Sedlock Farm
Lynn Center, IL. 309-521-8284
Seven Keys Company of Florida
Pompano Beach, FL 954-946-5010
Shawnee Canning Company
Cross Junction, VA 800-713-1414
Shenk's Foods
Lancaster, PA 717-393-4240
Shooting Star Farms
Bartlesville, OK 888-850-8540
Silver Palate Kitchens
Cresskill, NJ 800-872-5283
Skjodt-Barrett Foods
Mississauga, ON. 877-600-1200
St. Charles Trading
Lake Saint Louis, MO. 800-336-1333
Stickney & Poor Company
Peterborough, NH. 603-924-2259
Sugarman of Vermont
Hardwick, VT 800-932-7700
Summerland Sweets
Summerland, DC. 800-577-1277
Suzanne's Specialties
New Brunswick, NJ 800-762-2135
T.J. Blackburn Syrup Works
Jefferson, TX. 800-527-8630
T.W. Garner Food Company
Winston Salem, NC. 800-476-7383
Tait Farm Foods
Centre Hall, PA 800-787-2716
Terrapin Ridge
Clearwater, FL 800-999-4052
Tex-Mex Gourmet
Brenham, TX. 888-345-8467
The Great San Saba RiverPecan Company
San Saba, TX 800-621-9121
The Lollipop Tree, Inc
Auburn, NY. 800-842-6691
Thomson Food
Duluth, MN. 218-722-2529
Trailblazer Food Products
Portland, OR 800-777-7179
Trappist Preserves
Cleveland, OH 800-472-0425
Tropical Preserving Company
Los Angeles, CA. 213-748-5108
Uncle Fred's Fine Foods
Rockport, TX 361-729-8320
Valley View Blueberries
Vancouver, WA 360-892-2839
Vic Rossano Incorporated
Montreal, QC 514-766-5252
Wagner Gourmet Foods
Lenexa, KS 913-469-5411
Wax Orchards
Seattle, WA 800-634-6132
WCC Honey Marketing
City of Industry, CA 626-855-3086
Welch's Foods Inc
Kennewick, WA 509-582-2131
Welch's Foods Inc
Concord, MA 800-340-6870
Welch's Foods Inc.
North East, PA. 814-725-4577
Westport Rivers Vineyard& Winery
Westport, MA 800-993-9695
Wild Thyme Cottage Products
Pointe Claire, QC 514-695-3602

Spreads

A. Bauer's Mustard
Flushing, NY. 718-821-3570
A.M. Braswell Jr. Food Company
Statesboro, GA 800-673-9388
Aarhus United USA, Inc.
Newark, NJ 800-776-1338
Alaska Smokehouse
Woodinville, WA. 800-422-0852
Algood Food Company
Louisville, KY 502-637-1401
Allfresh Food Products
Evanston, IL 773-273-2343
Allied Old English
Port Reading, NJ. 732-636-2060
Amcan Industries
Elmsford, NY 914-347-4838
American Almond Products Company
Brooklyn, NY 800-825-6663
American Food Traders
Miami, FL. 305-273-7090
American Spoon Foods
Petoskey, MI 800-222-5886
Arbor Hill Grapery
Naples, NY 800-554-7553
Artichoke Kitchen
Hamilton, NC 252-798-2471
Assouline & Ting
Huntingdon Valley, PA 800-521-4491
Bainbridge Festive Foods
Tunica, MS 800-545-9205
Bakemark Ingredients Canada
Richmond, BC 800-665-9441
Baumer Foods
Metairie, LA 504-482-5761
Bear Meadow Farm
Colrain, MA 800-653-9241
Beaver Meadow Creamery
Du Bois, PA. 800-262-3711
Bel/Kaukauna USA
Kaukauna, WI. 800-558-3500
Berner Foods, Inc.
Roscoe, IL. 800-819-8199
Bestfoods
Englewood Cliffs, NJ 201-567-8000
Betty Lou's Golden Smackers
McMinnville, OR 800-242-5205
Black Bear
St Johnsbury, VT. 802-748-5888
Black Diamond Cheese
Toronto, ON 800-263-2858
Blue Jay Orchards
Bethel, CT. 203-748-0119
Bowman Apple Products Company
Mount Jackson, VA. 800-346-5382
BP Gourmet
Hauppauge, NY 631-234-5200
Bread Dip Company
Philadelphia, PA 215-563-9455
Butterball Farms
Grand Rapids, MI 616-243-0105
Butternut Mountain Farm
Morrisville, VT. 800-828-2376
California Dairies
Visalia, CA 559-625-2200
Carolina Cupboard
Hillsborough, NC 800-400-3441
Carriage House Companies
Fredonia, NY 800-462-8125
Castella Imports
Hauppauge, NY 866-227-8355
Chelsea Market Baskets
New York, NY 888-727-7887
Cheri's Desert Harvest
Tucson, AZ 800-743-1141
Cherry Hut
Traverse City, MI 888-882-4431
Chloe Foods Corporation
Brooklyn, NY 718-827-9000
Chocolaterie Bernard Callebaut
Calgary, AB. 800-661-8367
Chris' Farm Stand
Bradford, MA 978-994-4315
Chugwater Chili Corporation
Chugwater, WY 800-972-4454
Cinnabar Specialty Foods
Prescott, AZ 866-293-6433
Citadelle Maple Syrup Producers' Cooperative
Plessisville, QC. 819-362-3241
Clements Foods Company
Oklahoma City, OK 800-654-8355
Cold Hollow Cider Mill
Waterbury Center, VT. 800-327-7537
ConAgra Grocery Products
Irvine, CA 714-680-1000
Consumer Guild Foods
Toledo, OH 419-726-3406
Consumers Vinegar & Spice Company
Chicago, IL 773-376-4100
Cowboy Caviar
Berkeley, CA. 877-509-1796
Cugino's Gourmet Foods
Crystal Lake, IL 888-592-8446
Cumberland Packing Corporation
Brooklyn, NY 718-222-3233
Dawes Hill Honey Company
Nunda, NY 888-800-8075
Dean Distributing Inc
Green Bay, WI. 920-469-6500
Deer Mountain Berry Farms
Granite Falls, WA 360-691-7586
Dutch Gold Honey, Inc.
Lancaster, PA 800-338-0587
E. Waldo Ward & Son Corporation
Sierra Madre, CA 800-355-9273
East Wind Nut Butters
Tecumseh, MO 417-679-4682
Erba Food Products
Brooklyn, NY 718-272-7700
Esper Products DeLuxe
Kissimmee, FL 800-268-0892
Eva Gates Homemade Preserves
Bigfork, MT 800-682-4283
Fireside Kitchen
Halifax, NS. 902-454-7387
Flaum Appetizing
Brooklyn, NY 718-821-1970
Food Ingredients
Elgin, IL 800-500-7676
Food Specialties Company
Cincinnati, OH 513-761-1242
Forge Mountain Foods
Hendersonville, NC 800-823-6743
Fox Hollow Farm
Hanover, NH. 603-643-6002
From Oregon
Springfield, OR. 541-747-4222
G&G Foods
Santa Rosa, CA. 707-542-6300
Gardners Candies
Tyrone, PA. 800-242-2639
GEM Berry Products
Sandpoint, ID 800-426-0498
Gem Berry Products
Sandpoint, ID 800-426-0498
GFA Brands
Paramus, NJ 201-568-9300
Giovanni's Appetizing Food Products
Richmond, MI. 586-727-9355
Golden Heritage Foods
Hillsboro, KS 800-530-5827
Golden Valley Foods
Abbotsford, BC. 888-299-8855
Gourmet Central
Romney, WV. 800-984-3722
Graham Cheese Corporation
Elnoragton, IN 800-472-9178
Graves Mountain Lodge Inc.
Syria, VA. 540-923-4747
Graysmarsh Farm
Sequim, WA 800-683-4367
Great Garlic Foods
Bradley Beach, NJ 732-775-3311
Greaves Jams & Marmalades
Niagara-on-the-Lake, ON. 800-515-9939
Groeb Farms
Onsted, MI 517-467-2065
Groezinger Provisions
Neptune, NJ 800-927-9473
Grouse Hunt Farms
Tamaqua, PA. 570-467-2850
H&B Packing Company
Waco, TX 254-752-2506
Halben Food Manufacturing Company
Saint Louis, MO 800-888-4855
Harold Food Company
Charlotte, NC 704-588-8061
Hawaiian Fruit Specialties
Kalaheo, HI. 808-332-9333
Heinz Company of Canada
North York, ON. 877-574-3469
Heinz Portion Control
Mason, OH 800-547-8924
Herb Bee's Products
Colchester, VT 802-864-7387
Herkimer Foods
Herkimer, NY 315-895-7832
Hero of America
Amsterdam, NY 877-437-6526
Hillcrest Orchard
Lake Placid, FL. 865-397-5273
Hillside Lane Farm
Randolph, VT 802-728-0070
Hollman Foods
Chicago, IL 888-926-2879
Homemade By Dorothy
Boise, ID 208-375-3720
Honey Bear Fruit Basket
Denver, CO 888-330-2327
Honey Butter Products Company
Manheim, PA 717-665-9323
House of Webster
Rogers, AR 800-369-4641

Huckleberry Patch
Hungry Horse, MT 800-527-7340
Indi-Bel
Indianola, MS 662-887-1226
Indian Bay Frozen Foods
Centreville, NL 709-678-2844
J.M. Smucker Company
Orrville, OH 888-550-9555
JMS Specialty Foods
Ripon, WI 800-535-5437
John C. Meier Juice Company
Cincinnati, OH 800-346-2941
K&S Bakery Products
Edmonton, AB 780-481-8155
Kerr Jellies
Dana, NC. 877-685-8381
Kettle Foods
Salem, OR. 503-364-0399
Kind Snacks
New York, NY 800-732-2321
King Kelly Marmalade Company
Bellflower, CA 562-865-0291
Knott's Berry Farm Foods
Placentia, CA 800-289-9927
Knotts Whlse. Foods
Paris, TN. 731-642-1961
Knouse Foods Coop
Peach Glen, PA 717-677-8181
Kozlowski Farms
Forestville, CA 800-473-2767
Kraft Foods
Garland, TX 972-272-7511
Krema Nut Company
Columbus, OH 800-222-4132
Kretschmar
Don Mills, ON 800-561-4532
La Caboose Specialties
Sunset, LA. 337-662-5401
Laack Brothers Cheese Company
Greenleaf, WI 800-589-5127
Lancaster Packing Company
Lancaster, PA 717-397-9727
Land O'Lakes
Kent, OH. 800-328-9680
Land O'Lakes, Inc.
Arden Hills, MN. 800-328-9680
Landis Peanut Butter
Souderton, PA. 215-723-9366
Lawry's Foods
Monrovia, CA. 800-595-8917
Leavitt Corporation
Everett, MA. 617-389-2600
Leroux Creek Foods
Hotchkiss, CO. 877-970-5670
Let's Serve
Plattsburgh, NY
Level Valley Creamery
Antioch, TN 800-251-1292
Look's Gourmet Food Company
East Machias, ME. 800-962-6258
Lost Trail Root Beer Com
Louisburg, KS. 800-748-7765
Lov-It Creamery
Green Bay, WI. 800-344-0333
Love Creek Orchards
Medina, TX. 800-449-0882
Lynch Foods
North York, ON. 416-449-5464
Mad River Farm
Arcata, CA 707-822-0248
Madison Dairy Produce Company
Madison, WI 608-256-5561
Madison Foods
Saint Paul, MN 651-265-8212
Marantha Natural Foods
San Francisco, CA 866-972-6879
Marin Food Specialties
Byron, CA. 925-634-6126
McCutcheon's Apple Products
Frederick, MD. 800-888-7537
Merkts Cheese Company
Bristol, WI. 262-857-2316
Minnesota Specialty Crops
McGregor, MN 800-328-6731
Miss Scarlett's
Chandler, AZ. 800-345-6734
Mixon Fruit Farms
Bradenton, FL. 800-608-2525
Montana Mountain Smoked Fish
Montana City, MT. 800-649-2959
Moon Shine Trading Company
Woodland, CA. 800-678-1226

Mountainbrook of Vermont
Jeffersonville, VT 802-644-1988
Mrs. Annie's Peanut Patch
Floresville, TX 830-393-7845
National Grape Cooperative
Westfield, NY 716-326-5200
New Canaan Farms
Dripping Springs, TX 800-727-5267
Ocean Spray Cranberries
Kenosha, WI 262-694-5200
Old Country Farms
East Sandwich, MA 888-707-5558
Once Again Nut Butter
Nunda, NY 888-800-8075
Oregon Hill Farms
Saint Helens, OR. 800-243-4541
Organic Gourmet
Sherman Oaks, CA 800-400-7772
Pak Technologies
Milwaukee, WI 414-438-8600
Palmetto Canning Company
Palmetto, FL 941-722-1100
Parkers Farm
Coon Rapids, MN 800-869-6685
Peaceworks
New York, NY 212-897-3985
Penotti USA
Westport, CT. 877-720-0896
Pied-Mont/Dora
Ste Anne Des Plaines, QC 800-363-8003
Pine River Pre-Pack
Newton, WI. 920-726-4216
Plochman
Manteno, IL 815-468-3434
Private Harvest
El Dorado Hills, CA 916-933-7080
Producers Peanut Company
Suffolk, VA 800-847-5491
Protient (Land O Lakes)
St Paul, MN. 800-328-9680
Purity Factories
St.John's, NL. 800-563-3411
Purity Farms
Sedalia, CO 800-568-4433
Purity Products
Plainview, NY. 888-769-7873
Quality Choice Foods
Toronto, ON 416-650-9595
Quong Hop & Company
S San Francisco, CA. 650-553-9900
R. C. Bigelow
Fairfield, CT 888-244-3569
Rapazzini Winery
Gilroy, CA. 800-842-6262
Rapunzel Pure Organics
Bloomfield, NJ 800-225-1449
Regal Food Service
Houston, TX 281-477-3683
Reily Foods Company
New Orleans, LA 504-524-6131
Reily Foods/JFG Coffee Company
New Orleans, LA 800-535-1961
Restaurant Lulu Gourmet Products
San Francisco, CA 888-693-5800
Rocky Top Farms
Ellsworth, MI 800-862-9303
Roseland Manufacturing
Roseland, NJ. 973-228-2500
Rowena's
Norfolk, VA. 800-627-8699
Sabra Dipping Company
White Plains, NY 888-957-2272
Salmolux
Federal Way, WA 253-874-2026
Sarabeth's Kitchen
Bronx, NY. 800-773-7378
Sassafras Enterprises
Chicago, IL 800-537-4941
SBK Preserves
Bronx, NY. 800-773-7378
Schlotterbeck & Foss Company
Portland, ME. 800-777-4666
Schoolhouse Kitchen LLC
Brooklyn, NY 718-855-4990
Schreiber Foods Plant
Shippensburg, PA 717-530-5000
Scotsburn Dairy Group
Scotsburn, NS 902-485-8023
Scott-Bathgate
Winnipeg, MB. 800-216-2990
Sedlock Farm
Lynn Center, IL. 309-521-8284

Sessions Company
Enterprise, AL. 334-393-0200
Shawnee Canning Company
Cross Junction, VA 800-713-1414
Shenk's Foods
Lancaster, PA 717-393-4240
Silver Palate Kitchens
Cresskill, NJ 800-872-5283
Skjodt-Barrett Foods
Mississauga, ON. 877-600-1200
Sommer Maid Creamery
Doylestown, PA 215-345-6160
Southern Gold Honey CompAny
Vidor, TX 808-899-2494
Southern Peanut Company
Dublin, NC 910-862-2136
Springfield Smoked Fish Company
Springfield, MA 800-327-3412
St. Laurent Brothers
Bay City, MI 800-289-7688
Stello Foods
Punxsutawney, PA. 800-849-4599
Sugarman of Vermont
Hardwick, VT 800-932-7700
Summerland Sweets
Summerland, DC. 800-577-1277
Suzanne's Specialties
New Brunswick, NJ 800-762-2135
Sweet Mele's Hawaiian Products
Kailua, HI 800-990-8441
Synergy Foods
West Bloomfield, MI 313-849-2900
T Marzetti Company
Columbus, OH 614-846-2232
T.W. Garner Food Company
Winston Salem, NC. 800-476-7383
Tait Farm Foods
Centre Hall, PA 800-787-2716
Tara Foods
Atlanta, GA. 404-559-0605
Tarazi Specialty Foods
Chino, CA 909-628-3601
Terrapin Ridge Farms
Clearwater, FL 800-999-4052
The Great San Saba RiverPecan Company
San Saba, TX 800-621-9121
The Lollipop Tree, Inc
Auburn, NY. 800-842-6691
Thistledew Farm
Proctor, WV 800-854-6639
Thomson Food
Duluth, MN. 218-722-2529
Timber Crest Farms
Healdsburg, CA 888-374-9325
Trappist Preserves
Cleveland, OH 800-472-0425
Treasure Foods
West Valley, UT. 801-974-0911
Tribe Mediterranean Foods Company LLC
Taunton, MA. 774-961-0000
Tropical
Charlotte, NC 800-220-1413
Tropical Preserving Company
Los Angeles, CA. 213-748-5108
Valley View Blueberries
Vancouver, WA 360-892-2839
Ventura Foods
Ontario, CA. 323-262-9157
Ventura Foods
Salem, OR. 503-585-6423
Ventura Foods
Saginaw, TX 817-232-5450
Vic Rossano Incorporated
Montreal, QC 514-766-5252
Virginia & Spanish Peanut Company
Providence, RI 800-673-3562
Wagner Gourmet Foods
Lenexa, KS 913-469-5411
WCC Honey Marketing
City of Industry, CA 626-855-3086
Welch's Foods Inc
Kennewick, WA 509-582-2131
Welch's Foods Inc
Concord, MA 800-340-6870
Welch's Foods Inc.
North East, PA. 814-725-4577
Welcome Dairy
Colby, WI 800-472-2315
Westbrae Natural Foods
Melville, NY. 800-434-4246
Wild Thymes Farm
Greenville, NY 800-724-2877

WillowOak Farms
Woodland, CA. 888-963-2767
Wilsonhill Farm
South Bend, IN 802-899-2154
Wisconsin Wilderness Food Products
Milwaukee, WI 800-359-3039

Apple Butter

A.W. Jantzi & Sons
Wellesley, ON 519-656-2400
Bear Meadow Farm
Colrain, MA 800-653-9241
Betty Lou's Golden Smackers
McMinnville, OR 800-242-5205
Blue Jay Orchards
Bethel, CT. 203-748-0119
Bowman Apple Products Company
Mount Jackson, VA. 800-346-5382
Centennial Farms
Augusta, MO. 636-228-4338
Clements Foods Company
Oklahoma City, OK 800-654-8355
Cold Hollow Cider Mill
Waterbury Center, VT. 800-327-7537
Coutts Specialty Foods
Boxborough, MA 800-919-2952
Father's Country Hams
Bremen, KY 270-525-3554
Graves Mountain Lodge Inc.
Syria, VA. 540-923-4747
Hillcrest Orchard
Lake Placid, FL. 865-397-5273
House of Webster
Rogers, AR 800-369-4641
Kimes Cider Mill
Bendersville, PA 717-677-7539
Knouse Foods Coop
Peach Glen, PA 717-677-8181
Let's Serve
Plattsburgh, NY
Lost Trail Root Beer Com
Louisburg, KS. 800-748-7765
Love Creek Orchards
Medina, TX. 800-449-0882
McCutcheon's Apple Products
Frederick, MD. 800-888-7537
Shawnee Canning Company
Cross Junction, VA 800-713-1414
Shenk's Foods
Lancaster, PA 717-393-4240
Timber Crest Farms
Healdsburg, CA 888-374-9325
Tropical Preserving Company
Los Angeles, CA. 213-748-5108
Wilsonhill Farm
South Bend, IN 802-899-2154

Fruit Butter

A.M. Braswell Jr. Food Company
Statesboro, GA 800-673-9388
American Almond Products Company
Brooklyn, NY 800-825-6663
Applecreek Farms
Lexington, KY 800-747-8871
Betty Lou's Golden Smackers
McMinnville, OR 800-242-5205
Bowman Apple Products Company
Mount Jackson, VA. 800-346-5382
Clements Foods Company
Oklahoma City, OK 800-654-8355
Cold Hollow Cider Mill
Waterbury Center, VT. 800-327-7537
Dillman Farm
Bloomington, IN. 800-359-1362
Hollman Foods
Chicago, IL 888-926-2879
House of Webster
Rogers, AR 800-369-4641
JMS Specialty Foods
Ripon, WI 800-535-5437
Knouse Foods Coop
Peach Glen, PA 717-677-8181
Kozlowski Farms
Forestville, CA 800-473-2767
Lancaster Packing Company
Lancaster, PA 717-397-9727
Leroux Creek Foods
Hotchkiss, CO. 877-970-5670
Lost Trail Root Beer Com
Louisburg, KS. 800-748-7765
McCutcheon's Apple Products
Frederick, MD. 800-888-7537
Oregon Hill Farms
Saint Helens, OR. 800-243-4541
Scott Hams
Greenville, KY 800-318-1353
Shenk's Foods
Lancaster, PA 717-393-4240
Timber Crest Farms
Healdsburg, CA 888-374-9325
Tropical Preserving Company
Los Angeles, CA. 213-748-5108
Wilsonhill Farm
South Bend, IN 802-899-2154

Olive

A. Camacho
Plant City, FL 800-881-4534

Meats & Meat Products

Canned

Aunt Kitty's Foods
Vineland, NJ 856-691-2100
Broughton Cannery
Paulding, OH 419-399-3182
Calihan Pork Processing
Peoria, IL. 309-674-9175
Campbell Soup Company
Camden, NJ. 800-257-8443
Castleberry's
Vineland, NJ 856-691-2100
ConAgra Food Store Brands
Edina, MN. 952-469-4981
ConAgra Foods Trenton Plant
Trenton, MO 660-359-3913
ConAgra Foods/International Home Foods
Niagara Falls, ON 905-356-2661
Cordon Bleu International
Anjou, QC. 514-352-3000
Cumberland Gap Provision Company
Middlesboro, KY 800-331-7154
Dorina/So-Good
Union, IL. 815-923-2144
Fredericksburg Lockers/OPA's Smoke
Fredericksburg, TX. 800-543-6750
Gary's Frozen Foods
Lubbock, TX. 806-745-1933
Goya Foods of Florida
Miami, FL. 305-592-3150
Grabill Country Meats
Grabill, IN. 866-333-6328
Hormel Foods Corporation
Fremont, NE 402-721-2300
Hormel Foods Corporation
Orchard Park, NY 716-675-7700
Hormel Foods Corporation
Austin, MN 800-523-4635
Hsin Tung Yang Foods Co.
S San Francisco, CA 650-589-6789
J&B Sausage Company
Waelder, TX 830-788-7511
Kelly Foods
Jackson, TN 731-424-2255
Mertz Sausage Company
San Antonio, TX. 210-433-3263
O Chili Frozen Foods Inc
Northbrook, IL 847-562-1991
Triple U Enterprises
Fort Pierre, SD 605-567-3624
Vietti Foods Company Inc
Nashville, TN 800-240-7864

Cooked

Burke Corporation
Nevada, IA 800-654-1152

Always make it your best® with Burke fully cooked meats. We specialize in Italian sausage, beef, and pork toppings, meatballs, taco meats, shredded meats, pepperoni, bacon, Canadian-style bacon, chicken and beef strips. Additionally, we offer a variety of specialty products: Hand-Pinched Style® brand toppings, chorizo, gyro topping, andouille sausage, and breakfast patties and links.

Specialty Foods Group
Hampton, VA 800-238-0020

Dried

Alderfer Bologna
Harleysville, PA 800-341-1121
Asiago PDO & Speck Alto Adige PGI
New York, NY 646-258-0689
Breslow Deli Products
Philadelphia, PA 215-739-4200
Citterio USA Corporation
Freeland, PA 800-435-8888
Henningsen Foods
Omaha, NE 402-330-2500
High Country Snack Foods
Lincoln, MT 800-433-3916
Hoopeston Foods
Burnsville, MN 952-854-0903
Hsin Tung Yang Foods Co.
S San Francisco, CA 650-589-6789
Lone Star Beef Jerky Company
Lubbock, TX. 806-762-8833
Prime Smoked Meats
Oakland, CA 510-832-7167
Riverview Foods
Warsaw, KY 859-567-5211
Serv-Rite Meat Company
Los Angeles, CA. 323-227-1911
Shelton's Poultry
Pomona, CA 800-541-1833
Silver Star Meats
McKees Rocks, PA 800-548-1321
Sparrer Sausage Company
Chicago, IL 800-666-3287
Tupman-Thurlow Company
Deerfield Beach, FL 954-596-9989
Wolf Canyon Foods
Carmel, CA 831-626-1323

Frozen

Acme Steak & Seafood Company
Youngstown, OH. 330-270-8000
Ajinomoto Frozen Foods USA
Portland, OR 503-286-6548
Al Pete Meats
Muncie, IN 765-288-8817
Alphin Brothers
Dunn, NC 800-672-4502
AquaCuisine
Eagle, ID 208-323-2782
Armbrust Meats
Medford, WI 715-748-3102
Atlantic Meat Company
Savannah, GA 912-964-8511
Atlantic Veal & Lamb
Brooklyn, NY 800-222-8325
B&D Foods
Boise, ID 208-344-1183
Blakely Freezer Locker
Thomasville, GA. 229-723-3622
Bosell Foods
Cleveland, OH 216-991-7600
Bouma Meats
Provost, AB. 780-753-2092
Broadleaf Venison Usa
Vernon, CA 800-336-3844
Brook Locker Plant
Brook, IN 219-275-2611
Buono Beef Co
Philadelphia, PA 215-463-3600
Burke Corporation
Nevada, IA 800-654-1152

Always make it your best® with Burke fully cooked meats. We specialize in Italian sausage, beef, and pork toppings, meatballs, taco meats, shredded meats, pepperoni, bacon, Canadian-style bacon, chicken and beef strips. Additionally, we offer a variety of specialty products: Hand-Pinched Style® brand toppings, chorizo, gyro topping, andouille sausage, and breakfast patties and links.

Bush Brothers Provision Company
West Palm Beach, FL 800-327-1345
Butterfield Foods Company
Butterfield, MN. 507-956-5103
Buzz Food Service
Charleston, WV 304-925-4781
Calihan Pork Processing
Peoria, IL. 309-674-9175
Carando Gourmet Frozen Foods
Agawam, MA 888-227-2636
Cardinal Meat Specialists
Mississauga, ON. 800-363-1439
Caribbean Food Delights
Tappan, NY. 845-398-3000
Carriage House Foods
Ames, IA. 515-232-2273
Casa Di Bertacchi
Vineland, NJ 800-818-9261
Cedaredge Meats
Cedaredge, CO 970-856-6113
Centennial Food Corporation
Calgary, AB. 403-214-0044
Chef's Requested Foods
Oklahoma City, OK 800-256-0259
Cher-Make Sausage Company
Manitowoc, WI. 800-242-7679
Cheraw Packing
Cheraw, SC 843-537-7426
Completely Fresh Foods
Montebello, CA 323-722-9136
Conti Packing Company
Rochester, NY. 585-424-2500
Culinary Foods
Chicago, IL 800-621-4049
Culinary Standards Corporation
Louisville, KY 800-778-3434
Curly's Foods
Edina, MN. 800-722-1127
Davidson Meat Processing Plant
Waynesville, OH. 513-897-2971
Davidson Meat Products
New Bedford, MA 508-999-6293
Devault Foods
Devault, PA. 800-426-2874
Dold Foods
Wichita, KS. 316-838-9101
Duis Meat Processing
Concordia, KS. 800-281-4295
Duma Meats
Mogadore, OH 330-628-3438
El-Rey Foods
Ferguson, MO 314-521-3113
Florida Veal Processors
Wimauma, FL. 813-634-5545
Fuji Foods
Denver, CO 303-377-3738
Garden Protein International
Richmond, BC 877-305-6777
Gaucho Foods
Fayetteville, IL 877-677-2282
Gemini Food Industries
Charlton, MA 508-248-2730
Grecian Delight Foods
Elk Grove Village, IL 800-621-4387
Hall Brothers Meats
Cleveland, OH 440-235-3262
Hamm's Custom Meats
McKinney, TX. 972-562-7511
Hanover Foods Corporation
Hanover, PA 717-632-6000
Hatfield Quality Meats
Hatfield, PA. 800-523-5291
Heringer Meats
Covington, KY 859-291-2000
Holten Meats
Sauget, IL 800-851-4684
Hormel Foods Corporation
Columbia, MD 410-290-1916
Hormel Foods Corporation
Orchard Park, NY 716-675-7700
Hormel Foods Corporation
Austin, MN 800-523-4635
International Food Packers Corporation
Miami, FL. 305-669-1662
Jacob & Sons Wholesale Meats
Martins Ferry, OH. 740-633-3091
James Cowan & Sons
Worcester, MA 508-753-3259
Jbs Packerland Inc
Green Bay, WI
John Garner Meats
Van Buren, AR 800-543-5473
John Morrell & Company
Cincinnati, OH 712-279-7360
K&K Gourmet Meats
Leetsdale, PA 724-266-8400
Kelley Foods of Alabama
Elba, AL 334-897-5761
Kenosha Beef International
Kenosha, WI. 800-541-1685
King Kold Meats
Englewood, OH 800-836-2797
Kutztown Bologna Company
Leola, PA. 800-723-8824
L&H Packing Company
San Antonio, TX. 210-532-3241

Ladoga Frozen Food & Retail Meat
Ladoga, IN 765-942-2225
Leo G. Fraboni Sausage Company
Hibbing, MN. . . . 218-263-5074
MacFarlane Pheasants
Janesville, WI 877-269-8957
Mada'n Kosher Foods
Dania, FL 954-925-0077
Maid-Rite Steak Company
Dunmore, PA. . . . 800-233-4259
Maple Leaf Foods International
North York, ON. . . . 416-480-8900
Morrison Lamothe
Toronto, ON 877-677-6533
Mountain City Meat Company
Denver, CO 800-937-8325
North Side Foods Corporation
Arnold, PA 800-486-2201
O Chili Frozen Foods Inc
Northbrook, IL 847-562-1991
Omaha Steaks International
Omaha, NE 800-562-0500
Ottman Meat Company
New York, NY 212-879-4160
Otto & Son
West Jordan, UT 800-453-9462
P.A. Braunger Institutional Foods
Sioux City, IA. . . . 712-258-4515
Pacific Valley Foods
Bellevue, WA 425-643-1805
Paris Frozen Foods
Hillsboro, IL 217-532-3822
Pel-Freez
Rogers, AR 800-223-8751
Phoenix Agro-Industrial Corporation
Westbury, NY 516-334-1194
Pierceton Foods
Pierceton, IN. . . . 574-594-2344
Praters Foods
Lubbock, TX. . . . 806-745-2727
Prime Smoked Meats
Oakland, CA 510-832-7167
Provimi Foods, Inc
Seymour, WI. . . . 800-833-8325
R Four Meats
Chatfield, MN. . . . 507-867-4180
Redi-Serve Food Company
Fort Atkinson, WI. . . . 920-563-6391
Rogers Brothers
Galesburg, IL 309-342-2127
Rymer Foods
Chicago, IL. . . . 800-247-9637
Sanderson Farms
Collins, MS. . . . 601-765-0430
Sanderson Farms
Bryan, TX. . . . 979-778-5730
Sara Lee Corporation
Downers Grove, IL. . . . 630-598-8100
Scotsburn Dairy Group
Scotsburn, NS. . . . 902-485-8023
Shelley's Prime Meats
Jersey City, NJ 201-433-3434
Smith Packing Regional Meat
Utica, NY
Southeastern Meat Association
Oviedo, FL 407-365-5661
Specialty Brands
Carthage, MO 417-358-8104
Steak-Umm Company
Shillington, PA 860-928-5900
Stegall Smoked Turkey
Marshville, NC 800-851-6034
Sudlersville Frozen Food Locker
Sudlersville, MD. . . . 410-438-3106
Swissland Packing Company
Ashkum, IL. . . . 800-321-8325
Tenn Valley Ham Company
Paris, TN. . . . 731-642-9740
Thompson Packers
Slidell, LA. . . . 800-989-6328
Topps Meat Company
Elizabeth, NJ. . . . 877-998-6777
Travis Meats
Powell, TN 800-247-7606
Triple U Enterprises
Fort Pierre, SD 605-567-3624
Tucker Packing Company
Orrville, OH 330-683-3311
Tupman-Thurlow Company
Deerfield Beach, FL 954-596-9989
Tyson Fresh Meats Meat Packing Plant
Emporia, KS 620-343-3640
United Meat Company
San Francisco, CA 415-864-2118
Valley Meat Company
Modesto, CA. . . . 800-222-6328
Valley Meats
Coal Valley, IL 309-799-7341
W & G Marketing Company
Ames, IA. . . . 515-233-4774
Whitaker Foods
Waterloo, IA 800-553-7490
Zartic Inc
Rome, GA. . . . 800-241-0516

Ingredients

Burke Corporation
Nevada, IA 800-654-1152

Always make it your best® with Burke fully cooked meats. We specialize in Italian sausage, beef, and pork toppings, meatballs, taco meats, shredded meats, pepperoni, bacon, Canadian-style bacon, chicken and beef strips. Additionally, we offer a variety of specialty products: Hand-Pinched Style® brand toppings, chorizo, gyro topping, andouille sausage, and breakfast patties and links.

Cargill Texturizing Solutions
Cedar Rapids, IA. . . . 877-650-7080
GPI USA LLC.
Athens, GA 706-850-7826
Proliant Meat Ingredients
Harlan, IA 800-369-2672

Minced

Groff Meats
Elizabethtown, PA. . . . 717-367-1246
Reinhart Foods
Markham, ON. . . . 905-754-3500
Rohtstein Corporation
Woburn, MA 781-935-8300

Packers

A.C. Kissling Company
Philadelphia, PA 800-445-1943
A.L. Duck Jr Inc
Zuni, VA 757-562-2387
Abattoir Aliments Asta Inc.
St Alexandre Kamouraska, QC. . . . 418-495-2728
Agri Processors
Postville, IA 563-864-3013
AJM Meat Packing
San Juan, PR 787-787-4050
Al Safa Halal
Niagara Falls, NY. . . . 800-268-8174
Alaska Sausage and Seafood Company
Anchorage, AK. . . . 800-798-3636
Albert's Meats
Claysville, PA 800-522-9970
Alewel's Country Meats
Warrensburg, MO 800-353-8553
Alex Froehlich Packing Company
Johnstown, PA. . . . 814-535-7694
Alle Processing
Maspeth, NY. . . . 718-894-2000
Alle Processing Corporation
Maspeth, NY. . . . 800-245-5620
Amcan Industries
Elmsford, NY 914-347-4838
Appert's Foodservice
St Cloud, MN 800-225-3883
Arizona Sunland Foods
Tucson, AZ 520-624-7068
Atlantic Meat Company
Savannah, GA. . . . 912-964-8511
Atlantic Veal & Lamb
Brooklyn, NY 800-222-8325
B&D Foods
Boise, ID 208-344-1183
B&R Quality Meats
Waterloo, IA 319-232-6328
Bakalars Brothers Sausage Company
La Crosse, WI. . . . 608-784-0384
Ball Park Franks
Downers Grove, IL. . . . 630-598-8100
Bar-S Foods Company
Phoenix, AZ 602-264-7272
Baretta Provision
East Berlin, CT 860-828-0802
Barone Foods
Tucson, AZ 520-623-8571
Beef Packers, Inc.
Fresno, CA 559-268-5586
Bellville Meat Market
Bellville, TX. . . . 800-571-6328
Bierig Brothers
Vineland, NJ 856-691-8208
Big B Distributors
Evansville, IN. . . . 812-425-5235
Birchwood Foods
Kenosha, WI 800-541-1685
Blakely Freezer Locker
Thomasville, GA. . . . 229-723-3622
Blue Ribbon Meat Company
Sparks, NV 775-358-8116
Blue Ribbon Meats
Miami, FL. . . . 800-522-6115
Boesl Packing Company
Baltimore, MD 410-675-1071
Bowser Meat Processing
Meriden, KS 785-484-2454
Braham Food Locker Service
Braham, MN. . . . 320-396-2636
Brenntag Pacific
Santa Fe Springs, CA 562-903-9626
Breslow Deli Products
Philadelphia, PA 215-739-4200
Broadaway Ham Company
Jonesboro, AR. . . . 870-932-6688
Broadleaf Venison Usa
Vernon, CA 800-336-3844
Broken Bow Pack
Broken Bow, NE. . . . 308-872-2833
Brook Locker Plant
Brook, IN 219-275-2611
Brook Meadow ProvisionscCorporation
Hagerstown, MD. . . . 301-739-3107
Brown Packing Company
Gaffney, SC. . . . 864-489-5723
Bruce Packing Company
Silverton, OR 800-899-3629
Brush Locker
Fort Morgan, CO. . . . 970-842-2660
Bryant's Meats
Taylorsville, MS 601-785-6507
Buckhead Beef Company
Atlanta, GA. . . . 800-888-5578
Buono Beef Co
Philadelphia, PA 215-463-3600
Burgers Smokehouse
California, MO 800-624-5426
Burnett & Son Meat Company
Monrovia, CA. . . . 626-357-2165
Busseto Foods
Fresno, CA 800-628-2633
Buzz Food Service
Charleston, WV 304-925-4781
C&C Packing Company
Stamps, AR. . . . 870-533-2251
C&S Wholesale Meat Company
Atlanta, GA. . . . 404-627-3547
C. Roy Meat Products
Yale, MI. . . . 810-387-3957
Callaway Packing Company
Delta, CO 800-332-6932
Calumet Diversified Meat Company
Pleasant Prairie, WI 262-947-7200
Cambridge Packing Company
Boston, MA. . . . 800-722-6726
Carando Gourmet Frozen Foods
Agawam, MA 888-227-2636
Cardinal Meat Specialists
Mississauga, ON. . . . 800-363-1439
Cargill Meat Solutions
Timberville, VA 540-896-7041
Caribbean Food Delights
Tappan, NY. . . . 845-398-3000
Carl Streit & Son Company
Neptune, NJ 732-775-0803
Carl Venezia Meats
Plymouth Meeting, PA 610-239-6750
Carlton Farms
Carlton, OR. . . . 800-932-0946
Carolina By-Products Company
Winchester, VA. . . . 540-877-2590
Carolina Packers
Smithfield, NC 800-682-7675
Casa Di Bertacchi
Vineland, NJ 800-818-9261
Catelli Brothers
Camden, NJ. . . . 856-869-2200

Caughman's Meat Plant
Lexington, SC 803-356-0076
Cavens Meats
Conover, OH 937-368-3841
Caviness Packing Company
Hereford, TX 806-364-0900
Cedaredge Meats
Cedaredge, CO 970-856-6113
Centennial Food Corporation
Calgary, AB 403-214-0044
Center Locker Service Company
Center, MO 573-267-3343
Central Beef
Center Hill, FL 352-793-3671
Central Meat & Provision Company
San Diego, CA 619-239-1391
Charlie's Country Sausage
Minot, ND 701-838-6302
Charlie's Pride Meats
Vernon, CA 877-866-0982
Chef's Requested Foods
Oklahoma City, OK 800-256-0259
Chicago 58 Food Products
Woodbridge, ON 416-603-4244
Chino Meat Provision Corporation
Chino, CA 909-627-1997
Chisesi Brothers Meat Packing Company
New Orleans, LA 800-966-3550
Cibao Meat Product
Bronx, NY 718-993-5072
Cifelli & Sons
South River, NJ 732-238-0090
Clay Center Locker Plant
Clay Center, KS 785-632-5550
Cloud's Meat Processing
Carthage, MO 417-358-5855
Clyde's Italian & German Sausage
Denver, CO 303-433-8744
Collbran Locker Plant
Collbran, CO 970-487-3329
Community Market & Deli
Lindstrom, MN 651-257-1128
Con Agra Foods
Lincoln, NE 800-332-8400
ConAgra Beef Company
Greeley, CO 970-506-8000
ConAgra Foods Trenton Plant
Trenton, MO 660-359-3913
ConAgra Foods/Eckrich
Omaha, NE 800-327-4424
ConAgra Refrigerated Foods International
Omaha, NE 800-624-4724
ConAgra Refrigerated Prepared Foods
Naperville, IL 630-857-1000
Conecuh Sausage Company
Evergreen, AL 800-726-0507
Corfu Foods
Bensenville, IL 630-595-2510
Corte Provisions
Newark, NJ 201-653-7246
Country Butcher Shop
Palmyra, MO 573-769-2257
Country Smoked Meats
Bowling Green, OH 800-321-4766
Counts Sausage Company
Prosperity, SC 803-364-2392
Crater Meat Packing Company
Medford, OR 541-772-6966
Crofton & Sons
Brandon, FL 800-878-7675
Crystal Lake
Decatur, AR 800-382-4425
Cudlin's Market
Newfield, NY 607-564-3443
Culinary Standards Corporation
Louisville, KY 800-778-3434
Culver Duck
Middlebury, IN 800-825-9225
Curly's Foods
Edina, MN 800-722-1127
Custom-Pak Meats
Knoxville, TN 865-687-0871
Dakota Premium Foods
South Saint Paul, MN 651-552-8230
Dale T. Smith & Sons Meat Packing Corporation
Draper, UT 801-571-3611
Dallas City Packing
Dallas, TX 214-948-3901
David Mosner Meat Products
Bronx, NY 718-328-5600
Davidson Meat Products
New Bedford, MA 508-999-6293
Davis Custom Meat Processing
Overbrook, KS 785-665-7713
Dean Sausage Company
Attalla, AL 800-228-0704
Debragga & Spitler
New York, NY 212-924-1311
Dee's Cheesecake Factory/Dee's Foodservice
Albuquerque, NM 505-884-1777
Dennison Meat Locker
Dennison, MN 507-645-8734
Diggs Packing Company
Columbia, MO 573-449-2995
Dinner Bell Meat Product
Concord, VA
DiPasquale's
Baltimore, MD 410-276-6787
Dold Foods
Wichita, KS 316-838-9101
Dolores Canning Company
Los Angeles, CA 323-263-9155
Duis Meat Processing
Concordia, KS 800-281-4295
Dunham's Meats
Urbana, OH 937-653-6709
Dutterer's Home Food Service
Baltimore, MD 410-298-3663
Dynatabs
Brooklyn, NY 718-376-4508
E&H Packing Company
Detroit, MI 313-567-8286
E.E. Mucke & Sons
Hartford, CT 800-726-5598
E.W. Knauss & Son
Quakertown, PA 800-648-4220
East Dayton Meat & Poultry
Dayton, OH 937-253-6185
Edelman Meats
Antigo, WI 715-623-7686
Egon Binkert Meat Products
Baltimore, MD 410-687-5959
Ehresman Packing Company
Garden City, KS 620-276-3791
El Paso Meat Company
El Paso, TX 915-838-8600
El-Rey Foods
Ferguson, MO 314-521-3113

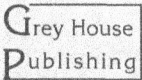

Elba Custom Meats
Elba, AL 334-897-2007
Ellsworth Locker
Ellsworth, MN 507-967-2544
Enslin & Son Packing Company
Hattiesburg, MS 800-898-4687
Excel Corporation
Wichita, KS. 800-835-2837
F&Y Enterprises
Wauconda, IL 847-526-0620
Fairbury Food Products
Fairbury, NE 402-729-3379
Fargo Packing & SausagecCompany
West Fargo, ND. 800-342-4250
Farm Boy Food Service
Evansville, IN 800-852-3976
Farmers Produce
Ashby, MN 218-747-2749
Farmington Food
Forest Park, IL 800-609-3276
Farmland Foods
Carroll, IA. 712-792-1660
Farmland Foods
Denison, IA. 800-831-1812
Ferko Meat Company
Milwaukee, WI 414-967-5500
Finchville Farms
Finchville, KY 502-834-7952
Fineberg Packing Company
Memphis, TN 901-458-2622
Fiorucci Foods
Colonial Heights, VA 800-524-7775
Fischer Meats
Issaquah, WA 425-392-3131
Flanders Provision Company
Waycross, GA. 912-283-5191
Flint Hills Foods
Alma, KS
Florida Veal Processors
Wimauma, FL. 813-634-5545
Foell Packing Company
Naperville, IL 919-776-0592
Fortenberry Ice Company
Kodak, TN. 865-933-2568
Foster Farms
Demopolis, AL 800-255-7227
Frank Wardynski & Sons
Buffalo, NY. 716-854-6083
Frank's Foods
Hilo, HI 808-959-9121
Freeze-Dry Products
Santa Rosa, CA. 707-547-1776
Fresh Mark
Canton, OH. 800-860-6777
Fricks Meat Products
Washington, MO. 800-241-2209
Fuji Foods
Denver, CO 303-377-3738
Fulton Provision Company
Portland, OR 800-333-6328
G Di Lullo & Sons
Westville, NJ. 856-456-3700
G&G Sheep Farm
Boston, KY 502-833-4863
Gaiser's European Style Provisions
Union, NJ 908-686-3421
GE Hawthorn Meat Company
Hot Springs, AR 501-623-8111
Gem Meat Packing Company
Boise, ID. 208-375-9424
Gemini Food Industries
Charlton, MA 508-248-2730
George L. Wells Meat Company
Philadelphia, PA 800-523-1730
Gibbon Packing
Gibbon, NE. 308-468-5771
Gilleshammer Thiele Farms
Saint Thomas, ND. 701-257-6634
Glasco Locker Plant
Glasco, KS 785-568-2364
Glazier Packing Company
Malone, NY. 518-483-4990
Glen's Packing Company
Hallettsville, TX 800-368-2333
Glier's Meats
Covington, KY 800-446-3882
Global Food Industries
Townville, SC 800-225-4152
Godshall's Quality Meats
Telford, PA 888-463-7425
Gold Cup Farms
Clayton, NY 800-752-1341
Gold Star Sausage Company
Denver, CO 800-258-7229
Grabill Country Meats
Grabill, IN. 866-333-6328
Grant Park Packing
Chicago, IL 312-421-4096
Greater Omaha Packing Company
Omaha, NE 402-731-1700
Grecian Delight Foods
Elk Grove Village, IL 800-621-4387
Griffin Industries
Cold Spring, KY 859-781-2010
Groezinger Provisions
Neptune, NJ 800-927-9473
Grote & Weigel
Bloomfield, CT. 860-242-8528
Gulf Packing Company
San Benito, TX 956-399-2631
Gunnoe Farms-Sausage & Salad Company
Charleston, WV 304-343-7686
Gwaltney of Smithfield
Portsmouth, VA. 757-465-0666
H&H Foods
Mercedes, TX 800-365-4632
H&K Packers Company
Winnipeg, NB 204-233-2354
Hahn Brothers
Westminster, MD 800-227-7675
Halal Transactions
Omaha, NE 402-572-6120
Hampton House J.D. Sweid Ltd
Burnaby, BC 800-665-4355
Hansen Packing Meat Company
Jerseyville, IL 618-498-3714
Harvest Direct
Knoxville, TN. 800-838-2727
Hastings Meat Supply
Hastings, NE. 402-463-9857
Hatfield Quality Meats
Hatfield, PA. 800-523-5291
Henningsen Foods
Omaha, NE 402-330-2500
Henry J Meat Specialties
Chicago, IL 800-242-1314
Herman Falter Packing Company
Columbus, OH 800-325-6328
Herring Brothers
Dover Foxcroft, ME 207-876-2631
High Country Snack Foods
Lincoln, MT 800-433-3916
Hightower's Packing
Minden, LA. 318-377-5459
Hilltop Meat Company
Andalusia, AL. 800-781-0053
Hoffman Sausage Company
Cincinnati, OH 513-621-4160
Holly Hill Locker Company
Holly Hill, SC. 803-496-3611
Holten Meats
Sauget, IL 800-851-4684
Holton Meat Processing
Holton, KS 785-364-2331
Home Delivery Food Service
Jefferson, GA 706-367-9551
Hoopeston Foods
Burnsville, MN. 952-854-0903
Hoople Country Kitchens
Rockport, IN 812-649-2351
Hormel Foods Corporation
Fremont, NE 402-721-2300
Hormel Foods Corporation
Maitland, FL. 407-660-1433
Hormel Foods Corporation
Columbia, MD 410-290-1916
Hormel Foods Corporation
Pittsburgh, PA. 412-921-7036
Hormel Foods Corporation
Franklin, MA 508-541-7101
Hormel Foods Corporation
Cincinnati, OH 513-563-0211
Hormel Foods Corporation
Des Moines, IA. 515-276-8872
Hormel Foods Corporation
Phoenix, AZ 602-230-2400
Hormel Foods Corporation
Orchard Park, NY. 716-675-7700
Hormel Foods Corporation
Austin, MN 800-523-4635
Hormel Foods Corporation
Arlington, TX 817-465-4735
Hormel Foods Corporation
Cordova, TN 901-753-4282
Hormel Foods Corporation
Lebanon, NJ 908-236-7009
Hormel Foods Corporation
Pleasanton, CA 925-734-9555
Hot Springs Packing Company
Hot Springs, AR 800-535-0449
Hsin Tung Yang Foods Co.
S San Francisco, CA. 650-589-6789
Hubbard Meat Company
Big Spring, TX 432-267-7781
Hughes Springs Frozen Food Center
Hughes Springs, TX 903-639-2941
Hughson Meat Company
San Marcos, TX 877-462-6328
Huisken Meat Center
Sauk Rapids, MN 320-259-0305
Humphrey Blue Ribbon Meats
Springfield, IL. 800-747-6328
Indian Valley Meats
Indian, AK. 907-653-7511
International Casing Group
Chicago, IL 800-825-5151
International Casings Group
Santa Fe Springs, CA 800-635-9518
International Food Packers Corporation
Miami, FL. 305-669-1662
International Meat Company
Chicago, IL 773-622-1400
Iowa Quality Meats
Clive, IA 800-677-6868
Isernio Sausage Company
Seattle, WA 888-495-8674
Ito Cariani Sausage Company
Hayward, CA 510-887-0882
Ittels Meats
Howard Lake, MN 320-543-2285
J Freirich Food Products
Long Island City, NY 800-221-1315
J.T. Ward Meats & Provisions
Vernon, CA 323-585-9935
J.W. Treuth & Sons
Baltimore, MD 410-465-4650
Jack's Wholesale Meat Company
Trenton, TX. 903-989-2293
Jackson Brothers Food Locker
Post, TX 806-495-3245
Jackson Frozen Food Center
Hutchinson, KS. 620-662-4465
Jacobsmuhlen's Meats
Cornelius, OR 503-359-0479
Jaindl's Turkey Farms
Orefield, PA 800-475-6654
Jbs Packerland Inc
Green Bay, WI
Jemm Wholesale Meat Company
Chicago, IL 773-523-8161
Jensen Meat Company
Vista, CA. 760-727-6700
Jesses Fine Meats
Cherokee, IA. 712-225-3637
John Garner Meats
Van Buren, AR 800-543-5473
John R. Daily
Missoula, MT 406-721-7007
John R. Morreale
Chicago, IL. 312-421-3664
John Volpi & Company
St Louis, MO. 800-288-3439
Johnson's Wholesale Meats
Opelousas, LA 337-948-4444
Johnson, Nash, & Sons Farms
Rose Hill, NC 800-682-6843
Johnsonville Food Company
Sheboygan Falls, WI. 888-556-2728
Jones Dairy Farm
Fort Atkinson, WI. 800-563-1004
Jordahl Meats
Manchester, MN. 507-826-3418
Joseph Kirschner & Company
Augusta, ME. 207-623-3544
Joseph Sanders
Custer, MI. 800-968-5035
Keeter's Meat Company
Tulia, TX. 800-456-5019
Kelley Foods of Alabama
Elba, AL 334-897-5761
Kelly Packing Company
Torrington, WY. 307-532-2210
Kenosha Beef International
Kenosha, WI. 800-541-1685
Kent Quality Foods
Grand Rapids, MI 800-748-0141

Kershenstine Beef Jerky
Eupora, MS 662-258-2049
Ketters Meat Market & Locker Plant
Frazee, MN 218-334-2351
Keystone Foods Corporation
West Conshohocken, PA 610-667-6700
Kiefer Company
Louisville, KY 502-587-7474
King Meat
Los Angeles, CA 323-582-7401
Kingsbury Country Market
Kingsbury, IN 219-393-3016
Kiolbassa Provision Company
San Antonio, TX 800-456-5465
Koegel Meats
Flint, MI 810-238-3685
Konetzkos Market
Browerville, MN 320-594-2915
Kowalski Sausage Company
Hamtramck, MI 800-482-2400
Kretschmar
Don Mills, ON 800-561-4532
Kruse & Son
Monrovia, CA 626-358-4536
Kruse Meat Products
Alexander, AR 501-316-2100
Kunzler & Company
Lancaster, PA 888-586-9537
Kutztown Bologna Company
Leola, PA 800-723-8824
L&H Packing Company
San Antonio, TX 210-532-3241
L&L Packing Company
Chicago, IL 800-628-6328
L&M Frosted Food Lockers
Belt, MT 406-277-3522
Lad's Smokehouse Catering
Needville, TX 979-793-6210
Ladoga Frozen Food & Retail Meat
Ladoga, IN 765-942-2225
Lakeside Foods
Plainview, MN 507-534-3141
Lampost Meats
Grimes, IA 515-288-6111
Land O'Frost
Searcy, AR 800-643-5654

Larsen Packers
Burwick, NS 902-538-8060
Lees Sausage Company
Orangeburg, SC 803-534-5517
Lengerich Meats
Zanesville, IN 260-638-4123
Leo G. Fraboni Sausage Company
Hibbing, MN 218-263-5074
Lindner Bison
Valencia, CA 866-247-8753
Lombardi Brothers Meat Packers
Denver, CO 800-421-4412
Lone Star Beef Jerky Company
Lubbock, TX 806-762-8833
Lords Sausage & CountryhHam
Dexter, GA 800-342-6002
Lynden Meat Company
Lynden, WA 360-354-2449
M K Meat Processing Plant
Burton, TX 979-289-4022
Mac's Meats Wholesale
Las Cruces, NM 575-524-2751
MacFarlane Pheasants
Janesville, WI 877-269-8957
MacGregors Meat & Seafood
Toronto, ON 888-383-3663
Maid-Rite Steak Company
Dunmore, PA 800-233-4259
Manger Packing Company
Baltimore, MD 800-227-9262
Maple Leaf Foods International
North York, ON 416-480-8900
Maple Leaf Meats
Motreal, QC 800-268-3708
Maple Leaf Pork
Montreal, QC 800-268-3708
Marburger Foods
Peru, IN 765-472-1139
Marcel et Henri Charcuterie Francaise
South San Francisco, CA 800-227-6436
Marks Meat
Canby, OR 503-266-2048
MBM Corporation
Rocky Mount, NC 252-985-7200
McLemore's Abattoir
Vidalia, GA 912-537-4476

Meal Mart
Maspeth, NY 800-245-5620
Meat Center
Edna, TX 361-782-3776
Meating Place
Buffalo, NY 716-885-3623
Medeiros Farms
Kalaheo, HI 808-332-8211
Merkley & Sons Packing
Jasper, IN 812-482-7020
Michael's Finer Meats & Seafoods
Columbus, OH 800-282-0518
Midway Meats
Centralia, WA 360-736-5257
Mike's Meats
Eitzen, MN 507-495-3336
Miller Brothers PackingcCompany
Sylvester, GA 229-776-2014
Mishler Packing Company
Lagrange, IN 260-768-4156
Moonlite Bar Bq Inn
Owensboro, KY 800-322-8989
Morrison Lamothe
Toronto, ON 877-677-6533
Morrison Meat Packers
Miami, FL 800-330-4267
Mountain City Meat Company
Denver, CO 800-937-8325
Mountain States Rosen
Bronx, NY 800-872-5262
Moyer Packing Company
Souderton, PA 800-967-8325
Napoleon Locker
Napoleon, IN 812-852-4333
National Beef Packing Co., LLC
Kansas City, MO 800-449-2333
National By-Products
Omaha, NE 402-733-8308
National Foods
Indianapolis, IN 800-683-6565
Neithart Meats
Sylmar, CA 818-361-7141
New City Packing & Provision Company
North Aurora, IL 630-851-8800
New Generation Foods
Omaha, NE 402-733-5755

New Glarus Foods
New Glarus, WI 800-356-6685
Nicky
Portland, OR 800-469-4162
Niemuth's Steak & Chop Shop
Waupaca, WI. 715-258-2666
North Star Foods
Saint Charles, MN 507-932-4831
O'Brien & Company
Bellevue, NE. 800-433-7567
O'Neill Packing Company
Omaha, NE 402-733-1200
Oh Boy! Corporation
San Fernando, CA. 818-361-1128
Ohio Packing Company
Columbus, OH 800-282-6403
Oklahoma City Meat
Oklahoma City, OK 405-235-3308
Olson Locker
Fairmont, MN 507-238-2563
Omaha Meat Processors
Omaha, NE 402-554-1965
Omaha Steaks International
Omaha, NE 800-562-0500
On-Cor Foods Products
Northbrook, IL 847-205-1040
Original Chili Bowl
Tulsa, OK 918-628-0225
Oscars Whlse. Meats
Ogden, UT. 801-394-6472
Ossian Seafood Meats
Ossian, IN 260-622-4191
Our Best Foods
Tewksbury, MA. 978-858-0077
Owens Country Sausage
Richardson, TX. 800-966-9367
Package Concepts & Materials Inc
Greenville, SC. 800-424-7264
Palmer Packing Company
Tremonton, UT 435-257-5329
Paradise Locker Company
Trimble, MO 816-370-6328
Pasqualichio Brothers
Scranton, PA 800-232-6233
PB&S Chemicals
Henderson, KY 800-950-7267
Peco Foods
Tuscaloosa, AL 205-345-4711
Peerless Packing Company
Beckley, WV. 304-252-4731
Pekarna's Meat Market
Jordan, MN 952-492-6101
Pel-Freez
Rogers, AR 800-223-8751
Pender Packing Company
Rocky Point, NC. 910-675-3311
Petschl's Quality Meats
Tukwila, WA. 206-575-4400
Pfeffer's Country Mkt.
Sauk Centre, MN 320-352-6490
Phoenix Agro-Industrial Corporation
Westbury, NY 516-334-1194
Pie Piper Products
Bensenville, IL 800-621-8183
Pierceton Foods
Pierceton, IN. 574-594-2344
Pierre Foods
Cincinnati, OH 513-874-8741
Piller Sausages & Delicatessens
Waterloo, ON 800-265-2628
Pinter's Packing Plant
Dorchester, WI 715-654-5444
Plumrose USA
Elkhart, IN. 574-295-8190
Plymouth Beef
Bronx, NY. 718-589-8600
PM Beef Holdings
Windom, MN 800-622-5213
Prairie Cajun Whlse.
Eunice, LA 337-546-6195
Premium Meat Company
Brigham City, UT 435-723-5944
Premium Standard Farms
Princeton, MO. 660-748-4647
Prime Smoked Meats
Oakland, CA 510-832-7167
Provimi Foods, Inc
Seymour, WI. 800-833-8325
Pruden Packing Company
Suffolk, VA 757-539-8773
Puueo Poi Factory
Hilo, HI 808-935-8435
Quality Beef Company
Providence, RI 877-233-3462
Quality Meats & Seafood
West Fargo, ND. 800-342-4250
Quality Sausage Company
Dallas, TX. 214-634-3400
Quantum Foods LLC
Bolingbrook, IL 800-334-6328
R Four Meats
Chatfield, MN. 507-867-4180
R.E. Meyer Company
Lincoln, NE. 888-990-2333
R.M. Felts Packing Company
Ivor, VA. 888-300-0971
Rabbit Barn
Turlock, CA. 209-632-1123
Raber Packing
Peoria, IL. 309-673-0721
Raemica
Highland, CA 909-864-1990
Ralph's Packing Company
Perkins, OK. 800-522-3979
Rancher's Lamb of Texas
San Angelo, TX 325-659-4004
Randolph Packing Corporation
Asheboro, NC 336-672-1470
Randy's Frozen Meats
Faribault, MN 800-354-7177
Ray's Sausage Company Inc
Cleveland, OH 216-921-8782
Real Kosher Sausage Company
Newark, NJ 973-690-5394
Redi-Serve Food Company
Fort Atkinson, WI. 920-563-6391
Register Meat Company
Cottondale, FL 850-352-4269
Rego's Purity Foods
Honolulu, HI 808-847-3717
Reser's Fine Foods
Beaverton, OR 800-333-6431
Rhone-Poulenc Food Ingredients
Cranbury, NJ 609-860-4000
Rinehart Meat Processing
Branson, MO. 417-334-2044
Ritchie Wholesale Meats
Piketon, OH 800-628-1290
Riverton Packing
Riverton, WY 307-856-3838
Robbins Packing Company
Statesboro, GA 912-764-7503
Robinsons Sausage Company
London, KY 606-864-2914
Rock River Provision Company
Rock Falls, IL 800-685-1195
Rocky Mountain Packing Company
Havre, MT. 406-265-3401
Roman Packing Company
Norfolk, NE. 800-373-5990
Roman Sausage Company
Santa Clara, CA 800-497-7462
Roode Packing Company
Fairbury, NE 402-729-2253
Rosa Brothers
Miami, FL. 305-324-1510
Rose Packing Company
South Barrington, IL. 800-323-7363
Rosen's Diversified
Fairmont, MN 800-798-2000
Royal Center Locker Plant
Royal Center, IN 574-643-3275
Royal Home Bakery
Newmarket, ON 905-715-7044
Royal Palate Foods
Inglewood, CA 310-330-7701
Rudolph's Market & Sausage Factory
Dallas, TX. 214-741-1874
Russer Foods
Buffalo, NY. 800-828-7021
Rymer Foods
Chicago, IL 800-247-9637
S.S. Logan Packing Company
Huntington, WV 800-642-3524
S.W. Meat & Provision Company
Phoenix, AZ 602-275-2000
Sadler's Smokehouse
Henderson, TX 903-657-5581
Sahlen Packing Company
Buffalo, NY. 716-852-8677
Sambol Meat Company
Overland Park, KS 913-334-8404
San Angelo Packing
San Angelo, TX 325-653-6951
San Antonio Packing Company
San Antonio, TX. 210-224-5441
Sanderson Farms
Bryan, TX 979-778-5730
Sara Lee Corporation
Downers Grove, IL. 630-598-8100
Sardinha Sausage
Somerset, MA. 800-678-0178
Saval Foods
Elkridge, MD 800-527-2825
Savoie's Sausage & Food Products
Opelousas, LA. 337-948-4115
Scalas Original Beef & Sausage Company LLC
Chicago, IL 866-467-2252
Scanga Meat Company
Salida, CO 719-539-3511
Schleswig Specialty Meats
Schleswig, IA 712-676-3324
Schumacher Wholesale Meats
Golden Valley, MN 800-432-7020
Seaboard Foods
Shawnee Mission, KS. 800-262-7907
Serv-Rite Meat Company
Los Angeles, CA. 323-227-1911
Shaker Valley Foods
Cleveland, OH 216-961-8600
Shamrock Slaughter Plant
Shamrock, TX. 806-256-3241
Shelley's Prime Meats
Jersey City, NJ 201-433-3434
Shelton's Poultry
Pomona, CA 800-541-1833
Shofar Kosher Foods
Linden, NJ. 888-874-6327
Siena Foods
Toronto, ON 800-465-0422
Silver Creek Specialty Meats
Oshkosh, WI 920-232-3581
Silver Star Meats
McKees Rocks, PA 800-548-1321
Sioux-Preme Packing Company
Sioux Center, IA 712-722-2555
Skylark Meats
Omaha, NE 800-759-5275
Smith Meat Packing
Port Huron, MI 810-985-5900
Smith Packing Regional Meat
Utica, NY
Smith Provision Company
Erie, PA. 800-334-9151
Smithfield Packing Company
Smithfield, VA 757-357-4321
SOPAKCO Foods
Mullins, SC. 800-276-9678
Souris Valley Processors
Melita, NB. 204-522-8210
Southchem
Durham, NC 800-849-7000
Southern Packing Corporation
Chesapeake, VA 757-421-2131
Sparrer Sausage Company
Chicago, IL 800-666-3287
Specialty Brands
Carthage, MO 417-358-8104
Specialty Steak Service
Erie, PA. 814-452-2281
Spencer Packing Company
Washington, NC 252-946-4161
Spring Hill Meat Market
Spring Hill, KS 913-592-3501
Springville Meat & ColdsStorage
Springville, UT 801-489-6391
Stampede Meat
Bridgeview, IL 800-353-0933
Standard Beef Company
Foxboro, MA 203-787-2164
Statewide Meats & Poultry
New Haven, CT 203-777-6669
Steak-Umm Company
Shillington, PA 860-928-5900
Stewarts Market
Yelm, WA 360-458-2091
Stock Yards Packing Company
Chicago, IL 800-621-1119
Stone Meat Processor
Ogden, UT. 801-782-9825
Stonies Sausage Shop Inc
Perryville, MO 888-546-2540
Strasburg Provision
Strasburg, OH 800-207-6009
Striplings
Moultrie, GA. 229-985-4226

Sudlersville Frozen Food Locker
Sudlersville, MD 410-438-3106
Sunergia Soyfoods
Charlottesville, VA 800-693-5134
Sunnydale Meats
Gaffney, SC 864-489-6091
Superior Meat Company
Vernal, UT 435-789-3274
Suzanna's Kitchen
Duluth, GA 800-241-2455
SW Red Smith
Davie, FL 954-581-1996
Swift & Company
Greeley, CO 970-506-8000
Swiss American Sausage Corporation
Lathrop, CA 209-858-5555
Swiss-American Sausage Company
Lathrop, CA 209-858-5555
Swissland Packing Company
Ashkum, IL 800-321-8325
T O Williams
Portsmouth, VA 757-397-0771
T.L. Herring & Company
Wilson, NC 252-291-1141
Taylor Meat Company
Taylor, TX 512-352-6357
Taylor Provisions Company
Trenton, NJ 609-392-1113
Temptee Specialty Foods
Denver, CO 800-842-1233
Tenn Valley Ham Company
Paris, TN 731-642-9740
Tennessee Valley PackingCompany
Columbia, TN 931-388-2623
Theriaults Abattoir
Van Buren, ME 207-868-3344
Thomas Brothers Ham Company
Asheboro, NC 336-672-0337
Thomas Packing Company
Columbus, GA 800-729-0976
Thompson Packers
Slidell, LA 800-989-6328
Thumann's
Carlstadt, NJ 201-935-3636
Tiger Meat Provisions
Miami, FL 305-324-0083
Tillamook Meat Company
Tillamook, OR 503-842-4802
Tooele Valley Meat
Grantsville, UT 435-884-3837
Topps Meat Company
Elizabeth, NJ 877-998-6777
Travis Meats
Powell, TN 800-247-7606
Triple U Enterprises
Fort Pierre, SD 605-567-3624
Troy Pork Store
Troy, NY 518-272-8291
Tupman-Thurlow Company
Deerfield Beach, FL 954-596-9989
Tyler Packing Company
Tyler, TX 903-593-9592
Tyson Foods
Fort Smith, AR 479-783-8996
Tyson Foods Tyson Technical Services Lab
Amarillo, TX 806-335-1531
Tyson Foods Plant
Santa Teresa, NM 800-351-8184
Tyson Fresh Meats
Dakota Dunes, SD 605-235-2061
Tyson Fresh Meats Meat Packing Plant
Emporia, KS 620-343-3640
Une-Viandi
St. Jean Sur Richelieu, NB 800-363-1955
United Meat Company
San Francisco, CA 415-864-2118
United Packing
Providence, RI 401-751-6935
United Provision Meat Company
Columbus, OH 614-252-1126
V & V Supremo Foods
Chicago, IL 888-887-8773
V.W. Joyner & Company
Smithfield, VA 757-357-2161
Valley Institutional Foods Company
Edinburg, TX 956-383-7620
Valley Meat Company
Modesto, CA 800-222-6328
Victor Ostrowski & Son
Baltimore, MD 410-327-8935
Vienna Meat Products
Scarborough, ON 800-588-1931
Vienna Sausage Company
Chicago, IL 800-366-3647
Vietti Foods Company Inc
Nashville, TN 800-240-7864
Vollwerth & Baroni Companies
Hancock, MI 800-562-7620
W & G Marketing Company
Ames, IA 515-233-4774
Waco Beef & Pork Processors
Waco, TX 254-772-4669
Wall Meat Processing
Wall, SD 605-279-2348
Wampler's Farm Sausage Company
Lenoir City, TN 800-728-7243
Wasatch Meats
Salt Lake City, UT 801-363-5747
Washington Beef
Toppenish, WA 800-289-2333
Watsons Quality Food Prooducts
Blackwood, NJ 800-257-7870
Wayco Ham Company
Goldsboro, NC 800-962-2614
Weber-Stephen Products Company
Palatine, IL 800-446-1071
Western Meats
Rapid City, SD 605-342-0322
Westport Locker Service
Westport, IN 877-265-0551
White Castle System
Columbus, OH 866-272-8372
White Packing Company
Fredericksburg, VA 540-898-2029
Whittaker & Associates
Atlanta, GA 404-266-1265
Wichita Packing Company
Chicago, IL 800-986-9742
Willcox Packing House
Willcox, AZ 520-384-2015
Willies Smoke House
Harrisville, PA 800-742-4184
Wimmer's Meat Products
West Point, NE 800-358-0761
Windcrest Meat Packers
Port Perry, ON 800-750-2542
Wolverine Packing
Detroit, MI 313-259-7500
Woodbine
Norfolk, VA 757-461-2731
World Casing Corporation
Maspeth, NY 800-221-4887
Wright Brand Foods
Vernon, TX 940-553-1888
XL Beef
Calgary, AB 403-236-2424
Y&T Packing
Springfield, IL 217-522-3345
Yoakum Packing Company
Yoakum, TX 361-293-3541
Zartic Inc
Rome, GA 800-241-0516
Zerna Packing
Labadie, MO 636-742-4190
Zummo Meat Company
Beaumont, TX 409-842-1810
Zweigle's
Rochester, NY 585-546-1740

Patties

Acme Steak & Seafood Company
Youngstown, OH 330-270-8000
Cargill Foods
Minneapolis, MN 800-227-4455
Caribbean Food Delights
Tappan, NY 845-398-3000
Chicago Meat Authority
Chicago, IL 773-254-3811
Corfu Foods
Bensenville, IL 630-595-2510
Dallas Dressed Beef
Dallas, TX 214-638-0142
Decker & Son Company
Colorado Springs, CO 719-634-8311
Holten Meats
Sauget, IL 800-851-4684
Karn Meats
Columbus, OH 800-221-9585
Kenosha Beef International
Kenosha, WI 800-541-1685
Kutztown Bologna Company
Leola, PA 800-723-8824
L&H Packing Company
San Antonio, TX 210-532-3241
Laurent Meat Market
Marrero, LA 504-341-1771
Les Trois Petits Cochons 3 Little Pigs
Brooklyn, NY 212-219-1230
Meating Place
Buffalo, NY 716-885-3623
Otto & Son
West Jordan, UT 800-453-9462
Redi-Serve Food Company
Fort Atkinson, WI 920-563-6391
Rego's Purity Foods
Honolulu, HI 808-847-3717
Roman Sausage Company
Santa Clara, CA 800-497-7462
S.W. Meat & Provision Company
Phoenix, AZ 602-275-2000
Springville Meat & ColdsStorage
Springville, UT 801-489-6391
Topps Meat Company
Elizabeth, NJ 877-998-6777
Travis Meats
Powell, TN 800-247-7606
Valley Meat Company
Modesto, CA 800-222-6328
Wisconsin Packing Company
Butler, WI 800-558-2000
Zartic Inc
Rome, GA 800-241-0516

Frozen

Birchwood Foods
Kenosha, WI 800-541-1685
Burke Corporation
Nevada, IA 800-654-1152

Always make it your best® with Burke fully cooked meats. We specialize in Italian sausage, beef, and pork toppings, meatballs, taco meats, shredded meats, pepperoni, bacon, Canadian-style bacon, chicken and beef strips. Additionally, we offer a variety of specialty products: Hand-Pinched Style® brand toppings, chorizo, gyro topping, andouille sausage, and breakfast patties and links.

Cardinal Meat Specialists
Mississauga, ON 800-363-1439
Caribbean Food Delights
Tappan, NY 845-398-3000
Chicago Meat Authority
Chicago, IL 773-254-3811
Corfu Foods
Bensenville, IL 630-595-2510
Edmonds Chile Company
St Louis, MO 314-772-1499
Flanders Provision Company
Waycross, GA 912-283-5191
Glenmark Food Processors
Chicago, IL 800-621-0117
Holten Meats
Sauget, IL 800-851-4684
Jemm Wholesale Meat Company
Chicago, IL 773-523-8161
John Garner Meats
Van Buren, AR 800-543-5473
Kenosha Beef International
Kenosha, WI 800-541-1685
King Kold Meats
Englewood, OH 800-836-2797
Kutztown Bologna Company
Leola, PA 800-723-8824
Leo G. Fraboni Sausage Company
Hibbing, MN 218-263-5074
Maid-Rite Steak Company
Dunmore, PA 800-233-4259
Mello's North End Manufacturings
Fall River, MA 800-673-2320
On-Cor Foods Products
Northbrook, IL 847-205-1040
Plymouth Beef
Bronx, NY 718-589-8600
Redi-Serve Food Company
Fort Atkinson, WI 920-563-6391
Thompson Packers
Slidell, LA 800-989-6328
Topps Meat Company
Elizabeth, NJ 877-998-6777
Valley Meat Company
Modesto, CA 800-222-6328

Wisconsin Packing Company
Butler, WI 800-558-2000
Zartic Inc
Rome, GA 800-241-0516

Portion Cuts

A to Z Portion Meats
Bluffton, OH 800-338-6328
Atlantic Veal & Lamb
Brooklyn, NY 800-222-8325
B&D Foods
Boise, ID 208-344-1183
Beef Products
North Sioux City, SD 605-217-8000
Blue Ribbon Meats
Miami, FL 800-522-6115
Boar's Head Provisions Company
Sarasota, FL 888-884-2627
Bouma Meats
Provost, AB 780-753-2092
Broadleaf Venison Usa
Vernon, CA 800-336-3844
Bruss Company
Chicago, IL 800-621-3882
Bush Brothers Provision Company
West Palm Beach, FL 800-327-1345
C&S Wholesale Meat Company
Atlanta, GA 404-627-3547
Cambridge Packing Company
Boston, MA 800-722-6726
Canal Fulton Provision
Canal Fulton, OH 800-321-3502
Caribbean Food Delights
Tappan, NY 845-398-3000
Carl Streit & Son Company
Neptune, NJ 732-775-0803
Carolina Pride Foods
Greenwood, SC 864-229-5611
Castleberry's Meats
Atlanta, GA 404-873-1804
Chicago Meat Authority
Chicago, IL 773-254-3811
Cloverdale Foods Company
Mandan, ND 800-669-9511
Corfu Foods
Bensenville, IL 630-595-2510
Dairy Fresh Foods
Taylor, MI 313-295-6300
Decker & Son Company
Colorado Springs, CO 719-634-8311
Devault Foods
Devault, PA 800-426-2874
Foodbrands America
Oklahoma City, OK 405-290-4000
Frank's Foods
Hilo, HI 808-959-9121
Henry J Meat Specialties
Chicago, IL 800-242-1314
James J. Derba Company
Boston, MA 800-732-3848
King Kold Meats
Englewood, OH 800-836-2797
L&L Packing Company
Chicago, IL 800-628-6328
Land O'Frost
Searcy, AR 800-643-5654
Loggins Meat Company
Tyler, TX 800-527-8610
Marshallville Packing Company
Marshallville, OH 330-855-2871
National Foods
Indianapolis, IN 800-683-6565
O Chili Frozen Foods Inc
Northbrook, IL 847-562-1991
Ottman Meat Company
New York, NY 212-879-4160
Otto W Liebold & Company
Flint, MI 800-999-6328
Pacific Poultry Company
Honolulu, HI 808-841-2828
Paris Frozen Foods
Hillsboro, IL 217-532-3822
Quality Meats & Seafood
West Fargo, ND 800-342-4250
Randy's Frozen Meats
Faribault, MN 800-354-7177
Robinsons Sausage Company
London, KY 606-864-2914
Russer Foods
Buffalo, NY 800-828-7021
S.W. Meat & Provision Company
Phoenix, AZ 602-275-2000
SOPAKCO Foods
Mullins, SC 800-276-9678
Standard Beef Company
Foxboro, MA 203-787-2164
Tenn Valley Ham Company
Paris, TN 731-642-9740
Triple U Enterprises
Fort Pierre, SD 605-567-3624
United Meat Company
San Francisco, CA 415-864-2118
Waco Beef & Pork Processors
Waco, TX 254-772-4669
Whitaker Foods
Waterloo, IA 800-553-7490
Wisconsin Packing Company
Butler, WI 800-558-2000

Prepared

Burke Corporation
Nevada, IA 800-654-1152

Always make it your best® with Burke fully cooked meats. We specialize in Italian sausage, beef, and pork toppings, meatballs, taco meats, shredded meats, pepperoni, bacon, Canadian-style bacon, chicken and beef strips. Additionally, we offer a variety of specialty products: Hand-Pinched Style® brand toppings, chorizo, gyro topping, andouille sausage, and breakfast patties and links.

Gutheinz Meats
Scranton, PA 570-344-1191
Specialty Foods Group
Hampton, VA 800-238-0020

Proteins

Burke Corporation
Nevada, IA 800-654-1152

Always make it your best® with Burke fully cooked meats. We specialize in Italian sausage, beef, and pork toppings, meatballs, taco meats, shredded meats, pepperoni, bacon, Canadian-style bacon, chicken and beef strips. Additionally, we offer a variety of specialty products: Hand-Pinched Style® brand toppings, chorizo, gyro topping, andouille sausage, and breakfast patties and links.

Proliant Meat Ingredients
Harlan, IA 800-369-2672

General

Aala Meat Market
Honolulu, HI 808-832-6650
Acme Farms
Seattle, WA 800-542-8309
Alexian Pates/GroezingerProvisions
Neptune, NJ 800-927-9473
Arnold's Meat Food Products
Brooklyn, NY 800-633-7023
Asiago PDO & Speck Alto Adige PGI
New York, NY 646-258-0689
Ballard Custom Meats
Manchester, ME 207-622-9764
Baltimore Poultry & Meats
Baltimore, MD 410-783-7361
Belleville Brothers Packing
North Baltimore, OH 419-257-3529
Bering Sea Raindeer Products
Mekoryuk, AK 907-827-8940
Bernard & Sons
Bakersfield, CA 661-327-4431
Blalock Seafood
Orange Beach, AL 251-974-5811
Bradley Technologies Canada Inc.
Delta, BC 800-665-4188
Broadbent's B&B Foods
Kuttawa, KY 800-841-2202
Brown Foods
Dallas, GA 770-445-4554
Burke Corporation
Nevada, IA 800-654-1152

Always make it your best® with Burke fully cooked meats. We specialize in Italian sausage, beef, and pork toppings, meatballs, taco meats, shredded meats, pepperoni, bacon, Canadian-style bacon, chicken and beef strips. Additionally, we offer a variety of specialty products: Hand-Pinched Style® brand toppings, chorizo, gyro topping, andouille sausage, and breakfast patties and links.

C&J Tender Meat
Anchorage, AK 907-562-2838
Casper Foodservice Company
Chicago, IL 312-226-2265
Chipper Snax
Salt Lake City, UT 801-977-0742
Chong Mei Trading
East Point, GA 404-768-3838
Cimpl Meats
Yankton, SD 605-665-1665
Coleman Purely Natural Brands
Golden, CO 800-442-8666
Completely Fresh Foods
Montebello, CA 323-722-9136
Conco Food Service
New Orleans, LA 800-488-3988
Country - Fed - Meats Company
Riverdale, GA 800-637-7559
Creminelli Fine Meats, LLC
Salt Lake City, UT 801-428-1820
Double B Distributors
Lexington, KY 859-255-8822
Dpi Specialty Foods, Inc
Evanston, IL 503-692-0662
Dutch Valley Veal
South Holland, IL 800-832-8325
E-Fish-Ent Fish Company
Sooke, BC 250-642-4007
Ellsworth Foods
Tifton, GA 229-386-8448
Evan's Food Products
Chicago, IL 773-254-7400
G&W Packing Company
Chicago, IL 773-847-5400
Garden Protein International
Richmond, BC 877-305-6777
Glenoaks Food
Sun Valley, CA 818-768-9091
GoodMark Foods
Stamford, CT 919-790-9940
Gopicnic
Chicago, IL 773-328-2490
Great West of Hawaii
Honolulu, HI 808-593-9981
Grennan Meats
Rochelle, IL 815-562-5565
Gulf Marine & Industrial Supplies
New Orleans, LA 800-886-6252
Hammons Meat Sales
Bakersfield, CA 661-831-9541
Harbison Wholesale Meats
Cullman, AL 256-739-5105
Hawkins Inc
Minneapolis, MN 800-328-5460
Hela Spice Company
Uxbridge, ON 877-435-2649
Higa Meat and Pork Market Limited
Honolulu, HI 808-531-3591
Hinojosa Bros Wholesale
Roma, TX 800-554-4119
International Farmers Market
Chamblee, GA 770-455-1777
JM Swank Company
North Liberty, IA 800-593-6375
Kern Meat Distributing
Brooksville, KY 606-756-2255
King Nut Company
Solon, OH 800-860-5464
Kunzler & Company
Lancaster, PA 888-586-9537
Levonian Brothers
Troy, NY 518-274-3610
Link Snacks
Minong, WI 800-346-6896
Manda Fine Meats
Baton Rouge, LA 225-344-7636
Manhattan Wholesale MeatCompany
Manhattan, KS 785-776-9203
Marathon Enterprises
Englewood, NJ 800-722-7388

Market Day Corporation
Itasca, IL 877-632-7753
McDowell Fine Meats 2
Phoenix, AZ 602-254-6022
McFarling Foods
Indianapolis, IN 317-635-2633
McKenzie of Vermont
Burlington, VT 802-864-4585
McRedmond Brothers
Nashville, TN 615-361-8997
Meat & Fish Fellas
Glendale, AZ 623-931-6190
Meat Corral Company
Gainesville, GA 770-536-9188
Miami Beef Company
Hialeah, FL 305-621-3252
My Favorite Jerky
Boulder, CO 303-444-2846
Naman's Meat Company
Mobile, AL 251-633-2700
Nash Finch Company
Statesboro, GA 912-681-4580
National Meat & Provision Company
Reserve, LA 985-479-4200
New Grass Bison
Shawnee, KS 866-422-5888
Northern Meats
Anchorage, AK 907-561-1729
Northwest Meat Company
Chicago, IL 312-733-1418
Oberto Sausage Company
Kent, WA 877-453-7591
Oberweis Dairy
North Aurora, IL 888-645-5868
Oscars Whlse. Meats
Ogden, UT 801-394-6472
Otto W Liebold & Company
Flint, MI 800-999-6328
Park 100 Foods
Tipton, IN 800-854-6504
Phenix Food Service
Phenix City, AL 334-298-6288
Piggie Park Enterprises
West Columbia, SC 800-628-7423
Pilot Meat & Sea Food Company
Galena, IL 319-556-0760
Pioneer Snacks
Farmington Hills, MI 248-862-1990
Pluester's Quality Meat Company
Hardin, IL 618-396-2224
Pon Food Corporation
Ponchatoula, LA 985-386-6941
Porkie Company of Wisconsin
Cudahy, WI 800-333-2588
Porrhoff Foods Company
Des Moines, IA 515-244-5271
Prime Cut Meat & Seafood Company
Phoenix, AZ 602-455-8834
Primera Meat Service
Harlingen, TX 956-423-4846
Protos Foods
Greensburg, PA 724-836-1802
Ready Portion Meat Company
Baton Rouge, LA 225-355-5641
Schenk Packing Company
Mount Vernon, WA 360-336-2128
Seafood Dimension International
Anaheim, CA 714-692-6464
Service Foods
Norcross, GA 770-448-5300
Shuffs Meat Company
Thurmont, MD 301-271-2231
Smoke House
Sagle, ID 208-263-6312
Snak King Corporation
City of Industry, CA 626-336-7711
Southeastern Meats
Birmingham, AL 205-923-8555
Speco
Schiller Park, IL 800-541-5415
SRA Foods
Birmingham, AL 205-323-7447
SSI Food Service
Caldwell, ID 208-482-7844
Stegall Smoked Turkey
Marshville, NC 800-851-6034
Surlean Foods
San Antonio, TX 800-999-4370
Teddy's Tasty Meats
Anchorage, AK 907-562-2320
Thumann's
Carlstadt, NJ 201-935-3636
Todd's
Vernon, CA 800-938-6337
Trail's Best Snacks
Memphis, TN 800-852-1863
Trenton Processing
Trenton, IL 618-224-7383
Troyer Foods
Goshen, IN 800-876-9377
Turkey Creek Snacks
Thomaston, GA 706-647-8841
United Universal Enterprises Corporation
Phoenix, AZ 623-842-9691
Utz Quality Foods
Hanover, PA 800-367-7629
Vac Pac Manufacturing Company
Baltimore, MD 800-368-2301
Vanee Foods Company
Berkeley, IL 708-449-7300
Vantage USA
Chicago, IL 773-247-1086
Vity Meat & Provisions Company
Phoenix, AZ 602-269-7768
W.L. Halsey Grocery Company
Huntsville, AL 256-772-9691
YB Meats of Wichita
Wichita, KS 316-942-1213

Beef & Beef Products

A to Z Portion Meats
Bluffton, OH 800-338-6328
A. Stein Meat Products
Brooklyn, NY 718-492-0760
A. Thomas Meats
Louisville, KY 800-253-2020
A.C. Kissling Company
Philadelphia, PA 800-445-1943
Abbott's Meat
Flint, MI 810-232-7128
Abbyland Foods
Abbotsford, WI 800-732-5483
Abeles & Heymann GourmetKosher Provisions, Inc.
Bronx, NY 718-589-0100
Acme Steak & Seafood Company
Youngstown, OH 330-270-8000
Adolf's Meats & Sausage Kitchen
Hartford, CT 860-522-1588
Advance Food Company
Enid, OK 888-723-8237
AFI-FlashGril'd Steak
Salt Lake City, UT 800-382-2862
Agri-Best Foods
Chicago, IL 773-247-5060
Al Safa Halal
Niagara Falls, NY 800-268-8174
Alderfer Bologna
Harleysville, PA 800-341-1121
Alle Processing
Maspeth, NY 718-894-2000
Allied Meat Service
Hayward, CA 800-794-2554
Alphin Brothers
Dunn, NC 800-672-4502
Alpine Cheese Company
Winesburg, OH 330-359-6291
Alpine Meats
Stockton, CA 800-399-6328
American Food Traders
Miami, FL 305-273-7090
American Foods Group
Green Bay, WI 920-436-4229
Amity Packing Company
Chicago, IL 800-837-0270
Arena & Sons
Hopkinton, MA 508-435-3673
Arizona Sunland Foods
Tucson, AZ 520-624-7068
Arlund Meat Company
Overland Park, KS 913-321-3450
Armbrust Meats
Medford, WI 715-748-3102
Atlantic Meat Company
Savannah, GA 912-964-8511
Atlantic Premium Brands
Northbrook, IL 847-412-6200
Aunt Kitty's Foods
Vineland, NJ 856-691-2100
Aurora Packing Company
North Aurora, IL 630-897-0551
B&R Quality Meats
Waterloo, IA 319-232-6328
B3R Country Meats
Childress, TX 940-937-3668

Bakalars Brothers Sausage Company
La Crosse, WI 608-784-0384
Ball Park Franks
Downers Grove, IL 630-598-8100
Bar-W Meat Company
Fort Worth, TX 817-831-0051
Baretta Provision
East Berlin, CT 860-828-0802
Barney Pork House
Decatur, AL 256-350-9988
Barone Foods
Tucson, AZ 520-623-8571
Bartlow Brothers
Rushville, IL 800-252-7202
Beef Packers, Inc.
Fresno, CA 559-268-5586
Beef Products
North Sioux City, SD 605-217-8000
Bellville Meat Market
Bellville, TX 800-571-6328
Berks Packing Company, Inc.
Reading, PA 800-882-3757
Berry Processing
Watseka, IL 815-432-3264
Best Kosher Foods
Chicago, IL 888-800-0072
Best Provision Co Inc.
Newark, NJ 800-631-4466
Big B Distributors
Evansville, IN 812-425-5235
Binkert's Meat Products
Baltimore, MD 410-687-5959
Birchwood Foods
Kenosha, WI 800-541-1685
Blakely Freezer Locker
Thomasville, GA 229-723-3622
Blue Ribbon Meats
Cleveland, OH 216-631-8850
Blue Ribbon Meats
Miami, FL 800-522-6115
Border's Market
Plymouth, OH 419-687-2634
Boulder Sausage
Louisville, CO 303-665-6302
Bouma Meats
Provost, AB 780-753-2092
Bouvry Exports Calgary
Calgary, AB 403-253-0717
Boyd Sausage Company
Washington, IA 319-653-5715
Braham Food Locker Service
Braham, MN 320-396-2636
Breslow Deli Products
Philadelphia, PA 215-739-4200
Brockton Beef & Provisions Corporation
Brockton, MA 508-583-4703
Brook Locker Plant
Brook, IN 219-275-2611
Brook Meadow ProvisionscCorporation
Hagerstown, MD 301-739-3107
Brookfield Farms Nationwide Foods
Chicago, IL 773-787-4900
Brown Foods
Dallas, GA 770-445-4554
Brown Packing Company
Gaffney, SC 864-489-5723
Brown Thompson & Sons
Fancy Farm, KY 270-623-6321
Bruce Foods Corporation
New Iberia, LA 337-365-8101
Bruss Company
Chicago, IL 800-621-3882
Bullock's Country Meats
Westminster, MD 410-848-6786

Burke Corporation
Nevada, IA 800-654-1152

Always make it your best® with Burke fully cooked meats. We specialize in Italian sausage, beef, and pork toppings, meatballs, taco meats, shredded meats, pepperoni, bacon, Canadian-style bacon, chicken and beef strips. Additionally, we offer a variety of specialty products: Hand-Pinched Style® brand toppings, chorizo, gyro topping, andouille sausage, and breakfast patties and links.

Burnett & Son Meat Company
Monrovia, CA 626-357-2165
Bush Brothers Provision Company
West Palm Beach, FL 800-327-1345
Buzz Food Service
Charleston, WV 304-925-4781
C&J Tender Meat
Anchorage, AK 907-562-2838
C&S Wholesale Meat Company
Atlanta, GA 404-627-3547
Caddo Packing Company
Marshall, TX 903-935-2211
Callaway Packing Company
Delta, CO 800-332-6932
Cambridge Slaughtering
Cambridge, IL 309-937-2455
Campbell Soup Company
Camden, NJ 800-257-8443
Campbell's Quality Cuts
Sidney, OH 937-492-2194
Camrose Packers
Camrose, AB 780-672-4887
Canal Fulton Provision
Canal Fulton, OH 800-321-3502
Candelari's Specialty Sausage
Houston, TX 800-953-5343
Capital Packers Inc
Edmonton, AB 800-272-8868
Capolla Food Inc
North York, ON 416-633-0389
Carando Gourmet Frozen Foods
Agawam, MA 888-227-2636
Cargill Foods
Minneapolis, MN 800-227-4455
Cargill Meats
Milwaukee, WI 800-558-4242
Caribbean Food Delights
Tappan, NY 845-398-3000
Caribbean Products
Baltimore, MD 410-235-7700
Carl Rittberger Sr.
Zanesville, OH 740-452-2767
Carl Streit & Son Company
Neptune, NJ 732-775-0803
Carmel Meat/Specialty Foods
Marina, CA 800-298-5823
Caro Foods
Houma, LA 985-858-2640
Castle Rock Meats
Denver, CO 303-292-0855
Castleberry's
Vineland, NJ 856-691-2100
Castleberry's Meats
Atlanta, GA 404-873-1804
Cattaneo Brothers
San Luis Obispo, CA 800-243-8537
Centennial Food Corporation
Calgary, AB 403-214-0044
Center Locker Service Company
Center, MO 573-267-3343
Central Beef
Center Hill, FL 352-793-3671
Central Meat & Provision Company
San Diego, CA 619-239-1391
Chandler Foods
Greensboro, NC 800-537-6219
Charles Smart Donair Submarine
Edmonton, AB 780-468-2099
Charlie's Pride Meats
Vernon, CA 877-866-0982
Chef's Requested Foods
Oklahoma City, OK 800-256-0259
Cher-Make Sausage Company
Manitowoc, WI 800-242-7679
Cheraw Packing
Cheraw, SC 843-537-7426
Chicago 58 Food Products
Woodbridge, ON 416-603-4244
Chicago Meat Authority
Chicago, IL 773-254-3811
Chicago Steaks
Chicago, IL 800-776-4174
Chip Steak & Provision Company
Mankato, MN 507-388-6277
Choice One Foods
Los Angeles, CA 323-231-7777
Cimpl Meats
Yankton, SD 605-665-1665
Circle V Meat Company
Spanish Fork, UT 801-798-3081
Clay Center Locker Plant
Clay Center, KS 785-632-5550
Clem's Refrigerated Foods
Lexington, KY 800-544-5571
Clover Valley Food
Pierce, NE 402-329-4025
Cloverdale Foods Company
Mandan, ND 800-669-9511
Cloverdale Packing
Parkersburg, WV 304-485-5409
Clovervale Farms
Amherst, OH 800-433-0146
Coleman Purely Natural Brands
Golden, CO 800-442-8666
Collbran Locker Plant
Collbran, CO 970-487-3329
Columbia Packing Company
Dallas, TX 800-460-8171
Community Market & Deli
Lindstrom, MN 651-257-1128
Completely Fresh Foods
Montebello, CA 323-722-9136
Comstock's Marketing
Barton, VT 802-754-2426
Con Agra Food Cooperative
Montgomery, AL 334-288-8660
ConAgra Beef Company
Hyrum, UT 435-245-6456
ConAgra Beef Company
Greeley, CO 970-506-8000
ConAgra Foods/Eckrich
Omaha, NE 800-327-4424
ConAgra Foods/International Home Foods
Niagara Falls, ON 905-356-2661
ConAgra Refrigerated Foods International
Omaha, NE 800-624-4724
Conti Packing Company
Rochester, NY 585-424-2500
Continental Deli Foods
Cherokee, IA 712-225-6529
Continental Sausage
Denver, CO 303-288-9787
Corfu Foods
Bensenville, IL 630-595-2510
Corte Provisions
Newark, NJ 201-653-7246
Couch's Country Style Sausages
Cleveland, OH 216-823-2332
Country Butcher Shop
Palmyra, MO 573-769-2257
Country Village Meats
Sublette, IL 815-849-5532
Creuzebergers Meats
Duncansville, PA 814-695-3061
Critchfield Meats
Lexington, KY 800-866-3287
Crofton & Sons
Brandon, FL 800-878-7675
Cropp Cooperative-Organic Valley
La Farge, WI 888-444-6455
Crown Point
St John, IN 219-365-3200
Cumberland Gap Provision Company
Middlesboro, KY 800-331-7154
Curly's Custom Meats
Jackson Center, OH 937-596-6518
Curly's Foods
Edina, MN 800-722-1127
Curtis Packing Company
Greensboro, NC 336-275-7684
Cyclone Enterprises
Houston, TX 281-872-0087
D'Artagnan
Newark, NJ 800-327-8246
Daily's Premium Meats
Salt Lake City, UT 800-328-7695
Dakota Premium Foods
South Saint Paul, MN 651-552-8230
Dale T. Smith & Sons Meat Packing Corporation
Draper, UT 801-571-3611
Dallas City Packing
Dallas, TX 214-948-3901
Dallas Dressed Beef
Dallas, TX 214-638-0142
Daniel Weaver Company
Lebanon, PA 800-932-8377
Darling International
Bellevue, NE 402-731-7600
David Berg & Company
Chicago, IL 773-278-5195
Davidson Meat Processing Plant
Waynesville, OH 513-897-2971
Day-Lee Foods
Santa Fe Springs, CA 800-329-5331
Dearborn Sausage Company
Dearborn, MI 866-900-4426
Debragga & Spitler
New York, NY 212-924-1311
Dee's Cheesecake Factory/Dee's Foodservice
Albuquerque, NM 505-884-1777
Deen Meat Company
Fort Worth, TX 800-333-3953
Devault Foods
Devault, PA 800-426-2874
Diggs Packing Company
Columbia, MO 573-449-2995
Dino's Sausage & Meat Company
Utica, NY 315-732-2661
DiPasquale's
Baltimore, MD 410-276-6787
Dom's Sausage Company
Malden, MA 781-324-6390
Donald E. Hunter Meat Company
Hillsboro, OH 937-466-2311
Dorina/So-Good
Union, IL 815-923-2144
Drier's Meats
Three Oaks, MI 269-756-3101
Dryden Provision Company
Louisville, KY 502-583-1777
Dugdale Beef Company
Indianapolis, IN 317-291-9660
Duma Meats
Mogadore, OH 330-628-3438
Dutch Packing Company
Miami, FL 305-871-3640
Dutch Valley Veal
South Holland, IL 800-832-8325
Dutterer's Home Food Service
Baltimore, MD 410-298-3663
Dynamic Foods
Lubbock, TX 806-747-2777
E&H Packing Company
Detroit, MI 313-567-8286
E.W. Knauss & Son
Quakertown, PA 800-648-4220
East Beauregard Meat Processing Center
Deridder, LA 337-328-7171
East Dayton Meat & Poultry
Dayton, OH 937-253-6185
Ed Miniat
South Holland, IL 708-589-2400
Ed Miniat Inc. Headquarters/Cooked Meat Plant
South Holland, IL 708-589-2400
Edelman Meats
Antigo, WI 715-623-7686
Edelmann Provision Company
Harrison, OH 513-881-5800
Edmonton Meat Packing Company
Edmonton, AB 800-361-6328
Eickman's Processing
Seward, IL 815-247-8451
Eiserman Meats
Slave Lake, AB 780-849-5507
El Paso Meat Company
El Paso, TX 915-838-8600
Ellsworth Locker
Ellsworth, MN 507-967-2544
Empire Beef & Redistribution
Rochester, NY 800-462-6804
Empire Kosher Foods
Mifflintown, PA 800-367-4734
Enjoy Foods International
Fontana, CA 909-823-2228
Eureka Lockers
Eureka, IL 309-467-2731
Eurocaribe Packing Company
Vega Baja, PR
Ezzo Sausage Company
Columbus, OH 800-558-8841
Fabbri Sausage Manufacturing
Chicago, IL 312-829-6363
Farley Candy Company
Chicago, IL 773-254-0900

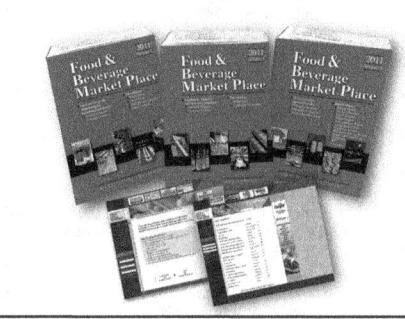

Farm Boy Food Service
Evansville, IN 800-852-3976
Farmland Foods
Kansas City, MO. . . . 888-327-6526
Ferko Meat Company
Milwaukee, WI 414-967-5500
First Original Texas Chili Company
Fort Worth, TX 817-626-0983
Flanders Provision Company
Waycross, GA 912-283-5191
Flint Hills Foods
Alma, KS
Fm Brown Sons
Reading, PA 800-345-3344
Foodbrands America
Oklahoma City, OK 405-290-4000
Foster Farms
Demopolis, AL 334-289-5082
Fred Usinger
Milwaukee, WI 800-558-9998
Freeze-Dry Ingredients
Berkeley, IL. 708-544-1880
Fremont Beef Company
Fremont, NE 402-727-7200
Frontier Beef Company
Huntingdon Valley, PA 215-663-2120
Fuji Foods
Denver, CO 303-377-3738
Gary's Frozen Foods
Lubbock, TX. 806-745-1933
Gaucho Foods
Fayetteville, IL 877-677-2282
GE Hawthorn Meat Company
Hot Springs, AR 501-623-8111
Gelsinger Food Products
Montrose, CA 818-248-7811
Gem Meat Packing Company
Boise, ID. 208-375-9424
Gemini Food Industries
Charlton, MA 508-248-2730
George L. Wells Meat Company
Philadelphia, PA 800-523-1730
Georgetown Farm
Free Union, VA. 888-328-5326
GFI Premium Foods
Minneapolis, MN 800-669-8996
Glasco Locker Plant
Glasco, KS 785-568-2364
Glenmark Industries
Chicago, IL 773-927-4800
Godshall's Quality Meats
Telford, PA 888-463-7425
Golden Locker Cooperative
Golden, IL. 217-696-4456
Grant Park Packing
Chicago, IL 312-421-4096
Greater Omaha Packing Company
Omaha, NE 402-731-1700
Grimm's Fine Food
Calgary, AB. 877-577-5220
Grimm's Locker Service
Sherwood, OH 419-899-2655
Groff Meats
Elizabethtown, PA. 717-367-1246
Gwinn's Foods
St Louis, MO. 314-521-8792
H&K Packers Company
Winnipeg, NB 204-233-2354
Hahn & Company
San Francisco, CA 415-394-6512
Hahn Brothers
Westminster, MD 800-227-7675
Halal Transactions
Omaha, NE 402-572-6120
Hall Brothers Meats
Cleveland, OH 440-235-3262
Ham I Am
Dallas, TX. 800-742-6426
Hamilos Brothers Inspected Meats
Madison, IL. 618-451-7877
Hamm's Custom Meats
McKinney, TX. 972-562-7511
Happy Acres Packing Company
Petal, MS. 601-584-8301
Harper's Country Hams
Clinton, KY. 888-427-7377
Harris Ranch Beef Company
Selma, CA. 800-742-1955
Hartford Provision Company
South Windsor, CT 860-583-3908
Harvin Choice Meats
Sumter, SC 803-775-9367
Hausman Foods
Corpus Christi, TX 800-364-5521
Heinke Industrial Park
Paradise, CA 530-877-1059
Henry J Meat Specialties
Chicago, IL 800-242-1314
Heringer Meats
Covington, KY 859-291-2000
Hickory Baked Food
Castle Rock, CO 303-688-2633
Hickory Farms
Maumee, OH. 419-893-7611
High Country Snack Foods
Lincoln, MT 800-433-3916
High Valley Farm
Castle Rock, CO 303-634-2944
Hillbilly Smokehouse
Rogers, AR 479-636-1927
Hoff's United Foods
Brownsville, WI 920-583-3734
Holly Hill Locker Company
Holly Hill, SC 803-496-3611
Holmes Foods
Nixon, TX. 830-582-1970
Holten Meats
Sauget, IL 800-851-4684
Holton Meat Processing
Holton, KS 785-364-2331
Home Market Foods
Norwood, MA. 781-948-1500
Honey Baked Ham Company
Cincinnati, OH 513-583-8792
Horlacher's Fine Meats
Logan, UT. 435-752-1287
Hormel Foods Corporation
Maitland, FL 407-660-1433
Hormel Foods Corporation
Austin, MN 800-523-4635
Houser Meats
Rushville, IL 217-322-4994
Hsin Tung Yang Foods Co.
S San Francisco, CA. 650-589-6789
Humeniuk's Meat Cutting
Ranfurly, AB 780-658-2381
Huse's Country Meats
Malone, TX. 254-533-2205
Idaho Beverages
Lewiston, ID 208-743-6535
Independent Master Casing Company
Santa Fe Springs, CA 800-635-9518
International Food Packers Corporation
Miami, FL. 305-669-1662
International Meat Company
Chicago, IL 773-622-1400
Isernio Sausage Company
Seattle, WA 888-495-8674
Ito Cariani Sausage Company
Hayward, CA 510-887-0882
Ittels Meats
Howard Lake, MN 320-543-2285
J.M. Schneider
Saint Anselme, QC 418-885-4474
Jack's Wholesale Meat Company
Trenton, TX. 903-989-2293
Jackson Brothers Food Locker
Post, TX 806-495-3245
Jacob & Sons Wholesale Meats
Martins Ferry, OH. 740-633-3091
Jacobs Meats
Defiance, OH 419-782-7831
Jacobsmuhlen's Meats
Cornelius, OR 503-359-0479
Jakes Brothers Country Meats
Joelton, TN 615-876-2911
Janowski's Hamburgers
Rockville Centre, NY 516-764-9591
Jay & Boots Meats
Knoxville, TN. 423-922-3213
Jbs Packerland Inc
Green Bay, WI
Jemm Wholesale Meat Company
Chicago, IL 773-523-8161
Jensen Meat Company
Vista, CA. 760-727-6700
Jesse's Best
Suffolk, VA. 757-489-8383
Jesses Fine Meats
Cherokee, IA. 712-225-3637
John Garner Meats
Van Buren, AR 800-543-5473
John R. Morreale
Chicago, IL 312-421-3664
Jones Packing Company
Harvard, IL 815-943-4488
Jordahl Meats
Manchester, MN 507-826-3418
Joseph Sanders
Custer, MI. 800-968-5035
K&K Gourmet Meats
Leetsdale, PA 724-266-8400
Karl Ehmer
Flushing, NY. 800-487-5275
Kelble Brothers
Berlin Heights, OH. 800-247-2333
Kelley Meats
Taberg, NY 315-337-4272
Kelly Kornbeef Company
Chicago, IL 773-588-2882
Kelly Packing Company
Torrington, WY. 307-532-2210
Kelly-Eisenberg Gourmet Deli Products
Chicago, IL 773-588-2882
Kenosha Beef International
Kenosha, WI 800-541-1685
Kent Meats
Grand Rapids, MI 800-748-0141
Kershenstine Beef Jerky
Eupora, MS 662-258-2049
Kessler Foods, Inc
Lemoyne, PA. 717-763-7162
Ketters Meat Market & Locker Plant
Frazee, MN 218-334-2351
Keystone Foods Corporation
West Conshohocken, PA. 610-667-6700

Keystone Foods Corporation
Huntsville, AL 800-327-6701
King Kold Meats
Englewood, OH 800-836-2797
King Meat
Los Angeles, CA. 323-582-7401
Kings Command Foods
Kent, WA. 800-247-3138
Kingsbury Country Market
Kingsbury, IN 219-393-3016
Kiolbassa Provision Company
San Antonio, TX. 800-456-5465
Klement Sausage Company
Milwaukee, WI. 800-553-6368
Korte Meat Processors
Highland, IL 618-654-3813
Kretschmar
Don Mills, ON 800-561-4532
Kroger Company
Cincinnati, OH 800-576-4377
Kulana Foods
Hilo, HI. 808-959-9144
Kutztown Bologna Company
Leola, PA. 800-723-8824
L&H Packing Company
San Antonio, TX. 210-532-3241
L&L Packing Company
Chicago, IL 800-628-6328
L&M Frosted Food Lockers
Belt, MT 406-277-3522
L&M Slaughtering
Georgetown, IL. 217-662-6841
Ladoga Frozen Food & Retail Meat
Ladoga, IN 765-942-2225
Lampost Meats
Grimes, IA. 515-288-6111
Land O'Frost
Lansing, IL 800-323-3308
Land O'Frost
Searcy, AR 800-643-5654
Landis Meat Company
Quakertown, PA 800-421-1565
Laxson Provision Company
San Antonio, TX. 210-226-8397
Lay Packing Company
Knoxville, TN. 865-922-4320
Leidy's
Souderton, PA. 800-222-2319
Lena Maid Meats
Lena, IL. 815-369-4522
Lengerich Meats
Zanesville, IN 260-638-4123
Leo G. Fraboni Sausage Company
Hibbing, MN. 218-263-5074
Levonian Brothers
Troy, NY 518-274-3610
Lilydale Foods
Edmonton, AB 800-661-5341
Lisbon Sausage Company
New Bedford, MA 508-993-7645
Lombardi Brothers Meat Packers
Denver, CO 800-421-4412
Lone Star Beef Jerky Company
Lubbock, TX. 806-762-8833
Long Food Industries
Fripp Island, SC 843-838-3205
Longview Meat & Merchandise Ltd
Longview, AB. 866-355-3759
Lowell Provision Company
Lowell, MA. 978-454-5603
M K Meat Processing Plant
Burton, TX 979-289-4022
Mac's Meats Wholesale
Las Cruces, NM 575-524-2751
MacGregors Meat & Seafood
Toronto, ON 888-383-3663
Mada'n Kosher Foods
Dania, FL 954-925-0077
Magnolia Beef Company
Elizabeth, NJ. 908-352-9412
Magnolia Meats
Shreveport, LA 318-221-2814
Maid-Rite Steak Company
Dunmore, PA. 800-233-4259
Malcolm Meat Company
Northwood, OH 800-822-6328
Manger Packing Company
Baltimore, MD 800-227-9262
Manley Meats
Decatur, IN 260-592-7313
Maple Leaf Foods & Scheider Foods
Saint Laurent, QC. 800-567-1890
Marie F
Markham, ON. 800-365-4464
Marks Meat
Canby, OR. 503-266-2048
Marshallville Packing Company
Marshallville, OH 330-855-2871
Matthiesen's Deer & Custom Processing
De Witt, IA 563-659-8409
Maurice's Gourmet Barbeque
West Columbia, SC. 800-628-7423
McKenzie of Vermont
Burlington, VT 802-864-4585
McLemore's Abattoir
Vidalia, GA. 912-537-4476
Meatco Sales
Mirror, AB 403-788-2292
Meating Place
Buffalo, NY. 716-885-3623
Meatland Packers
Medicine Hat, AB. 403-528-4321
Medeiros Farms
Kalaheo, HI. 808-332-8211
Merkley & Sons Packing
Jasper, IN 812-482-7020
Merrill's Meat Company
Encampment, WY. 307-327-5345
Metafoods, LLC
Atlanta, GA. 404-843-2400
Metropolitan Sausage Manufacturing Company
Flossmoor, IL 708-331-3232
Michael's Finer Meats & Seafoods
Columbus, OH 800-282-0518
Midway Meats
Centralia, WA 360-736-5257
Mike's Meats
Eitzen, MN 507-495-3336
Miko Meat
Hilo, HI. 808-935-0841
Miller Brothers PackingcCompany
Sylvester, GA 229-776-2014
Miller's Country Hams
Dresden, TN 800-622-0606
Miller's Meat Market
Red Bud, IL. 618-282-3334
Mims Meat Company
Houston, TX 713-453-0151
Mirasco
Atlanta, GA. 770-956-1945
Mishler Packing Company
Lagrange, IN. 260-768-4156
Montana Ranch Brand
Billings, MT 406-294-2333
Moo & Oink
Chicago, IL 773-493-7100
Mortimer's Fine Foods
Burlington, ON 905-336-0000
Mountain City Meat Company
Denver, CO 800-937-8325
Moweaqua Packing
Moweaqua, IL. 217-768-4714
Moyer Packing Company
Souderton, PA. 800-967-8325
Mr. Brown's Bar-B-Que
Portland, OR 503-274-0966
Munsee Meats
Muncie, IN 765-288-3645
Mutual Trading Company
Los Angeles, CA. 213-626-9458
Nagel Veal
San Bernardino, CA 909-383-7075
Napoleon Locker
Napoleon, IN. 812-852-4333
National Beef Packing Co., LLC
Kansas City, MO. 800-449-2333
National Foods
Indianapolis, IN 800-683-6565
National Steak & Poultry
Owasso, OK 800-366-6772
Natures Sungrown Foods
San Rafael, CA 415-491-4944
Nebraska Beef
Omaha, NE 402-734-6823
Nesbitt Processing
Aledo, IL. 309-582-5183
Nestle Pizza
Medford, WI 715-748-5550
New Braunfels Smokehouse
New Braunfels, TX. 800-537-6932
New Zealand Lamb Company
Wilton, CT 800-438-5262
Nodine's Smokehouse
Torrington, CT 800-222-2059
Nolechek's Meats
Thorp, WI 715-669-5580
North Star Foods
Saint Charles, MN 507-932-4831
Northern Packing Company
Brier Hill, NY. 315-375-8801
Nossack Fine Meats
Red Deer, AB 403-346-5006
Nueske's Applewood Smoked Meats
Wittenberg, WI. 800-386-2266
O Chili Frozen Foods Inc
Northbrook, IL 847-562-1991
O'Neill Packing Company
Omaha, NE 402-733-1200
Old Country Meat & Sausage Company
San Diego, CA 619-297-4301
Old Kentucky Hams
Cynthiana, KY 859-234-5015
Old Neighborhood Foods
Lynn, MA 781-595-1557
Old Wisconsin Sausage Company
Sheboygan, WI. 800-558-7840
Olson Locker
Fairmont, MN. 507-238-2563
Omaha Meat Processors
Omaha, NE 402-554-1965
Onoway Custom Packers
Onoway, AB 780-967-2207
Ossian Seafood Meats
Ossian, IN. 260-622-4191
Otto W Liebold & Company
Flint, MI 800-999-6328
P.G. Molinari & Sons
San Francisco, CA 415-822-5555
Palmer Packing Company
Tremonton, UT 435-257-5329
Palmyra Bologna
Palmyra, PA. 717-838-6336
Paradise Locker Company
Trimble, MO 816-370-6328
Paris Frozen Foods
Hillsboro, IL 217-532-3822
Pasqualichio Brothers
Scranton, PA 800-232-6233
Pat's Meat Discounter
Mills, WY 307-237-7549
Patrick Cudahy
Cudahy, WI. 800-486-6900
Paul Schafer Meat Products
Baltimore, MD 410-528-1250
Payne Packing Company
Artesia, NM. 575-746-2779
Pekarna's Meat Market
Jordan, MN. 952-492-6101
Pekarskis Sausage
South Deerfield, MA 413-665-4537
Penthouse Meat Company
Boston, MA. 570-563-1153
Petschl's Quality Meats
Tukwila, WA. 206-575-4400
Pierceton Foods
Pierceton, IN. 574-594-2344
Pierre Foods
Cincinnati, OH 513-874-8741
Pinter's Packing Plant
Dorchester, WI 715-654-5444
Piper Processing
Andover, OH. 440-293-7170
Plymouth Beef
Bronx, NY. 718-589-8600
PM Beef Holdings
Windom, MN 800-622-5213
Poche's Smokehouse
Breaux Bridge, LA 800-376-2437
Polarica
San Francisco, CA 800-426-3872
Pork Shop of Vermont
Charlotte, VT 800-458-3441
Premium Meat Company
Brigham City, UT 435-723-5944
Prime Pak Foods
Gainesville, GA 770-536-8708
Proliant Meat Ingredients
Harlan, IA. 800-369-2672
Provost Packers
Provost, AB. 780-753-2415
Quaker Maid Meats
Reading, PA 610-376-1500
Quality Beef Company
Providence, RI 877-233-3462
Quality Sausage Company
Dallas, TX. 214-634-3400

Quantum Foods LLC
Bolingbrook, IL 800-334-6328
R Four Meats
Chatfield, MN....................507-867-4180
R.E. Meyer Company
Lincoln, NE......................888-990-2333
R.I. Provision Company
Johnston, RI 401-831-0815
Raemica
Highland, CA 909-864-1990
Ralph's Packing Company
Perkins, OK......................800-522-3979
Ranch Oak Farm
Fort Worth, TX 800-888-0327
Randolph Packing Company
Streamwood, IL...................630-830-3100
Ray's Sausage Company Inc
Cleveland, OH 216-921-8782
Real Sausage Company
Chicago, IL......................312-842-5330
Red Deer Lake Meat Processing
Calgary, AB......................403-256-4925
Red Hot Chicago
Chicago, IL......................800-249-5226
Red Oak Farms
Red Oak, IA 712-623-9224
Red Steer Meats
Phoenix, AZ 602-272-6677
Redi-Serve Food Company
Fort Atkinson, WI.................920-563-6391
Redondo's Sausage Factory
Waipahu, HI 808-671-5444
Rinehart Meat Processing
Branson, MO.....................417-334-2044
Ritchie Wholesale Meats
Piketon, OH 800-628-1290
Riverside Packers
Drumheller, AB...................403-823-2595
Robbins Packing Company
Statesboro, GA 912-764-7503
Robertson's Country Meat Hams
Finchville, KY 800-678-1521
Robichaux's Meat Market
Crowley, LA 337-788-4124
Rock River Provision Company
Rock Falls, IL 800-685-1195
Rocky Mountain Meats
Rocky Mountain House, AB 403-845-3434
Rocky Mountain Natural Meats
Henderson, CO 800-327-2706
Rocky Mountain Packing Company
Havre, MT.......................406-265-3401
Roger Wood Foods
Savannah, GA....................800-849-9272
Rolet Food Products Company
Brooklyn, NY 718-497-0476
Roman Packing Company
Norfolk, NE......................800-373-5990
Romanian Kosher Sausage
Chicago, IL......................773-761-4141
Ron Tankersley Farms
Los Angeles, CA..................213-622-0724
Roode Packing Company
Fairbury, NE 402-729-2253
Rosa Brothers
Miami, FL.......................305-324-1510
Rose Packing Company
Chicago, IL......................800-323-7363
Rosen's Diversified
Fairmont, MN 800-798-2000
Royal Center Locker Plant
Royal Center, IN..................574-643-3275
Royal Palate Foods
Inglewood, CA 310-330-7701
Rubashkin
Brooklyn, NY 718-436-5511
Rude Custom Butchering
Mt Morris, IL 815-946-3795
Ruef's Meat Market
New Glarus, WI 608-527-2554
Rymer Foods
Chicago, IL......................800-247-9637
S.W. Meat & Provision Company
Phoenix, AZ 602-275-2000
Sadler's Smokehouse
Henderson, TX 903-657-5581
Safeway Inc
Pleasanton, CA...................877-723-3929
Sam Kane Beef Processors
Crp Christi, TX...................361-241-5000
Sampco
Chicago, IL......................800-767-1689

San Angelo Packing
San Angelo, TX 325-653-6951
San Francisco Sausage Company
S San Francisco, CA...............650-583-4993
Sangudo Custom Meat Packers
Sangudo, AB.....................888-785-3353
Sani-Dairy
Punxsutawney, PA.................814-938-7200
Sausage Kitchen
Oak Grove, OR...................503-656-9766
Saval Foods
Elkridge, MD 800-527-2825
Schneider Foods
Guelph, ON......................519-837-4848
Schneider Foods
Etobicoke, ON 800-268-0634
Sculli Brothers
Yeadon, PA 215-336-1223
Seltzer's Smokehouse Meats
Palmyra, PA......................814-928-5850
Shelley's Prime Meats
Jersey City, NJ 201-433-3434
Shirer Brothers Slaughter House
Adamsville, OH 740-796-3214
Shreve Meats Processing
Shreve, OH 330-567-2142
Silver Lake Sausage Shop
Providence, RI 401-944-4081
Simeus Foods International
Mansfield, TX....................888-772-3663
Sky Haven Farm
Cincinnati, OH 513-681-2303
Skylark Meats
Omaha, NE 800-759-5275
Slathars Smokehouse
Lake City, MN 507-753-2080
SMG
Crestview Hills, KY 859-344-3700
Smith Packing Regional Meat
Utica, NY
Smith Provision Company
Erie, PA.........................800-334-9151
Smokey Denmark Sausage
Austin, TX.......................512-385-0718
Souris Valley Processors
Melita, NB.......................204-522-8210
Southeastern Meat Association
Oviedo, FL 407-365-5661
Southern Packing Corporation
Chesapeake, VA 757-421-2131
Southtowns Seafood & Meats
Blasdell, NY 716-824-4900
Specialty Foods Group
Hampton, VA 800-238-0020
Spring Grove Foods
Miamisburg, OH..................937-866-4311
Springville Meat & ColdsStorage
Springville, UT...................801-489-6391
Square-H Brands
Vernon, CA......................323-267-4600
Stallings Headcheese Company
Houston, TX 713-523-1751
Standard Beef Company
Foxboro, MA 203-787-2164
Steak-Umm Company
Shillington, PA 860-928-5900
Stehlin & Sons Company
Cincinnati, OH 513-385-6164
Stettler Meats
Stettler, AB 403-742-1427
Stevison Ham Company
Portland, TN 800-844-4267
Stock Yards Packing Company
Chicago, IL......................800-621-1119
Stone Meat Processor
Ogden, UT.......................801-782-9825
Straub's
Clayton, MO.....................888-725-2121
Strauss Veal & Lamb International
Hales Corners, WI.................800-562-7775
Striplings
Moultrie, GA.....................229-985-4226
Sudlersville Frozen Food Locker
Sudlersville, MD..................410-438-3106
Sugardale Foods
Canton, OH......................330-455-5253
Sun-Rise
Alexandria, MN 320-846-5720
Sunnydale Meats
Gaffney, SC......................864-489-6091
Superior's Brand Meats
Massillon, OH....................330-830-0356

Suzanna's Kitchen
Duluth, GA......................800-241-2455
Swift & Company
Greeley, CO......................970-506-8000
Tankersley Food Service
Van Buren, AR 800-726-6182
Tanks Meat
Elmore, OH......................419-862-3312
Tarpoff Packing Company
Edwardsville, IL 618-656-4948
Taylor Meat Company
Taylor, TX.......................512-352-6357
Taylor's Sausage Company
Saint Louis, MO 314-652-3476
Tayse Meats
Cleveland, OH 216-664-1799
Temptee Specialty Foods
Denver, CO 800-842-1233
Terra's
Perham, MN 218-346-4100
Terrell Meats
Delta, UT........................435-864-2600
Texas Reds Steak House
Red River, NM 575-754-2922
Thompson Packers
Slidell, LA.......................800-989-6328
Thomson Meats ltd.
Melfort, SK......................306-752-2802
Tillamook Meat Company
Tillamook, OR 503-842-4802
Tom Clamon Foods
Palestine, TX.....................903-729-0138
Tooele Valley Meat
Grantsville, UT...................435-884-3837
Topper Meat Company
Belle Glade, FL...................561-996-6541
Topps Meat Company
Elizabeth, NJ.....................877-998-6777
Townsend-Piller Packing
Cumberland, WI 715-822-4910
Travis Meats
Powell, TN 800-247-7606
Tri-State Beef Company
Cincinnati, OH 513-579-1722
Troy Pork Store
Troy, NY........................518-272-8291
Troyer Foods
Goshen, IN 800-876-9377
Tucker Packing Company
Orrville, OH 330-683-3311
Tupman-Thurlow Company
Deerfield Beach, FL 954-596-9989
Turk Brothers Custom Meats
Ashland, OH 800-789-1051
Tyler Packing Company
Tyler, TX........................903-593-9592
Tyson Foods Tyson Technical Services Lab
Amarillo, TX.....................806-335-1531
Tyson Fresh Meats
Dakota Dunes, SD.................605-235-2061
Tyson Fresh Meats Meat Packing Plant
Emporia, KS 620-343-3640
Uncle Charley's Sausage Company
Vandergrift, PA...................724-845-3302
Une-Viandi
St. Jean Sur Richelieu, NB 800-363-1955
United Meat Company
San Francisco, CA 415-864-2118
United Provision Meat Company
Columbus, OH 614-252-1126
Universal Beef Products
Houston, TX 713-224-6043
Uvalde Meat Processing
Uvalde, TX 830-278-6247
Valley Meat Company
Modesto, CA.....................800-222-6328
Valley Meats
Coal Valley, IL 309-799-7341
Vantage USA
Chicago, IL......................773-247-1086
Victoria Fancy Sausage
Edmonton, AB 780-471-2283
Vienna Beef
Chicago, IL......................773-278-7800
Vienna Beef
Chicago, IL......................800-621-8183
Vienna Meat Products
Scarborough, ON 800-588-1931
Vietti Foods Company Inc
Nashville, TN 800-240-7864
Voget Meats
Hubbard, OR

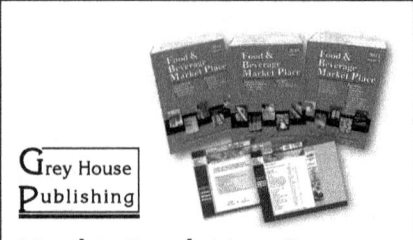

W & G Marketing Company
Ames, IA 515-233-4774
W.R. Delozier Sausage Company
Seymour, TN 865-577-5907
WA Bean & Sons
Bangor, ME 800-649-1958
Waco Beef & Pork Processors
Waco, TX 254-772-4669
Waken Meat Company
Atlanta, GA 404-627-3537
Walker Meats Corporation
Carrollton, GA 770-834-8171
Wall Meat Processing
Wall, SD 605-279-2348
Waltham Beef Company
Boston, MA 617-269-2250
Warren & Son Meat Processing
Whipple, OH 740-585-2421
Wasatch Meats
Salt Lake City, UT 801-363-5747
Washington Beef
Toppenish, WA 800-289-2333
Webster City Custom Meats
Webster City, IA 888-786-3287
Weiss Brothers Smoke House
Johnstown, PA 814-539-4085
West Liberty Foods
West Liberty, IA 888-511-4500
Westbrook Trading Company
Calgary, AB 800-563-5785
Western Meats
Tumwater, WA 360-357-6601
Western Meats
Rapid City, SD 605-342-0322
Westport Locker Service
Westport, IN 877-265-0551
White's Meat Processing
Peebles, OH 937-587-2930
Wildwood Natural Foods
Watsonville, CA 800-464-3915
Willcox Packing House
Willcox, AZ 520-384-2015
Wimmer's Meat Products
West Point, NE 800-358-0761
Windcrest Meat Packers
Port Perry, ON 800-750-2542
Winona Packing Company
Winona, MS 662-283-4317
Winter Sausage Manufacturing Company
Eastpointe, MI 586-777-9080
Wisconsin Packing Company
Butler, WI 800-558-2000
Wohrles Foods
Pittsfield, MA 800-628-6114
Wolverine Packing
Detroit, MI 313-259-7500
Woodbine
Norfolk, VA 757-461-2731
Woods Smoked Meats
Bowling Green, MO 800-458-8426
XL Beef
Calgary, AB 403-236-2424
Yewig Brothers Packing Company
Haubstadt, IN 812-768-6208
Yoakum Packing Company
Yoakum, TX 361-293-3541
Zartic Inc
Rome, GA 800-241-0516

Barbecued

Art's Tamales
Metamora, IL 309-367-2850
Bear Creek Smokehouse
Marshall, TX 800-950-2327
Burke Corporation
Nevada, IA 800-654-1152

Always make it your best® with Burke fully cooked meats. We specialize in Italian sausage, beef, and pork toppings, meatballs, taco meats, shredded meats, pepperoni, bacon, Canadian-style bacon, chicken and beef strips. Additionally, we offer a variety of specialty products: Hand-Pinched Style® brand toppings, chorizo, gyro topping, andouille sausage, and breakfast patties and links.

Curly's Foods
Edina, MN 800-722-1127
Dankworth Packing Company
Ballinger, TX 325-365-3552
Dorina/So-Good
Union, IL 815-923-2144
Gary's Frozen Foods
Lubbock, TX 806-745-1933
Gaucho Foods
Fayetteville, IL 877-677-2282
King Kold Meats
Englewood, OH 800-836-2797
Moonlite Bar Bq Inn
Owensboro, KY 800-322-8989
Sadler's Smokehouse
Henderson, TX 903-657-5581
Travis Meats
Powell, TN 800-247-7606
W & G Marketing Company
Ames, IA 515-233-4774

Frozen

Art's Tamales
Metamora, IL 309-367-2850
Burke Corporation
Nevada, IA 800-654-1152

Always make it your best® with Burke fully cooked meats. We specialize in Italian sausage, beef, and pork toppings, meatballs, taco meats, shredded meats, pepperoni, bacon, Canadian-style bacon, chicken and beef strips. Additionally, we offer a variety of specialty products: Hand-Pinched Style® brand toppings, chorizo, gyro topping, andouille sausage, and breakfast patties and links.

El-Rey Foods
Ferguson, MO 314-521-3113
Gary's Frozen Foods
Lubbock, TX 806-745-1933
Gaucho Foods
Fayetteville, IL 877-677-2282
Hormel Foods Corporation
Austin, MN 800-523-4635
Jesses Fine Meats
Cherokee, IA 712-225-3637
King Kold Meats
Englewood, OH 800-836-2797

Brisket

Bear Creek Smokehouse
Marshall, TX 800-950-2327
Farmland Foods
Kansas City, MO 888-327-6526
Nueces Canyon Texas Style Meat Seasoning
Brenham, TX 800-925-5058
Sara Lee Corporation
Downers Grove, IL 630-598-8100
Saval Foods
Elkridge, MD 800-527-2825

Canned with Natural Juices

Aunt Kitty's Foods
Vineland, NJ 856-691-2100
Crown Point
St John, IN 219-365-3200
International Food Packers Corporation
Miami, FL 305-669-1662
Tupman-Thurlow Company
Deerfield Beach, FL 954-596-9989

Chipped

Alderfer Bologna
Harleysville, PA 800-341-1121

Dinners

Campbell Soup Company
Camden, NJ 800-257-8443
ConAgra Foods/International Home Foods
Niagara Falls, ON 905-356-2661

Filet Mignon

Amana Meat Shop & Smokehouse
Amana, IA 800-373-6328
Chef's Requested Foods
Oklahoma City, OK 800-256-0259
Chicago Steaks
Chicago, IL 800-776-4174
Miami Beef Company
Hialeah, FL 305-621-3252

Fresh

Amity Packing Company
Chicago, IL 800-837-0270
Brook Locker Plant
Brook, IN 219-275-2611
Brookfield Farms Nationwide Foods
Chicago, IL 773-787-4900
Buckhead Beef Company
Atlanta, GA 800-888-5578
Cattleman's Meat Company
Detroit, MI 313-833-2700
Colorado Boxed Beef Company
Auburndale, FL 863-967-0636
Farmland Foods
Kansas City, MO 888-327-6526
International Meat Company
Chicago, IL 773-622-1400
Jbs Packerland Inc
Green Bay, WI
L&H Packing Company
San Antonio, TX 210-532-3241
Lengerich Meats
Zanesville, IN 260-638-4123
Mountain City Meat Company
Denver, CO 800-937-8325
National Beef Packing Co., LLC
Kansas City, MO 800-449-2333
Plymouth Beef
Bronx, NY 718-589-8600
R Four Meats
Chatfield, MN 507-867-4180
Schneider Foods
Etobicoke, ON 416-252-5790
Shelley's Prime Meats
Jersey City, NJ 201-433-3434
Smith Packing Regional Meat
Utica, NY
Temptee Specialty Foods
Denver, CO 800-842-1233
Thumann's
Carlstadt, NJ 201-935-3636
Topps Meat Company
Elizabeth, NJ 877-998-6777
Troy Pork Store
Troy, NY 518-272-8291

Tyson Fresh Meats Meat Packing Plant
Emporia, KS 620-343-3640
Waco Beef & Pork Processors
Waco, TX 254-772-4669

Frozen

Alphin Brothers
Dunn, NC 800-672-4502
Amity Packing Company
Chicago, IL 800-837-0270
Armbrust Meats
Medford, WI 715-748-3102
Art's Tamales
Metamora, IL 309-367-2850
Atlantic Meat Company
Savannah, GA 912-964-8511
Birchwood Foods
Kenosha, WI 800-541-1685
Birdie Pak Products
Chicago, IL 773-247-5293
Blakely Freezer Locker
Thomasville, GA 229-723-3622
Bob's Custom Cuts
Bonnyville, AB 780-826-2138
Brook Locker Plant
Brook, IN 219-275-2611
Brookfield Farms Nationwide Foods
Chicago, IL 773-787-4900
Brookview Farms
Archbold, OH 419-445-6366
Buckhead Beef Company
Atlanta, GA 800-888-5578
Buono Beef Co
Philadelphia, PA 215-463-3600
Burke Corporation
Nevada, IA 800-654-1152

Always make it your best® with Burke fully cooked meats. We specialize in Italian sausage, beef, and pork toppings, meatballs, taco meats, shredded meats, pepperoni, bacon, Canadian-style bacon, chicken and beef strips. Additionally, we offer a variety of specialty products: Hand-Pinched Style® brand toppings, chorizo, gyro topping, andouille sausage, and breakfast patties and links.

Bush Brothers Provision Company
West Palm Beach, FL 800-327-1345
Buzz Food Service
Charleston, WV 304-925-4781
Carando Gourmet Frozen Foods
Agawam, MA 888-227-2636
Caribbean Food Delights
Tappan, NY 845-398-3000
Caribbean Products
Baltimore, MD 410-235-7700
Carl Buddig & Company
Homewood, IL 800-621-0868
Cattleman's Meat Company
Detroit, MI 313-833-2700
Chip Steak & Provision Company
Mankato, MN 507-388-6277
City Foods
Chicago, IL 773-523-1566
Colorado Boxed Beef Company
Auburndale, FL 863-967-0636
Curly's Foods
Edina, MN 800-722-1127
Dallas Dressed Beef
Dallas, TX 214-638-0142
Davidson Meat Processing Plant
Waynesville, OH 513-897-2971
Devault Foods
Devault, PA 800-426-2874
Duma Meats
Mogadore, OH 330-628-3438
Dynamic Foods
Lubbock, TX 806-747-2777
Edmonds Chile Company
St Louis, MO 314-772-1499
El-Rey Foods
Ferguson, MO 314-521-3113
Farmland Foods
Kansas City, MO 888-327-6526
Fuji Foods
Denver, CO 303-377-3738
Gary's Frozen Foods
Lubbock, TX 806-745-1933
Gaucho Foods
Fayetteville, IL 877-677-2282
Gemini Food Industries
Charlton, MA 508-248-2730
Hall Brothers Meats
Cleveland, OH 440-235-3262
Hamm's Custom Meats
McKinney, TX 972-562-7511
Hausman Foods
Corpus Christi, TX 800-364-5521
Heringer Meats
Covington, KY 859-291-2000
Holten Meats
Sauget, IL 800-851-4684
Hormel Foods Corporation
Austin, MN 800-523-4635
International Food Packers Corporation
Miami, FL 305-669-1662
Jacob & Sons Wholesale Meats
Martins Ferry, OH 740-633-3091
Jbs Packerland Inc
Green Bay, WI
Jemm Wholesale Meat Company
Chicago, IL 773-523-8161
Jesses Fine Meats
Cherokee, IA 712-225-3637
K&K Gourmet Meats
Leetsdale, PA 724-266-8400
King Kold Meats
Englewood, OH 800-836-2797
Kutztown Bologna Company
Leola, PA 800-723-8824
L&H Packing Company
San Antonio, TX 210-532-3241
Ladoga Frozen Food & Retail Meat
Ladoga, IN 765-942-2225
Lengerich Meats
Zanesville, IN 260-638-4123
Leo G. Fraboni Sausage Company
Hibbing, MN 218-263-5074
Loggins Meat Company
Tyler, TX 800-527-8610
Maid-Rite Steak Company
Dunmore, PA 800-233-4259
Meat-O-Mat Corporation
Brooklyn, NY 718-965-7250
Mountain City Meat Company
Denver, CO 800-937-8325
National Beef Packing Co., LLC
Kansas City, MO 800-449-2333
Northern Packing Company
Brier Hill, NY 315-375-8801
Paris Frozen Foods
Hillsboro, IL 217-532-3822
Phoenix Agro-Industrial Corporation
Westbury, NY 516-334-1194
Pierceton Foods
Pierceton, IN 574-594-2344
Plymouth Beef
Bronx, NY 718-589-8600
R Four Meats
Chatfield, MN 507-867-4180
Redi-Serve Food Company
Fort Atkinson, WI 920-563-6391
Sam Kane Beef Processors
Crp Christi, TX 361-241-5000
Schneider Foods
Etobicoke, ON 416-252-5790
Shelley's Prime Meats
Jersey City, NJ 201-433-3434
Smith Packing Regional Meat
Utica, NY
Southeastern Meat Association
Oviedo, FL 407-365-5661
Steak-Umm Company
Shillington, PA 860-928-5900
Sudlersville Frozen Food Locker
Sudlersville, MD 410-438-3106
Thompson Packers
Slidell, LA 800-989-6328
Topps Meat Company
Elizabeth, NJ 877-998-6777
Travis Meats
Powell, TN 800-247-7606
Tucker Packing Company
Orrville, OH 330-683-3311
Tyson Fresh Meats Meat Packing Plant
Emporia, KS 620-343-3640
United Meat Company
San Francisco, CA 415-864-2118
Zartic Inc
Rome, GA 800-241-0516

Ground

Acme Steak & Seafood Company
Youngstown, OH 330-270-8000
American Foods Group
Green Bay, WI 920-436-4229
Atlantic Meat Company
Savannah, GA 912-964-8511
Blue Ribbon Meats
Miami, FL 800-522-6115
Brockton Beef & Provisions Corporation
Brockton, MA 508-583-4703
Caribbean Food Delights
Tappan, NY 845-398-3000
Centennial Food Corporation
Calgary, AB 403-214-0044
Chicago Steaks
Chicago, IL 800-776-4174
Chip Steak & Provision Company
Mankato, MN 507-388-6277
Cropp Cooperative-Organic Valley
La Farge, WI 888-444-6455
Devault Foods
Devault, PA 800-426-2874
Glenmark Industries
Chicago, IL 773-927-4800
Jensen Meat Company
Vista, CA 760-727-6700
John Garner Meats
Van Buren, AR 800-543-5473
Karn Meats
Columbus, OH 800-221-9585
Kenosha Beef International
Kenosha, WI 800-541-1685
Kessler Foods, Inc
Lemoyne, PA 717-763-7162
L&H Packing Company
San Antonio, TX 210-532-3241
Miami Beef Company
Hialeah, FL 305-621-3252
O Chili Frozen Foods Inc
Northbrook, IL 847-562-1991
Palmer Packing Company
Tremonton, UT 435-257-5329
Quality Beef Company
Providence, RI 877-233-3462
Rinehart Meat Processing
Branson, MO 417-334-2044
S.W. Meat & Provision Company
Phoenix, AZ 602-275-2000
Springville Meat & ColdsStorage
Springville, UT 801-489-6391
Stanley Provision Company
Manchester, CT 888-688-6347
Stone Meat Processor
Ogden, UT 801-782-9825
Thompson Packers
Slidell, LA 800-989-6328
Valley Meat Company
Modesto, CA 800-222-6328
Valley Meats
Coal Valley, IL 309-799-7341

Coarse Frozen

Devault Foods
Devault, PA 800-426-2874

Frozen

Acme Steak & Seafood Company
Youngstown, OH 330-270-8000
Caribbean Food Delights
Tappan, NY 845-398-3000
Chip Steak & Provision Company
Mankato, MN 507-388-6277
Kenosha Beef International
Kenosha, WI 800-541-1685
L&H Packing Company
San Antonio, TX 210-532-3241
Thompson Packers
Slidell, LA 800-989-6328

Hamburger

Acme Steak & Seafood Company
Youngstown, OH 330-270-8000
Alphin Brothers
Dunn, NC 800-672-4502
Atlantic Meat Company
Savannah, GA 912-964-8511
Bakalars Brothers Sausage Company
La Crosse, WI 608-784-0384

Birchwood Foods
Kenosha, WI 800-541-1685
Brockton Beef & Provisions Corporation
Brockton, MA 508-583-4703
Burke Corporation
Nevada, IA 800-654-1152

Always make it your best® with Burke fully cooked meats. We specialize in Italian sausage, beef, and pork toppings, meatballs, taco meats, shredded meats, pepperoni, bacon, Canadian-style bacon, chicken and beef strips. Additionally, we offer a variety of specialty products: Hand-Pinched Style® brand toppings, chorizo, gyro topping, andouille sausage, and breakfast patties and links.

Chicago Meat Authority
Chicago, IL 773-254-3811
Chicopee Provision Company
Chicopee, MA 800-924-6328
Crocetti Oakdale Packing
East Bridgewater, MA 508-587-0035
Devault Foods
Devault, PA 800-426-2874
Edmonds Chile Company
St Louis, MO 314-772-1499
Hormel Foods Corporation
Austin, MN 800-523-4635
Keystone Foods Corporation
West Conshohocken, PA 610-667-6700
Marathon Enterprises
Englewood, NJ 800-722-7388
Miami Beef Company
Hialeah, FL 305-621-3252
O Chili Frozen Foods Inc
Northbrook, IL 847-562-1991
Ossian Seafood Meats
Ossian, IN 260-622-4191
Otto & Son
West Jordan, UT 800-453-9462
Pierceton Foods
Pierceton, IN 574-594-2344
Rego's Purity Foods
Honolulu, HI 808-847-3717
Rinehart Meat Processing
Branson, MO 417-334-2044
Rymer Foods
Chicago, IL 800-247-9637
Thompson Packers
Slidell, LA 800-989-6328
Topps Meat Company
Elizabeth, NJ 877-998-6777
Travis Meats
Powell, TN 800-247-7606
Valley Meat Company
Modesto, CA 800-222-6328

Cooked Frozen

Burke Corporation
Nevada, IA 800-654-1152

Always make it your best® with Burke fully cooked meats. We specialize in Italian sausage, beef, and pork toppings, meatballs, taco meats, shredded meats, pepperoni, bacon, Canadian-style bacon, chicken and beef strips. Additionally, we offer a variety of specialty products: Hand-Pinched Style® brand toppings, chorizo, gyro topping, andouille sausage, and breakfast patties and links.

Maid-Rite Steak Company
Dunmore, PA 800-233-4259
On-Cor Foods Products
Northbrook, IL 847-205-1040

Uncooked Frozen

Al Safa Halal
Niagara Falls, NY 800-268-8174
Caribbean Food Delights
Tappan, NY 845-398-3000
Maid-Rite Steak Company
Dunmore, PA 800-233-4259
On-Cor Foods Products
Northbrook, IL 847-205-1040
Pierceton Foods
Pierceton, IN 574-594-2344

Italian

Burke Corporation
Nevada, IA 800-654-1152

Always make it your best® with Burke fully cooked meats. We specialize in Italian sausage, beef, and pork toppings, meatballs, taco meats, shredded meats, pepperoni, bacon, Canadian-style bacon, chicken and beef strips. Additionally, we offer a variety of specialty products: Hand-Pinched Style® brand toppings, chorizo, gyro topping, andouille sausage, and breakfast patties and links.

Liver

Caughman's Meat Plant
Lexington, SC 803-356-0076
D'Artagnan
Newark, NJ 800-327-8246
Dynamic Foods
Lubbock, TX 806-747-2777
Giovanni's Appetizing Food Products
Richmond, MI 586-727-9355
Lees Sausage Company
Orangeburg, SC 803-534-5517
Skylark Meats
Omaha, NE 800-759-5275
Stauber Performance Ingredients
Fullerton, CA 888-441-4233

London Broil

Burnett & Son Meat Company
Monrovia, CA 626-357-2165

NY Strip Steak

Amana Meat Shop & Smokehouse
Amana, IA 800-373-6328
Chef's Requested Foods
Oklahoma City, OK 800-256-0259
Cropp Cooperative-Organic Valley
La Farge, WI 888-444-6455

Patties

Burke Corporation
Nevada, IA 800-654-1152

Always make it your best® with Burke fully cooked meats. We specialize in Italian sausage, beef, and pork toppings, meatballs, taco meats, shredded meats, pepperoni, bacon, Canadian-style bacon, chicken and beef strips. Additionally, we offer a variety of specialty products: Hand-Pinched Style® brand toppings, chorizo, gyro topping, andouille sausage, and breakfast patties and links.

Miami Beef Company
Hialeah, FL 305-621-3252

Cooked Frozen

Loggins Meat Company
Tyler, TX 800-527-8610
O Chili Frozen Foods Inc
Northbrook, IL 847-562-1991

Frozen

Buzz Food Service
Charleston, WV 304-925-4781
Caribbean Food Delights
Tappan, NY 845-398-3000
Centennial Food Corporation
Calgary, AB 403-214-0044
Corfu Foods
Bensenville, IL 630-595-2510
Glenmark Food Processors
Chicago, IL 800-621-0117
Holten Meats
Sauget, IL 800-851-4684
John Garner Meats
Van Buren, AR 800-543-5473
Kenosha Beef International
Kenosha, WI 800-541-1685
King Kold Meats
Englewood, OH 800-836-2797
Kutztown Bologna Company
Leola, PA 800-723-8824
Maid-Rite Steak Company
Dunmore, PA 800-233-4259
Meat-O-Mat Corporation
Brooklyn, NY 718-965-7250
Patty Palace 732840 Ontario Limited
Scarborough, ON 416-297-0510
Topps Meat Company
Elizabeth, NJ 877-998-6777
Travis Meats
Powell, TN 800-247-7606
Valley Meat Company
Modesto, CA 800-222-6328
Wisconsin Packing Company
Butler, WI 800-558-2000

Jamacain

Royal Home Bakery
Newmarket, ON 905-715-7044

Porterhouse

Chef's Requested Foods
Oklahoma City, OK 800-256-0259
Chicago Steaks
Chicago, IL 800-776-4174

Pot Roast

Fontanini Italian Meats & Sausages
McCook, IL 800-331-6328

Processed

Al Safa Halal
Niagara Falls, NY 800-268-8174
Alderfer Bologna
Harleysville, PA 800-341-1121
Alewel's Country Meats
Warrensburg, MO 800-353-8553
Alpine Meats
Stockton, CA 800-399-6328
Aunt Kitty's Foods
Vineland, NJ 856-691-2100
Best Provision Co Inc.
Newark, NJ 800-631-4466
Big B Distributors
Evansville, IN 812-425-5235
Bruss Company
Chicago, IL 800-621-3882
Buckhead Beef Company
Atlanta, GA 800-888-5578
Bush Brothers Provision Company
West Palm Beach, FL 800-327-1345
Caddo Packing Company
Marshall, TX 903-935-2211
Campbell Soup Company
Camden, NJ 800-257-8443
Carando Gourmet Frozen Foods
Agawam, MA 888-227-2636
Cargill Meats
Milwaukee, WI 800-558-4242
Caribbean Food Delights
Tappan, NY 845-398-3000
Castleberry's
Vineland, NJ 856-691-2100
Castleberry's Meats
Atlanta, GA 404-873-1804
Cattaneo Brothers
San Luis Obispo, CA 800-243-8537
Central Beef
Center Hill, FL 352-793-3671
Central Meat & Provision Company
San Diego, CA 619-239-1391
Chandler Foods
Greensboro, NC 800-537-6219
Charlie's Pride Meats
Vernon, CA 877-866-0982
Cher-Make Sausage Company
Manitowoc, WI 800-242-7679
Cheraw Packing
Cheraw, SC 843-537-7426
Chip Steak & Provision Company
Mankato, MN 507-388-6277
Columbia Packing Company
Dallas, TX 800-460-8171
ConAgra Foods/Eckrich
Omaha, NE 800-327-4424
ConAgra Foods/International Home Foods
Niagara Falls, ON 905-356-2661
Conti Packing Company
Rochester, NY 585-424-2500

Continental Deli Foods
Cherokee, IA 712-225-6529
Corfu Foods
Bensenville, IL 630-595-2510
Darling International
Bellevue, NE 402-731-7600
David Berg & Company
Chicago, IL 773-278-5195
Dutterer's Home Food Service
Baltimore, MD 410-298-3663
E.W. Knauss & Son
Quakertown, PA 800-648-4220
F&Y Enterprises
Wauconda, IL 847-526-0620
Hahn Brothers
Westminster, MD 800-227-7675
Hamm's Custom Meats
McKinney, TX 972-562-7511
Henry J Meat Specialties
Chicago, IL 800-242-1314
High Country Snack Foods
Lincoln, MT 800-433-3916
Horlacher's Fine Meats
Logan, UT 435-752-1287
Hsin Tung Yang Foods Co.
S San Francisco, CA 650-589-6789
Jensen Meat Company
Vista, CA 760-727-6700
Jesses Fine Meats
Cherokee, IA 712-225-3637
John Garner Meats
Van Buren, AR 800-543-5473
Kershenstine Beef Jerky
Eupora, MS 662-258-2049
Keystone Foods Corporation
West Conshohocken, PA 610-667-6700
Kings Command Foods
Kent, WA 800-247-3138
Kutztown Bologna Company
Leola, PA 800-723-8824
Land O'Frost
Searcy, AR 800-643-5654
Lone Star Beef Jerky Company
Lubbock, TX 806-762-8833
Longview Meat & Merchandise Ltd
Longview, AB 866-355-3759
Lower Foods
Richmond, UT 435-258-2449
Moo & Oink
Chicago, IL 773-493-7100
Moyer Packing Company
Souderton, PA 800-967-8325
National Beef Packing Co., LLC
Kansas City, MO 800-449-2333
Nebraska Beef
Omaha, NE 402-734-6823
Nestle Pizza
Medford, WI 715-748-5550
Peoples Sausage Company
Los Angeles, CA 213-627-8633
Pierceton Foods
Pierceton, IN 574-594-2344
Plumrose USA
East Brunswick, NJ 800-526-4909
Plymouth Beef
Bronx, NY 718-589-8600
Red Oak Farms
Red Oak, IA 712-623-9224
Rinehart Meat Processing
Branson, MO 417-334-2044
Saval Foods
Elkridge, MD 800-527-2825
Smith Provision Company
Erie, PA 800-334-9151
Southtowns Seafood & Meats
Blasdell, NY 716-824-4900
Sunset Farm Foods
Valdosta, GA 800-882-1121
Temptee Specialty Foods
Denver, CO 800-842-1233
Terrell Meats
Delta, UT 435-864-2600
Thompson Packers
Slidell, LA 800-989-6328
Tri-State Beef Company
Cincinnati, OH 513-579-1722
Tupman-Thurlow Company
Deerfield Beach, FL 954-596-9989
Tyson Fresh Meats Meat Packing Plant
Emporia, KS 620-343-3640
Valley Meat Company
Modesto, CA 800-222-6328
Weaver Nut Company
Ephrata, PA 717-738-3781
Wimmer's Meat Products
West Point, NE 800-358-0761
Wisconsin Packing Company
Butler, WI 800-558-2000
Woods Smoked Meats
Bowling Green, MO 800-458-8426

Products

A. Stein Meat Products
Brooklyn, NY 718-492-0760
Alderfer Bologna
Harleysville, PA 800-341-1121
Alewel's Country Meats
Warrensburg, MO 800-353-8553
Bakalars Brothers Sausage Company
La Crosse, WI 608-784-0384
Big B Distributors
Evansville, IN 812-425-5235
Birchwood Foods
Kenosha, WI 800-541-1685
Bruss Company
Chicago, IL 800-621-3882
Buona Vita
Bridgeton, NJ 856-453-7972
Bush Brothers Provision Company
West Palm Beach, FL 800-327-1345
Caddo Packing Company
Marshall, TX 903-935-2211
Campbell Soup Company
Camden, NJ 800-257-8443
Caribbean Food Delights
Tappan, NY 845-398-3000
Carl Buddig & Company
Homewood, IL 800-621-0868
Castleberry's
Vineland, NJ 856-691-2100
Chicago Meat Authority
Chicago, IL 773-254-3811
Columbia Packing Company
Dallas, TX 800-460-8171
Counts Sausage Company
Prosperity, SC 803-364-2392
David Berg & Company
Chicago, IL 773-278-5195
Dino's Sausage & Meat Company
Utica, NY 315-732-2661
Dutterer's Home Food Service
Baltimore, MD 410-298-3663
E.W. Knauss & Son
Quakertown, PA 800-648-4220
Edmonds Chile Company
St Louis, MO 314-772-1499
El-Rey Foods
Ferguson, MO 314-521-3113
Elmwood Lockers
Elmwood, IL 309-742-8929
F&Y Enterprises
Wauconda, IL 847-526-0620
Flint Hills Foods
Alma, KS
Foodbrands America
Oklahoma City, OK 405-290-4000
G Di Lullo & Sons
Westville, NJ 856-456-3700
Glenmark Food Processors
Chicago, IL 800-621-0117
Groff Meats
Elizabethtown, PA 717-367-1246
Hahn Brothers
Westminster, MD 800-227-7675
Harris Ranch Beef Company
Selma, CA 800-742-1955
Hazle Park Packing Co
West Hazleton, PA 800-238-4331
Henry J Meat Specialties
Chicago, IL 800-242-1314
Holly Hill Locker Company
Holly Hill, SC 803-496-3611
Holten Meats
Sauget, IL 800-851-4684
Hormel Foods Corporation
Austin, MN 800-523-4635
Ito Cariani Sausage Company
Hayward, CA 510-887-0882
Ittels Meats
Howard Lake, MN 320-543-2285
John Garner Meats
Van Buren, AR 800-543-5473
Joseph Sanders
Custer, MI 800-968-5035
K&K Gourmet Meats
Leetsdale, PA 724-266-8400
Karn Meats
Columbus, OH 800-221-9585
Kelly Kornbeef Company
Chicago, IL 773-588-2882
Kenosha Beef International
Kenosha, WI 800-541-1685
Kershenstine Beef Jerky
Eupora, MS 662-258-2049
Keystone Foods Corporation
West Conshohocken, PA 610-667-6700
Kutztown Bologna Company
Leola, PA 800-723-8824
L&H Packing Company
San Antonio, TX 210-532-3241
Leo G. Fraboni Sausage Company
Hibbing, MN 218-263-5074
Lower Foods
Richmond, UT 435-258-2449
Maid-Rite Steak Company
Dunmore, PA 800-233-4259
Meating Place
Buffalo, NY 716-885-3623
Moo & Oink
Chicago, IL 773-493-7100
National Foods
Indianapolis, IN 800-683-6565
Nestle Pizza
Medford, WI 715-748-5550
Peer Foods Inc.
Chicago, IL 800-365-5644
Peoples Sausage Company
Los Angeles, CA 213-627-8633
Pinter's Packing Plant
Dorchester, WI 715-654-5444
Plumrose USA
East Brunswick, NJ 800-526-4909
Plymouth Beef
Bronx, NY 718-589-8600
Redi-Serve Food Company
Fort Atkinson, WI 920-563-6391
Rinehart Meat Processing
Branson, MO 417-334-2044
Rudolph Foods
Dallas, TX 214-638-2204
Rymer Foods
Chicago, IL 800-247-9637
S.W. Meat & Provision Company
Phoenix, AZ 602-275-2000
Sadler's Smokehouse
Henderson, TX 903-657-5581
Sara Lee Corporation
Downers Grove, IL 630-598-8100
Saval Foods
Elkridge, MD 800-527-2825
Sheinman Provision Company
Philadelphia, PA 215-473-7065
Steak-Umm Company
Shillington, PA 860-928-5900
Striplings
Moultrie, GA 229-985-4226
Temptee Specialty Foods
Denver, CO 800-842-1233
Terrell Meats
Delta, UT 435-864-2600
Tyson Fresh Meats Meat Packing Plant
Emporia, KS 620-343-3640
Une-Viandi
St. Jean Sur Richelieu, NB 800-363-1955
Vienna Meat Products
Scarborough, ON 800-588-1931
Weaver Nut Company
Ephrata, PA 717-738-3781
Wisconsin Packing Company
Butler, WI 800-558-2000
Woods Smoked Meats
Bowling Green, MO 800-458-8426
XL Beef
Calgary, AB 403-236-2424

Raw

Caribbean Food Delights
Tappan, NY 845-398-3000
Maid-Rite Steak Company
Dunmore, PA 800-233-4259

Rib Eye Roast

Cropp Cooperative-Organic Valley
La Farge, WI 888-444-6455

Rib Eye Steak

Amana Meat Shop & Smokehouse
Amana, IA. 800-373-6328
Chef's Requested Foods
Oklahoma City, OK 800-256-0259
Chicago Steaks
Chicago, IL 800-776-4174
Cropp Cooperative-Organic Valley
La Farge, WI 888-444-6455
Father's Country Hams
Bremen, KY 270-525-3554
Woods Smoked Meats
Bowling Green, MO 800-458-8426

Rib Steak

Chicago Steaks
Chicago, IL 800-776-4174

Roast Beef

Alderfer Bologna
Harleysville, PA 800-341-1121
Applegate Farms
Bridgewater, NJ 908-725-2768
Berks Packing Company, Inc.
Reading, PA 800-882-3757
Burnett & Son Meat Company
Monrovia, CA 626-357-2165
Carando Gourmet Frozen Foods
Agawam, MA 888-227-2636
Charlie's Pride Meats
Vernon, CA 877-866-0982
Chip Steak & Provision Company
Mankato, MN 507-388-6277
Curly's Foods
Edina, MN. 800-722-1127
David Berg & Company
Chicago, IL 773-278-5195
Dorina/So-Good
Union, IL. 815-923-2144
Dutterer's Home Food Service
Baltimore, MD 410-298-3663
El-Rey Foods
Ferguson, MO 314-521-3113
Hahn Brothers
Westminster, MD 800-227-7675
Henry J Meat Specialties
Chicago, IL 800-242-1314
Hormel Foods Corporation
Austin, MN 800-523-4635
Ito Cariani Sausage Company
Hayward, CA 510-887-0882
Lower Foods
Richmond, UT. 435-258-2449
Miami Beef Company
Hialeah, FL 305-621-3252
Ottman Meat Company
New York, NY 212-879-4160
Sara Lee Corporation
Downers Grove, IL 630-598-8100
Saval Foods
Elkridge, MD 800-527-2825
Sheinman Provision Company
Philadelphia, PA 215-473-7065
Upstate Farms Cooperative
Buffalo, NY. 716-892-2121
Vienna Meat Products
Scarborough, ON 800-588-1931

Rolls - Frozen

Alphin Brothers
Dunn, NC 800-672-4502
Columbia Packing Company
Dallas, TX. 800-460-8171
Travis Meats
Powell, TN 800-247-7606

Sirloin Cubes

Chicago Steaks
Chicago, IL 800-776-4174
Cropp Cooperative-Organic Valley
La Farge, WI 888-444-6455
Farmland Foods
Kansas City, MO. 888-327-6526

Sliced

E.W. Knauss & Son
Quakertown, PA 800-648-4220
Gemini Food Industries
Charlton, MA 508-248-2730
Plymouth Beef
Bronx, NY. 718-589-8600

Dried

Alderfer Bologna
Harleysville, PA 800-341-1121
E.W. Knauss & Son
Quakertown, PA 800-648-4220
Palmyra Bologna
Palmyra, PA. 717-838-6336
Red Oak Farms
Red Oak, IA 712-623-9224

Frozen

Burke Corporation
Nevada, IA 800-654-1152

Always make it your best® with Burke fully cooked meats. We specialize in Italian sausage, beef, and pork toppings, meatballs, taco meats, shredded meats, pepperoni, bacon, Canadian-style bacon, chicken and beef strips. Additionally, we offer a variety of specialty products: Hand-Pinched Style® brand toppings, chorizo, gyro topping, andouille sausage, and breakfast patties and links.

Gemini Food Industries
Charlton, MA 508-248-2730

Special Trim

Buckhead Beef Company
Atlanta, GA. 800-888-5578

Steak

Alaskan Gourmet Seafoods
Anchorage, AK. 800-288-3740
Bakalars Brothers Sausage Company
La Crosse, WI 608-784-0384
Bear Creek Smokehouse
Marshall, TX. 800-950-2327
Blue Ribbon Meats
Miami, FL 800-522-6115
Burnett & Son Meat Company
Monrovia, CA 626-357-2165
Campbell Soup Company
Camden, NJ. 800-257-8443
Castleberry's
Vineland, NJ 856-691-2100
ConAgra Foods/International Home Foods
Niagara Falls, ON 905-356-2661
Flint Hills Foods
Alma, KS
Jemm Wholesale Meat Company
Chicago, IL 773-523-8161
Joe Fazio's Famous Italian
Charleston, WV 304-344-3071
Karn Meats
Columbus, OH 800-221-9585
Kutztown Bologna Company
Leola, PA. 800-723-8824
Loggins Meat Company
Tyler, TX. 800-527-8610
Pine Point Seafood
Scarborough, ME 207-883-4701
Pinter's Packing Plant
Dorchester, WI 715-654-5444
Rymer Foods
Chicago, IL 800-247-9637
Steak-Umm Company
Shillington, PA 860-928-5900
Woods Smoked Meats
Bowling Green, MO 800-458-8426

Stew

Burnett & Son Meat Company
Monrovia, CA. 626-357-2165
Campbell Soup Company
Camden, NJ. 800-257-8443
Castleberry's
Vineland, NJ 856-691-2100
ConAgra Foods/International Home Foods
Niagara Falls, ON 905-356-2661
Johnston's Home Style Products
Charlottetown, PE. 902-629-1300
Miami Beef Company
Hialeah, FL 305-621-3252
Plymouth Beef
Bronx, NY. 718-589-8600

Frozen

Edmonds Chile Company
St Louis, MO. 314-772-1499

Tongue

A. Stein Meat Products
Brooklyn, NY 718-492-0760
Sara Lee Corporation
Downers Grove, IL. 630-598-8100
Saval Foods
Elkridge, MD 800-527-2825

Veal

A to Z Portion Meats
Bluffton, OH 800-338-6328
A. Stein Meat Products
Brooklyn, NY 718-492-0760
A. Thomas Meats
Louisville, KY 800-253-2020
A.C. Kissling Company
Philadelphia, PA 800-445-1943
Adolf's Meats & Sausage Kitchen
Hartford, CT 860-522-1588
Alphin Brothers
Dunn, NC 800-672-4502
Arena & Sons
Hopkinton, MA. 508-435-3673
Atlantic Veal
Olyphant, PA. 570-489-4781
Atlantic Veal & Lamb
Brooklyn, NY 800-222-8325
B&R Quality Meats
Waterloo, IA 319-232-6328
Baretta Provision
East Berlin, CT 860-828-0802
Border's Market
Plymouth, OH. 419-687-2634
Brook Locker Plant
Brook, IN 219-275-2611
Brown Packing Company
South Holland, IL 800-832-8325
Bruss Company
Chicago, IL 800-621-3882
Buckhead Beef Company
Atlanta, GA. 800-888-5578
Bush Brothers Provision Company
West Palm Beach, FL 800-327-1345
Buzz Food Service
Charleston, WV 304-925-4781
Canada West Foods
Innisfail, AB 403-227-3386
Capital Packers Inc
Edmonton, AB 800-272-8868
Carl Streit & Son Company
Neptune, NJ 732-775-0803

Carmel Meat/Specialty Foods
Marina, CA 800-298-5823
Castleberry's Meats
Atlanta, GA. 404-873-1804
Catelli Brothers
Camden, NJ. 856-869-2200
Central Meat & Provision Company
San Diego, CA 619-239-1391
Community Market & Deli
Lindstrom, MN 651-257-1128
Conti Packing Company
Rochester, NY. 585-424-2500
Country Village Meats
Sublette, IL 815-849-5532
Culinary Foods
Chicago, IL 800-621-4049
Cusack Wholesale Meat Company
Oklahoma City, OK 800-241-6328
D'Artagnan
Newark, NJ 800-327-8246
David Mosner Meat Products
Bronx, NY. 718-328-5600
Debragga & Spitler
New York, NY. 212-924-1311
Empire Beef & Redistribution
Rochester, NY. 800-462-6804
Ferko Meat Company
Milwaukee, WI 414-967-5500
Florida Veal Processors
Wimauma, FL 813-634-5545
George L. Wells Meat Company
Philadelphia, PA 800-523-1730
Glenmark Food Processors
Chicago, IL 800-621-0117
Godshall's Quality Meats
Telford, PA 888-463-7425
Heringer Meats
Covington, KY 859-291-2000
Holten Meats
Sauget, IL 800-851-4684
International Meat Company
Chicago, IL 773-622-1400
Jordahl Meats
Manchester, MN 507-826-3418
Kelley Meats
Taberg, NY 315-337-4272
King Kold Meats
Englewood, OH 800-836-2797
Kings Command Foods
Kent, WA. 800-247-3138
L&L Packing Company
Chicago, IL 800-628-6328
L&M Slaughtering
Georgetown, IL. 217-662-6841
Lay Packing Company
Knoxville, TN. 865-922-4320
Lombardi Brothers Meat Packers
Denver, CO 800-421-4412
Lowell Provision Company
Lowell, MA. 978-454-5603
Magnolia Beef Company
Elizabeth, NJ. 908-352-9412
Maid-Rite Steak Company
Dunmore, PA. 800-233-4259
Marcho Farms Veal
Harleysville, PA 215-721-7131
Meat-O-Mat Corporation
Brooklyn, NY 718-965-7250
Miami Beef Company
Hialeah, FL 305-621-3252
Michael's Finer Meats & Seafoods
Columbus, OH 800-282-0518
Mountain City Meat Company
Denver, CO 800-937-8325
Mountain States Rosen
Bronx, NY. 800-872-5262
Nagel Veal
San Bernardino, CA 909-383-7075
O Chili Frozen Foods Inc
Northbrook, IL 847-562-1991
Otto W Liebold & Company
Flint, MI 800-999-6328
Pasqualichio Brothers
Scranton, PA 800-232-6233
Petschl's Quality Meats
Tukwila, WA. 206-575-4400
Provimi Foods, Inc
Seymour, WI 800-833-8325
Quaker Maid Meats
Reading, PA 610-376-1500
Rancher's Lamb of Texas
San Angelo, TX 325-659-4004
Redi-Serve Food Company
Fort Atkinson, WI. 920-563-6391
Rendulic Packing
McKeesport, PA 412-678-9541
Sculli Brothers
Yeadon, PA 215-336-1223
Shelley's Prime Meats
Jersey City, NJ 201-433-3434
Smith Packing Regional Meat
Utica, NY
Southeastern Meat Association
Oviedo, FL 407-365-5661
Southern Packing Corporation
Chesapeake, VA 757-421-2131
Southtowns Seafood & Meats
Blasdell, NY 716-824-4900
Standard Beef Company
Foxboro, MA 203-787-2164
Stock Yards Packing Company
Chicago, IL 800-621-1119
Superior Farms
Davis, CA 800-228-5262
Suzanna's Kitchen
Duluth, GA 800-241-2455
Swissland Packing Company
Ashkum, IL. 800-321-8325
Thompson Packers
Slidell, LA. 800-989-6328
Tooele Valley Meat
Grantsville, UT 435-884-3837
Travis Meats
Powell, TN 800-247-7606
Tyler Packing Company
Tyler, TX. 903-593-9592
Une-Viandi
St. Jean Sur Richelieu, NB 800-363-1955
United Meat Company
San Francisco, CA 415-864-2118
United Provision Meat Company
Columbus, OH 614-252-1126
Valley Meats
Coal Valley, IL 309-799-7341
Vantage USA
Chicago, IL 773-247-1086
Wasatch Meats
Salt Lake City, UT 801-363-5747
Windcrest Meat Packers
Port Perry, ON. 800-750-2542
Wolverine Packing
Detroit, MI 313-259-7500

Breaded Frozen

Holten Meats
Sauget, IL 800-851-4684
Kings Command Foods
Kent, WA. 800-247-3138
Meat-O-Mat Corporation
Brooklyn, NY 718-965-7250
O Chili Frozen Foods Inc
Northbrook, IL 847-562-1991
Ottman Meat Company
New York, NY 212-879-4160
Redi-Serve Food Company
Fort Atkinson, WI. 920-563-6391
Valley Meats
Coal Valley, IL 309-799-7341

Burgers

Meat-O-Mat Corporation
Brooklyn, NY 718-965-7250

Cutlet

Redi-Serve Food Company
Fort Atkinson, WI. 920-563-6391

Fresh

Colorado Boxed Beef Company
Auburndale, FL. 863-967-0636
Florida Veal Processors
Wimauma, FL 813-634-5545
Jesse's Best
Suffolk, VA 757-489-8383
Provimi Foods, Inc
Seymour, WI 800-833-8325
Shelley's Prime Meats
Jersey City, NJ 201-433-3434
Smith Packing Regional Meat
Utica, NY
Swissland Packing Company
Ashkum, IL. 800-321-8325

Frozen

Atlantic Veal & Lamb
Brooklyn, NY 800-222-8325
Brook Locker Plant
Brook, IN 219-275-2611
Buckhead Beef Company
Atlanta, GA. 800-888-5578
Bush Brothers Provision Company
West Palm Beach, FL 800-327-1345
Buzz Food Service
Charleston, WV 304-925-4781
Colorado Boxed Beef Company
Auburndale, FL. 863-967-0636
Empire Beef & Redistribution
Rochester, NY. 800-462-6804
Florida Veal Processors
Wimauma, FL 813-634-5545
Glenmark Food Processors
Chicago, IL 800-621-0117
Heringer Meats
Covington, KY 859-291-2000
Holten Meats
Sauget, IL 800-851-4684
Jesse's Best
Suffolk, VA 757-489-8383
King Kold Meats
Englewood, OH 800-836-2797
Maid-Rite Steak Company
Dunmore, PA. 800-233-4259
Meat-O-Mat Corporation
Brooklyn, NY 718-965-7250
Montage Foods
Scranton, PA 800-521-8325
Mountain City Meat Company
Denver, CO 800-937-8325
O Chili Frozen Foods Inc
Northbrook, IL 847-562-1991
Omaha Steaks International
Omaha, NE 800-562-0500
Provimi Foods, Inc
Seymour, WI. 800-833-8325
Redi-Serve Food Company
Fort Atkinson, WI. 920-563-6391
Shelley's Prime Meats
Jersey City, NJ 201-433-3434
Smith Packing Regional Meat
Utica, NY
Southeastern Meat Association
Oviedo, FL 407-365-5661
Swissland Packing Company
Ashkum, IL. 800-321-8325
Thompson Packers
Slidell, LA. 800-989-6328
Travis Meats
Powell, TN 800-247-7606
United Meat Company
San Francisco, CA 415-864-2118

Ground

Buono Beef Co
Philadelphia, PA 215-463-3600
Dutch Valley Veal
South Holland, IL 800-832-8325

Loin Chop

Chicago Steaks
Chicago, IL 800-776-4174

Rib Chop

Chicago Steaks
Chicago, IL 800-776-4174

Frankfurters

Al Pete Meats
Muncie, IN 765-288-8817
Alle Processing Corporation
Maspeth, NY. 800-245-5620
Applegate Farms
Bridgewater, NJ 908-725-2768
AquaCuisine
Eagle, ID 208-323-2782
Ball Park Franks
Downers Grove, IL 630-598-8100
Bar-S Foods Company
Phoenix, AZ 602-264-7272
Best Provision Co Inc.
Newark, NJ 800-631-4466
Big City Reds
Omaha, NE 800-759-5275

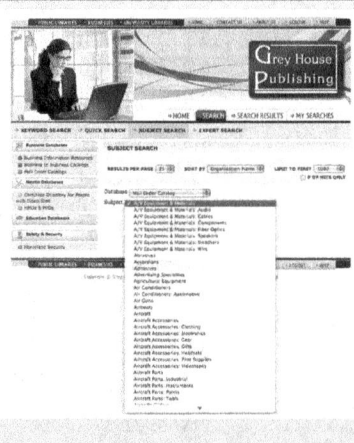

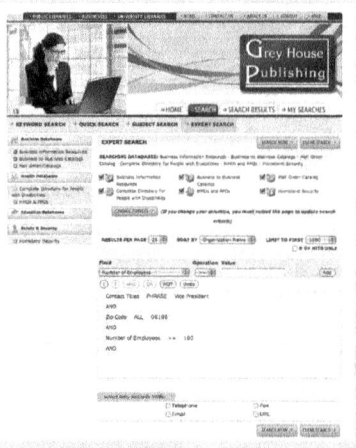

Boesl Packing Company
Baltimore, MD 410-675-1071
Carolina Packers
Smithfield, NC 800-682-7675
Chicago 58 Food Products
Woodbridge, ON. 416-603-4244
Chicago Steaks
Chicago, IL 800-776-4174
Chicopee Provision Company
Chicopee, MA. 800-924-6328
Chisesi Brothers Meat Packing Company
New Orleans, LA 800-966-3550
Cloverdale Foods Company
Mandan, ND 800-669-9511
ConAgra Foods Inc
Omaha, NE 402-595-7300
Continental Deli Foods
Cherokee, IA. 712-225-6529
Corte Provisions
Newark, NJ 201-653-7246
Country Village Meats
Sublette, IL 815-849-5532
Curtis Packing Company
Greensboro, NC 336-275-7684
David Berg & Company
Chicago, IL 773-278-5195
Dennison Meat Locker
Dennison, MN. 507-645-8734
Dietz & Watson
Philadelphia, PA 800-333-1974
Double B Foods
Arlington, TX 800-679-0349
Dutterer's Home Food Service
Baltimore, MD 410-298-3663
Farmland Foods
Kansas City, MO. 888-327-6526
Foodbrands America
Oklahoma City, OK 405-290-4000
Foster Farms
Livingston, CA 800-255-7227
Frank's Foods
Hilo, HI. 808-959-9121
Gary's Frozen Foods
Lubbock, TX. 806-745-1933
Georges Chicken
Edinburg, VA 866-444-2449
Glazier Packing Company
Malone, NY. 518-483-4990
Gold Star Sausage Company
Denver, CO 800-258-7229
Grote & Weigel
Bloomfield, CT. 860-242-8528
Gwaltney of Smithfield
Portsmouth, VA. 757-465-0666
Gwaltney of Smithfield
Smithfield, VA 800-888-7521
Hatfield Quality Meats
Hatfield, PA. 800-523-5291
Hazle Park Packing Co
West Hazleton, PA 800-238-4331
Health is Wealth Foods
Williamstown, NJ 856-728-1998
Hormel Foods Corporation
Fremont, NE 402-721-2300
Hormel Foods Corporation
Austin, MN 800-523-4635
Hummel Brothers
New Haven, CT 800-828-8978
Kayem Foods
Chelsea, MA 800-426-6100
Kelly Kornbeef Company
Chicago, IL 773-588-2882
Kent Quality Foods
Grand Rapids, MI 800-748-0141
Kessler Foods, Inc
Lemoyne, PA. 717-763-7162
Kilgus Meats
Toledo, OH 419-472-9721
Koegel Meats
Flint, MI 810-238-3685
Levonian Brothers
Troy, NY 518-274-3610
Little Rhody Brand Frankfurts
Johnston, RI 401-831-0815
Marathon Enterprises
Englewood, NJ 800-722-7388
Martin Rosol's
New Britain, CT 860-223-2707
Matthiesen's Deer & Custom Processing
De Witt, IA 563-659-8409
Milling Sausage Company
Milwaukee, WI 414-645-2677
National Foods
Indianapolis, IN 800-683-6565
O'Brien & Company
Bellevue, NE. 800-433-7567
Ohio Packing Company
Columbus, OH 800-282-6403
P & L Poultry
Spokane, WA. 509-892-1242
Pfeffer's Country Mkt.
Sauk Centre, MN 320-352-6490
Pie Piper Products
Bensenville, IL 800-621-8183
Porter's Food & Produce
Du Quoin, IL. 618-542-2155
Quong Hop & Company
S San Francisco, CA. 650-553-9900
R.L. Zeigler Company
Tuscaloosa, AL. 800-392-6328
Raemica
Highland, CA 909-864-1990
Rego's Purity Foods
Honolulu, HI. 808-847-3717
Saag's Products
San Leandro, CA. 800-352-7224
Sahlen Packing Company
Buffalo, NY. 716-852-8677
Sara Lee Corporation
Downers Grove, IL. 630-598-8100
Saugy Inc
Cranston, RI 866-467-2849
Schneider Foods
Kitchener, ON. 519-741-5000
Sechrist Brothers
Dallastown, PA 717-244-2975
Shelton's Poultry
Pomona, CA 800-541-1833
Simeus Foods International
Mansfield, TX. 888-772-3663
Smith Packing Regional Meat
Utica, NY
Smith Provision Company
Erie, PA. 800-334-9151
Stawnichy Holdings
Mundare, AB 888-764-7646
Stevens Sausage Company
Smithfield, NC 800-338-0561
Sunnydale Meats
Gaffney, SC. 864-489-6091
Tennessee Valley PackingCompany
Columbia, TN. 931-388-2623
Thomas Packing Company
Columbus, GA 800-729-0976
Thumann's
Carlstadt, NJ 201-935-3636
Troy Frozen Food
Troy, IL 618-667-6332
Vitasoy USA
Ayer, MA. 978-772-6880
Wimmer's Meat Products
West Point, NE 800-358-0761

Beef

Berks Packing Company, Inc.
Reading, PA 800-882-3757
Big City Reds
Omaha, NE 800-759-5275
Chicago Steaks
Chicago, IL 800-776-4174
D'Artagnan
Newark, NJ 800-327-8246
Farmland Foods
Kansas City, MO. 888-327-6526
Grote & Weigel
Bloomfield, CT. 860-242-8528
Health is Wealth Foods
Williamstown, NJ 856-728-1998
Hormel Foods Corporation
Austin, MN 800-523-4635
Kelly Kornbeef Company
Chicago, IL 773-588-2882
National Foods
Indianapolis, IN 800-683-6565
Pie Piper Products
Bensenville, IL 800-621-8183
Red Hot Chicago
Chicago, IL 800-249-5226
Wimmer's Meat Products
West Point, NE 800-358-0761

Chicken

Applegate Farms
Bridgewater, NJ 908-725-2768
Foster Farms
Livingston, CA 800-255-7227
Georges Chicken
Edinburg, VA 866-444-2449
P & L Poultry
Spokane, WA. 509-892-1242
Tyson Foods
Springdale, AR 800-643-3410

Corn Dogs

Al Pete Meats
Muncie, IN 765-288-8817
Foster Farms
Livingston, CA 800-255-7227
Hormel Foods Corporation
Austin, MN 800-523-4635
Porter's Food & Produce
Du Quoin, IL. 618-542-2155
Suzanna's Kitchen
Duluth, GA 800-241-2455

Hot Dogs

Specialty Foods Group
Hampton, VA 800-238-0020

Mini

Grote & Weigel
Bloomfield, CT. 860-242-8528
Hormel Foods Corporation
Austin, MN 800-523-4635

Pork

Hormel Foods Corporation
Fremont, NE 402-721-2300
Levonian Brothers
Troy, NY 518-274-3610

Soy

Lightlife Foods
Turners Falls, MA. 800-274-6001
Quong Hop & Company
S San Francisco, CA. 650-553-9900

Turkey

Applegate Farms
Bridgewater, NJ 908-725-2768
Foster Farms
Livingston, CA 800-255-7227
Georges Chicken
Edinburg, VA 866-444-2449
Longmont Foods
Longmont, CO 303-776-6611
P & L Poultry
Spokane, WA. 509-892-1242
Sardinha Sausage
Somerset, MA. 800-678-0178

Game

Alewel's Country Meats
Warrensburg, MO 800-353-8553
Bayou Land Seafood
Breaux Bridge, LA 337-667-6118
Bob's Custom Cuts
Bonnyville, AB. 780-826-2138
Bolner's Fiesta Products
San Antonio, TX. 210-734-6404
Boyd Sausage Company
Washington, IA. 319-653-5715
Broadleaf Venison Usa
Vernon, CA 800-336-3844
Brome Lake Ducks Ltd
Knowlton, QC. 888-956-1977
Bryant Preserving Company
Alma, AR 800-634-2413
Burgers Smokehouse
California, MO 800-624-5426
Burris Mill & Feed
Franklinton, LA 800-928-2782
Camrose Packers
Camrose, AB. 780-672-4887
Carolina Blueberry Association
Garland, NC 910-588-4355

Clay Center Locker Plant
Clay Center, KS 785-632-5550
Collbran Locker Plant
Collbran, CO..................... 970-487-3329
Community Market & Deli
Lindstrom, MN 651-257-1128
D'Artagnan
Newark, NJ 800-327-8246
Eickman's Processing
Seward, IL....................... 815-247-8451
Eiserman Meats
Slave Lake, AB................... 780-849-5507
Ellsworth Locker
Ellsworth, MN 507-967-2544
Farmers Meat Market
Viking, AB 780-336-3241
Fossil Farms
Boonton, NJ 201-651-1190
Georgetown Farm
Free Union, VA................... 888-328-5326
Goodheart Brand Specialty Foods
San Antonio, TX.................. 888-466-3992
Hickory Baked Food
Castle Rock, CO.................. 303-688-2633
Humeniuk's Meat Cutting
Ranfurly, AB..................... 780-658-2381
Indian Valley Meats
Indian, AK....................... 907-653-7511
Jewel Date Company
Thermal, CA...................... 760-399-4474
Ketters Meat Market & Locker Plant
Frazee, MN 218-334-2351
MacFarlane Pheasants
Janesville, WI 877-269-8957
Mahantongo Game Farms
Dalmatia, PA..................... 570-758-6284
Matthiesen's Deer & Custom Processing
De Witt, IA 563-659-8409
McLane's Meats
Wetaskiwin, AB 780-352-4321
Meat-O-Mat Corporation
Brooklyn, NY 718-965-7250
Meatco Sales
Mirror, AB 403-788-2292
Michael's Finer Meats & Seafoods
Columbus, OH 800-282-0518
Miller's Meat Market
Red Bud, IL...................... 618-282-3334
Musicon Deer Farm
Goshen, NY....................... 845-294-6378
Nicky
Portland, OR..................... 800-469-4162
Onoway Custom Packers
Onoway, AB....................... 780-967-2207
Oxford Frozen Foods Limited
Oxford, NS 902-447-2100
Palmetto Pigeon Plant
Sumter, SC 803-775-1204
Payne Packing Company
Artesia, NM...................... 575-746-2779
Pekarna's Meat Market
Jordan, MN....................... 952-492-6101
Pinter's Packing Plant
Dorchester, WI 715-654-5444
Prairie Cajun Whlse.
Eunice, LA 337-546-6195
Productos Alimenticios Tia Lencha
Cienega De Flores, NL............ 818-374-0774
Productos Medellin
Matehuala, SL.................... 488-882-1491
R Four Meats
Chatfield, MN.................... 507-867-4180
Rabbit Barn
Turlock, CA...................... 209-632-1123
Rocky Mountain Meats
Rocky Mountain House, AB 403-845-3434
Springville Meat & ColdsStorage
Springville, UT.................. 801-489-6391
Squab Producers of California
Modesto, CA...................... 209-537-4744
Stonies Sausage Shop Inc
Perryville, MO 888-546-2540
Thornbury Grandview Farms
Thornbury, ON 519-599-6368
Tofield Packers Ltd
Tofield, AB 780-662-4842
United Meat Company
San Francisco, CA 415-864-2118
Uvalde Meat Processing
Uvalde, TX 830-278-6247
Vantage USA
Chicago, IL 773-247-1086
Venison America
Hudson, WI....................... 800-310-2360
Victoria Fancy Sausage
Edmonton, AB 780-471-2283
Wall Meat Processing
Wall, SD 605-279-2348
Western Meats
Rapid City, SD 605-342-0322

Alligator

Acadian Ostrich Ranch
Clinton, LA...................... 800-350-0167
Bayou Land Seafood
Breaux Bridge, LA 337-667-6118
Bolner's Fiesta Products
San Antonio, TX.................. 210-734-6404
Burris Mill & Feed
Franklinton, LA 800-928-2782
Fish Breeders of Idaho
Boise, ID........................ 888-414-8818
Nicky
Portland, OR..................... 800-469-4162
Prairie Cajun Whlse.
Eunice, LA 337-546-6195

Boar

Broadleaf Venison Usa
Vernon, CA....................... 800-336-3844
D'Artagnan
Newark, NJ 800-327-8246
Nicky
Portland, OR..................... 800-469-4162
Thornbury Grandview Farms
Thornbury, ON 519-599-6368

Buffalo

Alewel's Country Meats
Warrensburg, MO.................. 800-353-8553
Broadleaf Venison Usa
Vernon, CA....................... 800-336-3844
Clay Center Locker Plant
Clay Center, KS 785-632-5550
D'Artagnan
Newark, NJ 800-327-8246
Miller's Meat Market
Red Bud, IL...................... 618-282-3334
Nicky
Portland, OR..................... 800-469-4162
Pinter's Packing Plant
Dorchester, WI 715-654-5444
Rocky Mountain Natural Meats
Henderson, CO.................... 800-327-2706
Springville Meat & ColdsStorage
Springville, UT.................. 801-489-6391
Superior Farms
Davis, CA........................ 800-228-5262
Triple U Enterprises
Fort Pierre, SD 605-567-3624
Vantage USA
Chicago, IL 773-247-1086
Wall Meat Processing
Wall, SD 605-279-2348
Western Meats
Rapid City, SD 605-342-0322
YB Meats of Wichita
Wichita, KS...................... 316-942-1213

Caribou

Thornbury Grandview Farms
Thornbury, ON 519-599-6368

Emu

Dino-Meat Company
White House, TN 877-557-6493
Thornbury Grandview Farms
Thornbury, ON.................... 519-599-6368
YB Meats of Wichita
Wichita, KS...................... 316-942-1213

Farm-Raised

Burris Mill & Feed
Franklinton, LA 800-928-2782
Clay Center Locker Plant
Clay Center, KS 785-632-5550
D'Artagnan
Newark, NJ 800-327-8246
Triple U Enterprises
Fort Pierre, SD 605-567-3624
Wall Meat Processing
Wall, SD 605-279-2348
Western Meats
Rapid City, SD 605-342-0322

Guinea Hen

D'Artagnan
Newark, NJ 800-327-8246

Meat & Poultry

Becker Food Company
Milwaukee, WI.................... 414-964-5353
Bolner's Fiesta Products
San Antonio, TX.................. 210-734-6404
Bon Secour Fisheries
Bon Secour, AL................... 800-633-6854
Broadleaf Venison Usa
Vernon, CA....................... 800-336-3844
Burris Mill & Feed
Franklinton, LA 800-928-2782
Clay Center Locker Plant
Clay Center, KS 785-632-5550
Community Market & Deli
Lindstrom, MN.................... 651-257-1128
Crescent Duck Farm
Aquebogue, NY 631-722-8700
Culinary Foods
Chicago, IL...................... 800-621-4049
Czimer's Game & Sea Foods
Homer Glen, IL................... 708-301-0500
D'Artagnan
Newark, NJ 800-327-8246
Eickman's Processing
Seward, IL....................... 815-247-8451
Ellsworth Locker
Ellsworth, MN 507-967-2544
Fox Deluxe Foods
Chicago, IL 312-421-3737
Grimaud Farms
Stockton, CA..................... 800-466-9955
Hickory Baked Food
Castle Rock, CO.................. 303-688-2633
Indian Valley Meats
Indian, AK....................... 907-653-7511
Ketters Meat Market & Locker Plant
Frazee, MN....................... 218-334-2351
Lindner Bison
Valencia, CA..................... 866-247-8753
MacFarlane Pheasants
Janesville, WI 877-269-8957
Metzer Farms
Gonzales, CA 800-424-7755
Miller Brothers PackingcCompany
Sylvester, GA 229-776-2014
Musicon Deer Farm
Goshen, NY....................... 845-294-6378
Palmetto Pigeon Plant
Sumter, SC 803-775-1204
Pekarna's Meat Market
Jordan, MN....................... 952-492-6101
Pel-Freez
Rogers, AR 800-223-8751
Pinter's Packing Plant
Dorchester, WI 715-654-5444
R Four Meats
Chatfield, MN.................... 507-867-4180
Schiltz Foods
Sisseton, SD 877-872-4458
Springville Meat & ColdsStorage
Springville, UT.................. 801-489-6391
Squab Producers of California
Modesto, CA...................... 209-537-4744
Stonies Sausage Shop Inc
Perryville, MO 888-546-2540
Thornbury Grandview Farms
Thornbury, ON 519-599-6368
Triple U Enterprises
Fort Pierre, SD 605-567-3624
United Meat Company
San Francisco, CA 415-864-2118
Uvalde Meat Processing
Uvalde, TX 830-278-6247
Wall Meat Processing
Wall, SD 605-279-2348
Wapsie Produce
Decorah, IA...................... 563-382-4271
Western Meats
Rapid City, SD 605-342-0322

Muscovy Duck

D'Artagnan
Newark, NJ 800-327-8246

Muskox

Thornbury Grandview Farms
Thornbury, ON 519-599-6368

Ostrich

Acadian Ostrich Ranch
Clinton, LA 800-350-0167
Broadleaf Venison Usa
Vernon, CA 800-336-3844
Clay Center Locker Plant
Clay Center, KS 785-632-5550
Community Market & Deli
Lindstrom, MN 651-257-1128
D'Artagnan
Newark, NJ 800-327-8246
Kingsbury Country Market
Kingsbury, IN 219-393-3016
Meat-O-Mat Corporation
Brooklyn, NY 718-965-7250
Nicky
Portland, OR 800-469-4162
Pokanoket Ostrich Farm
South Dartmouth, MA 508-992-6188
Prime Ostrich International
Morinville, AB 800-340-2311
Protos Foods
Greensburg, PA 724-836-1802
Struthious Ostrich Farm
Allentown, NJ 609-208-0702
Thornbury Grandview Farms
Thornbury, ON 519-599-6368
YB Meats of Wichita
Wichita, KS 316-942-1213

Partridge

D'Artagnan
Newark, NJ 800-327-8246

Peking Duck

D'Artagnan
Newark, NJ 800-327-8246

Pheasant

Burgers Smokehouse
California, MO 800-624-5426
D'Artagnan
Newark, NJ 800-327-8246
Hickory Baked Food
Castle Rock, CO 303-688-2633
MacFarlane Pheasants
Janesville, WI 877-269-8957
Mahantongo Game Farms
Dalmatia, PA 570-758-6284
Nicky
Portland, OR 800-469-4162
Squab Producers of California
Modesto, CA 209-537-4744

Quail (See also Eggs: Quail)

Burgers Smokehouse
California, MO 800-624-5426
D'Artagnan
Newark, NJ 800-327-8246
Manchester Farms
Columbia, SC 800-845-0421
Nicky
Portland, OR 800-469-4162
Nueces Canyon Texas Style Meat Seasoning
Brenham, TX. 800-925-5058
Squab Producers of California
Modesto, CA 209-537-4744

Rabbit

D'Artagnan
Newark, NJ 800-327-8246
Nicky
Portland, OR 800-469-4162
Rabbit Barn
Turlock, CA 209-632-1123

Fryer

Mahantongo Game Farms
Dalmatia, PA 570-758-6284
Squab Producers of California
Modesto, CA 209-537-4744
Tarazi Specialty Foods
Chino, CA 909-628-3601

Squab

Carmel Meat/Specialty Foods
Marina, CA 800-298-5823
D'Artagnan
Newark, NJ 800-327-8246
Palmetto Pigeon Plant
Sumter, SC 803-775-1204
Squab Producers of California
Modesto, CA 209-537-4744

Venison

Alewel's Country Meats
Warrensburg, MO 800-353-8553
Bellville Meat Market
Bellville, TX 800-571-6328
Blakely Freezer Locker
Thomasville, GA 229-723-3622
Boyd Sausage Company
Washington, IA 319-653-5715
Broadleaf Venison Usa
Vernon, CA 800-336-3844
Brookview Farms
Archbold, OH 419-445-6366
Collbran Locker Plant
Collbran, CO 970-487-3329
Community Market & Deli
Lindstrom, MN 651-257-1128
D'Artagnan
Newark, NJ 800-327-8246
Ellsworth Locker
Ellsworth, MN 507-967-2544
Houser Meats
Rushville, IL 217-322-4994
Indian Valley Meats
Indian, AK 907-653-7511
Jackson Brothers Food Locker
Post, TX 806-495-3245
Ketters Meat Market & Locker Plant
Frazee, MN 218-334-2351
Lena Maid Meats
Lena, IL 815-369-4522
MacGregors Meat & Seafood
Toronto, ON 888-383-3663
Matthiesen's Deer & Custom Processing
De Witt, IA 563-659-8409
Musicon Deer Farm
Goshen, NY. 845-294-6378
Nesbitt Processing
Aledo, IL 309-582-5183
New Zealand Lamb Company
Wilton, CT 800-438-5262
Nicky
Portland, OR 800-469-4162
R Four Meats
Chatfield, MN 507-867-4180
Smokey Denmark Sausage
Austin, TX 512-385-0718
Stonies Sausage Shop Inc
Perryville, MO 888-546-2540
Superior Farms
Davis, CA 800-228-5262
Thornbury Grandview Farms
Thornbury, ON 519-599-6368
Turner New Zealand
Aliso Viejo, CA 949-622-6181
United Meat Company
San Francisco, CA 415-864-2118
Uvalde Meat Processing
Uvalde, TX 830-278-6247
Venison America
Hudson, WI 800-310-2360
YB Meats of Wichita
Wichita, KS 316-942-1213

Canned

Indian Valley Meats
Indian, AK 907-653-7511

Frozen

Broadleaf Venison Usa
Vernon, CA 800-336-3844
Brookview Farms
Archbold, OH 419-445-6366
Indian Valley Meats
Indian, AK 907-653-7511
R Four Meats
Chatfield, MN 507-867-4180
United Meat Company
San Francisco, CA 415-864-2118

Wild

Clay Center Locker Plant
Clay Center, KS 785-632-5550
D'Artagnan
Newark, NJ 800-327-8246
Eickman's Processing
Seward, IL 815-247-8451
Triple U Enterprises
Fort Pierre, SD 605-567-3624
Wall Meat Processing
Wall, SD 605-279-2348
Western Meats
Rapid City, SD 605-342-0322

Wood Pigeon

D'Artagnan
Newark, NJ 800-327-8246

Goat

Braham Food Locker Service
Braham, MN 320-396-2636
Caribbean Food Delights
Tappan, NY 845-398-3000
Community Market & Deli
Lindstrom, MN 651-257-1128
D'Artagnan
Newark, NJ 800-327-8246
East Beauregard Meat Processing Center
Deridder, LA 337-328-7171
Halsted Packing House
Chicago, IL 312-421-4511
Jones Packing Company
Harvard, IL 815-943-4488
Nesbitt Processing
Aledo, IL 309-582-5183
Rancher's Lamb of Texas
San Angelo, TX 325-659-4004
Red Deer Lake Meat Processing
Calgary, AB 403-256-4925

Windcrest Meat Packers
Port Perry, ON. 800-750-2542

Horse

Bouvry Exports Calgary
Calgary, AB. 403-253-0717
Phoenix Agro-Industrial Corporation
Westbury, NY 516-334-1194

Lamb

A. Thomas Meats
Louisville, KY 800-253-2020
A.C. Kissling Company
Philadelphia, PA 800-445-1943
Acme Steak & Seafood Company
Youngstown, OH. 330-270-8000
Agri-Best Foods
Chicago, IL 773-247-5060
Alpine Meats
Stockton, CA. 800-399-6328
Blakely Freezer Locker
Thomasville, GA. 229-723-3622
Border's Market
Plymouth, OH. 419-687-2634
Brookview Farms
Archbold, OH 419-445-6366
Bruss Company
Chicago, IL 800-621-3882
Bush Brothers Provision Company
West Palm Beach, FL 800-327-1345
Buzz Food Service
Charleston, WV 304-925-4781
Callaway Packing Company
Delta, CO 800-332-6932
Cambridge Slaughtering
Cambridge, IL. 309-937-2455
Campbell's Quality Cuts
Sidney, OH 937-492-2194
Canada West Foods
Innisfail, AB 403-227-3386
Canal Fulton Provision
Canal Fulton, OH 800-321-3502
Carl Streit & Son Company
Neptune, NJ 732-775-0803
Carmel Meat/Specialty Foods
Marina, CA 800-298-5823
Castleberry's Meats
Atlanta, GA. 404-873-1804
Catelli Brothers
Camden, NJ. 856-869-2200
Center Locker Service Company
Center, MO 573-267-3343
Chicago Steaks
Chicago, IL. 800-776-4174
Clay Center Locker Plant
Clay Center, KS 785-632-5550
Coleman Purely Natural Brands
Golden, CO. 800-442-8666
Community Market & Deli
Lindstrom, MN 651-257-1128
ConAgra Beef Company
Greeley, CO. 970-506-8000
Conti Packing Company
Rochester, NY. 585-424-2500
Country Butcher Shop
Palmyra, MO. 573-769-2257
Country Village Meats
Sublette, IL 815-849-5532
Cusack Wholesale Meat Company
Oklahoma City, OK 800-241-6328
D'Artagnan
Newark, NJ 800-327-8246
Dale T. Smith & Sons Meat Packing Corporation
Draper, UT 801-571-3611
David Mosner Meat Products
Bronx, NY. 718-328-5600
Davidson Meat Processing Plant
Waynesville, OH. 513-897-2971
Debragga & Spitler
New York, NY. 212-924-1311
Dino's Sausage & Meat Company
Utica, NY 315-732-2661
Duma Meats
Mogadore, OH 330-628-3438
Eickman's Processing
Seward, IL. 815-247-8451
Eiserman Meats
Slave Lake, AB. 780-849-5507
Empire Beef & Redistribution
Rochester, NY. 800-462-6804
Eureka Lockers
Eureka, IL 309-467-2731
Ferko Meat Company
Milwaukee, WI 414-967-5500
G&G Sheep Farm
Boston, KY 502-833-4863
Glasco Locker Plant
Glasco, KS 785-568-2364
Godshall's Quality Meats
Telford, PA 888-463-7425
Halal Transactions
Omaha, NE 402-572-6120
Halsted Packing House
Chicago, IL 312-421-4511
Heringer Meats
Covington, KY 859-291-2000
Houser Meats
Rushville, IL 217-322-4994
International Meat Company
Chicago, IL 773-622-1400
Isernio Sausage Company
Seattle, WA 888-495-8674
Jones Packing Company
Harvard, IL 815-943-4488
Jordahl Meats
Manchester, MN 507-826-3418
Kelble Brothers
Berlin Heights, OH 800-247-2333
Kelly Packing Company
Torrington, WY. 307-532-2210
L&L Packing Company
Chicago, IL 800-628-6328
L&M Slaughtering
Georgetown, IL. 217-662-6841
Lay Packing Company
Knoxville, TN. 865-922-4320
Lena Maid Meats
Lena, IL. 815-369-4522
Lombardi Brothers Meat Packers
Denver, CO 800-421-4412
Lowell Provision Company
Lowell, MA. 978-454-5603
Magnolia Beef Company
Elizabeth, NJ. 908-352-9412
Maid-Rite Steak Company
Dunmore, PA. 800-233-4259
Manger Packing Company
Baltimore, MD 800-227-9262
Marks Meat
Canby, OR. 503-266-2048
Matthiesen's Deer & Custom Processing
De Witt, IA 563-659-8409
Meatland Packers
Medicine Hat, AB. 403-528-4321
Miami Beef Company
Hialeah, FL 305-621-3252
Miller Brothers PackingcCompany
Sylvester, GA 229-776-2014
Mountain City Meat Company
Denver, CO 800-937-8325
Mountain States Rosen
Bronx, NY. 800-872-5262
Nagel Veal
San Bernardino, CA 909-383-7075
Nesbitt Processing
Aledo, IL. 309-582-5183
New Zealand Lamb Company
Wilton, CT 800-438-5262
Old Neighborhood Foods
Lynn, MA 781-595-1557
Onoway Custom Packers
Onoway, AB 780-967-2207
Otto W Liebold & Company
Flint, MI 800-999-6328
Pasqualichio Brothers
Scranton, PA 800-232-6233
Petschl's Quality Meats
Tukwila, WA. 206-575-4400
Premium Meat Company
Brigham City, UT 435-723-5944
R Four Meats
Chatfield, MN. 507-867-4180
Ralph's Packing Company
Perkins, OK. 800-522-3979
Rancher's Lamb of Texas
San Angelo, TX 325-659-4004
Red Deer Lake Meat Processing
Calgary, AB. 403-256-4925
Rendulic Packing
McKeesport, PA 412-678-9541
Rocky Mountain Meats
Rocky Mountain House, AB 403-845-3434
Royal Center Locker Plant
Royal Center, IN 574-643-3275
Shelley's Prime Meats
Jersey City, NJ 201-433-3434
Smith Packing Regional Meat
Utica, NY
Southtowns Seafood & Meats
Blasdell, NY 716-824-4900
Springville Meat & ColdsStorage
Springville, UT. 801-489-6391
Standard Beef Company
Foxboro, MA 203-787-2164
Stock Yards Packing Company
Chicago, IL 800-621-1119
Superior Farms
Davis, CA 800-228-5262
Terrell Meats
Delta, UT. 435-864-2600
Thompson Packers
Slidell, LA. 800-989-6328
Tillamook Meat Company
Tillamook, OR 503-842-4802
Tooele Valley Meat
Grantsville, UT. 435-884-3837
Tucker Packing Company
Orrville, OH 330-683-3311
Turk Brothers Custom Meats
Ashland, OH 800-789-1051
Une-Viandi
St. Jean Sur Richelieu, NB 800-363-1955
United Meat Company
San Francisco, CA 415-864-2118
United Provision Meat Company
Columbus, OH 614-252-1126
Uvalde Meat Processing
Uvalde, TX 830-278-6247
Vantage USA
Chicago, IL 773-247-1086
Victoria Fancy Sausage
Edmonton, AB 780-471-2283
Wall Meat Processing
Wall, SD 605-279-2348
Warren & Son Meat Processing
Whipple, OH. 740-585-2421
Wasatch Meats
Salt Lake City, UT 801-363-5747
Westport Locker Service
Westport, IN 877-265-0551
White's Meat Processing
Peebles, OH. 937-587-2930
Willcox Packing House
Willcox, AZ 520-384-2015
Windcrest Meat Packers
Port Perry, ON. 800-750-2542
Wolverine Packing
Detroit, MI 313-259-7500
YB Meats of Wichita
Wichita, KS. 316-942-1213

Fresh

Mountain City Meat Company
Denver, CO 800-937-8325
R Four Meats
Chatfield, MN. 507-867-4180
Shelley's Prime Meats
Jersey City, NJ 201-433-3434
Smith Packing Regional Meat
Utica, NY

Frozen

Buzz Food Service
Charleston, WV 304-925-4781
Maid-Rite Steak Company
Dunmore, PA. 800-233-4259
Montage Foods
Scranton, PA 800-521-8325
Mountain City Meat Company
Denver, CO 800-937-8325
Phoenix Agro-Industrial Corporation
Westbury, NY 516-334-1194

R Four Meats
Chatfield, MN 507-867-4180
Shelley's Prime Meats
Jersey City, NJ 201-433-3434
Smith Packing Regional Meat
Utica, NY
Thompson Packers
Slidell, LA. 800-989-6328
United Meat Company
San Francisco, CA 415-864-2118

Leg of

Chicago Steaks
Chicago, IL 800-776-4174

Loin Chop

Chicago Steaks
Chicago, IL 800-776-4174

Rib Chop

Chicago Steaks
Chicago, IL 800-776-4174

Meat Meal

Carolina By-Products Company
Winchester, VA. 540-877-2590
McRedmond Brothers
Nashville, TN 615-361-8997

Mutton

Center Locker Service Company
Center, MO 573-267-3343

Packaged

Burke Corporation
Nevada, IA 800-654-1152

Always make it your best® with Burke fully cooked meats. We specialize in Italian sausage, beef, and pork toppings, meatballs, taco meats, shredded meats, pepperoni, bacon, Canadian-style bacon, chicken and beef strips. Additionally, we offer a variety of specialty products: Hand-Pinched Style® brand toppings, chorizo, gyro topping, andouille sausage, and breakfast patties and links.

Pates & Fois Gras

Foie Gras

Assouline & Ting
Huntingdon Valley, PA 800-521-4491
D'Artagnan
Newark, NJ 800-327-8246
DeChoix Specialty Foods
Woodside, NY. 800-332-4649

Pates

Alexian Pates/GroezingerProvisions
Neptune, NJ 800-927-9473
Caughman's Meat Plant
Lexington, SC. 803-356-0076
Cordon Bleu International
Anjou, QC. 514-352-3000
D'Artagnan
Newark, NJ. 800-327-8246
Dave's Gourmet Albacore
Kirkland, WA 800-454-8862

Ducktrap River Fish Farm
Belfast, ME 800-434-8727
Giovanni's Appetizing Food Products
Richmond, MI. 586-727-9355
Groezinger Provisions
Neptune, NJ 800-927-9473
Hickory Baked Food
Castle Rock, CO 303-688-2633
International Trading Company
Houston, TX 713-224-5901
Kretschmar
Don Mills, ON 800-561-4532
Les Trois Petits Cochons
Brooklyn, NY 800-537-7283
Marcel et Henri Charcuterie Francaise
South San Francisco, CA 800-227-6436
Michel's Magnifique
New York, NY 212-431-1070
Organic Gourmet
Sherman Oaks, CA 800-400-7772
Phoenicia Patisserie
Arlington, TX 817-261-2898
Salmolux
Federal Way, WA 253-874-2026
Sunset Farm Foods
Valdosta, GA. 800-882-1121
Taste of Gourmet
Indianola, MS 800-833-7731

Pork & Pork Products

A to Z Portion Meats
Bluffton, OH. 800-338-6328
A. Stein Meat Products
Brooklyn, NY 718-492-0760
A. Thomas Meats
Louisville, KY 800-253-2020
Abattoir Aliments Asta Inc.
St Alexandre Kamouraska, QC. 418-495-2728
Alaska Sausage and Seafood Company
Anchorage, AK. 800-798-3636
Alderfer Bologna
Harleysville, PA 800-341-1121
Alphin Brothers
Dunn, NC 800-672-4502
Amana Meat Shop & Smokehouse
Amana, IA. 800-373-6328
Armbrust Meats
Medford, WI 715-748-3102
Atlantic Pork & Provisions
Jamaica, NY 800-245-3536
B&D Foods
Boise, ID 208-344-1183
Bartlow Brothers
Rushville, IL. 800-252-7202
Bear Creek Smokehouse
Marshall, TX. 800-950-2327
Big B Distributors
Evansville, IN 812-425-5235
Bob Evans Farms
Hillsdale, MI. 517-437-3349
Bodin Foods
New Iberia, LA. 337-367-1344
Bruss Company
Chicago, IL. 800-621-3882
Burgers Smokehouse
California, MO 800-624-5426
Burke Corporation
Nevada, IA 800-654-1152

Always make it your best® with Burke fully cooked meats. We specialize in Italian sausage, beef, and pork toppings, meatballs, taco meats, shredded meats, pepperoni, bacon, Canadian-style bacon, chicken and beef strips. Additionally, we offer a variety of specialty products: Hand-Pinched Style® brand toppings, chorizo, gyro topping, andouille sausage, and breakfast patties and links.

Burnett & Son Meat Company
Monrovia, CA. 626-357-2165
Bush Brothers Provision Company
West Palm Beach, FL 800-327-1345
C. Roy Meat Products
Yale, MI. 810-387-3957
Caddo Packing Company
Marshall, TX. 903-935-2211
Calihan Pork Processing
Peoria, IL. 309-674-9175
Caribbean Products
Baltimore, MD 410-235-7700

Carmelita Provisions Company
Monterey Park, CA. 323-262-6751
Carolina Pride Foods
Greenwood, SC. 864-229-5611
Castleberry's
Vineland, NJ 856-691-2100
Castleberry's Meats
Atlanta, GA. 404-873-1804
Caughman's Meat Plant
Lexington, SC. 803-356-0076
Central Meat & Provision Company
San Diego, CA 619-239-1391
Chandler Foods
Greensboro, NC 800-537-6219
Chef's Requested Foods
Oklahoma City, OK 800-256-0259
Cheraw Packing
Cheraw, SC. 843-537-7426
Chicago Steaks
Chicago, IL. 800-776-4174
Chip Steak & Provision Company
Mankato, MN 507-388-6277
Chisesi Brothers Meat Packing Company
New Orleans, LA 800-966-3550
Cimpl Meats
Yankton, SD 605-665-1665
Circle V Meat Company
Spanish Fork, UT 801-798-3081
Clem Becker
Two Rivers, WI. 920-793-1391
Clougherty Packing Company
Vernon, CA. 323-583-4621
Cloverdale Foods Company
Mandan, ND 800-669-9511
Columbia Packing Company
Dallas, TX. 800-460-8171
Community Market & Deli
Lindstrom, MN 651-257-1128
Completely Fresh Foods
Montebello, CA 323-722-9136
ConAgra Foods/Eckrich
Omaha, NE 800-327-4424
Conti Packing Company
Rochester, NY. 585-424-2500
Continental Deli Foods
Cherokee, IA. 712-225-6529
Cordon Bleu International
Anjou, QC. 514-352-3000
Corte Provisions
Newark, NJ 201-653-7246
Country Butcher Shop
Palmyra, MO. 573-769-2257
Country Smoked Meats
Bowling Green, OH 800-321-4766
Country Village Meats
Sublette, IL 815-849-5532
Counts Sausage Company
Prosperity, SC 803-364-2392
Crawford Sausage Company
Chicago, IL. 866-653-2479
Crofton & Sons
Brandon, FL 800-878-7675
Cropp Cooperative-Organic Valley
La Farge, WI. 888-444-6455
Curtis Packing Company
Greensboro, NC 336-275-7684
Cusack Wholesale Meat Company
Oklahoma City, OK 800-241-6328
D'Artagnan
Newark, NJ 800-327-8246
Dietz & Watson
Philadelphia, PA 800-333-1974
Dohar Meats
Cleveland, OH 216-241-4197
Dolores Canning Company
Los Angeles, CA. 323-263-9155
Dreymiller & Kray
Hampshire, IL. 847-683-2271
Duma Meats
Mogadore, OH 330-628-3438
Dutch Valley Veal
South Holland, IL 800-832-8325
Edmonds Chile Company
St Louis, MO. 314-772-1499
Fabbri Sausage Manufacturing
Chicago, IL. 312-829-6363
Family Brand International
Lenoir City, TN. 865-986-8005
Fanestil Packing Company
Emporia, KS 620-342-6354
Fletcher's Fine Foods
Algona, WA. 253-735-0800

Foodbrands America
Oklahoma City, OK 405-290-4000
Fortenberry Ice Company
Kodak, TN. 865-933-2568
Fricks Meat Products
Washington, MO. 800-241-2209
Glazier Packing Company
Potsdam, NY. 315-265-2500
Grant Park Packing
Chicago, IL 312-421-4096
Groff Meats
Elizabethtown, PA. 717-367-1246
Gulf Marine & Industrial Supplies
New Orleans, LA 800-886-6252
Gwaltney Food Service Gwanltney+Smithfeild Ltd
Smithfield, VA 757-357-3131
Hahn Brothers
Westminster, MD 800-227-7675
Hamm's Custom Meats
McKinney, TX. 972-562-7511
Hancock's Old Fashioned
Franklinville, NC 336-824-2145
Hansel 'N Gretel
Flushing, NY. 718-326-0041
Hatfield Quality Meats
Hatfield, PA. 800-523-5291
Hazle Park Packing Co
West Hazleton, PA 800-238-4331
Hickory Baked Food
Castle Rock, CO 303-688-2633
Higa Meat and Pork Market Limited
Honolulu, HI. 808-531-3591
Hillbilly Smokehouse
Rogers, AR 479-636-1927
Holly Hill Locker Company
Holly Hill, SC. 803-496-3611
Hoople Country Kitchens
Rockport, IN 812-649-2351
Hormel Foods Corporation
Fremont, NE 402-721-2300
Hormel Foods Corporation
Austin, MN 800-523-4635
Humphrey Blue Ribbon Meats
Springfield, IL. 800-747-6328
Iowa Quality Meats
Clive, IA 800-677-6868
John Hofmeister & Son
Chicago, IL 800-923-4267
Johnsonville Food Company
Sheboygan Falls, WI. 888-556-2728
Joseph Sanders
Custer, MI 800-968-5035
Karn Meats
Columbus, OH 800-221-9585
Kelley Foods of Alabama
Elba, AL 334-897-5761
Kelley Meats
Taberg, NY 315-337-4272
Kessler Foods, Inc
Lemoyne, PA. 717-763-7162
Kilgus Meats
Toledo, OH 419-472-9721
Kowalski Sausage Company
Hamtramck, MI. 800-482-2400
Kubla Khan Food Company
Portland, OR 503-234-7494
Kutztown Bologna Company
Leola, PA. 800-723-8824
Land O'Frost
Searcy, AR 800-643-5654
Lay Packing Company
Knoxville, TN. 865-922-4320
Lees Sausage Company
Orangeburg, SC 803-534-5517
Leo G Fraboni Sausage Company
Hibbing, MN. 218-263-5074
Leona Meat Plant
Troy, PA. 570-297-3574
Levonian Brothers
Troy, NY 518-274-3610
Locustdale Meat Packing
Locustdale, PA 570-875-1270
Lords Sausage & CountryhHam
Dexter, GA 800-342-6002
Lowell Packing Company
Fitzgerald, GA 800-342-0313
Maple Leaf Foods
Winnipeg, NB 800-564-6253
Marshallville Packing Company
Marshallville, OH. 330-855-2871
McKenzie of Vermont
Burlington, VT 802-864-4585
Meating Place
Buffalo, NY. 716-885-3623
Mello's North End Manufacturings
Fall River, MA 800-673-2320
Metafoods, LLC
Atlanta, GA. 404-843-2400
Miami Beef Company
Hialeah, FL 305-621-3252
Mirasco
Atlanta, GA. 770-956-1945
Mitchell Foods
Barbourville, KY 888-202-9745
Montana Ranch Brand
Billings, MT 406-294-2333
Moo & Oink
Chicago, IL 773-493-7100
Morse's Sauerkraut
Waldoboro, ME. 866-832-5569
National Steak & Poultry
Owasso, OK 800-366-6772
New Braunfels Smokehouse
New Braunfels, TX. 800-537-6932
Niemuth's Steak & Chop Shop
Waupaca, WI. 715-258-2666
O Chili Frozen Foods Inc
Northbrook, IL 847-562-1991
Ossian Seafood Meats
Ossian, IN 260-622-4191
Owens Country Sausage
Richardson, TX. 800-966-9367
Parma Sausage Products
Pittsburgh, PA. 877-294-4207
Pasqualichio Brothers
Scranton, PA 800-232-6233
Payne Packing Company
Artesia, NM. 575-746-2779
Peer Foods Inc.
Chicago, IL 800-365-5644
Pierceton Foods
Pierceton, IN. 574-594-2344
Pioneer Packing Company
Bowling Green, OH 419-352-5283
Plumrose USA
East Brunswick, NJ. 800-526-4909
Premium Standard Farms
Dalhart, TX 806-377-3289
Proliant Meat Ingredients
Harlan, IA 800-369-2672
R.L. Zeigler Company
Tuscaloosa, AL. 800-392-6328
R.M. Felts Packing Company
Ivor, VA. 888-300-0971
Ray's Sausage Company Inc
Cleveland, OH 216-921-8782
Register Meat Company
Cottondale, FL 850-352-4269
Rego's Purity Foods
Honolulu, HI. 808-847-3717
Rendulic Packing
McKeesport, PA 412-678-9541
Rinehart Meat Processing
Branson, MO. 417-334-2044
Robertson's Country Meat Hams
Finchville, KY 800-678-1521
Rose Packing Company
South Barrington, IL. 800-323-7363
Rudolph Foods
Dallas, TX. 214-638-2204
Sadler's Smokehouse
Henderson, TX 903-657-5581
Safeway Inc
Pleasanton, CA 877-723-3929
Salaison Levesque
Montreal, QC 877- 53- 170
Sara Lee Corporation
Downers Grove, IL. 630-598-8100
Sausage Shoppe
Cleveland, OH 216-351-5213
Saval Foods
Elkridge, MD 800-527-2825
Savoie's Sausage & Food Products
Opelousas, LA. 337-948-4115
Schaller & Weber
Astoria, NY. 800-847-4115
Sculli Brothers
Yeadon, PA 215-336-1223
Seaboard Foods
Shawnee Mission, KS. 800-262-7907
Sechrist Brothers
Dallastown, PA 717-244-2975
Sheinman Provision Company
Philadelphia, PA 215-473-7065
Simeus Foods Internatio nal
Mansfield, TX. 888-772-3663
Smithfield Foods
Smithfield, VA 888-366-6767
Smolich Brothers
Joliet, IL 815-727-2144
Southtowns Seafood & Meats
Blasdell, NY 716-824-4900
Stevens Sausage Company
Smithfield, NC 800-338-0561
Stonies Sausage Shop Inc
Perryville, MO 888-546-2540
Striplings
Moultrie, GA. 229-985-4226
Sugar Creek Packing
Washington Court House, OH 800-848-8205
Suncrest Farms
Totowa, NJ 973-595-0214
Sunnydale Meats
Gaffney, SC. 864-489-6091
SW Red Smith
Davie, FL 954-581-1996
Swift & Company
Greeley, CO. 970-506-8000
Thomas Packing Company
Columbus, GA 800-729-0976
Tomasinos Sausage
Canton, OH. 330-454-4171
Troy Frozen Food
Troy, IL 618-667-6332
Troyers Trail Bologna
Dundee, OH 877-893-2414
Tupman-Thurlow Company
Deerfield Beach, FL 954-596-9989
V & V Supremo Foods
Chicago, IL 888-887-8773
V.W. Joyner & Company
Smithfield, VA 757-357-2161
Valley Meats
Coal Valley, IL 309-799-7341
Vantage USA
Chicago, IL 773-247-1086
Vollwerth & Baroni Companies
Hancock, MI 800-562-7620
WA Bean & Sons
Bangor, ME. 800-649-1958
Waco Beef & Pork Processors
Waco, TX 254-772-4669
Waken Meat Company
Atlanta, GA. 404-627-3537
Wayco Ham Company
Goldsboro, NC 800-962-2614
Whitaker Foods
Waterloo, IA 800-553-7490
William's Pork
Lumberton, NC. 910-608-2226
Willies Smoke House
Harrisville, PA. 800-742-4184
YB Meats of Wichita
Wichita, KS. 316-942-1213

Barbecued

Big B Distributors
Evansville, IN. 812-425-5235
Calumet Diversified Meat Company
Pleasant Prairie, WI 262-947-7200
Chandler Foods
Greensboro, NC 800-537-6219
Dankworth Packing Company
Ballinger, TX 325-365-3552
Dorina/So-Good
Union, IL. 815-923-2144
Moonlite Bar Bq Inn
Owensboro, KY 800-322-8989
Piggie Park Enterprises
West Columbia, SC. 800-628-7423
Sadler's Smokehouse
Henderson, TX 903-657-5581
W & G Marketing Company
Ames, IA. 515-233-4774
Woods Smoked Meats
Bowling Green, MO 800-458-8426

Frozen

Burke Corporation
Nevada, IA 800-654-1152

Always make it your best® with Burke fully cooked meats. We specialize in Italian sausage, beef, and pork toppings, meatballs, taco meats, shredded meats, pepperoni, bacon, Canadian-style bacon, chicken and beef strips. Additionally, we offer a variety of specialty products: Hand-Pinched Style® brand toppings, chorizo, gyro topping, andouille sausage, and breakfast patties and links.

Tenn Valley Ham Company
Paris, TN 731-642-9740

Breaded

Kings Command Foods
Kent, WA 800-247-3138
Simeus Foods International
Mansfield, TX 888-772-3663
Valley Meats
Coal Valley, IL 309-799-7341

Fresh

Abattoir A. Trahan Company
Yamachiche, QC 819-296-3791
Aliments Jolibec
St Jacques De Montcalm, QC 514-861-6082
Amity Packing Company
Chicago, IL 800-837-0270
Botsford Fisheries
Cap Pele, NB 506-577-4327
Brook Locker Plant
Brook, IN 219-275-2611
Buckhead Beef Company
Atlanta, GA 800-888-5578
Camrose Packers
Camrose, AB 780-672-4887
Charcuterie LaTour Eiffel
Vanier, QC 418-687-2840
Colorado Boxed Beef Company
Auburndale, FL 863-967-0636
Devro, Inc.
Swansea, SC 803-796-9730
Farmland Foods
Kansas City, MO 888-327-6526
J&M Meats
Warburg, AB 780-848-7598
John Morrell & Company
Cincinnati, OH 712-279-7360
John Morrell & Company
Cincinnati, OH 800-345-0743
Les Salaisons Brochu
St. Henri De Levis, QC 418-882-2282
Les Viandes Or-Fil
Laval, QC 450-687-5664
Maple Leaf Pork
Lethbridge, AB 403-328-1756
Mountain City Meat Company
Denver, CO 800-937-8325
Ontario Pork
Guelph, ON 877-668-7675
Quality Meat Packers
Toronto, ON 416-703-7675
R Four Meats
Chatfield, MN 507-867-4180
Schwab & Company
Oklahoma City, OK 800-888-8668
Shelley's Prime Meats
Jersey City, NJ 201-433-3434
Smith Packing Regional Meat
Utica, NY
Thomson Meats ltd.
Melfort, SK 306-752-2802
Trochu Meat Processors
Trochu, AB 403-442-4202
Troy Pork Store
Troy, NY 518-272-8291

Frozen

Abattoir A. Trahan Company
Yamachiche, QC 819-296-3791
Alcester Meats
Alcester, SD 605-934-2540
Aliments Jolibec
St Jacques De Montcalm, QC 514-861-6082
Amity Packing Company
Chicago, IL 800-837-0270
B&D Foods
Boise, ID 208-344-1183
Blakely Freezer Locker
Thomasville, GA 229-723-3622
Bob's Custom Cuts
Bonnyville, AB 780-826-2138
Botsford Fisheries
Cap Pele, NB 506-577-4327
Brook Locker Plant
Brook, IN 219-275-2611
Brookfield Farms Nationwide Foods
Chicago, IL 773-787-4900
Buckhead Beef Company
Atlanta, GA 800-888-5578
Buono Beef Co
Philadelphia, PA 215-463-3600
Burke Corporation
Nevada, IA 800-654-1152

Always make it your best® with Burke fully cooked meats. We specialize in Italian sausage, beef, and pork toppings, meatballs, taco meats, shredded meats, pepperoni, bacon, Canadian-style bacon, chicken and beef strips. Additionally, we offer a variety of specialty products: Hand-Pinched Style® brand toppings, chorizo, gyro topping, andouille sausage, and breakfast patties and links.

Buzz Food Service
Charleston, WV 304-925-4781
Charcuterie LaTour Eiffel
Vanier, QC 418-687-2840
Colorado Boxed Beef Company
Auburndale, FL 863-967-0636
Curly's Foods
Edina, MN 800-722-1127
Edmonds Chile Company
St Louis, MO 314-772-1499
El-Rey Foods
Ferguson, MO 314-521-3113
Farmland Foods
Kansas City, MO 888-327-6526
Fuji Foods
Denver, CO 303-377-3738
Gwaltney Food Service Gwanltney+Smithfeild Ltd
Smithfield, VA 757-357-3131
Hatfield Quality Meats
Hatfield, PA 800-523-5291
Holten Meats
Sauget, IL 800-851-4684
J&M Meats
Warburg, AB 780-848-7598
John Morrell & Company
Cincinnati, OH 712-279-7360
John Morrell & Company
Cincinnati, OH 800-345-0743
Kutztown Bologna Company
Leola, PA 800-723-8824
Ladoga Frozen Food & Retail Meat
Ladoga, IN 765-942-2225
Lengerich Meats
Zanesville, IN 260-638-4123
Les Salaisons Brochu
St. Henri De Levis, QC 418-882-2282
Les Viandes du Breton
Riviere-Du-Lup,, QC 418-863-6711
Les Viandes Or-Fil
Laval, QC 450-687-5664
Maid-Rite Steak Company
Dunmore, PA 800-233-4259
Maple Leaf Pork
Lethbridge, AB 403-328-1756
Mountain City Meat Company
Denver, CO 800-937-8325
Phoenix Agro-Industrial Corporation
Westbury, NY 516-334-1194
Pierceton Foods
Pierceton, IN 574-594-2344
Quality Meat Packers
Toronto, ON 416-703-7675
R Four Meats
Chatfield, MN 507-867-4180
Schwab & Company
Oklahoma City, OK 800-888-8668
Shelley's Prime Meats
Jersey City, NJ 201-433-3434
Smith Packing Regional Meat
Utica, NY
Springhill Farms
Neepawa, NB 204-476-3393
Steak-Umm Company
Shillington, PA 860-928-5900
Sudlersville Frozen Food Locker
Sudlersville, MD 410-438-3106
Tenn Valley Ham Company
Paris, TN 731-642-9740
Thompson Packers
Slidell, LA 800-989-6328
Thomson Meats ltd.
Melfort, SK 306-752-2802
Travis Meats
Powell, TN 800-247-7606

Loin Chop

Amana Meat Shop & Smokehouse
Amana, IA 800-373-6328
Chicago Steaks
Chicago, IL 800-776-4174

Loins

Bear Creek Smokehouse
Marshall, TX 800-950-2327
Black's Barbecue
Lockhart, TX 512-398-2712
Calumet Diversified Meat Company
Pleasant Prairie, WI 262-947-7200
Chicago Steaks
Chicago, IL 800-776-4174
Country Smoked Meats
Bowling Green, OH 800-321-4766
Farmland Foods
Kansas City, MO 888-327-6526
Father's Country Hams
Bremen, KY 270-525-3554
Pasqualichio Brothers
Scranton, PA 800-232-6233
Saval Foods
Elkridge, MD 800-527-2825

Pigs' Feet

Canned

Peer Foods Inc.
Chicago, IL 800-365-5644
SW Red Smith
Davie, FL 954-581-1996

Prepared

Frozen

Advance Food Company
Enid, OK 888-723-8237
Brookview Farms
Archbold, OH 419-445-6366
Buckhead Beef Company
Atlanta, GA 800-888-5578
Burke Corporation
Nevada, IA 800-654-1152

Always make it your best® with Burke fully cooked meats. We specialize in Italian sausage, beef, and pork toppings, meatballs, taco meats, shredded meats, pepperoni, bacon, Canadian-style bacon, chicken and beef strips. Additionally, we offer a variety of specialty products: Hand-Pinched Style® brand toppings, chorizo, gyro topping, andouille sausage, and breakfast patties and links.

Chicago Meat Authority
Chicago, IL 773-254-3811
Dallas Dressed Beef
Dallas, TX 214-638-0142
Davidson Meat Processing Plant
Waynesville, OH 513-897-2971
Empire Beef & Redistribution
Rochester, NY 800-462-6804
Hall Brothers Meats
Cleveland, OH 440-235-3262
Hamm's Custom Meats
McKinney, TX 972-562-7511
Holten Meats
Sauget, IL 800-851-4684
Jacob & Sons Wholesale Meats
Martins Ferry, OH 740-633-3091
Jesses Fine Meats
Cherokee, IA 712-225-3637
King Kold Meats
Englewood, OH 800-836-2797

Land O'Frost
Searcy, AR 800-643-5654
Larsen Packers
Burwick, NS 902-538-8060
O Chili Frozen Foods Inc
Northbrook, IL 847-562-1991
Paris Frozen Foods
Hillsboro, IL 217-532-3822
Pierceton Foods
Pierceton, IN 574-594-2344
Puueo Poi Factory
Hilo, HI 808-935-8435
Tucker Packing Company
Orrville, OH 330-683-3311
Whitaker Foods
Waterloo, IA 800-553-7490

Raw

Duma Meats
Mogadore, OH 330-628-3438

Rib Center Cut

Bear Creek Smokehouse
Marshall, TX 800-950-2327
Chicago Steaks
Chicago, IL 800-776-4174

Sausage

Alaska Sausage and Seafood Company
Anchorage, AK 800-798-3636
Arnold's Meat Food Products
Brooklyn, NY 800-633-7023
Battistoni Italina Specialty Meats
Buffalo, NY 800-248-2705
Bear Creek Smokehouse
Marshall, TX 800-950-2327
Bellville Meat Market
Bellville, TX 800-571-6328
Bob Evans Farms
Hillsdale, MI 517-437-3349
Broadbent's B&B Foods
Kuttawa, KY 800-841-2202
Burke Corporation
Nevada, IA 800-654-1152

Always make it your best® with Burke fully cooked meats. We specialize in Italian sausage, beef, and pork toppings, meatballs, taco meats, shredded meats, pepperoni, bacon, Canadian-style bacon, chicken and beef strips. Additionally, we offer a variety of specialty products: Hand-Pinched Style® brand toppings, chorizo, gyro topping, andouille sausage, and breakfast patties and links.

Caughman's Meat Plant
Lexington, SC 803-356-0076
Chisesi Brothers Meat Packing Company
New Orleans, LA 800-966-3550
Cimpl Meats
Yankton, SD 605-665-1665
Clougherty Packing Company
Vernon, CA 323-583-4621
ConAgra Foods/Eckrich
Omaha, NE 800-327-4424
Crofton & Sons
Brandon, FL 800-878-7675
Dutch Valley Veal
South Holland, IL 800-832-8325
Ebro Foods
Chicago, IL 773-696-0150
F.B. Purnell Sausage Company
Simpsonville, KY 800-626-1512
Fortenberry Ice Company
Kodak, TN 865-933-2568
Hahn Brothers
Westminster, MD 800-227-7675
Hoople Country Kitchens
Rockport, IN 812-649-2351
Hormel Foods Corporation
Fremont, NE 402-721-2300
Humphrey Blue Ribbon Meats
Springfield, IL 800-747-6328
Johnsonville Food Company
Sheboygan Falls, WI 888-556-2728
Kowalski Sausage Company
Hamtramck, MI 800-482-2400
Kramarczuk Sausage Company
Minneapolis, MN 612-379-3018
Kubisch Sausage Company
Shelby Twp, MI 586-566-4661
Lees Sausage Company
Orangeburg, SC 803-534-5517
Leo G. Fraboni Sausage Company
Hibbing, MN 218-263-5074
Lords Sausage & CountryhHam
Dexter, GA 800-342-6002
Magic Seasoning Blends
New Orleans, LA 800-457-2857
Manns Sausage Company
Blacksburg, VA 540-605-0867
Meating Place
Buffalo, NY 716-885-3623
Miami Beef Company
Hialeah, FL 305-621-3252
Morse's Sauerkraut
Waldoboro, ME 866-832-5569
New Braunfels Smokehouse
New Braunfels, TX 800-537-6932
Niemuth's Steak & Chop Shop
Waupaca, WI 715-258-2666
Nodine's Smokehouse
Torrington, CT 800-222-2059
Owens Country Sausage
Richardson, TX 800-966-9367
R.M. Felts Packing Company
Ivor, VA 888-300-0971
Ray's Sausage Company Inc
Cleveland, OH 216-921-8782
Register Meat Company
Cottondale, FL 850-352-4269
Rego's Purity Foods
Honolulu, HI 808-847-3717
Rinehart Meat Processing
Branson, MO 417-334-2044
Rose Packing Company
South Barrington, IL 800-323-7363
Sara Lee Corporation
Downers Grove, IL 630-598-8100
Savoie's Sausage & Food Products
Opelousas, LA 337-948-4115
Smith Provision Company
Erie, PA 800-334-9151
Specialty Foods Group
Hampton, VA 800-238-0020
Stonies Sausage Shop Inc
Perryville, MO 888-546-2540
Striplings
Moultrie, GA 229-985-4226
Sunnydale Meats
Gaffney, SC 864-489-6091
Sunset Farm Foods
Valdosta, GA 800-882-1121
SW Red Smith
Davie, FL 954-581-1996
Thomas Packing Company
Columbus, GA 800-729-0976
Tupman-Thurlow Company
Deerfield Beach, FL 954-596-9989
V & V Supremo Foods
Chicago, IL 888-887-8773
Vollwerth & Baroni Companies
Hancock, MI 800-562-7620
Waco Beef & Pork Processors
Waco, TX 254-772-4669
William's Pork
Lumberton, NC 910-608-2226
YB Meats of Wichita
Wichita, KS 316-942-1213

Ardouille

Burke Corporation
Nevada, IA 800-654-1152

Always make it your best® with Burke fully cooked meats. We specialize in Italian sausage, beef, and pork toppings, meatballs, taco meats, shredded meats, pepperoni, bacon, Canadian-style bacon, chicken and beef strips. Additionally, we offer a variety of specialty products: Hand-Pinched Style® brand toppings, chorizo, gyro topping, andouille sausage, and breakfast patties and links.

Magic Seasoning Blends
New Orleans, LA 800-457-2857
Sunset Farm Foods
Valdosta, GA 800-882-1121

Scrapple

Arnold's Meat Food Products
Brooklyn, NY 800-633-7023
Kirby & Holloway Provisions
Harrington, DE 800-995-4729

Spareribs

Farmland Foods
Kansas City, MO 888-327-6526
RJ Balson and Sons Inc
Fayetteville, AR 321-281-9473

Tenderloin Roast

Amana Meat Shop & Smokehouse
Amana, IA 800-373-6328
Bear Creek Smokehouse
Marshall, TX 800-950-2327
New Braunfels Smokehouse
New Braunfels, TX 800-537-6932

Poultry

50th State Poultry Processors
Honolulu, HI 808-845-5902
A. Thomas Meats
Louisville, KY 800-253-2020
Acme Farms
Seattle, WA 800-542-8309
Adolf's Meats & Sausage Kitchen
Hartford, CT 860-522-1588
AFC Enterprises
Atlanta, GA 800-222-5857
AJM Meat Packing
San Juan, PR 787-787-4050
Al Safa Halal
Niagara Falls, NY 800-268-8174
Alderfer Bologna
Harleysville, PA 800-341-1121
All-States Quality Foods
Charles City, IA 800-247-4195
Allen Family Foods
Seaford, DE 302-629-9136
American Egg Products
Blackshear, GA 912-449-5700
Amick Farms, LLC
Leesville, SC 800-926-4257
Applegate Farms
Bridgewater, NJ 908-725-2768
Arizona Sunland Foods
Tucson, AZ 520-624-7068
Armbrust Meats
Medford, WI 715-748-3102
Aspen Foods
Park Ridge, IL 847-384-5940
Atlantic Premium Brands
Northbrook, IL 847-412-6200
B&B Poultry Company
Norma, NJ 856-692-8893
B&D Foods
Boise, ID 208-344-1183
B&R Quality Meats
Waterloo, IA 319-232-6328
Baltimore Poultry & Meats
Baltimore, MD 410-783-7361
Barber Foods
Portland, ME 800-577-2595
Bear Creek Smokehouse
Marshall, TX 800-950-2327
Becker Food Company
Milwaukee, WI 414-964-5353
Bell & Evans
Fredericksburg, PA 717-865-6626
Bird-In-Hand Farms, Inc.
Lancaster, PA 717-291-5855
Birdie Pak Products
Chicago, IL 773-247-5293
Black's Barbecue
Lockhart, TX 512-398-2712
Blakely Freezer Locker
Thomasville, GA 229-723-3622
Blue Grass Dairy Foods
Glasgow, KY 270-651-2146
Blue Ridge Poultry
Athens, GA 706-546-6767
Bon Ton Products
Wheeling, IL 847-520-8300
Bowman & Landes Turkeys
New Carlisle, OH 877-466-9466
Brakebush Brothers
Westfield, WI 800-933-2121

Brook Locker Plant
Brook, IN 219-275-2611
Brown Foods
Dallas, GA.......................770-445-4554
Bryant's Meats
Taylorsville, MS 601-785-6507
Bullock's Country Meats
Westminster, MD 410-848-6786
Burgers Smokehouse
California, MO 800-624-5426
Burke Corporation
Nevada, IA 800-654-1152

Always make it your best® with Burke fully cooked meats. We specialize in Italian sausage, beef, and pork toppings, meatballs, taco meats, shredded meats, pepperoni, bacon, Canadian-style bacon, chicken and beef strips. Additionally, we offer a variety of specialty products: Hand-Pinched Style® brand toppings, chorizo, gyro topping, andouille sausage, and breakfast patties and links.

Bush Brothers Provision Company
West Palm Beach, FL 800-327-1345
Butterball Turkey Company
Carthage, MO 800-641-4228
Butterfield Foods Company
Butterfield, MN...................507-956-5103
Buzz Food Service
Charleston, WV 304-925-4781
Cadick Poultry Company
Grandview, IN....................812-649-4491
Cagle's Inc
Atlanta, GA.......................404-355-2820
Campbell Soup Company
Camden, NJ.......................800-257-8443
Canal Fulton Provision
Canal Fulton, OH 800-321-3502
Cargill Foods
Springdale, AR 479-750-6816
Cargill Meat Solutions
Timberville, VA 540-896-7041
Caribbean Food Delights
Tappan, NY.......................845-398-3000
Carl Streit & Son Company
Neptune, NJ 732-775-0803
Carmel Meat/Specialty Foods
Marina, CA.......................800-298-5823
Carolina By-Products Company
Winchester, VA....................540-877-2590
Carolina Culinary
West Columbia, SC.................803-739-8920
Case Farms of Ohio
Winesburg, OH....................330-359-7141
Castleberry's
Vineland, NJ 856-691-2100
Chandler Foods
Greensboro, NC 800-537-6219
Charles Poultry Company
Lancaster, PA 717-872-7621
Chef Hans Gourmet Foods
Monroe, LA.......................800-890-4267
Chef's Requested Foods
Oklahoma City, OK 800-256-0259
Chester Fried
Birmingham, AL...................800-288-1555
Chestertown Foods
Chestertown, MD 410-778-3131
Chick-Fil-A
Atlanta, GA.......................800-232-2677
Chisesi Brothers Meat Packing Company
New Orleans, LA 800-966-3550
Chloe Foods Corporation
Brooklyn, NY 718-827-9000
Choctaw Maid Farms
Carthage, MS 601-298-5300
College Hill Poultry
Fredericksburg, PA.................800-533-3361
Colorado Boxed Beef Company
Auburndale, FL....................863-967-0636
Community Market & Deli
Lindstrom, MN....................651-257-1128
Completely Fresh Foods
Montebello, CA 323-722-9136
ConAgra Frozen Foods Company
Omaha, NE 402-595-6107
ConAgra Frozen Foods Company
Macon, MO.......................660-385-3184
ConAgra Frozen Foods Company
Marshall, MO 660-886-3301
ConAgra Refrigerated Foods International
Omaha, NE 800-624-4724

Contigroup Companies
Oakwood, GA.....................770-538-2120
Cordon Bleu International
Anjou, QC........................514-352-3000
Corfu Foods
Bensenville, IL 630-595-2510
Couch's Country Style Sausages
Cleveland, OH 216-823-2332
Country Smoked Meats
Bowling Green, OH 800-321-4766
Crescent Duck Farm
Aquebogue, NY 631-722-8700
Crystal Lake
Decatur, AR 800-382-4425
Culinary Foods
Chicago, IL.......................800-621-4049
Culver Duck
Middlebury, IN 800-825-9225
Cusack Wholesale Meat Company
Oklahoma City, OK 800-241-6328
Danny's Poultry
Hamilton, OH 513-737-7780
David Elliott Poultry Farms
Scranton, PA 570-344-6348
Deb-El Foods
Elizabeth, NJ......................800-421-3447
Delphos Poultry Products
Delphos, OH 419-692-5816
Dietz & Watson
Philadelphia, PA 800-333-1974
DiPasquale's
Baltimore, MD 410-276-6787
Dno
Columbus, OH 800-686-2366
Double B Foods
Arlington, TX 800-679-0349
Draper Valley Farms
Mount Vernon, WA.................425-793-4135
Drohan Company
Huntington, NY 718-898-9672
Dutterer's Home Food Service
Baltimore, MD 410-298-3663
E&G Food
Brooklyn, NY 888-525-8855
E.C. Phillips & Son
Ketchikan, AK 907-225-3121
East Dayton Meat & Poultry
Dayton, OH.......................937-253-6185
East Poultry Company
Austin, TX........................512-476-5367
Eberly Poultry
Stevens, PA.......................717-336-6440
Edelman Meats
Antigo, WI 715-623-7686
Elwell Farms
Santa Ana, CA 800-698-5855
Empire Beef & Redistribution
Rochester, NY.....................800-462-6804
Empire Kosher Foods
Mifflintown, PA 800-367-4734
Equity Group
Reidsville, NC.....................336-342-6601
Exceldor Cooperative
St. Anselme, QC 877-320-8006
Fair Oaks Farms
Pleasant Prairie, WI 262-947-0320
Farbest Foods
Huntingburg, IN 812-683-4200
Farm T Market Company
Somerville, TN 901-465-2844
Farmers Produce
Ashby, MN 218-747-2749
Fieldale Farms
Gainesville, GA 800-241-5400
Fieldale Farms Corporation
Baldwin, GA......................800-241-5400
Forest Packing Company
Forest, MS........................601-469-3321
Foster Farms
Livingston, CA 800-255-7227
Freezer Queen Foods
Buffalo, NY.......................800-828-8383
Fried Provisions Company
Evans City, PA 724-538-3160
Galco Food Products
Toronto, ON 416-743-9671
Gemini Food Industries
Charlton, MA 508-248-2730
Gentry's Poultry Company
Ward, SC.........................800-926-2161
George L. Wells Meat Company
Philadelphia, PA 800-523-1730

George's
Springdale, AR 877-855-3447
Georges Chicken
Edinburg, VA 866-444-2449
Gerbers Poultry
Kidron, OH.......................800-362-7381
Giovanni's Appetizing Food Products
Richmond, MI.....................586-727-9355
Glenmark Industries
Chicago, IL.......................773-927-4800
Godshall's Quality Meats
Telford, PA 888-463-7425
Gold'n Plump Poultry
St Cloud, MN 800-328-2838
Golden Platter Foods
Newark, NJ 973-242-0290
Golden Rod Broilers
Cullman, AL......................256-734-0941
Grabill Country Meats
Grabill, IN........................866-333-6328
Grant Park Packing
Chicago, IL.......................312-421-4096
Gress Poultry
Scranton, PA 570-561-0150
Grimaud Farms
Stockton, CA......................800-466-9955
Hahn Brothers
Westminster, MD 800-227-7675
Halal Transactions
Omaha, NE 402-572-6120
Hall Brothers Meats
Cleveland, OH 440-235-3262
Hamilos Brothers Inspected Meats
Madison, IL.......................618-451-7877
Hampton House J.D. Sweid Ltd
Burnaby, BC 800-665-4355
Hanover Foods Corp
Hanover, PA 717-632-6000
Harrison Poultry
Bethlehem, GA....................770-867-9105
Health is Wealth Foods
Williamstown, NJ 856-728-1998
Heinkel's Packing Company
Decatur, IL 800-594-2738
Henningsen Foods
Purchase, NY 914-701-4020
Herb's Specialty Foods
Mount Holly, NJ 800-486-0276
Hickory Baked Food
Castle Rock, CO 303-688-2633
Hillbilly Smokehouse
Rogers, AR 479-636-1927
Hollman Foods
Chicago, IL.......................888-926-2879
Hormel Foods Corporation
Austin, MN.......................800-523-4635
House of Raeford Farms
Raeford, NC 800-888-7539
Indian Springs Fresh Poultry
Columbus, OH 614-443-7473
Indian Valley Meats
Indian, AK........................907-653-7511
International Home Foods
Parsippany, NJ.....................973-359-9920
International Meat Company
Chicago, IL.......................773-622-1400
J&G Poultry
Gainesville, GA 770-536-5540
J.R. Poultry
Fults, IL..........................618-476-7342
Jacob & Sons Wholesale Meats
Martins Ferry, OH.................740-633-3091
Jacobs Meats
Defiance, OH 419-782-7831

Jaindl's Turkey Farms
Orefield, PA 800-475-6654
James Cowan & Sons
Worcester, MA 508-753-3259
James J. Derba Company
Boston, MA. 800-732-3848
Janes Family Foods
Mississauga, ON. 800-565-2637
Jay Poultry Corporation
Voorhees, NJ. 856-435-0900
Jennie-O Turkey Store
Willmar, MN. 320-235-6080
Jitney Jungle Stores of America
Jackson, MS 800-647-2364
John Garner Meats
Van Buren, AR 800-543-5473
Johnson, Nash, & Sons Farms
Rose Hill, NC 800-682-6843
Jurgielewicz Duck Farm
Moriches, NY 800-543-8257
K&K Gourmet Meats
Leetsdale, PA 724-266-8400
Kauffman Turkey Farms
Waterman, IL 815-264-3470
Kelly Gourmet Foods
San Francisco, CA 415-648-9200
Keystone Foods
Camilla, GA 229-336-5211
Keystone Foods Corporation
West Conshohocken, PA. 610-667-6700
Keystone Foods Corporation
Huntsville, AL 800-327-6701
King Cole Ducks Limited
Aurora, ON 800-363-3825
Kings Command Foods
Kent, WA. 800-247-3138
Kings Delight
Gainesville, GA 770-536-5177
Koch Food
Chattanooga, TN. 423-266-0351
Koch Foods
Morristown, TN 423-586-3668
Koch Foods
Park Ridge, IL. 800-837-2778
Kretschmar
Don Mills, ON 800-561-4532
L&L Packing Company
Chicago, IL 800-628-6328
L. East Poultry Company
Austin, TX. 512-476-5367
Lake Charles Poultry
Lake Charles, LA 337-433-6818
Lamb-Weston
Kennewick, WA 800-766-7783
Land O'Frost
Lansing, IL 800-323-3308
Land O'Frost
Searcy, AR 800-643-5654
Lendy's
Virginia Beach, VA. 757-491-3511
Lilydale Foods
Edmonton, AB 800-661-5341
Locustdale Meat Packing
Locustdale, PA 570-875-1270
Loggins Meat Company
Tyler, TX. 800-527-8610
Long Food Industries
Fripp Island, SC 843-838-3205
Longmont Foods
Longmont, CO 303-776-6611
Lowell Provision Company
Lowell, MA. 978-454-5603
LSK Smoked Turkey Products
Bronx, NY. 718-792-1300
Lucks Food Decorating Company
Tacoma, WA 253-383-4815
M-G
Weimar, TX. 800-460-8581
MacFarlane Pheasants
Janesville, WI 877-269-8957
MacGregors Meat & Seafood
Toronto, ON 888-383-3663
Mada'n Kosher Foods
Dania, FL 954-925-0077
Mahantongo Game Farms
Dalmatia, PA. 570-758-6284
Maid-Rite Steak Company
Dunmore, PA. 800-233-4259
Manchester Farms
Columbia, SC 800-845-0421
Manger Packing Company
Baltimore, MD 800-227-9262
Manley Meats
Decatur, IN 260-592-7313
Maple Leaf Farms
Milford, IN 800-384-2812
Mar-Jac Poultry
Gainesville, GA 800-226-0561
Marshall Durbin Companies
Tarrant, AL 205-841-7315
Marshall Durbin Companies
Jackson, MS 601-969-1248
Marshall Durbin Companies
Birmingham, AL. 800-768-2456
Marshall Egg Products
Seymour, IN 812-497-2557
Marshallville Packing Company
Marshallville, OH. 330-855-2871
McFarland Foods
Riverton, UT. 209-869-6611
McFarland Foods
Riverton, UT. 800-441-9596
Meat-O-Mat Corporation
Brooklyn, NY 718-965-7250
Medeiros Farms
Kalaheo, HI. 808-332-8211
Metafoods, LLC
Atlanta, GA. 404-843-2400
Miami Beef Company
Hialeah, FL 305-621-3252
Miller Brothers PackingcCompany
Sylvester, GA 229-776-2014
Mirasco
Atlanta, GA. 770-956-1945
Molbert Brothers Poultry & Egg Company
Lake Charles, LA 337-439-2579
Montana Legacy Premium Ostrich Products
Billings, MT 406-656-6444
Moretti's Poultry
Columbus, OH 614-486-2333
Moroni Feed Company
West Liberty, IA 800-453-5327
Motz Poultry
Batavia, OH. 513-732-1381
Mountain Valley Poultry
Springdale, AR 479-751-7266
Mountaire Corporation
Millsboro, DE 877-887-1490
Murrays Chicken
South Fallsburg, NY. 800-770-6347
Mutual Trading Company
Los Angeles, CA. 213-626-9458
National Egg Products Company
Social Circle, GA 770-464-2652
New Braunfels Smokehouse
New Braunfels, TX. 800-537-6932
Nodine's Smokehouse
Torrington, CT 800-222-2059
North Star Foods
Saint Charles, MN 507-932-4831
O Chili Frozen Foods Inc
Northbrook, IL 847-562-1991
Oak Valley Farm
Voorhees, NJ. 856-435-0900
Ok Industries
Fort Smith, AR 800-635-9441
Olson Locker
Fairmont, MN. 507-238-2563
Olymel
Iberville, QC 450-542-9339
Omaha Steaks International
Omaha, NE 800-562-0500
Ottman Meat Company
New York, NY 212-879-4160
P & L Poultry
Spokane, WA. 509-892-1242
Pacific Poultry Company
Honolulu, HI. 808-841-2828
Paisano Food Products
Elk Grove Village, IL 800-672-4726
Palmetto Pigeon Plant
Sumter, SC 803-775-1204
Park Farms
Canton, OH 800-683-6511
Pasqualichio Brothers
Scranton, PA 800-232-6233
Peco Foods
Tuscaloosa, AL 205-345-4711
Peco Foods
Sebastopol, MS. 601-625-7432
Peco Foods
Canton, MS. 601-855-0925
Pennfield Corporation
Lancaster, PA 717-299-2561
Pennfield Farms
Mt Joy, PA. 800-732-0009
Perdue Farms
Salisbury, MD. 800-473-7383
Petaluma Poultry Processors
Petaluma, CA 800-556-6789
Peterson Farms
Decatur, AR 800-382-4425
Petschl's Quality Meats
Tukwila, WA. 206-575-4400
Pfeffer's Country Mkt.
Sauk Centre, MN 320-352-6490
Pierre Foods
Cincinnati, OH 513-874-8741
Pinty's Premium Foods
Burlington, ON. 800-263-7223
Pintys Delicious Foods
Burlington, ON. 800-263-9710
Plantation Foods
Waco, TX 800-733-0900
Pocono Foods
Mt Bethel, PA. 570-897-5000
Poultry Foods Industry
Springfield, AR. 800-643-3410
Prime Pak Foods
Gainesville, GA 770-536-8708
Puueo Poi Factory
Hilo, HI. 808-935-8435
Radlo Foods
Watertown, MA. 800-370-1439
Randall Farms
Vernon, CA 800-372-6581
Ray's Sausage Company Inc
Cleveland, OH 216-921-8782
Redi-Serve Food Company
Fort Atkinson, WI. 920-563-6391
Registry Steaks & Seafood
Bridgeview, IL 708-458-3100
Rhone-Poulenc Food Ingredients
Cranbury, NJ. 609-860-4000
Roman Sausage Company
Santa Clara, CA 800-497-7462
Rose Hill Distributors
Branford, CT. 203-488-7231
Rosebud Farms
Chicago, IL 773-928-5331
RusDun Farms
Collierville, TN. 901-853-0931
Rymer Foods
Chicago, IL 800-247-9637
Sadler's Smokehouse
Henderson, TX 903-657-5581
Sanderson Farms
Collins, MS. 601-765-0430
Sanderson Farms
Hazlehurst, MS. 601-894-3725
Sanderson Farms
Bryan, TX. 979-778-5730
Scanga Meat Company
Salida, CO. 719-539-3511
Schaller & Weber
Astoria, NY. 800-847-4115
Schiltz Foods
Sisseton, SD 877-872-4458
Schneider Foods
Kitchener, ON. 519-741-5000
Schneider Foods
Saint Marys, ON. 800-567-1890
Scotsburn Dairy Group
Scotsburn, NS. 902-485-8023
Selwoods Farm Hunting Preserve
Alpine, AL 256-362-7595
Serenade Foods
Milford, IN 574-658-4121
Seven K Feather Farm
Taylorsville, IN. 812-526-2651
Shelley's Prime Meats
Jersey City, NJ 201-433-3434
Shelton's Poultry
Pomona, CA 800-541-1833
Simeus Foods Internatio nal
Mansfield, TX. 888-772-3663
Simeus Foods International
Mansfield, TX. 888-772-3663
Simmons Foods
Siloam Springs, AR 888-831-7007
SJH Enterprises
Middleton, WI. 888-745-3845
Smith Packing Regional Meat
Utica, NY
Snow Ball Foods
Williamstown, NJ 856-629-4081

Somerset Industries
Spring House, PA 800-883-8728
SOPAKCO Foods
Mullins, SC 800-276-9678
Southeastern Meat Association
Oviedo, FL 407-365-5661
Southtowns Seafood & Meats
Blasdell, NY 716-824-4900
Springville Meat & ColdsStorage
Springville, UT 801-489-6391
Squab Producers of California
Modesto, CA 209-537-4744
Standard Beef Company
Foxboro, MA 203-787-2164
Starkel Poultry
Roy, WA 253-845-2876
Steak-Umm Company
Shillington, PA 860-928-5900
Stegall Smoked Turkey
Marshville, NC 800-851-6034
Sunnydale Meats
Gaffney, SC 864-489-6091
Sunshine Farms Poultry
West Palm Beach, FL 561-881-4500
Suzanna's Kitchen
Duluth, GA 800-241-2455
Sweet Sue Kitchens
Athens, AL 256-216-0500
Sylvest Farms Inc
Montgomery, AL 334-281-0400
Tampa Farm Services
Dover, FL 813-659-0605
Taylor's Poultry Place
Lexington, SC 803-356-3431
Tenn Valley Ham Company
Paris, TN 731-642-9740
Thomas Packing Company
Columbus, GA 800-729-0976
Tillamook Meat Company
Tillamook, OR 503-842-4802
Tip Top Poultry
Marietta, GA 800-241-5230
Troyer Foods
Goshen, IN 800-876-9377
Turkey Store Company
Faribault, MN 507-334-2050
Tyson Foods
Fort Smith, AR 479-783-8996
Tyson Foods
Bloomfield, MO 573-568-2153
Tyson Foods
Forest, MS 601-469-1712
Tyson Foods
Corydon, IN 800-223-3719
Tyson Foods
Springdale, AR 800-643-3410
Tyson Foods
Berryville, AR 870-423-3331
United Poultry Company
Los Angeles, CA 213-620-0498
United Provision Meat Company
Columbus, OH 614-252-1126
Universal Poultry Company
Athens, GA 706-546-6767
Vantage USA
Chicago, IL 773-247-1086
Vienna Meat Products
Scarborough, ON 800-588-1931
Vitale Poultry Company
Columbus, OH 614-267-1874
W & G Marketing Company
Ames, IA 515-233-4774
Waco Beef & Pork Processors
Waco, TX 254-772-4669
Walden Foods
Winchester, VA 800-648-7688
Walker Meats Corporation
Carrollton, GA 770-834-8171
Walt Koch
Decatur, GA 404-378-3666
Waltkoch
Decatur, GA 404-378-3666
Wapsie Produce
Decorah, IA 563-382-4271
Wasatch Meats
Salt Lake City, UT 801-363-5747
Watsons Quality Food Prooducts
Blackwood, NJ 800-257-7870
Wayco Ham Company
Goldsboro, NC 800-962-2614
Wayne Farms LLC
Union Springs, AL 334-738-2930
Wayne Farms LLC
Jack, AL 334-897-3435
Wayne Farms LLC
Laurel, MS 601-425-4721
Wayne Farms LLC
Pendergrass, GA 706-693-2271
Wayne Farms LLC
Oakwood, GA 800-392-0844
West Central Turkeys
Pelican Rapids, MN 218-863-6800
White Fence Farm Chicken
Romeoville, IL 630-739-1720
Whittaker & Associates
Atlanta, GA 404-266-1265
Will Poultry Company
Buffalo, NY 716-853-2000
Willies Smoke House
Harrisville, PA 800-742-4184
Willow Tree Poultry Farm
Attleboro, MA 508-222-2479
Wimmer's Meat Products
West Point, NE 800-358-0761
Wong Wing Foods
Montreal, QC 800-361-4820
Woods Smoked Meats
Bowling Green, MO 800-458-8426
World Flavors
Warminster, PA 215-672-4400
Wornick Company
Cincinnati, OH 800-860-4555
Yoakum Packing Company
Yoakum, TX 361-293-3541
Zacky Farms
Fresno, CA 800-888-0235
Zartic Inc
Rome, GA 800-241-0516

Chicken

50th State Poultry Processors
Honolulu, HI 808-845-5902
A. Stein Meat Products
Brooklyn, NY 718-492-0760
Al Safa Halal
Niagara Falls, NY 800-268-8174
All-States Quality Foods
Charles City, IA 800-247-4195
Atlantic Premium Brands
Northbrook, IL 847-412-6200
B&D Foods
Boise, ID 208-344-1183
Bear Creek Smokehouse
Marshall, TX 800-950-2327
Black's Barbecue
Lockhart, TX 512-398-2712
Blakely Freezer Locker
Thomasville, GA 229-723-3622
Brakebush Brothers
Westfield, WI 800-933-2121
Brook Locker Plant
Brook, IN 219-275-2611
Bryant's Meats
Taylorsville, MS 601-785-6507
Bullock's Country Meats
Westminster, MD 410-848-6786
Burgers Smokehouse
California, MO 800-624-5426
Burke Corporation
Nevada, IA 800-654-1152

Always make it your best® with Burke fully cooked meats. We specialize in Italian sausage, beef, and pork toppings, meatballs, taco meats, shredded meats, pepperoni, bacon, Canadian-style bacon, chicken and beef strips. Additionally, we offer a variety of specialty products: Hand-Pinched Style® brand toppings, chorizo, gyro topping, andouille sausage, and breakfast patties and links.

Buzz Food Service
Charleston, WV 304-925-4781
Cargill Meat Solutions
Timberville, VA 540-896-7041
Caribbean Food Delights
Tappan, NY 845-398-3000
Caribbean Products
Baltimore, MD 410-235-7700
Case Farms of North Carolina
Morganton, NC 800-437-6916
Cericola Farms
Bradford, ON 877-939-4449
Charles Poultry Company
Lancaster, PA 717-872-7621
Chef Hans Gourmet Foods
Monroe, LA 800-890-4267
Chester Fried
Birmingham, AL 800-288-1555
Chicago Steaks
Chicago, IL 800-776-4174
Chick-Fil-A
Atlanta, GA 800-232-2677
Chisesi Brothers Meat Packing Company
New Orleans, LA 800-966-3550
Choctaw Maid Farms
Carthage, MS 601-298-5300
Completely Fresh Foods
Montebello, CA 323-722-9136
ConAgra Foods Inc
Omaha, NE 402-595-7300
ConAgra Frozen Foods Company
Omaha, NE 402-595-6107
ConAgra Frozen Foods Company
Macon, MO 660-385-3184
ConAgra Frozen Foods Company
Marshall, MO 660-886-3301
Cordon Bleu International
Anjou, QC 514-352-3000
Corfu Foods
Bensenville, IL 630-595-2510
Crystal Lake
Decatur, AR 800-382-4425
Culver Duck
Middlebury, IN 800-825-9225
D'Artagnan
Newark, NJ 800-327-8246
Delphos Poultry Products
Delphos, OH 419-692-5816
Double B Foods
Arlington, TX 800-679-0349
E&G Food
Brooklyn, NY 888-525-8855
East Poultry Company
Austin, TX 512-476-5367
Equity Group
Reidsville, NC 336-342-6601
Exceldor Cooperative
St. Anselme, QC 877-320-8006
Farmers Produce
Ashby, MN 218-747-2749
Ferko Meat Company
Milwaukee, WI 414-967-5500
Fieldale Farms
Gainesville, GA 800-241-5400
Fieldale Farms Corporation
Baldwin, GA 706-778-5100
Fieldale Farms Corporation
Baldwin, GA 800-241-5400
Foster Farms
Livingston, CA 800-255-7227
Freezer Queen Foods
Buffalo, NY 800-828-8383
Galco Food Products
Toronto, ON 416-743-9671
Gemini Food Industries
Charlton, MA 508-248-2730
George L. Wells Meat Company
Philadelphia, PA 800-523-1730
Georges Chicken
Edinburg, VA 866-444-2449
Gress Poultry
Scranton, PA 570-561-0150
Hampton House J.D. Sweid Ltd
Burnaby, BC 800-665-4355
Health is Wealth Foods
Williamstown, NJ 856-728-1998
Henningsen Foods
Purchase, NY 914-701-4020
Home Delivery Food Service
Jefferson, GA 706-367-9551
Horizon Poultry
Toronto, ON 519-364-3200
Hormel Foods Corporation
Columbia, MD 410-290-1916
Hormel Foods Corporation
Cincinnati, OH 513-563-0211
Hormel Foods Corporation
Phoenix, AZ 602-230-2400
Hormel Foods Corporation
Orchard Park, NY 716-675-7700
Hormel Foods Corporation
Austin, MN 800-523-4635
Hormel Foods Corporation
Lebanon, NJ 908-236-7009

Hormel Foods Corporation
Pleasanton, CA 925-734-9555
House of Raeford Farms
Raeford, NC 800-888-7539
Hunter Food Inc
Anaheim, CA 714-666-1888
International Home Foods
Parsippany, NJ. 973-359-9920
Janes Family Foods
Mississauga, ON. 800-565-2637
Jesses Fine Meats
Cherokee, IA. 712-225-3637
K&K Gourmet Meats
Leetsdale, PA 724-266-8400
Karn Meats
Columbus, OH 800-221-9585
Kelly Gourmet Foods
San Francisco, CA 415-648-9200
Keystone Foods Corporation
West Conshohocken, PA. 610-667-6700
Keystone Foods Corporation
Huntsville, AL 800-327-6701
Kings Command Foods
Kent, WA. 800-247-3138
Koch Foods
Park Ridge, IL. 800-837-2778
Koch Poultry
Chicago, IL 800-837-2778
La Nova Wings
Buffalo, NY. 800-652-6682
Land O'Frost
Lansing, IL 800-323-3308
Land O'Frost
Searcy, AR 800-643-5654
Locustdale Meat Packing
Locustdale, PA 570-875-1270
Loggins Meat Company
Tyler, TX. 800-527-8610
Lucks Food Decorating Company
Tacoma, WA 253-383-4815
Magnolia Meats
Shreveport, LA 318-221-2814
Manger Packing Company
Baltimore, MD 800-227-9262
Maple Leaf Farms
Milford, IN 800-384-2812
Mar-Jac Poultry
Gainesville, GA 800-226-0561
McFarland Foods
Riverton, UT. 209-869-6611
Meat-O-Mat Corporation
Brooklyn, NY. 718-965-7250
Mexi-Frost Specialties Company
Brooklyn, NY 718-625-3324
Mitchell Foods
Barbourville, KY 888-202-9745
Moretti's Poultry
Columbus, OH 614-486-2333
Murrays Chicken
South Fallsburg, NY. 800-770-6347
North Country Smokehouse
Claremont, NH 800-258-4304
North Star Foods
Saint Charles, MN 507-932-4831
Ok Industries
Fort Smith, AR 800-635-9441
P & L Poultry
Spokane, WA. 509-892-1242
Paisano Food Products
Elk Grove Village, IL 800-672-4726
Palmetto Pigeon Plant
Sumter, SC 803-775-1204
Park Farms
Canton, OH. 800-683-6511
Pennfield Corporation
Lancaster, PA 717-299-2561
Perdue Farms
Salisbury, MD. 800-473-7383
Petaluma Poultry Processors
Petaluma, CA 800-556-6789
Petschl's Quality Meats
Tukwila, WA. 206-575-4400
Pinty's Premium Foods
Burlington, ON 800-263-7223
Plantation Foods
Waco, TX 800-733-0900
Prime Pak Foods
Gainesville, GA 770-536-8708
Proliant Meat Ingredients
Harlan, IA. 800-369-2672
Puueo Poi Factory
Hilo, HI 808-935-8435

Readyfoods
Denver, CO 800-748-1218
Redi-Serve Food Company
Fort Atkinson, WI. 920-563-6391
Roman Sausage Company
Santa Clara, CA 800-497-7462
Roy Dick Company
Griffin, GA 770-227-3916
Royal Palate Foods
Inglewood, CA 310-330-7701
Rymer Foods
Chicago, IL 800-247-9637
Safeway Inc
Pleasanton, CA 877-723-3929
Sanderson Farms
Hazlehurst, MS 601-894-3725
Sanderson Farms
Bryan, TX 979-778-5730
Schneider Foods
Guelph, ON. 519-837-4848
Simeus Foods Internatio nal
Mansfield, TX. 888-772-3663
Simeus Foods International
Mansfield, TX. 888-772-3663
Simmons Foods
Siloam Springs, AR 888-831-7007
SJH Enterprises
Middleton, WI. 888-745-3845
Smith Packing Regional Meat
Utica, NY
Snow Ball Foods
Williamstown, NJ 856-629-4081
SOPAKCO Foods
Mullins, SC. 800-276-9678
Steak-Umm Company
Shillington, PA 860-928-5900
Sunnydale Meats
Gaffney, SC. 864-489-6091
Suzanna's Kitchen
Duluth, GA 800-241-2455
Sweet Sue Kitchens
Athens, AL 256-216-0500
Thomson Meats ltd.
Melfort, SK. 306-752-2802
Tony Downs Foods Company
Madelia, MN. 507-642-3203
Tyson Foods
Wilkesboro, NC 336-838-0083
Tyson Foods
Bloomfield, MO 573-568-2153
Tyson Foods
Dexter, MO 573-624-4548
Tyson Foods
Star City, AR. 800-351-8184
Tyson Foods
Springdale, AR 800-643-3410
United Poultry Company
Los Angeles, CA. 213-620-0498
Vantage USA
Chicago, IL 773-247-1086
Waco Beef & Pork Processors
Waco, TX 254-772-4669
Waken Meat Company
Atlanta, GA. 404-627-3537
Wasatch Meats
Salt Lake City, UT 801-363-5747
Wayne Farms LLC
Union Springs, AL 334-738-2930
Wayne Farms LLC
Laurel, MS 601-425-4721
Wayne Farms LLC
Pendergrass, GA 706-693-2271
Wayne Farms LLC
Oakwood, GA. 800-392-0844
West Liberty Foods
West Liberty, IA 888-511-4500
Wong Wing Foods
Montreal, QC 800-361-4820
Wornick Company
Cincinnati, OH 800-860-4555
Zartic Inc
Rome, GA. 800-241-0516

Barbecued

Black's Barbecue
Lockhart, TX. 512-398-2712
Woods Smoked Meats
Bowling Green, MO 800-458-8426

Barbecued Frozen

Burke Corporation
Nevada, IA 800-654-1152

Always make it your best® with Burke fully cooked meats. We specialize in Italian sausage, beef, and pork toppings, meatballs, taco meats, shredded meats, pepperoni, bacon, Canadian-style bacon, chicken and beef strips. Additionally, we offer a variety of specialty products: Hand-Pinched Style® brand toppings, chorizo, gyro topping, andouille sausage, and breakfast patties and links.

Breaded

Delphos Poultry Products
Delphos, OH 419-692-5816
Gemini Food Industries
Charlton, MA 508-248-2730
Janes Family Foods
Mississauga, ON. 800-565-2637
Meat-O-Mat Corporation
Brooklyn, NY 718-965-7250
Schneider Foods
Ayr, ON. 519-632-7416

Broilers

Koala Moa Char Broiled Chicken
Honolulu, HI. 808-523-6701

Bulk - Leg Quarters - Legs - T

Pennfield Farms
Mt Joy, PA. 800-732-0009

Canned Boned

Criders Poultry
Stillmore, GA 800-342-3851
International Home Foods
Parsippany, NJ. 973-359-9920
Lucks Food Decorating Company
Tacoma, WA 253-383-4815

Capon

D'Artagnan
Newark, NJ. 800-327-8246
Wayne Farms LLC
Jack, AL 334-897-3435
Wayne Farms LLC
Laurel, MS 601-425-4721

Cooked - Breaded - Frozen

Advance Food Company
Enid, OK. 888-723-8237
Bear Creek Smokehouse
Marshall, TX. 800-950-2327
Loggins Meat Company
Tyler, TX. 800-527-8610

Cut-Up Frozen

Park Farms
Canton, OH. 800-683-6511
Wayne Farms LLC
Jack, AL 334-897-3435
Wayne Farms LLC
Laurel, MS 601-425-4721
Wayne Farms LLC
Oakwood, GA. 800-392-0844

Cut-Up IQF (Individually Quick Frozen)

Bell & Evans
Fredericksburg, PA 717-865-6626
Wayne Farms LLC
Laurel, MS 601-425-4721

Diced Frozen

Burke Corporation
Nevada, IA 800-654-1152

Always make it your best® with Burke fully cooked meats. We specialize in Italian sausage, beef, and pork toppings, meatballs, taco meats, shredded meats, pepperoni, bacon, Canadian-style bacon, chicken and beef strips. Additionally, we offer a variety of specialty products: Hand-Pinched Style® brand toppings, chorizo, gyro topping, andouille sausage, and breakfast patties and links.

Fajita Strips

Burke Corporation
Nevada, IA 800-654-1152

Always make it your best® with Burke fully cooked meats. We specialize in Italian sausage, beef, and pork toppings, meatballs, taco meats, shredded meats, pepperoni, bacon, Canadian-style bacon, chicken and beef strips. Additionally, we offer a variety of specialty products: Hand-Pinched Style® brand toppings, chorizo, gyro topping, andouille sausage, and breakfast patties and links.

Chef's Requested Foods
Oklahoma City, OK 800-256-0259

Fillets

Delphos Poultry Products
Delphos, OH 419-692-5816
Simeus Foods Internatio nal
Mansfield, TX 888-772-3663

Fresh

Becker Food Company
Milwaukee, WI 414-964-5353
Bell & Evans
Fredericksburg, PA 717-865-6626
Brook Locker Plant
Brook, IN 219-275-2611
Choctaw Maid Farms
Carthage, MS 601-298-5300
Exceldor Cooperative
St. Anselme, QC 877-320-8006
Fieldale Farms
Gainesville, GA 800-241-5400
Fieldale Farms Corporation
Baldwin, GA 800-241-5400
Foster Farms
Creswell, OR 541-895-2161
Galco Food Products
Toronto, ON 416-743-9671
Georges Chicken
Edinburg, VA 866-444-2449
Keystone Foods
Camilla, GA 229-336-5211
Perdue Farms
Salisbury, MD 800-473-7383
Petaluma Poultry Processors
Petaluma, CA 800-556-6789
Smith Packing Regional Meat
Utica, NY
Tyson Foods
Springdale, AR 800-643-3410
Wayne Farms LLC
Union Springs, AL 334-738-2930
Wayne Farms LLC
Jack, AL 334-897-3435
Wayne Farms LLC
Laurel, MS 601-425-4721
Wayne Farms LLC
Pendergrass, GA 706-693-2271
Wayne Farms LLC
Oakwood, GA 800-392-0844

Frozen

B&D Foods
Boise, ID 208-344-1183
Blakely Freezer Locker
Thomasville, GA 229-723-3622
Brakebush Brothers
Westfield, WI 800-933-2121
Brook Locker Plant
Brook, IN 219-275-2611
Burke Corporation
Nevada, IA 800-654-1152

Always make it your best® with Burke fully cooked meats. We specialize in Italian sausage, beef, and pork toppings, meatballs, taco meats, shredded meats, pepperoni, bacon, Canadian-style bacon, chicken and beef strips. Additionally, we offer a variety of specialty products: Hand-Pinched Style® brand toppings, chorizo, gyro topping, andouille sausage, and breakfast patties and links.

Buzz Food Service
Charleston, WV 304-925-4781
Caribbean Food Delights
Tappan, NY 845-398-3000
Caribbean Products
Baltimore, MD 410-235-7700
Choctaw Maid Farms
Carthage, MS 601-298-5300
ConAgra Frozen Foods Company
Macon, MO 660-385-3184
ConAgra Frozen Foods Company
Marshall, MO 660-886-3301
Draper Valley Farms
Mount Vernon, WA 425-793-4135
Equity Group
Reidsville, NC 336-342-6601
Exceldor Cooperative
St. Anselme, QC 877-320-8006
Fieldale Farms
Gainesville, GA 800-241-5400
Fieldale Farms Corporation
Baldwin, GA 706-778-5100
Fieldale Farms Corporation
Baldwin, GA 800-241-5400
Foster Farms
Creswell, OR 541-895-2161
Galco Food Products
Toronto, ON 416-743-9671
Gemini Food Industries
Charlton, MA 508-248-2730
Georges Chicken
Edinburg, VA 866-444-2449
Gress Poultry
Scranton, PA 570-561-0150
Health is Wealth Foods
Williamstown, NJ 856-728-1998
House of Raeford Farms
Raeford, NC 800-888-7539
Janes Family Foods
Mississauga, ON 800-565-2637
K&K Gourmet Meats
Leetsdale, PA 724-266-8400
Keystone Foods
Camilla, GA 229-336-5211
Koch Foods
Park Ridge, IL 800-837-2778
Manchester Farms
Columbia, SC 800-845-0421
Maple Leaf Farms
Milford, IN 800-384-2812
Mar-Jac Poultry
Gainesville, GA 800-226-0561
Mexi-Frost Specialties Company
Brooklyn, NY 718-625-3324
Paisano Food Products
Elk Grove Village, IL 800-672-4726
Palmetto Pigeon Plant
Sumter, SC 803-775-1204
Park Farms
Canton, OH 800-683-6511
Pennfield Corporation
Lancaster, PA 717-299-2561
Perdue Farms
Salisbury, MD 800-473-7383
Phoenix Agro-Industrial Corporation
Westbury, NY 516-334-1194
Pilgrim's
Greeley, CO 800-727-5366
Redi-Serve Food Company
Fort Atkinson, WI 920-563-6391
Rymer Foods
Chicago, IL 800-247-9637
Sanderson Farms
Hazlehurst, MS 601-894-3725
Sanderson Farms
Bryan, TX 979-778-5730
Simmons Foods
Siloam Springs, AR 888-831-7007
SJH Enterprises
Middleton, WI 888-745-3845
Smith Packing Regional Meat
Utica, NY
Snow Ball Foods
Williamstown, NJ 856-629-4081
Southeastern Meat Association
Oviedo, FL 407-365-5661
Steak-Umm Company
Shillington, PA 860-928-5900
Tony Downs Foods Company
Madelia, MN 507-642-3203
Tyson Foods
Bloomfield, MO 573-568-2153
Tyson Foods
Springdale, AR 800-643-3410
Wayne Farms LLC
Union Springs, AL 334-738-2930
Wayne Farms LLC
Jack, AL 334-897-3435
Wayne Farms LLC
Laurel, MS 601-425-4721
Wayne Farms LLC
Pendergrass, GA 706-693-2271
Wayne Farms LLC
Oakwood, GA 800-392-0844
Wong Wing Foods
Montreal, QC 800-361-4820
Zartic Inc
Rome, GA 800-241-0516

Grilled Patties

Chloe Foods Corporation
Brooklyn, NY 718-827-9000

Nuggets

Barber Foods
Portland, ME 800-577-2595
Bell & Evans
Fredericksburg, PA 717-865-6626
Equity Group
Reidsville, NC 336-342-6601
Hampton House J.D. Sweid Ltd
Burnaby, BC 800-665-4355
Health is Wealth Foods
Williamstown, NJ 856-728-1998
Pinty's Premium Foods
Burlington, ON 800-263-7223
Redi-Serve Food Company
Fort Atkinson, WI 920-563-6391
Snow Ball Foods
Williamstown, NJ 856-629-4081

Patties

Caribbean Food Delights
Tappan, NY 845-398-3000
Royal Caribbean Bakery
Mount Vernon, NY 888-818-0971

Patties Breaded

Meat-O-Mat Corporation
Brooklyn, NY 718-965-7250

Prepared

Cargill Meat Solutions
Timberville, VA 540-896-7041
Caribbean Food Delights
Tappan, NY 845-398-3000
Delphos Poultry Products
Delphos, OH 419-692-5816
Equity Group
Reidsville, NC 336-342-6601
House of Raeford Farms
Raeford, NC 800-888-7539
Lucks Food Decorating Company
Tacoma, WA 253-383-4815
Pasqualichio Brothers
Scranton, PA 800-232-6233
Pocono Foods
Mt Bethel, PA 570-897-5000
Snow Ball Foods
Williamstown, NJ 856-629-4081

Prepared Frozen

Burke Corporation
Nevada, IA 800-654-1152

Always make it your best® with Burke fully cooked meats. We specialize in Italian sausage, beef, and pork toppings, meatballs, taco meats, shredded meats, pepperoni, bacon, Canadian-style bacon, chicken and beef strips. Additionally, we offer a variety of specialty products: Hand-Pinched Style® brand toppings, chorizo, gyro topping, andouille sausage, and breakfast patties and links.

Caribbean Food Delights
Tappan, NY 845-398-3000
Chang Food Company
Garden Grove, CA 714-265-9990
Chef Hans Gourmet Foods
Monroe, LA 800-890-4267
ConAgra Frozen Foods Company
Marshall, MO 660-886-3301
Equity Group
Reidsville, NC 336-342-6601

Gemini Food Industries
Charlton, MA 508-248-2730
Hormel Foods Corporation
Austin, MN 800-523-4635
House of Raeford Farms
Raeford, NC 800-888-7539
Meat-O-Mat Corporation
Brooklyn, NY 718-965-7250
Morrison Lamothe
Toronto, ON 877-677-6533
Paisano Food Products
Elk Grove Village, IL 800-672-4726
SJH Enterprises
Middleton, WI 888-745-3845
Snow Ball Foods
Williamstown, NJ 856-629-4081
Tyson Foods
Springdale, AR 800-643-3410
Wong Wing Foods
Montreal, QC 800-361-4820

Raw

Caribbean Food Delights
Tappan, NY 845-398-3000
Kelly Gourmet Foods
San Francisco, CA 415-648-9200

Cornish Game Hens

Chicago Steaks
Chicago, IL 800-776-4174
Culinary Foods
Chicago, IL 800-621-4049
Tyson Foods
Springdale, AR 800-643-3410
Woods Smoked Meats
Bowling Green, MO 800-458-8426

Duck

Bear Creek Smokehouse
Marshall, TX 800-950-2327
Chicago Steaks
Chicago, IL 800-776-4174
Crescent Duck Farm
Aquebogue, NY 631-722-8700
Culver Duck
Middlebury, IN 800-825-9225
Maple Leaf Farms
Franksville, WI 262-878-1234
North Country Smokehouse
Claremont, NH 800-258-4304

Goose

Schiltz Foods
Sisseton, SD 877-872-4458
Wenk Foods Inc
Madison, SD 605-256-4569

Turkey

Alderfer Bologna
Harleysville, PA 800-341-1121
Amana Meat Shop & Smokehouse
Amana, IA 800-373-6328
Applegate Farms
Bridgewater, NJ 908-725-2768
Bear Creek Smokehouse
Marshall, TX 800-950-2327
Becker Food Company
Milwaukee, WI 414-964-5353
Bowman & Landes Turkeys
New Carlisle, OH 877-466-9466
Bullock's Country Meats
Westminster, MD 410-848-6786
Burgers Smokehouse
California, MO 800-624-5426
Burke Corporation
Nevada, IA 800-654-1152

Always make it your best® with Burke fully cooked meats. We specialize in Italian sausage, beef, and pork toppings, meatballs, taco meats, shredded meats, pepperoni, bacon, Canadian-style bacon, chicken and beef strips. Additionally, we offer a variety of specialty products: Hand-Pinched Style® brand toppings, chorizo, gyro topping, andouille sausage, and breakfast patties and links.

Buzz Food Service
Charleston, WV 304-925-4781
Campbell Soup Company
Camden, NJ 800-257-8443
Cargill Meat Solutions
Timberville, VA 540-896-7041
Carl Buddig & Company
Homewood, IL 800-621-0868
Carolina Turkeys
Mount Olive, NC 800-523-4559
Cericola Farms
Bradford, ON 877-939-4449
Charles Poultry Company
Lancaster, PA 717-872-7621
Chef's Requested Foods
Oklahoma City, OK 800-256-0259
Chicago Steaks
Chicago, IL 800-776-4174
Couch's Country Style Sausages
Cleveland, OH 216-823-2332
Country Smoked Meats
Bowling Green, OH 800-321-4766
Culinary Foods
Chicago, IL 800-621-4049
Dietz & Watson
Philadelphia, PA 800-333-1974
E&G Food
Brooklyn, NY 888-525-8855
Farbest Foods
Huntingburg, IN 812-683-4200
Foster Farms
Livingston, CA 800-255-7227
Freezer Queen Foods
Buffalo, NY 800-828-8383
Georges Chicken
Edinburg, VA 866-444-2449
Grabill Country Meats
Grabill, IN 866-333-6328
Heinkel's Packing Company
Decatur, IL 800-594-2738
Hickory Baked Food
Castle Rock, CO 303-688-2633
Hillbilly Smokehouse
Rogers, AR 479-636-1927
Hollman Foods
Chicago, IL 888-926-2879
Hormel Foods Corporation
Austin, MN 800-523-4635
House of Raeford Farms
Raeford, NC 800-888-7539
Iowa Ham Canning
Independence, IA 319-334-7134
Jaindl's Turkey Farms
Orefield, PA 800-475-6654
Jennie-O Turkey Store
Willmar, MN 320-235-6080
Kauffman Turkey Farms
Waterman, IL 815-264-3470
Land O'Frost
Searcy, AR 800-643-5654
Lindner Bison
Valencia, CA 866-247-8753
Locustdale Meat Packing
Locustdale, PA 570-875-1270
Longmont Foods
Longmont, CO 303-776-6611
Mada'n Kosher Foods
Dania, FL 954-925-0077
McFarland Foods
Riverton, UT 209-869-6611
Meat-O-Mat Corporation
Brooklyn, NY 718-965-7250
Moretti's Poultry
Columbus, OH 614-486-2333
Moroni Feed Company
West Liberty, IA 800-453-5327
New Braunfels Smokehouse
New Braunfels, TX 800-537-6932
Norbest
Midvale, UT 800-453-5327
North Star Foods
Saint Charles, MN 507-932-4831
Oak Valley Farm
Voorhees, NJ 856-435-0900
P & L Poultry
Spokane, WA 509-892-1242
Pasqualichio Brothers
Scranton, PA 800-232-6233
Perdue Farms
Salisbury, MD 800-473-7383
Piggie Park Enterprises
West Columbia, SC 800-628-7423
Plainville Farms
Memphis, NY 800-724-0206
Plantation Foods
Waco, TX 800-733-0900
Proliant Meat Ingredients
Harlan, IA 800-369-2672
Quaker Maid Meats
Reading, PA 610-376-1500
Raemica
Highland, CA 909-864-1990
Ray's Sausage Company Inc
Cleveland, OH 216-921-8782
Readyfoods
Denver, CO 800-748-1218
Riverside Packers
Drumheller, AB 403-823-2595
Roman Sausage Company
Santa Clara, CA 800-497-7462
Sahlen Packing Company
Buffalo, NY 716-852-8677
Selwoods Farm Hunting Preserve
Alpine, AL 256-362-7595
Smith Packing Regional Meat
Utica, NY
Snow Ball Foods
Williamstown, NJ 856-629-4081
Specialty Foods Group
Hampton, VA 800-238-0020
Standard Beef Company
Foxboro, MA 203-787-2164
Sunnydale Meats
Gaffney, SC 864-489-6091
Suzanna's Kitchen
Duluth, GA 800-241-2455
Sweet Sue Kitchens
Athens, AL 256-216-0500
Talisman Foods
Salt Lake City, UT 801-487-6409
Tenn Valley Ham Company
Paris, TN 731-642-9740
Thomas Packing Company
Columbus, GA 800-729-0976
Turkey Store Company
Faribault, MN 507-334-2050
Vantage USA
Chicago, IL 773-247-1086
Vienna Meat Products
Scarborough, ON 800-588-1931
W & G Marketing Company
Ames, IA 515-233-4774
Wayco Ham Company
Goldsboro, NC 800-962-2614
West Central Turkeys
Pelican Rapids, MN 218-863-6800
West Liberty Foods
West Liberty, IA 888-511-4500
Wimmer's Meat Products
West Point, NE 800-358-0761
Woods Smoked Meats
Bowling Green, MO 800-458-8426
Zacky Farms
Fresno, CA 800-888-0235

Breast

Alderfer Bologna
Harleysville, PA 800-341-1121
Amana Meat Shop & Smokehouse
Amana, IA 800-373-6328
Berks Packing Company, Inc.
Reading, PA 800-882-3757
Chicago Steaks
Chicago, IL 800-776-4174
Dietz & Watson
Philadelphia, PA 800-333-1974
Grote & Weigel
Bloomfield, CT 860-242-8528
Hickory Baked Food
Castle Rock, CO 303-688-2633
Rose Packing Company
South Barrington, IL 800-323-7363
Smith Packing Regional Meat
Utica, NY
Woods Smoked Meats
Bowling Green, MO 800-458-8426

Canned

Bowman & Landes Turkeys
New Carlisle, OH 877-466-9466
Grabill Country Meats
Grabill, IN 866-333-6328
Sweet Sue Kitchens
Athens, AL 256-216-0500

Fillets

Carolina Turkeys
Mount Olive, NC 800-523-4559

Fresh

Becker Food Company
Milwaukee, WI 414-964-5353
Blue Ridge Poultry
Athens, GA 706-546-6767
Carolina Turkeys
Mount Olive, NC 800-523-4559
Cooper Farms
Van Wert, OH 419-238-4056
Georges Chicken
Edinburg, VA 866-444-2449
Moroni Feed Company
West Liberty, IA 800-453-5327
Perdue Farms
Salisbury, MD 800-473-7383
Pilgrim's
Greeley, CO. 800-727-5366
Smith Packing Regional Meat
Utica, NY
Turkey Store Company
Faribault, MN 507-334-2050

Frozen

Burke Corporation
Nevada, IA 800-654-1152

Always make it your best® with Burke fully cooked meats. We specialize in Italian sausage, beef, and pork toppings, meatballs, taco meats, shredded meats, pepperoni, bacon, Canadian-style bacon, chicken and beef strips. Additionally, we offer a variety of specialty products: Hand-Pinched Style® brand toppings, chorizo, gyro topping, andouille sausage, and breakfast patties and links.

North Side Foods Corporation
Arnold, PA 800-486-2201

Ground

Carolina Turkeys
Mount Olive, NC 800-523-4559
Koch Foods
Park Ridge, IL. 800-837-2778

Leg

Karn Meats
Columbus, OH 800-221-9585

Raw

Carl Buddig & Company
Homewood, IL 800-621-0868
Foster Farms
Creswell, OR. 541-895-2161
Wayne Farms LLC
Jack, AL 334-897-3435

Sausage

Golden Platter Foods
Newark, NJ 973-242-0290
Hahn Brothers
Westminster, MD 800-227-7675

Whole Frozen

Hickory Baked Food
Castle Rock, CO 303-688-2633

Smoked, Cured & Deli Meats

Alphin Brothers
Dunn, NC 800-672-4502
Applegate Farms
Bridgewater, NJ 908-725-2768
Blue Grass Quality Meat
Covington, KY 859-331-7100
Boyd Sausage Company
Washington, IA 319-653-5715
Braham Food Locker Service
Braham, MN 320-396-2636
Burke Corporation
Nevada, IA 800-654-1152

Always make it your best® with Burke fully cooked meats. We specialize in Italian sausage, beef, and pork toppings, meatballs, taco meats, shredded meats, pepperoni, bacon, Canadian-style bacon, chicken and beef strips. Additionally, we offer a variety of specialty products: Hand-Pinched Style® brand toppings, chorizo, gyro topping, andouille sausage, and breakfast patties and links.

Caddo Packing Company
Marshall, TX 903-935-2211
Campbell Soup Company
Camden, NJ. 800-257-8443
Castleberry's
Vineland, NJ 856-691-2100
Castleberry's Meats
Atlanta, GA. 404-873-1804
Chicopee Provision Company
Chicopee, MA. 800-924-6328
Chip Steak & Provision Company
Mankato, MN 507-388-6277
Circle V Meat Company
Spanish Fork, UT 801-798-3081
Cloverdale Foods Company
Mandan, ND 800-669-9511
Columbia Packing Company
Dallas, TX. 800-460-8171
ConAgra Beef Company
Hyrum, UT 435-245-6456
Continental Deli Foods
Cherokee, IA. 712-225-6529
Crawford Sausage Company
Chicago, IL 866-653-2479
Curtis Packing Company
Greensboro, NC 336-275-7684
Cusack Wholesale Meat Company
Oklahoma City, OK 800-241-6328
Dallas Dressed Beef
Dallas, TX. 214-638-0142
Dankworth Packing Company
Ballinger, TX 325-365-3552
David Berg & Company
Chicago, IL 773-278-5195
Fredericksburg Lockers/OPA's Smoke
Fredericksburg, TX. 800-543-6750
Fricks Meat Products
Washington, MO. 800-241-2209
Gary's Frozen Foods
Lubbock, TX. 806-745-1933
H&B Packing Company
Waco, TX 254-752-2506
Harrington's In Vermont
Richmond, VT. 802-434-7500
Heringer Meats
Covington, KY 859-291-2000
Humboldt Sausage Company
Humboldt, IA 515-332-4121
Hummel Brothers
New Haven, CT 800-828-8978
Independent Meat Company
Twin Falls, ID 208-733-0980
J&B Sausage Company
Waelder, TX 830-788-7511
Kayem Foods
Chelsea, MA 800-426-6100
Kretschmar
Don Mills, ON 800-561-4532
Lay Packing Company
Knoxville, TN. 865-922-4320
Little Rhody Brand Frankfurts
Johnston, RI 401-831-0815
Lords Sausage & CountryhHam
Dexter, GA 800-342-6002
Mada'n Kosher Foods
Dania, FL 954-925-0077
Matthiesen's Deer & Custom Processing
De Witt, IA 563-659-8409
Mertz Sausage Company
San Antonio, TX. 210-433-3263
Miller's Meat Market
Red Bud, IL. 618-282-3334
Moo & Oink
Chicago, IL 773-493-7100
Murphy House
Louisburg, NC 919-496-6054
Neese Country Sausage
Greensboro, NC 800-632-1010
New Packing Company
Chicago, IL 312-666-1314
Patrick Cudahy
Cudahy, WI 800-486-6900
Peer Foods Inc.
Chicago, IL 800-365-5644
Plumrose USA
East Brunswick, NJ. 800-526-4909
R.M. Felts Packing Company
Ivor, VA. 888-300-0971
S. Abuin Packing
Elizabeth, NJ 908-354-2674
Sara Lee Corporation
Downers Grove, IL 630-598-8100
Stevens Sausage Company
Smithfield, NC 800-338-0561
Stonies Sausage Shop Inc
Perryville, MO 888-546-2540
Terrell Meats
Delta, UT. 435-864-2600
Thomas Packing Company
Columbus, GA 800-729-0976
Thumann's
Carlstadt, NJ 201-935-3636
Troy Frozen Food
Troy, IL 618-667-6332
Vermilion Packers Ltd
Vermilion, AB. 780-853-4622
Vienna Sausage Company
Chicago, IL 800-366-3647
Webster City Custom Meats
Webster City, IA 888-786-3287
Yoakum Packing Company
Yoakum, TX 361-293-3541

Bacon

Alderfer Bologna
Harleysville, PA 800-341-1121
Aliments Prince Foods
Anjou, QC 800-361-3898
Amana Meat Shop & Smokehouse
Amana, IA. 800-373-6328
Applegate Farms
Bridgewater, NJ 908-725-2768
Arnold's Meat Food Products
Brooklyn, NY 800-633-7023
Bacon America
Drummondville, QC 819-475-3030
Bear Creek Smokehouse
Marshall, TX. 800-950-2327
Blakely Freezer Locker
Thomasville, GA. 229-723-3622
Broadbent's B&B Foods
Kuttawa, KY 800-841-2202
Burke Corporation
Nevada, IA 800-654-1152

Always make it your best® with Burke fully cooked meats. We specialize in Italian sausage, beef, and pork toppings, meatballs, taco meats, shredded meats, pepperoni, bacon, Canadian-style bacon, chicken and beef strips. Additionally, we offer a variety of specialty products: Hand-Pinched Style® brand toppings, chorizo, gyro topping, andouille sausage, and breakfast patties and links.

Chef's Requested Foods
Oklahoma City, OK 800-256-0259
Chisesi Brothers Meat Packing Company
New Orleans, LA 800-966-3550
Cloverdale Foods Company
Mandan, ND 800-669-9511
Community Market & Deli
Lindstrom, MN 651-257-1128
Cropp Cooperative-Organic Valley
La Farge, WI 888-444-6455
D'Artagnan
Newark, NJ 800-327-8246
Farmland Foods
Kansas City, MO. 888-327-6526
Father's Country Hams
Bremen, KY 270-525-3554
Hahn Brothers
Westminster, MD 800-227-7675
Hickory Baked Food
Castle Rock, CO 303-688-2633
Hormel Foods Corporation
Fremont, NE 402-721-2300
Maple Leaf Consumer Foods
Fair Oaks, CA 800-999-7603
Niemuth's Steak & Chop Shop
Waupaca, WI. 715-258-2666

North Country Smokehouse
Claremont, NH 800-258-4304
Patrick Cudahy
Cudahy, WI 800-486-6900
R.L. Zeigler Company
Tuscaloosa, AL 800-392-6328
Rinehart Meat Processing
Branson, MO 417-334-2044
Rose Packing Company
South Barrington, IL 800-323-7363
Scott Hams
Greenville, KY 800-318-1353
Seaboard Foods
Shawnee Mission, KS 800-262-7907
Simeus Foods Internatio nal
Mansfield, TX 888-772-3663
Sugar Creek Packing
Washington Court House, OH 800-848-8205
Sunnydale Meats
Gaffney, SC 864-489-6091
Sunset Farm Foods
Valdosta, GA 800-882-1121
Thomas Packing Company
Columbus, GA 800-729-0976
V.W. Joyner & Company
Smithfield, VA 757-357-2161
Woods Smoked Meats
Bowling Green, MO 800-458-8426

Bits Imitation

American Key Food Products
Closter, NJ 800-767-0237
CHR Hansen
Elyria, OH 800-558-0802
CHS, Inc.
Inner Grove Heights, MN 800-232-3639
Con Yeager Spice Company
Zelienople, PA 800-222-2460
Fairbury Food Products
Fairbury, NE 402-729-3379
Feaster Foods
Omaha, NE 800-228-6098
Schiff Food Products
North Bergen, NJ 201-868-6800
Tova Industries
Louisville, KY 888-532-8682
Westin
Omaha, NE 800-228-6098

Bits Real

Burke Corporation
Nevada, IA 800-654-1152

Always make it your best® with Burke fully cooked meats. We specialize in Italian sausage, beef, and pork toppings, meatballs, taco meats, shredded meats, pepperoni, bacon, Canadian-style bacon, chicken and beef strips. Additionally, we offer a variety of specialty products: Hand-Pinched Style® brand toppings, chorizo, gyro topping, andouille sausage, and breakfast patties and links.

Con Yeager Spice Company
Zelienople, PA 800-222-2460
Sugar Creek Packing
Washington Court House, OH 800-848-8205
Tova Industries
Louisville, KY 888-532-8682

Canadian Style

Al & John's Glen Rock Ham
Paterson, NJ 800-969-4990
Burgers Smokehouse
California, MO 800-624-5426
Burke Corporation
Nevada, IA 800-654-1152

Always make it your best® with Burke fully cooked meats. We specialize in Italian sausage, beef, and pork toppings, meatballs, taco meats, shredded meats, pepperoni, bacon, Canadian-style bacon, chicken and beef strips. Additionally, we offer a variety of specialty products: Hand-Pinched Style® brand toppings, chorizo, gyro topping, andouille sausage, and breakfast patties and links.

Calihan Pork Processing
Peoria, IL 309-674-9175
Country Smoked Meats
Bowling Green, OH 800-321-4766
Foodbrands America
Oklahoma City, OK 405-290-4000
Hickory Baked Food
Castle Rock, CO 303-688-2633
Hormel Foods Corporation
Austin, MN 800-523-4635
Peer Foods Inc.
Chicago, IL 800-365-5644
Pioneer Packing Company
Bowling Green, OH 419-352-5283
Rose Packing Company
South Barrington, IL 800-323-7363

Slices

Carolina Pride Foods
Greenwood, SC 864-229-5611
ConAgra Foods/Eckrich
Omaha, NE 800-327-4424
Country Smoked Meats
Bowling Green, OH 800-321-4766
Jimmy Dean Foods
Cincinnati, OH 800-925-3326
Webster City Custom Meats
Webster City, IA 888-786-3287

Slices Thick

Healthy Oven
Croton on Hudson, NY 914-271-5458
Jimmy Dean Foods
Cincinnati, OH 800-925-3326
Westbrae Natural Foods
Melville, NY 800-434-4246

Beef Jerky

Alderfer Bologna
Harleysville, PA 800-341-1121
Alewel's Country Meats
Warrensburg, MO 800-353-8553
Amana Meat Shop & Smokehouse
Amana, IA 800-373-6328
Baier's Sausage & Meats
Red Deer, AB 403-346-1535
Better Made Snack Foods
Detroit, MI 800-332-2394
Big Chief Meat Snacks In
Calgary, AB 403-264-2641
Boyd Sausage Company
Washington, IA 319-653-5715
Cattaneo Brothers
San Luis Obispo, CA 800-243-8537
Chickasaw Trading Company
Denver City, TX 800-848-3515
David Berg & Company
Chicago, IL 773-278-5195
Debbie D's Jerky & Sausage
Tillamook, OR 503-842-2622
E.W. Knauss & Son
Quakertown, PA 800-648-4220
Eastside Deli Supply
Lansing, MI 800-349-6694
Eiserman Meats
Slave Lake, AB 780-849-5507
Enjoy Foods International
Fontana, CA 909-823-2228
F&Y Enterprises
Wauconda, IL 847-526-0620
High Country Snack Foods
Lincoln, MT 800-433-3916
Hsin Tung Yang Foods Co.
S San Francisco, CA 650-589-6789
Ittels Meats
Howard Lake, MN 320-543-2285
J&B Sausage Company
Waelder, TX 830-788-7511
Kershenstine Beef Jerky
Eupora, MS 662-258-2049
King B Meat Snacks
Minong, WI 800-346-6896
King Nut Company
Solon, OH 800-860-5464
Lone Star Beef Jerky Company
Lubbock, TX 806-762-8833
Longview Meat & Merchandise Ltd
Longview, AB 866-355-3759
Middlefield Cheese House
Middlefield, OH 800-327-9477
Mike's Meats
Eitzen, MN 507-495-3336
Nestle Pizza
Medford, WI 715-748-5550
New Braunfels Smokehouse
New Braunfels, TX 800-537-6932
Norpaco
Middletown, CT 800-252-0222
Palmer Packing Company
Tremonton, UT 435-257-5329
Peoples Sausage Company
Los Angeles, CA 213-627-8633
Red Oak Farms
Red Oak, IA 712-623-9224
Rinehart Meat Processing
Branson, MO 417-334-2044
Rudolph Foods
Dallas, TX 214-638-2204
Smokey Farm Meats
Carbon, AB 403-272-6587
Terrell Meats
Delta, UT 435-864-2600
Toxic Tommy's Beef Jerky & Spices
Wadsworth, OH 866-448-6942
WA Bean & Sons
Bangor, ME 800-649-1958
Weaver Nut Company
Ephrata, PA 717-738-3781
Western Beef Jerky
Edmonton, AB 780-469-4817
Wild Bill's Foods Monogram Snacks Martinsville, LLC
Martinsville, VA 800-848-3236
Willies Smoke House
Harrisville, PA 800-742-4184
Wimmer's Meat Products
West Point, NE 800-358-0761
Woods Smoked Meats
Bowling Green, MO 800-458-8426

Bologna

Alderfer Bologna
Harleysville, PA 800-341-1121
Atlantic Pork & Provisions
Jamaica, NY 800-245-3536
Boeckman JJ Wholesale Meats
Dayton, OH 937-222-4679
Boesl Packing Company
Baltimore, MD 410-675-1071
Boyd Sausage Company
Washington, IA 319-653-5715
C. Roy Meat Products
Yale, MI 810-387-3957
Cargill Meat Solutions
Timberville, VA 540-896-7041
Carolina Packers
Smithfield, NC 800-682-7675
Carolina Pride Foods
Greenwood, SC 864-229-5611
Chisesi Brothers Meat Packing Company
New Orleans, LA 800-966-3550
Curtis Packing Company
Greensboro, NC 336-275-7684
Farmland Foods
Kansas City, MO 888-327-6526
Foodbrands America
Oklahoma City, OK 405-290-4000
Frank Wardynski & Sons
Buffalo, NY 716-854-6083
Groff Meats
Elizabethtown, PA 717-367-1246
Grote & Weigel
Bloomfield, CT 860-242-8528
Hazle Park Packing Co
West Hazleton, PA 800-238-4331
Heritage Cheese House
Heuvelton, NY 315-344-2216
Hofmann Sausage Company
Syracuse, NY 800-724-8410
Ito Cariani Sausage Company
Hayward, CA 510-887-0882
Kessler Foods, Inc
Lemoyne, PA 717-763-7162
Kilgus Meats
Toledo, OH 419-472-9721
Kitts Meat Processing
Dedham, IA 712-683-5622
Larsen Packers
Burwick, NS 902-538-8060
Locustdale Meat Packing
Locustdale, PA 570-875-1270
Palmyra Bologna
Palmyra, PA 717-838-6336

Pfeffer's Country Mkt.
Sauk Centre, MN 320-352-6490
Raemica
Highland, CA 909-864-1990
Rego's Purity Foods
Honolulu, HI...................... 808-847-3717
Rendulic Packing
McKeesport, PA 412-678-9541
Sara Lee Corporation
Downers Grove, IL................. 630-598-8100
Sechrist Brothers
Dallastown, PA.................... 717-244-2975
Sheinman Provision Company
Philadelphia, PA.................. 215-473-7065
Silver Star Meats
McKees Rocks, PA.................. 800-548-1321
Spring Grove Foods
Miamisburg, OH.................... 937-866-4311
Stawnichy Holdings
Mundare, AB 888-764-7646
Sunset Farm Foods
Valdosta, GA...................... 800-882-1121
Tennessee Valley PackingCompany
Columbia, TN...................... 931-388-2623
Thumann's
Carlstadt, NJ..................... 201-935-3636
Troy Frozen Food
Troy, IL.......................... 618-667-6332
Troyers Trail Bologna
Dundee, OH 877-893-2414
Wimmer's Meat Products
West Point, NE.................... 800-358-0761

Bratwurst

Bob Evans Farms
Hillsdale, MI..................... 517-437-3349
Country Smoked Meats
Bowling Green, OH 800-321-4766
David Berg & Company
Chicago, IL....................... 773-278-5195
Elmwood Lockers
Elmwood, IL....................... 309-742-8929
Fontanini Italian Meats & Sausages
McCook, IL........................ 800-331-6328
Kilgus Meats
Toledo, OH 419-472-9721
Koegel Meats
Flint, MI 810-238-3685
Raemica
Highland, CA 909-864-1990
S.W. Meat & Provision Company
Phoenix, AZ 602-275-2000
Saugy Inc
Cranston, RI 866-467-2849
Silver Star Meats
McKees Rocks, PA.................. 800-548-1321
Smolich Brothers
Joliet, IL 815-727-2144
Sunset Farm Foods
Valdosta, GA...................... 800-882-1121
Waco Beef & Pork Processors
Waco, TX 254-772-4669
Wimmer's Meat Products
West Point, NE.................... 800-358-0761
Woods Smoked Meats
Bowling Green, MO................. 800-458-8426

Corned Beef

Alderfer Bologna
Harleysville, PA 800-341-1121
American Food Traders
Miami, FL......................... 305-273-7090
Art's Tamales
Metamora, IL 309-367-2850
Best Provision Co Inc.
Newark, NJ 800-631-4466
Burnett & Son Meat Company
Monrovia, CA...................... 626-357-2165
Carando Gourmet Frozen Foods
Agawam, MA 888-227-2636
Charlie's Pride Meats
Vernon, CA 877-866-0982
Chicopee Provision Company
Chicopee, MA...................... 800-924-6328
Curly's Foods
Edina, MN......................... 800-722-1127
D'Artagnan
Newark, NJ 800-327-8246
David Berg & Company
Chicago, IL....................... 773-278-5195

Dutterer's Home Food Service
Baltimore, MD 410-298-3663
Hahn Brothers
Westminster, MD 800-227-7675
Henry J Meat Specialties
Chicago, IL....................... 800-242-1314
Hormel Foods Corporation
Austin, MN........................ 800-523-4635
International Food Packers Corporation
Miami, FL......................... 305-669-1662
Kelly Foods
Jackson, TN 731-424-2255
Kelly Kornbeef Company
Chicago, IL....................... 773-588-2882
Levonian Brothers
Troy, NY.......................... 518-274-3610
Lower Foods
Richmond, UT...................... 435-258-2449
Nossack Fine Meats
Red Deer, AB 403-346-5006
Otto W Liebold & Company
Flint, MI 800-999-6328
Peer Foods Inc.
Chicago, IL....................... 800-365-5644
Plumrose USA
East Brunswick, NJ................ 800-526-4909
Sara Lee Corporation
Downers Grove, IL................. 630-598-8100
Saval Foods
Elkridge, MD 800-527-2825
Sheinman Provision Company
Philadelphia, PA.................. 215-473-7065
Stawnichy Holdings
Mundare, AB 888-764-7646
Thompson Packers
Slidell, LA....................... 800-989-6328
Tupman-Thurlow Company
Deerfield Beach, FL 954-596-9989
Vienna Meat Products
Scarborough, ON 800-588-1931

Deli Foods

American Food Traders
Miami, FL......................... 305-273-7090
Ask Foods
Palmyra, PA....................... 800-879-4275
Bagels By Bell
Brooklyn, NY 718-272-2780
Billingsgate Fish Company
Calgary, AB....................... 403-571-7700
Bloomfield Bakers
Los Alamitos, CA.................. 800-594-4111
Boeckman JJ Wholesale Meats
Dayton, OH........................ 937-222-4679
Bottomline Foods
Davie, FL 954-843-0562
Bouma Meats
Provost, AB....................... 780-753-2092
Boyd Sausage Company
Washington, IA.................... 319-653-5715
Bridgford Foods of North Carolina
Statesville, NC 704-878-2722
Carl Buddig & Company
Homewood, IL 800-621-0868
Carolina Packers
Smithfield, NC 800-682-7675
Charlie's Pride Meats
Vernon, CA 877-866-0982
Chicago 58 Food Products
Woodbridge, ON.................... 416-603-4244
Chloe Foods Corporation
Brooklyn, NY 718-827-9000
Cibao Meat Product
Bronx, NY......................... 718-993-5072
Continental Deli Foods
Cherokee, IA...................... 712-225-6529
Corfu Foods
Bensenville, IL 630-595-2510
Cumberland Gap Provision Company
Middlesboro, KY 800-331-7154
Curtis Packing Company
Greensboro, NC 336-275-7684
Czimer's Game & Sea Foods
Homer Glen, IL.................... 708-301-0500
Dairy Fresh Foods
Taylor, MI........................ 313-295-6300
Dan's Prize
Gainesville, GA 800-233-5845
Danner Salads
Peoria, IL........................ 309-691-0289

David Berg & Company
Chicago, IL....................... 773-278-5195
Dno
Columbus, OH 800-686-2366
Durrett Cheese Sales
Manchester, TN.................... 800-209-6792
Earth Island Natural Foods
Canoga Park, CA 818-725-2820
Eastside Deli Supply
Lansing, MI....................... 800-349-6694
Farmland Foods
Carroll, IA....................... 712-792-1660
Foodmark
Wellesley, MA..................... 781-237-7088
Freda Quality Meats
Philadelphia, PA 800-443-7332
Gilardi Foods
Sidney, OH 937-498-4511
Global Food Industries
Townville, SC..................... 800-225-4152
Gwaltney of Smithfield
Portsmouth, VA.................... 757-465-0666
Gwaltney of Smithfield
Smithfield, VA 800-888-7521
Harold M. Lincoln Company
Toledo, OH 800-345-4911
Heinkel's Packing Company
Decatur, IL 800-594-2738
HFI Foods
Redmond, WA....................... 425-883-1320
Home Made Brand Foods Company
Newburyport, MA................... 978-462-3663
Homestyle Foods Company
Hamtramck, MI..................... 313-874-3250
Hormel Foods Corporation
Columbia, MD 410-290-1916
Hormel Foods Corporation
Des Moines, IA.................... 515-276-8872
Hormel Foods Corporation
Austin, MN........................ 800-523-4635
Hormel Foods Corporation
Cordova, TN....................... 901-753-4282
Hormel Foods Corporation
Lebanon, NJ 908-236-7009
Hormel Foods Corporation
Pleasanton, CA 925-734-9555
Humboldt Sausage Company
Humboldt, IA 515-332-4121
Hummel Brothers
New Haven, CT 800-828-8978
Kay Foods Company
Detroit, MI 313-393-1100
Kelly Foods
Jackson, TN 731-424-2255
Kelly Kornbeef Company
Chicago, IL....................... 773-588-2882
Kitts Meat Processing
Dedham, IA........................ 712-683-5622
Klein's Kosher Pickles
Phoenix, AZ 602-269-2072
Landshire
Saint Louis, MO 800-468-3354
Lower Foods
Richmond, UT...................... 435-258-2449
Manda Fine Meats
Baton Rouge, LA 225-344-7636
Marshallville Packing Company
Marshallville, OH................. 330-855-2871
Meadows Country Products
Hollidaysburg, PA................. 888-499-1001
Murphy House
Louisburg, NC 919-496-6054
Norbest
Midvale, UT 800-453-5327
Ohio Packing Company
Columbus, OH 800-282-6403
Orval Kent Food Company
Wheeling, IL...................... 847-459-9000
Palmyra Bologna
Palmyra, PA....................... 717-838-6336
Plumrose USA
East Brunswick, NJ................ 800-526-4909
Randy's Frozen Meats
Faribault, MN..................... 800-354-7177
Real Kosher Sausage Company
Newark, NJ 973-690-5394
Russer Foods
Buffalo, NY....................... 800-828-7021
Schneider Foods
Kitchener, ON..................... 519-741-5000
Seneca Foods
Clyman, WI........................ 920-696-3331

Siena Foods
Toronto, ON 800-465-0422
Silver Star Meats
McKees Rocks, PA 800-548-1321
SMG
Crestview Hills, KY 859-344-3700
Smith Provision Company
Erie, PA 800-334-9151
Spring Glen Fresh Foods
Ephrata, PA 800-641-2853
Spring Grove Foods
Miamisburg, OH 937-866-4311
Springfield Smoked Fish Company
Springfield, MA 800-327-3412
Stevens Sausage Company
Smithfield, NC 800-338-0561
Swift & Company
Greeley, CO. 970-506-8000
Temptee Specialty Foods
Denver, CO 800-842-1233
Trebon European Specialties
South Hackensack, NJ 800-899-4332
Vegi-Deli
San Rafael, CA 888-473-3667

Deli Meats

Alderfer Bologna
Harleysville, PA 800-341-1121
Alle Processing Corporation
Maspeth, NY. 800-245-5620
American Food Traders
Miami, FL. 305-273-7090
Atlantic Pork & Provisions
Jamaica, NY 800-245-3536
Atlantic Premium Brands
Northbrook, IL 847-412-6200
Bar-S Foods Company
Phoenix, AZ 602-264-7272
Berks Packing Company, Inc.
Reading, PA 800-882-3757
Boar's Head Provisions Company
Sarasota, FL 888-884-2627
Boeckman JJ Wholesale Meats
Dayton, OH. 937-222-4679
Boesl Packing Company
Baltimore, MD 410-675-1071
Bridgford Foods of North Carolina
Statesville, NC 704-878-2722
Broadaway Ham Company
Jonesboro, AR. 870-932-6688
Burke Corporation
Nevada, IA 800-654-1152

Always make it your best® with Burke fully cooked meats. We specialize in Italian sausage, beef, and pork toppings, meatballs, taco meats, shredded meats, pepperoni, bacon, Canadian-style bacon, chicken and beef strips. Additionally, we offer a variety of specialty products: Hand-Pinched Style® brand toppings, chorizo, gyro topping, andouille sausage, and breakfast patties and links.

C. Roy Meat Products
Yale, MI. 810-387-3957
Cargill Meat Solutions
Timberville, VA 540-896-7041
Carl Buddig & Company
Homewood, IL 800-621-0868
Carolina Packers
Smithfield, NC 800-682-7675
Carolina Pride Foods
Greenwood, SC. 864-229-5611
Charlie's Country Sausage
Minot, ND. 701-838-6302
Charlie's Pride Meats
Vernon, CA 877-866-0982
Citterio USA Corporation
Freeland, PA 800-435-8888
ConAgra Foods Inc
Omaha, NE 402-595-7300
Continental Deli Foods
Cherokee, IA. 712-225-6529
Country Smoked Meats
Bowling Green, OH 800-321-4766
Curtis Packing Company
Greensboro, NC 336-275-7684
David Berg & Company
Chicago, IL 773-278-5195
Dietz & Watson
Philadelphia, PA 800-333-1974
Dohar Meats
Cleveland, OH 216-241-4197
Dutterer's Home Food Service
Baltimore, MD 410-298-3663
Egon Binkert Meat Products
Baltimore, MD 410-687-5959
Farmland Foods
Carroll, IA. 712-792-1660
Foodbrands America
Oklahoma City, OK 405-290-4000
Frank Wardynski & Sons
Buffalo, NY. 716-854-6083
Freda Quality Meats
Philadelphia, PA 800-443-7332
Fried Provisions Company
Evans City, PA 724-538-3160
Gaiser's European Style Provisions
Union, NJ 908-686-3421
Groff Meats
Elizabethtown, PA. 717-367-1246
Hansel 'N Gretel
Flushing, NY. 718-326-0041
Hazle Park Packing Co
West Hazleton, PA 800-238-4331
Heinkel's Packing Company
Decatur, IL 800-594-2738
Henry J Meat Specialties
Chicago, IL. 800-242-1314
Humboldt Sausage Company
Humboldt, IA 515-332-4121
Hummel Brothers
New Haven, CT 800-828-8978
Kelly Foods
Jackson, TN 731-424-2255
Kelly Kornbeef Company
Chicago, IL 773-588-2882
Kessler Foods, Inc
Lemoyne, PA. 717-763-7162
Kilgus Meats
Toledo, OH 419-472-9721
Kitts Meat Processing
Dedham, IA. 712-683-5622
Land O'Frost
Searcy, AR 800-643-5654
Lengerich Meats
Zanesville, IN 260-638-4123
Leona Meat Plant
Troy, PA. 570-297-3574
Levonian Brothers
Troy, NY 518-274-3610
Locustdale Meat Packing
Locustdale, PA 570-875-1270
Lowell Provision Company
Lowell, MA. 978-454-5603
Lower Foods
Richmond, UT. 435-258-2449
Manda Fine Meats
Baton Rouge, LA 225-344-7636
Marathon Enterprises
Englewood, NJ 800-722-7388
Marshallville Packing Company
Marshallville, OH 330-855-2871
Martin Rosol's
New Britain, CT 860-223-2707
Mishler Packing Company
Lagrange, IN. 260-768-4156
Murphy House
Louisburg, NC 919-496-6054
O'Brien & Company
Bellevue, NE. 800-433-7567
Otto W Liebold & Company
Flint, MI 800-999-6328
Parma Sausage Products
Pittsburgh, PA 877-294-4207
Pfeffer's Country Mkt.
Sauk Centre, MN 320-352-6490
Plumrose USA
East Brunswick, NJ. 800-526-4909
Queen City Sausage
Cincinnati, OH 877-544-5588
R.L. Zeigler Company
Tuscaloosa, AL. 800-392-6328
Raemica
Highland, CA 909-864-1990
Rego's Purity Foods
Honolulu, HI. 808-847-3717
Rendulic Packing
McKeesport, PA 412-678-9541
Robinsons Sausage Company
London, KY 606-864-2914
Roman Packing Company
Norfolk, NE. 800-373-5990
Russer Foods
Buffalo, NY. 800-828-7021
Saag's Products
San Leandro, CA. 800-352-7224
Sara Lee Corporation
Downers Grove, IL. 630-598-8100
Sausage Shoppe
Cleveland, OH 216-351-5213
Saval Foods
Elkridge, MD 800-527-2825
Schaller & Weber
Astoria, NY 800-847-4115
Sculli Brothers
Yeadon, PA 215-336-1223
Sechrist Brothers
Dallastown, PA 717-244-2975
Sheinman Provision Company
Philadelphia, PA 215-473-7065
Shofar Kosher Foods
Linden, NJ. 888-874-6327
Smith Packing Regional Meat
Utica, NY
Smith Provision Company
Erie, PA 800-334-9151
Snow Ball Foods
Williamstown, NJ 856-629-4081
Spring Grove Foods
Miamisburg, OH 937-866-4311
Standard Beef Company
Foxboro, MA 203-787-2164
Stawnichy Holdings
Mundare, AB 888-764-7646
Stevens Sausage Company
Smithfield, NC 800-338-0561
Stonies Sausage Shop Inc
Perryville, MO 888-546-2540
Swift & Company
Greeley, CO. 970-506-8000
Temptee Specialty Foods
Denver, CO 800-842-1233
Tennessee Valley PackingCompany
Columbia, TN 931-388-2623
Troy Frozen Food
Troy, IL 618-667-6332
Troyers Trail Bologna
Dundee, OH 877-893-2414
Tupman-Thurlow Company
Deerfield Beach, FL 954-596-9989
United Provision Meat Company
Columbus, OH 614-252-1126
Upstate Farms Cooperative
Buffalo, NY. 716-892-2121
V.W. Joyner & Company
Smithfield, VA 757-357-2161
Vienna Meat Products
Scarborough, ON 800-588-1931
Warren & Son Meat Processing
Whipple, OH. 740-585-2421
Wimmer's Meat Products
West Point, NE 800-358-0761

Ham

Aliments Prince Foods
Anjou, QC. 800-361-3898
Ashland Sausage Company
Carol Stream, IL 630-690-2600
Broadbent's B&B Foods
Kuttawa, KY. 800-841-2202
Chicago Steaks
Chicago, IL 800-776-4174
Chisesi Brothers Meat Packing Company
New Orleans, LA 800-966-3550
Cloverdale Foods Company
Mandan, ND 800-669-9511
Community Market & Deli
Lindstrom, MN 651-257-1128
ConAgra Foods/Eckrich
Omaha, NE 800-327-4424
D'Artagnan
Newark, NJ 800-327-8246
Farmland Foods
Kansas City, MO. 888-327-6526
Father's Country Hams
Bremen, KY 270-525-3554
Fricks Meat Products
Washington, MO. 800-241-2209
Grote & Weigel
Bloomfield, CT. 860-242-8528
Hancock's Old Fashioned
Franklinville, NC 336-824-2145

Hickory Baked Food
Castle Rock, CO 303-688-2633
Holly Hill Locker Company
Holly Hill, SC 803-496-3611
Hormel Foods Corporation
Fremont, NE 402-721-2300
Humphrey Blue Ribbon Meats
Springfield, IL 800-747-6328
Maple Leaf Consumer Foods
Fair Oaks, CA 800-999-7603
Niemuth's Steak & Chop Shop
Waupaca, WI 715-258-2666
Patrick Cudahy
Cudahy, WI 800-486-6900
Rinehart Meat Processing
Branson, MO 417-334-2044
Rose Packing Company
South Barrington, IL 800-323-7363
Scott Hams
Greenville, KY 800-318-1353
Silver Star Meats
McKees Rocks, PA 800-548-1321
Specialty Foods Group
Hampton, VA 800-238-0020
Stonies Sausage Shop Inc
Perryville, MO 888-546-2540
Thomas Packing Company
Columbus, GA 800-729-0976
Thumann's
Carlstadt, NJ 201-935-3636
Tupman-Thurlow Company
Deerfield Beach, FL 954-596-9989
V.W. Joyner & Company
Smithfield, VA 757-357-2161
Wayco Ham Company
Goldsboro, NC 800-962-2614

Canned

Badger Gourmet Ham
Milwaukee, WI 414-645-1756
Calihan Pork Processing
Peoria, IL 309-674-9175
ConAgra Foods/Eckrich
Omaha, NE 800-327-4424
Dold Foods
Wichita, KS 316-838-9101
Farmland Foods
Carroll, IA 712-792-1660
Hickory Baked Food
Castle Rock, CO 303-688-2633
Horlacher's Fine Meats
Logan, UT 435-752-1287
Hormel Foods Corporation
Fremont, NE 402-721-2300
International Trading Company
Houston, TX 713-224-5901
Levonian Brothers
Troy, NY 518-274-3610
S. Wallace Edward & Sons
Surry, VA 800-290-9213
Sara Lee Corporation
Downers Grove, IL 630-598-8100
Smithfield Packing Company
Smithfield, VA 757-357-4321
Stegall Smoked Turkey
Marshville, NC 800-851-6034
Tenn Valley Ham Company
Paris, TN 731-642-9740
Tupman-Thurlow Company
Deerfield Beach, FL 954-596-9989
Wayco Ham Company
Goldsboro, NC 800-962-2614

Cooked - Water-added Chilled

Madrange
Millington, NJ 908-647-6485

Fresh

Amana Meat Shop & Smokehouse
Amana, IA 800-373-6328
Gwaltney of Smithfield
Smithfield, VA 800-888-7521
Smith Provision Company
Erie, PA 800-334-9151

Frozen

Burke Corporation
Nevada, IA 800-654-1152

Always make it your best® with Burke fully cooked meats. We specialize in Italian sausage, beef, and pork toppings, meatballs, taco meats, shredded meats, pepperoni, bacon, Canadian-style bacon, chicken and beef strips. Additionally, we offer a variety of specialty products: Hand-Pinched Style® brand toppings, chorizo, gyro topping, andouille sausage, and breakfast patties and links.

Smoked

Alderfer Bologna
Harleysville, PA 800-341-1121
Badger Gourmet Ham
Milwaukee, WI 414-645-1756
Bear Creek Smokehouse
Marshall, TX 800-950-2327
Blakely Freezer Locker
Thomasville, GA 229-723-3622
Carolina Packers
Smithfield, NC 800-682-7675
Con Agra Foods
Lincoln, NE 800-332-8400
Continental Deli Foods
Cherokee, IA 712-225-6529
Cumberland Gap Provision Company
Middlesboro, KY 800-331-7154
Finchville Farms
Finchville, KY 502-834-7952
Fresh Mark
Canton, OH 800-860-6777
Fricks Meat Products
Washington, MO 800-241-2209
Gaiser's European Style Provisions
Union, NJ 908-686-3421
Groff Meats
Elizabethtown, PA 717-367-1246
Hillbilly Smokehouse
Rogers, AR 479-636-1927
Honeyville Grain
Rancho Cucamonga, CA 888-810-3212
Hormel Foods Corporation
Fremont, NE 402-721-2300
Humphrey Blue Ribbon Meats
Springfield, IL 800-747-6328
J&B Sausage Company
Waelder, TX 830-788-7511
John Hofmeister & Son
Chicago, IL 800-923-4267
Kelley Meats
Taberg, NY 315-337-4272
Kessler Foods, Inc
Lemoyne, PA 717-763-7162
Levonian Brothers
Troy, NY 518-274-3610
Manger Packing Company
Baltimore, MD 800-227-9262
North Country Smokehouse
Claremont, NH 800-258-4304
Nueske's Applewood Smoked Meats
Wittenberg, WI 800-386-2266
Ohio Packing Company
Columbus, OH 800-282-6403
Parma Sausage Products
Pittsburgh, PA 877-294-4207
Peer Foods Inc.
Chicago, IL 800-365-5644
Quality Meats & Seafood
West Fargo, ND 800-342-4250
R.M. Felts Packing Company
Ivor, VA 888-300-0971
Rinehart Meat Processing
Branson, MO 417-334-2044
Rose Packing Company
South Barrington, IL 800-323-7363
S. Wallace Edward & Sons
Surry, VA 800-290-9213
Sahlen Packing Company
Buffalo, NY 716-852-8677
Sechrist Brothers
Dallastown, PA 717-244-2975
Selwoods Farm Hunting Preserve
Alpine, AL 256-362-7595
Serv-Rite Meat Company
Los Angeles, CA 323-227-1911
Smith Provision Company
Erie, PA 800-334-9151
Swiss-American Sausage Company
Lathrop, CA 209-858-5555
Thomas Packing Company
Columbus, GA 800-729-0976
Troy Frozen Food
Troy, IL 618-667-6332
Tupman-Thurlow Company
Deerfield Beach, FL 954-596-9989
V.W. Joyner & Company
Smithfield, VA 757-357-2161
Webster City Custom Meats
Webster City, IA 888-786-3287
Willies Smoke House
Harrisville, PA 800-742-4184

Steak

Grote & Weigel
Bloomfield, CT 860-242-8528

Head Cheese

Ashland Sausage Company
Carol Stream, IL 630-690-2600
Chicopee Provision Company
Chicopee, MA 800-924-6328
Savoie's Sausage & Food Products
Opelousas, LA 337-948-4115
Sweet Traders
Huntington Beach, CA 714-903-6800
Wimmer's Meat Products
West Point, NE 800-358-0761

Knockwurst

Boesl Packing Company
Baltimore, MD 410-675-1071
Chicopee Provision Company
Chicopee, MA 800-924-6328
Country Smoked Meats
Bowling Green, OH 800-321-4766
David Berg & Company
Chicago, IL 773-278-5195
Matthiesen's Deer & Custom Processing
De Witt, IA 563-659-8409
Raemica
Highland, CA 909-864-1990
Rego's Purity Foods
Honolulu, HI 808-847-3717
Sunset Farm Foods
Valdosta, GA 800-882-1121

Liverwurst

Atlantic Pork & Provisions
Jamaica, NY 800-245-3536
Chicopee Provision Company
Chicopee, MA 800-924-6328
Gaiser's European Style Provisions
Union, NJ 908-686-3421
Grote & Weigel
Bloomfield, CT 860-242-8528
Silver Star Meats
McKees Rocks, PA 800-548-1321
Sunset Farm Foods
Valdosta, GA 800-882-1121

Luncheon Meat

Alderfer Bologna
Harleysville, PA 800-341-1121
Alle Processing Corporation
Maspeth, NY 800-245-5620
Atlantic Pork & Provisions
Jamaica, NY 800-245-3536
Atlantic Premium Brands
Northbrook, IL 847-412-6200
Bar-S Foods Company
Phoenix, AZ 602-264-7272
Berks Packing Company, Inc.
Reading, PA 800-882-3757
Birchwood Foods
Kenosha, WI 800-541-1685
Boar's Head Provisions Company
Sarasota, FL 888-884-2627
Boeckman JJ Wholesale Meats
Dayton, OH 937-222-4679
Boesl Packing Company
Baltimore, MD 410-675-1071
Boyd Sausage Company
Washington, IA 319-653-5715
Broadaway Ham Company
Jonesboro, AR 870-932-6688

C. Roy Meat Products
Yale, MI. 810-387-3957
Cargill Meat Solutions
Timberville, VA 540-896-7041
Carl Buddig & Company
Homewood, IL 800-621-0868
Carolina Packers
Smithfield, NC 800-682-7675
Carolina Pride Foods
Greenwood, SC. 864-229-5611
Charlie's Country Sausage
Minot, ND. 701-838-6302
Charlie's Pride Meats
Vernon, CA 877-866-0982
Chicopee Provision Company
Chicopee, MA. 800-924-6328
Chisesi Brothers Meat Packing Company
New Orleans, LA 800-966-3550
Cibao Meat Product
Bronx, NY. 718-993-5072
Citterio USA Corporation
Freeland, PA 800-435-8888
Country Smoked Meats
Bowling Green, OH 800-321-4766
Curtis Packing Company
Greensboro, NC 336-275-7684
David Berg & Company
Chicago, IL 773-278-5195
Dietz & Watson
Philadelphia, PA 800-333-1974
Dutterer's Home Food Service
Baltimore, MD 410-298-3663
Egon Binkert Meat Products
Baltimore, MD 410-687-5959
Evergood Sausage Company
San Francisco, CA 800-253-6733
Farmland Foods
Carroll, IA. 712-792-1660
Foodbrands America
Oklahoma City, OK 405-290-4000
Frank Wardynski & Sons
Buffalo, NY. 716-854-6083
Fried Provisions Company
Evans City, PA 724-538-3160
Groff Meats
Elizabethtown, PA. 717-367-1246
Gwaltney of Smithfield
Portsmouth, VA. 757-465-0666
Hansel 'N Gretel
Flushing, NY. 718-326-0041
Hazle Park Packing Co
West Hazleton, PA 800-238-4331
Henry J Meat Specialties
Chicago, IL 800-242-1314
Hoffman Sausage Company
Cincinnati, OH 513-621-4160
Hormel Foods Corporation
Austin, MN 800-523-4635
Humboldt Sausage Company
Humboldt, IA 515-332-4121
Hummel Brothers
New Haven, CT 800-828-8978
Ito Cariani Sausage Company
Hayward, CA 510-887-0882
John Volpi & Company
St Louis, MO. 800-288-3439
Kelly Kornbeef Company
Chicago, IL 773-588-2882
Kessler Foods, Inc
Lemoyne, PA. 717-763-7162
Kilgus Meats
Toledo, OH 419-472-9721
Kitts Meat Processing
Dedham, IA. 712-683-5622
Land O'Frost
Lansing, IL 800-323-3308
Land O'Frost
Searcy, AR 800-643-5654
Larsen Packers
Burwick, NS 902-538-8060
Lengerich Meats
Zanesville, IN 260-638-4123
Leona Meat Plant
Troy, PA. 570-297-3574
Levonian Brothers
Troy, NY 518-274-3610
Locustdale Meat Packing
Locustdale, PA 570-875-1270
Lower Foods
Richmond, UT. 435-258-2449
Manda Fine Meats
Baton Rouge, LA 225-344-7636
Marshallville Packing Company
Marshallville, OH 330-855-2871
Martin Rosol's
New Britain, CT 860-223-2707
Milan Salami Company
Oakland, CA 510-654-7055
Mishler Packing Company
Lagrange, IN. 260-768-4156
Murphy House
Louisburg, NC 919-496-6054
Norbest
Midvale, UT 800-453-5327
O'Brien & Company
Bellevue, NE. 800-433-7567
Ohio Packing Company
Columbus, OH 800-282-6403
Otto W Liebold & Company
Flint, MI 800-999-6328
Palmyra Bologna
Palmyra, PA. 717-838-6336
Parma Sausage Products
Pittsburgh, PA. 877-294-4207
Patrick Cudahy
Cudahy, WI. 800-486-6900
Pfeffer's Country Mkt.
Sauk Centre, MN 320-352-6490
Plumrose USA
East Brunswick, NJ. 800-526-4909
R.L. Zeigler Company
Tuscaloosa, AL. 800-392-6328
Raemica
Highland, CA 909-864-1990
Rego's Purity Foods
Honolulu, HI. 808-847-3717
Rendulic Packing
McKeesport, PA 412-678-9541
Robinsons Sausage Company
London, KY 606-864-2914
Roman Packing Company
Norfolk, NE. 800-373-5990
Russer Foods
Buffalo, NY. 800-828-7021
Saag's Products
San Leandro, CA. 800-352-7224
Sara Lee Corporation
Downers Grove, IL. 630-598-8100
Sausage Shoppe
Cleveland, OH 216-351-5213
Saval Foods
Elkridge, MD 800-527-2825
Schaller & Weber
Astoria, NY. 800-847-4115
Sculli Brothers
Yeadon, PA 215-336-1223
Sechrist Brothers
Dallastown, PA. 717-244-2975
Sheinman Provision Company
Philadelphia, PA 215-473-7065
Shofar Kosher Foods
Linden, NJ. 888-874-6327
Siena Foods
Toronto, ON 800-465-0422
Smith Packing Regional Meat
Utica, NY
Smith Provision Company
Erie, PA. 800-334-9151
Snow Ball Foods
Williamstown, NJ 856-629-4081
Spring Grove Foods
Miamisburg, OH. 937-866-4311
Standard Beef Company
Foxboro, MA 203-787-2164
Stevens Sausage Company
Smithfield, NC 800-338-0561
Stonies Sausage Shop Inc
Perryville, MO 888-546-2540
Sunset Farm Foods
Valdosta, GA. 800-882-1121
Superior's Brand Meats
Massillon, OH. 330-830-0356
Swift & Company
Greeley, CO. 970-506-8000
Tennessee Valley PackingCompany
Columbia, TN. 931-388-2623
Thumann's
Carlstadt, NJ 201-935-3636
Troy Frozen Food
Troy, IL 618-667-6332
Troyers Trail Bologna
Dundee, OH 877-893-2414
Tupman-Thurlow Company
Deerfield Beach, FL 954-596-9989
United Provision Meat Company
Columbus, OH 614-252-1126
Upstate Farms Cooperative
Buffalo, NY. 716-892-2121
V.W. Joyner & Company
Smithfield, VA 757-357-2161
Vienna Meat Products
Scarborough, ON 800-588-1931
Warren & Son Meat Processing
Whipple, OH. 740-585-2421
Wimmer's Meat Products
West Point, NE 800-358-0761

Canned

Continental Deli Foods
Cherokee, IA. 712-225-6529
Lowell Provision Company
Lowell, MA. 978-454-5603

Olive Loaf

Allen Canning Company
Siloam Springs, AR 800-234-2553
Bryant Preserving Company
Alma, AR 800-634-2413
Cajun Chef Products
Saint Martinville, LA 337-394-7112
Farmland Foods
Kansas City, MO. 888-327-6526
Grain Millers Eugene
Eugene, OR. 800-443-8972
McCain Foods USA
Colton, CA 800-938-7799
Wimmer's Meat Products
West Point, NE 800-358-0761

Pastrami

A. Stein Meat Products
Brooklyn, NY 718-492-0760
Alderfer Bologna
Harleysville, PA 800-341-1121
Best Provision Co Inc.
Newark, NJ 800-631-4466
Bottomline Foods
Davie, FL 954-843-0562
Carando Gourmet Frozen Foods
Agawam, MA 888-227-2636
Carl Buddig & Company
Homewood, IL 800-621-0868
Charlie's Pride Meats
Vernon, CA 877-866-0982
Chicago 58 Food Products
Woodbridge, ON. 416-603-4244
Curly's Foods
Edina, MN. 800-722-1127
David Berg & Company
Chicago, IL 773-278-5195
Dutterer's Home Food Service
Baltimore, MD 410-298-3663
Evergood Sausage Company
San Francisco, CA 800-253-6733
Henry J Meat Specialties
Chicago, IL 800-242-1314
Kelly Kornbeef Company
Chicago, IL 773-588-2882
Levonian Brothers
Troy, NY 518-274-3610
Lower Foods
Richmond, UT. 435-258-2449
Marathon Enterprises
Englewood, NJ 800-722-7388
Nossack Fine Meats
Red Deer, AB 403-346-5006
Otto W Liebold & Company
Flint, MI 800-999-6328
Sara Lee Corporation
Downers Grove, IL. 630-598-8100
Saval Foods
Elkridge, MD 800-527-2825
Snow Ball Foods
Williamstown, NJ 856-629-4081
Vienna Meat Products
Scarborough, ON 800-588-1931

Pepperoni

Big Chief Meat Snacks In
Calgary, AB. 403-264-2641

Burke Corporation
Nevada, IA 800-654-1152

Always make it your best® with Burke fully cooked meats. We specialize in Italian sausage, beef, and pork toppings, meatballs, taco meats, shredded meats, pepperoni, bacon, Canadian-style bacon, chicken and beef strips. Additionally, we offer a variety of specialty products: Hand-Pinched Style® brand toppings, chorizo, gyro topping, andouille sausage, and breakfast patties and links.

Busseto Foods
Fresno, CA 800-628-2633
Cattaneo Brothers
San Luis Obispo, CA 800-243-8537
Country Smoked Meats
Bowling Green, OH 800-321-4766
Farmland Foods
Kansas City, MO. 888-327-6526
Fiorucci Foods
Colonial Heights, VA 800-524-7775
Foodbrands America
Oklahoma City, OK 405-290-4000
Hormel Foods Corporation
Algona, IA. 515-295-8777
Hormel Foods Corporation
Austin, MN 800-523-4635
Humboldt Sausage Company
Humboldt, IA 515-332-4121
Ito Cariani Sausage Company
Hayward, CA 510-887-0882
Larsen Packers
Burwick, NS 902-538-8060
Milan Salami Company
Oakland, CA 510-654-7055
Quality Sausage Company
Dallas, TX. 214-634-3400
Sangudo Custom Meat Packers
Sangudo, AB. 888-785-3353
Sara Lee Corporation
Downers Grove, IL. 630-598-8100
Smokey Farm Meats
Carbon, AB 403-272-6587
Spring Grove Foods
Miamisburg, OH. 937-866-4311
Stawnichy Holdings
Mundare, AB 888-764-7646
Swift & Company
Greeley, CO. 970-506-8000
Swiss American Sausage Corporation
Lathrop, CA 209-858-5555
Swiss-American Sausage Company
Lathrop, CA 209-858-5555
Upstate Farms Cooperative
Buffalo, NY. 716-892-2121
Viau Foods
Laval, QC 800-663-5492

Prosciutto

Fiorucci Foods
Colonial Heights, VA 800-524-7775
Hormel Foods Corporation
Austin, MN 800-523-4635
Parma Sausage Products
Pittsburgh, PA. 877-294-4207
Santa Maria Foods
Branpton, ON 905-790-1991
Siena Foods
Toronto, ON 800-465-0422

Salami

Applegate Farms
Bridgewater, NJ 908-725-2768
Baier's Sausage & Meats
Red Deer, AB 403-346-1535
Boesl Packing Company
Baltimore, MD 410-675-1071
Burke Corporation
Nevada, IA 800-654-1152

Always make it your best® with Burke fully cooked meats. We specialize in Italian sausage, beef, and pork toppings, meatballs, taco meats, shredded meats, pepperoni, bacon, Canadian-style bacon, chicken and beef strips. Additionally, we offer a variety of specialty products: Hand-Pinched Style® brand toppings, chorizo, gyro topping, andouille sausage, and breakfast patties and links.

Busseto Foods
Fresno, CA 800-628-2633
Cargill Meat Solutions
Timberville, VA 540-896-7041
Charlie's Country Sausage
Minot, ND. 701-838-6302
Chicago 58 Food Products
Woodbridge, ON. 416-603-4244
Chicopee Provision Company
Chicopee, MA. 800-924-6328
Chisesi Brothers Meat Packing Company
New Orleans, LA 800-966-3550
Cibao Meat Product
Bronx, NY. 718-993-5072
Farmland Foods
Kansas City, MO. 888-327-6526
Fiorucci Foods
Colonial Heights, VA 800-524-7775
Foodbrands America
Oklahoma City, OK 405-290-4000
Hormel Foods Corporation
Austin, MN 800-523-4635
Humboldt Sausage Company
Humboldt, IA 515-332-4121
Ito Cariani Sausage Company
Hayward, CA 510-887-0882
John Volpi & Company
St Louis, MO. 800-288-3439
Kessler Foods, Inc
Lemoyne, PA. 717-763-7162
Larsen Packers
Burwick, NS 902-538-8060
Marathon Enterprises
Englewood, NJ 800-722-7388
Milan Salami Company
Oakland, CA 510-654-7055
Parma Sausage Products
Pittsburgh, PA. 877-294-4207
Patrick Cudahy
Cudahy, WI. 800-486-6900
Plumrose USA
East Brunswick, NJ. 800-526-4909
Raemica
Highland, CA 909-864-1990
Santa Maria Foods
Branpton, ON 905-790-1991
Sara Lee Corporation
Downers Grove, IL. 630-598-8100
Schaller & Weber
Astoria, NY. 800-847-4115
Sculli Brothers
Yeadon, PA 215-336-1223
Siena Foods
Toronto, ON 800-465-0422
Spring Grove Foods
Miamisburg, OH. 937-866-4311
Stawnichy Holdings
Mundare, AB 888-764-7646
Swift & Company
Greeley, CO. 970-506-8000
Swiss American Sausage Corporation
Lathrop, CA 209-858-5555
Swiss-American Sausage Company
Lathrop, CA 209-858-5555
Upstate Farms Cooperative
Buffalo, NY. 716-892-2121

Sausages

A.L. Duck Jr Inc
Zuni, VA 757-562-2387
Abbyland Foods
Abbotsford, WI. 800-732-5483
Adolf's Meats & Sausage Kitchen
Hartford, CT 860-522-1588
Aidell's Sausage Company
San Leandro, CA. 800-546-5795
Alaska Sausage and Seafood Company
Anchorage, AK. 800-798-3636
Alewel's Country Meats
Warrensburg, MO 800-353-8553
Alexian Pates/GroezingerProvisions
Neptune, NJ 800-927-9473
Aliments Prince Foods
Anjou, QC. 800-361-3898
Alpine Meats
Stockton, CA. 800-399-6328
Applegate Farms
Bridgewater, NJ 908-725-2768
AquaCuisine
Eagle, ID. 208-323-2782
Aries Prepared Beef
Burbank, CA. 818-526-4855
Armbrust Meats
Medford, WI 715-748-3102
Arnold's Meat Food Products
Brooklyn, NY 800-633-7023
Ashland Sausage Company
Carol Stream, IL 630-690-2600
Atlantic Premium Brands
Northbrook, IL 847-412-6200
Baier's Sausage & Meats
Red Deer, AB 403-346-1535
Baja Foods
Chicago, IL. 773-376-9030
Bakalars Brothers Sausage Company
La Crosse, WI. 608-784-0384
Bar-S Foods Company
Phoenix, AZ 602-264-7272
Berks Packing Company, Inc.
Reading, PA 800-882-3757
Big City Reds
Omaha, NE 800-759-5275
Black's Barbecue
Lockhart, TX. 512-398-2712
Blue Grass Quality Meat
Covington, KY 859-331-7100
Boesl Packing Company
Baltimore, MD 410-675-1071
Bouma Meats
Provost, AB. 780-753-2092
Bowser Meat Processing
Meriden, KS 785-484-2454
Boyd Sausage Company
Washington, IA. 319-653-5715
Braham Food Locker Service
Braham, MN. 320-396-2636
Bridgford Foods Corporation
Anaheim, CA 800-527-2105
Broadleaf Venison Usa
Vernon, CA. 800-336-3844
Brockton Beef & Provisions Corporation
Brockton, MA. 508-583-4703
Brook Meadow ProvisionscCorporation
Hagerstown, MD. 301-739-3107
Bryan Foods
West Point, MS. 662-494-3741
Bryant's Meats
Taylorsville, MS 601-785-6507
Burgers Smokehouse
California, MO 800-624-5426
Burke Corporation
Nevada, IA 800-654-1152

Always make it your best® with Burke fully cooked meats. We specialize in Italian sausage, beef, and pork toppings, meatballs, taco meats, shredded meats, pepperoni, bacon, Canadian-style bacon, chicken and beef strips. Additionally, we offer a variety of specialty products: Hand-Pinched Style® brand toppings, chorizo, gyro topping, andouille sausage, and breakfast patties and links.

Butcher Shop
Beaverlodge, AB. 780-354-8600
Camellia General Provision
Buffalo, NY. 716-893-5352
Caribbean Food Delights
Tappan, NY. 845-398-3000
Carl Buddig & Company
Homewood, IL 800-621-0868
Carl Streit & Son Company
Neptune, NJ 732-775-0803
Carolina Packers
Smithfield, NC 800-682-7675
Casa Di Bertacchi
Vineland, NJ 800-818-9261
Casa di Carfagna
Columbus, OH 614-846-6340
Casual Gourmet Foods
Clearwater, FL 727-298-8307
Cattaneo Brothers
San Luis Obispo, CA 800-243-8537
Caughman's Meat Plant
Lexington, SC. 803-356-0076
Cedaredge Meats
Cedaredge, CO 970-856-6113
Center Locker Service Company
Center, MO 573-267-3343
Charlie's Country Sausage
Minot, ND. 701-838-6302
Cher-Make Sausage Company
Manitowoc, WI. 800-242-7679

Chicopee Provision Company
Chicopee, MA. 800-924-6328
Chisesi Brothers Meat Packing Company
New Orleans, LA 800-966-3550
Cibao Meat Product
Bronx, NY. 718-993-5072
Cifelli & Sons
South River, NJ. 732-238-0090
Cimpl Meats
Yankton, SD 605-665-1665
Cloverdale Foods Company
Mandan, ND 800-669-9511
Clyde's Italian & German Sausage
Denver, CO 303-433-8744
Community Market & Deli
Lindstrom, MN 651-257-1128
ConAgra Foods Inc
Omaha, NE 402-595-7300
ConAgra Foods/Eckrich
Omaha, NE 800-327-4424
Conecuh Sausage Company
Evergreen, AL. 800-726-0507
Conti Packing Company
Rochester, NY. 585-424-2500
Corte Provisions
Newark, NJ 201-653-7246
Couch's Country Style Sausages
Cleveland, OH 216-823-2332
Country Pies
Coombs, BC 250-248-6415
Country Smoked Meats
Bowling Green, OH 800-321-4766
Counts Sausage Company
Prosperity, SC 803-364-2392
Crawford Sausage Company
Chicago, IL 866-653-2479
Crocetti Oakdale Packing
East Bridgewater, MA 508-587-0035
Crofton & Sons
Brandon, FL 800-878-7675
Cropp Cooperative-Organic Valley
La Farge, WI 888-444-6455
Culver Duck
Middlebury, IN 800-825-9225
Cumberland Gap Provision Company
Middlesboro, KY 800-331-7154
D'Artagnan
Newark, NJ 800-327-8246
Dallas City Packing
Dallas, TX. 214-948-3901
Dankworth Packing Company
Ballinger, TX 325-365-3552
David Berg & Company
Chicago, IL 773-278-5195
Dean Sausage Company
Attalla, AL 800-228-0704
Debbie D's Jerky & Sausage
Tillamook, OR 503-842-2622
Decker & Son Company
Colorado Springs, CO. 719-634-8311
Dennison Meat Locker
Dennison, MN. 507-645-8734
Diggs Packing Company
Columbia, MO 573-449-2995
DiGregorio Food Products
St Louis, MO. 314-776-1062
Dinner Bell Meat Product
Concord, VA
Dino's Sausage & Meat Company
Utica, NY 315-732-2661
Dohar Meats
Cleveland, OH 216-241-4197
Dreymiller & Kray
Hampshire, IL. 847-683-2271
Duis Meat Processing
Concordia, KS. 800-281-4295
Dutch Packing Company
Miami, FL. 305-871-3640
E.W. Knauss & Son
Quakertown, PA 800-648-4220
Edmonton Meat Packing Company
Edmonton, AB 800-361-6328
Egon Binkert Meat Products
Baltimore, MD 410-687-5959
Ellsworth Locker
Ellsworth, MN 507-967-2544
Elmwood Lockers
Elmwood, IL. 309-742-8929
Elore Enterprises
Miami, FL. 305-477-1650
Enslin & Son Packing Company
Hattiesburg, MS 800-898-4687

European Egg Noodle Manufacturing
Edmonton, AB 780-453-6767
Evergood Sausage Company
San Francisco, CA 800-253-6733
F&Y Enterprises
Wauconda, IL 847-526-0620
Fabbri Sausage Manufacturing
Chicago, IL 312-829-6363
Fanestil Packing Company
Emporia, KS 620-342-6354
Fargo Packing & SausagecCompany
West Fargo, ND. 800-342-4250
Farmland Foods
Kansas City, MO. 888-327-6526
Ferris Stahl-Meyer Packing Corporation
Bronx, NY. 718-328-0059
Foell Packing Company
Naperville, IL 919-776-0592
Fontanini Italian Meats & Sausages
McCook, IL. 800-331-6328
Foodbrands America
Oklahoma City, OK 405-290-4000
Fortenberry Ice Company
Kodak, TN. 865-933-2568
Foster Farms
Demopolis, AL 800-255-7227
Frank Wardynski & Sons
Buffalo, NY. 716-854-6083
Frank's Foods
Hilo, HI 808-959-9121
Fredericksburg Lockers/OPA's Smoke
Fredericksburg, TX. 800-543-6750
Fresh Mark
Canton, OH 800-860-6777
Fricks Meat Products
Washington, MO. 800-241-2209
Fried Provisions Company
Evans City, PA 724-538-3160
Gaiser's European Style Provisions
Union, NJ 908-686-3421
Gaspar's Sausage Company
North Dartmouth, MA 800-542-2038
Gem Meat Packing Company
Boise, ID 208-375-9424
Gerhard's Napa Valley Sausage
Napa, CA. 707-252-4116
Glazier Packing Company
Potsdam, NY. 315-265-2500
Glazier Packing Company
Malone, NY. 518-483-4990
Glier's Meats
Covington, KY 800-446-3882
Gold Star Sausage Company
Denver, CO 800-258-7229
Grant Park Packing
Chicago, IL 312-421-4096
Grimm's Fine Food
Calgary, AB. 877-577-5220
Grote & Weigel
Bloomfield, CT. 860-242-8528
Gunnoe Farms-Sausage & Salad Company
Charleston, WV 304-343-7686
Gwaltney of Smithfield
Portsmouth, VA. 757-465-0666
H&B Packing Company
Waco, TX 254-752-2506
Hahn Brothers
Westminster, MD 800-227-7675
Hansel 'N Gretel
Flushing, NY. 718-326-0041
Hatfield Quality Meats
Hatfield, PA. 800-523-5291
Hazle Park Packing Co
West Hazleton, PA 800-238-4331
Heinkel's Packing Company
Decatur, IL 800-594-2738
Hillbilly Smokehouse
Rogers, AR 479-636-1927
Hoffman Sausage Company
Cincinnati, OH 513-621-4160
Hofmann Sausage Company
Syracuse, NY 800-724-8410
Hoople Country Kitchens
Rockport, IN 812-649-2351
Hormel Foods Corporation
Fremont, NE 402-721-2300
Hormel Foods Corporation
Maitland, FL 407-660-1433
Hormel Foods Corporation
Austin, MN 800-523-4635
Hot Springs Packing Company
Hot Springs, AR 800-535-0449

Humboldt Sausage Company
Humboldt, IA 515-332-4121
Hummel Brothers
New Haven, CT 800-828-8978
Humphrey Blue Ribbon Meats
Springfield, IL. 800-747-6328
Huse's Country Meats
Malone, TX. 254-533-2205
Independent Meat Company
Twin Falls, ID 208-733-0980
Indian Valley Meats
Indian, AK. 907-653-7511
Isernio Sausage Company
Seattle, WA 888-495-8674
Ito Cariani Sausage Company
Hayward, CA 510-887-0882
Ittels Meats
Howard Lake, MN 320-543-2285
J&B Sausage Company
Waelder, TX 830-788-7511
Jody Maroni's Sausage Kingdom
Burbank, CA
John Morrell & Company
Cincinnati, OH 800-345-0743
Johnsonville Food Company
Sheboygan Falls, WI. 888-556-2728
Jones Dairy Farm
Fort Atkinson, WI. 800-563-1004
Kayem Foods
Chelsea, MA 800-426-6100
Kelley Foods of Alabama
Elba, AL 334-897-5761
Kelley Meats
Taberg, NY 315-337-4272
Kent Quality Foods
Grand Rapids, MI 800-748-0141
Kessler Foods, Inc
Lemoyne, PA. 717-763-7162
Kilgus Meats
Toledo, OH 419-472-9721
Kiolbassa Provision Company
San Antonio, TX. 800-456-5465
Kirby & Holloway Provisions
Harrington, DE 800-995-4729
Koegel Meats
Flint, MI 810-238-3685
Konetzkos Market
Browerville, MN. 320-594-2915
Kowalski Sausage Company
Hamtramck, MI. 800-482-2400
Lad's Smokehouse Catering
Needville, TX 979-793-6210
Larry's Sausage Corporation
Fayetteville, NC 910-483-5148
Larsen Packers
Burwick, NS 902-538-8060
Laurent Meat Market
Marrero, LA 504-341-1771
Le Pique-Nique
Oakland, CA 800-400-6454
Lebermuth Company
South Bend, IN 800-648-1123
Lee Kum Kee
Flushing, NY. 800-346-7562
Lees Sausage Company
Orangeburg, SC 803-534-5517
Leona Meat Plant
Troy, PA. 570-297-3574
Leone Provision Company
Cape Coral, FL 239-458-0013
Levonian Brothers
Troy, NY 518-274-3610
Lewis Sausage Corporation
Burgaw, NC. 910-259-2642
Little Rhody Brand Frankfurts
Johnston, RI 401-831-0815
Locustdale Meat Packing
Locustdale, PA 570-875-1270
Lords Sausage & CountryhHam
Dexter, GA 800-342-6002
Lowell Packing Company
Fitzgerald, GA 800-342-0313
Lucys Foods
Latrobe, PA. 724-539-1430
M K Meat Processing Plant
Burton, TX 979-289-4022
Mac's Farms Sausage Company
Newton Grove, NC. 910-594-0095
Manda Fine Meats
Baton Rouge, LA 225-344-7636
Marathon Enterprises
Englewood, NJ 800-722-7388

Marcel et Henri Charcuterie Francaise
South San Francisco, CA 800-227-6436
Marshallville Packing Company
Marshallville, OH 330-855-2871
McKenzie of Vermont
Burlington, VT 802-864-4585
McLane's Meats
Wetaskiwin, AB 780-352-4321
Meating Place
Buffalo, NY. 716-885-3623
Medeiros Farms
Kalaheo, HI 808-332-8211
Mello's North End Manufacturings
Fall River, MA 800-673-2320
Mertz Sausage Company
San Antonio, TX. 210-433-3263
Michael's Provision Company
Fall River, MA 508-672-0982
Michel's Magnifique
New York, NY 212-431-1070
Mike's Meats
Eitzen, MN 507-495-3336
Milan Provision Company
Flushing, NY. 718-899-7678
Milan Salami Company
Oakland, CA 510-654-7055
Miller Brothers PackingcCompany
Sylvester, GA 229-776-2014
Miller's Meat Market
Red Bud, IL. 618-282-3334
Milling Sausage Company
Milwaukee, WI 414-645-2677
Momence Packing Company
Momence, IL. 815-472-6485
Neese Country Sausage
Greensboro, NC 800-632-1010
Neto Sausage Company
Santa Clara, CA 888-482-6386
New Glarus Foods
New Glarus, WI 800-356-6685
New Packing Company
Chicago, IL 312-666-1314
Niemuth's Steak & Chop Shop
Waupaca, WI. 715-258-2666
Norpaco
Middletown, CT 800-252-0222
North Country Smokehouse
Claremont, NH 800-258-4304
North Side Foods Corporation
Arnold, PA 800-486-2201
Nossack Fine Meats
Red Deer, AB 403-346-5006
Nueske's Applewood Smoked Meats
Wittenberg, WI 800-386-2266
O'Brien & Company
Bellevue, NE. 800-433-7567
Odom's Tennessee Pride Sausage Company
Madison, TN. 800-327-6269
Ohio Packing Company
Columbus, OH 800-282-6403
Omaha Steaks International
Omaha, NE 800-562-0500
Ossian Seafood Meats
Ossian, IN 260-622-4191
Otto W Liebold & Company
Flint, MI 800-999-6328
Owens Country Sausage
Richardson, TX. 800-966-9367
Paris Frozen Foods
Hillsboro, IL 217-532-3822
Parma Sausage Products
Pittsburgh, PA 877-294-4207
Patrick Cudahy
Cudahy, WI 800-486-6900
Peer Foods Inc.
Chicago, IL 800-365-5644
Pekarna's Meat Market
Jordan, MN 952-492-6101
Pfeffer's Country Mkt.
Sauk Centre, MN 320-352-6490
Piller Sausages & Delicatessens
Waterloo, ON 800-265-2628
Pinter's Packing Plant
Dorchester, WI 715-654-5444
Pioneer Packing Company
Bowling Green, OH 419-352-5283
Pokanoket Ostrich Farm
South Dartmouth, MA 508-992-6188
Polka Home Style Sausage
Chicago, IL 773-221-0395
Quality Meats & Seafood
West Fargo, ND. 800-342-4250
Queen City Sausage
Cincinnati, OH 877-544-5588
R & D Sausage Company
Cleveland, OH 216-692-1832
Raemica
Highland, CA 909-864-1990
Ray's Sausage Company Inc
Cleveland, OH 216-921-8782
Real Kosher Sausage Company
Newark, NJ 973-690-5394
Register Meat Company
Cottondale, FL 850-352-4269
Rego's Purity Foods
Honolulu, HI 808-847-3717
Rinehart Meat Processing
Branson, MO. 417-334-2044
Riverside Packers
Drumheller, AB. 403-823-2595
Robbins Packing Company
Statesboro, GA 912-764-7503
Robinsons Sausage Company
London, KY 606-864-2914
Roma Packing Company
Chicago, IL 773-927-7371
Roman Packing Company
Norfolk, NE. 800-373-5990
Roman Sausage Company
Santa Clara, CA 800-497-7462
Roode Packing Company
Fairbury, NE 402-729-2253
Rudolph's Market & Sausage Factory
Dallas, TX. 214-741-1874
S. Wallace Edward & Sons
Surry, VA. 800-290-9213
S.W. Meat & Provision Company
Phoenix, AZ 602-275-2000
Saag's Products
San Leandro, CA. 800-352-7224
Sahlen Packing Company
Buffalo, NY. 716-852-8677
Sangudo Custom Meat Packers
Sangudo, AB. 888-785-3353
Sara Lee Corporation
Downers Grove, IL. 630-598-8100
Sardinha Sausage
Somerset, MA. 800-678-0178
Sausage Shoppe
Cleveland, OH 216-351-5213
Sausages by Amy
Chicago, IL 312-829-2250
Savoie's Sausage & Food Products
Opelousas, LA. 337-948-4115
Schaller & Weber
Astoria, NY. 800-847-4115
Schneider Foods
Surrey, BC. 604-576-1191
Scott Hams
Greenville, KY 800-318-1353
Sculli Brothers
Yeadon, PA 215-336-1223
Sechrist Brothers
Dallastown, PA 717-244-2975
Selecto Sausage Company
Houston, TX 713-926-1626
Serv-Rite Meat Company
Los Angeles, CA. 323-227-1911
Sheinman Provision Company
Philadelphia, PA 215-473-7065
Siena Foods
Toronto, ON 800-465-0422
Silver Creek Specialty Meats
Oshkosh, WI 920-232-3581
Silver Star Meats
McKees Rocks, PA 800-548-1321
Simeus Foods Internatio nal
Mansfield, TX. 888-772-3663
Smith Packing Regional Meat
Utica, NY
Smith Provision Company
Erie, PA 800-334-9151
Smokey Denmark Sausage
Austin, TX. 512-385-0718
Smokey Farm Meats
Carbon, AB 403-272-6587
Smolich Brothers
Joliet, IL 815-727-2144
Sparrer Sausage Company
Chicago, IL 800-666-3287
Spring Grove Foods
Miamisburg, OH 937-866-4311
Stanley Provision Company
Manchester, CT. 888-688-6347
Stauber Performance Ingredients
Fullerton, CA 888-441-4233
Stawnichy Holdings
Mundare, AB 888-764-7646
Stevens Sausage Company
Smithfield, NC 800-338-0561
Stewarts Market
Yelm, WA 360-458-2091
Stonies Sausage Shop Inc
Perryville, MO 888-546-2540
Strasburg Provision
Strasburg, OH 800-207-6009
Striplings
Moultrie, GA. 229-985-4226
Sunergia Soyfoods
Charlottesville, VA 800-693-5134
Sunnydale Meats
Gaffney, SC. 864-489-6091
SW Red Smith
Davie, FL 954-581-1996
Swiss American Sausage Corporation
Lathrop, CA 209-858-5555
Swiss-American Sausage Company
Lathrop, CA 209-858-5555
T.L. Herring & Company
Wilson, NC 252-291-1141
Tennessee Valley PackingCompany
Columbia, TN 931-388-2623
Texas Sausage Company
Austin, TX. 512-472-6707
Thomas Packing Company
Columbus, GA 800-729-0976
Tofield Packers Ltd
Tofield, AB 780-662-4842
Tomasinos Sausage
Canton, OH 330-454-4171
Troy Frozen Food
Troy, IL 618-667-6332
Tupman-Thurlow Company
Deerfield Beach, FL 954-596-9989
United Packing
Providence, RI 401-751-6935
Upstate Farms Cooperative
Buffalo, NY. 716-892-2121
Uvalde Meat Processing
Uvalde, TX 830-278-6247
V & V Supremo Foods
Chicago, IL 888-887-8773
Valenie Packers
Colinton, AB. 780-675-5881
Vermilion Packers Ltd
Vermilion, AB. 780-853-4622
Viau Foods
Laval, QC 800-663-5492
Victor Ostrowski & Son
Baltimore, MD 410-327-8935
Vienna Meat Products
Scarborough, ON 800-588-1931
Vienna Sausage Company
Chicago, IL 800-366-3647
Vollwerth & Baroni Companies
Hancock, MI 800-562-7620
WA Bean & Sons
Bangor, ME. 800-649-1958
Waco Beef & Pork Processors
Waco, TX 254-772-4669
Wampler's Farm Sausage Company
Lenoir City, TN. 800-728-7243
Warren & Son Meat Processing
Whipple, OH. 740-585-2421
Whitaker Foods
Waterloo, IA 800-553-7490
Willies Smoke House
Harrisville, PA. 800-742-4184
Wimmer's Meat Products
West Point, NE 800-358-0761
Wolfson Casing Corporation
Mount Vernon, NY 800-221-8042
Woods Smoked Meats
Bowling Green, MO 800-458-8426
Zummo Meat Company
Beaumont, TX. 409-842-1810

Andouille

Applegate Farms
Bridgewater, NJ 908-725-2768

Burke Corporation
Nevada, IA 800-654-1152

Always make it your best® with Burke fully cooked meats. We specialize in Italian sausage, beef, and pork toppings, meatballs, taco meats, shredded meats, pepperoni, bacon, Canadian-style bacon, chicken and beef strips. Additionally, we offer a variety of specialty products: Hand-Pinched Style® brand toppings, chorizo, gyro topping, andouille sausage, and breakfast patties and links.

D'Artagnan
Newark, NJ 800-327-8246
Grote & Weigel
Bloomfield, CT 860-242-8528
Laurent Meat Market
Marrero, LA 504-341-1771
Parma Sausage Products
Pittsburgh, PA 877-294-4207
Savoie's Sausage & Food Products
Opelousas, LA 337-948-4115
Thomas Packing Company
Columbus, GA 800-729-0976

Blood

Bavarian Meat Products
Seattle, WA 206-448-3540
Chicopee Provision Company
Chicopee, MA 800-924-6328
Rego's Purity Foods
Honolulu, HI 808-847-3717

Bockwurst

Chicopee Provision Company
Chicopee, MA 800-924-6328
Country Smoked Meats
Bowling Green, OH 800-321-4766
Koegel Meats
Flint, MI 810-238-3685

Boudin

Comeaux's
Lafayette, LA 800-323-2492
Marcel et Henri Charcuterie Francaise
South San Francisco, CA 800-227-6436
Savoie's Sausage & Food Products
Opelousas, LA 337-948-4115
Stallings Headcheese Company
Houston, TX 713-523-1751
Sunset Farm Foods
Valdosta, GA 800-882-1121
Woods Smoked Meats
Bowling Green, MO 800-458-8426
Zummo Meat Company
Beaumont, TX 409-842-1810

Bratwurst

Chicopee Provision Company
Chicopee, MA 800-924-6328
Country Smoked Meats
Bowling Green, OH 800-321-4766
Cropp Cooperative-Organic Valley
La Farge, WI 888-444-6455
Elmwood Lockers
Elmwood, IL 309-742-8929
F.B. Purnell Sausage Company
Simpsonville, KY 800-626-1512
Grote & Weigel
Bloomfield, CT 860-242-8528
Kayem Foods
Chelsea, MA 800-426-6100
Kilgus Meats
Toledo, OH 419-472-9721
Koegel Meats
Flint, MI 810-238-3685
New Braunfels Smokehouse
New Braunfels, TX 800-537-6932
Raemica
Highland, CA 909-864-1990
S.W. Meat & Provision Company
Phoenix, AZ 602-275-2000
Smolich Brothers
Joliet, IL 815-727-2144
Waco Beef & Pork Processors
Waco, TX 254-772-4669
Wimmer's Meat Products
West Point, NE 800-358-0761

Braunschweiger

Farmland Foods
Kansas City, MO 888-327-6526

Cajun

Fontanini Italian Meats & Sausages
McCook, IL 800-331-6328

Casings: Sausage, Pork, Beef

Austrade Food Ingredients
Palm Beach Gdns, FL 561-586-7145
Con Yeager Spice Company
Zelienople, PA 800-222-2460
Dewied International
San Antonio, TX 800-992-5600
Hofmann Sausage Company
Syracuse, NY 800-724-8410
International Casing Group
Chicago, IL 800-825-5151
International Casings Group
Santa Fe Springs, CA 800-635-9518
International Casings Group, Inc
Chicago, IL 800-825-5151
Koegel Meats
Flint, MI 810-238-3685
Marie F
Markham, ON 800-365-4464
Nitta Casings
Somerville, NJ 908-218-4400
Oversea Casing Company
Seattle, WA 800-682-6845
Package Concepts & Materials Inc
Greenville, SC 800-424-7264
Syracuse Casing Company
Syracuse, NY 315-475-0309
World Casing Corporation
Maspeth, NY 800-221-4887

Chicken

Bell & Evans
Fredericksburg, PA 717-865-6626
Kayem Foods
Chelsea, MA 800-426-6100
Lucys Foods
Latrobe, PA 724-539-1430
WA Bean & Sons
Bangor, ME 800-649-1958

Chorizo

Arnold's Meat Food Products
Brooklyn, NY 800-633-7023
Burke Corporation
Nevada, IA 800-654-1152

Always make it your best® with Burke fully cooked meats. We specialize in Italian sausage, beef, and pork toppings, meatballs, taco meats, shredded meats, pepperoni, bacon, Canadian-style bacon, chicken and beef strips. Additionally, we offer a variety of specialty products: Hand-Pinched Style® brand toppings, chorizo, gyro topping, andouille sausage, and breakfast patties and links.

Carmelita Provisions Company
Monterey Park, CA 323-262-6751
Corte Provisions
Newark, NJ 201-653-7246
Country Smoked Meats
Bowling Green, OH 800-321-4766
D'Artagnan
Newark, NJ 800-327-8246
F.B. Purnell Sausage Company
Simpsonville, KY 800-626-1512
Lucys Foods
Latrobe, PA 724-539-1430
Parma Sausage Products
Pittsburgh, PA 877-294-4207
Sunset Farm Foods
Valdosta, GA 800-882-1121
V & V Supremo Foods
Chicago, IL 888-887-8773
Waco Beef & Pork Processors
Waco, TX 254-772-4669

Chourico

Gaspar's Sausage Company
North Dartmouth, MA 800-542-2038
Mertz Sausage Company
San Antonio, TX 210-433-3263
Odessa Tortilla & TamaleFactory
Odessa, TX 800-753-2445
Sardinha Sausage
Somerset, MA 800-678-0178

Hot

Boesl Packing Company
Baltimore, MD 410-675-1071
Chicopee Provision Company
Chicopee, MA 800-924-6328
D'Artagnan
Newark, NJ 800-327-8246
E.W. Knauss & Son
Quakertown, PA 800-648-4220
Farmland Foods
Kansas City, MO 888-327-6526
Gecko Gary's
Scottsdale, AZ 877-994-3256
H&B Packing Company
Waco, TX 254-752-2506
Hofmann Sausage Company
Syracuse, NY 800-724-8410
Hormel Foods Corporation
Austin, MN 800-523-4635
Ray's Sausage Company Inc
Cleveland, OH 216-921-8782
Sheinman Provision Company
Philadelphia, PA 215-473-7065
Siena Foods
Toronto, ON 800-465-0422
Wy's Wings
Strasburg, VA 800-997-9464

Hot Italian

Atlantic Quality Spice &Seasonings
New Brunswick, NJ 800-584-0422
Decker & Son Company
Colorado Springs, CO 719-634-8311
Eagle Rock Food Company
Albuquerque, NM 505-323-1183
F.B. Purnell Sausage Company
Simpsonville, KY 800-626-1512
Grote & Weigel
Bloomfield, CT 860-242-8528
Siena Foods
Toronto, ON 800-465-0422

Kielbasa

Atlantic Quality Spice &Seasonings
New Brunswick, NJ 800-584-0422
Berks Packing Company, Inc.
Reading, PA 800-882-3757
Boesl Packing Company
Baltimore, MD 410-675-1071
Chicopee Provision Company
Chicopee, MA 800-924-6328
Country Smoked Meats
Bowling Green, OH 800-321-4766
Frank Wardynski & Sons
Buffalo, NY 716-854-6083
Gaspar's Sausage Company
North Dartmouth, MA 800-542-2038
Grote & Weigel
Bloomfield, CT 860-242-8528
Hot Springs Packing Company
Hot Springs, AR 800-535-0449
Leo G. Fraboni Sausage Company
Hibbing, MN 218-263-5074
Locustdale Meat Packing
Locustdale, PA 570-875-1270
Marathon Enterprises
Englewood, NJ 800-722-7388
Martin Rosol's
New Britain, CT 860-223-2707
Norpaco
Middletown, CT 800-252-0222
Otto W Liebold & Company
Flint, MI 800-999-6328
Parma Sausage Products
Pittsburgh, PA 877-294-4207
Raemica
Highland, CA 909-864-1990
Roma Packing Company
Chicago, IL 773-927-7371
Sardinha Sausage
Somerset, MA 800-678-0178
Silver Star Meats
McKees Rocks, PA 800-548-1321

Smith Packing Regional Meat
Utica, NY
Stanley Provision Company
Manchester, CT. 888-688-6347
Victor Ostrowski & Son
Baltimore, MD 410-327-8935
Wimmer's Meat Products
West Point, NE 800-358-0761

Knockwurst

Boesl Packing Company
Baltimore, MD 410-675-1071
Country Smoked Meats
Bowling Green, OH 800-321-4766
D'Artagnan
Newark, NJ 800-327-8246
Grote & Weigel
Bloomfield, CT. 860-242-8528
Raemica
Highland, CA 909-864-1990
Rego's Purity Foods
Honolulu, HI. 808-847-3717

Legonica (Thin Italian)

Gaspar's Sausage Company
North Dartmouth, MA 800-542-2038

Linguica

Burke Corporation
Nevada, IA 800-654-1152

Always make it your best® with Burke fully cooked meats. We specialize in Italian sausage, beef, and pork toppings, meatballs, taco meats, shredded meats, pepperoni, bacon, Canadian-style bacon, chicken and beef strips. Additionally, we offer a variety of specialty products: Hand-Pinched Style® brand toppings, chorizo, gyro topping, andouille sausage, and breakfast patties and links.

Swiss-American Sausage Company
Lathrop, CA 209-858-5555

Link

Bakalars Brothers Sausage Company
La Crosse, WI. 608-784-0384
Bellville Meat Market
Bellville, TX. 800-571-6328
Burke Corporation
Nevada, IA 800-654-1152

Always make it your best® with Burke fully cooked meats. We specialize in Italian sausage, beef, and pork toppings, meatballs, taco meats, shredded meats, pepperoni, bacon, Canadian-style bacon, chicken and beef strips. Additionally, we offer a variety of specialty products: Hand-Pinched Style® brand toppings, chorizo, gyro topping, andouille sausage, and breakfast patties and links.

Country Smoked Meats
Bowling Green, OH 800-321-4766
F.B. Purnell Sausage Company
Simpsonville, KY 800-626-1512
Father's Country Hams
Bremen, KY 270-525-3554
Fontanini Italian Meats & Sausages
McCook, IL. 800-331-6328
Fredericksburg Lockers/OPA's Smoke
Fredericksburg, TX. 800-543-6750
H&B Packing Company
Waco, TX 254-752-2506
Hormel Foods Corporation
Austin, MN 800-523-4635
Jimmy Dean Foods
Cincinnati, OH 800-925-3326
Mello's North End Manufacturings
Fall River, MA 800-673-2320
Ray's Sausage Company Inc
Cleveland, OH 216-921-8782
Upstate Farms Cooperative
Buffalo, NY. 716-892-2121

Mortadella

Fiorucci Foods
Colonial Heights, VA 800-524-7775
John Volpi & Company
St Louis, MO. 800-288-3439

Parma Sausage Products
Pittsburgh, PA. 877-294-4207
Siena Foods
Toronto, ON 800-465-0422
Swift & Company
Greeley, CO. 970-506-8000

Patti

F.B. Purnell Sausage Company
Simpsonville, KY 800-626-1512
Farmland Foods
Kansas City, MO. 888-327-6526
Father's Country Hams
Bremen, KY 270-525-3554
Fontanini Italian Meats & Sausages
McCook, IL. 800-331-6328
Hormel Foods Corporation
Austin, MN 800-523-4635
Jimmy Dean Foods
Cincinnati, OH 800-925-3326
Mello's North End Manufacturings
Fall River, MA 800-673-2320
Ray's Sausage Company Inc
Cleveland, OH 216-921-8782
Roman Sausage Company
Santa Clara, CA 800-497-7462

Polish

Fontanini Italian Meats & Sausages
McCook, IL. 800-331-6328

Pork

Farmland Foods
Kansas City, MO. 888-327-6526
Grote & Weigel
Bloomfield, CT. 860-242-8528
Lucys Foods
Latrobe, PA. 724-539-1430

Salmon

Aquatec Seafoods Ltd.
Comox, BC 250-339-6412

Sicilian Style (with Cheese)

Atlantic Quality Spice &Seasonings
New Brunswick, NJ 800-584-0422

Sweet

Chicopee Provision Company
Chicopee, MA. 800-924-6328
Farmland Foods
Kansas City, MO. 888-327-6526

Sweet Italian

Atlantic Quality Spice &Seasonings
New Brunswick, NJ 800-584-0422
Grote & Weigel
Bloomfield, CT. 860-242-8528

Turkey

Couch's Country Style Sausages
Cleveland, OH 216-823-2332
Eagle Rock Food Company
Albuquerque, NM 505-323-1183
Gaspar's Sausage Company
North Dartmouth, MA 800-542-2038
Lucys Foods
Latrobe, PA. 724-539-1430

Venison

Broadleaf Venison Usa
Vernon, CA 800-336-3844

Smoked Meat

Alewel's Country Meats
Warrensburg, MO 800-353-8553
Alpine Meats
Stockton, CA. 800-399-6328
Applegate Farms
Bridgewater, NJ 908-725-2768
Bellville Meat Market
Bellville, TX. 800-571-6328
Berks Packing Company, Inc.
Reading, PA 800-882-3757
Boesl Packing Company
Baltimore, MD 410-675-1071

Braham Food Locker Service
Braham, MN 320-396-2636
Brook Meadow ProvisionscCorporation
Hagerstown, MD. 301-739-3107
Burgers Smokehouse
California, MO 800-624-5426
Carolina Pride Foods
Greenwood, SC. 864-229-5611
Cedaredge Meats
Cedaredge, CO 970-856-6113
Chicago 58 Food Products
Woodbridge, ON. 416-603-4244
Cloud's Meat Processing
Carthage, MO 417-358-5855
Community Market & Deli
Lindstrom, MN 651-257-1128
Country Smoked Meats
Bowling Green, OH 800-321-4766
Crofton & Sons
Brandon, FL 800-878-7675
Duis Meat Processing
Concordia, KS. 800-281-4295
E.W. Knauss & Son
Quakertown, PA 800-648-4220
F&Y Enterprises
Wauconda, IL 847-526-0620
Fairbury Food Products
Fairbury, NE 402-729-3379
Fiorucci Foods
Colonial Heights, VA 800-524-7775
Fresh Mark
Canton, OH. 800-860-6777
Fricks Meat Products
Washington, MO. 800-241-2209
Gaiser's European Style Provisions
Union, NJ 908-686-3421
Hickory Baked Food
Castle Rock, CO 303-688-2633
Hollman Foods
Chicago, IL 888-926-2879
Hormel Foods Corporation
Fremont, NE 402-721-2300
Hormel Foods Corporation
Austin, MN 800-523-4635
Humphrey Blue Ribbon Meats
Springfield, IL. 800-747-6328
Ittels Meats
Howard Lake, MN 320-543-2285
John Hofmeister & Son
Chicago, IL 800-923-4267
John Volpi & Company
St Louis, MO. 800-288-3439
Kelley Meats
Taberg, NY 315-337-4272
Kessler Foods, Inc
Lemoyne, PA. 717-763-7162
Koegel Meats
Flint, MI 810-238-3685
Konetzkos Market
Browerville, MN. 320-594-2915
Laurent Meat Market
Marrero, LA 504-341-1771
Leo G. Fraboni Sausage Company
Hibbing, MN. 218-263-5074
Lords Sausage & CountryhHam
Dexter, GA 800-342-6002
Manger Packing Company
Baltimore, MD 800-227-9262
McKenzie of Vermont
Burlington, VT 802-864-4585
Mike's Meats
Eitzen, MN 507-495-3336
Mountain City Meat Company
Denver, CO 800-937-8325
Nestle Pizza
Medford, WI 715-748-5550
Nodine's Smokehouse
Torrington, CT 800-222-2059
Nueces Canyon Texas Style Meat Seasoning
Brenham, TX. 800-925-5058
Original Chili Bowl
Tulsa, OK 918-628-0225
Peoples Sausage Company
Los Angeles, CA. 213-627-8633
Pioneer Packing Company
Bowling Green, OH 419-352-5283
Quality Meats & Seafood
West Fargo, ND. 800-342-4250
R.M. Felts Packing Company
Ivor, VA. 888-300-0971
Raemica
Highland, CA 909-864-1990

Rinehart Meat Processing
Branson, MO. 417-334-2044
Robbins Packing Company
Statesboro, GA 912-764-7503
Rose Packing Company
South Barrington, IL. 800-323-7363
Saag's Products
San Leandro, CA. 800-352-7224
Sahlen Packing Company
Buffalo, NY. 716-852-8677
Sara Lee Corporation
Downers Grove, IL 630-598-8100
Sardinha Sausage
Somerset, MA. 800-678-0178
Savoie's Sausage & Food Products
Opelousas, LA. 337-948-4115
Schaller & Weber
Astoria, NY. 800-847-4115
Sechrist Brothers
Dallastown, PA 717-244-2975
Smith Meat Packing
Port Huron, MI 810-985-5900
Stonies Sausage Shop Inc
Perryville, MO 888-546-2540
Striplings
Moultrie, GA. 229-985-4226
Superior's Brand Meats
Massillon, OH. 330-830-0356
Swiss-American Sausage Company
Lathrop, CA 209-858-5555
Thomas Packing Company
Columbus, GA 800-729-0976
Tomasinos Sausage
Canton, OH. 330-454-4171
Triple U Enterprises
Fort Pierre, SD 605-567-3624
Troy Pork Store
Troy, NY 518-272-8291
Tupman-Thurlow Company
Deerfield Beach, FL 954-596-9989
V.W. Joyner & Company
Smithfield, VA 757-357-2161
Warren & Son Meat Processing
Whipple, OH. 740-585-2421
Wayco Ham Company
Goldsboro, NC 800-962-2614
Willies Smoke House
Harrisville, PA. 800-742-4184
Wimmer's Meat Products
West Point, NE 800-358-0761
Woods Smoked Meats
Bowling Green, MO 800-458-8426
Yoakum Packing Company
Yoakum, TX 361-293-3541
Zerna Packing
Labadie, MO. 636-742-4190

Poultry & Game

Selwoods Farm Hunting Preserve
Alpine, AL 256-362-7595

Tasso

Comeaux's
Lafayette, LA 800-323-2492
Savoie's Sausage & Food Products
Opelousas, LA. 337-948-4115

Turkey

Deli Breast - Fresh

Carolina Turkeys
Mount Olive, NC 800-523-4559
Farmland Foods
Kansas City, MO. 888-327-6526
Norbest
Midvale, UT 800-453-5327
Wimmer's Meat Products
West Point, NE 800-358-0761

Deli Breast - Frozen

Norbest
Midvale, UT 800-453-5327

Deli Breast - Smoked

Applegate Farms
Bridgewater, NJ 908-725-2768

Smoked

Applegate Farms
Bridgewater, NJ 908-725-2768
Burgers Smokehouse
California, MO 800-624-5426
Chickasaw Trading Company
Denver City, TX 800-848-3515
Crofton & Sons
Brandon, FL 800-878-7675
Hollman Foods
Chicago, IL 888-926-2879
North Country Smokehouse
Claremont, NH 800-258-4304
Ranch Oak Farm
Fort Worth, TX 800-888-0327
Selwoods Farm Hunting Preserve
Alpine, AL 256-362-7595
Thomas Packing Company
Columbus, GA 800-729-0976
Wayco Ham Company
Goldsboro, NC 800-962-2614

Steaks

B&D Foods
Boise, ID 208-344-1183
Bakalars Brothers Sausage Company
La Crosse, WI. 608-784-0384
Blue Ribbon Meats
Miami, FL. 800-522-6115

Burnett & Son Meat Company
Monrovia, CA. 626-357-2165
Buzz Food Service
Charleston, WV 304-925-4781
Cambridge Packing Company
Boston, MA. 800-722-6726
Centennial Food Corporation
Calgary, AB. 403-214-0044
Devault Foods
Devault, PA. 800-426-2874
Dynamic Foods
Lubbock, TX. 806-747-2777
Flint Hills Foods
Alma, KS
Glenmark Food Processors
Chicago, IL 800-621-0117
Kutztown Bologna Company
Leola, PA. 800-723-8824
Ossian Seafood Meats
Ossian, IN 260-622-4191
Pierceton Foods
Pierceton, IN. 574-594-2344
Pinter's Packing Plant
Dorchester, WI 715-654-5444
Rymer Foods
Chicago, IL 800-247-9637
S.W. Meat & Provision Company
Phoenix, AZ 602-275-2000
Stampede Meat
Bridgeview, IL 800-353-0933
Steak-Umm Company
Shillington, PA 860-928-5900
Valley Meats
Coal Valley, IL 309-799-7341

Tripe

Bradshaw's Food Products
Dighton, MA. 508-669-6088

Nuts & Nut Butters

Nut Butters

American Almond Products Company
Brooklyn, NY 800-825-6663
Amoretti
Oxnard, CA 800-266-7388
Brost International Trading Company
Chicago, IL 312-861-7100
Cache Creek Foods
Woodland, CA 530-662-1764
East Wind Nut Butters
Tecumseh, MO 417-679-4682
Fastachi
Watertown, MA 800-466-3022
Feridies/The Peanut Patch Inc.
Courtland, VA 866-732-6883
Food Mill
Oakland, CA 510-482-3848
Fresh Hemp Foods
Winnipeg, NB 800-665-4367
Jonny Almond Nut Company
Flint, MI 810-767-6886
Justin's Nut Butter
Boulder, CO 303-449-9559
Marin Food Specialties
Byron, CA 925-634-6126
Moon Shine Trading Company
Woodland, CA 800-678-1226
Once Again Nut Butter
Nunda, NY 888-800-8075
Seabrook Ingredients
Edenton, NC 252-482-2112
Sokol & Company
Countryside, IL 800-328-7656
SoyNut Butter Company
Glenview, IL 800-288-1012
Sungold Foods
Fargo, ND 800- 43- 553

Almond

Fastachi
Watertown, MA 800-466-3022
Marin Food Specialties
Byron, CA 925-634-6126

Hazelnut

Fastachi
Watertown, MA 800-466-3022

Peanut Butter

Algood Food Company
Louisville, KY 502-637-1401
American Almond Products Company
Brooklyn, NY 800-825-6663
American Food Traders
Miami, FL 305-273-7090
Azar Nut Company
El Paso, TX 800-592-8103
Bella Vista Farm
Lawton, OK 866-237-8526
Carriage House Companies
Fredonia, NY 800-462-8125
Clements Foods Company
Oklahoma City, OK 800-654-8355
ConAgra Grocery Products
Irvine, CA 714-680-1000
E.F. Lane & Son
Colton, CA 510-569-8980
East Wind Nut Butters
Tecumseh, MO 417-679-4682
Fastachi
Watertown, MA 800-466-3022
Food Ingredients
Elgin, IL 800-500-7676
Gardners Candies
Tyrone, PA 800-242-2639
Golden Foods
Commerce, CA 800-350-2462
Griffin Food Company
Muskogee, OK 800-580-6311
Groeb Farms
Onsted, MI 517-467-2065
Hershey Company
Hershey, PA 800-468-1714
JMS Specialty Foods
Ripon, WI 800-535-5437
Krema Nut Company
Columbus, OH 800-222-4132
Landis Peanut Butter
Souderton, PA 215-723-9366
Leavitt Corporation
Everett, MA 617-389-2600
Lynch Foods
North York, ON 416-449-5464
Marantha Natural Foods
San Francisco, CA 866-972-6879
Mrs. Annie's Peanut Patch
Floresville, TX 830-393-7845
Once Again Nut Butter
Nunda, NY 888-800-8075
Peanut Butter & Co
New York, NY 866-ILO-EPB
Producers Peanut Company
Suffolk, VA 800-847-5491
Ralcorp Holdings
St Louis, MO 800-772-6757
Reily Foods Company
New Orleans, LA 504-524-6131
Reily Foods/JFG Coffee Company
New Orleans, LA 800-535-1961
Scott-Bathgate
Winnipeg, MB 800-216-2990
Sessions Company
Enterprise, AL 334-393-0200
Simple Foods
Tonawanda, NY 800-234-8850
Southern Peanut Company
Dublin, NC 910-862-2136
St. Laurent Brothers
Bay City, MI 800-289-7688
Sunland Inc/Peanut Better
Portales, NM 575-356-6638
Synergy Foods
West Bloomfield, MI 313-849-2900
Tara Foods
Atlanta, GA 404-559-0605
Vic Rossano Incorporated
Montreal, QC 514-766-5252
Virginia & Spanish Peanut Company
Providence, RI 800-673-3562

Crunchy

Griffin Food Company
Muskogee, OK 800-580-6311
Groeb Farms
Onsted, MI 517-467-2065

No Additives

Groeb Farms
Onsted, MI 517-467-2065

Smooth

Griffin Food Company
Muskogee, OK 800-580-6311
Groeb Farms
Onsted, MI 517-467-2065

Nut Pastes

American Almond Products Company
Brooklyn, NY 800-825-6663
Amoretti
Oxnard, CA 800-266-7388
Georgia Nut Ingredients
Skokie, IL 877-674-2993
Sokol & Company
Countryside, IL 800-328-7656

Almond

Bear Stewart Corporation
Chicago, IL 800-697-2327
Georgia Nut Ingredients
Skokie, IL 877-674-2993
Putney Pasta Company
Brattleboro, VT 800-253-3683

Nuts

A La Carte
Chicago, IL 800-722-2370
A Southern Season
Chapel Hill, NC 877-929-7133
A. Battaglia Processing Company
Chicago, IL 773-523-5900
A.L. Bazzini Company
Bronx, NY 800-228-0172
Adams & Brooks, Inc
Los Angeles, CA 800-999-9808
Adkin & Son Associated Food Products
South Haven, MI 269-637-7450
Albanese Confectionery Group
Merrillville, IN 800-536-0581
All Wrapped Up
Plantation, FL 800-891-2194
Alldrin Brothers
Ballico, CA 209-667-1600
American Almond Products Company
Brooklyn, NY 800-825-6663
American Health & Nutrition
Ann Arbor, MI 734-677-5570
American Key Food Products
Closter, NJ 800-767-0237
American Nut & Chocolate Company
Boston, MA 800-797-6887
American Yeast/Lallemand
Pembroke, NH 866-920-9885
Ames International
Fife, WA 888-469-2637
AnaCon Foods Company
Atchison, KS 800-328-0291
Anderson Peanuts
Opp, AL 334-493-4591
Ann's House of Nuts, Inc.
Jessup, MD 301-498-4920
ARA Food Corporation
Miami, FL 800-533-8831
Archibald Candy Corporation
Chicago, IL 800-333-3629
Arizona Cowboy
Phoenix, AZ 602-956-4833
Arizona Pistachio Company
Tulare, CA 800-333-8575
Arway Confections
Chicago, IL 773-267-5770
Aunt Aggie De's Pralines
Sinton, TX 888-772-5463
Aurora Products
Stratford, CT 800-398-1048
Azar Nut Company
El Paso, TX 800-592-8103
Baldwin-Minkler Farms
Orland, CA 530-865-8080
Balsu
Bay Harbour Islands, FL 305-993-5045
Barcelona Nut Company
Baltimore, MD 800-292-6887
Bavarian Nut Company
Stockton, CA 209-465-9181
Beard's Quality Nut Company
Empire, CA 209-526-3590
Beer Nuts
Bloomington, IL 800-233-7688
Bened Food Corporation
Bronx, NY 718-842-8644
Berberian Nut Company
Chico, CA 530-891-4900
Beta Pure Foods
Aptos, CA 831-685-6565
Birdsong Corporation
Suffolk, VA 757-539-3456
Birdsong Peanuts
Blakely, GA 800-597-7688
Blue Diamond Growers
Sacramento, CA 916-442-0771
Brooks Peanut Company
Samson, AL 334-898-7194
Buchanan Hollow Nut Company
Le Grand, CA 800-532-1500
Buddy Squirrel LLC
Milwaukee, WI 800-972-2658
Byrd's Pecans
Butler, MO 866-679-5583

Cache Creek Foods
Woodland, CA....530-662-1764
Cajun Creole Products
New Iberia, LA....800-946-8688
Cal-Grown Nut Company
Hughson, CA....209-883-4081
California Almond Packers
Corning, CA....530-824-3836
California Fruit & Nut
Gustine, CA....888-747-8224
California Independent Almond Growers
Merced, CA....209-667-4855
California Wholesale Nut Company
Chico, CA....530-895-0512
Camilla Pecan Company
Camilla, GA....800-526-8770
Capay Canyon Ranch
Esparto, CA....530-662-2372
Capco Enterprises
East Hanover, NJ....800-252-1011
Carolina Cracker
Garner, NC....919-779-6899
Cheese Straws & More
Monroe, LA....800-997-1921
Cherrydale Farms
Allentown, PA....800-333-4525
Chico Nut Company
Chico, CA....530-891-1493
Chieftain Wild Rice Company
Spooner, WI....800-262-6368
China Doll Company
Saraland, AL....251-457-7641
CHS
Inver Grove Heights, MN....800-232-3639
CJ Dannemiller Company
Norton, OH....800-624-8671
Cloverland Sweets/Priester's Pecan Company
Fort Deposit, AL....800-523-3505
Columbia Empire Farms
Sherwood, OR....503-538-2156
Commodities Marketing, Inc.
Edison, NJ....732-603-5077
ConAgra Grocery Products
Irvine, CA....714-680-1000
Crain Ranch
Los Molinos, CA....530-527-1077
Crown Point
St John, IN....219-365-3200
D Steengrafe & Company
Pleasant Valley, NY....845-635-4067
Dakota Gourmet
Wahpeton, ND....800-727-6663
Dave's Gourmet
San Francisco, CA....800-758-0372
Del Rio Nut Company
Livingston, CA....209-394-7945
Derco Foods
Fresno, CA....559-435-2664
Diamond Foods
Fishers, IN....317-845-5534
Diamond Foods Inc
Stockton, CA....209-467-6000
Diamond of California
San Francisco, CA....415-912-3180
Durey-Libby Edible Nuts
Carlstadt, NJ....800-332-6887
E.F. Lane & Son
Colton, CA....510-569-8980
El Brands
Ozark, AL....334-445-2828
El Paso Chile Company
El Paso, TX....888-472-5727
Elegant Edibles
Houston, TX....800-227-3226
Energy Club
Pacoima, CA....800-688-6887
Fastachi
Watertown, MA....800-466-3022
Fine Foods Northwest
Seattle, WA....800-862-3965
Flanigan Farms
Culver City, CA....800-525-0228
Foley's Candies
Richmond, BC....888-236-5397
Ford's Fancy Fruit
Raleigh, NC....800-446-0947
Frazier Nut Farms
Waterford, CA....209-522-1406
Fresh Roasted Almond Company
Warren, MI....877-478-6887
Frito-Lay
Dallas, TX....800-352-4477

Fun Factory
Milwaukee, WI....877-894-6767
G Scaccianoce & Company
Bronx, NY....718-991-4462
Garry Packing
Del Rey, CA....800-248-2126
Germack Pistachio Company
Detroit, MI....800-872-4006
Glennys
Freeport, NY....888-864-1243
GNS Foods/Pacific Gold
Arlington, TX....817-795-4671
Golden Kernel Pecan Company
Cameron, SC....800-845-2448
Golden Peanut Company
Ashburn, GA....229-567-3311
Golden Peanut Company
Aulander, NC....252-345-1661
Golden Peanut Company
Alpharetta, GA....770-752-8160
Golden West Nuts
Ripon, CA....209-599-6193
Goodart Candy
Lubbock, TX....806-747-2600
Govadinas Fitness Foods
San Diego, CA....800-900-0108
Granite State Potato Chip Company
Salem, NH....603-898-2171
Great Northern Maple Products
Saint Honor, De Shenley, QC....418-485-7777
Green Valley Pecan Company
Sahuarita, AZ....800-533-5269
Guerra Nut Shelling Company
Hollister, CA....831-637-4471
Gurley's Foods
Willmar, MN....800-426-7845
H&S Edible Products Corporation
Mount Vernon, NY....800-253-3364
H. Naraghi Farms
Escalon, CA....209-577-5777
Hammons Products Company
Stockton, MO....888-429-6887
Hampton Farms
Severn, NC....800-313-2748
Hancock Peanut Company
Courtland, VA....757-653-9351
Harmony Foods Corporation
Fishers, IN....800-837-2855
Harris Farms
Coalinga, CA....800-742-1955
Haven's Candies
Westbrook, ME....800-639-6309
Hawaiian King Candies
Honolulu, HI....800-570-1902
Hazelnut Growers of Oregon
Cornelius, OR....503-648-4176
HempNut
Henderson, NV....707-576-7050
Herkimer Foods
Herkimer, NY....315-895-7832
Herr Foods
Chillicothe, OH....800-523-8468
Hershey
Mississauga, ON....800-468-1714
Hialeah Products Company
Hollywood, FL....800-923-3379
Hickory Harvest Foods
Akron, OH....330-644-6887
Honey Bar/Creme de la Creme
Kingston, NY....845-331-4643
Horriea 2000 Food Industries
Reynolds, GA....478-847-4186
HP Schmid
San Francisco, CA....415-765-5925
Hubbard Peanut Company
Sedley, VA....800-889-7688
Idaho Candy Company
Boise, ID....800-898-6986
International Harvest
Mt Vernon, NY....914-699-5600
International Service Group
Alpharetta, GA....770-518-0988
Jardine Organic Ranch Co
Paso Robles, CA....866-833-5050
Jason & Son Specialty Foods
Rancho Cordova, CA....800-810-9093
Jerry's Nut House
Denver, CO....888-214-0747
Jewel Date Company
Thermal, CA....760-399-4474
JF Braun & Sons Inc.
Elizabeth, NJ....800-997-7177

Jimbo's Jumbos
Edenton, NC....800-334-4771
John B Sanfilippo & Son
Garysburg, NC....252-536-5111
John B Sanfilippo & Son
Selma, TX....800-423-6546
John B Sanfilippo & Son
Elgin, IL....847-289-1800
John B Sanfilippo & Sons
Selma, TX....800-423-6546
John B. Sanfilippo & Son
Gustine, CA....800-218-3077
Kalustyan Corporation
Union, NJ....908-688-6111
Karl Bissinger French Confections
St Louis, MO....800-325-8881
Kenlake Foods
Murray, KY....800-632-6900
Kettle Foods
Salem, OR....503-364-0399
King Nut Company
Solon, OH....800-860-5464
Koeze Company
Wyoming, MI....800-555-3909
Krema Nut Company
Columbus, OH....800-222-4132
Krispy Kernels
Sainte Foy, QC....877-791-9986
L&S Packing Company
Farmingdale, NY....800-286-6487
LA Wholesale Produce Market
Los Angeles, CA....888-454-6887
Leavitt Corporation
Everett, MA....617-389-2600
Lee Seed Company
Inwood, IA....800-736-6530
Livingston Farmers Association
Livingston, CA....209-394-7941
Lodi Nut Company
Lodi, CA....800-234-6887
Lou-Retta's Custom Chocolates
Buffalo, NY....716-833-7111
Lowery's Home Made Candies
Muncie, IN....800-541-3340
MacFarms of Hawaii
Captain Cook, HI....808-328-2435
Majestic Foods
Huntington, NY....631-424-9444
Marantha Natural Foods
San Francisco, CA....866-972-6879
Mareblu Naturals
Anaheim, CA
Mariani Nut Company
Winters, CA....530-662-3311
Masterson Company
Milwaukee, WI....414-647-1132
Mayfair Sales
Buffalo, NY....800-248-2881
McCleskey Mills
Smithville, GA....229-846-2003
Meridian Nut Growers
Clovis, CA....559-458-7272
Merritt Pecan Company
Weston, GA....800-762-9152
Mezza
Lake Forest, IL....888-206-6054
Midwest/Northern
Minneapolis, MN....800-328-5502
Monsanto
St Louis, MO....314-694-1000
Monte Vista Farming Company
Denair, CA....209-874-1866
Mound City Shelled Nut Company
St Louis, MO....800-647-6887
Mrs May's Naturals
Carson, CA....877-677-6297
Mrs. Dog's Products
Grand Rapids, MI....800-2Mr-Dog
Natural Foods
Toledo, OH....419-537-1713
Nature's Candy
Fredericksburg, TX....800-729-0085
Nature's Select
Grand Rapids, MI....888-715-4321
Navarro Pecan Company
Corsicana, TX....800-333-9507
Naylor Candies
Mount Wolf, PA....717-266-2706
New England Natural Baker
Greenfield, MA....800-910-2884
Northwest Chocolate Factory
Salem, OR....503-362-1340

Northwest Hazelnut Company
Hubbard, OR. 503-982-8030
NSpired Natural Foods
Boulder, CO 800-434-4246
Nspired Natural Foods
Boulder, CO 800-434-4246
Nutorious
Green Bay, WI. 920-288-0483
Nuts + Nuts USA
Brooklyn, NY 347-513-9670
Nutsco Inc
Camden, NJ. 856-966-6400
Nutty Bavarian
Sanford, FL. 800-382-4788
Old Dominion Peanut Corporation
Norfolk, VA. 800-368-6887
Once Again Nut Butter
Nunda, NY 888-800-8075
Orangeburg Pecan Company
Orangeburg, SC 800-845-6970
Organic Planet
San Francisco, CA 415-765-5590
Osage Pecan Company
Butler, MO 660-679-6137
P-R Farms
Clovis, CA 559-299-0201
Pacific Gold Marketing
Fresno, CA
Panoche Creek Packing
Fresno, CA 559-449-1721
Pape's Pecan Company
Seguin, TX 888-688-7273
Paramount Farms
Los Angeles, CA. 877-450-9493
Patsy's Candies
Colorado Springs, CO. 866-372-8797
Peanut Patch
Courtland, VA. 866-732-6883
Peanut Roaster
Henderson, NC 800-445-1404
Pear's Coffee
Omaha, NE 800-317-1773
Pease's Candy Shoppe
Springfield, IL. 217-523-3721
Pecan Deluxe Candy Company
Dallas, TX. 800-733-3589
Pennsylvania Dutch Candies
Camp Hill, PA. 800-233-7082
Picard Peanuts
Simcoe, ON. 888-244-7688
Pippin Snack Pecans
Albany, GA 800-554-6887
Pippin Snack Pecans Incorporated
Albany, GA 229-432-9316
Pittsburgh Snax & Nut Company
Pittsburgh, PA. 800-404-6887
Planters LifeSavers Com pany
Fort Smith, AR 479-648-0100
Pleasant Grove Farms
Pleasant Grove, CA 916-655-3391
Porkie Company of Wisconsin
Cudahy, WI. 800-333-2588
Priester Pecan Company
Fort Deposit, AL. 800-277-3226
Prince of Peace Enterprises
Hayward, CA 800-732-2328
Producers Peanut Company
Suffolk, VA 800-847-5491
Ramos Orchards
Winters, CA 530-795-4748
Red River Foods
Richmond, VA. 800-443-6637
Reed Lang Farms
Rio Hondo, TX 956-748-2354
Regal Health Foods International
Chicago, IL 773-252-1044
Richard Green Company
Indianapolis, IN 317-972-0941
Roberts Ferry Nut Company
Waterford, CA. 209-874-3247
Ross-Smith Pecan Company
Thomasville, GA. 800-841-5503
Royal Wine Corp
Bayonne, NJ 718-384-2400
Ryan-Parreira Almond Company
Los Banos, CA 209-826-0272
Sachs Peanuts
Clarkton, NC. 800-732-6933
Sambets Cajun Deli
Austin, TX. 800-472-6238
Santa Clara Nut Company
San Jose, CA. 408-298-2425
Sara Lee Corporation
Downers Grove, IL 630-598-8100
Service Packing Company
Vancouver, BC 604-681-0264
Setton International Foods
Commack, NY 800-227-4397
Severn Peanut Company
Windsor, NC 252-794-3435
Severn Peanut Company
Severn, NC 800-642-4064
Shade Foods
New Century, KS 800-225-6312
Shields Date Gardens
Indio, CA. 800-414-2555
Sivetz Coffee
Corvallis, OR 541-753-9713
Snackerz
Commerce, CA 888-576-2253
Society Hill Snacks
Philadelphia, PA 800-595-0050
Solnuts
Hudson, IA 800-648-3503
South Georgia Pecan
Valdosta, GA. 800-627-6630
South Georgia Pecan Company
Valdosta, GA. 800-627-6630
South Valley Farms
Wasco, CA 661-391-9000
Southern Peanut Company
Dublin, NC 910-862-2136
Southern Style Nuts
Denison, TX 903-463-3161
Spice World
Orlando, FL. 800-433-4979
Spring Tree Maple Products
Brattleboro, VT. 802-254-8784
Sprucewood Handmade Cookie Company
Warkworth, ON. 877-632-1300
Squirrel Brand Company
McKinney, TX 800-624-8242
St. Laurent Brothers
Bay City, MI 800-289-7688
Stahmann Farms
La Mesa, NM 575-526-2453
Stapleton-Spence PackingCompany
San Jose, CA. 800-297-8815
Star Snacks Company
Jersey City, NJ 800-775-9909
Stone Mountain Pecan Company
Monroe, GA 800-633-6887
Sugai Kona Coffee
Kealakekua, HI 808-322-7717
Sun Empire Foods
Kerman, CA 800-252-4786
Sun Garden Growers
Bard, CA. 800-228-4690
Sun Ridge Farms
Pajaro, CA. 831-786-7000
Sunny South Pecan Company
Statesboro, GA 800-764-3687
Sunnyland Farms
Albany, GA. 800-999-2488
Sunopta Sunflower
Minnetonka, MN. 952-224-4764
Sunray Food Products Corporation
Bronx, NY. 718-548-2255
Sunridge Farms
Salinas, CA 831-755-1430
SunRise Commodities
Englewood Cliffs, NJ 201-947-1000
Sunwest Foods
Davis, CA 530-758-8550
Superior Nut & Candy Company
Chicago, IL 800-843-2238
Superior Nut Company
Cambridge, MA 800-251-6060
Superior Pecan
Eufaula, AL. 800-628-2350
Synergy Foods
West Bloomfield, MI 313-849-2900
T.M. Duche Company
Orland, CA 530-865-5511
Tejon Ranch
Lebec, CA. 661-248-5181
Terri Lynn
Elgin, IL 800-323-0775
The Peanut Butter Shop Of Williamsburg
Toano, VA. 800-831-1828
Timber Crest Farms
Healdsburg, CA 888-374-9325
Todd's
Vernon, CA 800-938-6337
Torn & Glasser
Los Angeles, CA. 800-282-6887
Torn Ranch
Novato, CA. 415-506-3000
Tracy Luckey Pecans
Harlem, GA. 800-476-4796
Treehouse Farms
Earlimart, CA 559-757-5020
Trophy Nut
Tipp City, OH 800-219-9004
Tropical
Charlotte, NC 800-220-1413
Tropical
Marietta, GA. 800-544-3762
Tropical Nut & Fruit Company
Orlando, FL. 800-749-8869
Tucker Pecan Company
Montgomery, AL. 800-239-6540
Twenty First Century Snacks
Ronkonkoma, NY. 800-975-2883
Utz Quality Foods
Hanover, PA 800-367-7629
Variety Foods
Warren, MI 586-268-4900
Vending Nut
Ft. Worth, TX 817-737-3071
Vic Rossano Incorporated
Montreal, QC 514-766-5252
Virginia & Spanish Peanut Company
Providence, RI 800-673-3562
Warner Candy
El Paso, TX. 847-928-7200
Waymouth Farms
New Hope, MN. 800-527-0094
Weaver Nut Company
Ephrata, PA. 717-738-3781
Westnut
Cornelius, OR
Whaley Pecan Company
Troy, AL 800-824-6827
Whitley's Peanut Factory
Hayes, VA 800-470-2244
Willamette Valley Walnuts
McMinnville, OR 503-472-3215
Willmar Cookie & Nut Company
Willmar, MN. 320-235-0600
Wise Foods
Kennesaw, GA 770-426-5821
Wolfies Roasted Nuts
Findlay, OH. 866-889-6887
Woodland Foods
Gurnee, IL. 847-625-8600
Young Pecan
Las Cruces, NM 575-524-4321
Young Pecan Company
Florence, SC 800-829-6864
Zenobia Company
Bronx, NY. 866-936-6242

Almonds

Alldrin Brothers
Ballico, CA. 209-667-1600
American Almond Products Company
Brooklyn, NY 800-825-6663
American Key Food Products
Closter, NJ. 800-767-0237
Baldwin-Minkler Farms
Orland, CA 530-865-8080
Buchanan Hollow Nut Company
Le Grand, CA 800-532-1500
Cache Creek Foods
Woodland, CA. 530-662-1764
Cal-Grown Nut Company
Hughson, CA 209-883-4081
California Almond Packers
Corning, CA 530-824-3836
California Independent Almond Growers
Merced, CA. 209-667-4855
Capco Enterprises
East Hanover, NJ. 800-252-1011
Charles H. Baldwin & Sons
West Stockbridge, MA 413-232-7785
Chico Nut Company
Chico, CA. 530-891-1493
Chieftain Wild Rice Company
Spooner, WI 800-262-6368
Chocolate Moon
Asheville, NC 800-723-1236
Commodities Marketing, Inc.
Edison, NJ. 732-603-5077

Del Rio Nut Company
Livingston, CA 209-394-7945
Diamond Foods Inc
Stockton, CA. . . . 209-467-6000
Durey-Libby Edible Nuts
Carlstadt, NJ 800-332-6887
Erba Food Products
Brooklyn, NY 718-272-7700
Fastachi
Watertown, MA. . . . 800-466-3022
Foley's Candies
Richmond, BC 888-236-5397
Frazier Nut Farms
Waterford, CA. . . . 209-522-1406
Fresh Roasted Almond Company
Warren, MI 877-478-6887
G Scaccianoce & Company
Bronx, NY. . . . 718-991-4462
Golden West Nuts
Ripon, CA. . . . 209-599-6193
H. Naraghi Farms
Escalon, CA 209-577-5777
Harris Farms
Coalinga, CA 800-742-1955
Hershey
Mississauga, ON. . . . 800-468-1714
Hialeah Products Company
Hollywood, FL 800-923-3379
Hughson Nut Company
Hughson, CA 209-883-0403
Jardine Organic Ranch Co
Paso Robles, CA. . . . 866-833-5050
Jasmine Vineyards
Delano, CA. . . . 661-792-2141
John B Sanfilippo & Son
Selma, TX. . . . 800-423-6546
John B Sanfilippo & Sons
Selma, TX. . . . 800-423-6546
John B. Sanfilippo & Son
Gustine, CA 800-218-3077
Krema Nut Company
Columbus, OH 800-222-4132
Livingston Farmers Association
Livingston, CA 209-394-7941
Lodi Nut Company
Lodi, CA. . . . 800-234-6887
Lou-Retta's Custom Chocolates
Buffalo, NY. . . . 716-833-7111
Mapled Nut Company
Montgomery, VT. . . . 800-726-4661
Mariani Nut Company
Winters, CA. . . . 530-662-3311
Masterson Company
Milwaukee, WI 414-647-1132
Meridian Nut Growers
Clovis, CA 559-458-7272
Monte Vista Farming Company
Denair, CA 209-874-1866
Nunes Farm Almonds
Newman, CA. . . . 209-862-3033
Nut Factory
Spokane Valley, WA 888-239-5288
Nutty Bavarian
Sanford, FL. . . . 800-382-4788
Omega Nutrition
Bellingham, WA 800-661-3529
Organic Planet
San Francisco, CA 415-765-5590
P-R Farms
Clovis, CA 559-299-0201
Pacific Gold Marketing
Fresno, CA
Panoche Creek Packing
Fresno, CA 559-449-1721
Paramount Farms
Los Angeles, CA. . . . 877-450-9493
Patterson Vegetable Company
Patterson, CA 209-892-2611
Planters LifeSavers Com pany
Fort Smith, AR 479-648-0100
Pleasant Grove Farms
Pleasant Grove, CA 916-655-3391
Ramos Orchards
Winters, CA 530-795-4748
Roberts Ferry Nut Company
Waterford, CA. . . . 209-874-3247
Rotteveel Orchards
Dixon, CA. . . . 707-678-1495
Ryan-Parreira Almond Company
Los Banos, CA 209-826-0272
Service Packing Company
Vancouver, BC 604-681-0264
Setton International Foods
Commack, NY 800-227-4397
Simple Foods
Tonawanda, NY 800-234-8850
South Valley Farms
Wasco, CA 661-391-9000
Southern Style Nuts
Denison, TX 903-463-3161
Spring Tree Maple Products
Brattleboro, VT. . . . 802-254-8784
Stapleton-Spence PackingCompany
San Jose, CA. . . . 800-297-8815
Sun Garden Growers
Bard, CA. . . . 800-228-4690
Sunwest Foods
Davis, CA 530-758-8550
T.M. Duche Company
Orland, CA 530-865-5511
Tejon Ranch
Lebec, CA. . . . 661-248-5181
Terri Lynn
Elgin, IL 800-323-0775
Timber Crest Farms
Healdsburg, CA 888-374-9325
Treehouse Farms
Earlimart, CA 559-757-5020
Unique Ingredients
Naches, WA. . . . 509-653-1991
Virginia Diner
Wakefield, VA. . . . 888-823-4637
Weaver Nut Company
Ephrata, PA. . . . 717-738-3781
Whitley's Peanut Factory
Hayes, VA. . . . 800-470-2244
Wolfies Roasted Nuts
Findlay, OH. . . . 866-889-6887

Salted

Cache Creek Foods
Woodland, CA. . . . 530-662-1764
Golden West Nuts
Ripon, CA. . . . 209-599-6193
Hialeah Products Company
Hollywood, FL 800-923-3379
Setton International Foods
Commack, NY 800-227-4397
Terri Lynn
Elgin, IL 800-323-0775

Brazil

American Almond Products Company
Brooklyn, NY 800-825-6663
Cache Creek Foods
Woodland, CA. . . . 530-662-1764
Chieftain Wild Rice Company
Spooner, WI 800-262-6368
Diamond Foods
Fishers, IN. . . . 317-845-5534
Diamond Foods Inc
Stockton, CA. . . . 209-467-6000
Durey-Libby Edible Nuts
Carlstadt, NJ 800-332-6887
Fastachi
Watertown, MA. . . . 800-466-3022
Hialeah Products Company
Hollywood, FL 800-923-3379
John B Sanfilippo & Sons
Selma, TX. . . . 800-423-6546
LA Wholesale Produce Market
Los Angeles, CA. . . . 888-454-6887
Setton International Foods
Commack, NY 800-227-4397
Stapleton-Spence PackingCompany
San Jose, CA. . . . 800-297-8815
Terri Lynn
Elgin, IL 800-323-0775
Weaver Nut Company
Ephrata, PA. . . . 717-738-3781
Woodland Foods
Gurnee, IL. . . . 847-625-8600

Cashews

American Almond Products Company
Brooklyn, NY 800-825-6663
American Health & Nutrition
Ann Arbor, MI 734-677-5570
American Key Food Products
Closter, NJ. . . . 800-767-0237
Cache Creek Foods
Woodland, CA. . . . 530-662-1764
California Fruit & Nut
Gustine, CA 888-747-8224
Chieftain Wild Rice Company
Spooner, WI 800-262-6368
Commodities Marketing, Inc.
Edison, NJ. . . . 732-603-5077
Diamond Foods
Fishers, IN. . . . 317-845-5534
Durey-Libby Edible Nuts
Carlstadt, NJ 800-332-6887
Fastachi
Watertown, MA. . . . 800-466-3022
Fresh Roasted Almond Company
Warren, MI 877-478-6887
Germack Pistachio Company
Detroit, MI 800-872-4006
Hialeah Products Company
Hollywood, FL 800-923-3379
John B Sanfilippo & Son
Selma, TX. . . . 800-423-6546
John B Sanfilippo & Sons
Selma, TX. . . . 800-423-6546
Koeze Company
Wyoming, MI 800-555-3909
Krema Nut Company
Columbus, OH 800-222-4132
LA Wholesale Produce Market
Los Angeles, CA. . . . 888-454-6887
Landies Candies Company
Buffalo, NY. . . . 800-955-2634
Lou-Retta's Custom Chocolates
Buffalo, NY. . . . 716-833-7111
Mapled Nut Company
Montgomery, VT. . . . 800-726-4661
Marantha Natural Foods
San Francisco, CA 866-972-6879
Maxwell's Gourmet Food
Raleigh, NC 800-952-6887
Meridian Nut Growers
Clovis, CA 559-458-7272
Naylor Candies
Mount Wolf, PA 717-266-2706
Nut Factory
Spokane Valley, WA 888-239-5288
Nuts & Stems
Rosharon, TX 281-464-6887
Nutsco Inc
Camden, NJ. . . . 856-966-6400
Nutty Bavarian
Sanford, FL. . . . 800-382-4788
Organic Planet
San Francisco, CA 415-765-5590
Pacific Gold Marketing
Fresno, CA
Planters LifeSavers Com pany
Fort Smith, AR 479-648-0100
Setton International Foods
Commack, NY 800-227-4397
Southern Style Nuts
Denison, TX 903-463-3161
Spring Tree Maple Products
Brattleboro, VT. . . . 802-254-8784
Stapleton-Spence PackingCompany
San Jose, CA. . . . 800-297-8815
Sunray Food Products Corporation
Bronx, NY. . . . 718-548-2255
Terri Lynn
Elgin, IL 800-323-0775
Tropical
Marietta, GA. . . . 800-544-3762
Virginia Diner
Wakefield, VA. . . . 888-823-4637
Weaver Nut Company
Ephrata, PA. . . . 717-738-3781
Wolfies Roasted Nuts
Findlay, OH. . . . 866-889-6887
Woodland Foods
Gurnee, IL. . . . 847-625-8600

Chestnuts

Adkin & Son Associated Food Products
South Haven, MI. . . . 269-637-7450
Chieftain Wild Rice Company
Spooner, WI 800-262-6368

Coated

Chocolate

A.L. Bazzini Company
Bronx, NY. . . . 800-228-0172

Karl Bissinger French Confections
St Louis, MO. 800-325-8881
Lowery's Home Made Candies
Muncie, IN 800-541-3340
Weaver Nut Company
Ephrata, PA. 717-738-3781

Yogurt

GKI Foods
Brighton, MI. 248-486-0055
Setton International Foods
Commack, NY 800-227-4397
Terri Lynn
Elgin, IL 800-323-0775

Filberts

American Almond Products Company
Brooklyn, NY 800-825-6663
Cache Creek Foods
Woodland, CA. 530-662-1764
Commodities Marketing, Inc.
Edison, NJ. 732-603-5077
Diamond Foods
Fishers, IN. 317-845-5534
Durey-Libby Edible Nuts
Carlstadt, NJ 800-332-6887
Erba Food Products
Brooklyn, NY 718-272-7700
Germack Pistachio Company
Detroit, MI 800-872-4006
Hialeah Products Company
Hollywood, FL 800-923-3379
Krema Nut Company
Columbus, OH 800-222-4132
Nut Factory
Spokane Valley, WA 888-239-5288
Organic Planet
San Francisco, CA 415-765-5590
Setton International Foods
Commack, NY 800-227-4397
Stapleton-Spence PackingCompany
San Jose, CA. 800-297-8815
Terri Lynn
Elgin, IL 800-323-0775
Weaver Nut Company
Ephrata, PA. 717-738-3781

Glazed & Coated

A.L. Bazzini Company
Bronx, NY. 800-228-0172
Archibald Candy Corporation
Chicago, IL 800-333-3629
Arway Confections
Chicago, IL 773-267-5770
Betty Lou's Golden Smackers
McMinnville, OR 800-242-5205
Cache Creek Foods
Woodland, CA. 530-662-1764
Candy Factory
Hayward, CA 800-736-6887
Cheese Straws & More
Monroe, LA. 800-997-1921
Chocolate Moon
Asheville, NC 800-723-1236
Cloverland Sweets/Priester's Pecan Company
Fort Deposit, AL. 800-523-3505
Columbia Empire Farms
Sherwood, OR. 503-538-2156
Crown Candy Corporation
Macon, GA 800-241-3529
Dillon Candy Company
Boston, GA 800-382-8338
Farr Candy Company
Idaho Falls, ID 208-522-8215
Foley's Candies
Richmond, BC 888-236-5397
G Scaccianoce & Company
Bronx, NY. 718-991-4462
GKI Foods
Brighton, MI. 248-486-0055
Goodart Candy
Lubbock, TX. 806-747-2600
Haven's Candies
Westbrook, ME 800-639-6309
Hershey
Mississauga, ON. 800-468-1714
Jason & Son Specialty Foods
Rancho Cordova, CA 800-810-9093
Karl Bissinger French Confections
St Louis, MO. 800-325-8881
Kay Foods Company
Detroit, MI 313-393-1100
King Nut Company
Solon, OH 800-860-5464
Laymon Candy Company
San Bernardino, CA 909-825-4408
Lowery's Home Made Candies
Muncie, IN 800-541-3340
MacFarms of Hawaii
Captain Cook, HI 808-328-2435
Marich Confectionery Company
Hollister, CA. 800-624-7055
Matangos Candies
Harrisburg, PA 717-234-0882
Midwest/Northern
Minneapolis, MN 800-328-5502
Moore's Candies
Baltimore, MD 410-426-2705
Mrs. Annie's Peanut Patch
Floresville, TX 830-393-7845
Muth Candies
Louisville, KY 502-585-2952
Nature's Candy
Fredericksburg, TX. 800-729-0085
Naylor Candies
Mount Wolf, PA 717-266-2706
New England Confectionery Company
Revere, MA. 781-485-4500
Northwest Chocolate Factory
Salem, OR. 503-362-1340
NSpired Natural Foods
Boulder, CO 800-434-4246
Nutty Bavarian
Sanford, FL. 800-382-4788
Old Dominion Peanut Corporation
Norfolk, VA. 800-368-6887
Pippin Snack Pecans
Albany, GA. 800-554-6887
Popcorn Connection
North Hollywood, CA 800-852-2676
Priester Pecan Company
Fort Deposit, AL. 800-277-3226
Prince of Peace Enterprises
Hayward, CA 800-732-2328
Randag & Associates Inc
Elmhurst, IL 630-530-2830
Setton International Foods
Commack, NY 800-227-4397
Shade Foods
New Century, KS 800-225-6312
Southern Style Nuts
Denison, TX 903-463-3161
St. Laurent Brothers
Bay City, MI 800-289-7688
Superior Nut & Candy Company
Chicago, IL. 800-843-2238
Terri Lynn
Elgin, IL 800-323-0775
Tom & Sally's Handmade Chocolates
Brattleboro, VT. 800-827-0800
Tonex
Wallington, NJ 973-773-5135
Tropical
Columbus, OH 800-538-3941
Warrell Corporation
Camp Hill, PA. 800-233-7082
Waymouth Farms
New Hope, MN. 800-527-0094
Weaver Nut Company
Ephrata, PA. 717-738-3781
Webbs Citrus Candy
Davenport, FL. 863-422-1051
Whitley's Peanut Factory
Hayes, VA. 800-470-2244

Hazelnuts

Balsu
Bay Harbour Islands, FL. 305-993-5045
Cache Creek Foods
Woodland, CA. 530-662-1764
Chieftain Wild Rice Company
Spooner, WI 800-262-6368
Columbia Empire Farms
Sherwood, OR. 503-538-2156
Commodities Marketing, Inc.
Edison, NJ. 732-603-5077
Fancy's Candy's
Rougemont, NC 888-403-2629
Fastachi
Watertown, MA. 800-466-3022
Hazelnut Growers of Oregon
Cornelius, OR. 503-648-4176
Hazy Grove Nuts
Lake Oswego, OR. 800-574-6887
Hialeah Products Company
Hollywood, FL 800-923-3379
Krema Nut Company
Columbus, OH 800-222-4132
LA Wholesale Produce Market
Los Angeles, CA. 888-454-6887
Meridian Nut Growers
Clovis, CA 559-458-7272
Northwest Chocolate Factory
Salem, OR. 503-362-1340
Northwest Hazelnut Company
Hubbard, OR. 503-982-8030
Omega Nutrition
Bellingham, WA 800-661-3529
Organic Planet
San Francisco, CA 415-765-5590
Purity Foods
Okemos, MI 800-997-7358
Setton International Foods
Commack, NY 800-227-4397
Terri Lynn
Elgin, IL 800-323-0775
Westnut
Cornelius, OR

Macadamia

American Key Food Products
Closter, NJ. 800-767-0237
Cache Creek Foods
Woodland, CA. 530-662-1764
Chieftain Wild Rice Company
Spooner, WI 800-262-6368
Diamond Foods
Fishers, IN. 317-845-5534
Durey-Libby Edible Nuts
Carlstadt, NJ 800-332-6887
Fastachi
Watertown, MA. 800-466-3022
Hawaiian Sun Products
Honolulu, HI 808-845-3211
Hialeah Products Company
Hollywood, FL 800-923-3379
Island Princess
Honolulu, HI 866-872-8601
John B Sanfilippo & Sons
Selma, TX. 800-423-6546
Koeze Company
Wyoming, MI 800-555-3909
Lodi Nut Company
Lodi, CA 800-234-6887
MacFarms of Hawaii
Captain Cook, HI 808-328-2435
Meridian Nut Growers
Clovis, CA 559-458-7272
Organic Planet
San Francisco, CA 415-765-5590
Prince of Peace Enterprises
Hayward, CA 800-732-2328
Setton International Foods
Commack, NY 800-227-4397
Stapleton-Spence PackingCompany
San Jose, CA. 800-297-8815
Sugai Kona Coffee
Kealakekua, HI. 808-322-7717
Terri Lynn
Elgin, IL 800-323-0775
Woodland Foods
Gurnee, IL. 847-625-8600

Mixed Nuts

Crazy Jerry's
Roswell, GA 770-993-0651
Mapled Nut Company
Montgomery, VT. 800-726-4661

Nut Meats

American Almond Products Company
Brooklyn, NY 800-825-6663
Baldwin-Minkler Farms
Orland, CA 530-865-8080
Cache Creek Foods
Woodland, CA. 530-662-1764
Durey-Libby Edible Nuts
Carlstadt, NJ 800-332-6887
Hammons Products Company
Stockton, MO 888-429-6887

Jerry's Nut House
Denver, CO 888-214-0747
King Nut Company
Solon, OH 800-860-5464
Mid-Valley Nut Company
Hughson, CA 209-883-4491
Mother Earth Enterprises
New York, NY 866-436-7688
Service Packing Company
Vancouver, BC 604-681-0264
Setton International Foods
Commack, NY 800-227-4397
South Georgia Pecan Company
Valdosta, GA 800-627-6630
Superior Nut & Candy Company
Chicago, IL 800-843-2238
Superior Pecan
Eufaula, AL 800-628-2350
Terri Lynn
Elgin, IL 800-323-0775
Waymouth Farms
New Hope, MN 800-527-0094
Whaley Pecan Company
Troy, AL 800-824-6827
Willamette Valley Walnuts
McMinnville, OR 503-472-3215
Young Pecan Company
Florence, SC 800-829-6864

Peanuts

American Health & Nutrition
Ann Arbor, MI 734-677-5570
Anderson Peanuts
Opp, AL 334-493-4591
Belmont Peanuts of Southampton Inc
Capron, VA 800-648-4613
E.F. Lane & Son
Colton, CA 510-569-8980
Fastachi
Watertown, MA 800-466-3022
Golden Peanuts Company
Alpharetta, GA 770-752-8205
Hardy Farms Peanuts
Hawkinsville, GA 888-368-6887
Koeze Company
Wyoming, MI 800-555-3909
Krema Nut Company
Columbus, OH 800-222-4132
Peanut Corporation of America
Lynchburg, VA 434-384-7098
Peanut Processors
Dublin, NC 910-862-2136
Peanut Shop of Williamsburg
Portsmouth, VA 800-637-3268
Queensway Foods Company
Burlingame, CA 650-871-7770
Richfield Foods
Cairo, GA 229-377-2102
Royal Oak Peanuts
Drewryville, VA 800-608-4590
Setton International Foods
Commack, NY 800-227-4397
Southern Peanut Company
Dublin, NC 910-862-2136
Terri Lynn
Elgin, IL 800-323-0775
Virginia Diner
Wakefield, VA 888-823-4637

Granulated

American Almond Products Company
Brooklyn, NY 800-825-6663
American Key Food Products
Closter, NJ 800-767-0237
Cajun Creole Products
New Iberia, LA 800-946-8688
Hialeah Products Company
Hollywood, FL 800-923-3379
Producers Peanut Company
Suffolk, VA 800-847-5491
Seabrook Ingredients
Edenton, NC 252-482-2112
Terri Lynn
Elgin, IL 800-323-0775

Raw

American Almond Products Company
Brooklyn, NY 800-825-6663
Birdsong Corporation
Suffolk, VA 757-539-3456
Birdsong Peanuts
Blakely, GA 800-597-7688
Cajun Creole Products
New Iberia, LA 800-946-8688
Hialeah Products Company
Hollywood, FL 800-923-3379
John B Sanfilippo & Son
Elgin, IL 847-289-1800
Krema Nut Company
Columbus, OH 800-222-4132
LA Wholesale Produce Market
Los Angeles, CA 888-454-6887
St. Laurent Brothers
Bay City, MI 800-289-7688

Raw & Shelled

American Health & Nutrition
Ann Arbor, MI 734-677-5570
American Key Food Products
Closter, NJ 800-767-0237
Cajun Creole Products
New Iberia, LA 800-946-8688
Golden Peanut Company
Ashburn, GA 229-567-3311
Hialeah Products Company
Hollywood, FL 800-923-3379
King Nut Company
Solon, OH 800-860-5464
McCleskey Mills
Smithville, GA 229-846-2003
Royal Oak Peanuts
Drewryville, VA 800-608-4590
Sachs Peanuts
Clarkton, NC 800-732-6933
Seabrook Ingredients
Edenton, NC 252-482-2112
Setton International Foods
Commack, NY 800-227-4397
Southern Peanut Company
Dublin, NC 910-862-2136
Terri Lynn
Elgin, IL 800-323-0775

Roasted

American Almond Products Company
Brooklyn, NY 800-825-6663
Cajun Creole Products
New Iberia, LA 800-946-8688
CJ Dannemiller Company
Norton, OH 800-624-8671
E.F. Lane & Son
Colton, CA 510-569-8980
John B Sanfilippo & Son
Elgin, IL 847-289-1800
King Nut Company
Solon, OH 800-860-5464
Naylor Candies
Mount Wolf, PA 717-266-2706
Queensway Foods Company
Burlingame, CA 650-871-7770
Southern Peanut Company
Dublin, NC 910-862-2136
St. Laurent Brothers
Bay City, MI 800-289-7688
Synergy Foods
West Bloomfield, MI 313-849-2900

Salted

American Health & Nutrition
Ann Arbor, MI 734-677-5570
Cajun Creole Products
New Iberia, LA 800-946-8688
Durey-Libby Edible Nuts
Carlstadt, NJ 800-332-6887
Hialeah Products Company
Hollywood, FL 800-923-3379
Koeze Company
Wyoming, MI 800-555-3909
LA Wholesale Produce Market
Los Angeles, CA 888-454-6887
Seabrook Ingredients
Edenton, NC 252-482-2112
Setton International Foods
Commack, NY 800-227-4397
Southern Peanut Company
Dublin, NC 910-862-2136
St. Laurent Brothers
Bay City, MI 800-289-7688
Terri Lynn
Elgin, IL 800-323-0775
Virginia & Spanish Peanut Company
Providence, RI 800-673-3562

Pecan

American Health & Nutrition
Ann Arbor, MI 734-677-5570
American Key Food Products
Closter, NJ 800-767-0237
Aunt Aggie De's Pralines
Sinton, TX 888-772-5463
Cache Creek Foods
Woodland, CA 530-662-1764
Carolina Cracker
Garner, NC 919-779-6899
Carolyn's Gourmet
Concord, MA 800-656-2940
Cheese Straws & More
Monroe, LA 800-997-1921
Chieftain Wild Rice Company
Spooner, WI 800-262-6368
Claxton Bakery
Claxton, GA 800-841-4211
Cloverland Sweets/Priester's Pecan Company
Fort Deposit, AL 800-523-3505
Columbus Gourmet
Columbus, GA 800-356-1858
Diamond Foods Inc
Stockton, CA 209-467-6000
Durey-Libby Edible Nuts
Carlstadt, NJ 800-332-6887
Elegant Edibles
Houston, TX 800-227-3226
Fancy's Candy's
Rougemont, NC 888-403-2629
Fastachi
Watertown, MA 800-466-3022
Fresh Roasted Almond Company
Warren, MI 877-478-6887
Golden Harvest Pecans
Cairo, GA 800-597-0968
Golden Kernel Pecan Company
Cameron, SC 800-845-2448
Green Valley Pecan Company
Sahuarita, AZ 800-533-5269
Hialeah Products Company
Hollywood, FL 800-923-3379
Indianola Pecan House
Indianola, MS 800-541-6252
Indianola Pecan House, Inc./Wheeler's Gourmet Pecans
Indianola, MS 800-541-6252
Jewel Date Company
Thermal, CA 760-399-4474
John B Sanfilippo & Son
Selma, TX 800-423-6546
John B Sanfilippo & Sons
Selma, TX 800-423-6546
Koeze Company
Wyoming, MI 800-555-3909
Krema Nut Company
Columbus, OH 800-222-4132
Landies Candies Company
Buffalo, NY 800-955-2634
Lane Packing Company
Fort Valley, GA 478-825-3362
Lou-Retta's Custom Chocolates
Buffalo, NY 716-833-7111
Mapled Nut Company
Montgomery, VT 800-726-4661
Maxwell's Gourmet Food
Raleigh, NC 800-952-6887
Meridian Nut Growers
Clovis, CA 559-458-7272
Merritt Pecan Company
Weston, GA 800-762-9152
Mingo River Pecan Company
Florence, SC 800-440-6442
Mountain States Pecan
Roswell, NM 575-623-2216
Navarro Pecan Company
Corsicana, TX 800-333-9507
Nuthouse Company
Mobile, AL 800-633-1306
Nutty Bavarian
Sanford, FL 800-382-4788
Orangeburg Pecan Company
Orangeburg, SC 800-845-6970
Pape's Pecan Company
Seguin, TX 888-688-7273
Pippin Snack Pecans
Albany, GA 800-554-6887
Pippin Snack Pecans Incorporated
Albany, GA 229-432-9316
Planters LifeSavers Com pany
Fort Smith, AR 479-648-0100
Priester Pecan Company
Fort Deposit, AL 800-277-3226
Reed Lang Farms
Rio Hondo, TX 956-748-2354
Ross-Smith Pecan Company
Thomasville, GA 800-841-5503
San Saba Pecan
San Saba, TX 800-683-2101
Santa Cruz Valley Pecan
Sahuarita, AZ 800-533-5269
Setton International Foods
Commack, NY 800-227-4397
South Georgia Pecan
Valdosta, GA 800-627-6630
South Georgia Pecan Company
Valdosta, GA 800-627-6630
Southern Style Nuts
Denison, TX 903-463-3161
Southwest Nut Co.
Fabens, TX 915-764-4949
Stahmann Farms
La Mesa, NM 575-526-2453
Stapleton-Spence PackingCompany
San Jose, CA 800-297-8815
Stone Mountain Pecan Company
Monroe, GA 800-633-6887
Sunny South Pecan Company
Statesboro, GA 800-764-3687
Sunnyland Farms
Albany, GA 800-999-2488
Sunshine Farms The Nut House Inc
Roseboro, NC 910-564-2421
Sunwest Foods
Davis, CA 530-758-8550
Superior Pecan
Eufaula, AL 800-628-2350
Terri Lynn
Elgin, IL 800-323-0775
Tracy Luckey Pecans
Harlem, GA 800-476-4796
Tucker Pecan Company
Montgomery, AL 800-239-6540
Weaver Nut Company
Ephrata, PA 717-738-3781
Whaley Pecan Company
Troy, AL 800-824-6827
Whitley's Peanut Factory
Hayes, VA 800-470-2244
Young Pecan
Las Cruces, NM 575-524-4321
Young Pecan Company
Florence, SC 800-829-6864

Salted

Stahmann Farms
La Mesa, NM 575-526-2453

Pignolias

Castella Imports
Hauppauge, NY 866-227-8355
L&S Packing Company
Farmingdale, NY 800-286-6487

Pine

American Importing Company
Minneapolis, MN 612-331-7000
American Key Food Products
Closter, NJ 800-767-0237
Chieftain Wild Rice Company
Spooner, WI 800-262-6368
Diamond Foods
Fishers, IN 317-845-5534
Diamond Foods Inc
Stockton, CA 209-467-6000
Durey-Libby Edible Nuts
Carlstadt, NJ 800-332-6887
Fastachi
Watertown, MA 800-466-3022
Grapevine Trading Company
Santa Rosa, CA 800-469-6478
Hialeah Products Company
Hollywood, FL 800-923-3379
John B Sanfilippo & Sons
Selma, TX 800-423-6546
Setton International Foods
Commack, NY 800-227-4397
Spring Tree Maple Products
Brattleboro, VT 802-254-8784
Stapleton-Spence PackingCompany
San Jose, CA 800-297-8815
Terri Lynn
Elgin, IL 800-323-0775
Woodland Foods
Gurnee, IL 847-625-8600

Pistachio

Arizona Pistachio Company
Tulare, CA 800-333-8575
Buchanan Hollow Nut Company
Le Grand, CA 800-532-1500
Cache Creek Foods
Woodland, CA 530-662-1764
California Fruit & Nut
Gustine, CA 888-747-8224
Capco Enterprises
East Hanover, NJ 800-252-1011
Chieftain Wild Rice Company
Spooner, WI 800-262-6368
Commodities Marketing, Inc.
Edison, NJ 732-603-5077
Diamond Foods
Fishers, IN 317-845-5534
Durey-Libby Edible Nuts
Carlstadt, NJ 800-332-6887
Fastachi
Watertown, MA 800-466-3022
Germack Pistachio Company
Detroit, MI 800-872-4006
H. Naraghi Farms
Escalon, CA 209-577-5777
Hialeah Products Company
Hollywood, FL 800-923-3379
Jardine Organic Ranch Co
Paso Robles, CA 866-833-5050
John B Sanfilippo & Sons
Selma, TX 800-423-6546
Kalustyan Corporation
Union, NJ 908-688-6111

Keenan Farms
Avenal, CA 559-945-1400
Koeze Company
Wyoming, MI 800-555-3909
Krema Nut Company
Columbus, OH 800-222-4132
LA Wholesale Produce Market
Los Angeles, CA................... 888-454-6887
Meridian Nut Growers
Clovis, CA 559-458-7272
Mrs. Dog's Products
Grand Rapids, MI 800-2Mr-Dog
Nunes Farm Almonds
Newman, CA...................... 209-862-3033
Nuts & Stems
Rosharon, TX 281-464-6887
Omega Nutrition
Bellingham, WA 800-661-3529
Organic Planet
San Francisco, CA 415-765-5590
Pacific Gold Marketing
Fresno, CA
Paramount Farms
Los Angeles, CA................... 877-450-9493
Planters LifeSavers Com pany
Fort Smith, AR 479-648-0100
Primex International Trading Corporation
Los Angeles, CA................... 310-568-8855
Santa Barbara Pistachio Company
Santa Barbara, CA 800-896-1044
Setton International Foods
Commack, NY 800-227-4397
South Valley Farms
Wasco, CA 661-391-9000
Spring Tree Maple Products
Brattleboro, VT.................... 802-254-8784
Stapleton-Spence PackingCompany
San Jose, CA...................... 800-297-8815
Sunray Food Products Corporation
Bronx, NY........................ 718-548-2255
Sunwest Foods
Davis, CA 530-758-8550
Tejon Ranch
Lebec, CA........................ 661-248-5181
Terri Lynn
Elgin, IL 800-323-0775
Timber Crest Farms
Healdsburg, CA 888-374-9325
Weaver Nut Company
Ephrata, PA....................... 717-738-3781
Woodland Foods
Gurnee, IL........................ 847-625-8600

Pralines (See also Confectionery)

Aunt Aggie De's Pralines
Sinton, TX........................ 888-772-5463
B&B Pecan Processors of NC
Turkey, NC 866-328-7322
Blueberry Store
Grand Junction, MI................. 877-654-2400
Creole Delicacies Pralines
New Orleans, LA 504-523-6425
Landies Candies Company
Buffalo, NY....................... 800-955-2634
Pecan Deluxe Candy Company
Dallas, TX........................ 800-733-3589

Roasted

Adkin & Son Associated Food Products
South Haven, MI................... 269-637-7450
American Almond Products Company
Brooklyn, NY 800-825-6663
Baker Candy Company
Snohomish, WA 425-422-6331
Bruno's Cajun Foods & Snacks
Slidell, LA........................ 985-726-0544
CJ Dannemiller Company
Norton, OH 800-624-8671
Dakota Gourmet
Wahpeton, ND..................... 800-727-6663
Osage Pecan Company
Butler, MO 660-679-6137
Solnuts
Hudson, IA 800-648-3503
Superior Nut & Candy Company
Chicago, IL 800-843-2238
Tropical
Charlotte, NC 800-220-1413
Tropical Nut & Fruit Company
Orlando, FL....................... 800-749-8869
Willmar Cookie & Nut Company
Willmar, MN...................... 320-235-0600
Wolfies Gourmet Nuts
Findlay, OH....................... 866-889-6887

Shelled

A. Battaglia Processing Company
Chicago, IL 773-523-5900
Alldrin Brothers
Ballico, CA 209-667-1600
Bruno's Cajun Foods & Snacks
Slidell, LA........................ 985-726-0544
Frazier Nut Farms
Waterford, CA..................... 209-522-1406
Jerry's Nut House
Denver, CO 888-214-0747
Pippin Snack Pecans
Albany, GA....................... 800-554-6887
Ross-Smith Pecan Company
Thomasville, GA................... 800-841-5503
Santa Clara Nut Company
San Jose, CA...................... 408-298-2425
Tracy Luckey Pecans
Harlem, GA....................... 800-476-4796
Whaley Pecan Company
Troy, AL 800-824-6827

Soy

Almost Nuts, LLC
Denmark, WI...................... 920-915-0152
American Health & Nutrition
Ann Arbor, MI 734-677-5570
American Importing Company
Minneapolis, MN 612-331-7000
Fastachi
Watertown, MA.................... 800-466-3022
Hialeah Products Company
Hollywood, FL 800-923-3379
Just Tomatoes Company
Westley, CA....................... 800-537-1985
Lee Seed Company
Inwood, IA 800-736-6530
Nature's Select
Grand Rapids, MI 888-715-4321
Solnuts
Hudson, IA 800-648-3503

Walnuts

American Almond Products Company
Brooklyn, NY 800-825-6663
American Health & Nutrition
Ann Arbor, MI 734-677-5570
Beard's Quality Nut Company
Empire, CA....................... 209-526-3590
Berberian Nut Company
Chico, CA 530-891-4900
Byrd's Pecans
Butler, MO 866-679-5583
Chieftain Wild Rice Company
Spooner, WI 800-262-6368
Crain Ranch
Los Molinos, CA 530-527-1077
Diamond Foods
Fishers, IN........................ 317-845-5534
Diamond Foods Inc
Stockton, CA...................... 209-467-6000
Durey-Libby Edible Nuts
Carlstadt, NJ 800-332-6887
Erba Food Products
Brooklyn, NY 718-272-7700
Fastachi
Watertown, MA.................... 800-466-3022
Frazier Nut Farms
Waterford, CA..................... 209-522-1406
Fresh Roasted Almond Company
Warren, MI 877-478-6887
Guerra Nut Shelling Company
Hollister, CA...................... 831-637-4471
H. Naraghi Farms
Escalon, CA 209-577-5777
Hammons Products Company
Stockton, MO 888-429-6887
Hialeah Products Company
Hollywood, FL 800-923-3379
John B Sanfilippo & Son
Selma, TX........................ 800-423-6546
John B. Sanfilippo & Son
Gustine, CA 800-218-3077
Lodi Nut Company
Lodi, CA 800-234-6887
Mapled Nut Company
Montgomery, VT................... 800-726-4661
Mariani Nut Company
Winters, CA....................... 530-662-3311
Meridian Nut Growers
Clovis, CA 559-458-7272
Mid-Valley Nut Company
Hughson, CA 209-883-4491
Nut Factory
Spokane Valley, WA 888-239-5288
Planters LifeSavers Com pany
Fort Smith, AR 479-648-0100
Ramos Orchards
Winters, CA 530-795-4748
Santa Clara Nut Company
San Jose, CA...................... 408-298-2425
Service Packing Company
Vancouver, BC 604-681-0264
Specialty Commodities
Fargo, ND 701-282-8222
Stapleton-Spence PackingCompany
San Jose, CA...................... 800-297-8815
Sunwest Foods
Davis, CA 530-758-8550
Tejon Ranch
Lebec, CA........................ 661-248-5181
Weaver Nut Company
Ephrata, PA....................... 717-738-3781
Wilbur Packing Company
Yuba City, CA..................... 530-671-4911
Willamette Valley Walnuts
McMinnville, OR 503-472-3215
Woodland Foods
Gurnee, IL........................ 847-625-8600

Black

American Health & Nutrition
Ann Arbor, MI 734-677-5570
American Key Food Products
Closter, NJ........................ 800-767-0237
Cache Creek Foods
Woodland, CA..................... 530-662-1764
Frazier Nut Farms
Waterford, CA..................... 209-522-1406
Guerra Nut Shelling Company
Hollister, CA...................... 831-637-4471
Hammons Products Company
Stockton, MO 888-429-6887
Hialeah Products Company
Hollywood, FL 800-923-3379
John B Sanfilippo & Son
Selma, TX........................ 800-423-6546
Lodi Nut Company
Lodi, CA 800-234-6887
Organic Planet
San Francisco, CA 415-765-5590
Setton International Foods
Commack, NY 800-227-4397
Terri Lynn
Elgin, IL 800-323-0775
Unique Ingredients
Naches, WA....................... 509-653-1991

Oils, Shortening & Fats

General

AAK USA
Port Newark, NJ 973-344-1300
Akicorp
N Miami Beach, FL 786-426-5750
American Hawaiian Soy Company
Honolulu, HI. 800-841-8435
Austrian Trade Commission
New York, NY 212-421-5250
Capa Di Roma, Inc
East Hartford, CT 860-282-0298
Central Soyfoods
Lawrence, KS 785-312-8698
CHS
Inver Grove Heights, MN. 800-232-3639
Columbus Oils
Des Plaines, IL 773-265-6500
Dee Bee's Feed
Milford, IA 712-262-4850
Denomega Nutritional Oils
Boulder, CO 303-581-9000
Diricom
1 Seccion, MC. 555-596-0898
Dpi Specialty Foods, Inc
Evanston, IL 503-692-0662
FINA LLC
Cicinnati, OH 814-218-3439
First Food International
Linden, NJ. 908-862-5558
Fruit of the Land Products
Thornhill, ON 877-311-5267
Frutech International
Pasadena, CA 626-844-0200
G Banis Company And Services, Inc.
Wilmington, DE 617-516-9092
Gourmet Mondiale
Ste-Catherine, QC. 450-638-6380
Heartland Flax
Valley City, ND. 866-599-3529
I Heart Olive Oil
Ft Lauderdale, FL. 954-607-1539
Italian Products USA Inc
Clark, NJ. 201-770-9130
JFG Coffee Co
Knoxville, TN. 865-546-2120
Marubeni America Corporation
New York, NY 212-450-0563
Maywood International Sales
Sante Fe, NM 505-982-2700
NAR
Nashua, NH. 603-888-5420
Nealanders Food Ingredients
Elgin, IL 847-468-0001
Oasis Foods Company
Hillside, NJ. 908-964-0477
Pacific Soybean & Grain
San Francisco, CA 415-433-0867
Paktec-100% Tunisian Olive Oil
Johnson City, TN 423-467-9864
Patrick Cudahy
Cudahy, WI. 800-486-6900
Pondini Imports, Inc
Somerset, NJ. 732-545-1255
Rallis Whole Foods
Windsor, ON. 519-796-9712
SIGCO Sun Products
Breckenridge, MN 800-654-4145
Ventura Foods
Philadelphia, PA 215-223-8700
Wannamaker Seeds
St. Matthews, SC 803-874-1381

Fats & Lard

Chicken

All-States Quality Foods
Charles City, IA 800-247-4195

Dried

Agri-Dairy Products
Purchase, NY 914-697-9580

Frozen

Clofine Dairy & Food Products
Linwood, NJ 800-441-1001
Henningsen Foods
Purchase, NY 914-701-4020
Proliant Meat Ingredients
Harlan, IA. 800-369-2672

Liquid

Agri-Dairy Products
Purchase, NY 914-697-9580
Clofine Dairy & Food Products
Linwood, NJ 800-441-1001
Henningsen Foods
Purchase, NY 914-701-4020

Powdered

Clofine Dairy & Food Products
Linwood, NJ 800-441-1001
Henningsen Foods
Purchase, NY 914-701-4020

Hydrogenated

AG Processing, Inc.
Omaha, NE 800-247-1345
Agri-Dairy Products
Purchase, NY 914-697-9580
Baker Commodities
Vernon, CA 800-427-0696
Blossom Farm Products
Ridgewood, NJ 800-729-1818
CBP Resources
Gastonia, NC. 704-864-9941
Columbus Foods Company
Des Plaines, IL 800-322-6457
Griffin Industries
Starke, FL 904-964-8083
Loders Croklaan
Channahon, IL 800-621-4710
Mallet & Company
Carnegie, PA. 800-245-2757
National Starch & Chemical Corporate Office
Bridgewater, NJ 908-685-5000
Theriaults Abattoir
Van Buren, ME 207-868-3344
Werling & Sons Slaughterhouse
Burkettsville, OH 937-338-3281

Lard

CanAmera Foods
Oakville, ON. 905-825-7900
Columbus Foods Company
Des Plaines, IL 800-322-6457

Cooking Compounds

Columbus Foods Company
Des Plaines, IL 800-322-6457
Wws
Spring Park, MN. 952-548-9306

Margarine

ADM Refined Oils
Decatur, IL 800-637-5866
Allfresh Food Products
Evanston, IL 773-273-2343
Beaver Meadow Creamery
Du Bois, PA. 800-262-3711
Bunge Canada
Oakville, ON. 800-361-3043
Bunge North America
St Louis, MO. 314-292-2000
Butterball Farms
Grand Rapids, MI 616-243-0105
CanAmera Foods
Oakville, ON. 905-825-7900
CHS
Inver Grove Heights, MN. 800-232-3639
Florida Shortening Corporation
Miami, FL. 305-691-2992
GFA Brands
Paramus, NJ 201-568-9300
JE Bergeron & Sons
Bromptonville, QC 800-567-2798
Keller's Creamery
Harleysville, PA 800-535-5371
Land O'Lakes
Kent, OH. 800-328-9680
Land O'Lakes, Inc.
Arden Hills, MN 800-328-9680
Lov-It Creamery
Green Bay, WI. 800-344-0333
Madison Dairy Produce Company
Madison, WI 608-256-5561
Madison Foods
Saint Paul, MN 651-265-8212
Oasis Foods Company
Hillside, NJ 908-964-0477
Parmalat Canada
Toronto, ON 800-563-1515
Protient (Land O Lakes)
St Paul, MN. 800-328-9680
Schneider's Dairy Holdings Inc
Pittsburgh, PA. 412-881-3525
Sommer Maid Creamery
Doylestown, PA 215-345-6160
Spring Tree Maple Products
Brattleboro, VT. 802-254-8784
Ventura Foods
Ontario, CA. 323-262-9157
Ventura Foods
Portland, OR 503-255-5512
Ventura Foods
Salem, OR. 503-585-6423
Ventura Foods
City of Industry, CA 800-327-3906
Ventura Foods
Saginaw, TX 817-232-5450

Oils

A M Todd Company
Kalamazoo, MI 800-968-2603
ACH Food Companies
Ankeny, IA
ACH Food Companies
Oakbrook Terrace, IL 800-691-1106
ADM Packaged Oils
Decatur, IL 800-637-1550
Agrusa, Inc.
Leonia, NJ. 201-592-5950
Akicorp
N Miami Beach, FL 786-426-5750
Alexander International (USA)
Brightwaters, NY 866-965-0143
American Hawaiian Soy Company
Honolulu, HI. 800-841-8435
American Mercantile Corporation
Memphis, TN 901-454-1900
American Yeast/Lallemand
Pembroke, NH. 866-920-9885
Aphrodisia Products
Brooklyn, NY 877-274-3677
Arista Industries
Wilton, CT 800-255-6457
Aroma Vera
Los Angeles, CA. 800-669-9514
Aroma-Life
Encino, CA 818-905-7761
ARRO Corporation
Hodgkins, IL. 708-352-8200
Astral Extracts Ltd.
Syosset, NY. 516-496-2505
Au Printemps Gourmet
Saint-Jerome, QC 800-663-0416
Avatar Corporation
University Park, IL 800-255-3181
Beta Pure Foods
Aptos, CA. 831-685-6565
Birdsong Peanuts
Blakely, GA. 800-597-7688
Bittersweet Herb Farm
Shelburne Falls, MA. 800-456-1599
Brand Aromatics International
Lakewood, NJ. 800-363-2080
Bunge North America
St Louis, MO. 314-292-2000

Bungy Oils
Pawtucket, RI 401-724-3800
Buon Italia Misono Food Ltd.
New York, NY 212-633-9090
C.F. Sauer Company
Richmond, VA. 800-688-5676
California Olive Oil Corporation
Berkeley, CA. 888-718-9830
CanAmera Foods
Oakville, ON. 905-825-7900
Cargill Refined Oils
Minneapolis, MN 800-323-6232
Cargill Vegetable Oils
Minneapolis, MN 612-378-0551
Carothers Research Laboratories
Flint, MI 810-235-2055
Catania-Spagna Corporation
Ayer, MA. 800-343-5522
Centflor Manufacturing Company
New York, NY 212-246-8307
Central Soya
Bradley, IL 800-556-6777
CHR Hansen
Elyria, OH. 800-558-0802
CHS
Inver Grove Heights, MN. 800-232-3639
Classic Flavors & Fragrances
New York, NY 212-777-0004
Clic International Inc
Laval, QC 450-669-2663
Coast Packing Company
Vernon, CA. 323-277-7700
Colonna Brothers
North Bergen, NJ 201-864-1115
Columbus Foods Company
Des Plaines, IL 800-322-6457
Columbus Vegetable Oils
Des Plaines, IL 800-322-6457
Consumer Guild Foods
Toledo, OH 419-726-3406
Consumers Vinegar & Spice Company
Chicago, IL 773-376-4100
Conway Import Company
Franklin Park, IL. 800-323-8801
Corn Products International
Westchester, IL 800-443-2746
Critelli Olive Oil
Fairfield, CA. 800-865-4836
Cw Resources
New Britain, CT 860-229-7700
Darling International
Bellevue, NE. 402-731-7600
Delicae Gourmet
Tarpon Springs, FL. 800-942-2502
Denomega Nutritional Oils
Boulder, CO 303-581-9000
East Coast Olive Oil
Utica, NY 315-797-3151
Ed Miniat Inc. Headquarters/Cooked Meat Plant
South Holland, IL. 708-589-2400
Erba Food Products
Brooklyn, NY 718-272-7700
Fauchon
New York, NY 877-605-0130
FINA LLC
Cicinnati, OH 814-218-3439
Flavorchem
Downers Grove, IL. 800-435-8867
Flora Manufacturing & Distributing
Burnaby, BC 888-436-6697
Florida Shortening Corporation
Miami, FL. 305-691-2992
Follmer Development/Americana
Newbury Park, CA 800-499-4668
Food Ingredients
Elgin, IL 800-500-7676
Freed, Teller & Freed
South San Francisco, CA 800-370-7371
Frutech International
Pasadena, CA 626-844-0200
GFA Brands
Paramus, NJ 201-568-9300
Golden Brands
Louisville, KY 800-622-3055
Golden Eagle Olive Products
Porterville, CA 559-784-3468
Golden Whisk
South San Francisco, CA 800-660-5222
Good Food
Honey Brook, PA 800-327-4406
Grapevine Trading Company
Santa Rosa, CA. 800-469-6478

Hartsville Oil Mill
Darlington, SC 843-393-2855
Herbal Products & Development
Aptos, CA 831-688-8706
HVJ International
Spring, TX. 877-730-3663
Hybco USA
Los Angeles, CA. 323-269-3111
II Sisters
Moss Beach, CA 800-282-7058
International Home Foods
Parsippany, NJ. 973-359-9920
Kalsec
Kalamazoo, MI 269-349-9711
Kalustyan Corporation
Union, NJ 908-688-6111
Kendall Citrus Corporation
Goulds, FL 305-258-1628
La Tourangelle
Richmond, CA 866-688-6457
Lesley Elizabeth
Lapeer, MI. 800-684-3300
Liberty Natural Products
Oregon City, OR. 800-289-8427
Liberty Vegetable Oil Company
Santa Fe Springs, CA 562-921-3567
Lorann Oils
Lansing, MI. 800-862-8620
Loriva Culinary Oils Worldpantry.Com, Inc
San Francisco, CA 866-972-6879
Lou Ana Foods
Opelousas, LA 800-723-3652
Lubriplate Lubricants
Newark, NJ. 800-733-4755
Lucini Italia Company
San Francisco, CA 888-558-2464
M. Brown & Sons
Bremen, IN 800-258-7450
Mallet & Company
Carnegie, PA. 800-245-2757
Marathon Packing Corporation
San Leandro, CA. 510-895-2000
Marnap Industries
Buffalo, NY. 716-897-1220
Maywood International Sales
Sante Fe, NM 505-982-2700
McLaughlin Oil Company
Columbus, OH 614-231-2518
Medallion Intl.
Pompton Plains, NJ. 973-616-3401
Mercado Latino
City of Industry, CA 626-333-6862
Minute Maid Company
Atlanta, GA. 800-438-2653
Monini North America, Inc
Norwalk, CT. 203-750-0531
Mott's
Elmsford, NY
Mountainbrook of Vermont
Jeffersonville, VT 802-644-1988
Napa Valley Kitchens
Napa, CA. 707-254-3700
National Products Company
Kalamazoo, MI. 269-344-3640
Natural Value Products
Sacramento, CA 916-427-7242
NatureMost Laboratories
Middletown, CT 800-234-2112
Naturex Inc.
South Hackensack, NJ 201-440-5000
Nealanders Food Ingredients
Elgin, IL 847-468-0001
Newport Flavours & Fragrances
Orange, CA. 714-744-3700
North American Enterprises
Tucson, AZ 800-817-8666
O Olive Oil
Petaluma, CA 888-827-7148
Omega Nutrition
Bellingham, WA 800-661-3529
Omega Protein
Houston, TX 877-866-3423
Pacifica Culinaria
Vista, CA. 800-622-8880
Pak Technologies
Milwaukee, WI. 414-438-8600
Paradise Products Corporation
Boca Raton, FL. 800-826-1235
Pastorelli Food Products
Chicago, IL 800-767-2829
Patsy's
New York, NY 212-247-3491

Perdue Farms
Salisbury, MD. 800-473-7383
Pompeian
Baltimore, MD 800-638-1224
Prairie Thyme
Santa Fe, NM 800-869-0009
Proacec USA
Santa Monica, CA. 310-996-7770
Purity Products
Plainview, NY. 888-769-7873
Rcb Intl.
Albany, OR 541-967-3814
Rising Sun Farms
Phoenix, OR 800-888-0795
Ron-Son Foods
Swedesboro, NJ 856-241-7333
Salute Sante! Food & Wine
Napa, CA. 707-251-3900
Santini Foods
San Lorenzo, CA. 800-835-6888
Sieco USA Corporation
Houston, TX 800-325-9443
Silver Palate Kitchens
Cresskill, NJ 800-872-5283
Source Food Technology
Durham, NC 866-277-3849
Sovena USA
Rome, NY. 315-797-7070
Sparboe Companies
Los Angeles, CA. 213-626-7538
Spectrum Organic Products
Petaluma, CA 800-995-2705
Star Fine Foods
Fresno, CA 559-498-2900
Steiner, S.S.
New York, NY 212-515-7200
Tait Farm Foods
Centre Hall, PA. 800-787-2716
Technical Oil
Easton, PA. 610-252-8350
Tee Pee Olives
Rye, NY. 800-431-1529
The Solae Company
Saint Louis, MO 800-325-7108
Tres Classique
Ukiah, CA. 888-644-5127
Tropical
Charlotte, NC 800-220-1413
Trotters Imports
Colrain, MA 800-863-8437
Unilever Bestfoods, Inc.
Englewood Cliffs, NJ 201-894-4000
Ventura Foods
Portland, OR 503-255-5512
Veronica Foods Company
Oakland, CA 800-370-5554
Vitamins
Chicago, IL 312-861-0700
Welch, Home & Clark Company
Newark, NJ. 973-465-1200
Wine Country Kitchens
Napa, CA. 707-252-9463
Wing Nien Company
Hayward, CA 510-487-8877
Wisconsin Cheese
Melrose Park, IL. 708-450-0074
Wws
Spring Park, MN. 952-548-9306

Almond

AG Processing, Inc.
Omaha, NE 800-247-1345
Aroma-Life
Encino, CA 818-905-7761
Astral Extracts Ltd.
Syosset, NY. 516-496-2505
Embassy Flavours Ltd.
Brampton, ON. 800-334-3371
Emerling International Foods
Buffalo, NY. 716-833-7381

Flavtek Geneva Flavors Inc.
Beloit, WI 800-562-5880
Flora
Lynden, WA. 800-446-2110

Gold Coast Ingredients
Commerce, CA 800-352-8673
Janca's Jojoba Oil & Seed Company
Mesa, AZ. 480-497-9494
K.L. Keller Imports
Oakland, CA 510-839-7890
Naturex Inc.
South Hackensack, NJ 201-440-5000
Pokonobe Industries
Santa Monica, CA. 310-392-1259
Pure Extracts Inc
Ronkonkoma, NY. 631-588-9727
Universal Preservachem Inc
Somerset, NJ. 732-568-1266
Welch, Home & Clark Company
Newark, NJ 973-465-1200

Anise or Aniseed

Astral Extracts Ltd.
Syosset, NY. 516-496-2505
Embassy Flavours Ltd.
Brampton, ON. 800-334-3371
Emerling International Foods
Buffalo, NY. 716-833-7381

We supply food manufacturers and food service customers worldwide (since 1988) with bulk ingredients including: Fruits & Vegetables; Juice Concentrates; Herbs & Spices; Oils & Vinegars; Flavors & Colors; Honey & Molasses. We also produce PURE MAPLE SYRUP.

Medallion Intl.
Pompton Plains, NJ. 973-616-3401
Naturex Inc.
South Hackensack, NJ 201-440-5000
Pure Extracts Inc
Ronkonkoma, NY. 631-588-9727

Avocado

Arista Industries
Wilton, CT 800-255-6457

Bean

ADM Refined Oils
Decatur, IL 800-637-5866
Avatar Corporation
University Park, IL. 800-255-3181
Irving R. Boody & Company
New York, NY 212-947-8300
JFG Coffee Co
Knoxville, TN. 865-546-2120
Pure Extracts Inc
Ronkonkoma, NY. 631-588-9727

Black Pepper

Medallion Intl.
Pompton Plains, NJ. 973-616-3401
Naturex Inc.
South Hackensack, NJ 201-440-5000
Pure Extracts Inc
Ronkonkoma, NY. 631-588-9727

Borage

Omega Nutrition
Bellingham, WA 800-661-3529

Canola

AAK USA
Port Newark, NJ 973-344-1300
ACH Food Companies
Ankeny, IA
ADM Food Oils
Decatur, IL 800-637-5866
ADM Refined Oils
Decatur, IL 800-637-5866
AG Processing, Inc.
Omaha, NE 800-247-1345
American Health & Nutrition
Ann Arbor, MI 734-677-5570
Avatar Corporation
University Park, IL. 800-255-3181
Bunge Canada
Oakville, ON. 800-361-3043
California Olive Oil Corporation
Berkeley, CA. 888-718-9830
Cargill Refined Oils
Minneapolis, MN 800-323-6232
Catania-Spagna Corporation
Ayer, MA. 800-343-5522
Central Soya
Bradley, IL 800-556-6777
Columbus Oils
Des Plaines, IL 773-265-6500
Emerling International Foods
Buffalo, NY. 716-833-7381

We supply food manufacturers and food service customers worldwide (since 1988) with bulk ingredients including: Fruits & Vegetables; Juice Concentrates; Herbs & Spices; Oils & Vinegars; Flavors & Colors; Honey & Molasses. We also produce PURE MAPLE SYRUP.

Flora
Lynden, WA. 800-446-2110
Gama Products
Medley, FL 305-883-1200
Good Food
Honey Brook, PA 800-327-4406
Heartland Gourmet Popcorn
Elk Grove Village, IL 866-945-5346
Intermountain Canola Cargill
Idaho Falls, ID 800-822-6652
Janca's Jojoba Oil & Seed Company
Mesa, AZ. 480-497-9494
Loriva Culinary Oils Worldpantry.Com, Inc
San Francisco, CA 866-972-6879
Marubeni America Corporation
New York, NY 212-450-0563
Maywood International Sales
Sante Fe, NM 505-982-2700
Montana Specialty Mills
Great Falls, MT. 406-761-2338
Nealanders Food Ingredients
Elgin, IL 847-468-0001
Omega Nutrition
Bellingham, WA 800-661-3529
Pokonobe Industries
Santa Monica, CA. 310-392-1259
Pure Extracts Inc
Ronkonkoma, NY. 631-588-9727
Universal Preservachem Inc
Somerset, NJ. 732-568-1266
Ventura Foods
Opelousas, LA 337-948-6561

Caraway

Emerling International Foods
Buffalo, NY. 716-833-7381

We supply food manufacturers and food service customers worldwide (since 1988) with bulk ingredients including: Fruits & Vegetables; Juice Concentrates; Herbs & Spices; Oils & Vinegars; Flavors & Colors; Honey & Molasses. We also produce PURE MAPLE SYRUP.

Medallion Intl.
Pompton Plains, NJ. 973-616-3401
Naturex Inc.
South Hackensack, NJ 201-440-5000
Pure Extracts Inc
Ronkonkoma, NY. 631-588-9727

Cardamom

Medallion Intl.
Pompton Plains, NJ. 973-616-3401
Naturex Inc.
South Hackensack, NJ 201-440-5000
Pure Extracts Inc
Ronkonkoma, NY. 631-588-9727

Cassia

Embassy Flavours Ltd.
Brampton, ON. 800-334-3371
Naturex Inc.
South Hackensack, NJ 201-440-5000
Pure Extracts Inc
Ronkonkoma, NY. 631-588-9727

Castor

Arista Industries
Wilton, CT 800-255-6457
Avatar Corporation
University Park, IL. 800-255-3181
Heritage Store
Virginia Beach, VA. 800-862-2923
Leatex Chemical Company
Philadelphia, PA 215-739-2000
Pure Extracts Inc
Ronkonkoma, NY. 631-588-9727
Salem Oil & Grease Company
Salem, MA 978-745-0585

Celery

Naturex Inc.
South Hackensack, NJ 201-440-5000
Pure Extracts Inc
Ronkonkoma, NY. 631-588-9727

Cinnamon - Leaf & Bark

Flavtek Geneva Flavors Inc.
Beloit, WI 800-562-5880
Medallion Intl.
Pompton Plains, NJ. 973-616-3401
Pure Extracts Inc
Ronkonkoma, NY. 631-588-9727

Citrus

Astral Extracts Ltd.
Syosset, NY. 516-496-2505
Boyajian, Inc.
Canton, MA 800-965-0665
California Olive Oil Corporation
Berkeley, CA. 888-718-9830
Diana's Specialty Foods
Pingree Grove, IL 847-683-1200
Embassy Flavours Ltd.
Brampton, ON. 800-334-3371
Emerling International Foods
Buffalo, NY. 716-833-7381

We supply food manufacturers and food service customers worldwide (since 1988) with bulk ingredients including: Fruits & Vegetables; Juice Concentrates; Herbs & Spices; Oils & Vinegars; Flavors & Colors; Honey & Molasses. We also produce PURE MAPLE SYRUP.

Flavtek Geneva Flavors Inc.
Beloit, WI 800-562-5880
Frutech International
Pasadena, CA 626-844-0200
Gold Coast Ingredients
Commerce, CA. 800-352-8673
Kendall Citrus Corporation
Goulds, FL 305-258-1628
Louis Dreyfus Citrus
Winter Garden, FL 800-549-4272
Medallion Intl.
Pompton Plains, NJ. 973-616-3401
Minute Maid Company
Atlanta, GA. 800-438-2653
O Olive Oil
Petaluma, CA 888-827-7148
Peace River Citrus Products
Vero Beach, FL. 772-467-1234
Prime Ingredients
Saddle Brook, NJ 888-791-6655
Pure Extracts Inc
Ronkonkoma, NY. 631-588-9727
Robertet Flavors
Piscataway, NJ 732-271-1804
Ungerer & Company
Lincoln Park, NJ. 973-628-0600

Clove

Pure Extracts Inc
Ronkonkoma, NY. 631-588-9727

Coconut

AAK USA
Port Newark, NJ 973-344-1300
Aarhus United USA, Inc.
Newark, NJ 800-776-1338
ADM Food Oils
Decatur, IL 800-637-5866
ADM Refined Oils
Decatur, IL 800-637-5866
AG Processing, Inc.
Omaha, NE 800-247-1345
Avatar Corporation
University Park, IL. 800-255-3181
Catania-Spagna Corporation
Ayer, MA. 800-343-5522

Central Soya
Bradley, IL 800-556-6777
Clofine Dairy & Food Products
Linwood, NJ 800-441-1001
Columbus Oils
Des Plaines, IL 773-265-6500
Emerling International Foods
Buffalo, NY. 716-833-7381

We supply food manufacturers and food service customers worldwide (since 1988) with bulk ingredients including: Fruits & Vegetables; Juice Concentrates; Herbs & Spices; Oils & Vinegars; Flavors & Colors; Honey & Molasses. We also produce PURE MAPLE SYRUP.

First Food International
Linden, NJ. 908-862-5558
Flavtek Geneva Flavors Inc.
Beloit, WI 800-562-5880
Gold Coast Ingredients
Commerce, CA 800-352-8673
Good Food
Honey Brook, PA 800-327-4406
Janca's Jojoba Oil & Seed Company
Mesa, AZ. 480-497-9494
Maywood International Sales
Sante Fe, NM 505-982-2700
Pokonobe Industries
Santa Monica, CA. 310-392-1259
Pure Extracts Inc
Ronkonkoma, NY. 631-588-9727
Ventura Foods
Opelousas, LA 337-948-6561
Welch, Home & Clark Company
Newark, NJ 973-465-1200

Cod Liver

Irving R. Boody & Company
New York, NY 212-947-8300
Jamieson Laboratories
Windosr, ON. 519-974-8482
JR Carlson Laboratories
Arlington Hts, IL 888-234-5656

Cooking

ACH Food Companies
Ankeny, IA
ACH Food Companies
Cordova, TN 800-691-1106
ADM Southern Cotton Oil
Decatur, IL 800-637-5843
Agrusa, Inc.
Leonia, NJ. 201-592-5950
Alberto-Culver Company
Melrose Park, IL. 708-450-3000
Allfresh Food Products
Evanston, IL 773-273-2343
Americana Marketing
Newbury Park, CA 800-742-7520
Arista Industries
Wilton, CT 800-255-6457
ARRO Corporation
Hodgkins, IL. 708-352-8200
Avatar Corporation
University Park, IL 800-255-3181
Butterbuds Food Ingredients
Racine, WI. 800-426-1119
C&T Refinery
Richmond, VA. 800-284-6457
California Oils Corporation
Richmond, CA 800-225-6457
California Olive Oil Corporation
Berkeley, CA. 888-718-9830
Capital City Processors
Oklahoma City, OK 800-473-2731
Cargill Refined Oils
Minneapolis, MN 800-323-6232
Cargill Specialty Oils
Minneapolis, MN 800-851-8331
Cargill Vegetable Oils
Minneapolis, MN 612-378-0551
Catania-Spagna Corporation
Ayer, MA. 800-343-5522
Central Soya
Bradley, IL 800-556-6777
Coast Packing Company
Vernon, CA 323-277-7700
Colonna Brothers
North Bergen, NJ 201-864-1115
ConAgra Grocery Products
Irvine, CA 714-680-1000
Deep South Products
Fitzgerald, GA. 229-423-1121
Diana's Specialty Foods
Pingree Grove, IL 847-683-1200
Dipasa
Brownsville, TX 956-831-5893
Embassy Flavours Ltd.
Brampton, ON. 800-334-3371
Emerling International Foods
Buffalo, NY. 716-833-7381

We supply food manufacturers and food service customers worldwide (since 1988) with bulk ingredients including: Fruits & Vegetables; Juice Concentrates; Herbs & Spices; Oils & Vinegars; Flavors & Colors; Honey & Molasses. We also produce PURE MAPLE SYRUP.

Flora
Lynden, WA. 800-446-2110
Follmer Development/Americana
Newbury Park, CA 800-499-4668
Gateway Food Products Company
Dupo, IL 877-220-1963
Good Food
Honey Brook, PA 800-327-4406
Intermountain Canola Cargill
Idaho Falls, ID 800-822-6652
Janca's Jojoba Oil & Seed Company
Mesa, AZ. 480-497-9494
Liberty Vegetable Oil Company
Santa Fe Springs, CA 562-921-3567
Loriva Culinary Oils Worldpantry.Com, Inc
San Francisco, CA 866-972-6879
Louis Dreyfus Citrus
Winter Garden, FL 800-549-4272
Mallet & Company
Carnegie, PA. 800-245-2757
Marathon Packing Corporation
San Leandro, CA. 510-895-2000
Mercado Latino
City of Industry, CA 626-333-6862
Milnot Company
Neosho, MO 800-877-6455
Morris J. Golombeck
Brooklyn, NY 718-284-3505
Mother Earth Enterprises
New York, NY 866-436-7688
Mott's
Elmsford, NY
Natural Oils International
Simi Valley, CA. 805-433-0160
Nick Sciabica & Sons
Modesto, CA. 800-551-9612
North American Enterprises
Tucson, AZ 800-817-8666
Our Thyme Garden
Cleburne, TX 800-482-4372
Par-Way Tryson
St Clair, MO 636-629-4545
Pastorelli Food Products
Chicago, IL 800-767-2829
Pokonobe Industries
Santa Monica, CA. 310-392-1259
Producers Cooperative Oil Mill
Oklahoma City, OK 405-232-7555
Progresso Quality Foods
Vineland, NJ 800-200-9377
Pure Extracts Inc
Ronkonkoma, NY. 631-588-9727
Purity Products
Plainview, NY. 888-769-7873
Ron-Son Foods
Swedesboro, NJ 856-241-7333
Sovena USA
Rome, NY 315-797-7070
Ventura Foods
Opelousas, LA 337-948-6561
Ventura Foods
Salem, OR. 503-585-6423
Viobin USA
Monticello, IL. 217-762-2561
Welch, Home & Clark Company
Newark, NJ 973-465-1200
Western Pacific Commodities
Henderson, NV 702-382-8880

Spray

ACH Food Companies
Ankeny, IA
Butterbuds Food Ingredients
Racine, WI. 800-426-1119
Follmer Development/Americana
Newbury Park, CA 800-499-4668
International Home Foods
Parsippany, NJ. 973-359-9920

Coriander Seed

Pure Extracts Inc
Ronkonkoma, NY 631-588-9727

Corn

ACH Food Companies
Ankeny, IA
ADM Food Oils
Decatur, IL 800-637-5866
ADM Refined Oils
Decatur, IL 800-637-5866
AG Processing, Inc.
Omaha, NE 800-247-1345
ARRO Corporation
Hodgkins, IL. 708-352-8200
Avatar Corporation
University Park, IL 800-255-3181
Cargill Dry Corn Ingredients
Paris, IL. 800-637-6481
Cargill Refined Oils
Minneapolis, MN 800-323-6232
Catania-Spagna Corporation
Ayer, MA. 800-343-5522
Central Soya
Bradley, IL 800-556-6777
Columbus Oils
Des Plaines, IL 773-265-6500
Corn Products International
Westchester, IL 800-443-2746
Dee Bee's Feed
Milford, IA 712-262-4850
Erba Food Products
Brooklyn, NY 718-272-7700
Gama Products
Medley, FL 305-883-1200
Good Food
Honey Brook, PA 800-327-4406
Mallet & Company
Carnegie, PA. 800-245-2757
Maywood International Sales
Sante Fe, NM 505-982-2700
Mercado Latino
City of Industry, CA 626-333-6862
Nealanders Food Ingredients
Elgin, IL 847-468-0001
Olde Tyme Food Corporation
East Longmeadow, MA 800-356-6533
Pacific Soybean & Grain
San Francisco, CA 415-433-0867
Pastorelli Food Products
Chicago, IL. 800-767-2829
Pokonobe Industries
Santa Monica, CA. 310-392-1259
Pure Extracts Inc
Ronkonkoma, NY. 631-588-9727
Purity Products
Plainview, NY. 888-769-7873
Sovena USA
Rome, NY. 315-797-7070
Universal Preservachem Inc
Somerset, NJ. 732-568-1266
Ventura Foods
Opelousas, LA 337-948-6561
Welch, Home & Clark Company
Newark, NJ 973-465-1200

Cottonseed

Aarhus United USA, Inc.
Newark, NJ. 800-776-1338
ADM Food Oils
Decatur, IL 800-637-5866
ADM Refined Oils
Decatur, IL 800-637-5866
AG Processing, Inc.
Omaha, NE 800-247-1345
Cargill Refined Oils
Minneapolis, MN 800-323-6232
Catania-Spagna Corporation
Ayer, MA. 800-343-5522
Central Soya
Bradley, IL 800-556-6777
Columbus Oils
Des Plaines, IL 773-265-6500

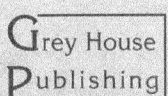

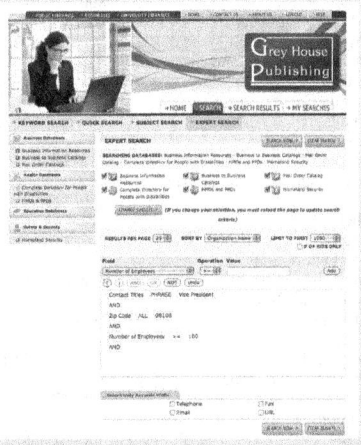

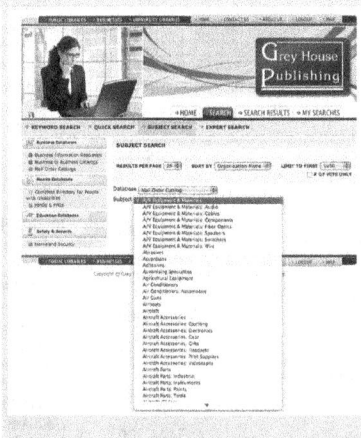

Emerling International Foods
Buffalo, NY....................716-833-7381

We supply food manufacturers and food service customers worldwide (since 1988) with bulk ingredients including: Fruits & Vegetables; Juice Concentrates; Herbs & Spices; Oils & Vinegars; Flavors & Colors; Honey & Molasses. We also produce PURE MAPLE SYRUP.

Golden Brands
Louisville, KY....................800-622-3055
Good Food
Honey Brook, PA....................800-327-4406
Lamesa Cotton Oil Mill
Chandler, AZ....................806-872-2166
Lubbock Cotton Oil Company
Lubbock, TX....................806-763-4371
Maywood International Sales
Sante Fe, NM....................505-982-2700
Nealanders Food Ingredients
Elgin, IL....................847-468-0001
Producers Cooperative Oil Mill
Oklahoma City, OK....................405-232-7555
Pure Extracts Inc
Ronkonkoma, NY....................631-588-9727
PYCO Industries
Lubbock, TX....................806-747-3434
Stevenson-Cooper
Philadelphia, PA....................215-223-2600
Ventura Foods
Opelousas, LA....................337-948-6561
Welch, Home & Clark Company
Newark, NJ....................973-465-1200

Dillweed

Pure Extracts Inc
Ronkonkoma, NY....................631-588-9727
Rcb Intl.
Albany, OR....................541-967-3814

Edible

Aarhus United USA, Inc.
Newark, NJ....................800-776-1338
ABITEC Corporation
Janesville, WI....................800-457-1977
Abitec Corporation
Columbus, OH....................800-555-1255
ACH Food Companies
Ankeny, IA
ADM Refined Oils
Decatur, IL....................800-637-5866
ADM Southern Cotton Oil
Decatur, IL....................800-637-5843
AG Processing, Inc.
Omaha, NE....................800-247-1345
Agri-Dairy Products
Purchase, NY....................914-697-9580
Agrusa, Inc.
Leonia, NJ....................201-592-5950
Alberto-Culver Company
Melrose Park, IL....................708-450-3000
Allfresh Food Products
Evanston, IL....................773-273-2343
American Health & Nutrition
Ann Arbor, MI....................734-677-5570
Americana Marketing
Newbury Park, CA....................800-742-7520
Arista Industries
Wilton, CT....................800-255-6457
ARRO Corporation
Hodgkins, IL....................708-352-8200
Avatar Corporation
University Park, IL....................800-255-3181
Barlean's
Ferndale, WA....................360-384-0325
Boyajian, Inc.
Canton, MA....................800-965-0665
Bungy Oils
Pawtucket, RI....................401-724-3800
Butterbuds Food Ingredients
Racine, WI....................800-426-1119
California Oils Corporation
Richmond, CA....................800-225-6457
California Olive Oil Corporation
Berkeley, CA....................888-718-9830
Capital City Processors
Oklahoma City, OK....................800-473-2731
Capitol Foods
Memphis, TN....................662-781-9021
Cargill Dry Corn Ingredients
Paris, IL....................800-637-6481
Cargill Vegetable Oils
Minneapolis, MN....................612-378-0551
Catania-Spagna Corporation
Ayer, MA....................800-343-5522
Central Soya
Bradley, IL....................800-556-6777
Colavita
Edison, NJ....................732-404-8300
Colonna Brothers
North Bergen, NJ....................201-864-1115
ConAgra Grocery Products
Irvine, CA....................714-680-1000
Consumer Guild Foods
Toledo, OH....................419-726-3406
CP Vegetable Oil
Fort Lauderdale, FL....................905-792-2309
Darling International
Bellevue, NE....................402-731-7600
Dipasa
Brownsville, TX....................956-831-5893
Embassy Flavours Ltd.
Brampton, ON....................800-334-3371
Emerling International Foods
Buffalo, NY....................716-833-7381

We supply food manufacturers and food service customers worldwide (since 1988) with bulk ingredients including: Fruits & Vegetables; Juice Concentrates; Herbs & Spices; Oils & Vinegars; Flavors & Colors; Honey & Molasses. We also produce PURE MAPLE SYRUP.

Energen Products
Norwalk, CA....................800-423-8837
Erba Food Products
Brooklyn, NY....................718-272-7700
Flora
Lynden, WA....................800-446-2110
Gama Products
Medley, FL....................305-883-1200
Gateway Food Products Company
Dupo, IL....................877-220-1963
Golden Whisk
South San Francisco, CA....................800-660-5222
Good Food
Honey Brook, PA....................800-327-4406
Grassland Dairy Products
Greenwood, WI....................800-428-8837
Herbal Products & Development
Aptos, CA....................831-688-8706
Intermountain Canola Cargill
Idaho Falls, ID....................800-822-6652
Irving R. Boody & Company
New York, NY....................212-947-8300
Janca's Jojoba Oil & Seed Company
Mesa, AZ....................480-497-9494
John I. Haas
Washington, DC....................202-777-4800
JR Carlson Laboratories
Arlington Hts, IL....................888-234-5656
Liberty Vegetable Oil Company
Santa Fe Springs, CA....................562-921-3567
Loders Croklaan
Channahon, IL....................800-621-4710
Loriva Culinary Oils Worldpantry.Com, Inc
San Francisco, CA....................866-972-6879
Lou Ana Foods
Opelousas, LA....................800-723-3652
Louis Dreyfus Citrus
Winter Garden, FL....................800-549-4272
Marina Foods
Dania, FL....................954-929-9047
Medallion Intl.
Pompton Plains, NJ....................973-616-3401
Mercado Latino
City of Industry, CA....................626-333-6862
Milnot Company
Neosho, MO....................800-877-6455
Morris J. Golombeck
Brooklyn, NY....................718-284-3505
Mother Earth Enterprises
New York, NY....................866-436-7688
Natural Oils International
Simi Valley, CA....................805-433-0160
Nick Sciabica & Sons
Modesto, CA....................800-551-9612
North American Enterprises
Tucson, AZ....................800-817-8666
Oils of Aloha
Waialua, HI....................800-367-6010
Ottens Flavors
Philadelphia, PA....................800-523-0767
Our Thyme Garden
Cleburne, TX....................800-482-4372
Paradise Products Corporation
Boca Raton, FL....................800-826-1235
Pastorelli Food Products
Chicago, IL....................800-767-2829
Perdue Farms
Salisbury, MD....................800-473-7383
Pokonobe Industries
Santa Monica, CA....................310-392-1259
Pompeian
Baltimore, MD....................800-638-1224
Progresso Quality Foods
Vineland, NJ....................800-200-9377
Pure Extracts Inc
Ronkonkoma, NY....................631-588-9727
Purity Products
Plainview, NY....................888-769-7873
Riceland Foods Rice Milling Operations
Stuttgart, AR....................870-673-5500
Ron-Son Foods
Swedesboro, NJ....................856-241-7333
Scally's Imperial Importing Company Inc
Staten Island, NY....................718-983-1938
Sessions Company
Enterprise, AL....................334-393-0200
Silver Palate Kitchens
Cresskill, NJ....................800-872-5283
Sovena USA
Rome, NY....................315-797-7070
Stuart Hale Company
Chicago, IL....................773-638-1800
Tropical
Charlotte, NC....................800-220-1413
Unilever Bestfoods, Inc.
Englewood Cliffs, NJ....................201-894-4000
Universal Preservachem Inc
Somerset, NJ....................732-568-1266
Ventura Foods
Opelousas, LA....................337-948-6561
Ventura Foods
Salem, OR....................503-585-6423
Veronica Foods Company
Oakland, CA....................800-370-5554
Viobin USA
Monticello, IL....................217-762-2561
Vogel Popcorn
Hamburg, IA....................800-831-5818
Welch, Home & Clark Company
Newark, NJ....................973-465-1200
Wisconsin Cheese
Melrose Park, IL....................708-450-0074

Essential

A M Todd Company
Kalamazoo, MI....................800-968-2603
AM Todd Company
Kalamazoo, MI....................800-968-2603
American Mercantile Corporation
Memphis, TN....................901-454-1900
Aphrodisia Products
Brooklyn, NY....................877-274-3677
Aroma Vera
Los Angeles, CA....................800-669-9514
Aroma-Life
Encino, CA....................818-905-7761
Aromachem
Brooklyn, NY....................718-497-4664
AVRI Companies
Richmond, CA....................800-883-9574
Blue California Company
Rcho Sta Marg, CA....................949-635-1990
Britannia Natural Products
New Windsor, NY....................845-534-1335
Cargill Juice Products
Frostproof, FL....................800-227-4455
Centflor Manufacturing Company
New York, NY....................212-246-8307
Classic Flavors & Fragrances
New York, NY....................212-777-0004
Colin Ingram
Comptche, CA....................707-937-1824
Consumers Flavoring Extract Company
Brooklyn, NY....................718-435-0201
Embassy Flavours Ltd.
Brampton, ON....................800-334-3371

Emerling International Foods
Buffalo, NY....................716-833-7381

We supply food manufacturers and food service customers worldwide (since 1988) with bulk ingredients including: Fruits & Vegetables; Juice Concentrates; Herbs & Spices; Oils & Vinegars; Flavors & Colors; Honey & Molasses. We also produce PURE MAPLE SYRUP.

Essential Products of America
Tampa, FL....................800-822-9698
Flavor Sciences
Lenior, NC....................800-535-2867
Flavorchem
Downers Grove, IL....................800-435-8867
Flavormatic Industries
Wappingers Falls, NY
Flavtek Geneva Flavors Inc.
Beloit, WI....................800-562-5880
Global Botanical
Barrie, ON....................705-733-2117
Green Turtle Bay Vitamin Company
Summit, NJ....................800-887-8535
Greenwood Associates
Highland Park, IL....................847-579-5500
H B Taylor Company
Chicago, IL....................773-254-4805
Heritage Store
Virginia Beach, VA....................800-862-2923
Hi-Country Corona
Selah, WA....................951-272-2600
Irving R. Boody & Company
New York, NY....................212-947-8300
Joseph Adams Corporation
Valley City, OH....................330-225-9135
Kalsec
Kalamazoo, MI....................269-349-9711
Lebermuth Company
South Bend, IN....................800-648-1123
Leeward Resources
Baltimore, MD....................410-837-9003
Loriva Culinary Oils Worldpantry.Com, Inc
San Francisco, CA....................866-972-6879
M. Brown & Sons
Bremen, IN....................800-258-7450
Maple Ridge Farms
Prince Albert, SK....................306-922-8056
Marnap Industries
Buffalo, NY....................716-897-1220
Medallion Intl.
Pompton Plains, NJ....................973-616-3401
Millennium Specialty Chemicals
Jacksonville, FL....................800-231-6728
Mother Earth Enterprises
New York, NY....................866-436-7688
Native Scents
Taos, NM....................800-645-3471
Naturex
South Hackensack, NJ....................201-440-5000
Now Foods
Bloomingdale, IL....................888-669-3663
Pure Extracts Inc
Ronkonkoma, NY....................631-588-9727
Robertet Flavors
Piscataway, NJ....................732-271-1804
Starwest Botanicals
Rancho Cordova, CA....................888-273-4372
SunPure
Lakeland, FL....................863-619-2222
Torre Products Company
New York, NY....................212-925-8989
Treatt USA
Lakeland, FL....................800-866-7704
Ungerer & Company
Lincoln Park, NJ....................973-628-0600
Whole Herb Company
Sonoma, CA....................707-935-1077

Fish

Daybrook Fisheries
Empire, LA....................504-657-8400
Eckhart Corporation
Novato, CA....................415-892-3880
Irving R. Boody & Company
New York, NY....................212-947-8300
Jamieson Laboratories
Windosr, ON....................519-974-8482
Jedwards International
Quincy, MA....................617-472-9300
JR Carlson Laboratories
Arlington Hts, IL....................888-234-5656
Nutraceutical Corporation
Park City, UT....................800-669-8877
Omega Pure
Irvine, CA....................562-429-3335
Scandinavian Laboratories
Mount Bethel, PA....................570-897-7735
Tabco Enterprises
Pomona, CA....................909-623-4565

Fruit

Arista Industries
Wilton, CT....................800-255-6457

Garlic

Astral Extracts Ltd.
Syosset, NY....................516-496-2505
California Olive Oil Corporation
Berkeley, CA....................888-718-9830
Diana's Specialty Foods
Pingree Grove, IL....................847-683-1200
Emerling International Foods
Buffalo, NY....................716-833-7381

We supply food manufacturers and food service customers worldwide (since 1988) with bulk ingredients including: Fruits & Vegetables; Juice Concentrates; Herbs & Spices; Oils & Vinegars; Flavors & Colors; Honey & Molasses. We also produce PURE MAPLE SYRUP.

Halladays Harvest Barn
Bellows Falls, VT....................802-463-3331
Lebermuth Company
South Bend, IN....................800-648-1123
Loriva Culinary Oils Worldpantry.Com, Inc
San Francisco, CA....................866-972-6879
Nutraceutical Corporation
Park City, UT....................800-669-8877
Our Thyme Garden
Cleburne, TX....................800-482-4372
Prime Ingredients
Saddle Brook, NJ....................888-791-6655
Pure Extracts Inc
Ronkonkoma, NY....................631-588-9727
Vegetable Juices
Chicago, IL....................888-776-9752

Ginger

Astral Extracts Ltd.
Syosset, NY....................516-496-2505
Pure Extracts Inc
Ronkonkoma, NY....................631-588-9727
Ungerer & Company
Lincoln Park, NJ....................973-628-0600

Grapefruit

Astral Extracts Ltd.
Syosset, NY....................516-496-2505
Emerling International Foods
Buffalo, NY....................716-833-7381

We supply food manufacturers and food service customers worldwide (since 1988) with bulk ingredients including: Fruits & Vegetables; Juice Concentrates; Herbs & Spices; Oils & Vinegars; Flavors & Colors; Honey & Molasses. We also produce PURE MAPLE SYRUP.

Flavtek Geneva Flavors Inc.
Beloit, WI....................800-562-5880
Gold Coast Ingredients
Commerce, CA....................800-352-8673
Pure Extracts Inc
Ronkonkoma, NY....................631-588-9727
SunPure
Lakeland, FL....................863-619-2222

Grapeseed

AG Processing, Inc.
Omaha, NE....................800-247-1345
Ameri-Kal Inc
Wichita Falls, TX....................940-322-5400
Arista Industries
Wilton, CT....................800-255-6457
Cuisine Perel
Richmond, CA....................800-887-3735
Diana's Specialty Foods
Pingree Grove, IL....................847-683-1200
Emerling International Foods
Buffalo, NY....................716-833-7381

We supply food manufacturers and food service customers worldwide (since 1988) with bulk ingredients including: Fruits & Vegetables; Juice Concentrates; Herbs & Spices; Oils & Vinegars; Flavors & Colors; Honey & Molasses. We also produce PURE MAPLE SYRUP.

Food & Vine
Napa, CA....................707-251-3900
Hormel Foods Corporation
Austin, MN....................507-437-5395
Lifestar Millennium
Sedona, AZ....................877-422-4739
Pokonobe Industries
Santa Monica, CA....................310-392-1259
Pure Extracts Inc
Ronkonkoma, NY....................631-588-9727
Queensway Foods Company
Burlingame, CA....................650-871-7770
Salute Sante! Food & Wine
Napa, CA....................707-251-3900
Tabco Enterprises
Pomona, CA....................909-623-4565

Hazelnut

K.L. Keller Imports
Oakland, CA....................510-839-7890
Loriva Culinary Oils Worldpantry.Com, Inc
San Francisco, CA....................866-972-6879
Pure Extracts Inc
Ronkonkoma, NY....................631-588-9727

Hemp Nut

Columbus Oils
Des Plaines, IL....................773-265-6500
Herbal Products & Development
Aptos, CA....................831-688-8706
Mother Earth Enterprises
New York, NY....................866-436-7688
Pure Extracts Inc
Ronkonkoma, NY....................631-588-9727

Lemon

AG Processing, Inc.
Omaha, NE....................800-247-1345
Astral Extracts Ltd.
Syosset, NY....................516-496-2505
Boyajian, Inc.
Canton, MA....................800-965-0665
Diana's Specialty Foods
Pingree Grove, IL....................847-683-1200
Embassy Flavours Ltd.
Brampton, ON....................800-334-3371
Emerling International Foods
Buffalo, NY....................716-833-7381

We supply food manufacturers and food service customers worldwide (since 1988) with bulk ingredients including: Fruits & Vegetables; Juice Concentrates; Herbs & Spices; Oils & Vinegars; Flavors & Colors; Honey & Molasses. We also produce PURE MAPLE SYRUP.

Flavtek Geneva Flavors Inc.
Beloit, WI....................800-562-5880
Gold Coast Ingredients
Commerce, CA....................800-352-8673
Prime Ingredients
Saddle Brook, NJ....................888-791-6655
Pure Extracts Inc
Ronkonkoma, NY....................631-588-9727
SunPure
Lakeland, FL....................863-619-2222
Ungerer & Company
Lincoln Park, NJ....................973-628-0600

Lemon Grass

Emerling International Foods
Buffalo, NY....................716-833-7381

We supply food manufacturers and food service customers worldwide (since 1988) with bulk ingredients including: Fruits & Vegetables; Juice Concentrates; Herbs & Spices; Oils & Vinegars; Flavors & Colors; Honey & Molasses. We also produce PURE MAPLE SYRUP.

Pure Extracts Inc
Ronkonkoma, NY 631-588-9727

Lime

Astral Extracts Ltd.
Syosset, NY. 516-496-2505
Boyajian, Inc.
Canton, MA 800-965-0665
Emerling International Foods
Buffalo, NY. 716-833-7381

We supply food manufacturers and food service customers worldwide (since 1988) with bulk ingredients including: Fruits & Vegetables; Juice Concentrates; Herbs & Spices; Oils & Vinegars; Flavors & Colors; Honey & Molasses. We also produce PURE MAPLE SYRUP.

Flavtek Geneva Flavors Inc.
Beloit, WI 800-562-5880
Gold Coast Ingredients
Commerce, CA 800-352-8673
Pure Extracts Inc
Ronkonkoma, NY 631-588-9727
Ungerer & Company
Lincoln Park, NJ 973-628-0600

Mustard

Emerling International Foods
Buffalo, NY. 716-833-7381

We supply food manufacturers and food service customers worldwide (since 1988) with bulk ingredients including: Fruits & Vegetables; Juice Concentrates; Herbs & Spices; Oils & Vinegars; Flavors & Colors; Honey & Molasses. We also produce PURE MAPLE SYRUP.

Hemisphere Associated
Huntington, NY 631-673-3840
Montana Specialty Mills
Great Falls, MT. 406-761-2338
Pure Extracts Inc
Ronkonkoma, NY. 631-588-9727

Nutmeg

Emerling International Foods
Buffalo, NY. 716-833-7381

We supply food manufacturers and food service customers worldwide (since 1988) with bulk ingredients including: Fruits & Vegetables; Juice Concentrates; Herbs & Spices; Oils & Vinegars; Flavors & Colors; Honey & Molasses. We also produce PURE MAPLE SYRUP.

Pure Extracts Inc
Ronkonkoma, NY. 631-588-9727
Whole Herb Company
Sonoma, CA 707-935-1077

Olive

A Southern Season
Chapel Hill, NC 877-929-7133
A. Camacho
Plant City, FL 800-881-4534
ACH Food Companies
Ankeny, IA
AG Processing, Inc.
Omaha, NE 800-247-1345
Agrocan
Ville St Laurent, QC 877-247-6226
Agrusa, Inc.
Leonia, NJ. 201-592-5950
Arista Industries
Wilton, CT 800-255-6457
Ariston Specialties
Bloomfield, CT. 860-224-7184
Arnabal International
Tustin, CA. 714-665-9477
Assouline & Ting
Huntingdon Valley, PA 800-521-4491
Avatar Corporation
University Park, IL 800-255-3181
B.R. Cohn Olive Oil
Glen Ellen, CA 800-330-4064
Bella Cucina Artful Food
Atlanta, GA. 866-350-9040
Bella Vista Farm
Lawton, OK. 866-237-8526
BR Cohn Winery
Glen Ellen, CA 707-938-4064
California Olive Growers
Fresno, CA 888-965-4837
California Olive Oil Corporation
Berkeley, CA. 888-718-9830
Calio Groves
Berkeley, CA. 800-865-4836
Castella Imports
Hauppauge, NY 866-227-8355
Catania-Spagna Corporation
Ayer, MA. 800-343-5522
Colavita
Edison, NJ. 732-404-8300
Colonna Brothers
North Bergen, NJ 201-864-1115
Continental Group
Huntington Beach, CA 858-391-5670
CreAgri
Hayward, CA 510-732-6478
Critelli Olive Oil
Fairfield, CA. 800-865-4836
Diana's Specialty Foods
Pingree Grove, IL 847-683-1200
East Coast Olive Oil
Utica, NY 315-797-3151
Emerling International Foods
Buffalo, NY. 716-833-7381

We supply food manufacturers and food service customers worldwide (since 1988) with bulk ingredients including: Fruits & Vegetables; Juice Concentrates; Herbs & Spices; Oils & Vinegars; Flavors & Colors; Honey & Molasses. We also produce PURE MAPLE SYRUP.

Erba Food Products
Brooklyn, NY 718-272-7700
Fantis Foods
Carlstadt, NJ 201-933-6200
GB Ratto & Company Int ernational
Oakland, CA 800-325-3483
Golden Eagle Olive Products
Porterville, CA 559-784-3468
Golden Whisk
South San Francisco, CA 800-660-5222
Good Food
Honey Brook, PA 800-327-4406
Good Health Natural Foods
Northport, NY. 631-261-2111
Gourmet Food Mall
Kenner, LA 800-903-7553
Goya Foods of Florida
Miami, FL. 305-592-3150
Grapevine Trading Company
Santa Rosa, CA. 800-469-6478
Greek Gourmet Limited
Mill Valley, CA. 415-480-8050
Hormel Foods Corporation
Austin, MN 507-437-5395
HVJ International
Spring, TX. 877-730-3663
Krinos Foods
Santa Barbara, CA 800-624-4896
La Piccolina
Decatur, GA 800-626-1624
Live Food Products
Santa Barbara, CA 800-446-1990
Loriva Culinary Oils Worldpantry.Com, Inc
San Francisco, CA 866-972-6879
Lucero Olive Oil
Corning, CA 877-330-2190
Lucini Italia Company
San Francisco, CA 888-558-2464
Mancini Packing Company
Zolfo Springs, FL 863-735-2000
Mancuso Cheese Company
Joliet, IL 815-722-2475
MNH Erickson Ranch
Orland, CA 530-865-9587
Moscahlades Brothers
New York, NY 212-226-5410
Mountainbrook of Vermont
Jeffersonville, VT 802-644-1988
Nick Sciabica & Sons
Modesto, CA. 800-551-9612
North American Enterprises
Tucson, AZ 800-817-8666
Olive Oil Factory
Waterbury, CT. 860-945-9549
Organic Planet
San Francisco, CA 415-765-5590
Our Thyme Garden
Cleburne, TX 800-482-4372
Paradise Products Corporation
Boca Raton, FL. 800-826-1235
Pastorelli Food Products
Chicago, IL 800-767-2829
Pokonobe Industries
Santa Monica, CA. 310-392-1259
Pompeian
Baltimore, MD 800-638-1224
Proacec USA
Santa Monica, CA. 310-996-7770
Pure Extracts Inc
Ronkonkoma, NY 631-588-9727
Purity Products
Plainview, NY. 888-769-7873
Queensway Foods Company
Burlingame, CA 650-871-7770
Ron-Son Foods
Swedesboro, NJ 856-241-7333
SilverLeaf International
Stafford, TX 800-442-7542
Sovena USA
Rome, NY. 315-797-7070
Sun Olive Oil Company
Templeton, CA 805-434-0626
Sweet Corn Products Company
Bloomfield, NE. 877-628-6115
Tee Pee Olives
Rye, NY. 800-431-1529
Trotters Imports
Colrain, MA 800-863-8437
Tutto Sicilia
New Britain, CT
Unilever Bestfoods, Inc.
Englewood Cliffs, NJ 201-894-4000
Valley Grain Products
Madera, CA. 559-675-3400
Veronica Foods Company
Oakland, CA 800-370-5554
Victoria Packing Corporation
Brooklyn, NY 718-927-3000
Vincent Formusa Company
Chicago, IL 312-421-0485

Extra Virgin

A. Camacho
Plant City, FL 800-881-4534
Adams Olive Ranch
Lindsay, CA 888-216-5483
Agrocan
Ville St Laurent, QC 877-247-6226
Agrusa, Inc.
Leonia, NJ. 201-592-5950
Arnabal International
Tustin, CA. 714-665-9477
Assouline & Ting
Huntingdon Valley, PA 800-521-4491
Calio Groves
Berkeley, CA. 800-865-4836
Castella Imports
Hauppauge, NY 866-227-8355
Colonna Brothers
North Bergen, NJ 201-864-1115
Critelli Olive Oil
Fairfield, CA. 800-865-4836
Golden Eagle Olive Products
Porterville, CA 559-784-3468
K.L. Keller Imports
Oakland, CA 510-839-7890
Lucini Italia Company
San Francisco, CA 888-558-2464
O Olive Oil
Petaluma, CA 888-827-7148
Paesana Products
East Farmingdale, NY. 631-845-1717
Paradise Products Corporation
Boca Raton, FL. 800-826-1235
Pastorelli Food Products
Chicago, IL 800-767-2829
Pepper Mill Imports
Carmel, CA 800-928-1744
Proacec USA
Santa Monica, CA. 310-996-7770
Queensway Foods Company
Burlingame, CA 650-871-7770
Robert Rothschild Berry Farm
Urbana, OH. 866-565-6790
Ron-Son Foods
Swedesboro, NJ 856-241-7333
Sabatino Truffles USA
Bronx, NY. 888-444-9971

Sieco USA Corporation
Houston, TX ... 800-325-9443

Specialty Foods International
Atlanta, GA ... 404-816-8268

Spruce Foods
San Clemente, CA ... 800-326-3612

Veronica Foods Company
Oakland, CA ... 800-370-5554

Pomace

A. Camacho
Plant City, FL ... 800-881-4534

Agrocan
Ville St Laurent, QC ... 877-247-6226

Onion

Astral Extracts Ltd.
Syosset, NY ... 516-496-2505

Naturex Inc.
South Hackensack, NJ ... 201-440-5000

Pure Extracts Inc
Ronkonkoma, NY ... 631-588-9727

Vegetable Juices
Chicago, IL ... 888-776-9752

Whole Herb Company
Sonoma, CA ... 707-935-1077

Orange

Astral Extracts Ltd.
Syosset, NY ... 516-496-2505

Boyajian, Inc.
Canton, MA ... 800-965-0665

Diana's Specialty Foods
Pingree Grove, IL ... 847-683-1200

Embassy Flavours Ltd.
Brampton, ON ... 800-334-3371

Emerling International Foods
Buffalo, NY ... 716-833-7381

Flavtek Geneva Flavors Inc.
Beloit, WI ... 800-562-5880

Gold Coast Ingredients
Commerce, CA ... 800-352-8673

Naturex Inc.
South Hackensack, NJ ... 201-440-5000

Pure Extracts Inc
Ronkonkoma, NY ... 631-588-9727

SunPure
Lakeland, FL ... 863-619-2222

Ungerer & Company
Lincoln Park, NJ ... 973-628-0600

V&E Kohnstamm
Brooklyn, NY ... 800-847-4500

Whole Herb Company
Sonoma, CA ... 707-935-1077

Palm

AAK USA
Port Newark, NJ ... 973-344-1300

Aarhus United USA, Inc.
Newark, NJ ... 800-776-1338

ADM Food Oils
Decatur, IL ... 800-637-5866

ADM Refined Oils
Decatur, IL ... 800-637-5866

AG Processing, Inc.
Omaha, NE ... 800-247-1345

Columbus Oils
Des Plaines, IL ... 773-265-6500

Emerling International Foods
Buffalo, NY ... 716-833-7381

We supply food manufacturers and food service customers worldwide (since 1988) with bulk ingredients including: Fruits & Vegetables; Juice Concentrates; Herbs & Spices; Oils & Vinegars; Flavors & Colors; Honey & Molasses. We also produce PURE MAPLE SYRUP.

FINA LLC
Cicinnati, OH ... 814-218-3439

Maywood International Sales
Sante Fe, NM ... 505-982-2700

Nealanders Food Ingredients
Elgin, IL ... 847-468-0001

Pokonobe Industries
Santa Monica, CA ... 310-392-1259

Pure Extracts Inc
Ronkonkoma, NY ... 631-588-9727

Stevenson-Cooper
Philadelphia, PA ... 215-223-2600

Ventura Foods
Opelousas, LA ... 337-948-6561

Welch, Home & Clark Company
Newark, NJ ... 973-465-1200

Kernel

ADM Food Oils
Decatur, IL ... 800-637-5866

Peanut

ADM Food Oils
Decatur, IL ... 800-637-5866

ADM Refined Oils
Decatur, IL ... 800-637-5866

AG Processing, Inc.
Omaha, NE ... 800-247-1345

ARRO Corporation
Hodgkins, IL ... 708-352-8200

Avatar Corporation
University Park, IL ... 800-255-3181

Birdsong Peanuts
Blakely, GA ... 800-597-7688

California Olive Oil Corporation
Berkeley, CA ... 888-718-9830

Cargill Refined Oils
Minneapolis, MN ... 800-323-6232

Catania-Spagna Corporation
Ayer, MA ... 800-343-5522

Central Soya
Bradley, IL ... 800-556-6777

Columbus Oils
Des Plaines, IL ... 773-265-6500

First Food International
Linden, NJ ... 908-862-5558

Good Food
Honey Brook, PA ... 800-327-4406

JFG Coffee Co
Knoxville, TN ... 865-546-2120

K.L. Keller Imports
Oakland, CA ... 510-839-7890

Loriva Culinary Oils Worldpantry.Com, Inc
San Francisco, CA ... 866-972-6879

Mallet & Company
Carnegie, PA ... 800-245-2757

Maywood International Sales
Sante Fe, NM ... 505-982-2700

Nealanders Food Ingredients
Elgin, IL ... 847-468-0001

Pastorelli Food Products
Chicago, IL ... 800-767-2829

Pokonobe Industries
Santa Monica, CA ... 310-392-1259

Pure Extracts Inc
Ronkonkoma, NY ... 631-588-9727

Purity Products
Plainview, NY ... 888-769-7873

Sessions Company
Enterprise, AL ... 334-393-0200

Sovena USA
Rome, NY ... 315-797-7070

Synergy Foods
West Bloomfield, MI ... 313-849-2900

Ventura Foods
Opelousas, LA ... 337-948-6561

Pepper

Pure Extracts Inc
Ronkonkoma, NY ... 631-588-9727

Whole Herb Company
Sonoma, CA ... 707-935-1077

Peppermint

AM Todd Company
Kalamazoo, MI ... 800-968-2603

Emerling International Foods
Buffalo, NY ... 716-833-7381

We supply food manufacturers and food service customers worldwide (since 1988) with bulk ingredients including: Fruits & Vegetables; Juice Concentrates; Herbs & Spices; Oils & Vinegars; Flavors & Colors; Honey & Molasses. We also produce PURE MAPLE SYRUP.

Gold Coast Ingredients
Commerce, CA ... 800-352-8673

Lebermuth Company
South Bend, IN ... 800-648-1123

Medallion Intl.
Pompton Plains, NJ ... 973-616-3401

Naturex Inc.
South Hackensack, NJ ... 201-440-5000

Pure Extracts Inc
Ronkonkoma, NY ... 631-588-9727

Ungerer & Company
Lincoln Park, NJ ... 973-628-0600

Pimiento

Naturex Inc.
South Hackensack, NJ ... 201-440-5000

Pure Extracts Inc
Ronkonkoma, NY ... 631-588-9727

Popping Corn

Acatris USA
Edina, MN ... 952-920-7700

ADM Refined Oils
Decatur, IL ... 800-637-5866

Avatar Corporation
University Park, IL ... 800-255-3181

Central Soya
Bradley, IL ... 800-556-6777

Delicious Popcorn Company
Waupaca, WI ... 715-258-7683

Great Western Products Company
Assumption, IL ... 217-226-3241

Great Western Products Company
Bismarck, MO ... 573-734-2210

Pure Extracts Inc
Ronkonkoma, NY ... 631-588-9727

Vogel Popcorn
Hamburg, IA ... 800-831-5818

Poppy Seed

Herbal Products & Development
Aptos, CA ... 831-688-8706

Pure Extracts Inc
Ronkonkoma, NY ... 631-588-9727

Whole Herb Company
Sonoma, CA ... 707-935-1077

Pumpkin Seed

Arista Industries
Wilton, CT ... 800-255-6457

Rice Bran

Arista Industries
Wilton, CT ... 800-255-6457

Safflower

AG Processing, Inc.
Omaha, NE ... 800-247-1345

American Health & Nutrition
Ann Arbor, MI ... 734-677-5570

Arista Industries
Wilton, CT ... 800-255-6457

California Oils Corporation
Richmond, CA ... 800-225-6457

Flora
Lynden, WA ... 800-446-2110

Loriva Culinary Oils Worldpantry.Com, Inc
San Francisco, CA ... 866-972-6879

Pokonobe Industries
Santa Monica, CA ... 310-392-1259

Pure Extracts Inc
Ronkonkoma, NY ... 631-588-9727

Welch, Home & Clark Company
Newark, NJ ... 973-465-1200

Sage

Astral Extracts Ltd.
Syosset, NY. 516-496-2505
Emerling International Foods
Buffalo, NY. 716-833-7381

We supply food manufacturers and food service customers worldwide (since 1988) with bulk ingredients including: Fruits & Vegetables; Juice Concentrates; Herbs & Spices; Oils & Vinegars; Flavors & Colors; Honey & Molasses. We also produce PURE MAPLE SYRUP.

Naturex Inc.
South Hackensack, NJ 201-440-5000
Pure Extracts Inc
Ronkonkoma, NY. 631-588-9727
Southeastern Wisconsin Products Company
Milwaukee, WI. 414-482-1730
Whole Herb Company
Sonoma, CA 707-935-1077

Salad

ADM Refined Oils
Decatur, IL 800-637-5866
Arista Industries
Wilton, CT 800-255-6457
ARRO Corporation
Hodgkins, IL. 708-352-8200
Avatar Corporation
University Park, IL 800-255-3181
Cargill Refined Oils
Minneapolis, MN 800-323-6232
Consumer Guild Foods
Toledo, OH 419-726-3406
Emerling International Foods
Buffalo, NY. 716-833-7381

We supply food manufacturers and food service customers worldwide (since 1988) with bulk ingredients including: Fruits & Vegetables; Juice Concentrates; Herbs & Spices; Oils & Vinegars; Flavors & Colors; Honey & Molasses. We also produce PURE MAPLE SYRUP.

Pure Extracts Inc
Ronkonkoma, NY. 631-588-9727
Sovena USA
Rome, NY. 315-797-7070
Ventura Foods
Ontario, CA. 323-262-9157
Ventura Foods
City of Industry, CA 800-327-3906

Sassafras

Astral Extracts Ltd.
Syosset, NY. 516-496-2505
Pure Extracts Inc
Ronkonkoma, NY. 631-588-9727
Whole Herb Company
Sonoma, CA 707-935-1077

Sesame

AG Processing, Inc.
Omaha, NE 800-247-1345
Arista Industries
Wilton, CT 800-255-6457
Avatar Corporation
University Park, IL 800-255-3181
California Olive Oil Corporation
Berkeley, CA. 888-718-9830
Columbus Foods Company
Des Plaines, IL 800-322-6457
Dipasa
Brownsville, TX 956-831-5893
Emerling International Foods
Buffalo, NY. 716-833-7381

We supply food manufacturers and food service customers worldwide (since 1988) with bulk ingredients including: Fruits & Vegetables; Juice Concentrates; Herbs & Spices; Oils & Vinegars; Flavors & Colors; Honey & Molasses. We also produce PURE MAPLE SYRUP.

Flora
Lynden, WA. 800-446-2110
Golden Gate Foods
Dallas, TX. 214-747-2223
Loriva Culinary Oils Worldpantry.Com, Inc
San Francisco, CA 866-972-6879
Organic Planet
San Francisco, CA 415-765-5590
Pokonobe Industries
Santa Monica, CA. 310-392-1259
Pure Extracts Inc
Ronkonkoma, NY. 631-588-9727
Universal Preservachem Inc
Somerset, NJ. 732-568-1266

Soybean

Aarhus United USA, Inc.
Newark, NJ 800-776-1338
ADM Food Oils
Decatur, IL 800-637-5866
ADM Refined Oils
Decatur, IL 800-637-5866
AG Processing, Inc.
Omaha, NE 800-247-1345
Agri-Dairy Products
Purchase, NY 914-697-9580
American Hawaiian Soy Company
Honolulu, HI. 800-841-8435
American Health & Nutrition
Ann Arbor, MI 734-677-5570
ARRO Corporation
Hodgkins, IL. 708-352-8200
Avatar Corporation
University Park, IL 800-255-3181
California Olive Oil Corporation
Berkeley, CA. 888-718-9830
Cargill Refined Oils
Minneapolis, MN 800-323-6232
Cargill Vegetable Oils
Minneapolis, MN 612-378-0551
Catania-Spagna Corporation
Ayer, MA. 800-343-5522
Central Soya
Bradley, IL 800-556-6777
Central Soyfoods
Lawrence, KS 785-312-8698
CHS
Inver Grove Heights, MN. 800-232-3639
Clofine Dairy & Food Products
Linwood, NJ 800-441-1001
Columbus Foods Company
Des Plaines, IL 800-322-6457
Columbus Oils
Des Plaines, IL 773-265-6500
Dee Bee's Feed
Milford, IA 712-262-4850
Dixie Usa
Tomball, TX 800-233-3668
Emerling International Foods
Buffalo, NY. 716-833-7381

We supply food manufacturers and food service customers worldwide (since 1988) with bulk ingredients including: Fruits & Vegetables; Juice Concentrates; Herbs & Spices; Oils & Vinegars; Flavors & Colors; Honey & Molasses. We also produce PURE MAPLE SYRUP.

First Food International
Linden, NJ. 908-862-5558
Gama Products
Medley, FL 305-883-1200
Golden Brands
Louisville, KY 800-622-3055
Mallet & Company
Carnegie, PA 800-245-2757
Marubeni America Corporation
New York, NY 212-450-0563
Maywood International Sales
Sante Fe, NM 505-982-2700
Nealanders Food Ingredients
Elgin, IL 847-468-0001
Organic Planet
San Francisco, CA 415-765-5590
Owensboro Grain Edible Oils
Owensboro, KY 270-273-5443
Pacific Soybean & Grain
San Francisco, CA 415-433-0867
Pastorelli Food Products
Chicago, IL 800-767-2829
Pokonobe Industries
Santa Monica, CA. 310-392-1259
Pure Extracts Inc
Ronkonkoma, NY. 631-588-9727
Purity Products
Plainview, NY. 888-769-7873
Sovena USA
Rome, NY. 315-797-7070
Universal Preservachem Inc
Somerset, NJ. 732-568-1266
Ventura Foods
Opelousas, LA 337-948-6561
Welch, Home & Clark Company
Newark, NJ 973-465-1200

Sunflower

Aarhus United USA, Inc.
Newark, NJ 800-776-1338
ACH Food Companies
Ankeny, IA
ADM Food Oils
Decatur, IL 800-637-5866
ADM Refined Oils
Decatur, IL 800-637-5866
AG Processing, Inc.
Omaha, NE 800-247-1345
American Health & Nutrition
Ann Arbor, MI 734-677-5570
Columbus Foods Company
Des Plaines, IL 800-322-6457
Columbus Oils
Des Plaines, IL 773-265-6500
Emerling International Foods
Buffalo, NY. 716-833-7381

We supply food manufacturers and food service customers worldwide (since 1988) with bulk ingredients including: Fruits & Vegetables; Juice Concentrates; Herbs & Spices; Oils & Vinegars; Flavors & Colors; Honey & Molasses. We also produce PURE MAPLE SYRUP.

First Food International
Linden, NJ. 908-862-5558
Flora
Lynden, WA. 800-446-2110
Loriva Culinary Oils Worldpantry.Com, Inc
San Francisco, CA 866-972-6879
Maywood International Sales
Sante Fe, NM 505-982-2700
Pacific Soybean & Grain
San Francisco, CA 415-433-0867
Pokonobe Industries
Santa Monica, CA. 310-392-1259
Pure Extracts Inc
Ronkonkoma, NY. 631-588-9727
SIGCO Sun Products
Breckenridge, MN 800-654-4145
Wannamaker Seeds
St. Matthews, SC 803-874-1381
Welch, Home & Clark Company
Newark, NJ 973-465-1200

Tangerine

Astral Extracts Ltd.
Syosset, NY. 516-496-2505
Emerling International Foods
Buffalo, NY. 716-833-7381

We supply food manufacturers and food service customers worldwide (since 1988) with bulk ingredients including: Fruits & Vegetables; Juice Concentrates; Herbs & Spices; Oils & Vinegars; Flavors & Colors; Honey & Molasses. We also produce PURE MAPLE SYRUP.

Gold Coast Ingredients
Commerce, CA 800-352-8673
Pure Extracts Inc
Ronkonkoma, NY. 631-588-9727

Thyme

Astral Extracts Ltd.
Syosset, NY. 516-496-2505
Emerling International Foods
Buffalo, NY. 716-833-7381

We supply food manufacturers and food service customers worldwide (since 1988) with bulk ingredients including: Fruits & Vegetables; Juice Concentrates; Herbs & Spices; Oils & Vinegars; Flavors & Colors; Honey & Molasses. We also produce PURE MAPLE SYRUP.

Naturex Inc.
South Hackensack, NJ 201-440-5000

Pure Extracts Inc
Ronkonkoma, NY 631-588-9727
Whole Herb Company
Sonoma, CA 707-935-1077

Vegetable

Aarhus United USA, Inc.
Newark, NJ 800-776-1338
Abitec Corporation
Columbus, OH 800-555-1255
ACH Food Companies
Ankeny, IA
Adams Vegetable Oils
Arbuckle, CA 530-668-2000
ADM Refined Oils
Decatur, IL 800-637-5866
ADM Southern Cotton Oil
Decatur, IL 800-637-5843
AG Processing, Inc.
Omaha, NE 800-247-1345
Allfresh Food Products
Evanston, IL 773-273-2343
American Chemical Service
Griffith, IN 219-924-4370
ARC Diversified
Cookeville, TN 800-239-9029
Arista Industries
Wilton, CT 800-255-6457
ARRO Corporation
Hodgkins, IL 708-352-8200
Avatar Corporation
University Park, IL 800-255-3181
Blue California Company
Rcho Sta Marg, CA 949-635-1990
Bunge Canada
Oakville, ON 800-361-3043
Bungy Oils
Pawtucket, RI 401-724-3800
C&T Refinery
Richmond, VA 800-284-6457
California Oils Corporation
Richmond, CA 800-225-6457
Cargill Specialty Oils
Minneapolis, MN 800-851-8331
Cargill Vegetable Oils
Minneapolis, MN 612-378-0551
Catania-Spagna Corporation
Ayer, MA 800-343-5522
CBS Food Products Corporation
Brooklyn, NY 718-452-2500
Central Soya
Bradley, IL 800-556-6777
CHS
Inver Grove Heights, MN 800-232-3639
Columbus Foods Company
Des Plaines, IL 800-322-6457
ConAgra Grocery Products
Irvine, CA 714-680-1000
CP Vegetable Oil
Fort Lauderdale, FL 905-792-2309
Emerling International Foods
Buffalo, NY 716-833-7381

We supply food manufacturers and food service customers worldwide (since 1988) with bulk ingredients including: Fruits & Vegetables; Juice Concentrates; Herbs & Spices; Oils & Vinegars; Flavors & Colors; Honey & Molasses. We also produce PURE MAPLE SYRUP.

Follmer Development/Americana
Newbury Park, CA 800-499-4668
Fuji Vegetable Oil
White Plains, NY 914-761-7900
Gateway Food Products Company
Dupo, IL 877-220-1963
Good Food
Honey Brook, PA 800-327-4406
Hybco USA
Los Angeles, CA 323-269-3111
Janca's Jojoba Oil & Seed Company
Mesa, AZ 480-497-9494
Liberty Vegetable Oil Company
Santa Fe Springs, CA 562-921-3567
Loriva Culinary Oils Worldpantry.Com, Inc
San Francisco, CA 866-972-6879
Mallet & Company
Carnegie, PA 800-245-2757
Mercado Latino
City of Industry, CA 626-333-6862
Milnot Company
Neosho, MO 800-877-6455
Montana Specialty Mills
Great Falls, MT 406-761-2338
Natural Oils International
Simi Valley, CA 805-433-0160
Oasis Foods Company
Hillside, NJ 908-964-0477
Ottens Flavors
Philadelphia, PA 800-523-0767
Pokonobe Industries
Santa Monica, CA 310-392-1259
Pure Extracts Inc
Ronkonkoma, NY 631-588-9727
Purity Products
Plainview, NY 888-769-7873
Riceland Foods Rice Milling Operations
Stuttgart, AR 870-673-5500
Spruce Foods
San Clemente, CA 800-326-3612
Starwest Botanicals
Rancho Cordova, CA 888-273-4372
Stepan Company
Maywood, NJ 800-523-3614
Technical Oil Products
Newton, NJ
The Solae Company
Saint Louis, MO 800-325-7108
Universal Preservachem Inc
Somerset, NJ 732-568-1266
Ventura Foods
Salem, OR 503-585-6423
Welch, Home & Clark Company
Newark, NJ 973-465-1200

Fortified Refined

ABITEC Corporation
Janesville, WI 800-457-1977

Vitamin

Arista Industries
Wilton, CT 800-255-6457
Columbus Foods Company
Des Plaines, IL 800-322-6457

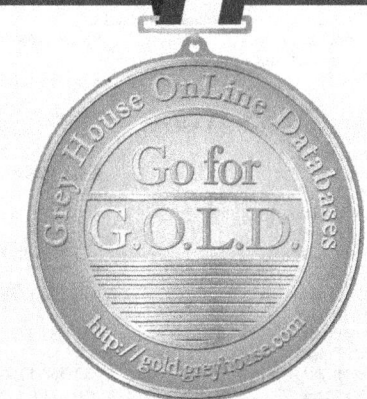

Green Turtle Bay Vitamin Company
Summit, NJ 800-887-8535
P.J. Noyes Company, Inc
Lancaster, NH 800-522-2469
Pure Extracts Inc
Ronkonkoma, NY 631-588-9727
Universal Preservachem Inc
Somerset, NJ 732-568-1266

Walnut

K.L. Keller Imports
Oakland, CA 510-839-7890
Loriva Culinary Oils Worldpantry.Com, Inc
San Francisco, CA 866-972-6879
Welch, Home & Clark Company
Newark, NJ 973-465-1200

Wheat Germ

Arista Industries
Wilton, CT 800-255-6457
Avatar Corporation
University Park, IL 800-255-3181
Energen Products
Norwalk, CA 800-423-8837
Pokonobe Industries
Santa Monica, CA 310-392-1259
Pure Extracts Inc
Ronkonkoma, NY 631-588-9727
Universal Preservachem Inc
Somerset, NJ 732-568-1266
VIOBIN
Monticello, IL 888-473-9645
Viobin USA
Monticello, IL 217-762-2561
Vitamins
Chicago, IL 312-861-0700

Pan Coatings & Sprays

Americana Marketing
Newbury Park, CA 800-742-7520
Technical Oil
Easton, PA 610-252-8350

Shortening

ACH Food Companies
Ankeny, IA
ADM Refined Oils
Decatur, IL 800-637-5866
Allfresh Food Products
Evanston, IL 773-273-2343
Brand Aromatics International
Lakewood, NJ 800-363-2080
Bunge North America
St Louis, MO 314-292-2000
Bungy Oils
Pawtucket, RI 401-724-3800
C.F. Sauer Company
Richmond, VA 800-688-5676
C.W. Brown & Company
Mount Royal, NJ 856-423-3700
CanAmera Foods
Oakville, ON 905-825-7900
Cargill Refined Oils
Minneapolis, MN 800-323-6232
Central Soya
Bradley, IL 800-556-6777
Clofine Dairy & Food Products
Linwood, NJ 800-441-1001
Coast Packing Company
Vernon, CA 323-277-7700
Columbus Foods Company
Des Plaines, IL 800-322-6457
Florida Shortening Corporation
Miami, FL 305-691-2992
Golden Brands
Louisville, KY 800-622-3055
JE Bergeron & Sons
Bromptonville, QC 800-567-2798
Mallet & Company
Carnegie, PA 800-245-2757
Mercado Latino
City of Industry, CA 626-333-6862
Mid Atlantic Vegetable Shortening Company
Kearny, NJ 800-966-1645
Pak Technologies
Milwaukee, WI 414-438-8600
Pastorelli Food Products
Chicago, IL 800-767-2829
Price's Creameries
El Paso, TX 915-565-2711
Riceland Foods Rice Milling Operations
Stuttgart, AR 870-673-5500
Source Food Technology
Durham, NC 866-277-3849
The Solae Company
Saint Louis, MO 800-325-7108
Ventura Foods
Ontario, CA 323-262-9157
Ventura Foods
Salem, OR 503-585-6423
Ventura Foods
City of Industry, CA 800-327-3906
Wells' Dairy
Le Mars, IA 800-942-3800

Fluid

Central Soya
Bradley, IL 800-556-6777
Mercado Latino
City of Industry, CA 626-333-6862
Pastorelli Food Products
Chicago, IL 800-767-2829
The Solae Company
Saint Louis, MO 800-325-7108

Vegetable

Bunge Canada
Oakville, ON 800-361-3043
Central Soya
Bradley, IL 800-556-6777
Gateway Food Products Company
Dupo, IL 877-220-1963
JE Bergeron & Sons
Bromptonville, QC 800-567-2798
Mercado Latino
City of Industry, CA 626-333-6862
Pastorelli Food Products
Chicago, IL 800-767-2829
The Solae Company
Saint Louis, MO 800-325-7108

Liquid

Central Soya
Bradley, IL 800-556-6777
Mallet & Company
Carnegie, PA 800-245-2757
Mercado Latino
City of Industry, CA 626-333-6862
Pastorelli Food Products
Chicago, IL 800-767-2829
The Solae Company
Saint Louis, MO 800-325-7108

Pasta & Noodles

General

A Zerega's Sons, Inc.
Fair Lawn, NJ 201-797-1400
Agrusa, Inc.
Leonia, NJ 201-592-5950
Al Dente
Whitmore Lake, MI 800-536-7278
Alaska Pasta Company
Anchorage, AK 907-276-2632
Alaska Smokehouse
Woodinville, WA 800-422-0852
American Italian Pasta Company
Kansas City, MO 816-584-5000
Archer Daniels Midland Company
Lincoln, NE 800-228-4060
Armanino Foods of Distinction
Hayward, CA 510-441-9300
Arrowhead Mills
Hereford, TX 800-749-0730
Associated Brands Inc.
Medina, NY 800-265-0050
Atlanta Bread Company
Smyrna, GA 800-398-3728
Belletieri Company
Allentown, PA 610-433-4334
Bernie's Foods
Brooklyn, NY 718-417-6677
Biagio's Banquets
Chicago, IL 800-392-2837
Borden Foods
Columbus, OH 614-233-3759
Borinquen Macaroni Corporation
Yauco, PR 787-856-1450
Boudreaux's Foods
New Orleans, LA 504-733-8440
Bruno Specialty Foods
West Sayville, NY 631-589-1700
Buon Italia Misono Food Ltd.
New York, NY 212-633-9090
Buona Vita
Bridgeton, NJ 856-453-7972
Burnette Foods
Elk Rapids, MI 231-264-8116
Caesar's Pasta Products
Blackwood, NJ 856-227-2585
Canasoy Enterprises
Vancouver, BC 800-663-1222
Canton Noodle Corporation
New York, NY 212-226-3276
Capone Foods
Somerville, MA 617-629-2296
Carando Gourmet Frozen Foods
Agawam, MA 888-227-2636
Carla's Pasta
South Windsor, CT 800-957-2782
Castella Imports
Hauppauge, NY 866-227-8355
Cedarlane Foods
Carson, CA 310-886-7720
Codino's Italian Foods
Scotia, NY 800-246-8908
Comet Rice
Houston, TX 281-272-8800
ConAgra Frozen Foods Company
Omaha, NE 402-595-6107
ConAgra Frozen Foods Company
Marshall, MO 660-886-3301
ConAgra Grocery Products
Irvine, CA 714-680-1000
Conte Luna Foods
Warminster, PA 215-441-5220
Conte Luna Foods
Philadelphia, PA 215-923-3141
Continental Group
Huntington Beach, CA 858-391-5670
Corsetti's Pasta Products
Woodbury, NJ 800-989-1188
Costa's Pasta
Kennesaw, GA 770-514-8814
Cottage Street Pasta
Barre, VT 802-476-4024
Country Foods
Polson, MT 406-883-4384
Cuizina Food Company
Woodinville, WA 425-486-7000
Cumberland Pasta
Cumberland, MD 800-572-7821
D'Orazio Foods
Bellmawr, NJ 888-328-7287
Dairy Maid Ravioli Manufacturing Corporation
Brooklyn, NY 718-449-2620
Dakota Growers Pasta Company
New Hope, MN 763-531-5360
De Cio Pasta Primo
Cave Creek, AZ 800-397-0770
Difiore Pasta Company
Hartford, CT 860-296-1077
Drakes Fresh Pasta Company
High Point, NC 336-861-5454
E.D. Smith Foods Ltd
Winona, ON 800-263-9246
Eden Foods Inc.
Clinton, MI 800-248-0320
Eden Organic Pasta Company
Detroit, MI 800-248-0320
El Peto Products
Cambridge, ON 800-387-4064
Elena's
Auburn Hills, MI 800-723-5362
Ener-G Foods
Seattle, WA 800-331-5222
Ethnic Gourmet Foods
West Chester, PA 610-692-7575
European Egg Noodle Manufacturing
Edmonton, AB 780-453-6767
Faribault Foods
Minneapolis, MN 612-333-6461
Fiori-Bruna Pasta Products
Hialeah, FL 305-621-0074
Florence Macaroni Manufacturing
Los Angeles, CA 323-232-7269
Florence Macaroni Manufacturing
Chicago, IL 800-647-2782
Florence Pasta & Cheese
Marshall, MN 800-533-5290
Florentyna's Fresh Pasta Factory
Vernon, CA 800-747-2782
Fontana's Casa De La Pasta
Vandergrift, PA 724-567-2782
Food City USA
Arvada, CO 303-321-4447
Food Source
Mc Kinney, TX 972-548-9001
Foulds
Libertyville, IL 847-362-3062
Freeze-Dry Ingredients
Berkeley, IL 708-544-1880
Fresh Market Pasta Company
Portland, ME 207-773-7146
Fun Foods
East Rutherford, NJ 800-507-2782
Gabriele Macaroni Company
City of Industry, CA 626-964-2324
Gaston Dupre
Excelsior Springs, MO 817-629-6275
Geetha's Gourmet of India
Las Cruces, NM 800-274-0475
Gentilini's Italian Products
Sunriver, OR 541-593-5053
German Village Products
Wauseon, OH 419-335-1515
Gilardi Foods
Sidney, OH 937-498-4511
Gilster-Mary Lee Corporation
Chester, IL 800-851-5371
Golden Grain
Pleasanton, CA 925-734-8800
Golden Grain Company
Bridgeview, IL 708-458-7020
Golden Whisk
South San Francisco, CA 800-660-5222
Good Old Dad Food Products
Sault Ste. Marie, ON 800-267-7426
Gourmets Fresh Pasta
Pasadena, CA 626-798-0841
Great Eastern Sun
Asheville, NC 800-334-5809
Greenfield Noodle & Specialty Company
Detroit, MI 313-873-2212
Haypress Gourmet Pasta
Haverstraw, NY 845-947-4580
Heartline Foods
Westport, CT 203-222-0381
Hershey Pasta Group
Louisville, KY 800-468-1714
HFI Foods
Redmond, WA 425-883-1320
Hodgson Mill Inc.
Effingham, IL 800-525-0177
Hong Tou Noodle Company
Los Angeles, CA 323-256-3843
Hung's Noodle House
Calgary, AB 403-250-1663
Hunt-Wesson Food Service Company
Rochester, NY 866-484-8676
Iltaco Food Products
Chicago, IL 800-244-8935
International Harvest
Mt Vernon, NY 914-699-5600
International Home Foods
Parsippany, NJ 973-359-9920
International Noodle Company
Madison Heights, MI 248-583-2479
Italia Foods
Schaumburg, IL 800-747-1109
Italian Gourmet Foods Canada
Calgary, AB 403-263-6996
Itarca
Los Angeles, CA 800-747-2782
J-N-D Company
Fort Wayne, IN 260-459-6206
J.B. Sons
Yonkers, NY 914-963-5192
Joseph's Gourmet Pasta & Sauces
Haverhill, MA 800-863-8998
Joseph's Pasta Company
Haverhill, MA 888-327-2782
JSL Foods
Los Angeles, CA 800-745-3236
Juno Chef's
Goshen, NY 845-294-5400
Kay Foods Company
Detroit, MI 313-393-1100
Kemach Food Products Corporation
Brooklyn, NY 888-453-6224

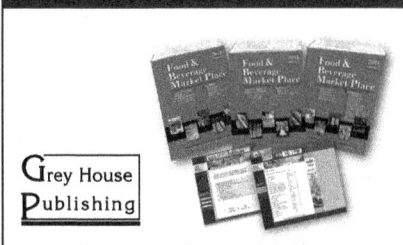

Koyo Foods
Richmond, CA 510-527-7066
Kozlowski Farms
Forestville, CA 800-473-2767
Kraft Foods
Springfield, MO 417-881-2701
La Moderna
Col Centro, TL
La Piccolina
Decatur, GA 800-626-1624
La Romagnola
Orlando, FL....................... 800-843-8359
La Spiga D'Oro Fresh Pasta Co
Pacifica, CA 800-847-2782
Ladson Homemade Pasta Company
Phoenix, AZ 480-353-0874
LaMonica Fine Foods
Millville, NJ 856-825-8111
Landolfi Food Products
Trenton, NJ 609-392-1830
Lapasta
Silver Spring, MD.................. 301-588-1111
Liberty Richter
Saddle Brook, NJ 201-291-8749
Lotsa Pasta
San Diego, CA 858-581-6777
Louis Severino Pasta
Collingswood, NJ 856-854-7666
Louisa Food Products
Saint Louis, MO 314-868-3000
Mama Del's Macacroni
East Haven, CT.................... 203-469-6255
Mama Mucci's Pasta
Canton, MI 734-453-4555
Mama Rosie's Ravioli Company
Charlestown, MA 888-246-4300
Mamma Lina Ravioli Company
San Diego, CA 858-535-0620
Marsan Foods
Toronto, ON 416-755-9262
Maruchan
Irvine, CA......................... 949-789-2300
McCain Foods USA
Lodi, NJ.......................... 800-938-7799
Michael Angelo's Gourmet Foods
Austin, TX........................ 877-482-5426
Midwest Foods
Chicago, IL 773-927-8870
Modern Macaroni Company
Honolulu, HI...................... 808-845-6841
Montreal Chop Suey Company
Montreal, QC 514-522-3134
Morrison Lamothe
Toronto, ON 877-677-6533
Mount Rose Ravioli & Macaroni Company
Farmingdale, NY
Mrs. Leeper's Pasta
Excelsior Springs, MO 800-848-5266
Muruchan
Irvine, CA........................ 949-789-2300
Mutual Trading Company
Los Angeles, CA................... 213-626-9458
Nantucket Pasta Company, Inc.
Nantucket, MA 508-494-5209
Napoli Pasta Manufacturers
Miami, FL........................ 305-666-1942
Natural Value Products
Sacramento, CA 916-427-7242
New World Pasta Company 7
Harrisburg, PA 800-730-5957
Nissin Foods USA Company
Gardena, CA...................... 310-327-8478
Nissin Foods USA Company
Lancaster, PA 717-291-1881
Nonna Foods
Woodbury, NY 516-234-9897
North American Enterprises
Tucson, AZ 800-817-8666
Oakland Noodle Company
Oakland, IL....................... 217-346-2322
OB Macaroni Company
Fort Worth, TX 800-555-4336
Oh Boy! Corporation
San Fernando, CA.................. 818-361-1128
Okahara Saimin Factory
Honolulu, HI...................... 808-949-0588
On-Cor Foods Products
Northbrook, IL 847-205-1040
Ore-Ida Foods
Pittsburgh, PA..................... 800-892-2401
Original Italian Pasta Poducts Company
Chelsea, MA 800-999-9603
P&S Ravioli Company
Philadelphia, PA 215-465-8888
Pak Technologies
Milwaukee, WI 414-438-8600
Pappardelle's Pasta Company
Denver, CO 800-607-2782
Pascucci Family Pasta
San Diego, CA 619-285-8000
Pasta Del Mondo
Carmel, NY....................... 800-392-8887
Pasta Factory
Melrose Park, IL................... 800-615-6951
Pasta International
Mississauga, ON................... 905-890-5550
Pasta Italiana
Massapequa, NY................... 800-536-5611
Pasta Mami
Smyrna, GA 770-438-6022
Pasta Mill
Edmonton, AB 780-454-8665
Pasta Montana
Great Falls, MT.................... 406-761-1516
Pasta Partners
Salt Lake City, UT 800-727-8284
Pasta Prima
Benicia, CA....................... 707-746-6888
Pasta Quistini
Toronto, ON 416-742-3222
Pasta Shoppe
Nashville, TN 800-247-0188
Pasta Sonoma
Rohnert Park, CA 707-584-0800
Pasta USA
Spokane, WA...................... 800-456-2084
Pastorelli Food Products
Chicago, IL 800-767-2829
PaStreeta Fresca
Dublin, OH 800-343-5266
Peace Village Organic Foods
Berkeley, CA...................... 510-524-4420
Pede Brothers
Schenectady, NY................... 518-356-3042
Peking Noodle Company
Los Angeles, CA................... 323-223-2023
Pennsylvania Macaroni Company
Pittsburgh, PA..................... 800-223-5928
Philadelphia Macaroni Company
Philadelphia, PA 215-923-3141
Pierino Frozen Foods
Lincoln Park, MI................... 313-928-0950
Pondini Imports, Inc
Somerset, NJ...................... 732-545-1255
Porinos Gourmet Food
Central Falls, RI 800-826-3938
Primo Foods
Toronto, ON 800-377-6945
Primo Piatto
Minneapolis, MN 763-531-9194
Pure Sales
Costa Mesa, CA 714-540-5455
Purity Foods
Okemos, MI 800-997-7358
Quality Choice Foods
Toronto, ON 416-650-9595
Queen Ann Ravioli & Macaroni Company
Brooklyn, NY 718-256-1061
Quinoa Corporation
Gardena, CA...................... 310-217-8125
Rahco International
St Augustine, FL................... 800-851-7681
Randag & Associates Inc
Elmhurst, IL 630-530-2830
Ravioli Store
Long Islnad City, NY 877-727-8269
Rice Innovations
Norval, ON 905-451-7423
Riviera Ravioli Company
Bronx, NY........................ 718-823-0260
Roccas Italian Foods
New Castle, PA.................... 724-654-3344
Ron-Son Foods
Swedesboro, NJ 856-241-7333
Ronzoni Foods Canada
Etobicoke, ON 800-387-5032
Rosa Food Products Co Inc
Philadelphia, PA 215-467-2214
Roses Ravioli
Oglesby, IL 815-883-8011
Rossi Pasta
Marietta, OH...................... 800-227-6774
S.T. Specialty Foods Inc
Brooklyn Park, MN................. 763-493-9600
Sabatino Truffles USA
Bronx, NY........................ 888-444-9971
Salt Lake Macaroni & Noodle Company
Salt Lake City, UT 801-969-9855
Savoia Foods
Chicago Heights, IL 800-867-2782
Sedlock Farm
Lynn Center, IL.................... 309-521-8284
Sfoglia Fine Pastas & Gourmet
Freeland, WA 360-331-4080
Shanghai Company
Portland, OR 503-235-2525
Shreveport Macaroni Company
Shreveport, LA 318-222-6857
Silver Palate Kitchens
Cresskill, NJ 800-872-5283
Silver State Foods
Denver, CO....................... 800-423-3351
Somerset Industries
Spring House, PA 800-883-8728
SOPAKCO Foods
Mullins, SC....................... 800-276-9678
SOUPerior Bean & Spice Company
Vancouver, WA.................... 800-878-7687
Specialty Brands
Carthage, MO 417-358-8104
Specialty Brands
Ontario, CA....................... 800-782-1180
SPI Foods
Fremont, NE 866-266-1304
Spring Glen Fresh Foods
Ephrata, PA....................... 800-641-2853
Spruce Foods
San Clemente, CA.................. 800-326-3612
ST Specialty Foods
Brooklyn Park, MN................. 763-493-9600
Star Ravioli Manufacturing Company
Moonachie, NJ 201-933-6427
Strom Products Ltd.
Bannockburn, IL................... 800-862-3311
Sun Ridge Farms
Pajaro, CA........................ 831-786-7000
Suns Noodle Company
Atlanta, GA....................... 770-448-7799
Swiss Colony
Monroe, WI....................... 608-328-8536
TAIF
Folcroft, PA....................... 610-522-0122
Taif Foods
Folcroft, PA....................... 610-522-0122
Tasty Mix Quality Foods
Brooklyn, NY................... 866-TAS-TYMX
TexaFrance
Round Rock, TX................... 800-776-8937
Tomasso Corporation
Baie D'Urfe, QC................... 514-325-3000
Tommaso's Fresh Pasta
Dallas, TX 972-869-1111
Tropical
Charlotte, NC 800-220-1413
Turris Italian Foods
Roseville, MI 586-773-6010
Twin Marquis
Brooklyn, NY 800-367-6868
Unilever
Harrisburg, PA 717-234-6215
Union
Irvine, CA........................ 800-854-7292
United Noodle Manufacturing Company
Salt Lake City, UT 801-485-0951
US Durum Products
Lancaster, PA 866-268-7268
Vantage USA
Chicago, IL 773-247-1086
Varco Brothers
Chicago, IL 312-642-4740
Viamar Foods
Glen Cove, NY 516-759-0652
Vitasoy USA
Ayer, MA......................... 978-772-6880
Wan Hua Foods
Seattle, WA 206-622-8417
Weiss Noodle Company
Solon, OH 440-248-4550
Willow Foods
Beaverton, OR 800-338-3609
Wine Country Pasta
Sonoma, CA 707-935-1366
Wing's Food Products
Etobicoke, ON 416-259-2662
Wisconsin Cheese
Melrose Park, IL................... 708-450-0074

Wisconsin Whey International
Juda, WI 608-233-5101
WMFB
Beaver Dam, WI 920-887-1771
Wonton Food
Brooklyn, NY 800-776-8889
Woodland Foods
Gurnee, IL 847-625-8600
Wornick Company
Cincinnati, OH 800-860-4555
Young's Noodle Factory
Honolulu, HI 808-533-6478

Agnolotti

Agrusa, Inc.
Leonia, NJ 201-592-5950
Caesar's Pasta Products
Blackwood, NJ 856-227-2585
ConAgra Foods/International Home Foods
Niagara Falls, ON 905-356-2661
Pasta Factory
Melrose Park, IL 800-615-6951
Putney Pasta Company
Brattleboro, VT 800-253-3683
Queen Ann Ravioli & Macaroni Company
Brooklyn, NY 718-256-1061
Supreme Dairy Farms Company
Warwick, RI 401-739-8180
Wisconsin Whey International
Juda, WI 608-233-5101

Angel Hair

Al Dente
Whitmore Lake, MI 800-536-7278
Caesar's Pasta Products
Blackwood, NJ 856-227-2585
Cipriani's Spaghetti & Sauce Company
Chicago Heights, IL 708-755-6212
Costa Macaroni Manufacturing
Los Angeles, CA 800-433-7785
Food City USA
Arvada, CO 303-321-4447
La Romagnola
Orlando, FL 800-843-8359
Lucys Foods
Latrobe, PA 724-539-1430
Mrs. Leeper's Pasta
Excelsior Springs, MO 800-848-5266
Noodles By Leonardo
Devil's Lake, ND 701-662-8300
Pascucci Family Pasta
San Diego, CA 619-285-8000
Pasta By Valente
Charlottesville, VA 888-575-7670
Pasta Factory
Melrose Park, IL 800-615-6951
Pasta USA
Spokane, WA 800-456-2084
Putney Pasta Company
Brattleboro, VT 800-253-3683

Canned

Canton Noodle Corporation
New York, NY 212-226-3276
ConAgra Foods/International Home Foods
Niagara Falls, ON 905-356-2661
ConAgra Grocery Products
Irvine, CA 714-680-1000
Heinz Company of Canada
North York, ON 877-574-3469
International Home Foods
Parsippany, NJ 973-359-9920
Midwest Foods
Chicago, IL 773-927-8870
Natural Value Products
Sacramento, CA 916-427-7242
Seneca Foods
Clyman, WI 920-696-3331
Shanghai Company
Portland, OR 503-235-2525

Cannelloni

Food Source
Mc Kinney, TX 972-548-9001
Louisa Food Products
Saint Louis, MO 314-868-3000
Marsan Foods
Toronto, ON 416-755-9262
Pasta Factory
Melrose Park, IL 800-615-6951
Pasta International
Mississauga, ON 905-890-5550
Riviera Ravioli Company
Bronx, NY 718-823-0260
Star Ravioli Manufacturing Company
Moonachie, NJ 201-933-6427
Tomasso Corporation
Baie D'Urfe, QC 514-325-3000
Turris Italian Foods
Roseville, MI 586-773-6010

Cavatappi

Costa Macaroni Manufacturing
Los Angeles, CA 800-433-7785

Cavatelli

Alfredo's Italian Foods Manufacturing Company
Quincy, MA 617-479-6360
Caesar's Pasta Products
Blackwood, NJ 856-227-2585
Fiori-Bruna Pasta Products
Hialeah, FL 305-621-0074
Italian Village Ravioli & Pasta Products
Portsmouth, NH 603-431-6865
J.B. Sons
Yonkers, NY 914-963-5192
Landolfi Food Products
Trenton, NJ 609-392-1830
Pasta Del Mondo
Carmel, NY 800-392-8887
Pasta Factory
Melrose Park, IL 800-615-6951
Pasta USA
Spokane, WA 800-456-2084
Queen Ann Ravioli & Macaroni Company
Brooklyn, NY 718-256-1061
Riviera Ravioli Company
Bronx, NY 718-823-0260
Star Ravioli Manufacturing Company
Moonachie, NJ 201-933-6427
Wisconsin Whey International
Juda, WI 608-233-5101

Elbow Macaroni

A Zerega's Sons, Inc.
Fair Lawn, NJ 201-797-1400
Archer Daniels Midland Company
Lincoln, NE 800-228-4060
Borinquen Macaroni Corporation
Yauco, PR 787-856-1450
Costa Macaroni Manufacturing
Los Angeles, CA 800-433-7785
Cuizina Food Company
Woodinville, WA 425-486-7000
Noodles By Leonardo
Devil's Lake, ND 701-662-8300
Pascucci Family Pasta
San Diego, CA 619-285-8000
Pasta USA
Spokane, WA 800-456-2084
Superior Pasta Company
Philadelphia, PA 215-922-7278

Farfalle

Costa Macaroni Manufacturing
Los Angeles, CA 800-433-7785
Italia Foods
Schaumburg, IL 800-747-1109
Pasta USA
Spokane, WA 800-456-2084

Fettuccine

Lucys Foods
Latrobe, PA 724-539-1430
Noodles By Leonardo
Devil's Lake, ND 701-662-8300
Pasta By Valente
Charlottesville, VA 888-575-7670

Gnocchi

Agrusa, Inc.
Leonia, NJ 201-592-5950
Dixie Usa
Tomball, TX 800-233-3668
Italian Foods Corporation
Raleigh, NC 888-516-7262
Lucys Foods
Latrobe, PA 724-539-1430
Queen Ann Ravioli & Macaroni Company
Brooklyn, NY 718-256-1061

Frozen

Lucys Foods
Latrobe, PA 724-539-1430
Queen Ann Ravioli & Macaroni Company
Brooklyn, NY 718-256-1061
Turris Italian Foods
Roseville, MI 586-773-6010

Lasagna

Noodles By Leonardo
Devil's Lake, ND 701-662-8300

Frozen

Alfredo's Italian Foods Manufacturing Company
Quincy, MA 617-479-6360
Bruno Specialty Foods
West Sayville, NY 631-589-1700
Caesar's Pasta Products
Blackwood, NJ 856-227-2585
Cedarlane Foods
Carson, CA 310-886-7720
Codino's Italian Foods
Scotia, NY 800-246-8908
D'Orazio Foods
Bellmawr, NJ 888-328-7287
Food Source
Mc Kinney, TX 972-548-9001
Foodbrands America
Oklahoma City, OK 405-290-4000

Gilardi Foods
Sidney, OH . . . 937-498-4511
Italia Foods
Schaumburg, IL. . . . 800-747-1109
LaMonica Fine Foods
Millville, NJ . . . 856-825-8111
Landolfi Food Products
Trenton, NJ . . . 609-392-1830
Mamma Lina Ravioli Company
San Diego, CA . . . 858-535-0620
Marcetti Frozen Pasta
Altoona, IA . . . 515-967-4254
Marsan Foods
Toronto, ON . . . 416-755-9262
McCain Foods Canada
Toronto, ON . . . 866-622-2461
Molinaro's Fine Italian Foods
Mississauga, ON. . . . 800-268-4959
Pasta Factory
Melrose Park, IL. . . . 800-615-6951
Pasta International
Mississauga, ON. . . . 905-890-5550
Riviera Ravioli Company
Bronx, NY. . . . 718-823-0260
Specialty Brands
Carthage, MO . . . 417-358-8104
Tomasso Corporation
Baie D'Urfe, QC. . . . 514-325-3000
Wisconsin Whey International
Juda, WI . . . 608-233-5101

Noodles

A Zerega's Sons, Inc.
Fair Lawn, NJ . . . 201-797-1400
Archer Daniels Midland Company
Lincoln, NE. . . . 800-228-4060
Borinquen Macaroni Corporation
Yauco, PR . . . 787-856-1450
Costa Macaroni Manufacturing
Los Angeles, CA. . . . 800-433-7785
Pasta USA
Spokane, WA. . . . 800-456-2084

Canned

Canton Noodle Corporation
New York, NY . . . 212-226-3276
ConAgra Grocery Products
Irvine, CA . . . 714-680-1000
Shanghai Company
Portland, OR . . . 503-235-2525
United Noodle Manufacturing Company
Salt Lake City, UT . . . 801-485-0951

Chow Mein

Everfresh Food Corporation
Minneapolis, MN . . . 612-331-6393
Nanka Seimen Company
Vernon, CA . . . 323-585-9967
Valdez Food
Philadelphia, PA . . . 215-634-6106
Wan Hua Foods
Seattle, WA . . . 206-622-8417
Willow Foods
Beaverton, OR . . . 800-338-3609
Wing Hing Noodle Company
Los Angeles, CA. . . . 888-223-8899
Wonton Food
Brooklyn, NY . . . 800-776-8889

Egg

A Zerega's Sons, Inc.
Fair Lawn, NJ . . . 201-797-1400
Costa Macaroni Manufacturing
Los Angeles, CA. . . . 800-433-7785
Cumberland Pasta
Cumberland, MD . . . 800-572-7821
Eden Organic Pasta Company
Detroit, MI . . . 800-248-0320
Foulds
Libertyville, IL . . . 847-362-3062
Hershey Pasta Group
Louisville, KY . . . 800-468-1714
Nanka Seimen Company
Vernon, CA . . . 323-585-9967
Noodles By Leonardo
Devil's Lake, ND . . . 701-662-8300
R.A.B. Food Group LLC
Secaucus, NJ . . . 201-553-1100
Reames Foods
Columbus, OH . . . 614-846-2232
Silver State Foods
Denver, CO . . . 800-423-3351
Strom Products Ltd.
Bannockburn, IL . . . 800-862-3311

Oriental

Allied Old English
Port Reading, NJ. . . . 732-636-2060
Annie Chun's
San Rafael, CA . . . 415-479-8272
Chieftain Wild Rice Company
Spooner, WI . . . 800-262-6368
Union
Irvine, CA . . . 800-854-7292
Vitasoy USA
Ayer, MA. . . . 978-772-6880
Wonton Food
Brooklyn, NY . . . 800-776-8889
Woodland Foods
Gurnee, IL. . . . 847-625-8600

Ramen

Maruchan
Irvine, CA . . . 949-789-2300
Union
Irvine, CA . . . 800-854-7292

Pasta

Borinquen Macaroni Corporation
Yauco, PR . . . 787-856-1450
Caesar's Pasta Products
Blackwood, NJ . . . 856-227-2585
Canada Bread
North Bay, ON . . . 800-461-6122
Conte's Pasta Company
Vineland, NJ . . . 800-211-6607
Costa Macaroni Manufacturing
Los Angeles, CA. . . . 800-433-7785
Cuizina Food Company
Woodinville, WA. . . . 425-486-7000
Fantis Foods
Carlstadt, NJ . . . 201-933-6200
Faribault Foods
Minneapolis, MN . . . 612-333-6461
Gia Russa
Coitsville, OH. . . . 800-527-8772
Krinos Foods
Santa Barbara, CA . . . 800-624-4896
La Romagnola
Orlando, FL. . . . 800-843-8359
Lapasta
Silver Spring, MD. . . . 301-588-1111
Lucys Foods
Latrobe, PA. . . . 724-539-1430
Mezza
Lake Forest, IL . . . 888-206-6054
Park 100 Foods
Tipton, IN . . . 800-854-6504
Pasta Prima
Benicia, CA. . . . 707-746-6888
Philadelphia Macaroni Company
Warminster, PA. . . . 215-441-5220
Plentiful Pantry
Salt Lake City, UT . . . 800-727-8284
Queen Ann Ravioli & Macaroni Company
Brooklyn, NY . . . 718-256-1061
Ragozzino Food
Meriden, CT . . . 800-348-1240
Reid Foods
Gurnee, IL. . . . 888-295-8478
Royal Angelus Macaroni
Chino, CA. . . . 909-627-7312
Superior Pasta Company
Philadelphia, PA . . . 215-922-7278
Turris Italian Foods
Roseville, MI . . . 586-773-6010
Viamar Foods
Glen Cove, NY. . . . 516-759-0652
Vincent Formusa Company
Chicago, IL. . . . 312-421-0485
Wisconsin Whey International
Juda, WI . . . 608-233-5101

Frozen

Homestead Ravioli Company
South San Francisco, CA . . . 650-615-0750
LaMonica Fine Foods
Millville, NJ . . . 856-825-8111
Lapasta
Silver Spring, MD. . . . 301-588-1111

Orzo

Chieftain Wild Rice Company
Spooner, WI . . . 800-262-6368
Woodland Foods
Gurnee, IL. . . . 847-625-8600

Polenta

Chieftain Wild Rice Company
Spooner, WI . . . 800-262-6368
Woodland Foods
Gurnee, IL. . . . 847-625-8600

Penne

A Zerega's Sons, Inc.
Fair Lawn, NJ . . . 201-797-1400
Costa Macaroni Manufacturing
Los Angeles, CA. . . . 800-433-7785
Cuizina Food Company
Woodinville, WA. . . . 425-486-7000
Noodles By Leonardo
Devil's Lake, ND . . . 701-662-8300
Pasta USA
Spokane, WA. . . . 800-456-2084
Turris Italian Foods
Roseville, MI . . . 586-773-6010

Ravioli

Agrusa, Inc.
Leonia, NJ. . . . 201-592-5950
Alfonso Gourmet Pasta
Pompano Beach, FL . . . 800-370-7278
Alfredo's Italian Foods Manufacturing Company
Quincy, MA. . . . 617-479-6360
Antoni Ravioli
North Massapequa, NY . . . 800-783-0350
Armanino Foods of Distinction
Hayward, CA . . . 510-441-9300
Bella Ravioli
Medford, MA . . . 781-396-0875
Borgattis Ravioli
Bronx, NY. . . . 718-367-3799
Bruno Specialty Foods
West Sayville, NY. . . . 631-589-1700
Caesar's Pasta Products
Blackwood, NJ . . . 856-227-2585
Campbell Soup Company
Camden, NJ. . . . 800-257-8443
Chinese Spaghetti Factory
Boston, MA. . . . 617-445-7714
Codino's Italian Foods
Scotia, NY. . . . 800-246-8908
ConAgra Foods/International Home Foods
Niagara Falls, ON . . . 905-356-2661
Cottage Street Pasta
Barre, VT . . . 802-476-4024
Cuizina Food Company
Woodinville, WA. . . . 425-486-7000
D'Orazio Foods
Bellmawr, NJ. . . . 888-328-7287
Dairy Maid Ravioli Manufacturing Corporation
Brooklyn, NY . . . 718-449-2620
Fiori-Bruna Pasta Products
Hialeah, FL . . . 305-621-0074
Fontana's Casa De La Pasta
Vandergrift, PA . . . 724-567-2782
Food Source
Mc Kinney, TX . . . 972-548-9001
International Home Foods
Parsippany, NJ. . . . 973-359-9920
Italia Foods
Schaumburg, IL. . . . 800-747-1109
J.B. Sons
Yonkers, NY . . . 914-963-5192
La Romagnola
Orlando, FL. . . . 800-843-8359
Landolfi Food Products
Trenton, NJ . . . 609-392-1830
Louisa Food Products
Saint Louis, MO . . . 314-868-3000
Lucys Foods
Latrobe, PA. . . . 724-539-1430
Mamma Lina Ravioli Company
San Diego, CA . . . 858-535-0620

Maria and Son Italian Products
Saint Louis, MO 866-481-9009
Mount Rose Ravioli & Macaroni Company
Farmingdale, NY
New York Ravioli & Pasta Company
New Hyde Park, NY 888-588-7287
Nuovo Pasta Productions
Stratford, CT 800-803-0033
O Chili Frozen Foods Inc
Northbrook, IL 847-562-1991
Pasta Del Mondo
Carmel, NY 800-392-8887
Pasta Factory
Melrose Park, IL 800-615-6951
Pasta International
Mississauga, ON 905-890-5550
Pasta Italiana
Massapequa, NY 800-536-5611
Pasta Mill
Edmonton, AB 780-454-8665
Pasta Prima
Benicia, CA 707-746-6888
Queen Ann Ravioli & Macaroni Company
Brooklyn, NY 718-256-1061
Roses Ravioli
Oglesby, IL 815-883-8011
Specialty Brands
Carthage, MO 417-358-8104
Star Ravioli Manufacturing Company
Moonachie, NJ 201-933-6427
Tomasso Corporation
Baie D'Urfe, QC 514-325-3000
Viamar Foods
Glen Cove, NY 516-759-0652
Wisconsin Whey International
Juda, WI 608-233-5101

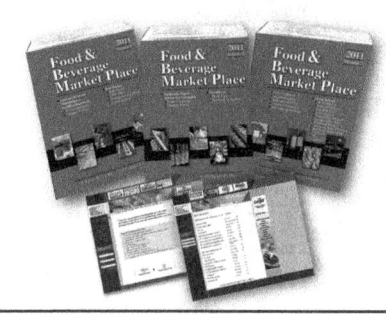

Canned

Alfredo's Italian Foods Manufacturing Company
Quincy, MA 617-479-6360
Campbell Soup Company
Camden, NJ 800-257-8443
ConAgra Foods/International Home Foods
Niagara Falls, ON 905-356-2661
Cuizina Food Company
Woodinville, WA 425-486-7000
International Home Foods
Parsippany, NJ 973-359-9920
Specialty Brands
Carthage, MO 417-358-8104

Cheese

Alfredo's Italian Foods Manufacturing Company
Quincy, MA 617-479-6360
Fiori-Bruna Pasta Products
Hialeah, FL 305-621-0074
La Romagnola
Orlando, FL 800-843-8359
Louisa Food Products
Saint Louis, MO 314-868-3000
Queen Ann Ravioli & Macaroni Company
Brooklyn, NY 718-256-1061

Frozen

Alfredo's Italian Foods Manufacturing Company
Quincy, MA 617-479-6360
Bruno Specialty Foods
West Sayville, NY 631-589-1700
Caesar's Pasta Products
Blackwood, NJ 856-227-2585
Codino's Italian Foods
Scotia, NY 800-246-8908
Cuizina Food Company
Woodinville, WA 425-486-7000
D'Orazio Foods
Bellmawr, NJ 888-328-7287
Fiori-Bruna Pasta Products
Hialeah, FL 305-621-0074
Food Source
Mc Kinney, TX 972-548-9001
Homestead Ravioli Company
South San Francisco, CA 650-615-0750
Italia Foods
Schaumburg, IL 800-747-1109
Italian Village Ravioli & Pasta Products
Portsmouth, NH 603-431-6865
J.B. Sons
Yonkers, NY 914-963-5192
LaMonica Fine Foods
Millville, NJ 856-825-8111
Landolfi Food Products
Trenton, NJ 609-392-1830
Louisa Food Products
Saint Louis, MO 314-868-3000
Mount Rose Ravioli & Macaroni Company
Farmingdale, NY
Pascucci Family Pasta
San Diego, CA 619-285-8000
Pasta Del Mondo
Carmel, NY 800-392-8887
Pasta Factory
Melrose Park, IL 800-615-6951
Pasta International
Mississauga, ON 905-890-5550
Pasta Italiana
Massapequa, NY 800-536-5611
Pasta Prima
Benicia, CA 707-746-6888
Specialty Brands
Carthage, MO 417-358-8104
Star Ravioli Manufacturing Company
Moonachie, NJ 201-933-6427
Tomasso Corporation
Baie D'Urfe, QC 514-325-3000
Turris Italian Foods
Roseville, MI 586-773-6010
Viamar Foods
Glen Cove, NY 516-759-0652
Wisconsin Whey International
Juda, WI 608-233-5101

Meat

La Romagnola
Orlando, FL 800-843-8359
Queen Ann Ravioli & Macaroni Company
Brooklyn, NY 718-256-1061

Seafood

La Romagnola
Orlando, FL 800-843-8359
Queen Ann Ravioli & Macaroni Company
Brooklyn, NY 718-256-1061

Vegetable

La Romagnola
Orlando, FL 800-843-8359
Queen Ann Ravioli & Macaroni Company
Brooklyn, NY 718-256-1061

Rigatoni

Al Dente
Whitmore Lake, MI 800-536-7278
Codino's Italian Foods
Scotia, NY 800-246-8908
Landolfi Food Products
Trenton, NJ 609-392-1830
Lucys Foods
Latrobe, PA 724-539-1430
Pascucci Family Pasta
San Diego, CA 619-285-8000
Pasta Factory
Melrose Park, IL 800-615-6951
Pasta USA
Spokane, WA 800-456-2084

Rotelle

Cuizina Food Company
Woodinville, WA 425-486-7000
Pascucci Family Pasta
San Diego, CA 619-285-8000
Pasta USA
Spokane, WA 800-456-2084

Rotini

A Zerega's Sons, Inc.
Fair Lawn, NJ 201-797-1400
Al Dente
Whitmore Lake, MI 800-536-7278
Archer Daniels Midland Company
Lincoln, NE 800-228-4060
Noodles By Leonardo
Devil's Lake, ND 701-662-8300
Pascucci Family Pasta
San Diego, CA 619-285-8000
Pasta USA
Spokane, WA 800-456-2084
Turris Italian Foods
Roseville, MI 586-773-6010

Semolina

Florence Macaroni Manufacturing
Chicago, IL 800-647-2782
Gabriele Macaroni Company
City of Industry, CA 626-964-2324
Pasta USA
Spokane, WA 800-456-2084

Shells

A Zerega's Sons, Inc.
Fair Lawn, NJ 201-797-1400
Borinquen Macaroni Corporation
Yauco, PR 787-856-1450
Costa Macaroni Manufacturing
Los Angeles, CA 800-433-7785
LaMonica Fine Foods
Millville, NJ 856-825-8111

Spaghetti

Archer Daniels Midland Company
Lincoln, NE 800-228-4060
Borinquen Macaroni Corporation
Yauco, PR 787-856-1450
Caesar's Pasta Products
Blackwood, NJ 856-227-2585
Campbell Soup Company
Camden, NJ 800-257-8443
ConAgra Foods/International Home Foods
Niagara Falls, ON 905-356-2661
Costa Macaroni Manufacturing
Los Angeles, CA 800-433-7785
Country Cupboard
Virginia City, NV 775-847-7300

De Cio Pasta Primo
Cave Creek, AZ 800-397-0770
Foulds
Libertyville, IL 847-362-3062
Heinz Company of Canada
North York, ON. 877-574-3469
Hershey Pasta Group
Louisville, KY 800-468-1714
International Home Foods
Parsippany, NJ. 973-359-9920
Iwamoto Natto Factory
Paia, HI 808-579-9933
La Romagnola
Orlando, FL. 800-843-8359
Ladson Homemade Pasta Company
Phoenix, AZ 480-353-0874
Landolfi Food Products
Trenton, NJ 609-392-1830
Lucys Foods
Latrobe, PA 724-539-1430
Marcetti Frozen Pasta
Altoona, IA 515-967-4254
Noodles By Leonardo
Devil's Lake, ND 701-662-8300
O Chili Frozen Foods Inc
Northbrook, IL 847-562-1991
Pasta Factory
Melrose Park, IL 800-615-6951
Pasta International
Mississauga, ON 905-890-5550
Shreveport Macaroni Company
Shreveport, LA 318-222-6857
Superior Pasta Company
Philadelphia, PA 215-922-7278
Taif Foods
Folcroft, PA. 610-522-0122
Varco Brothers
Chicago, IL 312-642-4740
Wisconsin Whey International
Juda, WI 608-233-5101

Canned

ConAgra Foods/International Home Foods
Niagara Falls, ON 905-356-2661
Heinz Company of Canada
North York, ON. 877-574-3469
International Home Foods
Parsippany, NJ. 973-359-9920
O Chili Frozen Foods Inc
Northbrook, IL 847-562-1991
Seneca Foods
Clyman, WI. 920-696-3331

Frozen

Caesar's Pasta Products
Blackwood, NJ 856-227-2585
Landolfi Food Products
Trenton, NJ 609-392-1830
Marcetti Frozen Pasta
Altoona, IA 515-967-4254
Pasta International
Mississauga, ON. 905-890-5550

Spelt

A Zerega's Sons, Inc.
Fair Lawn, NJ 201-797-1400
Costa Macaroni Manufacturing
Los Angeles, CA. 800-433-7785
Purity Foods
Okemos, MI 800-997-7358

Spinach

Cipriani's Spaghetti & Sauce Company
Chicago Heights, IL 708-755-6212
La Romagnola
Orlando, FL. 800-843-8359
Marsan Foods
Toronto, ON 416-755-9262
Pascucci Family Pasta
San Diego, CA 619-285-8000
Pasta USA
Spokane, WA. 800-456-2084
Wonton Food
Brooklyn, NY 800-776-8889

Stuffed Shells

Armanino Foods of Distinction
Hayward, CA 510-441-9300
Lucys Foods
Latrobe, PA 724-539-1430
Pasta USA
Spokane, WA. 800-456-2084
Queen Ann Ravioli & Macaroni Company
Brooklyn, NY 718-256-1061
Turris Italian Foods
Roseville, MI 586-773-6010

Tagliatelle

Costa Macaroni Manufacturing
Los Angeles, CA. 800-433-7785
Pasta USA
Spokane, WA. 800-456-2084

Tortellini

Agrusa, Inc.
Leonia, NJ. 201-592-5950
Alfredo's Italian Foods Manufacturing Company
Quincy, MA. 617-479-6360
Armanino Foods of Distinction
Hayward, CA 510-441-9300
Bruno Specialty Foods
West Sayville, NY. 631-589-1700
Costa Macaroni Manufacturing
Los Angeles, CA. 800-433-7785
Cuizina Food Company
Woodinville, WA. 425-486-7000
Dairy Maid Ravioli Manufacturing Corporation
Brooklyn, NY 718-449-2620
Fiori-Bruna Pasta Products
Hialeah, FL 305-621-0074
Italia Foods
Schaumburg, IL. 800-747-1109
LaMonica Fine Foods
Millville, NJ 856-825-8111
Landolfi Food Products
Trenton, NJ 609-392-1830
Lucys Foods
Latrobe, PA 724-539-1430
Mount Rose Ravioli & Macaroni Company
Farmingdale, NY
New York Ravioli & Pasta Company
New Hyde Park, NY 888-588-7287
Pascucci Family Pasta
San Diego, CA 619-285-8000
Pasta Del Mondo
Carmel, NY. 800-392-8887
Pasta Factory
Melrose Park, IL 800-615-6951
Pasta International
Mississauga, ON 905-890-5550
Pasta Mill
Edmonton, AB 780-454-8665
Pasta USA
Spokane, WA. 800-456-2084
Putney Pasta Company
Brattleboro, VT. 800-253-3683
Queen Ann Ravioli & Macaroni Company
Brooklyn, NY 718-256-1061
Riviera Ravioli Company
Bronx, NY. 718-823-0260
Roses Ravioli
Oglesby, IL 815-883-8011
Taif Foods
Folcroft, PA. 610-522-0122
Turris Italian Foods
Roseville, MI 586-773-6010
Viamar Foods
Glen Cove, NY 516-759-0652

Vermicelli

Archer Daniels Midland Company
Lincoln, NE. 800-228-4060
Cipriani's Spaghetti & Sauce Company
Chicago Heights, IL 708-755-6212
Costa Macaroni Manufacturing
Los Angeles, CA. 800-433-7785
Iwamoto Natto Factory
Paia, HI 808-579-9933
Pasta USA
Spokane, WA. 800-456-2084
Superior Pasta Company
Philadelphia, PA 215-922-7278

Prepared Foods

Battered

Simeus Foods International
Mansfield, TX....................888-772-3663

Refrigerated

Alderfer Bologna
Harleysville, PA..................800-341-1121
AquaCuisine
Eagle, ID........................208-323-2782
Atlantic Pork & Provisions
Jamaica, NY.....................800-245-3536
Avon Heights Mushrooms
Avondale, PA....................610-268-2092
Boesl Packing Company
Baltimore, MD...................410-675-1071
Bosell Foods
Cleveland, OH...................216-991-7600
Boudreaux's Foods
New Orleans, LA.................504-733-8440
Bridgford Foods of North Carolina
Statesville, NC...................704-878-2722
C. Roy Meat Products
Yale, MI.........................810-387-3957
Charlie's Country Sausage
Minot, ND.......................701-838-6302
Chicago 58 Food Products
Woodbridge, ON..................416-603-4244
Chisesi Brothers Meat Packing Company
New Orleans, LA.................800-966-3550
Citterio USA Corporation
Freeland, PA.....................800-435-8888
Corfu Foods
Bensenville, IL...................630-595-2510
Country Maid
Milwaukee, WI...................800-628-4354
Dairy Fresh Foods
Taylor, MI.......................313-295-6300
Danner Salads
Peoria, IL........................309-691-0289
Dietz & Watson
Philadelphia, PA..................800-333-1974
Dohar Meats
Cleveland, OH...................216-241-4197
Dole Fresh Vegetable Company
Soledad, CA.....................800-333-5454
Egon Binkert Meat Products
Baltimore, MD...................410-687-5959
F&S Produce Company
Rosenhayn, NJ...................800-886-3316
Foodbrands America
Oklahoma City, OK...............405-290-4000
Frank Wardynski & Sons
Buffalo, NY......................716-854-6083
Fried Provisions Company
Evans City, PA...................724-538-3160
Gilardi Foods
Sidney, OH......................937-498-4511
Green Garden Food Products
Kent, WA........................800-304-1033
Groff Meats
Elizabethtown, PA.................717-367-1246
Hansel 'N Gretel
Flushing, NY.....................718-326-0041
Hazle Park Packing Co
West Hazleton, PA................800-238-4331
Helens Pure Foods
Cheltenham, PA..................215-379-6433
Henry J Meat Specialties
Chicago, IL......................800-242-1314
Herold's Salad, Inc
Cleveland, OH...................800-427-2523
HFI Foods
Redmond, WA....................425-883-1320
Hoople Country Kitchens
Rockport, IN.....................812-649-2351
House of Thaller
Knoxville, TN....................800-462-3365
Ito Cariani Sausage Company
Hayward, CA....................510-887-0882
John Volpi & Company
St Louis, MO.....................800-288-3439
Kelly Kornbeef Company
Chicago, IL......................773-588-2882
Kessler Foods, Inc
Lemoyne, PA.....................717-763-7162
Kilgus Meats
Toledo, OH......................419-472-9721
Knotts Whlse. Foods
Paris, TN........................731-642-1961
Lakeside Foods
Manitowoc, WI...................920-684-3356
Land O'Frost
Searcy, AR......................800-643-5654
Lengerich Meats
Zanesville, IN....................260-638-4123
Leona Meat Plant
Troy, PA.........................570-297-3574
Levonian Brothers
Troy, NY........................518-274-3610
Litehouse
Sandpoint, ID....................208-263-7569
Locustdale Meat Packing
Locustdale, PA...................570-875-1270
Lowell Provision Company
Lowell, MA......................978-454-5603
Marshallville Packing Company
Marshallville, OH.................330-855-2871
Martin Rosol's
New Britain, CT..................860-223-2707
Meadows Country Products
Hollidaysburg, PA.................888-499-1001
Milan Salami Company
Oakland, CA.....................510-654-7055
Mishler Packing Company
Lagrange, IN.....................260-768-4156
Mrs. Grissom's Salad
Nashville, TN....................800-255-0571
Northern Star Company
Chaska, MN.....................612-339-8981
O'Brien & Company
Bellevue, NE.....................800-433-7567
Ohio Packing Company
Columbus, OH...................800-282-6403
Orval Kent Food Company
Wheeling, IL.....................847-459-9000
Otto W Liebold & Company
Flint, MI.........................800-999-6328
Parma Sausage Products
Pittsburgh, PA....................877-294-4207
Pfeffer's Country Mkt.
Sauk Centre, MN.................320-352-6490
Queen City Sausage
Cincinnati, OH...................877-544-5588
R.C. McEntire & Company
Columbia, SC....................803-799-3388
Real Kosher Sausage Company
Newark, NJ......................973-690-5394
Rego's Purity Foods
Honolulu, HI.....................808-847-3717
Rendulic Packing
McKeesport, PA..................412-678-9541
Reser's Fine Foods
Salt Lake City, UT................801-972-5633
Roman Packing Company
Norfolk, NE......................800-373-5990
Saag's Products
San Leandro, CA..................800-352-7224
Sandridge Food Corporation
Medina, OH......................800-627-2523
Sara Lee Corporation
Downers Grove, IL................630-598-8100
Sausage Shoppe
Cleveland, OH...................216-351-5213
Saval Foods
Elkridge, MD....................800-527-2825
Schaller & Weber
Astoria, NY......................800-847-4115
Sculli Brothers
Yeadon, PA......................215-336-1223
Sechrist Brothers
Dallastown, PA...................717-244-2975
Sheinman Provision Company
Philadelphia, PA..................215-473-7065
Smith Packing Regional Meat
Utica, NY
Snow Ball Foods
Williamstown, NJ.................856-629-4081
Spring Glen Fresh Foods
Ephrata, PA......................800-641-2853
Spring Grove Foods
Miamisburg, OH..................937-866-4311
Springfield Smoked Fish Company
Springfield, MA..................800-327-3412
Standard Beef Company
Foxboro, MA....................203-787-2164
Stawnichy Holdings
Mundare, AB....................888-764-7646
Stonies Sausage Shop Inc
Perryville, MO...................888-546-2540
Suter Company
Sycamore, IL.....................800-435-6942
Swift & Company
Greeley, CO......................970-506-8000
Tennessee Valley PackingCompany
Columbia, TN....................931-388-2623
Teti Bakery
Etobicoke, ON...................800-465-0123
Troy Frozen Food
Troy, IL.........................618-667-6332
Troyers Trail Bologna
Dundee, OH.....................877-893-2414
Tupman-Thurlow Company
Deerfield Beach, FL...............954-596-9989
United Provision Meat Company
Columbus, OH...................614-252-1126
Upstate Farms Cooperative
Buffalo, NY......................716-892-2121
Van Bennett Food Company
Reading, PA.....................800-423-8897
Vienna Meat Products
Scarborough, ON.................800-588-1931
Warren & Son Meat Processing
Whipple, OH.....................740-585-2421
Wimmer's Meat Products
West Point, NE...................800-358-0761
Wornick Company
Cincinnati, OH...................800-860-4555
Yarbrough Produce Company
Birmingham, AL..................205-324-4569

General

1-2-3 Gluten Inc
Orange, OH......................843-768-7231
A Gift Basket by Carmela
Longmeadow, MA................413-746-1400
A.C. Petersen Farms
West Hartford, CT.................860-233-8483
Acme Steak & Seafood Company
Youngstown, OH..................330-270-8000
Advance Food Company
Enid, OK.........................888-723-8237
Agrusa, Inc.
Leonia, NJ.......................201-592-5950
Al Pete Meats
Muncie, IN......................765-288-8817
Alderfer Bologna
Harleysville, PA..................800-341-1121
Alfonso Gourmet Pasta
Pompano Beach, FL...............800-370-7278
Alfonso Gourmet Pasta
Pompano Beach, FL...............800-370-7278
Alfonso Gourmet Pasta
Pompano Beach, FL...............800-370-7278
Alfredo's Italian Foods Manufacturing Company
Quincy, MA......................617-479-6360
Amberwave Foods
Oakmont, PA.....................412-828-3040
Armanino Foods of Distinction
Hayward, CA....................510-441-9300
Atlantic Pork & Provisions
Jamaica, NY.....................800-245-3536
Avalon Gourmet
Phoenix, AZ.....................602-253-0343
Avon Heights Mushrooms
Avondale, PA....................610-268-2092
Bake Crafters Food
Collegedale, TN..................800-296-8935
Barber Foods
Portland, ME.....................800-577-2595
Bay Cities Produce Company
San Leandro, CA..................510-346-4943
Beaver Street Fisheries
Jacksonville, FL..................800-874-6426
Bellisio Foods, Inc.
Duluth, MN......................800-368-7337
Bernardi Italian Foods Company
Bloomsburg, PA..................570-389-5500

Biagio's Banquets
Chicago, IL 800-392-2837
Biagio's Banquets
Chicago, IL 800-392-2837
Big B Distributors
Evansville, IN 812-425-5235
BlueWater Seafoods
Lachine, QC 888-560-2539
Boeckman JJ Wholesale Meats
Dayton, OH 937-222-4679
Boesl Packing Company
Baltimore, MD 410-675-1071
Bosell Foods
Cleveland, OH 216-991-7600
Bouma Meats
Provost, AB 780-753-2092
Boyd Sausage Company
Washington, IA 319-653-5715
Bridgford Foods of North Carolina
Statesville, NC 704-878-2722
Bruno Specialty Foods
West Sayville, NY 631-589-1700
Buxton Foods
Buxton, ND 800-726-8057
C. Roy Meat Products
Yale, MI 810-387-3957
Cajun Chef Products
Saint Martinville, LA 337-394-7112
Camino Real Foods
Vernon, CA 800-421-6201
Campbell Soup Company
Camden, NJ 800-257-8443
Campbell Soup Company
Camden, NJ 800-257-8443
Canada Bread
Etobicoke, ON 416-926-2000
Caribbean Food Delights
Tappan, NY 845-398-3000
Carl Buddig & Company
Homewood, IL 800-621-0868
Carolina Packers
Smithfield, NC 800-682-7675
Carrington Foods
Saraland, AL 251-675-9700
Casa Di Bertacchi
Vineland, NJ 800-818-9261
Castleberry's
Vineland, NJ 856-691-2100
Cedar Lake Foods
Cedar Lake, MI 800-246-5039
Cedarlane Foods
Carson, CA 310-886-7720
Chang Food Company
Garden Grove, CA 714-265-9990
Charlie's Country Sausage
Minot, ND 701-838-6302
Chateau Food Products
Cicero, IL 708-863-4207
Chef America
Chatsworth, CA 818-718-8111
Chef America East
Mount Sterling, KY 859-498-4300
Chef Hans Gourmet Foods
Monroe, LA 800-890-4267
Chicago 58 Food Products
Woodbridge, ON 416-603-4244
Chicago Meat Authority
Chicago, IL 773-254-3811
Chincoteague Seafood Company
Parsonsburg, MD 443-260-4800
Chisesi Brothers Meat Packing Company
New Orleans, LA 800-966-3550
Chloe Foods Corporation
Brooklyn, NY 718-827-9000
Chungs Gourmet Foods
Houston, TX 713-741-2118
Citterio USA Corporation
Freeland, PA 800-435-8888
ConAgra Foods
Boisbriand, QC 450-433-1322
ConAgra Foods Inc
Omaha, NE 402-595-7300
ConAgra Frozen Foods Company
Marshall, MO 660-886-3301
ConAgra Mexican Foods
Compton, CA 310-223-1499
Continental Deli Foods
Cherokee, IA 712-225-6529
Continental Mills
Seattle, WA 253-872-8400
Corfu Foods
Bensenville, IL 630-595-2510

Country Pies
Coombs, BC 250-248-6415
County Gourmet Foods, LLC
Sewickley, PA 412-741-8902
Cuisine Solutions
Alexandria, VA 888-285-4679
Culinary Foods
Chicago, IL 800-621-4049
Culinary Standards Corporation
Louisville, KY 800-778-3434
Cumberland Gap Provision Company
Middlesboro, KY 800-331-7154
Curtis Packing Company
Greensboro, NC 336-275-7684
D'Orazio Foods
Bellmawr, NJ 888-328-7287
Dairy Fresh Foods
Taylor, MI 313-295-6300
Danner Salads
Peoria, IL 309-691-0289
David Berg & Company
Chicago, IL 773-278-5195
Deep Foods
Union, NJ 908-810-7500
Depoe Bay Fish Company
Newport, OR 541-265-8833
Depoe Bay Fish Company
Newport, OR 541-265-8833
Devault Foods
Devault, PA 800-426-2874
Dietz & Watson
Philadelphia, PA 800-333-1974
Dippy Foods
Cypress, CA 800-819-8551
Dno
Columbus, OH 800-686-2366
Doerle Food Services
Broussard, LA 337-252-8551
Dohar Meats
Cleveland, OH 216-241-4197
Dole Fresh Vegetable Company
Soledad, CA 800-333-5454
Earth Island Natural Foods
Canoga Park, CA 818-725-2820
Earth Island Natural Foods
Canoga Park, CA 818-725-2820
Egon Binkert Meat Products
Baltimore, MD 410-687-5959
El Aguila Food Products
Salinas, CA 800-398-2929
Emerling International Foods
Buffalo, NY 716-833-7381

We supply food manufacturers and food service customers worldwide (since 1988) with bulk ingredients including: Fruits & Vegetables; Juice Concentrates; Herbs & Spices; Oils & Vinegars; Flavors & Colors; Honey & Molasses. We also produce PURE MAPLE SYRUP.

Enjoy Foods International
Fontana, CA 909-823-2228
Equity Group
Reidsville, NC 336-342-6601
Euro Source Gourmet
Cedar Grove, NJ 973-857-6000
F&S Produce Company
Rosenhayn, NJ 800-886-3316
F&S Produce Company
Rosenhayn, NJ 800-886-3316
Fast Food Merchandisers
Rocky Mount, NC 252-450-4000
Fine Choice Foods
Richmond, BC 604-522-3110
Fisher Rex Sandwiches
Raleigh, NC 919-901-0739
Flavor Right Foods Group
Columbus, OH 888-464-3734
Food Source
Mc Kinney, TX 972-548-9001
Foodbrands America
Oklahoma City, OK 405-290-4000
Frank Wardynski & Sons
Buffalo, NY 716-854-6083
Fried Provisions Company
Evans City, PA 724-538-3160
Garden Protein International
Richmond, BC 877-305-6777
George L. Wells Meat Company
Philadelphia, PA 800-523-1730
Gilardi Foods
Sidney, OH 937-498-4511

Glendora Quiche Company
San Dimas, CA 909-394-1777
Golden Gulf Coast Packing Company
Biloxi, MS 228-374-6121
Gonard Foods
Calgary, AB 403-277-0991
Gopicnic
Chicago, IL 773-328-2490
Great West of Hawaii
Honolulu, HI 808-593-9981
Grecian Delight Foods
Elk Grove Village, IL 800-621-4387
Green Garden Food Products
Kent, WA 800-304-1033
Green Garden Food Products
Kent, WA 800-304-1033
Groff Meats
Elizabethtown, PA 717-367-1246
Guiltless Gourmet®
Secaucus, NJ 512-389-0770
Gutheinz Meats
Scranton, PA 570-344-1191
Hansel 'N Gretel
Flushing, NY 718-326-0041
Harold Food Company
Charlotte, NC 704-588-8061
Hartselle Frozen Foods
Hartselle, AL 256-773-7261
Harvest Time Foods
Ayden, NC 252-746-6675
Hazle Park Packing Co
West Hazleton, PA 800-238-4331
Heinkel's Packing Company
Decatur, IL 800-594-2738
Heinz Company of Canada
North York, ON 877-574-3469
Heinz Company of Canada
North York, ON 877-574-3469
Helens Pure Foods
Cheltenham, PA 215-379-6433
Henry J Meat Specialties
Chicago, IL 800-242-1314
Herold's Salad, Inc
Cleveland, OH 800-427-2523
HFI Foods
Redmond, WA 425-883-1320
HFI Foods
Redmond, WA 425-883-1320
Holland American International Specialties
Bellflower, CA 562-925-6914
Homestead Fine Foods
S San Francisco, CA 650-615-0750
Homestead Fine Foods
S San Francisco, CA 650-615-0750
Hoople Country Kitchens
Rockport, IN 812-649-2351
Hormel Foods Corporation
Algona, IA 515-295-8777
Hot Potato Distributor
Chicago, IL 312-243-0640
House of Raeford Farms
Raeford, NC 800-888-7539
House of Thaller
Knoxville, TN 800-462-3365
House of Webster
Rogers, AR 800-369-4641
HSR Associates
Tarzana, CA 818-757-7152
Humboldt Sausage Company
Humboldt, IA 515-332-4121
Hummel Brothers
New Haven, CT 800-828-8978
Hunt-Wesson Food Service Company
Rochester, NY 866-484-8676
I & K Distributors
Delphos, OH 800-869-6337
Ians Natural Foods
Lawrence, MA 800-543-6637
Independent Packers Corporation
Seattle, WA 206-285-6000
Independent Packers Corporation
Seattle, WA 206-285-6000
ISE America, Inc.
Galena, MD 410-755-6300
ISE America, Inc.
Galena, MD 410-755-6300
Ito Cariani Sausage Company
Hayward, CA 510-887-0882
Jesses Fine Meats
Cherokee, IA 712-225-3637
John Volpi & Company
St Louis, MO 800-288-3439

Kanai Tofu Factory
Honolulu, HI 808-591-8205
Karam Elsaha Baking Company
Manlius, NY
Kay Foods Company
Detroit, MI 313-393-1100
Kelly Foods
Jackson, TN 731-424-2255
Kelly Kornbeef Company
Chicago, IL 773-588-2882
Kerala Curry
Pittsboro, NC 919-545-9401
Kessler Foods, Inc
Lemoyne, PA. 717-763-7162
Key Ingredients
Harrisburg, PA 800-227-4448
Kilgus Meats
Toledo, OH 419-472-9721
King Kold Meats
Englewood, OH 800-836-2797
Kitts Meat Processing
Dedham, IA. 712-683-5622
Knotts Whlse. Foods
Paris, TN. 731-642-1961
Kronos Products
Glendale Heights, IL. 800-621-0099
Kubla Khan Food Company
Portland, OR 503-234-7494
Lafitte Frozen Foods Corporation
Lafitte, LA. 504-689-2041
Lakeside Foods
Manitowoc, WI. 920-684-3356
Land O'Frost
Searcy, AR 800-643-5654
Landolfi Food Products
Trenton, NJ 609-392-1830
Lengerich Meats
Zanesville, IN 260-638-4123
Leona Meat Plant
Troy, PA. 570-297-3574
Levonian Brothers
Troy, NY 518-274-3610
Levonian Brothers
Troy, NY 518-274-3610
Lisa Shively's Kitchen Helpers, LLC
Eden, NC. 336-623-7511
Locustdale Meat Packing
Locustdale, PA 570-875-1270
Loggins Meat Company
Tyler, TX. 800-527-8610
Louisiana Packing Company
Westwego, LA. 800-666-1293
Love & Quiches Desserts
Freeport, NY. 800-525-5251
Lowell Provision Company
Lowell, MA. 978-454-5603
Lowell Provision Company
Lowell, MA. 978-454-5603
Lower Foods
Richmond, UT. 435-258-2449
Lucks Food Decorating Company
Tacoma, WA 253-383-4815
Macabee Foods
West Nyack, NY 845-623-1300
Made Rite Foods
Burlington, NC 336-229-5728
Mah Chena Company
Chicago, IL 312-226-5100
Manda Fine Meats
Baton Rouge, LA 225-344-7636
Manda Fine Meats
Baton Rouge, LA 225-344-7636
Manda Fine Meats
Baton Rouge, LA 225-344-7636
Maria and Son Italian Products
Saint Louis, MO 866-481-9009
Market Fare Foods
Phoenix, AZ 888-669-6420
Marsan Foods
Toronto, ON 416-755-9262
Marshallville Packing Company
Marshallville, OH 330-855-2871
Martin Rosol's
New Britain, CT 860-223-2707
Martin Rosol's
New Britain, CT 860-223-2707
Martin Seafood Company
Jessup, MD 410-799-5822
McFarling Foods
Indianapolis, IN 317-635-2633
McGrath's Frozen Foods
Streator, IL 815-672-2654
McLane Foods
Phoenix, AZ 602-275-5509
Meadows Country Products
Hollidaysburg, PA. 888-499-1001
Menemsha Fish Market
Chilmark, MA. 508-645-2282
Metafoods, LLC
Atlanta, GA. 404-843-2400
Mexi-Frost Specialties Company
Brooklyn, NY 718-625-3324
Michael Foods, Inc.
Minnetonka, MN. 952-258-4000
Michael Foods, Inc.
Minnetonka, MN. 952-258-4000
Milan Salami Company
Oakland, CA 510-654-7055
Mishler Packing Company
Lagrange, IN. 260-768-4156
Molinaro's Fine Italian Foods
Mississauga, ON. 800-268-4959
Molinaro's Fine Italian Foods
Mississauga, ON. 800-268-4959
Mrs. Grissom's Salad
Nashville, TN 800-255-0571
Murphy House
Louisburg, NC 919-496-6054
Naleway Foods
Winnipeg, MB. 800-665-7448
Naleway Foods
Winnipeg, MB. 800-665-7448
Nash Finch Company
Statesboro, GA 912-681-4580
Nestle Pizza
Medford, WI 715-748-5550
Nestle USA Inc
Glendale, CA 800-225-2270
Night Hawk Frozen Foods
Buda, TX. 800-580-4166
North Atlantic Fish Company
Gloucester, MA. 978-283-4121
Northern Star Company
Chaska, MN 612-339-8981
O Chili Frozen Foods Inc
Northbrook, IL 847-562-1991
O'Brien & Company
Bellevue, NE. 800-433-7567
Ohio Packing Company
Columbus, OH 800-282-6403
Old Fashioned Kitchen
Lakewood, NJ. 732-364-4100
On-Cor Foods Products
Northbrook, IL 847-205-1040
Orval Kent Food Company
Wheeling, IL. 847-459-9000
Otto W Liebold & Company
Flint, MI 800-999-6328
P.A. Braunger Institutional Foods
Sioux City, IA. 712-258-4515
Parma Sausage Products
Pittsburgh, PA. 877-294-4207
Pasta Factory
Melrose Park, IL. 800-615-6951
Pasta USA
Spokane, WA. 800-456-2084
Penguin Natural Foods
Commerce, CA 800-600-8448
Pfeffer's Country Mkt.
Sauk Centre, MN 320-352-6490
Pictsweet Frozen Foods
Bells, TN. 731-422-7600
Pinnacle Foods Group
Cherry Hill, NJ 877-852-7424
Plumrose USA
East Brunswick, NJ. 800-526-4909
Pocino Foods
City of Industry, CA 800-345-0150
Pon Food Corporation
Ponchatoula, LA. 985-386-6941
Preferred Meal Systems
Scranton, PA 570-457-8311
Prolimer Foods
Candiac, QC 877-535-4631
Queen International Foods
Monterey Park, CA. 800-423-4414
R.C. McEntire & Company
Columbia, SC 803-799-3388
R.L. Zeigler Company
Tuscaloosa, AL. 800-392-6328
Ramona's Mex. Food Produoducts
Gardena, CA. 310-323-1950
Ready Portion Meat Company
Baton Rouge, LA 225-355-5641
Real Kosher Sausage Company
Newark, NJ. 973-690-5394
Redi-Serve Food Company
Fort Atkinson, WI. 920-563-6391
Regal Food Service
Houston, TX 281-477-3683
Rego's Purity Foods
Honolulu, HI. 808-847-3717
Rendulic Packing
McKeesport, PA 412-678-9541
Request Foods
Holland, MI. 800-748-0378
Reser's Fine Foods
Salt Lake City, UT 801-972-5633
Reser's Fine Foods
Salt Lake City, UT 801-972-5633
Roman Packing Company
Norfolk, NE. 800-373-5990
Ruiz Food Products
Dinuba, CA. 800-477-6474
Saag's Products
San Leandro, CA. 800-352-7224
Salem Food Service
Salem, IN 812-883-2196
Sales Associates of Alaska
Fairbanks, AK. 907-458-0000
Salvage Sale
Houston, TX 800-856-7445
Samjin America
Vernon, CA 213-622-5111
Sana Foods
Bainbridge Island, WA 206-842-4741
Sanderson Farms
Bryan, TX. 979-778-5730
Sandridge Food Corporation
Medina, OH. 800-627-2523
Sara Lee Corporation
Downers Grove, IL. 630-598-8100
Sausage Shoppe
Cleveland, OH 216-351-5213
Saval Foods
Elkridge, MD 800-527-2825
Savannah Food Company
Savannah, TN 800-795-2550
Savannah Food Company
Savannah, TN 800-795-2550
Schaller & Weber
Astoria, NY. 800-847-4115
Sculli Brothers
Yeadon, PA 215-336-1223
Sechrist Brothers
Dallastown, PA 717-244-2975
Seneca Foods
Clyman, WI. 920-696-3331
Sheinman Provision Company
Philadelphia, PA 215-473-7065
Simco Foods
Los Angeles, CA. 310-284-8446
Simeus Foods International
Mansfield, TX. 888-772-3663
Sims Wholesale
Batesville, AR. 870-793-1109
Smith Packing Regional Meat
Utica, NY
Snow Ball Foods
Williamstown, NJ 856-629-4081
Somerset Food Service
Somerset, KY 606-274-4858
Somerset Industries
Spring House, PA 800-883-8728
Sonoco Wholesale Grocers
Houma, LA 985-851-0727
Specialty Brands
Carthage, MO 417-358-8104
Specialty Brands
Ontario, CA. 800-782-1180
Spring Glen Fresh Foods
Ephrata, PA. 800-641-2853
Spring Grove Foods
Miamisburg, OH. 937-866-4311
Springfield Smoked Fish Company
Springfield, MA 800-327-3412
Standard Beef Company
Foxboro, MA 203-787-2164
Star Ravioli Manufacturing Company
Moonachie, NJ 201-933-6427
Stawnichy Holdings
Mundare, AB 888-764-7646
Steak-Umm Company
Shillington, PA 860-928-5900
Stefano Gourmet A Taste of Italy
Rural Ridge, PA 888-781-4104

Stevens Sausage Company
Smithfield, NC 800-338-0561
Stonies Sausage Shop Inc
Perryville, MO 888-546-2540
Storheim's
Green Bay, WI. 920-498-2343
Sunburst Foods
Goldsboro, NC 919-778-2151
SunMeadow Family of Products
Saint Petersburg, FL 727-573-2211
Sunset Specialty Foods
Sunset Beach, CA 562-592-4976
Sunset Whlse.
Lebanon, PA 800-876-2123
Swift & Company
Greeley, CO. 970-506-8000
Swiss Colony
Monroe, WI. 608-328-8536
Symphony Foods
Berkeley, CA. 510-845-8275
Tampa Maid Foods
Lakeland, FL. 800-237-7637
Tasty Mix Quality Foods
Brooklyn, NY. 866-TAS-TYMX
Tennessee Valley PackingCompany
Columbia, TN 931-388-2623
Teti Bakery
Etobicoke, ON 800-465-0123
Theoworld
Fairfield, OH. 773-268-2800
Tomasso Corporation
Baie D'Urfe, QC. 514-325-3000
Tree Tavern Products
Paterson, NJ 973-279-1617
Trident Seafoods Corporation
Seattle, WA 800-426-5490
Troy Frozen Food
Troy, IL 618-667-6332
Troyers Trail Bologna
Dundee, OH 877-893-2414
Tupman-Thurlow Company
Deerfield Beach, FL 954-596-9989
Tyson Foods
Springdale, AR 800-643-3410
United Provision Meat Company
Columbus, OH 614-252-1126
Upstate Farms Cooperative
Buffalo, NY. 716-892-2121
Van Bennett Food Company
Reading, PA 800-423-8897
Vanee Foods Company
Berkeley, IL. 708-449-7300
Vantage USA
Chicago, IL 773-247-1086
Vienna Meat Products
Scarborough, ON 800-588-1931
Viking Seafoods Inc
Malden, MA 800-225-3020
WA Bean & Sons
Bangor, ME. 800-649-1958
Warren & Son Meat Processing
Whipple, OH. 740-585-2421
Wawona Frozen Foods
Clovis, CA 559-299-2901
William E. Caudle Company
Idaho Falls, ID 208-523-6637
Wimmer's Meat Products
West Point, NE 800-358-0761
Winkler
Winkler, MB 204-325-4771
Wong Wing Foods
Montreal, QC 800-361-4820
Woods Fabricators
Taylorsville, GA 770-684-5377
Wornick Company
Cincinnati, OH 800-860-4555
Wornick Company
Cincinnati, OH 800-860-4555
Wornick Company
Cincinnati, OH 800-860-4555
Yarbrough Produce Company
Birmingham, AL. 205-324-4569
Zartic Inc
Rome, GA. 800-241-0516
Zuccaro's Fruit & Produce Company
Minneapolis, MN 612-333-1122

Antipasto

Victoria Packing Corporation
Brooklyn, NY 718-927-3000

Appetizers

Anchor Appetizer Group
Appleton, WI 920-997-2200
Anchor Food Products/ McCain Foods
Appleton, WI 920-734-0627
Appetizers And
Chicago, IL 800-323-5472
B&D Foods
Boise, ID 208-344-1183
Barber Foods
Portland, ME. 800-577-2595
Belle River Enterprises
Belle River, PE 902-962-2248
Better Baked Foods
North East, PA. 814-725-8778
Biagio's Banquets
Chicago, IL 800-392-2837
Bocconcino Food Products
Moonachie, NJ 201-933-7474
Caribbean Food Delights
Tappan, NY 845-398-3000
Cateraid
Howell, MI 800-508-8217
Cathay Foods Corporation
Boston, MA. 617-427-1507
Chang Food Company
Garden Grove, CA 714-265-9990
Chateau Food Products
Cicero, IL 708-863-4207
Chinese Spaghetti Factory
Boston, MA. 617-445-7714
Chungs Gourmet Foods
Houston, TX 713-741-2118
ConAgra Grocery Products
Irvine, CA 714-680-1000
ConAgra Mexican Foods
Compton, CA 310-223-1499
Cordon Bleu International
Anjou, QC. 514-352-3000
Culinary Foods
Chicago, IL 800-621-4049
Dominex
St Augustine, FL. 904-810-2132
Dufour Pastry Kitchens
Bronx, NY. 800-439-1282
Egg Roll Fantasy
Auburn, CA. 530-887-9197
Excelline Foods
Chatsworth, CA 818-701-7710
Fillo Factory
Dumont, NJ. 800-653-4556
Fine Choice Foods
Richmond, BC. 604-522-3110
Foodbrands America
Oklahoma City, OK 405-290-4000
Frozen Specialties
Archbold, OH 419-445-9015
Fry Foods
Tiffin, OH 800-626-2294
Glendora Quiche Company
San Dimas, CA 909-394-1777
Golden Gate Foods
Dallas, TX. 214-747-2223
Goodwives Hors D'Oeuvres
Wilmington, MA. 800-521-8160
Great American Appetizers
Nampa, ID. 800-282-4834
Harvest Food Products Company
Concord, CA. 925-676-8208
Health is Wealth Foods
Williamstown, NJ 856-728-1998
Kretschmar
Don Mills, ON 800-561-4532
L&S Packing Company
Farmingdale, NY 800-286-6487
La Tang Cuisine Manufacturing
Houston, TX 713-780-4876
Lamb-Weston
Kennewick, WA 800-766-7783
LaMonica Fine Foods
Millville, NJ 856-825-8111
Lees Sausage Company
Orangeburg, SC 803-534-5517
Mama Amy's Quality Foods
Mississauga, ON. 905-456-0056
Matador Processors
Blanchard, OK 800-847-0797
McCain Foods USA
Lisle, IL. 800-938-7799
Mt. Olympus Specialty Foods
Buffalo, NY. 716-874-0771
Musco Olive Products
Tracy, CA 800-523-9828
Nancy's Specialty Foods
Newark, CA 510-494-1100
Omstead Foods Ltd
Wheatley, ON 905-315-8883
Pastene Companies
Canton, MA 781-830-8200
Perfect Bite Company
Glendale, CA 818-507-1527
Pie Piper Products
Bensenville, IL 800-621-8183
Plenus Group
Lowell, MA. 978-970-3832
Produits Belle Baie
Caraquet, NB 506-727-4414
Rubschlager Baking Corporation
Chicago, IL 773-826-1245
Sable & Rosenfeld Foods
Toronto, ON 416-929-4214
Sabra Dipping Company
White Plains, NY 888-957-2272
Shonna's Gourmet Goodies
West Bridgewater, MA 888-312-7868
Simeus Foods Internatio nal
Mansfield, TX. 888-772-3663
Simeus Foods International
Mansfield, TX. 888-772-3663
Sinbad Sweets
Fresno, CA 800-350-7933
Specialty Brands
Ontario, CA. 800-782-1180
Steak-Umm Company
Shillington, PA 860-928-5900
Tampa Maid Foods
Lakeland, FL. 800-237-7637
Thyme & Truffles Hors D'oeuvres
Dollard-Des-Ormeaux, QC. 877-785-9759
Tipiak
Stamford, CT. 203-961-9117
Tribe Mediterranean Foods Company LLC
Taunton, MA. 774-961-0000
Valdez Food
Philadelphia, PA 215-634-6106
Van-Lang Foods
Countryside, IL. 708-588-0800
Wayne Farms LLC
Pendergrass, GA 706-693-2271
William Poll
New York, NY 800-993-7655
Willow Foods
Beaverton, OR 800-338-3609
Windsor Foods
Houston, TX 713-843-5200
Wonton Food
Brooklyn, NY 800-776-8889

Fresh, Canned & Frozen

Anchor Food Products/ McCain Foods
Appleton, WI 920-734-0627
Barber Foods
Portland, ME. 800-577-2595
Belle River Enterprises
Belle River, PE 902-962-2248
Biagio's Banquets
Chicago, IL 800-392-2837
Caribbean Food Delights
Tappan, NY 845-398-3000
Cateraid
Howell, MI 800-508-8217
Cathay Foods Corporation
Boston, MA. 617-427-1507
Caughman's Meat Plant
Lexington, SC. 803-356-0076
Cedar Key Aquaculture Farms
Mango, FL. 888-252-6735
Chang Food Company
Garden Grove, CA 714-265-9990
Chateau Food Products
Cicero, IL 708-863-4207
Chinese Spaghetti Factory
Boston, MA. 617-445-7714
Chungs Gourmet Foods
Houston, TX 713-741-2118
Cordon Bleu International
Anjou, QC. 514-352-3000
Culinary Foods
Chicago, IL 800-621-4049
Dufour Pastry Kitchens
Bronx, NY. 800-439-1282

Fine Choice Foods
Richmond, BC. 604-522-3110
Foodbrands America
Oklahoma City, OK 405-290-4000
Frozen Specialties
Archbold, OH 419-445-9015
Glendora Quiche Company
San Dimas, CA 909-394-1777
Golden Gate Foods
Dallas, TX. 214-747-2223
Good Wives, Inc.
Wilmington, MA. 800-521-8160
Gourmet Foods
Compton, CA 310-632-3300
Great American Appetizers
Nampa, ID. 800-282-4834
Kabob's
Lake City, GA. 800-732-9484
Kretschmar
Don Mills, ON 800-561-4532
La Tang Cuisine Manufacturing
Houston, TX 713-780-4876
LaMonica Fine Foods
Millville, NJ 856-825-8111
Lees Sausage Company
Orangeburg, SC 803-534-5517
Matador Processors
Blanchard, OK 800-847-0797
Musco Olive Products
Tracy, CA 800-523-9828
Nancy's Specialty Foods
Newark, CA 510-494-1100
Pie Piper Products
Bensenville, IL 800-621-8183
Produits Belle Baie
Caraquet, NB 506-727-4414
Royal Palate Foods
Inglewood, CA 310-330-7701
Shonna's Gourmet Goodies
West Bridgewater, MA. 888-312-7868
SilverLeaf International
Stafford, TX 800-442-7542
Steak-Umm Company
Shillington, PA 860-928-5900
Tampa Maid Foods
Lakeland, FL. 800-237-7637
Thyme & Truffles Hors D'oeuvres
Dollard-Des-Ormeaux, QC. 877-785-9759
Tipiak
Stamford, CT. 203-961-9117
Van-Lang Foods
Countryside, IL. 708-588-0800
Victoria Packing Corporation
Brooklyn, NY 718-927-3000
VLR Food Corporation
Concord, ON. 800-387-7437
Windsor Foods
Houston, TX 713-843-5200

Frozen

Appetizers And
Chicago, IL. 800-323-5472
B&D Foods
Boise, ID 208-344-1183
Barber Foods
Portland, ME. 800-577-2595
Bocconcino Food Products
Moonachie, NJ 201-933-7474
Caribbean Food Delights
Tappan, NY. 845-398-3000
Cathay Foods Corporation
Boston, MA. 617-427-1507
Chang Food Company
Garden Grove, CA 714-265-9990
Chateau Food Products
Cicero, IL 708-863-4207
Clear Springs Foods
Cherry Hill, NJ 800-635-8211
Coastal Seafoods
Ridgefield, CT 203-431-0453
ConAgra Mexican Foods
Compton, CA 310-223-1499
Cordon Bleu International
Anjou, QC. 514-352-3000
Dufour Pastry Kitchens
Bronx, NY. 800-439-1282
Foodbrands America
Oklahoma City, OK 405-290-4000
Good Wives, Inc.
Wilmington, MA. 800-521-8160
Great American Appetizers
Nampa, ID. 800-282-4834
Health is Wealth Foods
Williamstown, NJ 856-728-1998
LaMonica Fine Foods
Millville, NJ 856-825-8111
Matador Processors
Blanchard, OK 800-847-0797
McCain Foods USA
Lisle, IL. 800-938-7799
Specialty Brands
Ontario, CA. 800-782-1180
Stacey's Famous Foods
Hayden, ID 800-782-2395
Steak-Umm Company
Shillington, PA 860-928-5900
Tampa Maid Foods
Lakeland, FL. 800-237-7637
Thyme & Truffles Hors D'oeuvres
Dollard-Des-Ormeaux, QC. 877-785-9759
Tipiak
Stamford, CT. 203-961-9117
William Poll
New York, NY 800-993-7655

Refrigerated

Cyclone Enterprises
Houston, TX 281-872-0087
Larsen Packers
Burwick, NS 902-538-8060
Reser's Fine Foods
Beaverton, OR 800-333-6431

Baked Beans (see also Pork & Beans)

Canned

Agland, Inc.
Eaton, CO 800-433-4688
Allen Canning Company
Siloam Springs, AR 800-234-2553
AlpineAire Foods
Rocklin, CA 800-322-6325
Amigos Canning Company
San Antonio, TX. 800-580-3477
B&M
Portland, ME. 207-772-7043
Beckman & Gast Company
Saint Henry, OH 419-678-4195
Blue Runner Foods
Gonzales, LA 225-647-3016
Burnette Foods
Elk Rapids, MI 231-264-8116
Bush Brothers & Co.
Augusta, WI 715-286-2211
California Fruit and Tomato Kitchens
Riverbank, CA 209-869-9300
Campbell Soup Company
Camden, NJ. 800-257-8443
Carriere Foods Inc
Saint-Denis-Sur-Richelie, QC 450-787-3411
ConAgra Grocery Products
Irvine, CA. 714-680-1000
Cordon Bleu International
Anjou, QC. 514-352-3000
Eden Foods Inc.
Clinton, MI 800-248-0320
Faribault Foods
Minneapolis, MN 612-333-6461
Grandma Brown's Beans Inc
Mexico, NY. 315-963-7221
H.K. Canning
Ventura, CA. 805-652-1392
Hanover Foods Corporation
Hanover, PA 717-632-6000
Heinz Company of Canada
North York, ON. 877-574-3469
Hoopeston Foods
Burnsville, MN 952-854-0903
International Home Foods
Parsippany, NJ. 973-359-9920
L&S Packing Company
Farmingdale, NY 800-286-6487
Lakeside Foods
Plainview, MN 507-534-3141
Lakeside Foods
Mondovi, WI. 715-926-5075
Lakeside Foods
Manitowoc, WI 920-684-3356
Lakeside Foods
Seymour, WI. 920-833-2371
Lucks Food Decorating Company
Tacoma, WA 253-383-4815
McCall Farms
Effingham, SC. 800-277-2012
Mercado Latino
City of Industry, CA 626-333-6862
Miyako Oriental Foods
Baldwin Park, CA. 877-788-6476
Morgan Food
Austin, IN 888-430-1780
Nationwide Canning
Cottam, ON. 519-839-4831
Natural Value Products
Sacramento, CA 916-427-7242
New Era Canning Company
New Era, MI 231-861-2151
New Harvest Foods
Pulaski, WI 920-822-2578
New Meridian
Eaton, IN. 765-396-3344
NORPAC Foods
Stayton, OR. 503-769-2101
NORPAC Foods
Lake Oswego, OR. 800-733-9311
Old Ranchers Canning Company
Upland, CA. 909-982-8895
Omstead Foods Ltd
Wheatley, ON 905-315-8883
Poynette Distribution Center
Poynette, WI 608-635-4396
Princeville Canning Company
Princeville, IL 309-385-4301
Red River Commodities
Fargo, ND 701-282-2600
Rio Valley Canning Company
Donna, TX. 956-464-7843
Seneca Foods
Cumberland, WI 715-822-2181
Sunrise Growers
Placentia, CA 714-630-6292
Truitt Brothers Inc
Salem, OR. 800-547-8712
United Intertrade Corporation
Houston, TX 800-969-2233
Wornick Company
Cincinnati, OH 800-860-4555

Breaded Vegetables

Al Pete Meats
Muncie, IN 765-288-8817
Anchor Food Products/ McCain Foods
Appleton, WI 920-734-0627
Brooks Food Group Corporate Office
Bedford, VA 800-873-4934
Great American Appetizers
Nampa, ID. 800-282-4834
Lake Erie Frozen Foods Company
Ashland, OH 800-766-8501
Omstead Foods Ltd
Wheatley, ON 905-315-8883
Ore-Ida Foods
Pittsburgh, PA 800-892-2401
Pictsweet Frozen Foods
Bells, TN. 731-422-7600
Trans Pecos Foods
San Antonio, TX. 210-228-0896
Westin
Omaha, NE 800-228-6098

Breakfast Foods: Instant

Agricore United
Winnipeg, MB. 800-661-4844
Bake Crafters Food
Collegedale, TN 800-296-8935
Bede Inc
Haledon, NJ 866-239-6565
California Cereal Products
Oakland, CA 510-452-4500
Campbell Soup Company
Camden, NJ. 800-257-8443
ConAgra Store Brands, Inc.
Lakeville, MN. 800-328-6286
Continental Mills
Seattle, WA 253-872-8400
Country Smoked Meats
Bowling Green, OH 800-321-4766
Cream of the West
Harlowton, MT 800-477-2383
GFA Brands
Paramus, NJ 201-568-9300

Gilster Mary Lee/Jasper Foods
Jasper, MO 800-777-2168
Hodgson Mill Inc.
Effingham, IL 800-525-0177
Homestead Mills
Cook, MN 800-652-5233
International Home Foods
Parsippany, NJ 973-359-9920
Jimmy Dean Foods
Cincinnati, OH 800-925-3326
Kellogg Canada Inc
Mississauga, ON 888-876-3750
Kellogg Company
Omaha, NE 402-331-7717
Kellogg Company
Hammonton, NJ 609-567-2300
Kellogg Company
Memphis, TN 901-743-0052
Little Crow Foods
Warsaw, IN 800-288-2769
Nestle Prepared Foods Company
Englewood, CO 800-225-2270
New England Natural Baker
Greenfield, MA 800-910-2884
Noodles By Leonardo
Devil's Lake, ND 701-662-8300
Northern Star Company
Chaska, MN 612-339-8981
Purity Foods
Okemos, MI 800-997-7358
Quaker Oats Company
Peterborough, ON 800-267-6287
Real Food Marketing
Kansas City, MO 816-221-4100
Rhodes Bake-N-Serv
Salt Lake City, UT 800-695-0122
Rich-Seapak Corporation
St Simons Island, GA 800-654-9731
Sturm Foods
Manawa, WI 800-347-8876
Tami Great Food
Monsey, NY 732-803-6366
Tova Industries
Louisville, KY 888-532-8682
US Mills
Bala Cynwyd, PA 800-422-1125

Broth

Canned,Frozen,Powdered

Blount Seafood Corporation
Fall River, MA 774-888-1300
Clofine Dairy & Food Products
Linwood, NJ 800-441-1001
Cordon Bleu International
Anjou, QC 514-352-3000
Fuji Foods
Browns Summit, NC 336-375-3111
Hormel Foods Corporation
Austin, MN 800-523-4635
International Dehydrate d Foods
Springfield, MO 800-641-6509
International Dehydrated Foods
Springfield, MO 800-525-7435
Old Ranchers Canning Company
Upland, CA 909-982-8895
Organic Gourmet
Sherman Oaks, CA 800-400-7772

Sentry Seasonings
Elmhurst, IL 630-530-5370

The product development experts of Sentry Seasonings are eager to offer the assistance and hands-on experience to food processors of all sizes. Sentry Seasonings will ensure the consistent high quality and repeat sales of your products, whether you choose one of our many off-the-shelf Bench Mark products or a modified version to meet your preferences. Sentry Seasonings can also duplicate and/or improve your present flavor profile; formulate, blend and package specifically for your requirements.

SOUPerior Bean & Spice Company
Vancouver, WA 800-878-7687
St. Ours & Company
Norwell, MA 781-331-8520
Sweet Sue Kitchens
Athens, AL 256-216-0500
Tova Industries
Louisville, KY 888-532-8682

Chicken

All-States Quality Foods
Charles City, IA 800-247-4195
Clofine Dairy & Food Products
Linwood, NJ 800-441-1001
Sentry Seasonings
Elmhurst, IL 630-530-5370

The product development experts of Sentry Seasonings are eager to offer the assistance and hands-on experience to food processors of all sizes. Sentry Seasonings will ensure the consistent high quality and repeat sales of your products, whether you choose one of our many off-the-shelf Bench Mark products or a modified version to meet your preferences. Sentry Seasonings can also duplicate and/or improve your present flavor profile; formulate, blend and package specifically for your requirements.

Sweet Sue Kitchens
Athens, AL 256-216-0500
Vanee Foods Company
Berkeley, IL 708-449-7300

Frozen

Proliant Meat Ingredients
Harlan, IA 800-369-2672

Powdered

Proliant Meat Ingredients
Harlan, IA 800-369-2672

Chili

Aunt Kitty's Foods
Vineland, NJ 856-691-2100
Baja Foods
Chicago, IL 773-376-9030
Bear Creek Kitchens
Marshall, TX 888-300-7687
Big B Distributors
Evansville, IN 812-425-5235
Bruce Foods Corporation
New Iberia, LA 800-299-9082
Burnett & Son Meat Company
Monrovia, CA 626-357-2165
Bush Brothers & Co.
Augusta, WI 715-286-2211
Buxton Foods
Buxton, ND 800-726-8057
Campbell Soup Company
Camden, NJ 800-257-8443
Castleberry's
Vineland, NJ 856-691-2100
Chandler Foods
Greensboro, NC 800-537-6219
Cherchies
Malvern, PA 800-644-1980
Culinary Standards Corporation
Louisville, KY 800-778-3434
Detroit Chili Company
Southfield, MI 248-440-5933
Edmonds Chile Company
St Louis, MO 314-772-1499
El-Rey Foods
Ferguson, MO 314-521-3113
Faribault Foods
Minneapolis, MN 612-333-6461
Harold Food Company
Charlotte, NC 704-588-8061
Health Valley Company
Irwindale, CA 800-334-3204
Hoopeston Foods
Burnsville, MN 952-854-0903
International Home Foods
Parsippany, NJ 973-359-9920
Kelly Foods
Jackson, TN 731-424-2255
Lees Sausage Company
Orangeburg, SC 803-534-5517
Mexisnax Corporation
El Paso, TX 915-779-5709
Mi Ranchito Foods
Bayard, NM 575-537-3868
Milnot Company
Litchfield, IL 800-877-6455
Milnot Company
Saint Louis, MO 888-656-3245
Moonlite Bar Bq Inn
Owensboro, KY 800-322-8989
Mr Jay's Tamales & Chili
Lynwood, CA 310-537-3932
North of the Border
Tesuque, NM 800-860-0681
O Chili Frozen Foods Inc
Northbrook, IL 847-562-1991
Original Chili Bowl
Tulsa, OK 918-628-0225
Pokanoket Ostrich Farm
South Dartmouth, MA 508-992-6188
Reser's Fine Foods
Salt Lake City, UT 801-972-5633
Stockpot
Woodinville, WA 800-468-1611
Supreme Frozen Products
Chicago, IL 773-622-3777
T.L. Herring & Company
Wilson, NC 252-291-1141
Taylor's Mexican Chili
Carlinville, IL 800-382-4454
Terra Sol Chile Company
Austin, TX 512-836-3525
Todd's Enterprises
Irvine, CA 949-250-4080
Torn & Glasser
Los Angeles, CA 800-282-6887
Wisconsin Packing Company
Butler, WI 800-558-2000
Yankee Specialty Foods
Boston, MA 617-951-0739

Canned

Blue Ribbon Meats
Cleveland, OH 216-631-8850
Milnot Company
Litchfield, IL 800-877-6455
Peco Foods
Canton, MS 601-855-0925
Pure Food Ingredients
Verona, WI 800-355-9601
Vanee Foods Company
Berkeley, IL 708-449-7300

Canned & Frozen

Aunt Kitty's Foods
Vineland, NJ 856-691-2100
Baja Foods
Chicago, IL 773-376-9030
Big B Distributors
Evansville, IN 812-425-5235
Campbell Company of Canada
Toronto, ON 800-410-7687
Castleberry's
Vineland, NJ 856-691-2100
Caughman's Meat Plant
Lexington, SC 803-356-0076
Chandler Foods
Greensboro, NC 800-537-6219
Culinary Standards Corporation
Louisville, KY 800-778-3434
Don Miguel Mexican Foods
Orange, CA 714-634-8441
Edmonds Chile Company
St Louis, MO 314-772-1499

First Original Texas Chili Company
Fort Worth, TX 817-626-0983
G Di Lullo & Sons
Westville, NJ 856-456-3700
Kelly Foods
Jackson, TN 731-424-2255
Marsan Foods
Toronto, ON 416-755-9262
Mi Ranchito Foods
Bayard, NM.......................575-537-3868
Milnot Company
Litchfield, IL......................800-877-6455
North of the Border
Tesuque, NM......................800-860-0681
O Chili Frozen Foods Inc
Northbrook, IL 847-562-1991
Old Ranchers Canning Company
Upland, CA.......................909-982-8895
SOPAKCO Foods
Mullins, SC.......................800-276-9678
Stauber Performance Ingredients
Fullerton, CA 888-441-4233
Todd's Enterprises
Irvine, CA........................949-250-4080
Vietti Foods Company Inc
Nashville, TN 800-240-7864
Westbrae Natural Foods
Melville, NY......................800-434-4246
Worthmore Food Product
Cincinnati, OH 513-559-1473

Frozen

Bueno Food Products
Albuquerque, NM..................800-888-7336
Original Texas Chili Company
Fort Worth, TX 800-507-0009

with Cheese

Mexisnax Corporation
El Paso, TX.......................915-779-5709

Chowder

Aunt Kitty's Foods
Vineland, NJ 856-691-2100
Blount Seafood Corporation
Fall River, MA 774-888-1300
Campbell Company of Canada
Toronto, ON 800-410-7687
Campbell Soup Company
Camden, NJ.......................800-257-8443
Cherchies
Malvern, PA 800-644-1980
Denzer's Food Products
Baltimore, MD 410-889-1500
Fish Hopper
Monterey, CA 831-372-2406
LaMonica Fine Foods
Millville, NJ 856-825-8111
Mid-Atlantic Foods
Easton, MD.......................800-922-4688
New England Marketers
Boston, MA.......................800-688-9904
Ronzoni Foods Canada
Etobicoke, ON 800-387-5032
Specialty Brands of America
Westbury, NY 516-997-6969
Triton Seafood Company
Medley, FL 305-888-8999
Valdez Food
Philadelphia, PA 215-634-6106
Yankee Specialty Foods
Boston, MA.......................617-951-0739

Clam & Fish

Aunt Kitty's Foods
Vineland, NJ 856-691-2100
Blount Seafood Corporation
Fall River, MA 774-888-1300
Campbell Company of Canada
Toronto, ON 800-410-7687
Campbell Soup Company
Camden, NJ.......................800-257-8443
Chincoteague Seafood Company
Parsonsburg, MD 443-260-4800
Fish Hopper
Monterey, CA 831-372-2406
Kettle Cuisine
Chelsea, MA 877-302-7687
LaMonica Fine Foods
Millville, NJ 856-825-8111
Mid-Atlantic Foods
Easton, MD.......................800-922-4688
New England Marketers
Boston, MA.......................800-688-9904
Sea Watch Intl.
Easton, MD.......................410-822-7500

Chutney

A Perfect Pear from NapaValley
Napa, CA.........................800-553-5753
Blue Jay Orchards
Bethel, CT........................203-748-0119
Blueberry Store
Grand Junction, MI.................877-654-2400
Chelsea Market Baskets
New York, NY 888-727-7887
Chicama Vineyards
West Tisbury, MA..................888-244-2262
Cinnabar Specialty Foods
Prescott, AZ 866-293-6433
Coastal Classics
Duxbury, MA 508-746-6058
Commissariat Imports
Los Angeles, CA...................310-475-5628
Creative Foodworks
San Antonio, TX...................210-212-4761
Cuizina Food Company
Woodinville, WA...................425-486-7000
Curry King Corporation
Waldwick, NJ 800-287-7987
Delicae Gourmet
Tarpon Springs, FL.................800-942-2502
Earth & Vine Provisions
Loomis, CA.......................888-723-8463
Graves Mountain Lodge Inc.
Syria, VA........................540-923-4747
Hawaiian Fruit Specialties
Kalaheo, HI......................808-332-9333
Jay Shah Foods
Mississauga, ON...................905-696-0172
Kozlowski Farms
Forestville, CA 800-473-2767
Outback Kitchens LLC
Huntington, VT....................802-434-5262
Schoolhouse Kitchen LLC
Brooklyn, NY 718-855-4990
Silver Palate Kitchens
Cresskill, NJ 800-872-5283
Sokol & Company
Countryside, IL....................800-328-7656
Spruce Mountain Blueberries
West Rockport, ME.................207-236-3538
Steel's Gourmet Foods, Ltd.
Bridgeport, PA 800-678-3357
Tait Farm Foods
Centre Hall, PA....................800-787-2716
Terrapin Ridge
Clearwater, FL 800-999-4052
Vermont Harvest Speciality Foods
Stowe, VT........................800-338-5354
Wild Thymes Farm
Greenville, NY 800-724-2877
Wisconsin Wilderness Food Products
Milwaukee, WI 800-359-3039

Convenience Food

Ailments E.D. Foods Inc.
Pointe Claire, QC 800-267-3333
American Wholesale Grocery
Mobile, AL 251-433-2500
Andalusia Distributing Company
Andalusia, AL.....................334-222-3671
Anmar Foods
Chicago, IL.......................312-421-6500
Arizona Institutional Foods
Tucson, AZ.......................520-624-8667
Biagio's Banquets
Chicago, IL.......................800-392-2837
Big B Distributors
Evansville, IN 812-425-5235
Camino Real Foods
Vernon, CA.......................800-421-6201
ConAgra Grocery Products
Fullerton, CA 800-736-2212
Crum Creek Mills
Springfield, PA 888-607-3500
Dorothy Dawson Foods Products
Jackson, MI.......................517-788-9830
Fantastic Foods
Napa, CA.........................800-288-1089
Frookie
Des Plaines, IL 847-699-3200
General Mills
Minneapolis, MN 800-248-7310
Gilroy Foods
Gilroy, CA........................800-921-7502
Grecian Delight Foods
Elk Grove Village, IL 800-621-4387
J&J Wholesale
Junction City, KS 785-238-4721
Kellogg Company
Hammonton, NJ 609-567-2300
Kelly Foods
Jackson, TN 731-424-2255
Kraft Canada Headquarters
Don Mills, ON 888-572-3806
Kraft Foods
Northfield, IL 800-323-0768
Lacassagne's
Baton Rouge, LA 225-218-0237
LD Foods
Annapolis, MD 410-216-9300
Lucks Food Decorating Company
Tacoma, WA 253-383-4815
McCain Foods Canada
Toronto, ON 866-622-2461
Michael Foods, Inc.
Minnetonka, MN...................952-258-4000
Movie Breads Food
Chateauguay, QC 450-692-7606
Naleway Foods
Winnipeg, MB.....................800-665-7448
Nancy's Specialty Foods
Newark, CA 510-494-1100
Natural Quick Foods
Seattle, WA.......................206-365-5757
Pasta USA
Spokane, WA......................800-456-2084
Sunburst Foods
Goldsboro, NC 919-778-2151
Suzanna's Kitchen
Duluth, GA.......................800-241-2455
U.S. Foodservice
Norcross, GA 800-554-8050
US Foods
Lincoln, NE.......................402-470-2021

Frozen

Advance Food Company
Enid, OK.........................888-723-8237
Agrusa, Inc.
Leonia, NJ........................201-592-5950
Al Pete Meats
Muncie, IN 765-288-8817
American Seafoods International
New Bedford, MA 800-343-8046
Applegate Farms
Bridgewater, NJ 908-725-2768
Barber Foods
Portland, ME......................800-577-2595
Bernardi Italian Foods Company
Bloomsburg, PA 570-389-5500
Biagio's Banquets
Chicago, IL.......................800-392-2837
Bocconcino Food Products
Moonachie, NJ 201-933-7474
Buxton Foods
Buxton, ND.......................800-726-8057
Camino Real Foods
Vernon, CA.......................800-421-6201
Campbell Soup Company
Camden, NJ.......................800-257-8443
Canada Bread
Etobicoke, ON 416-926-2000
Cedar Lake Foods
Cedar Lake, MI....................800-246-5039
Cedarlane Foods
Carson, CA 310-886-7720
Chloe Foods Corporation
Brooklyn, NY 718-827-9000
Chungs Gourmet Foods
Houston, TX 713-741-2118
ConAgra Foods
Richland, WA 800-766-7783
ConAgra Frozen Foods Company
Marshall, MO 660-886-3301
ConAgra Store Brands, Inc.
Lakeville, MN.....................800-328-6286

Culinary Standards Corporation
Louisville, KY 800-778-3434
Don Miguel Mexican Foods
Orange, CA 714-634-8441
Endico Potatoes
Mount Vernon, NY 914-664-1151
English Bay Batter
Columbus, OH 614-471-9994
Fine Choice Foods
Richmond, BC 604-522-3110
Food Source
Mc Kinney, TX 972-548-9001
Foodbrands America
Oklahoma City, OK 405-290-4000
Forte Stromboli Company
Philadelphia, PA 215-463-6336
Gemini Food Industries
Charlton, MA 508-248-2730
Gilardi Foods
Sidney, OH 937-498-4511
Gilroy Foods
Gilroy, CA 800-921-7502
Gonard Foods
Calgary, AB 403-277-0991
Harvest Time Foods
Ayden, NC 252-746-6675
Heinz Company of Canada
North York, ON 877-574-3469
High Liner Foods Inc
Lunenburg, NS 902-634-9475
Hormel Foods Corporation
Austin, MN 800-523-4635
House of Raeford Farms
Raeford, NC 800-888-7539
Ice Land Corporation
Pittsburgh, PA 412-441-9512
Juno Chef's
Goshen, NY 845-294-5400
Kellogg Canada Inc
Mississauga, ON 888-876-3750
Kellogg Company
Hammonton, NJ 609-567-2300
Lamb-Weston
Kennewick, WA 800-766-7783
Landolfi Food Products
Trenton, NJ 609-392-1830
Little Lady Foods
Elk Grove Vlg, IL 800-439-1440
Love & Quiches Desserts
Freeport, NY 800-525-5251
Macabee Foods
West Nyack, NY 845-623-1300
Made Rite Foods
Burlington, NC 336-229-5728
Maple Leaf Farms
Milford, IN 800-384-2812
Market Fare Foods
Phoenix, AZ 888-669-6420
Marsan Foods
Toronto, ON 416-755-9262
Martin Seafood Company
Jessup, MD 410-799-5822
McCain Foods USA
Easton, ME 800-938-7799
McLane Foods
Phoenix, AZ 602-275-5509
Michael Foods, Inc.
Minnetonka, MN 952-258-4000
Milnot Company
Litchfield, IL 800-877-6455
Morrison Lamothe
Toronto, ON 877-677-6533
Mrs. Smith's Bakeries
Spartanburg, SC 800-756-4746
Naleway Foods
Winnipeg, MB 800-665-7448
Nestle Pizza
Medford, WI 715-748-5550
Nestle Prepared Foods Company
Englewood, CO 800-225-2270
Nickabood's Company
Los Angeles, CA 213-746-1541
Night Hawk Frozen Foods
Buda, TX 800-580-4166
O Chili Frozen Foods Inc
Northbrook, IL 847-562-1991
Old Fashioned Kitchen
Lakewood, NJ 732-364-4100
Omstead Foods Ltd
Wheatley, ON 905-315-8883
Ore-Ida Foods
Pittsburgh, PA 800-892-2401
Pasta Factory
Melrose Park, IL 800-615-6951
Praters Foods
Lubbock, TX 806-745-2727
Queen International Foods
Monterey Park, CA 800-423-4414
Ragozzino Food
Meriden, CT 800-348-1240
Ramona's Mex. Food Produoducts
Gardena, CA 310-323-1950
Randy's Frozen Meats
Faribault, MN 800-354-7177
Redi-Serve Food Company
Fort Atkinson, WI 920-563-6391
Request Foods
Holland, MI 800-748-0378
Reser's Fine Foods
Salt Lake City, UT 801-972-5633
Ruiz Food Products
Dinuba, CA 800-477-6474
Specialty Brands
Carthage, MO 417-358-8104
Specialty Brands
Ontario, CA 800-782-1180
Steak-Umm Company
Shillington, PA 860-928-5900
Sunset Specialty Foods
Sunset Beach, CA 562-592-4976
Tami Great Food
Monsey, NY 732-803-6366
Thyme & Truffles Hors D'oeuvres
Dollard-Des-Ormeaux, QC 877-785-9759
Tomasso Corporation
Baie D'Urfe, QC 514-325-3000
Turris Italian Foods
Roseville, MI 586-773-6010
Van De Kamp Frozen Foods
Mountain Lake, NJ 973-541-6620
Wawona Frozen Foods
Clovis, CA 559-299-2901
Worthington Foods
Zanesville, OH 800-535-5644
Zartic Inc
Rome, GA 800-241-0516

Crepes

Culinary Foods
Chicago, IL 800-621-4049
Echo Lake Farm Produce Company
Burlington, WI 262-763-9551
Old Fashioned Kitchen
Lakewood, NJ 732-364-4100
Table De France
Ontario, CA 909-923-5205

Croquettes

Hanover Foods Corporation
Hanover, PA 717-632-6000
Heinz Company of Canada
North York, ON 877-574-3469

French Fries

Cavendish Farms
Jamestown, ND 888-284-5687
Cavendish Farms
Dieppe, NB 888-883-7437
ConAgra Foods
Kennewick, WA 509-735-4651
ConAgra Foods
Richland, WA 800-766-7783
Endico Potatoes
Mount Vernon, NY 914-664-1151
Hanover Potato Products
Hanover, PA 717-632-0700
J.R. Simplot Company
Boise, ID 208-336-2110
J.R. Simplot Company
Grand Forks, ND 701-746-6431
Lamb-Weston
Hermiston, OR 800-766-7783
McCain Foods Canada
Toronto, ON 866-622-2461
McCain Foods USA
Easton, ME 800-938-7799
Paris Foods Corporation
Trappe, MD 410-476-3185
Qualifresh Michel St. Arneault
St. Hubert, QC 800-565-0550
Terry Foods Inc
Idaho Falls, ID 208-604-8143
Twin City Foods
Stanwood, WA 208-743-5568
Yum Yum Potato Chips
Warwick, QC 800-567-5792

Canned

Emerling International Foods
Buffalo, NY 716-833-7381

We supply food manufacturers and food service customers worldwide (since 1988) with bulk ingredients including: Fruits & Vegetables; Juice Concentrates; Herbs & Spices; Oils & Vinegars; Flavors & Colors; Honey & Molasses. We also produce PURE MAPLE SYRUP.

McCain Foods Canada
Toronto, ON 866-622-2461

Frozen

Cavendish Farms
Laval, QC 450-973-1952
ConAgra Foods
Kennewick, WA 509-735-4651
ConAgra Foods
Richland, WA 800-766-7783
Emerling International Foods
Buffalo, NY 716-833-7381

We supply food manufacturers and food service customers worldwide (since 1988) with bulk ingredients including: Fruits & Vegetables; Juice Concentrates; Herbs & Spices; Oils & Vinegars; Flavors & Colors; Honey & Molasses. We also produce PURE MAPLE SYRUP.

Endico Potatoes
Mount Vernon, NY 914-664-1151
J.R. Simplot Company
Grand Forks, ND 701-746-6431
Lamb-Weston
Hermiston, OR 800-766-7783
Maple Leaf Potatoes
Lethbridge, AB 800-268-3708
McCain Foods Canada
Toronto, ON 866-622-2461
Ore-Ida Foods
Pittsburgh, PA 800-892-2401
Qualifresh Michel St. Arneault
St. Hubert, QC 800-565-0550
Twin City Foods
Stanwood, WA 208-743-5568

Shoestring

Emerling International Foods
Buffalo, NY 716-833-7381

We supply food manufacturers and food service customers worldwide (since 1988) with bulk ingredients including: Fruits & Vegetables; Juice Concentrates; Herbs & Spices; Oils & Vinegars; Flavors & Colors; Honey & Molasses. We also produce PURE MAPLE SYRUP.

Lamb-Weston
Hermiston, OR 800-766-7783
McCain Foods Canada
Toronto, ON 866-622-2461
Ore-Ida Foods
Pittsburgh, PA 800-892-2401

Tater Tots

Cavendish Farms
Jamestown, ND 888-284-5687

French Toast

Brooks Food Group Corporate Office
Bedford, VA 800-873-4934
Continental Mills
Seattle, WA 253-872-8400
Rich-Seapak Corporation
St Simons Island, GA 800-654-9731
Tami Great Food
Monsey, NY 732-803-6366

Frozen

Bake Crafters Food
Collegedale, TN 800-296-8935

Brooks Food Group Corporate Office
Bedford, VA 800-873-4934
Continental Mills
Seattle, WA 253-872-8400
Tami Great Food
Monsey, NY 732-803-6366

Fresh

Garden Protein International
Richmond, BC 877-305-6777

Frozen

Better Baked Foods
North East, PA. 814-725-8778
Blount Fine Foods
Fall River, MA 774-888-1300
Bridgford Foods of North Carolina
Statesville, NC 704-878-2722
Burke Corporation
Nevada, IA 800-654-1152

Always make it your best® with Burke fully cooked meats. We specialize in Italian sausage, beef, and pork toppings, meatballs, taco meats, shredded meats, pepperoni, bacon, Canadian-style bacon, chicken and beef strips. Additionally, we offer a variety of specialty products: Hand-Pinched Style® brand toppings, chorizo, gyro topping, andouille sausage, and breakfast patties and links.

Charles Rockel & Son
Cincinnati, OH 513-631-3009
Emerling International Foods
Buffalo, NY. 716-833-7381

We supply food manufacturers and food service customers worldwide (since 1988) with bulk ingredients including: Fruits & Vegetables; Juice Concentrates; Herbs & Spices; Oils & Vinegars; Flavors & Colors; Honey & Molasses. We also produce PURE MAPLE SYRUP.

Freeze-Dry Foods
Albion, NY 905-844-1471
Garden Protein International
Richmond, BC 877-305-6777
H.J. Heinz Company
Pittsburgh, PA. 800-872-2229
Old Fashioned Kitchen
Lakewood, NJ. 732-364-4100

Giardiniera

A. Camacho
Plant City, FL 800-881-4534
Castella Imports
Hauppauge, NY 866-227-8355
Colonna Brothers
North Bergen, NJ 201-864-1115
Fontanini Italian Meats & Sausages
McCook, IL. 800-331-6328
L&S Packing Company
Farmingdale, NY 800-286-6487
Orleans Packing Company
Hyde Park, MA. 617-361-6611
Victoria Packing Corporation
Brooklyn, NY 718-927-3000

Hash

Canned & Frozen

Aunt Kitty's Foods
Vineland, NJ 856-691-2100
Castleberry's
Vineland, NJ 856-691-2100
Caughman's Meat Plant
Lexington, SC. 803-356-0076
Hormel Foods Corporation
Austin, MN. 800-523-4635
Kelly Foods
Jackson, TN 731-424-2255
Lees Sausage Company
Orangeburg, SC 803-534-5517
Ninety Six Canning Company
Ninety Six, SC 864-543-2700
SOPAKCO Foods
Mullins, SC. 800-276-9678

Hush Puppies

Atkinson Milling Company
Selma, NC. 800-948-5707
Delta Pride Catfish
Indianola, MS 800-421-1045
Fry Krisp Food Products
Jackson, MI. 517-784-8531
Lakeside Mills
Rutherfordton, NC 828-286-4866
Lone Star Consolidated Foods
Dallas, TX. 800-658-5637
Savannah Food Company
Savannah, TN 800-795-2550
Shenandoah Mills
Lebanon, TN. 615-444-0841
Triton Seafood Company
Medley, FL 305-888-8999

Frozen & Mixes

Lone Star Consolidated Foods
Dallas, TX. 800-658-5637
Premier Blending
Wichita, KS. 316-267-5533
Savannah Food Company
Savannah, TN 800-795-2550
Tova Industries
Louisville, KY 888-532-8682
Triton Seafood Company
Medley, FL 305-888-8999
Weisenberger Mills
Midway, KY 800-643-8678

Individual Packets

Foodservice

Baldwin Richardson Foods
Frankfort, IL 866-644-2732

Liquid ingredient manufacturer specializing in signature sauces, dessert toppings, beverage/pancake syrups, specialty fruit fillings and condiments.

Heinz Portion Control
Mason, OH 800-547-8924
Magic Seasoning Blends
New Orleans, LA 800-457-2857
Star Packaging Corporation
Atlanta, GA. 404-763-2800
Sugar Foods
Lawrenceville, GA 800-732-8963

Individual Quick Frozen Food

Applegate Farms
Bridgewater, NJ 908-725-2768
Appleton Produce Company
Weiser, ID 208-414-3352
Bandon Bay Fisheries
Bandon, OR 541-347-4454
Beef Products
North Sioux City, SD 605-217-8000
Boardman Foods
Boardman, OR 541-481-3000
Burke Corporation
Nevada, IA 800-654-1152

Always make it your best® with Burke fully cooked meats. We specialize in Italian sausage, beef, and pork toppings, meatballs, taco meats, shredded meats, pepperoni, bacon, Canadian-style bacon, chicken and beef strips. Additionally, we offer a variety of specialty products: Hand-Pinched Style® brand toppings, chorizo, gyro topping, andouille sausage, and breakfast patties and links.

Cherryfield Foods
Cherryfield, ME 207-546-7573
Cuizina Food Company
Woodinville, WA. 425-486-7000
Cut Above Foods
Carlsbad, CA. 760-931-6777
Eckert Cold Storage
Escalon, CA 209-838-4040

Emerling International Foods
Buffalo, NY. 716-833-7381

We supply food manufacturers and food service customers worldwide (since 1988) with bulk ingredients including: Fruits & Vegetables; Juice Concentrates; Herbs & Spices; Oils & Vinegars; Flavors & Colors; Honey & Molasses. We also produce PURE MAPLE SYRUP.

FishKing
Glendale, CA 818-244-2161
Freezer Queen Foods
Buffalo, NY. 800-828-8383
Gay's Wild Maine Blueberries
Old Town, ME 207-570-3535
Guptill's Farms
Machias, ME. 207-255-8536
GYMA IQF
Stroudsburg, PA 888-496-2872
High Liner Foods Inc
Lunenburg, NS 902-634-9475
Hillman Shrimp & Oyster Company
Dickinson, TX. 800-582-4416
Icelandic USA
Newport News, VA. 757-820-4000
International Food Trade
Amherst, NS 902-667-3013
International Oceanic Enterprises of Alabama
Bayou La Batre, AL 800-816-1832
Jasper Wyman & Son
Milbridge, ME 800-341-1758
Jasper Wyman & Son Canada
Morell, PE. 902-961-5610
LaMonica Fine Foods
Millville, NJ 856-825-8111
Leach Farms Inc.
Berlin, WI. 920-361-1880
Lef Bleuges Marinor Incorporated
St-Felicien, QC 418-679-4577
Louisiana Packing Company
Westwego, LA. 800-666-1293
Merkel McDonald
Austin, TX. 800-356-0229
Merrill's Blueberry Farms
Ellsworth, ME. 800-711-6551
Mon Cuisine
Flushing, NY. 877-666-8348
Mr. Dell Foods
Kearney, MO. 816-628-4644
My Grandma's of New England®
Hyde Park, MA. 800-847-2636
Nature Quality
San Martin, CA. 408-683-2182
NorSun Food Group
West Chester, OH 800-886-4326
Northern Michigan Fruit Company
Omena, MI 231-386-5142
Ore-Cal Corporation
Los Angeles, CA. 800-827-7474
Rain Sweet
Salem, OR. 800-363-4293
Randag & Associates Inc
Elmhurst, IL 630-530-2830
Sea Snack Foods
Los Angeles, CA. 213-622-2204
Stahlbush Island Farms
Corvallis, OR 541-757-1497
Sun Harvest Foods
San Diego, CA 619-661-0909
Sun-Glo of Idaho
Sugar City, ID 208-356-7346
Sure Fresh Produce
Santa Maria, CA 888-423-5379
Unique Ingredients
Naches, WA. 509-653-1991

Washington Rhubarb Growers Association
Sumner, WA 800-435-9911

Winder Dairy
West Valley, UT 800-946-3371

Knishes

Chloe Foods Corporation
Brooklyn, NY 718-827-9000

Gabilas Knishes
Brooklyn, NY

Oceanside Knish Factory
Oceanside, NY 516-766-4445

Meat Balls

Armanino Foods of Distinction
Hayward, CA 510-441-9300

Buona Vita
Bridgeton, NJ 856-453-7972

Carando Gourmet Frozen Foods
Agawam, MA 888-227-2636

Casa Di Bertacchi
Vineland, NJ 800-818-9261

Cordon Bleu International
Anjou, QC 514-352-3000

DelGrosso Foods
Tipton, PA 800-521-5880

Devault Foods
Devault, PA 800-426-2874

Fontanini Italian Meats & Sausages
McCook, IL 800-331-6328

G Di Lullo & Sons
Westville, NJ 856-456-3700

Kings Command Foods
Kent, WA 800-247-3138

Maid-Rite Steak Company
Dunmore, PA 800-233-4259

Marcho Farms Veal
Harleysville, PA 215-721-7131

Oh Boy! Corporation
San Fernando, CA 818-361-1128

Quality Sausage Company
Dallas, TX 214-634-3400

Redi-Serve Food Company
Fort Atkinson, WI 920-563-6391

Specialty Brands
Carthage, MO 417-358-8104

Tupman-Thurlow Company
Deerfield Beach, FL 954-596-9989

Tyson Foods Plant
Santa Teresa, NM 800-351-8184

Canned

Acme Steak & Seafood Company
Youngstown, OH 330-270-8000

Campbell Soup Company
Camden, NJ 800-257-8443

Cordon Bleu International
Anjou, QC 514-352-3000

Leone Provision Company
Cape Coral, FL 239-458-0013

O Chili Frozen Foods Inc
Northbrook, IL 847-562-1991

On-Cor Foods Products
Northbrook, IL 847-205-1040

Specialty Brands
Carthage, MO 417-358-8104

Frozen

Burke Corporation
Nevada, IA 800-654-1152

Always make it your best® with Burke fully cooked meats. We specialize in Italian sausage, beef, and pork toppings, meatballs, taco meats, shredded meats, pepperoni, bacon, Canadian-style bacon, chicken and beef strips. Additionally, we offer a variety of specialty products: Hand-Pinched Style® brand toppings, chorizo, gyro topping, andouille sausage, and breakfast patties and links.

Carando Gourmet Frozen Foods
Agawam, MA 888-227-2636

Carolina Turkeys
Mount Olive, NC 800-523-4559

Casa Di Bertacchi
Vineland, NJ 800-818-9261

Devault Foods
Devault, PA 800-426-2874

Maid-Rite Steak Company
Dunmore, PA 800-233-4259

On-Cor Foods Products
Northbrook, IL 847-205-1040

Redi-Serve Food Company
Fort Atkinson, WI 920-563-6391

Specialty Brands
Carthage, MO 417-358-8104

Turris Italian Foods
Roseville, MI 586-773-6010

West Liberty Foods
West Liberty, IA 888-511-4500

Swedish

Burke Corporation
Nevada, IA 800-654-1152

Always make it your best® with Burke fully cooked meats. We specialize in Italian sausage, beef, and pork toppings, meatballs, taco meats, shredded meats, pepperoni, bacon, Canadian-style bacon, chicken and beef strips. Additionally, we offer a variety of specialty products: Hand-Pinched Style® brand toppings, chorizo, gyro topping, andouille sausage, and breakfast patties and links.

Rose Packing Company
South Barrington, IL 800-323-7363

Meat Loaf

Buona Vita
Bridgeton, NJ 856-453-7972

Burnett & Son Meat Company
Monrovia, CA 626-357-2165

Corfu Foods
Bensenville, IL 630-595-2510

Fontanini Italian Meats & Sausages
McCook, IL 800-331-6328

Kings Command Foods
Kent, WA 800-247-3138

Marcho Farms Veal
Harleysville, PA 215-721-7131

Mitchell Foods
Barbourville, KY 888-202-9745

Rymer Foods
Chicago, IL 800-247-9637

Sandridge Food Corporation
Medina, OH 800-627-2523

Sunset Farm Foods
Valdosta, GA 800-882-1121

Onion Rings

Agri-Pack
Pasco, WA 509-545-6181

Brooks Food Group Corporate Office
Bedford, VA 800-873-4934

Great American Appetizers
Nampa, ID 800-282-4834

Matador Processors
Blanchard, OK 800-847-0797

McCain Foods USA
Colton, CA 800-938-7799

Oxford Frozen Foods Limited
Oxford, NS 902-447-2100

Westin
Omaha, NE 800-228-6098

Yum Yum Potato Chips
Warwick, QC 800-567-5792

Frozen

Brooks Food Group Corporate Office
Bedford, VA 800-873-4934

Emerling International Foods
Buffalo, NY 716-833-7381

We supply food manufacturers and food service customers worldwide (since 1988) with bulk ingredients including: Fruits & Vegetables; Juice Concentrates; Herbs & Spices; Oils & Vinegars; Flavors & Colors; Honey & Molasses. We also produce PURE MAPLE SYRUP.

Fry Foods
Tiffin, OH 800-626-2294

Great American Appetizers
Nampa, ID 800-282-4834

Matador Processors
Blanchard, OK 800-847-0797

Oxford Frozen Foods Limited
Oxford, NS 902-447-2100

Westin
Omaha, NE 800-228-6098

Pancakes

ConAgra Store Brands, Inc.
Lakeville, MN 800-328-6286

Continental Mills
Seattle, WA 253-872-8400

Cook-In-The-Kitchen
White River Junction, VT 802-333-4141

Mama Mary's
Fairforest, SC 864-595-6262

Old Fashioned Kitchen
Lakewood, NJ 732-364-4100

Pamela's Products
Ukiah, CA 707-462-6605

Red Rose Trading Company
Wrightsville, PA 717-252-5500

Ungars Food Products
Elmwood Park, NJ 201-703-1300

Wagner Excello Food Products
Broadview, IL 708-338-4488

Frozen

ADM Edible Bean Specialies
Kinde, MI 989-874-4720

Bake Crafters Food
Collegedale, TN 800-296-8935

ConAgra Store Brands, Inc.
Lakeville, MN 800-328-6286

Continental Mills
Seattle, WA 253-872-8400

Crosby Molasses Company
St John, NB 506-634-7515

Old Fashioned Kitchen
Lakewood, NJ 732-364-4100

Tami Great Food
Monsey, NY 732-803-6366

Thomas Brothers Ham Company
Asheboro, NC 336-672-0337

Refrigerated

Echo Lake Farm Produce Company
Burlington, WI 262-763-9551

with Fruit

Continental Mills
Seattle, WA 253-872-8400

Pierogies

Aunt Kathy's Homestyle Products
Waldheim, SK 306-945-2181

Babci's Specialty Foods
Holyoke, MA 800-225-2023

Brom Food Group
St. Laurent, QC 514-744-5152

Giorgio Foods
Temple, PA 800-220-2139

Heritage Foods
Edmonton, AB 780-454-7383

Millie's Pierogi
Chicopee Falls, MA 800-743-7641

Mrs. Ts Pierogies
Shenandoah, PA 800-233-3170

Naleway Foods
Winnipeg, MB 800-665-7448

Old Fashioned Kitchen
Lakewood, NJ 732-364-4100

Pierogi Place
Mears, MI 23- 8-3 14

Pizza & Pizza Products

Al Safa Halal
Niagara Falls, NY 800-268-8174

Amberwave Foods
Oakmont, PA....................412-828-3040
Andre-Boudin Bakeries
San Francisco, CA 415-882-1849
Avanti Food Company
Walnut, IL......................800-243-3739
Baja Foods
Chicago, IL.....................773-376-9030
BBU Bakeries
Denver, CO......................303-691-6342
Bertucci's
Northborough, MA................508-351-2500
Biagio's Banquets
Chicago, IL.....................800-392-2837
Blue Planet Foods
Collegedale, TN 877-396-3145
Bocconcino Food Products
Moonachie, NJ 201-933-7474
Brownie Products Company
Terre Haute, IN
Burke Corporation
Nevada, IA 800-654-1152

Always make it your best® with Burke fully cooked meats. We specialize in Italian sausage, beef, and pork toppings, meatballs, taco meats, shredded meats, pepperoni, bacon, Canadian-style bacon, chicken and beef strips. Additionally, we offer a variety of specialty products: Hand-Pinched Style® brand toppings, chorizo, gyro topping, andouille sausage, and breakfast patties and links.

California Blending Corpany
El Monte, CA 626-448-1918
Calise & Sons Bakery
Lincoln, RI 800-225-4737
Canada Bread
Etobicoke, ON 416-926-2000
Capri Bagel & Pizza Corporation
Brooklyn, NY 718-497-4431
Chelsea Milling Company
Chelsea, MI......................734-475-1361
CHR Hansen
Elyria, OH.......................800-558-0802
ConAgra Foods
Boisbriand, QC...................450-433-1322
Continental Food Products
Flushing, NY.....................718-358-7894
Delgrosso Foods Inc.
Tipton, PA.......................800-521-5880
Dorothy Dawson Foods Products
Jackson, MI......................517-788-9830
Entenmann's-Oroweat/BestFoods
South San Francisco, CA 650-583-5828
Foodbrands America
Oklahoma City, OK 405-290-4000
Fresh Mark
Canton, OH......................800-860-6777
Frozen Specialties
Archbold, OH 419-445-9015
Furmano Foods
Northumberland, PA...............877-877-6032
Gold Standard Baking
Chicago, IL......................800-648-7904
Harbar Corporation
Canton, MA 800-881-7040
Heinz Company of Canada
North York, ON...................877-574-3469
Home Run Inn Frozen Foods
Woodridge, IL....................800-636-9696
I & K Distributors
Delphos, OH.....................800-869-6337
Ice Land Corporation
Pittsburgh, PA....................412-441-9512
Indian Foods Company
Minneapolis, MN 763-593-3000
Italian Baking Company
Youngstown, OH..................330-782-1358
Kamish Food Products
Chicago, IL......................773-725-6959
Kosto Food Products Company
Wauconda, IL 847-487-2600
L&S Packing Company
Farmingdale, NY 800-286-6487
Lamb-Weston
Weston, OR......................800-766-7783
Lamonaca Bakery
Windber, PA 814-467-4909
Leprino Foods Company
Denver, CO......................800-537-7466
Little Lady Foods
Elk Grove Vlg, IL.................800-439-1440
Livermore Falls Baking Company
Livermore Falls, ME...............207-897-3442
Longo's Bakery
Hazleton, PA.....................570-454-5825
Magic Seasoning Blends
New Orleans, LA 800-457-2857
Mama Amy's Quality Foods
Mississauga, ON..................905-456-0056
McCain Foods Canada
Toronto, ON 866-622-2461
Molinaro's Fine Italian Foods
Mississauga, ON..................800-268-4959
Nardone Brothers Baking Company
Hanover Township, PA.............800-822-5320
Nation Pizza Products
Schaumburg, IL...................847-397-3320
Nationwide Canning
Cottam, ON......................519-839-4831
Nestle Pizza
Medford, WI.....................715-748-5550
Northwestern Foods
Saint Paul, MN 800-236-4937
O Chili Frozen Foods Inc
Northbrook, IL 847-562-1991
O'Neal's Fresh Frozen Pizza Crust
Springfield, OH...................937-323-0050
Ore-Ida Foods
Pittsburgh, PA....................800-892-2401
Oroweat Baking Company
Montebello, CA 323-721-5161
Palmieri Food Products
New Haven, CT 800-845-5447
Pecoraro Dairy Products
Rome, NY.......................315-339-0101
Piqua Pizza Supply Company
Piqua, OH.......................800-521-4442
Pizzas of Eight
Saint Louis, MO 800-422-2901
Quality Sausage Company
Dallas, TX.......................214-634-3400
Red Gold
Elwood, IN 877-748-9798
Rosina Food Products
Buffalo, NY......................888-767-4621
Schwartz Meat Company
Sophia, WV......................304-683-4595
Sunset Farm Foods
Valdosta, GA.....................800-882-1121
Supreme Dairy Farms Company
Warwick, RI 401-739-8180
Swiss-American Sausage Company
Lathrop, CA 209-858-5555
Teeny Foods Corporation
Portland, OR 503-252-3006
Teti Bakery
Etobicoke, ON 800-465-0123
Tip Top Canning Company
Tipp City, OH 800-352-2635
TNT Crust
Green Bay, WI....................920-431-7240
Tomanetti Food Products
Oakmont, PA.....................800-875-3040
Tomaro's Bakery
Clarksburg, WV 304-622-0691
Triple K Manufacturing Company
Shenandoah, IA...................888-987-2824
Valdez Food
Philadelphia, PA 215-634-6106
Violet Packing
Williamstown, NJ 856-629-7428
Wanda's Nature Farm
Lincoln, NE......................800-735-6828
Weisenberger Mills
Midway, KY 800-643-8678
Welcome Dairy
Colby, WI 800-472-2315
Worthmore Food Product
Cincinnati, OH 513-559-1473

Pizza

Amy's Kitchen
Petaluma, CA 707-568-4500
Andre-Boudin Bakeries
San Francisco, CA 415-882-1849
Art's Tamales
Metamora, IL 309-367-2850
Atlanta Bread Company
Smyrna, GA 800-398-3728
Aunt Kathy's Homestyle Products
Waldheim, SK....................306-945-2181
Berkshire Mountain Bakery
Housatonic, MA 866-274-6124
Biagio's Banquets
Chicago, IL......................800-392-2837
Bocconcino Food Products
Moonachie, NJ 201-933-7474
Cafe Moak
Rockford, MI 800-757-8776
Cedarlane Foods
Carson, CA......................310-886-7720
Chelsea Milling Company
Chelsea, MI......................734-475-1361
Chicago Pizza & Brewery
Huntington Beach, CA 714-500-2400
Colors Gourmet Pizza
Carlsbad, CA.....................760-431-2203
Continental Food Products
Flushing, NY.....................718-358-7894
Dorothy Dawson Foods Products
Jackson, MI......................517-788-9830
European Egg Noodle Manufacturing
Edmonton, AB 780-453-6767
Frozen Specialties
Archbold, OH 419-445-9015
Gilardi Foods
Sidney, OH 937-498-4511
Ice Land Corporation
Pittsburgh, PA....................412-441-9512
Italian Baking Company
Youngstown, OH..................330-782-1358
Joe Corbis' Wholesale Pizza
Baltimore, MD 888-526-7247
Lamb-Weston
Kennewick, WA 800-766-7783
Lucia's Pizza Company
Saint Louis, MO 314-843-2553
Macabee Foods
West Nyack, NY 845-623-1300
McCain Foods Canada
Toronto, ON 866-622-2461
Molinaro's Fine Italian Foods
Mississauga, ON..................800-268-4959
Mozzicato De Pasquale Bakery Pastry
Hartford, CT 860-296-0426
Nardone Brothers Baking Company
Hanover Township, PA.............800-822-5320
Nestle Pizza
Medford, WI.....................715-748-5550
New York Pizza
Daytona Beach, FL................386-257-2050
Newman's Own
Westport, CT.....................203-222-0136
Oh Boy! Corporation
San Fernando, CA.................818-361-1128
Randy's Frozen Meats
Faribault, MN 800-354-7177
Richelieu Foods
Randolph, MA 781-961-1537
Rustic Crust
Pittsfield, NH 603-435-5119
Sunset Specialty Foods
Sunset Beach, CA.................562-592-4976
Superbrand Dairies
Montgomery, AL..................334-277-6010
Teeny Foods Corporation
Portland, OR 503-252-3006
Teti Bakery
Etobicoke, ON 800-465-0123

Cheese

Amberwave Foods
Oakmont, PA.....................412-828-3040
Avanti Food Company
Walnut, IL.......................800-243-3739
Leprino Foods Company
Denver, CO......................800-537-7466
Pecoraro Dairy Products
Rome, NY.......................315-339-0101
Schwartz Meat Company
Sophia, WV......................304-683-4595
Sun-Re Cheese
Sunbury, PA......................570-286-1511

Crust

Amberwave Foods
Oakmont, PA.....................412-828-3040
Baker & Baker, Inc.
Schaumburg, IL...................800-593-5777
Berkshire Mountain Bakery
Housatonic, MA 866-274-6124

Boboli Intl. Inc.
Stockton, CA 209-473-3507
Brownie Products Company
Terre Haute, IN
Calise & Sons Bakery
Lincoln, RI 800-225-4737
Chelsea Milling Company
Chelsea, MI 734-475-1361
Colors Gourmet Pizza
Carlsbad, CA 760-431-2203
Dorothy Dawson Foods Products
Jackson, MI 517-788-9830
Flamin' Red's Woodfired
Pawlet, VT 802-325-3641
Goglanian Bakeries
Santa Ana, CA 714-444-3500
Livermore Falls Baking Company
Livermore Falls, ME 207-897-3442
Lone Star Bakery
Round Rock, TX 512-255-3629
Mama Mary's
Fairforest, SC 864-595-6262
Molinaro's Fine Italian Foods
Mississauga, ON 800-268-4959
Northwestern Foods
Saint Paul, MN 800-236-4937
Pacific Ocean Produce
Santa Cruz, CA 831-423-2654
Pascucci Family Pasta
San Diego, CA 619-285-8000
Piqua Pizza Supply Company
Piqua, OH 800-521-4442
Richelieu Foods
Randolph, MA 781-961-1537
Rustic Crust
Pittsfield, NH 603-435-5119
Teeny Foods Corporation
Portland, OR 503-252-3006
Teti Bakery
Etobicoke, ON 800-465-0123
TNT Crust
Green Bay, WI 920-431-7240
Tomaro's Bakery
Clarksburg, WV 304-622-0691

Frozen

Badger Best Pizzas
Green Bay, WI 920-336-6464
Better Baked Foods
North East, PA 814-725-8778
Biagio's Banquets
Chicago, IL 800-392-2837
Bocconcino Food Products
Moonachie, NJ 201-933-7474
Calise & Sons Bakery
Lincoln, RI 800-225-4737
Cedarlane Foods
Carson, CA 310-886-7720
Chelsea Milling Company
Chelsea, MI 734-475-1361
Continental Food Products
Flushing, NY 718-358-7894
Gilardi Foods
Sidney, OH 937-498-4511
I & K Distributors
Delphos, OH 800-869-6337
Ice Land Corporation
Pittsburgh, PA 412-441-9512
Iltaco Food Products
Chicago, IL 800-244-8935
Lucia's Pizza Company
Saint Louis, MO 314-843-2553
Macabee Foods
West Nyack, NY 845-623-1300
Molinaro's Fine Italian Foods
Mississauga, ON 800-268-4959
Nestle Pizza
Medford, WI 715-748-5550
Randy's Frozen Meats
Faribault, MN 800-354-7177
Richelieu Foods
Randolph, MA 781-961-1537
Schwartz Meat Company
Sophia, WV 304-683-4595
Sunset Specialty Foods
Sunset Beach, CA 562-592-4976
Superbrand Dairies
Montgomery, AL 334-277-6010

Pizza Toppings

Avanti Food Company
Walnut, IL 800-243-3739
Baja Foods
Chicago, IL 773-376-9030
Buona Vita
Bridgeton, NJ 856-453-7972
Burke Corporation
Nevada, IA 800-654-1152

Always make it your best® with Burke fully cooked meats. We specialize in Italian sausage, beef, and pork toppings, meatballs, taco meats, shredded meats, pepperoni, bacon, Canadian-style bacon, chicken and beef strips. Additionally, we offer a variety of specialty products: Hand-Pinched Style® brand toppings, chorizo, gyro topping, andouille sausage, and breakfast patties and links.

Fontanini Italian Meats & Sausages
McCook, IL 800-331-6328
Fresh Mark
Canton, OH 800-860-6777
Moody Dunbar
Johnson City, TN 800-251-8202
O Chili Frozen Foods Inc
Northbrook, IL 847-562-1991
Patrick Cudahy
Cudahy, WI 800-486-6900
Quality Sausage Company
Dallas, TX 214-634-3400
Schwartz Meat Company
Sophia, WV 304-683-4595
Swiss-American Sausage Company
Lathrop, CA 209-858-5555

Shells

Bowness Bakery
Calgary, AB 403-250-9760
Lamonaca Bakery
Windber, PA 814-467-4909
Livermore Falls Baking Company
Livermore Falls, ME 207-897-3442
Longo's Bakery
Hazleton, PA 570-454-5825

Pork & Beans (see also Baked Beans)

ConAgra Grocery Products
Irvine, CA 714-680-1000
International Home Foods
Parsippany, NJ 973-359-9920
Morgan Food
Austin, IN 888-430-1780

Canned

Allen Canning Company
Siloam Springs, AR 800-234-2553
Bush Brothers & Co.
Augusta, WI 715-286-2211
Dankworth Packing Company
Ballinger, TX 325-365-3552
Grandma Brown's Beans Inc
Mexico, NY 315-963-7221
International Home Foods
Parsippany, NJ 973-359-9920

Porkskins

Fried

Cajun

Bruno's Cajun Foods & Snacks
Slidell, LA 985-726-0544

Portion Contol & Packaged Foods

A to Z Portion Meats
Bluffton, OH 800-338-6328
Acme Steak & Seafood Company
Youngstown, OH 330-270-8000
Advance Food Company
Enid, OK 888-723-8237
Al Pete Meats
Muncie, IN 765-288-8817
AlpineAire Foods
Rocklin, CA 800-322-6325

Arizona Sunland Foods
Tucson, AZ 520-624-7068
ASC Seafood
Largo, FL 800-876-3474
Associated Brands Inc.
Medina, NY 800-265-0050
Baldwin Richardson Foods
Frankfort, IL 866-644-2732

Liquid ingredient manufacturer specializing in signature sauces, dessert toppings, beverage/pancake syrups, specialty fruit fillings and condiments.

Beaver Meadow Creamery
Du Bois, PA 800-262-3711
Black Diamond Cheese
Toronto, ON 800-263-2858
Blue Ribbon Meats
Miami, FL 800-522-6115
Bouma Meats
Provost, AB 780-753-2092
Broadleaf Venison Usa
Vernon, CA 800-336-3844
Bruno Specialty Foods
West Sayville, NY 631-589-1700
Bruno's Cajun Foods & Snacks
Slidell, LA 985-726-0544
Bruss Company
Chicago, IL 800-621-3882
Buono Beef Co
Philadelphia, PA 215-463-3600
Bush Brothers Provision Company
West Palm Beach, FL 800-327-1345
C&S Wholesale Meat Company
Atlanta, GA 404-627-3547
Cal-Tex Citrus Juice
Houston, TX 800-231-0133
Cambridge Packing Company
Boston, MA 800-722-6726
Canal Fulton Provision
Canal Fulton, OH 800-321-3502
Cardinal Meat Specialists
Mississauga, ON 800-363-1439
Carl Streit & Son Company
Neptune, NJ 732-775-0803
Cloverdale Foods Company
Mandan, ND 800-669-9511
Cloverland Dairy
Saint Clairsville, OH 740-699-0509
Country Pure Foods
Akron, OH 330-753-2293
Country Pure Foods
Akron, OH 877-995-8423
Cuizina Food Company
Woodinville, WA 425-486-7000
Danish Baking Company
Van Nuys, CA 818-786-1700
Devault Foods
Devault, PA 800-426-2874
Dynamic Foods
Lubbock, TX 806-747-2777
Elwood International
Copiague, NY 631-842-6600
Fancy Farms Popcorn
Bernie, MO 800-833-8154
Flint Hills Foods
Alma, KS
Glenmark Food Processors
Chicago, IL 800-621-0117
Good Old Days Foods
Little Rock, AR 501-565-1257
Gregory's Box'd Beverages
Newark, NJ 973-465-1113

Heinz Company of Canada
North York, ON. 877-574-3469
Heinz Portion Control
Mason, OH 800-547-8924
Henry J Meat Specialties
Chicago, IL 800-242-1314
Holten Meats
Sauget, IL 800-851-4684
Instantwhip: Arizona
Phoenix, AZ 800-454-7878
Iowa Quality Meats
Clive, IA 800-677-6868
Italia Foods
Schaumburg, IL. 800-747-1109
Jemm Wholesale Meat Company
Chicago, IL 773-523-8161
John Garner Meats
Van Buren, AR 800-543-5473
Kenosha Beef International
Kenosha, WI 800-541-1685
Kessler Foods, Inc
Lemoyne, PA. 717-763-7162
King Kold Meats
Englewood, OH 800-836-2797
Kings Command Foods
Kent, WA. 800-247-3138
Knouse Foods Coop
Peach Glen, PA 717-677-8181
Koch Foods
Park Ridge, IL. 800-837-2778
Kutik's Honey Farm
Norwich, NY. 607-336-4105
Kutztown Bologna Company
Leola, PA. 800-723-8824
L&L Packing Company
Chicago, IL 800-628-6328
Lamb-Weston
Kennewick, WA 800-766-7783
Land O'Frost
Searcy, AR 800-643-5654
Leahy Orchards
Franklin Centre, QC 800-667-7380
Litehouse
Sandpoint, ID 208-263-7569
Love & Quiches Desserts
Freeport, NY 800-525-5251
Lynch Foods
North York, ON. 416-449-5464
Maid-Rite Steak Company
Dunmore, PA. 800-233-4259
Marcho Farms Veal
Harleysville, PA 215-721-7131
Mardale Specialty Foods
Waukegan, IL 847-336-4777
Maxim's Import Corporation
Miami, FL. 800-331-6652
Meat-O-Mat Corporation
Brooklyn, NY 718-965-7250
National Foods
Indianapolis, IN 800-683-6565
New Generation Foods
Omaha, NE 402-733-5755
North Side Foods Corporation
Arnold, PA 800-486-2201
O Chili Frozen Foods Inc
Northbrook, IL 847-562-1991
Ocean Beauty Seafoods
Seattle, WA 206-285-6800
Okuhara Foods
Honolulu, HI. 808-848-0581
Omaha Steaks International
Omaha, NE 800-562-0500
Ossian Seafood Meats
Ossian, IN 260-622-4191
Ottman Meat Company
New York, NY 212-879-4160
Otto & Son
West Jordan, UT 800-453-9462
Otto W Liebold & Company
Flint, MI 800-999-6328
Pacific Poultry Company
Honolulu, HI. 808-841-2828
Paris Frozen Foods
Hillsboro, IL 217-532-3822
Pascucci Family Pasta
San Diego, CA 619-285-8000
Peggy Lawton Kitchens
East Walpole, MA. 800-843-7325
Pierceton Foods
Pierceton, IN. 574-594-2344
Pierre Foods
Cincinnati, OH 513-874-8741

Plymouth Beef
Bronx, NY. 718-589-8600
Pokanoket Ostrich Farm
South Dartmouth, MA 508-992-6188
Preferred Meal Systems
Scranton, PA 570-457-8311
Premier Meats
Calgary, AB. 403-287-3550
Prime Ostrich International
Morinville, AB 800-340-2311
Quality Croutons
Chicago, IL 800-334-2796
Quality Meats & Seafood
West Fargo, ND. 800-342-4250
Quality Naturally! Foods
City of Industry, CA 888-498-6986
Randy's Frozen Meats
Faribault, MN 800-354-7177
Ready Portion Meat Company
Baton Rouge, LA 225-355-5641
Redi-Serve Food Company
Fort Atkinson, WI. 920-563-6391
Rego's Purity Foods
Honolulu, HI. 808-847-3717
Russer Foods
Buffalo, NY. 800-828-7021
Savannah Foods Industrial
Savannah, GA. 912-234-1261
Schneider's Dairy Holdings Inc
Pittsburgh, PA. 412-881-3525
Serv-Rite Meat Company
Los Angeles, CA. 323-227-1911
Skylark Meats
Omaha, NE 800-759-5275
Smith Packing Regional Meat
Utica, NY
Somerset Industries
Spring House, PA 800-883-8728
Southeastern Meat Association
Oviedo, FL 407-365-5661
Spilke's Baking Company
Brooklyn, NY 718-384-2150
Stampede Meat
Bridgeview, IL 800-353-0933
Stickney & Poor Company
Peterborough, NH. 603-924-2259
Sugar Foods
Lawrenceville, GA 800-732-8963
Swiss Colony
Monroe, WI. 608-328-8536
Taku Smokehouse
Juneau, AK 800-582-5122
Temptee Specialty Foods
Denver, CO 800-842-1233
Tiller Foods Company
Dayton, OH. 937-435-4601
Travis Meats
Powell, TN 800-247-7606
Trident Seafoods Corporation
Salem, NH. 603-893-3368
Triple U Enterprises
Fort Pierre, SD 605-567-3624
Tyson Foods
Springdale, AR 800-643-3410
Ultra Seal
New Paltz, NY 845-255-2490
United Meat Company
San Francisco, CA 415-864-2118
United Provision Meat Company
Columbus, OH 614-252-1126
Valley Meat Company
Modesto, CA. 800-222-6328
Waco Beef & Pork Processors
Waco, TX 254-772-4669
Wawona Frozen Foods
Clovis, CA 559-299-2901
Wayne Farms LLC
Pendergrass, GA 706-693-2271
Wing Nien Company
Hayward, CA 510-487-8877
Wing's Food Products
Etobicoke, ON 416-259-2662
Wolverine Packing
Detroit, MI 313-259-7500
Yarbrough Produce Company
Birmingham, AL. 205-324-4569

Pot Pies

Cedarlane Foods
Carson, CA 310-886-7720
Morrison Lamothe
Toronto, ON 877-677-6533

Real Food Marketing
Kansas City, MO. 816-221-4100
Stacey's Famous Foods
Hayden, ID 800-782-2395
Twin Hens
Princeton, NJ. 908-925-9040

Pot Stickers

Chang Food Company
Garden Grove, CA 714-265-9990
Golden Gate Foods
Dallas, TX. 214-747-2223
Harvest Food Products Company
Concord, CA. 925-676-8208
Health is Wealth Foods
Williamstown, NJ 856-728-1998
Kubla Khan Food Company
Portland, OR 503-234-7494
Peking Noodle Company
Los Angeles, CA. 323-223-2023
Shine Foods Inc
Torrance, CA. 310-533-6010
Wan Hua Foods
Seattle, WA 206-622-8417

Potato Products

Alexia Foods
Long Island City, NY 718-937-0100
Allen Canning Company
Siloam Springs, AR 800-234-2553
Bob Evans Farms
Hillsdale, MI. 517-437-3349
Chloe Foods Corporation
Brooklyn, NY 718-827-9000
ConAgra Foods
Kennewick, WA 509-735-4651
ConAgra Foods
Richland, WA 800-766-7783
Idahoan Foods, LLC
Lewisville, ID 800-635-6100
Lamb-Weston
Kennewick, WA 800-766-7783
Maple Leaf Foods International
North York, ON. 416-480-8900
McCain Foods USA
Colton, CA 800-938-7799
Noodles By Leonardo
Devil's Lake, ND 701-662-8300
Pacific Valley Foods
Bellevue, WA 425-643-1805
Rices Potato Chips
Biloxi, MS. 228-396-5775
Seneca Foods
Clyman, WI. 920-696-3331
Somerset Industries
Spring House, PA 800-883-8728
Sturm Foods
Manawa, WI 800-347-8876

Hash Browned Potatoes

Basic American Foods
Walnut Creek, CA. 800-722-2084
Bob Evans Farms
Hillsdale, MI. 517-437-3349
Cavendish Farms
Jamestown, ND. 888-284-5687
Emerling International Foods
Buffalo, NY. 716-833-7381

We supply food manufacturers and food service customers worldwide (since 1988) with bulk ingredients including: Fruits & Vegetables; Juice Concentrates; Herbs & Spices; Oils & Vinegars; Flavors & Colors; Honey & Molasses. We also produce PURE MAPLE SYRUP.

Idahoan Foods, LLC
Lewisville, ID 800-635-6100
McCain Foods Canada
Toronto, ON 866-622-2461
McCain Foods USA
Easton, ME 800-938-7799
Michael Foods, Inc.
Minnetonka, MN. 952-258-4000
Mr. Dell Foods
Kearney, MO. 816-628-4644
Northern Star Company
Chaska, MN 612-339-8981
Sun-Glo of Idaho
Sugar City, ID 208-356-7346

Puffs - Frozen

Lamb-Weston
Kennewick, WA ... 800-766-7783
McCain Foods USA
Easton, ME ... 800-938-7799

Prepared Meals

Amigos Canning Company
San Antonio, TX ... 800-580-3477
Aunt Kitty's Foods
Vineland, NJ ... 856-691-2100
Barber Foods
Portland, ME ... 800-577-2595
BlueWater Seafoods
Lachine, QC ... 888-560-2539
Castleberry's
Vineland, NJ ... 856-691-2100
Chandler Foods
Greensboro, NC ... 800-537-6219
Chef Hans Gourmet Foods
Monroe, LA ... 800-890-4267
Chloe Foods Corporation
Brooklyn, NY ... 718-827-9000
ConAgra Foods/International Home Foods
Niagara Falls, ON ... 905-356-2661
Culinary Foods
Chicago, IL ... 800-621-4049
Foodbrands America
Oklahoma City, OK ... 405-290-4000
Garden Protein International
Richmond, BC ... 877-305-6777
Heinz Company of Canada
North York, ON ... 877-574-3469
J.B. Sons
Yonkers, NY ... 914-963-5192
JTM Food Group
Harrison, OH ... 800-626-2308
La Tolteca Foods
Pueblo, CO ... 719-543-5733
Molinaro's Fine Italian Foods
Mississauga, ON ... 800-268-4959
Noodles By Leonardo
Devil's Lake, ND ... 701-662-8300
O Chili Frozen Foods Inc
Northbrook, IL ... 847-562-1991
Pasta USA
Spokane, WA ... 800-456-2084
Seneca Foods
Clyman, WI ... 920-696-3331
Snapdragon Foods
Oakland, CA ... 877-881-7627

Beef Dinner

Big B Distributors
Evansville, IN ... 812-425-5235
Bob Evans Farms
Hillsdale, MI ... 517-437-3349
Kelly Foods
Jackson, TN ... 731-424-2255
Simeus Foods International
Mansfield, TX ... 888-772-3663

Breakfast

Bob Evans Farms
Hillsdale, MI ... 517-437-3349
Gilster Mary Lee/Jasper Foods
Jasper, MO ... 800-777-2168
ISE America, Inc.
Galena, MD ... 410-755-6300
Jimmy Dean Foods
Cincinnati, OH ... 800-925-3326
Michael Foods, Inc.
Minnetonka, MN ... 952-258-4000

Burritos

Chimichangas

Camino Real Foods
Vernon, CA ... 800-421-6201
Queen International Foods
Monterey Park, CA ... 800-423-4414

Canned

Kelly Foods
Jackson, TN ... 731-424-2255
Lucks Food Decorating Company
Tacoma, WA ... 253-383-4815

Casseroles

Dynamic Foods
Lubbock, TX ... 806-747-2777
Good Old Days Foods
Little Rock, AR ... 501-565-1257
Marsan Foods
Toronto, ON ... 416-755-9262
Savannah Food Company
Savannah, TN ... 800-795-2550

Chicken

Kiev

Tyson Foods
Springdale, AR ... 800-643-3410

Convenience

Chef Hans Gourmet Foods
Monroe, LA ... 800-890-4267
ConAgra Frozen Foods Company
Marshall, MO ... 660-886-3301
Contessa Food Products
San Pedro, CA ... 310-832-8000
Gemini Food Industries
Charlton, MA ... 508-248-2730
Homegrown Naturals
Napa, CA ... 800-288-1089
Lucks Food Decorating Company
Tacoma, WA ... 253-383-4815

Corn Fritters

Tami Great Food
Monsey, NY ... 732-803-6366
Triton Seafood Company
Medley, FL ... 305-888-8999

Crab

Hancock Lobster Gourmet Company
Topsham, ME ... 800-266-1700

Stuffed

Boja's Foods
Bayou La Batre, AL ... 251-824-4186

Eggplant Parmigiana

Bruno Specialty Foods
West Sayville, NY ... 631-589-1700
Pasta Factory
Melrose Park, IL ... 800-615-6951

Eggs

Dixie Egg Company
Jacksonville, FL ... 800-394-3447
Great Valley Mills
Barto, PA ... 800-688-6455
ISE America, Inc.
Galena, MD ... 410-755-6300
Michael Foods, Inc.
Minnetonka, MN ... 952-258-4000
Sunnyslope Farms Egg Ranch
Cherry Valley, CA ... 951-845-1131

Entrees

Atlantic Premium Brands
Northbrook, IL ... 847-412-6200
Bellisio Foods, Inc.
Duluth, MN ... 800-368-7337
Bernardi Italian Foods Company
Bloomsburg, PA ... 570-389-5500
Blue Runner Foods
Gonzales, LA ... 225-647-3016
Boudreaux's Foods
New Orleans, LA ... 504-733-8440
Burnett & Son Meat Company
Monrovia, CA ... 626-357-2165
Carando Gourmet Frozen Foods
Agawam, MA ... 888-227-2636
ConAgra Foods Inc
Omaha, NE ... 402-595-7300
Culinary Revolution
La Jolla, CA ... 858-454-4390
Culinary Standards Corporation
Louisville, KY ... 800-778-3434
Deep Foods
Union, NJ ... 908-810-7500
Don Miguel Mexican Foods
Orange, CA ... 714-634-8441
Ethnic Gourmet Foods
West Chester, PA ... 610-692-7575
HFI Foods
Redmond, WA ... 425-883-1320
Home Made Brand Foods Company
Newburyport, MA ... 978-462-3663
Hormel Foods Corporation
Pittsburgh, PA ... 412-921-7036
Hormel Foods Corporation
Franklin, MA ... 508-541-7101
Hormel Foods Corporation
Cincinnati, OH ... 513-563-0211
Hormel Foods Corporation
Des Moines, IA ... 515-276-8872
Hormel Foods Corporation
Phoenix, AZ ... 602-230-2400
Hormel Foods Corporation
Arlington, TX ... 817-465-4735
Hormel Foods Corporation
Cordova, TN ... 901-753-4282
Hormel Foods Corporation
Lebanon, NJ ... 908-236-7009
Hormel Foods Corporation
Pleasanton, CA ... 925-734-9555
Hunt-Wesson Food Service Company
Rochester, NY ... 866-484-8676
JTM Food Group
Harrison, OH ... 800-626-2308
King Kold Meats
Englewood, OH ... 800-836-2797
Mann's International Meat Specialties
Omaha, NE ... 800-228-2170
Marsan Foods
Toronto, ON ... 416-755-9262
Natural Quick Foods
Seattle, WA ... 206-365-5757
Oh Boy! Corporation
San Fernando, CA ... 818-361-1128
Pasta USA
Spokane, WA ... 800-456-2084
Pinnacle Foods Group
Cherry Hill, NJ ... 877-852-7424
Plenus Group
Lowell, MA ... 978-970-3832
Quality Chef Foods
Cedar Rapids, IA ... 800-356-8307
Ragozzino Food
Meriden, CT ... 800-348-1240
Reser's Fine Foods
Beaverton, OR ... 800-333-6431
Ruggiero Seafood
Newark, NJ ... 866-225-2627
Sanderson Farms
Laurel, MS ... 800-844-4030
Spring Glen Fresh Foods
Ephrata, PA ... 800-641-2853
Steak-Umm Company
Shillington, PA ... 860-928-5900
Sugar Foods
Sun Valley, CA ... 818-768-7900
Tamarind Tree
Neshanic Station, NJ ... 800-432-8733
Thyme & Truffles Hors D'oeuvres
Dollard-Des-Ormeaux, QC ... 877-785-9759
Truesoups
Kent, WA ... 253-872-0403
Wong Wing Foods
Montreal, QC ... 800-361-4820

Frozen

Alfredo's Italian Foods Manufacturing Company
Quincy, MA ... 617-479-6360
Amy's Kitchen
Petaluma, CA ... 707-568-4500
Atlantic Premium Brands
Northbrook, IL ... 847-412-6200
Bellisio Foods, Inc.
Duluth, MN ... 800-368-7337
Bernardi Italian Foods Company
Bloomsburg, PA ... 570-389-5500
Campbell Soup Company of Canada
Listowel, ON ... 800-575-7687
Carando Gourmet Frozen Foods
Agawam, MA ... 888-227-2636
Cedarlane Natural Foods
Carson, CA ... 310-886-7720
ConAgra Mexican Foods
Compton, CA ... 310-223-1499
Contessa Food Products
San Pedro, CA ... 310-832-8000

Culinary Standards Corporation
Louisville, KY 800-778-3434
Deep Foods
Union, NJ 908-810-7500
Don Miguel Mexican Foods
Orange, CA 714-634-8441
Dynamic Foods
Lubbock, TX 806-747-2777
Fairfield Farm Kitchens
Tamworth, NH 508-584-9300
HFI Foods
Redmond, WA 425-883-1320
Hunt-Wesson Food Service Company
Rochester, NY 866-484-8676
Kelly Gourmet Foods
San Francisco, CA 415-648-9200
King Kold Meats
Englewood, OH 800-836-2797
Lenchner Bakery
Concord, ON 905-738-8811
Marsan Foods
Toronto, ON 416-755-9262
Milmar Food Group
Goshen, NY 845-294-5400
Oven Poppers
Manchester, NH 603-644-3773
Pasta USA
Spokane, WA 800-456-2084
Reser's Fine Foods
Beaverton, OR 800-333-6431
Royal Palate Foods
Inglewood, CA 310-330-7701
Ruggiero Seafood
Newark, NJ 866-225-2627
Sanderson Farms
Laurel, MS 800-844-4030
Simeus Foods Internatio nal
Mansfield, TX 888-772-3663
Steak-Umm Company
Shillington, PA 860-928-5900
Thyme & Truffles Hors D'oeuvres
Dollard-Des-Ormeaux, QC 877-785-9759
Wong Wing Foods
Montreal, QC 800-361-4820

Microwavable

Alle Processing Corporation
Maspeth, NY 800-245-5620
Atlantic Premium Brands
Northbrook, IL 847-412-6200

Shelf Stable

Associated Brands Inc.
Medina, NY 800-265-0050
California Creative Foods
Oceanside, CA 760-757-2622
Cordon Bleu International
Anjou, QC 514-352-3000
Dorina/So-Good
Union, IL 815-923-2144
Food Reserves
Concordia, MO 800-944-1511
Global Marketing Associates
Schaumburg, IL 847-397-2350
Hanover Foods Corporation
Hanover, PA 717-632-6000
Health Valley Company
Irwindale, CA 800-334-3204
Hormel Foods Corporation
Orchard Park, NY 716-675-7700
Hormel Foods Corporation
Austin, MN 800-523-4635
Lundberg Family Farm
Richvale, CA 530-882-4551
Mr Jay's Tamales & Chili
Lynwood, CA 310-537-3932
My Own Meals, Inc.
Chicago, IL 773-378-6505
SOPAKCO Foods
Mullins, SC 800-276-9678
Spring Glen Fresh Foods
Ephrata, PA 800-641-2853
Sugar Foods
Sun Valley, CA 818-768-7900
Truitt Brothers Inc
Salem, OR 800-547-8712
Vigo Importing Company
Tampa, FL 813-884-3491

Etoufee

Chef Hans Gourmet Foods
Monroe, LA 800-890-4267

Fish

American Seafoods International
New Bedford, MA 800-343-8046
Carrington Foods
Saraland, AL 251-675-9700
Cuizina Food Company
Woodinville, WA 425-486-7000
Icelandic USA
Newport News, VA 757-820-4000
Janes Family Foods
Mississauga, ON 800-565-2637
Menemsha Fish Market
Chilmark, MA 508-645-2282
Omstead Foods Ltd
Wheatley, ON 905-315-8883
Quinalt Pride Seafood
Taholah, WA 360-276-4431
Stacey's Famous Foods
Hayden, ID 800-782-2395
Trident Seafoods Corporation
Seattle, WA 800-426-5490

Stuffed

Anchor Frozen Foods
Westbury, NY 800-566-3474
Beaver Street Fisheries
Jacksonville, FL 800-874-6426
King & Prince Seafood Corporation
Brunswick, GA 800-841-0205
Sweet Water Seafood Corporation
Carlstadt, NJ 201-939-6622
Tampa Maid Foods
Lakeland, FL 800-237-7637

Fish & Chips

Viking Seafoods Inc
Malden, MA 800-225-3020

Fish Patties

Northwest Naturals
Olympia, WA 360-866-9661
Pacific Salmon Company
Edmonds, WA 425-774-1315
Viking Seafoods Inc
Malden, MA 800-225-3020

Fish Sticks

Icelandic USA
Newport News, VA 757-820-4000
North Atlantic Fish Company
Gloucester, MA 978-283-4121
Ungars Food Products
Elmwood Park, NJ 201-703-1300
Van De Kamp Frozen Foods
Mountain Lake, NJ 973-541-6620
Viking Seafoods Inc
Malden, MA 800-225-3020

Frozen

Al Safa Halal
Niagara Falls, NY 800-268-8174
Tichon Seafood Corporation
New Bedford, MA 508-999-5607
Van De Kamp Frozen Foods
Mountain Lake, NJ 973-541-6620
Viking Seafoods Inc
Malden, MA 800-225-3020

Fried Rice

Willow Foods
Beaverton, OR 800-338-3609
Wong Wing Foods
Montreal, QC 800-361-4820

Frozen

Bake Crafters Food
Collegedale, TN 800-296-8935
Biagio's Banquets
Chicago, IL 800-392-2837
Birds Eye Foods
Cherry Hill, NJ 800-999-5044
ConAgra Frozen Foods Company
Marshall, MO 660-886-3301
Cuizina Food Company
Woodinville, WA 425-486-7000
Food Source
Mc Kinney, TX 972-548-9001
Foodbrands America
Oklahoma City, OK 405-290-4000
Heinkel's Packing Company
Decatur, IL 800-594-2738
High Liner Foods Inc
Lunenburg, NS 902-634-9475
House of Spices
Flushing, NY 718-507-4900
McCain Foods Canada
Toronto, ON 866-622-2461
Pasta USA
Spokane, WA 800-456-2084
Philadelphia Cheese Steak Company
Philadelphia, PA 800-342-9771
Reser's Fine Foods
Beaverton, OR 800-333-6431

Gyros

Corfu Foods
Bensenville, IL 630-595-2510
Corfu Tasty Gyros
Bensenville, IL 630-595-2510

Lasagna

Alfredo's Italian Foods Manufacturing Company
Quincy, MA 617-479-6360
Foodbrands America
Oklahoma City, OK 405-290-4000
Homestead Fine Foods
S San Francisco, CA 650-615-0750
McCain Foods Canada
Toronto, ON 866-622-2461
Reames Foods
Columbus, OH 614-846-2232

Macaroni

Campbell Soup Company
Camden, NJ 800-257-8443
ConAgra Foods/International Home Foods
Niagara Falls, ON 905-356-2661
Gilster-Mary Lee Corporation
Chester, IL 800-851-5371
Molinaro's Fine Italian Foods
Mississauga, ON 800-268-4959
Pasta USA
Spokane, WA 800-456-2084
Strom Products Ltd.
Bannockburn, IL 800-862-3311

Mozzarella Sticks

Giorgio Foods
Temple, PA 800-220-2139
Matador Processors
Blanchard, OK 800-847-0797

Pasta & Noodle Dishes

Agrusa, Inc.
Leonia, NJ 201-592-5950
Alfredo's Italian Foods Manufacturing Company
Quincy, MA 617-479-6360
Antoni Ravioli
North Massapequa, NY 800-783-0350
Bernardi Italian Foods Company
Bloomsburg, PA 570-389-5500
Bruno Specialty Foods
West Sayville, NY 631-589-1700
Carando Gourmet Frozen Foods
Agawam, MA 888-227-2636
Casa Di Bertacchi
Vineland, NJ 800-818-9261
ConAgra Frozen Foods Company
Marshall, MO 660-886-3301
Cuizina Food Company
Woodinville, WA 425-486-7000
D'Orazio Foods
Bellmawr, NJ 888-328-7287
Dabruzzi's Italian Foods
Hudson, WI 715-386-3653
Food City USA
Arvada, CO 303-321-4447
Global Marketing Associates
Schaumburg, IL 847-397-2350

Kraft Foods
Springfield, MO 417-881-2701
Landolfi Food Products
Trenton, NJ 609-392-1830
Noodles By Leonardo
Devil's Lake, ND 701-662-8300
Pasta USA
Spokane, WA. 800-456-2084
Ragozzino Food
Meriden, CT 800-348-1240
Sandridge Food Corporation
Medina, OH. 800-627-2523
Specialty Brands
Carthage, MO 417-358-8104
ST Specialty Foods
Brooklyn Park, MN. 763-493-9600
Star Ravioli Manufacturing Company
Moonachie, NJ 201-933-6427

Rice

Amalgamated Produce
Bridgeport, CT 800-358-3808
Tony Chachere's Creole Foods
Opelousas, LA 800-551-9066

Salad

Classic Commissary
Binghamton, NY. 800-929-3486
Club Chef
Covington, KY 859-578-3100
Dole Fresh Vegetable Company
Soledad, CA 800-333-5454
Earth Island Natural Foods
Canoga Park, CA 818-725-2820
F&S Produce Company
Rosenhayn, NJ 800-886-3316
Lakeside Foods
Manitowoc, WI. 920-684-3356
Paisley Farms
Willoughby, OH 800-676-8656
R.C. McEntire & Company
Columbia, SC 803-799-3388
Ready-Pac Produce
Florence, NJ 609-499-1900
Reser's Fine Foods
Salt Lake City, UT 801-972-5633
Sandridge Food Corporation
Medina, OH. 800-627-2523
Suter Company
Sycamore, IL. 800-435-6942
Van Bennett Food Company
Reading, PA 800-423-8897

Sandwiches

B-S Foods Company
Oklahoma City, OK 405-949-9797
Bake Crafters Food
Collegedale, TN 800-296-8935
Black's Barbecue
Lockhart, TX. 512-398-2712
Bridgford Foods Corporation
Anaheim, CA 800-527-2105
Camino Real Foods
Vernon, CA 800-421-6201
Classic Delight
Saint Marys, OH 800-274-9828
Corfu Foods
Bensenville, IL 630-595-2510
Country Smoked Meats
Bowling Green, OH 800-321-4766
D&A Foodservice
Dartmouth, NS 902-468-4715
Deli Express/EA Sween Company
Eden Prairie, MN 800-328-8184
Eastside Deli Supply
Lansing, MI. 800-349-6694
Food Factory
Honolulu, HI 808-593-2633
Gilardi Foods
Sidney, OH 937-498-4511
Helens Pure Foods
Cheltenham, PA 215-379-6433
Honeybake Farms
Kansas City, KS 913-371-7777
Hormel Foods Corporation
Austin, MN 800-523-4635
JTM Food Group
Harrison, OH. 800-626-2308
Knotts Whlse. Foods
Paris, TN. 731-642-1961
Landshire
Saint Louis, MO 800-468-3354
Lilydale Foods
Edmonton, AB 800-661-5341
Made-Rite Sandwich Company
Ooltewah, TN 800-343-1327
Market Fare Foods
Phoenix, AZ 888-669-6420
Maui Bagel
Kahului, HI 808-270-7561
McLane Foods
Phoenix, AZ 602-275-5509
Oh Boy! Corporation
San Fernando, CA. 818-361-1128
Piemonte's Bakery
Rockford, IL 815-962-4833
Pierre Foods
Cincinnati, OH 513-874-8741
Randy's Frozen Meats
Faribault, MN 800-354-7177
Royal Touch Foods
Etobicoke, ON 416-213-1077
Southern Belle SandwichcCompany
Baton Rouge, LA 800-344-4670
Steak-Umm Company
Shillington, PA 860-928-5900
Sunburst Foods
Goldsboro, NC 919-778-2151
SunMeadow Family of Products
Saint Petersburg, FL 727-573-2211
Zartic Inc
Rome, GA. 800-241-0516

Pocket

Applegate Farms
Bridgewater, NJ 908-725-2768
Ore-Ida Foods
Pittsburgh, PA. 800-892-2401

Scampi

Shrimp Frozen

Contessa Food Products
San Pedro, CA. 310-832-8000

Seafood

AquaCuisine
Eagle, ID. 208-323-2782
Carnival Brands
New Orleans, LA 800-925-2774
Carrington Foods
Saraland, AL. 251-675-9700
Chincoteague Seafood Company
Parsonsburg, MD 443-260-4800
Contessa Food Products
San Pedro, CA. 310-832-8000
Cuizina Food Company
Woodinville, WA. 425-486-7000
FishKing
Glendale, CA 818-244-2161
Gemini Food Industries
Charlton, MA 508-248-2730
Gulf City Marine Supply
Bayou La Batre, AL 251-824-2516
Icelandic USA
Newport News, VA. 757-820-4000
International Oceanic Enterprises of Alabama
Bayou La Batre, AL 800-816-1832
King & Prince Seafood Corporation
Brunswick, GA. 800-841-0205
Menemsha Fish Market
Chilmark, MA. 508-645-2282
Neptune Fisheries
Newport News, VA. 800-545-7474
North Atlantic Fish Company
Gloucester, MA. 978-283-4121
Oven Poppers
Manchester, NH 603-644-3773
Ruggiero Seafood
Newark, NJ. 866-225-2627
Sanderson Farms
Bryan, TX. 979-778-5730
Sea Pearl Seafood
Bayou La Batre, AL 800-872-8804
Tex-Mex Cold Storage
Brownsville, TX 956-831-9433
Triton Seafood Company
Medley, FL 305-888-8999
Weyand Fisheries
Wyandotte, MI 800-521-9815

Spaghetti

Canned

Campbell Soup Company
Camden, NJ. 800-257-8443
Castleberry's
Vineland, NJ 856-691-2100
ConAgra Foods/International Home Foods
Niagara Falls, ON. 905-356-2661
Heinz Company of Canada
North York, ON. 877-574-3469
Hormel Foods Corporation
Austin, MN 800-523-4635
Seneca Foods
Clyman, WI. 920-696-3331

with Meatballs

Burnett & Son Meat Company
Monrovia, CA. 626-357-2165
JTM Food Group
Harrison, OH. 800-626-2308

Stuffed Cabbage

Morrison Lamothe
Toronto, ON 877-677-6533

Stuffed Peppers

L&S Packing Company
Farmingdale, NY 800-286-6487
Matador Processors
Blanchard, OK 800-847-0797
Norpaco
Middletown, CT 800-252-0222
Vega Food Industries
Cranston, RI 800-973-7737

Stuffed Shells

Antoni Ravioli
North Massapequa, NY 800-783-0350
Bruno Specialty Foods
West Sayville, NY. 631-589-1700
Caesar's Pasta Products
Blackwood, NJ 856-227-2585
Codino's Italian Foods
Scotia, NY. 800-246-8908
D'Orazio Foods
Bellmawr, NJ. 888-328-7287
J.B. Sons
Yonkers, NY 914-963-5192
Landolfi Food Products
Trenton, NJ 609-392-1830
Pasta Del Mondo
Carmel, NY. 800-392-8887
Pasta Factory
Melrose Park, IL. 800-615-6951
Star Ravioli Manufacturing Company
Moonachie, NJ 201-933-6427
Wisconsin Whey International
Juda, WI 608-233-5101

Turkey Dinner

Morrison Lamothe
Toronto, ON 877-677-6533

Vegetarian

Alle Processing
Maspeth, NY. 718-894-2000
Alle Processing Corporation
Maspeth, NY. 800-245-5620
Dixie Usa
Tomball, TX 800-233-3668
F&S Produce Company
Rosenhayn, NJ 800-886-3316
Garden Protein International
Richmond, BC 877-305-6777
Health Valley Company
Irwindale, CA 800-334-3204
Mortimer's Fine Foods
Burlington, ON. 905-336-0000
Tamarind Tree
Neshanic Station, NJ. 800-432-8733

Prepared Salads

Avon Heights Mushrooms
Avondale, PA 610-268-2092

Bay Cities Produce Company
San Leandro, CA. 510-346-4943
Black's Barbecue
Lockhart, TX. 512-398-2712
Bosell Foods
Cleveland, OH 216-991-7600
Chef Solutions
Wheeling, IL 800-877-1157
Chiquita Brands Intl. ional
Cincinnati, OH 800-438-0015
Chloe Foods Corporation
Brooklyn, NY 718-827-9000
Danner Salads
Peoria, IL. 309-691-0289
Giovanni's Appetizing Food Products
Richmond, MI. 586-727-9355
Hanover Foods Corporation
Hanover, PA 717-632-6000
Harold Food Company
Charlotte, NC 704-588-8061
Helens Pure Foods
Cheltenham, PA 215-379-6433
Herold's Salad, Inc
Cleveland, OH 800-427-2523
HFI Foods
Redmond, WA. 425-883-1320
Homestyle Foods Company
Hamtramck, MI. 313-874-3250
Honeybake Farms
Kansas City, KS 913-371-7777
Hoople Country Kitchens
Rockport, IN 812-649-2351
House of Thaller
Knoxville, TN. 800-462-3365
Kay Foods Company
Detroit, MI 313-393-1100
Kings Processing
Middleton, NS. 902-825-2188
L&S Packing Company
Farmingdale, NY 800-286-6487
Meadows Country Products
Hollidaysburg, PA. 888-499-1001
Mrs. Grissom's Salad
Nashville, TN 800-255-0571
Mrs. Stratton's Salads
Birmingham, AL. 205-940-9640
Orval Kent Food Company
Wheeling, IL 847-459-9000
Pastene Companies
Canton, MA 781-830-8200
PowerBar
Berkeley, CA. 800-587-6937
Reser's Fine Foods
Salt Lake City, UT 801-972-5633
Sandridge Food Corporation
Medina, OH. 800-627-2523
Sara Lee Corporation
Downers Grove, IL 630-598-8100
Spring Glen Fresh Foods
Ephrata, PA 800-641-2853
Thumann's
Carlstadt, NJ 201-935-3636
Vega Food Industries
Cranston, RI 800-973-7737
Yarbrough Produce Company
Birmingham, AL. 205-324-4569
Zuccaro's Fruit & Produce Company
Minneapolis, MN 612-333-1122

Antipasto

Giovanni's Appetizing Food Products
Richmond, MI. 586-727-9355
L&S Packing Company
Farmingdale, NY 800-286-6487
Pastene Companies
Canton, MA 781-830-8200

Chicken

Burnette Foods
Hartford, MI 616-621-3181
Mrs. Stratton's Salads
Birmingham, AL. 205-940-9640
Old Dutch Mustard Company
Great Neck, NY 516-466-0522
Orval Kent Food Company
Wheeling, IL 847-459-9000
Quality Brands
Deland, FL 888-676-2700
Sara Lee Corporation
Downers Grove, IL 630-598-8100

Cole Slaw

Avon Heights Mushrooms
Avondale, PA 610-268-2092
Black's Barbecue
Lockhart, TX. 512-398-2712
Chef Solutions
Wheeling, IL 800-877-1157
Flaum Appetizing
Brooklyn, NY 718-821-1970
Kay Foods Company
Detroit, MI 313-393-1100
Mrs. Stratton's Salads
Birmingham, AL. 205-940-9640
Orval Kent Food Company
Wheeling, IL 847-459-9000
Spring Glen Fresh Foods
Ephrata, PA 800-641-2853
Yarbrough Produce Company
Birmingham, AL. 205-324-4569

Iceberg Lettuce Based

Bay Cities Produce Company
San Leandro, CA. 510-346-4943
Chloe Foods Corporation
Brooklyn, NY 718-827-9000
Zuccaro's Fruit & Produce Company
Minneapolis, MN 612-333-1122

Macaroni

Black's Barbecue
Lockhart, TX. 512-398-2712
Chef Solutions
Wheeling, IL 800-877-1157
Hanover Foods Corporation
Hanover, PA 717-632-6000
Spring Glen Fresh Foods
Ephrata, PA 800-641-2853

Pasta

Chloe Foods Corporation
Brooklyn, NY 718-827-9000
Herold's Salad, Inc
Cleveland, OH 800-427-2523
HFI Foods
Redmond, WA. 425-883-1320
Homestyle Foods Company
Hamtramck, MI. 313-874-3250
Kay Foods Company
Detroit, MI 313-393-1100
Noodles By Leonardo
Devil's Lake, ND 701-662-8300
Sandridge Food Corporation
Medina, OH. 800-627-2523
Spring Glen Fresh Foods
Ephrata, PA 800-641-2853

Potato

Black's Barbecue
Lockhart, TX. 512-398-2712
Chef Solutions
Wheeling, IL 800-877-1157
Danner Salads
Peoria, IL. 309-691-0289
Hanover Foods Corporation
Hanover, PA 717-632-6000
Herold's Salad, Inc
Cleveland, OH 800-427-2523
Kay Foods Company
Detroit, MI 313-393-1100
Mrs. Stratton's Salads
Birmingham, AL. 205-940-9640
Orval Kent Food Company
Wheeling, IL 847-459-9000
Sandridge Food Corporation
Medina, OH. 800-627-2523
Spring Glen Fresh Foods
Ephrata, PA 800-641-2853

Salmon

Springfield Smoked Fish Company
Springfield, MA 800-327-3412

Seafood

Springfield Smoked Fish Company
Springfield, MA 800-327-3412

Tuna

Bumble Bee Foods
San Diego, CA 858-715-4000
Flaum Appetizing
Brooklyn, NY 718-821-1970
Mrs. Stratton's Salads
Birmingham, AL. 205-940-9640
Orval Kent Food Company
Wheeling, IL 847-459-9000
Sara Lee Corporation
Downers Grove, IL 630-598-8100

Turkey

Sara Lee Corporation
Downers Grove, IL 630-598-8100

Quiche

Culinary Foods
Chicago, IL 800-621-4049
Glendora Quiche Company
San Dimas, CA 909-394-1777
Goodwives Hors D'Oeuvres
Wilmington, MA. 800-521-8160
Love & Quiches Desserts
Freeport, NY 800-525-5251
Nancy's Specialty Foods
Newark, CA 510-494-1100
Naturally Fresh Foods
Atlanta, GA. 800-765-1950
Pie Piper Products
Bensenville, IL 800-621-8183
Quelle Quiche
Brentwood, MO 314-961-6554
Quiche & Tell
Flushing, NY. 718-381-7562
Stacey's Famous Foods
Hayden, ID 800-782-2395

Soups & Stews

Abbey Road Farms
Tallahassee, FL 850-878-7677
AFP Advanced Food Products, LLC
Visalia, CA 559-627-2070
Ailments E.D. Foods Inc.
Pointe Claire, QC 800-267-3333
Alaska Smokehouse
Woodinville, WA. 800-422-0852
All American Foods, Inc.
Mankato, MN 800-833-2661
Andersen's Pea Soup
Buellton, CA. 805-688-5581
Anke Kruse Organics
Guelph, ON. 519-824-6161
Annie Chun's
San Rafael, CA 415-479-8272
Associated Brands Inc.
Medina, NY. 800-265-0050
Atlanta Bread Company
Smyrna, GA 800-398-3728
Aunt Kitty's Foods
Vineland, NJ 856-691-2100
Baycliff Company
New York, NY 212-772-6078
Bear Creek Country Kitchens
Heber City, UT 800-516-7286
Bear Creek Kitchens
Marshall, TX. 888-300-7687
Belleisle Foods Aliments Wong Wing Inc
Belleisle Creek, NB 506-485-2564
Bellisio Foods, Inc.
Duluth, MN. 800-368-7337
Blount Seafood Corporation
Fall River, MA 774-888-1300
Blue Crab Bay Company
Melfa, VA 800-221-2722
Bombay Breeze Specialty Foods
Mississauga, ON. 416-410-2320
Boston Chowda Company
Lowell, MA. 800-992-0054
Boudreaux's Foods
New Orleans, LA 504-733-8440
Brinkley Dryer and Storage
Brinkley, AR. 870-734-1616
Cagnon Foods Company
Brooklyn, NY 718-647-2244
Cajun Fry Company
Pierre Part, LA 888-272-2586
California Natural Products
Lathrop, CA 209-858-2525

California Wild Rice Growers
Fall River Mills, CA 800-626-4366
Caltex Foods
Canoga Park, CA 800-522-5839
Cambridge Food
Monterey, CA 800-433-2584
Campbell Company of Canada
Toronto, ON 800-410-7687
Campbell Soup Company
Camden, NJ. 800-257-8443
Campbell Soup Company of Canada
Listowel, ON. 800-575-7687
Cape Cod Chowders
Hyannis, MA. 508-771-0040
Chef Francisco of Pennsylvania
King of Prussia, PA. 610-265-7400
Chef Hans Gourmet Foods
Monroe, LA. 800-890-4267
Cherchies
Malvern, PA 800-644-1980
Chicopee Provision Company
Chicopee, MA. 800-924-6328
Chincoteague Seafood Company
Parsonsburg, MD 443-260-4800
Christie Food Products
Randolph, MA 800-727-2523
Cibolo Junction Food & Spice
Albuquerque, NM. 505-888-1987
Clarmil Manufacturing Corporation
Hayward, CA 888-252-7645
Colonna Brothers
North Bergen, NJ 201-864-1115
Comfort Foods
Albuquerque, NM. 800-460-5803
ConAgra Grocery Products
Fullerton, CA 800-736-2212
Conifer Specialties Inc
Woodinville, WA. 800-588-9160
Cooke Tavern Ltd
Spring Mills, PA 866-422-7687
Country Cupboard
Virginia City, NV 775-847-7300
Cugino's Gourmet Foods
Crystal Lake, IL 888-592-8446
Culinary Standards Corporation
Louisville, KY 800-778-3434
Custom Culinary
Lombard, IL 800-621-8827
Daily Soup
New York, NY 888-393-7687
Daniel Webster Hearth N Kettle
Hyannis, MA. 888-774-5511
David Berg & Company
Chicago, IL 773-278-5195
Denzer's Food Products
Baltimore, MD 410-889-1500
Diversified Foods & Seasoning
Metairie, LA 504-846-5090
Dorothy Dawson Foods Products
Jackson, MI. 517-788-9830
Dr McDougall's Right Foods
South San Francisco, CA 650-583-4993
Eatem Foods Company
Vineland, NJ 800-683-2836
Edmonds Chile Company
St Louis, MO. 314-772-1499
El Peto Products
Cambridge, ON. 800-387-4064
Erba Food Products
Brooklyn, NY 718-272-7700
Fair Scones
Medina, WA 800-588-9160
Fantastic Foods
Napa, CA. 800-288-1089
Fish Hopper
Monterey, CA 831-372-2406
Flavor House
Adelanto, CA 760-246-9131
Food Source
Mc Kinney, TX 972-548-9001
Foodbrands America
Oklahoma City, OK 405-290-4000
Gemini Food Industries
Charlton, MA 508-248-2730
George F Brocke & Sons
Kendrick, ID 208-289-4231
Global Express Gourmet
Bozeman, MT 406-587-5571
Grace Foods International
Astoria, NY. 718-433-4789
Grandma Brown's Beans Inc
Mexico, NY. 315-963-7221
Grandma Pat's Products
Albin, WY. 307-631-0801
Great Eastern Sun
Asheville, NC 800-334-5809
Griffith Laboratories Worldwide
Alsip, IL 800-346-4743
H.K. Canning
Ventura, CA. 805-652-1392
Hains Celestial Group
Melville, NY 877-612-4246
Hale & Hearty Soups
New York, NY 646-214-5700
Hanover Foods Corporation
Hanover, PA 717-632-6000
Health Valley Company
Irwindale, CA 800-334-3204
Heartline Foods
Westport, CT. 203-222-0381
Hega Food Products
Cranbury, NJ. 800-345-7742
Heinz Company of Canada
North York, ON. 877-574-3469
Hirzel Canning Company &Farms
Northwood, OH 419-693-0531
Home Made Brand Foods Company
Newburyport, MA. 978-462-3663
Hoopeston Foods
Burnsville, MN 952-854-0903
Hormel Foods Corporation
Pittsburgh, PA 412-921-7036
Hormel Foods Corporation
Cincinnati, OH 513-563-0211
Hormel Foods Corporation
Des Moines, IA 515-276-8872
Hormel Foods Corporation
Phoenix, AZ 602-230-2400
Hormel Foods Corporation
Orchard Park, NY 716-675-7700
Hormel Foods Corporation
Austin, MN 800-523-4635
Hormel Foods Corporation
Arlington, TX 817-465-4735
Hormel Foods Corporation
Cordova, TN 901-753-4282
Hormel Foods Corporation
Lebanon, NJ 908-236-7009
Idaho Pacific Corporation
Ririe, ID 800-238-5503
Indian Harvest
Colusa, CA 800-294-2433
Jager Foods
Sauk Centre, MN 800-358-7251
JC World Foods
Brooklyn, NY 347-386-1130
JMAC Trading, Inc.
Torrance, CA. 877-566-4569
Juanita's Foods
Wilmington, CA 310-834-5339
Just Delicious Gourmet Foods
Seal Beach, CA 800-871-6085
Jyoti Cruisine India Gourmail Inc
Berwyn, PA 610-296-4620
K&S Riddle
Buzzards Bay, MA 508-563-7333
K.B. Specialty Foods
Greensburg, IN 812-663-8184
Karlsburger Foods
Monticello, MN 800-383-6549
Kay Foods Company
Detroit, MI 313-393-1100
Kettle Cooked Food
Fort Worth, TX 817-615-4500
Kettle Cuisine
Chelsea, MA 877-302-7687
Leonard Mountain Trading
Leonard, OK 918-366-2800
Les Aliments Ramico Foods
St. Leonard, QC 514-329-1844
Liberty Richter
Saddle Brook, NJ 201-291-8749
Locus Foods
Findlay, OH. 41- 4-3 49
Loffredo Produce
Rock Island, IL 800-397-2096
Marburger Foods
Peru, IN 765-472-1139
Marsan Foods
Toronto, ON 416-755-9262
Meat-O-Mat Corporation
Brooklyn, NY 718-965-7250
Mercer Processing
Modesto, CA. 209-529-0150
Mid-Atlantic Foods
Easton, MD. 800-922-4688
Montana Soup Company
Helena, MT. 800-862-7687
Moonlite Bar Bq Inn
Owensboro, KY 800-322-8989
Morgan Food
Austin, IN 888-430-1780
Near East Food Products
Leominster, MA 800-822-7423
New England Marketers
Boston, MA. 800-688-9904
Nissin Foods USA Company
Lancaster, PA 717-291-1881
North Aire Market
Shakopee, MN 800-662-3781
North of the Border
Tesuque, NM. 800-860-0681
Old Ranchers Canning Company
Upland, CA 909-982-8895
Organic Gourmet
Sherman Oaks, CA 800-400-7772
Overhill Farms
Vernon, CA 800-859-6406
Park 100 Foods
Tipton, IN 800-854-6504
Pasta USA
Spokane, WA. 800-456-2084
Perez Food Products
Kansas City, MO. 816-931-8761
Phillips Foods
Baltimore, MD 888-234-2722
Pioneer Foods Industries
Stuttgart, AR 870-673-4444
Plenus Group
Lowell, MA. 978-970-3832
Progresso Quality Foods
Vineland, NJ 800-200-9377
Quality Chef Foods
Cedar Rapids, IA. 800-356-8307
R.A.B. Food Group LLC
Secaucus, NJ 201-553-1100
R.L. Schreiber Company
Pompano Beach, FL 800-624-8777
Ragozzino Food
Meriden, CT 800-348-1240
Rapunzel Pure Organics
Bloomfield, NJ 800-225-1449
Reily Foods Company
New Orleans, LA 504-524-6131
RL Schreiber
Pompano Beach, FL 954-972-7102
Ronzoni Foods Canada
Etobicoke, ON 800-387-5032
Royal Palate Foods
Inglewood, CA 310-330-7701
Sallock International Foods
Millbury, OH. 419-838-7223
Sams Food Group
Chicago, IL 800-852-0283
San-J International
Richmond, VA. 800-446-5500
Sanderson Farms
Laurel, MS 800-844-4030
Sandridge Food Corporation
Medina, OH. 800-627-2523
Sea Watch Intl.
Easton, MD. 410-822-7500
Shelton's Poultry
Pomona, CA 800-541-1833
Simeus Foods Internatio nal
Mansfield, TX. 888-772-3663
Simeus Foods International
Mansfield, TX. 888-772-3663
SOUPerior Bean & Spice Company
Vancouver, WA 800-878-7687
Spice Hunter
San Luis Obispo, CA 800-444-3061
Sprague Foods
Belleville, ON. 613-966-1200
Spring Glen Fresh Foods
Ephrata, PA 800-641-2853
St. Ours & Company
Norwell, MA. 781-331-8520
Stinson Seafood Company
San Diego, CA
Stockpot
Woodinville, WA. 800-468-1611
Stokes Canning Company
Denver, CO 303-292-4018
Sudbury Soups and Salads
Sudbury, MA. 888-783-7687

Sweet Earth Natural Foods
Pacific Grove, CA.................800-737-3311
Sweet Sue Kitchens
Athens, AL.......................256-216-0500
Swiss Food Products
Chicago, IL......................312-829-0100
Tabatchnick's Fine Foods
Somerset, NJ.....................732-247-6668
Tex-Mex Gourmet
Brenham, TX......................888-345-8467
Thumann's
Carlstadt, NJ....................201-935-3636
Timber Peaks Gourmet
Parker, CO.......................800-982-7687
Truesoups
Kent, WA.........................253-872-0403
Turtle Island Foods
Hood River, OR...................800-508-8100
Twin Marquis
Brooklyn, NY.....................800-367-6868
Unilever
Lisle, IL.........................877-995-4483
Unilever Canada
Saint John, NB...................800-565-7273
Ventura Foods
Philadelphia, PA.................215-223-8700
Vermont Sprout House
Bristol, VT......................802-453-3098
Vienna Sausage Company
Chicago, IL......................800-366-3647
Vigor Cup Corp
Long Beach, NY...................516-785-6352
Vince's Seafoods
Gretna, LA.......................504-368-1544
VIP Foods
Flushing, NY.....................718-821-5330
Westbrae Natural Foods
Melville, NY.....................800-434-4246
White Coffee Corporation
Astoria, NY......................800-221-0140
William Poll
New York, NY.....................800-993-7655
Williams-West & Witt Products
Michigan City, IN
Worthmore Food Product
Cincinnati, OH...................513-559-1473
Yankee Specialty Foods
Boston, MA.......................617-951-0739

Beef Soup

Country Cupboard
Virginia City, NV.................775-847-7300
Culinary Standards Corporation
Louisville, KY...................800-778-3434
Erba Food Products
Brooklyn, NY.....................718-272-7700
Williams-West & Witt Products
Michigan City, IN

Beef Stew

Aunt Kitty's Foods
Vineland, NJ.....................856-691-2100
Caltex Foods
Canoga Park, CA..................800-522-5839
Campbell Company of Canada
Toronto, ON......................800-410-7687
Castleberry's
Vineland, NJ.....................856-691-2100
Cibolo Junction Food & Spice
Albuquerque, NM..................505-888-1987
Cleugh's Frozen Foods
Buena Park, CA...................714-521-1002
ConAgra Foods/International Home Foods
Niagara Falls, ON................905-356-2661
Heinz Company of Canada
North York, ON...................877-574-3469
Hoopeston Foods
Burnsville, MN...................952-854-0903
Kelly Foods
Jackson, TN......................731-424-2255
Marsan Foods
Toronto, ON......................416-755-9262
Midwest Foods
Chicago, IL......................773-927-8870
Old Ranchers Canning Company
Upland, CA.......................909-982-8895
Sanderson Farms
Bryan, TX........................979-778-5730
Spring Glen Fresh Foods
Ephrata, PA......................800-641-2853

Sweet Sue Kitchens
Athens, AL.......................256-216-0500

Borscht

Gold Pure Foods Products Company
Hempstead, NY....................800-422-4681

Canned Soup

Amy's Kitchen
Petaluma, CA.....................707-568-4500
Caltex Foods
Canoga Park, CA..................800-522-5839
Campbell Sales Company
Schaumburg, IL...................847-885-7164
Carriere Foods Inc
Saint-Denis-Sur-Richelie, QC.....450-787-3411
Chef Hans Gourmet Foods
Monroe, LA.......................800-890-4267
Chincoteague Seafood Company
Parsonsburg, MD..................443-260-4800
Colonna Brothers
North Bergen, NJ.................201-864-1115
Dynamic Foods
Lubbock, TX......................806-747-2777
Faribault Foods
Minneapolis, MN..................612-333-6461
Hoopeston Foods
Burnsville, MN...................952-854-0903
Look's Gourmet Food Company
East Machias, ME.................800-962-6258
Marburger Foods
Peru, IN.........................765-472-1139
Mid-Atlantic Foods
Easton, MD.......................800-922-4688
Old Ranchers Canning Company
Upland, CA.......................909-982-8895
Overhill Farms
Vernon, CA.......................800-859-6406
Progresso Quality Foods
Vineland, NJ.....................800-200-9377
Sea Watch Intl.
Easton, MD.......................410-822-7500
Shelton's Poultry
Pomona, CA.......................800-541-1833
Stinson Seafood Company
San Diego, CA
Sweet Sue Kitchens
Athens, AL.......................256-216-0500
Unilever
Lisle, IL.........................877-995-4483
Vanee Foods Company
Berkeley, IL.....................708-449-7300
Worthmore Food Product
Cincinnati, OH...................513-559-1473

Canned Stew

Aunt Kitty's Foods
Vineland, NJ.....................856-691-2100
Caltex Foods
Canoga Park, CA..................800-522-5839
Campbell Company of Canada
Toronto, ON......................800-410-7687
Campbell Soup Company
Camden, NJ.......................800-257-8443
Castleberry's
Vineland, NJ.....................856-691-2100
ConAgra Foods/International Home Foods
Niagara Falls, ON................905-356-2661
Cordon Bleu International
Anjou, QC........................514-352-3000
Faribault Foods
Minneapolis, MN..................612-333-6461
Glenmark Food Processors
Chicago, IL......................800-621-0117
Hoopeston Foods
Burnsville, MN...................952-854-0903
Kelly Foods
Jackson, TN......................731-424-2255
Midwest Foods
Chicago, IL......................773-927-8870
Old Ranchers Canning Company
Upland, CA.......................909-982-8895
On-Cor Foods Products
Northbrook, IL...................847-205-1040
Sweet Sue Kitchens
Athens, AL.......................256-216-0500
Vietti Foods Company Inc
Nashville, TN....................800-240-7864

Chicken & Dumplings

Culinary Standards Corporation
Louisville, KY...................800-778-3434

Chicken & Noodles

Aunt Kathy's Homestyle Products
Waldheim, SK.....................306-945-2181
Country Cupboard
Virginia City, NV.................775-847-7300
Culinary Standards Corporation
Louisville, KY...................800-778-3434
Shelton's Poultry
Pomona, CA.......................800-541-1833
Swagger Foods Corporation
Vernon Hills, IL.................847-913-1200

Chowder

Culinary Standards Corporation
Louisville, KY...................800-778-3434
Fish Hopper
Monterey, CA.....................831-372-2406
LaMonica Fine Foods
Millville, NJ....................856-825-8111
Look's Gourmet Food Company
East Machias, ME.................800-962-6258
Mid-Atlantic Foods
Easton, MD.......................800-922-4688
Phillips Foods
Baltimore, MD....................888-234-2722
Plenus Group
Lowell, MA.......................978-970-3832
Ronzoni Foods Canada
Etobicoke, ON....................800-387-5032
Sea Watch Intl.
Easton, MD.......................410-822-7500
Vanee Foods Company
Berkeley, IL.....................708-449-7300
Yankee Specialty Foods
Boston, MA.......................617-951-0739

Manhattan

Culinary Standards Corporation
Louisville, KY...................800-778-3434
LaMonica Fine Foods
Millville, NJ....................856-825-8111

New England

Cagnon Foods Company
Brooklyn, NY.....................718-647-2244
Campbell Company of Canada
Toronto, ON......................800-410-7687
Culinary Standards Corporation
Louisville, KY...................800-778-3434
Custom Culinary
Lombard, IL......................800-621-8827
Hormel Foods Corporation
Austin, MN.......................800-523-4635
LaMonica Fine Foods
Millville, NJ....................856-825-8111
Vanee Foods Company
Berkeley, IL.....................708-449-7300

Cream of Broccoli

Culinary Standards Corporation
Louisville, KY...................800-778-3434

Cream of Mushroom

Culinary Standards Corporation
Louisville, KY...................800-778-3434
Vanee Foods Company
Berkeley, IL.....................708-449-7300

Cream of Potato

Culinary Standards Corporation
Louisville, KY...................800-778-3434

Dehydrated Soup

Associated Brands Inc.
Medina, NY.......................800-265-0050
Atlantic Quality Spice &Seasonings
New Brunswick, NJ................800-584-0422
Borden Foods
Columbus, OH.....................614-233-3759
Chef Merito
Encino, CA.......................800-637-4861

Dorothy Dawson Foods Products
Jackson, MI 517-788-9830
Flavor House
Adelanto, CA 760-246-9131
Frontier Soups
Waukegan, IL 800-300-7867
Henningsen Foods
Purchase, NY 914-701-4020
Maruchan
Irvine, CA 949-789-2300
Mayacamas Fine Foods
Sonoma, CA 800-826-9621
Northwestern Foods
Saint Paul, MN 800-236-4937
Sentry Seasonings
Elmhurst, IL 630-530-5370

The product development experts of Sentry Seasonings are eager to offer the assistance and hands-on experience to food processors of all sizes. Sentry Seasonings will ensure the consistent high quality and repeat sales of your products, whether you choose one of our many off-the-shelf Bench Mark products or a modified version to meet your preferences. Sentry Seasonings can also duplicate and/or improve your present flavor profile; formulate, blend and package specifically for your requirements.

Serv-Agen Corporation
Cherry Hill, NJ 856-663-6966
SOUPerior Bean & Spice Company
Vancouver, WA 800-878-7687
Tropical
Columbus, OH 800-538-3941
VIP Foods
Flushing, NY 718-821-5330
Vogue Cuisine
Sunnyvale, CA 888-236-4144
Williams-West & Witt Products
Michigan City, IN

Fresh Stew

Heinz Company of Canada
North York, ON 877-574-3469
Midwest Foods
Chicago, IL 773-927-8870
On-Cor Foods Products
Northbrook, IL 847-205-1040
Vietti Foods Company Inc
Nashville, TN 800-240-7864

Frozen Soup

Ajinomoto Frozen Foods USA
Portland, OR 503-286-6548
Bellisio Foods, Inc.
Duluth, MN 800-368-7337
Blount Fine Foods
Fall River, MA 774-888-1300
Campbell Soup Company of Canada
Listowel, ON 800-575-7687
Chef Francisco of Pennsylvania
King of Prussia, PA 610-265-7400
Chincoteague Seafood Company
Parsonsburg, MD 443-260-4800
Culinary Standards Corporation
Louisville, KY 800-778-3434
Dorothy Dawson Foods Products
Jackson, MI 517-788-9830
Edmonds Chile Company
St Louis, MO 314-772-1499
Fairfield Farm Kitchens
Tamworth, NH 508-584-9300
Food Source
Mc Kinney, TX 972-548-9001
Gemini Food Industries
Charlton, MA 508-248-2730
Mann's International Meat Specialties
Omaha, NE 800-228-2170
Marburger Foods
Peru, IN 765-472-1139
Marsan Foods
Toronto, ON 416-755-9262
Progresso Quality Foods
Vineland, NJ 800-200-9377
Shelton's Poultry
Pomona, CA 800-541-1833
Truesoups
Kent, WA 253-872-0403
William Poll
New York, NY 800-993-7655

Frozen Stew

Ajinomoto Frozen Foods USA
Portland, OR 503-286-6548
Campbell Soup Company
Camden, NJ 800-257-8443
Cleugh's Frozen Foods
Buena Park, CA 714-521-1002
Edmonds Chile Company
St Louis, MO 314-772-1499
Glenmark Food Processors
Chicago, IL 800-621-0117
Heinz Company of Canada
North York, ON 877-574-3469
Marsan Foods
Toronto, ON 416-755-9262
Midwest Foods
Chicago, IL 773-927-8870
On-Cor Foods Products
Northbrook, IL 847-205-1040
Sanderson Farms
Bryan, TX 979-778-5730

Gumbo

Bear Creek Kitchens
Marshall, TX 888-300-7687
Cajun Crawfish Distributors
Mansura, LA 800-525-6813
Cajun Fry Company
Pierre Part, LA 888-272-2586
Chef Hans Gourmet Foods
Monroe, LA 800-890-4267
Cuizina Food Company
Woodinville, WA 425-486-7000
Gazin's
New Orleans, LA 800-262-6410
Kajun Kettle Foods
New Orleans, LA 504-733-8800
Louisiana Gourmet Enterprises
La Place, LA 985-783-2446
Vince's Seafoods
Gretna, LA 504-368-1544
Yankee Specialty Foods
Boston, MA 617-951-0739

Lentil Soup

Colonna Brothers
North Bergen, NJ 201-864-1115
Country Cupboard
Virginia City, NV 775-847-7300

Wonton Soup

Maruchan
Irvine, CA 949-789-2300
Wong Wing Foods
Montreal, QC 800-361-4820

Stuffing

Meat

Texas Crumb & Food Products
Farmers Branch, TX 800-522-7862
World Flavors
Warminster, PA 215-672-4400

Relishes & Pickled Products

Pickled Products

A-1 Eastern Home Made Pickle Company
Los Angeles, CA....323-223-1141
A.M. Braswell Jr. Food Company
Statesboro, GA....800-673-9388
Baensch Food
Milwaukee, WI....800-562-8234
Big B Distributors
Evansville, IN....812-425-5235
Bob Gordon & Associates
Oak Park, IL....708-524-9611
Bryant Preserving Company
Alma, AR....800-634-2413
Cajun Chef Products
Saint Martinville, LA....337-394-7112
Campbell Soup Company
Camden, NJ....800-257-8443
Carson City Pickle Company
Carson City, MI....989-584-3148
Chloe Foods Corporation
Brooklyn, NY....718-827-9000
Commissariat Imports
Los Angeles, CA....310-475-5628
Cordon Bleu International
Anjou, QC....514-352-3000
Corsair Pepper Sauce
Gulfport, MS....228-452-0311
David Berg & Company
Chicago, IL....773-278-5195
Dolores Canning Company
Los Angeles, CA....323-263-9155
F&S Produce Company
Rosenhayn, NJ....800-886-3316
Feature Foods
Etobicoke, ON....416-675-7350
Fjord Pacific Marine Industries
Richmond, BC....604-270-3393
Food City Pickle Company
Chicago, IL
Foster Family Farm
South Windsor, CT....860-648-9366
Freestone Pickle Company
Bangor, MI....877-874-2553
G. L. Mezzetta
American Canyon, CA....707-648-1050
Giovanni's Appetizing Food Products
Richmond, MI....586-727-9355
Granny Blossom Specialty Foods
Wells, VT....802-645-0507
Great Lakes Kraut Company
Bear Creek, WI....715-752-4105
Hell on the Red
Telephone, TX....903-664-2573
Hermann Pickle Farm
Garrettsville, OH....800-245-2696
HVJ International
Spring, TX....877-730-3663
L&S Packing Company
Farmingdale, NY....800-286-6487
Lakeside Packing Company
Harrow, ON....519-738-2314
Lancaster Packing Company
Lancaster, PA....717-397-9727
McCutcheon's Apple Products
Frederick, MD....800-888-7537
Money's Mushrooms
Vancouver, BC....800-669-7992
Musco Olive Products
Orland, CA....530-865-4111
Ocean Beauty Seafoods
Taunton, MA....774-961-0000
Papetti's Egg Products
Elizabeth, NJ....800-328-5474
Paradise Products Corporation
Boca Raton, FL....800-826-1235
Peer Foods Inc.
Chicago, IL....800-365-5644
Pepperland Farms
Denham Springs, LA....225-665-3555
Porinos Gourmet Food
Central Falls, RI....800-826-3938
S&G Products
Nicholasville, KY....800-826-7652
Sara Lee Corporation
Downers Grove, IL....630-598-8100
Seneca Foods
Clyman, WI....920-696-3331
Springfield Smoked Fish Company
Springfield, MA....800-327-3412
Stanchfield Farms
Milo, ME....207-732-5173
Star Fine Foods
Fresno, CA....559-498-2900
Sumida Pickle Products
Honolulu, HI....808-593-2487
SW Red Smith
Davie, FL....954-581-1996
Talk O'Texas Brands
San Angelo, TX
Tribe Mediterranean Foods Company LLC
Taunton, MA....774-961-0000
Troy Pork Store
Troy, NY....518-272-8291
Tucker Cellars
Sunnyside, WA....509-837-8701
United Pickle Products Corporation
Bronx, NY....718-933-6060
Wetta Egg Farm
Andale, KS....316-445-2231
Yergat Packing Co Inc
Fresno, CA....559-276-9180

Cauliflower

Bloch & Guggenheimer
Hurlock, MD....800-541-2809
S&G Products
Nicholasville, KY....800-826-7652

Eggs

Cordon Bleu International
Anjou, QC....514-352-3000
Feature Foods
Etobicoke, ON....416-675-7350
Papetti's Egg Products
Elizabeth, NJ....800-328-5474
SW Red Smith
Davie, FL....954-581-1996
Wetta Egg Farm
Andale, KS....316-445-2231

Meats

Sara Lee Corporation
Downers Grove, IL....630-598-8100
Troy Pork Store
Troy, NY....518-272-8291

Peppers

Apecka
Rockwall, TX....972-772-2654
Bloch & Guggenheimer
Hurlock, MD....800-541-2809
F&S Produce Company
Rosenhayn, NJ....800-886-3316
G. L. Mezzetta
American Canyon, CA....707-648-1050
Porinos Gourmet Food
Central Falls, RI....800-826-3938
S&G Products
Nicholasville, KY....800-826-7652
Star Fine Foods
Fresno, CA....559-498-2900

Pickles

A-1 Eastern Home Made Pickle Company
Los Angeles, CA....323-223-1141
A.M. Braswell Jr. Food Company
Statesboro, GA....800-673-9388
Alimentaire Whyte's Inc
Laval, QC....800-625-1979
Allen's Pickle Works
Glen Cove, NY....516-676-0640
Artichoke Kitchen
Hamilton, NC....252-798-2471
B&G Foods
Parsippany, NJ....973-401-6500
Bainbridge Festive Foods
Tunica, MS....800-545-9205
Batampte Pickle Foods, Inc.
Brooklyn, NY....718-251-2100
Bay Valley Foods
Platteville, WI....800-236-1119
Bessinger Pickle Company
Au Gres, MI....989-876-8008
Blazzin Pickle Company
McAllen, TX....956-630-0733
Bloch & Guggenheimer
Hurlock, MD....800-541-2809
Cains Foods LP/Olde CapeCod
Ayer, MA....651-698-6832
Caltex Foods
Canoga Park, CA....800-522-5839
Campbell Soup Company
Camden, NJ....800-257-8443
Carson City Pickle Company
Carson City, MI....989-584-3148
Chloe Foods Corporation
Brooklyn, NY....718-827-9000
Claussen Pickle Company
Woodstock, IL....800-435-2817
Clic International Inc
Laval, QC....450-669-2663
Commissariat Imports
Los Angeles, CA....310-475-5628
Country Cupboard
Virginia City, NV....775-847-7300
David Berg & Company
Chicago, IL....773-278-5195
Dean Distributing Inc
Green Bay, WI....920-469-6500
Erba Food Products
Brooklyn, NY....718-272-7700
Flaum Appetizing
Brooklyn, NY....718-821-1970
Florida Deli Pickle
Fort Lauderdale, FL....954-463-0222
Forge Mountain Foods
Hendersonville, NC....800-823-6743
GFA Brands
Paramus, NJ....201-568-9300
Gielow Pickles
Lexington, MI....810-359-7680
GWB Foods Corporation
Brooklyn, NY....877-977-7610
Hausbeck Pickle Company
Saginaw, MI....866-754-4721
Heinz Company of Canada
North York, ON....877-574-3469
Hermann Pickle Farm
Garrettsville, OH....800-245-2696
Hilltop Herb Farm & Restaurant
Cleveland, TX....832-397-4020
House of Spices India
Flushing, NY....718-507-4900
Howard Foods
Danvers, MA....978-774-6207
Hurd Orchards
Holley, NY....585-638-8838
Island Spring
Vashon, WA....206-463-9848
J. G. Van Holten & Son
Waterloo, WI....800-256-0619
Jane Specialty Foods
Green Bay, WI....800-558-4700
Kaiser Pickles
Cincinnati, OH....888-291-0608
Kaplan & Zubrin
Camden, NJ....800-334-0002
Klein's Kosher Pickles
Phoenix, AZ....602-269-2072
Kruger Foods
Stockton, CA....209-941-8518
L&S Packing Company
Farmingdale, NY....800-286-6487
Lakeside Packing Company
Harrow, ON....519-738-2314
Lancaster Packing Company
Lancaster, PA....717-397-9727
Liberty Richter
Saddle Brook, NJ....201-291-8749
Limited Edition
Midland, TX....432-686-2008
Maine Coast Sea Vegetables
Franklin, ME....207-565-2907

Miramar Pickles & Food Products
Fort Lauderdale, FL 954-351-8030
Miss Ginny's Orginal Vermont Pickle Works
Northfield, VT 802-485-3057
Mixon Fruit Farms
Bradenton, FL. 800-608-2525
Mount Olive Pickle Company
Mount Olive, NC 800-672-5041
Mr. Pickle
Brooklyn, NY
Mt. Olive Pickle Company
Mt Olive, NC 800-672-5041
Olde Tyme Mercantile
Arroyo Grande, CA. 805-489-7991
Our Enterprises
Oklahoma City, OK 800-821-6375
Paisley Farms
Willoughby, OH 800-676-8656
Paradise Products Corporation
Boca Raton, FL. 800-826-1235
Pemberton's Gourmet Foods
Gray, ME. 800-255-8401
Picklesmith
Taft, TX. 800-499-3401
Pinnacle Foods Group
Cherry Hill, NJ 877-852-7424
Porter's Pick-A-Dilly
Stowe, VT. 802-253-6338
Precision Foods
Saint Louis, MO 800-647-8170
Purity Products
Plainview, NY. 888-769-7873
Ralph Sechler & Son Inc
St Joe, IN. 800-332-5461
Regal Crown Foods
Worcester, MA 508-752-2679
Ripon Pickle Company
Ripon, WI 800-324-5493
S&G Products
Nicholasville, KY. 800-826-7652
Sambets Cajun Deli
Austin, TX. 800-472-6238
Sargent's Bear Necessities
North Troy, VT 802-988-2903
Schwartz Pickle Company
Chicago, IL 773-927-7700
Shawnee Canning Company
Cross Junction, VA. 800-713-1414
Stan-Mark Food Products
Chicago, IL 800-651-0994
Strub Pickles
Brantford, ON. 519-751-1717
Sumida Pickle Products
Honolulu, HI. 808-593-2487
Sunshine Fresh
Totowa, NJ 800-832-8081
Texas Sassy Foods
Austin, TX. 512-215-4022
Tony Packo Food Company
Toledo, OH 866-472-2567
Topor's Pickle Company
Detroit, MI 313-237-0288
United Pickle Products Corporation
Bronx, NY. 718-933-6060
Vaughn Rue Produce
Wilson, NC 800-388-8138
Vienna Sausage Company
Chicago, IL 800-366-3647
Whyte's Food Corporation
Mississauga, ON. 905-624-5065
William Harrison Vineyar
Saint Helena, CA 800-913-9463

Dill

Allen's Pickle Works
Glen Cove, NY 516-676-0640
Bessinger Pickle Company
Au Gres, MI 989-876-8008
Food City Pickle Company
Chicago, IL
Hausbeck Pickle Company
Saginaw, MI 866-754-4721
Hermann Pickle Farm
Garrettsville, OH. 800-245-2696
Schwartz Pickle Company
Chicago, IL 773-927-7700
Sechler's Fine Pickles
Saint Joe, IN 800-332-5461
Strub Pickles
Brantford, ON. 519-751-1717
United Pickle Products Corporation
Bronx, NY. 718-933-6060

Gherkins

Paradise Products Corporation
Boca Raton, FL. 800-826-1235
S&G Products
Nicholasville, KY 800-826-7652
Sechler's Fine Pickles
Saint Joe, IN 800-332-5461

Kosher

Kaplan & Zubrin
Camden, NJ. 800-334-0002

Sweet

Food City Pickle Company
Chicago, IL
Hausbeck Pickle Company
Saginaw, MI 866-754-4721
Schwartz Pickle Company
Chicago, IL 773-927-7700
Sechler's Fine Pickles
Saint Joe, IN 800-332-5461
United Pickle Products Corporation
Bronx, NY. 718-933-6060

Vegetables

Apecka
Rockwall, TX 972-772-2654
Bloch & Guggenheimer
Hurlock, MD. 800-541-2809
Bob Gordon & Associates
Oak Park, IL 708-524-9611
Carson City Pickle Company
Carson City, MI. 989-584-3148
F&S Produce Company
Rosenhayn, NJ 800-886-3316
Foster Family Farm
South Windsor, CT 860-648-9366
G. L. Mezzetta
American Canyon, CA 707-648-1050
Hell on the Red
Telephone, TX. 903-664-2573
Hermann Pickle Farm
Garrettsville, OH. 800-245-2696
HVJ International
Spring, TX. 877-730-3663
Johnson Canning Company
Sunnyside, WA 509-837-4188
L&S Packing Company
Farmingdale, NY 800-286-6487
Lancaster Packing Company
Lancaster, PA 717-397-9727
Landry's Pepper Company
Saint Martinville, LA 337-394-6097
Miramar Pickles & Food Products
Fort Lauderdale, FL 954-351-8030
Money's Mushrooms
Vancouver, BC 800-669-7992
Musco Olive Products
Orland, CA 530-865-4111
Paradise Products Corporation
Boca Raton, FL. 800-826-1235
Pepperland Farms
Denham Springs, LA 225-665-3555
RES Food Products International
Green Bay, WI. 800-255-3768
Star Fine Foods
Fresno, CA 559-498-2900
Sumida Pickle Products
Honolulu, HI. 808-593-2487
Talk O'Texas Brands
San Angelo, TX
Tucker Cellars
Sunnyside, WA 509-837-8701
Yergat Packing Co Inc
Fresno, CA 559-276-9180

Relishes

A. Bauer's Mustard
Flushing, NY. 718-821-3570
A.M. Braswell Jr. Food Company
Statesboro, GA 800-673-9388
Alimentaire Whyte's Inc
Laval, QC 800-625-1979
Aloha from Oregon
Eugene, OR. 800-241-0300
Alto Rey Food Corporation
Studio City, CA. 323-969-0178
American Culinary GardenNoble Communications Co
Springfield, MO 888-831-2433
American Fine Food Corporation
Doral, FL. 305-392-5000
Amigos Canning Company
San Antonio, TX. 800-580-3477
Arizona Pepper Products
Mesa, AZ. 800-359-3912
Artichoke Kitchen
Hamilton, NC 252-798-2471
Assouline & Ting
Huntingdon Valley, PA 800-521-4491
Au Printemps Gourmet
Saint-Jerome, QC 800-663-0416
Baldwin Richardson Foods
Frankfort, IL 866-644-2732

Liquid ingredient manufacturer specializing in signature sauces, dessert toppings, beverage/pancake syrups, specialty fruit fillings and condiments.

Bay Valley Foods
Platteville, WI 800-236-1119
BBQ Bunch
Kansas City, MO. 816-941-4534
Best Provision Co Inc.
Newark, NJ 800-631-4466
Big B Distributors
Evansville, IN 812-425-5235
Blue Jay Orchards
Bethel, CT. 203-748-0119
Blue Ridge Farms
Brooklyn, NY 718-827-9000
Boca Grande Foods
Duluth, GA 800-788-8026
Boetje Foods
Rock Island, IL 877-726-3853
Bogland
Pembroke, MA 781-829-9549
Brede
Detroit, MI 313-273-1079
Brockles Foods Company
Garland, TX 972-272-5593
Bryant Preserving Company
Alma, AR 800-634-2413
Burleson's
Waxahachie, TX 972-937-4810
C&E Canners
Hammonton, NJ 609-561-1078
C.F. Sauer Company
Richmond, VA. 800-688-5676
Cafe Terra Cotta
Tucson, AZ 800-492-4454
Cains Foods LP/Olde CapeCod
Ayer, MA. 651-698-6832
Cajun Chef Products
Saint Martinville, LA 337-394-7112
Califrance
Los Angeles, CA. 310-440-0729
Campbell Soup Company
Camden, NJ. 800-257-8443
Carolina Treet
Wilmington, NC 800-616-6344
Carolyn's Caribbean Heat
Malvern, PA 610-647-0336
Castleberry's
Vineland, NJ 856-691-2100
Catskill Mountain Specialties
Saugerties, NY 800-311-3473
Chandler Foods
Greensboro, NC 800-537-6219
Cherith Valley Gardens
Fort Worth, TX 800-610-9813
Chicago Sweeteners
Des Plaines, IL 847-299-1999
Chipotle Chile Company
Milford, MI. 248-496-8308
Chloe Foods Corporation
Brooklyn, NY 718-827-9000
Christie Food Products
Randolph, MA 800-727-2523
Cinnabar Specialty Foods
Prescott, AZ 866-293-6433
Claussen Pickle Company
Woodstock, IL. 800-435-2817
Clements Foods Company
Oklahoma City, OK 800-654-8355
Commissariat Imports
Los Angeles, CA. 310-475-5628
ConAgra Grocery Products
Irvine, CA 714-680-1000
Conroy Foods
Pittsburgh, PA 412-781-1446

Consumer Guild Foods
Toledo, OH 419-726-3406
Consumers Vinegar & Spice Company
Chicago, IL 773-376-4100
Corfu Foods
Bensenville, IL 630-595-2510
Cosmopolitan Foods
Glen Ridge, NJ 973-680-4560
Country Cupboard
Virginia City, NV 775-847-7300
Curry King Corporation
Waldwick, NJ 800-287-7987
Cyclone Enterprises
Houston, TX 281-872-0087
Daisy Brand
Dallas, TX 877-292-9830
Danisco USA
Lakeland, FL 863-646-0165
Darling International
Cleveland, OH 216-651-9300
Davis Food Company
Plantation, FL 954-791-5868
Dean Distributing Inc
Green Bay, WI 920-469-6500
Delallo Italian Foods
Jeannette, PA 724-523-5000
Delgrosso Foods Inc.
Tipton, PA 800-521-5880
Dhidow Enterprises
Oxford, PA 610-932-7868
Dickson's Pure Honey
San Angelo, TX 915-655-9233
E. Waldo Ward & Son Corporation
Sierra Madre, CA 800-355-9273
Earth Island Natural Foods
Canoga Park, CA 818-725-2820
Ehmann Olive Company
Oroville, CA 530-533-3303
Elwood International
Copiague, NY 631-842-6600
Embasa Foods MegaMex Foods, LLC
Chino, CA 888-236-2272
Europa Foods
Saddle Brook, NJ 201-368-8929
Firth Maple Products
Spartansburg, PA 814-654-7265
Flamm Pickle & Packing Company
Eau Claire, MI 269-461-6916
Flavormatic Industries
Wappingers Falls, NY
Flavors of the Heartland
Rocheport, MO 800-269-3210
Fliinko
South Dartmouth, MA 508-996-9609
Florida Deli Pickle
Fort Lauderdale, FL 954-463-0222
Food City Pickle Company
Chicago, IL
Forge Mountain Foods
Hendersonville, NC 800-823-6743
Fountain Valley Foods
Colorado Springs, CO 719-573-6012
Fox Hollow Farm
Hanover, NH 603-643-6002
Garden Row Foods
St Charles, IL 800-505-9999
Garden Row Foods
Franklin Park, IL 800-555-9798
Gerkens Cacao Wilbur Chocolate Company
Lititz, PA 800-233-0139
Gil's Gourmet Gallery
Sand City, CA 800-438-7480
Glen Rose Meat Company
Vernon, CA 323-589-3393
Golding Farms Foods
Winston Salem, NC 336-766-6161
Graves Mountain Lodge Inc.
Syria, VA 540-923-4747
Green Garden Food Products
Kent, WA 800-304-1033
Groeb Farms
Onsted, MI 517-467-2065
Grouse Hunt Farms
Tamaqua, PA 570-467-2850
Growth Products
Racine, WI 262-637-9287
Half Moon Bay Trading Company
Atlantic Beach, FL 888-447-2823
Halifax Group
Doraville, GA 770-452-8828
Hanson Thompson Honey Farms
Redfield, SD 605-472-0474

Hartford City Foam Pack aging & Converting
Hartford City, IN 765-348-2500
Haus Barhyte
Pendleton, OR 800-407-9241
Hausbeck Pickle Company
Saginaw, MI 866-754-4721
Heintz & Weber Company
Buffalo, NY 716-852-7171
Heinz Company of Canada
North York, ON 877-574-3469
Heller Seasonings
Chicago, IL 800-323-2726
Heluva Good Cheese
Sodus, NY 315-483-6971
Hendon & David
Millbrook, NY 845-677-9696
Herlocher Foods
State College, PA 800-437-5624
Hilltop Herb Farm & Restaurant
Cleveland, TX 832-397-4020
Honey Acres
Ashippun, WI 800-558-7745
Honeypot Treats
Camden, NY 800-223-1024
Howard Foods
Danvers, MA 978-774-6207
Hudson Valley Homestead
Craryville, NY 518-851-7336
Hume Specialties
Chester, VT 802-875-3117
IMEX Enterprises
Hatboro, PA 215-672-2887
Imus Ranch Foods
Darien, CT 505-892-0883
Isabel's Country Mustard
Columbia, MO 877-441-9188
J. G. Van Holten & Son
Waterloo, WI 800-256-0619
J.N. Bech
Elk Rapids, MI 800-232-4583
J.W. Raye & Company
Eastport, ME 800-853-1903
Jalapeno Foods Company
Brea, CA 800-863-9198
Jalapeno Foods Company
The Woodlands, TX 800-896-2318
Jardine Foods
Buda, TX 800-544-1880
Jay Shah Foods
Mississauga, ON 905-696-0172
Joe Hutson Foods
Jacksonville, FL 904-731-9065
Joseph Bertman Foods
Cleveland, OH 216-431-4460
Kaiser Pickles
Cincinnati, OH 888-291-0608
Kaplan & Zubrin
Camden, NJ 800-334-0002
Keller's Creamery
Harleysville, PA 800-535-5371
Khatsa & Company
Bellevue, WA 888-542-8728
Kid's Pantry
Grants Pass, OR 800-452-9551
Kitchen Kettle Foods
Intercourse, PA 800-732-3538
Klein Pickle Company
Phoenix, AZ 602-269-2072
Klein's Kosher Pickles
Phoenix, AZ 602-269-2072
Kozlowski Farms
Forestville, CA 800-473-2767
Kruger Foods
Stockton, CA 209-941-8518
La Vencedora Products
Los Angeles, CA 800-327-2572
Lakeside Packing Company
Harrow, ON 519-738-2314
Lancaster Packing Company
Lancaster, PA 717-397-9727
Landry's Pepper Company
Saint Martinville, LA 337-394-6097
Laredo Mexican Foods
Fort Wayne, IN 800-252-7336
Letraw Manufacturing Company
Rockford, IL 815-987-9670
Lochhead Manufacturing Company
Fenton, MO 888-776-2088
Lounsbury Foods
Toronto, ON 416-656-6330
M&G Honey Farms
Bushton, KS 620-562-3643

M.A. Hatt & Sons
Lunenburg, NS 902-634-8407
Marburger Foods
Peru, IN 765-472-1139
Mardale Specialty Foods
Waukegan, IL 847-336-4777
McCutcheon's Apple Products
Frederick, MD 800-888-7537
Mendocino Mustard
Fort Bragg, CA 800-964-2270
Mo Hotta-Mo Betta
Pooler, GA 912-748-6111
Monticello Canning Company
Crossville, TN 931-484-3696
Mount Olive Pickle Company
Mount Olive, NC 800-672-5041
Mrs. Dog's Products
Grand Rapids, MI 800-2Mr-Dog
National Vinegar Company
Houston, TX 713-223-4214
Nature Quality
San Martin, CA 408-683-2182
Nestelles's
Tangent, OR 50- 2-1 12
New Canaan Farms
Dripping Springs, TX 800-727-5267
New England Natural Baker
Greenfield, MA 800-910-2884
NPC Dehydrators
Eden, NC 336-635-5190
NutraSweet Company
Chicago, IL 800-323-5321
O'Garvey Sauces
New Braunfels, TX 830-620-6127
Oasis Foods Company
Hillside, NJ 908-964-0477
Ocean Spray Cranberries
Kenosha, WI 262-694-5200
Ocean Spray Cranberries
Lakeville-Middleboro, MA 800-662-3263
Ojai Cook
Los Angeles, CA 886-571-1551
Old Dutch Mustard Company
Great Neck, NY 516-466-0522
Olds Products Company
Pleasant Prairie, WI 800-233-8064
Olives & Foods Inc
Hialeah, FL 305-821-3444
Orleans Packing Company
Hyde Park, MA 617-361-6611
Paisley Farms
Willoughby, OH 800-676-8656
Palmieri Food Products
New Haven, CT 800-845-5447
Peaceworks
New York, NY 212-897-3985
Pepper Creek Farms
Lawton, OK 800-526-8132
Peter's Mustards
Sharon, CT 860-364-0842
Plochman
Manteno, IL 815-468-3434
PM AG Products
Homewood, IL 800-323-2663
Precise Food Ingredients
Carrollton, TX 972-323-4951
Quaker Sugar Company
Brooklyn, NY 718-387-6500
R.B. Morriss Company
Diamond Bar, CA 909-861-8671
R.E. Kimball & Company
Amesbury, MA 978-388-1826
Ragsdale-Overton Food Traditions
Smithfield, NC 888-424-8863
Red Gold
Elwood, IN 877-748-9798
Red Pelican Food Products
Detroit, MI 313-881-4095
Refined Sugars
Yonkers, NY 800-431-1020
Reily Foods Company
New Orleans, LA 504-524-6131
Reily Foods/JFG Coffee Company
New Orleans, LA 800-535-1961
Renfro Foods
Fort Worth, TX 817-336-3849
Rex Wine Vinegar Company
Newark, NJ 973-589-6911
Ripon Pickle Company
Ripon, WI 800-324-5493
Robert & James Brands
Birmingham, MI 248-646-0578

Ruby Apiaries
Milnor, ND 701-427-5263
Sal's Caesar Dressing
Novato, CA 415-897-0605
Salad Oils International Corporation
Chicago, IL 773-261-0500
Savannah Food Company
Savannah, TN 800-795-2550
Seminole Foods
Springfield, OH 800-881-1177
Seneca Foods
Clyman, WI 920-696-3331
Shenk's Foods
Lancaster, PA 717-393-4240
Smiling Fox Pepper Company
North Aurora, IL 630-337-3734
Snowizard Extracts
New Orleans, LA 800-366-9766
Somerset Industries
Spring House, PA 800-883-8728
Sperry Apiaries
Kindred, ND 701-428-3000
St. Martin Sugar Cooperative
St Martinville, LA 33- 3-4 37
St. Mary Sugar Cooperative
Jeanerette, LA 337-276-6761
Stage Coach Sauces
Palatka, FL 386-328-6330
Stan-Mark Food Products
Chicago, IL 800-651-0994
Stickney & Poor Company
Peterborough, NH 603-924-2259
Strub Pickles
Brantford, ON 519-751-1717
Sun Valley Mustard
Hailey, ID 800-628-7124
Sunshine Fresh
Totowa, NJ 800-832-8081
Sweet Baby Ray's
Chicago, IL 877-729-2229
T Hasegawa Flavors USA
Cerritos, CA 714-670-1586
T Marzetti Company
Columbus, OH 614-846-2232
T. Marzetti Company
Columbus, OH 614-846-2232
Tapatio Hot Sauce
Vernon, CA 323-587-8933
Target Flavors
Brookfield, CT 800-538-3350
Terrapin Ridge
Clearwater, FL 800-999-4052
Terrapin Ridge Farms
Clearwater, FL 800-999-4052
Thistledew Farm
Proctor, WV 800-854-6639
Tipp Distributors
El Paso, TX 888-668-2639
Tony Packo Food Company
Toledo, OH 866-472-2567
Topper Food Products
East Brunswick, NJ 800-377-2823
Ultimate Gourmet
Belle Mead, NJ 908-359-4050
United Pickle Products Corporation
Bronx, NY 718-933-6060
Van De Walle Farms
San Antonio, TX 210-436-5551
Ventura Foods
Philadelphia, PA 215-223-8700
Ventura Foods
Saginaw, TX 817-232-5450
Vidalia Sweets Brand
Lyons, GA 912-565-8881
Welch's Foods Inc
Kennewick, WA 509-582-2131
Wild Thyme Cottage Products
Pointe Claire, QC 514-695-3602
Wing's Food Products
Etobicoke, ON 416-259-2662
Wing-Time
Steamboat Springs, CO 970-871-1198
Wisconsin Wilderness Food Products
Milwaukee, WI 800-359-3039
Yangtze Agribusiness Group
Great Neck, NY 516-466-1996
Ye Olde Pepper Company
Salem, MA 866-393-6533

Beets

Beetroot Delights
Foothill, ON 888-842-3387

Relishes & Condiments

Baldwin Richardson Foods
Frankfort, IL 866-644-2732

Liquid ingredient manufacturer specializing in signature sauces, dessert toppings, beverage/pancake syrups, specialty fruit fillings and condiments.

Grandma Hoerner's Foods
Alma, KS 785-765-2300
Howard Foods
Danvers, MA 978-774-6207
Marathon Enterprises
Englewood, NJ 800-722-7388
Shawnee Canning Company
Cross Junction, VA 800-713-1414
Texas Sassy Foods
Austin, TX 512-215-4022
Virginia Chutney Company
Washington, VA 540-675-1984

Sauerkraut

A.C. Kissling Company
Philadelphia, PA 800-445-1943
Alimentaire Whyte's Inc
Laval, QC 800-625-1979
Bush Brothers & Co.
Shiocton, WI 920-986-3816
Dietz & Watson
Philadelphia, PA 800-333-1974
Emerling International Foods
Buffalo, NY 716-833-7381

We supply food manufacturers and food service customers worldwide (since 1988) with bulk ingredients including: Fruits & Vegetables; Juice Concentrates; Herbs & Spices; Oils & Vinegars; Flavors & Colors; Honey & Molasses. We also produce PURE MAPLE SYRUP.

Flaum Appetizing
Brooklyn, NY 718-821-1970
Fremont Authentic Brands
Fremont, OH 419-334-8995
Great Lakes Kraut Company
Bear Creek, WI 715-752-4105
Hirzel Canning Company &Farms
Northwood, OH 419-693-0531
Kaiser Pickles
Cincinnati, OH 888-291-0608
Kruger Foods
Stockton, CA 209-941-8518
Lakeside Foods
Seymour, WI 920-833-2371
Lakeside Packing Company
Harrow, ON 519-738-2314
Marathon Enterprises
Englewood, NJ 800-722-7388
Miramar Pickles & Food Products
Fort Lauderdale, FL 954-351-8030
New Harvest Foods
Pulaski, WI 920-822-2578
Red Pelican Food Products
Detroit, MI 313-881-4095
Ripon Pickle Company
Ripon, WI 800-324-5493
Schwartz Pickle Company
Chicago, IL 773-927-7700
Strub Pickles
Brantford, ON 519-751-1717
United Pickle Products Corporation
Bronx, NY 718-933-6060
Victor Preserving Company
Ontario, NY 315-524-2711

Juice

Claussen Pickle Company
Woodstock, IL 800-435-2817
Fremont Authentic Brands
Fremont, OH 419-334-8995
Gwaltney of Smithfield
Smithfield, VA 800-888-7521
Hirzel Canning Company &Farms
Northwood, OH 419-693-0531
Kaiser Pickles
Cincinnati, OH 888-291-0608
Leo G. Fraboni Sausage Company
Hibbing, MN 218-263-5074
M.A. Hatt & Sons
Lunenburg, NS 902-634-8407

Sauces, Dips & Dressings

Condiments

3Gyros Inc
Windsor, ON 519-257-8668
A Taste of the Kingdom
Kingdom City, MO 888-592-5080
A.M. Braswell Jr. Food Company
Statesboro, GA 800-673-9388
Alimentaire Whyte's Inc
Laval, QC 800-625-1979
Allied Old English
Port Reading, NJ 732-636-2060
Aloha Shoyu Company LTD.
Pearl City, HI 808-456-5929
American Spoon Foods
Petoskey, MI 800-222-5886
Appledore Cove LLC
North Berwick, ME 207-676-4088
Ashman Manufacturing & Distributing Company
Virginia Beach, VA 800-641-9924
Atlantic Quality Spice &Seasonings
New Brunswick, NJ 800-584-0422
Au Printemps Gourmet
Saint-Jerome, QC 800-663-0416
August Kitchen
Armonk, NY 914-589-6477
Bartush-Schnitzius Foods Company
Lewisville, TX 972-219-1270
Baumer Foods
Metairie, LA 504-482-5761
Bear Meadow Farm
Colrain, MA 800-653-9241
Beetroot Delights
Foothill, ON 888-842-3387
Bel/Kaukauna USA
Kaukauna, WI 800-558-3500
Bessinger Pickle Company
Au Gres, MI 989-876-8008
Best Boy
Fort Wayne, IN 260-426-2474
Bettah Buttah, LLC
Kansas City, KS 800-568-8468
Betty Lou's Golden Smackers
McMinnville, OR 800-242-5205
Big B Distributors
Evansville, IN 812-425-5235
Bob Gordon & Associates
Oak Park, IL 708-524-9611
Bobby D'S
Minnetonka, MN 954-240-9108
Boetje Foods
Rock Island, IL 877-726-3853
Bone Doctors' BBQ,LLC
Charlottesville, VA 434-296-7766
Border Foods Inc
Deming, NM 888-737-7752
Brad's Taste of New York
Floral Park, NY 516-354-9004
Bradley Technologies Canada Inc.
Delta, BC 800-665-4188
Brede
Detroit, MI 313-273-1079
Brothers Sauces
Fort Worth, TX 817-821-3374
Bryant Preserving Company
Alma, AR 800-634-2413
Bush Brothers & Co.
Shiocton, WI 920-986-3816
C&E Canners
Hammonton, NJ 609-561-1078
Cains Foods
Ayer, MA 800-225-0601
CaJohns Fiery Foods
Westerville, OH 888-703-3473
Cajun Chef Products
Saint Martinville, LA 337-394-7112
California Creative Foods
Oceanside, CA 760-757-2622
Caltex Foods
Canoga Park, CA 800-522-5839
Capa Di Roma, Inc
East Hartford, CT 860-282-0298
Carol Hall's Hot Pepper Jelly
Fort Bragg, CA 866-737-7379
Carolina Treet
Wilmington, NC 800-616-6344
Carolyn's Caribbean Heat
Malvern, PA 610-647-0336
Carriage House Companies
Fredonia, NY 800-462-8125
Casa Visco Finer Food Company
Schenectady, NY 888-607-2823
Castleberry's
Vineland, NJ 856-691-2100
Cedarvale Food Products Lounsbury Food Ltd
Toronto, ON 416-656-3331
Chandler Foods
Greensboro, NC 800-537-6219
Charles Faraud C/O Pramex
New York, NY
Chef Silvio's of Wooster Street
Guilford, CT 203-453-1064
Chef Tim Foods, LLC
Etters, PA 717-802-0350
Chicago 58 Food Products
Woodbridge, ON 416-603-4244
Chloe Foods Corporation
Brooklyn, NY 718-827-9000
Christie Food Products
Randolph, MA 800-727-2523
Christopher Ranch
Gilroy, CA 408-847-1100
CHS, Inc.
Inner Grove Heights, MN 800-232-3639
Cinnabar Specialty Foods
Prescott, AZ 866-293-6433
Clements Foods Company
Oklahoma City, OK 800-654-8355
Cold Hollow Cider Mill
Waterbury Center, VT 800-327-7537
Commissariat Imports
Los Angeles, CA 310-475-5628
Consumers Vinegar & Spice Company
Chicago, IL 773-376-4100
Cordoba Foods LLC
Hialeah, FL 786-925-9072
Corfu Foods
Bensenville, IL 630-595-2510
Creative Foodworks
San Antonio, TX 210-212-4761
Creole Fermentation Industries
Abbeville, LA 337-898-9377
Cuizina Food Company
Woodinville, WA 425-486-7000
Cumberland Packing Corporation
Brooklyn, NY 718-222-3233
Dave's Gourmet
San Francisco, CA 800-758-0372
Deer Mountain Berry Farms
Granite Falls, WA 360-691-7586
Diamond Crystal Brands
Savannah, GA 800-654-5115
Doral International
Bayside, NY 718-224-7413
Dorina/So-Good
Union, IL 815-923-2144
Dragunara LLC
Palos Verdes Estate, CA 310-618-8818
Earth Island Natural Foods
Canoga Park, CA 818-725-2820
Edward & Sons Trading Company
Carpinteria, CA 805-684-8500
El Paso Chile Company
El Paso, TX 888-472-5727
El Toro Food Products
Watsonville, CA 831-728-9266
Elwood International
Copiague, NY 631-842-6600
Enrico's/Ventre Packing
Syracuse, NY 888-472-8237
Erba Food Products
Brooklyn, NY 718-272-7700
Famous Chili
Fort Smith, AR 479-782-0096
Fernandez Chili Company
Alamosa, CO 719-589-6043
Fireside Kitchen
Halifax, NS 902-454-7387
Ford's Fancy Fruit
Raleigh, NC 800-446-0947
Ford's Foods, Inc.
Raleigh, NC 800-446-0947
Fountain Valley Foods
Colorado Springs, CO 719-573-6012
Freda Quality Meats
Philadelphia, PA 800-443-7332
Fremont Authentic Brands
Fremont, OH 419-334-8995
French's Flavor Ingredients
Springfield, MO 800-437-3624
Garden Complements
Kansas City, MO 800-966-1091
GE Barbour
Sussex, NB 506-432-2300
GFA Brands
Paramus, NJ 201-568-9300
GFF
City of Industry, CA 323-846-2700
Gibbons Bee Farm
Ballwin, MO 877-736-8607
Gingras Vinegar
Rougemont, QC 514-293-4591
Girard's Food Service Dressings
City of Industry, CA 888-327-8442
Golden Gate Foods
Dallas, TX 214-747-2223
Golden Specialty Foods
Norwalk, CA 562-802-2537
Golden Valley Foods
Abbotsford, BC 888-299-8855
Golden Whisk
South San Francisco, CA 800-660-5222
Gourmet Central
Romney, WV 800-984-3722
Goya Foods
Secaucus, NJ 201-348-4900
Graysmarsh Farm
Sequim, WA 800-683-4367
Greaves Jams & Marmalades
Niagara-on-the-Lake, ON 800-515-9939
Green Garden Food Products
Kent, WA 800-304-1033
Griffin Food Company
Muskogee, OK 800-580-6311
GWB Foods Corporation
Brooklyn, NY 877-977-7610
H.J. Heinz Company
Pittsburgh, PA 800-872-2229
Halben Food Manufacturing Company
Saint Louis, MO 800-888-4855
Happy Goat
Menlo Park, CA 650-922-8667
Harpo's
Honolulu, HI 808-735-6456
Hawaiian Fruit Specialties
Kalaheo, HI 808-332-9333
Heinz Company of Canada
North York, ON 877-574-3469
Heinz Portion Control
Mason, OH 800-547-8924
Hell on the Red
Telephone, TX 903-664-2573
Hipard International
Tinguindin, MC
Hombres Foods
Cedar Creek, TX 877-446-6273
Homegrown Naturals
Napa, CA 800-288-1089
Hoople Country Kitchens
Rockport, IN 812-649-2351
Hormel Foods Corporation
Austin, MN 800-523-4635
House of Spices India
Flushing, NY 718-507-4900
House of Webster
Rogers, AR 800-369-4641
Howjax
Pembroke Pines, FL 954-441-2491
HSR Associates
Tarzana, CA 818-757-7152
HVJ International
Spring, TX 877-730-3663
Hyde & Hyde
Corona, CA 951-817-2300
I Heart Olive Oil
Ft Lauderdale, FL 954-607-1539
Instantwhip: Florida
Tampa, FL 813-621-3233

International Food Products Corporation
Saint Louis, MO 314-421-6151
International Home Foods
Parsippany, NJ. . . . 973-359-9920
J.N. Bech
Elk Rapids, MI 800-232-4583
Jalapeno Foods Company
The Woodlands, TX 800-896-2318
Jasmine & Bread
South Royalton, VT 802-763-7115
Jayone Foods, Inc/G. East Co., LTD
Paramount, CA 562-633-7400
JMS Specialty Foods
Ripon, WI 800-535-5437
John Volpi & Company
St Louis, MO. . . . 800-288-3439
Junuis Food Products
Palatine, IL 847-359-4300
Kamish Food Products
Chicago, IL 773-725-6959
Kari-Out Company
White Plains, NY 800-433-8799
Kathy's Gourmet Specialties
Mendocino, CA. . . . 707-937-1383
KC Innovations
Kansas City, KS 816-506-9023
Ken's Foods
Marlborough, MA. . . . 800-633-5800
Kitchen Kettle Foods
Intercourse, PA 800-732-3538
Knese Enterprise
Bellerose, NY 516-354-9004
Kozlowski Farms
Forestville, CA 800-473-2767
Kraft Foods
Garland, TX 972-272-7511
Krinos Foods
Santa Barbara, CA 800-624-4896
Kruger Foods
Stockton, CA. . . . 209-941-8518
L&S Packing Company
Farmingdale, NY 800-286-6487
La Ferme Martinette
Coaticook, QC 819-849-7089
La Morena
Huamantla, TL 222-211-0515
Lakeside Foods
Seymour, WI. . . . 920-833-2371
Lakeside Packing Company
Harrow, ON. . . . 519-738-2314
Landry's Pepper Company
Saint Martinville, LA 337-394-6097
Le Caramel
La Mesa, CA. . . . 619-562-0713
Lea & Perrins
Fair Lawn, NJ 800-289-5797
Lee Kum Kee
Flushing, NY. . . . 800-346-7562
Lefty Spices
Waldorf, MD. . . . 301-885-1817
Letterman Enterprises Inc.
State College, PA 814-574-4339
Li'l Guy Foods
Kansas City, MO. . . . 800-886-8226
Liberty Richter
Saddle Brook, NJ 201-291-8749
Litehouse Foods
Sandpoint, ID 800-669-3169
Lounsbury Foods
Toronto, ON 416-656-6330
M.A. Gedney
Chaska, MN 952-448-2612
Mad Will's Food Company
Auburn, CA. . . . 888-275-9455
Marathon Enterprises
Englewood, NJ 800-722-7388
Mardale Specialty Foods
Waukegan, IL 847-336-4777
Marsa Specialty Products
Vernon, CA 800-628-0500
Marukan Vinegar (U.S.A.) Inc.
Paramount, CA 562-630-6060
McIlhenny Company
Avery Island, LA. . . . 800-634-9599
Miguel's Stowe Away
Stowe, VT. . . . 800-448-6517
Mizkam Americas
Kansas City, MO. . . . 816-483-1700
Modern Packaging
Duluth, GA 770-622-1500
Morgan Food
Austin, IN 888-430-1780
Morse's Sauerkraut
Waldoboro, ME. . . . 866-832-5569
Mother Shucker's Original Cocktail Sauce
Columbia, SC 803-261-3802
Mullins Food Products
Broadview, IL. . . . 708-344-3224
Musco Olive Products
Orland, CA 530-865-4111
Nature Quality
San Martin, CA. . . . 408-683-2182
New Canaan Farms
Dripping Springs, TX. . . . 800-727-5267
New England Natural Baker
Greenfield, MA. . . . 800-910-2884
Oasis Foods Company
Hillside, NJ 908-964-0477
Oberweis Dairy
North Aurora, IL. . . . 888-645-5868
Olde Tyme Mercantile
Arroyo Grande, CA. . . . 805-489-7991
Olympia International
Belvidere, IL. . . . 815-547-5972
Once Again Nut Butter
Nunda, NY 888-800-8075
Pacific Choice Brands
Fresno, CA 559-237-5583
Palmieri Food Products
New Haven, CT 800-845-5447
Paradise Products Corporation
Boca Raton, FL. . . . 800-826-1235
Passage Foods LLC
Collinsville, CT. . . . 800-860-1045
Pastene Companies
Canton, MA 781-830-8200
Phamous Phloyd's Barbeque Sauce
Denver, CO. . . . 303-757-3285
Piknik Products Company Inc
Montgomery, AL. . . . 334-240-2218
Pilgrim Foods
Greenville, NH 603-878-2100
Pineland Farms
New Gloucester, ME. . . . 207-688-8085
Pondini Imports, Inc
Somerset, NJ. . . . 732-545-1255
Porinos Gourmet Food
Central Falls, RI 800-826-3938
Prairie Thyme
Santa Fe, NM 800-869-0009
Productos Del Plata, Inc
Miami, FL. . . . 786-357-8261
Progress Industries
Mansfield, OH 419-756-0044
Purity Farms
Sedalia, CO. . . . 800-568-4433
Purity Products
Plainview, NY. . . . 888-769-7873
Ralph Sechler & Son Inc
St Joe, IN. . . . 800-332-5461
Rapazzini Winery
Gilroy, CA. . . . 800-842-6262
Ready Foods
Denver, CO 720-889-1104
Reser's Fine Foods
Salt Lake City, UT 801-972-5633
Restaurant Lulu Gourmet Products
San Francisco, CA 888-693-5800
REX Pure Foods
New Orleans, LA 800-344-8314
Richardson Foods Corporation
Macedon, NY 315-986-2807
River Run
Burlington, VT 802-863-0499
Rod's Food Products
City of Industry, CA 909-839-8925
Roller Ed
Rochester, NY. . . . 585-458-8020
Rowena's
Norfolk, VA. . . . 800-627-8699
Royal Food Products
Indianapolis, IN 317-782-2660
S&G Products
Nicholasville, KY 800-826-7652
Sambets Cajun Deli
Austin, TX. . . . 800-472-6238
San Benito Foods
Hollister, CA. . . . 831-637-4434
Santa Barbara Olive Company
Santa Barbara, CA 800-624-4896
Savannah Food Company
Savannah, TN 800-795-2550
Savoie's Sausage & Food Products
Opelousas, LA. . . . 337-948-4115
Schlotterbeck & Foss Company
Portland, ME. . . . 800-777-4666
Schoolhouse Kitchen LLC
Brooklyn, NY 718-855-4990
Schwartz Pickle Company
Chicago, IL 773-927-7700
Scott-Bathgate
Winnipeg, MB. . . . 800-216-2990
Seneca Foods
Clyman, WI. . . . 920-696-3331
Shenk's Foods
Lancaster, PA 717-393-4240
Silver Palate Kitchens
Cresskill, NJ 800-872-5283
Silver Spring Gardens
Eau Claire, WI 800-826-7322
Sir Kensington's Gourmet Scooping Kitchen
New York, NY 646-450-5735
Sisler's Ice & Ice Cream
Ohio, IL. . . . 888-891-3856
Skillet Street Food
Seattle, WA 425-998-9817
Skjodt-Barrett Foods
Mississauga, ON. . . . 877-600-1200
Somerset Industries
Spring House, PA 800-883-8728
Spanish Gardens Food Manufacturing
Kansas City, KS 913-831-4242
Spectrum Organic Products
Petaluma, CA 800-995-2705
Sprague Foods
Belleville, ON. . . . 613-966-1200
Steel's Gourmet Foods, Ltd.
Bridgeport, PA 800-678-3357
Stickney & Poor Company
Peterborough, NH. . . . 603-924-2259
Stonewall Kitchen
York, ME. . . . 800-207-5267
Strub Pickles
Brantford, ON. . . . 519-751-1717
Sue Bee Honey
Sioux City, IA. . . . 712-258-0638
Sumida Pickle Products
Honolulu, HI. . . . 808-593-2487
T. Marzetti Company
Columbus, OH 614-846-2232
Tamarind Tree
Neshanic Station, NJ. . . . 800-432-8733
Target Flavors
Brookfield, CT 800-538-3350
Taste Teasers
Dallas, TX. . . . 800-526-1840
Terrell's Potato Chip Company
Syracuse, NY 315-437-2786
Texas Heat
San Antonio, TX. . . . 800-656-5916
The Lollipop Tree, Inc
Auburn, NY. . . . 800-842-6691
Thompson's Fine Foods
Shoreview, MN. . . . 800-807-0025
Thor-Shackel HorseradishCompany
Eau Claire, WI 800-826-7322
Thumann's
Carlstadt, NJ 201-935-3636
Trappist Preserves
Cleveland, OH 800-472-0425
Tribe Mediterranean Foods Company LLC
Taunton, MA. . . . 774-961-0000
Tropical
Charlotte, NC 800-220-1413
Tulkoff Food Products
Baltimore, MD 800-638-7343
Tutto Sicilia
New Britain, CT
Twang
San Antonio, TX. . . . 800-950-8095
Two Chefs on a Roll
Carson, CA 800-842-3025
Ultra Seal
New Paltz, NY 845-255-2490
Unette Corporation
Randolph, NJ 973-328-6800
Unilever United States
Englewood Cliffs, NJ 201-894-4000
V & V Supremo Foods
Chicago, IL 888-887-8773
Ventura Foods
Ontario, CA. . . . 323-262-9157
Ventura Foods
Salem, OR. . . . 503-585-6423
Vienna Sausage Company
Chicago, IL 800-366-3647

Village Imports
Brisbane, CA.......................888-865-8714
Wagner Gourmet Foods
Lenexa, KS.......................913-469-5411
Walker Foods
Los Angeles, CA.......................800-966-5199
Wei-Chuan
Bell Gardens, CA.......................562-372-2020
Welch's Foods Inc
Concord, MA.......................800-340-6870
Welch's Foods Inc.
North East, PA.......................814-725-4577
Westbrae Natural Foods
Melville, NY.......................800-434-4246
Westin
Omaha, NE.......................800-228-6098
Westport Rivers Vineyard& Winery
Westport, MA.......................800-993-9695
Wild Thymes Farm
Greenville, NY.......................800-724-2877
Wing Nien Company
Hayward, CA.......................510-487-8877
Wings Foods of Alberta
Edmonton, AB.......................780-433-6406
Wisconsin Spice
Berlin, WI.......................920-361-3555
Woeber Mustard Manufacturing
Springfield, OH.......................800-548-2929
Wood Brothers
West Columbia, SC.......................803-796-5146
Woodlake Ranch
Woodlake, CA.......................559-564-2161
Woody's Bar-B-Q Sauce Company
Waldenburg, AR.......................870-579-2251
World Harbors
Auburn, ME.......................800-355-6221
York Mountain Winery
Templeton, CA.......................805-237-7575
Zatarain's
Gretna, LA.......................800-435-6639

Dips

A.M. Braswell Jr. Food Company
Statesboro, GA.......................800-673-9388
Abraham's Natural Foods
Long Branch, NJ.......................800-327-9903
Amigos Canning Company
San Antonio, TX.......................800-580-3477
Anderson Erickson Dairy
Des Moines, IA.......................515-265-2521
Appledore Cove LLC
North Berwick, ME.......................207-676-4088
Arbor Hill Grapery
Naples, NY.......................800-554-7553
Ashman Manufacturing & Distributing Company
Virginia Beach, VA.......................800-641-9924
Ask Foods
Palmyra, PA.......................800-879-4275
Au Printemps Gourmet
Saint-Jerome, QC.......................800-663-0416
Baptista's Bakery
Franklin, WI.......................877-261-3157
Barber's Dairy
Birmingham, AL.......................205-942-2351
Bear Creek Country Kitchens
Heber City, UT.......................800-516-7286
Bear Creek Kitchens
Marshall, TX.......................888-300-7687
Bel/Kaukauna USA
Kaukauna, WI.......................800-558-3500
Blount Fine Foods
Fall River, MA.......................774-888-1300
Bread Dip Company
Philadelphia, PA.......................215-563-9455
Bread Dip Company
Friday Harbor, WA.......................360-378-6070
Bruno's Cajun Foods & Snacks
Slidell, LA.......................985-726-0544
Byrne Dairy
Syracuse, NY.......................800-899-1535
Cass Clay Creamery
Fargo, ND.......................701-293-6455
Chelten House Products
Bridgeport, NJ.......................856-467-1600
Consun Food Industries
Elyria, OH.......................440-322-6301
Country Cupboard
Virginia City, NV.......................775-847-7300
Crazy Jerry's
Roswell, GA.......................770-993-0651
Creamland Dairies
Albuquerque, NM.......................505-247-0721

Creative Foodworks
San Antonio, TX.......................210-212-4761
Crowley Foods
Binghamton, NY.......................800-637-0019
Culinary Standards Corporation
Louisville, KY.......................800-778-3434
Custom Ingredients
New Braunfels, TX.......................800-457-8935
Dairy Fresh Corporation
Greensboro, AL.......................800-239-5114
DCI Cheese Company
Richfield, WI.......................262-677-3407
Dixie Dew Products
Erlanger, KY.......................800-867-8548
Dorina/So-Good
Union, IL.......................815-923-2144
El Toro Food Products
Watsonville, CA.......................831-728-9266
Flamous Brands
San Gabriel, CA.......................626-551-3201
Fountain Valley Foods
Colorado Springs, CO.......................719-573-6012
Franklin Foods
Enosburg Falls, VT.......................800-933-6114
Garden Complements
Kansas City, MO.......................800-966-1091
Golden Specialty Foods
Norwalk, CA.......................562-802-2537
Goldwater's Food's Of Arizona
Fredericksburg, TX.......................800-488-4932
Gourmet Village
Morin Heights, QC.......................800-668-2314
Guiltless Gourmet The Manischewitz Company
Secaucus, NJ.......................201-553-1100
Halladays Harvest Barn
Bellows Falls, VT.......................802-463-3331
Havana's Limited
Titusville, FL.......................321-267-0513
Havoc Maker Products
Guilford, CT.......................800-681-3909
Helens Pure Foods
Cheltenham, PA.......................215-379-6433
Heluva Good Cheese
Sodus, NY.......................315-483-6971
Herb Patch of Vermont
Bellows Falls, VT.......................800-282-4372
Herkimer Foods
Herkimer, NY.......................315-895-7832
Herlocher Foods
State College, PA.......................800-437-5624
Hiland Dairy Foods Company
Branson, MO.......................417-334-0090
Hirzel Canning Company &Farms
Northwood, OH.......................419-693-0531
Hombres Foods
Cedar Creek, TX.......................877-446-6273
Innovative Ingredients
Reisterstown, MD.......................888-403-2907
Intercorp Excelle Foods
North York, ON.......................416-226-5757
Jalapeno Foods Company
The Woodlands, TX.......................800-896-2318
Kentucky Beer Cheese
Nicholasville, KY.......................859-887-1645
Knese Enterprise
Bellerose, NY.......................516-354-9004
Kraft Foods
Walton, NY.......................607-865-7131
Leigh Olivers
Tyler, TX.......................903-245-9183
Litehouse
Sandpoint, ID.......................208-263-7569
Litehouse Foods
Sandpoint, ID.......................800-669-3169
Look's Gourmet Food Company
East Machias, ME.......................800-962-6258
Lost Trail Root Beer Com
Louisburg, KS.......................800-748-7765
Low Country Produce
Lobeco, SC.......................800-935-2792
Martin's Famous Pastry Shoppe, Inc
Chambersburg, PA.......................800-548-1200
Mayfield Dairy Farms
Athens, TN.......................800-362-9546
Mid States Dairy
Hazelwood, MO.......................314-731-1150
Mixon Fruit Farms
Bradenton, FL.......................800-608-2525
Naturally Fresh Foods
Atlanta, GA.......................800-765-1950
New Canaan Farms
Dripping Springs, TX.......................800-727-5267

Outta The Park Eats, Inc
Cary, NC.......................919-462-0012
Penn Maid Crowley Foods
Philadelphia, PA.......................800-247-6269
Phillips Foods
Baltimore, MD.......................888-234-2722
Pied-Mont/Dora
Ste Anne Des Plaines, QC.......................800-363-8003
Prairie Farms Dairy
Carlinville, IL.......................217-854-2547
Prairie Farms Dairy Inc.
Carlinville, IL.......................217-854-2547
Productos Del Plata, Inc
Miami, FL.......................786-357-8261
Quality Foods
San Pedro, CA.......................877-833-7890
Refrigerated Foods Association
Chamblee, GA.......................770-452-0660
Renfro Foods
Fort Worth, TX.......................817-336-3849
Reser's Fine Foods
Beaverton, OR.......................800-333-6431
Road's End Organics
Stowe, VT.......................877-247-3373
Robert Rothschild Berry Farm
Urbana, OH.......................866-565-6790
Rod's Food Products
City of Industry, CA.......................909-839-8925
Sabra Dipping Company
White Plains, NY.......................888-957-2272
Sabra-Go Mediterranean
Dallas, TX.......................888-957-2272
Sambets Cajun Deli
Austin, TX.......................800-472-6238
Schneider Valley Farms Dairy
Williamsport, PA.......................570-326-2021
Sea Gold Seafood Products
New Bedford, MA.......................508-993-3060
Sentry Seasonings
Elmhurst, IL.......................630-530-5370

The product development experts of Sentry Seasonings are eager to offer the assistance and hands-on experience to food processors of all sizes. Sentry Seasonings will ensure the consistent high quality and repeat sales of your products, whether you choose one of our many off-the-shelf Bench Mark products or a modified version to meet your preferences. Sentry Seasonings can also duplicate and/or improve your present flavor profile; formulate, blend and package specifically for your requirements.

Sheila's Select Gourmet Recipe
Heber City, UT.......................800-516-7286
Shine Companies
Spring, TX.......................281-353-8392
Shooting Star Farms
Bartlesville, OK.......................888-850-8540
Simeus Foods International
Mansfield, TX.......................888-772-3663
Sinton Dairy Foods Company
Colorado Springs, CO.......................800-388-4970
Sterzing Food Company
Burlington, IA.......................800-754-8467
Texas Heat
San Antonio, TX.......................800-656-5916
Thompson's Fine Foods
Shoreview, MN.......................800-807-0025
Tova Industries
Louisville, KY.......................888-532-8682
Tribe Mediterranean Foods Company LLC
Taunton, MA.......................774-961-0000
Two Chefs on a Roll
Carson, CA.......................800-842-3025
US Chocolate Corporation
Brooklyn, NY.......................718-788-8555
Ventre Packing Company
Syracuse, NY.......................888-472-8237
Victoria Packing Corporation
Brooklyn, NY.......................718-927-3000
Wells' Dairy
Le Mars, IA.......................800-942-3800
Wild West Spices
Cody, WY.......................888-587-8887
William Poll
New York, NY.......................800-993-7655

Bean

Garden Complements
Kansas City, MO.......................800-966-1091

Hormel Foods Corporation
Austin, MN 800-523-4635
Sentry Seasonings
Elmhurst, IL 630-530-5370

The product development experts of Sentry Seasonings are eager to offer the assistance and hands-on experience to food processors of all sizes. Sentry Seasonings will ensure the consistent high quality and repeat sales of your products, whether you choose one of our many off-the-shelf Bench Mark products or a modified version to meet your preferences. Sentry Seasonings can also duplicate and/or improve your present flavor profile; formulate, blend and package specifically for your requirements.

Ventre Packing Company
Syracuse, NY 888-472-8237

Cheese

Better Made Snack Foods
Detroit, MI 800-332-2394
Hell on the Red
Telephone, TX. 903-664-2573
Hormel Foods Corporation
Austin, MN 800-523-4635
Kentucky Beer Cheese
Nicholasville, KY 859-887-1645
Sentry Seasonings
Elmhurst, IL 630-530-5370

The product development experts of Sentry Seasonings are eager to offer the assistance and hands-on experience to food processors of all sizes. Sentry Seasonings will ensure the consistent high quality and repeat sales of your products, whether you choose one of our many off-the-shelf Bench Mark products or a modified version to meet your preferences. Sentry Seasonings can also duplicate and/or improve your present flavor profile; formulate, blend and package specifically for your requirements.

Southernfood Specialties
Atlanta, GA. 800-255-5323
Texas Heat
San Antonio, TX. 800-656-5916
Ventre Packing Company
Syracuse, NY 888-472-8237

Chili

Food Processor of New Mexico
Albuquerque, NM. 877-634-3772
Golden Specialty Foods
Norwalk, CA. 562-802-2537
Sentry Seasonings
Elmhurst, IL 630-530-5370

The product development experts of Sentry Seasonings are eager to offer the assistance and hands-on experience to food processors of all sizes. Sentry Seasonings will ensure the consistent high quality and repeat sales of your products, whether you choose one of our many off-the-shelf Bench Mark products or a modified version to meet your preferences. Sentry Seasonings can also duplicate and/or improve your present flavor profile; formulate, blend and package specifically for your requirements.

Chip

Amigos Canning Company
San Antonio, TX. 800-580-3477
Consun Food Industries
Elyria, OH. 440-322-6301
Dorina/So-Good
Union, IL. 815-923-2144
Rod's Food Products
City of Industry, CA 909-839-8925

Sentry Seasonings
Elmhurst, IL 630-530-5370

The product development experts of Sentry Seasonings are eager to offer the assistance and hands-on experience to food processors of all sizes. Sentry Seasonings will ensure the consistent high quality and repeat sales of your products, whether you choose one of our many off-the-shelf Bench Mark products or a modified version to meet your preferences. Sentry Seasonings can also duplicate and/or improve your present flavor profile; formulate, blend and package specifically for your requirements.

Guacamole

Jalapeno Foods Company
The Woodlands, TX 800-896-2318
Sentry Seasonings
Elmhurst, IL 630-530-5370

The product development experts of Sentry Seasonings are eager to offer the assistance and hands-on experience to food processors of all sizes. Sentry Seasonings will ensure the consistent high quality and repeat sales of your products, whether you choose one of our many off-the-shelf Bench Mark products or a modified version to meet your preferences. Sentry Seasonings can also duplicate and/or improve your present flavor profile; formulate, blend and package specifically for your requirements.

Salsa

Alicita-Salsa
Great Falls, VA 703-406-1275
Allied Old English
Port Reading, NJ. 732-636-2060
Arizona Beverage Company
Woodbury, NY 800-832-3775
Bachman Company
Reading, PA 800-523-8253
Bel/Kaukauna USA
Kaukauna, WI. 800-558-3500
Bettah Buttah, LLC
Kansas City, KS 800-568-8468
Bingo Salsa, LLC
Poulsbo, WA 360-779-6746
Border Foods Inc
Deming, NM. 888-737-7752
Bread Dip Company
Friday Harbor, WA 360-378-6070
Casa Visco Finer Food Company
Schenectady, NY. 888-607-2823
Choice of Vermont
Destin, FL 800-444-6261
Colorado Salsa Company
Littleton, CO. 303-932-2617
El Paso Chile Company
El Paso, TX. 888-472-5727
Fountain Valley Foods
Colorado Springs, CO. 719-573-6012
Franklin Foods
Enosburg Falls, VT. 800-933-6114
Frontera Foods
Chicago, IL 800-509-4441
Golden Specialty Foods
Norwalk, CA. 562-802-2537
Golden Valley Foods
Abbotsford, BC. 888-299-8855
Granny Blossom Specialty Foods
Wells, VT 802-645-0507
Green Mountain Gringo
Winston Salem, NC
Herlocher Foods
State College, PA 800-437-5624
Jalapeno Foods Company
The Woodlands, TX 800-896-2318
Kind Snacks
New York, NY 800-732-2321
Li'l Guy Foods
Kansas City, MO. 800-886-8226
Maggie's Salsa
Charleston, WV 304-550-5460
Native South Services
Fredericksburg, TX. 800-236-2848
New Canaan Farms
Dripping Springs, TX 800-727-5267
North of the Border
Tesuque, NM. 800-860-0681

Old Home Foods
Saint Paul, MN 800-309-9035
Pacific Choice Brands
Fresno, CA 559-237-5583
Quality Foods
San Pedro, CA. 877-833-7890
Ready Foods
Denver, CO 720-889-1104
Royal Resources
New Orleans, LA 800-888-9932
Sentry Seasonings
Elmhurst, IL 630-530-5370

The product development experts of Sentry Seasonings are eager to offer the assistance and hands-on experience to food processors of all sizes. Sentry Seasonings will ensure the consistent high quality and repeat sales of your products, whether you choose one of our many off-the-shelf Bench Mark products or a modified version to meet your preferences. Sentry Seasonings can also duplicate and/or improve your present flavor profile; formulate, blend and package specifically for your requirements.

Shooting Star Farms
Bartlesville, OK 888-850-8540
T.W. Garner Food Company
Winston Salem, NC. 800-476-7383
Terrell's Potato Chip Company
Syracuse, NY 315-437-2786
Ventre Packing Company
Syracuse, NY 888-472-8237

Glazes

A Taste of the Kingdom
Kingdom City, MO 888-592-5080
Abel & Schafer
Ronkonkoma, NY. 800-443-1260
Ashman Manufacturing & Distributing Company
Virginia Beach, VA. 800-641-9924
Bakemark Ingredients Canada
Richmond, BC 800-665-9441
Baker & Baker, Inc.
Schaumburg, IL. 800-593-5777
Genarom International
Cranbury, NJ 609-409-6200
Gracious Gourmet
Bridgewater, CT 860-350-1213
Howard Foods
Danvers, MA. 978-774-6207
Newly Weds Foods
Chicago, IL 800-621-7521
Newport Flavours & Fragrances
Orange, CA. 714-744-3700
Puratos Canada
Mississauga, ON. 905-362-3668
Sentry Seasonings
Elmhurst, IL 630-530-5370

The product development experts of Sentry Seasonings are eager to offer the assistance and hands-on experience to food processors of all sizes. Sentry Seasonings will ensure the consistent high quality and repeat sales of your products, whether you choose one of our many off-the-shelf Bench Mark products or a modified version to meet your preferences. Sentry Seasonings can also duplicate and/or improve your present flavor profile; formulate, blend and package specifically for your requirements.

Valley View Blueberries
Vancouver, WA 360-892-2839

Gravy

Ailments E.D. Foods Inc.
Pointe Claire, QC 800-267-3333
Atlantic Seasonings
Kinston, NC 800-433-5261
Aunt Kitty's Foods
Vineland, NJ 856-691-2100
Cagnon Foods Company
Brooklyn, NY 718-647-2244
Campbell Soup Company
Camden, NJ. 800-257-8443
Castleberry's
Vineland, NJ 856-691-2100
Cordon Bleu International
Anjou, QC. 514-352-3000

Custom Culinary
Lombard, IL 800-621-8827

Diversified Foods & Seasoning
Metairie, LA 504-846-5090

Edmonds Chile Company
St Louis, MO 314-772-1499

Griffith Laboratories Worldwide
Alsip, IL 800-346-4743

Mayacamas Fine Foods
Sonoma, CA 800-826-9621

O Chili Frozen Foods Inc
Northbrook, IL 847-562-1991

Praters Foods
Lubbock, TX 806-745-2727

R.L. Schreiber
Pompano Beach, FL 800-624-8777

R.L. Schreiber Company
Pompano Beach, FL 800-624-8777

Sambets Cajun Deli
Austin, TX 800-472-6238

Savannah Food Company
Savannah, TN 800-795-2550

Schlotterbeck & Foss Company
Portland, ME 800-777-4666

Select Food Products
Toronto, ON 800-699-8016

Sentry Seasonings
Elmhurst, IL 630-530-5370

The product development experts of Sentry Seasonings are eager to offer the assistance and hands-on experience to food processors of all sizes. Sentry Seasonings will ensure the consistent high quality and repeat sales of your products, whether you choose one of our many off-the-shelf Bench Mark products or a modified version to meet your preferences. Sentry Seasonings can also duplicate and/or improve your present flavor profile; formulate, blend and package specifically for your requirements.

Stockpot
Woodinville, WA 800-468-1611

Taste Maker Foods
Memphis, TN 800-467-1407

Vanee Foods Company
Berkeley, IL 708-449-7300

Prepared

Ailments E.D. Foods Inc.
Pointe Claire, QC 800-267-3333

Aunt Kitty's Foods
Vineland, NJ 856-691-2100

Campbell Soup Company
Camden, NJ 800-257-8443

Castleberry's
Vineland, NJ 856-691-2100

Cordon Bleu International
Anjou, QC 514-352-3000

Custom Culinary
Lombard, IL 800-621-8827

Lawry's Foods
Monrovia, CA 800-595-8917

Mayacamas Fine Foods
Sonoma, CA 800-826-9621

O Chili Frozen Foods Inc
Northbrook, IL 847-562-1991

Praters Foods
Lubbock, TX 806-745-2727

Savannah Food Company
Savannah, TN 800-795-2550

Sentry Seasonings
Elmhurst, IL 630-530-5370

The product development experts of Sentry Seasonings are eager to offer the assistance and hands-on experience to food processors of all sizes. Sentry Seasonings will ensure the consistent high quality and repeat sales of your products, whether you choose one of our many off-the-shelf Bench Mark products or a modified version to meet your preferences. Sentry Seasonings can also duplicate and/or improve your present flavor profile; formulate, blend and package specifically for your requirements.

Williams Foods, Inc
Lenexa, KS 800-255-6736

Ketchup

Alimentaire Whyte's Inc
Laval, QC 800-625-1979

Baldwin Richardson Foods
Frankfort, IL 866-644-2732

Liquid ingredient manufacturer specializing in signature sauces, dessert toppings, beverage/pancake syrups, specialty fruit fillings and condiments.

Brown Family Farm
Brattleboro, VT 86- 2-4 87

C&E Canners
Hammonton, NJ 609-561-1078

Carriage House Companies
Fredonia, NY 800-462-8125

Deep South Products
Fitzgerald, GA 229-423-1121

E.D. Smith Foods Ltd
Winona, ON 800-263-9246

Erba Food Products
Brooklyn, NY 718-272-7700

Fremont Special Brands
Fremont, OH 419-334-8995

Golden State Foods
Irvine, CA 949-252-2000

Heinz Company of Canada
North York, ON 877-574-3469

Heinz Portion Control
Mason, OH 800-547-8924

Kari-Out Company
White Plains, NY 800-433-8799

Mountain Fire Foods
Huntington, VT 802-434-2685

Mucky Duck Mustard Company
Ferndale, MI 248-544-4610

New Business Corporation
Gary, IN 800-742-8435

San Benito Foods
Hollister, CA 831-637-4434

Sir Kensington's Gourmet Scooping Kitchen
New York, NY 646-450-5735

Somerset Industries
Spring House, PA 800-883-8728

Stickney & Poor Company
Peterborough, NH 603-924-2259

Ultra Seal
New Paltz, NY 845-255-2490

Westport Rivers Vineyard& Winery
Westport, MA 800-993-9695

Wing's Food Products
Etobicoke, ON 416-259-2662

World's Best
Norwood, MA 888-690-8766

Marinades

A Perfect Pear from NapaValley
Napa, CA 800-553-5753

A. Lassonde, Inc.
Rougemont, QC 888-477-6663

Allegro Fine Foods
Paris, TN 731-642-6113

Annie's Naturals
East Calais, VT 800-434-1234

Applecreek Farms
Lexington, KY 800-747-8871

Appledore Cove LLC
North Berwick, ME 207-676-4088

Ashman Manufacturing & Distributing Company
Virginia Beach, VA 800-641-9924

Atlantic Quality Spice &Seasonings
New Brunswick, NJ 800-584-0422

B&G Foods
Parsippany, NJ 973-401-6500

Barhyte Specialty Foods Inc
Pendleton, OR 503-691-7858

Bea & B Foods
San Diego, CA 800-952-2117

Blendex Company
Jeffersontown, KY 800-626-6325

Blue Smoke Salsa
Ansted, WV 888-725-7298

CaJohns Fiery Foods
Westerville, OH 888-703-3473

Cajun Injector
Clinton, LA 800-221-8060

CHS
Inver Grove Heights, MN 800-232-3639

Cinnabar Specialty Foods
Prescott, AZ 866-293-6433

Colonna Brothers
North Bergen, NJ 201-864-1115

Con Yeager Spice Company
Zelienople, PA 800-222-2460

Creative Foodworks
San Antonio, TX 210-212-4761

Cugino's Gourmet Foods
Crystal Lake, IL 888-592-8446

Cuizina Food Company
Woodinville, WA 425-486-7000

Delta BBQ Sauce Company
Stockton, CA 209-472-9284

Dixie Trail Farms
Wilmington, NC 800-665-3968

Don Tango Foods
Sterling, VA 877-406-4064

Dorothy Dawson Foods Products
Jackson, MI 517-788-9830

Dr Pete's
Savannah, GA 888-599-0047

Dr. Pete's
Savannah, GA 912-233-3035

Fords Gourmet Foods
Raleigh, NC 800-446-0947

Fox Hollow Farm
Hanover, NH 603-643-6002

FunniBonz
West Windsor, NJ 877-300-2669

Garden Complements
Kansas City, MO 800-966-1091

Geetha's Gourmet of India
Las Cruces, NM 800-274-0475

Gemini Food Industries
Charlton, MA 508-248-2730

Genarom International
Cranbury, NJ 609-409-6200

General Spice
South Plainfield, NJ 800-345-7742

GFF
City of Industry, CA 323-846-2700

Girard's Food Service Dressings
City of Industry, CA 888-327-8442

Golden West Specialty Foods
Brisbane, CA 800-584-4481

Havana's Limited
Titusville, FL 321-267-0513

Intercorp Excelle Foods
North York, ON 416-226-5757

J.T. Pappy's Sauce
Los Angeles, CA 323-969-9605

Judicial Flavors
Auburn, CA 530-885-1298

L&S Packing Company
Farmingdale, NY 800-286-6487

Lawry's Foods
Monrovia, CA 800-595-8917

Love'n Herbs
Waterbury, CT 203-756-4932

Mad Will's Food Company
Auburn, CA 888-275-9455

Magic Seasoning Blends
New Orleans, LA 800-457-2857

Maple Grove Farms of Vermont
St Johnsbury, VT 800-525-2540

Marin Food Specialties
Byron, CA 925-634-6126

McIlhenny Company
Avery Island, LA 800-634-9599

Montebello Kitchens
Gordonsville, VA 800-743-7687

Mountain Fire Foods
Huntington, VT 802-434-2685

Mt. Olympus Specialty Foods
Buffalo, NY 716-874-0771

Nantucket Off-Shore Seasoning
Nantucket, MA 508-994-1300

Napa Valley Kitchens
Napa, CA 707-254-3700

Newly Weds Foods
Decatur, AL 800-521-6189

Newly Weds Foods
Chicago, IL 800-621-7521

Newly Weds Foods
Chicago, IL 800-647-9314

Newman's Own
Westport, CT 203-222-0136

North Coast Processing
North East, PA 814-725-9617

Old Mansion Foods
Petersburg, VA 800-476-1877

Original Cajun Injector
New Iberia, LA 337-367-1344

Parthenon Food Products
Ann Arbor, MI 734-994-1012
Phamous Phloyd's Barbeque Sauce
Denver, CO 303-757-3285
Porinos Gourmet Food
Central Falls, RI 800-826-3938
Produits Ronald
St. Damase, QC 800-465-0118
Quality Foods
San Pedro, CA 877-833-7890
Red Creek Marinade Company
Amarillo, TX 800-687-9114
Restaurant Lulu Gourmet Products
San Francisco, CA 888-693-5800
Rivertown Foods
Saint Louis, MO 800-844-3210
Rosmarino Foods/R.Z. Humbert Company
Odessa, FL 888-926-9053
Sambets Cajun Deli
Austin, TX 800-472-6238
Santa Barbara Salsa/California Creative
Oceanside, CA 800-748-5523
Schoolhouse Kitchen LLC
Brooklyn, NY 718-855-4990
Sentry Seasonings
Elmhurst, IL 630-530-5370

The product development experts of Sentry Seasonings are eager to offer the assistance and hands-on experience to food processors of all sizes. Sentry Seasonings will ensure the consistent high quality and repeat sales of your products, whether you choose one of our many off-the-shelf Bench Mark products or a modified version to meet your preferences. Sentry Seasonings can also duplicate and/or improve your present flavor profile; formulate, blend and package specifically for your requirements.

Southern Ray's Foods
Miami Beach, FL 800-972-8237
Soy Vay Enterprises
Felton, CA 800-600-2077
Surlean Foods
San Antonio, TX 800-999-4370
Swagger Foods Corporation
Vernon Hills, IL 847-913-1200
Sweetwater Spice Company
Austin, TX 800-531-6079
T. Marzetti Company
Columbus, OH 614-846-2232
Thorough Fare Gourmet
Marlboro, VT 802-257-5612
Tillie's Gourmet
Doylestown, PA 215-272-8326
Tova Industries
Louisville, KY 888-532-8682
Trailblazer Food Products
Portland, OR 800-777-7179
Ultimate Gourmet
Belle Mead, NJ 908-359-4050
Uncle Bum's Gourmet Foods
Riverside, CA 800-486-2867
Vita Food Products
Chicago, IL 312-738-4500
Vita Specialty Foods
Inwood, WV 800-974-4778
Wicker's Food Products
Hornersville, MO 800-847-0032
Wild Thymes Farm
Greenville, NY 800-724-2877
Wine Country Chef LLC
Hidden Valley Lake, CA 707-322-0406

Beef

Lawry's Foods
Monrovia, CA 800-595-8917
Sentry Seasonings
Elmhurst, IL 630-530-5370

The product development experts of Sentry Seasonings are eager to offer the assistance and hands-on experience to food processors of all sizes. Sentry Seasonings will ensure the consistent high quality and repeat sales of your products, whether you choose one of our many off-the-shelf Bench Mark products or a modified version to meet your preferences. Sentry Seasonings can also duplicate and/or improve your present flavor profile; formulate, blend and package specifically for your requirements.

Chicken

Delphos Poultry Products
Delphos, OH 419-692-5816
Gemini Food Industries
Charlton, MA 508-248-2730
Sentry Seasonings
Elmhurst, IL 630-530-5370

The product development experts of Sentry Seasonings are eager to offer the assistance and hands-on experience to food processors of all sizes. Sentry Seasonings will ensure the consistent high quality and repeat sales of your products, whether you choose one of our many off-the-shelf Bench Mark products or a modified version to meet your preferences. Sentry Seasonings can also duplicate and/or improve your present flavor profile; formulate, blend and package specifically for your requirements.

Sunchef Farms
Vernon, CA 323-588-5800

Fajita

Magic Seasoning Blends
New Orleans, LA 800-457-2857
Sentry Seasonings
Elmhurst, IL 630-530-5370

The product development experts of Sentry Seasonings are eager to offer the assistance and hands-on experience to food processors of all sizes. Sentry Seasonings will ensure the consistent high quality and repeat sales of your products, whether you choose one of our many off-the-shelf Bench Mark products or a modified version to meet your preferences. Sentry Seasonings can also duplicate and/or improve your present flavor profile; formulate, blend and package specifically for your requirements.

Tova Industries
Louisville, KY 888-532-8682
Van De Walle Farms
San Antonio, TX 210-436-5551

Lamb

Sentry Seasonings
Elmhurst, IL 630-530-5370

The product development experts of Sentry Seasonings are eager to offer the assistance and hands-on experience to food processors of all sizes. Sentry Seasonings will ensure the consistent high quality and repeat sales of your products, whether you choose one of our many off-the-shelf Bench Mark products or a modified version to meet your preferences. Sentry Seasonings can also duplicate and/or improve your present flavor profile; formulate, blend and package specifically for your requirements.

Meat

A. Lassonde, Inc.
Rougemont, QC 888-477-6663
Allegro Fine Foods
Paris, TN 731-642-6113
American Culinary GardenNoble Communications Co
Springfield, MO 888-831-2433
Atlantic Quality Spice &Seasonings
New Brunswick, NJ 800-584-0422
Booneway Farms
Knoxville, TN 865-521-9500
Centennial Food Corporation
Calgary, AB 403-214-0044
Cinnabar Specialty Foods
Prescott, AZ 866-293-6433
Con Yeager Spice Company
Zelienople, PA 800-222-2460
D & D Foods
Columbus, GA 706-322-4507
Delta BBQ Sauce Company
Stockton, CA 209-472-9284
Favorite Foods
Burnaby, BC 604-420-5100
Fuji Foods
Denver, CO 303-377-3738
Genarom International
Cranbury, NJ 609-409-6200
L&S Packing Company
Farmingdale, NY 800-286-6487
Lawry's Foods
Monrovia, CA 800-595-8917
Magic Seasoning Blends
New Orleans, LA 800-457-2857
Mrs. Dog's Products
Grand Rapids, MI 800-2Mr-Dog
Newly Weds Foods
Chicago, IL 800-621-7521
Newly Weds Foods
Chicago, IL 800-647-9314
Original Cajun Injector
New Iberia, LA 337-367-1344
Parthenon Food Products
Ann Arbor, MI 734-994-1012
Passetti's Pride
Hayward, CA 800-521-4659
Produits Ronald
St. Damase, QC 800-465-0118
Red Creek Marinade Company
Amarillo, TX 800-687-9114
Rob Salamida Company
Johnson City, NY 607-770-7046
Sentry Seasonings
Elmhurst, IL 630-530-5370

The product development experts of Sentry Seasonings are eager to offer the assistance and hands-on experience to food processors of all sizes. Sentry Seasonings will ensure the consistent high quality and repeat sales of your products, whether you choose one of our many off-the-shelf Bench Mark products or a modified version to meet your preferences. Sentry Seasonings can also duplicate and/or improve your present flavor profile; formulate, blend and package specifically for your requirements.

Southern Ray's Foods
Miami Beach, FL 800-972-8237
Stanchfield Farms
Milo, ME 207-732-5173
Tova Industries
Louisville, KY 888-532-8682
Van De Walle Farms
San Antonio, TX 210-436-5551

Mayonaise

Bestfoods
Englewood Cliffs, NJ 201-567-8000
C.F. Sauer Company
Richmond, VA 800-688-5676
Cains Foods LP/Olde CapeCod
Ayer, MA 651-698-6832
Carriage House Companies
Fredonia, NY 800-462-8125
Clements Foods Company
Oklahoma City, OK 800-654-8355
Consumer Guild Foods
Toledo, OH 419-726-3406
Consumers Vinegar & Spice Company
Chicago, IL 773-376-4100
Conway Import Company
Franklin Park, IL 800-323-8801
Cuisine Perel
Richmond, CA 800-887-3735
Dave's Gourmet
San Francisco, CA 800-758-0372
Deep South Products
Fitzgerald, GA 229-423-1121
Earth Island Natural Foods
Canoga Park, CA 818-725-2820
Erba Food Products
Brooklyn, NY 718-272-7700
Food Specialties
Indianapolis, IN 317-271-0862
Food Specialties Company
Cincinnati, OH 513-761-1242
GFA Brands
Paramus, NJ 201-568-9300
GFF
City of Industry, CA 323-846-2700
Girard's Food Service Dressings
City of Industry, CA 888-327-8442
Green Garden Food Products
Kent, WA 800-304-1033
Heinz Company of Canada
North York, ON 877-574-3469
Heinz Portion Control
Mason, OH 800-547-8924

IFM
New York, NY 212-229-1633
Kraft Foods
Garland, TX 972-272-7511
Litehouse Foods
Sandpoint, ID 800-669-3169
Mardale Specialty Foods
Waukegan, IL 847-336-4777
Mrs. Clark's Foods
Ankeny, IA 800-736-5674

Juices, salad dressings and sauces.

Oasis Foods Company
Hillside, NJ 908-964-0477
Olde Tyme Mercantile
Arroyo Grande, CA 805-489-7991
Piknik Products Company Inc
Montgomery, AL 334-240-2218
Purity Products
Plainview, NY 888-769-7873
Rapazzini Winery
Gilroy, CA 800-842-6262
Reily Foods Company
New Orleans, LA 504-524-6131
Reily Foods/JFG Coffee Company
New Orleans, LA 800-535-1961
Restaurant Lulu Gourmet Products
San Francisco, CA 888-693-5800
Royal Food Products
Indianapolis, IN 317-782-2660
San Gennaro Foods
Kent, WA 800-462-1916
Stickney & Poor Company
Peterborough, NH 603-924-2259
T Marzetti Company
Columbus, OH 614-846-2232
T. Marzetti Company
Columbus, OH 614-846-2232
Ventura Foods
Ontario, CA 323-262-9157
Ventura Foods
Salem, OR 503-585-6423
Ventura Foods
Saginaw, TX 817-232-5450
Wood Brothers
West Columbia, SC 803-796-5146

Mustard

G.S. Dunn Limited
Hamilton, ON 905-522-0833

Brown

G.S. Dunn Limited
Hamilton, ON 905-522-0833
Groeb Farms
Onsted, MI 517-467-2065
Stickney & Poor Company
Peterborough, NH 603-924-2259

Oriental

G.S. Dunn Limited
Hamilton, ON 905-522-0833
GS Dunn & Company
Hamilton, ON 905-522-0833

Yellow

Bestfoods
Englewood Cliffs, NJ 201-567-8000
Country Cupboard
Virginia City, NV 775-847-7300
G.S. Dunn Limited
Hamilton, ON 905-522-0833
Griffin Food Company
Muskogee, OK 800-580-6311
Groeb Farms
Onsted, MI 517-467-2065
GS Dunn & Company
Hamilton, ON 905-522-0833
Marathon Enterprises
Englewood, NJ 800-722-7388
Stickney & Poor Company
Peterborough, NH 603-924-2259

Salad Dressings

A Perfect Pear from NapaValley
Napa, CA 800-553-5753
Allied Old English
Port Reading, NJ 732-636-2060
American Spoon Foods
Petoskey, MI 800-222-5886
Annie's Naturals
East Calais, VT 800-434-1234
Arbor Hill Grapery
Naples, NY 800-554-7553
Argee Corporation
Santee, CA 800-449-3030
Argo Century
Charlotte, NC 800-446-7108
Arizona Sunland Foods
Tucson, AZ 520-624-7068
Ashman Manufacturing & Distributing Company
Virginia Beach, VA 800-641-9924
Atlantic Seasonings
Kinston, NC 800-433-5261
B&G Foods
Parsippany, NJ 973-401-6500
Baldwin Richardson Foods
Frankfort, IL 866-644-2732

Liquid ingredient manufacturer specializing in signature sauces, dessert toppings, beverage/pancake syrups, specialty fruit fillings and condiments.

Bartush-Schnitzius Foods Company
Lewisville, TX 972-219-1270
Baycliff Company
New York, NY 212-772-6078
Bear Meadow Farm
Colrain, MA 800-653-9241
Betty Lou's Golden Smackers
McMinnville, OR 800-242-5205
Boudreaux's Foods
New Orleans, LA 504-733-8440
BP Gourmet
Hauppauge, NY 631-234-5200
Brown Family Farm
Brattleboro, VT 86- 2-4 87
Buckhead Gourmet
Atlanta, GA 800-673-6338
C.F. Sauer Company
Richmond, VA 800-688-5676
Cains Foods
Ayer, MA 800-225-0601
Cains Foods LP/Olde CapeCod
Ayer, MA 651-698-6832
California Style Gourmet Products
San Diego, CA 800-243-5226
Carole's Cheesecake Company
Toronto, ON 416-256-0000
Carriage House Companies
Fredonia, NY 800-462-8125
Chelten House Products
Bridgeport, NJ 856-467-1600
Chicama Vineyards
West Tisbury, MA 888-244-2262
Christie Food Products
Randolph, MA 800-727-2523
CHS
Inver Grove Heights, MN 800-232-3639
CHS, Inc.
Inner Grove Heights, MN 800-232-3639
Clements Foods Company
Oklahoma City, OK 800-654-8355
Columbus Foods Company
Des Plaines, IL 800-322-6457
Consumer Guild Foods
Toledo, OH 419-726-3406
Conway Import Company
Franklin Park, IL 800-323-8801
Corsair Pepper Sauce
Gulfport, MS 228-452-0311
Country Fresh Food & Confections, Inc.
Oliver Springs, TN 800-545-8782
Creative Foodworks
San Antonio, TX 210-212-4761
Cuisine Perel
Richmond, CA 800-887-3735
Cw Resources
New Britain, CT 860-229-7700
D & D Foods
Columbus, GA 706-322-4507
Dave's Gourmet
San Francisco, CA 800-758-0372
Del Sol Food Company
Brenham, TX 979-836-5978
Delicae Gourmet
Tarpon Springs, FL 800-942-2502
Dorina/So-Good
Union, IL 815-923-2144
Drusilla Seafood Packing & Processing Company
Baton Rouge, LA 800-364-8844
Dynamic Foods
Lubbock, TX 806-747-2777
Earth Island Natural Foods
Canoga Park, CA 818-725-2820
Food Source Company
Mississauga, ON 905-625-8404
Food Specialties
Indianapolis, IN 317-271-0862
Food Specialties Company
Cincinnati, OH 513-761-1242
GFA Brands
Paramus, NJ 201-568-9300
GFF
City of Industry, CA 323-846-2700
Girard's Food Service Dressings
City of Industry, CA 888-327-8442
Gold Pure Foods Products Company
Hempstead, NY 800-422-4681
Golden Specialty Foods
Norwalk, CA 562-802-2537
Golden State Foods
Irvine, CA 949-252-2000
Gourmet Central
Romney, WV 800-984-3722
Greek Gourmet Limited
Mill Valley, CA 415-480-8050
Green Garden Food Products
Kent, WA 800-304-1033
Griffith Laboratories Worldwide
Alsip, IL 800-346-4743
Grouse Hunt Farms
Tamaqua, PA 570-467-2850
Hagerty Foods
Orange, CA 714-628-1230
Halben Food Manufacturing Company
Saint Louis, MO 800-888-4855
Harpo's
Honolulu, HI 808-735-6456
Heinz Company of Canada
North York, ON 877-574-3469
Hell on the Red
Telephone, TX 903-664-2573
HVJ International
Spring, TX 877-730-3663
IFM
New York, NY 212-229-1633
Instantwhip Foods
San Antonio, TX 800-544-9447
Instantwhip: Florida
Tampa, FL 813-621-3233
International Food Products Corporation
Saint Louis, MO 314-421-6151
J.D. Mullen Company
Palestine, IL 618-586-2727
Jed's Maple Products
Westfield, VT 866-478-7388
Kauai Organic Farms
Kilauea, HI 808-651-1777
Ken's Foods
Marlborough, MA 800-633-5800
Key Ingredients
Harrisburg, PA 800-227-4448
Knott's Berry Farm Foods
Placentia, CA 800-289-9927
Kosto Food Products Company
Wauconda, IL 847-487-2600
Kozlowski Farms
Forestville, CA 800-473-2767
Kraft Foods
Allentown, PA 610-398-0311
Kraft Foods
Garland, TX 972-272-7511
L&S Packing Company
Farmingdale, NY 800-286-6487
Litehouse
Sandpoint, ID 208-263-7569
Litehouse Foods
Sandpoint, ID 800-669-3169
Live A Little Gourmet Foods
Newark, CA 888-744-2300
Love'n Herbs
Waterbury, CT 203-756-4932
Lynch Foods
North York, ON 416-449-5464
M.A. Gedney
Chaska, MN 952-448-2612
Mad Will's Food Company
Auburn, CA 888-275-9455
Maple Grove Farms of Vermont
St Johnsbury, VT 800-525-2540

Mardale Specialty Foods
Waukegan, IL 847-336-4777
Marie's Quality Foods
Brea, CA 800-339-1051
Marie's Refrigerated Dressings
Thornton, IL 800-441-3321
Marjon Specialty Foods, Inc
Plant City, FL 813-752-3482
Marukan Vinegar (U.S.A.) Inc.
Paramount, CA 562-630-6060
Mayacamas Fine Foods
Sonoma, CA 800-826-9621
McCutcheon's Apple Products
Frederick, MD 800-888-7537
Mermaid Spice Corporation
Fort Myers, FL 239-693-1986
Milo's Whole World Gourmet
Athens, OH 866-589-6456
Mixon Fruit Farms
Bradenton, FL 800-608-2525
Mother Teresa's
Clute, TX 888-265-7429
Mrs. Clark's Foods
Ankeny, IA 800-736-5674

Juices, salad dressings and sauces.

Mucky Duck Mustard Company
Ferndale, MI 248-544-4610
Mullins Food Products
Broadview, IL 708-344-3224
Napa Valley Kitchens
Napa, CA 707-254-3700
Naturally Fresh Foods
Atlanta, GA 800-765-1950
North American Enterprises
Tucson, AZ 800-817-8666
North Coast Processing
North East, PA 814-725-9617
O'Brian Brothers Food
Cincinnati, OH 513-791-9909
Oasis Foods Company
Hillside, NJ 908-964-0477
Ocean Spray Cranberries
Lakeville-Middleboro, MA 800-662-3263
Olde Tyme Mercantile
Arroyo Grande, CA 805-489-7991
Ott Food Products
Carthage, MO 800-866-2585
Pacific Harvest Products
Bellevue, WA 425-401-7990
Pacific Westcoast Foods
Beaverton, OR 800-874-9333
Parthenon Food Products
Ann Arbor, MI 734-994-1012
Pearlco of Boston
Canton, MA 781-821-1010
Pfeiffer's Foods
Columbus, OH 614-846-2232
Piknik Products Company Inc
Montgomery, AL 334-240-2218
Porinos Gourmet Food
Central Falls, RI 800-826-3938
Precision Foods
Melrose Park, IL 800-333-0003
Purity Products
Plainview, NY 888-769-7873
Quality Foods
San Pedro, CA 877-833-7890
Quong Hop & Company
S San Francisco, CA 650-553-9900
Reily Foods Company
New Orleans, LA 504-524-6131
Rivertown Foods
Saint Louis, MO 800-844-3210
Robert Rothschild Berry Farm
Urbana, OH 866-565-6790
Rod's Food Products
City of Industry, CA 909-839-8925
Rosmarino Foods/R.Z. Humbert Company
Odessa, FL 888-926-9053
Royal Food Products
Indianapolis, IN 317-782-2660
Royal Kedem Food & Wine Company
Bayonne, NJ 201-437-9131
Royal Resources
New Orleans, LA 800-888-9932
Sal's Caesar Dressing
Novato, CA 415-897-0605
Sallock International Foods
Millbury, OH 419-838-7223
San Diego Soy Dairy
El Cajon, CA 619-447-8638
San Fernando Creamery Farmdale Creamery
San Bernardino, CA 909-889-3002
San Gennaro Foods
Kent, WA 800-462-1916
San-J International, Inc
Richmond, VA 800-446-5500
Schlotterbeck & Foss Company
Portland, ME 800-777-4666
Select Food Products
Toronto, ON 800-699-8016
Sentry Seasonings
Elmhurst, IL 630-530-5370

The product development experts of Sentry Seasonings are eager to offer the assistance and hands-on experience to food processors of all sizes. Sentry Seasonings will ensure the consistent high quality and repeat sales of your products, whether you choose one of our many off-the-shelf Bench Mark products or a modified version to meet your preferences. Sentry Seasonings can also duplicate and/or improve your present flavor profile; formulate, blend and package specifically for your requirements.

Shawnee Canning Company
Cross Junction, VA 800-713-1414
Silver Palate Kitchens
Cresskill, NJ 800-872-5283
Sprague Foods
Belleville, ON 613-966-1200
Stearns & Lehman
Mansfield, OH 800-533-2722
Stickney & Poor Company
Peterborough, NH 603-924-2259
Stubb's Legendary Kitchen
Austin, TX 800-883-3238
Swagger Foods Corporation
Vernon Hills, IL 847-913-1200
Sweet Earth Natural Foods
Pacific Grove, CA 800-737-3311
T Marzetti Company
Columbus, OH 614-846-2232
T. Marzetti Company
Columbus, OH 614-846-2232
Tasty-Toppings
Columbus, NE 800-228-4148
Tex-Mex Gourmet
Brenham, TX 888-345-8467
TexaFrance
Round Rock, TX 800-776-8937
The Lollipop Tree, Inc
Auburn, NY 800-842-6691
Thistledew Farm
Proctor, WV 800-854-6639
Thorough Fare Gourmet
Marlboro, VT 802-257-5612
Tillie's Gourmet
Doylestown, PA 215-272-8326
Trader Vic's Food Products
Emeryville, CA 877-762-4824
Tulocay & Company
Napa, CA 888-627-2859
Unilever Bestfoods
Englewood Cliffs, NJ 201-567-8000
Unilever Bestfoods, Inc.
Englewood Cliffs, NJ 201-894-4000
Unilever United States
Englewood Cliffs, NJ 201-894-4000
Valley Grain Products
Madera, CA 559-675-3400
Vanlaw Food Products
Fullerton, CA 714-870-9091
Ventura Foods
Philadelphia, PA 215-223-8700
Ventura Foods
Ontario, CA 323-262-9157
Ventura Foods
Opelousas, LA 337-948-6561
Ventura Foods
Portland, OR 503-255-5512
Ventura Foods
Salem, OR 503-585-6423
Ventura Foods
City of Industry, CA 800-327-3906
Ventura Foods
Saginaw, TX 817-232-5450
Vincent Formusa Company
Chicago, IL 312-421-0485
Virginia Honey Company
Inwood, WV 304-267-8500
Vita Food Products
Chicago, IL 312-738-4500
Vita Specialty Foods
Inwood, WV 800-974-4778
Vitasoy USA
Ayer, MA 978-772-6880
Walden Farms
Linden, NJ 800-229-1706
Westin
Omaha, NE 800-228-6098
Wild Thymes Farm
Greenville, NY 800-724-2877
WillowOak Farms
Woodland, CA 888-963-2767
Wine Country Kitchens
Napa, CA 707-252-9463
Wizards Cauldron, LTD
Yanceyville, NC 336-694-5665
Wood Brothers
West Columbia, SC 803-796-5146
World Flavors
Warminster, PA 215-672-4400
York Mountain Winery
Templeton, CA 805-237-7575

Balsamic Vinegar

Adams Olive Ranch
Lindsay, CA 888-216-5483
Atlantic Quality Spice &Seasonings
New Brunswick, NJ 800-584-0422
Buckhead Gourmet
Atlanta, GA 800-673-6338
Colonna Brothers
North Bergen, NJ 201-864-1115
Newman's Own
Westport, CT 203-222-0136

Blue Cheese

Wood Brothers
West Columbia, SC 803-796-5146

Ceasar

Knott's Berry Farm Foods
Placentia, CA 800-289-9927
Newman's Own
Westport, CT 203-222-0136
Sal's Caesar Dressing
Novato, CA 415-897-0605

French

Heinz Company of Canada
North York, ON 877-574-3469
O'Brian Brothers Food
Cincinnati, OH 513-791-9909
Ott Food Products
Carthage, MO 800-866-2585
Wood Brothers
West Columbia, SC 803-796-5146

Gourmet

Betty Lou's Golden Smackers
McMinnville, OR 800-242-5205
Olde Tyme Mercantile
Arroyo Grande, CA 805-489-7991

Italian Style

Newman's Own
Westport, CT 203-222-0136
O'Brian Brothers Food
Cincinnati, OH 513-791-9909
Olde Tyme Mercantile
Arroyo Grande, CA 805-489-7991
Ott Food Products
Carthage, MO 800-866-2585
Wood Brothers
West Columbia, SC 803-796-5146

Mixes

Atlantic Quality Spice &Seasonings
New Brunswick, NJ 800-584-0422
CHS
Inver Grove Heights, MN 800-232-3639
House of Thaller
Knoxville, TN 800-462-3365
Kokopelli's Kitchen
Phoenix, AZ 888-943-9802

RC Fine Foods
Belle Mead, NJ 800-526-3953

Blue Cheese

Atlantic Quality Spice &Seasonings
New Brunswick, NJ 800-584-0422

Ceasar

Atlantic Quality Spice &Seasonings
New Brunswick, NJ 800-584-0422

Creamy Dijon

Atlantic Quality Spice &Seasonings
New Brunswick, NJ 800-584-0422

Dijon

Atlantic Quality Spice &Seasonings
New Brunswick, NJ 800-584-0422

French

Atlantic Quality Spice &Seasonings
New Brunswick, NJ 800-584-0422

Italian Style

Atlantic Quality Spice &Seasonings
New Brunswick, NJ 800-584-0422

Oil & Vinegar

Atlantic Quality Spice &Seasonings
New Brunswick, NJ 800-584-0422
Marukan Vinegar (U.S.A.) Inc.
Paramount, CA 562-630-6060

Parmesan

Atlantic Quality Spice &Seasonings
New Brunswick, NJ 800-584-0422

Peppercorn

Atlantic Quality Spice &Seasonings
New Brunswick, NJ 800-584-0422

Ranch

Atlantic Quality Spice &Seasonings
New Brunswick, NJ 800-584-0422
Ott Food Products
Carthage, MO 800-866-2585

Raspberry Vinegrette

Atlantic Quality Spice &Seasonings
New Brunswick, NJ 800-584-0422

Reduced-Calorie

Atlantic Quality Spice &Seasonings
New Brunswick, NJ 800-584-0422

Thousand Island

Atlantic Quality Spice &Seasonings
New Brunswick, NJ 800-584-0422

Non-Fat

Betty Lou's Golden Smackers
McMinnville, OR 800-242-5205
Marukan Vinegar (U.S.A.) Inc.
Paramount, CA 562-630-6060
Naturally Fresh Foods
Atlanta, GA 800-765-1950
Walden Farms
Linden, NJ 800-229-1706

Oil & Vinegar

Au Printemps Gourmet
Saint-Jerome, QC 800-663-0416
Gourme' Mist
Coral Springs, FL 866-502-8472
Marukan Vinegar (U.S.A.) Inc.
Paramount, CA 562-630-6060
Newman's Own
Westport, CT 203-222-0136
Ventura Foods
Philadelphia, PA 215-223-8700

Ranch

Newman's Own
Westport, CT 203-222-0136
O'Brian Brothers Food
Cincinnati, OH 513-791-9909

Raspberry Vinegrette

Knott's Berry Farm Foods
Placentia, CA 800-289-9927
Rising Sun Farms
Phoenix, OR 800-888-0795

Thousand Island

Heinz Company of Canada
North York, ON 877-574-3469
Wood Brothers
West Columbia, SC 803-796-5146

Salsa

Alimentaire Whyte's Inc
Laval, QC 800-625-1979
Alimentos Naturales Sabrosa, SA de CV
San Antonio, TX 210-545-1792
Allied Old English
Port Reading, NJ 732-636-2060
American Spoon Foods
Petoskey, MI 800-222-5886
Amigos Canning Company
San Antonio, TX 800-580-3477
Anna's Unlimited, Inc
Austin, TX 800-849-7054
Appledore Cove LLC
North Berwick, ME 207-676-4088
Arizona Cowboy
Phoenix, AZ 602-956-4833
Ashman Manufacturing & Distributing Company
Virginia Beach, VA 800-641-9924
ATA International
Belton, TX 816-221-0660
B&G Foods
Parsippany, NJ 973-401-6500
Bartush-Schnitzius Foods Company
Lewisville, TX 972-219-1270
BBQ Bunch
Kansas City, MO 816-941-4534
Bear Creek Kitchens
Marshall, TX 888-300-7687
Bel/Kaukauna USA
Kaukauna, WI 800-558-3500
Better Made Snack Foods
Detroit, MI 800-332-2394
Bien Padre Foods
Eureka, CA 707-442-4585
Big B Distributors
Evansville, IN 812-425-5235
Blueberry Store
Grand Junction, MI 877-654-2400
Border Foods Inc
Deming, NM 888-737-7752
CaJohns Fiery Foods
Westerville, OH 888-703-3473
California Creative Foods
Oceanside, CA 760-757-2622
California Fresh Salsa
Woodland, CA 530-662-0512
California Style Gourmet Products
San Diego, CA 800-243-5226
California-Antilles Trading Consortium
San Diego, CA 800-330-6450
Casa Visco Finer Food Company
Schenectady, NY 888-607-2823
Catamount Specialties ofVermont
Stowe, VT 800-820-8096
Cervantes Foods Products
Albuquerque, NM 877-982-4453
Charlie Beigg's Sauce Company
Windham, ME 888-502-8595
Chelten House Products
Bridgeport, NJ 856-467-1600
Chile Today
San Francisco, CA 800-758-0372
Choice of Vermont
Destin, FL 800-444-6261
Cibolo Junction Food & Spice
Albuquerque, NM 505-888-1987
Cinnabar Specialty Foods
Prescott, AZ 866-293-6433
Circle R Ranch Gourmet Foods
Flower Mound, TX 800-247-3077
Ciro Foods
Pittsburgh, PA 412-771-9018
Colorado Salsa Company
Littleton, CO 303-932-2617
Country Cupboard
Virginia City, NV 775-847-7300
Cowgirl Chocolates
Moscow, ID 888-882-4098
Creative Foodworks
San Antonio, TX 210-212-4761
Cuizina Food Company
Woodinville, WA 425-486-7000
Custom Food Solutions
Louisville, KY 800-767-2993
Cw Resources
New Britain, CT 860-229-7700
Dave's Gourmet
San Francisco, CA 800-758-0372
Dei Fratelli
Toledo, OH 800-837-1631
DelGrosso Foods
Tipton, PA 800-521-5880
Delgrosso Foods Inc.
Tipton, PA 800-521-5880
Deneen Company
Belen, NM 505-988-1515
Dockside Market
Key Largo, FL 800-813-2253
Dorina/So-Good
Union, IL 815-923-2144
E.D. Smith Foods Ltd
Winona, ON 800-263-9246
El Paso Chile Company
El Paso, TX 888-472-5727
El Toro Food Products
Watsonville, CA 831-728-9266
Famous Chili
Fort Smith, AR 479-782-0096
Fiesta Gourmet of Tejas
Canyon Lake, TX 800-585-8250
Fischer & Wieser Specialty Foods, Inc.
Fredericksburg, TX 800-880-8526
Food Processor of New Mexico
Albuquerque, NM 877-634-3772
Food Specialties Company
Cincinnati, OH 513-761-1242
Ford's Fancy Fruit
Raleigh, NC 800-446-0947
Forge Mountain Foods
Hendersonville, NC 800-823-6743
Fountain Valley Foods
Colorado Springs, CO 719-573-6012
Fremont Authentic Brands
Fremont, OH 419-334-8995
Frog Ranch Foods
Glouster, OH 800-742-2488
Galena Canning Company
Galena, IL 815-777-2882
Garden Complements
Kansas City, MO 800-966-1091
Garden Fresh Salsa
Ferndale, MI 866-725-7239
Geetha's Gourmet of India
Las Cruces, NM 800-274-0475
Gingro Corp
Manchester Center, VT 802-362-0836
Giovanni Food Company
Syracuse, NY 315-457-2373
Gold Pure Foods Products Company
Hempstead, NY 800-422-4681
Golden Specialty Foods
Norwalk, CA 562-802-2537
Golden Valley Foods
Abbotsford, BC 888-299-8855
Gourmet Central
Romney, WV 800-984-3722
Green Mountain Gringo
Winston Salem, NC
Groeb Farms
Onsted, MI 517-467-2065
Guiltless Gourmet The Manischewitz Company
Secaucus, NJ 201-553-1100
Gumpert's Canada
Mississauga, ON 800-387-9324
Hagerty Foods
Orange, CA 714-628-1230
Hains Celestial Group
Melville, NY 877-612-4246
Hartford City Foam Pack aging & Converting
Hartford City, IN 765-348-2500
Havana's Limited
Titusville, FL 321-267-0513

Hirzel Canning Company &Farms
Northwood, OH 419-693-0531
Holy Mole
Austin, TX. 877-310-8453
Hombres Foods
Cedar Creek, TX. 877-446-6273
Hormel Foods Corporation
Austin, MN 800-523-4635
Hot Licks Hot Sauces
Spring Valley, CA 888-766-6468
Hot Wachula's
Lakeland, FL. 877-883-8700
House of Webster
Rogers, AR 800-369-4641
Hume Specialties
Chester, VT 802-875-3117
HVJ International
Spring, TX. 877-730-3663
Iguana Tom's
Fremont, CA 888-827-2572
Imus Ranch Foods
Darien, CT. 505-892-0883
Indel Food Products
El Paso, TX. 800-472-0159
Jalapeno Foods Company
The Woodlands, TX 800-896-2318
JC's Midnite Salsa
Tucson, AZ 800-817-2572
Jillipepper
Albuquerque, NM. 505-344-2804
Joe Hutson Foods
Jacksonville, FL 904-731-9065
Kettle Master
Hillsville, VA 276-728-7571
Kind Snacks
New York, NY 800-732-2321
Kozlowski Farms
Forestville, CA 800-473-2767
La Vencedora Products
Los Angeles, CA. 800-327-2572
La Victoria Foods
Rosemead, CA 800-523-4635
Laredo Mexican Foods
Fort Wayne, IN 800-252-7336
Leigh Olivers
Tyler, TX. 903-245-9183
Li'l Guy Foods
Kansas City, MO. 800-886-8226
Los Chileros de Nuevo Mexico
Santa Fe, NM 888-EAT-CHIL
M.A. Gedney
Chaska, MN 952-448-2612
Mad Will's Food Company
Auburn, CA. 888-275-9455
Mexisnax Corporation
El Paso, TX. 915-779-5709
Miguel's Stowe Away
Stowe, VT. 800-448-6517
Mixon Fruit Farms
Bradenton, FL. 800-608-2525
Mojave Foods Corporation
Commerce, CA 323-890-8900
Native Kjalii Foods
San Francisco, CA 415-522-5580
O'Garvey Sauces
New Braunfels, TX. 830-620-6127
Ocean Spray Cranberries
Lakeville-Middleboro, MA 800-662-3263
Our Enterprises
Oklahoma City, OK 800-821-6375
Paisley Farms
Willoughby, OH 800-676-8656
Palmieri Food Products
New Haven, CT 800-845-5447
Paradise Products Corporation
Boca Raton, FL. 800-826-1235
Pepper Creek Farms
Lawton, OK. 800-526-8132
Plocky's Fine Snacks
Hinsdale, IL 630-323-8888
Quality Foods
San Pedro, CA. 877-833-7890
Rapazzini Winery
Gilroy, CA. 800-842-6262
Ready Foods
Denver, CO 720-889-1104
Red Gold
Elwood, IN 877-748-9798
Reser's Fine Foods
Salt Lake City, UT 801-972-5633
Riba Foods
Houston, TX 800-327-7422
Robert Rothschild Berry Farm
Urbana, OH. 866-565-6790
Royal Resources
New Orleans, LA 800-888-9932
Ruffner's
Wayne, PA. 610-687-9800
Sabra-Go Mediterranean
Dallas, TX. 888-957-2272
Sambets Cajun Deli
Austin, TX. 800-472-6238
Santa Barbara Olive Company
Santa Barbara, CA 800-624-4896
Santa Barbara Salsa/California Creative
Oceanside, CA 800-748-5523
Sechler's Fine Pickles
Saint Joe, IN 800-332-5461
Select Food Products
Toronto, ON 800-699-8016
Shawnee Canning Company
Cross Junction, VA 800-713-1414
Smiling Fox Pepper Company
North Aurora, IL. 630-337-3734
Southern Bar-B-Que
Jennings, LA. 866-612-2586
Southwest Spirit
Socorro, NM 800-838-0773
Soylent Brand
Irving, TX. 972-255-4747
Spruce Foods
San Clemente, CA. 800-326-3612
Steel's Gourmet Foods, Ltd.
Bridgeport, PA 800-678-3357
Stello Foods
Punxsutawney, PA. 800-849-4599
Sun Harvest Foods
San Diego, CA 619-661-0909
T.W. Garner Food Company
Winston Salem, NC. 800-476-7383
Terrell's Potato Chip Company
Syracuse, NY 315-437-2786
Texas Heat
San Antonio, TX. 800-656-5916
The Brooklyn Salsa Co LLC
Ridgewood, NY 609-680-9319
Thomson Food
Duluth, MN. 218-722-2529
Timber Peaks Gourmet
Parker, CO. 800-982-7687
Topper Food Products
East Brunswick, NJ. 800-377-2823
Uncle Bum's Gourmet Foods
Riverside, CA 800-486-2867
Uncle Fred's Fine Foods
Rockport, TX 361-729-8320
Van De Walle Farms
San Antonio, TX. 210-436-5551
Vegetable Juices
Chicago, IL 888-776-9752
Victoria Packing Corporation
Brooklyn, NY 718-927-3000
Vita Food Products
Chicago, IL 312-738-4500
Vita Specialty Foods
Martinsburg, WV 800-989-8482
Walker Foods
Los Angeles, CA. 800-966-5199
Wing Nien Company
Hayward, CA 510-487-8877
Xochitl
Dallas, TX. 214-800-3551
Ynrico's Food Products Company
Syracuse, NY 888-472-8237
Zuni Foods
San Antonio, TX. 800-906-3876

Canned

Hartford City Foam Pack aging & Converting
Hartford City, IN. 765-348-2500
Kozlowski Farms
Forestville, CA 800-473-2767
Palmieri Food Products
New Haven, CT 800-845-5447
T.W. Garner Food Company
Winston Salem, NC. 800-476-7383

Chunky

Newman's Own
Westport, CT. 203-222-0136
T.W. Garner Food Company
Winston Salem, NC. 800-476-7383

Mild

California Creative Foods
Oceanside, CA 760-757-2622
Garden Fresh Salsa
Ferndale, MI 866-725-7239
Hot Wachula's
Lakeland, FL. 877-883-8700
Iguana Tom's
Fremont, CA 888-827-2572
JC's Midnite Salsa
Tucson, AZ 800-817-2572
T.W. Garner Food Company
Winston Salem, NC. 800-476-7383

Picante

Bartush-Schnitzius Foods Company
Lewisville, TX 972-219-1270
Garden Fresh Salsa
Ferndale, MI 866-725-7239
Hormel Foods Corporation
Austin, MN 800-523-4635
Hot Wachula's
Lakeland, FL. 877-883-8700
Iguana Tom's
Fremont, CA 888-827-2572
JC's Midnite Salsa
Tucson, AZ 800-817-2572
T.W. Garner Food Company
Winston Salem, NC. 800-476-7383
Texas Heat
San Antonio, TX. 800-656-5916

with Cheese

Amigos Canning Company
San Antonio, TX. 800-580-3477

Cactus-Creek
Dallas, TX........800-471-7723
Delgrosso Foods Inc.
Tipton, PA........800-521-5880
Groeb Farms
Onsted, MI........517-467-2065

Sauces

A.M. Braswell Jr. Food Company
Statesboro, GA........800-673-9388
AFP Advanced Food Products, LLC
Visalia, CA........559-627-2070
Ajinomoto Food Ingredients LLC
Chicago, IL........773-714-1436
Al Dente
Whitmore Lake, MI........800-536-7278
Alimentaire Whyte's Inc
Laval, QC........800-625-1979
Allegro Fine Foods
Paris, TN........731-642-6113
Allied Old English
Port Reading, NJ........732-636-2060
Amboy Specialty Foods Company
Dixon, IL........800-892-0400
American Culinary GardenNoble Communications Co
Springfield, MO........888-831-2433
American Saucery
Oak Park, MI........877-728-2379
American Spoon Foods
Petoskey, MI........800-222-5886
Amigos Canning Company
San Antonio, TX........800-580-3477
Amy's Kitchen
Petaluma, CA........707-568-4500
Anke Kruse Organics
Guelph, ON........519-824-6161
Ankle Deep Foods
Norfolk, NE........402-371-2991
Annie Chun's
San Rafael, CA........415-479-8272
Annie's Naturals
East Calais, VT........800-434-1234
Apecka
Rockwall, TX........972-772-2654
Archie Moore's Foods Products
Milford, CT........203-876-5088
Argo Century
Charlotte, NC........800-446-7108
Armanino Foods of Distinction
Hayward, CA........510-441-9300
Aromont USA
Southlake, TX........817-552-5544
Ashley Foods
Sudbury, MA........800-617-2823
Ashman Manufacturing & Distributing Company
Virginia Beach, VA........800-641-9924
Ask Foods
Palmyra, PA........800-879-4275
Athena Oil
Long Island City, NY........718-956-8893
Atlanta Burning
Newnan, GA........800-665-5611
Atlantic Seasonings
Kinston, NC........800-433-5261
Au Printemps Gourmet
Saint-Jerome, QC........800-663-0416
Aunt Aggie De's Pralines
Sinton, TX........888-772-5463
Aunt Jenny's Sauces/Melba Foods
Brooklyn, NY........718-383-3192
Austin Slow Burn
Austin, TX........877-513-3192
B&B Pecan Processors of NC
Turkey, NC........866-328-7322
B&G Foods
Parsippany, NJ........973-401-6500
Bainbridge Festive Foods
Tunica, MS........800-545-9205
Baldwin Richardson Foods
Frankfort, IL........866-644-2732

Liquid ingredient manufacturer specializing in signature sauces, dessert toppings, beverage/pancake syrups, specialty fruit fillings and condiments.

Barefoot Contessa Pantry
York, ME........800-826-1752
Barhyte Specialty Foods Inc
Pendleton, OR........503-691-7858
Bartush-Schnitzius Foods Company
Lewisville, TX........972-219-1270
Basic Food Flavors
North Las Vegas, NV........702-643-0043
Baumer Foods
Metairie, LA........504-482-5761
Bay Valley Foods
Platteville, WI........800-236-1119
Baycliff Company
New York, NY........212-772-6078
BBQ Bunch
Kansas City, MO........816-941-4534
BBQ Shack
Paola, KS........913-294-5908
BBQ'n Fools
Bend, OR........800-671-8652
Beaverton Foods
Beaverton, OR........800-223-8076
Bel/Kaukauna USA
Kaukauna, WI........800-558-3500
Bellisio Foods, Inc.
Duluth, MN........800-368-7337
Berner Cheese Corporation
Dakota, IL........800-819-8199
Bettah Buttah, LLC
Kansas City, KS........800-568-8468
Bien Padre Foods
Eureka, CA........707-442-4585
Big B Distributors
Evansville, IN........812-425-5235
Bittersweet Herb Farm
Shelburne Falls, MA........800-456-1599
Blackberry Patch
Thomasville, GA........800-853-5598
Blair's Death Sauces & Snacks
Highlands, NJ........732-872-0755
Blount Fine Foods
Fall River, MA........774-888-1300
Blue Jay Orchards
Bethel, CT........203-748-0119
Blue Smoke Salsa
Ansted, WV........888-725-7298
Bodin Foods
New Iberia, LA........337-367-1344
Borden Foods
Columbus, OH........614-233-3759
Border Foods Inc
Deming, NM........888-737-7752
Bove's of Vermont
Burlington, VT........802-862-7235
Bowman Apple Products Company
Mount Jackson, VA........800-346-5382
Brateka Enterprises
Ocala, FL........877-549-3227
Brede
Detroit, MI........313-273-1079
Brockles Foods Company
Garland, TX........972-272-5593
Brother Bru Bru's Produce
Venice, CA........310-396-9033
Brown Family Farm
Brattleboro, VT........86- 2-4 87
Brown Family Farm
Brattleboro, VT........866-254-8718
Bruno Specialty Foods
West Sayville, NY........631-589-1700
Buckhead Gourmet
Atlanta, GA........800-673-6338
Buddy's
Pocatello, ID........208-233-1172
Buffalo Wild Wings
Minneapolis, MN........763-546-1891
Burnette Foods
Hartford, MI........616-621-3181
C&E Canners
Hammonton, NJ........609-561-1078
C.F. Sauer Company
Richmond, VA........800-688-5676
Cafe Chilku
Colchester, VT........802-878-4645
Cafe Tequila
San Francisco, CA........415-264-0106
Cains Foods
Ayer, MA........800-225-0601
CaJohns Fiery Foods
Westerville, OH........888-703-3473
Cajun Chef Products
Saint Martinville, LA........337-394-7112
California Creative Foods
Oceanside, CA........760-757-2622
Campagna
Lebanon, OR........800-959-4372
Campbell Soup Company
Camden, NJ........800-257-8443
Canada Bread
Etobicoke, ON........416-926-2000
Canada Bread
North Bay, ON........800-461-6122
Cantisano Foods
Fairport, NY........585-377-7700
Capone Foods
Somerville, MA........617-629-2296
Captain Bob's Jet Fuel
Fort Wayne, IN........877-486-6468
Carando Gourmet Frozen Foods
Agawam, MA........888-227-2636
Carmela's Gourmet
Monterey, CA........831-373-6291
Carol's Country Cuisine
Glen Ellen, CA........707-996-1124
Carole's Cheesecake Company
Toronto, ON........416-256-0000
Carolina Cupboard
Hillsborough, NC........800-400-3441
Carolina Treet
Wilmington, NC........800-616-6344
Carolyn's Caribbean Heat
Malvern, PA........610-647-0336
Carriage Charles
Fredonia, NY........800-462-125
Carriage House Companies
Fredonia, NY........800-462-8125
Carriere Foods Inc
Saint-Denis-Sur-Richelie, QC........450-787-3411
Cary Randall's Sauces & Dressings
Highlands, NJ........732-872-6353
Casa di Carfagna
Columbus, OH........614-846-6340
Casa DiLisio Products
Mt Kisco, NY........800-247-4199
Casa Visco Finer Food Company
Schenectady, NY........888-607-2823
Castleberry's
Vineland, NJ........856-691-2100
Catamount Specialties ofVermont
Stowe, VT........800-820-8096
Catskill Mountain Specialties
Saugerties, NY........800-311-3473
Cattle Boyz Foods
Calgary, AB........888-662-9366
Cedarvale Food Products Lounsbury Food Ltd
Toronto, ON........416-656-3331
Certified Savory
Countryside, IL........800-328-7656
Cervantes Foods Products
Albuquerque, NM........877-982-4453
Charlie Palmer Group
New York, NY........888-287-3653
Charlie Trotter Foods
Chicago, IL........773-248-6228
Chef Merito
Encino, CA........800-637-4861
Chef Shells Catering & Roadside Cafe
Port Huron, MI........810-966-8371
Chef-A-Roni
East Greenwich, RI........401-884-8798
Chelten House Products
Bridgeport, NJ........856-467-1600
Cherchies
Malvern, PA........800-644-1980
Cherry Hut
Traverse City, MI........888-882-4431
Chincoteague Seafood Company
Parsonsburg, MD........443-260-4800
Chocolaterie Bernard Callebaut
Calgary, AB........800-661-8367
Chocolatique
Los Angeles, CA........310-479-3849
Christie Food Products
Randolph, MA........800-727-2523
Christopher Ranch
Gilroy, CA........408-847-1100
CHS, Inc.
Inner Grove Heights, MN........800-232-3639
Chukar Cherries
Prosser, WA........800-624-9544
Cinnabar Specialty Foods
Prescott, AZ........866-293-6433
Cipriani's Spaghetti & Sauce Company
Chicago Heights, IL........708-755-6212
Ciro Foods
Pittsburgh, PA........412-771-9018
Clarmil Manufacturing Corporation
Hayward, CA........888-252-7645
Classy Delites
Austin, TX........800-440-2648

Clement Pappas & Company
Carneys Point, NJ 800-257-7019
Clements Foods Company
Oklahoma City, OK 800-654-8355
Clofine Dairy & Food Products
Linwood, NJ 800-441-1001
Cold Hollow Cider Mill
Waterbury Center, VT. 800-327-7537
Colgin Companies
Dallas, TX. 888-226-5446
Colonna Brothers
North Bergen, NJ 201-864-1115
Colorado Salsa Company
Littleton, CO 303-932-2617
ConAgra Foods
Boisbriand, QC 450-433-1322
ConAgra Grocery Products
Archbold, OH 419-445-8015
ConAgra Grocery Products
Irvine, CA 714-680-1000
Consumers Vinegar & Spice Company
Chicago, IL 773-376-4100
Continental Seasoning
Teaneck, NJ. 800-631-1564
Conway Import Company
Franklin Park, IL. 800-323-8801
Cookies Food Products
Wall Lake, IA 800-331-4995
Cordon Bleu International
Anjou, QC. 514-352-3000
Corfu Foods
Bensenville, IL 630-595-2510
Corsair Pepper Sauce
Gulfport, MS. 228-452-0311
Costa Deano's Gourmet Foods
Canton, OH 800-337-2823
Couch's Original Sauce
Jonesboro, AR. 800-264-7535
Country Bob's
Centralia, IL 800-373-2140
Country Fresh Food & Confections, Inc.
Oliver Springs, TN 800-545-8782
Country Village Meats
Sublette, IL 815-849-5532
Cowboy Foods
Bozeman, MT 800-759-5489
Crave Natural Foods
Northampton, MA. 413-587-7999
Crazy Jerry's
Roswell, GA 770-993-0651
Creative Foodworks
San Antonio, TX. 210-212-4761
Crustacean Foods
Los Angeles, CA. 866-263-2625
Cucina Antica Foods Corp
Mount Kisco, NY 877-728-2462
Cugino's Gourmet Foods
Crystal Lake, IL 888-592-8446
Cuizina Food Company
Woodinville, WA. 425-486-7000
Culinary Foods
Chicago, IL 800-621-4049
Culinary Standards Corporation
Louisville, KY 800-778-3434
Curry King Corporation
Waldwick, NJ 800-287-7987
Custom Culinary
Lombard, IL 800-621-8827
Custom Food Solutions
Louisville, KY 800-767-2993
Custom Ingredients
New Braunfels, TX. 800-457-8935
Cyclone Enterprises
Houston, TX 281-872-0087
D & D Foods
Columbus, GA 706-322-4507
D'Oni Enterprises
San Juan Capistrano, CA 800-809-8298
Dabruzzi's Italian Foods
Hudson, WI. 715-386-3653
Dahm's Foods
Skokie, IL 847-673-0653
Daregal Gourmet
Princeton, NJ. 609-375-2312
Dean Distributors
Burlingame, CA 800-792-0816
Deep South Products
Fitzgerald, GA. 229-423-1121
Del Mar Food Products Corporation
Watsonville, CA 831-722-3516
Delgrosso Foods Inc.
Tipton, PA 800-521-5880

Dell'Amore Enterprises
Colchester, VT 800-962-6673
Delta BBQ Sauce Company
Stockton, CA. 209-472-9284
Dhidow Enterprises
Oxford, PA 610-932-7868
DiGregorio Food Products
St Louis, MO. 314-776-1062
Dillard's Bar-B-Q Sauce
Durham, NC 919-544-1587
Dipasa
Brownsville, TX 956-831-5893
Diversified Foods & Seasoning
Metairie, LA 504-846-5090
Divine Foods
Elizabethtown, NC 910-862-2576
Dixie Trail Farms
Wilmington, NC 800-665-3968
Dolefam Corporation
Arlington Hts, IL 847-577-2122
Dorina/So-Good
Union, IL. 815-923-2144
Dorothy Dawson Foods Products
Jackson, MI 517-788-9830
Dr Pete's
Savannah, GA 888-599-0047
Dressed in Style/Chase Chase Food Company
Atlanta, GA. 888-368-2698
Drew's
Chester, VT. 800-228-2980
Drew's All Natural
Chester, VT. 800-228-2980
E. Waldo Ward & Son Corporation
Sierra Madre, CA 800-355-9273
E.D. Smith Foods Ltd
Winona, ON 800-263-9246
E.M.D. Sales, Inc.
Baltimore, MD 301-322-4503
Earth & Vine Provisions
Loomis, CA. 888-723-8463
East Wind Nut Butters
Tecumseh, MO 417-679-4682
Eastern Food Industries
East Greenwich, RI. 401-884-8798
Eastern Foods Naturally Fresh
College Park, GA 404-765-9000
Eatem Foods Company
Vineland, NJ 800-683-2836
Eden Foods Inc.
Clinton, MI 800-248-0320
Edmonds Chile Company
St Louis, MO. 314-772-1499
El Charro Mexican Food Industries
Roswell, NM. 575-622-8590
El Paso Chile Company
El Paso, TX. 888-472-5727
El Rancho Tortilla
San Antonio, TX. 210-922-8411
El Toro Food Products
Watsonville, CA 831-728-9266
El-Rey Foods
Ferguson, MO. 314-521-3113
Escalon Premier Brand
Escalon, CA 209-838-7341
Essen Nutrition
Romeoville, IL 630-739-6700
Ethnic Gourmet Foods
West Chester, PA. 610-692-7575
Europa Foods
Saddle Brook, NJ 201-368-8929
Excalibur Seasoning Company
Pekin, IL 800-444-2169
Famous Chili
Fort Smith, AR 479-782-0096
Farmacopia
Saratoga, CA. 888-827-3623
Father's Country Hams
Bremen, KY 270-525-3554
Favorite Foods
Burnaby, BC 604-420-5100
Felbro Food Products
Los Angeles, CA. 800-335-2761
Fernandez Chili Company
Alamosa, CO. 719-589-6043
Festive Foods
Virginia Beach, VA. 757-490-9186
Fiesta Canning Company
Mc Neal, AZ 520-642-3376
Figaro Company
Mesquite, TX 972-288-3587
Fireside Kitchen
Halifax, NS 902-454-7387

Fischer & Wieser Specialty Foods, Inc.
Fredericksburg, TX. 800-880-8526
Flavor House
Adelanto, CA 760-246-9131
Food Concentrate Corporation
Oklahoma City, OK 405-840-5633
Food Masters
Griffin, GA 888-715-4394
Food Source
Mc Kinney, TX 972-548-9001
Food Source Company
Mississauga, ON. 905-625-8404
Foodbrands America
Oklahoma City, OK 405-290-4000
Fool Proof Gourmet Products
Grapevine, TX 817-329-1839
Ford's Fancy Fruit
Raleigh, NC 800-446-0947
Fords Gourmet Foods
Raleigh, NC 800-446-0947
Fountain Valley Foods
Colorado Springs, CO. 719-573-6012
Fox Hollow Farm
Hanover, NH. 603-643-6002
Freedom Gourmet Sauce
Nashville, TN 615-333-9063
Fremont Authentic Brands
Fremont, OH. 419-334-8995
French's Flavor Ingredients
Springfield, MO 800-437-3624
Frontera Foods
Chicago, IL 800-509-4441
Furmano Foods
Northumberland, PA 877-877-6032
Fusion Gourmet
Gardena, CA 310-532-8938
Fuzzy's Wholesale Bar-B-Q
Madison, NC. 336-548-2283
G Di Lullo & Sons
Westville, NJ. 856-456-3700
Galena Canning Company
Galena, IL 815-777-2882
Garden Complements
Kansas City, MO. 800-966-1091
Garden Row Foods
Franklin Park, IL. 800-555-9798
Garlic Festival Foods
Hollister, CA. 888-427-5423
Garlic Survival Company
San Francisco, CA 415-822-7112
Gator Hammock
Felda, FL. 800-664-2867
Gayle's Sweet 'N Sassy Foods
Beverly Hills, CA 310-246-1792
Geetha's Gourmet of India
Las Cruces, NM 800-274-0475
Gehl Foods, Inc.
Germantown, WI. 800-521-2873
Gehl Guernsey Farms
Germantown, WI. 800-434-5713
Gemini Food Industries
Charlton, MA 508-248-2730
Genarom International
Cranbury, NJ 609-409-6200
Geneva Ingredients
Waunakee, WI. 800-828-5924
Gentilini's Italian Products
Sunriver, OR 541-593-5053
GFF
City of Industry, CA 323-846-2700
Gia Russa
Coitsville, OH. 800-527-8772
Gingro Corp
Manchester Center, VT. 802-362-0836
Giovanni Food Company, Inc
Liverpool, NY. 315-457-2373
Girard's Food Service Dressings
City of Industry, CA 888-327-8442
Glencourt
Napa, CA. 707-944-4444
GMB Specialty Foods
San Juan Cpstrno, CA. 800-809-8098
Gold Dollar Products
Memphis, TN 800-971-8964
Gold Pure Foods Products Company
Hempstead, NY. 800-422-4681
Golden Specialty Foods
Norwalk, CA. 562-802-2537
Golden State Foods
Irvine, CA. 949-252-2000
Golden Valley Foods
Abbotsford, BC. 888-299-8855

Golden West Specialty Foods
Brisbane, CA......................800-584-4481
Golden Whisk
South San Francisco, CA............800-660-5222
Goldrush Sourdough
San Jose, CA......................408-288-4090
Goldwater's Food's Of Arizona
Fredericksburg, TX.................800-488-4932
Gourmet Central
Romney, WV......................800-984-3722
Gourmet Conveniences Ltd
Litchfield, CT.....................866-793-3801
Gourmet's Secret
North Highlands, CA...............916-334-6161
Grain Processing Corporation
Muscatine, IA.....................800-448-4472
Gravymaster, Inc.
Canajoharie, NY...................800-839-8938
Great American Barbecue Company
Weimar, TX.......................510-865-3133
Green Garden Food Products
Kent, WA.........................800-304-1033
Griffin Food Company
Muskogee, OK.....................800-580-6311
Griffith Laboratories Worldwide
Alsip, IL.........................800-346-4743
Groeb Farms
Onsted, MI.......................517-467-2065
Grouse Hunt Farms
Tamaqua, PA......................570-467-2850
Guido's International Foods
Pasadena, CA.....................877-994-8436
Gumpert's Canada
Mississauga, ON...................800-387-9324
Gunther's Gourmet
Richmond, VA.....................804-240-1796
H.J. Heinz Company
Pittsburgh, PA.....................800-872-2229
Habby Habanero's Food Products
Jacksonville, FL...................904-333-9758
Hagerty Foods
Orange, CA.......................714-628-1230
Hains Celestial Group
Melville, NY......................877-612-4246
Halben Food Manufacturing Company
Saint Louis, MO...................800-888-4855
Halifax Group
Doraville, GA.....................770-452-8828
Hampton Chutney Company
Amagansett, NY
Hanan Products Company
Hicksville, NY....................516-938-1000
Hanover Foods Corporation
Hanover, PA......................717-632-6000
Harry's Cafe
Mount Holly, VT...................802-259-2996
Hartford City Foam Pack aging & Converting
Hartford City, IN...................765-348-2500
Hartville Kitchen
Hartville, OH.....................330-877-9353
Hartville Locker
Hartville, OH.....................330-877-9547
Harvest-Pac Products
Chatham, ON.....................519-436-0446
Haus Barhyte
Pendleton, OR.....................800-407-9241
Havana's Limited
Titusville, FL.....................321-267-0513
Havoc Maker Products
Guilford, CT......................800-681-3909
Hawaiian Fruit Specialties
Kalaheo, HI.......................808-332-9333
Heartline Foods
Westport, CT......................203-222-0381
Heffy's BBQ Company
Kansas City, MO..................816-200-2271
Heintz & Weber Company
Buffalo, NY.......................716-852-7171
Heinz Company of Canada
North York, ON....................877-574-3469
Heinz Portion Control
Mason, OH.......................800-547-8924
Heluva Good Cheese
Sodus, NY........................315-483-6971
Heritage Family Specialty Foods
Grand Prairie, TX..................800-648-2837
Heronwood Farm
Kent, WA.........................877-203-5908
Hillside Lane Farm
Randolph, VT.....................802-728-0070
Hirzel Canning Company &Farms
Northwood, OH...................419-693-0531
Hoffman Aseptic Packaging Company
Hoffman, MN.....................320-986-2084
Hogtowne B-B-Q Sauce Company
Gainesville, FL....................352-375-6969
Hollman Foods
Chicago, IL.......................888-926-2879
Homestead Fine Foods
S San Francisco, CA................650-615-0750
Honey Bear Fruit Basket
Denver, CO.......................888-330-2327
Honeydrop Foods
Bridgewater, NJ...................908-203-1577
HongryHawg Products
Prairieville, LA....................888-772-4294
Hoopeston Foods
Burnsville, MN....................952-854-0903
Hopkins Inn
Warren, CT.......................860-868-7295
Hormel Foods Corporation
Columbia, MD....................410-290-1916
Hormel Foods Corporation
Orchard Park, NY..................716-675-7700
Hormel Foods Corporation
Austin, MN.......................800-523-4635
House of Webster
Rogers, AR.......................800-369-4641
Howjax
Pembroke Pines, FL................954-441-2491
Hume Specialties
Chester, VT.......................802-875-3117
Hunt-Wesson Food Service Company
Rochester, NY.....................866-484-8676
HV Food Products Company
Oakland, CA......................800-537-2823
HVJ International
Spring, TX.......................877-730-3663
Illes Seasonings & Flavors
Carrollton, TX....................800-683-4553
Imus Ranch Foods
Darien, CT.......................505-892-0883
Inter-State Cider & Vinegar Company
Baltimore, MD....................410-947-1529
Intercorp Excelle Foods
North York, ON...................416-226-5757
International Bar-B-Que
Unionville, IN.....................812-988-6150
International Diverse Foods
Nashville, TN.....................615-889-8345
International Food Products Corporation
Saint Louis, MO...................314-421-6151
International Foods & Confections
Alpharetta, GA....................770-887-0201
International Home Foods
Parsippany, NJ....................973-359-9920
Island Spices
Miami, FL........................786-208-2066
Italia Foods
Schaumburg, IL...................800-747-1109
Ittella Foods
Los Angeles, CA..................213-746-6201
J&R Foods
Long Branch, NJ..................732-229-4020
J.A.M.B. Low Carb Distributor
Pompano Beach, FL................800-708-6738
J.D. Mullen Company
Palestine, IL......................618-586-2727
J.N. Bech
Elk Rapids, MI....................800-232-4583
J.T. Pappy's Sauce
Los Angeles, CA...................323-969-9605
J.W. Raye & Company
Eastport, ME......................800-853-1903
J.W. Raye & Company
Mira Loma, CA...................909-428-8630
Jack Miller's Food Products
Ville Platte, LA...................800-646-1541
Jalapeno Foods Company
The Woodlands, TX................800-896-2318
Jet's Le Frois Foods Corporation
Brockport, NY....................585-637-5003
Jillipepper
Albuquerque, NM.................505-344-2804
Jimtown Store
Healdsburg, CA...................707-433-1212
JMS Specialty Foods
Ripon, WI........................800-535-5437
Joe Hutson Foods
Jacksonville, FL...................904-731-9065
Johnny Harris Famous Barbecue Sauce
Savannah, GA.....................912-354-8828
Joseph's Pasta Company
Haverhill, MA.....................888-327-2782
Juanita's Foods
Wilmington, CA...................310-834-5339
Judyth's Mountain
San Jose, CA......................408-264-3330
Jyoti Cuisine India
Berwyn, PA.......................610-296-4620
Kagome
Los Banos, CA....................209-826-8850
Kajun Kettle Foods
New Orleans, LA..................504-733-8800
Kari-Out Company
White Plains, NY..................800-433-8799
Kathy's Gourmet Specialties
Mendocino, CA....................707-937-1383
Kelchner's Horseradish
Dublin, PA........................215-249-3439
Kemach Food Products Corporation
Brooklyn, NY.....................888-453-6224
Ken's Foods
Marlborough, MA..................800-633-5800
Kentucky Bourbon
Westport, KY.....................866-472-7797
Kerala Curry
Pittsboro, NC.....................919-545-9401
Kettle Cooked Food
Fort Worth, TX....................817-615-4500
Kettle Master
Hillsville, VA.....................276-728-7571
Key Ingredients
Harrisburg, PA....................800-227-4448
Kikkoman International
San Francisco, CA.................415-956-7750
Kilwons Foods
Santa Cruz, CA....................831-426-9670
Kind Snacks
New York, NY....................800-732-2321
King's Cupboard
Red Lodge, MT....................800-962-6555
Kitchen Products
Gloucester, MA....................978-283-1384
Knott's Berry Farm Foods
Placentia, CA.....................800-289-9927
Knouse Foods Coop
Peach Glen, PA....................717-677-8181
Knudsen's Candy
Hayward, CA.....................800-736-6887
Kozlowski Farms
Forestville, CA....................800-473-2767
Kraus & Company
Commerce Township, MI............800-662-5871
Kroger Company
Cincinnati, OH....................800-576-4377
L & S Packing Company
Farmingdale, NY..................877-879-6453
L&S Packing Company
Farmingdale, NY..................800-286-6487
La Piccolina
Decatur, GA......................800-626-1624
La Vencedora Products
Los Angeles, CA..................800-327-2572
LaMonica Fine Foods
Millville, NJ......................856-825-8111
Lang Naturals
Newport, RI......................401-848-7700
Laredo Mexican Foods
Fort Wayne, IN....................800-252-7336
Le Frois Foods Corporation
Brockport, NY....................585-637-5003
Lea & Perrins
Fair Lawn, NJ.....................800-289-5797
Leams
Hutchinson, KS...................316-662-4287
Lee Kum Kee
City of Industry, CA................800-654-5082
Lees Sausage Company
Orangeburg, SC...................803-534-5517
Lemmes Company
Coventry, RI......................401-821-2575
Lendy's
Virginia Beach, VA................757-491-3511
Leroux Creek Foods
Hotchkiss, CO....................877-970-5670
Les Aliments Livabec Foods
Sherrington, QC...................450-454-7971
Li'l Guy Foods
Kansas City, MO..................800-886-8226
Litehouse Foods
Sandpoint, ID.....................800-669-3169
Lloyd's Barbeque Company
Eagan, MN.......................651-688-6000
Longmeadow
Longmeadow, MA.................413-565-4153

Louis Maull Company
Saint Louis, MO 314-241-8410
Louisa Food Products
Saint Louis, MO 314-868-3000
Louisiana Gourmet Enterprises
La Place, LA 985-783-2446
Lounsbury Foods
Toronto, ON 416-656-6330
Lynch Foods
North York, ON 416-449-5464
Lyons-Magnus
Fresno, CA 559-268-5966
M.A. Gedney
Chaska, MN 952-448-2612
Mad Chef Enterprise
Mentor, OH 800-951-2433
Mad Will's Food Company
Auburn, CA 888-275-9455
Madison Foods
Saint Paul, MN 651-265-8212
Maggie Gin's
San Francisco, CA 415-221-6080
Magic Seasoning Blends
New Orleans, LA 800-457-2857
Mandarin Soy Sauce
Middletown, NY 845-343-1505
Mansmith's Barbecue
San Jn Bautista, CA 800-626-7648
Maple Grove Farms of Vermont
St Johnsbury, VT 800-525-2540
Mar-K Anchor Bar Hot Sauces
Buffalo, NY 71- 8-6 89
Marsan Foods
Toronto, ON 416-755-9262
Martha Olson's Great Foods
Sutter Creek, CA 800-973-3966
Matouk International USAInc
Sunrise, FL 954-742-2204
Mayacamas Fine Foods
Sonoma, CA 800-826-9621
McCutcheon's Apple Products
Frederick, MD 800-888-7537
McLane Foods
Phoenix, AZ 602-275-5509
Mcllhenny Company
New Orleans, LA 504-523-7370
Meditalia
New York, NY 212-616-3006
Mercado Latino
City of Industry, CA 626-333-6862
Mexisnax Corporation
El Paso, TX 915-779-5709
Michele's Original Gourmet Tofu Products
Philadelphia, PA 215-922-2588
Mid-Atlantic Foods
Easton, MD 800-922-4688
Miguel's Stowe Away
Stowe, VT 800-448-6517
Millflow Spice Corporation
Hauppauge, NY 866-227-8355
Minnesota Specialty Crops
McGregor, MN 800-328-6731
Mix-A-Lota Stuff LLC
Fort Pierce, FL 772-468-4688
Miyako Oriental Foods
Baldwin Park, CA 877-788-6476
Mizkam Americas
Kansas City, MO 816-483-1700
Mo Hotta-Mo Betta
Pooler, GA 912-748-6111
Mojave Foods Corporation
Commerce, CA 323-890-8900
Molinaro's Fine Italian Foods
Mississauga, ON 800-268-4959
Mom's Barbeque Sauce
Stow, OH 330-929-7290
Montebello Kitchens
Gordonsville, VA 800-743-7687
Monterrey Products Company
San Antonio, TX 210-435-2872
Monterrey Products Company
San Antonio, TX 800-872-1652
Moonlite Bar Bq Inn
Owensboro, KY 800-322-8989
More Than Gourmet
Akron, OH 800-860-9385
Morgan Food
Austin, IN 888-430-1780
Morning Star Packing Company
Los Banos, CA 209-826-8000
Mother Teresa's
Clute, TX 888-265-7429

Mott's
Elmsford, NY
MPK Sonama Corporation
Sonoma, CA 707-996-3931
Mrs. Clark's Foods
Ankeny, IA 800-736-5674

Juices, salad dressings and sauces.

Mrs. Dog's Products
Grand Rapids, MI 800-2Mr-Dog
Mullins Food Products
Broadview, IL 708-344-3224
Multi Foods
Portland, OR 800-666-8998
Myron's Fine Foods
Millers Falls, MA 800-730-2820
Nana Mae's Organics
Sebastopol, CA 707-829-7359
Nationwide Canning
Cottam, ON 519-839-4831
Native Kjalii Foods
San Francisco, CA 415-522-5580
Naturally Fresh Foods
Atlanta, GA 800-765-1950
New Business Corporation
Gary, IN 800-742-8435
New Canaan Farms
Dripping Springs, TX 800-727-5267
New England Natural Baker
Greenfield, MA 800-910-2884
New Era Canning Company
New Era, MI 231-861-2151
Newly Weds Foods
Chicago, IL 800-647-9314
Nog Incorporated
Dunkirk, NY 800-332-2664
Noh Foods of Hawaii
Honolulu, HI 808-944-0655
North American Enterprises
Tucson, AZ 800-817-8666
North Coast Processing
North East, PA 814-725-9617
Nuovo Pasta Productions
Stratford, CT 800-803-0033
O'Brian Brothers Food
Cincinnati, OH 513-791-9909
O'Garvey Sauces
New Braunfels, TX 830-620-6127
Ocean Spray Cranberries
Kenosha, WI 262-694-5200
Ocean Spray Cranberries
Lakeville-Middleboro, MA 800-662-3263
Ojai Cook
Los Angeles, CA 886-571-1551
Old Mansion Foods
Petersburg, VA 800-476-1877
Old World Spices & Seasonings, Inc.
Overland Park, KS 800-241-0070
On the Verandah
Highlands, NC 828-526-2338
Original Italian Pasta Poducts Company
Chelsea, MA 800-999-9603
Ott Food Products
Carthage, MO 800-866-2585
Our Enterprises
Oklahoma City, OK 800-821-6375
Overhill Farms
Vernon, CA 800-859-6406
Pacific Choice Brands
Fresno, CA 559-237-5583
Pacific Harvest Products
Bellevue, WA 425-401-7990
Pacific Poultry Company
Honolulu, HI 808-841-2828
Pak Technologies
Milwaukee, WI 414-438-8600
Palmieri Food Products
New Haven, CT 800-845-5447
Papa Leone Food Enterprises
Beverly Hills, CA 310-552-1660
Paradise Products Corporation
Boca Raton, FL 800-826-1235
Park 100 Foods
Tipton, IN 800-854-6504
Parthenon Food Products
Ann Arbor, MI 734-994-1012
Passetti's Pride
Hayward, CA 800-521-4659
Pasta Factory
Melrose Park, IL 800-615-6951
Pasta Partners
Salt Lake City, UT 800-727-8284

Pastor Chuck Orchards
Portland, ME 207-773-1314
Pastorelli Food Products
Chicago, IL 800-767-2829
PaStreeta Fresca
Dublin, OH 800-343-5266
Peaceworks
New York, NY 212-897-3985
Peaceworks
New York, NY 800-732-2321
Pearlco of Boston
Canton, MA 781-821-1010
Pearson's Homestyle
Bowden, AB 877-224-3339
Pecan Deluxe Candy Company
Dallas, TX 800-733-3589
Pemberton's Gourmet Foods
Gray, ME 800-255-8401
Pepper Creek Farms
Lawton, OK 800-526-8132
Pepper Town
Van Nuys, CA 800-973-7738
Peppers
Rehoboth Beach, DE 302-644-6900
Pett Spice Products
Atlanta, GA 404-691-5235
Pierino Frozen Foods
Lincoln Park, MI 313-928-0950
Piggie Park Enterprises
West Columbia, SC 800-628-7423
Pino's Pasta Veloce
Staten Island, NY 718-273-6660
Plentiful Pantry
Salt Lake City, UT 800-727-8284
Plenus Group
Lowell, MA 978-970-3832
Poison Pepper Company
Floral City, FL 888-539-5540
Pomodoro Fresca Foods
Millburn, NJ 973-467-6609
Porinos Gourmet Food
Central Falls, RI 800-826-3938
Porky's Gourmet
Gallatin, TN 800-767-5911
Prairie Thyme
Santa Fe, NM 800-869-0009
Presco Food Seasonings
Flemington, NJ 800-526-1713
Pride of White River Valley
Gaysville, VT 802-234-9115
Private Harvest
El Dorado Hills, CA 916-933-7080
Private Harvest Gourmet Specialities
Lakeport, CA 800-463-0594
Private Label Foods
Rochester, NY 585-254-9205
Produits Ronald
St. Damase, QC 800-465-0118
Progresso Quality Foods
Vineland, NJ 800-200-9377
Purity Products
Plainview, NY 888-769-7873
Quality Assured Packing
Stockton, CA 209-931-6700
Quality Chef Foods
Cedar Rapids, IA 800-356-8307
Quality Foods
San Pedro, CA 877-833-7890
R&R Homestead Kitchen
Saumico, WI 888-779-8245
R.L. Schreiber
Pompano Beach, FL 800-624-8777
R.L. Schreiber Company
Pompano Beach, FL 800-624-8777
R.W. Knudsen
Chico, CA 530-899-5000
Raggy-O Chutney
Smithfield, NC 888-424-8863
Ragozzino Food
Meriden, CT 800-348-1240
Ragsdale-Overton Food Traditions
Smithfield, NC 888-424-8863
Rahco International
St Augustine, FL 800-851-7681
Rancho's
Memphis, TN 901-276-8820
Randag & Associates Inc
Elmhurst, IL 630-530-2830
Rao's Specialty Foods
New York, NY 212-269-0151
Ray's Sausage Company Inc
Cleveland, OH 216-921-8782

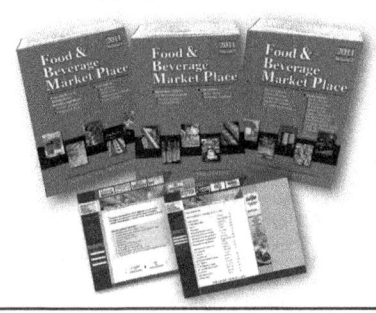

Red Lion Spicy Foods Company
Red Lion, PA 717-309-8303
Reily Foods Company
New Orleans, LA 504-524-6131
Renfro Foods
Fort Worth, TX 817-336-3849
Restaurant Lulu Gourmet Products
San Francisco, CA 888-693-5800
REX Pure Foods
New Orleans, LA 800-344-8314
Reynolds Sugar Bush
Aniwa, WI. 715-449-2057
Riba Foods
Houston, TX 800-327-7422
Richardson Foods Corporation
Macedon, NY 315-986-2807
Richelieu Foods
Randolph, MA 781-961-1537
Rio Valley Canning Company
Donna, TX. 956-464-7843
River Run
Burlington, VT 802-863-0499
Rivertown Foods
Saint Louis, MO 800-844-3210
Robert Rothschild Farm
Urbana, OH. 866-565-6790
Robinson Barbecue Sauce Company
Oak Park, IL 800-836-6750
Robinson's Barbecue Sauce Company
Oak Park, IL 708-383-8452
Ronzoni Foods Canada
Etobicoke, ON 800-387-5032
Rosa Mexicano Kitchen
New York, NY 212-397-0666
Roses Ravioli
Oglesby, IL 815-883-8011
Rosmarino Foods/R.Z. Humbert Company
Odessa, FL 888-926-9053
Rossi Pasta
Marietta, OH. 800-227-6774
Rowena's
Norfolk, VA. 800-627-8699
Royal Baltic
Brooklyn, NY 718-385-8300
Royal Food Products
Indianapolis, IN 317-782-2660
Ruskin Redneck Trading Company
Ruskin, FL 813-645-7710
S.D. Mushrooms
Avondale, PA 610-268-8082
Sabatino Truffles USA
Bronx, NY. 888-444-9971
Sable & Rosenfeld Foods
Toronto, ON 416-929-4214
Sadler's Smokehouse
Henderson, TX 903-657-5581
Sambets Cajun Deli
Austin, TX. 800-472-6238
San Benito Foods
Hollister, CA. 831-637-4434
Santa Barbara Olive Company
Santa Barbara, CA 800-624-4896
Santa Barbara Salsa/California Creative
Oceanside, CA 800-748-5523
Santa Cruz Chili & SpiceCompany
Tumacacori, AZ 520-398-2591
Sau-Sea Foods
Tarrytown, NY 914-631-1717
Sauces 'n Love
Lynn, MA 866-772-8237
Savannah Food Company
Savannah, TN 800-795-2550
Savoie's Sausage & Food Products
Opelousas, LA. 337-948-4115

Schiavone's Casa Mia
Middletown, OH. 513-422-8650
Schlotterbeck & Foss Company
Portland, ME. 800-777-4666
Scott's Sauce Company
Goldsboro, NC 800-734-7282
Seeds of Change
Santa Fe, NM 888-762-7333
Select Food Products
Toronto, ON 800-699-8016
Seminole Foods
Springfield, OH. 800-881-1177
Senba USA
Hayward, CA 888-922-5852
Seneca Foods
Clyman, WI. 920-696-3331
Sentry Seasonings
Elmhurst, IL 630-530-5370

The product development experts of Sentry Seasonings are eager to offer the assistance and hands-on experience to food processors of all sizes. Sentry Seasonings will ensure the consistent high quality and repeat sales of your products, whether you choose one of our many off-the-shelf Bench Mark products or a modified version to meet your preferences. Sentry Seasonings can also duplicate and/or improve your present flavor profile; formulate, blend and package specifically for your requirements.

Sieco USA Corporation
Houston, TX 800-325-9443
Silver Palate Kitchens
Cresskill, NJ 800-872-5283
Silver Spring Gardens
Eau Claire, WI 800-826-7322
Silver State Foods
Denver, CO. 800-423-3351
Simeus Foods Internatio nal
Mansfield, TX. 888-772-3663
Simeus Foods International
Mansfield, TX. 888-772-3663
Simply Delicious
Cedar Grove, NC 919-732-5294
SK Foods
Lemoore, CA. 559-924-6527
Skjodt-Barrett Foods
Mississauga, ON. 877-600-1200
Slather Brand Foods LLC
Charleston, SC 843-513-1750
Sokol & Company
Countryside, IL. 800-328-7656
Solana Gold Organics
Sebastopol, CA 800-459-1121
SOPAKCO Foods
Mullins, SC. 800-276-9678
Sopakco Foods
Mullins, SC. 843-464-7851
Sophia's Sauce Works
Carson City, NV 800-718-7769
South Ceasar Dressing Company
Novato, CA. 415-897-0605
Southern Delight Gourmet Foods
Bowling Green, KY 866-782-9943
Southern Ray's Foods
Miami Beach, FL 800-972-8237
Southwest Specialty Food
Goodyear, AZ 800-536-3131
Soy Vay Enterprises
Felton, CA. 800-600-2077
Spanarkel Company
Neptune City, NJ. 732-775-4144

Spanish Gardens Food Manufacturing
Kansas City, KS 913-831-4242
Specialty Brands
Carthage, MO 417-358-8104
Spring Tree Maple Products
Brattleboro, VT. 802-254-8784
Stage Coach Sauces
Palatka, FL 386-328-6330
Stanislaus Food Products
Modesto, CA. 800-327-7201
Starport Foods
San Francisco, CA 866-206-9343
Stello Foods
Punxsutawney, PA. 800-849-4599
Stickney & Poor Company
Peterborough, NH. 603-924-2259
Stonewall Kitchen
York, ME. 800-207-5267
Stubb's Legendary Kitchen
Austin, TX. 800-227-2283
Sun Harvest Foods
San Diego, CA 619-661-0909
Super Smokers BBQ
Dardenne, IL 636- 61- 118
Surlean Foods
San Antonio, TX. 800-999-4370
Swatt Baking Company
Olean, NY 800-370-6656
Sweet Baby Ray's
Chicago, IL 877-729-2229
Sweetwater Spice Company
Austin, TX. 800-531-6079
Swift & Company
Greeley, CO. 970-506-8000
Swiss Food Products
Chicago, IL 312-829-0100
T Marzetti Company
Columbus, OH 614-846-2232
T. Marzetti Company
Columbus, OH 614-846-2232
T.W. Garner Food Company
Winston Salem, NC. 800-476-7383
Tait Farm Foods
Centre Hall, PA. 800-787-2716
Tantos Foods International
Markham, ON. 905-943-9993
Tapatio Hot Sauce
Vernon, CA 323-587-8933
Tasty Tomato
San Antonio, TX. 210-822-2443
Tex-Mex Gourmet
Brenham, TX. 888-345-8467
Texas Heat
San Antonio, TX. 800-656-5916
Thistledew Farm
Proctor, WV 800-854-6639
Thomas Gourmet Foods
Greensboro, NC 800-867-2823
Thompson's Fine Foods
Shoreview, MN. 800-807-0025
Thomson Food
Duluth, MN. 218-722-2529
Thor-Shackel HorseradishCompany
Eau Claire, WI 800-826-7322
Thornton Foods Company
Eden Prairie, MN 952-944-1735
Timber Crest Farms
Healdsburg, CA 888-374-9325
Timeless Traditions
Pittsford, VT. 802-483-6024
Tip Top Canning Company
Tipp City, OH 800-352-2635
Todd's
Des Moines, IA. 800-247-5363

Tomasso Corporation
Baie D'Urfe, QC. 514-325-3000
Tommaso's Fresh Pasta
Dallas, TX. 972-869-1111
Top Hat Company
Wilmette, IL 847-256-6565
Topper Food Products
East Brunswick, NJ. 800-377-2823
Trader Vic's Food Products
Emeryville, CA. 877-762-4824
Trappey's Fine Foods
New Iberia, LA. 337-365-8281
Tree Top
Selah, WA 800-367-6571
Tree Top
Selah, WA 800-542-4055
Tres Classique
Ukiah, CA. 888-644-5127
Triple H Food Processors
Riverside, CA 951-352-5700
Triple K Manufacturing Company
Shenandoah, IA. 888-987-2824
Truesoups
Kent, WA. 253-872-0403
Tulkoff Food Products
Baltimore, MD 800-638-7343
Twin Marquis
Brooklyn, NY 800-367-6868
Two Chefs on a Roll
Carson, CA 800-842-3025
Ultimate Gourmet
Belle Mead, NJ 908-359-4050
Uncle Bum's Gourmet Foods
Riverside, CA 800-486-2867
Valley Grain Products
Madera, CA. 559-675-3400
Vanlaw Food Products
Fullerton, CA 714-870-9091
Vegetable Juices
Chicago, IL 888-776-9752
Ventre Packing Company
Syracuse, NY 888-472-8237
Ventura Foods
Philadelphia, PA 215-223-8700
Vermont BS
Hinesburg, VT. 802-482-2152
Victoria Packing Corporation
Brooklyn, NY 718-927-3000
Vidalia Brands
Reidsville, GA 800-752-0206
Vidalia Sweets Brand
Lyons, GA. 912-565-8881
Vietti Foods Company Inc
Nashville, TN 800-240-7864
Village Imports
Brisbane, CA. 888-865-8714
Vincent's Food Corporation
Carle Place, NY 516-481-3544
Violet Packing
Williamstown, NJ 856-629-7428
Vivienne Dressings
St Louis, MO. 800-827-0778
Wagner Gourmet Foods
Lenexa, KS 913-469-5411
Walker Foods
Los Angeles, CA. 800-966-5199
Webbpak
Trussville, AL 800-655-3500
Wei-Chuan
Bell Gardens, CA 562-372-2020
Weir Sauces
Napa, CA. 415-884-5849
Welcome Dairy
Colby, WI 800-472-2315
Well Dressed Food Company
Tupper Lake, NY 866-567-0845
West Pac
Idaho Falls, ID 800-973-7407
Westbrae Natural Foods
Melville, NY. 800-434-4246
Western Dressing
Grundy Center, IA. 319-824-3304
Westin
Omaha, NE 800-228-6098
WFI
Linden, NJ. 800-229-1706
Whole in the Wall
Binghamton, NY. 607-722-5138
Whyte's Food Corporation
Mississauga, ON. 905-624-5065
Wicker's Food Products
Hornersville, MO 800-847-0032
Widow's Mite Vinegar Company
Washington, DC 877-678-5854
WILD Flavors (Canada)
Mississauga, ON. 800-263-5286
Wild Thymes Farm
Greenville, NY 800-724-2877
William B. Reily & Company
Baltimore, MD 410-675-9550
William Poll
New York, NY 800-993-7655
Williams Foods, Inc
Lenexa, KS 800-255-6736
Williams-West & Witt Products
Michigan City, IN
Williamsburg Chocolatier
Williamsburg, VA 757-253-1474
WillowOak Farms
Woodland, CA. 888-963-2767
Wing It
Falmouth, MA. 508-540-9860
Wing Nien Company
Hayward, CA 510-487-8877
Wing-Time
Steamboat Springs, CO. 970-871-1198
Wizards Cauldron, LTD
Yanceyville, NC 336-694-5665
Woeber Mustard Manufacturing
Springfield, OH. 800-548-2929
Wong Wing Foods
Montreal, QC 800-361-4820
Wood Brothers
West Columbia, SC. 803-796-5146
World Flavors
Warminster, PA 215-672-4400
World Harbors
Auburn, ME 800-355-6221
World Herbs Gourmet Company
Hadlyme, CT. 860-526-1908
Worthmore Food Product
Cincinnati, OH 513-559-1473
Wy's Wings
Strasburg, VA 800-997-9464
Yair Scones/Canterbury Cuisine
Medina, WA 800-588-9160
Yamasa Corporation
Torrance, CA. 310-944-3883
Yellow Emperor Pepper Sauce Company
Los Angeles, CA. 608-238-2991
Ynrico's Food Products Company
Syracuse, NY 888-472-8237
Yoshida Food International
Portland, OR 800-653-1114
Zarda Bar-B-Q & Catering Company
Blue Springs, MO. 800-776-7427

Alfredo

Al Dente
Whitmore Lake, MI 800-536-7278
Casa DiLisio Products
Mt Kisco, NY 800-247-4199
Classy Delites
Austin, TX. 800-440-2648
Cuizina Food Company
Woodinville, WA. 425-486-7000
Genarom International
Cranbury, NJ 609-409-6200
Marsan Foods
Toronto, ON 416-755-9262
Newman's Own
Westport, CT. 203-222-0136
Pasta Factory
Melrose Park, IL. 800-615-6951
Sargento Foods Inc.
Plymouth, WI 800-243-3737
Tomasso Corporation
Baie D'Urfe, QC. 514-325-3000
Topper Food Products
East Brunswick, NJ. 800-377-2823
Williams Foods, Inc
Lenexa, KS 800-255-6736

Barbecue

A. Camacho
Plant City, FL 800-881-4534
A. Lassonde, Inc.
Rougemont, QC 888-477-6663
Allied Old English
Port Reading, NJ. 732-636-2060
Annie's Naturals
East Calais, VT. 800-434-1234
Arbor Hill Grapery
Naples, NY 800-554-7553
Ashley Foods
Sudbury, MA. 800-617-2823
Ashman Manufacturing & Distributing Company
Virginia Beach, VA. 800-641-9924
Baker's Rib
Dallas, TX. 214-748-5433
Baldwin Richardson Foods
Frankfort, IL 866-644-2732

Liquid ingredient manufacturer specializing in signature sauces, dessert toppings, beverage/pancake syrups, specialty fruit fillings and condiments.

Bartush-Schnitzius Foods Company
Lewisville, TX 972-219-1270
Baumer Foods
Metairie, LA 504-482-5761
BBQ Bunch
Kansas City, MO. 816-941-4534
BBQ'n Fools
Bend, OR. 800-671-8652
BBS Bodacious BBQ Company
Coral Springs, FL 800-537-5928
Bear Creek Kitchens
Marshall, TX. 888-300-7687
Bettah Buttah, LLC
Kansas City, KS 800-568-8468
Big B Distributors
Evansville, IN 812-425-5235
Blueberry Store
Grand Junction, MI. 877-654-2400
Buffalo Wild Wings
Minneapolis, MN 763-546-1891
Cafe Chilku
Colchester, VT 802-878-4645
Cafe Tequila
San Francisco, CA 415-264-0106
CaJohns Fiery Foods
Westerville, OH. 888-703-3473
California-Antilles Trading Consortium
San Diego, CA 800-330-6450
Captain Bob's Jet Fuel
Fort Wayne, IN 877-486-6468
Carolina Cupboard
Hillsborough, NC 800-400-3441
Carolina Treet
Wilmington, NC 800-616-6344
Casa Visco Finer Food Company
Schenectady, NY. 888-607-2823
Castleberry's
Vineland, NJ 856-691-2100
Catamount Specialties ofVermont
Stowe, VT. 800-820-8096
Catskill Mountain Specialties
Saugerties, NY 800-311-3473
Charlie Beigg's Sauce Company
Windham, ME. 888-502-8595
CHS
Inver Grove Heights, MN. 800-232-3639
CHS, Inc.
Inner Grove Heights, MN. 800-232-3639
Cinnabar Specialty Foods
Prescott, AZ 866-293-6433
Clements Foods Company
Oklahoma City, OK 800-654-8355
Colgin Companies
Dallas, TX. 888-226-5446
Cookies Food Products
Wall Lake, IA 800-331-4995
Cookshack
Ponca City, OK 800-423-0698
Couch's Original Sauce
Jonesboro, AR. 800-264-7535
Country Bob's
Centralia, IL 800-373-2140
Country Cupboard
Virginia City, NV 775-847-7300
Crazy Mary's
Tacoma, WA 253-536-8690

Creative Foodworks
San Antonio, TX … 210-212-4761
Cugino's Gourmet Foods
Crystal Lake, IL … 888-592-8446
Cuisine Perel
Richmond, CA … 800-887-3735
Cuizina Food Company
Woodinville, WA … 425-486-7000
Culver Duck
Middlebury, IN … 800-825-9225
D & D Foods
Columbus, GA … 706-322-4507
Delta BBQ Sauce Company
Stockton, CA … 209-472-9284
Dillard's Bar-B-Q Sauce
Durham, NC … 919-544-1587
Dorina/So-Good
Union, IL … 815-923-2144
Douglas Cross Enterprises
Seattle, WA … 206-448-1193
Dynamic Foods
Lubbock, TX … 806-747-2777
E.D. Smith Foods Ltd
Winona, ON … 800-263-9246
El Paso Chile Company
El Paso, TX … 888-472-5727
El-Rey Foods
Ferguson, MO … 314-521-3113
Favorite Foods
Burnaby, BC … 604-420-5100
Felbro Food Products
Los Angeles, CA … 800-335-2761
Fiesta Gourmet of Tejas
Canyon Lake, TX … 800-585-8250
Figaro Company
Mesquite, TX … 972-288-3587
Food Concentrate Corporation
Oklahoma City, OK … 405-840-5633
Food Ingredients Solutions
Blauvelt, NY … 845-353-8501
Food Processor of New Mexico
Albuquerque, NM … 877-634-3772
Food Specialties
Indianapolis, IN … 317-271-0862
Fremont Authentic Brands
Fremont, OH … 419-334-8995
Fremont Special Brands
Fremont, OH … 419-334-8995
French's Flavor Ingredients
Springfield, MO … 800-437-3624
FunniBonz
West Windsor, NJ … 877-300-2669
Garden Complements
Kansas City, MO … 800-966-1091
Gayle's Sweet 'N Sassy Foods
Beverly Hills, CA … 310-246-1792
Giovanni Food Company
Syracuse, NY … 315-457-2373
Golden Specialty Foods
Norwalk, CA … 562-802-2537
Golden West Specialty Foods
Brisbane, CA … 800-584-4481
Golden Whisk
South San Francisco, CA … 800-660-5222
Golding Farms Foods
Winston Salem, NC … 336-766-6161
Gormly's Orchard
South Burlington, VT … 800-639-7604
Gumpert's Canada
Mississauga, ON … 800-387-9324
Havana's Limited
Titusville, FL … 321-267-0513
Head Country Food Products
Ponca City, OK … 888-762-1227
Heartland Farms
Fort Wayne, IN … 888-747-7423
Heinz Company of Canada
North York, ON … 877-574-3469
Heinz Portion Control
Mason, OH … 800-547-8924
Hollman Foods
Chicago, IL … 888-926-2879
Hormel Foods Corporation
Austin, MN … 800-523-4635
Hot Licks Hot Sauces
Spring Valley, CA … 888-766-6468
Hot Wachula's
Lakeland, FL … 877-883-8700
House of Webster
Rogers, AR … 800-369-4641
J. K Marley's Llc
Rockford, IL
J.N. Bech
Elk Rapids, MI … 800-232-4583
JMS Specialty Foods
Ripon, WI … 800-535-5437
Johnny Harris Famous Barbecue Sauce
Savannah, GA … 912-354-8828
Judicial Flavors
Auburn, CA … 530-885-1298
Kozlowski Farms
Forestville, CA … 800-473-2767
Kraft Foods
Garland, TX … 972-272-7511
L&S Packing Company
Farmingdale, NY … 800-286-6487
Lang Naturals
Newport, RI … 401-848-7700
Lea & Perrins
Fair Lawn, NJ … 800-289-5797
Lees Sausage Company
Orangeburg, SC … 803-534-5517
Lendy's
Virginia Beach, VA … 757-491-3511
Lounsbury Foods
Toronto, ON … 416-656-6330
M.A. Gedney
Chaska, MN … 952-448-2612
Mad Will's Food Company
Auburn, CA … 888-275-9455
Mansmith's Barbecue
San Jn Bautista, CA … 800-626-7648
Mar-K Anchor Bar Hot Sauces
Buffalo, NY … 71- 8-6 89
McCutcheon's Apple Products
Frederick, MD … 800-888-7537
Millflow Spice Corporation
Hauppauge, NY … 866-227-8355
Mrs. Clark's Foods
Ankeny, IA … 800-736-5674

Juices, salad dressings and sauces.

Mucky Duck Mustard Company
Ferndale, MI … 248-544-4610
Nantucket Off-Shore Seasoning
Nantucket, MA … 508-994-1300
New Business Corporation
Gary, IN … 800-742-8435
Newly Weds Foods
Chicago, IL … 800-647-9314
Noh Foods of Hawaii
Honolulu, HI … 808-944-0655
North of the Border
Tesuque, NM … 800-860-0681
O'Brian Brothers Food
Cincinnati, OH … 513-791-9909
Old Mansion Foods
Petersburg, VA … 800-476-1877
Ott Food Products
Carthage, MO … 800-866-2585
Pacific Choice Brands
Fresno, CA … 559-237-5583
Pacific Poultry Company
Honolulu, HI … 808-841-2828
Palmetto Canning Company
Palmetto, FL … 941-722-1100
Palmieri Food Products
New Haven, CT … 800-845-5447
Paradise Products Corporation
Boca Raton, FL … 800-826-1235
Passetti's Pride
Hayward, CA … 800-521-4659
Piggie Park Enterprises
West Columbia, SC … 800-628-7423
Porinos Gourmet Food
Central Falls, RI … 800-826-3938
PorkRubbers BBQ Specialty Products
Lombard, IL … 630-424-8200
Private Harvest Gourmet Specialities
Lakeport, CA … 800-463-0594
Produits Ronald
St. Damase, QC … 800-465-0118
Randag & Associates Inc
Elmhurst, IL … 630-530-2830
Red Gold
Elwood, IN … 877-748-9798
Rivertown Foods
Saint Louis, MO … 800-844-3210
Rob Salamida Company
Johnson City, NY … 607-770-7046
Robbie's Natural Products
Altadena, CA … 626-798-9944
Robinson's Barbecue Sauce Company
Oak Park, IL … 708-383-8452
Rosmarino Foods/R.Z. Humbert Company
Odessa, FL … 888-926-9053
Sadler's Smokehouse
Henderson, TX … 903-657-5581
Sambets Cajun Deli
Austin, TX … 800-472-6238
San Gennaro Foods
Kent, WA … 800-462-1916
Savoie's Sausage & Food Products
Opelousas, LA … 337-948-4115
Schlotterbeck & Foss Company
Portland, ME … 800-777-4666
Scott's Sauce Company
Goldsboro, NC … 800-734-7282
Southern Bar-B-Que
Jennings, LA … 866-612-2586
Southern Delight Gourmet Foods
Bowling Green, KY … 866-782-9943
Southern Ray's Foods
Miami Beach, FL … 800-972-8237
Stanchfield Farms
Milo, ME … 207-732-5173
Steel's Gourmet Foods, Ltd.
Bridgeport, PA … 800-678-3357
Subco Foods Inc
Sheboygan, WI … 800-473-0757
Sweet Baby Ray's
Chicago, IL … 877-729-2229
T. Marzetti Company
Columbus, OH … 614-846-2232
T.W. Garner Food Company
Winston Salem, NC … 800-476-7383
Thompson's Fine Foods
Shoreview, MN … 800-807-0025
Todd's
Des Moines, IA … 800-247-5363
Triple H Food Processors
Riverside, CA … 951-352-5700
Valley Grain Products
Madera, CA … 559-675-3400
Ventre Packing Company
Syracuse, NY … 888-472-8237
Ventura Foods
Philadelphia, PA … 215-223-8700
Vidalia Sweets Brand
Lyons, GA … 912-565-8881
Vietti Foods Company Inc
Nashville, TN … 800-240-7864
Vita Specialty Foods
Martinsburg, WV … 800-989-8482
VT Made Richard's Sauces
Saint Albans, VT … 802-524-3196
Webbpak
Trussville, AL … 800-655-3500
Wei-Chuan
Bell Gardens, CA … 562-372-2020
West Pac
Idaho Falls, ID … 800-973-7407
Westin
Omaha, NE … 800-228-6098
Wine Country Chef LLC
Hidden Valley Lake, CA … 707-322-0406
Wing Nien Company
Hayward, CA … 510-487-8877
Wing-Time
Steamboat Springs, CO … 970-871-1198
Wizards Cauldron, LTD
Yanceyville, NC … 336-694-5665
Wood Brothers
West Columbia, SC … 803-796-5146
World Flavors
Warminster, PA … 215-672-4400
Zarda Bar-B-Q & Catering Company
Blue Springs, MO … 800-776-7427

Black Bean

Favorite Foods
Burnaby, BC … 604-420-5100
Lee Kum Kee
City of Industry, CA … 800-654-5082

Cheese

AFP Advanced Food Products, LLC
Visalia, CA … 559-627-2070
Amboy Specialty Foods Company
Dixon, IL … 800-892-0400
Berner Cheese Corporation
Dakota, IL … 800-819-8199
Berner Foods, Inc.
Roscoe, IL … 800-819-8199

Clofine Dairy & Food Products
Linwood, NJ 800-441-1001
Cuizina Food Company
Woodinville, WA. 425-486-7000
Fountain Valley Foods
Colorado Springs, CO. 719-573-6012
Gehl Guernsey Farms
Germantown, WI. 800-434-5713
Genarom International
Cranbury, NJ. 609-409-6200
Knouse Foods Coop
Peach Glen, PA 717-677-8181
Mann Packing
Salinas, CA 831-422-7405
Marsan Foods
Toronto, ON 416-755-9262
Sargento Foods Inc.
Plymouth, WI 800-243-3737
Thornton Foods Company
Eden Prairie, MN 952-944-1735
Tulkoff Food Products
Baltimore, MD 800-638-7343

Nacho

Associated Milk Producers
Rochester, MN 507-282-7401
Bel/Kaukauna USA
Kaukauna, WI. 800-558-3500
Knouse Foods Coop
Peach Glen, PA 717-677-8181
Olde Tyme Food Corporation
East Longmeadow, MA 800-356-6533
Tulkoff Food Products
Baltimore, MD 800-638-7343
Vanee Foods Company
Berkeley, IL. 708-449-7300

Chili

Baldwin Richardson Foods
Frankfort, IL 866-644-2732

Liquid ingredient manufacturer specializing in signature sauces, dessert toppings, beverage/pancake syrups, specialty fruit fillings and condiments.

Big B Distributors
Evansville, IN 812-425-5235
Cervantes Foods Products
Albuquerque, NM. 877-982-4453
Commodities Marketing, Inc.
Edison, NJ. 732-603-5077
El Charro Mexican Food Industries
Roswell, NM. 575-622-8590
Fernandez Chili Company
Alamosa, CO. 719-589-6043
Fiesta Canning Company
Mc Neal, AZ. 520-642-3376
First Original Texas Chili Company
Fort Worth, TX 817-626-0983
Hurd Orchards
Holley, NY 585-638-8838
Ingleby Farms
Dublin, PA. 877-728-7277
Lee Kum Kee
Flushing, NY. 800-346-7562
Lee Kum Kee
City of Industry, CA 800-654-5082
Mexisnax Corporation
El Paso, TX. 915-779-5709
Miguel's Stowe Away
Stowe, VT 800-448-6517
Mrs. Auld's Gourmet Foods
Reno, NV 800-322-8537
North of the Border
Tesuque, NM. 800-860-0681
Old Mansion Foods
Petersburg, VA 800-476-1877
Red Gold
Elwood, IN 877-748-9798
Santa Cruz Chili & SpiceCompany
Tumacacori, AZ 520-398-2591
T.W. Garner Food Company
Winston Salem, NC. 800-476-7383

Clam

Casa DiLisio Products
Mt Kisco, NY 800-247-4199
Chincoteague Seafood Company
Parsonsburg, MD 443-260-4800
Colonna Brothers
North Bergen, NJ 201-864-1115
Cuizina Food Company
Woodinville, WA. 425-486-7000
Look's Gourmet Food Company
East Machias, ME. 800-962-6258
Mid-Atlantic Foods
Easton, MD. 800-922-4688
Pasta Factory
Melrose Park, IL. 800-615-6951
Topper Food Products
East Brunswick, NJ. 800-377-2823

Cocktail

Baldwin Richardson Foods
Frankfort, IL 866-644-2732

Liquid ingredient manufacturer specializing in signature sauces, dessert toppings, beverage/pancake syrups, specialty fruit fillings and condiments.

Cedarvale Food Products Lounsbury Food Ltd
Toronto, ON 416-656-3331
Clements Foods Company
Oklahoma City, OK 800-654-8355
ConAgra Grocery Products
Irvine, CA 714-680-1000
Cuizina Food Company
Woodinville, WA. 425-486-7000
E. Waldo Ward & Son Corporation
Sierra Madre, CA 800-355-9273
Golden West Specialty Foods
Brisbane, CA. 800-584-4481
Golding Farms Foods
Winston Salem, NC. 336-766-6161
Joe Hutson Foods
Jacksonville, FL 904-731-9065
Kelchner's Horseradish
Dublin, PA. 215-249-3439
Lounsbury Foods
Toronto, ON 416-656-6330
Palmieri Food Products
New Haven, CT 800-845-5447
Paradise Products Corporation
Boca Raton, FL. 800-826-1235
Roller Ed
Rochester, NY. 585-458-8020
Sau-Sea Foods
Tarrytown, NY 914-631-1717
Silver Spring Gardens
Eau Claire, WI 800-826-7322
T. Marzetti Company
Columbus, OH 614-846-2232
T.W. Garner Food Company
Winston Salem, NC. 800-476-7383
Thor-Shackel HorseradishCompany
Eau Claire, WI 800-826-7322
Tulkoff Food Products
Baltimore, MD 800-638-7343
Vegetable Juices
Chicago, IL 888-776-9752

Curry

Baldwin Richardson Foods
Frankfort, IL 866-644-2732

Liquid ingredient manufacturer specializing in signature sauces, dessert toppings, beverage/pancake syrups, specialty fruit fillings and condiments.

Bo-Ling's Products
Overland Park, KS 913-888-8223
Curry King Corporation
Waldwick, NJ 800-287-7987
Lang Naturals
Newport, RI. 401-848-7700

Dessert

Amoretti
Oxnard, CA. 800-266-7388
Applecreek Farms
Lexington, KY 800-747-8871

Duck

Allied Old English
Port Reading, NJ. 732-636-2060
Kari-Out Company
White Plains, NY 800-433-8799
L&S Packing Company
Farmingdale, NY 800-286-6487

Fish

Certified Savory
Countryside, IL. 800-328-7656
Stacey's Famous Foods
Hayden, ID 800-782-2395

Fra Diavolo

Cuizina Food Company
Woodinville, WA. 425-486-7000
L&S Packing Company
Farmingdale, NY 800-286-6487
Palmieri Food Products
New Haven, CT 800-845-5447
Papa Leone Food Enterprises
Beverly Hills, CA 310-552-1660

Frozen

Bellisio Foods, Inc.
Duluth, MN. 800-368-7337
Campbell Soup Company of Canada
Listowel, ON. 800-575-7687
Carando Gourmet Frozen Foods
Agawam, MA 888-227-2636
Casa DiLisio Products
Mt Kisco, NY 800-247-4199
ConAgra Grocery Products
Archbold, OH 419-445-8015
Cuizina Food Company
Woodinville, WA. 425-486-7000
Culinary Standards Corporation
Louisville, KY 800-778-3434
Dynamic Foods
Lubbock, TX. 806-747-2777
Food Source
Mc Kinney, TX 972-548-9001
Gemini Food Industries
Charlton, MA 508-248-2730
Hunt-Wesson Food Service Company
Rochester, NY. 866-484-8676
Louisa Food Products
Saint Louis, MO 314-868-3000
Marsan Foods
Toronto, ON 416-755-9262
McLane Foods
Phoenix, AZ 602-275-5509
Original Italian Pasta Poducts Company
Chelsea, MA 800-999-9603
Overhill Farms
Vernon, CA 800-859-6406
Pierino Frozen Foods
Lincoln Park, MI. 313-928-0950
Specialty Brands
Carthage, MO 417-358-8104
Tomasso Corporation
Baie D'Urfe, QC. 514-325-3000
Topper Food Products
East Brunswick, NJ. 800-377-2823
Two Chefs on a Roll
Carson, CA 800-842-3025
Vegetable Juices
Chicago, IL 888-776-9752

Fudge

Paradigm Food Works
Lake Oswego, OR. 503-595-4360

Garlic

Baldwin Richardson Foods
Frankfort, IL 866-644-2732

Liquid ingredient manufacturer specializing in signature sauces, dessert toppings, beverage/pancake syrups, specialty fruit fillings and condiments.

Captain Bob's Jet Fuel
Fort Wayne, IN 877-486-6468

CHS
Inver Grove Heights, MN 800-232-3639
Cuizina Food Company
Woodinville, WA. 425-486-7000
Garlic Survival Company
San Francisco, CA 415-822-7112
Golden Whisk
South San Francisco, CA 800-660-5222
L&S Packing Company
Farmingdale, NY 800-286-6487
Lang Naturals
Newport, RI. 401-848-7700
Lee Kum Kee
City of Industry, CA 800-654-5082
Marsan Foods
Toronto, ON 416-755-9262
Pasta Factory
Melrose Park, IL. 800-615-6951
Robbie's Natural Products
Altadena, CA 626-798-9944
Silver Spring Gardens
Eau Claire, WI 800-826-7322
Southern Ray's Foods
Miami Beach, FL 800-972-8237
Soy Vay Enterprises
Felton, CA. 800-600-2077
Vegetable Juices
Chicago, IL 888-776-9752

Ginger

Baldwin Richardson Foods
Frankfort, IL 866-644-2732

Liquid ingredient manufacturer specializing in signature sauces, dessert toppings, beverage/pancake syrups, specialty fruit fillings and condiments.

Cuizina Food Company
Woodinville, WA. 425-486-7000
Lang Naturals
Newport, RI. 401-848-7700
Southern Ray's Foods
Miami Beach, FL 800-972-8237
Vegetable Juices
Chicago, IL 888-776-9752

Gourmet

Vita Food Products
Chicago, IL 312-738-4500
Wildly Delicious
Toronto, ON 888-545-9995

Habanero

Baldwin Richardson Foods
Frankfort, IL 866-644-2732

Liquid ingredient manufacturer specializing in signature sauces, dessert toppings, beverage/pancake syrups, specialty fruit fillings and condiments.

Captain Bob's Jet Fuel
Fort Wayne, IN 877-486-6468
Catskill Mountain Specialties
Saugerties, NY 800-311-3473
Chili Dude
Dallas, TX. 214-354-9906
Havana's Limited
Titusville, FL. 321-267-0513
Lendy's
Virginia Beach, VA 757-491-3511
Mo Hotta-Mo Betta
Pooler, GA. 912-748-6111
Mrs. Dog's Products
Grand Rapids, MI 800-2Mr-Dog
New Canaan Farms
Dripping Springs, TX 800-727-5267
Porky's Gourmet
Gallatin, TN 800-767-5911
Tex-Mex Gourmet
Brenham, TX. 888-345-8467
Vegetable Juices
Chicago, IL 888-776-9752
Wing-Time
Steamboat Springs, CO. 970-871-1198

Hoisin

Baldwin Richardson Foods
Frankfort, IL 866-644-2732

Liquid ingredient manufacturer specializing in signature sauces, dessert toppings, beverage/pancake syrups, specialty fruit fillings and condiments.

Cuizina Food Company
Woodinville, WA. 425-486-7000
Hormel Foods Corporation
Austin, MN 800-523-4635
Lee Kum Kee
City of Industry, CA 800-654-5082
Miyako Oriental Foods
Baldwin Park, CA. 877-788-6476
Soy Vay Enterprises
Felton, CA. 800-600-2077
Wei-Chuan
Bell Gardens, CA 562-372-2020

Hollandaise

Cuizina Food Company
Woodinville, WA. 425-486-7000
W&G Flavors
Hunt Valley, MD. 410-771-6606

Horseradish

Bartush-Schnitzius Foods Company
Lewisville, TX 972-219-1270
Beaverton Foods
Beaverton, OR 800-223-8076
Cedarvale Food Products Lounsbury Food Ltd
Toronto, ON 416-656-3331
Chicopee Provision Company
Chicopee, MA. 800-924-6328
Grouse Hunt Farms
Tamaqua, PA. 570-467-2850
Hoople Country Kitchens
Rockport, IN 812-649-2351
Kelchner's Horseradish
Dublin, PA. 215-249-3439

Lounsbury Foods
Toronto, ON ... 416-656-6330
Mothers Mountain Mustard
Falmouth, ME ... 800-440-9891
Mrs. Clark's Foods
Ankeny, IA ... 800-736-5674

Juices, salad dressings and sauces.

Penn Maid Crowley Foods
Philadelphia, PA ... 800-247-6269
Roller Ed
Rochester, NY ... 585-458-8020
Sau-Sea Foods
Tarrytown, NY ... 914-631-1717
Seminole Foods
Springfield, OH ... 800-881-1177
Silver Spring Gardens
Eau Claire, WI ... 800-826-7322
Southwest Specialty Food
Goodyear, AZ ... 800-536-3131
Strub Pickles
Brantford, ON ... 519-751-1717
T. Marzetti Company
Columbus, OH ... 614-846-2232
Thor-Shackel HorseradishCompany
Eau Claire, WI ... 800-826-7322
Tulkoff Food Products
Baltimore, MD ... 800-638-7343
Ventura Foods
Philadelphia, PA ... 215-223-8700
Westin
Omaha, NE ... 800-228-6098
Woeber Mustard Manufacturing
Springfield, OH ... 800-548-2929

Hot

Archie Moore's Foods Products
Milford, CT ... 203-876-5088
Arizona Cowboy
Phoenix, AZ ... 602-956-4833
Ashley Foods
Sudbury, MA ... 800-617-2823
Ashman Manufacturing & Distributing Company
Virginia Beach, VA ... 800-641-9924
B&G Foods
Parsippany, NJ ... 973-401-6500
Baldwin Richardson Foods
Frankfort, IL ... 866-644-2732

Liquid ingredient manufacturer specializing in signature sauces, dessert toppings, beverage/pancake syrups, specialty fruit fillings and condiments.

Baumer Foods
Metairie, LA ... 504-482-5761
BBQ'n Fools
Bend, OR ... 800-671-8652
Boston Spice & Tea Company
Boston, VA ... 800-966-4372
Bruce Foods Corporation
New Iberia, LA ... 800-299-9082
Buds Kitchen
New Castle, PA ... 724-654-9216
Buffalo Wild Wings
Minneapolis, MN ... 763-546-1891
Cafe Tequila
San Francisco, CA ... 415-264-0106
CaJohns Fiery Foods
Westerville, OH ... 888-703-3473
Cajun Chef Products
Saint Martinville, LA ... 337-394-7112
California Creative Foods
Oceanside, CA ... 760-757-2622
California-Antilles Trading Consortium
San Diego, CA ... 800-330-6450
Cannon's Sweets Hots
Albuquerque, NM ... 877-630-7026
Captain Bob's Jet Fuel
Fort Wayne, IN ... 877-486-6468
Carolyn's Caribbean Heat
Malvern, PA ... 610-647-0336
Carriere Foods Inc
Saint-Denis-Sur-Richelie, QC ... 450-787-3411
Chile Today
San Francisco, CA ... 800-758-0372
Colorado Salsa Company
Littleton, CO ... 303-932-2617
ConAgra Grocery Products
Archbold, OH ... 419-445-8015
Country Bob's
Centralia, IL ... 800-373-2140

Cyclone Enterprises
Houston, TX ... 281-872-0087
Dave's Gourmet
San Francisco, CA ... 800-758-0372
Dhidow Enterprises
Oxford, PA ... 610-932-7868
Dockside Market
Key Largo, FL ... 800-813-2253
Favorite Foods
Burnaby, BC ... 604-420-5100
Festive Foods
Virginia Beach, VA ... 757-490-9186
Forge Mountain Foods
Hendersonville, NC ... 800-823-6743
French's Flavor Ingredients
Springfield, MO ... 800-437-3624
Garden Complements
Kansas City, MO ... 800-966-1091
Garden Row Foods
Franklin Park, IL ... 800-555-9798
Hartford City Foam Pack aging & Converting
Hartford City, IN ... 765-348-2500
Havana's Limited
Titusville, FL ... 321-267-0513
Heintz & Weber Company
Buffalo, NY ... 716-852-7171
Hormel Foods Corporation
Austin, MN ... 800-523-4635
Hot Licks Hot Sauces
Spring Valley, CA ... 888-766-6468
Hot Wachula's
Lakeland, FL ... 877-883-8700
HVJ International
Spring, TX ... 877-730-3663
Ingleby Farms
Dublin, PA ... 877-728-7277
Joe Hutson Foods
Jacksonville, FL ... 904-731-9065
Juanita's Foods
Wilmington, CA ... 310-834-5339
Judicial Flavors
Auburn, CA ... 530-885-1298
Kari-Out Company
White Plains, NY ... 800-433-8799
L&S Packing Company
Farmingdale, NY ... 800-286-6487
Lang Naturals
Newport, RI ... 401-848-7700
Lendy's
Virginia Beach, VA ... 757-491-3511
Lounsbury Foods
Toronto, ON ... 416-656-6330
Mad Will's Food Company
Auburn, CA ... 888-275-9455
Magic Seasoning Blends
New Orleans, LA ... 800-457-2857
MAK Enterprises
Palmdale, CA ... 661-272-1867
Maple Grove Farms of Vermont
St Johnsbury, VT ... 800-525-2540
Mar-K Anchor Bar Hot Sauces
Buffalo, NY ... 71- 8-6 89
McIlhenny Company
New Orleans, LA ... 504-523-7370
Mexisnax Corporation
El Paso, TX ... 915-779-5709
Millflow Spice Corporation
Hauppauge, NY ... 866-227-8355
Mizkam Americas
Kansas City, MO ... 816-483-1700
Mo Hotta-Mo Betta
Pooler, GA ... 912-748-6111
Mrs. Dog's Products
Grand Rapids, MI ... 800-2Mr-Dog
Native Kjalii Foods
San Francisco, CA ... 415-522-5580
Natural Value Products
Sacramento, CA ... 916-427-7242
North of the Border
Tesuque, NM ... 800-860-0681
O'Garvey Sauces
New Braunfels, TX ... 830-620-6127
Paradise Products Corporation
Boca Raton, FL ... 800-826-1235
Pepper Creek Farms
Lawton, OK ... 800-526-8132
Pepper Island Beach
Lawrence, PA ... 724-746-2401
Peppered Palette
Bellingham, WA ... 866-829-7101
Peppers
Rehoboth Beach, DE ... 302-644-6900

Porky's Gourmet
Gallatin, TN ... 800-767-5911
Quality Foods
San Pedro, CA ... 877-833-7890
Ray's Sausage Company Inc
Cleveland, OH ... 216-921-8782
Red Hot Foods
Santa Paula, CA ... 805-258-3650
Reily Foods Company
New Orleans, LA ... 504-524-6131
Robinson's Barbecue Sauce Company
Oak Park, IL ... 708-383-8452
Royal Resources
New Orleans, LA ... 800-888-9932
Sambets Cajun Deli
Austin, TX ... 800-472-6238
Sams-Leon Mexican Supplies
Omaha, NE ... 402-733-3809
Simmons Hot Gourmet Products
Lethbridge, AB ... 403-327-9087
Southwest Specialty Food
Goodyear, AZ ... 800-536-3131
Spice House International Specialties
Hicksville, NY ... 516-942-7248
Sweet Baby Ray's
Chicago, IL ... 877-729-2229
T.W. Garner Food Company
Winston Salem, NC ... 800-476-7383
Tantos Foods International
Markham, ON ... 905-943-9993
Tapatio Hot Sauce
Vernon, CA ... 323-587-8933
Thistledew Farm
Proctor, WV ... 800-854-6639
Thompson's Fine Foods
Shoreview, MN ... 800-807-0025
Tomorrow Enterprise
New Iberia, LA ... 337-783-2666
Topper Food Products
East Brunswick, NJ ... 800-377-2823
Ukuva Africa
Kirkland, WA ... 888-280-1003
Uncle Bum's Gourmet Foods
Riverside, CA ... 800-486-2867
Van De Walle Farms
San Antonio, TX ... 210-436-5551
Vegetable Juices
Chicago, IL ... 888-776-9752
Whitfield Foods
Montgomery, AL ... 800-633-8790
Wing It
Falmouth, MA ... 508-540-9860
Wing-Time
Steamboat Springs, CO ... 970-871-1198
Wizards Cauldron, LTD
Yanceyville, NC ... 336-694-5665

Jerk

Baldwin Richardson Foods
Frankfort, IL ... 866-644-2732

Liquid ingredient manufacturer specializing in signature sauces, dessert toppings, beverage/pancake syrups, specialty fruit fillings and condiments.

Buffalo Wild Wings
Minneapolis, MN ... 763-546-1891
Catskill Mountain Specialties
Saugerties, NY ... 800-311-3473
Chieftain Wild Rice Company
Spooner, WI ... 800-262-6368
Cinnabar Specialty Foods
Prescott, AZ ... 866-293-6433
Cuizina Food Company
Woodinville, WA ... 425-486-7000
Mix-A-Lota Stuff LLC
Fort Pierce, FL ... 772-468-4688
Ventura Foods
Philadelphia, PA ... 215-223-8700

Lemon

Baldwin Richardson Foods
Frankfort, IL ... 866-644-2732

Liquid ingredient manufacturer specializing in signature sauces, dessert toppings, beverage/pancake syrups, specialty fruit fillings and condiments.

Genarom International
Cranbury, NJ ... 609-409-6200

Wei-Chuan
Bell Gardens, CA 562-372-2020

Marinara

Baldwin Richardson Foods
Frankfort, IL 866-644-2732

Liquid ingredient manufacturer specializing in signature sauces, dessert toppings, beverage/pancake syrups, specialty fruit fillings and condiments.

Campbell Soup Company
Camden, NJ 800-257-8443
Casa DiLisio Products
Mt Kisco, NY 800-247-4199
CHS
Inver Grove Heights, MN 800-232-3639
Colonna Brothers
North Bergen, NJ 201-864-1115
ConAgra Foods
Boisbriand, QC 450-433-1322
Cowboy Caviar
Berkeley, CA 877-509-1796
Cuizina Food Company
Woodinville, WA 425-486-7000
Dell'Amore Enterprises
Colchester, VT 800-962-6673
Hartford City Foam Pack aging & Converting
Hartford City, IN 765-348-2500
Hot Wachula's
Lakeland, FL 877-883-8700
J&R Foods
Long Branch, NJ 732-229-4020
Kozlowski Farms
Forestville, CA 800-473-2767
L&S Packing Company
Farmingdale, NY 800-286-6487
Mad Will's Food Company
Auburn, CA 888-275-9455
Mamma Lombardi's All Natural Sauces
Holbrook, NY 631-471-6609
Marsan Foods
Toronto, ON 416-755-9262
Molinaro's Fine Italian Foods
Mississauga, ON 800-268-4959
Newman's Own
Westport, CT 203-222-0136
Palmieri Food Products
New Haven, CT 800-845-5447
Pasta By Valente
Charlottesville, VA 888-575-7670
Pasta Factory
Melrose Park, IL 800-615-6951
Pastorelli Food Products
Chicago, IL 800-767-2829
Red Gold
Elwood, IN 877-748-9798
Sargento Foods Inc.
Plymouth, WI 800-243-3737
Stanislaus Food Products
Modesto, CA 800-327-7201
T. Marzetti Company
Columbus, OH 614-846-2232
Topper Food Products
East Brunswick, NJ 800-377-2823
Vanee Foods Company
Berkeley, IL 708-449-7300
Ventre Packing Company
Syracuse, NY 888-472-8237
Violet Packing
Williamstown, NJ 856-629-7428
Webbpak
Trussville, AL 800-655-3500

Meat

Victoria Packing Corporation
Brooklyn, NY 718-927-3000
Woods Smoked Meats
Bowling Green, MO 800-458-8426

Mediterranean

Baldwin Richardson Foods
Frankfort, IL 866-644-2732

Liquid ingredient manufacturer specializing in signature sauces, dessert toppings, beverage/pancake syrups, specialty fruit fillings and condiments.

Cookies Food Products
Wall Lake, IA 800-331-4995
Cuizina Food Company
Woodinville, WA 425-486-7000
L&S Packing Company
Farmingdale, NY 800-286-6487
Papa Leone Food Enterprises
Beverly Hills, CA 310-552-1660
Parthenon Food Products
Ann Arbor, MI 734-994-1012

Mexican Food

B&G Foods
Parsippany, NJ 973-401-6500
Big B Distributors
Evansville, IN 812-425-5235
Border Foods Inc
Deming, NM 888-737-7752
Casa Visco Finer Food Company
Schenectady, NY 888-607-2823
ConAgra Grocery Products
Irvine, CA 714-680-1000
Fernandez Chili Company
Alamosa, CO 719-589-6043
Garden Complements
Kansas City, MO 800-966-1091
Golden Specialty Foods
Norwalk, CA 562-802-2537
Golding Farms Foods
Winston Salem, NC 336-766-6161
Heluva Good Cheese
Sodus, NY 315-483-6971
Jalapeno Foods Company
The Woodlands, TX 800-896-2318
New Canaan Farms
Dripping Springs, TX 800-727-5267
Palmieri Food Products
New Haven, CT 800-845-5447
Pepper Creek Farms
Lawton, OK 800-526-8132
Subco Foods Inc
Sheboygan, WI 800-473-0757
Topper Food Products
East Brunswick, NJ 800-377-2823

Ventura Foods
Philadelphia, PA 215-223-8700
Walker Foods
Los Angeles, CA. 800-966-5199

Mint

Baldwin Richardson Foods
Frankfort, IL 866-644-2732

Liquid ingredient manufacturer specializing in signature sauces, dessert toppings, beverage/pancake syrups, specialty fruit fillings and condiments.

Cedarvale Food Products Lounsbury Food Ltd
Toronto, ON 416-656-3331
Lounsbury Foods
Toronto, ON 416-656-6330
Top Hat Company
Wilmette, IL 847-256-6565

Mixes

Breakfast at Brennan's
New Orleans, LA 800-888-9932
CHS
Inver Grove Heights, MN. 800-232-3639
Lawry's Foods
Monrovia, CA. 800-595-8917
Premier Blending
Wichita, KS. 316-267-5533
Produits Alimentaires Berthelet
Laval, QC 450-665-6100
RC Fine Foods
Belle Mead, NJ 800-526-3953
Serv-Agen Corporation
Cherry Hill, NJ 856-663-6966
Spice Advice
Ankeny, IA 800-247-5251
Superior Quality Foods
Ontario, CA. 800-300-4210
UFL Foods
Mississauga, ON. 905-670-7776
W&G Flavors
Hunt Valley, MD. 410-771-6606

Mole

Juanita's Foods
Wilmington, CA 310-834-5339

Mushroom

Cipriani's Spaghetti & Sauce Company
Chicago Heights, IL 708-755-6212
Cuizina Food Company
Woodinville, WA. 425-486-7000
Vanee Foods Company
Berkeley, IL. 708-449-7300
Vegetable Juices
Chicago, IL 888-776-9752
Worthmore Food Product
Cincinnati, OH 513-559-1473

Orange

Papa Leone Food Enterprises
Beverly Hills, CA 310-552-1660
Southern Ray's Foods
Miami Beach, FL 800-972-8237

Organic

Clement Pappas & Company
Carneys Point, NJ 800-257-7019

Oyster

Favorite Foods
Burnaby, BC 604-420-5100
Lee Kum Kee
City of Industry, CA 800-654-5082
Wei-Chuan
Bell Gardens, CA 562-372-2020

Pasta

Dei Fratelli
Toledo, OH 800-837-1631
Giovanni Food Company
Syracuse, NY 315-457-2373
Milo's Whole World Gourmet
Athens, OH 866-589-6456
Mondiv/Division of Lassonde Inc
Boisbriand, QC 450-979-0717
Newman's Own
Westport, CT. 203-222-0136
Pacific Choice Brands
Fresno, CA 559-237-5583
Paesana Products
East Farmingdale, NY. 631-845-1717
Patsy's Brands
New York, NY 212-247-3491

Peanut

Golden Whisk
South San Francisco, CA 800-660-5222
Lang Naturals
Newport, RI. 401-848-7700
Rowena's
Norfolk, VA. 800-627-8699

Pepper

Colibri Pepper Company LLC
Elmer, LA 316-730-6528
Genarom International
Cranbury, NJ 609-409-6200
Judicial Flavors
Auburn, CA. 530-885-1298
Landry's Pepper Company
Saint Martinville, LA 337-394-6097
McIlhenny Company
New Orleans, LA 504-523-7370
Pepper Source
Rogers, AR 479-246-1030
Pepper Source
Van Buren, AR 479-474-5178
Pepper Source
Metairie, LA 504-885-3223
Porky's Gourmet
Gallatin, TN 800-767-5911
T.W. Garner Food Company
Winston Salem, NC. 800-476-7383
Vermont Pepper Works
South Burlington, VT 802-598-6419

Hot

Mothers Mountain Mustard
Falmouth, ME. 800-440-9891
Porky's Gourmet
Gallatin, TN 800-767-5911

Pesto

Al Dente
Whitmore Lake, MI 800-536-7278
Armanino Foods of Distinction
Hayward, CA 510-441-9300
Bella Cucina Artful Food
Atlanta, GA. 866-350-9040
Casa DiLisio Products
Mt Kisco, NY 800-247-4199
Christopher Ranch
Gilroy, CA. 408-847-1100
Cuizina Food Company
Woodinville, WA. 425-486-7000
Delectable Gourmet LLC
Lindenhurst, NY 800-696-1350
Golden Specialty Foods
Norwalk, CA. 562-802-2537
Golden West Specialty Foods
Brisbane, CA. 800-584-4481
Gracious Gourmet
Bridgewater, CT 860-350-1213
Great Garlic Foods
Bradley Beach, NJ 732-775-3311
Kind Snacks
New York, NY 800-732-2321
La Maison Le Grand
St-Joseph-du-Lac, QC. 450-623-3000
Les Aliments Livabec Foods
Sherrington, QC 450-454-7971
Maison Le Grand
St Joseph du Lac, QC 450-623-3000
Millflow Spice Corporation
Hauppauge, NY 866-227-8355
Mondiv/Division of Lassonde Inc
Boisbriand, QC 450-979-0717
North American Enterprises
Tucson, AZ 800-817-8666
Pasta Factory
Melrose Park, IL 800-615-6951
Peaceworks
New York, NY 212-897-3985
Peaceworks
New York, NY 800-732-2321
Pestos with Panache by Lauren
Brooklyn, NY 917-656-3082
Red Gold
Elwood, IN 877-748-9798
Rising Sun Farms
Phoenix, OR 800-888-0795
Sauces 'n Love
Lynn, MA 866-772-8237
TexaFrance
Round Rock, TX. 800-776-8937
Topper Food Products
East Brunswick, NJ. 800-377-2823
Tulkoff Food Products
Baltimore, MD 800-638-7343
Waterfield Farms
Amherst, MA 413-549-3558

Pizza

Alimentaire Whyte's Inc
Laval, QC 800-625-1979
Baldwin Richardson Foods
Frankfort, IL 866-644-2732

Liquid ingredient manufacturer specializing in signature sauces, dessert toppings, beverage/pancake syrups, specialty fruit fillings and condiments.

Big B Distributors
Evansville, IN 812-425-5235
Canada Bread
Etobicoke, ON 416-926-2000
Cuizina Food Company
Woodinville, WA. 425-486-7000
DelGrosso Foods
Tipton, PA. 800-521-5880
Delgrosso Foods Inc.
Tipton, PA. 800-521-5880
Dorothy Dawson Foods Products
Jackson, MI. 517-788-9830
Furmano Foods
Northumberland, PA. 877-877-6032
Furmano's Foods
Northumberland, PA. 877-877-6032
Giovanni Food Company
Syracuse, NY 315-457-2373
Hartford City Foam Pack aging & Converting
Hartford City, IN. 765-348-2500
Heinz Company of Canada
North York, ON. 877-574-3469
Hirzel Canning Company &Farms
Northwood, OH 419-693-0531
Mama Mary's
Fairforest, SC 864-595-6262
Nationwide Canning
Cottam, ON. 519-839-4831
Old Mansion Foods
Petersburg, VA 800-476-1877
Palmieri Food Products
New Haven, CT 800-845-5447
Paradise Tomato Kitchens
Louisville, KY 502-637-1700
Pastorelli Food Products
Chicago, IL 800-767-2829
Rustic Crust
Pittsfield, NH 603-435-5119
Sargento Foods Inc.
Plymouth, WI 800-243-3737
Sassafras Enterprises
Chicago, IL 800-537-4941
Stanislaus Food Products
Modesto, CA. 800-327-7201
Tip Top Canning Company
Tipp City, OH 800-352-2635
Triple K Manufacturing Company
Shenandoah, IA. 888-987-2824
Violet Packing
Williamstown, NJ 856-629-7428
Worthmore Food Product
Cincinnati, OH 513-559-1473

Plum

Baldwin Richardson Foods
Frankfort, IL 866-644-2732

Liquid ingredient manufacturer specializing in signature sauces, dessert toppings, beverage/pancake syrups, specialty fruit fillings and condiments.

Cuizina Food Company
Woodinville, WA. . . . 425-486-7000
Favorite Foods
Burnaby, BC 604-420-5100
Lee Kum Kee
City of Industry, CA 800-654-5082
Wei-Chuan
Bell Gardens, CA 562-372-2020
Wing's Food Products
Etobicoke, ON 416-259-2662
Wong Wing Foods
Montreal, QC 800-361-4820

Primavera

Cuizina Food Company
Woodinville, WA. . . . 425-486-7000
L&S Packing Company
Farmingdale, NY 800-286-6487
Topper Food Products
East Brunswick, NJ. . . . 800-377-2823

Puttanesca

Baldwin Richardson Foods
Frankfort, IL 866-644-2732

Liquid ingredient manufacturer specializing in signature sauces, dessert toppings, beverage/pancake syrups, specialty fruit fillings and condiments.

Casa DiLisio Products
Mt Kisco, NY 800-247-4199
Cuizina Food Company
Woodinville, WA. . . . 425-486-7000
L&S Packing Company
Farmingdale, NY 800-286-6487
Papa Leone Food Enterprises
Beverly Hills, CA 310-552-1660

Seafood

Blue Crab Bay Company
Melfa, VA 800-221-2722
Chincoteague Seafood Company
Parsonsburg, MD 443-260-4800
Clements Foods Company
Oklahoma City, OK 800-654-8355
Cuizina Food Company
Woodinville, WA. . . . 425-486-7000
E. Waldo Ward & Son Corporation
Sierra Madre, CA 800-355-9273
Heinz Portion Control
Mason, OH 800-547-8924
Look's Gourmet Food Company
East Machias, ME. . . . 800-962-6258
Lounsbury Foods
Toronto, ON 416-656-6330
Mid-Atlantic Foods
Easton, MD. . . . 800-922-4688
Myron's Fine Foods
Millers Falls, MA 800-730-2820
New Business Corporation
Gary, IN. . . . 800-742-8435
New Canaan Farms
Dripping Springs, TX 800-727-5267
Palmieri Food Products
New Haven, CT 800-845-5447
Paradise Products Corporation
Boca Raton, FL. . . . 800-826-1235
Red Gold
Elwood, IN 877-748-9798
Rosmarino Foods/R.Z. Humbert Company
Odessa, FL 888-926-9053
T. Marzetti Company
Columbus, OH 614-846-2232
T.W. Garner Food Company
Winston Salem, NC. . . . 800-476-7383
Woeber Mustard Manufacturing
Springfield, OH. . . . 800-548-2929

Soy

Ajinomoto Food Ingredients LLC
Chicago, IL 773-714-1436
Alimentaire Whyte's Inc
Laval, QC 800-625-1979
American Culinary GardenNoble Communications Co
Springfield, MO 888-831-2433
Baldwin Richardson Foods
Frankfort, IL 866-644-2732

Liquid ingredient manufacturer specializing in signature sauces, dessert toppings, beverage/pancake syrups, specialty fruit fillings and condiments.

Bartush-Schnitzius Foods Company
Lewisville, TX 972-219-1270
Basic Food Flavors
North Las Vegas, NV 702-643-0043
Baumer Foods
Metairie, LA 504-482-5761
Baycliff Company
New York, NY 212-772-6078
Castella Imports
Hauppauge, NY 866-227-8355
Clements Foods Company
Oklahoma City, OK 800-654-8355
Commodities Marketing, Inc.
Edison, NJ. . . . 732-603-5077
ConAgra Grocery Products
Archbold, OH 419-445-8015
Dixie Usa
Tomball, TX 800-233-3668
Edward & Sons Trading Company
Carpinteria, CA. . . . 805-684-8500
Favorite Foods
Burnaby, BC 604-420-5100
Felbro Food Products
Los Angeles, CA. . . . 800-335-2761
Flavor House
Adelanto, CA 760-246-9131
Golden Gate Foods
Dallas, TX. . . . 214-747-2223
Hormel Foods Corporation
Austin, MN 800-523-4635
Inter-American Products
Cincinnati, OH 800-645-2233
Kari-Out Company
White Plains, NY 800-433-8799
Kikkoman International
San Francisco, CA 415-956-7750
Kikkoman International
Oakbrook Terrace, IL 630-954-1244
Kikkoman International
Tucker, GA 770-496-0605
Kikkoman International
Dallas, TX. . . . 972-267-4207
Lee Kum Kee
City of Industry, CA 800-654-5082
Lee's Food Products
Toronto, ON 416-465-2407
Mandarin Soy Sauce
Middletown, NY. . . . 845-343-1505
McIlhenny Company
Avery Island, LA. . . . 800-634-9599
McIlhenny Company
New Orleans, LA 504-523-7370
Millflow Spice Corporation
Hauppauge, NY 866-227-8355
Myron's Fine Foods
Millers Falls, MA 800-730-2820
Nikken Foods Company
Saint Louis, MO 636-532-1019
Randag & Associates Inc
Elmhurst, IL 630-530-2830
San-J International, Inc
Richmond, VA. . . . 800-446-5500
Serv-Agen Corporation
Cherry Hill, NJ 856-663-6966
Sobaya
Cowansville, QC. . . . 800-319-8808
Tomasso Corporation
Baie D'Urfe, QC. . . . 514-325-3000
Wei-Chuan
Bell Gardens, CA 562-372-2020
Wing Nien Company
Hayward, CA 510-487-8877
Wing's Food Products
Etobicoke, ON 416-259-2662
Wizards Cauldron, LTD
Yanceyville, NC 336-694-5665
Yamasa Corporation
Torrance, CA. . . . 310-944-3883

Spaghetti

Alimentaire Whyte's Inc
Laval, QC 800-625-1979
Baldwin Richardson Foods
Frankfort, IL 866-644-2732

Liquid ingredient manufacturer specializing in signature sauces, dessert toppings, beverage/pancake syrups, specialty fruit fillings and condiments.

Campbell Soup Company
Camden, NJ. . . . 800-257-8443
Casa Visco Finer Food Company
Schenectady, NY. . . . 888-607-2823
Chef-A-Roni
East Greenwich, RI. . . . 401-884-8798
Cipriani's Spaghetti & Sauce Company
Chicago Heights, IL 708-755-6212
ConAgra Foods
Boisbriand, QC 450-433-1322
Cuizina Food Company
Woodinville, WA. . . . 425-486-7000
DelGrosso Foods
Tipton, PA. . . . 800-521-5880
Delgrosso Foods Inc.
Tipton, PA. . . . 800-521-5880
Eden Foods Inc.
Clinton, MI 800-248-0320
Furmano's Foods
Northumberland, PA. . . . 877-877-6032
G Di Lullo & Sons
Westville, NJ. . . . 856-456-3700
Gumpert's Canada
Mississauga, ON. . . . 800-387-9324
Hagerty Foods
Orange, CA. . . . 714-628-1230
Hanover Foods Corporation
Hanover, PA 717-632-6000
Heinz Company of Canada
North York, ON. . . . 877-574-3469
Hirzel Canning Company &Farms
Northwood, OH 419-693-0531
Key Ingredients
Harrisburg, PA 800-227-4448
Knott's Berry Farm Foods
Placentia, CA 800-289-9927
L&S Packing Company
Farmingdale, NY 800-286-6487
Marsan Foods
Toronto, ON 416-755-9262
Molinaro's Fine Italian Foods
Mississauga, ON. . . . 800-268-4959
Nationwide Canning
Cottam, ON. . . . 519-839-4831
Nicola Pizza
Rehoboth Beach, DE 302-226-2654
Palmieri Food Products
New Haven, CT 800-845-5447
Peaceworks
New York, NY 212-897-3985
Pino's Pasta Veloce
Staten Island, NY 718-273-6660
Porinos Gourmet Food
Central Falls, RI 800-826-3938
Progresso Quality Foods
Vineland, NJ 800-200-9377
Ragozzino Food
Meriden, CT 800-348-1240
Red Gold
Elwood, IN 877-748-9798
Seneca Foods
Clyman, WI. . . . 920-696-3331
Silver State Foods
Denver, CO 800-423-3351
Specialty Brands
Carthage, MO 417-358-8104
Thomson Food
Duluth, MN. . . . 218-722-2529
Todd's
Des Moines, IA. . . . 800-247-5363
Vietti Foods Company Inc
Nashville, TN 800-240-7864
Violet Packing
Williamstown, NJ 856-629-7428
Westin
Omaha, NE 800-228-6098
Williams Foods, Inc
Lenexa, KS 800-255-6736

Worthmore Food Product
Cincinnati, OH 513-559-1473
Ynrico's Food Products Company
Syracuse, NY 888-472-8237

Meat

Campbell Soup Company
Camden, NJ. 800-257-8443
Chef-A-Roni
East Greenwich, RI. 401-884-8798
Cipriani's Spaghetti & Sauce Company
Chicago Heights, IL 708-755-6212
ConAgra Foods
Boisbriand, QC. 450-433-1322
Gaucho Foods
Fayetteville, IL 877-677-2282
Vanee Foods Company
Berkeley, IL. 708-449-7300

Meatless

Campbell Soup Company
Camden, NJ. 800-257-8443
Chef-A-Roni
East Greenwich, RI. 401-884-8798
Molinaro's Fine Italian Foods
Mississauga, ON. 800-268-4959

Steak

Ashman Manufacturing & Distributing Company
Virginia Beach, VA. 800-641-9924
Baumer Foods
Metairie, LA 504-482-5761
Creative Foodworks
San Antonio, TX. 210-212-4761
Golding Farms Foods
Winston Salem, NC. 336-766-6161
Inter-State Cider & Vinegar Company
Baltimore, MD 410-947-1529
Joe Hutson Foods
Jacksonville, FL 904-731-9065
Kozlowski Farms
Forestville, CA 800-473-2767
L&S Packing Company
Farmingdale, NY 800-286-6487
Lea & Perrins
Fair Lawn, NJ 800-289-5797
Magic Seasoning Blends
New Orleans, LA 800-457-2857
McIlhenny Company
New Orleans, LA 504-523-7370
Myron's Fine Foods
Millers Falls, MA 800-730-2820
Newman's Own
Westport, CT. 203-222-0136
Paradise Products Corporation
Boca Raton, FL. 800-826-1235
Private Harvest Gourmet Specialities
Lakeport, CA 800-463-0594
Quality Foods
San Pedro, CA. 877-833-7890
Webbpak
Trussville, AL. 800-655-3500
Wine Country Chef LLC
Hidden Valley Lake, CA. 707-322-0406
Wizards Cauldron, LTD
Yanceyville, NC 336-694-5665

Stir-Fry

Baldwin Richardson Foods
Frankfort, IL 866-644-2732

Liquid ingredient manufacturer specializing in signature sauces, dessert toppings, beverage/pancake syrups, specialty fruit fillings and condiments.

Cuizina Food Company
Woodinville, WA. 425-486-7000
Flavor House
Adelanto, CA 760-246-9131
Hormel Foods Corporation
Austin, MN. 800-523-4635
L&S Packing Company
Farmingdale, NY 800-286-6487
Mandarin Soy Sauce
Middletown, NY. 845-343-1505
Marjon Specialty Foods, Inc
Plant City, FL 813-752-3482
Myron's Fine Foods
Millers Falls, MA 800-730-2820
Wei-Chuan
Bell Gardens, CA 562-372-2020
Wing Nien Company
Hayward, CA 510-487-8877
Wizards Cauldron, LTD
Yanceyville, NC 336-694-5665

Sweet & Sour

Baldwin Richardson Foods
Frankfort, IL 866-644-2732

Liquid ingredient manufacturer specializing in signature sauces, dessert toppings, beverage/pancake syrups, specialty fruit fillings and condiments.

Big B Distributors
Evansville, IN 812-425-5235
ConAgra Grocery Products
Archbold, OH 419-445-8015
Cuizina Food Company
Woodinville, WA. 425-486-7000
Garden Complements
Kansas City, MO. 800-966-1091
Gumpert's Canada
Mississauga, ON. 800-387-9324
Kari-Out Company
White Plains, NY 800-433-8799
L&S Packing Company
Farmingdale, NY 800-286-6487
Lang Naturals
Newport, RI. 401-848-7700
Lee Kum Kee
City of Industry, CA 800-654-5082
Robbie's Natural Products
Altadena, CA 626-798-9944
Vanee Foods Company
Berkeley, IL. 708-449-7300
Wei-Chuan
Bell Gardens, CA 562-372-2020
Wing Nien Company
Hayward, CA 510-487-8877

Szechuan

Baldwin Richardson Foods
Frankfort, IL 866-644-2732

Liquid ingredient manufacturer specializing in signature sauces, dessert toppings, beverage/pancake syrups, specialty fruit fillings and condiments.

Favorite Foods
Burnaby, BC 604-420-5100
Myron's Fine Foods
Millers Falls, MA 800-730-2820

Taco

Amigos Canning Company
San Antonio, TX. 800-580-3477
Baldwin Richardson Foods
Frankfort, IL 866-644-2732

Liquid ingredient manufacturer specializing in signature sauces, dessert toppings, beverage/pancake syrups, specialty fruit fillings and condiments.

Bartush-Schnitzius Foods Company
Lewisville, TX 972-219-1270
Bien Padre Foods
Eureka, CA 707-442-4585
Big B Distributors
Evansville, IN 812-425-5235
ConAgra Grocery Products
Irvine, CA 714-680-1000
Cookies Food Products
Wall Lake, IA 800-331-4995
El Rancho Tortilla
San Antonio, TX. 210-922-8411
Famous Chili
Fort Smith, AR 479-782-0096
Fernandez Chili Company
Alamosa, CO. 719-589-6043
Golden Specialty Foods
Norwalk, CA. 562-802-2537
Golding Farms Foods
Winston Salem, NC. 336-766-6161
Hagerty Foods
Orange, CA. 714-628-1230
Heluva Good Cheese
Sodus, NY. 315-483-6971
Hirzel Canning Company &Farms
Northwood, OH 419-693-0531
Hormel Foods Corporation
Austin, MN. 800-523-4635
Hume Specialties
Chester, VT 802-875-3117
Imus Ranch Foods
Darien, CT. 505-892-0883
Jalapeno Foods Company
The Woodlands, TX 800-896-2318
Judicial Flavors
Auburn, CA. 530-885-1298
La Vencedora Products
Los Angeles, CA. 800-327-2572
La Victoria Foods
Rosemead, CA 800-523-4635
Laredo Mexican Foods
Fort Wayne, IN 800-252-7336
Li'l Guy Foods
Kansas City, MO. 800-886-8226
New Canaan Farms
Dripping Springs, TX. 800-727-5267
Palmieri Food Products
New Haven, CT 800-845-5447
Pepper Creek Farms
Lawton, OK. 800-526-8132
Red Gold
Elwood, IN 877-748-9798
Spanish Gardens Food Manufacturing
Kansas City, KS 913-831-4242
Topper Food Products
East Brunswick, NJ. 800-377-2823
Ventura Foods
Philadelphia, PA 215-223-8700

Tahini

Dipasa
Brownsville, TX 956-831-5893
East Wind Nut Butters
Tecumseh, MO 417-679-4682
Vic Rossano Incorporated
Montreal, QC 514-766-5252

Tartar

Baldwin Richardson Foods
Frankfort, IL 866-644-2732

Liquid ingredient manufacturer specializing in signature sauces, dessert toppings, beverage/pancake syrups, specialty fruit fillings and condiments.

Bestfoods
Englewood Cliffs, NJ 201-567-8000
Cedarvale Food Products Lounsbury Food Ltd
Toronto, ON 416-656-3331
Cuizina Food Company
Woodinville, WA. 425-486-7000
Food Specialties Company
Cincinnati, OH 513-761-1242
Golding Farms Foods
Winston Salem, NC. 336-766-6161
Heinz Portion Control
Mason, OH 800-547-8924
Kelchner's Horseradish
Dublin, PA. 215-249-3439

Lounsbury Foods
Toronto, ON 416-656-6330
Mrs. Clark's Foods
Ankeny, IA 800-736-5674

Juices, salad dressings and sauces.

Private Harvest Gourmet Specialities
Lakeport, CA 800-463-0594
Sau-Sea Foods
Tarrytown, NY 914-631-1717
Schlotterbeck & Foss Company
Portland, ME 800-777-4666
Silver Spring Gardens
Eau Claire, WI 800-826-7322
T. Marzetti Company
Columbus, OH 614-846-2232
Ventura Foods
Philadelphia, PA 215-223-8700
Westin
Omaha, NE 800-228-6098
Wood Brothers
West Columbia, SC 803-796-5146

Teriyaki

Argo Century
Charlotte, NC 800-446-7108
Baldwin Richardson Foods
Frankfort, IL 866-644-2732

Liquid ingredient manufacturer specializing in signature sauces, dessert toppings, beverage/pancake syrups, specialty fruit fillings and condiments.

Baycliff Company
New York, NY 212-772-6078
BBQ'n Fools
Bend, OR 800-671-8652
Buffalo Wild Wings
Minneapolis, MN 763-546-1891
Cuizina Food Company
Woodinville, WA 425-486-7000
Dynamic Foods
Lubbock, TX 806-747-2777
Favorite Foods
Burnaby, BC 604-420-5100
Golden Specialty Foods
Norwalk, CA 562-802-2537
Hormel Foods Corporation
Austin, MN 800-523-4635
Kikkoman International
San Francisco, CA 415-956-7750
Kikkoman International
Oakbrook Terrace, IL 630-954-1244
Kikkoman International
Tucker, GA 770-496-0605
Kikkoman International
Dallas, TX 972-267-4207
L&S Packing Company
Farmingdale, NY 800-286-6487
Mandarin Soy Sauce
Middletown, NY 845-343-1505
Miyako Oriental Foods
Baldwin Park, CA 877-788-6476
Myron's Fine Foods
Millers Falls, MA 800-730-2820
Passetti's Pride
Hayward, CA 800-521-4659
Sagawa's Savory Sauces
Tualatin, OR 503-692-4334
San-J International, Inc
Richmond, VA 800-446-5500
T. Marzetti Company
Columbus, OH 614-846-2232
Valley Grain Products
Madera, CA 559-675-3400
Vanlaw Food Products
Fullerton, CA 714-870-9091
Wong Wing Foods
Montreal, QC 800-361-4820
World Flavors
Warminster, PA 215-672-4400
Yamasa Corporation
Torrance, CA 310-944-3883

Tomato

Furmano's Foods
Northumberland, PA 877-877-6032
Mamma Lombardi's All Natural Sauces
Holbrook, NY 631-471-6609

Canned

Bartush-Schnitzius Foods Company
Lewisville, TX 972-219-1270
Bruno Specialty Foods
West Sayville, NY 631-589-1700
Cajun Chef Products
Saint Martinville, LA 337-394-7112
Casa DiLisio Products
Mt Kisco, NY 800-247-4199
Casa Visco Finer Food Company
Schenectady, NY 888-607-2823
Colonna Brothers
North Bergen, NJ 201-864-1115
Costa Deano's Gourmet Foods
Canton, OH 800-337-2823
Cucina Antica Foods Corp
Mount Kisco, NY 877-728-2462
Cuizina Food Company
Woodinville, WA 425-486-7000
Escalon Premier Brand
Escalon, CA 209-838-7341
Golden Valley Foods
Abbotsford, BC 888-299-8855
Gumpert's Canada
Mississauga, ON 800-387-9324
Hanover Foods Corporation
Hanover, PA 717-632-6000
Hartford City Foam Pack aging & Converting
Hartford City, IN 765-348-2500
Heinz Company of Canada
North York, ON 877-574-3469
Hirzel Canning Company &Farms
Northwood, OH 419-693-0531
International Home Foods
Parsippany, NJ 973-359-9920
J&R Foods
Long Branch, NJ 732-229-4020
Kozlowski Farms
Forestville, CA 800-473-2767
L&S Packing Company
Farmingdale, NY 800-286-6487
Molinaro's Fine Italian Foods
Mississauga, ON 800-268-4959
Nationwide Canning
Cottam, ON 519-839-4831
Palmieri Food Products
New Haven, CT 800-845-5447
Papa Leone Food Enterprises
Beverly Hills, CA 310-552-1660
Pasta Factory
Melrose Park, IL 800-615-6951
Pastorelli Food Products
Chicago, IL 800-767-2829
Progresso Quality Foods
Vineland, NJ 800-200-9377
San Benito Foods
Hollister, CA 831-637-4434
Seneca Foods
Clyman, WI 920-696-3331
Specialty Brands
Carthage, MO 417-358-8104
Tip Top Canning Company
Tipp City, OH 800-352-2635
Tomasso Corporation
Baie D'Urfe, QC 514-325-3000
Topper Food Products
East Brunswick, NJ 800-377-2823
Walker Foods
Los Angeles, CA 800-966-5199
Williams Foods, Inc
Lenexa, KS 800-255-6736

Frozen

Cajun Chef Products
Saint Martinville, LA 337-394-7112
Casa DiLisio Products
Mt Kisco, NY 800-247-4199
Cuizina Food Company
Woodinville, WA 425-486-7000
Hanover Foods Corporation
Hanover, PA 717-632-6000
Marsan Foods
Toronto, ON 416-755-9262
Molinaro's Fine Italian Foods
Mississauga, ON 800-268-4959
Progresso Quality Foods
Vineland, NJ 800-200-9377
Seneca Foods
Clyman, WI 920-696-3331
Specialty Brands
Carthage, MO 417-358-8104
Topper Food Products
East Brunswick, NJ 800-377-2823

with Spices

Heinz Company of Canada
North York, ON 877-574-3469
Palmieri Food Products
New Haven, CT 800-845-5447
Patsy's
New York, NY 212-247-3491

Worcestershire

A. Lassonde, Inc.
Rougemont, QC 888-477-6663
Annie's Naturals
East Calais, VT 800-434-1234
Baldwin Richardson Foods
Frankfort, IL 866-644-2732

Liquid ingredient manufacturer specializing in signature sauces, dessert toppings, beverage/pancake syrups, specialty fruit fillings and condiments.

Baumer Foods
Metairie, LA 504-482-5761
Big B Distributors
Evansville, IN 812-425-5235
Cajun Chef Products
Saint Martinville, LA 337-394-7112
Clements Foods Company
Oklahoma City, OK 800-654-8355
Felbro Food Products
Los Angeles, CA 800-335-2761
Gold Coast Ingredients
Commerce, CA 800-352-8673
Illes Seasonings & Flavors
Carrollton, TX 800-683-4553
Inter-American Products
Cincinnati, OH 800-645-2233
Inter-State Cider & Vinegar Company
Baltimore, MD 410-947-1529
Lea & Perrins
Fair Lawn, NJ 800-289-5797
McIlhenny Company
Avery Island, LA 800-634-9599
Millflow Spice Corporation
Hauppauge, NY 866-227-8355
New Business Corporation
Gary, IN 800-742-8435
Robbie's Natural Products
Altadena, CA 626-798-9944
Serv-Agen Corporation
Cherry Hill, NJ 856-663-6966
T.W. Garner Food Company
Winston Salem, NC 800-476-7383
Uncle Ben's
Greenville, MS 800-548-6253
Vegetable Juices
Chicago, IL 888-776-9752

Vinegar

A Perfect Pear from NapaValley
Napa, CA 800-553-5753
A Southern Season
Chapel Hill, NC 877-929-7133
Agrusa, Inc.
Leonia, NJ 201-592-5950
American Culinary GardenNoble Communications Co
Springfield, MO 888-831-2433
Arbor Hill Grapery
Naples, NY 800-554-7553
Arnabal International
Tustin, CA 714-665-9477
Assouline & Ting
Huntingdon Valley, PA 800-521-4491
Au Printemps Gourmet
Saint-Jerome, QC 800-663-0416
B.R. Cohn Olive Oil
Glen Ellen, CA 800-330-4064
Baycliff Company
New York, NY 212-772-6078
Belton Foods
Dayton, OH 800-443-2266
Big B Distributors
Evansville, IN 812-425-5235
Bittersweet Herb Farm
Shelburne Falls, MA 800-456-1599
Blueberry Store
Grand Junction, MI 877-654-2400

Boston Spice & Tea Company
Boston, VA 800-966-4372
Boyajian, Inc.
Canton, MA 800-965-0665
BR Cohn Winery
Glen Ellen, CA 707-938-4064
Buon Italia Misono Food Ltd.
New York, NY 212-633-9090
California Olive Oil Corporation
Berkeley, CA. 888-718-9830
Castella Imports
Hauppauge, NY 866-227-8355
Chicama Vineyards
West Tisbury, MA. 888-244-2262
Clements Foods Company
Oklahoma City, OK 800-654-8355
Colonna Brothers
North Bergen, NJ 201-864-1115
Consumers Vinegar & Spice Company
Chicago, IL. 773-376-4100
Creole Fermentation Industries
Abbeville, LA. 337-898-9377
Cw Resources
New Britain, CT 860-229-7700
Dark Tickle Company
St Lunaire-Griquet, NL. 709-623-2354
Delicae Gourmet
Tarpon Springs, FL. 800-942-2502
Eden Foods Inc.
Clinton, MI 800-248-0320
Emerling International Foods
Buffalo, NY. 716-833-7381

We supply food manufacturers and food service customers worldwide (since 1988) with bulk ingredients including: Fruits & Vegetables; Juice Concentrates; Herbs & Spices; Oils & Vinegars; Flavors & Colors; Honey & Molasses. We also produce PURE MAPLE SYRUP.

Fleischmann's Vinegar
Cerritos, CA 800-443-1067
Fleischmann's Yeast
Chesterfield, MO 800-247-7473
Fleischmanns Vinegar
Cerritos, CA 800-443-1067
Four Chimneys Farm Winery Trust
Himrod, NY 607-243-7502
Fredericksburg Herb Farm
Fredericksburg, TX. 800-259-4372
Gold Pure Foods Products Company
Hempstead, NY. 800-422-4681
Golden Whisk
South San Francisco, CA 800-660-5222
Grapevine Trading Company
Santa Rosa, CA. 800-469-6478
Gregory-Robinson Speas
Dallas, TX. 214-352-1761
Halladays Harvest Barn
Bellows Falls, VT. 802-463-3331
Heinz Company of Canada
North York, ON. 877-574-3469
Herb Bee's Products
Colchester, VT 802-864-7387
Hinzerling Winery
Prosser, WA. 800-722-6702
Hormel Foods Corporation
Austin, MN. 507-437-5395
Hudson Valley Fruit Juice
Highland, NY 845-691-8061
Hurd Orchards
Holley, NY 585-638-8838
II Sisters
Moss Beach, CA. 800-282-7058
Inter-State Cider & Vinegar Company
Baltimore, MD 410-947-1529
K.L. Keller Imports
Oakland, CA 510-839-7890
Kari-Out Company
White Plains, NY 800-433-8799
Ken's Foods
Marlborough, MA. 800-633-5800
Knouse Foods Coop
Paw Paw, MI. 269-657-5524
Knouse Foods Coop
Peach Glen, PA 717-677-8181
Kozlowski Farms
Forestville, CA 800-473-2767
Lesley Elizabeth
Lapeer, MI. 800-684-3300
Lounsbury Foods
Toronto, ON 416-656-6330

M.A. Gedney
Chaska, MN 952-448-2612
Mandarin Soy Sauce
Middletown, NY. 845-343-1505
Marukan Vinegar (U.S.A.) Inc.
Paramount, CA 562-630-6060
Mizkam Americas
Kansas City, MO. 816-483-1700
Modena Fine Foods
Clifton, NJ. 201-842-8900
Morehouse Foods
City of Industry, CA 626-854-1655
Myron's Fine Foods
Millers Falls, MA 800-730-2820
National Vinegar Company
St Louis, MO. 314-962-4111
National Vinegar Company
Alton, IL 618-465-6532
National Vinegar Company
Houston, TX 713-223-4214
North American Enterprises
Tucson, AZ 800-817-8666
O Olive Oil
Petaluma, CA 888-827-7148
Oasis Foods Company
Hillside, NJ 908-964-0477
Old Dutch Mustard Company
Great Neck, NY 516-466-0522
Olds Products Company
Pleasant Prairie, WI 800-233-8064
Our Thyme Garden
Cleburne, TX 800-482-4372
Pastorelli Food Products
Chicago, IL 800-767-2829
Patsy's
New York, NY 212-247-3491
Pilgrim Foods
Greenville, NH 603-878-2100
Pompeian
Baltimore, MD 800-638-1224
Prairie Thyme
Santa Fe, NM 800-869-0009
Proacec USA
Santa Monica, CA. 310-996-7770
Purity Products
Plainview, NY. 888-769-7873
Rahco International
St Augustine, FL. 800-851-7681
Red Pelican Food Products
Detroit, MI 313-881-4095
Reinhart Foods
Markham, ON. 905-754-3500
Restaurant Lulu Gourmet Products
San Francisco, CA 888-693-5800
REX Pure Foods
New Orleans, LA 800-344-8314
Rex Wine Vinegar Company
Newark, NJ 973-589-6911
Roanoke Apple Products
Salem, VA 540-375-3782
Robert Rothschild Berry Farm
Urbana, OH. 866-565-6790
Robert Rothschild Farm
Urbana, OH. 866-565-6790
S&G Products
Nicholasville, KY 800-826-7652
Santa Barbara Olive Company
Santa Barbara, CA 800-624-4896
Satiety
Davis, CA 530-757-2699
Sedlock Farm
Lynn Center, IL. 309-521-8284
Sherrill Orchards
Arvin, CA 661-858-2035
Sieco USA Corporation
Houston, TX 800-325-9443
Silver Palate Kitchens
Cresskill, NJ 800-872-5283
Sister's Kitchen
Rutland, VT 802-775-2457
Solana Gold Organics
Sebastopol, CA 800-459-1121
Spruce Mountain Blueberries
West Rockport, ME. 207-236-3538
Star Fine Foods
Fresno, CA 559-498-2900
Stickney & Poor Company
Peterborough, NH. 603-924-2259
Thistledew Farm
Proctor, WV 800-854-6639
Todhunter Foods
Lake Alfred, FL. 863-956-1116

Tres Classique
Ukiah, CA. 888-644-5127
Tropical
Charlotte, NC 800-220-1413
Unilever Bestfoods, Inc.
Englewood Cliffs, NJ 201-894-4000
Victoria Packing Corporation
Brooklyn, NY 718-927-3000
Village Imports
Brisbane, CA. 888-865-8714
Vincent Formusa Company
Chicago, IL 312-421-0485
Walker Foods
Los Angeles, CA. 800-966-5199
Webbpak
Trussville, AL 800-655-3500
White House Foods
Winchester, VA 540-662-3401
Widow's Mite Vinegar Company
Washington, DC 877-678-5854
Wild Thymes Farm
Greenville, NY 800-724-2877
Wing's Food Products
Etobicoke, ON 416-259-2662
Wisconsin Cheese
Melrose Park, IL. 708-450-0074
Woeber Mustard Manufacturing
Springfield, OH. 800-548-2929

Apple Cider

Eden Foods Inc.
Clinton, MI 800-248-0320
Emerling International Foods
Buffalo, NY. 716-833-7381

We supply food manufacturers and food service customers worldwide (since 1988) with bulk ingredients including: Fruits & Vegetables; Juice Concentrates; Herbs & Spices; Oils & Vinegars; Flavors & Colors; Honey & Molasses. We also produce PURE MAPLE SYRUP.

Fleischmanns Vinegar
Cerritos, CA 800-443-1067
Gregory-Robinson Speas
Dallas, TX. 214-352-1761
Knouse Foods Coop
Peach Glen, PA 717-677-8181
Live Food Products
Santa Barbara, CA 800-446-1990
Mizkam Americas
Kansas City, MO. 816-483-1700
Nana Mae's Organics
Sebastopol, CA 707-829-7359
National Vinegar Company
St Louis, MO. 314-962-4111
Pastorelli Food Products
Chicago, IL 800-767-2829
Reinhart Foods
Markham, ON 905-754-3500
Roanoke Apple Products
Salem, VA 540-375-3782
Sieco USA Corporation
Houston, TX 800-325-9443
Solana Gold Organics
Sebastopol, CA 800-459-1121
Walker Foods
Los Angeles, CA. 800-966-5199
Webbpak
Trussville, AL 800-655-3500
White House Foods
Winchester, VA 540-662-3401
Widow's Mite Vinegar Company
Washington, DC 877-678-5854

Balsamic

Agrusa, Inc.
Leonia, NJ. 201-592-5950
California Olive Oil Corporation
Berkeley, CA. 888-718-9830
Emerling International Foods
Buffalo, NY. 716-833-7381

We supply food manufacturers and food service customers worldwide (since 1988) with bulk ingredients including: Fruits & Vegetables; Juice Concentrates; Herbs & Spices; Oils & Vinegars; Flavors & Colors; Honey & Molasses. We also produce PURE MAPLE SYRUP.

Fleischmanns Vinegar
Cerritos, CA 800-443-1067

Golden Whisk
South San Francisco, CA 800-660-5222
Modena Fine Foods
Clifton, NJ. 201-842-8900
North American Enterprises
Tucson, AZ 800-817-8666
Olive Oil Factory
Waterbury, CT. 860-945-9549
Organic Planet
San Francisco, CA 415-765-5590
Pastorelli Food Products
Chicago, IL 800-767-2829
Proacec USA
Santa Monica, CA. 310-996-7770
Reinhart Foods
Markham, ON 905-754-3500
Restaurant Lulu Gourmet Products
San Francisco, CA 888-693-5800
Rex Wine Vinegar Company
Newark, NJ 973-589-6911
Sieco USA Corporation
Houston, TX 800-325-9443
Unilever Bestfoods, Inc.
Englewood Cliffs, NJ 201-894-4000
Valley Grain Products
Madera, CA. 559-675-3400
Victoria Packing Corporation
Brooklyn, NY 718-927-3000
Wild Thymes Farm
Greenville, NY 800-724-2877

Liquid

Assouline & Ting
Huntingdon Valley, PA 800-521-4491
Clements Foods Company
Oklahoma City, OK 800-654-8355
Colonna Brothers
North Bergen, NJ 201-864-1115

Flavored

Assouline & Ting
Huntingdon Valley, PA 800-521-4491

Malt

Eden Foods Inc.
Clinton, MI 800-248-0320
Fleischmanns Vinegar
Cerritos, CA 800-443-1067
Reinhart Foods
Markham, ON 905-754-3500

Raspberry

Reinhart Foods
Markham, ON 905-754-3500
Thistledew Farm
Proctor, WV 800-854-6639

Sherry

National Vinegar Company
St Louis, MO. 314-962-4111

White Distilled

Big B Distributors
Evansville, IN 812-425-5235
Creole Fermentation Industries
Abbeville, LA 337-898-9377
Emerling International Foods
Buffalo, NY. 716-833-7381

We supply food manufacturers and food service customers worldwide (since 1988) with bulk ingredients including: Fruits & Vegetables; Juice Concentrates; Herbs & Spices; Oils & Vinegars; Flavors & Colors; Honey & Molasses. We also produce PURE MAPLE SYRUP.

Fleischmanns Vinegar
Cerritos, CA 800-443-1067
Gregory-Robinson Speas
Dallas, TX. 214-352-1761
Knouse Foods Coop
Peach Glen, PA 717-677-8181
Mizkam Americas
Kansas City, MO. 816-483-1700
National Vinegar Company
St Louis, MO. 314-962-4111
National Vinegar Company
Alton, IL 618-465-6532
Pastorelli Food Products
Chicago, IL 800-767-2829
Reinhart Foods
Markham, ON 905-754-3500
Roanoke Apple Products
Salem, VA 540-375-3782
Walker Foods
Los Angeles, CA. 800-966-5199
Webbpak
Trussville, AL 800-655-3500
White House Foods
Winchester, VA 540-662-3401
Wisconsin Cheese
Melrose Park, IL 708-450-0074

Wine

B&G Foods
Parsippany, NJ. 973-401-6500
Eden Foods Inc.
Clinton, MI 800-248-0320
Fleischmanns Vinegar
Cerritos, CA 800-443-1067
Gregory-Robinson Speas
Dallas, TX. 214-352-1761
Hansen's Juices
Azusa, CA. 800-426-7367
Knouse Foods Coop
Peach Glen, PA 717-677-8181
Mizkan Americas
Mt Prospect, IL 800-323-4358
Modena Fine Foods
Clifton, NJ. 201-842-8900
National Vinegar Company
St Louis, MO. 314-962-4111
Pastorelli Food Products
Chicago, IL 800-767-2829
Pompeian
Baltimore, MD 800-638-1224
Reinhart Foods
Markham, ON 905-754-3500
Roanoke Apple Products
Salem, VA 540-375-3782
Satiety
Davis, CA 530-757-2699
Sieco USA Corporation
Houston, TX 800-325-9443
Star Fine Foods
Fresno, CA 559-498-2900
Tres Classique
Ukiah, CA. 888-644-5127
Victoria Packing Corporation
Brooklyn, NY 718-927-3000
Wine Country Kitchens
Napa, CA. 707-252-9463

Snack Foods

General

34 Degrees
Denver, CO 303-861-4818
Alimentos Bermudez
Brooklyn, NY 347-533-2230
America's Classic Foods
Cambria, CA 805-927-0745
American Importing Company
Minneapolis, MN 612-331-7000
Arico Natural Foods
Beaverton, OR 503-259-0871
Bake Crafters Food
Collegedale, TN 800-296-8935
Barbara's Bakery
Petaluma, CA 707-765-2273
Bazaar
River Grove, IL 800-736-1888
Betsy's Cheese Straws
Chattanooga, TN 877-902-3141
Big Steer Enterprises
Beaumont, TX 800-421-4951
Blue Crab Bay Company
Melfa, VA 800-221-2722
Brothers International Food Corp
Rochester, NY 888-842-7477
CGI Desserts
Sugar Land, TX 281-240-1200
ConAgra Food Store Brands
Edina, MN 952-469-4981
Cornfields, Inc.
Waukegan, IL 847-263-7000
DCL
Honolulu, HI 808-845-3834
Divvies
South Salem, NY 914-533-0333
Double B Distributors
Lexington, KY 859-255-8822
East Kentucky Foods
Winchester, KY 859-744-2218
Eat Your Heart Out
New York, NY 212-989-8303
Enjoy Life Foods
Schiller Park, IL 888-503-6569
Excelline Foods
Chatsworth, CA 818-701-7710
GeniSoy
Tulsa, OK 800-228-4656
GKI Foods
Brighton, MI 248-486-0055
Gourmet Basics
Brooklyn, NY 718-509-9366
Gourmet Kitchen, Inc.
Neptune, NJ 800-492-3663
Govadinas Fitness Foods
San Diego, CA 800-900-0108
H.J. Heinz Company
Pittsburgh, PA 800-872-2229
Happy Herberts Food Company
Jersey City, NJ 800-764-2779
Husman Snack Food Company
Cincinnati, OH 859-282-7490
Ideal Snacks
Liberty, NY 845-292-7000
Internacional De Productos Y Semillas
Apodaca, NL 811-160-0700
Inventure Foods
Phoenix, AZ 623-932-6200
Jonny Almond Nut Company
Flint, MI 810-767-6886
Kateri Foods
Hopkins, MN 800-330-8351
Kettle Foods
Salem, OR 503-364-0399
Kind Snacks
New York, NY 800-732-2321
King Henry's Inc.
Valencia, CA 661-295-5566
King Nut Company
Solon, OH 800-860-5464
Kraft Foods
Northfield, IL 800-323-0768
Krema Nut Company
Columbus, OH 800-222-4132
L. Craven & Sons
Melrose Park, IL 800-453-4303
Late July Organic Snacks
Barnstable, MA 508-362-5859
Laurel Hill Foods
Attleboro, MA 877-759-8141
LesserEvil Snacks
Greenwich, CT
Lisanatti Foods
Oregon City, OR 866-864-3922
Lost Trail Root Beer Com
Louisburg, KS 800-748-7765
Lynard Company
Stamford, CT 203-323-0231
McIlhenny Company
Avery Island, LA 800-634-9599
Mezza
Lake Forest, IL 888-206-6054
Mister Bee Potato Chip Company
Parkersburg, WV 304-428-6133
Nebraska Popcorn
Clearwater, NE 800-253-6502
Nu-World Amaranth
Naperville, IL 630-369-6819
Ozark Mountain Trading
Westfield, NJ 908-232-6365
Papa Dean's Popcorn
San Antonio, TX 877-855-7272
Peeled Snacks
Brooklyn, NY 212-706-2001
Pippin Snack Pecans
Albany, GA 800-554-6887
Poore Brothers
Boulder, CO 303-546-9939
R.A.B. Food Group LLC
Secaucus, NJ 201-553-1100
Ramsey Popcorn Company
Ramsey, IN 800-624-2060
Rudolph Foods Company
Lima, OH 419-648-3611
Ryt Way Industries
Lakeville, MN 952-469-1417
Sargento Foods Inc.
Plymouth, WI 800-243-3737
Seapoint Farms
Huntington Beach, CA 888-722-7098
Setton International Foods
Commack, NY 800-227-4397
Simply 7 Snacks
Houston, TX 877-682-2359
Snack Works/Metrovox Snacks
Orange, CA 800-783-9870
Snikdiddy
Boulder, CO 303-444-4405
Snyder's of Hanover
Hanover, PA 717-632-4477
Snyder's-Lance Inc.
Charlotte, NC 800-438-1880
Squire Boone Village
New Albany, IN 888-934-1804
Sugar Foods Corporation
New York, NY 212-753-6900
Sunridge Farms
Salinas, CA 831-755-1430
Terrell's Potato Chip Company
Syracuse, NY 315-437-2786
Terri Lynn
Elgin, IL 800-323-0775
Thatcher's Special Popcorn
San Francisco, CA 800-926-2676
The Hampton Popcorn Company Inc.
Mineola, NY 888-947-6726
The Humphrey Co
Lockport, NY 716-597-1974
The Mediterranean Snack Food Company
Boonton, NJ 973-333-4888
Touche Bakery
London, ON 518-455-0044
Tri-Sum Potato Chip Company
Leominster, MA 978-697-2447
Wyandot Inc.
Marion, OH 800-992-6368
Your Bar Factory
LaSalle, QC 888-366-0258

Cheese Curls

Barbara's Bakery
Petaluma, CA 707-765-2273
Better Meat North
Bay City, MI 989-684-6271
Cheeze Kurls
Grand Rapids, MI 616-784-6095
Elmer's Fine Foods
New Orleans, LA 504-949-2716
Golden Flake Snack Foods
Birmingham, AL 800-239-2447
Happy's Potato Chip Company
Minneapolis, MN 612-781-3121
Hartley's Potato Chip Company
Lewistown, PA 717-248-0526
Herr Foods
Chillicothe, OH 800-523-8468
Hostess Frito-Lay Company
Swift Current, SK 306-773-9621
Martin's Famous Pastry Shoppe, Inc
Chambersburg, PA 800-548-1200
McCleary
South Beloit, IL 800-523-8644
Medallion Foods
Newport, AR 870-523-3500
Tri-Sum Potato Chip Company
Leominster, MA 978-697-2447
Variety Foods
Warren, MI 586-268-4900
Wyandot Inc.
Marion, OH 800-992-6368

Cheese Twists

Aileen Quirk & Sons
Kansas City, MO 816-471-4580
Alamo Masa Company
Uvalde, TX 800-568-9651
Allen Canning Company
Siloam Springs, AR 800-234-2553
American Blanching Company
Fitzgerald, GA 229-423-4098
American Nut & Chocolate Company
Boston, MA 800-797-6887
American Skin LLC
Burgaw, NC 800-248-7463
Amsnack
Stockton, CA 209-982-5545
Archie Moore's Foods Products
Milford, CT 203-876-5088
Arizona Brands
Phoenix, AZ 602-273-7139
Arizona Pistachio Company
Tulare, CA 800-333-8575
Art's Mexican Products
Kansas City, KS 913-371-2163
Ateeco
Shenandoah, PA 800-233-3170
Austinuts
Austin, TX 877-329-6887
B. Lloyd's Pecans
Barwick, GA 800-322-6887
Bachman Company
Reading, PA 800-523-8253
Backer's Potato Chip Company
Fulton, MO 573-642-2833
Baldwin-Minkler Farms
Orland, CA 530-865-8080
Ballreich's Potato Chips
Tiffin, OH 800-323-2447
Barrel O'Fun Snacks Foods Company
Perham, MN 218-346-7000
Berberian Nut Company
Chico, CA 530-891-4900
Bickels Snacks
York, PA 717-843-0738
Bimbo Bakeries
Horsham, PA 800-984-0989
Birds Eye Foods
Berlin, PA 814-267-4641
Birmhall Foods Company
Memphis, TN 901-377-9016
Black Jewell®Popcorn
St Francisville, IL 800-948-2302
Boyd Sausage Company
Washington, IA 319-653-5715

Brandmeyer Popcorn Company
Ankeny, IA 800-568-8276
Bremner Biscuit Company
Denver, CO 800-722-1871
Brennan Snacks Manufacturing
Bogalusa, LA 800-290-7486
Browns' Ice Cream Company
Bowling Green, KY 270-843-9882
Buffalo Bill's Snack Foods
Denver, CO 303-298-0705
C.J. Distributing
Surf City, NC 800-990-2366
Cafe Fanny
Berkeley, CA 800-441-5413
Calbee America
Fairfield, CA 707-427-2500
California Fruit & Nut
Gustine, CA 888-747-8224
California Garden Products
Lake Forest, CA 949-215-0000
California Snack Foods
South El Monte, CA 626-444-4508
Capri Bagel & Pizza Corporation
Brooklyn, NY 718-497-4431
Carolina Fine Snack Foods
Greensboro, NC 336-605-0773
Cattaneo Brothers
San Luis Obispo, CA 800-243-8537
Central Snacks
Carthage, MS 601-267-3112
Chappaqua Crunch
Marblehead, MA 781-631-8118
Cheese Straws & More
Monroe, LA 800-997-1921
Chelsea Milling Company
Chelsea, MI 734-475-1361
Cher-Make Sausage Company
Manitowoc, WI 800-242-7679
Chickasaw Foods
Memphis, TN 901-323-5467
Chocolate Potpourri
Glenview, IL 888-680-1600
Chooljian Brothers Packing Company
Sanger, CA 559-875-5501
City Farm/Rocky Peanut Company
Detroit, MI 800-437-6825
Cloud Nine
San Leandro, CA 201-358-8588
Colorado Cereal
Fort Collins, CO 970-282-9733
Colorado Popcorn Company
Sterling, CO 800-238-2676
Columbia Empire Farms
Sherwood, OR 503-538-2156
Columbia Snacks
Columbia, SC 803-776-0133
Commonwealth Brands
Bowling Green, KY 270-781-9100
Community Orchard
Fort Dodge, IA 515-573-8212
ConAgra Foods
Boisbriand, QC 450-433-1322
Conn's Potato Chip Company
Zanesville, OH 866-486-4615
Consolidated Biscuit Company
Michigan City, IN 219-873-1880
Corbin Foods-Edibowls
Santa Ana, CA 800-695-5655
Corn Poppers
San Diego, CA 858-231-2617
Country Estate Pecans
Sahuarita, AZ 800-473-2267
Cuisinary Fine Foods
Irving, TX 888-283-5303
Dan-Dee Pretzel & Chip Company
Columbus, OH 614-322-0376
Dare Foods
Spartanburg, SC 1 8-0 6-8 32
Dare Foods
Kitchener, ON 800-265-8225
Dellaco Classic Confections
Burlington, WI 262-537-2656
Dieffenbach Potato Chips
Womelsdorf, PA 610-589-2385
Dole Nut Company
Orland, CA 530-865-5511
Door Country Potato Chips
Milwaukee, WI 414-964-1428
Durey-Libby Edible Nuts
Carlstadt, NJ 800-332-6887
Durham/Ellis Pecan Country Store
Comanche, TX 325-356-5291
Eddy's Bakery
Boise, ID 208-377-8100
El Grano De Oro
Pacifica, CA 650-355-8417
Elegant Edibles
Houston, TX 800-227-3226
Ellis Popcorn Company
Murray, KY 800-654-3358
Europa Foods
Saddle Brook, NJ 201-368-8929
Evans Food Products Com pany
Chicago, IL 866-254-7400
Exquisita Tortillas
Edinburg, TX 956-383-6712
Fairchester Snacks Corporation
White Plains, NY 914-761-2824
Fairmont Snacks Group
Independence, OH 216-573-2777
Farmers Investment Company
Sahuarita, AZ 520-625-8809
Fastachi
Watertown, MA 800-466-3022
Fisher's Popcorn
Ocean City, MD 888-395-0335
Foley's Candies
Richmond, BC 888-236-5397
Fontazzi/Metrovox Snacks
Orange, CA 800-428-0522
Food Products Corporation
Phoenix, AZ 602-273-7139
Fortella Fortune Cookies
Chicago, IL 312-567-9000
Fresh Roasted Almond Company
Warren, MI 877-478-6887
Fun City Popcorn
Las Vegas, NV 800-423-1710
Furukawa Potato Chip Factory
Captain Cook, HI 808-323-3785
Garrett Popcorn Shops
Chicago, IL 888-476-7267
Germack Pistachio Company
Detroit, MI 800-872-4006
GH Bent Company
Milton, MA 617-698-5945
Gilda Industries
Hialeah, FL 305-887-8286
Glacial Ridge Foods
Redford, MI 612-239-2215
Golden Peanut Company
Alpharetta, GA 770-752-8160
Govatos
Wilmington, DE 888-799-5252
Great Western Products Company
Assumption, IL 217-226-3241
Great Western Products Company
Bismarck, MO 573-734-2210
Gulf Pecan Company
Gulf Shores, AL 251-943-4320
Guy's Food
Liberty, MO 800-821-2405
Guylian USA Inc.
Englewood Cliffs, NJ 800-803-4123
Haby's Alsatian Bakery
Castroville, TX 830-931-2118
Hammond's Candies
Denver, CO 888-226-3999
Happy Herberts Food Company
Jersey City, NJ 800-764-2779
Hazelnut Growers of Oregon
Cornelius, OR 503-648-4176
Hillson Nut Company
Cleveland, OH 800-333-2818
Hirsch Brothers & Company
Holland, MI 616-335-5806
Hoody Corporation
Newark, MD 410-632-1766
Hume Specialties
Chester, VT 802-875-3117
Humphrey Company
Cleveland, OH 800-486-3739
Hungry Sultan
Lake Forest, CA 949-215-0000
Imus Ranch Foods
Darien, CT 505-892-0883
Inventure Foods
Phoenix, AZ 623-932-6200
Ira Middleswarth & Son
Middleburg, PA 570-837-1431
J&B Sausage Company
Waelder, TX 830-788-7511
J.R. Short Milling Company
Kankakee, IL 800-457-3547
J.W. Haywood & Sons Dairy
Louisville, KY 502-774-2311
Jack Link Snack Foods
Minong, WI 715-466-2234
Jay Shah Foods
Mississauga, ON 905-696-0172
Jay's Foods
Chicago, IL 800-621-6152
Jenkins Foods
Detroit, MI 800-800-3286
Jerrell Packaging
Bessemer, AL 205-426-8930
JMS Specialty Foods
Ripon, WI 800-535-5437
Joel Harvey Distributing
Brooklyn, NY 718-629-2690
John B. Sanfilippo & Son
Gustine, CA 800-218-3077
John Wm. Macy's Cheesesticks
Elmwood Park, NJ 800-643-0573
Judy's Cream Caramels
Sherwood, OR 503-625-7161
Kendrick Gourmet Products
Columbus, GA 800-356-1858
Kettle Foods
Salem, OR 503-364-0399
Kevton Gourmet Tea
Streetman, TX 888-538-8668
Kid's Kookie Company
San Clemente, CA 800-350-7577
Kitty Clover Snacktime Company
Omaha, NE 402-342-7342
La Fronteriza
Toledo, OH 800-897-1772
La Vencedora Products
Los Angeles, CA 800-327-2572
Lamb-Weston
Kennewick, WA 800-766-7783
Laredo Mexican Foods
Fort Wayne, IN 800-252-7336
LaRosa's Bakery
Shrewsbury, NJ 800-527-6722
Longleaf Plantation
Lumberton, MS 800-421-7370
Longview Meat & Merchandise Ltd
Longview, AB 866-355-3759
Los Angeles Nut House Brands
Los Angeles, CA 213-481-0134
Louis Trauth Dairy
Newport, KY 800-544-6455
Louise's
Shelbyville, KY 502-633-9700
Ludwick's Frozen Donuts
Grand Rapids, MI 800-366-8816
Mac's Snacks
Arlington, TX 817-640-5626
MacFarms of Hawaii
Captain Cook, HI 808-328-2435
Madhouse Munchies
Colchester, VT 802-655-6662
Mama Amy's Quality Foods
Mississauga, ON 905-456-0056
Marantha Natural Foods
San Francisco, CA 866-972-6879
Mauna Loa Macadamia Nut Corporation
Keaau, HI 800-832-9993
Maxin Marketing Corporation
Aliso Viejo, CA 949-362-1177
Meadow Gold Dairies
Englewood, CO 800-525-3289
Mental Process
Atlanta, GA 404-875-7440
Mex. Accent
New Berlin, WI 262-784-4422
Mexisnax Corporation
El Paso, TX 915-779-5709
Mitchum Potato Chips
Charlotte, NC 704-372-6744
Molinaro's Fine Italian Foods
Mississauga, ON 800-268-4959
Mrs. Dog's Products
Grand Rapids, MI 800-2Mr-Dog
Mrs. Rio's Corn Products
San Angelo, TX 325-653-5640
Natchez Pecan Shelling Company
Taylorsville, MS 601-785-4333
National Foods
Bronx, NY 800-683-6565
Nichols Pistachio
Hanford, CA 559-584-6811
Nips Potato Chips
Honolulu, HI 808-593-8549

Noah's Potato Chip Company
Alexandria, LA 318-445-0283
Noble Popcorn Farms
Sac City, IA 800-537-9554
Northwest Candy Emporium
Everett, WA 800-404-7266
Nustef Foods
Mississauga, ON 905-896-3060
Nut House
Mobile, AL 800-633-1306
Nutty Bavarian
Sanford, FL 800-382-4788
Oasis Mediterranean Cuisine
Toledo, OH 419-269-1516
Odessa Tortilla & TamaleFactory
Odessa, TX 800-753-2445
Old Dutch Foods
Roseville, MN 800-989-2447
Old Sacramento Popcorn Company
Sacramento, CA 916-446-1980
Our Thyme Garden
Cleburne, TX 800-482-4372
Packaged Products Division
Largo, FL 888-833-2247
Paddack Enterprises
Escalon, CA 209-838-1536
Pape's Pecan Company
Seguin, TX 888-688-7273
Pepes Mexican Foods
Etobicoke, ON 416-674-0882
Perfections by Allan
Owings Mills, MD 800-581-8670
Peterson's Ventures
Salt Lake City, UT 80- 4-8 03
Picard Peanuts
Simcoe, ON 888-244-7688
Pickle Cottage
Bucklin, KS 316-826-3502
Pioneer Snacks
Mankato, MN 507-388-1661
Pizza Products
Farmington Hills, MI 800-600-7482
Plantation Pecan Company
Waterproof, LA 800-477-3226
Plehn's Bakery
Louisville, KY 502-896-4438
Pond Brothers Peanut Company
Suffolk, VA 757-539-2356
Poore Brothers
Bluffton, IN 260-824-2800
Poore Brothers
Phoenix, AZ 800-279-2250
Popcorner
Swansea, IL 618-277-2676
Poppee's Popcorn Company
Elyria, OH 440-327-0775
Poppin Popcorn
Naples, FL 941-262-1691
Premiere Packing Company
Greenacres, WA 888-239-5288
Quality Snack Foods
Alsip, IL 708-396-8826
RDO Foods Company
Grand Forks, ND 701-775-3154
Reed's Original Beverage Corporation
Los Angeles, CA 800-997-3337
Rices Potato Chips
Biloxi, MS 228-396-5775
Ricos Candy Snacks & Bakery
Hialeah, FL 305-885-7392
Ripensa A/S
Lehigh Acres, FL 941-561-5882
Ritts-Chavelle Snack Company
North Hills, CA 818-830-3305
Rolet Food Products Company
Brooklyn, NY 718-497-0476
Route 11 Potato Chips
Middletown, VA 800-294-7783
Rudy's Tortillas
Dallas, TX 800-878-2401
Rupari Food Service
Deerfield Beach, FL 800-578-7274
Rural Route 1 Popcorn
Livingston, WI 800-828-8115
Rygmyr Foods
South Saint Paul, MN 800-545-3903
Sachs Nut Company
Clarkton, NC 800-732-6933
Saint Amour/Powerline Foods
Costa Mesa, CA 714-754-1900
San Saba Pecan
San Saba, TX 800-683-2101
Sanarak Paper & Popcorn Supplies
Buffalo, NY 716-874-5662
Savory Foods
Portsmouth, OH 740-354-6655
Scotsburn Dairy Group
Scotsburn, NS 902-485-8023
Sesaco Corporation
San Antonio, TX 800-737-2260
Severance Foods
Hartford, CT 860-724-7063
Shallowford Farms
Yadkinville, NC 800-892-9539
Shearer's Foods
Brewster, OH 330-767-3426
SLB Snacks
Lynn, MA 781-593-4422
Snack Factory
Princeton, NJ 888-683-5400
SnackMasters
Ceres, CA 800-597-9770
Snappy Popcorn Company
Breda, IA 800-742-0228
Snelgrove Ice Cream Company
Salt Lake City, UT 800-569-0005
Sommer's Food Products
Salisbury, MO 660-388-5511
South Georgia Pecan Company
Valdosta, GA 800-627-6630
Southern Popcorn Company
Memphis, TN 901-362-5238
Southern Roasted Nuts
Fitzgerald, GA 912-423-5616
Sparta Foods
Saint Paul, MN 800-700-0809
Spilke's Baking Company
Brooklyn, NY 718-384-2150
Stateline Boyd
Lynn, MA 781-593-4422
Story's Popcorn Company
Charleston, MO 573-649-2727
Sunnyside Farms
Neligh, NE 402-791-2210
Texas Tito's
San Antonio, TX 830-626-1123
Tim's Cascade Chips
Algona, WA 800-533-8467
Tom Sturgis Pretzels
Reading, PA 800-817-3834
Trinidad Benham Company
Denver, CO 303-220-1400
Tuscan Bakery
Portland, OR 800-887-2261
Twin Valley Products
Greenleaf, KS 800-748-7416
Uncle Ralph's Cookie Company
Frederick, MD 800-422-0626
Uncle Ray's Potato Chips
Detroit, MI 313-834-0800
Universal Blanchers
Blakely, GA 229-723-4181
Van-Lang Foods
Countryside, IL 708-588-0800
Vande Walle's Candies
Appleton, WI 920-738-7799
Variety Foods
Warren, MI 586-268-4900
Vic's Gourmet Popping Corn Company
Omaha, NE 402-331-2822
Vogel Popcorn
Hamburg, IA 800-831-5818
Wabash Valley Farms
Monon, IN 800-270-2705
Wachusett Potato Chip Company
Fitchburg, MA 800-551-5539
Warden Peanut Company
Portales, NM 575-356-6691
Weaver Popcorn Company
Noblesville, IN 800-634-8161
Wells' Dairy
Le Mars, IA 800-942-3800
Wise Foods
Carlstadt, NJ 201-507-0015
Wise Foods
Berwick, PA 570-759-4000
Wise Foods
Bristol, TN 864-585-9011
Wynnewood Pecan Company
Wynnewood, OK 800-892-4985
Yarnell Ice Cream Company
Searcy, AR 800-766-2414
Yick Lung Company
Honolulu, HI 808-841-3611
Young Pecan
Las Cruces, NM 575-524-4321
Young Pecan Company
Florence, SC 800-829-6864
Zapp's Chips
Gramercy, LA 800-349-2447
Zapp's Potato Chips
Gramercy, LA 800-349-2447

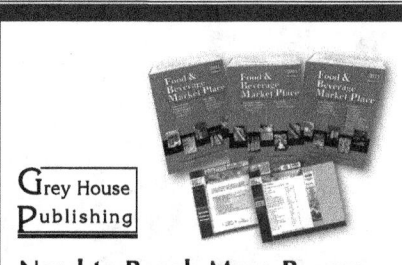

Chips

Bagel Chips

Harlan Bakeries
Avon, IN 317-272-3600
Soloman Baking Company
Denver, CO 303-371-2777
Weaver Nut Company
Ephrata, PA 717-738-3781

Baked

Abuelita Mexican Foods
Manassas Park, VA 703-369-0232
Azteca Foods
Summit Argo, IL 708-563-6600
C.J. Vitner Company
Chicago, IL 773-523-7900
Golden Flake Snack Foods
Ocala, FL 800-239-2447
Golden Fluff Popcorn Company
Lakewood, NJ 732-367-5448
Harlan Bakeries
Avon, IN 317-272-3600
Hostess Frito-Lay Company
Swift Current, SK 306-773-9621
Humpty Dumpty Snack Foods
Lachine, QC 800-361-6440
Imus Ranch Foods
Darien, CT 505-892-0883
Kettle Foods
Salem, OR 503-364-0399
La Canasta Mexican Food Products
Phoenix, AZ 855-269-7721
La Fronteriza
Toledo, OH 800-897-1772
La Mexicana
Chicago, IL 773-247-5443
Laredo Mexican Foods
Fort Wayne, IN 800-252-7336

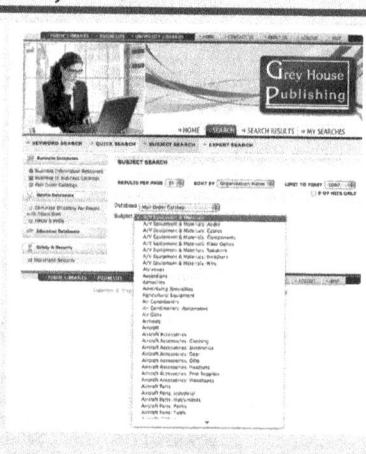

Li'l Guy Foods
Kansas City, MO 800-886-8226
Luna's Tortillas
Dallas, TX 214-747-2661
Medallion Foods
Newport, AR 870-523-3500
Mex. Accent
New Berlin, WI 262-784-4422
Olde Tyme Food Corporation
East Longmeadow, MA 800-356-6533
Ozuna Food Products Corporation
Sunnyvale, CA 408-400-0495
Pepes Mexican Foods
Etobicoke, ON 416-674-0882
Puebla Foods
Passaic, NJ 973-473-4494
R&J Farms
West Salem, OH 419-846-3179
Rubschlager Baking Corporation
Chicago, IL 773-826-1245
Rudy's Tortillas
Dallas, TX 800-878-2401
Severance Foods
Hartford, CT 860-724-7063
Shallowford Farms
Yadkinville, NC 800-892-9539
Spanish Gardens Food Manufacturing
Kansas City, KS 913-831-4242
Tom's Snacks Company
Charlotte, NC 800-995-2623
Troyer Farms
Waterford, PA 800-458-0485
Westbrae Natural Foods
Melville, NY 800-434-4246
Wyandot
Marion, OH 800-992-6368

Banana

American Importing Company
Minneapolis, MN 612-331-7000

Cassava

Arico Natural Foods
Beaverton, OR 503-259-0871
Tantos Foods International
Markham, ON 905-943-9993

Chocolate

Ghirardelli Chocolate Company
San Leandro, CA 800-877-9338
NSpired Natural Foods
Boulder, CO 800-434-4246
Sheryl's Chocolate Creations
Hicksville, NY 888-882-2462
St. Charles Trading
Lake Saint Louis, MO 800-336-1333
Wilbur Chocolate
Lititz, PA 800-233-0139

Corn

Abuelita Mexican Foods
Manassas Park, VA 703-369-0232
C.J. Vitner Company
Chicago, IL 773-523-7900
Delicious Popcorn Company
Waupaca, WI 715-258-7683
Golden Flake Snack Foods
Birmingham, AL 800-239-2447
Hostess Frito-Lay Company
Swift Current, SK 306-773-9621
Jay's Foods
Chicago, IL 800-621-6152
La Mexicana
Chicago, IL 773-247-5443
McCleary
South Beloit, IL 800-523-8644
Oak Creek Farms
Edgar, NE 402-224-3038
Pippin Snack Pecans
Albany, GA 800-554-6887
Tom's Snacks Company
Charlotte, NC 800-995-2623
Wyandot
Marion, OH 800-992-6368
Xochitl
Dallas, TX 214-800-3551

Fried

Abuelita Mexican Foods
Manassas Park, VA 703-369-0232
Archie Moore's Foods Products
Milford, CT 203-876-5088
Better Meat North
Bay City, MI 989-684-6271
Bickel's Potato Chip Company
Manheim, PA 717-665-2002
Birds Eye Foods
Berlin, PA 814-267-4641
C.J. Vitner Company
Chicago, IL 773-523-7900
Calbee America
Fairfield, CA 707-427-2500
Delicious Popcorn Company
Waupaca, WI 715-258-7683
El-Milagro
Chicago, IL
Elmer's Fine Foods
New Orleans, LA 504-949-2716
Golden Flake Snack Foods
Ocala, FL 800-239-2447
Granite State Potato Chip Company
Salem, NH 603-898-2171
Happy's Potato Chip Company
Minneapolis, MN 612-781-3121
Hartley's Potato Chip Company
Lewistown, PA 717-248-0526
Hostess Frito-Lay Company
Swift Current, SK 306-773-9621
Humpty Dumpty Snack Foods
Lachine, QC 800-361-6440
Jones Potato Chip Company
Mansfield, OH 800-466-9424
Kettle Foods
Salem, OR 503-364-0399
Kitch'n Cook'd Potato Chip Company
Staunton, VA 800-752-1535
La Fronteriza
Toledo, OH 800-897-1772
La Mexicana
Chicago, IL 773-247-5443
La Vencedora Products
Los Angeles, CA 800-327-2572
Laredo Mexican Foods
Fort Wayne, IN 800-252-7336
Maui Potato Chips
Kahului, HI 808-877-3652
Medallion Foods
Newport, AR 870-523-3500
Mex. Accent
New Berlin, WI 262-784-4422
Middleswarth Potato Chips
Wilkes Barre, PA 570-288-2447
Miguel's Stowe Away
Stowe, VT 800-448-6517
Mrs. Fisher's
Rockford, IL 815-964-9114
Olde Tyme Food Corporation
East Longmeadow, MA 800-356-6533
Ozuna Food Products Corporation
Sunnyvale, CA 408-400-0495
Peerless Potato Chips
Gary, IN 219-885-6843
Pepes Mexican Foods
Etobicoke, ON 416-674-0882
Puebla Foods
Passaic, NJ 973-473-4494
Randag & Associates Inc
Elmhurst, IL 630-530-2830
Revonah Pretzel Bakery
Hanover, PA 717-630-2883
Route 11 Potato Chips
Middletown, VA 800-294-7783
Rubschlager Baking Corporation
Chicago, IL 773-826-1245
Seasons' Enterprises
Addison, IL 630-628-0211
Severance Foods
Hartford, CT 860-724-7063
Shearer's Foods
Brewster, OH 330-767-3426
Spanish Gardens Food Manufacturing
Kansas City, KS 913-831-4242
Sun Pac Foods
Brampton, ON 905-792-2700
Terrell's Potato Chip Company
Syracuse, NY 315-437-2786
Tim's Cascade Chips
Algona, WA 800-533-8467
Tom's Foods
Charlotte, NC 800-995-2623
Tom's Snacks Company
Charlotte, NC 800-995-2623
Troyer Farms
Waterford, PA 800-458-0485
Westbrae Natural Foods
Melville, NY 800-434-4246
Wyandot
Marion, OH 800-992-6368
Yum Yum Potato Chips
Warwick, QC 800-567-5792

Nacho

Arizona Beverage Company
Woodbury, NY 800-832-3775
Luna's Tortillas
Dallas, TX 214-747-2661
Olde Tyme Food Corporation
East Longmeadow, MA 800-356-6533
Ozuna Food Products Corporation
Sunnyvale, CA 408-400-0495

Pita

Argo Fine Foods
Saint James, NY 631-703-0443
Regco Corporation
Haverhill, MA 978-521-4370
Regenie's All Natural and Organic Snacks
Haverhill, MA 877-Reg-nie
Sensible Portions
Boulder, CO 800-913-6637
Soloman Baking Company
Denver, CO 303-371-2777

Plantain

Alimentos Bermudez
Brooklyn, NY 347-533-2230
Lam's Foods Inc
Queens, NY 718-271-0476

Potato

All American Snacks
Midland, TX 800-840-2455
ARA Food Corporation
Miami, FL 800-533-8831
Bachman Company
Reading, PA 800-523-8253
Barbara's Bakery
Petaluma, CA 707-765-2273
Better Made Snack Foods
Detroit, MI 800-332-2394
Better Meat North
Bay City, MI 989-684-6271
Bickel's Potato Chip Company
Manheim, PA 717-665-2002
Bickel's Snack Foods Inc
York, PA 800-233-1933
Birds Eye Foods
Berlin, PA 814-267-4641
Brad's Taste of New York
Floral Park, NY 516-354-9004
Cactus-Creek
Dallas, TX 800-471-7723
Covered Bridge Potato Chip Company
Waterville, NB 506-375-2447
Deep River Snacks
Old Lyme, CT 860-434-7347
Delicious Popcorn Company
Waupaca, WI 715-258-7683
Eli's Bread
New York, NY 866-354-3547
Elmer's Fine Foods
New Orleans, LA 504-949-2716
Go-Rachel.com
Minneapolis, MN 952-884-2305
Golden Flake Snack Foods
Birmingham, AL 800-239-2447
Grippo's Food Products
Cincinnati, OH 513-923-1900
H.E. Butt Grocery Company
San Antonio, TX 800-432-3113
Hanover Foods Corporation
Hanover, PA 717-632-6000
Happy's Potato Chip Company
Minneapolis, MN 612-781-3121
Hartley's Potato Chip Company
Lewistown, PA 717-248-0526

Herr Foods
Chillicothe, OH....................800-523-8468
Herr's Foods
Nottingham, PA....................800-344-3777
Hostess Frito-Lay Company
Swift Current, SK..................306-773-9621
Humpty Dumpty Snack Foods
Scarborough, ME..................877-228-2273
Husman Snack Food Company
Cincinnati, OH....................859-282-7490
Jay's Foods
Chicago, IL.......................800-621-6152
Jones Potato Chip Company
Mansfield, OH....................800-466-9424
Kitch'n Cook'd Potato Chip Company
Staunton, VA......................800-752-1535
Knese Enterprise
Bellerose, NY.....................516-354-9004
Martin's Potato Chips
Thomasville, PA...................800-272-4477
Maui Potato Chips
Kahului, HI.......................808-877-3652
McCleary
South Beloit, IL...................800-523-8644
Middleswarth Potato Chips
Wilkes Barre, PA..................570-288-2447
Mike-Sell's Potato Chip Company
Dayton, OH.......................800-853-9437
Mister Bee Potato Chip Company
Parkersburg, WV..................304-428-6133
Mrs. Fisher's
Rockford, IL......................815-964-9114
Ole Salty's of Rockford
Loves Park, IL
Osem USA, Inc
Englewood Cliffs, NJ...............800-200-6736
Pippin Snack Pecans
Albany, GA.......................800-554-6887
Poore Brothers
Boulder, CO.......................303-546-9939
Popchips
San Francisco, CA.................866-217-9327
Proctor & Gamble Company
Cincinnati, OH....................513-983-1100
Randag & Associates Inc
Elmhurst, IL......................630-530-2830
Revonah Pretzel Bakery
Hanover, PA......................717-630-2883
Rock-N-Roll Gourmet
Marina Del Ray, CA................800-518-3891
Route 11 Potato Chips
Mount Jackson, VA.................800-294-7783
Snak King Corporation
City of Industry, CA................626-336-7711
Snyder's of Hanover
Hanover, PA......................717-632-4477
Snyder's-Lance Inc.
Charlotte, NC.....................800-438-1880
Sterzing Food Company
Burlington, IA.....................800-754-8467
Terrell's Potato Chip Company
Syracuse, NY.....................315-437-2786
The Mediterranean Snack Food Company
Boonton, NJ......................973-333-4888
Thomasson's Potato Chip Company
Mansfield, OH....................800-466-9424
Tom's Foods
Charlotte, NC.....................800-995-2623
Tom's Snacks Company
Charlotte, NC.....................800-995-2623
Tri-Sum Potato Chip Company
Leominster, MA...................978-697-2447
Troyer Farms
Waterford, PA.....................800-458-0485
Troyer Potato Products
Waterford, PA.....................814-796-2611
Utz Quality Foods
Hanover, PA......................800-367-7629
Wachusett Potato Chip Company
Fitchburg, MA....................800-551-5539
Westbrae Natural Foods
Melville, NY......................800-434-4246
Wise Foods
Kennesaw, GA....................770-426-5821
Wyandot
Marion, OH.......................800-992-6368
Wysong Corporation
Midland, MI......................800-748-0188
Yum Yum Potato Chips
Warwick, QC......................800-567-5792

Alternative

The Mediterranean Snack Food Company
Boonton, NJ......................973-333-4888

Baked

Wyandot Inc.
Marion, OH.......................800-992-6368

Barbecue

Martin's Potato Chips
Thomasville, PA...................800-272-4477
Mister Bee Potato Chip Company
Parkersburg, WV..................304-428-6133
Wachusett Potato Chip Company
Fitchburg, MA....................800-551-5539

Low-Fat

Snack Appeal
Fairfax, VA.......................540-383-0561

No Salt

Wachusett Potato Chip Company
Fitchburg, MA....................800-551-5539

Ridges

Wachusett Potato Chip Company
Fitchburg, MA....................800-551-5539

Salt & Vinegar

Wachusett Potato Chip Company
Fitchburg, MA....................800-551-5539

Salted

International Trading Company
Houston, TX......................713-224-5901
The Mediterranean Snack Food Company
Boonton, NJ......................973-333-4888

Sour Cream & Onion

Martin's Potato Chips
Thomasville, PA...................800-272-4477
Mister Bee Potato Chip Company
Parkersburg, WV..................304-428-6133
Wachusett Potato Chip Company
Fitchburg, MA....................800-551-5539

Taco

Li'l Guy Foods
Kansas City, MO..................800-886-8226

Tortilla

Abuelita Mexican Foods
Manassas Park, VA.................703-369-0232
ARA Food Corporation
Miami, FL........................800-533-8831
Arizona Cowboy
Phoenix, AZ......................602-956-4833
Azteca Foods
Summit Argo, IL...................708-563-6600
Bachman Company
Reading, PA......................800-523-8253
Bake Crafters Food
Collegedale, TN...................800-296-8935
Better Made Snack Foods
Detroit, MI.......................800-332-2394
C.J. Vitner Company
Chicago, IL.......................773-523-7900
Cactus-Creek
Dallas, TX........................800-471-7723
Deep River Snacks
Old Lyme, CT.....................860-434-7347
El Matador Foods
Baytown, TX......................281-424-4555
El-Milagro
Chicago, IL
Festida Food
Cedar Springs, MI.................616-696-0400
Food Should Taste Good
Needham Heights, MA..............781-455-8500
Frog Ranch Foods
Glouster, OH.....................800-742-2488
Golden Flake Snack Foods
Birmingham, AL...................800-239-2447
Golden Fluff Popcorn Company
Lakewood, NJ.....................732-367-5448
Herr Foods
Chillicothe, OH....................800-523-8468
Herr's Foods
Nottingham, PA....................800-344-3777
Hostess Frito-Lay Company
Swift Current, SK..................306-773-9621
Husman Snack Food Company
Cincinnati, OH....................859-282-7490
La Canasta Mexican Food Products
Phoenix, AZ......................855-269-7721
La Mexicana
Chicago, IL.......................773-247-5443
Los Amigos Tortilla Manufacturing
Atlanta, GA.......................800-969-8226
McCleary
South Beloit, IL...................800-523-8644
Medallion Foods
Newport, AR......................870-523-3500
Mexi-Snax
Addison, IL.......................630-628-0211
Miguel's Stowe Away
Stowe, VT........................800-448-6517
Mike-Sell's Potato Chip Company
Dayton, OH.......................800-853-9437
Mission Foodservice
Oldsmar, FL......................800-443-7994
Nature Star Foods
Hinsdale, IL......................630-323-8888
Ozuna Food Products Corporation
Sunnyvale, CA....................408-400-0495
Plocky's Fine Snacks
Hinsdale, IL......................630-323-8888
Puebla Foods
Passaic, NJ.......................973-473-4494
R.W. Garcia
San Jose, CA......................408-287-4616
RW Garcia Company
San Jose, CA......................408-287-4616
Snak King Corporation
City of Industry, CA................626-336-7711
Snyder's of Hanover
Hanover, PA......................717-632-4477
Snyder's-Lance Inc.
Charlotte, NC.....................800-438-1880
Spanish Gardens Food Manufacturing
Kansas City, KS...................913-831-4242
Sun Pac Foods
Brampton, ON.....................905-792-2700
T.W. Garner Food Company
Winston Salem, NC................800-476-7383
Tom's Snacks Company
Charlotte, NC.....................800-995-2623
Troyer Farms
Waterford, PA.....................800-458-0485
Tumaro's Gourmet Tortillas & Snacks
Edison, NJ........................800-777-6317
Utz Quality Foods
Hanover, PA......................800-367-7629
Variety Foods
Warren, MI.......................586-268-4900
Westbrae Natural Foods
Melville, NY......................800-434-4246
Wise Foods
Kennesaw, GA....................770-426-5821
Wyandot
Marion, OH.......................800-992-6368
Wyandot Inc.
Marion, OH.......................800-992-6368

Corn Nuts

California Nuggets
Ripon, CA........................209-599-7131
Dakota Gourmet
Wahpeton, ND.....................800-727-6663
Hialeah Products Company
Hollywood, FL....................800-923-3379
Setton International Foods
Commack, NY.....................800-227-4397

Popcorn

A La Carte
Chicago, IL.......................800-722-2370
American Pop Corn Company
Sioux City, IA.....................712-239-1232
Angelic Gourmet Inc
Naples, NY
Bachman Company
Reading, PA......................800-523-8253
Better Made Snack Foods
Detroit, MI.......................800-332-2394

Better Meat North
Bay City, MI 989-684-6271
Birds Eye Foods
Berlin, PA 814-267-4641
Black Jewell®Popcorn
St Francisville, IL 800-948-2302
Black Shield
Albuquerque, NM 800-653-9357
Brandmeyer Popcorn Company
Ankeny, IA 800-568-8276
Buddy Squirrel LLC
Milwaukee, WI 800-972-2658
C&F Foods
City of Industry, CA 626-723-1000
C.J. Vitner Company
Chicago, IL 773-523-7900
Cape Cod Potato Chip Company
Hyannis, MA 508-775-3358
Carmadhy's Foods
Waterloo, ON 519-746-0551
Casa De Oro Foods
Omaha, NE 402-339-7740
Cheeze Kurls
Grand Rapids, MI 616-784-6095
Chester Inc.
Valparaiso, IN 800-778-1131
China Doll Company
Saraland, AL 251-457-7641
CJ Dannemiller Company
Norton, OH 800-624-8671
Cloud Nine
San Leandro, CA 201-358-8588
Clutter Farms
Gambier, OH 740-427-3515
Colorado Cereal
Fort Collins, CO 970-282-9733
Colorado Popcorn Company
Sterling, CO 800-238-2676
ConAgra Foods/International Home Foods
Niagara Falls, ON 905-356-2661
ConAgra Store Brands, Inc.
Lakeville, MN 800-328-6286
Convenience Food Suppliers
Durham, NC 800-922-1586
Corn Poppers
San Diego, CA 858-231-2617
Crickle Company
Thomasville, GA 800-237-8689
Deep River Snacks
Old Lyme, CT 860-434-7347
Delicious Popcorn Company
Waupaca, WI 715-258-7683
Ellis Popcorn Company
Murray, KY 800-654-3358
Elmer's Fine Foods
New Orleans, LA 504-949-2716
Fancy Farms Popcorn
Bernie, MO 800-833-8154
Fernando C Pujals & Bros
Guaynabo, PR 787-792-3080
Fireworks Popcorn Company
Belgium, WI 877-668-4800
Fizzle Flat Farm
Yale, IL 618-793-2060
Frankford Candy & Chocolate Company
Philadelphia, PA 800-523-9090
Frito-Lay
Dallas, TX 800-352-4477
Fun City Popcorn
Las Vegas, NV 800-423-1710
Funkychunky Inc.
Edina, MN 888-473-8659
Gaslamp Popcorn Company
Riverside, CA 877-237-8276
General Mills
Minneapolis, MN 800-248-7310
Gilster Mary Lee/Jasper Foods
Jasper, MO 800-777-2168
Gilster-Mary Lee Corporation
Chester, IL 800-851-5371
Golden Fluff Popcorn Company
Lakewood, NJ 732-367-5448
Good Health Natural Foods
Northport, NY 631-261-2111
Grandpa Po's Nutra Nuts
Commerce, CA 323-260-7457
Granite State Potato Chip Company
Salem, NH 603-898-2171
Great American Popcorn Works of Pennsylvania
Telford, PA 800-542-2676
Great Western Products Company
Assumption, IL 217-226-3241
Great Western Products Company
Bismarck, MO 573-734-2210
Hain Celestial Group
Melville, NY 800-434-4246
Happy Herberts Food Company
Jersey City, NJ 800-764-2779
Happy's Potato Chip Company
Minneapolis, MN 612-781-3121
Heartland Gourmet Popcorn
Elk Grove Village, IL 866-945-5346
Herr Foods
Chillicothe, OH 800-523-8468
Herr's Foods
Nottingham, PA 800-344-3777
Hostess Frito-Lay Company
Swift Current, SK 306-773-9621
Houston Harvest
Franklin Park, IL 800-548-5896
Humpty Dumpty Snack Foods
Lachine, QC 800-361-6440
Humpty Dumpty Snack Foods
Scarborough, ME 877-228-2273
International Home Foods
Parsippany, NJ 973-359-9920
International Service Group
Alpharetta, GA 770-518-0988
Jerry's Nut House
Denver, CO 888-214-0747
Jess Jones Farms
Dixon, CA 707-678-3839
John J. Nissen Baking Company
Wareham, MA 508-295-2337
Kernel Fabyan's Gourmet Popcorn
St Charles, IL 847-483-1377
Kernel Season's LLC
Elk Grove Village, IL 866-328-7672
Kettle Foods
Salem, OR 503-364-0399
Keystone Food Products
Easton, PA 800-523-9426
Kloss Manufacturing Company
Allentown, PA 800-445-7100
Koeze Company
Wyoming, MI 800-555-3909
Kornfections
Chantilly, VA 800-469-8886
Krispy Kernels
Sainte Foy, QC 877-791-9986
Lincoln Snacks Company
Stamford, CT 800-872-7622
Lucks Food Decorating Company
Tacoma, WA 253-383-4815
Martin's Famous Pastry Shoppe, Inc
Chambersburg, PA 800-548-1200
Martin's Potato Chips
Thomasville, PA 800-272-4477
Metzger Popcorn Company
Delphos, OH 800-819-6072
Michele's Chocolate Truffles
Clackamas, OR 800-656-7112
Midwest/Northern
Minneapolis, MN 800-328-5502
Mike-Sell's Potato Chip Company
Dayton, OH 800-853-9437
Mills Brothers International
Tukwila, WA 206-575-3000
Morrison Farms
Clearwater, NE 402-887-5335
Nebraska Popcorn
Clearwater, NE 800-253-6502
Newman's Own
Westport, CT 203-222-0136
Noble Popcorn Farms
Sac City, IA 800-537-9554
Nutra Nuts
Commerce, CA 323-260-7457
Old Sacramento Popcorn Company
Sacramento, CA 916-446-1980
Olson Livestock & Seed
Haigler, NE 308-297-3283
Oogie's Snacks LLC
Denver, CO 303-455-2107
Organic Planet
San Francisco, CA 415-765-5590
Papa Dean's Popcorn
San Antonio, TX 877-855-7272
Patsy's Candies
Colorado Springs, CO 866-372-8797
Pleasant Grove Farms
Pleasant Grove, CA 916-655-3391
Popcorn Connection
North Hollywood, CA 800-852-2676

Popcorn Palace
Schiller Park, IL 800-873-2686
Popcorn World
Sedalia, MO 800-443-8226
Popcorner
Swansea, IL 618-277-2676
Poppers Supply Company
Allentown, PA 800-457-9810
Preston Farms
Palmyra, IN 866-767-7464
Purity Foods
Okemos, MI 800-997-7358
R&J Farms
West Salem, OH 419-846-3179
Ramsey Popcorn Company
Ramsey, IN 800-624-2060
Randag & Associates Inc
Elmhurst, IL 630-530-2830
Reist Popcorn Company
Mount Joy, PA 717-653-8078
Richard Green Company
Indianapolis, IN 317-972-0941
Rivard Popcorn Products
Lancaster, PA 717-393-1074
Roberts Ferry Nut Company
Waterford, CA 209-874-3247
Rock-N-Roll Gourmet
Marina Del Ray, CA 800-518-3891
Rocky Mountain Popcorn Company
Centennial, CO 303-744-8850
Rygmyr Foods
South Saint Paul, MN 800-545-3903
Sahagian & Associates
Oak Park, IL 800-327-9273
Shallowford Farms
Yadkinville, NC 800-892-9539
Shepherd Farms
Hillsboro, IL 800-383-2676
Sheryl's Chocolate Creations
Hicksville, NY 888-882-2462
Snack Works/Metrovox Snacks
Orange, CA 800-783-9870
Snak King Corporation
City of Industry, CA 626-336-7711
Snappy Popcorn Company
Breda, IA 800-742-0228
Snyder's-Lance Inc.
Charlotte, NC 800-438-1880
Stock Popcorn Company
Lake View, IA 712-657-2811
Sugar Plum
Forty Fort, PA 800-447-8427
Tee Lee Popcorn, Inc
Shannon, IL 800-578-2363
Todd's
Vernon, CA 800-938-6337
Treier Popcorn Farms
Bloomdale, OH 419-454-2811
Tri-Sum Potato Chip Company
Leominster, MA 978-697-2447
Trinidad Benham Company
Denver, CO 303-220-1400
Troyer Farms
Waterford, PA 800-458-0485
Utz Quality Foods
Hanover, PA 800-367-7629
Vande Walle's Candies
Appleton, WI 920-738-7799
Variety Foods
Warren, MI 586-268-4900
Velvet Creme Popcorn Company
Westwood, KS 888-553-6708
Vogel Popcorn
Lake View, IA 712-657-8561

Vogel Popcorn
Hamburg, IA 800-831-5818
Wabash Valley Farms
Monon, IN. 800-270-2705
Wachusett Potato Chip Company
Fitchburg, MA 800-551-5539
Weaver Popcorn Company
Noblesville, IN 800-634-8161
Westbrae Natural Foods
Melville, NY. 800-434-4246
Westlam Foods
Chino, CA 800-722-9519
Widman Popcorn Company
Chapman, NE 308-986-2293
Yaya's
Corona Del Mar, CA. 949-675-7708

Coated

Black Shield
Albuquerque, NM. 800-653-9357
Bruno's Cajun Foods & Snacks
Slidell, LA. 985-726-0544
Golden Fluff Popcorn Company
Lakewood, NJ. 732-367-5448
Kernel Season's LLC
Elk Grove Village, IL 866-328-7672
Lou-Retta's Custom Chocolates
Buffalo, NY. 716-833-7111
Popcorn Palace
Schiller Park, IL 800-873-2686

Flavored

Black Shield
Albuquerque, NM. 800-653-9357
Dale and Thomas Popcorn
Englewood, NJ 800-767-4444
DGZ Chocolates
Houston, TX 877-949-9444
Eda's Sugarfree Candies
Philadelphia, PA 215-324-3412
Golden Fluff Popcorn Company
Lakewood, NJ. 732-367-5448
Happy's Potato Chip Company
Minneapolis, MN 612-781-3121
Jody's Gourmet Popcorn
Virginia Beach, VA. 866-797-5639
Kernel Season's LLC
Elk Grove Village, IL 866-328-7672
Middlefield Cheese House
Middlefield, OH 800-327-9477
Midwest/Northern
Minneapolis, MN 800-328-5502
Mini Pops, Inc
Stoughton, MA 781-436-5864
Oogie's Snacks LLC
Denver, CO 303-455-2107
Popcorn Palace
Schiller Park, IL 800-873-2686
Popcorn World
Sedalia, MO 800-443-8226
Rivard Popcorn Products
Lancaster, PA 717-393-1074
Tri-Sum Potato Chip Company
Leominster, MA 978-697-2447
Troyer Potato Products
Waterford, PA 814-796-2611
Velvet Creme Popcorn Company
Westwood, KS. 888-553-6708
Victoria's Catered Traditions
Manteca, CA 877-272-5208
Yaya's
Corona Del Mar, CA. 949-675-7708

Pork Rinds

Better Made Snack Foods
Detroit, MI 800-332-2394
Better Meat North
Bay City, MI 989-684-6271
Bruno's Cajun Foods & Snacks
Slidell, LA. 985-726-0544
Golden Flake Snack Foods
Birmingham, AL. 800-239-2447
Herr Foods
Chillicothe, OH. 800-523-8468
Jay's Foods
Chicago, IL 800-621-6152
Rudolph Foods
Dallas, TX. 214-638-2204
Rudolph Foods Company
Lima, OH. 419-648-3611
Sau-Sea Foods
Tarrytown, NY 914-631-1717
Tom's Snacks Company
Charlotte, NC 800-995-2623

Bacon

Rudolph Foods Company
Lima, OH. 419-648-3611

Potato Sticks

Golden Fluff Popcorn Company
Lakewood, NJ. 732-367-5448
Wachusett Potato Chip Company
Fitchburg, MA 800-551-5539

Pretzels

All American Snacks
Midland, TX 800-840-2455
All Wrapped Up
Plantation, FL 800-891-2194
Amoroso's Baking Company
Philadelphia, PA 800-377-6557
Anderson Bakery Company
Lancaster, PA 800-732-0089
Angelic Gourmet Inc
Naples, NY
Bachman Company
Reading, PA 800-523-8253
Bake Crafters Food
Collegedale, TN 800-296-8935
Benzel's Pretzel Bakery
Altoona, PA. 800-344-4438
Better Made Snack Foods
Detroit, MI 800-332-2394
Brad's Taste of New York
Floral Park, NY. 516-354-9004
Buckeye Pretzel Company
Williamsport, PA. 800-257-6029
Buddy Squirrel LLC
Milwaukee, WI. 800-972-2658
Candy Cottage Company
Huntingdon Valley, PA 215-953-8288
Cape Cod Potato Chip Company
Hyannis, MA. 508-775-3358
Chile Today
San Francisco, CA 800-758-0372
Clara Foods
Clara City, MN 888-844-8518
Dream Confectioners
Teaneck, NJ. 201-836-9000
Frito-Lay
Dallas, TX. 800-352-4477
GKI Foods
Brighton, MI. 248-486-0055
Golden Flake Snack Food
Birmingham, AL. 800-239-2447
Good Health Natural Foods
Northport, NY. 631-261-2111
GWB Foods Corporation
Brooklyn, NY 877-977-7610
Happy Herberts Food Company
Jersey City, NJ 800-764-2779
Hartley's Potato Chip Company
Lewistown, PA 717-248-0526
Herr Foods
Chillicothe, OH. 800-523-8468
Herr's Foods
Nottingham, PA. 800-344-3777
Hialeah Products Company
Hollywood, FL 800-923-3379
J&J Snack Foods Corporation
Pennsauken, NJ. 800-486-9533
J&J Snack Foods Corporation
Pennsauken, NJ. 856-665-9533
Jay's Foods
Chicago, IL 800-621-6152
Julius Sturgis Pretzel House
Lititz, PA. 717-626-4354
K&R Pretzel Bakery
Dayton, OH. 937-299-2231
Karl Bissinger French Confections
St Louis, MO. 800-325-8881
Key III Candies
Fort Wayne, IN 800-752-2382
Keystone Food Products
Easton, PA. 800-523-9426
Keystone Pretzel Bakery
Lititz, PA. 888-572-4500
Kim & Scott's Gourmet Pretzels
Chicago, IL 800-578-9478
Knese Enterprise
Bellerose, NY 516-354-9004
Krispy Kernels
Sainte Foy, QC 877-791-9986
Martin's Famous Pastry Shoppe, Inc
Chambersburg, PA 800-548-1200
Martin's Potato Chips
Thomasville, PA 800-272-4477
McCleary
South Beloit, IL 800-523-8644
Mike-Sell's Potato Chip Company
Dayton, OH. 800-853-9437
Palmer Candy Company
Sioux City, IA. 800-831-0828
Porkie Company of Wisconsin
Cudahy, WI. 800-333-2588
Pretzels
Bluffton, IN. 800-456-4838
Quinlan Pretzels
Denver, PA 717-336-7571
R&J Farms
West Salem, OH 419-846-3179
SB Global Foods
Lansdale, PA. 877-857-1727
Sheryl's Chocolate Creations
Hicksville, NY 888-882-2462
Shultz Company
Hanover, PA 717-633-4585
Snack Works/Metrovox Snacks
Orange, CA. 800-783-9870
Snak King Corporation
City of Industry, CA 626-336-7711
Snyder's of Hanover
Hanover, PA 717-632-4477
Sporting Colors LLC
St. Louis, MO 888-394-2292
Sweet City Supply
Virginia Beach, VA. 888-793-3824
Tell City Pretzel Company
Tell City, IN. 812-547-4631
Todd's
Vernon, CA 800-938-6337
Tom Sturgis Pretzel Inc
Reading, PA 610-775-0335
Triple-C
Hamilton, ON 800-263-9105
Utz Quality Foods
Hanover, PA 800-367-7629
Vermont Pretzel
Bellows Falls, VT. 888-671-4774
Weaver Nut Company
Ephrata, PA. 717-738-3781
Wege Pretzel Company
Hanover, PA 800-233-1933
Westbrae Natural Foods
Melville, NY. 800-434-4246
Wise Foods
Kennesaw, GA 770-426-5821

Flavored

Grippo's Food Products
Cincinnati, OH 513-923-1900
Kim & Scott's Gourmet Pretzels
Chicago, IL 800-578-9478
Sunflower Food and Spice Company
Riverside, MO. 800-377-4693

Nubs

Kim & Scott's Gourmet Pretzels
Chicago, IL 800-578-9478

Soft

Bakers' Best Snack Food Corporation
Hatfield, PA. 215-822-3511
Federal Pretzel Baking Company
Bridgeport, NJ. 215-467-0505
Hammond Pretzel Bakery
Lancaster, PA 717-392-7532
J&J Snack Foods Corporation
Pennsauken, NJ. 800-486-9533
Kim & Scott's Gourmet Pretzels
Chicago, IL 800-578-9478
Kim and Scott's Gourmet Pretzels
Chicago, IL 800-578-9478
New York Pretzel Makkos of Brooklyn Ltd
Brooklyn, NY 718-366-9800
Vermont Pretzel
Bellows Falls, VT. 888-671-4774

Sticks or Rods

Confectionately Yours
Buffalo Grove, IL 800-875-6978
Handy Pax
Randolph, MA 781-963-8300
Kim & Scott's Gourmet Pretzels
Chicago, IL 800-578-9478
McCleary
South Beloit, IL 800-523-8644
Sheryl's Chocolate Creations
Hicksville, NY 888-882-2462

Twists

Kim & Scott's Gourmet Pretzels
Chicago, IL 800-578-9478
Sheryl's Chocolate Creations
Hicksville, NY 888-882-2462

Rice Cakes

GWB Foods Corporation
Brooklyn, NY 877-977-7610
Hawaii Candy
Honolulu, HI 808-836-8955
Lundberg Family Farm
Richvale, CA 530-882-4551
Ohta Wafer Factory
Honolulu, HI 808-949-2775
Quaker
Barrington, IL 800-333-8027
Westbrae Natural Foods
Melville, NY 800-434-4246

Snack Pellets

Preformed

Kerry Ingredients
Blue Earth, MN 507-526-7575
Rudolph Foods Company
Lima, OH 419-648-3611

Trail Mix

American Importing Company
Minneapolis, MN 612-331-7000
Big Steer Enterprises
Beaumont, TX 800-421-4951
C.J. Vitner Company
Chicago, IL 773-523-7900
East Kentucky Foods
Winchester, KY 859-744-2218
El Paso Chile Company
El Paso, TX 888-472-5727
Inn Maid Food
Lenox, MA 413-637-2732
King Nut Company
Solon, OH 800-860-5464
Lehi Valley Trading Company
Mesa, AZ 480-684-1402
Marin Food Specialties
Byron, CA 925-634-6126
Midwest/Northern
Minneapolis, MN 800-328-5502
Mister Snacks
Amherst, NY 800-333-6393
Nature Kist Snacks
Stockton, CA 209-944-7200
New England Natural Baker
Greenfield, MA 800-910-2884
Nspired Natural Foods
Boulder, CO 800-434-4246
Nut Factory
Spokane Valley, WA 888-239-5288
Pittsburgh Snax & Nut Company
Pittsburgh, PA 800-404-6887
Randag & Associates Inc
Elmhurst, IL 630-530-2830
Setton International Foods
Commack, NY 800-227-4397
Sonne
Wahpeton, ND 800-727-6663
Sun Ridge Farms
Pajaro, CA 831-786-7000
Sunridge Farms
Salinas, CA 831-755-1430
Superior Nut & Candy Company
Chicago, IL 800-843-2238
Terri Lynn
Elgin, IL 800-323-0775
Timber Peaks Gourmet
Parker, CO 800-982-7687
Tropical
Charlotte, NC 800-220-1413
Valley View Blueberries
Vancouver, WA 360-892-2839
Variety Foods
Warren, MI 586-268-4900
Weaver Nut Company
Ephrata, PA 717-738-3781
Wysong Corporation
Midland, MI 800-748-0188

Specialty & Organic Foods

General

Arico Natural Foods
Beaverton, OR 503-259-0871
Fallwood Corp
White Plains, NY 914-304-4065
Global Organics
Arlington, MA 781-648-8844
Heartland Mill
Marienthal, KS 620-379-4472
Heartland Mill
Marienthal, KS 620-379-4472

Aquaculture

Bayou Land Seafood
Breaux Bridge, LA 337-667-6118
Bays English Muffin Corporation
Chicago, IL 800-367-2297
Bourbon Barrel Foods
Louisville, KY 502-333-6103
Burris Mill & Feed
Franklinton, LA 800-928-2782
Chef Silvio's of Wooster Street
Guilford, CT 203-453-1064
Farm Fresh Catfish Company
Hollandale, MS 800-647-8264
G.S. Gelato and Desserts, Inc.
Fort Walton Beach, FL 850-243-5455
Idaho Trout Company
Buhl, ID 866-878-7688
Marion's Smart Delights
Arlington, VA 703-593-3450
Red Lake Fisheries Associates
Redby, MN 218-679-3513
Silver Streak Bass Company
El Campo, TX 979-543-6343
Southern Pride Catfish Company
Seattle, WA 800-343-8046
Treats Island Fisheries
Scaly Mountain, NC 207-733-4580

Dietary Products

Alfred L. Wolff, Inc.
Park Ridge, IL 847-759-8888
Personal Edge Nutrition
Ballwin, MO 877-982-3343

Diet & Weight Loss Aids

Action Labs
Park City, UT 800-669-8877
Alkinco
New York, NY 800-424-7118
American Supplement Technologies
Phoenix, AZ 888-469-0242
Body Ammo Research Center
Byron, CA 925-513-8514
Body Breakthrough
Deer Park, NY 800-874-6299
Eckhart Corporation
Novato, CA 415-892-3880
Himalayan Heritage
Fredonia, WI 888-414-9500
Innovative Food Solutions LLC
Columbus, OH 800-884-3314
Natural Balance
Englewood, CO 800-624-4260
Nature's Plus
Long Beach, CA 562-494-2500
Nellson Candies
Irwindale, CA 626-334-4508
Pro Form Labs
Orinda, CA 925-299-9000
Russo Farms
Vineland, NJ 856-692-5942
Soluble Products Company
Lakewood, NJ 732-364-8855
Tova Industries
Louisville, KY 888-532-8682
USA Laboratories
Burns, TN 800-489-4872
Zevia
Culver City, CA 855-469-3842

Dietary Supplements

Acta Health Products
Sunnyvale, CA 408-732-6830
Alacer Corporation
Foothill Ranch, CA 800-854-0249
Archon Vitamin Corporation
Irvington, NJ 800-349-1700
Balanced Health Products
New York, NY 212-794-9878
BetaStatin Nutritional Rsearch
Toms River, NJ 800-660-9570
Cargill Texturizing Solutions
Cedar Rapids, IA 877-650-7080
Century Foods International
Sparta, WI 800-269-1901
Edom Laboratories
Deer Park, NY 800-723-3366
ImmuDyne
Florence, KY 888-246-6839
Integrated Therapeutics
Lake Oswego, OR 800-648-4755
Kabco
Amityville, NY 631-842-3600
Life Extension Foods
Fort Lauderdale, FL 800-678-8989
Maat Nutritionals
Los Angeles, CA 888-818-6228
Montana Naturals
Park City, UT 800-672-8349
Nature's Herbs
Merritt, BC 800-437-2257
North West Marketing Company
Brea, CA 714-529-0980
Now Foods
Bloomingdale, IL 888-669-3663
Omni-Pak Industries
Anaheim, CA 714-765-8323
Paragon Laboratories
Torrance, CA 800-231-3670
QBI
South Plainfield, NJ 908-668-0088
Rainbow Light Nutritional Systems
Santa Cruz, CA 800-635-1233
Schiff Nutrition International
Salt Lake City, UT 800-526-6251
Source Naturals
Scotts Valley, CA 800-815-2333
Trace Mineral Research
Roy, UT 800-624-7145
Twinlab
New York, NY 800-645-5626
Valentine Enterprises
Lawrenceville, GA 770-995-0661
Vita-Pure
Roselle, NJ 908-245-1212
Vitamer Laboratories
Irvine, CA 800-432-8355
Wilke International
Shawnee Mission, KS 800-779-5545

Health Products

Abita Brewing Company
Abita Springs, LA 800-737-2311
Abunda Life Laboratories
Asbury Park, NJ 732-775-7575
Acta Health Products
Sunnyvale, CA 408-732-6830
Action Labs
Placentia, CA 800-400-5696
Action Labs
Park City, UT 800-669-8877
Adee Honey Farm
Bruce, SD 605-627-5621
ADH Health Products
Congers, NY 845-268-0027
Advanced Nutritional Research, Inc.
Ellicottville, NY 800-836-0644
Agger Fish
Brooklyn, NY 718-855-1717
Alacer Corporation
Foothill Ranch, CA 800-854-0249
Alamance Foods/Triton Water Company
Burlington, NC 800-476-9111
Albion Laboratories
Clearfield, UT 866-243-5283
Alfer Laboratories
Chatsworth, CA 818-709-0737
Alkinco
New York, NY 800-424-7118
Aloe Farms
Harlingen, TX 800-262-6771
Aloe Laboratories, Inc.
Harlingen, TX 800-258-5380
AlpineAire Foods
Rocklin, CA 800-322-6325
Alternative Health & Herbs
Albany, OR 800-345-4152
Amberwave Foods
Oakmont, PA 412-828-3040
Amcan Industries
Elmsford, NY 914-347-4838
American Almond Products Company
Brooklyn, NY 800-825-6663
American Spoon Foods
Petoskey, MI 800-222-5886
Amerifit Brands, Inc.
Cromwell, CT 800-722-3476
Amerifit Nutrition
Bloomfield, CT 800-722-3476
Anabol Naturals
Santa Cruz, CA 800-426-2265
Annie's Naturals
East Calais, VT 800-434-1234
Apotheca Naturale
Woodbine, IA 800-736-3130
Archon Vitamin Corporation
Irvington, NJ 800-349-1700
Arizona Natural Products
Phoenix, AZ 602-997-6098
ARRO Corporation
Hodgkins, IL 708-352-8200
Atkins Nutritionals
Melville, NY 800-628-5467
Atlantic Laboratories
Waldoboro, ME 207-832-5376
Atrium Biotech
Fairfield, NJ 866-628-2355
Bake'n Joy Foods
North Andover, MA 800-666-4937
Bay State Milling Company
Winona, MN 800-533-8098
BBS Bodacious BBQ Company
Coral Springs, FL 800-537-5928
Bede Inc
Haledon, NJ 866-239-6565
Beehive Botanicals, Inc.
Hayward, WI 800-233-4483
Bel/Kaukauna USA
Kaukauna, WI 800-558-3500
Betty Lou's Golden Smackers
McMinnville, OR 800-242-5205
Bevco
Surrey, BC 800-663-0090
Beverly International Nutrition
Cold Spring, KY 800-888-3364
Bio San Laboratories/MegaFood
Derry, NH 800-848-5022
Bio-Foods
Pine Brook, NJ 973-808-5856
Black Ranch Organic Grains
Etna, CA 530-467-3387
Blessed Herbs
Oakham, MA 800-489-4372
Blue Planet Foods
Collegedale, TN 877-396-3145
Blue Sky Natural Beverage Company
Corona, CA 800-426-7367
Body Ammo Research Center
Byron, CA 925-513-8514
Botanical Products
Springville, CA 559-539-3432
Bragg-Live Food Products
Santa Barbara, CA 800-446-1990
Broughton Foods
Marietta, OH 800-283-2479
Browns Dairy
Valparaiso, IN 219-464-4141
Brucia Plant Extracts
Shingle Springs, CA 530-676-2774
Buckhead Gourmet
Atlanta, GA 800-673-6338

Butterbuds Food Ingredients
Racine, WI. 800-426-1119
Cactu Life Inc
Corona Del Mar, CA. 800-500-1713
California Fruit
Sanger, CA 559-266-7117
California Natural Products
Lathrop, CA 209-858-2525
California Olive Oil Corporation
Berkeley, CA. 888-718-9830
Caltex Foods
Canoga Park, CA 800-522-5839
Canada Dry Bottling Company
Flushing, NY. 718-762-5967
Canasoy Enterprises
Vancouver, BC .800-663-1222
Carbolite Foods
Evansville, IN 888-524-3314
Carole's Cheesecake Company
Toronto, ON 416-256-0000
Carriage House Companies
Fredonia, NY 800-462-8125
Cascade Fresh
Seattle, WA 800-511-0057
Cedar Crest Specialties
Cedarburg, WI. .800-877-8341
Cedar Lake Foods
Cedar Lake, MI. 800-246-5039
Cedarlane Foods
Carson, CA 310-886-7720
Cemac Foods Corporation
Harrison, NY. 800-724-0179
Central Coca-Cola Bottling Company
Richmond, VA. .800-359-3759
Champlain Valley Milling Corporation
Westport, NY. 518-962-4711
Chase Brothers Dairy
Oxnard, CA. 800-438-6455
China Mist Tea Company
Scottsdale, AZ. .800-242-8807
Christopher Ranch
Gilroy, CA. 408-847-1100
CHS, Inc.
Inner Grove Heights, MN. 800-232-3639
Cliff Bar
Emeryville, CA. 800-884-5254
Coating Place
Verona, WI 608-845-9521
Coburg Dairy
North Charleston, SC 843-554-4870
Coca-Cola Bottling Company
Honolulu, HI. 808-839-6711
Coffee Bean International
Portland, OR 800-877-0474
Con Agra Foods
Holly Ridge, NC. 910-329-9061
ConAgra Grocery Products
Irvine, CA 714-680-1000
Consun Food Industries
Elyria, OH. 440-322-6301
Contact International
Skokie, IL 847-324-4411
Continental Culture Specialists
Los Angeles, CA. 818-240-7400
Cookie Tree Bakeries
Salt Lake City, UT. 800-998-0111
Country Pure Foods
Akron, OH. 877-995-8423
Creme Glacee Gelati
Montreal, QC 888-322-0116
Crystal Geyser Roxanne LLC
Pensacola, FL 850-476-8844
CVC Specialties
Vernon, CA 800-421-6175
Cyanotech Corporation
Kailua Kona, HI 800-395-1353
Dahlgren & Company
Crookston, MN .800-346-6050
Dairy Farmers of America
East Syracuse, NY 315-431-1352
Dairy Farmers of America
Medina, OH. 330-670-7800
Dairy Maid Dairy
Frederick, MD. .301-695-0431
Dannon Company
Fort Worth, TX .800-211-6565
Dave's Hawaiian Ice Cream
Pearl City, HI 808-453-0500
Dean Distributors
Burlingame, CA 800-792-0816
Delavau LLC
Philadelphia, PA 215-671-1400
Devansoy
Carroll, IA. 800-747-8605
Diamond Crystal Brands
Savannah, GA 800-654-5115
Dolphin Natural Chocolates
Cambria, CA. 800-236-5744
Dorothy Dawson Foods Products
Jackson, MI. 517-788-9830
Dulce de Leche Delcampo Products
Hialeah, FL 877-472-9408
Earth Island Natural Foods
Canoga Park, CA 818-725-2820
Eda's Sugarfree Candies
Philadelphia, PA 215-324-3412
Edner Corporation
Hayward, CA 510-441-8504
Elwood International
Copiague, NY 631-842-6600
Emkay Trading Corporation
Elmsford, NY 914-592-9000
Ener-G Foods
Seattle, WA 800-331-5222
Energen Products
Norwalk, CA. 800-423-8837
Essential Nutrients
Cerritos, CA 800-767-8585
Faber Foods and Aeronautics
Evergreen, CO. .800-237-3255
Fairmont Products
Belleville, PA 717-935-2121
Falcone's Cookieland
Brooklyn, NY 718-236-4200
Fieldbrook Farms
Dunkirk, NY 800-333-0805
First District Association
Litchfield, MN .320-693-3236
Flagship Atlanta Dairy
Belleview, FL 800-224-0669
Food Reserves/Good For You America
Concordia, MO .800-944-1511
Fortitech
Schenectady, NY. 800-950-5156
Freeda Vitamins
Long Island City, NY 800-777-3737
Fresh Dairy Direct/Morningstar
Dallas, TX. 800-395-7004
FW Witt & Company
Yorkville, IL 630-553-6366
G&J Pepsi-Cola Bottlers
Cicinnati, OH 513-785-6060
Gabriele Macaroni Company
City of Industry, CA 626-964-2324
Garratt & Gunn
Santa Rosa, CA. 707-578-8192
Garuda International
Lemon Cove, CA 559-594-4380
Germack Pistachio Company
Detroit, MI 800-872-4006
Gertrude & Bronner's Magic Alpsnack
Escondido, CA .760-743-2211
Gifford's Dairy
Skowhegan, ME 207-474-9821
Ginseng Up Corporation
Rockleigh, NJ 201-660-8081
Global Health Laboratories
Amityville, NY .631-777-2134
Glover's Ice Cream
Frankfort, IN 800-686-5163
Go Lightly Candy
Hillside, NJ 800-524-1304
Govadinas Fitness Foods
San Diego, CA .800-900-0108
Great Circles
Bellows Falls, VT 877-877-2120
Green Foods Corporation
Oxnard, CA. 800-777-4430
Green Options
San Rafael, CA .888-473-3667
Grow Company
Ridgefield, NJ. .201-941-8777
GWB Foods Corporation
Brooklyn, NY 877-977-7610
H&K Products-Pappy's Sassafras Teas
Columbus Grove, OH 877-659-5110
H. Fox & Company
Brooklyn, NY 718-385-4600
H. Reisman Corporation
Orange, NJ 973-677-9200
Hagelin & Company
Branchburg, NJ. 800-229-2112
Harvest Valley Bakery
La Salle, IL 815-224-9030
Haydenergy Health
New York, NY .800-255-1660
Health Valley Company
Irwindale, CA 800-334-3204
Healthy Grain Foods
Northbrook, IL .847-272-5576
Healthy Oven
Croton on Hudson, NY. 914-271-5458
Healthy Times
Poway, CA 858-513-1550
Heart to Heart Foods
Logan, UT. 435-753-9602
Heavenly Hemp Foods
Nederland, CO .888-328-4367
Heini's Cheese Company
Millersburg, OH 800-253-6636
Herb Connection
Springville, UT .801-489-4254
Herbal Products & Development
Aptos, CA 831-688-8706
Heritage Farms Dairy
Murfreesboro, TN. 615-895-2790
Heritage Store
Virginia Beach, VA. 800-862-2923
Heterochemical Corporation
Valley Stream, NY 516-561-8225
HFI Foods
Redmond, WA. .425-883-1320
Hillestad Pharmaceuticals
Woodruff, WI 800-535-7742
Hinckley Springs Water Company
Chicago, IL 773-586-8600
Holistic Products Corporation
Englewood, NJ .800-221-0308
Home Baked Group
Boca Raton, FL. 561-995-0767
Homestead Mills
Cook, MN 800-652-5233
Hormel Foods Corporation
Austin, MN 800-523-4635
Hospitality Mints
Boone, NC. 800-334-5181
House Foods America Corporation
Garden Grove, CA 714-901-4350
Howard Foods
Danvers, MA. 978-774-6207
Hsu's Ginseng Enterprises
Wausau, WI. 800-826-1577
Humco
Texarkana, TX. .903-334-6200
Increda-Meal
Cato, NY 315-626-2111
Innovative Food Solutions LLC
Columbus, OH .800-884-3314
Innovative Health Products
Largo, FL 800-654-2347
Interbake Foods Corporate Office
Richmond, VA. .804-755-7107
InterHealth
Benicia, CA. 800-783-4636
International Casings Group, Inc
Chicago, IL 800-825-5151
Isabella's Healthy Bakery
Cuyahoga Falls, OH 800-476-6328
Island Spring
Vashon, WA. 206-463-9848
IVC American Vitamin
Freehold, NJ 800-666-8482
J&J Snack Foods Corporation
Vernon, CA 800-486-7622
J&J Snack Foods Corporation
Pennsauken, NJ. 800-486-9533
J.N. Bech
Elk Rapids, MI .800-232-4583
Jackson Ice Cream Company
Denver, CO 303-534-2454
Jamieson Laboratories
Windosr, ON 519-974-8482
Janet's Own Home Sweet Home
Austin, TX. 512-385-4708
Jason & Son Specialty Foods
Rancho Cordova, CA 800-810-9093
Jason Pharmaceuticals
Owings Mills, MD 800-638-7867
JMS Specialty Foods
Ripon, WI 800-535-5437
John Gust Foods & Products Corporation
Batavia, IL. 800-756-5886
Jonathan's Sprouts
Rochester, MA .508-763-2577
JR Carlson Laboratories
Arlington Hts, IL 888-234-5656

Kapaa Poi Factory
Kapaa, HI 808-822-5426
KDK Inc
Draper, UT 801-571-3506
Kemach Food Products Corporation
Brooklyn, NY 888-453-6224
Keto Foods
Neptune, NJ 732-922-0009
Klinke Brothers Ice Cream Company
Memphis, TN 901-743-8250
Knott's Berry Farm Foods
Placentia, CA 800-289-9927
Knouse Foods Coop
Peach Glen, PA.................... 717-677-8181
Kolb-Lena Cheese Company
Lena, IL.......................... 815-369-4577
Kozlowski Farms
Forestville, CA 800-473-2767
Kraft Foods
Walton, NY....................... 607-865-7131
Land-O-Sun Dairies
O Fallon, IL....................... 314-436-6820
Lassen Foods
Santa Barbara, CA 805-683-7696
Le Bleu Corporation
Advance, NC...................... 800-854-4471
Life Extension Foods
Fort Lauderdale, FL 800-678-8989
Lifeway Foods Inc
Morton Grove, IL 877-281-3874
Lifewise Ingredients
Lake Zurich, IL.................... 847-550-8270
Living Farms
Tracy, MN........................ 507-629-3517
Lucas Meyer
Decatur, IL 800-769-3660
Lukas Confections
York, PA 717-843-0921
Mafco Natural Products
Richmond, VA..................... 804-222-1600
Magnetic Springs Water Company
Columbus, OH 800-572-2990
Main Street Gourmet
Cuyahoga Falls, OH 800-533-6246
Main Street Muffins
Cuyahoga Falls, OH 800-533-6246
Maple Grove Farms of Vermont
St Johnsbury, VT.................. 800-525-2540
Marsa Specialty Products
Vernon, CA 800-628-0500
Marsan Foods
Toronto, ON 416-755-9262
Masala Chai Company
Santa Cruz, CA.................... 831-475-8881
Master Mix
Placentia, CA 714-524-1698
Master Peace Food Imports
Pleasantville, NY 914-769-7148
Mayway Corporation
Oakland, CA 800-262-9929
McCutcheon's Apple Products
Frederick, MD..................... 800-888-7537
Meadow Brook Dairy
Erie, PA.......................... 800-352-4010
Meadow Gold Dairies
Tulsa, OK 800-742-7349
Mei Shun Tofu Products Company
Chicago, IL 312-842-7000
Merlino Italian Baking Company
Seattle, WA 800-207-2997
Michigan Dairy
Livonia, MI....................... 734-367-5390
Michigan Dessert Corporation
Oak Park, MI...................... 800-328-8632
Microsoy Corporation
Jefferson, IA 515-386-2100
Mid States Dairy
Hazelwood, MO 314-731-1150
Midwest/Northern
Minneapolis, MN 800-328-5502
Mills Brothers International
Tukwila, WA...................... 206-575-3000
Modoc Orchard Company
Medford, OR...................... 541-535-1437
Monarch Beverage Company
Atlanta, GA 800-241-3732
Morinaga Nutritional Foods
Torrance, CA...................... 310-787-0200
Morningland Dairy CheeseCompany
Mountain View, MO 417-469-3817
Mountain High Yogurt
Minneapolis, MN 303-761-2210

Mrs. Leeper's Pasta
Excelsior Springs, MO 800-848-5266
Mrs. Malibu Foods
Malibu, CA 800-677-6254
Murray Cider Company Inc
Roanoke, VA...................... 540-977-9000
Mustard Seed
Central, SC 877-621-2591
National Enzyme Company
Forsyth, MO 800-825-8545
National Vinegar Company
Houston, TX 713-223-4214
Natural Balance
Englewood, CO.................... 800-624-4260
Natural Company
Baltimore, MD 410-628-1262
Natural Food Supplements
Canoga Park, CA 818-341-3375
Natural Food World
Culver City, CA 310-836-7770
Naturally Fresh Foods
Atlanta, GA....................... 800-765-1950
Nature's Herbs
Merritt, BC 800-437-2257
Nature's Plus
Long Beach, CA 562-494-2500
Naturex Inc
South Hackensack, NJ 201-440-5000
NBTY
Ronkonkoma, NY................. 800-920-6090
Nellson Candies
Irwindale, CA 626-334-4508
Nestle Pizza
Medford, WI 715-748-5550
New England Country Bakers
Watertown, CT 800-225-3779
New England Natural Baker
Greenfield, MA.................... 800-910-2884
Nomolas Corp-Jarret Specialties
Woodbridge, NJ 732-634-5565
Norimoor Company
Astoria, NY....................... 718-423-6667
North Country Natural Spring Water
Port Kent, NY..................... 518-834-9400
North Peace Apiaries
Fort St. John, BC.................. 250-785-4808
Now & Zen
Mill Valley, CA.................... 800-335-1959
Now Foods
Bloomingdale, IL 888-669-3663
Nut Factory
Spokane Valley, WA 888-239-5288
Nutrilabs
San Francisco, CA 877-468-8745
Nutritional International Enterprises Company
Irvine, CA 949-854-4855
Nutriwest
Douglas, WY...................... 800-443-3333
O'Boyle's Ice Cream Company
Bristol, PA........................ 215-788-3882
O'Donnell Formula
San Marcos, CA 800-736-1991
Old Fashioned Natural Products
Santa Ana, CA 800-552-9045
Olde Tyme Mercantile
Arroyo Grande, CA................ 805-489-7991
Once Again Nut Butter
Nunda, NY 888-800-8075
Oorganik
Houston, TX 281-240-7992
Optimum Nutrition
Walterboro, SC 800-763-3444
Organic Gourmet
Sherman Oaks, CA 800-400-7772
Organic Milling Company
San Dimas, CA 800-638-8686
Oroweat Baking Company
Montebello, CA 323-721-5161
Orval Kent Food Company
Wheeling, IL...................... 847-459-9000
Ota Tofu Company
Portland, OR 503-232-8947
P.J. Noyes Company, Inc
Lancaster, NH..................... 800-522-2469
Palm Apiaries
Fort Myers, FL 239-334-6001
Particle Dynamics
Saint Louis, MO 800-452-4682
Pasta USA
Spokane, WA...................... 800-456-2084
Pecan Deluxe Candy Company
Dallas, TX........................ 800-733-3589

Pechters Baking
Harrison, NJ 800-525-5779
Pecoraro Dairy Products
Rome, NY........................ 315-339-0101
Peggy Lawton Kitchens
East Walpole, MA.................. 800-843-7325
Penta Manufacturing Company
Livingston, NJ..................... 973-740-2300
Perfect Foods
Goshen, NY....................... 800-933-3288
Perry's Ice Cream Company
Akron, NY........................ 800-873-7797
Phillips Syrup Corporation
Westlake, OH 800-350-8443
Pied-Mont/Dora
Ste Anne Des Plaines, QC 800-363-8003
Pines International
Lawrence, KS 800-697-4637
Plainview Milk Products Cooperative
Plainview, MN 507-534-3872
Pleasant View Dairy
Highland, IN 219-838-0155
Pleasoning Gourment Seasonings
La Crosse, WI..................... 800-279-1614
Poland Spring Water
Stamford, CT...................... 800-955-4426
Prairie Farms Dairy
Carlinville, IL 217-854-2547
Premium Water
Orange Springs, FL................. 800-243-1163
Pro Form Labs
Orinda, CA 925-299-9000
Pro Portion Food
Sayville, NY 631-567-4494
Progenix Corporation
Wausau, WI....................... 800-233-3356
Proper-Chem
Dix Hills, NY 631-420-8000
Protein Research Associates
Livermore, CA 800-948-1991
Protient
Woodland, CA..................... 651-638-2600
Purity Dairies
Nashville, TN 615-244-1900
Purity Foods
Okemos, MI 800-997-7358
Quaker Oats Company
Danville, IL....................... 217-443-4995
Quaker Oats Company
Mountain Top, PA.................. 800-367-6287
Quality Naturally! Foods
City of Industry, CA 888-498-6986
Quong Hop & Company
S San Francisco, CA................ 650-553-9900
R.J. Corr Naturals
Posen, IL......................... 708-389-4200
Ramos Orchards
Winters, CA 530-795-4748
Ramsen
Lakeville, MN..................... 952-431-0400
Randag & Associates Inc
Elmhurst, IL 630-530-2830
Randal Nutritional Products
Santa Rosa, CA.................... 800-221-1697
Red Willow Natural Foods
River Falls, WI 715-425-1489
Regal Health Foods International
Chicago, IL 773-252-1044
Reiter Dairy
Springfield, OH.................... 937-323-5777
Rinehart Meat Processing
Branson, MO...................... 417-334-2044
Rio Syrup Company
Saint Louis, MO 800-325-7666
Roberts Dairy Foods
Kansas City, MO................... 800-279-1692
Roquette America
Keokuk, IA 800-553-7035
Royal Body Care
Irving, TX 972-893-4000
Royal Products
Scottsdale, AZ..................... 480-948-2509
Russo Farms
Vineland, NJ 856-692-5942
Safeway Inc
Pleasanton, CA 877-723-3929
Sahadi Fine Foods
Brooklyn, NY 800-724-2341
Sally Lane's Candy Farm
Paris, TN......................... 731-642-5801
San-J International, Inc
Richmond, VA..................... 800-446-5500

Saratoga Beverage Group
Saratoga Springs, NY 888-426-8642
Schiff Nutrition International
Salt Lake City, UT 800-526-6251
Schneider's Dairy Holdings Inc
Pittsburgh, PA 412-881-3525
Schreiber Foods Plant
Shippensburg, PA 717-530-5000
Schulze & Burch Biscuit Company
Chicago, IL 773-927-6622
Seasons' Enterprises
Addison, IL 630-628-0211
Sells Best
Mishawaka, IN 800-837-8368
Setton International Foods
Commack, NY 800-227-4397
Shenk's Foods
Lancaster, PA 717-393-4240
Sisler's Ice & Ice Cream
Ohio, IL 888-891-3856
Smith Dairy Products Company
Orrville, OH 800-776-7076
Solana Gold Organics
Sebastopol, CA 800-459-1121
Solnuts
Hudson, IA 800-648-3503
Source Naturals
Scotts Valley, CA 800-815-2333
Southwestern Wisconsin Dairy Goat Products
Mt Sterling, WI 608-734-3151
Sovena USA
Rome, NY 315-797-7070
SPI Nutritional
Covina, CA 626-915-1151
Spring Tree Maple Products
Brattleboro, VT 802-254-8784
Staff of Life Natural Foods
Santa Cruz, CA 831-423-8632
Stapleton-Spence PackingCompany
San Jose, CA 800-297-8815
Star of the West MillingCompany
Frankenmuth, MI 989-652-9971
Stevia LLC
Valley Forge, PA 888-878-3842
Strom Products Ltd.
Bannockburn, IL 800-862-3311
Subco Foods Inc
Sheboygan, WI 800-473-0757
Sunergia Soyfoods
Charlottesville, VA 800-693-5134
Sunray Food Products Corporation
Bronx, NY 718-548-2255
Sunsweet Growers
Yuba City, CA 800-417-2253
Superior Trading Company
San Francisco, CA 415-982-8722
Superstore Industries
Fairfield, CA 707-864-0502
Suzanne's Specialties
New Brunswick, NJ 800-762-2135
Swagger Foods Corporation
Vernon Hills, IL 847-913-1200
Sweet Productions
Amityville, NY 631-842-0548
Swiss Valley Farms Company
Davenport, IA 563-468-6600
Tastee Apple Inc
Newcomerstown, OH 800-262-7753
Thornton Foods Company
Eden Prairie, MN 952-944-1735
Timber Crest Farms
Healdsburg, CA 888-374-9325
Toft Dairy
Sandusky, OH 800-521-4606
Tova Industries
Louisville, KY 888-532-8682
Tree of Life
St Augustine, FL 904-940-2100
Tree of Life North Bergen
North Bergen, NJ 800-735-5175
Trophic International
Salt Lake City, UT 800-878-0099
Tropical
Charlotte, NC 800-220-1413
Tropical
Marietta, GA 800-544-3762
Tulkoff Food Products
Baltimore, MD 800-638-7343
Turtle Mountain
Eugene, OR 541-338-9400
Twinlab
New York, NY 800-645-5626
Unique Ingredients
Naches, WA 509-653-1991
Upstate Farms Cooperative
Buffalo, NY 716-892-2121
Valley View Blueberries
Vancouver, WA 360-892-2839
Vance's Foods
Gilmer, TX 800-497-4834
Varni Brothers/7-Up Bottling
Modesto, CA 209-521-1777
Vaxa International
Tampa, FL 800-248-8292
Ventre Packing Company
Syracuse, NY 888-472-8237
Venus Wafers
Hingham, MA 800-545-4538
Vermont Bread Company
Brattleboro, VT 877-293-0876
VIP Foods
Flushing, NY 718-821-5330
Vitamer Laboratories
Irvine, CA 800-432-8355
Vitamins
Chicago, IL 312-861-0700
Vitasoy USA
Ayer, MA 978-772-6880
VitaTech International
Tustin, CA 714-832-9700
Vitatech International
Tustin, CA 714-832-9700
Vogue Cuisine
Sunnyvale, CA 888-236-4144
Wah Yet Group
Hayward, CA 800-229-3392
Walden Farms
Linden, NJ 800-229-1706
Wax Orchards
Seattle, WA 800-634-6132
Wellington Foods
Corona, CA 562-989-0111
Wengert's Dairy
Lebanon, PA 800-222-2129
Westin
Omaha, NE 800-228-6098
White Rock Products Corporation
Flushing, NY 800-969-7625
White Wave
Broomfield, CO 800-488-9283
Whitey's Ice Cream Manufacturing
Moline, IL 888-594-4839
Whole Herb Company
Sonoma, CA 707-935-1077
Wilke International
Shawnee Mission, KS 800-779-5545
Williams-West & Witt Products
Michigan City, IN
Wilson's Fantastic Candy
Memphis, TN 901-767-1900
Wing Nien Company
Hayward, CA 510-487-8877
Winmix/Natural Care Products
Englewood, FL 941-475-7432
World Flavors
Warminster, PA 215-672-4400
World Ginseng Center
San Francisco, CA 800-747-8808
World Organics Corporation
Huntington Beach, CA 714-893-0017
Yoplait USA
Minneapolis, MN 800-248-7310
Yoshida Food International
Portland, OR 800-653-1114
YZ Enterprises
Maumee, OH 800-736-8779

Low-Calorie Desserts

T. Marzetti Company
Columbus, OH 614-846-2232

Sugar-Free Foods

American Instants
Flanders, NJ 973-584-8811
Aunt Gussie Cookies & Crackers
Garfield, NJ 800-422-6654
Bissinger's Handcrafted Chocolatier
St Louis, MO 800-325-8881
California Custom Fruits & Flavors
Irwindale, CA 877-558-0056
Clemmy's
Randcho Mirage, CA 877-253-6698
Dresden Stollen Company
Albertson, NY 516-746-5802
Eda's Sugarfree Candies
Philadelphia, PA 215-324-3412
GKI Foods
Brighton, MI 248-486-0055
Golden Apples Candy Company
Southport, CT 800-776-0393
Home Baked Group
Boca Raton, FL 561-995-0767
Howard Foods
Danvers, MA 978-774-6207
Inn Maid Food
Lenox, MA 413-637-2732
International Brownie
East Weymouth, MA 800-230-1588
Isabella's Healthy Bakery
Cuyahoga Falls, OH 800-476-6328
John Gust Foods & Products Corporation
Batavia, IL 800-756-5886
Kinnikinnick Foods
Edmonton, AB 877-503-4466
Main Street Gourmet
Cuyahoga Falls, OH 800-533-6246
Maple Grove Farms of Vermont
St Johnsbury, VT 800-525-2540
McCutcheon's Apple Products
Frederick, MD 800-888-7537
Michigan Dessert Corporation
Oak Park, MI 800-328-8632
Mrs. Leeper's Pasta
Excelsior Springs, MO 800-848-5266
Nancy's Pies
Rock Island, IL 800-480-0055
Olde Tyme Mercantile
Arroyo Grande, CA 805-489-7991
Perry's Ice Cream Company
Akron, NY 800-873-7797
Sally Lane's Candy Farm
Paris, TN 731-642-5801
Sells Best
Mishawaka, IN 800-837-8368
Setton International Foods
Commack, NY 800-227-4397
Shenk's Foods
Lancaster, PA 717-393-4240
Silver Tray Cookies
Fort Lauderdale, FL 305-883-0800
Tova Industries
Louisville, KY 888-532-8682

Gourmet & Specialty Foods

Gourmet & Specialty Foods

A Natural Harvest Restaurant
Chicago, IL 773-363-3939
A Southern Season
Chapel Hill, NC 877-929-7133
A.M. Braswell Jr. Food Company
Statesboro, GA 800-673-9388
AgriCulver Seeds
Trumansburg, NY 800-836-3701
Ailments E.D. Foods Inc.
Pointe Claire, QC 800-267-3333
Al Safa Halal
Niagara Falls, NY 800-268-8174
Alfonso Gourmet Pasta
Pompano Beach, FL 800-370-7278
Allen's Naturally
Farmington, MI 800-352-8971
Amaranth Resources
Albert Lea, MN 800-842-6689
Amberwave Foods
Oakmont, PA 412-828-3040
American Lecithin Company
Oxford, CT 800-364-4416
American Marketplace Foods
Paterson, NJ 800-683-3464
Ames International
Fife, WA 888-469-2637
Ancora Coffee Roasters
Madison, WI 800-260-0217
Andre-Boudin Bakeries
San Francisco, CA 415-882-1849
Annie's Homegrown
Napa, CA 800-288-1089
Applecreek Farms
Lexington, KY 800-747-8871
Arbor Hill Grapery
Naples, NY 800-554-7553

Arbuckle Coffee
Pittsburgh, PA 800-533-8278

Art CoCo Chocolate Company
Denver, CO 800-779-8985

Ashland Plantation Gourmet
Bunkie, LA 318-346-6600

Ashley Foods
Sudbury, MA 800-617-2823

Ashman Manufacturing & Distributing Company
Virginia Beach, VA 800-641-9924

Asian Brands
Hayward, CA 510-523-7474

Aspen Foods
Park Ridge, IL 847-384-5940

Assouline & Ting
Huntingdon Valley, PA 800-521-4491

Autocrat Coffee & Extracts
Lincoln, RI 800-288-6272

Avary Farms
Odessa, TX 432-332-4139

Babe Farms
Santa Maria, CA 800-648-6772

Barn Stream Natural Foods
Walpole, NH 800-654-2882

Barrie House Gourmet Coffee
Yonkers, NY 800-876-2233

Basketfull
New York, NY 800-645-4438

Bella Cucina Artful Food
Atlanta, GA 866-350-9040

Berardi's Fresh Roast
Cleveland, OH 800-876-9109

Biagio's Banquets
Chicago, IL 800-392-2837

Big Steer Enterprises
Beaumont, TX 800-421-4951

Blue Crab Bay Company
Melfa, VA 800-221-2722

Boetje Foods
Rock Island, IL 877-726-3853

Bombay Breeze Specialty Foods
Mississauga, ON 416-410-2320

Boston's Best Coffee Roasters
South Easton, MA 800-898-8393

Boyd Coffee Company
Portland, OR 800-545-4077

Brad's Taste of New York
Floral Park, NY 516-354-9004

Brandmeyer Popcorn Company
Ankeny, IA 800-568-8276

Brass Ladle Products
Concordville, PA 800-955-2353

Brateka Enterprises
Ocala, FL 877-549-3227

Brazos Legends/Texas Tamale Co
Houston, TX 800-882-6253

Bread Dip Company
Friday Harbor, WA 360-378-6070

Breaktime Snacks
Paramount, CA 800-677-1868

Bremner Biscuit Company
Denver, CO 800-722-1871

Brier Run Farm
Birch River, WV 304-649-2975

British American Tea & Coffee
Durham, NC 919-471-1357

Brutocao Cellars
Hopland, CA 800-433-3689

BTS Company/Hail Caesar Dressings
Nashville, TN 800-617-8899

Bubbles Baking Company
Van Nuys, CA 800-777-4970

Buckmaster Coffee
Hillsboro, OR 800-962-9148

Buona Vita
Bridgeton, NJ 856-453-7972

Busseto Foods
Fresno, CA 800-628-2633

Buxton Foods
Buxton, ND 800-726-8057

Buzzn Bee Farms
West Palm Beach, FL 561-881-1551

Byrd Cookie Company
Savannah, GA 800-291-2973

Cafe Sark's Gourmet Coffee
Yorba Linda, CA 626-579-6000

Cafe Terra Cotta
Tucson, AZ 800-492-4454

Caffe D'Oro
Chino, CA 800-200-5005

Cal Trading Company
Burlingame, CA 650-697-4615

California Oils Corporation
Richmond, CA 800-225-6457

California Orchards
Danville, CA 925-648-1500

California Specialty Farms
Los Angeles, CA 800-437-2702

California Treats
South El Monte, CA 800-966-5501

Calistoga Food Company
New York, NY 212-879-4940

Caltex Foods
Canoga Park, CA 800-522-5839

Candy Factory
Hayward, CA 800-736-6887

Cape Cod Specialty Foods
Sagamore, MA 508-888-7099

Cappuccine
Palm Springs, CA 800-511-3127

Carando Gourmet Frozen Foods
Agawam, MA 888-227-2636

Carbon's Golden Malted Pancake & Waffle Flour Mix
Buchanan, MI 800-253-0590

Carl Buddig & Company
Homewood, IL 800-621-0868

Carolyn's Gourmet
Concord, MA 800-656-2940

Cateraid
Howell, MI 800-508-8217

Cedarlane Foods
Carson, CA 310-886-7720

Champignon North America
Englewood Cliffs, NJ

Chatz Roasting Company
Ceres, CA 800-792-6333

Chef Hans Gourmet Foods
Monroe, LA 800-890-4267

Chef Zachary's Gourmet Blended Spices
Detroit, MI 313-226-0000

Cherchies
Malvern, PA 800-644-1980

Cheryl & Company
Westerville, OH 614-776-1500

Chewys Rugulach
San Diego, CA 800-241-3456

Chex Finer Foods
Attleboro, MA 800-322-2434

Chieftain Wild Rice Company
Spooner, WI 800-262-6368

Chile Today
San Francisco, CA 800-758-0372

Chocolate Street of Hartville
Hartville, OH 888-853-5904

Chocolates by Mark
La Porte, TX 832-736-2626

Choice of Vermont
Destin, FL 800-444-6261

Christie Food Products
Randolph, MA 800-727-2523

Christopher Ranch
Gilroy, CA 408-847-1100

Citterio USA Corporation
Freeland, PA 800-435-8888

Clem's Seafood & Specialties
Buckner, KY 502-222-7571

Clements Pastry Shop
Hyattsville, MD 800-444-7428

Cloud Nine
San Leandro, CA 201-358-8588

Coffee Masters
Spring Grove, IL 800-334-6485

Cold Fusion Foods
West Hollywood, CA 310-287-3244

Colorado Popcorn Company
Sterling, CO 800-238-2676

Colors Gourmet Pizza
Carlsbad, CA 760-431-2203

Coltsfoot/Golden Eagle Herb
Grants Pass, OR 800-736-8749

Columbus Foods Company
Des Plaines, IL 800-322-6457

ConAgra Foods
Boisbriand, QC 450-433-1322

Cook's Gourmet Foods
Riverside, CA 951-352-5700

Cookie Tree Bakeries
Salt Lake City, UT 800-998-0111

Cordon Bleu International
Anjou, QC 514-352-3000

Corfu Foods
Bensenville, IL 630-595-2510

Corn Poppers
San Diego, CA 858-231-2617

Cosentino Winery Vintage Grapevine, Inc.
Yountville, CA 800-764-1220

Costa Deano's Gourmet Foods
Canton, OH 800-337-2823

Costadeanos Gourmet Foods
Canton, OH 330-453-1555

Cottonwood Canyon Winery
Santa Maria, CA 805-937-8463

Cowboy Caviar
Berkeley, CA 877-509-1796

Creative Confections
Northbrook, IL 608-455-1448

Creole Delicacies Pralines
New Orleans, LA 504-523-6425

Crown Pacific Fine Foods
Kent, WA 425-251-8750

Crustacean Foods
Los Angeles, CA 866-263-2625

CTC Manufacturing
Calgary, AB 800-668-7677

Cugino's Gourmet Foods
Crystal Lake, IL 888-592-8446

Cuisinary Fine Foods
Irving, TX 888-283-5303

Culinary Foods
Chicago, IL 800-621-4049

Culinary Masters Corporation
Alpharetta, GA 800-261-5261

Custom House Coffee RoasJodyana Corporation
Miami, FL 888-563-5282

Cw Resources
New Britain, CT 860-229-7700

Cyclone Enterprises
Houston, TX 281-872-0087

Davis Bakery & Delicatessen
Cleveland, OH 216-464-5599

Dean & Deluca
New York, NY 800-221-7714

Dean Distributors
Burlingame, CA 800-792-0816

DeChoix Specialty Foods
Woodside, NY 800-332-4649

Dee's All Natural Baking Company
Bettendorf, IA 800-358-8099

Deep Foods
Union, NJ 908-810-7500

Delftree Farm
North Adams, MA 800-243-3742

DeMedici Imports
Elizabeth, NJ 908- 37- 096

Deneen Foods
Santa Fe, NM 80- 8-6 46

Desserts by David Glass
South Windsor, CT 860-462-7520

Diana's Specialty Foods
Pingree Grove, IL 847-683-1200

Dinkel's Bakery
Chicago, IL 800-822-8817

Dobake
Oakland, CA 800-834-3134

Dole & Bailey
Woburn, MA 781-935-1234

Dolores Canning Company
Los Angeles, CA 323-263-9155

Don Alfonso Foods
Austin, TX 800-456-6100

Don Francisco Coffee Traders
Los Angeles, CA 800-697-5282

Dorina/So-Good
Union, IL 815-923-2144

Dowd & Rogers
Park City, UT 800-669-8877

Dr. Tima Natural Products
Los Angeles, CA 310-472-2181

Dufour Pastry Kitchens
Bronx, NY 800-439-1282

Dummbee Gourmet Foods
Albany, GA 800-569-1657

Dunford Bakers
Fayetteville, AR 479-521-3000

Dutchie Sales Corporation
Hanover, PA 717-632-9343

E. Waldo Ward & Son Corporation
Sierra Madre, CA 800-355-9273

Eagle Coffee Company
Baltimore, MD 800-545-4015

Earth & Vine Provisions
Loomis, CA 888-723-8463

East Indies Coffee & Tea Company
Lebanon, PA 800-220-2326

East Shore Specialty Foods
Hartland, WI 800-236-1069

Egg Roll Fantasy
Auburn, CA....................530-887-9197
Eilenberger Bakery
Palestine, TX....................800-831-2544
Emerald Valley Kitchen
Salinas, CA....................831-536-62
Emkay Trading Corporation
Elmsford, NY....................914-592-9000
Endangered Species Chocolate
Indianapolis, IN....................800-293-0160
Enjoy Life Foods
Schiller Park, IL....................888-503-6569
Europa Foods
Saddle Brook, NJ....................201-368-8929
Eweberry Farms
Brownsville, OR....................541-466-3470
Fabe's Natural Gourmet
San Francisco, CA....................818-838-6633
Fairwinds Gourmet Coffee
Lincoln, CA....................1 8-0 8-9 13
Fantasy Chocolates
Delray Beach, FL....................800-804-4962
Fantis Foods
Carlstadt, NJ....................201-933-6200
Fife Vineyards
Redwood Valley, CA....................707-485-0323
Fillo Factory
Dumont, NJ....................800-653-4556
Fiorucci Foods
Colonial Heights, VA....................800-524-7775
First District Association
Litchfield, MN....................320-693-3236
Fliinko
South Dartmouth, MA....................508-996-9609
Foodbrands America
Oklahoma City, OK....................405-290-4000
Fox Hollow Farm
Hanover, NH....................603-643-6002
Fox Meadow Farm
Chester Springs, PA....................610-827-9731
Fox's Fine Foods
Laguna Beach, CA....................888-522-3697
France Delices
Montreal, QC....................800-663-1365
Fratello Coffee Roasters
Calgary, AB....................800-465-7227
Frontera Foods
Chicago, IL....................800-509-4441
Fun Foods
East Rutherford, NJ....................800-507-2782
Future Bakery & Cafe
Etobicoke, ON....................416-231-1491
Gadsden Coffee/Caffe
Arivaca, AZ....................888-514-5282
Garry Packing
Del Rey, CA....................800-248-2126
General Mills
Federalsburg, MD....................410-754-5000
Geneva Foods
Sanford, FL....................800-240-2326
Gerhard's Napa Valley Sausage
Napa, CA....................707-252-4116
Germain-Robin/Alambic
Ukiah, CA....................707-462-0314
Gift Basket Supply World
Jacksonville, FL....................800-786-4438
Gillies Coffee Company
Brooklyn, NY....................800-344-5526
Gindi Gourmet
Boulder, CO....................303-473-9177
Giovanni's Appetizing Food Products
Richmond, MI....................586-727-9355
Giusto's Specialty Foods
S San Francisco, CA....................650-873-6566
GKI Foods
Brighton, MI....................248-486-0055
Glacial Ridge Foods
Redford, MI....................612-239-2215
Global Express Gourmet
Bozeman, MT....................406-587-5571
Gold Seal Fruit Bouquet
Milwaukee, WI....................800-558-5558
Golden Moon Tea
Herndon, VA....................877-327-5473
Golden West Specialty Foods
Brisbane, CA....................800-584-4481
Golden Whisk
South San Francisco, CA....................800-660-5222
Gondwanaland
Corrales, NM....................505-899-2843
Good Fortunes & Edible Art
Canoga Park, CA....................800-644-9474
Good Health Natural Foods
Northport, NY....................631-261-2111
Gourmet Concepts International
Suwanee, GA....................800-241-4166
Gourmet Food Mall
Kenner, LA....................800-903-7553
Gourmet Foods Market
Knoxville, TN....................865-584-8739
Gourmet Products
Thomaston, CT....................860-283-5147
Goya Foods
Secaucus, NJ....................201-348-4900
Grace Tea Company
Acton, MA....................978-635-9500
Grande Cheese Company
Brownsville, WI....................800-678-3122
Granowska's
Toronto, ON....................416-533-7755
Great American Popcorn Works of Pennsylvania
Telford, PA....................800-542-2676
Green Mountain Gringo
Winston Salem, NC
Greenwell Farms
Morganfield, KY....................270-389-3289
Grey Owl Foods
Grand Rapids, MN....................800-527-0172
Groezinger Provisions
Neptune, NJ....................800-927-9473
Grounds for Thought
Bowling Green, OH....................419-354-2326
GWB Foods Corporation
Brooklyn, NY....................877-977-7610
Habby Habanero's Food Products
Jacksonville, FL....................904-333-9758
Happy & Healthy Products
Boca Raton, FL....................561-367-0739
Harbar Corporation
Canton, MA....................800-881-7040
Harrington's In Vermont
Richmond, VT....................802-434-7500
Harrison Napa Valley
Saint Helena, CA....................707-963-8762
Haus Barhyte
Pendleton, OR....................800-407-9241
Hawthorne Valley Farm
Ghent, NY....................518-672-5808
Haypress Gourmet Pasta
Haverstraw, NY....................845-947-4580
Hearthstone Whole Grain Bakery
Bozeman, MT....................800-757-7919
Hendricks Apiaries
Englewood, CO....................303-789-3209
Heritage Fancy Foods Marketing
Erlanger, KY....................859-282-3782
Hialeah Products Company
Hollywood, FL....................800-923-3379
Hickory Baked Food
Castle Rock, CO....................303-688-2633
High Liner Foods Inc
Lunenburg, NS....................902-634-9475
Hollman Foods
Chicago, IL....................888-926-2879
Homestead Baking Company
Rumford, RI....................800-556-7216
Honeybake Farms
Kansas City, KS....................913-371-7777
Hongar Farm Gourmet Foods
Tucker, GA....................888-296-7191
Hop Kee
Chicago, IL....................312-791-9111
Hospitality Mints
Boone, NC....................800-334-5181
House of Coffee Beans
Houston, TX....................800-422-1799
Humphrey Blue Ribbon Meats
Springfield, IL....................800-747-6328
Hunt Country Foods
Middleburg, VA....................540-364-2622
Hye Cuisine
Del Rey, CA....................559-834-3000
Hye Quality Bakery
Fresno, CA....................877-445-1778
I. Epstein & Sons
East Brunswick, NJ....................800-237-5320
Impromtu Gourmet
New York, NY....................212-475-4640
Indian Foods Company
Minneapolis, MN....................763-593-3000
Indigo Coffee Roasters
Florence, MA....................800-447-5450
Intermountain Canola Cargill
Idaho Falls, ID....................800-822-6652
International Brownie
East Weymouth, MA....................800-230-1588
International Trading Company
Houston, TX....................713-224-5901
Isabella's Healthy Bakery
Cuyahoga Falls, OH....................800-476-6328
Ivy Foods
Phoenix, AZ....................877-223-5459
J.A.M.B. Low Carb Distributor
Pompano Beach, FL....................800-708-6738
J.B. Peel Coffee Roasters
Red Hook, NY....................800-231-7372
J.N. Bech
Elk Rapids, MI....................800-232-4583
Jalapeno Foods Company
The Woodlands, TX....................800-896-2318
James Frasinetti & Sons
Sacramento, CA....................916-383-2444
Jason & Son Specialty Foods
Rancho Cordova, CA....................800-810-9093
Jay Shah Foods
Mississauga, ON....................905-696-0172
Jeremiah's Pick Coffee Company
San Francisco, CA....................800-537-3642
Jesses Fine Meats
Cherokee, IA....................712-225-3637
Jim's Cheese Pantry
Waterloo, WI....................800-345-3571
Joy's Specialty Foods
Mancos, CO....................800-831-5697
Joyva Corporation
Brooklyn, NY....................718-497-0170
Just Desserts
San Francisco, CA....................415-602-9245
Karen's Fabulous Biscotti
White Plains, NY....................914-682-2165
Karen's Wine Country Cafe
Sonoita, AZ....................800-453-5650
Kay Foods Company
Detroit, MI....................313-393-1100
Kelly Gourmet Foods
San Francisco, CA....................415-648-9200
Kennedy Gourmet
Houston, TX....................800-882-6253
Kevton Gourmet Tea
Streetman, TX....................888-538-8668
Keystone Coffee Company
San Jose, CA....................408-998-2221
Kid's Kookie Company
San Clemente, CA....................800-350-7577
King David's All NaturalFood
Syracuse, NY....................315-471-5000
Knese Enterprise
Bellerose, NY....................516-354-9004
Knott's Berry Farm Foods
Placentia, CA....................800-289-9927
Knox Mountain Farm
Franklin, NH....................800-943-2822
Koch Foods
Park Ridge, IL....................800-837-2778
Koegel Meats
Flint, MI....................810-238-3685
Kokopelli's Kitchen
Phoenix, AZ....................888-943-9802
Kolb-Lena Cheese Company
Lena, IL....................815-369-4577
Kornfections
Chantilly, VA....................800-469-8886
Krinos Foods
Santa Barbara, CA....................800-624-4896
L&S Packing Company
Farmingdale, NY....................800-286-6487
L'Esprit de Campagne
Winchester, VA....................800-692-8008
La Cookie
Houston, TX....................713-784-2722
La Rosa
Addison, IL....................630-916-9552
La Vigne Enterprises
Fallbrook, CA....................760-723-9997
LaRosa's Bakery
Shrewsbury, NJ....................800-527-6722
Laska Stuff
Rochester, MI....................248-652-8473
Lay's Fine Foods
Knoxville, TN....................800-251-9636
Leech Lake Wild Rice
Deer River, MN....................877-246-0620
Legumes Plus
Fairfield, WA....................800-845-1349
Les Trois Petits Cochons
Brooklyn, NY....................800-537-7283

Lesley Elizabeth
Lapeer, MI. 800-684-3300
Let's Serve
Plattsburgh, NY
Liberty Richter
Saddle Brook, NJ 201-291-8749
Lindsay Farms
Cave Spring, GA. 706-777-9797
Little Lady Foods
Elk Grove Vlg, IL. 800-439-1440
Live A Little Gourmet Foods
Newark, CA 888-744-2300
Lodi Nut Company
Lodi, CA 800-234-6887
Longmeadow Foods
Gray, ME. 800-255-8401
Lotus Brands
Silver Lake, WI. 800-824-6396
Louisiana Fish Fry Products
Baton Rouge, LA 800-356-2905
Louisiana Gourmet Enterprises
La Place, LA 985-783-2446
Love Creek Orchards
Medina, TX. 800-449-0882
Lucile's Creole Foods
Boulder, CO 303-442-4743
Lusitania Bakery
Blandon, PA 610-926-1311
M&L Gourmet Ice Cream
Baltimore, MD .410-276-4880
M. Marion & Company
Santa Rosa, CA. 707-836-0551
Mad Chef Enterprise
Mentor, OH. 800-951-2433
Mad Will's Food Company
Auburn, CA. 888-275-9455
Madhava Honey
Longmont, CO .800-530-2900
Madrona Specialty Foods
Tukwila, WA. 425-814-2500
Maggie Gin's
San Francisco, CA 415-221-6080
Magic Ice Products
Cincinnati, OH .800-776-7923
Magnum Coffee Roastery
Nunica, MI 888-937-5282
Main Street Custom Foods
Cuyahoga Falls, OH 800-533-6246
Main Street Gourmet
Cuyahoga Falls, OH 800-533-6246
Main Street Gourmet Fundraising
Cuyahoga Falls, OH 800-533-6246
Main Street Muffins
Cuyahoga Falls, OH 800-533-6246
Main Street's Cambritt Cookies
Cuyahoga Falls, OH 800-533-6246
Maitake Products
East Rutherford, NJ 800-747-7418
Mama Lee's Gourmet Hot Chocolate
Nashville, TN. . . . . .1 8-8 m-male
Mama Rose's Gourmet Foods
Phoenix, AZ 877-325-4477
Mama Vida
Randallstown, MD 877-521-0742
Mancini Packing Company
Zolfo Springs, FL 863-735-2000
Manitok Food & Gifts
Callaway, MN 800-726-1863
Maple Leaf Foods International
North York, ON. 416-480-8900
Marantha Natural Foods
San Francisco, CA 866-972-6879
Marcel et Henri Charcuterie Francaise
South San Francisco, CA 800-227-6436
Mardi Gras
Verona, NJ. 973-857-3777
Marich Confectionery Company
Hollister, CA. 800-624-7055
Marin Food Specialties
Byron, CA. 925-634-6126
Market Square Food Company
Highland Park, IL 800-232-2299
Marukai Corporation
Gardena, CA 310-660-6300
Meat-O-Mat Corporation
Brooklyn, NY 718-965-7250
Mendocino Mustard
Fort Bragg, CA .800-964-2270
Mercado Latino
City of Industry, CA 626-333-6862
Merlino Italian Baking Company
Seattle, WA 800-207-2997
Metropolis Sambeve Specialty Foods
Lawrence, MA .978-683-2873
Mille Lacs MP Company
Madison, WI 800-843-1381
Mills Brothers International
Tukwila, WA. 206-575-3000
Minnestalgia
McGregor, MN .800-328-6731
Modern Baked Products
Oakdale, NY 877-727-2253
Moody Dunbar
Johnson City, TN 800-251-8202
Moon Shine Trading Company
Woodland, CA. .800-678-1226
Morningland Dairy CheeseCompany
Mountain View, MO. 417-469-3817
Mother Earth Enterprises
New York, NY .866-436-7688
Mrs. Auld's Gourmet Foods
Reno, NV 800-322-8537
Mrs. Leeper's Pasta
Excelsior Springs, MO 800-848-5266
MSRF, Inc.
Chicago, IL 773-227-1115
Mt. Olympus Specialty Foods
Buffalo, NY. 716-874-0771
Murvest Fine Foods
Fort Lauderdale, FL 954-772-6440
Mustard Seed
Central, SC 877-621-2591
My Sister's Caramels
Redlands, CA 909-792-6242
Nancy's Specialty Foods
Newark, CA 510-494-1100
Naron Mary Sue Candy Company
Baltimore, MD .800-662-2639
National Foods
Liberal, KS 620-624-1851
National Importers
Richmond, BC .888-894-6464
Natural Exotic Tropicals
Pompano Beach, FL 800-756-5267
Natural Quick Foods
Seattle, WA 206-365-5757
Nature's Finest Products
Dallas, TX. 800-237-5205
Neilsen-Massey Vanillas
Waukegan, IL 800-525-7873
Nell Baking Company
Kenedy, TX. 800-215-9190
Neshaminy Valley Natural Foods
Warminster, PA .215-745-3773
Nest Eggs
Chicago, IL 773-525-4952
New Canaan Farms
Dripping Springs, TX 800-727-5267
New England Marketers
Boston, MA. 800-688-9904
New Glarus Foods
New Glarus, WI 800-356-6685
Newmarket Foods
Petaluma, CA 707-778-3400
Niche Import Company
Cedar Knolls, NJ. 800-548-6882
Nina's Gourmet Dip
Mc Lean, VA. 703-356-1667
NorCal Wild Rice
Davis, CA 530-758-8550
North American Enterprises
Tucson, AZ 800-817-8666
Northern Flair Foods
Mound, MN 888-530-4453
Northwest Candy Emporium
Everett, WA. 800-404-7266
Nostalgic Specialty Foods
Baca Raton, FL. 561-237-8086
Nueske's Applewood Smoked Meats
Wittenberg, WI .800-386-2266
Nutty Bavarian
Sanford, FL 800-382-4788
OH Chocolate
Calgary, AB. 800-887-3959
Olde Tyme Mercantile
Arroyo Grande, CA. 805-489-7991
Olympic Specialty Foods
Tonawanda, NY 716-874-0771
Oregon Hill Farms
Saint Helens, OR. 800-243-4541
Oregon Pride
The Dalles, OR .888-697-4767
Organic By Nature
Long Beach, CA 800-452-6884
Organic Gourmet
Sherman Oaks, CA 800-400-7772
Orleans Packing Company
Hyde Park, MA. 617-361-6611
P & M Staiger Vineyard
Boulder Creek, CA 831-338-0172
Pacific Ocean Producers
Honolulu, HI 808-537-2905
Pacific Westcoast Foods
Beaverton, OR .800-874-9333
Palmetto Pigeon Plant
Sumter, SC 803-775-1204
Palmieri Food Products
New Haven, CT 800-845-5447
Panola Pepper Corporation
Lake Providence, LA 800-256-3013
Papa Dean's Popcorn
San Antonio, TX. 877-855-7272
Paradise Products Corporation
Boca Raton, FL. 800-826-1235
Parma Sausage Products
Pittsburgh, PA. .877-294-4207
Parny Gourmet
Miami, FL. 305-798-5177
Pastene Companies
Canton, MA 781-830-8200
PaStreeta Fresca
Dublin, OH 800-343-5266
Pastry Chef
Pawtucket, RI 800-639-8606
Pati-Petite Cookies
Bridgeville, PA .800-253-5805
Paulaur Corporation
Cranbury, NJ. 888-398-8844
Peanut Patch
Courtland, VA. .866-732-6883
Pearl Coffee Company
Akron, OH. 800-822-5282
Peerless Coffee Company
Oakland, CA 800-310-5662
Pelican Bay
Dunedin, FL 800-826-8982
Phipps Desserts
Toronto, ON 416-481-9111
Piantedosi Baking Company
Malden, MA 800-339-0080
Picard Peanuts
Simcoe, ON. 888-244-7688
Pickwick Catfish Farm
Counce, TN. 731-689-3805
Pidy Gourmet Pastry Shells
Inwood, NY. 800-231-7439
PJ's Coffee & Tea
New Orleans, LA 800-527-1055
Plaidberry Company
Vista, CA. 760-727-5403
Plaza de Espana Gourmet
Sunny Isles Beach, FL 305-971-3468
Pontiac Coffee Break
Pontiac, MI 248-332-9403
Popcorn Connection
North Hollywood, CA 800-852-2676
Popcorner
Swansea, IL. 618-277-2676
Porinos Gourmet Food
Central Falls, RI 800-826-3938
Power-Selles Imports
Lynnwood, WA. 425-398-9761
Prairie Thyme
Santa Fe, NM 800-869-0009
Premium Brands
Bardstown, KY .502-348-0081
Prince of Peace Enterprises
Hayward, CA 800-732-2328
Private Harvest
El Dorado Hills, CA 916-933-7080
Purely American
Norfolk, VA. 800-359-7873
Purity Farms
Sedalia, CO 800-568-4433
R.L. Schreiber
Pompano Beach, FL 800-624-8777
Rabbit Barn
Turlock, CA. 209-632-1123
Rainbow Valley Frozen Yogurt
White Lake, MI. 800-979-8669
Rainforest Company
Maryland Heights, MO. 314-344-1000
Rao's Specialty Foods
New York, NY .212-269-0151
Raymond-Hadley Corporation
Spencer, NY 800-252-5220

RC Fine Foods
Belle Mead, NJ 800-526-3953
Reading Coffee Roasters
Birdsboro, PA 800-331-6713
Regency Coffee & VendingCompany
Olathe, KS. 913-829-1994
Restaurant Lulu Gourmet Products
San Francisco, CA 888-693-5800
Rich Products of Canada
Buffalo, NY. 800-457-4247
Righetti Specialties
Santa Maria, CA 800-268-1041
Rio Trading Company
Baltimore, MD 443-384-2500
Robert Rothschild Farm
Urbana, OH. 866-565-6790
Ron-Son Foods
Swedesboro, NJ 856-241-7333
Rosmarino Foods/R.Z. Humbert Company
Odessa, FL 888-926-9053
Rossi Pasta
Marietta, OH. 800-227-6774
Rowena's
Norfolk, VA. 800-627-8699
Royal Baltic
Brooklyn, NY 718-385-8300
Royal Coffee & Tea Company
Mississauga, ON. 800-667-6226
Royal Palm Popcorn Company
Edison, NJ. 800-526-8865
Royal Wine Corp
Bayonne, NJ 718-384-2400
Rubschlager Baking Corporation
Chicago, IL 773-826-1245
Rudolph's Specialty Bakery
Toronto, ON 800-268-1589
Russ & Daughters
New York, NY 800-787-7229
Russian Chef
New York, NY 212-249-1550
Saguaro Food Products
Tucson, AZ 800-732-2447
Sambets Cajun Deli
Austin, TX. 800-472-6238
San Francisco Popcorn Works
San Francisco, CA 800-777-2676
San Gennaro Foods
Kent, WA. 800-462-1916
Sandridge Food Corporation
Medina, OH. 800-627-2523
Santa Barbara Olive Company
Santa Barbara, CA 800-624-4896
Santa Barbara Salsa
Oceanside, CA 800-748-5523
Santa Fe Seasons
Belen, NM. 800-264-5535
Sara Lee Corporation
Downers Grove, IL 630-598-8100
Sardinha Sausage
Somerset, MA 800-678-0178
Sassafras Enterprises
Chicago, IL 800-537-4941
Savannah Cinnamon & Cookie Company
Bradenton, FL 800-288-0854
Schwan Food Company
Marshall, MN 800-533-5290
Scooty's Wholesome Foods
Boulder, CO 303-440-4025
Seawind Trading International
Carlsbad, CA. 760-438-5600
Selma's Cookies
Apopka, FL 800-922-6654
Senor Felix's Gourmet Mexican
Baldwin Park, CA. 626-960-2800

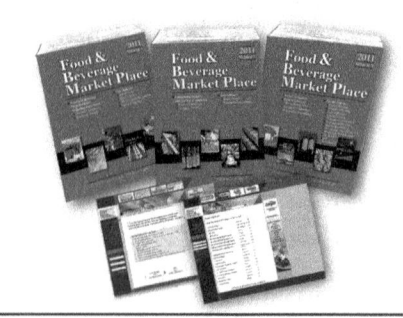

Serranos Salsa
Austin, TX. 512-328-9200
Sfoglia Fine Pastas & Gourmet
Freeland, WA 360-331-4080
Shady Grove Orchards
Onalaska, WA 360-985-7033
Sheila's Select Gourmet Recipe
Heber City, UT 800-516-7286
Shine Foods Inc
Torrance, CA. 310-533-6010
Shonfeld's
South Hackensack, NJ 800-462-3464
Signature Foods
Miami, FL. 305-436-5392
Silver Palate Kitchens
Cresskill, NJ 800-872-5283
Simply Divine
New York, NY 212-541-7300
Simpson & Vail
Brookfield, CT 800-282-8327
Sonoma Gourmet
Sonoma, CA 707-939-3700
Southern Gold Honey CompAny
Vidor, TX 808-899-2494
Southern Heritage Coffee Company
Indianapolis, IN 800-486-1198
Southern Style Nuts
Denison, TX 903-463-3161
Spanarkel Company
Neptune City, NJ. 732-775-4144
Spartan Imports
Endicott, NY. 607-785-0239
Specialty Coffee Roasters
Delray Beach, FL 800-253-9363
Specialty Foods South
Charleston, SC 800-538-0003
Spring Creek Natural Foods
Spencer, WV. 304-927-3780
Sprout House
Ramona, CA 800-777-6887
Star of the West MillingCompany
Frankenmuth, MI 989-652-9971
Star Ravioli Manufacturing Company
Moonachie, NJ 201-933-6427
Stearns & Lehman
Mansfield, OH 800-533-2722
Steel's Gourmet Foods, Ltd.
Bridgeport, PA 800-678-3357
Sticky Fingers Bakeries
Spokane, WA. 800-458-5826
Stirling Foods
Renton, WA. 800-332-1714
Sugar Plum Farm
Plumtree, NC. 888-257-0019
Summerfield Farm Products
Orange, VA 800-898-3276
Sunset Specialty Foods
Sunset Beach, CA 562-592-4976
Sweet Shop
Mount Pleasant, TX 800-222-2269
Sweety Novelty
Monterey Park, CA. 626-282-4482
Swiss Chalet Fine Foods
Doral, FL. 800-347-9477
Swiss Colony
Monroe, WI. 608-328-8536
Swiss-American
St Louis, MO. 800-325-8150
T.W. Garner Food Company
Winston Salem, NC. 800-476-7383
Table De France
Ontario, CA. 909-923-5205
Tabor Hill/CHI Company
Buchanan, MI 80- 2-3 33

Taft Street Winery
Sebastopol, CA 707-823-2049
Tait Farm Foods
Centre Hall, PA 800-787-2716
Takara Sake
Berkeley, CA. 510-540-8250
Tarzai Specialty Foods
Chino, CA 909-628-3601
Teeccino Caffe
Santa Barbara, CA 800-498-3434
Texas Traditions
Georgetown, TX 800-547-7062
Thackery & Company
Bolinas, CA. 415-868-1781
Thistledew Farm
Proctor, WV 800-854-6639
Tipiak
Stamford, CT. 203-961-9117
Tokunaga Farms
Selma, CA. 559-896-0949
Tom & Sally's Handmade Chocolates
Brattleboro, VT. 800-827-0800
Too Good Gourmet
San Lorenzo, CA. 877-850-4663
Topolos at Russian River Vine
Forestville, CA 707-887-1575
Torn Ranch
Novato, CA. 415-506-3000
Torrefazione Italia
Seattle, WA 800-827-2333
Tostino Coffee Roasters
Tucson, AZ 800-678-3519
Tova Industries
Louisville, KY 888-532-8682
Town & Country Foods
Greene, ME. 207-946-5489
Trader Joe's Company
Monrovia, CA. 626-599-3700
Treat Ice Cream Company
San Jose, CA. 408-292-9321
Tree of Life
St Augustine, FL. 904-940-2100
Tres Classique
Ukiah, CA 888-644-5127
Trinity Spice
Midland, TX 800-460-1149
Tropical
Charlotte, NC 800-220-1413
Tropical
Marietta, GA 800-544-3762
Tropical Nut & Fruit Company
Orlando, FL. 800-749-8869
Tuscan Hills
El Dorado Hills, CA 916-939-3814
Two Chefs on a Roll
Carson, CA 800-842-3025
Uncle Ralph's Cookie Company
Frederick, MD. 800-422-0626
Unibroue/Unibrew Sleeman Unibroue
Chambly, QC. 450-658-7658
Unique Foods
Raleigh, NC 919-779-5600
United Natural Foods
Chesterfield, NH. 800-451-2525
Valley View Blueberries
Vancouver, WA 360-892-2839
Van-Lang Foods
Countryside, IL. 708-588-0800
Vega Food Industries
Cranston, RI 800-973-7737
Ventura Foods
Salem, OR. 503-585-6423
Venus Wafers
Hingham, MA. 800-545-4538

Vermont Country Store
Manchester Center, VT. 802-362-4667
Vermont Food Experience
Shelburne, VT. 802-985-8101
Vermont Natural Company
Jacksonville, VT 802-368-2231
Vigneri Confections
Rochester, NY. 877-843-6374
Vine Village
Napa, CA. 707-255-4099
Viola's Gourmet Goodies
Los Angeles, CA. 323-731-5277
Volcano Island Honey Company
Honokaa, HI 888-663-6639
W.J. Clark & Co
Chicago, IL 312-329-0830
W.S. Wells & Sons
Wilton, ME 207-645-3393
Wagner Gourmet Foods
Lenexa, KS 913-469-5411
Walden Foods
Winchester, VA 800-648-7688
Warren & Son Meat Processing
Whipple, OH 740-585-2421
Weaver Nut Company
Ephrata, PA 717-738-3781
Wechsler Coffee Corporation
Moonachie, NJ 800-800-2633
Wenner Bread Products
Bayport, NY 800-869-6262
Westbrae Natural Foods
Melville, NY 800-434-4246
Western Pacific Commodities
Henderson, NV 702-382-8880
White Wave Foods
Jacksonville, FL 800-874-6765
Wild Rice Exchange
Woodland, CA. 800-223-7423
Wildwood Natural Foods
Watsonville, CA 800-464-3915
Will-Pak Foods
Ontario, CA. 800-874-0883
Woeber Mustard Manufacturing
Springfield, OH. 800-548-2929
Wong Wing Foods
Montreal, QC 800-361-4820
World of Coffee, World of Tea
Stirling, NJ 908-647-1218
Yair Scones/Canterbury Cuisine
Medina, WA 800-588-9160
Yankee Specialty Foods
Boston, MA. 617-951-0739
Yayin Corporation
Valley Village, CA 707-829-5686
Yorktown Baking Company
Yorktown Heights, NY 800-235-3961
Your Bar Factory
LaSalle, QC. 888-366-0258
Yvonne's Gourmet Sensations
Marlton, NJ. 856-985-7677
Zitos Specialty Foods
Port Charlotte, FL. 941-625-0806

Health & Dietary

Energy Bars

Abbott Laboratories Nutritionals/Ross Products
Abbott Park, IL. 847-937-6100
Eat Your Heart Out
New York, NY 212-989-8303
Gertrude & Bronner's Magic Alpsnack
Escondido, CA 760-743-2211
Kettle Valley Fruits SunOpta Inc
Summerland, BC. 888-297-6944
Optimum Nutrition
Walterboro, SC 800-763-3444

Organic Foods

Abunda Life Laboratories
Asbury Park, NJ 732-775-7575
Adrienne's Gourmet Foods
Santa Barbara, CA 800-937-7010
AgriCulver Seeds
Trumansburg, NY 800-836-3701
Alliston Creamery & Dairy
Alliston, ON 705-435-6751
Alta Dena Certified Dairy
City of Industry, CA 800-535-1369
Amberwave Foods
Oakmont, PA. 412-828-3040
American Health & Nutrition
Ann Arbor, MI 734-677-5572
American Natural & Organic Spices
Fremont, CA 510-440-1044
Amy's Kitchen
Petaluma, CA 707-568-4500
Andre-Boudin Bakeries
San Francisco, CA 415-882-1849
Ankeny Lakes Wild Rice
Salem, OR. 800-555-5380
Annie's Naturals
East Calais, VT 800-434-1234
Applegate Farms
Bridgewater, NJ 908-725-2768
Atlantic Quality Spice &Seasonings
New Brunswick, NJ 800-584-0422
Avalon Organic Coffees
Albuquerque, NM 800-662-2575
Barrows Tea Company
New Bedford, MA 800-832-5024
Bedrock Farm Certified Organic Medicinal Herbs
Wakefield, RI 401-789-9943
Bel/Kaukauna USA
Kaukauna, WI 800-558-3500
Belgravia Imports
Portsmouth, RI 800-848-1127
Bella Vista Farm
Lawton, OK. 866-237-8526
Berardi's Fresh Roast
Cleveland, OH 800-876-9109
Beta Pure Foods
Aptos, CA 831-685-6565
Beth's Fine Desserts
Mill Valley, CA. 415-464-1891
Blessed Herbs
Oakham, MA. 800-489-4372
Blue Marble Brands
Providence, RI 401-528-8634
Boehringer Ingelheim
Saint Charles, IL. 630-377-5150
Bombay Breeze Specialty Foods
Mississauga, ON. 416-410-2320
Brad's Organic
Haverstraw, NY. 845-429-9080
Brass Ladle Products
Concordville, PA. 800-955-2353
Bread Alone Bakery
Boiceville, NY 800-769-3328
Brewster Dairy
Brewster, OH 800-874-8874
Brier Run Farm
Birch River, WV. 304-649-2975
Buchanan Hollow Nut Company
Le Grand, CA 800-532-1500
Buns & Roses Organic Wholegrain Bakery
Edmonton, AB 780-438-0098
Butterbuds Food Ingredients
Racine, WI. 800-426-1119
Buywell Coffee
Colorado Springs, CO. 719-598-7870
C&H Sugar Company
Crockett, CA 800-729-4840
C.F. Burger Creamery
Detroit, MI 800-229-2322
Cafe Society Coffee Company
Dallas, TX. 800-717-6000
California Custom Fruits & Flavors
Irwindale, CA 877-558-0056
California Independent Almond Growers
Merced, CA. 209-667-4855
California Olive Oil Corporation
Berkeley, CA. 888-718-9830
Candone Fine Natural Foods
Atlanta, GA. 404-469-2348
Carob Tree
Arcadia, CA 626-445-0215
Cascadian Farm & MUIR Glen
Sedro Woolley, WA. 360-855-0100
Caudill Seed Company
Louisville, KY 800-626-5357
Cedarlane Foods
Carson, CA 310-886-7720
Century Foods International
Sparta, WI. 800-269-1901
Champlain Valley Milling Corporation
Westport, NY. 518-962-4711
Chelten House Products
Bridgeport, NJ. 856-467-1600
Cherith Valley Gardens
Fort Worth, TX 800-610-9813
Chino Valley Ranchers
Arcadia, CA 626-652-0890
Chris' Farm Stand
Bradford, MA 978-994-4315
Christopher Ranch
Gilroy, CA. 408-847-1100
Chunco Foods Inc
Kansas City, MO. 816-283-0716
Citrus Service
Winter Garden, FL 407-656-4999
Clean Foods
Santa Paula, CA 800-526-8328
Clear Mountain Coffee Company
Silver Spring, MD. 301-587-2233
Coleman Purely Natural Brands
Golden, CO 800-442-8666
College Hill Poultry
Fredericksburg, PA 800-533-3361
Columbus Foods Company
Des Plaines, IL 800-322-6457
Contact International
Skokie, IL 847-324-4411
Country Choice Naturals
Eden Prairie, MN 952-829-8824
Crystal Geyser Roxanne LLC
Pensacola, FL 850-476-8844
Cuizina Food Company
Woodinville, WA. 425-486-7000
Cyanotech Corporation
Kailua Kona, HI 800-395-1353
Dagoba Organic Chocolate
Hershey, PA. 717-534-4200
Dakota Growers Pasta Company
New Hope, MN. 763-531-5360
Dakota Organic Products
Watertown, SD 800-243-7264
Dakota Prairie Organic Flour Company
Harvey, ND 701-324-4330
Dancing Paws
Chatsworth, CA 888-644-7297
Daymar Select Fine Coffees
El Cajon, CA. 800-466-7590
Dorothy Dawson Foods Products
Jackson, MI. 517-788-9830
Dr. Kracker
Plano, TX. 97- 63- 110
Driscoll Strawberry Associates
Watsonville, CA 831-763-5100
Earth Fire Products
Viroqua, WI. 608-735-4711
East Wind Nut Butters
Tecumseh, MO 417-679-4682
Eatem Foods Company
Vineland, NJ 800-683-2836
Eberly Poultry
Stevens, PA 717-336-6440
Eco-Cuisine
Boulder, CO 303-444-6634
Eden Foods Inc.
Clinton, MI 800-248-0320
Eden Organic Pasta Company
Detroit, MI 800-248-0320
Eggology
Canoga Park, CA 818-610-2222
Extracts and Ingredients Ltd
Union, NJ 908-688-9009
Fairhaven Cooperative Flour Mill
Burlington, WA
FarmGro Organic Foods
Regina, SK 306-522-0092
Fearn Natural Foods
Thiensville, WI 800-877-8935
Fine Dried Foods International
Santa Cruz, CA. 831-426-1413
Fireside Kitchen
Halifax, NS 902-454-7387
Florence Macaroni Manufacturing
Chicago, IL 800-647-2782
Florida Food Products
Eustis, FL 800-874-2331
Food Reserves/Good For You America
Concordia, MO 800-944-1511
French Meadow Bakery
Eagan, MN 877-669-3278
Fresh Tofu, Inc
Allentown, PA. 610-433-4711
Frontier Ingredients
Norway, IA 800-669-3275
FungusAmongUs Inc
Snohomish, WA 360-568-3403
Gabriele Macaroni Company
City of Industry, CA 626-964-2324
Garuda International
Exeter, CA. 559-594-4380

Gelato Fresco
Toronto, ON 416-785-5415
George Chiala Farms
Morgan Hill, CA. 408-778-0562
Gerber Products Company
Parsippany, NJ. 800-443-7237
Ginseng Up Corporation
Rockleigh, NJ 201-660-8081
Golden Harvest Pecans
Cairo, GA 800-597-0968
Grandpa Po's Nutra Nuts
Commerce, CA 323-260-7457
Great Eastern Sun
Asheville, NC 800-334-5809
Guayaki Sustainable Rainforest Products
Sebastopol, CA 888-482-9254
H&K Products-Pappy's Sassafras Teas
Columbus Grove, OH 877-659-5110
Hallcrest Vineyards
Felton, CA. 831-335-4441
Harbar Corporation
Canton, MA 800-881-7040
Hawkhaven Greenhouse International
Wautoma, WI 800-745-4295
Health Valley Company
Irwindale, CA 800-334-3204
Heini's Cheese Company
Millersburg, OH 800-253-6636
HempNut
Henderson, NV 707-576-7050
Herbal Magic
Forest Knolls, CA 415-488-9488
Heritage Shortbread
Hilton Head Island, SC. 843-342-7268
Highland Sugarworks, Inc
Websterville, VT. 800-452-4012
Homestead Mills
Cook, MN 800-652-5233
HP Schmid
San Francisco, CA 415-765-5925
Indigo Coffee Roasters
Florence, MA 800-447-5450
Ineeka Inc
Chicago, IL 312-733-8327
International Casing Group
Chicago, IL 800-825-5151
Internatural Foods
Bloomfield, NJ 800-225-1449
Island Spring
Vashon, WA. 206-463-9848
Johnson Fruit Company
Sunnyside, WA 509-837-4600
Kerry Ingredients
Blue Earth, MN. 507-526-7575
Kopali Organics
Miami, FL. 305-751-7341
Kozlowski Farms
Forestville, CA 800-473-2767
Kraft Foods
Springfield, MO 417-881-2701
La Brea Bakery
Van Nuys, CA 818-742-4242
Lakeview Bakery
Calgary, AB. 403-246-6127
Late July Organic Snacks
Barnstable, MA. 508-362-5859
Lifeway Foods Inc
Morton Grove, IL 877-281-3874
Lowell Farms
El Campo, TX. 888-484-9213
Lundberg Family Farm
Richvale, CA. 530-882-4551
Made in Nature
Fresno, CA 800-906-7426
Magnum Coffee Roastery
Nunica, MI 888-937-5282
Mandarin Soy Sauce
Middletown, NY. 845-343-1505
McFadden Farm
Potter Valley, CA 800-544-8230
Mercantile Food Company
Philmont, NY 518-672-0190
Merlino Italian Baking Company
Seattle, WA 800-207-2997
Mills Brothers International
Tukwila, WA. 206-575-3000
Minnesota Specialty Crops
McGregor, MN 800-328-6731
Miyako Oriental Foods
Baldwin Park, CA. 877-788-6476
Mom's Gourmet, LLC
Chagrin Falls, OH. 440-564-9702

Mountain Sun Organic & Natural Juices
Boulder, CO. 1 8-0 4-4 42
Mr. Espresso
Oakland, CA 510-287-5200
Mrs. Leeper's Pasta
Excelsior Springs, MO 800-848-5266
Mrs. Miller's Homeade Noodles
Fredericksburg, OH 800-227-4487
Mushroom Company
Cambridge, MD 410-221-8971
Mustard Seed
Central, SC 877-621-2591
Najla's
Louisville, KY 877-962-5527
Native American Natural Foods
Kyle, SD 800-416-7212
Natural Way Mills
Middle River, MN. 218-222-3677
Nature's Candy
Fredericksburg, TX. 800-729-0085
Nature's Hand
Burnsville, MN 952-890-6033
Nature's Nutrition
Melbourne, FL 800-242-1115
Naturel
Rancho Cucamonga, CA 877-242-8344
Natures Sungrown Foods
San Rafael, CA 415-491-4944
New England Natural Baker
Greenfield, MA. 800-910-2884
North American Seasonings
Lake Oswego, OR. 503-636-7043
North Bay Trading Company
Brule, WI. 800-348-0164
North Country Natural Spring Water
Port Kent, NY 518-834-9400
NSpired Natural Foods
Melville, NY 631-845-4689
NSpired Natural Foods
Boulder, CO 800-434-4246
Nutra Nuts
Commerce, CA 323-260-7457
Nutrex Hawaii, Inc
Kailua Kona, HI 800-453-1187
O Olive Oil
Petaluma, CA 888-827-7148
Omega Nutrition
Bellingham, WA 800-661-3529
Once Again Nut Butter
Nunda, NY 888-800-8075
Organic Gourmet
Sherman Oaks, CA 800-400-7772
Organic Valley
La Farge, WI. 608-625-2602
Organic Wine Company
San Francisco, CA 888-326-9463
Oskri Organics
Lake Mills, WI 800-628-1110
Pacari Organic Chocolate
Miami, FL. 561-214-4726
Pack Ryt, Inc.
La Quinta, CA. 770-771-8880
Pak Technologies
Milwaukee, WI 414-438-8600
Palmieri Food Products
New Haven, CT 800-845-5447
Panos Brands
Saddle Brook, NJ 201-843-8900
Parthenon Food Products
Ann Arbor, MI 734-994-1012
Pasta Prima
Benicia, CA. 707-746-6888
Pasta USA
Spokane, WA. 800-456-2084
Peace Mountain Natural Beverages Corporation
Springfield, MA 413-567-4942
Peace Village Organic Foods
Berkeley, CA. 510-524-4420
Pearl Valley Cheese Company
Fresno, OH 740-545-6002
Personal Edge Nutrition
Ballwin, MO 877-982-3343
Phillips Gourmet, Inc
Kennett Square, PA. 610-925-0520
Pleasant Grove Farms
Pleasant Grove, CA 916-655-3391
Prairie Mills Company
Rochester, IN 574-223-3177
Prairie Sun Grains
Calgary, AB. 800-556-6807
Progenix Corporation
Wausau, WI. 800-233-3356

Purity Farms
Sedalia, CO. 800-568-4433
Purity Foods
Okemos, MI 800-997-7358
R&J Farms
West Salem, OH 419-846-3179
R.J. Corr Naturals
Posen, IL. 708-389-4200
Rajbhog Foods
Jersey City, NJ 201-395-9400
Rapunzel Pure Organics
Bloomfield, NJ 800-225-1449
Ravioli Store
Long Islnad City, NY 877-727-8269
Red River Commodities
Fargo, ND. 701-282-2600
Regenie's All Natural and Organic Snacks
Haverhill, MA 877-Reg-nie
Rocky Mountain Honey Company
Salt Lake City, UT 801-355-2054
Run-A-Ton Group
Chester, NJ 800-247-6580
Rustic Crust
Pittsfield, NH 603-435-5119
SafeTrek Foods
Bozeman, MT. 406-586-4840
Season Harvest Foods
Sunnyvale, CA 408-749-8018
Shariann's Organics
Melville, NY. 800-434-4246
Sierra Madre Organic Coffee
Denver, CO 303-446-0050
Silver Creek Specialty Meats
Oshkosh, WI. 920-232-3581
SJH Enterprises
Middleton, WI. 888-745-3845
Slim Fast Foods Company
West Palm Beach, FL 561-833-9920
Solana Gold Organics
Sebastopol, CA 800-459-1121
Solnuts
Hudson, IA 800-648-3503
Sophia's Sauce Works
Carson City, NV 800-718-7769
Springfield Creamery
Eugene, OR. 541-689-2911
Stevia LLC
Valley Forge, PA. 888-878-3842
Straus Family Creamery
Petaluma, CA 800-572-7783
Sun Garden Growers
Bard, CA. 800-228-4690
Sun Ridge Farms
Pajaro, CA. 831-786-7000
Sunergia Soyfoods
Charlottesville, VA 800-693-5134
Sunridge Farms
Salinas, CA 831-755-1430
Sunwest Foods
Davis, CA 530-758-8550
Sustainable Sourcing
Great Barrington, MA. 413-528-5141
Suzanne's Specialties
New Brunswick, NJ 800-762-2135
Tastybaby
Malibu, CA 866-588-8278
Tea Room
San Leandro, CA. 866-515-8866
Tea-n-Crumpets
San Rafael, CA 415-457-2495
Teeny Tiny Spice Company of Vermont LLC
Shelburne, VT. 802-598-6800
Templar Food Products
New Providence, NJ 800-883-6752
The Mediterranean Snack Food Company
Boonton, NJ 973-333-4888
Thomas Canning/Maidstone
Maidstone, ON 519-737-1531
Tova Industries
Louisville, KY 888-532-8682
Travel Chocolate
New York, NY 718-841-7030
Tree of Life
St Augustine, FL. 904-940-2100
Treehouse Farms
Earlimart, CA 559-757-5020
Triple Springs Spring Water
Meriden, CT 203-235-8374
Tripper
Oxnard, CA. 888-336-8747
True Organic Products International
Miami, FL. 800-487-0379

Twin Marquis
Brooklyn, NY 800-367-6868
Vegetable Juices
Chicago, IL 888-776-9752
Ventre Packing Company
Syracuse, NY 888-472-8237
Vermont Bread Company
Brattleboro, VT 877-293-0876
Vic Rossano Incorporated
Montreal, QC 514-766-5252
Vienna Bakery
Edmonton, AB 780-489-4142
Vogue Cuisine
Sunnyvale, CA 888-236-4144
WCC Honey Marketing
City of Industry, CA 626-855-3086
Westbrae Natural Foods
Melville, NY 800-434-4246
Wholesome Sweeteners
Sugar Land, TX 800-680-1896
Wild Rice Exchange
Woodland, CA 800-223-7423
Wing Nien Company
Hayward, CA 510-487-8877
Wizards Cauldron, LTD
Yanceyville, NC 336-694-5665
World Casing Corporation
Maspeth, NY 800-221-4887
Xochitl
Dallas, TX 214-800-3551
Your Bar Factory
LaSalle, QC 888-366-0258
YZ Enterprises
Maumee, OH 800-736-8779
Zhena's Gypsy Tea
Commerce, CA 800-448-0803

Certified

American Health & Nutrition
Ann Arbor, MI 734-677-5570
American Purpac Technologies, LLC
Beloit, WI 877-787-7221
Brier Run Farm
Birch River, WV 304-649-2975
Briess Industries
Chilton, WI 920-849-7711
California Custom Fruits & Flavors
Irwindale, CA 877-558-0056
Clofine Dairy & Food Products
Linwood, NJ 800-441-1001
Emerling International Foods
Buffalo, NY 716-833-7381

We supply food manufacturers and food service customers worldwide (since 1988) with bulk ingredients including: Fruits & Vegetables; Juice Concentrates; Herbs & Spices; Oils & Vinegars; Flavors & Colors; Honey & Molasses. We also produce PURE MAPLE SYRUP.

Frontier Natural Co-op
Norway, IA 303-449-8137
Hains Celestial Group
Melville, NY 877-612-4246
Hoyt's Honey Farm
Baytown, TX 281-576-5383
Innovative Food Solutions LLC
Columbus, OH 800-884-3314
J.W. Raye & Company
Eastport, ME 800-853-1903
Jonathan's Sprouts
Rochester, MA 508-763-2577
Kozlowski Farms
Forestville, CA 800-473-2767
Lily of the Desert
Denton, TX 800-229-5459
Marukan Vinegar (U.S.A.) Inc.
Paramount, CA 562-630-6060
Mediterranean Delights
Contoocook, NH 800-347-5850
National Vinegar Company
Houston, TX 713-223-4214
Nu-World Amaranth
Naperville, IL 630-369-6819
Once Again Nut Butter
Nunda, NY 888-800-8075
Organic Gourmet
Sherman Oaks, CA 800-400-7772
Organic Planet
San Francisco, CA 415-765-5590
RFI Ingredients
Blauvelt, NY 800-962-7663
Roberts Seed
Axtell, NE 308-743-2565
Royal Angelus Macaroni
Chino, CA 909-627-7312
St Mary's & Ankeny Lakes Wild Rice Company
Salem, OR 503-363-3241
Sun Garden Growers
Bard, CA 800-228-4690
Sure Fresh Produce
Santa Maria, CA 888-423-5379
Tuscarora Organic Growers Cooperative
Hustontown, PA 814-448-2173
Wood's Sugar Bush
Spring Valley, WI 715-772-4656

Beef

Sunnyside Organics
Washington, VA 540-675-2627

Fruit

Kozlowski Farms
Forestville, CA 800-473-2767
Sun Garden Growers
Bard, CA 800-228-4690

Poultry

Horizon Organic Dairy
Bloomfield, CO 888-494-3020

Produce

Argee Corporation
Santee, CA 800-449-3030
Pack Ryt, Inc.
La Quinta, CA 770-771-8880
Price Cold Storage & Packing Company
Yakima, WA 509-966-4110

Fruits

Atwater Foods
Lyndonville, NY
California Custom Fruits & Flavors
Irwindale, CA 877-558-0056
Emerling International Foods
Buffalo, NY 716-833-7381

We supply food manufacturers and food service customers worldwide (since 1988) with bulk ingredients including: Fruits & Vegetables; Juice Concentrates; Herbs & Spices; Oils & Vinegars; Flavors & Colors; Honey & Molasses. We also produce PURE MAPLE SYRUP.

Fine Dried Foods International
Santa Cruz, CA 831-426-1413
Global Organics
Arlington, MA 781-648-8844
Golden Town Apple Products
Rougemont, QC 519-599-6300
Hallcrest Vineyards
Felton, CA 831-335-4441
Hialeah Products Company
Hollywood, FL 800-923-3379
Made in Nature
Fresno, CA 800-906-7426
Organic Planet
San Francisco, CA 415-765-5590
Price Cold Storage & Packing Company
Yakima, WA 509-966-4110
Setton International Foods
Commack, NY 800-227-4397
Solana Gold Organics
Sebastopol, CA 800-459-1121
Sunshine Farm & Gardens
Renick, WV 304-497-2208
Unique Ingredients
Naches, WA 509-653-1991

Ingredients

Garuda International
Exeter, CA 559-594-4380
Global Organics
Arlington, MA 781-648-8844
Harten Corporation
Fairfield, NJ 866-642-7836
Marroquin Organic International
Santa Cruz, CA 831-423-3442
SK Foods International
Fargo, ND 701-356-4106

Natural

American Health & Nutrition
Ann Arbor, MI 734-677-5570
Arico Natural Foods
Beaverton, OR 503-259-0871
Baker
Milford, NJ 800-995-3989
Cache Creek Foods
Woodland, CA 530-662-1764
California Custom Fruits & Flavors
Irwindale, CA 877-558-0056
Clofine Dairy & Food Products
Linwood, NJ 800-441-1001
Earthrise Nutritionals
Irvine, CA 800-949-7473
Ethical Naturals
San Anselmo, CA 415-459-4454
GKI Foods
Brighton, MI 248-486-0055
Global Organics
Arlington, MA 781-648-8844
Horner International
Raleigh, NC 919-787-3112
Innovative Food Solutions LLC
Columbus, OH 800-884-3314
International Foods
Bloomfield, NJ 800-225-1449
Larabar
Denver, CO 800-543-2147
Main Street Gourmet
Cuyahoga Falls, OH 800-533-6246
Main Street Muffins
Cuyahoga Falls, OH 800-533-6246
Organic Planet
San Francisco, CA 415-765-5590
Pasta Prima
Benicia, CA 707-746-6888
Quality Naturally! Foods
City of Industry, CA 888-498-6986
Seitenbacher America LLC
Odessa, FL 727-376-3000
Sure Fresh Produce
Santa Maria, CA 888-423-5379
Unique Ingredients
Naches, WA 509-653-1991
Vegetable Juices
Chicago, IL 888-776-9752
Wine Country Chef LLC
Hidden Valley Lake, CA 707-322-0406
Your Bar Factory
LaSalle, QC 888-366-0258

Antioxidants

A&B Ingredients
Fairfield, NJ 973-227-1390

Rice Starch

A&B Ingredients
Fairfield, NJ 973-227-1390

Flour

A&B Ingredients
Fairfield, NJ 973-227-1390
Domino Specialty Ingredients
West Palm Beach, FL 800-446-9763

Vegetables

Emerling International Foods
Buffalo, NY 716-833-7381

We supply food manufacturers and food service customers worldwide (since 1988) with bulk ingredients including: Fruits & Vegetables; Juice Concentrates; Herbs & Spices; Oils & Vinegars; Flavors & Colors; Honey & Molasses. We also produce PURE MAPLE SYRUP.

Global Organics
Arlington, MA 781-648-8844
Made in Nature
Fresno, CA 800-906-7426
Organic Valley
La Farge, WI 608-625-2602
Pleasant Grove Farms
Pleasant Grove, CA 916-655-3391
R&J Farms
West Salem, OH 419-846-3179
Sno Pac Foods
Caledonia, MN 800-533-2215

Vegetable Juices
Chicago, IL 888-776-9752

Survival Foods

AlpineAire Foods
Rocklin, CA 800-322-6325
Food Reserves
Concordia, MO 800-944-1511
Hialeah Products Company
Hollywood, FL 800-923-3379

Vegetarian Products

Adventist Book & Food
Trenton, NJ 800-765-6955
Caribbean Food Delights
Tappan, NY 845-398-3000
CHS
Inver Grove Heights, MN 800-232-3639
Cricklewood Soyfoods
Mertztown, PA 610-682-4109
Dixie Usa
Tomball, TX 800-233-3668
Earth Island Natural Foods
Canoga Park, CA 818-725-2820
Eco-Cuisine
Boulder, CO 303-444-6634
Franklin Farms
North Franklin, CT 800-204-1503
Innovative Food Solutions LLC
Columbus, OH 800-884-3314
Jyoti Cruisine India Gourmail Inc
Berwyn, PA 610-296-4620
Lisanatti Foods
Oregon City, OR 866-864-3922
Local Tofu
Nyack, NY 845-727-6393
Marjon Specialty Foods, Inc
Plant City, FL 813-752-3482
Mon Cuisine
Flushing, NY 877-666-8348
ND Labs Inc
Lynbrook, NY 888-263-5227
Oogolow Enterprises
Chico, CA 800-816-6873
Pasta USA
Spokane, WA 800-456-2084
Pulmuone Wildwood
Fullerton, CA 641-236-5170
Salvati Foods
Hicksville, NY 516-932-8300
Savannah Food Company
Savannah, TN 800-795-2550
Sweet Earth Natural Foods
Pacific Grove, CA 800-737-3311
Turtle Island Foods
Hood River, OR 800-508-8100
Twin Oaks Community Foods
Louisa, VA 540-894-4062
Unique Ingredients
Naches, WA 509-653-1991
Vegetable Juices
Chicago, IL 888-776-9752
VeggieLand
Parsippany, NJ 888-808-5540
Vegi-Deli
San Rafael, CA 888-473-3667
Vitasoy USA
Ayer, MA 978-772-6880
Wine Country Chef LLC
Hidden Valley Lake, CA 707-322-0406
Worthington Foods
Zanesville, OH 800-535-5644
Your Bar Factory
LaSalle, QC 888-366-0258

Burgers

Dixie Usa
Tomball, TX 800-233-3668
Quaker Maid Meats
Reading, PA 610-376-1500
Sunshine Burger Company
Fort Atkinson, WI
Ungars Food Products
Elmwood Park, NJ 201-703-1300
Vitasoy USA
Ayer, MA 978-772-6880

Patties

Caribbean Food Delights
Tappan, NY 845-398-3000
ConAgra Beef Company
Hyrum, UT 435-245-6456
Gardenburger
Clearfield, UT 801-773-8855
Hampton House J.D. Sweid Ltd
Burnaby, BC 800-665-4355
Innovative Food Solutions LLC
Columbus, OH 800-884-3314
Neese Country Sausage
Greensboro, NC 800-632-1010
Tami Great Food
Monsey, NY 732-803-6366
Vitasoy USA
Ayer, MA 978-772-6880

Specialty Processed Foods

Barbecue Products (See also Specific Foods)

A. Lassonde, Inc.
Rougemont, QC ... 888-477-6663

Allied Old English
Port Reading, NJ ... 732-636-2060

Arbor Hill Grapery
Naples, NY ... 800-554-7553

Art's Tamales
Metamora, IL ... 309-367-2850

Aunt Kitty's Foods
Vineland, NJ ... 856-691-2100

Baker's Rib
Dallas, TX ... 214-748-5433

Bartush-Schnitzius Foods Company
Lewisville, TX ... 972-219-1270

Baumer Foods
Metairie, LA ... 504-482-5761

BBQ Bunch
Kansas City, MO ... 816-941-4534

Big B Distributors
Evansville, IN ... 812-425-5235

Black's Barbecue
Lockhart, TX ... 512-398-2712

Broadaway Ham Company
Jonesboro, AR ... 870-932-6688

Cafe Tequila
San Francisco, CA ... 415-264-0106

California-Antilles Trading Consortium
San Diego, CA ... 800-330-6450

Calumet Diversified Meat Company
Pleasant Prairie, WI ... 262-947-7200

Captain Bob's Jet Fuel
Fort Wayne, IN ... 877-486-6468

Carolina Cupboard
Hillsborough, NC ... 800-400-3441

Carolina Treet
Wilmington, NC ... 800-616-6344

Casa Visco Finer Food Company
Schenectady, NY ... 888-607-2823

Castleberry's
Vineland, NJ ... 856-691-2100

Catskill Mountain Specialties
Saugerties, NY ... 800-311-3473

Caughman's Meat Plant
Lexington, SC ... 803-356-0076

Chandler Foods
Greensboro, NC ... 800-537-6219

CHS, Inc.
Inner Grove Heights, MN ... 800-232-3639

Cinnabar Specialty Foods
Prescott, AZ ... 866-293-6433

Clements Foods Company
Oklahoma City, OK ... 800-654-8355

Colgin Companies
Dallas, TX ... 888-226-5446

Consumers Vinegar & Spice Company
Chicago, IL ... 773-376-4100

Cookies Food Products
Wall Lake, IA ... 800-331-4995

Corky's Bar-B-Q
Memphis, TN ... 800-926-7597

Couch's Original Sauce
Jonesboro, AR ... 800-264-7535

Creative Foodworks
San Antonio, TX ... 210-212-4761

Culinary Standards Corporation
Louisville, KY ... 800-778-3434

Curly's Foods
Edina, MN ... 800-722-1127

D & D Foods
Columbus, GA ... 706-322-4507

Dankworth Packing Company
Ballinger, TX ... 325-365-3552

Delta BBQ Sauce Company
Stockton, CA ... 209-472-9284

Dillard's Bar-B-Q Sauce
Durham, NC ... 919-544-1587

Dorina/So-Good
Union, IL ... 815-923-2144

Dorothy Dawson Foods Products
Jackson, MI ... 517-788-9830

El-Rey Foods
Ferguson, MO ... 314-521-3113

Favorite Foods
Burnaby, BC ... 604-420-5100

Felbro Food Products
Los Angeles, CA ... 800-335-2761

Figaro Company
Mesquite, TX ... 972-288-3587

Food Concentrate Corporation
Oklahoma City, OK ... 405-840-5633

Food Specialties
Indianapolis, IN ... 317-271-0862

Fremont Authentic Brands
Fremont, OH ... 419-334-8995

French's Flavor Ingredients
Springfield, MO ... 800-437-3624

Fry Krisp Food Products
Jackson, MI ... 517-784-8531

Garden Complements
Kansas City, MO ... 800-966-1091

Gary's Frozen Foods
Lubbock, TX ... 806-745-1933

Gaucho Foods
Fayetteville, IL ... 877-677-2282

Gayle's Sweet 'N Sassy Foods
Beverly Hills, CA ... 310-246-1792

Golden Specialty Foods
Norwalk, CA ... 562-802-2537

Golden Whisk
South San Francisco, CA ... 800-660-5222

Golding Farms Foods
Winston Salem, NC ... 336-766-6161

Gumpert's Canada
Mississauga, ON ... 800-387-9324

Hampton House J.D. Sweid Ltd
Burnaby, BC ... 800-665-4355

Harold Food Company
Charlotte, NC ... 704-588-8061

Head Country Food Products
Ponca City, OK ... 888-762-1227

Heinz Portion Control
Mason, OH ... 800-547-8924

Hollman Foods
Chicago, IL ... 888-926-2879

Hormel Foods Corporation
Austin, MN ... 800-523-4635

House of Webster
Rogers, AR ... 800-369-4641

J&B Sausage Company
Waelder, TX ... 830-788-7511

J.D. Mullen Company
Palestine, IL ... 618-586-2727

J.N. Bech
Elk Rapids, MI ... 800-232-4583

JMS Specialty Foods
Ripon, WI ... 800-535-5437

Johnny Harris Famous Barbecue Sauce
Savannah, GA ... 912-354-8828

King Kold Meats
Englewood, OH ... 800-836-2797

Kozlowski Farms
Forestville, CA ... 800-473-2767

Kraft Foods
Garland, TX ... 972-272-7511

Kubla Khan Food Company
Portland, OR ... 503-234-7494

L&S Packing Company
Farmingdale, NY ... 800-286-6487

Lea & Perrins
Fair Lawn, NJ ... 800-289-5797

Lees Sausage Company
Orangeburg, SC ... 803-534-5517

Lendy's
Virginia Beach, VA ... 757-491-3511

Lounsbury Foods
Toronto, ON ... 416-656-6330

M.A. Gedney
Chaska, MN ... 952-448-2612

Mad Will's Food Company
Auburn, CA ... 888-275-9455

Magic Seasoning Blends
New Orleans, LA ... 800-457-2857

Mansmith's Barbecue
San Jn Bautista, CA ... 800-626-7648

Mar-K Anchor Bar Hot Sauces
Buffalo, NY ... 71- 8-6 89

McCutcheon's Apple Products
Frederick, MD ... 800-888-7537

Mitchell Foods
Barbourville, KY ... 888-202-9745

Moonlite Bar Bq Inn
Owensboro, KY ... 800-322-8989

Mrs. Clark's Foods
Ankeny, IA ... 800-736-5674

Juices, salad dressings and sauces.

New Business Corporation
Gary, IN ... 800-742-8435

Newly Weds Foods
Chicago, IL ... 800-647-9314

Ninety Six Canning Company
Ninety Six, SC ... 864-543-2700

O'Brian Brothers Food
Cincinnati, OH ... 513-791-9909

Original Chili Bowl
Tulsa, OK ... 918-628-0225

Ott Food Products
Carthage, MO ... 800-866-2585

Ottman Meat Company
New York, NY ... 212-879-4160

Pacific Poultry Company
Honolulu, HI ... 808-841-2828

Palmieri Food Products
New Haven, CT ... 800-845-5447

Paradise Products Corporation
Boca Raton, FL ... 800-826-1235

Piggie Park Enterprises
West Columbia, SC ... 800-628-7423

Porinos Gourmet Food
Central Falls, RI ... 800-826-3938

Produits Ronald
St. Damase, QC ... 800-465-0118

Randag & Associates Inc
Elmhurst, IL ... 630-530-2830

Red Gold
Elwood, IN ... 877-748-9798

Rivertown Foods
Saint Louis, MO ... 800-844-3210

Riverview Foods
Warsaw, KY ... 859-567-5211

Robinson's Barbecue Sauce Company
Oak Park, IL ... 708-383-8452

Roos Foods
Kenton, DE ... 800-343-3642

Rosmarino Foods/R.Z. Humbert Company
Odessa, FL ... 888-926-9053

Sadler's Smokehouse
Henderson, TX ... 903-657-5581

Savoie's Sausage & Food Products
Opelousas, LA ... 337-948-4115

Schiff Food Products
North Bergen, NJ ... 201-868-6800

Schlotterbeck & Foss Company
Portland, ME ... 800-777-4666

Scott's Sauce Company
Goldsboro, NC ... 800-734-7282

Southern Ray's Foods
Miami Beach, FL ... 800-972-8237

Steel's Gourmet Foods, Ltd.
Bridgeport, PA ... 800-678-3357

Suzanna's Kitchen
Duluth, GA ... 800-241-2455

Sweet Baby Ray's
Chicago, IL ... 877-729-2229

T. Marzetti Company
Columbus, OH ... 614-846-2232

T.W. Garner Food Company
Winston Salem, NC ... 800-476-7383

Tenn Valley Ham Company
Paris, TN ... 731-642-9740

Thompson's Fine Foods
Shoreview, MN ... 800-807-0025

Todd's
Des Moines, IA ... 800-247-5363

Travis Meats
Powell, TN ... 800-247-7606

Triple H Food Processors
Riverside, CA ... 951-352-5700

Triple K Manufacturing Company
Shenandoah, IA ... 888-987-2824

Triple U Enterprises
Fort Pierre, SD ... 605-567-3624

Tyson Foods Plant
Santa Teresa, NM ... 800-351-8184

Valley Grain Products
Madera, CA....559-675-3400
Vanlaw Food Products
Fullerton, CA....714-870-9091
Ventura Foods
Philadelphia, PA....215-223-8700
Vidalia Sweets Brand
Lyons, GA....912-565-8881
Vietti Foods Company Inc
Nashville, TN....800-240-7864
W & G Marketing Company
Ames, IA....515-233-4774
Webbpak
Trussville, AL....800-655-3500
Wei-Chuan
Bell Gardens, CA....562-372-2020
West Pac
Idaho Falls, ID....800-973-7407
Westin
Omaha, NE....800-228-6098
Wing Nien Company
Hayward, CA....510-487-8877
Wood Brothers
West Columbia, SC....803-796-5146
Woods Smoked Meats
Bowling Green, MO....800-458-8426
Zarda Bar-B-Q & Catering Company
Blue Springs, MO....800-776-7427

Dehydrated Food (See also Specific Foods)

Agvest
Cleveland, OH....216-464-3737
Ailments E.D. Foods Inc.
Pointe Claire, QC....800-267-3333
Alkinco
New York, NY....800-424-7118
American Nut & Chocolate Company
Boston, MA....800-797-6887
Amport Foods
Minneapolis, MN....800-989-5665
Anderson Custom Processing
New Ulm, MN....877-588-4950
Associated Brands Inc.
Medina, NY....800-265-0050
Atlantic Quality Spice &Seasonings
New Brunswick, NJ....800-584-0422
Atrium Biotech
Fairfield, NJ....866-628-2355
Basic American Foods
Blackfoot, ID....800-227-4050
Basic American Foods
Walnut Creek, CA....800-722-2084
Blossom Farm Products
Ridgewood, NJ....800-729-1818
Boghosian Raisin Packing Company
Fowler, CA....559-834-5348
Cagnon Foods Company
Brooklyn, NY....718-647-2244
California Fruit
Sanger, CA....559-266-7117
Caltex Foods
Canoga Park, CA....800-522-5839
Casados Farms
San Juan Pueblo, NM....505-852-2433
Challenge Dairy Products
Dublin, CA....800-733-2479
Chef Merito
Encino, CA....800-637-4861
Chia I Foods Company
South El Monte, CA....626-401-3038
Chooljian Brothers Packing Company
Sanger, CA....559-875-5501
Chukar Cherries
Prosser, WA....800-624-9544
Clofine Dairy & Food Products
Linwood, NJ....800-441-1001
Colorado Bean Company/ Greeley Trading
Greeley, CO....888-595-2326
Commercial Creamery Company
Spokane, WA....800-541-0850
Consumers Vinegar & Spice Company
Chicago, IL....773-376-4100
Country Cupboard
Virginia City, NV....775-847-7300
Crystal Foods
Brick, NJ....732-477-0073
Dairy Farmers of America
East Syracuse, NY....315-431-1352
Dairy Farmers of America
Medina, OH....330-670-7800
Dairy King Milk Farms/Foodservice
Whitter, CA....800-900-6455
Dairy-Mix
St Petersburg, FL....727-525-6101
DeFrancesco & Sons
Firebaugh, CA....209-364-7000
Del Rey Packing Company
Del Rey, CA....559-888-2031
Desert Valley Date
Coachella, CA....760-398-0999
Devansoy
Carroll, IA....800-747-8605
Diamond Foods
Fishers, IN....317-845-5534
Dietrich's Milk Products
Reading, PA....800-526-6455
Dismat Corporation
Toledo, OH....419-531-8963
Emerling International Foods
Buffalo, NY....716-833-7381

We supply food manufacturers and food service customers worldwide (since 1988) with bulk ingredients including: Fruits & Vegetables; Juice Concentrates; Herbs & Spices; Oils & Vinegars; Flavors & Colors; Honey & Molasses. We also produce PURE MAPLE SYRUP.

Fig Garden Packing
Fresno, CA....559-275-2191
Fine Dried Foods International
Santa Cruz, CA....831-426-1413
First District Association
Litchfield, MN....320-693-3236
Food Reserves
Concordia, MO....800-944-1511
Foremost Farms
Wilson, WI....715-772-4211
Freeman Industries
Tuckahoe, NY....800-666-6454
Fuji Foods
Browns Summit, NC....336-375-3111
Garden Valley Foods
Sutherlin, OR....541-459-9565
Gilroy Foods
Gilroy, CA....800-921-7502
Global Food Industries
Townville, SC....800-225-4152
Golden Town Apple Products
Rougemont, QC....519-599-6300
Graf Creamery
Bonduel, WI
Green House Fine Herbs
Encinitas, CA....760-942-5371
Henningsen Foods
Omaha, NE....402-330-2500
Henningsen Foods
Purchase, NY....914-701-4020
Henry Broch & Company/APK, Inc.
Libertyville, IL....847-816-6225
Hialeah Products Company
Hollywood, FL....800-923-3379
Honeyville Grain
Salt Lake City, UT....801-972-2168
Humco
Texarkana, TX....903-334-6200
Idaho Pacific Corporation
Ririe, ID....800-238-5503
Idaho Supreme Potatoes
Firth, ID....208-346-6841
Ittels Meats
Howard Lake, MN....320-543-2285
Jasper Wyman & Son
Milbridge, ME....800-341-1758
Jones Produce
Quincy, WA....509-787-3537
Kamish Food Products
Chicago, IL....773-725-6959
Kelley Bean Company
Scottsbluff, NE....308-635-6438
Kozlowski Farms
Forestville, CA....800-473-2767
Kraft Foods
Albany, MN....320-845-2131
Land O'Lakes, Inc.
Arden Hills, MN....800-328-9680
Larsen Farms
Hamer, ID....208-662-5501
Larsen of Idaho
Hamer, ID....800-767-6104
Leroux Creek Foods
Hotchkiss, CO....877-970-5670
Lone Star Beef Jerky Company
Lubbock, TX....806-762-8833
Made in Nature
Fresno, CA....800-906-7426
Main Street Ingredients
La Crosse, WI....800-359-2345
Maine Wild Blueberry Company
Cherryfield, ME....800-243-4005
Maruchan
Irvine, CA....949-789-2300
Master Mix
Placentia, CA....714-524-1698
Mayacamas Fine Foods
Sonoma, CA....800-826-9621
Mercer Processing
Modesto, CA....209-529-0150
Mojave Foods Corporation
Commerce, CA....323-890-8900
Morris J. Golombeck
Brooklyn, NY....718-284-3505
Niagara Foods
Middleport, NY....716-735-7722
North Bay Trading Company
Brule, WI....800-348-0164
Northern Feed & Bean Company
Lucerne, CO....800-316-2326
Oakland Bean Cleaning & Storage
Knights Landing, CA....530-735-6203
Ontario Foods Exports
Mississauga, ON....888-466-2372
Oregon Potato Company
Boardman, OR....800-336-6311
Pack Ryt, Inc.
La Quinta, CA....770-771-8880
Paisano Food Products
Elk Grove Village, IL....800-672-4726
Pasta USA
Spokane, WA....800-456-2084
Pines International
Lawrence, KS....800-697-4637
Plainview Milk Products Cooperative
Plainview, MN....507-534-3872
Pro Form Labs
Orinda, CA....925-299-9000
Producers Cooperative
Olathe, CO....970-874-9736
Produits Alimentaires Berthelet
Laval, QC....450-665-6100
Protient (Land O Lakes)
St Paul, MN....800-328-9680
Quality Brands
Deland, FL....888-676-2700
Quality Ingredients Corporation
Burnsville, MN....952-898-4002
Ramos Orchards
Winters, CA....530-795-4748
Ramsen
Lakeville, MN....952-431-0400
Red River Foods
Richmond, VA....800-443-6637
Reinhart Foods
Markham, ON....905-754-3500
Rinehart Meat Processing
Branson, MO....417-334-2044
Russell E. Womack
Lubbock, TX....877-787-3559
Schiff Food Products
North Bergen, NJ....201-868-6800
Seneca Foods
Marion, NY....315-926-8100
Serv-Agen Corporation
Cherry Hill, NJ....856-663-6966
Shields Date Gardens
Indio, CA....800-414-2555
Smeltzer Orchard Company
Frankfort, MI....231-882-4421
Smuggler's Kitchen
Dundee, FL....800-604-6793
Solana Gold Organics
Sebastopol, CA....800-459-1121
Somerset Industries
Spring House, PA....800-883-8728
SOUPerior Bean & Spice Company
Vancouver, WA....800-878-7687
South Mill Distribution
Kennett Square, PA....610-444-4800
Spice Hunter
San Luis Obispo, CA....800-444-3061
Spreda Group
Louisville, KY....502-426-9411
St. Ours & Company
Norwell, MA....781-331-8520

Stapleton-Spence PackingCompany
San Jose, CA....................800-297-8815
Sterigenics International
Los Angeles, CA....................800-472-4508
Sugar Foods
Sun Valley, CA....................818-768-7900
Tastee Apple Inc
Newcomerstown, OH....................800-262-7753
Total Ultimate Foods
Columbus, OH....................800-333-0732
Tova Industries
Louisville, KY....................888-532-8682
Trinidad Benham Company
Denver, CO....................303-220-1400
Trinidad/Benham Corporation
Patterson, CA....................209-892-9051
Triple U Enterprises
Fort Pierre, SD....................605-567-3624
Tropical
Charlotte, NC....................800-220-1413
Tropical
Columbus, OH....................800-538-3941
Tropical
Marietta, GA....................800-544-3762
Unique Ingredients
Naches, WA....................509-653-1991
United Dairymen of Arizona
Tempe, AZ....................480-966-7211
Ursula's Island Farms
Seattle, WA....................206-762-3113
US Foods
Lincoln, NE....................402-470-2021
Valley View Packing Company
San Jose, CA....................408-289-8300
Van Drunen Farms
Momence, IL....................815-472-3537
Verhoff Alfalfa Mills
Ottawa, OH....................800-834-8563
VIP Foods
Flushing, NY....................718-821-5330
Vogue Cuisine
Sunnyvale, CA....................888-236-4144
Vrymeer Commodities
St Charles, IL....................630-584-0069
W&G Flavors
Hunt Valley, MD....................410-771-6606
WA Bean & Sons
Bangor, ME....................800-649-1958
Washington Potato Company
Warden, WA....................509-349-8803
Welsh Farms
Edison, NJ....................800-221-0663
Westin
Omaha, NE....................800-228-6098
Westlam Foods
Chino, CA....................800-722-9519

Fermented Products (See also Specific Foods)

Roland Industries
Saint Louis, MO....................800-325-1183

Freeze Dried Food (See also Specific Foods)

Emerling International Foods
Buffalo, NY....................716-833-7381

We supply food manufacturers and food service customers worldwide (since 1988) with bulk ingredients including: Fruits & Vegetables; Juice Concentrates; Herbs & Spices; Oils & Vinegars; Flavors & Colors; Honey & Molasses. We also produce PURE MAPLE SYRUP.

Food Reserves
Concordia, MO....................800-944-1511
Freeze-Dry Products
Santa Rosa, CA....................707-547-1776
Hanover Foods Corp
Hanover, PA....................717-632-6000
Hanover Foods Corporation
Hanover, PA....................717-632-6000
L.K. Bowman Company
Hanover, PA....................800-853-1919
Mark-Lynn Foods
Bremen, GA....................800-327-0162
SafeTrek Foods
Bozeman, MT....................406-586-4840
Unique Ingredients
Naches, WA....................509-653-1991
Van Drunen Farms
Momence, IL....................815-472-3537
Vivolac Cultures Corporation
Indianapolis, IN....................317-356-8460

Frozen Foods (See also Specific Foods)

A Natural Harvest Restaurant
Chicago, IL....................773-363-3939
A&G Food & Liquors
Chicago, IL....................773-994-1541
A.C. Petersen Farms
West Hartford, CT....................860-233-8483
Abbotsford Growers Co-operative
Abbotsford, BC....................604-864-0022
Ace Food
Bayou La Batre, AL....................800-884-0741
Acme Steak & Seafood Company
Youngstown, OH....................330-270-8000
Aglamesis Brothers
Cincinnati, OH....................513-531-5196
Agland, Inc.
Eaton, CO....................800-433-4688
Agripac
Denver, CO....................503-363-9255
Agropur Cooperative Agro-Alimentaire
Granby, QC....................800-363-5686
Agvest
Franklin, ME....................207-565-3303
Agvest
Cleveland, OH....................216-464-3737
Ajinomato Frozen Foods USA
Portland, OR....................503-286-5869
Ajinomoto Frozen Foods USA
Portland, OR....................503-286-6548
Al Gelato Bornay
Franklin Park, IL....................847-455-5355
Al Pete Meats
Muncie, IN....................765-288-8817
Al-Rite Fruits & Syrups
Miami, FL....................305-652-2540
Aladdin Bakers
Brooklyn, NY....................718-499-1818
Alamance Foods/Triton Water Company
Burlington, NC....................800-476-9111
Alaska Seafood Company
Los Angeles, CA....................213-626-1212
Alaskan Gourmet Seafoods
Anchorage, AK....................800-288-3740
Alati-Caserta Desserts
Montreal, QC....................514-271-3013
Alexia Foods
Long Island City, NY....................718-937-0100
Alfredo's Italian Foods Manufacturing Company
Quincy, MA....................617-479-6360
Aliotti Wholesale Fish Company
Monterey, CA....................831-375-2881
All Round Foods
Westbury, NY....................516-338-1888
Alle Processing Corporation
Maspeth, NY....................800-245-5620
Allen Canning Company
Siloam Springs, AR....................800-234-2553
Allen Family Foods
Seaford, DE....................302-629-9136
Allen's Blueberry Freezer
Ellsworth, ME....................207-667-5561
Alpenrose Dairy Farms
Portland, OR....................503-244-1133
Alphin Brothers
Dunn, NC....................800-672-4502
Alyeska Seafoods
Seattle, WA....................206-547-2100
Amano Fish Cake Factory
Hilo, HI....................808-935-5555
Amberwave Foods
Oakmont, PA....................412-828-3040
American Classic Ice Cream Company
Bay Shore, NY....................631-666-1000
American Seafoods Group
Seattle, WA....................800-275-2019
American Seafoods International
New Bedford, MA....................800-343-8046
Anchor Food Products/ McCain Foods
Appleton, WI....................920-734-0627
Andrew & Williamson Sales Company
San Diego, CA....................619-661-6000
Angy's Food Products Inc.
Westfield, MA....................413-572-1010
Annie's Frozen Yogurt
Minneapolis, MN....................800-969-9648
Appert's Foodservice
St Cloud, MN....................800-225-3883
Appleton Produce Company
Weiser, ID....................208-414-3352
AquaCuisine
Eagle, ID....................208-323-2782
Arista Industries
Wilton, CT....................800-255-6457
Arkansas Poly
N Little Rock, AR....................800-364-5036
Arkansas Refrigerated Services
Fort Smith, AR....................479-783-1006
Armbrust Meats
Medford, WI....................715-748-3102
Arrowac Fisheries
Seattle, WA....................206-282-5655
Art's Tamales
Metamora, IL....................309-367-2850
Artuso Pastry Foods Corp
Mt Vernon, NY....................914-663-8806
Artuso Pastry Shop
Bronx, NY....................718-367-2515
ASC Seafood
Largo, FL....................800-876-3474
Aspen Foods
Park Ridge, IL....................847-384-5940
Assouline & Ting
Huntingdon Valley, PA....................800-521-4491
Athens Pastries & Frozen Foods
Cleveland, OH....................800-837-5683
Atkinson Milling Company
Selma, NC....................800-948-5707
Atlantic Blueberry Company
Hammonton, NJ....................609-561-8600
Atlantic Meat Company
Savannah, GA....................912-964-8511
Atlantic Premium Brands
Northbrook, IL....................847-412-6200
Atlantic Queen Seafoods Limited
St Josephs, NL....................709-739-6668
Atlantic Veal & Lamb
Brooklyn, NY....................800-222-8325
Aurora Frozen Foods Division
Saint Louis, MO....................314-801-2300
Austin Packaging Company
Austin, MN....................507-433-6623
Austin Special Foods Company
Austin, TX....................866-372-8663
Avalon Foodservice, Inc.
Canal Fulton, OH....................800-362-0622
Avanti Food Company
Walnut, IL....................800-243-3739
Avo King Intl.
Orange, CA....................800-286-5464
Awrey Bakeries
Livonia, MI....................800-950-2253
B&D Foods
Boise, ID....................208-344-1183
Badger Best Pizzas
Green Bay, WI....................920-336-6464
Baja Foods
Chicago, IL....................773-376-9030
Baker Boy Bake Shop
Dickinson, ND....................800-437-2008
Baker Boys
Calgary, AB....................877-246-6036
Baker's Point Fisheries
Oyster Pond Jeddore, NS....................902-845-2347
Bakery Chef
Louisville, KY....................800-594-0203
Balboa Dessert Company
Santa Ana, CA....................800-974-9699
Ballas Egg Products Corporation
Zanesville, OH....................740-453-0386
Bama Frozen Dough
Tulsa, OK....................800-756-2262
Bandon Bay Fisheries
Bandon, OR....................541-347-4454
Barber Foods
Portland, ME....................800-577-2595
Barnes Ice Cream Company
Manchester, ME
Barnum & Bagel Frozen Soup
Skokie, IL....................847-676-4466
Basic American Foods
Blackfoot, ID....................800-227-4050
Bavarian Specialty Foods
Sun Valley, CA....................310-212-6199
Bay Oceans Sea Foods
Garibaldi, OR....................503-322-3316
Bayou Land Seafood
Breaux Bridge, LA....................337-667-6118

Beaver Street Fisheries
Jacksonville, FL 800-874-6426
Beck's Waffles of Oklahoma
Shawnee, OK 800-646-6254
Becker Food Company
Milwaukee, WI 414-964-5353
Behm Blueberry Farms
Grand Haven, MI 616-846-1650
Bell Buoy Crab Company
Seaside, OR. 800-529-2722
Bellisio Foods, Inc.
Duluth, MN. 800-368-7337
Ben E. Keith DFW
Fort Worth, TX 877-317-6100
Bensons Bakery
Bogart, GA 800-888-6059
Bernardi Italian Foods Company
Bloomsburg, PA 570-389-5500
Bernie's Foods
Brooklyn, NY 718-417-6677
Best Maid Cookie Company
River Falls, WI 888-444-0322
Beta Pure Foods
Aptos, CA 831-685-6565
BG Smith Sons Oyster
Sharps, VA 877-483-8279
Biagio's Banquets
Chicago, IL 800-392-2837
Bill Mack's Homemade Ice Cream
Dover, PA 717-292-1931
Birch Street Seafoods
Digby, NS 902-245-6551
Birchwood Foods
Kenosha, WI 800-541-1685
Birdie Pak Products
Chicago, IL 773-247-5293
Birdsall Ice Cream Company
Mason City, IA 641-423-5365
Blakely Freezer Locker
Thomasville, GA. 229-723-3622
Bland Farms
Reidsville, GA 800-752-0206
Blend Pak
Bloomfield, KY 502-252-8000
Blount Seafood Corporation
Fall River, MA 774-888-1300
Blue Ridge Poultry
Athens, GA 706-546-6767
Blue Wave Seafoods
Port Mouton, NS. 902-683-2044
BlueWater Seafoods
Lachine, QC 888-560-2539
Bob's Custom Cuts
Bonnyville, AB 780-826-2138
Boboli Intl. Inc.
Stockton, CA. 209-473-3507
Bocconcino Food Products
Moonachie, NJ 201-933-7474
Bodin Foods
New Iberia, LA 337-367-1344
Boekhout Farms
Ontario, NY. 315-524-4041
Bolner's Fiesta Products
San Antonio, TX. 210-734-6404
Bon Secour Fisheries
Bon Secour, AL. 800-633-6854
Bonnie Doon Ice Cream Corporation
Elkhart, IN. 574-264-3390
Bornstein Seafoods
Bellingham, WA 360-734-7990
Bosell Foods
Cleveland, OH 216-991-7600
Boston Chowda Company
Lowell, MA. 800-992-0054
Bottineau Coop Creamery
Bottineau, ND. 701-228-2216
Brady Farms
West Olive, MI 616-842-3916
Brakebush Brothers
Westfield, WI 800-933-2121
Braun Seafood Company
Cutchogue, NY 631-734-6700
Breakfast at Brennan's
New Orleans, LA 800-888-9932
Bridgford Foods Corporation
Anaheim, CA 800-527-2105
Brighams
Arlington, MA 800-274-4426
Bright Harvest Sweet Potato Company
Clarksville, AR 800-793-7440
Broadleaf Venison Usa
Vernon, CA 800-336-3844

Brom Food Group
St. Laurent, QC. 514-744-5152
Brook Locker Plant
Brook, IN 219-275-2611
Brooklyn Bagel Company
Staten Island, NY 800-349-3055
Brooks Food Group Corporate Office
Bedford, VA 800-873-4934
Brookview Farms
Archbold, OH 419-445-6366
Broughton Foods
Marietta, OH. 800-283-2479
Brown Produce Company
Farina, IL. 618-245-3301
Brown's Ice Cream
Minneapolis, MN 612-378-1075
Brownie Products Company
Terre Haute, IN
Browns Dairy
Valparaiso, IN 219-464-4141
Browns' Ice Cream Company
Bowling Green, KY 270-843-9882
Bruno Specialty Foods
West Sayville, NY. 631-589-1700
Bubbies Homemade Ice Cream
Aiea, HI. 808-487-7218
Buck's Spumoni Company
Milford, CT. 203-874-2007
Bueno Food Products
Albuquerque, NM. 800-888-7336
Bullock's Country Meats
Westminster, MD 410-848-6786
Buns & Things Bakery
Charlottetown, PE. 902-892-2600
Buono Beef Co
Philadelphia, PA 215-463-3600
Burke Corporation
Nevada, IA 800-654-1152

Always make it your best® with Burke fully cooked meats. We specialize in Italian sausage, beef, and pork toppings, meatballs, taco meats, shredded meats, pepperoni, bacon, Canadian-style bacon, chicken and beef strips. Additionally, we offer a variety of specialty products: Hand-Pinched Style® brand toppings, chorizo, gyro topping, andouille sausage, and breakfast patties and links.

Bush Brothers Provision Company
West Palm Beach, FL 800-327-1345
Butterfield Foods Company
Butterfield, MN. 507-956-5103
Buxton Foods
Buxton, ND. 800-726-8057
Buzz Food Service
Charleston, WV 304-925-4781
C.F. Gollott & Son Seafood
Biloxi, MS. 866-846-3474
Caesar's Pasta Products
Blackwood, NJ 856-227-2585
Cahoon Farms
Wolcott, NY 315-594-8081
California Brands Flavors
Oakland, CA 800-348-0111
Callis Seafood
Lancaster, VA 804-462-7634
Camino Real Foods
Vernon, CA 800-421-6201
Campbell Soup Company
Camden, NJ. 800-257-8443
Campbell Soup Company of Canada
Listowel, ON. 800-575-7687
Canada Safeway Limited
Abbotsford, BC. 604-854-1191
Captain Ken's Foods
St Paul, MN. 651-298-0071
Captain Ottis Seafood
Morehead City, NC. 252-247-3569
Carando Gourmet Frozen Foods
Agawam, MA 888-227-2636
Carbolite Foods
Evansville, IN 888-524-3314
Caribbean Food Delights
Tappan, NY. 845-398-3000
Caribbean Products
Baltimore, MD 410-235-7700
Carla's Pasta
South Windsor, CT 800-957-2782
Carolina Blueberry Association
Garland, NC 910-588-4355
Carolina Foods
Charlotte, NC 800-234-0441

Carousel Cakes
Nanuet, NY 800-659-2253
Carriere Foods Inc
Saint-Denis-Sur-Richelie, QC 450-787-3411
Carrington Foods
Saraland, AL. 251-675-9700
Casa Di Bertacchi
Vineland, NJ 800-818-9261
Casa di Carfagna
Columbus, OH 614-846-6340
Casa DiLisio Products
Mt Kisco, NY 800-247-4199
Castleberry's
Vineland, NJ 856-691-2100
Cateraid
Howell, MI 800-508-8217
Cathay Foods Corporation
Boston, MA. 617-427-1507
Cavendish Farms
Jamestown, ND. 888-284-5687
Cavendish Farms
Dieppe, NB 888-883-7437
CBC Foods
Little River, KS. 800-276-4770
Cedar Crest Specialties
Cedarburg, WI. 800-877-8341
Cedar Key Aquaculture Farms
Mango, FL. 888-252-6735
Cedar Lake Foods
Cedar Lake, MI. 800-246-5039
Cedaredge Meats
Cedaredge, CO 970-856-6113
Cedarlane Foods
Carson, CA 310-886-7720
Centreside Dairy
Renfrew, ON. 613-432-2914
Challenge Dairy Products
Dublin, CA 800-733-2479
Chandler Foods
Greensboro, NC 800-537-6219
Chang Food Company
Garden Grove, CA 714-265-9990
Chases Lobster Pound
Port Howe, NS 902-243-2408
Chateau Food Products
Cicero, IL 708-863-4207
Chef America
Chatsworth, CA. 818-718-8111
Chef America East
Mount Sterling, KY 859-498-4300
Chef Francisco of Pennsylvania
King of Prussia, PA. 610-265-7400
Chef Hans Gourmet Foods
Monroe, LA. 800-890-4267
Cher-Make Sausage Company
Manitowoc, WI. 800-242-7679
Cherbogue Fisheries
Yarmouth, NS 902-742-9157
Cherry Growers
Grawn, MI. 231-276-9241
Cherry Hill Orchards Pelham
Fenwick, ON. 905-892-3782
Cherry Lane Frozen Fruits
Vineland Station, ON 877-243-7796
Chester W. Howeth & Brother
Crisfield, MD 410-968-1398
Chewys Rugulach
San Diego, CA 800-241-3456
Chicago Meat Authority
Chicago, IL 773-254-3811
Chill & Moore
Fort Worth, TX 800-676-3055
Chincoteague Seafood Company
Parsonsburg, MD 443-260-4800
Chloe Foods Corporation
Brooklyn, NY 718-827-9000
Chocolate Shoppe Ice Cream Company
Madison, WI. 608-221-8640
Chocolaterie Bernard Callebaut
Calgary, AB. 800-661-8367
Choctaw Maid Farms
Carthage, MS 601-298-5300
CHR Foods
Watsonville, CA 831-728-0157
Christie Cookie Company
Nashville, TN 615-242-3817
Chungs Gourmet Foods
Houston, TX 713-741-2118
Ciao Bella Gelato Company
Irvington, NJ. 800-435-2863
Cinderella Cheese Cake Company
Riverside, NJ. 856-461-6302

Citrico
Northbrook, IL 888-625-8516
Citrus Citrosuco North America
Lake Wales, FL 800-356-4592
Citrus Service
Winter Garden, FL 407-656-4999
Clark Foodservice
Elk Grove Vlg, IL 800-504-3663
Clark Foodservice
Elk Grove Vlg, IL 847-956-1730
Classic Delight
Saint Marys, OH 800-274-9828
Clear Springs Foods
Buhl, ID 800-635-8211
Clearwater Fine Foods
Bedford, NS 902-443-0550
Cleugh's Frozen Foods
Buena Park, CA 714-521-1002
Clydes Delicious Donuts
Addison, IL 630-628-6555
Coastal Seafoods
Ridgefield, CT 203-431-0453
Codino's Italian Foods
Scotia, NY 800-246-8908
Cohen's Bakery
Buffalo, NY 716-892-8149
Cole's Quality Foods
Grand Rapids, MI 616-975-0081
Coloma Frozen Foods
Coloma, MI 800-642-2723
Columbia Foods
Snohomish, WA 360-568-0838
Columbia Foods
Quincy, WA 509-787-1585
Con Agra Foods
Holly Ridge, NC 910-329-9061
ConAgra Foods
Boisbriand, QC 450-433-1322
ConAgra Foods
Kennewick, WA 509-735-4651
ConAgra Foods
Sidney, OH 800-736-2212
ConAgra Foods
Richland, WA 800-766-7783
ConAgra Foods/Eckrich
Omaha, NE 800-327-4424
ConAgra Frozen Foods Company
Omaha, NE 402-595-6107
ConAgra Frozen Foods Company
Macon, MO 660-385-3184
ConAgra Frozen Foods Company
Marshall, MO 660-886-3301
ConAgra Grocery Products
Archbold, OH 419-445-8015
ConAgra Mexican Foods
Compton, CA 310-223-1499
ConAgra Store Brands, Inc.
Lakeville, MN 800-328-6286
Consolidated Mills
Houston, TX 713-896-4196
Consun Food Industries
Elyria, OH 440-322-6301
Contact International
Skokie, IL 847-324-4411
Contessa Food Products
San Pedro, CA 310-832-8000
Continental Food Products
Flushing, NY 718-358-7894
Continental Mills
Seattle, WA 253-872-8400
Cook Inlet Processing
Nikiski, AK 907-776-8174
Cookie Tree Bakeries
Salt Lake City, UT 800-998-0111
Corky's Bar-B-Q
Memphis, TN 800-926-7597
Country Fresh
Grand Rapids, MI 800-748-0480
Country Fresh Golden Valley
Livonia, MI 734-261-7980
Country Pies
Coombs, BC 250-248-6415
Country Pure Foods
Akron, OH 330-753-2293
Cozy Harbor Seafood
Portland, ME 800-225-2586
Cream O'Weaver Dairy
Salt Lake City, UT 801-973-9922
Creighton Brothers
Atwood, IN 574-267-3101
Creme Curls Bakery
Hudsonville, MI 800-466-1219
Creme D'Lite
Irving, TX 972-255-7255
Creme Glacee Gelati
Montreal, QC 888-322-0116
Crescent Duck Farm
Aquebogue, NY 631-722-8700
Crest International Corporation
San Diego, CA 800-548-1232
Crestar Crusts
Washington Ct Hs, OH 740-335-4813
Crevettes Du Nord
Gaspe, QC 418-368-1414
Crowley Foods
Binghamton, NY 800-637-0019
Crown Point
St John, IN 219-365-3200
Crystal Cream & Butter Company
Sacramento, CA 916-447-6455
Cuisine Solutions
Alexandria, VA 888-285-4679
Cuizina Food Company
Woodinville, WA 425-486-7000
Culinary Foods
Chicago, IL 800-621-4049
Culinary Standards Corporation
Louisville, KY 800-778-3434
Culver Duck
Middlebury, IN 800-825-9225
Curly's Foods
Edina, MN 800-722-1127
Cut Above Foods
Carlsbad, CA 760-931-6777
Cutie Pie Corporation
Salt Lake City, UT 800-453-4575
Cutler Egg Products
Abbeville, AL 334-585-2268
Cyclone Enterprises
Houston, TX 281-872-0087
D'Orazio Foods
Bellmawr, NJ 888-328-7287
Dairy Fresh Corporation
Greensboro, AL 800-239-5114
Dairy Fresh Foods
Taylor, MI 313-295-6300
Dairy King Milk Farms/Foodservice
Whitter, CA 800-900-6455
Dairy Land
Macon, GA 478-742-6461
Dairy Queen of Georgia
Decatur, GA 404-292-3553
Dakota Brands Intl. nal
Jamestown, ND 800-844-5073
Dallas Dressed Beef
Dallas, TX 214-638-0142
Danish Baking Company
Van Nuys, CA 818-786-1700
Dave's Hawaiian Ice Cream
Pearl City, HI 808-453-0500
Davidson Meat Processing Plant
Waynesville, OH 513-897-2971
Dawn Food Products
Louisville, KY 800-626-2542
De-Iorio's Frozen Dough
Utica, NY 800-649-7612
Deconna Ice Cream
Orange Lake, FL 800-824-8254
Dee's Cheesecake Factory/Dee's Foodservice
Albuquerque, NM 505-884-1777
Deep Creek Custom Packing
Ninilchik, AK 800-764-0078
Deep Foods
Union, NJ 908-810-7500
Deep Sea Foods
Bayou La Batre, AL 251-824-7000
Del Campo Baking Company
Wilmington, DE 302-656-6676
Del's Lemonade & Refreshments
Cranston, RI 401-463-6190
Del's Seaway Shrimp & Oyster Company
Biloxi, MS 228-432-2604
Delta Pride Catfish
Indianola, MS 800-421-1045
Deluxe Ice Cream Company
Salem, OR 800-304-7172
Depoe Bay Fish Company
Newport, OR 541-265-8833
Desserts of Distinction
Milwaukie, OR 503-654-8370
Detroit Chili Company
Southfield, MI 248-440-5933
Devault Foods
Devault, PA 800-426-2874
Devine Foods
Media, PA 888-338-4631
Diamond Blueberry
Hammonton, NJ 609-561-3661
Dick & Casey's Gourmet Seafoods
Harbor, OR 800-662-9494
Dickinson Frozen Foods
Fruitland, ID 208-452-5200
Dillman Farm
Bloomington, IN 800-359-1362
Dimitria Delights
North Grafton, MA 800-763-1113
Diversified Avocado Products
Mission Viejo, CA 800-879-2555
Division Baking Corporation
New York, NY 800-934-9238
Dol Cice' Gelato Company
Yardley, PA 215-499-5661
Dold Foods
Wichita, KS 316-838-9101
Don Miguel Mexican Foods
Orange, CA 714-634-8441
Dorothy Dawson Foods Products
Jackson, MI 517-788-9830
Dr. Praeger's Sensible Foods
Elmwood Park, NJ 877-PRA-GER
Draper Valley Farms
Mount Vernon, WA 425-793-4135
Dreyer's Grand Ice Cream
Oakland, CA 877-437-3937
Drohan Company
Huntington, NY 718-898-9672
Dufour Pastry Kitchens
Bronx, NY 800-439-1282
Duma Meats
Mogadore, OH 330-628-3438
Dunkin Brands Inc.
Canton, MA 800-458-7731
Dutch Ann Foods Company
Natchez, MS 601-445-5566
Dwayne Keith Brooks Company
Orangevale, CA 916-988-1030
Dynamic Foods
Lubbock, TX 806-747-2777
E. Gagnon & Fils
St Therese-De-Gaspe, QC 418-385-3011
E.W. Bowker Company
Pemberton, NJ 609-894-9508
Eastern Fish Company
Teaneck, NJ 800-526-9066
Eastern Shore Seafood Products
Mappsville, VA 800-466-8550
Eberhard Creamery
Redmond, OR 541-548-5181
Eckert Cold Storage
Escalon, CA 209-838-4040
Edmonds Chile Company
St Louis, MO 314-772-1499
Edner Corporation
Hayward, CA 510-441-8504
Edwards Baking Company
Atlanta, GA 800-241-0559
Edy's Dreyers Grand Ice Cream
Rockaway, NJ 800-362-7899
Edy's Grand Ice Cream
Glendale Heights, IL 888-377-3397
El Paso Meat Company
El Paso, TX 915-838-8600
El-Rey Foods
Ferguson, MO 314-521-3113
Elena's Food Specialties
S San Francisco, CA 800-376-5368
Eli's Cheesecake Company
Chicago, IL 800-999-8300
Empire Beef & Redistribution
Rochester, NY 800-462-6804
Endico Potatoes
Mount Vernon, NY 914-664-1151
Enfield Farms
Lynden, WA 360-354-3019
English Bay Batter
Columbus, OH 614-471-9994
Entenmann's-Oroweat/BestFoods
South San Francisco, CA 650-583-5828
Enterprises Pates et Croutes
Boucherville, QC 450-655-7790
Enway/Northwood
Clackamas, OR 503-657-9334
Equity Group
Reidsville, NC 336-342-6601
Evans Bakery
Cozad, NE 800-222-5641

Evans Properties
Dade City, FL 352-567-5662
Ever Fresh Fruit Company
Boring, OR 800-239-8026
Exceldor Cooperative
St. Anselme, QC 877-320-8006
Fairmont Foods of Minnesota
Fairmont, MN 507-238-9001
Faith Dairy
Tacoma, WA 253-531-3398
Fantasia
Sedalia, MO 660-827-1172
Farm Fresh Catfish Company
Hollandale, MS 800-647-8264
Farr Candy Company
Idaho Falls, ID 208-522-8215
Fendall Ice Cream Company
Salt Lake City, UT 801-355-3583
Ferroclad Fishery
Batchawana Bay, ON 705-882-2295
Field's
Pauls Valley, OK 800-286-7501
Fieldale Farms
Gainesville, GA 800-241-5400
Fieldale Farms Corporation
Baldwin, GA 706-778-5100
Fieldale Farms Corporation
Baldwin, GA 800-241-5400
Fieldbrook Farms
Dunkirk, NY 800-333-0805
Fiera Foods
Toronto, ON 416-744-1010
Fine Choice Foods
Richmond, BC 604-522-3110
Fiori-Bruna Pasta Products
Hialeah, FL 305-621-0074
First Original Texas Chili Company
Fort Worth, TX 817-626-0983
Fishery Products International
Danvers, MA 800-374-4700
Fishery Products International
Seattle, WA 800-374-4770
FishKing
Glendale, CA 818-244-2161
Fishmarket Seafoods
Louisville, KY 502-587-7474
Flagship Atlanta Dairy
Belleview, FL 800-224-0669
Flavors from Florida
Bartow, FL 863-533-0408
Fleischer's Bagels
Macedon, NY 315-986-9999
Florentyna's Fresh Pasta Factory
Vernon, CA 800-747-2782
Florida Veal Processors
Wimauma, FL 813-634-5545
Florida's Natural Growers
Lake Wales, FL 888-657-6600
Food City USA
Arvada, CO 303-321-4447
Food Source
Mc Kinney, TX 972-548-9001
Foodbrands America
Oklahoma City, OK 405-290-4000
Foodmark
Wellesley, MA 781-237-7088
Foothills Creamery
Calgary, AB 800-661-4909
Forte Stromboli Company
Philadelphia, PA 215-463-6336
Fran's Healthy Helpings
Burlingame, CA 650-652-5772
France Croissant
New York, NY 212-888-1210
France Delices
Montreal, QC 800-663-1365
Freeze-Dry Products
Santa Rosa, CA 707-547-1776
Freezer Queen Foods
Buffalo, NY 800-828-8383
French Gourmet
Honolulu, HI 808-524-4000
Fresh Dairy Direct/Morningstar
Dallas, TX 800-395-7004
Fresh Frozen Foods
Jefferson, GA 800-277-9851
Fresh Juice Company
Newark, NJ 973-465-7100
Friendly Ice Cream Corporation
Wilbraham, MA 800-966-9970
Frio Foods
San Antonio, TX 210-278-4525
Frostbite
Toledo, OH 800-968-7711
Frozen Specialties
Archbold, OH 419-445-9015
Frozfruit Corporation
Gardena, CA 310-217-1034
Frozsun Foods
Placentia, CA 714-630-6292
Fruit a Freeze
Norwalk, CA 562-407-2881
Fruit Belt Foods
Lawrence, MI 269-674-3939
Fruithill
Yamhill, OR 503-662-3926
Fry Foods
Tiffin, OH 800-626-2294
FSI/MFP
Archbold, OH 419-446-6528
Fuji Foods
Denver, CO 303-377-3738
G. M. Allen & Son
Orland, ME 207-469-7060
Gabilas Knishes
Brooklyn, NY
Gad Cheese Company
Medford, WI 715-748-4273
Galco Food Products
Toronto, ON 416-743-9671
Galliker Dairy
Johnstown, PA 800-477-6455
Galloway Company
Neenah, WI 800-722-8903
Garber Ice Cream Company
Winchester, VA 800-662-5422
Gardenburger
Clearfield, UT 801-773-8855
Gardner Pie Company
Akron, OH 330-245-2030
Garelick Farms
Lynn, MA 800-487-8700
Gary's Frozen Foods
Lubbock, TX 806-745-1933
Gaucho Foods
Fayetteville, IL 877-677-2282
Gelato Fresco
Toronto, ON 416-785-5415
Gemini Food Industries
Charlton, MA 508-248-2730
George Chiala Farms
Morgan Hill, CA 408-778-0562
George L. Wells Meat Company
Philadelphia, PA 800-523-1730
George Robberecht Seafood
Montross, VA 804-472-3556
Georges Chicken
Edinburg, VA 866-444-2449
Georgia Sun
Newnan, GA 770-251-2500
Gesco ENR
Gaspe, QC 418-368-1414
Gifford's Dairy
Skowhegan, ME 207-474-9821
Gilardi Foods
Sidney, OH 937-498-4511
Gilroy Foods
Gilroy, CA 800-921-7502
Glacier Foods
Sanger, CA 559-875-3354
Glazier Packing Company
Potsdam, NY 315-265-2500
Glendora Quiche Company
San Dimas, CA 909-394-1777
Glenmark Food Processors
Chicago, IL 800-621-0117
Global Citrus Resources
Lakeland, FL 863-647-9020
Global Trading
Buena Park, CA
Glover's Ice Cream
Frankfort, IN 800-686-5163
Gold Standard Baking
Chicago, IL 800-648-7904
Golden Gulf Coast Packing Company
Biloxi, MS 228-374-6121
Golden Platter Foods
Newark, NJ 973-242-0290
Golden Town Apple Products
Rougemont, QC 519-599-6300
Gonard Foods
Calgary, AB 403-277-0991
Gonnella Baking Company
Chicago, IL 312-733-2020
Gonnella Frozen Products
Schaumburg, IL 847-884-8829
Good Harbor Fillet Company
Gloucester, MA 978-675-9100
Good Humor Breyers Ice Cream Company
Green Bay, WI 920-499-5151
Good Old Days Foods
Little Rock, AR 501-565-1257
Good Wives, Inc.
Wilmington, MA 800-521-8160
Gordon Food Service
Plant City, FL 813-703-6500
Gorton's Seafood
Gloucester, MA 978-283-3000
Gourmet Croissant
Brooklyn, NY 718-499-4911
Gourmet Organics
Waynesville, NC 828-452-7700
Goya Foods
Secaucus, NJ 201-348-4900
Goya Foods of Florida
Miami, FL 305-592-3150
Granny's Kitchens
Frankfort, NY 315-735-5000
Great American Appetizers
Nampa, ID 800-282-4834
Great American Foods Commissary
Ore City, TX 903-968-8630
Great Northern Baking Company
Minneapolis, MN 612-331-1043
Great Northern Products
Warwick, RI 401-490-4590
Great Valley Mills
Barto, PA 800-688-6455
Grecian Delight Foods
Elk Grove Village, IL 800-621-4387
Gregory's Box'd Beverages
Newark, NJ 973-465-1113
Gregory's Foods
Eagan, MN 800-231-4734
Gress Poultry
Scranton, PA 570-561-0150
Grimaud Farms
Stockton, CA 800-466-9955
Grimmway Frozen Foods
Arvin, CA 661-854-2132
Grossinger's Home Bakery
New York, NY 800-479-6996
Grosso Foods
Swedesboro, NJ
Grow-Pac
Cornelius, OR 503-357-9691
Gulf Pride Enterprises
Biloxi, MS 888-689-0560
Guttenplan's Frozen Dough
Middletown, NJ 888-422-4357
GWB Foods Corporation
Brooklyn, NY 877-977-7610
Gyma
East Stroudsburg, PA 570-422-6311
H&H Bagels
New York, NY 800-692-2435
H&H Fisheries Limited
Eastern Passage, NS 902-465-6330
H.C. Brill Company
Tucker, GA 800-241-8526
Haas Baking Company
St Louis, MO 800-325-3171
Hall Brothers Meats
Cleveland, OH 440-235-3262
Hallmark Fisheries
Charleston, OR 541-888-3253
Hamm's Custom Meats
McKinney, TX 972-562-7511
Handy International
Salisbury, MD 800-426-3977
Hanover Foods Corp
Hanover, PA 717-632-6000
Hanover Foods Corporation
Hanover, PA 717-632-6000
Happy Refrigerated Services
Fairport, NY 585-388-0080
Harker's Distribution
Le Mars, IA 800-798-7700
Harlan Bakeries
Avon, IN 317-272-3600
Harold Food Company
Charlotte, NC 704-588-8061
Harold M. Lincoln Company
Toledo, OH 800-345-4911
Harrisburg Dairies
Harrisburg, PA 800-692-7429

Hartog Rahal Foods
New York, NY 212-687-2000
Harvest Time Foods
Ayden, NC. . . . 252-746-6675
Hatfield Quality Meats
Hatfield, PA. . . . 800-523-5291
Hawaii Coffee Company
Honolulu, HI. . . . 800-338-8353
Hazelwood Farms Bakery
Rochester, NY. . . . 585-424-1240
Health is Wealth Foods
Williamstown, NJ 856-728-1998
Heidi's Gourmet Desserts
Tucker, GA 800-241-4166
Heinz Company of Canada
North York, ON. . . . 877-574-3469
Henry J's Hashtime
Chicago, IL 800-242-1313
Herbs Seafood
Mount Holly, NJ 800-486-0276
Heringer Meats
Covington, KY 859-291-2000
Hermann Pickle Farm
Garrettsville, OH. . . . 800-245-2696
Hershey Creamery Company
Harrisburg, PA 888-240-1905
HFI Foods
Redmond, WA. . . . 425-883-1320
Hi Point Industries
Vernon, CA 800-959-7292
Hi-Country Corona
Selah, WA 951-272-2600
Higgins Seafood
Lafitte, LA. . . . 504-689-3577
High Liner Foods USA
Danvers, MA. . . . 888-860-3664
Hillard Bloom Packing Co
Port Norris, NJ 856-785-0120
Hillman Shrimp & Oyster Company
Dickinson, TX. . . . 800-582-4416
Hiscock Enterprises
Brigus, NL. . . . 709-528-4577
Holten Meats
Sauget, IL 800-851-4684
Holton Food Products Company
La Grange, IL 708-352-5599
Home Delivery Food Service
Jefferson, GA 706-367-9551
Home Run Inn Frozen Foods
Woodridge, IL. . . . 800-636-9696
Homer's Ice Cream
Wilmette, IL 847-251-0477
Honeybake Farms
Kansas City, KS 913-371-7777
Hormel Foods Corporation
Columbia, MD 410-290-1916
Hormel Foods Corporation
Franklin, MA 508-541-7101
Hormel Foods Corporation
Cincinnati, OH 513-563-0211
Hormel Foods Corporation
Des Moines, IA. . . . 515-276-8872
Hormel Foods Corporation
Phoenix, AZ 602-230-2400
Hormel Foods Corporation
Austin, MN. . . . 800-523-4635
Hormel Foods Corporation
Arlington, TX 817-465-4735
Hormel Foods Corporation
Cordova, TN. . . . 901-753-4282
Hormel Foods Corporation
Lebanon, NJ 908-236-7009
Horst Alaskan Seafood
Juneau, AK 877-518-4300
Houdini
Fullerton, CA 714-525-0325
House of Flavors
Ludington, MI. . . . 800-930-7740
House of Raeford Farms
Raeford, NC 800-888-7539
House of Spices India
Flushing, NY. . . . 718-507-4900
Hudsonville Creamery & Ice Cream
Holland, MI. . . . 616-546-4005
Humble Cremery
Fortuna, CA 800-697-9925
Humboldt Creamery Association
Fortuna, CA 707-725-6182
Hunt-Wesson Food Service Company
Rochester, NY. . . . 866-484-8676
Hunter Farms
High Point, NC 800-446-8035

I & K Distributors
Delphos, OH 800-869-6337
Ice Cream & Yogurt Club
Boynton Beach, FL. . . . 561-731-3331
Ice Cream Specialties
Saint Louis, MO 314-962-2550
Ice Cream Specialties
Lafayette, IN 765-474-2989
Ice Land Corporation
Pittsburgh, PA 412-441-9512
Icelandic USA
Newport News, VA. . . . 757-820-4000
Icicle Seafoods
Seattle, WA 206-282-0988
Icy Bird
Sparta, TN. . . . 931-738-3557
Ideal Dairy
Richfield, UT 435-896-5061
Il Gelato
Astoria, NY. . . . 800-899-9299
Imagine Foods
Melville, NY. . . . 800-333-6339
Incredible Cheesecake Company
San Diego, CA 619-563-9722
Independent Packers Corporation
Seattle, WA 206-285-6000
Indian Ridge Shrimp Company
Chauvin, LA 985-594-3361
Indian River Foods
Fort Pierce, FL 772-462-2222
Indian Valley Meats
Indian, AK. . . . 907-653-7511
Inn Foods
Watsonville, CA 831-724-2026
Inshore Fisheries
Middle West Pubnico, NS. . . . 902-762-2522
International Cuisine
East Palatka, FL 904-325-0002
International Food Packers Corporation
Miami, FL. . . . 305-669-1662
International Food Trade
Amherst, NS 902-667-3013
International Multifoods Corporation
Orrville, OH 800-664-2942
International Oceanic Enterprises of Alabama
Bayou La Batre, AL 800-816-1832
International Yogurt Company
Portland, OR. . . . 800-962-7326
Isabella's Healthy Bakery
Cuyahoga Falls, OH 800-476-6328
Island Marine Products
Clarks Harbour, NS. . . . 902-745-2222
Island Oasis Frozen Cocktail Company
Walpole, MA. . . . 800-777-4752
Island Scallops
Qualicum Beach, BC 250-757-9811
It's It Ice Cream Company
Burlingame, CA 800-345-1928
Italia Foods
Schaumburg, IL. . . . 800-747-1109
Itarca
Los Angeles, CA. . . . 800-747-2782
J&J Snack Foods Corporation
Pennsauken, NJ. . . . 800-486-9533
J&J Wall Baking Company
Sacramento, CA 916-381-1410
J. Matassini & Sons Fish Company
Tampa, FL. . . . 813-229-0829
J.B. Sons
Yonkers, NY 914-963-5192
J.H. Verbridge & Son
Williamson, NY 315-589-2366
J.R. Simplot Company
Boise, ID 208-336-2110
J.R. Simplot Company
Grand Forks, ND. . . . 701-746-6431
J.S. McMillan Fisheries
Vancouver, BC 604-255-5191
J.W. Haywood & Sons Dairy
Louisville, KY. . . . 502-774-2311
Jack & Jill Ice Cream Company
Moorestown, NJ 856-813-2300
Jack's Lobsters
Musquodoboit Harbor, NS 902-889-2771
Jackson Ice Cream Company
Denver, CO 303-534-2454
Jackson Milk & Ice CreamCompany
Hutchinson, KS. . . . 620-663-1244
Jacob & Sons Wholesale Meats
Martins Ferry, OH. . . . 740-633-3091
James Cowan & Sons
Worcester, MA 508-753-3259

James Skinner Company
Omaha, NE 800-358-7428
Janca's Jojoba Oil & Seed Company
Mesa, AZ. . . . 480-497-9494
Janes Family Foods
Mississauga, ON. . . . 800-565-2637
Jasper Wyman & Son
Milbridge, ME 800-341-1758
Jazz Fine Foods
Montreal, QC 514-255-0110
Jbs Packerland Inc
Green Bay, WI
JBS Packing Company
Port Arthur, TX. . . . 409-982-3216
Jecky's Best
Santa Clarita, CA 888-532-5972
Jel-Sert Company
West Chicago, IL 800-323-2592
Jemm Wholesale Meat Company
Chicago, IL 773-523-8161
Jenport International Distributors
Coquitlam, BC 604-464-9888
Jesses Fine Meats
Cherokee, IA. . . . 712-225-3637
Jessie's Ilwaco Fish Company
Ilwaco, WA 360-642-3773
John Garner Meats
Van Buren, AR 800-543-5473
John Morrell & Company
Cincinnati, OH 712-279-7360
Johnson's Real Ice Cream
Columbus, OH 614-231-0014
Joseph Foodservice
Valdosta, GA. . . . 800-333-2261
Josh & John's Ice Cream
Colorado Springs, CO. . . . 800-530-2855
JR Wood/Big Valley
Atwater, CA 209-358-5643
JRL
Vineland, NJ 856-690-9000
Jubilee Foods
Emmitsburg, MD 301-447-6688
Juno Chef's
Goshen, NY. . . . 845-294-5400
Junuis Food Products
Palatine, IL 847-359-4300
Jurgielewicz Duck Farm
Moriches, NY 800-543-8257
K&K Gourmet Meats
Leetsdale, PA 724-266-8400
Kan-Pac
Arkansas City, KS. . . . 620-442-6820
Karn Meats
Columbus, OH 800-221-9585
Karp's
Georgetown, MA 800-373-5277
Katrina's Tartufo
Port Jeffrsn Sta, NY 800-480-8836
Kelley Foods of Alabama
Elba, AL 334-897-5761
Kellogg Canada Inc
Mississauga, ON. . . . 888-876-3750
Kellogg Company
Hammonton, NJ 609-567-2300
Kenosha Beef International
Kenosha, WI 800-541-1685
Kent Foods
Gonzales, TX 830-672-7993
Key Largo Fisheries
Key Largo, FL. . . . 800-432-4358
Keyser Brothers
Lottsburg, VA 804-529-6837
Keystone Foods
Camilla, GA 229-336-5211
King Cole Ducks Limited
Aurora, ON 800-363-3825
King Kold
Lakewood, NJ. . . . 732-730-2157
King Kold Meats
Englewood, OH 800-836-2797
Kitchens Seafood
Plant City, FL 800-327-0132
Klinke Brothers Ice Cream Company
Memphis, TN 901-743-8250

Koch Foods
Park Ridge, IL. 800-837-2778
Kodiak Salmon Packers
Larsen Bay, AK. 907-847-2250
Kohler Mix Specialties
White Bear Lake, MN. 651-426-1633
Kohler Mix Specialties
Newington, CT 860-666-1511
Kokinos Purity Ice CreamCompany
Monroe, LA. 318-322-2930
Kona Cold Lobsters Ltd
Kailua Kona, HI 808-329-4332
Konto's Foods
Paterson, NJ 973-278-2800
KT's Kitchens
Carson, CA 310-764-0850
Kubla Khan Food Company
Portland, OR 503-234-7494
Kutztown Bologna Company
Leola, PA. 800-723-8824
Kyger Bakery Products
Lafayette, IN. 765-447-1252
L&C Fisheries
Kensington, PE 902-886-2770
L&H Packing Company
San Antonio, TX. 210-532-3241
L.K. Bowman Company
Hanover, PA 800-853-1919
La Cookie
Houston, TX 713-784-2722
La Francaise Bakery
Melrose Park, IL. 800-654-7220
La Nova Wings
Buffalo, NY. 800-652-6682
La Tolteca Foods
Pueblo, CO 719-543-5733
Ladoga Frozen Food & Retail Meat
Ladoga, IN 765-942-2225
Lady Gale Seafood
Baldwin, LA 337-923-2060
Lafitte Frozen Foods Corporation
Lafitte, LA. 504-689-2041
Lake Packing Company
Lottsburg, VA 804-529-6101
Lake Shore Frozen Foods
Lake City, PA 877-774-3668
Lakeside Foods
Brooten, MN 320-346-2900
Lakeside Foods
Plainview, MN 507-534-3141
Lakeside Foods
Seymour, WI. 920-833-2371
Lamb-Weston
Hermiston, OR 800-766-7783
LaMonica Fine Foods
Millville, NJ 856-825-8111
Land O'Lakes, Inc.
Arden Hills, MN. 800-328-9680
Landolfi Food Products
Trenton, NJ 609-392-1830
LBA
Seatac, WA 800-522-1185
Le Notre, Alain & Marie Baker
Houston, TX 800-536-6873
Leach Farms
Berlin, WI 920-361-1880
Leader Candies
Brooklyn, NY 718-366-6900
Leelanau Fruit Company
Suttons Bay, MI 231-271-3514
Leidenheimer Baking Company
New Orleans, LA 504-525-1575
Lenchner Bakery
Concord, ON. 905-738-8811
Lender's Bagel Bakery
Mattoon, IL. 217-235-3181
Lengerich Meats
Zanesville, IN 260-638-4123
Lennox Farm
Shelburne, ON 519-925-6444
Leon's Bakery
North Haven, CT. 800-223-6844
Leonetti's Frozen Food
Philadelphia, PA 215-729-4200
Lewis Packing Company
Sandy, OR 503-668-8122
Little Lady Foods
Elk Grove Vlg, IL. 800-439-1440
Lombardi's Seafood
Orlando, FL. 800-879-8411
Lone Star Bakery
Round Rock, TX. 512-255-3629
Lone Star Consolidated Foods
Dallas, TX. 800-658-5637
Long Beach Seafoods
Long Beach, CA 562-435-5357
Longmont Foods
Longmont, CO 303-776-6611
Lougheed Fisheries
Owen Sound, ON 519-376-1586
Louis Dreyfus Citrus
Winter Garden, FL 800-549-4272
Louis Trauth Dairy
Newport, KY. 800-544-6455
Louisa Food Products
Saint Louis, MO 314-868-3000
Louisiana Packing Company
Westwego, LA. 800-666-1293
Love & Quiches Desserts
Freeport, NY. 800-525-5251
Lucerne Foods
Lethbridge, AB 403-328-5501
Lucia's Pizza Company
Saint Louis, MO 314-843-2553
Ludwick's Frozen Donuts
Grand Rapids, MI 800-366-8816
Ludwig Fish & Produce Company
La Porte, IN. 219-362-2608
M&L Gourmet Ice Cream
Baltimore, MD 410-276-4880
M&M Shrimp Company
Biloxi, MS. 228-435-4915
M-G
Weimar, TX. 800-460-8581
M.A. Johnson Frozen Foods
Marion, IN 76- 66- 802
Macabee Foods
West Nyack, NY 845-623-1300
MacFarlane Pheasants
Janesville, WI 877-269-8957
Mack's Homemade Ice Cream
York, PA 717-741-2027
Mackie Intl.
Riverside, CA 800-733-9762
Mada'n Kosher Foods
Dania, FL 954-925-0077
Maid-Rite Steak Company
Dunmore, PA. 800-233-4259
Main Street Custom Foods
Cuyahoga Falls, OH 800-533-6246
Main Street Gourmet
Cuyahoga Falls, OH 800-533-6246
Main Street Gourmet Fundraising
Cuyahoga Falls, OH 800-533-6246
Main Street Muffins
Cuyahoga Falls, OH 800-533-6246
Main Street's Cambritt Cookies
Cuyahoga Falls, OH 800-533-6246
Maine Wild Blueberry Company
Cherryfield, ME 800-243-4005
Majestic Foods
Huntington, NY 631-424-9444
Mama Rosie's Ravioli Company
Charlestown, MA 888-246-4300
Mamma Lina Ravioli Company
San Diego, CA 858-535-0620
Manchester Farms
Columbia, SC 800-845-0421
Mancuso Cheese Company
Joliet, IL 815-722-2475
Mannhardt Inc
Sheboygan Falls, WI. 920-467-1027
Maola Milk & Ice Cream Company
New Bern, NC. 252-514-2792
Maple Leaf Farms
Milford, IN 800-384-2812
Maple Leaf Foods International
North York, ON. 416-480-8900
Maplehurst Bakeries
Brownsburg, IN 317-858-9000
Mar-Jac Poultry
Gainesville, GA 800-226-0561
Mar-Key Foods
Vidalia, GA. 912-537-4204
Marburger Foods
Peru, IN. 765-472-1139
Marcetti Frozen Pasta
Altoona, IA 515-967-4254
Marche Tramsatlantique
Montreal, QC 514-287-3530
Mardi Gras
Verona, NJ. 973-857-3777
Mariner Seafoods
Montague, PE 902-838-2481
Mario's Gelati
Vancouver, BC 604-879-9411
Market Fare Foods
Phoenix, AZ 888-669-6420
Marsan Foods
Toronto, ON 416-755-9262
Martin Brothers Distributing Company
Cedar Falls, IA 319-266-1775
Martin Brothers SeafoodcCompany
Westwego, LA. 504-341-2251
Martin Seafood Company
Jessup, MD 410-799-5822
MAS Sales
Northlake, IL. 800-615-6951
Mason County Fruit Packers Cooperative
Ludington, MI. 231-845-6248
Matador Processors
Blanchard, OK 800-847-0797
Maui Pineapple Company
Concord, CA. 925-798-0240
Maxim's Import Corporation
Miami, FL. 800-331-6652
Mayfield Farms
Caledon, ON 905-846-0506
McArthur Dairy
Miami, FL. 877-803-6565
McCain Foods Canada
Toronto, ON 866-622-2461
McCain Foods USA
Colton, CA 800-938-7799
McConnell's Fine Ice Cream
Santa Barbara, CA 805-963-2958
McLane Foods
Phoenix, AZ 602-275-5509
Meadow Gold Dairies
Englewood, CO. 800-525-3289
Meat-O-Mat Corporation
Brooklyn, NY 718-965-7250
Mehaffie Pies
Dayton, OH. 937-253-1163
Meleddy Cherry Plant
Sturgeon Bay, WI 920-743-2858
Menemsha Fish Market
Chilmark, MA. 508-645-2282
Merrill's Blueberry Farms
Ellsworth, ME. 800-711-6551
Mersey Seafoods
Liverpool, NS 902-354-3467
Mexi-Frost Specialties Company
Brooklyn, NY 718-625-3324
Meyer's Bakeries
Hope, AR 800-643-1542
Mi Ranchito Foods
Bayard, NM. 575-537-3868
Mia Products
Scranton, PA 570-457-7431
Michael Foods, Inc.
Minnetonka, MN. 952-258-4000
Michael's Cookies
San Diego, CA 800-822-5384
Michele's Family Bakery
York, PA 717-741-2027
Michelle Chocolatiers
Colorado Springs, CO. 888-447-3654
Michigan Dairy
Livonia, MI. 734-367-5390
Mid States Dairy
Hazelwood, MO 314-731-1150
Mid-Atlantic Foods
Easton, MD. 800-922-4688
Mikawaya Bakery
Vernon, CA
Mike & Jean's Berry Farm
Mount Vernon, WA. 360-424-7220
Miles J H & Company
Norfolk, VA. 757-622-9264
Milfico Foods
Elk Grove Vlg, IL. 847-427-0491
Mill Cove Lobster Pound
Boothbay Harbor, ME. 207-633-3340
Millers Ice Cream
Houston, TX 713-861-3138
Milmar Food Group
Goshen, NY. 845-294-5400
Milne Fruit Products
Prosser, WA. 509-786-2611
Minh Food Corporation Schwan's Food Company
Pasadena, TX 800-344-7655
Minor Fisheries
Port Colborne, ON 905-834-9232
Minterbrook Oyster Company
Gig Harbor, WA 253-857-5251

Minute Maid Company
Atlanta, GA 800-438-2653
Mister Cookie Face
Lakewood, NJ 732-370-5533
Mobile Processing
Mobile, AL 251-438-6944
Model Dairy
Reno, NV 800-433-2030
Model Diary
El Paso, TX 1 8-0 3-5 70
Molinaro's Fine Italian Foods
Mississauga, ON 800-268-4959
Momence Packing Company
Momence, IL 815-472-6485
Monterey Mushrooms
Watsonville, CA 800-333-6874
Mooresville Ice Cream Company
Mooresville, NC 704-664-5456
Morey's Seafood Intl. ional
Motley, MN 218-352-6345
Morgan Food
Austin, IN 888-430-1780
Moroni Feed Company
West Liberty, IA 800-453-5327
Morrison Lamothe
Toronto, ON 877-677-6533
Morrison Meat Pies
West Valley, UT 801-977-0181
Morrison Milling Company
Denton, TX 800-580-5487
Mortimer's Fine Foods
Burlington, ON 905-336-0000
Mother's Kitchen
Burlington, NJ 800-566-8437
Mothers Kitchen Inc
Burlington, NJ 609-589-3026
Motivatit Seafoods
Houma, LA 985-868-7191
Mount Baker Vineyards
Everson, WA 800-441-8263
Mount Rose Ravioli & Macaroni Company
Farmingdale, NY
Mountain City Meat Company
Denver, CO 800-937-8325
Mozzicato De Pasquale Bakery Pastry
Hartford, CT 860-296-0426
Mushroom Company
Cambridge, MD 410-221-8971
Mutual Fish Company
Seattle, WA 206-322-4368
Myers Frozen Food Provisions
Saint Paul, IN 765-525-6304
Naleway Foods
Winnipeg, MB 800-665-7448
Nan Sea Enterprises of Wisconsin
Waukesha, WI 262-542-8841
Nancy's Specialty Foods
Newark, CA 510-494-1100
National Beef Packing Co., LLC
Kansas City, MO 800-449-2333
National Fish & Oysters Company
Olympia, WA 360-491-5550
National Fish and Seafood Limited
Brownsville, TX 956-546-5525
National Frozen Foods Corporation
Seattle, WA 206-322-8900
Natural Feast Corporation
Dover, MA 508-785-3322
Natural Fruit Corporation
Hialeah, FL 305-887-7525
Natural Wonder Foods Inc
Brooklyn, NY
Nature Quality
San Martin, CA 408-683-2182
Nelson Crab
Tokeland, WA 800-262-0069
Nelson's Ice Cream
Royersford, PA 610-948-3000
Neptune Fisheries
Newport News, VA 800-545-7474
Nestle Pizza
Medford, WI 715-748-5550
Nestle Prepared Foods Company
Englewood, CO 800-225-2270
New England Muffin Company
Fall River, MA 508-675-2833
New York Frozen Foods
Cleveland, OH 216-292-5655
Newfound Resources
St Josephs, NL 709-579-7676
Niagara Foods
Middleport, NY 716-735-7722

Nickabood's Company
Los Angeles, CA 213-746-1541
Night Hawk Frozen Foods
Buda, TX 800-580-4166
Nor-Cliff Farms
Port Colborne, ON 905-835-0808
Norbest
Midvale, UT 800-453-5327
Nordic Group
Boston, MA 800-486-4002
Norfood Cherry Growers
Simcoe, ON 519-426-5784
NORPAC Foods
Stayton, OR 503-769-2101
NORPAC Foods
Lake Oswego, OR 800-733-9311
North Atlantic Fish Company
Gloucester, MA 978-283-4121
North Star Foods
Saint Charles, MN 507-932-4831
Northern Michigan Fruit Company
Omena, MI 231-386-5142
Northern Products Corporation
Seattle, WA 206-448-6677
Northern Wind
New Bedford, MA 888-525-2525
Northland Frozen Foods
Sugar City, ID 800-886-4326
Notre Dame Seafood
Comfort Cove, NL 709-244-5511
O Chili Frozen Foods Inc
Northbrook, IL 847-562-1991
O'Boyle's Ice Cream Company
Bristol, PA 215-788-3882
O'Hara Corporation
Rockland, ME 207-594-0405
Oak Leaf Confections
Scarborough, ON 877-261-7887
Oasis Foods
Planada, CA 209-382-0263
Ocean Beauty Seafoods
Seattle, WA 206-285-6800
Ocean Beauty Seafoods
Monroe, WA 425-482-2923
Ocean Food Company
Scarborough, ON 416-285-6487
Ocean Spray Cranberries
Lakeville-Middleboro, MA 800-662-3263
Ocean Springs Seafood
Ocean Springs, MS 228-875-0104
Oceana Foods
Shelby, MI 231-861-2141
Okuhara Foods
Honolulu, HI 808-848-0581
Old Fashioned Kitchen
Lakewood, NJ 732-364-4100
Olymel
Iberville, QC 450-542-9339
Omaha Steaks International
Omaha, NE 800-562-0500
Omstead Foods Ltd
Wheatley, ON 905-315-8883
On-Cor Foods Products
Northbrook, IL 847-205-1040
Orange Bakery
Huntersville, NC 704-875-3003
Orange Bakery
Irvine, CA 949-863-1377
Ore-Ida Foods
Pittsburgh, PA 800-892-2401
Oregon Cherry Growers
Salem, OR 800-367-2536
Oregon Fruit Products Company
Salem, OR 800-394-9333
Oregon Potato Company
Boardman, OR 800-336-6311
Original Italian Pasta Poducts Company
Chelsea, MA 800-999-9603
Original Ya-hoo! Baking Company
Sherman, TX 800-575-9373
Oroweat Baking Company
Montebello, CA 323-721-5161
Otis Spunkmeyer
San Leandro, CA 800-938-1900
Otter Valley Foods
Tillsonburg, ON 800-265-5731
Ottman Meat Company
New York, NY 212-879-4160
Otto & Son
West Jordan, UT 800-453-9462
Out of a Flower
Lancaster, TX 800-743-4696

Oven Poppers
Manchester, NH 603-644-3773
Overhill Farms
Vernon, CA 800-859-6406
Overlake Foods Corporation
Olympia, WA 800-683-1078
Oxford Frozen Foods Limited
Oxford, NS 902-447-2100
P&J Oyster Company
New Orleans, LA 504-523-2651
P. Janes & Sons
Hant's Harbor, NL 709-586-2252
Pacific Alaska Seafoods
Seattle, WA 206-587-0002
Pacific American Fish Co.,Inc.
Vernon, CA 800-625-2525
Pacific Blueberries
Rochester, WA 360-273-5405
Pacific Coast Fruit Company
Portland, OR 503-234-6411
Pacific Ocean Produce
Santa Cruz, CA 831-423-2654
Pacific Salmon Company
Edmonds, WA 425-774-1315
Pacific Seafoods International
Port Hardy, BC 250-949-8781
Pacific Shrimp Company
Newport, OR 541-265-4215
Pacific Valley Foods
Bellevue, WA 425-643-1805
Paisano Food Products
Elk Grove Village, IL 800-672-4726
Palermo's Frozen Pizza
Milwaukee, WI 414-643-0919
Palmetto Pigeon Plant
Sumter, SC 803-775-1204
Pamlico Packing Company
Grantsboro, NC 800-682-1113
Paradise Island Foods
Nanaimo, BC 800-889-3370
Parco Foods
Blue Island, IL 708-371-9200
Paris Foods Corporation
Trappe, MD 410-476-3185
Paris Frozen Foods
Hillsboro, IL 217-532-3822
Park Farms
Canton, OH 800-683-6511
Pascucci Family Pasta
San Diego, CA 619-285-8000
Pasta Del Mondo
Carmel, NY 800-392-8887
Pasta Factory
Melrose Park, IL 800-615-6951
Pasta International
Mississauga, ON 905-890-5550
Pasta Italiana
Massapequa, NY 800-536-5611
Pastry Chef
Pawtucket, RI 800-639-8606
Patterson Frozen Foods
Patterson, CA 209-892-2611
Paul Piazza & Sons
New Orleans, LA 504-524-6011
Peco Foods
Canton, MS 601-855-0925
Pede Brothers
Schenectady, NY 518-356-3042
PEI Mussel King
Morrell, PE 800-673-2767
Pel-Freez
Rogers, AR 800-223-8751
Pellman Foods
New Holland, PA 717-354-8070
Penguin Frozen Foods
Northbrook, IL 847-291-9400
Peninsula Fruit Exchange
Traverse City, MI 231-223-4282
Pennfield Corporation
Lancaster, PA 717-299-2561
Penobscot McCrum
Belfast, ME 800-435-4456
Pepe's Mexican Restaurants
Chicago, IL 312-733-2500
Pepes Mexican Foods
Etobicoke, ON 416-674-0882
Perdue Farms
Salisbury, MD 800-473-7383
Perfect Addition
Newport Beach, CA 949-640-0220
Perfect Foods
Goshen, NY 800-933-3288

Perry's Ice Cream Company
Akron, NY 800-873-7797
Pet Dairy
Portsmouth, VA 757-397-2387
Pet Dairy
Spartanburg, SC 864-576-6280
Peter Pan Seafoods
Seattle, WA 206-728-6000
Petersburg Fisheries
Petersburg, AK 877-772-4294
Petersen Ice Cream Company
Oak Park, IL 708-386-6130
Pevely Dairy Company
Hazelwood, MO 314-771-4400
Pfeffers Country Market
Sauk Centre, MN 320-352-6490
Phillips Foods
Baltimore, MD 888-234-2722
Phoenix Agro-Industrial Corporation
Westbury, NY 516-334-1194
Phranil Foods
Spokane, WA 509-534-7770
Pictsweet Frozen Foods
Bells, TN 731-422-7600
Piemonte Foods
Greenville, SC 864-242-0424
Pierceton Foods
Pierceton, IN 574-594-2344
Pierino Frozen Foods
Lincoln Park, MI 313-928-0950
Pilgrim's
Greeley, CO 800-727-5366
Pinocchio Italian Ice Cream Company
Edmonton, AB 780-455-1905
Piqua Pizza Supply Company
Piqua, OH 800-521-4442
Plains Creamery
Amarillo, TX 806-374-0385
Platte Valley Creamery
Scottsbluff, NE 308-632-4225
Plehn's Bakery
Louisville, KY 502-896-4438
Plymouth Beef
Bronx, NY 718-589-8600
POG
Grand Bend, ON 519-238-5704
Port Chatham Smoked Seafood
Everett, WA 800-872-5666
Portland Shellfish Company
South Portland, ME 207-799-9290
Positively Third Street Bakery
Duluth, MN 218-724-8619
Poudre Valley Creamery
Fort Collins, CO 970-237-7000
Prairie Cajun Whlse.
Eunice, LA 337-546-6195
Prairie Farms Dairy
Carlinville, IL 217-854-2547
Prairie Farms Dairy Inc.
Carlinville, IL 217-854-2547
Praters Foods
Lubbock, TX 806-745-2727
Preferred Meal Systems
Scranton, PA 570-457-8311
Price Seafood
Chauvin, LA 985-594-3067
Price's Creameries
El Paso, TX 915-565-2711
Prime Pastry
Brooklyn, NY 888-771-2464
Prime Smoked Meats
Oakland, CA 510-832-7167
Provimi Foods, Inc
Seymour, WI 800-833-8325
Puritan/ATZ Ice Cream
Kendallville, IN 260-347-2700
Purity Dairies
Nashville, TN 615-244-1900
Purity Ice Cream Company
Ithaca, NY 607-272-1545
Quality Brands
Deland, FL 888-676-2700

Quality Chef Foods
Cedar Rapids, IA 800-356-8307
Quality Foods Products
Chicago, IL 312-666-4559
Quality Seafood
Apalachicola, FL 850-653-9696
Queen International Foods
Monterey Park, CA 800-423-4414
Quelle Quiche
Brentwood, MO 314-961-6554
R Four Meats
Chatfield, MN 507-867-4180
Radar Farms
Lynden, WA 360-354-6574
Ragozzino Food
Meriden, CT 800-348-1240
Rain Sweet
Salem, OR 800-363-4293
Rainbow Farms
Upper Rawdon, NS 902-632-2548
Ralph's Italian Ices
Babylon, NY 631-893-5646
Ramona's Mex. Food Produoducts
Gardena, CA 310-323-1950
Ranaldi Bros Frozen Food Products Inc
Warwick, RI 401-738-3444
Randag & Associates Inc
Elmhurst, IL 630-530-2830
Randy's Frozen Meats
Faribault, MN 800-354-7177
Ready Bake Foods
Mississauga, ON 905-567-0660
Ready Foods
Denver, CO 720-889-1104
Reames Foods
Columbus, OH 614-846-2232
Reames Foods
Altoona, IA 800-247-4194
Redi-Serve Food Company
Fort Atkinson, WI 920-563-6391
Reinhold Ice Cream Company
Pittsburgh, PA 412-321-7600
Reiter Dairy
Akron, OH 800-362-0825
Request Foods
Holland, MI 800-748-0378
Reser's Fine Foods
Beaverton, OR 800-333-6431
Reser's Fine Foods
Salt Lake City, UT 801-972-5633
Resource Trading Company
Portland, ME 207-772-2299
Restaurant Systems International
Staten Island, NY 718-494-8888
Rhodes Bake-N-Serv
Salt Lake City, UT 800-695-0122
Rhodes International
Salt Lake City, UT 800-695-0122
Rhodes International
Columbus, WI 800-876-7333
Rich Ice Cream Company
West Palm Beach, FL 561-833-7585
Rich Products Corporation
Winchester, VA 540-667-1955
Rich Products Corporation
Fresno, CA 559-486-7380
Rich Products Corporation
Hilliard, OH 614-771-1117
Rich Products Corporation
Cameron, WI 715-458-4556
Rich Products Corporation
Buffalo, NY 800-356-7094
Rich Products Corporation
Buffalo, NY 800-828-2021
Rich Products of Canada
Buffalo, NY 800-457-4247
Rich-Seapak Corporation
Brownsville, TX 956-542-0001
Riviera Ravioli Company
Bronx, NY 718-823-0260
Roberts Dairy Foods
Omaha, NE 402-371-3660
Roberts Dairy Foods
Kansas City, MO 800-279-1692
Robinson Cold Storage
Ridgefield, WA 360-887-3501
Robinson Dairy
Denver, CO 800-332-6355
Rosati Italian Water Ice
Clifton Heights, PA 610-626-1818
Rose Frozen Shrimp
Los Angeles, CA 213-626-8251

Roselani Tropics Ice Cream
Wailuku, HI 808-244-7951
Rowena's
Norfolk, VA 800-627-8699
Royal Harvest Foods
Springfield, MA 413-737-8392
Royal Madera
Madera, CA 559-486-6666
Royal Seafood
Monterey, CA 831-655-8326
Rubschlager Baking Corporation
Chicago, IL 773-826-1245
Ruggiero Seafood
Newark, NJ 866-225-2627
Ruiz Food Products
Dinuba, CA 800-477-6474
Rymer Foods
Chicago, IL 800-247-9637
S&E Organic Farms
Bakersfield, CA 661-325-2644
S.D. Mushrooms
Avondale, PA 610-268-8082
Safeway Dairy Products
Capitol Heights, MD 301-341-9555
Safeway Stores
Tempe, AZ 480-966-0295
Sahadi Fine Foods
Brooklyn, NY 800-724-2341
Sal-Serve
Mobile, AL 251-438-6944
Sanderson Farms
Collins, MS 601-765-0430
Sanderson Farms
Hazlehurst, MS 601-894-3725
Sanderson Farms
Laurel, MS 800-844-4030
Sanderson Farms
Bryan, TX 979-778-5730
Sara Lee Corporation
Downers Grove, IL 630-598-8100
Sargeant's Army Marketing
Bowmanville, ON 905-623-2888
Savannah Food Company
Savannah, TN 800-795-2550
Savino's Italian Ices
Deerfield Beach, FL 954-426-4119
Saxby Foods
Edmonton, AB 780-440-4179
Scenic Fruit Company
Gresham, OR 800-554-5578
Schneider Foods
Saint Marys, ON 800-567-1890
Schneider Valley Farms Dairy
Williamsport, PA 570-326-2021
Schneider's Dairy Holdings Inc
Pittsburgh, PA 412-881-3525
Schoep's Ice Cream Company
Madison, WI 800-236-0032
Schwartz Meat Company
Sophia, WV 304-683-4595
Scotsburn Dairy Group
Scotsburn, NS 902-485-8023
Sea Pearl Seafood
Bayou La Batre, AL 800-872-8804
Sea Safari
Belhaven, NC 800-688-6174
Sea Safari Ltd.
Belhaven, NC 800-688-6174
Sea Snack Foods
Los Angeles, CA 213-622-2204
Sea Watch Intl.
Easton, MD 410-822-7500
Seaberghs Frozen Foods
White Plains, NY 914-948-6377
Seabrook Brothers & Sons
Seabrook, NJ 856-455-8080
Seafood Producers Coop ative
Bellingham, WA 360-733-0120
Seapoint Farms
Huntington Beach, CA 888-722-7098
Seatech Corporation
Lynnwood, WA 425-487-3231
Seneca Foods
Marion, NY 315-926-8100
Serendipity 3
New York, NY 800-805-5493
Sesinco Foods
New York, NY 212-243-1306
Seviroli Foods
Garden City, NY
Seymour & Sons Seafood
Diberville, MS 228-392-4020

Shamrock Foods Company
Phoenix, AZ 800-289-3663
Shaw's Southern Belle Frozen
Jacksonville, FL 888-742-9772
Shawmut Fishing Company
Anchorage, AK. 709-334-2559
Shelley's Prime Meats
Jersey City, NJ 201-433-3434
Shonna's Gourmet Goodies
West Bridgewater, MA 888-312-7868
Sidari's Italian Foods
Cleveland, OH 216-431-3344
Sill Farms Market
Lawrence, MI 269-674-3755
Silver Lining Seafood
Ketchikan, AK 907-225-9865
Silver State Foods
Denver, CO 800-423-3351
Simeus Foods International
Mansfield, TX. 888-772-3663
Simmons Foods
Siloam Springs, AR 888-831-7007
Sisler's Ice & Ice Cream
Ohio, IL. 888-891-3856
Sitka Sound Seafoods
Sitka, AK. 907-747-6662
Smart Ice
Fort Myers, FL 239-334-3123
Smeltzer Orchard Company
Frankfort, MI 231-882-4421
Smith Dairy Products Company
Orrville, OH 800-776-7076
Smith Frozen Foods
Weston, OR. 541-566-3515
Smith Frozen Foods
Weston, OR. 800-547-0203
Smith Packing Regional Meat
Utica, NY
Snelgrove Ice Cream Company
Salt Lake City, UT 800-569-0005
Sno-Co Berry Pak
Marysville, WA. 360-659-3555
Snow Ball Foods
Williamstown, NJ 856-629-4081
Snowbear Frozen Custard
W Lafayette, IN. 765-746-2930
Snowcrest Packer
Abbotsford, BC. 800-265-5332
Somerset Industries
Spring House, PA 800-883-8728
Sonstegard Foods Company
Sioux Falls, SD. 800-533-3184
Southeastern Meat Association
Oviedo, FL 407-365-5661
Southern Ice Cream Specialties
Marietta, GA. 770-428-0452
Southtowns Seafood & Meats
Blasdell, NY 716-824-4900
Sparboe Companies
Los Angeles, CA. 213-626-7538
Specialty Brands
Carthage, MO 417-358-8104
Squab Producers of California
Modesto, CA. 209-537-4744
St. Ours & Company
Norwell, MA. 781-331-8520
Star Foods
Cleveland, OH 800-837-0992
Star Ravioli Manufacturing Company
Moonachie, NJ 201-933-6427
Starbucks Coffee Company
Seattle, WA 800-782-7282
Starkel Poultry
Roy, WA 253-845-2876
Steak-Umm Company
Shillington, PA 860-928-5900
Stegall Smoked Turkey
Marshville, NC 800-851-6034
Stewart's Ice Cream
Saratoga Springs, NY 518-581-1300
Stinson Seafood Company
San Diego, CA
Stolt SeaFarm
Elverta, CA 800-525-0333
Stone Crabs
Miami Beach, FL 800-260-2722
Stone's Home Made Candy Shop
Oswego, NY 888-223-3928
Strathroy Foods
Strathroy, ON 519-245-4600
Strebin Farms
Troutdale, OR 503-665-8328

Sudlersville Frozen Food Locker
Sudlersville, MD. 410-438-3106
Sugar Creek/Eskimo Pie
Russellville, AR 800-445-2715
Sun-Glo of Idaho
Sugar City, ID 208-356-7346
Sungarden Sprouts
Cookeville, TN 931-526-1106
SunMeadow Family of Products
Saint Petersburg, FL 727-573-2211
Sunny Avocado
Jamul, CA 800-999-2862
Sunnyslope Farms Egg Ranch
Cherry Valley, CA. 951-845-1131
Sunset Specialty Foods
Sunset Beach, CA 562-592-4976
Sunshine Dairy Foods
Portland, OR 503-234-7526
Sunshine Food Sales
Miami, FL. 305-696-2885
Super Snooty Sea Food Corporation
Boston, MA. 617-426-6390
Superbrand Dairies
Montgomery, AL. 334-277-6010
Superior Foods
Watsonville, CA 831-728-3691
Superstore Industries
Fairfield, CA 707-864-0502
Supreme Frozen Products
Chicago, IL 773-622-3777
Sutherland's Foodservice
Forest Park, GA 404-366-8550
Suzanna's Kitchen
Duluth, GA 800-241-2455
Sweet Fortunes of America
Woodstock, NY. 845-679-7327
Sweet Shop
La Crosse, WI 608-784-7724
Sweet Water Seafood Corporation
Carlstadt, NJ 201-939-6622
Sweety Novelty
Monterey Park, CA. 626-282-4482
Swissland Packing Company
Ashkum, IL. 800-321-8325
Switzer's
East Saint Louis, IL 618-271-6336
Symons Frozen Foods
Galvin, WA 360-736-1321
Sysco Central Illinois
Lincoln, IL 217-735-6100
Sysco Indianapolis
Indianapolis, IN 317-291-2020
Sysco Louisville
Louisville, KY 800-669-1236
T. Marzetti Company
Columbus, OH 614-846-2232
Table De France
Ontario, CA. 909-923-5205
TAIF
Folcroft, PA. 610-522-0122
Taku Smokehouse
Juneau, AK 800-582-5122
Tami Great Food
Monsey, NY 732-803-6366
Tampa Maid Foods
Lakeland, FL. 800-237-7637
Tantos Foods International
Markham, ON. 905-943-9993
Tasty Mix Quality Foods
Brooklyn, NY. 866-TAS-TYMX
Tasty Selections
Concord, ON. 905-760-2353
Taylor Shellfish Farms
Shelton, WA 360-426-6178
Tebay Dairy Company
Parkersburg, WV. 304-422-1014
Tech Pak Solutions
Westbrook, ME 207-878-6667
Tenn Valley Ham Company
Paris, TN. 731-642-9740
Tex-Mex Cold Storage
Brownsville, TX 956-831-9433
The Bama Company
Tulsa, OK 800-756-2262
The Pillsbury Company
Chelsea, MA 800-370-7834
Thompson Packers
Slidell, LA. 800-989-6328
Thoms-Proestler Company
Rock Island, IL 309-787-1234
Threshold RehabilitationServices
Reading, PA 610-777-7691

Thrifty Ice Cream
El Monte, CA 626-571-0122
Thyme & Truffles Hors D'oeuvres
Dollard-Des-Ormeaux, QC. 877-785-9759
Tichon Seafood Corporation
New Bedford, MA 508-999-5607
Tillamook County Creamery Association
Tillamook, OR 503-815-1300
Tipiak
Stamford, CT. 203-961-9117
TNT Crust
Green Bay, WI. 920-431-7240
Toft Dairy
Sandusky, OH 800-521-4606
Tom's Ice Cream Bowl
Zanesville, OH 740-452-5267
Tomasso Corporation
Baie D'Urfe, QC. 514-325-3000
Tony Downs Foods Company
Saint James, MN 507-375-3111
Tony's Ice Cream Company
Gastonia, NC. 704-867-7085
Topper Food Products
East Brunswick, NJ. 800-377-2823
Topps Meat Company
Elizabeth, NJ. 877-998-6777
Totino's
Minneapolis, MN 800-248-7310
Trade Winds Pizza
Green Bay, WI. 920-336-7810
Trans Pecos Foods
San Antonio, TX. 210-228-0896
Trappe Packing Corporation
Trappe, MD. 410-476-3185
Travis Meats
Powell, TN 800-247-7606
Tree Top
Selah, WA 800-367-6571
Tri-State Processing Company
Kokomo, IN 317-452-4008
Trident Seafoods Corporation
Salem, NH. 603-893-3368
Trident Seafoods Corporation
Seattle, WA 800-426-5490
Triple D Orchards
Empire, MI 866-781-9410
Triple U Enterprises
Fort Pierre, SD 605-567-3624
Tripp Bakers
Wheeling, IL. 800-621-3702
Triton Seafood Company
Medley, FL 305-888-8999
Tropical Illusions
Trenton, MO 660-359-5422
Tropical Treets
North York, ON. 888-424-8229
Tropicana
Bradenton, FL. 800-237-7799
Tru-Blu Cooperative Associates
New Lisbon, NJ 609-894-8717
Tucson Frozen Storage
Tucson, AZ 520-623-0660
Tupman-Thurlow Company
Deerfield Beach, FL 954-596-9989
Turano Pasty Shops
Berwyn, IL 708-788-5320
Turk Brothers Custom Meats
Ashland, OH 800-789-1051
Turkey Store Company
Faribault, MN 507-334-2050
Turris Italian Foods
Roseville, MI 586-773-6010
Turtle Mountain
Eugene, OR. 541-338-9400
Twin City Foods
Stanwood, WA 208-743-5568
Two Chefs on a Roll
Carson, CA 800-842-3025
Tyson Foods
Wilkesboro, NC 336-838-0083
Tyson Foods
Bloomfield, MO 573-568-2153
Tyson Foods
Dexter, MO 573-624-4548
Tyson Foods
Springdale, AR 800-643-3410
Tyson Foods
Berryville, AR. 870-423-3331
Tyson Foods Plant
Santa Teresa, NM 800-351-8184
Tyson Fresh Meats Meat Packing Plant
Emporia, KS 620-343-3640

Umpqua Dairy Products Company
Roseburg, OR 541-672-2638
Uncle Ralph's Cookie Company
Frederick, MD. 800-422-0626
Unilever
Lisle, IL. 877-995-4483
Unique Ingredients
Naches, WA. 509-653-1991
United Dairy
Martins Ferry, OH. 800-252-1542
United Dairy
Uniontown, PA 800-966-6455
United Meat Company
San Francisco, CA 415-864-2118
United Shellfish Company
Grasonville, MD 410-827-8171
Valley Dairy Fairview Dairy
Windber, PA 814-467-1384
Valley Meat Company
Modesto, CA. 800-222-6328
Valley Meats
Coal Valley, IL 309-799-7341
Van De Kamp Frozen Foods
Mountain Lake, NJ 973-541-6620
Van Drunen Farms
Momence, IL. 815-472-3537
Van Oriental Foods
Dallas, TX. 214-630-0333
Van-Lang Foods
Countryside, IL. 708-588-0800
Velda Farms
Winter Haven, FL 800-279-4166
Velda Farms
North Miami Beach, FL 800-795-4649
Velvet Ice Cream Company
Utica, OH 800-589-5000
Venison America
Hudson, WI. 800-310-2360
Vie de France Yamazaki
Vernon, LA 323-582-1241
Viking Seafoods Inc
Malden, MA 800-225-3020
Vince's Seafoods
Gretna, LA 504-368-1544
Vincent Piazza Jr & Sons
Harahan, LA 800-259-5016
Virginia Trout Company
Monterey, VA 540-468-2280
Vita-Pakt Citrus Company
Covina, CA 626-332-1101
Vitamilk Dairy
Bellingham, WA 206-529-4128
Vivolac Cultures Corporation
Indianapolis, IN 317-356-8460
VMI Corporation
Omaha, NE 800-228-2248
W & G Marketing Company
Ames, IA. 515-233-4774
W.L. Petrey Wholesale Company
Luverne, AL 334-230-5674
Walt Koch
Decatur, GA 404-378-3666
Waltkoch
Decatur, GA 404-378-3666
Wanchese Fish Company
Suffolk, VA. 757-673-4500
Wapsie Produce
Decorah, IA. 563-382-4271
Ward Cove Packing Company
Seattle, WA 206-323-3200
Warwick Ice Cream Company
Warwick, RI 401-821-8403
Washington Potato Company
Warden, WA 509-349-8803
Washington Rhubarb Growers Association
Sumner, WA 800-435-9911
Waugh Foods
East Peoria, IL. 309-427-8000
Wawona Frozen Foods
Clovis, CA 559-299-2901
Wayfield Foods
Atlanta, GA. 404-559-3200
Wayne Dairy Products
Richmond, IN 800-875-9294
Wayne Farms LLC
Jack, AL 334-897-3435
Webster Farms
Cambridge Station, NS 902-538-9492
Welch's Foods Inc
Concord, MA 800-340-6870
Welch's Foods Inc.
North East, PA. 814-725-4577
Weldon Ice Cream Company
Millersport, OH. 740-467-2400
Wells' Dairy
Le Mars, IA. 800-942-3800
Welsh Farms
Edison, NJ. 800-221-0663
Welsh Farms
Clifton, NJ. 973-772-2388
Wenk Foods Inc
Madison, SD 605-256-4569
Wenner Bread Products
Bayport, NY 800-869-6262
Westco-Bake Mark
Pico Rivera, CA 562-949-1054
Western Foods
Little Rock, AR. 501-562-4646
Westin
Omaha, NE 800-228-6098
Weyand Fisheries
Wyandotte, MI 800-521-9815
Wham Food & Beverage
Hollywood, FL 954-920-7857
Whitaker Foods
Waterloo, IA 800-553-7490
White Cap Fish Company
Islip, NY 631-581-0125
White Toque
Perth Amboy, NJ. 800-237-6936
Whitey's Ice Cream Manufacturing
Moline, IL. 888-594-4839
Wick's Pies
Winchester, IN 800-642-5880
Wild Rice Exchange
Woodland, CA. 800-223-7423
Williams Institutional Foods
Douglas, GA 912-384-5270
Windatt Farms
Picton, ON. 613-393-5289
Winder Dairy
West Valley, UT 800-946-3371
Windsor Foods
Houston, TX 713-843-5200
Winmix/Natural Care Products
Englewood, FL 941-475-7432
Winter Garden Citrus
Winter Garden, FL 407-656-4423
Wolferman's
Medford, OR
Wolfgang Puck Food Company
Santa Monica, CA. 310-432-1350
Wong Wing Foods
Montreal, QC 800-361-4820
Wornick Company
Cincinnati, OH 800-860-4555
Wrangell Fisheries
Wrangell, AK 907-874-3346
Wright Ice Cream
Cayuga, IN 800-686-9561
Yamasa Fish Cake Company
Los Angeles, CA. 213-626-2211
Yarnell Ice Cream Company
Searcy, AR 800-766-2414
Yorktown Baking Company
Yorktown Heights, NY 800-235-3961
Zartic Inc
Rome, GA. 800-241-0516
Ziegenfelder Company
Wheeling, WV 304-232-6360

Spices, Seasonings & Seeds

General

DEKO International
Earth City, MO 314-298-0910
Mexnutri
San Luis Potosi, ... 444-841-5625

Herbs

A M Todd Company
Kalamazoo, MI 800-968-2603
Agrexco USA
Jamaica, NY 718-481-8700
Agrinom LLC
Hakalau, HI 808-963-6771
Agrocosa
Meoqui, CH 639-573-1611
Allen & Cowley SpecialtyFoods
Phoenix, AZ 800-279-1634
American Botanicals
Eolia, MO 800-684-6070
American Mercantile Corporation
Memphis, TN 901-454-1900
Anna's Unlimited, Inc
Austin, TX 800-849-7054
Aphrodisia Products
Brooklyn, NY 877-274-3677
Ashland Sausage Company
Carol Stream, IL 630-690-2600
Assets Health Foods
Hillsborough, NJ 888-849-2048
Atlantic Quality Spice &Seasonings
New Brunswick, NJ 800-584-0422
August Kitchen
Armonk, NY 914-589-6477
Badia Spices
Miami, FL 305-629-8000
BDS Natural Products, Inc.
Carson, CA 310-518-2227
Belmont Chemicals
Clifton, NJ 800-722-5070
Beta Pure Foods
Aptos, CA 831-685-6565
Better Living Products
Princeton, TX 972-736-6691
Bijol & Spices, Inc.
Miami, FL 888-BIJ-L 70
Bolner's Fiesta Products
San Antonio, TX 210-734-6404
Brewster Foods TestLab
Reseda, CA 818-881-4268
Castella Imports
Hauppauge, NY 866-227-8355
Chef Tim Foods, LLC
Etters, PA 717-802-0350
Cinnabar Specialty Foods
Prescott, AZ 866-293-6433
Colorado Spice
Boulder, CO 800-677-7423
Connection Source
Alpharetta, GA 770-667-1051
Crystal Star Herbal Nutrition
Salinas, CA 831-422-7500
Cyclone Enterprises
Houston, TX 281-872-0087
Daregal Gourmet
Princeton, NJ 609-375-2312
Dion Herbs & Spices
St-Jerome, QC 877-569-8001
Dizzy Pig Barbeque Company
Manassas, VA 703-273-3580
Dragunara LLC
Palos Verdes Estate, CA 310-618-8818
DynaPro International
Kaysville, UT 800-877-1413
Eckhart Corporation
Novato, CA 415-892-3880
Fantis Foods
Carlstadt, NJ 201-933-6200
FDP
Santa Rosa, CA 707-547-1776
Freed, Teller & Freed
South San Francisco, CA 800-370-7371
Frontier Cooperative Herbs
Boulder, CO 800-669-3275
Georgia Spice Company
Atlanta, GA 800-453-9997
Gloria's Gourmet
New Britain, CT 860-225-9196
Great Spice Company
Reno, NV 800-730-3575
Green House
San Luis Rey, CA 760-439-6515
Green House Fine Herbs
Encinitas, CA 760-942-5371
Guayaki Sustainable Rainforest Products
Sebastopol, CA 888-482-9254
Hari Om Farms
Eagleville, TN 615-368-7778
Health Concerns
Oakland, CA 800-233-9355
Health Products Corporation
Yonkers, NY 914-423-2900
HealthBest
San Marcos, CA 760-752-5230
Heffy's BBQ Company
Kansas City, MO 816-200-2271
Herb Connection
Springville, UT 801-489-4254
Herb Patch of Vermont
Bellows Falls, VT 800-282-4372
Herbs, Etc.
Santa Fe, NM 888-694-3727
Jodie's Kitchen
Pinellas Park, FL 800-728-3704
Kalustyan Corporation
Union, NJ 908-688-6111
La Flor Spices
Hauppauge, NY 631-885-9601
Leeward Resources
Baltimore, MD 410-837-9003
Lefty Spices
Waldorf, MD 301-885-1817
M. Brown & Sons
Bremen, IN 800-258-7450
McCormick & Company
Sparks, MD 800-632-5847
Mermaid Spice Corporation
Fort Myers, FL 239-693-1986
Mezza
Lake Forest, IL 888-206-6054
Modern Day Masala, LLC
Marietta, GA 866-611-3757
Mojave Foods Corporation
Commerce, CA 323-890-8900
Mom's Gourmet, LLC
Chagrin Falls, OH 440-564-9702
Morris J. Golombeck
Brooklyn, NY 718-284-3505
Mother Shucker's Original Cocktail Sauce
Columbia, SC 803-261-3802
Nature's Sunshine Products Company
Provo, UT 800-223-8225
Nature's Way
Lehi, UT 800-962-8873
Now Foods
Bloomingdale, IL 888-669-3663
Pacific Spice Company
Commerce, CA 800-281-0614
Pereg Gourmet Spices
Flushing, NY 718-261-6767
Phamous Phloyd's Barbeque Sauce
Denver, CO 303-757-3285
Pots de Creme
Lexington, KY 859-299-2254
Prince of Peace Enterprises
Hayward, CA 800-732-2328
QBI
South Plainfield, NJ 908-668-0088
Realsalt
Heber City, UT 800-367-7258
Red Monkey Foods
Mount Vernon, MI 417-466-9109
Republic of Tea
Novato, CA 80- 2-8 48
Rodelle Vanillas
Fort Collins, CO 800-898-5457
Sampac Enterprises
South San Francisco, CA 650-876-0808
San Francisco Herb & Natural Food Company
Fremont, CA 800-227-2830
San Francisco Urban Naturals
Fremont, CA 510-770-1215
Sentry Seasonings
Elmhurst, IL 630-530-5370

The product development experts of Sentry Seasonings are eager to offer the assistance and hands-on experience to food processors of all sizes. Sentry Seasonings will ensure the consistent high quality and repeat sales of your products, whether you choose one of our many off-the-shelf Bench Mark products or a modified version to meet your preferences. Sentry Seasonings can also duplicate and/or improve your present flavor profile; formulate, blend and package specifically for your requirements.

Specialty Food America
Hopkinsville, KY 888-881-1633
Spice House International Specialties
Hicksville, NY 516-942-7248
Spice World
Orlando, FL 800-433-4979
Sunshine Farm & Gardens
Renick, WV 304-497-2208
Superior Trading Company
San Francisco, CA 415-982-8722

SupHerb Farms
Turlock, CA 800-787-4372

Frozen culinary herb and specialty vegetable ingredients.

Universal Formulas
Kalamazoo, MI 800-342-6960
Van Eeghen International Inc
St Laurent, QC 514-332-6455
Vantage USA
Chicago, IL 773-247-1086
Wagner Gourmet Foods
Lenexa, KS 913-469-5411
Whole Herb Company
Sonoma, CA 707-935-1077
Wisdom Natural Brands
Gilbert, AZ 800-899-9908
Woodland Foods
Gurnee, IL 847-625-8600
World Spice
Roselle, NJ 800-234-1060
Xcell International Corporation
Lemont, IL 800-722-7751
Yellow Emperor
Eugene, OR 877-485-6664
Young Winfield
Kleinburg, ON 905-893-9682

Herbal Supplements

A M Todd Company
Kalamazoo, MI 800-968-2603
Abunda Life Laboratories
Asbury Park, NJ 732-775-7575
Acta Health Products
Sunnyvale, CA 408-732-6830
ADH Health Products
Congers, NY 845-268-0027
Advanced Spice & Trading
Carrollton, TX 800-872-7811
Agumm
Coral Springs, FL 954-344-0607
Alfred L. Wolff, Inc.
Park Ridge, IL 847-759-8888
Allen & Cowley SpecialtyFoods
Phoenix, AZ 800-279-1634
Alta Health Products
Idaho City, ID 800-423-4155
Alternative Health & Herbs
Albany, OR 800-345-4152
Amazing Herbs Nutraceuticals
Stone Mountain, GA 800-241-9138
Ameri-Kal Inc
Wichita Falls, TX 940-322-5400

American Biosciences
Blauvelt, NY 888-884-7770
Aphrodisia Products
Brooklyn, NY 877-274-3677
Arise & Shine Herbal Products
Medford, OR...... 800-688-2444

Asiamerica Ingredients
Westwood, NJ 201-497-5531

Processor, importer, exporter and distributor of bulk vitamins, amino acids, nutraceuticals, aromatic chemicals, food additives, herbs, mineral nutrients and pharmaceuticals.

Auroma International, Inc.
Silver Lake, WI...... 262-889-8569
Bedrock Farm Certified Organic Medicinal Herbs
Wakefield, RI 401-789-9943
Bionutritional Research Group
Irvine, CA
Blessed Herbs
Oakham, MA...... 800-489-4372
Bodyonics Limited
Farmingdale, NY 516-822-1230
Botanical Products
Springville, CA...... 559-539-3432
Brewster Foods TestLab
Reseda, CA...... 818-881-4268
Brucia Plant Extracts
Shingle Springs, CA 530-676-2774
Cinnabar Specialty Foods
Prescott, AZ 866-293-6433
Country Life
Hauppauge, NY 800-645-5768
Cyanotech Corporation
Kailua Kona, HI 800-395-1353
Dr. Christopher's Original Foods
Spanish Fork, UT 800-453-1406
Dreamous Corporation
Torrance, CA...... 800-251-7543
EB Botanicals
Montclair, NJ 973-655-9585
Eclectic Institute
Sandy, OR...... 503-668-4120
Edge Labs
Trenton, NJ 866-334-3522
Emerling International Foods
Buffalo, NY...... 716-833-7381

We supply food manufacturers and food service customers worldwide (since 1988) with bulk ingredients including: Fruits & Vegetables; Juice Concentrates; Herbs & Spices; Oils & Vinegars; Flavors & Colors; Honey & Molasses. We also produce PURE MAPLE SYRUP.

Empire Spice Mills
Winnipeg, NB 204-786-1594
En Garde Health Products
Reseda, CA
Essential Flavors & Fragrances, Inc
Corona, CA...... 888-333-9935
Essiac Canada International
Ottawa, ON 613-729-9111
Fmali Herb
Santa Cruz, CA...... 831-423-7913
Frank Capurro & Son
Moss Landing, CA 831-728-3904
Freeman Industries
Tuckahoe, NY...... 800-666-6454
Functional Products LLC
Atlantic Beach, FL 800-628-5908
Fungi Perfecti
Olympia, WA 800-780-9126
Gaia Herbs
Brevard, NC 800-831-7780
GCI Nutrients (USA)
Foster City, CA...... 650-697-4700
Generation Farms
Rice, TX 903-326-4263
Geni
Noblesville, IN 888-656-4364
Ginco International
Simi Valley, CA...... 800-423-5176
Ginkgoton
Gardena, CA...... 310-538-8383
Global Botanical
Barrie, ON...... 705-733-2117
Global Express Gourmet
Bozeman, MT...... 406-587-5571
Global Health Laboratories
Amityville, NY 631-777-2134
Graminex
Saginaw, MI 877-472-6469
Green Gold Group
Marathon, WI 888-533-7288
Green Grown Products Inc
Marina Del Ray, CA 310-828-1686
Green Turtle Bay Vitamin Company
Summit, NJ...... 800-887-8535
H. Reisman Corporation
Orange, NJ 973-677-9200
Health & Nutrition Systems International
Boynton Beach, FL...... 561-433-0733
Health Plus
Chino, CA...... 800-822-6225
Health Products Corporation
Yonkers, NY 914-423-2900
Heart Foods Company
Minneapolis, MN 800-229-3663
Herb Connection
Springville, UT...... 801-489-4254
Herbal Magic
Forest Knolls, CA...... 415-488-9488
Herbal Products & Development
Aptos, CA...... 831-688-8706
Herbalist & Alchemist
Washington, NJ...... 908-689-9020
HerbaSway Laboratories
Wallingford, CT 800-672-7322
Herbco International
Duvall, WA...... 425-788-7903
Herbs from China
Chicago, IL 866-823-4372
Herbs, Etc.
Santa Fe, NM 888-433-1212
Hill Nutritional Products
Cherry Hill, NJ 856-857-0811
Himalaya
Houston, TX 800-869-4640
Himalayan Heritage
Fredonia, WI...... 888-414-9500

Honso USA
Chandler, AZ....................888-461-5808
Humco
Texarkana, TX....................903-334-6200
IL HWA American Corporation
Worcester, MA....................800-446-7364
Indena USA
Seattle, WA....................206-340-6140
Indiana Botanic Gardens
Hobart, IN....................219-947-4040
IVC American Vitamin
Freehold, NJ....................800-666-8482
Jaguar Yerba Company
Ashland, OR....................800-839-0775
Janca's Jojoba Oil & Seed Company
Mesa, AZ....................480-497-9494
Jarrow Industries
Santa Fe Springs, CA....................562-906-1919
JBS Natural Products
Dallas, PA....................800-565-6207
JR Laboratories Cc 13 Herbs Inc
Honesdale, PA....................570-253-5826
Kalustyan Corporation
Union, NJ....................908-688-6111
Kingchem
Allendale, NJ....................800-211-4330
Kombucha Wonder Drink
Portland, OR....................877-224-7331
LA Lifestyle NutritionalProducts
Santa Ana, CA....................800-387-4786
LifeTime Nutritional Specialties
Orange, CA....................714-634-9340
Local Tofu
Nyack, NY....................845-727-6393
Mafco Natural Products
Richmond, VA....................804-222-1600
Maharishi Ayurveda Products International
Fairfield, IA....................800-255-8332
Mayway Corporation
Oakland, CA....................800-262-9929
McCormick & Company
Sparks, MD....................800-632-5847
McFadden Farm
Potter Valley, CA....................800-544-8230
Meridian Trading
Boulder, CO....................303-442-8683
Michael's Naturopathic
San Antonio, TX....................800-525-9643
Mincing Overseas Spice Company
Dayton, NJ....................732-355-9944
Mix Industries
Richton Park, IL....................708-339-6692
Motherland International Inc
Rancho Cucamonga, CA....................800-590-5407
Nature's Herbs
Merritt, BC....................800-437-2257
NatureMost Laboratories
Middletown, CT....................800-234-2112
NBTY
Ronkonkoma, NY....................800-920-6090
NorSun Food Group
West Chester, OH....................800-886-4326
North West Marketing Company
Brea, CA....................714-529-0980
Northridge Laboratories
Chatsworth, CA....................818-882-5622
Nutritional Life Support Systems
, OH....................800-533-4372
Paragon Laboratories
Torrance, CA....................800-231-3670
Pendery's
Dallas, TX....................800-533-1870
Pharmline
Florida, NY....................845-651-4443
Phyto-Technologies
Woodbine, IA....................877-809-3404
Prairie Sun Grains
Calgary, AB....................800-556-6807
Prince of Peace Enterprises
Hayward, CA....................800-732-2328
Pro Form Labs
Orinda, CA....................925-299-9000
Pro. Pac. Labs
Ogden, UT....................888-277-6722
Progenix Corporation
Wausau, WI....................800-233-3356
Rainbow Light Nutritional Systems
Santa Cruz, CA....................800-635-1233
Restaurant Lulu Gourmet Products
San Francisco, CA....................888-693-5800
Sadkhin Complex
Brooklyn, NY....................800-723-5446
San Francisco Herb & Natural Food Company
Fremont, CA....................800-227-2830
Sandbar Trading Corporation
Louisville, CO....................303-499-7480
Schiff Food Products
North Bergen, NJ....................201-868-6800
Schiff Nutrition International
Salt Lake City, UT....................800-526-6251
Silva International
Momence, IL....................815-472-3535
Soft Gel Technologies
Commerce, CA....................800-360-7484
Soolim
Buffalo Grove, IL....................847-357-8515
Spice World
Orlando, FL....................800-433-4979
Starwest Botanicals
Rancho Cordova, CA....................888-273-4372
Stevia LLC
Valley Forge, PA....................888-878-3842
Sundial Gardens
Higganum, CT....................860-345-4290
Superior Trading Company
San Francisco, CA....................415-982-8722
Swagger Foods Corporation
Vernon Hills, IL....................847-913-1200
Tova Industries
Louisville, KY....................888-532-8682
Turtle Island Herbs
Boulder, CO....................800-684-4060
Tusitala
Grand Bay, AL....................251-865-6240
United Society of Shakers
New Gloucester, ME....................888-624-6345
Van Drunen Farms
Momence, IL....................815-472-3537
Vitamer Laboratories
Irvine, CA....................800-432-8355
Vitarich Laboratories
Naples, FL....................800-817-9999
VitaTech International
Tustin, CA....................714-832-9700
Whole Herb Company
Sonoma, CA....................707-935-1077
World Ginseng Center
San Francisco, CA....................800-747-8808
World Organics Corporation
Huntington Beach, CA....................714-893-0017
Yerba Prima
Ashland, OR....................800-488-4339

for Beef

Sentry Seasonings
Elmhurst, IL....................630-530-5370

for Pork

Sentry Seasonings
Elmhurst, IL....................630-530-5370

for Poultry

Sentry Seasonings
Elmhurst, IL....................630-530-5370

for Seafood

Hsu's Ginseng Enterprises
Wausau, WI....................800-826-1577
Sentry Seasonings
Elmhurst, IL....................630-530-5370

Salt

Adluh Flour Mill
Columbia, SC....................800-692-3584
Agri-Dairy Products
Purchase, NY....................914-697-9580
Ajinomoto Food Ingredients LLC
Chicago, IL....................773-714-1436
Atlantic Quality Spice &Seasonings
New Brunswick, NJ....................800-584-0422
Blue Chip Group
Salt Lake City, UT....................800-878-0099
Cabo Rojo Enterprises
Boqueron, PR....................787-254-0015
Canadian Salt Company Limited
Pointe Claire, QC....................514-630-0900
CHR Hansen
Elyria, OH....................800-558-0802
Con Yeager Spice Company
Zelienople, PA....................800-222-2460
Dr. Paul Lohmann Inc.
Islandia, NY....................631-851-8810
Franco's Cocktail Mixes
Pompano Beach, FL....................800-782-4508
Heinz Portion Control
Mason, OH....................800-547-8924
ICL Performance Products
St. Louis, MO....................800-244-6169
Java-Gourmet/Keuka Lake Coffee Roaster
Penn Yan, NY....................888-478-2739
Jungbunzlauer
Newton, MA....................800-828-0062
Lawry's Foods
Monrovia, CA....................800-595-8917
Morton Salt
Chicago, IL....................800-789-7258
Morton Salt Company
Chicago, IL....................312-807-2000
North American Salt Company
Overland Park, KS....................913-344-9100
Nutricepts
Burnsville, MN....................800-949-9060
Oregon Flavor Rack
Eugene, OR....................541-342-2085
Rapunzel Pure Organics
Bloomfield, NJ....................800-225-1449
Redi-Froze
South Bend, IN....................574-237-5111
Stickney & Poor Company
Peterborough, NH....................603-924-2259
Swagger Foods Corporation
Vernon Hills, IL....................847-913-1200
Twang
San Antonio, TX....................800-950-8095
United Salt Corporation
Houston, TX....................800-554-8658

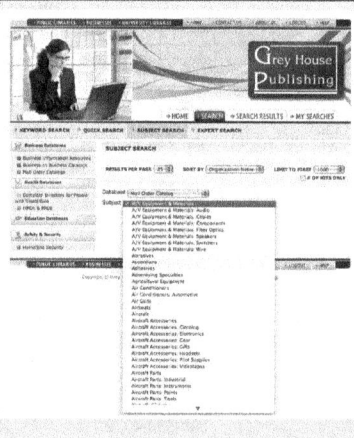

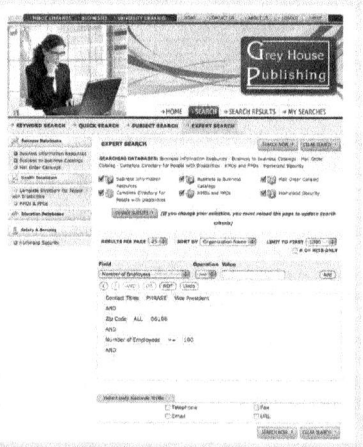

Active

Dr. Paul Lohmann Inc.
Islandia, NY 631-851-8810
Particle Dynamics
Saint Louis, MO 800-452-4682

Celery

American Key Food Products
Closter, NJ. 800-767-0237
Gel Spice Company, Inc
Bayonne, NJ 800-922-0230

Garlic

American Key Food Products
Closter, NJ. 800-767-0237
Gel Spice Company, Inc
Bayonne, NJ 800-922-0230

MSG & Salt Mixture

American Food Ingredients
Oceanside, CA 760-929-9505
Compass Minerals
Overland Park, KS 877-462-7258
DeSouza International
Beaumont, CA. 800-373-5171
Dr. Paul Lohmann Inc.
Islandia, NY 631-851-8810

Onion

American Key Food Products
Closter, NJ. 800-767-0237
Atlantic Quality Spice &Seasonings
New Brunswick, NJ 800-584-0422
Gel Spice Company, Inc
Bayonne, NJ 800-922-0230

Rock

Morton Salt Company
Chicago, IL. 312-807-2000

Sea

Blue Crab Bay Company
Melfa, VA 800-221-2722
Chieftain Wild Rice Company
Spooner, WI 800-262-6368
D'Artagnan
Newark, NJ 800-327-8246
Heartland Gourmet Popcorn
Elk Grove Village, IL 866-945-5346
Redmond Minerals
Redmond, UT 800-367-7258
Sea Salt Superstore
Lynnwood, WA. 866-999-7258
Selina Naturally
Arden, NC. 800-867-7258
Spice Lab
Oakland Park, PA 954-275-4478

Substitutes

Ajinomoto Food Ingredients LLC
Chicago, IL 773-714-1436
Mermaid Spice Corporation
Fort Myers, FL 239-693-1986
Morre-Tec Industries
Union, NJ 908-688-9009
Morton Salt
Chicago, IL 800-789-7258
Spice Hunter
San Luis Obispo, CA 800-444-3061

Tablets

Dr. Paul Lohmann Inc.
Islandia, NY 631-851-8810

Enriched

Dr. Paul Lohmann Inc.
Islandia, NY 631-851-8810

Seasonings

A M Todd Company
Kalamazoo, MI. 800-968-2603
AC Legg
Calera, AL. 800-422-5344
Adluh Flour Mill
Columbia, SC 800-692-3584
Advanced Food Systems Inc.
Somerset, NJ. 732-873-6776
Ailments E.D. Foods Inc.
Pointe Claire, QC 800-267-3333
Alberto-Culver Company
Melrose Park, IL. 708-450-3000
All American Seasonings
Denver, CO 303-574-9223
Alpine Touch Spices
Choteau, MT. 877-755-2525
American Food Ingredients
Oceanside, CA 760-929-9505
American Key Food Products
Closter, NJ. 800-767-0237
Ampacco
Sparks, MD 800-632-5847
Andy's Seasoning
St Louis, MO. 800-305-3004
Aphrodisia Products
Brooklyn, NY 877-274-3677
Ariake USA, Inc.
Harrisonburg, VA 888-201-5885
Arizona Natural Products
Phoenix, AZ 602-997-6098
Atlantic Quality Spice &Seasonings
New Brunswick, NJ 800-584-0422
Atlantic Seasonings
Kinston, NC 800-433-5261
Au Printemps Gourmet
Saint-Jerome, QC 800-663-0416
Autin's Cajun Cookery
Covington, LA 800-877-7290
Badia Spices
Miami, FL. 305-629-8000
Baker's Rib
Dallas, TX. 214-748-5433
Bakon Yeast
Scottsdale, AZ. 480-595-9370
Barataria Spice Company
Barataria, LA. 800-793-7650
BBQ'n Fools
Bend, OR. 800-671-8652
Bell Flavors & Fragrances
Northbrook, IL 800-323-4387
Benson's Gourmet Seasonings
Azusa, CA. 800-325-5619
Bettah Buttah, LLC
Kansas City, KS 800-568-8468
Bittersweet Herb Farm
Shelburne Falls, MA. 800-456-1599
BKW Seasonings Inc
Knoxville, TN. 865-466-8365
Blend Pak
Bloomfield, KY 502-252-8000
Blendex Company
Jeffersontown, KY 800-626-6325
Blue Crab Bay Company
Melfa, VA 800-221-2722
Boston Spice & Tea Company
Boston, VA 800-966-4372
Braswell Food Company
Statesboro, GA 800-673-9388
C.F. Sauer Company
Richmond, VA. 800-688-5676
Cabo Rojo Enterprises
Boqueron, PR 787-254-0015
Cajun Boy's Louisiana Products
Baton Rouge, LA 800-880-9575
Cajun Chef Products
Saint Martinville, LA 337-394-7112
California Blending Corpany
El Monte, CA 626-448-1918
Canadian Salt Company Limited
Pointe Claire, QC 514-630-0900
Caribbean Food Delights
Tappan, NY. 845-398-3000
Catamount Specialties ofVermont
Stowe, VT. 800-820-8096
Char Crust
Chicago, IL 800-311-9884
Chef Hans Gourmet Foods
Monroe, LA. 800-890-4267
Chef Merito
Encino, CA 800-637-4861
Chef Paul Prudhomme's Magic Seasonings Blends
Harahan, LA 800-457-2857
Chef Shells Catering & Roadside Cafe
Port Huron, MI 810-966-8371
Cherchies
Malvern, PA 800-644-1980
Chester Fried
Birmingham, AL. 800-288-1555
Chieftain Wild Rice Company
Spooner, WI 800-262-6368
CHR Hansen
Gainesville, FL 352-332-9455
CHR Hansen
Elyria, OH. 440-324-6060
CHR Hansen
Milwaukee, WI. 800-343-4680
CHR Hansen
Elyria, OH. 800-558-0802
Christie Food Products
Randolph, MA 800-727-2523
Christopher Ranch
Gilroy, CA. 408-847-1100
Chugwater Chili Corporation
Chugwater, WY 800-972-4454
Cibolo Junction Food & Spice
Albuquerque, NM. 505-888-1987
Colonna Brothers
North Bergen, NJ 201-864-1115
Colorado Spice
Boulder, CO 800-677-7423
Commercial Creamery Company
Spokane, WA. 800-541-0850
Common Folk Farm
Naples, ME 207-787-2764
Con Yeager Spice Company
Zelienople, PA. 800-222-2460
ConAgra Food Ingredients
Omaha, NE 877-266-2472
ConAgra Grocery Products
Irvine, CA. 714-680-1000
Continental Seasoning
Teaneck, NJ. 800-631-1564
Creative Seasonings
Wakefield, MA 617-246-1461
Crest Foods Company
Ashton, IL. 800-435-6972
Custom Culinary
Lombard, IL 800-621-8827
Dean Distributors
Burlingame, CA 800-792-0816
DeFrancesco & Sons
Firebaugh, CA. 209-364-7000
DEKO International
Earth City, MO 314-298-0910
Demitri's Bloody Mary Seasonings
Seattle, WA 800-627-9649
Dismat Corporation
Toledo, OH 419-531-8963
Dona Yiya Foods
San Sebastian, PR. 787-896-4007
Dorothy Dawson Foods Products
Jackson, MI. 517-788-9830
Earthen Vessels Herb Company
Hockessin, DE 302-234-7667
Elite Spice
Jessup, MD 800-232-3531
Enrico's/Ventre Packing
Syracuse, NY 888-472-8237
Erba Food Products
Brooklyn, NY 718-272-7700
Everglades Foods
Labelle, FL 800-689-2221
Everson Spice Company
Long Beach, CA 800-421-3753
Excalibur Seasoning Company
Pekin, IL 800-444-2169
Fernandez Chili Company
Alamosa, CO. 719-589-6043
First Spice Mixing Company
Long Island City, NY 800-221-1105
Five Star Food Base Company
St Paul, MN. 800-505-7827
Flavor Dynamics
South Plainfield, NJ 888-271-8424
Flavorbank Company
Tucson, AZ 800-835-7603
Fmali Herb
Santa Cruz, CA. 831-423-7913
Food Concentrate Corporation
Oklahoma City, OK 405-840-5633
Food Ingredients Solutions
Blauvelt, NY. 845-353-8501
Foran Spice Company
Oak Creek, WI 800-558-6030
Fox Meadow Farm of Vermont
Rutland, VT 888-754-4204
FW Witt & Company
Yorkville, IL 630-553-6366

Garden of the Gods Seasonings
Colorado Springs, CO. 877-229-1548
Georgia Spice Company
Atlanta, GA. 800-453-9997
Gilroy Foods
Gilroy, CA. 800-921-7502
Golden Specialty Foods
Norwalk, CA. 562-802-2537
Gravymaster, Inc.
Canajoharie, NY 800-839-8938
Green Mountain Gringo
Winston Salem, NC
Griffith Laboratories
Alsip, IL 800-346-9494
Grouse Hunt Farms
Tamaqua, PA 570-467-2850
Guapo Spices Company
Los Angeles, CA. 213-322-8900
Guido's International Foods
Pasadena, CA 877-994-8436
Halladays Harvest Barn
Bellows Falls, VT 802-463-3331
Harris Farms
Coalinga, CA 800-742-1955
Head Country Food Products
Ponca City, OK 888-762-1227
Heartline Foods
Westport, CT. 203-222-0381
Herb Society of America
Willoughby, OH 440-256-0514
Hollman Foods
Chicago, IL 888-926-2879
Homegrown Naturals
Napa, CA. 800-288-1089
Illes Seasonings & Flavors
Carrollton, TX. 800-683-4553
Ingredients Corporationoof America
Memphis, TN 888-242-2669
International Food
Germantown, WI. 800-558-8696
J. Dickerson
Birmingham, AL. 205-956-0881
Jagulana Herbal Products
Badger, CA 559-337-2188
Jensen Luhr & Sons
Hood River, OR 541-386-3811
JM All Purpose Seasoning
Lincoln, NE. 402-421-8326
Kikkoman International
San Francisco, CA 415-956-7750
La Flor Spices
Hauppauge, NY 631-885-9601
Lawry's Foods
Monrovia, CA 800-595-8917
Louisiana Gourmet Enterprises
La Place, LA 985-783-2446
Lucile's Famous Creole Seasonings
Boulder, CO 800-727-3653
Lynch Supply
Lenexa, KS 913-492-8500
Mad Chef Enterprise
Mentor, OH. 800-951-2433
Magic Seasoning Blends
New Orleans, LA 800-457-2857
Maharishi Ayurveda Products International
Fairfield, IA 800-255-8332
Mane Inc.
Milford, OH 513-248-9876
Mansmith Enterprises
San Jn Bautista, CA 800-626-7648
Mansmith's Barbecue
San Jn Bautista, CA 800-626-7648
Marin Food Specialties
Byron, CA. 925-634-6126
Marion-Kay Spices
Brownstown, IN 800-627-7423
Marnap Industries
Buffalo, NY. 716-897-1220
Mayacamas Fine Foods
Sonoma, CA 800-826-9621
McClancy Seasoning Company
Fort Mill, SC. 800-843-1968
McCormick & Company
Sparks, MD 800-632-5847
Meat-O-Mat Corporation
Brooklyn, NY 718-965-7250
Mermaid Spice Corporation
Fort Myers, FL 239-693-1986
Metarom Corporation
Newport, VT 888-882-5555
Mild Bill's Spices
Bulverde, TX 830-980-4124

Misty
Lincoln, NE. 402-466-8424
Modern Products/Fearn Natural Foods
Mequon, WI 800-877-8935
Moderncuts
Mequon, WI 262-242-2400
Mojave Foods Corporation
Commerce, CA 323-890-8900
Morris J. Golombeck
Brooklyn, NY 718-284-3505
Morton Salt
Chicago, IL 800-789-7258
Morton Salt Company
Chicago, IL 312-807-2000
Mrs. McGarrigle's Fine Foods
Merrickville, ON. 877-768-7827
Mulligan Sales
City of Industry, CA 626-968-9621
Newly Weds Foods
Decatur, AL. 800-521-6189
Newly Weds Foods
Chicago, IL 800-621-7521
Newly Weds Foods
Chicago, IL 800-647-9314
North Coast Processing
North East, PA. 814-725-9617
Nu Products Seasoning Company
South Hackensack, NJ 800-836-7692
Old Mansion Foods
Petersburg, VA 800-476-1877
Old World Spices & Seasonings, Inc.
Overland Park, KS 800-241-0070
One Source
Concord, MA 800-554-5501
Oregon Flavor Rack
Eugene, OR. 541-342-2085
Oregon Flavor Rack Spice
Eugene, OR. 800-725-8373
Oregon Spice Company
Portland, OR 800-565-1599
Organic Gourmet
Sherman Oaks, CA 800-400-7772
Original Cajun Injector
New Iberia, LA. 337-367-1344
Pacific Foods
Kent, WA. 800-347-9444
Pappy Meat Company
Fresno, CA 559-291-0218
Pearson's Homestyle
Bowden, AB 877-224-3339
Pelican Bay
Dunedin, FL 800-826-8982
Pemberton's Gourmet Foods
Gray, ME. 800-255-8401
Pleasoning Gourment Seasonings
La Crosse, WI. 800-279-1614
Precise Food Ingredients
Carrollton, TX. 972-323-4951
Presco Food Seasonings
Flemington, NJ. 800-526-1713
Produits Alimentaires Berthelet
Laval, QC 450-665-6100
RC Fine Foods
Belle Mead, NJ 800-526-3953
Rector Foods
Brampton, ON. 888-314-7834
Red Lion Spicy Foods Company
Red Lion, PA. 717-309-8303
Reggie Ball's Cajun Foods
Lake Charles, LA 337-436-0291
Restaurant Lulu Gourmet Products
San Francisco, CA 888-693-5800
REX Pure Foods
New Orleans, LA 800-344-8314
Rezolex
Las Cruces, NM 505-527-1730
Robinson's Barbecue Sauce Company
Oak Park, IL 708-383-8452
Royal Foods & Flavors
Elk Grove Vlg, IL. 847-595-9166
S&B International Corporation
Torrance, CA. 310-257-0177
Salmolux
Federal Way, WA 253-874-2026
San Francisco Herb & Natural Food Company
Fremont, CA. 800-227-2830
San-J International, Inc
Richmond, VA. 800-446-5500
Saratoga Food Specialties
Bolingbrook, IL 800-451-0407
Schiff Food Products
North Bergen, NJ 201-868-6800

Secret Garden
Park Rapids, MN. 800-950-4409
Sentry Seasonings
Elmhurst, IL 630-530-5370

The product development experts of Sentry Seasonings are eager to offer the assistance and hands-on experience to food processors of all sizes. Sentry Seasonings will ensure the consistent high quality and repeat sales of your products, whether you choose one of our many off-the-shelf Bench Mark products or a modified version to meet your preferences. Sentry Seasonings can also duplicate and/or improve your present flavor profile; formulate, blend and package specifically for your requirements.

Shine Companies
Spring, TX. 281-353-8392
Silver Palate Kitchens
Cresskill, NJ 800-872-5283
Soteria
Fairburn, GA. 404-768-5161
SOUPerior Bean & Spice Company
Vancouver, WA 800-878-7687
Southern Delight Gourmet Foods
Bowling Green, KY 866-782-9943
Spice Advice
Ankeny, IA 800-247-5251
Spice Hunter
San Luis Obispo, CA 800-444-3061
Spice King Corporation
Beverly Hills, CA 310-836-7770
Spice World
Orlando, FL. 800-433-4979
St Charles Trading
Batavia, IL. 630-377-0608
Sterigenics International
Los Angeles, CA. 800-472-4508
Sun-Rype Products
Kelowna, BC. 888-786-7973
Superior Quality Foods
Ontario, CA. 800-300-4210
Swagger Foods Corporation
Vernon Hills, IL 847-913-1200
T Hasegawa
Cerritos, CA 714-522-1900
Tampico Spice Company
Los Angeles, CA. 323-235-3154
Taste Maker Foods
Memphis, TN 800-467-1407
Texas Coffee Company
Beaumont, TX. 800-259-3400
Texas Crumb & Food Products
Farmers Branch, TX 800-522-7862
Texas Traditions
Georgetown, TX 800-547-7062
Todd's
Des Moines, IA. 800-247-5363
Tommy Tang's Thai Seasonings
Los Angeles, CA. 818-442-0219
Tony Chachere's Creole Foods
Opelousas, LA 800-551-9066
Trader Vic's Food Products
Emeryville, CA. 877-762-4824
Triple H
Riverside, CA 951-352-5700
Tropical
Charlotte, NC 800-220-1413
UFL Foods
Mississauga, ON. 905-670-7776
Unilever United States
Englewood Cliffs, NJ 201-894-4000
US Ingredients
Naperville, IL 630-820-1711
Vanns Spices
Baltimore, MD 800-583-1693
Victoria Gourmet
Woburn, MA 866-972-6879
Victoria Packing Corporation
Brooklyn, NY 718-927-3000
Wagner Gourmet Foods
Lenexa, KS 913-469-5411
West Pac
Idaho Falls, ID 800-973-7407
Whole Herb Company
Sonoma, CA 707-935-1077
WILD Flavors (Canada)
Mississauga, ON. 800-263-5286
Wildly Delicious
Toronto, ON 888-545-9995

William E. Martin & Sons Company
Jamaica, NY 718-291-1300
Williams Foods, Inc
Lenexa, KS 800-255-6736
Williams-West & Witt Products
Michigan City, IN
Wixon/Fontarome
St Francis, WI 414-769-3000
Woodland Foods
Gurnee, IL 847-625-8600
Woody's Bar-B-Q Sauce Company
Waldenburg, AR 870-579-2251
World Flavors
Warminster, PA 215-672-4400
World Harbors
Auburn, ME 800-355-6221
Wynn Starr Flavors
Allendale, NJ 800-996-7827
Xcell International Corporation
Lemont, IL 800-722-7751
Young Winfield
Kleinburg, ON 905-893-9682
Zatarain's
Gretna, LA 800-435-6639

Baking

Atlantic Quality Spice &Seasonings
New Brunswick, NJ 800-584-0422
Sentry Seasonings
Elmhurst, IL 630-530-5370

The product development experts of Sentry Seasonings are eager to offer the assistance and hands-on experience to food processors of all sizes. Sentry Seasonings will ensure the consistent high quality and repeat sales of your products, whether you choose one of our many off-the-shelf Bench Mark products or a modified version to meet your preferences. Sentry Seasonings can also duplicate and/or improve your present flavor profile; formulate, blend and package specifically for your requirements.

World Spice
Roselle, NJ 800-234-1060

Barbecue

Applecreek Farms
Lexington, KY 800-747-8871
Mansmith's Barbecue
San Jn Bautista, CA 800-626-7648
Sentry Seasonings
Elmhurst, IL 630-530-5370

The product development experts of Sentry Seasonings are eager to offer the assistance and hands-on experience to food processors of all sizes. Sentry Seasonings will ensure the consistent high quality and repeat sales of your products, whether you choose one of our many off-the-shelf Bench Mark products or a modified version to meet your preferences. Sentry Seasonings can also duplicate and/or improve your present flavor profile; formulate, blend and package specifically for your requirements.

Blackening

Atlantic Quality Spice &Seasonings
New Brunswick, NJ 800-584-0422
Sentry Seasonings
Elmhurst, IL 630-530-5370

The product development experts of Sentry Seasonings are eager to offer the assistance and hands-on experience to food processors of all sizes. Sentry Seasonings will ensure the consistent high quality and repeat sales of your products, whether you choose one of our many off-the-shelf Bench Mark products or a modified version to meet your preferences. Sentry Seasonings can also duplicate and/or improve your present flavor profile; formulate, blend and package specifically for your requirements.

Cajun Style

Atlantic Quality Spice &Seasonings
New Brunswick, NJ 800-584-0422
Cajun Creole Products
New Iberia, LA 800-946-8688
Reggie Ball's Cajun Foods
Lake Charles, LA 337-436-0291
Sentry Seasonings
Elmhurst, IL 630-530-5370

The product development experts of Sentry Seasonings are eager to offer the assistance and hands-on experience to food processors of all sizes. Sentry Seasonings will ensure the consistent high quality and repeat sales of your products, whether you choose one of our many off-the-shelf Bench Mark products or a modified version to meet your preferences. Sentry Seasonings can also duplicate and/or improve your present flavor profile; formulate, blend and package specifically for your requirements.

Slap Ya Mama Cajun Seasoning
Ville Platte, LA 800-485-5217

Cheese

Atlantic Quality Spice &Seasonings
New Brunswick, NJ 800-584-0422
Sentry Seasonings
Elmhurst, IL 630-530-5370

The product development experts of Sentry Seasonings are eager to offer the assistance and hands-on experience to food processors of all sizes. Sentry Seasonings will ensure the consistent high quality and repeat sales of your products, whether you choose one of our many off-the-shelf Bench Mark products or a modified version to meet your preferences. Sentry Seasonings can also duplicate and/or improve your present flavor profile; formulate, blend and package specifically for your requirements.

Chinese Style

Atlantic Quality Spice &Seasonings
New Brunswick, NJ 800-584-0422
San Francisco Herb & Natural Food Company
Fremont, CA 800-227-2830
Sentry Seasonings
Elmhurst, IL 630-530-5370

The product development experts of Sentry Seasonings are eager to offer the assistance and hands-on experience to food processors of all sizes. Sentry Seasonings will ensure the consistent high quality and repeat sales of your products, whether you choose one of our many off-the-shelf Bench Mark products or a modified version to meet your preferences. Sentry Seasonings can also duplicate and/or improve your present flavor profile; formulate, blend and package specifically for your requirements.

Curd

Atlantic Quality Spice &Seasonings
New Brunswick, NJ 800-584-0422
Sentry Seasonings
Elmhurst, IL 630-530-5370

The product development experts of Sentry Seasonings are eager to offer the assistance and hands-on experience to food processors of all sizes. Sentry Seasonings will ensure the consistent high quality and repeat sales of your products, whether you choose one of our many off-the-shelf Bench Mark products or a modified version to meet your preferences. Sentry Seasonings can also duplicate and/or improve your present flavor profile; formulate, blend and package specifically for your requirements.

Dairy Products

Atlantic Quality Spice &Seasonings
New Brunswick, NJ 800-584-0422
Sentry Seasonings
Elmhurst, IL 630-530-5370

The product development experts of Sentry Seasonings are eager to offer the assistance and hands-on experience to food processors of all sizes. Sentry Seasonings will ensure the consistent high quality and repeat sales of your products, whether you choose one of our many off-the-shelf Bench Mark products or a modified version to meet your preferences. Sentry Seasonings can also duplicate and/or improve your present flavor profile; formulate, blend and package specifically for your requirements.

Fajita

Atlantic Quality Spice &Seasonings
New Brunswick, NJ 800-584-0422
Sentry Seasonings
Elmhurst, IL 630-530-5370

The product development experts of Sentry Seasonings are eager to offer the assistance and hands-on experience to food processors of all sizes. Sentry Seasonings will ensure the consistent high quality and repeat sales of your products, whether you choose one of our many off-the-shelf Bench Mark products or a modified version to meet your preferences. Sentry Seasonings can also duplicate and/or improve your present flavor profile; formulate, blend and package specifically for your requirements.

Fried Rice

Atlantic Quality Spice &Seasonings
New Brunswick, NJ 800-584-0422
Sentry Seasonings
Elmhurst, IL 630-530-5370

The product development experts of Sentry Seasonings are eager to offer the assistance and hands-on experience to food processors of all sizes. Sentry Seasonings will ensure the consistent high quality and repeat sales of your products, whether you choose one of our many off-the-shelf Bench Mark products or a modified version to meet your preferences. Sentry Seasonings can also duplicate and/or improve your present flavor profile; formulate, blend and package specifically for your requirements.

Greek Style

Atlantic Quality Spice &Seasonings
New Brunswick, NJ 800-584-0422
Sentry Seasonings
Elmhurst, IL 630-530-5370

The product development experts of Sentry Seasonings are eager to offer the assistance and hands-on experience to food processors of all sizes. Sentry Seasonings will ensure the consistent high quality and repeat sales of your products, whether you choose one of our many off-the-shelf Bench Mark products or a modified version to meet your preferences. Sentry Seasonings can also duplicate and/or improve your present flavor profile; formulate, blend and package specifically for your requirements.

Italian Herbs

Atlantic Quality Spice &Seasonings
New Brunswick, NJ 800-584-0422
Sentry Seasonings
Elmhurst, IL 630-530-5370

The product development experts of Sentry Seasonings are eager to offer the assistance and hands-on experience to food processors of all sizes. Sentry Seasonings will ensure the consistent high quality and repeat sales of your products, whether you choose one of our many off-the-shelf Bench Mark products or a modified version to meet your preferences. Sentry Seasonings can also duplicate and/or improve your present flavor profile; formulate, blend and package specifically for your requirements.

Italian Style

Atlantic Quality Spice &Seasonings
New Brunswick, NJ 800-584-0422
Schiff Food Products
North Bergen, NJ 201-868-6800
Sentry Seasonings
Elmhurst, IL 630-530-5370

The product development experts of Sentry Seasonings are eager to offer the assistance and hands-on experience to food processors of all sizes. Sentry Seasonings will ensure the consistent high quality and repeat sales of your products, whether you choose one of our many off-the-shelf Bench Mark products or a modified version to meet your preferences. Sentry Seasonings can also duplicate and/or improve your present flavor profile; formulate, blend and package specifically for your requirements.

Lemon & Basil

Atlantic Quality Spice &Seasonings
New Brunswick, NJ 800-584-0422
Sentry Seasonings
Elmhurst, IL 630-530-5370

The product development experts of Sentry Seasonings are eager to offer the assistance and hands-on experience to food processors of all sizes. Sentry Seasonings will ensure the consistent high quality and repeat sales of your products, whether you choose one of our many off-the-shelf Bench Mark products or a modified version to meet your preferences. Sentry Seasonings can also duplicate and/or improve your present flavor profile; formulate, blend and package specifically for your requirements.

Lemon & Dill

Atlantic Quality Spice &Seasonings
New Brunswick, NJ 800-584-0422
Sentry Seasonings
Elmhurst, IL 630-530-5370

The product development experts of Sentry Seasonings are eager to offer the assistance and hands-on experience to food processors of all sizes. Sentry Seasonings will ensure the consistent high quality and repeat sales of your products, whether you choose one of our many off-the-shelf Bench Mark products or a modified version to meet your preferences. Sentry Seasonings can also duplicate and/or improve your present flavor profile; formulate, blend and package specifically for your requirements.

Lemon Pepper

Atlantic Quality Spice &Seasonings
New Brunswick, NJ 800-584-0422
Chieftain Wild Rice Company
Spooner, WI 800-262-6368
Sentry Seasonings
Elmhurst, IL 630-530-5370

The product development experts of Sentry Seasonings are eager to offer the assistance and hands-on experience to food processors of all sizes. Sentry Seasonings will ensure the consistent high quality and repeat sales of your products, whether you choose one of our many off-the-shelf Bench Mark products or a modified version to meet your preferences. Sentry Seasonings can also duplicate and/or improve your present flavor profile; formulate, blend and package specifically for your requirements.

Meat Products

AC Legg
Calera, AL. 800-422-5344
All American Seasonings
Denver, CO 303-574-9223
Atlantic Quality Spice &Seasonings
New Brunswick, NJ 800-584-0422
JM All Purpose Seasoning
Lincoln, NE. 402-421-8326
Lynch Supply
Lenexa, KS 913-492-8500
Nueces Canyon Texas Style Meat Seasoning
Brenham, TX. 800-925-5058
Rector Foods
Brampton, ON. 888-314-7834
Robinson's Barbecue Sauce Company
Oak Park, IL 708-383-8452
Sentry Seasonings
Elmhurst, IL 630-530-5370

The product development experts of Sentry Seasonings are eager to offer the assistance and hands-on experience to food processors of all sizes. Sentry Seasonings will ensure the consistent high quality and repeat sales of your products, whether you choose one of our many off-the-shelf Bench Mark products or a modified version to meet your preferences. Sentry Seasonings can also duplicate and/or improve your present flavor profile; formulate, blend and package specifically for your requirements.

Spice of Life
Merritt Island, FL 321-453-5727
Wixon/Fontarome
St Francis, WI. 414-769-3000
World Flavors
Warminster, PA 215-672-4400

Mexican Style

Atlantic Quality Spice &Seasonings
New Brunswick, NJ 800-584-0422
Bea & B Foods
San Diego, CA 800-952-2117
El Ranchito
Portland, OR 503-665-4919
Golden Specialty Foods
Norwalk, CA. 562-802-2537
Schiff Food Products
North Bergen, NJ 201-868-6800
Sentry Seasonings
Elmhurst, IL 630-530-5370

The product development experts of Sentry Seasonings are eager to offer the assistance and hands-on experience to food processors of all sizes. Sentry Seasonings will ensure the consistent high quality and repeat sales of your products, whether you choose one of our many off-the-shelf Bench Mark products or a modified version to meet your preferences. Sentry Seasonings can also duplicate and/or improve your present flavor profile; formulate, blend and package specifically for your requirements.

Pizza

Atlantic Quality Spice &Seasonings
New Brunswick, NJ 800-584-0422
California Blending Corpany
El Monte, CA 626-448-1918
CHR Hansen
Elyria, OH. 800-558-0802
Dorothy Dawson Foods Products
Jackson, MI. 517-788-9830
Sentry Seasonings
Elmhurst, IL 630-530-5370

The product development experts of Sentry Seasonings are eager to offer the assistance and hands-on experience to food processors of all sizes. Sentry Seasonings will ensure the consistent high quality and repeat sales of your products, whether you choose one of our many off-the-shelf Bench Mark products or a modified version to meet your preferences. Sentry Seasonings can also duplicate and/or improve your present flavor profile; formulate, blend and package specifically for your requirements.

Rib Rub

Atlantic Quality Spice &Seasonings
New Brunswick, NJ 800-584-0422
Sentry Seasonings
Elmhurst, IL 630-530-5370

The product development experts of Sentry Seasonings are eager to offer the assistance and hands-on experience to food processors of all sizes. Sentry Seasonings will ensure the consistent high quality and repeat sales of your products, whether you choose one of our many off-the-shelf Bench Mark products or a modified version to meet your preferences. Sentry Seasonings can also duplicate and/or improve your present flavor profile; formulate, blend and package specifically for your requirements.

Swagger Foods Corporation
Vernon Hills, IL 847-913-1200

Sausage

Sentry Seasonings
Elmhurst, IL 630-530-5370

The product development experts of Sentry Seasonings are eager to offer the assistance and hands-on experience to food processors of all sizes. Sentry Seasonings will ensure the consistent high quality and repeat sales of your products, whether you choose one of our many off-the-shelf Bench Mark products or a modified version to meet your preferences. Sentry Seasonings can also duplicate and/or improve your present flavor profile; formulate, blend and package specifically for your requirements.

Andouille

Sentry Seasonings
Elmhurst, IL 630-530-5370

The product development experts of Sentry Seasonings are eager to offer the assistance and hands-on experience to food processors of all sizes. Sentry Seasonings will ensure the consistent high quality and repeat sales of your products, whether you choose one of our many off-the-shelf Bench Mark products or a modified version to meet your preferences. Sentry Seasonings can also duplicate and/or improve your present flavor profile; formulate, blend and package specifically for your requirements.

Hot Italian

Sentry Seasonings
Elmhurst, IL 630-530-5370

The product development experts of Sentry Seasonings are eager to offer the assistance and hands-on experience to food processors of all sizes. Sentry Seasonings will ensure the consistent high quality and repeat sales of your products, whether you choose one of our many off-the-shelf Bench Mark products or a modified version to meet your preferences. Sentry Seasonings can also duplicate and/or improve your present flavor profile; formulate, blend and package specifically for your requirements.

Kielbasa

Sentry Seasonings
Elmhurst, IL 630-530-5370

The product development experts of Sentry Seasonings are eager to offer the assistance and hands-on experience to food processors of all sizes. Sentry Seasonings will ensure the consistent high quality and repeat sales of your products, whether you choose one of our many off-the-shelf Bench Mark products or a modified version to meet your preferences. Sentry Seasonings can also duplicate and/or improve your present flavor profile; formulate, blend and package specifically for your requirements.

Sweet Italian

Sentry Seasonings
Elmhurst, IL 630-530-5370

The product development experts of Sentry Seasonings are eager to offer the assistance and hands-on experience to food processors of all sizes. Sentry Seasonings will ensure the consistent high quality and repeat sales of your products, whether you choose one of our many off-the-shelf Bench Mark products or a modified version to meet your preferences. Sentry Seasonings can also duplicate and/or improve your present flavor profile; formulate, blend and package specifically for your requirements.

Snack

Butter

Atlantic Quality Spice &Seasonings
New Brunswick, NJ 800-584-0422
Sentry Seasonings
Elmhurst, IL 630-530-5370

The product development experts of Sentry Seasonings are eager to offer the assistance and hands-on experience to food processors of all sizes. Sentry Seasonings will ensure the consistent high quality and repeat sales of your products, whether you choose one of our many off-the-shelf Bench Mark products or a modified version to meet your preferences. Sentry Seasonings can also duplicate and/or improve your present flavor profile; formulate, blend and package specifically for your requirements.

Cajun Spice

Atlantic Quality Spice &Seasonings
New Brunswick, NJ 800-584-0422
Sentry Seasonings
Elmhurst, IL 630-530-5370

The product development experts of Sentry Seasonings are eager to offer the assistance and hands-on experience to food processors of all sizes. Sentry Seasonings will ensure the consistent high quality and repeat sales of your products, whether you choose one of our many off-the-shelf Bench Mark products or a modified version to meet your preferences. Sentry Seasonings can also duplicate and/or improve your present flavor profile; formulate, blend and package specifically for your requirements.

Cheddar

Atlantic Quality Spice &Seasonings
New Brunswick, NJ 800-584-0422
Sentry Seasonings
Elmhurst, IL 630-530-5370

The product development experts of Sentry Seasonings are eager to offer the assistance and hands-on experience to food processors of all sizes. Sentry Seasonings will ensure the consistent high quality and repeat sales of your products, whether you choose one of our many off-the-shelf Bench Mark products or a modified version to meet your preferences. Sentry Seasonings can also duplicate and/or improve your present flavor profile; formulate, blend and package specifically for your requirements.

Cinnamon Toast

Atlantic Quality Spice &Seasonings
New Brunswick, NJ 800-584-0422
Sentry Seasonings
Elmhurst, IL 630-530-5370

The product development experts of Sentry Seasonings are eager to offer the assistance and hands-on experience to food processors of all sizes. Sentry Seasonings will ensure the consistent high quality and repeat sales of your products, whether you choose one of our many off-the-shelf Bench Mark products or a modified version to meet your preferences. Sentry Seasonings can also duplicate and/or improve your present flavor profile; formulate, blend and package specifically for your requirements.

Mesquite BBQ

Atlantic Quality Spice &Seasonings
New Brunswick, NJ 800-584-0422
Bickel's Snack Foods Inc
York, PA 800-233-1933
Middleswarth Potato Chips
Wilkes Barre, PA. 570-288-2447
Mrs. Fisher's
Rockford, IL 815-964-9114
Sentry Seasonings
Elmhurst, IL 630-530-5370

The product development experts of Sentry Seasonings are eager to offer the assistance and hands-on experience to food processors of all sizes. Sentry Seasonings will ensure the consistent high quality and repeat sales of your products, whether you choose one of our many off-the-shelf Bench Mark products or a modified version to meet your preferences. Sentry Seasonings can also duplicate and/or improve your present flavor profile; formulate, blend and package specifically for your requirements.

Nacho Cheese

Atlantic Quality Spice &Seasonings
New Brunswick, NJ 800-584-0422
Sentry Seasonings
Elmhurst, IL 630-530-5370

The product development experts of Sentry Seasonings are eager to offer the assistance and hands-on experience to food processors of all sizes. Sentry Seasonings will ensure the consistent high quality and repeat sales of your products, whether you choose one of our many off-the-shelf Bench Mark products or a modified version to meet your preferences. Sentry Seasonings can also duplicate and/or improve your present flavor profile; formulate, blend and package specifically for your requirements.

Ranch

Atlantic Quality Spice &Seasonings
New Brunswick, NJ 800-584-0422
Sentry Seasonings
Elmhurst, IL 630-530-5370

The product development experts of Sentry Seasonings are eager to offer the assistance and hands-on experience to food processors of all sizes. Sentry Seasonings will ensure the consistent high quality and repeat sales of your products, whether you choose one of our many off-the-shelf Bench Mark products or a modified version to meet your preferences. Sentry Seasonings can also duplicate and/or improve your present flavor profile; formulate, blend and package specifically for your requirements.

Sour Cream & Onion

Atlantic Quality Spice &Seasonings
New Brunswick, NJ 800-584-0422
Bickel's Snack Foods Inc
York, PA 800-233-1933
Middleswarth Potato Chips
Wilkes Barre, PA. 570-288-2447
Mrs. Fisher's
Rockford, IL 815-964-9114
Sentry Seasonings
Elmhurst, IL 630-530-5370

The product development experts of Sentry Seasonings are eager to offer the assistance and hands-on experience to food processors of all sizes. Sentry Seasonings will ensure the consistent high quality and repeat sales of your products, whether you choose one of our many off-the-shelf Bench Mark products or a modified version to meet your preferences. Sentry Seasonings can also duplicate and/or improve your present flavor profile; formulate, blend and package specifically for your requirements.

Southwest

Atlantic Quality Spice &Seasonings
New Brunswick, NJ 800-584-0422
Sentry Seasonings
Elmhurst, IL 630-530-5370

The product development experts of Sentry Seasonings are eager to offer the assistance and hands-on experience to food processors of all sizes. Sentry Seasonings will ensure the consistent high quality and repeat sales of your products, whether you choose one of our many off-the-shelf Bench Mark products or a modified version to meet your preferences. Sentry Seasonings can also duplicate and/or improve your present flavor profile; formulate, blend and package specifically for your requirements.

Tomato Pesto

Atlantic Quality Spice &Seasonings
New Brunswick, NJ 800-584-0422
Sentry Seasonings
Elmhurst, IL 630-530-5370

The product development experts of Sentry Seasonings are eager to offer the assistance and hands-on experience to food processors of all sizes. Sentry Seasonings will ensure the consistent high quality and repeat sales of your products, whether you choose one of our many off-the-shelf Bench Mark products or a modified version to meet your preferences. Sentry Seasonings can also duplicate and/or improve your present flavor profile; formulate, blend and package specifically for your requirements.

for Corned Beef

Atlantic Quality Spice &Seasonings
New Brunswick, NJ 800-584-0422

Sentry Seasonings
Elmhurst, IL 630-530-5370

The product development experts of Sentry Seasonings are eager to offer the assistance and hands-on experience to food processors of all sizes. Sentry Seasonings will ensure the consistent high quality and repeat sales of your products, whether you choose one of our many off-the-shelf Bench Mark products or a modified version to meet your preferences. Sentry Seasonings can also duplicate and/or improve your present flavor profile; formulate, blend and package specifically for your requirements.

for Tacos

Atlantic Quality Spice &Seasonings
New Brunswick, NJ 800-584-0422
Badia Spices
Miami, FL 305-629-8000
Sentry Seasonings
Elmhurst, IL 630-530-5370

The product development experts of Sentry Seasonings are eager to offer the assistance and hands-on experience to food processors of all sizes. Sentry Seasonings will ensure the consistent high quality and repeat sales of your products, whether you choose one of our many off-the-shelf Bench Mark products or a modified version to meet your preferences. Sentry Seasonings can also duplicate and/or improve your present flavor profile; formulate, blend and package specifically for your requirements.

Seeds

AgriCulver Seeds
Trumansburg, NY 800-836-3701
American Mercantile Corporation
Memphis, TN 901-454-1900
Ann's House of Nuts, Inc.
Jessup, MD 301-498-4920
Atlantic Quality Spice &Seasonings
New Brunswick, NJ 800-584-0422
Birdsong Peanuts
Blakely, GA 800-597-7688
Brock Seed Company
Finley, TN 760-353-1632
Buddy Squirrel LLC
Milwaukee, WI 800-972-2658
CHS Sunflower
Grandin, ND 701-484-5313
Con Yeager Spice Company
Zelienople, PA 800-222-2460
Diamond Foods
Fishers, IN 317-845-5534
Dipasa
Brownsville, TX 956-831-5893
Eden Foods Inc.
Clinton, MI 800-248-0320
El Brands
Ozark, AL 334-445-2828
Energy Club
Pacoima, CA 800-688-6887
Fernando C Pujals & Bros
Guaynabo, PR 787-792-3080
Fresh Hemp Foods
Winnipeg, NB 800-665-4367
Frito-Lay
Dallas, TX 800-352-4477
Golden Valley Seed
El Centro, CA 760-337-3100
Govadinas Fitness Foods
San Diego, CA 800-900-0108
Gurley's Foods
Willmar, MN 800-426-7845
H B Taylor Company
Chicago, IL 773-254-4805
Harmony Foods Corporation
Fishers, IN 800-837-2855
HempNut
Henderson, NV 707-576-7050
Hialeah Products Company
Hollywood, FL 800-923-3379
Hinojosa Bros Wholesale
Roma, TX 800-554-4119
Honey Bar/Creme de la Creme
Kingston, NY 845-331-4643
HP Schmid
San Francisco, CA 415-765-5925
International Harvest
Mt Vernon, NY 914-699-5600
Interstate Seed Company
West Fargo, ND 800-437-4120
Kalustyan Corporation
Union, NJ 908-688-6111
King Nut Company
Solon, OH 800-860-5464
Krispy Kernels
Sainte Foy, QC 877-791-9986
Mayfair Sales
Buffalo, NY 800-248-2881
Mezza
Lake Forest, IL 888-206-6054
Midwest/Northern
Minneapolis, MN 800-328-5502
Mincing Overseas Spice Company
Dayton, NJ 732-355-9944
Minn-Dak Growers Ltd.
Grand Forks, ND 701-746-7453
Natural Foods
Toledo, OH 419-537-1713
Nature's Candy
Fredericksburg, TX 800-729-0085
Nature's Select
Grand Rapids, MI 888-715-4321
Nestle USA Inc
Glendale, CA 800-225-2270
Nu-World Amaranth
Naperville, IL 630-369-6819
Occidental International Foods Llc
Randolph, NJ 973-970-9220
Osage Pecan Company
Butler, MO 660-679-6137
Patsy's Candies
Colorado Springs, CO 866-372-8797
Plantation Products
Norton, MA 508-285-5800
PYCO Industries
Lubbock, TX 806-747-3434
R&J Farms
West Salem, OH 419-846-3179
Red River Commodities
Fargo, ND 701-282-2600
Schiff Food Products
North Bergen, NJ 201-868-6800
Scott-Bathgate
Winnipeg, MB 800-216-2990
Snackerz
Commerce, CA 888-576-2253
Sonne
Wahpeton, ND 800-727-6663
Specialty Commodities
Fargo, ND 701-282-8222
Spitz USA
Loveland, CO 970-613-9319
Stapleton-Spence PackingCompany
San Jose, CA 800-297-8815
Sun Ridge Farms
Pajaro, CA 831-786-7000
Sunray Food Products Corporation
Bronx, NY 718-548-2255
Sunshine Farm & Gardens
Renick, WV 304-497-2208
Tantos Foods International
Markham, ON 905-943-9993
Tasty Seeds Ltd
Winkler, NB 888-632-6906
Texas Coffee Company
Beaumont, TX 800-259-3400
Todd's
Vernon, CA 800-938-6337
Torn & Glasser
Los Angeles, CA 800-282-6887
Trophy Nut
Tipp City, OH 800-219-9004
Tropical
Charlotte, NC 800-220-1413
Tropical
Marietta, GA 800-544-3762
Tropical Nut & Fruit Company
Orlando, FL 800-749-8869
US Foods
Lincoln, NE 402-470-2021
Weaver Nut Company
Ephrata, PA 717-738-3781
Westin
Omaha, NE 800-228-6098
Whole Herb Company
Sonoma, CA 707-935-1077
Willmar Cookie & Nut Company
Willmar, MN 320-235-0600
Woodland Foods
Gurnee, IL 847-625-8600
Zenobia Company
Bronx, NY 866-936-6242

Alfalfa

Woodland Foods
Gurnee, IL 847-625-8600

Anise or Aniseed

Chesapeake Spice Company
Baltimore, MD 410-391-2100
Chieftain Wild Rice Company
Spooner, WI 800-262-6368
Commodities Marketing, Inc.
Edison, NJ 732-603-5077
Morris J. Golombeck
Brooklyn, NY 718-284-3505

Annatto

Chieftain Wild Rice Company
Spooner, WI 800-262-6368
Gel Spice Company, Inc
Bayonne, NJ 800-922-0230
Morris J. Golombeck
Brooklyn, NY 718-284-3505
Organic Planet
San Francisco, CA 415-765-5590
Schiff Food Products
North Bergen, NJ 201-868-6800

Cabbage

Abbott & Cobb, Inc.
Langhorne, PA 800-345-7333

Caraway

Chesapeake Spice Company
Baltimore, MD 410-391-2100
Chieftain Wild Rice Company
Spooner, WI 800-262-6368
Organic Planet
San Francisco, CA 415-765-5590

Cardamom

Advanced Spice & Trading
Carrollton, TX 800-872-7811
American Key Food Products
Closter, NJ 800-767-0237
Atlantic Quality Spice &Seasonings
New Brunswick, NJ 800-584-0422
Con Yeager Spice Company
Zelienople, PA 800-222-2460
Organic Planet
San Francisco, CA 415-765-5590
Schiff Food Products
North Bergen, NJ 201-868-6800

Celery

Advanced Spice & Trading
Carrollton, TX 800-872-7811
American Key Food Products
Closter, NJ 800-767-0237
Atlantic Quality Spice &Seasonings
New Brunswick, NJ 800-584-0422
Chieftain Wild Rice Company
Spooner, WI 800-262-6368
Con Yeager Spice Company
Zelienople, PA 800-222-2460
Schiff Food Products
North Bergen, NJ 201-868-6800
Unique Ingredients
Naches, WA 509-653-1991
Whole Herb Company
Sonoma, CA 707-935-1077

Ground

Chesapeake Spice Company
Baltimore, MD 410-391-2100

Coriander

Naturex Inc.
South Hackensack, NJ 201-440-5000

Cumin

Con Yeager Spice Company
Zelienople, PA....................800-222-2460

Dill

Advanced Spice & Trading
Carrollton, TX....................800-872-7811
Con Yeager Spice Company
Zelienople, PA....................800-222-2460
Organic Planet
San Francisco, CA................415-765-5590
Schiff Food Products
North Bergen, NJ.................201-868-6800
Vegetable Juices
Chicago, IL......................888-776-9752

Fennel

Acatris USA
Edina, MN........................952-920-7700
Advanced Spice & Trading
Carrollton, TX....................800-872-7811
American Key Food Products
Closter, NJ......................800-767-0237
Atlantic Quality Spice &Seasonings
New Brunswick, NJ...............800-584-0422
Commodities Marketing, Inc.
Edison, NJ.......................732-603-5077
Con Yeager Spice Company
Zelienople, PA....................800-222-2460
Organic Planet
San Francisco, CA................415-765-5590
Schiff Food Products
North Bergen, NJ.................201-868-6800

Fenugreek

Acatris USA
Edina, MN........................952-920-7700
Naturex Inc.
South Hackensack, NJ.............201-440-5000

Flax

American Health & Nutrition
Ann Arbor, MI....................734-677-5570
Dixie Usa
Tomball, TX......................800-233-3668
Gel Spice Company, Inc
Bayonne, NJ......................800-922-0230
Hialeah Products Company
Hollywood, FL....................800-923-3379
Minn-Dak Growers Ltd.
Grand Forks, ND..................701-746-7453
Montana Specialty Mills
Great Falls, MT...................406-761-2338
Natural Way Mills
Middle River, MN.................218-222-3677
Organic Planet
San Francisco, CA................415-765-5590
Pizzey's Milling & Baking Company
Angusville, NB...................204-773-2575
Red River Commodities
Fargo, ND........................701-282-2600
Woodland Foods
Gurnee, IL.......................847-625-8600

Mustard

American Health & Nutrition
Ann Arbor, MI....................734-677-5570
American Key Food Products
Closter, NJ......................800-767-0237
Commodities Marketing, Inc.
Edison, NJ.......................732-603-5077
Con Yeager Spice Company
Zelienople, PA....................800-222-2460
Demeter Agro
Lethbridge, AB...................800-661-1450
Phamous Phloyd's Barbeque Sauce
Denver, CO.......................303-757-3285

Peanut

Adkin & Son Associated Food Products
South Haven, MI..................269-637-7450
Birdsong Peanuts
Blakely, GA......................800-597-7688

Poppy

Advanced Spice & Trading
Carrollton, TX....................800-872-7811
American Health & Nutrition
Ann Arbor, MI....................734-677-5570
American Key Food Products
Closter, NJ......................800-767-0237
Atlantic Quality Spice &Seasonings
New Brunswick, NJ...............800-584-0422
Chieftain Wild Rice Company
Spooner, WI......................800-262-6368
Con Yeager Spice Company
Zelienople, PA....................800-222-2460
HP Schmid
San Francisco, CA................415-765-5925
Organic Planet
San Francisco, CA................415-765-5590
Patisserie Wawel
Montreal, QC.....................614-524-3348
Schiff Food Products
North Bergen, NJ.................201-868-6800
Texas Coffee Company
Beaumont, TX.....................800-259-3400

Pumpkin

Advanced Spice & Trading
Carrollton, TX....................800-872-7811
American Health & Nutrition
Ann Arbor, MI....................734-677-5570
American Key Food Products
Closter, NJ......................800-767-0237
Atlantic Quality Spice &Seasonings
New Brunswick, NJ...............800-584-0422
Cache Creek Foods
Woodland, CA.....................530-662-1764
Chieftain Wild Rice Company
Spooner, WI......................800-262-6368
Diamond Foods
Fishers, IN.......................317-845-5534
Durey-Libby Edible Nuts
Carlstadt, NJ.....................800-332-6887
Emerling International Foods
Buffalo, NY......................716-833-7381

We supply food manufacturers and food service customers worldwide (since 1988) with bulk ingredients including: Fruits & Vegetables; Juice Concentrates; Herbs & Spices; Oils & Vinegars; Flavors & Colors; Honey & Molasses. We also produce PURE MAPLE SYRUP.

Fastachi
Watertown, MA....................800-466-3022
Hialeah Products Company
Hollywood, FL....................800-923-3379
Mental Process
Atlanta, GA......................404-875-7440
Midwest/Northern
Minneapolis, MN..................800-328-5502
Organic Planet
San Francisco, CA................415-765-5590
Sunray Food Products Corporation
Bronx, NY........................718-548-2255
Woodland Foods
Gurnee, IL.......................847-625-8600

Rape

American Health & Nutrition
Ann Arbor, MI....................734-677-5570
American Key Food Products
Closter, NJ......................800-767-0237
Continental Grain/ContiGroup Companies
New York, NY.....................212-207-5200

Sesame

American Health & Nutrition
Ann Arbor, MI....................734-677-5570
American Key Food Products
Closter, NJ......................800-767-0237
Chesapeake Spice Company
Baltimore, MD....................410-391-2100
Chieftain Wild Rice Company
Spooner, WI......................800-262-6368
Organic Planet
San Francisco, CA................415-765-5590
Setton International Foods
Commack, NY......................800-227-4397
Spice & Spice
Rolling Hills Estates, CA.........866-729-7742
Woodland Foods
Gurnee, IL.......................847-625-8600

Black

Atlantic Quality Spice &Seasonings
New Brunswick, NJ...............800-584-0422

White

Atlantic Quality Spice &Seasonings
New Brunswick, NJ...............800-584-0422
Spice & Spice
Rolling Hills Estates, CA.........866-729-7742

Spice

Advanced Spice & Trading
Carrollton, TX....................800-872-7811
American Key Food Products
Closter, NJ......................800-767-0237
Atlantic Quality Spice &Seasonings
New Brunswick, NJ...............800-584-0422
Fantis Foods
Carlstadt, NJ.....................201-933-6200
Stan-Mark Food Products
Chicago, IL......................800-651-0994

Sunflower

American Health & Nutrition
Ann Arbor, MI....................734-677-5570
American Importing Company
Minneapolis, MN..................612-331-7000
American Key Food Products
Closter, NJ......................800-767-0237
Cache Creek Foods
Woodland, CA.....................530-662-1764
Chieftain Wild Rice Company
Spooner, WI......................800-262-6368
CHS Sunflower
Grandin, ND......................701-484-5313
Commodities Marketing, Inc.
Edison, NJ.......................732-603-5077
ConAgra Foods Inc
Omaha, NE........................402-595-7300
Dahlgren & Company
Crookston, MN....................800-346-6050
Diamond Foods
Fishers, IN.......................317-845-5534
Durey-Libby Edible Nuts
Carlstadt, NJ.....................800-332-6887
Eden Foods Inc.
Clinton, MI......................800-248-0320
Fastachi
Watertown, MA....................800-466-3022
Heartland Mill
Marienthal, KS...................800-232-8533
Hialeah Products Company
Hollywood, FL....................800-923-3379
HP Schmid
San Francisco, CA................415-765-5925
Inn Maid Food
Lenox, MA........................413-637-2732
Marantha Natural Foods
San Francisco, CA................866-972-6879
Midwest/Northern
Minneapolis, MN..................800-328-5502
Minn-Dak Growers Ltd.
Grand Forks, ND..................701-746-7453
Organic Planet
San Francisco, CA................415-765-5590
Purity Foods
Okemos, MI.......................800-997-7358
R&J Farms
West Salem, OH...................419-846-3179
Red River Commodities
Fargo, ND........................701-282-2600
Scott-Bathgate
Winnipeg, MB.....................800-216-2990
Setton International Foods
Commack, NY......................800-227-4397
Sonne
Wahpeton, ND.....................800-727-6663
Sunray Food Products Corporation
Bronx, NY........................718-548-2255
Trinidad/Benham Corporation
Patterson, CA....................209-892-9051
Westin
Omaha, NE........................800-228-6098

Vegetable

Abbott & Cobb, Inc.
Langhorne, PA 800-345-7333
Atlantic Quality Spice &Seasonings
New Brunswick, NJ 800-584-0422
Golden Valley Seed
El Centro, CA 760-337-3100
Harris Moran Seed Company
Modesto, CA. 209-579-7333
McKenna Brothers
Cardigan, PE. 902-583-2951
Plantation Products
Norton, MA. 508-285-5800
Seminis Vegetable Seeds
Oxnard, CA. 805-647-1572

Spices

A M Todd Company
Kalamazoo, MI 800-968-2603
Abunda Life Laboratories
Asbury Park, NJ 732-775-7575
AC Legg
Calera, AL. 800-422-5344
Adventure Foods
Whittier, NC 828-497-4113
Alberto-Culver Company
Melrose Park, IL. 708-450-3000
All American Seasonings
Denver, CO 303-574-9223
Allen & Cowley SpecialtyFoods
Phoenix, AZ 800-279-1634
American Food Ingredients
Oceanside, CA 760-929-9505
American Key Food Products
Closter, NJ. 800-767-0237
American Mercantile Corporation
Memphis, TN 901-454-1900
American Natural & Organic Spices
Fremont, CA 510-440-1044
Amfit Spices
Orlando, FL. 407-352-5290
Ampacco
Sparks, MD 800-632-5847
Aphrodisia Products
Brooklyn, NY 877-274-3677
Arizona Natural Products
Phoenix, AZ 602-997-6098
Ashley Foods
Sudbury, MA. 800-617-2823
Astor Products
Jacksonville, FL 904-783-5000
Atlantic Quality Spice &Seasonings
New Brunswick, NJ 800-584-0422
Au Printemps Gourmet
Saint-Jerome, QC 800-663-0416
Badia Spices
Miami, FL. 305-629-8000
Barataria Spice Company
Barataria, LA. 800-793-7650
Bell Flavors & Fragrances
Northbrook, IL 800-323-4387
Bi Nutraceuticals
Long Beach, CA 310-669-2100
Big B Distributors
Evansville, IN 812-425-5235
Bijol & Spices, Inc.
Miami, FL. 888-BIJ-L 70
Bloch & Guggenheimer
Hurlock, MD. 800-541-2809
Boston Spice & Tea Company
Boston, VA 800-966-4372
Boyd Coffee Company
Portland, OR 800-545-4077
Bruno's Cajun Foods & Snacks
Slidell, LA. 985-726-0544
Bueno Food Products
Albuquerque, NM. 800-888-7336
C.F. Sauer Company
Richmond, VA. 800-688-5676
California Blending Corpany
El Monte, CA 626-448-1918
Canadian Salt Company Limited
Pointe Claire, QC 514-630-0900
Castella Imports
Hauppauge, NY 866-227-8355
Chef Hans Gourmet Foods
Monroe, LA. 800-890-4267
Chef Merito
Encino, CA 800-637-4861
Chef Paul Prudhomme's Magic Seasonings Blends
Harahan, LA 800-457-2857
Chef Zachary's Gourmet Blended Spices
Detroit, MI 313-226-0000
Chesapeake Spice Company
Baltimore, MD 410-391-2100
Chia I Foods Company
South El Monte, CA 626-401-3038
Chieftain Wild Rice Company
Spooner, WI 800-262-6368
CHR Hansen
Elyria, OH. 440-324-6060
Christopher Ranch
Gilroy, CA. 408-847-1100
Chugwater Chili Corporation
Chugwater, WY 800-972-4454
Cibolo Junction Food & Spice
Albuquerque, NM. 505-888-1987
Colonna Brothers
North Bergen, NJ 201-864-1115
Colorado Spice
Boulder, CO 800-677-7423
Commodities Marketing, Inc.
Edison, NJ. 732-603-5077
Con Yeager Spice Company
Zelienople, PA. 800-222-2460
ConAgra Foods Inc
Omaha, NE 402-595-7300
Consolidated Mills
Houston, TX 713-896-4196
Consumers Vinegar & Spice Company
Chicago, IL 773-376-4100
Continental Seasoning
Teaneck, NJ. 800-631-1564
Creole Delicacies Pralines
New Orleans, LA 504-523-6425
Cut Above Foods
Carlsbad, CA. 760-931-6777
Cyclone Enterprises
Houston, TX 281-872-0087
D Steengrafe & Company
Pleasant Valley, NY 845-635-4067
Davidsons
Reno, NV 800-882-5888
De Coty Coffee Company
San Angelo, TX 800-588-8001
DeFrancesco & Sons
Firebaugh, CA. 209-364-7000
Delicae Gourmet
Tarpon Springs, FL. 800-942-2502
Dona Yiya Foods
San Sebastian, PR. 787-896-4007
Drusilla Seafood Packing & Processing Company
Baton Rouge, LA 800-364-8844
Earthen Vessels Herb Company
Hockessin, DE 302-234-7667
Ecom Manufacturing Corporation
Markham, ON. 905-477-2441
El Paso Chile Company
El Paso, TX. 888-472-5727
El Ranchito
Portland, OR 503-665-4919
Elite Spice
Jessup, MD 800-232-3531
Emerling International Foods
Buffalo, NY. 716-833-7381

We supply food manufacturers and food service customers worldwide (since 1988) with bulk ingredients including: Fruits & Vegetables; Juice Concentrates; Herbs & Spices; Oils & Vinegars; Flavors & Colors; Honey & Molasses. We also produce PURE MAPLE SYRUP.

Empire Spice Mills
Winnipeg, NB 204-786-1594
Enrico's/Ventre Packing
Syracuse, NY 888-472-8237
Erba Food Products
Brooklyn, NY 718-272-7700
Excalibur Seasoning Company
Pekin, IL 800-444-2169
Farmer Brothers Company
Torrance, CA. 800-735-2878
FDP
Santa Rosa, CA. 707-547-1776
Feature Foods
Etobicoke, ON 416-675-7350
Fernandez Chili Company
Alamosa, CO. 719-589-6043
First Spice Mixing Company
Long Island City, NY 800-221-1105
Flavorbank Company
Tucson, AZ 800-835-7603
Florida Shortening Corporation
Miami, FL. 305-691-2992
Fmali Herb
Santa Cruz, CA. 831-423-7913
Food Ingredients Solutions
Blauvelt, NY. 845-353-8501
Fool Proof Gourmet Products
Grapevine, TX 817-329-1839
Foran Spice Company
Oak Creek, WI 800-558-6030
Fox Meadow Farm of Vermont
Rutland, VT 888-754-4204
Freed, Teller & Freed
South San Francisco, CA 800-370-7371
Frontier Cooperative Herbs
Boulder, CO 800-669-3275
Frontier Ingredients
Norway, IA 800-669-3275
Ful-Flav-R Foods
Alamo, CA 925-838-0300
FW Witt & Company
Yorkville, IL 630-553-6366
Garlic Survival Company
San Francisco, CA 415-822-7112
GB Ratto & Company Int ernational
Oakland, CA 800-325-3483
George Chiala Farms
Morgan Hill, CA. 408-778-0562
Georgia Spice Company
Atlanta, GA. 800-453-9997
Gilroy Foods
Gilroy, CA. 800-921-7502
Global Botanical
Barrie, ON. 705-733-2117
Gloria's Gourmet
New Britain, CT 860-225-9196
Golden Whisk
South San Francisco, CA 800-660-5222
Gourmantra Foods
Markham, ON 416-225-6711
Gourmet Food Mall
Kenner, LA 800-903-7553
Great Lakes Tea & Spice Company
Glen Arbor, MI. 877-645-9363
Great Spice Company
Reno, NV 800-730-3575
Green Mountain Gringo
Winston Salem, NC
Griffith Laboratories
Alsip, IL 800-346-9494
Griffith Laboratories Worldwide
Alsip, IL 800-346-4743
GS Dunn & Company
Hamilton, ON 905-522-0833
Guapo Spices Company
Los Angeles, CA. 213-322-8900
Harbor Spice Company
Forest Hill, MD. 410-893-9500
Harris Farms
Coalinga, CA 800-742-1955
HealthBest
San Marcos, CA 760-752-5230
Henry Broch & Company/APK, Inc.
Libertyville, IL 847-816-6225
Herb Connection
Springville, UT. 801-489-4254
Herb Society of America
Willoughby, OH 440-256-0514
Hermann Laue Spice Company
Uxbridge, ON 905-852-5100
Hollman Foods
Chicago, IL 888-926-2879
Homegrown Naturals
Napa, CA. 800-288-1089
House of Spices
Flushing, NY. 718-507-4900
Ingretec
Lebanon, PA 717-273-1360
Instant Products of America
Columbus, IN 812-372-9100
Italian Rose Garlic Products
West Palm Beach, FL 800-338-8899
Jagulana Herbal Products
Badger, CA 559-337-2188
Jodie's Kitchen
Pinellas Park, FL
Kalsec
Kalamazoo, MI 269-349-9711
Kalustyan Corporation
Union, NJ 908-688-6111
La Flor Spices
Hauppaugue, NY 631-885-9601

La Flor Spices Company
Hauppauge, NY 631-851-9601
Lakeside Mills
Rutherfordton, NC 828-286-4866
Lawry's Foods
Monrovia, CA. 800-595-8917
Lebermuth Company
South Bend, IN 800-648-1123
Leeward Resources
Baltimore, MD 410-837-9003
Li'l Guy Foods
Kansas City, MO. 800-886-8226
Lost Trail Root Beer Com
Louisburg, KS. 800-748-7765
Lucerne Foods
Taber, AB 403-223-3546
Magic Seasoning Blends
New Orleans, LA 800-457-2857
Mansmith Enterprises
San Jn Bautista, CA 800-626-7648
Mansmith's Barbecue
San Jn Bautista, CA 800-626-7648
Maple Grove Farms of Vermont
St Johnsbury, VT. 800-525-2540
Marin Food Specialties
Byron, CA. 925-634-6126
Marion-Kay Spices
Brownstown, IN 800-627-7423
Marnap Industries
Buffalo, NY. 716-897-1220
McClancy Seasoning Company
Fort Mill, SC. 800-843-1968
McCormick & Company
Sparks, MD. 800-632-5847
Mercado Latino
City of Industry, CA 626-333-6862
Mermaid Spice Corporation
Fort Myers, FL 239-693-1986
Mezza
Lake Forest, IL 888-206-6054
Mild Bill's Spices
Bulverde, TX 830-980-4124
Milton A. Klein Company
New York, NY 800-221-0248
Mincing Overseas Spice Company
Dayton, NJ 732-355-9944
Modern Products/Fearn Natural Foods
Mequon, WI 800-877-8935
Moderncuts
Mequon, WI 262-242-2400
Mojave Foods Corporation
Commerce, CA. 323-890-8900
Mojave Foods Corporation
Commerce, CA. 800-995-8906
Monterrey Products Company
San Antonio, TX. 210-435-2872
Morris J. Golombeck
Brooklyn, NY 718-284-3505
Morton & Bassett Spices
Novato, CA. 866-972-6879
Morton Salt Company
Chicago, IL 312-807-2000
Natural Foods
Toledo, OH 419-537-1713
Nature Quality
San Martin, CA. 408-683-2182
Naturex Inc.
South Hackensack, NJ 201-440-5000
Newly Weds Foods
Chicago, IL 800-647-9314
Noh Foods International
Torrance, CA. 310-618-2092
North American Seasonings
Lake Oswego, OR. 503-636-7043
Northwestern Coffee Mills
La Pointe, WI 800-243-5283
Oak Grove Smokehouse
Prairieville, LA 225-673-6857
Occidental International Foods Llc
Randolph, NJ 973-970-9220
Ocean Cliff Corporation
New Bedford, MA 508-990-7900
Old Mansion Foods
Petersburg, VA 800-476-1877
Old World Spices & Seasonings, Inc.
Overland Park, KS 800-241-0070
One Source
Concord, MA 800-554-5501
Oregon Flavor Rack
Eugene, OR. 541-342-2085
Oregon Flavor Rack Spice
Eugene, OR. 800-725-8373

Oregon Spice Company
Portland, OR 800-565-1599
Organic Planet
San Francisco, CA 415-765-5590
Ottens Flavors
Philadelphia, PA 800-523-0767
Paca Foods
Tampa, FL. 800-388-7419
Pacific Spice Company
Commerce, CA. 800-281-0614
Pak Technologies
Milwaukee, WI 414-438-8600
Palmieri Food Products
New Haven, CT 800-845-5447
Pappy Meat Company
Fresno, CA 559-291-0218
Papy's Foods
McHenry, IL 815-385-3313
Particle Dynamics
Saint Louis, MO 800-452-4682
Pearson's Homestyle
Bowden, AB 877-224-3339
Pecos Valley Spice Company
Corrales, NM 505-243-2622
Pelican Bay
Dunedin, FL 800-826-8982
Pemberton's Gourmet Foods
Gray, ME. 800-255-8401
Pendery's
Dallas, TX. 800-533-1870
Pereg Gourmet Spices
Flushing, NY. 718-261-6767
Pett Spice Products
Atlanta, GA. 404-691-5235
Precise Food Ingredients
Carrollton, TX. 972-323-4951
Precision Blends
Baldwin Park, CA. 800-836-9979
Premier Blending
Wichita, KS. 316-267-5533
Presco Food Seasonings
Flemington, NJ 800-526-1713
Proacec USA
Santa Monica, CA. 310-996-7770
R&S Mexican Food Products
Glendale, AZ. 602-272-2727
R.L. Schreiber
Pompano Beach, FL 800-624-8777
R.L. Schreiber Company
Pompano Beach, FL 800-624-8777
Randag & Associates Inc
Elmhurst, IL 630-530-2830
Rapazzini Winery
Gilroy, CA. 800-842-6262
Raymond-Hadley Corporation
Spencer, NY 800-252-5220
RC Fine Foods
Belle Mead, NJ 800-526-3953
Red Lion Spicy Foods Company
Red Lion, PA. 717-309-8303
Reggie Ball's Cajun Foods
Lake Charles, LA 337-436-0291
REX Pure Foods
New Orleans, LA 800-344-8314
RL Schreiber
Pompano Beach, FL 954-972-7102
Sambets Cajun Deli
Austin, TX. 800-472-6238
San Francisco Herb & Natural Food Company
Fremont, CA 800-227-2830
Sandbar Trading Corporation
Louisville, CO. 303-499-7480
Santa Cruz Chili & SpiceCompany
Tumacacori, AZ 520-398-2591
Saratoga Food Specialties
Bolingbrook, IL 800-451-0407
Schiff Food Products
North Bergen, NJ 201-868-6800
Sea Salt Superstore
Lynnwood, WA. 866-999-7258
Selecto Sausage Company
Houston, TX 713-926-1626

Sentry Seasonings
Elmhurst, IL 630-530-5370

The product development experts of Sentry Seasonings are eager to offer the assistance and hands-on experience to food processors of all sizes. Sentry Seasonings will ensure the consistent high quality and repeat sales of your products, whether you choose one of our many off-the-shelf Bench Mark products or a modified version to meet your preferences. Sentry Seasonings can also duplicate and/or improve your present flavor profile; formulate, blend and package specifically for your requirements.

Serv-Agen Corporation
Cherry Hill, NJ 856-663-6966
Shanks Extracts
Lancaster, PA 800-346-3135
SJH Enterprises
Middleton, WI. 888-745-3845
Somerset Industries
Spring House, PA 800-883-8728
SOUPerior Bean & Spice Company
Vancouver, WA. 800-878-7687
South Texas Spice Company
San Antonio, TX. 210-436-2280
Spanish Gardens Food Manufacturing
Kansas City, KS 913-831-4242
Specialty Food America
Hopkinsville, KY 888-881-1633
Spice & Spice
Rolling Hills Estates, CA 866-729-7742
Spice Advice
Ankeny, IA 800-247-5251
Spice Hunter
San Luis Obispo, CA 800-444-3061
Spice O' Life
Seattle, WA 206-789-4195
Spiceco
Avenel, NJ. 732-499-9070
Spiceland
Chicago, IL 800-352-8671
St Charles Trading
Batavia, IL. 630-377-0608
St. John's Botanicals
Bowie, MD 301-262-5302
Stan-Mark Food Products
Chicago, IL 800-651-0994
Starwest Botanicals
Rancho Cordova, CA 888-273-4372
Sterigenics International
Los Angeles, CA. 800-472-4508
Stickney & Poor Company
Peterborough, NH. 603-924-2259
Sundial Gardens
Higganum, CT. 860-345-4290
Sunflower Restaurant Supply
Salina, KS 316-267-9881

SupHerb Farms
Turlock, CA 800-787-4372

Frozen culinary herb and specialty vegetable ingredients.

Sustainable Sourcing
Great Barrington, MA. 413-528-5141
Swagger Foods Corporation
Vernon Hills, IL 847-913-1200
Tampico Spice Company
Los Angeles, CA. 323-235-3154
Taste Maker Foods
Memphis, TN 800-467-1407
Teeny Tiny Spice Company of Vermont LLC
Shelburne, VT. 802-598-6800
Texas Coffee Company
Beaumont, TX. 800-259-3400
Texas Traditions
Georgetown, TX 800-547-7062
To Market-To Market
West Linn, OR 970-278-1000
Tommy Tang's Thai Seasonings
Los Angeles, CA. 818-442-0219
Trader Vic's Food Products
Emeryville, CA. 877-762-4824

Transa
Libertyville, IL 847-281-9582
Trinity Spice
Midland, TX 800-460-1149
Triple H
Riverside, CA 951-352-5700
Tripper
Oxnard, CA. 888-336-8747
Tropical
Charlotte, NC 800-220-1413
Tropical Nut & Fruit Company
Orlando, FL. 800-749-8869
Two Guys Spice Company
Jacksonville, FL 800-874-5656
Uncle Fred's Fine Foods
Rockport, TX 361-729-8320
Urban Accents
Chicago, IL 877-872-7742
US Spice Mills
Chicago, IL 773-378-6800
Van Eeghen International Inc
St Laurent, QC 514-332-6455
Van Roy Coffee
Cleveland, OH 877-826-7669
Vanns Spices
Baltimore, MD 800-583-1693
Vegetable Juices
Chicago, IL 888-776-9752
Victoria Packing Corporation
Brooklyn, NY 718-927-3000
Vincent Formusa Company
Chicago, IL 312-421-0485
W&G Flavors
Hunt Valley, MD. 410-771-6606
Wabash Heritage Spices
Vincennes, IN 812-895-0059
Wagner Gourmet Foods
Lenexa, KS 913-469-5411
Weaver Nut Company
Ephrata, PA 717-738-3781
West Pac
Idaho Falls, ID 800-973-7407
Wheeling Coffee & SpicecCompany
Wheeling, WV 800-500-0141
Whole Herb Company
Sonoma, CA 707-935-1077
Wild West Spices
Cody, WY 888-587-8887
William Bounds
Torrance, CA. 800-473-0504
William E. Martin & Sons Company
Jamaica, NY 718-291-1300
Wine Country Chef LLC
Hidden Valley Lake, CA. 707-322-0406
Wisconsin Cheese
Melrose Park, IL. 708-450-0074
Wisconsin Spice
Berlin, WI 920-361-3555
Wixon/Fontarome
St Francis, WI. 414-769-3000
World Flavors
Warminster, PA. 215-672-4400
World Harbors
Auburn, ME 800-355-6221
World of Spices
Stirling, NJ 908-647-1218
World Spice
Roselle, NJ 800-234-1060
Xcell International Corporation
Lemont, IL 800-722-7751
Young Winfield
Kleinburg, ON. 905-893-9682
Zatarain's
Gretna, LA 800-435-6639

Allspice

Atlantic Quality Spice &Seasonings
New Brunswick, NJ 800-584-0422
Chesapeake Spice Company
Baltimore, MD 410-391-2100
Chieftain Wild Rice Company
Spooner, WI 800-262-6368
Commodities Marketing, Inc.
Edison, NJ. 732-603-5077
Ecom Manufacturing Corporation
Markham, ON. 905-477-2441
Emerling International Foods
Buffalo, NY. 716-833-7381

We supply food manufacturers and food service customers worldwide (since 1988) with bulk ingredients including: Fruits & Vegetables; Juice Concentrates; Herbs & Spices; Oils & Vinegars; Flavors & Colors; Honey & Molasses. We also produce PURE MAPLE SYRUP.

Erba Food Products
Brooklyn, NY 718-272-7700
Gel Spice Company, Inc
Bayonne, NJ 800-922-0230
Morris J. Golombeck
Brooklyn, NY 718-284-3505
Organic Planet
San Francisco, CA 415-765-5590
Schiff Food Products
North Bergen, NJ 201-868-6800
Texas Coffee Company
Beaumont, TX. 800-259-3400
Tova Industries
Louisville, KY 888-532-8682
Victoria Packing Corporation
Brooklyn, NY 718-927-3000
Whole Herb Company
Sonoma, CA 707-935-1077

Ground

Con Yeager Spice Company
Zelienople, PA. 800-222-2460
Schiff Food Products
North Bergen, NJ 201-868-6800
Wabash Heritage Spices
Vincennes, IN 812-895-0059
Whole Herb Company
Sonoma, CA 707-935-1077

Whole

Con Yeager Spice Company
Zelienople, PA. 800-222-2460
Whole Herb Company
Sonoma, CA 707-935-1077

Anise - Star

Ground

Chesapeake Spice Company
Baltimore, MD 410-391-2100

Basil

Advanced Spice & Trading
Carrollton, TX. 800-872-7811
American Key Food Products
Closter, NJ. 800-767-0237
Atlantic Quality Spice &Seasonings
New Brunswick, NJ 800-584-0422
Chesapeake Spice Company
Baltimore, MD 410-391-2100
Chieftain Wild Rice Company
Spooner, WI 800-262-6368
Con Yeager Spice Company
Zelienople, PA. 800-222-2460
Emerling International Foods
Buffalo, NY. 716-833-7381

We supply food manufacturers and food service customers worldwide (since 1988) with bulk ingredients including: Fruits & Vegetables; Juice Concentrates; Herbs & Spices; Oils & Vinegars; Flavors & Colors; Honey & Molasses. We also produce PURE MAPLE SYRUP.

Gel Spice Company, Inc
Bayonne, NJ 800-922-0230
Green House Fine Herbs
Encinitas, CA 760-942-5371
Lebermuth Company
South Bend, IN 800-648-1123
Morris J. Golombeck
Brooklyn, NY 718-284-3505
Schiff Food Products
North Bergen, NJ 201-868-6800
Specialty Food America
Hopkinsville, KY 888-881-1633
Spiceco
Avenel, NJ. 732-499-9070

SupHerb Farms
Turlock, CA 800-787-4372

Frozen culinary herb and specialty vegetable ingredients.

Tova Industries
Louisville, KY 888-532-8682
Van Drunen Farms
Momence, IL. 815-472-3537
Vegetable Juices
Chicago, IL 888-776-9752
Victoria Packing Corporation
Brooklyn, NY 718-927-3000
Waterfield Farms
Amherst, MA 413-549-3558
Whole Herb Company
Sonoma, CA 707-935-1077

Basil Leaf

Morris J. Golombeck
Brooklyn, NY 718-284-3505
Schiff Food Products
North Bergen, NJ 201-868-6800

Bay Leaves

Advanced Spice & Trading
Carrollton, TX. 800-872-7811
American Key Food Products
Closter, NJ. 800-767-0237
Atlantic Quality Spice &Seasonings
New Brunswick, NJ 800-584-0422
Chesapeake Spice Company
Baltimore, MD 410-391-2100
Chieftain Wild Rice Company
Spooner, WI 800-262-6368
Con Yeager Spice Company
Zelienople, PA. 800-222-2460
Gel Spice Company, Inc
Bayonne, NJ 800-922-0230
Pendery's
Dallas, TX. 800-533-1870
Spiceco
Avenel, NJ. 732-499-9070
Tova Industries
Louisville, KY 888-532-8682
Vegetable Juices
Chicago, IL 888-776-9752
Victoria Packing Corporation
Brooklyn, NY 718-927-3000
Wabash Heritage Spices
Vincennes, IN 812-895-0059
Whole Herb Company
Sonoma, CA 707-935-1077

Ground

Emerling International Foods
Buffalo, NY. 716-833-7381

We supply food manufacturers and food service customers worldwide (since 1988) with bulk ingredients including: Fruits & Vegetables; Juice Concentrates; Herbs & Spices; Oils & Vinegars; Flavors & Colors; Honey & Molasses. We also produce PURE MAPLE SYRUP.

Black Pepper - Ground

Chesapeake Spice Company
Baltimore, MD 410-391-2100
Spice & Spice
Rolling Hills Estates, CA 866-729-7742
Swagger Foods Corporation
Vernon Hills, IL 847-913-1200

Capers

Alimentaire Whyte's Inc
Laval, QC 800-625-1979
Castella Imports
Hauppauge, NY 866-227-8355

Emerling International Foods
Buffalo, NY 716-833-7381

We supply food manufacturers and food service customers worldwide (since 1988) with bulk ingredients including: Fruits & Vegetables; Juice Concentrates; Herbs & Spices; Oils & Vinegars; Flavors & Colors; Honey & Molasses. We also produce PURE MAPLE SYRUP.

G. L. Mezzetta
American Canyon, CA 707-648-1050
L&S Packing Company
Farmingdale, NY 800-286-6487
Les Trois Petits Cochons
Brooklyn, NY 800-537-7283
Orleans Packing Company
Hyde Park, MA 617-361-6611
Paradise Products Corporation
Boca Raton, FL 800-826-1235
Proacec USA
Santa Monica, CA 310-996-7770
Ron-Son Foods
Swedesboro, NJ 856-241-7333
Star Fine Foods
Fresno, CA 559-498-2900
Vegetable Juices
Chicago, IL 888-776-9752
Victoria Packing Corporation
Brooklyn, NY 718-927-3000

Cardamom

Fiesta Gourmet of Tejas
Canyon Lake, TX 800-585-8250
Flavouressence Products
Mississauga, ON 866-209-7778
Goodnature Products
Orchard Park, NY 800-875-3381
Min Tong Herbs
Oakland, CA 800-562-5777
Sill Farms Market
Lawrence, MI 269-674-3755
Sunja's Oriental Foods
Waterbury, VT 802-244-7644

Ground

Chesapeake Spice Company
Baltimore, MD 410-391-2100
Chieftain Wild Rice Company
Spooner, WI 800-262-6368
Wabash Heritage Spices
Vincennes, IN 812-895-0059

Carob Powder

American Key Food Products
Closter, NJ 800-767-0237
Gel Spice Company, Inc
Bayonne, NJ 800-922-0230

Cassia (Cinnamon)

American Key Food Products
Closter, NJ 800-767-0237
Commodities Marketing, Inc.
Edison, NJ 732-603-5077
Naturex Inc.
South Hackensack, NJ 201-440-5000

Cayenne

Chesapeake Spice Company
Baltimore, MD 410-391-2100
Chieftain Wild Rice Company
Spooner, WI 800-262-6368
Vegetable Juices
Chicago, IL 888-776-9752
Victoria Packing Corporation
Brooklyn, NY 718-927-3000

Cayenne Pepper

American Key Food Products
Closter, NJ 800-767-0237
Atlantic Quality Spice &Seasonings
New Brunswick, NJ 800-584-0422
El Ranchito
Portland, OR 503-665-4919
Herb Connection
Springville, UT 801-489-4254
Morris J. Golombeck
Brooklyn, NY 718-284-3505
Naturex Inc.
South Hackensack, NJ 201-440-5000
Pepper Creek Farms
Lawton, OK 800-526-8132
Tova Industries
Louisville, KY 888-532-8682
Wabash Heritage Spices
Vincennes, IN 812-895-0059

Dried

Naturex Inc.
South Hackensack, NJ 201-440-5000

Ground

Naturex Inc.
South Hackensack, NJ 201-440-5000

Whole

Texas Coffee Company
Beaumont, TX 800-259-3400

Celery Flakes

Swagger Foods Corporation
Vernon Hills, IL 847-913-1200

Chervil

American Key Food Products
Closter, NJ 800-767-0237
Chieftain Wild Rice Company
Spooner, WI 800-262-6368
Muirhead Canning Company
The Dalles, OR 541-298-1660

SupHerb Farms
Turlock, CA 800-787-4372

Frozen culinary herb and specialty vegetable ingredients.

Chile Pepper

Chesapeake Spice Company
Baltimore, MD 410-391-2100
Chieftain Wild Rice Company
Spooner, WI 800-262-6368
Chugwater Chili Corporation
Chugwater, WY 800-972-4454
Mexnutri
San Luis Potosi, 444-841-5625
Pendery's
Dallas, TX 800-533-1870

Chili Crush

Spice & Spice
Rolling Hills Estates, CA 866-729-7742

Chili Pods

Whole & Dried

Spice & Spice
Rolling Hills Estates, CA 866-729-7742

Chili Powder

Mezza
Lake Forest, IL 888-206-6054
Spice & Spice
Rolling Hills Estates, CA 866-729-7742

Chinese

Harvest 2000
Pomona, CA 909-622-8039
San Francisco Herb & Natural Food Company
Fremont, CA 800-227-2830

Chives

Advanced Spice & Trading
Carrollton, TX 800-872-7811
American Key Food Products
Closter, NJ 800-767-0237
Atlantic Quality Spice &Seasonings
New Brunswick, NJ 800-584-0422
Chesapeake Spice Company
Baltimore, MD 410-391-2100
Chieftain Wild Rice Company
Spooner, WI 800-262-6368
Gel Spice Company, Inc
Bayonne, NJ 800-922-0230
Green House Fine Herbs
Encinitas, CA 760-942-5371
Schiff Food Products
North Bergen, NJ 201-868-6800

SupHerb Farms
Turlock, CA 800-787-4372

Frozen culinary herb and specialty vegetable ingredients.

Van Drunen Farms
Momence, IL 815-472-3537

Cinnamon

Advanced Spice & Trading
Carrollton, TX 800-872-7811
American Key Food Products
Closter, NJ 800-767-0237
Atlantic Quality Spice &Seasonings
New Brunswick, NJ 800-584-0422
Chesapeake Spice Company
Baltimore, MD 410-391-2100
Chieftain Wild Rice Company
Spooner, WI 800-262-6368
Con Yeager Spice Company
Zelienople, PA 800-222-2460
Emerling International Foods
Buffalo, NY 716-833-7381

We supply food manufacturers and food service customers worldwide (since 1988) with bulk ingredients including: Fruits & Vegetables; Juice Concentrates; Herbs & Spices; Oils & Vinegars; Flavors & Colors; Honey & Molasses. We also produce PURE MAPLE SYRUP.

Erba Food Products
Brooklyn, NY 718-272-7700
Lebermuth Company
South Bend, IN 800-648-1123
Morris J. Golombeck
Brooklyn, NY 718-284-3505
Organic Planet
San Francisco, CA 415-765-5590
Pendery's
Dallas, TX 800-533-1870
Schiff Food Products
North Bergen, NJ 201-868-6800
Spice & Spice
Rolling Hills Estates, CA 866-729-7742
Swagger Foods Corporation
Vernon Hills, IL 847-913-1200
Texas Coffee Company
Beaumont, TX 800-259-3400
Tova Industries
Louisville, KY 888-532-8682
Tripper
Oxnard, CA 888-336-8747
Victoria Packing Corporation
Brooklyn, NY 718-927-3000

Cassia

Advanced Spice & Trading
Carrollton, TX 800-872-7811
Atlantic Quality Spice &Seasonings
New Brunswick, NJ 800-584-0422
Morris J. Golombeck
Brooklyn, NY 718-284-3505
Schiff Food Products
North Bergen, NJ 201-868-6800
Tova Industries
Louisville, KY 888-532-8682

Ground

Con Yeager Spice Company
Zelienople, PA 800-222-2460

Wabash Heritage Spices
Vincennes, IN 812-895-0059

Whole

Spice & Spice
Rolling Hills Estates, CA 866-729-7742

Citron

Emerling International Foods
Buffalo, NY. 716-833-7381

We supply food manufacturers and food service customers worldwide (since 1988) with bulk ingredients including: Fruits & Vegetables; Juice Concentrates; Herbs & Spices; Oils & Vinegars; Flavors & Colors; Honey & Molasses. We also produce PURE MAPLE SYRUP.

Seald Sweet Growers & Packers
Vero Beach, FL. 772-569-2244
Victoria Packing Corporation
Brooklyn, NY 718-927-3000

Cloves

Atlantic Quality Spice &Seasonings
New Brunswick, NJ 800-584-0422
Chesapeake Spice Company
Baltimore, MD 410-391-2100
Chieftain Wild Rice Company
Spooner, WI 800-262-6368
Con Yeager Spice Company
Zelienople, PA. 800-222-2460
Emerling International Foods
Buffalo, NY. 716-833-7381

We supply food manufacturers and food service customers worldwide (since 1988) with bulk ingredients including: Fruits & Vegetables; Juice Concentrates; Herbs & Spices; Oils & Vinegars; Flavors & Colors; Honey & Molasses. We also produce PURE MAPLE SYRUP.

Schiff Food Products
North Bergen, NJ 201-868-6800
Tova Industries
Louisville, KY 888-532-8682
Victoria Packing Corporation
Brooklyn, NY 718-927-3000

Ground

Con Yeager Spice Company
Zelienople, PA. 800-222-2460
Schiff Food Products
North Bergen, NJ 201-868-6800
Texas Coffee Company
Beaumont, TX. 800-259-3400
Wabash Heritage Spices
Vincennes, IN 812-895-0059

Coriander (Cilantro)

Advanced Spice & Trading
Carrollton, TX. 800-872-7811
Atlantic Quality Spice &Seasonings
New Brunswick, NJ 800-584-0422
Chesapeake Spice Company
Baltimore, MD 410-391-2100
Chieftain Wild Rice Company
Spooner, WI 800-262-6368
Con Yeager Spice Company
Zelienople, PA. 800-222-2460
El Ranchito
Portland, OR 503-665-4919
Gel Spice Company, Inc
Bayonne, NJ 800-922-0230
Morris J. Golombeck
Brooklyn, NY 718-284-3505
Naturex Inc.
South Hackensack, NJ 201-440-5000
Schiff Food Products
North Bergen, NJ 201-868-6800
Spice & Spice
Rolling Hills Estates, CA 866-729-7742
Tova Industries
Louisville, KY 888-532-8682

Cumin

Advanced Spice & Trading
Carrollton, TX. 800-872-7811
American Key Food Products
Closter, NJ. 800-767-0237
Atlantic Quality Spice &Seasonings
New Brunswick, NJ 800-584-0422
Chesapeake Spice Company
Baltimore, MD 410-391-2100
Chieftain Wild Rice Company
Spooner, WI 800-262-6368
Commodities Marketing, Inc.
Edison, NJ. 732-603-5077
Con Yeager Spice Company
Zelienople, PA. 800-222-2460
Emerling International Foods
Buffalo, NY. 716-833-7381

We supply food manufacturers and food service customers worldwide (since 1988) with bulk ingredients including: Fruits & Vegetables; Juice Concentrates; Herbs & Spices; Oils & Vinegars; Flavors & Colors; Honey & Molasses. We also produce PURE MAPLE SYRUP.

Famarco
Virginia Beach, VA. 757-460-3573
Gel Spice Company, Inc
Bayonne, NJ 800-922-0230
Spice & Spice
Rolling Hills Estates, CA 866-729-7742
Tova Industries
Louisville, KY 888-532-8682
Victoria Packing Corporation
Brooklyn, NY 718-927-3000
Wabash Heritage Spices
Vincennes, IN 812-895-0059

Curry Powder

Chieftain Wild Rice Company
Spooner, WI 800-262-6368
Texas Coffee Company
Beaumont, TX. 800-259-3400

Dill

Atlantic Quality Spice &Seasonings
New Brunswick, NJ 800-584-0422
Chesapeake Spice Company
Baltimore, MD 410-391-2100
Chieftain Wild Rice Company
Spooner, WI 800-262-6368
Con Yeager Spice Company
Zelienople, PA. 800-222-2460
Gel Spice Company, Inc
Bayonne, NJ 800-922-0230
Green House Fine Herbs
Encinitas, CA 760-942-5371

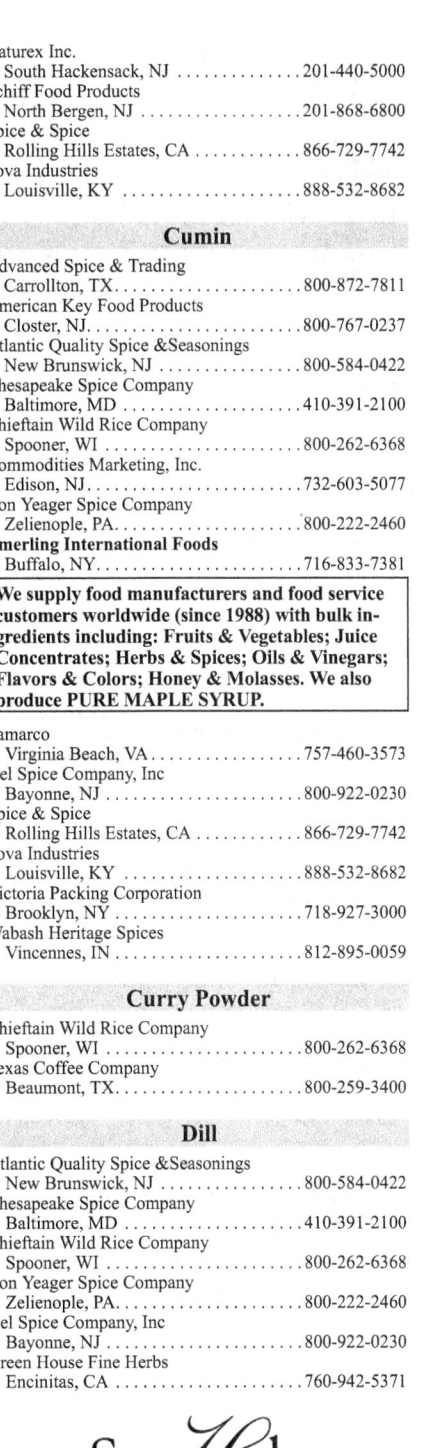

SupHerb Farms
Turlock, CA 800-787-4372

Frozen culinary herb and specialty vegetable ingredients.

Tova Industries
Louisville, KY 888-532-8682
Van Drunen Farms
Momence, IL. 815-472-3537
Victoria Packing Corporation
Brooklyn, NY 718-927-3000

Dill Weed

Con Yeager Spice Company
Zelienople, PA. 800-222-2460

SupHerb Farms
Turlock, CA 800-787-4372

Frozen culinary herb and specialty vegetable ingredients.

Dried

Island Spices
Miami, FL. 786-208-2066
Van Drunen Farms
Momence, IL. 815-472-3537

Endive

Frank Capurro & Son
Moss Landing, CA 831-728-3904

Epazote Herb

Chieftain Wild Rice Company
Spooner, WI 800-262-6368

Escarole

Frank Capurro & Son
Moss Landing, CA 831-728-3904

Extracts

Norac Technologies
Edmonton, AB 780-414-9595

Fennel

Chesapeake Spice Company
Baltimore, MD 410-391-2100
Chieftain Wild Rice Company
Spooner, WI 800-262-6368

SupHerb Farms
Turlock, CA 800-787-4372

Frozen culinary herb and specialty vegetable ingredients.

Wabash Heritage Spices
Vincennes, IN 812-895-0059

Fenugreek

Advanced Spice & Trading
Carrollton, TX. 800-872-7811
Chesapeake Spice Company
Baltimore, MD 410-391-2100
Chieftain Wild Rice Company
Spooner, WI 800-262-6368
Gel Spice Company, Inc
Bayonne, NJ 800-922-0230

Garlic

Arizona Natural Products
Phoenix, AZ 602-997-6098
Atlantic Quality Spice &Seasonings
New Brunswick, NJ 800-584-0422
Badia Spices
Miami, FL. 305-629-8000
Beaverton Foods
Beaverton, OR 800-223-8076
Bio-Nutritional Products
Northvale, NJ 201-784-8200
California Garlic Co
San Diego, CA 951-506-8883
Chieftain Wild Rice Company
Spooner, WI 800-262-6368
Christopher Ranch
Gilroy, CA. 408-847-1100
Con Yeager Spice Company
Zelienople, PA. 800-222-2460
DeFrancesco & Sons
Firebaugh, CA. 209-364-7000

Derlea Foods
Pickering, ON 888-430-7777
Ecom Manufacturing Corporation
Markham, ON 905-477-2441
Florida Shortening Corporation
Miami, FL 305-691-2992
Freeda Vitamins
Long Island City, NY 800-777-3737
Ful-Flav-R Foods
Alamo, CA 925-838-0300
Garlic Company
Bakersfield, CA 661-393-4212
Garlic Valley Farms Inc
Glendale, CA 800-424-7990
George Chiala Farms
Morgan Hill, CA 408-778-0562
Gilroy Foods
Gilroy, CA 800-921-7502
Golden Whisk
South San Francisco, CA 800-660-5222
Haliburton International Corporation
Ontario, CA 877-980-4295
Harris Farms
Coalinga, CA 800-742-1955
Herb Connection
Springville, UT 801-489-4254
Kimball Enterprise International
Hacienda Heights, CA 213-276-8898
L&S Packing Company
Farmingdale, NY 800-286-6487
Lawry's Foods
Monrovia, CA 800-595-8917
Lebermuth Company
South Bend, IN 800-648-1123
Marin Food Specialties
Byron, CA 925-634-6126
Morris J. Golombeck
Brooklyn, NY 718-284-3505
Nature Quality
San Martin, CA 408-683-2182
Naturex Inc.
South Hackensack, NJ 201-440-5000
NuNaturals
Eugene, OR 800-753-4372
Nutraceutical Corporation
Park City, UT 800-669-8877
Pacific Choice Brands
Fresno, CA 559-237-5583
Pendery's
Dallas, TX 800-533-1870
Rapazzini Winery
Gilroy, CA 800-842-6262
San Francisco Herb & Natural Food Company
Fremont, CA 800-227-2830
Schiff Food Products
North Bergen, NJ 201-868-6800
Specialty Food America
Hopkinsville, KY 888-881-1633
Spice World
Orlando, FL 800-433-4979
Spiceco
Avenel, NJ 732-499-9070

SupHerb Farms
Turlock, CA 800-787-4372

Frozen culinary herb and specialty vegetable ingredients.

Swagger Foods Corporation
Vernon Hills, IL 847-913-1200
Texas Coffee Company
Beaumont, TX 800-259-3400
Three Springs Farm
Prospect, VA 804-574-2314
Tova Industries
Louisville, KY 888-532-8682
Trout Lake Farm
Trout Lake, WA 509-395-2025
Tulkoff Food Products
Baltimore, MD 800-638-7343
Vessey & Company
Holtville, CA 760-356-0130

Chopped

California Garlic Co
San Diego, CA 951-506-8883
Ful-Flav-R Foods
Alamo, CA 925-838-0300
L&S Packing Company
Farmingdale, NY 800-286-6487
San Francisco Herb & Natural Food Company
Fremont, CA 800-227-2830
Spice World
Orlando, FL 800-433-4979
Tulkoff Food Products
Baltimore, MD 800-638-7343

Granulated

Advanced Spice & Trading
Carrollton, TX 800-872-7811
Gel Spice Company, Inc
Bayonne, NJ 800-922-0230
Naturex Inc.
South Hackensack, NJ 201-440-5000
San Francisco Herb & Natural Food Company
Fremont, CA 800-227-2830
Spice & Spice
Rolling Hills Estates, CA 866-729-7742
Tova Industries
Louisville, KY 888-532-8682
Wabash Heritage Spices
Vincennes, IN 812-895-0059

Minced

Con Yeager Spice Company
Zelienople, PA 800-222-2460
San Francisco Herb & Natural Food Company
Fremont, CA 800-227-2830
Spice World
Orlando, FL 800-433-4979
Wabash Heritage Spices
Vincennes, IN 812-895-0059

Powdered

Con Yeager Spice Company
Zelienople, PA 800-222-2460
Erba Food Products
Brooklyn, NY 718-272-7700
San Francisco Herb & Natural Food Company
Fremont, CA 800-227-2830
Texas Coffee Company
Beaumont, TX 800-259-3400
Victoria Packing Corporation
Brooklyn, NY 718-927-3000
Whole Herb Company
Sonoma, CA 707-935-1077

Garlic Salt

San Francisco Herb & Natural Food Company
Fremont, CA 800-227-2830
Texas Coffee Company
Beaumont, TX 800-259-3400

Ginger

Advanced Spice & Trading
Carrollton, TX 800-872-7811
American Key Food Products
Closter, NJ 800-767-0237
Atlantic Quality Spice &Seasonings
New Brunswick, NJ 800-584-0422
California Garlic Co
San Diego, CA 951-506-8883
Chesapeake Spice Company
Baltimore, MD 410-391-2100
Chieftain Wild Rice Company
Spooner, WI 800-262-6368
Christopher Ranch
Gilroy, CA 408-847-1100
Con Yeager Spice Company
Zelienople, PA 800-222-2460
D Steengrafe & Company
Pleasant Valley, NY 845-635-4067
Erba Food Products
Brooklyn, NY 718-272-7700
Gel Spice Company, Inc
Bayonne, NJ 800-922-0230
Herb Connection
Springville, UT 801-489-4254
Hialeah Products Company
Hollywood, FL 800-923-3379
Morris J. Golombeck
Brooklyn, NY 718-284-3505
Naturex Inc.
South Hackensack, NJ 201-440-5000
Pendery's
Dallas, TX 800-533-1870
Royal Pacific Foods/The Ginger People
Marina, CA 800-551-5284
Specialty Food America
Hopkinsville, KY 888-881-1633

SupHerb Farms
Turlock, CA 800-787-4372

Frozen culinary herb and specialty vegetable ingredients.

Texas Coffee Company
Beaumont, TX 800-259-3400
Tova Industries
Louisville, KY 888-532-8682
Wabash Heritage Spices
Vincennes, IN 812-895-0059

Crystallized

Hialeah Products Company
Hollywood, FL 800-923-3379

Ground

Con Yeager Spice Company
Zelienople, PA 800-222-2460

Pieces

Ful-Flav-R Foods
Alamo, CA 925-838-0300

Ginseng

Alternative Health & Herbs
Albany, OR 800-345-4152
Atkins Ginseng Farms
Waterford, ON 800-265-0239
Fmali Herb
Santa Cruz, CA 831-423-7913
Ginco International
Simi Valley, CA 800-423-5176
Ginseng America
Roxbury, NY 607-326-3123
Heise's Wausau Farms
Wausau, WI 800-764-1010
IL HWA American Corporation
Worcester, MA 800-446-7364
Madys Company
San Francisco, CA 415-822-2227
Master Mix
Placentia, CA 714-524-1698
Naturex Inc.
South Hackensack, NJ 201-440-5000
Penn Herb Company
Philadelphia, PA 800-523-9971
Prince of Peace Enterprises
Hayward, CA 800-732-2328
Progenix Corporation
Wausau, WI 800-233-3356
San Francisco Herb & Natural Food Company
Fremont, CA 800-227-2830
St. John's Botanicals
Bowie, MD 301-262-5302
Sun Wellness/Sun Chlorel
Torrance, CA 800-829-2828
Superior Trading Company
San Francisco, CA 415-982-8722
Triple Leaf Tea
S San Francisco, CA 800-552-7448
Yellow Emperor
Eugene, OR 877-485-6664

Heather

Chieftain Wild Rice Company
Spooner, WI 800-262-6368

Herbes de Provence

Chieftain Wild Rice Company
Spooner, WI 800-262-6368

SupHerb Farms
Turlock, CA 800-787-4372

Frozen culinary herb and specialty vegetable ingredients.

Horseradish

Buedel Food Products
Bridgeview, IL 708-496-3500
Feature Foods
Etobicoke, ON 416-675-7350
Gold Pure Foods Products Company
Hempstead, NY. 800-422-4681
Heintz & Weber Company
Buffalo, NY. 716-852-7171
Junuis Food Products
Palatine, IL 847-359-4300
Palmieri Food Products
New Haven, CT 800-845-5447
Red Pelican Food Products
Detroit, MI 313-881-4095
Strub Pickles
Brantford, ON. 519-751-1717
Thor-Shackel HorseradishCompany
Eau Claire, WI 800-826-7322
United Pickle Products Corporation
Bronx, NY. 718-933-6060

Juniper Berries

Chieftain Wild Rice Company
Spooner, WI 800-262-6368

Lavender

Chieftain Wild Rice Company
Spooner, WI 800-262-6368

Lavender Flowers

Wabash Heritage Spices
Vincennes, IN 812-895-0059

Lemon Grass

SupHerb Farms
Turlock, CA 800-787-4372

Frozen culinary herb and specialty vegetable ingredients.

Lemon Peel

Chieftain Wild Rice Company
Spooner, WI 800-262-6368

Liquid

Emerling International Foods
Buffalo, NY. 716-833-7381

We supply food manufacturers and food service customers worldwide (since 1988) with bulk ingredients including: Fruits & Vegetables; Juice Concentrates; Herbs & Spices; Oils & Vinegars; Flavors & Colors; Honey & Molasses. We also produce PURE MAPLE SYRUP.

Jogue Inc
Northville, MI. 800-521-3888
Sentry Seasonings
Elmhurst, IL 630-530-5370

The product development experts of Sentry Seasonings are eager to offer the assistance and hands-on experience to food processors of all sizes. Sentry Seasonings will ensure the consistent high quality and repeat sales of your products, whether you choose one of our many off-the-shelf Bench Mark products or a modified version to meet your preferences. Sentry Seasonings can also duplicate and/or improve your present flavor profile; formulate, blend and package specifically for your requirements.

Vegetable Juices
Chicago, IL 888-776-9752
World Flavors
Warminster, PA 215-672-4400

Mace (See also Nutmeg)

Advanced Spice & Trading
Carrollton, TX. 800-872-7811
American Key Food Products
Closter, NJ. 800-767-0237
Chesapeake Spice Company
Baltimore, MD 410-391-2100
Chieftain Wild Rice Company
Spooner, WI 800-262-6368
Con Yeager Spice Company
Zelienople, PA. 800-222-2460
Emerling International Foods
Buffalo, NY. 716-833-7381

We supply food manufacturers and food service customers worldwide (since 1988) with bulk ingredients including: Fruits & Vegetables; Juice Concentrates; Herbs & Spices; Oils & Vinegars; Flavors & Colors; Honey & Molasses. We also produce PURE MAPLE SYRUP.

Gel Spice Company, Inc
Bayonne, NJ 800-922-0230
Specialty Food America
Hopkinsville, KY 888-881-1633
Tova Industries
Louisville, KY 888-532-8682

Ground

Con Yeager Spice Company
Zelienople, PA. 800-222-2460

Marjoram

American Key Food Products
Closter, NJ. 800-767-0237
Chieftain Wild Rice Company
Spooner, WI 800-262-6368
Con Yeager Spice Company
Zelienople, PA. 800-222-2460
Emerling International Foods
Buffalo, NY. 716-833-7381

We supply food manufacturers and food service customers worldwide (since 1988) with bulk ingredients including: Fruits & Vegetables; Juice Concentrates; Herbs & Spices; Oils & Vinegars; Flavors & Colors; Honey & Molasses. We also produce PURE MAPLE SYRUP.

Gel Spice Company, Inc
Bayonne, NJ 800-922-0230
Naturex Inc.
South Hackensack, NJ 201-440-5000

SupHerb Farms
Turlock, CA 800-787-4372

Frozen culinary herb and specialty vegetable ingredients.

Tova Industries
Louisville, KY 888-532-8682
Van Drunen Farms
Momence, IL. 815-472-3537
Victoria Packing Corporation
Brooklyn, NY 718-927-3000
Wabash Heritage Spices
Vincennes, IN 812-895-0059

Mint

Whole Herb Company
Sonoma, CA 707-935-1077

Mint Leaves

Advanced Spice & Trading
Carrollton, TX. 800-872-7811
Atlantic Quality Spice &Seasonings
New Brunswick, NJ 800-584-0422
Charles H. Baldwin & Sons
West Stockbridge, MA 413-232-7785
Emerling International Foods
Buffalo, NY. 716-833-7381

We supply food manufacturers and food service customers worldwide (since 1988) with bulk ingredients including: Fruits & Vegetables; Juice Concentrates; Herbs & Spices; Oils & Vinegars; Flavors & Colors; Honey & Molasses. We also produce PURE MAPLE SYRUP.

Victoria Packing Corporation
Brooklyn, NY 718-927-3000

Spearmint

Gel Spice Company, Inc
Bayonne, NJ 800-922-0230

SupHerb Farms
Turlock, CA 800-787-4372

Frozen culinary herb and specialty vegetable ingredients.

Mulled Wine Spice

Chieftain Wild Rice Company
Spooner, WI 800-262-6368

Mulling

Aspen Mulling Company Inc.
Aspen, CO. 800-622-7736

Mustard

Dry - Prepared

American Key Food Products
Closter, NJ. 800-767-0237
Assouline & Ting
Huntingdon Valley, PA 800-521-4491
Au Printemps Gourmet
Saint-Jerome, QC 800-663-0416
Baldwin Richardson Foods
Frankfort, IL 866-644-2732

Liquid ingredient manufacturer specializing in signature sauces, dessert toppings, beverage/pancake syrups, specialty fruit fillings and condiments.

Catamount Specialties ofVermont
Stowe, VT. 800-820-8096
Food Specialties
Indianapolis, IN 317-271-0862
Groeb Farms
Onsted, MI 517-467-2065
GS Dunn & Company
Hamilton, ON 905-522-0833
Herlocher Foods
State College, PA 800-437-5624
Honey Acres
Ashippun, WI 800-558-7745
J.N. Bech
Elk Rapids, MI 800-232-4583
J.W. Raye & Company
Eastport, ME. 800-853-1903
Kozlowski Farms
Forestville, CA 800-473-2767
Minn-Dak Growers Ltd.
Grand Forks, ND. 701-746-7453
New Canaan Farms
Dripping Springs, TX 800-727-5267
Pepper Creek Farms
Lawton, OK. 800-526-8132
T. Marzetti Company
Columbus, OH 614-846-2232
Victoria Packing Corporation
Brooklyn, NY 718-927-3000

Prepared

Walker Foods
Los Angeles, CA. 800-966-5199

Mustard Powder

Wabash Heritage Spices
Vincennes, IN 812-895-0059

Mustards

Chesapeake Spice Company
Baltimore, MD 410-391-2100
Con Yeager Spice Company
Zelienople, PA. 800-222-2460

Natural Flavorings

Spice King Corporation
Beverly Hills, CA 310-836-7770

Nutmeg (See also Mace)

Advanced Spice & Trading
Carrollton, TX. 800-872-7811
American Key Food Products
Closter, NJ. 800-767-0237
Atlantic Quality Spice &Seasonings
New Brunswick, NJ 800-584-0422
Commodities Marketing, Inc.
Edison, NJ. 732-603-5077

Con Yeager Spice Company
Zelienople, PA. 800-222-2460
Emerling International Foods
Buffalo, NY. 716-833-7381

We supply food manufacturers and food service customers worldwide (since 1988) with bulk ingredients including: Fruits & Vegetables; Juice Concentrates; Herbs & Spices; Oils & Vinegars; Flavors & Colors; Honey & Molasses. We also produce PURE MAPLE SYRUP.

Gel Spice Company, Inc
Bayonne, NJ 800-922-0230
Schiff Food Products
North Bergen, NJ 201-868-6800
Spice & Spice
Rolling Hills Estates, CA 866-729-7742
Texas Coffee Company
Beaumont, TX. 800-259-3400
Tripper
Oxnard, CA. 888-336-8747
Victoria Packing Corporation
Brooklyn, NY 718-927-3000

Ground

Con Yeager Spice Company
Zelienople, PA. 800-222-2460

Whole

Con Yeager Spice Company
Zelienople, PA. 800-222-2460

Onion

Con Yeager Spice Company
Zelienople, PA. 800-222-2460
Ful-Flav-R Foods
Alamo, CA 925-838-0300
Gel Spice Company, Inc
Bayonne, NJ 800-922-0230
Marin Food Specialties
Byron, CA. 925-634-6126
Texas Coffee Company
Beaumont, TX. 800-259-3400

Chopped

Con Yeager Spice Company
Zelienople, PA. 800-222-2460
Ful-Flav-R Foods
Alamo, CA 925-838-0300

Granulated

Con Yeager Spice Company
Zelienople, PA. 800-222-2460
Victoria Packing Corporation
Brooklyn, NY 718-927-3000
Wabash Heritage Spices
Vincennes, IN 812-895-0059

Minced

Con Yeager Spice Company
Zelienople, PA. 800-222-2460
Erba Food Products
Brooklyn, NY 718-272-7700

Oregano

Advanced Spice & Trading
Carrollton, TX. 800-872-7811
Atlantic Quality Spice &Seasonings
New Brunswick, NJ 800-584-0422
Castella Imports
Hauppauge, NY 866-227-8355
Chesapeake Spice Company
Baltimore, MD 410-391-2100
Chieftain Wild Rice Company
Spooner, WI 800-262-6368
Con Yeager Spice Company
Zelienople, PA. 800-222-2460
Emerling International Foods
Buffalo, NY. 716-833-7381

We supply food manufacturers and food service customers worldwide (since 1988) with bulk ingredients including: Fruits & Vegetables; Juice Concentrates; Herbs & Spices; Oils & Vinegars; Flavors & Colors; Honey & Molasses. We also produce PURE MAPLE SYRUP.

Morris J. Golombeck
Brooklyn, NY 718-284-3505
Schiff Food Products
North Bergen, NJ 201-868-6800
Specialty Food America
Hopkinsville, KY 888-881-1633
Spiceco
Avenel, NJ. 732-499-9070

SupHerb FARMS®

SupHerb Farms
Turlock, CA 800-787-4372

Frozen culinary herb and specialty vegetable ingredients.

Texas Coffee Company
Beaumont, TX. 800-259-3400
Trout Lake Farm
Trout Lake, WA. 509-395-2025
Van Drunen Farms
Momence, IL. 815-472-3537
Vegetable Juices
Chicago, IL 888-776-9752
Victoria Packing Corporation
Brooklyn, NY 718-927-3000
Whole Herb Company
Sonoma, CA 707-935-1077

Greek

Agrocan
Ville St Laurent, QC 877-247-6226

Mexican

Wabash Heritage Spices
Vincennes, IN 812-895-0059

Paprika

Advanced Spice & Trading
Carrollton, TX. 800-872-7811
American Key Food Products
Closter, NJ. 800-767-0237
Atlantic Quality Spice &Seasonings
New Brunswick, NJ 800-584-0422
Chesapeake Spice Company
Baltimore, MD 410-391-2100
Chieftain Wild Rice Company
Spooner, WI 800-262-6368
Con Yeager Spice Company
Zelienople, PA. 800-222-2460
Emerling International Foods
Buffalo, NY. 716-833-7381

We supply food manufacturers and food service customers worldwide (since 1988) with bulk ingredients including: Fruits & Vegetables; Juice Concentrates; Herbs & Spices; Oils & Vinegars; Flavors & Colors; Honey & Molasses. We also produce PURE MAPLE SYRUP.

Erba Food Products
Brooklyn, NY 718-272-7700
Gel Spice Company, Inc
Bayonne, NJ 800-922-0230
Gilroy Foods
Gilroy, CA. 800-921-7502
Heartline Foods
Westport, CT. 203-222-0381
Morris J. Golombeck
Brooklyn, NY 718-284-3505
Naturex Inc.
South Hackensack, NJ 201-440-5000
Pendery's
Dallas, TX. 800-533-1870
Schiff Food Products
North Bergen, NJ 201-868-6800
SJH Enterprises
Middleton, WI. 888-745-3845
Spice & Spice
Rolling Hills Estates, CA 866-729-7742
Spiceco
Avenel, NJ. 732-499-9070
Swagger Foods Corporation
Vernon Hills, IL 847-913-1200
Victoria Packing Corporation
Brooklyn, NY 718-927-3000

Wabash Heritage Spices
Vincennes, IN 812-895-0059

Parsley

Bifulco Farms
Pittsgrove, NJ 856-692-0707
Chesapeake Spice Company
Baltimore, MD 410-391-2100
Chieftain Wild Rice Company
Spooner, WI 800-262-6368
Frank Capurro & Son
Moss Landing, CA 831-728-3904
Specialty Food America
Hopkinsville, KY 888-881-1633

SupHerb Farms
Turlock, CA 800-787-4372

Frozen culinary herb and specialty vegetable ingredients.

Dehydrated

Alfred L. Wolff, Inc.
Park Ridge, IL. 847-759-8888
American Key Food Products
Closter, NJ. 800-767-0237
Emerling International Foods
Buffalo, NY. 716-833-7381

We supply food manufacturers and food service customers worldwide (since 1988) with bulk ingredients including: Fruits & Vegetables; Juice Concentrates; Herbs & Spices; Oils & Vinegars; Flavors & Colors; Honey & Molasses. We also produce PURE MAPLE SYRUP.

Gel Spice Company, Inc
Bayonne, NJ 800-922-0230
Unique Ingredients
Naches, WA. 509-653-1991

Pepper

Advanced Spice & Trading
Carrollton, TX. 800-872-7811
American Key Food Products
Closter, NJ. 800-767-0237
Con Yeager Spice Company
Zelienople, PA. 800-222-2460
Eatem Foods Company
Vineland, NJ 800-683-2836
Lawry's Foods
Monrovia, CA. 800-595-8917
Morris J. Golombeck
Brooklyn, NY 718-284-3505
Pepper Mill Imports
Carmel, CA. 800-928-1744
Schiff Food Products
North Bergen, NJ 201-868-6800
Spice & Spice
Rolling Hills Estates, CA 866-729-7742
Swagger Foods Corporation
Vernon Hills, IL 847-913-1200
Texas Coffee Company
Beaumont, TX. 800-259-3400
Tripper
Oxnard, CA. 888-336-8747
Victoria Packing Corporation
Brooklyn, NY 718-927-3000
Walker Foods
Los Angeles, CA. 800-966-5199
Wine Country Chef LLC
Hidden Valley Lake, CA. 707-322-0406

Black - White - Red

Spice & Spice
Rolling Hills Estates, CA 866-729-7742

White Ground

Chesapeake Spice Company
Baltimore, MD 410-391-2100
Chieftain Wild Rice Company
Spooner, WI 800-262-6368

Pepper Mash

Emerling International Foods
Buffalo, NY. 716-833-7381

We supply food manufacturers and food service customers worldwide (since 1988) with bulk ingredients including: Fruits & Vegetables; Juice Concentrates; Herbs & Spices; Oils & Vinegars; Flavors & Colors; Honey & Molasses. We also produce PURE MAPLE SYRUP.

Vegetable Juices
Chicago, IL 888-776-9752

Peppercorns

Wabash Heritage Spices
Vincennes, IN 812-895-0059

Peppermint

Trout Lake Farm
Trout Lake, WA. 509-395-2025

Pickling Spices

Texas Coffee Company
Beaumont, TX. 800-259-3400

Red Pepper

Crushed

Swagger Foods Corporation
Vernon Hills, IL 847-913-1200
Victoria Packing Corporation
Brooklyn, NY 718-927-3000

Rosemary

Advanced Spice & Trading
Carrollton, TX. 800-872-7811
American Key Food Products
Closter, NJ. 800-767-0237
Atlantic Quality Spice &Seasonings
New Brunswick, NJ 800-584-0422
Chesapeake Spice Company
Baltimore, MD 410-391-2100
Chieftain Wild Rice Company
Spooner, WI 800-262-6368
Con Yeager Spice Company
Zelienople, PA. 800-222-2460
Emerling International Foods
Buffalo, NY. 716-833-7381

We supply food manufacturers and food service customers worldwide (since 1988) with bulk ingredients including: Fruits & Vegetables; Juice Concentrates; Herbs & Spices; Oils & Vinegars; Flavors & Colors; Honey & Molasses. We also produce PURE MAPLE SYRUP.

Gel Spice Company, Inc
Bayonne, NJ 800-922-0230
Morris J. Golombeck
Brooklyn, NY 718-284-3505
Naturex Inc.
South Hackensack, NJ 201-440-5000
RFI Ingredients
Blauvelt, NY. 800-962-7663
Schiff Food Products
North Bergen, NJ 201-868-6800

SupHerb Farms
Turlock, CA 800-787-4372

Frozen culinary herb and specialty vegetable ingredients.

Universal Preservachem Inc
Somerset, NJ. 732-568-1266
Victoria Packing Corporation
Brooklyn, NY 718-927-3000
Wabash Heritage Spices
Vincennes, IN 812-895-0059

Cut

RFI Ingredients
Blauvelt, NY. 800-962-7663

Ground

Con Yeager Spice Company
Zelienople, PA. 800-222-2460
RFI Ingredients
Blauvelt, NY. 800-962-7663
Schiff Food Products
North Bergen, NJ 201-868-6800

Saffron

Advanced Spice & Trading
Carrollton, TX. 800-872-7811
American Key Food Products
Closter, NJ. 800-767-0237
Atlantic Quality Spice &Seasonings
New Brunswick, NJ 800-584-0422
Chesapeake Spice Company
Baltimore, MD 410-391-2100
Chieftain Wild Rice Company
Spooner, WI 800-262-6368
Emerling International Foods
Buffalo, NY. 716-833-7381

We supply food manufacturers and food service customers worldwide (since 1988) with bulk ingredients including: Fruits & Vegetables; Juice Concentrates; Herbs & Spices; Oils & Vinegars; Flavors & Colors; Honey & Molasses. We also produce PURE MAPLE SYRUP.

Gel Spice Company, Inc
Bayonne, NJ 800-922-0230
Naturex Inc.
South Hackensack, NJ 201-440-5000
Schiff Food Products
North Bergen, NJ 201-868-6800
Shanks Extracts
Lancaster, PA 800-346-3135
Whole Herb Company
Sonoma, CA 707-935-1077

Whole Threads

Chieftain Wild Rice Company
Spooner, WI 800-262-6368

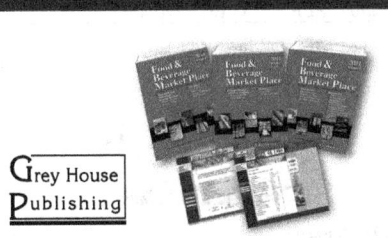

Sage

Castella Imports
Hauppauge, NY 866-227-8355
Chesapeake Spice Company
Baltimore, MD 410-391-2100
Chieftain Wild Rice Company
Spooner, WI 800-262-6368
Con Yeager Spice Company
Zelienople, PA. 800-222-2460

SupHerb Farms
Turlock, CA 800-787-4372

Frozen culinary herb and specialty vegetable ingredients.

Leaves

Advanced Spice & Trading
Carrollton, TX. 800-872-7811
Atlantic Quality Spice &Seasonings
New Brunswick, NJ 800-584-0422
Con Yeager Spice Company
Zelienople, PA. 800-222-2460
Emerling International Foods
Buffalo, NY. 716-833-7381

We supply food manufacturers and food service customers worldwide (since 1988) with bulk ingredients including: Fruits & Vegetables; Juice Concentrates; Herbs & Spices; Oils & Vinegars; Flavors & Colors; Honey & Molasses. We also produce PURE MAPLE SYRUP.

Gel Spice Company, Inc
Bayonne, NJ 800-922-0230

SupHerb Farms
Turlock, CA 800-787-4372

Frozen culinary herb and specialty vegetable ingredients.

Rubbed

Con Yeager Spice Company
Zelienople, PA. 800-222-2460

Savory

All American Foods, Inc.
Mankato, MN 800-833-2661
American Key Food Products
Closter, NJ. 800-767-0237
Certified Savory
Countryside, IL. 800-328-7656
Chieftain Wild Rice Company
Spooner, WI 800-262-6368
David Michael & Company
Philadelphia, PA 800-363-5286
Flavor House
Adelanto, CA 760-246-9131
Silver Palate Kitchens
Cresskill, NJ 800-872-5283
Swagger Foods Corporation
Vernon Hills, IL 847-913-1200

Shallots

SupHerb Farms
Turlock, CA 800-787-4372

Frozen culinary herb and specialty vegetable ingredients.

Sorrel

SupHerb Farms
Turlock, CA 800-787-4372

Frozen culinary herb and specialty vegetable ingredients.

Spearmint

SupHerb Farms
Turlock, CA 800-787-4372

Frozen culinary herb and specialty vegetable ingredients.

Trout Lake Farm
Trout Lake, WA. 509-395-2025

Star Anise

Chesapeake Spice Company
Baltimore, MD 410-391-2100

Sumac Berries

Chieftain Wild Rice Company
Spooner, WI 800-262-6368

Tandoori

Chieftain Wild Rice Company
Spooner, WI 800-262-6368

Tarragon

Advanced Spice & Trading
Carrollton, TX. 800-872-7811
Atlantic Quality Spice &Seasonings
New Brunswick, NJ 800-584-0422
Chesapeake Spice Company
Baltimore, MD 410-391-2100
Con Yeager Spice Company
Zelienople, PA. 800-222-2460
Schiff Food Products
North Bergen, NJ 201-868-6800
Specialty Food America
Hopkinsville, KY 888-881-1633

SupHerb Farms
Turlock, CA 800-787-4372

Frozen culinary herb and specialty vegetable ingredients.

Wabash Heritage Spices
Vincennes, IN 812-895-0059

Tartar

Cream

Chieftain Wild Rice Company
Spooner, WI 800-262-6368
Universal Preservachem Inc
Somerset, NJ 732-568-1266

Teas

Castella Imports
Hauppauge, NY 866-227-8355
O'Neill Coffee Company
West Middlesex, PA 724-528-9281

Thyme

Advanced Spice & Trading
Carrollton, TX. 800-872-7811
American Key Food Products
Closter, NJ. 800-767-0237
Atlantic Quality Spice &Seasonings
New Brunswick, NJ 800-584-0422
Chesapeake Spice Company
Baltimore, MD 410-391-2100
Chieftain Wild Rice Company
Spooner, WI 800-262-6368
Con Yeager Spice Company
Zelienople, PA. 800-222-2460
Emerling International Foods
Buffalo, NY. 716-833-7381

We supply food manufacturers and food service customers worldwide (since 1988) with bulk ingredients including: Fruits & Vegetables; Juice Concentrates; Herbs & Spices; Oils & Vinegars; Flavors & Colors; Honey & Molasses. We also produce PURE MAPLE SYRUP.

Morris J. Golombeck
Brooklyn, NY 718-284-3505
Schiff Food Products
North Bergen, NJ 201-868-6800
Specialty Food America
Hopkinsville, KY 888-881-1633

SupHerb Farms
Turlock, CA 800-787-4372

Frozen culinary herb and specialty vegetable ingredients.

Ground

Schiff Food Products
North Bergen, NJ 201-868-6800
Wabash Heritage Spices
Vincennes, IN 812-895-0059

Turmeric

Agri-Dairy Products
Purchase, NY 914-697-9580
American Key Food Products
Closter, NJ. 800-767-0237
Atlantic Quality Spice &Seasonings
New Brunswick, NJ 800-584-0422
Chieftain Wild Rice Company
Spooner, WI 800-262-6368
Con Yeager Spice Company
Zelienople, PA. 800-222-2460

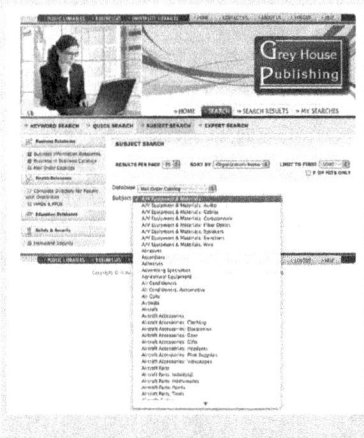

Emerling International Foods
Buffalo, NY....................... 716-833-7381

We supply food manufacturers and food service customers worldwide (since 1988) with bulk ingredients including: Fruits & Vegetables; Juice Concentrates; Herbs & Spices; Oils & Vinegars; Flavors & Colors; Honey & Molasses. We also produce PURE MAPLE SYRUP.

Schiff Food Products
North Bergen, NJ 201-868-6800
SJH Enterprises
Middleton, WI..................... 888-745-3845

Ground

Schiff Food Products
North Bergen, NJ 201-868-6800
Wabash Heritage Spices
Vincennes, IN 812-895-0059

Vanilla

Agri-Dairy Products
Purchase, NY 914-697-9580
Chieftain Wild Rice Company
Spooner, WI 800-262-6368
Naturex Inc.
South Hackensack, NJ 201-440-5000
Nielsen-Massey Vanillas
Waukegan, IL 800-525-7873
Texas Coffee Company
Beaumont, TX..................... 800-259-3400
Triple H
Riverside, CA 951-352-5700
Tripper
Oxnard, CA....................... 888-336-8747
Wabash Heritage Spices
Vincennes, IN 812-895-0059

Vanilla Beans

Ambassador Foods
Van Nuys, CA..................... 800-338-3369
Atlantic Quality Spice &Seasonings
New Brunswick, NJ 800-584-0422

Emerling International Foods
Buffalo, NY....................... 716-833-7381

We supply food manufacturers and food service customers worldwide (since 1988) with bulk ingredients including: Fruits & Vegetables; Juice Concentrates; Herbs & Spices; Oils & Vinegars; Flavors & Colors; Honey & Molasses. We also produce PURE MAPLE SYRUP.

Naturex Inc.
South Hackensack, NJ 201-440-5000
Zink & Triest Company
Montgomeryville, PA 800-537-5070

Wasabi

Chieftain Wild Rice Company
Spooner, WI 800-262-6368

White Pepper

Ground

Spice & Spice
Rolling Hills Estates, CA 866-729-7742

Sugars, Syrups & Sweeteners

General

ADM Food Ingredients
Olathe, KS. 800-255-6637
Bear Stewart Corporation
Chicago, IL 800-697-2327
Burleson's Honey, Inc
Waxahachie, TX 972-937-4810
Cocoline Chocolate Company
Brooklyn, NY 718-522-4500
Colorado Sweet Gold
Lakewood, CO 303-384-1101
Crosby Molasses Company
St John, NB 506-634-7515
Deborah's Kitchen Inc.
Littleton, MA 617-216-9908
Deer Creek Honey Farms
London, OH 740-852-0899
E.F. Lane & Son
Colton, CA 510-569-8980
Escalade Ltd
Huntington, NY 631-659-3374

Evergreen Sweeteners, Inc
Hallandale Beach, FL 305-931-1321

Evergreen Sweeteners is a full service sweetener distributor serving the entire Southeastern United States. From bulk liquid sweeteners to bagged sweeteners, Evergreen provides its customers with industry-leading service and unsurpassed quality.

Glorybee Natural Sweeteners
Eugene, OR. 800-456-7923
Hoyt's Honey Farm
Baytown, TX. 281-576-5383
Indiana Sugar
Burr Ridge, IL. 630-986-9150
JK SucraLose Inc
Edison, NJ
Kerry Ingredients
Blue Earth, MN. 507-526-7575
Maple Products
Sherbrooke, QC 819-569-5161
Particle Control
Albertville, MN. 763-497-3075
Paulaur Corporation
Cranbury, NJ. 888-398-8844
Rogers Sugar
Montreal, QC 514-527-8686
Savannah Foods & Industries
Savannah, GA. 800-241-3785
Stearns & Lehman
Mansfield, OH 800-533-2722
Unilever
Lisle, IL. 877-995-4483
W&G Flavors
Hunt Valley, MD. 410-771-6606
Western New York Syrup Corporation
Lakeville, NY 585-346-2311
Whitfield Foods
Montgomery, AL. 800-633-8790
Wholesome Sweeteners
Sugar Land, TX. 800-680-1896

Artificial

Merisant
Chicago, IL 312-840-6000
Silver Ferm Chemical
Seattle, WA 206-282-3376
Universal Preservachem Inc
Somerset, NJ. 732-568-1266
US Sugar Company
Buffalo, NY. 716-828-1170

Fructose

ADM Corn Processing
Decatur, IL 800-553-8411
Agri-Dairy Products
Purchase, NY 914-697-9580
Brady Farms
West Olive, MI 616-842-3916
Cargill Corn Milling
Naperville, IL 800-344-1633

EVERGREEN sweeteners
Your Total Sweetener Solution.

Evergreen Sweeteners, Inc
Hallandale Beach, FL 305-931-1321

Evergreen Sweeteners is a full service sweetener distributor serving the entire Southeastern United States. From bulk liquid sweeteners to bagged sweeteners, Evergreen provides its customers with industry-leading service and unsurpassed quality.

H. Interdonati
Cold Spring Harbor, NY. 800-367-6617
Hunter Farms
High Point, NC 800-446-8035
Malt Products Corporation
Saddle Brook, NJ 800-526-0180
Oxford Frozen Foods Limited
Oxford, NS 902-447-2100
Scenic Fruit Company
Gresham, OR. 800-554-5578
St. Lawrence Starch
Mississauga, ON. 905-271-8396
Wells' Dairy
Le Mars, IA. 800-942-3800

Crystalline

Farbest-Tallman Foods Corporation
Montvale, NJ. 201-573-4900

Honey

Alaska Herb Tea Company
Anchorage, AK. 800-654-2764
Ambrosia Honey
Longmont, CO 970-625-3382
Babe's Honey Farm
Victoria, BC 250-658-8319
Barkman Honey Company
Hillsboro, KS 800-530-5827
Bee-Raw Honey
New York, NY 888-660-0090
Bella Vista Farm
Lawton, OK. 866-237-8526
Castella Imports
Hauppauge, NY 866-227-8355
Country Cupboard
Virginia City, NV 775-847-7300
Davidson of Dundee
Dundee, FL. 800-294-2266
Domino Specialty Ingredients
West Palm Beach, FL 800-446-9763
Ed's Honey Company
Dickinson, ND 701-225-9223
Emerling International Foods
Buffalo, NY. 716-833-7381

We supply food manufacturers and food service customers worldwide (since 1988) with bulk ingredients including: Fruits & Vegetables; Juice Concentrates; Herbs & Spices; Oils & Vinegars; Flavors & Colors; Honey & Molasses. We also produce PURE MAPLE SYRUP.

Fisher Honey Company
Lewistown, PA 717-242-4373
Glorybee Natural Sweeteners
Eugene, OR. 800-456-7923
Gold Sweet Company
Lake Wales, FL. 863-676-0963
Golden Heritage Food
Latty, OH. 888-233-6446
Govadinas Fitness Foods
San Diego, CA 800-900-0108
Hanna's Honey
Salem, OR. 503-393-2945
Heritage Cheese House
Heuvelton, NY 315-344-2216
Honey Bee Company
Alpharetta, GA 800-572-8838
Hoyt's Honey Farm
Baytown, TX. 281-576-5383
Island of the Moon Apiaries
Esparto, CA. 530-787-3993
John Paton
Doylestown, PA 215-348-7050
Klein Foods
Marshall, MN 800-657-0174
Laney Family Honey Company
North Liberty, IN 574-656-8701
Life Force Winery
Moscow, ID. 208-882-9158
Merrimack Valley Apiaries
Billerica, MA 978-667-5380
Miller's Honey Company
Colton, CA 909-825-1722
Mixon Fruit Farms
Bradenton, FL. 800-608-2525
Round Rock Honey Co, LLC
Round Rock, TX. 512-828-5416
Savannah Bee Company
Savannah, GA. 800-955-5080
Scott Hams
Greenville, KY 800-318-1353
Shawnee Canning Company
Cross Junction, VA 800-713-1414
Sutton Honey Farms
Lancaster, KY. 859-792-4277
Sweet Harvest Foods
Cannon Falls, MN. 612-803-1995
Tropical Blossom Honey Company
Edgewater, FL. 386-428-9027
Virginia Honey Company
Inwood, WV 304-267-8500
Vita Food Products
Chicago, IL 312-738-4500
Vita Specialty Foods
Inwood, WV 800-974-4778

Bee Pollen & Propolis

Alfred L. Wolff, Inc.
Park Ridge, IL. 847-759-8888
Babe's Honey Farm
Victoria, BC 250-658-8319
CC Pollen Company
Phoenix, AZ 800-875-0096
Green Grown Products Inc
Marina Del Ray, CA 310-828-1686
Hsu's Ginseng Enterprises
Wausau, WI. 800-826-1577
Island of the Moon Apiaries
Esparto, CA. 530-787-3993
Lenny's Bee Productions
Bearsville, NY 845-679-4514
Madhava Honey
Longmont, CO 800-530-2900
Miller's Honey Company
Colton, CA 909-825-1722
Moon Shine Trading Company
Woodland, CA. 800-678-1226
Natural Foods
Toledo, OH 419-537-1713
Nature Cure Northwest
Poulsbo, WA 800-957-8048
Naturex Inc.
South Hackensack, NJ 201-440-5000
Nicola Valley Apiaries
Merritt, BC 250-378-5208
North Peace Apiaries
Fort St. John, BC. 250-785-4808
Paradis Honey
Girouxville, AB 780-323-4283
Penauta Products
Stouffville, ON 905-640-1564
QBI
South Plainfield, NJ 908-668-0088
Rocky Mountain Honey Company
Salt Lake City, UT 801-355-2054

Southern Gold Honey CompAny
Vidor, TX 808-899-2494
Thistledew Farm
Proctor, WV 800-854-6639

Bees Wax

Adee Honey Farm
Bruce, SD 605-627-5621
Babe's Honey Farm
Victoria, BC 250-658-8319
D Steengrafe & Company
Pleasant Valley, NY 845-635-4067
Madhava Honey
Longmont, CO 800-530-2900
Miller's Honey Company
Colton, CA 909-825-1722
Moon Shine Trading Company
Woodland, CA.................... 800-678-1226
Paradis Honey
Girouxville, AB 780-323-4283
Pure Food Ingredients
Verona, WI 800-355-9601
Rocky Mountain Honey Company
Salt Lake City, UT 801-355-2054
Silverbow Honey Company
Moses Lake, WA.................. 866-444-6639
Southern Gold Honey CompAny
Vidor, TX 808-899-2494
Thistledew Farm
Proctor, WV 800-854-6639
Wixson Honey
Dundee, NY 607-243-8583

Butter

Davidson of Dundee
Dundee, FL...................... 800-294-2266
Honey Butter Products Company
Manheim, PA 717-665-9323
Limited Edition
Midland, TX...................... 432-686-2008
Treasure Foods
West Valley, UT................... 801-974-0911

Dried

Domino Specialty Ingredients
West Palm Beach, FL 800-446-9763

Granules

Natural

ADM Food Ingredients
Olathe, KS........................ 800-255-6637
Groeb Farms
Onsted, MI 517-467-2065

Liquid

ADM Food Ingredients
Olathe, KS........................ 800-255-6637
Burleson's Honey, Inc
Waxahachie, TX 972-937-4810
Champlain Valley Apiaries Company
Middlebury, VT.................... 800-841-7334
Deer Creek Honey Farms
London, OH 740-852-0899
E.F. Lane & Son
Colton, CA 510-569-8980
Groeb Farms
Onsted, MI 517-467-2065
Hoyt's Honey Farm
Baytown, TX..................... 281-576-5383
Western New York Syrup Corporation
Lakeville, NY 585-346-2311

Molasses

ADM Food Ingredients
Olathe, KS........................ 800-255-6637
Alexander & Baldwin
Honolulu, HI..................... 808-525-6611
Alma Plantation
Lakeland, LA 225-627-6666
Amalgamated Sugar Company
Boise, ID......................... 208-383-6500
American Health & Nutrition
Ann Arbor, MI 734-677-5570
B&G Foods
Parsippany, NJ.................... 973-401-6500
Baldwin Richardson Foods
Frankfort, IL 866-644-2732

Liquid ingredient manufacturer specializing in signature sauces, dessert toppings, beverage/pancake syrups, specialty fruit fillings and condiments.

C&H Sugar Company
Crockett, CA...................... 510-787-2121
C.S. Steen's Syrup Mill
Abbeville, LA..................... 800-725-1654
CHR Hansen
Gretna, LA 504-367-7727
CHR Hansen
Chicago, IL....................... 773-646-2203
Consumers Vinegar & Spice Company
Chicago, IL....................... 773-376-4100
Cora-Texas Manufacturing Company
White Castle, LA 225-545-3679
Crosby Molasses Company
St John, NB....................... 506-634-7515
Deer Creek Honey Farms
London, OH 740-852-0899
Domino Foods
West Palm Beach, FL 561-366-5150
Domino Specialty Ingredients
West Palm Beach, FL 800-446-9763
Domino Sugar Corporation
Baltimore, MD 410-752-6150
Emerling International Foods
Buffalo, NY....................... 716-833-7381

We supply food manufacturers and food service customers worldwide (since 1988) with bulk ingredients including: Fruits & Vegetables; Juice Concentrates; Herbs & Spices; Oils & Vinegars; Flavors & Colors; Honey & Molasses. We also produce PURE MAPLE SYRUP.

Glorybee Foods
Eugene, OR....................... 800-456-7923
Golding Farms Foods
Winston Salem, NC................ 336-766-6161
Groeb Farms
Onsted, MI 517-467-2065

Imperial Sugar Company
Port Wentworth, GA ... 800-727-8427
Jones Dairy Farm
Fort Atkinson, WI ... 800-563-1004
Lafourche Sugar Corporation
Thibodaux, LA ... 985-447-3210
Louisiana Sugar Cane Cooperation
Saint Martinville, LA ... 337-394-3255
Louisiana Sugar Cane Cooperative
Saint Martinville, LA ... 337-394-3255
Malt Products Corporation
Saddle Brook, NJ ... 800-526-0180
Malt-Diastase Company
Garfield, NJ ... 800-772-0416
Michigan Dessert Corporation
Oak Park, MI ... 800-328-8632
Michigan Sugar Company
Bay City, MI ... 989-686-0161
Mid-Eastern Molasses Company
Oceanport, NJ ... 732-462-1868
Mott's
Elmsford, NY
Osceola Farms
Pahokee, FL ... 561-924-7156
Pacific Westcoast Foods
Beaverton, OR ... 800-874-9333
Pure Foods
Sultan, WA ... 360-793-2241
Pure Sweet Honey Farm
Verona, WI ... 800-355-9601
Raceland Raw Sugar Corporation
Raceland, LA ... 985-537-3533
Rogers Sugar Inc
Vancouver, BC ... 800-661-5350
Savoie Industries
Belle Rose, LA ... 225-473-9293
Scott Hams
Greenville, KY ... 800-318-1353
Southern Minnesota Beet Sugar Cooperative
Renville, MN ... 320-329-8167
St. James Sugar Coop ive
Saint James, LA ... 225-265-4056
Stanley Drying Company
Stanley, WI ... 715-644-5827
Sugar Cane Growers Cooperative of Florida
Belle Glade, FL ... 561-996-6146
Suzanne's Specialties
New Brunswick, NJ ... 800-762-2135
Tate & Lyle North American Sugars
Decatur, IL ... 217-423-4411
Tova Industries
Louisville, KY ... 888-532-8682
WCC Honey Marketing
City of Industry, CA ... 626-855-3086
Westway Trading Corporation
Mapleton, ND ... 701-282-5010
Whitfield Foods
Montgomery, AL ... 800-633-8790
Wholesome Sweeteners
Sugar Land, TX ... 800-680-1896

Dried

Domino Specialty Ingredients
West Palm Beach, FL ... 800-446-9763

Natural Sweeteners

Abunda Life Laboratories
Asbury Park, NJ ... 732-775-7575
Adee Honey Farm
Bruce, SD ... 605-627-5621
ADM
Marshall, MN ... 800-328-4150
ADM Corn Processing
Decatur, IL ... 800-553-8411
ADM Food Ingredients
Olathe, KS ... 800-255-6637
Alfred L. Wolff, Inc.
Park Ridge, IL ... 847-759-8888
Alma Plantation
Lakeland, LA ... 225-627-6666
Amalgamated Sugar Company
Boise, ID ... 208-383-6500
American Crystal Sugar Company
Moorhead, MN ... 218-236-4400
American Health & Nutrition
Ann Arbor, MI ... 734-677-5570
Artesian Honey Producers
Artesian, SD ... 605-527-2423
Atlantic Sugar Association
West Palm Beach, FL ... 877-835-2828
Babe's Honey Farm
Victoria, BC ... 250-658-8319
Barkman Honey Company
Hillsboro, KS ... 800-530-5827
Briess Industries
Chilton, WI ... 920-849-7711
Burleson's Honey, Inc
Waxahachie, TX ... 972-937-4810
C&H Sugar Company
Crockett, CA ... 800-729-4840
C&H Sugar/Sweetener Products
Crocket, CA ... 800-773-803
C.S. Steen's Syrup Mill
Abbeville, LA ... 800-725-1654
California Natural Products
Lathrop, CA ... 209-858-2525
Cargill Corn Milling
Naperville, IL ... 800-344-1633
Champlain Valley Apiaries Company
Middlebury, VT ... 800-841-7334
CHR Hansen
Gretna, LA ... 504-367-7727
CHR Hansen
Chicago, IL ... 773-646-2203
CHR Hansen
Elyria, OH ... 800-558-0802
Cleveland Syrup Corporation
Cleveland, OH ... 216-883-1845
Clover Blossom Honey
La Fontaine, IN ... 765-981-4443
Consumers Vinegar & Spice Company
Chicago, IL ... 773-376-4100
Cora-Texas Manufacturing Company
White Castle, LA ... 225-545-3679
Corn Products International
Westchester, IL ... 800-443-2746
Crockett-Stewart Honey Company
Tempe, AZ ... 480-731-3936
Crosby Molasses Company
St John, NB ... 506-634-7515
Dakota Organic Products
Watertown, SD ... 800-243-7264
Dawes Hill Honey Company
Nunda, NY ... 888-800-8075
Deer Creek Honey Farms
London, OH ... 740-852-0899
Dixie Usa
Tomball, TX ... 800-233-3668
Domino Foods
West Palm Beach, FL ... 561-366-5150
Domino Specialty Ingredients
West Palm Beach, FL ... 800-446-9763
Domino Sugar Corporation
Baltimore, MD ... 410-752-6150
Doyon & Doyon
Toronto, ON ... 888-851-3110
Dutch Gold Honey, Inc.
Lancaster, PA ... 800-338-0587
E.F. Lane & Son
Colton, CA ... 510-569-8980
Eastman Chemical Company
Kingsport, TN ... 800-327-8626
Eden Foods Inc.
Clinton, MI ... 800-248-0320

Farbest-Tallman Foods Corporation
Montvale, NJ ... 201-573-4900
Fischer Honey Company
North Little Rock, AR ... 501-758-1123
Garuda International
Lemon Cove, CA ... 559-594-4380
Gateway Food Products Company
Dupo, IL ... 877-220-1963
GlobeTrends
Morris Plains, NJ ... 800-416-8327
Golden Heritage Foods
Hillsboro, KS ... 800-530-5827
Golding Farms Foods
Winston Salem, NC ... 336-766-6161
Grain Processing Corporation
Muscatine, IA ... 800-448-4472
Great Eastern Sun
Asheville, NC ... 800-334-5809
Greenwood Associates
Highland Park, IL ... 847-579-5500
Groeb Farms
Onsted, MI ... 517-467-2065
H. Interdonati
Cold Spring Harbor, NY ... 800-367-6617
Hanna's Honey
Salem, OR ... 503-393-2945
Heinz Portion Control
Mason, OH ... 800-547-8924
Hendricks Apiaries
Englewood, CO ... 303-789-3209
Honey Acres
Ashippun, WI ... 800-558-7745
Honey World
Parker, SD ... 605-297-4188
Hoyt's Honey Farm
Baytown, TX ... 281-576-5383
Iberia Sugar Coop
New Iberia, LA ... 337-367-2230
Imperial Sugar Company
Gramercy, LA ... 800-727-8427
Indiana Sugar
Burr Ridge, IL ... 630-986-9150
Jogue Inc
Northville, MI ... 800-521-3888
Kutik's Honey Farm
Norwich, NY ... 607-336-4105
Lafourche Sugar Corporation
Thibodaux, LA ... 985-447-3210
Leighton's Honey
Haines City, FL ... 863-422-1773
Leprino Foods Company
Denver, CO ... 800-537-7466
Les Industries Bernard Et Fils
Saint Victor, QC ... 418-588-3590
Louisiana Sugar Cane Cooperation
Saint Martinville, LA ... 337-394-3255
Louisiana Sugar Cane Cooperative
Saint Martinville, LA ... 337-394-3255
M.A. Patout & Son
Jeanerette, LA ... 337-276-4592
Madhava Honey
Longmont, CO ... 800-530-2900
Malt Products Corporation
Saddle Brook, NJ ... 800-526-0180
Maple Products
Sherbrooke, QC ... 819-569-5161
Michele's Foods
South Holland, IL ... 708-331-7316
Michigan Sugar Company
Bay City, MI ... 989-686-0161
Miller's Honey Company
Colton, CA ... 909-825-1722
Minn-Dak Farmers Cooperative
Wahpeton, ND ... 701-642-8411
Minnesota Specialty Crops
McGregor, MN ... 800-328-6731
Mississippi Blending Company
Keokuk, IA ... 800-758-4080
Moon Shine Trading Company
Woodland, CA ... 800-678-1226
Nickabood's Company
Los Angeles, CA ... 213-746-1541
Nicola Valley Apiaries
Merritt, BC ... 250-378-5208
Norris Brothers Syrup Company
West Monroe, LA ... 318-396-1960
North Peace Apiaries
Fort St. John, BC ... 250-785-4808
Nu-Tek Foods
Wapakoneta, OH ... 800-837-0160
Once Again Nut Butter
Nunda, NY ... 888-800-8075
Organic Planet
San Francisco, CA ... 415-765-5590
Osceola Farms
Pahokee, FL ... 561-924-7156
Palm Apiaries
Fort Myers, FL ... 239-334-6001
Particle Control
Albertville, MN ... 763-497-3075
Paulaur Corporation
Cranbury, NJ ... 888-398-8844

Pied-Mont/Dora
Ste Anne Des Plaines, QC . . . 800-363-8003

Pot O'Gold Honey Company
Hemingway, SC . . . 843-558-9598

Pure Food Ingredients
Verona, WI . . . 800-355-9601

Pure Foods
Sultan, WA . . . 360-793-2241

Pure Sweet Honey Farm
Verona, WI . . . 800-355-9601

Raceland Raw Sugar Corporation
Raceland, LA . . . 985-537-3533

Rio Grande Valley Sugar Growers
Santa Rosa, TX . . . 956-636-1411

Rocky Mountain Honey Company
Salt Lake City, UT . . . 801-355-2054

Rogers Sugar
Montreal, QC . . . 514-527-8686

Roquette America
Keokuk, IA . . . 800-553-7035

Sandt's Honey Company
Easton, PA . . . 800-935-3960

Savannah Foods & Industries
Savannah, GA . . . 800-241-3785

Savannah Foods Industrial
Savannah, GA . . . 912-234-1261

Savoie Industries
Belle Rose, LA . . . 225-473-9293

Shady Maple Farm
Mississauga, ON . . . 905-206-1455

Silverbow Honey Company
Moses Lake, WA . . . 866-444-6639

Sno-Shack
Rexburg, ID . . . 888-766-7425

Southern Minnesota Beet Sugar Cooperative
Renville, MN . . . 320-329-8167

Specialty Ingredients
Watertown, WI . . . 920-261-4229

St. James Sugar Coop ive
Saint James, LA . . . 225-265-4056

St. John Levert
St Martinville, LA . . . 337-394-9694

Stanley Drying Company
Stanley, WI . . . 715-644-5827

Stearns & Lehman
Mansfield, OH . . . 800-533-2722

Stickney & Poor Company
Peterborough, NH . . . 603-924-2259

Sue Bee Honey
Sioux City, IA . . . 712-258-0638

Sugar Cane Growers Cooperative of Florida
Belle Glade, FL . . . 561-996-6146

Sugar Cane Industry Glades Correctional Institution
Belle Glade, FL . . . 561-829-1400

Sugar Foods
Lawrenceville, GA . . . 800-732-8963

Suzanne's Specialties
New Brunswick, NJ . . . 800-762-2135

Tate & Lyle North American Sugars
Decatur, IL . . . 217-423-4411

Thistledew Farm
Proctor, WV . . . 800-854-6639

Tropical Blossom Honey Company
Edgewater, FL . . . 800-324-8843

Unilever
Lisle, IL . . . 877-995-4483

Unique Ingredients
Naches, WA . . . 509-653-1991

United Canadian Malt
Peterborough, ON . . . 800-461-6400

Universal Preservachem Inc
Somerset, NJ . . . 732-568-1266

Valentine Sugars
Lockport, LA . . . 985-532-2541

Valley View Blueberries
Vancouver, WA . . . 360-892-2839

VIP Foods
Flushing, NY . . . 718-821-5330

WCC Honey Marketing
City of Industry, CA . . . 626-855-3086

Weaver R. Apiaries
Navasota, TX . . . 936-825-2333

Western New York Syrup Corporation
Lakeville, NY . . . 585-346-2311

Westway Trading Corporation
Mapleton, ND . . . 701-282-5010

Whitfield Foods
Montgomery, AL . . . 800-633-8790

Wholesome Sweeteners
Sugar Land, TX . . . 800-680-1896

Wixson Honey
Dundee, NY . . . 607-243-8583

Woodworth Honey Company
Halliday, ND . . . 701-938-4647

Sucrose

Evergreen Sweeteners, Inc
Hallandale Beach, FL . . . 305-931-1321

Rogers Sugar Inc
Vancouver, BC . . . 800-661-5350

Universal Preservachem Inc
Somerset, NJ . . . 732-568-1266

Sugar

Adirondack Maple Farms
Fonda, NY . . . 518-853-4022

ADM Food Ingredients
Olathe, KS . . . 800-255-6637

Agri-Dairy Products
Purchase, NY . . . 914-697-9580

Alexander & Baldwin
Honolulu, HI . . . 808-525-6611

Alma Plantation
Lakeland, LA . . . 225-627-6666

Amalgamated Sugar Company
Boise, ID . . . 208-383-6500

Atlantic Sugar Association
West Palm Beach, FL . . . 877-835-2828

Bateman Products
Rigby, ID . . . 208-745-9033

Beneo Palatinit
Morris Plains, NJ . . . 800-476-6258

C&H Sugar Company
Crockett, CA . . . 510-787-2121

C&H Sugar Company
Crockett, CA . . . 800-729-4840

Caravan Products Company
Totowa, NJ . . . 800-526-5261

Cleveland Syrup Corporation
Cleveland, OH . . . 216-883-1845

Cora-Texas Manufacturing Company
White Castle, LA . . . 225-545-3679

Domino Foods
West Palm Beach, FL . . . 561-366-5150

Domino Specialty Ingredients
West Palm Beach, FL . . . 800-446-9763

Domino Sugar Corporation
Baltimore, MD . . . 410-752-6150

EpicCure Princess of Yum
San Luis Obispo, CA . . . 805-466-3655

Erba Food Products
Brooklyn, NY . . . 718-272-7700

Evergreen Sweeteners, Inc
Hallandale Beach, FL . . . 305-931-1321

Franco's Cocktail Mixes
Pompano Beach, FL . . . 800-782-4508

Gay & Robinson
Kaumakani, HI . . . 808-335-3133

Global Organics
Arlington, MA . . . 781-648-8844

Greenwell Farms
Morganfield, KY . . . 270-389-3289

Heinz Portion Control
Mason, OH . . . 800-547-8924

Honey Ridge Farms
Brush Prairie, WA . . . 360-256-0086

Iberia Sugar Coop
New Iberia, LA . . . 337-367-2230

Imperial Sugar Company
Port Wentworth, GA . . . 800-727-8427

Indiana Sugar
Burr Ridge, IL . . . 630-986-9150

Jakeman's Maple ProductsAuvergne Farms Limited
Beachville, ON . . . 800-382-9795

Lafourche Sugar Corporation
Thibodaux, LA . . . 985-447-3210

Lantic Sugar
Montreal, QC . . . 514-527-8686

Louisiana Sugar Cane Cooperation
Saint Martinville, LA . . . 337-394-3255

Louisiana Sugar Cane Cooperative
Saint Martinville, LA . . . 337-394-3255

M.A. Patout & Son
Jeanerette, LA . . . 337-276-4592

Maple Products
Sherbrooke, QC . . . 819-569-5161

Michigan Sugar Company
Bay City, MI . . . 989-686-0161

Minn-Dak Farmers Cooperative
Wahpeton, ND . . . 701-642-8411

Organic Planet
San Francisco, CA . . . 415-765-5590

Osceola Farms
Pahokee, FL . . . 561-924-7156

Particle Control
Albertville, MN . . . 763-497-3075

Paulaur Corporation
Cranbury, NJ . . . 888-398-8844

Penta Manufacturing Company
Livingston, NJ . . . 973-740-2300

Quaker Sugar Company
Brooklyn, NY . . . 718-387-6500

Raceland Raw Sugar Corporation
Raceland, LA . . . 985-537-3533

Rapunzel Pure Organics
Bloomfield, NJ . . . 800-225-1449

Refined Sugars
Yonkers, NY . . . 800-431-1020

Rice Company
Roseville, CA . . . 916-784-7745

Rio Grande Valley Sugar Growers
Santa Rosa, TX . . . 956-636-1411

Rogers Sugar
Montreal, QC . . . 514-527-8686

Rogers Sugar Inc
Vancouver, BC . . . 800-661-5350

Savannah Foods & Industries
Savannah, GA . . . 800-241-3785

Savannah Foods Industrial
Savannah, GA . . . 912-234-1261

Savoie Industries
Belle Rose, LA . . . 225-473-9293

Shady Maple Farm
Mississauga, ON . . . 905-206-1455

South Louisiana Sugars
Saint James, LA . . . 225-265-4056

Southern Minnesota Beet Sugar Cooperative
Renville, MN . . . 320-329-8167

Specialty Ingredients
Watertown, WI . . . 920-261-4229

St. James Sugar Coop ive
Saint James, LA . . . 225-265-4056

Stearns & Lehman
Mansfield, OH . . . 800-533-2722

Sugar Foods
Lawrenceville, GA . . . 800-732-8963

Sugar Foods
Sun Valley, CA . . . 818-768-7900

Suzanne's Specialties
New Brunswick, NJ . . . 800-762-2135

Tate & Lyle North American Sugars
Decatur, IL . . . 217-423-4411

US Sugar Company
Buffalo, NY . . . 716-828-1170

Valentine Sugars
Lockport, LA . . . 985-532-2541

Western Pacific Commodities
Henderson, NV . . . 702-382-8880

Western Sugar Cooperative
Denver, CO . . . 303-830-3939

Westin
Omaha, NE . . . 800-228-6098

William Bounds
Torrance, CA . . . 800-473-0504

Brown

Agri-Dairy Products
Purchase, NY 914-697-9580
C&H Sugar Company
Crockett, CA 510-787-2121
C&H Sugar Company
Crockett, CA 800-729-4840
Domino Foods
West Palm Beach, FL 561-366-5150
Domino Specialty Ingredients
West Palm Beach, FL 800-446-9763
Domino Sugar Corporation
Baltimore, MD 410-752-6150

Evergreen Sweeteners, Inc
Hallandale Beach, FL 305-931-1321

Evergreen Sweeteners is a full service sweetener distributor serving the entire Southeastern United States. From bulk liquid sweeteners to bagged sweeteners, Evergreen provides its customers with industry-leading service and unsurpassed quality.

Savannah Foods Industrial
Savannah, GA 912-234-1261
Tate & Lyle North American Sugars
Decatur, IL 217-423-4411
US Sugar Company
Buffalo, NY 716-828-1170
Westin
Omaha, NE 800-228-6098

Cane

A. Duda Farm Fresh Foods
Belle Glade, FL 561-996-7621
Agri-Dairy Products
Purchase, NY 914-697-9580
American Health & Nutrition
Ann Arbor, MI 734-677-5570
Atlantic Sugar Association
West Palm Beach, FL 877-835-2828
C&H Sugar Company
Crockett, CA 510-787-2121
C&H Sugar Company
Crockett, CA 800-729-4840
Domino Specialty Ingredients
West Palm Beach, FL 800-446-9763

Evergreen Sweeteners, Inc
Hallandale Beach, FL 305-931-1321

Evergreen Sweeteners is a full service sweetener distributor serving the entire Southeastern United States. From bulk liquid sweeteners to bagged sweeteners, Evergreen provides its customers with industry-leading service and unsurpassed quality.

Florida Crystals
West Palm Beach, FL 877-835-2828
Global Organics
Arlington, MA 781-648-8844
Imperial Sugar Company
Port Wentworth, GA 800-727-8427
M.A. Patout & Son
Jeanerette, LA 337-276-4592
Organic Planet
San Francisco, CA 415-765-5590
Rio Grande Valley Sugar Growers
Santa Rosa, TX 956-636-1411
Rogers Sugar
Montreal, QC 514-527-8686
St. John Levert
St Martinville, LA 337-394-9694
Sugar Cane Industry Glades Correctional Institution
Belle Glade, FL 561-829-1400
Wholesome Sweeteners
Sugar Land, TX 800-680-1896

Fondant

Domino Specialty Ingredients
West Palm Beach, FL 800-446-9763

Granulated

Amalgamated Sugar Company
Boise, ID 208-383-6500
American Crystal Sugar Company
Moorhead, MN 218-236-4400
C&H Sugar Company
Crockett, CA 800-729-4840
Domino Foods
West Palm Beach, FL 561-366-5150
Domino Sugar Corporation
Baltimore, MD 410-752-6150

Evergreen Sweeteners, Inc
Hallandale Beach, FL 305-931-1321

Evergreen Sweeteners is a full service sweetener distributor serving the entire Southeastern United States. From bulk liquid sweeteners to bagged sweeteners, Evergreen provides its customers with industry-leading service and unsurpassed quality.

Michigan Sugar Company
Bay City, MI 989-686-0161
Paulaur Corporation
Cranbury, NJ 888-398-8844
Rogers Sugar Inc
Vancouver, BC 800-661-5350
US Sugar Company
Buffalo, NY 716-828-1170
Westin
Omaha, NE 800-228-6098

Icing

BakeMark USA
Schaumburg, IL 562-949-1054
Baker & Baker
Schaumburg, IL 800-593-5777
Domino Specialty Ingredients
West Palm Beach, FL 800-446-9763
Lantic Sugar
Montreal, QC 514-527-8686
Signature Brands
Ocala, FL 800-456-9573

Invert

Agri-Dairy Products
Purchase, NY 914-697-9580
Domino Foods
West Palm Beach, FL 561-366-5150
Domino Specialty Ingredients
West Palm Beach, FL 800-446-9763

Evergreen Sweeteners, Inc
Hallandale Beach, FL 305-931-1321

Evergreen Sweeteners is a full service sweetener distributor serving the entire Southeastern United States. From bulk liquid sweeteners to bagged sweeteners, Evergreen provides its customers with industry-leading service and unsurpassed quality.

Malt Products Corporation
Saddle Brook, NJ 800-526-0180
Paulaur Corporation
Cranbury, NJ 888-398-8844
Tate & Lyle North American Sugars
Decatur, IL 217-423-4411

Liquid

Amalgamated Sugar Company
Boise, ID 208-383-6500
American Crystal Sugar Company
Moorhead, MN 218-236-4400
C&H Sugar Company
Crockett, CA 800-729-4840
Domino Foods
West Palm Beach, FL 561-366-5150

EVERGREEN sweeteners
Your Total Sweetener Solution.

Evergreen Sweeteners, Inc
Hallandale Beach, FL 305-931-1321

Evergreen Sweeteners is a full service sweetener distributor serving the entire Southeastern United States. From bulk liquid sweeteners to bagged sweeteners, Evergreen provides its customers with industry-leading service and unsurpassed quality.

Flavouressence Products
Mississauga, ON 866-209-7778
Lantic Sugar
Montreal, QC 514-527-8686
Paulaur Corporation
Cranbury, NJ 888-398-8844
Tate & Lyle North American Sugars
Decatur, IL 217-423-4411

Liquid & Granulated

Agri-Dairy Products
Purchase, NY 914-697-9580
Amalgamated Sugar Company
Boise, ID 208-383-6500
American Crystal Sugar Company
Moorhead, MN 218-236-4400
C&H Sugar Company
Crockett, CA 510-787-2121
C&H Sugar Company
Crockett, CA 800-729-4840

Evergreen Sweeteners, Inc
Hallandale Beach, FL 305-931-1321

Evergreen Sweeteners is a full service sweetener distributor serving the entire Southeastern United States. From bulk liquid sweeteners to bagged sweeteners, Evergreen provides its customers with industry-leading service and unsurpassed quality.

Lantic Sugar
Montreal, QC 514-527-8686
Michigan Sugar Company
Bay City, MI 989-686-0161
Rogers Sugar
Montreal, QC 514-527-8686
Savannah Foods Industrial
Savannah, GA 912-234-1261
South Louisiana Sugars
Saint James, LA 225-265-4056

Specialty Ingredients
Watertown, WI 920-261-4229

Maple

Brown Family Farm
Alstead, NH. 866-254-8718

Butternut Mountain Farm
Morrisville, VT. 800-828-2376

Citadelle Maple Syrup Producers' Cooperative
Plessisville, QC. 819-362-3241

Emerling International Foods
Buffalo, NY. 716-833-7381

We supply food manufacturers and food service customers worldwide (since 1988) with bulk ingredients including: Fruits & Vegetables; Juice Concentrates; Herbs & Spices; Oils & Vinegars; Flavors & Colors; Honey & Molasses. We also produce PURE MAPLE SYRUP.

Maple Hollow
Merrill, WI 715-536-7251

Maple Products
Sherbrooke, QC 819-569-5161

Richards Maple Products
Chardon, OH. 800-352-4052

Shady Maple Farm
Mississauga, ON. 905-206-1455

Vermont Country Naturals
Charlotte, VT 800-528-7021

Whitfield Foods
Montgomery, AL. 800-633-8790

Butter

Butternut Mountain Farm
Morrisville, VT. 800-828-2376

Choice of Vermont
Destin, FL 800-444-6261

Whitfield Foods
Montgomery, AL. 800-633-8790

Organic

Domino Specialty Ingredients
West Palm Beach, FL 800-446-9763

Powdered

Agri-Dairy Products
Purchase, NY 914-697-9580

C&H Sugar Company
Crockett, CA. 510-787-2121

C&H Sugar Company
Crockett, CA. 800-729-4840

Cleveland Syrup Corporation
Cleveland, OH 216-883-1845

Domino Foods
West Palm Beach, FL 561-366-5150

EVERGREEN sweeteners
Your Total Sweetener Solution.

Evergreen Sweeteners, Inc
Hallandale Beach, FL. 305-931-1321

Evergreen Sweeteners is a full service sweetener distributor serving the entire Southeastern United States. From bulk liquid sweeteners to bagged sweeteners, Evergreen provides its customers with industry-leading service and unsurpassed quality.

Flavouressence Products
Mississauga, ON. 866-209-7778

Michigan Sugar Company
Bay City, MI 989-686-0161

Savannah Foods Industrial
Savannah, GA. 912-234-1261

US Sugar Company
Buffalo, NY. 716-828-1170

Vermont Country Naturals
Charlotte, VT 800-528-7021

Westin
Omaha, NE 800-228-6098

Sugar Substitutes

Abunda Life Laboratories
Asbury Park, NJ 732-775-7575

Agri-Dairy Products
Purchase, NY 914-697-9580

Amcan Industries
Elmsford, NY 914-347-4838

Associated Brands Inc.
Medina, NY. 800-265-0050

Cumberland Packing Corporation
Brooklyn, NY 718-222-3233

Eastman Chemical Company
Kingsport, TN. 800-327-8626

EMD Chemicals
Gibbstown, NJ 800-364-4535

Fasweet Company
Jonesboro, AR. 870-932-1562

Franco's Cocktail Mixes
Pompano Beach, FL 800-782-4508

GLG Life Tech Corporation
Vancouver, BC 604-641-1368

Great Eastern Sun
Asheville, NC 800-334-5809

H. Interdonati
Cold Spring Harbor, NY. 800-367-6617

Hoechst Food Ingredients
Edison, NJ. 800-344-5807

Jungbunzlauer
Newton, MA 800-828-0062

M. Licht & Son
Knoxville, TN. 865-523-5593

Malt Products Corporation
Saddle Brook, NJ 800-526-0180

McNeil Nutritionals
Fort Washington, PA. 215-273-7000

McNeil Specialty Products Company
New Brunswick, NJ 732-524-3799

Miller's Honey Company
Colton, CA 909-825-1722

Minnesota Specialty Crops
McGregor, MN 800-328-6731

Nickabood's Company
Los Angeles, CA. 213-746-1541

North Peace Apiaries
Fort St. John, BC. 250-785-4808

Once Again Nut Butter
Nunda, NY 888-800-8075

Paulaur Corporation
Cranbury, NJ. 888-398-8844

PMC Specialties Group
Cincinnati, OH 800-543-2466

Rit-Chem Company
Thornwood, NY 914-769-9110

Rocky Mountain Honey Company
Salt Lake City, UT 801-355-2054

Roquette America
Keokuk, IA 800-553-7035

Savannah Foods & Industries
Savannah, GA. 800-241-3785

St. Lawrence Starch
Mississauga, ON. 905-271-8396

Stickney & Poor Company
Peterborough, NH. 603-924-2259

Sugar Foods
Lawrenceville, GA 800-732-8963

Sugar Foods
Sun Valley, CA 818-768-7900

Suzanne's Specialties
New Brunswick, NJ 800-762-2135

Sweet Green Field LLC
Bellingham, WA 360-483-4555

Universal Preservachem Inc
Somerset, NJ. 732-568-1266

VIP Foods
Flushing, NY. 718-821-5330

WCC Honey Marketing
City of Industry, CA 626-855-3086

Westin
Omaha, NE 800-228-6098

Wholesome Sweeteners
Sugar Land, TX. 800-680-1896

Aspartame

Ajinomoto Food Ingredients LLC
Chicago, IL 773-714-1436

Holland Sweeteners N A
Merietta, GA. 770-956-8443

McNeil Nutritionals
Fort Washington, PA. 215-273-7000

Saccharin

Jungbunzlauer
Newton, MA. 800-828-0062

PMC Specialties Group
Cincinnati, OH 800-543-2466

Roquette America
Keokuk, IA 800-553-7035

Sugar Alternatives

Consumers Vinegar & Spice Company
Chicago, IL. 773-376-4100

GLG Life Tech Corporation
Vancouver, BC 604-641-1368

McNeil Nutritionals
Fort Washington, PA. 215-273-7000

Syrups

A.C. Calderoni & Company
Brisbane, CA. 866-468-1897

A.W. Jantzi & Sons
Wellesley, ON. 519-656-2400

Abunda Life Laboratories
Asbury Park, NJ 732-775-7575

ADM
Marshall, MN 800-328-4150

Advanced Ingredients, Inc.
Capitola, CA 888-238-4647

Al-Rite Fruits & Syrups
Miami, FL. 305-652-2540

Alaska Herb Tea Company
Anchorage, AK. 800-654-2764

Alimentaire Whyte's Inc
Laval, QC 800-625-1979

Amalgamated Sugar Company
Boise, ID. 208-383-6500

American Health & Nutrition
Ann Arbor, MI 734-677-5570

Aunt Aggie De's Pralines
Sinton, TX. 888-772-5463

Autocrat Coffee & Extracts
Lincoln, RI 800-288-6272

Baldwin Richardson Foods
Frankfort, IL 866-644-2732

Liquid ingredient manufacturer specializing in signature sauces, dessert toppings, beverage/pancake syrups, specialty fruit fillings and condiments.

Bay Valley Foods
Platteville, WI. 800-236-1119

Belton Foods
Dayton, OH. 800-443-2266

Blueberry Store
Grand Junction, MI. 877-654-2400

Bosco Products
Towaco, NJ 800-438-2672

Boyd Coffee Company
Portland, OR 800-545-4077

Braswell Food Company
Statesboro, GA 800-673-9388

Briess Industries
Chilton, WI 920-849-7711

C.S. Steen's Syrup Mill
Abbeville, LA 800-725-1654

California Natural Products
Lathrop, CA 209-858-2525

Cameron Birch Syrup & Confections
Wasilla, AK. 800-962-4724

Carbonator Rental Service
Philadelphia, PA 800-220-3556

Cargill Corn Milling
Naperville, IL 800-344-1633

Carolina Beverage Corporation
Salisbury, NC 704-637-5881

Carolina Treet
Wilmington, NC 800-616-6344

Carriage House Companies
Fredonia, NY 800-462-8125

Castella Imports
Hauppauge, NY 866-227-8355

Cheri's Desert Harvest
Tucson, AZ 800-743-1141

Citadelle Maple Syrup Producers' Cooperative
Plessisville, QC. 819-362-3241

Classic Tea
Libertyville, IL 630-680-9934

Clear Mountain Coffee Company
Silver Spring, MD. 301-587-2233

Clements Foods Company
Oklahoma City, OK 800-654-8355

Cleveland Syrup Corporation
Cleveland, OH 216-883-1845

Coca-Cola Bottling Company
Kapolei, HI 800-682-5778
Coca-Cola Bottling Company
Honolulu, HI 808-839-6711
Coca-Cola North America
Columbus, OH 614-492-6414
Coffee Bean International
Portland, OR 800-877-0474
Coffee Concepts
Dallas, TX 214-363-9331
Cold Hollow Cider Mill
Waterbury Center, VT 800-327-7537
Con Yeager Spice Company
Zelienople, PA 800-222-2460
Confectionery Treasures
Cumberland, MD 301-478-2245
Consolidated Mills
Houston, TX 713-896-4196
Consumers Vinegar & Spice Company
Chicago, IL 773-376-4100
Conway Import Company
Franklin Park, IL 800-323-8801
Cora Italian Specialties
La Grange, IL 800-969-2672
Cora-Texas Manufacturing Company
White Castle, LA 225-545-3679
Corn Products International
Westchester, IL 800-443-2746
Crosby Molasses Company
St John, NB 506-634-7515
Da Vinci Gourmet
Seattle, WA 800-640-6779
Daily Juice Products
Verona, PA 800-245-2929
Daymar Select Fine Coffees
El Cajon, CA 800-466-7590
Dean Distributors
Burlingame, CA 800-792-0816
Deer Creek Honey Farms
London, OH 740-852-0899
Domino Sugar Corporation
Baltimore, MD 410-752-6150
E.D. Smith Foods Ltd
Winona, ON 800-263-9246
Emerling International Foods
Buffalo, NY 716-833-7381

We supply food manufacturers and food service customers worldwide (since 1988) with bulk ingredients including: Fruits & Vegetables; Juice Concentrates; Herbs & Spices; Oils & Vinegars; Flavors & Colors; Honey & Molasses. We also produce PURE MAPLE SYRUP.

Entner-Stuart Premium Syrups
Albany, OR 800-926-6886
Eva Gates Homemade Preserves
Bigfork, MT 800-682-4283

Evergreen Sweeteners, Inc
Hallandale Beach, FL 305-931-1321

Evergreen Sweeteners is a full service sweetener distributor serving the entire Southeastern United States. From bulk liquid sweeteners to bagged sweeteners, Evergreen provides its customers with industry-leading service and unsurpassed quality.

Eweberry Farms
Brownsville, OR 541-466-3470
Felbro Food Products
Los Angeles, CA 800-335-2761
Ferrara Bakery & Cafe
New York, NY 212-226-6150
Flavor Consortium
Los Angeles, CA 323-724-1010
Flavors from Florida
Bartow, FL 863-533-0408
Flavors of Hawaii
Honolulu, HI 808-597-1727
Flavouressence Products
Mississauga, ON 866-209-7778
Florida Citrus
Bartow, FL 863-537-3999
Folklore Foods
Toppenish, WA 509-865-4772

Forge Mountain Foods
Hendersonville, NC 800-823-6743
Foxtail Foods
Fairfield, OH 800-487-2253
Gateway Food Products Company
Dupo, IL 877-220-1963
GEM Berry Products
Sandpoint, ID 800-426-0498
Gem Berry Products
Sandpoint, ID 800-426-0498
Golden Cheese Company of California
Corona, CA 951-493-4700
Golden Eagle Syrup Manufacturing Company
Fayette, AL 205-932-5294
Golden Foods
Commerce, CA 800-350-2462
Golden State Foods
Irvine, CA 949-252-2000
Great Valley Mills
Barto, PA 800-688-6455
Great Western Juice Company
Maple Heights, OH 800-321-9180
Great Western Products Company
Assumption, IL 217-226-3241
Great Western Products Company
Bismarck, MO 573-734-2210
Groeb Farms
Onsted, MI 517-467-2065
H&H Products Company
Orlando, FL 407-299-5410
H. Fox & Company
Brooklyn, NY 718-385-4600
Hawaiian Fruit Specialties
Kalaheo, HI 808-332-9333
Heinz Portion Control
Mason, OH 800-547-8924
Henry & Henry
Lancaster, NY 800-828-7130
Hershey
Mississauga, ON 800-468-1714
Hershey Company
Hershey, PA 800-468-1714
Highland Sugarworks, Inc
Websterville, VT 800-452-4012
Homemade By Dorothy
Boise, ID 208-375-3720
HoneyRun Winery
Chico, CA 530-345-6405
Howard Foods
Danvers, MA 978-774-6207
Huckleberry Patch
Hungry Horse, MT 800-527-7340
I Rice & Company
Philadelphia, PA 800-232-6022
Instant Products of America
Columbus, IN 812-372-9100
International Food Products Corporation
Saint Louis, MO 314-421-6151
J.M. Smucker Company
Orrville, OH 888-550-9555
Jakeman's Maple ProductsAuvergne Farms Limited
Beachville, ON 800-382-9795
JMS Specialty Foods
Ripon, WI 800-535-5437
Jogue Inc
Northville, MI 800-521-3888
John Gust Foods & Products Corporation
Batavia, IL 800-756-5886
Josef Aaron Syrup Company
Redmond, WA 425-820-7221
Jus-Made
Dallas, TX 800-969-3746
Kalva Corporation
Gurnee, IL 800-525-8220
Kemach Food Products Corporation
Brooklyn, NY 888-453-6224

Kloss Manufacturing Company
Allentown, PA 800-445-7100
Knott's Berry Farm Foods
Placentia, CA 800-289-9927
Kozlowski Farms
Forestville, CA 800-473-2767
Lafourche Sugar Corporation
Thibodaux, LA 985-447-3210
Lancaster Packing Company
Lancaster, PA 717-397-9727
Les Industries Bernard Et Fils
Saint Victor, QC 418-588-3590
Limpert Brothers
Vineland, NJ 800-691-1353
Lost Trail Root Beer Com
Louisburg, KS 800-748-7765
Louisiana Sugar Cane Cooperation
Saint Martinville, LA 337-394-3255
Louisiana Sugar Cane Cooperative
Saint Martinville, LA 337-394-3255
Lowery's Premium Roast Coffee
Snohomish, WA 800-767-1783
Lynch Foods
North York, ON 416-449-5464
Lyons-Magnus
Fresno, CA 559-268-5966
M.A. Gedney
Chaska, MN 952-448-2612
Magic Ice Products
Cincinnati, OH 800-776-7923
Malt-Diastase Company
Garfield, NJ 800-772-0416
Maple Grove Farms of Vermont
St Johnsbury, VT 800-525-2540
Maple Products
Sherbrooke, QC 819-569-5161
Mardale Specialty Foods
Waukegan, IL 847-336-4777
Marsa Specialty Products
Vernon, CA 800-628-0500
Masterson Company
Milwaukee, WI 414-647-1132
Melchers Flavors of America
Indianapolis, IN 800-235-2867
Michele's Foods
South Holland, IL 708-331-7316
Michigan Sugar Company
Bay City, MI 989-686-0161
Minnesota Specialty Crops
McGregor, MN 800-328-6731
Monin
Clearwater, FL 800-966-5225
National Fruit Flavor Company
New Orleans, LA 800-966-1123
National Products Company
Kalamazoo, MI 269-344-3640
Naturally Fresh Foods
Atlanta, GA 800-765-1950
Naturel
Rancho Cucamonga, CA 877-242-8344
New Chapter
Brattleboro, VT 800-543-7279
Newport Flavours & Fragrances
Orange, CA 714-744-3700
Nog Incorporated
Dunkirk, NY 800-332-2664
Northwestern Extract Company
Germantown, WI 800-466-3034
NSpired Natural Foods
Melville, NY 541-488-2747
Orange Bang
Sylmar, CA 818-833-1000
Oregon Hill Farms
Saint Helens, OR 800-243-4541
Osceola Farms
Pahokee, FL 561-924-7156
Pacific Westcoast Foods
Beaverton, OR 800-874-9333
Paradigm Food Works
Lake Oswego, OR 503-595-4360
Paulaur Corporation
Cranbury, NJ 888-398-8844
Phillips Syrup Corporation
Westlake, OH 800-350-8443
Pied-Mont/Dora
Ste Anne Des Plaines, QC 800-363-8003
Pinnacle Foods Group
Cherry Hill, NJ 877-852-7424
Poppers Supply Company
Allentown, PA 800-457-9810
Pride of Dixie Syrup Company
Jonesboro, AR 800-530-7654

Prima Foods International
Silver Springs, FL 800-774-8751
Pure Foods
Sultan, WA 360-793-2241
Purity Factories
St.John's, NL 800-563-3411
Quaker Oats Company
Cedar Rapids, IA 319-362-0200
Raceland Raw Sugar Corporation
Raceland, LA 985-537-3533
Richards Maple Products
Chardon, OH 800-352-4052
Richfield Foods
Cairo, GA 229-377-2102
Rio Syrup Company
Saint Louis, MO 800-325-7666
Rogers Sugar
Montreal, QC 514-527-8686
Roquette America
Keokuk, IA 800-553-7035
Routin America
New York, NY 800-367-1883
Royal Crown Bottling Company
Bowling Green, KY 270-842-8106
Royal Wine Corp
Bayonne, NJ 718-384-2400
Santini Foods
San Lorenzo, CA 800-835-6888
Savoie Industries
Belle Rose, LA 225-473-9293
SBK Preserves
Bronx, NY 800-773-7378
Sea Breeze Fruit Flavors
Towaco, NJ 800-732-2733
Sethness Products Company
Lincolnwood, IL 847-329-2080
Shady Maple Farm
Mississauga, ON 905-206-1455
Shanks Extracts
Lancaster, PA 800-346-3135
Shawnee Canning Company
Cross Junction, VA 800-713-1414
Singer Extract Laboratory
Livonia, MI 313-345-5880
Skjodt-Barrett Foods
Mississauga, ON 877-600-1200
Somerset Syrup & Beverage
Edison, NJ 800-526-8865
Southern Minnesota Beet Sugar Cooperative
Renville, MN 320-329-8167
Spring Tree Maple Products
Brattleboro, VT 802-254-8784
St. James Sugar Coop ive
Saint James, LA 225-265-4056
Stanley Drying Company
Stanley, WI 715-644-5827
Star Kay White
Congers, NY 800-874-8518
Stasero International
KENT, WA 888-929-2378
Stearns & Lehman
Mansfield, OH 800-533-2722
Steel's Gourmet Foods, Ltd.
Bridgeport, PA 800-678-3357
Stevens Tropical Plantation
West Palm Beach, FL 561-683-4701
Stirling Foods
Renton, WA 800-332-1714
Sugar Cane Growers Cooperative of Florida
Belle Glade, FL 561-996-6146
Sugar Plum Farm
Plumtree, NC 888-257-0019
Sugarman of Vermont
Hardwick, VT 800-932-7700
Superior Trading Company
San Francisco, CA 415-982-8722
Suzanne's Specialties
New Brunswick, NJ 800-762-2135
T. Marzetti Company
Columbus, OH 614-846-2232
T.J. Blackburn Syrup Works
Jefferson, TX 800-527-8630
Tate & Lyle North American Sugars
Decatur, IL 217-423-4411
Thomson Food
Duluth, MN 218-722-2529
Tone Products Company
Melrose Park, IL 708-681-3660
Torani Syrups
S San Francisco, CA 800-775-1925
Tova Industries
Louisville, KY 888-532-8682

Trader Vic's Food Products
Emeryville, CA 877-762-4824
Trailblazer Food Products
Portland, OR 800-777-7179
Triple H Food Processors
Riverside, CA 951-352-5700
Tulkoff Food Products
Baltimore, MD 800-638-7343
Turtle Island Herbs
Boulder, CO 800-684-4060
Uncle Bum's Gourmet Foods
Riverside, CA 800-486-2867
United Canadian Malt
Peterborough, ON 800-461-6400
Valley Grain Products
Madera, CA 559-675-3400
Valley View Blueberries
Vancouver, WA 360-892-2839
Van Tone Creative Flavors Inc
Terrell, TX 800-856-0802
Vanlaw Food Products
Fullerton, CA 714-870-9091
Ventura Foods
Ontario, CA 323-262-9157
Vita Food Products
Chicago, IL 312-738-4500
Wagner Excello Food Products
Broadview, IL 708-338-4488
WCC Honey Marketing
City of Industry, CA 626-855-3086
Webbpak
Trussville, AL 800-655-3500
Western Syrup Company
Santa Fe Springs, CA 562-921-4485
Westin
Omaha, NE 800-228-6098
Westway Trading Corporation
Mapleton, ND 701-282-5010
White-Stokes Company
Chicago, IL 800-978-6537
Whitfield Foods
Montgomery, AL 800-633-8790
Wing Nien Company
Hayward, CA 510-487-8877
Zumbro
Hayfield, MN 800-365-2409

Bar

Da Vinci Gourmet
Seattle, WA 800-640-6779

Beverages

Andresen Ryan Coffee Com
Superior, WI 715-395-3793
Coca-Cola North America
Columbus, OH 614-492-6414
Da Vinci Gourmet
Seattle, WA 800-640-6779
Flavouressence Products
Mississauga, ON 866-209-7778
Folklore Foods
Toppenish, WA 509-865-4772
Great Western Juice Company
Maple Heights, OH 800-321-9180
Lenox-Martell
Jamaica Plain, MA 617-442-7777
Rio Syrup Company
Saint Louis, MO 800-325-7666
Skjodt-Barrett Foods
Mississauga, ON 877-600-1200
Van Tone Creative Flavors Inc
Terrell, TX 800-856-0802

Cane

Agri-Dairy Products
Purchase, NY 914-697-9580
American Health & Nutrition
Ann Arbor, MI 734-677-5570

Evergreen Sweeteners, Inc
Hallandale Beach, FL 305-931-1321

Evergreen Sweeteners is a full service sweetener distributor serving the entire Southeastern United States. From bulk liquid sweeteners to bagged sweeteners, Evergreen provides its customers with industry-leading service and unsurpassed quality.

Malt Products Corporation
Saddle Brook, NJ 800-526-0180
Norris Brothers Syrup Company
West Monroe, LA 318-396-1960
Rogers Sugar
Montreal, QC 514-527-8686
Suzanne's Specialties
New Brunswick, NJ 800-762-2135
Webbpak
Trussville, AL 800-655-3500

Corn

Evergreen Sweeteners, Inc
Hallandale Beach, FL 305-931-1321

Evergreen Sweeteners is a full service sweetener distributor serving the entire Southeastern United States. From bulk liquid sweeteners to bagged sweeteners, Evergreen provides its customers with industry-leading service and unsurpassed quality.

Quaker Oats Company
Cedar Rapids, IA 319-362-0200
Whitfield Foods
Montgomery, AL 800-633-8790

Blends

Evergreen Sweeteners, Inc
Hallandale Beach, FL 305-931-1321

Evergreen Sweeteners is a full service sweetener distributor serving the entire Southeastern United States. From bulk liquid sweeteners to bagged sweeteners, Evergreen provides its customers with industry-leading service and unsurpassed quality.

Dextrose

Evergreen Sweeteners, Inc
Hallandale Beach, FL 305-931-1321

Evergreen Sweeteners is a full service sweetener distributor serving the entire Southeastern United States. From bulk liquid sweeteners to bagged sweeteners, Evergreen provides its customers with industry-leading service and unsurpassed quality.

Glucose - Etc.

ADM
Marshall, MN 800-328-4150

ADM Corn Processing
Decatur, IL ... 800-553-8411

American Health & Nutrition
Ann Arbor, MI ... 734-677-5570

Baldwin Richardson Foods
Frankfort, IL ... 866-644-2732

Liquid ingredient manufacturer specializing in signature sauces, dessert toppings, beverage/pancake syrups, specialty fruit fillings and condiments.

Cargill Corn Milling
Naperville, IL ... 800-344-1633

Cargill Sweeteners
Minneapolis, MN ... 800-227-4455

Con Yeager Spice Company
Zelienople, PA ... 800-222-2460

Corn Products International
Westchester, IL ... 800-443-2746

Evergreen Sweeteners, Inc
Hallandale Beach, FL ... 305-931-1321

Evergreen Sweeteners is a full service sweetener distributor serving the entire Southeastern United States. From bulk liquid sweeteners to bagged sweeteners, Evergreen provides its customers with industry-leading service and unsurpassed quality.

Gateway Food Products Company
Dupo, IL ... 877-220-1963

Malt Products Corporation
Saddle Brook, NJ ... 800-526-0180

Paulaur Corporation
Cranbury, NJ ... 888-398-8844

PepsiCo Chicago
Chicago, IL ... 312-821-1000

Roquette America
Keokuk, IA ... 800-553-7035

WCC Honey Marketing
City of Industry, CA ... 626-855-3086

Westin
Omaha, NE ... 800-228-6098

High Fructose

Corn Products International
Westchester, IL ... 800-443-2746

Evergreen Sweeteners, Inc
Hallandale Beach, FL ... 305-931-1321

Evergreen Sweeteners is a full service sweetener distributor serving the entire Southeastern United States. From bulk liquid sweeteners to bagged sweeteners, Evergreen provides its customers with industry-leading service and unsurpassed quality.

Fruit

Al-Rite Fruits & Syrups
Miami, FL ... 305-652-2540

Baker & Baker, Inc.
Schaumburg, IL ... 800-593-5777

Baldwin Richardson Foods
Frankfort, IL ... 866-644-2732

Liquid ingredient manufacturer specializing in signature sauces, dessert toppings, beverage/pancake syrups, specialty fruit fillings and condiments.

Blackberry Patch
Thomasville, GA ... 800-853-5598

California Custom Fruits & Flavors
Irwindale, CA ... 877-558-0056

Cold Hollow Cider Mill
Waterbury Center, VT ... 800-327-7537

ConAgra Grocery Products
Irvine, CA ... 714-680-1000

Da Vinci Gourmet
Seattle, WA ... 800-640-6779

Eva Gates Homemade Preserves
Bigfork, MT ... 800-682-4283

GEM Berry Products
Sandpoint, ID ... 800-426-0498

Great Valley Mills
Barto, PA ... 800-688-6455

H&H Products Company
Orlando, FL ... 407-299-5410

H. Fox & Company
Brooklyn, NY ... 718-385-4600

Hawaiian Fruit Specialties
Kalaheo, HI ... 808-332-9333

Hershey
Mississauga, ON ... 800-468-1714

Hungerford J Smith Company
Humboldt, TN ... 731-784-3461

I Rice & Company
Philadelphia, PA ... 800-232-6022

Inn Maid Food
Lenox, MA ... 413-637-2732

J.M. Smucker Company
Orrville, OH ... 888-550-9555

Jogue Inc
Northville, MI ... 800-521-3888

Knott's Berry Farm Foods
Placentia, CA ... 800-289-9927

Maple Grove Farms of Vermont
St Johnsbury, VT ... 800-525-2540

Minnesota Specialty Crops
McGregor, MN ... 800-328-6731

Orange Bang
Sylmar, CA ... 818-833-1000

Pacific Westcoast Foods
Beaverton, OR ... 800-874-9333

Phillips Syrup Corporation
Westlake, OH ... 800-350-8443

Purity Factories
St.John's, NL ... 800-563-3411

Royal Wine Corp
Bayonne, NJ ... 718-384-2400

Sea Breeze Fruit Flavors
Towaco, NJ ... 800-732-2733

Sugar Plum Farm
Plumtree, NC ... 888-257-0019

Summerland Sweets
Summerland, DC ... 800-577-1277

Three Vee Food & Syrup Company
Brooklyn, NY ... 800-801-7330

Valley View Blueberries
Vancouver, WA ... 360-892-2839

Van Tone Creative Flavors Inc
Terrell, TX ... 800-856-0802

Vermont Specialty Food Association
Randolph, VT ... 802-728-0070

Western Syrup Company
Santa Fe Springs, CA ... 562-921-4485

Malt Extract

Briess Industries
Chilton, WI ... 920-849-7711

CHR Hansen
Gretna, LA ... 504-367-7727

CHR Hansen
Chicago, IL ... 773-646-2203

Grounds for Thought
Bowling Green, OH ... 419-354-2326

Lake Country Foods
Oconomowoc, WI ... 262-567-5521

Malt Products Corporation
Saddle Brook, NJ ... 800-526-0180

Premier Malt Products
Warren, MI ... 586-443-3355

Roquette America
Keokuk, IA ... 800-553-7035

Suzanne's Specialties
New Brunswick, NJ ... 800-762-2135

United Canadian Malt
Peterborough, ON ... 800-461-6400

Maple

A Perfect Pear from NapaValley
Napa, CA ... 800-553-5753

Adirondack Maple Farms
Fonda, NY ... 518-853-4022

B&G Foods
Parsippany, NJ ... 973-401-6500

Baldwin Richardson Foods
Frankfort, IL ... 866-644-2732

Liquid ingredient manufacturer specializing in signature sauces, dessert toppings, beverage/pancake syrups, specialty fruit fillings and condiments.

Brown Family Farm
Brattleboro, VT ... 86- 2-4 87

Brown Family Farm
Alstead, NH ... 866-254-8718

Butternut Mountain Farm
Morrisville, VT ... 800-828-2376

Citadelle Maple Syrup Producers' Cooperative
Plessisville, QC ... 819-362-3241

Confectionery Treasures
Cumberland, MD ... 301-478-2245

Conway Import Company
Franklin Park, IL ... 800-323-8801

Coombs Vermont Gourmet
Brattleboro, VT ... 888-266-6271

Couture's Maple Shop
Westfield, VT ... 800-845-2733

Dole Pond Maple Products
Jackman, ME ... 418-653-5322

Emerling International Foods
Buffalo, NY ... 716-833-7381

We supply food manufacturers and food service customers worldwide (since 1988) with bulk ingredients including: Fruits & Vegetables; Juice Concentrates; Herbs & Spices; Oils & Vinegars; Flavors & Colors; Honey & Molasses. We also produce PURE MAPLE SYRUP.

Glorybee Foods
Eugene, OR ... 800-456-7923

Green River Chocolates
Hinesburg, VT ... 802-482-6727

Heritage Cheese House
Heuvelton, NY ... 315-344-2216

Highland Sugarworks, Inc
Websterville, VT ... 800-452-4012

Hillside Lane Farm
Randolph, VT ... 802-728-0070

Howard Foods
Danvers, MA ... 978-774-6207

Jed's Maple Products
Westfield, VT ... 866-478-7388

JMS Specialty Foods
Ripon, WI ... 800-535-5437

Les Industries Bernard Et Fils
Saint Victor, QC ... 418-588-3590

Maple Acres
Kewadin, MI ... 231-264-9265

Maple Grove Farms of Vermont
St Johnsbury, VT ... 800-525-2540

Maple Hollow
Merrill, WI ... 715-536-7251

Maple Products
Sherbrooke, QC ... 819-569-5161

Mclure's Honey & Maple Products
Littleton, NH ... 603-444-6246

Middlefield Cheese House
Middlefield, OH ... 800-327-9477

Minnesota Specialty Crops
McGregor, MN ... 800-328-6731

Moosewood Hollow LLC
Morrisville, VT ... 800-828-2376

Phillips Syrup Corporation
Westlake, OH ... 800-350-8443

Pride of Dixie Syrup Company
Jonesboro, AR ... 800-530-7654

Richards Maple Products
Chardon, OH ... 800-352-4052

Sea Breeze Fruit Flavors
Towaco, NJ ... 800-732-2733

Shady Maple Farm
Mississauga, ON ... 905-206-1455

Spring Tree Maple Products
Brattleboro, VT ... 802-254-8784

Subco Foods Inc
Sheboygan, WI ... 800-473-0757

Sugarman of Vermont
Hardwick, VT ... 800-932-7700

Sugarwoods Farm
Glover, VT ... 800-245-3718

Suzanne's Specialties
New Brunswick, NJ ... 800-762-2135

Swisser Sweet Maple
Castorland, NY ... 315-346-1034

Turkey Hill Sugarbush
Waterloo, QC 450-539-4822
Vermont Specialty Food Association
Randolph, VT 802-728-0070
Wagner Excello Food Products
Broadview, IL 708-338-4488
Webbpak
Trussville, AL 800-655-3500

Pancake

Golden Eagle Syrup Manufacturing Company
Fayette, AL 205-932-5294
John Gust Foods & Products Corporation
Batavia, IL 800-756-5886
Knott's Berry Farm Foods
Placentia, CA 800-289-9927
Pride of Dixie Syrup Company
Jonesboro, AR 800-530-7654
Royal Crown Bottling Company
Bowling Green, KY 270-842-8106
Sea Breeze Fruit Flavors
Towaco, NJ 800-732-2733
Spring Tree Maple Products
Brattleboro, VT 802-254-8784
T. Marzetti Company
Columbus, OH 614-846-2232
Tone Products Company
Melrose Park, IL 708-681-3660
Vanlaw Food Products
Fullerton, CA 714-870-9091
Vermont Country Naturals
Charlotte, VT 800-528-7021
Whitfield Foods
Montgomery, AL 800-633-8790

Toppings

Sundae

California Custom Fruits & Flavors
Irwindale, CA 877-558-0056
Hungerford J Smith Company
Humboldt, TN 731-784-3461
I Rice & Company
Philadelphia, PA 800-232-6022

Waffle

Golden Eagle Syrup Manufacturing Company
Fayette, AL 205-932-5294
Pride of Dixie Syrup Company
Jonesboro, AR 800-530-7654
Royal Crown Bottling Company
Bowling Green, KY 270-842-8106
T. Marzetti Company
Columbus, OH 614-846-2232

Food & Beverage Manufacturers, including Ingredients

A to Z Profiles

1 **1-2-3 Gluten Inc**
125 Orange Tree Drive
Orange, OH 44022 843-768-7231
Fax: 216-378-9234 info@123glutengfree.com
www.123glutenfree.com
Gluten-free, wheat-free, nut-free, peanut-free, dairy-free baking mixes.

2 **21st Century Products**
2692 Gravel Dr
Bldg 5
Fort Worth, TX 76118-6976 817-284-8299
Fax: 817-284-4844
Processor and exporter of vitamins; also, mineral and weight loss drinks
President: Greg Harris
Vice President: Dixon Ray
National Sales Director: Richard Fabose
Estimated Sales: $100,000
Number Employees: 2
Type of Packaging: Consumer, Food Service, Private Label, Bulk

3 **34 Degrees**
3507 Ringsby Court
Suite 106
Denver, CO 80216 303-861-4818
Fax: 303-484-4664 sales@34-degrees.com
www.34-degrees.com
Lightier, crispier, all-natural crackers.
Marketing: Craig Lieberman
Western Regional Sales Manager: Robert Harrison
Public Relations Director: Jennifer Strailey
General Manager: Jennifer Margoles

4 **3Gyros Inc**
5131 Halford Rd
Windsor, ON N9A 6J6 519-257-8668
Fax: 888-678-8584 timf@3gyros.com
www.3gyros.com
Gluten-free, sugar-free, other condiments, salad dressing, other sauces, seasonings and cooking enhancers.
Marketing: Tim Fittler

5 **479 Popcorn**
3450 Sacramento Street
Suite 101
San Fransisco, CA 94118 415-876-7600
Fax: 415-358-8518 888-479-9866
jean@479popcorn.com www.479popcorn.com
Popcorn.
Marketing: Jean Arnold

6 **4C Foods Corporation**
580 Fountain Ave
Brooklyn, NY 11208-6002 718-272-4242
Fax: 718-272-2899 inthekitchen@4c.com
www.4c.com
Manufacturer and exporter of a variety of food products including iced tea, soft drink mix; imported cheese; bread crumbs and soup mix.
Founder and President: John Celauro
SVP Operations: Wayne Celauro
Number Employees: 100-249
Sq. footage: 210000
Type of Packaging: Food Service, Private Label

7 **50th State Poultry Processors**
P.O.Box 29490
Honolulu, HI 96820-1890 808-845-5902
Fax: 808-847-7040
Processor of poultry
President: Darryl Uezu
VP: Linda Uezu
Estimated Sales: $ 10 - 20 Million
Number Employees: 20-49
Type of Packaging: Consumer, Food Service

8 **A Gift Basket by Carmela**
64 Magnolia Cir
Longmeadow, MA 01106-2525 413-746-1400
Fax: 413-746-1441
Manufacturer of customized gift baskets; importer of plum tomatoes, olive oil, balsamic vinegar, coffee, cookies, cakes, artichokes and gourmet foods from Italy
President: Carmela Daniele
Estimated Sales: Less than $500,000
Number Employees: 1-4
Sq. footage: 8200
Brands:
Gift Baskets By Carmela

9 **A La Carte**
5610 W Bloomingdale Ave
Chicago, IL 60639-4110 773-237-3000
Fax: 773-237-3075 800-722-2370
service@alacarteline.com www.alacarteline.com
Custom promotional products including hard candy and popcorn in decorative tins, jars, boxes, etc.
President: Michael Shulkin
CEO: Adam Robins
Sales Director: James Janowski
Purchasing: Marly Robins
Estimated Sales: $ 10 - 20 Million
Number Employees: 50-99
Parent Co: David Scott Industries
Type of Packaging: Food Service, Private Label, Bulk

10 **A M Todd Company**
1717 Douglas Avenue
Kalamazoo, MI 49007 269-343-2603
Fax: 269-343-3399 800-968-2603
info@amtodd.com www.amtodd.com
Processor and exporter of natural flavor extracts including alfalfa, black walnut hulls, wild cherry bark, dandelion, spice, oleoresins, xanthan gum, agar agar, fruit aromas (essences), essential oils, ethyl vanillin, papain, coffeeechinacea and ginseng
President: Jeffrey Spencer
CEO: Scotty McConnell
CFO: Catherine Hnatin
VP Sales/Marketing: Anthony Williard
VP Operations: Scott Pearsall
Plant Manager: Chuck Bell
Estimated Sales: $ 50 - 100 Million
Number Employees: 265
Sq. footage: 95000
Type of Packaging: Bulk
Brands:
Foenugreek
Mountain Maple
Peeled Chinese Ginger
St. John's Bread

11 **A Natural Harvest Restaurant**
7122 S Jeffery Blvd
Chicago, IL 60649-2426 773-363-3939
Fax: 773-363-7101
Frozen foods with soy products
General Manager: Cheryl Simms
Estimated Sales: Less than $500,000
Number Employees: 5-9
Type of Packaging: Private Label
Brands:
Natural Harvest
Vegetarian Cornmeal
Vegetarian Tamale

12 **A Perfect Pear from NapaValley**
1283 Monticello Rd
Napa, CA 94558 707-251-8532
Fax: 707-257-6830 800-553-5753
info@aperfectpear.net www.aperfectpear.net
All natural pear products to include vinegars, preserves, jellies, chutneys, marinades, salad dressings and maple syrup

13 **A Southern Season**
201 S Estes Dr
University Mall
Chapel Hill, NC 27514-6118 919-929-7133
Fax: 919-942-9274 877-929-7133
customerservice@southernseason.com
www.southernseason.com
Chocolates, preserves, relishes, hams, cookware
Owner: Michael Cooper Barefoot
VP Public Relations: Jay White
Estimated Sales: $25 Million
Number Employees: 250
Sq. footage: 59000
Other Locations:
A Southern Season
Hillsborough NC
Brands:
A SOUTHERN SEASON
ALASKA SMOKED SALMON
ASHBY'S
BARBERA FRANTIOIA
CALIFORNIA HARVEST
CAROLINA CUPBOARD
CROOK'S
FRESCOBALDI LAUDEMIO
GODIVA
JOHNSTON COUNTY HAMS
LINDT
MCEVOY RANCH
MY GRANDMA'S OF NEW ENGLAND
NUNEZ DE PRADO
SPARROW LANE
TERRE D'OLIVIER

14 **A Sprinkle and A Dash**
32 Woodland Drive
PO Box 733
Port Washington, NY 11050-1141 516-767-6431
Fax: 516-767-5139
sales@asprinkleandadash.com
www.asprinkleandadash.com
Manufacturer of individual servings of Belgium chocolate souffle cakes.
Type of Packaging: Consumer, Private Label

15 **A Taste of the Kingdom**
3773 County Road 210
Kingdom City, MO 65262-2018
USA 573-592-7373
Fax: 573-642-8680 888-592-5080
hotstuff@tasteofkingdom.com
www.tasteofkingdom.com
Natural, kosher condiments and glazes
Owner: Julie Price
Estimated Sales: $ 3 - 5 Million
Number Employees: 5-9

16 **A Zerega's Sons, Inc.**
20-01 Broadway
Fair Lawn, NJ 7410 201-797-1400
Fax: 201-797-0148 sales@zerega.com
www.zerega.com
Dry pasta
President: John Vermylen
VP: Rob Vermylen
Quality Assurance: Gary Rivers
Assistant Production Manager: P Lee
Purchasing Manager: Gus Deocampo
Estimated Sales: $100 Million
Number Employees: 225
Sq. footage: 130000
Type of Packaging: Consumer, Food Service, Private Label, Bulk
Brands:
ANTOINE'S
COLUMBIA

17 **A to Z Portion Meats**
201 N Main St
Bluffton, OH 45817-1283 419-358-2926
Fax: 419-358-8876 800-338-6328
toddb@atozmeats.com www.atozmeats.com
Processor of beef, veal and pork including portion cut.
President/CEO: Lee Ann Kagy
Product Specialist: Lois Bender
VP/Plant Operations: Terry Strahm
Production Manager: Ed Bucher
Shipping & Receiving: Chris Sterling
Estimated Sales: $20-50 Million
Number Employees: 20-49
Type of Packaging: Consumer, Food Service, Private Label, Bulk

18 **A&A Marine & Drydock Company**
10417 Front Line
Blenheim, ON N0P 1A0
Canada 519-676-2030
Fax: 519-676-4343 aamarine@kent.net
Manufacturer and exporter of fresh water fish and fresh, frozen perch and pickerel
President: George Anderson
Vice President: Sherry Anderson
Estimated Sales: $3.5 Million
Number Employees: 25
Type of Packaging: Consumer, Food Service

19 **A&B Ingredients**
24 Spielman Rd
Fairfield, NJ 07004 973-227-1390
Fax: 973-227-0172 gbakal@abingredients.com
www.abic-consulting.com
Supplier of technical ingredients including rice based starches for the food industry
President: Abraham Bakal
VP: Jim Smith
Estimated Sales: $3 Million
Number Employees: 10
Sq. footage: 20000
Type of Packaging: Bulk

Brands:
GRS
MIRENAT
ORIGANOX
REMY
REMYLINE
TOMESSENCE

20 **A&C Quinlin Fisheries**
1220 Highway 330
McGray, NS B0W 2G0
Canada 902-745-2742
Fax: 902-745-1788
Processor of salted fish and seafood
President: Aaron Quinlin
Estimated Sales: $5-10 Million
Number Employees: 20
Type of Packaging: Consumer, Food Service
Brands:
A&C
CHELSEA

21 **A&G Food & Liquors**
6945 S State St
Chicago, IL 60637-4528 773-994-1541
Fax: 773-994-9623
Manufacturer of frozen foods and liquor
President: Louis Kocsis
Estimated Sales: $ 3 - 5 Million
Number Employees: 5-9

22 **A&M Cookie Company Canada**
135 Otonabee Drive
Kitchener, ON N2C 1L7
Canada 519-893-6400
Fax: 519-893-9223 800-265-6508
www.parmalat.ca
Processor of cookies
President, Bakery Division: Ray Kingdon
President: John Stephens
Senior VP Finance Bakery Division: Brian Paluch

VP Sales: Richard Bordwell
VP Sales/Marketing: Ted Clarke
Number Employees: 500-999
Parent Co: Parmalat Bakery Group North America
Type of Packaging: Consumer
Brands:
A & M Cookie

23 **A-1 Eastern Home MadePickle Company**
1832 Johnston St
Los Angeles, CA 90031-3447 323-223-1141
Fax: 323-227-8951
Processor of kosher pickles and assorted pickle products
President: Martin Morhar
Vice President: Murray Berger
Estimated Sales: $3.6 Million
Number Employees: 29
Type of Packaging: Food Service
Brands:
A-1 Pickle

24 **A-Treat Bottling Company**
2001 Union Blvd
Allentown, PA 18109 610-434-6139
Fax: 610-434-5511 800-220-1531
www.a-treat.com
Soft drinks
President: Joseph Garvey
VP: Curt Thomas
Estimated Sales: $9 Million
Number Employees: 68
Brands:
A-TREAT
BIG BLUE
GREEN SPOT
TREAT-UP

25 **A. Battaglia ProcessingCompany**
3048 W 48th Place
Chicago, IL 60632-2000 773-523-5900
Fax: 773-523-6469 augbatt@aol.com
www.beatricepeanuts.com
Processor and exporter of in-shell and shelled peanuts; processor of fresh caramel apples and garlic; importer of Brazil nuts
President: Joseph Battaglia
Marketing: John Roschie
Sales Director: August Battaglia
Estimated Sales: $20-50 Million
Number Employees: 50-99
Type of Packaging: Consumer, Food Service, Private Label, Bulk
Brands:
Battaglia
Beatrice
Eatable Nuts & Snacks

26 **A. Bauer's Mustard**
5340 Metropolitan Ave
Flushing, NY 11385-1218 718-821-3570
Fax: 718-366-3055 bart@abauersmustard.com
www.abauesmustard.com
Processor of prepared mustard and mustard with horseradish
President: Bart Druery
Number Employees: 1-4
Type of Packaging: Consumer, Food Service
Brands:
A. BAUER'S

27 **A. Camacho**
2502 Walden Woods Dr
Plant City, FL 33566 813-305-4534
Fax: 813-305-4546 800-881-4534
www.acamacho-usa.com
Manufacturer of olives
President: Ang Alvarez
CEO: Brett Milligan
VP of Sales: John Nordquist
Estimated Sales: $92 Million
Number Employees: 34
Parent Co: Angel Camacho Group
Other Locations:
Plant City FL
Erlanger KY
Chicago IL
Antioch TN
Atlanta GA
Fond Du Lac WI
Preston MD
City of Commerce CA
Houston TX
Garland TX
Portland OR
Dayton NJ
Manteca CA
Brands:
BULERIAS
CHRISTOS
FRAGATA
PRIDE OF SPAIN
THE JUG

28 **A. Duda & Sons**
P.O.Box 620257
Oviedo, FL 32762 407-365-2111
Fax: 407-365-2010 www.duda.com
Fruits and vegetables
President/COO: Dan Duda
VP Customer Development: Mark Bassetti
Category R&D Director: John Castro
VP Operations: Dean Diefenthaler
Estimated Sales: $500 Million to $1 Billion
Number Employees: 500-999

29 **A. Duda & Sons**
P.O.Box 2386
Salinas, CA 93902-2386 831-424-6408
Fax: 831-424-1863 gdo@duda.com
www.duda.com
Vegetables; foodservice and export.
President: Bob Gray
Sales Manager: Grant Oswalt
Estimated Sales: $ 20 - 50 Million
Number Employees: 20-49
Parent Co: A. Duda & Sons

30 **(HQ)A. Duda & Sons**
P.O.Box 620257
Oviedo, FL 32762 407-365-2111
Fax: 407-365-2010 acd@duda.com
www.duda.com
Celery: diced, canned, frozen. Grower, shipper, marketer and exporter of citrus, vegetables, fruit, sugarcane and cattle.
President/CEO: Joseph Duda
VP: Richard Hanas
Industrial Sales Manager: Amy Duda
COO: Barton Weeks
Estimated Sales: $425 Million
Number Employees: 1,000 +
Parent Co: A. Duda & Sons
Type of Packaging: Consumer, Food Service

31 **A. Duda & Sons**
6000 State Road 29 S
Labelle, FL 33935 863-675-0336
Fax: 863-675-0231 800-440-3265
sjk@duda.com www.duda.com
Citrus nurseries and groves, frozen citrus juice concentrate plant, vegetables
President/CEO: Joseph Duda
Branch Manager: Chuck Harvey
COO: Ralph Hayes
Plant Manager: Henry Hiesler
Estimated Sales: $10-20 Million
Number Employees: 150
Parent Co: A Duda & Sons
Brands:
A.P. Duda
Dandy

32 **A. Duda Farm Fresh Foods**
P.O.Box 2015
Belle Glade, FL 33430-7015 561-996-7621
Fax: 561-996-1354 info@duda.com
www.duda.com
Manufacturer, marketer and exporter of fresh and processed vegetables and citrus, as well as sugarcane
President: Ferdinand Duda
VP: Ed Hamilton
Sales Manager: Les Crocker
Estimated Sales: $2.5-5 Million
Number Employees: 100-249
Type of Packaging: Consumer, Food Service, Private Label, Bulk
Brands:
DANDY

33 **A. Gagliano Company**
300 N Jefferson St
Milwaukee, WI 53203 414-272-1515
Fax: 414-272-7215 800-272-1516
info@agagliano.com www.agagliano.com
Ripener, packer and importer of fresh fruits and vegetables. Warehouse providing cold storage
President: Tony Gagliano
VP: Mike Gagliano
Manager, Legal and Finance: Rick Kollauf
Warehouse Manager: Rick Alsum
Estimated Sales: $20 Million
Number Employees: 20-49
Number of Brands: 1
Number of Products: 500
Sq. footage: 200000
Type of Packaging: Consumer, Food Service, Private Label, Bulk
Brands:
A. GAGLIANO

34 **A. Lassonde, Inc.**
755 Principale St
Rougemont, QC J0L 1M0
Canada 450-469-4926
Fax: 450-469-1366 888-477-6663
info@a-lassonde.com www.lassonde.com
Manufactures and processes fruit juices and drinks.
President/Chief Executive Officer: Jean Gattuso
Chairman/CEO: Pierre-Paul Lassonde
VP/Finance & Treasurer: Jean Tessier
VP/Information Technologies: Pierre Brault
Deputy CEO Research & Development/QC: Yves Dumont
Executive VP Sales & Marketing: Peter Mattson
Public Relations Director: Mario Allaire
VP/General Manager Operations: Sylvain Mayrand
Deputy CEO/HR/Communications/IT: Michel Simard
Estimated Sales: $500 Million- 1 Billion
Number Employees: 1,000-4,999
Type of Packaging: Food Service
Brands:
Allen's
Bright's
Fruite
Graves
Martins
Mont Rouge Nature's Best
Oasis Classic
Oasis Collection Premium
Oasis Del Sol
Rich n' Ready
Rougemont
Sun-Maid
SunLike
Sunkist

Tetley
Tropical Grove
Tropical Oasis

35 **A. Nonini Winery**
2640 N Dickenson Ave
Fresno, CA 93723 559-275-1936
Fax: 209-241-7119 www.noiniwinery.com
Wine
President: James Jordan
Sales Representative: James Jordan
GM: Thomas Nonini
Estimated Sales: $1-2.5 Million
Number Employees: 1-4
Type of Packaging: Private Label
Brands:
A NONINI

36 **A. Rafanelli Winery**
4685 W Dry Creek Rd
Healdsburg, CA 95448 707-433-1385
Fax: 707-433-3836 www.arafanelliwinery.com
Manufacturer of wines which include; Zinfandel, Cabernet Sauvignon and Merlot
Owner: David Rafanelli
Estimated Sales: $500,000-$1 Million
Number Employees: 5-9
Number of Brands: 1
Number of Products: 1
Type of Packaging: Private Label
Brands:
A. Rafanelli

37 **A. Smith Bowman Distillery**
1 Bowman Dr
Fredericksburg, VA 22408 540-373-4555
Fax: 540-371-2236 www.asmithbowman.com
Processor and exporter of bourbon, scotch, rum, tequila, whiskey, gin and vodka
President/CEO: Mark Brown
CFO/COO: Kent Broussard
VP Production and Distiller: Joseph Dangler
Estimated Sales: $20-50 Million
Number Employees: 20-49
Number of Brands: 2
Number of Products: 9
Brands:
BOWMAN'S
VIRGINIA GENTLEMAN

38 **A. Stein Meat Products**
5600 1st Ave # 22
Brooklyn, NY 11220-2551 718-492-0760
Fax: 718-439-0065 www.steinmeat.com
Processor of beef, veal, tongue, pastrami, chicken and pork.
President: Abraham Mora
VP: Howard Mora
VP: Alan Buxbaum
Purchasing: Alan Buxbaum
Estimated Sales: $20-50 Million
Number Employees: 20-49
Type of Packaging: Consumer

39 **A. Thomas Meats**
2055 Nelson Miller Pkwy
Louisville, KY 40223-2185 502-253-2000
Fax: 502-253-2020 800-253-2020
jathomas@athomasfoodservice.com
www.athomasmeats.com
Supplier of the finest butcher shop quality meats
President: Anthony Thomas
Estimated Sales: $100+ Million
Number Employees: 50-99
Sq. footage: 89000
Type of Packaging: Food Service

40 **A.C. Calderoni & Company**
P.O.Box 486
Brisbane, CA 94005-0486 415-468-2282
Fax: 415-468-5967 866-468-1897
calderoni@value.net www.accalderoni.com
Juices, juice concentrates, and cocktail mixes
President: Bob Baciocco
Purchasing: Scott Hawley
Estimated Sales: $2.5-5 Million
Number Employees: 1-4
Brands:
A.C. CALDERONI

41 **A.C. Kissling Company**
161 E Allen St
Philadelphia, PA 19125-4194 215-423-4700
Fax: 215-425-0525 800-445-1943
Manufacturer and wholesaler/distributor of sauerkraut
President: R W Kissling Jr
Estimated Sales: $2 Million
Number Employees: 10-19
Type of Packaging: Consumer
Brands:
Kissling

42 **A.C. Petersen Farms**
240 Park Rd
West Hartford, CT 06119-2040 860-233-8483
Fax: 860-233-8483 cadenton@comcast.net
www.whchamber.com/acpetersen
Processor of ice cream
Owner: Catherine Denton
President: Allen Petersen
Executive VP: Raymond Petersen
Estimated Sales: $20-50 Million
Number Employees: 10-19
Type of Packaging: Consumer, Food Service, Private Label, Bulk

43 **(HQ)A.L. Bazzini Company**
200 Food Center Dr
Bronx, NY 10474-7030 718-842-8644
Fax: 718-842-8582 800-228-0172
bazzininut@aol.com www.bazzininuts.com
Nuts, seed, dried fruit and chocolates
Owner/President: Rocco Damato
VP: JoAnn Marino
Marketing: Rob Zanger
Estimated Sales: $45 Million
Number Employees: 200
Sq. footage: 70000
Other Locations:
Allentown PA
Brands:
Bazzini
Candy Club
House of Bazzini
Natures Club
Nut Club

44 **A.L. Duck Jr Inc**
26231 River Run Trail
Zuni, VA 23898-3215 757-562-2387
Manufacturer of smoked sausages
President: Brenda Redd
Estimated Sales: $1-2.5 Million
Number Employees: 5-9
Type of Packaging: Consumer, Food Service

45 **(HQ)A.M. Braswell Jr. Food Company**
226 N Zetterower Ave
Statesboro, GA 30458 912-764-6191
Fax: 912-489-1572 800-673-9388
customerservice@braswells.com
www.braswells.com
Manufacturer of pear and fig preserves, fruit butter, artichoke pickles and relish and dipping sauces
President: Andy Oliver
VP: Stuart Saussy
R&D: Joanne Nobel
Director of Marketing: Jeff Baraswell
Manufacturing/Operations: Frank Farr
Director of Purchasing: Penny Coffey
Estimated Sales: $12.6 Million
Number Employees: 95
Number of Brands: 4
Number of Products: 200
Sq. footage: 50000
Type of Packaging: Consumer, Food Service, Private Label
Brands:
BRASWELL'S
CITRUS CREATIONS
SOUTHERN TRADITIONS
THE GIFT OF FLORIDA

46 **A.T. Gift Company**
RR 3
Box 802
Harpers Ferry, WV 25425-9310 304-876-6680
Fax: 304-876-2757
Manufacturer of wine related products
President: Angela Gift
Sales Manager: Frank Gift
Estimated Sales: Less than $500,000
Number Employees: 2

47 **A.W. Jantzi & Sons**
3800 Nafziger Rd
Wellesley, ON N0B 2T0
Canada 519-656-2400
Fax: 519-656-3370 info@wellappleproducts.com
www.wellappleproducts.com
Manufacturer of apple cider and apple butter
President: Steve Jantzi
Vice President: Kevin Jantzi
Number Employees: 15
Sq. footage: 10000
Type of Packaging: Consumer, Bulk
Brands:
Wellesley

48 **AAK USA**
131 Marsh Street
Port Newark, NJ 07114 973-344-1300
Fax: 973-344-9049 kurt.faudel@aak.com
www.aak.com
Oil & fats manufacturer including canola, coconut and palm oils.
Supply Chain Director: Kurt Faudel
Plant Manager: Tom Winter
Parent Co: AAK Group

49 **ABC Tea House**
14520 Arrow Hwy
Baldwin Park, CA 91706 626-813-1333
Fax: 626-813-1338 888-220-3988
info@teaone.com www.teaone.com
Tea and teabags
President: Thomas Shu
Production Manager: West Huang
Estimated Sales: $ 5-10 Million
Number Employees: 6
Parent Co: Cathay International
Brands:
Abc Tea (A Better Choice)

50 **ABITEC Corporation**
P.O.Box 1759
Janesville, WI 53547-1759 608-752-9007
Fax: 608-755-9842 800-457-1977
wi.logistics@abiteccorp.com
www.abiteccorp.com
Manufacturer and exporter of surfactants and vegetable oils
Eastern Regional Sales Manager: Anish Parker
VP Sales/Food Director: Larry Werner
Plant Manager: Ed Becerra
Estimated Sales: $10-20 Million
Number Employees: 20-49
Parent Co: Associated British Foods
Other Locations:
Janesville IL
Wisconsin IL
Paris IL
Brands:
Acconon
Accoquet
Caplube
Capmul
Caprol

51 **AC Gunter**
790 Welltown Road
Clear Brook, VA 22624-1720 540-662-5484
Sport and other beverages
Estimated Sales: Less than $500,000
Number Employees: 1-4

52 **AC Legg**
6330 Highway 31
Calera, AL 35040 205-324-3451
Fax: 205-668-7835 800-422-5344
sales@ACLegg.com www.aclegg.com
Processor of custom-blended seasonings for meat, poultry, seafood and snack foods
President: James Purvis
CEO: James Purvis
VP: Sandra Purvis
Estimated Sales: $20-50 Million
Number Employees: 100-249
Sq. footage: 130000
Type of Packaging: Food Service, Private Label, Bulk
Brands:
Legg's Old Plantation

53 **(HQ)ACH Food Companies**
7171 Goodlett Farms Parkway
Cordova, TN 38016 901-377-9016
Fax: 901-377-0476 800-691-1106
www.achfood.com
New product development; rice side dishes, shortening, cooking oils, regular and flavored nondairy creamers, cooking spray, balsamic vinegar, aerosol cheese products
CEO: Richard Rankin
CFO: Jeffery Atkins
Director Quality Assurance: Brian Gardner
Chief Marketing Officer: Charles Martin III
Director Sales Development: Gary Storm
SVP Program Management: Jack Straton
SVP Supply Chain: James House
Director Purchasing: John Hougendobler
Estimated Sales: $20 - $50 Million
Number Employees: 1990
Sq. footage: 700000
Parent Co: Associated British Foods

54 **ACH Food Companies**
2301 SE Tone's Drive
Ankeny, IA 50021
www.achfood.com
Manufacturer of ACH's spice and seasonings brands - Spice Islands, Durkee, Weber Seasongins, Tone's, French's and Patak's.
Manager: Marlene Bialecki
General Manager: Steve Hunt
Estimated Sales: $ 20 - 50 Million
Number Employees: 20-49
Sq. footage: 768000
Type of Packaging: Consumer, Food Service, Private Label

55 **ACH Food Companies**
1 Parkview Plaza
Suite 500
Oakbrook Terrace, IL 60181 901-381-3000
Fax: 901-381-2968 800-691-1106
contact@achfood.com www.achfood.com
Manufacturer of oil-based products and specialty products
Manager: Tim Weston
CFO: Jeffrey Atkins
Senior VP: Carmen Sciackitano
Estimated Sales: $100+ Million
Number Employees: 250-499
Sq. footage: 417000
Parent Co: Associated British Foods

56 **(HQ)ADH Health Products**
215 N Route 303
Congers, NY 10920 845-268-0027
Fax: 845-268-2988 info@adhhealth.com
www.adhhealth.com
Manufacturer of all-natural vitamins, minerals, botanicals and high-quality health supplements.
President: Balu Advani
Chairman/CEO: Balram Advani
CFO: Navin Advani
VP/Vice Chairman/Human Resource Director: Maya Advani
COO: Ashwin Advani
VP Production: Arun Deshpande
Estimated Sales: $12.6 Million
Number Employees: 70
Sq. footage: 50000
Type of Packaging: Private Label
Brands:
Centra-Vit
Daily Multiple S/C
One Daily Essential With Iron
Prenatal Formula
Stress Formula With Zinc
Thera-M Multiple

57 **ADM**
701 N 7th St
Marshall, MN 56258 507-532-5404
Fax: 507-537-2643 800-328-4150
www.admworld.com
Manufacturer of unmodified corn starch and unmodified and high fructose corn syrup
Chairman/CEO: G Allen Andreas
President/COO: Paul Mulhollem
Purchasing Agent: Brad Mortland
Number Employees: 200
Type of Packaging: Bulk

58 **(HQ)ADM Cocoa**
12500 W Carmen Ave
Milwaukee, WI 53225 414-358-5700
Fax: 414-358-5880 800-558-9958
www.adm.com
Manufacturer and exporter of chocolate and cocoa products
Managing Director: Dennis Whalen
Senior VP: William Camp
Estimated Sales: $50-100 Million
Parent Co: Archer Daniels Midland Company
Type of Packaging: Consumer, Private Label, Bulk
Brands:
Ambrosia
De Zaan
Merckens

59 **ADM Cocoa**
12500 W Carmen Ave
Milwaukee, WI 53225 414-358-5700
Fax: 414-358-5880 800-558-9958
admcocoa@admworld.com www.admworld.com
Product line includes a full range of natural and dutched powders, chocolate and compound chips and chunks, as well as chocolate and confectionery coatings
VP: Dennis Whalen
Confectionary Sales/Marketing: John Zima
Sales: Anthony Sepich
Purchasing Agent: Bob Redman
Estimated Sales: Below $ 500,000
Number Employees: 250-499
Parent Co: Archer Daniels Midland Company
Type of Packaging: Private Label, Bulk
Brands:
Ambrosia
De Zaan
Merckens

60 **ADM Cocoa**
150 Oakland St
Mansfield, MA 02048 508-339-8921
Fax: 508-261-8921 800-637-2536
www.admworld.com
Plant Manager: Frank O'Korn
Estimated Sales: $ 50 - 100 Million
Number Employees: 50-99
Parent Co: Archer Daniels Midland Company
Brands:
AMBROSIA
MERCKENS

61 **ADM Cocoa**
600 Ellis St
Glassboro, NJ 8028 856-881-4000
Fax: 856-881-0462 www.admworld.com
Manufacturers of chocolate liquor in powdered form for use in wet or dry mix; natural and alkalized cocoa powder in all fat ranges
Plant Manager: Allison Piers
Estimated Sales: $20-50 Million
Number Employees: 50-99
Parent Co: Archer Daniels Midland Company
Type of Packaging: Bulk

62 **ADM Corn Processing**
P.O.Box 1470
Decatur, IL 62525-1820 217-451-8411
Fax: 217-424-2572 800-553-8411
info@admworld.com www.admworld.com
Manufacturer of dextrose, crystalline fructose, maltodextrins, corn syrups, high fructose corn syrups, corn starches, alcohol food grade(190 proofs)
Chairman/President/CEO: Patricia Woertz
Senior Advisor Corn: Dennis Riddle
VP Corn Processing Operations: Randall Kampfe
Estimated Sales: $1.1 Billion
Number Employees: 10,000+
Parent Co: Archer Daniels Midland Company
Type of Packaging: Bulk
Brands:
Clintose
Cornsweet

63 **ADM Edible Bean Specialies**
4950 Railroad St
Kinde, MI 48445 989-874-4720
Fax: 989-874-4720
Manufacturer of dried beans including, pinto, lima and black turtle
Manager: John Schmidt
Estimated Sales: $20-50 Million
Number Employees: 1-4
Type of Packaging: Private Label, Bulk

64 **ADM Ethanol Sales**
4666 E Faries Parkway
Decatur, IL 62526-5666 217-424-5200
Fax: 217-424-6196 800-637-5843
www.admworld.com
Provide grain neutral spirits (GNS) to the food industry. These alcohols are 192 proof and are further processed by alcohol bottling companies to meet their specifications
President: Patricia Woertz
EVP: Juan Luciano
Number Employees: 600
Parent Co: Archer Daniels Midland Company
Type of Packaging: Bulk

65 **ADM Food Ingredients**
100 S Paniplus Roadway
Olathe, KS 66061 913-782-8800
Fax: 913-782-8801 800-255-6637
bcriss@admworld.com www.admworld.com
Food ingredients: dough conditioners, cake and donut conditioners, yeast foods, milk replacers, emulsifiers, diglycerides, enzymes, release agents, leavening agents, stabilizers, flavors/colors, mixes/bases/concentrates, and enrichmentproducts. Also produces wheat glutens, wheat starches, liquid honey, liquid molasses, and dry honeys.
President: Terry Myers
Estimated Sales: $ 20 - 50 Million
Number Employees: 50-99
Parent Co: Archer Daniels Midland Company
Type of Packaging: Bulk

66 **ADM Food Oils**
4666 E Faries Parkway
Decatur, IL 62526-5666 217-424-5467
Fax: 217-424-5467 800-637-5866
www.admworld.com
Producer of vegetable oils and shortenings made from soybean, canola, corn, cottonseed, sunflower, peanut, coconut, palm kernel and palm oil
President: Terry Myers

67 **ADM Lecithin & Monoglycerides**
4666 E Faries Parkway
Decatur, IL 62526-5666 217-451-4119
Fax: 217-451-4119 800-637-5843
lechithinsales@corp.admworld.com
www.admworld.com
Product line includes standard, complexed, modified and deoiled lecithins, and is anchored by Ultralec, an innovative deoiled lecithin that offers bland flavor and clean smell. Our distilled monoglycerides are widely used in foodapplications as an emulsifier or starch complexing agent
President: Terry Myers

68 **(HQ)ADM Milling Company**
P.O.Box 7007
Shawnee Mission, KS 66207 913-491-9400
Fax: 913-491-0035 www.admmilling.com
Manufacturer and exporter of pancake mixes, hard wheat flour, Canadian wheat flour, specialty wheat flours, specialty products, and corn meal, including yellow and white
President: Craig Hamlin
Vice President: D J Schmalz
VP-Exports: James Brainard
VP Sales: Michael Marsh
Estimated Sales: $50-100 Million
Number Employees: 1,000-4,999
Parent Co: Archer Daniels Midland Company
Type of Packaging: Consumer, Food Service, Private Label, Bulk
Brands:
Pillsbury Flour

69 **ADM Milling Company**
P.O.Box 609
Jackson, TN 38302-0609 731-424-3535
Fax: 731-423-1652 c_coughlin@admworld.com
www.admworld.com
Manufacturer of corn
Telecommunications: Myles Grant
Production Manager: David Maness
Plant Manager: Chip Coughlin
Purchasing Manager: Mike Sadler
Estimated Sales: $100-500 Million
Number Employees: 100-249
Number of Brands: 9
Number of Products: 25
Sq. footage: 150000
Parent Co: Archer Daniels Midland Company

Type of Packaging: Consumer, Food Service, Private Label, Bulk

70 **ADM Milling Company**
1200 S Mill Rd
Arkansas City, KS 67005 620-442-6200
Fax: 620-442-2309 www.admworld.com
Manufacturer and exporter of wheat flour
President: Doug Goff
Plant Manager: Doug Goff
Purchasing Agent: Chris Taylor
Estimated Sales: $20-50 Million
Number Employees: 50-99
Parent Co: Archer Daniels Midland Company
Type of Packaging: Food Service, Bulk

71 **ADM Milling Company**
1120 King St Ste 1
Chattanooga, TN 37403 423-756-0503
Fax: 423-265-6745 www.adm.com
Manufacturer of bakery flour
GM: Lawrence Guenther
Human Resources: Shannon Hayes
Sales/Marketing Executive: Jack McMenus
Estimated Sales: $50-100 Million
Number Employees: 50-99
Parent Co: Archer Daniels Midland Company
Type of Packaging: Bulk

72 **ADM Milling Company**
P.O.Box 3268
Cleveland, TN 37320 423-476-7551
Fax: 423-478-2023 www.adm.com
Manufacturer of flour
Office/Lab Manager: Darrell Cooper
Plant Manager: Brett Poland
Estimated Sales: $10-20 Million
Number Employees: 10-19
Parent Co: Archer Daniels Midland Company
Type of Packaging: Consumer, Food Service

73 **ADM Milling Company**
3501 Hiawatha Ave
Minneapolis, MN 55406 612-729-8381
Fax: 612-729-9321 800-528-7877
www.adm.com
Manufacturer of wheat flour
Chairman: Jeffrey Skiba
Plant Manager: Larry Glerum
Estimated Sales: $20-50 Million
Number Employees: 20-49
Sq. footage: 36000
Parent Co: Archer Daniels Midland Company
Type of Packaging: Food Service

74 **ADM Milling Company**
P.O.Box 427
Carthage, MO 64836-0427 417-358-2197
Fax: 417-358-6632 www.admworld.com
Manufacturer of wheat flour
Owner/President: Craig Hamlin
Operations Manager: Steve Peterson
Plant Manager: Jeremy Rupp
Estimated Sales: $ 20 - 50 Million
Number Employees: 20-49
Parent Co: Archer Daniels Midland Company
Type of Packaging: Bulk

75 **ADM Milling Company**
P.O.Box 7007
Shawnee Mission, KS 66207 913-491-9400
Fax: 913-491-0035 www.admworld.com
Processor and exporter of flour
President: Craig Fisher
Plant Manager: Les Voth
Number Employees: 1,000-4,999
Parent Co: Archer Daniels Midland Company
Type of Packaging: Consumer, Bulk

76 **ADM Milling Company**
7585 Danbro Crescent
Mississauga, ON L5N 6P9
Canada 905-819-7001
Fax: 905-819-9768 800-267-8492
www.admworld.com
Manufacturer of flour including hard and soft wheat, also mix products
Director: Dave Newhook
Quality Control: Sheliagh Arney
Sales: Robin Beatty
Number Employees: 22
Parent Co: Archer Daniels Midland Company

77 **ADM Milling Company**
P.O.Box 31155
Charlotte, NC 28231-1155 704-332-3165
Fax: 704-333-1926 www.admworld.com
Manufacturer of soft and hard wheat flour
Commercial Manager: Dennis Tucker
Plant Manager: Brandon Cornwell
Estimated Sales: $20-50 Million
Number Employees: 20-49
Parent Co: Archer Daniels Midland Company
Type of Packaging: Bulk

78 **ADM Milling Company**
210 NE 3rd St
Abilene, KS 67410 785-263-1631
Fax: 785-263-7583 www.admmilling.com
Processor and exporter of bulgur wheat and malted barley flour
Manager: Brenda Frey
Plant Superintendent: Ken Huston
Estimated Sales: $20-50 Million
Number Employees: 30
Parent Co: Archer Daniels Midland Company
Type of Packaging: Consumer, Private Label, Bulk

79 **ADM Milling Company**
2301 E Trent Ave
Spokane, WA 99202-3867 509-534-2636
Fax: 509-534-1040 www.admworld.com
Processor and exporter of flour
Manager: Shawn Lindhorst
Plant Supervisor: Terry Jones
Purchasing Agent: Bill Parr
Estimated Sales: $20-50 Million
Number Employees: 50-99
Parent Co: Archer Daniels Midland Company
Type of Packaging: Consumer, Food Service, Bulk

80 **ADM Milling Company**
1300 W Carroll Ave
Floor 2
Chicago, IL 60607 312-666-2465
Fax: 312-666-4277 www.admmilling.com
Processor of flour including cookie, pastry, cake and bread
General Manager: Brad Hammond
Sales Director: Stephanie Karau
Operations Manager: Charles Adams
Plant Superintendent: George Madrago
Estimated Sales: $20-50 Million
Number Employees: 50
Sq. footage: 187000
Parent Co: Archer Daniels Midland Company
Type of Packaging: Bulk

81 **ADM Milling Company**
P.O.Box 7007
Shawnee Mission, KS 66207 913-491-9400
Fax: 913-491-0035 800-422-1688
jim-brainard@admworld.com
www.admworld.com
Processes enough wheat, oats, rice, barley, corn and sorghum to produce more than 400 ingredients, primarily for the baking and food industries. Mills wheat flour for breads, cakes, pasta, cookies, and crackers. Mills specialty cornflours including masa that is used in tortillas and other Mexican specialty foods
President: Craig Fisher
CFO: Steven Mills
Executive VP: David Smith
Number Employees: 1,000-4,999
Parent Co: Archer Daniels Midland Company
Type of Packaging: Bulk

82 **ADM Nutraceuticals**
4666 E Faries Parkway
Decatur, IL 62526-5666 217-451-4112
Fax: 217-451-4510 800-510-2178
nutrition@admworld.com www.novasoy.com
Nutraceutical products derived from all-natural sources
President: Molly Wilson
Parent Co: Archer Daniels Midland Company
Brands:
Cardioaid
Natural-Source Vitamin E
Novasoy

83 **ADM Packaged Oils**
4666 E Faries Parkway
Decatur, IL 62526-5666 217-451-6112
Fax: 217-451-2689 800-637-1550
info@admworld.com www.admworld.com
Packaged oils
President: Todd Saathoff
R&D: Tom Tiffany
Quality Control: Kelly Singelton
Estimated Sales: Below $ 5 Million
Number Employees: 25
Parent Co: Archer Daniels Midland Company
Type of Packaging: Consumer, Food Service, Bulk
Brands:
Gold' N Flavor
Golden Chef
Superb
Superb Select
Tastee Pop

84 **ADM Refined Oils**
PO Box 1470
Decatur, IL 62525-1820 217-424-5463
Fax: 217-424-5467 800-637-5866
info@admworld.com www.admworld.com
Food grade oils for the food industry. Grains used and oil types include corn, soy, peanut, canola, sunflower, cottonseed, palm and coconut
CEO: Paul Mulhollem
Technical Service Manager: Frank Friend
Parent Co: Archer Daniels Midland Company
Type of Packaging: Bulk

85 **ADM Southern Cotton Oil**
4666 E Faries Pkwy
Decatur, IL 62526 217-424-5200
Fax: 217-424-6196 800-637-5843
www.admworld.com
Manufacturer of vegetable oil
Chairman/President/CEO: Patricia Woertz
EVP/CFO: Steven Mills
Estimated Sales: K
Number Employees: 28,200
Parent Co: Archer Daniels Midland Company
Type of Packaging: Bulk

86 **AFC Enterprises**
5555 Glenrdg Conn NE Ste 200
Atlanta, GA 30342 404-459-4450
Fax: 404-459-4530 800-222-5857
popeyescommunications@popeyes.com
www.afce.com
Restaurant,beverages,coffee roast
Chairman: Frank J Belatti
CFO: Frederick B Beilstein
Executive VP/CFO: Gerald Wilkins
CEO: Cheryl A Bachelder
Public Relations: Sherrie Rabford
Plant Manager: Mary Townsend-Smith
Estimated Sales: I
Number Employees: 1,000-4,999
Brands:
Church's Chicken
Cinnabon
Popeyes
Torrefazione Italia

87 **AFF International**
1265 Kennestone Circle
Marietta, GA 30066-6037 770-427-8177
Fax: 770-427-0964 800-241-7764
Processor and exporter of aromatic flavors and fragrances
President/Owner: Richard Neill
Operations:
Estimated Sales: $10-20 Million
Number Employees: 20-49
Type of Packaging: Bulk

88 **AFI-FlashGril'd Steak**
780 Layton Ave
Salt Lake City, UT 84104-1727 801-972-0055
Fax: 801-972-2050 800-382-2862
afisteak@aol.com
Frozen sandwich steaks
Manager: Goran Cvetkovic
CFO: Eugene Hill
VP, Marketing: Noel Working
Estimated Sales: $5-10 Million
Number Employees: 20-49
Brands:
FlashGril'd

89 **AFP Advanced Food Products, LLC**
P.O. Box 1551
Visalia, CA 93279-1551 559-627-2070
Fax: 559-627-2196 www.afpllc.com

Milk, cheese sauce, coconut juice, soup, pudding and dessert bases
President: Miroslav Hosek
Estimated Sales: $ 20 - 50 Million
Sq. footage: 98000
Type of Packaging: Consumer, Food Service, Private Label

90 **AG Processing, Inc.**
6501 N 9th St
Omaha, NE 68112-3529 402-455-2845
Fax: 402-492-7721 800-247-1345
info@agp.com www.agp.com
Processor and exporter of emulsifiers, lecithin, vegetable fats, soybean flours, soy proteins and oils including vegetable, almond, amaranth, avocado, canola, coconut, corn, cottonseed, grapeseed, lemon, olive, palm, peanut, rapeseedrice, safflower, etc.
CEO: Martin Reagan
CFO: J Keith Spackler
CEO: Martin P Reagan
Estimated Sales: $250,000
Number Employees: 4
Parent Co: AGP
Other Locations:
AG Processing Plant
Eagle Grove IA
AG Processing Plant
Emmetsburg IA
AG Processing Plant
Manning IA
AG Processing Plant
Mason City IA
AG Processing Plant
Sergeant Bluff IA
AG Processing Plant
Sheldon IA
AG Processing Plant
Dawson MN
AG Processing Plant
St. Joseph MO
AG Processing Plant
Hastings NE
Brands:
AEP
AGP GRAIN LTD
AGP GRAIN MARKETING
AMINOPLUS
MASTERFEEDS
SOYGOLD

91 **AHD International, LLC**
3340 Peachtree Rd NE
Suite 1685
Atlanta, GA 30326-1143 404-233-4022
Fax: 404-233-4041 info@ahdintl.com
www.ahdintl.com
Contract manufacturer of vitamins and nutritional products; Importer and exporter of nutritional raw materials and oils
President: John Alkire
Estimated Sales: $ 10 - 20 Million
Number Employees: 10-19
Type of Packaging: Bulk

92 **AIYA**
60 E 42nd St
New York, NY 10165-0006 212-499-0610
Fax: 212-661-7811 takeo@aiya-america.com
www.aiya-america.com
Japanese green tea
Sales Division Manager: Takeo Sugita

93 **AJM Meat Packing**
PO Box 13922
San Juan, PR 00908-3922 787-787-4050
Fax: 787-787-2445
Manufactures approved USDA, FDA, and AMS meat and poultry for the industry which processes products for the school lunch program
VP of Operations: Sabah Yassin

94 **ALDI**
220 E 4th St
Cincinnati, OH 45202-4102 513-421-1671
Fax: 513-421-1671 www.wendys.com
Manager: Amy Denny
Marketing Director: Bill Still
Estimated Sales: Under $500,000
Number Employees: 20-49

95 **AM Todd Company**
1717 Douglas Ave
Kalamazoo, MI 49007-1600 269-343-2603
Fax: 269-343-3399 800-968-2603
info@amtodd.com www.amtodd.com
Manufacturer of peppermint, spearmint and lime oils
President: Jeffrey Spencer
CEO: Scotty McConnell
CFO: Catherine Hnatin
VP Marketing/Sales/Business Development: Tony Willard
Director Innovation: Tim Chambers
VP Operations: Scott Pearsall
Plant Manager: Chuck Bell
Estimated Sales: $100+ Million
Number Employees: 265
Sq. footage: 95000
Parent Co: Frutarom USA
Other Locations:
Eugene OR
Montgomeryville PA
Mill Valley CA
Brands:
Crystal White
Rose Mitcham

96 **AOI Tea Company - NorthAmerica Office**
16651 Gothard Street
Unit M
Huntington Beach, CA 92647 714-841-2716
877-264-0877
consumer@AOItea.com www.aoitea.com
Manufacturer and distributor of matcha green tea.
Madam President: Ayano Honda

97 **ARA Food Corporation**
8025 NW 60th St
Miami, FL 33166 305-592-5558
Fax: 305-599-1385 800-533-8831
salesdep@arafood.com www.arafood.com
Plantain, taro and cassava tropical chips
President: Alberto Abrante
VP: Alberto Abrante Jr
Sales Manager: Michael Loriga
Estimated Sales: $10-20 Million
Number Employees: 1-4
Type of Packaging: Private Label
Brands:
ARA
BANANITAS
DONITA
MARIQUITAS
REAL
TROPICAL CHIPS

98 **ARC Diversified**
445 Universal Dr
Cookeville, TN 38506-4603
Fax: 931-432-5987 800-239-9029
thearc@arcmis.com www.arcmis.com/arcd.htm
Vegetable oils
President: Terri McRai
Number Employees: 100-249
Brands:
ARC

99 **AREL Group**
1279 Collier Road NW
Atlanta, GA 30318-2308 404-355-3001
Fax: 404-355-0770 800-737-3094
President: John Freebairn
Public Relations: Elviana Candoni De Zan
Estimated Sales: $10-20 Million
Number Employees: 20-49
Brands:
Arel

100 **ARRO Corporation**
7440 Santa Fe Dr Ste A
Hodgkins, IL 60525 708-352-8200
Fax: 708-352-5293 arroliquid@aol.com
www.arro.com
Processor of corn, peanut, salad, soybean and vegetable oils; warehouse providing dry storage for food and food related products. Rail siding available
Owner: Pat Gaughn
Estimated Sales: $500,000-1 Million
Number Employees: 1 to 4
Type of Packaging: Food Service, Private Label, Bulk
Other Locations:
Chicago IL
Hodgkins IL

101 **ASC Seafood**
6340 118th Ave
Largo, FL 33773 727-541-6896
Fax: 727-545-0582 800-876-3474
www.ascseafood.com
Manufacturer of quality seafood products
Owner: Steve Annas
VP Sales/Marketing: Fred Kunder
Estimated Sales: $4 Million
Number Employees: 18
Brands:
Gulf-Maid

102 **ASV Wines**
1998 Road 152
Delano, CA 93215 661-792-3159
Fax: 661-792-3995 sales@asvwines.com
www.asvwines.com
Wines
CEO: Marko Zaninovich
VP: William Nakata
Plant Manager: John Sleeman
Estimated Sales: $3.2 Million
Number Employees: 25
Type of Packaging: Food Service, Private Label, Bulk
Other Locations:
Marketing & Sales
Napa CA
San Martin Winery
San Martin CA
Brands:
CANYON OAKS
CROW CANYON
MUIRWOOD
STEEL CREEK

103 **ATA International**
RR 4
Box 4048g
Belton, TX 76513-9408 254-939-2695
Fax: 254-939-2695 816-221-0660
logic7777@aol.com
Chairman: Herb Hardwick
General Manager: Mark Huffer

104 **AVEBE America, Inc.**
305 College Rd E
Princeton, NJ 8540
brains@avebe.com
www.avebe.com
Producer and marketer of starch specialties to food industry: improving texture, stability and appearance.
Research/Development Manager: Dale Bertrand
Estimated Sales: $20-50 Million
Number Employees: 20-49
Parent Co: AVEBE Group

105 **AVRI Companies**
1080 Essex Avenue
Richmond, CA 94801-2113 510-223-0633
Fax: 510-233-0636 800-883-9574
avrico@avrico.com
Flavoring supplies, flavors, fragrances, essential oils
President: Carl Arvold
Estimated Sales: Less than $1 Million
Number Employees: 6
Brands:
AVRI Companies

106 **Aala Meat Market**
751 Waiakamilo Rd
Honolulu, HI 96817-4312 808-832-6650
Fax: 808-832-6659
President: Donald Chong
Estimated Sales: $ 1 - 3 Million
Number Employees: 10-19

107 **Aaland Potato Company**
P.O.Box 304
Hoople, ND 58243 701-894-6144
Fax: 701-894-6423
Manufacturer of potatoes
Manager: Jim Bailey
Estimated Sales: $2.5-5 Million
Number Employees: 10-19
Type of Packaging: Consumer
Brands:
AALAND

108 **Aarhus United USA, Inc.**
131 Marsh St
Newark, NJ 07114-3238 973-344-1300
Fax: 973-344-9049 800-776-1338
us.sales@aarhusunited.com www.aarhususa.com
Processor and importer of cocoa butter substitutes and oils including coconut, cottonseed, palm, soybean, sunflower, vegetable, etc.; exporter of lauric oil products
Sales Manager: Ed Wilson
Estimated Sales: $50-100 Million
Number Employees: 20-49
Parent Co: Aarhus Oliefabrik
Type of Packaging: Bulk

109 **Abattoir A. Trahan Company**
860 Chemin Des Acadiens
Yamachiche, QC G0X 3L0
Canada 819-296-3791
Fax: 819-296-3364
Processor of fresh and frozen pork
President: Rene Trahan
Marketing Director: Dennis Trahan
Number Employees: 50-99
Type of Packaging: Consumer, Food Service, Private Label, Bulk

110 **Abattoir Aliments AstaInc.**
511 Av De La Gare
St Alexandre Kamouraska, QC G0L 2G0
Canada 418-495-2728
Fax: 418-495-2879
Manufacturer of pork. Slaughtering services available
President: Jacques Poitras
Number Employees: 405
Type of Packaging: Bulk

111 **Abbey Road Farms**
1 Abbey Road
Tallahassee, FL 32309-9276 850-878-7677
President: Lucia Maxwell
Plant Manager: Chad Armstrong
Estimated Sales: $2.5-5 Million
Number Employees: 5-9
Brands:
Abbey

112 **Abbotsford Growers Co-operative**
31825 Marshall Road
Abbotsford, BC V2T 5Z8
Canada 604-864-0022
Fax: 604-864-0020 info@abbotsfordgrowers.com
www.abbotsfordgrowers.com
Growers and processors of raspberries used in sauces, desserts, jams, yogurts, pie filings, muffins and many other products.
President: Gurnaib Gill
Quality Assurance Supervisor: Dan Sigfusson
Sales/Plant/Production: Stephen Evans
Estimated Sales: $3.5 Million
Number Employees: 120
Sq. footage: 25000
Type of Packaging: Bulk
Brands:
ABBOTSFORD GROWERS CO-OP

113 **(HQ)Abbott & Cobb, Inc.**
4151 E Street Rd
Langhorne, PA 19053 215-245-6666
Fax: 215-245-9043 800-345-7333
acseed@abbottcobb.com www.abbottcobb.com
Processor and exporter of vegetable seeds
Owner: Art Abbott
Estimated Sales: $ 10 - 20 Million
Number Employees: 20-49
Other Locations:
Bakersfield CA
Brawley CA
Caldwell ID
Valdosta GA
Immokalee FL
West Palm Beach FL
Nogales AZ
McAllen TX
Brands:
SUMMER
SUMMER SWEET

114 **Abbott Laboratories Nutritionals/Ross Products**
100 Abbott Park Rd
Abbott Park, IL 60064-3500 847-937-6100
Fax: 847-937-9555 www.abbott.com
Offers a variety of pediatric and adult nutritional products, pharmaceuticals and enteral feeding products. Processor of evaporated and condensed milk.
Chairman/CEO: Miles White
CFO: Thomas Freyman
Senior VP: Gary McCullough
Director Public Affairs: Tracy Noe
Number Employees: 1,000-4,999
Parent Co: Abbott Laboratories
Type of Packaging: Consumer
Brands:
Similac Toddler's Best

115 **Abbott's Candy Shop**
48 E Walnut St
Hagerstown, IN 47346 765-489-4442
Fax: 765-489-5501 877-801-1200
abbottscandy@abbottscandy.com
www.abbottscandy.com
Gourmet chocolates and caramels
President: Suanna Goodnight
Vice President: Gordon Goodnight
Estimated Sales: $780,000
Number Employees: 20
Sq. footage: 7
Type of Packaging: Private Label
Brands:
Abbott's Candy

116 **Abbott's Meat**
3623 Blackington Ave
Flint, MI 48532 810-232-7128
Fax: 810-232-7960
Beef and beef products
President: Edward Abbott
Estimated Sales: $5-10 Million
Number Employees: 10-19
Brands:
Abbotts Meat

117 **(HQ)Abbyland Foods**
P.O.Box 69
Abbotsford, WI 54405 715-223-6386
Fax: 715-223-6388 800-732-5483
abbyland@abbyland.com www.abbyland.com
Meat, sausage and boneless beef
President: Harland Schraufnagel
CFO: Paul Hess
Sales Representative: Patricia Patterson
Estimated Sales: $127 Million
Number Employees: 250
Sq. footage: 122000
Type of Packaging: Food Service, Private Label, Bulk
Brands:
ABBULAND
LONDON CLASSIC BROIL
TAILGATE

118 **Abdallah Candies**
3501 County Road 42 West
Burnsville, MN 55306 952-890-4770
Fax: 952-890-3664 800-348-7328
service@abdallahcandies.com
www.abdallahcandies.com
Confectionery products including boxed chocolates.
President: Steven Hegedus Jr
Sales: MaDonna Schmitz
Estimated Sales: $2.5-5 Million
Number Employees: 20-49
Sq. footage: 6500
Type of Packaging: Consumer, Food Service, Private Label, Bulk
Brands:
Alligators
Bare Paws
Chocolate Angel Mint
Downtowner Assortment
TOFFEE-ETTES

119 **Abel & Schafer**
20 Alexander Ct
Ronkonkoma, NY 11779 631-737-2220
Fax: 631-737-2335 800-443-1260
info@kompletusa.com www.abelandschafer.com
Processor of mixes including bread, cake, muffin, dough conditioners, glazes and fillings
President: Martin Schafer
VP: Frank Triedman
QA: Christopher Gaumet
Production Manager: Christopher Weber
Estimated Sales: $ 20 - 25 Million
Number Employees: 50-99
Parent Co: Abel & Schafer Group
Type of Packaging: Private Label
Other Locations:
Abel & Schafer
VoLklingen, Germany
KOMPLET Berlin
Berlin
KOMPLET Italia
Grassobbio, Italy
KOMPLET Mantler
Rosenburg
Ste COMPLET
Forbach, France
KOMPLET Iberica
Barcelona, Spain
Abel & Schafer
Coulsdon, Surrey UK
Quality Bakery Products
Houston TX
KOMPLET Benelux
Luxembourg, Belium
KOMPLET Polska
Suchy Las, Poland

120 **Abeles & Heymann GourmetKosher Provisions, Inc.**
3498 3rd Ave
Bronx, NY 10456 718-589-0100
Fax: 718-589-0102 sleav16311@aol.com
www.abeles-heymann.com
Producer of salami, pastrami, corned beef, brisket, hot dogs, beef fry, smoked turkey, and knockwurst.
President: Seth Leavitt
Estimated Sales: $5-10 Million
Number Employees: 5-9

121 **Abimco USA, Inc.**
43 Hampshire Dr
Mendham, NJ 7945 973-543-7393
Fax: 973-543-2948 abimcous@ix.netcom.com
www.home.netcom.com/~ambicous
Processor of fruit juice concentrates; importer and exporter of dried and frozen fruits and vegetables; Importer of juice concentrates, honey and tomato paste; exporter of fresh mushrooms
President: Paulette Krelman
General Manager: Arthur Kupperman
Number Employees: 1-4
Type of Packaging: Bulk

122 **Abingdon Vineyard & Winery**
20308 Alvarado Rd
Abingdon, VA 24211 276-623-1255
Fax: 276-623-0125 info@abingdonwinery.com
www.abingdonwinery.com
Wines
Owner: Bob Carlson
Co-Owner: Bob Carlson
Vineyard Manager: Kevin Sutherland
Estimated Sales: $ .5 - 1 million
Number Employees: 1-4

123 **Abita Brewing Company**
PO Box 1510
Abita Springs, LA 70420 985-893-3143
Fax: 985-898-3546 800-737-2311
friends@abita.com www.abita.com
Lager and ale and caffeine-free root beer.
President: David Blossman
Estimated Sales: $20-50 Million
Number Employees: 10-19
Sq. footage: 14000
Type of Packaging: Consumer, Private Label
Brands:
Abita
Golden
Purple Haze
Turbodog

124 **Abita Springs Water Company**
P.O.Box 867
Metairie, LA 70004-0867 504-828-2500
Fax: 504-828-2520 abitman@abitasprings.com
www.abitasprings.com
Spring water
Chairman: Bill Roohi
CEO: George Mayer
Estimated Sales: $12,700,000
Number Employees: 100-249
Brands:
ABITA GOLDEN
ABITA PURPLE
ABITA ROOT BEER
ABITA SEASMALS
ABITA TURBODAY

125 **(HQ)Abitec Corporation**
501 West 1st Avenue
PO Box 569
Columbus, OH 43215 614-429-6464
Fax: 614-421-7996 800-555-1255
www.abiteccorp.com
Vegetable oil refining and processing
CEO: Jeff Walton
CFO: Susan Tayloe
Vice President: Frank Detrano
Research & Development: Jim Williams
VP Sales: Larry Warner
Plant Manager: Jeff Fulton
Purchasing Manager: Rick Laws
Estimated Sales: $50-100 Million
Number Employees: 50-99
Other Locations:
Abitec Corporation
Janesville WI
Abitec Corporation
Paris IL
Brands:
Abitec

126 **Abkit Camocare Nature Works**
61 Broadway
Room 1310
New York, NY 10006-2722 212-292-1550
Fax: 212-292-1542 800-226-6227
info@abkit.com www.abkit.com
Natural products, vitamins, etc
President: Claus Ghringer
Director International Sales: Alison Carley
Estimated Sales: $ 3 - 5 Million
Number Employees: 10-19
Brands:
Catuama
Kwai
Nature Works

127 **Abraham's Natural Foods**
P.O.Box 89
Long Branch, NJ 7740 732-229-5799
Fax: 732-571-0890 800-327-9903
www.abrahamsnatural.com
Processor of natural gourmet dips, salads and cookies, and kosher and Middle Eastern foods
President: Louis Fellman
Estimated Sales: $1 Million
Number Employees: 7
Brands:
Baba Ghannouj
Hummos

128 **(HQ)Absopure Water Company**
8835 General Dr
Plymouth, MI 48170 734-459-8000
800-422-7678
www.absopure.com
Manufacturer of bottled water.
President: William Young
Estimated Sales: $20-50 Million
Number Employees: 100-249
Type of Packaging: Consumer, Food Service
Brands:
ABSOPURE ARTESIAN SPRING WATER
ABSOPURE DRINKING WATER
ABSOPURE SPARKLING SPRING WATER
ABSOPURE STEAM DISTILLED WATER
CAP 10 MINERAL WATER (ALL FLAVORS)

129 **Absopure Water Company**
3201 W Clark Rd
Champaign, IL 61822 217-398-5011
Fax: 734-451-0055 800-422-7678
service@absopure.com www.absopure.com
Processor of bottled water including deionized natural and distilled.
Manager: Bo Wagner
Estimated Sales: $1-2.5 Million
Number Employees: 20-49
Brands:
Greensbriar Farms
Mountain Valley
Quality

130 **Absopure Water Company**
425 36th St SW
Grand Rapids, MI 49548-2161 616-455-5700
Fax: 734-451-0055 800-422-7678
service@absopure.com www.absopure.com
Manufacturer of bottled water.
President/CEO: William Young
Estimated Sales: $22.9 Million
Number Employees: 50-99
Type of Packaging: Consumer, Bulk

131 **Absopure Water Company -Pine Valley**
8845 General Drive
Plymouth, MI 48170 618-624-6730
Fax: 618-624-8648 800-422-7678
service@absopure.com www.absopure.com
Processor of bottled water.
Plant Manager: Ken Barnhill
Estimated Sales: $ 1 - 3 Million
Number Employees: 20-49
Type of Packaging: Consumer, Food Service

132 **Abuelita Mexican Foods**
9209 Enterprise Ct
Manassas Park, VA 20111 703-369-0232
Fax: 703-369-0875 abuelitask@aol.com
www.abuelita.com
Corn tortillas and corn tortilla chips
President: Eugene Suarez Sr
GM/Finance Executive/Human Resources: Peggy Suarez
VP: Eugene Suarez
Marketing Manager: Steve Dill
Sales Director: Marie Forman
Plant Manager: Paul Hammond
Estimated Sales: $4.7 Million
Number Employees: 46
Number of Brands: 3
Number of Products: 45
Sq. footage: 26500
Type of Packaging: Consumer, Food Service, Private Label
Brands:
Abuelita
Casa De Carmen
Nana's Cocina

133 **(HQ)Abunda Life Laboratories**
208 3rd Ave
Asbury Park, NJ 07712-6016 732-775-7575
Fax: 732-502-0899 naturaldoc@abundalife.com
www.abundalife.com/labs.asp
Manufacturer exporter of natural health products including vitamins, goat milk powder, fiber supplements, herbal spices, herbal teas, rice bran syrups and sweeteners including: banana, grape, pineapple and orange
Founder: Dr Robert Sorge
Estimated Sales: $300,000-500,000
Number Employees: 1-4
Sq. footage: 4200
Type of Packaging: Consumer, Private Label
Brands:
24 Super Amino Acids
Abunda Body
Blood Building Broth
Blood Building Powder
Brain Invigoration Powder
Cholesterol Solve
Cram For Students
Dieters Tea
Energy Powder
Essaic Formula
Fruit Fiber
Live Plant Juice
Liver Detox Formula
Parasite Annihilation Powder
Royal Pollen Complex
Super Bowl Cleanse
Super C Active
Super Detox
Super Green
Super Salad Oil
Super Tonic

134 **Acacia Vineyard**
2750 Las Amigas Rd
Napa, CA 94559-9715 707-226-9991
Fax: 707-226-1685
acacia.info@acaciawinery.com
www.diageo.com
Manufacturer of wines
Owner: Matthew Glynn
Estimated Sales: $ 10 - 20 Million
Number Employees: 20-49
Parent Co: Chalone Wine Group
Brands:
Acacia

135 **Acadian Fine Foods**
228 Saint Charles Ave # 1323
New Orleans, LA 70130-2646 504-581-2355
Fax: 504-525-9841
Frozen stuffed chicken, seafood pies, canned blue crabmeat, frozen crabs, crawfish
President: Charles Williams
VP: Russell Raelston
Estimated Sales: $ .5 - 1 million
Number Employees: 5-9

136 **Acadian Ostrich Ranch**
9010 Highway 961
Clinton, LA 70722 225-683-9988
Fax: 225-683-9988 800-350-0167
acadianostrichrh@cs.com
www.acadianostrich.com
Manufacturer of ostrich and alligator meats
President: Marco Dermody

137 **(HQ)Acadian Seaplants**
30 Brown Avenue
Dartmouth, NS B3B 1X8
Canada 902-468-2840
Fax: 902-468-3474 800-575-9100
info@acadian.ca www.acadianseaplants.com
Manufacturer and exporter of natural, specialty fertilizers, feed, food, food ingredients and brewery supplies
President: Jean Paul Deveau
CFO: Perry Bevin
Research & Development: Franklin Evans
Quality Control: Barry Galbraith
Marketing Director: John Sewuster
VP Sales: Patrick Bennett
Marketing/Communications Manager: Linda Theriault
Production Manager: Paul Empey
Purchasing Manager: Ian Rennie
Estimated Sales: $32 Million
Number Employees: 300
Type of Packaging: Private Label, Bulk
Brands:
Drewclar
Hana-Nori
Nutramer

138 **Acatris**
3300 Edinborough Way # 300
Edina, MN 55435-5959 952-835-9590
Fax: 952-835-9063 info@us.acatris.com
www.great-expectations.net
Leading supplier of special health ingredients including SoyLife, FenuLife and LinumLife
Manager: Joni Johnson
Sales Manager: Cherie Jones
Estimated Sales: $ 5 - 10 Million
Number Employees: 20-49
Number of Brands: 3
Number of Products: 3
Parent Co: Royal Schouten Group
Type of Packaging: Bulk
Brands:
FENULIFE
LINUMLIFE
SOYLIFE

139 **Acatris USA**
3300 Edinborough Way # 712
Edina, MN 55435-5963 952-920-7700
Fax: 952-920-7704 info@us.acatris.com
www.frutarom.com
Blended dough conditioners, antioxidant solutions, release agents and lubricants; wholesaler/distributor of soy flour, vitamin/mineral blends and oils including soybean and canola
President: Laurent Leduc
Estimated Sales: $5 Million
Number Employees: 5-9
Sq. footage: 16000
Parent Co: Royal Schouten Group
Type of Packaging: Bulk
Brands:
ALUBE
DADEX
DAEDOL
DAEJEL
DAELUBE
DAMINAIDE
DAMINCO
DAMINET
EXTOL
FENULIFE
LESOY

LINUMLIFE
MYVACET
MYVEROL
SOYLIFE

140 **Accucaps Industries Limited**
2125 Ambassador Drive
Windsor, ON N9C 3R5
Canada 519- 96- 540
Fax: 51- 25- 332 800-665-7210
info@accucaps.com www.accucaps.com
President: Dwight Goraham
Marketing Director: Peter Wares
CFO: Ed Kanters
Brands:
Accucaps

141 **Accuplace**
1800 NW 69th Ave Ste 102
Plantation, FL 33313 866-820-0434
Fax: 954-791-1501 www.accuplace.com
Owner: Jamie Schlinkmann
Estimated Sales: $ 10 - 20 Million
Number Employees: 50-99

142 **Accurate Ingredients**
160 Eileen Way Ste 100
Syosset, NY 11791 516-496-2500
Fax: 516-496-2516 www.acing-iri.com
Manufacturer, Importer/Exporter of food ingredients
Owner: Jack Sollazzo
Executive Sales Manager: Frank Wells
Estimated Sales: $10-20 Million
Number Employees: 20-49
Other Locations:
Accurate Ingredients
Santa Ana CA

143 **Ace Baking Company**
PO Box 535
Wadsworth, IL 60083-0535 920-497-1893
Fax: 920-497-1893 800-879-2231
Ice cream cones including waffle, sugar and cake, and waffle bowls
Number Employees: 250-499

144 **Ace Development**
31194 State Highway 51
Bruneau, ID 83604-5076 208-845-2487
Fax: 208-845-2274 copakarobert@hotmail.com
Presiden: Robert Williams
Estimated Sales: $800,000
Number Employees: 1-4

145 **Ace Food**
P.O.Box 962
Bayou La Batre, AL 36509-0962 251-824-4367
Fax: 251-824-7950 800-884-0741
Owner: Russell Collier
Estimated Sales: $ .5 - 1 million
Number Employees: 1-4
Brands:
Ace Seafood

146 **Acharice Specialties**
PO Box 690
Greenville, MS 38702-0690 800-432-4901
Fax: 901-381-3287 www.achafood.com
Rice and grain products
President/CEO: Jack Stratol
Research & Development: Bill Land
Sales/Marketing: Nelson Wurth
Operations/Production: Mike Well
Plant Manager: Pat Roy
Number Employees: 500-999
Type of Packaging: Private Label

147 **Ackerman Winery**
4406 220th Trl
Amana, IA 52203-8035 319-622-3379
Fax: 319-622-6513 sales@ackermanwinery.com
www.ackermanwinery.com
Wine
President: Les Ackerman
Estimated Sales: $1-2.5 Million
Number Employees: 10-19
Type of Packaging: Bulk

148 **Acme Candy Company**
2109 E Division Street
Arlington, TX 76011-7817 254-634-2825
President: Malcolm Cohen

149 **Acme Farms**
P.O.Box 3065
Seattle, WA 98114-3065 206-323-4300
Fax: 206-235-1910 800-542-8309
Manufacturer of Chicken, turkey and other poultry products.
Manager: Tom Perry
VP/Sales: Edward Shane
Marketing Manager: Jerry Ryder
Estimated Sales: $40 Million
Number Employees: 5-9
Parent Co: Acme Poultry Company
Type of Packaging: Consumer, Food Service, Private Label, Bulk
Brands:
ACME
MT PARK
PEAK QUALITY
PILGRIM
SILVER BEAUTY

150 **Acme Smoked Fish Corporation**
30 Gem St
Brooklyn, NY 11222 718-383-8585
Fax: 718-383-9115 800-221-0795
acmefish@aol.com www.acmesmokedfish.com
Processor and importer of smoked fish and herring
President: Eric Caslow
Controller: Nathan Sudakoff
VP, Operations: Robert Caslow
Marketing Director: Richard Schiff
Estimated Sales: $20-50 Million
Number Employees: 100-249
Type of Packaging: Consumer, Food Service, Private Label, Bulk
Brands:
ACME
BLUE HILL BAY

151 **Acme Steak & Seafood Company**
P.O.Box 688
Youngstown, OH 44501 330-270-8000
Fax: 330-270-8006
Importer and processor of sausage, hamburgers and portion controlled meat
Owner: Michael Mike Iii III
Marketing/National Accounts: Michael Mike III
Sales Manager: Michael Mike III
Secretary/Treasurer: M Charlotte Mike
Estimated Sales: $20-50 Million
Number Employees: 10-19
Sq. footage: 68000
Type of Packaging: Consumer, Food Service, Private Label

152 **Acqua Blox LLC**
12000 Slauson Ave # 3
Santa Fe Springs, CA 90670-8663 562-693-9599
Fax: 562-945-3133 info@aquablox.com
www.aquablox.com
Purified and bacteria free water products specifically designed for emergency preparedness, first responders, and disaster victims
Manager: Mike Harris
Estimated Sales: Below $ 5 Million
Number Employees: 1-4
Type of Packaging: Consumer, Bulk
Brands:
Aqua Blox®

153 **Across Foods, LLC**
608 Coach Drive
New Hope, PA 18938 215-693-6274
Fax: 267-895-6311 mjmsas@acrossfoods.com
www.acrossfoods.com
Kosher, organic/natiral, cookies, full-line candy, gummies/jellies/pates de fruits, licorice, health, fitness and energy bars, dried fruit.

154 **Acta Health Products**
380 N Pastoria Avenue
Sunnyvale, CA 94085-4108 408-732-6830
Fax: 408-732-0208 davidc@actaproducts.com
www.actaproducts.com
Processor and exporter of vitamins, minerals, herbal extracts and other dietary supplements; importer of raw materials
President: David Chang
VP: K Y Chang
Director Quality Control: Michael Chang
Director Marketing/Sales: Cal Bewicke
Director Purchasing: Leo Liu
Estimated Sales: $3 Million
Number Employees: 30
Sq. footage: 31000
Type of Packaging: Private Label, Bulk

155 **Action Labs**
1400 Kearns Blvd # 2
Park City, UT 84060-7228 435-655-6106
Fax: 800-767-8514 800-669-8877
info@nutrceutical.com
www.thomasregister.com/olc/actionlabs
Manufacturer and exporter of vitamins, minerals and nutritional supplements
President: Bruce Hough
CEO/Director/Chairman: Frank Gay II
CFO/Senior VP Finance: Leslie Brown Jr
CEO: Bill Gay
VP Marketing/Sales: Christopher Neuberger
COO/Director/Executive VP: Jeffrey Hinrichs
Estimated Sales: $500,000-$1 Million
Number Employees: 5-9
Type of Packaging: Consumer, Private Label, Bulk
Brands:
Fentinel
Keep
Natural Health
Un-Soap

156 **Action Labs**
P.O.Box 1090
Placentia, CA 92871-1090 714-630-5941
Fax: 714-630-8221 800-400-5696
actionvit@aol.com www.actionlab.com
Specialty Supplements for men, women, diet, energy, and specialty.
President: James R Bailey
Marketing: Mandy Ray
Sales: John Russo
Brands:
GINSENG 4X
MADE FOR MEN
SUPER FAT BURNER
YOHIMBE ACTION
YOHIMBE FOR MEN

157 **Active Organics**
1097 Yates St
Lewisville, TX 75057 972-221-7500
Fax: 972-221-3324 info@activeorganics.com
www.activeorganics.com
Manufacturer of botanical extracts
Owner: Kim Wandell
CFO: Glen Guthmann
VP: Bill Hynes
Maarketing Executive: Linda Defratus
Human Resources Executive: Angi Rene
VP Operations: Bill Heinz
Estimated Sales: $9.9 Million
Number Employees: 70
Sq. footage: 121000

158 **Acushnet Fish Corporation**
46 Middle Street
Fairhaven, MA 02719-3086 508-997-7482
Fax: 508-999-6697
President: Ralph Parsons

159 **Adair Vineyards**
52 Alhusen Rd
New Paltz, NY 12561 845-255-1377
adairwines@aol.com
www.adairwine.com
Wines
Owner: Mark Stopkie
Estimated Sales: $500,000-$1 Million
Number Employees: 1-4
Type of Packaging: Private Label

160 **Adam Matthews, Inc.**
2104 Plantside Dr
Jeffersontown, KY 40299 502-499-2253
Fax: 502-499-8331 patriciat@adammatthews.com
www.adammatthews.com
Processor of bakery products including cheesecakes, Festival Pie and other miscellaneous desserts
President: Adam Burckle
VP Operations: Cathy Fleig
Estimated Sales: $1-2.5 Million
Number Employees: 23
Sq. footage: 20000
Brands:
Adam Matthews

161 **Adam Puchta Winery**
1947 Frene Creek Rd
Hermann, MO 65041 573-486-5596
Fax: 573-486-2361 apuchta@centurytel.net
www.adampuchtawine.com
Wines
President: Timothy Puchta
Estimated Sales: $1-2.5 Million
Number Employees: 1-4
Type of Packaging: Private Label

162 **Adams & Brooks, Inc**
1915 South Hoover St
Po Box 7303
Los Angeles, CA 90007 213-737-2955
Fax: 213-737-2951 800-999-9808
shelly.clarey@adams-brooks.com
www.adams-brooks.com
Processor and exporter of bagged candy including: chocolate cups, candy bars, lollypops, novelty, nut, caramel and taffy. Also vending, fund raising and theatre packaging
President: John Brooks Sr
Business Development Manager: John Brooks Jr
Human Resources Manager/Corp. Secretary: Tempe Brooks
Product Manager: Cindy Brooks
Estimated Sales: $10-20 Million
Number Employees: 50-99
Type of Packaging: Consumer, Private Label, Bulk
Brands:
ADAMS & BROOKS
COFFEE RIO
COMIC ANIMAL
CUP-O-GOLD
FAIRTIME
P-NUTTLES
P-NUTTLES BUTTER TOFFEE PEANUTS
PSYCHO POPS
PSYCHO PSOURS
UNICORN POPS

163 **Adams County Winery**
251 Peach Tree Rd
Orrtanna, PA 17353
Fax: 717-334-4026
vintner@adamscountywinery.com
www.adamscountywinery.com
Wines
Owner: John Kramb
Estimated Sales: $1-2.5 Million
Number Employees: 1-4

164 **Adams Fisheries Ltd**
617 Bear Point Rd
Shag Harbour, NS B0W 3B0
Canada 902-723-2435
Fax: 902-723-2325 adamfish@auracom.com
Processor, importer and exporter of salted cod, pollack and haddock and live lobster
President: Donald Adams
Estimated Sales: $3.2 Million
Number Employees: 8
Sq. footage: 8500

165 **Adams Foods**
146 Industrial Dr
Box 143a
Dothan, AL 36303 334-983-4233
Fax: 334-983-5596
Manufacturer of cakes including pound, sheet and decorated
President: Ted Adams
Manager: Larry Nowkaiski
Manager: Joy Pettis
Estimated Sales: $5-10 Million
Number Employees: 5-9
Parent Co: Adams Milling Company
Type of Packaging: Consumer, Food Service, Private Label, Bulk
Brands:
Adams
Avery
Baker's Best
Home Style
Mother's

166 **Adams Olive Ranch**
1200 S Aster Ave
Lindsay, CA 93247 559-562-2882
Fax: 559-562-2272 888-216-5483
www.adamsoliveranch.com
Manufacturer of olives
Owner: Denis Bonfilio
Estimated Sales: Less than $500,000
Number Employees: 10-19
Sq. footage: 6000
Type of Packaging: Consumer, Private Label
Brands:
Adam's Ranch
RAW EARTH ORGANICS
Smith Home Cured

167 **Adams USA**
235 East 42nd Street
New York, NY 10017 212-733-2323
Fax: 800-946-4102 www.pfizer.com
Health products
CEO: Ian Read

168 **Adams Vegetable Oils**
7301 John Galt Way
PO Box 956
Arbuckle, CA 95912 530-668-2000
Fax: 530-668-2006 info@adamsgrp.com
www.adamsvegetableoils.com
Processor of specialty vegetable oils, cotton
President: Mike Adams
VP: William Adams
Sales Manager/Plant Manager: David Hoffsten
Estimated Sales: $100+ Million
Number Employees: 7
Sq. footage: 5889
Type of Packaging: Bulk

169 **Adee Honey Farm**
P.O.Box 368
Bruce, SD 57220-0368 605-627-5621
Fax: 605-627-5622 sales@adeehoneyfarms.com
www.adeehoneyfarms.com
Processor of honey and beeswax. Pollination services also available
Owner: Richard Adee
Owner: Kelvin Adee
Owner: Bret Adee
Estimated Sales: $ 20 - 50 Million
Number Employees: 50-99
Type of Packaging: Bulk
Other Locations:
Bakersfield CA
Cedar Rapids NE
Roscoe SD
Woodville MS

170 **Adelaida Cellars**
5805 Adelaida Rd
Paso Robles, CA 93446 805-239-8980
Fax: 805-239-4671 800-676-1232
wines@adelaida.com www.adelaida.com
Wines
Owner: Elizabeth Vansteenwyk
National Sales: Paul Sowerby
Production: Lalo Escalante
Estimated Sales: $1-2.5 Million
Number Employees: 10-19

171 **Adelsheim Vineyard**
16800 NE Calkins Ln
Newberg, OR 97132 503-538-3652
Fax: 503-538-2248 info@adelsheim.com
www.adelsheim.com
Wines
Owner: David Adelsheim
CFO: Kathi Neal
Quality Control: Erik Kramer
Marketing: Leah Jorgensen
National Sales: Michael Adelsheim
Vineyard Manager: Andy Hemphrey
Estimated Sales: $10-20 Million
Number Employees: 20-49
Brands:
Adelsheim Vineyard

172 **Adirondack Beverages**
701 Corporation Park
Scotia, NY 12302 518-370-3621
Fax: 518-370-3762 800-316-6096
www.adirondackbeverages.com
Processor of carbonated and noncarbonated beverages including cola, ginger ale, tonic, fruit drink, seltzer and sparkling and still water
President: Douglas Martin
Estimated Sales: $500,000-1 Million
Number Employees: 5-9
Sq. footage: 750000
Parent Co: Polar Corporation
Type of Packaging: Consumer, Food Service, Private Label
Brands:
Adironack
Clear 'n' Natural
Waist Watcher

173 **Adirondack Maple Farms**
490 Persse Rd
Fonda, NY 12068 518-853-4022
Fax: 518-853-3791
Processor and packer of pure maple syrup, sugar and candy
Owner: Robert Roblee
Estimated Sales: Less than $100,000
Number Employees: 1-4
Type of Packaging: Private Label
Brands:
ADIRONDACK MAPLE FARMS

174 **Adkin & Son Associated Food Products**
6645 107th Ave
South Haven, MI 49090-9366 269-637-7450
Fax: 269-637-2636
Manufacturer of edible fresh chestnut; chestnut tree production
President: Roy Adkin
National Accounts: L Adkin
Research & Development: Shelly Newton
Marketing Director: K Johnson
Production/Quality Control: Harold Bennett
Estimated Sales: $15 Million
Number Employees: 5-9
Sq. footage: 22000
Type of Packaging: Food Service, Bulk
Brands:
Adkin's
Adkin's Royal Blue

175 **Adler Fels Vineyards & Winery**
980 Airway Ct # D
Santa Rosa, CA 95403-2000 707-569-1493
Fax: 707-569-8301 info@adlerfels.com
www.adlerfels.com
Wines
Manager: Steve Lindsey
GM: Steve Lindsay
Estimated Sales: $20 Million
Number Employees: 20-49
Parent Co: Adams Wine Group

176 **(HQ)Adluh Flour Mill**
P.O.Box 1437
Columbia, SC 29202-1437 803-779-2460
Fax: 803-252-0014 800-692-3584
info@adluh.com www.adluh.com
Manufacturer of flour and corn meal
President: Jack Edgerton Jr
Estimated Sales: $5 Million
Number Employees: 10-19
Type of Packaging: Food Service
Brands:
ADLUH
CAROLINA GEM
EATMOR
GOLD BOND

177 **Admiral Beverages**
P.O.Box 726
Worland, WY 82401-0726 307-347-4201
Fax: 307-347-3571 www.admiralbeverage.com
Manufacturer of soft drinks
President: F Clay
VP Operations: Kelly Clay
Estimated Sales: $ 20 - 50 Million
Number Employees: 50-99
Parent Co: Pepsi Company
Type of Packaging: Consumer, Food Service

178 **Admiral Wine Merchants**
603 S 21st Street
Irvington, NJ 07111-4201 973-371-2211
Fax: 973-371-8521 800-582-9463
www.admiralwine.com
Wines
President: Michael Zeiger
Principal: Chet Zeiger
Number Employees: 1-4
Brands:
Alain Jungueovet ions
Arden Woods
Bodegas Gurpegui
Casa De Pancas
Castillo Perlada
Cattani

Caves Dom Teodosio
Cerca Aguardente
Chateau Haut Brisson
Chatonet
Conde De Amarante
Dantello
Dantello
Donte Riveth
Hopler
J.P. Vinhos
Lanson Champagne
Le Ginestre
Marble Crest
Societe Donatien Bahaud
Star Hill
Staton Hill
Tamega
Teobar
Valdamaror
Velhissima
Villa Dante - Italy

179 **Adobe Creek Packing**
P.O.Box 335
Kelseyville, CA 95451 707-279-4204
Fax: 707-279-0366 shirleyacp@aol.com
www.adobecreekpacking.com
Manufacturer and exporter of Bartlett pears
President/CEO: Kenneth Barr
Controller: Shirley Campbell
Shipping Manager: Floyd Saderlund
Office Manager: Lisa Fronsman
Estimated Sales: $2.7 Million
Number Employees: 250-499
Type of Packaging: Consumer, Food Service, Bulk
Brands:
BLAZING STAR

180 **Adobe Springs**
PO Box 1417
Patterson, CA 95363-1417 408-897-3023
Fax: 408-897-3028 magnesum@ix.netcom.com
www.mgwater.com
Bulk magnesium rich mineral water
President: Paul Mason
Co-Owner: Janet Mason
Brands:
HiOSpring
Noah's Spring Water
Seven-Up

181 **(HQ)Adolf's Meats & SausageKitchen**
35 New Britain Ave
Hartford, CT 06106 860-522-1588
Manufacturer and importer of beef, pork, veal, sausage and chicken
President: Joseph Gorski
Estimated Sales: Less than $500,000
Number Employees: 1-4
Type of Packaging: Consumer, Food Service, Bulk
Other Locations:
Adolf's Meat & Sausage
Norwalk CT

182 **Adrienne's Gourmet Foods**
849 Ward Dr
Santa Barbara, CA 93111 805-964-6848
Fax: 805-964-8698 800-937-7010
www.adriennes.com
Manufacturer, importer and exporter of the finest organic and kosher cookies, crackers and high protein pastas
President: John O'Donnell
Vice President: Adrienne O'Donnell
Estimated Sales: $5-10 Million
Number Employees: 20-49
Type of Packaging: Consumer, Food Service, Private Label, Bulk
Brands:
Appeteasers
California Crisps
Courtney's
Courtney's Organic Water Crackers
Darcia's Organic Crostini
Lavosh Hawaii
Lavosh-Hawaii
Papadina Pasta
Papadini Hi-Protein

183 **Advance Food Company**
301 W Broadway Ave
Enid, OK 73701 580-237-6656
Fax: 580-231-4587 888-723-8237
tmclaughlin@advancefoodcompany.com
www.advance-food.com
Manufacturer or breaded pre-portion, ready-to-cook, fully cooked beef, pork, veal, chicken and turkey
President/CEO: Greg Allen
Co-Founder: David McLaughlin
Co-Founder: Paul Allen
SVP Sales: Mark Allen
VP/Corporate Accounts: Tim McLaughlin
VP/Product Management: Rob McLaughlin
Estimated Sales: $194 Million
Number Employees: 50-99
Type of Packaging: Consumer, Food Service, Private Label
Other Locations:
Advance Food Company
Caryville TN
Advance Food Company
Scanton PA
Advance Food Company - Sales
Oklahoma City OK
Brands:
54TH STREET DELI
CERTIFIED ANGUS BEEF
CHEESEBURGER FRIES
EASY BEGINNINGS
FAST FIXON
KITCHEN SENSATIONS
SHORTY'S
SMART SERVE
STEAK EZE
VINCELLO LAMB AND VEAL

184 **Advanced Aquacultural Technologies**
14792 Cr 52
Syracuse, IN 46567 574-457-5802
Fax: 219-457-5887
Hybrid striped bass
President: Gary Miller
Vice President: Barbara Miller
Estimated Sales: $65,000
Number Employees: 5

185 **Advanced Food Services**
9807 Lackman Rd
Shawnee Mission, KS 66219-1209 913-888-8088
Fax: 913-888-8075 info@advancedfood.com
www.advancedfood.com
President: Raju Shah

186 **(HQ)Advanced Food Systems Inc.**
21 Roosevelt Ave
Somerset, NJ 8873 732-873-6776
Fax: 732-873-4177 info@afsnj.com
www.afsnj.com
Develops and manufactures customized ingredient systems for meat and poultry products, frozen foods, sauces and marinades, and more
President: Yongkeun Joh
CFO: Pamela Cooper
EVP: Warren Love
Sales Executive: Chris Kelly
Operations Director: Bob Lijana
Purchasing Director: Mike Walker
Estimated Sales: $6.5 Million
Number Employees: 50
Sq. footage: 26800

187 **Advanced Food Technology**
11252 W Cooper Dr
Littleton, CO 80127-5845 303-980-5221
Fax: 303-799-1262
Coffee extract (concentrate), coffee filters, flavors

188 **Advanced Ingredients, Inc.**
331 Capitola Ave Ste F
Capitola, CA 95010 831-464-9891
Fax: 831-464-9895 888-238-4647
info@advancedingredients.com
www.advancedingredients.com
Processor and exporter of specialty ingredients
President: Fred Greenland
Estimated Sales: $ 1 - 3 Million
Number Employees: 5-9
Brands:
BAKESMART®
ENERGYSMART®
ENERGYSOURCE®
FRUITRIM®
FRUITSAVR®
FRUITSOURCE®
MOISTURLOK®
PLUS AND MOISTURIOK®

189 **Advanced Nutritional Research, Inc.**
1 W Washington St
Ellicottville, NY 14731 716-699-2020
Fax: 716-699-2036 800-836-0644
info@advancednutritionalresearch.com
www.anrminerals.com
Processor of vitamin and mineral supplements
President: Nancy Jemison
Estimated Sales: $1-2.5 Million
Number Employees: 1-4
Type of Packaging: Consumer, Private Label

190 **Advanced Spice & Trading**
1808 Monetary Ln Ste 100
Carrollton, TX 75006 972-242-8580
Fax: 972-242-6920 800-872-7811
sales@advancedspice.com
www.advancedspice.com
Importer, processor and full line distributor of spices and manufacturing ingredients used in the food industry
Owner: Greg Hank
Office Manager: Genie Wolf
Vice President: Douglas Hanks
Estimated Sales: $2.3 Million
Number Employees: 15
Sq. footage: 67200
Type of Packaging: Consumer, Food Service, Private Label, Bulk
Brands:
Santaka Chili Pods
Supper Topper

191 **Advent Machine Company**
6815 E Washington Blvd
Commerce, CA 90040-1905 323-728-5367
Fax: 323-728-2443 800-846-7716
info@adventmachine.net
www.adventmachine.net
Manufacturer of pressure-sensitive or plain paper labels
Owner: Richard G Ealy
Estimated Sales: $ 1 - 3 Million
Number Employees: 5-9

192 **Adventist Book & Food**
2160 Us Highway 1
Trenton, NJ 08648-4447 609-392-8010
Fax: 609-392-4477 800-765-6955
njabc@erols.com www.adventistbookcenter.com
Vegetarian meat substitutes
Manager: Herb Shiroma
CFO: Herb Shiroma
Owner: New Jersey
Estimated Sales: $ .5 - 1 million
Number Employees: 1-4

193 **Adventure Foods**
481 Banjo Lane
Whittier, NC 28789-7999 828-497-4113
Fax: 828-497-7529
CustomerService@adventurefoods.com
www.adventurefoods.com
Manufacturer a complete line of freeze-dried, dehydrated, shelf stable foods and instant food items for the food service, food storage programs, health food markets and the outdoor market. Also offered are baking mixes, bulk spices andingredients, specialty foods and special packing for vegetarian, diabetics, gluten intolerance and for other food or health restrictions
President: Jean Spangenberg
CEO: Sam Spangenberg
Number Employees: 5-9
Parent Co: Jean's Garden Greats
Type of Packaging: Consumer, Food Service, Private Label, Bulk
Brands:
ADVENTURE FOODS
BAKE PACKERS
GSI
HEARTTLINE
LUMEN
OPEN COUNTRY
WELL SEASONED TRAVELER

194 **Aegean Cheese**
2606 W Oakland Avenue
Austin, MN 55912 507-433-1292
Fax: 507-433-1909
Cheese
President: Roger Enstad
VP Marketing: Steve Enstad
Estimated Sales: $20-50 Million
Number Employees: 20-49

195 **Aetna Springs Cellars**
7227 Pope Valley Rd
Pope Valley, CA 94567 707-965-2675
Fax: 707-965-2675 skimsey@napanet.net
www.aetnaspringscellars.com
Wines
General Partner: Sally Kimsey
Partner: Jim Watson
Partner: Margaret Ann Watson
Winemaker/Partner: Paul Kimsey
Estimated Sales: $500,000-$1 Million
Number Employees: 1-4
Brands:
AETNA SPRINGS CELLARS

196 **Affiliated Rice Milling**
715 N 2nd St
Alvin, TX 77511 281-331-6176
Fax: 281-585-0336
Processor and exporter of rice and rice flour
Manager: Johnny Dunham
VP, Operations: Johnny Dunham
Estimated Sales: $20-50 Million
Number Employees: 10-19
Sq.footage: 130000
Parent Co: Rice Belt Warehouse
Brands:
Eminence

197 **Afton Mountain Vineyards**
234 Vineyard Ln
Afton, VA 22920 540-456-8667
Fax: 540-456-8002
finewines@aftonmountainvineyards.com
www.aftonmountainvineyards.com
Wines
President: Tom Corpora
VP: Shinko Corpora
Estimated Sales: $1-2.5 Million
Number Employees: 5-9
Type of Packaging: Private Label

198 **AgSource Milk Analysis Laboratory**
403 Cedar Ave W
Menomonie, WI 54751-1300 715-235-1128
Fax: 715-235-8680 menomlab@agsource.com
www.agsource.com
Co-Owner: Don Niles
Co-Owner: John Pagel
VP: Joel Amdall
Personnel Manager: Bruce Cornish
General Manager: C Smith
Estimated Sales: $ 1 - 3 Million
Number Employees: 20-49
Brands:
Ag Co-Op

199 **Agger Fish**
63 Flushing Ave Unit 313
Brooklyn, NY 11205 718-855-1717
Fax: 718-855-4545 marcagger@gmail.com
www.monkfish.net
Manufacturer and importer and exporter of monkfish, fluke, monkfish liver and shark fins, bones and cartilage for food supplements and ingredients
President: Mark Agger
Estimated Sales: $500,000-$1 Million
Number Employees: 500-999
Sq.footage: 3000
Type of Packaging: Bulk

200 **(HQ)Agilex Flavors & Fragrances, Inc.**
140 Centennial Avenue
Piscataway, NJ 08854-3908 800-542-7662
Fax: 732-393-7378 info@agilexfandf.com
www.aromatec.com
Manufacturer of Flavors and Fragrances
President: Thomas Damiano
Chairman/Ceo: Thomas Lamb
Senior VP/CFO: Richard Green Jr Jr.
Estimated Sales: $5-10 Million
Number Employees: 162
Other Locations:
Flavor Division Headquarters
Rancho Santa Margarita CA
Fragrance Division Headquarters
Piscataway NJ

201 **Aglamesis Brothers**
3046 Madison Rd
Cincinnati, OH 45209 513-531-5196
Fax: 513-531-5403 www.aglamesis.com
Processor of ice cream and confectionery products
President: James Aglamesis
Estimated Sales: $2.5-5 Million
Number Employees: 10-19
Type of Packaging: Consumer, Food Service

202 **Agland, Inc.**
P.O.Box 338
Eaton, CO 80615 970-454-3391
Fax: 970-454-2144 800-433-4688
www.aglandinc.com
Processor of pinto beans and grain
President: William McKay
CEO: Mitch Anderson
CFO: Rob Lyons
CEO: Mitch Anderson
Estimated Sales: $10-20 Million
Number Employees: 100-249
Type of Packaging: Consumer
Brands:
RED BIRD

203 **AgraWest Foods**
PO Box 760
Souris
Prince Edward Island, NS C0A 2B0
Canada 902-687-1400
Fax: 902-687-1401 877-687-1400
agrawest@agrawest.com www.agrawest.com
Manufacturer and exporter of dehydrated potato granules
President: Richard Zirkelback
CEO: Richard Nickel
VP/GM: Todd Sutton
Quality Assurance Manager: Kendra Deagle
Sales Manager: Mary Croucher
Production Manager: Jamie Trainor
Parent Co: Idaho Pacific Corporation
Type of Packaging: Food Service, Bulk
Brands:
Chef Master

204 **Agrexco USA**
15012 132nd Ave
Jamaica, NY 11434 718-481-8700
Fax: 718-481-8710 amoso@agrexco.com
www.agrexco.com
Processor and importer of fruits including dried dates, grapefruits and oranges as well as fresh cut herbs
President: Yoram Shalev
CFO/VP, Quality Control: Jack Aschkeigi
Estimated Sales: $20-50 Million
Number Employees: 20-49
Brands:
Alesia
Carmel

205 **Agri Processors**
10001 Aspen Ave
Postville, IA 52162 563-864-3013
Fax: 563-864-7890
Processor of kosher meat
Owner: Aaron Rubashkin
CEO: Bernard Feldman
Estimated Sales: $50-100 Million
Number Employees: 500-999

206 **Agri-Best Foods**
4430 S Tripp Ave
Chicago, IL 60632 773-247-5060
Fax: 773-247-7247
President: Bill Koulch
Estimated Sales: $100+ Million
Number Employees: 100-249

207 **Agri-Dairy Products**
3020 Westchester Ave
Purchase, NY 10577 914-697-9580
Fax: 914-697-9586
customerservice@agridairy.com
www.agridairy.com
A full service manufacturer distributor of dairy and food ingredients including whey and lactose, milkfat, milk powders, casein, milk proteins, cheese
President: Frank Reeves
CFO: Maryellen Storino
VP: Steve Bronfield
Sales Manager: Cliff Lang
Estimated Sales: $32 Million
Number Employees: 12
Number of Products: 50+
Sq. footage: 1600
Type of Packaging: Bulk

208 **Agri-Mark**
P.O.Box 5800
Lawrence, MA 1842 978-689-4442
Fax: 978-794-8304 information@agrimark.net
www.agrimark.net
Manufacturer of dairy products including butter and nonfat, skim and condensed milk; exporter of butter powder
President: Paul Johnston
Estimated Sales: $20-50 Million
Number Employees: 100-249
Type of Packaging: Private Label, Bulk
Other Locations:
Agri-Mark Manufacturing Plant
West Springfield MA
Agri-Mark Manufacturing Plant
Middlebury VT
Agri-Mark Manufacturing Plant
Cabot VT
Agri-Mark Manufacturing Plant
Chateaugay NY
Brands:
Cabot
McCADAM

209 **(HQ)Agri-Mark**
P.O.Box 5800
Lawrence, MA 1842 978-689-4442
Fax: 978-794-8304 info@agrimark.net
www.agrimark.net
Milk, cream and butter
President: Paul Johnston
Senior VP: Robert Wellington
VP/Marketing: John Burke
Plant Manager: Gary Carlow
Estimated Sales: $20-50 Million
Number Employees: 50-99
Other Locations:
Agri-Mark
Middlebury VT
Agri-Mark
Cabot VT
Agri-Mark
Chateaugay NY

210 **Agri-Mark**
P.O.Box 5800
Lawrence, MA 01842 978-689-4442
Fax: 978-794-8304 ddimento@agrimark.net
www.agrimark.net
Dairy products
President: Paul P Johnston
CEO: Paul Johnston
Executive VP/COO: Dr. Richard Stammer
Director Communications: Douglas DiMento
Estimated Sales: $1-500 Million
Number Employees: 100-249
Parent Co: Agri-Mark
Brands:
CABOT DAIRIES
McCADAM

211 **(HQ)Agri-Northwest**
7404 W Hood Pl
Kennewick, WA 99336-6718 509-734-1195
Fax: 509-734-1092
Potatoes
President: Don Sleight
CFO: R Thomas Mackay
Estimated Sales: $65 Million
Number Employees: 10-19

212 **Agri-Pack**
P.O.Box 2086
Pasco, WA 99302 509-545-6181
Fax: 509-545-5748 steve@agri-pack.com
Processor of onions including whole, rings, diced and strips
Manager: Tim Sessions
Account Executive: Jon Josephson
Director Sales/Marketing: Steve Shepard
Plant Manager: Todd Daniko

Estimated Sales: $2.5-5 Million
Number Employees: 20-49
Sq. footage: 150000
Parent Co: Agri Pack
Type of Packaging: Food Service, Bulk

213 **AgriCulver Seeds**
2059 State Route 96
Trumansburg, NY 14886-9129 607-387-5788
Fax: 607-387-5789 800-836-3701
info@agriculverseeds.com
www.agriculverseeds.com
Manufacturer, packager, exporter and wholesaler/distributor of specialty organic grains including wheat, spelt, barley, buckwheat and alfalfa
Manager: Wayne Brown
GM: Rod Porter
Office Manager/Customer Service: Nancy Fraboni
Estimated Sales: $2.5-5 Million
Number Employees: 10-19
Sq. footage: 32000
Brands:
DAIRY BANQUET

214 **Agricor**
P.O.Box 807
Marion, IN 46952-0807 765-662-0606
Fax: 765-662-7189 sales@agricor.org
www.agricor.info
Processor and exporter of corn grits, flour and meal
President: Steve Wickes
Sales Coordinator: Duane Hudson
Operations Manager: Bill Cramer
Plant Manager: Jack Jones
Estimated Sales: $20-50 Million
Number Employees: 20-49
Type of Packaging: Bulk
Brands:
Agricor

215 **Agricore United**
CanWest Global Place 201 Portage Avenue
28th Floor
Winnipeg, MB R3C 3A7
Canada 204-944-5411
Fax: 204-944-5454 800-661-4844
infomaster@agricoreunited.com
www.agricoreunited.com
Manufacturer and exporter of wheat, barley, oats, 3-grain and instant cereals, pancake mix, organic flour and herb food bars and beans including; pinto, black, Great Northern and lentil
President/Ceo: Mayo Schmidt
Chairman: Terry Baker
CFO: David Carefoot
Senior VP: Ronald Enns
VP Human Resources: Gerald Valois
VP Operations: S MacKay
Estimated Sales: $2 Billion
Number Employees: 2,800
Type of Packaging: Consumer, Food Service, Bulk
Other Locations:
Manitoba
Saskatchewan
Alberta
British Columbia

216 **Agrinom LLC**
P.O.Box 267
Hakalau, HI 96710 808-963-6771
Fax: 808-963-6143 mail@agrinom.com
www.agrinom.com
President: Jay Ram
Marketing: Jay Ram
Brands:
Agrinom

217 **(HQ)Agrinorthwest**
7404 W Hood Pl
Kennewick, WA 99336 509-734-1195
Fax: 509-734-1092
Manufacturer and packer of produce including apples, potatoes, onions, etc.
President: Don Sleight
CFO: Thomas MacKay
Manager: Mark Larsen
Estimated Sales: $65 Million
Number Employees: 150
Type of Packaging: Consumer, Food Service, Private Label, Bulk

218 **Agripac**
PO Box 5110
Denver, CO 80217-5110 503-363-9255
Fax: 503-371-5682 consultas@agripac.com.ar
www.agripac.com
Frozen red raspberries, strawberries, marionberries, rhubarb, snap beans, broccoli, cauliflower, corn, whole onions, peas and carrots, squash, mixed vegetables, prepared vegetables
Director: Pablo Adreani
Senior VP: Patrick Monaghan
Senior VP, Operations: Russ Grubb
Brands:
Agripac

219 **Agro Farma Inc.**
669 County Road 25
New Berlin, NY 13411 607-847-6181
Fax: 607-847-8847 877-847-6181
tiffany.gray@agro-farma.com www.chobani.com
Greek Yogurt
Chairman: Hamdi Ulukaya
Controller: Besnik Fetoski
Estimated Sales: $15.8 Million
Number Employees: 60

220 **Agro Foods, Inc.**
3531 SW 13th St
Miami, FL 33145 305-361-7200
Fax: 305-361-7639 agro@agrofoods.com
www.agrofoods.com
Manufacturer, packer, wholesaler/distributor, importer and exporter of Spanish olives
Manager: Isa Knight
Estimated Sales: $1-2.5 Million
Number Employees: 5-9
Sq. footage: 131500
Parent Co: Agro Aceitunera SA
Type of Packaging: Consumer, Food Service, Private Label, Bulk
Brands:
Candelita
Exporsevilla
Lola

221 **AgroCepia**
9703 Dixie Highway
Suite 3
Miami, FL 33156 305-704-3488
Fax: 305-666-6930 acusa_us@bellsouth.net
www.agrocepia.cl
Low moisture colored apple flakes and nuggets, evaporated apple dices, grinds, rings and wedges, low moisture powders, dehydrated tomato, green bell pepper, red bell pepper and jalapeno pepper dices and granules
Sales Director: Mike Zobel
Estimated Sales: $ 3 - 5 Million
Number Employees: 1-4

222 **(HQ)Agrocan**
176 Benjamin Hudon
Ville St Laurent, QC H4N 1H8
Canada 514-272-2512
Fax: 514-270-6370 877-247-6226
info@agrocanfoods.com www.agrocanfoods.com
Manufacturer and exporter of fruit, olives, oil, vegetables and miscellaneous products
President: John Karellis
Number Employees: 3
Type of Packaging: Private Label
Other Locations:
Agrocan
Aeginion, N. Pierias
Brands:
SUNMED

223 **Agrocomplex**
1100 E. Main Cross
Suite 23
Findlay, OH 45840 419-420-1800
Fax: 419-420-1800 bill@agrocomplex.us
www.agrocomplex.us
Supplier of dairy products such as milk powder & milk powder blends, whey blends, casein and caseinates and butter.

224 **Agrocosa**
Calle Morelos 11
Meoqui, CH 33130
Mexico 639-573-1611
Fax: 639-473-1658 elizagomc.@agrocosa.com
www.agrocosa.com
Kosher, Spices
Marketing: Elizabeth Gomez

225 **Agropur**
2701 Freedom Road
Appleton, WI 54913 608-441-3030
Fax: 608-441-3031 kevin.thomson@agropur.com
www.agropur.com
Cheese and cheese products manufacturer
Director of Sales: Kevin Thomson
Parent Co: Agropur

226 **(HQ)Agropur Cooperative Agro-Alimentaire**
510 Rue Principale
Granby, QC J2G 2X2
Canada 450-375-1991
Fax: 450-375-7160 800-363-5686
jarollan@agropur.com
Manufacturer, importer and exporter of milk, cream, ice cream, butter, cheese and yogurt
Chairman: Jacques Cartier
CEO: Claude Menard
Secretary: Andre Gauthier
Number Employees: 650
Type of Packaging: Consumer, Food Service
Other Locations:
Agropur Coop. Agro-Alimentair
Markham ON

227 **Agrusa, Inc.**
PO Box 267
Leonia, NJ 07605-7244 201-592-5950
Fax: 201-585-7244 agrusa@agrusainc.com
www.agritalia.com
Manufacturer and importer of Italian foods, both conventional and organic including: pasta, olive oil, balsamic vinegar, tomatoes, risotto, rice and frozen pizza.
President: Jill Bush
Number Employees: 5
Sq. footage: 2000
Type of Packaging: Consumer, Food Service, Private Label, Bulk
Brands:
Bella Italia
Celio
Don Peppe
Private Label

228 **Agumm**
10636 NW 49th Street
Coral Springs, FL 33076-2702 954-344-0607
Fax: 305-341-6667 bfjelde@corpcomm.net
Baked products, batters, breading, confectionery, dry mixes
President: Matthew Rutter

229 **Agvest**
7 Winter Rd
Franklin, ME 4634 207-565-3303
Fax: 207-565-3303 www.agvest.com
Processor and exporter of frozen blueberries and cranberries; also, sugar-infused blueberries.
EVP: Holace Hills
Sales/Marketing: Barry Schneider
Plant Manager: Anthony Kelley
Estimated Sales: $20-50 Million
Number Employees: 12
Sq. footage: 18728
Parent Co: Agvest
Type of Packaging: Consumer, Food Service
Brands:
North Eastern

230 **(HQ)Agvest**
7589 First Pl Ste 2
Cleveland, OH 44146 216-464-3737
Fax: 440-735-1680 www.agvest.com
Processor and exporter of frozen apples, elderberries, bilberries, sugar infused blueberries, cranberries and cherries, and fruit flakes and powders.
President/CEO: Barry Schneider
CFO: Steve Hamilton
Estimated Sales: $1-2.5 Million
Number Employees: 5-9
Type of Packaging: Food Service
Brands:
North Eastern
Quality

231 **Ah Dor Kosher Fish Corporation**
25 Main St
Monsey, NY 10952-3707 845-425-7776

Fish
President: Joseph Neuman
Estimated Sales: Less than $500,000
Number Employees: 1-4
Type of Packaging: Private Label

232 **Ahlgren Vineyard**
20320 Highway 9
Boulder Creek, CA 95006 831-338-6071
Fax: 831-338-9111 800-338-6071
ahlgren@cruzio.com www.ahlgrenvineyard.com
Processor of wines
Co-Owner: Valerie Ahlgren
Co-Owner/CEO/Winemaker: Dexter Ahlgren
Estimated Sales: $1-2.5 Million
Number Employees: 1-4
Type of Packaging: Food Service, Private Label
Brands:
AHLGREN VINEYARD
TRE VINI ROSSI

233 **Ahmad Tea London**
P.O.Box 876
Deer Park, TX 77536 281-478-0957
Fax: 281-479-0521 800-637-7704
info@ahmadteausa.com www.ahmadtea.com
Tea and tea gift producer
Marketing: Karim Afshar

234 **Aidell's Sausage Company**
1625 Alvarado St
San Leandro, CA 94577-2636 510-614-5450
Fax: 510-614-2287 800-546-5795
info@aidells.com www.aidells.com
Manufacturer of sausage products
Founder: Chef Bruce Aidells
CEO: Bob Mc Henry
Number Employees: 20-49
Type of Packaging: Consumer, Food Service, Bulk
Brands:
Aidell's

235 **Aileen Quirk & Sons**
235 W 12th Ave
Kansas City, MO 64116 816-471-4580
Fax: 816-842-8063
Packages a wide variety of dried edible beans and sell them to wholesalers and grocery stores
President: Kelly Quirk
CEO: Larry Quirk
Traffic Manager: Leslie Quirk
Office Manager: Frances Kuhn
Estimated Sales: $3 Million
Number Employees: 15
Type of Packaging: Food Service, Private Label, Bulk
Brands:
Pdq Puncher Dry Edible Bean

236 **Ailments E.D. Foods Inc.**
6200 Trans Canada Highway
Pointe Claire, QC H9R 1B9
Canada 514-695-3333
Fax: 514-695-0281 800-267-3333
leslie@ed.ca www.ed.ca
Manufacturer and exporter of dehydrated soup and gravy bases, specialty seasonings and dehydrated mixes including soup, gravy and side dishes; also, consultant specializing in research, development and processing of custom recipes
President: Victor Eiser
Number Employees: 50-99
Sq. footage: 50000
Type of Packaging: Consumer, Food Service, Private Label, Bulk
Brands:
Easily Done
Inspiration
Luda
Top & Toss

237 **Aimonetto and Sons**
720 N 10th St
Renton, WA 98057 206-767-2777
Fax: 206-762-6792 866-823-2777
Manufacturer of milk, juice, cottage cheese, sour cream and yogurt; wholesaler/distributor of dairy products
Owner: Jim Aimonetto
Estimated Sales: $10-20 Million
Number Employees: 10-19
Type of Packaging: Consumer, Food Service

238 **(HQ)Aina Hawaiian Tropical Products**
175 E Kawailani St
Hilo, HI 96720-5606 808-981-0771
Fax: 808-981-2644 877-961-4774
trinag@alohablooms.com
www.hawaiitropicals.com
Ethnic foods
Owner: Steven Parente
Manager: Steven Parente
Estimated Sales: $ .5 - 1 million
Number Employees: 5-9
Brands:
Hawaii Gourmet
Kona Coffee

239 **Airlie Winery**
15305 Dunn Forest Rd
Monmouth, OR 97361 503-838-6013
Fax: 503-838-6279 airlie@airliewinery.com
www.airliewinery.com
Wines
Owner: Mary Olson
Marketing/Sales VP: Barry Glassman
Winemaker: Elizabeth Ogg
Estimated Sales: $500,000-$1 Million
Number Employees: 1-4
Type of Packaging: Private Label
Brands:
Airlie

240 **Aiya America Inc.**
2807 Oregon Ct Ste D5
Unit 104
Torrance, CA 90503-2635
Fax: 310-212-1386 info@aiya-america.com
www.aiya-america.com
Wholesaler and distributor of matcha green tea and premium leaf teas used in many types of food and beverage applications.

241 **Ajinomato Frozen Foods USA**
7124 N Marine Dr
Portland, OR 97203-6480 503-286-5869
Fax: 503-286-7089 yoshimineh@ajiusa.com
www.ajinomato-usa.com
Frozen vegetables
President/CEO: Yoshio Ishii
Director Research: T Arima
Production Manager: Bruce Jenson
Plant Manager: Dan Trainer
Estimated Sales: $20-50 Million
Number Employees: 100-249

242 **Ajinomoto Food Ingredients LLC**
8430 W Bryn Mawr Ave Ste 635
Chicago, IL 60631 773-714-1436
Fax: 773-380-7006 naultyb@ajiusa.com
www.lysine.com
Processor of flavorings including aspartame, enzymes, monosodium glutamate, nucleotides, glutamic salts, soy oligosaccharides and amino acids. Also liquid and dry sauces, including soy sauce, sesame oil
President: Tommy Teshima
Director Sales: David Barbour
Estimated Sales: $ 600,000
Number Employees: 5
Parent Co: Ajinomoto Company
Type of Packaging: Bulk
Brands:
ACTIVA TG
KOJI-AJI
TRANSGLUTAMINASE

243 **Ajinomoto Frozen Foods USA**
7124 N Marine Dr
Portland, OR 97203 503-286-6548
info@ajifrozenusa.com
www.ajifrozenusa.com
Manufacturer and exporter of frozen foods including sauteed and fried (tempura) meats, vegetables and seafood, soups, fried rice and pilafs, stews, roux, chowders and Oriental dishes; importer of noodles and spices
President, Ajinomoto Frozen Foods USA: Haruo Kurata
CIO: Brandon Sullivan
Sales Director: David Barbour
General Manager: Tomo Shiojima
Estimated Sales: $50 Million
Number Employees: 170
Sq. footage: 264000
Parent Co: Ajinomoto Company
Type of Packaging: Consumer, Food Service, Private Label
Other Locations:
Los Angeles CA
Portland OR
Honolulu HI
Brands:
Ajinomoto

244 **(HQ)Ajinomoto USA**
400 Kelby St Ste 78
Fort Lee, NJ 7024 201-292-3200
Fax: 201-261-7343 www.ajinomoto-usa.com
Provides consumer foods, amino acids, and food ingredients.
President/CEO: Shinichi Suzuki
SVP/Secretary/Treasurer: Hideki Nagano
Estimated Sales: $ 12 Billion
Number Employees: 400
Sq. footage: 264000
Parent Co: Ajinomoto Company
Type of Packaging: Consumer, Food Service, Private Label

245 **Ajiri Tea Company**
Po Box 244
Upper Black Eddy, PA 18972-0244 610-982-5075
Fax: 610-982-9346 sara@ajiritea.com
www.ajiritea.com
Tea
Marketing: Sara Holby

246 **Ak-Mak Bakeries**
89 Academy Ave
Sanger, CA 93657 559-875-5511
Fax: 559-875-2472
Armenian cracker bread
President: Manoog Soojian
VP: Hagop Soojian
Controller: Tanya Hodge
Estimated Sales: $20-50 Million
Number Employees: 20-49
Brands:
Ak Mak
Country Style
Round Cracker Bread

247 **Akay USA, LLC**
500 Hartle Street
Suite E
Sayreville, NJ 08872 732-254-7177
Fax: 732-254-7178 akayusallc@gmail.com
www.akay-group.com
Manufacturer and supplier of paprika and spices.

248 **Akicorp**
20145 NE 21st CT
N Miami Beach, FL 33179 786-426-5750
ysaac@akinin.com
www.akicorp.com
Oilseeds manufacturer and supplier
Manager: Ysaac Akinin

249 **Al & John's Glen Rock Ham**
444 Marshall St
Paterson, NJ 07503-2909 973-742-4990
Fax: 973-742-5141 800-969-4990
Processor of Canadian bacon and fresh ham including cooked, ready-to-eat, fat-free, semi-boneless, smoked boneless, honey, Virginia, maple, apple cinnamon, black forest, etc.
President/CEO: Alex Oldja
VP: Jennifer Oldja
Plant Manager: Alex Oldja, Jr.
Estimated Sales: $20-50 Million
Number Employees: 100-249

250 **Al Dente**
9815 Main St
Whitmore Lake, MI 48189 734-449-8522
Fax: 734-449-8511 800-536-7278
info@aldentepasta.com www.aldentepasta.com
Processor of specialty flavored pasta: linguine, fettuccine, angel hair, rigatoni, penne, fusilli, farfalle and rotini. Sauces: pesto and alfredo
President: Monique Deschaine
VP: Dennis Deschaine
Estimated Sales: $5-10 Million
Number Employees: 16
Brands:
Al Dente
Al Dente Pasta Selecta
Al Dente Sure Success
Monique's Pasta Sauces

251 **Al Gelato Bornay**
9133 Belden Ave
Franklin Park, IL 60131 847-455-5355
Fax: 847-455-7553 www.algelato.com
Importer, exporter and processor of ice cream, sorbet, spumoni, natural fruit sorbets, and frozen desserts
President: Paula DiNardo
Estimated Sales: $500,000- 1 Million
Number Employees: 6
Sq. footage: 5000
Type of Packaging: Food Service, Private Label, Bulk
Brands:
Al Gelato

252 **(HQ)Al Pete Meats**
2100 E Willard St
Muncie, IN 47302-3737 765-288-8817
Fax: 765-281-2759
Processor of frozen portion control foods; including corn dogs, breaded meat and cheese, raw and cooked breaded mushrooms and cauliflower; Exporter of frozen portion controlled breaded meat products
President: Arlin Mann
CEO: John Hartmeyer
Purchasing Manager: Paul Whitechair
Estimated Sales: $10-20 Million
Number Employees: 20-49
Sq. footage: 150000
Type of Packaging: Consumer, Food Service, Private Label
Brands:
Al Pete
Pete's Pride

253 **Al Richards Chocolates**
851 Broadway
Bayonne, NJ 07002-3018 201-436-0915
Fax: 201-436-0485 888-777-6964
fstancampl@aol.com
www.alrichardschocolates.com
Chocolates and ceramics
Estimated Sales: $300,000-500,000
Number Employees: 1-4

254 **Al Safa Halal**
P.O.Box 1076
Niagara Falls, NY 14303 301-649-5778
Fax: 519-654-9245 800-268-8174
info@alsafahalal.com www.alsafahalal.com
Processor and exporter of halal processed foods including pizza, beef burgers, chicken nuggets, fish sticks, etc.
President: David Muller
VP: Steve Hahn
Number Employees: 10-19
Number of Brands: 40
Parent Co: Al Safa Halal
Type of Packaging: Consumer, Food Service
Other Locations:
Al Safa Halal
Cambridge, Ontario
Brands:
Al Safa Halal

255 **Al's Beverage Company**
3 Revay Rd
East Windsor, CT 06088 860-627-7003
Fax: 860-627-8067 888-257-7632
mfeldman@alsbeverage.com
www.alsbeverage.com
Fountain soft drinks
Owner: Marjorie Feldman
Sr. VP Sales: John Martin
VP: William Melcher
Marketing Consultant: Todd Lemieux
Sales Director: Art Gallegos
Operations Manager: Michael McCarthy
Estimated Sales: $3-5 Million
Number Employees: 50-99
Type of Packaging: Private Label
Brands:
Al's
Barrel Head
Canada Dry
RC
Stewarts
Sunkist

256 **Al-Rite Fruits & Syrups**
18524 NE 2nd Ave
Miami, FL 33179-4427 305-652-2540
Fax: 305-652-4478 alrite@icanect.net
www.al-rite.com
Processor and exporter of kosher products including isotonic iced tea, fountain and slush beverage, ice cream and nondairy bases. Also fudge and chocolate syrups, toppings, frozen cocktail/bar mixes and extracts and flavors forbeverages and desserts
Manager: Alfredo Faubel
Estimated Sales: $5-10 Million
Number Employees: 10-19
Type of Packaging: Consumer, Food Service, Private Label, Bulk
Brands:
Al-Rite
Iso-Sport
Tropical

257 **Alabama Catfish**
P.O.Box 769
Uniontown, AL 36786-0769 334-628-3474
Fax: 334-628-2122 www.harvestselect.com
Catfish
President: Jerry Whittington
President: George Smelley
Estimated Sales: $ 20 - 50 Million
Number Employees: 250-499

258 **Alabama Seafood Producers**
9280 Seafood House Rd
Bayou La Batre, AL 36509 251-824-4396
Fax: 251-824-7579
http://www.alabamaseafood.org
President: Richard Gazzier
Vice President: Donna Gazzier
Estimated Sales: $ 5 - 10 Million
Number Employees: 10-19

259 **Alacer Corporation**
80 Icon
Foothill Ranch, CA 92610 949-916-5698
Fax: 949-951-7235 800-854-0249
asolorzano@alacer.com www.alacercorp.com
Processor and exporter of dietary supplements, mineral ascorbates, vitamins and distilled water
President: Ron Fugate
Director Marketing: Bruce Sweyd
Executive Administration: Vernon Peck
Estimated Sales: $20-50 Million
Number Employees: 50-99
Sq. footage: 57000
Type of Packaging: Consumer
Brands:
Emer'gen-C
Miracle

260 **Aladdin Bakers**
240 25th St
Brooklyn, NY 11232 718-499-1818
Fax: 718-788-5174
kasindorf@aladdinbakers.com
www.aladdinbakers.com
Baker of sandwich wraps and gourmet flour tortillas, pita, panini and specialty breads, bagels, bread sticks, toast, croutons, and flatbreads
President: Joseph Ayoub
CFO/GM: Donald Guzzi
Quality Control Director: Javier Vasquez
VP Sales/Marketing: Paul Kasindorf
Human Resources Director: Barbara Adams
COO/Plant Manager: Arkadi Karachun
Production Manager: Ed Curran
Estimated Sales: $20-50 Million
Number Employees: 125
Sq. footage: 9774
Type of Packaging: Consumer, Food Service, Private Label, Bulk
Brands:
Aladdin

261 **Alakef Coffee Roasters**
1330 E Superior St Ste 1
Duluth, MN 55805 218-724-6849
Fax: 218-724-7727 800-438-9228
info@alakef.com www.alakef.com
Roasted coffee
President: Nessim Bohbot
VP: Deborah Bohbot
Estimated Sales: $1.7 Million
Number Employees: 12
Type of Packaging: Private Label

262 **Alamance Foods/Triton Water Company**
804 Plantation Drive
Burlington, NC 27215 336-226-6392
Fax: 336-229-9768 800-476-9111
info@alamancefoods.com
www.alamancefoods.com
Manufactures private label and branded water, flavored drinks, freeze pops and aerosol whipped cream.
President: Bill Scott Jr
Chairman/CEO: Bill Scott Sr
R&D: Dollie Rollins
VP Sales: Jeff Parker
Plant Manager: Gene Smith
Estimated Sales: $20-50 Million
Number Employees: 180
Sq. footage: 40000
Type of Packaging: Private Label
Brands:
CLASSIC CREAM
FUN POPS
FUN WHIP
HAPPY DRINKS
TRITON WATER

263 **Alamo Masa Company**
318 E Nopal Street
Uvalde, TX 78801-5331 210-732-9651
Fax: 210-735-5236 800-568-9651
Tortillas
President: Joe Martinez III
Estimated Sales: $10-20 Million
Number Employees: 10-19

264 **Alamo Onions**
PO Box 1126
Pharr, TX 78577-1621 210-281-0962
Refrigerated whole peeled onions
President: Chris Torres
VP: Manuel Rodriguez
Estimated Sales: $5-10 Million
Number Employees: 20-49

265 **(HQ)Alamo Tamale Corporation**
3713 Jensen Dr
Houston, TX 77026 713-228-6446
Fax: 713-228-7513 800-252-0586
alamotam@texas.net www.alamotamale.com
Manufacturer of tamales
President: Louis Webster
VP: Shirleen Webster
Estimated Sales: $10-20 Million
Number Employees: 50-99
Sq. footage: 25000
Type of Packaging: Consumer, Food Service, Private Label
Brands:
Alamo

266 **Alaska Aquafarms**
P.O.Box 7
Moose Pass, AK 99631-0007 907-288-3667
Fax: 907-288-3667 jjh@seward.net
www.ternlakeinn.com
Shellfish culture gear
Owner: James Hetrick
President/CEO: Willard Fehr
Estimated Sales: $300,000-500,000
Number Employees: 1-4

267 **Alaska Bounty Seafoods & Smokery**
110 Jarvis Street
Sitka, AK 99835-9806 907-966-2927
Processor of smoked salmon
Partner: Carol Petraborg
Partner: Gerold Brager
Estimated Sales: $1-2.5 Million
Number Employees: 5-9
Type of Packaging: Consumer, Food Service, Bulk

268 **Alaska Coffee Company**
6436 Homer Dr # A
Anchorage, AK 99518-1900 907-333-3626
Fax: 907-333-3690 coffcats@alaska.net
www.espressoconsultants.com
Coffee
Owner: Lori Brewer
Estimated Sales: $280,000
Number Employees: 10-19

269 **Alaska Fresh Seafoods**
105 E Marine Way
Kodiak, AK 99615 907-486-5749
Fax: 907-486-6417
Seafood
Owner: Dave Woodruff
Treasurer: Gary Painter
Vice President: David Woodruff
Estimated Sales: $ 20 - 50 Million
Number Employees: 50-99

270 **Alaska General Seafood**
6425 NE 175th St
Kenmore, WA 98028 425-485-7755
Fax: 425-485-5172
www.alaskageneralseafoods.com
Frozen herring, canned and frozen salmon
President: Doug Souter
VP: Gordon Linquist
Estimated Sales: $20-50 Million
Number Employees: 20
Parent Co: Jim Pattison Group
Brands:
Gold Seal

271 **Alaska Herb Tea Company**
6710 Weimer Dr
Anchorage, AK 99502 907-245-3499
Fax: 907-245-3499 800-654-2764
herbtea@alaska.net www.alaskaherbtea.com
Manufacturer of tea, honey, syrups, jams and jellies, cocoa, vinegars
President: Charles Walsh
VP: Sandra Fongemie
Operations Manager: Ann Stewart
Production Manager: Maria Salizar
Estimated Sales: Less than $500,000
Number Employees: 1-4
Sq. footage: 1
Type of Packaging: Private Label
Brands:
ALASKA WILD TEAS
ALASKAN BOREAL BOUQUET
ALASKAN FIREWEED
ALASKAN GOLD
COCOALASKA

272 **Alaska Jack's Trading Post**
6251 Tuttle Pl # 102
Anchorage, AK 99507-2099 907-248-9999
Fax: 907-243-2044 888-660-2257
jack@alaskajack.com www.alaskajacks.com
Smoked salmon, chocolate, taffy, jams and jellies, salmon, gold crunch, chikoot chews, klondike krisp, sourdough starters, earthquake bar
President: Starr Horton
Sales Manager: Dave Berry
Estimated Sales: $5-10 Million
Number Employees: 20-49
Brands:
Alaska Jack's
Alaska Tea Traders

273 **Alaska Ocean Trading**
4101 Westland Cir
Anchorage, AK 99517-1430 907-243-4399
Fax: 907-243-4399
Fish and seafood
Owner: I Park
CFO: Roger Park
Estimated Sales: Under $500,000
Number Employees: 1-4

274 **Alaska Pacific Seafood**
627 Shelikof St
Kodiak, AK 99615 907-486-3234
Fax: 907-486-5164
www.northpacificseafoods.com
President: Bob Mickinovich
Plant Manager: Matthew Moir
Estimated Sales: $ 50 - 100 Million
Number Employees: 100-249
Brands:
Alaska Pacific Seafood

275 **Alaska Pasta Company**
511 W 41st Ave Ste A
Anchorage, AK 99503 907-276-2632
Fax: 907-276-2632
Pasta
Owner: Hope Nelson
Estimated Sales: $1-2.5 Million
Number Employees: 5-9

276 **Alaska Sausage and Seafood Company**
2914 Arctic Blvd
Anchorage, AK 99503 907-562-3636
Fax: 907-562-7343 800-798-3636
aks@ak.net www.alaskasausage.com
Processor of sausage, processed meats and smoked fish; exporter of smoked salmon
President: Herbert Eckmann
Secretary/Treasurer: Eva Eckmann
Quality Control Manager: Martin Eckmann
Estimated Sales: $10-20 Million
Number Employees: 20-49
Sq. footage: 10000
Type of Packaging: Consumer, Food Service, Private Label, Bulk
Brands:
Alaskan

277 **Alaska Sea Pack**
1020 M Street
Anchorage, AK 99501-3317 907-272-3474
Seafood
President: Dennis Winfree
Vice President: Robert Winfree
Estimated Sales: $10.6 Million
Number Employees: 16

278 **Alaska Seafood Company**
441 Gladys Ave
Los Angeles, CA 90013-1728 213-626-1212
Fax: 213-626-0924
Processor and wholesaler/distributor of frozen fish
President: J Joseph
Estimated Sales: $5-10 Million
Number Employees: 10-19

279 **Alaska Seafood Company**
5731 Concrete Way
Juneau, AK 99801 907-780-5111
Fax: 907-780-5140 800-451-1400
info@alaskaseafoodcompany.com
www.alaskaseafoodcompany.com
Manufacturer, wholesale co=pack, smoking, canning, retort pouches, jars
President: James Hand
Plant Manager: Jason Wiard
Estimated Sales: $1 Million
Number Employees: 10-19
Sq. footage: 10000
Type of Packaging: Consumer, Private Label
Brands:
Alaska Cannery & Smokehouse
Alaska Gold
North Pass

280 **Alaska Seafood International**
111 W 16th Ave # 200
Anchorage, AK 99501-6206 907-770-8300
Fax: 907-770-8374 800-478-2903
info@alaska-seafood.com
www.alaska-seafood.com
Organization that generically markets Alaska seafood globally
Manager: Willie Redemaker
CFO: Naresh Shrestha
Director Food Service: Claudia Hogue
Director Retail Marketing: Wain Jackson
Director Public Relations: Laura Fleming
Number Employees: 20-49
Type of Packaging: Private Label
Brands:
Alaska Seafood Products

281 **Alaska Smokehouse**
21616 87th Ave SE
Woodinville, WA 98072 360-668-9404
Fax: 360-668-1005 800-422-0852
jackp@alaskasmokehouse.com
www.alaskasmokehouse.com
Manufacturer of shelf stable smoked salmon, spreads, jerky, cookies, fruit purees and coffee.
President: Richard Anderson
SVP: Tiffany Andriesen
Estimated Sales: $1.5 Million
Number Employees: 12
Sq. footage: 15000
Type of Packaging: Consumer, Private Label
Brands:
Alaska Smokehouse
SLEEPLESS IN SEATTLE COFFEE
THE FAMOUS PACIFIC DESSERT COMPANY

282 **Alaskan Brewing Company**
5429 Shaune Dr
Juneau, AK 99801 907-780-5866
Fax: 907-780-4514 info@alaskanbeer.com
www.alaskanbeer.com
Beer
President: Geoffrey Larson
CFO/VP: Marcy Larson
COO: Linda Thomas
Plant Manager: Curtis Holmes
Estimated Sales: $20-50 Million
Number Employees: 56
Type of Packaging: Private Label
Brands:
ALASKAN AMBER
ALASKAN IPA
ALASKAN PALE
ALASKAN SMOKED PORTER
ALASKAN STOUT
ALASKAN SUMMER ALE
ALASKAN WINTER ALE

283 **Alaskan Glacier**
P.O.Box 209
Petersburg, AK 99833-0209 907-772-3333
Fax: 907-772-3330 www.norquest.com
Plant Manager: Dave Ohmer
Estimated Sales: $ 50 - 100 Million
Number Employees: 100-249

284 **Alaskan Gourmet Seafoods**
1020 International Airport Road
Anchorage, AK 99518-1005 907-563-3752
Fax: 907-563-2592 800-288-3740
akfoods@alaska.net www.alaska.net/~akfoods
Manufacturer and exporter of frozen and canned smoked halibut and salmon
President: Paul Schilling
Public Relations: John Brace
Estimated Sales: $5-10 Million
Number Employees: 18
Sq. footage: 10000
Brands:
Alaskan Gourmet

285 **Alaskan Leader Fisheries**
8874 Bender Rd Ste 201
Lynden, WA 98264 360-318-1280
Fax: 306-318-1440
www.alaskanleaderfisheries.com
Owner: Rob Wurm
Partner: Kevin O'Leary
Partner: Richard Thummel
Estimated Sales: $ .5 - 1 million
Number Employees: 1-4
Brands:
Alaskan Leader Fisheries

286 **Alaskan Smoked Salmon International**
8430 Laviento Dr
Anchorage, AK 99515-1914 907-349-8234
Fax: 907-344-7666 fis.com/alaskansmoked.com
Manufacturer of smoked salmon
President: Christopher Rosauer
Estimated Sales: $200,000
Number Employees: 4
Type of Packaging: Consumer, Food Service

287 **Alati-Caserta Desserts**
277 Rue Dante
Montreal, QC H2S 1K3
Canada 514-271-3013
Fax: 514-277-5860 info@alaticaserta.com
www.alaticaserta.com
Processor and exporter of desserts including almond cakes, cannoli ricotta and chocolate mousse
President: Vittorio Caldarone
Co-Owner: Marco Caldarone
Estimated Sales: $243,000
Number Employees: 6
Type of Packaging: Food Service
Brands:
Alati-Casserta

288 **Alba Vineyard**
269 Route 627
Milford, NJ 08848-1771 908-995-7800
Fax: 908-995-7155 albavineyard@enter.net
www.albavineyard.com
Wines
President/Owner: Thomas Sharko
Partner: Rudy Marchesi

Estimated Sales: $2.5-5 Million
Number Employees: 5-9
Type of Packaging: Private Label, Bulk
Brands:
ALBA

289 **Albanese Confectionery Group**
5441 E Lincoln Hwy
Merrillville, IN 46410 219-769-6887
Fax: 219-769-6897 800-536-0581
sales@albaneseconfectionery.com
www.albaneseconfectionery.com
Chocolate covered nut candies and gummi's
President: Scott Albanese
Vice President: Richard Albanese
Purchasing: Alan Levinson
Estimated Sales: $5-10 Million
Number Employees: 10-19
Other Locations:
Hobart Manufacturing Facility
Hobart IN

290 **Albert's Meats**
2992 Green Valley Rd
Claysville, PA 15323 724-948-3321
Fax: 724-948-3340 800-522-9970
brian@albertsmeats.com www.albertsmeats.com
Fresh and cooked sausage, lower sodium hams and lunch meats
Owner: George P Weiss
Sales Manager: Brian Weiss
Estimated Sales: $20-50 Million
Number Employees: 50-99
Type of Packaging: Consumer

291 **Alberta Cheese Company**
8420 26th Street SE
Calgary, AB T2C 1C7
Canada 403-279-4353
Fax: 403-279-4795
Manufacturer of cheese including specialty, mozzarella, ricotta, cheddar, feta, provolone and monterey jack
President: Frank Talarico
Sales Manager/GM: Michael Talarico
Estimated Sales: E
Number Employees: 20
Type of Packaging: Consumer, Food Service
Brands:
Franco's
Sorento

292 **(HQ)Alberto-Culver Company**
2525 Armitage Ave
Melrose Park, IL 60160 708-450-3000
Fax: 708-450-3409 crelations@alberto.com
www.alberto.com
Manufactures cooking spray, butter, sour cream, cheese and sugar substitutes.
President/CEO/Director: V James Marino
EVP/CFO: Ralph Nicoletti
SVP/General Counsel: Gary Schmidt
Estimated Sales: $1.6 Billion
Number Employees: 2,600
Number of Brands: 5
Type of Packaging: Consumer
Brands:
BAKER'S JOY
MOLLY MCBUTTER
MRS DASH
SUGAR TWIN

293 **Albertson's Bakery**
42095 Washington St
Palm Desert, CA 92211-8017 760-360-6322
Fax: 760-345-6842 www.albertsons.com
Manager: Andrea Balmer
Member: Virginia Surrell
Estimated Sales: $ 20 - 50 Million
Number Employees: 100-249
Brands:
Albertson's

294 **Albion Laboratories**
101 N Main St
Clearfield, UT 84015 801-773-4631
Fax: 801-773-4633 866-243-5283
albionlabs@aol.com www.albionlabs.com
Manufacturer and exporter of nutritional mineral supplements including amino acid chelates, vitamin complexes, etc.
President: Duane Ashmead
CFO: Charles Whiting
Sales/Marketing: Ronald Wheelwright
Purchasing Manager: Brett Ashmead
Number Employees: 20-49
Type of Packaging: Consumer, Bulk
Brands:
Albion
Chela-Zone
Chelavite
Chelazome
Metalosate

295 **Alca Trading Co.**
5301 Blue Lagoon Dr Ste 570
Miami, FL 33126 305-265-8331
Supplier of banana juices and mango purees.

296 **Alcan Chemical**
333 Ludlow St # 6
Stamford, CT 06902-6991 203-541-9000
Fax: 203-541-9191 800-736-7893
chemicals@alcan.com www.alcan.com
Processor and exporter of Chemical Products, Active Pharmaceutical Ingredients (APIs), to the Pharmaceutical, Personal Care, Cosmetic, Nutritional and Industrial markets
President: Jeanpierre Paillot
Estimated Sales: $ 10 - 20 Million
Number Employees: 100-249
Parent Co: Alcan International Network USA

297 **Alcester Meats**
PO Box 472
Alcester, SD 57001-0472 605-934-2540
Fax: 605-934-2616 qualitypork@acsnet.com
Fresh and frozen pork products
President/Owner: Doug Thompson
General Sales Manager: Doug Jensen
Accounts Manager: Gloria Thompson
Estimated Sales: $20-50 Million
Number Employees: 50-99
Number of Brands: 1

298 **Alder Springs Smoked Salmon**
PO Box 97
Sequim, WA 98382-0097 360-683-2829
Fax: 360-683-5359 alder@olypen.com
Manufacturer of smoked salmon, salmon jerky, oysters, cod and trout
Owner: Robert Bearden
Estimated Sales: Less than $500,000
Number Employees: 1-4
Type of Packaging: Private Label
Brands:
Alder Springs

299 **Alderfer Bologna**
382 Main Street
PO Box 2
Harleysville, PA 19438 215-256-8818
Fax: 215-256-6120 800-341-1121
comments@alderfermeats.com
www.alderfermeats.com
Pork, beef and turkey products
President/CEO: Jim Van Stone
CFO: Sandy Sloyer
Marketing Manager: Samantha Alderfer
Sales Executive: Chet Dudzinski
Human Resources Manager: Janise Stauffer
Plant Manager: Brent Shoemaker
Purchasing Manager: Ray Ganser
Estimated Sales: $12 Million
Number Employees: 120
Number of Brands: 1
Number of Products: 300
Sq. footage: 30000
Type of Packaging: Consumer, Food Service, Private Label, Bulk
Brands:
ALDERFER
LEIDY'S

300 **AleSmith Brewing Company**
9368 Cabot Dr
San Diego, CA 92126 858-549-9888
Fax: 858-549-1052 peter@alesmith.com
www.alesmith.com
Manufacturer of ale including seasonal
Owner: Peter Zien
Estimated Sales: $ 3 - 5 Million
Number Employees: 1-4
Sq. footage: 3200
Type of Packaging: Food Service, Bulk

301 **Alessi Bakery**
2909 W Cypress St
Tampa, FL 33609 813-879-4544
Fax: 813-872-9103 www.alessibakeries.com
Manufacturer of tortes, pastry desserts, cakes, cookies
President: Phil Alessi
CFO: Debrah Herman
Estimated Sales: $5-10 Million
Number Employees: 70
Sq. footage: 15000
Type of Packaging: Consumer, Food Service
Brands:
Alessi Bakery

302 **Alewel's Country Meats**
911 N Simpson Dr
Warrensburg, MO 64093 660-747-8261
Fax: 660-747-1857 800-353-8553
alewels@sprintmail.com
www.country-meats.com
Manufacturer of dry, shelf stable, game and summer sausage, and game jerky including deer and buffalo. Cured meat mail order operation, custom processing and catering-whole hog specialties available
President: Roger Alewel
Estimated Sales: $2.5-5 Million
Number Employees: 5-9
Sq. footage: 5000
Type of Packaging: Consumer, Food Service, Private Label, Bulk
Brands:
Alewel's Country Meats
Grandpa A'S

303 **Alex Froehlich Packing Company**
77 D Street Ext
Johnstown, PA 15906 814-535-7694
Fax: 814-535-7695
Livestock processor
President: E Froehlich
VP: David Froehlich
Estimated Sales: $5-10 Million
Number Employees: 10-19
Type of Packaging: Bulk
Other Locations:
Alex Froelich Packing Company
Johnstown PA

304 **(HQ)Alexander & Baldwin**
822 Bishop St
Honolulu, HI 96813 808-525-6611
Fax: 808-525-6652 www.alexanderbaldwin.com
Manufacturer of molasses, raw sugar and coffee
President: Norbert Buelsing
Pres/Ceo: Stanley Kuriyama
Sr VP/CFO: Christopher Benjamin
Estimated Sales: $1.6 Billion
Number Employees: 14,400
Type of Packaging: Consumer, Food Service, Bulk
Brands:
Kauai Coffee
Maui Sugar

305 **Alexander Gourmet Imports**
16431 Airport Road
Caledon, ON L7C 2Y2
Canada 905-361-2577
Fax: 905-282-0601 800-265-5081
info@alexanderstea.com
www.alexanderstea.com
Full range of tea production: flavouring, blending, tea bagging, loose tea packaging and gift selections. Experienced in packing flavoured, estate, herbal, medicinal and organic teas.
President: Dave Elliott
Estimated Sales: $3.5 Million
Number Employees: 60+
Number of Brands: 6
Sq. footage: 30000
Type of Packaging: Consumer, Food Service, Private Label, Bulk
Brands:
Alexander's Gourmet Tea
Cocoa Creations
Herbal Teazers

306 **Alexander International(USA)**
132 Concourse East
Brightwaters, NY 11718 866-965-0143
service@alexander-usa.com
www.alexander-usa.com
Drink mixes, herbs and spices, olive and other oils

307 **Alexander Johnson's Valley Wines**
8333 Highway 128
Healdsburg, CA 95448-9639 707-433-2319
Fax: 707-433-5302 800-888-5532
johnsons@funvacation.net
www.johnsonsavwines.com
Wines
President: Ellen Johnson
Estimated Sales: $1-2.5 Million
Number Employees: 1-4
Brands:
Johnson's Alexander Valley

308 **Alexandra & Nicolay**
2607 Nostrand Ave # 2
Brooklyn, NY 11210-4695 718-253-9400
Fax: 718-331-4986
info@alexandraandnicolay.com
www.alexandraandnicolay.com
Manufacturer of chocolates in milk, white and dark
Founder: Alexandra Mazhirov
Founder: Nicolay Mazhirov
Estimated Sales: $300,000-500,000
Number Employees: 5-9

309 **Alexia Foods**
5102 21st St Ste 3b
Long Island City, NY 11101 718-937-0100
Fax: 718-937-0110 info@alexiafoods.com
www.alexiafoods.com
Manufacturer of frozen potato products including artisan breads, oven blends, onion rings, organic products, mashed potatoes, oven fries and oven reds, julienne fries, and appetizers.
President: Alex Dzieduszycki
CEO: Alex Dzieduscycki
Estimated Sales: G
Type of Packaging: Food Service

310 **Alexian Pates/GroezingerProvisions**
1200 7th Ave
Neptune, NJ 07753-5190 732-775-3220
Fax: 732-775-3223 800-927-9473
donna@alexianpate.com www.alexianpate.com
Specialty meats and sausages. All natural preservative free pates and mousses; pork, poultry, vegetarian and vegan pates.
President: Laurie Groezinger
Estimated Sales: $10-20 Million
Number Employees: 10-19
Type of Packaging: Private Label

311 **Alexis Bailly Vineyard**
18200 Kirby Ave S
Hastings, MN 55033 651-437-1413
www.abvwines.com
Wines
Founder: David Bailly
Owner/CEO: Nan Bailly
Master Winemaker: Nan Bailly
Estimated Sales: $500,000-$1 Million
Number Employees: 1-4
Type of Packaging: Consumer, Private Label
Brands:
ALEXIS BAILLY

312 **Alfer Laboratories**
9566 Vassar Ave
Chatsworth, CA 91311-4141 818-709-0737
Fax: 818-709-5360
Processor of nutritional supplements and vitamins including liquid cal-mag, acidophilus cultures and aloe vera gels/juices
President: Ines Gutierrez
Purchasing Manager: Ines Gutierrez
Estimated Sales: $2.5-5 Million
Number Employees: 5-9
Type of Packaging: Private Label

313 **Alfonso Gourmet Pasta**
2211 NW 30th Pl
Pompano Beach, FL 33069 954-960-1010
Fax: 954-974-2773 800-370-7278
customerservice@alfonsogourmetpasta.com
www.alfonsogourmetpasta.com
Manufacturer and exporter of gourmet ravioli and prepared foods including fresh, frozen and processed
President: David Ruiz
Estimated Sales: $2.5 Million
Number Employees: 22
Sq. footage: 12000
Type of Packaging: Food Service
Brands:
ALFONSO GOURMET PASTA

314 **Alfred & Sam Italian Bakery**
17 Fairview Ave
Lancaster, PA 17603 717-392-6311
Fax: 717-392-6311
Manufacturer of rolls, breads, cannolis and cookies
President: Salvatore Borsellino
Owner: Sam Borsellino
Estimated Sales: $500,000-$1 Million
Number Employees: 10-19
Type of Packaging: Consumer
Brands:
Alfred & Sam's

315 **Alfred L. Wolff, Inc.**
1440 N Northwest Hwy # 230
Park Ridge, IL 60068 847-759-8888
Fax: 312-265-9888 tmwolffus@sbcglobal.net
www.alwolff.com
Importer of dehydrated vegetables, herbs, honey and other bee products including royal jelly, bee pollen and propolis; also, gum arabic, acidulating agents and nutritional fiber
General Manager: Magnus von Buddenbrock
Estimated Sales: $5 Million
Number Employees: 3
Parent Co: Alfred L. Wolff GmbH
Type of Packaging: Bulk
Brands:
BIG ONION
FINEST HONEY ORGANIC
FINEST HONEY SELECTION
QSLIC
QUICK ACID
QUICK CHEW
QUICK COAT
QUICK FIBRE
QUICK GLANZ
QUICK GUM
QUICK LAC
QUICK OIL
QUICK SHINE
SHELLAC

316 **Alfred Louie**
4501 Shepard St
Bakersfield, CA 93313 661-831-2520
Fax: 805-833-9197
Fruits and vegetables, pasta, and Chinese canned goods and vegetables.
President: Susan Louie
Estimated Sales: $5,115,628
Number Employees: 12

317 **Alfredo's Italian FoodsManufacturing Company**
122 Water St
Quincy, MA 02169-6661 617-479-6360
Fax: 617-773-3342 www.aapasta.com
Processor of fresh lasagna, ravioli, cavatelli, tortellini, fettuccini
President: Peter Aiello
Operations Manager: Lino Aiello
Purchasing Manager: John Lucca
Estimated Sales: $5-10 Million
Number Employees: 20-49
Type of Packaging: Consumer, Food Service, Private Label, Bulk
Brands:
ALFREDO

318 **Algood Food Company**
7401 Trade Port Dr
Louisville, KY 40258 502-637-1401
Fax: 502-637-1502 wphilpot@algoodfood.com
www.algoodfood.com
Processor and exporter of peanut butter, jams, jellies and preserves
President: Cecil Barnett
VP: Kathy Powell
CEO: Kathy Powell
VP: Nicolas Melhuish
Quality/Technical Service: Dan Schmidt
VP Sales: Melhuish
VP Sales: Nick Melhuish
Plant Manager: David Temple
Purchasing Manager: David Frantz
Estimated Sales: $100+ Million
Number Employees: 100-249
Sq. footage: 100000
Brands:
ALGOOD BLUE LABEL
ALGOOD JELLY
ALGOOD MARMALADE
ALGOOD OLD FASHIONED
ALGOOD PRESERVES
ALGOOD RED LABEL
CAP 'N KID

319 **Alicita-Salsa**
737 Walker Road
Suite 2, Po Box 1064
Great Falls, VA 22066 703-406-1275
Fax: 703-406-1276 www.alicitasalsa.com
Dairy-free, gluten-free, sugar-free, vegetarian, salsa/dips, other sauces, seasonings and cooking enhancers, other snacks, other vegetables/fruit.
Marketing: Suzanne Fields

320 **Alimentaire Whyte's Inc**
1540 Rue Des Patriotes
Laval, QC H7L 2N6
Canada 450-625-1976
Fax: 450-625-9295 800-625-1979
www.whytes.ca
Sauces, cherries, olives, condiments, relish, cooking oils, and table syrup
President: Paul Kawaja
Estimated Sales: $32.52 Million
Number Employees: 100
Sq. footage: 250000

321 **Alimentos Bermudez**
1900 Linden Boulevard
Brooklyn, NY 11207 347-533-2230
cphilip@bermudezcaribbean.com
Chips and a full line of snacks
Marketing Contact: Caleb Philip

322 **Alimentos Naturales Sabrosa, SA de CV**
2935 Thousand Oaks Drive
Suite 6-142
San Antonio, TX 78247-3312 210-545-1792
Fax: 210-545-1792 foodtek@satx.rr.com
www.lasabrosa.com

323 **Aliments Jolibec**
149 Montee Allard
St Jacques De Montcalm, QC J0K 2R0
Canada 514-861-6082
Manufacturer of fresh and frozen pork
President: Roger Ethier
Number Employees: 43
Type of Packaging: Bulk

324 **Aliments Prince Foods**
11053 Louis H Lafontaine
Anjou, QC H1S 2Z4
Canada 450-771-0400
Fax: 450-771-4872 800-361-3898
princef@odyssee.net www.princefoods.com
Manufacturer of bacon, ham and sausages
President: Marcel Heroux
GM: Alain Heroux
Director Sales: Sylvain Blais
Number Employees: 800
Type of Packaging: Consumer, Food Service, Private Label

325 **Aliments Trigone**
93 Ch De L'Aqueduc Rr 1
St-Francois-De-La-Rivier, QC G0R 3A0
Canada 418-259-7414
Fax: 418-259-2417 877-259-7491
bio@alimentstrigone.com
www.alimentstrigone.com
Manufacturer of buckwheat and shelled hempseeds.
President: Jacques Cote

Estimated Sales: $1.3 Million
Number Employees: 9
Brands:
Trigone

326 **Aliotti Wholesale Fish Company**
2 Wharf II
Monterey, CA 93940 831-375-2881
Fax: 831-375-4285
Processor and exporter of frozen squid
President: Jospeh Aliotii
Purchasing: Joe Aliotti
Estimated Sales: $2.7 Million
Number Employees: 8
Type of Packaging: Food Service
Brands:
PRIMA QUALITY

327 **Alkinco**
129 W 29th St # 5
New York, NY 10001-5105 212-719-3070
Fax: 212-764-7804 800-424-7118
custser@alkincohair.com www.alkincohair.com
Processor of beverage mixes including sugared, chocolate and weight control; also, protein supplements
President: Julius Klugman
VP: Stewart Hoffman
Estimated Sales: $5-10 Million
Number Employees: 20-49
Sq. footage: 50000
Type of Packaging: Consumer, Private Label
Brands:
Alkinco

328 **All About Lollipops**
12155 Kirkham Road
Poway, CA 92064-6870 208-333-9896
Fax: 208-333-9938 866-475-6554
Candy
Owner: Robert Maire
Sales Manager: Lannie Davis
Plant Manager: Bill Cole
Number Employees: 25
Brands:
BIG BUNNY POP
BIG FAT TOAD POP
BIG HEART POP
BIG LIPS POP
BIG PUMPKIN POP
BIG SKULL POP
DOUBLE DIP POP
HAND MADE BALL POP
JOLLY SANTA POP
LUCKY POP
SOUR BALL POP
SOUR BRAINS POP

329 **All American Foods, Inc.**
121 Mohr Drive
Box 8242
Mankato, MN 56002-8242 507-387-6480
Fax: 507-387-6111 800-833-2661
info@aafoods.com www.aafoods.com
One-for-one replacements for dairy commodities, dairy blends, nondairy blends, kosher parve, milk replacers and dry dairy ingredients
President: Keith Brekke
CEO: Jeff Thom
CFO: Kevin Olson
CEO: Jeff Thom
QA Director: Shawn Schlueter
Market Development Director: Rod Mitchell
National Sales Manager: Chad Anderson
Operations Director: Connie Stokman
Estimated Sales: $20 Million
Number Employees: 100-249
Number of Brands: 1
Number of Products: 150
Sq. footage: 80000
Parent Co: All American Foods
Type of Packaging: Private Label, Bulk

330 **All American Seasonings**
10600 E 54th Ave Unit B
Denver, CO 80239 303-574-9223
Fax: 303-623-1920
info@allamericanseasonings.com
www.allamericanseasonings.com
Manufacturer of custom blended seasonings and spices
Manager: Eric Willy
Marketing Director: Joseph Gallagher
Estimated Sales: $12 Million
Number Employees: 20-49
Sq. footage: 40000
Type of Packaging: Consumer, Food Service, Private Label, Bulk
Brands:
ALL AMERICAN

331 **All American Snacks**
P.O.Box 3
Midland, TX 79702 432-687-6666
Fax: 915-699-2305 800-840-2455
www.allamericansnacks.com
White chocolate hand-stirred into crisp cereals, pretzels and pecan halves
Owner/Public Relations: Lexie Kauffman
Co-Owner/Manager: Sheri Brockett
Sales Director: Kimberlea Bryand
Estimated Sales: $5-10 Million
Number Employees: 20-49
Brands:
All American Afternoon Delight
All American Precious Stones
All American White Trash

332 **All Goode Organics**
PO Box 61256
Santa Barbara, CA 93160-1256 805-683-3370
Fax: 805-683-7669 k-everard@home.com
www.allgoodorganics.com
Organic foods, herbal teas

333 **All Juice Food & Beverage**
352 Jet St
Hendersonville, NC 28792 828-685-8821
Fax: 828-685-8495 800-736-5674
www.mrsclarks.com
Beverages, apple juice
President: Ron Kahrer
Plant Manager: John Weber
Number Employees: 20-49

334 **All Round Foods**
437 Railroad Ave
Westbury, NY 11590-4314 516-338-1888
Fax: 516-939-2338
Processor and exporter of frozen doughnuts including plain, glazed, sugar, cinnamon, jelly, etc.
Owner: Glen Wolther
Executive VP: Robert Glasser
VP: Glenn Wolther
Purchasing: Steven Finkelstein
Estimated Sales: $ 3 - 5 Million
Number Employees: 1-4
Sq. footage: 84000
Type of Packaging: Food Service
Brands:
ALL ROUND FOODS

335 **All Seasons International Distributors**
650 Park East Blvd
New Albany, IN 47150 812-949-1898
President: Michael Tao
Vice President: Richard Tao
Estimated Sales: $ 2.60 Million

336 **All Wrapped Up**
801 W Tropical Way
Plantation, FL 33317 954-587-2111
Fax: 954-587-2144 800-891-2194
info@allwrappedup-gifts.com
www.allwrappedup-gifts.com
Candies, cookies, chocolates, nuts, and pretzels, professionally wrapped
President/CEO: Pam Schwimmer
VP: Donna Merill
VP Marketing: Donna Merill
Operations Manager: Pam Schwimmer
Estimated Sales: Less than $500,000
Number Employees: 5-9
Type of Packaging: Consumer, Private Label

337 **All-States Quality Foods**
901 N Main Street
Charles City, IA 50616-0365 641-228-5023
Fax: 641-228-2624 800-247-4195
Processor of chicken products including broth, rendered fat, diced cooked meat and turkey and chicken quesadillas.
President: Elliot Jones
Marketing Director: Steve Tenney
Operations Manager: Dan Anderegg
Estimated Sales: $17 Million
Number Employees: 150
Number of Products: 10
Type of Packaging: Consumer, Food Service, Private Label, Bulk

338 **Allann Brothers Coffee Company**
1852 Fescue St SE
Albany, OR 97322 541-812-8000
Fax: 541-812-8010 800-926-6886
info@entnerstuartsyrups.com
www.allannbroscoffee.com
Coffee and teas
President: A Stuart
Sales Director: Michael Harris
Estimated Sales: Less than $500,000
Number Employees: 10-19
Type of Packaging: Consumer, Food Service, Private Label, Bulk

339 **Alldrin Brothers**
P.O.Box 10
Ballico, CA 95303-0010 209-667-1600
Fax: 209-667-0463 sales@almondcafe.com
www.almondcafe.com
Processor and exporter of almonds
President: Gary Alldrin
Purchasing Manager: Gary Alldrin
Estimated Sales: $1-2.5 Million
Number Employees: 50-99
Type of Packaging: Bulk
Brands:
ALLDRIN

340 **(HQ)Alle Processing**
5620 59th St
Maspeth, NY 11378 718-894-2000
Fax: 718-326-4642 www.alleprocessing.com
Processor of kosher fresh and frozen beef, lamb, veal and poultry, fish, vegetables and frozen vegetarian entrees; importer of puff pastry products; exporter of kosher frozen vegetable entrees
President: Albert Weinstock
CEO: Sam Hollander
VP Sales/Marketing: Shlomi Pilo
Estimated Sales: $44 Million
Number Employees: 250
Sq. footage: 150000
Type of Packaging: Consumer, Food Service, Private Label, Bulk
Other Locations:
Alle Processing
Maspeth NY
Brands:
GLATT KOSHER
MEAL MART
MON CUISINE
NEW YORK KOSHER DELI
PASSOVER
SCHREIBER

341 **Alle Processing Corporation**
5620 59th St
Maspeth, NY 11378 718-894-2000
Fax: 718-326-4642 800-245-5620
ezs@alleprocessing.com
www.alleprocessing.com
Processor and exporter of kosher food products including meat analogs, luncheon meats, frankfurters and microwaveable vegetarian meals
President: Albert WeinStreetock
CEO: Sam Hollander
Vice President: Shlomi Pilo
Chief Technology Officer: Israel Gross
Estimated Sales: $44 Million
Number Employees: 250
Sq. footage: 150000
Type of Packaging: Food Service
Brands:
Meal Mart
New York Kosher Deli
Schrieber Meatless Meats

342 **Alleghany's Fish Farm**
2755 Route 281
Saint Philemon, QC G0R 4A0
Canada 418-469-2823
Fax: 418-469-2872 alleghan@globetrotter.net
Manufacturer of live trout eggs
GM: Yves Boulanger
Estimated Sales: $1-5 Million
Number Employees: 22
Type of Packaging: Consumer, Food Service

Brands:
Alleghanys

343 **Allegria**
233 E Weddell Dr Ste I
Sunnyvale, CA 94089 408-734-4300
Fax: 408-734-2444 800-467-8648
Bakers of traditional ethnic specialties since 1984.
President: G Giurlani
CFO: Claire Baxter
Marketing Director: R Giurlani
Plant Manager: G Portida
Purchasing Manager: G Giurlani
Estimated Sales: $ 5 - 10 Million
Number Employees: 10-19
Type of Packaging: Consumer, Food Service, Private Label, Bulk

344 **Allegro Coffee Company**
12799 Claude Ct
Thornton, CO 80241 303-444-4844
Fax: 303-920-5468 800-666-4869
prodinfo@allegro-coffee.com
www.allegrocoffee.com
Manufacturer, importer and wholesaler/distributor of roasted specialty coffees; importer of green coffee beans
President/General Manager: Jeff Teter
CFO: Clarence Peterson
VP: David Kubena
Marketing Director: Tara Cross
Sales Director: Glenda Chamberlain
Human Resources Director: Mimi Fins
Plant Operations Manager: Alejandro Rodolfo
Marketing/Purchasing Manager: Susan Drexel
Estimated Sales: F
Number Employees: 50
Sq. footage: 25000
Brands:
Allegro Coffee
Allegro Tea
Organic Coffee

345 **Allegro Fine Foods**
1595 Highway 218 Bypass
PO Box 1262
Paris, TN 38242 731-642-6113
Fax: 731-642-6116 info@allegromarinade.com
www.allegromarinade.com
Processor and exporter of meat and vegetable marinades
President: John Fuqua
VP: Thomas Harrison
Quality Assurance Manager: Marti Jones
Marketing Manager: Tim Phifer
VP Operations: Stan Nelms
Purchasing: Melanie Mathis
Estimated Sales: $3 Million
Number Employees: 30
Sq. footage: 20000
Type of Packaging: Consumer, Food Service, Private Label, Bulk
Brands:
ALLEGRO

346 **Allegro Vineyards**
3475 Sechrist Rd
Brogue, PA 17309 717-927-9148
Fax: 717-927-1521 info@allegrowines.com
www.allegrowines.com
Wines
Owner: Kris Miller
Owner: Carl Helrich
Estimated Sales: $500,000-$1 Million
Number Employees: 1-4
Sq. footage: 4000
Brands:
ALLEGRO

347 **Allen & Cowley SpecialtyFoods**
4053 E Washington St
Phoenix, AZ 85034-1819 602-275-9211
Fax: 602-275-9600 800-279-1634
info@allen-cowley.com www.allen-cowley.com
Crackers, croutons, herbs, spices and spreads.
Owner: Allen Sweat
Vice President: Michael Cowley
Sales Manager: Lindsey Wescott
Production Manager: JT Howard
Purchasing Manager: Lee Allen
Estimated Sales: $500,000-$1 Million
Number Employees: 20-49
Type of Packaging: Consumer, Food Service
Brands:
DUST
STARR RIDGE

348 **Allen Canning Company**
305 E Main St
Siloam Springs, AR 72761 479-524-6431
Fax: 479-524-3291 800-234-2553
www.allencanning.com
Processor and exporter of canned beans, carrots, peas, greens, hominy, kale, lentils, okra, potatoes, spinach, squash, turnips and snack foods
President: Rick Allen, Jr.
Chairman/CEO: Rick Allen
Executive Vice President: Nick Allen
Executive Vice President: Josh Allen
Quality Control: Earl Wells
Senior VP Sales/Marketing: Mike Hubbard
Government Relations: Robert Stephenson
COO: Jim Robason
Estimated Sales: $50-100 Million
Number Employees: 1,000-4,999
Number of Brands: 13
Type of Packaging: Consumer, Food Service, Private Label, Bulk
Brands:
ALLENS
ALLENS ITALIAN GREEN BEANS
BUTTERFIELD
EAST TEXAS FAIR
FRESHLIKE
POPEYE
PRINCELLA
ROYAL PRINCE
SUGARY SAM
SUNSHINE
TRAPPEYS
VEG-ALL
WAGON MASTER

349 **(HQ)Allen Family Foods**
126 N Shipley St
Seaford, DE 19973 302-629-9136
Fax: 302-629-5081
affeob@allenfamilyfoods.com
www.allenfamilyfoods.com
Processor of poultry products including frozen parts and whole birds; exporter of frozen poultry items
President: Charles C Allen Iii III
Chairman/CEO: Charles Allen
Quality Control: Sharen Nowak
VP Sales/Marketing: Chuck Kucharik
Plant Manager (Cordova, MD): Terry Nichols
Plant Manager (Harbeson, DE): Buck Korneman
Purchasing Agent: Gary Lacher
Estimated Sales: $400 Million
Number Employees: 100-249
Type of Packaging: Consumer, Food Service, Private Label, Bulk
Other Locations:
Allen Family Foods
Delmar DE
Allen Family Foods
Hurlock MD
Allen Family Foods
Linkwood MD
Brands:
ALLENS

350 **(HQ)Allen Flavors**
23 Progress St
Edison, NJ 8820 908-561-5995
Fax: 908-561-4164 info@allenflavors.com
www.allenflavors.com
Tea Essences, Instant Teas, Instant Coffees and Coffee Extracts.
President: Joseph Allen
VP: Michele Allen
Research Director: Harvey Krohn
Quality Control Director: Dr Donald Mull
VP Sales: Joe Moran
VP Operations: Al Handel
Plant Manager: Tony Parada
Estimated Sales: $10-20 Million
Number Employees: 20-49
Sq. footage: 4000
Brands:
ALLEN

351 **Allen's Blueberry Freezer**
244 Main Street
Ellsworth, ME 04605 207-667-5561
Fax: 207-667-8315 www.allensblueberries.com
Frozen wild blueberries.
President: Roy Allen II
Secretary: Kim Allen
Sales: Kim Allen-Wadman
Estimated Sales: $ 10 - 20 Million
Number Employees: 10-19
Type of Packaging: Consumer, Food Service
Brands:
ALLEN'S

352 **Allen's Blueberry Freezer**
244 Main St
Ellsworth, ME 4605 207-667-5561
Fax: 207-667-8315 info@allensblueberries.com
www.allensblueberries.com
Frozen blueberries
President/CEO: George Allen
CEO/Plant Manager: Roy Allen
Estimated Sales: $10-20 Million
Number Employees: 25
Type of Packaging: Private Label
Brands:
ALLEN'S

353 **Allen's Naturally**
PO Box 514
Farmington, MI 48332-0514
Fax: 248-449-7709 800-352-8971
info@allensnaturally.com
www.allensnaturally.com
Biodegradable dishwashing liquid
Purchasing Manager: W Allen Conlon
Estimated Sales: $2.5-5 Million
Number Employees: 1-4
Brands:
ALLENS NATURALLY

354 **Allen's Pickle Works**
36 Garvies Point Rd
Glen Cove, NY 11542 516-676-0640
Fax: 516-759-5780 bgpickl@aol.com
Processor of cold packed sour dill and half sour pickles including whole, spears and chips
President: Ronald Horman
Purchasing: Ronald Horman
Estimated Sales: $2.5-5 Million
Number Employees: 10-19
Sq. footage: 18000
Type of Packaging: Private Label
Brands:
ALLENS
ALMA
BUTTERFIELD
CLEAR SAILING

355 **Alley Kat Brewing Co, Lt**
9929-60th Avenue
Edmonton, AB T6E 0C7
Canada 780-436-8922
Fax: 780-430-7363 thekats@alleykatbeer.com
www.alleykatbeer.com
Manufacturer of beer, ale, lager and stout
Co-Owner: Neil Herbst
Co-Owner: Lavonne Herbst
Sales Director: Christopher Ducharme
Estimated Sales: B
Number Employees: 8
Sq. footage: 3750
Type of Packaging: Consumer, Food Service
Brands:
Alley Kat Amber
Aprikat
CHARLIE FLINT'S ORIGINAL LAGER
EIN PROSIT!
FULL MOON PALE ALE
OLDE DEUTERONOMY
RAZZYKAT
SMOKED PORTER
ST. PADDY'S
WEIHNACHTSKATZE

356 **Allfresh Food Products**
2156 Green Bay Rd
Evanston, IL 60201 773-273-2343
Fax: 847-869-3103
Processor of butter blends, margarine, shortening and vegetable oil
President: Gulshan Wadhwa
VP: Anil Wadhwa
Purchasing Manager: Gulshan Wadhwa
Estimated Sales: $5-10 Million
Number Employees: 5-9
Parent Co: Food Corporation of America
Type of Packaging: Consumer, Food Service

Brands:
ALL FRESH
BIG BOY
BUCKSON
FARMER BROTHERS
TOP NOTCH

357 **Allied Blending & Ingredients**
121 Royal Road
Keokuk, IA 52632 319-526-6448
Fax: 319-538-0178 800-526-8102
www.alliedblending.com
Anti-caking agents, food stabilizers, preservative & shelf life extenders, specialty starches and tortilla blends and concentrates.
President: Randy Schmelzel
Vice President Technical Services: John Fannon, PhD
Vice President, Operations: Matt Stelzer
Vice President], Purchasing: Stephanie Slattery
Number Employees: 50-99
Sq. footage: 1200

358 **(HQ)Allied Custom Gypsum Company**
1550 Double C Dr
Norman, OK 73069-8288
Fax: 405-366-9515 800-624-5963
customerservice@alliedcustomgypsum.com
www.alliedcustomgypsum.com
Food and pharmaceutical grade calcium sulfate-odorless, tasteless white powder from a select high purity gypsum deposit. Used as a calcium fortificant, dough conditioner, yeast food, water conditioner, brewing aid, in specialty mixesand dry blended products, tofu, milk replacers, and dietary supplements.
Manager: Tracy Shirley
CFO: Tracy Shirley III
Executive VP: Dan Northcutt
VP Operations: Kris Kinder
Estimated Sales: $1-5 Million
Number Employees: 10-19
Number of Products: 1
Sq. footage: 50000
Parent Co: Harrison Gypsum
Type of Packaging: Food Service
Brands:
ACG
ACG BROADCAST GYPSUM
TERRA ALBA
VALU-FIL

359 **Allied Food Products**
251 Saint Marks Ave
Brooklyn, NY 11238
www.alliedfoodproducts.com
Manager: Ernest Stern
Estimated Sales: $1-2.5 Million
Number Employees: 5-9
Brands:
E&S Vanilla Sugar

360 **Allied Meat Service**
25447 Industrial Blvd
Hayward, CA 94545-2931 510-351-6677
Fax: 510-481-7877 800-794-2554
tremington@alliedmeatservice.com
www.alliedmeatservice.com
Beef and beef products
President: Greg Nigro
Marketing Director: Akane Nigro
CEO: Greg Nigro
Estimated Sales: $20-50 Million
Number Employees: 20-49
Brands:
Aidells
Farmland
Millers
Saralee
Silva
Simplot

361 **Allied Old English**
100 Markley St
Port Reading, NJ 7064 732-636-2060
Fax: 732-636-2538 info@alliedoldenglish.com
www.alliedoldenglish.com
Processor and exporter of Oriental prepared foods including noodles and sauces; also, pancake syrup, molasses, salad dressings, jams, jellies, preserves, salsa and barbecue sauce
CEO: Sharon O'Brien
CFO: Frank Gatti
Director of Quality Control: Josie Alves
National Sales Manager: Dale Allen
Human Resources Manager: JoAnn Tedesco
COO: Steve Owens
Production Supervisor: Eddie Richardson
Plant Engineer: Rick McGlynn
VP Purchasing: Bobbi James
Estimated Sales: $8 Million
Number Employees: 70
Sq. footage: 63000
Type of Packaging: Consumer, Food Service, Private Label, Bulk
Brands:
Ah-So
China Pride
Dai Dairy
Mee Tu
Plantation
Polynesian
Rio Grande
Saucy Susan

362 **Allied Wine Corporation**
2 Fairground Rd
Monticello, NY 12701 845-796-4160
Fax: 845-796-4161 armonwine@verizon.net
http://www.verizon.net
Processor, importer and exporter of kosher wines and spirits
Manager: David Fieldman
VP: Herman Schwartz
Estimated Sales: $500,000-$1 Million
Number Employees: 1-4
Type of Packaging: Food Service, Private Label
Brands:
Armon

363 **Alliston Creamery & Dairy**
26 Dominion Street
Alliston, ON L9R 1L5
Canada 705-435-6751
Fax: 705-435-6797
Manufacturer of butter; organic butter, whey butter and occassionally goat butter
President: David Kennedy
Number Employees: 9
Sq. footage: 15000
Type of Packaging: Consumer, Food Service, Private Label, Bulk
Brands:
Golden Dawn

364 **(HQ)Alljuice**
352 Jet St
Hendersonville, NC 28792-8004 828-685-8821
Fax: 828-685-8495 800-736-5674
www.mrsclarks.com
Processor of shelf-stable juices, salad dressings, and sauces
President: Ron Kahrer
QC: Ned Williams
Plant Manager: John Weber
Purchasing: Ron Mathis
Estimated Sales: $450,000
Number Employees: 4
Number of Brands: 12
Number of Products: 50
Sq. footage: 60000
Parent Co: AGRI Industries
Type of Packaging: Consumer, Food Service, Private Label
Brands:
ALLJUICE
NATURE'S CHOICE

365 **Alltech Natural Food Division**
3031 Catnip Hill Rd
Nicholasville, KY 40356-9765 859-885-9613
Fax: 859-887-3223 info@alltech.com
www.alltech.com
Meat tenderizers, gelating agents, flavor bases and sequestrants
President: T Pearse Lyons
Marketing Manager: Clare Flannery
Estimated Sales: $ 20 - 50 Million
Number Employees: 250-499

366 **Alma Plantation**
4612 Alma Rd
Lakeland, LA 70752 225-627-6666
Fax: 225-627-5138 DavidStewart@Bellsouth.net
Blackstrap molasses and sugar.
President: David Stewart
Sec-Treasurer: John S Campbell
Purchasing Agent: Stuart Carter
Estimated Sales: $20-50 Million
Number Employees: 50-99
Type of Packaging: Bulk

367 **Alma-Leo**
485 E Half Day Rd
Buffalo Grove, IL 60089-8806 847-821-0411
Fax: 847-291-1541
Brands:
Alma Leo
Count Duckula
Slime Slurps
Treasure Trolls
World Wrestling Fede

368 **Almark Foods**
2118 Centennial Dr
Gainesville, GA 30504 770-536-4520
Fax: 770-536-4793 800-849-3447
almarkfoods@msn.com www.almarkeggs.com
Processor of egg products
President: Don Stoner
CEO: Mark Papp
Operations Manager: Paul Heard
Estimated Sales: $5-10 Million
Number Employees: 90
Sq. footage: 15000
Type of Packaging: Food Service
Brands:
ALMARK

369 **Almarla Vineyards & Winery**
Highway 510
Shubuta, MS 39360 601-687-5548
Wines
President: Timothy Dunbar
Brands:
Almarla Black Lightning
Almarla Soul Train
Sautene
Thunder McCloud

370 **Almondina®/YZ Enterprises, Inc.**
1930 Indian Wood Cir
Maumee, OH 43537-4053 419-893-8777
Fax: 419-893-8825 800-736-8779
linda@almondina.com www.almondina.com
Cookies, biscuits. No artificial colors, flavors or preservatives
President/CEO: Yuval Zaliouk
Marketing: Jeff Wolff
Public Relations: Linda Semer
Estimated Sales: $5-10 Million
Number Employees: 10-19
Type of Packaging: Consumer, Food Service, Private Label
Brands:
ALMONDINA BISCUITS

371 **Almost Nuts, LLC**
PO Box 19
Denmark, WI 54208 920-915-0152
sales@soyalmostnuts.com
soyalmostnuts.com
Dry roasted soybeans covered in dark chocolate.
Owner: Darren Kornowske
Estimated Sales: $80,000
Number Employees: 2
Sq. footage: 1945

372 **Aloe Commodities International**
1270 Champion Circle
Suite 100
Carrollton, TX 75006-8333 972-241-4251
Fax: 972-243-4705 800-701-2563
flauterbach@acinatural.com
www.aloeonline.com
Processor and exporter of aloe vera products, cosmetics and dietary supplement drinks
President: Mark McKnight
CEO: L Scott McKnight
CFO: Richard Ellis
General Manager: Fred Lauterbach
Estimated Sales: $ 20 - 50 Million
Number Employees: 20-49
Number of Brands: 20

Number of Products: 100
Sq. footage: 64000
Type of Packaging: Consumer, Private Label
Brands:
AVERA SPORT
CARBMATE
EL TORO LOCO
KATAHNA
NATURALLY ALOE

373 **Aloe Farms**
3102 W Wilson Rd
Harlingen, TX 78552 956-425-1289
Fax: 956-425-3390 800-262-6771
aloefarms@earthlink.net
www.aloeverafarms.com
Manufacturer and supplier of aloe vera juice, gel and capsules.
President: Mark Berry
VP: Elvia Berry
Estimated Sales: $750,000
Number Employees: 10
Sq. footage: 1056
Type of Packaging: Consumer, Private Label, Bulk
Brands:
Aloe Farms

374 **Aloe Laboratories, Inc.**
P.O.Box 831
Harlingen, TX 78551 956-428-8416
Fax: 956-428-8482 800-258-5380
lrodriguez@aloelabs.com www.aloelabs.com
Manufacturer and exporter of organic and conventional aloe vera gel, juice, concentrates and powder.
President: Luis Rodriguez
CEO: Hide Aragaki
Operations and Logistics: Mike Hernandez
Estimated Sales: $3-5 Million
Number Employees: 50-99
Sq. footage: 40000
Brands:
Aloe Burst
Aloe Labs

375 **Aloe'Ha Drink Products**
1908 Augusta Drive
Suite 2
Houston, TX 77057-3717 713-978-6359
Fax: 713-978-6858 info@aloeha.com
www.aloeha.com
Manufacturer and exporter of carbonated fruit drinks including rasberry, kiwi-strawberry, peach, lemon-lime, etc.
Operations Manager: Doyle Gaskamp
Number Employees: 5
Type of Packaging: Consumer, Food Service
Brands:
Aloe'ha

376 **Aloecorp**
46 Pako Ave
Keene, NH 03431 603-352-0650
Fax: 800-733-6290 jeff@aloecorp.com
www.aloecorp.com
Grower and manufacturer of aloe vera ingredients
Sales Manager: Jeff Barrie
Number Employees: 5-9
Parent Co: Aloecorp

377 **Aloha Distillers**
5 Sand Island Rd Unit 118
Honolulu, HI 96819 808-841-5787
Fax: 808-847-2903
alohadistillers@gyello.com/site/
Processor and exporter of liqueurs including coffee, chocolate-coconut and chi-chi
President: Dave Fazendin
Marketing: Ann Fazendin
Purchasing Manager: Dave Fazendin
Estimated Sales: $1-2.5 Million
Number Employees: 1-4
Number of Brands: 1
Number of Products: 1
Type of Packaging: Consumer
Brands:
COFFEE
GOLD
KONA
LIQUEUR

378 **Aloha Poi Factory**
800 Lower Main St
Wailuku, HI 96793 808-244-3536
Fax: 808-244-1914
Processor of poi
President: Les Nakama
Estimated Sales: $2.5-5 Million
Number Employees: 10-19
Type of Packaging: Consumer, Food Service

379 **Aloha Shoyu Company LTD.**
96-1205 Waihona Street
Pearl City, HI 96782 808-456-5929
Fax: 808-456-5903 bahquin@alohashoyu.com
www.alohashoyu.com
Manufacturer of sauces.

380 **Aloha Tofu Factory**
961 Akepo Lane
Honolulu, HI 96817-4503 808-845-2669
Fax: 808-848-4607 www.aloha-tofu.com
Soft and firm tofu
President: Paul Uyehara
VP/Office Manager: Jane Uyehara
Estimated Sales: $2.3 Million
Number Employees: 24
Sq. footage: 22000

381 **Aloha from Oregon**
P.O.Box 42077
Eugene, OR 97404 541-343-5519
Fax: 541-343-5499 800-241-0300
office@alohafromoregon.com
www.alohafromoregon.com
Pepper jellies, chutneys, and other specialty items.
President: Judi Dodson
Estimated Sales: $ 5 - 10 Million
Number Employees: 5-9
Type of Packaging: Consumer, Food Service, Private Label

382 **Alois J. Binder Bakery**
940 Frenchmen St
New Orleans, LA 70116 504-947-1111
Fax: 504-947-1122
Manufacturer of bread and other bakery products
Owner: Alois Binder Jr Jr.
Treasurer: Joseph Binder
Estimated Sales: $4 Million
Number Employees: 50-99
Type of Packaging: Consumer, Food Service, Private Label, Bulk

383 **Alouette Cheese USA**
400 S Custer Ave
New Holland, PA 17557 717-355-8500
www.alouettecheese.com
Manufacturer of dairy products, cheese
CFO: Ulrich Strietholt
Sales Executive: Michael Cobb
Warehouse Operations: Rusty Rutter
Number Employees: 200
Parent Co: Segur Developpment

384 **Alpen Cellars**
Hc 2 Box 3966
Trinity Center, CA 96091-9500 530-266-9513
Fax: 530-266-3363 winemaker@alpencellars.com
www.alpencellars.com
Wine
Owner: Mark Groves
Winemaker: Keith Grooves
Estimated Sales: Less than $500,000
Number Employees: 10-19
Brands:
Alpen Cellars

385 **Alpen Sierra Coffee Company**
2222 Park Pl Ste 1a
Minden, NV 89423 775-783-7263
Fax: 775-783-7293 800-531-1405
coffeentea@alpensierra.com
www.alpensierra.com
Roast and manufactures coffee and tea
President: Christian Waskiewicz
Marketing: Megan Waskiewicz
Estimated Sales: $1-2.5 Million
Number Employees: 5-9
Brands:
ALPEN SIERRA

386 **Alpenglow Beverage Company**
4675 John Marshall Highway
Linden, VA 22642 540-635-2118
Fax: 304-229-4377 terry@alpenglow.net
www.alpenglow.net
Kosher, organic/natural, juice/cider, non-alcoholic beverages, RTD-ready to drink (coffee, tea, concentrates, powders).
Marketing: Terry Hess

387 **Alpenrose Dairy Farms**
P.O.Box 25030
6149 Sw Shattuck Rd
Portland, OR 97298-0030 503-244-1133
Fax: 503-452-2139 alpenrose@alpenrose.com
www.alpenrose.com
Processor of ice cream and milk farm eggs,yogurt,orange juice,butter
President: Carl Cadanau Iii
Operations: Tom Nieradka
Purchasing: Rocky Amick
Estimated Sales: $1.6 Million
Number Employees: 100-249
Type of Packaging: Consumer, Food Service
Brands:
ALPENROSE

388 **Alpha Baking Company**
5001 W Polk St
Chicago, IL 60644 773-261-6000
Fax: 773-489-2711 ebickhem@alphabaking.com
www.alphabaking.com
Processor of baked goods including fresh bread.
Chairman/CEO: Michael Marcucci
CFO: Mark Zawicki
CEO: Michael L Marcucci
VP/Sales & Marketing: Gary Narcisi
VP/Sales: Mark Marcucci
Operations: David Granger
Production: George Pohelos
Plant Manager: Steve Rosen
Purchasing: Bill Harp
Estimated Sales: $170 Million
Number Employees: 1,000-4,999
Number of Products: 300
Sq. footage: 135000
Type of Packaging: Consumer, Food Service, Private Label, Bulk
Brands:
CABLE CAR
CASTLE
GOLDEN HEARTH
KREAMO
MARYANN
NATIONAL
S. ROSEN

389 **Alpha Baking Company**
360 N Fail Rd
La Porte, IN 46350 219-324-7440
Fax: 219-324-9863 contact@alphabaking.com
www.alphabaking.com
Processor of bread and buns
President: Michael Marcucci
EVP Operations: Robert Cruice
Controller: Sheryl Smith
Plant Manager: Dirk Peterson
Estimated Sales: $100+ Million
Number Employees: 100-249
Parent Co: Alpha Baking Company
Type of Packaging: Consumer, Food Service, Private Label

390 **Alphin Brothers**
2302 Us Highway 301 S
Dunn, NC 28334 910-892-8751
Fax: 910-892-2709 800-672-4502
alphin@alphinbrothers.com
www.alphinbrothers.com
Wholesaler/distributor of frozen seafood, beef and pork.
President: Jesse Alphin Jr
VP/Financial Officer: Ernest Alphin
Production Manager: John Hyland
Estimated Sales: $2 Million
Number Employees: 26
Type of Packaging: Consumer, Food Service

391 **Alpine Cheese Company**
P.O.Box 181
Winesburg, OH 44690 330-359-6291
Fax: 330-359-0035
Dairy products, natural cheeses and deli
President: Robert Ramseyer
Manager: Joe Nisley
Plant Manager: Brian Barbey
Purchasing Manager: Donald Fudge
Estimated Sales: $35 Million
Number Employees: 45

Type of Packaging: Private Label

392 **Alpine Coffee Roasters**
894 Us Highway 2
Leavenworth, WA 98826-1340 509-548-3313
Fax: 509-548-4251 800-246-2761
java@alpinecoffeeroasters.com
www.alpinecoffeeroasters.com
Coffee
Co-Owner: Dale Harrison
Co-Owner: Veronica Harrison
Roastmaster: Bill Harrison
Estimated Sales: $2.5-5 Million
Number Employees: 5-9
Brands:
Alpine Coffee

393 **Alpine Meats**
9900 Lower Sacramento Rd
Stockton, CA 95210-3912 209-477-2691
Fax: 209-477-1994 800-399-6328
info@alpinemeats.com
www.alpinepackingco.com
Manufacturer of Frankfurters, sausages and hams, private brands.
President: Jerry Singer
Quality Control: James Sturgeon
Controller: Cecil McKie
Production: Dennis Saragoza
Purchasing: Robby Jaynes
Estimated Sales: $8 Million
Number Employees: 50-99
Sq. footage: 49000
Type of Packaging: Consumer, Food Service, Private Label, Bulk
Brands:
ALPINE

394 **Alpine Pure USA**
33 Richdale Avenue
Cambridge, MA 02140 617-548-8301
Fax: 888-311-6541 866-832-7997
info@teaspree.com www.teaspree.com
Teas

395 **Alpine Touch Spices**
P.O.Box 864
Choteau, MT 59422-0864 406-466-2063
Fax: 406-466-2076 877-755-2525
sales@alpinetouch.com www.alpinetouch.com
Seasonings
President: Mark Southard
Co-Owner: Vicki Southard
Estimated Sales: $500,000-$1 Million
Number Employees: 1-4

396 **Alpine Valley Water**
16900 Lathrop Ave
Harvey, IL 60426 708-333-3910
Fax: 708-333-3921
sales@AlpineValleyWater.com
www.alpinevalleywater.com
A manufacturer of distilled and bottled water
Owner: Tim Rausch
Estimated Sales: Less than $500,000
Number Employees: 1-4
Sq. footage: 10000
Type of Packaging: Food Service
Brands:
Alpine Valley

397 **Alpine Vineyards**
25904 Green Peak Rd
Monroe, OR 97456 541-424-5851
Fax: 541-424-5891
www.oregonwine.org/wine/alpine
Wines
Owner: Daniel Jepsen
Winemaker: Daniel Jepsen
Estimated Sales: $1-2.5 Million
Number Employees: 1-4

398 **AlpineAire Foods**
PO Box 1799
Rocklin, CA 95677-7799 916-624-6050
Fax: 916-624-1604 800-322-6325
info@aa-foods.com www.aa-foods.com
Manufacturer and exporter of health, backpacking, self-heating and emergency prepared foods, freeze-dried and no cooking required foods including; pre-packed beans, cereals, desserts, dried fruits and vegetables, grains and meatsubstitutes
President: Don Gearing
Sq. footage: 50000
Parent Co: TyRy, Inc
Type of Packaging: Consumer, Private Label, Bulk
Brands:
Alpineaire
Gourmet Reserves

399 **(HQ)Alsum Produce**
N9083 Cty Hwy EF
Friesland, WI 53935 920-348-5127
800-236-5127
alsum@alsum.com www.alsum.com
Grower, packer and shipper of potatoes and onions; wholesale distributor of fresh fruits and vegetables.
Owner: Larry Alsum
CFO: Jan Braaksma
Quality Control: Dave Breiwa
Sales/Marketing Director: Rick Kantner
Human Resources: Matt Smith
Production: Randy Fischer
Plant Manager: Steve Tillema
Estimated Sales: $44 Million
Number Employees: 100
Sq. footage: 135000
Parent Co: Alsum Farms
Type of Packaging: Consumer, Food Service, Private Label, Bulk
Brands:
WINDMILL
WOODEN SHOE

400 **Alta Dena Certified Dairy**
17637 Valley Blvd
City of Industry, CA 91744 626-964-6401
Fax: 626-913-9062 800-535-1369
Mary_Larrowe@deanfoods.com
www.altadenadairy.com
Manufacturer of dairy products including butter, cheese, ice cream, kefir, yogurt, frozen yogurt, milk, eggnog and yogurt drinkables
Manager: John Keith
CFO: Keith Anderson
Vice President: Bob Pettigrew
Quality Control: Steve Okada
Sales Director: Mike Dobbs
Plant Manager: Stuart Saito
Estimated Sales: $100-500 Million
Number Employees: 500-999
Parent Co: Dean Foods Company
Brands:
ALTA DENA CLASSIC
CARIBBEAN CHILL
CRAZY COW
DAIRY MART
DECADENT TEMPTATIONS
LE YOUNGHURT
OLD TYME

401 **Alta Health Products**
2137 E Summersweet Dr
Boise, ID 83716 208-344-0852
Fax: 208-367-0089 800-423-4155
altavpdebbie@aol.com
www.altahealthproducts.com
Herbal supplements
Owner/CEO: Judy Haswell
Estimated Sales: $ 1 - 3 Million
Number Employees: 1-4
Brands:
Alta Health

402 **Alta Health Products**
P.O.Box 990
Idaho City, ID 83631-0990 208-392-4170
Fax: 208-392-4185 800-423-4155
altavpdebbie@aol.com
www.altahealthproducts.com
Processor of herbal supplements, teas and minerals
President: Judy Haswell
Founder: Richard Barmakian
Vice President: Deborah Saw Kims
Product Promotion: Kelli Fischer
Estimated Sales: $3-5 Million
Number Employees: 1-4
Brands:
Alta

403 **Alta Vineyard Cellar**
PO Box 980
Calistoga, CA 94515-0980 707-942-6708
Fax: 707-942-5065
Wines
President: Benjamin Falk
Estimated Sales: $500,000-$1 Million
Number Employees: 1-4
Brands:
Alta

404 **Alta-Dena Certified Dairy**
17637 Valley Blvd
City of Industry, CA 91744 626-964-6401
Fax: 626-913-9062 800-535-1369
Mary_Larrowe@deanfoods.com
www.altadenadairy.com
Manager: John Keith
Number Employees: 500-999
Brands:
Alta Dena

405 **Altamura Vineyards & Winery**
P.O.Box 3209
Napa, CA 94558-0320 707-253-2000
Fax: 707-255-3937 altamurawinery@aol.com
www.altamura.com
Wines
President: Frank C Altamura
Estimated Sales: $ 3 - 5 Million
Number Employees: 5-9
Number of Brands: 1
Number of Products: 2

406 **Alternative Health & Herbs**
425 Jackson St SE
Albany, OR 97321 541-791-8400
Fax: 541-791-8401 800-345-4152
healthinfo@healthherbs.com
www.healthherbs.com
Processor of liquid herbal formulations and herbal teas and vitamins; wholesaler/distributor of air and water filters, herbs and vitamins; exporter of herbs and herbal tinctures; importer of herbs. Custom formulations available
Owner: Truman Berst
Estimated Sales: Less than $500,000
Number Employees: 1-4
Sq. footage: 3000
Type of Packaging: Consumer, Private Label, Bulk
Brands:
AMERICAN HEALTH & HERBS MINISTRY
American Naturals
Truman's

407 **Alto Dairy Cooperative**
N3545 County Road Ee
Waupun, WI 53963 920-346-2215
Fax: 920-346-2377 www.altodairy.com
Manufacturer of natural cheese products. Manufacturer and exporter of whey.
CEO: Rich Scheuerman
CFO: Greg Pollesch
Executive: Kurt Sonnleitner
Director Quality Control: Theresa Hurd
Marketing: Rachel Bradley
VP Sales: Dennis Kasuboski
Piblic Relations: Karen Endres
Director Operations: John Smedema
Director Engineering: Hans Horetzki
Plant Manager: David Schmidt
Purchasing: Pam Ferch
Estimated Sales: $430 Million
Number Employees: 250-499
Number of Brands: 3
Number of Products: 12
Sq. footage: 270000
Type of Packaging: Food Service, Bulk

408 **Alto Dairy Cooperative**
307 N Clark St
Black Creek, WI 54106 920-984-3331
Fax: 920-346-2377 www.altodairy.com
Cheese and cheese products, dry whey
President: Rich Scheuerman
CEO: Rich Scheuerman
VP: Larry Lemmenes
VP Sales: Dennis Kasuboski
Estimated Sales: Under $500,000
Number Employees: 50-99
Brands:
Black Creek Classic

409 **Alto Rey Food Corporation**
11468 Dona Teresa Dr
Studio City, CA 91604 323-969-0178
Fax: 323-969-0197
Condiments, dips, salsas, dressings
President: David Ufberg

Estimated Sales: $1-2.5 Million
Number Employees: 5-9
Brands:
Alto Rey

410 **Alto Vineyards**
P.O.Box 51
Alto Pass, IL 62905-0051 618-893-4898
Fax: 618-893-4935 altovin@midwest.net
www.altovineyards.net
Producers of red, white and port wines.
Owner: Paul Renzaglia
Estimated Sales: $5-10 Million
Number Employees: 5-9
Type of Packaging: Bulk
Other Locations:
Alto Vineyards
Champaign IL

411 **Alum-A-Lift**
7909 Highway 78
Winston, GA 30187 770-489-0328
Fax: 770-489-7247 applications@alum-a-lift.com
www.alum-a-lift.com
Manufacture custom egronomic lifting solutions.
President: Stanley Bressner
CFO: Niels Bressner
Vice President: Eric Bressner
Marketing Director: Cheri Pounds
Number Employees: 50-99
Number of Brands: 4

412 **Alvarado Street Bakery**
2225 S McDowell Boulevard Ext
Petaluma, CA 94954 707-283-0300
Fax: 707-283-0350
info@alvaradostreetbakery.com
www.alvaradostreetbakery.com
Processor of organic goods including sprouted wheat bread, kosher bagels, tortillas and whole grain and oil-free granola; exporter of frozen organic wheat bread and kosher bagels
President: Michael Girkout
VP: John Ponnceu
VP Marketing: Doug Radi
Sales Executive: Scott Young
Human Resources Executive: Gregg Sisneros
Plant Manager: Bryan Long
Purchasing: Jamie Mitchell
Estimated Sales: $23 Million
Number Employees: 127
Number of Brands: 2
Number of Products: 27
Sq. footage: 75000
Type of Packaging: Consumer, Private Label
Brands:
ALVARADO STREET BAKERY

413 **Alyeska Seafoods**
P.O.Box 31359
Seattle, WA 98103-1359 206-547-2100
Fax: 206-547-1808
Fresh and frozen seafoods
President: Ken Tippett
VP: Murry Simpson
Purchasing Agent: Cynthia Swazo
Estimated Sales: $50-100 Million
Number Employees: 5-9

414 **AmRhein Wine Cellars**
9243 Patterson Dr
Bent Mountain, VA 24059-2215 540-929-4632
Fax: 540-929-4632 info@amrheins.com
www.roanokewine.com
Wines
Owner: Russel Amrhein
Estimated Sales: $ 1 - 3 Million
Number Employees: 1-4

415 **AmTech Ingredients**
573 County Route A
Suite 102
Hudson, WI 54016 715-381-5746
www.amtechingredients.com
Producer/distributor of specialty food ingredients, primarily in powdered form.
Estimated Sales: $330,000
Number Employees: 3
Sq. footage: 3367

416 **Amador Foothill Winery**
12500 Steiner Rd
Plymouth, CA 95669 209-245-6307
Fax: 209-245-3580 800-778-9463
info@amadorfoothill.com
www.amadorfoothill.com
Wines
Owner/President: Ben Zeitman
Owner/Winemaker: Katie Quinn
Estimated Sales: $1-$2.5 Million
Number Employees: 1-4
Type of Packaging: Private Label
Brands:
Amador Foothill

417 **Amalfitano's Italian Bakery**
29 E Commons Blvd # 700
New Castle, DE 19720-1740 302-324-9005
Fax: 302-324-9008
Bakery products
Owner: Ralph Jacobs
Estimated Sales: $2.5-5 Million
Number Employees: 20-49

418 **Amalgamated Produce**
P.O.Box 5159
Bridgeport, CT 6610-159
Fax: 203-339-3773 800-358-3808
Processor of bean soup mixes, dried fruits, stuffings, sprout products and wild rice dishes
CEO/President: Richard Blackwell
Vice President: Adriana Alvarez
Estimated Sales: $ 10 - 20 Million
Number Employees: 20-49
Sq. footage: 12000
Brands:
SPECIALTY FARMS

419 **Amalgamated Sugar Company**
1951 S Saturn Way
Suite 100
Boise, ID 83709 208-383-6500
Fax: 208-383-6688 www.amalgamatedsugar.com
Manufacturer of liquid and granulated sugar, molasses and livestock feed products.
President/CEO: Victor Jaro
VP Finance: Wayne Neeley
VP Marketing: Bill Smith
VP Operations: Joe Huff
Purchasing Agent: Nasser Shoaee
Estimated Sales: $656 Million
Number Employees: 1,500
Parent Co: Snake River Sugar Company
Type of Packaging: Consumer, Food Service, Private Label, Bulk
Brands:
WHITE SATIN

420 **Amalthea Cellars Farm Winery**
209 Vineyard Rd
Apt A
Atco, NJ 8004 856-767-8890
Winery@amaltheacellars.com
www.amaltheacellars.com
Wines
Owner: Louis Caracciolo
Manager: Virginia Caracciolo
Estimated Sales: $1-2.5 Million
Number Employees: 5-9

421 **Amana Meat Shop & Smokehouse**
4513 F St
Amana, IA 52203 319-622-7586
Fax: 319-622-6245 800-373-6328
info@amanameatshop.com
www.amanameatshop.com
Manufacturer and wholesaler/distributor of hickory-smoked meats including sausage, ham, bacon, pork tenderloin and bratwurst
Manager: Greg Hergert
Director: Mike Shoup
Estimated Sales: Less than $500,000
Number Employees: 20-49
Parent Co: Amana Society Corporation
Type of Packaging: Consumer, Food Service
Brands:
Amana Meats

422 **Amanda Hills Spring Water**
431 W Broad St
Pataskala, OH 43062 740-927-3422
Fax: 740-927-1856 800-375-0885
info@amandahills.com www.amandahills.com
Manufacturer of spring water
Owner: David Betts
Estimated Sales: $300,000-500,000
Number Employees: 1-4
Number of Brands: 1
Sq. footage: 10000
Type of Packaging: Private Label
Brands:
Amanda Hills

423 **Amano Artisan Chocolate**
496 S 1325 W
Orem, UT 84058 801-655-1996
amano@amanochocolate.com
www.amanochocolate.com
Chocolate bars
President: Arthur Pollard
VP: Clark Goble
Sales Director: Rick Raile

424 **Amano Enzyme USA Company, Ltd**
2150 Point Blvd Ste 100
Elgin, IL 60123 847-649-0101
Fax: 847-649-0205 800-446-7652
sales@amanoenzymeusa.com
www-amano-enzyme.co.jp
Supplies the North and South American markets with non—animal and non-GMO enzymes for the dietary supplement, nutraceutical, food, diagnostic and pharmaceutical industries.
President: Motoyuki Amano
VP Science/Technology: James Jolly
Estimated Sales: $15 Million
Number Employees: 440
Sq. footage: 25000
Parent Co: Amano Enzyme

425 **Amano Fish Cake Factory**
30 Holomua St
Hilo, HI 96720 808-935-5555
Fax: 808-961-2154
Processor of frozen and canned fish cakes
Owner: Hiroshi Mathubara
Purchasing Manager: Hiroshi Matsubara
Estimated Sales: $1-2.5 Million
Number Employees: 5-9
Type of Packaging: Consumer
Brands:
AMANO

426 **Amaranth Resources**
139 E William Street
Suite 325
Albert Lea, MN 56007-2535 310-370-2500
Fax: 507-373-4753 800-842-6689
edward@dm.deskmedia.com
http://www.dm.deskmedia.com
Grains, cereals, spices, seasonings, condiments, allergy free products
President: Edward Hubbard
CEO: Edward Hubbard
Vice President: R Merrell
Estimated Sales: $2.5-5 Million
Brands:
Ambake
Amban
Amburst
Amgrain
Best of Health

427 **Amazing Candy Craft Company**
18408 Jamaica Avenue
Hollis, NY 11423-2431 718-264-3031
Fax: 718-264-8437 800-429-9368
www.axxent.net
Candy
President: Frank Salacuse
VP: Catherine Salacuse
VP Marketing/Sales: Brad Demsky
Brands:
CANDY ACTIVITY
MAKE YOUR OWN GUMMIES

428 **Amazing Herbs Nutraceuticals**
1960 Parker Ct # F
Stone Mountain, GA 30087-3450 770-982-4780
800-241-9138
info@amazingherbs.com
www.amazingherbs.com
Manufactuers of nutritional supplements and natural products made from herbs and botanicals from around the globe.
Owner: Tony Goreja

Brands:
AMAZING HERBS
THERAMUNE NUTRITIONALS

429 **Ambassador Foods**
16625 Saticoy St
Van Nuys, CA 91406-2837 818-787-2000
Fax: 818-778-6464 800-338-3369
info@ambassadorfoods.com
www.ambassadorfoods.com
A national distributor of premium imported and domestic products for the pastry and bakery trade. We supply the finest chocolate from Belgium and Switzerland, mousse cake bases and dessert pastes from Germany, jams and glazes fromBelgium, domestic fruit fillings, delicate chocolate cups and decorations from Holland, marzipan from Germany, all part of our exciting and innovative line of ingredients
Owner: Peter Seeger
Estimated Sales: $ 50 - 100 Million
Number Employees: 20-49
Parent Co: Qzina Specialty Foods
Type of Packaging: Consumer, Bulk
Other Locations:
Clifton NJ
Chicago IL
Miami FL
San Francisco CA
Vancouver BC
Toronto ON
Brands:
Ambassador

430 **Amberg Wine Cellars**
2412 Castle Rd
Clifton Springs, NY 14432 585-526-6742
Fax: 315-462-6512 info@ambergwine.com
www.ambergwine.com
Wines
Owner: Ute Amberg
President: Herman Amberg
CFO: Eric Amberg
Marketing Manager: Debbie Amberg
Plant Manager: Eric Amberg
Estimated Sales: $500,000-$1 Million
Number Employees: 1-4
Type of Packaging: Private Label
Brands:
Amberg Wine Cellars

431 **Amberland Foods**
2972 25th St NE
Harvey, ND 58341 701-324-4804
Fax: 701-324-4805 800-950-4558
amberlandfoods@gondto.com
www.dakotaseasonings.com
Processor of dehydrated soup mixes, scone and dip mixes, jams, jellies, seasonings, syrups and toppings
Owner/Manager: Susan K Schwarz
Operations Manager: Elreen Olson
Estimated Sales: $1-2.5 Million
Number Employees: 10-19
Number of Brands: 1
Number of Products: 50
Sq. footage: 4000
Type of Packaging: Consumer, Private Label
Brands:
DAKOTA SEASONINGS

432 **Amberwave Foods**
625 Allegheny Avenue
Oakmont, PA 15139-2003 412-828-3040
Fax: 412-828-2282 www.tomanetti.com
Processor of gourmet pizza products including cheese analogs, crusts and focaccia; also, whole wheat pizzas
President: George Michel
Purchasing Manager: Tammy Carroll
Estimated Sales: $ 10 - 20 Million
Number Employees: 20-49
Parent Co: Tomanetti Foods
Type of Packaging: Consumer, Food Service, Private Label, Bulk
Brands:
GRAINDANCE
SOYDANCE

433 **Ambootia Tea Estate**
PO Box 11696
Chicago, IL 60611-0696 312-661-1550
Fax: 312-661-1523 goels@worldnet.att.net
www.teareport.com
Beverages
Chairman: Shashank Goel
Director: Shashank Goel
Estimated Sales: Less than $500,000
Number Employees: 5-9
Brands:
Ambootia

434 **Amboy Specialty Foods Company**
P.O.Box 529
Dixon, IL 61021-0529 815-288-4097
Fax: 815-288-5022 800-892-0400
www.bayvalleyfoods.com
Processor of canned ready-made cheese sauces and puddings
President: Randy Smith
VP of Sales: Robert Doeseckle
Plant Manager: Jerry Petrasko
Estimated Sales: $25-50 Million
Number Employees: 100-249
Parent Co: Dean Foods Company
Type of Packaging: Consumer, Food Service, Private Label, Bulk

435 **Ambrosia Honey**
14300 E I-25 Frontage Rd
Longmont, CO 80504-9626 970-625-3382
Fax: 970-625-0555 www.madhavasweeteners.com
Honey
President: Craig Gerbore
Estimated Sales: $ 1-2.5 Million
Number Employees: 3
Type of Packaging: Private Label
Brands:
Ambrosia Honey

436 **Ambrosial Granola**
Po Box 090712
Brooklyn, NY 11209 718-491-1335
Fax: 718-425-9932 info@ambrosialgranola.com
www.ambrosialgranola.com
Granola cereals
President: Hariclia Makoulis

437 **Amcan Industries**
570 Taxter Road
Elmsford, NY 10523-2356 914-347-4838
Fax: 914-347-4960 salesus@amcan-online.com
www.amcan-online.com
Meat, jam, jelly, preserves, health food, nutriceuticals, confectionery, fish, seafood, dairy, beverage and juices, bakery and cereal, natural and artificial sweeteners
President: Bowes Dempsey
VP: Benjamin Dempsey
Estimated Sales: $5-10 Million
Number Employees: 7

438 **Amelia Bay Beverage Systems**
11800 Wills Rd
Suite 120
Alpharetta, GA 30004 770-772-6360
Fax: 770-772-4766 800-650-8327
info@ameliabay.com www.ameliabay.com
Manufacture and formulate high fold liquid concentrates for coffees, teas, cappucinos, chais, and other ready - to- drink products, as well as custom formulations
President: John Crandall
Sales Manager: Ralph Lane
Estimated Sales: $ 5 - 10 Million
Number Employees: 10-19
Type of Packaging: Food Service

439 **Amendt Corporation**
317 W Front St
Monroe, MI 48161 734-242-2411
Fax: 734-242-9407 amendtcorp@teleweb.net
www.amendt.com
Flour, frosting, cake and donut mixes
Estimated Sales: $5-10 Million
Number Employees: 20-49

440 **Ameri Color Corporation**
341 S Melrose St # C
Placentia, CA 92870-5974 714-996-1820
Fax: 714-996-7422 800-556-0233
info@americolorcorp.com
www.americolorcorp.com
Manufacturer of food colors for the bakery industry
President: Ernie Molina
CFO: Fay Molina
Estimated Sales: $500,000-$1 Million
Number Employees: 1-4
Brands:
Ameri Color

441 **Ameri-Kal Inc**
5405 Centime Dr
Suite 400
Wichita Falls, TX 76305-5271 940-322-5400
sales@amerikal.com
www.amerikal.com
Processor and exporter domestic of nutritional supplements, vitamins, minerals, herbal formulations, sports nutrition products, herb flavored grapeseed oil, capsules, tablets, bulk powder, liquids, soft gel, etc.; also, packaging, Q/Aand R/D labs and custom formulation
Director: Djoko Soejoto
CEO: Tom Soejoto
Director/Of Marketing: Ron Soejoto
Purchasing Agent: Ron Soejoto
Number Employees: 18
Sq. footage: 35500
Type of Packaging: Private Label, Bulk

442 **Ameri-Suisse Group**
1348 South Ave
Plainfield, NJ 07062-1900 908-222-1001
Fax: 732-222-1929
Novelty candies
Owner: Lew Demeter

443 **AmeriCandy Company**
3618 Saint Germaine Ct
Louisville, KY 40207-3722 502-583-1776
Fax: 502-583-1176 omar@americandybar.com
www.americandybar.com
AmeriCandy has designed 3 packages of gourmet chocolates known as the State 10-piece, the Regional 10-piece, and the Signature Collection containing all 50 state chocolates. There are also three AmeriCandy stores and kiosks.Information is available upon request.
Owner: Omar Tatum
Estimated Sales: 1 Million
Number Employees: 1
Type of Packaging: Consumer, Private Label, Bulk
Brands:
Americandy
Asher
Jim Candy
Rooster Run

444 **AmeriGift**
P.O.Box 5767
Oxnard, CA 93031-5767 805-988-0350
Fax: 805-988-4668 800-421-9039
dneff@ameri-gift.com www.ameri-gift.com
Candy gift items
Owner: Lionel Meff
Estimated Sales: $2.5-5 Million
Number Employees: 50-99
Brands:
AMERIGIFT SWEET TOOTH ORIGINALS
GHIRARDELLI

445 **AmeriPure Processing Company**
803 Willow St
Franklin, LA 70538-6030 337-413-8000
Fax: 337-413-8003 800-328-6729
staff@ameripure.com www.ameripure.com
Processor of raw in-shell and shucked, vibrio-free oysters
President: John Jestvich
Estimated Sales: $5 Million
Number Employees: 80
Type of Packaging: Consumer, Food Service, Private Label
Brands:
Ameripure

446 **America's Classic Foods**
1298 Warren Rd
Cambria, CA 93428-4642 805-927-0745
Fax: 805-927-2280 webmail@amcf.com
www.amcf.com
Manufacturer and exporter of powdered ice cream mix, ice cream freezers, processor and exporter of mixes including ice cream, baking, doughnut, etc. Other product lines include bread & roll mixes, drink mixes and donut mixes.
President: Monty Rice
Estimated Sales: $1 Million
Sq. footage: 30000
Type of Packaging: Food Service, Private Label, Bulk
Brands:
AMERICA'S CLASSIC FOODS
AMERICAN CREAMERY

EMPOWER
MOMMY'S CHOICE
SMOOTH & CREAMY

447 **American Almond Products Company**
103 Walworth St
Brooklyn, NY 11205-2898 718-875-8310
Fax: 718-935-1505 800-825-6663
info@americanalmond.com
www.americanalmond.com
Processed nuts, natural nut butters & pastes, specialty pastes, marzipan, lekvar, poppy butter, piping gelee, crunch toppings and coconut macaroon mix.
President: Victor Frumolt
Customer Service: Priscilla Morales
Estimated Sales: $5-10 Million
Number Employees: 20-49
Sq. footage: 40000
Type of Packaging: Consumer, Food Service, Private Label, Bulk
Brands:
AMERICA ALMOND
AMERICAN ALMOND

448 **(HQ)American Beverage Marketers**
810 Progress Blvd
New Albany, IN 47150 812-941-0072
Fax: 812-949-7344 www.finestcall.com
Processor and exporter of alcoholic and nonalcoholic cocktail mixes including margarita, pina colada, strawberry daiquiri, bloody mary, etc.
Owner: Charles Wagner
President/CEO: George Wagner
VP Marketing: Bill Hinkebein
Operations Manager: Ernie Adams
Plant Manager: Mark Maraman
Estimated Sales: $ 20 - 50 Million
Number Employees: 52
Sq. footage: 110000
Type of Packaging: Consumer, Food Service, Private Label
Other Locations:
American Beverage Marketers
Overland Park KS
Brands:
FINEST CALL
MASTER OF MIXES

449 **American Beverage Marketers**
6900 College Blvd
Suite 650
Leawood, KS 66211-1875 913-451-8311
Fax: 913-451-8655
finestcallinfo@abmcocktails.com
www.abmcocktails.com
Manufacturer of cocktail mixes including margarita, Bloody Mary and whiskey sour
Manager: Joe Armanees
Sr. VP: Joe Armaneef
Estimated Sales: $99,000
Number Employees: 2
Type of Packaging: Food Service
Brands:
Finest Call
Master of Mix

450 **American Biosciences**
560 Bradley Pkwy # 4
Blauvelt, NY 10913 845-727-0800
888-884-7770
info@americanbiosciences.com
www.americanbiosciences.com
Herbs and supplements.
President: David Wales
Estimated Sales: $ 5 - 10 Million
Number Employees: 5-9
Type of Packaging: Consumer

451 **American Blanching Company**
155 Rip Wiley Rd
Fitzgerald, GA 31750 229-423-4098
Fax: 229-423-3842
sales@americanblanching.com
Blanched peanuts
President: Allen A Conger
CEO: Allen A Conger
Marketing Director: David J Conger

452 **American Botanicals**
PO Box 158
Eolia, MO 63344-0158 573-485-2400
Fax: 573-485-3801 800-684-6070
info@americanbotanicals.com
www.americanbotanicals.com
Manufacturer and exporter of whole, cut, powder, kosher, organic, and wild crafted American herbs.
President: Allen Lockard
Quality Control: Denise Kunzweiler
Sales: Becky Johnson
Operations: Chris Zumwalt
Milling Production: Ron Kunzweiler
Purchasing Agent: Tom Duncan
Purchasing Agent: Gennie Martinez
Estimated Sales: $12 Million
Number Employees: 25
Number of Products: 200
Sq. footage: 35000
Type of Packaging: Bulk

453 **American Bottling & Beverage**
1756 Industrial Rd
Walterboro, SC 29488 843-538-7937
Fax: 801-975-7185
Sport beverages

454 **American Brittle**
1034 Hancock St
Sandusky, OH 44870-3616 419-626-8080
Fax: 419-626-8330 800-274-8853
Candy
Specialty Sales: John Cayten
Estimated Sales: $ 10 - 20 Million
Number Employees: 20-49

455 **American Canadian Fisheries**
6069 Hannegan Rd
Bellingham, WA 98226 360-398-1117
Fax: 360-398-8801 800-344-7942
Fresh salmon, red snapper, true cod, halibut, a variety of frozen seafood, shellfish and salmon and gift boxes made
President: Andy Vitaljic
Estimated Sales: $500,000-$1 Million
Number Employees: 1-4
Brands:
Hannegan Seafoods

456 **American Casein Company**
109 Elbow Ln
Burlington, NJ 08016 609-387-3130
Fax: 609-387-7204 sales@109elbow.com
www.americancasein.com
Manufacturer of powdered protein ingredients for the food, beverage, and nutraceutical industries
President: Michael Geiger
Account Executive: Jane Macey Jr
Estimated Sales: $ 50 - 100 Million
Number Employees: 50-99
Sq. footage: 40000
Type of Packaging: Bulk

457 **American Chalkis Intl.Foods Company**
20120 Paseo Del Prado Ste A
Walnut, CA 91789 909-595-5358
Fax: 909-992-3334 info@chalkistomato.us
www.chalkistomato.us
Supplier of tomato products & tomato paste, apricot puree, pomegranate, apple & grape concentrates.

458 **American Cheesemen**
PO Box 261
Clear Lake, IA 50428-0261 641-357-7176
Fax: 641-357-7177
Cheese
President: Paul Austin
Estimated Sales: $5-10 Million
Number Employees: 1-4
Brands:
American Cheesemen
Choppin N Block
E-Z Keep

459 **American Chemical Service**
PO Box 190
Griffith, IN 46319 219-924-4370
Fax: 219-924-5298 www.acs-chem.com
Bromainated vegetable oil
President: James Tarpo
Customer Service: Mike Burge
Sales Manager: David Cole
Estimated Sales: $10-20 Million
Number Employees: 20-49

460 **American Classic Ice Cream Company**
1565 5th Industrial Ct Unit D
Bay Shore, NY 11706 631-666-1000
Fax: 631-666-1319
Manufacturer of ice cream and novelties including sandwiches, cups, pies, etc.; also, toppings
Owner: Edgar Williams
Owner/VP: Gregory Kronrad
General Manager: Theresa Bellizzi
Estimated Sales: Under $500,000
Number Employees: 5-9
Type of Packaging: Consumer, Food Service

461 **American Coffee Company**
P.O.Box 52018
New Orleans, LA 70152-2018 504-581-7234
Fax: 504-581-7518 800-554-7234
info@frenchmarketcoffee.com
www.frenchmarketcoffee.com
Manufacturer and packer of coffee
President: Fraser Bartlett
Estimated Sales: $2.5-5 Million
Number Employees: 20-49
Type of Packaging: Consumer
Brands:
FRENCH MARKET

462 **American Copak Corporation**
9175 Eton Ave
Chatsworth, CA 91311-5806 818-576-1000
Fax: 818-882-1637 info@americancopak.com
www.americancopak.com
Manufacturer of bakers' and confectioners' supplies, beverages, candy, cereals, snack foods, condiments, dairy products, spreads, kosher foods, mixes, pasta, sauces, soups, sugar, syrups, etc.
President: Steven Brooker
Business Development: Wanda Walk
Estimated Sales: $ 5 - 10 Million
Number Employees: 50-99
Sq. footage: 100000

463 **(HQ)American Crystal Sugar Company**
101 3rd St N
Moorhead, MN 56560 218-236-4400
Fax: 218-236-4422 www.crystalsugar.com
Largest producer of beet sugar sweetners,starch,vegetables.
President/CEO: David Berg
VP Finance/CFO: Thomas Astrup
Treasurer Of Operations: Lisa Maloy
Estimated Sales: $1.2 Billion
Number Employees: 1,361
Type of Packaging: Consumer, Private Label, Bulk
Other Locations:
Crookston MN
Drayton ND
East Grand Forks MN
Hillsboro ND
Moorhead MN
Brands:
ALBERTSON
Crystal

464 **American Culinary GardenNoble Communications Co**
3508 E Division Street
Springfield, MO 65802-2499 417-799-1410
Fax: 417-831-9933 888-831-2433
www.acgardens.com
Processor and exporter of balsamic vinegar and soy sauce and also dessert glazes and burgundy soy marinade
Manager: Gary Anderson
Vice President: Judy Sipe
Sales Director: Gary Anderson
Order Desk: Lisa Clifford
Estimated Sales: $2.5-5 Million
Number Employees: 1
Type of Packaging: Consumer, Food Service
Brands:
American Culinary Gardens
Teatro

465 **(HQ)American Dehydrated Food, Inc.**
3801 E. Sunshine
Springfield, MO 65809 417-881-7755
Fax: 417-881-4963 800-456-3447
info@adf.com www.adfinc.com
Dehydrated foods.
Chairman: Thomas Slaight
President: Kurt Hellweg
VP Engineering/Process Design: Mike Gerke
Plant Manager: Mike Scabarozi
Estimated Sales: $ 20 - 50 Million
Number Employees: 232

466 **American Egg Products**
375 Pierce Industrial Blvd
Blackshear, GA 31516 912-449-5700
Fax: 912-449-2438
www.americaneggproducts.com
Egg products
President: James Hull
CEO: Ken Looper
CFO: Richard Looper
Office Manager: Michelle Kersey
Estimated Sales: $7 Million
Number Employees: 65

467 **American Fine Food Corporation**
3600 NW 114th Ave
Doral, FL 33178-1842 305-392-5000
Fax: 305-392-5400 affco@affcointl.com
Processor and exporter of fine foods
President: Sam Amoudi
Marketing/Export Manager: Fadi Ladki
Estimated Sales: $5-10 Million
Number Employees: 5-9

468 **American Flatbread**
46 Lareau Rd
Waitsfield, VT 05673 802-496-8856
Fax: 802-496-8886
flatbread@americanflatbread.com
www.americaflatbread.com
Flatbreads
President: George Schenk
VP: Camilla Behn
Marketing Director: Jennifer Moffroid
Manager: Paul Krcmar
Purchasing: Amy Troiano
Estimated Sales: $13.9 Million
Number Employees: 100

469 **American Food & Equipment**
1301 N Miami Ave
Miami, FL 33136
US 305-377-8991
Fax: 305-358-4328
michael@americanfoodequipment.com
www.americanfoodequipment.com
Manufacturer of coolers, freezers, ice machines, tomato paste, asparagus, ice cream mixes, wheat gluten, veggie burgers, frozen fruit, coffee, etc.; importer of tomato paste, asparagus, etc.; exporter of ice cream mix and powderedwhole and fat-free milk,make all necessary products for resteraunts,sell glassware,bakeware,cookware,small appliances,and janitorial items.
President: Robert Green
Estimated Sales: $460.00k
Number Employees: 5
Sq. footage: 7000
Parent Co: American Grinding And Equipment Company.
Type of Packaging: Consumer, Private Label, Bulk

470 **American Food Ingredients**
4021 Ave De La Plata Ste 501
Suite 501
Oceanside, CA 92056 760-929-9505
Fax: 760-967-1952 amerfood@aol.com
www.americanfoodingredients.com
Dehydrated fruits and vegetables, mushrooms, truffles, non GMO ingredients, salt and salt mixtures, seasonings, spices and herbs
Owner: Karen Koppenhaver
CEO: Karen Koppenhaver
Estimated Sales: $5-10 Million
Number Employees: 5-9
Brands:
American Food

471 **American Food Products**
983 Riverside Dr
Methuen, MA 01844 978-682-1855
Fax: 978-687-0476
Repackage candy for other companies.
President: Tom Reilly
Estimated Sales: $ 50 - 100 Million
Number Employees: 50-99
Type of Packaging: Private Label, Bulk

472 **American Food Traders**
10661 N Kendall Dr Ste 206a
Apt 313
Miami, FL 33176 305-273-7090
Fax: 305-670-6468
customerservice@americanfoodtraders.com
www.americanfoodtraders.com
Wholesaler/distributor, importer and exporter of corned beef, peanut butter, juices, foam, plastic and paper disposable goods and sodas
President: Freddy Olcese
Number Employees: 1-4
Type of Packaging: Consumer, Food Service, Private Label, Bulk

473 **(HQ)American Foods Group**
500 South Washington Street
Green Bay, WI 54301-4219 920-436-4229
Fax: 920-436-6510
akohlbeck@americanfoodsgroup.com
www.americanfoodsgroup.com
Manufacturer and exporter of beef products. Rosen's Diversified has merged with American Foods and will operate as American Foods Group
CEO: Tom Rosen
President/COO: Greg Benedict
CFO: Robert Hovde
Estimated Sales: $500 Million-$1 Billion
Number Employees: 4000
Sq. footage: 60000
Type of Packaging: Consumer, Food Service
Other Locations:
Mitchell SD
Sharonville OH
Brands:
AMERICAN FOODS
AMERICAN FOODS SPECIALTIES
BLACK ANGUS RESERVE
DAKOTA SUPREME
GREEN BAY DRESSED BEEF

474 **(HQ)American Fruit Processors**
10725 Sutter Ave
Pacoima, CA 91331-2553 818-899-9574
Fax: 818-899-6042 sales@americanfruit.com
www.americanfruits-flavors.com
Manufacturer and exporter of fruit juice and custom blended concentrates and natural fruit sweeteners
President: Fred Farago
VP Marketing: Richard Linn
Purchasing Manager: Jack Haddad
Estimated Sales: $50-100 Million
Number Employees: 50-99
Sq. footage: 40000
Parent Co: American Fruit & Flavors
Type of Packaging: Bulk
Other Locations:
American Fruit Processors
Los Angeles CA
Brands:
Juicy Moo
Moose Juice
Phytoceuticals
Pound-4-Pound Powdered

475 **(HQ)American Fruits and Flavors**
1547 North Knowles Ave
Los Angeles, CA 90063 323-264-7790
Fax: 323-264-9506 sales@americanfruit.com
www.americanfruit.com
Processor of natural and artificial flavoring ingredients, bases and emulsions; also, spray dried flavors
President: Fred Farago
Chief Information Officer: Ron Velis
Estimated Sales: $13.7 Million
Number Employees: 100
Sq. footage: 20000

476 **American Hawaiian Soy Company**
274 Kalihi Street
Honolulu, HI 96819 808-841-8435
800-841-8435
Soybean manufacturer
President: Thomas Morita

477 **American Health**
2100 Smithtown Ave
Ronkonkoma, NY 11779-7347 631-244-2021
Fax: 631-244-1777 800-445-7137
infi@americanhealthus.com
www.americanhealthus.com
American Health is the largest American-owned prime manufacturer of quality vitamins, minerals, food supplements, health and beauty aids.
President/CEO: Dorie Greenblatt
Vice President: Robert Silverman
Estimated Sales: $ 3 - 5 Million
Number Employees: 5-9
Type of Packaging: Consumer

478 **American Health & Nutrition**
3990 Varsity Dr
Ann Arbor, MI 48108 734-677-5570
Fax: 734-677-5572 www.neworganics.com
Organic Ingredient Supplier-grains, sweetners, oils, soy powders
President: Jethren Phillips
CEO: Thomas Bunkley
VP: David Singsank
Purchasing: Shane Rohan
Estimated Sales: $18 Million
Number Employees: 30
Number of Brands: 3
Number of Products: 100
Sq. footage: 25000
Type of Packaging: Bulk
Other Locations:
American Health & Nutrition
Eaton Rapids MI
Brands:
ORGANIC GARDEN
ORGANIC HARVEST
SOY-N-ERGY SOY POWDERS

479 **American Health & Nutrition**
3990 Varsity Dr
Ann Arbor, MI 48108 734-677-5572
Fax: 734-677-5572 sales@organictrading.com
www.organicharvest.com
Organic soy snacks and cereals
President: Dennis Singsank
Account Manager: Kevin Lockwood
CFO: Martha Carlton
International Trade Representative: Catherine Peckham
Public Relations: Cindy Maynard
Estimated Sales: $ 10 Million
Number Employees: 20-49
Brands:
Organic Garden

480 **American Importing Company**
550 Kasota Ave SE
Minneapolis, MN 55414 612-331-7000
Fax: 612-331-1122 customers@amportfoods.com
www.amportfoods.com
Manufacturer and an importer/exporter of dates, full line of extruded dried fruit based bits
President: Andrew Stillman
CEO: Ralph Stillman
VP Marketing: Jeff Vogel
Estimated Sales: $20-50 Million
Number Employees: 20-49
Number of Brands: 2
Number of Products: 50
Sq. footage: 65000
Type of Packaging: Consumer, Private Label, Bulk
Brands:
AMPORT FOODS
DESSERT JEWELL
SALAD EXPRESSIONS

481 **American Instants**
P.O.Box 817
Flanders, NJ 7836 973-584-8811
Fax: 973-584-0444 sales@americaninstants.com
www.americaninstants.com
A private label packer of instant coffee and tea. Also a full line manufacturer of cappuccino, granita, chai, fresh brew tea, hot chocolate, drink mixes and liquid coffee extract.
President: Marty Wagner
CEO: Christopher Roche
CEO: Chris Roche
Research and Development: Henry Spanier
Quality Control: Mary Short
Estimated Sales: $15 Million
Number Employees: 50-99
Sq. footage: 72000

Type of Packaging: Food Service, Private Label
Brands:
CAPPUCCINO SUPREME
DEEP RICH
HOT CHOCOLATE SUPREME

482 **(HQ)American Italian Pasta Company**
4100 N Mulberry Drive
Suite 200
Kansas City, MO 64116-1787 816-584-5000
Fax: 816-584-5100 consumeraffairs@aipc.com
www.aipc.com
Manufacturer, importer and exporter of dry pasta
Chairman: William Patterson
President: Walter George
CFO: Paul Geist
CEO: John P Kelly
VP Quality/Research & Development: Jayne Hoover
VP Marketing: Drew Lericos
VP Information Systems: Chrystal Johnson
EVP/Operations & Supply Chain: Wayne George
Estimated Sales: $600 Million
Number Employees: 600
Sq. footage: 300000
Parent Co: Ralcorp
Type of Packaging: Consumer, Food Service, Private Label, Bulk
Other Locations:
Exeisior Springs MO
Columbia SC
Kenosha WI
Brands:
AMERICAN ITALIAN
ANTHONY'S
CALABRIA
GLOBE A-1
LUXURY
MONTALCINO
MRS. GRASS
MUELLER'S
PASTA AMERICAN ITALIAN
PASTA LABELLA
PENNYSYLVANIA DUTCH NOODLES
R&F
RONCO

483 **American Key Food Products**
1 Reuten Dr
Closter, NJ 7624 201-767-8022
Fax: 201-767-9124 800-767-0237
www.akfponline.com
American Key Food products supplies bulk quantity starches, spices and ingredients to a variety of food industries such as baking, snacks, soup, spices, meats and dairy. We have an extensive product list which can be seen on ourwebsite www.AmericanKeyFood.com along with product specification sheets and Kosher Certificates.
Manager: Luis Mansueto Jr
VP: Ivan Sarda
Sales: Mel Festejo
Operations: Edwin Pacia
Purchasing: Connie Ponce de Leon
Number Employees: 20-49
Type of Packaging: Bulk
Brands:
EMSLAND
KING LION

484 **American Laboratories**
4410 S 102nd St
Omaha, NE 68127 402-339-2494
Fax: 402-339-0801
sales@americanlaboratories.com
www.americanlaboratories.com
American Laboratories Inc has more than 35 years of expertise in manufacturing pancreatin and pepsin enzymes as well as more than 200 biologically derived products, and are now a leading supplier of fungal and plant enzymes for thefoid, human nutritional, pharmaceutical, veterinary, and disgnostic industries. a combination of versatile facilities, continuous expansion, and strict adherence to FDA/USDA regulations ensures quality products and service.
President/CEO: Jeff Jackson
VP Sales: Rod Schake
Chief Operating Officer: Kenny Soejoto
Purchasing Manager: Tom Hall
Number Employees: 50-99
Number of Products: 960
Type of Packaging: Bulk

485 **American Lecithin Company**
115 Hurley Rd Ste 2b
Oxford, CT 06478 203-262-7100
Fax: 203-262-7101 800-364-4416
customerservice@americanlecithin.com
www.americanlecithin.com
Manufacturer and exporter of lecithin products and specialty phospholipids; importer of lecithin
President: Randall Zigmont
CEO: Matthias Rebmann
Estimated Sales: $ .5 - 1 million
Number Employees: 5-9
Sq. footage: 7000
Type of Packaging: Consumer, Bulk
Brands:
ALCOLEC

486 **(HQ)American Licorice Company**
2796 NW Clearwater Dr
Bend, OR 97701 541-617-0800
Fax: 541-617-0224 800-220-2399
www.americanlicorice.com
Licorice candy
CEO: John Kretchman
CEO: John Kretchmer
VP Sales: Michael MacDonald
Type of Packaging: Consumer
Brands:
Red Vines
Snaps
Sour Punch
Super Ropes

487 **American Licorice Company**
PO Box 826
Union City, CA 94587 219-362-5790
Fax: 219-979-2055 866-442-2783
consumerfeedback@amerlic.com
www.americanlicorice.com
Manufacturer of licorice and licorice candy products
CEO: John Kretchmer
National Sales Manager: Michael MacDonald
SVP, Supply Chain: Edward Gerdow
Corporate Procurement Director: Ed Gerdow
Estimated Sales: $100 Million
Number Employees: 250-499
Type of Packaging: Consumer, Food Service, Private Label, Bulk
Brands:
AMERICAN
BLACK LICORICE VINES
LICORICE ROPES
RED ROPES
RED VINES
SNAPS
SOUR PUNCH
SUGAR FREE VINES
SUPER ROPES
TWISTY PUNCH

488 **American Licorice Company**
PO Box 826
Union City, CA 94587 510-487-5500
Fax: 510-487-2517 866-442-2783
info@americanlicorice.com
www.americanlicorice.com
Manufacturer and exporter of licorice confections
President/CEO: James Kretchmer
VP: Karen Bettencourt
Quality Control Manager: Ed Silva
Sales Director: Marty Cline
President/Human Resources Manager: John Nelson
VP Manufacturing: Paul Silvey
Estimated Sales: $50-100 Million
Number Employees: 350
Sq. footage: 126521
Type of Packaging: Consumer, Private Label, Bulk
Brands:
NATURAL VINES
RED VINES
SNAPS
SOUR PUNCH
SUPER ROPES

489 **American Marketplace Foods**
359 McLean Boulevard
Paterson, NJ 07513-1039 201-278-9060
Fax: 201-684-0174 800-683-3464
www.biscottithins.com
President: Jack Galione
Executive VP: Thomas Morgan
VP, Retail Sales: Elisabeth Hill
Sales Director: Chuck Flemballa
Operations Manager: Robert Bauet
Estimated Sales: $2.5-5 Million
Number Employees: 10-19
Brands:
Biscotti Thins
Cool Cakes
Our Daily Muffin

490 **American Mercantile Corporation**
P.O.Box 2165
Windermere, FL 34786-2165
Fax: 901-454-0207 dsa@memphi.net
www.americanmercantile.net
Manufacturer of citrus juice including orange, grapefruit, tangerine, etc
President/Marketing Director: Damon Arney
VP Operations: Tom Resler
Estimated Sales: $1-2.5 Million
Number Employees: 20-49
Type of Packaging: Consumer, Food Service, Bulk

491 **American Mercantile Corporation**
P.O.Box 240654
Memphis, TN 38124 901-454-1900
Fax: 901-454-0207 amc@memphi.net
www.americanmercantile.net
Spices, seeds, herbs, botanicals, extracts, essential oils and related natural products
President: Damond Arney
Marketing Director: Damond Arney

492 **American Micronutrients**
PO Box 7129
Kansas City, MO 64113-0129 816-254-6000
Fax: 816-254-6004 impdavison@worldnet.att.net
Manufacturer of chelated calcium
President: Mike Davison
Brands:
American Micronutrients

493 **American Mint**
727 Avenue of the Americas
New York, NY 10010-2731 212-929-1410
Fax: 212-929-1235 800-401-6468
www.theamericanmint.com
Processor of natural mints
Owner: Sam Hamirani
Estimated Sales: Less than $500,000
Number Employees: 1-4
Type of Packaging: Private Label, Bulk

494 **American Natural & Organic Spices**
4180 Business Center Dr
Fremont, CA 94538-6354 510-440-1044
Fax: 510-440-1008 info@organicspices.com
www.spicely.com
organic spices
CEO: Bijan Chansari
Marketing: John Chansari
Estimated Sales: $1.2 Million
Number Employees: 9

495 **American Nut & Chocolate Company**
121 Newmarket Sq
Boston, MA 02118 617-427-1510
Fax: 617-427-1805 800-797-6887
info@amnut.com www.amnut.com
hand roasted nuts, chocolates, dried fruits and candies.
Manager: Robert Novack
Estimated Sales: $1-2.5 Million
Number Employees: 1-4
Sq. footage: 16000
Type of Packaging: Food Service, Bulk
Brands:
HARVARD

496 **American Pop Corn Company**
P.O.Box 178
Sioux City, IA 51102-0178 712-239-1232
Fax: 712-239-1268 email@jollytime.com
www.jollytime.com

Manufacturer of popcorn
Founder: Cloid Smith
President: Garrett Smith
VP Marketing: Tom Elsen
VP Sales: Steve Huisenga
Facilities Manager: Damon Lohry
Purchasing Manager: Brett Hegarty
Estimated Sales: $ 20 - 50 Million
Number Employees: 100-249
Type of Packaging: Consumer, Bulk
Brands:
JOLLY TIME

497 **American Purpac Technologies, LLC**
2924 Wyetta Dr
Beloit, WI 53511-3964 608-362-5012
Fax: 608-362-5028 877-787-7221
www.purpac.com
American Purpac Technologies (APT) is a leading aseptic/hot fill contract manufacturer providing bulk blending, ingredient processing an dfilling for the food and beverage industries. Through the use of the latest in aseptic processing(HTST) and packaging technologies we process perishable high acid liquid ingredients into ready to use concentrates for the food and beverage industries.
Manager: Tony Rebello
CEO: D Scott Eckman
CFO: John Saladino
VP: Dan Lang
Quality Control: Dave Flora
Sales: Kevin Farrell
Plant Manager: David Devine
Purchasing: Luke Seibert
Number Employees: 50-99
Sq. footage: 65000
Type of Packaging: Consumer, Food Service, Private Label, Bulk

498 **American Raisin Packers**
2335 Chandler St
PO Box 30
Selma, CA 93662 559-896-4760
Fax: 559-896-8942 americanraisin@sbcglobal.net
americanraisinpacking.com
Packers of raisins
Owner: John Paboojian
Estimated Sales: $2.5 Million
Number Employees: 16
Sq. footage: 30000
Type of Packaging: Consumer, Bulk
Brands:
American Raisin Packers

499 **American Saucery**
10750 Capital St
Oak Park, MI 48237-3134
US 248-544-4574
Fax: 248-544-4384 877-728-2379
americansaucery@midasfoods.com
www.americansaucery.com
Processor of dry mix foods and bases including gravies, sauces, cheese sauce, soup bases, batter products .They manufacturer dry powdered mixes for food processing and national restauraunt chains.
Owner: Richard Elias
Number Employees: 5-9
Sq. footage: 45000
Parent Co: MiDAS Foods International
Type of Packaging: Food Service, Bulk
Brands:
American Saucery

500 **(HQ)American Seafoods Group**
2025 1st Ave Ste 900
Seattle, WA 98121 206-374-1515
Fax: 206-374-1516 800-275-2019
info@americanseafoods.com
www.americanseafoods.com
Manufacturer and exporter of frozen seafood
President: Inge Andreassen
CEO: Bernt Bodal
CFO: Brad Bodenman
Estimated Sales: $430 Million
Number Employees: 1,000
Type of Packaging: Bulk
Other Locations:
Seattle WA
Dutch Harbor AK
New Bedford MA
Greensboro AL

501 **American Seafoods International**
40 Herman Melville Blvd
New Bedford, MA 02740-7344 508-997-0031
Fax: 508-991-6432 800-343-8046
john.cummings@americanprideseafoods.com
www.americanprideseafoods.com
Manufacturer of the Frionor brand; prepared seafood products. Battered, breaded, precooked, coated, glazed, marinated groundfish portions, and natural fillets
President: John Cummings
VP Finance/Administration: Bob Myatt
VP Retail Sales: Robert Hatcher
Estimated Sales: $ 20 - 50 Million
Number Employees: 100-249
Number of Brands: 5
Number of Products: 500+
Sq. footage: 240000
Parent Co: American Seafoods Group
Type of Packaging: Consumer, Food Service, Private Label, Bulk
Brands:
FRIONOR USA
SOUTHERN PRIDE CATFISH LLC

502 **American Skin LLC**
140 Industrial Dr
Burgaw, NC 28425 910-259-2232
Fax: 910-259-2535 800-248-7463
americanskinllc@bellsouth.net
www.pork-rinds.com
Processor of pork rings and pork rinds
Manager: Wes Blake
Estimated Sales: $300,000-500,000
Number Employees: 1-4

503 **American Soy Products**
1474 Woodland Dr
Saline, MI 48176 734-429-2310
Fax: 734-429-2112 infoasp@ameicansoy.com
www.americansoy.com
Aseptic packer of juices, teas and soy products
President: Ron Roller
Estimated Sales: $2.5-5 Million
Number Employees: 20-49
Sq. footage: 65000
Type of Packaging: Consumer, Private Label

504 **American Specialty Confections**
888 County Road D W Ste 100
Saint Paul, MN 55112 651-251-7000
Fax: 651-251-7070 800-776-2085
Candy
President: Jeff Haynes
Marketing Director: Chris Dusk
Sales Manager: Mike Gardener
Number Employees: 100

505 **American Specialty Foods**
2320 Norman Road
Lancaster, PA 17601 717-397-9578
Fax: 717-397-9578 800-335-6663
info@asfbrands.com www.asfbrands.com
Gluten-free, full-line baking mixes and ingredients, tea, full-line condiments, other frozen, full-line spices, dessert toppings (i.e. fudge sauce, caramel sauce, whipped cream, etc.), co-packing.
Marketing: Doug Harris

506 **American Spoon Foods**
1668 Clarion Ave
PO Box 566
Petoskey, MI 49770 231-347-9030
Fax: 800-647-2512 800-222-5886
info@spoon.com www.spoon.com
Jams, jellies, salsas and condiments.
President: Justin Rashid
VP: Larry Forgione
Human Resources Manager: Dorothy Felton
Plant Manager: Paul Ramey
Purchasing Director: John Kafer
Estimated Sales: $10-20 Million
Number Employees: 45
Sq. footage: 12000
Type of Packaging: Consumer, Food Service
Other Locations:
American Spoon Foods
Petosky MI
American Spoon Foods
Charlevoix MI
American Spoon Foods
Traverse City MI
American Spoon Foods
Harbor Springs MI
American Spoon Foods
Saugatuck MI
American Spoon Foods
Northville MI
American Spoon Foods
Ann Arbor MI
Brands:
American Chef Larry Forgione's
American Fruit Butters
American Fruit Toppings
American Salad Dazzlers
American Spoon Foods
American Spoon Fruits
Salad Dazzlers
Spoon Fruit
Spoon Toppers

507 **American Supplement Technologies**
3312 E Broadway Rd
Phoenix, AZ 85040 602-680-1650
Fax: 602-680-1601 888-469-0242
info@americansupplement.com
www.americansupplement.com
Manufacturer of nutritional supplements in capsule and tablet form
President: Bradley Grossman
Estimated Sales: $ 50 - 100 Million
Number Employees: 50-99
Type of Packaging: Private Label, Bulk

508 **American Tartaric Products**
1865 Palmer Ave Ste 207
Larchmont, NY 10538 914-834-1881
Fax: 914-834-4611 atp@americantartaric.com
www.americantartaric.com
Processor of tartaric acid, cream of tartar and baking powder
President: Emilio Zanin
Vice President: Luca Zanin
Estimated Sales: $5-10 Million
Number Employees: 27
Other Locations:
American Tartaric Products
Windsor CA

509 **American Ultraviolet Company**
212 S Mount Zion Rd
Lebanon, IN 46052 765-483-9514
Fax: 765-483-9525 800-288-9288
mstines@auvco.com
www.americanultraviolet.com
Founded in 1960, American Ultraviolet Company is a manufacturer of UV curing and UV disinfection systems that includes indoor air quality, water purification, liquid sugar/syrup storage and germicidal sterilization.
CEO: Meredith Stines
Germicidal HVAC/International: Jeffrey Stines
UV Curing/International: Rafael Hernandez
UV Curing & Germicidal HVAC: Sam Guzman
Germicidal HVAC: Donna Wieder

510 **American Vintage Wine Biscuits**
4003 27th St
Long Island City, NY 11101 718-361-1003
Fax: 718-361-0204 info@americanvintage.com
www.americanvintage.com
Manufacturer of cracker/snack made with wine and pepper
President: Mary-Lynn Mondich
Estimated Sales: Less than $500,000
Number Employees: 1-4
Type of Packaging: Consumer

511 **American Wholesale Grocery**
131 New Jersey Street
Mobile, AL 36603-2111 251-433-2500
Fax: 251-432-7982
President: Harold Owens
Secretary/Treasurer: James Statter
Vice President: John Carpenter

512 **American Yeast/Lallemand**
319 Commerce Way # 2
Pembroke, NH 03275-3718 603-228-8454
Fax: 603-228-6745 866-920-9885
asbe@asbe.org www.lallemand.com

Baking enzymes, baking ingredients, dough conditioners, such as bromate replacers, chocolate, cocoa, egges, fruit, nuts, oils, oxidizers, raisisns, spices, sweetners, yeast foods
Manager: Bud Spooner
First Vice Chairwoman: Theresa S Cogswell
VP: Christine Merenova
Second Vice-Chairman: Eddie Perrou
Estimated Sales: $5-10 Million
Number Employees: 20-49
Brands:
Essential
Fermaid

513 **Americana Marketing**
850 Tourmaline Dr
Newbury Park, CA 91320-1205 805-499-0451
Fax: 805-499-4668 800-742-7520
ami@follmerdevelopment.com
www.follmerdevelopment.com
Manufacturer of aerosol nonstick cooking, baking and flavor sprays
President/CEO: Garrett Follmer
Sales/Marketing VP: David McKenzie
Number Employees: 50-99
Type of Packaging: Consumer, Food Service, Private Label
Brands:
NATURAL LITE
PURE & SIMPLE

514 **Americana Vineyards**
4367 E Covert Rd
Interlaken, NY 14847 607-387-6801
Fax: 607-387-3852 wineinny@aol.com
www.americanavineyards.com
Wines
President: Joseph Gober
Estimated Sales: $840,000
Number Employees: 10-19
Brands:
Americana

515 **(HQ)Americas Catch**
P.O.Box 584
Itta Bena, MS 38941 662-254-7207
Fax: 662-254-9776 800-242-0041
solons@catfish.com www.catfish.com
Processor of fresh and frozen farm-raised catfish
President: Solon Scott
VP Sales: John Nelms
Plant Manager: Bill Martin
Estimated Sales: $20-50 Million
Number Employees: 250-499
Type of Packaging: Consumer, Food Service, Private Label, Bulk
Brands:
AMERICA'S CATCH

516 **(HQ)Amerifit Brands, Inc.**
55 Sebethe Dr
Suite 102
Cromwell, CT 06416-1016 860-242-3476
Fax: 860-243-9400 800-722-3476
martyherman@amerifit.com www.amerifit.com
Processor and exporter of vitamins, supplements and health food
CEO: Cyrill Siewert
CFO: Victor Emerson Jr.
CEO: Cyrill Siewert
Executive VP Sales/Marketing: Doug Meyer
VP Operations: Ernesto Martinez
Estimated Sales: $463 Million
Number Employees: 65
Sq. footage: 50000
Other Locations:
Amerifit/Strength Systems USA
Bloomfield CT
Brands:
AZO
CULTURELLE
DHEA
ESTROVEN
FLEX ABLE
SOOTHERBS
VITABALL

517 **Amerifit Nutrition**
166 Highland Park Drive
Bloomfield, CT 06002-5306 860-242-3476
Fax: 860-243-9400 800-722-3476
www.Amerifit.com
Health foods
Chairman/President: Cyrill Siewert
Sr. VP Marketing: David D Belaga
Estimated Sales: $ 10-100 Million
Number Employees: 99
Parent Co: Amerifit/Strength Systems
Brands:
Estroven
Vitazll

518 **Amerilab Technologies**
2765 Niagara Ln N
Plymouth, MN 55447 763-525-1262
Fax: 763-525-1285 800-445-6468
sales@amerilabtech.com www.amerilabtech.com
Amerilab Technologies is a private label and contract manufacturer who specializes in the development and production of effervescent tablets. We manufacture products for a large number of industries including both domestic andinternational markets. Amerilab Technologies, Inc. is a leader in the development, manufacturing and packing of effervescent tablets and powders.
President: Fred Wehling
CFO: Wes Peterson
Research & Development: Mary Aldritt
Quality Control: Terry Wehling
Operations Manager: Dawn Poellinger
Estimated Sales: 8,000,000
Number Employees: 20-49
Type of Packaging: Private Label

519 **Ameripec**
6965 Aragon Cir
Buena Park, CA 90620 714-994-2990
Fax: 714-562-0849 www.ameripecinc.com
Contract packing of PET bottles and glass bottles of juices, juice drink, flavored drink and water at acidified pH
President: Ping Wu
Operations: Mike Lin
Estimated Sales: $20-50 Million
Number Employees: 150
Sq. footage: 130000
Type of Packaging: Private Label

520 **Ameripure Processing Company**
803 Willow Street
Franklin, LA 70538 504-467-0474
Fax: 337-413-8003 800-328-6729
pfahey@ameripure.com
http://www.ameripure.com
President: John Tesvich

521 **Ameriqual Foods**
18200 Highway 41 N
Evansville, IN 47725 812-867-1444
Fax: 812-867-0278 info@ameriqual.com
www.ameriqual.com
Supplier of pre-made food items and manufacturer of heat-sealed microwavable bowls, trays and flexible pouches
CEO: Steve Chancellor
CFO: Sandra Rasche
Finance: Dave Barnes
Estimated Sales: $50-100 Million
Number Employees: 510

522 **Amerivacs**
1518 Lancaster Point Way
San Diego, CA 92154-7700
Fax: 619-498-8227 info@amerivacs.com
www.amerivacs.com
President: Peter Tadlock
Estimated Sales: $800,000
Number Employees: 1-4
Brands:
Amerivacs

523 **Amerol Corporation**
71 Carolyn Blvd
Farmingdale, NY 11735
Fax: 631-694-9177
cmonteleone@amerolcorp.com
www.amerolcorp.com
Manufacturer and custom blender of synthetic and natural antioxidants such as BHA, BHT, TBHQ, propyl gallate and mixed tocopherols
President: C J Monteleone
CEO: D Sartorio
CFO: A Diaz
R&D: Y Liang
Marketing: S Jean Charles
Operations: F Monteleone
Production: D Ghiglieri
Purchasing Director: D Raleigh
Estimated Sales: $10 Million
Number Employees: 1-4
Sq. footage: 23000
Type of Packaging: Private Label, Bulk

524 **(HQ)Amerol Corporation**
71 Carolyn Blvd
Farmingdale, NY 11735
Fax: 631-694-9177 info@amerolcorp.com
www.amerolcorp.com
Manufacturer and exporter of antioxidants and antioxidant blends including potassium sorbate and sorbic acid
CFO: Tony Diaz
EVP: Charles Monteleone
Director New Product Development: Ora Roitberg
Estimated Sales: $300,000-500,000
Number Employees: 1-4
Sq. footage: 18000
Type of Packaging: Private Label
Brands:
Amerol

525 **(HQ)Ames Company**
PO Box 46
New Ringgold, PA 17960-0046 570-386-2131
Fax: 413-604-0541 info@amescompany.com
www.amescompany.com
Contract manufacturer, exporter and importer of vegetarian meat analogs and dry mixes; broker of soy concentrates, phosphates, flavors, hydrolyzed protein, autolyzed and torula yeast; consultant specializing in product development fordry and frozen foods
Owner: Joseph Ames, Sr.
Number Employees: 5-9

526 **Ames International**
4401 Industry Dr E # A
Fife, WA 98424-1832 253-946-4779
Fax: 253-926-4147 888-469-2637
questions@emilyschocolates.com
www.emilyschocolates.com
Processor and exporter of nut products, and gourmet chocolates and cookies
President: George Paulose
VP: Susan Paulose
Marketing: Amy Paulose
Estimated Sales: $5-10 Million
Number Employees: 50-99
Sq. footage: 55000
Type of Packaging: Private Label, Bulk
Brands:
Amy's
EcoSnax
Emily's
Orchard Hills
Santa Cruz
Seven Seas

527 **Amfit Spices**
7380 W Sand Lake Rd Ste 500
Orlando, FL 32819 407-352-5290
Fax: 407-351-1901
Spices
Estimated Sales: Less than $500,000
Number Employees: 1-4

528 **Amick Farms, LLC**
P.O.Box 2309
Leesville, SC 29070-0309 803-532-1400
Fax: 803-532-1492 800-926-4257
www.amickfarms.com
Manufacturer and exporter of poultry
CEO: Bill Amick
President: Jimmy Riggs
CFO: Marcus Miller
VP: Fred West
SVP Marketing: Norah Morley
VP Operations: Fred West
Estimated Sales: $200 Million
Number Employees: 1500

Sq. footage: 11000
Parent Co: OSI Group
Type of Packaging: Consumer, Food Service, Private Label, Bulk
Brands:
AMICK FARMS

529 **Amigos Canning Company**
600 Carswell
San Antonio, TX 78226 210-798-5360
Fax: 210-798-5365 800-580-3477
osaenz@amigoscanning.com
www.amigosfoods.com
Mexican Foods including hot filled sauces, canned products and fried corn products
Manager: Clint Mc New
Controller: Ivan Kerr
Sales Manager: Tom Murrin
COO: Gene Welka
Plant Manager: Carlos Menchaca
Estimated Sales: $11.5 Million
Number Employees: 90
Sq. footage: 39000
Parent Co: Durrset Amigos
Type of Packaging: Consumer, Private Label
Brands:
Amigos
Firehouse

530 **Amity Packing Company**
210 N Green St
Chicago, IL 60607 312-942-0270
Fax: 312-942-0413 800-837-0270
info@amitypacking.com
www.amitypacking.com
Manufacturer of fresh and frozen pork and beef products.
President: Richard T Samuel
Vice President: Matt Buol
VP Sales/Marketing: Tom Laplant
Operations Manager: Jim Stamm
Estimated Sales: $110,000
Number Employees: 2
Sq. footage: 2806

531 **Amity Vineyards**
18150 SE Amity Vineyards Rd
Amity, OR 97101 503-835-2362
Fax: 503-835-6451 888-264-8966
amity@amityvineyards.com
www.amityvineyards.com
Wines
President: Myron Redford
Sales/Manager: Peter Higbee
Estimated Sales: $830,000
Number Employees: 10
Sq. footage: 15

532 **Amizetta Vineyards**
1099 Greenfield Rd
Saint Helena, CA 94574 707-963-1460
Fax: 707-963-1460 cab@amizetta.com
www.amizetta.com
Wines
President: Spencer Clark
Operations/Winemaker: Robert Egelhoff
Estimated Sales: $1-2.5 Million
Number Employees: 1-4

533 **(HQ)Amoretti**
451 Lombard St
Oxnard, CA 93030-5143 805-983-2903
Fax: 805-718-0204 800-266-7388
info@amoretti.com www.amoretti.com
Manufacturer and exporter of nut flour, paste and butter; also, marzipan, ganache, fruit extracts and dessert sauces
Owner: Jack Barsoumian
CEO: Jack Barsoumian
Marketing President: Maral Barsoumian
Manufacturing President: Ara Barsoumian
Estimated Sales: $20+ Million
Number Employees: 1-4
Type of Packaging: Food Service, Bulk
Brands:
Amoretti
Baristella
Capriccio

534 **Amoroso's Baking Company**
845 S 55th St
Philadelphia, PA 19143 215-471-4740
Fax: 215-472-5299 800-377-6557
info@amorosobaking.com
www.amorosobaking.com
Manufacturer of rolls, breads, bagels, jewish bread and pretzels
VP: Leonard Amoroso
Sales Director: Len Constantino
Estimated Sales: $50-100 Million
Number Employees: 250-499
Type of Packaging: Consumer, Food Service, Private Label
Brands:
AMOROSO

535 **Amour Chocolates**
2416 San Mateo Pl NE
Albuquerque, NM 87110-4057 505-881-2803
Fax: 505-884-8189
amourchocolates@comcast.net
www.amourchocolates.com
Chocolates
President: Lori Swanson

536 **Ampac Packaging, LLC**
12025 Tricon Road
Cincinnati, OH 45246 513-671-1777
Fax: 513-671-2920 800-543-7030
www.ampaconline.com
Manufacturer of flexible packaging and bags
Brands:
AB SEALERS
ALL PACKAGING MACHINERY
CHANTLAND
FISCHBEIN BAG CLOSING
FUJY
HIGHLIGHT STRETCH RAPPERS
LIFT PRODUCTS
NEW LONDON ENG
VACULET USA

537 **Ampacco**
18 Loveton Circle
Sparks, MD 21152 410-771-7301
Fax: 410-771-7462 800-632-5847
www.mccormick.com
Spices, extracts, seasonings, dry seasoning mixes
President: Allen Wilson
EVP, CFO, and Director: Gordon Stetz
Vice President: Bob Lawless
Managing Director: James Brady
Estimated Sales: $ 3.34 Billion
Number Employees: 200
Brands:
McCormick

538 **Amport Foods**
560 Kasota Avenue SE
Minneapolis, MN 55414-2811 612-331-7000
Fax: 612-331-1122 800-989-5665
customers@amportfoods.com
www.amportfoods.com
Dates, dried fruits whole and pressed
President: Andrew Stillman
Vice President: Jeff Vogel
Production Manager: Mike McIvor
Estimated Sales: $ 20 - 50 Million
Number Employees: 20-49
Type of Packaging: Bulk

539 **Amrion**
6565 Odell Place
Boulder, CO 80301-3306 303-530-4554
Fax: 303-530-2592 800-627-7775
Manufacturer of nutritional supplements including capsules, powders and softgels
CEO: Mark Crossen
Sales Manager: Tom Weaver
Estimated Sales: $68 Million
Number Employees: 250-499
Sq. footage: 400000
Parent Co: WholeFoods Market
Type of Packaging: Consumer

540 **Amros the Second, Inc.**
69 Veronica Ave # 69
Somerset, NJ 08873-3467 732-846-7755
Fax: 732-846-4956
Processor of Russian-style chocolate and marshmallow candy; importer of European food products including packaged grains, beans and kasha
Owner: Leom Mogilezer
Estimated Sales: $20-50 Million
Number Employees: 20-49
Type of Packaging: Consumer, Food Service
Brands:
Amros

541 **Amsnack**
7770 Longe Street
Stockton, CA 95206-3925 209-982-5545
Fax: 209-982-4955
Rice crackers, cookies crackers and chips
President: Satoshi Yamada
Shipping Coordinator: Karen Valterza
Estimated Sales: $5-9.9 Million
Number Employees: 20-49

542 **Amstell Holding**
209 Theodore Rice Boulevard
New Bedford, MA 02745-1213 508-995-6100
Fax: 508-995-2912
Provides state-of-the-art, Grade A Dairy, FDA- and LACF -approved processing of shelf-stable nonrefrigerated milk, nutritional supplements, juices, teas, and drink beverages. Provides Tetra Brik packs with pull tab or strawapplication
Director Operations: Cindy Aldrich

543 **Amster-Kirtz Company**
2830 Cleveland Ave NW
Canton, OH 44709 330-535-6021
Fax: 330-437-2015 800-257-9338
www.amsterkirtzco.net
Candy and confectionery
President: Joe Bauer
Estimated Sales: $50-100 Million
Number Employees: 50-99

544 **Amsterdam Brewing Company**
21 Bathurst Street
Toronto, ON M5V 2N6
Canada 416-504-1040
Fax: 416-504-1043 info@amsterdambeer.com
www.amsterdambeer.com
Manufacturer of beer, lager and ale including stout
President: Jeff Carefoote
Number Employees: 12
Type of Packaging: Consumer, Food Service

545 **Amt Labs**
680 N 700 W
North Salt Lake, UT 84054 801-299-1661
Fax: 801-299-0220 customercare@amtlabs.net
www.amtlabs.net
Processor and exporter of food supplements including mineral supplements, amino acid chelates, ascorbates, citrates, etc.
President: Bing Fang
VP/Research & Development: Oliver Fang
VP Manufacturing: Todd Rasmussen
Estimated Sales: $8.2 Million
Number Employees: 58
Sq. footage: 100000
Type of Packaging: Private Label, Bulk

546 **Amurol Confections Company**
2800 State Route 47
Yorkville, IL 60560-9441 630-553-4800
Fax: 630-553-4801 www.confections.com
Bubble gum, suckers and candy
Executive Director: Lupe Alvarez
CEO: A G Atwater Jr
VP Marketing: Bruce Thompson
VP Sales: Steve Howard
Estimated Sales: $50-100 Million
Number Employees: 10-19
Brands:
BIG LEAGUE CHEW
BLASTERS
BUBBLE BEEPER
BUBBLE CANE
BUBBLE JUG
BUBBLE TAPE
BUBBLE TAPE HOLIDAY STRIPE
BUBBLE TAPE MEGA ROLL
BUG CITY
BUNGEE
CANDY MOUSE
CARAMEL APPLE BUBBLE GUM
CLUCKERS
EVEREST
FRESH SQUEEZED
NEON BEACH
OUCH!
REED'S

RUGRATS BUBBLE GUM BABIES
RUGRATS COMIC BOOK
RUGRATS COOKIE JAR
RUGRATS TOY BAG
SANTA DISPENSER
SANTA'S COAL
SQUEEZE POP
SQUEEZE POP LAVA LICK
SQUEEZE POP SPORTS BOTTLE
SUGARFREE BUBBLE TAPE
TAPE SPARKLERS
TAPE TWISTERS
THUMB SUCKERS
ZING ZANG

547 **Amwell Valley Vineyard**
80 Old York Rd
Ringoes, NJ 8551 908-788-5852
Fax: 908-788-1030
jefferyfisher@amwellvalleyvineyard.com
www.amwellvalleyvineyard.com
Wines
Owner: Jeff Fischer
VP: Jeffrey Fisher
Operations Manager: Scott Gares
Estimated Sales: $1-2.5 Million
Number Employees: 1-4
Number of Brands: 1
Number of Products: 20
Type of Packaging: Consumer
Brands:
Amwell Valley Vineyard

548 **Amy's Kitchen**
P.O.Box 449
Petaluma, CA 94953-0449 707-568-4500
Fax: 707-578-7995 amy@amyskitchen.net
www.amys.com
Manufacturer and exporter of frozen organic meals and entrees; also, canned soups and bottled pasta sauces.
Co-Owner: Rachel Berliner
Co-Owner: Andy Berliner
Sourcing Manager: Joel Humphries
Estimated Sales: $250 Million
Number Employees: 1600
Number of Brands: 1
Number of Products: 146
Sq. footage: 105000
Type of Packaging: Consumer, Food Service
Brands:
AMYS KITCHEN

549 **AnaCon Foods Company**
1145 Main St
Atchison, KS 66002 913-367-2885
Fax: 913-367-1794 800-328-0291
anacon@journey.com www.wheatnuts.com
Processor and exporter of simulated nut and fruit particulates and analogs
Executive Director: Tom Miller
VP Sales/Marketing: Jane Hallas
Director Operations: Marvin Mikkelson
Estimated Sales: $2.5-5 Million
Number Employees: 20-49
Brands:
Bits'N'Pops
Bowlby's Bits
Mix-Ups
Nuts'N'Pops
Wheat Nuts

550 **Anabol Naturals**
1550 Mansfield St
Santa Cruz, CA 95062 831-479-1403
Fax: 831-479-1406 800-426-2265
service@anabol.com www.anabol.com
Manufacturer and exporter of sports nutrition supplements including free-form amino acids, GH releasers, muscle octane, muscle mass and fat burner kits and life extension nutrients
President: Roger Prince
Estimated Sales: $500,000-$1 Million
Number Employees: 5-9
Sq. footage: 5000
Brands:
Anabol Naturals

551 **Anastasia Confections Inc.**
1815 Cypress Lake Dr
Orlando, FL 32837 407-816-9944
Fax: 407-816-9901 800-329-7100
jlascano@anastasiaconfections.com
www.anastasiaconfections.com
Specialty Candy
President: Mike Constantine
Marketing: James Lascano
Purchasing Director: Mike Constantine
Estimated Sales: $2 Million

552 **Anchor Appetizer Group**
555 N Hickory Farm Ln
Appleton, WI 54914-3037 920-997-2200
Fax: 920-734-2828 www.anchorfoods.com
Appetizers
President: Mark Follett
Vice President: Scott Follet
Estimated Sales: $ 6 Million
Parent Co: McCain Foods USA/H.J. Heinz Company
Type of Packaging: Consumer, Food Service
Brands:
BREW CITY
CHEESE SENASATIONS
GOLDEN CRISP
GOLDEN CRISP
MOORE'S
MOZZALUNA
MOZZAMIA
OLIVENOS
POPPERS
PRIMASAMO CUBES
PROVAGO WHEELS
QUESO TRIANGULOS
WRAPPETIZERS

553 **Anchor Brewing Company**
1705 Mariposa St
San Francisco, CA 94107 415-863-8350
Fax: 415-552-7094 info@anchorbrewing.com
www.anchorbrewing.com
Processor and exporter of beer and ale, products of which include Anchor Steam; Liberty Ale; Anchor Porter; Summer Beer; Old Foghorn; Anchor Small, and Christmas Ale.
President/Brewmaster: Fritz Maytag
Director of Sales and Marketing: John Dannerbeck
Head Brewer: Mike Lee
Estimated Sales: $20-50 Million
Number Employees: 50-99
Type of Packaging: Consumer, Private Label

554 **(HQ)Anchor Food Products/ McCain Foods**
555 N Hickory Farm Lane
Appleton, WI 54914-3037 920-734-0627
mberg@anchorfoods.com
www.mccainusa.com
Processor and exporter of frozen breaded appetizers including cauliflower, mushrooms, okra, squash, zucchini, cheese, onion rings and stuffed jalapenos.
Chairman: Allison McCain
President/CEO: Dale Morrison
VP/CFO: Thomas Tranetzki
COO: Greg Brook
Purchasing Director: Janet Evans
Chairman: Mack Follett
VP Procurement: Brian Follett
Plant Manager: Steven Hesseling
Estimated Sales: $10-100 Million
Number Employees: 250-499
Parent Co: McCain Foods
Type of Packaging: Food Service, Private Label, Bulk
Other Locations:
Anchor Food Products
Pecos TX
Brands:
All Kitchens
Anchor
Comsource
Nugget
Pocahontas
Poppers
Sysco
WRAPPETIZERS

555 **Anchor Frozen Foods**
32 Urban Ave
Westbury, NY 11590 516-333-6344
Fax: 516-997-1823 800-566-3474
info@anchorfrozenfoods.com
www.anchorfrozenfoods.com
Manufacturer of seafood including stuffed sole, conch, shrimp, lobster tails, octopus, calamari and king crab legs.
President: Roy Tuccillo
Estimated Sales: $500,000- 1 Million
Number Employees: 5-9
Type of Packaging: Consumer, Food Service, Bulk

556 **Anco Foods**
P.O.Box 2010
Caldwell, NJ 7007 973-808-7148
Fax: 973-575-5010 800-526-2596
www.ancofinecheese.com
Cheese
President: Alain Boss
Estimated Sales: $2.5-5 Million
Number Employees: 5-9
Type of Packaging: Bulk

557 **Ancora Coffee Roasters**
3701 Orin Rd
Madison, WI 53704 608-255-2900
Fax: 608-255-2901 800-260-0217
service@ancoracoffee.com
www.ancoracoffee.com
Specialty coffees, espresso coffee, whole bean and ground, loose leaf teas including black, green, oolong, herbal and decaffinated
President/CEO: George Krug
Quality Control/Production: Rob Jeffries
Marketing: Christy Gibbs
Estimated Sales: $1-5 Million
Number Employees: 10-19
Sq. footage: 15000
Type of Packaging: Consumer, Food Service, Bulk
Brands:
ANCORA COFFEE
ANCORA D'ORO
ANCORA ESPRESSO

558 **Andalan Confections**
PO Box 2149
Fort Oglethorpe, GA 30742-0149 706-858-4640
Fax: 706-858-4642 877-263-2526
www.andalan.com
President: Anita Loizeaux
Brands:
EDO

559 **Andalusia Distributing Company**
117 Allen Ave
Andalusia, AL 36420 334-222-3671
Fax: 334-222-6575
President: Michael Jones
Vice President: Richard Jones
Estimated Sales: $ 50 - 100 Million
Number Employees: 50-99

560 **Andersen's Pea Soup**
376 Avenue of the Flags
Buellton, CA 93427 805-688-5581
Fax: 805-686-5670 info@peasoupandersens.net
www.peasoupandersens.net
Gourmet canned split pea soup
Manager: Tony Picard
Purchasing Director: Brinda Wolf
Estimated Sales: $2.5-5 Million
Number Employees: 50-99

561 **Anderson Bakery Company**
2060 Old Philadelphia Pike
Lancaster, PA 17602 717-299-2321
Fax: 717-393-3511 800-732-0089
www.andersonpretzel.com
Processor and exporter of pretzels including salted and no-salt, gems, logs, twists, peanut butter filled, bread sticks and snack mixes
President: Richard Dwinell
Executive VP: Norman Randall
Research & Development: Michael Bockman
Quality Control: Michael Bockman
Sales Director: Dan Walker
Purchasing Manager: Carol Maxey
Estimated Sales: $20-50 Million
Number Employees: 250-499
Sq. footage: 175000
Type of Packaging: Consumer, Food Service, Private Label, Bulk
Brands:
ANDERSON
NATIONAL

562 **Anderson Custom Processing**
P.O.Box 279
New Ulm, MN 56073 507-233-2800
Fax: 507-233-2806 877-588-4950
acpi@newulmtel.net
www.andersonprocessing.com

Custom manufacturer of spray-dried food products including whey, starches, cheese and cream powders
President: Brian Anderson
Production Manager: Jerome Braun
Estimated Sales: $ 3 - 5 Million
Number Employees: 1-4
Type of Packaging: Bulk
Other Locations:
Sleepy Eye MN
Little Falls WI
Belleville WI

563 **Anderson Dairy**
801 Searles Ave
Las Vegas, NV 89101 702-642-7507
Fax: 702-642-3480 www.andersondairy.com
Milk, dairy products
President: Harold Bellanger
Manager: Catherine Boman
VP, Sales: Dave Coon
Estimated Sales: $76 Million
Number Employees: 200
Brands:
Anderson Dairy

564 **(HQ)Anderson Erickson Dairy**
2420 E University Ave
Des Moines, IA 50317 515-265-2521
Fax: 515-263-6301 aedairy@aedairy.com
www.aedairy.com
Processing and bottling dairy products
CEO: Jim Erickson
CEO: Miriam Erickson Brown
Estimated Sales: $100+ Million
Number Employees: 250-499
Type of Packaging: Food Service

565 **Anderson Peanuts**
P.O.Box 810
Opp, AL 36467 334-493-4591
Fax: 334-493-7767 andpeanut@alaweb.com
www.alaweb.com
Manufacturer of peanuts
Division Manager: Dennis Finch
Estimated Sales: $1-2.5 Million
Number Employees: 5-9
Type of Packaging: Bulk

566 **Anderson Seafoods**
P.O.Box 17636
Anaheim, CA 92817-7636 714-777-7100
Fax: 714-777-7116 www.andersonseafoods.com
Manufacturer and wholesaler/distributor of fresh and frozen seafood; serving the food service market and supermarkets
President: Dennis Anderson
Secretary/Treasurer: Leean Anderson
Vice President: Todd Anderson
Estimated Sales: $20-50 Million
Number Employees: 20-49
Sq. footage: 20000

567 **Anderson Valley Brewing**
P.O.Box 505
Boonville, CA 95415 707-895-2337
Fax: 707-895-2353 avbc@pacific.net
www.avbc.com
Processor of seasonal beer, ale, porter, stout, lager and pilsner
VP Sales: David Gatlin
Estimated Sales: $7 Million
Number Employees: 45
Sq. footage: 20000
Type of Packaging: Consumer
Brands:
Barney Flats Oatmeal Stout
Beik's Esb
Boont Amber
High Rollers Wheat
Hop Ottin' Ipa
Poleeko Gold
Winter Solstice

568 **Anderson's Conn Valley Vineyards**
680 Rossi Rd
Saint Helena, CA 94574 707-963-8600
Fax: 707-963-7818 800-946-3497
cvvinfo@connvalleyvineyards.com
www.connvalleyvineyards.com
Wines
President: Todd Anderson
Operations: Mac Sawyer
Estimated Sales: $2.5-5 Million
Number Employees: 5-9

569 **(HQ)Andes Candy**
7401 S Cicero Ave
Chicago, IL 60629-5885 773-838-3400
Fax: 773-838-3435 www.tootsie.com
Manufacturer and exporter of chocolate mints
President/COO: Ellen Gordon
Chairman/CEO: Melvin Gordon
VP Finance/CFO: G Howard Ember Jr
Research & Development Manager: Terry Sons
Research/Q&A Director: Gordon Brown
VP Marketing/Sales: Thomas Corr
Public Relations Director: Janet Vasilenko
VP Manufacturing: John Newlin Jr
Estimated Sales: $521 Million
Number Employees: 1,000-4,999
Type of Packaging: Consumer, Food Service, Bulk
Brands:
ANDES

570 **Andre French Bakery Retail**
12901 McGregor Blvd
Fort Myers, FL 33919-4587 239-482-2011
Fax: 941-482-1178
Bakery products
Estimated Sales: $300,000-500,000
Number Employees: 5-9

571 **Andre Prost**
680 Middlesex Tpke
Old Saybrook, CT 6475 860-388-0838
Fax: 860-388-0830 800-243-0897
prostinc@andreprost.com www.andreprost.com
Candy, confectionery, seasonings and spices.
Owner: Frank Landrey
Vice President: Peter Cumings
VP Finance: Charles Landrey
Estimated Sales: $2 Million
Number Employees: 13
Brands:
A TASTE OF CHINA
A TASTE OF INDIA
A TASTE OF THAI
GINGER SNAPS
HONEES
NOTTA PASTA
ODENSE
ZOTZ

572 **Andre's Confiserie Suisse**
5018 Main St
Kansas City, MO 64112-2755 816-561-3440
Fax: 816-561-2922 800-892-1234
customer service@andreschocolates.com
www.andreschocolates.com
Processor of Swiss style chocolate candies
President: Macel Bollier
CEO: Rene Bollier
CFO: Connie Bollier
Estimated Sales: $2.5-5 Million
Number Employees: 50-99
Type of Packaging: Consumer
Other Locations:
Andre's Confiserie Suisse
Overland Park KS
Andre's Confiserie Suisse
Denver CO

573 **Andre-Boudin Bakeries**
221 Main St Ste 1230
San Francisco, CA 94105 415-882-1849
Fax: 415-913-1818 boudin@boudinbakery.com
www.boudinbakery.com
Manufacturer of sourdough bread, specialty breads, and sweet goods
Owner: Sharon Duvall
VP Sales/Marketing: Terry Wight
Plant Manager: Rick Rodrick
Estimated Sales: $300,000-500,000
Number Employees: 1,000-4,999
Type of Packaging: Private Label, Bulk
Other Locations:
Boudin Cafe
San Francisco CA
Boudin Cafe
San Mateo CA
Boudin Cafe
Santa Clara CA
Boudin Cafe
Palo Alto CA
Boudin Cafe
Corte Madera CA
Boudin Cafe
Walnut Creek CA
Boudin Cafe
Costa Mesa CA
Boudin Cafe
San Diego CA
Boudin Cafe
Escondido CA
Brands:
Boudin

574 **Andresen Ryan Coffee Com**
2206 Winter St
Superior, WI 54880-1437 715-395-3793
Fax: 715-392-4776 ruby@superior-wi.com
www.arcocoffee.com
Processor of coffee and coffee syrups
Owner: John Andresen
President: B Fleming
Director Manufacturing: Vern Suby
Estimated Sales: Less than $500,000
Number Employees: 1-4
Type of Packaging: Consumer, Food Service
Brands:
Arco

575 **Andrew & Williamson Sales Company**
9940 Marconi Dr
San Diego, CA 92154 619-661-6000
Fax: 619-661-6007
accounting@andrew-williamson.com
www.andrew-williamson.com
Frozen strawberries
President: Fred Williamson
Estimated Sales: $2.5-5 Million
Number Employees: 20-49
Brands:
A&W

576 **Andrew Peller Limited**
697 S Service Road
Grimsby, ON L3M 4E8
Canada 905-643-4131
Fax: 905-643-4944 info@andreswines.com
www.andrewpeller.com
Leading producer and marketer of quality wines in Canada with wineries in British Columbia, Ontario and Nova Scotia. Products include award winning premium VQA wines, table wines, sparkling wines, Icewine, and premium craft beers.7
President Winexpert Inc./Vineco Intl.: Robert Van Wely
President/CEO: John Peller
Key Account Director: Steve Azzopardi
VP Marketing: Shari Niles
VP Sales: Chris Zarafonitis
Estimated Sales: 211.8 Million
Number Employees: 1,400
Type of Packaging: Consumer, Food Service, Bulk
Brands:
CALONA VINEYARDS
GRANVILLE ISLAND
HILLEBRAND
PELLER ESTATES
RED ROOSTER
SANDHILL
THIRTY BENCH
TRIUS
VINECO
WINEXPERT

577 **Andrew's Brewing**
353 High St
Lincolnville, ME 04849 207-763-3305
Beer
Owner: Andrew Hazen
Estimated Sales: $500,000-$1 Million
Number Employees: 1-4
Brands:
Brown Ale
English Pale Ale
St. Nicks Poter
Summer Golden Ale

578 **Andrews Caramel Apples**
5001 W Belmont Ave
Chicago, IL 60641 773-286-2224
Fax: 773-286-2258 800-305-3004
Info@AndysSeasoning.com
www.andysseasoning.com
Processor of caramel apples
President: Daniel De Marco
Treasurer: Sylvia Schuman
Purchasing: Rick Walker

Estimated Sales: $2.5-5 Million
Number Employees: 10-19
Type of Packaging: Consumer
Brands:
Andrews
Ms. Kays

579 **Andy's Seasoning**
2829 Chouteau Ave
St Louis, MO 63103-3016 314-664-2149
Fax: 314-664-2149 800-305-3004
Info@AndysSeasoning.com
www.andysseasoning.com
Seasoned salt, breadings for fish and chicken
President: Katherine Anderson
Estimated Sales: $20-50 Million
Number Employees: 1-4
Sq. footage: 27000
Type of Packaging: Consumer, Food Service, Private Label, Bulk
Brands:
Andy's Custom Blended Breading
Andy's Hot Spicey Chicken Breading
Andy's Mild Chicken Breading
Andy's Red Fish Breading
Andy's Seasoned Salt
Andy's Yellow Fish Breading

580 **Anette's Chocolate Factory**
1321 First Street
Napa, CA 94559 707-252-4228
Fax: 707-252-8074 mary@anettes.com
www.anettes.com
Truffles, creams, brittles, chews, chocolate sauces, caramel sauces, traditional and unique seasonal specialties.
President: Anette Madsen
VP: Brent Madsen
Marketing: Mary Stornetta
Number Employees: 15

581 **Angel's Bakeries**
29 Norman Avenue
Brooklyn, NY 11222 718-389-1400
Fax: 718-389-3928 joe@angelsbakery.com
www.angelsbakery.com
Cookies, muffin tops, muffins, florentines, cakes and cake slices.
President: Joseph Angel
Marketing Director: Bill McNamee
Production Manager: Eloy Rojas
Estimated Sales: $4.1 Million
Number Employees: 45

582 **Angelic Gourmet Inc**
P.O.Box 127
Naples, NY 14512
Fax: 585-374-9753 www.angelicgourmet.com
Chocolate dipped pretzels and chocolate drizzled popcorn.
President: Sher Kemp
Estimated Sales: $1.8 Million
Number Employees: 20

583 **Anglo American Trading**
P.O.Box 97
Harvey, LA 70059-0097 504-341-5631
Fax: 504-341-5635
Manager: Dennis Skrmetta
CEO: Eric Skrmetta

584 **Angy's Food Products Inc.**
77 Servistar Industrial Way
Westfield, MA 1085 413-572-1010
Fax: 413-572-4785 www.angysfood.com
Processor of frozen tortellini, gnocchi, cavatelli, stuffed shells, manicotti and ravioli
President: Jack Fu
CFO: Liz Campanini
VP: Steve Campanini
Number Employees: 20-49
Sq. footage: 23000
Type of Packaging: Consumer, Food Service, Private Label, Bulk
Brands:
Angy's
Big Y
Finast
Introvigne's
Shaw's

585 **Anheuser-Busch**
15800 Roscoe Blvd
Van Nuys, CA 91406 818-989-5300
Fax: 818-908-5685 www.anheuser-busch.com
Manufacturer of beer including light.
Manager: Gary Lee IV
VP/Chief Legal Officer: Mark Bobak
VP/Chief Financial Officer: W Randolph Baker
Manager/Quality Assurance: Tanya Towns
VP/Communications & Consumer Affairs: Francine Katz
VP/Chief Information Officer: Joseph Castellano
VP/Corporate Human Resources: John Farrell
Plant Manager: Gary Lee
Estimated Sales: $500 Million-$1 Billion
Number Employees: 1,000-4,999
Parent Co: Anheuser-Busch Companies
Type of Packaging: Consumer, Food Service, Bulk

586 **Anheuser-Busch**
775 Gellhorn Dr
Houston, TX 77029 713-675-2311
Fax: 713-670-1690 www.anheuser-busch.com
Manufacturer, bottler, canner and exporter of beer including light and nonalcoholic.
President/CEO: Augusta Busch IV
VP/Chief Legal Officer: Mark Bobak
VP/Chief Financial Officer: W Randolph Baker
CIO: Steve Edler
VP/Communications & Consumer Affairs: Francine Katz
VP Human Resources: Robert Alvarez
COO/General Manager/Plant Manager: Steve Ghiglieri
Estimated Sales: $500 Million-$1 Billion
Number Employees: 1,000-4,999
Parent Co: Anheuser-Busch Companies
Type of Packaging: Consumer, Food Service, Bulk

587 **Anheuser-Busch**
2885 Belgium Rd
Baldwinsville, NY 13027 315-638-0365
Fax: 315-635-4404 www.anheuser-busch.com
Manufacturer of bottled regular and light beer.
President/Owner: Rus Adams
VP/Chief Legal Officer: Mark Bobak
VP/Chief Financial Officer: W Randolph Baker
VP/Communications & Consumer Affairs: Francine Katz
Public Relations: Larry Harmon
Plant Manager: Brian McNelis
Estimated Sales: $500 Million-$1 Billion
Number Employees: 1,000-4,999
Parent Co: Anheuser-Busch Companies
Type of Packaging: Consumer

588 **Anheuser-Busch**
700 Schrock Rd
Columbus, OH 43229 614-888-6644
Fax: 614-847-6497 www.anheuserbusch.com
Manufacturer of bottled and canned beer, ale, malt liquor and lager.
President: David Peacock
VP Finance: David Almeida
VP/Communications & Consumer Affairs: Franice Katz
VP/Chief Information Officer: Joseph Castellano
VP/Corporate Human Resources: John Farrell
Estimated Sales: $500 Million-$1 Billion
Number Employees: 500
Parent Co: Anheuser-Busch Companies
Type of Packaging: Consumer

589 **Anheuser-Busch**
P.O.Box 200248
Cartersville, GA 30120-9029 770-386-2000
Fax: 770-606-3111 www.anheuser-busch.com
Manufacturer of canned and bottled beer.
President/CEO: Augusta Busch IV
VP/Chief Legal Officer: Mark Bobak
VP/Chief Financial Officer: W Randolph Baker
VP/Communications & Consumer Affairs: Francine Katz
VP/Chief Information Officer: Joseph Castellano
VP/Corporate Human Resources: John Farrell
Plant Manager: Greg Kellerman
Estimated Sales: $2.5-5 Million
Number Employees: 10-19
Parent Co: Anheuser-Busch Companies
Type of Packaging: Consumer, Food Service, Bulk

590 **Anheuser-Busch**
3101 Busch Dr
Fairfield, CA 94534 707-429-2000
Fax: 707-429-7517 www.anheuser-busch.com
Manufacturer of canned and bottled beer.
Manager: Kevin Finger IV
VP/Chief Legal Officer: Mark Bobak
VP/Chief Financial Officer: W Randolph Baker
VP/Communications & Consumer Affairs: Francine Katz
VP/Chief Information Officer: Joseph Castellano
VP/Corporate Human Resources: John Farrell
Estimated Sales: $100-500 Million
Number Employees: 250-499
Parent Co: Anheuser-Busch Companies
Type of Packaging: Bulk

591 **Anheuser-Busch**
111 Busch Dr
Jacksonville, FL 32218 800-342-5283
Fax: 904-751-8120 www.buschjobs.com
Manufacturer of canned and bottled beer.
President/CEO: Augusta Busch IV
VP/Chief Legal Officer: Mark Bobak
VP/Chief Financial Officer: W Randolph Baker
VP/Communications & Consumer Affairs: Francine Katz
VP/Chief Information Officer: Joseph Castellano
VP/Corporate Human Resources: John Farrell
Plant Manager: Syl Robinson
Estimated Sales: $100-500 Million
Number Employees: 500-999
Parent Co: Anheuser-Busch Companies
Type of Packaging: Bulk

592 **(HQ)Anheuser-Busch Inc.**
1 Busch Pl
Saint Louis, MO 63118 314-577-2000
Fax: 314-577-2900 800-342-5283
douglas.muhleman@anheuser-busch.com
www.anheuser-busch.com/ABInc.html
Beer, adventure park entertainment and packaging; also interests in aluminum beverage container recycling, malt production, rice milling, real estate, turf farming, creative services, metalized paper label printing and transportation.Processor, importer and exporter of beer, malt liquor, ales, lagers and non-alcoholic brews.
President: David Peacock
Zone President/North America: Luiz Fernando Edmond
VP Finance: David Almeida
VP Information & Business Services: Odilon Queiroz
VP Logistics: Pablo Gonzalez
VP Corporate Affairs & Communications: James Villeneuve
VP Supply: Peter Kraemer
VP Procurement: Lee Keathley
Estimated Sales: $36 Billion
Number Employees: 116,000
Type of Packaging: Consumer, Food Service, Bulk
Other Locations:
Baldwinsville NY
Cartersville GA
Columbus OH
Fairfield CA
Fort Collins CO
Houston TX
Jacksonville FL
Los Angeles CA
Merrimack NH
St. Louis MO
Williamsburg VA
Newark NJ
Brands:
180
Anheuser World Select
BE
Bacardi Silver
Bacardi Silver Limon
Bacardi Silver Low Carb BlackCherry
Bacardi Silver O3
Bacardi Silver Raz
Bare Knuckle Stout
Bud Dry
Bud Ice
Bud Ice Light
Bud Light
Budweiser
Busch
Busch Ice
Busch Light
Busch NA
Hurricane Ice

Hurricane Malt Liquor
King Cobra
Michelob
Michelob Amber Bock
Michelob Golden Draft
Michelob Golden Draft Light
Michelob Hefeweizen
Michelob Honey Lager
Michelob Light
Michelob Ultra
Natural Ice
Natural Light
O'Douls
O'Douls Amber
Redhook Ale
Tequiza
Tilt
Widmer Brothers
ZiegenLight

593 **Anheuser-Busch North Brewery**
200 Us Highway 1 and 9
Newark, NJ 7114 973-645-7700
Fax: 973-645-7950 www.anheuser-busch.com
Manufacturer and exporter of canned and bottled beer.
President/CEO: Augusta Busch IV
VP/Chief Legal Officer: Mark Bobak
VP/Chief Financial Officer: W Randolph Baker
VP/Communications & Consumer Affairs: Francine Katz
VP/Chief Information Officer: Joseph Castellano
VP/Corporate Human Resources: John Farrell
Plant Manager: Bob Rogers
Estimated Sales: $500 Million-$1 Billion
Number Employees: 500-999
Parent Co: Anheuser-Busch Companies
Type of Packaging: Bulk

594 **Anita's Mexican Foods Corporation**
686 S Allen St
San Bernardino, CA 92408 909-890-4647
www.anitafoods.com
Manufacturer and exporter of Mexican foods including tortilla chips and taco and tostada shells, plus organic snacks, chips and popcorn
President: Jose Gomez
Plant Manager: Frank Coser
Estimated Sales: $20-50 Million
Number Employees: 100-249
Sq. footage: 30000
Parent Co: La Reina
Type of Packaging: Consumer, Food Service, Private Label, Bulk
Brands:
ANITA'S
GO-MEX
LA REINA
OLD PUEBLO RANCH

595 **Anke Kruse Organics**
#9-685 Speedvale Avenue W
Guelph, ON N1K 1E6
Canada 519-824-6161
Fax: 519-853-5155 info@ankekruseorganics.ca
www.ankekruseorganics.ca
President: Anke Kruse
Brands:
Anke Kruse Organics

596 **Ankeny Lakes Wild Rice**
9594 Sidney Rd S
Salem, OR 97306-9448 503-363-3241
Fax: 503-371-9080 800-555-5380
info@wildriceonline.com
www.wildriceonline.com
Grower, processor, packer and importer of certified organic wild rice and nonorganic and wild rice blends
Co-Owner: Larry Payne
Co-Owner: Sharon Jenkins-Payne
Sales Director: Larry Payne
Purchasing Manager: Larry Payne
Estimated Sales: $500,000
Number Employees: 1-4
Sq. footage: 3000
Type of Packaging: Consumer, Food Service, Private Label, Bulk
Brands:
Canadian Jumbo Lake
Idaho Lake Wild Rice
Oregon
Wild & Ricey

597 **Ankle Deep Foods**
912 W Omaha Avenue
Norfolk, NE 68701-5842 402-371-2991
wings@buffalomaid.com
www.buffalomaid.com
Manufacturer of hot suaces and marinades
Brands:
Buffalo Maid

598 **Anmar Foods**
2150 W Carroll Ave
Chicago, IL 60612-1604 312-421-6500
Fax: 312-421-4765 www.anmarfoods.com
Owner: Bob Martinelli
Estimated Sales: $ 20 - 50 Million
Number Employees: 20-49

599 **Anmar Nutrition**
P.O.Box 2343
Bridgeport, CT 06608-0343 203-336-8330
Fax: 203-336-5508 blancoanmar@snet.net
www.anmarinternational.com
A distributor and contract manufacturer specializing in vitamins, nutritional products, excipients, non-prescription pharmaceutical products, herbs, and amino acids. We offer expertise in sourcing granulations, triturations, millingand custom blends
President: John Blanco
VP: Hongbing Deng
Sales Director: Allan Pollard
Production Manager: John Blanco
Estimated Sales: $ 10 - 20 Million
Number Employees: 10-19
Number of Products: 100+
Sq. footage: 15000
Type of Packaging: Bulk

600 **Ann Hemyng Candy**
P.O.Box 567
Trumbauersville, PA 18970-0567 215-536-7004
Fax: 215-536-6848 800-779-7004
chocolat@fast.net www.chocolateshop.com
Manufacturer of molded chocolate including lollypops, novelties in chocolates, custom corporate logos
President/Owner: Louise Spindler
Estimated Sales: $ .5 - 1 million
Number Employees: 5-9

601 **Ann's House of Nuts, Inc.**
8221 Preston Court
Jessup, MD 20794-8613 301-498-4920
Fax: 301-317-6248
Processor of various nuts, dried fruits, and mixes
President: Edward Zinke
Estimated Sales: $2.5-5 Million
Number Employees: 50-99
Sq. footage: 200000
Type of Packaging: Consumer, Food Service, Private Label

602 **Anna's Oatcakes**
988 Route 100
Weston, VT 05161-5414 802-824-3535
abjordan@vermontel.net
www.snackvermont.com
Oatcakes

603 **Anna's Unlimited, Inc**
PO Box 141154
Austin, TX 78714-1154 512-837-2203
Fax: 512-837-0003 800-849-7054
jim.u@anasfoods.com www.anasfoods.com
Ana's Foods is a gourmet food product development and marketing company. It sells Anna's salsa, a fresh, refrigerated salsa picante, and Ana's herbs, a dry blend of eight spices.
President: Anna Olvera - Ullrich
COO/VP: Jim Ullrich
VP: James A Ullrich
Marketing: James Ullrich Jr
Estimated Sales: $500,000
Number Employees: 1-4
Number of Brands: 3
Number of Products: 8
Type of Packaging: Consumer, Food Service, Bulk
Brands:
Ana's

604 **Annabelle Candy Company**
P.O.Box 3665
Hayward, CA 94540-3665 510-783-2900
Fax: 510-785-7675 info@annabelle-candy.com
www.annabelle-candy.com
Processor of confectionery products including chocolate truffles, candy bars, nougats and taffy
President/CEO: Susan Gamson Karl
Director of Finance: Shelley Craft
CEO: Susan G Karl
VP Quality Control/Production/Purchasing: Carlos Osorio
Direcotr of Sales/Marketing: David Klabunde
Estimated Sales: $20-50 Million
Number Employees: 50-99
Type of Packaging: Consumer, Bulk
Brands:
Abba-Zaba
Big Hunk
Look!
Rocky Road
U-No

605 **Annabelle Lee**
70 Rear Mills Road
Cape Porpoise, ME 04014 207-967-4611
Fax: 207-832-7795
President: Frank Minio
Number Employees: 30

606 **Annapolis Produce & Restaurant Supply**
15 Lee St
Annapolis, MD 21401 410-266-5211
Fax: 410-266-0568
President: Timothy Campbell
Estimated Sales: $ 50 - 100 Million
Number Employees: 50-99

607 **Annapolis Winery**
26055 Soda Springs Rd
Annapolis, CA 95412 707-886-5460
Fax: 707-886-5460
annapoliswinery@starband.net
www.annapoliswinery.com
Wines
President: Basil Scalabrini
Estimated Sales: $2.5-5 Million
Number Employees: 5-9

608 **Annette Island Packing Company**
P.O.Box 10
Metlakatla, AK 99926-0010 907-886-4661
Fax: 907-886-4660 info@metlakatlaseafood.com
www.metlakatlaseafood.com
Salmon and cured seafood
Manager: Freeman Mc Gilton
Estimated Sales: $50-100 Million
Number Employees: 100-249

609 **Annie Chun's**
4340 Redwood Hwy
Suite B60
San Rafael, CA 94903 415-479-8272
Fax: 415-479-8274 info@anniechun.com
www.anniechun.com
All natural Pan-Asian soup bowls, noodle bowls, noodle express, rice express and organic noodles and sauce kits.
Owner: Annie Chun
CEO: Mike Keeland
CFO: Han Kim
Estimated Sales: Less than $500,000
Number Employees: 5-9

610 **Annie's Frozen Yogurt**
5200 W 74th St Ste A
Minneapolis, MN 55439 952-835-2110
Fax: 952-835-2378 800-969-9648
www.anniesyogurt.com
Processor of frozen yogurt - many delicious flavors
President: Lawrence Serf
Estimated Sales: $500,000-$1 Million
Number Employees: 5-9

611 **Annie's Homegrown**
564 Gateway Dr
Napa, CA 94558 707-254-3700
Fax: 781-224-9728 800-288-1089
bernie@annies.com www.annies.com
Gourmet foods
President: John Foraker
CEO: John Foraker
CFO: Steven Jackson
VP Research/Development: Bob Kaake
VP Marketing: Sarah Bird
Senior VP Sales: Mark Mortimer
Estimated Sales: $2.5-5 Million
Number Employees: 5-9

Type of Packaging: Private Label
Brands:
Annie's Macaroni & Cheese
Tamarind Tree

612 **Annie's Naturals**
792 Foster Hill Rd
East Calais, VT 05650 802-456-8866
Fax: 802-456-8865 800-434-1234
info@anniesnaturals.com
www.anniesnaturals.com
Manufacturer and exporter of natural dressings and vinigrettes, BBQ sauces, marinades and worcestershire sauce
Owner/Production Development: Annie Christopher
Owner/Sales/Marketing: Peter Backman
Number Employees: 10-19
Type of Packaging: Consumer, Food Service, Private Label
Brands:
Annie's Naturals
Annie's Naturals Magic Sauces
Annie's Naturals Salad Dressings

613 **Antelope Valley Winery**
42041 20th St W
Lancaster, CA 93534 661-722-0145
Fax: 661-722-6035 800-282-8332
wines@avwinery.com www.avwinery.com
Wines
Owner: Cyndee Donato
Winemaker: Cecil McLester
Estimated Sales: $2.5-5 Million
Number Employees: 5-9
Type of Packaging: Private Label
Brands:
Antelope Valley

614 **Anthony & Sons Italian Bakery**
1275 Bloomfield Ave
Fairfield, NJ 07004-2708 973-244-9669
Fax: 973-244-1298 anthonyandsons@aol.com
Bread
Owner: Anthony Pio Costa
Plant Manager: Robert Tobia
Estimated Sales: Less than $500,000
Number Employees: 5-9

615 **Anthony Road Wine Company**
1225 Anthony Rd
Penn Yan, NY 14527 315-536-2182
Fax: 315-536-5851 800-559-2182
info@anthonyroadwine.com
www.anthonyroadwine.com
Wines
President: John Martini
VP: Ann Martini
Operations Manager: Peter Martini
Production Manager: Johannes Reinhardt
Estimated Sales: $2.5-5 Million
Number Employees: 10-19

616 **Anthony-Thomas Candy Company**
1777 Arlingate Lane
Columbus, OH 43228 614-274-8405
Fax: 614-274-0019 877-226-3921
dougwheeler@anthony-thomas.com
www.anthony-thomas.com
Manufacturer of gourmet-style chocolate in prepackaged boxes including truffles, real butter creams, cordial cherries, creams, peanut butter cups, pecans and English Toffee
President: Joe Zanetos
EVP Administration/Finance: Greg Zanetos
Marketing/Sales Manager: Clara Davis
EVP Production: Tim Zanetos
Plant Manager: Paul Reeder
Estimated Sales: $10-20 Million
Number Employees: 191
Sq. footage: 152000
Type of Packaging: Consumer
Brands:
ANTHONY-THOMAS CHOCOLATES

617 **Anton Caratan & Son**
P.O.Box 2797
Bakersfield, CA 93303-2797
Fax: 661-725-5829 www.acaratan.com
Processor and exporter of table grapes
President: Anton Caratan
Sales Manager: George Ann Caratan
Estimated Sales: $10-20 Million
Number Employees: 250-499
Type of Packaging: Consumer
Brands:
Good Times
Prosperity

618 **Antoni Ravioli**
879 N Broadway
North Massapequa, NY 11758 516-799-0350
Fax: 516-799-0357 800-783-0350
info@antoniravioli.com www.antoniravioli.com
Manufacturer of ravioli, stuffed shells and manicotti, tortellini, cavatelli and gnocchi, fresh pasta, also gluten free products.
President: Eugene Saucci
Human Resources Director: Ann Saucci
Estimated Sales: $1.5 Million
Number Employees: 10
Sq. footage: 3000
Type of Packaging: Food Service, Private Label, Bulk
Brands:
Antoni Ravioli

619 **Antonio Mozzarella Factory**
631 Frelinghuysen Ave # 2
Newark, NJ 07114 973-353-9411
Fax: 973-353-0996 antoniomozz@verizon.net
www.antoniomozzarella.com
Fresh mozarella
Presdient: Tom Pugliese
Estimated Sales: $7.1 Million
Number Employees: 25

620 **Antonio's Bakery**
9616 Atlantic Ave
Jamaica, NY 11416 718-322-1314
Fax: 718-322-1475
President: Peter Backman
Estimated Sales: $20-50 Million
Number Employees: 20-49

621 **Apac Chemical Corporation**
150 N Santa Anita Ave Ste 850
Arcadia, CA 91006 626-203-0066
Fax: 626-203-0067 866-849-2722
sales@apacchemical.com
www.apacchemical.com
Manufacturer of potassium sorbate and sorbic acid
President: Sun Chang
Vice President: Tom Kusaka
Account Executive: Dave Plowman
Estimated Sales: $4 Million
Number Employees: 7

622 **Apani Southwest**
5401 N 1st St
Abilene, TX 79603 325-690-1550
Fax: 325-690-1412 drinkapak@sbcglobal.net
www.apanisw.com
Premium purified drinking water
Owner/President: Jay Pickens
VP: Glenda Pickens
Estimated Sales: $2 Million
Number Employees: 1-4
Type of Packaging: Private Label

623 **Apecka**
371 Stevens Road
Rockwall, TX 75032-6754 972-772-2654
Fax: 973-772-2655 apecka1@aol.com
Peppered pickles, pickled okra and garlic, green chile sauce
President: Sharon Eisenbraun
Estimated Sales: Less than $500,000
Number Employees: 1-4

624 **Apex Marketing Group**
7835 S Rainbow Blvd
Suite 17-300
Las Vegas, NV 89139 866-610-6165
Fax: 805-499-4204 888-990-2739
apexmktg@earthlink.net www.hairnomore.com
Manufacturer of natural products for personal care in the food industry
President/CEO: Mel Landyn
Vice President: Carole Landyn
Marketing Director: Mark Landyn
Operations Manager: Armen Grigorian Jr.
Product Manager: Mel Landyn
Estimated Sales: $5 Million
Number Employees: 25
Number of Brands: 2
Number of Products: 6
Sq. footage: 16000
Parent Co: Health Tec Labs
Type of Packaging: Consumer, Private Label, Bulk
Other Locations:
Apex Marketing Group
Newbury Park CA

625 **Aphrodisia Products**
62 Kent St
Brooklyn, NY 11222-1517 718-383-3677
Fax: 718-383-6618 877-274-3677
info@aphrodisiaproducts.com
www.aphrodisiaproducts.com
Manufacturer and exporter of bulk herbs, spices, botanical extracts and essential oils
President: James Adelson
Estimated Sales: $2.5-5 Million
Number Employees: 1-4
Sq. footage: 40000
Type of Packaging: Bulk

626 **Apotheca Naturale**
201 Apple Boulevard
Woodbine, IA 51579 712-647-3133
Fax: 712-647-2573 800-736-3130
Manufacturer of homeopathics, botanical extracts, capsules, tablets and sports nutritionals
President: Kathryn Simon
Estimated Sales: $10-20 Million
Number Employees: 100
Sq. footage: 70000

627 **Appert's Foodservice**
900 Highway 10 S
St Cloud, MN 56304-1807 320-251-3200
Fax: 320-259-0747 800-225-3883
info@apperts.com www.apperts.com
Processor of meat, fish and seafood, canned and dry groceries, chemicals; wholesaler/distributor of fresh and frozen produce and general line items
President: Joe Omann
President: Tim Appert
Owner: Chris Appert
Quality Control: Duane Du Monceaux
Production Manager: Adrian Seguin
Purchasing Director: Wayne Harrison
Estimated Sales: $20-50 Million
Number Employees: 100-249
Sq. footage: 93000
Type of Packaging: Consumer, Food Service, Bulk

628 **Appetizers And**
2555 N Elston Ave
Chicago, IL 60647 773-227-0400
Fax: 773-227-0448 800-323-5472
emailus@appetizersandinc.com
www.appetizersandinc.com
Manufacturer of frozen hors d'oeuvres
President/CEO/Co-Owner: George King
EVP/Co-Owner: Patricia Domanik
CFO: Scott Forester
SVP Operations/COO: Kristine Holtz
VP Manufacturing: John Trellicoso
Number Employees: 250-499
Type of Packaging: Consumer, Food Service

629 **Apple & Eve**
P.O.Box K
Roslyn, NY 11576-0410 516-621-1122
Fax: 516-621-2164 800-969-8018
info@appleandeve.com www.appleandeve.com
Manufacturer and exporter 100% pure and natural juices and juice blends; importer of fruit concentrates
Founder/CEO: Gordon Crane
VP Sales/Marketing: Cary Crane
Operations Manager: John Donlon
Estimated Sales: $90+ Million
Number Employees: 1-4
Sq. footage: 6000
Type of Packaging: Consumer
Brands:
Apple & Eve
Made in the Shade
Sesame Street
Tribal

630 **Apple Acres**
4633 Us Route 20
La Fayette, NY 13084 315-677-5144
Fax: 315-677-5143

Grower, packer and exporter of apples.
Owner: Walter Blackler
CEO: Walter Blackler
Estimated Sales: $4 Million
Number Employees: 20-49
Sq. footage: 32000
Type of Packaging: Consumer

631 **Apple Flavor & FragranceUSA Corp.**
55 Carter Dr Ste 103
Edison, NJ 8817 732-356-3800
Fax: 732-393-1933
Flavor ingredients and enhancers.

632 **Apple Valley Market**
9067 Us Highway 31 # A
Berrien Springs, MI 49103-1806 269-471-3234
Fax: 269-471-6035 800-237-7436
avnf@avnf.com www.avnf.com
Vitamins and vegetarian groceries
Manager: George Schmidt
CEO: Frank Williams
Marketing Director: Frank Williams
Estimated Sales: $ 5 - 10 Million
Number Employees: 100-249
Sq. footage: 50000

633 **Applecreek Farms**
PO Box 8383
Lexington, KY 40533 859-881-8010
Fax: 877-869-9184 800-747-8871
bhall@mis.net www.applecreek.net
Preserves, fruit butters, marinade, salsa, relish, caramel and chocolate fidge dessert sauces, dressings, BBQ seasonings and homemade candies.
Owner: Buddy Hall
Operations Manager: Lynn Abshear
Estimated Sales: $ 1 - 3 Million
Number Employees: 1-4
Brands:
Applecreek Orchards

634 **Appledore Cove LLC**
19 Buffum Rd Unit 6
North Berwick, ME 03906 207-676-4088
Fax: 207-636-8100 info@appledorecove.com
www.appledorecove.com
Salsas, condiments & dips, sauces & marinades, preserves & dessert sauces
President: Jeff Garstka

635 **Applegate Farms**
750 Us Highway 202 # 300
Bridgewater, NJ 08807-5530 908-725-2768
Fax: 908-725-3383 help@applegatefarms.com
www.applegatefarms.com
Manufacturer and distributor natural (ABF) and organic meat including beef, chicken, turkey and pork. Also cheese, sausage and hotdogs.
Owner: Seven McDonald
Co-Founder: Chris Ely
Number Employees: 50-99
Sq. footage: 7000
Type of Packaging: Consumer, Food Service, Private Label, Bulk
Brands:
APPLEGATE FARMS
GREAT ORGANIC HOTDOG
JOY STICK

636 **Appleton Produce Company**
1408 Weiser River Road
PO Box 110
Weiser, ID 83672 208-414-3352
Fax: 208-414-1862
onions@appletonproduce.com
www.appletonproduce.com
Packer and Shipper of fresh onions.
President: C. Robert Woods
President/Owner: Steve Woods
Marketing/Sales Manager: Steve Walker
Purchasing Manager: Dave Price
Estimated Sales: $12 Million
Number Employees: 50
Type of Packaging: Consumer, Food Service, Private Label, Bulk
Brands:
APCO
Appleton
Gold Nugget

637 **Applewood Orchards**
2998 Rodesiler Hwy
Deerfield, MI 49238 517-447-3002
Fax: 517-447-3006 800-447-3854
scottaoi@cass.net www.applewoodapples.com
Processor and exporter of apples
President: Jim Swindeman
VP: Scott Swindeman
Estimated Sales: $5-10 Million
Number Employees: 20-49
Type of Packaging: Consumer

638 **April Hill**
190 28th St SE
Grand Rapids, MI 49548 616-245-0595
Fax: 616-245-2368
Breads, rolls
Plant Manager: William MacKenzie
Estimated Sales: $2.5-5 Million
Number Employees: 10-19

639 **Aqua Clara Bottling & Distribution**
1315 Cleveland Street
Clearwater, FL 33755-5102 727-446-2999
Fax: 727-446-3999 info@aquaclara.com
www.aquaclara.com
Bottles and distributes oxygen-enriched premium drinking water 0-2 parts total dissolved solids, bottled with over 55 parts pure oxygen
Chairman: E Douglas Cifers
President: Jack Plunkett
CEO: Jack Plunkett
Number Employees: 5-9
Brands:
Aqua Clara

640 **Aqua Vie Beverage Corporation**
PO Box 6759
Ketchum, ID 83340-6759 208-622-7792
Fax: 208-622-8829 800-744-7500
contact@aquavie.com www.aquavie.com
Natural falvored water without carbonation, low-calorie and exotic flavors
President: Thomas Gillespie
Estimated Sales: $1-2.5 Million
Number Employees: 20-49
Type of Packaging: Bulk
Brands:
Avalanche

641 **(HQ)AquaCuisine**
1065 E Winding Creek Dr, #275
Eagle, ID 83616-7243 208-323-2782
Fax: 208-323-4730 mgoforth@aquacuisine.com
www.aquacuisine.com
Processor of value added seafood products including fresh and frozen burgers, franks and refrigerated seafood entrees
President: Mark Goforth
Estimated Sales: $5 Million
Number Employees: 1-4
Number of Products: 7
Sq. footage: 5000
Type of Packaging: Consumer
Brands:
AQUACUISINE

642 **AquaTec Development**
1543 Locke Ln
Sugar Land, TX 77478 281-491-0808
Fax: 281-242-7771 stern4@alltel.net
Bulk production of algae and nutraceutical extracts and concentrates. Algae food supplements and food fortificial bulk only
President: Howard Stern
Number Employees: 1-4
Type of Packaging: Bulk

643 **Aquafina**
700 Anderson Hill Road
Purchase, NY 10577-1444 914-253-2000
Fax: 914-253-2070 willard.walker@pepsi.com
www.aquafina.com OR www.pepsico.com
Manufacturer of bottled water
Chairman/Chief Executive Officer: Indra Nooyi
EVP Global Operations: Richard Goodman
Chief Financial Officer: Hugh Johnston
VP: Joe Schuler
SVP/Corporate Strategy & Development: Wahid Hamid
Chief Communications Officer: Julie Hamp
Sales & Marketing: A Salman Amin
General Manager: Bill Mikulka
Estimated Sales: $100 Million
Number Employees: 250-499
Sq. footage: 40000
Parent Co: PepsiCo North America
Type of Packaging: Consumer, Food Service
Brands:
Aquafina
Aquafina Alive
Aquafina FlavorSplash
Aquafina Sparkling

644 **Aquatec Seafoods Ltd.**
820 Shamrock Place
Comox, BC V9M 4G4
Canada 250-339-6412
Fax: 250-339-4951 info@aquatec.bc.ca
www.aquatec.bc.ca
Manufacturer of fresh and frozen salmon and oysters
President: Malena Tutte
Estimated Sales: $2.7 Million
Number Employees: 20
Sq. footage: 7000
Type of Packaging: Consumer, Food Service, Private Label, Bulk

645 **Aquatech**
6221 Petersburg St
Anchorage, AK 99507 907-563-1387
Fax: 907-563-1852
Partner: Miki Ballard
Partner: Lamar Ballard
General Manager: Sarah Ballard
Estimated Sales: $ 3 - 5 Million
Number Employees: 1-4

646 **Aralia Olive Oils**
1105 Massachusetts Avenue
Suite 2E
Cambridge, MA 02138 617-354-8556
Fax: 617-249-1855 877-585-9510
www.araliaoliveoils.com
Olive Oils
President: Emmanuel Daskalakis
Number Employees: 2

647 **Arbor Crest Wine Cellars**
4705 N Fruit Hill Rd
Spokane, WA 99217 509-927-9463
Fax: 509-927-0574 info@arborcrest.com
www.arborcrest.com
Wine
Manager: Jim Van Loven Sels
Marketing Director: Joe Algeo
General Manager: James van Loben Sels
Production Manager: Kristine Mielke-van Loben Sels
Estimated Sales: $1.25 Million
Number Employees: 10-19
Type of Packaging: Private Label
Brands:
Arbor Crest

648 **Arbor Hill Grapery**
6461 State Route 64
Naples, NY 14512-9726 585-374-2870
Fax: 585-374-9198 800-554-7553
js@thegrapey.com www.thegrapery.com
Gourmet wines, grape and fruit based products, fruit preservatives, wine jellies, dressings, vinegars, barbeque sauces, mustard, spreadable sauce and dips, pretzel dips, wine sauces and tea concentrates
CEO: John Brahm III
VP: Katharine Brahm
Public Relations: Sherry Brahm-Orlando
Estimated Sales: Less than $5 Million
Number Employees: 5-9
Type of Packaging: Consumer, Private Label
Brands:
Arbor Hill Wine
Brahm's Wine Country
Mrs. Brahms

649 **Arbor Mist Winery**
116 Buffalo Street
Canandaigua, NY 14424-1012 866-396-7394
www.arbormist.com
Fruit flavored wines

650 **(HQ)Arbor Springs Water Company**
855 E Cambourne St
Ferndale, MI 48220 248-543-7150
Fax: 248-543-0488 800-343-7003
sales@aswaterco.com www.aswaterco.com

Bottled Spring and Purified water.
Estimated Sales: $5-10 Million
Number Employees: 10-19
Other Locations:
Arbor Springs Water Company
Ann Arbor MI
Brands:
Arbor Springs Drinking Water
Arbor Springs Purified Water
Arbor Springs Spring Water

651 **Arboris, Llc**
1101 W Lathrop Ave
Garden City, GA 31415 912-238-7537
Fax: 912-238-7454 www.arboris-us.com
Supplier of sterols used in yogurt, milks, juices and breads.
Vice President/General Manager: Peter Acton
Sales: Peter Acton
Purchasing: Jeanne Anderson

652 **(HQ)Arbre Farms Corporation**
6362 N 192nd Avenue
Walkerville, MI 49459 231-873-3337
Fax: 231-873-5699 www.arbrefarms.com
Provides food service and frozen food manufacturing industries with the finest quality frozen fruits and vegetables.
President: C.O. Johnson
Quality Control: Robert Anderson
Marketing: Tripper Showell
Sales: Jean Hovey
Plant Manager: Vince Miskosky
Type of Packaging: Food Service, Bulk

653 **Arbuckle Coffee**
275 Curry Hollow Road
Pittsburgh, PA 15236-4631 412-653-8878
800-533-8278
www.arbucklecoffee.com
Specialty coffee and tea.
President: Denney Willis
VP: Josh Willis
Estimated Sales: $500,000-$1 Million
Number Employees: 5-9
Brands:
Arbuckle

654 **Arcadia Dairy Farms**
P.O.Box 631
Arden, NC 28704 828-684-3556
Fax: 828-684-7988 info@arcadiadairyfarms.com
www.arcadiadairyfarms.com
Processor of juices including orange, apple, strawberry and grape; also, water
President: James Arthur
Vice President: Carolyn Arthur
Estimated Sales: $1 Million
Number Employees: 9
Type of Packaging: Consumer
Brands:
Arcadia
Sunrise

655 **Arcadian Estate Winery**
4184 State Route 14
Rock Stream, NY 14878 607-535-2068
Fax: 607-535-4692 800-298-1346
info@arcadianwine.com www.arcadianwine.com
Manufacturer of red, white and fruit wines.
Owner: John Dalonzo
Number Employees: 10-19
Type of Packaging: Consumer

656 **Arcee Sales Company**
30 Gem St
Brooklyn, NY 11222 718-383-0107
Fax: 718-383-9115
Processor of fresh fish
Controller: Leo Sumera
Manager: Eric Caslow
Estimated Sales: $20-50 Million
Number Employees: 100-249
Type of Packaging: Consumer, Food Service

657 **(HQ)Archer Daniels Midland Company**
4666 Faries Parkway
Decatur, IL 62526 217-424-5200
Fax: 217-424-6196 800-637-5843
info@admworld.com www.adm.com
Processors of soybeans, corn, wheat and cocoa
Chairman/President/CEO: Paticia woertz
Vice Chairman: John Rice
SVP/CFO: Ray Young
EVP/Performance & Growth: Steven Mills
VP/Chief Communications Officer: Victoria Podesta
Estimated Sales: $69 Billion
Number Employees: 28,200
Type of Packaging: Bulk
Other Locations:
ADM
Canada
ADM do Brasil Ltda
Sao Paulo, Brasil
ADM Paraguay S.A.E.C.A
Mingua Guaz£, Paraguay
ADM SAO S.A. Bolivia
Santa Cruz de la Sierra
ADM
Europe
ADM
Middle East
ADM
Africa
ADM Australia
Sydney, Australia
ADM Hong Kong
Wanchai, Hong Long
ADM Trading Company Ltd
Shanghai, China
ADM Tianjin
Tianjin, China
ADM Dalian
Dalian, China
ADM Far East
Bunkyo-Ku Tokyo, Japan
Brands:
AMRBOSIA®
ARCON®
BEAKIN
CAPSULEC
CLINTOSER
CORNSWEET®
DE ZAAN®
FIBERSOL-2™
MERCKENS®
NOVALIPID™
NOVASOY®
NOVAXAN™
NUSUN®
NUTRISOY®
NUTRIsOY® NEXT™
OPTIXAN™
PFL™
PRO-FAM®
SUPERB®
THERMOLEC
ULTRALEC®
YELKIN®

658 **Archer Daniels Midland Company**
P.O.Box 29268
Lincoln, NE 68529 402-464-9131
Fax: 402-464-5956 800-228-4060
www.adm.com
Processor of flour and pancake mix
President: John Baumgartner
Plant Manager: Jeramy Fisher
Estimated Sales: $100+ Million
Number Employees: 100-249
Parent Co: Archer Daniels Midland Company
Type of Packaging: Consumer, Food Service, Private Label, Bulk
Brands:
Budget
Larosa
Martha Gooch
Russo
Soy7 Soy Enriched Pasta

659 **Archibald Candy Corporation**
6700 N Northwest Hwy
Chicago, IL 60631 773-631-6171
Fax: 312-243-3921 800-333-3629
customerservice@archibaldcandy.com
www.fanniemaycandies.com
Manufacturer and exporter of confectionery products including chocolates, hard candy and nuts
President: Ted Shepherd
Number Employees: 1-4
Parent Co: Fannie May
Type of Packaging: Consumer, Food Service, Private Label, Bulk
Brands:
Fannie May
Fanny Farmer
Laura Secord
Sweet Factory

660 **Archie Moore's Foods Products**
15 Factory Ln
Milford, CT 06460-3306 203-876-5088
Fax: 203-876-0525 www.archiemoores.com
Manufacturer and exporter of buffalo wing sauce and flavored potato chips
President: Todd Ressler
Estimated Sales: $ .5 - 1 million
Number Employees: 20-49
Sq. footage: 2500
Parent Co: Archie Moore's Bar & Restaurant
Type of Packaging: Consumer, Food Service, Private Label, Bulk
Brands:
Archie Moore's

661 **Archon Vitamin Corporation**
209 40th Street
Irvington, NJ 07111
Fax: 973-371-1277 800-349-1700
purchasing@archonvitamin.com
www.archonvitamin.com
Established manufacturer of vitamins, minerals, herbs, and other nutritionals.
President: Tom Pugsley
VP Products Division: Paul Stevens
Quality Assurance Manager: Susan Jackson
Sales Manager: Rick McNall
Operations Executive: Jose Camaano
Purchasing Director: Tracy Daniiel
Estimated Sales: $ 5 - 10 Million
Number Employees: 50-99
Number of Brands: 1
Sq. footage: 50000
Type of Packaging: Consumer, Private Label, Bulk
Brands:
BIONUTRIENT

662 **Archway & Mother's Cookie Company**
810 81st Avenue
Oakland, CA 94621-2583 510-569-2323
Fax: 510-569-6604 800-369-3997
www.archway
Manufacturer of cookies and crackers
Plant Manager: Terry Goodman
Estimated Sales: $250 Million
Number Employees: 200
Parent Co: Catterton Partners
Type of Packaging: Consumer, Food Service, Bulk

663 **Archway Cookies**
2041 Claremont Ave
Ashland, OH 44805 419-289-0787
Fax: 419-289-1289 888-427-2492
www.archwaycookies.com
Processor of cookies
President: John Stevens
VP Operations: Tom Seddon
Plant Manager: Jeremy Bowman
Purchasing Manager: Brenda Marker
Estimated Sales: $ 50 - 100 Million
Number Employees: 500-999
Sq. footage: 170000
Parent Co: Parmalat Bakery Group North America
Type of Packaging: Consumer

664 **(HQ)Archway Cookies**
87 Michigan Avenue W
Suite 608
Battle Creek, MI 49017-3605 269-962-6205
Fax: 616-962-8149 888-427-2492
archie@archwaycookies.com
www.archwaycookies.com
Manufacturer of cookies
President: Patrick O'Dey
CFO: Nicola Melillo
Marketing: William Klump
Sales: Mark O'Toole
Public Relations: Dan Keefe
Operations: Peter Lowes
Number Employees: 20-49
Parent Co: Parmalat Bakery Group North America
Type of Packaging: Private Label
Brands:
ARCHWAY

665 **Arcobasso Foods Inc**
8014 N Broadway
St Louis, MO 63147-2417 314-381-8083
Fax: 314-381-4522 800-284-0620
pat@arcobasso.com www.arcobasso.com
Arcobasso Foods is a full-service custom manufacturer and bottler of salad dressings, sauces and marinades.
President: Tom Newsham
Vice President: Pat Newsham
Type of Packaging: Food Service

666 **Arcor USA**
6205 Blue Lagoon Dr Ste 350
Miami, FL 33126-6034
Fax: 305-592-1081 800-572-7267
www.arcor.com.ar
Candies
President: Sergio Limonti
National Sales Manager: Michael Figueras
Product Manager: Damian Cordova
Estimated Sales: $ 10 - 20 Million
Number Employees: 20-49
Type of Packaging: Private Label
Brands:
ARCOR PREMIUM HARD FILLED CANDIES
ARCOR VALUE LINE HARD CANDIES
ROCKLETS
WHISPER CHOCOLATE BON BONS

667 **(HQ)Arctic Beverages**
314 Green Street
Flin Flon, MB R8A 0H2
Canada 204-687-7517
Fax: 204-687-7940
Wholesaler/distributor and bottler of soft drinks and juices for vending, fountains and coolers; also, installation services available
President: Allan McLeod
Estimated Sales: $6 Million
Number Employees: 44
Sq. footage: 17000
Parent Co: Pepsi
Other Locations:
Arctic Beverages Ltd.
The Pas MB
Arctic Beverages Ltd.
Thompson MB
Arctic Beverages Ltd.
Winnipeg MB

668 **Arctic Glacier**
625 Henry Avenue
Winnipeg, MB R3A 0V1 204-772-2473
Fax: 204-783-9857 888-573-9237
info@arcticglacierinc.com
www.arcticglacierinc.com
Manufacture ice
President, CEO: Keith McMahon
Chief Financial Officer: Douglas Bailey
Manager: Sharon Douglass
Equipment Sales/Leasing: Jeff Hendler
Estimated Sales: $ 10 - 20 Million
Number Employees: 20-49
Parent Co: Arctic Glacier
Other Locations:
Happy Ice
Buffalo NY

669 **Arctic Glacier**
20 Wells Ave
Utica, NY 13502-2520 315-732-4148
Fax: 315-793-8851 800-792-5958
info@arcticglacierinc.com
www.arcticglacierinc.com
Manufactures ice
Owner: Dave Dubiel
Chief Financial Officer: Douglas Bailey
Manager: Sharon Douglass
Equipment Sales/Leasing: Jeff Hendler
Estimated Sales: $ 3 - 5 Million
Number Employees: 1-4
Parent Co: Arctic Glacier
Other Locations:
Happy Ice
Utica NY

670 **Arctic Glacier**
234 Barker Street
Corning, NY 14830 607-936-4511
800-937-4423
info@arcticglacierinc.com
www.arcticglacierinc.com
Manufactures ice
President/CEO: Keith McMahon
Chief Financial Officer: Dougals Bailey
Manager: Sharon Douglass
Equipment Sales/Leasing: Jeff Hendler
Estimated Sales: $ 1 - 3 Million
Number Employees: 1-4
Parent Co: Arctic Glacier
Other Locations:
Happy Ice
Corning NY

671 **Arctic Glacier**
2 Commerce Avenue
Albany, NY 12206-2016 518-438-2070
518-438-2082
info@arcticglacierinc.com
www.arcticglacierinc.com
Manufactures ice
President/CEO: Keith McMahon
Chief Financial Officer: Douglas Bailey
Manager: Sharon Douglass
Equipment Sales/Leasing: Jeff Hendler
Estimated Sales: $ 10 - 20 Million
Number Employees: 20-49
Parent Co: Arctic Glacier
Other Locations:
Happy Ice
Albany NY

672 **Arctic Ice Cream Company**
22 Arctic Pkwy
Ewing, NJ 8638 609-393-4264
Fax: 609-392-3663 astephens@chartermi.net
www.acticicecreamco.com
Ice cream
President: Thomas Green
Vice President: Christine Green
Estimated Sales: $1 Million
Number Employees: 18

673 **Arctic Seas**
21 Burchard Ave
Little Compton, RI 2837 401-635-4000
Fax: 401-635-9158 brian@arcticseas.com
www.arcticseas.com
Manufacturer of frozen fish and seafood including whitefish, crab meat, scallops, shrimp, squid and surimi
President: Brian Eliason
Estimated Sales: $20-50 Million
Number Employees: 5-9
Type of Packaging: Consumer, Food Service, Private Label
Brands:
Arctic Iceland
Arctic Seas
Arctic Sprays

674 **Ardmore Cheese Company**
P.O.Box 888
Shelbyville, TN 37162 931-427-2191
Fax: 931-427-4116
Manufacturer of cheddar cheese including sliced, diced and shredded
Manager: Abby Woods
VP: Joe Madeo
Plant Manager: Brad Jackson
Estimated Sales: $500-1 Million appx.
Number Employees: 1-4
Sq. footage: 10000
Type of Packaging: Consumer, Private Label
Brands:
Ardmore
Avalon

675 **Arena & Sons**
159 Ash St
Hopkinton, MA 01748-1903 508-435-3673
Fax: 508-435-2457
Manufacturer of veal and beef
President: Frank Arena
Estimated Sales: $2.5-5 Million
Number Employees: 5-9
Type of Packaging: Bulk

676 **Argee Corporation**
9550 Pathway St
Santee, CA 92071 619-449-5050
Fax: 619-449-8392 800-449-3030
argee@tsn.net www.argeecorp.com
CEO: Robert Oldman
Marketing Director: Ruth Oldman
CEO: Robert Goldman
President: Robert Oldman
Estimated Sales: $ 10 - 20 Million
Number Employees: 50-99

677 **Argo Century**
4913 Chastain Ave
Suite 17
Charlotte, NC 28217-3116 704-525-6180
Fax: 704-525-6280 800-446-7108
info@tontonsauce.com www.tontonsauce.com
Manufacturer of ginger dressing, teriyaki sauce and vinaigrettes.
President: Yoshi Shioda
Estimated Sales: $ 1 - 3 Million
Number Employees: 1-4
Type of Packaging: Consumer

678 **Argo Fine Foods**
PO Box 2077
Saint James, NY 11780 631-703-0443
cdeblasio@argofinefoods.com
www.argofinefoods.com
Tzatziki (yogurt sauce), pita snacks
President/Owner: Christel DeBlasio-Pavlidis

679 **Argonaut Winery**
13825 Willow Creek Rd
Ione, CA 95640 800-704-9463
Fax: 209-245-5567 argonautwnry@cdepot.net
Wines
Owner: Mark McMaster
CEO: Debe Fake
Vice President: Steve Fale
Marketing Director: Jennifer Marston
Operations Manager: Brian Marston
Estimated Sales: $1-2.5 Million
Number Employees: 1-4

680 **(HQ)Argyle Wines**
P.O.Box 280
Dundee, OR 97115-0280 503-538-8520
Fax: 503-538-2055 888-427-4953
tastingroom@argylewinery.com
www.argylewinery.com
Wines
President: Rollin Soles
General Manager: Allen Holstein
Estimated Sales: $20-50 Million
Number Employees: 50-99
Type of Packaging: Private Label
Brands:
Argyle Brut
Nuthouse Pinot Noir

681 **(HQ)Ariake USA, Inc.**
1711 N Liberty St
Harrisonburg, VA 22802 540-432-6550
Fax: 540-432-6549 888-201-5885
polansky@ariake.com www.ariakeusa.com
Manufacturer of Stocks, Broths, Bases, Seasonings, Flavor Systems
Manager: Kyle Wellsford
Marketing/Sales Manager: Aaron Robinson
Sales Manager: Joe Brisby
Estimated Sales: $10-20 Million
Number Employees: 20-49
Sq. footage: 58000
Other Locations:
Ariake USA
China
Ariake USA
Japan
Ariake USA
France
Ariake USA
Belgium

682 **Arico Natural Foods**
3720 Sw 141st Ave
Suite 210
Beaverton, OR 97005 503-259-0871
www.crisproot.com
Manufacturer of Casava root chips and other natural snacks
President/CEO: Angela Ichwan
CFO/VP: Hermanto Hidajat
Vice President of Sales and Marketing: Duke Field
Estimated Sales: $500,000-1 Million
Number Employees: 5-9

683 **Ariel Natural Foods**
13400 N 20th St
Suite 32
Bellevue, WA 98005 425-637-3345
Fax: 425-637-8655 contactus@arielfoods.com
www.arielfoods.com
Sugar-free, dairy-free and gluten-free premium freeze dried snacks.

684 **Ariel Vineyards**
860 Napa Valley Corporate Way
Napa, CA 94558 707-258-8048
Fax: 707-258-8052 800-456-9472
info@arielvineyards.com
www.arielvineyards.com
Processors and exporter of nonalcoholic wine
Manager: Craig Rosser
VP Operations: Jeff Meier
Estimated Sales: $5-10 Million
Number Employees: 1-4
Sq. footage: 64000
Parent Co: J. Lohr Vineyards & Wines
Brands:
Ariel
Ariel Blanc
Ariel Brut Cuve
Ariel Cabernet
Ariel Chardonnay
Ariel Merlot
Ariel Rouge
Ariel White Zinfandel

685 **Aries Prepared Beef**
17 W Magnolia Blvd
Burbank, CA 91502-1719 818-526-4855
Fax: 818-845-3041
Processor of cooked and smoked beef and sausage
Owner: Fred Scholder
Sales Manager: Fred Weiss
Estimated Sales: $50-100 Million
Number Employees: 20-49
Type of Packaging: Consumer, Food Service

686 **Arise & Shine Herbal Products**
P.O.Box 400
Medford, OR 97501 541-282-0891
Fax: 541-773-8866 800-688-2444
admin@ariseandshine.com
www.ariseandshine.com
Processor and exporter of digestive aids and herbal supplements for complete body detoxification and follow-up nourishment
Founder: Dr. Richard Anderson
CEO: Avona L'Carttier
Brands:
Chomper
Flora Grow
Herbal Nutrition
Super Antioxidant Blend
Ultimate Food Complex

687 **Arista Industries**
557 Danbury Rd
Wilton, CT 06897 203-761-1009
Fax: 203-761-4980 800-255-6457
info@aristaindustries.com
www.aristaindustries.com
Processor, exporter and wholesaler/distributor of oils, frozen shrimp, lobster tails and octopus; serving the food service market; importer of octopus, shrimp, squid, lobster tails, oils and surimi products
President: Charles Hillyer
CEO: Stephen Weitzer
Sales Manager: Nick Collins
Estimated Sales: $2.5-5 Million
Number Employees: 20-49
Type of Packaging: Consumer, Food Service
Brands:
Arista
Pacific Treasures
Sea Devils

688 **Ariston Specialties**
PO Box 306
Bloomfield, CT 06002 860-224-7184
Fax: 860-726-1263
aristonspecialties@hotmail.com
www.aristonoliveoil.com
Olive Oils
Owner: Thomas Doukas

689 **Ariza Cheese Company**
7602 Jackson St
Paramount, CA 90723 562-630-4144
Fax: 562-630-4174 800-762-4736
www.mexicancheese.com
Processor of Mexican cheese
General Manager: Ernestina Mariscal
Estimated Sales: $5.5 Million
Number Employees: 40
Type of Packaging: Consumer, Food Service

690 **Arizona Beverage Company**
60 Crossways Park Dr W
Woodbury, NY 11797-2003
Fax: 516-326-4988 800-832-3775
info@arizonabev.com www.arizonabev.com
Manufacturer of flavored beverages including teas, juices and iced coffees
President: John Ferolito
VP Business Development: John Balboni
VP National Sales: Paul O'Donnell
Estimated Sales: $ 5 - 10 Million
Number Employees: 500-999
Brands:
Arizona
Ferolito, Vultaggio & Sons
Rx Extreme Energy Shot

691 **Arizona Brands**
3121 E Washington St
Phoenix, AZ 85034-1519 602-273-7139
Fax: 602-275-9429
Prepared Foods and Specialties
President: Ken Charbonneau
Sales Manager: Bob Stephens
VP Operations: Mike Depinto
Plant Manager: Joaquin Amaro
Estimated Sales: $20-50 Million
Number Employees: 50-99

692 **(HQ)Arizona Chemical Company**
P.O.Box 550850
Jacksonville, FL 32255 904-928-8700
Fax: 904-928-8779 800-526-5294
www.arizonachemical.com
Manufacturer of pine chemicals
CEO: Cornelis Verhaar
Number Employees: 1,000-4,999
Other Locations:
Dover OH
Panama City FL
Pensacola FL
Port St. Joe FL
Savannah GA
Valdosta GA
Miami FL

693 **(HQ)Arizona Cowboy**
3010 N 24th St
Phoenix, AZ 85016-7816 602-956-4833
Fax: 602-381-0248 amelio@cactuscandy.com
www.arizonacowboy.net
Processor and exporter of salsa, jellies, hot sauces, tortilla chips, honey, candy and nuts
Owner/President: Amelio Casciato
Estimated Sales: $500,000-1 Million
Number Employees: 5-9
Sq. footage: 1650
Type of Packaging: Consumer, Food Service, Private Label

694 **Arizona Institutional Foods**
1922 E 18th St
Tucson, AZ 85719-6910 520-624-8667
Fax: 520-629-4377 www.shamrockfoods.com
Manager: Paul Sedon
Estimated Sales: $ 20 - 50 Million
Number Employees: 20-49

695 **Arizona Natural Products**
12815 N Cave Creek Road
Phoenix, AZ 85022-5834 602-997-6098
Fax: 602-288-8331 info@arizonanatural.com
www.arizonanatural.com
Processor and exporter of herbal and vitamin supplements
President: Michael Hanna
Estimated Sales: $1-2.5 Million
Number Employees: 5-9
Sq. footage: 10000
Brands:
Allirich

696 **Arizona Nutritional Supplements**
210 S Beck Ave
Chandler, AZ 85226-3311 480-966-9630
Fax: 480-966-9640 888-742-7675
www.aznutritional.com
Contract manufacturer and packer, custom nutritional and dietary supplements
Owner: Jonathan Pinkus
Estimated Sales: $ 10 - 20 Million
Number Employees: 100-249
Sq. footage: 50000

697 **Arizona Pepper Products**
P.O.Box 40605
Mesa, AZ 85274 480-833-1908
Fax: 480-833-0309 800-359-3912
info@azgunslinger.com www.azgunslinger.com
Hot sauces, olives, spices and pistachios
President: Bill Marko
Purchasing Director: William Marco
Estimated Sales: $2.5-5 Million
Number Employees: 5-9

698 **Arizona Pistachio Company**
26487 N Highway 99
Tulare, CA 93274-9317 520-746-0880
Fax: 520-741-9797 800-333-8575
salesapc@azpistachio.com www.azpistachio.com
Grower and processor of pistachios
President: Henry Mollner
Estimated Sales: $2.5-5 Million
Number Employees: 5-9
Type of Packaging: Consumer, Food Service, Bulk

699 **Arizona Sunland Foods**
3752 S Broadmont Dr
Tucson, AZ 85713-5256 520-624-7068
info@sunlandfoods.com
www.sunlandfoods.com
Processor of portion-controlled salad dressings, chicken, beef and shrimp
Owner: Arnie L Jacobsen
VP: Josh Jacobson
Estimated Sales: $20-50 Million
Number Employees: 20-49
Type of Packaging: Food Service

700 **Arizona Sunland Foods**
3752 S Broadmont Dr
Tucson, AZ 85713-5256 520-624-7068
info@sunlandfoods.com
www.azsunlandfoods.com
Beef, poultry and seafood products manufactured to customer specifications, as well as custom sauce and dressing portion control.
Owner: Arnie L Jacobsen
CFO/VP: Tony Jacobson
Estimated Sales: $3.2 Million
Number Employees: 25
Number of Brands: 1
Number of Products: 30
Type of Packaging: Food Service

701 **Arizona Vineyards**
1830 E Patagonia Hwy
Nogales, AZ 85621 520-287-7972
Fax: 520-287-7597
Wines
Owner/President: Arthur Ocheltree
Owner/CEO: Tino Ocheltree
Estimated Sales: Less than $150,000
Number Employees: 1-4
Brands:
Arizona Vineyards

702 **Arkansas Poly**
309 Phillips Rd
N Little Rock, AR 72117-4105 501-945-5763
Fax: 501-945-0276 800-364-5036
sales@arkpoly.com www.allampoly.com
Manager: Jim Wilson
VP Sales/Marketing: Kip Johnson
Controller: Dave Robertson
Estimated Sales: $ 20 - 50 Million
Number Employees: 50-99
Brands:
Arkansas Poly

703 **Arkansas Refrigerated Services**
P.O.Box 2554
Fort Smith, AR 72902 479-783-1006
Fax: 479-783-1008
info@arkansasrefrigeratedservices.com
www.arkansasrefrigerated.com

Warehouse providing frozen storage for food products; also, rail siding available
President: Mike Group
Number Employees: 50-99

704 **Arla Foods Inc**
675 Rivermede Road
Concord, ON L4K 2G9
Canada 905-669-9393
Fax: 905-669-5614
Processor, wholesaler/distributor and importer of cheese
President: Douglas Smith
Estimated Sales: $19 Million
Number Employees: 120
Sq. footage: 100000
Type of Packaging: Consumer, Food Service, Private Label, Bulk
Brands:
Tre Stelle

705 **Arla Foods Ingredients**
645 Martinsville Road
Basking Ridge, NJ 07920 908-604-8551
Fax: 908-604-9310 peter.hassing@arlafoods.com
www.arlafoodsingredients.com
The specialist provider of advanced innovative solutions withing the milk-based ingredients industry such as dairy, ice cream, meat, ready meals/fine foods, bakery, infant nutrition and functional foods applications.
General Manager: Peter Hassing
CEO: Peter Tuborgh
CFO: Jeff Brauner
Marketing: Mikael Horsboll
Sales Director: Sten Nielsen
Product Manager: Adam Criscione
Estimated Sales: $5-10 Million
Number Employees: 5-9
Sq. footage: 1000
Parent Co: Arla Foods Ingredients AMBA
Type of Packaging: Bulk
Brands:
CAPOLAC®
DANO®
LACPRODAN®
MILEX®
MIPRODAN®
MULTILAC®
NUTRILAC®
PERLAC®
PIPTIGEN®
VARIOLAC®

706 **Arlington City Market**
301 Burnside Street
Annapolis, MD 21403-2471 703-527-7100
Fax: 703-527-7101
Owner: Leif Klasson

707 **Arlund Meat Company**
PO Box 23443
Overland Park, KS 66283-0443 913-321-3450
Fax: 913-321-5029
Beef, beef products
President: Charles Arlund
Estimated Sales: $10-20 Million
Number Employees: 5-9

708 **Armand's Coffee Flavors**
3765 Atlanta Industrial Dr NW
Atlanta, GA 30331-1031 404-696-4178
Fax: 404-696-4003
Flavoring supplies and flavors
Owner: Armand Hammer
Estimated Sales: $500,000-$1 Million
Number Employees: 50-99

709 **Armanino Foods of Distinction**
30588 San Antonio St
Hayward, CA 94544-7102 510-441-9300
Fax: 510-441-0101
customerservice@armanino.biz
www.armaninofoods.com
Manufacturer and exporter of Italian foods including sauces, pasta, meat balls and bread; importer of Italian cheeses
President/CEO: William Armanino
Secretary/Treasurer/COO: Edmond Pera
CEO: Edmond J Pera
Controller: Edgar Estonina
Director of Sales: Deborah Armanino
Operations Manager: Georgianne Stephen
Estimated Sales: F
Number Employees: 20-49
Type of Packaging: Consumer, Food Service
Brands:
Armanino

710 **Armbrust Meats**
224 S Main St
Medford, WI 54451 715-748-3102
Fax: 715-748-6399
Processor of fresh and frozen sausage, beef, pork and poultry
President: Thomas Armbrust
Estimated Sales: $500,000-$1 Million
Sq. footage: 33000
Type of Packaging: Consumer, Bulk

711 **(HQ)Armenia Coffee Corporation**
2975 Westchester Ave Ste 210
Purchase, NY 10577 914-694-6100
Fax: 914-694-5622 agcofy@aol.com
Coffee
President: Joseph Apuzzo Jr.
Owner: John Randall
Estimated Sales: $1.4 Million
Number Employees: 9

712 **Armeno Coffee Roasters**
75 Otis St
Northborough, MA 01532 508-393-2821
Fax: 508-393-2818 beans@armeno.com
www.armeno.com
Coffee
Owner: Chuck Koffman
Co-Owner: John Parks
Estimated Sales: Under $1 Million
Number Employees: 5-9
Sq. footage: 5000
Type of Packaging: Consumer, Private Label
Brands:
Armeno

713 **Armistead Citrus Company**
1057 N Greenfield Rd
Mesa, AZ 85205 480-830-2491
Processing citrus
Owner: Ken Armistead
Estimated Sales: Under $500,000
Number Employees: 1-4
Brands:
Armistead Citrus Products

714 **Arnabal International**
13459 Savanna
Tustin, CA 92782 714-665-9477
Fax: 714-665-9477 armen@arnabel.com
www.arnabal.com
Oils and vinegars
Owner: Nairy Balian
Estimated Sales: $ .5 - 1 million
Number Employees: 1-4

715 **Arnhem Group**
25 Commerce Dr
Cranford, NJ 07016-3605 908-709-4045
Fax: 908-709-4045 800-851-1052
info@arnhemgroup.com OR
Sylva@arnhemgroup.com
www.arnhemgroup.com
Products include binders and extenders, fat replacers, flavor enhancers, milk products, stabilizers. Arnhem's Flavonoid technology division features natural botanical powdered extracts, bioflavonoids, and isolated flavonoids for thenutraceutical, wellness, food, pharmaceutical and cosmetics industries.
President, Chairman, CEO: Michael Bonner
National Accounts Manager: Sandra Lyna
Estimated Sales: $1-2.5 Million
Number Employees: 1-4

716 **Arnold Foods Company**
10 Hamilton Ave
Greenwich, CT 6830 203-531-4770
Fax: 203-531-2170 www.gwbakeries.com
Manufactures baked goods
Vice President: Rod Cuha
Manager: Vinnie Greco
Number Employees: 1-4
Brands:
Beck's
Beck's Dark
Beck's For Oktoberfest
Haake Beck Non-Alcoholic

717 **Arnold's Meat Food Products**
274 Heyward St
Brooklyn, NY 11206 718-963-1400
Fax: 718-963-2303 800-633-7023
quality@arnolds-sausage.com
www.arnolds-sausage.com
Smoked sausage, scrapple, chorizos, kielbasa and bacon.
President: Sheldon Dosik
Chief Executive: Shelly Dosik
VP: Jason Judd
Estimated Sales: $3.6 Million
Number Employees: 25
Sq. footage: 8485
Type of Packaging: Consumer, Food Service, Private Label, Bulk
Brands:
ARNOLD'S MEATS
CAROLINE'S SAUSAGE
EL CERDITO

718 **Arns Winery**
P.O.Box 652
Saint Helena, CA 94574 707-963-3429
Fax: 707-963-5780 arnswine@napanet.net
www.arnswinery.com
A 1000cs production of high end mountain fruit grown organic methods. Arns Estate grown 100% Cabernet Sauvignon and Arns Napa Valley Cabernet Sauvignon.
President: John Arns
CEO/Winemaker: Sandi Belcher
Marketing: Sandi Belcher
Sales: Kathi Belcher
Estimated Sales: $100,000
Number Employees: 2
Number of Brands: 1
Number of Products: 1
Sq. footage: 1200
Type of Packaging: Consumer
Brands:
Arns

719 **Aroma Coffee Company**
7650 Industrial Dr
Forest Park, IL 60130 708-488-8340
Fax: 708-488-8366
Manufacturer and packager of roasted whole bean coffee in french and chicory and demitasse coffee, also teas
President: Gust Papanicholas
Estimated Sales: $5-10 Million
Number Employees: 5-9
Type of Packaging: Consumer, Food Service, Private Label, Bulk
Brands:
AROMA CUISINER'S CHOICE
AROMA SOUTHERN MAISON
AROMA TURKISH
CUISINIERS CHOICE

720 **Aroma Coffee Roasters**
1601 Madison St
Hoboken, NJ 7030 201-792-1730
Fax: 201-659-1883
Coffee
Manager: Ruth Santuccio
Purchasing Director: Ruth Santuccio
Estimated Sales: $1-2.5 Million
Number Employees: 20-49

721 **Aroma Ridge**
1831 West Oak Parkway
Suite C
Marietta, GA 30062 770-421-9600
Fax: 770-421-9116 800-528-2123
contact@aromaridge.com www.aromaridge.com
coffee

722 **Aroma Vera**
5310 Beethoven St
Los Angeles, CA 90066-7015 310-574-6920
Fax: 310-306-5873 800-669-9514
cservice@aromavera.com www.aromavera.com
Processor, importer and exporter of essential oils
President: Marcel Lavabre
CEO: Klee Irwin
Estimated Sales: $59,000
Number Employees: 1
Sq. footage: 50000
Brands:
Aroma Vera

723 **Aroma-Life**
16161 Ventura Boulevard
Encino, CA 91436-2522 818-905-7761
Fax: 818-905-0292 mzwan@aol.com
Processor, importer and exporter of essential, almond and macadamia oils
President: Moshe Zwang
CEO: Diana Zwang
Estimated Sales: $300,000-500,000
Number Employees: 1-4
Number of Brands: 18
Number of Products: 16
Sq. footage: 27500
Type of Packaging: Private Label, Bulk
Brands:
Aroma-Life

724 **Aromachem**
599 Johnson Ave
Brooklyn, NY 11237 718-497-4664
Fax: 718-419-4507
Processor, importer and exporter of flavors, essential oils and fragrances
President: M Edwards
CEO: Leona Levine
Estimated Sales: $3 Million
Number Employees: 30
Sq. footage: 25000
Type of Packaging: Bulk

725 **Aromatech USA**
5770 Hoffner Avenue
Suite 103
Orlando, FL 32822 407-277-5727
Fax: 407-277-5725 www.aromatech.fr
manufacturer of flavorings for beverages, candies, baking, snacks and pastries

726 **Arome Fleurs & Fruits**
850 Pierre-Caisse
Suite 400
St-Jean-Sur-Richelie, QC J3B 7YS
Canada 450-349-3282
Fax: 450-348-3518 877-349-3282
info@floralfood.com www.floralfood.com
Floral products incorporated into spreads, jellies and syrups.

727 **Aromi d'Italia**
5 N Calhoun St
Baltimore, MD 21223-1814 410-761-5215
Fax: 410-761-5216 877-435-2869
ashworth@ashworth.com www.aromiditalia.com
Manufacturer and provider of the highest quality gelato products originating from Italy.
Owner: Boris Ghazarian
Estimated Sales: $200,000
Number Employees: 5-9
Brands:
Aromi d'Italia

728 **Aromont USA**
1800 E Highway 114 # 102
Southlake, TX 76092-6529 817-552-5544
Fax: 817-552-5539 aromont@aromontusa.com
www.texasepicenter.com
Naturally processed stocks and concentrated sauces
Manager: Whitney Otto
Estimated Sales: $10-20 Million
Number Employees: 1-4

729 **Aromor Flavors & Fragrances**
560 Sylvan Ave Ste 61
Englewood Cliffs, NJ 7632 201-503-1662
Fax: 201-503-1663 sales@aromorinc.com
www.aromor.com
Supplier of Flavors and Fragrances, Raw Materials
Manager: Carol Feldman
General Manager: Gary Romans
Number Employees: 50-99

730 **Aron Streit Inc.**
150 Rivington St
New York, NY 10002 212-475-7000
Fax: 212-505-7650 lburke@StreitsMatzos.com
www.streitsmatzos.com
Manufacturer of matzos and other fine kosher foods.
President: Aron Yagoda
Executive VP: Aron Yogoda
Marketing: Laura Burke
Sales: Mel Gross
Production: Alan Adler
Estimated Sales: $5-10 Million
Number Employees: 50-99
Brands:
ETHNIC DELIGHTS
STREITS

731 **(HQ)Arrowac Fisheries**
Fisherman's Commerce Building
4039 21st Avenue W, Suite 200
Seattle, WA 98199 206-282-5655
Fax: 206-282-9329 info@arrowac-merco.com
www.arrowac-merco.com
fresh and frozen seafood
President: Frank Mercker
VP: Waltrout Yanagisawa
Sales Manager: Anthony Weber
VP Production & Operations/Plant Manager: R Anthony Blore
Estimated Sales: $25 Million
Number Employees: 3
Number of Brands: 3
Number of Products: 15
Sq. footage: 2000
Type of Packaging: Consumer, Food Service, Private Label, Bulk
Brands:
Arrow
Merco
Ocean Dawn

732 **(HQ)Arrowhead Mills**
110 S Lawton Ave
Hereford, TX 79045 806-364-0730
Fax: 806-364-8242 800-749-0730
www.arrowheadmills.com
Pasta
President/CEO: Irwin Simon
Operations: Gary Schultz
Purchasing: Dale Hollingswoth
Number Employees: 50-99
Parent Co: Hain Food Group

733 **Arrowood Vineyards & Winery**
P.O.Box 1240
Glen Ellen, CA 95442-1240 707-935-2600
Fax: 707-938-5947 800-938-5170
hospitality@arrowoodvineyards.com
www.arrowoodvineyards.com
Wines
Manager: Patty Mullins
VP: Alis Demers Arrowood
Retail Operations Manager: Claudia DiClemente
Estimated Sales: $10-20 Million
Number Employees: 20-49
Type of Packaging: Private Label
Brands:
ARROWOOD
GRAND ARCHER

734 **Art CoCo Chocolate Company**
2660 Walnut St
Denver, CO 80205-2231 303-292-6364
Fax: 303-292-6365 800-779-8985
mbonick@artcoco.com www.artcoco.com
Chocolate boxes, hand foiled chocolate novelties, specialty molded chocolates
President: Kenneth Wolf
VP: Gail Zucker
National Retail Sales Director: Michele Bonnick
Production Manager: Charles Martinez
Estimated Sales: $5-9.9 Million
Number Employees: 5-9
Parent Co: Silvestri Sweets, Inc.
Type of Packaging: Private Label
Brands:
Art Coco
Art Fidos Cookies
Art Topo

735 **Art's Fisheries**
305 E Buchanan Street
Phoenix, AZ 85004-2520 602-252-9550
Fax: 602-340-0335
President: E Steven Ansel
Estimated Sales: $ 10 - 20 Million
Number Employees: 20-49

736 **Art's Mexican Products**
615 Kansas Ave
Kansas City, KS 66105-1311 913-371-2163
Fax: 913-371-2052 www.artsmexican.com
Mexican food specialties
President: Bob Gutierrez
President: Robert Gutierrez
Estimated Sales: $10-20 Million
Number Employees: 10-19

737 **Art's Tamales**
1453 Hickory Point Rd
Metamora, IL 61548 309-367-2850
www.artstamales.com
beef tamales and bbq
President: David Chinuge
CEO: Zack Fosdyck
Public Relations: Robin Fosdyck
Production Manager: Bill Sanders
Estimated Sales: $300,000-500,000
Number Employees: 5
Sq. footage: 5000
Type of Packaging: Consumer, Food Service, Private Label
Brands:
Art's Tamales
Party Time

738 **Artek USA**
5700 Corsa Avenue
Suite 202f
Westlake Village, CA 91362-7332 626-333-3939
Fax: 626-333-3308 866-278-3501
President: Larry Jones
Estimated Sales: $ .5 - 1 million
Number Employees: 5

739 **Artesa Vineyards & Winery**
1345 Henry Rd
Napa, CA 94559-9705 707-224-1668
Fax: 707-224-1672 Info@artesawinery.com
www.artesawinery.com
Wines
President: Michael Kenton
CFO: Tim O'Leary
VP Production: Dave Dobson
Estimated Sales: $20-50 Million
Number Employees: 50-99
Type of Packaging: Private Label

740 **Artesian Honey Producers**
P.O.Box 6
Artesian, SD 57314 605-527-2423
Processor of honey
Owner: John Zen
Estimated Sales: $1-2.5 Million
Number Employees: 5-9
Type of Packaging: Bulk

741 **Arthur Schuman, Inc.**
40 New Dutch Lane
Fairfield, NJ 07004 973-227-0630
Cheese
Marketing: Melissa Shore

742 **Artic Ice Cream Novelties**
1901 23rd Avenue S
Seattle, WA 98144-4615 206-324-0414
Fax: 206-323-0259 paddy@articicecream.com
Ice cream
President/CEO: Bill Dinsmore
Sales Manager: Jerry Gregory
General Manager: S Paddy Narayan
Estimated Sales: $20-50 Million
Number Employees: 50-99
Type of Packaging: Private Label

743 **Artichoke Kitchen**
P.O.Box 159
Hamilton, NC 27840 252-798-2471
Pickles, relish, jams, jellies
President: Ellen Jackson
Estimated Sales: $570,000
Number Employees: 5-9

744 **Artist Coffee**
51 Harvey Road
Londonderry, NH 03053-7414 603-434-9385
Fax: 603-216-8029 866-440-4511
dan@artistcoffee.com www.artistcoffee.com
Producer of gourmet coffee, tea and candy for promotional trade. Specializing in Custom Labeling with very special products.
President: Tom Rushton
Marketing Director: Dan Sewell
Estimated Sales: $ 3 - 5 Million
Number Employees: 1-4
Type of Packaging: Consumer, Private Label
Other Locations:
Lambent Technologies
Gurnee IL
Brands:
Cirashine
Erucical

Hodag
Lamchem
Lumisolve
Lumisorb
Lumulse
Oleocal
Polycal

745 **Arturo's Bakery**
53 Interstate Ln
Waterbury, CT 06705-2658 203-754-3056
Cookies
President: Fred Napolitano
Estimated Sales: $1-2.5 Million appx.
Number Employees: 5-9

746 **Artuso Pastry Foods Corp**
158 S 12th Ave
Mt Vernon, NY 10550-2915 914-663-8806
Fax: 914-663-8815 sales@artusopastry.com
www.artusopastry.com
Cannoli shells and cream, spogliatelle, lobster tails, tiramisu, pastry shells, assorted italian pastries.
CEO: Anthony Artuso Jr
Estimated Sales: $ 10 - 20 Million
Number Employees: 20-49
Type of Packaging: Food Service, Private Label, Bulk
Brands:
ARTUSO

747 **Artuso Pastry Shop**
670 E 187th St
Bronx, NY 10458-6802 718-367-2515
Fax: 718-367-2553 sales@artusopastry.com
www.artusopastry.com
Italian pastry ingredients, fresh and frozen
Owner: Anthony Artuso Sr
CEO: Anthony Artuso Jr
Estimated Sales: $3 Million
Number Employees: 25
Brands:
ARTUSO

748 **Arway Confections**
3425 N Kimball Ave
Chicago, IL 60618 773-267-5770
Fax: 773-267-0610
cragileva@arwayconfections.com
www.arwayconfections.com
Manufacturer of candy including brittles, butter toffee, panned and enrobed products, sponge candy and glazed nuts
President: James Resnick
President/Marketing Manager: Craig Leva
General Manager/Purchasing: Rick Johnson
Estimated Sales: $5-10 Million
Number Employees: 100
Sq. footage: 80000
Type of Packaging: Bulk

749 **Arylessence**
1091 Lake Drive
Marietta, GA 30066 770-924-3775
Fax: 770-928-5671 800-553-2440
customerservice@arylessence.com
www.arylessence.com
Manufactures fragrance and flavors
President: Steve Tanner
Executive Vice President: Cynthia Reichard
Estimated Sales: $23 Million
Number Employees: 84
Type of Packaging: Private Label

750 **Asael Farr & Sons Company (Russells Ice Cream)**
P.O.Box 651250
Salt Lake City, UT 84165-1250 801-484-8724
Fax: 801-484-8768
michael.farr@farrsicecream.com
www.farrsicecream.com
Processor of ice creams, yogurts, sorbets, ice cream and yogurt mixes, specialty foods, etc
President: Dexter Farr
CEO: Michael Farr
Estimated Sales: $ .5 - 1 million
Number Employees: 1-4
Brands:
Farr
Russell's

751 **Aseltine Cider Company**
533 Lamoreaux Dr NW
Comstock Park, MI 49321 616-784-7676
Fax: 616-784-7676
Bottled apple products
Owner: John Klamt
General Manager: John Klant
Estimated Sales: $2.5-5 Million
Number Employees: 10-19

752 **Asher Candy**
1803 Research Blvd # 201
Rockville, MD 20850-6106 301-309-6161
Fax: 301-309-6162 sales@sherwoodbrands.com
www.sherwoodbrands.com
Flavored candy canes
President: Uziel Frydman
Estimated Sales: G
Number Employees: 50-99
Brands:
ASHER

753 **Asher's Chocolates**
80 Wambold Rd
Souderton, PA 18964 866-310-3008
Fax: 215-721-3265 800-223-4420
dbruno@asherschocolates.com www.ashers.com
chocolate and confections, including chocolate-covered pretzels potato chips, and graham crackers. The company also produces boxed assortments (including truffles, chews, nuts, cordials, and creams) and gift baskets, fudgepecan-caramel patties, almond bark, and sugar-free and low-carb assortments.
President/CEO: David Asher
CFO: Charles Clark
VP Sales/Marketing: Jeff Asher
VP Operations: Steve Marcanello
Estimated Sales: $17.7 Million
Number Employees: 120

754 **Ashers Chocolates**
19 Susquehanna Ave
Lewistown, PA 17044-2332 717-248-8613
Fax: 717-248-8637 800-343-0520
Processor and exporter of chocolates
President: John Asher
Estimated Sales: $10-24.9 Million
Number Employees: 50-99
Sq. footage: 46000
Type of Packaging: Consumer, Food Service, Private Label, Bulk

755 **Ashland Milling**
P.O.Box 1775
Ashland, VA 23005 804-798-8329
Fax: 804-798-9357 amc@ashlandmilling.com
www.byrdmill.com
Manufacturer of flour, cornmeal and mixes
President: Todd Attkisson
General Manager: Lynwood Atkinson
Estimated Sales: $ 10 - 20 Million
Number Employees: 20-49
Brands:
BLUE BARN
DIAMOND
EUKANUBA
HYLAND
KALMBACH
PURINA

756 **Ashland Plantation Gourmet**
133 Highway 1177
Bunkie, LA 71322-9773 318-346-6600
Fax: 318-346-4666
President: Kim White
Estimated Sales: Less than $500,000
Number Employees: 1-4

757 **Ashland Sausage Company**
280 S Westgate Dr
Carol Stream, IL 60188 630-690-2600
Fax: 630-690-2612
Processor of sausage
President: Stanley Podgorski
Purchasing: Stanley Podgorski
Estimated Sales: $1-2.5 Million
Number Employees: 10-19
Type of Packaging: Consumer, Food Service
Brands:
ASHLAND

758 **Ashland Vineyards**
2775 E Main St
Ashland, OR 97520-9781 541-488-0088
Fax: 541-488-5857 www.winenet.com
Wines
Owner/President: Philip Kodak
Owner/CEO: Kathleen Kodak
Estimated Sales: Less than $400,000
Number Employees: 1-4
Brands:
Ashland

759 **Ashley Food Company, Inc.**
P.O.Box 912
Sudbury, MA 01776 781-251-9775
Fax: 978-579-8989 800-617-2823
maddog@ashleyfood.com www.ashleyfood.com
President: David Ashley
Estimated Sales: $1-2.5 Million
Number Employees: 1-4
Brands:
JOE PERRY'S
MAD CAT
MAD DOG
WEIR'S

760 **Ashley Foods**
P.O.Box 912
Sudbury, MA 01776-0912 978-579-8988
Fax: 978-579-8989 800-617-2823
maddog@ashleyfood.com www.ashleyfood.com
Sauces
President: David Ashley
Marketing Director: David Ashley
New Product Development: David Ashley
Estimated Sales: $5-10 Million
Number Employees: 5-9
Type of Packaging: Consumer, Private Label
Brands:
Madcat
Maddog

761 **Ashman Manufacturing & Distributing Company**
P.O.Box 1068
Virginia Beach, VA 23451-0068 757-428-6734
Fax: 757-437-0398 800-641-9924
admin@ashmanco.com www.ashmanco.com
Manufacturer of a wide variety of gourmet sauces, salsas, hot sauces, dry blends, marinades, dessert sauces and drink mixes
President: Tim Ashman
Sales Manager: Joel Lutchin
Estimated Sales: $5-10 million
Number Employees: 10-19
Type of Packaging: Consumer, Private Label
Brands:
Ashman Armbruster's
Ashman Bodean's
Ashman Boli's
Ashman Boulevard Cafe
Ashman Chili Peppers
Ashman Coastal Cactus
Ashman Deathwish
Ashman Edwards Surry Sopping Sauce
Ashman Four Corners
Ashman Fuller's
Ashman George's
Ashman Hog Heaven Sooee Sauce
Ashman Hog Wild Bbq Sauce
Ashman Hot Wing Sauce
Ashman House
Ashman House London Broil Sauce
Ashman Jimmy Sauce
Ashman Joni's
Ashman King Street Blues
Ashman Little Red Raspberry Dijon
Ashman London House
Ashman Magnolia
Ashman Mini Malbon's Bbq Sauce
Ashman Nana's
Ashman Old Hickory Grille & Dip
Ashman Pass Out
Ashman Pigman's
Ashman Red Hot Rooster Sauce
Ashman Rockland's Bbq Sauce
Ashman St. Ann's Bay Jamaican Jerk
Ashman Tailgate
Ashman Tuscan Gardens Caponata
Ashman Virginia Gentleman
Ashman Whitley's
Ashman an Original Marinade
Ashman the Jewish Mother

762 **Asiago PDO & Speck AltoAdige PGI**
26 West 23rd Street
New York, NY 10010 646-258-0689
Fax: 646-624-2893 dchiarini@colangelopr.com
www.genuinetaste.org
Cheese, cured meats i.e. prosciutto/bacon.
Marketing: Flavio Innocenzi

763 **Asiamerica Ingredients**
245 Old Hood Rd #3
Westwood, NJ 07675-3174 201-497-5993
Fax: 201-497-5994 201-497-5531
info@asiamericaingredients.com
www.asiamericaingredients.com

Processor, importer, exporter and distributor of bulk vitamins, amino acids, nutraceuticals, aromatic chemicals, food additives, herbs, mineral nutrients and pharmaceuticals.

President: Mark Zhang
Estimated Sales: $5-10 Million
Number Employees: 5
Type of Packaging: Bulk

764 **Asian Brands**
2733 McCone Avenue
Hayward, CA 94545-1614 510-523-7474
Fax: 510-523-4817 info@asianbrands.com
www.asianbrands.com
Processor, importer and exporter of natural gourmet rice pilafs, Indian basmati and Thai jasmine rice; importer of spices and botanical herbs
President: Alok Mohan
Estimated Sales: $2.5-5 Million
Number Employees: 5-9
Sq. footage: 14000
Type of Packaging: Consumer, Food Service, Private Label, Bulk
Brands:
BAHAAR
GOURMET GURU
GOURMET GURU ALL NATURALL SPECIALTY
Gourmet Guru
Gourmet Guru All-Natural Specialty
SEVEN STAR
Seven Star
TOHFA

765 **Asian Foods**
1300 L Orient St
Saint Paul, MN 55117 651-558-2400
Fax: 651-558-2404 afiinfo@asianfoods.com
www.asianfoods.com
Supplier of Asian products
Owner: Quyen Ngyun
Owner: Avlina Litchnegger
Executive Director: Julie Howden
Estimated Sales: $50-100 Million
Number Employees: 200
Parent Co: Sysco
Type of Packaging: Food Service, Private Label
Other Locations:
Kansas City MO
Hampshire IL
Brands:
Heartland

766 **Ask Foods**
P.O.Box 388
Palmyra, PA 17078 717-838-6356
Fax: 717-838-7458 800-879-4275
wdimatteo@askfoods.com www.askfoods.com
Processor of desserts, dips, deli salads, sauces, soups and entrees
CEO: Wendy Holsinger
CFO: Rich Rutkowski
Director: Maxine Smith
Estimated Sales: $10-20 Million
Number Employees: 180
Sq. footage: 200
Type of Packaging: Consumer, Food Service, Private Label, Bulk
Brands:
Ask Foods
Homestyle

767 **Askinosie Chocolate**
514 E Commercial St
Springfield, MO 65803 417-862-9900
Fax: 417-862-9904 lawren@askinosie.com
www.askinosie.com
Chocolate/cocoa products
Owner: Shawn Askinosie
Operations Manager: Jill Tilman
Number Employees: 6

768 **Aspen Foods**
1300 Higgins Rd # 100
Park Ridge, IL 60068-5766 847-384-5940
Fax: 847-384-5961 www.kochfoods.com
Manufacturer and exporter of gourmet frozen poultry products
President: Michael Fields
CEO: Joseph C Grendys
National Sales Manager: Mike Fields
Director Plant Operation: Ken Springer
Estimated Sales: $20-50 Million
Number Employees: 20-49
Sq. footage: 45000
Parent Co: Koch Foods
Type of Packaging: Consumer, Food Service, Private Label
Brands:
ANTIOCH FARMS
Chef Maxlotte

769 **Aspen Mulling Company Inc.**
302 A.A.B.C.
Aspen, CO 81611 970-925-5027
Fax: 970-925-5408 800-622-7736
aspenmulling@sopris.net www.aspenspices.com
Manufacturer and exporter of mulling spices
Manager: Leo Varade
Marketing: David Kallen
Estimated Sales: Under $5 Million
Number Employees: 5-9
Type of Packaging: Consumer, Food Service

770 **Assets Grille & Southwest Brewing Company**
6910 Montgomery Boulevard NE
Albuquerque, NM 87109-1406 505-889-6400
Fax: 505-889-0264
Brewer of beer, ale and stout
Owner: Mark Devesti
Estimated Sales: $2.5-5 Million
Number Employees: 50-99
Parent Co: Assets Brewing Company
Type of Packaging: Consumer, Food Service, Bulk

771 **Assets Health Foods**
909 Merritt Drive
Apt C
Hillsborough, NJ 08844-5310 908-874-8004
Fax: 908-874-8668 888-849-2048
frisinanatfoods@rcn.com
Natural flavors, herbs, botanicals, nutraceuticals, soya products, product development
Estimated Sales: $3 Million
Number Employees: 5-9

772 **Associated Bakers Products**
7 High St Ste 400
Huntington, NY 11743 631-673-3841
Fax: 631-673-3870
Manufactures dried replacement supply fruit juice blends to bakeries.
Owner: Louis Mayoka
VP: Louis Mayoka
Estimated Sales: $ 5 - 10 Million
Number Employees: 5-9
Sq. footage: 10000
Type of Packaging: Bulk
Brands:
ALBUMIX
NO-TEG
OVO-TEG
VITEG

773 **Associated Brands Inc.**
4001 Salt Works Rd
Medina, NY 14103 585-798-3475
Fax: 585-798-1931 800-265-0050
info@associatedbrands.com
www.associatedbrands.com
Processor and exporter of dehydrated and packaged food mixes including instant tea, meals in a cup, soup, bouillon, hot cocoa, noodles and sauce, artificial sweeteners and fruit drinks; importer of sugar; also, dry food packagingavailable
Finance Manager: Jim Dimatteo
VP: Donald Albrecht
R&D Director: Judi Hogg
Quality Assurance Director: Sharon Power
VP Marketing: Shane Silver
SVP Sales: Tom Studer
Human Resources Executive: Marylou Porter
VP Manufacturing/Operations: Richard Cook
Plant Manager: Rick Gambling
Purchasing Manager: Lowell Behm
Estimated Sales: $ 50 - 100 Million
Number Employees: 185
Sq. footage: 340000
Parent Co: Associated Brands, Inc.
Type of Packaging: Consumer, Food Service, Private Label, Bulk
Brands:
COOKS
GOLDEN KETTLE
NELSON
PRO-SEAL
SADANO'S
SWEET * 10
SWEET SPRINKLES
THIRST QUENCH'R

774 **Associated Fruit Company**
3721 Colver Rd
Phoenix, OR 97535 541-535-1787
Fax: 541-535-6936
Manufacturer and exporter of fresh fruit including plums and pears
President: David Lowry
Purchasing: Scott Martinez
Estimated Sales: $1-2.5 Million
Number Employees: 5-9
Type of Packaging: Bulk

775 **(HQ)Associated Milk Producers**
315 N Broadway St
PO Box 455
New Ulm, MN 56073 507-354-8295
Fax: 507-359-8651 800-533-3580
meshkes@ampi.com www.ampi.com
Manufacturer of cheese and dairy products products include: cheese, butter, cheese sauce, pudding,milk.
President/CEO: Ed Welch
Chairman: Steve Schlangen
Marketing: Jim Walsh
SVP Public Affairs & Corp Strategy: Sheryl Doering Meshke
Estimated Sales: $1.7 Billion
Number Employees: 3,000
Type of Packaging: Consumer, Food Service, Private Label
Brands:
CASS-CLAY®

776 **Associated Milk Producers**
1864 311th Avenue
P.O. Box 1013
Dawson, MN 56232 320-769-2994
Fax: 320-769-4692 www.ampi.com
Dairy
Manager: Joe Vaske
Production Manager: Richard Johnson
Estimated Sales: K
Number Employees: 100
Parent Co: Associated Milk Producers
Brands:
CASS-CLAY®

777 **Associated Milk Producers**
3281 40th St
Arlington, IA 50606 563-933-4521
www.ampi.com
Dairy
Manager: Gary Johnson

Estimated Sales: K
Number Employees: 71
Parent Co: Associated Milk Producers
Brands:
CASS-CLAY®

778 **Associated Milk Producers**
220 E Center St
P.O. Box 6
Blair, WI 54616 608-989-2535
www.ampi.com
Dairy
Manager: Mark Frederexion
Estimated Sales: K
Number Employees: 80
Parent Co: Associated Milk Producers
Brands:
CASS-CLAY®

779 **Associated Milk Producers**
4107 W Michigan Street
P.O. Box 16387
Duluth, MN 55816 218-624-4803
www.ampi.com
Dairy
Manager: Matt Quade
Estimated Sales: K
Number Employees: 5
Parent Co: Associated Milk Producers
Brands:
CASS-CLAY®

780 **Associated Milk Producers**
200 20th Street North
P.O. Box 3126
Fargo, ND 58108-3126 701-293-6455
www.ampi.com
Dairy
Estimated Sales: K
Number Employees: 5-9
Parent Co: Associated Milk Producers
Brands:
CASS-CLAY®

781 **Associated Milk Producers**
136 East Railway
PO Box 430
Freeman, SD 57029 605-925-4234
www.ampi.com
Dairy
Manager: Sandy Hilbret
Estimated Sales: K
Number Employees: 38
Parent Co: Associated Milk Producers
Brands:
CASS-CLAY®

782 **Associated Milk Producers**
127 Commercial Avenue West
P.O. Box 825
Hoven, SD 57450 605-948-2211
www.ampi.com
Dairy
Estimated Sales: K
Number Employees: 38
Parent Co: Associated Milk Producers
Brands:
CASS-CLAY®

783 **Associated Milk Producers**
14193 County Highway S
Jim Falls, WI 54748 715-382-4113
www.ampi.com
Dairy
Manager: John Breene
Estimated Sales: K
Number Employees: 150
Parent Co: Associated Milk Producers
Brands:
CASS-CLAY®

784 **Associated Milk Producers**
1305 19th St SW
Mason City, IA 50401 641-424-6111
www.ampi.com
Dairy
Manager: Sylvia Brainard
Marketing Manager: Jim Walsh
Estimated Sales: K
Number Employees: 58
Parent Co: Associated Milk Producers
Brands:
CASS-CLAY®

785 **Associated Milk Producers**
200 W Railroad St
P.O. Box 205
Paynesville, MN 56362 320-243-3794
www.ampi.com
Dairy
Manager: Matt Quade
Estimated Sales: K
Number Employees: 78
Parent Co: Associated Milk Producers
Brands:
CASS-CLAY®

786 **Associated Milk Producers**
301 Brooks St
Portage, WI 53901 608-742-2114
www.ampi.com
Dairy
Manager: Don Weideman
Estimated Sales: K
Number Employees: 50-99
Parent Co: Associated Milk Producers
Brands:
CASS-CLAY®

787 **Associated Milk Producers**
101 W 1st St
Sanborn, IA 51248 712-729-3255
www.ampi.com
Dairy
Manager: Ed Welch
Estimated Sales: K
Number Employees: 70
Parent Co: Associated Milk Producers
Brands:
CASS-CLAY®

788 **Associated Milk Producers**
700 First Avenue SE
Rochester, MN 55904 507-282-7401
www.ampi.com
Dairy
Plant Manager: William Swan
Director, Purchasing: John Russell
Estimated Sales: K
Number Employees: 50
Parent Co: Associated Milk Producers
Brands:
CASS-CLAY®

789 **(HQ)Associated Potato Growers, Inc.**
2001 N 6th St
Grand Forks, ND 58203 701-775-4614
Fax: 701-746-5767 800-437-4685
www.apgspud.com
Potatoes and potato products
President: Mike Loyland
General Manager: Paul Dolan
Director Sales: Greg Holtman
Estimated Sales: $26 Million
Number Employees: 25
Other Locations:
Associated Potato Growers
Grafton ND
Associated Potato Growers
Drayton ND
Brands:
APG
Dole
Holsom
Natives Pride
Nodark
Potato Mity Red

790 **Assouline & Ting**
P.O.Box 1103
Huntingdon Valley, PA 19006 215-427-0806
Fax: 215-627-3517 800-521-4491
info@caviar.com www.assoulineandting.com
Processor, wholesaler/distributor, importer and exporter of gourmet foods including snails, mustard, chocolate, caviar, frozen fruits and purees, flavored vinegar, etc
President: Joel Assouline
Operations Manager: S Schwartz
Estimated Sales: $10-20 Million
Number Employees: 1-4
Sq. footage: 45000
Other Locations:
Caviar Assouline
Philadelphia PA
Brands:
ABASA
AMPHORA
CAVIAR ASSOULINE
CORICELLI
MAXIM'S
ROMEO Y GUILIETA
VALRHONA
VILLA VITTORIA
VOSS

791 **Asti Holdings Ltd**
320 Stewardson Way
Unit 2-3
New Westminster, BC V3M 6C3
Canada 604-523-6866
Fax: 604-523-6880 info@goldenbonbon.com
www.goldenbonbon.com
Candy
President: Ricardo Mazzucco
Estimated Sales: $1.7 Million
Number Employees: 20

792 **Astor Chocolate**
651 New Hampshire Ave
Lakewood, NJ 08701 732-901-1000
Fax: 732-415-1150 info@astorchocolate.com
www.astorchocolate.com
Manufacturer, importer and exporter of chocolate including fund raising, foiled novelties, bars, truffles, mints, shells and boxed.
President: Erwin Grunhut
President: David Grunhut
CFO: Nat Vernaci
CFO: George Klopacs
Sales Director: Howard Cubberly
Human Resource Executive: Arie Lax
Purchasing Manager: Karen Garrison
Estimated Sales: $25,000
Number Employees: 120
Sq. footage: 22054
Type of Packaging: Consumer, Food Service, Private Label, Bulk
Brands:
AFTER DARK
LE BELGE CHOCOLATIER
PARTY FAVORS BY ASTOR
PASTRY ESSENTIALS
SQUARE ONE

793 **Astor Products**
5244 Edgewood CT.
Jacksonville, FL 32254 904-783-5000
Fax: 904-783-5294
Manufactures teas, coffees and spices.
President: James Kufeldt
Vice President: JH Childers
Manager: Denny Courson
Estimated Sales: $ 26 Million
Number Employees: 204
Parent Co: Winn-Dixie Stores
Type of Packaging: Consumer
Brands:
DIXIE
FISHER

794 **Astral Extracts Ltd.**
160 Eileen Way Ste 100
Syosset, NY 11791 516-496-2505
Fax: 516-496-4248 info@astralextracts.com
www.astralextracts.com
Processor, wholesaler, distributor, importer and exporter of fruit juice concentrates, essential oils and citrus products
President: Cynthia Astrack
General Manager: Joan Pace
Estimated Sales: $5-10 Million
Number Employees: 10
Sq. footage: 30000
Type of Packaging: Food Service, Private Label, Bulk

795 **Astro Dairy Products**
25 Rakely Court
Etobicoke, ON M9C 5G2
Canada 416-622-2811
Fax: 416-622-4180 www.astro.ca
/www.parmalat.ca
Manufacturer of dairy products including yogurt, cottage cheese, sour cream and cream cheese
President: James Biltekoff
Number Employees: 200
Parent Co: Parmalat Canada
Type of Packaging: Consumer, Food Service, Private Label, Bulk

Brands:
Astro
Biobest

796 **At Last Naturals**
401 Columbus Ave
Valhalla, NY 10595-1325 914-747-3599
Fax: 914-747-3791 800-527-8123
info@atlastnaturals.com www.atlastnaturals.com
Manufacturer and exporter of laxative tea and natural herbal health products.
VP: Fred Rosen
Estimated Sales: $ 1 - 3 Million
Number Employees: 5-9
Sq. footage: 37000
Type of Packaging: Consumer
Brands:
DHEA
INNERCLEAN
SUL-RAY
VALERIAN

797 **(HQ)Ateeco**
600 E Centre St
Shenandoah, PA 17976 570-462-2745
Fax: 570-462-1392 800-233-3170
ConsumerContact@pierogies.com
www.pierogies.com
Frozen pierogies, specialty foods, pasta, potatoes
President: Thomas Twardzik
Executive VP: Tim Twardzik
Director Finance: John Witkin
Sales Director: John Putney
Public Relations: Wayne Holben
Director Operations: Ray Stasulli
Estimated Sales: $20-50 Million
Number Employees: 40
Sq. footage: 350
Type of Packaging: Private Label

798 **Athena Oil**
3082 36th St
Long Island City, NY 11103 718-956-8893
Fax: 718-956-5813 m.scoullis@att.net
www.athenaoil.com
Olive oil
President: Moschos Scoullis
Estimated Sales: $1.2 Million
Number Employees: 10-19

799 **Athena's Silverland®Desserts**
439 Des Plaines Ave
Forest Park, IL 60130-1763 708-488-0800
Fax: 708-488-0894 800-737-3636
peter@silverlanddesserts.com
www.silverlanddesserts.com
Tortes, dessert bars, brownies, cookies, cakes fat-free and low-fat brownies
President/Owner: Athena Uslander
Sales: Peter Wodek
Operations: Chris Ogden
Estimated Sales: $2.5-5 Million
Number Employees: 10-19
Number of Brands: 1
Type of Packaging: Consumer, Food Service, Private Label
Brands:
Silverland

800 **Athens Baking Company**
4589 W Jacquelyn Ave
Fresno, CA 93722 559-485-3024
Fax: 559-485-4156 www.athensbaking.com
Manufacturer of filo dough and filo products
Owner: Dave Smart
Estimated Sales: $5-10 Million
Type of Packaging: Consumer, Food Service, Private Label
Brands:
ATHENS

801 **Athens Pastries & Frozen Foods**
13600 Snow Rd
Cleveland, OH 44142-2546 216-676-8500
Fax: 216-676-0609 800-837-5683
www.athens.com
Processor of pastries, frozen strudel and pita bread
CFO: Bob Tansing
VP Sales/Marketing: Bill Buckingham
VP Operations: Jeff Swint
Plant Manager: Jeff Swint
Estimated Sales: $10-24.9 Million
Number Employees: 100-249
Number of Brands: 2
Number of Products: 200
Sq. footage: 120000
Type of Packaging: Consumer, Food Service, Private Label, Bulk
Brands:
APOLLO
ATHENS

802 **Atka Pride Seafoods**
234 Gold St
Juneau, AK 99801-1211 907-586-0161
Fax: 907-586-0165 www.apicda.com
Chairman: George Dirks
CEO: Larry Cotter
Number Employees: 1-4

803 **Atkins Elegant Desserts**
11852 Allisonville Rd
Fishers, IN 46038-2312 317-570-1850
Fax: 317-773-3766 800-887-8808
latkins@atkins-intl-foods.com
www.atkins-intl-foods.com/home.html
Processor of frozen cheesecakes, pies, cakes and pastries.
Manager: Debbie Llewellyn
CEO: Tom Atkins Jr
CFO: Tom Atkins
R&D: Darrell Bell
Quality Control: John Parent
Canadian National Manager: Wayne Barefoot
VP Sales & Marketing: Bob Barry
National Accounts Manager: Lisa Atkins Miller
Operations: Bill Beglin
Production: Jeff Fascko
Plant Manager: Terry Graves
Purchasing: Denise Miller
Estimated Sales: $12-13 Million
Number Employees: 50-99
Sq. footage: 35000
Type of Packaging: Consumer, Food Service, Private Label
Brands:
ATKINS

804 **Atkins Ginseng Farms**
RR 1
Waterford, ON NOE 1Y0
Canada 519-443-4433
Fax: 519-443-4565 800-265-0239
info@atkinsginseng.com
Manufacturer, importer and exporter of ginseng products including capsules, also grower of american ginseng
Owner/President: Micheal Atkins
Number Employees: 5-9
Sq. footage: 1500
Type of Packaging: Consumer, Private Label, Bulk
Brands:
Atkins
Gin Ultimate
Golden Dreams
Golden Grower
Northern Serenitea
Northern Spirit

805 **Atkins Nutritionals**
105 Maxess Road
Melville, NY 11747-3854 631-953-4000
800-628-5467
www.atkins.com
Atkins diet food, candy and nutritional bars.
CEO: Christopher Smith
Senior VP/CFO: Joel Shiff
VP Sales: Jason Shiver
Estimated Sales: $ 5 - 10 Million
Number Employees: 50-99
Type of Packaging: Consumer, Food Service
Brands:
ATKINS
ATKINS ADVANTAGE
ATKINS BAKERY
ATKINS ENDULGE
ATKINS KITCHEN

806 **Atkinson Candies Company**
PO Box 150220
Lufkin, TX 75915 936-639-2333
Fax: 936-639-2337 contact@atkinsoncandy.com
www.atkinsoncandy.com
Manufacturer of candy
President/CEO: Eric Atkinson
VP: Amy Atkinson Voltz
VP Sales/Marketing: Doyle Huntsman
Human Resources Manager: Sonia Cardenaz
Marketing/Operations Manager: Sara Ramirez
Plant Manager: Mark Love
Purchasing Manager: Michael Morgan
Estimated Sales: $21.8 Million
Number Employees: 170
Sq. footage: 100000
Type of Packaging: Consumer, Food Service

807 **Atkinson Candy Company**
P.O.Box 150220
Lufkin, TX 75915 936-639-2333
Fax: 936-639-2337 800-231-1203
www.atkinsoncandy.com
Manufacturer and exporter of candy, including peanut butter and peppermint candies
President: Basil Atkinson III
Estimated Sales: $25-49.9 Million
Number Employees: 100-249
Sq. footage: 100000
Type of Packaging: Consumer, Bulk
Brands:
CHICK-O-STICK
COCONUT LONGBOYS
CRUNCHY PEANUT BUTTER BARS
MINT TWISTS
PECO BRITTLE
RAINBOW COCONUT
RAINBOW STICKS

808 **Atkinson Milling Company**
95 Atkinson Mill Rd
Selma, NC 27576-9067 919-965-3547
Fax: 919-202-0523 800-948-5707
information@atkinsonmilling.com
www.atkinsonmilling.com
Processor of: corn meal, hushpuppy mixes, breaders, biscuit mixes, frozen hushpuppies, cornbread sticks, chicken dumplings
President: Glenn Wheeler
CEO: Ray Wheeler
VP: Ben Wheeler
Estimated Sales: $5 Million
Number Employees: 20-49
Type of Packaging: Consumer, Food Service, Private Label, Bulk
Brands:
ATKINSON'S
BODDIE
CATTAIL
ELLIS DAVIS

809 **(HQ)Atlanta Bread Company**
4490 B South Cobb Dr
Smyrna, GA 30082 770-438-6800
Fax: 770-438-6848 800-398-3728
www.atlantabread.com
Processor of bread, pastries, bagels, rolls,muffins,sandwiches,salads and desserts. Also featuring expanded coffee selection
President/CEO: Jerry Couvaras
CFO: Alan Sack
Estimated Sales: $1-2.5 Million
Number Employees: 50-99
Type of Packaging: Consumer, Food Service
Brands:
ATLANTA BREAD

810 **Atlanta Brewing Company**
15 Knox Rd
Bar Harbor, ME 04609-7770 207-288-2337
Fax: 207-288-2589 800-475-5417
realale@atlanticbrewing.com
www.atlantabrewing.com
Processor of seasonal beer, ale, stout, lager and pilsner
Owner: Douglas Maffucci
CEO: Robet Budd
Estimated Sales: $10-20 Million
Number Employees: 10-19
Type of Packaging: Consumer, Food Service
Brands:
RED BRICK

811 **Atlanta Burning**
3781 Happy Valley Cir
Newnan, GA 30263 770-253-8100
Fax: 770-253-9941 800-665-5611
information@atlantaburning.com
www.atlantaburning.com

Manufacturer of hot sauces, BBQ sauce. Supplier of food related products
Owner: Marilyn Witt
Estimated Sales: $500,000-$1,000,000
Number Employees: 1-4
Type of Packaging: Consumer, Bulk
Brands:
Atlanta Burning

812 **Atlanta Coffee & Tea Company**
5400 Truman Dr
Decatur, GA 30035 770-981-6774
Fax: 770-981-6697 800-426-4781
sales@atlantacoffeeandtea.com
www.atlantacoffeeandtea.com
Processor and importer of coffee and tea; coffee roaster and tea packer, private label packaging available
President: Mary Black
VP: Harris Carver
Estimated Sales: $5-9.9 Million
Number Employees: 10-19
Type of Packaging: Food Service, Private Label

813 **Atlanta Coffee Roasters**
2205 Lavista Rd NE Ste F
Atlanta, GA 30329 404-636-1038
Fax: 404-255-1189 800-252-8211
info@atlantacoffeeroasters.com
www.atlantacoffeeroasters.com
Coffee
Owner: William Letbetter
CFO: Stephen Burress
Estimated Sales: $910,000
Number Employees: 5-9
Brands:
Brazil Celebes
Celebes
Columbian
Costa rica
Jamaica Bluemountain
Laminita

814 **Atlanta Fish Market**
265 Pharr Rd NE
Atlanta, GA 30305 404-262-3165
Fax: 404-240-6665
Seafood
Manager: Jason Zaleski
Estimated Sales: $ 5 - 10 Million
Number Employees: 100-249

815 **Atlantic Aqua Farms**
918 Brush Wharf Rd
Vernon Bridge, PE C0A 2E0
Canada 902-651-2563
Fax: 902-651-2513
Manufacturer and exporter of fresh mussels, oysters and clams-hardshell
GM: Brian Fortune
Number Employees: 50
Type of Packaging: Consumer, Food Service, Private Label, Bulk

816 **Atlantic Blueberry Company**
7201 Weymouth Rd Ste A
Hammonton, NJ 8037 609-561-8600
Fax: 609-561-5033 art@atlanticblueberry.com
www.atlanticblueberry.com
Processor and exporter of fresh and frozen blueberries
President/CEO: Arthur Galletta
Director: Paul Galletta
Operations: Robert Galletta
Plant Manager: Denny Doyle
Estimated Sales: $5-10 Million
Number Employees: 40
Number of Brands: 1
Number of Products: 1
Sq. footage: 80000
Type of Packaging: Private Label
Brands:
ATLANTIC BLUEBERRY

817 **(HQ)Atlantic Capes Fisheries**
985 Ocean Dr
Cape May, NJ 08204-1855 609-884-3000
Fax: 609-884-3261 jtirello@atlanticcapes.com
www.atlanticcapes.com
Processor of fresh and frozen scallops, fish, clams, mackerel, squid and monkfish; importer of scallops; exporter of fresh and frozen scallops, squid, butterfish and mackerel
President: Daniel Cohen
VP Sales/Marketing: Jeff Bolton
Sales Manager: Peter Hughes
General Manager: John Tirello
Estimated Sales: $15 Million
Number Employees: 20-49
Sq. footage: 20000
Other Locations:
ACF Production Facility
Point Pleasant Beach NJ
ACF Sales/Marketing Office
New Bedford MA
Brands:
ATLANTIC CAPES
CAPE MAY SALT

818 **Atlantic Chemicals Trading of North America, Inc.**
116 N Maryland Ave Ste 210
Glendale, CA 91206 818-246-0077
Fax: 818-246-0079 www.act.de
Manufacturer and distributor of flavors such as peppermint & menthol, sweeteners, acidifiers and preservatives.

819 **Atlantic Fish Specialties**
17 Walker Drive
Charlottetown, PE C1A 8S5
Canada 902-894-7005
Fax: 902-566-3546
Manufacturer and exporter of smoked salmon, mackerel and trout
President: Glenn Cooke
GM: Doug Galen
Number Employees: 40
Type of Packaging: Consumer, Food Service, Private Label, Bulk

820 **(HQ)Atlantic Foods**
1771 Front St Ste B
307
Scotch Plains, NJ 7076 908-322-9900
Fax: 909-322-9993 www.atlanticfds.com
Manufacturer of seafood
President: Derek Ivey
Estimated Sales: $3 Million
Number Employees: 40
Type of Packaging: Consumer, Food Service, Private Label, Bulk

821 **Atlantic Laboratories**
41 Cross St
Waldoboro, ME 04572 207-832-5376
Fax: 207-832-6905 nak@noamkelp.com
www.noamkelp.com
Processor and exporter of kelp meal and powder
President: Robert Morse
Sales: Foster Stroup
Estimated Sales: $ 3 - 5 Million
Number Employees: 5-9
Number of Brands: 1
Number of Products: 4
Sq. footage: 15000
Type of Packaging: Bulk
Brands:
SEA LIFE

822 **Atlantic Meat Company**
2600 Louisville Rd
Savannah, GA 31415 912-964-8511
Fax: 912-964-6831
Processor, importer and exporter of fresh and frozen ground beef, including hamburger patties
President/CEO: Lee Javetz
Sales Manager: James Rourke
Purchasing Agent: Marc Javetz
Estimated Sales: $20-50 Million
Number Employees: 50
Sq. footage: 30000
Type of Packaging: Consumer, Food Service, Private Label, Bulk
Brands:
Atlantic Meat
Circle a Brands Beef Patties
Circlea Beef Patties

823 **Atlantic Mussel GrowersCorporation**
PO Box 70
Point Pleasant, PE C0A 1W0
Canada 902-962-3089
Fax: 902-962-3741 800-838-3106
www.atlanticmusselgrowers.pe.ca
Manufacturer and exporter of fresh mussels
President: Wayne Sonerr
Marketing Manager: Rollie McInnis
Manager: Marjorie Henderson
Number Employees: 25
Type of Packaging: Consumer, Food Service, Private Label, Bulk

824 **Atlantic Pork & Provisions**
14707 94th Ave
Jamaica, NY 11435-4513 718-272-9550
Fax: 718-272-9630 800-245-3536
Manufacturer of fresh hams; also, bologna and liverwurst loaves
President/Ceo: Jack Antinori
Number Employees: 50
Type of Packaging: Consumer
Brands:
Atlantic
Eidelweiss
Laurel Hill
Lifeline

825 **Atlantic Premium Brands**
1033 Skokie Blvd Ste 600
Northbrook, IL 60062 847-412-6200
Fax: 847-412-9766
info@atlanticpremiumbrands.com
www.atlanticpremiumbrands.com
Manufacturer of bacon, sausage, luncheon meats, boxed beef, pork and chicken and entrees including barbecue, cooked, microwaveable, frozen and Cajun
President/CEO: Thomas Dalton
CFO: Michael Lambright
Human Resources Corporate Manager: Jennifer Farwell
Estimated Sales: I
Number Employees: 250-499
Type of Packaging: Consumer, Private Label
Brands:
BLUE RIBBON
CARLTON
JC POTTER
RICHARD'S

826 **Atlantic Quality Spice &Seasonings**
9 Elkins Rd
New Brunswick, NJ 08816 732-574-3200
Fax: 732-574-3344 800-584-0422
info@aqspice.com www.aqspice.com
Imports, processes and packs conventional and organic spices and blends thousands of seasoning formulations.
President: Stanley Gorski
COO: Robert Ferguson
Quality Control: Bob Machemer
Sales: Tom Schmidt
Plant Manager: Hector Herrera
Purchasing: Hector Herrera
Estimated Sales: $25 Million
Number Employees: 100
Sq. footage: 150000
Type of Packaging: Consumer, Food Service, Private Label, Bulk
Brands:
KINGRED
ROSERED
SUNRED
Saigon Select

827 **Atlantic Queen SeafoodsLimited**
84 Airport Rd
St Josephs, NL A1A 4Y3
Canada 709-739-6668
Fax: 709-739-6620 www.luxurycrab.com
Manufacturer and exporter of frozen crab and crab claws
President: Scott Boland
Estimated Sales: $40 Million
Number Employees: 25
Other Locations:
Toronto ON
Winnipeg MB
Calgary AB
Vancouver BC

Danvers MA
Seattle WA
Brands:
Atlantic Queen
Classic
Luxury

828 **Atlantic Salmon of Maine**
57 Little River Dr
Belfast, ME 04915 207-338-9028
Fax: 207-338-6288 800-508-7861
sales@us.fjord.com www.majesticsalmon.com
Manufacturer of fresh salmon
GM: David Peterson
CFO: John Thibodeau
Sales Manager: Mary Warner
Receptionist: Becky Darres
Number Employees: 200
Type of Packaging: Food Service
Other Locations:
Atlantic Salmon of Maine
Swan Island ME

829 **Atlantic Sea Pride**
400 Dorchester Ave
South Boston, MA 2127 617-269-7700
Fax: 617-269-7766
Processor and wholesaler/distributor of fresh fish and fillets; serving the food service market
President: Anthony Corenti
Estimated Sales: $ 20 - 50 Million
Number Employees: 20-49
Type of Packaging: Consumer, Food Service, Bulk

830 **Atlantic Seacove**
20 Newmarket Sq
Boston, MA 2118 617-442-6206
Fax: 617-442-6258 info@atlanticseacove.com
www.atlanticseacove.com
Wholesale dealers in fresh and frozen fish
President: John Wojitasinski
Owner: Andrew Bunten
Treasurer: Mitchell Wojitasinski
Estimated Sales: $3.3 Million
Number Employees: 14

831 **Atlantic Seafood Direct**
PO Box 1128
Rockland, ME 04841-1128 207-596-7152
Fax: 207-594-4042
Seafood

832 **Atlantic Seasonings**
417 E Vernon Ave
Kinston, NC 28501 252-522-1515
800-433-5261
Processor of salad dressing and drink mixes, gravies, seasoning and flour blends and sauces; custom blending available
President: Jay Neuhoff
VP Marketing: Ken Neuhoff
Estimated Sales: $2.5-5 Million
Number Employees: 10-19
Sq. footage: 18000
Type of Packaging: Food Service, Private Label, Bulk
Brands:
ATLANTIC SEASONINGS

833 **Atlantic Sugar Association**
One North Clematis Street
Suite 200
West Palm Beach, FL 33401 561-366-5100
Fax: 561-366-5158 877-835-2828
www.floridacrystals.com
Manufacturer of sugar cane
President: Donald Carson
Estimated Sales: $50-100 Million
Number Employees: 100-249
Parent Co: Florida Crystals
Type of Packaging: Consumer, Bulk

834 **Atlantic Veal**
218 Hull Ave
Olyphant, PA 18447 570-489-4781
Fax: 570-489-2544
Processor and exporter of veal
Plant Manager: Ken Thomas
Estimated Sales: $2.5-5 Million
Number Employees: 20-49
Type of Packaging: Consumer
Brands:
ATLANTIC VEAL

835 **Atlantic Veal & Lamb**
275 Morgan Ave
Brooklyn, NY 11211 718-599-6400
Fax: 718-599-6400 800-222-8325
info@atlanticveal.com atlanticveal.com
Processor and exporter of individually vacuumed frozen veal including portion controlled, hand sliced, leg cutlets, roasts and cubed
CEO: Phil Peerless
CFO: Joe Saccardi
VP: Martin Weiner
VP Sales/Marketing: Glenn Ermoian
Human Resources Director: Steve Kaiser
Estimated Sales: $20-50 Million
Number Employees: 150
Sq. footage: 8571
Type of Packaging: Consumer, Food Service
Brands:
FARM FED VEAL
PLUME DE VEAU
THE EPICUREAN

836 **Atlantis Pak USA**
75 Valencia Ave, Ste 701
Coral Gables, FL 33134 305-403-2603
Fax: 786-249-0454
customerservice@atlantis-pak.com
www.atlantis-pak.com
Food ingredients; textured soy flour
Principle: Vladimir Zhamgotsev
Number Employees: 5-9
Parent Co: Atlantis Pak

837 **Atlas Biscuit Company**
155 Pompton Ave Ste 107
Verona, NJ 7044 973-239-8300
Fax: 973-239-8301
Cookies and candies
President: Steve Koplin
Estimated Sales: 750,000
Number Employees: 5-9
Type of Packaging: Private Label, Bulk
Brands:
Stephans

838 **Atlas Peak Vineyards**
PO Box 182
Sonoma, CA 95476 866-522-9463
Fax: 707-226-2306 866-522-9463
wineclub@atlaspeak.com www.atlaspeak.com
Red and white wines
CFO: Chris Stenzel
VP Operations: Darren Procsal
VP Production: Tony Fernandez
Estimated Sales: $5-10 Million
Number Employees: 20-49
Type of Packaging: Consumer, Food Service
Brands:
ATLAS PEAK
CONSENSO

839 **Atoka Cranberries, Inc.**
3025, Route 218
Manseau, Quebec, CN G0X 1V0
Canada 819-356-2001
Fax: 819-356-2111 infoatoka@atoka.qc.ca
www.atoka.qc.ca
Distributor of fresh and dried cranberries, and cranberry juice concentrate for industrial applications.

840 **(HQ)Atrium Biotech**
9 Commerce Road
Fairfield, NJ 07004-1601 866-628-2355
Fax: 866-628-6661 info@biotherapies.com
www.atrium-bio.com
Processor, importer and exporter of shark cartilage, nutritional supplements and powders
President: Richard Bordeleau
CEO: Luc Dupont
Vice President: Jocelyn Harvey
Development: Serge Yelle
Sales: Johan Aerts
Purchasing: Rene Augstburger
Estimated Sales: $1.5 Million
Number Employees: 20
Number of Brands: 3
Number of Products: 20
Sq. footage: 100000
Brands:
2-MIX
BIOMEGA
CARTCELT
CARTILADE
DERMANEX
GENISTA
NATCELT
PEPOGEST
PHYTO-EST
PROSTACARE
PROSTAVITE

841 **Attala Company**
P.O. Box 9
Kosciusko, MS 39090-0009 662-289-6641
Fax: 662-289-2733 800-824-2691
Processor of corn flour meal and blended wheat flour
Manager: David Bain
Purchasing: Joe Cain
Estimated Sales: $20-50 Million
Number Employees: 20-49
Type of Packaging: Consumer, Private Label
Brands:
MAGNOLIA

842 **Atwater Block Brewing Company**
237 Joseph Campau St
Detroit, MI 48207-4107 313-877-9205
Fax: 313-877-9241 atwater@atwaterbeer.com
www.atwaterbeer.com
Processor of German-style lager, ale and beer; importer of malt and hops
President: Mark Rieth
Estimated Sales: $ .5 - 1 million
Number Employees: 10-19
Sq. footage: 20000
Type of Packaging: Consumer, Food Service, Private Label
Brands:
ATWATER
STONEY

843 **Atwater Foods**
10190 Roosevelt Hwy
Lyndonville, NY 14098
Fax: 585-765-9443 sales@atwaterfoods.com
www.atwaterfoods.com
Manufacturer, exporter and wholesaler of many kinds of dried fruit, including apples, cherries, cranberries, blueberries and strawberries. Star-K Kosher. Our customer service support is responsive to timelines and responsible forkeeping everything on track
Manager: Randy Atwater
Quality Control: Chris Fraser
Sales/Marketing: Jim Palmer
GM: Randall Atwater
Plant Manager: Steve Mohr
Purchasing Manager: Pat Glidden
Estimated Sales: 15-20 Million
Number Employees: 50-99
Number of Products: 50+
Sq. footage: 90000
Type of Packaging: Private Label, Bulk
Brands:
ATWATER
ATWATER DRIED FRUITS
SHORELINE FRUIT

844 **Atwood Cheese Company**
Rural Route 1
Atwood, ON N0G 1B0
Canada 519-356-2271
Fax: 519-356-2170
Manufacturer of cheeses including mozzarella, feta, fontina, emmental and parmesan
Manager: Samuel Cadeddo
Number Employees: 19
Sq. footage: 30000
Type of Packaging: Bulk

845 **Au Bon Climat Winery**
P.O.Box 440
Los Olivos, CA 93441-0440 805-937-9801
Fax: 805-937-2539 info@aubonclimat.com
www.qupe.com
Wines
Owner: Robert Lindquist
Estimated Sales: $ .5 - 1 million
Number Employees: 1-4
Type of Packaging: Private Label

846 **Au Printemps Gourmet**
680 Rue Labelle
Saint-Jerome, QC J7Z 5L5
Canada 450-224-8221
Fax: 450-224-7943 800-663-0416
news@printempsgourmet.com
www.printempsgourmet.com
Manufacturer of vinegars, jams, jelly seasonings and gift sets
President/Co-Owner: Hyman Weisbord
Co-Owner: A O'Grady
Brands:
Au Printemps Gourmet

847 **(HQ)Au'some Candies**
2031 US Highway 130
Suite E, Building A
Monmouth Junction, NJ 08852-3014 732-951-8818
Fax: 732-951-8828 info@ausomecandy.com
www.ausomecandy.com
Candy
President: Carlos Yeung
CEO: David Tsu
VP Operations: Rose Downey
Estimated Sales: $ 5 - 10 Million
Number Employees: 10-19
Other Locations:
Au'some Candies
Mission Viejo CA
Au'some Candies
Coppell TX
Au'Some Candies
Mississauga, Ontario
Au'Some Candies Europe S.L.
Sitges, Spain
Au'Some Candy Asia
Kowloon, Hong Kong
Brands:
CANDY YO-YO
GUMMI ALIEN INVADERS
POP MAGIC
SUPER SUCKER

848 **Auburn Dairy Products**
702 W Main St
Auburn, WA 98001-5299 253-833-3400
Fax: 253-833-3751 800-950-9264
customerservice@yamiyogurt.com
www.yamiyogurt.com
Processor of sour cream, half and half and yogurt including plain, orange, cherry, strawberry, blueberry and lemon.
Manager: Jerry Dinsmore
Executive Director: Martin Lavine
Plant Manager: Marv Query
Purchasing: Marv Query
Estimated Sales: $10-20 Million
Number Employees: 20-49
Parent Co: Instantwhip Foods
Type of Packaging: Consumer, Food Service
Brands:
AUBURN
YAMI

849 **August Food Limited**
4820 Avenue Q
Lubbock, TX 79412-2210 806-744-1918
Fax: 806-744-4934
Fried pies
President: August Moeller
Estimated Sales: $750
Number Employees: 17
Sq. footage: 3600
Brands:
AUGUST'S FRIED

850 **August Foods**
4820 Avenue Q
Lubbock, TX 79412 806-744-1918
Fax: 806-744-4934 www.augustpies.com
Manufacturer of fresh pies
Partner: August Moeller
Purchasing: Ken Moeller
Estimated Sales: $10-20 Million
Number Employees: 10-19
Sq. footage: 2600
Parent Co: Excel
Type of Packaging: Consumer, Food Service
Brands:
AUGUST'S FRIED

851 **August Kitchen**
Po Box 54
Armonk, NY 10504-1232 914-589-6477
Fax: 914-219-5249
Marinades, other sauces, seasonings and cooking enhancers.
Marketing: Zina Ovchinnikoff/Santos

852 **August Schell Brewing Company**
1860 Schells Rd
New Ulm, MN 56073 507-354-5528
Fax: 507-359-9119 800-770-5020
schells@schellsbrewery.com
www.schellsbrewery.com
Manufacturer of beer, ale and lager.
President: Ted Marti
Marketing Director: Bob Andersen
Operations/Plant Manager: Jeremy Kral
Estimated Sales: $21 Million
Number Employees: 20-49
Type of Packaging: Consumer, Private Label
Brands:
GRAIN BELT
SCHELL'S

853 **Augusta Winery**
P.O.Box 8
Augusta, MO 63332 636-228-4301
Fax: 636-228-4683 888-667-9463
info@augustawinery.com
www.augustawinery.com
Wines
President: Tony Kooyumjian
Estimated Sales: $2.5-5 Million
Number Employees: 5-9
Type of Packaging: Bulk

854 **Augustin's Waffles**
51 Glen Ridge Drive
Long Valley, NJ 07853 908-684-0830
Fax: 908-684-4878 info@augustinswaffles.com
augustinswaffles.com
Waffles

855 **Ault Foods**
405 The West Mall
Toronto, ON M9C 5J1
Canada 416-626-1973
Fax: 416-620-3666 www.parmalat-ingredients.com
Manufacturer, importer and exporter of bulking agents, fat/oil substitutes, hydrolyzed animal proteins, nonfat and nonfat hydrolyzed milk solids, proteins, sweeteners, whey and whey products
Chairman: D E Loadman
President/CEO: G P M Freeman
CFO: J J Hamilton
Treasurer: P C Quintiliani
Secretary: P L Ferraro
Parent Co: Parmalat Finanziaria SpA.
Brands:
Ault-Pro
Prestige
Protelac

856 **Aunt Aggie De's Pralines**
311 W Sinton St
Sinton, TX 78387 361-364-2711
Fax: 361-364-3775 888-772-5463
sales@auntaggiede.com www.auntaggiede.com
Processor of original, chocolate and chewy pecan pralines and hot fudge, and pecan praline sauces
President: Eleanor Harren
Estimated Sales: $5-10 Million
Number Employees: 20-49
Sq. footage: 2200
Brands:
AUNT AGGIE DE'S PRALINES

857 **Aunt Gussie Cookies & Crackers**
141 Lanza Ave
Bldg 8
Garfield, NJ 07026-3538 973-340-4480
Fax: 973-340-3501 800-422-6654
info@auntgussies.com www.auntgussies.com
Processor of cookies and crackers including sugar-free
President: David Caine
VP: Marilyn Caine
Estimated Sales: $2.5-5 Million
Number Employees: 5-9
Number of Brands: 1
Number of Products: 45
Sq. footage: 15000
Type of Packaging: Consumer, Private Label, Bulk
Brands:
AUNT GUSSIE'S COOKIES & CRACKERS

858 **Aunt Heddy's Bakery**
234 N 9th Street
Brooklyn, NY 11211-2012 718-782-0582
Fax: 718-782-5583
Breads, babka
President: Richards Habrarki
Purchasing: Rich Zablocki
Estimated Sales: $10-20 Million
Number Employees: 10-19

859 **Aunt Jenny's Sauces/Melba Foods**
186 Huron St
Brooklyn, NY 11222-1706 718-383-3192
Fax: 718-383-3191 admin@melbafoods.com
http://www.melbafoods.com
Sauces, melba foods
President: Marie Cuoco
Estimated Sales: $2.5-5 Million
Number Employees: 10-19
Type of Packaging: Private Label

860 **Aunt Kathy's Homestyle Products**
PO Box 279
Waldheim, SK S0K 4R0
Canada 306-945-2181
Fax: 306-945-2043
Manufacturer of cabbage rolls, filled perogies, pizza, borscht and chicken noodle soup
Owner: Kathy Fehr
Owner: Gerald Fehr
Estimated Sales: Under $500,000
Number Employees: 5-9
Sq. footage: 7560
Type of Packaging: Consumer, Bulk

861 **Aunt Kitty's Foods**
270 N Mill Road
Vineland, NJ 08360 856-691-2100
Fax: 856-696-1295 www.auntkittys.com
Chili, hot dog chili, beef stew, brunswick stew
Vice President: Gary Knisely
General Manager: John Vaeth
Sales: Roy Bryant
Director Operations: Jack Bowersox
Plant Manager: J Keith Griffis
Estimated Sales: $ 1 - 3 Million
Number Employees: 120
Sq. footage: 120000
Parent Co: Hanover Foods Corp
Type of Packaging: Consumer, Food Service, Private Label
Brands:
AUNT KITTY'S
AUSTEX
BUNKER HILL
CASTLEBERRY
VENICE MAID

862 **Aunt Lizzie's**
1531 Overton Park Ave
Memphis, TN 38112-5138 901-274-2966
Fax: 901-274-2902 800-993-7788
www.auntlizzie.com
Different flavored cheese straws and other products
President: Ginna Kelley
Co-Owner: Ginna Kelly
Founder: Elizabeth Harwell
Estimated Sales: Under $500,000
Number Employees: 5-9
Type of Packaging: Private Label
Brands:
Aunt Lizzie's
Lemon Shortbread
Libby's Pecan Cookies
Sharp Cheddar Cheese
Sun-Dried Tomato Str
Wind & Willow Key Lime Cheeseball

863 **(HQ)Aunt Millies Bakeries**
350 Pearl St
Fort Wayne, IN 46802-1508 260-424-8245
Fax: 260-424-5047 www.auntmillies.com
Manufacturer of breads, buns, English muffins, rolls, as well as bread and muffin mixes
President: John Popp
VP Finance: Jay Miller
Estimated Sales: $10-15 Million
Number Employees: 1,000-4,999
Type of Packaging: Consumer, Food Service
Other Locations:
Brands:
Aunt Millie's
Sumbeam

864 **Aunt Sally's Praline Shops, Inc.**
2831 Chartres St
New Orleans, LA 70117 504-944-6090
Fax: 504-944-5925 800-642-7257
ceo@auntsallys.com www.auntsallys.com
Manufacturer of New Orleans style creamy praline candies in four flavors, and other specialty food items.
Manager: Bethany Gex
CEO: Frank Simoncioni
Sales: Becky Hebert
Sales: Cherie Cunningham
Director Of Operations: Karl Schmidt
Materials Management: Bethany Gex
Estimated Sales: $5 Million+
Number Employees: 20-49
Sq. footage: 10000
Type of Packaging: Consumer, Food Service, Private Label, Bulk
Brands:
AUNT SALLY'S CREAMY PRALINES
AUNT SALLY'S GOURMET

865 **Auroma International, Inc.**
1100 E Lotus Dr
Silver Lake, WI 53170 262-889-8569
Fax: 262-889-2461 auroma@lotuspress.com
www.auromaintl.com
Dietary supplements, herbs and herbal formulas.
CEO: Santosh Krinsky

866 **Aurora Alaska Premium Smoked Salmon & Seafood**
PO Box 211376
Anchorage, AK 99521-1376 800-653-3474
Fax: 907-338-2228
Seafood products
Owner: Bill Dornberger
Owner: Gloria Dornberger

867 **Aurora Frozen Foods Division**
11432 Lackland Road
Suite 300
Saint Louis, MO 63146-3516 314-801-2300
Fax: 314-801-2550 mourdla@vdkff.com
www.aurorafoods.com
Frozen sea food, pizza and breakfast products, including waffles, french toast
Chairman: Dale F Morrison
COO: Eric D Brenk
CFO: William R McManaman
Number Employees: 5-9
Brands:
Aunt Jemima
Celeste
Duncan Hines
Lender's
Log Cabin
Mrs Butterworth's
Mrs Paul's
Van de Kamp's

868 **Aurora Packing Company**
P.O.Box 209
North Aurora, IL 60542 630-897-0551
Fax: 630-897-0647 www.aurorasafety.com
Processor and exporter of beef
President/CEO: Marvin Fagel
CFO: Nicholas Venneman
Plant Manager: Marty Gilbert
Estimated Sales: $41 Million
Number Employees: 250
Type of Packaging: Consumer, Food Service, Private Label

869 **Aurora Products**
400 Long Beach Blvd Ste 4
Stratford, CT 06615 203-375-9956
Fax: 203-375-9734 800-398-1048
orders@auroraproduct.com
www.auroraproduct.com
Manufacturer of trail mixes, nuts, dried fruits and candy
Owner: Stephanie Blackwell
Estimated Sales: $ 30 - 40 Million
Number Employees: 100+

870 **Aussie Crunch**
1865 Air Lane Drive
Suite 4
Nashville, TN 37210-3814 615-535-5575
Fax: 615-261-9055 800-401-6534
tim@aussiecrunch.com www.aussiecrunch.com
Makers of gourmet popcorn.

871 **Austin Chase Coffee**
4001 21st Ave W
Seattle, WA 98199-1201 206-282-7045
Fax: 206-282-5218 888-502-2333
www.austinchasecoffee.com
Coffee
President: Phil Sancken
VP of Sales/Marketing: Tucker McHugh
Estimated Sales: $5-10 Million
Number Employees: 50-99
Type of Packaging: Private Label

872 **Austin Packaging Company**
1118 N Main St
Austin, MN 55912 507-433-6623
Fax: 507-433-9717 mail@austinpackaging.com
www.austinpackaging.com
Contract packager of meal kits, meat pouches, frozen liquid sauces, pizza and portion control products; exporter of frozen liquid sauces
CEO: Bob Thatcher
EVP: Jeff Thatcher
Plant Manager: Jon Vietor
Estimated Sales: $20 Million
Number Employees: 300
Sq. footage: 125000
Type of Packaging: Consumer, Food Service, Private Label

873 **Austin Slow Burn**
P.O.Box 150042
Austin, TX 78715-0042 512-282-7140
Fax: 512-282-7140 877-513-3192
austinslowburn@austin.rr.com
www.austinslowburn.com
Marinades, jams, jellies, hot pepper sauce, red sauce, green sauce and special variety sauces.
President: Jill Lewis
VP: Kevin Lewis
Estimated Sales: $300,000-500,000
Number Employees: 1-4

874 **Austin Special Foods Company**
11400 Burnet Rd # 200
Austin, TX 78758-3406 512-652-2600
Fax: 512-652-2699 866-372-8663
austinspec@aol.com www.convio.com
All natural and kosher dairy biscotti, cookies and frozen cookie dough. Many biscotti flavors
Owner: Laura Logan
CEO: Gene Austin
Estimated Sales: $ 10 - 20 Million
Number Employees: 250-499

875 **Austinuts**
2900 W Anderson Ln Ste 19b
Austin, TX 78757 512-323-6887
Fax: 512-323-6889 877-329-6887
info@austinuts.com www.austinuts.com
Dry Roasted Gourmet Nuts and Seeds, Dried Fruits, Chocolates, Candy, Trail Mixes, Gourmet Food, Go Texan Products, Gift Baskets & Corporate Gifts.
President: Cipi Ilai
Estimated Sales: $650,000
Number Employees: 5-9
Sq. footage: 2
Type of Packaging: Private Label
Brands:
Austinuts

876 **Austrade Food Ingredients**
3309 Northlake Blvd # 201
Palm Beach Gdns, FL 33403-1705 561-586-7145
Fax: 561-585-7164 info@austradeinc.com
www.austradeinc.com
The leader in importing fine chemicals and food products.
President: Garry Bartl
VP: Stephen Bartl
Marketing: Joseph Schantl
Sales: Sandra Bartl
Estimated Sales: Less than $500,000
Number Employees: 3

877 **Austrian Trade Commission**
120 West 45th Street, 9th Floor
New York, NY 10036 212-421-5250
Fax: 212-421-5251
newyork@advantageaustria.org
www.advantageaustria.org/us
Non-alcoholic beverages, water, beer, salad dressing, full-line vinegar, full-line chcoolate, cheese, agency/trade organization.

878 **Authentic Marotti Biscotti**
749 Red Wing Dr
Lewisville, TX 75067 972-221-7295
Fax: 972-436-4547 biscotti@mbiscotti.com
www.mbiscotti.com
Processor of gourmet biscotti, brownies and bar cookies.
Owner: Joann Mancini
VP: Glenn Mancini
Estimated Sales: $2.5-5 Million
Number Employees: 1-4
Type of Packaging: Consumer, Private Label, Bulk
Brands:
MAROTTI BISCOTTI

879 **Autin's Cajun Cookery**
804 W 8th Ave
Covington, LA 70433-2306 985-871-1199
Fax: 985-871-7290 800-877-7290
autinskjun@aol.com
www.autinscajuncookery.com
Manufacturer of Cajun dinner mixes and seasonings including jambalaya, etouffee, dirty rice, chili, gumbo, etc
President: Gibson Autin II
Estimated Sales: $500,000-$1 Million
Number Employees: 1-4
Type of Packaging: Consumer, Food Service, Private Label, Bulk
Brands:
Autin's

880 **Autocrat Coffee & Extracts**
10 Blackstone Valley Pl
Lincoln, RI 02865-1145 401-333-3300
Fax: 401-334-5972 800-288-6272
info@autocrat.com www.autocrat.com
Roaster and extractor of gourmet coffee; also, coffee extracts, syrups, concentrates, iced cappuccino, iced coffee, espresso and smoothies available; services include retail, distributor, OCS, food service and food ingredients
President: Richard M Field Jr
VP/Owner: Cynthia Wall
Director Technical Services: Susan Maiocchi
Director Food Ingredient Sales: Noreen Carroll
Marketing Director: Kimberly Cipriano
Plant Manager: Scott Tittle
Number Employees: 100-249
Sq. footage: 45000
Type of Packaging: Consumer, Food Service, Private Label
Brands:
AUTOCRAT
ECLIPSE
NEWPORT COFFEE TRADERS

881 **Automatic Rolls of New Jersey**
1 Gourmet Ln Ste 4
Edison, NJ 8837 732-549-2243
Fax: 732-494-4980
Manufacturer of soft hamburger rolls; serving McDonalds chains
Manager: John Lyons
Plant Manager: John Lyons
Estimated Sales: $50-100 Million
Number Employees: 50-99
Parent Co: Northeast Foods
Type of Packaging: Food Service

882 **Autumn Hill Vineyards/Blue Ridge Wine**
301 River Dr
Stanardsville, VA 22973 434-985-6100
autumnhill@mindspring.com
www.autumnhillwine.com
Wine
Owner: Avra Schwab
Owner: Ed Schwab
Estimated Sales: $ 1 - 3 Million
Number Employees: 1-4

883 **Autumn Wind Vineyard**
15225 NE North Valley Rd
Newberg, OR 97132 503-538-6931
Fax: 503-538-6931
chat@autumnwindwinery.com

Wines
Estimated Sales: $500,000-$1 Million
Number Employees: 1-4
Sq. footage: 3
Type of Packaging: Private Label
Brands:
Patricia Green Cellars

884 **Avalon Foodservice, Inc.**
P.O.Box 536
Canal Fulton, OH 44614-0536 330-854-4551
Fax: 330-854-7108 800-362-0622
marketing@avalonfoods.com
www.avalonfoods.com
Fresh and frozen foods, dry and canned goods, produce, juices, ice cream, fresh dairy products, coffee and beverage programs, fresh and custom cut meats.
President: Andy Schroer

885 **Avalon Gourmet**
1051 E Broadway Rd
Phoenix, AZ 85040 602-253-0343
Fax: 480-253-0432
President: Richard Du Pree
VP: Dolores DuPree
Estimated Sales: $ 5 - 10 Million
Number Employees: 5-9

886 **Avalon Organic Coffees**
8308 Corona Loop NE
Albuquerque, NM 87113-1665 505-856-5588
Fax: 505-856-5588 800-662-2575
e-mail@avalonorganic.com
www.avalonorganic.com
Organic coffee

887 **Avanti Food Company**
109 Depot Street
Walnut, IL 61376 815-379-2155
Fax: 815-379-9357 800-243-3739
info@avantifoods.com www.avantifoods.com
Frozen pizzas and walnut cheeses
Owner/Sales: Bob Linley
VP Finance/Operations: Anton Zueger
Executive VP: Mike LePine
Estimated Sales: $6 Million
Number Employees: 45
Type of Packaging: Consumer, Food Service, Private Label, Bulk
Brands:
GINO'S
SWISS PARTY
WALNUT CHEESE

888 **Avary Farms**
S Highway 385
Odessa, TX 79761 432-332-4139
Fax: 915-332-4130
Owner: Bob Avary
Sales/Marketing Manager: Angela Avery
Estimated Sales: $300,000-500,000
Number Employees: 1-4

889 **Avatar Corporation**
500 Central Ave
University Park, IL 60484 708-534-5511
Fax: 708-534-0123 800-255-3181
inquiries@avatarcorp.com www.avatarcorp.com
Manufacture, refine and supply raw materials and ingrdients for the food, drug and personal care industries.
Owner: Wallace Duvall
Owner/President/CEO: Michael Shamie
VP Marketing: David Darwin
Chief Operating Officer: Phil Ternes
Plant Manager: Kent Taylor
Purchasing: Kristina Gutyan
Estimated Sales: $9 Million
Number Employees: 49
Sq. footage: 40000
Type of Packaging: Private Label, Bulk
Brands:
AROL
AROX
AVOX
Avagel
Avapol
Avatar
Avatech
Brown 'n' Serve
Citation
DPO
LSC
PROTROLLEY
Paneze
Pankote
Pinnacle
Probio
Prochill
Procon
Prokote
Prophos
Prosyn
Protech
SNOW WHITE
SOFT WHITE
TROKOTE
WINTREX

890 **Avent Luvel Dairy Products**
P.O.Box 1229
Kosciusko, MS 39090-1229 662-289-2511
Fax: 662-289-2572 800-281-1307
luvelsales@hypercon.net www.luvel.com
Dairy products
Owner: Jimmy Biscoe
COO: Larry Crockett
Vice President: Richard Briscoe
Controller: Charles Terry
Quality Control: Rodney Smith
South Sales Manager: Ance Cascio
North Sales Manager: Paul Ables
General Manager: G Tucker Arrington
Estimated Sales: $5-10 Million
Number Employees: 10-19

891 **Aventine Renewable Energy**
P.O.Box 1800
Pekin, IL 61555 309-347-9200
Fax: 309-346-0742 www.aventinerei.com/
Beverage alcohol, food grade yeast
CEO/COO: Thomas Manuel
CFO/Secretary: John Castle
VP Human Resources: Ray Godbout
Estimated Sales: $ 500 Million
Number Employees: 100-249

892 **Avenue Gourmet**
Po Box 628
Reistertown, MD 21136-0628 410-902-5701
Fax: 410-902-0600

893 **Avery Brewing Company**
5763 Arapahoe Ave Ste E
Boulder, CO 80303 303-440-4324
Fax: 303-786-8790 877-844-5679
info@averybrewing.com
www.averybrewing.com
Beers
President: Adam Avery
CEO/CFO: Larry Avery
Vice President: Thomas Boogaard
Quality Control Manager: Matt Thrall
Operations Manager: Steve Breezley
Chief Technology Officer: Shaun Nanavati
Estimated Sales: $5-10 Million
Number Employees: 9
Brands:
14'ER ESB
AVERY
ELLIE'S BROWN
HOG HEAVEN
OUT OF BOUNDS
REDPOINT
SALVATION
THE REVEREND
WHITE RASCAL

894 **Avo King Intl.**
2140 W Chapman Ave Ste 240
Orange, CA 92868 714-937-1551
Fax: 714-937-1974 800-286-5464
information@avoking.com www.avo-king.com
Processor and importer of frozen guacamole and avocado pulp
Owner: Guido Doddoli
Vice President: Pablo Doddoli
Estimated Sales: $5.5 Million
Number Employees: 5-9
Parent Co: Doddoli Hermanos Group
Brands:
AVO-KING

895 **Avoca**
P.O.Box 129
Merry Hill, NC 27957 252-482-2133
Fax: 252-482-8622 www.avocainc.com
Manufacturer and exporter of flavors and fragrances
President: David Peele
COO: Danny White
Research & Development: Richard Teague
Marketing Director: Shannon Sloan
Plant Manager: Danny White
Number Employees: 50-99

896 **Avon Heights Mushrooms**
48 Old Baltimore Pike
Avondale, PA 19311 610-268-2092
Fax: 610-268-8706
Manufacturer of coleslaw and salad mixes; also, packer of spinach
Owner: Philip Pusey Jr
Estimated Sales: $2 Millio
Number Employees: 20
Sq. footage: 8000

897 **Avonmore Ingredients**
523 6th St
Monroe, WI 53566-1065 608-329-2800
Fax: 608-329-2828 800-336-2183
nutrition@glanbiausa.com
http://www.glanbiafoods.com/
Manufacturers of dairy ingredients
President: Jerry O'Dea
CFO: Frank Stephnson
General Manager/VP: Jerry O'Dea
Marketing Manager: Fiona O'Keeffe
Number Employees: 25
Type of Packaging: Bulk
Brands:
Avonmore Ingredients

898 **Avron Resources**
1080 Essex Ave
Richmond, CA 94801 510-233-0633
Fax: 510-233-0636 800-883-9574
avron@avron.com
Flavors
President: Carl Arvold
Estimated Sales: $5-10 Million
Number Employees: 5-9
Type of Packaging: Private Label

899 **Award Baking International**
206 State Ave S
New Germany, MN 55367-9521 952-353-2533
Fax: 952-353-8066 800-333-3523
awardbaking@oblaten.com www.oblaten.com
Manufacturer of biscottis
Co-Owner: Tim Kraft
Co-Owner: Ken Barron
Marketing: Rhonda Kossack
Estimated Sales: $1-2.5 Million
Number Employees: 10-19
Sq. footage: 10000
Parent Co: Kenny B's Cookie
Brands:
Auer
Award Auer/Blaschke
Award Crunchy Dunkers
Biscotti Di Roma
Carlsbad Oblaten

900 **Awrey Bakeries**
12301 Farmington Rd
Livonia, MI 48150 734-522-1100
Fax: 734-522-1585 800-950-2253
personnel@awrey.com www.awrey.com
Manufacturer of frozen baked goods including cakes, sweet rolls, bagels, muffins, doughnuts, danish, croissants, biscuits, rolls, english muffins, browniesand marquise desserts
President/CEO: Robert A. Wallace
CFO: Gregory Gallagher
Marketing Director: Leslie Davidson
Public Relations: Betty Jean Awrey
Plant Manager: Belanger
Estimated Sales: $75 Million
Number Employees: 250-499
Number of Brands: 4
Number of Products: 200
Sq. footage: 280000
Type of Packaging: Consumer, Food Service, Private Label
Brands:
Awrey's Maestro
Grande
Marquise

901 **Axelsson & Johnson Fish Company**
PO Box 180
Cape May, NJ 08204-0180 609-884-8426
Fax: 609-898-0221
Seafood
Manager: Andrew Axelsson
Estimated Sales: $5-10 Million
Number Employees: 10-19

902 **Azar Nut Company**
1800 Northwestern
El Paso, TX 79912 915-298-3091
Fax: 915-877-1186 800-592-8103
kim@azarnutco.com www.azarnutco.com
Processor of peanuts, almonds, pecans, walnuts, pine and mixed nuts, dried fruit, candy and snack mixes
CEO: Richard Condie
Director Logistics: Randy Meeks
Marketing: Kim Williams Kennedy
VP Sales/Marketing: Gary Stewart
Operations Manager: James Jamison
Warehouse Manager: Art Romero
Estimated Sales: $50-100 Million
Number Employees: 100-249
Other Locations:
Sunlight Plant
Juarez, Mexico

903 **Azteca Foods**
P.O.Box 427
Summit Argo, IL 60501-0427 708-563-6600
Fax: 708-563-0331
arthur.velasquez@aztecafoods.com
www.aztecafoods.com
Manufacturer of Mexican food products including salad shells, tortilla chips and tortillas
President: Arthur R Velasquez
Estimated Sales: $50 Million
Number Employees: 100-249
Type of Packaging: Consumer, Food Service

904 **Azteca Milling**
1159 Cottonwood Ln # 130
Irving, TX 75038-6118 972-232-5300
Fax: 972-232-5370 800-364-0040
maseca_sales@aztecamilling.com
www.aztecamilling.com
Manufacturer of corn tortilla flours; snack flours; retail flours, and speciality flours.
President: Ignacio Hernandez
Vice President: Don Schleppegrell
Corporate Sales Manager: Rick Norton
Snack Manager Sales: Alan Davis
Estimated Sales: $40 Million
Number Employees: 100-249
Parent Co: Gruma Corporation
Type of Packaging: Bulk
Brands:
MASA MIXTA
MASECA

905 **(HQ)Azuma Foods International**
20201 Mack St
Hayward, CA 94545-1224
Fax: 510-782-1188 www.azumafoods.com
Processor, exporter and importer of frozen seafood, caviar and ready-made sushi
President: Takahiro Tamura
CEO: Toshinobu Azuma
Estimated Sales: $5-10 Million
Number Employees: 50-99
Other Locations:
New York Branch
East Rutherford NJ
Hawaii Sales Office
Honolulu HI
West Coast American Division Sales
Novato CA
East Coast American Division Sales
Boston MA
Brands:
ICHIBAN DELIGHT®
MY-DOL®
SEA SALAD
TAKOHACHI
TASTE OF ISLAND LEGENDS
TOBIKKO®

906 **B&A Bakery**
1820 Ellesmere Road
Scarborough, ON M1H 2V5
Canada 416-752-7436
www.breadsource.com
Processor of homestyle sandwich bread and rolls including hamburger, submarine, hot dog, dinner and kaiser
Proprietor: Arif Sunderji
Estimated Sales: $1.4 Million
Number Employees: 10
Sq. footage: 12000
Type of Packaging: Food Service

907 **B&B Caramel Apple Company**
2151 W 21st Street
Chicago, IL 60608-2607 773-927-7559
Fax: 773-927-7446
Processor of caramel apples
President: John Ramondi
Estimated Sales: $1-2.5 Million
Number Employees: 5-9
Type of Packaging: Consumer, Food Service
Brands:
B&B

908 **B&B Food Distributors**
724 S 13th St
Terre Haute, IN 47807 812-238-1438
Fax: 812-232-0670 800-264-1438
www.bandbfoods.net
Manufacturer of general merchandise and foodservice equipment
President: R Scott Isles
Estimated Sales: $ 10 - 20 Million
Number Employees: 50-99

909 **B&B Pecan Processors ofNC**
106 Thomson Ave
Turkey, NC 28393 910-533-2229
Fax: 910-553-4610 866-328-7322
info@elizabethspecans.com
www.elizabethspecans.com
Manufacturer of pecan praline, brittle, chocolate covered pecans, butter-roasted pecans and BBQ sauce
Owner: Alan Bundy
Estimated Sales: $ .5 - 1 million
Number Employees: 5-9
Brands:
ELIZABETH'S

910 **B&B Poultry Company**
P.O.Box 307
Norma, NJ 8347 856-692-8893
Fax: 856-455-7681 www.bandbpoultry.com
Refrigerated chickens, whole and parts
Treasurer: Dorothy Fisher
Vice President: Mark Fisher
Estimated Sales: $25 Million
Number Employees: 175

911 **B&B Produce**
2778 Nc Highway 50 S
Benson, NC 27504 919-894-2527
Fax: 919-894-2127 800-633-4902
Processor of sweet potatoes
President: Bob Bassetti
Estimated Sales: $20-50 Million
Number Employees: 50-99
Brands:
Sun Beauty

912 **B&C Seafood Market**
2155 Highway 18
Vacherie, LA 70090 225-265-8356
Fax: 225-265-9960 info@bandcseafood.com
www.bandcseafood.com
Processor of vacuum packed, fresh and frozen alligator and seafood
Owner: Jeremy Laudry
Estimated Sales: Under $1 Million
Number Employees: 8
Type of Packaging: Consumer, Food Service

913 **B&D Food Corporation**
575 Madison Ave # 1006
New York, NY 10022-8511 212-937-8456
Fax: 212-412-9034 info@bdfcorp.com
www.bdfcorp.com
Manufacturer of roasted, ground coffee; chocolate beverages and cappaccinos; and spray dried agglomerated soluble coffee and powdered tea.
Chief Executive Officer/Board Directors: Yaron Arbell
Chief Financial Officer/Board Directors: Yossi Haras
CEO: Daniel Ollech
Board of Directors: Daniel Ollech
Number Employees: 1-4
Type of Packaging: Food Service

914 **B&D Foods**
3275 S Federal Way
Boise, ID 83705 208-344-1183
Fax: 208-344-6825 sales@banddfoods.net
www.banddfoods.net
Processor of frozen finger steaks, pork and chicken strips and battered mozzarella cheese sticks
Estimated Sales: $10-20 Million
Number Employees: 5-9
Sq. footage: 12000
Type of Packaging: Food Service, Private Label

915 **B&G Foods**
4 Gatehall Dr Ste 110
Parsippany, NJ 07054 973-401-6500
Fax: 973-364-1037 www.bgfoods.com
Hot cereals, jams, jellies and fruit spreads, canned meats and beans, spices, seasonings, marinades, hot sauces, wine vinegar, maple syrup, molasses, salad dressings, Mexican-style sauces, taco shells, and kits, salsas, pickles andpeppers.
Chairman of the Board: Stephen Sherrill
President/CEO/Director: David Wennerr
EVP/Chief Financial Officer/Director: Robert Cantwell
CEO: David L Wenner
EVP/ Marketing & Strategic Planning: Albert Soricelli
Executive Vice President Sales: Vanessa Maskal
VP General Counsel & Secretary: Scott Lerner
Executive Vice President/Manufacturing: James Brown
Estimated Sales: $20-50 Million
Number Employees: 500-999
Sq. footage: 200000
Type of Packaging: Consumer, Food Service
Brands:
AC'CENT
AC'CENT SA-SON
B&G
B&M
BRER RABBIT
EMERIL'S
JOAN OF ARC
LAS PALMAS
MAPLE GROVE FARMS OF VERMONT
ORTEGA
POLANER
RED DEVIL
REGINA
SAN DEL
TRAPPERY'S
UNDERWOOD
UP COUNTRY ORGANICS
VERMONT MAID
WRIGHT'S

916 **B&J Seafood Company**
P.O.Box 3321
New Bern, NC 28560 252-637-1552
Fax: 252-633-0775
Canned, frozen and refrigerated blue crabmeat, frozen and refrigerated flounder fillets
President: Brent Fulcher
Manager: Catherine Fulcher
Estimated Sales: $14 Million
Number Employees: 85
Type of Packaging: Private Label
Brands:
Upper Bay

917 B&M
1 Beanpot Circle
Portland, ME 04103-5304 207-772-7043
info@bmbeans.com
www.bmbeans.com
Manufacturer of canned baked beans and brown bread
Principal: John Manoush
Manufacturing Director: Johnathan Tupper
Estimated Sales: $350,000
Number Employees: 5
Parent Co: B&G Foods
Type of Packaging: Consumer
Brands:
B&M BAKED BEANS

918 B&M Enterprises
9111 Brocklehurst Lane
Charlotte, NC 28215-8705 704-566-9332
Fax: 704-566-9332
Owner: Marson Berry
Estimated Sales: Under $500,000
Number Employees: 5-9

919 B&M Fisheries
15 Pingree Farm Rd
Georgetown, MA 01833 978-352-6663
Fax: 978-352-7565

920 B&R Quality Meats
200 Park Rd
Waterloo, IA 50703 319-232-6328
Fax: 319-232-8623
Processor and wholesaler/distributor of meat including beef, pork, veal and poultry; serving the foodservice market
President: Mark Ratkovich
VP: Dennis Brennan
Estimated Sales: $5-10 Million
Number Employees: 5-9
Sq. footage: 6000
Type of Packaging: Consumer, Food Service, Bulk

921 B-S Foods Company
1000 Cornell Pkwy # 600
Oklahoma City, OK 73108-1800 405-949-9797
Fax: 405-949-9802
Processor of pre-packaged luncheon meats and sandwiches
Owner: Sandra Henager
Sales Manager: Dave Heinecke
Estimated Sales: $2.5-5 Million
Number Employees: 5-9
Parent Co: B-S Foods Company
Type of Packaging: Consumer

922 B. Lloyd's Pecans
PO Box 354
Barwick, GA 31720 770-358-0782
Fax: 40- 7-9 24 800-322-6887
blloyds@gowebway.com
http://www.blloyds.com/contact_us/info.php
Pecans and pecan confections
President: Bobby Fowler
Executive Secretary: Janice Fowler
Estimated Sales: $500-1 Million appx.
Number Employees: 10-19
Type of Packaging: Food Service

923 B. Martinez & Sons Company
P.O.Box 830159
San Antonio, TX 78283 210-226-6772
Fax: 210-226-5262
Processor of corn tortillas, nacho chips and chalupa and taco shells
Owner: Ariel Berrueto
VP: David Garcia
Estimated Sales: $20-50 Million
Number Employees: 20-49

924 B.B. Bean Coffee
583 County Line Rd
Monument, CO 80132 719-481-1170
Fax: 719-488-2001 bbcoffee@aol.com
Coffee
President: Elizabeth Kawczynski
CEO: Elizabeth Kawczynski
Marketing Director: Elizabeth Kawczynski
Roastmaster: Bob Polito
Brands:
Bean Coffee

925 B.B.S. Lobster Company
141 Smalls Point Rd
Machiasport, ME 04655 207-255-8888
Fax: 207-255-3987
Fish and seafoods.
President: Susan West
Estimated Sales: $1,600,000
Number Employees: 5-9

926 B.C. Fisheries
P.O.Box 334
Hancock, ME 04640-0334 207-422-8205
Fax: 207-422-8206
Seafood
Manager: Pete Daley

927 B.K. Coffee
P.O.Box 1238
Oneonta, NY 13820-5238 607-432-1499
Fax: 607-432-1592 800-432-1499
www.bkcoffee.com
Coffee
Owner: Paul Karabins
Estimated Sales: $10-24.9 Million
Number Employees: 20-49
Type of Packaging: Private Label
Brands:
B.K. COFFEE

928 (HQ)B.M. Lawrence & Company
601 Montgomery St # 1115
San Francisco, CA 94111-2614 415-981-3650
Fax: 415-981-2926 info@bmlawrence.com
Processor and exporter of soft drinks, nonalcoholic beer, canned fruits, vegetables, juices and fish
President: B Lawrence
Purchasing Agent: Hugh Ditzler
Estimated Sales: $5-10 Million
Number Employees: 5-9
Sq. footage: 2000
Brands:
CALIFORNIA FARMS
GRAPEFRUIT
LEMON-LIME
US COLA
US SELECT

929 B.N.W. Industries
7930 N 700 E
Tippecanoe, IN 46570 574-353-7855
Fax: 574-353-8152 sales@belt-o-matic.com
www.belt-o-matic.com
Manufacturer of dryers, roasters, and coolers for the food industry.
President: Dan Norris
Founder/Consultant: Lee Norris
Regional Sale Engineer: Dick Garner
Export Department: Les Haspl
Vice President Sales: Aaron Norris
Estimated Sales: $ 1 - 3 Million
Number Employees: 5-9

930 B.R. Cohn Olive Oil
1500 Sonoma Highway
Glen Ellen, CA 95442 707-938-4064
Fax: 707-938-4585 800-330-4064
info@brcohn.com www.brcohnoliveoil.com
Olive oils and vinegars

931 B3R Country Meats
PO Box 374
Childress, TX 79201-0374 940-937-3668
Fax: 940-937-6657
All natural beef
President: Mary Lou Bradley
General Manager: James Henderson
Purchasing: Kathleen Lewis
Estimated Sales: $20-50 Million
Number Employees: 50-99
Type of Packaging: Consumer, Food Service
Brands:
B 3 R
B C NATURAL

932 (HQ)BASF Corporation
100 Campus Dr
Florham Park, NJ 7932 973-245-6000
Fax: 973-895-8002 800-526-1072
www.basf.com
Manufacturer of vitamins including A, B, C, D, E, K, Omega-3 and pre-mixed liquid blends
Chairman/CEO: Klaus Peter Lobbe
EVP/CFO: Hans Engel Dr.
CEO: Kurt Bock
Estimated Sales: 100+ Million
Number Employees: 10,000+
Other Locations:
Geismar LA
Shreveport LA
Livonia MI
Wyandotte MI
Sparks GA
Aberdeen MI
Palmyra MO
Belvidere NJ
Jamesburg NJ
Washington NJ
Enka NC
Morganton NC
Wilmington NC

933 BBQ Bunch
13100 Woodland Avenue
Kansas City, MO 64146-1801 816-941-4534
Fax: 816-941-0263 lewieb@aol.com
Processor of BBQ and mustard sauce; wholesaler/distrinutor of BBQ products; marketing consultant to the BBQ industry.
Owner: Lewis Bunch
Estimated Sales: $500,000-$1 Million
Number Employees: 1-4
Type of Packaging: Food Service, Private Label, Bulk
Brands:
Jazzy Barbecue Sauce

934 BBQ Shack
1613 E Peoria St
Paola, KS 66071 913-294-5908
pitmaster@thebbqshack.com
www.thebbqshack.com
Barbacue meats
Owner: Rick Schoenberger
Director Marketing/Sales: Debbie McCrackin
Brands:
BBQ Shack

935 BBQ'n Fools
61535 S Highway 97
9-367
Bend, OR 97702-2154 541-312-9227
Fax: 800-671-8652 800-671-8652
tom@bbqnfools.com www.bbqnfools.com
Owner: Tom Brohamer
Co-Owner: Kurt Weidmann
Estimated Sales: $ 40.00 K
Number Employees: 3
Brands:
BBQ'n Fools
Papa Dan's World Famous Jerky

936 BBS Bodacious BBQ Company
8411 Forest Hills Dr Apt 303
Coral Springs, FL 33065 954-752-0909
Fax: 954-345-3482 800-537-5928
bbsbbq@aol.com www.800jerky2u.com
Processor of natural and fat-free barbecue sauces, spicy jellies and steak, turkey jerky
President/CEO: Susan Sheldon
Estimated Sales: $500,000-$1 Million
Number Employees: 10-19
Brands:
AUNT JAYNE'S
BBS BODACIOUS
SAMMYE'S SUMPTUOUS

937 BBU Bakeries
5050 E Evans Ave
Denver, CO 80222-5218 303-691-6342
Fax: 303-757-4332
Manufacturer of cakes, pies, muffins, doughnuts, breads, pizza dough and bagels
Plant Manager: Ron Schulthies
Estimated Sales: $300,000-500,000
Number Employees: 5-9
Type of Packaging: Consumer

938 BCGA Concept Corporation
39 Canal Street
New York, NY 10002 212-488-0661
Fax: 212-488-0700 info@freshgingerale.com
www.freshgingerale.com
Soft Drinks, Non Alcoholic.
Marketing: Jenny Chen

939 **BDS Natural Products, Inc.**
2779 El Presidio Street
Carson, CA 90810 310-518-2227
Fax: 310-518-2577 info@bdsnatural.com
www.bdsnatural.com
Manufacturer and distributor of spices and seasoning blends.
Co-Founder: Steve Brennis
Director Of Sales: Shauna Walker
Director Of Operations: Kevin Witt

940 **BG Smith Sons Oyster**
P.O.Box 69
Sharps, VA 22548-0069 804-394-2721
Fax: 804-394-2741 877-483-8279
Manufacturer and exporter of fresh and frozen oysters; processor and packager of ice
President/CEO: B Smith Jr
Estimated Sales: $2.5-5 Million
Number Employees: 10-19
Number of Brands: 3
Number of Products: 1
Sq. footage: 100000
Type of Packaging: Consumer, Food Service, Private Label
Brands:
Chesapeake Bay Ice
Chesapeake Pride
Ocean Spray
Perch Creek

941 **BGS Jourdan & Sons**
1415 Stafford Rd
Darlington, MD 21034 410-457-4904
Processor of canned whole tomatoes
Owner: Scott Reezes
Estimated Sales: Less than $120,000
Number Employees: 1-4
Type of Packaging: Consumer, Private Label
Brands:
Point Pleasant

942 **BK Giulini Corporation**
3695 Alamo Street
Suite 203
Simi Valley, CA 93063-2188 805-581-1979
Fax: 805-581-2139 800-526-2688
mail@bkgiulinicorp.com
www.bkgiulinicorp.com
Manufacturer of Phosphate-based food ingredients for further processed meat, poultry, dairy and seafood.
CEO: Sandy Stone
Finace Manager/Sales & Marketing Manager: Marilyn Cheshire
Sales Director: Walter Bonell
Human Resources: Marilyn Hems
Estimated Sales: $24 Million
Number Employees: 15
Sq. footage: 4129
Parent Co: BK Giulini GmbH
Brands:
BEKAPLUS®
BRIFISOL®
JOHR®
TURRISIN®

943 **BKW Seasonings Inc**
10065 Double Tree Road
Knoxville, TN 37932 865-466-8365
Fax: 865-966-6963 matt@bkwseasonings.com
www.bkwseasonings.com
Various types of seasonings

944 **BN Soda**
60 Birmingham Pkwy
Boston, MA 02135-1123 617-782-7888
Fax: 240-536-3079
tommy@tommysnakedsoda.com
www.tommysnakedsoda.com
Manufacturer of soda made of natural flavors and cane sugar, also caffeine-free
Founder: Tom Bleier

945 **BP Gourmet**
135 Ricefield Ln
Hauppauge, NY 11788-2046 631-234-5200
Fax: 631-234-8200 info@bpgourmet.com
www.bpgourmet.com
Fat-free and organic cookies, sugar free cookies, fruit spreads and salad dressing. Also produces bread sticks and croutons
President: Florence Boris
Estimated Sales: $2.5-5 Million
Number Employees: 20-49
Brands:
Bp Gourmet
Freida's Kitchen
Monte Carlo Bake Shop
Sweet Nothings

946 **BR Cohn Winery**
15000 Hwy 12
Glen Ellen, CA 95442 707-938-4064
Fax: 707-938-4585 stephanie@brcohn.com
www.brcohn.com
Wine, olive oils, vinegars
Owner: Bruce Cohn
President: Greg Reisinger
VP Sales/Marketing: Deborah Mazzaferro
Purchasing: Bruce Cohn
Estimated Sales: $2.5-5 Million
Number Employees: 10-19
Type of Packaging: Private Label
Brands:
BALSAMIC AND HERB DIPPING OIL
BALSAMIC VINEGAR OF MODENA
CABERNET VINEGAR
CARNEROS CHARDONNAY
CHAMPAGNE VINEGAR
CHARDONNAY VINEGAR
MENDOCINO CTY. SAUVIGNON BLANC
OLIVE HILL CABERNET SAUVIGNON
OLIVE HILL CABERNET SAUVIGNON
OLIVE HILL PINOT NOIR
ORGANIC EXTRA VIRGIN OLIVE OIL
RASPBERRY CHAMPAGNE VINEGAR
RESERVE CARNEROS CHARDONNAY
SILVER LABEL CABERNET SAUVIGNO
SONOMA EXTRA VIRGIN OLIVE OIL
SONOMA VALLEY MERLOT
SONOMA VALLEY ZINFANDEL

947 **BRJ Coffee & Tea**
1731 Aviation Blvd
Lincoln, CA 95648-9317 916-258-8000
Fax: 510-632-0839 800-829-1300
sfbay_service@rogersfamilyco.com
www.rogersfamilyco.com
Roasted coffee
President: Jon B Rogers
VP Sales: Jim Rogers
VP: Barbra Rogers
Sales Director: Mike Carlin
Operations Manager: Pete Rogers
Purchasing Manager: Tom Garber
Estimated Sales: $ 10-24.9 Million
Number Employees: 100
Type of Packaging: Private Label
Brands:
Fairwinds Coffee
Jbr Coffee
Organic Coffee Compa

948 **BTS Company/Hail CaesarDressings**
PO Box 218015
Nashville, TN 37221-8015 615-226-6868
Fax: 615-226-6867 800-617-8899
hail.caesar@home.com
www.hailcaesardressings.com
Gourmet dressings, pasta sauces, marinades. Available in Original, Low-Fat and Fat Free, Wide variety of flavors & sizes.
Owner: Bunny Sundock
Estimated Sales: $ 1 - 3 Million
Number Employees: 1-4

949 **Babci's Specialty Foods**
115 Clemente Street
Holyoke, MA 01040-5644 413-594-7111
Fax: 413-594-7111 800-225-2023
at@a-tsurgical.com www.a-tsurgical.com
Bahcis pierogies, kapusta, chrust
President: Eugene Kirejczyk
Type of Packaging: Food Service, Private Label

950 **Babcock Winery & Vineyards**
P.O.Box 637
Lompoc, CA 93438-0637 805-736-1455
Fax: 805-736-3886 info@babcockwinery.com
www.babcockwinery.com
Producers of red and white wines.
Owner: Bryan Babcock
Estimated Sales: $5-10 Million
Number Employees: 20-49
Type of Packaging: Private Label

951 **Babe Farms**
1485 N Blosser Rd
Santa Maria, CA 93458 805-925-4144
Fax: 805-922-3950 800-648-6772
www.babefarms.com
Processor and exporter of specialty and baby produce items including peeled carrots and root vegetables
CEO: Judy Lundberg
Office Manager: Kerry Jordan
Operations: Jeff Lundberg
Estimated Sales: $7 Million
Number Employees: 10
Type of Packaging: Food Service, Private Label
Brands:
Babe Farms

952 **Babe's Honey Farm**
334 Walton Place
Victoria, BC V9E 2A4
Canada 250-658-8319
Fax: 250-658-8149
Manufacturer of fireweed and wild flower honey; also, beeswax
President: Mark Pitcher
Estimated Sales: $585,000
Number Employees: 60
Sq. footage: 12000
Type of Packaging: Food Service
Brands:
Babe's

953 **Baby's Coffee**
3178 Us Highway 1
Key West, FL 33040 305-744-9866
Fax: 305-744-9843 800-523-2326
info@babyscoffee.com www.babyscoffee.com
Processor of coffee
Manager: Mary Browman
Co-Owner: Olga Teplitsky
Marketing Manager: Alfonse Manosalvas
Estimated Sales: Less than $500,000
Number Employees: 1-4
Type of Packaging: Private Label
Brands:
Baby's Breakfast Roast
Baby's Private Buzz
Baby's Wrelker's Roa
Hemingway's Hair of
Killer Joe
Old Town Roast
Sexpresso

954 **Bacardi Canada, Inc.**
1000 Steeles Avenue E
Brampton, ON L6T 1A1
Canada 905-451-6100
Fax: 905-451-6753 www.bacardi.com
Manufacturer and importer of premium alcoholic beverages including rum, vodka, scotch, gin, vermouth, carbonated low proof beverages, and liqueurs.
Executive Manager: Manuel Diaz
CEO: Paul Beggan
Estimated Sales: 250-499
Number Employees: 100
Parent Co: Bacardi Limited
Type of Packaging: Consumer, Food Service
Brands:
1873 RUM
BACARDI 151 RUM
BACARDI 8 RUM
BACARDI BIG APPLE RUM
BACARDI BLACK RUM
BACARDI BREEZER
BACARDI COCO RUM
BACARDI GOLD RUM
BACARDI LIMON
BACARDI RAZZ
BACARDI SUPERIOR RUM
BOMBAY GIN
GREY GOOSE VODKA
MARTINI & ROSSI ASTI
MARTINI & ROSSI VERMOUTHS
RUSSIAN PRINCE VODKA

955 **(HQ)Bacardi USA**
2701 Le Jeune Rd
Coral Gables, FL 33134 305-573-8511
Fax: 305-573-0756 800-222-2734
hrbmusa@bacardi.com www.bacardi.com

Processor and importer of tropical drink flavored coolers, rum, vodka, prepared mixed drinks
President/CEO: Eduardo Sardina
CEO: John Esposito
Vice President: Doug Watson
Estimated Sales: $650 Million
Number Employees: 220
Parent Co: Bacardi International
Type of Packaging: Consumer, Food Service
Brands:
Anejo
B&B/Benedictine
Bacardi Breezers
Bacardi Limon
Bacardi Rum
Bacardi Spice
Bombay
Castillo Rums
Dewar's Scotch
Hatuey Beers
Martini & Rossi Asti
Martini & Rossi Vermouth
O
Pommeroy

956 **Bacci Chocolate Design**
17 Columbia Street
Swampscott, MA 01907 781-595-1511
Fax: 781-595-1544 888-725-2877
sales@baccichocolatedesign.com
www.baccichocolatedesign.com
Chocolate bars, other chocolate, toffee.
Marketing: Carlo Bacci

957 **Bachman Company**
1 Park Plaza
Reading, PA 19610-1301 610-320-7800
Fax: 610-320-7897 800-523-8253
customerserv@thebachmancompany.com
www.bachmanco.com
Pretzels, jax, tortilla chips, popcorn, potato chips, party mix and onion rings.
President: Joseph Welch
CEO: Joanne Millisock
CFO: Roy Emery
VP Sales: Frank Kunkel
Director of Human Resources: Deanna Williams
VP Manufacturing/Operations: Mark Miller
VP Manufacturing: Daniel Meyers
Purchasing Director: Lisa George
Estimated Sales: $10-20 Million
Number Employees: 350
Sq. footage: 20000
Type of Packaging: Consumer, Food Service
Brands:
Bachman
KIDZELS
TREAT
VALLEY MAID

958 **Back Bay Trading**
11800 Wills Rd # 120
Alpharetta, GA 30009-2080 770-772-6360
Fax: 770-772-4766 800-650-8327
ralph@ameliabay.com www.ameliabay.com
Liquid tea and Coffee Bag-N-box
President/CEO: John Crandall
CFO: Sherry Harder
Vice President: Jason Crandall
Sales Director: Marshall Cartmill
Public Relations: Jackie Hewitt
Operations Manager: Dudley Blizzard
Estimated Sales: $ 5 - 10 Million
Number Employees: 5-9
Type of Packaging: Private Label
Brands:
AMELIA BAY
PRIVATE LABEL

959 **Backer's Potato Chip Company**
P.O.Box 128
Fulton, MO 65251-0128 573-642-2833
Fax: 573-642-7617
Processors of potato chips.
President/Purchasing: Vicki McDaniel
Chairman: William Backer
Estimated Sales: $10-20 Million
Number Employees: 50-99

960 **Bacon America**
255 Rue Rocheleau
Drummondville, QC J2C 7G2
Canada 819-475-3030
Fax: 819-475-3031
Processor, importer and exporter of bacon
President: Marcel Heroux
Number Employees: 500-999
Parent Co: J.M. Schneider
Type of Packaging: Consumer, Food Service, Private Label

961 **Bad Frog Brewing**
1093 A1A Beach Blvd
Suite 346
Saint Augustine, FL 32080
Fax: 734-629-1777 888-223-3764
badfrog@badfrog.com www.badfrog.com
Beers
President: Jim Wauldron
Estimated Sales: $2.5-5 Million
Number Employees: 20-49
Type of Packaging: Private Label
Brands:
BAD FROG AMBER LAGER
BAD FROG BAD LIGHT
BAD FROG MICRO MALT

962 **Badger Best Pizzas**
1548 Deckner Avenue
Green Bay, WI 54302-2618 920-336-6464
Frozen pizza
President: Herm Fredericks
Plant Manager: Peggy Seefeldt
Estimated Sales: $2.5-5 Million
Number Employees: 5-9

963 **Badger Gourmet Ham**
3521 W Lincoln Ave
Milwaukee, WI 53215-2394 414-645-1756
Fax: 414-645-5189 www.badgergourmetham.com
Processors of ham.
President: Mark Schwellinger
Estimated Sales: $10-20 Million
Number Employees: 20-49

964 **Badger Island Shell-Fish & Lobster**
2 Badgers Is W
Kittery, ME 03904-1601 207-439-3820
Fax: 207-439-7080
Seafood, shellfish, lobster
Owner: Ed Gokey
Estimated Sales: $ .5 - 1 million
Number Employees: 1-4

965 **Badia Spices**
1400 NW 93rd Avenue
Miami, FL 33172 305-629-8000
Fax: 305-629-8100 info@badiaspices.com
www.badiaspices.com
Manufacturer and exporter of herbs, spices and seasonings including garlic, buboric, jalapeno, lindo and taco flavoring
Owner/President/CFO: Joseph Badia
Marketing Director: Dakota Badia
COO: Nancy Fredriksen- Badi
Purchasing Manager: Alina Lastra
Estimated Sales: $20 Million
Number Employees: 102
Sq. footage: 64770
Type of Packaging: Consumer, Food Service, Private Label, Bulk
Brands:
Arrowroot
Chili Powder
Cinnamon Korintje Ground
Pepper Black Butcher
Seasoning Complete

966 **Baensch Food**
1025 E Locust St
Milwaukee, WI 53212 414-562-4643
Fax: 414-562-5525 800-562-8234
order@mabaensch.com www.mabaensch.com
Manufacturer of herring that is pickled and creamed
Owner/President: Kim Wall
GM: David Jackson
Estimated Sales: $610 Million
Number Employees: 6
Sq. footage: 30000
Parent Co: Wild Foods
Type of Packaging: Consumer, Food Service, Private Label, Bulk
Brands:
MA BAENSCH
MA BAENSCH HERRING

967 **Bagai Tea Company**
PO Box 1046
San Marcos, CA 92079-1046 760-591-3084
Fax: 760-510-1904 sales.chaya@juno.com
www.chaya.com
Tea
President: Arun Bagai
CFO: Sanjay Bagai
VP: Vik Bagai
Production Manager: Maria Bagai
Purchasing Manager: Arun Bagai
Estimated Sales: $1-5 Million
Number Employees: 5-9
Type of Packaging: Private Label
Brands:
Chaya
Emerald Green
Golden Amber

968 **Bagel Factory**
3640 Woodvale Rd
Mountain Brk, AL 35223 205-967-6931
Bagel manufacturers
CEO: Jay Epstein
Estimated Sales: $500,000-$1 Million
Number Employees: 10-19
Sq. footage: 2500

969 **Bagel Guys**
102 Willoughby Street
Brooklyn, NY 11201-5318 718-222-4361
Fax: 718-222-4362 bagelguyscorp@AOL.com
www.bagelguys.com
Processor of bagels
President: Jeffrey Gargiulo
Estimated Sales: $120,000
Number Employees: 3

970 **Bagel Works**
8177 glades rd #1
Boca Raton, FL 33434 561-852-8992
Fax: 704-553-0222
Processor and exporter of bagels
President: Sadiah Hinnawi
VP: Steven Goldstein
Estimated Sales: $500,000 appx.
Number Employees: 5-9

971 **Bagels By Bell**
10013 Foster Ave
Brooklyn, NY 11236-2117 718-272-2780
Fax: 718-272-2789 info@bialy.com
www.bialy.com
Bakery and deli specializing in bagels and bialy
President: Warren Bell
Estimated Sales: $1 Million
Number Employees: 10-19
Type of Packaging: Private Label
Brands:
Bell Bialy
Bell Mini Bagel
bagel by bell

972 **(HQ)Bagelworks**
1229 1st Ave
New York, NY 10065-6314 212-744-6444
Fax: 718-358-3076
Processor of muffins and bagels including oat bran, sesame, poppy, cinnamon raisin, sundried tomato, chocolate, sourdough, spinach, herb, wholewheat, cheese, broccoli, rye, peanut butter, etc. including fat free
President: Saadiah Hinnawi
CEO: Aliyeh Hinnawi
CFO: Joseph Hinnawi
VP: Ramsey Hinnawi
Estimated Sales: $720,000
Number Employees: 5-9
Sq. footage: 850
Other Locations:
Bagelworks
New York NY

973 **Baier's Sausage & Meats**
6022 67a Street
Red Deer, AB T4P 3E8
Canada 403-346-1535
Fax: 403-346-1773
Processor of ham, sausage, beef jerky, bacon and salami
President: Keith Baires
CEO: Keith Baires
Marketing: Keith Baires
Type of Packaging: Consumer, Food Service, Bulk

Brands:
Baier's

974 **Bailey Street Bakery**
165 Bailey Street SW
Atlanta, GA 30314-4801 404-584-9540
Fax: 404-584-9526 800-822-4634
www.flowersfoods.com
Processor of baked goods including breads and buns.
President: Wayne Chandler
Chairman: George Deese
Director of Finance: Keith Williams
Sales Manager: Williard Fowler
VP/Communications: Mary Krier
SVP/Supply Chain: Michael Beaty
Estimated Sales: $26 Million
Number Employees: 200
Sq. footage: 5000
Parent Co: Flowers Baking Company
Type of Packaging: Consumer

975 **Bailey's Basin Seafood**
1683 Front Street
Morgan City, LA 70381-3523 985-384-4926
Fax: 985-384-4928
Prepared, packaged fish and seafood
President: Nolton Bailey Sr
Estimated Sales: $2.6 Million
Number Employees: 30
Type of Packaging: Consumer, Food Service

976 **Baily Vineyard & Winery**
33440 La Serena Way
Temecula, CA 92591 951-676-9463
Fax: 951-676-1276 contact@bailywinery.com
www.bailywinery.com
Wines
Owner: Phillip Baily
Owner: Carol Baily
Estimated Sales: $2,800,000
Number Employees: 1-4
Brands:
Baily

977 **Bainbridge Festive Foods**
PO Box 305
Tunica, MS 38676-0305 662-363-9891
Fax: 662-363-9895 800-545-9205
bainbridge@tecinfo.com
Jellies, pickles, preserves, spice tea mix, and parsley mustard sauce
President: Bobbie Hood
Estimated Sales: $150,000
Number Employees: 1-4
Number of Products: 12
Sq. footage: 3500
Type of Packaging: Private Label

978 **Baird Dairies**
110 N Randolph Ave
Clarksville, IN 47129-2761 812-283-3345
Fax: 812-283-8701
Processor of ice cream mixes
Owner: Randall Baird
Estimated Sales: $500,000-$1 Million
Number Employees: 1-4
Type of Packaging: Consumer

979 **Baja Foods**
636 W Root St
Chicago, IL 60609 773-376-9030
Fax: 773-376-9245 www.bajafoodsllc.com
Processor and exporter of frozen tamales, quesadillas, chimichangas, burritos, enchiladas, taco meat and chili; processor of pizza toppings and meat crumbles
Owner: Art Velasquez
Sales/Marketing: Jeff Rothschild
General Manager: Timothy Poisson
Purchasing Manager: Cheryl Canning
Estimated Sales: $ 10 - 20 Million
Number Employees: 20-49
Sq. footage: 30000
Type of Packaging: Consumer, Food Service, Private Label, Bulk
Brands:
AMIGO
CAFE AMIGO
LA MARCA
TANGO

980 **Bakalars Brothers Sausage Company**
P.O. Box 1943
La Crosse, WI 54602-1943 608-784-0384
Fax: 608-784-8361 www.bakalarssausage.com
Manufacturer of sausage, beef, fish, pork, hamburger meat, steak, etc
President: Michael Bakalars
Purchasing Manager: Mike Bakalars
Estimated Sales: $15 Million
Number Employees: 20-49
Type of Packaging: Consumer, Food Service, Private Label, Bulk
Brands:
BAKALARS

981 **Bake Crafters Food**
P.O.Box 489
Collegedale, TN 37315-0489 423-396-3392
Fax: 423-396-9604 800-296-8935
support@bakecrafters.com
www.bakecrafters.com
Bake Crafters is a wholesaler baking company servicing the continental Unite States with fully baked, par baked, and frozen dough products. Currently we make a wonderful line of donuts, muffins, cookies, croissants, Danish, wrapsEnglish muffins, breadsticks, Tortillas and many other baked goods. Want to develop a new product? We specialize in custom product development and would be happy to work with you to develop a signature product
President: Michael Byrd
Sales Manager: Bob Richmand
General Manager: Michael Byrd
Estimated Sales: $20 Million
Number Employees: 1-4
Number of Brands: 1
Type of Packaging: Consumer, Food Service, Private Label, Bulk
Brands:
BAKE CRAFTERS

982 **Bake Mark**
7351 Crider Ave
Pico Rivera, CA 90660-3705 562-949-1054
Fax: 562-948-2655 ibie-mgr@bakemarkwest.com
www.bakemark.com
VP: Bruce Reynolds
Estimated Sales: $ 20 - 50 Million
Number Employees: 250-499

983 **Bake Rite Rolls**
2945 Samuel Dr
Bensalem, PA 19020 215-638-2400
Fax: 215-638-1662
Manufacturer of soft sandwich rolls, english muffins, hamburger and hot dog rolls.
Manager: Bob Cranmer
Plant Manager: Bob Cranmer
Estimated Sales: $20-50 Million
Number Employees: 100-249
Parent Co: Northeast Foods
Type of Packaging: Private Label

984 **Bake'n Joy Foods**
351 Willow St
North Andover, MA 1845 978-683-1414
Fax: 978-683-1713 800-666-4937
productinfo@bakenjoy.com www.bakenjoy.com
Processor of low-fat, fat-free and frozen batters, bakery mixes, fillings, toppings, icings and ready-to-bake items
President/CEO: Robert Ogan
EVP/COO: Jack Waldron
VP Finance: Alice Shephard
Estimated Sales: $20-50 Million
Number Employees: 100-249
Type of Packaging: Food Service, Bulk
Other Locations:
Bake'n Joy Foods
Chuluota FL
Brands:
FRESHBAKES
STRAWBERRY COLADA FROZEN BATTER
TRIPLE BERRY BLAST FROZEN BATTER

985 **BakeMark Canada**
2345 Francis-Hughes Avenue
Laval, QC H7S 1N5
Canada 450-667-8888
Fax: 450-667-3342 800-361-4998
www.bakemarkcanada.com
Processor and exporter of bakers' and confectioners' supplies including fondants, cocoa chips and pieces, apricot and strawberry glazes, rainbow and chocolate sprinkles and fruit pie fillings
President: Larry Sullivan
Number Employees: 10-19
Sq. footage: 70000
Parent Co: CSM Bakery Supplies North America
Type of Packaging: Food Service, Private Label
Brands:
GOLDEN
LAFAVE

986 **BakeMark USA**
1933 N Meacham Road
Suite 530
Schaumburg, IL 60173-4342 562-949-1054
Fax: 562-949-1257 www.bakemarkusa.com
Manufacturer of bakery products
President/CEO: Robert Wallace
CFO: Herman Brons
VP: Tom Gumkowski
Plant Manager: Karen Werner
Estimated Sales: $4 Million
Type of Packaging: Private Label
Other Locations:
Phoenix AZ
Burlington NJ
Pico Rivera CA
North Las Vegas NV
Rancho Cordova CA
Reno NV
Union City CA
Buffalo NY
Denver CO
Saratoga Springs NY
Altanta GA
Fairfield OH
Carol Stream IL
Brands:
BAKEQWIK
BAKESENSE
FLOUR BRANDS
PRODUITS MARGUERITE
TRIGAL DORADO
WESTCO

987 **Bakehouse**
834 W Hallandale Beach Blvd
Hallandale Beach, FL 33009-5239 954-458-1600
Fax: 954-458-0126 bakehouse@mailcity.com
Processor of dough, yeasts and breads including pumpernickel, kalamata olive, focaccia, challah, wholewheat, chocolate cherry, sesame semolina, etc
President: Ed Robertson
Purchasing: Harris Ross
Estimated Sales: $10-20 Million
Number Employees: 10-19

988 **Bakemark Ingredients Canada**
2480 Viking Way
Richmond, BC V6V 1N2
Canada 604-303-1700
Fax: 604-303-1705 800-665-9441
sales@bakemarkcanada.com
www.bakemarkcanada.com
Bakemark Canada; manufacturers and suppliers of fine bakery and food ingredients
President: Larry Sullivan
Vice President: Michael Armstrong
Marketing: Linda McKenzie-Low
Sales Manager: Jeff Bligh
General Manager: Rick Barnes
Purchasing: Linda McKenzie-Low
Estimated Sales: $23 Million
Number Employees: 160
Number of Brands: 12
Number of Products: 2000
Type of Packaging: Private Label, Bulk
Brands:
BAKEMARK
BIB ULMER SPATZ
BRILL
CARAVAN
DEGOEDE
DIAMALT
DREIDOPPEL
MARQUERITE
MEISTERMARKEN

989 **Baker**
60 Bridge St
Milford, NJ 8848 908-995-4040
Fax: 908-995-9669 800-995-3989
sales@the-baker.com www.the-baker.com

Manufacturer of breads and rolls, organic breads, pita, cereals and grains such as wheat, oats, corn, rice, barley, rye, millet and buckwheat.
Estimated Sales: $1-3 Million
Number Employees: 20-49
Brands:
THE BAKER

990 **Baker & Baker**
1933 N Meacham Rd Ste 530
Schaumburg, IL 60173 847-593-5700
Fax: 847-925-5171 800-593-5777
www.csm.nl/index3.html
Manufacturer and exporter of mixes, frozen dough and fruit fillings
President/CEO: Paul Barron
Estimated Sales: $100+ Million
Number Employees: 100-249
Sq. footage: 100000
Parent Co: CSM
Type of Packaging: Food Service, Private Label, Bulk
Brands:
KARP'S

991 **Baker & Baker, Inc.**
1933 N Meacham Rd Ste 530
Schaumburg, IL 60173 847-593-5700
Fax: 847-925-5171 800-593-5777
www.csm.nl/index3.html
Frozen muffin batters, cookies, puff pastries, pie fillings, cobblers, icings, and glazes
Purchasing: Carmella Vasquez
Estimated Sales: $100-500 Million
Number Employees: 100-249
Brands:
BAKER & BAKER
BESTOVALL
KARP'S
ORTH
SCOOP-N-BAKE

992 **Baker Boy Bake Shop**
170 GTA Drive
Dickinson, ND 58601 701-225-4444
Fax: 701-225-7981 800-437-2008
loril@bakerboy.com www.bakerboy.com
Processor of frozen dough products; wholesaler/distributor of bakery supplies including flour, sugar, etc.; serving the foodservice market
President/CEO: Guy Moos
QA Manager: Lisa Buesh
Marketing Manager/Sales Executive: Carrie Elkin

Human Resources Director: Lori Luptak
Production/Manufacturing: Bob Thompson
Plant Manager: Michael Crawford
Estimated Sales: $29 Million
Number Employees: 225
Sq. footage: 86000
Type of Packaging: Consumer, Food Service, Private Label
Brands:
BAKER BOY

993 **Baker Boys**
2140 Pegasus Road NE
Calgary, AB T2E 8G8
Canada 403-255-4556
Fax: 403-259-5124 877-246-6036
info@bakerboys.net www.bakerboys.net
Processor of cinnamon rolls including thaw and serve, pre-proofed and frozen
President: Berry Walton
VP of Sales: Barry Wolton
Number Employees: 20-49
Type of Packaging: Consumer, Food Service
Brands:
Baker Boys

994 **Baker Candy Company**
12345 139th St Se
Snohomish, WA 98290 425-422-6331
Fax: 206-361-7009
Manufacturer of roasted nuts, chocolates and hard candy
Owner: Randy Spoo
VP: Ronald Prevele
Treasurer: Ronald Prevele
VP: Lee Prevele
Estimated Sales: $5-10 Million
Number Employees: 10-19
Sq. footage: 15000
Type of Packaging: Consumer, Bulk

995 **Baker Cheese Factory**
N5279 County Road G
Saint Cloud, WI 53079 920-477-7871
Fax: 920-477-2404 dick@bakercheese.com
www.bakercheese.com
Manufacturer of string cheese
President: Richard Baker
Vice President: John Baker
VP Sales: Brian Baker
Operations Manager: Brian Baker
Purchasing: Richard Baker
Estimated Sales: $25-50 Million
Number Employees: 100-249
Type of Packaging: Consumer, Private Label
Brands:
BAKER

996 **(HQ)Baker Commodities**
4020 Bandini Blvd
Vernon, CA 90058 323-268-2801
Fax: 323-268-0598 800-427-0696
dluckey@bakercommodities.com
www.bakercommodities.com
Manufacturer of protein meal and feeding fats
President: Jim Andreoli
CFO: Jim Reynolds
Executive VP: Dennis Luckey
VP Operations: Bill Sikes
Estimated Sales: $10-20 Million
Number Employees: 500-999
Type of Packaging: Bulk
Other Locations:
Seattle WA
Spokane WA
Kerman CA
Phoenix AZ
Rochester NY
North Billerica MA

997 **Baker Maid Products, Inc.**
P.O.Box 50424
New Orleans, LA 70150-0424 504-827-5500
Fax: 504-827-5400 bakermaid@bellsouth.net
Sliced, individually-wrapped dark brandied fruit cake, chunky chocolate cookies including almond toffee crunch, pecan praline and double chocolate raspberry
President: Darryl Sorrensen
CEO: Darell Sorensen
Estimated Sales: $1-2.5 Million
Number Employees: 20-49

998 **Baker Produce Company**
P.O.Box 6757
Kennewick, WA 99336 509-586-6174
Fax: 509-582-3694 800-624-7553
pbeamer@bakerproduce.com
www.bakerproduce.com
Grower and exporter of produce including apples, asparagus, cherries, onions, potatoes and sweet corn.
Manager: Pam Beamer
Sales Manager: Pam Beamer
Sales Representative: Diana Hawkins
Sales Representative: Tyler Saunders
Shipping: Savannah Davis
Estimated Sales: $100-500 Million
Number Employees: 250-499
Type of Packaging: Consumer, Food Service, Bulk
Brands:
BAKER SUPREME
BAKERS BEAUTIES
RED CHIP
YOU LIKE MORE

999 **Baker's Coconut**
8000 Horizon Center Blvd
Memphis, TN 38133-5197 901-381-6500
Fax: 901-381-6524 800-323-1092
www.kraftfoodscompany.com
Processor and exporter of cheese, coconut, flavors and cheese powders
Marketing/Sales Executive: Mike Malone
National Sales Manager: Greg Leininger
Number Employees: 100-249
Parent Co: Kraft Foods
Type of Packaging: Bulk

1000 **Baker's Dozen**
225 E State St
Herkimer, NY 13350 315-866-6770
Manufacturer of baked goods including bread, rolls and doughnuts
Owner: Tom Watkins
Manager: Tony Durso
Estimated Sales: $ 1 - 3 Million
Number Employees: 10-19

1001 **Baker's Point Fisheries**
33 Bakers Point Rd East
Oyster Pond Jeddore, NS B0J 1W0
Canada 902-845-2347
Fax: 902-845-2770
Processor and exporter of fresh and frozen haddock, cod, pollack, hake and cusk
Co-Owner: Janette Faulkner
Co-Owner: Wyman Baker
Number Employees: 50-99
Type of Packaging: Bulk

1002 **Baker's Rib**
2724 Commerce St
Dallas, TX 75226-1404 214-748-5433
Fax: 214-748-8544 www.bakersribs.com
Processor of BBQ sauces and seasonings
Manager: Julie Richter
Estimated Sales: Less than $500,000
Number Employees: 5-9
Type of Packaging: Consumer, Food Service
Brands:
Baker's Rib Inc

1003 **Bakerhaus Veit Limited**
70 Whitmore Road
Woodbridge, ON L4L 7Z4
Canada 905-850-9229
Fax: 905-850-9292 800-387-8860
info@backerhausveit.com
www.backerhausveit.com
Handcrafted artisan breads.
President/CEO: Sabine C Veit
CEO: Karen Reissmann
Brands:
Bakerhaus Veit

1004 **Bakers Breakfast Cookie**
4208 Meridian St
Bellingham, WA 98226 360-714-9585
Fax: 360-715-8011 877-889-1090
info@bbcookies.com www.bbcookies.com
Manufacturer of all natural cookies
Owner: Erin Baker
Estimated Sales: $ 5 - 10 Million
Number Employees: 20-49
Sq. footage: 4000

1005 **Bakers Candy**
P.O.Box 88
Greenwood, NE 68366-0088 402-789-2700
Fax: 402-789-2013 800-804-7330
Manufacturer of fine chocolates, including our chocolate meltaways in seven flavors
Owner: Kevin Baker
VP: Patty Baker
Sales Manager: Todd Baker
Estimated Sales: $ 3 - 5 Million
Number Employees: 5-9
Type of Packaging: Consumer

1006 **Bakers of Paris**
99 Park Ln
Brisbane, CA 94005 415-468-9100
Fax: 415-468-4320
customer-service@bakersofparis.com
www.bakersofparis.com
Manufacturer of all natural French bread and French pastries
Owner: Lionel Robbe-Jeadu
VP: Gilles Wicker

Estimated Sales: $5-10 Million

1007 **Bakers' Best Snack FoodCorporation**
1880 N Penn Rd
Hatfield, PA 19440 215-822-3511
Fax: 215-997-2049 www.jj snacks.com
Processor of soft pretzels
Manager: Wayne Childs
VP: Bob Radano
Marketing Manager: Michael Karaban
G.M.: Wayne Childs
Number Employees: 50-99
Parent Co: J&J Snack Foods Company
Type of Packaging: Consumer
Brands:
Chill Smooth Ice
Pretzel Fillers
Super Pretzel

1008 **Bakery Chef**
4501 W Fullerton Ave
Chicago, IL 60639-1933 773-384-1900
Fax: 773-384-3661 www.ralcorpfrozen.com
Processor and co-packer of baked goods including muffins, pound and crumb cakes.
Executive Director: Laura Rivera
VP Sales: Larry Gordon
General Manager: Ronald Krass
Estimated Sales: $9-14 Million
Number Employees: 1-4
Type of Packaging: Consumer, Food Service, Private Label, Bulk

1009 **Bakery Chef**
12650 Westport Rd
Louisville, KY 40245 502-423-8944
Fax: 502-423-9348 800-594-0203
information@bakerychef.com
www.bakerychef.com
Processor of frozen ready to serve biscuits, breads, muffins, pancakes, french toast and waffles.
Customer Development VP: Terry Rice
Director Operations: David Jerome
Manager: John Bischoff
Purchasing Agent: Jim Jupin
Estimated Sales: $100-500 Million
Number Employees: 250-499
Sq. footage: 320000
Parent Co: Ralcorp Holdings
Type of Packaging: Food Service, Private Label
Brands:
CHEF SUPREME
KRUSTEAZ
WAFFLE STICKS

1010 **Bakery Corp**
15625 NW 15th Ave
Miami, FL 33169 305-623-3838
Fax: 305-626-9189 800-521-4345
info@bakerycorp.com www.bakerycorp.com
Manufacturers of breads and cakes
President: Luis Lacal
Estimated Sales: $10-20 Million
Number Employees: 10-19

1011 **Bakery Crafts**
P.O.Box 37
West Chester, OH 45071 513-942-0862
Fax: 513-942-3835 800-543-1673
Manufacturer, wholesaler, importer and exporter of cake decoration supplies
President: Sam Guttman
CFO: Bill Biddinger
Director: Victor Dupre
VP Marketing: Laura Guder
Estimated Sales: $ 20 - 50 Million
Number Employees: 100-249
Sq. footage: 150000
Parent Co: Jack Guttman
Type of Packaging: Bulk
Brands:
Bakery CraftS
Copy Confection

1012 **Bakery Europa**
500 Alakawa Street
Honolulu, HI 96817-4593 808-845-5011
Fax: 808-847-6263
Processor of breads, croissants, pastries and desserts
President: Dennis Dolim
Cntllr.: Stuart Kimura
CFO: Walter Lum
Estimated Sales: $50-100 Million
Number Employees: 100-249
Sq. footage: 18000
Parent Co: Global Operations Pacific
Type of Packaging: Consumer, Food Service, Private Label, Bulk
Brands:
Bakery Europa
Bakery Iwilei
Bakery Weilei
Coach House Bakeries
Old Vienna Bake Shop

1013 **Bakery Management Corporation**
15625 NW 15th Ave
Miami, FL 33169-5601 305-623-3838
Fax: 305-626-9189 info@bakerycorp.com
www.bakerycorp.com
Baked goods including danish, muffins, croissant, cakes, bagels, rolls, bread and buns.
President: Luis Lacal
Vice President: Juan Lacal
Estimated Sales: $1.7 Million
Number Employees: 21

1014 **Bakon Yeast**
33415 N 64th Place
Scottsdale, AZ 85266-7363 480-595-9370
Fax: 480-595-9371 bakonyeast@aol.com
bakonyeast.samsbiz.com
Processor of vegetable derived bacon flavored seasonings and hickory smoked torula yeast; exporter of hickory smoked torula yeast
President: Phyll Ray
VP: Larry Ray
Plant Manager: Rebecca Schaefer
Estimated Sales: $600,000
Number Employees: 1
Sq. footage: 10000
Parent Co: Bakon Yeast
Type of Packaging: Consumer, Food Service, Bulk
Brands:
Bakon Seasonings
Bakon Yeast

1015 **Balagna Winery Company**
223 Rio Bravo Dr
Los Alamos, NM 87544 505-672-3678
Fax: 505-672-1482
Wines
Proprietor: John Balagna
Operations Manager: John Balagna
Estimated Sales: $ .5 - 1 million
Number Employees: 20
Brands:
Balagna Winery

1016 **Balanced Health Products**
215 E 68th St Ste 33a
New York, NY 10065 212-794-9878
Fax: 212-794-5108 nikkistar@worldnet.att.net
www.starcaps.com
Processor of dietetic candy and supplements
President: Nikki Haskell
Estimated Sales: $790,000
Number Employees: 1-4
Sq. footage: 1000
Brands:
Nikki Bars
Star Blend
Star Caps
Star Sucker Sour
Star Suckers

1017 **Balboa Dessert Company**
1760 E Wilshire Ave
Santa Ana, CA 92705 714-972-4972
Fax: 714-972-0605 800-974-9699
www.balboadessert.com
Processor and exporter of desserts including frozen cakes, cheesecakes and tortes
President: Maryknoll Benner
Vice President: Dan Hamilton
Estimated Sales: $4 Million
Number Employees: 50
Type of Packaging: Food Service

1018 **Baldinger Bakery**
215 Eva St
Saint Paul, MN 55107 651-224-5761
Fax: 651-224-9047 www.baldingerbakery.com
Breads, breadsticks, buns, rolls, bagels and more
Partner: Bob Baldinger
Partner: Steve Baldinger
Asst General Manager: Paul Chan
Estimated Sales: $22 Million
Number Employees: 140
Sq. footage: 36000
Type of Packaging: Consumer, Food Service
Brands:
Old World

1019 **Baldwin Richardson Foods**
20201 S La Grange Rd, Ste 200
Frankfort, IL 60423 815-464-9994
Fax: 815-464-9995 866-644-2732
www.brfoods.com

Liquid ingredient manufacturer specializing in signature sauces, dessert toppings, beverage/pancake syrups, specialty fruit fillings and condiments

President/CEO: Eric Johnson
CFO: Evelyn White
Director: Michele Salva
Purchasing: Paula Bell
Estimated Sales: $ 5 - 10 Million
Number Employees: 200
Sq. footage: 900000
Type of Packaging: Consumer, Food Service, Private Label, Bulk
Brands:
Baldwin Ice Cream
Mrs Richardson Toppings
Nance's Mustards
Nance's Wing Sauce & Condiments

1020 **Baldwin Vineyards**
176 Hardenburgh Rd
Pine Bush, NY 12566 845-744-2226
Fax: 845-744-6321
baldwin_Vineyards@frontiernet.net
www.baldwinvineyards.com
Processor of wines
Owner/CEO: Patricia Baldwin
Owner/President: Jack Baldwin
VP: John Baldwin
Estimated Sales: $500,000-$1 Million
Number Employees: 1-4
Brands:
Baldwin

1021 **Baldwin-Minkler Farms**
320 E South St
Orland, CA 95963-9111 530-865-8080
Fax: 530-865-8085 djsoetaert@aol.com
Processor of almonds
Owner: Roderick Minkler
General Manager: Bill Minkler
Estimated Sales: $20-50 Million
Number Employees: 50-99
Type of Packaging: Bulk

1022 **Balic Winery**
6623 Harding Hwy
Mays Landing, NJ 8330 609-625-1903
Fax: 609-625-1904 www.balicwinery.com
Wine
Owner: Bojan Boskodich
Estimated Sales: Less than $200,000
Number Employees: 5-9

1023 **Ball Park Franks**
3500 Lacey Road
Downers Grove, IL 60515-5424 630-598-8100
Fax: 630-598-8482 www.ballparkfranks.com

Hot dogs, packaged meat products, kosher hot dogs, kosher packaged meat products
Chairman: Jon Bennink
CEO: Marcel Smits
CFO/North America: Maria Henry
SVP/CIO: Steve Merry
SVP/Global Communications: Jon Harris
Estimated Sales: $100-500 Million
Number Employees: 1-4
Parent Co: Sara Lee Corporation
Brands:
Ball Park Fat Free Franks
Ball Park Franks

1024 **(HQ)Ballantine Produce Company**
P.O.Box 756
Reedley, CA 93654 559-875-2583
Fax: 559-637-2159 info@ballantineproduce.com
www.ballantineproduce.com
Manufacturer and processor of over 200 varieties of plums, peaches, nectarines, pluots, white flesh, apricots, grapes, Asian pears, quince, pomegranates, persimmons and apples.
President: Virgil Rasmussen
CFO: Richard Graham
Estimated Sales: $10-20 Million
Type of Packaging: Consumer, Food Service
Other Locations:
Reedley Sales Office
Reedley CA
Brands:
Ballantine

1025 **Ballard Custom Meats**
55 Myrtle St
Manchester, ME 04351-3251 207-622-9764
Fax: 207-621-0242
Meats
President: Kenneth Ballard Jr
Estimated Sales: $2,000,000
Number Employees: 10-19

1026 **Ballas Egg Products Corporation**
PO Box 2217
Zanesville, OH 43702-2217 740-453-0386
Fax: 740-453-0491 www.ballasegg.com
Manufacturer of frozen, dried and liquid egg products
President: Leonard Ballas
CEO: J Saliba
VP: Craig Ballas
Estimated Sales: $25 Million
Number Employees: 100-249
Sq. footage: 100000
Brands:
BALLAS

1027 **Ballreich's Potato Chips**
186 Ohio Ave
Tiffin, OH 44883 419-447-1814
Fax: 419-447-5635 800-323-2447
chips@ballreich.com www.ballreich.com
Snacks including potato chips; flavors include BBQ, sour cream and onion, southwestern BBQ, salt and vinegar, no salt added, and marcelled
President: Brian Reis
VP: Linda Reis
Estimated Sales: $5 Million
Number Employees: 44
Number of Brands: 1
Number of Products: 52
Sq. footage: 50000
Type of Packaging: Private Label
Brands:
Ballreich
Ballreich's Caramel Corn
Ballreich's Cheese Curls
Ballreich's Cheese Popcorn
Ballreich's Party Mix
Ballreich's Pork Rinds
Ballreich's Pretzels
Ballreich's Tortilla Chips
Ballreich's Triple Mix

1028 **Balsu**
P.O.Box 545838
1160 Kane Concourse Ste 403
Bay Harbour Islands, FL 33154
US 305-993-5045
Fax: 305-993-5047 balsusa@aol.com
www.balsusa.com
Processor and exporter of hazelnuts
President/CHR: H. Zapsu
Director/Sales And Marketing: Sezen Donmezer
Sales Director: Karim Azzaoui
Estimated Sales: A
Number Employees: 1-4
Type of Packaging: Bulk

1029 **Balticshop.Com LLC**
2842 Main Street
Glastonbury, CT 06033-1077
Fax: 201-300-0146 margita@balticshop.com
www.balticshop.com
Bread, candy & cookies.

1030 **Baltimore Bakery**
1140 Kingwood Ave
Norfolk, VA 23502-5603 757-855-4731
Fax: 757-855-2568 www.mamakayersbakery.com
Baked goods
President: Jason Mathis
COO: Robert Fall
Estimated Sales: $10-20 Million
Number Employees: 50-99

1031 **Baltimore Brewing Company**
104 Albemarle St
Baltimore, MD 21202 410-837-5000
Fax: 410-837-5024 theo@degroens.com
www.degroens.com
Processor of seasonal beer and lager
President: Theo De Groen
Secretary: Imtraud De Groen
Estimated Sales: Under $500,000
Number Employees: 1-4
Brands:
De Groen's

1032 **Baltimore Coffee & Tea Company**
9 W Aylesbury Rd Ste T
Timonium, MD 21093 410-561-1080
Fax: 410-561-4816 800-823-1408
orders@baltcoffee.com
www.baltimorecoffee.com
Manufacturer of coffee and tea
President: Stanley Constantine
VP: Norman Loverde
Estimated Sales: $2.5-5 Million
Number Employees: 50-99
Type of Packaging: Private Label
Brands:
Easten Shore Tea

1033 **Baltimore Poultry & Meats**
1552 Ridgely Street
Baltimore, MD 21230-2013 410-783-7361
Fax: 410-783-7740
Manufacturer of poultry and meats
President: Hong Kim

1034 **Bama Fish Atlanta**
3113 Main Street
East Point, GA 30344-4802 404-765-9896
Fax: 404-765-9874
Fresh and frozen fish

1035 **Bama Frozen Dough**
2745 East 11th Street
Tulsa, OK 74104 918-732-2600
Fax: 918-592-7499 800-756-2262
dwilson@bama.com www.bama.com
Manufacturer of frozen pizza, yeast, pastry sheet dough
CEO: Paula Marshall-Chapman
VP Operations: Ted Easton
Estimated Sales: $20-50 Million
Number Employees: 100-249
Parent Co: Bama Companies
Other Locations:
Bama Companies
Tulsa OK
Bama Foods Ltd.
Tulsa OK
Beijing Bama Food Processing Co.
Daxing County, Beijing

1036 **Banana Distributing Company**
1500 S Zarzamora St Unit 326
San Antonio, TX 78207 210-227-8285
Fax: 210-227-8287 mj@banana-distributing.com
www.banana-distributing.com
Manufacturer and wholesaler/distributor of bananas and plantains
Owner: Jim Scarsdale
Sales Manager: Augie Aguilar
Operations Manager: Leo Aguilar
Estimated Sales: $ 5 - 10 Million
Number Employees: 10-19
Parent Co: Barshop Enterprises
Type of Packaging: Consumer, Food Service, Bulk

1037 **Bandiera Winery**
155 Cherry Creek Road
Cloverdale, CA 95425-3807 707-894-4295
Fax: 707-894-2563 info@bandiera.com
www.bandiera.com
Wines
President: Cathy Delfava
Estimated Sales: $10-20 Million
Number Employees: 20-49
Parent Co: California Winery

1038 **Bandon Bay Fisheries**
PO Box 485
Bandon, OR 97411-0485 541-347-4454
Fax: 541-347-4313
Processor of IQF shrimp meat and crab meat
Manager: Graydon Stinnett
Number Employees: 50-99
Sq. footage: 10000
Parent Co: S&S Seafood
Type of Packaging: Private Label

1039 **Banfi Vintners**
1111 Cedar Swamp Rd
Glen Head, NY 11545 516-626-9200
Fax: 516-626-9218 800-645-6511
info@banfivintners.com www.banfivintners.com
Manufacturer and importer of Wines
President: James Mariani
CEO: Cristina Mariani-May
Marketing Director: Gary Clayton
VP Public Relations: Lars Leicht
Estimated Sales: $ 100-500 Million
Number Employees: 50-99
Brands:
ALMAVIVA
BELL' AGIO
BORGOGNO
CECCHI
CONCHA Y TORO
CONO SUR
COSTELLO BANFI
ENTREE
FLORIO
OLD BROOKVILLE
PLACIDO
RIUNITE
SARTORI
SINCERITY
STONE HAVEN
STONE HAVEN
STONE'S
SUNRISE
VIGNE REGALI
WALNUT CREST
WISDOM & WARTER

1040 **Banner Candy Manufacturing Company**
700 Liberty Avenue
Brooklyn, NY 11208-2197 718-647-4747
Fax: 718-647-7192
Candy
President: Michael Smith
Plant Manager: Rose Grunther
Estimated Sales: $10-20 Million
Number Employees: 50-99
Type of Packaging: Bulk

1041 **(HQ)Banner Pharmacaps**
4100 Mendenhall Oaks Pkwy Ste 301
High Point, NC 27265 336-812-3442
Fax: 336-812-7030 globalinfo@banpharm.com
www.banpharm.com
Manufacturer and exporter of soft gel and vitamins
President/CEO: Roger Gordon PhD
CFO Banner: Robert Gretton
Global VP/R&D/Operations: Aqeel Fatmi
Global VP/Legal/Human Resources: Charles Cain

Global VP/Commercial Operations: Timothy Doran
Estimated Sales: $114 Million
Number Employees: 250-499

Sq. footage: 250000
Parent Co: Sobel-Holland
Other Locations:
Banner Pharmacaps
Chatsworth CA
Banner Pharmacaps
Alberta, Canada
Gelcaps Exportadora De Mexico
Naucalpan, Edo. de Mexico
Banner Pharmacaps Europe BV
Tilburg, The Netherlands
Banner Pharmacaps India Pvt. Ltd.
Bangalore, India
Brands:
BANNER SOFLET

1042 **Banquet Schuster Bakery**
115 E Abriendo Ave
Pueblo, CO 81004-4201 719-544-1062
Manufacturer of baked goods including bread, pies, cakes, pastries, etc.
President: Janet Monack
Estimated Sales: $1-2.5 Million
Number Employees: 10-19
Type of Packaging: Consumer

1043 **Baptista's Bakery**
P.O.Box 321010
Franklin, WI 53132-6161 414-409-2000
Fax: 414-423-4375 877-261-3157
mdavis@baptistas.com
Manufacturer of bread products and dipping sauces
President: Thomas Howe
CEO: Nannette Gardetto
Estimated Sales: $ 10 - 20 Million
Number Employees: 50-99
Brands:
BAPTISTA'S
GARDETTO'S

1044 **Bar Harbor Brewing Company**
8 Mount Desert St
Bar Harbor, ME 04609 207-288-4592
orders@barharborbrewing.com
www.barharborbrewing.com
Brewers
President: Andre Lozano
Operations: Tod Foster
Estimated Sales: $1-2.5 Million
Number Employees: 1-4
Brands:
BAR HARBOR GINGER ALE
BAR HARBOR PEACH ALE
CADILLAC MOUNTAIN STOUT
HARBOR LIGHTHOUSE ALE
THUNDER HOLE ALE
TRUE BLUE

1045 **(HQ)Bar-S Foods Company**
P.O.Box 29049
Phoenix, AZ 85038 602-264-7272
Fax: 602-285-5252 www.bar-s.com
Refrigerated frankfurters, bacon, hams, luncheon meats and sausages
CEO: Timothy T Day
VP Sales/Marketing: Linda Boodman
General Manager: Max Pyron
Estimated Sales: $400 Million
Number Employees: 1,000-4,999
Type of Packaging: Consumer, Food Service, Private Label, Bulk
Other Locations:
Bar-S
Clinton OK
Bar-S
Altus OK
Bar-S
Lawton OK
Bar-S
Elk City OK
Brands:
BAR-S BRANDS
BIGGIES
CHUNKWAGON
CORONADO
EXTRA LEAN
LITE
PRESIDENT'S PRIDE
REX
THRIFTY
VIRGINIA REEL

1046 **Bar-W Meat Company**
3517 Conway St
Fort Worth, TX 76111 817-831-0051
Fax: 817-834-6766
Meat
President: John Wehba
Vice President: Paul Weahper
Estimated Sales: $12 Million
Number Employees: 60

1047 **Baraboo Candy Company**
E10891 Coop Ln
Baraboo, WI 53913 608-356-7425
Fax: 608-356-1815 800-967-1690
sales@baraboocandy.com
www.baraboocandy.com
Chocolate candy sugar free, dark, milk and white chocolate
President: Michael Ford
CEO: Walter Smith
Chief Executive: Dennis Roney
Estimated Sales: $1 Million
Number Employees: 16
Type of Packaging: Private Label, Bulk
Brands:
CHEWY GOOEY PRETZEL STICKS
COW LICK
COW PIE
GREEN BAY PUDDLES
LICK-A-PIG
MOO CHEW
UPPER FINGERS
WALLY WALLEYE

1048 **Barataria Spice Company**
2317 Privateer Blvd
Barataria, LA 70036 504-689-7650
800-793-7650
www.seasoningspice.com
Spices
Co-Owner/President: Mike Hymel
Co-Owner/CEO: Cynthia Hymel
Estimated Sales: Less than $500,000
Number Employees: 1-4
Type of Packaging: Consumer, Food Service
Brands:
Captain Mike's

1049 **Barbara's Bakery**
3900 Cypress Dr
Petaluma, CA 94954 707-765-2273
Fax: 707-765-2927 info@barbarabakery.com
www.barbarasbakery.com
Manufacturer of organic and natural cereals. crackers, cookies, bars, puffs and chips
President: Barabara Jaffe
Executive VP: Chuck Marble
Quality Control: Erik Smitt
Director/Marketing: Kent Spalding
Director/Sales: Linda Gerwig
Purchasing: Laura Barberio
Estimated Sales: $20-50 Million
Number Employees: 50-99
Sq. footage: 102500
Type of Packaging: Consumer, Private Label
Other Locations:
Barbara's Bakery
Sacramento CA
Brands:
BARBARA'S BAKERY
NATURE'S CHOICE
WEETABIX

1050 **Barbe's Dairy**
1420 Fourth Street
PO Box 186
Westwego, LA 70094 504-347-6201
Fax: 504-347-6201
Processor of orange juice, ice milk mix, fruit drinks and dairy products including fresh cream and regular and chocolate milk
General Manager: Laurent Barbe Jr
Estimated Sales: $50-100 Million
Number Employees: 100-249
Parent Co: Suiza Dairy Group
Type of Packaging: Consumer, Food Service, Private Label, Bulk

1051 **Barber Foods**
56 Milliken St
Portland, ME 04103 207-482-5500
Fax: 207-797-0286 800-577-2595
Customer_relations@barberfoods.com
www.barberfoods.com
Manufacturer and exporter of frozen chicken including stuffed breasts, entrees, appetizers, chicken fingers, nuggets, fillets and patties
CEO: Bruce Wagner
CFO: Vicki Manner
Vice President: David Barber
Estimated Sales: $ 3 - 5 Million
Sq. footage: 150000
Type of Packaging: Consumer, Food Service
Other Locations:
Barber Foods Production Plant
Portland ME
Brands:
BARBER FOODS

1052 **Barber Pure Milk Ice Cream Company**
36 Barber Ct
Birmingham, AL 35209-6435 205-942-2351
Fax: 205-943-0296
edmonia_anderson@deanfoods.com
www.barbersdairy.com
Manufacturer of dairy products, such as; egg nog, Mexican coffee, coffee parfaits
General Manager/VP: P Flagg
Plant Manager: Valerie Meyers
Estimated Sales: $5-10 Million
Number Employees: 100-249
Parent Co: Dean Foods Company
Type of Packaging: Consumer, Food Service, Private Label, Bulk

1053 **Barber's Dairy**
36 Barber Ct
Birmingham, AL 35209 205-942-2351
Fax: 205-943-0296 www.barbersdairy.com
Manufacturer of dairy products including ice cream and milk
VP of Sales/Marketing: Bruce Williamson
Plant Manager: Valerie Meyers
Number Employees: 100-249
Parent Co: Dean Foods Company
Type of Packaging: Consumer, Food Service, Private Label

1054 **Barbero Bakery, Inc.**
61 Conrad St
Trenton, NJ 8611 609-394-5122
Fax: 609-394-5567 info@barberobakery.com
www.barberobakery.com
Manufacturer of specialty cakes, pastries, italian cookies, deserts, deli breads and rolls
President: Gerardo Barbero
Estimated Sales: $2.5-5 Million
Number Employees: 20-49

1055 **Barboursville Vineyards**
P.O.Box 136
Barboursville, VA 22923 540-832-3824
Fax: 540-832-7572 bvvy@barboursvillewine.com
www.barboursvillecellar.com
Manufacturer of wines
Manager: Luca Paschina
Number Employees: 20-49

1056 **Barca Wine Cellars**
PO Box 1150
Roseville, CA 95678 916-967-0770
Fax: 916-784-7575
barcaintlwines@barcawines.net
barcawines.net
Wines
General Manager: Gino Barca
Estimated Sales: $ 3 - 5 Million
Number Employees: 5-9
Brands:
Barbousville Vineyards

1057 **Barcelona Nut Company**
502 S Mount St
Baltimore, MD 21223 410-233-5252
Fax: 410-233-6555 800-292-6887
sales@barcelonanut.com www.barcelonanut.com
Over 150 different snack food items including packaged nuts, trail mixes, snack mixes, 2 for $1.00 candy and cotton candy.
President/CEO: Tony Tsonis
Marketing Executive/VP Sales: Mike Adams
VP & Director Of Sales: Mike Adams
Estimated Sales: $20-50 Million
Number Employees: 100-249
Sq. footage: 50000
Type of Packaging: Consumer, Food Service, Private Label, Bulk

Brands:
BARCELONA
CANDYMAN LANE
HEALTHNUT
SNACKNUT

1058 Bard Valley Medjool Date Growers
2575 E 23rd Lane
Yuma, AZ 85365 928-726-0901
Fax: 928-726-9413 edwardo@datepac.com
www.datepac.com
Medjool date packing and marketing
President: Edward O'Malley
President of Sales Operations: Dave Nelson
Production Manager: Camen Wilson
General Manager: Glen Vandervoort

1059 Barefoot Contessa Pantry
2 Stonewall Lane
York, ME 03909 207-351-2712
Fax: 207-351-2715 800-826-1752
kbouchie@stonewallkitchen.com
www.stonewallkitchen.com
French citrus, dessert baking mixes, breakfast baking mixes, dessert toppings, sauces and marinades, pancakes and syrups, preserves and lemon curd, coffee and hot chocolate
President/Owner: Jonathan King
CEO: James Stott

1060 Baretta Provision
172 Commerce St
East Berlin, CT 06023 860-828-0802
Fax: 860-828-8699
Manufacturer and packer of meats including beef, pork and veal
President: William Baretta
VP: Daniel Baretta
Estimated Sales: $3-5 Million
Number Employees: 10-19
Type of Packaging: Food Service
Brands:
LENORA

1061 Bargetto's Winery
3535 N Main St
Soquel, CA 95073-2530 831-475-2258
Fax: 831-475-2664 800-422-7438
customerservice@bargetto.com
www.bargetto.com
Wines
President: Martin Bargetto
Operations: Michael Sones
Estimated Sales: $5-9.9 Million
Number Employees: 20-49
Type of Packaging: Private Label
Brands:
BARGETTO
CHAUCERS
LAVITA

1062 Barhyte Specialty Foods Inc
912 Airport Rd
Po Box 1499
Pendleton, OR 97801 503-691-7858
Fax: 503-691-8918 chris@barhyte.com
www.barhyte.com
Sauces, dressings, marinades, mustards
President/Owner: Susan Barhyte
CEO: Chris Barhyte
CFO: Irene Barhyte
Estimated Sales: $5.7
Number Employees: 43

1063 Bari & Gail
24 Walpole Park S
Walpole, MA 02081-2541 508-668-5629
Fax: 508-850-9555 800-828-9318
info@bariandgail.com bariandgail.com
Chocolates
President: Joseph Sesnovich
Owner: Barrie Steinberg
Vice President: Lisa Gail Sesnovich
Estimated Sales: $2.5-5 Million
Number Employees: 5-9
Type of Packaging: Bulk

1064 Barilla America Inc.
1200 Lakeside Dr
Deerfield, IL 60015 847-405-7500
Fax: 847-405-7505 connie.lee@wasa-barilla.com
www.wasa-usa.com
Manufacturer of pasta, pasta sauces, biscuits, toasts, snacks, and soft breads, short pastry, cakes and crispbread.
President: Kirk Trofholz
CEO: Gianluca Bolla
Product Development Manager: Judy Glass
VP Marketing: Sergio Pereira
Public Relations: Catherine Franklin
Estimated Sales: 113,400,000
Number Employees: 1,000-4,999
Type of Packaging: Food Service

1065 Barker System Bakery
209 S Oak St
Mt Carmel, PA 17851-2147 570-339-3380
President: Cathy Saukatis
Estimated Sales: Less than $500,000
Number Employees: 1-4

1066 Barkman Honey Company
120 Santa Fe St
Hillsboro, KS 67063-9688 620-947-3173
Fax: 620-947-3640 800-530-5827
www.ghfllc.com
Manufacturer of pure and clear honey featuring distinctive flavors, including clover honey, wildflower honey, orange blossom honey, and honey spread
President: Dwight Stroller
CEO: Brent Barkman
CEO: Dwight Stoller
Estimated Sales: $20-50 Million
Number Employees: 50-99
Type of Packaging: Consumer, Food Service
Other Locations:
Latty OH

1067 Barlean's
4936 Lake Terrell Rd
Ferndale, WA 98248-9014 360-384-0325
Fax: 360-384-1746 orders@barleans.com
www.barleansfishery.com
Produces the world's finest and freshest organic flaxseed oil, fish oil, green food supplement and other premium essential fatty acid products.
Owner: Cindy Smith
CEO: Jane Beutler
Marketing Director: Andreas Koch
Number Employees: 1-4

1068 Barn Stream Natural Foods
PO Box 896
Walpole, NH 03608-0896 800-654-2882
Fax: 603-756-9000
Gourmet food
Owner: Nicholas Raynor
Estimated Sales: $10-20 Million
Number Employees: 10-19
Brands:
Zapit-Za Bread

1069 Barnes & Watson Fine Teas
270 S Hanford St Ste 211
Seattle, WA 98134 206-625-9435
Fax: 206-625-0345 800-447-8832
tea@barnesandwatson.com
www.barnesandwatson.com
Whole leaf tea bags
Owner: Ken Rudee
Estimated Sales: $1-2.5 Million
Number Employees: 1-4
Number of Products: 50+
Type of Packaging: Consumer, Food Service, Bulk
Brands:
Barnes
Watson Fine Teas

1070 Barnes Farming Corporation
7840 Old Bailey Hwy
Spring Hope, NC 27882 252-459-9380
Fax: 252-459-9020 information@farmpak.com
www.farmpak.com
President: Carson Barnes
VP: John Barnes
Packhouse Manager: Frank Salinas
Estimated Sales: $100-500 Million
Number Employees: 500-999
Brands:
Farm Pak
Heart of Carolina
Queen Ann

1071 Barnes Ice Cream Company
475 Pond Rd
Manchester, ME 04351-3612
Manufacturer of ice cream
Owner: Richard Barnes
Owner: Carl Barnes
Estimated Sales: $500,000-$1 Million
Number Employees: 1-4
Type of Packaging: Consumer

1072 Barney Pork House
433 Johnston St SE
Decatur, AL 35601-3007 256-350-9988
Fax: 256-350-9940
Sausage
Partner: Billy C Burney Ii
Estimated Sales: $ .5 - 1 million
Number Employees: 5-9

1073 Barnie's Coffee & Tea Company
2126 W Landstreet Rd Ste 300
Orlando, FL 32809 407-854-6600
Fax: 407-854-6601 800-284-1416
customerservice@barniescoffee.com
www.barniescoffee.com
Coffee and tea
CEO: Neil Leach
CFO: Glorian Leach
Vice President: Robert Kalafut
Estimated Sales: $10-20 Million
Number Employees: 40

1074 Barnum & Bagel Frozen Soup
4700 Dempster Street
Skokie, IL 60076-2045 847-676-4466
Fax: 847-676-4546
Restaurant
President: George Mellos
Estimated Sales: $1-2.5 Million
Number Employees: 50-99

1075 Barnum-Goodfriend Farms
4938 State Route 52
Jeffersonville, NY 12748-5620 845-482-4123
Fax: 845-482-4124 jgoodfriend@zelacom.com
Owner: Mike Barber
Number Employees: 20-49

1076 Baron Vineyards
PO Box 624
Paso Robles, CA 93447-0624 805-239-3313
Fax: 805-239-2789 tombaron@webtv.net
Wines
Owner: Tom Baron
Co-Owner: Sharon Baron
Number Employees: 20-49
Brands:
Baron

1077 Barone Foods
345 S Kino Pkwy
Tucson, AZ 85719 520-623-8571
Fax: 520-622-1599
Manufacturer of cooked and processed meats including sausage
General Manager: Tim Barone
Estimated Sales: $ 5 - 10 Million
Number Employees: 10-19
Parent Co: City Meat
Type of Packaging: Consumer, Food Service, Private Label, Bulk

1078 Barone Foods
345 S Kino Pkwy
Tucson, AZ 85719 520-623-8571
Fax: 520-622-1599
Beef, beef products, sausage, deli products, meat packing
General Manager: Tim Barone
Estimated Sales: $5-10 Million
Number Employees: 20-49

1079 Baronet Coffee
P.O.Box 987
Hartford, CT 06143-0987 860-527-7253
Fax: 860-524-9130 800-227-6638
baronet@cyberusa.net www.baronetcoffee.com
Manufacturer and importer of coffee
President: Bruce Goldsmith
Estimated Sales: $10-20 Million
Number Employees: 10-19
Brands:
Baronet Coffees

1080 **Barrel O'Fun Snacks Foods Company**
P.O.Box 230
Perham, MN 56573-0230 218-346-7000
Fax: 218-346-7003 www.redtwist.com
Dry snack foods, potato chips, popcorn
President: Ken Nelson
VP/COO: Mike Holper
VP Sales/Marketing: Randy Johnson
Production: Mike Bormann
Estimated Sales: $20-50 Million
Number Employees: 250-499
Parent Co: KLN Enterprises, Inc
Type of Packaging: Private Label

1081 **Barricini Chocolate**
P.O.Box 5189
Avoca, PA 18641-0189 570-457-6756
Fax: 570-457-8276
customerservice@barricini.com
www.barricini.com
Manufacturer of dark and milk chocolates with hazelnuts, cashews, peanut butter confections and more.
Manager: Barnett Tessler
Estimated Sales: $20-50 Million
Number Employees: 50-99
Brands:
BARRICINI
BARRICINI CHATEAU
BARRICINI DREAM
BARRICINI EDDY LEON
BARRICINI HOLIDAY
BARRICINI ROYAL

1082 **Barrie House Gourmet Coffee**
945 Nepperhan Ave
Yonkers, NY 10703-1727 914-423-8437
Fax: 914-423-8499 800-876-2233
sales@barriehouse.com www.barriehouse.com
Complete selection of coffees, teas, accesories and equipment, to serve the specialty coffee and tea industry
President: Paul Goldstein
CEO: Barry Goldstein
CFO: Stephen Eccles
Estimated Sales: $20-50 Million
Number Employees: 20-49
Number of Products: 200
Type of Packaging: Food Service, Private Label, Bulk
Brands:
BARRIE HOUSE
CAFE BODEGA
CAFE EXCELLENCE
DONUT SHOP

1083 **Barrington Coffee Roasting Company**
165 Quarry Hill Rd
Lee, MA 01238-9623 413-243-3008
Fax: 413-528-0614 800-528-0998
coffee@barringtoncoffee.com
www.barringtoncoffee.com
Quality coffees from around the world.
Owner: Barth Anderson
Owner: Gregg Charbonneau
Manager: Christina Stanton
Estimated Sales: $2.5-5 Million
Number Employees: 1-4
Type of Packaging: Private Label
Brands:
BARRINGTON ESTATE
BARRINGTON GOLD
DARK ROAST
LIMITED EDITION
ORGANIC/FAIR TRADE
SINGLE ORIGIN

1084 **Barrington Nutritionals**
500 Mamaroneck Ave # 201
Harrison, NY 10528-1636 914-381-3500
Fax: 914-381-2232 800-684-2436
info@barringtonchem.com
www.barringtonchem.com
Barrington Nutritionals offers custom granulation, blending and particle size reduction of products for the Vitamin/Nutrition, and Pharmaceutical industries.
Owner: Stuart Gelbard
National Sales Manager: Nelson Fretwell

1085 **(HQ)Barrows Tea Company**
PO Box 40278
New Bedford, MA 02744-0003 774-488-8684
Fax: 508-990-2760 800-832-5024
madhatter@barrowstea.com
www.barrowstea.com
Processor and importer of round unbleached tea bags and natural and organic teas
President: Sam Barrows
Estimated Sales: $1-2.5 Million
Number Employees: 1-4
Number of Brands: 1
Number of Products: 15
Type of Packaging: Consumer, Food Service
Brands:
Barrows

1086 **Barry Callebaut USA LLC**
903 Industrial Highway
Eddystone, PA 19022 610-872-4528
Fax: 610-872-4527 www.barry-callebaut.com
Manufacturer and supplier of chocolate, cocoa powders, ready to use fillings, coatings and decorations.

1087 **Barry Callebaut USA LLC**
400 Industrial Park Road
Saint Albans, VT 05478-1875 802-524-9711
Fax: 802-524-5148 800-556-8845
stalbans@barry-callebaut.com
www.barry-callebaut.com
High quality Belgium chocolate ingredients
Director Sales: Joe Lucas
Estimated Sales: $50-100 Million
Number Employees: 7500
Parent Co: Barry Callebaut
Brands:
BARRY CALLEBAUT
BENSDORP
CACAO BARRY
CALLEBAUT
CARMA
VAN HOUTEN
VAN LEER

1088 **(HQ)Barry Callebaut USA LLC**
600 West Chicago Aveneu
Suite 860
Chicago, IL 60654 312-496-7300
Fax: 312-496-7399 866-443-0460
stablans@barry-callebaut.com
www.barry-callebaut.com
Producer of cocoa and chocolate products
CEO: Juergen Steinemann
Estimated Sales: $5 Billion
Number Employees: 7500
Parent Co: Barry Callebaut AG
Brands:
Cacaobarry
Carma
Cenleer
Kalibert

1089 **Barry Callebaut USA, Inc.**
1500 Suckle Hwy
Pennsauken, NJ 8110 856-663-2260
Fax: 856-665-0474 800-836-2626
pennsauken@barry-callebaut.com
www.barry-callebaut.com
Manufacturer of cocoa and chocolate products
Owner: Ted Bertran
Manager: Michelle Trembley
Estimated Sales: $4.9 Billion
Number Employees: 7,500
Parent Co: Barry Callebaut

1090 **Barry Group**
415 Griffin Drive
Corner Brook, NL A2H 7T2
Canada 709-785-7387
Fax: 709-785-5365 bgi@barrygroupinc.com
www.barrygroupinc.com
Processor and exporter of frozen fish and seafood including lobster, coldwater shrimp, opilio crab, red fish, Greenland turbot, cod, hat-fish, crab sections, herring, mackerel and capelan, frozen imitation crab meat and sticks. Alsoimporter of frozen grenadier fillets
President: William Barry
Vice President: James Barry
Director: Joseph Barry
Director Marketing: David Middleton
Estimated Sales: $300 Million
Number Employees: 720
Parent Co: Westfish International
Type of Packaging: Consumer, Food Service, Private Label, Bulk
Brands:
Icelandic
Ocean Leader
Pacific
Seafreez
Seafreez/Shawmut

1091 **Bartek Ingredients, Inc.**
421 Seaman Street
Stoney Creek, ON L8E 3J4
Canada 905-662-3292
Fax: 905-662-8849 800-263-4165
sales@bartek.ca www.bartek.ca
Manufacturer and exporter of acidulants including malic and fumaric acid; also, FCC-NF
President/Board Member: Raffaele Brancato
Estimated Sales: $40 Million
Number Employees: 80
Sq. footage: 40000

1092 **Bartlett Dairy & Food Service**
10503 150th St
Jamaica, NY 11435-5017 718-658-2299
Fax: 718-725-2527 www.bartlettny.com
Distributor of dairy products and other perishable foods for grocery and foodservice.
President: Thomas Malave Jr.
VP Sales: Jimmy Malave
Estimated Sales: $75 Million
Number Employees: 20-49

1093 **Bartlett Milling Company**
1307 Maple St
Coffeyville, KS 67337 620-251-4650
Fax: 620-251-4390
Flour milling
Manager: Mark Bastian
Principal: John Gilquist
Principal: Rod Geiger
Plant Manager: Gene Horton
Estimated Sales: $20-50 Million
Number Employees: 50
Parent Co: Barlett and Company

1094 **Bartlow Brothers**
P.O.Box 207
Rushville, IL 62681 217-322-3365
Fax: 217-322-2560 800-252-7202
http://agj3240.cafnr.missouri.edu/w06/reynoldsk/mp/index.htm
Manufacturer of beef and pork products including: sliced lunchmeats; sliced bacon; deli meats; dinner sausages; bone-in hams; hot dogs and sausages; BBQ specialty meats.
President: Dan Reynolds
Manager: Jim Foster
Manager: Bob Black
Estimated Sales: $50-100 Million
Number Employees: 50-99
Type of Packaging: Food Service
Brands:
KORNTOP

1095 **Bartolini Ice Cream**
967 E 167th St
Bronx, NY 10459 718-589-5151
Fax: 718-893-3171
Distributers of ice cream
Owner: Michael Bartolini
Estimated Sales: $3 Million
Number Employees: 20

1096 **Barton Brands**
10401 Linn Station Rd Ste 300
Louisville, KY 40223-3825
Fax: 312-855-1220 800-598-6352
www.bartoninc.com
Manufacturer and exporter of bourbon, scotch, whiskey, gin and vodka; importer of scotch
President/CEO: Alexander Berk
CFO: Troy Christensen
CEO: Alexander Berke
EVP/Marketing Barton Brands: Ed Gaultieri
Estimated Sales: $158 Million
Number Employees: 100-249
Parent Co: Constellation Brands
Brands:
99 SCHNAPPS
BARTON
BLACK VELVET
CANADIAN LTD

CHI-CHI'S
FLEISCHMANN'S
MONTE ALBAN
MONTEZUMA
MR BOSTON
NORTHERN LIGHT CANADIAN
THOR'S HAMMER
di AMORE

1097 **Bartons Fine Foods**
Highway 460
Denniston, KY 40316 606-768-3750
Fax: 606-768-3737 888-810-3750
Processor of jellies, jams, mustards, barbecue sauces, molasses and relishes
President: Bryan Allphin
Operations Director: Phil Madrio
Estimated Sales: $2.5-5 Million
Number Employees: 5-9
Sq. footage: 6000
Type of Packaging: Consumer, Food Service, Private Label

1098 **(HQ)Bartush-Schnitzius Foods Company**
P.O.Box 396
Lewisville, TX 75067-0396 972-219-1270
Fax: 972-436-5719 sales@bartushfoods.com
www.bartushfoods.com
Processor of bar mixes, salad dressing and sauces including horseradish, salsa, barbecue, taco, picante and tomato and sugar based
President/CEO: John Rubi
Estimated Sales: $12 Million
Number Employees: 50-99
Number of Products: 200+
Sq. footage: 50000
Type of Packaging: Consumer, Food Service, Private Label
Brands:
BAR-SNITZ
FAIRWAY
MELCER
SCHNITZIUS
TEXAS

1099 **Basciani Foods**
8876 Gap Newport Pike
Avondale, PA 19311 610-268-3610
Fax: 610-268-2186 michael@bascianifoods.com
www.bascianifoods.com
Fresh mushrooms
President: Mario Basciani Sr
Estimated Sales: $ 20 - 50 Million
Number Employees: 100-249

1100 **Basic American Foods**
415 W Collins Rd
Blackfoot, ID 83221 208-785-3200
Fax: 208-785-8776 800-227-4050
rgansie@baf.com www.baf.com
Manufacturer and exporter of dehydrated potatoes and beans, canned and frozen green chiles and vegetable extracts/nutraceuticals
President: Brad Johnson
Chief Information Officer: Mike Hart
EVP: Gordon Lewis
Director Procurement: Steve Henricksman
Director Raw Materials: Mark Klompien
Estimated Sales: $100-500 Million
Number Employees: 140
Sq. footage: 13000
Parent Co: Basic American
Type of Packaging: Consumer, Food Service, Private Label, Bulk
Brands:
CLASSIC CASSEROLES
GOLDEN GRILL
NATURE'S OWN
POTATO PEARLS
POTATO PEARLS EXCEL
QUIK START
REDI SHRED
REGIONAL RECIPE
SANTIAGO

1101 **(HQ)Basic American Foods**
2121 North California Blvd
Suite 400
Walnut Creek, CA 94596 925-472-4000
Fax: 925-472-4360 800-722-2084
www.baf.com
Processor of dehydrated potatoes
President/CEO: Loren Kimura
Chairman: George Hume
VP/CFO: John Argent
Corporate Communications: Jennifer Hamann
Plant Manager: Mark Klompien
Estimated Sales: $160 Million
Number Employees: 1500
Type of Packaging: Consumer, Food Service, Private Label, Bulk
Brands:
CLASSIC CASSEROLE®
GOLDEN GRILL RUSSET™
GOLDEN GRILL®
HUNGRY JACK®
NANA'S OWN®
NATURALLY POTATOES®
NATURE'S OWN®
POTATO PEARLS EXCEL®
POTATO PEARLS®
QUICK-START®
REDI-SHRED®
SANTIAGO®
WHIPP®

1102 **Basic Food Flavors**
3950 E Craig Rd
North Las Vegas, NV 89030 702-643-0043
Fax: 702-643-6149 info@basicfoodflavors.com
www.basicfoodflavors.com
Manufacturer and exporter of industrial ingredients including hydrolyzed vegetable proteins, processed flavors, soy sauce and soy bases
President: Kanu Patel
CFO/VP: Bill Robertson
Sales Executive: David Wood
Operations Director/HR Executive: Ruben Nestares
Estimated Sales: $10 Million
Number Employees: 65
Sq. footage: 30000
Type of Packaging: Food Service, Bulk

1103 **Basic Grain Products**
300 E Vine St
Coldwater, OH 45828-1399 419-678-2304
Fax: 419-678-4647 info@tastemorr.com
www.tastemorr.com
Dry rice cakes
President: Carol Knapke
Estimated Sales: $ 20 - 50 Million
Number Employees: 100-249
Brands:
Taste More Snacks

1104 **Basignani Winery**
15722 Falls Rd
Sparks Glencoe, MD 21152 410-472-0703
Fax: 410-472-2536 basignaniwinery.com
Wines
President: Bertero Basignani
CEO: Lynn Basignani
Estimated Sales: Less than $300,000
Number Employees: 5-9

1105 **Basin Crawfish Processors**
P.O.Box 25
Breaux Bridge, LA 70517-0025 337-332-6655
Fax: 337-332-5917 www.bbcrawfest.com
Crawfish, seafood
President: Brayon Blanchard
Estimated Sales: $300,000-500,000
Number Employees: 1-4

1106 **Basketfull**
276 5th Ave Rm 201
New York, NY 10001 212-686-2175
Fax: 212-255-9019 800-645-4438
baskefull@aol.com, info@basketfullinc.com
www.basketfullinc.com
Manufacturer and exporter of gourmet food and fruit baskets
President: Nancy Forest
Estimated Sales: Less than $500,000
Number Employees: 5-9

1107 **Baskin-Robbins Flavors**
109 E Alameda Ave
Burbank, CA 91502-2004 818-558-4000
Fax: 818-558-1844 800-859-5339
www.baskinrobbins.com
High quality premium ice cream, specialty frozen desserts, bases for dairy beverages, nondairy; flavors
Manager: Alex Lee
CFO: Kate Lavelle
Estimated Sales: $50 Million
Number Employees: 10-19
Parent Co: Dunkin' Brands, Inc.
Type of Packaging: Consumer, Food Service

1108 **Basque French Bakery**
2625 Inyo St
Fresno, CA 93721 559-268-7088
Fax: 559-268-0510
Baked goods, breads and rolls
President: Al Lewis
Vice President: Rita Ingmire
Production Manager: Ed Kwiecien
Estimated Sales: $2.5-5 Million
Number Employees: 20-49

1109 **Bass Lake Cheese Factory**
598 Valley View Trl
Somerset, WI 54025 715-247-5586
Fax: 715-549-6617 800-368-2437
blcheese@blcheese.com www.blcheese.com
Manufacturer of cheese including colby, cheddar, cheddar curds, jack, goat's and sheep's milk
Co-Owner/President: Scott Erickson
Co-Owner: Julie Erickson
Estimated Sales: $5-9.9 Million
Number Employees: 5-9
Type of Packaging: Consumer
Brands:
MASTER'S MARK

1110 **(HQ)Bassett's**
1211 Chestnut St # 410
Philadelphia, PA 19107-4114 215-864-2771
Fax: 215-864-2766 888-999-6314
bassettsic@aol.com www.bassettsicecream.com
Premium ice cream, yogurt, sorbet
President: Michael Strange
CEO: Ann Bassett
Estimated Sales: $5-10 Million
Number Employees: 5-9
Other Locations:
Bassetts Ice Cream
Philadelphia PA

1111 **Batampte Pickle Foods, Inc.**
77 Brooklyn Terminal Market
Brooklyn, NY 11236-1511 718-251-2100
Fax: 718-531-9212
Manufacturers of pickles.
President/CEO: Barry Silberstein
Vice President: Scott Silberstein
Estimated Sales: $20-50 Million
Number Employees: 50-99

1112 **Batavia Wine Cellars**
235 N Bloomfield Road
Canandaigua, NY 14424-1059 585-396-7600
Fax: 585-396-7833
Processor, bottler and exporter of wine, salted cooking wine and sparkling fruit juices, plus bulk wines for the food industry
President: Ned Cooper
Ceo/Vice President: Tim Richenberg
Number Employees: 100-249
Parent Co: Canandaigua Wine Company
Type of Packaging: Consumer, Food Service, Private Label, Bulk
Brands:
CAPRI
HENRI MERCHANT
VINTER'S CHOICE

1113 **Batdorf and Bronson Roasters**
200 Market St NE
Olympia, WA 98501 360-754-5282
Fax: 360-754-5283 800-955-5282
javatalk@batdorf.com www.batdorf.com
Coffee roaster, mail order & wholesale
President: Larry Challain
CFO: Dave Wasson
Vice President: Scott Merle
Quality Control: Michael Elvin
Public Relations: Lois Maffeo
Operations Manager: Heather Ringwood
Production Manager: Brian Meyers
Plant Manager: Shelia Smith
Estimated Sales: $5-10 Million
Number Employees: 50-99

Type of Packaging: Consumer, Food Service, Private Label, Bulk

1114 **Bateman Products**
251 W Main Street
Rigby, ID 83442-1351 208-745-9033
Fax: 208-357-5317 www.mrsbateman.com
Fat products and sugar and egg replacements in the food and health industry
Owner: Mrs Bateman
Estimated Sales: $ .5 - 1 million
Number Employees: 5-9

1115 **Batko Flavors LLC**
772 Cranbury Crossroad
North Brunswick, NJ 08092 732-991-3462
Fax: 732-932-9441 daphnahf@baktoflavors.com
www.baktoflavors.com
Production, commercialization and distribution of natural products, such as flavors, fragrances and preservatives.
President: Prof Chaim Frenkel
VP/R&D Director: Dr Daphna Havkin Frenkel
Number Employees: 7

1116 **Battistoni Italina Specialty Meats**
81 Dingens St
Buffalo, NY 14206-2307 716-826-2700
Fax: 716-826-0603 800-248-2705
www.battistonibrand.com
Manufacturer of Italian Meat products including salami, pepperoni, capocollo, chorizo
President: Alvino Battistoni Jr.
Executive VP: Tina Battistoni
Estimated Sales: $10-24.9 Million
Number Employees: 20-49
Parent Co: Rich Products
Brands:
RICH PRODUCTS

1117 **Bauducco Foods Inc.**
1530 NW 98th Court
Suite 103
Doral, FL 33172 305-477-9270
Fax: 305-477-4703 sales@bauduccofoods.com
www.bauduccofoods.com
bars, bite-sized cookies, butter cookies, cakes, cookies, corn flour cookies, cream-filled cookies, finger cakes, food service, grissini, savory biscuits, toast, wafer
President: Stefano Mozzi
Marketing: Fred Rodrigues
Estimated Sales: $5 Million
Number Employees: 10

1118 **Bauhaven Lobster**
280 Chases Pond Rd
York, ME 03909 207-363-5265
Fax: 907-486-6417
Lobster
Partner: Randy Small
Estimated Sales: $ 1 - 3 Million
Number Employees: 5-9

1119 **(HQ)Baumer Foods**
2424 Edenborn Ave
Suite 510
Metairie, LA 70001 504-482-5761
info@baumerfoods.com
www.baumerfoods.com
Manfacturer and exporter of sauces including hot, steak, soy and barbecue; also, mustard, preserves and peppers including tabasco and cortido
Chairman/President/CEO: Alvin Baumer Jr
EVP/COO: Terry Hanes
CFO: Ronald Wendel
R&D/Quality Control: Javed Rashid
VP Operations: Doug Wakefield
Estimated Sales: $50 Million
Number Employees: 250-499
Number of Brands: 1
Number of Products: 11
Sq. footage: 220000
Type of Packaging: Consumer, Food Service, Private Label
Brands:
AB
BAUMER
CRYSTAL
FIREY
FLAME

1120 **Bautista Organic Dates**
P.O.Box 726
Mecca, CA 92254-0726 760-396-2337
Dates and grapefruits
Owner: Enrique Bautista
Estimated Sales: $500,000 appx.
Number Employees: 1-4

1121 **Bavaria Corporation**
515 Cooper Commerce Dr Ste 100
Apopka, FL 32703 407-880-0322
Fax: 407-880-1932 bavaria@fdn.com
www.bavariacorp.com
Manufacturer of specialty blends, the injection, marinades, and dips for better color, yields and shelf-life in beef, pork, poultry, and seafood
President/CEO: Peter Schaeflein
VP: Dennis Koo
Estimated Sales: $5-$10 Million
Number Employees: 10-19
Type of Packaging: Food Service, Bulk
Brands:
BAFOS

1122 **Bavarian Meat Products**
2934 Western Ave
Seattle, WA 98121 206-448-3540
Fax: 206-956-0526
Processor of sausage
President: Manny Dupper
Co-Owner: Robert Hofstatter
Vice President: Lynn Stewart
Estimated Sales: $2.5-5 Million
Number Employees: 10-19
Type of Packaging: Consumer, Food Service

1123 **Bavarian Nut Company**
1503 S Fresno Avenue
Stockton, CA 95206-1179 209-465-9181
Fax: 360-465-6008
Dry walnuts
Manager: Rex Lewis
Plant Manager: Ben Fairbanks
Estimated Sales: $ 20 - 50 Million
Number Employees: 50-99

1124 **Bavarian Specialty Foods**
11450 Sheldon Street
Sun Valley, CA 91352-1121 310-212-6199
Fax: 310-781-9149
Frozen baked goods
President: Richard Tan
CFO: Les Starnes
General Manager: Jack Samaras
Production Manager: Paul Trujillo
Plant Manager: Mike Engel
Estimated Sales: $10-24.9 Million
Number Employees: 100-249
Type of Packaging: Private Label

1125 **Baxter's Vineyard**
P.O.Box 342
Nauvoo, IL 62354-0342 217-453-2528
Fax: 217-453-6600 800-854-1396
baxters@nauvoo.net www.nauvoowinery.com
Wines
Owner/President: Kelly Logan
Owner/CEO: Brenda Logan
Estimated Sales: $500,000-$1 Million
Number Employees: 1-4
Brands:
Baxters Old Nauvoo

1126 **(HQ)Bay Cities Produce Company**
2109 Williams St
San Leandro, CA 94577 510-346-4943
Fax: 510-832-1509 www.baycitiesproduce.com
Manufacturer and wholesaler/distributor of fresh, frozen and prepared fruits and vegetables
Owner: Al Del Matso
SVP: Steve Del Masso
Secretary/Treasurer: Diana Del Masso
Vice President: Steve Del Masso
GM: Rick Onstad
Sales Manager: Tony D'Amato
Estimated Sales: $20-50 Million
Number Employees: 20-49
Sq. footage: 55000
Type of Packaging: Food Service

1127 **Bay Hawk Ales**
2000 Main St
Irvine, CA 92614-7202 949-442-7565
Fax: 949-442-7566 info@bayhawkales.com
www.bayhawkales.com
Processor of seasonal beer, ale, lager and porter
Manager: Carl Zappa
Sales: Robert Fischer
General Manager: Karl Zappa
Estimated Sales: $2.5-5 Million
Number Employees: 5-9
Type of Packaging: Consumer, Food Service, Private Label
Brands:
AMBER ALE
BAYHAWK IPA
BAYHAWK STOUT
BEACH BLONDE
CALIFORNIA PALE ALE (CPA)
CHOCOLATE PORTER
HEFE WEIZEN
HONEY BLONDE
O.C. LAGER

1128 **Bay Hundred Seafood**
P.O.Box 10
McDaniel, MD 21647-0010 410-745-9329
Fax: 410-745-9176
Processor and packer of oysters and crabs including soft and meat
President: Joseph Spurry
VP: Joseph Spurry, Jr.
Estimated Sales: $10-20 Million
Number Employees: 10-19
Type of Packaging: Consumer
Brands:
Miles River

1129 **Bay Oceans Sea Foods**
P.O.Box 348
Garibaldi, OR 97118-0348 503-322-3316
Fax: 503-322-0049
customerservice@bayoceanseafood.com
www.bayoceanseafood.com
Products include gourmet albacore tuna, chinook salmon, dungeness crab and shrimp, as well as canned tuna and salmon.
Owner: Jeff Princehouse
Estimated Sales: $ 10 - 20 Million
Number Employees: 20-49
Type of Packaging: Consumer, Food Service

1130 **Bay Pac Beverages**
1150 Civic Drive
Suite 300
Walnut Creek, CA 94596-8221 925-279-0800
Fax: 925-279-0804 baypac@pacbell.net
www.sportsenergy.com/baypaccorp
Sports drink beverages
President: Jackson Bays
Manager of Export Sales: Alan Wirsig
Estimated Sales: $2.5-5 Million
Number Employees: 5-9
Type of Packaging: Bulk

1131 **Bay Star Baking Company**
1222 Lincoln Ave
Alameda, CA 94501-2326 510-523-4202
Fax: 925-449-1224
Bread, rolls
Estimated Sales: $10-20 Million
Number Employees: 100-249

1132 **(HQ)Bay State Milling Company**
100 Congress St Ste 2
Quincy, MA 02169 617-328-4423
Fax: 617-479-8910 800-553-5687
info@bsm.com www.bsm.com
Manufacturer of flour
Chairman: Bernard Rothwell
President: Brian Rothwell
Estimated Sales: $100+ Million
Number Employees: 20-49
Type of Packaging: Consumer, Food Service, Private Label, Bulk
Other Locations:
Tolleson AZ
Platteville CO
Minneapolis MN
Winona MN
Indiantown FL
Mooresville NC
Clifton NJ

1133 **Bay State Milling Company**
55 Franklin St
Winona, MN 55987 507-452-1770
Fax: 507-452-1776 800-533-8098
larryo.wn@bsm.com www.bsm.com
Miller of wheat and rye flour
Plant Manager: Tony Wasinger
VP: Mark Norton
Sales Manager: Larry Overhaug
Plant Manager: Tony Wasinger
Estimated Sales: $50-100 Million
Number Employees: 50-99
Parent Co: Bay State Milling Company
Type of Packaging: Consumer, Food Service, Private Label, Bulk

1134 **(HQ)Bay Valley Foods**
1555 East Highway 151
Platteville, WI 53818 920-497-9893
Fax: 920-497-7131 800-236-1119
www.bayvalleyfoods.com
Manufacturer of shelf stable pickles, relish, peppers, syrups, powdered non-dairy coffee creamers, liquid non-dairy coffee creamers, egg substitutes, cheese sauces, puddings, special sauces, soups, broths, gravies and infant foods.
President: Joe Coning
VP Finance: Greg Lewandowski
SVP/CAO: Alan Gambrel
Sr. VP Retail Sales/Marketing: Kevin Holden
VP Bulk Ingredients/International Sales: Mike Cooney
VP Foodservice Sales/Marketing: Gary Schachter
Sr. VP Operations/Supply Chain: George Jurkovich
SVP Corporate Development: Erik Kahler
Estimated Sales: $94 Million
Number Employees: 1,000
Sq. footage: 50000
Parent Co: TreeHouse Foods
Type of Packaging: Consumer, Food Service, Private Label, Bulk
Brands:
BENNETT'S
CREMORA
FARMANS
GRACIAS
HEIFETZ
HOFFMAN HOUSE
MOCHA MIX
NALLEY
NATURE'S GOODNESS
NORTHWOODS
PETER PIPER
PRIVATE LABEL
SECOND NATURE
STEINFELD'S
THANK YOU

1135 **Bay View Farm**
P.O.Box 680
Honaunau, HI 96726-0680 808-328-9658
Fax: 808-328-8693 800-662-5880
bayview@aloha.net
www.bayviewfarmcoffees.com
Coffees, Flavored Coffees and gourmet foods
President: Andrew Roy
VP: Roslyn Roy
Estimated Sales: $5-10 Million
Number Employees: 10-19

1136 **Baycliff Company**
242 E 72nd St
New York, NY 10021 212-772-6078
Fax: 212-472-8980 aj@sushichef.com
www.sushichef.com
Processor, exporter and importer of Japanese food products including rice vinegar, soy sauces, soy salad dressing, teriyaki sauce, rice, rice cracker mix, green tea, and soups
President: Helen Chandler
VP: Alan Johnson
Estimated Sales: $20-50 Million
Number Employees: 20
Type of Packaging: Consumer, Food Service
Brands:
Sushi Chef

1137 **Bayley Quality Seafoods**
21 Snow Canning Rd
Scarborough, ME 04074-5001 207-883-4581
Fax: 207-883-2872
Seafood
President/Treasurer: Stanley Bayley
CEO: Nancy Bayley
Vice President: Nancy Bayley
Estimated Sales: $1.5 Million
Number Employees: 5-9

1138 **Bayley's Lobster Pound**
9 Jones Creek Dr
Scarborough, ME 04074 207-883-4571
Fax: 207-883-4797 800-932-6456
bayleys@bayleys.com www.bayleys.com
Fresh and frozen shrimp and clams
President/Treasurer: Stanley Bayley
Estimated Sales: $1,500,000
Number Employees: 5-9

1139 **Bayou Cajun Foods**
PO Box 8460
Monroe, LA 71211-8460 318-388-2383
Fax: 318-361-5036
Cajum foods
President: Vicki Roark

1140 **Bayou Crab**
10380 Foots Rd
Grand Bay, AL 36541-6491 251-824-2076
Fax: 251-824-2615
Cajum foods
Owner: Dan Viravong
Estimated Sales: $ 3 - 5 Million
Number Employees: 10-19

1141 **Bayou Foods**
949 Industry Rd
Kenner, LA 70062-6848 504-469-1745
Fax: 504-469-1852 800-516-8283
bayoufoods@hughes.com
Fillet fish, crabs and peeled and headless shrimp; importer of shrimp; wholesaler/distributor of frozen foods, provisions, beef, pork, poultry and seafood;serving the food service market
President/Owner: Miu Lin Kong
CEO: Arthur Mitchell
Estimated Sales: $5-10 Million
Number Employees: 10-19
Sq. footage: 13600
Type of Packaging: Food Service

1142 **Bayou Gourmet**
412 Palm Avenue
Houma, LA 70364-3400 504-872-4825
Fax: 504-868-7472
President: Ernest Voisin

1143 **Bayou Land Seafood**
1008 Vincent Berard Rd
Breaux Bridge, LA 70517 337-667-6118
Fax: 337-667-6059 bayoulandseafood@aol.com
Processor and wholesaler/distributor of seafood including fresh and frozen crawfish, fish, crabs and shrimp; also, alligator and turtle
Owner/Human Resource Manager: Adam Johnson

VP: Sharon Difatta
Plant Manager: Jeff Guidry
Estimated Sales: $2 Million
Number Employees: 10
Number of Products: 100
Sq. footage: 9600
Type of Packaging: Consumer, Food Service, Bulk
Brands:
Bayou Land Seafood

1144 **Bays English Muffin Corporation**
PO Box 1455
Chicago, IL 60690-1455 312-346-5757
Fax: 316-226-3435 800-367-2297
www.bays.com
Aqua culture
President: George Bay
Estimated Sales: $1-2.5 Million
Number Employees: 20-49

1145 **Baywood Cellars**
5573 W Woodbridge Rd
Lodi, CA 95242 209-334-0137
Fax: 209-334-0132 800-214-0445
mail@baywood-cellars.com
www.baywood-cellars.com
Wines
Founder: Joe Cotta Jr
President: John Cotta
Co-Owner: James Cotta
Estimated Sales: Under $500,000
Number Employees: 1-4
Brands:
Baywood Cellars

1146 **Bazaar**
1900 5th Ave
River Grove, IL 60171 708-583-1800
Fax: 708-583-9782 800-736-1888
Supplier of closeout packaged foods including candy, snacks and spices
Pres: Robert Nardick
Finance Executive: Tony Ligenza
VP: Arlene Nardick
Sales Manager: Arnie Fishbain
VP Purchasing: Gene Wisniewski
Estimated Sales: $15 Million
Number Employees: 70
Sq. footage: 295000

1147 **Be-Bop Biscotti**
601 NE 1st St
Bend, OR 97701 888-545-7487
Fax: 541-389-6185 888-545-7487
mlee@be-bop.net www.be-bop.net
biscotti
President/Owner: Robert Golden
Number Employees: 99

1148 **Bea & B Foods**
1771 Bervy St
San Diego, CA 92110 619-276-6534
Fax: 619-276-9254 800-952-2117
pilarcitas@aol.com www.pilarcitas.com
Mexican seasonings and marinades
President: Bea Knapp
Estimated Sales: $ 3 - 5 Million
Number Employees: 1-4
Brands:
Pilarcitas

1149 **Beach Bagel Bakeries**
915 NW 72nd Street
Miami, FL 33150-3616 305-691-3514
Fax: 305-836-0959
Bagels and bakery products
President: Harold Greenblatt
Vice President: David Greenblatt
Estimated Sales: $20-50 Million
Number Employees: 20-49

1150 **Beachaven Vineyards & Winery**
1100 Dunlop Ln
Clarksville, TN 37040 931-645-8867
Fax: 931-645-3522
thefolks@beachavenwinery.com
www.beachavenwinery.com
Wines
President/Owner: Louisa Cooke
VP: Edward Cooke
Estimated Sales: $2.5-5 Million
Number Employees: 10-19

1151 **Beacon Drive In**
255 John B White Sr Blvd
Spartanburg, SC 29306-6047 864-585-9387
Fax: 864-585-2888 www.beacondriveinn.com
Iced Tea
Manager: Kenny Church
CEO: Steve McManus
Estimated Sales: $ 3 - 5 Million
Number Employees: 50-99
Sq. footage: 5000
Type of Packaging: Food Service, Private Label
Brands:
Beacon Drive-In Iced Tea

1152 **Beal's Lobster Pier**
182 Clark Point Rd
Southwest Harbor, ME 04679 207-244-3202
Fax: 207-244-9479 800-244-7178
beals@arcadia.net www.bealslobster.com
Lobster, all types of seafood
President: Elmer Beal
Estimated Sales: $ 1 - 3 Million
Number Employees: 10-19

1153 **Beam Global Spirits &Wine**
510 Lake Cook Road
Deerfield, IL 60015-4964 847-948-8888
Fax: 847-948-8610 www.beamglobal.com

Cognac, bourbon and bourbon mixes, whisky, rum, and tequila.
President & CEO: Matthew Shattock
CFO: Robert Probst
President Beam Global Spirits & Wine USA: William Newlands
SVP & Global CMO: A Rory Finlay
SVP Operations & Supply Chain: Ian Gourlay
Estimated Sales: $2.5 Billion
Number Employees: 3,452
Parent Co: Fortune Brands
Type of Packaging: Consumer, Food Service
Other Locations:
Jim Beam Brands Co.
Geyserville CA
Brands:
ANIS CASTELLANA
ARDMORE
BAKER'S
BASIL HAYDEN'S
BOOKER'S
CALVERT EXTRA
CALVERT GIN
CANADIAN CLUB
COURVOISIER
CRUZAN
D-Y-C
DEKUYPER
FUNDADOR
GILBY'S
JIM BEAM
KAMCHATKA
KAMORA
KESSLER
KNOB CREEK
LAPHROAIG
LORD CALVERT
MAKER'S MARK
OLD CROW
OLD GRAND DAD WHISKY
OLD OVERHOLT
RED STAG
RI
SAUZA
SOURZ APPLE
TANGLE RIDGE
TEACHER'S
TERRY CENTENARIO
TOSORO
VOX VODKA
WINDSOR CANADIAN
WOLFSCHMIDT VODKA

1154 **Beamon Brothers**
3392 Us Highway 117 N
Goldsboro, NC 27530 919-734-4931
Fax: 919-736-1849
Fresh potatoes
President: Robert Rackley
Estimated Sales: Under $500,000
Number Employees: 1-4
Brands:
Mount Herman
Stoney Hill

1155 **Bean Buddies**
1804 Plaza Avenue
New Hyde Park, NY 11040-4937 516-775-3726
Fax: 516-775-3706
Chocolate, coffee candy
President: Nina Cole
Estimated Sales: $2.5-5 Million
Number Employees: 5-9

1156 **Bean Forge**
ÿ93753 Coos Sumner Lane
Coos Bay, OR 97420-1614 541-267-5191
Fax: 88- 35- 094 sales@thebeanforge.com
www.thebeanforge.com
Manager: Adam Hinkle
Owner: David Herold
Estimated Sales: $500,000-$1 Million
Number Employees: 5-9
Brands:
Bean Forge
Guido & Sals Old Chicago
Kenya AA
Lighthouse
Menehune Magic
Tanzanian Peaberry
Whiskey Run

1157 **Bear Creek Country Kitchens**
325 W 600 S
Heber City, UT 84032-2230 435-654-2660
Fax: 435-654-4525 800-516-7286
brianb@bearcreekfoods.com
www.sbamerica.com
Manufacturer of powdered dips and soups
Owner: Donald White
President/CEO: Kevin Ruda
CFO: Al Van Leeuwen
Director R&D: Brian Brinkerhoff
VP Sales/Marketing: Stephen White
VP Operations: Kevin Kowalski
Purchasing Manager: Mark Hartman
Estimated Sales: $40 Million
Number Employees: 100-249
Sq. footage: 180000
Parent Co: American Capital Strategies
Type of Packaging: Consumer, Food Service
Brands:
Bear Creek Country Kitchens
Sheila's Select Gourmet Recipes

1158 **Bear Creek Kitchens**
10857 State Highway 154
Marshall, TX 75670 903-935-0253
Fax: 903-935-5560 888-300-7687
twostep@internetwork.net
Bottled soup mix in six flavors, seasonings, BBQ mixes
Owner: Robbie Shoults
Director: Kim Shoults
Estimated Sales: $1 Million
Number Employees: 9
Brands:
Bear Creek Pandhandler Pasta
Bear Creek Panhandler Brand
Bear Creek the Texas Two Step

1159 **Bear Creek Smokehouse**
10857 State Highway 154
Marshall, TX 75670 903-935-5217
Fax: 903-935-2871 800-950-2327
info@bearcreeksmokehouse.com
www.bearcreeksmokehouse.com
Manufacturer of smoked chicken, turkey and turkey products, smoked and cured ham, salted pork, soup mixes, smoked bacon, sausages, pork ribs and desserts
President: Charles Shoults
VP: Robbie Shoults
Secretary/Treasurer: Brenda Shoults
Estimated Sales: $10-20 Million
Number Employees: 20-49
Sq. footage: 20000
Type of Packaging: Consumer
Brands:
Bear Creek Brand

1160 **Bear Creek Winery**
4210 Holland Loop Road
PO Box609
Cave Junction, OR 97523-9714 541-592-4688
Fax: 541-592-2127 877-273-4843
bvw@bridgeviewwine.com
www.bridgeviewwine.com
Wines
President: Rene Eichmann
CEO: Rene Eichmann
Marketing: Lorie Eichmann
Estimated Sales: Less than $500,000
Number Employees: 1
Brands:
Dijon Clone
Rogue Valley

1161 **Bear Meadow Farm**
248 Greenfield Rd
Colrain, MA 01340 413-624-0291
Fax: 413-664-8373 800-653-9241
retail.info@bearmeadowfarm.com
www.bearmeadowfarm.com
Manufacturer of quality food condiments such as; jellies, preserves, jams, salad dressings
Principal Owner/GM: Matt Shearer
Estimated Sales: $1-2.5 Million
Number Employees: 1-4
Sq. footage: 3000
Type of Packaging: Consumer, Food Service, Private Label
Brands:
Bear Meadow Farm
Rt 66 Foods

1162 **Bear Stewart Corporation**
1011 N Damen Ave
Chicago, IL 60622 773-276-0400
Fax: 773-276-3512 800-697-2327
info@bearstewart.com www.bearstore.com
Processor and exporter of ingredients for bakers and confectioners including flavoring extracts, dry and meringue cake/pie fillings, cake mix, jellies and almond paste.
Owner: Clifford Brooks
Executive VP: Cliff Brooks
VP of Sales: Michael Hoffman
Estimated Sales: $5-10 Million
Number Employees: 20-49
Sq. footage: 50000
Type of Packaging: Food Service

1163 **Beard's Quality Nut Company**
3006 Yosemite Blvd
Empire, CA 95319 209-526-3590
Fax: 209-526-8110
Processor of in-shell and shelled walnuts
Owner: Rodney Beard
Estimated Sales: $ 1 - 3 Million
Number Employees: 50
Type of Packaging: Consumer, Food Service

1164 **Beatrice Bakery Company**
201 S 5th St
Beatrice, NE 68310 402-223-2358
Fax: 402-223-4465 800-228-4030
ron@beatricebakery.com
www.beatricebakery.com
Processor and exporter of dessert cakes, fruit cakes, and liqueur-filled cakes
President: Greg Leach
Quality Control: Robin Dickinson
Sales Manager: Connie Warnsing
Public Relations: Brooklyn Soft
Production Manager: Robin Dickinson
Estimated Sales: $ 5-10 Million
Number Employees: 20-49
Number of Brands: 10
Number of Products: 125
Sq. footage: 50000
Type of Packaging: Private Label
Brands:
GRANDMA'S BAKE SHOPPE
GRANDMA'S FRUIT CAKE
INNKEEPER'S OWN
YE OLDE ENGLISH

1165 **(HQ)Beatrice Bakery Company/Grandma's Bake Shoppe**
201 S 5th Street
PO Box 457
Beatrice, NE 68310-0457
Fax: 402-223-4465 800-228-4030
www.beatricebakery.com
Manufacturer of fruit and nut cake, baked goods
President: Greg Leech
Estimated Sales: $ 20 - 50 Million
Number Employees: 20-34

1166 **Beaucanon Estate Wines**
1006 Monticello Rd
Napa, CA 94558-2032 707-254-1460
Fax: 707-254-1462 800-660-3520
www.beaucanonestate.com
Wines
President: Louis De Coninck
Estimated Sales: $2.5-5 Million
Number Employees: 10-19

1167 **Beaulieu Vineyard**
P.O.Box 219
Rutherford, CA 94573 707-967-5200
Fax: 707-967-1066 800-264-6918
bvinfo@bvwines.com www.bvwines.com
Processor of wines
Executive Director: Armond Rist
Vice President Winemaking: Joel Aiken
Winemaker: Robert Masvczek
Purchasing Manager: Marisa Licata
Estimated Sales: $50-100 Million
Number Employees: 100-249
Parent Co: International Distillers
Type of Packaging: Bulk
Brands:
BV BEAUTOUR
BV CAMENOS PINOT NOIR
BV CARNEROS CHARDONNAY

BV ENSEMBLE
BV NAPA SERIES
BV NAPA VALLEY SAUVIGNON BLANC
BV NAPA VALLEY ZINFANDEL
BV RESERVE
BV RUTHERFORD/NAPA VALLEY CABERNET
BV SIGNET COLLECTION
BV SYRAH
BV TAPESTRY
BV VIN GRIS DE PINOT NOIR
BV VROGNIER

1168 **Beaumont Products**
1560 Big Shanty Dr NW
Kennesaw, GA 30144 770-514-7400
Fax: 770-514-7400 800-451-7096
citrusii@citrusii@beaumontpr
www.citrusmagic.com

President: Hank Picken
Estimated Sales: $ 3 - 5 Million
Number Employees: 20-49

1169 **Beaumont Rice Mills**
1800 Pecos St
Beaumont, TX 77701 409-832-2521
Fax: 409-832-6927 info@bmtricemills.com
www.bmtricemills.com
Manufacturer and exporter of brewers' rice and rice bran
President: Louis Broussard Jr
VP: Martin Broussard
Secretary: Fred Adams Jr
Assistant Secretary/Treasurer: Brenda Cook
Estimated Sales: $ 20 - 50 Million
Number Employees: 50-99
Type of Packaging: Consumer

1170 **Beaver Enterprises**
1 Gordon Dr
Rockland, ME 04841 207-596-2900
Fax: 207-596-2922

Owner: Wayne Stinson
Estimated Sales: $800,000
Number Employees: 5-9

1171 **Beaver Meadow Creamery**
415 Maple Ave
Du Bois, PA 15801 814-371-3711
Fax: 814-371-3713 800-262-3711
bmbutter@comcast.net
Processor and exporter of portion control butter, margarine and blends
President: J Kirk
Vice President: R Kirk
Estimated Sales: $20 - 50 Million
Sq. footage: 30000
Type of Packaging: Food Service, Private Label, Bulk
Brands:
BEAVER MEADOW

1172 **Beaver Street Brewery**
11 S Beaver St # 1
Flagstaff, AZ 86001-5500 928-779-0079
Fax: 928-779-0029
info@beaverstreetbrewery.com
www.beaverstreetbrewery.com
Processor of seasonal beers and porter
President/Owner: Evan Hanseth
VP: Winnie Hanseth
Estimated Sales: $2.5-5 Million
Number Employees: 100-249
Type of Packaging: Consumer, Food Service
Brands:
BRAMBLE BERRY BREW
HEFE WEIZEN
INDIA PALE ALE
MARZEN LAGER
PILSENER
R&r OATMEAL STOUT
RAIL HEAD RED ALE
VIENNA LAGER

1173 **Beaver Street Fisheries**
P.O.Box 41430
Jacksonville, FL 32203-1430 904-354-8533
Fax: 904-354-2607 800-874-6426
www.beaverfish.com
Processor, exporter and importer of frozen fish and seafood including stuffed shrimp, crabs and crab meat
President: Jeff Edwards
VP: Harry Frisch
Sales Manager: Carlos Sanchez
Estimated Sales: $$50-100 Million
Number Employees: 100-249
Parent Co: Beaver Street Fisheries
Type of Packaging: Consumer, Food Service, Private Label, Bulk

1174 **Beaverton Foods**
P.O.Box 687
Beaverton, OR 97075 503-646-8138
Fax: 503-644-9204 800-223-8076
dombg@beavertonfoods.com
www.beavertonfoods.com
Processor and exporter of horseradish, mustard, garlic and sauces.
President: Gene Biggi
CEO: Bill Small
Foodservice Manager: Domonic Biggi
CEO: Bill Small
Marketing/Advertising Manager: Barbara Lutheran
Retail Grocery Sales Manager: Tom Murphy
Private Label Manager: Jan Westfall
Business/Customer Service Manager: Roger Klingsporn
Mail Order Manager: Mark Vander Yacht
Estimated Sales: $10-20 Million
Number Employees: 50-99
Sq. footage: 65000
Type of Packaging: Consumer, Food Service, Private Label, Bulk
Brands:
BEAVER
INGLEHOFFER
NAPA VALLEY
OLD SPICE

1175 **Beaverton Foods**
7100 Northwest Century Boulevard
Hillsboro, OR 97124 503-646-8138
Fax: 503-644-9204 800-223-8076
dbiggi@beavertonfoods.com
www.beavertonfoods.com
Processor and exporter of horseradish, mustard, garlic and sauces.
President: Gene Biggi
CEO: Bill Small
Foodservice Manager: Domonic Biggi
CEO: Bill Small
Marketing/Advertising Manager: Barbara Lutheran
Retail Grocery Sales Manager: Tom Murphy
Private Label Manager: Jan Westfall
Business/Customer Service Manager: Roger Klingsporn
Mail Order Manager: Mark Vander Yacht
Estimated Sales: $10-20 Million
Number Employees: 50-99
Sq. footage: 65000
Type of Packaging: Consumer, Food Service, Private Label, Bulk

1176 **Beck Farms**
RR #8 12-7
Lethbridg, AB T1J 4P4
Canada 403-227-1020
Fax: 403-227-5414 Beck@tellesplanet.net
www.beckfarms.com
Processor and packer of carrots and parsnips
President: Peter Edgar
CEO: Peter Edgar
VP: Rod Bradsha
Sales Manager: Shelley Bradsha
Estimated Sales: A
Number Employees: 1-4
Brands:
Beck Farms
Beck Gourmet

1177 **Beck Flavors**
411 Gano Ave
Saint Louis, MO 63147 314-436-7624
Fax: 314-436-1049 800-851-8100
usa.info@danisco.com www.danisco.com
Manufacturer and exporter of vanilla and coffee extracts and flavors; also, sweet flavors
HR Administrator: Kim Hopkins
Operations Manager: Andy Zook
Estimated Sales: $ 20 - 50 Million
Number Employees: 50-99
Sq. footage: 120000
Type of Packaging: Bulk
Other Locations:
Ardsley NY
Bakersfield CA
Lakeland FL
New Century KS
Brands:
Beck Cafe
Beck Flavors

1178 **Beck's Ice Cream**
830 Roosevelt Ave
York, PA 17404-2830 717-848-8400
Fax: 717-846-5121

Ice cream
Owner: Jerry Beck
CEO: Lynne Beck
CFO: Kerry Beck
Estimated Sales: $250,000
Number Employees: 5-9
Brands:
Becks Ice Cream

1179 **Beck's Waffles of Oklahoma**
101 S Kickapoo Ave
Shawnee, OK 74801-7686 405-878-0615
Fax: 405-878-8546 800-646-6254
wafflman@swbell.net www.beckswaffles.com
Processor of frozen Belgian waffles; wholesaler/distributor of waffle mix and irons
Sales: Doyle Beck
Estimated Sales: $1-3 Million
Number Employees: 20-49
Sq. footage: 20000
Type of Packaging: Consumer, Food Service

1180 **Becker Food Company**
4160 N Port Washington Rd
Milwaukee, WI 53212 414-964-5353
Fax: 414-964-4523
Manufacturer, importer and wholesaler/distributor of meats, frozen foods, poultry and seafood; serving the food service market
President: Stephen Becker
Estimated Sales: $100+ Million
Number Employees: 80
Sq. footage: 60000
Type of Packaging: Food Service

1181 **Beckman & Gast Company**
P.O.Box 307
Saint Henry, OH 45883 419-678-4195
Fax: 419-678-3005 infobg@beckmangast.com
www.beckmangast.com
Processor of canned goods including tomato juice, tomatoes and cut green beans.
President: William Gast
Agriculture Manager: Bo Gast
Secretary/Treasurer: Trish Albers
Vice President: Nicholas Gast
Production: Gary Broering
Estimated Sales: $5-9.9 Million
Number Employees: 10-19
Type of Packaging: Consumer, Private Label
Brands:
BECKMAN'S

1182 **Beckmann's Old World Bakery**
2341 Mission St
Santa Cruz, CA 95060 831-423-2566
Fax: 831-457-2269

Bread and baked goods
Manager: Beth Taiva
VP: Sharon May
Marketing Manager: Doug Eckley
Estimated Sales: $100-500 Million
Number Employees: 100-249

1183 **Beckmen Vineyards**
P.O.Box 542
Los Olivos, CA 93441-0542 805-688-8664
Fax: 805-688-9983 info@beckmenvineyards.com
www.beckmenvineyards.com
Wines
President: Tom Beckmen
Operations Manager: Steve Beckmen
Estimated Sales: $500-1 Million appx.
Number Employees: 1-4

1184 **Bede Inc**
PO Box 8263
Haledon, NJ 07538-0263 973-956-2900
Fax: 973-956-0600 866-239-6565
bedeinc@aol.com www.bedenj.com
Processor and exporter of instant hot cereals including peanut porridge, banana, plantain, etc.; also, peanut-based health beverage mixes
President: Jasseth Cummings
CFO: Gloria Johnson
Buyer: Sam Cummings
Quality Control: King H
Estimated Sales: $2.5-5 Million
Number Employees: 1-4
Brands:
Cream of Peanut
Crema De Many
Malted Peanut
Quick Peanut Porridge
Vigorteen

1185 **Bedell North Fork, LLC**
36225 Main Rd
Cutchogue, NY 11935-1346 631-734-7537
Fax: 631-734-5788 wine@bedellcellars.com
www.bedellcellars.com
Wines
Manager: Trent Prezler
CEO: Michael Lynne
Senior VP Sales/Marketing: Jim Silver
COO: Trent Preszler
Plant Manager: Dave Thompson
Estimated Sales: $1-2.5 Million
Number Employees: 5-9
Other Locations:
Corey Creek Vineyards(Tasting Room)
Southold NY
Brands:
BEDELL CELLARS
COREY CREEK

1186 **Bedoukian Research, Inc.**
21 Finance Drive
Danbury, CT 06810 203-830-4000
Fax: 203-830-4010
customerservice@bedoukian.com
www.bedoukian.com
Manufactures flavors
President: Robert Bedoukian
Regulatory and Technical Services: Joseph Bania
Number Employees: 20-49

1187 **Bedrock Farm Certified Organic Medicinal Herbs**
106 Woodland Trl
Wakefield, RI 02879-1926 401-789-9943
ageary@bedrockfarmherbs.com
www.bedrockfarmherbs.com
Organic medicinal herbs
President: Angie Geary

1188 **Bee Int'l., Inc**
2311 Boswell Rd
Suite 1
Chula Vista, CA 91914 619-710-1800
Fax: 619-710-1822 800-421-6465
www.beeinc.com
Manufacturer and importer of Easter, Valentine, Halloween, Christmans and novelty candy items
Owner/CEO: Louis Block
Quality Assurance Manager: Martin Quezada
VP Operations: Charles Block
Estimated Sales: $18 Million
Number Employees: 30
Sq. footage: 55000
Type of Packaging: Consumer
Brands:
CHICLE CHIPS
MICRO BMX BIKE
MICRO SCOOTER

1189 **Bee-Raw Honey**
PO Box 1343
New York, NY 10013 212-941-1932
Fax: 646-607-2060 888-660-0090
beeraw@worldpantry.com www.beeraw.com
honey
President/Owner: Zeke Freeman
CEO: Sam Yocum

1190 **Beech-Nut Nutrition Corporation**
100 S 4th Street
Saint Louis, MO 63102-1800 314-655-2100
Fax: 314-436-7679 800-233-2468
beech-nut@beech-nut.com www.beech-nut.com
Baby food formulated to supplement baby's diet of breast milk or formula. With no refined sugar, no added salt and no harsh spices. Juices and waters
President/CEO: Christoph Rudolph
Estimated Sales: $ 10 - 20 Million
Number Employees: 20-49
Parent Co: Hero Group
Brands:
CEREALS
STAGE 1
STAGE 2
TABLE TIME

1191 **Beef Packers, Inc.**
P.O.Box 12503
Fresno, CA 93778-2503 559-268-5586
Fax: 559-268-1352 www.beefpackers.com
Processor of beef; slaughtering services available
VP: Roger Hall
General Manager: Dennis Roth
Estimated Sales: $50-100 Million
Number Employees: 1,000-4,999
Sq. footage: 201550
Parent Co: Cargill Meat Solutions
Brands:
ANGUS PRIDE
CIRCLE T BEEF™
EXCEL
HONEYSUCKLE WHITE
MEADOWLAND FARMS™GROUND BEEF
PRAIRIE GROVE FARMS
PREFERRED ANGUS®BEEF
RANCHERS REGISTRY ANGUS® BEEF
RUMBA™
SHADY BROOK FARMS
STERLING SILVER
TENDER CHOICE
TENDER RIDGE™ANGUS BEEF
VALLEY™TRADITION BEEF

1192 **(HQ)Beef Products**
891 Two Rivers Dr
North Sioux City, SD 57049-5391 605-217-8000
Fax: 605-217-8001 sales@beefproducts.com
www.beefproducts.com
Manufacturer of partially de-fatted chopped beef and chopped pork; also, fat-reduced beef and pork
President/CEO: Eldon Roth
CFO/VP: Regina Roth
VP: Richard Jochum
Sales & Marketing: Bruce Smith
Estimated Sales: I
Number Employees: 100-249
Type of Packaging: Consumer, Food Service
Other Locations:
BPI Plant
South Sioux City NE
BPI Plant
Amarillo TX
BPI Plant
Garden City KS
BPI Plant
Waterloo IA
BPI Plant
Finney County KS

1193 **Beehive Botanicals, Inc.**
16297 W Nursery Rd
Hayward, WI 54843 715-634-4274
Fax: 715-634-3523 800-233-4483
e-mail@beehivebotanicals.com
www.beehivebotanicals.com
Processor and exporter of health supplements derived from honey, propolis, pollen and royal jelly; also, sugar-free propolis chewing gum
President/CEO: Linda Graham
Quality Control Manager: Denise Gregory
Purchasing Manager: Lisa Johnson
Estimated Sales: $6.5 Million
Number Employees: 38
Sq. footage: 6000
Brands:
Beehive Botanicals
Honey Silk

1194 **Beer Nuts**
P.O.Box 1549
Bloomington, IL 61702-1549 309-827-8580
Fax: 309-827-0914 800-233-7688
info@beernuts.com www.beernuts.com
Processor of numerous nut products including: original peanuts; glazed old fashioned peanuts; almonds; cashews; macadamia nuts; honey mustard crunch nuts; sesame crunch nuts; bar mix; pecans, barbeque crunch nuts; chocolate coverednuts; spicy & hot peanuts; mixes; kettle cooked peanuts; and cajun crunch nuts.
Manager: James A Shirk
Marketing Manager: Cindy Shirk
Public Relations: Tom Foster
Media Relations: Georgia Dawson
Estimated Sales: $20-50 Million
Number Employees: 50-99
Type of Packaging: Food Service
Brands:
Beer Nuts

1195 **Beetroot Delights**
72 Spruceside Crescent
Foothill, ON L0S 1E1
Canada 888-842-3387
Fax: 905-892-1080 info@beetrootdelights.com
www.beetrootdelights.com
Manufacturer and exporter of beetroot condiments including cherry beet pepper and ginger beet jelly, spiced beet ketchup and beet relish
President: Grace Lallemand
Number Employees: 3
Sq. footage: 800
Type of Packaging: Consumer, Food Service
Brands:
BEETROOT DELIGHTS

1196 **Behm Blueberry Farms**
14904 Canary Drive
Grand Haven, MI 49417-8663 616-846-1650
Fresh blueberries
President: Howard Behm
VP: Sharon Behm
Estimated Sales: $ 3 - 5 Million
Number Employees: 10-19
Brands:
Blueberry King

1197 **Bel/Kaukauna USA**
P.O.Box 1974
Kaukauna, WI 54130-7074 920-788-3524
Fax: 920-788-9725 800-558-3500
customerservicekk@belkauusa.com
www.kaukaunacheese.com
Manufacturer of nacho sauce, salsa and cheeses including cold pack, natural, mini goudas and processed spreads; importer of natural cheeses
President: Robert Gilbert
VP Finance: Alan Patz
VP: Al Patz
Director Marketing: Becky Ryan
VP Sales: David Peterson
Director Operations: Bob Eger
Estimated Sales: $258.6 Million
Number Employees: 250-499
Sq. footage: 120000
Parent Co: Fromageries Bel SA
Type of Packaging: Consumer, Food Service, Bulk
Brands:
CONNOISSEUR
KAUKAUNA
LAUGHING COW
MERKETS
MINI BABYBEL
OWLS NEST
PRICE'S
WISPRIDE

1198 **Belcolade**
8030 National Hwy
Pennsauken, NJ 8110 856-661-9123
Fax: 856-665-0005 kzimmermann@puratos.com
belcolade@aol.com
Manufacturer of couverture chocolate
Estimated Sales: $5-10 Million
Number Employees: 5-9
Parent Co: Belcolade NV/SA
Brands:
BELCOLADE
BELCOLADE
CARAT

1199 **Belgioioso Cheese**
5810 County Rd NN
Denmark, WI 54208 920-863-2123
Fax: 920-863-8791 877-863-2123
info@belgioioso.com www.belgioioso.com

Manufacturer of Italian cheeses including provolone, parmesan, romano, asiago, fontina, kasseri, mascarpone, gorgonzola, fresh mozzarella, pepato, peperoncino, parveggiano
President: Errico Auricchio
VP/CFO: Thomas Krueger
Marketing Director: Francis Wall
VP Sales: Gaetano Auricchio
Operations Manager: Mark Schleitwiler
Production Manager: Mauro Rozzi
Estimated Sales: $50-99.9 Million
Number Employees: 100-249
Number of Brands: 1
Number of Products: 15
Type of Packaging: Consumer, Food Service, Bulk
Brands:
BELGIOIOSO

1200 **Belgravia Imports**
275 Highpoint Ave
Portsmouth, RI 2871 401-683-3323
Fax: 401-683-2717 800-848-1127
belgravia@belgraviaimports.com
www.belgraviaimports.com
Organic and natural foods
President: Donald Dick
Estimated Sales: $1-2.5 Million
Number Employees: 5-9

1201 **Bell & Evans**
P.O.Box 39
Fredericksburg, PA 17026 717-865-6626
Fax: 717-865-7046 info@bellandevans.com
www.bellandevans.com
Processor and exporter of fresh chicken, chicken nuggets, sausages, burgers, and diced IQF chicken breast
President/Owner: Scott Sechler
CEO: Bruno Schmalhofer
CEO: Mike Good
Estimated Sales: $50-100 Million
Number Employees: 1,000
Sq. footage: 100000
Brands:
Bell & Evans the Excellent Chicken
Farmers Pride Natural

1202 **Bell Buoy Crab Company**
PO Box 680
Seaside, OR 97138
Fax: 503-738-8325 800-529-2722
bellbuoy@pacifier.com
www.bellbuoyofseaside.com
canned and fresh seafood

Estimated Sales: $240,000
Number Employees: 4
Type of Packaging: Consumer, Food Service, Private Label, Bulk

1203 **Bell Dairy Products**
201 University Ave
Lubbock, TX 79415 806-293-1367
Fax: 806-765-5192
Processor of milk and buttermilk
VP: Bill Murphy
Plant Manager: Damon Mc Dermott
Estimated Sales: $50-100 Million
Number Employees: 100-249
Parent Co: Dean Foods Company
Type of Packaging: Consumer, Food Service, Private Label

1204 **(HQ)Bell Flavors & Fragrances**
500 Academy Dr
Northbrook, IL 60062 847-291-8300
Fax: 847-291-1217 800-323-4387
infousa@bellff.com www.bellff.com
Manufacturer and exporter of natural and artificial flavoring extracts for food and beverages; also, spice compounds
President/CEO: James Heinz
Controller: Julie Fox
VP/Technical Director: Mike Bloom
R & D: Robert Barrera
Director of Marketing: Mike Natale
VP Plant Operations: Mike Bianco
Estimated Sales: $150 Million
Number Employees: 50-99
Sq. footage: 100000
Type of Packaging: Consumer, Food Service
Brands:
YUCCAFOAM

1205 **Bell Mountain Vineyards**
P.O.Box 756
Fredericksburg, TX 78624-0756 830-685-3297
Fax: 830-685-3657
contactus@bellmountainwine.com
www.bellmountainwine.com
Wines
Owner: Robert P Oberhelman
VP: Ames Morrison
Estimated Sales: $2.5-5 Million
Number Employees: 5-9

1206 **Bell-Carter Foods**
3742 Mt Diablo Blvd
Lafayette, CA 94549 925-284-5933
Fax: 925-284-1289 800-252-3557
contactus@bellcarter.com www.bellcarter.com
Manufacturer and marketer of black ripe, spanish, sicilian, kalamota, and other specialty olive products
President: H Judson Carater
CEO: Ken Wienholz
CFO: Patti Davis
Corporate QA/R&D: Julia Workman
VP Marketing: Robin Robinson
VP Sales: Paul McGinty
VP Operations: Pat Campbell
Plant Superintendent: Steve Henderson
Estimated Sales: $ 20 - 50 Million
Number Employees: 450
Type of Packaging: Consumer, Food Service, Private Label, Bulk
Brands:
LINDSAY OLIVES

1207 **Bella Chi-Cha Products**
216-B Fern Street
Santa Cruz, CA 95060 831-423-1851
Fax: 831-423-0212 ccrusso@pacbell.net
www.bellachicha.com
Pesto and layered tortas
President/Owner: Chi-Cha Russo

1208 **Bella Coola Fisheries**
3133 188 St
Surrey, BC V3S 9V5
Canada 604-541-0339
Fax: 604-541-0370 info@belcofish.com
www.belcofish.com
Processor and exporter of fresh and frozen herring roe and salmon
General Manager: Frank Taylor
Number Employees: 10-19
Type of Packaging: Consumer, Food Service, Private Label, Bulk

1209 **Bella Cucina Artful Food**
1870 Murphy Avenue
Atlanta, GA 30310 678-539-8400
Fax: 678-539-8401 866-350-9040
alisa@bellacucina.com www.bellacucina.com
Manufacturer of quality Mediterranean inspired food, such as olive oils and pestos
Manager: Reginald Weekes
Estimated Sales: $2.5-5 Million
Number Employees: 20-49
Type of Packaging: Private Label

1210 **Bella Napoli Italian Bakery**
721 River St
Troy, NY 12180 518-274-8277
Fax: 518-274-2625 888-800-0103
www.bellanapolibakery.com
Manufacturer of Italian specialties
President: Dominic Mainella
Estimated Sales: $2.5-5 Million
Number Employees: 50-99
Other Locations:
Bella Napoli Italian Bakery
Latham NY

1211 **Bella Ravioli**
369 Main St
Medford, MA 02155 781-396-0875
Fax: 781-396-0876
Processor of pasta
Owner: Mario De Pasquale
Estimated Sales: Less than $100,000
Number Employees: 1-4
Brands:
Bella Ravioli

1212 **Bella Vista Farm**
1002 SW Ard St
Lawton, OK 73505-9660 580-536-1300
Fax: 580-536-4886 866-237-8526
craig@peppercreekfarms.com
www.peppercreekfarms.com
Organic jams, honey, peanut butter, popcorn, all nautral pasta sauces, organic pasta and organic olive oil.
Owner: Craig Weissman
Estimated Sales: Less than $500,000
Number Employees: 5-9
Brands:
Bella Vista

1213 **Bella Viva Orchards**
3019 S Quincy Rd
Denair, CA 95316 209-883-4146
Fax: 209-883-0215 800-552-8218
CustomerCare@BellaViva.com
www.bellaviva.com
Kosher dried fruit and chocolate fruits packaged for gifts
Owner: Victor Martino
Estimated Sales: $1-2.5 Million
Number Employees: 20-49

1214 **Belle Plaine Cheese Factory**
N3473 Wisconsin Ave
Shawano, WI 54166 715-526-2789
866-245-5924
Retailer of cheese including colby, cheddar, monterey jack, rainbow and pepper jack
President: Donald Brandl
Estimated Sales: $50,000
Number Employees: 1-4
Type of Packaging: Consumer

1215 **Belle River Enterprises**
RR 3
Belle River, PE C0A 1B0
Canada 902-962-2248
Fax: 902-962-4276
Processor and exporter of rock crab combo and minced crab, cocktail claws and salad meat
President: Howard Hancock
Vice President: Dean Hancock
Estimated Sales: $10 Million
Number Employees: 60
Sq. footage: 8000
Brands:
Belle River

1216 **BelleHarvest Sales**
11900 Fisk Rd
Belding, MI 48809 616-794-0320
Fax: 616-794-3961 800-452-7753
bellehar@iserv.net www.belleharvest.com
Manufacturer, wholesaler/distributor, exporter and packer of fresh fruits and vegetables
President: Mike Rothwell
Sales/Marketing: Tom Pletcher
Number Employees: 10-19
Parent Co: Belding Fruit Storage

1217 **Belleisle FoodsAliments Wong Wing Inc**
880 Route 870
Belleisle Creek, NB E5P 1G4
Canada 506-485-2564
Fax: 506-485-2566
tellmemore@belleislefoods.com
www.belleislefoods.com
Manufacturer of frozen Chinese food and meat pies and entrees
EVP: Peter Pope
Quality Assurance: Jeanette Sprague
Marketing/Sales: Shelly Bronnum
Number Employees: 100
Sq. footage: 33000
Type of Packaging: Consumer, Food Service, Private Label, Bulk
Brands:
BELLEISLE

1218 **Bellerose Vineyard**
435 W Dry Creek Rd
Healdsburg, CA 95448 707-433-1637
Fax: 707-433-7024 www.everettridge.com
Wines
President: Charles Richard
Founder/Owner: Charles Richard
Co-Owner: Charles Richard

Estimated Sales: $500,000 appx.
Number Employees: 5-9
Brands:
Bellerose

1219 **(HQ)Belletieri Company**
1207 W Chew St
Allentown, PA 18102-3751 610-433-4334
Italian specialty foods
President: Louie Belletieri
Treasurer: Peter Belletieri
Estimated Sales: Under $500,000
Number Employees: 6

1220 **Belleville Brothers Packing**
2545 Insley Rd
North Baltimore, OH 45872 419-257-3529
Fax: 419-257-3529
Processor of meat products
President: James Belleville
Estimated Sales: $500,000
Number Employees: 1-4
Type of Packaging: Consumer, Bulk

1221 **(HQ)Bellisio Foods, Inc.**
PO Box 16630
Duluth, MN 55816 612-371-8222
800-368-7337
info@bellisiofoods.com www.bellisiofoods.com
Processor of frozen entrees, sauces and soups
CEO: Joel Conner
CFO: Danette Bucsko
Senior VP Sales/Marketing: Charlie Pountney
Senior VP Operations: Jeff Wilson
Estimated Sales: $300 Million
Number Employees: 1400
Sq. footage: 60000
Type of Packaging: Consumer, Food Service
Brands:
AUTHENTICO®
BUDGET GOURMET®
MICHELINA'S GRANDE
MICHELINA'S LEAN GOURMET®
MICHELINA'S PIZZA SNACK ROLLS
MICHELINA'S SIGNATURE®
ZAP'EMS®

1222 **Bellville Meat Market**
36 S Front St
Bellville, TX 77418 979-865-5782
Fax: 979-865-0550 800-571-6328
sara@bellvillemeatmarket.com
www.bellvillemeatmarket.com
Processor of regular and flavored beef and pork smoked sausage links including garlic, jalapeno, cayenne pepper, etc.; also, fresh pork links, dry, all beef summer and pan sausages and venison products available
Owner/Manager: Daniel Poffenberger Jr.
Plant Manager: Jerrod Poffenberger
Estimated Sales: $2.5-5 Million
Number Employees: 20-49
Sq. footage: 1500
Type of Packaging: Consumer, Food Service, Private Label, Bulk
Brands:
Poffenberger's Bellville

1223 **Bellwether Farms**
PO Box 299
Valley Ford, CA 94972-0299 707-763-0993
Fax: 707-763-2443 info@bellwethercheese.com
www.bellwethercheese.com
Fresh and aged cheese
Owner: Cynthia Callahan
Founder: Cindy Callahan
Vice President: Liam Callahan
Estimated Sales: Under $500,000
Number Employees: 5-9
Type of Packaging: Private Label
Brands:
Bellwether

1224 **Belmar Spring Water Company**
410 Grove St
Glen Rock, NJ 7452 201-444-1010
Fax: 973-423-4503
service@belmarspringwater.com
www.belmarspringwater.com
Processor and bottler of spring water
President: Wesley Outwater
Estimated Sales: $1-2.5 Million
Number Employees: 10-19
Type of Packaging: Consumer, Private Label

1225 **Belmont Brewing Company**
25 39th Pl
Long Beach, CA 90803 562-433-3891
Fax: 562-434-0604 www.belmontbrewing.com
Beer and micro brews
Owner: David Hansen
VP: Tom Avila
Estimated Sales: $2.5-5 Million
Number Employees: 50-99
Brands:
BITBURGER
BLACK & TAN
FRANZISKANER HEFE-WEISSE
GROWLER
LONG BEACH CRUDE
MARATHON
PENNY FOGGER
SHANDY
STRAWBERRY BLONDE
TOP SAIL AMBER
WOODCHUCK PEAR CIDER

1226 **Belmont Chemicals**
50 Mount Prospect Ave
Clifton, NJ 07013 973-777-2225
Fax: 973-777-6384 800-722-5070
www.belmontchemicals.com
Processor and exporter of vitamins, nutritional and protein supplements, herbs and amino acids
Owner/President: Paul Egyes
Sales Manager: Paul Egyes
Public Relations: Mary Apuzzo
Estimated Sales: $4.5 Million
Number Employees: 4
Number of Products: 50
Sq. footage: 1000
Type of Packaging: Bulk

1227 **Belmont Peanuts of Southampton Inc**
23195 Popes Station Rd
Capron, VA 23829 800-648-4613
info@belmontpeanuts.com
www.belmontpeanuts.com
Peanut and peanut products
President/Owner: Patsy Marks
VP: Robert Marks

1228 **Belton Foods**
P.O.Box 13605
Dayton, OH 45413 937-890-7768
Fax: 937-890-7780 800-443-2266
dsipos@beltonfoods.com www.belton.com
Beverages, concentrates, pancake and table syrups, vinegars, drink mixes, enhancing syrups and slush base
President: David Sipos
Vice President: Cynthia Gillespie
Sales Director: Don Fox
Production Manager: Joe Reece
Manager: Tony Dudon
Estimated Sales: $3.4 Million
Number Employees: 27
Number of Brands: 20
Number of Products: 120
Sq. footage: 24
Type of Packaging: Consumer, Food Service, Private Label, Bulk

1229 **Belvedere Vineyards & Winery**
250 Center St
Healdsburg, CA 95448-4402 707-431-4442
Fax: 707-433-2429 800-433-8296
www.belvederewinery.com
Wines
CFO: Tom Christenson
Winemaker: Alison Rosenelum
Plant Manager: Proy McEndry
Estimated Sales: $10-20 Million
Number Employees: 20-49
Sq. footage: 24
Type of Packaging: Private Label
Brands:
Belvedere
Grove Street
Hambrecht Vineyards

1230 **(HQ)Ben & Jerry's Homemade**
30 Community Drive
South Burlington, VT 5403 802-846-1500
Fax: 802-846-1610 www.benjerry.com
Processor of ice cream, frozen yogurt, sorbet and smoothies
President/CEO: Perry Odak
CEO: Jostein Solheim
CFO: Michael Graning
Marketing Director: David Stever
Public Relations Manager: Sean Greenwood
Senior Director Operations: Bruce Bowman
Plant Manager: Janette Cole
Purchasing: Daniel Scheidt
Estimated Sales: $50-99.9 Million
Number Employees: 841
Sq. footage: 69000
Parent Co: Unilever USA
Type of Packaging: Consumer
Other Locations:
Ben & Jerry's
Waterbury VT
Brands:
Ben & Jerry's
Ben & Jerry's Frozen Smoothies
Ben & Jerry's Ice Cream

1231 **Ben B. Schwartz & Sons**
7201 W Fort St. #27
Detroit, MI 48209 313-841-8300
Fax: 313-841-1253 www.benbdetroit.com
Grower of fruits and vegetables including apples, peaches, pears, cucumbers, lettuce and potatoes
Owner: Chris Billmeyer
Manager: Gary Schwartz
Estimated Sales: $10-20 Million
Number Employees: 20-49
Type of Packaging: Consumer

1232 **Ben E. Keith DFW**
7650 Will Rogers Blvd
Fort Worth, TX 76140 817-759-6000
Fax: 817-759-6238 877-317-6100
dfwinfo@benekeith.com www.benekeith.com
Wholesaler/distributor of frozen food, produce, groceries, dairy products, meats, etc.; serving the food service market
President: Howard Hallam
CEO: Robert Hallam
CFO: Mel Cockrell
Estimated Sales: $100-500 Million
Number Employees: 20-49
Sq. footage: 591000
Parent Co: Ben E. Keith Company
Type of Packaging: Food Service, Private Label, Bulk
Brands:
ADMIRAL OF THE FLEET™
BEKO®
CEYLON TEA GARDENS®
CORTONA®
ELLINGTON ROASTING COMPANY®
FRESH FROM KEITH'S®
GOLDEN HARVEST®
KEITH'S CHOICE
KEITH'S ESSENTIALS
KEITH'S EXCLUSIVE
KEITH'S HOMESTYLE
KEITH'S PREMIUM
MARKRON COOPERATIVE®
SWEET D'LITE®

1233 **Ben Heggy's Candy Company**
743 Cleveland Ave NW
Canton, OH 44702 330-455-7703
Fax: 330-455-9865 info@heggys.com
www.heggys.com
Manufacturer of Old Fashioned Candies and Handcrafted Chocolates
President/Owner: Richard Wollenberg
Estimated Sales: $10-20 Million
Number Employees: 20-49
Type of Packaging: Private Label

1234 **Ben Hill Griffin, Inc.**
700 S Scenic Hwy
Frostproof, FL 33843 863-635-2251
Fax: 863-635-7333
Manufacturer of fresh citrus fruits including grapefruit and oranges
President: Ben Hill Griffin
CFO: Stewart Hurst
CEO: Ben Hill Griffin Iii
Sales: Steve Maxwell
Operations: Larry Gray
Purchasing Manager: Dick Peavy
Estimated Sales: I
Number Employees: 250-499

Type of Packaging: Consumer, Bulk

1235 **Ben-Bud Growers Inc.**
One North Federal Highway
Suite 203
Boca Raton, FL 33432 561-347-3120
Fax: 561-347-3101 www.ben-bud.com
Processor and importer of vegetables
President: Ben Litowich
Estimated Sales: $20-50 Million
Number Employees: 10-19
Type of Packaging: Consumer, Bulk

1236 **Benbow's Coffee Roasters**
8 Access Alley
Bar Harbor, ME 04609-1717 207-288-5271
Fax: 207-288-8227 ron@Benbows.com
www.benbows.com
Coffee roasters and jams
President: Ron Greenberg
CEO: Jaren Greenberg
Estimated Sales: Less than $500,000
Number Employees: 1-4
Type of Packaging: Private Label
Brands:
Benbow's

1237 **Bened Food Corporation**
200 Food Center Dr
Bronx, NY 10474-7030 718-842-8644
Fax: 718-842-8582 www.bazzinionline.com
Nuts and dried fruits
President: Rocco Damato
Estimated Sales: $25-49.9 Million
Number Employees: 100-249

1238 **Beneo Palatinit**
2740 Rt 10 West
Suite 205
Morris Plains, NJ 07950-1258 973-867-2140
Fax: 973-867-2141 800-476-6258
info.usa@beneo.com www.beneo-palatinit.com
Supplier of Isomalt a bulk sugar replacer
President: Peter Strater
VP: Cees Boon
Estimated Sales: $170,000
Number Employees: 1-4
Brands:
Isomalt

1239 **Benmarl Wine Company**
156 Highland Ave
Marlboro, NY 12542 845-236-4265
Fax: 845-236-7271 www.benmarl.com
Processor of wines including white, blended red, rose and Chardonnay
Owner: Victor Spaccerelli
Estimated Sales: $2.5-5 Million
Number Employees: 5-9
Type of Packaging: Consumer, Food Service
Brands:
Marlboro Village

1240 **Bennett's Apples & Cider**
944 Garners Road E
Ancaster, ON L9G 3K9
Canada 905-648-6878
Fax: 905-648-3647
Processor of sweet and mulled apple and apple cranberry cider, apples, pumpkins and sweet corn; contract packaging available
CEO/President: Todd Bennett
Vice President: Richard Bennett
Estimated Sales: $3 Million
Number Employees: 27
Sq. footage: 10000
Type of Packaging: Consumer, Food Service, Private Label, Bulk
Brands:
Bennett's

1241 **Bens Seafood Company**
P.O.Box 276
Crescent, GA 31304-0276 912-832-5121
Fax: 912-832-2722
Fresh, frozen, smoked, live roe
Owner: Ben H Cox Jr

1242 **Benson's Gourmet Seasonings**
P.O.Box 638
Azusa, CA 91702-0638 626-969-4443
Fax: 626-969-2912 800-325-5619
bensons4u@aol.com
www.bensonsseasonings.com
Manufacturer of kosher, salt-free and sugar-free seasoning blends including herb/pepper, natural salty flavor, Southwestern, Jamaican, lemon and garlic/herb, big game, game bird and chili
President: Debbie Benson
Estimated Sales: Less than $500,000
Number Employees: 1-4
Sq. footage: 1000
Type of Packaging: Consumer, Food Service, Bulk

1243 **Bensons Bakery**
134 Elder St
Bogart, GA 30622 770-725-5711
Fax: 770-725-5888 800-888-6059
larrybenson@home.com
www.bensonsbakery.com
Processor of frozen and sourdough bread and pound and fruit cakes.
President: Larry Benson
Controller: Bob Mills
VP Sales/Marketing: Browning Adair
Plant Manager: Rich Preller
Estimated Sales: $10-20 Million
Number Employees: 50-99
Sq. footage: 100000
Parent Co: Benson's
Type of Packaging: Consumer, Food Service, Private Label, Bulk
Other Locations:
Benson's Old Home Kitchens
Athens GA
Brands:
BENSON'S
BENSON'S OLD HOME KITCHENS
HOLIDAY ISLAND
PERKINS WILLIAMS
SPECIALTY BREADS
SUN MAID
SUN-MAID FRUIT
VILLAGE FAIR
WES HEADLEY

1244 **Bensons Bakery**
134 Elder St
Bogart, GA 30622 770-725-5711
Fax: 770-725-5888 800-888-6059
sales@bensonsbakery.com
www.bensonsbakery.com
Manufacturer of cakes and fruit cake
President: Larry Benson
Estimated Sales: $10-20 Million
Number Employees: 50-99
Type of Packaging: Private Label

1245 **Benton's Seafood Center**
711 Central Ave S
Tifton, GA 31794-5212 229-382-4976
Fax: 229-382-0779
Seafood
President: Timothy Benton
Estimated Sales: $ 1 - 3 Million
Number Employees: 1-4

1246 **Benzel's Pretzel Bakery**
5200 6th Ave
Altoona, PA 16602-1435 814-942-5062
Fax: 814-942-4133 800-344-4438
pretzels@benzels.com www.benzels.com
Processor of pretzels
President: Ann Benzel
Vice President: William Benzel
Sales Director: Shaun Benzel
Production Manager: Erkin McCaulley
Plant Manager: Don Gority
Purchasing Manager: Angela Decker
Estimated Sales: $ 10 - 20 Million
Number Employees: 50-99
Number of Products: 36
Sq. footage: 180000
Type of Packaging: Consumer, Food Service, Private Label, Bulk
Brands:
BENZEL'S BRAND
PENNYSTICKS BRAND

1247 **Benziger Family Winery**
1883 London Ranch Rd
Glen Ellen, CA 95442 707-935-3000
Fax: 707-935-3016 888-490-2739
greatwine@benziger.com www.benziger.com
Wines
President: Tim Wallace
VP Winegrowing: Mark Burningham
National Sales Manager: Chris Benziger
General Manager: Mike Benziger
Estimated Sales: $20-50 Million
Number Employees: 30

1248 **Bequet Confections**
8235 Huffine Lane
Bozeman, MT 59718 406-586-2191
Fax: 406-586-7003 877-423-7838
sales@bequetconfections.com
www.bequetconfections.com
caramels and flavored caramels
President: Joe Sharber
Number Employees: 6

1249 **Berardi's Fresh Roast**
12029 Abbey Rd
Cleveland, OH 44133-2637 440-582-4303
Fax: 440-582-4359 800-876-9109
www.berardis.com
Specialty coffees, estates, organic, signature blends, espresso and espresso pods. Green, black, organic and herbal teas
Manager: Sean Leneghan
Estimated Sales: $2.5-5 Million
Number Employees: 20-49
Type of Packaging: Private Label
Brands:
Berardi's
Berardi's Bodum
Berardi's Bunn
Berardi's Effie Mari
Berardi's Estate Col
Berardi's Estate-Dir
Berardi's Harvest Te
Berardi's Jet Tea Fr
Berardi's Joe To Go
Berardi's Melitta
Berardi's Miniminits
Berardi's Monin
Berardi's Monin
Berardi's Nissan
Berardi's Oregon Cha
Berardi's Senza
Berardi's Technibrew
Berardi's Toddy
Berardi's Vita-Mix

1250 **Berberian Nut Company**
6100 Wilson Landing Rd
Chico, CA 95973-8902 530-891-4900
Fax: 209-465-6008
Processor and exporter of walnuts, dry beans and rice
Principal: Pete Turner
General Manager: Terry Turner
Plant Manager: Ren Fairbanks
Estimated Sales: $20-50 Million
Number Employees: 50-99
Parent Co: Farm Management Company
Type of Packaging: Consumer, Food Service, Private Label, Bulk

1251 **Bergen Marzipan & Chocolate**
205 S Washington Ave
Bergenfield, NJ 07621 201-385-8343
Fax: 201-385-0042
bergenmarzipan@optonline.net
Confections, marzipan and chocolate
Owner: Eddie Sarpon
Estimated Sales: Under $500,000
Number Employees: 1-4

1252 **Bergey's Dairy Farm**
2221 Mt Pleasant Rd
Chesapeake, VA 23322 757-482-4711
Fax: 757-482-5439
Milk, ice cream and butter
President: Leonard Bergey
Vice President: Elsa Bergey
Estimated Sales: $5-10 Million
Number Employees: 20-49

1253 **Berghausen Corporation**
4524 Este Ave
Cincinnati, OH 45232 513-541-5631
Fax: 513-541-1169 800-648-5887
info@berghausen.com www.berghausen.com

Processor and finisher of quillaja and yucca extracts (powder and liquid forms) and food colors
President: Fritz Berghausen
Quality Control Manager: Tom Davlin
Estimated Sales: Below $5 Million
Number Employees: 10-19

1254 **Bering Sea Fisheries**
4413 83rd Avenue SE
Snohomish, WA 98290-5204 425-334-1498
Processor and exporter of frozen salmon
President: H Bodey
Vice President: Russell Bodey
Estimated Sales: $780,000
Number Employees: 10
Type of Packaging: Private Label

1255 **Bering Sea Raindeer Products**
PO Box 42
Mekoryuk, AK 99630-0042 907-827-8940
Fax: 907-827-8514

1256 **Berke-Blake Fancy Foods, Inc.**
150 National Pl # 140
Longwood, FL 32750-6431 407-831-7288
Fax: 407-831-7065 888-386-2253
info@anniepiesbakery.com
www.anniepiesbakery.com
Manufacturer of cakes including cheesecakes, and pies
CEO: Anne Resnick
CEO: Ann Resnick
Executive VP Sales/Marketing: Marnie Blake Zahn
General Manager: Mark Hanft
Production Manager: Daniele Sansone
Estimated Sales: $ 5 - 10 Million
Number Employees: 5-9
Number of Brands: 1
Number of Products: 100
Sq. footage: 9000
Type of Packaging: Food Service
Brands:
Annie Pie's

1257 **Berkeley Farms**
25500 Clawiter Rd
Hayward, CA 94545 510-265-8600
Fax: 510-265-8748 www.berkeleyfarms.com
Manufacturer of dairy products
Manager: Nick Kelble
VP Sales/Marketing: Mike Lasky
Number Employees: 500-999
Parent Co: Dean Foods Company

1258 **Berks Packing Company, Inc.**
319 Bingaman St
Reading, PA 19602 610-376-7291
Fax: 610-378-1210 800-882-3757
marketingdept@berksfoods.com
www.berksfoods.com
Processor of beef frankfurters, smoked sausage and kielbasa, roast beef, turkey breast, regular and reduced-sodium ham, deli meats, etc
President: Mike Boylan
Purchasing Director: David Boylan
Estimated Sales: $50-100 Million
Number Employees: 100-249

1259 **Berkshire Brewing Company, Inc.**
12 Railroad St
South Deerfield, MA 1373 413-665-6600
Fax: 413-665-7837 877-222-7468
frontdesk@berkshirebrewingcompany.com
www.berkshirebrewingcompany.com
Processor of ale and seasonal beer
Owner: Gary Bogoff
CEO: Christopher Lalli
Director: Julia Dvorko
Estimated Sales: $1.2 Million
Number Employees: 14
Type of Packaging: Consumer, Food Service
Brands:
BERKSHIRE ALE
CABIN FEVER ALE
COFFEEHOUSE PORTER
DRAYMAN'S PORTER
GOLD SPIKE ALE
HEFEWEIZEN
HOLIDALE BARLEY WINE
IMPERIAL STOUT
LOST SAILOR INDIA PALE ALE
MAILBOCK LAGER
OKTOBERFEST LAGER
RASPBERRY BARLEY WINE
RIVER ALE
SHABADOO BLACK AND TAN ALE
STEEL RAIL EXTRA PALE ALE

1260 **Berkshire Dairy & Food Products**
1258 Penn Ave Ofc
Wyomissing, PA 19610 610-378-9999
Fax: 610-378-4975 888-654-8008
info@berkshiredairy.com
www.berkshiredairy.com
Manufacturer, importer and exporter of analog extenders, dehydrated dairy products, powders, cheese, creamers, lactose, milk and whey, whole milk powder, Anhydreos milkfat butter, nonfat dry milk, permeate
President: Dale Mills
Sales Manager: Deb Haretty
Operations Manager: Steve Cinegi
Controller: Mark Moyer
Estimated Sales: $200 Million
Number Employees: 10-19
Sq. footage: 6000
Type of Packaging: Private Label, Bulk
Brands:
Berk-Cap

1261 **Berkshire Mountain Bakery**
P.O.Box 785
Housatonic, MA 01236 413-274-3412
Fax: 413-274-6124 866-274-6124
info@berkshiremountainbakery.com
www.berkshiremountainbakery.com
Manufacturer of baked goods such as; sourdough bread, ciabatta bread, bread w/chocolate, oat pecan cookies, pizza crusts and pizza's
President: Richard Bourdon
Estimated Sales: Less than $500,000
Number Employees: 10-19

1262 **Berlin Natural Bakery**
P.O.Box 311
Berlin, OH 44610 330-893-2734
Fax: 330-893-2157 800-686-5334
www.berlinnaturalbakery.com
Manufacturer of bakery products made with spelt
Manager: Cindy Widder
Owner: Joy Schrock
Estimated Sales: $1.3 Million
Number Employees: 21
Type of Packaging: Private Label

1263 **Bernadette Baking Company**
85 Commercial St
Medford, MA 2155 781-393-8700
Fax: 781-393-0414 info@bernadettebaking.com
www.bernadettebaking.com
Crunchy biscotti dipped in brews, coffeees, teas, or wines
President: Bernadette De Vergilio
Vice President: Marie Cooke
Plant Manager: Mario Ruiz
Estimated Sales: Under $500,000
Number Employees: 7
Type of Packaging: Private Label
Brands:
Bernadette's Biscotti
Bernadette's Biscotti Soave
Bernadette's Cookies

1264 **Bernard & Sons**
4011 Jewett Ave
Bakersfield, CA 93301 661-327-4431
Fax: 661-327-7461 www.bernardandsons.com
Meat
President: Dennis Bernard
General Manager: Hal Ulmer
Estimated Sales: $11,100,000
Number Employees: 20-49

1265 **Bernard Food Industries**
P.O.Box 1497
Evanston, IL 60204-1497 847-869-5222
Fax: 800-962-1546 800-323-3663
bernardfoods@bernardfoods.com
www.bernardfoods.com
Manufacturer and exporter of mixes including dessert, soup, drink, baking, etc.; also, soup bases and gravy, textured vegetable protein, gelatin, syrup dessert toppings, dietary foods, etc.
Owner: Steve Bernard
CEO: Steven Bernard
Vice President: Jules Bernard
Purchasing Director: Steven Bernardi
Estimated Sales: $20-50 Million
Number Employees: 50-99
Sq. footage: 60000
Type of Packaging: Consumer, Food Service, Private Label, Bulk
Brands:
BERNARD
BETA-CARE
CALORIE CONTROL
HOLA
KWIK-DISH
LITE-95
LONGHORN GRILL
SANS SUCRE
TEX-PRO
THIXX

1266 **Bernard Marcantel Company**
PO Box 1149
Kinder, LA 70648-1149 318-738-5122
Fax: 401-783-2759
Owner: Bernard Marcantel

1267 **Bernardi Italian Foods Company**
595 W 11th St
Bloomsburg, PA 17815 570-389-5500
Fax: 570-784-0293 www.windsorfoods.com
Processor of frozen and prepared Italian dinners and cheese foods
Manager: Howard Teufel
Q/A Manager: Julie Simcox
Plant Manager: Howard Toufel
Purchasing: Sharon Lawrence
Estimated Sales: $20-50 Million
Number Employees: 100-249
Sq. footage: 70000
Parent Co: Windsor Frozen Foods
Type of Packaging: Consumer, Food Service, Private Label, Bulk

1268 **Bernardo Winery**
13330 Paseo Del Verano Norte
San Diego, CA 92128 858-487-1866
Fax: 858-673-5376 jim@bernardowinery.com
www.bernardowinery.com
Manufacturer of wine
Owner/President: Ross Rizzo
CEO/VP: Rossi Rizzo
Event Manager: Kathy Lieber
Estimated Sales: $500,000-$1 Million
Number Employees: 1-4
Type of Packaging: Private Label
Brands:
Bernardo

1269 **Bernardus Winery & Vineyards**
P.O.Box 1800
Carmel Valley, CA 93924-1800 831-659-1900
Fax: 831-659-1676 888-648-9463
www.bernardus.com
Wines
Owner: Ben Pon
Operations Manager: Dean DeKorth
Plant Manager: Matthew Shea
Estimated Sales: $5-10 Million
Number Employees: 20-49
Type of Packaging: Private Label
Brands:
Bernardus

1270 **Berner Cheese Corporation**
10010 N Rock City Rd
Rock City, IL 61070 815-865-5136
Fax: 815-563-4017 rickz@bernerfoods.com
Processor of cheese
President: Steve Kneubehl
Office Manager: Nancy Germain
Purchsiding Director: Melody Fuchs
Estimated Sales: $2.5-5 Million
Number Employees: 20-49
Parent Co: Berner Cheese Corporation
Type of Packaging: Consumer

1271 **(HQ)Berner Cheese Corporation**
2034 E Factory Rd
Dakota, IL 61018 815-563-4222
Fax: 815-563-4017 800-819-8199
sales@bernercheese.com www.bernercheese.com

Processor of shelf stable, refrigerated and pasteurized cheese sauces
President: Steve Kneubuehl
CFO: William Marchido
Vice President: Edward Kneubuehl
Research & Development: Laura Flores
Quality Control: Deanna Ritschard
Marketing Manager: Donna Noenning
Estimated Sales: $65 Million
Number Employees: 195
Type of Packaging: Food Service, Bulk
Other Locations:
Berner Cheese Corp.
Rock City IL

1272 **Berner Foods, Inc.**
11447 2nd St Ste 6
Roscoe, IL 61073 815-623-1722
Fax: 815-623-1622 800-819-8199
berner.sales@bernerfoods.com
www.bernerfoods.com
Processor of shelf stable cheese sauces and spreads, shelf stable dips, and milk based retort beverages.
Executive VP: Steve Fay
Quality Control: Tammy Jacobs
Marketing Manager: Dani Amman
Estimated Sales: $ 10 - 20 Million
Number Employees: 10-19
Parent Co: Illini Protein
Type of Packaging: Food Service, Private Label
Other Locations:
Rock City IL
Dakota IL
Brands:
DAKOTA
STEADFAST

1273 **Bernheim Distilling Company**
1416 S 3rd Street
Louisville, KY 40208-2117 502-638-1387
Fax: 502-585-9110 800-303-0053
Reservations@BernheimMansion.com
www.bernheimmansion.com
Spirits
Owner: Bernard Bernheim
Estimated Sales: $300,000-500,000
Number Employees: 5-9

1274 **Bernie's Foods**
263 Classon Ave
Brooklyn, NY 11205-4321 718-417-6677
Fax: 718-417-0932 berniesfoods@aol.com
www.ratners.com
Ice-cream, sorbets and frozen pasta
President: Abraham Ostreicher
Number Employees: 20-49
Number of Brands: 3
Number of Products: 50
Sq. footage: 10000
Type of Packaging: Consumer, Food Service, Private Label
Brands:
Frankel's Homestyle
Tovli

1275 **Berry Processing**
522 E Elm St
Watseka, IL 60970 815-432-3264
Processor of beef and pork
President: Catherine Berry
Estimated Sales: $500,000-$1 Million
Number Employees: 1-4
Type of Packaging: Consumer, Food Service, Private Label, Bulk

1276 **Bertucci's**
155 Otis St
Northborough, MA 01532 508-351-2500
Fax: 508-393-1231 www.bertuccis.com
Pizza restaurant chain, and manufacturer and grocer
President: Rick Barbick
CEO: Stephen Clark
Purchasing Manager: Artie Morris
Estimated Sales: $100-500 Million
Number Employees: 5,000-9,999
Parent Co: NE Restaurant Company
Type of Packaging: Consumer

1277 **Bessinger Pickle Company**
537 N Court St
Au Gres, MI 48703 989-876-8008
Fax: 989-876-8028
Manufacturer of dill pickles
President: Craig Carruthers
Estimated Sales: $1 Million
Number Employees: 50-99
Sq. footage: 26000
Type of Packaging: Consumer

1278 **Best Boy**
5120 Investment Drive
Fort Wayne, IN 46808-3600 260-426-2474
Fax: 260-426-2475 shive@bestboyandco.com
Other chocolate, BBQ sauce, herbs, rubs.
Marketing: Wayne Shive

1279 **(HQ)Best Brands Corporation**
111 Cheshire Lane
Suite 100
Minnetonka, MN 55305 952-404-7500
Fax: 952-404-7501 800-866-3300
www.bestbrandscorp.com
Manufacturer of cakes, cookies, pies and rolls.
President/CEO: Scott Humphrey
CFO: Jody Anderson
Data Processing: Mike Hayden
SVP Sales: Mike Schultz
Estimated Sales: $156 Million
Number Employees: 1000
Sq. footage: 170000
Parent Co: CSM

1280 **Best Chocolate In Town**
880 Massachusetts Ave
Indianapolis, IN 46204 317-636-2800
Fax: 317-636-2822 888-294-2378
info@bestchocolateintown.com
www.bestchocolateintown.com
Manufacturer of hand-made chocolates
Founder/President: Elizabeth Garber
Estimated Sales: $100,000
Number Employees: 5-9

1281 **Best Ever Bake Shop**
52 North Street
Mount Vernon, NY 10550-1150 914-665-7005
Fax: 914-665-7005
Processor of sweet potato and pecan pie
President/Owner: Connie Williams
Estimated Sales: A
Number Employees: 1-4
Type of Packaging: Consumer

1282 **Best Foods Baking Group**
4613 Wedgewood Blvd
Frederick, MD 21703-7120 301-631-8185
800-635-1700
Controller: Clarence Jenkins
Operations Manager: Mark Baugher
Plant Manager: Gary Willis
Estimated Sales: $20-50 Million
Number Employees: 1-4
Parent Co: Unilever USA

1283 **(HQ)Best Harvest Bakeries**
530 S 65th St
Kansas City, KS 66111 913-287-6300
Fax: 913-287-5408 800-811-5715
info@bestharvest.com www.bestharvest.com
Processor of buns and rolls
President/COO: Ed Honesty Jr.
Chairman/CEO: Robert Beavers
VP: Brandon Beavers
Quality Assurance Supervisor: Jason McConico
Plant Manager: Brad Wolf
Purchasing: Rich Lingo
Estimated Sales: $3.4 Million
Number Employees: 52
Sq. footage: 32000
Type of Packaging: Consumer, Food Service

1284 **Best Kosher Foods**
1000 W Pershing Rd
Chicago, IL 60609 773-650-6330
Fax: 773-650-9046 888-800-0072
slfconsumeraffairs@saralee.com
www.bestkosherfoods.com
Kosher meats
Manager: Damon Williams
Sr Manager Facilities: John Empen
Engineering: Roger Savastano
Plant Manager: Robert Worth
Estimated Sales: $100+ Million
Number Employees: 250-499
Parent Co: Sara Lee Meat Group
Brands:
Best's Kosher
Oscherwitz
Shofar
Sinai Kosher

1285 **Best Maid Cookie Company**
1147 Benson St
River Falls, WI 54022 715-426-2090
Fax: 715-426-1950 888-444-0322
customerservice@bestmaid.com
www.bestmaidcookie.com
Processor of pre-formed frozen cookie dough and baked cookies; also specialty products available.
Co-President: Deb Dartsch
Co-President: Ron Thielen
Number Employees: 50-99
Sq. footage: 20000
Type of Packaging: Food Service, Private Label

1286 **Best Provision Co Inc.**
144 Avon Ave
Newark, NJ 07108 973-242-5000
Fax: 973-648-0041 800-631-4466
bestprovco@aol.com www.bestprovision.com
Processor and exporter of beef including corned, roast, frankfurters, pastrami and bacon
Co-Owner: Leonard Karp
Co-Owner: Kevin Karp
Co-Owner: Richard Dolinko
Human Resource Director: Clara Mendez
Estimated Sales: $35 Million
Number Employees: 105
Sq. footage: 65000
Type of Packaging: Consumer, Food Service

1287 **BestSweet**
288 Mazeppa Rd
Mooresville, NC 28115 704-664-4300
Fax: 704-664-7493 888-211-5530
www.bestsweet.com
Manufacturer of confectinery products, nutritional supplements and cough drops
CEO: Richard Zulman
VP Marketing: Steve Berkowitz
Estimated Sales: $ 50 - 100 Million
Number Employees: 100-249
Type of Packaging: Private Label
Brands:
BASKIN-ROBBINS SMOOTH & CREAMY
HARD
CANDY
FIRE ANTZ
GUMMY GUARD
GUMMY WATCH
SANTA PANTS

1288 **(HQ)Bestfoods**
800 Sylvan Avenue
Englewood Cliffs, NJ 07632-3201 201-567-8000
Fax: 201-894-2244 www.bestfoods.com
Pasta/noodles, ice cream, spaghetti sauce, butter, mayonaise, peanut butter, salad dressings
CEO: John Rice
President: Neil Beckerman
Chief Information Officer: Paul Slator
Chief Engineer: TH Floyd
SVP: Ian Ramsey
VP Sales: Robert Jackson
Estimated Sales: $8.4 Billion
Number Employees: 15000
Sq. footage: 6500
Parent Co: Unilever
Type of Packaging: Consumer, Food Service
Brands:
BEN & JERRY'S
BERTOLLI
BREYERS
GOOD HUMOR
HELLMAN'S
I CAN'T BELIEVE IT'S NOT BUTTER
KLONDIKE
KNORR
KNORR (LIPTON) SIDES
LIPTON
POPSICLE
PROMISE
RAGU
SHEDD'S SPREAD COUNTRY CROCK
SKIPPY
SLIM-FAST
WISH-BONE

1289 **Beta Pure Foods**
335 Spreckels Dr # D
Aptos, CA 95003-3952 831-685-6565
Fax: 831-685-6569 nate.morr@sunopta.com
www.betapure.com
Organic frozen fruits and vegetables, concentrates and purees, sweeteners.
President/CEO: Nate Morr
Number Employees: 5-9
Parent Co: SunOpta
Type of Packaging: Food Service, Private Label, Bulk

1290 **BetaStatin Nutritional Rsearch**
1187 Washington Street
Toms River, NJ 08753-6833 203-869-7778
Fax: 203-869-7774 800-660-9570
sales@betastatin.com www.betastatin.com
Managing Director: Dr Stephen L Newman

1291 **Beth's Fine Desserts**
34 Miller Avenue
Mill Valley, CA 94941 415-464-1891
Fax: 415-925-9941 info@beths.com
www.beths.com
Manufacturer of bite-sized cookies and savory cheese wafers, gourmet gift items, gingerbreads
Brands:
Beth's
Beth's Baking Basics
Heavenly Little Cookies

1292 **Bethel Heights Vineyard Inc.**
6060 Bethel Heights Rd NW
Salem, OR 97304 503-581-2262
Fax: 503-581-0943 info@bethelheights.com
www.bethelheights.com
Wines
President: Pat Dudley
Vice President: Ted Casteel
Director: Pat Dudley
Estimated Sales: $2 Million
Number Employees: 27
Type of Packaging: Private Label

1293 **Betsy's Cheese Straws**
P.O.Box 111
Chattanooga, TN 37401 334-285-1354
Fax: 800-625-9700 877-902-3141
elizabeth@moonpie.com
www.betsyscheesestraws.com
Cheese straws
President/Owner: Betsy Parker
Number Employees: 6

1294 **Bettah Buttah, LLC**
111 Southwest Blvd
Kansas City, KS 66103-2132 913-432-5228
Fax: 913-432-5880 800-568-8468
jpolo@originaljuan.com www.bettahbuttah.com
Manufacturer of Specialty foods, snacks, hot sauces, condiments, seasonings, salsas, barbeque sauces
President: Joe Polo
Estimated Sales: Less than $500,000
Number Employees: 20-49
Brands:
CAJUN BAYOU
CALIDO CHILE TRADERS
FIESTA
JOSE GOLDSTEIN
ORIGINAL JUAN
PANISGOOD
TEXAS LONGHORN
WILD AND MILD

1295 **Bette's Diner Products**
1807 4th St
Berkeley, CA 94710-1910 510-644-3230
Fax: 510-644-3209 bettesdiner@worldpantry.com
www.bettesdiner.com
Manufacturer and exporter of pancake mixes including buttermilk, oatmeal and buckwheat; also, scone mixes including raisin, cranberry and lemon currant
President: Manfred Kroening
VP: Bette Kroening
Number Employees: 5-9
Type of Packaging: Consumer, Food Service
Brands:
Bette's Oceanview Diner

1296 **Better Bagel Bakery**
4854 S Tamiami Trl
Sarasota, FL 34231-4352 941-924-0393
Fax: 941-924-0358
Processor of baked goods such as; breads, rolls, bagels, etc
Owner: Jun Park
Estimated Sales: Less than $100,000
Number Employees: 1-4

1297 **Better Baked Foods**
56 Smedley St
North East, PA 16428 814-725-8778
Fax: 814-725-5021 www.betterbaked.com
French bread pizza, panini sandwiches, appetizers, garlic breads, breakfast items, and desserts.
President/COO: Joseph Pacinelli
CEO: Chris Miller
Quality Assurance: Connie Dibacco
Marketing Director: Chad Lindholm
VP Sales: David Elchynski
Human Resources Director: Mike Kostelnik
Plant Operations Director: Gerard Pacinelli
Production Manager: Rose Baybrook
Plant Manager: Scott Carpenter
Purchasing Manager: John Shifler
Estimated Sales: $20-50 Million
Number Employees: 400
Sq. footage: 200000
Type of Packaging: Private Label

1298 **Better Beverages**
10624 Midway Ave
Cerritos, CA 90703 562-924-8321
Fax: 562-924-6204 www.betbev.com
Processor of soft drinks; wholesaler/distributor of soft drinks and juices; serving the food service market
Owner: Ronald Harris
CEO: G Harris
Estimated Sales: $ 20 - 50 Million
Number Employees: 40
Type of Packaging: Consumer, Food Service
Brands:
Rc Cola

1299 **Better Living Products**
208 Harvard Drive
Princeton, TX 75407 972-736-6691
Fax: 903-298-0014 zetawize@yahoo.com
www.betterlivingusa.com
Processor, importer of kava kava powder, aloe vera juice and herbs
COO: Ed Carter
Estimated Sales: Less than $500,000
Number Employees: 1-4
Parent Co: Zeta Wize LLC Company
Brands:
KAVA KAVA
NONI NONU

1300 **Better Made Snack Foods**
10148 Gratiot Ave
Detroit, MI 48213 313-925-4774
Fax: 313-925-6028 800-332-2394
info@bettermadesnackfoods.com bmchips.com
Potato chips, popcorn, crunchy chips, pretzels, pork rinds, tortilla chips, beef jerky, chocolate covered potato chips and pretzels, salsas and cheese dips.
Owner: Patti Hughes
President: Sam Cipriano
CFO: Mark Winkleman
VP: Salvatore Cipriano
Quality Manager: Monna Via
Marketing Manager: Mike Esseltine
Sales Director/Marketing Manager: Mark Costello
Chief of Operations/General Manager: Michael Schena
Production Manager: Alan Lee
Estimated Sales: $20-50 Million
Number Employees: 152
Sq. footage: 34000
Type of Packaging: Consumer, Food Service
Brands:
Better Made

1301 **Better Meat North**
P.O.Box 1100
Bay City, MI 48706-0100 989-684-6271
Fax: 989-684-6390
Processor of potato chips, popcorn and cheese curls and puffs; wholesaler/distributor of snack foods including pork rinds, puffs and tortillas; private labeling and co-packing available
Manager: Mike Esseltine
Estimated Sales: $ 20 - 50 Million
Number Employees: 20-49
Parent Co: Cross & Peters
Type of Packaging: Consumer, Private Label
Brands:
Made Rite

1302 **BetterBody Foods & Nutrition LLC**
1762 W 20 S Ste 500
Lindon, UT 84042-1762
Fax: 801-456-2601 866-404-6582
info@xagave.com www.xagave.com
President/Owner: Stephen Richards

1303 **(HQ)Betty Jane Homemade Candies**
3049 Asbury Rd
Dubuque, IA 52001 563-582-4668
Fax: 563-582-2150 800-642-1254
www.bettyjanecandies.com
Manufacturer of candy
President/CEO: John Heinz Jr
Vice President: George Hagge
Estimated Sales: $5-10 Million
Number Employees: 15
Type of Packaging: Consumer
Brands:
GREMLINS

1304 **Betty Lou's Golden Smackers**
P.O.Box 537
McMinnville, OR 97128-0537 503-434-5205
Fax: 503-472-8643 800-242-5205
bettylous@.onlinemac.com
www.bettylousinc.com
Processor and exporter of oil and, low-fat oven baked apple butter, low-fat and wheat-free fruit bars and fat-free cookies, snack foods and candies, protein bars
Owner: Betty Carrier
VP Sales: John Sizemore
Estimated Sales: $2.5-5 Million
Number Employees: 20-49
Sq. footage: 9000
Type of Packaging: Consumer, Private Label
Brands:
Betty Lou's

1305 **Bevco**
9354 - 194th Street
Surrey, BC V4N 4E9
Canada 604-888-1455
Fax: 604-888-2887 800-663-0090
info@bevco.net www.bevco.net
Processor and co-packer of fruit juices, citrus drinks and bottled water
President/Board Member: Brian Fortier
Board Member: Donna Fortier
Estimated Sales: $5-10 Million
Number Employees: 10-19
Type of Packaging: Consumer, Private Label
Brands:
Juicetyme Delites
O-Jay
Watertyme
Wild Springs

1306 **(HQ)Beverage America**
545 E 32nd St
Holland, MI 49423-5495 616-396-1281
Fax: 616-396-8121
Bottled water, fruit beverages, Snapple
Plant Manufacturing: Dale Stein
Estimated Sales: $ 5 - 10 Million
Number Employees: 5-9

1307 **Beverage Capital Corporation**
2209 Sulphur Spring Rd
Baltimore, MD 21227-2933 410-242-7003
Fax: 410-247-2977 info@beveragecapital.com
www.beveragecapital.com
Processor and exporter of bottled and canned soft and juice drinks and juice; also, seltzer water; contract packaging available
President: Jim Sheridan
VP: Rick Smith
Estimated Sales: $50-100 Million
Number Employees: 100-249
Sq. footage: 400000
Type of Packaging: Consumer, Private Label
Other Locations:
Whitehead Court Manufacturing
Baltimore MD

30th Street Manufacturing
Baltimore MD
Brands:
BEVNET
CADBURY SCHWEPPES
CANADA DRY
ENERGY BRAND
MISTIC
SNAPPLE

1308 **Beverage House**
400 High Point Rd SE
Cartersville, GA 30120 770-387-0451
Fax: 770-387-1809 888-367-8327
info@beveragehouse.com
www.beveragehouse.com
Coffee, tea and beverage concentrates
Manager: Jimmy Garren
Marketing Manager: Robbin McCool
Number Employees: 10-19
Type of Packaging: Private Label
Brands:
NEW SOUTHERN TRADITION TEAS
REEDY BREW TEAS

1309 **Beverage Specialties**
196 Newton St
Fredonia, NY 14063-1354 716-673-1000
Fax: 716-679-7702 800-462-8125
www.carriagehousecos.com
Non-alcoholic cocktail mixes and Bloody Mary mix under the Major Peters & Jero labels.
President: David Skarie
Quality Control: Joe Woloseyn
Marketing: Dan Bensur
Director Sales: Kevin Dress
Public Relations: Mary Jane Knight
Operations: Mark Chamberlain
Estimated Sales: I
Number Employees: 1500
Number of Brands: 2
Parent Co: The Carriage House Companies/Ralcorp
Type of Packaging: Consumer, Food Service, Private Label
Brands:
JERO
MAJOR PETERS

1310 **Beverage Technologies**
5 Connerty Court
East Brunswick, NJ 08816-1633 888-204-4299
Fax: 732-254-5736
Processor of coffee concentrates
Type of Packaging: Food Service
Brands:
La Spezzia

1311 **Beverly International Nutrition**
1768 Industrial Rd
Cold Spring, KY 41076-8610 859-781-3474
Fax: 859-781-7590 800-888-3364
support@beverlyintl.com
www.bodybuildingworld.com
Manufacturer and exporter of multiple vitamin and mineral packs; also, protein powders
Owner: Roger Riedinger
Owner: Sandy Riedinger
Estimated Sales: Less than $500,000
Number Employees: 10-19
Type of Packaging: Consumer, Food Service, Private Label
Brands:
BEVERLY INTERNATIONAL

1312 **Bi Nutraceuticals**
2550 E El Presidio St
Long Beach, CA 90810 310-669-2100
Fax: 310-637-3644 www.binutraceuticals.com
Manufacturer and distributor of water soluable extracts, pre-mixes, herb powders and teas.

1313 **Bi-O-Kleen Industry**
PO Box 2679
Clackamas, OR 97015-2679 360-260-1587
Fax: 503-557-7818 crluvearth@msn.com

1314 **Biagio's Banquets**
4242 N Central Ave
Chicago, IL 60634-1810 773-736-9009
Fax: 773-587-3011 800-392-2837
rperrye@aol.com www.suparossa.com
Processor and exporter of pasta, breaded appetizers and pizza including deep dish, thin crust, pan and self-rising
President: Samuel Cirrincione
General Manager: Tom Cirrincione
Estimated Sales: $10-20 Million
Number Employees: 20-49
Sq. footage: 30000
Brands:
Suparossa

1315 **Bianchi Winery**
3380 Branch Road
Paso Robles, CA 93446 805-226-9922
Fax: 805-226-8230 sales@bianchiwine.com
www.bianchiwine.com
Manufacturer and exporter of red and white wines
Owner: Glenn Bianchi
CFO: Mike Gardnier
Vice President: Albert Paul
Estimated Sales: $5 Million
Number Employees: 10-19
Number of Brands: 3
Number of Products: 20
Type of Packaging: Consumer, Food Service, Bulk
Brands:
Bianchi Vineyards
Chateau Cellars
Domaine Noel
Vista Verde

1316 **Bias Vineyards & Winery**
3166 Highway B
Berger, MO 63014 573-834-5475
Fax: 573-834-2046 www.biaswinery.com
Wines
President: Carol Grass
VP: Kirk Grass
Purchasing Director: Carol Grass
Estimated Sales: $1-2.5 Million
Number Employees: 1-4
Type of Packaging: Private Label

1317 **Biazzo Dairy Products**
1145 Edgewater Ave
Ridgefield, NJ 7657 201-941-6800
Fax: 201-941-4151 info@biazzo.com
www.biazzo.com
Processor and exporter of fresh, chunk and shredded mozzarella, ricotta and string cheese.
President: John Iapichino Jr
Vice President: John Iapichino, Jr.
Sales Director: Tim Holden
Plant Manager: Joe Iapichino
Estimated Sales: $ 20 - 50 Million
Number Employees: 20-49
Sq. footage: 58000
Type of Packaging: Consumer, Food Service, Private Label, Bulk
Brands:
BIAZZO BRAND
PRIVATE LABEL

1318 **Bickel's Potato Chip Company**
51 N Main St
Manheim, PA 17545-1503 717-665-2002
Fax: 717-665-5449 www.bickelssnacks.com
Warehouse location for Bickel's potato chips.
President: John Wareheine
Controller: Gary Knisely
Director Sales: Ed Dobkel
Plant Manager: Jay Epstein
Purchasing Director: Nellie Redding
Estimated Sales: $10-24.9 Million
Number Employees: 5-9
Type of Packaging: Consumer
Brands:
Bickel's

1319 **(HQ)Bickel's Snack Foods Inc**
PO Box 2427
York, PA 17405
800-233-1933
www.bickelssnacks.com
Potato chips, pretzels and other snack foods.
Manager: Jeff Warhime
Controller: Gary Knisely
Sales: Michael Carter
Operations: Wade Fitzkee
Purchasing: Allen Young
Estimated Sales: $20-50 Million
Number Employees: 1,000-4,999
Parent Co: Hanover Foods
Type of Packaging: Private Label, Bulk
Brands:
BICKEL'S
BON-TON
CABANA
GOLDEN GOURMET
WEGE

1320 **Bickels Snacks**
P.O.Box 2427
York, PA 17405-2427 717-843-0738
Fax: 717-843-5192
customerservice@bickelsnacks.com
www.bickelssnacks.com
Snack food products
Manager: Jeff Warhime
Marketing/Advertising Manager: Jerry Neidigh
Sales Manager: Ed Doekel
Plant Manager: Gary Glatselter
Estimated Sales: $ 20-50 Million
Number Employees: 1,000-4,999
Type of Packaging: Private Label
Brands:
Bickle Snacks

1321 **Bickford Daniel LobsterCompany**
Lanes Is
Vinalhaven, ME 04863 207-863-4688
Fax: 207-863-4525
Lobster
Estimated Sales: $ 1 - 3 Million
Number Employees: 5-9

1322 **Bickford Flavors**
19007 Saint Clair Ave
Cleveland, OH 44117 216-531-6006
Fax: 216-531-2006 800-283-8322
orders@bickfordflavors.com
www.bickfordflavors.com
Processor of extracts including vanilla and assorted flavoring
President: Scott Sofer
Operations: Heather Noel
Estimated Sales: $2.5-5 Million
Number Employees: 5-9
Number of Brands: 1
Number of Products: 150
Sq. footage: 15000
Type of Packaging: Private Label
Brands:
Bickford

1323 **Bidwell Candies**
1610 Broadway Ave
Mattoon, IL 61938 217-234-3858
Fax: 217-234-3856 barbara@bidwellcandies.com
www.bidwellcandies.com
Manufactures chocolates and candies
Owner: Greg Kuhl
Plant Manager: Judy Brown
Estimated Sales: Less than $500,000
Number Employees: 5-9

1324 **Bidwell Vineyard**
18910 Middle Rd # 48
Cutchogue, NY 11935-1069 631-734-5200
Fax: 631-734-6763
Wines
Owner: Rose Pipia
Purchasing Director: James Bidwell
Estimated Sales: $1-2.5 Million appx.
Number Employees: 1-4
Brands:
CARBERNET SAUVIGNON
CHARDONNAY
COUNTRY GARDENS BLUSH BANQUET
MERLOT
SAUVIGNON BLANC
WHITE RIESLING

1325 **Bien Padre Foods**
P.O.Box 3748
Eureka, CA 95502-3748 707-442-4585
Fax: 707-442-4584 sales@bienpadre.com
www.bienpadre.com
Manufacturer and exporter of tortilla chips, corn and flour tortillas and salsas
President: Benito Lim
Estimated Sales: $1-2.5 Million
Number Employees: 20-49
Sq. footage: 14000
Type of Packaging: Consumer, Food Service, Private Label, Bulk

1326 **Bieri's Jackson Cheese**
3271 County Road P
Jackson, WI 53037 262-677-3227
Fax: 262-677-3480 annette@bierischeese.com
www.bierischeese.com
Retailers of the finest Wisconsin cheeses
Owner: Annette Du Bois
Co-Owner/CEO: Wayne Dubois
Estimated Sales: $300,000-500,000
Number Employees: 5-9
Type of Packaging: Bulk

1327 **Bierig Brothers**
3539 Reilly Ct
Vineland, NJ 8360 856-691-8208
Fax: 856-692-7869 sales@bierigbros.com
www.bierigbros.com
Processor of veal
President: Herbert Bierig
Manager: Danny Bierig
Purchasing Director: Herbert Bierig
Estimated Sales: $10-20 Million
Number Employees: 10

1328 **Biery Cheese Company**
6544 Paris Ave
Louisville, OH 44641 330-875-3381
Fax: 330-875-5896 800-243-3731
www.bierycheese.com
Processor of cheese
President: Jeff Fairless
CEO: Dennis Biery
Finance Director: Louanne Kiko
Quality Control Executive: Scott Schillig
Marketing Manager: Bob Bollas
Human Resources Director: Mike Fairless
Operations Manager: Ben Biery
Production Manager: Todd Hadorn
Purchasing Manager: Jeff Linerode
Estimated Sales: $40 Million
Number Employees: 250
Sq. footage: 110000
Type of Packaging: Consumer, Food Service, Private Label, Bulk
Brands:
Biery

1329 **Bifulco Farms**
590 Almond Rd
Pittsgrove, NJ 8318 856-692-0707
Fax: 856-696-5445 www.bifulco.com
Manufacturer of parsley, peppers, tomatoes and zucchini
Secretary: Mrs. Bifulco
Estimated Sales: $2.5-5 Million
Number Employees: 5-9
Type of Packaging: Consumer, Bulk
Brands:
Tall-Boy

1330 **Big Al's Seafood**
P.O.Box 293
Bozman, MD 21612 410-745-2637
Fax: 410-745-9046
Manufacturer of wholesaler/distributor of crabs, clams, fish and oysters
Owner: Alan Poore
Estimated Sales: Less than $500,000
Number Employees: 5-9
Sq. footage: 6000
Type of Packaging: Consumer

1331 **Big B Distributors**
P.O.Box 996
Evansville, IN 47706-0996 812-425-5235
Fax: 812-428-8432
Manufacturer of sauces, pepperoncinis, chili, pork barbecue, sloppy joes, vinegar, salsa and pickled products
President: Bob Bonenberger
CEO: Rich Bonenberger
Estimated Sales: $5-9.9 Million
Number Employees: 10-19
Type of Packaging: Consumer, Food Service, Private Label, Bulk
Brands:
Big B
Frontier Gold

1332 **Big Bucks Brewery & Steakhouse**
P.O.Box 7049
Bloomfield Hills, MI 48302-7049
Fax: 989-732-3990 information@bigbuck.com
www.bigbuck.com
Processor of beer, ale, lager and stout
Manager: Tracy Dalman
Estimated Sales: $2.5-5 Million
Number Employees: 1-4
Type of Packaging: Consumer, Food Service

1333 **Big Chief Meat Snacks In**
3900 52 Ave NW
Calgary, AB T3J 3X4
Canada 403-264-2641
Fax: 403-262-9053
snacks@bigchiefbeefjerky.com
www.bigchiefbeefjerky.com
Manufacturer of snack meats including pepperoni and teriyaki sticks, beef jerky and kippered beef
Founder: William Klein
Estimated Sales: C
Number Employees: 17
Type of Packaging: Consumer
Brands:
Big Chief
Old Dutch

1334 **Big City Reds**
4430 S 110th Street
Omaha, NE 68137-1217 847-714-1640
Fax: 847-714-1647 800-759-5275
info@bigcityreds.com www.bigcityreds.com
Manufacturer of all beef hotdogs, frankfurters and sausage including Polish and cocktail
President: Michael Sternberg
VP Marketing: Rebecca Sternberg
National Sales Manager: Robin Warren
Estimated Sales: $5-10 Million
Number Employees: 5-9
Type of Packaging: Consumer, Food Service, Private Label
Brands:
Big City Reds

1335 **Big Fatty's Flaming Foods**
639 County Road 240
Valley View, TX 76272 940-726-3741
Fax: 940-726-6257 888-248-6332
whatscookin@bigfattys.com www.bigfattys.com
Spicy foods; biscotti, spice rubs and cornbread.
President/Owner: Gail Patterson
VP: Ricky Patterson
Estimated Sales: $300,000-500,000
Number Employees: 1-4

1336 **Big Island Candies**
585 Hinano Street
Hilo, HI 96720 808-935-8890
Fax: 808-961-0659 800-935-5510
contactus@bigislandcandies.com
www.bigislandcandies.com
Manufacturer if macadamia nut cookies and chocolates
President/CEO: Allan Ikawa
CFO: Paul Pakele
Marketing/PR/Retail Operations Manager: Lance Duyao
COO/VP Sales/Marketing: Sherrie Holi
Estimated Sales: $58 Million
Number Employees: 90

1337 **Big Island Seafood, LLC**
1201 University Drive NE
Atlanta, GA 30306-2504 404-366-8667
Fax: 404-366-9129
Tuna, swordfish, snapper, grouper, sea bass, mahi-mahi, tilapia, seafood

1338 **Big J. Milling & Elevato Company**
733 W Forest St
Brigham City, UT 84302 435-723-3459
Fax: 435-723-3450
Manufacturer of grain and flour
President: John Reese
Owner: Mike Chadwick
Owner: Ken Sutton
Vice President: Ray Reese
Estimated Sales: $2.6 Million
Number Employees: 20
Type of Packaging: Consumer, Food Service, Private Label

1339 **Big Red Bottling**
6500 River Place Boulevard
Building 1
Austin, TX 78730 254-772-7791
Fax: 254-772-2441 www.bigredltd.com
Manufacturer of carbonated soft drinks
CEO: Don Sharp
CEO: Gary Smith
Estimated Sales: $20-50 Million
Number Employees: 20-49

1340 **Big River Seafood**
PO Box 77980
Baton Rouge, LA 70879-7980 225-751-1116
Fax: 225-751-1108
Seafood
President: Lisa Porsche

1341 **Big Rock Brewery**
5555 76th Avenue SE
Calgary, AB T2C 4L8
Canada 403-720-3239
Fax: 403-236-7523 800-242-3107
beer@bigrockbeer.com www.bigrockbeer.com
Processor of beer, ale, stout and lager
President: E McNally
Marketing Director: Jessica Barrie
CFO: Tim Duffin
Estimated Sales: G
Number Employees: 100-249
Type of Packaging: Consumer, Food Service
Brands:
Traditional

1342 **Big Shoulders Baking**
4014 N Rockwell St
Chicago, IL 60618-3721 773-463-6328
Fax: 773-463-7101 800-456-9328
kat@littlemissmuffin.com
www.bigshouldersbaking.com
Four flavors of cookies
Owner: Staci Minic Mintz
Estimated Sales: $ 20 - 50 Million
Number Employees: 20-49

1343 **(HQ)Big Sky Brands**
3289 Lenworth Drive, Unit A
Mississauga, ON L4X 2H1
Canada 416-599-5415
Fax: 416-599-0392 888-624-4759
luke@bigskybrands.com www.bigskybrands.com
Candy and mints.
President/Owner: Ron Cheng
VP: Steve Yacht
Type of Packaging: Private Label
Other Locations:
Big Sky Brands
Chicago IL
Big Sky Brands
Buffalo NY
Big Sky Brands
Los Angeles CA
Brands:
CO2 HARD CANDY
DIABLO IGNITED SOURS
DRIVE ACTIVATED
GREEN-T ENERGY MINTS
JONES SODA CARBONATED CANDY
JONES SODA CARBONATED SOURS
JONES SODA ENERGY BOOSTERS
JONES SOURS
LOVE MINTS
MAKE OUT MINTS
PLAYBOY MINTS
WARP ENERGY MINTS
WARP MICRO HYPER CHARGED MINTS

1344 **Big Sky Brewing Company**
P.O.Box 17170
Missoula, MT 59808 406-549-2777
Fax: 406-549-1919 800-559-2774
info@bigskybrew.com www.bigskybrew.com
Processor of ale and stout
President: Neal Leathers
VP: Bjorn Nabozney
VP Production: Kris Nabozney
Estimated Sales: $3 Million
Number Employees: 32
Sq. footage: 24000
Type of Packaging: Consumer, Food Service, Bulk
Brands:
BIG SKY IPA
MOOSE DROOL BROWN ALE
POWDER HOUND WINTER ALE
SCAPE GOAT PALE ALE
SUMMER HONEY SEASONAL ALE
TROUT SLAYER ALE

1345 **Big Steer Enterprises**
P.O.Box 5413
Beaumont, TX 77726 409-866-3198
Fax: 409-866-0734 800-421-4951
juwhi4@aol.com www.bigsteer.biz
Manufacturer microwave fudge and gourmet snack mixes
President: Grant Nichols
Estimated Sales: $1-2.5 Million
Number Employees: 1-4
Type of Packaging: Private Label

1346 **Big Train Inc**
25392 Commercentre Dr
Lake Forest, CA 92630 949-340-8800
Fax: 949-707-1000 800-244-8724
info@bigtrain.com www.bigtrain.com
Processor of ice blended coffees and flavored syrups.
Manager: Steve Schartg
CEO: Mike Dunn
CFO: Kevin Smith
VP, Supply Chain: Steve Scharetg
International Sales: Rachel Pena
Customer Service Supervisor: Shannon Haskill
Estimated Sales: $10-12 Million
Number Employees: 1-4
Sq. footage: 18000
Type of Packaging: Bulk

1347 **Bigelow Tea**
201 Black Rock Turnpike
Fairfield, CT 06825 203-929-2254
Fax: 203-926-0916 888-244-3569
sales@imsfood.com
www.bigelowtea.com/foodservice
Processor of tea bags and tea including organic, loose, hot and iced
President: Cynthia Bigelow
Co-CEO: David Bigelow Jr.
Co-CEO: Eunice Bigelow
Estimated Sales: $ 5 - 10 Million
Number Employees: 20-49
Brands:
Bigelow

1348 **Bijol & Spices, Inc.**
2154 NW 22nd Court
Miami, FL 33242 305-634-9030
Fax: 305-634-7454 888-BIJ-L 70
www.bijol.com
Contract packager and exporter of spices and herbs
President: Idi Borges
Estimated Sales: $2.5-5 Million
Number Employees: 10-19
Type of Packaging: Consumer

1349 **Bilgore's Groves**
PO Box 1958
Clearwater, FL 33757-1958 727-442-2171
Fax: 727-446-3998
Fruits
Manager: Evelyn Tumber
Estimated Sales: $500-1 Million appx.
Number Employees: 1-4

1350 **Bill Lowden Seafood**
PO Box 327
Warren, ME 04864-0327 207-273-2162
Fax: 207-273-1162
Seafood
Principal: Bill Lowden

1351 **Bill Mack's Homemade Ice Cream**
3890 Carlisle Rd
Dover, PA 17315-4418 717-292-1931
Manufacturer of ice cream including chocolate, vanilla, oreo cookie, peanut butter, raspberry, banana, caramel, strawberry, etc.
Owner: Todd Mc Daniel
Estimated Sales: $500,000-$1 Million
Number Employees: 20-49
Type of Packaging: Consumer
Brands:
Bill Mack's

1352 **Bill's Seafood**
9016 Belair Rd
Baltimore, MD 21236 410-256-9520
Fax: 410-256-3491
Seafood
Owner: Bill Paulshock
Estimated Sales: $ 5 - 10 Million
Number Employees: 20-49

1353 **(HQ)Billingsgate Fish Company**
630 7th Avenue SE
Calgary, AB T2G 0J7
Canada 403-571-7700
Fax: 403-571-7717 www.billingsgate.com
Processor and packager of fish, meat and deli products; wholesaler/distributor of meats and seafood; serving the food service market
President: Bryan Fallwell
Sales Representative: Brenda Shreindorfer
Operations Manager: Mark Puffer
Estimated Sales: $2.8 Million
Number Employees: 20
Sq. footage: 35000
Type of Packaging: Consumer, Food Service
Other Locations:
Billingsgate Fish Company
Edmonton, Alberta
Billingsgate Fish Company
St. Albert, Alberta
Brands:
Billingsgate
King of Fish
Plough Boy

1354 **Billy's Seafood**
16780 River Rd
Bon Secour, AL 36511 251-949-6288
Fax: 251-949-6505 www.billys-seafood.com
Seafood
Owner: Billy Parks
Estimated Sales: $2,000,000
Number Employees: 5-9

1355 **Biltmore Estate Wine Company**
1 Antler Hill Road
Asheville, NC 28803 828-225-1776
Fax: 828-225-6383 800-411-3812
snowak@biltmore.com www.biltmore.com
Wines
President/CEO: William Cecil
EVP: Stephen Miller
Executive Director: Beth Poslusny
Operations: Bernard Delille
Estimated Sales: $10-20 Million
Number Employees: 120

1356 **Biltmore Trading LLC**
4818 E Peak View Rd
Cave Creek, AZ 85331 480-502-7500
Fax: 480-502-7503
Food broker
Estimated Sales: $ 3 - 5 Million
Number Employees: 1-4

1357 **(HQ)Bimbo Bakeries**
255 Business Center Drive
Horsham, PA 19044-2861
Fax: 610-320-9286 800-984-0989
contactBBU@bimbobakeriesusa.com
www.bimbobakeriesusa.com
Breads, rolls, buns, tortillas, chips, snack cakes, cookies, donuts, cakes and pastries.
President: Gary Prince
Brand Manager: Cristina Torres
Sales Director: Phil Harley
SVP/Operations: Dan Babin
Estimated Sales: $4 Billion
Number Employees: 18000
Sq. footage: 11000
Parent Co: Grupo Bimbo
Brands:
ARNOLD
BIMBO
BOBOLI
BROWNBERRY
ENTENMANN'S
FRANCISCO
FREIHOFER'S
MARINELA
MRS BAIRD'S
OLD COUNTRY BREAD
OROWEAT
STROEHMANN
THOMAS'
TIA ROSA

1358 **Binding Brauerei USA**
194 Main St
Norwalk, CT 06851-3502 203-229-0111
Fax: 203-229-0105 bbusa@optonline.net
www.clausthaler.com
Beer and ale.
President: Hans Schliebs
CEO: Dilip Mehta
VP Sales: Dave Deuser
COO: Dilip Mehta
Estimated Sales: $5-10 Million
Number Employees: 10-19
Parent Co: Radeberger Gruppe GmbH
Brands:
CLAUSTHALER
DAB
KRUSOVICE
RADEBERGER
TUCHER

1359 **Bingo Salsa, LLC**
2001 Nw Swanlund Street
Poulsbo, WA 98370-9528 360-779-6746
Fax: 360-930-8377 bingosalsa67@yahoo.com
www.bingosalsas.com
Makers of salsa.

1360 **Binkert's Meat Products**
8805 Philadelphia Rd
Baltimore, MD 21237 410-687-5959
Fax: 410-687-5023
Sausage and other prepared meats
Owner: Sonya Weber
President: Sonya Weber
Estimated Sales: $300,000-$310,000
Number Employees: 1-4
Brands:
Binkert's

1361 **Binns Vineyards & Winery**
1501 S Don Roser Dr
Las Cruces, NM 88011-4538 575-522-2211
Fax: 575-522-1112
Wines
Owner: Eddie Binns
Vice President: Glenn Binns
Estimated Sales: $1-4.9 Million
Number Employees: 5-9
Type of Packaging: Private Label

1362 **Bio San Laboratories/MegaFood**
P.O.Box 325
Derry, NH 03038-0325 603-432-5022
Fax: 603-434-4736 800-848-5022
info@biosan.net www.biosanlabs.com
Processor of food nutrients; exporter of food supplements
President: Carl Jackson
V.P. Mfg.: Richard Lafond
Estimated Sales: $20-50 Million
Number Employees: 50-99
Type of Packaging: Consumer
Brands:
Daily Foods
Essentials
Megafood
Nutritional Therapeutix

1363 **Bio-Foods**
P.O.Box 622
Pine Brook, NJ 7058 973-808-5856
Fax: 973-396-2999 bobkoetzner@aol.com
www.biofoodsltd.com
Manufacturer and exporter of nutrients
President: Bharat Patel
Vice President: Robert Koetzner
Number Employees: 6
Sq. footage: 9000
Type of Packaging: Bulk
Brands:
BIO-FOODS

1364 **Bio-Hydration Research Lab**
1900 Avenue of the Stars Fl 7
Los Angeles, CA 90067 760-438-6686
Fax: 760-268-0808 800-531-5088
www.pentawater.com
Manufacturer of Bio-Hydration; a molecular restructured water that hydrates faster and provides enhanced performance and healthy living
CEO: Bill Holloway
CEO: Dennis O'Bryan
Public Relations Manager: Jeffrey Pizzino
Estimated Sales: $ 5 - 10 Million
Number Employees: 50-99
Number of Brands: 1
Number of Products: 2
Sq. footage: 110000
Type of Packaging: Consumer

Brands:
PENTA

1365 Bio-K + International
495 Boulevard Armand - Frappier
Laval, QC H7V 4B3
Canada 450-978-2465
Fax: 450-978-9729 800-593-2465
info@biokplus.com www.biokplus.com
President: Claude Chevalier
Marketing Director: Michael Sirdemt
CFO: Michael Rheault
Brands:
Bio K

1366 Bio-Nutritional Products
119 Rockland Ave
Northvale, NJ 07647-2144 201-784-8200
Fax: 201-784-8201
President: Stephen Difolco
Brands:
Eugalan
Lacto

1367 Bio-Tech Pharmacal
P.O.Box 1927
Fayetteville, AR 72702-1927 479-443-9148
Fax: 479-443-5643 800-345-1199
service@bio-tech-pharm.com
www.bio-tech-pharm.com
Manufacturer of hypo-allergenic nutraceuticals, vitamins, minerals, herbals, anti-oxidants, amino acids, etc
Owner: Dale Benedict
CFO: Martha Bendike
Estimated Sales: $ 10 - 20 Million
Number Employees: 10-19
Type of Packaging: Consumer, Private Label, Bulk
Brands:
Bio-Tech Pharmacal

1368 BioSynergy
P.O.Box 16833
Boise, ID 83715-6833 208-342-6660
Fax: 208-342-0880 800-554-7145
email@biosynergy.com www.biosynergy.com
Processor of health related products
President: Ted Kremer
Marketing Director: Hidemi Kremer
Estimated Sales: $200,000
Number Employees: 1-4
Brands:
Nojo

1369 (HQ)BioTech Corporation
107 Oakwood Dr Ste E
Glastonbury, CT 06033 860-633-8111
Fax: 860-682-6863 800-880-7188
info@biotechcorp.com www.biotechcorp.com
Nutraceuticals and nutritional supplements.
President: Gregory Kelly
Estimated Sales: $ 5 - 10 Million
Number Employees: 10-19

1370 Bioforce USA
6 Grandinetti Drive
Ghent, NY 12075 518-828-9111
Fax: 888-798-7555 800-641-7555
Info@BioforceUSA.com www.bioforceusa.com
Natural products, vitamins, etc.
President: Paul Ross
Sales Manager: Rich Manziello
Operations Manager: Roberts Sheets
Estimated Sales: $300,000-500,000
Number Employees: 1-4
Brands:
A. Vogel

1371 Bionutritional ResearchGroup
15375 Barranca Pkwy Ste C104
Irvine, CA 92618-2206
Fax: 714-427-6998 nadine@bnrg.com
www.bnrg.com
Nutritional products, protein powder and bars, supplements.
President/CEO: Kevin Lawrence
VP Sales: Ken Braunstein
VP Operations: Tom Williams
Estimated Sales: $15 Million
Number Employees: 5-9
Brands:
ALPHA GLUTAMINE
CELL CHARGE®
POWER CRUNCH®
PROTO WHEY®

1372 Biotec AZ Laboratories
20809 N 19th Avenue
Suite 1
Phoenix, AZ 85027-3519 800-218-6979
Fax: 623-576-2285 www.biotechazlabs.com
Supplements and vitamins.
President: Tyler Rosales

1373 Biothera
3388 Mike Collins Dr Ste A
Saint Paul, MN 55121 651-675-0300
Fax: 651-657-0400 info@biotheraoharma.com
www.biopolymer.com
Markets food-grade immune-enhancing ingredients for the nutritional supplement, functional food, cosmetic and the animal feed nutrition markets.
Founder: Dan Conners
President/CEO: Richard G Mueller
CFO: Julie R Streed
CEO: Richard Mueller
VP Sales and Marketing: Allen F Porter
Estimated Sales: $ 3 - 5 Million
Number Employees: 10-19
Type of Packaging: Bulk

1374 Birch Street Seafoods
31 Birch St
Digby, NS B0V 1A0
Canada 902-245-6551
Fax: 902-245-6554
Processor and exporter of fresh and frozen salted groundfish
Vice President: William Cottreau
Plant Manager: Alan Frankland
Estimated Sales: $12 Million
Number Employees: 32
Type of Packaging: Consumer, Food Service, Private Label, Bulk

1375 Birchwood Foods
P.O.Box 639
Kenosha, WI 53141 262-859-2881
Fax: 262-859-2078 800-541-1685
bwinfo@bwfoods.com www.bwfoods.com
Manufactuer and exporter of cryogenically frozen and vacuum-packed fresh ground beef in bulk and patties; importer of boneless beef
President/CEO: Dennis Vignieri
CFO: Jerry King
VP Sales/National Accounts: David Van Kampen
Corporate HR/Safety Director: Phyllis Murray
EVP Operations & Procurement: John Ruffolo
Estimated Sales: $300 Million
Number Employees: 250-499
Parent Co: Kenosha Beef International
Type of Packaging: Consumer, Food Service, Private Label, Bulk
Other Locations:
Frankfort Manufacturing Facility
Frankfort IN
Columbus Manufacturing Facility
Columbus OH
Atlanta Manufacturing Facility
Atlanta GA

1376 Bird-In-Hand Farms, Inc.
1708 Columbia Ave
Lancaster, PA 17603-4550 717-291-5855
Fax: 717-291-1990 ted.bloom@bihfarms.com
www.bihfarms.com
Poultry
President: Fred Bloom
VP Sales: Ted Bloom
Estimated Sales: $5-10 Million
Number Employees: 5-9
Type of Packaging: Private Label
Other Locations:
Bird-In-Hand Farms
Chapin SC
Bird-In-Hand Farms
Jackson MI
Bird-In-Hand Farms
Huntington IN
Bird-In-Hand Farms
Nacogdoches TX
Bird-In-Hand Farms
Monett MO
Bird-In-Hand Farms
Topsail Beach NC
Bird-In-Hand Farms
Russellville AR
Bird-In-Hand Farms
Southern Pines NC
Brands:
BIRD-IN-HAND
TRULY DUTCH

1377 Birdie Pak Products
3925 W 31st St
Chicago, IL 60623 773-247-5293
Fax: 773-247-4280 Kevin@birdiepak.com
www.birdiepak.com
Processor and distributor of frozen beef, poultry and fish
President: Thomas Krueger
VP: Kevin Krueger
Estimated Sales: $2.5-5 Million
Number Employees: 10-19
Type of Packaging: Consumer, Food Service, Private Label
Brands:
Birdie Pak

1378 (HQ)Birds Eye Foods
121 Woodcrest Rd
Cherry Hill, NJ 8003 585-383-1850
Fax: 585-385-2857 800-999-5044
www.birdseyefoods.com
Frozen vegetables and prepared meals
President/COO: Christopher Puma
Chairman/CEO: Neil Harrison
EVP/CFO: Linda Nelson
Estimated Sales: $930 Million
Number Employees: 1,000-4,999
Parent Co: Pinnacle Foods Group LLC
Type of Packaging: Consumer, Food Service, Bulk
Other Locations:
Fennville MI
Waseca MN
Fulton NY
Berlin PA
Algona WA
Tacoma WA
Darien WI
Green Bay WI
Brands:
BERNSTEIN'S
BIRDS EYE
BIRDS EYE C&W
BIRDS EYE FRESHLIKE
BIRDS EYE STEAMFRESH
BROOKS
COMSTOCK WILDERNESS
FRESHLIKE
GREENWOOD
HUSMAN'S
LARSEN FRESHLIKE FOODS
MARINER'S COVE CLAM CHOWDER
MCKENZIE'S
MCKENZIE'S
NALLEY
NALLEY'S CHILI & STEWS
NALLEY'S DRESSINGS
NALLEY'S PICKLES
NATURALLY GOOD FRUITS & VEGETABLES
ORCHARD FARM CANNED VEGETABLES
ORCHARD FRESH FROZEN FRUITS
OREGON'S FINEST
PIXIE CANNED CORN & CHUTNEYS
POPEYE POPCORN
POPS RITE POPCORN
PUFF-N-CORN
QUALITY BRAND
QUE PASA CHEESE SAUCE & SALSA
RIVIERA
RIVIERA CANNED ITALIAN SOUPS
SAVORAL SALT & OILS
SILVER FLOSS SAUERKRAUT
SNYDER OF BERLIN
SNYDER OF BERLIN SNACK PRODUCTS
SOUTH LAND FROZEN FOODS
SOUTHERN FARMS PRODUCE
SPOON BRAND
STIR CRAZY
THANK YOU FRUIT FILLINGS
TIM'S CASCADE CHIPS
TIM'S CASCADE SNACKS
TROPIC ISLE FROZEN COCONUT
VICTOR SAUERKRAUT
VIOLA
WEST BAY PIE FILLINGS
WILDERNESS

1379 **Birds Eye Foods**
1313 Stadium St
Berlin, PA 15530-1401 814-267-4641
Fax: 814-267-5648 rhayman@birdseyefoods.com
www.birdseyefoods.com/snyder
Manufacturer of pretzels, potato chips and chips, cheese curls and popcorn
Chairman/President/CEO: Neil Harrison
VP: John Blough
VP Human Resources/Purchasing: John Blough
Production Manager: John Lahm
Plant Engineer: Dennis Brant
Estimated Sales: $50 Milion
Number Employees: 250-499
Parent Co: Agrilink Foods
Type of Packaging: Consumer
Brands:
BERNSTEIN'S
BIRD'S EYE
BIRD'S EYE VOILA
BROOKS
C&W
COMSTOCK
FRESHLIKE
GREENWOOD BEETS
HUSMAN'S
MARINER'S COVE
MCKENZIE'S
NALLEY PRODUCTS
RIVIERA
SYNDER OF BERLIN
TIM'S CASCADE SNACKS
WILDERNESS

1380 **Birdsall Ice Cream Company**
518 N Federal Ave
Mason City, IA 50401 641-423-5365
Manufacturer of ice cream
Owner: Vaughn Escher
Owner: Dave Escher
Estimated Sales: $1 Million
Number Employees: 10-19
Type of Packaging: Consumer, Food Service

1381 **Birdseye Dairy**
2325 Memorial Dr
Green Bay, WI 54303 920-494-5388
Fax: 920-494-4388
Processor of apple and orange juice; wholesaler/distributor of dairy products including milk, ice cream, butter and sour cream; serving the food service market
President: Steven Williams
Estimated Sales: $10-20 Million
Number Employees: 10-19
Type of Packaging: Consumer, Food Service, Private Label, Bulk
Brands:
Birdseye
Morning Glory

1382 **(HQ)Birdsong Corporation**
612 Madison Avenue
Suffolk, VA 23434 757-539-3456
Fax: 757-539-7360 www.bird-song.com
Manufacturer and exporter of raw peanuts
President: Jeff Johnson
CEO: George Birdsong
CFO: Stephen Huber
Estimated Sales: $395.4 Million
Number Employees: 700
Sq. footage: 10000
Type of Packaging: Food Service
Other Locations:
Birdsong Corp.
Gorman TX

1383 **Birdsong Peanuts**
230 North Bay Street
Blakely, GA 31723 229-723-3641
800-597-7688
pduke@birdsong-peanuts.com
www.birdsong-peanuts.com
Manufacturer of raw peanuts and peanut products including seeds, meal and oil, shellers and crushers
President: Jeff Johnson
CEO: George Birdsong
VP/General Manager: Max Grice
VP Sales/Officer Manager: D Presley Duke Jr
Estimated Sales: $100-500 Million
Number Employees: 125
Parent Co: Birdsong Corporation
Type of Packaging: Bulk
Other Locations:
Birdsong Peanuts
Blakely GA
Birdsong Peanuts
Suffolk VA

1384 **Birkett Mills**
P.O.Box 440
Penn Yan, NY 14527 315-536-4112
Fax: 315-536-6740 service@theberkettmills.com
www.thebirkettmills.com
Processor of flour
President: Jeff Gifford
COO: Jeff Giffond
VP Marketing: Cliff Orr
Estimated Sales: $1-2.5 Million
Number Employees: 20-49
Type of Packaging: Consumer, Private Label, Bulk
Brands:
Bessie
Pocono
Puritan
Wolffs

1385 **Birkholm's Jr Danish Bakery**
1555 Mission Drive
Solvang, CA 93463-2607 805-688-3872
Fax: 805-693-1027 www.birkholms.com
Breads, rolls, pastries, cakes
Owner: Danish Birkholm Jr
Estimated Sales: Less than $500,000
Number Employees: 5-9
Brands:
Birkholm's Jr. Danish

1386 **Birmhall Foods Company**
P.O.Box 34232
Memphis, TN 38184-0232 901-377-9016
Fax: 901-377-0476 ps139@brimsnacks.com
www.brimsnacks.com
President: Terry Brimhall
VP: Becki Brimhall
General Manager: Michael Patrick
Estimated Sales: $ 20 - 50 Million
Number Employees: 50-99
Brands:
Brim's

1387 **Birnn Chocolates**
314 Cleveland Ave
Highland Park, NJ 8904 732-545-4400
Fax: 732-545-4494 info@birnnchocolates.com
www.birnnchocolates.com
Chocolate confections
President: John Cunnell
Estimated Sales: $500,000-$1 Million
Number Employees: 10-19
Type of Packaging: Private Label

1388 **Birnn Chocolates of Vermont**
102 Kimball Ave Ste 4
South Burlington, VT 5403 802-860-1047
Fax: 802-860-1256 800-338-3141
www.birnn.com
Manufacturer of premium wholesale truffles
President/Owner: Jeff Birnn
VP: Bill Birnn
Estimated Sales: $2 Million
Number Employees: 17
Type of Packaging: Private Label

1389 **(HQ)Biscomerica Corporation**
P.O.Box 1070
Rialto, CA 92377-1070 909-877-5997
Fax: 909-877-3593 info@biscomerica.com
www.biscomerica.com
Cookies and candy
President: Nadi Soltan
CEO: Nadi Soltan
Estimated Sales: $30 Million
Number Employees: 250-499
Sq. footage: 225000
Brands:
CHECKERS COOKIES
GRANNY'S OVEN
KNOTT'S BERRY FARMS

1390 **(HQ)Biscoti Di Suzy**
1070 40th St
Oakland, CA 94608-3617 510-923-0446
Fax: 510-923-0344 800-211-5903
info@crunchyfoods.com
www.crunchyfoods.com
Cookies, other baked goods.
Owner: Karen Jackson
CEO: Karen Jackson
Marketing: Will Tassi
Estimated Sales: $5-9.9 Million
Number Employees: 5-9
Type of Packaging: Consumer, Food Service, Private Label, Bulk
Brands:
BISCOTTI DI SUZY™

1391 **Biscottea**
23216 SE 135th Ct
Issaquah, WA 98027 425-313-1993
Fax: 425-427-0709 info@biscottea.net
www.biscottea.net
Organic, all natural flavored shortbread
President/Owner: Laurance Milner
Number Employees: 2

1392 **Biscotti Goddess**
3910 Amberleigh Blvd
Richmond, VA 23236 804-745-9490
jan@biscotti-goddess.com
www.biscotti-goddess.com
Biscotti

1393 **Biscotti Goddess**
12500 Eagles Nest Road
Charles City, VA 23030 855-745-9490
Fax: 804-829-2119
wheeler@biscotti-goddess.com
www.biscotti-goddess.com
Organic/natural, bread/biscuits, cookies, other snacks.
Marketing: Wheeler Wood

1394 **Bishop Baking Company**
1335 S Ocoee St
Cleveland, TN 37311 423-472-1561
Fax: 423-472-6355 info@bishoptaboli.com
www.flowersfoods.com
Processor and exporter of snack cakes
President: Kent Feagans
Controller: Craig Parrish
Estimated Sales: $50-100 Million
Number Employees: 250-499
Parent Co: Flower Roods
Type of Packaging: Consumer, Private Label

1395 **Bishop Brothers**
113 W 5th Ave
Bristow, OK 74010 918-367-2270
Fax: 918-367-2270 800-859-8304
info@bishoptaboli.com www.bishoptaboli.com
Wholesaler/distributor of bulgur wheat including tabbouleh; custom packaging services available
Owner: Eddie Bishop
Estimated Sales: $2.5-5 Million
Number Employees: 5-9
Type of Packaging: Consumer, Food Service, Bulk

1396 **Bishop Farms Winery**
500 S Meriden Rd
Cheshire, CT 06410-2968 203-272-8243
Fax: 203-272-7344
Wines
President: John Romanik
Marketing Director: Mary Romanik
Estimated Sales: $500,000-$1 Million
Number Employees: 1-4

1397 **Bison Brewing Company**
PO Box 4821
Berkeley, CA 94704-4821 510-697-1537
Fax: 510-217-4332 info@bisonbrew.com
www.bisonbrew.com
Organic Beer
Owner: Dan DelGarande
Sales Representative: Rich Schwanbeck
Estimated Sales: $5-10 Million
Number Employees: 10-19
Brands:
BARLEY WINE ALE
BELGIAN ALE
CHOCOLATE STOUT
FARMHOUSE SAISON
GINGERBREAD ALE
HONEY BASIL ALE
INDIA PALE ALE
RED ALE
WINTER WARMER

1398 **Bissett Produce Company**
P.O.Box 279
Spring Hope, NC 27882-0279 252-478-4158
Fax: 252-478-7798 800-849-5073
Bissettproducecompanyinc@msn.com
Grower, packer and exporter of sweet potatoes, pickling cucumbers and banana and specialty peppers and seedless watermelons
Manager: Don Sparks II
Vice President: Lee Bissett II
Sales Director: Don Sparks
Estimated Sales: $2.5-5 Million
Number Employees: 20-49
Sq. footage: 60000
Type of Packaging: Consumer, Food Service, Private Label, Bulk
Brands:
Bissett's
Rue's Choice

1399 **Bissinger's HandcraftedChocolatier**
3983 Gratiot Street
St Louis, MO 63110 314-534-2401
Fax: 314-534-2419 800-325-8881
sales@bissingers.com www.bissingers.com
boxed chocolates, sugar free chocolate and classic gourmet candies
Number Employees: 50-99

1400 **Bittersweet Herb Farm**
635 Mohawk Trl
Shelburne Falls, MA 01370-9775 413-625-6523
Fax: 413-625-0166 800-456-1599
dave@bittersweetherbfarm.com
www.bittersweetherbfarm.com
Wasabi ginger sauce, lemon garlic sauce, strawberry jam and all natural seasonings. Also flavored oils and balsamic vinegars
President: David Wallace
Estimated Sales: $1-2.5 Million
Number Employees: 10-19

1401 **Bittersweet Pastries**
385 Chestnut St
Norwood, NJ 07648-2001
US 973-227-2800
Fax: 973-882-6998 800-217-2938
salesinfo@bittersweetpastries.com
www.bittersweetpastries.com
Processor of desserts including tarts, layer cakes, and flourless chocolate truffle cakes. Also sold frozen and dessert bars.
President: Phyllis Trier
VP: Louis Florencia
Estimated Sales: $1-5 Million
Number Employees: 20-49
Sq. footage: 4500
Parent Co: Fairfield Gourmet Foods Corporation
Type of Packaging: Food Service

1402 **Bjorneby Potato Company**
P.O.Box 317
Minto, ND 58261-0317 701-248-3482
Fax: 701-248-3508 lonewolf@uslink.net
www.lonewolffarms.com
Supplier of potatoes
President: Keith Bjorneby
VP: Dean Bjorneby
Sales Manager: Chris Bjorneby
Production Manager: Chris Bjorneby
Estimated Sales: $ 10 - 20 Million
Number Employees: 16
Type of Packaging: Consumer, Bulk

1403 **Black Bear**
PO Box 296
St Johnsbury, VT 05819-0296 802-748-5888
Fruit spreads

1404 **Black Diamond Cheese**
405 The West Mall
10th Floor
Toronto, ON M9C 5J1
Canada 416-626-1973
Fax: 416-620-3666 800-263-2858
www.blackdiamond.ca
Cheese, processed slices, shredded and portion packs
President/CEO: Alnashir Lakha
National VP Sales: Tom Shurrie
National VP Supply Chain: Steve Wuthmann
Estimated Sales: $2 Billion
Number Employees: 1000
Sq. footage: 100000
Type of Packaging: Food Service, Private Label
Brands:
BLACK DIAMOND

1405 **Black Duck Cove Lobster**
PO Box 42
Beals, ME 04611-0042 207-497-2232
Fax: 215-925-1779
Lobster
President: Marianne Beal

1406 **Black Garlic Inc**
2499 American Ave
Hayward, CA 94546
888-811-9065
info@blackgarlic.com www.blackgarlic.com
Garlic

1407 **Black Hound New York**
111 N 10th St
Brooklyn, NY 11211-1942 718-782-0154
Fax: 718-782-1608 800-344-4417
customerservice@blackhoundny.com
www.blackhoundny.com
Hard, soft and chocolate candies, cakes and delectibles
President: Amiram Dror
Estimated Sales: $500,000-$1 Million
Number Employees: 10-19

1408 **Black Jewell®Popcorn**
Rr 1
St Francisville, IL 62460 618-948-2303
Fax: 618-948-2505 800-948-2302
bjsales@blackjewell.com www.blackjewell.com
Black and red popcorn
President: Carole Klein
Estimated Sales: $2.5-5 Million
Number Employees: 10-19
Type of Packaging: Private Label
Brands:
BLACK JEWELL®
CRIMSON JEWELL®

1409 **Black Mesa Winery**
P.O.Box 432
Velarde, NM 87582 505-852-2820
Fax: 505-852-2820 800-852-6372
www.blackmesawinery.com
Processor of wine
Co-Owner: Jerry Burd
Co-Owner: Lynda Burd
Estimated Sales: $500,000-$1 Million
Number Employees: 1-4
Type of Packaging: Private Label
Brands:
Black Mesa
Coyote Wine

1410 **Black Mountain Brewing Company**
6245 E Cave Creek Rd
Cave Creek, AZ 85331-8655 480-488-3553
Fax: 480-488-0482 chili1!ix.netcom.com
www.chilibeer.com
Beer
Owner: Glory Agenter
VP: Dick Chilleen
Operations Manager: Juan Olguin
Estimated Sales: $10-20 Million
Number Employees: 5-9
Type of Packaging: Private Label
Brands:
BLACK MOUNTAIN GOLD
CAVE CREEK CHILI BEER
FROG LIGHT
JUANDERFUL WHEAT
OCOTILLO AMBER
SOUTH OF THE BORDER PORTER

1411 **Black Prince Distillery Inc.**
691 Clifton Avenue
PO Box 1999
Clifton, NJ 07011 973-365-2050
Fax: 973-365-0746 rickn@blackprincedist.com
www.blackprincedistillery.com
Processor of liquor, liqueurs and cordials
President: Robert Guttag
Operations Manager: Rick Noone
Estimated Sales: $3.2 Million
Number Employees: 50-99
Sq. footage: 120000
Brands:
BLACK PRINCE
DEVILS SPRING
DORADO
LLORD'S
TJ TOAD

1412 **Black Ranch Organic Grains**
5917 Eastside Road
Etna, CA 96027-9753 530-467-3387
Processor of seven grain cereals including wheat and barley
Owner: Dave Black
Co-Owner: Dawn Black
Estimated Sales: Under $500,000
Number Employees: 1-4
Type of Packaging: Consumer, Food Service
Brands:
Black Ranch Gourmet Grains

1413 **Black Sheep Vintners**
P.O.Box 1851
Murphys, CA 95247 209-728-2157
Fax: 209-728-2157 info@blacksheepwinery.com
www.blacksheepwinery.com
Wines
Owner: Steve Millier
CEO: David Olson
Marketing Director: Janis Olson
Estimated Sales: Less than $500,000
Number Employees: 1-4
Type of Packaging: Private Label

1414 **Black Shield**
5356 Pan American E Freeway NE
Albuquerque, NM 87109-2306 505-880-1112
Fax: 505-884-5643 800-653-9357
Specialty gourmet popcorn
President: Marc Moore
Estimated Sales: Less than $500,000
Number Employees: 1-4

1415 **Black's Barbecue**
215 N Main St
Lockhart, TX 78644 512-398-2712
Fax: 512-398-6000 blacksbbq@sbcglobal.net
www.blacksbbq.com
Manufacturer of barbequed sausage; wholesaler/distributor of meats including brisket, ribs, chicken, pork and loin.
Manager: Steve Cloud
CEO: Terry Black
Estimated Sales: $300,000-500,000
Number Employees: 20-49
Type of Packaging: Bulk

1416 **Blackbear Coffee Company**
318 N Main St
Hendersonville, NC 28792-0407 828-692-6333
Fax: 828-692-6333
www.mountainshops.com/bear.html
Coffee
Manager: Bo Rodriquez
Estimated Sales: Less than $500,000
Number Employees: 5-9

1417 **Blackberry Patch**
Po Box 1639
Thomasville, GA 31799
Fax: 229-558-9998 800-853-5598
fruittreats@blackberrypatch.com
www.blackberrypatch.com
Manufacturer of natural fruit syrups, jams, jellies, chocolate sauces and pancake mixes
Owner: Harry Jones
Secretary: Randy Harvey
Estimated Sales: $870,000
Number Employees: 11
Number of Brands: 2
Number of Products: 48
Type of Packaging: Consumer, Private Label

1418 **Blackey's Bakery**
639 22nd Ave NE
Minneapolis, MN 55418 612-789-5326
Fax: 612-789-2924
Processor of bakery products
Owner: Rob Reding
Estimated Sales: $1-2.5 Million
Number Employees: 10-19

1419 **Blair's Death Sauces & Snacks**
188 Bay Ave
Highlands, NJ 07732-1624 732-872-0755
Fax: 732-872-2035 www.extremefood.com
Sauces and snack foods
Owner: Blair Lazar
Estimated Sales: $ 10 - 20 Million
Number Employees: 10-19

1420 **Blake's Creamery**
46 Milford St
Manchester, NH 3102 603-623-7242
Fax: 603-623-7244 info@blakesicecream.com
www.blakesicecream.com
Manufacturer of ice cream and frozen yogurt
Owner: Ann Mirageas
Owner: Richard Marquis
VP: Raymond Boucher
Estimated Sales: $20-50 Million
Number Employees: 150
Type of Packaging: Consumer, Food Service, Private Label, Bulk

1421 **Blakely Freezer Locker**
PO Box 7055
Thomasville, GA 31758-7055 229-723-3622
Fax: 229-723-9156
sales@blakelyfreezerlocker.com
www.blakelyfreezerlocker.com
Manufacturer of frozen beef, pork and chicken
Owner: Douglas Huey Johnson
Owner: Deeann Benton Johnson
Estimated Sales: $2.5-5 Million
Number Employees: 5-9
Type of Packaging: Consumer
Other Locations:
Blakely GA

1422 **Blalock Seafood**
24822 Canal Rd
Orange Beach, AL 36561-3894 251-974-5811
Fax: 251-974-5812 www.blalockseafood.com
Seafood
President: Peter Blalock
Estimated Sales: $4,000,000
Number Employees: 10-19
Type of Packaging: Consumer

1423 **Blanc Industries**
88 King St Ste 1
Dover, NJ 7801 973-537-0090
Fax: 973-537-0906 888-332-5262
email@blancind.com www.blancind.com
Manufacture, design and print point of sale promotional signage, displays and fixtures for the food and retail industry.
President: Didier Blanc

1424 **Bland Farms**
6054 Ga Highway 121
Reidsville, GA 30453 912-654-2726
Fax: 912-654-4280 800-752-0206
Frozen foods

1425 **Blansh International**
6560 Rolling Oaks Dr
San Jose, CA 95120 408-997-2325
Fax: 408-279-8444
Ethnic foods
President: Atoor Eliasnia
Estimated Sales: $250,000
Number Employees: 1-4

1426 **Blanton's**
246 Jarco Dr
Sweetwater, TN 37874 423-337-3487
Fax: 423-337-3487
Manufacturer of hard stick candy, molded and regular chocolate; also, seasonal products available
Owner: Harld Blanton
Vice President: Betty Blanton
Estimated Sales: $500,000
Number Employees: 5-9
Type of Packaging: Consumer
Brands:
Blanton's

1427 **Blaser's USA, Inc.**
Us Highway 63
Comstock, WI 54826-0036 715-822-2437
Fax: 715-822-8459 mail@blasersusa.com
www.blasersusa.com
Cheese
President: Anthony Curella
VP of Sales: Jim Grande
National VP Sales/Marketing: Jim Grande
Operations Manager: Thomas Messicci
Estimated Sales: $500,000-$1 Million
Number Employees: 1-4
Type of Packaging: Private Label
Brands:
BLASER'S

1428 **Blau Oyster Company**
11317 Blue Heron Rd
Bow, WA 98232 360-766-6171
Fax: 360-766-6115 contact@blauoyster.com
www.blauoyster.com
Processor and exporter of oysters.
President: Paul Blau
Marketing Manager: Pete Nordlund
Director of Operations: Paul Blau
Estimated Sales: $2.5-5 Million
Number Employees: 10-19
Type of Packaging: Consumer, Food Service, Private Label, Bulk

1429 **Blazzin Pickle Company**
6105 N 32nd Street
McAllen, TX 78504-5006 956-630-0733
Processor of pickles including chips and spears
President: Craig Johnson
VP: Kathy Johnson
Number Employees: 1-4
Sq. footage: 2000
Type of Packaging: Consumer, Food Service
Brands:
Blazzin

1430 **Blend Pak**
10039 High Grove Rd
PO Box 458
Bloomfield, KY 40008 502-252-8000
Fax: 502-252-8001 vickie@blendpak.com
www.blendpak.com
Manufactures batter, breaders, marinades, seasoning blends, specialty mixes, and custom blended dry formulas.
CEO/Human Resources Director: Dan Sutherland
EVP: Sue Sutherland
R&D: Linda Mikels
Quality Control: Rob Elkin
Plant Manager: Matt Elder
Estimated Sales: $10 Million
Number Employees: 25
Sq. footage: 22000
Type of Packaging: Food Service, Private Label, Bulk
Brands:
Blend Pak
Bloomfield Farms
Pier Fresh

1431 **Blendco**
8 J M Tatum Industrial Dr
Hattiesburg, MS 39401 601-544-9800
Fax: 601-544-5634 800-328-3687
csr@blendcoinc.com www.blendcoinc.com
Dry food manufacturer, do customize blending and packaging as well as private labeling and contract packaging
President: Charles N Mc Caffrey Jr
Public Relations: Ken Hrdlica
Purchasing Director: Charles Prescott
Estimated Sales: $10-20 Million
Number Employees: 20-49
Type of Packaging: Consumer, Food Service, Private Label, Bulk
Brands:
EZY TIME
HOME SENSATIONS

1432 **Blendex Company**
11208 Electron Dr
Jeffersontown, KY 40299 502-267-1003
Fax: 502-267-1024 800-626-6325
sales@blendex.com www.blendex.com
Breadings, seasonings, flavors and marinades
President: Jacquelyn Bailey
CEO: Ronald Pottinger
CEO: Ronald W Pottinger
VP Research/Development: Jordan Stivers
Chief Marketing Officer: Olin Cook
VP Operations: Wayne McDowell
Estimated Sales: $10-20 Million
Number Employees: 50-99

1433 **Blenheim Bottling Company**
N Highway 301 & I-95
Hamer, SC 29547 843-774-0322
Fax: 843-774-4018 800-270-9344
blenheimga@aol.com
Jamaican ginger ale
President: Alan Schafer
CEO: Mackie Hayes
Sales Director: Sheila McDowell
Estimated Sales: $2.5-5 Million
Number Employees: 5-9
Brands:
Blenheim

1434 **Blessed Herbs**
109 Barre Plains Rd
Oakham, MA 01068 508-882-3839
Fax: 508-882-3755 800-489-4372
info@blessedherbs.com www.blessedherbs.com
Manufacturer, importer and exporter of organic and wildcrafted dried herbs, extracts, formulas and tablets; also, echinacea angustifolia root; exporter and importer of dried herbs
Co-Founder: Michael Volchok
Co-Founder: Martha Volchok
Marketing Director: Shalom Volchok
Estimated Sales: $500,000-$1 Million
Number Employees: 5-9
Sq. footage: 6000
Type of Packaging: Consumer, Bulk

1435 **Bletsoe's Cheese**
8281 3rd Ln
Marathon, WI 54448-9522 715-443-2526
Fax: 715-443-6407
Cheese
President: David Bletsoe
Marketing Director: Bonnie Bletsoe
Estimated Sales: $5-10 Million
Number Employees: 10-19
Type of Packaging: Consumer
Brands:
Bletsoe's Cheese

1436 **Bliss Brothers Dairy, Inc.**
P.O.Box 2288
Attleboro, MA 02703 508-222-2884
Fax: 508-226-6320 800-622-8789
www.blissdairy.com
Manufacturers of ice cream, frozen yogurt, sherbert, sorbet, and ice cream mixes
President: David Bliss
Estimated Sales: $1-2.5 Million
Number Employees: 50-99

1437 **Blk Enterprises**
214 W 39th Street
Suite 202
New York, NY 10018-4404 212-764-3331
Fax: 212-764-3338 c.laurita@blkbeverages.com
Beverages

1438 **Bloch & Guggenheimer**
P.O.Box 850
Hurlock, MD 21643-0850 410-943-4933
Fax: 410-943-4729 800-541-2809
www.bgfoods.com
Roasted peppers, pickles, relishes, pickled cauliflower, pickled onions, pickled peppers, spices
CFO: Robert C Cantwell
CEO: David L Wenner
VP Operations: Jim DePrima
Estimated Sales: $50-100 Million
Number Employees: 100-249
Brands:
Ac'cent
B&G
Joan of Arc
Ortega
Polaner
Red Devil
Regina
Vermont Maid

1439 **(HQ)Blommer Chocolate Company**
600 W Kinzie St
Chicago, IL 60654 312-226-7700
Fax: 312-226-4141 800-621-1606
www.blommer.com

Processor and exporter of chocolate ingredients for the bakery, dairy and confectionery industries including milk and dark chocolate, confectioner and pastel coatings, cookie drops, chocolate liquor, cocoa butter, cocoa powder, icecream ingredients, etc
CFO: Linda Melampy
VP: Rich Blommer
Estimated Sales: $500 Million +
Number Employees: 358
Sq. footage: 500000
Type of Packaging: Bulk

1440 **Blommer Chocolate Company**
1101 Blommer Dr
East Greenville, PA 18041 215-679-4472
Fax: 215-679-4196 800-825-8181
klhicks@uc.blommer.com www.blommer.com
Manufacturer of chocolate
President: Peter Blommer
Estimated Sales: Less than $500,000
Number Employees: 100-249
Type of Packaging: Bulk
Other Locations:
Chicago IL
Union City CA

1441 **Bloomer Candy Company**
2200 Linden Ave.
Po Box 905
Zanesville, OH 43702-0905 740-452-7501
Fax: 740-452-7865 800-452-7501
feedback@bloomercandy.com
www.bloomercandy.com
Manufacturer and wholesaler/distributor of chocolate candy
President: Bill Barry
VP Sales: Bob Barry
Estimated Sales: $20-50 Million
Number Employees: 100-249
Type of Packaging: Food Service, Private Label, Bulk
Brands:
STAR
STARLINE SWEETS

1442 **Bloomfield Bakers**
10711 Bloomfield St
Los Alamitos, CA 90720 562-594-4411
Fax: 562-742-0408 800-594-4111
info@bloomfieldbakers.com
www.bloomfieldbakers.com
Cookies, cereals, crackers, bars and mixes.
President: Sam Calderon
Owner/CEO: William Ross
Research & Development Manager: Christina Lates
Quality Control Manager: Steve Huber
National Sales Manager: Russ Case
Human Resources Manager: Evangelina Garza
COO: Gary Marx
Plant/Production Manager: Ricardo Gonzalez
Estimated Sales: $5-10 Million
Number Employees: 850
Sq. footage: 75000
Type of Packaging: Private Label

1443 **Bloomington Brewing Company**
1795 E 10th St
Bloomington, IN 47408 812-339-2256
Fax: 812-333-3200
Processor of ale and stout
Manager: Michael Fox
CFO: Lennie Busch
Marketing Director: Sera Shikh
Number Employees: 1-4
Parent Co: One World Enterprises
Type of Packaging: Consumer, Food Service, Bulk
Brands:
Bloomington Brewing
Quarrymen Pale

1444 **Bloomsberry & Co**
92 Jackson St
Salem, MA 01970 978-745-9100
Fax: 978-745-9150 800-745-5154
sales@bloomsberry.com www.bloomsberry.com
chocolates
President/Owner: Paul Pruett
VP: Kerry Francis
Number Employees: 5

1445 **Blossom Farm Products**
545 State Rt 17 Ste 2003
Ridgewood, NJ 7450 201-493-2626
Fax: 201-493-2666 800-729-1818
kblossom@rcn.com
Processor, importer and exporter of dairy products including milk powders, dry blends, whey, caseinates, lactose, butter fats, etc.
Manager: Kathy Oviedo
VP: Paul Podell
Operations Manager: Kathy Oviedo
Number Employees: 5-9
Type of Packaging: Consumer, Food Service, Bulk

1446 **Blount Fine Foods**
630 Currant Road
Fall River, MA 02720 774-888-1300
Fax: 774-888-1399 info@blountfinefoods.com
www.blountfinefoods.com
Refrigerated and frozen gourmet soups, sauces, dips and spreads; also clam meat products and breaded seafood
President: Todd Blount
CEO/CFO: Louise Goodman
VP: John Durkin
EVP Sales/Marketing: Bob Sewall
VP Operations: Jonathan Arena
Number Employees: 225
Sq. footage: 65000

1447 **(HQ)Blount Seafood Corporation**
630 Currant Rd
Fall River, MA 2720 774-888-1300
Fax: 774-888-1399 info@blountseafood.com
www.blountseafood.com
Processor of frozen seafood products including chopped clams, lobster bisque, clam chowder, meat and hearty soups.
President/CEO: Todd Blount
President: George Richardson
Vice President of Operations: Jonathan Arena
Marketin: David Vittorio
VP Sales/Marketing: Bob Sewald
Operations: Jonathan Areno
Purchasing: Ed Sheehan
Estimated Sales: $20-50 Million
Number Employees: 100-249
Type of Packaging: Consumer, Food Service, Private Label, Bulk
Brands:
BLOUNT
GOURMET STUFFED CLAMS
POINT JUDITH
SAMS CLAMS
WHITE CAP

1448 **Blue Bell Creameries**
P.O.Box 1807
Brenham, TX 77834 979-836-7977
Fax: 979-830-7398 www.bluebell.com
Manufacturer of ice milk mix, ices, ice cream and frozen yogurt
President/CEO: Paul Kruse
CEO: Paul W Kruse
Number Employees: 1,000-4,999
Type of Packaging: Consumer, Food Service
Other Locations:
Sylacauga AL
Broken Arrow OK
Brenham TX
Brands:
Blue Bell

1449 **(HQ)Blue California Company**
30111 Tomas
Rcho Sta Marg, CA 92688 949-635-1990
Fax: 949-635-1988
info@bluecal-ingredients.com
www.bluecal-ingredients.com
Manufacturer of botanical extracts and specialty ingredients
President: Steven Chen
Quality Control Manager: Carl Lai
VP Sales/Marketing: Cecilia McCollum
Estimated Sales: $ 10 - 20 Million
Number Employees: 5-9
Other Locations:
Rockaway NJ

1450 **Blue Chip Group**
432 W 3440 S
Salt Lake City, UT 84115 801-263-6667
Fax: 801-269-9666 800-878-0099
customerservice@bluechipgroup.net
www.bluechipgroup.net
Processor of milk drinks including tofu, rice and soy
President: George Moo
CFO: Mike Leonard
R&D: Jeff Lund
Quality Control: Jeff Olsen
CIO: Gary Johnson
Estimated Sales: $5 Million
Number Employees: 23
Number of Brands: 16
Number of Products: 160
Sq. footage: 17500
Type of Packaging: Consumer, Food Service, Private Label, Bulk
Brands:
BLUE CHIP BAKER
BLUE CHIP GROUP
MORNING MOO'S
SWISS WHEY D'LITE

1451 **Blue Crab Bay Company**
Accomack Airport Industrial Park
29368 Atlantic Drive
Melfa, VA 23410 757-787-3602
Fax: 757-787-3430 800-221-2722
sales@baybeyond.net www.baybeyond.net
Processor and exporter of Bloody Mary mixes, seafood soups, seasonings, snacks, preserves, crab meat; sea salt, and sweet potato chips
President: Pamela Barefoot
Treasurer: Dawn Colona
Marketing: Amy Savona
Estimated Sales: $1-3 Million
Number Employees: 10-19
Sq. footage: 12400
Parent Co: Bay Beyond
Type of Packaging: Consumer
Brands:
Barnacles Snack Mix
Blue Crab Bay
Crab House Nuts
Salmonberry
Sting Ray Bloody Mary Mixer
Watts Island Trading

1452 **Blue Crab Bay Company**
29368 Atlantic Dr
Melfa, VA 23410 757-787-3602
Fax: 757-787-3430 800-221-2722
sales@bluecrabbay.com www.bluecrabbay.com
Specialty foods
President: Pamela Barefoot
CFO: Dawn Colona
Public Relations: Susan Tyler
Product Manager: Linda Nyborg
Estimated Sales: $2.6 Million
Number Employees: 22
Sq. footage: 24000
Type of Packaging: Private Label
Brands:
BARNACLES®
CRAB HOUSE CRUNCH™
CRAB HOUSE NUTS®
SEA SALT NUTS™
SHUCKERS™
SKIPJACKS™
STING RAY®

1453 **Blue Diamond Growers**
1802 C St
Sacramento, CA 95811 916-442-0771
Fax: 916-446-8461 feedback@bdgrowers.com
www.bluediamond.com
Processor, grower and exporter of almonds, macadamians, pistachios and hazelnuts. Two thousand almond products in many cuts, styles, sizes and shapes for use in confectionery, bakery, dairy and processed foods. In house R/D for customproducts
President/CEO: Douglas Youngdahl
CFO: Robert Donovan
Estimated Sales: $709 Million
Number Employees: 1100
Type of Packaging: Consumer, Food Service, Private Label, Bulk
Brands:
ALMOND BREEZE
ALMOND TOPPERS
BLUE DIAMOND
BLUE DIAMOND ALMONDS

BLUE DIAMOND HAZELNUT
BLUE DIAMOND MACADAMIAS
BREEZE
NUT THINS
SMOKEHOUSE

1454 **Blue Dog Bakery**
1210 E Shelby St Unit D
Seattle, WA 98102 206-323-6958
Fax: 206-666-3835 888-749-7229
BlueDog@bluedogbakery.com
www.bluedogbakery.com
Company produces a variety of premium, natural, low fat dog biscuits and treats.
President/Owner: Margot Kenly
Estimated Sales: $ 1 - 3 Million
Number Employees: 1-4
Type of Packaging: Private Label
Brands:
Mariner Biscuits
Original Sesame Low Fat Crackers
Parmesan Low Fat Crackers
Sweet Onion Low Fat Crackers
Sweet Pepper Low Fat Crackers

1455 **Blue Gold Mussels**
39 Allston Ave
Suite 40
Middletown, RI 2842-5801
Fax: 508-994-9508
Processor of fresh and frozen mussel products and calamari salad
Director Marketing: Joe Jeffrey
Type of Packaging: Consumer, Food Service, Private Label
Brands:
Blue Gold

1456 **Blue Grass Dairy Foods**
1117 Cleveland Ave
Glasgow, KY 42141-1011 270-651-2146
Fax: 270-651-8844 www.bluegrassdairy.com
Dairy and nondairy foods
CEO: Billy Joe Williams
Plant Manager: Mike Caron
Estimated Sales: $10-24.9 Million
Number Employees: 50-99

1457 **Blue Grass Quality Meat**
P.O.Box 17658
Covington, KY 41017-0658 859-331-7100
Fax: 859-331-4273
www.bluegrassqualitymeats.com
Manufacturer of smoked meats and sausage
President: Paul Rice
Estimated Sales: $10-24.9 Million
Number Employees: 50-99
Type of Packaging: Consumer, Food Service, Private Label, Bulk

1458 **Blue Hills Spring WaterCompany**
80 Washington St Bldg L
Norwell, MA 02061-1742
Fax: 617-770-2720 www.monadnock.com
Bottled water
President: Mike Verachi
COO: Mark Okum
Estimated Sales: $2.5-5 Million
Number Employees: 50-99
Brands:
Monadnock Mountain Spring Water

1459 **Blue Jay Orchards**
125 Plumtrees Rd
Bethel, CT 6801 203-748-0119
Fax: 203-748-4814 www.bluejayorchardsct.com
Processor of apple butter, sauce and chutney; also, pear butter
President: Paul Patterson
VP: Mary Patterson
Estimated Sales: $500,000
Number Employees: 5
Sq. footage: 10000
Type of Packaging: Consumer, Private Label
Brands:
Blue Jay Orchards

1460 **Blue Lakes Trout Farm**
133 Warm Creek Rd
Jerome, ID 83338 208-734-7151
Fax: 208-733-0325
Rainbow trout
Estimated Sales: $2.5-5 Million
Number Employees: 20-49
Type of Packaging: Consumer, Food Service
Brands:
GREENE'S

1461 **Blue Marble Brands**
313 Iron Hrose Way
Providence, RI 02908 401-528-8634
Fax: 732-650-9969 http://www.unfi.com
Organic, natural, specialty, ethnic and functional foods.
President/CEO: Steven Spinner
Estimated Sales: K
Number Employees: 250-499

1462 **Blue Moon Foods**
568 N Main Street
White River Junction, VT 05001-7026 802-295-1165
Fax: 802-295-2553
Ice cream and frozen desserts.
President: John Donaldson
Estimated Sales: $440,000
Number Employees: 7
Brands:
Blue Moon Tea

1463 **Blue Mountain Flavors**
4000 Commerce Dr
Kinston, NC 28504-7906 252-522-1544
Fax: 252-522-2599 800-522-1544
bluemountainflavors@embarqmail.com
www.bluemountainflavors.com
Manufacturer of savory flavors for the food industry, also contract manufacturing and packaging
President: William Baugher PhD
Corporate Secretary/Treasurer: Teresa Baugher
Quality Control: Margaret Jones
Customer Service: Maureen Suggs
Operations Manager: Laura Keys
Estimated Sales: $3 Million
Number Employees: 15
Number of Products: 150
Sq. footage: 37838
Parent Co: Blue Mountain Enterprises
Type of Packaging: Bulk

1464 **Blue Mountain Vineyards**
7627 Grape Vine Dr
New Tripoli, PA 18066 610-298-3068
Fax: 610-298-8616 info@bluemountainwine.com
www.bluemountainwine.com
Wines
President/Owner: Joseph Greff
VP: Vickie Greff
Estimated Sales: $2.5-5 Million
Number Employees: 10-19

1465 **(HQ)Blue Pacific Flavors & Fragrances**
1354 Marion Ct
City of Industry, CA 91745 626-934-0099
Fax: 626-934-0089 800-248-7499
www.bluepacificflavors.com
Basic manufacturer of natural flavors, extracts, essences and functional ingredients to the beverage, dairy, confectionery, baking and pharmaceutical industries
President: Donald Wilkes
Estimated Sales: $ 10 - 20 Million
Number Employees: 20-49
Sq. footage: 40000
Type of Packaging: Food Service, Private Label, Bulk
Other Locations:
Blue Pacific Asia
Malaysia
Blue Pacific China
Beijing, China
Blue Pacific Korea
Seoul, Korea
Brands:
Cafe Extract
Instacafe
Naturessence
Sun-Ripened
Synature

1466 **Blue Planet Foods**
P.O.Box 2178
Collegedale, TN 37315 423-396-3145
Fax: 423-396-3479 877-396-3145
sales@blueplanetfoods.net
www.blueplanetfoods.net
Manufacturer of grain based products, granola, nutrition and granola bar components, bread bases and nutritional fillers; exporter of granola products
President/CFO: Deris Bagli
Sales Director/Manager: Deris Bagli
Industrial/Co-Packaging Sales Assistant: Sherry Poole
Plant Manager: Frank Park
Estimated Sales: $100 Million
Number Employees: 250-499
Number of Products: 5
Sq. footage: 250000
Parent Co: McKee Foods Corporation
Type of Packaging: Consumer, Food Service, Private Label, Bulk

1467 **Blue Ribbon Dairy**
827 Exeter Ave
Exeter, PA 18643-1728 570-655-5579
Fax: 570-655-5637
Ice cream
President: Ken Sorick
Estimated Sales: $5-10 Million
Number Employees: 10-19

1468 **Blue Ribbon Meat Company**
P.O. Box 633
Sparks, NV 89432-0633 775-358-8116
Fax: 775-358-0992 www.blueribbonmeat.com
Processor and wholesaler/distributor of meat; serving the food service market.
Owner: Scott Taylor
Owner: Aaron Taylor
Estimated Sales: $20-50 Million
Number Employees: 20-49

1469 **Blue Ribbon Meats**
3316 W 67th Pl
Cleveland, OH 44102 216-631-8850
Fax: 216-631-8934
Meats
President: Albert Radis
Estimated Sales: $28.6 Million
Number Employees: 100-249

1470 **Blue Ribbon Meats**
200 S Biscayne Blvd
Miami, FL 33131-2310 305-960-2244
Fax: 305-888-3917 800-522-6115
www.brmeatsinc.com
Processor and exporter of portion controlled ground beef products, steaks and chops
VP: Ira Bregman
Estimated Sales: $20-50 Million
Number Employees: 100-249
Type of Packaging: Consumer, Food Service, Private Label, Bulk
Brands:
BLUE RIBBON
QUALITY CUTS

1471 **Blue Ridge Farms**
3301 Atlantic Ave
Brooklyn, NY 11208 718-827-9000
Fax: 718-647-0052 www.blueridgefarms.com
Processor of specialty foods including salads, pickles, desserts and frozen foods.
CEO: Andrew Themis
CEO: Seymour Siegel
Sales Manager: David Charif
Estimated Sales: $5-10 Million
Number Employees: 10-19
Brands:
Chloe

1472 **Blue Ridge Poultry**
145 Oneta St
Athens, GA 30601 706-546-6767
Processor of fresh and frozen poultry including turkey; wholesaler/distributor of poultry and eggs
President: Robert Harris
Estimated Sales: $ 1 - 3 Million
Number Employees: 5-9
Sq. footage: 4500
Type of Packaging: Consumer

1473 **Blue Ridge Tea & Herb Company**
26 Woodhull St
Brooklyn, NY 11231 718-625-3100
Fax: 718-935-1874 pr@blueridgetea.com
www.blueridgetea.com

Custom herbal and teabag formulations for private label. Also sales agent for teabags with ten vitamins; flavored
President: Roger Rigolli
Vice President: Paulette Rigolli
Estimated Sales: $4.5 Million est.
Type of Packaging: Private Label
Brands:
Blue Ridge Teas

1474 **Blue Runner Foods**
726 South Burnside Ave
Gonzales, LA 70737 225-647-3016
Fax: 225-647-4017
customerservice@bluerunnerfoods.com
www.bluerunnerfoods.com
Processor and canner of Cajun and Creole creamed beans, peas and heat and serve entrees
Estimated Sales: $5-10 Million
Number Employees: 20-49
Type of Packaging: Consumer, Food Service
Brands:
Blue Runner

1475 **Blue Sky Natural Beverage Company**
550 Monica Circle
Suite 201
Corona, CA 92880 505-995-9761
Fax: 505-982-4004 800-426-7367
heather@bleuskysoda.com
www.blueskysoda.com
Manufacturer and exporter of natural and energy sodas; also sparkling and artesian drinking water
Chairman/CEO: Rodney Sacks
President/Coo/Cfo: Hilton Schlosberg
Estimated Sales: $1.3 Billion
Number Employees: 1,186
Brands:
Blue Sky
Blue Sky Artesian Water
Blue Sky Natural Soda
True Seltzer

1476 **Blue Smoke Salsa**
119 East Main Street
Po Box 244
Ansted, WV 25812 304-658-3800
Fax: 304-658-5400 888-725-7298
bluesmokesalsa@hotmail.com
www.bluesmokedsalsa.com
Jams and jellys, barbecue sauces, sparkling cider, honey, gourmet mustards, specialty butters, pickles, marinades and sauces, salsa, hot and spicy foods, seasonings, and dry mixes
President: Robin Hildebrand
Estimated Sales: $300,000
Number Employees: 7

1477 **Blue Wave Seafoods**
413 Central Port Mouton
Port Mouton, NS B0T 1T0
Canada 902-683-2044
Fax: 902-683-2366
Processor of fresh and frozen groundfish and shellfish
President: Sylvain D'Eon
CEO: Sylvain D'Eon
Marketing: Sylvain D'Eon
Estimated Sales: $13 Million
Number Employees: 96
Type of Packaging: Consumer, Food Service, Private Label, Bulk

1478 **Blue Willow Tea Company**
4059 Emery Street
Emeryville, CA 94608-3601 510-420-5777
800-328-0353
info@bluewillowtea.com
www.bluewillowtea.com
Manufacturer of teas
President/CEO: Lynn Mallard
Estimated Sales: Under $500,000
Number Employees: 5-9
Brands:
BLUE WILLOW
WU WEI

1479 **BlueWater Seafoods**
1640 Brandon Crescent
Lachine, QC H8T 2N1
Canada 514-637-1171
Fax: 514-637-5250 888-560-2539
www.bluewaterfish.com
haddock and sole, shrimp temptations, five star tilapia, grill fillets, grill salmon and haddock, natural cut fillets, popcorn shrimp, classic family favorites, seasoned fillets and shrimp bowls
Sales/Marketing Director: Guy Emard
Number Employees: 225
Parent Co: Gortons USA
Type of Packaging: Consumer, Food Service

1480 **Blueberry Hill Foods**
7 Zane Grey St
El Paso, TX 79906-5213 915-779-8807
Fax: 915-779-8181 800-451-8664
sales@blueberryhillfoods.com
www.blueberryhillfoods.com
Manufacturer of confectioneries, jaw breakers, jellyies and more
SVP Sales/Marketing: Scott Frey
National Sales Manager: Jim Kelm
Estimated Sales: $ 10 - 20 Million
Number Employees: 10-19
Brands:
ARBOR
BLUEBERRY HILL
BRADFORD FINE CANDIES
SIMPLY SMART

1481 **(HQ)Blueberry Store**
04726 County Road 215
Grand Junction, MI 49056 269-434-8341
Fax: 269-434-6997 877-654-2400
jvannatter@blueberries.com
www.theblueberrystore.com
Manufacturer of all natural blueberry preserve, blueberry salsa, blueberry BBQ sauce, blueberry juice, chocolate covered blueberries, blueberry syrup, blueberry mustard, blueberry vinegar and chutney
CEO: Jennifer Montgomery
CFO: Jeff Van Natter
Estimated Sales: $300,000-500,000
Number Employees: 1-4
Number of Products: 20
Parent Co: Michigan Blueberry Growers Association

1482 **Bluebird**
P.O.Box 378
Peshastin, WA 98847-0378 509-548-1700
Fax: 509-548-0288
Manufacturer and exporter of apples and pears
President: Ron Gonvales
Estimated Sales: $35 Million
Number Employees: 500-999
Brands:
Blue Bird
Skookum

1483 **Bluebird Restaurant**
19 N Main St
Logan, UT 84321 435-752-3155
Candy and confectionery
Owner: Ansheng Xu
Estimated Sales: $1-2.5 Million
Number Employees: 20-49

1484 **Bluegrass Brewing Company**
3929 Shelbyville Rd
St Matthews, KY 40207 502-899-7070
Fax: 502-899-7051 pathagan@bbcbrew.com
www.bbcbrew.com
Brewer of ale, stout and lager
Owner: Pat Hagan
Estimated Sales: $10-20 Million
Type of Packaging: Consumer, Food Service, Bulk
Brands:
ALTBIER
AMERICAN PALE ALE
BLUEBIRD RESTAURANT
DARK STAR PORTER
NUT BROWN ALE

1485 **Bluepoint Bakery**
1721 E 58th Ave
Denver, CO 80216 303-298-1100
Fax: 303-298-9797 sales@bluepointbakery.com
www.bluepointbakery.com
Bakery products
President: Fred Bramhall
Estimated Sales: $20-50 Million
Number Employees: 50-99

1486 **Blumenhof Vineyards-Winery**
P.O.Box 30
Dutzow, MO 63342 800-419-2245
Fax: 636-433-5224 800-419-2245
info@blumenhof.com www.blumenhof.com
Wines
President: Mark Blumenberg
Estimated Sales: $1-2.5 Million
Number Employees: 10-19

1487 **Blundell Seafoods**
11351 River Road
Richmond, BC V6X 1Z6
Canada 604-270-3300
Fax: 604-270-6513 www.blundellseafoods.com
Processor and exporter of fresh and frozen salmon and wall fish
President: Ian Tak Yen Law
Vice President: Russ Kitaura
Manager: Bill Leung
Estimated Sales: $30 Million
Number Employees: 75
Type of Packaging: Consumer, Food Service, Private Label, Bulk

1488 **Bo-Ling's Products**
9000 Bond Street
Overland Park, KS 66214-1723 913-888-8223
Vegetarian, Chinese curry
Estimated Sales: Less than $500,000
Number Employees: 1-4

1489 **Boar's Head Provision Company**
1819 Main Street
Suite 800
Sarasota, FL 34236 941-955-0994
Fax: 888-884-2627 www.boarshead.com
Processor of premium deli meats and cheeses.
Number Employees: 100-249
Type of Packaging: Consumer, Food Service

1490 **Boar's Head Provisions Company**
17 Parkway Pl
Edison, NJ 08837-3717 732-225-3111
Fax: 732-225-3748 800-794-7180
www.boarshead.com
Processor of premium deli meats and cheeses.
Estimated Sales: $ 1 - 3 Million
Number Employees: 5-9

1491 **Boar's Head Provisions Company**
P.O.Box 929
Forrest City, AR 72336 870-630-1638
Fax: 870-630-0274 www.boarshead.com
Gourmet meat and poultry products.
Manager: Ken Bosnert
Estimated Sales: $100+ Million
Number Employees: 500-999

1492 **Boar's Head Provisions Company**
1950 Industry Pl
Petersburg, VA 23805 804-722-4100
Fax: 804-863-1409 www.boarshead.com
Processor of premium deli meats and cheeses.
Plant Manager: Rachelle Harris
Estimated Sales: $100+ Million
Number Employees: 250-499

1493 **Boar's Head Provisions Company**
4434 Wyatts Mill Rd
Jarratt, VA 23867 434-535-0129
Fax: 434-535-8255 www.boarshead.com
Premium deli meats and cheeses, sausage.
Plant Manager: Jeff Szymanski

1494 **(HQ)Boar's Head Provisions Company**
7025 Professional Pkwy E
Sarasota, FL 34240-8412 941-907-4192
Fax: 941-907-3981 888-884-2627
www.boarshead.com
Processor of premium deli meats and cheeses.
Owner: Robert Fox
CEO: Robert Martin
CFO: Alex Baruch
Director Marketing: RuthAnn LaMore
Estimated Sales: $300,000-500,000
Number Employees: 1-4
Type of Packaging: Consumer
Brands:
BOAR'S HEAD

1495 **Boardman Foods**
P.O.Box 786
Boardman, OR 97818 541-481-3000
Fax: 801-881-8999
debbieradie@boardmanfoodsinc.com
www.boardmanfoodsinc.com
Processor of onions including IQF and peeled
President: Brian Maag
Quality Control: Deanna Goodeve
VP Sales: Thomas Flaherty
VP Operations: Debbie Radie
Estimated Sales: $20-50 Million
Number Employees: 100
Type of Packaging: Bulk

1496 **Bob Evans Farms**
200 N Wolcott St
Hillsdale, MI 49242 517-437-3349
www.bobevans.com
Manufacturer of fresh sausage, refrigerated mashed potatoes and side dishes and frozen breakfast
Manager: Dave Brummett
Manager: Tery Camp
Number Employees: 100
Type of Packaging: Consumer, Bulk
Other Locations:
Food Production Facilities
Hillsdale MI
Galva IL
Bidwell OH
Springfield OH
Xenia OH
Richardson TX
Sulphur Springs TX
Distribution Center
Springfield OH
Brands:
BOB EVANS®
BOB EVANS® RESTAURANT
MIMIS CAFE
OWENS®

1497 **(HQ)Bob Evans Farms**
3776 S High St
Columbus, OH 43207 614-491-2225
Fax: 614-492-4949 800-939-2338
www.bobevans.com
Manufacturer of fresh sausage, refrigerated mashed potatoes and side dishes and frozen breakfast
President/Chief Restaurant Oper. Officer: Harvey Brownlee
Chairman, CEO: Stephen Davis
CFO: Paul DeSantiser
President/Bob Evans Foods: Mike Townsley
Chief Concept Officer: Randall Hicks
Estimated Sales: $1.75 Billion
Number Employees: 44,086
Type of Packaging: Consumer, Bulk
Brands:
BOB EVANS
BOB EVANS RESTAURANTS
MIMIS CAFE
OWENS

1498 **Bob Evans Farms**
1001 Sw 2nd Street
Galva, IL 61434-1605 309-932-2194
www.bobevans.com
Manufacturer of fresh sausage, refrigerated mashed potatoes and side dishes and frozen breakfast
Plant Manager: David Swanson
Secretary/Vice President: Larry Beckwith
Number Employees: 62
Type of Packaging: Consumer, Bulk

1499 **Bob Evans Farms**
363 Green Valley Drive
Bidwell, OH 45614-9240 740-446-2612
www.bobevans.com
Manufacturer of fresh sausage, refrigerated mashed potatoes and side dishes and frozen breakfast
Manager: Dave Morgan
Secretary/Manager: Jim Bush
Number Employees: 90
Type of Packaging: Consumer, Bulk

1500 **Bob Evans Farms**
2110 W Jefferson Street
Springfield, OH 45506-1122 937-324-3356
www.bobevans.com
Manufacturer of fresh sausage, refrigerated mashed potatoes and side dishes and frozen breakfast
Manager: Roger Burnett
Number Employees: 50
Type of Packaging: Consumer, Bulk

1501 **Bob Evans Farms**
640 Birch Road
Xenia, OH 45385-7600 937-372-8067
www.bobevans.com
Manufacturer of fresh sausage, refrigerated mashed potatoes and side dishes and frozen breakfast
Manager: Thomas Sefton
Number Employees: 7
Type of Packaging: Consumer, Bulk

1502 **Bob Evans Farms**
3776 South High Street
Columbus, OH 43207
800-939-2338
www.bobevans.com
Manufacturer of fresh sausage, refrigerated mashed potatoes and side dishes and frozen breakfast
Project Manager: Ismael Martinez
Number Employees: 50
Type of Packaging: Consumer, Bulk

1503 **Bob Gordon & Associates**
940 Linden Avenue
Oak Park, IL 60302-1349 708-524-9611
Processor and importer of green and black olives, maraschino cherries, pickled onions, pickled mushrooms and Greek pepperoncini
President: Roberta Seefeldt
Vice President: Aaron Seefeldt
VP of Sales: Marcel Seefeldt
Controller: James Gosling
Estimated Sales: $1.2 Million
Number Employees: 10-19
Type of Packaging: Food Service, Private Label, Bulk
Brands:
Marquis
Splinter

1504 **Bob's Candies**
PO Box 3170
Albany, GA 31706-3170 229-430-8300
Fax: 229-430-8331 800-841-3602
info@bobscandies.coms www.bobscandies.com
Peppermint candy and candy.
President: Gregory McCormack
VP: Julie Roth
VP Sales: Ed Hudson
Purchasing Director: Mary Helen Dykes
Estimated Sales: $20-50 Million
Number Employees: 500-999
Type of Packaging: Private Label
Brands:
BOBS CANDY CANES
BOBS SUGAR FREE
OLD TIMEY
SWEET STRIPES

1505 **Bob's Custom Cuts**
PO Box 6189
Bonnyville, AB T9N 2G4
Canada 780-826-2138
Fax: 780-826-2138
Processor of fresh and frozen beef, pork, lamb, elk, jerky, deer, buffalo, wild boar, ostrich and game sausage
President: Paulette Dargis
Plant Manager: Ken Wychopen
Estimated Sales: A
Number Employees: 1-4
Sq. footage: 9500
Parent Co: Dargis Land & Cattle
Type of Packaging: Consumer, Food Service, Private Label, Bulk

1506 **(HQ)Bob's Red Mill Natural Foods**
13521 SE Pheasant Court
Milwaukie, OR 97222 503-654-3215
Fax: 503-653-1339 800-553-2258
www.bobsredmill.com
Processor of milled whole grain flours, cereals and corn meal; also, mixes, bean flour and fat replacers
President: Bob Moore
CEO: Dennis Gilliam
CFO: John Wagner
Estimated Sales: $25-50 Million
Number Employees: 200
Sq. footage: 320000
Type of Packaging: Consumer, Food Service, Bulk
Brands:
Bob's Red Mill

1507 **Bobby D'S**
4737 County Road 101 # 222
Minnetonka, MN 55345-2634 954-240-9108
tiffany@bobbyds.com
www.bobbyds.com
Manufacturer of sauces.

1508 **Boboli Intl. Inc.**
3439 Brookside Rd Ste 104
Stockton, CA 95219 209-473-3507
Fax: 209-473-0492 bobint@mail.com
www.boboli-intl.com
Frozen and unfrozen bakery products, pizza crusts
President/CEO: George Visgilio
EVP: Wellington Henderson
VP Sales: Angela Rosenquist
Estimated Sales: $12.3 Million
Number Employees: 75
Type of Packaging: Food Service
Brands:
AMBRETTA
DUTCH CHOCK FACTORY
PATISSA
TULIP STREET BAKERY
VAN DIERMAN

1509 **Boca Bons East,LLC.**
5190 Lake Worth Road
Greenacres, FL 33463 954-346-0494
Fax: 954-346-0497 800-314-2835
skanter@bocabons.com www.bocabons.com
Manufacturer and exporter of a certified kosher chocolate that is a combination of a truffle, fudge, and a brownie.
President: Susan Kanter
Estimated Sales: $1-3 Million
Number Employees: 10-19
Sq. footage: 5000
Type of Packaging: Consumer, Food Service, Private Label, Bulk
Brands:
Boca Bons

1510 **Boca Foods Company**
910 Mayer Ave
Madison, WI 53704 608-285-3311
Fax: 608-285-6741 www.bocafoods.com
Manufacturer of meatless burgers
President: Kevin Scott
Director: Heather Fries
Brand Manager: Gary Berger
Estimated Sales: $20-50 Million
Number Employees: 35
Parent Co: Kraft Foods
Brands:
BOCA®

1511 **Boca Grande Foods**
3245 N Berkeley Lake Rd NW
Duluth, GA 30096-3054 770-622-1500
Fax: 770-814-0046 800-788-8026
customerservice@bocagrandefoods.com
Portion control packaging
President: Herb Sodel
Marketing: Mark Katz
Office Manager: Melinda England
Estimated Sales: $5-10 Million
Number Employees: 100-249
Type of Packaging: Bulk
Brands:
GRANDE GOURMET
POCO PAC

1512 **Bocconcino Food Products**
140 W Commercial Ave
Moonachie, NJ 07074-1703 201-933-7474
Fax: 201-933-1530
Processor of frozen pizza and pizza bagels including regular and bite-size; exporter of pizza bagels
Owner: Frank Lagalia
VP: Eric Silbeerman
Office Manager: Fay Campisi
Production Manager: Dan D'Amico
Estimated Sales: $5-10 Million
Number Employees: 20-49
Sq. footage: 19000
Type of Packaging: Consumer, Food Service, Private Label
Brands:
Bocconcino

1513 **Bodacious Food Company**
339 Gennett Dr
Jasper, GA 30143 706-253-1153
Fax: 706-253-1156 800-391-1979
cathy@bodaciousfoods.com
www.bodaciousfoods.com
Processor of cheese straws and shortbread, gingerbread, key lime, chocolate and sugar-free brownie bites
President: Cathy Cunningham Hays
Purchasing Manager: Dave Hays
Estimated Sales: $1.4 Million
Number Employees: 20-49
Sq. footage: 8000
Type of Packaging: Consumer
Brands:
Geraldine's Bodacious

1514 **Bodega Chocolates**
17290 Newhope St Ste A A
Fountain Valley, CA 92708 714-432-0708
Fax: 714-432-1537 888-326-3342
customerinfo@bodegachocolates.com
www.bodegachocolates.com
Manufacturer of fudge truffle bars and confections
Principal: Gary Khazanovich
Co-Owner: Martucci Angiano
Estimated Sales: Under $500,000
Number Employees: 8
Type of Packaging: Consumer, Food Service
Brands:
Fudgescotti

1515 **Bodek Kosher Produce**
1294 E 8th St
Brooklyn, NY 11230 718-377-4163
Fax: 718-377-0782 mail@bodek.com
www.bodek.com
Grade A, California grown produce, strictly supervised from seedling to harvest to production under the Central Rabbinical Congress, OU, and Rabbi Gissinger.
Owner: Jack Whyman
Estimated Sales: $1-$2.5 Million
Number Employees: 5-9

1516 **Bodin Foods**
704 Avenue D
New Iberia, LA 70560-0527 337-367-1344
Fax: 337-364-4968 daniel@cajun-recipes.com
www.cajun-recipes.com
Manufacturer of frozen Cajun foods, browning/seasoning sauce, pork boudin, shrimp boudin, crawfish boudin, dressing mix, crawfish pies, meat pies, shrimp and crabmeat pies, and crawfish and crabmeat pies
Owner: Dennis Higginebotham
CEO: Madine Pacetti
Estimated Sales: $500,000
Number Employees: 5-9
Number of Brands: 2
Number of Products: 11
Sq. footage: 8545
Type of Packaging: Consumer, Food Service, Private Label
Brands:
Bodin's
Brown Kwik
Cajun Bites

1517 **Body Ammo Research Center**
2014 Cypress Pt
Byron, CA 94505-9300 925-513-8514
customerservice@bodyammoproducts.com
www.bodyammoproducts.com
Processor and exporter of energy food powder, weight loss systems and health and nutritional supplements, including anabolic, joint rehab formulas, etc
Number Employees: 1-4
Sq. footage: 30000
Brands:
ACTI VIN
BODY AMMO

1518 **Body Breakthrough**
561 Acorn St # I
Deer Park, NY 11729-3600 631-243-2443
Fax: 631-243-2464 800-874-6299
trimaxx@earthlink.com
www.bodybreakthrough.com
Processor and exporter of teas including herbal, dietary and antioxidant; also, weight loss aids
President: Cori Lichter
Executive Director: Glenn Lichter
Estimated Sales: $2.5-5 Million
Number Employees: 5-9
Sq. footage: 5000
Type of Packaging: Consumer, Private Label
Brands:
ANTI OXIDANT EDGE
TRIM MAXX
YOHIMBE

1519 **Bodyonics Limited**
200 Adams Blvd
Farmingdale, NY 11735-6615 516-822-1230
Fax: 516-822-1252 www.greatearth.com
Sports nutrition, vitamins, herbs and supplements.
President: Mel Rich
Sales/Marketing: Andy Fishman
Number Employees: 50-99

1520 **Boeckman JJ Wholesale Meats**
1218 N Keowee St
Dayton, OH 45404-1546 937-222-4679
Manufacturer of ham and bologna
President: James Weller
Estimated Sales: $1-2.5 Million
Number Employees: 1-4
Type of Packaging: Consumer, Food Service, Private Label, Bulk

1521 **Boeger Winery**
1709 Carson Rd
Placerville, CA 95667 530-622-8094
Fax: 530-622-8112 800-655-2634
sue@boegerwinery.com www.boegerwinery.com
Wines
President: Greg Boeger
Vice President: Susan Boeger
Sales Director: Carl Keinert
Estimated Sales: $2.5-5 Million
Number Employees: 20-49
Type of Packaging: Private Label

1522 **Boehringer Ingelheim**
39w879 Hoeweed Lane
Saint Charles, IL 60175-6979 630-377-5150
Fax: 630-377-5150 tomgush@avenew.com
Organic mineral salts

1523 **(HQ)Boekhout Farms**
2592 Ridge Rd
Ontario, NY 14519 315-524-4041
Fax: 315-524-4041
Grower of peaches, plums, rhubarb and apples. Distributer of frozen fruits; raspberries, strawberries, blackberries, blueberries, cherries, aplles, peaches and rhubarb.
President: William Schwarz
Estimated Sales: $10 Million
Number Employees: 1-4
Number of Brands: 1
Number of Products: 30
Sq. footage: 15900
Type of Packaging: Consumer, Private Label, Bulk
Brands:
BOEKHOUT FARM

1524 **Boesl Packing Company**
2322 Belair Rd
Baltimore, MD 21213 410-675-1071
Fax: 410-327-4131
Manufacturer and packer of meat products including smoked frankfurters, knockwurst, bologna, salami and bacon; pig tails, neck bones and chitterlings; sausage: hot, smoked and Polish
Owner: Jeffery Burton
Vice President: Robert Barrett
Estimated Sales: $5.6 Million
Number Employees: 20-49
Type of Packaging: Consumer

1525 **Boetje Foods**
2736 12th St
Rock Island, IL 61201 309-788-4352
Fax: 309-788-4365 877-726-3853
boetje1889@aol.com www.boetjefoods.com
Processor of gourmet mustard
President: Robert Kropp
Treasurer: Dorothy Kropp
General Manager: Will Kropp
Production Manager: Stuart Soliz
Estimated Sales: $2.5-5 Million
Number Employees: 1-4
Sq. footage: 6000
Type of Packaging: Consumer, Food Service, Private Label, Bulk
Brands:
DUTCH BOY

1526 **Bogdon Candy Company**
101 Erie Blvd
Canajoharie, NY 13317-1148
Fax: 888-673-2451 800-839-8938
info@richardsonbrands.com
www.bogdonschocolates.com
Manufacturer of mint, lemon, orange and cinnamon flavored candy sticks dipped in dark chocolate and individually wrapped
President: Mr. Bogdon
Supply Chain Manager: Rebecca Woodruff
Estimated Sales: $5-10 Million
Number Employees: 20-49
Type of Packaging: Consumer, Food Service, Private Label, Bulk

1527 **Boggiatto Produce**
P.O.Box 2266
Salinas, CA 93902 831-424-4864
Fax: 831-424-1974 produce@boggiatto.com
www.boggiattoproduce.com
Processor of artichokes, broccoli, Brussels sprouts, cabbage, celery, cilantro, squash, lettuce, romaine lettuce hearts, kale, onions, leeks, peas, parsley, beets, green beans, rapini, spinach, etc
Owner: Michael Boggiatto
Sales Manager: Kraig Kuska
Sales: Don Day
Estimated Sales: $2.5-5 Million
Number Employees: 10-19
Type of Packaging: Consumer, Food Service
Brands:
Boggiatto
Garden Hearts

1528 **Boghosian Raisin Packing Company**
726 S 8th Street
PO Box 338
Fowler, CA 93625 559-834-5348
Fax: 559-834-1419 philipbrp@aol.com
www.boghosianraisin.com
Processor of raisins
Owner: Philip Boghosian
Owner: Peter Boghosian
Owner: Paul Boghosian
Human Resource Executive: Roger Stiles
Manufacturing Supervisor: Richard Lokey
Plant Manager: Richard Lokey
Estimated Sales: $7 Million
Number Employees: 60
Sq. footage: 11000
Type of Packaging: Consumer, Bulk

1529 **Bogland**
300 Oak Street
Pembroke, MA 02359-1984 781-829-9549
Fax: 781-829-9567 janbaird@costalclassics.com
Cranberry chutney, cranberry mustard, cranberry grill sauce, cranberry cabernet vinaigrette, cranberry orange marmalade, cranberry blueberry preserves, Szechuan peanut sauce, margarita madness mustard, port mustard, seafood mustard
President: Jan Baird
Estimated Sales: $2.5-5 Million
Number Employees: 1-4
Brands:
Bogland
Bogland By the Sea
Boglandish

1530 **Bogle Vineyards**
37783 County Road 144
Clarksburg, CA 95612-5009 916-744-1139
Fax: 916-744-1187 info@boglewinery.com
www.boglewinery.com
Wine
President: Patty Bogle
VP: Warren Bogle
Marketing Manager: Christopher Catterton
Public Relation Manager: Kristen Alling
Winemaker: Christopher Smith
Estimated Sales: $2.5-5 Million
Number Employees: 10-19
Type of Packaging: Private Label

1531 **Bohemian Biscuit Company**
258 Littlefield Avenue
South San Francisco, CA 94080-6922650-952-2226
Fax: 650-952-2439 jhsosnick@sosnick.com
Wholesaler/distributor and importer of candy including sugar-free, gourmet chocolate, lollipops and gummies
President: Jeffrey Sosnick
Vice President: Martin Sosnick
Sales Director: Wayne Sosnick
Estimated Sales: $15 Million
Number Employees: 85
Sq. footage: 35000
Parent Co: J. Sosnick & Son
Type of Packaging: Consumer, Food Service, Private Label, Bulk
Brands:
Droste
Ferrero
Ghirardelli
Haribo
La Vosigienne
Lindt
Royal Flush
Walkers

1532 **Bohemian Brewery**
94 Fort Union Blvd
Midvale, UT 84047 801-566-5474
Fax: 801-566-5321
jpetras@bohemianbrewery.com
www.bohemianbrewery.com
Manufacturer of ale and lager
Owner: Joe Petras
Vice President: Helen Petras
Estimated Sales: Under $500,000
Number Employees: 10
Type of Packaging: Consumer, Food Service
Brands:
Bohemian

1533 **Boisset America**
2320 Marinship Way
Suite 140
Sausalito, CA 94965-2830 415-339-9393
Fax: 415-979-0305 800-878-1123
info@ boissetamerica.com
www.boissetamerica.com
Wines
President: Jean Charles Boisset
CFO: Kelley Nowrouzk
VP: Alain Leonnet
Marketing: Lisa Heisinger
Sales: Raymond Nantel
Operations: Alain Leonnet
Estimated Sales: $10-20 Million
Number Employees: 5-9
Brands:
BOUCHARD AINE FILS
Boisset Classic
Boisset Mediterranee
Charles De Fere
Christophe Cellars
Evoluna Estate
Fog Mountain
J MOREAU FILS
Jean-Claude Boisset
Joliesse Vineyards
LES DOMAINES BERNARD
Lyeth Estate
Oceana Coastal
Ropiteall
Summerlake
Vienot
William Wheeler Winery

1534 **Boisson Slow Cow Inc**
3023 Boul Wilfrid-Hamel Est
Suite 116
Canada 418-266-0432
Fax: 418-877-1596 info@slowcowdrink.com
www.slowcowdrink.com
Relaxation beverage

1535 **Boissons Miami Pomor**
704 Boulevard Guimond
Longueuil, QC J4G 1T5
Canada 450-677-3744
Fax: 450-677-7826 877-977-3744
administration@boissonsmiami.com
www.boissonsmiami.com
Processor of juices, concentrates and crystals
Administration: Lise Huneault
Administration: Yves Brisebois
Administration: Andre Brisebois
Number Employees: 12
Sq. footage: 6750

1536 **Boja's Foods**
13120 N Wintzell Ave
Bayou La Batre, AL 36509 251-824-4186
Fax: 251-824-7339
Crab meat stuffing
President: Kay Kramer
CFO: Nancy West
Vice President: John Malone
Estimated Sales: $2 Million
Number Employees: 20
Brands:
Boja's
Boja's Chef's Delight
Paulines

1537 **Bold Coast Smokehouse**
224 County Rd
Lubec, ME 04652 207-733-8912
Fax: 207-733-8986 888-733-0807
vinny@boldcoastsmokehouse.com www.rier.com
Processor of hot and cold smoked Atlantic salmon, smoked salmon, smoked salmon pate and lox, smoked trout pate, finnan haddie, smoked mackeral, smoked salmon kabobs, graulax, smoked lobster products, smoked mussels and smokescallops.
President/Owner: Vinny Gartmayer
Estimated Sales: $ 1 - 3 Million
Number Employees: 5-9
Type of Packaging: Consumer, Private Label

1538 **Bolner's Fiesta Products**
426 Menchaca St
San Antonio, TX 78207 210-734-6404
Fax: 210-734-7866 info@fiestaspices.com
www.fiestaspices.net
Processor and importer of dehydrated vegetables, liquid extracts and spices, herbs and seasonings, including: bay leaves, cinnamon, cloves, cumin, sage, nutmeg, oregano, paprika, onion salt, anise, caraway, garlic, celery and mustardseeds, black pepper.
President: Timothy Bolner
CEO: Rosalie Bolner
CFO: George Paz
Marketing Director: Chris Bolner
VP of Sales & Marketing: Michael Bolner
Operations Manager: Tim Bolner
Plant Manager: James Morris
Estimated Sales: $10-24.9 Million
Number Employees: 100-249
Type of Packaging: Consumer, Food Service, Private Label, Bulk
Brands:
FIESTA
LYNWOOD FARMS
PAPA JOE'S
RIVER ROAD
SPICE CHOICE
SPICE RANCH
SPICE STAR

1539 **Bolthouse Farms**
7200 E Brundage Ln
Bakersfield, CA 93307 661-366-7205
Fax: 661-366-7289 800-467-4683
raust@bolthouse.com www.bolthouse.com
President/CEO: Andre Hdant
VP: Tim McCorkle
Marketing Director: Bryan Reese
Sales Director: Tim McCorkle
Estimated Sales: $ 5 - 10 Million
Number Employees: 20-49
Brands:
Earth Unt Farm
Green Gaint

1540 **Bombay Breeze Specialty Foods**
Box 67019
Mississauga, ON L5L 5V4
Canada 416-410-2320
Fax: 416-410-2320 bombaybreeze@usa.com
www.bombaybreeze.com
Exotic tropical fruit juices, jams, chutney, sauce, organic soups, and Indian curries.
President: Raju Tripathi
Brands:
SAHARA

1541 **Bon Secour Fisheries**
P.O.Box 60
Bon Secour, AL 36511 251-949-7411
Fax: 251-949-6478 800-633-6854
bonsec@bonsecourfisheries.com
www.bonsecourfisheries.com
Manufacturer, exporter and wholesaler of fresh and frozen flounder, whiting, snapper, shrimp, oysters, scallops, crawfish, snow, soft shell and king crab, lobster, cod, catfish, tuna, grouper, pollock, shark, mahi, talapia, etc.; alsoalligator meat.
CEO: John Ray Nelson
CFO/Secretary/Treasurer: Frank Bailey
Vice President: Christopher Nelson
Sales: Kenny Crawford
Purchasing Director: Carl Haynes
Estimated Sales: $20-50 Million
Number Employees: 100-249
Sq. footage: 60000
Type of Packaging: Consumer, Food Service, Bulk
Brands:
BON SECOUR
NELSON'S

1542 **Bon Ton Products**
275 E Hintz Rd
Wheeling, IL 60090 847-520-8300
Fax: 847-520-8396
Meat buyer, boxed beef and pork cuts.
Manager: James Cristy
Marketing Director: Dave Centino
Estimated Sales: $17 Million
Number Employees: 5-9

1543 **Bone Doctors' BBQ,LLC**
534 Park Street
Charlottesville, VA 22902-4748 434-296-7766
Fax: 434-977-6613 sales@bonedoctorsbbq.com
www.bonedoctorsbbq.com
BBQ sauce, grilling sauces, marinades, spices.
Marketing: David Heilbronner

1544 **Bonert's Slice of Pie**
2727 S Susan St
Santa Ana, CA 92704 714-540-3535
Fax: 714-540-9615 susanm@bonertspies.com
www.bonertspies.com
Manufacturer of fruit, creme, meringue, no sugar added, and no top-ready to finish pies.
CEO: Michael Bonert
Sales Rep: Susan Mahoney
Estimated Sales: $ 5 - 10 Million
Number Employees: 5-9

1545 **Bongard's Creameries**
110 3rd Ave NE
Perham, MN 56573 218-346-4680
Fax: 218-346-4684
Processor of dairy products including cheese and whey
Number Employees: 100-249
Parent Co: Land O'Lakes
Type of Packaging: Consumer, Private Label

1546 **Bongards Creameries**
13200 County Road 51
Norwood, MN 55368 952-466-5521
Fax: 952-466-5556 800-877-6417
customerservice@bongards.com
www.bongardscheese.com
Manufacturer of butter, cheese and whey powder
President: Curtis Wolter
CEO: Roger Engelman
Sales Manager: Stu Kringen
Estimated Sales: $172 Million
Number Employees: 250-499
Type of Packaging: Private Label

1547 **(HQ)Bongrain Cheese**
400 S Custer Ave
New Holland, PA 17557-9220 717-355-8500
Fax: 717-355-8561 www.bongrain.com
Cheese and cream cheese
President: Frank Otis
President: James Williams
Marketing Director: Jon Gutknecht
Purchasing Manager: Nancy Henry
Estimated Sales: $ 20 - 50 Million
Number Employees: 50-99
Brands:
Aloutte
Chaumes
Creme De Brie
Cremeux

Gerard
La Cheesierie
Mamie
New Hoolland
Quaker
Real Fresh
Short Cuts
St. Albray
Tartare
Ultra Delight
Zausner

1548 **Bongrain North America**
One International Blvd Ste 400
Mahwah, NJ 07495-0025 201-512-8825
Fax: 201-512-8718 bna1@aol.com
Processor of cheese and cheese products
President/CFO: Tom Swartele
Estimated Sales: 1 Billion
Number Employees: 1-4
Parent Co: Bongrain USA
Type of Packaging: Consumer, Food Service
Brands:
Allouette
Charrie
Delico
Fleur De Lait
Isle de Francis
Montracheti
Real Fresh

1549 **Bonnie Baking Company**
P.O.Box 426
La Porte, IN 46352-0426 219-362-4561
Fax: 219-325-0030
Bread, rolls
Manager: John West
Estimated Sales: $ 20 - 50 Million
Number Employees: 100-249

1550 **Bonnie Doon Ice Cream Corporation**
2941 Moose Trl
Elkhart, IN 46514 574-264-3390
Fax: 574-264-6208
Manufacturer of ice cream
President: Samuel Dugan II
Vice President: Jim Otis
Estimated Sales: $ 10 - 20 Million
Number Employees: 20-49
Type of Packaging: Food Service, Bulk

1551 **Bonnie's Ice Cream**
21 Leaman Road
Paradise, PA 17562-9660 717-687-9301
President: Lou Termini
Estimated Sales: $1-2.5 Million
Number Employees: 10-19

1552 **Bonnie's Jams**
Cambridge, MA 02138-4729 617-714-5380
bonnie@bonniesjams.com
www.bonniesjams.com
Jams, jellies
Marketing: Bonnie Shershow

1553 **Bonny Doon Vineyard**
328 Ingalls St
Santa Cruz, CA 95060-5849 831-425-3625
Fax: 831-425-3856
grahmcru@bonnydoonvineyard.com
www.bonnydoonvineyard.com
Wines
General Manager: David Amadia
Marketing Manager: Ted Pearson
Controller-Operations: Jim Fullmer
President/CEO: Randall Graham
Estimated Sales: $10 Million
Number Employees: 20-49
Type of Packaging: Private Label

1554 **Bonterra Vineyard**
12625 E Side Road
Hopland, CA 95449 707-744-7575
Fax: 707-744-1844
Wines
Brands:
Bonterra

1555 **Booneway Farms**
2810 Hoitt Ave
Knoxville, TN 37917-4865 865-521-9500
Fax: 859-986-3583
Processor of mustards, hamburger marinades, jellies, preserves, seasonings and spices
President: Williams Arant, Jr.
Estimated Sales: $2.5-5 Million
Number Employees: 20-49
Type of Packaging: Private Label

1556 **Boordy Vineyards**
12820 Long Green Pike
Hydes, MD 21082 410-592-5015
Fax: 410-592-5385 wineinfo@boordy.com
www.boordy.com
Wines
President/Owner: Robert Deford
Marketing Director: Susan Daniels
Public Relations: Rory Calhoun
Production Manager: Tom Burns
Estimated Sales: $2.5-5 Million
Number Employees: 10-19
Type of Packaging: Private Label
Brands:
Boordy Vineyards

1557 **Boothbay Region Lobsterman**
97 Atlantic Ave
Boothbay Harbor, ME 04538 207-633-4900
Fax: 207-633-4077
Lobster
Estimated Sales: $ 3 - 5 Million
Number Employees: 10-19

1558 **Boquet's Oyster House**
6645 Highway 56
Chauvin, LA 70344-2630 504-594-5574
Fax: 253-761-0504
Fresh, frozen, shucked oysters
President: Lawrenece Bouquet, Jr.

1559 **Borden**
P.O.Box 3047
Tulsa, OK 74101-3047 918-587-2471
Fax: 918-582-4605 800-733-2230
Manufacturer of dairy products
Sales Director: Joan Farmer
General Manager: George Streetman
Plant Manager: Dave Schirmer
Number Employees: 50-99
Parent Co: Suiza Dairy Group
Type of Packaging: Consumer, Bulk

1560 **Borden Foods**
2001 Polaris Parkway
Columbus, OH 43240-2000 614-233-3759
Fax: 614-233-3701 www.prince.com
Manufacturer of dry pasta, jarred pasta sauce, dry soups and boullion
VP Quality/Purchasing: Lloyd Moberg
Parent Co: Suiza Dairy Group
Brands:
PRINCE

1561 **Borden's Bread**
1771 Winnipeg Street
Regina, SK S4P 1G1
Canada 306-525-3341
Fax: 306-522-5303
Manufacturer of baked goods including bread, rolls, cakes, cookies, pies and pastries
Co-Owner: Leif Ellefson
Co-Owner: Ruth Ellefson
Type of Packaging: Consumer, Food Service

1562 **Border Foods Inc**
4065 J St SE
Deming, NM 88030 575-546-8863
Fax: 575-546-8676 888-737-7752
customerservice@borderfoodsinc.com
www.borderfoodsinc.com
Manufacturer of canned Mexican food including green chile peppers, sauces and salsa.
President: John Bowman
Chief Financial Officer: Leslie Berriman
Senior VP: Bob Gats
SVP/Marketing & Sales: Bob Gats
Customer Service: Dela King
Estimated Sales: $100-500 Million
Number Employees: 250-499
Sq. footage: 7000
Parent Co: Border Foods
Type of Packaging: Food Service, Private Label, Bulk
Other Locations:
Basic American Foods
Vacaville CA
Brands:
CLASSIC CASSEROLE
GOLDEN GRILL
NATURE'S OWN
POTATOE PEARLS
QUICK START
REDI SHRED
REGIONAL RECIPE
SANTIAGO

1563 **Border's Market**
3798 State Route 603
Plymouth, OH 44865 419-687-2634
Processor of beef, pork, veal and lamb
Owner: Mike Bauer
Owner: Sandy Bauer
President: Mary Ganzhorn
Estimated Sales: $1-2.5 Million
Number Employees: 5-9
Type of Packaging: Consumer

1564 **Bordoni Vineyards**
RR 4
Box 885k
Vallejo, CA 94591-9802 707-642-1504
Wines
President: Jim Bordoni
Estimated Sales: $5-10 Million
Number Employees: 1-4

1565 **Borgattis Ravioli**
632 E 187th St
Bronx, NY 10458 718-367-3799
Fax: 718-367-2229 www.borgattis.com
Pasta
Owner: Mario Borgatti
Estimated Sales: $1-2.5 Million
Number Employees: 1-4

1566 **Borgnine Beverage Company**
4355 Sepulveda Boulevard
Apt 215
Sherman Oaks, CA 91403-3961 818-501-5312
Fax: 818-788-6096 borg9cs@aol.com
www.borgininescoffesoda.com
Manufacturer of Coffee, soda
Number Employees: 1-4

1567 **Borinquen Biscuit Corporation**
Carr 376 Km 0 1 St Ca
Yauco, PR 00698 787-856-3030
Fax: 787-856-5339 www.prtc.net
Manufacturers of quality soda crackers, cookies and biscuits.
President: Antonio Rodriguez Zamora
Vice President: Antonio Morales
Purchasing Manager: Antonio Rodriguez Morales
Number Employees: 140
Sq. footage: 58000
Type of Packaging: Consumer, Private Label
Brands:
Cien En Boca
Florecitas
Rica
Royal Borinquen Export
Vanilla Imperial

1568 **Borinquen Macaroni Corporation**
Carr 376 Km 0 2 Almacigo St Ca
Yauco, PR 00698 787-856-1450
Fax: 787-856-5630 pexcelsior@coqui.net
www.pastasexcelsior.com
Manufacturer of pasta: spaghetti, macaroni, lasagna, elbow, ditali, shells and ziti
President: Antonio Rodriguez-Zamor
Estimated Sales: $5 Million
Number Employees: 85
Type of Packaging: Private Label
Brands:
Excelsior
Pastas Exelsior

1569 **Bornstein Seafoods**
1001 Hilton Avenue
Bellingham, WA 98225 360-734-7990
Fax: 360-734-5732 www.bornstein.com
Processor of canned fish and fresh and frozen dungeness crab
President: Jay Bornstein
Sales: Colin Bornstein
Number Employees: 5-9
Parent Co: Bornstein Seafoods
Type of Packaging: Consumer, Food Service

Brands:
Pacific Best
Stormy

1570 **Bornstein Seafoods**
1001 Hilton Ave
Bellingham, WA 98225 360-734-7990
Fax: 360-734-5732 doug@bornstein.com
www.bornstein.com
Live, fresh and frozen seafood
President: Jay Bornstein
Marketing: Meyer Bornstein
Manager: Chris Lubtice
Estimated Sales: $20-50 Million
Number Employees: 75
Brands:
Bornstein

1571 **Bornt Family Farms**
2307 E Us Highway 98
Holtville, CA 92250 760-356-2233
Fax: 760-356-1066
Organic vegetables
Owner: Alan Bornt
CFO: Mary Bornt
Office Manager: Sandra Gaskin
VP Marketing/Sales: John Prock
Estimated Sales: $3.2 Million
Number Employees: 13
Brands:
Bornt Family Farms
Ocean Organics

1572 **Borra Vineyards**
1301 E Armstrong Rd
Lodi, CA 95242-9423 209-368-2446
Fax: 209-369-5116 info@borravineyards.com
www.borrawinery.com
Manufacturer of wine
Owner: Steve Borra Sr
CEO: Beverly Borra
VP Marketing: Gina Granlees
Estimated Sales: $ 1 - 3 Million
Number Employees: 1-4
Type of Packaging: Private Label
Brands:
BORRA

1573 **Borthwicks Flavors**
330 Motor Pkwy # 102
Hauppauge, NY 11788-5117 631-273-6200
Fax: 631-273-6346 800-255-6837
Flavors
Estimated Sales: $50-100 Million
Number Employees: 1-4

1574 **Bos Smoked Fish Inc**
1175 Patullo Avenue E
Woodstock, ON N4S 7W3
Canada 519-537-5000
Fax: 519-537-5522 bossmokedfish@bellnet.ca
Procesor and exporter of smoked herring, trout, salmon, whitefish, mackerel fillets, mackerel, (various spices) marinated products
President: Pieter Bos
VP: Klaas Bos
Estimated Sales: $6 Million
Number Employees: 15
Type of Packaging: Consumer, Food Service, Private Label, Bulk

1575 **Bosco Products**
441 Main Rd
Towaco, NJ 7082 973-334-7534
Fax: 973-334-2617 800-438-2672
boscomail@earthlink.net www.boscoworld.com
Chocolate and flavored syrup and drink products
President: Steven Sanders
Number Employees: 50-99
Brands:
Bosco

1576 **Boscoli Foods**
2254 Greenwood Street
Kenner, LA 70062 504-469-5500
Fax: 504-469-5548 edmontaldo@yahoo.com
www.boscoli.com
manufacturer of fine Italian gourmet foods.

1577 **Bosell Foods**
17212 Miles Ave
Cleveland, OH 44128 216-991-7600
Fax: 216-991-7739 questions@bosellfoods.com
www.bosellfoods.com
Processor of fresh and frozen prepared salads and meats
President/Owner: Bernie Polen
CEO: Jack Lain
Sales Executive: Alisa Capriottschrei
Estimated Sales: $1.3 Million
Number Employees: 12
Type of Packaging: Consumer, Food Service, Private Label
Brands:
Bosell
Brookside
Homestead

1578 **Boskovich Farms**
P.O.Box 1352
Oxnard, CA 93032 805-487-2299
Fax: 805-487-5189
marketing@boskovichfarms.com
www.boskovichfarms.com
Processor and exporter of fresh and frozen vegetables and strawberries
President: Joe Boskovich
CEO: George Boskovich Jr
Marketing Manager: Lindy Martinez
Estimated Sales: $50-100 Million
Number Employees: 205
Type of Packaging: Consumer, Food Service

1579 **Boskydel Vineyard**
7501 E Otto Rd
Lake Leelanau, MI 49653 231-256-7272
userg@jimrink.com
www.boskydel.com
Wines
Owner: Bernard Rink
President: Jim Rink
Vineyard Manager: Andrew Rink
Estimated Sales: Less than $500,000
Number Employees: 1-4
Type of Packaging: Private Label
Brands:
Boskydel

1580 **Boston America Corporation**
325 New Boston St Unit 17
Woburn, MA 01801 617-923-1111
Fax: 617-923-8839
customerservice@bostonamerica.com
www.bostonamerica.com
Manufacturer of tinned candies and cookies
Estimated Sales: $ 1 - 3 Million
Number Employees: 20-49
Brands:
BUBBLEGUM
GRINCH
MY LITTLE PONY
POWERPUFF GIRLS
SCOOBY DOO
SPIDER-MAN
STRAWBERRY SHORTCAKE

1581 **(HQ)Boston Beer Company**
50 Franklin St # 408
Boston, MA 02110-1306
US 617-422-0009
Fax: 617-368-5500 800-372-1131
www.bostonbeer.com
www.samueladams.com
Manufacturer and exporter of beer mainly sam adams.
Owner: Alex Bok
CFO: Richard Lindsay
VP Brand Development: Robert Hall
COO: Jeffrey White
Estimated Sales: $190 Million
Number Employees: 750
Parent Co: Samuel Adams Beer Company
Type of Packaging: Consumer, Food Service
Brands:
HARDCORE
SAMUEL ADAMS
TWISTED TEA
UTOPIAS

1582 **Boston Chowda Company**
101 Phoenix Ave
Lowell, MA 1852 978-970-1144
Fax: 978-970-0450 800-992-0054
www.bostonchowda.com
Processor and exporter of frozen soups and chowders
President: Richard Lamattina
Director: Paul Cassidy
Director: John Leroy
Director: Alan Katz
Estimated Sales: $20-50 Million
Number Employees: 13
Sq. footage: 13000
Brands:
Bay State Chowda

1583 **Boston Direct Lobster**
207 Iris Avenue
New Orleans, LA 70121-2807 504-834-6404
Fax: 504-834-6402
Lobsters
President: Earl Duke III

1584 **Boston Fruit Slice & Confectionery Corporation**
250 Canal St
Lawrence, MA 01840-1642 978-686-2699
Fax: 978-686-5898 rick@bostonfruitslice.com
www.bostonfruitslice.com
Manufacturer of jellied fruit slices
Manager: Richard Hiera
Estimated Sales: $5 Million
Number Employees: 20-49
Brands:
BOSTON FRUIT SLICES
POLLY ORCHARD

1585 **Boston Seafarms**
119 Malborough Street
Boston, MA 02116 617-784-4777
Fax: 800-692-9907 seafarms@ziplink.net
www.bostonseafarm.com
Processor, wholesaler/distributor, importer and exporter of seafood including fish and shellfish
President/CEO: Adam Weinberg
Estimated Sales: $300,000-500,000
Number Employees: 5-9
Sq. footage: 18000

1586 **Boston Spice & Tea Company**
12207 Obannons Mill Rd
Boston, VA 22713 540-547-3907
Fax: 540-547-3656 800-966-4372
bst@erols.com
Processor of herbal tea, vinegar, seasonings, mustard, sherry-pepper hot sauce, wassil, mulling and corned beef spices and dry bean soup mixes
President: Joann Neal
Marketing Director: Greaner Neal
Manager Sales: Greaner Neal
Estimated Sales: $ .5 - 1 million
Number Employees: 5-9
Type of Packaging: Consumer
Brands:
Boston spices
Logyan's Garden
Logyn's Garden Soups
O'Bannon's
Stews and Sauces

1587 **Boston Stoker**
P.O.Box 548
Vandalia, OH 45377 937-890-6401
Fax: 937-890-6403 800-745-5282
Coffee
President: Donald Dean
CFO: Sally Dean
Sales Manager: Ed Dunn
Plant Manager: John McWilliams
Estimated Sales: $500,000-$1 Million
Number Employees: 10,000+
Type of Packaging: Private Label

1588 **Boston Tea Company**
560 Hudson St
Suite 3
Hackensack, NJ 07601 201-440-3004
Fax: 201-440-3005
customerservice@bostontea.com
www.bostontea.com
Manufacturer of teas
President: Andy Jacobs
Vice President: Mary Jacobs
Marketing: Michael Lapointe
Estimated Sales: Under $500,000
Number Employees: 1-4
Brands:
Beddy By

Lemon Dew
Magic Mountain
Ming Cha
Natco
Pick O' the Bushel
Razzle Dazzle
Spice Bouquet

1589 **Boston's Best Coffee Roasters**
43 Norfolk Ave
South Easton, MA 02375 508-238-8393
Fax: 508-238-6835 800-898-8393
sales@bostonsbestcoffee.com
www.bostonsbestcoffee.com
Manufacturer, importer and exporter of coffee mixers and filters; processor, importer and exporter of coffee including freeze-dried, spray-dried, agglomerated, decaffeinated, whole bean, ground gourmet, spray dried, agglomen, flavoredand instant
President: Michael Dovner
CEO: Stephen Fortune
Production Manager: Rocky Raposa
Estimated Sales: $220,000
Number Employees: 2
Sq. footage: 2846
Type of Packaging: Consumer, Food Service, Private Label, Bulk
Brands:
DAVID'S GOURMET COFFEE
GOLD STAR COFFEE
PREMIER COFFEE
TROPICAL COFFEE

1590 **Botanical Bakery, LLC**
PO Box 11083
Napa, CA 94581 707-344-8103
Fax: 707-863-8949 info@botanicalbakery.com
www.botanicalbakery.com
Manufacturer of shortbread cookies.
CEO: Sondra Wells

1591 **(HQ)Botanical Laboratories**
1441 W Smith Rd
Ferndale, WA 98248 360-384-5656
Fax: 360-384-1140 800-232-4005
info@botlab.com www.botlab.com
Processor, exporter and contract packager of herbal and homeopathic food supplements in liquid, tablet and topical forms
President/CEO: Jim Coyne
CEO: Brian Halverson
CEO: Jim Thornton
Director R&D: Mary Beth Watkins
Quality Control: John McKnight
Marketing Director: Jeff Kuklenski
Estimated Sales: $100-500 Million
Number Employees: 50-99
Type of Packaging: Consumer, Private Label
Brands:
Bioallers
CompliMed
Natrabio
Nico-Rx
Symtec
Zand Hebs For Kids

1592 **Botanical Products**
34725 Bogart Dr
Springville, CA 93265 559-539-3432
Fax: 559-539-2058
desertprideyuca@onemain.com
Processor and exporter of tablets, capsules, extracts and powders made from yucca and melatonin
President: Gordon Bean
VP: Joyce Bean
Estimated Sales: $1-2.5 Million
Number Employees: 1-4
Sq. footage: 2000
Type of Packaging: Consumer
Brands:
Desert Pride
Desert Wonder

1593 **Botsford Fisheries**
Po Box 1093
Cap Pele, NB E4N 3B3
Canada 506-577-4327
Fax: 506-577-2846 botsford@nbnet.nb.ca
Processor and exporter of fresh and smoked herring
President: William LeBlanc
Export Sales Manager: Janice Ryan
Plant Manager: Clement LeBlanc
Estimated Sales: $2.5 Million
Number Employees: 50-99
Sq. footage: 40000
Type of Packaging: Consumer, Food Service, Private Label, Bulk

1594 **Bottineau Coop Creamery**
517 Thompson St
Bottineau, ND 58318 701-228-2216
Fax: 701-228-3426
Manufacturer of dairy products including butter, milk and ice cream
President: Daniel Managelo
Vice President: Floyd Slaughbaugh
Plant Manager: Jeff Byer
Plant Manager: Jeff Byer
Estimated Sales: $ 10 - 20 Million
Number Employees: 5-9
Type of Packaging: Consumer, Food Service, Bulk
Brands:
Pride

1595 **Bottle Green Drinks Company**
2375 Tedlost
Unit 1
Mississauga, ON L5A 3W7
Canada 905-273-6137
Fax: 905-273-3186 info@bottle-green.com
www.bottlegreendrinks.com
Processor of nonalcoholic and carbonated beverages including limeflower, elderflower, cranberry and lemongrass
President: Andrew James
CFO: Corrie James
Number Employees: 5-9
Number of Brands: 2
Number of Products: 9
Type of Packaging: Consumer, Food Service, Private Label
Brands:
Bottle Green

1596 **Bottomline Foods**
12401 Orange Drive
Suite 123
Davie, FL 33330 954-843-0562
Fax: 954-843-0568 info@blf.com
www.blf.com
Distributor and packer, exporter for frozen foods, meats, cheese, groceries, seafood, spices, etc.
President: Howard Blitz
CEO: Larry Blitz
CFO: Bob Blitz
Purchasing Manager: Mark Roberts
Number Employees: 5-9
Sq. footage: 2000
Type of Packaging: Food Service, Private Label, Bulk

1597 **Bouchaine Vineyards**
1075 Buchli Station Rd
Napa, CA 94559 707-252-9065
Fax: 707-252-0401 800-654-9463
www.bouchaine.com
Wines
Manager: Mike Richmond
Marketing Director: Carole Loomis
Sales Director: Jan Novotny
Controller: Steven Stoner
Winemaker: David Stevens
Estimated Sales: $2.5-5 Million
Number Employees: 10-19

1598 **Bouchard Family Farm**
3 Strip Rd
Fort Kent, ME 04743 207-834-3237
Fax: 207-834-7422 800-239-3237
bouchard@ployes.com www.ployes.com
Processor and exporter of buckwheat pancake mixes and flour
President: Joseph Bouchard
Sales/Marketing Executive: Elaine Mininger
Estimated Sales: $500,000-$1 Million
Number Employees: 5-9
Sq. footage: 110000
Type of Packaging: Consumer, Food Service
Brands:
Bouchard Family Farm

1599 **Boudreaux's Foods**
5401 Toler St
New Orleans, LA 70123 504-733-8440
Fax: 504-866-1965 bfoods@bellsouth.net
www.boudreauxsfoods.com
Processor of refrigerated entrees, salad dressings, breads, whole wheat pasta, soups, etc
President: Vince Hayward
Estimated Sales: $ 1 - 3 Million
Number Employees: 1-4
Sq. footage: 2000
Type of Packaging: Consumer
Brands:
Author's Choice
Boudreaux's

1600 **Boulder Beer Company**
2880 Wilderness Place
Boulder, CO 80301 303-444-8448
Fax: 303-444-4796 boulderbeer@aol.com
www.boulderbeer.com
Processor of beer and ale
President/CEO: Jeff Brown
Finance Manager: Ellen Leonard
Public Relations Director: Tess McFadden
VP Brewing Operations: David Zuckerman
Estimated Sales: $6 Million
Number Employees: 50
Number of Brands: 9
Number of Products: 1
Sq. footage: 18000
Brands:
Boulder
Boulder Amber Ale
Boulder Brews
Boulder Extra Pale
Boulder Pale Ale
Boulder Porter
Boulder Stout
Brown
Buffalo Gold
Cliffhanger
Fall Fest
Igloo
Porter
Rockies Brewing
Rockies Premium Draft
Stout

1601 **Boulder Creek Brewing Company**
13040 Highway 9
Boulder Creek, CA 95006-9154 831-338-7882
Fax: 831-338-7583 brewco@hwy9.com
www.bouldercreekbrewery.net
Beer, ale, lager
Owner: Nancy Long
Estimated Sales: Less than $500,000
Number Employees: 10-19
Brands:
Boulder Creek
Redwood Ale

1602 **Boulder Sausage**
513 S Pierce Ave
Louisville, CO 80027 303-665-6302
Fax: 303-665-3109 www.bouldersausage.com
Meat
President: Herm Schempp
Vice President: Donald Gullickson
Office Manager: Suzanne Richards
Estimated Sales: $2.4 Million
Number Employees: 20
Number of Products: 14
Type of Packaging: Consumer, Food Service, Private Label, Bulk
Brands:
Boulder Sausage Products
Private Label Products
Rocky Mountain Products

1603 **Boulder Street Coffee Roaster**
332 N Tejon St
Colorado Springs, CO 80903-1224 719-577-4291
Fax: 719-577-4291
www.coloradospringsfictionwritersgroup.org
Coffee
Owner: Iwao Green
Estimated Sales: $5-10 Million
Number Employees: 10-19

1604 **Boulevard Brewing Company**
2501 Southwest Blvd
Kansas City, MO 64108 816-474-7095
Fax: 816-474-1722 fineales@blvdbeer.com
www.blvdbeer.com

Processor of ale, lager, stout and seasonal beer
Manager: Steven Pauwels
CFO: Jeff Krum
Marketing Director: Bob Sullivan
Production Manager: Larry Dunaway
Estimated Sales: $7 Million
Number Employees: 20-49
Type of Packaging: Consumer, Food Service

1605 **Bouma Meats**
5017 50 St
Provost, AB T0B 3S0
Canada 780-753-2092
Fax: 780-753-4939
www.provostnews.ca/boumameats/
Processor of beef and pork including fresh, frozen, portion controlled, sausage and deli cuts; also, bacon and ham
President: Ben Richter
Co-Owner: Tim Rachinski
Number Employees: 10-19
Type of Packaging: Consumer, Food Service, Private Label, Bulk
Brands:
Bouma

1606 **Bountiful Pantry**
6 Gay St
Nantucket, MA 02554 508-325-0203
Fax: 508-325-0203 888-832-6466
judy@bountifulpantry.com
www.bountifulpantry.com
Manufacturer of soup mixes, side dishes, waffle mixes, bread, roll, scone and biscuit mixes, cookie and dessert mixes and teas and coffees

1607 **Bourbon Ball**
P.O.Box 4215
Louisville, KY 40204-0215 502-634-3300
Fax: 502-895-4403 800-280-0888
www.thebourbonball.com
Processor of chocolate liquor-filled candy
President: Jim Patton
Estimated Sales: $250,000
Number Employees: 5-9
Type of Packaging: Private Label
Brands:
Bourbon Ball

1608 **Bourbon Barrel Foods**
1201 Story Avenue
Suite 175
Louisville, KY 40206 502-333-6103
Fax: 502-333-6104
matt@bourbonbarrelfoods.com
www.bourbonbarrelfoods.com
Manufacturer of gourmet foods.

1609 **Boutique Seafood**
1326 White St SW
Atlanta, GA 30310-1648 404-752-8852
Fax: 404-752-6634
Seafood, red snapper, sea bass, lobster meat, crabmeat, grouper
President: Pano Karatassos
Estimated Sales: $1.3 Million
Number Employees: 5-9

1610 **Bouvry Exports Calgary**
222 58 Avenue SW
Suite 312
Calgary, AB T2H 2S3
Canada 403-253-0717
Fax: 403-259-3568
103241.2622@compuserve.com
www.egsood-alliance.ab.ca
Processor of horse meat, bison and beef
President: Claude Bouvry
CEO: John McNaughton
General Manager: Darin Sjonger
Sales: Alain Bouvry
Estimated Sales: $17.4 Million
Number Employees: 150
Type of Packaging: Consumer, Bulk

1611 **Bove's of Vermont**
68 Pearl St
Burlington, VT 05401-4332 802-862-7235
Fax: 802-651-9371 sauceboy@Boves.com
www.boves.com
Marinara sauce, roasted garlic sauce, chianti mushroom sauce, romano pomodoro sauce.
Owner: Richard Bove
Estimated Sales: $500,000-$1 Million
Number Employees: 20-49
Brands:
Bove's of Vermont

1612 **Bow Valley Brewing Company**
109 Boulder Crescent
Canmore, AB T1W 1L4
Canada 403-678-2739
Fax: 403-678-8813 bvbc@telusplanet.net
www.beerexpedition.com
Processor of lager
President: Hugh Hancock
Number Employees: 5-9
Type of Packaging: Consumer, Food Service
Brands:
Bow Valley

1613 **Bowman & Landes Turkeys**
6490 E Ross Rd
New Carlisle, OH 45344 937-845-9466
Fax: 937-845-9998 877-466-9466
info@bowmanlandes.com
www.bowmanlandes.com
Free range turkeys
CEO/President: Dan Landes
Estimated Sales: $10-20 Million
Number Employees: 100-249
Type of Packaging: Consumer, Bulk

1614 **Bowman Apple Products Company**
10119 Old Valley Pike
PO Box 817
Mount Jackson, VA 22842 540-477-3111
Fax: 540-477-2320 800-346-5382
sales@bowmanandros.com
www.bowmanappleproducts.com
Applesuace, apple juice, apple butter and apple cider
President: Gordon D Bowman Ii
President: Gordon Bowman
CFO: Benjamin Amoss II
Point of Sale Manager: Sam Wenger
Production Manager: George Hollida
Plant Manager: Gene Bodkin
Purchasing Manager: Timothy Proctor
Estimated Sales: $20-50 Million
Number Employees: 100-249
Type of Packaging: Consumer, Private Label
Brands:
Bowman
Bowman's
New Yorker
Old Virginia

1615 **Bowness Bakery**
4280-23rd Street NE
Calgary, AB T2E 6X7
Canada 403-250-9760
Fax: 403-291-9129
Processor of specialty breads, pretzels and pizza shells
President: Shams Habib
CEO: Shams Habib
Marketing Manager: Shams Habib
General Manager: Sm\Hams Habib
Estimated Sales: D
Number Employees: 50-99
Type of Packaging: Consumer, Food Service, Bulk
Brands:
Bowness Baker
Frisches Brot
Pretzeland

1616 **Bowser Meat Processing**
513 S Palmberg St
Meriden, KS 66512 785-484-2454
Processor of meat including sausage
Manager: Kirsti Petesch
Manager: Kirsti Petesch
Estimated Sales: $1-2.5 Million
Number Employees: 5-9
Type of Packaging: Consumer

1617 **Boyajian, Inc.**
144 Will Dr
Canton, MA 2021 781-828-9966
Fax: 781-828-9922 800-965-0665
customerservice@boyajianinc.com
www.boyajianinc.com
Processor and importer of flavored vinegars, infused oils including olive, garlic, lemon, lime, orange, peanut, pepper, sesame and pure Asian and natural flavorings including strawberry, raspberry, cherry, spearmint, clove, peppermintcinnamon and wintergreen, etc
Owner: John Boyajian
Estimated Sales: $1 Million
Number Employees: 12
Sq. footage: 20000
Type of Packaging: Consumer, Food Service, Private Label, Bulk
Brands:
Boyajian

1618 **(HQ)Boyd Coffee Company**
19730 NE Sandy Blvd
Portland, OR 97230 503-666-4545
Fax: 503-669-2223 800-545-4077
info@boyds.com www.boyds.com
Manufacturer of coffees teas, cocoa, hot and frozen beverages, soups, sauces, gravies and flour products.
Co-President/Co-CEO: David Boyd
Co-President/Co-CEO: Dick Boyd
President & CEO: Jeffrey Newman
SVP: Doug McKay
Estimated Sales: $59 Million
Number Employees: 500-999
Type of Packaging: Food Service
Other Locations:
Boyd Coffee Company
Coeur D Alene ID
Brands:
BOYD'S COFFEE
COFFEE HOUSE ROASTERS
ISLAND MIST ICED TEA
ITALIA D'ORO COFFEE
TECHNI-BREW
TODAY
VIAGGIO COFFEE

1619 **Boyd Sausage Company**
626 Highway 1 S
Washington, IA 52353 319-653-5715
Manufacturer of beef jerky, bologna and deer meat products including sausage
Owner: George Statler
GM: Brandon Statler
Estimated Sales: Under $400,000
Number Employees: 5-9
Sq. footage: 3500
Type of Packaging: Consumer, Bulk

1620 **Boyer Candy Company**
821 17th St
Altoona, PA 16601 814-944-9401
Fax: 814-944-4923 www.boyercandies.com
Processor of chocolate confectionery products including shell molded chocolates, cup candy and seasonal novelities
CEO: Robert Faith
Estimated Sales: $13 Million
Number Employees: 100
Sq. footage: 150000
Type of Packaging: Consumer, Private Label, Bulk
Brands:
Bartons
Boxer
Boyer
Casanova
Hill of Westchester
Kron
Schrafft's
Winters

1621 **Boyer Coffee Company**
7295 N Washington St
Denver, CO 80229-6707 303-289-3345
Fax: 303-289-2133 800-452-5282
boyers@usa.net www.boyerscoffee.com
Coffee
President: W Boyer
Marketing Director: Bonnie Rine
Plant Manager: L Smith
Purchasing Manager: L Smith
Estimated Sales: $2.5-5 Million
Number Employees: 20-49
Type of Packaging: Private Label

1622 **Boylan Bottling Company**
74 Lee Avenue
Haledon, NJ 07508-1202 973-790-7093
Fax: 973-790-9097 800-289-7978
boylan@cybernex.net

Bottled soft drinks
President/CEO: Ronald Fiorina
Executive VP: Mark Fiorina
COO: David Fiorina, Jr.
Estimated Sales: $1-2.5 Million
Number Employees: 20-49

1623 **Boyle Meat Company**
1638 Saint Louis Ave
Kansas City, MO 64101-1130 816-221-6283
Fax: 816-221-3888 800-821-3626
christysteaks@worldnet.att.net
www.boylescornedbeef.com
Steaks, corn beef, pastrami and pot roast
President: Don Wendl
VP: Christy Chester
Estimated Sales: $20-50 Million
Number Employees: 20-49
Sq. footage: 10000
Type of Packaging: Food Service, Private Label, Bulk

1624 **Boyton Shellfish**
RR 2
Box 85a
Ellsworth, ME 04605 207-667-8580
Fax: 619-474-6103
Shellfish
Owner: Dean Smith

1625 **(HQ)Brach's Confections**
3921 Vero Rd
Halethorpe, MD 21227-1564 443-872-2094
www.brachs.com
Manufacturer of candy
President/CEO: Charles Haak
CFO: James Hagedorn
Estimated Sales: $ 20 - 50 Million
Number Employees: 20-49
Parent Co: Barry-Callebaut
Type of Packaging: Consumer
Brands:
Brach's
DOUBLE DIPPERS
FRUTIO'S
SPECIAL TREASURES
STAR BRITES
STARS

1626 **Brad's Organic**
7 Hoover Ave
Haverstraw, NY 10927 845-429-9080
Fax: 845-429-9089 sales@bradsorganic.com
www.bradorganic.com
Organic, all-natural salsa, tortilla chips, honey, jams and peanut butter
Administration: Lisa Salia

1627 **Brad's Taste of New York**
P.O.Box 20475
Floral Park, NY 11002-0475 516-354-9004
Fax: 516-354-9004 bradstasteofny@aol.com
www.bradstasteofny.com
Manufacturer of gourmet mustard, pretzel dip, honey wheat pretzel, sourdough honey mustard nuggets, and kettle potato chips
Owner: Bradley Knese
Estimated Sales: $ 1 - 3 Million
Number Employees: 5-9

1628 **Bradley Creek Seafood**
2700 Gregory St Ste 200
Savannah, GA 31404 912-484-3510
Fax: 912-897-7815 tastycrab@mindspring.com
www.bradleycreek.com
Manufacturer of crab au gratin pastries; deviled crab; and crab cakes.
President/CEO: Michael Simmons
Type of Packaging: Food Service

1629 **Bradley TechnologiesCanada Inc.**
1609 Derwent Way
Delta, BC V3M 6K8 604-524-3848
Fax: 604-524-3839 800-665-4188
michael@bradleysmoker.com
www.bradleysmoker.com
Other meat/game/pate. other sauces, seasonings and cooking enhancers, private label, cooking implements,housewares.
Marketing: Michael Tostowaryk

1630 **Bradshaw's Food Products**
1425 Somerset Avenue
Dighton, MA 02715-1215 508-669-6088
Processor of pickled beef tripe
Partner: D Bradshaw
Partner: R Bradshaw
Estimated Sales: $1-2.5 Million
Number Employees: 1-4

1631 **Brady Farms**
14786 Winans St
West Olive, MI 49460 616-842-3916
Fax: 616-842-8357
Processor of blueberries including fresh, frozen and puree
President: Robert Brady
CEO: Myron Brady
Sales: Ronald Benson
Plant Manager: Juana Chavez
Estimated Sales: $14.5 Million
Number Employees: 112
Type of Packaging: Consumer, Food Service, Private Label, Bulk

1632 **Bradye P. Todd & Son**
2 Sunset Ln
Cambridge, MD 21613-1308 410-228-8633
www.toddseafood.com
Manufacturer of seafood including crabs, seafood delicatessen and restaurant
Owner: Roy Todd
Estimated Sales: $3 Million
Number Employees: 20-49
Sq. footage: 4000
Parent Co: T.A. Ocean Odyssey
Type of Packaging: Consumer

1633 **Bragg-Live Food Products**
P.O.Box 7
Santa Barbara, CA 93102 805-968-1020
Fax: 805-968-1001 800-446-1990
info@bragg.com www.bragg.com
Health foods
President: Patricia Bragg
Estimated Sales: $3-4 Million
Number Employees: 20-49
Brands:
Bragg Raw Organic Cider Vinegar

1634 **Braham Food Locker Service**
P.O.Box 554
Braham, MN 55006-0554 320-396-2636
Processor of meat products including beef, goat and pork; also, smoked and cured sausage
President: Nicholas Grote
CEO: Diane Grote
Estimated Sales: $250,000
Number Employees: 5-9
Type of Packaging: Consumer

1635 **Brakebush Brothers**
N4993 6th Dr
Westfield, WI 53964 608-296-3192
Fax: 608-296-3192 800-933-2121
brakebushrep@brakebush.com
www.brakebush.com
Manufacturer of frozen chicken
President: William Brakebush Jr
EVP: Carl Brakebush
QA Manager: Donna Halbach
Marketing Manager: Steve Ross
Director Sales/Marketing: Scott Sanders
Production Manager: Dave Robinson
Purchasing Manager: Chris Brakebrush
Estimated Sales: $100-500 Million
Number Employees: 500-999
Number of Brands: 1
Type of Packaging: Consumer, Food Service

1636 **Brand Aromatics International**
1600 Oak Street
Lakewood, NJ 08701 732-706-3411
Fax: 732-363-8041 800-363-2080
flavors@brandaromatics.com
http://www.brandaromatics.com/
Flavors and seasonings
President: Karl Brand
VP: Dennis Shea
Number Employees: 7

1637 **Brandborg Cellars**
PO Box 506
Elkton, OR 97436-0506 510-215-9553
Fax: 415-282-6179 terryb@nbn.com
Wine
President: Terry Brandborg
Number Employees: 20-49

1638 **Brander Vineyard**
P.O.Box 92
Los Olivos, CA 93441 805-688-2455
Fax: 805-688-8010 800-970-9979
info@Brander.com www.brander.com
Manufacturer of red and white wines
Owner/Winemaker: C Frederic Brander
Office Manager: Kathy Forner
Operations Assistant: Drew Horton
Estimated Sales: $900,000
Number Employees: 5-9
Type of Packaging: Consumer, Food Service
Brands:
Brander

1639 **Brandmeyer Popcorn Company**
3785 NE 70th Ave
Ankeny, IA 50021 515-262-3243
Fax: 866-400-8884 800-568-8276
www.lottapop.com
Processor and exporter of popcorn including gift boxes and specialty items
President: Arlie Brandmeyer
Estimated Sales: Less than $100,000
Number Employees: 1-4
Brands:
Iowa State
Lotta-Pop

1640 **Brandt Farms**
6040 Avenue 430
Reedley, CA 93654 559-638-6961
Fax: 559-638-6964 sales@treeripe.com
www.treeripe.com
Processor, exporter and importer of fresh fruits including kiwifruit, apricots, nectarines, plums, peaches and table grapes
President: Wayne Brandt
CEO: Eleanor Brandt
CFO: Jack Brandt
Domestic Sales: Michael Reimer
Public Relations: Dave Maddox
Estimated Sales: $ 50 - 100 Million
Number Employees: 100-249
Sq. footage: 30000
Brands:
BRANDT
CRYSTAL FOODS
CRYSTAL R-BEST

1641 **Brandt Mills**
607 Race Street
Mifflinville, PA 18631 570-752-4271
Fax: 570-752-8712
Manufacturer of flour including pastry and whole wheat
President: Richard Brandt Jr
Estimated Sales: $1.3 Million
Number Employees: 12
Sq. footage: 12000

1642 **Braren Pauli Winery**
7051 N State St
Redwood Valley, CA 95470-9629 707-485-0322
Fax: 707-485-6784 800-423-6519
info@brarenpauli.com www.brarenpauli.com
Wines
President: Charlie Barra
Co-Owner/CEO: Bill Pauli
Marketing Director: Larry Braren
Sales Director: Larry Braren
Winemaker: Larry Braren
Estimated Sales: $ .5 - 1 million
Number Employees: 20-49
Brands:
Braren Pauli

1643 **Brass Ladle Products**
P.O.Box 39
Concordville, PA 19331 610-565-8664
Fax: 610-565-8665 800-955-2353
frontdesk@brassladle.com www.brassladle.com
Manufacturer of all-natural gourmet cake mixes including carrot, mocha mud(chocolate) and lemon poppy seed.
Owner: Skip Achuff
Estimated Sales: $1,000,000
Number Employees: 1-4
Number of Brands: 1
Number of Products: 3
Sq. footage: 3000
Type of Packaging: Consumer, Food Service, Private Label, Bulk

Brands:
Brass Ladle
Mocha Mud
Mocha Mud Cake Mix

1644 **Brasserie Brasel Brewery**
8477 Rue Cordner
Lasalle, QC H8N 2X2
Canada 514-365-5050
Fax: 514-365-2954 800-463-2728
Processor and exporter of lager beers
President: Marcel Jagermann
Managing Director: Stan Jagermann
Number Employees: 10-19
Sq. footage: 12000
Type of Packaging: Consumer, Food Service, Private Label
Brands:
Brasal Bock
Brasal Legere
Brasal Special Amber
Hopps Aux Pommes
Hopps Brau

1645 **Brassica Protection Products**
2400 Boston St Ste 300
Baltimore, MD 21224 877-747-1277
Fax: 410-732-1980 877-747-1277
mail@brassica.com www.brassica.com
Food ingredients, supplements, nutraceuticals, functional foods (cander preventive products)
CEO: Anthony Talalay
CEO: Antony Talalay
VP Business Development: Earl Hauserman
Estimated Sales: $2,000,000
Number Employees: 5-9
Brands:
Brassica
Brassica Teas with SGS
BroccoSprouts

1646 **Braswell Food Company**
Po Box 485
Statesboro, GA 30459 912-764-6191
Fax: 912-489-1572 800-673-9388
andy.oliver@braswells.com www.braswells.com
Preserves, special teas, seafood collection, braswell's organics, braswell's select, flavoring mixes, dressings, salsas and dips, sauces, hot sauces, seasonings and rubs, marinades, jams, jellies, hors d'oeuvre jellies, fruit buttersfruit spreads, marmalades, mustards, pickles, relishes, syrups, honeys, toppings, chutneys, chow chows
President/Owner: Andy Oliver
Cfo: Jimmy Cobb
Production: Frank Farr
Estimated Sales: $12.4 Million
Number Employees: 95

1647 **Braswell's Winery**
7556 Bankhead Highway
Dora, AL 35062-2041 205-648-8335
Fax: 205-648-8335
Wines
President: Wayne Braswell
Owner: Ruth Braswell
Estimated Sales: $1-4.9 Million
Number Employees: 1-4

1648 **Brateka Enterprises**
15680 SW 23rd Avenue
Ocala, FL 34473-4278 352-307-5459
Fax: 352-307-5459 877-549-3227
brateka@aol.com www.lizabbasauce.com
Processor of gourmet sauces in gift baskets
CEO: Hyacinth Thomas
Number Employees: 10-19
Brands:
Lize Jamaican Style Gourmet BBQ

1649 **(HQ)Braum's Inc**
PO Box 25429
Oklahoma City, OK 73125-0429 405-478-1656
Fax: 405-475-2460 www.braums.com
Frozen desserts, dairy and milk
CEO: Drew Braum
CFO: Mark Godwin
Marketing Director: Terry Holden
Purchasing Manager: Kenny McDonald
Type of Packaging: Food Service

1650 **Braun Seafood Company**
30840 Main Rd
Cutchogue, NY 11935 631-734-6700
Fax: 631-734-7462 info@braunseafood.com
www.braunseafood.com
Processor of oysters and frozen scallops
President: Kenneth Homan
VP: Wayne Phillips
Estimated Sales: $7 Million
Number Employees: 35
Brands:
Peconic Bay
Robins Island

1651 **Bravard Vineyards & Winery**
15000 Overton Rd
Hopkinsville, KY 42240-9451 270-269-2583
jbravard@apex.net
www.commercecenter.org/visitors/bravard/
Processor of wines including dry, semi-dry, semi-sweet and sweet in white, blush, rose and red
Owner: Jim Bravard
Estimated Sales: $500,000-$1 Million
Number Employees: 1-4
Sq. footage: 250
Type of Packaging: Private Label
Brands:
Bravard
Countryside Red
Foch
Fruit Hill White
Lady Genevieve
Pennyroyal

1652 **Brazilian Home Collection**
249 Monree Street
Passaic, NJ 07055 973-365-5800
worldwide@wwiec.com
Brazil handicraft.

1653 **Brazos Legends/Texas Tamale Co**
9087 Knight Rd
Houston, TX 77054-4305 713-795-5500
Fax: 713-795-5534 800-882-6253
sbailey@texastamale.com www.texastamale.com
Gourmet food products
Manager: Shirley Bailey
Sales Director: Shirley Bailey
Operations Manager: Shirley Bailey
Plant Manager: Ana Flores
Estimated Sales: $3-5 Million
Number Employees: 20-49
Number of Brands: 5
Number of Products: 125
Sq. footage: 25000
Type of Packaging: Consumer, Food Service, Private Label, Bulk
Brands:
Brazos Legends
Red Eye

1654 **Bread & Chocolate**
1538 Industrial Park Road
Po Box 692
Wells River, VT 05081 802-429-2920
Fax: 802-429-2990 800-524-6715
breadcho@together.net
www.burnhamandmills.com
Manufacturer of gourmet lemonade, cocoa, pancake mixes, jams, mustards and iced tea mixes
President: Jonathan Rutstein
Vice President: Fran Rutstein
Estimated Sales: $500,000-900,000
Number Employees: 1-4
Brands:
BEAR RIVER
BREAD & CHOCOLATE
MOOSE MOUNTAIN
SNOWMAN
STORYTIME

1655 **Bread Alone Bakery**
3962 Route 28
Boiceville, NY 12412 845-657-3328
Fax: 845-657-6228 800-769-3328
info@breadalone.com www.breadalone.com
Processor of whole grain and organic bread
Owner/President: Daniel Leader
Co Owner: Sharon Burns-Leader
Estimated Sales: $20-50 Million
Number Employees: 20-49
Brands:
Bread Alone

1656 **Bread Box**
445 7th Avenue S
Virden, NB R0M 2C0
Canada 204-748-1513
Processor of bread and buns
President: Debby Andrews
Co-Owner: Irene Plaisier
Co-Owner: Dianna Careme
Number Employees: 1-4
Sq. footage: 1000
Type of Packaging: Consumer

1657 **Bread Dip Company**
PO Box 42782
Philadelphia, PA 19101-2782 215-563-9455
Fax: 215-563-9144 laura@breaddipcompany.com
www.breaddipcompany.com
Manufacturer of gourmet spreads
Owner: Laura Sterbenz
Number Employees: 1-4

1658 **Bread Dip Company**
378 Terrace Drive
Friday Harbor, WA 98250-8931 360-378-6070
breaddip@interisland.net
Flavored bread dips: sun-dried tomato, olive and herb, artichoke and caper, peppers and spice and feta and pink peppercorn
President: Laura Sterbenz
Estimated Sales: Under $500,000
Number Employees: 2

1659 **Breadsmith**
9871 Montgomery Rd
Cincinnati, OH 45242-6424 513-791-8817
Fax: 513-791-8851 www.breadsmith.com
Baked goods
Owner: Bob Harris
Estimated Sales: Less than $500,000
Number Employees: 20-49
Type of Packaging: Consumer

1660 **Breadworks Bakery & Deli**
923 Preston Ave # A
Charlottesville, VA 22903-4446 434-296-4663
Fax: 434-971-6740 info@breadworks.com
www.breadworks.org
Processor of breads including American and French sourdough, twelve grain, Jewish rye, challah, semolina, Irish soda and baguettes; also, cookies, muffins, scones, danish, pies, cakes and deli products
Manager: Jim Baber
Chairman: Marc Bridenhagen
Vice President: John Satoski
Manager: Jim Baber
Production/Sales: Priscilla Fox
Estimated Sales: $ 1 - 3 Million
Number Employees: 10-19
Parent Co: Worksource Enterprises
Type of Packaging: Consumer, Food Service

1661 **Breakfast at Brennan's**
417 Royal St
New Orleans, LA 70130-2191 504-525-9711
Fax: 504-525-2302 800-888-9932
brennansno@aol.com
www.brennansneworleans.com
Coffees, muffins, jellies, Bananas Foster sauce mix, Royal Delite cookies, Coffee-on-the-Rocks concentrate, beignet mix, frozen drink mixes
Owner: Owen Brennan
Owner: Ted Brennan
Co-Owner: Jimmy Brennan
Estimated Sales: $ 5 - 10 Million
Number Employees: 100-249
Brands:
Breakfast At Brennan's

1662 **Breaktime Snacks**
7723 Somerset Blvd
Paramount, CA 90723-4104 562-633-6200
Fax: 562-633-8789 800-677-1868
popcornconnection@earthlink.net
www.popcornconnection.com
Gourmet popcorn
President/CEO: Roger Glade
Estimated Sales: $1-2.5 Million
Number Employees: 5-9
Brands:
Corn Appetit

1663 **Breakwater Fisheries**
14 O'Briens Hill
St Josephs, NL A1B 4G4
Canada 709-754-1999
Fax: 709-754-9712 rrbarnes@nf-sympatico.ca
Processor and exporter of frozen snow crab, capelin, turbot, cod, mackerel, herring, squid and shrimp; importer of frozen squid
President: Randy Barnes
CEO: Lemuel C White
Vice President: Ken White
Estimated Sales: $72 Million
Number Employees: 500
Sq. footage: 75000
Brands:
Breakwater

1664 **Breakwater Seafoods**
306 S F St
Aberdeen, WA 98520 360-532-5693
Fax: 360-533-6488
Seafoods
Owner: Don Henry
Estimated Sales: $2 Million
Number Employees: 5-9

1665 **Breaux Vineyards**
36888 Breaux Vineyards Ln
Purcellville, VA 20132 540-668-6299
Fax: 540-668-6283 800-492-9961
info@breauxvineyards.com
www.breauxvineyards.com
Manufacturer of wines
Owner: Paul Breaux
Co-Owner: Alexis Breaux
Sales Director: Jennifer Breaux Blosser
Operations Manager: Chris Blosser
Wine Maker: Dave Collins
Estimated Sales: $ .5 - 1 million
Number Employees: 20-49
Sq. footage: 20000
Type of Packaging: Consumer, Private Label, Bulk

1666 **Brechet & Richter Company**
6005 Golden Valley Rd
Minneapolis, MN 55422-4439 763-545-0201
Fax: 763-545-0201
Baking ingredient doughnut and cake mixtures
President: Tom Moore
Estimated Sales: $10-20 Million
Number Employees: 20-49
Type of Packaging: Private Label

1667 **Breckenridge Brewery**
471 Kalamath St
Denver, CO 80204 303-573-0431
Fax: 303-573-4877 www.breckenridge.com
Processor of ale and stout
Owner: Ed Cerkovnik
General Manager: Graham Squire
Estimated Sales: $1-2.5 Million
Number Employees: 20-49
Parent Co: Breckenridge Brewery
Type of Packaging: Consumer, Food Service, Bulk
Brands:
AUTUMN ALE
AVALANCHE ALE
CHRISTMAS ALE
HEFE PROPER
OATMEAL STOUT
PANDORA'S BOCK
SUMMERBRIGHT ALE
TRADEMARK PALE ALE

1668 **Brede**
19000 Glendale St
Detroit, MI 48223 313-273-1079
Fax: 313-273-4110 info@bredefoods.com
www.bredefoods.com
Processor and exporter of horseradish and horseradish sauce.
President/CEO: Michael Brede
Vice Presiddent: Craig Brede
Estimated Sales: $1-2.5 Million
Number Employees: 5-9
Sq. footage: 12000
Type of Packaging: Consumer, Food Service, Private Label, Bulk
Brands:
BREDE OLD FASHIONED
FARMERS
HI PRAIZE
OLD FASHIONED
POZNANSKI

1669 **Breitenbach Wine Cellars**
5934 Old Route 39 NW
Dover, OH 44622-7787 330-343-3603
Fax: 330-343-8290 amishwine@tusco.net
www.breitenbachwine.com
Wines
President/CEO: Cynthia Bixler
Director Manufacturing: Dalton Bixler
Estimated Sales: $2.5-5 Million
Number Employees: 10-19
Brands:
Breitenbach
Charming Nancy
Dardenella
Dusty Miller
Festival
First Crush
Frost Fire
Roadhouse Red
Rosebarb
Silver Seyual

1670 **Bremner Biscuit Company**
4600 Joliet St
Denver, CO 80239 303-371-8180
Fax: 303-371-8185 800-722-1871
bremmer@worldpantry.com
www.bremnerbiscuitco.com
Processor and exporter of gourmet, snack and oyster crackers
Manager: Neil Bremner
Estimated Sales: $5-10 Million
Number Employees: 20-49
Sq. footage: 42000
Parent Co: Dare Foods
Type of Packaging: Consumer, Food Service, Private Label, Bulk
Brands:
BREMNER
BREMNER WAFERS
BREWSKI SNACK

1671 **Bremner Company**
400 Industrial Blvd
Poteau, OK 74953 918-647-8630
Fax: 918-647-8518
www.bremnercookies-crackers.com
Processor and exporter of cookies and crackers
Quality Director: Garry Caufield
Operations Director: Steve Hickman
Plant Manager: Jeff Hollis
Purchasing Manager: Becky Broussard
Estimated Sales: $100+ Million
Number Employees: 250-499
Sq. footage: 250000
Parent Co: Ralcorp Holdings
Type of Packaging: Consumer, Food Service, Private Label

1672 **Brennan Snacks Manufacturing**
1220 W 7th Street
Bogalusa, LA 70427-3406 800-290-7486
Fax: 985-732-5397
Processor of snacks and cotton candy
Co-Owner: Bernie Brennan, Jr.
Co-Owner: Christi Brennan
Number Employees: 20-49
Type of Packaging: Food Service, Private Label
Brands:
Oboy's

1673 **Brenntag**
5083 Pottsville Pike
Reading, PA 19605 610-926-6100
Fax: 610-926-4160 888-926-4151
northeast.salesadmin@brenntag.com
www.brenntagnortheast.com
Distributor of food ingredients and specialty chemicals
Chairman/President: Markus Klaehn
President: Anthony Medaglia
VP: Dennis Eisenhofer
Estimated Sales: K
Number Employees: 500

1674 **Brenntag Pacific**
10747 Patterson Pl
Santa Fe Springs, CA 90670 562-903-9626
Fax: 562-906-5287 brenntag@brenntag.com
Beverages, confectionery, canned foods, processed cheese, bakery, meat, seafood, dairy
President: Steven M Pozzi
VP, National Accounts: Robert L Moser Jr
Estimated Sales: $ 50-100 Million
Number Employees: 50-99
Brands:
Brenntag Pacific

1675 **Brent & Sam's Cookies**
30 Collins Industrial Pl
N Little Rock, AR 72113-6555 501-562-4300
Fax: 501-568-9777 800-825-1613
perfectcookies@brentandsams.com
www.brentandsams.com
Gourmet cookies.
President: Brent Bumpers
VP Sales: John Merck
Estimated Sales: $10-20 Million
Number Employees: 20-49
Type of Packaging: Private Label
Brands:
BUTTER PECAN WITH CINN. OATS, RAIS.
CARIBBEAN CRUNCH
CHOCOLATE CHIP WITH PECANS
EXTRA CHOCOLATE CHIP NO NUTS
KEY LIME WHITE CHOCOLATE
LEMON WHITE CHOCOLATE
RASPBERRY CHOCOLATE CHIP
WHITE CHOCOLATE MACADAMIA NUT

1676 **Breslow Deli Products**
1209 N Hancock Street
Philadelphia, PA 19122-4505 215-739-4200
Fax: 215-423-4199
Processor of beef including smoked and dried
President: Jon Breslow
Estimated Sales: $1-2.5 Million
Number Employees: 5-9
Type of Packaging: Consumer, Food Service

1677 **Brewfresh Coffee Company**
2375 S West Temple
South Salt Lake, UT 84115 801-486-3334
Fax: 801-486-9714 888-486-3334
info@BrewFresh.com www.brewfresh.com
Manufacturer of the largest coffee roaster in Utah. We also produce; hot cocoa mixes, powder coffee creamers and powdered shake mixes
President: Larry Brog
Sales/Marketing Manager/EVP: Anton Broq
Estimated Sales: $500,000-$1 Million
Number Employees: 10-19

1678 **(HQ)Brewster Dairy**
800 S Wabash Avenue
Brewster, OH 44613 330-767-3492
Fax: 330-767-3386 800-874-8874
www.brewstercheese.com
All natural swiss cheese.
President: Brad Nelson
CEO: Fritz Leeman
CFO: Emil Alecusan
R&D Manager: Gene Hong, Ph.D.
Human Resources Executive: Beth Young
Operations Manager: Jim Barnard
Purchasing Manager: Valerie Marvich
Estimated Sales: $50-100 Million
Number Employees: 310
Sq. footage: 78914
Type of Packaging: Consumer, Food Service, Private Label, Bulk
Other Locations:
Brewster Dairy
Stockton IL

1679 **Brewster Foods TestLab**
7121 Canby Avenue
Reseda, CA 91335-4304 818-881-4268
Fax: 818-881-6370 rob@testlabinc.com
www.testlabinc.com
Processor and exporter of enzymes, flavors and ingredients.
President: Gregory Brewster
Estimated Sales: $1100000
Number Employees: 15
Sq. footage: 4000
Brands:
Brewster
Testlab
Vitalfa

1680 **Briar's USA**
P.O.Box 7092
North Brunswick, NJ 08902 732-821-7600
Fax: 732-821-2898 887-327-4277
info@hgbev.com www.highgradebeverage.com

Manufacturer of soft drinks
President: Anthony Demarco

1681 **Briceland Vineyards**
5959 Briceland Thorn Rd
Redway, CA 95560 707-923-2429
Wines and champagnes
President: Margaret Carey
Estimated Sales: $1-2.5 Million
Number Employees: 1-4

1682 **Brick Brewery**
181 King Street S
Waterloo, ON N2J 1P7
Canada 519-576-9100
Fax: 519-576-0470 800-505-8971
info@brickbeer.com www.brickbeer.com
Manufacturer and exporter of light and dark lager beers; also, ale
Chairman: Peter Schwartz
President/CEO: George Croft
CFO: Jason Pratt
VP Operations: Michael Baumken
Director Brewing, Quality and Logistics: Bill Henry
VP Marketing: Norm Pickering
VP Sales: Craig Prentice
VP Operations: Mike Baumken
Estimated Sales: $20-50 Million
Number Employees: 20-49
Sq. footage: 45000
Type of Packaging: Consumer
Brands:
ALGONQUIN HONEYBROWN
ANDECHS
ANNIVERSARY BOCK
BRICK PREMIUM
CONNERS BEST BITTER
FIX
FORMOSA DRAFT
HENNINGER KAISER PILS
LAKER FAMILY OF BEERS
PACIFIC REAL DRAFT
RED BARON
RED CAP
WATERLOO DARK

1683 **Bricker Labs**
3305 N. Delaware St
Chandler, AZ 85225 262-334-7047
Fax: 262-334-7651 800-274-2537
www.brickerlabs.com
Processor of nutritional supplements
Sales/Marketing Manager: Tami Dechairo
Estimated Sales: $1-2.5 Million
Number Employees: 20-49
Type of Packaging: Consumer, Food Service, Private Label, Bulk

1684 **Bridenbaughs Orchards**
316 Orchard Ln
Martinsburg, PA 16662-8145 814-793-2364
Grower and packer of apples, peaches, cherries, strawberries and raspberries; exporter of apples
Co-Owner: Glenn Bridenbaugh
Co-Owner: David Bridenbaugh
Estimated Sales: Less than $500,000
Number Employees: 1-4
Sq. footage: 4000
Type of Packaging: Consumer, Bulk

1685 **Bridge Brand Chocolate**
286 12th Street
San Francisco, CA 94103 415-677-9194
Fax: 415-362-2080 888-732-4626
www.sfchocolate.com
gourmet chocolates

1686 **Bridgetown Coffee**
2330 NW 31st Ave
Portland, OR 97210 503-224-3330
Fax: 503-224-9529 800-726-0320
www.bridgetowncoffee.com
Processor and exporter of coffee; wholesaler/distributor and exporter of tea; serving the food service market
President/Owner: Don Jensen
CEO: Timothy Timmins
Treasurer: Susan Jensen
Estimated Sales: $3 Million
Number Employees: 20
Number of Brands: 6
Number of Products: 21
Sq. footage: 40000
Type of Packaging: Consumer, Food Service, Private Label, Bulk
Brands:
BRIDGETOWN

1687 **Bridgeview Winery**
P.O.Box 609
Cave Junction, OR 97523-0609 541-592-4688
Fax: 541-592-2127 877-273-4843
www.bridgeviewwine.com.
www.bridgeviewwine.com
Wine
President: Robert Kerivan
Estimated Sales: $ 10 - 20 Million
Number Employees: 20-49

1688 **(HQ)Bridgford Foods Corporation**
1308 North Patt Street
Box 3773
Anaheim, CA 92803 714-526-5533
Fax: 714-526-4360 800-527-2105
info@bridgford.com www.bridgford.com
Manufacturer of frozen dough, pre-baked biscuits, shelf-stable dry and semi-dry sausage products and an assortment of frozen micro-ready sandwiches
Senior Chairman: Allan Bridgford
President: John Simmons
EVP/CFO: Raymond Lancy
Vice President: Bruce Bridgford
Estimated Sales: $117 Million
Number Employees: 550
Sq. footage: 100000
Type of Packaging: Consumer, Food Service
Other Locations:
Bridgford Foods Plant
Dallas TX
Bridgford Foods Plant
Chicago IL
Bridgford Foods Plant
Statesville NC

1689 **Bridgford Foods of North Carolina**
112 Progress Place
Statesville, NC 28677 704-878-2722
info@bridgford.com
www.bridgford.com
Manufacturer and distributor of frozen products, refrigerated and snack food products such as; biscuits, bread dough, dry sausage, various sandwiches and sliced luncheon meats.
Senior Chairman: Allan Bridgford
President: John Simmons
EVP/CFO: Raymond Lancy
Vice President: Bruce Bridgford
Estimated Sales: $117 Million
Number Employees: 550
Parent Co: Bridgford Foods Corporation
Type of Packaging: Consumer, Food Service
Other Locations:
Bridgford Plant
Dallas TX
Bridgford Plant
Chicago IL
Bridgford Plant
Statesville NC
Brands:
BRIDGFORD JERKY

1690 **Brier Run Farm**
Hc 32
Box 73
Birch River, WV 26610-9729 304-649-2975
Manufacturer of certified organic fresh chevre cheese
Co-Owner: Greg Sava
Co-Owner: Verena Sava
Estimated Sales: $110,000
Number Employees: 6
Sq. footage: 2000
Type of Packaging: Consumer, Food Service
Brands:
Brier Run
Brier Run Chevre

1691 **(HQ)Briess Industries**
P.O.Box 229
Chilton, WI 53014 920-849-7711
Fax: 920-849-4277 info@briess.com
www.briess.com
Manufacturer of all-natural food ingredients including malts, natural sweeteners (grain and starch-based), natural colorants, tapioca maltodextrins, reduced cook-time grains, pregelatinized flakes, and toasted grains. Many are wholegrain. Non-GMO, Kosher Certified, USDA Certified Organics.
President: Gordon Lane
CEO: Monica Briess
CFO: Craig Kennedy
Research & Development: Bob Hansen
Purchasing: Leana Prupson
Number Employees: 125
Type of Packaging: Bulk
Other Locations:
Briess Ingredients Company
Chilton WI
Waterloo WI
Brands:
BRIESS
CBW
INSTA GRAINS
MALTOFERM
MALTOROSE

1692 **Briggs Ice Cream**
5110 Buchanan St
Hyattsville, MD 20781 301-277-8787
Fax: 301-927-4527 info@briggsicecream.com
www.rosinco.com
Ice cream
Owner, President: David Rosin
Sales Manager: Steve Williams
General Manager: Robert Strahorn
Estimated Sales: $5.3 Million
Number Employees: 26
Brands:
ELAN FROZEN YOGURT

1693 **Brighams**
30 Mill Street
Arlington, MA 02476 781-648-9000
Fax: 781-646-0507 800-274-4426
brighams-mail@brighams.com
www.brighams.com
Processor of ice cream, frozen yogurt, whipped cream and fudge topping
President/Coo: Charles Green
Vice President/Cfo: Greg Welch
Operations: Claudia Kost
Estimated Sales: $2.5-5 Million
Number Employees: 50
Sq. footage: 110000
Type of Packaging: Consumer, Private Label, Bulk
Brands:
BRIGHAM'S
ELAN

1694 **Bright Harvest Sweet Potato Company**
P.O.Box 528
Clarksville, AR 72830 479-754-6313
Fax: 479-754-7794 800-793-7440
swinter@brightharvest.com
www.brightharvest.com
Sweet potato patties, mashed sweet potatoes, sweet potato sticks, center cut sweet potatoes, sweet potato casserole
President: Rex King
President: Rex King
VP Finance: Ken Golden
Quality Control: Jeff Hannon
VP Marketing/Sales: Sam Winterberg
Regional Sales Representative: John Coniglio
VP Operations: John Eyberg
Customer Service: Patricia Melton
Estimated Sales: $20-50 Million
Number Employees: 50-99
Sq. footage: 22000
Type of Packaging: Consumer, Food Service

1695 **Brimstone Hill Vineyard**
61 Brimstone Hill Rd
Pine Bush, NY 12566 845-744-2231
Fax: 845-744-4782 bhvwine@frontiernet.net
brimstonehillwine.com
Manufacturer of still and sparkling wines
Owner: Richard Eldridge
Owner: Valerie Eldridge
Estimated Sales: $500,000-750,000
Number Employees: 1-4
Type of Packaging: Food Service
Brands:
Brimstone Hill

1696 **Brinkley Dryer and Storage**
P.O.Box 744
Brinkley, AR 72021 870-734-1616
Fax: 870-734-2113 www.achfood.com
Rice specialties
Manager: Donnie Parsley
Marketing Director: Nelson Wurth
Operations Manager: Rick Wade
Production Manager: Patrick Roy
Plant Manager: Donnie Parsley
Estimated Sales: $50 Million
Number Employees: 100-249
Sq. footage: 50
Parent Co: Riviana Foods
Type of Packaging: Private Label
Brands:
FIESTA BRAND
ISLAND GIRL BRAND

1697 **Briny Sea Delicacies**
715 78th Avenue SW
Tumwater, WA 98501-5700 360-956-1797
Fax: 360-956-1986 888-772-5666
www.brinysea.net
Processor of seafood including fresh, vacuum-packed smoked salmon
President: Jay Garrison
Estimated Sales: Less than $500,000
Number Employees: 1-4
Type of Packaging: Consumer, Food Service

1698 **Brisk Coffee Company**
402 N 22nd St
Tampa, FL 33605 813-248-6264
Fax: 813-248-2947 800-899-5282
rperez@briskcoffee.com www.briskcoffee.com
Processor and exporter of roasted coffee; also, leasing of coffee equipment available
President/CEO: Richard Perez
VP/COO: Denise Reddick
VP Production: Randall Gonzalez
Estimated Sales: $10-20 Million
Number Employees: 30
Sq. footage: 20000
Type of Packaging: Food Service
Brands:
BRISK
GOLD PLUS
INNKEEPERS CHOICE

1699 **Bristle Ridge Vineyard**
P.O.Box 95
Knob Noster, MO 65336-0095 660-422-5646
800-994-9463
edward@brvwine.com www.brvwine.com
Wines
President: Edward Smith
Co-Owner: Vickie Smith
General Manager: Todd Smith
Estimated Sales: $5-9.9 Million
Number Employees: 5-9
Brands:
Bristle Ridge

1700 **Bristol Brewing Company**
1647 S Tejon St
Colorado Springs, CO 80905 719-633-2555
Fax: 719-633-2145 info@bristolbrewing.com
www.bristolbrewing.com
Processor of ale and stout
Owner: Mike Bristol
Operations: Josh Osterhoudt
Estimated Sales: $1 Million
Number Employees: 16
Type of Packaging: Consumer, Food Service, Bulk
Brands:
BEEHIVE
EDGE CITY IPA
EDGE CITY PILSNER
LAUGHING LAB
MASS TRANSIT
OLD NO.23
RED ROCKET
SCOTTISH
WINTER WARLOCK

1701 **(HQ)Bristol Myers-Squibb Company**
345 Park Ave
New York, NY 10154 212-546-2852
Fax: 212-546-4020 www.bms.com
Manufacturer of pharmaceuticals and related health care products
Chairman: James Cornelius
President/CEO: Lamberto Andreotti
CFO: Charles Bancroft
Estimated Sales: $19 Billion
Number Employees: 28,000
Brands:
ENFACARE LIPIL
ENFALYTE
ENFAMIL GENTLE EASE LIPIL
ENFAMIL LIPIL LOW IRON
ENFAMIL WITH IRON
EXPECTA LIPIL
FER-IN SOL
KINDERCAL
LOCTOFREE LIPIL
NEXT STEP LIPIL
NEXT STEP PROSOBEE LIPIL
NUTRAMIGEN LIPIL
POLY-VI-SOL
PROGESTIMIL
PROSOBEE LIPIL
TRI-VI-SOL LIQUID

1702 **Britannia Natural Products**
PO Box 4554
New Windsor, NY 12553-0554 845-534-1335
Fax: 845-534-1312 bnpusa@aol.com
Beverage ingredients, fruit, essential oils, natural chemicals, flavors, concentrates
Estimated Sales: $500,000-$1 Million
Number Employees: 1-4

1703 **British American Tea & Coffee**
1320 Old Oxford Road
Durham, NC 27704-2470 919-471-1357
Fax: 919-471-1357
Tea and coffee.
President: Christopher Hulbert
CFO: Elizabeth Albert
Estimated Sales: Under $500,000
Number Employees: 20-49
Sq. footage: 2
Type of Packaging: Private Label

1704 **Brittle Bark Company**
215 W Main Street
PO Box 1064
Mechanicsburg, PA 17055-1064 717-697-6950
Fax: 717-731-9081 diane@brittlebark.com
www.brittlebark.com
Brittle candy made with assorted nuts, dried fruits and premium chocolate.
President/Owner: Diane Krulac

1705 **Brittle Kettle**
16285 Sw 85th #101
Tigard, OR 97224 503-639-9037
Fax: 615-449-6263 800-447-2128
bkettle@bellsouth.net www.brittlekettle.com
Processor of peanut brittle
President: Deanna Wilson
VP: Howard Wilson
Estimated Sales: $1-2.5 Million
Number Employees: 5-9
Type of Packaging: Consumer

1706 **Brix Chocolates**
PO Box 9111
Youngstown, OH 44513 330-657-5864
Fax: 330-726-0749 866-613-2749
sales@brixchocolate.com
www.brixchocolate.com
Chocolate
Estimated Sales: A
Number Employees: 1-4

1707 **Broad Run Vineyards**
10601 Broad Run Rd
Louisville, KY 40299 502-231-0372
finewine@iclou.com
www.broadrunvineyards.com
Dry table and dessert wines
Owner/Grower/Vintner: Gerald Kushner
Manager of Sales/Marketing: Marilyn Kushner
Assistant Vintner: Lloyd Hyatt
Estimated Sales: $1-2.5 Million
Number Employees: 1-4
Sq. footage: 2000
Type of Packaging: Food Service
Brands:
BROAD RUN VINEYARDS

1708 **Broad Street Coffee Roasers**
302 E Pettigrew Street
Suite 104
Durham, NC 27701-3796 919-688-5668
Fax: 919-683-6377 800-733-9916
www.broadstreetcoffee.com
Coffee
Founder, President: Larry Hayes
VP Administration: Terry Mancour
VP Operations, Roastmaster: Mark Leatherwood
Production: Jasmine Page
Estimated Sales: $2.5-5 Million
Number Employees: 1-4
Type of Packaging: Private Label

1709 **Broadaway Ham Company**
500 N Culberhouse St
Jonesboro, AR 72401-1690 870-932-6688
Fax: 870-932-6683 ham-man@sbcglobal.net
Manufacturer of meat products including deli barbecued ham and snack sticks
Owner: Bruce Broadway
Plant Manager: John Collins
Estimated Sales: $1-3 Million
Number Employees: 1-4
Sq. footage: 5000
Type of Packaging: Consumer
Brands:
CROWLEY RIDGE

1710 **Broadbent's B&B Foods**
257 Mary Blue Rd
Kuttawa, KY 42055-6299 270-388-0609
Fax: 270-388-0613 800-841-2202
manager@broadbenthams.com
www.broadbenthams.com
Manufacturer of cured ham, bacon and sausage
Owner: Ronny Drennan
Estimated Sales: Less Than $1 Million
Number Employees: 10-19

1711 **Broadleaf Venison Usa**
5600 S Alameda St
Vernon, CA 90058 323-826-9890
Fax: 323-826-9830 800-336-3844
mm@broadleafgame.com
www.broadleafgame.com
Specialty and exotic meats; Wagyu Beef, Buffalo, Cervena Venison, kurobuta Pork
President: Mark Mitchell
CEO: Pat McGowan
CFO: Ara Temuryan
Vice President: Annie Mitchell
Sales Director: Nathan Cooney
Operations Manager: Pierre La Breton
Plant Manager: Jose Madera
Purchasing Manager: Jamie Ferguson
Estimated Sales: $20-30 Million
Number Employees: 20-49
Sq. footage: 56000
Type of Packaging: Consumer, Food Service
Brands:
BROADLEAF
BROADLEAF CERVENA

1712 **Broadley Vineyards**
25158 Orchard Tract Rd
Monroe, OR 97456-9455 541-847-5934
Fax: 541-847-6018 broadley@peak.org
www.broadleyvineyards.com
Wines
President: Craig Broadley
Estimated Sales: $1-2.5 Million
Number Employees: 1-4

1713 **Broadmoor Labs**
4564 Telephone Rd
Ventura, CA 93003-5661 805-650-0996
Fax: 805-650-0997 800-822-3712
lfp@jetlink.net www.happyhealth.net
Processor, exporter and importer of health products including nutritional supplements
Owner: Larry Permen
VP: Larry Permen
Estimated Sales: $ 3 - 5 Million
Number Employees: 1-4
Brands:
Bread, Rice & Pasta Lovers Diet
Dermagest
Natragest
Sound Sleep

1714 **Brock Seed Company**
75 Richwood Rd
Finley, TN 38030-3051 760-353-1632
Fax: 760-353-1693 brockasparagus@prodigy.net
www.brockaspargus.com
Manufacturer and exporter of asparagus and asparagus seed
Owner: Clark Brock
Manager: Don Brock
Estimated Sales: $230,000
Number Employees: 3
Type of Packaging: Consumer, Food Service, Private Label
Brands:
Brock

1715 **Brockles Foods Company**
322 E Buckingham Road
Garland, TX 75040-4712 972-272-5593
Mayonnaise and sauces
President: Grover Howard
Estimated Sales: $5-9.9 Million
Number Employees: 5-9
Brands:
Brockles

1716 **Brockmann Chocolates**
7863 Progress Way
Delta, BC V4G 1A3
Canada 604-946-4111
Fax: 604-946-4114 888-494-2270
info@brockmannchocolate.com
www.brockmannchocolate.com
Manufacturer of chocolates
Founder: Willy Brockmann
President: Norbert Brockmann
CEO: Marianne Brockmann
Type of Packaging: Private Label
Brands:
TRUFFINI

1717 **Brockton Beef & Provisions Corporation**
994 Crescent Street
Brockton, MA 02302-3409 508-583-4703
Manufacturer of hamburgers and sausage; Retail Sales
President: Alan D'Ambrosio
Estimated Sales: $100,000-$150,000
Number Employees: 1-4

1718 **Brokay Products**
9999 Gantry Road
Philadelphia, PA 19115-1001 215-676-4800
Fax: 215-677-1973
Candy and confectionery, bulk supplier

1719 **Broken Bow Pack**
518 E South E St
Broken Bow, NE 68822-2716 308-872-2833
Processor of meat products
Owner: Gary Voss
Estimated Sales: $2.5-5 Million
Number Employees: 1-4
Type of Packaging: Consumer

1720 **Brolite Products**
1900 S Park Ave
Streamwood, IL 60107 630-830-0340
Fax: 630-830-0356 888-276-5483
info@bakewithbrolite.com
www.bakewithbrolite.com
Processor of flavors, stabilizers, yeast foods, dough accelerators and conditioners, egg yolk and whole egg substitutes and fudge, English muffin and bread bases; exporter of white and rye sour dough flavors
President: Virgil Delghingaro
Executive VP: David Del Ghingaro
R&D: Daniel Garcia
Marketing/Sales VP: Tom MacDonald
Estimated Sales: $2.5-5 Million
Number Employees: 50-99
Sq. footage: 36000
Type of Packaging: Bulk
Brands:
ALL SOFT
B5000
BRO EGCELLENT
BRO WHITE SOUR
BROLITE IA
BROSOFT
EGG-O-LITE
FEVER SOURS
VITA PLUS

1721 **Brom Food Group**
5595 Cote De Liesse
St. Laurent, QC H4M 1V2
Canada 514-744-5152
Fax: 514-744-8195
Processor, importer and exporter of frozen foods and frozen and fresh pierogies including cheese, potato/onion, beef and chicken
Director Marekting: Tom Luczak
Director Operations: Bruce Luczak, M.B.A.
Sq. footage: 18000
Type of Packaging: Consumer, Food Service, Private Label, Bulk
Brands:
Granny's
Ogi's

1722 **Brome Lake Ducks Ltd**
40 Centre Road
PO Box 3430
Knowlton, QC J0E 1V0
Canada 450-242-3825
Fax: 450-243-0497 888-956-1977
info@bromelakeducks.com
www.bromelakeducks.com
Duck products
President: Claude Trottier
CFO: Genevieve Grenier CMA
R&D Director: Jennifer Caron
Quality Control: Jennifer Caron
Marketing Coordinator: Pier-Luc Fiest
VP Sales/Marketing: Bruno Giuliani
Human Resources Director: Michele Cote
COO: Claude Trottier
Plant Manager: Guy Ducharme

1723 **Bronco Wine Company**
6342 Bystrum Road
Ceres, CA 95307-0789 209-538-3131
Fax: 209-538-4634 800-692-5780
info@broncowine.com www.broncowine.com
Manufacturer of wine
CEO: Fred Franzia
Co-President: Joseph Franzia
Co-President: John Franzia Jr
Estimated Sales: $250 Million
Number Employees: 300
Sq. footage: 10000
Type of Packaging: Private Label
Brands:
CHARLES SHAW
ESTRELLA
FORESTVILLE
FOXHOLLOW
GRAND CRU
HACIENDA
MONTPELLIER
NAPA RIDGE
RUTHERFORD VINTNERS
SILVER RIDGE

1724 **Brook Locker Plant**
243 W Main St
Brook, IN 47922 219-275-2611
Processor of meat products and fresh and frozen foods including beef, pork, chicken and veal; also, slaughtering available
Owner: Jeff Laffoon
Vice President: Chris Schoonveld
Estimated Sales: $1-2.5 Million
Number Employees: 5-9
Type of Packaging: Consumer, Bulk

1725 **Brook Meadow ProvisionscCorporation**
716 Security Rd
Hagerstown, MD 21740 301-739-3107
Manufacturer of pork, beef and sausage
Owner: Donald Hoffman
Estimated Sales: $5-10 Million
Number Employees: 1-4
Type of Packaging: Consumer

1726 **Brookema Company**
1100 Commerce Dr
West Chicago, IL 60185 630-562-2290
Fax: 630-562-2291
Processor and contract packager of dry mixes including cake, soup, cocoa, coffee and coffee creamer
President: Dan Clery
Estimated Sales: $2.5-5 Million
Number Employees: 20-49
Type of Packaging: Bulk

1727 **Brookfield FarmsNationwide Foods**
700 E 107th St
Chicago, IL 60628-3806 773-787-4900
Fax: 708-660-0990 www.brookfieldfarm.org
Processor and exporter of fresh and frozen pork and beef
President/Ceo: Frank Swan
President/Ceo: Dennis Gleason
Estimated Sales: $125 Million
Number Employees: 500
Type of Packaging: Consumer, Food Service

1728 **Brooklyn Bagel Company**
PO Box 120027
Staten Island, NY 10312-0027 718-349-3055
Fax: 718-349-1107 800-349-3055
Processor of frozen bagels
Sales Manager: Stanley Silverman
Sales Manager: Arnie Lichtenstein
General Manager: Donald Santman
Estimated Sales: $1-2.5 Million
Number Employees: 20-49
Sq. footage: 20000
Type of Packaging: Consumer, Food Service, Bulk

1729 **Brooklyn Baking Company**
8 John St
Waterbury, CT 06708 203-574-9198
Manufacturer of baked goods including sourdough, white and rye bread and cookies
Manager: Art Lessier
Estimated Sales: Less than $500,000
Number Employees: 5-9
Type of Packaging: Consumer, Bulk
Brands:
Brooklyn Baking Pumpernickel Bread
Brooklyn Baking Rye Bread

1730 **Brooklyn Bottling Company**
P.O.Box 808
Milton, NY 12547 845-795-2171
Fax: 845-795-2589 emiller@nsbottle.com
www.brooklynbottling.com
Processor and bottler of juice drinks, apple juice and cider, iced tea and carbonated beverages including Latin American soda
President: Eric Miller
Quality Control: Luis Gonzalez
Sales Director: Tom Marigliano
Estimated Sales: $10-20 Million
Number Employees: 100-249
Number of Brands: 25
Number of Products: 200
Type of Packaging: Private Label, Bulk
Brands:
APPLE DANDY
COUNTRY CLUB
D&G
NATURE'S OWN
POSTOBON
TROPICAL FANTASY

1731 **Brooklyn Brewery**
79 N 11th St
Brooklyn, NY 11211 718-486-7422
Fax: 718-486-7440 www.fansforfairplay.com
Processor of ale, stout and lager
President/CEO: Tom Potter
Principal: Sherwin Chang
Controller: Debra Bascome
Estimated Sales: $20-50 Million
Number Employees: 22
Type of Packaging: Consumer, Food Service, Bulk
Brands:
BROOKLYN
CHIMAY
DUVEL
PAULANER
SAMUEL SMITH
SIERRA NEVADA

1732 **Brookmere Vineyards**
107 Brookmere Farm Ln
Belleville, PA 17004-9303 717-935-5380
Fax: 717-935-5349 brookemere@nittanylink.com
www.brookmerewine.com
Wines
Owner: Cheryl Glick
Estimated Sales: $2.5-5 Million
Number Employees: 5-9
Type of Packaging: Bulk

1733 **(HQ)Brooks Food Group Corporate Office**
940 Orange St
Bedford, VA 24523-3303 540-586-8284
Fax: 540-587-3137 800-873-4934
customerservice@brooksfoodgroup.com
www.brooksfoodgroup.com
Manufacturer of frozen foods including onion rings, french toast, breaded vegetables and cheese sticks; also, protein products including nuggets, patties, sticks, strips; exporter of onion rings
Chairman/CEO: Robin Brooks
Estimated Sales: $20-50 Million
Number Employees: 250-499
Sq. footage: 90000
Other Locations:
Brooks Food Group Plant
Monroe NC
Brands:
GOLDEN WEST FOODS

1734 **Brooks Food Group, Inc**
2701 Simpson St
Monroe, NC 28112 704-289-8300
Fax: 704-283-7623 800-873-4934
sales@brooksfoodgroup.com
www.brooksfoodgroup.com
Battered and breaded beef steak patties, chicken patties, mozzarella cheese sticks, breaded okra
President: Harold Marshall
VP Finance: Alan Kolody
Executive VP: Jolene Belk
Quality Control: John Schultz
Plant Manager: Harold Marshall
Purchasing Manager: Libby Lawrence
Estimated Sales: $100-500 Million
Number Employees: 100-249
Type of Packaging: Private Label, Bulk

1735 **Brooks Peanut Company**
P.O.Box 305
Samson, AL 36477 334-898-7194
Fax: 334-898-7196
Processor of peanuts
Owner: Fleming G Brooks
Vice President: Barrett Brooks
Estimated Sales: $1-2.5 Million
Number Employees: 5-9
Type of Packaging: Bulk

1736 **Brooks Tropicals**
18400 Sw 256th St
Homestead, FL 33090 305-247-3544
Fax: 305-246-5827 800-327-4833
maryo@brookstropicals.com
www.brookstropicals.com
Grower, packer and shipper of papayas, avocados, starfruit, limes, passion fruit, mangos, guavas, uglyfruit and other tropical produce.
President: Neil Brooks
.EO: Craig Wheeling
Director Marketing: Mary Ostlund
VP Sales Management: Bill Brindle
VP Human Resources: Susan Kruse
Estimated Sales: $42 Million
Number Employees: 200
Type of Packaging: Bulk

1737 **Brooks Tropicals**
P.O.Box 900160
Homestead, FL 33090-0160 305-247-3544
Fax: 305-242-7393 800-327-4833
info@brookstropicals.com
www.brookstropicals.com
Tropical foods and vegetables
President: Neal Brooks
VP Sales Management: Bill Brindle
R & D: Frank Sesto
CEO: Craig Wheeling
Quality Control: Billy Pritchett
Marketing Manager: Mary Ostlund
Estimated Sales: $ 30-50 Million
Number Employees: 100-249
Type of Packaging: Bulk

1738 **Brookside Foods**
3899 Mt. Lehman Road
Abbotsford, BC V4X 2N1
Canada 604-607-6650
Fax: 604-607-7046 877-793-3866
info@brooksidefoods.com
www.brooksidefoods.com
Processor of base concentrates, fruit fillings, custom ice cream inclusions, confectionery coatings, and panned and deposited chocolate confections, etc. Importer of cocoa butter, cocoal powder, chocolate liquer, etc. Exporter of realfruit chips, chocolate, panned and deposited chocolate confections, etc. Custom dry blending and private labeling.
President: Kenneth Shaver
Director Sales: Alan Whitteker
Estimated Sales: $19 Million
Number Employees: 150
Parent Co: Brookside Foods
Type of Packaging: Consumer, Private Label, Bulk

1739 **Brookview Farms**
V354 County Road 24
Archbold, OH 43502-9502 419-445-6366
Fax: 419-445-0503
Processor of fresh and frozen meat including beef, pork, lamb and venison
President: Jack Lugbill
Estimated Sales: $5-10 Million
Number Employees: 10-19
Sq. footage: 7000
Type of Packaging: Consumer, Food Service, Bulk

1740 **Brost International Trading Company**
180 N Stetson Ave # 3400
Chicago, IL 60601-6740 312-861-7100
Fax: 312-225-4444
Processor and exporter of nuts, cheese flavored balls, nacho cheese, potato and corn chips, potato sticks and canned whole kernel corn and diced carrots
President: David Brost
VP: Elayne Brost
Estimated Sales: $ 3 - 5 Million
Number Employees: 20-49
Sq. footage: 10000
Type of Packaging: Consumer, Private Label
Brands:
Regal
Regal Farms

1741 **Brother Bru Bru's Produce**
PO Box 2964
Venice, CA 90294-2964 310-396-9033
Fax: 301-455-7221 brobrubru@aol.com
Natural salt-free sauces
President: Bruce Langhorne
Vice President: Janet Bachelor
Sales Director: Cynthia Riddle
Estimated Sales: $ 5 - 10 Million
Number Employees: 5-9
Type of Packaging: Private Label

1742 **Brotherhood Winery**
P.O.Box 190
Washingtonville, NY 10992 845-496-3661
Fax: 845-496-8720 wine@frontiernet.net
www.brotherhoodwinery.net
Wines
President/Owner: Cesar Baeza
Owner: Robert Markovits
Treasurer: Michael Venieri
Estimated Sales: $4 Million
Number Employees: 35
Type of Packaging: Private Label
Brands:
BROTHERHOOD

1743 **Brothers International Desserts**
1682 Kettering
Irvine, CA 92614-5614 949-655-0080
Fax: 949-655-0081 www.brothersdesserts.com
Processor sorbet, fruit bars and ice cream including vanilla, chocolate and strawberry; importer of chocolate and fruits; exporter of fruit bars
President: Gary Winkler
Number Employees: 50-99
Sq. footage: 30000
Type of Packaging: Food Service, Private Label
Brands:
Big Kahuna
Brothers
Kid Kobruno
Le Gourmet Sorbet
The Classic Sundae
Tropical Treat

1744 **Brothers International Food Corp**
P.O.Box 60679
Rochester, NY 14606-679
Fax: 585-343-4218 888-842-7477
info@brothersallnatural.com
www.brothersallnatural.com
All-natural, freeze dried fruit and potato Crisps
CEO: Travis Betters
CFO: Matthew Betters
Estimated Sales: $4.1 Million
Number Employees: 22

1745 **Brothers International Food Corporation**
1175 Lexington Ave
Rochester, NY 14606 585-343-3007
Fax: 585-343-4218
mbetters@brothersinternational.com
www.brothersinternational.com
Fruit juice traders and brokers; importer of wines; manufacturer of all-natural freeze-dried fruit snacks
President/CEO: Matt Betters
CFO: Travis Betters
VP Sales and Marketing: James Betters
National/International Sales Manager: Christopher Schmitz
Estimated Sales: $4.3 Million
Number Employees: 20-49

1746 **Brothers Sauces**
2617 Museum Way
Fort Worth, TX 76107 817-821-3374
Fax: 877-754-3488
barry.king@brotherssauces.com
www.brotherssauces.com
Gluten-free, organic/natural, BBQ sauce, dessert toppings (i.e. fudge sauce, caramel sauce, whipped cream, etc.), foodservice, private label.
Marketing: Barry King

1747 **Broughton Cannery**
7909 Broughton Pike
Paulding, OH 45879 419-399-3182
Fax: 419-399-3189
Processor of canned meat
Partner: Rex Bowersock
Estimated Sales: $5-10 Million
Number Employees: 10-19
Sq. footage: 14700
Type of Packaging: Consumer, Food Service, Private Label

1748 **Broughton Foods**
P.O.Box 656
Marietta, OH 45750 740-373-4121
Fax: 740-373-2861 800-283-2479
www.deanfoods.com
Manufacturer and distributor of dairy products including milk, ice cream, cottage cheese, half and half, whipping cream, creamers, yogurt and dips, also; nondairy aerosol whipped topping
GM: David Broughton
Controller: Mike McIlyar
Marketing Director: Tim Duty
Production Manager: Tracy Augenstein
Plant Manager: Mike DePue
Estimated Sales: $75 Million
Number Employees: 250-499
Parent Co: Dean Foods Company
Type of Packaging: Food Service
Brands:
BROUGHTON
DAIRYLANE

1749 **Brown & Haley**
P.O.Box 1596
Tacoma, WA 98401 253-620-3000
Fax: 253-272-6742 info@brown-haley.com
www.brown-haley.com
Manufacturer and exporter of confectionery items including Almond Roca.
President: Pierson Clair
CEO: Pierson E Clair Iii
VP Sales: Mark Greenhall
Number Employees: 100-249
Type of Packaging: Consumer, Private Label, Bulk
Brands:
MOUNTAIN BAR
ROCA
ZINGOS MINTS

1750 **Brown & Jenkins TradingCompany**
P.O.Box 236
Cambridge, VT 05444-0236 802-862-2395
Fax: 802-864-7336 800-456-5282
coffee@brownjenkins.com
www.brownjenkins.com
Coffee
Owner: Sandy Riggens
Marketing Director: Sarah Squirrell
Estimated Sales: $1-2.5 Million
Number Employees: 1-4
Brands:
Brown & Jenkins Fresh Roasted

1751 **Brown County Wine Company**
4520 State Road 46 E
Nashville, IN 47448 812-988-6144
Fax: 812-988-8285 888-298-2984
bcwinfo@browncountywinery.com
www.browncountywinery.com
Wines
President: David Schrodt
Marketing Manager: Cynthia Schrodt
Estimated Sales: $1-2.5 Million
Number Employees: 1-4
Sq. footage: 5000
Type of Packaging: Bulk

1752 **Brown Cow Farm**
3810 Delta Fair Blvd
Antioch, CA 94509-4008 925-757-9209
Fax: 925-757-9160 888-429-5459
www.browncowfarm.com
Processor of yogurt
Manager: Steve Jerkins
Office Manager: Jennifer Wyneken
Estimated Sales: $10-20 Million
Number Employees: 20-49
Type of Packaging: Consumer
Brands:
Brown Cow Farm

1753 **Brown Dairy**
P.O.Box 98
Coalville, UT 84017-0098 435-336-5952
Fax: 435-355-6079
Dairy products
Owner: Glen Brown

1754 **Brown Family Farm**
56 Sugar House Road
Alstead, NH 03602-4307 802-387-8718
Fax: 802-387-4759 866-254-8718
maple@sover.net
www.brownfamilyfarmmaple.com
Maple products
Estimated Sales: $1-2.5 Million
Number Employees: 10-19

1755 **Brown Family Farm**
74 Cotton Mill Hill
Suite A106, Po Box 117
Brattleboro, VT 05302 866-254-8718
Fax: 802-254-5022
wendyg@bascomfamilyfarmmaple.com
www.brownfamilyfarmmaple.com
Maple products, gourmet foods, confections
Executive Director: Arnold Coombs
CFO: Nancy Adams
Estimated Sales: $ 3 - 5 Million
Number Employees: 10-19
Brands:
BROWN FAIRY FARM

1756 **Brown Family Farm**
P.O. Box 117
Brattleboro, VT 05302 802-254-4554
Fax: 802-254-5022 86- 2-4 87
info@brownfamilyfarmmaple.com
www.brownfamilyfarmmaple.com
Processor of maple syrup, flavored syrups, pancake mixes, salad dressings, roasting sauces and ketchups
CEO: Bruce Bascom
Estimated Sales: $ 5-10 Million
Number Employees: 10-19

1757 **Brown Foods**
P.O.Box 953
Dallas, GA 30132-0017 770-445-4554
Fax: 770-445-5349
Poultry, pork, seafood, produce, beef
Owner: Graham Kirkman

1758 **Brown Packing Company**
P.O.Box 130
Gaffney, SC 29342-0130 864-489-5723
Fax: 864-487-3210
Processor and exporter of meat products including beef carcasses and primal cuts
President: Walter Brown
Sales/Transportation Manager: Johnny Price
Purchasing Agent: Sloan Bradford
Estimated Sales: $50-100 Million
Number Employees: 250-499
Type of Packaging: Consumer, Bulk

1759 **Brown Packing Company**
1 Dutch Valley Drive
South Holland, IL 60473 708-849-7990
Fax: 708-849-8094 800-832-8325
Processor and exporter of veal
President/CEO: John Oedzes
Operations/Quality Assurance Director: Mike Jedlica
COO: Bryan Scott
Operations/Purchasing Director: Jim Sowinski
Estimated Sales: $15 Million
Number Employees: 70
Sq. footage: 50000
Type of Packaging: Consumer, Food Service, Private Label

1760 **Brown Produce Company**
P.O.Box 265
Farina, IL 62838 618-245-3301
Fax: 618-245-3552
Processor and exporter of eggs and egg products including frozen, liquid, whites, whole and yolk
President: Larry Seger
Vice President: Larry Pemberton
Plant Supervisor: Larry Jahraus
Estimated Sales: $10-20 Million
Number Employees: 50-99
Sq. footage: 10000000
Type of Packaging: Consumer, Bulk

1761 **Brown Thompson & Sons**
139 State Route 339 N
Fancy Farm, KY 42039 270-623-6321
Fax: 270-623-6928
Beef, beef products
Owner: Penny Lamb
Estimated Sales: $ .5 - 1 million
Number Employees: 1-4

1762 **Brown's Bakery**
505 Downs St
Defiance, OH 43512 419-784-3330
Fax: 419-784-5346
Processor of baked goods including breads and rolls
President: David Graham
CEO: Richard Graham
Sales Manager: Glenn Vinz
Treasurer: Bill Franzdorf
Plant Manager: Ernest Lopshire
Estimated Sales: $10-20 Million
Number Employees: 100-249
Sq. footage: 49720
Type of Packaging: Consumer, Food Service, Private Label, Bulk
Brands:
Bunny
Country Kitchen

1763 **(HQ)Brown's Dairy**
P.O.Box 52559
New Orleans, LA 70152-2559 504-529-2221
Fax: 504-529-9267 info@brownsdairy.com
www.brownsdairy.com
Milk
President: Kennon Davis
Sales Director: Lauren Barre
Plant Manager: John Brousard
Estimated Sales: $300,000-500,000
Number Employees: 1-4
Parent Co: Suiza Dairy Group
Type of Packaging: Consumer
Brands:
Brown's Dairy
Bulgarian Style
Hershey's Milkshake
Luzianne Ready-to-Drink
Nesquik

1764 **Brown's Ice Cream**
3501 Marshall St NE Ste 150
Minneapolis, MN 55418 612-378-1075
Fax: 612-331-9273
Manufacturer of ice cream
Owner: Robert Nelson
Estimated Sales: $3 Million
Number Employees: 1-4
Parent Co: Upper Lakes Foods
Type of Packaging: Consumer, Food Service, Bulk

1765 **(HQ)Brown-Forman Corporation**
850 Dixie Highway
Louisville, KY 40210 502-585-1100
Fax: 502-774-7876 brown-forman@b-f.com
www.brown-forman.com
Manufacturer, importer and exporter of wine, tequila, champagne, whiskey, gin, vodka, and liqueurs.
Chairman & CEO: Paul Varga
Executive VP/CFO: Don Berg
Vp Evp Garvin Brown Iv: Phil Lynch
SVP/Global Human Resources: Lisa Steiner
Executive VP/COO: James Bareuther
SVP/Chief Production Officer: Jill Jones
Estimated Sales: $2.6 Billion
Number Employees: 4120
Number of Brands: 25
Type of Packaging: Consumer
Other Locations:
Toronto, Ontario, Canada
Louisville KY
Versailles KY
Braintree MA
Dallas TX
Lebanon TN
Lynchburg TN
Nashville TN
Atlanta GA
Hopland CA
Newport Beach CA
San Rafael CA
Windsor CA
Brands:
BEL ARBOR® WINES
BONTERRA® VINEYARDS
CAHMBORD® LIQUEUR
CANADIAN MIST®
DON EDUARDO® TEQUILAS
EARLY TIMES® KENTUCKY WHISKY
EL JIMADOR® TEQUILAS
FETZER® WINES
FINLANDIA® VODKAS
FIVE RIVERS® WINES
GENTLEMAN JACK® RARE TN WHISKY
HERRADURA® TEQUILAS
JACK DANIEL'S® COUNTRY COCKTAIL
JACK DANIEL'S® SINGLE BARREL
JACK DANIEL'S® TN WHISKY
JEKEL® VINEYARDS
KORBEL® CALIFORNIA CHAMPAGNES
LITTLE BLACK DRESS® WINES
OLD FORESTER® KY STRAIGHT B-W
PEPE LOPEZ® TEQUILAS
SANCTUARY® WINES
SONOMA-CUTRER® WINES
SOUTHERN COMFORT®
TUACA® LIQUEUR
WOODFORD RESERVE® KY STRAIGHT

1766 **Brownie Baker**
4870 W Jacquelyn Ave
Fresno, CA 93722 559-277-7070
Fax: 559-277-7077 800-598-6501
RWRoss1222@aol.com www.browniebaker.com
Manufacturer of baking products such as; muffins, cakes, brownies, cookies, danish, mexican pastries, poundcake slices and cheesecakes
President: Dennis Perkins
Director Business Development: Adam Maples
VP Sales: Bob Ross
Estimated Sales: $ 20 - 50 Million
Number Employees: 50-99
Sq. footage: 45000
Brands:
PRO TREATS
THE BROWNIE BAKER

1767 **Brownie Products Company**
9445 E Us Highway 40
Terre Haute, IN 47803-9218
Fax: 815-237-2644 www.kelloggs.com
Processor of frozen pizza crusts
President: Ronald Westman
CEO: Don Wilson
Quality Assurance Manager: Marion Baranski
Controller: Jeff Grober
Estimated Sales: $20-50 Million
Number Employees: 50-99
Type of Packaging: Consumer, Food Service, Private Label

1768 **Browniepops LLC**
12008 Wenonga
Leawood, KS 66209 816-797-0715
Fax: 913-491-0788 email@browniepops.com
www.browniepops.com
Brownies with a crisp chocolate exterior on a stick lik lollipops. Available in 11 unique flavors.
President/Owner: Marsha Pener Johnston

1769 **Browns Dairy**
55 Monroe St
Valparaiso, IN 46383-5535 219-464-4141
Fax: 219-462-9785
Manufacturer of ice cream, frozen yogurt and sherbet
President: Mike Brown
VP: Mark Brown
Estimated Sales: $500,000
Number Employees: 10-19
Sq. footage: 2000
Parent Co: Valpo Velvet Ice Cream Company
Type of Packaging: Consumer, Food Service
Brands:
Valpo Velvet

1770 **Browns' Ice Cream Company**
P.O.Box 269
Bowling Green, KY 42102-0269 270-843-9882
Distributor of ice cream
Owner: Jerry Conder
Estimated Sales: $500,000
Number Employees: 5-9
Type of Packaging: Consumer, Food Service, Bulk

1771 **Bruce Baking Company**
229 Union Avenue
New Rochelle, NY 10801-6048 914-636-0808
Fax: 914-636-0808
Baked goods, macrobiotic food
Owner: Bruce Merbaum
Estimated Sales: Under $500,000
Number Employees: 5-9
Brands:
Bruce Baking
Tahini Crunch

1772 **Bruce Church**
1341 Merrill St
Salinas, CA 93901 831-424-1543
Fax: 831-422-6714 800-538-2861
Grower of lettuce
CEO: Steve Taylor
Estimated Sales: $100-500 Million
Number Employees: 100-249
Parent Co: Fresh International
Type of Packaging: Consumer, Food Service, Bulk
Brands:
Friendly
Red Coach

1773 **Bruce Foods Corporation**
P.O.Box 1030
New Iberia, LA 70562-1030 337-365-8101
Fax: 337-364-3742 800-299-9082
info@brucefoodsla.com www.brucefoods.com
Manufacturer of true Cajun and Tex Mex food products such as; hot sauce, peppers, chili mix, chili powder, burrito seasoning mix, cajun seafood seasonings, canned yams and injectable flavoring
Owner: Si Brown
CEO: Joseph S Brown Jr
Estimated Sales: $10-20 Million
Number Employees: 100-249
Sq. footage: 250000
Type of Packaging: Consumer, Food Service, Bulk
Other Locations:
Bruce Foods Plant
El Paso TX
Bruce Foods Plant
Wilson NC
Bruce Foods Plant
Lozes LA
Bruce Foods Plant
Kerkrade, Netherlands
Brands:
BRUCE'S SWEET POTATO PANCAKE MIX
BRUCE'S YAMS
CAJUN INJECTOR
CAJUN KING
CASA FIESTA
LOUISIANA GOLD
MEXENE
THE ORIGINAL LOUISIANA

1774 **Bruce Foods Corporation**
P.O.Box 1030
New Iberia, LA 70562-1030 337-365-8101
Fax: 337-364-3742 info@brucefoodsla.com
www.brucefoods.com
Manufacturer of Cajun and Tex Mex products
CEO: Joseph S Brown Jr
Estimated Sales: $50-100 Million
Number Employees: 100-249
Number of Brands: 9
Number of Products: 350
Parent Co: Bruce Foods Corporation
Other Locations:
Bruce Foods Corporation
Lozes LA
Bruce Foods Corporation
Wilson NC
Bruce Foods Corporation
El Paso TX
Brands:
BRUCE'S
BRUCE'S YAMS
CAJUN INJECTOR
CAJUN KING
CASA FIESTA
LOUISIANA GOLD
LOUISIANA WING SAUCE
MEXENE CHILI
ORIGINAL

1775 **Bruce Packing Company**
P.O.Box 540
Silverton, OR 97381-0540 503-874-3000
Fax: 503-769-5081 800-899-3629
info@brucepac.com www.brucepac.com
Cooked and seasoned meats
President: Larry Bruce
VP: Rob Bruce
Marketing Manager: Jay Hansen
COO: Peter Larson
Production Manager: Cameron Cooper
Purchasing Manager: Duane Tipton
Estimated Sales: $5-10 Million
Number Employees: 100-249
Brands:
Brucepac
Early West
World Kitchen's

1776 **Brucia Plant Extracts**
3855 Dividend Dr
Shingle Springs, CA 95682 530-676-2774
Fax: 530-676-0574 brucia@naturex.com
www.naturex.com
A leading manufacturer of high quality natural antioxidants, colors, herbs & spices oleoresins and essential oils, and botanical extracts for the food, flavor and nutraceutical industries
President: Jacques Dikansky
VP: Stephane Ducroux
Marketing: Thomas Capogis
Sales: David Yuengniaux
Plant Manager: Chris Young
Purchasing Manager: Romain Bayzelon
Estimated Sales: $45 Million
Number Employees: 20-49
Number of Brands: 10
Number of Products: 400
Sq. footage: 85000
Parent Co: Naturex
Type of Packaging: Bulk
Brands:
Theraplant

1777 **Brum's Dairy**
631 Bruham Ave
Pembroke, ON K8A 4Z8
Canada 613-735-2325
Fax: 613-735-2068 bdairy@webhart.net
http://www.webhart.net
Process and distribute fresh dairy products as well as fresh juice
President: Stanley Brum
Vice President: Steven Brum
Estimated Sales: $12 Million +
Number Employees: 46
Sq. footage: 20000
Type of Packaging: Consumer, Private Label
Brands:
Nature's Pride

1778 **Brunkow Cheese Company**
17975 County Road F
Darlington, WI 53530-9310 608-776-3716
Fax: 608-776-3716
Processor of natural, cold pack and raw milk cheeses including cheddar, colby, monterey jack, mild, sharp, garlic, bacon, onion, dill, wine, jalapeno, Italian herb, smoked, etc
Owner/CEO: Karl Geissbuhler
Estimated Sales: $1-2.5 Million
Number Employees: 5-9
Sq. footage: 3200
Type of Packaging: Bulk
Brands:
Brunkow Cheese

1779 **Bruno Specialty Foods**
208 Cherry Ave
West Sayville, NY 11796-1223 631-589-1700
Fax: 631-589-6357 info@brunofoods.com
www.brunofoods.com
Processor of frozen kosher and nonkosher Italian food products including tomato sauces, tortellini, regular and vegetable lasagnas, eggplant parmagiana, ravioli, manicotti and stuffed shells
President: Louis D'Agrosa
Estimated Sales: $5-10 Million
Number Employees: 20-49
Number of Brands: 2
Number of Products: 150
Sq. footage: 10000
Type of Packaging: Consumer, Food Service, Private Label, Bulk
Brands:
Bruno
Tova's Best

1780 **Bruno's Cajun Foods & Snacks**
210 Provosty Drive
Slidell, LA 70461-1413 985-726-0544
Fax: 985-726-0532 cause4paws@charter.net
Manufacturer and Distributor of Cajun Food Snacks, Porkskins and Cracklins' Caramel Popcorn, Cotton Candy, Roasted Peanuts, and candy
President: Brandon Halligan
CEO: Melody Halligan
VP: Everett Halligan
Marketing: Erin Halligan
Sales: Michael Halligan
Public Relations: Tracy Stricklin
Plant Manager: Katie Halligan
Purchasing Director: Everett Halligan
Estimated Sales: $70 Million
Number Employees: 6
Number of Products: 8
Sq. footage: 2000
Type of Packaging: Consumer, Private Label

Brands:
BRUNO'S

1781 **Brush Locker**
14250 County Road 15
Fort Morgan, CO 80701-8610 970-842-2660
Fax: 970-842-4831
Processor and packer of meat
Owner: Aslom Khan
Plant Manager: Iram Khan
Estimated Sales: $5-10 Million
Number Employees: 10-19

1782 **Bruss Company**
3548 N Kostner Ave
Chicago, IL 60641 773-282-2900
Fax: 773-282-6966 800-621-3882
customer.bruss@tyson.com www.bruss.com
Manufacturer of portion controlled steaks, pork, lamb and veal
President/CEO: Jeff DeLapp
CFO: Mike Porcaro
VP: Gary Heymann
Director Marketing: Al Iverhouse
National Account Sales: Frank Cardone
Estimated Sales: $85.6 Million
Number Employees: 10-19
Sq. footage: 52000
Parent Co: Tyson Foods
Type of Packaging: Consumer, Food Service
Brands:
GOLDEN TROPHY STEAKS

1783 **Brutocao Cellars**
P.O.Box 780
Hopland, CA 95449 707-895-2152
Fax: 707-744-1046 800-433-3689
brutocoa@netdex.com www.brutocaocellars.com
Wines, gourmet foods
President: Len Brutocao
Estimated Sales: $1-2.5 Million
Number Employees: 20-49

1784 **Bryan Foods**
PO Box 1177
West Point, MS 39773-1177 662-494-3741
Fax: 662-495-4501 www.bryanfoods.com
Processor of fresh and frozen sausage
CEO/President: John Bryan III
VP/CFO: Cal Jenness
R&D: Frank Mello
Number Employees: 1,000-4,999
Parent Co: Sara Lee Packaged Meats
Type of Packaging: Consumer, Food Service
Brands:
Bryan
Picnic
Prairie Belt
Redbird
Savoy
Smoky Hollow
Sweet Sue

1785 **Bryant Preserving Company**
P.O.Box 367
Alma, AR 72921 479-632-2401
Fax: 479-632-2505 800-634-2413
sales@bryantpreserving.com www.oldsouth.com
Processor of pickled fruits and vegetables including sweet watermelon rinds and cucumber relish, baby carrots, green tomatoes and mild and hot okra.
President: Morgan Bryant
General Manager: Steve Bryant
Sales Manager: Leguetta Yates
Secretary/Treasurer: Morgan Bryant
COO: Steve Bryant
Plant Manager: Morgan Bryant
Estimated Sales: $1-2.5 Million
Number Employees: 5-9
Sq. footage: 25000
Type of Packaging: Consumer, Food Service, Private Label, Bulk
Brands:
OLD SOUTH

1786 **Bryant Vineyard**
1454 Griffitt Bend Road
Talladega, AL 35160-7255 256-268-2638
Wines
President: Susan Bryant
Co-Owner: Dan Bryant
Vice President: Kelly Bryant
Number Employees: 20-49

Brands:
Bryant Autumn Blush
Bryant Country White
Bryant Dixie Blush
Bryant Festive Red
Bryant Vineyard

1787 **Bryant's Meats**
104 Fellowship
Taylorsville, MS 39168 601-785-6507
Fax: 601-785-6507
Processor of meat products including smoked sausage, pork and chicken
Owner: Robert Hunt
Co-Owner: Robert Hunt
Estimated Sales: $5-10 Million
Number Employees: 20-49
Type of Packaging: Consumer
Brands:
River Road
Sunrise

1788 **Bt. McElrath Chocolatier**
2010 E Hennepin Ave # 78
Minneapolis, MN 55413 612-331-8800
Fax: 612-331-2881 info@btmcelrath.com
www.btmcelrath.com
Manufacturer of chocolates
President: Brian T Mc Elrath
Partner/Chief Taster: Christine McElrath
Marketing: Nancy Gross
Estimated Sales: $ 3 - 5 Million
Number Employees: 5-9

1789 **Bubbies Homemade Ice Cream**
99-1267 Waiua Pl
Aiea, HI 96701 808-487-7218
Fax: 808-484-5800
bubbiesicecream@hawaii.rr.com
www.bubbiesicecream.com
Mocha ice cream
President: Keith Robbins
CFO: Sandra Robbins
VP: Gertrude Robbins
Quality Control: Jayci Robbins
Marketing: Cara Nagao
Public Relations: Jo Lacar
Estimated Sales: $2.5-5 Million
Number Employees: 5-9
Sq. footage: 18000
Type of Packaging: Bulk
Brands:
Bubbies Homemade Ice Cream
Mountain Apple
Tutus

1790 **Bubbles Baking Company**
15215 Keswick St
Van Nuys, CA 91405-1050 818-786-1700
Fax: 818-786-3617 800-777-4970
Bubbles@aol.com
Gourmet baked goods
Manager: Torben Jensen
Manager: Torben Jenson
Plant Manager: Armando Berumen
Estimated Sales: $10-20 Million
Number Employees: 50-99
Brands:
Bubbles
Granny Gourmet Goodi

1791 **Bubbles of San Francisco**
2940 Chauncy Cir
Stockton, CA 95209-1617 209-951-6071
Fax: 209-957-9413 info@bubbies.com
www.bubbies.com
Kosher pickle products
Co-Owner/CEO: John Gray
Co-Owner/COO: Kathy Gray
Estimated Sales: $500,000-$1 Million
Number Employees: 1-4
Type of Packaging: Private Label, Bulk

1792 **Buccia Vineyard**
518 Gore Rd
Conneaut, OH 44030 440-593-5976
bucciwin@suite224.net
www.bucciavineyard.com
Wine
Owner/President: Alfred Bucci
Owner: Joanna Bucci
Estimated Sales: Under $1 Million
Number Employees: 1-4
Type of Packaging: Bulk

1793 **Buchanan Hollow Nut Company**
6510 Minturn Rd
Le Grand, CA 95333 209-389-4594
Fax: 209-389-4321 800-532-1500
sharleen@bhnc.com www.bhnc.com
Manufacturer and grower of organic pistachio, almonds, variety of nuts, dried fruit and candies
Owner: Sharleen Robson
Owner: Bob Robson
Estimated Sales: $500,000-$1 Million
Number Employees: 5-9
Sq. footage: 4000
Type of Packaging: Bulk

1794 **Buck's Spumoni Company**
229 Pepes Farm Rd
Milford, CT 06460-3671 203-874-2007
Fax: 203-877-5777
Manufacturer of ice cream specialties including nut roll, spumoni and tortoni
President: Charles A Buck Jr
Estimated Sales: $ 10 - 20 Million
Number Employees: 20-49
Type of Packaging: Food Service, Bulk

1795 **Buckeye Pretzel Company**
1253 Deerfield Drive
Williamsport, PA 17701-9307 570-547-6295
Fax: 570-547-6719 800-257-6029
Pretzels
President: John Best
Executive VP: Susan Best
Number Employees: 30
Brands:
BUCKEYE

1796 **Buckhead Beef Company**
2194 Marietta Blvd NW
Atlanta, GA 30318 404-355-4400
Fax: 404-355-4541 800-888-5578
info@buckheadbeef.com
www.buckheadbeef.com
Manufacturer and wholesaler/distributor of fresh and frozen specialty cut meat products including beef, veal, lamb and pork for food service operators
Founder/CEO: Howard Halpern
President: John Foster
CFO: Clay Jordan
Number Employees: 250-499
Type of Packaging: Food Service

1797 **Buckhead Gourmet**
4060 Peachtree Rd NE # D-272
Atlanta, GA 30319-3020 404-256-1399
Fax: 404-256-1335 800-673-6338
customerservice@buckheadgourmet.com
www.buckheadgourmet.com
Manufacturer of prepared sauces including fat-free gourmet, barbecue, bordeaux, hunter, peppercorn, maderia, marinades, spice ribs, salad dressings, jams, relishes and salsas
President: Stephan Gosch
CEO: Rupert Crawford
Estimated Sales: $1,000,000
Number Employees: 1-4
Number of Brands: 1
Number of Products: 35
Type of Packaging: Consumer, Food Service, Private Label, Bulk
Brands:
Buckhead Gourmet

1798 **Buckingham Valley Vineyards**
P.O.Box 371
Buckingham, PA 18912 215-794-7188
Fax: 215-794-3606 ask@pawine.com
www.pawine.com
Wine
President: Kathy Forest
Vice President: Gerald Forest
Winemaker: Jon Forest
Plant Manager: Kevin Forest
Estimated Sales: Under $500,000
Number Employees: 5-9
Brands:
Buckingham

1799 **(HQ)Buckmaster Coffee**
4893 NW 235th Ave Ste 101
Hillsboro, OR 97124 503-693-0796
Fax: 503-681-0944 800-962-9148

Processor of roasted whole bean gourmet coffee
VP: Joe Schlichte
Sales Manager: Paul Hoffmann
VP of Sales: Joe Schlichte
Estimated Sales: $2.5-5 Million
Number Employees: 5-9
Type of Packaging: Consumer

1800 **Bucks County Coffee Company**
2250 W Cabot Boulevard
Langhorne, PA 19047 215-741-1855
Fax: 215-741-1799 800-844-8790
help@buckscountycoffee.com
www.buckscountycoffee.com
Coffee
President: Rodger Owen
CFO: Debby Prentice
VP/Retail Operations: Kathy Owen
Sales Director: Roseann O'Connel
Purchasing Manager: Chris Vacearella
Estimated Sales: $19,600,000
Number Employees: 5-9
Type of Packaging: Private Label
Brands:
Bucks County Coffee

1801 **Buddy Squirrel LLC**
P.O.Box 070581
Milwaukee, WI 53207 414-483-4500
Fax: 414-483-4137 800-972-2658
jayb@qcbs.com www.qcbs.com
Processor, exporter and packer of candy including regular and sugar-free boxed, chocolates, brittles, toffees, holiday, mints, molded novelties, etc.; also, nuts, nut mixes and gourmet popcorn
President: Margaret Gile
Number Employees: 50-99
Number of Brands: 2
Number of Products: 2000
Sq. footage: 60000
Parent Co: Quality Candy Shoppes
Type of Packaging: Consumer, Food Service, Private Label, Bulk
Brands:
BUDDY SQUIRREL
FAIRY FOOD
QUALITY CANDY

1802 **Buddy's**
626 E Lewis St
Pocatello, ID 83201 208-233-1172
President: Steve Piper
Estimated Sales: $1-2.5 Million
Number Employees: 20-49

1803 **Buds Kitchen**
826 Gardner Center Road
New Castle, PA 16101-6020 724-654-9216
Fax: 724-654-9216 bud301@libcom.com
Hot sauce

1804 **(HQ)Buedel Food Products**
7661 S 78th Ave
Bridgeview, IL 60455 708-496-3500
Fax: 708-496-8369 www.buedelfoods.com
Processor of refrigerated horseradish and frozen smoked fish
Owner: Pat Bedolla
Vice President: Kristin Buedel
Sales Director: Fred Buedel
Estimated Sales: $ 3 - 5 Million
Number Employees: 10-19
Type of Packaging: Consumer, Private Label
Brands:
Prince Gourmet Foods

1805 **Buehler Vineyards**
820 Greenfield Rd
Saint Helena, CA 94574 707-963-2155
Fax: 707-963-3747 buehlers@pacbell.net
www.buehlervineyards.com
Wine
President: John Buehler
Manager Sales/Marketing: Misha Chelini
Winemaker: David Tronin
Office Manager: Lori Sax
Estimated Sales: $2.5-5 Million
Number Employees: 5-9
Type of Packaging: Private Label

1806 **Buena Vista Carneros Winery**
18000 Old Winery Rd
Sonoma, CA 95476 707-265-1472
Fax: 707-252-0392 800-678-8504
estate@buenavistawinery.com
www.buenavistawinery.com
Manufacturer, importer and exporter of wine and also, importer of champagne
President/CEO: Harry Parsley
CFO/VP: Peter Kasper
Human Resources: Dorothy Kines
Estimated Sales: $5-10 Million
Number Employees: 5-9
Sq. footage: 80000
Type of Packaging: Consumer, Private Label
Brands:
CARNEROS

1807 **Bueno Food Products**
P.O.Box 293
Albuquerque, NM 87103-0293 505-243-2722
Fax: 505-242-1680 800-888-7336
info@buenofoods.com www.buenofoods.com
Manufacturer of frozen Mexican food including green chile and corn and flour tortillas, chile peppers, spices and dry chile powders
President: Jacqueline Baca
VP: Gene Baca
R&D: Catherine Baca
Public Relations: Ana Baca
Estimated Sales: $10-100 Million
Number Employees: 20-49
Parent Co: El Encanto
Type of Packaging: Consumer, Food Service, Private Label
Brands:
Bueno
Chimayo

1808 **Buffalo Bill Brewing Company**
1082 B St
Hayward, CA 94541-4108 510-886-9823
Fax: 510-886-8157
Processor of ale, stout and lager
President: Jeff Harries
Co-Owner: Jeff Harries
Estimated Sales: $20-50 Million
Number Employees: 50-99
Type of Packaging: Consumer, Food Service, Bulk
Brands:
Alimony Ale
Billy Bock
Buffalo Brew
Pumpkin Ale
Tasmanian Devil
White Buffalo

1809 **Buffalo Bill's Snack Foods**
P.O.Box 16346
Denver, CO 80216-0346 303-298-0705
Fax: 303-298-0216 info@tortilla-chips.com
www.tortilla-chips.com
Tortilla chips in a variety of stone-ground and natural flavors, salsa and hot sauce
President: William A Ralston
Estimated Sales: $ 20 - 50 Million
Number Employees: 50-99
Brands:
Buffalo Bill's
Wild West

1810 **Buffalo Trace Distillery**
113 Great Buffalo Trace
Frankfort, KY 40601-2091 502-223-7641
Fax: 502-875-5553 800-654-8471
thunder@buffalotrace.com
www.buffalotrace.com
Bourbon and rum; importer of wine
President: Mark Brown
Vice President/Coo: Richard Wolf
VP of Operations: Joseph Darmand
Estimated Sales: $100-500 Million
Number Employees: 100-249
Parent Co: Sazerac Company
Type of Packaging: Bulk

1811 **Buffalo Wild Wings**
600 Highway 169 S
Suite 1919
Minneapolis, MN 55426-1205 763-546-1891
Fax: 952-593-9787 info@buffalowildwings.com
www.buffalowildwings.com
Buffalo wings
Owner: Jim Disbrow
Co-Owner: Scott Lowery
Estimated Sales: $300,000-500,000
Number Employees: 10-19

1812 **Bull Run Roasting Company**
16790 W Us Highway 63
Hayward, WI 54843-7214 715-634-3646
Fax: 715-634-8336 info@bullrunroasters.com
www.bullrunroasters.com
Produce three outstanding families of coffee blends for coffeehouses and restaurants plus two premium teas. Offer the following roasting degrees: Full City, Vienna, French and Italian
Owner: Granville Harlow
Owner: Greg Hoyt
Estimated Sales: $10-24.9 Million
Number Employees: 5-9

1813 **Bullock's Country Meats**
2020 Sykesville Rd
Westminster, MD 21157 410-848-6786
Fax: 410-848-8685
Manufacturer of beef, pork, chicken and turkey; also, frozen seafood; slaughtering services available
Owner: Clyde Hirt
Estimated Sales: $3 Million
Number Employees: 10-19

1814 **Bully Hill Vineyards**
8843 GHT Mem Drive
Hammondsport, NY 14840 607-868-3610
Fax: 607-868-3205 generalinfo@bullyhill.com
www.bullyhillvineyards.com
Wines, champagne and grape juice
President: Lillian Taylor
VP Quality Control: Gregg Learned
Sales: Adam LaPierre
Operations: Gregg Learned
Estimated Sales: $5-9.9 Million
Number Employees: 5-9
Type of Packaging: Consumer
Brands:
AURORA BLANC
BANTY RED
BARNYARD RED
BULLDOG BACO NOIR
CHAMBOURCIN
CHARDONNAY ELISE
EQUINOX
EQUINOX
ESTATE RED
FELICITY
FISH MARKET WHITE
FOCH
FUSION
GARNET
GOAT WHITE
GROWER'S RED
GROWERS BLUSH
GROWERS WHITE
HARBOR LIGHTS
IVES
LE GOAT BLUSH
LIGHTHOUSE WHITE
LOVE MY GOAT RED
MEAT MARKET RED
MISS LOVE WHITE
MOTHER SHIP OVER PARIS CHAMPAGNE
NIAGARA
OH, BE JOYFUL
PINOT NOIR
RAVAT BLANC
RIELSING
SEASONS
SEYVAL BLANC
SEYVAL BLANC BRUT CHAMPAGNE
SPACE SHUTTLE RED
SPACE SHUTTLE WHITE
SPECIAL RESERVE RED
SPECIAL RESERVE WHITE
SPRING BLUSH
SPRING WHITE
STATE CAPITAL RED
SWEET WALTER RED
SWEET WALTER WHITE
VERDELET BLANC
WALTER S. RED

1815 **Bumble Bee Foods**
9655 Granite Ridge Drive
Suite 100
San Diego, CA 92123-2674 858-715-4000
Fax: 858-202-4766 www.bumblebee.com
Manufacturer, importer and exporter of canned tuna, chicken, salmon, shrimp, crab, sardines & mackerel, oysters, clams; also ready to eat meals
President/CEO: Christopher Lischewski
EVP/CFO: Kent McNeil
EVP/COO: J Douglas Hines
Estimated Sales: $700 Million
Number Employees: 1700
Sq. footage: 40000
Parent Co: Lion Capital LLP
Type of Packaging: Consumer, Food Service, Private Label, Bulk
Other Locations:
Bumble Bee Canning Facility
Mayaguez, PR
Bumble Bee Canning Facility
Sante Fe Springs CA
Brands:
BEACH CLIFF
BRUNSWICK
BUMBLE BEE
CLOVER LEAF
CORAL
KING OSCAR
LIBBY'S
ORLEANS
SNOW'S

1816 **Bungalow Brand Foods**
1310 Panchita Place
Santa Barbara, CA 93103-2223 805-899-4747
Fax: 805-899-4747 800-899-5267
bungalo@silcom.com
Spreadable fruits, tropical fruit butters, jellies, chutney and scone mixes
President: Diane Bock
CFO: John Bock
Vice President: Bryan Bock
Estimated Sales: $75,000
Number Employees: 1-4
Type of Packaging: Private Label

1817 **Bunge Canada**
2190 S Service Road West
Oakville, ON L6L 5N1
Canada 905-825-7930
Fax: 905-469-2018 800-361-3043
onpack@canamerafoods.com
www.canamerafoods.com
Oil seeds, protein meals and edible oil products
President/CEO: Carl Hausmann
R&D: Dave Forster
Quality Control: Rolf Mantei
National Manager (Packaged Products): Larry Sigmundson
Sales Manager: Liz Micallef
Public Relations: Jim Francis
VP Operations: Herb Schafer
Plant Manager: Calvin Eyben
Number Employees: 500-999
Parent Co: Central Soya
Brands:
Canaplus

1818 **Bunge Foods**
15601 Mosher Ave
Tustin, CA 92780-6426 714-258-1223
Fax: 714-258-1520
Bread and rolls.
Manager: Joe Barsotti
Quality Control Manager: Peter Fadul
Plant Manager: Joe Barsotti
Estimated Sales: $ 20 - 50 Million
Number Employees: 100-249

1819 **Bunge Milling**
845 Kentucky Ave
Woodland, CA 95695 530-668-3909
Fax: 530-661-6028 800-747-4764
Manufacturer, packager and exporter of packaged and bulk rice and rice bran
President/CEO: Steve Malin
Director of National Accounts: John Gardias
Estimated Sales: $20.4 Million
Number Employees: 100
Number of Products: 10
Parent Co: Bunge Limited
Type of Packaging: Consumer, Food Service, Private Label, Bulk
Brands:
CALROSE
KAHO MAI
MARUYU
PACIFIC INTERNATIONAL

1820 **(HQ)Bunge North America**
11720 Borman Dr
St Louis, MO 63146 314-292-2000
Fax: 314-292-2110 bna.ebusiness@bunge.com
www.bungenorthamerica.com
Manufacturer and exporter of a wide range of shortenings, oils, margarines, mixes, frozen products, toppings and fillings for the foodservice, food processor and bakery industries
President/CEO: Soren Schroder
VP/CFO: Todd Bastean
Evp: Tim Gallagher
Sr. VP/GM, Oilseed Processing Division: Larry Clarke
Sr. VP/GM, Bunge Milling: Fred Luckey
Sr. VP/GM, Bunge Oils: Richard Goodman
VP, Bunge Grain, Fertilizer & Biofuels: Bailey Ragan
Estimated Sales: $100-500 Million
Number Employees: 4700
Parent Co: Bunge Limited
Type of Packaging: Consumer, Food Service, Private Label, Bulk
Other Locations:
Bradley IL
Chattanooga TN
Effingham IL
Fort Worth TX
Mexico MO
Modesto CA
Pawtucket RI
Seattle WA
St. Louis MO
Tustin CA
Decatur AL
Danville IL
Crete NE
Brands:
VILLA SIERRA

1821 **Bungy Oils**
38 Colfax St
Pawtucket, RI 02860-3422 401-724-3800
Fax: 401-724-4313 www.centralsoya.com
Edible vegetable oil and shortening
CEO: Soren Schroder
Plant Manager: David Parrillo
Estimated Sales: $50-100 Million
Number Employees: 20-49
Number of Products: 1
Parent Co: Central Soya
Type of Packaging: Private Label, Bulk

1822 **Bunny Bread**
418 E 1st St
Deridder, LA 70634-4204 337-463-7522
Fax: 504-241-0953 www.bunnybread.net
Processor of bread.
President: Daniel Brinson
VP: Darryl Trainer
Plant Manager: Daryl Mitchell
Estimated Sales: $17 Million
Number Employees: 240
Type of Packaging: Consumer

1823 **Bunny Bread Company**
833 Broadway St
Cape Girardeau, MO 63701 573-332-7349
www.bunnybread.net
Processor of sweet rolls, fruit bread, doughnuts and danish; wholesaler/distributor of bread
President: Jack Lewis
Estimated Sales: $5-10 Million
Number Employees: 5-9
Parent Co: Flowers Foods
Type of Packaging: Consumer, Food Service, Private Label

1824 **Buns & Roses Organic Wholegrain Bakery**
6519-111th Street NW
Edmonton, AB T5K 3M6
Canada 780-438-0098
Fax: 780-437-8805
Processor of breads and specialty baked products including organic whole grain and gluten-free
President: Dhammika Jayawickrama
Marketing Manager: Dhammika Jayawickrama
Owner: Dhammika Jayawickrama
Estimated Sales: A
Number Employees: 1-4
Sq. footage: 2400
Type of Packaging: Consumer, Food Service
Brands:
Buns & Roses

1825 **Buns & Things Bakery**
25 Brackley Point Road
Charlottetown, PE C1A 6Y1
Canada 902-892-2600
Fax: 902-892-2620
Processor of baked goods including danish, cinnamon rolls, bread, cookies, bagels, pies, rolls, etc
President/CEO: Robert DeBlois
Secretary: Elaine DeBlois
Number Employees: 10-19
Sq. footage: 2600

1826 **Buns Master Bakery**
2 East Beaver Rd Bldg 1
Richmond Hill, ON L4B 2N3
Canada 905-764-7066
Fax: 905-764-0476 800-563-6688
info@countrystyle.ca www.countrystyle.ca
Manufacturer of baked goods such as; breads and bakery products
President: Rick Martens
Estimated Sales: 2.5-5 Million
Number Employees: 10-19
Sq. footage: 6000
Type of Packaging: Consumer, Food Service, Bulk

1827 **Buns Master Bakery**
405 Stafford Drive N
Lethbridge, AB T1H 2A7
Canada 403-320-2966
Fax: 403-320-1080
Processor of baked goods including bread and rolls food prep,food products,deli.
President: Hugh McKee
Estimated Sales: 1-5 Million
Number Employees: 10-19
Parent Co: Buns Master Bakery Systems
Type of Packaging: Consumer, Food Service
Brands:
Buns Master

1828 **Buon ItaliaMisono Food Ltd.**
75 9th Ave # 17
New York, NY 10011-7029 212-633-9090
Fax: 212-633-9717 info@buonitalia.com
www.buonitalia.com
Processor and importer of gourmet Italian foods including pasta, rice, mushrooms, truffles, flour, jams, oils, cheeses, vinegar, fruit mustard, cookies, biscuits and sweets
Owner: Mimmo Majiulo
Estimated Sales: $3.8 Million
Number Employees: 20
Sq. footage: 10000
Parent Co: Misono Food
Type of Packaging: Consumer, Food Service, Private Label, Bulk

1829 **Buona Vita**
1 S Industrial Blvd
Bridgeton, NJ 08302-3401 856-453-7972
Fax: 856-453-7978 info@buonavitainc.com
www.buonavitainc.com
Processor of Italian specialties including meatballs, meatloaf, beef bracioli, eggplant, pasta and pizza toppings
President: Paul Infranco
VP: John Taormina
Production Manager: Blake Christy
Estimated Sales: $20-50 Million
Number Employees: 20-49
Sq. footage: 25000
Type of Packaging: Consumer, Food Service, Private Label, Bulk
Brands:
Buona Vita
Mama Mia

1830 **Buono Beef Co**
3650 S 3rd St
Philadelphia, PA 19148-5311 215-463-3600
Fax: 215-463-3481 www.buonobeef.com
Processor of frozen portion-controlled beef and pork
President: Michael Buono
Estimated Sales: D
Number Employees: 20-49

Brands:
Colonial Beef

1831 **Burch Farms**
P.O.Box 399
Faison, NC 28341 910-267-5781
Fax: 910-267-1133 800-466-9668
butch@intrastar.net www.burchfarms.com
Processor of sweet potatoes
President: Jimmy Burch
Partner: Ted Burch
Marketing Director: Jimmy Burch Jr
Estimated Sales: $5 Million
Number Employees: 90
Brands:
Candy Yams
Georgiana
Sugar & Spice

1832 **Burger Dairy**
3535 Rolling Hills Dr
Cleveland, OH 44124-5802 216-896-9100
Fax: 219-831-3494
Fluid and condensed milk
President: Alan Berger
Sales Manager: Gary Protsman
Controller: Mark Niezgodski
Production Manager: Terry Wuthrich
Plant Manager: Marty Crook
Estimated Sales: $25-49.9 Million
Number Employees: 1-4
Parent Co: Suiza Dairy Group

1833 **Burgers Smokehouse**
32819 Highway 87
California, MO 65018-3227 573-796-3134
Fax: 573-796-3137 800-624-5426
service@smokehouse.com
www.smokehouse.com
Smoked meats, country cured ham, spare ribs, St. Louis ribs, baby back ribs, pork chops, canadian bacon, spiral sliced ham, smoked bacon, summer sausage, smoked turkey, smoked chicken, smoked quail, smoked pheasant, and smoked duck
President: Steven Burger
CEO: Morris Burger
CFO: Ted Rohrbach
Vice President: Philip Burger
Marketing Director: Chris Mouse
Operations Manager: Keith Fletcher
Production Manager: Jeffery Kilgore
Plant Manager: Kenneth Phillips
Estimated Sales: $20-50 Million
Number Employees: 250-499
Sq. footage: 200000
Type of Packaging: Consumer, Food Service, Private Label, Bulk

1834 **Burke Brands**
521 NE 189th St
Miami, FL 33179-3909
Fax: 305-651-6018 877-436-6722
info@cafedonpablo.com www.cafedonpablo.com
Manufacturer of fine specialty coffee and gourmet food products.
President: Darron Burke
Vice President: Eliana Burke
Sales: Wilma Perez
Production: Gladys Menjura
Estimated Sales: $1.3 Million
Number Employees: 5-9
Number of Brands: 4
Number of Products: 27
Sq. footage: 10000
Type of Packaging: Consumer, Food Service, Private Label, Bulk
Other Locations:
Burke Brands
N Miami Beach FL
Brands:
Cafe Don Pablo

1835 **Burke Candy & Ingredient Corporation**
3840 N Fratney St
Milwaukee, WI 53212-1341 414-241-4369
Fax: 414-964-7644 888-287-5350
info@burkecandy.com www.burkecandy.com
Manufacturer of chocolate candies and confectionery. Products are certified kosher
Owner/Chef: Julia Burke
Owner/Chef: Tim Burke
Estimated Sales: Less than $500,000
Number Employees: 1-4

1836 **Burke Corporation**
1516 S D Ave
Nevada, IA 50201 515-382-3575
Fax: 515-382-2834 800-654-1152
sales_info@burkecorp.com www.burkecorp.com

Always make it your best® with Burke fully cooked meats. We specialize in Italian sausage, beef, and pork toppings, meatballs, taco meats, shredded meats, pepperoni, bacon, Canadian-style bacon, chicken and beef strips.Additionally, we offer a variety of specialty products: Hand-Pinched Style® brand toppings, chorizo, gyro topping, andouille sausage, and breakfast patties and links.

Marketing Director: Liz Hertz
VP Sales/Marketing: Doug Cooprider
Number Employees: 350
Type of Packaging: Food Service, Private Label, Bulk
Brands:
Burke
MagniFoods®
NaturaSelect™
Premoro®
Tezzata®

1837 **Burleigh Brothers Seafoods**
224 Burleigh Rd
Ellerslie, PE C0B 1J0
Canada 902-831-2349
Fax: 902-831-3072
Processor of fresh shellfish, mollusk, trout and smelt
CEO: Roger Burleigh
President: Proy Burleigh
Marketing Director: Tom Bradstaw
Number Employees: 100-249
Type of Packaging: Consumer, Food Service, Private Label, Bulk

1838 **Burleson's**
P.O.Box 578
Waxahachie, TX 75168-0578 972-937-4810
Fax: 972-937-8711 jimcburlesons-honey.com
www.burlesons-honey.com
Honey
President: Thomas E Burleson Jr
CEO: T Burleson
CFO: Walter Shugart
Marketing Director: Jim Phillips
Public Relations: Nina Swen-Kohler
Office Manager: Walter Shugert
Production Manager: Tim Burleson
Plant Manager: Steve Chambers
Purchasing Manager: LaWanna Ford
Estimated Sales: $10-20 Million
Number Employees: 20-49
Sq. footage: 45
Type of Packaging: Private Label
Brands:
Burleson Pure Honey

1839 **Burleson's Honey, Inc**
PO Box 578
Waxahachie, TX 75168 972-937-4810
Fax: 972-937-8711 jim@burlesons-honey.com
www.burlesons-honey.com
Processor and exporter of extracted honey
President: Thomas Burleson Jr
Marketing Staff Director: Jim Phillips
Estimated Sales: $860,000
Number Employees: 5
Type of Packaging: Consumer, Food Service, Private Label, Bulk
Brands:
BURLESON'S
NATURAL PURE

1840 **Burlington Bio-Medical Corporation**
71 Carolyn Blvd
Farmingdale, NY 11735-1527 631-694-4700
Fax: 631-694-9177 800-532-4808
bscchemny@aol.com www.amerolcorp.com
Processor and exporter of bittering agents and colors
President: Melvin Blum
VP Operations: Bill Rudy
Estimated Sales: $7.5 Million
Number Employees: 20-49
Sq. footage: 7
Type of Packaging: Bulk
Brands:
Bitter Guard

1841 **Burn Brae Farms**
5434 Tomken Rd
Mississauga, ON L4W 1P2
Canada 519-245-1630
Fax: 519-245-1690 General@burnbraefarms.com
www.burnbraefarms.com
Packager of eggs
President: Joe Hudson
Marketing Director: Margaret Hudson
COO: Bob Anderson
General Manager: Earl Powers
Estimated Sales: $29 Million
Number Employees: 100
Parent Co: Burnbrae Farm
Type of Packaging: Consumer, Food Service
Brands:
Free Run
Nature's Best
Omega Pro
Organic Shell Eggs

1842 **Burnett & Son Meat Company**
1420 S Myrtle Ave
Monrovia, CA 91016-4153 626-357-2165
Fax: 626-357-7115 info@burnettandson.com
www.burnettandson.com
Processor of meat including taco, London broil, shredded beef and pork, corned and roast beef, pot roast, steak, pork loin, etc; also, entrees including beef stew, chile, meat loaf, corned beef and cabbage, spaghetti and meatballsetc
Principal: Don Burnett
Principal: David Kruse
Estimated Sales: $20-50 Million
Number Employees: 50-99
Type of Packaging: Consumer, Food Service

1843 **Burnette Dairy Cooperative**
11631 State Road 70
Grantsburg, WI 54840-7135 715-689-2468
Fax: 715-689-2135 cheese@win.bright.net
www.burnettdairy.com
Processor of cheese including mozzarella, provolone, colby, cheddar and monterey jack
President: Dale Olson
Director: Gary Peterson
Estimated Sales: $20-50 Million
Number Employees: 100-249
Type of Packaging: Consumer, Food Service, Private Label, Bulk
Brands:
Fancy Brand

1844 **Burnette Foods**
701 Us Highway 31
Elk Rapids, MI 49629 231-264-8116
Fax: 231-264-9597 info@burnettefoods.com
www.burnettefoods.com
Pasta products, pie fillings, apple sauce, apple juice, vegetables and maraschinos.
Owner/Manager: William Sherman
Owner/Manager: Fred Sherman
Estimated Sales: $ 40 Million
Number Employees: 50-99
Type of Packaging: Consumer, Food Service, Private Label, Bulk
Brands:
Burnetti's
Mother's Maid
Romeo

1845 **Burnette Foods**
87171 County Road 687
Hartford, MI 49057-8602 616-621-3181
Fax: 616-621-4504 info@burnettefoods.com
www.burnettefoods.com
Processor of canned and glass packed apple sauce, potatoes, pie fillings and juices including tomato and apple
Manager: Bill Sherman
Operations Manager: Jack Wyatt
Estimated Sales: $10-20 Million
Number Employees: 50-99
Type of Packaging: Consumer, Food Service, Private Label, Bulk
Brands:
Mother's Maid

1846 **(HQ)Burnette Foods**
701 US Highway 31
Elk Rapids, MI 49629 231-264-8116
Fax: 231-264-9597 info@burnettefoods.com
www.burnettefoods.com
Manufacturer and exporter of canned fruits and vegetables including cherries, apples, plumbs, kidney beans, asparagus, green beans and potatoes
Owner/President: Teresa Amato
CFO: Jennifer Sherman
Quality Manager/Sales Executive: Jennifer Boyer
Operations Manager: Dave Schroderus
Production Manager: Eric Rockafellow
Plant Manager: Gary Wilson
Estimated Sales: $40-$50 Million
Number Employees: 200
Sq. footage: 12066
Type of Packaging: Consumer, Food Service
Other Locations:
Burnette Foods Plant
East Jordan MI
Burnette Foods Plant
Hartford MI
Brands:
BURNETTI'S
MOTHERS MAID
ROMEO

1847 **Burnley Vineyards and Daniel Cellars**
4500 Winery Ln
Barboursville, VA 22923-1833 540-832-2828
Fax: 540-832-2280 info@burnleywines.com
www.burnleywines.com
Wines
Owner/President: C Reeder
Owner: Lee Reeder
Sales Manager: Pat Reeder
Customer Service Manager: Dawn Reeder
Estimated Sales: $5-9.9 Million
Number Employees: 1-4

1848 **Burris Mill & Feed**
1012 Pearl St
Franklinton, LA 70438-1804 985-839-3400
Fax: 985-839-3404 800-928-2782
burris@burrismill.com www.cargill.com
Processor and exporter shrimp, alligator, redfish, etc
Manager: Pedro Curry
Manufacturing/Production: Robert Burris
Estimated Sales: $10-20 Million
Number Employees: 20-49
Type of Packaging: Private Label, Bulk

1849 **(HQ)Bush Boake Allen**
521 W 57th Street
New York, NY 10019-2929 212-765-5500
Fax: 212-708-7132 iff.information@iff.com
www.iff.com
Manufacturer and exporter of essential oils, flavors, fragrances, aroma chemicals, vanilla extract, enzyme modified dairy ingredients, spices and seasonings
Chairman/CEO: Richard Goldstein
COO: Jim Dunsdon
Sr. VP/CFO: Douglas Wetmore
EVP Global Operations: D Wayne Howard
Number Employees: 1900

1850 **Bush Brothers & Co.**
W7841 Smith Street
Shiocton, WI 54170-8640 920-986-3816
Fax: 920-986-3476 www.bushbeans.com
Processor of sauerkraut
General Manager: King Pharr
Estimated Sales: $5-10 Million
Number Employees: 20-49
Parent Co: Bush Brothers & Company
Type of Packaging: Consumer, Food Service
Brands:
Bush's Best

1851 **Bush Brothers & Co.**
3304 Chestnut Hill Rd
Dandridge, TN 37725 865-509-2361
Fax: 865-509-2339 www.bushbeans.com
Processor and exporter of dry packed beans, greens and hominy
President: Ronnie Scott
Estimated Sales: $2.5-5 Million
Number Employees: 250-499

1852 **Bush Brothers & Co.**
600 S Bush Brothers Dr
Augusta, WI 54722 715-286-2211
Fax: 715-286-1179 www.bushbeans.com
Manufacturer of canned beans and baked beans
Chairman/CEO: Jim Ethier
Finance Director: Mark Vankampen
Quality Assurance Manager: Jean Finger
Human Resources Director: Tim Haldeman
Operations Director: Joe Breid
Plant Manager: Joe Bried
Purchasing Director: Mike Coffey
Estimated Sales: $ 50 - 100 Million
Number Employees: 130
Sq. footage: 75698
Type of Packaging: Consumer, Food Service, Private Label
Other Locations:
Chestnut Hill TN
Brands:
Bush's Best
Showboat

1853 **Bush Brothers & Company**
1016 E Weisgarber Rd
Knoxville, TN 37909 865-588-7685
Fax: 865-584-9429 www.bushbeans.com
Dry edible beans and other value-added food products
President: James Ethier
Estimated Sales: $ 50 - 100 Million
Number Employees: 100-249

1854 **Bush Brothers Provision Company**
1931 N Dixie Hwy
West Palm Beach, FL 33407 561-832-6666
Fax: 561-832-1460 800-327-1345
Harry@bushbrothers.org
http://www.bushbrothers.org
Processor and exporter of fresh and frozen portion cut beef, veal, lamb, pork and poultry; wholesaler/distributor of dairy products; serving the food service market.
President: Harry Bush
VP: John Bush
Estimated Sales: $10-20 Million
Number Employees: 10-19
Sq. footage: 10000
Type of Packaging: Consumer, Food Service, Private Label, Bulk

1855 **Busken Bakery**
2675 Madison Rd
Cincinnati, OH 45208 513-871-5330
Fax: 513-871-2662 www.busken.com
Cookies, cakes, doughnuts, breads, rolls, pies and muffins.
President: Dan Busken
CEO: Page Busken
SVP: Brian Busken
Catering Operations: Larry Bossert
Production Manager: Tom Rinear
Estimated Sales: $10.5 Million
Number Employees: 90

1856 **Busseto Foods**
1351 N Crystal Ave
Fresno, CA 93728 559-485-9882
Fax: 559-485-9926 800-628-2633
www.busseto.com
Processor of specialty meats, salami, peperoni, prosciutto, chubs, pancetta and genoa
President/CEO: G Michael Grazier
CFO: C Laizure
Estimated Sales: $10-20 Million
Number Employees: 20-49
Parent Co: IBIS
Type of Packaging: Consumer, Food Service, Private Label, Bulk
Brands:
Busseto
Busseto Special Reserve

1857 **Bustelo Coffee RoastingCompany**
P.O.Box 520845
Miami, FL 33152-0845 305-592-7302
Fax: 305-592-9471 www.javacabana.com
Processor, importer and exporter of coffee; importer and wholesaler/distributor of coffee equipment and supplies including filters
President: Jose Souto
General Manager of Sales: Angeo Soupo
Estimated Sales: $2.5-5 Million
Number Employees: 20-49
Sq. footage: 25000
Parent Co: Tetley USA
Type of Packaging: Consumer, Food Service, Private Label
Brands:
Cafe Bustelo

1858 **Butcher Shop**
PO Box 698
Beaverlodge, AB T0H 0C0
Canada 780-354-8600
Fax: 780-354-8418
Processor of beef and pork sausages
Manager: Bob Geib
President: Bob Geib
Marketing Director: Bob Geib
Estimated Sales: B
Number Employees: 10-19
Sq. footage: 2000
Type of Packaging: Consumer, Bulk

1859 **Butler Winery**
1022 N College Ave
Bloomington, IN 47404-3589 812-339-7233
vineyard@butlerwinery.com
www.butlerwinery.com
Manufacturer of wine and wine making supplies
President/CEO: James Butler
Estimated Sales: $500,000-$1 Million
Number Employees: 1-4
Brands:
Butler

1860 **Butter Baked Goods**
4321 Dunbar Street
Vancouver, BC V6S 2G2 604-221-4333
Fax: 604-685-8563 info@butterbakedgoods.com
www.butterbakedgoods.com
Scones, muffins, cinnamon buns, cookies, bars, cupcakes, cakes, pies, tarts and mini tarts, loaves, and marshmallow

1861 **Butter Krust Baking Company**
249 N 11th St
Sunbury, PA 17801 570-286-5846
Fax: 570-286-6975 800-282-8093
www.butterkrust.com
Manufacturer of bread, rolls and donuts
President: James G Apple
Estimated Sales: $300,000-500,000
Number Employees: 5-9
Type of Packaging: Consumer, Private Label, Bulk
Other Locations:
Northumberland PA
Brands:
BUTTER-KRUST COUNTRY
HOLSUM
MILANO

1862 **(HQ)Butterball Farms**
1435 Buchanan Ave SW
Grand Rapids, MI 49507 616-243-0105
Fax: 616-243-9169 ron.s@butterballfarms.com
www.butterballfarms.com
Processor of butter and margarine; embossed designs available. Butter pats and butter balls certified kosher and dairy; Halal certification
President/CEO: Mark Peters
CFO: David Riemersma
Vice President: Tina Collins
Research & Development: Kasey Komdeur
Marketing/Sales: Kelly Andrus
Customer Service Manager: Ron Schalow
Operations Manager: Carol Schipper
Estimated Sales: $100+ Million
Number Employees: 250-499
Type of Packaging: Food Service, Private Label
Brands:
BUTTERBALL

FIGURE-MAID
PACK OF THE ROSES
POP-OUT
SWEETCORN

1863 **Butterball Turkey Company**
411 N Main St
Carthage, MO 64836 417-359-2000
Fax: 417-358-6553 800-641-4228
www.butterball.com
Frozen and refrigerated turkeys
President: Timothy Harris
COO: Randy Counts
Plant Manager: Jerry Lankford
Estimated Sales: Under $500,000
Number Employees: 20-49
Parent Co: ConAgra Refigerated Prepared Foods
Brands:
Butterball
Cook's
Crunch'n Munch
David
Decker
Gilroy
Golden Cuisine
Hunt's
Libbys
Louis Kemp
Luck's
Pen Rose
Peter Pan

1864 **Butterbuds Food Ingredients**
2330 Chicory Rd
Racine, WI 53403-4113 262-598-9900
Fax: 262-598-9999 800-426-1119
bbfi@bbuds.com www.bbuds.com
Processor and exporter of cholesterol-free butter flavored oils and sprays; also, natural dairy concentrates including butter, cheese and cream
President: Allen Buhler
VP: John Buhler
Applications Scientist: Adam Small
International Marketing Manager: Thomas Buhler
Estimated Sales: $5-10 Million
Number Employees: 20-49
Sq. footage: 5000
Parent Co: Cumberland Packing Corporation
Type of Packaging: Consumer, Food Service, Private Label, Bulk
Brands:
ALFREDOBUDS
BUTTER FLO
BUTTERBUDS
BUTTERMIST
CHEESEBUDS

1865 **Butterfield Foods Company**
225 Hubbard Ave
Butterfield, MN 56120 507-956-5103
Fax: 507-956-5751
mdowns@downsfoodgroup.com
www.tonydownsfoods.com
Processor of poultry including fresh and frozen chicken; also, slaughtering services available.
President: Mike Downs
Finance Director: Patty Johnson
Vice President: Greg Cook
Vice President: Mitch Forstie
Sales & Marketing: Leo Zachman
Estimated Sales: $5-10 Million
Number Employees: 100-249
Parent Co: Tony Downs Foods
Type of Packaging: Consumer, Food Service

1866 **Butterfields Brewing Company**
777 E Olive Ave
Fresno, CA 93728-3350 559-264-5521
Fax: 559-264-6033 www.sequoiabrewing.com
Processor of seasonal beer, ale, stout, lager and pilsner
President: Scott Kendall
Operations Manager: Holly Bragg
Director Manufacturing: Kevin Cox
Estimated Sales: $1-2.5 Million
Number Employees: 50-99
Type of Packaging: Consumer, Food Service
Brands:
Bridalveil Ale
San Joaquin Golden Ale
Tower Dark Ale

1867 **Butterfields/Sweet Concepts**
2155 S Old Franklin Rd
Nashville, NC 27856-8952 252-459-7771
Fax: 252-459-7606 800-945-5957
Processor of hard candy.
President: Brooks West
Estimated Sales: Under $500,000
Number Employees: 5-9

1868 **Butterfly Creek Winery**
4063 Triangle Rd
Mariposa, CA 95338-9031 209-966-2097
Fax: 209-742-5019 wine@yosemite.net
www.yosemite.com
Wines
President: John Gerken
General Manager: Bob Gerken
Estimated Sales: $500-$1 Million
Number Employees: 1-4
Type of Packaging: Private Label

1869 **Butternut Breads**
12 East Armour Blvd
Kansas City, MO 64111
Fax: 816-701-4781 800-483-7253
www.butternutbreads.com
Processor of bread including white, rye and whole wheat
Chairman: Leo Benatar
President/CEO: Michael J Anderson
Chief Marketing Officer: Richard C Seban
General Sales Manager: Rob Plough
Plant Manager: Daniel Hawkins
Estimated Sales: $100+ Million
Number Employees: 500-999
Parent Co: Interstate Bakeries Corporation
Type of Packaging: Consumer, Private Label
Brands:
Bread du Jour
Colombo
Cotton's
Eddy's Sweetheart
Holsum Di Carlo
J.J. Nissen
Millbrook
Mrs. Cubbison's
Parisian

1870 **Butternut Mountain Farm**
37 Industrial Park Dr
Morrisville, VT 05661 802-888-3491
Fax: 802-888-5909 800-828-2376
stuart@vermontmaplesugarcompany.com
www.butternutmountainfarm.com
Manufacturer of pure maple syrup, handmade maple candy, maple sugar, maple butter, maple spreads, cake mixes, honey, and honey spreads
Owner/President: David Marvin
CFO: John Kingston
VP Sales: Stuart Macfarland
Purchasing Manager: Stuart Macfarland
Estimated Sales: $1-2.5 Million
Number Employees: 65
Sq. footage: 50000
Parent Co: The Vermont Maple Syrup Company

1871 **Buttonwood Farm Winery**
1500 Alamo Pintado Rd
Solvang, CA 93463 805-688-3032
Fax: 805-688-6168 800-715-1404
imbibers@buttonwoodwinery.com
www.buttonwoodwinery.com
Wines
President: Bret Davenport
CFO: Elizabeth Williams
VP: Seyburn Zorthian
Estimated Sales: $500,000-$1 Million
Number Employees: 20-49

1872 **Buxton Foods**
401 Broadway
Buxton, ND 58218-4003 701-847-2110
800-726-8057
Manufacturer of gourmet frozen pinto beans and chili fully cooked and packaged in oven/microwaveable trays and boil-in-bags
President: Paul Siewert
CEO: Eileen Siewert
Estimated Sales: $ 10 - 20 Million
Number Employees: 1-4
Sq. footage: 4500
Type of Packaging: Consumer, Food Service
Brands:
Paul's Pintos

1873 **Buywell Coffee**
4850 North Park Drive
Colorado Springs, CO 80918 719-598-7870
Fax: 877-294-6246 main@buywellcoffee.com
www.buywellcoffee.com
organic coffee
Marketing: Christopher Aaby

1874 **Buzz Food Service**
4818 Kanawha Blvd E
Charleston, WV 25306-6328 304-925-4781
Fax: 304-925-1502 buzzfood@charter.net
www.buzzfoodsvc.com
Manufacturer of frozen beef, chicken, ribs, pork, turkey, veal and lamb
President: Dick Gould
GM: John Haddy
Estimated Sales: $50-100 Million
Number Employees: 50-99
Sq. footage: 25000
Type of Packaging: Consumer, Food Service

1875 **Buzzards Bay Trading Company**
PO Box 600
Fairhaven, MA 02719-0600 508-996-0242
Fax: 508-996-2421
Fresh and frozen seafood

1876 **Buzzn Bee Farms**
4700 N Flagler Dr
West Palm Beach, FL 33407-2907 561-881-1551
Fax: 561-881-7023 www.buzznbee.com
Honey
Owner/Beekeeper: David Rukin
Estimated Sales: $2.5-5 Million
Number Employees: 1-4
Brands:
Buzzn Bee Farms
Sweet Squeeze

1877 **Byblos Bakery**
2479 23rd Street NE
Calgary, AB T2E 8J8
Canada 403-250-3711
Fax: 403-291-4095 info@byblosbakery.com
www.byblosbakery.com
Processor of Middle Eastern baked goods including pita bread, bagels, baklava and tortilla wraps
President: Sal Daklala
VP: George Daklala
Estimated Sales: D
Number Employees: 50-99
Number of Brands: 1
Type of Packaging: Consumer, Food Service, Private Label, Bulk
Brands:
Byblos

1878 **Byesville Aseptics**
100 Hope Ave
Byesville, OH 43723 740-685-2548
Fax: 740-685-6550
Cocktail mixes, citrus juices, noncitrus fruit juices, vegetable juices
President: Vicky Meigh
Vice President: Jeff Campbell
General Manager: Thomas Szymaniak
Plant Manager: Bill Flynn
Purchasing Agent: George Bussington
Estimated Sales: $50-100 Million
Number Employees: 115
Type of Packaging: Bulk

1879 **Byington Winery & Vineyards**
21850 Bear Creek Rd
Los Gatos, CA 95033 408-354-1111
Fax: 408-354-2782 tastingroom@byington.com
www.byington.com
Wines
Manager: Frank Ashton
VP: Sheryl Byington Brissenden
General Manager: Rod Bravo
Estimated Sales: $1-2.5 Million
Number Employees: 5-9
Sq. footage: 15
Type of Packaging: Private Label
Brands:
Byington

1880 **Byrd Cookie Company**
P.O.Box 13086
Savannah, GA 31416-0086 912-355-1716
Fax: 912-355-4431 800-291-2973
custserv@byrdcookiecompany.com
www.byrdcookiecompany.com
Cookies
President: Jeff Repella
Vice President: Geoff Repella
Research & Development: Shawn Curl
Marketing Director: Amy Waddell
Sales Director: Geoff Repella
Public Relations: Amy Waddell
Operations/Plant Manager: Shawn Curl
Production Manager: Shawn Curl
Purchasing Manager: Shawn Curl
Estimated Sales: $5-10 Million
Number Employees: 50-99
Number of Brands: 3
Number of Products: 75
Sq. footage: 65000
Type of Packaging: Consumer, Private Label
Brands:
BYRD BASICS
BYRD COOKIE COMPANY
SECKINGER-LEE BISCUITS

1881 **Byrd Mill Company**
14471 Washington Hwy
Ashland, VA 23005 804-798-3627
Fax: 804-798-9357 888-897-3336
sales@byrdmill.com www.byrdmill.com
Manufacturer of specialty mixes including bread, pound cake, cookie, fruit cobbler, biscuit, pancake, waffle, muffin, spoon bread, shortbread, corn bread, hushpuppy, stoneground grits, etc
President: Todd Attkisson
Estimated Sales: $300,000-$500,000
Number Employees: 1-4
Sq. footage: 1650
Type of Packaging: Consumer, Food Service, Private Label, Bulk

1882 **Byrd's Pecans**
Rr 3 Box 196
Butler, MO 64730-9418 660-679-5583
Fax: 660-679-3783 866-679-5583
goodbye1@ckt.net byrdspecans.com
Pecans
Owner: Loyle Byrd
Owner: Mary Byrd
Estimated Sales: Less than $500,000
Number Employees: 1-4
Type of Packaging: Private Label
Brands:
Byrd Missouri Grown
Byrd's Hoot Owl Pecan Ranch Pecans

1883 **Byrd's Seafood**
101 Potomac St
Crisfield, MD 21817-1448 410-968-0990
Fax: 410-968-1424 www.byrdsseafood.com
Crabmeat
Manager: Patti Marshall
Estimated Sales: $ 3 - 5 Million
Number Employees: 5-9

1884 **Byrne & Carlson**
121 State St
Portsmouth, NH 03801-3825 603-559-9778
Fax: 603-559-9778 888-559-9778
info@byrneand carlson.com
www.byrneandcarlson.com
Manufacturer of chocolates and confections
Owner: Chris Carlson
Owner: Christopher Carlson
Estimated Sales: Less than $500,000
Number Employees: 1-4

1885 **Byrne Dairy**
240 Oneida St
Syracuse, NY 13202 315-475-2111
Fax: 315-471-0930 800-899-1535
mary.fietkiewicz@byrnedairy.com
www.byrnedairy.com
Processor of dairy products including fresh milk, cream and juice, UP milk and creams and ice cream.
President: William Byrne
Production: Nick Marsella
Estimated Sales: $100 Million
Number Employees: 100-249
Type of Packaging: Consumer, Food Service, Private Label, Bulk
Brands:
Byrne Dairy

1886 **Byrnes & Kiefer Company**
P.O.Box L
Callery, PA 16024 724-538-5200
Fax: 724-538-9292 877-444-2240
www.bkcompany.com
Baked goods
President: Jay Thier
Vice President: Tom Byrnes
Controller: Kathy Hoover
Estimated Sales: $18.5 Million
Number Employees: 25
Type of Packaging: Private Label

1887 **Byrnes Packing**
P.O.Box 8
Hastings, FL 32145-0008 904-692-1643
Fax: 904-692-2002
Grower and packer of whole potatoes
Owner: Danny Byrnes
Estimated Sales: $2.5-5 Million
Number Employees: 10-19
Type of Packaging: Consumer

1888 **Byron Vineyard & Winery**
5475 Chardonnay Ln
Santa Maria, CA 93454 805-934-4770
Fax: 805-938-1581 info@byronwines.com
www.byronwines.com
Manufacturer of wines
Manager: Jonathan Nagy
Winemaker/General Manager: Ken Brown
VP Winemaker: Byron Brown
Estimated Sales: $5-10 Million
Number Employees: 10-19
Type of Packaging: Private Label

1889 **C C Conway Seafoods**
2567 Conway Oyterhouse Road
Wicomico, VA 23184 804-642-2853
Fish and seafood
President: C Conway III
Estimated Sales: $500,000-$1 Million
Number Employees: 1-4
Type of Packaging: Food Service, Bulk

1890 **C&C Packing Company**
P.O.Box 157
Stamps, AR 71860 870-533-2251
Fax: 870-533-4309 www.candcpacking.com
Processor of meat
Owner: Randy Camp
Estimated Sales: $1-2.5 Million
Number Employees: 5-9
Type of Packaging: Consumer

1891 **C&E Canners**
P.O.Box 229
Hammonton, NJ 8037 609-561-1078
Fax: 609-567-2776
Processor, exporter and canner of sauces and ketchup
President: Robert Cappuccio
COO: David Cappuccio
Vice President: Joseph Cappuccio II
Director Manufacturing: Stephen Cappuccio
Purchasing: Robert Cappuccio
Estimated Sales: $5-10 Million
Number Employees: 20-49
Sq. footage: 80000
Type of Packaging: Consumer
Brands:
C & E SUGAR
CAPPUCCIO
NA PO'OKELA O HONAUNAU

1892 **(HQ)C&F Foods**
15620 Valley Blvd
City of Industry, CA 91744 626-723-1000
Fax: 626-723-1212 www.cnf-foods.com
Processor and exporter of dried beans, lentils, pop-corn, peas and rice
President: Luis Faura
CEO/Chairman: Manuel Fernandez
CFO: Jose Fernandez
Estimated Sales: $32.6 Million
Number Employees: 100-249
Type of Packaging: Consumer, Food Service, Private Label
Other Locations:
C&F Foods
Hansen ID
C&F Foods
Sikeston MO
C&F Foods
Manvel ND
C&F Food
Raleigh NC
Brands:
EL ORGULLO DE MI TIERRA
KANGA BEANS
PREMIER FIELDS

1893 **C&G Salsa**
P.O.Box 6085
Fishers, IN 46038 317-569-9099
Fax: 317-569-8666 sales@cgsalsa.com
www.cgsalsa.com
Produces a variety of salsa (mild/medium/hot) and chili sauce (mild/zesty) products.
Co-Owner: Charlie Ferguson
Co-Owner: Glenda Ferguson
Type of Packaging: Food Service

1894 **(HQ)C&H Sugar Company**
830 Loring Ave
Crockett, CA 94525 510-787-2121
Fax: 510-787-1791 800-729-4840
steve.tan@chsugar.com www.chsugar.com
Manufacturer of refined pure cane sugar including granulated, brown, powedered, liquid, cubes, raw and organic sugars, exporter of pure cane sugar
President/CEO: David Koncelik
CFO: Robert Guilbualt
VP: William Duff
VP Sales: William Duff
Estimated Sales: $500 Million-$1 Billion
Number Employees: 500-999
Type of Packaging: Consumer, Food Service, Private Label, Bulk
Brands:
C&H BAKER'S SUGAR
C&H DARK BROWN SUGAR
C&H GOLDEN BROWN SUGAR
C&H GRANULATED SUGAR
C&H POWDERED SUGAR
C&H SUPERFINE SUGAR
C&H WASHED RAW SUGAR

1895 **(HQ)C&H Sugar Company**
830 Loring Ave
Crockett, CA 94525 510-787-2121
Fax: 510-787-1791 edgn.orr@cgsugar.com
www.chsugar.com
Manufacturer of cane sugar and molasses
President/CEO: David Koncelik
CFO: Robert Guilbualt
VP: William Duff
Estimated Sales: $169 Million
Number Employees: 500-999
Type of Packaging: Consumer, Food Service, Private Label, Bulk
Brands:
C&H

1896 **C&H Sugar/Sweetener Products**
830 Loring Avenue
Crocket, CA 94525 714-475-2665
Fax: 949-475-2677 800-773-803
mkh4665@home.com www.chsugar.com
Sugar products
President: David G Koncelik
CEO: David G Koncelik
CFO: Robert Guilbualt
Brands:
C&H Sugar

1897 **C&J Tender Meat**
324 E Intl Airport Rd
Anchorage, AK 99518 907-562-2838
Fax: 907-561-5846
Owner: Steve Jones
Vice President: Arlita Jones
Estimated Sales: $1,300,000
Number Employees: 5-9

1898 **C&J Trading**
1140 Revere Ave
San Francisco, CA 94124-3423 415-822-8910
Fax: 415-822-7526
Oriental food
Owner: C Wo
Estimated Sales: $1-2.5 Million
Number Employees: 5-9
Type of Packaging: Private Label

1899 **C&S Wholesale Meat Company**
973 Confederate Ave SE
Atlanta, GA 30312-3799 404-627-3547
Fax: 404-627-3549
Processor of portion cut meat including pork and beef
President: Jay Bernath
CEO: Stanley Berneth
Chairman of the Board: Stanley Bernath
Marketing Administrator: Ronnie Berneth
Estimated Sales: $10-20 Million
Number Employees: 20-49
Type of Packaging: Food Service, Bulk
Brands:
C&S

1900 **C&T Refinery**
7110 Forest Ave Ste 200
Richmond, VA 23226 804-287-1340
Fax: 804-285-9168 800-284-6457
jonathan_gilbert@ctrefinery.com
www.cargill.com
Processor and exporter of vegetable oil
President: C Sauer IV
VP: Robert Holden
Parent Co: C.F. Sauer Company
Type of Packaging: Consumer, Food Service, Private Label, Bulk
Brands:
C&T

1901 **C. Gould Seafoods**
PO Box 14566
Scottsdale, AZ 85267-4566 480-314-9250
Fax: 480-314-9240
Seafood
President: Carla Gould
Secretary/Treasurer: Helen Sambrano
Vice President: Robert Llewellyn
Estimated Sales: $600,000

1902 **C. Howard Company**
1007 Station Rd
Bellport, NY 11713 631-286-7940
Fax: 631-286-7947
apratz@chowardcompany.com
www.chowardcompany.com
Processor of confectionery products including hard candy, mints and chewing gum
President: Kenneth Pratz
Treasurer: Gene Pratz
Vice President: Arthur Pratz
Estimated Sales: $570,000
Number Employees: 9
Sq. footage: 10000
Type of Packaging: Consumer, Private Label
Brands:
Chowards

1903 **C. Roy Meat Products**
444 Roy Dr
Yale, MI 48097-3461 810-387-3957
Fax: 810-387-3957
Processor of meat products including bologna
Owner: Richard Roy
Manager: Nancy Roy
Estimated Sales: $ 10 - 20 Million
Number Employees: 20-49
Type of Packaging: Consumer

1904 **C.B.S. Lobster Company**
41 Union Wharf
Portland, ME 04101 207-775-2917
Fax: 207-772-0169 www.mainelobsterdirect.com
Lobster
Owner: Lee Kressbach
Estimated Sales: $ 5 - 10 Million
Number Employees: 20-49

1905 **C.C. Graber Company**
P.O.Box 511
Ontario, CA 91762-8511 909-983-1761
Fax: 909-984-2180 800-996-5483
info@graberolives.com www.graberolives.com
Vegetables, gourmet foods, olives
President: Clifford Graber
Co-Owner: Robert Graber
Estimated Sales: $20-50 Million
Number Employees: 100-249
Brands:
Graber Olives

1906 **C.E. Fish Company**
P.O.Box 128
Jonesboro, ME 04648 207-434-2631
Fax: 207-434-6940
Processor and exporter of seafood including shucked soft shelled and steamer clams
President: Barbara Fish
Estimated Sales: $300,000
Number Employees: 5-9
Sq. footage: 3500
Type of Packaging: Consumer
Brands:
UNI

1907 **C.F. Burger Creamery**
8101 Greenfield Rd
Detroit, MI 48228-2296 313-584-4040
Fax: 313-584-9870 800-229-2322
www.cfburger.com
Processor of aerosol whip cream, ready-to-drink milkshakes, coconut beverages and natural Swiss goat's milk
Co-Chairman: Thomas "Angott, Sr"
CEO: Larry Angott
COO: Larry Angott
VP: James Brackett
Quality Control: Arvind Patel
Sales Manager: chris Angott
COO: Larry Angott
Estimated Sales: $20-50 Million
Number Employees: 50-99
Type of Packaging: Consumer, Food Service, Private Label, Bulk
Brands:
C.F. Burger
Goody Shake
Natures Fountain

1908 **C.F. Gollott & Son Seafood**
P.O.Box 1191
Biloxi, MS 39533-1191 228-392-3340
Fax: 228-392-8848 866-846-3474
www.gollottseafoodmarket.com
Importer of frozen shrimp
President: Armond Gollott
Secretary/Treasurer: Arny Gollot, Jr.
VP Sales/Marketing: Arnie Gollott Jr.
Estimated Sales: $20-50 Million
Number Employees: 50-99
Sq. footage: 7800
Type of Packaging: Consumer, Food Service, Private Label
Brands:
Gollott
Gollott's Brand
Merimaid Supreme
Mermaid Supreme

1909 **(HQ)C.F. Sauer Company**
2000 W Broad St
Richmond, VA 23220-2000 804-359-5786
Fax: 804-358-4396 800-688-5676
www.cfsauer.com
Processor of condiments, relishes, oils, shortenings, salad dressings, mayonnaise, sauces, spices and seasonings
President: Conrad F Sauer Iv
CFO: Richard Coppolo
Vice President: Richard Winger
Quality Control: Chuck Adams
SVP/Sales & Marketing: Frank Pyszkowski
Purchasing Agent: Anne Reager
Estimated Sales: $250 Million
Number Employees: 900
Sq. footage: 80000
Type of Packaging: Consumer, Food Service, Private Label
Other Locations:
C.F. Sauer Company
San Luis Obispo CA
Brands:
BAMA
C.F. SAUER COMPANY
DUKE'S MAYONAISE
GOLD MEDAL
MRS. FILBERTS
SAUER'S EVERYDAY SPICES
THE SPICE HUNTER

1910 **C.H. Guenther & Son**
129 E Guenther Street
San Antonio, TX 78204-1402 210-227-1401
Fax: 210-227-1409 800-531-7912
respinoza@chguenther.com
www.chguenther.com
Flour meal and prepared mixes, frozen bakery products
President/CEO: C.H. Guenther
CFO: Walter Moede
President/CEO, CHG: Dale W Tremblay
Research & Development: Ron Spies
Quality Control: Ron Spies
SVP/Operations: Chris Redkey
Corporate Accounts VP: Mike Toti
Food Service President: Steve Stroud
Sr. VP Supply Chair: Dennis Daniels
Plant Manager: Paul Chupp
Purchasing Manager: Jim Sharp
Estimated Sales: $100+ Million
Number Employees: 250-499
Type of Packaging: Consumer, Food Service, Private Label, Bulk
Brands:
MORRISON
PETER PAN
PIONEER
SAN ANTONIO RIVER MILL
WHITE LILY
WHITE WINGS

1911 **C.H. Guenther & Son, Inc**
129 E Guenther Street
San Antonio, TX 78204 210-227-1401
Fax: 210-227-1409 www.chguenther.com
Mixes (white gravy, flavored gravy, sauce, biscuits, pancake and waffle, dessert, cornbread and muffin, tortillas, flour and corn meal)
President/CEO: Dale Tremblay
SVP/CFO: Janelle Sykes
VP/General Counsel: Thomas McRae
R&D Director: John Gick
Quality Assurance Director: Michael Martinez
VP Sales/Marketing: Ronald Brown
VP Corporate Human Resources: Stephen Philips
SVP Operations: Chris Redkey
Manufacturing Manager: Ismael Cantu
VP Purchasing: James Sharp
Number Employees: 750
Sq. footage: 22869
Type of Packaging: Consumer, Food Service
Brands:
MORRISON
PIONEER BRAND
WHITE WINGS

1912 **C.J. Distributing**
P.O.Box 2344
Surf City, NC 28445 910-329-1681
Fax: 910-329-1286 800-990-2366
peanutsrus@aol.com
Processor of peanuts and snack food items
CEO: E Howell
Number Employees: 1-4
Sq. footage: 5000
Type of Packaging: Consumer, Private Label, Bulk

1913 **C.J. Vitner Company**
4202 W 45th St
Chicago, IL 60632 773-523-7900
Fax: 773-523-9143 vinnie@vitners.com
www.vitners.com
Processor of pretzels, popcorn and tortilla, corn and potato chips
President/COO: Edward Cepa
CEO: William Vitner
CFO: Steve Reusz
Human Resources: Jeanne McGreal Cassidy
Warehouse Manager: Phil Ceropski

Estimated Sales: $20-50 Million
Number Employees: 447
Sq. footage: 77000
Parent Co: C.J. Vitner Company
Type of Packaging: Consumer, Food Service, Private Label, Bulk

1914 C.L. Deveau & Son
PO Box 1
Salmon River, NS B0W 2Y0
Canada 902-649-2812
Fax: 902-649-2838
Processor and exporter of salted hake, cusk, pollack and cod; also, frozen herring roe
President: Irvan Paul Deveau
Number Employees: 10-19
Type of Packaging: Consumer, Food Service, Private Label, Bulk

1915 C.N.L. Trading
1117 Westminster Avenue
Alhambra, CA 91803-1234 626-282-1938
Fax: 626-282-1908
Proprietor: John Chan

1916 C.S. Steen's Syrup Mill
119 N Main St
Abbeville, LA 70510-4603 337-893-1654
Fax: 337-893-2478 800-725-1654
steens@steensyrup.com www.steensyrup.com
Processor of molasses and syrup
Owner: Charlie Steen
Marketing Director: Cole Thompson
General Manager: Charley Steen
Estimated Sales: $ 5 - 10 Million
Number Employees: 20-49
Type of Packaging: Bulk
Brands:
Steen's Cane Cured Pheasant

1917 C.W. Brown & Company
161 Kings Highway
Mount Royal, NJ 08061-1011 856-423-3700
Fax: 856-423-8894
Processor of sausage and lard
President: Robert Botto
Estimated Sales: $10-20 Million
Number Employees: 20-49
Type of Packaging: Consumer, Bulk
Brands:
BOTTO'S ITALIAN

1918 CA Fortune
141 Covington Dr
Bloomingdale, IL 60108-3107
Fax: 608-634-2400
Producers of dairy products, specialty foods, pizza toppings, pizza crusts and bread.
Administrator: Rhonda Powers
Purchasing: Ralph Johnson
Estimated Sales: $1-2.5 Million
Number Employees: 1-4
Type of Packaging: Private Label
Brands:
BURLLE MEATS
NEW HOLSTEIN CHEESE
ROTELLA BREAD

1919 CAL Sun Produce Company
511 Mountain View Ave
Oxnard, CA 93030 805-985-2262
Fax: 805-486-5022 www.calsunproduce.com
Processor of strawberries
Owner: S Taylor
CFO: T Burt
Purchasing Agent: Rick Meck
Estimated Sales: $10-20 Million
Number Employees: 500-999
Sq. footage: 48000
Type of Packaging: Bulk

1920 CB Beverage Corporation
P.O.Box 49
Hopkins, MN 55343 952-935-9905
Fax: 952-938-2731 www.cocknbull.com
Beverages; ginger beer, sarsaparilla, sparkling juice, root beer, etc.
President: Daniel Meyers
Estimated Sales: Less than $300,000
Number Employees: 1-4

1921 CB Seafoods
PO Box 299
Inverness, NS B0E 1N0
Canada 902-895-8181
Fax: 902-895-8180
Processor and exporter of fresh and frozen lobster, mackerel and sea urchins
President/CEO: Bernard MacLennan
Number Employees: 50-99
Type of Packaging: Consumer, Food Service, Private Label, Bulk

1922 CBC Foods
305 Main St
PO Box 396
Little River, KS 67457 620-897-6665
Fax: 620-897-5599 800-276-4770
carolyn@cookiehouse.com
Manufacture frozen cookie dough
President: Carolyn Wright
Estimated Sales: $1 Million
Number Employees: 6
Sq. footage: 5000
Type of Packaging: Consumer, Food Service, Private Label, Bulk

1923 CBP Resources
5533 York Hwy
Gastonia, NC 28052 704-864-9941
Fax: 704-861-9252
Processor of hydrogenated fats
President: Jj Smith
Plant Manager: Rick Stradtman
Estimated Sales: $ 20 - 50 Million
Number Employees: 100-249
Parent Co: Carolina By-Products Company

1924 CBS Food Products Corporation
770 Chauncey St
Brooklyn, NY 11207 718-452-2500
Fax: 718-452-2516
Vegetable oil
President: Chaim Stein
CEO: Bernard Steinberg
Vice President: Phillip Shapiro
Purchasing Agent: Bob Green
Estimated Sales: $2 Million
Number Employees: 15
Type of Packaging: Consumer, Food Service, Private Label
Brands:
CBS

1925 CC Pollen Company
3627 E Indian School Rd # 209
Phoenix, AZ 85018-5134 602-957-0096
Fax: 602-381-3130 800-875-0096
royden@earthlink.net www.ccpollen.com
Bee pollen and beehive products
President: Bruce Brown
CEO: C Brown
CFO: I Pettit
Marketing Director: M Hudnall
Purchasing: Bruce Brown
Estimated Sales: $10-20 Million
Number Employees: 20-49
Type of Packaging: Consumer, Food Service, Private Label, Bulk
Brands:
24-HOUR ROYAL JELLY
ALLER BEE-GONE
BEE PROPOLIS
BUZZ BARS
DYNAMIC TRIO
HIGH DESERT
POLLENERGY

1926 CCPI/Valley Foods
525 E Lindmore St
Lindsay, CA 93247-2559 559-562-5169
Fax: 559-562-5691
Orange juice concentrate
Owner: Tommy Elliott
CEO: John Barkley
Purchasing Agent: Tommy Elliott
Estimated Sales: $9 Million
Number Employees: 20-49
Sq. footage: 40000

1927 CE International Trading Corporation
13450 SW 134th Ave
Miami, FL 33186-4530 305-254-3448
Fax: 305-254-3182 800-827-1169
info@ceinternationaltrading.com
http://ceinternational.marcorojas.com/index.htm
Manufacturer of vibratory and separation systems. Food and beverage usage includes batch operations to screen and scalp powders, granules, or liquids in different locations.
Sales Representative: Edwin Rojas

1928 CGI Desserts
1 King Arthurs Ct
Sugar Land, TX 77478-3145 281-240-1200
Fax: 281-240-1242
Dessert manufacturer: layer cakes, sheet cakes, cheesecake, ice cream cake, mousse cakes, pies, single serve desserts, bars, brownies and minipuffs.
President: Sam Stolbun
Vice President: Mike Newlin
VP/Director Marketing: Cindy Newlin
Estimated Sales: $65 Million
Number Employees: 500
Type of Packaging: Consumer, Food Service, Private Label, Bulk

1929 CHR Foods
P.O.Box 608
Watsonville, CA 95077-0608 831-728-0157
Fax: 831-728-0459
Processor of frozen mixed vegetables and strawberries including whole and puree
President/CEO: Ray Rodriguez
CFO: Julis Skelton
Estimated Sales: $ 5 - 10 Million
Number Employees: 5-9
Type of Packaging: Food Service
Brands:
CHR
New Harvest Foods

1930 CHR Hansen
440 Business Park Cir
Stoughton, WI 53589 608-877-8970
Fax: 608-877-8984 www.chr-hansen.com
Tablet excipients and coating for pharmaceuticals and dietary supplements.
Parent Co: Chr Hansen

1931 CHR Hansen
P.O.Box 483
Gretna, LA 70054-0483 504-367-7727
Fax: 504-367-8832 www.chr-hansen.com
Specialty sweeteners, molasses and fondants. Certified organic facility.
Manager: Cory Breaux
Estimated Sales: $ 10 - 20 Million
Number Employees: 10-19
Parent Co: Chr Hansen

1932 CHR Hansen
2400 E 130th St
Chicago, IL 60633 773-646-2203
Fax: 773-646-6346 www.ch-humanhealth.com
Sweeteners, rice syrups, malt syrups and molasses. Certified organic facility.
Vice President: Knud Vindfeldt
Sales Director: Robert Ciero
Plant Manager: Chuck Stader
Estimated Sales: $ 5 - 10 Million
Number Employees: 20-49
Parent Co: Chr Hansen

1933 CHR Hansen
110 Liberty Court
Elyria, OH 44035-2237 440-324-6060
Fax: 440-324-2747 800-558-0802
www.chr-hansen.com
Manufacturer and exporter of seasonings, mixes, bacon bits, flour, oils, salt, binders, etc
President: John Cole
Estimated Sales: $3-5 Million
Number Employees: 1-4
Type of Packaging: Food Service, Private Label, Bulk

1934 CHR Hansen
3558 NW 97th Boulevard
Gainesville, FL 32606-7323 352-332-9455
Fax: 352-332-9939

Processor of meat and poultry starter cultures, spice extracts, seasoning blends and natural antioxidants.
FID Industry Group Leader: Kim Bright
Senior Applications Advisor: Jim Bacus
Estimated Sales: $500,000-$1 Million
Number Employees: 5-9
Parent Co: Chr. Hansen Group
Type of Packaging: Bulk

1935 **CHR Hansen**
110 Liberty Court
Elyria, OH 44035-2237 440-324-6060
Fax: 440-324-2747 www.chr-hansen.com
Liquid and dry seasonings and spice blends.
Sales Manager: Don Bachourus
Estimated Sales: Under $500,000
Number Employees: 1-4

1936 **CHR Hansen**
9015 W Maple St
Milwaukee, WI 53214 414-476-3632
Fax: 414-607-5959 800-343-4680
www.ch-humanhealth.com
Health nutritionals and savory, sweet, dairy and compound blend flavors.
Human Resources: Chris Beaudry
Estimated Sales: $50-100 Million
Number Employees: 1,000-4,999

1937 **(HQ)CHS**
5500 Cenex Drive
Inver Grove Heights, MN 55077 651-355-6000
800-232-3639
lani.jordan@chsinc.com www.chsinc.com
Miller and exporter of semolina, durum and bakery flours; producer of refined vegetable oils, textured soy protein, confectionary sunflower seeds, small grains and processed nut ingredients.crop nutri - ents,livestock feed,grain.
President & CEO: John Johnson
CEO: John Johnson
Executive VP & CFO: John Schmitz
Executive VP & COO Ag Business: Mark Palmquist
Manager: Dave Strum
Executive VP & COO Processing: Jay Debertin
Estimated Sales: $32+ Billion
Number Employees: 50,000
Type of Packaging: Consumer, Food Service, Private Label, Bulk

1938 **CHS Sunflower**
P.O.Box 169
Grandin, ND 58038-0169 701-484-5313
Fax: 701-484-5657 sunflower@chsinc.com
www.chssunflower.com
Processor of sunflower kernels, in-shell sunflower, flax, millet, buckwheat, pumpkin seeds, and soybean.
President/CEO: James Krogh
Research & Development: Joel Schaefer
Sales Director: Wes Dick
Sales Director: Bruce Fjelde
Plant Superintendent: Arvid Terry
Controller: Chuck Schmidt
Estimated Sales: $100+ Million
Number Employees: 100-249
Parent Co: CHS, Inc.
Type of Packaging: Consumer, Food Service, Private Label, Bulk

1939 **CHS, Inc.**
3500 Cenex Drive
Inner Grove Heights, MN 55077-1099651-355-6000
800-232-3639
www.chsinc.com
Flavored condiments, sauces and dressings, barbacue sauce and imitation bacon bits
President/CEO: John Johnson
Estimated Sales: Below $ 5 Million
Number Employees: 50-99
Brands:
Curley's Famous
I Magic
Imagic Baken
Imagic Imitation Sau
Imagic Meat Mix
Imagic Sloppy Joe Mi
Imitation Bacon Chip
Imitation Chicken Flavor
Imitation Ham Flavor
Imitation Pepperoni
Imitation Pepperoni
Imitation Pepperoni
Imitation Pepperoni
RK
TSP
Ultra-Soy

1940 **CJ America**
3500 Lacey Road
Suite 230
Downers Grove, IL 60515 630-241-0112
Fax: 630-241-2502 glickley@cj.net
www.cjamerica.com
Korean foods
President: Joonmo Suh
Vice President: Stephen Chang
National Sales Manager: Gene Moon
Product Manager: Chris Lee
Purchasing Agent: Jane Cho
Estimated Sales: $ .5 - 1 million
Number Employees: 10
Sq. footage: 7826
Parent Co: Cheiljedang

1941 **CJ Dannemiller Company**
5300 S Hametown Rd
Norton, OH 44203-6199 330-825-7808
Fax: 330-825-3793 800-624-8671
www.cjdannemiller.com
Processor of roasted nuts and popcorn
President: JA Dannemiller
Secretary: TW Dannemiller
Purchasing Manager: JA Dannemiller
Estimated Sales: $5-10 Million
Number Employees: 20-49
Sq. footage: 22000
Type of Packaging: Bulk

1942 **CJ Omni**
4591 Firestone Blvd
South Gate, CA 90280 323-567-8171
info@cjomni.com
www.cjomni.com
Manufacturer of Korean foods; specialize in mini wontons and korean sauces
President: James Chae
Estimated Sales: $ 3.5 Million
Number Employees: 50

1943 **CJ's Seafood**
125 Dixie Drive
Des Allemands, LA 70030-3320 985-758-1237
Processor of fresh and frozen catfish
President: Curtis Matherne
Number Employees: 1-4
Sq. footage: 280
Type of Packaging: Consumer, Food Service

1944 **CK Mondavi Vineyards**
P.O.Box 191
2800 Main Street
St Helena, CA 94574-0191 707-967-2200
Fax: 707-967-2291 info@ckmondavi.com
www.charleskrug.com
Manufacturer of wines
President: Peter Mondavi Sr
CFO: Tom Fossey
Sales Director: Larry Challacombe
Estimated Sales: $5-9.9 Million
Number Employees: 100-249
Type of Packaging: Private Label
Brands:
CK Mondavi Cabernet
CK Mondavi Chardonnay
CK Mondavi MERLOT
CK Mondavi WHITE ZIN
CK MondaviSAUVIGNON
CK MondaviZINFANDEL

1945 **CMT Packaging & Designs,Inc.**
312 Amboy Ave
Metuchen, NJ 08840-1833 732-321-4029
Fax: 732-549-3615 info@cmtpackaging.com
www.cmtpackaging.com
A custom packaging company for the food and perfume industry.
President: Preshal Iyar
Estimated Sales: $5,000
Sq. footage: 5000

1946 **CNS Confectionery Products**
33 Hook Rd
Bayonne, NJ 7002 201-823-1400
Fax: 201-823-2452 888-823-4330
sales@cnscoinc.com www.cnscoinc.com
Importer, processor and national distributor of sweetened, toasted and desiccated coconut as well as other sweet, dry baking ingredients. Certified kosher.
Chief, Production/Purchasing: Eva Deutsch
CFO: Irene Fishman
VP Sales: Miriam Gross
Estimated Sales: $1-2.5 Million
Number Employees: 10-19
Type of Packaging: Private Label
Brands:
CNS

1947 **COBE Chem Labs**
8616 Slauson Ave
Pico Rivera, CA 90660-4435 562-942-2426
Fax: 562-942-9985 sales@cobechem.com
www.cobechem.com
President: Sergio Quinones
CEO: Sergio Quinones
Marketing Manager: Sergio Quinones
Estimated Sales: $ 20 - 50 Million
Number Employees: 50-99
Brands:
Cobe

1948 **CP Kelco**
Cumberland Center II
3100 Cumberland Blvd, Suite 600
Atlanta, GA 30339 678-247-7300
Fax: 678-247-2797 800-535-2687
solutions@cpkelco.com www.cpkelco.com
Manufactures and sells a broad spectrum of texturizing and stabilizing ingredients. Food ingredi - ents include pectin, carrageenan, xanthan gum and gellan gum, locust bean gum and microparticulated whey protein concentrate.
President/Chief Executive Officer: Don Rubright
Vice President/Chief Financial Officer: Torben Wetche
CEO: Thomas B Lamb
Vice President Research & Development: Akvia Gross Ph.D
Vice President Business Management: Didier Viala
Vice President Commercial Operations: Rick Calk
Vice President & General Counsel: Edward Castorina
Vice President Operations: Russ Jordan
Global Marketing Director: Jane Schulenburg
Vice President Supply Chain & Services: Gerald Coughlin
Estimated Sales: $480 Million
Number Employees: 1500
Number of Brands: 10
Number of Products: 24
Parent Co: J.M. Huber Company
Other Locations:
CP Kelco Production Plant
Okmulgee OK
CP Kelco Production Plant
San Diego CA
Brands:
CEKOL
GENU
GENU PLUS
GENUGEL
GENULACTA
GENULACTA
GENUTINE
GENUVISCO
KELCOGEL
KELGUM
KELTROL
SIMPLESSE
SPLENDID

1949 **CP Vegetable Oil**
601 Sw 21st Ter
Suite 1
Fort Lauderdale, FL 33312-2278
Canada 905-792-2309
Fax: 905-792-9461 ngonsalves@cpvegoil.com
www.cpvegoil.com
Processor of vegetable oils
Ceo: Christian Pellerin
Number Employees: 15
Type of Packaging: Food Service, Bulk
Brands:
C.P.

1950 **CTC International**
11 York Ave
West Caldwell, NJ 07006-6486 973-228-2300
Fax: 973-228-7076 info@ctcint.com
www.ctcint.com
President: E L Herbert
Estimated Sales: $ 10 - 20 Million
Number Employees: 20-49

1951 **CTC Manufacturing**
416 Meridian Road SE
Suite B12
Calgary, AB T2A 1X2
Canada 403-235-2428
Fax: 403-272-9558 800-668-7677
candytree@sprint.ca
Processor and exporter of gourmet lollypops
President: G Paul Allen
Sales Manager: David Skultety
Plant Manager: Malcolm Steel
Number Employees: 10-19
Sq. footage: 3450
Parent Co: Candy Tree Company
Type of Packaging: Consumer, Food Service, Private Label
Brands:
The Candy Tree

1952 **CTL Foods**
507 Pine St
Colfax, WI 54730 715-962-3121
Fax: 715-962-4030 800-962-5227
foods@ctlcolfax.com www.ctlcolfax.com
Processor of malted milk powder, dry-form syrup bases and flavored slush drinks and bases; manufacturer of dry powder dispensers; also, custom blending and packaging services available
President: Michael Bean
Estimated Sales: $1.5 Million
Number Employees: 5-9
Sq. footage: 10000
Type of Packaging: Food Service, Private Label
Brands:
Glacier Ice
Soda Fountain

1953 **CVC Specialties**
4510 S Boyle Ave
Vernon, CA 90058 323-581-0178
Fax: 323-589-6667 800-421-6175
ronald@cvc4health.com www.cvc4health.com
Processor of vitamins, supplements and energy products
President: Ron Beckfield
VP Sales: Greg Faull
VP Operations: Bill Swan
Estimated Sales: $2.5-5 Million
Number Employees: 20-49
Sq. footage: 100000
Type of Packaging: Consumer, Private Label, Bulk
Brands:
Pep'n Energy
Unit Pac

1954 **CVP Systems**
2518 Wisconsin Ave
Downers Grove, IL 60515 630-852-1190
Fax: 630-852-1386 800-422-4720
sales@cvpsystems.com www.cvpsystems.com
Owner: Wes Bork
CFO: Wes Bork
COO: Chris Van Wandelen
Estimated Sales: $ 10 - 20 Million
Number Employees: 20-49
Brands:
C.V.P. Systems

1955 **CaJohns Fiery Foods**
816 Green Crest Dr
Westerville, OH 43081-2839
Fax: 614-418-0800 888-703-3473
cajohns@cajohns.com www.cajohns.com
Salsas, hot sauce, barbecue sauce, rubs, spice blends, mixes and mustards.
President/Owner: John Hard
Estimated Sales: $125,000
Number Employees: 1-4
Brands:
CaJohns
Nate Dog's

1956 **Cable Car Beverage Corporation**
555 17th Street
Denver, CO 80202-3950 303-298-9038
Fax: 303-298-1150
Beverages
Chairman/President: Samuel Simpson
Number Employees: 20-49
Brands:
Stewart's Cherries N' Cream
Stewart's Classic Ke
Stewart's Cream Soda
Stewart's Diet Cream
Stewart's Diet Orang
Stewart's Diet Root
Stewart's Ginger Bee
Stewart's Grape Soda
Stewart's Lemon Meri
Stewart's Orange N'
Stewart's Root Beer

1957 **Cabo Rojo Enterprises**
3301 Combate
Boqueron, PR 00622 787-254-0015
Fax: 787-254-2048
Processor and importer of salt
President: Jeffrey Montero
Number Employees: 20
Type of Packaging: Consumer

1958 **Cabot Creamery**
One Home Farm Way
Montpelier, VT 05602 802-229-9361
Fax: 802-371-1200 888-792-2268
info@cabotcheese.com www.cabotcheese.com
Processor of cheddar cheese, specialty and flavored cheeses, Monterey Jack and light chesses, plus a variety of other dairy products.
President/CEO: Rich Stammer
Master Cheddar Maker: Marcel Gravel
Marketing: Jack O'Halloran
Estimated Sales: $ 10 - 20 Million
Number Employees: 50-99
Sq. footage: 150000
Parent Co: Agri-Mark
Type of Packaging: Consumer, Food Service, Private Label, Bulk
Brands:
CABOT

1959 **Cache Cellars**
RR 2 Box 2780
Davis, CA 95616-9604 530-756-6068
Fax: 530-756-6463
Wines
President: Charles Lowe
Estimated Sales: $1-2.5 Million
Number Employees: 5-9
Type of Packaging: Private Label

1960 **Cache Creek Foods**
411 N Pioneer Ave
Woodland, CA 95776 530-662-1764
Fax: 530-662-2529 matt@cachecreekfoods.com
www.cachecreekfoods.com
Custom flavoring and wholesale manufacturing of almond, cashew, pistachio, nut products and nut butters
Manager: Matthew Moorehart
CEO: Matthew Morehart
Estimated Sales: $3-5 Million
Number Employees: 10-19
Number of Products: 75
Sq. footage: 30000
Type of Packaging: Consumer, Food Service, Private Label, Bulk
Brands:
PRIVATE LABEL

1961 **(HQ)Cacique**
14940 Proctor Ave
City of Industry, CA 91746 626-961-3399
Fax: 626-369-5780 www.caciqueusa.com
Processor and exporter of mozzarella and fresco cheese
President: Gilbert L De Cardenas
Vice President: Will Parker
Marketing Director: Alberto Fernandez
Estimated Sales: $50-100 Million
Number Employees: 250-499
Sq. footage: 200000
Other Locations:
Cacique
Cedar City UT
Brands:
Black & Gold
Cacique
Nochebuena
Ranchero
Yonique

1962 **Cactu Life Inc**
PO Box 349
Corona Del Mar, CA 92625-0349 949-640-8991
Fax: 949-640-8992 800-500-1713
info@cactulife.com www.cactulife.com
Health food supplements
President: Jeff Liebfreid
Estimated Sales: $500,000
Number Employees: 1-4
Brands:
Cactu Life

1963 **Cactus-Creek**
PO Box 671169
Dallas, TX 75367-1169 972-869-4600
Fax: 972-869-8050 800-471-7723
info@truco.com www.cactus-creek.com
Manufactures a variety of salsas, mixes, tortilla chips and candies.
Estimated Sales: $2.5-5 Million
Number Employees: 20-49
Parent Co: Truco Enterprises
Brands:
CACTUS CREEK BRAND

1964 **Cadbury Adams**
5000 Yonge Street
Toronto, ON M2N 7E9
Canada 416-590-5000
Fax: 416-590-5600
consumer.relations@brandspeoplelove.com
www.chocolate.ca/
Manufacturer of a variety of confectionery products.
President/ Canada: Dino Bianco
Chief Executive Officer: Todd Stitzer
Chief Financial Officer: Ken Hanna
Chief Legal Officer: Michael Clark
Chief Science & Technology Officer: David MacNair
President Americas Beverages: Gil Cassagne
President Europe/Middle East/Africa: Matt Shattock
Group Strategy Director: Mark Reckitt
Chief Legal Officer: Hank Udow
Chief Human Resources Officer: Bob Stack
Group Secretary: Hester Blanks
President Americas Confectionery: Jim Chambers

President Global Supply Chain: Steve Drive
Number Employees: 1,000-4,999
Parent Co: Cadbury Schweppes
Type of Packaging: Consumer, Food Service, Bulk

1965 **Cadbury Beverages Canada**
30 Eglinton Avenue W
Mississauga, ON L5R 3E7
Canada 905-712-4121
Fax: 905-712-8635
consumer.relations@brandspeoplelove.com
www.cadburyschweppes.com
Beverage brands include 7 UP, Canada Dry, Clamato, Dr. Pepper, Hawaiian Punch, Mott's, Schweppes and Snapple.
President/CEO: Irene Rosenfeld
Vice President/ CFO: David Brearton
Chief Financial Officer: Ken Hanna
Chief Legal Officer: Michael Clark
Chief Science & Technology Officer: David MacNair
President Americas Beverages: Gil Cassagne
President Europe/Middle East/Africa: Matt Shattock
Group Strategy Director: Mark Reckitt
Chief Legal Officer: Hank Udow
Chief Human Resources Officer: Bob Stack
Group Secretary: Hester Blanks
President Americas Confectionery: Jim Chambers

President Global Supply Chain: Steve Drive
Number Employees: 1,000-4,999
Parent Co: Cadbury Schweppes
Type of Packaging: Consumer, Food Service, Bulk
Brands:
CADBURY CHOCOLATE
CADBURY DAIRY MILK
CADBURY DARK
CADBURY FAVOURITES

CADBURY THINS
CARAMILK

1966 **Cadbury Schweppes**
P.O.Box 869077
Plano, TX 75086-9077 972-673-7000
Fax: 972-673-7980 800-696-5891
consumer.relations@brandspeoplelove.com
www.drpeppersnapplegroup.com
Beverage concentrates and confections.
Executive Chairman: John Sunderland
Chief Executive Officer: Todd Stitzer
Chief Financial Officer: Ken Hanna
CEO: Larry Young
Chief Science & Technology Officer: David MacNair
President Americas Beverages: Gil Cassagne
President Europe/Middle East/Africa: Matt Shattock
Chief Legal Officer: Hank Udow
Chief Human Resources Officer: Bob Stack
Group Secretary: Hester Blanks
President Americas Confectionery: Jim Chambers

President Global Supply Chain: Steve Drive
Estimated Sales: $50-100 Million
Number Employees: 10,000+
Parent Co: Cadbury Schweppes
Type of Packaging: Consumer, Food Service, Bulk
Brands:
7 UP
BASSETT'S
BUBBAS
BUTTERKIST
CADBURY
CADBURY CREME EGG
CADBURY DAIRY MILK
CADBURY ECLAIRS
CADBURY ROSES
CANADA DRY
CLAMATO
DENTYNE
DENTYNE ICE
DIET DR PEPPER
DR PEPPER
HALLS
HAWAIIAN PUNCH
HOLLYWOOD
MAYNARDS
MOTT'S
ORANGINA
PIBB ZERO
SCHWEPPES
SNAPPLE
SOUR PATCH KIDS
STIMOROL
TREBOR
TRIDENT

1967 **Cadbury Trebor Allan**
277 Gladstone Avenue
Toronto, ON M6J 3L9
Canada 416-530-0060
Fax: 416-530-0048 800-565-6541
Chocolate
President: Rinaldo Alfinito
Number Employees: 2700

1968 **(HQ)Cadbury Trebor Allan**
850 Industrial Boulevard
Granby, QC J2J 1B8
Canada 450-372-1080
Fax: 450-378-4256 800-387-3267
consumer.relations@brandspeoplelove.com
www.cadburyschweppes.com
Manufacturer of candy including hard, filled hard, toffee, mints, licorice, gums, taffy kisses, penny goods, cough drops, jellies and lollypops, chocolates
Chairman And Ceo: Irene Rosenfeld
Number Employees: 3030
Parent Co: Cadbury Schweppes PLC
Type of Packaging: Consumer, Food Service, Private Label, Bulk
Brands:
Trebor

1969 **Caddo Packing Company**
P.O. Box 327
Marshall, TX 75671-0327 903-935-2211
Processors and butchers of beef and pork.
President: Pat Parrish
Estimated Sales: $2.5-5 Million
Number Employees: 5-9
Type of Packaging: Consumer

1970 **Cadick Poultry Company**
1311 Main St
Grandview, IN 47615 812-649-4491
Fax: 812-649-5327 www.troyers.com
Processor of poultry.
President/Purchasing: John Cadick
Estimated Sales: $50-100 Million
Number Employees: 50-99
Type of Packaging: Consumer

1971 **Cadillac Coffee Company**
1801 Michael St
Madison Heights, MI 48071 248-545-2266
Fax: 248-584-4184 800-438-6900
info@cadillaccoffee.com
www.cadillaccoffee.com
Coffee, specialty teas, iced teas, flavored syrups, blended drink mixes, iced cappuccino and more.
President: Guy Gehlert
Chairman: John Gehlert
VP Finance: Timothy Mantyla
VP Operations: Doug Bachman
Purchasing Director: John Hunter
Estimated Sales: $30 Million
Number Employees: 95
Sq. footage: 6580
Type of Packaging: Consumer, Food Service, Private Label, Bulk
Brands:
Cadillac Coffee

1972 **Cady Cheese Factory**
126 State Road 128
Wilson, WI 54027 715-772-4218
Fax: 715-772-4224 info@cadycheese.com
www.cadycheese.com
Cheese
President: Dale Marcott
Treasurer: Wendy Marcott
Marketing Manager: Dale Marcott
Office Manager: Gay Wang
Production Manager: Sandy Lee
Plant Manager: John Pechmiller
Estimated Sales: $7 Million
Number Employees: 45
Brands:
GOLD'N JACK
HOT PEPPER
VEG'Y JACK

1973 **Caesar's Pasta Products**
1001 Lower Landing Rd # 311
Blackwood, NJ 08012-3124 856-227-2585
Fax: 856-227-1910 www.caesarspasta.com
Processor of frozen pre-cooked and raw pasta specialties including ravioli, stuffed shells, manicotti with crepes, gnocchi, cavatelli, spaghetti, fettuccine, linguine, angel hair, agnolotti, ravioletti, tortelloni, cheese lasagnaetc
President: Michael Lodato
Secretary: Raymond Lodato
VP: Ronald Lodato
Purchasing Manager: Ronald Lodato Sr
Estimated Sales: $1-2.5 Million
Number Employees: 20-49
Sq. footage: 30000
Parent Co: Sicilian Chef's
Type of Packaging: Consumer, Food Service, Private Label, Bulk
Brands:
CAESAR'S
SICILIAN CHEFS

1974 **Cafe Appassionato Coffee Company**
4001 21st Ave W
Seattle, WA 98199-1201 206-281-8040
Fax: 206-282-5218 888-522-2333
www.caffeappassionato.com
Coffee
President/CEO: Phil Sancken
CFO: Tim Schondelmayer
Vice President: Tucker McHugh
VP of Marketing: Tucker McHugh
Roastmaster: Richard Oakes
Production Manager: David Crumb
Plant Manager: Jeffrey Craig
Purchasing Manager: Phil Sancken
Estimated Sales: $5-10 Million
Number Employees: 50-99
Type of Packaging: Private Label
Brands:
CAFE APPASSIONATO

1975 **Cafe Bustelo**
5605 Nw 82nd Avenue
Miami, FL 33166 786-336-8048
Fax: 305-594-7603 800-990-9039
jcoleman@rowlandcoffee.co
www.javacabana.com
Roasted coffee
President: Jose Souto
Marketing: Fernando Acosta
Estimated Sales: $ 2.5-5 Million
Number Employees: 5-9

1976 **Cafe Cartago**
3835 Elm St Ste D
Denver, CO 80207 303-297-1212
Fax: 303-316-3325 800-443-8666
www.cafecartago.com
Coffee
Owner: Steve Larsen
Partner: Chuck Ask
Purchasing Manager: Steve Larsen
Estimated Sales: $2.5-5 Million
Number Employees: 5-9
Type of Packaging: Private Label, Bulk

1977 **Cafe Chilku**
433 Bar Road, Unit 2
Colchester, VT 05446-7916 802-878-4645
Producer of BBQ sauces and dipping sauce
Owner: Chilku Yi

1978 **Cafe Del Mundo**
229 E 51st Ave
Anchorage, AK 99503 907-562-2326
Fax: 907-562-3278 www.cafedelmundo.com
Coffee, espresso equipment
Owner: Perry Merkel
Purchasing: Perry Merkel
Estimated Sales: $1 Million
Number Employees: 12
Type of Packaging: Private Label, Bulk
Brands:
CAFE DEL MUNDO

1979 **Cafe Descafeinado de Chiapas**
3625 NW 82nd Avenue
Suite 404
Doral, FL 33166-7602 305-499-9775
Fax: 305-499-9776 www.deschiusa.com
Coffee importers
President: Daniel Robles
Director: Arandio Muguira
Director: Luis Demetrio
Estimated Sales: $500,000-$1 Million
Number Employees: 1-4
Type of Packaging: Private Label

1980 **Cafe Du Monde**
1039 Decatur St
New Orleans, LA 70116 504-587-0835
Fax: 504-587-0847 office@cafedumonde.com
www.cafedumonde.com
Processor and exporter of beignet doughnut mix, coffee and roasted chicory for coffee flavoring
Manager: Burt Benrud
CFO: J Roman III
Manager: Robert Maher
Estimated Sales: $500,000 appx.
Number Employees: 5-9
Sq. footage: 15000
Other Locations:
Cafe Du Monde-French Market
New Orleans LA
Cafe Du Monde-Riverwalk Marketplace
New Orleans LA
Care Du Monde-New Orleans Centre
New Orleans LA
Cafe Du Monde-Oakwood Mall
Gretna LA
Cafe Du Monde-Lakeside Mall
Metairie LA
Cafe Du Monde-Esplanade Mall
Kenner LA
Cafe Du Monde-Veterans Boulevard
Metairie LA
Brands:
Cafe Du Monde

1981 **Cafe Fanny**
1619 5th St
Berkeley, CA 94710-1714 510-526-7664
Fax: 510-526-7486 800-441-5413
www.cafefanny.com

Organic granola.
Owner: James Maser
Manager: Leslie Wilson
Estimated Sales: $1-2.5 Million
Number Employees: 20-49

1982 **Cafe La Semeuse**
55 Nassau Ave
Brooklyn, NY 11222-3143 718-387-9696
Fax: 718-782-2471 800-242-6333
contactus@cafelasemeuse.com
www.cafelasemeuse.com
Coffee
Manager: Andi Billow
Estimated Sales: Under $500,000
Number Employees: 1-4
Brands:
Cafe La Semeuse
Classique
Espresso

1983 **Cafe Moak**
509 E Division Street
Rockford, MI 49341-1342 616-866-7625
Fax: 616-866-6422 800-757-8776
russos@russospizza.com www.russospizza.com
Processor of bread sticks, subs, pizzas and coffee; importer of coffee
Owner: Sal Russo
Administrative Assistant: Becky Fate
Brands:
Russo's

1984 **Cafe Moto**
2619 National Ave
San Diego, CA 92113 619-239-6686
Fax: 619-239-9344 800-818-3363
www.cafemoto.com
Imported tea and roasted coffee
President: Torrey Lee
CFO: Kimberly Lee
Production Manager: Michael Figgins
Estimated Sales: Under $500,000
Number Employees: 20-49
Type of Packaging: Private Label

1985 **Cafe Sark's Gourmet Coffee**
22800 Savi Ranch Parkway
Yorba Linda, CA 92887-4623 626-579-6000
Gourmet coffee
President: Jeff Shamburger
Estimated Sales: Under $500,000
Number Employees: 5-9

1986 **Cafe Society Coffee Company**
2910 N Hall St
Dallas, TX 75204 214-922-8888
Fax: 214-922-0280 800-717-6000
info@cafesocietycoffee.net
Flavored and organic coffee and tea
President: Lauri Sanderfer
Sales Representative: Byron Laszlo
General Manager: Jessie Nickerson
Estimated Sales: $1-$1.4 Million
Number Employees: 11
Type of Packaging: Private Label

1987 **Cafe Tequila**
967 N Point Street
San Francisco, CA 94109-1111 415-264-0106
Fax: 415-674-1740 jfielder@cafetequila.com
www.cafetequila.com
Manufacturer of tequila sauces
President/CEO: John Fielder
Sales/Marketing Executive: Julie Fielder
Number Employees: 1-4
Type of Packaging: Consumer, Food Service
Brands:
Cafe Tequila

1988 **Cafe Terra Cotta**
6064 N Pinnacle Ridge Dr
Tucson, AZ 85718 520-577-8100
Fax: 520-577-9015 800-492-4454
feedback@terracotta.com
www.cafeterracotta.com
Contemporary Southwest cuisine
President: Don Luria
Vice President: Donna Nordin
Marketing Director: Michael Luria
Purchasing: Michael Luria
Estimated Sales: $2.5-5 Million
Number Employees: 100-249
Type of Packaging: Private Label

Brands:
CREATIVE CONDIMENTS

1989 **Cafe Yaucono/Jimenez & Fernandez**
1103 Avenue Fernandez Juncos
Po Box 13097
Santurce, PR 00907-4713 787-721-3337
Fax: 787-722-5590 info@yaucono.com
www.yaucono.com
Processor of coffee
President: Jose Jimenez
VP: Julio Torres
Comp/Treasurer: Julio Torres
Marketing Manager: Joaquin Class
Number Employees: 20
Sq. footage: 25000
Type of Packaging: Consumer
Brands:
Yaucono

1990 **Caffe D'Amore**
1107 S Mountain Ave
Po Box 1047
Monrovia, CA 91016 626-792-9146
Fax: 626-932-0152 800-999-0171
dhodgson@caffedamore.com
www.caffedamore.com
Processor of instant cappuccino
President: Chris Julius
Director Marketing: Cheri Hays
President: Chris Julius
Estimated Sales: $ 1 - 3 Million
Number Employees: 20-49
Type of Packaging: Consumer, Food Service

1991 **Caffe D'Amore Gourmet Beverages**
1107 S Mountain Ave
Monrovia, CA 91016-4258 626-792-9146
Fax: 626-792-4382 800-999-0171
support@caffeedamore.com
www.caffedamore.com
Manufacturer: Frap Freeze specialty coffee beverages, Green Tea Smoothies, Botanica Fruitea, Bellagio Coffee, Espresso, Sipping Chocolate and European-style cocoas.
President: Paul Comi
CEO: Chris Julius
Estimated Sales: $ 30 - 50 Million
Number Employees: 50-99

1992 **Caffe D'Oro**
14020 Central Avenue
Suite 580
Chino, CA 91710-5524 909-591-9493
Fax: 909-522-8844 800-200-5005
info@caffedoro.com www.caffedoro.com
Processor of specialty coffee and cappuccino
President: Pamela Abbadessa
V P Marketing: Frank Abbadessa
Number Employees: 5-9
Parent Co: Brad Barry Company
Type of Packaging: Private Label
Brands:
Caffe D'Oro Cappuccino & Cocoa

1993 **Caffe D'Vita**
14020 Central Avenue
Suite 580
Chino, CA 91710-5524 909-591-9493
Fax: 909-627-3747 800-200-5005
info@caffedvita.com www.caffedvita.com
Processor of instant cappuccino
President: Al Greene
CFO: Bob Greene
Vice President: Frank Abbadessa
Marketing Director: Frank Greene
Operations Manager: Frank Abbadessa
Estimated Sales: Under $500,000
Number Employees: 20-49
Parent Co: Brad Barry Company
Type of Packaging: Private Label
Brands:
Chai Delite
Chill-A-Ccino
Enhanted Chai
Horchata D'Vita

1994 **Caffe Darte**
719 S Myrtle St
Seattle, WA 98108 206-762-4381
Fax: 206-763-4665 800-999-5334
sales@caffedarte.com www.caffedarte.com
Coffee beans
Manager: Joe Mancuso
Vice President: Mauro Cipolla
Coffee Roaster: Sergio Barella
Estimated Sales: $5-10 Million
Number Employees: 5-9
Type of Packaging: Private Label
Brands:
CAFFE DARTE

1995 **Caffe Luca**
885 Industry Dr
Tukwila, WA 98188-3411 206-575-2720
Fax: 206-575-0537 800-728-9116
www.caffeluca.com
Processor, exporter and importer of espresso and blended coffee; also, custom roasting available
Owner: Carol Dema
Estimated Sales: $2.5-5 Million
Number Employees: 1-4
Sq. footage: 2000
Type of Packaging: Consumer, Food Service
Brands:
ANTONIO
CASA LUCA
GIOVANNI
GREGORIO
LEONARDO
MISTO
MISTO DARK

1996 **Caffe Trieste Superb Coffees**
1465 25th St
San Francisco, CA 94107-3403 415-550-1107
Fax: 415-550-1239 info@caffetrieste.com
www.caffetrieste.com
Coffee
President: F Giotta
Estimated Sales: $10-20 Million
Number Employees: 10-19
Type of Packaging: Private Label
Brands:
CAFFE TRIESTE COFFEE BEANS

1997 **(HQ)Cagle's Inc**
1385 Coller Road NW
Atlanta, GA 30318 404-355-2820
Fax: 404-350-9605 marketing@caglesinc.com
www.cagles.net
Processor of poultry products
President/CEO: J Douglas Cagle
EVP/CFO: Mark M Ham IV
VP: G Doug Cagle
VP: J David Cagle
Sales Director: Jared Mitchell
VP/Sales & Marketing: Dale Tolbert
VP/Live Operations: Brad Harp
Estimated Sales: $300 Million
Number Employees: 1900
Sq. footage: 22000
Type of Packaging: Consumer, Food Service, Private Label, Bulk

1998 **(HQ)Cagnon Foods Company**
206 Crescent St
Brooklyn, NY 11208 718-647-2244
Processor of soup and gravy bases; also, dehydrated soups and vegetables
Partner: Jeffrey Posner
Estimated Sales: $300,000-500,000
Number Employees: 1-4
Sq. footage: 5000
Type of Packaging: Consumer, Food Service, Bulk

1999 **Cahoon Farms**
10951 Lummisville Rd
Wolcott, NY 14590 315-594-8081
Fax: 315-594-1678 www.cahoonfarms.com
Processor of frozen apples and cherries
President: Donald D. Cahoon Jr
Vice President: William Cahoon
Operations/Sales Manager: Chuck Frederick
Estimated Sales: $10-20 Million
Number Employees: 100-249
Type of Packaging: Consumer

2000 **Caiazza Candy Company**
202 W Washington Street
New Castle, PA 16101-3945 724-652-9492
800-651-1171
sales@caiazzausa.com www.caiazzausa.com
Manufacturer of chocolate, raspberry, mint and peanut butter
Partner: Matt Caiazza
Marketing Director: Felicia Fincesel
Estimated Sales: $10-20 Million
Number Employees: 20-49
Type of Packaging: Private Label
Brands:
Caiazza
Millennium Meltaways
Pretzel Smooth

2001 **Cain Vineyard & Winery**
3800 Langtry Rd
St Helena, CA 94574-9772 707-963-1616
Fax: 707-963-7952 winery@cainfive.com
www.cainfive.com
Wines
Manager: Christopher Howell
Owner: Nancy Meadlock
Marketing Coordinator: Shari Coloumbe
General Manager/Winemaker: Christopher Howell
Production Manager: Francois Bugue
Purchasing Agent: Francois Bugue
Estimated Sales: $5-10 Million
Number Employees: 20-49

2002 **Cain's Coffee Company**
540 N Cedarbrook Ave # A
Springfield, MO 65802-6324 417-865-7414
Fax: 417-869-1201 800-641-4025
www.saralee.com
Processor of roasted coffee
Owner: Steve Flowers
Regional Manager: Stephen Flwoer
Purchasing Manager Assoc.: Steve McCreary
Estimated Sales: $500,000-$1 Million
Number Employees: 5-9
Type of Packaging: Consumer, Food Service
Brands:
Cains
Superior

2003 **Cains Foods**
Po Box 347
Ayer, MA 01432-0347 978-772-0300
Fax: 978-772-9254 800-225-0601
www.cainsfoods.com
Manufacturer of dressings, condiments, sauces and crackers
President: Denis Keaveny
CFO: Ronald Adams
VP Operations: Rick Duggan
Estimated Sales: $10-20 Million
Number Employees: 50-99
Type of Packaging: Food Service, Bulk
Brands:
CAINS
CAROLINE'S
OLDE CAPE COD
WESTMINSTER

2004 **(HQ)Cains Foods LP/Olde CapeCod**
114 Eats Main Street
Ayer, MA 01432 410-827-6845
Fax: 410-827-6846 651-698-6832
retail@cainsfoods.com www.cainsfoods.com
Manufacturer of mayonnaise, dressings, tartar sauce, cocktail sauce, barbecue sauces and other related products.
President/CEO: Denis Keaveny
CFO: Ronald Adams
Marketing: Michael Rossbach
VP Operations: Rick Dugan
Number Employees: 50-99
Number of Brands: 4
Sq. footage: 70000
Type of Packaging: Consumer, Food Service, Private Label, Bulk
Brands:
Cains
Cole Farms
Olde Cape Cod
Westminster

2005 **Caito Fisheries**
19400 Harbor Ave
Fort Bragg, CA 95437 707-964-6368
Fax: 707-964-6439 www.caitofisheries.com
Processor of fresh and frozen ground fish
President: Joe Caito
Estimated Sales: $20-50 Million
Number Employees: 100-249
Type of Packaging: Consumer, Food Service, Private Label, Bulk
Brands:
CAITO

2006 **Cajun Boy's Louisiana Products**
6413 Airline Highway
Baton Rouge, LA 70805-3212 225-929-7269
Fax: 225-357-6888 800-880-9575
hicks3421@aol.com
Processor and exporter of seasoned beans, blended seasonings and mixes
Owner/President: Gerald Hicks
Number Employees: 1-4
Type of Packaging: Consumer
Brands:
Cajun Boy's Louisiana

2007 **Cajun Chef Products**
519 Joseph Rd
Saint Martinville, LA 70582 337-394-7112
Fax: 337-394-7115 www.cajunchef.org
Processor of peppers including pickled, sport, tobasco, cherry, jalapeno, yellow chile, banana and serrano; also, prepared mustard, pure and imitation pepper and flavoring extracts, pickled okra and tomatoes and sauces including hotworcestershire, etc.
President: James Bulliard
Vice President: Daniel Bulliard
Estimated Sales: $10-20 Million
Number Employees: 100-249
Type of Packaging: Consumer, Food Service, Private Label, Bulk
Brands:
BIG CHIEF
CAJUN CHEF
EVANGELINE
TIFFE'S

2008 **Cajun Crawfish Distributors**
379 Industrial Blvd
Mansura, LA 71350-4210
Fax: 504-341-7627 800-525-6813
Processor of popcorn crawfish tail and seafood gumbo; wholesaler/distributor of seafood
Owner/President: Elton Bernard
Estimated Sales: $30 Million
Number Employees: 4

2009 **Cajun Creole Products**
5610 Daspit Rd
New Iberia, LA 70563 337-229-8464
Fax: 337-229-4814 800-946-8688
info@cajuncreole.com www.cajuncreole.com
Processor of coffee, peanuts and seasoning
President: Joel Wallins
VP: Sandra Wallins
Estimated Sales: $5-10 Million
Number Employees: 5-9
Type of Packaging: Consumer, Food Service, Bulk
Brands:
CAJUN CREOLE
CAJUN CREOLE COFFEE
CAJUN CREOLE HOT NUTS
CAJUN CREOLE JALAPEANUTS
JALAPEANUTS

2010 **Cajun Fry Company**
107 Mike St
Pierre Part, LA 70339 985-252-6438
Fax: 985-252-8010 888-272-2586
cajunfrycompany@aol.com www.cajunfry.com
Cajun rice mixes, jambalaya, spices
President: Clarence Cavalier Jr Jr
Vice President: Marilyn Cavalier
Estimated Sales: $1-2.5 Million
Number Employees: 5-9
Brands:
Cajun Creole Coffee & Chicory
Jalapeanuts
Smokeless Blackened Seasoning

2011 **Cajun Injector**
Highway 67 Street
Clinton, LA 70722 225-683-4490
Fax: 225-683-4401 800-221-8060
www.cjuninjecter.com
Marinades, honey praline ham kit
President: Reece William
CEO: Reece William
Vice President: Don Pallie
Estimated Sales: $5-10 Million
Number Employees: 20-49
Brands:
Cajun Injector
Flavors of the World

2012 **Cajun Seafood Enterprises**
9650 Highway 52 E
Murrayville, GA 30564-6901 706-864-9688
Fax: 706-864-9688
www.cajunseafoodenterprises.com
Seafood

2013 **Cakebread Cellars**
8300 St Helena Hwy
Rutherford, CA 94573 707-963-5221
Fax: 707-967-8620 800-588-0298
cellars@cakebread.com www.cakebread.com
Wines
President: John Cakebread
Director Sales: Dennis Cakebread
Purchasing Agent: Cathy Baldwin
Estimated Sales: $20-50 Million
Number Employees: 50-99
Brands:
CAKEBREAD

2014 **Cal India Foods International**
13591 Yorba Ave
Chino, CA 91710-5071 909-613-1660
Fax: 909-613-1663 infospecialityenzymes.com
www.systemicenzymetherapy.com
Processor and exporter of fruit juices, purees and concentrates including apple and pineapple; also, enzymes including papain, bromelin, proteases, amylases and cellulases; importer of juice concentrates including apple, grapepineapple and mango puree
President: Vic Rathi
Quality Control: Vilas Amin
Purchasing Agent: Priscilla Ferreri
Estimated Sales: $5-7 Million
Number Employees: 20-49
Sq. footage: 12000
Parent Co: Specialty Enzymes and Biochemicals Company
Type of Packaging: Bulk
Brands:
CAL INDIA

2015 **Cal Java International**
19519 Business Center Dr
Northridge, CA 91324-3402 818-718-2707
Fax: 818-718-2715 800-207-2750
caljava@hotmail.com www.cakevisions.com
Cake decorating supplies
Owner: Daniel Budiman
Estimated Sales: $ 5 - 10 Million
Number Employees: 5-9

2016 **Cal Trading Company**
32 Adrian Ct
Burlingame, CA 94010-2101 650-697-4615
Fax: 650-692-1049
Green coffee
Manager: Rick Johnson
Purchasing Agent: Steven McLaughlin
Estimated Sales: $10-100 Million
Number Employees: 5-9
Type of Packaging: Private Label
Brands:
100% KONA COFFEE

2017 **Cal-Grown Nut Company**
P.O.Box 69
Hughson, CA 95326-0069 209-883-4081
Fax: 209-883-0305
frankassali@californiagrown.com
www.californiagrown.com
Processor and exporter of almonds
President: Frank Assali
Vice President: Marie Assali
Office Manager: Linda Thomas
Estimated Sales: $ .5 - 1 million
Number Employees: 5-9

2018 **Cal-Harvest Marketing**
8700 Fargo Ave
Hanford, CA 93230-9771 559-582-4000
Fax: 559-582-0683 www.calharvest.com
Fresh fruits and vegetables
Owner: John Sagundes
Purchasing: John Fagundes
Estimated Sales: $5-10 Million
Number Employees: 5-9
Type of Packaging: Consumer, Private Label, Bulk
Brands:
CAL-KING
FRESH HARVEST
GOLDEN HARVEST

2019 **Cal-Maine Foods**
3320 Woodrwo Wilson Drive
Jackson, MS 39209 601-948-6813
Fax: 601-969-0905 IR@cmfoods.com
www.calmainefoods.com
Manufacturer and exporter of shell eggs
President/CEO/Director: Adolphus Baker
Vice President/CFO: Fred Adams Jr
VP/CFO/Treasurer/Secretary/Director: Timothy Dawson
CEO: Fred R Adams Jr
Estimated Sales: $375 Million
Number Employees: 1,000-4,999
Type of Packaging: Food Service, Private Label, Bulk

2020 **Cal-Maine Foods**
263 Cal Maine Rd
Pine Grove, LA 70453 225-222-4148
Fax: 225-222-4154 www.calmainefoods.com
Processor of eggs
President/CEO/Director: Adolphus Baker
VP/CFO: Timothy Dawson
VP Sales: Jeff Hardin
VP/COO: Sherman Miller
VP Operations/Production: Jack Self
Purchasing Agent: Robert Lewis
Estimated Sales: $50-100 Million
Number Employees: 52
Sq. footage: 15634
Parent Co: Cal-Maine Foods
Type of Packaging: Consumer, Food Service, Private Label, Bulk

2021 **Cal-Sun Produce Company**
511 Mountain View Ave
Oxnard, CA 93030 805-985-2262
Fax: 805-486-5022
Strawberries
President: Steve Taylor
General Manager: Jim Nahas
Purchasing: Rick Meck
Estimated Sales: $10-20 Million
Brands:
CAL-SUN

2022 **Cal-Tex Citrus Juice**
402 Yale Street
Houston, TX 77007 713-869-3471
Fax: 713-869-3277 800-231-0133
gary.van.liew@cal-texjuice.com
www.cal-texjuice.com
Package fruit juices and fruit drinks from concentrate.
President: Gary Van Lieu
Quality Control: Alvaro Falquez
Sales: Vicki White
Operations: Danny Teague
Purchasing: Kory Mason
Estimated Sales: $40 Million
Number Employees: 50-99
Number of Brands: 3
Number of Products: 63
Type of Packaging: Consumer, Food Service, Private Label
Brands:
CAL-TEX
CITRUS PRIDE
VITA-FRESH
VITA-MOST

2023 **CalSungold**
P.O.Box 1540
Indio, CA 92202-1540 760-399-5646
Fax: 760-399-1968 info@calsungold.com
www.calsungold.com
Dates and fruitbaskets.
Plant Manager: Jim Carter
Estimated Sales: $50-100 Million
Number Employees: 20-49

2024 **Calabro Cheese Corporation**
P.O.Box 120186
East Haven, CT 06512-0186 203-469-1311
Fax: 203-469-6929 salvatore@colabrocheese.com
www.calabrocheese.com
Processor of ricotta, mozzarella and grated cheese
CEO: Joseph Calabro
Purchasing Agent: Frank Angeloni
Estimated Sales: $50-100 Million
Number Employees: 100-249
Sq. footage: 54000
Type of Packaging: Consumer, Food Service, Private Label, Bulk
Brands:
CALABRO

2025 **Calafia Cellars**
629 Fulton Ln
Saint Helena, CA 94574 707-963-0114
Fax: 707-963-0114
Wines
President: Randle Johnson
VP Marketing: Mary Lee Johnson
Operations Manager: Randle Johnson
Estimated Sales: Less than $500,000
Number Employees: 1-4
Brands:
Calafia Wines

2026 **(HQ)Calavo Growers**
1141A Cummings Road
Santa Paula, CA 93060 805-525-1245
Fax: 805-921-3219 800-422-5280
www.calavo.com
Avacado pulp and puree, fresh avacado, papaya
Chairman/President/CEO: Lecil Cole
COO/CFO: Arthur Bruno
VP/Fresh Sales & Marketing: Rob Wedin
VP/Processed Product Sales: Al Ahmer
Fresh Operations: Mike Browne
Purchasing Agent: Mario Guizar
Estimated Sales: $398 Million
Number Employees: 1150
Type of Packaging: Consumer, Food Service, Bulk
Other Locations:
Temecula Packinghouse
Temecula CA
Santa Paula Packinghouse
Santa Paula CA
Calavo Processing Plant
Santa Paula CA
Brands:
CALAVO

2027 **Calbee America**
2600 Maxwell Way
Fairfield, CA 94534 707-427-2500
Fax: 707-428-2900 tkatsunoi@aol.com
http://www.calbeeamerica.com
Processor and exporter of potato chips
President/Ceo: Masanori Yasunaga
Vice President: Yoshi Ishiquro
Sales Manager: Hiroshi Kosuge
Purchasing Manager: Taka Katsunoi
Estimated Sales: $15 Million
Number Employees: 504

2028 **Calcium Springs Water Company**
2442 Lily Langtree Ct
Park City, UT 84060 435-615-7600
Fax: 435-615-7600 cool@calciumsprings.com
www.calciumsprings.com
Water
Owner: Lavelle Klobes

2029 **Calco of Calgary**
Bay C 1007 55th Avenue NE
Calgary, AB T2E 6W1
Canada 403-295-3578
Fax: 403-516-0286 calco1@telus.net
www.calcoofcalgary.com
Processor and packer of bean sprouts, pre-cut vegetables, frozen Chinese dumplings, spring and egg rolls and steamed noodles
President: Wing Tam
General Manager: May Yu
Production: Grace Tam
Number Employees: 10-19
Parent Co: Fung Nin Fine Foods
Type of Packaging: Consumer, Food Service
Brands:
Calgo
Mr. Egg Roll
Noodle Delights

2030 **Caleb Haley & Company**
14 Fulton Fish Market
New York, NY 10038-1903 212-732-7474
Fax: 212-349-2991
Seafood, seafood products
President: Neil Smith
Vice President: Michael Driansky
Production Manager: Joseph Serrantonio
Estimated Sales: $20-50 Million
Number Employees: 20-49
Brands:
Angel
Callaway
Ocean Harvest

2031 **Calera Wine Company**
11300 Cienega Rd
Hollister, CA 95023 831-637-9170
Fax: 831-637-9070 info@calerawine.com
www.calerawine.com
Wines
President: Josh Jensen
COO: Diana Vita
Number Employees: 20-49
Brands:
CALERA
Central Coast
Doe Mill
Mills
Mt. Harlan
Reed
Selleck
VIOGNIER

2032 **Calgary Italian Bakery**
5304 5th Street SE
Calgary, AB T2H 1L2
Canada 403-255-3515
Fax: 403-255-7016 800-661-6868
http://calgaryitalian.foodpages.ca
Processor of baked goods including bread, buns, pastries and English muffins
President: Luigi Bontorin
CEO: Luigi Bontorin
Marketing Manager: Ralph Knipsthilb
Office Manager: Louis Bontorin
Plant Manager: Dave Bontorin
Estimated Sales: D
Number Employees: 50-99
Sq. footage: 30000
Type of Packaging: Consumer, Food Service
Brands:
Calgary Italian
Country Boy
Golden Rich

2033 **Calhoun Bend Mill**
7603 Highway 71 S
Alexandria, LA 71302-9272 318-640-0060
Fax: 318-339-9099 800-519-6455
info@calhounbendmill.com
www.calhounbendmill.com
Products include mixes for Peach Cobbler mix, Apple Cinnamon Crisp mix, Cherry Oatmeal Crunch mix, Awesome Onion Coating mix, Fish Fry & Seafood coating, Stoneground Cornmeal, Cornbread & Muffin mix, Mexican Cornbread mix, Honey ButterCornbread mix, Pecan Pie mix and Sopapilla mix. Food services sizes in Fruit Cobblers, Cornmeal and Fish Fry & Seafood coating.
President/CEO: Patrick Calhoun
Vice President: Nathan Martin
Sales Manager: Emma Cash
Estimated Sales: 10-19
Number Employees: 20-49
Number of Brands: 2
Number of Products: 25
Sq. footage: 17000
Type of Packaging: Consumer, Food Service, Private Label, Bulk
Brands:
CALHOUN BEND MILL
ORCHARD MILLS

2034 **Calico Cottage**
210 New Highway
Amityville, NY 11701 631-841-2100
Fax: 631-841-2401 800-645-5345
info@calicocottage.com www.calicocottage.com

Equipment, ingredients and merchandising concepts for a profitable, small-space, fudge marketing program
President: Mark Wurzel
CFO: Michael Lobaccaro
VP: Larry Wurzel
Marketing: Andrew Vella
Estimated Sales: $5 Million
Number Employees: 50
Sq. footage: 45000
Brands:
CALICO COTTAGE FUDGE MIX
MISTER FUDGE

2035 **Calidad Foods**
PO Box 535008
Grand Prairie, TX 75053-5008 972-933-4100
Fax: 972-933-4120
Tortillas and other mexican food products.
CEO/President: Bing Graffunder
CFO: Sam Hillin
V.P Sales/Marketing: Gary Fraizer

2036 **California Almond Packers**
21275 Simpson Rd
Corning, CA 96021 530-824-3836
Fax: 530-824-3899 capex@dm-tech.net
www.almondboard.com
Processor of almonds
Manager: Mathieu Esteve
Estimated Sales: Less than $500,000
Number Employees: 50-99
Brands:
California Almond

2037 **California Blending Company**
2603 Seaman Ave
El Monte, CA 91733 626-448-1918
califblending@earthlink.net
www.californiablending.com
Processor of pizza spices, dough mixes, dressing mixes, steak salts, and garlic blends. Also provided; custom blending
President: Bill Morehart
VP: William Morehart, Jr.
Estimated Sales: Less than $500,000
Number Employees: 1-4
Sq. footage: 7300
Type of Packaging: Private Label, Bulk

2038 **California Brands Flavors**
411 Pendleton Way
Oakland, CA 94621-2115 510-562-2371
Fax: 510-562-1279 800-348-0111
webinfo@mane.com www.mane.com
Processor of customized natural and artificial flavors, flavor extracts, beverages bases and frozen dessert variegates
Manager: Gina Pinales
President: Michel Mane
VP: John Ashby
VP Sales: William Painter
Estimated Sales: $20-50 Million
Number Employees: 20-49
Parent Co: Mane
Type of Packaging: Food Service, Bulk

2039 **California Cereal Products**
1267 14th St
Oakland, CA 94607 510-452-4500
Fax: 510-452-4545
Processor and exporter of rice, cereal and flour
Owner: Sterling Savely
Chairman: Robert Sterling Savely
Number Employees: 50-99
Sq. footage: 150000
Type of Packaging: Consumer, Private Label, Bulk

2040 **California Citrus Producer**
525 E Lindmore St
Lindsay, CA 93247-2559 559-562-5169
Fax: 559-562-5691
Processor of citrus fruits including oranges
President: Tomy Elliott
Estimated Sales: $ 5 - 10 Million
Number Employees: 20-49
Brands:
Citrus Juices

2041 **California Citrus Pulp Company**
PO Box 667
Lindsay, CA 93247-0667 626-332-1101
Fax: 559-562-1014
Orange peel, citrus ingredients
President: Jim Boyles
CEO: Jim Boyles
Marketing Director: Jim Boyles
General Manager: Paul Gottschall

2042 **California Creative Foods**
649 Benet Rd
Oceanside, CA 92058-1208 760-757-2622
Fax: 760-721-2600 info@chachies.com
www.sbsalsa.com
Processor of refrigerated salsa, shelf stable foods and sauces. Co-packer of specialty foods.
President: Doug Pearson
VP Purchasing: Patrick Hickey
Estimated Sales: $10-15 Million
Number Employees: 1-4
Sq. footage: 19000
Type of Packaging: Consumer, Food Service
Brands:
CHACHIES
CON GUSTO
SAN DIEGO SALSA
SANTA BARBARA SALSA
TIO TIO

2043 **California Custom Fruits & Flavors**
15800 Tapia St
Irwindale, CA 91706 626-736-4130
Fax: 626-736-4145 877-558-0056
info@ccff.com www.ccff.com
California Custom Fruits and Flavors, in Irwindale, CA is an industry leader in the manufacture of fruit products and flavors. With an in-house flavor department and fully staffed lab, California Custom can respond to any flavorrequest. Employing the latest trends and technology, CCFF can bring your ideas to fruition
Owner: Rose Ann Hall
President: Mike Mulhausen
Marketing Manager: Christine Long
Director Operations: Jack Miller
Production Manager: Eric Nielsen
Director of Flavor Development: Phillip Barone
Purchasing Director: Phyllis Ferguson
Estimated Sales: $20-35 Million
Number Employees: 50-99
Sq. footage: 33000
Type of Packaging: Bulk
Brands:
B2B
CCFF
PRIVATE LABEL

2044 **California Dairies**
2000 N Plaza Drive
Visalia, CA 93291 559-625-2200
Fax: 559-625-5433 info@californiadairies.com
www.californiadairies.com
Co-op/processor of dairy products including butter, buttermilk, skim milk and powdered milk
Chairman: Tony Mendes
Vice Chairman: Gerben Leyendekker
Vice Chairman: John Bidart
VP Operations: Dave Bush
Estimated Sales: $3 Billion
Number Employees: 750
Type of Packaging: Consumer, Food Service, Bulk
Brands:
Challenge
Dairy America
Danish Creamery

2045 **(HQ)California Day Fresh**
935 W 8th St
Asusa, CA 91702 626-812-6022
Fax: 626-334-6439 877-858-4237
consumeraffairs@nakedjuice.com
www.nakedjuice.com
Processor of fresh and frozen fruit and vegetable juices
Vp/General Manager: Chris Lansing
VP Purchasing: Richard Ziff
Controller: Wendy Morgan
Quality Control: Dominic Marlia
Sales Director: Paul Johnson
PR/Promotions Manager: Heidi Meinholz
Director Operations: Tom Guenther
Purchasing Manager: Ron Marks
Estimated Sales: $50-100 Million
Number Employees: 250-499
Sq. footage: 61000
Type of Packaging: Consumer, Food Service, Private Label, Bulk
Brands:
Ferraro's Earth Juice
Mojave Magic
Naked Juice

2046 **California Fresh Salsa**
P.O.Box 948
Woodland, CA 95776 530-662-0512
Fax: 530-662-9418
Manufacturer of condiments, beans and sprouts
President: Steve Mendez
Estimated Sales: $2.5-5 Million
Number Employees: 10-19

2047 **California Fruit**
2730 S De Wolf Ave
Sanger, CA 93657-9770 559-266-7117
Fax: 559-266-0988 www.californiafruitbasket.com
Processor of dried apricots, peaches, pears and nectarines
President: Mark Melkonian
Estimated Sales: $2.5-5 Million
Number Employees: 10-19
Type of Packaging: Bulk

2048 **California Fruit & Nut**
295 South Avenue
Gustine, CA 95322 209-854-6887
Fax: 209-854-1819 888-747-8224
fruitnnut@fruitnnut.com www.fruitnnut.com
Processor of flavored nuts including pistachios, peanuts and cashews; also, dried fruit and fruit rolls including apricot
President: Zaher Shahbaz
Estimated Sales: Less than $500,000
Number Employees: 5-9
Sq. footage: 5400
Type of Packaging: Consumer, Food Service
Brands:
Cal-Fruit

2049 **California Fruit Processors**
2851 Bozzano Rd
Stockton, CA 95215 209-931-1760
Fax: 209-931-0784 vfo@lightspeed.net
Brined cherries
President: Alan Corradi
Manager: Allan Corradi

2050 **California Fruit and Tomato Kitchens**
2906 Santa Fe Street
Riverbank, CA 95367-2223 209-869-9300
Fax: 209-869-9060 bethclare@calfruittom.com
www.calfruittom.com
Manufacturer of canned goods including tomato products and peaches
President: Barbara Langum
Plant Manager: Ed Harmon
Estimated Sales: $ 10 - 20 Million
Number Employees: 20-49
Type of Packaging: Food Service, Private Label
Brands:
Dinapoli
Flotta
Paradise

2051 **California Garden Products**
14 Rancho Cir
Lake Forest, CA 92630-8325 949-215-0000
www.hungrysultan.com
Canned beans
President: Fouad El-Abd
Public Relations: Laura El-Adb
Estimated Sales: $5-9.9 Million
Number Employees: 1-4

2052 **California Garlic Co**
2707 Boston Avenue
San Diego, CA 92113 951-506-8883
Fax: 951-699-9155 info@garlicking.net
www.garlicking.net
Garlic, ginger, shallots, green onion, herbs and other
President: John Rosingana
Vice President: Peter Tarantino
Quality Control/Production: Larry George
Marketing: Jeff Crace
Sales Director: John Rosingana
Estimated Sales: $5 Million
Number Employees: 35
Number of Brands: 4

Number of Products: 60
Sq. footage: 24000
Type of Packaging: Consumer, Food Service, Private Label, Bulk

2053 California Independent Almond Growers
13000 Newport Road
Merced, CA 95303-9704 209-667-4855
Fax: 209-667-4854
Growers, packers, processors and shippers worldwide. California grown whole natural almonds direct from the source. State-of-the-art equipment
President: Karen Barstow
Estimated Sales: $2.5-5 Million
Number Employees: 50-99
Sq. footage: 30000
Type of Packaging: Consumer, Food Service, Private Label, Bulk
Brands:
California Independent Brand

2054 California Natural Products
1250 Lathrop Rd
Lathrop, CA 95330 209-858-2525
Fax: 209-858-2556
joehall@californianatural.com
www.californianatural.com
Processor of rice starch, oligodextrin, syrup/syrup solids, protein, etc.; also, soy milk and low acid aseptic beverages and soups; co-packer of low acid and aseptic beverages, soups, and teas; exporter of rice syrup, protein andoligodextrin
President: Pat Mitchell
VP, Head R&D: Cheryl Mitchell
Technical Sales Manager: John Ashby
VP Operations: Marc Weinstein
Estimated Sales: $5-10 Million
Number Employees: 100-249
Type of Packaging: Private Label
Brands:
DACOPA

2055 California Nuggets
23073 S Frederick Rd
Ripon, CA 95366 209-599-7131
Fax: 209-599-6320 info@californianuggets.com
www.californianuggets.com
President: Steve Gikas
Marketing Director: Diana Gikas
CFO: Nancy Knocks
Estimated Sales: $ 5 - 10 Million
Number Employees: 20-49
Brands:
California Nuggets

2056 California Oils Corporation
1145 Harbour Way S
Richmond, CA 94804 510-233-7660
Fax: 510-233-1329 800-225-6457
sales1@caloils.com www.caloils.com
Processor of vegetable oils and meal; exporter of corn and safflower oils
President: Sihira Ito
VP Sales & Trading: Joevic Fabregas
Number Employees: 20-49
Parent Co: Mitsubishi

2057 California Olive Growers
8427 N Millbrook Avenue
Suite 101
Fresno, CA 93720-2197 559-674-8741
Fax: 559-673-3960 888-965-4837
info@californiaolivegrowers.com
www.californiaolivegrowers.com
Packer of canned California ripe olives, olive oil, tomatoes and pizza sauce
President: Lewis Johnson
CEO: Tom Lindemann
CEO: Fred Avalli
Quality Control: Larry Newby
Production Manager: Bob Marshall
Estimated Sales: $10 Million
Number Employees: 100-249
Number of Brands: 2
Number of Products: 10
Sq. footage: 300000
Type of Packaging: Consumer, Food Service, Private Label, Bulk
Brands:
MADERA
OBERTI

2058 California Olive Oil Corporation
801 Camelia Street
Suite D
Berkeley, CA 94710 510-524-4523
Fax: 510-898-1530 888-718-9830
oliveoil@cooc.com www.cooc.com
Processor and exporter of oils including garlic, sesame, peanut, olive, canola, mineral, soybean, citrus, infused, organic, cold pressed and unrefined; also, balsamic vinegar and cooking wines; importer of kosher certified soy sauce
Owner: Claudia Siniawski
Vice President: Robert Mandia
CFO: Dave Lofgren
Marketing: Patricia Darragh
VP Sales/Marketing: Mark Moffitt
Estimated Sales: $10-20 Million
Number Employees: 10-19
Sq. footage: 38000
Parent Co: East Coast Olive Corporation
Type of Packaging: Consumer, Food Service, Private Label, Bulk
Brands:
California Classics
Montebello
Oishii
Virginia

2059 California Orchards
9000 Crow Canyon Road
Suite S-384
Danville, CA 94506-1189 925-648-1500
Fax: 925-648-4471
Dried fruits, nuts and chocolate
President: Ali Hashemian
Estimated Sales: $5-10 Million
Number Employees: 50-99
Type of Packaging: Private Label

2060 California Pie Company
7066 Las Positas Rd # G
Livermore, CA 94551-5134 925-373-7700
Fax: 925-373-8303 www.horizonsnackfoods.com
Pies
Owner: Bob Sharp
Controller: Brett Howell
Estimated Sales: $2.5-5 Million
Number Employees: 10-19

2061 California Prune Packing Company
P.O.Box 37
Live Oak, CA 95953 530-671-4200
Fax: 530-695-3654
Processor and packer of dried fruits including prunes
Number Employees: 10
Type of Packaging: Private Label

2062 California Shellfish Company
P.O.Box 2028
San Francisco, CA 94126-2028 415-923-7400
Fax: 415-923-1677
Processor of crab, smoked salmon, halibut and snapper
President: Eugene Bugatto
Manager: Richard Amundsen
Estimated Sales: $5-10 Million
Number Employees: 5-9
Type of Packaging: Consumer, Food Service, Private Label, Bulk

2063 California Smart Foods
2565 3rd St # 341
San Francisco, CA 94107-3159 415-826-0449
Fax: 415-826-0435
Breads, rolls, baked goods
Owner: Rudy Melnitzer
Estimated Sales: $20-50 Million
Number Employees: 20-49

2064 California Snack Foods
2131 Tyler Ave
South El Monte, CA 91733 626-444-4508
Fax: 626-579-3038 info@calsnacks.com
www.cal-snacks.com
Snack food
President: Steve Nelson
Manager: Alva Dallas
Production Manager: John Ohms
Estimated Sales: $5 Million
Number Employees: 45

2065 California Specialty Farms
2421 E 16th St Unit 1
Los Angeles, CA 90021 323-587-2200
Fax: 323-587-0050 800-437-2702
specfarms@aol.com
www.californiaspecialtyfarms.com
Processor of gourmet specialty produce; importer and exporter of baby squash, French beans and fresh herbs
General Manager: Joel Bixler
Manager: James Macec
Estimated Sales: $4 Million
Number Employees: 45
Brands:
California Specialty Farms

2066 California Style Gourmet Products
6161 El Cajon Boulevard
Suite 200
San Diego, CA 92115-3922 619-265-1988
Fax: 619-265-0893 800-243-5226
castylegor@aol.com
Processor, importer, exporter and co-packer of barbecue/raspberry and dessert sauces, mustards, salad dressings, salsas, jams, preserves and fudge
President: John Payne
Research & Development: Marielaina Payne
Marketing: John Payne
Estimated Sales: $750,000
Number Employees: 1-4
Sq. footage: 5000
Type of Packaging: Consumer, Food Service, Private Label
Brands:
A Taste of the West
California Style Gourmet

2067 California Treats
2131 Tyler Ave
South El Monte, CA 91733-2754 626-444-4508
Fax: 626-579-3038 800-966-5501
info@caltreats.com www.cal-snacks.com
Gourmet foods
Owner: Ken Wong
Estimated Sales: $2.5-5 Million
Number Employees: 20-49
Type of Packaging: Private Label
Brands:
Betty Clark's Confections
Harmon's Gourmet

2068 California Watercress
P.O.Box 874
Fillmore, CA 93016-0874 805-524-4808
Fax: 805-524-5295
Processor of herbal supplements and herbs including cilantro and chives; also, vegetables including mixed, watercress and leeks
President: Alfred Beserra
Office Manager: Susan Barbera
Estimated Sales: $ 10 - 20 Million
Number Employees: 50-99
Type of Packaging: Consumer, Food Service, Bulk
Brands:
Al's Best

2069 California Wholesale Nut Company
1925 Manzanita Ave
Chico, CA 95926 530-895-0512
Fax: 530-345-1263
Processor of nuts
Owner: Naomi Mc Dermott
Estimated Sales: $100,000
Number Employees: 1-4

2070 California Wild Rice Growers
41577 Osprey Rd
Fall River Mills, CA 96028-9750 530-336-5222
Fax: 530-336-5265 800-626-4366
info@frwr.com www.frwr.com
Wild Rice
Manager: Walt Oiler
Manager: Hiram Oilar
PLant Manager: Tony Knight
Estimated Sales: $ 3 - 5 Million
Number Employees: 5-9
Brands:
Fall River

2071 **California-Antilles Trading Consortium**
3735 Adams Ave
San Diego, CA 92116 619-283-4834
Fax: 619-283-4834 800-330-6450
caliantilles@worldnet.att.net
www.calantilles.com
Hot sauces, salsas, barbecue sauces
President: Richard E Gardner
Operations: Tevor Dyer
Production: Robert Davis
Estimated Sales: $2.5-5 Million
Number Employees: 1-4
Number of Brands: 2
Number of Products: 25
Type of Packaging: Consumer, Private Label

2072 **Califrance**
P.O.Box 491327
Los Angeles, CA 90049 310-440-0729
Fax: 310-440-0879 califrance@formula9.com
www.formula9.com
Ketchups
Brands:
Formula 9

2073 **Calihan Pork Processing**
1 South St
Peoria, IL 61602 309-674-9175
Fax: 309-674-3003 calihanpork@aol.com
www.calihanpork.com
Processor of pork products including pre-rigor, boneless hams, Canadian bacon, back ribs and offals.
President: Tom Landon
Co-Owner: Lou Landon
General Manager: Jim Forbes
Manufacturing/Operations Director: Bill Murphy
Plant Supervisor: Bill Murphy
Estimated Sales: $20 Million
Number Employees: 60
Type of Packaging: Bulk

2074 **Calio Groves**
675 Cedar Street
Berkeley, CA 94710-1731 707-402-4700
Fax: 707-402-4747 800-865-4836
letters@caliogroves.com www.caliogroves.com
Processor of olive oil and extra virgin olive oil; importer of olive oil
President: Brendan Frasier
VP Production & Farming: Bob Singletary
Estimated Sales: $20-50 Million
Number Employees: 20-49
Parent Co: NVK Realty
Type of Packaging: Consumer, Food Service, Private Label, Bulk
Brands:
Calio Groves
EVO
Olio Santo
Stutz Olive Oil
VG Buck California Foods

2075 **Calise & Sons Bakery**
2 Quality Dr
Lincoln, RI 02865 401-334-3444
Fax: 401-334-0938 800-225-4737
Info@calisebakery.com www.calisebakery.com
Processor of fresh Italian bread, rolls and pizza shells.
Founder: Francesco Calise
Treasurer: Joseph Calise
CEO: Peter Petrocelli
Sales/Marketing Manager: Michael Calise
Production Manager: James Fontaine
Purchasing Manager: Anthony Capuzli
Estimated Sales: $15 Million
Number Employees: 100-249
Number of Products: 150
Sq. footage: 70000
Type of Packaging: Consumer, Food Service, Private Label
Brands:
CALISE
SUN RAY

2076 **Calistoga Food Company**
171 E 74th Street
New York, NY 10021-3221 212-879-4940
Fax: 212-879-5005
President: Martin Kreinik
Estimated Sales: $2.5-5,000,000
Number Employees: 5-9
Brands:
Calistoga Food

2077 **Calkins & Burke**
1500 Georgia St W
Suite 800
Vancouver, BC V6G 2Z6
Canada 604-669-3741
Fax: 604-699-9732 http://www.calbur.com
Processor and exporter of fresh and frozen halibut, salmon and crab
Director: David Calkins
VP: Micheal Kolinn
Head of Marketing: Ken Jonn
Estimated Sales: $8.6 Million
Number Employees: 60
Type of Packaging: Consumer, Food Service, Private Label
Brands:
Astra
Norden
Royal Canadian

2078 **Callard & Bowser-Suchard**
Ei-3 250 N Street
White Plains, NY 10573 914-345-3311
Fax: 914-345-3303 877-226-3900
President: Jerry Finard
National Sales Manager: John Kernan
Senior Product Manager: Mark Sugden
Estimated Sales: $5-10 Million appx.
Number Employees: 10-19

2079 **Callaway Packing Company**
663 W 4th St
Delta, CO 81416 970-874-9743
Fax: 970-874-7842 800-332-6932
calpack@montrose.net
Meat packer of beef, pork and lamb
President: David Dillie
Contact: Erlene Grover
Estimated Sales: $20-50 Million
Number Employees: 10-19
Type of Packaging: Consumer

2080 **Callaway Vineyards & Winery**
32720 Rancho California Road
Temecula, CA 92591 951-676-4001
Fax: 951-676-5209 800-472-2377
www.callawaywinery.com
Processor of red and white wine
President: Mike Jellison
Director: Lori Lyn Narlock
VP/Winemaker: Dwayne Helmuth
Associate Public Relations Manager: Kelly Keagy

Vineyard Manager: Craig Weaver
Cellar Foreman: Joe Vera
Plant Manager: Jose Ceja
Estimated Sales: $20-50 Million
Number Employees: 50-99
Parent Co: Hiram Walker-Allied Domeq.
Type of Packaging: Consumer, Food Service

2081 **Callie's Charleston Biscuits LLC**
498-A Meeting Street
Charleston, SC 29403 843-577-1198
carrie@calliesbiscuits.com
www.calliesbiscuits.com
Bread/biscuits, cakes/pastries, full line of baked goods and frozen desserts.
Owner: Callie White

2082 **Callis Seafood**
353 Callis Rd
Lancaster, VA 22503 804-462-7634
Fax: 804-435-6808 callissfd@rivernet.net
www.callissfd.net
Processor of oysters, crabs and frozen shrimp
President: Diane Callis-Haydon
CEO/VP: Diane Haydon
Estimated Sales: $200,000
Number Employees: 1-4
Type of Packaging: Consumer

2083 **Calmar Bakery**
PO Box 585
Calmar, AB T20 2J2
Canada 780-985-3583
Fax: 780-985-3583
Processor of baked goods including fruit cakes and Danish almond rings and wedding cakes
President: Doug Campbell
CEO: Doug Campbell
Marketing Director: Doug Campbell
Manager: Tork Kristiansen
Estimated Sales: A
Number Employees: 1-4
Type of Packaging: Consumer, Food Service
Brands:
Calmar Bakery

2084 **Calpro Ingredients**
1138 W Rincon Street
Corona, CA 92880-9601 909-493-4890
Fax: 909-493-4845 cnorthup@dfamilk.com
www.goldencheese.com
Processor and exporter of whey protein concentrates
President: Garry Johns
Operations: Carole Northup
Number Employees: 5-9
Sq. footage: 3000
Parent Co: Golden Cheese Company of California
Type of Packaging: Bulk
Brands:
Calpro

2085 **Caltex Foods**
9045-A Eton Ave
Canoga Park, CA 91304 818-700-8657
Fax: 818-700-0285 800-522-5839
info@aasanfoods.com www.aasanfoods.com
Ready made meals, Kosher ready made foods, Halal ready made foods, Mediterrenean foods, Middle Eastern Foods.
President/Secretary: Mehrdad Pakravan
Estimated Sales: $3 Million
Number Employees: 8
Sq. footage: 5000
Parent Co: Caltex Trading
Type of Packaging: Consumer, Private Label
Brands:
Aasan
Aviva
Beit Hashita
Jaffer

2086 **Calumet Diversified Meat Company**
10000 80th Ave
Pleasant Prairie, WI 53158 262-947-7200
Fax: 262-947-7209 chops.com
www.porkchops.com
Processor of pork including cutlets, loin, barbecued ribs, tenderloins, chops, etc
President: Larry Becker
National Accounts Manager: Joy Huskey
Estimated Sales: $24 Million
Number Employees: 125

2087 **Calvert's**
PO Box 1761
El Paso, TX 79949 915-544-3434
Fax: 915-544-7552 888-472-5727
info@elpasochile.com www.elpasochile.com
Lemonade mix
Owner: William Parker
Estimated Sales: $ 10 - 20 Million
Number Employees: 20-49

2088 **Camara Raisin Packing Company**
8427 N Millbrook Avenue
Suite 101
Fresno, CA 93720-2197 559-661-3780
Fax: 559-661-8123
Dried raisins
Owner: Ronald Camara
Estimated Sales: $20-50 Million
Number Employees: 20-49
Type of Packaging: Bulk

2089 **Camas Prairie Winery**
110 S Main St
Moscow, ID 83843-2806 208-882-0214
Fax: 208-882-0214 800-616-0214
scottcamas@turbonet.com
www.camasprairiewinery.com
Processor of wine
Co-Owner/President: Stuart Scott
Co-Owner/CFO: Susan Scott
Estimated Sales: $150,000
Number Employees: 1-4
Number of Products: 22
Type of Packaging: Private Label

Brands:
Camas

2090 Cambria Winery & Vineyard
5475 Chardonnay Ln
Santa Maria, CA 93454-9600 805-937-8091
Fax: 805-934-3589 888-339-9463
www.cambriawines.com
Wines
President: Barbara Banke
Marketing: Holly Evans
Customer Relations: Karen Readey
Public Relations: Elaine Mellis
General Manager: Keith W Moak
Vineyard Manager: Pat Huguenard
Winemaker: Denise Shurtleff
Estimated Sales: $5-10 Million
Number Employees: 50-99
Brands:
CAMBRIA

2091 Cambridge Brands
810 Main St
Cambridge, MA 02139 617-491-2500
Fax: 617-547-2381
Manufacturer of candy: bagged, bars, caramels, chocolate, chocolate covered cherries, fudge, holiday, gums and jellies, hard, jelly beans, licorice, lollypops, mints, nougats and coated nuts; also, chocolate and cocoa products forbakers, confectioners, etc.
VP: John "Newlin,"
President: Ellen Gordon
VP Finance: G Howard Ember Jr
Plant Manager: Gerald Chesser
Number Employees: 100-249
Parent Co: Tootsie Roll Industries
Type of Packaging: Consumer, Food Service
Brands:
Charleston Chew
Chuckles
Junior Mints,
Pearson
Pom Poms
Sugar Babies
Sugar Daddy
Sugar Mama

2092 Cambridge Food
2801 Salinas Hwy # F
Monterey, CA 93940-6401 831-373-2300
Fax: 831-373-7167 800-433-2584
info@cambridgedietusa.com
www.cambridgedietusa.com
Meal replacement formulas, cereals, soups, nutrition bars
Manager: Janet Bishop
Research & Development: Dr Robert Nesheim
Estimated Sales: $300,000-500,000
Number Employees: 1-4
Brands:
Cambridge Food

2093 Cambridge Packing Company
41 Food Mart Rd
Boston, MA 2118 617-464-6000
Fax: 617-269-0266 800-722-6726
info@campcosteaks.com
www.cambridgepacking.com
Processor of portion controlled steaks; wholesaler/distributor of fine meats and fresh and frozen seafood; serving the food service market
President/CEO: Bruce Rodman
CFO: Donald Kingston
Estimated Sales: $45 Million
Number Employees: 62
Sq. footage: 30000

2094 Cambridge Slaughtering
110 N East Rd
Cambridge, IL 61238 309-937-2455
Processor of beef, pork and lamb
Owner: Sharon Helg
Estimated Sales: $2.5-5 Million
Number Employees: 1-4

2095 Camellia Beans
5401 Toler Street
Harahan, LA 70183 504-733-8480
Fax: 504-733-8155 info@camelliabeans.com
www.lhhco.com
Manufacturer and exporter of dried beans, peas and lentils
Partner: Ken Hayward
Partner: Connely Hayward
Estimated Sales: $10-20 Million
Number Employees: 20-49
Type of Packaging: Consumer, Food Service, Bulk
Brands:
Camellia

2096 Camellia General Provision
1333 Genesee St
Buffalo, NY 14211 716-893-5352
Fax: 716-895-7713 contact@camelliafoods.com
www.camelliafoods.com
Processor of meat including smoked, sausage and ham
President: Peter Cichocki
Vice President: Eric Cichocki
Estimated Sales: $5-10 Million
Number Employees: 20-49

2097 Cameo Confections
543 Juneway Drive
Bay Village, OH 44140-2606 440-871-5732
Fax: 440-892-8656
Confections
President: Gail Barker

2098 Cameo Metal Products Inc
127 12th St
Brooklyn, NY 11215 718-788-1106
Fax: 718-788-3761 cameosales@cameometal.com
OR beverage@cameometal.com
www.cameometal.com
Cameo Metal Products Manufactures metal closures for the food and beverage industry.
President: Vito Di Maio
Director of Operations: Anthony Di Maio
Sq. footage: 100000

2099 Cameron Birch Syrup & Confections
951 Hermon Road
Suite 6
Wasilla, AK 99654-7379 907-373-6275
Fax: 907-373-6274 800-962-4724
admin@birchsyrup.com www.birchsyrup.com
Processor and exporter of birch syrup, marinades, salad dressing and candy
President: Marlene Cameron
Number Employees: 1-4
Sq. footage: 2500
Type of Packaging: Consumer, Food Service, Private Label, Bulk
Brands:
Birch Bark
Birch Logs
Black Tie
Cameron
Cameron's
Sesame Birch Sticks

2100 Cameron Seafood Processors
PO Box 1228
Cameron, LA 70631-1228 318-775-5510
Fax: 318-755-5529 www.cameronseafood.com
Seafood
President: Bruce Bang

2101 Camilla Pecan Company
P.O.Box 508
275 Industrial Blvd
Camilla, GA 31730-3911 229-336-7282
Fax: 229-336-1177 800-526-8770
info@harrellnut.com www.harrellnut.com
Pecans
President: Marty Harrell
Estimated Sales: $1-2.5 Million
Number Employees: 10-19
Number of Brands: 3
Brands:
Camilla Pecan
Harrell Nut
Ole' Henry's Nuthouse

2102 Camino Real Foods
2638 E Vernon Ave
Vernon, CA 90058 323-585-6599
Fax: 323-585-5420 800-421-6201
customerservice@crfoods.com
www.crfoods.com
Processor of frozen burritos and stuffed microwaveable sandwiches
President: Howard Wang
Marketing: Clark Metcalf
CFO: Stephen Wilson
CEO: Robert Cross
VP Sales: Terry McMartin
Parent Co: Nissan Foods
Type of Packaging: Consumer, Food Service
Brands:
Taxco
Tina's Las Campanas

2103 Camp Holly Springs
4100 Diamond Springs Dr
Richmond, VA 23231 804-795-2096
Fax: 804-795-1280 www.campholly springs.com
Bottled spring water, bulk spring water
Owner: Dusty Dowdy
General Manager: Roland Dowey, Jr.
CFO: Jeannie Pierce
Estimated Sales: $500,000-$1 Million
Number Employees: 5-9

2104 Campagana Winery
10950 West Road
Redwood Valley, CA 95470-9741 707-485-1221
Fax: 707-485-1225
george@campagnawinery.com
Winery
Chairman: Joseph Campagna
CEO: Tony Coturri
CFO/COO: George Pruden
Marketing Director: Paul White
Sales Director: Paul White
Production Manager: Nic Coturri
Estimated Sales: $3 Million
Number Employees: 8
Type of Packaging: Private Label
Brands:
GABRIELLI
GABRIELLI WINERY

2105 Campagna
P.O.Box 2403
Lebanon, OR 97355-0995 541-258-6806
Fax: 541-258-7806 800-959-4372
mgpcampagna@msn.com
www.campagnagourmet.com
Processor of cooking sauces, fruit, savory, and mustard flavors; hot pepper and garlic jellies
President: Marlene Peterson
CFO: Joseph Peterson
Estimated Sales: $1-2.5 Million
Number Employees: 5-9
Type of Packaging: Private Label

2106 Campagna-Turano Bakery
6501 Roosevelt Rd
Berwyn, IL 60402-1100 708-788-9220
Fax: 708-788-3075 info@turano-baking.com
www.turanobaking.com
Baked goods, bread
President: Renato Turano
VP Sales: Bill Carlson
Quality Control Manager: Les Messina
Executive VP Sales/Marketing: Giarcarto Turano
Operations Manager: Umberto Turano
Executive VP Production/Operations: Tony Turano
Estimated Sales: $10-20 Million
Number Employees: 250-499
Type of Packaging: Private Label

2107 Campari
55 E 59th St # 9
New York, NY 10022-1112 212-891-3600
Fax: 212-891-3661 www.mps.it
Alcoholic beverages
Manager: Gennaro Miccoli
Estimated Sales: $2.5-5 Million
Number Employees: 10-19
Parent Co: Campari
Brands:
Campari

2108 Campbell Company of Canada
60 Birmingham Street
Toronto, ON M8V 2B8
Canada 416-251-1131
Fax: 416-253-8611 800-410-7687
www.campbellsoup.ca

Manufacturer of canned foods including condensed soups, broth, chili and ready to serve soups.
President: Phillip Donne
VP/CFO: Earl Ellis
VP/Marketing: M Childs
President Food Service: K Matier
Number Employees: 800
Type of Packaging: Consumer, Food Service, Private Label
Brands:
BISTO
BROTHS
CAMPBELLS READY TO ENJOY SOUPS
CAMPBELLS SOUP AT HAND
CHUNKY READY TO GO BOWLS
CHUNKY READY TO SERVE SOUPS/CHILI
GARDENNAY
GODIVA
HABITANT
HEALTHY REQUEST READY TO SERVE SOUP
PACE
PEPPERIDGE FARM
RED & WHITE CONDENSED SOUPS
V8
V8 SPLASH
V8 VGO

2109 **Campbell Sales Company**
68 Fulbright Lane
Schaumburg, IL 60194-5168 847-885-7164
Processor of canned soup
Manager: John Prestia
Manager: Pete Barber
Number Employees: 1
Parent Co: Campbell Soup Company
Type of Packaging: Consumer, Food Service

2110 **(HQ)Campbell Soup Company**
1 Campbell Pl
Camden, NJ 08103
US 800-257-8443
Fax: 856-342-3878 800-257-8443
www.campbellsoup.com
Manufacturer of prepared convenience foods, baked goods, instant breakfast foods, soups, chili, chowders, stew, spaghetti, vegetable juice, gravies, relishes, sauces, beans, candy, etc.; importer of cooked beef; exporter of preparedentrees and soups. some pepridge farm products goldfish and crackers.
President & CEO: Denise Morrison
President/Campbell International: Mark Alexander
SVP/Finance: Anthony DiSilvestro
SVP/CFO/CAO: B Craig Owens
SVP Global R&D/Quality: George Dowdie
SVP/Chief Information Officer: Joseph Spagnoletti
SVP/Chief Strategy Officer: Irene Chang Britt
SVP/Public Affairs: Jerry Buckley
SVP/Human Resources & Communications: Nancy Reardon
SVP/Global Supply Chain: David White
Estimated Sales: $7.5 Billion
Number Employees: 18,700
Type of Packaging: Consumer, Food Service, Bulk
Other Locations:
Campbell Soup Co.
Redmond WA
Beverage Plant
Napoleon OH
Pepperidge Farms HQ
Norwalk CT
Brands:
CAMPBELL'S
PACE SAUCES
PEPPERIDGE FARMS
PREGO ITALIAN SAUCES
SWANSON BROTHS AND STOCKS
V8

2111 **Campbell Soup Company of Canada**
1400 Mitchell Avenue
Listowel, ON N4W 3B3
Canada 519-291-3410
Fax: 519-291-2551 800-575-7687
Processor and co-packer of frozen dinners, entrees, pastries, soups and sauces; also, powder gravy mixes and bottled sauces; exporter of frozen entrees, soup and meat balls
President: Philip Donne
VP, CFO: G J Arnold
Director R&D: S Graham
VP Marketing: R Weyersberg
Director Corporate Communications: J Nelson
Purchasing Director: Paul Martin
Number Employees: 500-999
Parent Co: Campbell Soup Company
Type of Packaging: Consumer, Private Label
Other Locations:
Campbell Heat Process Plant
Listowel ON
Campbell Frozen Foodservice Plant
Etobicoke ON
Brands:
CAMPBELLS

2112 **Campbell's Quality Cuts**
2551 Michigan St
Sidney, OH 45365-9083 937-492-2194
Fax: 937-492-4044
Processor of lamb, beef and pork
Owner: Dennis Campbell
Estimated Sales: $300,000-$500,000
Number Employees: 1-4
Type of Packaging: Consumer, Bulk

2113 **Camrose Packers**
5320 47th Street
Camrose, AB T4V 1K6
Canada 780-672-4887
Processor of fresh beef and pork and wild game including deer, elk and moose
Owner: Andrew Anderson
Manager: Debilyn Witvoet Parent
Number Employees: 5-9
Type of Packaging: Consumer
Brands:
Camrose

2114 **Can Am Seafood**
972 County Road
Lubec, ME 04652 207-733-2267
Fax: 207-733-0927
Seafood
President: William Jackson

2115 **Can-Oat Milling**
Box 520
Portage la Prairie, MB R1N 3W1
Canada 204-857-9700
Fax: 204-857-9500 800-663-6287
www.can-oat.com
Processor and exporter of oats including rolled, bran, instant, steel cut, whole groats and flour; importer of whole oat groats
President: Karl Gerrand
Number Employees: 100-249
Parent Co: Saskatchewan Wheat Pool
Type of Packaging: Bulk

2116 **CanAmera Foods**
2190 South Service Rd W
Oakville, ON L6L 5N1
Canada 905-825-7900
Fax: 905-847-1336
Processor of shortenings, margarines, oils, lard, whipped toppings, stabilizers and emulsifiers including lecithin
President: Murray Davis

2117 **Canada Bread**
1704 Seymour Street
North Bay, ON P1B 8G4
Canada 705-474-3970
Fax: 705-474-6847 800-461-6122
www.canadabread.ca
Manufacturer and distributor of fresh bakery products, frozen partially baked and fresh pasta and sauces
GM: Greg Chadbourn
Number Employees: 7,000
Parent Co: Maple Leaf
Type of Packaging: Consumer, Food Service
Brands:
BEN'S
DEMPSTERS
OLAFSON'S
OLIVIERI
POM

2118 **Canada Bread**
10 Four Seasons Place
Etobicoke, ON M9B 6H7
Canada 416-926-2000
Fax: 416-926-2018 www.canadabread.ca
Processor and exporter of pre-baked pizzas, shells and sauces
President/CEO: Richard Lan
Chairman: Michael McCain
CFO: Michael Vels
Senior VP Finance: Steve Attridge
Number Employees: 100-249
Sq. footage: 46000
Parent Co: Maple Leaf Foods Inc.
Type of Packaging: Consumer, Food Service, Private Label, Bulk
Brands:
Denpster
Dough Delight
Olivieri

2119 **Canada Bread Atlantic**
67 O'Leary Avenue
PO Box 8245
St. John's, NL A1B 3N4
Canada 709-722-5410
Fax: 709-722-7802
Manufacturer of bread and rolls
Operations Manager: Weldon Peddle
Type of Packaging: Consumer, Food Service

2120 **Canada Bread Company**
9850 62 Ave Nw
Edmonton, AB T6E 0E3
Canada 780-435-2240
Fax: 780-435-3556
Processor of bread and rolls
Parent Co: Maple Leaf Foods Inc.
Brands:
Country
Homestead

2121 **Canada Bread Company**
6350 203 Street
Langley, BC V2Y 1L9
Canada 604-532-8200
Fax: 604-532-8204 800-465-5515
investorrelations@mapleleaf.ca
www.canadabread.ca
Processor of baked goods including bread, rolls and English muffins
President: Michael McCain
Chairman: John L Bragg
COO: Richard A Lan
Parent Co: Corporate Foods/Canada Bread Company
Type of Packaging: Consumer, Food Service, Private Label, Bulk
Brands:
Ben
Dempsters
Olafsons
Olivieri
POM
Tenderflake

2122 **Canada Dry Bottling Company**
11202 15th Ave
Flushing, NY 11356 718-762-5967
Fax: 718-353-5235
consumer_relations@dpsu.com
www.dpsu.com
Manufacturer/bottler of sodas, seltzer and mineral water including diet
President: Dennis Berberich
Estimated Sales: $100-500 Million
Number Employees: 250-499
Parent Co: Cadbury Schweppes
Type of Packaging: Consumer, Food Service, Private Label
Brands:
A&W
CANADA DRY
COUNTRY TIME
DIET RITE
DR. PEPPER
HAWAIIAN PUNCH
HIRES ROOT BEER
RC COLA
SCHWEPPES
SEVEN UP
SLUSH PUPPIE
SQUIRT
SUNDROP

SUNKIST
VERNORS
WELCH'S

2123 **Canada Safeway Limited**
31122 S Fraser Way
Abbotsford, BC V2T 6L5
Canada 604-854-1191
Fax: 604-850-1179
Processor of frozen fruits and vegetables including blueberries, cranberries, whole beans, peas and brussels sprouts; exporter of frozen brussels sprouts, whole beans and cranberries
Plant Manager: Vic Giesbrecht
Number Employees: 150
Sq. footage: 64000
Parent Co: Safeway
Type of Packaging: Consumer, Food Service, Private Label, Bulk
Brands:
Bel-Air

2124 **Canada West Foods**
4312 51st Street
Innisfail, AB T4G 1A3
Canada 403-227-3386
Fax: 403-227-1661
Processor of case-ready lamb, veal and bison; also, custom processing available (very little)
President: Gary Haley
CEO: Gary Haley
Vice President: Don Finstad
Plant Manager: Miles Kliner
Number Employees: 100-249
Parent Co: Canada West Foods
Type of Packaging: Consumer

2125 **Canadian Fish Exporters**
PO Box 411
Watertown, MA 02471-0411 617-924-8300
Fax: 617-926-8214 800-225-4215
cfe@cfeboston.com www.cfeboston.com
Processor, importer and exporter of saltfish including bacalao, pollock, hake, cusk, haddock, herring, mackerel and cod; importer of Italian cheeses and canned tomatoes
President: Robert Metafora
CEO: Robert Metafora
CFO/Treasurer: Janelle Calamari
VP: James Scannell
Estimated Sales: $ 10 - 20 Million
Number Employees: 10-19
Type of Packaging: Consumer, Private Label, Bulk
Brands:
BACALA RICO
BUENA VENTURA
CRISTOBAL

2126 **(HQ)Canadian Harvest**
1001 Cleveland St S
Cambridge, MN 55008-1150 763-689-5800
Fax: 763-689-5949 888-689-5800
miker@skypoint.com www.sunopta.com
Processor of stabilized fiber ingredients including bleached oat fibers, red and white wheat brans, corn brans, oat blends, wheat germs and customized grain blends
Marketing Manager: Mike Rudquist
General Manager: John White
Plant Manager: Paul Empanger
Estimated Sales: $10-20 Million
Number Employees: 20-49
Other Locations:
Canadian Harvest
St. Thomas ON
Brands:
Snowite

2127 **Canadian Mist Distillers**
202 MacDonald Road
Collingwood, ON L9Y 4J2
Canada 705-445-4690
Fax: 705-445-7948 www.b-f.com
Processor and exporter of whiskey
Manager Admin./Commodities: Steve Sly
Manager Production: Don Jaques
Plant Manager: Harold Ferguson
Estimated Sales: $13 Million
Number Employees: 35
Sq. footage: 500000
Parent Co: Brown-Forman Corporation
Type of Packaging: Consumer, Food Service
Brands:
Canadian Mist

2128 **Canadian Salt Company Limited**
Pointe Claire, QC H9R 5M9
Canada 514-630-0900
Fax: 514-694-2451 tferrara@windsorsalt.com
www.windsorsalt.com
Manufacaturer and exporter of salt including table, food processing, water conditioning and ice melting
President/CEO: Guy Leblanc
VP Finance: Francois Allard
Marketing Manager: Michel Prevost
VP Sales/Marketing: Luc Savoic
Human Resources Manager: Nicole Gagnon
Estimated Sales: $300+ Million
Number Employees: 700
Parent Co: Morton International
Type of Packaging: Consumer, Food Service, Bulk
Other Locations:
Canadian Salt Company
Pugwash, Nova Scoti
Canadian Salt Company
Mines Seleine, Quebec
Canadian Salt Company-Warehouse
Goderich, Ontario
Canadian Salt Company-Warehouse
Clarkson, Ontario
Canadian Salt Company-Warehouse
Anjou, Quebec
Canadian Salt Company
Ojibway, Ontario
Canadian Salt Company
Windsor, Ontario
Canadian Salt Company
Regina, Saskatchewan
Canadian Salt Company
Lindbergh, Alberta
Brands:
WINDSOR

2129 **Canadian Silver Herring**
2181 Route 950
Petit-Cap, NB E4N 2H8
Canada 506-577-6426
Fax: 506-577-2846
Processor and exporter of smoked herring
Owner: Janice Ryan
Number Employees: 20-49
Type of Packaging: Bulk

2130 **Canal Fulton Provision**
2014 Locust St S
Canal Fulton, OH 44614 330-854-3502
Fax: 330-854-3502 800-321-3502
www.canalfultonpro.com
Processor of portion cut poultry and meats including beef, lamb and pork
President: George Mizarek
Estimated Sales: $5 Million
Number Employees: 22
Sq. footage: 27000
Type of Packaging: Consumer, Food Service, Private Label, Bulk
Brands:
Corn King
Flavor Pack
Weaver

2131 **Canasoy Enterprises**
57 Lakewood Drive
Vancouver, BC V5L 4W4
Canada 604-255-1304
Fax: 604-255-5659 800-663-1222
info@canasoy.com www.canasoy.com
Processor, importer and exporter of health foods, including grains and pasta
President: Hau Cheong Chau
Marketing/Sales: Gregory Chan
Number Employees: 10-19
Number of Products: 3000
Sq. footage: 25000
Type of Packaging: Consumer, Food Service, Private Label

2132 **Candelari's Specialty Sausage**
6002 Washington Ave
Houston, TX 77007-5015 832-200-1474
Fax: 281-568-8098 800-953-5343
emaillist@candelaris.com www.candelaris.com
Sausage
President: Michael May
CFO: Michael Freeman
Estimated Sales: $500,000-$1 Million
Number Employees: 5-9
Type of Packaging: Private Label
Brands:
Candelari's

2133 **Candone Fine Natural Foods**
3343 Peachtree Road NE
Suite 1115
Atlanta, GA 30326-1430 404-469-2348
Fax: 404-364-3499
President: Elvaina Candoni De Zan

2134 **Candy Bouquet of Elko**
3362 Dux Avenue
Elko, NV 89801-4432 775-777-9866
Fax: 775-777-3200 888-855-3391
hopkins@sierra.net
Manufacturer of candy bouquets
Co-Owner: Judy Hopkins
Co-Owner: Diane Noble
Manager: Angie Demars
Number Employees: 1-4

2135 **Candy Cottage Company**
465 Pike Rd Ste 103
Huntingdon Valley, PA 19006 215-953-8288
Fax: 215-357-3035 info@candycottageco.com
www.candycottageco.com
Manufacturer of chocolate covered pretzels
Co-Owner: Al Palagruto
Co-Owner: Joan Palagruto
Estimated Sales: Under $500,000
Number Employees: 3
Type of Packaging: Consumer, Food Service, Private Label, Bulk
Brands:
Ultimate Petite Pretzels
Ultimate Pretzel
Ultimate Pretzel Rods
Ultimate Pretzel Sculptures

2136 **Candy Factory**
25067 Viking St
Hayward, CA 94545-2703 510-293-6887
Fax: 510-293-6890 800-736-6887
www.knudsens.com
Processor of gourmet chocolates including bon bons, creams, regular and caramel nut clusters, truffles, etc.; also, private labeling available
President: Gary Love
Chairman: David Knudsen
Treasurer/Secretary: Kathy Knudsen
Vice President: Tod Knudsen
Marketing Director: Tod Knudsen
Purchasing Manager: Tod Knudsen
Number Employees: 20-49
Sq. footage: 36000
Type of Packaging: Consumer, Private Label
Brands:
Enjoymints
Tropical Wonders

2137 **(HQ)Candy Flowers**
9350 Mercantile Drive
Mentor, OH 44060-4525 888-476-6467
Fax: 508-842-3065 www.candyflowersinc.com
Processor of chocolate and candy flowers, chocolate covered pretzels, coffee spoons and cookies and theme wrapped chocolate bars; exporter of candy flowers; importer of chocolates
President: Joanne Henry
Marketing: Anthony Henry
Estimated Sales: $50,000
Number Employees: 2
Sq. footage: 21000
Type of Packaging: Food Service
Brands:
CANDY FLOWER BOUQUETS
SPOONFUL OF FLAVORS
SWEET BLOSSOMS

2138 **Candyrific**
3738 Lexington Rd
Louisville, KY 40207-3010 502-893-3626
Fax: 502-893-3951 sales@candyrific.com
www.candyrific.com
Candy
Brands:
COOL POPS
CRAYOLA
ETCH-A-SKETCH
MARVEL
PEEPS
SLINKY BRAND CANDY

2139 **Canelake's**
414 Chestnut St
Virginia, MN 55792-2526 218-741-1557
Fax: 218-741-1557 888-928-8889
candy@canelakes.com www.canelakes.com
Processor and exporter of candies and chocolates; importer of nuts
President: James Cina
Estimated Sales: $1-2.5 Million
Number Employees: 10-19
Sq. footage: 2000
Type of Packaging: Consumer

2140 **Cangel**
60 Paton Road
Toronto, ON M6H 1R8
Canada 416-532-5111
Fax: 416-532-6231 800-267-4795
b.imai@cangel.com
Manufacturer and exporter of food, hydrolyzed and technical gelatins
President: Richard Manka
Number Employees: 50-99
Sq. footage: 80000
Type of Packaging: Bulk

2141 **Cannery Row**
PO Box 120
Cordova, AK 99574-0120 907-424-5920
Fax: 907-424-5923
Seafood

2142 **Cannoli Factory**
75 Wyandanch Ave
Wyandanch, NY 11798 631-643-2700
Fax: 631-643-2777 www.cannolifactory.net
Processor and exporter of Italian and New York style cheesecake, tiramisu, lobster tail pastries and cannoli products including chocolate covered shells, cream and tarts
Owner: Michael Zucaro
Estimated Sales: $4 Million
Number Employees: 50
Type of Packaging: Food Service

2143 **Cannon Potato Company**
P.O.Box 880
Center, CO 81125-0880 719-754-3445
Fax: 719-754-2227 sales@canonpotato.com
www.canonpotato.com
Potato packer and shipper
President: Jim Tonso
Sales Manager: David Tonso
Estimated Sales: $10-20 Million
Number Employees: 20-49
Type of Packaging: Private Label

2144 **Cannon's Sweets Hots**
2724 Tennessee Street NE
Albuquerque, NM 87110-3732 505-294-7018
Fax: 505-292-4581 877-630-7026
sweethot@sweethots.com www.sweethots.com
Hot sauces and chili
Co-Owner/President: John Cannon
Co-Owner/CEO: Diane Cannon
Estimated Sales: Under $500,000
Number Employees: 1-4

2145 **Canoe Lagoon Oyster Company**
118 Bayview Ave
Coffman Cove, AK 99918 907-329-2253
Fax: 425-643-7266
Oyster
Owner: Sharon Gray
Owner: Don Nicholson
Estimated Sales: $500,000
Number Employees: 1-4
Type of Packaging: Consumer, Food Service, Bulk

2146 **Cantare Foods**
7651 St Andrews Ave
San Diego, CA 92154 619-690-7550
Fax: 619-690-7551 www.cantarefoods.com
Manufacturer of fresh mozzarella, ricotta, mascarpone, burratta, and baked brie en croute
President: Bob Fisher
CEO: Olivier Fischer
COO: Christopher Megevan
Estimated Sales: $7.6 Million
Number Employees: 60

2147 **(HQ)Cantisano Foods**
815 Whitney Rd W
Fairport, NY 14450 585-377-7700
Fax: 716-377-8150
Pizza sauce, tomato sauce, meatless spaghetti sauce, kosher spaghetti sauce, barbecue sauce
President: Giovanni LiDestri
CFO: John Vetere
EVP/COO: Edward Salzano
Production Manager: Santi LiDestri
Estimated Sales: $50-100 Million
Number Employees: 400
Brands:
Cantisano
Francesco Rinaldi

2148 **Canton Noodle**
481 W 26th St
Chicago, IL 60616 312-842-4900
Fax: 312-225-2262
Chinese foods and noodles
President: Mitta Moy
Estimated Sales: $2.5-5 Million
Number Employees: 10-19

2149 **Canton Noodle Corporation**
101 Mott St
New York, NY 10013 212-226-3276
Fax: 212-226-8037
Processor of Chinese canned noodles
Estimated Sales: $1-2.5 Million
Number Employees: 5-9
Type of Packaging: Consumer

2150 **Cantrell's Seafood**
Sabino Road
Bath, ME 04530 207-442-7261
Fax: 207-770-1600
Seafood
President: S C Cantrell

2151 **Cantwell's Old Mill Winery**
403 S Broadway
Geneva, OH 44041-1844 440-466-5560
Fax: 440-466-2099 winedoc@ncweb.com
www.oldmillwinery.com
Gourmet foods, wines
Owner: Dave Froelich
Winemaker: Bill Turgeon
Marketing Director: Shirley Barnett
Estimated Sales: $1-2.5 Million appx.
Number Employees: 1-4

2152 **Canus Fisheries**
PO Box 149
Clark's Harbour, NS B0W 1P0
Canada 902-745-2888
Fax: 902-745-2526 canus@auracom.com
Processor and exporter of fresh lobster and salted and fresh fish
President: Margot Swim
Number Employees: 50-99
Type of Packaging: Consumer, Food Service, Private Label, Bulk

2153 **Canyon Specialty Foods**
PO Box 35154
Dallas, TX 75235-0154 214-352-1771
Fax: 214-352-3118 877-815-3663
aconally@canyonfoods.com
www.canyonfoods.com
Gourmet shelf and frozen food, salsa and sauces
Owner, President: Anne Connally
Production Manager: Tara McConnell
Estimated Sales: $10-20 Million
Number Employees: 10-19
Type of Packaging: Private Label

2154 **Cap Candy**
50 Technology Court
Napa, CA 94558-7519 707-251-9321
Fax: 707-251-9482
Candy
VP of Marketing: Deirdre Gonzalez
General Manager: Tom Pritchard
Number Employees: 250-499
Parent Co: Hasbro

2155 **Cap Rock Winery**
408 E Woodrow Rd
Lubbock, TX 79423 806-863-2704
Fax: 806-863-2712 800-546-9463
www.caprockwinery.com
Wines
President: Don Roark
CEO: Todd Graham
Plant Manager: Kim McPherson
Estimated Sales: $1.5 Million
Number Employees: 12
Type of Packaging: Private Label

2156 **Capa Di Roma, Inc**
358 Burnside Avenue
East Hartford, CT 06108-2405 860-282-0298
Fax: 860-289-6211 ecrest@aol.com
www.capadiroma.com
Olive oil, balsamic vinegar, pasta sauce.
Marketing: Emilia Capaccio

2157 **Capalbo's Gift Baskets**
350 Allwood Rd
Clifton, NJ 07012 800-252-6262
Fax: 973-450-1199 800-252-6262
www.capalbosonline.com
Gift baskets for the specialty food industry
Owner: Frank Capalbo
President: J Capalbo
Vice President: Susan Capalbo
Estimated Sales: $5 Million
Number Employees: 40
Brands:
Capalbo's

2158 **Caparone Winery**
2280 San Marcos Rd
Paso Robles, CA 93446 805-467-3827
info@caparone.com
www.caparone.com
Wines
President: M Caparone
Estimated Sales: Under $500,000
Number Employees: 20-49

2159 **Capay Canyon Ranch**
P.O.Box 508
Esparto, CA 95627-0508 530-662-2372
Fax: 530-662-2306
Processor and exporter of almonds, walnuts and grapes, and inshell chandler walnuts.
President/Owner: Stan Barth
Quality Control: Todd Barth
Sales Director: Leslie Barth
Operations Manager: Javier Quiroz
Production: Todd Barth
Plant Manager: Todd Barth
Estimated Sales: $14 Million
Number of Brands: 2
Number of Products: 8
Sq. footage: 10000
Type of Packaging: Bulk
Brands:
Capay Canyon Ranch
STAN BARTH FARMS

2160 **Capco Enterprises**
34 Deforest Ave # 3
East Hanover, NJ 07936-2832 973-884-0044
Fax: 973-884-8711 800-252-1011
www.capcoenterprisesinc.com
Almonds, licorice, baked beans, sugar-coated pistachios and chick peas
Owner: Carole Lapone
Estimated Sales: $2.5-5 Million
Number Employees: 5-9

2161 **Cape Ann Seafood**
44 Grapevine Road
Gloucester, MA 01930-4241 978-283-0687
Fax: 978-282-1870
Seafood
President: Nickolas Avelis
VP: James Douglass
Estimated Sales: $ 2.0 Million
Number Employees: 2

2162 **Cape Ann Tuna**
11 Parker St
Gloucester, MA 01930 978-283-8188
Fax: 978-281-6584
Tuna
Owner: William Raymond
Estimated Sales: $ .5 - 1 million
Number Employees: 1-4

2163 **Cape Cod Chowders**
141 Falmouth Rd
Hyannis, MA 02601-2755 508-771-0040
Fax: 508-771-0883
www.cataniahospitalitygroup.com
Chowder
President: Vincent J Catania
Vice President: Richard Catenia
Sales Director: Dan Sheehan
Purchasing Manager: Paul Rumel
Estimated Sales: F
Number Employees: 500-999
Type of Packaging: Private Label
Brands:
Cape Cod Clam Chowder
Cape Cod Lobster Cho

2164 **Cape Cod Coffee Roasters**
348 Main St
Mashpee, MA 2649 508-477-2400
Fax: 508-477-2989 www.cccoffee.com
Coffee
Owner: Demos Young
Office Manager: Jean Pagano
Estimated Sales: Under $500,000
Number Employees: 7

2165 **Cape Cod Potato Chip Company**
100 Breeds Hill Rd
Hyannis, MA 02601 508-775-3358
Fax: 508-775-2808
customer.service@capecodchips.com
www.capecodchips.com
Processor and exporter of popcorn including white cheddar cheese, natural and butter; also, kettle-cooked potato chips
President: Margaret Wicklund
Estimated Sales: $20-50 Million
Number Employees: 140
Sq. footage: 30000
Parent Co: Lance
Type of Packaging: Consumer
Brands:
Cape Cod

2166 **Cape Cod Provisions**
31 Jonathan Bourne Dr
Unit 1
Pocasset, MA 02559 508-564-5840
Fax: 508-564-5844 mail@capecodprovisions.com
www.capecodprovisions.com
Chocolate covered cranberries, chocolate covered fruit, fruit truffles
Owner: Susan Faria
Estimated Sales: $1 Million
Number Employees: 10

2167 **Cape Cod Specialty Foods**
PO Box 519
11 Cranberry Hwy
Sagamore, MA 02561 508-888-7099
Fax: 508-888-6616 bogbeans@rcn.com
www.bogbeans.com
Wholesaler/distributor of gourmet condiments including lemon pepper mustard, cranberry chutney, relish and sauces, schnappy peach preserves, chocolate covered cranberries, bog beans, etc.; also mail order available
President: Mike Duryea
Estimated Sales: $2.5-5 Million
Number Employees: 1-4
Sq. footage: 2000
Type of Packaging: Consumer, Food Service

2168 **Capital Brewery**
7734 Terrace Ave
Middleton, WI 53562-3163 608-836-7100
Fax: 608-831-9155 capital@capital-brewery.com
www.capital-brewery.com
Brewer of lager and ale
President, CEO: Carl Nolen
Brewmaster: Kirby Nelson
Estimated Sales: $5-10 Million
Number Employees: 20-49
Type of Packaging: Consumer, Food Service, Bulk
Brands:
Gartenbrau

2169 **Capital City Processors**
P.O.Box 94148
Oklahoma City, OK 73143 405-232-5511
800-473-2731
Processor of cooking oils
Manager: Randal McKiddie
Treasurer: Richard Jerome
Estimated Sales: $20-50 Million
Number Employees: 10-19
Type of Packaging: Bulk

2170 **Capital Packers Inc**
12907-57th Street
Edmonton, AB T5A 0E7
Canada 780-476-1391
Fax: 780-478-0083 800-272-8868
info@capitalpackers.ca www.capitalpackers.ca
Processor of cooked and smoked meats including beef, pork and veal
President: Brent Komarnicki
Sales Manager: Peter Andreassen
Plant Manager: Cor Van Miltenburg
Estimated Sales: F
Number Employees: 100-249
Number of Brands: 3
Number of Products: 850
Type of Packaging: Food Service, Private Label, Bulk
Brands:
Bavarian Brand Sausage
Cajun Brand Sausage
Ham Sausage
Polish Sausage

2171 **Capital Seaboard**
8005 Rappahanock Ave
Jessup, MD 20794-9438 443-755-1733
Fax: 443-755-0282
Seafood
Owner: Troy Geller

2172 **Capitol Foods**
PO Box 751541
Memphis, TN 38175-1541 662-781-9021
Fax: 662-781-0697
Processor of canned vegetables, diced peaches, mixed fruits and edible oils; exporter of canned vegetables; wholesaler/distributor of bakery, dairy and grocery products, soups and bases, produce, syrups, oils, pasta, meats; serving thefood service markets
President: Kenneth Porter
CFO: Phillip Duncan
Number Employees: 10-19
Sq. footage: 10000
Type of Packaging: Consumer, Food Service
Brands:
Capitol Foods
Orchard Naturals

2173 **Capolla Food Inc**
25 Lepage Court
North York, ON M3J 3M3
Canada 416-633-0389
Fax: 416-633-7718 www.coppolafood.com
Processor of packaged luncheon meats including beef and pork
President: Rick De Vincenzo
CEO: Rick De Vincenzo
Marketing Director: Francefca Ivas
Sales/Marketing: Dion McGuire
Purchasing Agent: John Capolla
Number Employees: 50-99
Parent Co: J.M. Schneider
Type of Packaging: Consumer
Brands:
Capolla Foods

2174 **Capone Foods**
14 Bow St
Somerville, MA 2143 617-629-2296
Fax: 617-776-0318 albert@caponefoods.com
www.caponefoods.com
Pasta and sauces
Owner: Albert Capone
Estimated Sales: $5-10 Million
Number Employees: 5-9

2175 **Caporale Winery**
910 Enterprise Way
Napa, CA 94558-6209 707-253-9230
Fax: 707-253-9232
Wines
President: Mark Caporale
Estimated Sales: $500,000- 1 Million
Number Employees: 20-49

2176 **Cappiello Dairy Products**
534 Broadway
Schenectady, NY 12305 518-374-5064
Fax: 518-374-4015 info@Cappiello.com
www.cappiello.com
Processor of cheeses including ricotta, mozzarella, scamorza and Italian hand-crafted
Owner: Peter Cappiello
VP Marketing: Julianne Cappiello-Miranda
VP Sales: Julianne Cappiello-Miranda
Director Of Operations: Peter Cappiello
Estimated Sales: $20-50 Million
Number Employees: 50-99
Type of Packaging: Consumer, Private Label, Bulk
Brands:
Cappiello

2177 **Cappola Foods**
25 Lappage Ct
Toronto, ON M3J 3M3
Canada 416-633-0389
Fax: 416-787-1535 sales@cappolafood.com
www.cappolafood.com
Processor and exporter of Italian flavored ices
Owner: Dom Cappola
Type of Packaging: Consumer, Food Service

2178 **Cappuccine**
1285 N Valdivia Way
Palm Springs, CA 92262 760-864-7355
Fax: 760-864-7360 800-511-3127
sales@cappuccine.net www.cappuccine.net
Gourmet instant powder beverage mixes in chai, vanilla, chocolate, fruit, toffes and coconut flavors
Founder/President/CEO: Michael Rubin
General Manager/COO: John Strohm
Executive VP: Charles Jennings
Sales Manager: Alan Dossey
Operations Manager: Kayvon McMains
Estimated Sales: $5 Million
Number Employees: 5-9
Number of Brands: 1
Number of Products: 18
Sq. footage: 3600
Type of Packaging: Consumer, Food Service, Private Label, Bulk
Brands:
Cappuccine
Cappuccino Exotic Island Smoothies

2179 **Capri Bagel & Pizza Corporation**
215 Moore St
Brooklyn, NY 11206-3745 718-497-4431
Fax: 718-497-7567
Manufacturer and exporter of pizza, pizza bagels and mini pizzas
President: Adrian Cooper
Plant Manager: Ikey Tuachi
Estimated Sales: $500,000-$1 Million
Number Employees: 20-49
Sq. footage: 31000
Type of Packaging: Consumer, Food Service, Private Label
Brands:
Big Time
Boardwalk

2180 **Capriccio**
10021 1/2 Canoga Avenue
Chatsworth, CA 91311-0981 818-718-7620
Fax: 818-718-0204 capriccio@worldnet.att.net
Manufacturer and exporter of food ingredients
CEO: Jack Barsoumian
Estimated Sales: $500,000-$1 Million
Number Employees: 1-4
Type of Packaging: Food Service

2181 **Capricorn Coffees**
353 10th St
San Francisco, CA 94103 415-621-8500
Fax: 415-621-9875 800-541-0758
www.capricorncoffees.com
Coffee
Manager: Megan Patterson
Estimated Sales: $1-2.5 Million
Number Employees: 10-19
Type of Packaging: Private Label

2182 **Caprine Estates**
3669 Centerville Road
Bellbrook, OH 45305-0307 937-848-7406
Fax: 937-848-7437 info@caprineestates.com

Processor of goat milk cheese, fudge and bottled milk
President: Dennis Dean
VP: Patti Dean
Sales/Marketing VP: Ron Best
Estimated Sales: $250,000
Number Employees: 5
Sq. footage: 15000
Type of Packaging: Consumer, Food Service, Private Label, Bulk

2183 **Capsule Works**
10 Vitamin Dr
Bayport, NY 11705
Fax: 631-472-2817 800-920-6090
sales@capsuleworks.com
www.capsuleworks.com
Vitamins
President: Kazuo Kawabata
CFO: Jean-Marc Huët
Estimated Sales: $ 10 - 20 Million
Number Employees: 20-49
Brands:
Capsule Works

2184 **Captain Alex Seafood**
8874 N Milwaukee Ave
Niles, IL 60714 847-803-8833
Fax: 847-803-9854
Seafood
Owner: Alex Malidis
Estimated Sales: $680,000
Number Employees: 5-9

2185 **Captain Bob's Jet Fuel**
2216 Ladue Ln
Fort Wayne, IN 46804-2794 260-436-3895
877-486-6468
customerservice@captainbobs.com
www.captainbobs.com
Processor of hot sauces including habanero-garlic, smoked serrano jalapeno and chile de arbol; also, hot barbecue sauces
President: Robert Kitto
Estimated Sales: $1-2.5 Million
Number Employees: 1-4
Brands:
Captain Bob's Jet Fuel

2186 **Captain Collier Seafood**
14733 Tom Johnson Ave
Coden, AL 36523 251-824-4925
Fax: 251-824-2374
Seafood
Owner: Phil Brannon
Estimated Sales: $ 3 - 5 Million
Number Employees: 5-9

2187 **Captain Cook Coffee Company**
P.O.Box 818
Captain Cook, HI 96704 808-488-1776
Fax: 808-322-2087 captaincoffee@hawaii.rr.com
www.captaincoffee.com
Coffee
President/CEO: Steven McLaughlin
Estimated Sales: $5-10 Million
Number Employees: 10-19

2188 **Captain Joe & Sons**
95 E Main St
Gloucester, MA 01930 978-283-1454
Fax: 978-283-1466 www.wholesalelobster.com
Seafood
Co-Owner: Joe Ciaramitaro
Co-Owner: Frank Ciaramitaro
Estimated Sales: $300,000-500,000
Number Employees: 1-4

2189 **Captain Ken's Foods**
344 Robert St S
St Paul, MN 55107-2200 651-298-0071
Fax: 651-298-0849 jtraxler@captainkens.com
www.captainkens.com
Processor of frozen foods including chili, oven baked beans and au gratin potatoes, taco meat, meatloaf, macaroni and beef
President, CEO: John Traxler
Chairman, Owner: Mike Traxler
Controller: Linda Traxler
VP Business Development: Tom Traxler
VP Sales: Don Keis
Operations Manager: Kevin Kosel
Plant Manager: Richard Gavin
Estimated Sales: $5-9.9 Million
Number Employees: 20-49
Sq. footage: 62000
Type of Packaging: Consumer, Food Service
Brands:
Captain Ken's

2190 **Captain Ottis Seafood**
711 Shepard Street
Morehead City, NC 28557-4206 252-247-3569
Fax: 252-726-7097
Frozen flounder, scallops, shrimp
President: Doug Brady
Estimated Sales: $5-10 Million
Number Employees: 10-19

2191 **Captain's Choice**
29629 11th Pl S
Federal Way, WA 98003 253-941-1184
Fax: 253-946-2852 captainschoice@juno.com
www.captains-choice.com
Honey brine smoked salmon products and gift packages
President: Donald Buchanan
Public Relations: Rosalie Buchanan
Estimated Sales: Under $300,000
Number Employees: 1-4
Type of Packaging: Consumer, Food Service, Private Label
Brands:
Captain's Choice Honey Brine
Smoked Salmon
Smoked Spices

2192 **Captiva**
45 Us Highway 206 Ste 104
Augusta, NJ 7822 973-579-7883
Fax: 973-579-2509
Processor and exporter of bottled water including stilled, carbonated and flavored; also, sports/health drinks
Owner: Don Destefano
VP: Mary Ann Bell
Estimated Sales: $ 3 - 5 Million
Number Employees: 1-4
Sq. footage: 3000
Type of Packaging: Consumer, Food Service, Private Label, Bulk
Brands:
Nature's Mist
Pro-Life

2193 **Captn's Pack Products**
7135 Minstrel Way Ste 203
Columbia, MD 21045 410-720-6668
Fax: 410-381-6868
Seafood
President: Benjamin Sha
Estimated Sales: $ 5 - 10 Million
Number Employees: 5-9

2194 **Cara Mia Foods**
10838 Cara Mia Parkway
PO Box 1307
Castroville, CA 95012-3211 831-633-2423
Fax: 831-633-9025
Frozen artichokes and artichoke hearts
Purchasing Manager: Robert Epperson
Estimated Sales: $20-50 Million
Number Employees: 250-499

2195 **Cara Mia Products**
2680 W Shaw Lane
Fresno, CA 93725 559-498-2900
Fax: 559-498-2910 www.starfinefoods.com
Processor of artichokes, brussels sprouts and mushrooms; contract packager of vegetables
President: Jerry Maynard
VP Marketing: Jim Scattini
Estimated Sales: $10-25 Million
Number Employees: 20-49
Type of Packaging: Consumer, Food Service, Private Label, Bulk
Brands:
Cara Mia

2196 **Caracollillo Coffee Mills**
4419 N Hesperides St
Tampa, FL 33614-7618 813-876-0302
Fax: 813-875-6407 800-682-0023
info@ccmcoffee.com www.ccmcoffee.com
Coffee
President: Michael Faedo
VP/Owner: Julian Faedo
Estimated Sales: $ 3 - 5 Million
Number Employees: 5-9
Type of Packaging: Consumer, Food Service, Private Label
Brands:
CAFE QUISQUEVA
Cafe Caracolillo Decafe
Cafe Caracolillo Expresso
Cafe Caracolillo Gourmet
Cafe Regil
Cafe Rico Rico
Cafe Riquisimo

2197 **Carando Gourmet Frozen Foods**
175 Main Street
Agawam, MA 01001 413-730-4205
Fax: 413-789-1653 888-227-2636
www.carandogourmet.com
Processor of frozen food and entrees including roast beef, corned beef, pastrami, sauces, Italian stuffed pastas, gourmet meatballs, cabbage and sweet peppers
Owner: Peter Carando Jr
Director Sales: Brian Kelly
Parent Co: Carando Gourmet
Type of Packaging: Consumer, Food Service, Private Label, Bulk
Brands:
Carando Gourmet

2198 **Caraquet Ice Company**
20 Rue Du Quai
Caraquet, NB E1W 1B6
Canada 506-727-7211
Fax: 506-727-6769
Processor of fresh and frozen seafood
President: Richard Albert
Type of Packaging: Bulk
Brands:
Caraquet

2199 **Caravan Company**
237 Chandler St
Worcester, MA 01609 508-752-3777
Fax: 508-753-4717 www.caravanco.com
Manufacturer of coffee
President: George Drapos
Estimated Sales: $10 Million
Number Employees: 10-19

2200 **(HQ)Caravan Products Company**
P.O.Box 1004
Totowa, NJ 07512 973-256-8886
Fax: 973-256-8395 800-526-5261
info@caravanproducts.com
www.caravaningredients.com
Manufacturer, wholesaler and exporter of bakery ingredients
President: John Stone
VP: Joseph Solimini
Quality Control: Mark Carlson
Estimated Sales: $20-50 Million
Number Employees: 100-249
Other Locations:
Caravan Products Co.
Totowa NJ
Brands:
DABUBE SEVEN
HEART OF RYE
SURFAX

2201 **Caravan Trading Company**
33300 Western Ave
Union City, CA 94587-2211 510-487-2600
Fax: 510-487-4100
Baked goods
President: Joseph Maroun Sr
VP Operations: William Maroun
Estimated Sales: $20-50 Million
Number Employees: 250-499

2202 **Carberry's Home Made Ice Cream**
3831 W Vine St
Kissimmee, FL 34741-4659
US 407-933-7343
jc@carberrysbakery.com
Processor of ice cream including pies and cheesecake
Owner: Sal Colaci
Estimated Sales: Less than $100,000
Number Employees: 1-4
Type of Packaging: Consumer, Food Service

2203 Carbolite Foods
1325 Newton Ave
Evansville, IN 47715 812-485-0002
Fax: 812-485-0002 888-524-3314
consumer@carbolitefoods.com
Manufacturer of low-carb items such as ice cream, soy shakes, zero-carb bake mix and low carb bread mix as well as low-carb candy bars, snack bars, candies and protein shakes.
President: Gerry Morrison
CEO: Jeff Greder
CFO: Mike Lish
VP: Roeland Polet
R&D/Quality Control: Gordon Brown
Marketing: William Dugan
Operations Manager: Scott Gagnon
Number Employees: 24
Number of Products: 75
Type of Packaging: Food Service
Brands:
Jolle Desserts

2204 Carbon's Golden Malted
4101 William Richardson Dr
South Bend, IN 46628-9485 574-247-2270
Fax: 574-247-2280 800-686-6258
retail@goldenmalted.com
www.goldenmalted.com
Manufacturer and market flour mix for pancakes and waffles
President: Rick Mc Keel
CFO: Robert Spencer
National Account Sales Manager: Thomas Anderson
VP Sales/Marketing: Robert Coquillard
Number Employees: 1-4

2205 Carbon's Golden Malted Pancake & Waffle Flour Mix
PO Box 71
Buchanan, MI 49107-0071 574-247-2270
Fax: 574-247-2280 800-253-0590
newcarbon@goldenmalted.com
www.goldenmalted.com
Manufacturer of gourmet malted pancake and waffle flour mixes.
President/CEO: Rick McKeel
CFO: Robert Spencer
VP Sales/Marketing: Robert Coquillard
National Account Sales Manager: Thomas Anderson
Estimated Sales: $10-20 Million
Number Employees: 1-4

2206 Carbonator Rental Service
6500 Eastwick Ave
Philadelphia, PA 19142 215-726-9100
Fax: 215-726-6367 800-220-3556
info@carbonatorrental.com
www.carbonatorrental.com
Processor of soda water syrups and bar mixes; wholesaler/distributor of beverage dispensing equipment
Chairman: Herbert Pincus
President: Andrew Pincus
Corporate Secretary: Susan Pincus
Estimated Sales: $4 Million
Number Employees: 32
Sq. footage: 40000

2207 Cardi Foods
1003 Sethcreek Drive
Fuquay Varina, NC 27526-5156 973-983-8818
Fax: 973-627-6273 schwcscs@cs.com
Yeast extracts, kosher flavors
Vice President: Charles Schweizer
Estimated Sales: $150,000
Number Employees: 1
Number of Brands: 5
Number of Products: 10
Type of Packaging: Consumer, Food Service
Brands:
CARDI C

2208 Cardinal Meat Specialists
2396 Stanfield Road
Mississauga, ON L4Y 1S1
Canada 905-672-1411
Fax: 905-672-0450 800-363-1439
www.cardinalmeats.com
Processor of hamburger patties and steaks
President: Brent Cator
Estimated Sales: $5-10 Million
Number Employees: 50-99
Type of Packaging: Food Service
Brands:
Cardinal Kettle
Roadhouse

2209 Cardinale Winery
7600 St. Helena Highway
Oakville, CA 94562-0328 707-948-2643
Fax: 707-944-2824 800-588-0279
info@cardinale.com www.cardinale.com
Wines
Manager: Chantal Leruitte
Winemaker: Christopher Carpenter
Vineyard Manager: Pete Richmond
Estimated Sales: $20-50 Million
Number Employees: 50-99

2210 Care Ingredients
3141 W North Ave
Melrose Park, IL 60160-1108 708-450-3260
Fax: 708-450-1034 www.kerryingredients.com
Processor of dry breading and baking mixes
Manager: Jim Braglia
Plant Manager: Jim Cisler
Estimated Sales: $20-50 Million
Number Employees: 100-249
Type of Packaging: Consumer, Food Service, Private Label, Bulk

2211 Caremoli USA
23959 580th Ave
Ames, IA 50010 515-233-1255
Fax: 515-233-2933
j.brandquist@caremoli-usa.com
www.caremoligroup.com
Ingredients of naturally processed grains, flours and fibers
President: Andrea Caremoli
Vice President: David Vitale
Director: Barry Nadler
Sales Manager: John Brandquist
Estimated Sales: $24 Million
Number Employees: 33

2212 Cargill
PO Box 9300
Minneapolis, MN 55440-9300 952-742-7575
Fax: 952-742-7393 800-227-4455
www.cargill.com
An international provider of food, agricultural and risk management products and services.
President: David MacLennan
Senior VP/CFO: David MacLennan
Corporate VP, Corporate Affairs: Bonnie Raquet
Number Employees: 10,000+
Parent Co: Cargill, Inc
Type of Packaging: Consumer, Food Service, Private Label, Bulk
Brands:
ANGUS PRIDE
BREAKFAST TAC-GO
CARMEL APPLE CINAMMON FRENCH TOAST
CERTIFIED ANGUS BEEF
CIRCLE T BEEF
COUNTRY CLASSIC
CULINARY EDGE
EGGS ASAP
ESL
EXCEL
EXCEL SUPREME
HONEYSUCKLE WHITE
JOBE'S
MEADOWLAND FARMS
OUR OWN KITCHEN
PECK/EXCEL
PRAIRIE GROVE FARMS
PREFERRED ANGUS BEEF
RANCHER'S REGISTRY ANGUS BEEF
RUMBA
SHADY BROOK FARMS
SKILLET FRITTATAS
SKILLET OMELETS
STERLING SILVER
STONESIDE PORK
SUN BREAK SCRAMBLED EGG MIX
SUNNY FRESH
SUNNY FRESH FREE
TENDER CHOICE
TENDER RIDGE ANGUS BEEF
THE BREAKFAST CLUB
TNT
VALLEY TRADITION BEEF
WIS-PAK FOODS

2213 Cargill Corn Milling
400 E Diehl Rd # 330
Naperville, IL 60563-3533 630-505-7788
Fax: 630-505-7840 800-344-1633
bill_gruber@cargill.com www.cargill.com
Processor of liquid and dry dextrose corn syrups, high fructose and high maltose corn syrups, sodium and potassium citrates, sodium and potassium benzoates, citric acid, starches and CO2; exporter of citric products
VP: Pete Richter
Marketing Manager: Diane Pederson
Estimated Sales: $ 20 - 50 Million
Number Employees: 20-49
Parent Co: Cargill Foods
Type of Packaging: Bulk

2214 Cargill Dry Corn Ingredients
616 S Jefferson St
Paris, IL 61944 217-465-5331
Fax: 217-463-1644 800-637-6481
www.cargill.com
Processor and exporter of milled corn products including crude oil, pre-gelatinized flour, meal, grits, masa, bran, etc
Manager: Rick Sims
Vice President: Mary Thompson
Research/Development Scientist: Dr. Ansui Xu
Quality Assurance Manager: Keith Smith
Estimated Sales: $50-100 Million
Number Employees: 250-499
Parent Co: Cargill Foods
Type of Packaging: Food Service, Private Label, Bulk
Other Locations:
Paris IL
Indianapolis IN
Minneapolis MN

2215 Cargill Flour Milling
12700 Whitewater Drive
Minneapolis, MN 55440 952-742-7575
Fax: 612-742-7934 800-227-4455
www.cargill.com
Processor and exporter of wheat flour
Chairman/CEO: Gregory Page
SVP/CFO: David MacLennan
Corporate VP R&D: Mallett
Corporate VP Human Resources: Peter Vrijsen
Estimated Sales: K
Number Employees: 10,000+
Parent Co: Cargill Foods
Type of Packaging: Consumer, Food Service, Private Label, Bulk

2216 (HQ)Cargill Foods
P.O.Box 9300
Minneapolis, MN 55440-9300 952-742-7575
Fax: 952-742-7393 800-227-4455
info@cargill.com www.cargill.com
Cargill has operations in about 70 countries. It has five business units- Agriculture Services; Food Ingredients and Applications; Industrial, Origination and Processing; Risk Management and Financial; and Industrial.
Chairman/CEO: Gregory Page
SVP/CFO: David MacLennan
Estimated Sales: $100-500 Million
Number Employees: 10,000 +
Type of Packaging: Food Service, Private Label

2217 Cargill Foods
505 S Old Missouri Road
Springdale, AR 72764-4715 479-750-6816
www.honeysucklewhite.com
Turkey products
President: John O'Carroll
Controller: Mike Peirson
Director Sales/Marketing: Lin Lauve
Operations Manager: Andy Southerly
Estimated Sales: $ 10 - 20 Million
Number Employees: 10-19
Type of Packaging: Private Label
Brands:
HONEYSUCKLE WHITE
MEDALLION
PLANTATION
RIVERSIDE

2218 Cargill Juice Products
100 E 6th Street
Frostproof, FL 33843-2300 863-635-2211
Fax: 863-635-8180 800-227-4455
jon_hysell@cargill.com www.carillfoods.com

Juice and juice ingredients, essential oils and orange essence
President: Martin Dudley
VP: Tom Abrahamson
Sales Director: Pat Rain
Estimated Sales: $100-500 Million
Number Employees: 100-249
Type of Packaging: Private Label

2219 **Cargill Meat Solutions**
480 Coop Dr
Timberville, VA 22853 540-896-7041
Fax: 540-896-6625 www.cargill.com
Processor and exporter of cooked turkey and chicken products including salami, bologna and ham; also, breasts
Plant Manager: Wesley Carter
Operations Manager: Milt McPike
Purchasing Agent: George Miller
Estimated Sales: $300,000-500,000
Number Employees: 1-4
Sq. footage: 112708
Parent Co: Rocco
Type of Packaging: Consumer, Food Service, Private Label
Other Locations:
Rocco Quality Foods
Edinburg VA

2220 **Cargill Meats**
4700 North 132nd St
Milwaukee, WI 53201-2006 414-645-6500
Fax: 414-645-6762 800-558-4242
www.cargill.com
Manufacturer, importer and exporter of boxed and processed beef
President: Bill Rupp
Controller: Richard Cundy
VP R&D: Thomas Rourke PhD
VP Public Affairs: Robert Segel
Estimated Sales: $100-500 Million
Number Employees: 1,000-4,999
Parent Co: Excel Corporation
Type of Packaging: Consumer, Food Service
Brands:
BERNHARDT PECK
COUNTRY CLASSICS
DELI RITE
EMMBER CLASSIC
EMMBER COUNTRY CLASSIC
EMMBER COUNTRY MAGIC
EMMBER DELI RITE
EMMBER FAT FREE LEAN 'N TENDER
EMMBER HEARTY CLASSIC
EMMBER LEAN 'N TENDER
EMMBER OUR OWN KITCHEN
EMMBER REDI-ROAST
EMMBER THICK 'N TENDER
EMMBER TONIGHT'S CHOICE
HEARTY CLASSICS
OUR OWN KITCHEN
PECK MEAT PACKING
THICK N' TENDER
TONIGHT'S CHOICE

2221 **Cargill Refined Oils**
PO Box 5625
Minneapolis, MN 55440-5625 952-742-6782
Fax: 208-522-0794 800-323-6232
willie_loh@cargill.com
www.clearvalleyoils.com
Salad and cooking oils, frying and baking shortenings, soybean, winterized soybean, corn, cottonseed, canola, creamy liquid soybean and canola oil, pan and grill oil, peanut oil, all-purpose, animal and vegetable blends, and flavoredroll-in
Sales: Stephanie Quah

2222 **Cargill Specialty Oils**
P.O.Box 9300
Minneapolis, MN 55440-9300 952-742-7575
Fax: 952-742-5503 800-851-8331
www.cargill.com
Manufacturer of specialty cooking and ingredient oils
CEO: Gregory R Page
Marketing Director: Connie Tobin
Estimated Sales: K
Number Employees: 10,000+
Parent Co: Cargill Foods
Type of Packaging: Food Service, Bulk
Brands:
Clear Valley Oils
Elitra Premium Vegtable Oils
Odessey Oils
Popwise Oils

2223 **Cargill Sweeteners**
P.O.Box 5621
Minneapolis, MN 55440-5621 952-984-8280
Fax: 952-984-3256 800-227-4455
cargillfoods@cargill.com www.cargillsalt.com
Dry sweeteners, food starches, high fructose corn syrup
President: Mike Venker
President/COO: Gregory Page
Senior VP/Director Corporate Affairs: Robin Johnson
C.V.P. Public Affairs: Bonnie Raquet
Estimated Sales: less than $ 500,000
Number Employees: 10,000+
Number of Products: 19

2224 **Cargill Texturizing Solutions**
308 6th Avenue SE
Cedar Rapids, IA 52401 319-399-3627
Fax: 319-399-6170 877-650-7080
For Cultures & Enzymes: 800-342-5724; For Hydrocolloids & Blends: 800-241-9485
www.cargilltexturizing.com
Supplier of texturizing and emulsifiers to the global food and beverage industry, as well as the pharmaceutical and cosmetics markets.
President: Ralph Apple
R&D: Joe Holtwick
Marketing: Jim Kubczak
Sales: Andy Dederich
Operations: Bernard Cerles
Plant Manager: Mike Rizor
Number Employees: 100-249
Parent Co: Cargill Inc
Type of Packaging: Food Service, Bulk
Brands:
ActiStar
Amylogel
Aubygum
Battercrisp
Biogarde
Cargill Dry MD
Cargill Dry Set
Cargill Gel
Cargill Set
Cargill Tex
Clean Set
Cream Gel
Cream Tex
Daritech
Deli Tex
EZ Fill
Em Cap
Em Tex
Emulfluid
Emulpur
Flanogen
HiForm
Polar Tex
Prolia
Prosante
Pulp Tex
Salioca
Satiagel
Satialgine
Satiaxane
Stabi Tex
Topcithin
Unipectine
ViscoGum

2225 **Cargill Vegetable Oils**
5858 Park Ave
Minneapolis, MN 55417-3120 612-378-0551
Fax: 612-742-5503 www.crcmeetings.com
Processor of vegetable and soybean oils; also, soybean meal
Owner: Lisa Cargill
National Accounts Sales: Bill Bohmer
Estimated Sales: $300,000-500,000
Number Employees: 1-4
Parent Co: Cargill Foods
Type of Packaging: Bulk

2226 **Cargill Worldwide Acidulants**
400 E Diehl Rd # 330
Naperville, IL 60563-3533 630-505-7788
Fax: 630-505-7840 800-344-1633
tim_bauer@cargill.com www.cargill.com
Food acidulants
VP: Pete Richter
Director Sales/Marketing: Tim Bauer
Estimated Sales: $100-500 Million
Number Employees: 20-49
Parent Co: Cargill Foods
Type of Packaging: Bulk

2227 **Caribbean Coffee Company**
495 Pine Ave, Ste A
Goleta, CA 93117 805-962-3201
Fax: 805-692-2600 800-932-5282
info@caribbeancoffee.com
www.caribbeancoffee.com
Specialty coffee and tea
President: John Goerke
Marketing Manager: Putnam Fairbanks
Estimated Sales: $20-50 Million
Number Employees: 10-19
Type of Packaging: Private Label

2228 **Caribbean Cookie Company**
515 Central Drive
Suite 103
Virginia Beach, VA 23454-5274 757-631-6767
Fax: 757-631-1725 800-326-5200
jumbia@norfold.infi.net
www.caribbeancookie.com
Gourmet cookies
President: Charles Phelps
Marketing Director: Leo Palomo
Estimated Sales: $1-2.5 Million
Number Employees: 10-19

2229 **Caribbean Food Delights**
117 Route 303
Suite B
Tappan, NY 10983 845-398-3000
Fax: 845-398-3001
customerservice@caribbeanfooddelights.com
www.caribbeanfooddelights.com
Manufacturer and exporter of Jamaican baked goods including breads, fruit cakes and buns; also, beef, chicken and vegetable patties, jerk chicken, sausage, curried goat, rice, peas, etc
President, CEO: Vincent HoSang
CEO: Vincent Hosang
Estimated Sales: $10-20 Million
Number Employees: 20-49
Sq. footage: 60000
Parent Co: Royal Caribbean Bakery
Type of Packaging: Consumer, Food Service, Private Label, Bulk

2230 **Caribbean Products**
3624 Falls Rd Ste 2
Baltimore, MD 21211 410-235-7700
Fax: 410-235-1513 www.loyoladonsalumni.com
Manufacturer and also processor and packager of beef and pork products.
President: Brian Hartman
Vice President: Mark Sheubrooks
Controller: Alan Wilner
Estimated Sales: $ 13 Million
Number Employees: 20-49
Type of Packaging: Consumer, Food Service

2231 **Caribou Coffee Company**
9638 Colorado Ln N
Brooklyn Ctr, MN 55445 763-488-1506
Fax: 763-592-2300 888-227-4268
www.cariboucoffee.com
Coffee
CEO: Michael Coles
CFO: George Mileusnic
CEO: Michael Tattersfield
VP R&D: Eddie Boyle
VP Marketing: Chris Toal
Sales Director: Henry Stein
Estimated Sales: $10-20 Million
Number Employees: 14
Parent Co: Arcapita Inc

2232 **(HQ)Carl Buddig & Company**
950 175th St
Homewood, IL 60430 708-798-0900
Fax: 708-798-3178 800-621-0868
buddigconsumers@buddig.com
www.buddig.com

Processor and exporter of luncheon meats including chipped beef, ham, turkey, chicken, pastrami and turkey ham; also, specialty sausage and meat snacks
President: John Buddig
CEO: Robert Buddig
Executive VP: Tom Budding
Quality Control: Joe Buchanan
Estimated Sales: $200-250 Million
Number Employees: 800
Number of Brands: 6
Type of Packaging: Consumer, Food Service, Private Label, Bulk
Brands:
BUDDIG ORIGINAL
BUDDIG PREMIUM LEAN SLICES
BUDDIG VALUE PACK

2233 **Carl Colteryahn Dairy**
1601 Brownsville Rd
Pittsburgh, PA 15210 412-881-1408
Fax: 412-881-0460 www.colteryahndairy.com
Milk, cream and juices
Owner: Carl Colteryahn
Director: Frank Dean
Estimated Sales: $1 Million
Number Employees: 50

2234 **Carl Rittberger Sr.**
1900 Lutz Ln
Zanesville, OH 43701 740-452-2767
Fax: 740-452-6001 info@rittbergermeats.com
www.rittbergermeats.com
Processor of beef and pork
President: Andrew Rittberger
VP: George Rittberger
VP Sales: Mark McCabe
Estimated Sales: $4.5 Million
Number Employees: 32
Sq. footage: 100000
Type of Packaging: Consumer, Bulk

2235 **Carl Streit & Son Company**
P.O.Box 157
Neptune, NJ 7754 732-775-0803
Fax: 732-775-2274 www.carlstreit.com
Processor and wholesaler/distributor of poultry, Italian sausage and special cuts of beef, lamb, veal and pork
Owner: Jim Robinson Jr Jr
VP: Judith Robinson
Estimated Sales: $10-20 Million
Number Employees: 5-9
Sq. footage: 4000
Brands:
Allen
Hatfield

2236 **Carl Venezia Meats**
1007 Germantown Pike
Plymouth Meeting, PA 19462-2449 610-239-6750
Fax: 610-239-6751 www.carlveneziameats.com
Processor and packer of meat
President: Carl Venezia
Sales Manager: Don Venezia
Estimated Sales: $500,000
Number Employees: 1-4

2237 **Carla's Pasta**
50 Talbot Ln
South Windsor, CT 06074 860-436-4042
Fax: 860-436-4073 800-957-2782
info@carlaspasta.com www.carlaspasta.com
Processor of frozen pastas including ravioli and lasagna as well as sauces
President: Carla Squatrito
Director Sales: Sandro Squatrito
Manager, Productions: Sergio Squatrito
Estimated Sales: $21.20 Million
Number Employees: 50-99
Sq. footage: 13000
Type of Packaging: Food Service, Private Label, Bulk

2238 **Carlisle Cereal Company**
P.O.Box 2775
Bismarck, ND 58502 701-222-3531
Fax: 701-222-3531 800-809-6018
chuck@hometownstars.com
www.hometownstars.com
Cereal
President: Charles Fleming
Estimated Sales: $1 Million
Number Employees: 5-9
Type of Packaging: Private Label
Brands:
Hometown Stars

2239 **Carlson Vineyards**
461 35 Rd
Palisade, CO 81526-9518 970-464-5554
Fax: 970-464-5442 888-464-5554
www.carlsonvineyards.com
Wines
President: Parker Carlson
Estimated Sales: $1-2.5 Million
Number Employees: 5-9

2240 **Carlson Vitamins**
15 W College Dr
Arlington Hts, IL 60004-1985 847-255-1600
Fax: 847-255-1605 888-234-5656
carlson@carlsonlabs.com www.carlsonlabs.com
Full line of nutritional food supplements and fish oils
President: John Carlson
CEO: Susan Carlson
CFO: Trish Lange
Vice President: Robert Meyer
Quality Control: Melissa Wilson
Marketing Coordinator: Carilyn Anderson
Sales Director: Vicki Accardi
Public Relations: Kirsten Meyer
Operations Manager: Robert Meyer
Production Manager: Michael Anderson
Purchasing Manager: Lindy Eck
Estimated Sales: $ 50 - 100 Million
Number Employees: 100-249
Number of Brands: 2
Number of Products: 275
Sq. footage: 40000

2241 **Carlton Farms**
P.O.Box 580
Carlton, OR 97111 503-852-7166
Fax: 503-852-6263 800-932-0946
www.carltonfarms.com
Processor of meats
President, CEO: John Duyn
Director Food Safety & Food Quality: Jacob Burns
Sales Manager: Forrest Peterson
Plant Manager: Bill Orton
Estimated Sales: $10 Million
Number Employees: 75

2242 **Carmadhy's Foods**
282 Marsland Drive
Waterloo, ON N2J 3Z1
Canada 519-746-0551
Fax: 519-746-0280 carol@carmadhys.ca
www.carmadhys.ca
Processor of flavored popcorn including caramel, butter, cheese, white cheddar, pizza, barbecue, ranch, salt and vinegar, sour cream and onion, dill pickle, jalapeno, custom packaging and popcorn seasoning
Proprietor: Dave Charlton
Number Employees: 5-9
Sq. footage: 4500
Type of Packaging: Consumer, Private Label, Bulk
Brands:
Country Style
Olde Fashioned

2243 **Carmel Meat/Specialty Foods**
3345 Paul Davis Dr
Marina, CA 93933 831-883-3555
Fax: 831-883-3599 800-298-5823
www.sierrameat.com
Processor of lamb, beef, poultry, veal, game and seafood
Manager: Jim Pryor
VP Marketing: Janetta Lucas
VP Sales: Bob Furter
Estimated Sales: $50-100 Million
Number Employees: 50-99
Type of Packaging: Food Service

2244 **Carmela Vineyards**
P.O.Box 790
Glenns Ferry, ID 83623 208-366-2313
Fax: 208-366-2458 info@carmelavineyards.com
www.carmelawinery.com
Wines
Manager: Neil Glancey
Winemaker: Neil Glancy
Estimated Sales: $1-2.5 Million
Number Employees: 20-49

2245 **Carmela's Gourmet**
415 English Ave
Monterey, CA 93940-3810 831-373-6291
Fax: 831-375-5313
carmelasgourmet@comcast.net
www.carmelasgourmet.com
Salad dressings
Owner: Carmela Cantisani
Co-Owner: Carmela Cantisani
Estimated Sales: Under $500,000
Number Employees: 1-4
Type of Packaging: Private Label
Brands:
Carmela's

2246 **Carmelita Provisions Company**
2901 W Floral Dr
Monterey Park, CA 91754-3626 323-262-6751
Fax: 323-262-3503 www.carmelitachorizo.com
Processor of pigs' feet including crackling and pickled; also, chorizo
Owner: Mario Lopez
Estimated Sales: $ .5 - 1 million
Number Employees: 20-49
Type of Packaging: Consumer, Food Service

2247 **(HQ)Carmi Flavor & Fragrance Company**
6030 Scott Way
City of Commerce, CA 90040 323-888-9240
Fax: 323-888-9339 800-421-9647
sales@carmiflavors.com www.carmiflavors.com
Manufacturer of high quality natural and artificial flavors in liquid or powder form; supplier of packaging products.
President: Eliot Carmi
CEO: Frank Carmi
Sales: Bruce Rutenburg
Plant Manager: Roger Speakman
Purchasing Director: Judy Montgomery
Estimated Sales: $12 Million
Number Employees: 40
Number of Brands: 1
Number of Products: 500
Sq. footage: 30000
Type of Packaging: Private Label, Bulk
Other Locations:
Carmi Flavor & Fragrance
Port Coquitlam, Canada
Carmi Flavor & Fragrance
Waverly LA
Brands:
CARMI FLAVORS
FLAVOR DEPOT

2248 **Carmine's Bakery**
2100 Country Club Road
Sanford, FL 32771-4051 407-324-1200
Fax: 407-324-1209 marlafrede@aol.com
Baked goods

2249 **Carneros Creek Winery**
P.O.Box 6828
Napa, CA 94581-1828 707-253-9464
Fax: 707-253-9465 wineinfo@carneroscreek.com
www.mahoneyvineyards.com
Wines
President: Francis Mahoney
Winemaker: Ken Foster
Vice President: Scot Rich
Sales Director: Hadden Guridie
Plant Manager: Greg Opitz
Estimated Sales: $5-10 Million
Number Employees: 10-19
Type of Packaging: Bulk
Brands:
CARNEROS
CARNEROS CREEK
COTE DE CARNEROS
FLEUR DE CARNEROS

2250 **Carnival Brands**
535 S Clark St
New Orleans, LA 70119-7007 504-734-8851
Fax: 504-734-5886 800-925-2774
gumboking@aol.com www.carnivalbrands.com

Processor of French bisques, alligator sauce piquante, dry seasoning, boneless stuffed chicken, sauce mix and seafood entrees including gumbo, crab and shrimp cakes, shrimp Creole and crawfish etouffee
President: Raymond Rathle Jr
Vice President: Stephen Scott
Marketing: E Alexander Stafford
Public Relations: Simone Rathle
Estimated Sales: $1-2.5 Million
Number Employees: 12
Sq. footage: 7000
Type of Packaging: Consumer, Food Service
Brands:
Baby Cakes
Carnival Cajun Classics
Chef Creole
Zipp

2251 **Caro Foods**
2324 Bayou Blue Rd
Houma, LA 70364 985-858-2640
Fax: 985-876-0825 www.carofoods.com
Fresh meat and produce, canned and dry goods.
President: Ricky Thibodaux
Human Resources: Mike Latour
Number Employees: 100-249
Parent Co: Performance Food Group Company
Brands:
HERITAGE OVENS

2252 **Carob Tree**
1008 N Santa Anita Ave
Arcadia, CA 91006 626-445-0215
Fax: 626-445-0215 thecarobtree@earthlink.net
Natural groceries and vitamins
Owner: Hyun Chung
Estimated Sales: $160,000
Number Employees: 1-4
Type of Packaging: Consumer, Bulk

2253 **Carol Hall's Hot PepperJelly**
330 N Main St
Fort Bragg, CA 95437-3406 707-961-1899
Fax: 707-961-0879 866-737-7379
hall@mcn.org www.hotpepperjelly.com
Jams and condiments
President: Carol Hall
CFO: Albert Hall
Marketing Director: John Temples
Production Manager: Bill Hall
Estimated Sales: $1-2.5 Million
Number Employees: 5-9
Type of Packaging: Private Label

2254 **Carol Lee Products**
920 E 30th St
Lawrence, KS 66046 785-842-5489
Processor of blended mixes for bakery products including yeast raised and cake doughnuts, danish, breads and cookies
President: O Lee Scott
VP: Agnes Scott
Number Employees: 4
Sq. footage: 9330
Type of Packaging: Consumer
Brands:
Carol Lee

2255 **Carol's Country Cuisine**
2546 Warm Springs Road
Glen Ellen, CA 95442-8712 707-996-1124
Fax: 707-996-1124 carolco@vom.com
www.carolscountrycuisine.com
Marinades, dressings, sauces
Partner: Carol Frankenfield
Sales Director: Susan Wise
Production Manager: Carol Frankenfield
Estimated Sales: $5-10 Million
Number Employees: 5-9
Type of Packaging: Private Label

2256 **Carole's Cheesecake Company**
1272 Castlefield Avenue
Toronto, ON M6B 1G3
Canada 416-256-0000
Fax: 416-256-0001 info@carolescheesecake.com
www.carolescheesecake.com
Processor of cheesecakes including praline, lemon, blueberry, raspberry and strawberry; also, pies, low-fat salad dressings, pasta sauces and toppings for cakes and ice cream; exporter of cakes and salad dressings; vegetarian soups
President: Carole Ogus
CFO: Alexander Ogus
Executive VP: Michael Ogus
Estimated Sales: $1-5 Million
Number Employees: 30
Number of Brands: 2
Number of Products: 160
Sq. footage: 15000
Type of Packaging: Consumer, Food Service, Private Label, Bulk
Brands:
CAROLE'S
CAROLE'S TOPS
POSITIVELY BLUEBERRY
POSITIVELY PRALINES
POSITIVELY STRAWBERRY

2257 **Carolina Atlantic Seafood Enterprises**
PO Box 158
Beaufort, NC 28516-0158 252-504-2663
Fax: 252-726-7097 case@mail.clis.com
Processor of frozen seafood
President: Doug Brady
CEO: Walter C Brady
Estimated Sales: $5-10 Million
Number Employees: 10-19
Type of Packaging: Private Label
Brands:
Carolina Atlantic Seafood

2258 **(HQ)Carolina Beverage Corporation**
1413 Jake Alexander Blvd S
Salisbury, NC 28146 704-637-5881
Fax: 704-633-7491 custserv@cheerwine.com
www.cheerwine.com
Processor of syrups and beverage concentrates; exporter of soft drinks and concentrates; wholesaler/distributor of soft drinks and water
President: Cliff Ritchie
CFO: Tommy Page
CIO: Bill Barten
VP Operations: David Swaim
Estimated Sales: $10-20 Million
Number Employees: 25
Sq. footage: 25000
Parent Co: Cheerwine & Diet Cheerwine
Type of Packaging: Consumer
Other Locations:
Carolina Beverage Corp.
Hickory NC
Carolina Beverage Corp.
Greenville SC
Brands:
CHEERWINE
CHEERWINE SOFT DRINK
DIET CHEERWINE
SAVAGE ENERGY

2259 **Carolina Blueberry Association**
11421 Us Highway 701 N
Garland, NC 28441 910-588-4355
Fax: 910-588-4093
dennis@carolinablueberry.com
www.carolinablueberry.com
Manufacturer of fresh and frozen blueberries
General Manager: Dennis Harrell
Process Manager: Steve Kuepker
Estimated Sales: Under $500,000
Number Employees: 1-4
Type of Packaging: Consumer, Food Service, Bulk
Brands:
BONNIE BLUE

2260 **Carolina Brewery**
460 W Franklin St
Chapel Hill, NC 27516 919-942-1800
Fax: 919-942-1809 www.carolinabrewery.com
Processor of ale, stout and lager
Owner: Robert Poitras
Co-Owner: Chris Rice
Estimated Sales: $2.5-5 Million
Number Employees: 50-99
Sq. footage: 8000
Type of Packaging: Consumer, Food Service, Bulk
Brands:
Copperline Amber
Franklin Street
Old North State

2261 **Carolina By-Products Company**
P.O. Box 3588
Winchester, VA 22604-2586 540-877-2590
Fax: 540-877-3215 www.valleyproteins.com
Processor and exporter of rendering meats including poultry and bone meal; also, by-products
President: Gerald Smith Jr.
Vp Finance: Kirby Brown
Vice President: Michael Smith
Estimated Sales: $ 50 - 100 Million
Number Employees: 20-49
Parent Co: Valley Proteins, Inc.
Type of Packaging: Food Service, Bulk

2262 **Carolina Classic Catfish**
P.O.Box 10
Ayden, NC 28513-0010 252-746-2818
Fax: 252-746-3947 www.cccatfish.com
Processor of fresh and frozen catfish
President: Robert Mayo
Sales Manager: Doug Doering
Sales Manager: Jeff Betcher
General Manager: Mike McCready
Controller: Mark Lomis
Estimated Sales: $20-50 Million
Number Employees: 100-249
Type of Packaging: Consumer, Food Service
Brands:
Carolina Classics

2263 **Carolina Cookie Company**
1010 Arnold Street
Greensboro, NC 27405 336-294-2100
Fax: 336-294-9537 800-447-5797
gary@carolinacookie.com
www.carolinacookie.com
Cookies
Owner/President: Gary Smith
Estimated Sales: $3,000,000
Number Employees: 20
Sq. footage: 12000

2264 **Carolina Cracker**
P.O.Box 374
Garner, NC 27529-0374 919-779-6899
Fax: 919-779-6899 www.carolinacracker.net
Manufacturer of nut crackers for soft shell nuts, shelled pecans in bulk
President: Dot Woodruff
CEO: Harold Woodruff
Estimated Sales: $1-2.5 Million
Number Employees: 10-19
Number of Brands: 3
Sq. footage: 1
Type of Packaging: Bulk
Brands:
The Carolina Cracker

2265 **Carolina Culinary**
1964 Old Dunbar Road
West Columbia, SC 29172-3922 803-739-8920
Fax: 843-739-8920
Processor of value-added poultry and cooked bone-in, breaded and roasted chicken
President: Sheldon Phillips
Manager: Ellen Burgin
Manager: Bob Harris
Estimated Sales: $50 Million
Number Employees: 300

2266 **Carolina Cupboard**
505 Eno St
Hillsborough, NC 27278 919-245-1654
Fax: 800-646-1118 800-400-3441
customerservice@carolinacupboard.com
www.southernseason.com
Cheesestraws, BBQ sauces, lemon drops, cookies, jams and jellies
Owner: Michael Barefoot
Marketing Director: Deborah Miller
Brands:
Carolina Cupboard

2267 **Carolina Fine Snack Foods**
209 Citation Ct
Greensboro, NC 27409-9026 336-605-0773
Fax: 336-605-0721
Nutrional snacks
President: Phil Kosak
Estimated Sales: $2.5-5 Million
Number Employees: 5-9

2268 **Carolina Foods**
1807 S Tryon St
Charlotte, NC 28203 704-333-9812
Fax: 704-940-0040 800-234-0441
Processor of baked goods including sweet rolls, fresh and frozen fried pies, yeast raised doughnuts and cakes, fruit turnovers and pie dough.
President: Kathryn Scarborough
Vice President: Paul Scarborough
Marketing Director: Paul Deer
Plant Manager/Operations: Bob Schumacher
General Manager: Kent Byrom
Purchasing Manager: Joanna Houchins
Estimated Sales: $20-50 Million
Number Employees: 250-499
Sq. footage: 110000
Type of Packaging: Consumer, Food Service, Private Label
Brands:
DUCHESS
O'BOY
SUNBEAM

2269 **Carolina Ingredients**
1595 Cedar Line Drive
Rock Hill, SC 29730 803-323-6550
Fax: 803-323-6535
sales@carolinaingredients.com
www.carolinaingredients.com
ingredients
President: Doug Meyer-Cuno
Sales/Marketing Direcotr: Allen Heavey
Production Manager: Richard Dawes
Purchasing Director: Glenn Shishido

2270 **Carolina Packers**
P.O.Box 1109
Smithfield, NC 27577 919-934-2181
Fax: 919-989-6794 800-682-7675
info@carolinapackers.com
www.carolinapackers.com
Processor of hot dogs, bologna and smoked sausage and ham.
President: John Johnes Jr
Controller: Linwood Thornton II
VP: Hilton Byrd
Plant Manager: Johnny Hayes
Estimated Sales: $20-50 Million
Number Employees: 50-99
Type of Packaging: Consumer
Brands:
BRIGHTLEAF

2271 **Carolina Pride Foods**
1 Packer Avenue
Greenwood, SC 29646-3460 864-229-5611
Fax: 864-330-1118 cpridesales@emeraldis.com
www.carolinaprideonline.com
Manufacturer of fresh pork and bacon, smoked meats and processed luncheon meats including deli loaves and bologna; exporter of skinned jowls, pork kidneys, liver and stomachs, flat belly skins, etc
CEO/President: William Barnette Jr
CFO: Mark Litts
Vice President: Lee Miles
VP Procurement: Thomas Jackson
Estimated Sales: $100 Million
Number Employees: 850
Sq. footage: 450000
Type of Packaging: Consumer, Food Service, Private Label, Bulk
Brands:
CAROLINA PRIDE
COTTAGE BRAND
GREENWOOD
GREENWOOD FARMS

2272 **Carolina Pride Products**
24488 Nc Highway 561
Enfield, NC 27823 252-445-3154
Fax: 252-445-1033
Processor of sweet potatoes
President: Jake Taylor
Estimated Sales: $1-2.5 Million
Number Employees: 1-4
Brands:
Carolina Pride

2273 **Carolina Products**
1990 Hood Rd
Greer, SC 29650-1011 864-879-3084
Fax: 864-877-5736 cliffstar@cliffstar.com
www.cliffstar.com
Processor of bottled apple juice
President, CEO: Sean McGirr
Branch Manager: Chris Nielson
Quality Control: Angela Lewis
VP Human Resources: Dawn Vousboukis
Purchasing: Dennis Jones
Estimated Sales: $10-20 Million
Number Employees: 20-49
Sq. footage: 29000
Parent Co: Cliffstar
Type of Packaging: Consumer, Private Label
Brands:
CAROLINA GOLD

2274 **Carolina Seafoods**
P.O.Box 396
Mc Clellanville, SC 29458 843-887-3713
Fax: 843-887-3318
Manufacturer and importer of seafood including shrimp, oysters and clams
President: Rutledge Leland
Estimated Sales: $5-10 Million
Number Employees: 10-19
Sq. footage: 10000
Type of Packaging: Consumer

2275 **Carolina Treet**
Po Box 1017
Wilmington, NC 28402 910-762-1950
Fax: 910-762-1438 800-616-6344
info@carolinatreet.com www.carolinatreet.com
Processor and importer of barbecue sauce, condiments, syrups, brewed tea, bar mixes and beverage concentrates
President: Joe King
Vice President: Lenwood King
General Manager: Allen Finberg
Estimated Sales: $1.4 Million
Number Employees: 13
Number of Brands: 5
Number of Products: 20
Sq. footage: 20000
Type of Packaging: Consumer, Food Service, Private Label, Bulk
Brands:
AUNT BERTIE'S
CAROLINA TREET

2276 **Carolina Turkeys**
1628 Garner Chapel Rd
Mount Olive, NC 28365 919-658-6743
Fax: 919-658-5865 800-523-4559
jcoleman@carolinaturkeys.com
www.carolinaturkeys.com
Manufacturer and exporter of fresh and frozen turkey
President/CEO: C Daniel Blackshear
CFO: Ed Kascuta
CEO: Keith Shoemaker
Estimated Sales: $330 Million
Number Employees: 1,000-4,999
Type of Packaging: Consumer, Food Service
Brands:
CAROLINA TURKEYS

2277 **Carolyn Candies**
PO Box 120861
Clermont, FL 34712-0861 352-394-8555
Fax: 877-394-3452

2278 **Carolyn's Caribbean Heat**
283 Boot Road
Malvern, PA 19355-3315 610-647-0336
Processor of hot sauces and condiments; also, importer of sauces, condiments and ingredients for production
Owner: Carolyn Thomas
Sales Manager: Robert Thomas
Number Employees: 1-4
Sq. footage: 500
Brands:
Carolyn's Caribbean Heat

2279 **Carolyn's Gourmet**
40 Beharrell St Ste 2
Concord, MA 1742 978-369-2940
Fax: 978-371-0639 800-656-2940
Pecans, walnuts, peanuts, English toffee, chocolate bars
President: Hans van Putten
Executive VP: Tracey van Putten
Estimated Sales: $5-10 Million
Number Employees: 5-9
Parent Co: 40ParkLake, LLC
Type of Packaging: Consumer, Private Label, Bulk
Brands:
TULIP

2280 **Carothers Research Laboratories**
2438 Corunna Rd
Flint, MI 48503-3359 810-235-2055
Edible fats and oils
Manager: Marie Killein
Estimated Sales: $5-9.9 Million
Number Employees: 1-4

2281 **Carousel Cakes**
11 Seeger Dr
Nanuet, NY 10954 845-627-2323
Fax: 845-627-0258 800-659-2253
www.carouselcakes.com
Processor of fresh and frozen cakes, mousse, cheesecakes and pies, kosher pdairy and non-dairy products
Owner: David Finkelstein
Estimated Sales: $500,000-$1 Million
Number Employees: 10-19
Type of Packaging: Consumer, Food Service
Brands:
Carousel Cakes

2282 **Carousel Candies**
2248 Gary Lane
Geneva, IL 60134 630-232-2500
Fax: 630-232-2528 888-656-1552
info@silvestrisweets.com
www.carouselcandy.com
Processor of candy including caramel, caramel apples, caramel sauce, chocolates, chocolate covered strawberries, gift boxes, gift baskets, assortments, bulk, and special occasion gift bags for holidays and special events.
President/CEO: Mary Jane Silvestri
Vice President: Andy Silvestri
Estimated Sales: $2.5-5 Million
Number Employees: 10-19
Type of Packaging: Food Service, Bulk
Brands:
CAROUSEL

2283 **Carr Cheese Factory/GileCheese Company**
116 N Main St
Cuba City, WI 53807 608-744-8455
Fax: 608-744-3457
Cheese and cheese products
Owner: John Gile
Owner: Diane Gile
Estimated Sales: $2.5-5 Million
Number Employees: 1-4

2284 **Carr Valley Cheese Company**
S3797 County Road G
La Valle, WI 53941 608-986-2781
Fax: 608-986-2906 800-462-7258
www.carrvalleychesse.com
Monterey jack, cheddar and colby cheese
President: Sid Cook
Vice President: Nancy Cook
Estimated Sales: $15 Million
Number Employees: 25

2285 **Carrabassett Coffee Roasters**
P.O.Box 197
Kingfield, ME 04947 207-265-2326
Fax: 207-265-3527 888-292-2326
info@carrabassettcoffee.com
www.carrabassettcoffee.com
Roaster and wholesaler of coffee
President: Tom Hildreth
CEO: Steve Skaling
Estimated Sales: $450,000
Number Employees: 5-9
Number of Brands: 35
Number of Products: 1
Sq. footage: 1800
Type of Packaging: Bulk
Brands:
35

2286 **Carriage Charles**
196 Newton St
Fredonia, NY 14063-1354 716-673-1000
Fax: 716-679-702 800-462-125
www.carriagehousecos.com
Sauces and dressings
President: Richard Koulouris
President, Co-CEO: David Skarie

Estimated Sales: $50-100 Million
Number Employees: 900
Parent Co: Ralcorp
Brands:
BEAZUR
FARM KING
RED WING

2287 **Carriage House Companies**
196 Newton St
Fredonia, NY 14063 716-673-1000
Fax: 716-679-7702 800-462-8125
klanacm@carriagehousecos.com
www.carriagehousecos.com
Manufacturer and exporter of preserves and jellies, peanut butter, pasta sauce, salad dressing, table syrup, flavored syrup, barbecue sauce, mexican sauce, steak sauce/marinade, and cocktail sauce.
President: Richard Koulouris
VP/Controller: Daniel Zoellner
VP/Operations: Tim Bender
Director/Information Technology: G A Woznak
VP/Quality & Product Safety: Dan Ludwig
VP/Marketintg: Mike Klanac
VP/Retail Sales: David Funk
Corporate VP/Director Human Resources: Jack Owczarczak
VP/Manufacturing: Mark Chamberlain
Director/Purchasing: Robert Vojslavek
Estimated Sales: $389.2 Million
Number Employees: 1500
Sq. footage: 16000
Parent Co: Ralcorp Holdings, Inc.
Type of Packaging: Consumer, Food Service, Private Label, Bulk
Other Locations:
Carriage House Companies - Plant Dunkirk NY
Carriage House Companies - Plant Streator IL
Carriage House Companies - Plant Buckner KY
Brands:
BOB WHITE
CHICKEN 'N' RIBS
CHICKEN 'N' RIBS PREMIUM
KING SYRUP
MAPLE RICH
ROBB ROSS DRESSINGS
SAUCE ARTURO

2288 **Carriage House Foods**
1131 Dayton Ave
Ames, IA 50010 515-232-2273
Fax: 515-232-3003 www.carriagehousefoods.com
Processor of frozen meat products
President: Jerry Grauf
Plant Manager: Jim Ringelstetter
Estimated Sales: $7.5 Million
Number Employees: 35
Type of Packaging: Consumer, Food Service, Private Label
Brands:
Carriage House

2289 **Carrie's Chocolates**
9216-63 Avenue
Edmonton, AB T6E 0G3
Canada 780-435-7900
877-778-2462
carrie@compusmart.ab.ca
www.candybarwrapper.ca
Processor and exporter of handmade novelty and gift chocolates, promotional bars, and wedding candy
Owner: Carrie MacKenzie
Number Employees: 2
Sq. footage: 450
Type of Packaging: Consumer, Food Service, Private Label, Bulk

2290 **Carriere Foods Inc**
540 Chemin Des Patriotes
Saint-Denis-Sur-Richelie, QC J0H 1K0
Canada 450-787-3411
Fax: 450-787-3537
marketing@carrierefoods.com
www.bonduelle.ca
Manufacturer and exporter of frozen and canned vegetables and fruits including peas, waxed beans, chick peas, green beans, asparagus and corn, dried beans, blueberries, cranberries, rasberries, rhubarb, strawberries, soups and sauces;importer of asparagus, carrots and spinach
President: Marcel Ostiguy
Number Employees: 990perm 180
Type of Packaging: Consumer, Private Label
Brands:
ARCTICA GARDENS
Avon
Carriere
Festino
Graves
Paula
SUNNY FARM
Stokely

2291 **Carrington Foods**
200 Jacintoport Blvd
Saraland, AL 36571 251-675-9700
Fax: 251-679-8721 www.carringtonfoods.com
Processor of frozen seafood including stuffed flounder, crab and shrimp
President: David Carrington Sr
Secretary: Sally Carrington
Estimated Sales: $10-20 Million
Number Employees: 100-249
Type of Packaging: Consumer, Food Service
Brands:
MISS SALLY'S

2292 **Carrousel Cellars**
2825 Day Road
Gilroy, CA 95020-8827 408-847-2060
Fax: 831-424-1077
Wines
Winemaker: John DeSantis
Number Employees: 20-49

2293 **Carson & Company**
16749 River Rd
Bon Secour, AL 36511 251-949-7474
Fax: 251-949-5042
President: Carson Kimbrough
Estimated Sales: $ 10 - 20 Million
Number Employees: 100-249
Brands:
Carson & Co.

2294 **Carson City Pickle Company**
7451 S Garlock Rd
Carson City, MI 48811 989-584-3148
Fax: 517-879-2146
Processor of produce including cucumbers, pickles and pickled and brined vegetables
Manager: Mike Zwerk
Manager: Rudy Montoya
Estimated Sales: $1-2.5 Million
Number Employees: 1-4
Parent Co: Funk Enterprises
Type of Packaging: Consumer, Food Service, Bulk

2295 **Carta Blanca**
3912 Frutas Ave
El Paso, TX 79905-1316 915-544-6367
Fax: 915-544-0109
Beer
Manager: Carmen Bitar
General Manager: Miriam De La Vega
Estimated Sales: $ 1 - 3 Million
Number Employees: 1-4

2296 **Cary Randall's Sauces &Dressings**
PO Box 363
Highlands, NJ 07732-0363 732-872-6353
Fax: 732-872-2035 www.deathsauce.com
Fat-free all natural salad dressing, hot sauce
Contact: Cary Lazon
Estimated Sales: Under $500,000
Number Employees: 1-4

2297 **Cary's of Oregon**
413 Union Ave
Grants Pass, OR 97527 541-474-0030
Fax: 541-474-5924 888-822-9300
purchases@carysoforegon.com
www.carysoforegon.com
English toffee in 7 different flavors.
Number Employees: 14

2298 **Casa De Oro Foods**
4433 S 94th St
Omaha, NE 68127 402-339-7740
Fax: 402-339-0140 www.cdof.com
Producer of corn and flour tortillas, tortilla chips, taco shells, pre-cut chips, gordidas, flatbreads, tostadas, mexican dinner kits and low carbohydrate products.
President: Ted Longacre
CEO: Ray Murphy
VP: Charles Kraut
VP Product Development/Quality Assurance: Charles Kraut PhD
Director/Quality Assurance: Greg Power
VP Sales: Chuck Sinon
VP Operations: John Heussner
Plant Manager: Rod Hardenbergh
Estimated Sales: $100+ Million
Number Employees: 250-499
Brands:
CHI-CHI'S
Casa de Oro
Mesa

2299 **Casa Di Bertacchi**
1910 Gallagher Dr
Vineland, NJ 8360 856-696-5600
Fax: 856-696-3341 800-818-9261
consumerrelations@rich-seapak.com
www.richs.com
Processor and exporter of frozen Italian meat balls, filled pasta and sausage
Chairman/Founder: Robert E Rich
President: Robert E Rich Jr
Executive VP Innovation: Mindy Rich
COO: Bill Gisel
Plant Manager: James Shradick
Purchasing Director: Steve Owens
Estimated Sales: $ 20 - 50 Million
Number Employees: 100-249
Sq. footage: 100000
Parent Co: Rich Products Corporation
Type of Packaging: Consumer, Food Service

2300 **Casa DiLisio Products**
486 Lexington Ave
Mt Kisco, NY 10549-2758 914-666-5021
Fax: 914-666-7209 800-247-4199
casadi@aol.com www.casadilisio.com
Processor, importer and exporter of frozen Italian sauces including walnut and sun dried tomato pesto, clam, marinara, puttanesca, basil pesto, cilantro pesto provencal,alfredo and roasted red peppers pest
Owner: Lou Dilisio
VP: Lucy DiLisio
Sales: Linda DiLisio
Estimated Sales: $ 20 - 50 Million
Number Employees: 50-99
Number of Brands: 1
Number of Products: 25
Sq. footage: 4000
Type of Packaging: Consumer, Food Service, Private Label, Bulk
Brands:
Casa Dilisio

2301 **Casa Larga Vineyards**
P.O.Box 400
Fairport, NY 14450 585-223-4210
Fax: 585-223-8899 info@casalarga.com
www.casalarga.com
Wines
President: John Colaruotolo
Vineyard Manager: Andrew Colaruotolo
CFO: Ann Colaruotolo
Sales Director: Cathy Fabretti
Estimated Sales: $10-20 Million
Number Employees: 30
Sq. footage: 20
Type of Packaging: Private Label

2302 **Casa Nuestra**
3451 Silverado Trl N
St Helena, CA 94574-9662 707-963-5783
Fax: 707-963-3174 866-844-9463
info@casanuestra.com www.casanuestra.com
Wine
Owner: Gene Kirkham
Marketing Manager/Apprentice Winemaker: Stephanie Zacharia
Chief Winemaker: Allen Price
Vineyard Manager/Cellar Master: Rigoberto Nava
Estimated Sales: $500,000
Number Employees: 5-9
Brands:
Casa Nuestra

2303 **Casa Valdez**
502 E Chicago St
Caldwell, ID 83605 208-459-6461
Fax: 208-459-4154 www.casavaldez.com
Corn and flour tortillas
Owner: Jose Valdez
Sales/Marketting: Joe Romero
Estimated Sales: $2 Million
Number Employees: 69

2304 **(HQ)Casa Visco Finer Food Company**
819 Kings Rd
Schenectady, NY 12303-2627 518-377-8814
Fax: 518-377-8269 888-607-2823
info@casavisco.com www.casavisco.com
Processor of kosher products including spaghetti and barbecue sauces, salsa and mustard; exporter of spaghetti sauce
President: Joseph Viscusi
VP: Michael Viscusi
Marketing Director: Adine Gallo
Production Manager: Michael Viscusi, Jr.
Estimated Sales: $1-2.5 Million
Number Employees: 5-9
Sq. footage: 25000
Parent Co: Casa Visco Finer Food
Type of Packaging: Consumer, Food Service, Private Label, Bulk
Brands:
CASA VISCO
MY COUNTRY SWEET
SCHABERS

2305 **Casa di Carfagna**
1405 E Dublin Granville Rd
Columbus, OH 43229-3357 614-846-6340
Fax: 614-846-0937 www.carfagnas.com
Manufacturer of Italian sausages, frozen Italian meals and sauces
President: Sam Carfagna
Estimated Sales: $ 5 - 10 Million
Number Employees: 50-99
Brands:
Carfagna

2306 **Casados Farms**
P.O.Box 852
San Juan Pueblo, NM 87566 505-852-2433
Manufacturer of dried and dehydrated fruits
President: Peter Casados
Estimated Sales: $200,000
Number Employees: 10-19
Type of Packaging: Consumer

2307 **Casani Candy Company**
5301 Tacony St Ste 208
Philadelphia, PA 19137 215-535-0110
Fax: 215-535-8110
Confectionery ingredients
Manager: John Lees
VP: Joseph Lees
Estimated Sales: $2.5-5 Million
Number Employees: 10-19

2308 **Cascade Cheese Company**
P.O.Box 188
Cascade, WI 53011 920-528-8221
Fax: 920-528-7473
Provolone, mozzarella
President: Keith Babler
Treasurer: Elizabeth Babler
Estimated Sales: $2.4 Million
Number Employees: 22

2309 **Cascade Clear Water**
1600 Port Drive
Burlington, WA 98233-3106 360-757-4441
Fax: 360-757-3534 www.clearly.ca
Clear water
President, CEO: Douglas Mason
Managing Director International Div: Robert Allen
Estimated Sales: $2.5-5 Million
Number Employees: 20-49
Parent Co: Cleary Canadian Beverage Company

2310 **Cascade Coffee**
1525 75th St SW Ste 100
Everett, WA 98203 425-347-3995
Fax: 425-347-5076 www.cascadecoffeeinc.com
Coffee
President: Luther Jonson
Director: Philip Johnson
Director: Greg Jacobson
Estimated Sales: $20-50 Million
Number Employees: 70
Brands:
ORGANIC ALTURA
ORGANIC MEXICAN ALTURA
ORGANIC SIERRA MADRE BLEND

2311 **Cascade Cookie Company**
P.O.Box 618
St Louis, MO 63188-0618 314-877-7000
Fax: 314-877-7797
investorrelations@ralcorp.com
www.ralstonfoods.com
Manufacture of store brand products
President: Kevin Hunt
Estimated Sales: $1-3 Million
Number Employees: 1,000-4,999
Parent Co: Ralcorp Holdings
Brands:
Bremner
CARRIAGE HOUSE
Cascade Cookie
NUTCRACKER BRANDS

2312 **Cascade Fresh**
14300 Greenwood Ave N Ste E
Seattle, WA 98133 206-363-0991
Fax: 206-363-8191 800-511-0057
yogurt@cascadefresh.com
www.cascadefresh.com
Fat free, low fat and whole milk yogurts, as well as Greek and Mediterranean style yogurts, sour cream and acai, peach, raspberry and strawberry smoothies.
President: Satshakti Khalsa
Estimated Sales: $2,600,000
Number Employees: 10-19
Brands:
Cascade Fresh

2313 **Cascade Mountain Winery & Restaurant**
835 Cascade Mountain Rd
Amenia, NY 12501 845-373-9021
Fax: 845-373-7869 cascademt@mohawk.net
www.cascademt.com
Processor and exporter of dry and semi-dry and nonsweet table wines
Owner: William Wathmore
CEO: Margaret Wetmore
Estimated Sales: $ 3 - 5 Million
Number Employees: 5-9
Number of Products: 8
Sq. footage: 6000
Type of Packaging: Consumer

2314 **Cascade Specialties**
P.O.Box 583
Boardman, OR 97818-0583 541-481-2522
Fax: 541-481-2640 www.cascadespec.com
Dehydrated onions
Owner: Fraser Hawley
VP: Mike Kilfoy
Quality Assurance: Jeff Hermanson
Sales: Dan Biondi
Estimated Sales: $5-10 Million
Number Employees: 20-49
Brands:
CASCADE SPECIALTIES

2315 **Cascadian Farm & MUIR Glen**
719 Metcalf St
Sedro Woolley, WA 98284-1456 360-855-0100
Fax: 360-855-0444 www.smallplanetfoods.com
Processor, importer, manufacturer and marketer of frozen organic foods including fruits, vegetables and juice concentrates; also pickles and fruit spreads.
President: Maria Morgan
CEO: Steve Sanger
Estimated Sales: $10-20 Million
Number Employees: 50-99
Sq. footage: 14465
Parent Co: Small Planet Foods
Type of Packaging: Consumer, Food Service, Bulk
Other Locations:
Cascadian Farm
Napa CA
Brands:
CASCADIAN FARM
FANTASTIC FOODS
MUIR GLEN
SMALL PLANET FOODS

2316 **Casco Bay Brewing**
386 Fore St # 302
Portland, ME 004101-740 207-797-2020
Fax: 207-797-4495 cascobaybrewing@msn.com
www.cascobaybrewing.com
Beer
Owner/President: Bryan Smith
Brewmaster: Bryan Smith
Production: Jim Walters
Estimated Sales: $1 Million
Number Employees: 10-19
Type of Packaging: Private Label
Brands:
Carrabassett
Casco Bay

2317 **(HQ)Case Farms of North Carolina**
121 Rand Street
PO Box 308
Morganton, NC 28655 828-438-6900
Fax: 828-437-8566 800-437-6916
corpsales@casefarms.com www.casefarms.com
Processor of fresh, partially-cooked and frozen-for-export poultry products
Chairman/CEO: Thomas Shelton
President/COO: David Van Hoose
CFO: Mike Popowycz
International Sales Manager: David Turner
Plant Manager: Tom Shelton Jr
Estimated Sales: $250 Million
Number Employees: 2500

2318 **Case Farms of Ohio**
1818 County Road 160
Winesburg, OH 44690-0185 330-359-7141
Fax: 330-359-6482 www.casefarms.com
Processor of fresh ice and tray packed poultry
President: John Turner
Vice President: Wayne Jones
General Manager: Wayne Jones
Plant Manager: Paul Nelson
Sq. footage: 32500
Parent Co: Case Foods
Type of Packaging: Private Label
Brands:
CASE FARMS AMISH COUNTRY

2319 **Case Side Holdings Company**
37 Garden Dr
Kensington, PE C0B 1M0
Canada 902-836-4214
Fax: 902-836-3297 www.marysbakeshoppe.com
Processor of bread, muffins, biscuits, scones, doughnuts, cookies, pastries, cakes and pies
President: Don Caseley
VP: Trudy Caseley
Secretary: Roy Hogan
Managing Director: Trudy Caseley
Estimated Sales: $752,000
Number Employees: 15
Type of Packaging: Private Label

2320 **Casey Fisheries**
146 Water St
Digby, NS B0V 1A0
Canada 902-245-5801
Fax: 902-245-5552
Processor and exporter of fresh and frozen scallops and salmon
President: Joseph Casey
Plant Manager: Duncan Casey
Estimated Sales: $1.6 Million
Number Employees: 15
Type of Packaging: Consumer, Food Service, Private Label, Bulk

2321 **Casey's Seafood**
807 Jefferson Ave
Newport News, VA 23607-6117 757-928-1979
Fax: 757-928-0257 caseyseafood@prodigy.net
www.caseysseafood.com
Processor of canned and frozen blue crab meat; also, heat and serve gourmet crab cakes and deviled crabs and crawfish cakes
Owner: Jim Casey
Marketing Director: Mike Casey
Estimated Sales: $3 Million
Number Employees: 50-99
Sq. footage: 10000
Type of Packaging: Consumer, Food Service

Brands:
CASEY'S
CHESAPEAKE BAY'S FINEST

2322 **Casino Bakery**
P.O.Box 5828
Tampa, FL 33675 813-242-0311
Fax: 813-242-4691
Processor of Cuban bread
Owner: Mark N Muhsen
Estimated Sales: $1-2.5 Million
Number Employees: 10-19
Type of Packaging: Consumer, Food Service

2323 **Casper Foodservice Company**
1041 W Carroll Ave
Chicago, IL 60607-1201 312-226-2265
Fax: 312-226-2686
President: Thomas Casper
Estimated Sales: $ 1 - 3 Million
Number Employees: 10-19

2324 **Casper's Ice Cream**
11805 N 200 E
Richmond, UT 84333 435-258-2477
Fax: 435-258-5633 800-772-4182
fatboy@fatboyicecream.com
www.fatboyicecream.com
Manufacturer of ice cream novelties including sandwiches and nut sundaes on a stick
President: Keith Merrill
CEO: Gayle Smith
Vice President: Paul Merrill
Estimated Sales: $8 Million
Number Employees: 50
Sq. footage: 46000
Type of Packaging: Consumer
Brands:
FAT BOY

2325 **Cass Clay**
200 20 Th St N
Fargo, ND 58108-3126 701-293-6455
Fax: 701-241-9154 chadf@cassclay.com
www.cassclay.com
Processor of parmesan cheese
President: Jim Hageman
Quality Control: Chad Flores
VP Sales: Greg Hansen
VP Production: Al Nielson
VP/Procurement: Tom Kludt
Estimated Sales: $20-50 Million
Number Employees: 340
Type of Packaging: Consumer

2326 **Cass Clay Creamery**
P.O.Box 3126
Fargo, ND 58108 701-293-6455
Fax: 701-241-9154 salesinfo@cassclay.coom
www.cassclay.com
ice cream, dips, sour cream, cream and butter, juice, cottage cheese and yogurt
CEO: Keith Pagel
CFO: Chuck Schmidt
Quality Assurance Manager: Steve Lieser
Sales Director: Paul Morlock
Plant Manager: Troy Anderson
Estimated Sales: $50-100 Million
Number Employees: 125
Type of Packaging: Consumer, Food Service, Private Label, Bulk
Brands:
CASS-CLAY

2327 **Castella Imports**
60 Davids Dr
Hauppauge, NY 11788 631-231-5500
Fax: 631-777-1022 866-227-8355
info@castellaimports.com
www.castellaimports.com
Castella Imports, Inc. is one of the country's largest importer, manufacturer and distributor of specailty foods; bringing gourmet flavor to your table from around the world. From cheeses and spices to olives and olive oils, CastellaImports offers only the best in quality, service and price. Through hard work and dedication, Castella is continually adding to and improving to this extensive line of quality products.
Owner: Bill Valsamos
Estimated Sales: $100+ Million
Number Employees: 100-249
Sq. footage: 66000

2328 **(HQ)Castellini Company**
P.O.Box 721610
Newport, KY 41072-1610 859-442-4600
Fax: 859-442-4266 800-233-8560
info@castellinicompany.com
www.castellinicompany.com
Processor of produce; also, transportation company offering a 48 state authority of transporting
Owner: William Schuler
President: Bill Schuler
Number Employees: 20-49
Type of Packaging: Consumer, Food Service, Bulk

2329 **Castello Di Borghese**
17150 County Road 48
Cutchogue, NY 11935 631-734-5111
Fax: 631-734-5485 800-734-5158
info@castellodiborghese.com
www.castellodiborghese.com
Vineyard and winery
Owner: Marco Borghese
Owner: Ann Marie Borghese
Estimated Sales: $500-1 Million appx.
Number Employees: 10-19
Type of Packaging: Private Label
Brands:
Hargrave Vineyards

2330 **Castle Beverages**
105 Myrtle Ave
Ansonia, CT 06401 203-734-0883
Carbonated beverages
President: David Pantalone
General Manager: David Pantalone
Estimated Sales: $2.5-5 Million
Number Employees: 5-9
Brands:
Castle Beverages
Castle Carbonated Beverages

2331 **(HQ)Castle Cheese**
2850 Perry Hwy
Slippery Rock, PA 16057 724-368-3022
Fax: 724-368-9456 800-252-4373
castlecheese@adelphia.net
www.castlecheeseinc.com
Processor and exporter of cheese foods including substitutes, imitation and natural blends
President: George Myrter
Purchasing Manager: Michelle Sabol
Estimated Sales: $370,000
Number Employees: 2
Sq. footage: 3278
Type of Packaging: Consumer, Food Service, Private Label, Bulk
Other Locations:
Castle Cheese
Vernon BC
Brands:
CASTLE CHEESE
VERNON BC

2332 **Castle Hill Lobster**
333 Linebrook Rd # R
Ipswich, MA 01938-1146 978-356-3947
Fax: 978-356-9883
Whole seafoods; lobsters
Owner: Robert Marcaurelle
Estimated Sales: $2 Million
Number Employees: 1-4
Type of Packaging: Food Service

2333 **Castle Rock Meats**
P.O.Box 16323
Denver, CO 80216-0323 303-292-0855
Fax: 303-292-0680
Meats
President: Michael Andrade
Plant Manager: Allen Rigby
Estimated Sales: $20-50 Million
Number Employees: 20-49

2334 **(HQ)Castleberry's**
270 North Mill Road
Vineland, NJ 08360 856-691-2100
Fax: 856-696-1295 info@castleberrys.com
www.castleberrys.com
Manufacturer and exporter of canned meat products, sloppy joe sauce, chili, gravy, stew, hash, chicken and noodles, barbecue products, pork and canned chicken.
President/CEO: Robert Kirby
Vice President: Mike Davis
VP Marketing and Strategic Planning: David Melbourne Jr
Estimated Sales: $330 Million
Number Employees: 120
Sq. footage: 100000
Parent Co: Hanover Foods
Type of Packaging: Consumer, Food Service, Private Label
Brands:
CASTLEBERRY
SNOW'S

2335 **Castleberry's Meats**
748 Donald Lee Hollowell Pkwy
Atlanta, GA 30318-6775 404-873-1804
Fax: 404-873-4736
Manufacturer of beef, pork, veal and lamb
Owner: Russell Paulsen
Estimated Sales: $1-2.5 Million
Number Employees: 5-9
Sq. footage: 20000
Type of Packaging: Consumer, Food Service, Private Label

2336 **Casual Gourmet Foods**
4500 140th Avenue N
Suite 113
Clearwater, FL 33762-3827 727-298-8307
Fax: 727-298-0616 info@cgfoods.com
www.cgfoods.com
Fully-cooked, all-natural chicken sausages and chicken burgers. Turkey sausage
Marketing/Sales: David Canarelli
Public Relations: Ben Rizzo
Operations/Production/Plant Manager: Robert Hapanowicz
Number Employees: 5-9

2337 **Catahoula Crawfish**
1006 Pete Guidry Rd
Saint Martinville, LA 70582 337-394-4223
Fax: 337-394-4236
Crawfish
Owner: Terry Guidry
Estimated Sales: $ 3 - 5 Million
Number Employees: 10-19

2338 **Catamount Specialties ofVermont**
1880 Mountain Rd
Stowe, VT 05672-4638 802-253-4525
Fax: 802-253-6933 800-820-8096
greenmt@warwick.net
www.catamountspecialties.com
Produces mustards, salsas, BBQ sauces, pepper jellies, pasta sauces and seasonings
Co-Owner: Don Mugford
Co-Owner: George Gooss
Estimated Sales: $ .5 - 1 million
Number Employees: 1-4

2339 **Catania Bakery**
1404 N Capitol St NW
Washington, DC 20002 202-332-5135
info@cataniabakery.com
www.cataniabakery.com
Italian bread and biscotti
President: Nicole Tramonte
General Manager: Carolyn Craig
Estimated Sales: $630,000
Number Employees: 10

2340 **Catania-Spagna Corporation**
1 Nemco Way
Ayer, MA 01432 978-772-7900
Fax: 978-772-7970 800-343-5522
oils@cataniausa.com www.cataniausa.com
Processor, packer, importer and exporter of oils including canola, coconut, cooking, corn, cottonseed, vegetable, olive, peanut and soybean
President: Anthony Basile
VP: Robert Basile
Quality Control: Paul Sampson
Marketing: David Masciolli
Sales: Joseph Basile
Production: Sam Bellino
Plant Manager: Steve Sampson
Director Purchasing: Brad Eisold

Estimated Sales: $40-60 Million
Number Employees: 50-99
Sq. footage: 55000
Type of Packaging: Consumer, Food Service, Private Label, Bulk
Brands:
Atlantic Organic
Atlantic Rose
La Spagnola
Marconi
Sicilia

2341 Catawissa Bottling Company
450 Fisher Ave
Catawissa, PA 17820 570-356-2301
Fax: 570-356-2304 800-892-4419
www.catawissabottlingco.com
Soft drinks
Partner: Joseph Gregorowicz
Controller: Michael Gregorowicz
Plant Manager: Stephen Gregorowicz
Purchasing: Paula Clark
Estimated Sales: $10-20 Million
Number Employees: 20-49

2342 Catelli Brothers
50 Ferry Ave
Camden, NJ 8103 856-869-2200
Fax: 856-869-9488 www.catellibrothers.com
Processor of veal and lamb
President: Anthony Catelli
Estimated Sales: $100+ Million
Number Employees: 250-499
Brands:
American Lamb
Ami
Namp

2343 Cateraid
1167 Fendt Dr
Howell, MI 48843 517-546-8217
Fax: 517-546-8674 800-508-8217
cateraidinc@provide.net www.cateraidinc.com
Processor of frozen European style tortes, cakes, cheesecakes, miniature pastries and hors d'oeuvres
Owner: Rob Katz
Co-Founder/VP Marketing: Robert Katz
Plant Manager: Lise Holman
Purchasing Manager: Suanne Brow
Estimated Sales: $2.5-5 Million
Number Employees: 20-49
Number of Brands: 2
Number of Products: 85
Sq. footage: 17000
Type of Packaging: Food Service, Private Label
Brands:
CATERAID
CATERED GOURMET

2344 Cates Addis Company
P.O.Box 146
Parkton, NC 28371 910-865-5386
Fax: 910-858-3074 800-423-1883
Manufacturer and exporter of fresh and brined cucumbers for pickles
President: John Cates
VP/Treasurer: John Cates
Estimated Sales: $2.5-5 Million
Number Employees: 5-9
Type of Packaging: Bulk

2345 Catfish Wholesale
P.O.Box 759
Abbeville, LA 70511 337-643-6700
Fax: 337-643-1396 800-334-7292
jimrich@catfishewholesale.com
www.catfishwholesale.com
Processor and distributor of catfish, garfish, crawfish, shrimp, crabs, flounder and trout
President: James Rich
Sales Executive: Shab Calahan
Sales Manager: David Lowery
Estimated Sales: $2.5 Million
Number Employees: 60
Number of Brands: 1
Sq. footage: 8000
Type of Packaging: Consumer, Food Service, Private Label, Bulk

2346 Cathay Foods Corporation
960 Massachusetts Ave Ste 2
Boston, MA 02118 617-427-1507
Fax: 617-427-4083
Processor of frozen spring, cocktail and full sized egg rolls including shrimp, lobster, vegetable, pizza, spinach and cheese; also, egg roll wrappers and crab rangoons
President: Victor Wong
Sales: Nancy Tashjian
Estimated Sales: $5-10 Million
Number Employees: 20-49
Sq. footage: 18000
Type of Packaging: Consumer, Food Service, Private Label, Bulk
Brands:
CATHAY FOODS

2347 Catoctin Vineyards
805 Greenbridge Rd
Brookeville, MD 20833 301-774-2310
Fax: 301-774-2310 wineman1@starpower.net
Wines
President: Bob Lyon
Estimated Sales: Less than $500,000
Number Employees: 1

2348 Catoris Candy
981 5th Ave
New Kensington, PA 15068-6307 724-335-4371
Fax: 724-335-1759
Processor of confectionery items
Owner: John Gentile
Estimated Sales: $5-10 Million
Number Employees: 10-19
Type of Packaging: Consumer

2349 Catskill Mountain Specialties
1411 Route 212
Saugerties, NY 12477-3040 845-246-0900
Fax: 845-246-5313 800-311-3473
mtmanfire@aol.com
www.newworldhomecooking.com
Processor of condiments including roasted habanero, chipotle, barbecue, Jamaican jerk, etc.; importer of hot peppers, spices, etc.; also, co-packer of acidified foods
Owner: Liz Corrado
VP: Edward Palluth
Number Employees: 1-4
Sq. footage: 2000
Type of Packaging: Consumer, Food Service, Private Label, Bulk
Brands:
Mountainman
New World Home Cooking Co.

2350 Cattaneo Brothers
797 Caudill St
San Luis Obispo, CA 93401 805-543-8166
Fax: 805-543-4698 800-243-8537
catteneo@cattaneobros.com
www.cattaneobros.com
Processor of jerky, pepperoni sticks and sausage
Owner: Mike Kanney
Marketing Director: Katelyn Kaney
Operations Manager: Jim Douglass
Estimated Sales: $2.5-5 Million
Number Employees: 20-49
Number of Brands: 1
Number of Products: 50
Sq. footage: 8500
Type of Packaging: Consumer, Food Service, Private Label
Brands:
CATTANEO BROTHERS

2351 Cattle Boyz Foods
1735 33rd Avenue SW
Calgary, AB T2T 148
Canada 403-262-9366
Fax: 403-262-5829 888-662-9366
sales@cattleboyzsauce.com
www.cattleboyzsauce.com
Manufacturer and exporter of unique latchtop bottle containing versatile gourmet sauces for barbecuing, marinades, glaze for all meats and seafoods. Available in 17 and 35 oz. sizes
Managing Partner/Owner: Karen Hope
Managing Partner: Joe Ternes
Quality Control: Roxanne Quest
Sales: Karen Hope
Number Employees: 1-4
Number of Brands: 1
Number of Products: 4
Type of Packaging: Consumer, Food Service, Private Label, Bulk
Brands:
Cattle Boyz

2352 Cattle Canada
PO Box 277
GD
Bentley, AB T0C 0J0
Canada 403-748-2474
Fax: 403-748-2474
Fresh vegetables, frozen chopped rhubarb, beef jerky, rhubarb juice and more.
President: David Thevenaz
Vice President: Brenda Thevenaz
Estimated Sales: A
Number Employees: 1-25
Type of Packaging: Consumer, Food Service
Brands:
Alberta Brand
The Salad Ranch

2353 Cattleman's Meat Company
1825 Scott St
Detroit, MI 48207-2031 313-833-2700
Fax: 313-833-7164 www.cattlemansmeat.com
Processor of fresh and frozen beef; exporter of frozen beef
Chairman, Treasurer: Markus Rothbart
CEO/President: David Rothbart
Comptroller: Jerry Fowler
CEO: David S Rohtbart
Estimated Sales: $20-50 Million
Number Employees: 340
Sq. footage: 65000
Type of Packaging: Bulk
Brands:
CATTLEMEN'S

2354 Caudill Seed Company
1402 W Main St
Louisville, KY 40203 502-583-4402
Fax: 502-583-4405 800-626-5357
hf@caudillseed.com www.caudillseed.com
Manufactures organic and kosher foods, dried fruits, nuts, snacks, popcorn and basic foods
President: Dan Caudill
CFO: Iris Mudd
Vice President: Edgar Caudill
Sales Director: Jack Donahoe
Estimated Sales: $20 Million
Number Employees: 20-49
Number of Brands: 5
Number of Products: 400
Sq. footage: 275000
Type of Packaging: Private Label, Bulk
Brands:
WHOLE ALTERNATIVES

2355 Caughman's Meat Plant
P.O.Box 457
Lexington, SC 29071-0457 803-356-0076
Fax: 803-356-4413
Manufacturer of sausage, liver pudding, barbecue hash and beef chili
President: Marguerite Caughman
VP: Ronald Caughman
Estimated Sales: $20-50 Million
Number Employees: 20-49
Type of Packaging: Consumer
Brands:
LEXINGTON

2356 (HQ)Cave Creek Coffee Company
P.O.Box 4390
Cave Creek, AZ 85327 480-488-0603
Fax: 480-595-1565 info@cavecreekcoffee.com
www.cavecreekcoffee.com
Processor of coffee
Owner: Todd Newman
Co-Owner/Roastmaster: David Anderson
Estimated Sales: $5-10 Million
Number Employees: 20-49

2357 Cavender Castle Winery
142 Mitchell Street SW
Suite 300
Atlanta, GA 30303-3432 706-864-4759
Wines
Vineyard Manager: Gerry Carty
Number Employees: 20-49

2358 **Cavendish Farms**
100 Midland Drive
Dieppe, NB E1A 6X4
Canada 506-858-7777
Fax: 506-858-9107 888-883-7437
webadmin@cavendishfarms.com
www.cavendishfarms.com
Processor and exporter of frozen potato products
President: Robert Irving
VP Finance: Michael Fox
Parent Co: Irving Group
Type of Packaging: Consumer, Food Service
Brands:
CAVENDISH FARMS
DOUBLE R
FAIR ISLE
SCOTCH MAID

2359 **Cavendish Farms**
25 Mall Rd Ste 608
Burlington, MA 1803 781-273-2777
Fax: 781-221-2154 888-88 -7437
webadmin@cavendishfarms.com
www.cavendishfarms.com
Processor of potato products
President: Robert Irving
Vice President: Michael Zieger
Estimated Sales: $500 Million
Number Employees: 25
Parent Co: The Irving Group
Brands:
Always Crips
Cavendish Farms
County Fair
Double R
Scotch Maid

2360 **Cavendish Farms**
1200 boul Chomedy
Bureau 825
Laval, QC H7V 3Z3
Canada 450-973-1952
Fax: 450-973-1955 www.cavendishfarms.com
Processor of frozen French fries
General Manager: Michael Johnston Johnston
VP Operations: Ron Clow
VP: Claude Valler
Sr. Account Manager: Greg Foster
Number Employees: 10-19
Parent Co: Cavendish Farms
Type of Packaging: Consumer, Food Service, Private Label
Brands:
Always Crisp
Cavendish Farms

2361 **Cavendish Farms**
5855 3rd St SE
Jamestown, ND 58401 701-252-5222
Fax: 701-252-6863 888-284-5687
www.cavendishfarms.com
Processor of frozen potatoes
President: Robert Irving
Vice President: Steve Gort
COO: Ron Clow
Estimated Sales: $50-100 Million
Number Employees: 225
Parent Co: J.D. Irving
Brands:
DAKOTA GOLD
DAKOTA SKINS
NORTHERN GROWN
PRAIRIE SELECT

2362 **Cavens Meats**
Us Rt 36
Conover, OH 45317-0400 937-368-3841
Fax: 937-368-3849
Processor and wholesaler/distributor of meat products; serving the food service market
President: Victor Caven
VP: Dean Caven
Estimated Sales: $10-20 Million
Number Employees: 10-19
Sq. footage: 15000
Type of Packaging: Consumer, Food Service

2363 **Caver Shellfish**
PO Box 187
Beals, ME 04611-0187 207-497-2629
Fax: 207-497-2770
Shellfish
President: Albert Carver

2364 **Caves Of Faribault/SwissValley**
222 3rd St NE
Faribault, MN 55021 507-334-5260
Fax: 507-332-9011
jeff.jirik@cavesoffaribault.com
www.faribaultdairy.com
cheese
President/Owner: Sarah Arhameault
CEO: Jeff Jirik
VP: Michael Gilbertson
Estimated Sales: $3.5 Million
Number Employees: 21

2365 **Caviness Packing Company**
P.O.Box 790
Hereford, TX 79045 806-364-0900
Fax: 806-357-2277 www.cavinessbeefpackers.com
Manufacturer of meat products; slaughtering services available
President: Terry Caviness
VP: Trevor Caviness
Estimated Sales: $150-200 Million
Number Employees: 100-249

2366 **Cawy Bottling Company**
2440 NW 21st Ter
Miami, FL 33142 305-634-2291
Fax: 305-634-2291 877-917-2299
cawy@cawy.net www.cawy.net
Manufacturer of soft drinks
President: Vincent Cossio
CEO/VP/Public Relations: Vincent Cossio Jr
Quality Control: Ramon Mesa
Marketing Director: Vincent Cossio
Sales Director: Harris Padron
Public Relations: Vincent Cossio Jr
Operations Manager: Mayra Alfonsin
Production Manager: Carlos Garcia
Plant Manager: Carlos Garcia
Purchasing Manager: Harris Padron
Estimated Sales: $10-20 Million
Number Employees: 20-49
Sq. footage: 60000
Type of Packaging: Consumer, Food Service
Brands:
CAWY CC
CAWY LEMON-LIME
CAWY WATERMELON
CHAMP'S COLA
COCO SOLO
JUPINA
MALTA CAWY
MALTA RICA
MATERVA
QUINABEER
RICA MALT TONIC
TRIMALTA

2367 **Caymus Vineyards**
P.O.Box 268
Rutherford, CA 94573 707-963-4204
Fax: 707-963-5958 www.caymus.com
Wines
President: Chuck Wagner
VP: Karen Perry
Public Relations: Phyllis Turner
Estimated Sales: $300,000-500,000
Number Employees: 1-4
Number of Brands: 1
Number of Products: 2
Brands:
CAYMUS

2368 **Cayuga Grain**
P.O.Box 336
Cayuga, IN 47928 765-492-3324
Processor of grain
Manager: Nancy Martin
Estimated Sales: $500,000-$1 Million
Number Employees: 5-9
Type of Packaging: Food Service, Bulk

2369 **Cayuga Ridge Estate Winery**
6800 State Route 89
Ovid, NY 14521 607-869-5158
Fax: 607-869-3412 800-598-9463
crew@fitg.net www.cayugaridgewinery.com
Wines
Owner: Tom Challen
Owner: Susie Challen
Estimated Sales: $1-2.5 Million
Number Employees: 1-4

2370 **Ce De Candy**
1091 Lousons Rd
Union, NJ 07083 908-964-0660
Fax: 908-964-0911 800-631-7968
cede@smarties.com www.smarties.com
Processor and exporter of lollypops and novelty candy items including lipsticks, fruit, money and watches; also, sweet and sour wafers; importer of candy necklaces
Owner: Jonathan Dee
VP: Michael Dee
VP Sales/Marketing: Eric Ostrow
VP Operations: Karen Connell
Estimated Sales: $20-50 Million
Number Employees: 100-249
Type of Packaging: Consumer
Brands:
SMARTIES

2371 **Cebro Frozen Foods**
2100 Orestimba Rd
Newman, CA 95360 209-862-0150
Fax: 209-862-0717 cffrich@inreach.com
www.cebrofrozenfoods.com
Frozen foods
President: Richard Brown
Estimated Sales: $2.5-5 Million
Number Employees: 10-19

2372 **Cecchetti Sebastiani Cellar**
PO Box 1607
Sonoma, CA 95476-1607 707-996-8463
Fax: 707-996-0424
Processor of wine
Owner/President: Roy Cecchetti
CEO: Don Sebastiani
SVP Sales: Jim O'Connor
SVP/Winemaker: Bob Broman
Estimated Sales: Less than $500,000
Number Employees: 1-4
Type of Packaging: Private Label
Brands:
Brandy
Cecchetti Sebastiani Napa Valley
Pepperwood Grove
Quatro
Wines

2373 **Cedar Creek Winery**
N70w6340 Bridge Rd
Cedarburg, WI 53012 262-377-8020
Fax: 262-375-9428 800-827-8020
info@cedarcreekwinery.com
www.cedarcreekwinery.com
Manufacturer of bottler of wine
Manager: Steve Danner
Estimated Sales: $5-9.9 Million
Number Employees: 10-19
Sq. footage: 12000
Type of Packaging: Consumer, Food Service, Private Label
Brands:
CEDAR CREEK

2374 **Cedar Crest Specialties**
7269 State Road 60 Stop 4
Cedarburg, WI 53012 262-377-7252
Fax: 262-377-5554 800-877-8341
info@cedarcresticecream.com
www.cedarcresticecream.com
Processor of premium ice cream and no-fat ice cream, frozen yogurt, sherbet and Tom and Jerry mix
President: Ken Kohlwey
CEO: Bill Kohlwey
VP: Robert Kohlwey
Marketing Manager: Charlene Leach
Sales: Robert Kohlwey
Purchasing: Nadine Schmitt
Estimated Sales: $16 Million
Number Employees: 50-99
Number of Brands: 2
Number of Products: 400
Sq. footage: 45000
Parent Co: Cedar Crest Specialties
Type of Packaging: Consumer, Food Service, Private Label, Bulk
Brands:
CEDAR CREST
GUSTAFSON'S

2375 **Cedar Grove Cheese**
E5904 Mill Rd
Plain, WI 53577 608-546-5284
Fax: 608-546-2805 800-200-6020
cheese@cedargrovecheese.com
www.cedargrovecheese.com
Organic cheese and specialty artisan crafted cheese
President: Robert Wills
Vice President: Beth Nachreiner
Marketing Director: Robert Wills
General Manager: Peter DeWaard
Estimated Sales: $2.5-5 Million
Number Employees: 20-49
Number of Brands: 3
Number of Products: 50
Type of Packaging: Consumer, Food Service, Private Label, Bulk
Brands:
CEDAR GROVE
FAMILY FARMER
SQUEAKS

2376 **Cedar Hill Seasonings**
P.O.Box 4055
Edmond, OK 73034 405-340-1119
Fax: 405-340-7673 800-342-1986
info@cedarhillseasonings.com
www.cedarhillseasonings.com
Manufacturer of seasonings, bottled products and packaged mixes, Cedar Hill Seasonings produces a variety of food items including taco mixes; dip mix with seasonings; cheese ball mixes; marinara and sauce mixes, in addition to offeringgift packages and combo samplers.
Co-Owner: Felicia Schaefer
Co-Owner: Helen Schaefer
Type of Packaging: Food Service

2377 **Cedar Key Aquaculture Farms**
Po Box 428
Mango, FL 33550-0428 352-543-9131
Fax: 352-543-9132 888-252-6735
custserv@cedarkeyclams.com
www.cedarkeyclams.com
Processor of fresh and frozen clams including hors d'oeuvres
President: Dan Solano
Operations Manager: Mike Smith
Type of Packaging: Food Service
Brands:
Cedar Key

2378 **Cedar Lake Foods**
P.O.Box 65
Cedar Lake, MI 48812 989-427-5143
Fax: 989-427-5392 800-246-5039
cedarlakemgm@nethawk.com
www.cedarlakefoods.com
Processor and exporter of canned and frozen vegetable protein entrees including meat analogs; also, dry soy milk and vegetarian foods
President: Alejo Pizzaro
Contact: Cheri Graves
Production Manager: John Sias
Plant Manager: John Sias
Purchasing Manager: Ann Britten
Estimated Sales: $5-9.9 Million
Number Employees: 10-19
Type of Packaging: Consumer, Food Service, Private Label, Bulk
Brands:
CEDAR LAKE
MGM

2379 **Cedar Mountain Winery**
7000 Tesla Rd
Livermore, CA 94550 925-373-6636
Fax: 925-373-6694 cedarmtn@neal.verio.com
www.cedarmountainwinery.com
Wines
President: Linda Ault
Co-Owner: Earl Ault
Marketing Manager: Sigrid Laing
VP Operations/Production Manager: R Michael Hasbrouck
Estimated Sales: $840,000
Number Employees: 12
Type of Packaging: Private Label
Brands:
Cedar Grove
Cedar Mountain

2380 **Cedar Valley Cheese**
W3111 Jay Rd
Belgium, WI 53004 920-994-4415
Fax: 920-994-2317
contact@cedarvalleycheese.com
www.cedarvalleycheese.com
Cheese
President: Jeff Hiller
Sec: William Peterson
Estimated Sales: $6.5 Million
Number Employees: 46

2381 **Cedar Valley Fish Market**
218 Division St
Waterloo, IA 50703 319-236-2965
Fax: 253-761-0504
Seafood
Owner: Marilyn Ruvino
Estimated Sales: $370,000
Number Employees: 5-9

2382 **Cedaredge Meats**
230 E Main St
Cedaredge, CO 81413 970-856-6113
Fax: 970-856-3517
Manufacturer of frozen sausage; custom cut meat available
General Manager: Randy Sunderland
Estimated Sales: $1-2.5 Million
Number Employees: 12-15
Type of Packaging: Consumer, Food Service, Private Label
Brands:
COLORADO CLASSIC

2383 **Cedarlane Foods**
1135 E Artesia Blvd
Carson, CA 90746 310-886-7720
Fax: 310-886-7755
feedback@cedarlanefoods.com
www.cedarlanefoods.com
Processor of natural refrigerated and frozen foods including enchiladas, burritos, pot pies, tortillas, specialty breads, pizza and lasagna; varieties include vegetarian, low-fat and cholesterol and lactose-free
President: Robert Atallah
Vice President: Terry Mayo
Number Employees: 300
Sq. footage: 16000
Type of Packaging: Consumer, Food Service, Private Label
Brands:
CEDARLANE
SOYPREME

2384 **Cedarlane Natural Foods**
1135 E Artesia Blvd
Carson, CA 90746-1602 310-886-7720
Fax: 310-886-7733 www.cedarlanefoods.com
Natural foods
Owner: Robert Atallah
Estimated Sales: $ 50 - 100 Million
Number Employees: 250-499

2385 **Cedarvale Food ProductsLounsbury Food Ltd**
11 Wiltshire Avenue
Toronto, ON M6N 2V7
Canada 416-656-3331
Fax: 416-656-6803 lounsbury@lounsbury.ca
Processor of mustard and sauces including horseradish, cocktail, mint and tartar; importer of tomato paste
VP: David Higgins
Manager Export Sales/Marketing: Tim Higgins
General Manager: Gil Marks
Estimated Sales: $487,000
Number Employees: 12
Sq. footage: 15000
Parent Co: Lounsbury Foods
Type of Packaging: Consumer, Food Service, Private Label, Bulk
Brands:
CEDARVALE
LOUNSBURY
WILTSHIRE

2386 **Ceilidh Fisherman's Cooperative**
158 Main St
Port Hood, NS B0E 2W0
Canada 902-787-2666
Fax: 902-787-2388
Processor and exporter of salted cod, live lobster and crab
Gerneral Manager: Bernie MacDonald
Estimated Sales: $6 Million
Number Employees: 35
Type of Packaging: Consumer, Food Service, Private Label, Bulk

2387 **Celebration Foods**
1 Celebration Way
New Britain, CT 6053-1480 800-322-4848
Fax: 860-257-8859 800-322-4848
cranaldi@carvelcorp.com
www.celebrationfoods.com
Ice cream, frozen desserts
President: Steve Fellingham
CFO: George Brooks-Gonyer
Director: Jayne Minigell
Marketing Coordinator: Maggie Collin
Sales Director: Tom Fuchs
Public Relations: Melody Macary
Operations Manager: Greg Demadis
Purchasing Manager: Richard Carlo
Estimated Sales: $10-$100 Million
Number Employees: 50-99
Brands:
CARVEL
FLYING SAUCERS

2388 **Celebrity Cheesecake**
655 Nova Drive
Suite 304
Davie, FL 33317
877-986-2253
Cheesecakes, pies, cakes
Owner: Anita Phillips
President: Susie Bernstein
Estimated Sales: $500,000-$1 Million
Number Employees: 10-19
Sq. footage: 6000
Brands:
Celebrity Cheesecakes

2389 **Celestial Seasonings Teas**
4600 Sleepytime Dr
Boulder, CO 80301 800-434-4246
Fax: 303-581-1332 www.celestialseasonings.com
Processor and exporter of black and herbal teas including powdered and bags; also, bottled iced teas
President: Steve Hughes
CEO/Chairman: Mo Siegel
VP: Michael A Bloom
Estimated Sales: $300,000-500,000
Number Employees: 10-19
Parent Co: Hain Food Group
Type of Packaging: Consumer, Food Service
Brands:
Celestial Seasonings

2390 **Cell Tech International**
565 Century Ct
Klamath Falls, OR 97601 541-882-5406
Fax: 541-885-5458 strausj@celltech.com
www.celltech.com
Processor and exporter of blue green algae products
President/CEO: Marta Carpenter
COO: Justin Straus
CEO: Bob Underwood
VP Marketing/Strategy: Victor Bond
Number Employees: 20-49
Sq. footage: 250000
Brands:
ALPHA GOLD
ELZ SUPER ENZYMES
OMEGA GOLD
OMEGA SURO
PLANET FOOD
SPECTRABIOTIC
SUPER BLUE GREEN ENZYMES
SUPER Q10

2391 **Cella's Confections**
7401 S Cicero Ave
Chicago, IL 60629 773-838-3400
Fax: 773-838-3435 www.tootsie.com
Processor of confectionery products including boxed chocolates, chocolate covered cherries and holiday novelties
CEO: Melvin J Gordon
Plant Manager: Charles Musso
Estimated Sales: I
Number Employees: 1,000-4,999
Parent Co: Tootsie Roll Industries
Type of Packaging: Consumer, Food Service, Bulk

2392 **Cellone Bakery**
P.O.Box 16288
Pittsburgh, PA 15242 412-922-5335
Fax: 412-922-6940 800-334-8438
cellone@cellonebakery.net
www.cellonebakery.com
Bread and rolls
President: Jay Cellone
Owner: Randy Cellone
Management Info Systems Manager: Lori Edward

Operations Manager: Gary Cellone
Production Manager: Dean Cellone
Estimated Sales: $7 Million
Number Employees: 85
Type of Packaging: Private Label

2393 **Cellu-Con**
P.O.Box 185
Strathmore, CA 93267-0185 559-568-0190
Fax: 559-568-0271 cellucon@ocsnet.net
www.cellucon.com
Processor of natural yucca extract
Owner: John Yale
VP R&D: John Yale
Administrative Assistant: Kelly Smith
Estimated Sales: $1-3 Million
Number Employees: 10-19
Sq. footage: 10000

2394 **Celplast Metallized Products Limited**
67 Commander Boulevard
Unit 4
Toronto, ON M1S-3M7 416-293-4330
Fax: 416-293-9198 800-866-0059
jim@celplast.com http://cmp.celplast.com
Producer and manufacturer of metallized films for the food industry.
President/Founder: Chuck Larsen
Vice President: Bill Hellings
Technical Representative: Dante Ferrari
Sales Representative: Jim Lush
Sales Representative: Naomi Otta

2395 **Cemac Foods Corporation**
8 Cayuga Trl
Suite 1402
Harrison, NY 10528-1820
Fax: 212-869-6177 800-724-0179
info@cemacfoods.com www.cemacfoods.com
Processor and exporter of cheese blends and analogs including soy cheese; importer of health foods including dairy products, pastas and snack chips. Manufacturer of full fat and low-fat cheesecake. Private labels
President: Tom May
CFO: Mildred Nash
VP: Mel Persily
Quality Control/Operations: Josef Zahal
Marketing: David Abuschinow
Contact: Kate Stoughton
Type of Packaging: Consumer, Food Service, Private Label, Bulk
Brands:
NU TOFU
ORGRAN PASTAS
SOY CHEESE
UNBELIEVABLE CHEESECAKE

2396 **Cemac Foods Corporation**
1821 E Sedgley Ave
Philadelphia, PA 19124 215-288-7440
Fax: 215-533-8993 800-724-0179
Processor of cheesecake and cut and shredded cheese; also, soy protein cheese substitutes: importer of soy chips and organic pasta
Director R&D/Plant Manager: Yoseph Zahal
National Sales Manager: Zachary Scott
VP Plant Operations: Morris Lowenthal
Number Employees: 20-49
Sq. footage: 28000
Brands:
Nutofu
Organ Pastas
Soy Cheese
Soy-A-King Soy Chips
Unbelievable Brand

2397 **Centennial Farms**
199 Jackson St
Augusta, MO 63332 636-228-4338
centfarmaug@aol.com
www.centennialfarms.biz
Apple butters
Owner: Robert Knoernschild
Estimated Sales: $125,000
Number Employees: 5-9
Number of Brands: 1
Number of Products: 8
Type of Packaging: Consumer, Private Label

2398 **(HQ)Centennial Food Corporation**
4412 Manilla Rd
Calgary, AB T2G 4A7
Canada 403-214-0044
Fax: 403-214-1656
www.centennialfoodservice.com
Processor and exporter of fresh and frozen meat products including spiced and formed ground beef, beef patties, battered and breaded steaks and cutlets, vacuum sealed and aged beef cuts, bacon wrapped scallops and marinated short ribs;importer of beef and seafood
Chairman: Ron Kovitz
CEO/President: J Kalef
VP/General Manager: Nashir Vasanji
Number Employees: 250-499
Type of Packaging: Consumer, Food Service, Private Label, Bulk
Other Locations:
Centennial Food Corp.
Calgary AB
Brands:
Canadian Gourmet
Centennial
Mastercut

2399 **Centennial Mills**
601 1st St
Cheney, WA 99004-1653 509-235-6216
Fax: 509-235-2144
Processor of flour
Manager: Luke Burger
Estimated Sales: Under $500,000
Number Employees: 10-19
Parent Co: Archer Daniels Midland Company
Type of Packaging: Consumer, Food Service, Bulk

2400 **Center Locker Service Company**
108 N Public St
Center, MO 63436 573-267-3343
Fax: 573-267-3392
Processor of beef, pork, sausage and meat and meat products
Owner: Dennis Mc Millen
Co-Owner: Debby McMillen
Estimated Sales: $500,000-$1 Million
Number Employees: 1-4
Type of Packaging: Food Service, Bulk

2401 **Centflor Manufacturing Company**
545 W 45th St Fl 8
New York, NY 10036 212-246-8307
Fax: 212-262-9717
Processor and exporter of essential oils and aromatic chemicals
President: Robert Beller
General Manager: Gloria Rose
Estimated Sales: $1.5 Million
Number Employees: 9
Sq. footage: 12000

2402 **Central Bakery**
711 Pleasant St
Fall River, MA 02723 508-675-7620
Fax: 508-677-4523
Processor of bread & other bakery products
Owner: Tibeiro Lopes
Estimated Sales: $2.3 Million
Number Employees: 10-19

2403 **Central Bean Company**
P.O.Box 215
Quincy, WA 98848-0215 509-787-1544
Fax: 509-787-4040 info@centralbean.com
www.centralbean.com
Processor of dry beans including pinto, black, navy, small red, great northern, light red kidney, pink, dry bean flour and seven bean soup mix.
President: Tom Grebb
Estimated Sales: $20-50 Million
Number Employees: 10-19
Sq. footage: 62000
Type of Packaging: Consumer, Food Service, Private Label, Bulk

2404 **Central Beef**
P.O. Box 399
Center Hill, FL 33514-0399 352-793-3671
Fax: 352-793-2227
Processor of beef
Owner: Thomas Bryan
Estimated Sales: $ 20 - 50 Million
Number Employees: 50-99
Type of Packaging: Consumer, Food Service

2405 **Central California Raisin Packers**
5316 S Del Rey Ave
Del Rey, CA 93616 559-888-2195
Fax: 559-888-2298
Dried apricots, mixed fruit, peaches, prunes, raisins
President: Dan Milinovich
Estimated Sales: $10-20 Million
Number Employees: 10-19
Brands:
DEL CARA

2406 **Central Coast Coffee Roasting**
1172 Los Olivos Ave
Los Osos, CA 93402 805-528-7317
Fax: 805-528-1150 800-382-6837
www.slowroasted.com
Coffee
Owner: Norman Galloway
Owner: Chirs Galloway
Owner: Joe Galloway
Estimated Sales: Less than $500,000
Number Employees: 10-19
Type of Packaging: Food Service

2407 **(HQ)Central Coast Seafoods**
5495 Traffic Way
Atascadero, CA 93422 805-462-3474
Fax: 805-466-6613 800-273-4741
info@ccseafood.com www.ccseafood.com
Wholesaler/distributor and exporter of fresh seafood; serving the food service market in California
Owner/President: Giovanni Comin
Owner/Executive Officer: Molly Comin
VP Sales/Marketing: Nancy Osorio
Operations Manager: Jorge Sanchez
Estimated Sales: $5.9 Million
Number Employees: 27
Sq. footage: 10000
Other Locations:
Central Coast Seafoods
Morro Bay CA

2408 **Central Coca-Cola Bottling Company**
1706 Roseneath Road
Richmond, VA 23230-4436 804-359-3759
Fax: 804-358-5822 800-359-3759
Processor and bottler of flavored and regular iced teas, soft drinks, bottled and soda waters, fruit juices and drinks including sport, fruit and chocolate
Chairman Board/President: Betty Sams
Estimated Sales: $10-20 Million
Number Employees: 20-49
Type of Packaging: Consumer

2409 **Central Dairies**
PO Box 8588
Station A
St Johns, NL A1B 3P2
Canada 709-364-7531
Fax: 709-364-8714 800-563-6455
customer.service@centraldairies.com
www.centraldairies.com
Milk, cultured products, frozen desserts, cheese, spreads, juices and drinks
VP: Deve Collins
CEO: Kennetch Peacock
VP/General Manager: David Collins
Manager Sales/Marketing: Ron Croke
Plant Manager: Clarence Chaytor
Parent Co: Farmers Co-op Dairy
Type of Packaging: Consumer
Brands:
Farmers Ice Cream
Flavoured Milk

2410 **Central Dairy Company**
610 Madison St
Jefferson City, MO 65101 573-635-6148
Fax: 573-634-3028

Milk and ice cream
President: Gale Hackman
CEO: Chris Hackman
VP: Steve Raithel
Controller: Mike Fennewald
Estimated Sales: $20-50 Million
Number Employees: 100

2411 **Central Grocers, Inc.**
2600 W Haven Ave
Joliet, IL 60433 815-553-8800
Fax: 815-553-8710 sales@central-grocers.com
www.central-grocers.com
Wholesaler/distributor of equipment and fixtures, frozen foods, general line items, produce, meat products, etc
President/CEO: James Denges
CFO: Tim Kubis
Estimated Sales: 1 Billion +
Number Employees: 1,000-4,999

2412 **Central Meat & Provision Company**
1603 National Ave
San Diego, CA 92113 619-239-1391
Fax: 619-239-1634
Processor of beef, pork and veal
Owner/President: Robert Kuhlken
VP Operations: Bert Risley
Estimated Sales: $10-20 Million
Number Employees: 20-49

2413 **Central Milling Company**
122 E Center St
Logan, UT 84321 435-752-6625
Fax: 435-753-7960 www.centralmilling.com/
Processor of pancake flour, Golden West All Purpose Flour, Red Rose All Purpose Flour, whole wheat flour, and Germade.
President: H Roscoe Weston
Controller: Shaun Owen
Quality Control: Jeff Daniels
Mill Manager: Manuel Solis
Mill Manager: Nathan Shumway
Mill Manager: Melvin Alberta
Secretary: James Weston
Mill Manager/Electrician: Kurtis Williams
Plant Manager: Fred Weston
Estimated Sales: $10-20 Million
Number Employees: 10-19
Type of Packaging: Consumer, Food Service
Brands:
GOLDEN WEST
RED ROSE

2414 **Central Snacks**
1700 N Pearl St
Carthage, MS 39051 601-267-3112
Fax: 601-267-5249 porkskin@aol.com
Pork skins
President: N Carson
Estimated Sales: $2.5-5 Million
Number Employees: 10-19

2415 **Central Soya**
885 N Kinzie Ave
Bradley, IL 60915 401-724-3800
Fax: 401-724-4313 800-556-6777
www.centralsoya.com
Processor of shortenings and edible oils including corn, canola, peanut, cottonseed, coconut, vegetable and soybean; exporter and importer of popcorn and frying oils and shortenings
President: Sidney Dressler
VP Sales/Marketing: Larry Dressler
Plant Manager: David Parrillo
Estimated Sales: $50-100 Million
Number Employees: 20-49
Type of Packaging: Bulk
Brands:
COLFAX
GOLDLINE
POPSIT

2416 **Central Soya Company**
4300 Duncan Ave
Saint Louis, MO 63110 314-659-3000
Fax: 314-629-5749 800-325-7108
www.solae.com
Develops innovative soy technologies and ingredients for food, meat and industrial products.
Chairman: Craig Binetti
CEO: Torkel Rhenman
CFO: Steve Fray
VP/General Counsel: Cornel Fuerer
Senior Director Research & Development: Phil Kerr PhD
Estimated Sales: $1 Billion
Number Employees: 2,400
Other Locations:
Central Soya Company
Fort Wayne IN

2417 **Central Soyfoods**
710 East 22nd Street
Suite C
Lawrence, KS 66046 785-312-8698
www.centralsoyfoods.com
Soybean oil manufacturer
General Partner: Jim Cooley
Plant Manager: Lori Kruger
Estimated Sales: $700,000
Number Employees: 12

2418 **Central Valley Dairymen**
PO Box 576767
Modesto, CA 95357-6767 209-551-2667
Fax: 209-551-2672
Cooperative of dairy product processors
Chairman Board: Joe Machado
Controller: Dee Wooldridge
Number Employees: 1-4

2419 **Centreside Dairy**
61 Lorne Street N
Renfrew, ON K7V 1K8
Canada 613-432-2914
Fax: 613-432-5157
Processor of ice cream; wholesaler/distributor of dairy products
President: Mark Tracey
General Manager: Melany Tracey
Estimated Sales: $2 Million
Number Employees: 15
Type of Packaging: Consumer, Food Service, Private Label
Brands:
ECONOMY
PREMIUM
TRACEY'S

2420 **Century Foods International**
400 Century Ct
Sparta, WI 54656 608-269-1900
Fax: 608-269-1910 800-269-1901
info@centuryfoods.com www.centuryfoods.com
Century Foods International is a manufacturer of nutritional powders and ready-to-drink beverages under private label and contract manufacturing agreements for food, sports, health and nutritional supplement industries. Other servicesprovided include agglomeration, blending and instantizing, research and development, analytical testing, and packaging from bulk to consumer size.
President: Tom Miskowski
VP R&D: Julie Wagner
VP Sales/Marketing: Kevin Meyer
VP Operations: Wade Nolte
Number Employees: 250-499
Sq. footage: 420000
Parent Co: Hormel Foods Corporation
Type of Packaging: Private Label, Bulk
Brands:
CENPREM
LACEY DELITE
PIZAZZ
READY CHEESE

2421 **(HQ)Cereal Food Processors**
2001 Shawnee Msn Pkwy Ste 110
Mission Woods, KS 66205 913-890-6300
Fax: 913-890-6382 info@cerealfood.com
www.cerealfood.com
Manufacturer and exporter of flour
President: J Breck Barton
CFO: Steven J. Heeney
Vice President: J. Brent Wall
VP Sales: Bruce King
VP Operations: John Erker
Estimated Sales: $20-50 Million
Number Employees: 20-49
Type of Packaging: Consumer
Other Locations:
Cereal Food Processors Plant
Los Angeles CA
Cereal Food Processors Plant
Kansas City MO
Cereal Food Processors Plant
McPherson KS
Cereal Food Processors Plant
Billings MT
Cereal Food Processors Plant
Great Falls MT
Cereal Food Processors Plant
Cleveland OH
Cereal Food Processors Plant
Portland OR
Cereal Food Processors Plant
Ogden UT
Cereal Food Processors Plant
Salt Lake City UT
Cereal Food Processors Plant
Montreal QC

2422 **Cereal Food Processors**
425 W 500 S
Salt Lake City, UT 84101-2206 801-355-2981
info@cerealfood.com
www.cerealfood.com
Processor of wheat flour
Owner: Jaymie B Carroll
Plant Superintendant: Max Horrocks
Estimated Sales: $10-24.9 Million
Number Employees: 10-19
Parent Co: Cereal Food Processors

2423 **Cereal Food Processors**
2001 Shawnee Msn Pkwy Ste 110
Mission Woods, KS 66205 913-890-6300
Fax: 913-890-6382 info@cerealfood.com
www.cerealfood.com
Processor of flour
President: Breck Barton
Chairman: Fred Merrill
Vice Chairman: David Mattson
VP Operations: John Erker
Estimated Sales: $20-50 Million
Number Employees: 20-49
Parent Co: Cereal Food Processors
Type of Packaging: Consumer, Food Service, Private Label, Bulk

2424 **Cereal Food Processors**
1635 Merwin Street
Cleveland, OH 44113 216-621-3206
Fax: 216-621-0404 j.blanton@cerealfood.com
www.cerealfood.com
Processor of flour
President: J Breck Barton
EVP Administration/Finance: Steven Heeney
VP: J Brent Wall
EVP/General Sales Manager: Mark Dobbins
VP Operations: John Erker
Plant Manager: Joe Blanton
Estimated Sales: $20-50 Million
Number Employees: 27
Sq. footage: 20000
Type of Packaging: Private Label, Bulk

2425 **Cereal Food Processors**
2001 Shawnee Msn Pkwy Ste 110
Mission Woods, KS 66205 913-890-6300
Fax: 913-890-6382 info@cerealfood.com
www.cerealfood.com
Cereals
President: J Breck Barton
Sales: Mark Dobbins
Estimated Sales: $20-50 Million
Number Employees: 20-49

2426 **Cereal Ingredients**
10835 N Ambassador Dr
Kansas City, MO 64153 816-891-1055
Fax: 816-891-7606 cereal@cerealingredients.com
www.cerealingredients.com
Proprietary, specialized ingredients developed from wheat fiber concentrates
Chairman, CEO: Bob Hatch
Executive VP Sales/Marketing: James Thomasson
Estimated Sales: $1-2.5 Million
Number Employees: 50-99

2427 **Ceres Fruit Juices**
7270 Woodbine Avenue
Suite 201
Markham, ON L3R 4B9
Canada 905-474-4450
Fax: 905-474-2536 800-905-1116
www.ceresjuices.com
All natural, 100% pure fruit juice

2428 **Cericola Farms**

Bradford, ON L3Z 2A4
Canada 905-939-2962
Fax: 905-939-8423 877-939-4449
Processor of chicken and turkey also, fresh and frozen eggs and egg products
President: Amedeo Cericola
VP: Anthony Cericola
Co-Owner: Anthony Cericola
Co-Owner/VP: Mary Cericola
Marketing Director: Amedeo Cericola
Estimated Sales: $146,000
Number Employees: 1
Type of Packaging: Consumer, Food Service, Private Label, Bulk
Brands:
SureFresh Foods

2429 **Certi-Fresh Foods**
7410 Scout Ave
Bell Gardens, CA 90201 562-806-1100
Fax: 562-806-2047 info@certi-fresh.com
www.certi-fresh.com
seafood processing and distribution
President/CEO/Owner: Nino Palma
President: Larry Cirin
CFO: Jerry Saenz
Quality Control: Michael Jamehdor
VP Marketing and Merchandising: Dave Versak
Sales: Pete Palma
Plant Manager: Tom Dukescherer
Purchasing: Revi Ayla
Estimated Sales: $75 Million
Number Employees: 130
Type of Packaging: Consumer, Food Service
Brands:
CERTI-FRESH

2430 **Certified Grocers Midwest**
1 Certified Dr
Hodgkins, IL 60525 708-579-2100
Fax: 708-354-7502 www.certisaver.com
President: James Bradley
CEO: Jim Denges
Number Employees: 100-249

2431 **Certified Processing Corporation**
184 Us Highway 22
Hillside, NJ 07205-1837 973-923-5200
Processor of caffeine
President: Paul Iacono
Estimated Sales: $ 1 - 3 Million
Number Employees: 1-4
Sq. footage: 35000

2432 **Certified Savory**
5315 Dansher Road
Countryside, IL 60525-3101 800-328-7656
Fax: 847-244-5612 800-328-7656
dgoral@certifiedsavory.com
www.certifiedsavory.com
Processor of anchovy pastes, anchovy powders, fish sauces
President: John Novak Jr.
CFO: Luigi Buffone
VP: Ralph Pirritano
Quality Control: Galina Mann
Sales: Dan Goral
Production: Tracy Swanson
Plant Manager: Galvin Reynolds
Purchasing: Andrew Kaminski
Estimated Sales: $ 20 - 50 Million
Number Employees: 50-99
Number of Brands: 2
Sq. footage: 25000
Parent Co: Sokol and Company
Type of Packaging: Food Service, Bulk

2433 **Cervantes Foods Products**
5801 Gibson Blvd SE
Albuquerque, NM 87108-4833 505-262-2253
Fax: 505-262-2253 877-982-4453
nmchile@earthlink.net
www.nmchileproducts.com
Chiles: red and green; fresh, dried, canned, frozen
Owner: Roberta Finley
Estimated Sales: $ 1 - 3 Million
Number Employees: 20-49

2434 **Chaddsford Winery**
632 Baltimore Pike
Chadds Ford, PA 19317 610-388-6221
Fax: 610-388-0360 cfwine@chaddsford.com
www.chaddsford.com
Wines
Owner: Eric Miller
Winemaker: Eric Miller
Special Events Planner: Betsie Williamson
Marketing Director: Lee Miller
Sales Director: William Harris
Public Relations: Larry D'Antonio
Operations Manager: James Osborn
Estimated Sales: $1-2.5 Million
Number Employees: 5-9
Type of Packaging: Private Label
Brands:
CHADDSFORD

2435 **Chadler**
400 Eagle Ct
Swedesboro, NJ 08085-1758 856-467-0099
Fax: 856-467-8024 www.barry-callebaut.com
Processor and exporter of cocoa products, including powder, butter and liqueur
President: Bill Mahaffy
Estimated Sales: $50-100 Million
Number Employees: 50-99
Parent Co: Chadley

2436 **Chalet Cheese Coope**
N4858 County Road N
Monroe, WI 53566 608-325-4343
Fax: 608-325-4409
Cheese
Manager: Myron Olson
Owner: Hans Wampfler
Estimated Sales: $2.5 Million
Number Employees: 24
Type of Packaging: Private Label

2437 **Chalet Debonne Vineyards**
7743 Doty Rd
Madison, OH 44057-9512 440-466-3485
Fax: 440-466-6753 info@debonne.com
www.debonne.com
Wines and vineyard
Owner: Anthony Debevc
Treasurer: Rose Debevc
Vice President: Tony Debevec
Estimated Sales: $2.5-5 Million
Number Employees: 10-19

2438 **Chalk Hill Estate Vineyards & Winery**
10300 Chalk Hill Rd
Healdsburg, CA 95448 707-838-4306
Fax: 707-838-9687 www.chalkhill.com
Wines
President: Frederick Furth
CEO: Kenneth Born
CFO: Melina Hobby
VP Winemaker: Mark Lingenfelder
Marketing Director: Nancy Bailey
VP Sales: Craige Bennett
VP Vineyard Operations: Mark Lingenfelder
Estimated Sales: $10-20 Million
Number Employees: 20-49
Type of Packaging: Private Label
Brands:
CHALK HILL ESTATE BOTTLED
CHALK HILL ESTATE SELECTION

2439 **Challenge Dairy Products**
11875 Dublin Blvd Ste B230
Dublin, CA 94568 925-828-6160
Fax: 925-551-7591 800-733-2479
www.challengedairy.com
Processor and exporter of butter and dehydrated milk; wholesaler/distributor of butter and frozen foods; serving the food service market
President, CEO: John Whetten
CFO: Alan Maag
CEO: Irv Holmes
VP of Retail: Bud Tuohy
Estimated Sales: $100+ Million
Number Employees: 50-99
Type of Packaging: Consumer, Food Service, Private Label, Bulk
Brands:
CHALLENGE
CHALLENGE DANISH

2440 **Champignon North America**
456 Sylvan Ave
Englewood Cliffs, NJ 07632
Fax: 201-871-7214
renata.araujo@champignon-usa.com
www.champignon-usa.com
Gourmet cheeses.
President: Birgit Bernhard
VP: Olaf Glaser
Estimated Sales: $8 Million
Number Employees: 5-9
Number of Brands: 2
Brands:
BRIE W/GARLIC DE LUXE
CAMBOZOLA
CHAMPIGNON
HOFMEISTER
MIRABO
MONTAGNOLO
ROUGETTE
ROYAL BAVARIAN

2441 **Champion Beverages**
44 Talmadge Hill Road
Darien, CT 06820-2125 203-655-9026
Fax: 203-655-0676
Beer, dairy drinks
President/CEO: Joseph Tighe
COO: Elaine Tighe
Estimated Sales: Under $500,000
Number Employees: 1-4
Brands:
ERIN'S ROCK AMBER AND STOUT
SMOOTHIE SPARKLING CHOC.EGG CREAM
STALLION X MALT LIQUOR

2442 **Champion Nutrition**
1301 Sawgrass Corporate Pkwy
Sunrise, FL 33323
Fax: 925-689-0821 800-225-4831
admin@champion-nutrition.com
www.champion-nutrition.com
Processor and exporter of sports nutrition supplements
Principal: Michael Zumpano
VP Finance: Jannie Motta
Industry Contact: Christy Olson
Estimated Sales: $10-20 Million
Number Employees: 30
Sq. footage: 9094
Brands:
HEAVYWEIGHT GAINER 900
MET-MAX
METABOLOL
MUSCLE NITRO
OXI PRO METABOLOL
REVENGE

2443 **Champlain Valley Apiaries Company**
504 Washington Street Ext
Middlebury, VT 05753 802-388-7724
Fax: 802-388-1653 800-841-7334
cva@together.net
www.champlainvalleyhoney.com
Processor of liquid and natural crystallized honey
Owner: Charles Mraz
Office Manager: Sue Synder
Bee Keeper: James Gabriel
Estimated Sales: $2.5-5 Million
Number Employees: 1-4
Type of Packaging: Consumer

2444 **Champlain Valley Milling Corporation**
P.O.Box 454
Westport, NY 12993-0454 518-962-4711
Fax: 518-962-8799 cvm@westelcom.com
http://www.westelcom.com
Processor of organic and kosher whole grain flour including spring wheat, stone ground, soy, rye, white, whole pastry, pancake, etc
President: Samuel Sherman
Vice President: Paul Barton
Operations Manager: Donald White
Estimated Sales: $5-9.9 Million
Number Employees: 5-9
Type of Packaging: Private Label

Brands:
CHAMP

2445 **Champoeg Wine Cellars**
10375 Champoeg Rd NE
Aurora, OR 97002 503-678-2144
Fax: 503-678-1024
champoeg@champoegwine.com
www.champoegwine.com
Wines
Owner: Lounna Eggert
Estimated Sales: $1-2.5 Million
Number Employees: 1-4

2446 **Chandler Foods**
2727 Immanuel Rd
Greensboro, NC 27407 336-299-1934
Fax: 336-854-4649 800-537-6219
cfoods@triad.rr.com www.carolinabarbecue.com
Manufacturer of barbecue products including pork, chicken and beef; also, chili products including frozen, hot dog and con carne
CEO: John Chandler
EVP: Jeff Chandler
Estimated Sales: $5-9.9 Million
Number Employees: 20-49
Sq. footage: 39900
Type of Packaging: Food Service
Brands:
CHANDELR FOODS

2447 **Chang Food Company**
13941 Nautilus Dr
Garden Grove, CA 92843 714-265-9990
Fax: 714-265-9996
Processor of process frozen egg rolls, spring rolls, soba noodle, egg noodle bowls (stir fried tofu, vegetable, etc)
President: Van Ntuyen
Manager: Nhuan Nguyen
Estimated Sales: $2.5-$3 Million
Number Employees: 20-49
Sq. footage: 9800
Type of Packaging: Consumer, Food Service, Private Label, Bulk
Brands:
Chang Food

2448 **Channel Fish ProcessingcCompany**
18 Food Mart Rd
Roxbury, MA 02118 617-464-3366
Fax: 617-464-3377 info@channelfish.com
www.channelfish.com
Fresh and frozen seafood
President: John Zaffiro
Inventory Control: Paul D'Agostino
COO: Roy Zaffiro
Production Supervisor: James Gallagher
Manager: Even Silvester
Estimated Sales: $45 Million
Number Employees: 75

2449 **Channing Rudd Cellars**
PO Box 426
Middletown, CA 95461-0426 707-987-2209
Wines
President: J Rudd
Number Employees: 20-49

2450 **Chappaqua Crunch**
65 Tedesco St
Marblehead, MA 01945-1039 781-631-8118
Fax: 781-631-8113
Granola, snack foods
President: Debbie Waugh
Estimated Sales: Under $500,000
Number Employees: 1-4

2451 **Chappellet Winery**
1581 Sage Canyon Rd
Saint Helena, CA 94574 707-286-4268
Fax: 707-963-7445 800-494-6379
info@chappellet.com www.chappellet.com
Wines
Founder/President: Donn Chappellet
Founder: Molly Chappallet
Marketing/Sales: Cyril Chappellet
Director National Sales: Steve Tamburelli
Winery/Vineyard Operations: Jon Mark
Winemaker: Phillip Corallo-Titus
Vineyard Manager: David Pirio
Purchasing Manager: Carissa Chappellet
Estimated Sales: $2.5 Million
Number Employees: 35
Type of Packaging: Private Label
Brands:
CHAPPALLET

2452 **Chappellet Winery**
1581 Sage Canyon Rd
Saint Helena, CA 94574 707-963-7136
Fax: 707-963-7445 800-494-6379
winery@chappellet.com www.chappellet.com
Wines
Founder: Donn Chappellet
Co-Founder: Molly Chappellet
Director National Sales: Steve Tamburelli
Estimated Sales: $ 10 - 20 Million
Number Employees: 20-49

2453 **Char Crust**
3017 N Lincoln Ave
Chicago, IL 60657-4242 773-528-0600
Fax: 773-472-1101 800-311-9884
charcrust@charcrust.com www.charcrust.com
Dry-rub seasonings for all meat and fish
President: Bernard Silver
Marketing: Susan Eriksen
Estimated Sales: $500,000-$1 Million
Number Employees: 5-9
Brands:
CHAR CRUST

2454 **Char-Wil Canning Company**
6818 Hunting Creek Road
Hurlock, MD 21643-3318 410-943-3580
Fax: 410-943-3580
Processor and canner of whole and peeled tomatoes
Owner/Partner: Charles Adams
Number Employees: 6
Type of Packaging: Consumer, Food Service, Private Label, Bulk
Brands:
Char-Wil

2455 **Charcuterie LaTour Eiffel**
485 Rue Lavoie
Vanier, QC G1M 2J8
Canada 418-687-2840
Fax: 418-688-9558
Processor and exporter of fresh and frozen pork
Marketing Director: Francois Couture
Parent Co: McCain Foods USA
Type of Packaging: Bulk
Brands:
Bilopage
Tour Eiffel

2456 **Charles B. Mitchell Vineyards**
8221 Stoney Creek Rd
Somerset, CA 95684 530-620-3467
Fax: 530-620-1005 800-704-9463
cbmvwine@inforum.net
www.charlesbmitchell.com
Wine
Owner: Michael Conti
Estimated Sales: $2.5-5 Million
Number Employees: 5-9
Type of Packaging: Private Label

2457 **Charles Boggini**
733 Bread and Milk St
Coventry, CT 06238-1014 860-742-2652
Fax: 860-742-7903 glen@bogginicola.com
www.chasbcola.com
Manufacturer and exporter of flavoring extracts
President: Glen Boggini
VP: David Boggini
Estimated Sales: $5-10 Million
Number Employees: 5-9
Type of Packaging: Consumer

2458 **Charles FaraudC/O Pramex**
1251 Avenue Of The Americas
34th Floor
New York, NY 10020
catherine.chavrier@charlesfaraud.com
www.charlesfaraud.com
Health, fitness and energy bars, dessert toppings (i.e. fudge sauce, caramel sauce, whipped cream, etc.), canned or preserved vegetables/fruit.
Marketing: Catherine Chavrier

2459 **Charles H. Baldwin & Sons**
P.O.Box 372
West Stockbridge, MA 01266 413-232-7785
Fax: 413-232-0114 www.baldwinextracts.com
Manufacturer of flavoring extracts and flavors, maple table syrup and supplier of baking supplies.
Owner: Earl Moffatt
Estimated Sales: $500,000-$1 Million
Number Employees: 1-4
Brands:
Baldwin

2460 **Charles H. Parks & Company**
P.O.Box 100
Fishing Creek, MD 21634 410-397-3400
Fax: 410-397-3400
Manufacturer of fresh, canned and pasteurized crabmeat; also, fresh crabs
President: Virgil Ruark Jr Jr
Estimated Sales: $3-5 Million
Number Employees: 10-19
Sq. footage: 3000
Type of Packaging: Consumer
Brands:
CAPTAIN CHARLIE

2461 **Charles Heitzman Bakery**
4749 Dixie Hwy
Louisville, KY 40216-2653
Fax: 502-634-1197
Baked goods
President: Tony Osting
Estimated Sales: $500,000-$1 Million
Number Employees: 5-9

2462 **Charles J. Ross**
401 Egle Road
Reading, PA 19601 610-685-5161
Fax: 717-843-0592
Estimated Sales: $300,000-500,000
Number Employees: 1-4

2463 **Charles Jacquin Et Cie**
2633 Trenton Ave
Philadelphia, PA 19125 215-425-9300
Fax: 215-425-9438 800-523-3811
feedback@ou.org www.chambordonline.com
Wines and liquors
President: Norton Cooper
CFO: Mark Small
V.P., National Sales Manager: Kevin O'Brien
VP: John Cooper
Sales Director: Mark Small
Operations Manager: Paul Stefan
Plant Manager: William Heinz
Estimated Sales: $50-100 Million
Number Employees: 110
Type of Packaging: Private Label
Brands:
BIRELL
Bocador
Botticelli
Canadian Whiskey
Devonshire Royal
Royale Montaine
Savory & James
Witenheim

2464 **Charles Krug Winery**
P.O.Box 191
St Helena, CA 94574-0191 707-967-2200
Fax: 707-967-2291 charleskmg@pmondavi.com;
information@pmondavi.com
www.charleskrug.com
Processor of wines
Proprietor: Peter Mondavi, Jr.
CEO/President: Peter Mondavi, Sr.
Proprietor: Marc Mondavi
CEO: Peter Mondavi Sr
Estimated Sales: $20 Million
Number Employees: 100-249
Brands:
Charles Krug
Ck Mondavi

2465 **Charles Poultry Company**
2931 Charlestown Road
Lancaster, PA 17603 717-872-7621
Fax: 717-872-9571 sales@charlespoultry.com
www.charlespoultry.com

Processor of free range and all natural chicken and turkey including whole cut up, cutlets, legs, wings, whole breasts, drums, thighs, etc
President: Ken Charles
VP: Richard Charles
Estimated Sales: $20-50 Million
Number Employees: 20-49
Sq. footage: 9000
Parent Co: Charles Poultry Live Broker
Type of Packaging: Consumer, Food Service, Private Label, Bulk

2466 **Charles Rockel & Son**
4303 Smith Rd
Cincinnati, OH 45212-4236 513-631-3009
Fax: 513-631-3083
Food brokers of dairy/deli products, frozen foods, general merchandise, groceries, industrial ingredients, etc
President: Charles Rockel
CFO: Don Rockel
Estimated Sales: $2.5-5 Million
Number Employees: 3

2467 **Charles Smart Donair Submarine**
8952 82nd Avenue NW
Edmonton, AB T6C 0Z3
Canada 780-468-2099
Fax: 780-462-4647
Processor of raw, cooked, fresh and frozen spiced beef
President: Chawki El Homeira
Number Employees: 5-9
Type of Packaging: Food Service
Brands:
Son Bake Kita
Son's Bun

2468 **Charles Spinetta Winery**
12557 Steiner Road
Plymouth, CA 95669-9510 209-245-3384
Fax: 209-245-3386
www.charlesspinettawinery.com
Table wine including wines for bulk market
Owner: Charles Spinetta
Estimated Sales: $1-2.5 Million
Number Employees: 1-4
Brands:
Charles Spinetta Barbera
Charles Spinetta Primitivo
Charles Spinetta Zinfanel

2469 **Charleston Tea Plantation**
6617 Maybank Hwy
Wadmalaw Island, SC 29487 843-559-0383
Fax: 843-559-3049 800-443-5987
chastea@awod.com
Tea
Co-President: Bill Hall
Estimated Sales: $2,900,000
Number Employees: 20-49
Brands:
American Classic Tea

2470 **Charlie Beigg's Sauce Company**
4 Heritage Lane
Windham, ME 04062-4984 888-502-8595
sales@charliebeiggs.com
www.charliebeiggs.com
Manufacturer of BBQ sauce and salsa.
Head of Sales/Marketing: Paula Standley
Parent Co: Equitythink Holdings, LLC

2471 **Charlie Palmer Group**
372 5th Ave
New York, NY 10018-8106 212-967-6942
Fax: 212-750-8613 888-287-3653
info@charliepalmer.com
www.charliepalmer.com
Pan sauces, dessert sauces
Owner: Charlie Lee
Estimated Sales: $2.5-5 Million
Number Employees: 50-99
Brands:
Charlie Palmer

2472 **Charlie Trotter Foods**
816 W Armitage Ave
Chicago, IL 60614-4308 773-248-6228
Fax: 773-248-6088 info@charlietrotters.com
www.charlietrotters.com
Sauces, smoked salmon and natural products
Owner, Chef: Charlie Trotter
Estimated Sales: $ 1 - 3 Million
Number Employees: 50-99

2473 **Charlie's Country Sausage**
4005 Burdick Expy E
Minot, ND 58701 701-838-6302
Manufacturer of meat products including salami, honey ham and sausage
Owner: Charles Weiskopf
Estimated Sales: $1-2.5 Million
Number Employees: 6

2474 **Charlie's Pride Meats**
2959 E 50th St
Vernon, CA 90058 323-585-3358
Fax: 323-587-7317 877-866-0982
info@cpmhotline.com www.cpmhotline.com
Processor and exporter of roast beef, corned beef, pastrami, entrees, au jus, dipping sauces and gravies
Co-President: Jim Dickman
Co-President: Robert Dickman
Operations Director: Jim Miller
Plant Manager: James Miller
Estimated Sales: $23 Million
Number Employees: 120
Number of Products: 50
Sq. footage: 25000
Type of Packaging: Consumer, Food Service, Private Label, Bulk

2475 **Charlie's Specialties**
2500 Freedland Rd
Hermitage, PA 16148 724-346-2350
Fax: 724-346-1110
Fancy cookies
President: John Thier
Owner: Thomas Carpenter
Sales: Joe Webb
Plant Manager: Frank Keck
Estimated Sales: $5-10 Million
Number Employees: 80
Number of Products: 45
Sq. footage: 24000

2476 **Charlotte's Confections**
1395 El Camino Real
Millbrae, CA 94030-1410 650-589-1126
Fax: 650-589-1923 800-798-2427
lisa@charlottesconfections.com
www.charlottesconfections.com
Boxed chocolates, taffy, caramel, brittle, fudge, marshmallow, and holiday specialties.
President: Jeffrey Sosnick
Vice President: Sean Callaway
Marketing Director: Susan Muniak
Production Coordinator: Jim Macintire
Purchasing Manager: Jim Macintire
Estimated Sales: $5 Million
Number Employees: 50-99
Sq. footage: 24000
Type of Packaging: Consumer, Food Service, Private Label, Bulk

2477 **Charlton Deep Sea Charters**
P.O.Box 637
Warrenton, OR 97146-0637 503-338-0569
Fax: 503-861-3229 www.charltoncharters.com
Seafood, including halibut, salmon, sturgeon, tuna, bottomfish
President: Mark Charlton
Purchasing Manager: Mark Charlton
Estimated Sales: $2.5-5 Million
Number Employees: 1-4

2478 **Chase Brothers Dairy**
595 S Wolff Rd
Oxnard, CA 93033-2101 805-487-4981
Fax: 805-487-2529 800-438-6455
Processor of milk and related products including fluid, half and half, chocolate, low-fat, nonfat, buttermilk, eggnog and shakes; also, juices, concentrates and drinks including orange, etc
President: Glywn Chase Jr
Vice President: S Chase
Estimated Sales: $5-10 Million
Number Employees: 20-49
Sq. footage: 7000
Parent Co: Hailwood
Type of Packaging: Consumer, Food Service
Brands:
CHASE BROTHERS
GOLD COAST

2479 **Chase Candy Company**
P.O.Box 698
Saint Joseph, MO 64502 816-279-1625
Fax: 816-279-1997 800-786-1625
info@cherrymash.com www.cherrymash.com
Processor of candy including bagged, bar, brittle, chocolate, coconut, fund raising, multi-pack, vending, Christmas, Easter, Halloween and Valentine
President: Barry Yantis
Purchasing Manager: Barry Yantis
Estimated Sales: $ 10 - 20 Million
Number Employees: 20-49
Sq. footage: 20000
Type of Packaging: Consumer, Bulk
Brands:
CHERRY MASH
POE BRANDS

2480 **Chases Lobster Pound**
PO Box 1
Port Howe, NS B0K 1K0
Canada 902-243-2408
Fax: 902-243-3334
Processor and exporter of fresh and frozen lobster
Owner/Manager: Earl Chase
Number Employees: 10-19
Type of Packaging: Consumer, Food Service, Private Label, Bulk

2481 **Chateau Anne Marie**
6580 NE Mineral Springs Rd
Carlton, OR 97111-9529 503-864-2991
Fax: 503-864-2203 www.anneamie.com
Wines
Owner: Robert Pamplin Jr
Purchasing: Scott Huffman
Estimated Sales: $5-10 Million
Number Employees: 20-49

2482 **Chateau Boswell**
3468 Silverado Trl N
St Helena, CA 94574-9662 707-963-5472
josh@chateauboswellwinery.com
www.chateauboswellwinery.com
Manufacturer of wines
President: Dr Thronton Boswell
COO: Susan Boswell
Operations Manager: Joshua Peeples
Estimated Sales: Less than $500,000
Number Employees: 1-4
Type of Packaging: Consumer
Brands:
Chateau Boswell
Chateau Boswell Estate
Jacquelynn Cuv'e
Jacquelynn Syrah

2483 **Chateau Chevre Winery**
2030 Hoffman Ln
Napa, CA 94558 707-944-2184
Fax: 707-944-2408
Wines
Owner: Jerry Hazen
Estimated Sales: Less than $100,000
Number Employees: 1-4
Type of Packaging: Private Label

2484 **Chateau Diana Winery**
6195 Dry Creek Rd
Healdsburg, CA 95448 707-433-6992
Fax: 707-433-0401 info@chateaud.com
www.chateaudiana.com
Wines
President: Corey Manning
VP Marketing: Dawn Manning
Quality Control: Nicole Martineau
Estimated Sales: $5-10 Million
Number Employees: 18
Brands:
Chateau Diana

2485 **Chateau Food Products**
6137 W Cermak Rd
Cicero, IL 60804 708-863-4207
Fax: 708-863-5806 www.chateaufoods.com
Processor of frozen potato and bread dumplings
President: Donald Shotola
VP: Anita Shotola
Production: Jon Shotola
Estimated Sales: $1 Million
Number Employees: 5-9
Sq. footage: 10000
Type of Packaging: Consumer, Food Service

Brands:
Chateau
Mihel

2486 **Chateau Grand Traverse**
12239 Center Rd
Traverse City, MI 49686 231-223-7355
Fax: 231-223-4105 www.cgtwines.com
Wines
Owner: Ed Okeefe
Founder/CEO: Edward O'Keefe, Sr
VP/Trade Relations: Sean O'Keefe
Operations Manager/Controller: Terrie McClelland
Productions/shipping/Warehouse: Mark Groenevelt
Purchasing Manager: Mark Groenevelt
Estimated Sales: $2.5-5 Million
Number Employees: 10-19

2487 **Chateau Julien Winery**
8940 Carmel Valley Rd
Carmel, CA 93923 831-624-2600
Fax: 831-624-6138 www.chateaujulien.com
Wines
Owner: Robert Brower
VP National Sales: Tom Kencheloe
Winemaker: Bill Anderson
Estimated Sales: $1-2.5 Million
Number Employees: 10-19
Brands:
CHATEAU JULIEN
EMERALD BAY COASTAK
GARLAND RANCH

2488 **Chateau Lafayette Reneau**
P.O.Box 238
Hector, NY 14841 607-546-2062
Fax: 607-546-2069 800-469-9463
support@clrwine.com www.clrwine.com
Wine
Owner: Dick Reno
Vice President: Betty Reno
General Manager: Heather Lodge
Purchasing Manager: Dick Reno
Estimated Sales: $1.4 Million
Number Employees: 25
Type of Packaging: Private Label

2489 **Chateau Montelena Winery**
1429 Tubbs Ln
Calistoga, CA 94515 707-942-5105
Fax: 707-942-4221
customer-service@montelena.com
www.montelena.com
Wines
President: James Barrett
Marketing Director: Greg Ralston
Public Relations: Tom Inlay
Operations Manager: Bo Barrett
Estimated Sales: $10-20 Million
Number Employees: 20-49
Brands:
Chateau Montelena
Silverado Cellars

2490 **Chateau Morisette Winery**
P.O.Box 766
Meadows of Dan, VA 24120-0766 540-593-2865
Fax: 540-593-2868 info@thedogs.com
www.chateaumorrisette.com
Wines
President: David Morrisette
Purchasing Manager: Nora Cooper
Estimated Sales: $10-20 Million
Number Employees: 20-49

2491 **Chateau Potelle Winery**
4 Blackberry Dr
Napa, CA 94558-7016 707-255-9440
Fax: 707-255-9444 info@chateaupotelle.com
www.chateaupotelle.com
Wines
President: Jean Noel Fourmeaux
Purchasing Manager: Ulysses Montre
Estimated Sales: $2.5-5 Million
Number Employees: 5-9
Brands:
CHATEAU POTELLE

2492 **Chateau Ra-Ha**
P.O.Box 428
Jerseyville, IL 62052-0428 618-639-4841
Fax: 618-639-0510 866-639-4832
chateauraha@gtec.com www.gtec.com
Wines
Owner: Paul Arnold
Estimated Sales: $500,000-$1 Million
Number Employees: 1-4

2493 **Chateau Souverain**
P.O.Box 245
Cloverdale, CA 95425-245
Fax: 707-433-5174 www.chateausouverain.com
Processor of cabernet sauvignon, merlot, sauvignon blanc, chardonnay and zinfandel
President: Dan Leese
Purchasing Manager: John Peavey
Estimated Sales: $20-50 Million
Number Employees: 50-99
Type of Packaging: Private Label
Brands:
CHATEAU SOUVERAIN

2494 **Chateau St. Jean Vineyards**
P.O.Box 293
Kenwood, CA 95452-0293 707-833-4134
Fax: 707-833-4200 www.chateaustjean.com
Processor of table wine
Manager: Margo Van Stafvaren
Winemaker/Operation Director: Margo Anstaavern
Public Relations Manager: Nicole Breier
Wine Maker: Steven Reeder
Estimated Sales: $10-24.9 Million
Number Employees: 50-99
Parent Co: Beringer Wine Estates
Type of Packaging: Consumer

2495 **Chateau Thomas Winery**
6291 Cambridge Way
Plainfield, IN 46168 317-837-9463
Fax: 317-837-8464 888-761-9463
info@chateauthomas.com
www.chateauthomas.com
Premium vinifera wines made from West Coast grapes
President: Charles Thomas
Purchasing Manager: Tommy England
Estimated Sales: $5-10 Million
Number Employees: 20-49
Type of Packaging: Private Label
Brands:
CHATEAU THOMAS

2496 **Chateau des Charmes Wines**
PO Box 280
St. Davids, ON L0S 1P0
Canada 905-262-4219
Fax: 905-262-5548 800-263-2541
www.chateaudescharmes.com
Processor of wines and champagnes, ice wine
President: Paul Bosc
Secretary: Rodger Gordon
Director Marketing: Paul-Andre Bosc
Estimated Sales: $1-2.5 Million
Number Employees: 100-249

2497 **Chatila's Bakery**
254 N Broadway
Salem, NH 03079-2132 603-898-5459
Fax: 603-893-1586
customercare@chatilasbakery.com
www.chatilasbakery.com
All sugar-free items. Chatila's muffins, cookies, pastries, cheesecakes, donuts, bagels, pies, breads, chocolates and ice cream. All items sweetend with Splenda and/or Melltitol, low carb, low cal, low fat, low cholestrol, notrans-fat.
President: Mohamad Chatila
Sales: Jennifer Marks
Estimated Sales: $650,000-700,000
Number Employees: 10-19
Number of Brands: 1
Number of Products: 100+
Sq. footage: 12000
Type of Packaging: Consumer, Food Service, Private Label, Bulk

2498 **Chatom Vineyards**
P.O.Box 2730
Murphys, CA 95247-2730 209-736-6500
Fax: 209-736-6507 800-435-8852
info@chatomvineyards
www.chatomvineyards.com
Wines
President: Gay Callan
Production Manager: Scott Klann
Purchasing Manager: Mari Wells
Estimated Sales: $1-2.5 Million
Number Employees: 10-19
Number of Products: 7
Sq. footage: 4200
Brands:
SANGIOVESE
SYRAH

2499 **Chattanooga Bakery**
P.O.Box 111
Chattanooga, TN 37401 423-267-3351
Fax: 423-266-2169 800-251-3404
linda@moonpie.com www.moonpie.com
Manufacturer of marshmallow snack cakes and sandwiches
President/CEO: Sam Campbell IV
CEO: Sam H Campbell Iv
VP Marketing: Tory Johnston
VP Sales: John Campbell
VP Operations: Guy Callahan
Estimated Sales: $20-50 Million
Number Employees: 100-249
Type of Packaging: Consumer
Brands:
MOON PIE

2500 **Chattem Chemicals**
3708 Saint Elmo Ave
Chattanooga, TN 37409 423-822-5001
Fax: 423-825-0507
eva.edwards@chattemchemicals.com
www.chattemchemicals.com
Manufacturer of glycine and creatine monohydrate
President: Jitendra Doshi
CFO: Ed Rusk
VP/General Manager: Jason Allen
Research & Development: Nilesh Patel
Quality Assurance/Quality Control: Frank Seymour
Human Resources: Wanda Lowe
VP Operations/Production/Manufacturing: Ray Smith
Manufacturing Director: Scott Newton
Purchasing Director: Ellen Werkau
Estimated Sales: $5-10 Million
Number Employees: 65
Sq. footage: 12987
Parent Co: Elcat
Type of Packaging: Bulk

2501 **Chatz Roasting Company**
PO Box 2765
Ceres, CA 95307-7765 510-265-1600
Fax: 510-265-1734 800-792-6333
chatzcoffee@linkline.com www.chatz.com
Gourmet coffee, tea, cocoa
President: Linda Blaney
CEO: Robert Heinz
DirecterMarketing: Robert Heinz
Estimated Sales: $10-20 Million
Number Employees: 20-49
Brands:
Chatz

2502 **Chaucer Foods**
160 Eileen Way
Syosset, NY 11791 516-496-2500
Fax: 516-496-2516
charles.carlson@chaucerfoods.com
www.chaucerfoods.com
Manufacturers freeze dried ingredients, croutons & bread based products, clusters and mushroom extract
National Broker/ Distributor Manager: Charles Carlson
Number Employees: 5-9
Parent Co: Chaucer Foods Ltd

2503 **Chauvin Coffee Corporation**
4160 Meramec St
Saint Louis, MO 63116 314-772-0700
Fax: 314-772-0722 800-455-5282
info@chauvincoffee.com
www.chauvincoffee.com

Coffee
President: Dave Charleville
Sales Manager: Sonya Miller
Estimated Sales: $ 1 - 3 Million
Number Employees: 10-19
Type of Packaging: Private Label

2504 **Chazy Orchards**
P.O. Box 147
Chazy, NY 12921-0147 518-846-7171
Fax: 518-846-8171 chazyapples@westel.com
www.chazy.com
Grower of apples
Owner: Donald F Green Iii III
Estimated Sales: $ 5 - 10 Million
Number Employees: 20-49

2505 **Cheddar Box Cheese House**
264 Alpine Dr
Shawano, WI 54166 715-526-5411
Fax: 715-524-9930 info@cheddarbox.com
www.cheddarbox.com
Processor of cheese spreads
President: James O'Betts
Estimated Sales: $400,000
Number Employees: 1-4
Brands:
CHEDDAR BOX CHEESE

2506 **(HQ)Cheese Factory**
19724 Huber Road
Borden, IN 47106-8309 812-923-8861
Cheese
President: Pat Huffman
General Manager: LaDonna Mitchell
Estimated Sales: $5-9.9 Million
Number Employees: 1-4

2507 **Cheese Smokers**
360 Johnson Ave
Brooklyn, NY 11206
Fax: 718-381-0534
Processor of naturally smoked cheeses including Swiss, kosher, cheddar, mozzarella and provolone; also, bars and deli loaves; contract smoking available
President: Irving Binik
VP: Bary Binik
VP Sales: Barry Binik
Estimated Sales: $1-2.5 Million
Number Employees: 10-19
Sq. footage: 12000
Type of Packaging: Consumer, Food Service, Private Label, Bulk
Brands:
Hic-O-Ree
La-natural

2508 **Cheese Straws & More**
5717 Desiard Street
Monroe, LA 71203-4793 318-343-4666
Fax: 318-343-6333 800-997-1921
schwab@cheesestraws.com
www.cheesestraws.com
Processor of straws including Cajun cheese and southern tea; also, pecan pralines, candied pecans and pecan brittle
President: Brenda Schwab
Number Employees: 1-4

2509 **CheeseLand**
P.O.Box 22230
Seattle, WA 98122-0230 206-709-1220
Fax: 206-709-1818
Cheese
President: Jan Kos
Estimated Sales: $1-2.5 Million
Number Employees: 1-4

2510 **Cheesecake Aly**
530 S Broad St
Glen Rock, NJ 7452 201-444-8590
Fax: 201-444-8454 800-555-8862
chzcakealy@aol.com www.cheesecakealy.com
Processor of cheesecakes and desserts
President: Aly Boyd
Estimated Sales: $1-3 Million
Number Employees: 10-19
Sq. footage: 4000
Type of Packaging: Consumer, Food Service, Bulk
Brands:
Cheesecake Aly

2511 **Cheesecake Etc. Desserts**
400 Swallow Dr
Miami Springs, FL 33166 305-887-0258
Fax: 305-888-5463
Cheesecakes, key lime pies, diner style layer cakes, individual dessert cups; including all varieties of layer cakes, cheesecake, and key lime pie
President: Francesco Romano
Office Manager: Rachelle Romano
Estimated Sales: Under $500,000
Number Employees: 1-4
Number of Brands: 3
Number of Products: 25
Sq. footage: 10000
Type of Packaging: Food Service
Brands:
Florida Key Lime Pie

2512 **Cheesecake Factory**
26901 Malibu Hills Rd
Calabasas Hills, CA 91301-5354 818-871-3000
Fax: 818-871-3100 www.cheesecakefactory.net
Cheesecakes
President/CEO: David Overton
Estimated Sales: $37,800,000
Number Employees: 10,000+
Brands:
Cheesecake Factory

2513 **Cheesecake Momma**
200 W Henry St
Ukiah, CA 95482 707-462-2253
Fax: 707-468-9056 momma@pacific.net
www.cheesecakemomma.com
Processor and wholesaler of cheesecake including all natural and 100% organic
President: Robin Collier
Vice President: Alana Rouse
Purchasing Manager: Robin Collier
Estimated Sales: $2.5-5 Million
Number Employees: 20-49

2514 **Cheeze Kurls**
3711 Dykstra Drive NW
Grand Rapids, MI 49544-9745 616-784-6095
Fax: 616-784-7445 www.cksnacks.com
Processor of snack foods including popcorn and cheese curls
President: Ed DeDinas
VP: Bob Franzak
Number Employees: 20-49
Sq. footage: 30000
Type of Packaging: Consumer, Food Service, Private Label, Bulk
Brands:
CK

2515 **Cheezwhse.Com**
111 Business Park Dr
Armonk, NY 10504 914-273-1400
Fax: 914-273-2052 800-922-4337
sales@cheezwhse.com www.cheezwhse.com
Dairy products
President/Owner: Joseph Gellert
Estimated Sales: $6.2 Million
Number Employees: 30

2516 **Chef America**
9601 Canoga Ave
Chatsworth, CA 91311 818-718-8111
www.chefamerica.com
Processor of prepared frozen foods including stuffed sandwiches and croissants, pizza snacks and waffles
CEO: Paul Merage
CFO: Glenn Lee
VP: Larry Johnson
Research & Development: Phil Mason
V P Finance: Glenn Lee
Manufacturing Development Manager: John Spinner
Purchasing Director: George Turner
Purchasing Manager: Russ Shroyer
Plant Manager: Mike Crawford
Number Employees: 500-999
Type of Packaging: Consumer, Food Service

2517 **Chef America East**
150 Oak Grove Drive
Mount Sterling, KY 40353-9087 859-498-4300
www.chefamerica.com
Processor of prepared frozen foods including stuffed sandwiches and croissants, pizza snacks and waffles
CEO: Paul Merage
CFO: Glenn Lee
VP: Larry Johnson
Research & Development: Phil Mason
V P Finance: Glenn Lee
Manufacturing Development Manager: John Spinner
Purchasing Director: George Turner
Purchasing Manager: Russ Shroyer
Plant Manager: Mike Crawford
Purchasing Manager: George Turner
Number Employees: 100-249
Type of Packaging: Consumer, Food Service

2518 **Chef Francisco of Pennsylvania**
250 Hansen Access Road
King of Prussia, PA 19406-2448 610-265-7400
Fax: 610-265-0153 www.cheffrancisco.com
Processor of frozen soups
Manager: Suzann Shreck
Plant Manager: Thomas Butler
Estimated Sales: $50-100 Million
Number Employees: 250-499
Parent Co: Heinz USA
Type of Packaging: Food Service, Private Label

2519 **Chef Hans Gourmet Foods**
310 Walnut St
Monroe, LA 71201 318-322-2334
Fax: 318-322-2340 800-890-4267
ckorrodi@bayou.com
www.chefhansgourmetfoods.com
Processor and exporter of soup bases, batter, spices, seafood, breading, seasonings, wild rice pilaf, rice, desserts, bran, jambalaya, gumbo, etouffee, etc.
President: Hans Korrodi
Estimated Sales: $1-2.5 Million
Number Employees: 5-9
Sq. footage: 22000
Brands:
Chef Hans

2520 **Chef Merito**
PO Box 260948
Encino, CA 91426-0948 800-637-4861
info@chefmerito.com
www.chefmerito.com
Processor, importer and exporter of dried spices, seasonings, seasoned rice, batters, breading mixes, soups and sauces
President/CEO: Plinio Garcia, Jr
Estimated Sales: $10-20 Million
Number Employees: 20-49
Sq. footage: 30000
Type of Packaging: Consumer, Food Service, Bulk
Brands:
CHEF MERITO
PIKOS PIKOSOS
PPEPPERS
SABROSITO

2521 **Chef Paul Prudhomme's Magic Seasonings Blends**
P.O.Box 23342
Harahan, LA 70123 504-731-3590
Fax: 504-731-3576 800-457-2857
info@chefpaul.com www.chefpaul.com
Seasonings and spices
President: Shawn Mc Bride
President/CEO: Shawn McBride
CFO: Paula LaCour
Marketing VP: John McBride
Production Manager: David Hickey
Purchasing Agent: Carol Mauthe
Estimated Sales: $10-20 Million
Number Employees: 50-99
Sq. footage: 30000
Type of Packaging: Private Label
Brands:
CHEF PAUL PRUDHOMME'S

2522 **Chef Shells Catering & Roadside Cafe**
2639 24th St
Port Huron, MI 48060-6418 810-966-8371
Fax: 810-966-8372 info@jabars.com
www.chefshells.com
Processor of wine vinaigrettes, sauces, seasonings and dip mixes; gourmet catering available
Owner: Michelle Wrubel

Estimated Sales: $1-2.5 Million
Number Employees: 5-9
Number of Products: 45
Sq. footage: 1800
Type of Packaging: Consumer, Food Service, Private Label, Bulk

2523 **Chef Silvio's of Wooster Street**
69 Brookward Road
Guilford, CT 06437-1804 203-453-1064
Fax: 203-453-1064 newmedfoods@aol.com
www.chefsilvios.com
Manufacturer of gourmet foods and sauces.

2524 **Chef Solutions**
120 W Palatine Rd
Wheeling, IL 60090 847-325-7500
Fax: 847-325-7594 800-877-1157
www.chefsolutions.com
Manufacturers of fresh, refrigerated foods such as deli-style salads, compnent kit salads, mashed potatoes and side dishes, fresh cut fruit, dips and salad dressing.
CEO: Steven Silk
Chief Food Safety Officer: William Schwartz
VP Human Resources: Bryan Glancy
Plant Engineer: Mike Wilcox
Purchasing Agent: Debbie Shafer
Estimated Sales: $500+ Million
Number Employees: 150
Sq. footage: 60000
Parent Co: Questor
Type of Packaging: Consumer, Food Service
Brands:
ORVAL KENT

2525 **Chef Tim Foods, LLC**
65 Sam Snead Circle
Etters, PA 17319-9565 717-802-0350
cheftim@ptd.net
www.cheftimfoods.com
Gluten-free, kosher, organic/natural, salad dressing, marinades, other sauces, seasonings and cooking enhancers.

2526 **Chef Zachary's Gourmet Blended Spices**
216 Bagley Street
Detroit, MI 48221-0053 313-226-0000
Fax: 313-226-0000 zach4spice@aol.com
www.chefzachary.com
Natural, gourmet spice blends
Owner/President: Chef Zachary Smith
Estimated Sales: $300,000-500,000
Number Employees: 1-4
Type of Packaging: Consumer
Brands:
Blackening Spice
Chelsea Spice
Mediterranean
Shana Spice

2527 **Chef's Requested Foods**
P.O.Box 82096
Oklahoma City, OK 73148-0096 405-239-2610
Fax: 405-239-2616 800-256-0259
customerservice@chefsrequested.com
www.chefsrequested.com
Processor of fresh and frozen meats
President: John Williams
Estimated Sales: $50-100 Million
Number Employees: 100-249
Type of Packaging: Food Service

2528 **Chef-A-Roni**
2832 S County Trl
East Greenwich, RI 02818-1742 401-884-8798
Fax: 401-884-3552 www.chefaroni.com
Processor of spaghetti sauce
President: Henry Caniglia
Vice President: Lillian Caniglia
Estimated Sales: $500,000-$1 Million
Number Employees: 5-9
Type of Packaging: Consumer, Food Service
Brands:
Chef-A-Roni

2529 **Chefmaster**
10871 Forbes Ave Ste A
Garden Grove, CA 92843 714-554-4000
Fax: 714-554-4410 800-333-7443
Chefmaster@BKCOMPANY.COM
www.bkcompany.com
Manufacturer of ingredients for the bakery, confectionery and food industries. Items such as; gels, liqua-gels, airbrush and candy colors, as well as other decorating items such as piping gel, pastry bags and meringue powders
Manager: Ed Larrarte
Estimated Sales: $10-20 Million
Number Employees: 20-49
Sq. footage: 60000
Type of Packaging: Food Service, Private Label
Brands:
CHEFMASTER

2530 **Chelan Fresh**
317 Johnson St
Chelan, WA 98816 509-682-5133
Fax: 509-923-2329 www.chelanfresh.com
Grower of apples and pears
CEO: David Green
Office Manager: Susan Campbell
Sales Manager: Doug McClellan
Sales: Troy Burnett
General Manager: Gerald Mineard
Estimated Sales: $ 10 - 20 Million
Number Employees: 100-249
Type of Packaging: Consumer
Brands:
Chelan Fresh
Frutrition

2531 **Chella's Dutch Delicacies**
6024 Jean Road
Suite C150
Lake Oswego, OR 97035-5330 503-534-9888
Fax: 503-635-1399 800-458-3331
Shortbread pastry and bread
Purchasing Agent: Jake Raymond
Estimated Sales: $10-20 Million
Number Employees: 10-19

2532 **Chelsea Market Baskets**
75 9th Ave # 1
New York, NY 10011-7047 212-727-1111
Fax: 212-727-1778 888-727-7887
info@chelseamarketbaskets.com
www.chelseamarketbaskets.com
Custom made gift baskets for various occasions
President: David Porat
Estimated Sales: $500,000-$1 Million
Number Employees: 10-19
Brands:
Chelsea Market Baskets
Cottage Delight
Shortbread Housf

2533 **(HQ)Chelsea Milling Company**
201 W North St
Chelsea, MI 48118 734-475-1361
Fax: 734-475-4630 www.jiffymix.com
Processor of mixes including cake, frosting, muffin, brownie, pizza crust, biscuit, etc.
President: Howard Holmes
Vice President: Jack Kennedy
Plant Manager: Mike Williamson
Purchasing Manager: Ed Hofpstadter
Estimated Sales: $50-100 Million
Number Employees: 250-499
Type of Packaging: Consumer
Other Locations:
Chelsea Milling Co.
Marshall MI
Brands:
JIFFY MIX

2534 **Chelten House Products**
607 Heron Dr
Bridgeport, NJ 08014 856-467-1600
Fax: 856-467-4769 info@cheltenhouse.com
www.cheltenhouse.com
Manufacturer of organic and all-natural dressings, sauces, marinades, salsa and ketchup. QAI certified and OU approved.
CEO: Steven Dabrow
Estimated Sales: $40 Million
Number Employees: 20-49
Sq. footage: 140000
Type of Packaging: Consumer, Food Service, Private Label
Brands:
CHELTEN HOUSE
MARINADE BAY
SIMPLY NATURAL

2535 **Chempacific Corporation**
6200 Freeport Ctr
Baltimore, MD 21224-6524 410-633-5771
Fax: 410-633-5808 sales@ChemPacific.com
www.chempacific.com
President: Dr Dean Wei
COO: Tony Liang
CEO: Rebecca Chiu
VP Sales/Marketing: Jim Havlin
Director Sales: Tony Liang
Estimated Sales: $ 3 - 5 Million
Number Employees: 20-49

2536 **(HQ)Cher-Make Sausage Company**
2915 Calumet Ave
Manitowoc, WI 54220-5550 920-683-5980
Fax: 920-682-2588 800-242-7679
www.cher-make.com
Processor and exporter of kippered beef, sausage and meat snacks; importer of frozen meat.
President: Arthur Chermak Jr
Executive Dir: Betty Hoefner
Director Finance/Vp Fin: Lawrence Franke
Director Sales/Marketing: Rod Nedvedr
Plant Manager: Chuck Hoefner
Purchasing Manager: Jim Coulson
Estimated Sales: $10-20 Million
Number Employees: 100-249
Sq. footage: 80000
Type of Packaging: Consumer, Private Label
Brands:
CHER-MAKE SAUSAGE
HOME GAME
SMOKEY MESQUITE
SMOKY VALLEY

2537 **Cheraw Packing**
578 Highway 1 S
Cheraw, SC 29520-3812 843-537-7426
Fax: 843-537-6699
Processor of beef and pork
President: John Weeks
Purchasing: John Weeks
Estimated Sales: $5-10 Million
Number Employees: 10-19
Type of Packaging: Consumer, Food Service, Private Label, Bulk

2538 **Cherbogue Fisheries**
PO Box 326
Yarmouth, NS B5A 4B3
Canada 902-742-9157
Fax: 902-742-7708
Processor and exporter of fresh and frozen seafood
VP: Alfred LeBlanc
Number Employees: 20-49
Type of Packaging: Bulk

2539 **Cherchies**
1 N Bacton Hill Rd Ste 107
Malvern, PA 19355 610-640-9440
Fax: 610-644-7937 800-644-1980
staff@cherchies.com www.cherchies.com
Processor of gourmet foods including mustard, peppers, pepper jellies, sauces, soups, chowders, preserves and seasonings; also, chili and freeze-dried soup and chowder mixes
President: Anthony Spallone
VP: Patti Spallone
Marketing: Joe Shrum
Operations: Lori Hughes
Purchasing: Gayle Snyder
Estimated Sales: $1-2.5 Million
Number Employees: 10-19
Number of Brands: 1
Number of Products: 60
Sq. footage: 1400
Type of Packaging: Consumer, Food Service, Private Label
Brands:
CHERCHIES

2540 **Cheri's Desert Harvest**
1840 E Winsett St
Tucson, AZ 85719 520-623-4141
Fax: 520-623-7741 800-743-1141
help@cherisdesertharvest.com
www.cherisdesertharvest.com
Jellies, marmalade, bread, candies, syrup
Owner: Cheri Romanoski
Vice President: Jon Romanaski
Production Manager: Nancy Howes
Purchasing Manager: Cheryl Romanaski

Estimated Sales: $1-2.5 Million
Number Employees: 5-9
Brands:
CHERI'S DESERT HARVEST

2541 **Cheribundi**
500 Technology Farm Drive
Geneva, NY 14456 315-781-7308
Fax: 315-282-2317 brian.ross@cherrypharm.com
www.cheribundi.com
Juice/cider.
Marketing: Brian Ross

2542 **Cherith Valley Gardens**
P.O.Box 12040
Fort Worth, TX 76110 817-922-8822
Fax: 817-922-8884 800-610-9813
terriw@cherithvalley.com
www.cherithvalley.com
Processor, importer and exporter of gourmet pickles, pickled vegetables, salsas, jellies, fruit toppings, peppers, relishes and hors d'oeuvres
President: Alan Werner
Public Relations: Terri Werner
Operations Manager: Christa Werner
Estimated Sales: $ 5 - 10 Million
Number Employees: 10-19
Sq. footage: 6000
Type of Packaging: Consumer, Food Service
Brands:
Cherith Valley Gardens

2543 **Cherokee Trout Farms**
P.O.Box 525
Cherokee, NC 28719-0525 828-497-9227
Fax: 828-497-4330 800-732-0075
Processor of fresh and frozen trout including rainbow, hickory and smoked; also, trout cakes and dip
Owner: Dale Owen
Processing Mgr.: James Pheasant
Farm Manager: Ron Blankenship
Estimated Sales: $ .5 - 1 million
Number Employees: 1-4
Sq. footage: 8000
Type of Packaging: Consumer, Bulk
Brands:
Native American Foods

2544 **Cherry Central Cooperative Inc**
P.O.Box 988
Traverse City, MI 49685 231-946-1860
Fax: 231-941-4167 info@cherrycentral.com
www.cherrycentral.com
Manufacturer and exporter of canned, frozen and dried blueberries, cherries, apples and plums.
President/General Manager: Richard Bogard
Chairman: Claude Rowley
Controller: Laura Reed
VP Sales: James Giannestras
Estimated Sales: $100-500 Million
Number Employees: 50-99
Sq. footage: 15500
Type of Packaging: Consumer, Food Service, Private Label, Bulk
Brands:
CHERRY CENTRAL
FRUIT PATCH
GRAND TRAVERSE
INDIAN SUMMER
MONTMORENCY
NORTH BAY
REDDI MAID
TRAVERSE BAY
WILDERNESS

2545 **Cherry Growers**
6331 US Highway 31
PO Box 90
Grawn, MI 49637 231-276-9241
Fax: 231-276-7075 orders@cherrygrowers.net
www.cherrygrowers.net
Processor and exporter of canned and frozen cherries, apples and juices.
President: Thomas Rochford
VP/Director of Sales: Tim Daly
Human Resources Director: Tom Spencer
Plant Manager: Charlie Roderick
Purchasing Director: John Harrigan
Estimated Sales: $49 Million
Number Employees: 125
Number of Brands: 2
Sq. footage: 125000
Type of Packaging: Consumer, Food Service, Private Label, Bulk
Brands:
VERMONT JACK'S
VERMONT VILLAGE

2546 **Cherry Hill Orchards Pelham**
333 Hwy 20 W
Fenwick, ON L0S 1C0
Canada 905-892-3782
Fax: 905-892-7808
Processor and packer of fresh and frozen red tart cherries for pies and desserts.
President: Lawrence Haun
Secretary: Mary Lou Haun
Plant Manager: Stephen Haun
Number Employees: 24
Sq. footage: 25000
Type of Packaging: Consumer, Food Service
Brands:
Tree Ripe

2547 **Cherry Hut**
2345 N Us Highway 31 N
Traverse City, MI 49686-3755 231-938-8888
Fax: 231-938-3333 888-882-4431
www.cherrytreeinn.com
Products made from cherries, including sauces, jams, jellies, conserves, preserves
Manager: Jonathan Pack
Owner: Brenda Case
Production VP: Leonard Case
Estimated Sales: Less than $500,000
Number Employees: 1-4

2548 **Cherry Lane Frozen Fruits**
4230 Victoria Avenue
Vineland Station, ON L0R 2E0
Canada 905-562-4337
Fax: 905-562-5577 877-243-7796
www.cherrylane.net
Processor of cherries and peaches
President: John Smith
Number Employees: 100
Type of Packaging: Consumer, Food Service

2549 **Cherry Point Products**
54 Wyman Rd
Milbridge, ME 04658 207-546-7056
Fax: 207-546-7079
Canned and cured fish and seafood
Owner: Drusilla Ray

2550 **Cherrybrook Kitchen Inc**
20 Mall Rd
Suite 410
Burlington, MA 01803 781-272-0400
Fax: 781-272-4460 866-I L-V CB
www.cherrybrookkitchen.com
Peanut free, dairy free, egg free and nut free cake, cookie and brownie mixes, cookies, frostings, breakfast mixes, and wheat free and gluten free mixes
President/Owner: Chip Rosenberg
Founder: Patsy Rosenberg
VP Marketing: Laura Kuykendall
VP Sales: Sallie Bowling
Finance/HR Manager: Sue Giannetti
Number Employees: 7

2551 **Cherrydale Farms**
1035 Mill Rd
Allentown, PA 18106-3101 610-366-1606
Fax: 610-391-9284 800-333-4525
info@cherrydale.com www.cherrydalefarms.com
Manufacturer of chocolate and confections featuring nuts, caramel, creams, crunch products and more; packaged in a variety of tin shapes, sizes and designs for fundraising programs.
President: Richard Toltzis
Co-President: Richard Toltzis
Vice President: Jack Bucchioni
Senior Sales Representative: Larry Brown
Vice President Manufacturing: John Cooke
Estimated Sales: 10-100 Million
Number Employees: 500-999
Type of Packaging: Consumer, Private Label, Bulk

2552 **Cherryfield Foods**
P.O.Box 128
Cherryfield, ME 04622-0128 207-546-7573
Fax: 207-546-2713
sales@oxfordfrozenfoods.com
www.oxfordfrozenfoods.com
Blueberries
COO: Jeff Vose
Estimated Sales: $ 50 - 100 Million
Number Employees: 100-249
Parent Co: Oxford Frozen Foods

2553 **Cheryl & Company**
646 McCorkle Blvd
Westerville, OH 43082 614-776-1500
Fax: 614-891-8799 www.cherylandco.com
Cookies, brownies, cakes and pies
President: Cheryl Krueger
CFO: Dennis Hicks
Marketing Director: Lisa Henry
Production Planner: Scott Miller
Manager: Elisabeth Allwein
Estimated Sales: $50-100 Million
Number Employees: 225
Parent Co: 1-800-Flowers
Type of Packaging: Private Label
Brands:
CHERYL & CO.

2554 **Chesapeake Bay Gourmet**
8805 Kelso Dr
Essex, MD 21221-3112 410-780-0444
Fax: 800-858-6547 800-432-2722
info@cbgourmet.com www.cbcrabcake.com
A specialty line of handmade, hand picked Jumbo Lump crab cakes and other gourmet seafood products.
President: Ron Kauffman
CEO: Margie Kauffman
CEO: Steve Cohen
Estimated Sales: $ 20 - 50 Million
Number Employees: 100-249
Sq. footage: 35000

2555 **Chesapeake Feed Company**
PO Box 23
Beltsville, MD 20704-0023 301-419-2433
Feed
President: Lingard Klein
Estimated Sales: $1-2.5 Million appx.
Number Employees: 1-4

2556 **Chesapeake Spice Company**
9341 Philadelphia Rd.
Baltimore, MD 21237
US 410-391-2100
Fax: 410-391-2596 csc@chesapeakespice.com
www.chesapeakespice.com
Processor and importers of spices and seasoning. including the following types of herbs..anise,cumin,sage and sage oil,black pepper,paprika,cinnamon,saffron ,thyme,and ginger.
Estimated Sales: $5-10 Million
Number Employees: 20-49
Sq. footage: 50000
Type of Packaging: Bulk

2557 **Chester Dairy Company**
1915 State St
Chester, IL 62233 618-826-2394
Fax: 618-826-2395
Dairy
President: Jason Ohlau
Plant Manager: Doyle Lueders
Estimated Sales: $10-20 Million
Number Employees: 17
Parent Co: ConAgra

2558 **Chester Fried**
3500 Colonnade Parkway
Suite 325
Birmingham, AL 35243-8300 334-272-3528
Fax: 334-272-3561 800-288-1555
jenniferp@gilesent.com www.chesterfried.com
Manufacturer and exporter of fried chicken products including breading mixes, seasonings, packaging supplies, deep fryers, fry kettles, marinades, warmers, breading tables, etc
President/CEO: Ted Giles
Vice President: Richard Davis
Purchasing: Bryan Gonseth
Estimated Sales: $10-100 Million
Number Employees: 52
Sq. footage: 100000
Brands:
CHESTER FRIED CHICKEN
CHESTERFRIED

2559 **Chester Inc.**
P.O.Box 2237
Valparaiso, IN 46384-2237 219-465-7555
Fax: 219-462-2652 800-778-1131
clark@chesterinc.com www.buy.chesters.com
Processor and exporter of popcorn
Chairman/CEO: Peter Peuquet
President: Larry Holt
EVP: Leonard Clark
Estimated Sales: $5-10 Million
Number Employees: 50-99
Type of Packaging: Consumer, Private Label
Other Locations:
Francesville IN
Gary IN
Troy MI
Brands:
Chester Farms
Chester Farms Popping Corn
Golden

2560 **Chester River Clam Co, Inc**
305 Roe Ingleside Rd
Centreville, MD 21617 410-758-3810
Fax: 410-758-4089
Clams
President: Melvin Hickman
Estimated Sales: $2,100,000
Number Employees: 5-9

2561 **Chester W. Howeth & Brother**
P.O.Box 446
Crisfield, MD 21817-0446 410-968-1398
Fax: 410-968-0670
Processor of fresh and frozen seafood
Manager: Arthur Tawes
Estimated Sales: $5-10 Million
Number Employees: 20-49
Sq. footage: 4200
Type of Packaging: Food Service
Brands:
Chas. W. Howeth & Bro.

2562 **Chestertown Foods**
27030 Morgnec Rd
Chestertown, MD 21620-3112 410-778-3131
Fax: 410-778-6386 cfoods@crosslink.net
www.chestertownfoods.com
Poultry
Manager: Jack Laird
CEO: Louis Rothman
Vice President: William Schroeder
Manager Industrial Sales: Michael Carrow
Plant Manager: Jack Laird
Estimated Sales: $5-10 Million
Number Employees: 250-499
Type of Packaging: Private Label
Brands:
Chestertown

2563 **Chestnut Mountain Winery**
1123 Highway 124
Hoschton, GA 30548-3421 770-867-6914
Fax: 770-867-6914
Wines
President: James Laikam
General Manager: Jim O'Dell
Estimated Sales: $1-2.5 Million
Number Employees: 1-4

2564 **Chevalier Chocolates**
39 Eastgate Lane
Enfield, CT 06082-6213 860-741-3330
gifts@chevalierchoc.com
www.chevalier.ws
Belgian chocolates, pralines, truffles, mints, also chocolate, cordial, and brandy covered cherries
President: Linda Chevalier
Brands:
Chevalier Chocolates

2565 **Chewys Rugulach**
7795 Arjons Dr
San Diego, CA 92126 858-271-1234
Fax: 858-271-1346 800-241-3456
chewy123@aol.com www.chewys.com
Processor of filled rugulach including baked, unbaked and frozen
President: Ahmad Paksima
Vice President: Emily Paksima
Marketing Director: Shahriar Paksima
Purchasing Manager: Shahriar Paksima
Estimated Sales: $2.5-5 Million
Number Employees: 20-49
Sq. footage: 6240
Parent Co: Ahuramazda
Type of Packaging: Consumer, Food Service, Private Label, Bulk
Brands:
CHEWY'S

2566 **Chex Finer Foods**
39 Franklin R McKay Rd
Attleboro, MA 02703 508-226-0660
Fax: 508-226-7060 800-322-2434
www.chexfoods.com
Processor and importer of gourmet foods including biscuits, confectionery items, specialties, etc
President: David Isenberg
Controller: Donald Robillard
Purchasing: Dan Powers
Estimated Sales: $10-20 Million
Number Employees: 5-9
Type of Packaging: Consumer

2567 **Chi & Hing Food Service**
4545 N 43rd Ave
Phoenix, AZ 85031-1509 623-939-8889
Fax: 623-340-8887
President: Chi Tsang
Estimated Sales: $28,010,403

2568 **Chi Company/Tabor Hill Winery**
185 Mount Tabor Rd
Buchanan, MI 49107-8326 269-422-1165
Fax: 269-422-2787 800-283-3363
www.taborhill.com
Wines and champagnes
President: David Upton
Purchasing Manager: Patsy Wyman
Estimated Sales: $10-20 Million
Number Employees: 50-99

2569 **Chia I Foods Company**
2131 Tyler Avenue
South El Monte, CA 91733-2754 626-401-3038
Fax: 626-579-3038
Spices and dehydrated fruits
President: Ann Huang
Vice President: Steve Huang
Purchasing Manager: Mary Nelson
Estimated Sales: $10-24.9 Million
Number Employees: 10-19

2570 **Chianti Cheese Company**
P.O.Box 157
Wapakoneta, OH 45895-157 609-894-0900
Fax: 609-894-4206 800-220-3503
info@chianticheese.com www.chianticheese.com
Manufacturer of hard grated cheese, parmesan and romano cheese, in all sizes. Also available fresh mozzarella, ricotta, pecorino romano, provolone, pizza cheese, impastata, parmigiano, grana panado, grated or shredded, domestic orimported cheese
Sales: Jack Salemi
Estimated Sales: $20 Million
Number Employees: 90
Number of Brands: 10
Number of Products: 200
Sq. footage: 80000
Parent Co: Kantner Group
Type of Packaging: Consumer, Food Service, Private Label, Bulk
Other Locations:
Chianti Cheese Company
Phila PA
Brands:
CHIANTI
PAISANO MIO
PARMILLANO

2571 **Chicago 58 Food Products**
135 Haist Ave
Woodbridge, ON L4L 5V6
Canada 416-603-4244
Fax: 905-265-0566
Processor of meat products including beef, pastrami, smoked salami, frankfurters; also, herring, condiments and cheese; importer of beef cuts
President: Sidney Starkman
Secretary: Harold Bernholtz
VP: Max Reiken
Estimated Sales: $3.8 Million
Number Employees: 12
Sq. footage: 15000
Type of Packaging: Consumer, Food Service, Private Label, Bulk
Brands:
Chicago 58
Deli-Dogs
Lanky Franky

2572 **Chicago Baking Company**
40 E Garfield Boulevard
Chicago, IL 60615-4603 773-536-7700
Fax: 773-536-7692
Bread and rolls
Controller: Richard Wilson
VP/General Manager: Larry Anaszewicz
Production Manager: Kevin Koenig
Estimated Sales: $50-100 Million
Number Employees: 250-499

2573 **Chicago Coffee Roastery**
11880 Smith Ct
Huntley, IL 60142 847-669-1156
Fax: 847-669-1114 800-762-5402
sales@chicagocoffee.com
www.chicagocoffee.com
Coffee, instant cocoa, instant cappuccio, tea
Owner: Sandra Knight
Vice President: Brian Gosell
Purchasing Manager: Brian Gosell
Estimated Sales: $2 Million
Number Employees: 5-9
Sq. footage: 8000
Type of Packaging: Consumer, Food Service, Private Label, Bulk

2574 **Chicago Food Market**
2245 S Wentworth Ave
Chicago, IL 60616 312-842-4361
Fax: 312-842-6448
President: Matthew Chan
Estimated Sales: $2,500,000
Number Employees: 10-19

2575 **Chicago Meat Authority**
1120 W 47th Pl
Chicago, IL 60609 773-254-3811
Fax: 773-254-5841 www.chicagomeat.com
Pork and pork products as well as beef and beef products
President/CEO: Jordan Dorfman
VP: Peter Bozzo
Quality Control Manager: Chung Wu
Marketing Manager: Renee Twardowski
Human Resource Director: Kristyn Olson
Operations Manager: John Nault
Production/Plant & Facilities Manager: Lee Koepke
Purchasing Director: Armando Ortiz
Estimated Sales: $46 Million
Number Employees: 360
Sq. footage: 24000
Type of Packaging: Consumer, Food Service, Private Label, Bulk

2576 **Chicago Oriental Wholesale**
2160 S Archer Ave
Chicago, IL 60616-1514 312-842-9993
Fax: 312-808-1787
Manager: Phil Chen
Estimated Sales: $ 20 - 50 Million
Number Employees: 20-49

2577 **Chicago Pizza & Brewery**
7755 Center Ave
Suite 300
Huntington Beach, CA 92647 714-500-2400
dianne@bjsbrewhouse.com
www.bjsbrewhouse.com
Processor of beer, ale and lager; also, pizza
President/CEO: Gerald Deitchle
Cfo/Evp: Gregory Levin
Estimated Sales: 513,000
Number Employees: 10-19
Parent Co: BJ's Restaurants Inc
Brands:
BJ Beer

2578 **Chicago Steaks**
824 W Exchange Ave
Chicago, IL 60609 773-847-5400
Fax: 773-847-3364 800-776-4174
blackangus@chicagosteaks.com
www.chicagosteaks.com
Manufacturer of meat products, value added products, and gift steaks
President/CEO: Tom Campbell

Estimated Sales: $9 Million
Number Employees: 20-49
Number of Brands: 5
Sq. footage: 1640
Type of Packaging: Food Service, Private Label
Brands:
CHICAGO STEAK

2579 **Chicago Sweeteners**
1700 E Higgins Rd # 610
Des Plaines, IL 60018-5615 847-299-1999
Fax: 847-299-6217 rfriedman@chisweet.com
www.chisweet.com
Manufacturer of sugar
President: Abel Friedman
Quality Assurance: Kate Capek
Ingredient Sales: Brian Abendroth
Estimated Sales: $50-100 Million
Number Employees: 50-99
Parent Co: Dot Foods, Inc

2580 **Chicama Vineyards**
PO Box 430
West Tisbury, MA 02575-0430 508-693-0309
Fax: 508-693-5628 888-244-2262
info@chicamavineyards.com
www.chicamavineyards.com
Wines, vinegar and dressings
President: Catherine Mathiesen
Co-Owner: George Mathiesen
Purchasing Manager: Catherine Mathiesen
Estimated Sales: $5-9.9 Million
Number Employees: 1-4
Brands:
CHICAMA

2581 **Chick-Fil-A**
PO Box 500367
Atlanta, GA 31150-0367 404-765-8000
Fax: 404-765-8140 800-232-2677
www.chick-fil-a.com
Manufacturer of chicken
Founder/Chairman: S Truett Cathy
President/COO: Dan Cathy
SVP: Donald Cathy
SVP/General Counsel: Bureon Ledbetter Jr.
SVP Finance/CFO: James McCabe
Sr. Manager Public Relations: Jerry Johnston
SVP Operations: Tim Tassopoulos
Number Employees: 250-499
Brands:
Chick-Fil-A

2582 **Chickasaw Foods**
335 Cumberland Street
Memphis, TN 38112-3350 901-323-5467
Potato chips
President: Jon M Buhler
Estimated Sales: $5-10,000,000 appx.
Number Employees: 20-49

2583 **Chickasaw Trading Company**
P.O.Box 1418
Denver City, TX 79323 806-592-3515
Fax: 806-592-3460 800-848-3515
joe@texaslean.com
Processor and exporter of lean beef jerky and smoked turkey breast strips
Co-Owner: Linda Kay
Co-Owner: Joe Kay
Number Employees: 1-4
Sq. footage: 5000
Type of Packaging: Private Label
Brands:
Texas Lean

2584 **Chicken of the Sea International**
P.O.Box 85568
San Diego, CA 92186-5568 858-558-9662
Fax: 858-597-4566 800-678-8862
www.chickenofthesea.com
Canner and importer of tuna, salmon, shrimp, crab, oysters, clams, mackerel and sardines
President/CEO: Dennis Mussell
CEO: Shue Wing Chan
Senior VP Marketing: Don George
Senior VP Sales: Tony Montoya
Estimated Sales: $600 Million
Number Employees: 1,000-4,999
Parent Co: Tri-Union Seafoods
Type of Packaging: Consumer, Food Service, Private Label
Brands:
CHICKEN OF THE SEA
CHICKEN OF THE SEA SINGLES
CHICKEN OF THE SEA TUNA SALAD KIT
GENOVA TONNO
JACK MACKEREL

2585 **Chico Nut Company**
2020 Esplanade
Chico, CA 95926 530-891-1493
Fax: 530-893-5381 almonds@chiconut.com
www.chiconut.com
Processor, exporter and packer of almonds
Owner: Peter D Peterson
Estimated Sales: $ 3 - 5 Million
Number Employees: 20-49
Type of Packaging: Bulk

2586 **Chicopee Provision Company**
19 Sitarz Ave
Chicopee, MA 01013 413-594-4765
Fax: 413-594-2584 800-924-6328
info@bluesealkielbasa.com
www.bluesealkielbasa.com
Manufacturer of kielbasa and table ready meats, including polish kielbasa, baked loaf, hot dogs, cold cuts, and sausage
President: Fred Mamuszka
Office Manager: Carolyn Donnelly
Operations/Marketing: Thomas Bardon
Estimated Sales: $4.5 Million
Number Employees: 20-49
Number of Brands: 220
Number of Products: 610
Sq. footage: 24000
Type of Packaging: Consumer, Food Service, Private Label, Bulk
Brands:
BLUE SEAL

2587 **Chief Wenatchee**
1705 N Miller St
Wenatchee, WA 98801 509-662-5197
Fax: 509-662-9415
Grower and exporter of apples, cherries and pears
President: Brian Birsall
Operations Manager: Skip Coonfield
Number Employees: 250-499
Type of Packaging: Bulk
Brands:
Chief Chelan
Chief Supreme
Chief Wenatchee
Wenatchee Gold

2588 **Chieftain Wild Rice Company**
1210 Basswood Ave
Spooner, WI 54801 715-635-6401
Fax: 715-635-6415 800-262-6368
info@chieftainwildrice.com
www.chieftainwildrice.com
Processor of wild rice and blends; also, specialty beans and grains. Rice River Farms is a retail line sold to specialty stores, Chieftian Wild Rice is a food service line for restaurants
President: Donald Richards
CEO: Jim Deutsch
Marketing Director: Keith Kappel
General Manager: Joan Gerland
Plant Manager: Jim Deutsch
Estimated Sales: $2-5 Million
Number Employees: 20-49
Number of Brands: 2
Sq. footage: 16000
Type of Packaging: Consumer, Food Service
Brands:
AUTUMN HARVEST
BANQUET BLEND
CALICO BLEND
CHIEFTAIN WILD RICE
COUNTRY HARVEST
FESTIVAL BLEND
HOUSE BLEND
LOWER CARB BLEND
MIDWEST MEDLEY
PASTA RICE BLEND
QUINOA CONFETTI
RICE RIVER FARMS
SAVORY BLEND
SPECIAL BASMATI

2589 **ChildLife-Nutrition forKids**
5335 McConnell Avenue
Los Angeles, CA 90066 310-305-4640
Fax: 310-305-4680 800-993-0332
mailroom@childlife.net www.childlife.net
Liquid supplements & vitamins for infants to children up to twelve years old
Founder: Dr. Murray C Clarke
VP: Helen Mauchi
Estimated Sales: $300,000-500,000
Number Employees: 1-4
Number of Products: 9

2590 **Chile Today**
2000 McKinnon Ave.,Bldg. 428,#5
San Francisco, CA 94124-1621 800-758-0372
Fax: 415-401-9107 800-758-0372
chiletoday@aol.com www.chiletoday.com
Processor of trail mixes, gourmet hot sauce, salsa, seasoned pretzels, dried chiles and chile powders
President: Rob Polishook
VP: David Lipson
Purchasing Manager: David Lipson
Estimated Sales: $1-2.5 Million
Number Employees: 1-4
Sq. footage: 7000
Type of Packaging: Consumer, Food Service
Brands:
CHILE
FIRE NUGGET
SMOKED HABANERO PRETZELS

2591 **Chili Dude**
745 Kirkwood Drive
Dallas, TX 75218 214-354-9906
info@thechilidude.com
www.thechilidude.com
Chili
Director: Corrine Lovato
Brands:
Chili Dude

2592 **Chill & Moore**
3221 May Street
Fort Worth, TX 76110-4124 505-769-2649
Fax: 505-762-0571 800-676-3055
steph2@airmail.net
Processor of frozen ices
Sales Manager (Food Service): Bob Moore
Sales Manager (Retail): Jay Jackson
Type of Packaging: Consumer, Food Service

2593 **Chimere**
1800 Sequoia Drive
Santa Maria, CA 93454-7645 805-922-9097
Fax: 805-922-9143
Wines
President: Gary Mosby
Estimated Sales: $1-2.5 Million
Number Employees: 5-9

2594 **China Doll Company**
100 Jacintoport Boulevard
Saraland, AL 36571-3304 251-457-7641
Fax: 251-457-4569
gbagget@achfoodcompany.com
Processor and exporter of rice, dried beans and peas, lentils, popcorn and raw shelled peanuts
CEO: Dan Antonelli
CFO: Daryl Vrbas
VP: Steve Robinson
Marketing/Sales: Gerald Baggett
Manager: Gerald Baggett
Production: Deprest Turner
Plant Manager: Gordan McElhenney
Purchasing: Gerald Bagget
Estimated Sales: $1-2.5 Million
Number Employees: 20-49
Number of Brands: 4
Number of Products: 38
Sq. footage: 40000
Parent Co: ACH Food Companies
Type of Packaging: Consumer, Food Service, Private Label, Bulk
Brands:
China Boy
China Doll
Jocko
Paddy
Silver King
Southern Charm

2595 **China Mist Tea Company**
7435 E Tierra Buena Ln
Scottsdale, AZ 85260 480-998-8807
Fax: 480-443-8384 800-242-8807
info@chinamist.com www.chinamist.com

China mist and leaves pure teas
Owner: Richard Gusauskas
CEO: John Martinson
President/CEO/Finance Executive: Rommie Flammer
Marketing Coordinator: Kiley Biggins
Human Resource Manager: Wade McKesson
Plant Manager: Kevin McCullough
Estimated Sales: $3.8 Million
Number Employees: 27
Sq. footage: 17500
Brands:
CHINA MIST
FRENZY MIST
GREEN STAR

2596 **China Pharmaceutical Enterprises**
8323 Ohara Court
Baton Rouge, LA 70806-6513 225-924-1423
Fax: 225-924-4154 800-345-1658
Processor and importer of ascorbic acid, caffeine anhydrous and vitamin B-12
Office Manager: Susan Giska
Type of Packaging: Bulk

2597 **(HQ)Chincoteague Seafood Company**
7056 Forest Grove Rd
Po Box 88
Parsonsburg, MD 21849 443-260-4800
Fax: 443-260-4900 gourmetsoups@hotmail.com
www.chincoteagueseafood.com
Processor and distributor of gourmet specialty seafood items: canned and frozen products including fried clams, stuffed clams, New England/Manhattan clam chowders, corn chowder, lobster/clam/shrimp/lobster and cheddar bisques, cream ofcrab/vegetable crab/crab and cheddar soups, white/red clam sauces, chopped clams, clam juice
President: Leonard Rubin
CEO: Bernard Rubin
CFO: Toby Rubin
Estimated Sales: $1-2.5 Million
Number Employees: 5-9
Number of Brands: 4
Number of Products: 25
Sq. footage: 6000
Type of Packaging: Consumer, Food Service, Private Label, Bulk
Brands:
CAPE COD
CAPT'N DON'S
CAPT'N EDS
CHINOTEAQUE

2598 **Chinese Spaghetti Factory**
83 Newmarket Sq
Boston, MA 2118 617-445-7714
Fax: 617-427-5918 www.chinesespaghetti.com
Processor of Peking ravioli, chicken and pork dumplings, scallops with bacon and shrimp spring rolls
President: Lai Fou Sou
General Manager: Henry Moy
Operations Manager: Ken Moy
Estimated Sales: $1 Million
Number Employees: 10
Sq. footage: 16000
Type of Packaging: Consumer, Food Service, Private Label, Bulk

2599 **Chino Meat Provision Corporation**
13564 Central Ave
Chino, CA 91710-5105 909-627-1997
Fax: 909-628-5147
Processor and packer of meat products
Owner: Orestes Blanco
Estimated Sales: $2.5-5 Million
Number Employees: 10-19
Sq. footage: 6000
Brands:
El Paso

2600 **Chino Valley Ranchers**
5611 Peck Rd
Arcadia, CA 91006 626-652-0890
Fax: 626-652-0893
david@chinovalleyranchers.com
www.chinovalleyranchers.com
Processor of fresh organic, cage free, free range and fertile white and brown eggs
Marketing Director: David Will
Plant Manager: Mario Gonzalez
Type of Packaging: Consumer, Food Service, Private Label
Brands:
Chino Valley
Humane Harvest
Mothers Free Range
Nutrifresh
Veg-A-Fed

2601 **Chip Steak & Provision Company**
232 Dewey St
Mankato, MN 56001 507-388-6277
Fax: 507-388-6279
Wholesales meat & meat products; wholesales packaged frozen foods
President: Michael Miller
Secertary: Mike Miller
Estimated Sales: $5-9.9 Million
Number Employees: 5-9
Sq. footage: 4000
Type of Packaging: Consumer, Food Service, Bulk

2602 **Chipotle Chile Company**
510 Highland Avenue
174
Milford, MI 48381-1516 248-496-8308
www.dancingcow.com
Peppers
Brands:
Dancing Cow Steak Sauce

2603 **Chipper Snax**
1750 S 500 W Ste 700
Salt Lake City, UT 84115 801-977-0742
Fax: 801-977-0743 info@chipperjerky.com
www.chipperjerky.com
Beef jerky
Manager: Jeffrey Labrum
Executive Vice President: Jeffrey Labrum
National Sales Manager: Steve Pich
Estimated Sales: $ 10 - 20 Million
Number Employees: 20-49
Brands:
CHIPPER BEEF JERKY

2604 **(HQ)Chiquita Brands Intl**
250 E 5th St
Cincinnati, OH 45202 513-784-8000
Fax: 513-784-8030 800-438-0015
www.chiquita.com
Grower, processor, importer and exporter of bananas; processor of fruits, fresh and canned vegetables, wet and dry salads, and fruit juices for consumer, manufacturing, and food service industries
Chairman, President & CEO: Fernando Aquirre
President, North America: Joe Huston
SVP & CFO: Michael Sims
SVP Chief People Officer: Kevin Holland
SVP General Counsel: James Thompson
VP Food Safety & Quality: Mike Burness
Pres. Global Innovation/Emerg Mkts & CMO: Tanios Viviani
SVP Coporate Responsibility: Manuel Rodriquez
SVP Product Supply Organization: Waheed Zaman
Estimated Sales: $3.23Billion
Number Employees: 21,000
Type of Packaging: Consumer, Food Service, Private Label, Bulk
Brands:
CHIQUITA
FRESH EXPRESS

2605 **Chiquita Processed Foods**
Rr 1
Markesan, WI 53946 920-398-2386
Fax: 920-398-3924
Processor, packager and exporter of canned corn
Plant Manager: Richard Koehler
Purchasing Agent: Craig Giese
Estimated Sales: $ 1 - 3 Million
Number Employees: 5-9
Type of Packaging: Consumer, Private Label

2606 **Chisesi Brothers Meat Packing Company**
5221 Jefferson Hwy
New Orleans, LA 70123 504-822-3550
Fax: 504-822-3916 800-966-3550
www.chisesibros.com
Manufacturer of hams, frankforters, and sausage
President: Phillip Chisesi
Estimated Sales: $15-20 Million
Number Employees: 100-249
Type of Packaging: Consumer, Food Service

2607 **Chisholm Bakery**
128 8th Street NW
Chisholm, MN 55719-1656 218-254-4006
Baked goods
Owner: Todd Renke
Estimated Sales: $500,000-$1 Million
Number Employees: 5-9

2608 **(HQ)Chloe Foods Corporation**
3301 Atlantic Ave
Brooklyn, NY 11208 718-827-9000
Fax: 718-647-0052 www.blueridgefarms.com
Manufacturer of nonkosher, kosher and parve salads, knishes, cream cheeses, frozen hot entrees, desserts, pickles, and other ready-to-eat foods.
President: Andrew Themis
CEO: Andrew Themis
CFO: Annette Apergis
VP Sales North American: Ronnie Loeb
Estimated Sales: $80 Million
Number Employees: 250-499
Brands:
BLUE RIDGE FARMS
CHLOE FARMS
EZ CUISINE
JOSHUA'S KOSHER KITCHEN
TEXAS SUPERIOR MEATS
THE COOKIE STORE

2609 **Chmuras Bakery**
14 Pulaski St
Indian Orchard, MA 01151 413-543-2521
Fax: 413-543-2507
Rye bread and bakery products
President: Joe Albes
CEO: Joe Albes
Estimated Sales: $1-2.5 Million
Number Employees: 20-49

2610 **Chock Full O'Nuts**
370 Lexington Ave
New York, NY 10017 212-532-0300
Fax: 212-532-0864 888-246-2598
cad@saralee.com www.chockfullonuts.com
Manufacturer of regular, decaffeinated, ground roast, instant and specialty coffees
President: Peter Wirth
VP: Richard Walker
Estimated Sales: $100-500 Million
Number Employees: 1,275
Parent Co: Sara Lee
Type of Packaging: Consumer, Food Service, Private Label
Other Locations:
Chock Full O'Nuts Corp.
Brooklyn NY
Brands:
CHOCK FULL O'NUTS
NEW YORK CLASSICS

2611 **Chocoholics Divine Desserts**
14400 E Highway 26
Linden, CA 95236-9744
Fax: 209-759-3350 800-760-2462
info@gourmetchocolate.com
www.gourmetchocolate.com
Processor of chocolate dessert toppings, carmel sauces, double fudge cookies, truffles and chocolate novelties
President: Ernie Schenone
VP Sales & Operations: Mary Schenone
Estimated Sales: $5-10 Million
Number Employees: 10-19
Type of Packaging: Private Label

2612 **Chocolat**
2039 Bellevue Sq
Bellevue, WA 98004-5028 425-452-1141
Fax: 425-452-1142 800-808-2462
www.globalgourmet.com
Beverages
President: Will Deeg
Director Marketing: Rob Scott
Brands:
Neuhaus
Teuscher

2613 **Chocolat Belge Heyez**
16 Ch De La Rabastaliere E
St-Lazare-De-Bellechasse, QC J3V 2A5
Canada 450-653-5616
Fax: 450-653-1445
Processor and importer of chocolates
President: Hubert Heyez
VP: Janine Heyez
Estimated Sales: $371,000
Number Employees: 6
Sq. footage: 4000
Type of Packaging: Consumer, Private Label

2614 **Chocolat Jean Talon**
4620 Boul Thimens
Montreal, QC H4R 2B2
Canada 514-333-8540
Fax: 514-333-8540 888-333-8540
info@jtalon.ca
Processor of molded hollow chocolates for Easter
President: Robert Poirier
VP/Marketing: Richard Poirier
Sales Manager: Johanne Lavallee
Plant Manager: Lyne Lacharite
Purchasing Manager: Marc Plante
Estimated Sales: $6 Million
Number Employees: 93
Number of Products: 100
Sq. footage: 55000
Type of Packaging: Food Service
Brands:
Chocolat Jean Talon

2615 **Chocolate By Design**
700-4 Union Parkway
Ronkonkoma, NY 11779 631-737-0082
Fax: 631-737-0188 800-536-3618
chocobd@aol.com www.cbdontheweb.com
Processor of gourmet chocolate novelties and coins; also, custom molding available
President: Ellen Motlin
CEO: Richard Motlin
Estimated Sales: $500,000
Number Employees: 5-9
Number of Products: 350
Sq. footage: 5000
Type of Packaging: Consumer, Private Label

2616 **Chocolate Chix**
501 N College Street
Waxahachie, TX 75165-3361 214-744-2442
Fax: 214-744-2449 csurana@chocolatechix.com
www.chocolatechix.com
Processor of meringue cookies
President: Cheryl Surana
Estimated Sales: Less than $500,000
Number Employees: 1-4
Brands:
Just Meringues
Mushroom Meringue Cookies

2617 **Chocolate Creations**
3016 Annita Dr
Glendale, CA 91206 323-340-1576
Fax: 323-340-4021 800-229-4140
sales@chocolateart.com www.chocolateart.com
Full line of specialty and seasonal chocolate gifts
Owner: Jean Girard
Purchasing Manager: J Dirard
Estimated Sales: $5-10 Million
Number Employees: 5-9

2618 **Chocolate Fantasies**
340 Shore Drive
Burr Ridge, IL 60527 630-572-0045
Fax: 630-572-0039
contactus@espressosecrets.net
www.espressosecrets.net
all natural darck chocolate confections married to rich espresso coffee.
CEO: Leonard Defranco

2619 **Chocolate House**
4121 S 35th St
Milwaukee, WI 53221 414-281-7803
Fax: 414-423-2484 800-236-2022
candy@chocolatehouse.com
www.chocolatehouse.com
Manufacturer and exporter of chocolate
Manager: Irene Hyducki
Executive Vice President: Gary Winder
Estimated Sales: $10-20 Million
Number Employees: 50-99
Type of Packaging: Consumer
Brands:
ABSOLUTELY ALMOND
CHOCOLATE MINT MELTAWAYS
FUDGIE BEARS
POSITIVELY PECAN

2620 **Chocolate Moon**
2002 Riverside Dr Ste 42f
Asheville, NC 28804 828-253-6060
Fax: 828-253-1020 800-723-1236
info@chocolatemoon.com
www.bluemoonwater.com
Chocolate covered dried cherries, blueberries and apricots, toffee, cocoa and cappuccino chocolate almonds and pistachios
Owner: Chris Mathis
Operations Manager: Jennifer Donnell
Purchasing Manager: Jennifer Donnell
Estimated Sales: $1-2.5 Million
Number Employees: 10-19
Brands:
DAVINCI GOURMET
GHIARDELLI
GUITTARD
LINDT
MARICH
OREGON CHAI

2621 **Chocolate Potpourri**
1814 Johns Dr
Glenview, IL 60025 847-729-8878
Fax: 847-729-8879 888-680-1600
micheal@chocolatetruffles.com
www.chocolatetruffles.com
Processor of Pretzel rod dipped in caramel, rolled in fresh pecans and drizzled with rich, thick streams of chocolate, freshly popped corn dusted with white chocolate
President: Richard Gordan
VP: Marsha Gordon
Sales Staff Director: Michael Gordon
Estimated Sales: $ 5 - 10 Million
Number Employees: 10-19
Brands:
Dipped Oreos
Pop Au Chocolat
Pretzel Twists

2622 **Chocolate Shoppe Ice Cream Company**
2221 Daniels St
Madison, WI 53718 608-221-8640
Fax: 608-221-8650
www.chocolateshoppeicecream.com
Frozen desserts
Owner: C B Deadman
Vice President: Dave Deadman
Purchasing Manager: Dave Deadman
Estimated Sales: $2.5-5 Million
Number Employees: 20-49

2623 **Chocolate Soup**
2300 Mount Werner Circle
Unit C-1
Steamboat Springs, CO 80487 970-870-0224
Fax: 970-870-0378 lisa@chocolatesoupcafe.com
www.chocolatesoupcafe.com
Organic/natural, cakes/pastries, cookies, crackers, other baked goods, other chocolate, other snacks, private label.
Marketing: Lisa Ciraldo

2624 **Chocolate Street of Hartville**
1116 Woodland St SW
Hartville, OH 44632 330-877-3000
Fax: 330-877-1100 888-853-5904
Processor of custom chocolate products including 3-D corporate logos, bars and personalized gold foil wrapped coins; also, private label available; exporter of chocolate processing equipment including cooling tunnels, vibration tablesmeasuring pumps, etc
General Manager: Robert Barton
Estimated Sales: $ 10 - 20 Million
Number Employees: 20-49
Sq. footage: 13000
Type of Packaging: Consumer, Food Service, Private Label, Bulk
Brands:
Chocolate Street of Hartville

2625 **Chocolate Studio**
142 W Germantown Pike # A
Norristown, PA 19401 610-272-3872
Fax: 610-272-3872
sales@ChocolateStudioOnline.com
www.chocolatestudioonline.com
Chocolates
Owner: John Giaimo
Estimated Sales: $2.5-5 Million
Number Employees: 5-9
Type of Packaging: Consumer, Bulk

2626 **Chocolaterie Bernard Callebaut**
1313 1st SE
Calgary, AB T2G 5L1
Canada 403-265-5777
Fax: 403-265-7738 800-661-8367
www.bernardcallebaut.com
Processor and exporter of quality chocolates and chocolate products, including spreads, sauces and ice cream bars
President/CEO: Bernard Callebaut
Number Employees: 20-49
Type of Packaging: Consumer, Private Label
Brands:
Chocolaterie Bernard Callebaut

2627 **Chocolaterie Stam**
2814 Ingersoll Ave
Des Moines, IA 50312 515-282-9575
Fax: 515-282-9763 877-782-6246
chocolate@stamchocolate.com
www.stamchocolate.com
Quality Dutch chocolates
President: Ton Stam
Estimated Sales: $500,000-$1 Million
Number Employees: 10-19
Brands:
Stam

2628 **Chocolates El Rey**
P.O.Box 853
Fredericksburg, TX 78624-0853 830-997-2200
Fax: 830-997-2417 www.chocolateselrey.com
Premium chocolates. Retail/wholesale, block, discos and chips
President: Randall Turner
Estimated Sales: $2.5-5 Million
Number Employees: 1-4
Brands:
CARENERO
EL REY
RIO CARIBE

2629 **Chocolates Turin**
Granite Parkway
Suite 200
Plano, TX 75024 972-731-6771
Fax: 972-731-6774
customerservice@turin.com.mx
www.turin.com.mx
Chocolates
National Sales Manager: Jim Hutchins

2630 **Chocolates a La Carte**
28455 Livingston Ave
Valencia, CA 91355 661-257-3700
Fax: 661-257-4999 800-818-2462
orders@candymaker.com
www.chocolatesalacarte.com
Processor, importer and exporter of chocolate designs for desserts, amenities and gifts including pianos, swans, sea shells, etc
President: Rena Pocrass
CEO/VP: Richard Pocrass
VP Finance and Administration: Michael Pocrass
Marketing Manager: Diane Rudman
EVP/Head of Operations: Frank Geukens
Estimated Sales: $26 Million
Number Employees: 165
Sq. footage: 110000
Type of Packaging: Food Service
Brands:
CHOCOLATES A LA CARTE

2631 **Chocolates by Mark**
210 W Main
La Porte, TX 77571 832-736-2626
Fax: 603-925-8000 mark@chocolatesbymark.com
www.chocolatesbymark.com
Processor of custom chocolate wedding/party favors, gifts
President: Mark Caffey

Number Employees: 1-4
Sq. footage: 2200
Type of Packaging: Private Label, Bulk

2632 Chocolates by Mr. Robert
505 NE 20th St
Boca Raton, FL 33431-8141 561-392-3007
Fine chocolates and truffles, chocolate-covered fruit
Owner: Heinz Robert Goldschneider
Estimated Sales: Less than $500,000
Number Employees: 1-4

2633 Chocolati Handmade Chocolates
7708 Aurora Ave N
Seattle, WA 98103-4752 206-784-5212
Fax: 206-525-4574 information@chocolati.com
www.chocolati.com
Processor of candy including mint truffles
President: Christian Wong
VP: John Berg
Estimated Sales: $100000
Number Employees: 5-9
Sq. footage: 5100
Type of Packaging: Consumer, Private Label, Bulk

2634 Chocolatier
27 Water St
Exeter, NH 03833 603-772-5253
Fax: 603-772-0793 888-246-5528
the.chocolatier@verizon.net
www.the-chocolatier.com
Molded corporate chocolate candy
Owner: Jayne Welcome
Estimated Sales: $220,000
Number Employees: 5-9

2635 Chocolatique
11030 Santa Monica Blvd
#301
Los Angeles, CA 90025 310-479-3849
Fax: 310-479-8448 www.choclatique.com
chocolates, bars, marshmallows, nuts and novelties, sauces, ganaches and beverages, and baking ingredients
Co-Founder: Ed Engoron
Co-Founder: Joan Vieweger

2636 Chocolove
P.O.Box 18357
Boulder, CO 80308 303-786-7888
Fax: 303-440-8850 888-246-2656
info@chocolove.com www.chocolove.com
Belgian chocolate bars
President: Timothy Moley
CEO: Timothy Moley
Marketing: Kerri Gedert
Estimated Sales: $2.5-5 Million
Number Employees: 5-9
Brands:
CHOCOLOVE

2637 Choctaw Maid Farms
3865 Highway 35 N
Carthage, MS 39051 601-298-5300
Fax: 601-298-5497
Processor, importer and exporter of fresh and frozen chicken parts
Owner: Tammy Etheridge
Purchasing Agent: Ruthie Harper
Number Employees: 250-499
Type of Packaging: Bulk

2638 Choice One Foods
4020 Compton Ave
Los Angeles, CA 90011 323-231-7777
Fax: 323-231-2007
Poultry and meats
CEO: Gary Rodkin
Estimated Sales: $101 Million
Number Employees: 100-249
Parent Co: ConAgra

2639 Choice Organic Teas
2414 SW Andover St
Seattle, WA 98106-1153 206-525-0051
Fax: 206-523-9750 choice@granum-inc.com
www.choiceorganicteas.com
Processor and exporter of organic teas including black, green and herbal
Owner: Blake Rankin
Estimated Sales: $1-$2.5 Million
Number Employees: 20-49
Type of Packaging: Consumer, Food Service, Private Label, Bulk
Brands:
Choice
Choice Organic Teas
Granum
Kaiseki Select
Mitoku Macrobiotic
Sound Sea Vegetables

2640 Choice of Vermont
305 Tequesta Drive
Destin, FL 32541-5715 802-888-6261
Fax: 802-888-6244 800-444-6261
gourmetfood@vtusa.net
Processor of mustard, hummus, black bean salsa, bruschetta toppings, maple pumpkin butter, pesto sauce and horseradish jam
President: Jim Peterson
Sales Director: Kevin Butler
Operations Manager: Robert Nelson
Estimated Sales: $1 Million
Number Employees: 5-9
Number of Brands: 1
Number of Products: 28
Sq. footage: 10000
Type of Packaging: Consumer, Food Service, Private Label
Brands:
Choice of Vermont

2641 Chong Mei Trading
1130 Oakleigh Dr
East Point, GA 30344 404-768-3838
Fax: 404-768-0008
Pork, beef, seafood, chicken, dry goods, dairy, produce, Oriental grocery items
President: Kai Chen Wong
Estimated Sales: $ 1 - 3 Million
Number Employees: 10-19

2642 Chooljian Brothers Packing Company
3192 S Indianola Ave
Sanger, CA 93657 559-875-5501
Fax: 559-875-6618 raisinnic@aol.com
www.californiaraisins.com
Processor and exporter of raisins
President: Leo Chooljian
Sales Manager: Nicholas Boghosian
Estimated Sales: $500,000
Number Employees: 50-99
Parent Co: Chooljian Brothers Packing Company
Type of Packaging: Consumer, Food Service, Private Label, Bulk
Brands:
Chooljian
Prize

2643 Chouinard Vineyards
33853 Palomares Rd
Castro Valley, CA 94552 510-582-9900
Fax: 510-733-6274 www.chouinard.com
Wines
President: George Chouinard
Estimated Sales: $1-2.5 Million
Number Employees: 1-4
Brands:
ALICANTE BOUSCHET
CALIFORNIA CHAMPAGNE
CENTRAL COAST CHARDONNAY
CHOUINARD RED
CHOUINARD ROSE
GRANNY SMITH APPLE
LODI ZINFANDEL
MONTEREY CABERNET SAUVIGNON
MONTEREY CHARDONNAY
MONTEREY PETITE SYRAH
PASO ROBLES CABERNET SAUVIGNON
PASO ROBLES ORANGE MUSCAT

2644 Choyce Produce
3140 Ualena St # 206
Honolulu, HI 96819-1965 808-839-1502
President: Edmund Choy
Estimated Sales: $ 5 - 10 Million
Number Employees: 5-9

2645 Chozen Ice Cream
171 W 12th Street
Suite 6C
New York, NY 10011-8210 212-675-4191
Fax: 212-675-4191 meredith@chozen.com
www.chozen.com
Kosher, organic/natural, frozen desserts. ice cream/sorbet.
Marketing: Meredith Fisher

2646 Chris A. Papas & Son Company
921 Baker St
Covington, KY 41011 859-431-0499
Fax: 859-431-0499
Candy and confectionery
President: Carl Papas
Vice President: Chris Papas
Estimated Sales: $1-2.5 Million
Number Employees: 1-4
Number of Products: 15
Sq. footage: 12000
Type of Packaging: Consumer, Private Label, Bulk
Brands:
Chocolate Marshmallow
It's a Boy
It's a Girl
Sugar Sticks

2647 Chris Candies
1557 Spring Garden Ave
Pittsburgh, PA 15212 412-322-9400
Fax: 412-322-9402 sales@chriscandies.com
www.chriscandies.com
Processor of chocolate bars and novelties; also, custom molds, labels and imprints available. Organic and kosher certified
President: Timothy Rogers
VP/CIO: Dave Byard
Human Resources Manager: Lori Cipkins
Operations Executive: Mike Gefert
Estimated Sales: $5-9.9 Million
Number Employees: 50
Sq. footage: 32000
Type of Packaging: Consumer, Food Service, Private Label

2648 Chris Hansen Seafood
134 Chris Ln
Port Sulphur, LA 70083 504-564-2888
Fax: 580-564-2888
Seafood
Owner: Chris Hansen

2649 Chris Parker Company
55 Hearthstone Drive
Stockbridge, GA 30281-2801 770-474-6091
Fax: 770-474-7091

2650 Chris' Farm Stand
22 South Cross Rd
Bradford, MA 01835 978-994-4315
www.chrisfarmstand.com
Processor of organic produce and jams and jellies
President: Thomas Holopainen
Estimated Sales: Less than $500,000
Number Employees: 5-9
Type of Packaging: Consumer

2651 Christensen Ridge
489 Gabriel Ln
Madison, VA 22727 540-923-4800
info@christensenridge.com
www.christensenridge.com
Wine
President/Owner: J D Hartman
Estimated Sales: $ 3 - 5 Million
Number Employees: 5-9

2652 Christie Cookie Company
1205 3rd Ave N
Nashville, TN 37208 615-242-3817
Fax: 615-242-5572 www.christiecookies.com
Gourmet cookies and frozen ready to bake dough
President: Fleming Wilt
CFO: Bob Turner
Plant Manager: Steve Meyers
Purchasing Manager: Robert Shefton
Estimated Sales: $10-20 Million
Number Employees: 40

2653 Christie Food Products
Po Bxo 341
Randolph, MA 02368 781-341-3341
Fax: 781-341-3340 800-727-2523
hlemovitz@christiefoods.com
www.christiefoods.com

Processor and contract packager of drink mixes, condiments, salad dressings, specialty foods, sauces and seasonings.
Dried/Dehydrated Fruits Vegetables
VP: Raymond Smith
General Manager: Raymond Smith
Estimated Sales: $1-2.5 Million
Number Employees: 20-49
Sq. footage: 30000
Parent Co: Vision Specialty Foods
Type of Packaging: Consumer, Food Service, Private Label, Bulk
Brands:
Christie's Instant-Chef

2654 **Christie-Brown**
200 Deforest Avenue
East Hanover, NJ 07936-2833 973-503-4000
Fax: 973-503-3660
President: Chip Clothier
CEO: Chip Clothier
Estimated Sales: Under $500,000
Number Employees: 5-9

2655 **Christine & Rob's**
41103 Stayton Scio Rd SE
Stayton, OR 97383-9400 503-769-2993
Fax: 503-769-1291 bartell@wvi.com
www.christineandrobs.com
Manufacturer of old-fashioned oatmeal and preserves
Owner: Christine Bartell
Owner: Rob Bartell
Estimated Sales: $200,000
Number Employees: 1-4

2656 **Christine Woods Winery**
3155 Highway 128
Philo, CA 95466 707-895-2115
Fax: 707-895-2748 sales@christinewoods.com
www.christinewoods.com
Wines
Owner: Vernon Rose
Owner: Jo Rose
Partner: Edward Rose
Partner: Lisa Rose
Estimated Sales: $500,000-$1 Million
Number Employees: 1-4
Type of Packaging: Private Label

2657 **Christmas Point Wild Rice Company**
14803 Edgewood Dr
Baxter, MN 56425 218-828-0603
Fax: 218-828-0543 www.christmaspoint.com
Wild rice products
Manager: Scott Goehring
Public Relations: Scott Goehring
Estimated Sales: $500,000-$1 Million
Number Employees: 20-49

2658 **Christopher Creek Winery**
641 Limerick Ln
Healdsburg, CA 95448 707-431-8243
Fax: 707-431-0183 chriscrk@ix.netcom.com
www.christophercreek.com
Wines
Owner: Fred Wasserman
Estimated Sales: $500,000
Number Employees: 6
Sq. footage: 3
Type of Packaging: Private Label

2659 **Christopher Joseph Brewing Company**
6812 E Valley Vista Ln
Paradise Valley, AZ 85253 480-948-7882
Beer
President: Joseph Mocca
Estimated Sales: Under $500,000
Number Employees: 10-19
Brands:
Bandersnatch Milk Stout
Big Horn Premium
Cardinal Pale Ale

2660 **Christopher Norman Chocolates**
60 New St
New York, NY 10004 212-402-1243
Fax: 212-402-1249
sales@ChristopherNormanChocolates.com
www.christophernormanchocolates.com
Manufacturers of hand made chocolates
Founder/Owner: John Down
Estimated Sales: $300,000-500,000
Number Employees: 1-4
Brands:
Christopher Norman Chocolates

2661 **Christopher Ranch**
305 Bloomfield Ave
Gilroy, CA 95020 408-847-1100
Fax: 408-847-0139
garlicia@christopherranch.com
www.christopherranch.com
Processor, importer and exporter of garlic, ginger, bell peppers, corn, cherries, shallots, horseradish, and dried chiles.
President/CEO: Bill Christopher
VP Marketing: Patsy Ross
Sales Director: Jeff Stokes
Human Resources Executive: Janette Codiga
Purchasing Manager: Bridgette Dunning
Estimated Sales: $135 Million
Number Employees: 200
Sq. footage: 220000
Type of Packaging: Consumer, Food Service, Bulk

2662 **Chuao Chocolatier**
2345 Camino Vida Roble
Carlsbad, CA 92011 760-476-1668
Fax: 760-476-1355 888-635-1444
sales@chuaochocolatier.com
www.chuaochocolatier.com
Chocolates
President: Michael Antonorsi
Ceo: Sergio Alvarez
Chairman: Richard Antonorsi
Marketing: Thomas Pineda
Number Employees: 30

2663 **Chuck's Seafoods**
P.O.Box 5502
Charleston, OR 97420-0616 541-888-5525
Fax: 541-888-2121 www.chuckseafoods.com
Processor and canner of seafood including salmon, tuna, clams, crabs and shrimp
President: Jack Hampel
Secretary: Diana Hampel
Estimated Sales: $5-10 Million
Number Employees: 5-9
Type of Packaging: Consumer
Brands:
Vandon Sea-Pack

2664 **Chudleigh's**
8501 Chudleigh Way
Milton, ON L9T 0L9
Canada 905-878-8781
Fax: 905-878-6979 farm@chudleighs.com
www.chudleighs.com
Processor of fresh fruit pies and baked fruits
President: Dean Chudleigh
VP: Scott Chudleigh
Estimated Sales: $4.8 Million
Number Employees: 120
Brands:
Chudleigh's

2665 **Chugwater Chili Corporation**
P.O.Box 92
Chugwater, WY 82210 307-422-3345
Fax: 307-422-3357 800-972-4454
chugchili@direcway.com
www.chugwaterchili.com
Processor of chili products including dip and dressing mixes, chili nuts red pepper jelly and ingredients including spices, seasoning blends and peppers, and also steak rub which is new.
Owner: Marcelyn Brown
CEO: Del Ficanz
VP: Karl Wilkerson
Marketing Director: Raece Wilkerson
Sales Director: Raece Wilkerson
Public Relations: Marcelyn Brown
Estimated Sales: $2.5-5 Million
Number Employees: 10-19
Number of Brands: 1
Number of Products: 5
Sq. footage: 2560
Type of Packaging: Consumer, Food Service
Brands:
Chugwater Chili

2666 **Chukar Cherries**
P.O.Box 510
Prosser, WA 99350-0510 509-786-2055
Fax: 509-786-2591 800-624-9544
sales@chukar.com www.chukar.com
Cherries, dried fruit, trail mixes, chocolates, preserves, sauces, baking mixes, tea and fresh cherries
President: Pam Auld
Head of Production: Kathlene Yound
Estimated Sales: $20-50 Million
Number Employees: 20-49

2667 **Chula Vista Cheese Company**
2923 Mayer Rd
Browntown, WI 53522 608-439-5211
Fax: 608-439-5295
Cheese
Manager: James Meives
Estimated Sales: $10-20 Million
Number Employees: 20
Parent Co: V & V Supremo Foods

2668 **Chunco Foods Inc**
1400 E 2nd Street
Kansas City, MO 64106-1301 816-283-0716
Fax: 816-362-8097 contact@chuncofoods.com
www.chuncofoods.com
Fresh tofu, mung bean sprouts, alfalfa sprouts, radish sprouts, authentic koream kim chee, broccoli sprouts, onion sprouts, crispy sprouts and soy milk
Estimated Sales: $660,000
Number Employees: 6
Sq. footage: 4000
Type of Packaging: Food Service

2669 **Chung's Gourmet Foods**
3907 Dennis St
Houston, TX 77004 713-741-2118
Fax: 713-741-2330 800-824-8647
www.chungsfoods.com
Processor of juice, drinks, beverages and cranberry sauce products
President: David Huddle
CEO: Tarrus Richardson
CEO: Vreij A Kolandjian
Sr. VP: Michael Cooper
Estimated Sales: $ 10 - 20 Million
Number Employees: 100-249
Type of Packaging: Consumer, Food Service, Private Label
Brands:
Chung's

2670 **Chungs Gourmet Foods**
3907 Dennis St
Houston, TX 77004-2520 713-741-2118
Fax: 713-741-2330 www.chungsfoods.com
Processor and importer of Oriental frozen entrees and appetizers including egg rolls
President: Gene Chung
CEO: Vreij A Kolandjian
Production Manager: Bob Lee
Purchasing Manager: Lynn Tri
Estimated Sales: $10-20 Million
Number Employees: 100-249

2671 **Chupa Chups USA**
1200 Abernathy Rd NE
Atlanta, GA 30328-5662 770-730-6200
Fax: 678-443-3157 800-843-1858
Candy
President: Xavier Bernat
VP/General Manager: Allan Slimming
Director of Trade Marketing: Mike Grindstaff
VP Sales: Jeff Goodman
Brand Manager: Kimberly Liss
Estimated Sales: $50 Million
Brands:
CHUPA CHUPS
CRAZY DIPS
POP ROCKS
SMINT
WHISTLE POPS

2672 **(HQ)Church & Dwight Company**
469 N Harrison St
Princeton, NJ 8540 609-683-5900
Fax: 609-497-7269 800-221-0453
www.churchdwight.com

Manufacturer and exporter of leavening agents including sodium, ammonium and potassium bicarbonates; including Arm & Hammer Baking Soda. bathroom cleaners, antiperspirants, trojan condoms,cat litter,toothpaste.
Chairman/President/CEO: James Craigie
Ceo: James Craigie
EVP Finance & CFO: Matthew Farrell
R&D: Paul Siracusa Phd
EVP & CMO: Bruce Fleming
VP Human Resources: Dennis Moore
EVP Global Operations: Mark Conish
Estimated Sales: $2.589 Million
Number Employees: 3600 all sites
Type of Packaging: Consumer, Food Service, Bulk
Other Locations:
Lakewood NJ
London OH
Green River WY
Old Fort OH
Madera CA
Oskaloosa IA
Princeton NJ
Colonial Heights VA
North Brunswick NJ
Harrisonville MO
Brands:
ARM & HAMMER®

2673 **Churny Company**
705 W Fulton St
Waupaca, WI 54981 715-258-4040
Fax: 715-258-4046 www.philipmorrisusa.com
Processor of cheese
Sr. VP: Pascal Fernandez
Controller: Mark Hausman
Asset Manager: Dave Edel
Operations/Plant Manager: Michael Spence
Estimated Sales: $10-20 Million
Number Employees: 100-249
Sq. footage: 42000
Parent Co: Kraft Foods
Type of Packaging: Consumer, Food Service, Private Label
Brands:
Hoffmans

2674 **(HQ)Ciao Bella Gelato Company**
25 Vreeland Rd, #A-104
Irvington, NJ 07040 973-373-1200
Fax: 973-373-1224 800-435-2863
info@ciaobellagelato.com
www.ciaobellagelato.com
Processor of gelato and sorbet
CFO: Stan Fabian
VP, Finance: Ray Bialick
Estimated Sales: $5-10 Million
Number Employees: 50
Sq. footage: 10000
Type of Packaging: Consumer, Food Service, Private Label, Bulk
Other Locations:
Ciao Bella Gelato Co.
San Francisco CA
Ciao Bella Gelato Co.
Los Angeles CA
Brands:
Ciao Bella
Gelato
Gotham Dairy
Sarabeth's

2675 **Ciao Bella Gellato Company**
25a Vreeland Rd Ste 104
Florham Park, NJ 7932-1918
Fax: 323-965-8692 info@ciaobellagelato.com
www.ciaobellagelato.com
Processor of gelato and sorbet
Manager: Enrique Lerma
Estimated Sales: $ 3 - 5 Million
Number Employees: 1-4
Parent Co: Ciao Bella Gelato
Other Locations:
Ciao Bella Gelato Company
Los Angeles CA

2676 **Cibao Meat Product**
630 Saint Anns Ave
Bronx, NY 10455-1404 718-993-5072
Fax: 718-993-5638 info@cibaomeat.com
www.cibaomeat.com
Processor and exporter of Spanish sausage and salami.
CEO: Heinz Vielus
Estimated Sales: $5-10 Million
Number Employees: 20-49
Type of Packaging: Food Service, Bulk
Brands:
CAMPESINO JAMONETA
DON PEDRO JAMONADA
INDUVECA
LONGANIZA CIBAO
PAVOLAMI
SALAMI CAMPESINO
SALAMI DEL PUEBLO
SALAMI SOSUA
SALAPENO SALAMI
VER-MEX
VILLA MELLA

2677 **Cibolo Junction Food & Spice**
3013 Aztec Road NE
Albuquerque, NM 87107-4301 505-888-1987
Fax: 505-888-1972 info@chimayotogo.com
www.chimayotogo.com
Soup, stew and bread mixes, salsas, pretzels, herbs, spices and seasonings
President: Brian McKinsey
Vice President: Susan McKinsey
Estimated Sales: $1-4.9 Million
Number Employees: 5-9
Type of Packaging: Private Label

2678 **Cienega Valley Winery/DeRose**
9970 Cienega Rd
Hollister, CA 95023 831-636-9143
Fax: 831-636-1435 info@derosewine.com
www.derosewine.com
Producers of red, white and port wines.
Owner: Pat De Rose
Winemaker: Al DeRose
Assistant Winemaker: Ralph Hurd IV
Estimated Sales: $500,000-1 Million
Number Employees: 1-4
Type of Packaging: Private Label
Brands:
DE ROSE VINEYARDS

2679 **Cifelli & Sons**
38 Obert St
South River, NJ 8882 732-238-0090
Fax: 732-238-7768
Processor of Italian sausage
President: J Cifelli
Estimated Sales: $2.5 Million
Number Employees: 14
Sq. footage: 3500
Type of Packaging: Private Label

2680 **Cimarron Cellars**
P.O.Box 8
Caney, OK 74533 580-889-5997
Fax: 580-889-6312 cimcel@atoka.net
Wine
Owner/Winemaker: Dwayne Pool
Owner: Suze Pool
President: Linda Pool
Estimated Sales: $1-2.5 Million
Number Employees: 1-4
Brands:
Cimarron Cellars

2681 **Cimpl Meats**
P.O.Box 80
Yankton, SD 57078-0080 605-665-1665
Fax: 605-665-8908
Manufacturer and packer of sausage and beef
VP: Dave Frankforter
Estimated Sales: $50-100 Million
Number Employees: 100-249

2682 **Cincinnati Preserves Company**
3015 E Kemper Rd
Cincinnati, OH 45241-1514
US 513-771-2000
Fax: 513-771-8381 800-222-9966
www.clearbrookfarms.com
Processor of fruit preserves ,jams,jellies,canned fruit,pie fillings,fruit pie mixes.
Owner: Andrew Liscow
CEO: Andy Liscow
VP: Dan Cohen
Estimated Sales: 1.8 Million
Number Employees: 18
Sq. footage: 30000
Parent Co: Cincinatti Preserving Company
Type of Packaging: Consumer
Brands:
Clearbrook Frams
Spreadable Fruit

2683 **Cinderella Cheese Cake Company**
208 N Fairview St
Riverside, NJ 8075 856-461-6302
Fax: 856-461-5813
Processor/Manufacturer of frozen cheesecake
President/CEO: Joseph Makin
VP: Alfred Rezende
Estimated Sales: $1 Million
Number Employees: 15
Sq. footage: 20000
Type of Packaging: Consumer, Food Service
Brands:
Cinderella

2684 **Cinnabar Specialty Foods**
1134 Haining St Ste C
Prescott, AZ 86305 928-778-3687
Fax: 928-778-4289 866-293-6433
info@cinnabarfoods.com
www.cinnabarfoods.com
Processor and exporter of sauces including ethnic and barbecue; also, fruit chutneys, dry spice blends, Caribbean salsa, kashmiri marinade, rice mixes, soup enhancers, etc
President: Neera Tandon
Vice President: Ted Schleicher
Estimated Sales: $1-4.9 Million
Number Employees: 1-4
Sq. footage: 1000
Type of Packaging: Consumer, Food Service, Private Label, Bulk
Brands:
Cinnabar Specialty Foods
Neera's

2685 **Cinnabar Vineyards & Winery**
P.O.Box 245
Saratoga, CA 95071-0245 408-741-5858
Fax: 408-741-5860 www.cinnabarwine.com
Wines
President: Suzanne Frontz
General Manager: Suzan Franz
Estimated Sales: $2.5-5 Million
Number Employees: 5-9

2686 **Cinnamon Bakery**
121 Hancock Street
Braintree, MA 02184-7040 781-843-2867
Fax: 781-849-0015 800-886-2867
cinbak@aol.com www.cinnamonbakery.com
Processor of cinnamon, raspberry and chocolate sticks, pecan sticky buns and cinnamon rolls
President: Tom Pattavina
Treasurer: Frances Pattavina
Estimated Sales: $2.5-5 Million
Number Employees: 5-9
Brands:
Boston Bakers Exchange
Cinnamon Bakery

2687 **Cipriani's Spaghetti & Sauce Company**
1025 W End Ave
Chicago Heights, IL 60411-2742 708-755-6212
Fax: 708-755-6272 www.cipspasta.com
Processor and exporter of pasta including angel hair, vermicelli, linguine, fettuccine, lasagna, spinach, etc.; also, pasta sauces
President: Annett Johnson
Executive VP: Arthur Petrarca
Purchasing Manager: Annette Johnson
Estimated Sales: $5-10 Million
Number Employees: 10-19
Sq. footage: 10893
Type of Packaging: Consumer, Food Service, Private Label, Bulk
Brands:
Cipriani's Classic Italian
Cipriani's Premium

2688 **Circle Packaging Machinery Inc**
2020 American Blvd
De Pere, WI 54115 920-983-3420
Fax: 920-983-3421
dstelzer@circlepackaging.com
www.circlepackaging.com

Manufacturer of vertical and horizontal form/fill/seal machines. F/F/S machines can be used to package a wide verity of liquids, tablet, capsules and other food and beverage products.
President: John Dykema
VP Marketing & Sales: Don Stelzer
Product Manager: Craig Stelzer
Production Manager: Steve Joosten
Parts & Service Manager: Ralph Ruggiero
Estimated Sales: Less than $ 500,000
Number Employees: 20-49
Type of Packaging: Consumer

2689 **Circle R Ranch Gourmet Foods**
5901 Cross Timbers Rd
Flower Mound, TX 75022-3142 817-430-1561
Fax: 817-430-8108 800-247-3077
www.circlerranch.org
Processor of sauces including black bean salsa, jalapeno jelly, green chili salsa, cheese and spice blend, corn relish and mesquite barbecue; also, snacks including jalapeno popcorn, habanero popcorn and snack mix
Manager: Wendy Foster
CEO: Alan Powdermaker
Estimated Sales: Less than $500,000
Number Employees: 10-19
Parent Co: Sunset Trails
Type of Packaging: Consumer, Private Label
Brands:
Circle R Gourmet Foods

2690 **Circle V Meat Company**
609 Arrowhead Trail Rd
Spanish Fork, UT 84660 801-798-3081
Fax: 801-798-8671 www.circlevmeat.com
Manufacturer of beef and pork including roasts, ham and bacon
Owner: Cliff Voorhees
Estimated Sales: $3 Million
Number Employees: 10-19

2691 **Circle Valley Produce**
P.O.Box 51260
Idaho Falls, ID 83405 208-524-2628
Fax: 208-524-2630
Processor and exporter of potatoes
President: Kent Cornelison
Purchasing: Dave Owens
Estimated Sales: $8.8 Million
Number Employees: 90
Type of Packaging: Consumer, Bulk
Brands:
Throughbred
Valley Gold

2692 **Circus Man Ice Cream Corporation**
1000 Fulton St
Farmingdale, NY 11735-4245 516-249-4400
Fax: 516-249-4435
Processor of ice cream
Owner: Blaise Graziano
Estimated Sales: $1.8 Million
Number Employees: 10-19
Brands:
CIRCUS MAN

2693 **Ciro Foods**
PO Box 44096
Pittsburgh, PA 15205-0296 412-771-9018
Fax: 412-771-9018 cirofoods@usa.net
Processor of roasted red pepper spread, Italian salsa, sauces including pizza, barbecue and cooking and hot honey mustard; wholesaler/distributor of hot pepper sauce; serving the food service market; importer of vinegar; exporter ofhot honey mustard
President: Robert Pasquarelli
VP: Josephine Proto
Marketing Executive: Armand Pasquarelli
Number Employees: 20
Type of Packaging: Consumer, Food Service, Private Label

2694 **Cisco Brewers**
P.O.Box 2928
Nantucket, MA 02584-2928 508-325-5929
Fax: 508-325-5209 brewers@nantucket.net
www.ciscobrewers.com
Processor and exporter of ale and lager
Owner: Randy Hudson
Estimated Sales: $600,000
Number Employees: 1-4
Sq. footage: 3200
Type of Packaging: Consumer
Brands:
Baggywrinkle
Bailey's
Captain Swain's Extra
Celebration Libation
Dubbel Felix Caspian
Moor
Nobadeer Ginger
Summer of Lager
Whale's Tale

2695 **(HQ)Citadelle Maple Syrup Producers' Cooperative**
2100 St-Laurent, CP 310
Plessisville, QC G6L 2Y8
Canada 819-362-3241
Fax: 819-362-2830 citadelle@citadelle.coop
www.citadelle.coop
Processor and exporter of fruit spreads, honey, pure maple syrup and maple sugar
CEO: Luc Lussier
Financial Services Director/Treasurer: Andre Bouffard
Operations/Quality Control Director: Denis Lajoie
Marketing Director: Sylvie Chapron
Human Resources Director: Richard Cote
Number Employees: 150
Sq. footage: 90000
Type of Packaging: Consumer, Food Service, Private Label, Bulk
Other Locations:
Brands:
Camp
Canada Gold
Citadelle
O'Canada

2696 **Citrico**
155 Revere Dr # 1
Northbrook, IL 60062-1558 847-835-4368
Fax: 847-945-7405 888-625-8516
rtv2@citrico.com www.creativeimpactgroup.com
An independent manufacturer of citrus products for the food, beverage, pharmaceutical and nutraceutical industries. Citrico operates companies in the Cayman Islands, United States, Mexico, Argentina, Ireland, Germany and South Africa.Our two largest prod
Owner: Joanne Brooks
VP Technical Sales: Robert Vieregg
Sales: Timothy Grano
Estimated Sales: $4.8 Million
Number Employees: 10-19
Number of Brands: 20
Parent Co: Citrico International
Brands:
Citrico

2697 **Citrop**
5707 W Sligh Ave
Tampa, FL 33634 813-249-5955
Fax: 813-249-5956
Suppliers of natural flavoring
President/CEO: Jorge Figueredo
Estimated Sales: $1-2.5 Million
Number Employees: 5-9

2698 **Citrus Citrosuco North America**
5937 State Road 60 E
Lake Wales, FL 33898-9279 863-696-7400
Fax: 863-696-1303 800-356-4592
Processor of orange juice and concentrates; importer of frozen orange and apple concentrates and not from concentrate orange juice; exporter of frozen orange juice concentrates and not from concentrate orange juice
President: Nick Emanuel
Secretary: Dennis Helms
Sales Manager: Michael DuBrul
Estimated Sales: $ 50 - 100 Million
Number Employees: 100-249
Type of Packaging: Bulk

2699 **Citrus International**
210 Salvador Sq
Winter Park, FL 32789-5619 407-629-8037
Fax: 407-629-8195
Citrus juice
President: Brian Albertson
Estimated Sales: Under $500,000
Number Employees: 1-4

2700 **Citrus Service**
120 S Dillard St
Winter Garden, FL 34787-3560 407-656-4999
Fax: 407-656-4999 beroper@iag.net
Manufacturer and exporter of frozen organic citrus juices and frozen juice concentrates
President: Bert Roper
CEO: Charles Roper
Estimated Sales: $4 Million
Number Employees: 20-49
Sq. footage: 14000
Type of Packaging: Bulk
Brands:
GROVE SWEET

2701 **Citrus and Allied Essences**
3000 Marcus Ave, Ste 3e11
New Hyde Park, NY 11042 516-354-1200
Fax: 516-354-1502 www.citrusandallied.com
Supplier of essential oils, oleoresins, aromatic chemicals and specialty flavor ingredients.
President/CEO/Owner: Richard Pisano Jr.
CFO: Nancy McDonald
Executive Vice President: Stephen Pisano
Director Purchasing: Rob Haedrich
Number Employees: 100+
Type of Packaging: Food Service, Bulk

2702 **Citterio USA Corporation**
2008 State Route 940
Freeland, PA 18224-3256 570-636-3171
Fax: 570-636-1267 800-435-8888
sales@citteriousa.com www.citteriousa.com
Processor and importer of Italian Speciality deli meat products
President/COO: Osvaldo Vanucci
Chairman/CEO: Enrico Citterio
CEO: Nick Dei Tos
VP Sales: Joseph Petruce
VP Manufacturing: Michael Zieminski
Estimated Sales: $5-10 Million
Number Employees: 100-249
Parent Co: Giuseppe Citterio Spa
Type of Packaging: Consumer, Food Service, Private Label, Bulk

2703 **City Baker**
906 1st Avenue NE
Calgary, AB T2E 0C5
Canada 403-263-8578
Fax: 403-237-0453 www.waymarking.com
Processor of baked goods including breads, pastries, cakes and frozen proofed dough products
President: George Weston
VP Operations: ED HOLIK
Sales Manager: Rick San Salvador
Number Employees: 50-99
Type of Packaging: Consumer, Food Service
Brands:
City Bakery

2704 **City Bakery**
3 West 18th Street
New York, NY 10011-4610 212-366-1414
Fax: 212-645-0810 877-328-3687
allison@thecitybakery.com
www.thecitynakery.com
Pretzel croissants and baked goods
Owner: Maury R Rubin
Marketing: Allison Dees
Estimated Sales: $ .5 - 1 million
Number Employees: 10-19
Brands:
Maury's Cookie Dough
The City Bakery

2705 **City Bean**
26042 Tennyson Lane
Stevenson Ranch, CA 91381-1018 310-208-0108
Fax: 310-208-4554 888-248-9232
info@citybean.com www.citybean.com
Coffee, tea
President: James Marcotte
Estimated Sales: $500,000-$1 Million
Number Employees: 5-9

2706 **City Brewery Latrobe**
119 Jefferson St
Latrobe, PA 15650 724-537-5545
Fax: 724-537-4035 www.rollingrock.com
Manufacturer and exporter of beer
the new company brews iron city beer.duquesne bottle company took over the city brewery.
Brewer: Joe Gruss

Estimated Sales: $3 Billion
Number Employees: 1000
Parent Co: Duquesne Bottle Company
Type of Packaging: Consumer

2707 **City Brewing Company**
925 3rd St S
La Crosse, WI 54601 608-785-4200
Fax: 608-785-4333 contact@citybrewery.com
www.citybrewery.com
Processor of beer and malt beverages
Manager: Julie Ann Wilkins
Sales/Marketing Executive: Randy Hull
Brewmaster: Randy Hughes
Purchasing Director: Jeff Glynn
Estimated Sales: $10-20 Million
Number Employees: 10-19
Type of Packaging: Consumer
Brands:
CITY LAGER
CITY LIGHT
CITY SLICKER
KUL
LACROSS LAGER
LACROSS LIGHT

2708 **City Cafe Bakery**
215 Glynn St S
Fayetteville, GA 30214 770-461-6800
Fax: 770-461-2161 www.citycafeandbakery.com
Bakery products
Owner: Jorg Schatte
Estimated Sales: $ 3 - 5 Million
Number Employees: 20-49

2709 **City Farm/Rocky Peanut Company**
1545 Clay Street
Detroit, MI 48211-1911 313-871-5100
Fax: 313-871-5106 800-437-6825
info@rockypeanut.com
rocky-peanut.com/city-farm.com
Holiday snack items
President: Joe Russo
Purchsing Director: Joe Russo
Estimated Sales: $2.5-5 Million
Number Employees: 5-9

2710 **City Foods**
4230 S Racine Ave
Chicago, IL 60609 773-523-1566
Fax: 773-523-1414 www.beasbest.com
Processor, importer and exporter of frozen beef products including corned beef brisket, short ribs, corned, sliced, roast beef, pastrami,and beef bacon
President: Kenneth Kohn
Marketing Director: Steven Bash
Controller: Jerry Kohn
Estimated Sales: $15 Million
Number Employees: 95
Sq. footage: 43000
Type of Packaging: Consumer, Food Service, Private Label, Bulk
Brands:
Bea's Best Corned beef
Chef's Pride
SILVER LABEL

2711 **City Market**
1508 Gloucester St
Brunswick, GA 31520 912-265-4430
Fax: 912-261-2191
Fish and seafood
Manager: Frank Owens
Estimated Sales: $3,500,000
Number Employees: 5-9

2712 **City Seafood Company ofMonroe**
1508 Siddon Street
Monroe, LA 71201-5026 318-323-3281
Fax: 318-388-4539
President: Carey Messina

2713 **Clabber Girl Corporation**
900 Wabash Ave
Terre Haute, IN 47807-3208 812-232-9446
Fax: 812-478-7181 info@clabbergirl.com
www.clabbergirlb2b.com
Processor and exporter of single and double-acting baking powder, cornstarch, baking soda, baking mixes
President: Gary Morris
Vice President: Eric Gloe
R&D: Mark Bormann
Quality Control: Keith Lee
Marketing: Lori Danielson
Sales: Eric Gloe
Plant Manager: Archie Kappel
Purchasing Manager: Bruce West
Number Employees: 100-249
Number of Products: 50
Parent Co: Hulman & Company
Type of Packaging: Consumer, Food Service, Private Label, Bulk
Brands:
Clabber Girl
Rumford

2714 **Claeys Candy**
P.O.Box 1535
South Bend, IN 46634-1535 574-287-1818
Fax: 574-287-4184 800-348-2239
claeysinc@aol.com www.claeyscandy.com
Candy, old fashioned hard candies, cream fudge, gourmet peanut brittle, chocolate charlie gift boxes, bulk, private label
President: Gregg Claeys
Plant Manager: Brian Machalleck
Estimated Sales: $10-20 Million
Number Employees: 20-49
Type of Packaging: Consumer, Private Label, Bulk
Brands:
CHOCOLATE CHARLIE
CLAEYS GOURMET CREAM FUDGE
CLAEYS GOURMET PEANUT BRITTLE
CLAEYS OLD FASHION HARDS CANDIES

2715 **Claiborne & Churchill Vintners**
2649 Carpenter Canyon Rd
San Luis Obispo, CA 93401 805-544-4066
Fax: 805-544-7012 info@claibornechurchill.com
www.claibornechurchill.com
Wines
Owner/President: Claiborne Thompson
Owner/CEO: Fredericka Churchill
Estimated Sales: $500,000-$1 Million
Number Employees: 1-4
Brands:
Claiborne & Churchill

2716 **Claire's Grand River Winery**
5750 Madison Rd
Madison, OH 44057-9001 440-298-9838
Fax: 440-298-1861
Wines
Manager: Cindy Lindberg
Vice-President: William Worthy
Estimated Sales: $2.5-5 Million
Number Employees: 5-9

2717 **Clara Foods**
100 First Avenue SE
Clara City, MN 56222-0457 320-847-3680
Fax: 320-847-3939 888-844-8518
snacks@hcnet.net
Processor of snack foods, pretzels, cereal, baking ingredients and extruded products
President: Massoud Kazemzadeh
Research & Development: Massoud Kazemzadeh
VP Sales/Marketing: Tom Condon
Purchasing Manager: Joe Jeanotte
Estimated Sales: $1.5 Million
Number Employees: 40

2718 **Clarendon Flavor Engineering**
P.O.Box 21069
Louisville, KY 40221-0069 502-634-9215
Fax: 502-634-1438 info@clarendonflavors.com
www.clarendonflavors.com
Manufactures natural and artificial flavors to food and beverage industry. Specializes in natural soft drinks, juice added and flavored sparkling waters
President: Richard Rigney
Estimated Sales: $5-10 Million
Number Employees: 5-9
Sq. footage: 20000
Type of Packaging: Bulk

2719 **Clark Foodservice**
950 Arthur Ave
Elk Grove Vlg, IL 60007-5217 847-956-1730
Fax: 847-956-1064
Wholesaler/distributor of groceries, meats, produce, dairy/frozen foods and seafood; serving the food service market
President: Steven Schallert
VP: Daniel Dunne
Estimated Sales: $100+ Million
Number Employees: 500-999
Number of Products: 8000
Sq. footage: 165000
Parent Co: Clark Foodservice
Type of Packaging: Food Service

2720 **(HQ)Clark Foodservice**
950 Arthur Ave
Elk Grove Vlg, IL 60007-5217 847-956-1730
Fax: 847-956-1064 800-504-3663
Wholesaler/distributor of general line products and general merchandise including food, paper products and chemicals; serving the food service market
President: Steven Schallert
VP: Daniel Dunne
Estimated Sales: $50-100 Million
Number Employees: 50-99
Other Locations:
Clark Foodservice
West Palm Beach FL

2721 **Clark Spring Water Company**
319 Clark St
Pueblo, CO 81003 719-543-1594
Fax: 719-543-6334 info.clark@aol.com
Processor and bottler of water
President: William Clark
CEO: William Clark
Marketing Director: William Clark
Estimated Sales: $2.5-5 Million
Number Employees: 5-9
Type of Packaging: Consumer
Brands:
Alpine

2722 **(HQ)Clarks Joe Fund RaisingCandies & Novelties**
621 E 1st Ave
Tarentum, PA 15084-2005 724-226-0866
888-459-9520
ourcard@nuwavemedia.com
Processor of chocolate candy including mints, nougats, boxed and fund raising; also, importer of raw chocolate
Owner: Bob Clark
Estimated Sales: $ 3 - 5 Million
Number Employees: 5-9
Type of Packaging: Consumer
Brands:
Joe Clark's Candies, Inc.

2723 **Clarkson Scottish Bakery**
1715 Lakeshore Road W
Mississauga, ON L5J 1J4
Canada 905-823-1500
Processor of Scottish baked goods including pies, pastries and breads; importer of Scottish and English meats, candies and chocolates
Proprietor: Catherine Whitelaw
Number Employees: 1-4
Sq. footage: 450

2724 **Clarmil Manufacturing Corporation**
30865 San Clemente St
Hayward, CA 94544 510-476-0700
Fax: 510-476-0707 888-252-7645
info@clarmilmfg.com www.goldilocks-usa.com
Manufacturers a full line of breads, rolls, buns, filled buns and pies, pastries, sweet goods, cookies, crackers and snack items. Cakes-pound cake, sponge, devil, chiffon, snack cakes and other specialty cake items. Processes soupssauces, side dishes, stews, processed meat products, meat and vegetable fillings, hors d'ouvers, specialty snacks and appetizers.
President: Marion Ortiz Luis
Estimated Sales: Less than $500,000
Number Employees: 5-9
Number of Products: 200+
Sq. footage: 57000
Type of Packaging: Consumer, Food Service, Private Label, Bulk

2725 **Clasen Quality Coatings**
5126 West Terrance Drive, Ste 100
Madison, WI 53718 630-584-2851
Fax: 331-442-0957 877-459-4500
info@clasen.us www.clasen.us

Manufacturer of pure chocolate and confectionery coatings. Product line includes milk, dark, white, yogurt, peanut, colored and flavored
President: Jay Jensen
CFO: Andy Gitter
VP: Dennis Tagarelli
National Account Manager: Claudia Davis
Estimated Sales: Under $500,000
Number Employees: 5-9
Sq. footage: 2807
Type of Packaging: Consumer, Bulk
Brands:
CLASEN

2726 **Classic Commissary**
126 E Arterial Highway
Binghamton, NY 13901-1656 800-929-3486
Fax: 607-722-1415 classiccommissary@aol.com
www.classiccommissary.com
Processor of fresh salads and fruits; also, frozen dinners, sandwiches and bagels; for the vending and convenience food industry
Owner: Tara Gianfrate
Manager: Cataldo Gianfrate
Number Employees: 50-99
Number of Products: 125
Sq. footage: 22000
Type of Packaging: Food Service, Private Label, Bulk
Brands:
Classic Commissary

2727 **Classic Confectionery**
PO Box 573
Fort Worth, TX 76101-0573 847-674-4490
Fax: 847-674-4435 800-674-4435
TomDetective@yahoo.com
www.candydetective.com
Candy and confectionery
President: Cory Rogin
Co-Founder: Thomas Allen
President: Gail Robinson
General Manager: Trevor Toppen
Number Employees: 50-99

2728 **Classic Delight**
310 S Park Dr
Saint Marys, OH 45885 419-394-7955
Fax: 419-394-3199 800-274-9828
classicdelight@classicdelight.com
www.classicdelight.com
Processor and co-packer of USDA and FDA frozen and refrigerated sandwiches, meat and entrees
President: D Harkleroad
Quality Control: Thresia Buscher
Estimated Sales: $8 Million
Number Employees: 50-99
Number of Brands: 25
Number of Products: 60
Sq. footage: 18500
Type of Packaging: Consumer, Food Service, Private Label, Bulk
Brands:
CLASSIC DELIGHT
EXPRESS DELIGHTS
SENSIBLE DELIGHTS

2729 **Classic Flavors & Fragrances**
878 W End Ave Apt 12b
New York, NY 10025 212-777-0004
Fax: 212-353-0404 cffi125@aol.com
Manufacturer, importer and exporter of flavors, essential oils, aromatics, etc
Owner: George Ivolin
CEO: George Ivolin
Estimated Sales: $2.5-5 Million
Number Employees: 5-9
Sq. footage: 1800
Type of Packaging: Bulk

2730 **Classic Foods**
1592 Union Street
49
San Francisco, CA 94123-4531 800-574-8122
Fax: 866-235-9993 custserv@kettleclassics.com
www.kettleclassics.com
Family owned manufacturer of top quality branded snack foods distributed throughout the United States and Canada.
President: Florencio Cuetara
VP of Sales - Food Service: Shane Gray
Director of Sales - Vending: Lynn Marie Robles
Public Relations: Army Nix
Estimated Sales: $5-10 Million
Number Employees: 100-249
Brands:
Baked Classics
Kettle Classics
Kids Klassics
Stoned Classics

2731 **(HQ)Classic Tea**
649 Innsbruck Court
Libertyville, IL 60048-1845 630-680-9934
Processor, importer and exporter of ceylon (black) tea, liquid tea syrup and iced tea concentrates
Managing Dir.: Thomas Rielly
Dir.: F Court Bailey
Number Employees: 20-49
Sq. footage: 20000
Type of Packaging: Consumer, Food Service, Private Label, Bulk
Other Locations:
Classic Tea Ltd.
Chicago IL
Brands:
Ceylon Classic
Classic Ceylon
Pearl

2732 **Classy Delites**
P.O.Box 340189
Austin, TX 78734-0004 512-266-7157
Fax: 512-266-7198 800-440-2648
classydelites@calssydelites.com
www.classydelites.com
Processor of all-natural, artichoke marvelous melody, basalmic bean sauce, reduced carbs tweed tortilla chips, jamaican sauce, spinach - avacado sauce and portabella sauce.
Owner: Debbie Westbrook
CEO: Drew Westbrook
Estimated Sales: $1-2.5 Million
Number Employees: 1-4
Type of Packaging: Consumer
Brands:
Classy Delites

2733 **Claudia B Chocolates**
663 W Rhapsody Dr
San Antonio, TX 78216 210-366-0319
Fax: 800-375-4602
customerservice@claudiab.com
www.claudiab.com
Chocolates
President: Don Bankler
Estimated Sales: $ 1 - 3 Million
Number Employees: 1-4
Sq. footage: 4000
Type of Packaging: Consumer, Private Label, Bulk

2734 **Claudio Corallo Chocolate**
2122 Westlake Ave
Seattle, WA 98121-2717
Fax: 206-204-0629
chocolate@claudiocorallo.com
www.claudiocorallochocolate.com
chocolates

2735 **Claudio Pastry Company**
7308 W North Avenue
Elmwood Park, IL 60707-4234 708-453-0598
Fax: 708-453-9043
Cakes and pastries
President/Owner: John Golella
Estimated Sales: Less than $500,000
Number Employees: 5-9

2736 **Claussen Pickle Company**
1300 Claussen Dr
Woodstock, IL 60098-2155 815-338-7000
Fax: 815-338-9244 800-435-2817
www.kraft.com
Processor and exporter of kosher sauerkraut, tomatoes and pickles including garlic-free, whole, spears, halves, slices, mini, chips and sweet and sour
President: Richard Lerner
Maintenance Manager: Jim Darby
Production Manager: Paul Homola
Plant Manager: Gerry Lales
Estimated Sales: $100-500 Million
Number Employees: 250-499
Sq. footage: 200000
Parent Co: Kraft Foods
Type of Packaging: Consumer, Food Service
Brands:
BREAD 'N BUTTER
BURGER SLICES
DELI STYLE HEARTY
KOSHER DILLS
NEW YORK DELI HALF SOURS

2737 **Claxton Bakery**
203 W Main St
P.O. Box 367
Claxton, GA 30417 912-739-3441
Fax: 912-739-3097 800-841-4211
service@claxtonfruitcake.com
www.claxtonfruitcake.com
Manufacturer and exporter of fruit cake and pecans
President: Delorease Parker
Controller: Joe Miller
Vice President: Middleton Parker
COO: Mid Parker
Estimated Sales: $20-50 Million
Number Employees: 100-249
Type of Packaging: Consumer
Brands:
Claxton

2738 **Clay Center Locker Plant**
212 6th St
Clay Center, KS 67432 785-632-5550
Fax: 785-632-5550
Processor of beef, pork, lamb, buffalo and ostrich
Owner: Brad Dieckmann
Estimated Sales: $ 3 - 5 Million
Number Employees: 5-9
Type of Packaging: Consumer, Food Service

2739 **Clayton's Coffee & Tea**
1016 H St
Modesto, CA 95354-2317 209-522-7811
Fax: 209-576-1123 sales@claytoncoffee.com
www.claytonrestaurant.com
Coffee and tea
Owner: Mitch Maiseti
Estimated Sales: $1-2.5 Million
Number Employees: 1-4
Type of Packaging: Bulk
Brands:
Clayton Coffee & Tea

2740 **Claytons Crab Company**
5775 Us Highway 1
Rockledge, FL 32955-5729 321-639-0161
Fax: 321-636-4631
Processor of crab meat; wholesaler/distributor of fresh, frozen and canned seafood and meat; serving the food service market
Owner: Clayton M Korecky Jr
Estimated Sales: $1-3 Million
Number Employees: 20-49

2741 **Clean Foods**
760 E Santa Maria St
Santa Paula, CA 93060 805-933-3027
Fax: 805-933-9367 800-526-8328
contact@cafealtura.com www.cafealtura.com
Processor, importer and exporter of organic coffee
President: Chris Shepard
Sales Manager: Elizabeth Blatz
Estimated Sales: $2.5-5 Million
Number Employees: 5-9
Sq. footage: 1000
Parent Co: Clean Foods
Brands:
Cafe Altura

2742 **Clear Creek Distillery**
2389 NW Wilson St
Portland, OR 97210 503-248-9470
Fax: 503-248-0490
steve@clearcreekdistillery.com
www.clearcreekdistillery.com
Wine and liquor
President: Stephen McCarthy
Vice President: Rachel Showaiter
Estimated Sales: $700,000
Number Employees: 7
Type of Packaging: Private Label
Brands:
BARTLETT
BLUE PLUMB BRANDY
CLEAR CREEK GRAPPAS
FLAMBOISE
KIRSCHWASSER (CHERRY BRANDY)
MCCARTHY'S OREGON SINGLE MALT
PEAR BRANDY
PURE FRUITE

2743 **Clear Lake Bakery**
8400 Maryland Avenue
Saint Louis, MO 63105-3647 641-357-5264
Fax: 641-357-7911
Bakery products
President: Jim McQuaid
Sales/Marketing Manager: Matthwe Miller
General Manager: Terry Olinger
Estimated Sales: $5-9.9 Million
Number Employees: 20-49

2744 **Clear Mountain Coffee Company**
9155 Brookville Rd
Silver Spring, MD 20910 301-587-2233
Fax: 301-587-7158 www.clearmountaincoffee.com
Fourteen varieties of organic and wood roasted coffees, syrups, Choice Tea, Ghiradelli Chocolate
President: Robert Dasilva
Estimated Sales: $1-2.5 Million
Number Employees: 10-19
Number of Brands: 10
Brands:
10

2745 **Clear Springs Foods**
1500 E 4424 N
Buhl, ID 83316 208-543-4316
Fax: 208-543-5608 800-635-8211
csf@clearsprings.com www.tommytrout.com
Processor of fresh and frozen rainbow trout; breaded trout portions, shapes and melts
President: Keith Quigley
VP Operations: Ed White
Division Manager: Dennis Knapp
Estimated Sales: $50 Million
Number Employees: 325
Sq. footage: 43000
Parent Co: Clear Springs Foods
Type of Packaging: Consumer, Food Service, Private Label
Brands:
CLEAR SPRINGS KITCHEN®
CLEAR SPRINGS®
CLEARùCUTS®
SPLASH®

2746 **Clear Springs Foods**
14 Oakley Court
Cherry Hill, NJ 08003-2225 856-424-9412
Fax: 856-751-0147 800-635-8211
csf@clearsprings.com www.clearsprings.com
Processor of fresh and frozen rainbow trout, appetizers, roulades, and breaded portions and has its own fish farm,hatched and raised.
President: Larry Cope
CFO: Keith Quigly
Research & Development: Randy McMillan
Quality Control: Julie Sradleman
Marketing Director: Chris Howard
Sales Director: Don Riffle
Operations Manager: Tim Harrifan
Estimated Sales: $ .5 - 1 million
Number Employees: 1-5
Parent Co: Clear Springs Foods
Type of Packaging: Food Service, Private Label

2747 **Clear-Vu Industries**
200 Homer Avenue
Suite 3
Ashland, MA 01721-1716 508-881-9100
Fax: 508-881-9111 info@clear-vuindustries.com
www.clear-vuindustries.com
Bulk Candy System
President: Robert McCann
Estimated Sales: $1-2.5 Million
Number Employees: 10-19

2748 **Clearly Canadian Beverage Corporation**
220 Viceroy Rd
Units 11/12
Vanghan, ON L4K 3CA
Canada 905-761-0597
Fax: 607-742-5301 800-735-7180
info@clearly.ca www.clearly.ca
Processor and exporter of water including sparkling fruit, carbonated mineral and artesian
President: David Reingold
CEO/CHR: Bobby Genovese
VP Operations And Brand Manager: Renella Zahler
Estimated Sales: $10.62million
Number Employees: 20
Type of Packaging: Consumer, Food Service
Brands:
CLEARLY CANADIAN
CLEARLY CANADIAN O+2
ORBITZ
QUENCHER
TRE' LIMONE

2749 **Clearwater Coffee Company**
711 Rose Rd
Lake Zurich, IL 60047-1542 847-540-7711
Fax: 847-540-7719
Coffee
President: Jim Ludwig

2750 **Clearwater Fine Foods**
757 Bedford Highway
Bedford, NS B4A 3Z7
Canada 902-443-0550
Fax: 902-443-8367 www.clearwater.ca
Processor and exporter of frozen shrimp, lobster, scallops, crabs and clams
Chairman: Colin MacDonald
CEO: Ian Smith
Number Employees: 100-249
Type of Packaging: Consumer, Food Service

2751 **Clem Becker**
2720 Lincoln Ave
Two Rivers, WI 54241 920-793-1391
Fax: 920-793-1393 clembeckerinc@lakefield.net
Processor of smoked pork products
President: Peter Becker
VP: Oliver Skrivanie
Business Manager: Jan Eycke
Estimated Sales: $ 5 - 10 Million
Number Employees: 25
Type of Packaging: Consumer, Food Service, Private Label

2752 **Clem's Refrigerated Foods**
181 Virginia Ave
Lexington, KY 40508 859-233-0821
Fax: 859-233-0868 800-544-5571
Processor of beef and pork products
Owner: William Clem
Sales Manager: Bill Mahan
Estimated Sales: $4 Million
Number Employees: 25
Type of Packaging: Consumer, Food Service, Bulk
Brands:
Clem's Custom Cut Cattle

2753 **Clem's Seafood & Specialties**
4505 Mattingly Ct
Buckner, KY 40010-8830 502-222-7571
Fax: 502-222-7598
Owner: Michael Mc Alister
Estimated Sales: $ 3 - 5 Million
Number Employees: 1-4

2754 **Clement Pappas & Company**
1 Collins Drive
Suite 200
Carneys Point, NJ 08069 856-455-1000
Fax: 856-455-8746 800-257-7019
customerservice@clementpappas.com
www.clementpappas.com
Manufacturer and exporter of juices including apple, blueberry, grape, papaya and cranberry sauce
President: Peter Pappas
Vice President: Michael Strickland
Estimated Sales: $100+ Million
Number Employees: 106
Sq. footage: 170000
Type of Packaging: Consumer, Private Label, Bulk
Other Locations:
Clement Pappas Food Plant
Springdale AR
Clement Pappas Food Plant
Seabrook NJ
Clement Pappas Food Plant
Mountain Home NC
Clement Pappas Food Plant
Ontario CA
Brands:
CLEMENT PAPPAS

2755 **(HQ)Clements Foods Company**
P.O.Box 14538
Oklahoma City, OK 73113-0538 405-842-3308
Fax: 405-843-6894 800-654-8355
www.clementsfoods.com
Processor of apple butter, preserves, jellies, salad dressings, pie fillings, mayonnaise, mustard, sauces, syrups, vinegar, peanut butter and imitation vanilla; exporter of salad dressings and mustards
President/CEO: Edward Clements
CEO: Robert Clements
Vice President: Gunnar Anderson
Quality Control: Tom Johnson
Operations Manager: Richard Meadors
Plant Manager: Louis LeFlore
Estimated Sales: $ 50 - 100 Million
Number Employees: 100-249
Sq. footage: 150000
Type of Packaging: Consumer, Food Service, Private Label
Other Locations:
Clements Foods Company
Lewisville TX
Brands:
American
Delicious
Dorcheste
Garden Club
Little Pig
PAR
Savory
Win You

2756 **Clements Pastry Shop**
3355 52nd Ave Ste B
Hyattsville, MD 20781 301-277-6300
Fax: 301-277-2897 800-444-7428
www.clementspastry.com
Custom manufacturing of specialty dessert and pastry items
CEO: Teresa Walls
VP of Sales: John Barrazotto
Estimated Sales: $100+ Million
Number Employees: 100-249
Number of Brands: 1
Number of Products: 200
Type of Packaging: Food Service, Private Label
Brands:
CLEMENTS PASTRY SHOP

2757 **Clemmy's**
PO Box 1746
Randcho Mirage, CA 92270
877-253-6698
www.clemmysicecream.com
lactose free, 100% sugar free and gluten free ice cream.
Founder/Owner: Jon Gordon
Number Employees: 6
Sq. footage: 2187
Type of Packaging: Consumer

2758 **Clermont**
PO Box 604
Hillsboro, OR 97123-0604 503-648-8544
Fax: 503-861-8054
Produces frozen fruits, fruit juice concentrate and fruit purees
Estimated Sales: $10-25 Million
Number Employees: 100-249

2759 **Cleugh's Frozen Foods**
6571 Altura Blvd
Buena Park, CA 90620-1019 714-521-1002
Fax: 714-670-1731
Manufacturer and importer of frozen produce including strawberries, red, yellow and green bell peppers, rhubarb, small whole potatoes, brussels sprouts and exporter of strawberries and peppers
President: Serge Verela
Estimated Sales: $50 Million
Number Employees: 20-49
Sq. footage: 45000
Parent Co: Sunopta, Inc.
Type of Packaging: Consumer, Food Service, Private Label, Bulk
Brands:
Cleugh's

2760 **Cleveland Syrup Corporation**
P.O.Box 91959
Cleveland, OH 44101 216-883-1845
Fax: 216-883-6204
Processor of syrup and powdered sugar
Manager: Jim Chaney
VP: James Chaney
President: Virginia Chaney
Estimated Sales: $1-2.5 Million
Number Employees: 1-4

Type of Packaging: Food Service, Bulk

2761 **Clic International Inc**
2185 Avenue Francis Hugues
Laval, QC H7S 1N5
Canada 450-669-2663
Fax: 450-667-6799 clic@clicfoods.com
www.clicfoods.com
Rice, beans and lentils, cereals, spices, dried fruits, oil and shortenings, gravy, cans and juices, milk products, pickles, Asiatic, Indian and African, coffee, nuts and desserts
President/Owner: M Assaad Abelnour
Estimated Sales: $24.5
Number Employees: 123

2762 **Cliff Bar**
1451 66th St
Emeryville, CA 94608-1004
Fax: 510-558-7872 800-884-5254
Healthy energy bars
Owner: Gary Erickson
Marketing/Sales: Terrye Parker
Estimated Sales: $ .5 - 1 million
Number Employees: 1-4
Type of Packaging: Private Label
Brands:
Cliff Bars
Luna Bars

2763 **Cline Cellars**
24737 Arnold Dr
Sonoma, CA 95476 707-940-4000
Fax: 707-940-4034 800-543-2070
www.clinecellars.com
Wines
Owner: Frederic Cline
CFO: Nancy Cline
Production Manager: Matt Cline
Estimated Sales: Under $500,000
Type of Packaging: Private Label
Brands:
Cline Cellars

2764 **Clinton Milk Company**
353 Morris Avenue
Newark, NJ 07103-2695 973-642-3000
Fax: 973-642-3457
Milk and juices
President: Kelly Marx
VP: Dan Marx
Plant Manager: Lawrence Dineen
Estimated Sales: $50-100 Million
Number Employees: 50-99

2765 **Clinton Vineyards**
450 Schultzville Rd
Clinton Corners, NY 12514 845-266-5372
Fax: 845-266-3395 info@clintonvineyards.com
www.clintonvineyards.com
Processor of white, dessert and sparkling wines
President: Ben Feder
VP: Phyllis Feder
Marketing Director: Phyllis Rich Feder
Production Manager: Mike Kelsey
Plant Manager: Bill Wentzel
Estimated Sales: $ 1 - 3 Million
Number Employees: 1-4
Type of Packaging: Consumer
Brands:
Clinton Victory
DUET
Embrace
NUIT
PEACH GAL
Romance
Seyval Blanc
Seyval Naturel

2766 **Clipper City Brewing**
4615 Hollins Ferry Rd Ste B
Baltimore, MD 21227 410-247-7822
Fax: 410-247-7829 www.ccbeer.com
Brewer of beer and ale
Manager: Jonathan McIntire
Manager: Kevin Fox
Packaging Manager: John Eugeni
Estimated Sales: $2 Million
Number Employees: 20
Type of Packaging: Consumer, Food Service

2767 **(HQ)Clofine Dairy & Food Products**
P.O.Box 335
Linwood, NJ 08221 609-653-1000
Fax: 609-653-0127 800-441-1001
fsmith@clofinedairy.com www.clofinedairy.com
Manufacturer and distributor of a full line of fluid and dried dairy products, proteins, cheeses, milk replacement blends, tofu and soymilk powders, vital wheat gluten, etc.
President/CEO: Fredrick Smith
VP Finance: Butch Harmon
Marketing - Fluid Products: Dawn Sink
VP Sales: Rich Eluk
Manager-manufactured Products: Jennifer Ingram
Estimated Sales: $20-50 Million
Number Employees: 10-19
Number of Brands: 2
Number of Products: 100
Type of Packaging: Food Service, Private Label, Bulk
Brands:
Fine-Mix Dairy
Food Blends
Soy Products
Soyfine
Soymilk

2768 **Clos Du Bois**
P.O. Box 940
Geyserville, CA 95441-0940 707-857-1651
Fax: 707-857-1667 800-222-3189
thewinespot.com www.closdubois.com
Wines
President: Bill Newlands
VP: Jan Casebeer
Product Manager: Charles Stewart
Estimated Sales: $50-100 Million
Number Employees: 100-249

2769 **Clos Du Muriel**
27230 Madison Ave # A
Temecula, CA 92590-5639 951-296-5400
Fax: 909-676-9606
Wines
Manager: Mike Stasi

2770 **Clos Pegase Winery**
1060 Dunaweal Ln
Calistoga, CA 94515-9642 707-942-4981
Fax: 707-942-4993 800-866-8583
cp@clospeggase.com www.clospegase.com
Wines
President: Jon Shrem
Controller/Business Manager: Abbe Bailon
VP: Theodore Sanford
Sales Director: Shannon Beglin
Winemaker: Steven Rogstad
Purchsing Manager: Theodore Sanford
Estimated Sales: $5-10 Million
Number Employees: 10-19

2771 **Clos du Lac Cellars**
P.O.Box 1164
Ione, CA 95640 209-274-2238
Fax: 209-274-4147 www.closdulac.com
Wines
President/CEO: Timothy Evans
CFO: Robert Neumann
Vice President: Peter Evans
Winemaker: Francois Cardesse
Cellar Manager: Kelly Evans
Estimated Sales: $2.5-5 Million
Number Employees: 5-9

2772 **Clos du Val Wine Company**
P.O.Box 4350
Napa, CA 94558-0567 707-259-2200
Fax: 707-252-6125 800-993-9463
cdv@closduval.com www.closduval.com
Producer and exporter of wines
CFO: Bill Cambron
VP: Robert Saiz
VP/Marketing: Debra Eagle
VP/Sales: Robert Salz
PR Manager: Michaela Baltasar
Estimated Sales: $ 50 - 100 Million
Number Employees: 100-249
Brands:
Clos Du Val

2773 **Cloud Nine**
14855 Wicks Boulevard
San Leandro, CA 94577-6605 201-358-8588
Fax: 201-216-0383 cloud9choc@aol.com
www.cloudninecandy.com
Processor and exporter of hard candy, organic breath mints, caramel popcorn and natural, gourmet, dairy, nondairy, low-fat and organic chocolate bars
President: Josh Taylor
CFO: Lana Nguyen
Marketing Director: Robert Wagg
Sales Director: Sharon Desser
Director Operations: Andrew Spector
Number Employees: 10-19
Sq. footage: 2000
Type of Packaging: Consumer, Private Label
Brands:
Cloud Nine
Cloud Nine All-Natural Chocolate
Environments
Sorrento Valley Organics
Tropical Source
Tropical Source Dairy-Free Gourmet
Tropical Source Organic

2774 **Cloud's Meat Processing**
2051 S Paradise Ln
Carthage, MO 64836-8452 417-358-5855
Fax: 417-358-7639
Processor of smoked meat; slaughtering services available
President: Mike Cloud
Marketing Director: Mike Cloud
Estimated Sales: $ 5 - 10 Million
Number Employees: 20-49

2775 **Cloudstone Vineyards**
27345 Deer Springs Way
Los Altos Hills, CA 94022-4352 650-948-8621
Wines
President: Peter Wolken
CEO: Judith Wolken
Number Employees: 1-4

2776 **Clougherty Packing Company**
3049 E Vernon Ave
Vernon, CA 90058 323-583-4621
Fax: 323-584-1699 farmerjohn@farmerjohn.com
www.farmerjohn.com
Manufacturer of pork and pork products including a full line of lean, fresh cut pork, sausages, weiners, franks, Polish sausage, bacon in varied thicknesses, boneless smoked fully cooked ham, liver spreads, pre-packaged ready to eatlunch meats and more.
President: Greg N Longstreet
VP Finance: James Stephenson
VP Technical Services: Bob Delmore
VP Marketing: Steve Kolodin
Director Public Relations: Ronald Smith
Estimated Sales: $420 Million
Number Employees: 1,000-4,999
Parent Co: Hormel Foods
Type of Packaging: Consumer, Bulk
Brands:
FARMER JOHN
FARMER JOHN MEATS

2777 **Clover Blossom Honey**
4279 E State Road 218
La Fontaine, IN 46940 765-981-4443
Fax: 765-981-4086
Manufacturer of honey
President/Co-Owner: David Shenefield
VP/Co-Owner: Don Shenefield
Estimated Sales: $5-10 Million
Number Employees: 5-9
Type of Packaging: Consumer, Food Service, Private Label, Bulk

2778 **Clover Farms Dairy Company**
P.O.Box 14627
Reading, PA 19612 610-921-9111
Fax: 610-921-9913 800-323-0123
contact@cloverfarms.com www.cloverfarms.com
Milk
President/CEO: Richard Hartman
VP: Richard Rothenberger
Treasurer: John Rothenberger
VP of Sales: Thomas Mullery
Manager Plant Operations: Dennis Dietrich
Plant Manager: Royce Haag
Purchasing Manager: Craig Saul
Estimated Sales: $50-100 Million
Number Employees: 260

2779 **Clover Hill Vineyards &Winery**
9850 Newtown Rd
Breinigsville, PA 18031 610-395-2468
Fax: 610-366-1246 800-256-8374
www.cloverhillwinery.com
Wines
Owner: John Skrip Jr
Owner: Pat Skrip
Estimated Sales: $2.5-5 Million
Number Employees: 10-19

2780 **Clover Leaf Cheese**
1201 45th Avenue NE
Calgary, AB T2E 2P2
Canada 403-250-3780
Fax: 403-291-9782 888-835-0126
chris@cheese-please.com
Packer and wholesaler/distributor of cheese
President: John Downey
Sales Manager: Chris Cameron
General Manager: John Downey
Plant Manager: Brad Lake
Estimated Sales: F
Number Employees: 50-99

2781 **Clover Stornetta Farms**
P.O.Box 750369
Petaluma, CA 94975-0369 707-778-8448
Fax: 707-778-0509 800-237-3315
www.clover-stornetta.com
Dairy products
President: Marcus Benedetti
CEO: Gary Imm
CEO: Kevin Imm
Sales Director: Mike Keefer
Estimated Sales: $50-100 Million
Number Employees: 100-249

2782 **Clover Valley Food**
RR 2
Box 134
Pierce, NE 68767-9668 402-329-4025
Fax: 402-329-4993
Canner of beef
President: Lawrence Polt
Estimated Sales: $500,000-$1 Million
Number Employees: 1-4
Type of Packaging: Consumer, Food Service

2783 **(HQ)Cloverdale Foods Company**
P.O.Box 667
Mandan, ND 58554 701-663-9511
Fax: 701-663-0690 800-669-9511
www.cloverdalefoods.com
Manufacturer and wholesaler/distributor of meat products including hickory smoked franks, bacon, ham and sausages, along with other quality pork products.
President/CEO: TJ Russell
Executive Vice President: Jim Miller
CFO: Kirk Olson
VP Sales/Marketing: Scott Russell
Estimated Sales: $50-100 Million
Number Employees: 250-499
Sq. footage: 114000
Type of Packaging: Consumer, Food Service, Private Label, Bulk
Other Locations:
Cloverdale Foods Plant
Minot ND
Brands:
Cloverdale
Teardrop

2784 **Cloverdale Packing**
PO Box 3346
Parkersburg, WV 26103-3346 304-485-5409
Fax: 304-428-3091
Meats
President: Jack Kincaid
Owner: David Winans
Estimated Sales: $5-9.9 Million
Number Employees: 10-19

2785 **Cloverhill Bakery-Vend Corporation**
2035 N Narragansett Ave
Chicago, IL 60639-3842 773-745-9800
Fax: 773-745-1647 bakery@cloverhill.com
www.cloverhill.com
Processor and exporter of sweet goods, doughnuts, cakes and muffins.
President: William Gee
Executive VP: Edward Gee
Quality Control: Dan Gee
VP Sales: Robert Gee
Production Manager: Richard Salkowski
Estimated Sales: $20-50 Million
Number Employees: 100-249
Sq. footage: 140000
Type of Packaging: Consumer, Food Service
Brands:
CLOVER HILL

2786 **Cloverland Dairy**
PO Box 329
Saint Clairsville, OH 43950-0329 740-699-0509
www.cloverlanddairy.com
Processor of portion controlled butter and buttermilk
President: Robert Hyest
Estimated Sales: $ .5 - 1 million
Number Employees: 300
Type of Packaging: Consumer, Private Label, Bulk

2787 **Cloverland Green Spring Dairy**
2701 Loch Raven Rd
Baltimore, MD 21218 410-235-4477
Fax: 410-889-3690 800-876-6455
www.cloverlanddairy.com
Manufacturer of fluid milk and dairy
President: Ralph Kemp
VP: John Kemp
Purchasing Director: John Evens
Estimated Sales: $100-499.9 Million
Number Employees: 250-499
Brands:
CLOVERLAND

2788 **Cloverland Sweets/Priester's Pecan Company**
P.O. Box 381
Fort Deposit, AL 36032-0381 334-227-4301
Fax: 334-227-4294 800-523-3505
www.priesterpecans.com
Pecan candies, pies, baked goods, and chocolates. Pecan shellers
President: Ned T Ellis Jr
Owner: Ellen Burkett
Vice President: Ellen Burkett
Public Relations: Faye Hood
Plant Manager: Jim Wheeler
Estimated Sales: $ 20 - 50 Million
Number Employees: 50-99
Type of Packaging: Food Service, Private Label, Bulk
Brands:
Cloverland Sweets
Priester's Pecans

2789 **Cloverleaf Dairy**
W10903 County Road N
Stanley, WI 54768 715-669-3145
Fax: 715-720-9332
Colby, cheddar, monterey jack cheeses
President: Daeo Paul
VP: Erlene Paul
Estimated Sales: $10-20 Million
Number Employees: 10-19
Type of Packaging: Private Label
Brands:
Cloverleaf

2790 **Clovervale Farms**
1833 Cooper Foster Park Rd
Amherst, OH 44001 440-960-0146
800-433-0146
sales@clovervale.com www.clovervale.com
Provides nutritious, pure, and safe food products. Product line includes; individual preportioned servings of entrees, vegetables, sandwiches, fruits, cobblers, butter and jelly bars, frozen yogurts, sherbets, italian ices, frozenjuice pops and milk
CEO: Don Russel
Executive VP: Jim Miller
Marketing/Sales Manager: Ray Kautzman
VP Sales: Anne Williams
Purchasing Manager: Angela Viglas
Estimated Sales: $20-50 Million
Number Employees: 100
Brands:
CHEF'S PASTRY
CLOVERDALE

2791 **Clown-Gysin Brands**
3184 Doolittle Dr
Northbrook, IL 60062-2409 847-564-5950
Fax: 847-564-9076 800-323-5778
info@clown-gysin.com www.clown-gysin.com
Producer and importer of marshmallows, snack foods, breadsticks, toasted onion bits, sesame dots, confectionery, and caramel apple dip items; importer of toasted onion bits and breadsticks
President: Herb Horn
Estimated Sales: $7-10 Million
Number Employees: 5-9
Number of Brands: 2
Sq. footage: 2000
Parent Co: Food Network
Type of Packaging: Food Service

2792 **Club Chef**
3776 Lake Park Dr Unit 1
Covington, KY 41017 859-578-3100
Fax: 859-578-3374 http://www.clubchef.com
Processor of wet and dry chopped salad items including lettuce, onions and cabbage
Owner: Bob Castelline
VP Retail Sales: Jeff Klare
Estimated Sales: $1-2.5 Million
Number Employees: 250-499
Sq. footage: 90000
Parent Co: Castellini Company
Type of Packaging: Consumer, Food Service, Private Label, Bulk
Brands:
Club Chef
Farm Fresh
Readypac

2793 **Clutter Farms**
7283 Millersburg Rd
Gambier, OH 43022 740-427-3515
Processor of popcorn including microwaveable
President: Gordon Clutter
V.P.: Larry Clutter
V.P.: Larry Clutter
Sq. footage: 7000
Type of Packaging: Consumer
Brands:
Clutters Indian Fields

2794 **Clyde's Italian & German Sausage**
3655 Inca St
Denver, CO 80211-3030 303-433-8744
Manufacturer of Italian and German sausage
President: Clyde Archer
Estimated Sales: $10 Milion
Number Employees: 1-4
Type of Packaging: Consumer

2795 **Clydes Delicious Donuts**
1120 W Fullerton Ave
Addison, IL 60101-4304 630-628-6555
Fax: 630-628-6838 www.clydesdonuts.com
Baked goods, bagels, danish, coffee cakes, sweet rolls, frozen and fresh yeast and cake donuts. Also apple, blueberry, maple, and cherry fritters
President: Kent Bickford
COB: William Bickford
Vice President: Kim Bickford
Research & Development: Mike Faherty
Quality Control: Rob LaScola
Marketing Director: Sue Nieues
Sales Director: Dave Bennett
Operations Manager: Larry Frank
Purchasing Manager: Dave Kells
Estimated Sales: $16-20 Million
Number Employees: 100-249
Number of Products: 125
Sq. footage: 160000
Type of Packaging: Consumer, Food Service, Private Label, Bulk

2796 **Coach Farm Enterprises**
105 Mill Hill Rd
Pine Plains, NY 12567 518-398-5325
Fax: 518-398-5329 800-999-4628
info@coachfarm.com www.coachfarm.com
Processor of goat's milk products including soft cheese and yogurt
President: Miles Cahn
Marketing: Steve Margarites
General Manager: Phil Peeples
Plant Manager: Rosie Parsons
Estimated Sales: $10-20 Million
Number Employees: 20-49

Type of Packaging: Private Label
Brands:
Coach Farm
Yo-Goat

2797 **Coach's Oats**
22735 La Palma Ave
Yorba Linda, CA 92887 714-692-6885
Fax: 714-692-6887 www.coachsoats.com
Oats
Owner: Lynn Rogers
Estimated Sales: $ 1 - 3 Million
Number Employees: 5-9

2798 **Coast Packing Company**
3275 E Vernon Ave
Vernon, CA 90058 323-277-7700
Fax: 323-277-7712 www.coastpacking.com
Manufacturer of quality shortening products for the restaurant, baking and food industries. Also the leading supplier of animal fats and vegetable oil shortenings.
President: Ronald R Gustafson
Sales: Dieter Rehnberg
Estimated Sales: $50-100 Million
Number Employees: 50-99
Type of Packaging: Consumer, Food Service

2799 **Coast Seafoods Company**
14711 NE 29th Pl Ste 111
Bellevue, WA 98007 425-702-8800
Fax: 425-702-0400 800-423-2303
info@coastseafoods.com
www.coastseafoods.com
Processor and exporter of fresh oysters and clams
President: John Petrie
CFO: Kay Christopher
Manager: Jim Donaldson
Estimated Sales: $2.5-5 Million
Number Employees: 1-4
Parent Co: Coast Seafoods Company
Type of Packaging: Consumer, Food Service

2800 **Coast to Coast Seafood**
9803 19th Avenue NE
Seattle, WA 98115-2311 425-889-2862
Fax: 425-822-3960
Seafood, seafood products
Estimated Sales: $50-100 Million
Number Employees: 20-49

2801 **Coastal Classics**
380 Church St
Duxbury, MA 02332 508-746-6058
Fax: 508-746-6063 info@ciastalclassics.com
www.coastalclassics.com
Processor of cranberry chutney, cranberry mustard, cranberry preserves, cranberry hot sauce, cranberry orange marmalade, cranberry blueberry grilling sauce, peanut sauce
President: Jan Baird
Brands:
Bogland
Bogland By the Sea
Coastal Gourmet

2802 **Coastal Cocktails**
18242 McDurmott Street
Irvine, CA 92614 949-250-3129
Fax: 949-250-9787
bbartels@coastalcocktails.com

2803 **Coastal Goods**
44 Old Jail Lane
Barnstable, MA 02630 508-375-1050
Fax: 508-375-1052 nigel@coastalgoods.com
Juice/cider, herbs, rubs, salt, spices, foodservice.

2804 **Coastal Promotions**
251 Champion Ct
Destin, FL 32541 561-626-6384
Fax: 561-626-8961 info@tasteoffl.com
www.tasteoffl.com
Manufacturer of beverage mixers
President: Doug McWhorter
Operations Manager: Kevin Blankenship
Number of Brands: 3
Number of Products: 21
Type of Packaging: Consumer, Food Service
Brands:
Taste of Florida
Wild Olive

2805 **Coastal Seafood Partners**
4647 N Lincoln Ave
Chicago, IL 60625-2024 773-989-7788
Fax: 773-989-7799
Seafood
President: Chris Costello
Estimated Sales: $ 1 - 3 Million
Number Employees: 20-49

2806 **Coastal Seafood Processors**
134 Brookhollow Esplanade
Harahan, LA 70123 504-734-9444
Fax: 504-736-9447
Seafood
President: Brian Quartano

2807 **Coastal Seafoods**
39 Acre Ln
Ridgefield, CT 06877 203-431-0453
Fax: 203-438-7099
Seafood
President: Robert Iseley
CFO/Secretary: Linda Iseley
Operations: Manuel Reyes
Plant Manager: Manuel Reyes
Estimated Sales: $2.5-5 Million
Number Employees: 20-49
Sq. footage: 2500
Type of Packaging: Food Service, Private Label

2808 **Coastlog Industries**
45380 W 10 Mile Rd
Novi, MI 48375-3000 248-344-9556
Fax: 248-344-9559
Aseptic shelf stable juice and milk products
President: R K Sridharan
VP Sales: Andy Larkin
Type of Packaging: Food Service
Brands:
Coastlog

2809 **Coastside Lobster Company**
P.O.Box 151
Stonington, ME 04681-0151 207-367-2297
Fax: 207-367-5929
Lobster
President: Peter Collin
Purchsing Director: Karen Rains
Number Employees: 5-9

2810 **Coating Place**
200 Paoli St
Verona, WI 53593 608-845-9521
Fax: 608-845-9526 info@encap.com
www.encap.com
Contract manufacturer specializing in wurster fluid bed coating services for encapsulation of solid particulate materials such as powders, grenules, crystals and capsules
President: Tim Breuning
R&D: Charles Frey
Quality Control: Scott Young
Purchasing Director: Kurt Schmidt
Estimated Sales: $10-20 Million
Number Employees: 20-49
Sq. footage: 110000
Type of Packaging: Bulk

2811 **Cobb Hill Chesse**
5 Linden Rd
Hartland, VT 05048-8104 802-436-1612
gailholmes@cobbhill.org
www.vermontcheese.com
Cheese
President: Gail Holmes

2812 **Cobraz Brazilian Coffee**
450 Park Ave
New York, NY 10022-2644 212-759-7700
Fax: 212-725-1170
Coffee
Managing Director: Francisco Barreto
Estimated Sales: $500,000-$1 Million
Number Employees: 5-9

2813 **Cobscook Bay Seafood**
PO Box 252
Perry, ME 04667-0252 207-853-2890
Fax: 208-459-3712
Seafood
President: Joyce Pottle

2814 **Coburg Dairy**
50001 LaCross Road
North Charleston, SC 29419 843-554-4870
Fax: 843-745-5502 marv.ervin@coburgmilk.com
www.coburgmilk.com
Milk, flavored milk, juice, cream
President: Robert Cotet
Finance Executive: Robert Garrett
VP: Kathy Turner
General Sales Manager: Dennis Roberts
General Manager: Gary Rackley
Estimated Sales: $ 20 - 50 Million
Number Employees: 265
Sq. footage: 100000
Type of Packaging: Consumer, Food Service, Bulk
Brands:
Coburg

2815 **(HQ)Coby's Cookies**
17 Vickers Rd
Toronto, ON M9B 1C1
Canada 416-633-1567
Fax: 416-633-9812
Processor and exporter of frozen cookie dough, muffin and brownie batter; also, retail pack rice crispy squares and brownies
President: Michael Topolinkski
Executive VP: Jay Punwasee
Estimated Sales: $9.3 Million
Number Employees: 150
Sq. footage: 15000
Type of Packaging: Consumer, Food Service, Private Label
Other Locations:
Coby's Cookies
Downsview ON
Brands:
Coby's Cookies, Inc.
Just Great Bakers, Inc.

2816 **Coca-Cola Bottling Company**
949 Mapunapuna St
Honolulu, HI 96819 808-839-6711
Fax: 808-834-7718 schow@na.cokecce.com
www.cokecce.com
Processor of fruit juices, bottled water, soft drinks and fountain syrup.
President: Dan Whitford Jr
SVP/Corporate Chief Information Officer: Jean Michel Ares
Quality Control: Clint Iziuka-Sheeley
SVP/Corporate External Affairs Director: Ingrid Saunders Jones
General Manager: Stanley Chow
Estimated Sales: $50-100 Million
Number Employees: 100-249
Parent Co: Coca-Cola Bottling Company
Type of Packaging: Consumer

2817 **Coca-Cola Bottling Company**
91-233 Kalaeloa Blvd
Kapolei, HI 96707-1817 808-682-5778
Fax: 808-682-4123 800-682-5778
www.cokecce.com
Processor of syrups for soft drinks.
President/COO North America Operations: J Alexander Douglas Jr
SVP/Corporate Chief Information Officer: Jean Michel Ares
SVP/Corporate External Affairs Director: Ingrid Saunders Jones
General Manager: Jim Hood
Estimated Sales: $5-10 Million
Number Employees: 10,000+
Parent Co: Coca-Cola Bottling Company
Type of Packaging: Consumer, Food Service, Bulk

2818 **Coca-Cola Bottling Company**
1 Coca-Cola Plaza
Atlanta, GA 30313-2499
Canada 404-676-2121
800-438-2653
www.cokecce.com
Processor of soft drinks.
Chairman/CeO: Muhtar Kent Jr
Evp/Cfo: Gary Fayard
Number Employees: 275
Parent Co: Coca-Cola Bottling Company
Type of Packaging: Consumer, Food Service

2819 Coca-Cola Bottling Company
4100 Coca Cola Plz Ste 100
Charlotte, NC 28211 704-557-4400
Fax: 704-551-4646 800-777-2653
www.cokebottling.com
Processor of soft drinks
Chairman/CEO: J Frank Harrison III
President/COO: William Elmore
SVP/CFO: Steven Westphal
CEO: J Frank Harrison Iii
SVP/Chief Marketing Officer: Melvin Landis III
SVP/Sales: C Ray Mayhall Jr
SVP/Chief Information Officer: Jolanta Zwirek
SVP/Human Resources: Kevin Henry
Estimated Sales: $1.4 Billion
Number Employees: 6000
Parent Co: Coca-Cola Bottling Company
Type of Packaging: Consumer, Food Service
Brands:
Coca-Cola

2820 Coca-Cola Bottling Company
9000 Marshall Dr
Lenexa, KS 66215 913-492-8100
Fax: 913-599-9364 ccemail@na.cokecce.com
www.cokecce.com
Processor of regular and diet soft drinks.
Manager: Kevin Shea Jr
SVP/Corporate Chief Information Officer: Jean Michel Ares
SVP/Corporate External Affairs Director: Ingrid Saunders Jones
Plant Manager: Karen Marshall
Estimated Sales: $100+ Million
Number Employees: 100-249
Parent Co: Coca-Cola Enterprises
Type of Packaging: Consumer, Food Service
Brands:
Coca-Cola

2821 Coca-Cola Bottling Company
11001 Gateway Blvd W
El Paso, TX 79935 915-593-2657
Fax: 915-594-6977 800-288-3228
ccemail@na.cokecce.com www.cokecce.com
Processor of soft drinks.
Chairman/Interim CEO: Lowry F Kline
Branch Manager: John Chavarria
Telecommunications: Fred Calderon
Branch Manager: Lui Rivera
Operations Manager: Dave Kurzweg
Estimated Sales: $100-500 Million
Number Employees: 250-499
Parent Co: Coca-Cola Enterprises
Type of Packaging: Food Service
Brands:
Coca-Cola

2822 Coca-Cola Bottling Company
1400 Rainer Rd
West Memphis, AR 72301 870-732-1460
Fax: 870-732-3018 www.cokecce.com
Canner of soft drinks
Manager: Larry Colbert Jr
SVP/Corporate Chief Information Officer: Jean Michel Ares
Estimated Sales: $20-50 Million
Number Employees: 50-99
Parent Co: Coca-Cola Bottling Company
Type of Packaging: Consumer
Brands:
Coke

2823 (HQ)Coca-Cola Enterprises
2500 Win Rdg Pkwy SE Ste 700
Atlanta, GA 30339
US 770-989-3000
Fax: 770-989-3788 800-233-7210
www.cokecce.com/
Manufacturer, marketer and distributor of a full range of beverage categories, including sodas, energy drinks, still and sparkling waters, juices, sports drinks, milk-based products, fruit drinks, coffee-based beverages and teas.
President: Donna James
Chairman & CEO: John Brock
EVP/CFO: William Douglas III
Svp: Calvin Draden
Marketing Officer: Katie Bayne
SVP Human Resources: Pamela Kimmet
Estimated Sales: $7.4 Billion
Number Employees: 11,000
Type of Packaging: Consumer, Food Service, Bulk
Brands:
5-ALIVE
ANDINA
APPOLLINARIS
AQUANA
AQUARIUS
BACARDI MIXERS
BARQ'S
BEAT
BISTRONE
BODY STYLE WATER
BONAQUA
BRIGHT & EARLY
BURN
BUZZ
CAMPBELL'S V8
CANADA DRY
CANNING'S
CARIBOU COFFEE
CHAUDFONTAINE
CHERRY COKE
COCA-COLA
CRUSH
DASANI
DELAWARE PUNCH
DIET COKE
DR PEPPER
EARTH & SKY
ENVIGA
EVIAN
FANTA
FAR COAST
FRESCA
FRUITOPIA
FULL THROTTLE
FUZE
GALCEAU FRUIT WATER
GODIVA BELGIAN BLENDS
GOLD PEAK
HI-C
KINLEY
LIFT
MELLO YELLO
MINUTE MAID JUICES
MONSTER
MR PIBB
NESTEA
NORTHERN NECK
NOS
ODWALLA
POWERade
RED FLASH
REHAB
SEAGRAM'S
SIMPLY JUICES
SMARTWATER
SPRITE
SUPER CAFFEINATED CANNED COFFEE
SUPER CAFFEINATED COFFEE
THE WELLNESS FROM COCA-COLA
VITAMINWATER

2824 Coca-Cola North America
2455 Watkins Rd
Columbus, OH 43207 614-492-6414
Fax: 614-491-0342 www.coca-cola.com
Processor of beverage syrups.
Manager: Willie Peet Jr
SVP/Chief Corporate Information Officer: Navel Idell
CFO: Gary Fayard
Vice President: Lisa Lowe
SVP/Corporate External Affairs Director: Ingrid Saunders Jones
General Manager: Terry McGann
Purchasing Agent: Sherry Smailes
Estimated Sales: $100-500 Million
Number Employees: 100-249
Parent Co: Coca-Cola Enterprises
Type of Packaging: Consumer, Bulk
Brands:
Coca-Cola
Sugar Free Full Throttle

2825 Cocina de Mino
P.O.Box 851280
Yukon, OK 73085 405-632-1036
Fax: 405-632-1394 www.cocinademino.com
Ethnic foods
Owner: Tim Wagner
Marketing Manager: Emeleo Perez
Estimated Sales: $ 1 - 3 Million
Number Employees: 20-49
Brands:
Cocina de Mino

2826 Coco Lopez
3401 SW 160th Ave Ste 350
Miramar, FL 33027 954-450-3100
Fax: 954-450-3111 800-341-2242
customerservice@cocolopez.com
www.cocolopez.com
Canned fruits and vegetables, preserves, jams and jellie. Also manufacturer of cream of coconut, coconut milk, and coconut juice.
President: Leonardo Vargas
VP: Gisela Sanchez
Estimated Sales: $1,888,884
Number Employees: 10-19
Brands:
Coco Lopez

2827 Coco Rico
3907 St. Laurent Boulevard
Montreal, QC H2W 1X9
Canada 514-849-5554
Fax: 514-849-6677
Processor, importer and exporter of coconut extract
President: Carlos M Fuertes
Plant Manager: Roberto Villafana

2828 Cocolalla Winery
463254 Highway 95 N
Cocolalla, ID 83813 208-263-3774
Fax: 208-263-7605 cocolalla@idahowine.com
Wines
President/Owner: Mike Wagoner
VP: Vivian Merkeley
Estimated Sales: $1-4.9 Million
Number Employees: 1-4
Brands:
Cocolalla

2829 (HQ)Cocoline Chocolate Company
689 Myrtle Ave
Brooklyn, NY 11205-3984 718-522-4500
Fax: 718-522-4500 cocolichoc@aol.com
Processor and exporter of chocolate products including bars, boxed, bagged, jimmies, chips and coatings; also, cocoa powder, carob candy, etc.; importer of cocoa beans

Estimated Sales: $2.5-5 Million
Number Employees: 10-19
Sq. footage: 100000
Type of Packaging: Consumer, Food Service, Private Label, Bulk
Brands:
America's Best
Coveretts
Greeting Bars
Topping King

2830 Cocomira Confections
321 Evans Avenue
Toronto, ON M8Z 1K2
Canada 416-253-4867
Fax: 416-946-1749 866-413-9049
info@cocomira.com www.cocomira.com
Chocolates, hazelnut crunch, dark chocolate crunch, espresso crunch and maple crunch.
President/Owner: Anna Janes

2831 Codino's Italian Foods
704 Corporation Park Ste 5
Scotia, NY 12302 518-372-3308
Fax: 518-372-2787 800-246-8908
teresa@codinos.com www.codinos.com
Processor of frozen pasta including lasagna, manicotti, stuffed shells and rigatoni, ravioli, gnocchi and cavatelli
Owner: Leno Codino
Marketing Director: Scott DeVantier
Estimated Sales: $5-10 Million
Number Employees: 35
Type of Packaging: Consumer, Food Service, Private Label, Bulk
Brands:
Codino's

2832 (HQ)Coffee & Tea
2000 NE Court
Bloomington, MN 55425 952-854-2883
Fax: 952-853-0590

Coffee and tea
President: Lee Cone
Vice President: Jim Cone
Estimated Sales: Less than $500,000
Number Employees: 5-9
Type of Packaging: Private Label

2833 **(HQ)Coffee Associates**
178 River Rd
Edgewater, NJ 7020 201-945-1060
Fax: 201-945-4887 www.themis.com
Coffee
President/CEO: William Callas
Treasurer: Constantine Callas
Estimated Sales: $1.4 Million
Number Employees: 8

2834 **Coffee Barrel**
2446 Jolly Rd
Okemos, MI 48864-3514 517-349-3888
Fax: 517-349-3036 www.thecoffeebarrel.com
Coffee
President: William DeGrow
Manager: Mary Vegrow
CEO: Tim Brenner
Estimated Sales: $2.5-5 Million
Number Employees: 5-9
Type of Packaging: Private Label
Brands:
Bis Train
David Rio
Ghiradelli Syrup
Guidparg Chocolates
Stirling Syrup

2835 **Coffee Bean**
1630 W Evans Ave
Englewood, CO 80110-1098 303-922-1238
Fax: 303-937-6336
Coffee
Owner: Carlo Rondn
Estimated Sales: Under $500,000
Number Employees: 1-4
Brands:
Country Spice Tea
Panache Cocoa and Blender Mix
Panache Gourmet Coffee
Xanadu Exotic Tea

2836 **Coffee Bean & Tea Leaf**
1945 S La Cienega Blvd
Los Angeles, CA 90034 310-237-2326
800-832-5323
info@coffeebean.com www.coffeebean.com
Coffee, tea and blended drinks
Manager: Amber Rivero
CEO: Sunny Sassoon
VP of Finance: Kenneth A DiLillo
VP of Real Estate and Construction: Paul Goldman
Production Manager and Tea Buyer: David DeCandida
General Counsel/Sr. Director: Terry Phillip Mansky
Sr. Director, Marketing/Strategic All.: Tami Clark

Sr. Director of Store Operationa: Jay McDonald
Sr. Director/Green Coffee Mft/Distrib.: John 'Jay' Anthony Isais
Estimated Sales: $300,000-500,000
Number Employees: 10-19

2837 **Coffee Bean International**
9120 NE Alderwood Rd
Portland, OR 97220-1366 503-227-4490
Fax: 503-225-9604 800-877-0474
products@coffeebeanintl.com
www.coffeebeanintl.com
Processor of roasted coffee, teas, cocoa, syrups and confectionery products; manufacturer of coffee equipment; importer of coffee beans and teas
President: Patrick Critecer
CFO: Kevin Burton
Vice President: Karen Hunt
Marketing Director: Kusa Wakjer
Estimated Sales: $10-20 Million
Number Employees: 50-99
Sq. footage: 125000
Type of Packaging: Consumer, Food Service, Private Label, Bulk
Brands:
BLUE PARROT AUSSIE-STYLE TEA
CAFE TIERRA
COUNTRY SPICE TEA
PANACHE

2838 **Coffee Bean of Leesburg**
110 S King St # A
Leesburg, VA 20175-3009 703-777-9556
Fax: 703-777-4515 800-232-6872
dion@mindspring.com www.beanusa.com
Coffee
Manager: Juanita Frye
Estimated Sales: $250,000
Number Employees: 5-9

2839 **Coffee Beanery**
3429 Pierson Pl
Flushing, MI 48433 810-733-1020
Fax: 810-733-1536 800-728-2326
kevins@beanerysupport.com
www.coffeebeanery.com
Coffee
President: Joann Shaw
CFO: Kenneth Coxen
VP Development: Kevin Shaw
Marketing Director: Dee Kasmier
Purchasing Manager: Audrey Brown
Estimated Sales: $20 Million
Number Employees: 100
Type of Packaging: Private Label
Brands:
Coffee Beanery Franchise

2840 **Coffee Brothers**
1204 Via Roma
Colton, CA 92324 909-370-1100
Fax: 909-370-1101 888-443-5282
ilcaffe@aol.com www.coffeebrothers.com
Processor of coffee and espresso; importer and wholesaler/distributor of espresso machines
Owner: Cal Amodemo
General Manager: Max Amodeo
Estimated Sales: $2.5-5 Million
Number Employees: 1-4
Sq. footage: 11000
Type of Packaging: Private Label, Bulk
Brands:
Coffee Brothers
Il Caffe
Sigma

2841 **Coffee Butler Service**
3660 Wheeler Avenue
Alexandria, VA 22304-6403 703-823-0028
Fax: 703-823-6943
Coffee
President: H Steve Swink, Ph.D.
COO: Mike Kelsey

2842 **Coffee Concepts**
10836 Grissom Lane
Suite 110
Dallas, TX 75229-3544 214-363-9331
Fax: 972-241-1619 espresso@ont.com
www.coffeeconcepts.com
Roaster of arabica coffees, flavor syrups, granita machines and mixes, espresso bar supplies, consulting, employee training, private labeling and unique customized signature blends
Estimated Sales: $ 1 - 5 Million
Number Employees: 20-49

2843 **Coffee Creations**
PO Box 10765
Portland, OR 97296-0765 503-224-9798
Fax: 503-224-9796 800-245-5856
Manufacturer of coffee products including carbonated coffee sodas and Latte mixes
Estimated Sales: $5-10 Million
Number Employees: 5-9

2844 **Coffee Culture-A House**
1311 O Street
Lincoln, NE 68508-1512 402-438-8456
Fax: 402-474-3535
Coffee
General Manager: Terrance Alan Reis
Operations Manager: Gregory Looney
Estimated Sales: Less than $500,000
Number Employees: 1-4

2845 **Coffee Enterprises**
286 College St
Burlington, VT 05401 802-865-4480
Fax: 802-865-3364 800-375-3398
info@coffee-ent.com www.coffee-ent.com
Processor of coffee extracts and chilled coffee-based beverage concentrates; laboratory specializing in the testing and analyzing services for coffee; consultant specializing in the marketing and promotion of coffee
Owner/President: Dan Cox
Director Coffee Operations: Paul Songer
Estimated Sales: $ 1 - 3 Million
Number Employees: 10-19
Sq. footage: 3500
Type of Packaging: Bulk

2846 **Coffee Exchange**
207 Wickenden St
Providence, RI 2903 401-273-1198
Fax: 401-273-4440 800-263-3339
coffeex@ids.net www.coffeexchange.com
Processor and importer of regular and decaffeinated whole bean organic coffee; gift baskets available
President: Charles Fishbein
CEO: Susan Wood
Estimated Sales: $1-2.5 Million
Number Employees: 20-49
Brands:
Coffee Exchange
Mel's
Roasting Coffee Daily

2847 **Coffee Express Company**
47722 Clipper St
Plymouth, MI 48170-2437 734-459-4900
Fax: 734-459-5511 800-466-9000
info@coffeeexpressco.com
www.coffeeexpressco.com
Wholesaler roaster of specialty coffees; distributors of associated products.
President: Tom Isaia
Production: Scott Novak
Number Employees: 10-19
Number of Brands: 8
Number of Products: 20
Sq. footage: 8000
Type of Packaging: Consumer, Food Service, Private Label, Bulk
Brands:
Coffee Express
Mountain Country

2848 **Coffee Grounds**
1579 Hamline Ave N
St Paul, MN 55108-2107 651-644-9959
Fax: 651-776-1143
dave.coffeegrounds@comcast.net
http://www.thecoffeegrounds.net/
Coffee flavorings
Owner: David Lawrence
Estimated Sales: $420,000
Number Employees: 5-9

2849 **Coffee Holding Company**
3475 Victory Blvd07
Staten Island, NY 10314 718-832-0800
Fax: 718-832-0892 800-458-2233
sales@coffeeholding.com
www.coffeeholding.com
Roaster, vemdor and packer of regular and green coffee; also, packer of instant coffees
President: Andrew Gordon
CFO: David Gordon
Quality Control: S Gordon
Marketing, Specialty Coffee: Karen Gordon
Food Service Sales: Dominic Caruso
Plant Manager: D Rodriguez
Estimated Sales: $25 Million
Number Employees: 50-99
Number of Brands: 6
Sq. footage: 22000
Type of Packaging: Consumer, Food Service, Private Label, Bulk
Brands:
5th Avenue
Cafe Caribe
Cafe Supremo
Don Manuel 100% Colombian
S&W
Via Roma

2850 **Coffee Masters**
P.O.Box 460
Spring Grove, IL 60081 312-527-4980
Fax: 815-675-3166 800-334-6485
cmaster@coffeemasters.com
www.coffeemasters.com

Gourmet coffee, tea and cocoa
Owner: Mike Ebert
President: Mike Ebert
Marketing Director: Betsy Summers
Sales Director: Alan Denek
Operations Manager: Tony Nowak
Number Employees: 50-99
Sq. footage: 46500
Type of Packaging: Consumer, Food Service, Private Label, Bulk
Brands:
ASHBY'S ICED TEAS
ASHBY'S TEAS OF LONDON
BELLA CREMA
BREW-A-CUP: PERFECT POTFULS
COCOA AMORE
COFFEE MASTERS

2851 **Coffee Mill Roastery**
108 Branchwood Drive
Elon, NC 27244-9384 919-929-1727
Fax: 919-929-5899 800-729-1727
coffeemill@bellsouth.net
Coffee and tea
Owner: Jan Lawrence
Estimated Sales: $1-2.5 Million
Number Employees: 10-19
Type of Packaging: Private Label

2852 **Coffee Mill Roasting Company**
598 Falconbridge Road
Sudbury, ON P3A 5K6
Canada 705-525-2700
Fax: 705-525-2790
Processor and packer of coffee
President: Geoff Hong
Number Employees: 1-4
Type of Packaging: Food Service
Brands:
The Coffee Mill

2853 **Coffee Millers & Roasting**
926 SE 9th Ln # B
Cape Coral, FL 33990-3121 239-573-6800
Fax: 239-573-3693 ed@coffeemillers.com
www.coffeemillers.com
Domestic and European coffees and blends. Over 150 varieties
President: Marcell Miller
Estimated Sales: $1-2.5 Million
Number Employees: 1-4

2854 **Coffee People**
4130 SW 117th Ave Ste P
Beaverton, OR 97005 503-643-3053
Fax: 503-672-9013 800-354-5282
customerservice@coffeepeople.com
www.coffeepeople.com
Specialty coffees and teas
Customer Service: Patti Graves
Estimated Sales: $ .5 - 1 million
Parent Co: Diedrich Coffee

2855 **Coffee Process Technology**
6005 N Shepherd Dr # G1
Houston, TX 77091-4253 713-695-7530
Fax: 713-695-7530 www.emperorcoffee.com
Coffee
Owner: Carlos De Aldecoa
CFO: Larissa De Aldeco
Vice President: Maria Carmen De Aldecoa
Estimated Sales: $1-2.5 Million
Number Employees: 10-19
Type of Packaging: Private Label
Brands:
Uvvw Decaff

2856 **Coffee Reserve**
2030 W Quail Ave
Phoenix, AZ 85027 623-434-0939
Fax: 623-434-0946 java@coffeereserve.com
www.coffeereserve.com
Coffee roasting
President/CEO: Richard Grayson Jr
Production Manager: Jeff Jackson
Estimated Sales: $5-10 Million
Number Employees: 10-19
Type of Packaging: Bulk

2857 **Coffee Roasters**
29 Edison Ave Ofc 2a
Oakland, NJ 7436 201-337-8221
Fax: 201-337-0622 www.coffeeroastersinc.com
Coffees
President: Lance Wetzel
Estimated Sales: $1,300,000
Number Employees: 10-19

2858 **Coffee Roasters of New Orleans**
712 Orleans Avenue
New Orleans, LA 70116-3111 504-827-0878
Fax: 800-743-5711 800-737-5464
nolajava@iomenca.net www.orleanscoffee.com
Coffee
President: Bill Fiamers
Director Sales/Marketing: Kathleen Siemers
General Manager: William Siemers
Production Supervisor: Robert Arceneaux
Estimated Sales: $5-9.9 Million
Number Employees: 5-9

2859 **Coffee Up**
2201 S Halsted Street
Chicago, IL 60608-4585 847-288-9330
Fax: 847-288-9334
Coffee
President: Chris Chacko
Estimated Sales: Under $500,000
Number Employees: 1-4

2860 **Coffee Works**
3418 Folsom Blvd
Sacramento, CA 95816
Fax: 916-452-9134 800-275-3335
js@coffeeworks.com www.coffeeworks.com
Coffee
President: John Shahabian
Sales: Greg Ward
Estimated Sales: $1-2.5 Million
Number Employees: 20-49
Brands:
Balthazar's Blend
Dark Star
Jump Start
Sweetfire

2861 **Cognis**
4900 Este Ave
Cincinnati, OH 45232 513-641-4355
Fax: 513-482-5503 www.cognis.com
Suppliers of bulk nutritional raw materials for the food industry
Manager: Paul Allen
CEO: Antonio Trius
CFO: Klaus Edelmann
Vice President: Paul Allen
Managing Director: Paul Allen
Estimated Sales: $1-2.5 Million
Number Employees: 500-999

2862 **Cohen's Bakery**
1132 Broadway St
Buffalo, NY 14212-1502 716-892-8149
Fax: 716-892-8150
Manufacturer of fresh bread, rolls and pastries; also, frozen raw bread, pizza and roll dough
President: John J Blando
Estimated Sales: $20-50 Million
Number Employees: 20-49
Sq. footage: 25000
Brands:
Al Cohen's

2863 **Cohen's Original Tasty Coddie**
6639 Chippewa Dr
Baltimore, MD 21209-1542 410-539-0111
Snack foods including potato chips.
President: Esther Cohen
Estimated Sales: Under $500,000
Number Employees: 1-4

2864 **Colavita**
1 Runyons Lane
Edison, NJ 08817 732-404-8300
Fax: 732-287-9401 usa@colavita.com
www.colavita.com
Processor, importer and wholesaler/distributor of olive and blended oils, pasta and grains.
President/CEO: John Profaci
CFO: John Profaci Jr
VP Sales/Marketing: John Manginelli
Marketing: Giovanni Colavita
Estimated Sales: $50-100 Million
Number Employees: 50-99
Brands:
COLAVITA 25-STAR GRAN RISERVA VIN.
COLAVITA BALSAMIC VINEGAR
COLAVITA CLASSIC HOT SAUCE
COLAVITA EXTRA VIRGIN OLIVE OIL
COLAVITA FAT FREE CLASSIC HOT SAUCE
COLAVITA FAT FREE GARDEN STYLE SAU.
COLAVITA FAT FREE MARINARA SAUCE
COLAVITA FAT FREE MUSHROOM SAUCE
COLAVITA GARDEN STYLE SAUCE
COLAVITA HEALTHY SAUCE
COLAVITA MARINARA SAUCE
COLAVITA MARINATED VEGETABLES
COLAVITA MUSHROOM SAUCE
COLAVITA PASTA
COLAVITA PASTA PLUS
COLAVITA PUTTANESCA SAUCE
COLAVITA RED CLAM SAUCE
COLAVITA WHITE CLAM SAUCE

2865 **Colchester Bakery**
96 Lebanon Ave
Colchester, CT 06415 860-537-2415
Fax: 860-537-4742 info@colchesterbakery.com
www.colchesterbakery.com
Manufacturer of baked breads
Owner: Ursula Paredes
Estimated Sales: $1-2.5 Million
Number Employees: 20-49
Type of Packaging: Consumer

2866 **Colchester Foods**
17 Schwartz Rd
Bozrah, CT 06334 860-886-2445
Fax: 860-886-1138 800-243-0469
Processor and exporter of brown and white eggs
VP: Kevin O'Brien
Number Employees: 50-99
Parent Co: Kofkoff Egg Farm
Type of Packaging: Consumer, Food Service, Private Label
Brands:
New England Farms Eggs

2867 **Cold Fusion Foods**
8787 Shoreham Drive
Apt 308
West Hollywood, CA 90069-2227 310-287-3244
Fax: 310-287-3242 react@colfusionfoods.com
www.coldfusionfoods.com
Processor of protein enriched frozen juice bars
President: Collin Madden

2868 **Cold Hollow Cider Mill**
P.O.Box 420
Waterbury Center, VT 05677-8020 802-244-8771
Fax: 802-244-7212 800-327-7537
info@coldhollow.com www.coldhollow.com
Processor of apple products including cider, cider jelly, butters, syrup, sauce, preserves and juices; exporter of cider jelly; wholesaler/distributor of health and specialty foods, general merchandise, private label items andproduce
President: Paul Brown
Vice President: Gayle Brown
Estimated Sales: $ 5 - 10 Million
Number Employees: 20-49
Sq. footage: 10000
Type of Packaging: Consumer, Food Service, Bulk
Brands:
Cold Hollow Cider Mill

2869 **Cold Spring Bakery**
308 Main St
Cold Spring, MN 56320 320-685-8681
Fax: 320-685-3634 www.coldspringbakery.com
Bakery goods
President: Dale Schurman
Vice President: Brian Schurman
Estimated Sales: $2.2 Million
Number Employees: 60

2870 **Cold Spring Brewing Company**
219 Red River Ave N
Cold Spring, MN 56320 320-685-8686
Fax: 320-685-8318 info@coldspringbrewery.com
www.coldspringbrewery.com
Processor and exporter of beer and soda - 8oz & 16oz energy drinks
Owner: John Lenore
President: Maurice Bryan
Sr VP Marketing: Dave Pergl
Sr VP Sales: Dave Pergl
Head Brewmaster: Mike Kneip
Estimated Sales: $50-99.9 Million
Number Employees: 250-499
Type of Packaging: Private Label

Brands:
Doppelbock
Dunkel
Gluek Golden Light
Gluek Golden Pilsner
Gluek Honey Bock
Hefe Weiss
Marzen
Stite

2871 **Coldwater Fish Farms**
PO Box 1
Lisco, NE 69148-0001 308-772-3474
Fax: 308-772-3845 800-658-4450
cwsalmon@btigate.com
www.wheatbelt.com/cwfish_farm.htm
Fish
President: Walter Queen
Sales Director: Molly Vogler
Production Manager: Lloyd Harding
Estimated Sales: $5-10 Million
Number Employees: 20-49
Type of Packaging: Private Label

2872 **Cole's Quality Foods**
25 Ottawa SW
4th Floor
Grand Rapids, MI 49503 616-975-0081
Fax: 616-975-0267 info@coles.com
www.coles.com
Processor of fresh and frozen garlic bread.
President/CEO: John Sammavilla
Chairman: W Scott Devon
Quality Control: Robert Lewandoski
SVP Sales: Ray Peuller
Human Resources Director: Karen Frazier
COO: Cynthia Harvard
SVP Production: Jeffrey Lewandoski
Plant Manager: Monty Annis
Estimated Sales: $20-50 Million
Number Employees: 100-249
Type of Packaging: Consumer, Food Service
Brands:
Home Style

2873 **Coleman Dairy**
6901 Interstate 30
Little Rock, AR 72209 501-568-6237
Fax: 501-568-9581 www.colemandairy.com
Processor of milk
President: W Coleman
Principal: Steve Turner
Vice President: Don Hunt
Estimated Sales: $20-50 Million
Number Employees: 100-249
Parent Co: Turner Holdings
Type of Packaging: Consumer, Food Service

2874 **(HQ)Coleman Purely Natural Brands**
1667 Cole Blvd
Building 19 Suite 300
Golden, CO 80401 303-273-9444
Fax: 303-297-0426 800-442-8666
info@colemannatural.com
www.colemannatural.com
Processor and exporter of natural and organic beef and lamb.
President: Mel Coleman Sr
Ceo: Mark McKay Jr
VP: Chuck Fletcher
Media: Ken Trantowski
Media: Robyn Nick
Plant Manager: Phil Wieke
Purchasing Manager: Ann DuPilka
Estimated Sales: $1 million
Number Employees: 2,300
Sq. footage: 25000
Type of Packaging: Food Service
Brands:
Coleman Natural Angus
Coleman Natural Beef

2875 **Colgin Companies**
2230 Valdina St
Dallas, TX 75207 214-951-8687
Fax: 214-951-8668 888-226-5446
www.colgin.com
Processor of barbecue sauces including mesquite, apple and hickory liquid smoke
President: Elizabeth Thornhill
CEO: Kerry Thornhill
Estimated Sales: $2.5-5 Million
Number Employees: 5-9
Type of Packaging: Consumer, Bulk
Brands:
Chigarid
Colgin

2876 **Colibri Pepper CompanyLLC**
21 Burrough Cemetery Rd
Elmer, LA 71424 316-730-6528
millereric@bellsouth.net
www.colibrihotsauce.com
Pepper sauce
President: Eric Miller
Estimated Sales: $25,000
Number Employees: 2
Number of Brands: 1
Number of Products: 1
Sq. footage: 700
Type of Packaging: Consumer

2877 **Colin Ingram**
P.O.Box 146
Comptche, CA 95427-0146 707-937-1824
Fax: 707-937-5834
Manufacturer, importer and exporter of essential oils
President: John Weir
Estimated Sales: $2.5-5 Million
Number Employees: 1-4
Type of Packaging: Consumer, Food Service, Private Label, Bulk

2878 **Collbran Locker Plant**
P.O.Box 122
Collbran, CO 81624 970-487-3329
Processor of meat products including beef, deer and elk
Owner: Frank Jones
Estimated Sales: Less than $500,000
Number Employees: 1-4

2879 **College Coffee Roasters**
115 N Donerville Rd Ste I
Mountville, PA 17554 717-285-9561
Fax: 717-872-8554
www.collegecoffeeroasters.com
Coffee
President/Owner: Susan Lithgoe
VP: George Kerekgyarto
Estimated Sales: Less than $500,000
Number Employees: 1-4

2880 **College Hill Poultry**
P.O.Box 10
Fredericksburg, PA 17026-0010 717-865-2136
Fax: 717-865-0302 800-533-3361
info@raisedright.com www.raisedright.com
Manufacturer of fresh organic chicken. The Hain Celestial Group acquired the poultry processing facility assets of College Hill Poultry
VP Sales: Mike Yourison
Plant Manager: Lee Lebbon
Estimated Sales: $25-49.9 Million
Number Employees: 5-9
Parent Co: Hain Celestial Group, Inc.
Type of Packaging: Food Service
Brands:
RAISED RIGHT

2881 **Collier's Fisheries**
102 Bayou Road
Des Allemands, LA 70030-4433 985-758-7481
Fax: 985-454-8669
Seafood
President: Glay Collier

2882 **Collin Street Bakery**
P.O.Box 79
Corsicana, TX 75151-0079 903-872-8111
Fax: 903-872-6879 800-504-1896
cbsinfo@collinstreet.com
www.collinstreetbakery.com
Processor and exporter of fruit cakes.
President: Bob McNutt
CFO: Scott Holloman
VP Marketing: John Crawford
Operations: Jerry Grimmett
Plant Manager: John Watson
Purchasing: Marcia Lougo
Estimated Sales: $20-50 Million
Number Employees: 50-99
Sq. footage: 125000
Brands:
APPLE CINNAMON PECAN CAKE
APRICOT PECAN CAKE
BRITTLE DUET
CHEESECAKE SLICER
CINCHONA COFFEE
DEEP DISH PECAN PIKE
DELUXE FRUITCAKE
DOUBLE DEEP FUDGE PECAN PIE
GOLDEN RUM CAKE
KEY LIME CHEESECAKE
LEMON POPPY SEED CAKE
NEW YORK STYLE CHEESECAKE
ORANGE PARADISE CAKE
PECAN COFFEE CAKE
PECAN DUET
PECAN HALVES & PIECES
PINEAPPLE PECAN CAKE
PRALINE PECAN CHEESECAKE
TRIO OF CHEESECAKE
TRIPLE CHOCOLATE CAKE

2883 **Collins Caviar Company**
113 York St
Michigan City, IN 46360 219-809-8100
Fax: 219-809-8105 cavco@collinscaviar.com
www.collinscaviar.com
American freshwater caviar, caviar creme spreads and custom compound butters
President/Owner: Carolyn Collins
CEO: Carolyn Collins
VP: Rachel Collins
Estimated Sales: $500,000-$1 Million
Number Employees: 1-4
Type of Packaging: Private Label

2884 **Coloma Frozen Foods**
4145 Coloma Rd
Coloma, MI 49038 269-849-0500
Fax: 269-849-0415 800-642-2723
info@colomafrozen.com
www.colomafrozen.com
Frozen fruits, vegetables, juices and juice concentrates.
President: Brad Wendzel
COO/CFO: Terry Harris
Quality Assurance Manager: Jennifer Brighton
Sales Manager: Brad Wendzel
Plant Production Manager: Kevin Metz
Plant Manager: Larry Endfield
Purchasing Manager: George Cuthbert
Estimated Sales: $20-50 Million
Number Employees: 170
Sq. footage: 52000
Type of Packaging: Food Service, Bulk
Brands:
Coloma

2885 **Colombo Bakery**
1329 Fee Dr
Sacramento, CA 95815-3911 916-648-1011
Fax: 916-649-2534
Processor of bread, buns and rolls
Plant Manager: Paul Gonzalez
Estimated Sales: $300,000-500,000
Number Employees: 5-9
Parent Co: Metz Group
Type of Packaging: Consumer, Food Service, Private Label, Bulk

2886 **Colonial Coffee Roasters**
3250 NW 60th St
Miami, FL 33142 305-634-1843
Fax: 305-634-2538 info@colonialcoffee.com
www.colonial-coffee.com
Coffee roaster
Owner/President: Rafael Acevedo
Vice President: Melvin Weinkle
Operations Manager: Al Reyes
Estimated Sales: $6 Million
Number Employees: 13
Number of Brands: 3
Sq. footage: 30000
Type of Packaging: Food Service, Private Label, Bulk
Brands:
Cafe Europa
Cafe Latino
Colonial International

2887 **Colonna Brothers**
4102 Bergen Tpke
North Bergen, NJ 7047 201-864-1115
Fax: 201-864-0144
customerservice@colonnabrothers.com
www.colonnabrothers.com

Manufacturer of bread crumbs, grated cheese, sauces, olive oil & vinegar, soups, stuffing mix, roasted peppers, marinated mushrooms, pepperoncini, chopped garlic, artichoke hearts and bread sticks
President: Peter Colonna
Secretary/Treasurer: Diane Maniscalco
VP: Mark Colonna
Estimated Sales: $5.6 Million
Number Employees: 100-249
Type of Packaging: Consumer, Food Service
Brands:
COLONNA

2888 Colony Foods
439 Haverhill St
Lawrence, MA 01841 978-682-9677
Fax: 978-687-8448 www.colonyfoods.net
Frozen, fresh and special order food items.
President: Dereck Barbagallo
Estimated Sales: $ 10 - 20 Million
Number Employees: 20-49

2889 (HQ)Colorado Baking Company
3333 WARRENVILLE RD., SUITE 200
Lisle, IL 60532-1579 630-799-8195
Fax: 630-799-8101
Bakery products
Chairman/CEO: Steve Beaman
Estimated Sales: $2.6 Million
Number Employees: 4
Type of Packaging: Private Label, Bulk

2890 Colorado Bean Company/Greeley Trading
14574 County Road 64
Greeley, CO 80631-9317 970-356-1032
Fax: 970-351-6003 888-595-2326
wayne@coloradobeancompany.com
www.coloradobeancompany.com
Processor of dried and refried beans
Owner: Andrew Orris
Estimated Sales: 10,500,000
Number Employees: 100-249
Type of Packaging: Consumer, Food Service, Bulk

2891 (HQ)Colorado Boxed Beef Company
302 Progress Rd
Auburndale, FL 33823 863-967-0636
Fax: 863-965-2222 j.rattigan@cbbcorp.com
www.coloradoboxedbeef.com
Processor, exporter and wholesaler/distributor of fresh and frozen beef, veal, pork, lamb and poultry; also, portion control available; importer of lamb; transportation service and warehouse providing storage for meat products
President and CEO: John Rattigan
Senior VP: Bryan Saterbo
COO: John Rattigan Jr.
Number Employees: 500-999
Type of Packaging: Consumer, Food Service, Private Label, Bulk
Other Locations:
Colorado Boxed Beef Co.
North Miami Beach FL
Brands:
CASTRICUM BROTHERS
CEDAR CREEK
COLORADO GOLD
COLORADO SUPREME
DUTCH VALLEY VEAL
EXCEL
GREAT FISH COMPANY
GWALTNEY
IBP
NATIONAL BEEF
PACKERLAND PACKING
PROVIMI VEAL
SMITHFIELD PORK

2892 Colorado Cellars Winery
3553 E Rd
Palisade, CO 81526-9588 970-464-7921
Fax: 970-464-0574 www.coloradocellars.com
Wines
President: Richard Turley
Treasurer: Padte Turley
Estimated Sales: $1-2.5 Million
Number Employees: 1-4

2893 Colorado Cereal
4129 Shoreline Dr
Fort Collins, CO 80526-4818 970-282-9733
Fax: 970-223-4302 rmpop@webaccess.net
www.coloradocereal.com
Processor and distributor of breakfast cereals in boxes and bags
President: Bernie Blach
Secretary: Cindy Blach
Estimated Sales: Less than $150,000
Number Employees: 1-4
Sq. footage: 20000
Type of Packaging: Consumer, Food Service, Private Label, Bulk
Brands:
Colorado's Kernels
Las Palomas Grandes
Pop'n Snak

2894 Colorado Mountain Jams & Jellies
3573 G Rd
Palisade, CO 81526 970-464-0745
www.plumdaisy.com
fruit jams and wine jellies

2895 Colorado Popcorn Company
320 Oak St
Sterling, CO 80751 970-522-7612
Fax: 970-522-8630 800-238-2676
popcorn@coloradopopcorn.com
www.coloradopopcorn.com
Processor of gourmet popcorn
Owner: Kathleen Littler
Estimated Sales: $100,000
Number Employees: 1-4
Number of Products: 13
Type of Packaging: Consumer, Food Service

2896 Colorado Salsa Company
1228 W Littleton Blvd
Littleton, CO 80120-5800 303-932-2617
Fax: 303-297-7752
info_salsacolorado@yahoo.com
www.salsacolorado.com
Processor of salsa
Owner: David Karas
CEO: Patricia Parkos
Estimated Sales: $1-2.5 Million
Number Employees: 1-4
Sq. footage: 1500
Type of Packaging: Consumer
Brands:
Denver

2897 Colorado Spice
6350 Gunpark Dr
Boulder, CO 80301-3588 303-581-9586
Fax: 303-581-9288 800-677-7423
tzieglerne@prodigy.net
Processor of custom packed spice and herb blends; also, tea and tea blends
President: Tim Ziegler
CEO: Rod Smith
Estimated Sales: $900,000 appx.
Number Employees: 20-49
Sq. footage: 10200
Type of Packaging: Food Service, Private Label, Bulk
Brands:
Cinnamon Ridge
Shadow Mountain Foods, Inc.
The Colorado Spice Co.
The Spice Box
The Spice Co.

2898 Colorado Sweet Gold
1722 S Golden Road
Lakewood, CO 80401 303-384-1101
Fax: 303-384-1118 www.coloradosweetgold.com
Manufacturers of sweeteners and food ingredients
President: Charlie Gilbert
Executive: Tom Herrmann
Estimated Sales: $500,000-$1 Million
Number Employees: 1-4
Number of Products: 6
Type of Packaging: Private Label

2899 Colors Gourmet Pizza
6106 Avenida Encinas Ste F
Carlsbad, CA 92011 760-431-2203
Fax: 760-431-0914 martial@colorspizza.com
www.colorspizza.com
Manufacturer of gourmet pizza, handmade crusts, focaccia and panini bread
President: Martial Bricnet
Director of Sales/Distribution: James Tuckwell
Estimated Sales: $ 1 - 3 Million
Number Employees: 20
Sq. footage: 7500
Brands:
Colors Gourmet Pizza

2900 Colts Chocolates
609 Overton St
Nashville, TN 37203 615-251-0100
Fax: 615-251-0120
information@coltschocolates.com
www.coltschocolates.com
Chocolate candy and pies
President: MacKenzie Colt
Estimated Sales: $1-2.5 Million
Number Employees: 20-49
Brands:
Animal Crackers
Brownies & Roses
Butter Grahams
Chocolate Covered Marshmallows
Colts Bolts
Gooey Butter Bar, NEW!
Happy Trails T-Shirts
Marie McGhee's
Roy Rogers Happy Trails
Truffle Babies

2901 Coltsfoot/Golden Eagle Herb
P.O.Box 5205
Grants Pass, OR 97527-0205 541-476-8267
Fax: 541-476-0205 800-736-8749
gldneagle@grantspass.com
www.goldeneaglechew.com
Herbs
Owner: Robert Anderson
Owner: Joni Anderson
Estimated Sales: $ 3 - 5 Million
Number Employees: 5-9

2902 Columbia Coffee & Tea Company
4-505 Clayton Road
Weston, ON M9M 2G7
Canada 416-745-4235
Fax: 416-745-4560
Processor and importer of coffee; importer and wholesaler/distributor of gourmet syrups; wholesaler/distributor of tea, hot chocolate, drink crystals and hot beverage equipment, groceries, meats, etc.; serving the food servicemarket
President/CEO: Maria McLean
Number Employees: 10-19
Sq. footage: 12000
Type of Packaging: Food Service, Private Label
Brands:
Columbia

2903 Columbia County Fruit Processors
204 E Washington Street
Hanson, MA 02341-1137 508-763-5257
Fax: 508-763-3830 www.northeastcranberry.com
Cranberries and cranberry products
Plant Manager: Michael Kelly

2904 Columbia Empire Farms
31461 NE Bell Rd
Sherwood, OR 97140 503-538-2156
Fax: 503-537-9693
moreinfo@columbiaempirefarms.com
www.columbiaempirefarms.com
Manufacturer of hazelnuts, hazelnut candies, strawberries, red and black raspberries, Marion blackberries, honey, preserves and Oregon wines
President: Floyd Aylor
VP: Janet Pendergrass
Estimated Sales: $5-10 Million
Number Employees: 20-49
Number of Brands: 5
Number of Products: 15
Sq. footage: 50000
Type of Packaging: Consumer, Food Service, Private Label, Bulk
Brands:
AMERICA NORTHWEST
COLUMBIA EMPIRE FARMS
DOODLEBERRY
FILBERT ACRES
NORTHWEST GOURMAT
NUTWORLD

2905 **(HQ)Columbia Empire Farms**
31461 NE Bell Rd
Sherwood, OR 97140 503-538-2156
Fax: 503-538-4393
jpendergrass@columbiaempirefarms.com
www.columbiaempirefarms.com
Processor of Salted and roasted hazelnuts
Partner: Linda Strand
Finance Manager: Janet Pendergrass
Number Employees: 100
Type of Packaging: Private Label
Brands:
America's Northwest
Chateau Beniot
Columbia Empire Farms
Doodleberry
Northwest Gourmet
Nutworld

2906 **Columbia Foods**
P.O.Box 249
Snohomish, WA 98291-0249 360-568-0838
Fax: 360-568-4202
Processor and exporter of frozen vegetables
President: Jay Cedergreen
VP Sales: Ky Carlton
Estimated Sales: $1-2.5 Million
Number Employees: 5-9
Type of Packaging: Consumer, Food Service, Private Label, Bulk

2907 **Columbia Foods**
10504 State Route 28 W
Quincy, WA 98848 509-787-1585
Fax: 509-787-1735
Processor and exporter of frozen vegetables including peas, corn and carrots
President: Jay Cedergreen
Plant Manager: John Cedergreen
Estimated Sales: $20-50 Million
Number Employees: 100-249
Type of Packaging: Consumer, Food Service, Private Label

2908 **Columbia Packing Company**
2807 E 11th St
Dallas, TX 75203 214-946-8171
Fax: 214-946-2424 800-460-8171
info@columbiapacking.com
www.columbiapacking.com
Meat packers, cattle and hog slaughterers and distributors of boxed beef, boxed pork and sausage items
Pesident: Joseph Ondrusek
Estimated Sales: $20-50 Million
Number Employees: 50-99

2909 **Columbia Snacks**
P.O.Box 90424
Columbia, SC 29290-1424 803-776-0133
Fax: 803-776-0145
Snack products
Owner: Steve Mims
Estimated Sales: $1-2.5 Million
Number Employees: 10-19

2910 **Columbia Winery**
14030 NE 145th St
Woodinville, WA 98072 425-488-2776
Fax: 425-488-3460
contact@columbiawinery.com
www.columbiawinery.com
Processor and exporter of wine
CEO: Jon Moramarco
VP: Glenn Coogan
Quality Control: Bruce Watson
Marketing: Mike Jaeger
Sales: Jim Icocoloski
Public Relations: Lisa Farrell
Estimated Sales: $20-50 Million
Number Employees: 50-99
Parent Co: Canandaigua Wine Company
Type of Packaging: Consumer

2911 **Columbus Bakery**
4093 Cleveland Ave
Columbus, OH 43224-1699 614-645-2275
Fax: 614-462-2043
Processor of bread, buns, danish pastry, crackers and cookies.
QA/QC Manager: Ronald Kamer
QA/QC Manager: Danielle Swineheart
Sales Manager: Greg Mallory
Product Manager: Tim Hatem
General Manager: John Masa
Estimated Sales: $ .5 - 1 million
Number Employees: 1-4
Type of Packaging: Consumer, Private Label

2912 **Columbus Brewing Company**
525 Short St
Columbus, OH 43215 614-464-2739
Fax: 614-221-3316 www.columbusbrewingco.com
Beer
Manager: Doug Griggs
Vice President: Ben Pridgeon
Estimated Sales: $500,000-$1 Million
Number Employees: 20-49
Brands:
1859 Porter
Apricot Ale
Columbus Pale Ale
Nut Brown Ale

2913 **Columbus Foods Company**
30 E Oakton St
Des Plaines, IL 60018 773-265-6500
Fax: 773-265-6985 800-322-6457
info@columbusfoods.com
www.columbusfoods.com
Vegetable oils, and vegetable and animal shortenings.
President: Paulette Gagliardo
CFO: Rick Gerbatsch
Quality Control: Rick Cumminsford
Sales: Bob Bartilotta
Public Relations: Kathy Miller
Manufacturing Director: Joe Feely
Estimated Sales: $75-100 Million
Number Employees: 50-99
Sq. footage: 150000
Type of Packaging: Consumer, Food Service, Private Label, Bulk
Brands:
BUTCHER BOY
CODE 123
EAGLE BRAND
ENVIRO SAVER
GOLDEN BUTCHER BOY
LA SPAGNOLA
MIKE
NATURE'S SECRET
PENOLA
SORRENTO
SUN
SUNRISE 2000

2914 **Columbus Gourmet**
302 Brown Ave
Columbus, GA 31903-1253 706-687-0161
Fax: 706-682-1528 800-356-1858
www.columbusgourmet.com
Supplier of gourmet spirit cakes, pecans and cookies.
President/CEO: Brian Stone
General Manager: Stacey Chambers
Accounting: Karl McLure
Sales Manager: Brad Arnholt
COO: Jonothan Field
Sq. footage: 60000
Type of Packaging: Food Service, Private Label
Other Locations:
Atlanta GA
Cartersville GA
Jacksonville FL
Evansville IN
Columbus GA
Brands:
DODGE CITY STEAKS
KENDRICK PECAN
LA PICCOLINA

2915 **Columbus Oils**
30 East Oakton Ave
Des Plaines, IL 60018 773-265-6500
Fax: 773-265-6985 sales@columbusfoods.net
www.columbusfoods.com
Manufacturer of edible foods and oils
Vice President: John Healy
Plant Manager: Joe Freely
Number Employees: 100

2916 **Columbus Vegetable Oils**
30 E. Oakton Avenue
Des Plaines, IL 60018 773-265-6500
Fax: 773-265-6985 800-322-6457
www.columbusvegoils.com
Manufacturer and supplier of vegetable oils, liquid & solid shortenings, bakery, specialty & organic oils, and balsamic vinegar.

2917 **Comanche Tortilla Factory**
107 S Nelson St
Fort Stockton, TX 79735 432-336-3245
Processor of Mexican products including peppers, tortillas and tamales
President: Joe Ben Gallegos
Estimated Sales: $2.5-5 Million
Number Employees: 1-4
Type of Packaging: Consumer

2918 **Comanzo & Company Specialty Bakers**
10 Industrial Dr
Smithfield, RI 02917-1500 401-231-2361
Fax: 401-232-9826 888-352-5455
licette@comanzobiscotti.com
www.comanzosbiscotti.com
Biscotti, European style shortbread
President: Liz Walker
Estimated Sales: Less than $500,000
Number Employees: 1-4

2919 **Comax Flavors**
130 Baylis Rd
Melville, NY 11747-3808 63- 2-9 05
Fax: 631-249-9255 800-992-0629
info@comaxflavors.com
http://www.comaxflavors.com
Flavors
President: Peter Calabretta
CFO: Virginia Wyan
Vice President: Paul Calabretta
Research & Development: Agneta Weisz
Quality Control: Frank Vollaro
Marketing Director: Catherine Armstrong
Sales Director: Norman Katz
PR/Communications Manager: Laura Ferrante
Production Manager: Jorge Quintanilla
Plant Manager: Marion Cunningham
Purchasing Manager: Michael Keppel
Estimated Sales: $15 Million
Number Employees: 55

2920 **Comeau's Sea Foods**
60 Saulnierville Rd
Saulnierville, NS B0W 2Z0
Canada 902-769-2101
Fax: 902-769-3594 www.comeauseafoods.com
Processor and exporter of fresh, frozen and processed sea foods, herring, smoked salmon
President: Marcel Comeau
Vice President: Kim d'Entremont
VP Marketing: Sandy Clark
Number Employees: 150
Type of Packaging: Consumer, Food Service, Private Label, Bulk

2921 **Comeaux's**
2807 Kaliste Saloom Rd
Lafayette, LA 70508-7141 337-988-0516
Fax: 337-989-0091 800-323-2492
Sonja@comeaux.com www.comeaux.com
Processor of vacuum packed seafood including crawfish boudin, oysters, seafood boudin, shrimp, pork and tasso
Owner: Ray Comeaux
Co-Owner: Sonja Comeaux
Estimated Sales: $300,000-500,000
Number Employees: 5-9
Type of Packaging: Consumer, Food Service
Brands:
Comeaux's Andouille Sausage
Comeaux's Crawfish Tails
Comeaux's Tasso

2922 **Comet Rice**
P.O.Box 2587
Houston, TX 77252-2587 281-272-8800
Fax: 281-272-9707 www.amrice.com
Processor and exporter of rice, pasta and olives
President: Lee Adams
Estimated Sales: $ 20 - 50 Million
Number Employees: 50-99
Type of Packaging: Consumer, Food Service

Brands:
AA BRAND
ADOLPHUS
BLUE RIBBON
BLUE RIBBON GOLDEN
COLUSA RICE
COMET RICE
DRAGON RICE
GREEN PEACOCK
PEAR BLOSSOM
WONDER RICE

2923 **Comfort Foods**
25 Commerce Way Ste 5
North Andover, MA 01845 978-557-0009
Fax: 978-557-0131 800-514-3663
www.harmonybaycoffee.com
Coffee
President/CEO: Michael Sullivan
VP of Marketing: Stephan Liff
Operations Manager: John Sullivan
Estimated Sales: $5-10 Million
Number Employees: 10-19
Type of Packaging: Private Label
Brands:
Benley's Irish Creme
Harmony Bay

2924 **Comfort Foods**
9900 Montgomery Blvd Ne
Albuquerque, NM 87111-3554 505-281-7083
Fax: 505-281-4626 800-460-5803
http://www.comfortfoods.com
Soups and dip mixes
President/CEO: Mark Harden
VP: Dawn Johnson
Handles Marketing/Sales: Matthew Coxler
Plant Manager: Debbie Holm
Estimated Sales: $3 Million
Number Employees: 24
Number of Brands: 2
Number of Products: 80
Sq. footage: 35000
Type of Packaging: Private Label
Brands:
COUNTRY GARDENS CUISINE
DESERT GARDENS CHILE AND SPICE

2925 **Comidas Y Bebidas Fermentadas**
Av. San Jeronimo #200
Col. San Jeronimo, MO 64640
Mexico
ecastellanos@aguadepiedra.com
www.aguadepeidra.com
Water, beer.

2926 **Commercial Creamery Company**
159 S Cedar St
Spokane, WA 99204 509-747-4131
Fax: 509-838-2271 800-541-0850
megan@cheesepowder.com
www.cheesepowder.com
Processor of dried cheese and yogurt powders; processor and exporter of snack seasoning and spray dried dairy flavors
President: Michael Gilmartin
CFO: David Foedisch
VP: Peter Gilmartin
R&D: Staurt Terhune
Senior Project Leader: Kelly Curry
Estimated Sales: $10-20 Million
Number Employees: 5-9

2927 **Commissariat Imports**
PO Box 643025
Los Angeles, CA 90064-0271 310-475-5628
Fax: 310-475-8246 info@bombaybrand.com
www.bombaybrand.com
Processor, importer and exporter of indian chutneys, pickles, curry powder and pastes including curry, biryani, ginger, garlic and tandoori; certified kosher available
President/CEO: Parvez Commissariat
VP: Aban Commissariat
Estimated Sales: Over $500,000
Number Employees: 2
Type of Packaging: Food Service, Private Label
Brands:
Bombay

2928 **Commodities Marketing, Inc.**
2 Stephenville Pkwy
Edison, NJ 08820-3024
USA 732-603-5077
Fax: 732-603-5037 weldonrice@usa.net
www.weldonfoods.com
Importer and Wholesaler distributors of private label, specialty and ethnic food products to retail markets, national distributors and food service companies. Jasmine rice, Basmati rice, Coconut drinks, Coconut milk, Fruits, BeansGuar gum, Fruit juices and Cashews, Almonds, Saffron (Spain) White Rice/Parboiled Rice. We pack any size in rice.
President: Harbinder Sahni
CEO: Gagandeep Sahni
CFO: Soena Sahni
VP: Avneet Sodhi
R&D: Manoj Hedge
Marketing: Harbinder Singh Sahni & Melvin Medina
Sales: Avneet Sodhi
Public Relations: Mr. Dough & Harshida Shaw
Operations: Harshida Shah
Production: Mr Nobpsaul
Plant Manager: Mr Chandej
Estimated Sales: $10+ Million
Number Employees: 10-19
Number of Brands: 3
Number of Products: 6
Sq. footage: 1800
Type of Packaging: Consumer, Food Service, Private Label, Bulk
Brands:
MEHER
PRIVATE LABEL
WELDON

2929 **Common Folk Farm**
PO Box 141
Naples, ME 04055-0141 207-787-2764
Fax: 207-787-3894 www.commonfolk.com
Processor and exporter of herbal teas, seasonings and culinary mixes
Owner: Betz Golon
Owner: Dale Golon
Type of Packaging: Consumer, Private Label, Bulk
Brands:
Common Folk Farm, Inc.

2930 **Commonwealth Brands**
P.O.Box 51587
Bowling Green, KY 42102-5887 270-781-9100
Fax: 270-843-8607
www.commonwealthbrands.com
President: Bill Milton
CEO: John C Poling Ii
Estimated Sales: $2.5-5 Million
Number Employees: 20-49

2931 **Commonwealth Brewing Company**
138 Portland Street
Boston, MA 02114-1706 617-523-8383
Fax: 617-523-1037 www.commfish.com
Beer
Owner: Joe Quappeski
Estimated Sales: $1-2.5 Million
Number Employees: 50-99

2932 **Commonwealth Fish & Beer Company**
138 Portland St
Boston, MA 02114 617-523-8383
Fax: 617-523-1037
Brewer of beer
President: Austin O'Connor
Chef: Gwen Jordan
General Manager: Bill Goodwin
Chef: Gwen Jordan
Estimated Sales: $1-2.5 Million
Number Employees: 50-99
Sq. footage: 8000

2933 **Community Bakeries**
4501 W Fullerton Ave
Chicago, IL 60639-1933 773-384-1900
Fax: 773-384-3661 www.ralcorpfrozen.com
Muffins
Executive Director: Laura Rivera
Estimated Sales: $5-9.9 Million
Number Employees: 1-4
Brands:
Community Bakeries

2934 **Community Coffee Specialty**
P.O.Box 2311
Baton Rouge, LA 70821-2311 800-525-5583
Fax: 800-643-8199 www.communitycoffee.com
Processor of coffee and tea; importer of green coffee; wholesaler/distributor of coffee creamer; serving the food service market
President: Randall Russ
CFO: Stephen Smith
CEO: Matthew Saurage
Director Green Coffee: George Guthrie
Sales Director: Kevin Stevenson
Purchasing Manager: Judy Landry
Number Employees: 1,000-4,999
Type of Packaging: Consumer, Food Service, Private Label, Bulk

2935 **Community Market & Deli**
P.O.Box 454
Lindstrom, MN 55045-0454 651-257-1128
Fax: 651-257-3069
Manufacturer of beef, pork, lamb, goat, veal, venison, elk, ostrich, buffalo, smoked poultry, bacon, ham and sausage; private labeling available
Owner: Martin Ziegler
Estimated Sales: $300,000
Number Employees: 10-19
Type of Packaging: Consumer, Private Label

2936 **Community Mill & Bean**
267 State Route 89
Savannah, NY 13146-9711 315-365-2664
Fax: 315-365-2690 800-755-0554
cmbs@mail.teds.net www.crusoeisland.com
Organic flour milling
President: Richard Corichi
CEO: Richard Corichi
Estimated Sales: $1-2.5 Million
Number Employees: 1-4

2937 **Community Orchard**
2237 160th St
Fort Dodge, IA 50501-8547 515-573-8212
Fax: 515-576-0489 www.communityorchards.com
Processor of apple cider, pie and dumplings
President: Greg Baedke
Estimated Sales: $2.5-5 Million
Number Employees: 20-49

2938 **Company of a Philadelphia Gentleman**
2824 N 2nd St
Philadelphia, PA 19133-3515 215-427-2827
Fax: 215-739-0871 sim4033@aol.com
Teas
Owner: Morton Simkins
Estimated Sales: $500,000-$1 Million
Number Employees: 5-9

2939 **Compass Minerals**
9900 W 109th St
Suite 100
Overland Park, KS 66210-1436 913-344-9200
Fax: 913-338-7932 877-462-7258
pressrelations@compassminerals.com
www.compassminerals.com
Food grade salt products
President/CEO: Angelo Brisimitzakis
VP/CFO: Rodney Underdown
VP/CIO: Jerry Smith
VP/Supply Chain & Technology: David Bergeson
VP/Environmental, Health, Safety: James Wolf
VP/Strategic Development: David Goadby
VP/GM, North America Highway: Keith Clark
VP/GM, Consumer & Industrial Business: Jerry Bucan
VP/Manufacturing & Engineering: Jack Leunig
VP/GM, Specialty Fertilizer: Ronald Bryan
Estimated Sales: $1 Billion
Number Employees: 1,792
Type of Packaging: Consumer, Food Service, Private Label, Bulk

2940 **Completely Fresh Foods**
1117 West Olympic Blvd
Montebello, CA 90640 323-722-9136
Fax: 323-722-9139
www.completelyfreshfoods.com
Processor and distributor of fresh and frozen beef, poultry, pork and seafood products
President: Josh Solovy
Vice President: Eric Litmanovich
COO: Shaun Oshita

Estimated Sales: $60 Million
Number Employees: 200

2941 **Compton Dairy**
25 Walker Street
Shelbyville, IN 46176-1332 317-398-8621
Fax: 317-392-9777
Milk, dairy products-noncheese
President: Dan Compton
Estimated Sales: $2.5-5 Million
Number Employees: 10-19

2942 **Comstock's Marketing**
PO Box 424
Barton, VT 05822-0424 802-754-2426
Fax: 802-754-2428
Beef, beef products
President: Dean Comstock
Estimated Sales: $2.5-5 Million
Number Employees: 1-4

2943 **Con Agra Food Coperative**
4530 Mobile Highway
Montgomery, AL 36108-5110 334-288-8660
Fax: 334-286-6770 webmaster@conagra.com
www.conagra.com
Beef processing
CEO: Ronald Roskens
Plant Manager: Richard Schulcz
Quality Control: Patrick Trygstad
Estimated Sales: $ 100-500 Million
Number Employees: 300
Brands:
Act II
Butterball
David
Decker
Fernando's
FireCrackers
Gilroy

2944 **Con Agra Foods**
P.O.Box 116
Holly Ridge, NC 28445-0116 910-329-9061
Fax: 910-329-1999
denise.queen@lambweston.com
www.lambweston.com
Processor of frozen turnovers including apple, cherry, peach, lemon, blueberry, chocolate, sweet potato, pumpkin, pineapple and meat/vegetable; also, custom formulations available
VP Sales: Ed Buchanan
VP Manufacturing: Allen Padgett
Plant Manager: Charlie Jennings
Estimated Sales: $ 20 - 50 Million
Number Employees: 100-249
Sq. footage: 22000
Parent Co: ConAgra Foods
Type of Packaging: Food Service, Private Label
Brands:
Pixie Pie
Pocket Taco

2945 **Con Agra Foods**
200 S 2nd St
Lincoln, NE 68508 402-475-6700
Fax: 402-475-4772 800-332-8400
www.cooksham.com
Processor of smoked ham
COO: Gene Dimkowski
Sales: Rick Ruge
Sales/Marketing Executive: Rick Ruge
VP Operations: Joe Gallagher
Estimated Sales: I
Number Employees: 1,000-4,999
Parent Co: ConAgra Refrigerated Prepared Foods
Type of Packaging: Consumer, Food Service

2946 **Con Agro Food**
3311 S State Road 19
Peru, IN 46970-7476 765-473-3086
Fax: 765-473-5147
Canned meat spreads, bacon bits, bacon chips, bacon ipzza topping, meat analogs
CEO: Bruce Rhode
Plant Manager: Mike Firtz
Estimated Sales: $100+ Million
Number Employees: 250-499

2947 **Con Piacere Italian Specialty**
3110 Mission Beach Road
Tulalip, WA 98271-9735 360-653-7563
Fax: 360-659-0729 800-204-3594
Italian foods
President: Karen Mitchelli

2948 **Con Yeager Spice Company**
144 Magill Rd
Zelienople, PA 16063 724-452-4120
Fax: 724-452-6171 800-222-2460
sales@yeagerspice.com www.yeagerspice.com
Processor of seasonings and meat cures and binders; wholesaler/distributor of meat casings and spices
President: William Kreuer
Research & Development: Rodney Schaffer
Sales Rep.: Rod Schaffer
Production Manager: William Wolford
Estimated Sales: $1-2.5 Million
Number Employees: 10-19
Sq. footage: 18000
Type of Packaging: Consumer, Food Service, Private Label, Bulk
Brands:
Con Yeager Spices

2949 **ConAgra Beef Company**
410 N 200 W
Hyrum, UT 84319-1024 435-245-6456
Fax: 435-245-6634 www.eamiller.com
Processor, packer and exporter of beef
President: Ted Miller
Sales Manager: Bruce Miller
Estimated Sales: $ 50 - 100 Million
Number Employees: 250-499
Type of Packaging: Consumer, Private Label, Bulk

2950 **ConAgra Beef Company**
1770 Promontory Cir
Greeley, CO 80634-9039 970-506-8000
Fax: 970-506-8307 www.jbsswift.com
Processor and exporter of beef
President: Wesley Bagista
VP (East): John DeMoney
Director Merchandising: John Lichtfuss
Estimated Sales: $100+ Million
Number Employees: 10,000+
Parent Co: ConAgra Foods
Type of Packaging: Consumer, Food Service

2951 **ConAgra Beef Company**
1770 Promontory Circle
Greeley, CO 80634 970-506-8000
http://www.conagrafoods.com
Processor and exporter of angus beef,pork,lamb
President: Wesley Batista
CFO: Andre Souza
EVP: Ted Miller
Estimated Sales: H
Number Employees: 9,600
Parent Co: ConAgra Foods
Type of Packaging: Consumer, Food Service, Private Label, Bulk
Other Locations:
ConAgra Beef Co.
Grand Island NE

2952 **ConAgra Flour Milling**
2201 E 7th St
Oakland, CA 94606-5301 510-536-9555
Fax: 510-536-9593 www.conagrafoods.com
Processor of flour including potato, wheat, rye and rice, yellow corn meal and oat. Daily capacity 1.15 million pounds of flour.
Manager/Plant Manager: Bart Hahlweg
Estimated Sales: $5-10 Million
Number Employees: 10-19
Type of Packaging: Food Service, Bulk
Brands:
American Beauty
Kyrol
Magnifico Special
Occident

2953 **ConAgra Flour Milling**
4545 E 64th Ave
Commerce City, CO 80022-3107 303-289-6141
Fax: 303-287-4942 www.conagra.com
Manufacturer and exporter of milled flour
President: Darek Nowakowski
VP Sales: Don Brown
Plant Manager: John Mason
Estimated Sales: $50-100 Million
Number Employees: 100-249
Parent Co: ConAgra Foods
Type of Packaging: Consumer, Food Service, Private Label, Bulk

2954 **ConAgra Flour Milling**
P.O.Box 280
Macon, GA 31202-0280 478-743-5424
Fax: 478-745-4116 www.conagra.com
Processor of soft wheat flour
Milling Superintendent: Scott Freebern
Plant Manager: Charles Dawson
Estimated Sales: $10-20 Million
Number Employees: 10-19
Parent Co: ConAgra Foods
Type of Packaging: Bulk

2955 **ConAgra Flour Milling**
2201 E 7th St
Oakland, CA 94606-5301 510-536-9555
Fax: 510-536-9593
Processor of flour including wheat
Manager: Bart Hahlweg
Estimated Sales: $10-20 Million
Number Employees: 10,000+
Type of Packaging: Bulk

2956 **ConAgra Flour Milling**
P.O.Box 369
Chester, IL 62233-0369 618-826-2371
Fax: 618-826-4154 www.conagrafoods.com
Processor of wheat flour
Manager: Alan Bindel
VP Sales/Marketing: Bruce Rohde
Executive VP/CFO: Frank S Sklarsky
Plant Manager: Eric Schmidt
Estimated Sales: $20-50 Million
Number Employees: 20-49
Parent Co: ConAgra Trading & Processing Companies
Type of Packaging: Bulk
Brands:
Andy Capp's
Armour
Banquet
Big Mama
Blue Bonnet
Butterball
Cook's
David
Decker
Eckrich
Fernando's
Firecracker
Gilroy
Golden Cuisine
Louis Kemp
Parkay
Peter Pan
Singleto
Slim Jim
Swiss Miss
Wesson
Wolfgang Puck

2957 **ConAgra Flour Milling**
125 S Broad St
Fremont, NE 68025-5658 402-721-4200
Fax: 402-721-1016 www.conagra.com
Processor of wheat flour
Manager: D Zongker
EVP/Legal & External Affairs: Rob Sharpe Jr
EVP/Chief Financial Officer: Andre Hawaux
EVP Research/Quality/Innovation: Al Bolles PhD
EVP/Chief Marketing Officer: Joan Chow
EVP/Human Resources: Pete Perez
Plant Superintendent: Todd Peterson
Plant Manager: Travis Kapusta
Estimated Sales: $10-20 Million
Number Employees: 20-49
Parent Co: ConAgra Trading & Processing Companies
Type of Packaging: Bulk

2958 **ConAgra Flour Milling**
P.O.Box 193
Martins Creek, PA 18063-0193 610-253-9341
Fax: 610-250-2003 www.conagra.com
Processor of milled wheat flour
Manager: Scott Dillingham
EVP Research/Quality/Innovation: Al Bolles PhD
EVP/Chief Marketing Officer: Joan Chow
General Manager: John Mason
Estimated Sales: $20-50 Million
Number Employees: 50-99
Parent Co: ConAgra Trading & Processing Companies
Type of Packaging: Consumer, Bulk

2959 **ConAgra Flour Milling**
321 Taylor Ave
Red Lion, PA 17356-2211 717-244-4559
Fax: 717-244-8072 www.conagra.com
Processor of wheat flour
Chief Executive Officer: Gary Rodkin
EVP Chief Financial Officer: Andre Hawaux
EVP Research/Quality/Innovation: Al Bolles PhD
Chief Marketing Officer: Joan Chow
Office Manager: Timothy Royer
Plant Manager: Matthew Fanshier
Purchasing Agent: Gus Gentzler
Estimated Sales: $5-10 Million
Number Employees: 5-9
Parent Co: ConAgra Trading & Processing Companies
Type of Packaging: Food Service, Bulk

2960 **ConAgra Flour Milling**
2800 Black Bridge Rd
York, PA 17406 717-846-7773
Fax: 717-845-9534 www.conagra.com
Processor of wheat flour
Chief Executive Officer: Gary Rodkin
EVP/Chief Financial Officer: Andre Hawaux
EVP Research/Quality/Innovation: Al Bolles PhD
Chief Marketing Officer: Joan Chow
Plant Manager: Curt Aarons
Estimated Sales: $10-20 Million
Number Employees: 10-19
Sq. footage: 10000
Parent Co: ConAgra Trading & Processing Companies
Type of Packaging: Bulk

2961 **ConAgra Flour Milling**
408 E Magnolia St
Sherman, TX 75090-7049 903-893-8111
Fax: 903-892-7711
Processor and exporter of wheat flour
Plant Manager: Randy Garvert
Estimated Sales: $20-50 Million
Number Employees: 50-99
Parent Co: ConAgra Foods
Type of Packaging: Consumer, Food Service, Private Label, Bulk

2962 **(HQ)ConAgra Food Ingredients**
1 Conagra Dr
Omaha, NE 68102-5003 402-595-4000
Fax: 402-595-4707 877-266-2472
www.conagrafoods.com
Manufacturer of savory flavors, seasonings, food bases, advanced flavoring systems
President: Paul Maass
President/COO: Gregory Heckman
Estimated Sales: $75-100 Million
Number Employees: 10,000+
Number of Brands: 60
Number of Products: 3000
Sq. footage: 104000
Parent Co: ConAgra Foods
Type of Packaging: Bulk
Brands:
SPICETEC

2963 **ConAgra Food Store Brands**
7700 France Ave S # 200
Edina, MN 55435-5867 952-469-4981
Fax: 952-469-5550
www.conagrafoodscompany.com
Fruit snack, chewy granola bars, crisp rice bars, fruit and grain bars, graham cracker pie crust, ready - to - eat cereal, marshmallows; canned meats, beans, chili, pasta, beef stew
Plant Manager: Robert Marando

2964 **ConAgra Foods**
570 Boul Cure Boivin
Boisbriand, QC J7G 2A7
Canada 450-433-1322
Fax: 450-433-9276 www.conagra.com
Canned and frozen fruits and vegetables
President: John Geminari
VP: Anthony Parent
Marketing Manager: William Wong
Number Employees: 250
Type of Packaging: Consumer, Food Service, Private Label, Bulk
Brands:
ARTEL
CUISIEXPRESS
FINE TABLE
POGO
QUICK MEALS
YIN YANG

2965 **ConAgra Foods**
8701 W Gage Blvd
Kennewick, WA 99336-1034 509-735-4651
Fax: 509-736-0448
herb.sprinkel@conagrafoods.com
www.lamb-weston.com / www.conagra.com
Manufacturer of frozen potato products including French fries
President/Ceo: Jeffrey Delapp
Chairman/Director: Richard Porter
Vp Of Finance: Steve Rummel
Regional Sales Manager: Herb Sprinkel
Manager: Don Odegard
Estimated Sales: $100+ Million
Number Employees: 4,500
Parent Co: ConAgra Foods
Type of Packaging: Consumer, Food Service, Private Label, Bulk
Brands:
GENERATION 7 FRIES
LAMBS SUMPREME
LW PRIVATE
STEALTH FRIES
SUPREME STARZ
SWEET THINGS
TIMESAVOR
aMAIZEing

2966 **ConAgra Foods**
2005 Saint St
Richland, WA 99354-5302 509-375-4181
Fax: 509-375-5808 800-766-7783
herb.sprinkel@conagrafoods.com
www.lambweston.com / www.conagrafoods.com
Manufacturer of frozen seasoned and regular French fries
Vice President: Larry Shipp
Vice President Marketing: Andy Johnston
Plant Manager: Rick Gardner
Estimated Sales: $100+ Million
Parent Co: ConAgra Foods
Type of Packaging: Consumer, Food Service, Private Label, Bulk
Brands:
LAMB WESTON

2967 **ConAgra Foods**
PO Box 2819
Tampa, FL 33601-2819 813-241-1500
Fax: 813-247-2019
www.conagrafoods.com/index.jsp
Processor of frozen oysters, scallops, shrimp, crab and fish
President/CEO: Gary Rodkin
EVP/Chief Financial Officer: Andre Hawaux
EVP/Research & Development & Quality: Al Bolles Ph.D
EVP/Chief Marketing Officer: Joan Chow
Plant Manager: Steve Marlette
Estimated Sales: $300,000-500,000
Parent Co: ConAgra Foods Inc
Type of Packaging: Consumer, Food Service, Private Label
Brands:
Florida Sea
Gulf Harvest
Peninsular

2968 **ConAgra Foods**
1910 Fair Rd
Sidney, OH 45365 937-492-9155
Fax: 937-497-8786 800-736-2212
www.conagrafoods.com
Italian, frozen entrees and pizza
President: Bill Mackin
COO: Mike Gilardi
VP Sales: Mike Keenan
Estimated Sales: $10-20 Million
Brands:
Gilardi's
Mama Rosa
Old Italian
Spanky's

2969 **(HQ)ConAgra Foods Inc**
9 Conagra Dr
Omaha, NE 68102 402-595-7300
Fax: 402-240-4707
consumeraffairs@conagrafoods.com
www.conagrafoods.com
Processor, importer and exporter of stir fry dinners, entrees, fish, seafood, sausage, hot dogs, cold cuts, chicken, grains, spices, prepared foods, canned goods, etc.
President/CEO: Gary Rodkin
EVP/CFO: John Gehring
EVP Chief Administrative Officer: Owen Johnson

EVP Research/Development/Quality: Al Bolles Ph.D
EVP Chief Marketing Officer: Joan Chow
Senior VP Communications: Timothy McMahon
President Sales Division: Doug Knudsen
EVP Legal and External Affairs: Rob Sharpe Jr
President/COO Consumer Foods Division: Dean Hollis
President/COO Commerical Products: Greg Heckman
Estimated Sales: $12 Billion
Number Employees: 25,600
Type of Packaging: Consumer, Food Service
Other Locations:
ConAgra
Los Angeles CA
Brands:
ACT II
ANDY CAPP'S
ANGELA MIA
ARMOUR
AWARD
BANQUET
BIG MAMA SAUSAGE
BLUE BONNET
BROWN 'N SERVE
BUTTERBALL
CHEF BOYARDEE
CHUN KING
COOK'S
COUNTRY LINE
CRUNCH 'N MUNCH
CULTURELLE
DAVID
DECKER
DENNISON'S
ECKRICH
EGG BEATERS
FERNADO'S
FIRE CRACKER
FLEISCHMANN'S
GEBHARDT
GILARDI FOODS
GILROY BRAND
GOLDEN CUISINE
GOLDEN'S
HEALTHY CHOICE
HEBREW NATIONAL
HOMESTYLE BAKES
HUNT'S
HUNT'S SNACK PACK
ISLAND VALLEY
JHS - J. HUNGERFORD SMITH
JIFFY POP
KID CUISINE
KNOTT'S BERRY FARM
LA CHOY
LAMB WESTON
LIBBY'S
LIGHTLIFE
LONGMONT
LOUIS KEMP
LUCK'S
LUNCH MARKERS
MAMA ROSA'S
MANWICH
MARGHERITA
MARIE CALLENDER'S
MERIDEN
MOVE OVER BUTTER
ORVILLE REDENBACHER'S
PAM
PARKEY
PATIO
PEMMICAN
PENROSE
PETER PAN
RANCH STYLE
READY CRISP
REDDI-WIP
RO*TEL
ROSARITA
SINGLETON
SLIM JIM
ROSARITA
SINGLETON

SLIM JIM
SQUEEZE 'N GO
SWISS MISS
WOLFGANG PUCK'S

2970 ConAgra Foods Trenton Plant
1401 Harris Ave
Trenton, MO 64683-1963 660-359-3913
Fax: 660-359-4260 www.conagra.com
Manufacturer and exporter of canned meats
President/CEO: Gary Rodkin
EVP/Chief Financial Offficer: Andre Hawaux
Human Resources: Teresa Morse
EVP/Research & Development & Quality: Al Bolles Ph.D
EVP/Chief Marketing Officer: Joan Chow
Plant Manager: James Waits
Estimated Sales: $100+ Million
Number Employees: 500-999
Parent Co: Conagra Grocery Products
Type of Packaging: Consumer, Food Service, Private Label

2971 ConAgra Foods/Eckrich
1 Conagra Dr
Omaha, NE 68102 402-595-4000
Fax: 402-240-4707 800-327-4424
www.conagrafoods.com
Processor and exporter of sausage, sliced bacon, boneless ham and processed beef
President/CEO: Gary Rodkin
Chairman: Steven Goldstone
EVP/CFO: John Gehring
EVP/Chief Marketing Officer: Joan Chow
Plant Manager: Buz Sameuelson
EVP/Product Supply: Jim Hardy Jr
Estimated Sales: $12.8 Billion
Number Employees: 24,400
Sq. footage: 167260
Parent Co: ConAgra Foods Inc
Type of Packaging: Consumer, Food Service

2972 ConAgra Foods/International Home Foods
4825 Pettit Avenue
Niagara Falls, ON L2E 7B8
Canada 905-356-2661
Fax: 905-356-2633 www.congrafoods.com
Manufacturer and exporter of popcorn, stews and canned macaroni dinners including ravioli and spaghetti
Chairman/CEO: C Dean Metropoulas
EVP, Operational/Support Information: Kevin Adams
Number Employees: 250
Parent Co: ConAgra Foods
Type of Packaging: Consumer
Brands:
BUMBLE BEE
CHEF BOYARDEE
GULDEN'S
PAM

2973 ConAgra Frozen Foods Company
204 Vine St
Macon, MO 63552-1657 660-385-3184
Fax: 660-385-3566
www.conagrafoods.com/index.jsp
Processor and exporter of frozen chicken
President/CEO: Gary Rodkin
EVP/Chief Financial Officer: Andre Hawaux
Human Resources: Bonnie Seehase
EVP/Research & Development & Quality: Al Ph.D
EVP/Chief Marketing Officer: Joan Chow
Office Manager: Dave Ripley
Plant Manager: Kevin Arlin
Purchasing Agent: Dean Van Sickle
Estimated Sales: $50-100 Million
Number Employees: 250-499
Parent Co: ConAgra Frozen Foods
Type of Packaging: Consumer, Food Service, Private Label, Bulk

2974 ConAgra Frozen Foods Company
200 N Banquet Dr
Marshall, MO 65340-1718 660-886-3301
Fax: 660-886-3301
brian.lovell@conagrafoods.com
www.conagrafoods.com
Manufacturer of frozen and prepared meals; as well as snacks, mustard, whip cream and cooking oils.
CEO: Gary Rodkin
EVP/CFO: John Gehring
EVP/General Counsel: Colleen Batcheler
EVP Research & Quality: Al Bolles PhD
EVP/Chief Marketing Officer: Joan Chow
Manager: Brian Cooke
Purchasing Director: Aaron Pemberton
Estimated Sales: $1.5billion
Number Employees: 60
Parent Co: ConAgra Foods Inc.
Type of Packaging: Consumer
Brands:
ACT II
BANQUET
CHEF BOYARDEE
CRUNCH 'N MUNCH
DAVID SEEDS
EGG BEEATERS
GULDEN'S
HEALTHY CHOICE
HEBREW NATIONAL
HUNT'S
KID CUISINE
LA CHOY
MANWICH
MARIE CALLENDER'S
ORVILLE REDENBACHER'S
PAM
PARKAY
PETER PAN
REDDI-WIP
RO*TEL
SLIM JIM
SNACK PACK
SWISS MISS
VAN CAMP'S
WESSON

2975 ConAgra Frozen Foods Company
6 Conagra Dr
Omaha, NE 68102 402-595-6107
Fax: 402-595-4447 www.conagrafoods.com
Processor of prepared frozen foods including seafood, pasta, chicken, meat and Mexican
CEO: Gary Rodkin
EVP/CFO: John Gehring
EVP/General Counsel: Colleen Batcheler
EVP Research/Quality & Development: Al Bolles PhD
EVP/Chief Marketing Officer: Joan Chow
Estimated Sales: $2 Billion
Number Employees: 10,000+
Type of Packaging: Consumer, Food Service, Private Label, Bulk

2976 ConAgra Grocery Products
1645 W Valencia Drive
Fullerton, CA 92833-3860 714-680-1000
Fax: 714-680-2269 800-736-2212
info@conagrafoods.com www.conagrafoods.com
CEO: Gary Rodkin
CFO: John Gehring
Executive Vice President, Research, Qual: Al Bolles
Executive Vice President and Chief Mark: Joan Chow
COO: Dennis F O'Brien
Sales Director: Doug Knudsen
Estimated Sales: $ 3 - 5 Million
Number Employees: 1-4
Brands:
Andy Capps's
Angela Mia
Armour
Banquet
Cook's Ham
Fernando's

2977 ConAgra Grocery Products
901 Stryker St
Archbold, OH 43502 419-445-8015
Fax: 419-446-9278 www.conagra.com
Processor and exporter of canned and frozen Chinese food including chop suey, chow mein, egg rolls, sauces and vegetables
President/CEO: Gary Rodkin
EVP/Research Development & Quality: Al Bolles Ph.D
EVP/Chief Marketing Officer: Joan Chow
Plant Manager: Ron Corkins
Estimated Sales: $100+ Million
Number Employees: 250-499
Parent Co: ConAgra Grocery Products
Type of Packaging: Consumer, Food Service
Brands:
La Choy

2978 ConAgra Grocery Products
3353 Michelson Drive
Irvine, CA 92612-7622 714-680-1000
www.conagra.com
Processor and exporter of beans, ketchup, dessert preparations and mixes, egg rolls, gravies, tomato juice, mustard, noodles, nuts, oils, tomato paste, canned and frozen fruits, jalapeno peppers, popcorn, sauces, cocoa mixes, etc
President: Ronald Roskens
Vice President: Rob Sharpe
Sales Director: Doug Knudsen
Director Corporate Communications: Kay Carpenter
Number Employees: 1,000-4,999
Parent Co: ConAgra Foods
Type of Packaging: Consumer, Food Service, Private Label, Bulk

2979 ConAgra Grocery Products
1 Conagra Dr
Omaha, NE 68102-5003 402-595-4000
Fax: 402-595-4447 www.conagrafoods.com
Canned sliced apples, baked beans w/meat, pork and beans, dry beans, greens, dried peas, chicken and noodles, pizza sauce, packaged stovetop popcorn
CEO: Bruce Rhode
CFO: James O'Donnell
CEO: Gary M Rodkin
Estimated Sales: $27.1 Million
Number Employees: 10,000+
Number of Brands: 1
Number of Products: 50
Other Locations:
Conagra Grocery Products
Irvine CA
Brands:
Chef Boy-Ar-Dee
Jiffy Pop
Luck's Country Style

2980 ConAgra Mexican Foods
1805 N Santa Fe Ave
Compton, CA 90221 310-223-1499
Fax: 310-223-1698 http://www.conagrafoods.com
Processor of frozen Mexican entrees and appetizers
Manager: Roger Mucino
Senior VP Sales/Marketing: Brett Schrock
General Manager: Abe Haymahmoud
Estimated Sales: $25-49.9 Million
Number Employees: 250-499
Parent Co: ConAgra Foods
Type of Packaging: Consumer, Food Service, Bulk

2981 ConAgra Mills
110 S Nebraska Ave
Tampa, FL 33602-5530 813-223-4741
Fax: 813-221-5284 800-582-1483

www.conagrafoodingredients.com/products/conagramills.jsp
Processor of multi-purpose flours including ultragrain, whole grains, bakery flours, cake and pastry flours, and durum flours.
Manager: Alan Mersnick
EVP/Chief Financial Officer: Andre Hawaux
EVP/Chief Administrative Officer: Owen Johnson

EVP/Research & Development & Quality: Al Bolles Ph.D
EVP/Chief Marketing Officer: Joan Chow
EVP/Legal And External Affairs: Rob Sharpe Jr
President/COO Consumer Foods Division: Dean Hollis
EVP/Product Supply: Jim Hardy Jr
Plant Manager: Joseph Doyle
Estimated Sales: $ 20 - 50 Million
Number Employees: 20-49
Sq. footage: 100000
Parent Co: ConAgra Food Ingredients/ConAgra Foods Inc
Type of Packaging: Private Label, Bulk

2982 **ConAgra Mills**
1 ConAgra Dr.
Omaha, NE 68103-0500
US 402-240-4000
Fax: 402-595-4111 800-851-9618
www.conagramills.com
Processor and exporter of grain and flour including wheat, oat, barley and corn conagra mills provide whole grains to breads,bagels,soft pret- zels,doughs,pastas,cakes.
CEO: Bruce Rhode
Estimated Sales: $1 Billion+
Number Employees: 250-499
Parent Co: ConAgra Foods
Brands:
ARMOUR
CONAGRA FOODS
GILROY
SPICETEC

2983 **ConAgra Refrigerated Foods International**
1 Conagra Drive
Omaha, NE 68102-5003 402-595-4000
Fax: 970-506-8309 800-624-4724
www.conagra.com
Manufacturer and exporter of beef, pork, chicken and turkey products, processed meats, cheeses and refrigerated dessert toppings.
President/COO: Gary Rodkin
EVP/Chief Financial Officer: Andre Hawaux
EVP/Research & Development & Quality: Al Bolles Ph.D
EVP/Chief Marketing Officer: Joan Chow
Estimated Sales: $70 Million
Number Employees: 50-99
Parent Co: ConAgra Foods
Type of Packaging: Consumer, Food Service, Bulk

2984 **(HQ)ConAgra Refrigerated Prepared Foods**
215 W Diehl Rd
Naperville, IL 60563-1278 630-857-1000
Fax: 630-512-1133 www.conagra.com
Manufacturer and exporter of meat products including ham, poultry, beef, pork, veal
President/CEO: Richard Scalise
Vice President: Julie Deyoung
VP, Marketing: Bob Wallach
VP, Sales: Paul Burger
Number Employees: 10,000 +
Parent Co: ConAgra Foods
Type of Packaging: Consumer, Food Service, Private Label, Bulk
Brands:
Armour Swift-Eckrich
Butterball Turkey
Cook Family Foods
El Extremo
Lightlife
National Foods
The Max

2985 **ConAgra Shrimp Companies**
PO Box 2819
Tampa, FL 33601-2819 813-241-1501
Fax: 813-248-6030
Processor of frozen seafood including shrimp, clams, crabs, lobsters, oysters, scallops, fish patties and cakes and stir fry seafood dinners
President: Jesse Gonzalez
Parent Co: ConAgra Frozen Foods
Type of Packaging: Consumer, Food Service, Private Label, Bulk

2986 **ConAgra Store Brands, Inc.**
21340 Hayes Ave
Lakeville, MN 55044-6802 952-835-6900
Fax: 952-469-5550 800-328-6286
www.actii.com OR www.conagrafoods.com
Processor and exporter of microwaveable popcorn
President: Paul Lapadat
President: Scott Lutz
Vice President: Jeff Schellinger
Number Employees: 500-999
Parent Co: ConAgra Grocery Products
Type of Packaging: Consumer, Food Service, Private Label, Bulk
Brands:
ACT II POPCORN

2987 **ConAgra Trading and Processing**
11 Conagra Dr
Omaha, NE 68102-5011 402-595-4581
402-595-5775
www.conagrafoods.com
Processor of dry beans; also, cleaning services available
Operations Manager: Greg Konsor
Director: Bill Liebermann
Estimated Sales: K
Number Employees: 10,000+
Sq. footage: 1010000
Parent Co: ConAgra Foods

2988 **Concannon Vineyard**
4590 Tesla Rd
Livermore, CA 94550 925-456-2505
Fax: 925-583-1160 800-258-9866
info@concannonvineyard.com
www.concannonvineyard.com
Processor and exporter of bottled wines; grower of grapes
General Manager: Adam Richardson
CEO: Jim Concannon
CFO: Jim Page
Marketing Manager: Jim Ryan
Sales Director: Jeremy Levenberg
Wine Maker/General Manager: Tom Lane
Estimated Sales: $1.6 Million
Number Employees: 15
Sq. footage: 7478
Parent Co: Wine Group
Type of Packaging: Consumer, Private Label
Brands:
Concannon Vineyard

2989 **Concept 2 Bakers**
7350 Commerce Lane NE
Minneapolis, MN 55432-3113 800-266-2782
Fax: 763-574-2210 heidi.wolter@c2b
www.c2b.com
Frozen baked goods.
Parent Co: McGlynn Bakeries
Brands:
EARL OF SANDWICH
PANNE' PROVINCIO

2990 **Conco Food Service**
918 Edwards Ave
New Orleans, LA 70123 504-733-5200
Fax: 504-734-5270 800-488-3988
www.concofoods.com
Wholesaler/distributor of frozen foods, groceries, dairy products, general line items, general merchandise, produce, meats, seafood and equipment and fixtures; serving the food service market
President: Winn Chadwick
VP Procurement: Dick Bachtell
VP Sales: Robert Breaux
Estimated Sales: $100-500 Million
Number Employees: 100-249
Sq. footage: 200000
Parent Co: Consolidated Companies

2991 **Concord Brewery**
199 Cabot St
Lowell, MA 01854 978-937-1200
Fax: 978-937-1423 www.concordbrew.com
Processor of ale
President: Brett Pacheco
Estimated Sales: $1-2.5 Million
Number Employees: 1-4
Number of Brands: 4
Sq. footage: 5000
Type of Packaging: Consumer
Brands:
Concord Grape Ale
Concord Junction Porter
Concord North Woods Ale
Concord Pale Ale

2992 **Concord Confections**
7401 South Cicero Avenue
Chicago, IL 60629
Canada 773-838-3400
800-267-0037
info@dubblebubble.com
www.concordconfectionsinc.com
Processor and exporter of gum including bubble, chewing, filled and balls; also, dextrose and novelty candy
President/Coo/Director: Ellen Gordon
Chairman/Ceo: Melvin Gordon
Vp Finance/Cfo: G. Howard Ember Jr
VP Sales: Virgil Lloyd
Plant Manager: Howard Smuschkowitz
Estimated Sales: $860 Million
Number Employees: 2,200
Sq. footage: 300000
Brands:
DUBBLE BUBBLE
RAZZLES
TEAR JERKERS
TONGUE SPLASHERS
TWINKLES

2993 **Concord Farms**
2811 Faber St
Union City, CA 94587 510-429-8855
Fax: 510-429-8844 www.concordfarms.com
Grower of fresh shiitake and oyster mushrooms
Owner: Grace Tung
Owner: David Tung
Number Employees: 10-19
Type of Packaging: Consumer, Private Label, Bulk
Brands:
Oringer
Reddy Glaze

2994 **Concord Foods**
10 Minuteman Way
Brockton, MA 02301 508-580-1700
Fax: 508-584-9425 roringer@concordfoods.com
www.concordfoods.com
Variegated fruit purees, stabilized fruit, caramel for frozen desserts, bakery and confectionery including sugar free, flavors systems — dry mixes for seafood, chicken
President: Peter Nevell
Sales Manager: Rich Renna
Research & Development: Diane Douglas
Quality Control: Scott Lufz
Sales Director: Rod Oringer
VP of Manufacturing: Jesse Salfia
Estimated Sales: $10-20 Million
Number Employees: 249
Sq. footage: 190000
Type of Packaging: Bulk
Brands:
Concord Foods
Concord Mills
Oringer
Red E Made
Tempo

2995 **Condaxis Coffee Company**
1805 W Beaver St
Jacksonville, FL 32209 904-356-5330
Fax: 904-358-2027
Coffee
President: Peter Condaxis
Estimated Sales: $500,000-$1 Million
Number Employees: 5-9

2996 **Conecuh Sausage Company**
200 Industrial Cir
Evergreen, AL 36401 251-578-3380
Fax: 251-578-5408 800-726-0507
sales@conecuhsausage.com
www.conecuhsausage.com
Processor of meat products including sausage
President/CEO/Owner: John Sessions
Manager: Ronny Elliot
Estimated Sales: $10-20 Million
Number Employees: 50-99
Type of Packaging: Consumer
Brands:
Cajun Smoked Sausage
Hickory Smoked Sausage
Original Smoked Sausage
Spicy and Hot Hickory Sausage

2997 **Confection Solutions**
12428 Gladstone Ave
Sylmar, CA 91342-5320 818-365-6619
Fax: 818-365-8519 800-284-2422
info@confectionsolutions.com
www.confectionsolutions.com

Manufacturer and exporter of truffle, fruit juice sweetened and chocolate chip cookies, cashew clusters, peanut brittle and crunch, chocolate spoons, chocolate covered graham crackers, etc
President: Scott Goodspeed
Estimated Sales: $5-9.9 Million
Number Employees: 10-19
Sq. footage: 10000
Type of Packaging: Consumer, Food Service, Private Label, Bulk
Brands:
Beverly Hills Confection Line
Coffee Companions
Gourmet Delight
More Than a Box

2998 **Confectionately Yours**
160 Lexington Drive
Suite D
Buffalo Grove, IL 60089-6929 847-537-3535
Fax: 847-537-7178 800-875-6978
info@confectionately-yours.com
www.confectionately-yours.com
Processor of pretzel rods, English toffee and other homemade style candies
President: Kathy Fish
VP: Tom Fish
Estimated Sales: $600,000
Number Employees: 1-4
Number of Products: 35
Sq. footage: 4000
Type of Packaging: Consumer, Food Service, Private Label, Bulk
Brands:
Big Yummy
Blasting Powder
Bola Pop's
Fizz Wiz
Fun Stuff
Joy Stiks
Lumpy Logs
Lumpy Lous
Monster
Monster Chews
Nasty Tricks
Ninja Sticks
Oogly Eyes
Rock 'n Roll Chews
Stickers
Sweet Stirrings
Tuesday Toffee

2999 **Confectionery Treasures**
PO Box 418
Cumberland, MD 21501-0418 301-478-2245
Fax: 301-478-2245
Syrups and maple products
Sales Manager: Alan Grub

3000 **Confish**
P.O.Box 271
Isola, MS 38754 662-962-3101
Fax: 662-962-0114 800-228-3474
Processor and exporter of farm raised catfish
Owner/President: Dick Stevens
VP Sales/Marketing: Jack Perkins
VP Operations: Frank Davis
Estimated Sales: $10-20 Million
Sq. footage: 240000
Type of Packaging: Consumer, Food Service, Private Label, Bulk
Brands:
Country Select

3001 **Confish**
P.O.Box 271
Isola, MS 38754 662-962-3101
Fax: 662-962-0114
Sea food
President: Richard Stevens
Member: David Gray
Estimated Sales: $59 Million
Number Employees: 600
Brands:
Country Skillet

3002 **Congdon Orchards**
W Nob Hill Blvd
Yakima, WA 98902 509-965-2886
Fax: 509-966-4447
Processor of apples and pears
President: Richard Woodin Jr
CFO: Paul Pert
Marketing Director: Tim Maddin

Estimated Sales: $100-500 Million
Number Employees: 250-499
Type of Packaging: Consumer, Food Service

3003 **Conifer Specialties Inc**
15500 Woodinville-Redmond Rd
Suite C-400
Woodinville, WA 98072 425-486-3334
Fax: 425-398-0301 800-588-9160
ldolstad@conifer-inc.com www.conifer-inc.com
Soups, breads, desserts and Fisher scones
CEO: Mike Maher
Estimated Sales: $2.7 Million
Number Employees: 75

3004 **Conlin Food Sales**
PO Box 489
Placentia, CA 92871-0489 714-572-1088
Fax: 800-429-1137 800-429-1136
conbrokbill3@prodigy.net
Cheese, bacon, sour cream, various meats
President: Walter Conlin
Estimated Sales: Under $500,000
Number Employees: 5-9

3005 **Conn Creek Winery**
8711 Silverado Trl S
Saint Helena, CA 94574 707-963-5133
Fax: 707-963-7840 800-793-7960
Wines
President: Allen Shoup
COO: David Lawrence
Estimated Sales: $5-10 Million
Number Employees: 10-19

3006 **(HQ)Conn's Potato Chip Company**
1805 Kemper Ct
Zanesville, OH 43701 740-452-4615
Fax: 740-452-9272 866-486-4615
conns@connschips.com www.connschips.com
Potato chips
Owner: Monte Hunter
Vice President: Thomas George
Estimated Sales: $11 Million
Number Employees: 30
Brands:
CONN'S BBQ PORK RINDS
CONN'S BEAN DIP
CONN'S CARAMEL POPCORN
CONN'S CHEESE CORN POPCORN
CONN'S CHEESE CURLS
CONN'S CHEESE DIP
CONN'S CORN CHIPS
CONN'S CORN POPS POPCORN
CONN'S GREEN ONION
CONN'S HONEY BBQ JERKY
CONN'S HONEY MUSTARD DIP
CONN'S JALAPENO DIP
CONN'S NACHO TORTILLA CHIPS
CONN'S OAT BRAN PRETZELS
CONN'S ORIGINAL
CONN'S ORIGINAL BEEF JERKY
CONN'S PARTY MIX
CONN'S PICANTE DIP
CONN'S PORK RINDS
CONN'S PRETZEL RODS
CONN'S PRETZEL STICKS
CONN'S PRETZEL THINS
CONN'S PRETZEL TWISTS
CONN'S RESTAURANT TORTILLA CHIPS
CONN'S ROUND TORTILLA CHIPS
CONN'S SALSA SUPREME DIP
CONN'S SALT & VINEGAR
CONN'S SOUR CREAM
CONN'S WAVY

3007 **Conneaut Cellars Winery**
P.O.Box 5075
Conneaut Lake, PA 16316 814-382-3999
Fax: 814-382-6151 877-229-9463
www.ccw-wine.com
Wines
President: Joel Wolf
Sales/Office Manager: Jackie Elliot
Estimated Sales: $2.5-5 Million
Number Employees: 5-9

3008 **Connection Source**
5515 Taylor Road
Alpharetta, GA 30022-2600 770-667-1051
Fax: 770-667-1283

Manufacturer of vitamins, minerals, herbs, soft gelatin capsules and amino acids; manufacturer of printed folding cartons; private label packaging available
President: Andrew Compain
Type of Packaging: Private Label, Bulk
Brands:
Q GEL

3009 **Connors Aquaculture**
Estes Head
Eastport, ME 04631 207-853-6081
Fax: 207-853-6056
Fish hatchery
President: Ken Hirtle
Network Administrator: Tony Irving
Plant Manager: David Morang

3010 **Conrad Rice Mill**
307 Ann St
New Iberia, LA 70560 337-364-7242
Fax: 337-365-5806 800-551-3245
sales@conradricemill.com
www.conradricemill.com
Manufacturer of packed rice including yellow, herb, curry, ranch and wild; also, rice mixes including paella, long grain and wild
President: Michael Davis
Estimated Sales: $20-50 Million
Number Employees: 20-49
Type of Packaging: Consumer, Food Service
Brands:
CONRAD-DAVIS
HOL GRAIN
KONRIKO
R.M.QUIGGS

3011 **Conrotto A. Winery**
1690 Hecker Pass Road
Gilroy, CA 95020-8800 408-847-2233
Wine
President: James Burr
Estimated Sales: $1-2.5 Million
Number Employees: 1-4

3012 **Conroy Foods**
906 Old Freeport Rd
Pittsburgh, PA 15238-4163 412-781-1446
Fax: 412-781-1409 beanos@conroyfoods.com
www.conroyfoods.com
Deli and seafood condiments
President: Jon Conroy
CEO: Jon Conroy
Estimated Sales: $2.5-5 Million
Number Employees: 10-19
Brands:
Beanos's

3013 **(HQ)Consolidated Biscuit Company**
312 Rader Rd
Mc Comb, OH 45858 419-293-2911
Fax: 419-293-3366 800-537-9544
dan.bash@cbcbakery.com
Manufacturer and exporter of cookies, crackers, biscuits, nuts and snack foods; exporter of cookies; contract packaging available
President/Owner: Jim Appold
Vice President: Walter Kinsey
Estimated Sales: $100-500 Million
Number Employees: 1,000-4,999
Type of Packaging: Consumer, Food Service, Private Label, Bulk
Other Locations:
Consolidated Biscuit Facility
Michigan City IN
Consolidated Biscuit Facility
London KY
Consolidated Biscuit Facility
Willmar MN
Consolidated Biscuit Facility
Louisville KY
Brands:
Fireside
Gurley
Gurley Golden Recipe
Royal Crest

3014 **Consolidated Biscuit Company**
502 W Us Highway 20
Michigan City, IN 46360-6836 219-873-1880
Fax: 219-873-1882 info@cbiscuits.com
www.cbiscuits.com

Nut brittle
President: Jeff Schuster
VP: William Varney
Vice President: Martin Seidler
CEO: Michael Rienhard
Estimated Sales: $10-20 Million
Number Employees: 250-499
Brands:
Tal-Furnar
Venezini

3015 **Consolidated Brands**
821 17th Street
Altoona, PA 16601-2074 814-941-2200
Fax: 814-943-2354
Chocolate candy
President: Roger Raybuck
Manager Sales/Marketing: Lorretta Brown
Estimated Sales: $50-100 Million
Number Employees: 100-249

3016 **Consolidated Distilled Products**
2600 W 35th Street
Chicago, IL 60632-1602 773-927-4161
Fax: 773-927-8105
Distributor of liquor
President/CEO: John Wittert
CFO: Steve O'Malley
Number Employees: 100-249
Brands:
Amaretto Corso
Bambuca
Barbarossa
Benevento
Canadian Reserve
Chila
Classic
Conte
Desert Island
Dimitri
E.S.T.
Georgia
Grand Suzette
Grommes & Ullrich
Gusano Grande
Hannah & Hogg
Kampai
Karlof
Lautrec
McGuires Original
Merlin
Mme Lautrec
Monastery
Royal Islander
Schranck's
Sunset
Vogue

3017 **(HQ)Consolidated Factors**
2959 Monterey Salinas Highway
Monterey, CA 93940-6400 831-375-5121
Fax: 831-375-0754 max@confacto.com
Fresh and frozen fish, seafood, fruits and vegetables
President/CEO: Warren Nobusada
Executive VP/COO: Alan Nobusada
VP of Sales: Max Boland
Estimated Sales: $50 Million+
Number Employees: 10-19
Brands:
Crescent
Red Rose Farms
Sea Diamond
Sea Jade
Sea Pearl

3018 **Consolidated Mills**
7190 Brittmoore Rd Ste 150
Houston, TX 77041 713-896-4196
Fax: 713-896-4199 cto@hypercon.com
www.consolidatedmills.com
Processor of frozen drink bases, slush flavors, flavoring extracts, sundae toppings, sno-cone syrups and custom spice blends
Owner: Chuck Rodner
Vice President: Mark Estep
Estimated Sales: $1-3 Million
Number Employees: 10-19
Sq. footage: 15000
Parent Co: Consolidated Mills
Type of Packaging: Consumer, Food Service
Brands:
C&D
COOL & DELICIOUS
SOUTHERN FLAVORS

3019 **Consolidated Sea Products**
250 N Water St
Mobile, AL 36602-4000 251-433-3240
Fax: 251-433-6721
Manufacturer of seafood
Owner: Paul William
Estimated Sales: $ .5 - 1 million
Number Employees: 1-4

3020 **Consolidated Seafood Enterprises**
4718 E Cactus Road
188
Phoenix, AZ 85032-7706 480-348-9548
Fax: 480-348-9587
President: Karen Lamarche Blyth
Vice President: David Phelps

3021 **Consolidated Simon Distributor**
1835 Burnet Ave
Suite 1
Union, NJ 07083-4282 973-674-2124
Fax: 973-687-9132 www.candycentral.com
Candy and confections
President: Ken Simon
CEO: Herbert Lefkowitz
CFO: William German
Estimated Sales: $23 Million
Number Employees: 50-99

3022 **Consolidated Tea Company**
300 Merrick Rd Ste 202
Lynbrook, NY 11563 516-887-1144
Fax: 516-887-1643
Tea
President: Elliot Labiner
Estimated Sales: $1 Million
Number Employees: 10

3023 **Consumer Guild Foods**
5035 Enterprise Blvd
Toledo, OH 43612-3839 419-726-3406
Fax: 419-726-8771
Processor of salad dressings and oils, mayonnaise, condiments and relishes
President: W Ascham
Quality Control: R Fuller
VP Production: R Petrick
Estimated Sales: $10-20 Million
Number Employees: 20-49
Type of Packaging: Consumer, Food Service, Private Label, Bulk
Brands:
Amhurst Kitchens
Annie's Supreme
Cg Supreme

3024 **Consumer Packing Company**
Plum & Liberty Streets
Lancaster, PA 17604 717-397-6141
Fax: 717-397-0322
wanda.hart@handoverfoods.com
General grocery
Estimated Sales: $ 1 - 3 Million
Number Employees: 5-9
Type of Packaging: Private Label

3025 **Consumers Flavoring Extract Company**
921 McDonald Ave
Brooklyn, NY 11218 718-435-0201
Processor and exporter of flavoring extracts and essential oils including vanilla
President: L Fontana
Estimated Sales: $10-20 Million
Number Employees: 10-19

3026 **Consumers Packing Company**
1301 Carson Dr
Melrose Park, IL 60160 708-345-6780
Fax: 708-345-9052 800-356-9876
www.consumerspacking.com
Meat products
President: William Schutz
Estimated Sales: $ 10 - 20 Million
Number Employees: 20-49

3027 **Consumers Vinegar & Spice Company**
4723 S Washtenaw Ave
Chicago, IL 60632-2097 773-376-4100
Fax: 773-376-6224
Processor of vinegar, spices and dehydrated garlic and onion
President: Stanley Zarno
Estimated Sales: $5-10 Million
Number Employees: 10-19
Sq. footage: 40000
Type of Packaging: Consumer, Food Service, Private Label, Bulk
Brands:
Burma
Consumers

3028 **Consun Food Industries**
123 N Gateway Blvd
Elyria, OH 44035-4923 440-322-6301
Fax: 440-322-8196
Processor of dairy products including buttermilk, whipped cream, cottage cheese, sour cream and ice cream; also, dips, sherbet and soft-serve mixes, fruit drinks, orange juice, etc
Owner: Jeff Coonrod
Director of Manufacturing: Paul Meiss
Facilities Manager: Mike Sedevik
Estimated Sales: $30 Million
Number Employees: 180
Type of Packaging: Consumer, Food Service, Private Label, Bulk
Brands:
Sunshine Farms

3029 **Consun Food Industries**
123 N Gateway Blvd
Elyria, OH 44035 440-322-6301
Fax: 440-322-8196
Packaged milk, fruit juices and ice cream
President: Dennis Walter
CFO: Steve Cannon
Controller: Brad Essex
Marketing Director: Jerry Lattimer
Operations Manager: Ron Lattimer
Plant Manager: Paul Meiss
Estimated Sales: $30 Million
Number Employees: 12
Number of Brands: 1
Type of Packaging: Consumer, Food Service, Private Label, Bulk

3030 **Consup North America**
170 Beaverbrook Rd
Lincoln Park, NJ 07035 973-628-7330
Fax: 973-628-2919 customerservice@consup.us
Candy
President: Maarten Moog
Marketing: Russ Harlock
Estimated Sales: $ 5-10 Million
Number Employees: 5-9

3031 **Contact International**
8001 Lincoln Ave
Skokie, IL 60077-3695 847-324-4411
Fax: 847-229-1386 info@contactamt.com
Processor of liquid and powder flavor extracts, natural spring water, liquid tea, juices and carbonated soft drinks, RTD Beverages, CSD
President: Sumner Katz
VP: Phillip Ross
VP: Robert Goodman
Estimated Sales: $5-10 Million
Number Employees: 10-19
Type of Packaging: Private Label
Brands:
Artica

3032 **Conte Luna Foods**
760 S 11th St
Philadelphia, PA 19147-2614
US 215-923-3141
Fax: 215-925-4298 Sales@ConteLuna.com
www.conteluna.com
Processor and exporter of pasta and noodles for soups, frozen foods and shelf-stable foods, etc types of noodles produced...fusili,lisci,cut ziti,rigatini,rigatoni,rotelle,tri-vein rotini,salad rotini,spiretti,penne.
President: Luke Marano
Director Of Marketing And Sales: Joe Viviani
EVP Sales: Bill Stabert
Estimated Sales: $ 5 - 10 Million
Number Employees: 5-9
Type of Packaging: Bulk

3033 **Conte Luna Foods**
40 Jacksonville Rd
Warminster, PA 18974 215-441-5220
Fax: 215-441-8934 Sales@ConteLuna.com
www.conteluna.com

President: Max Powell
VP: John Briggs
EVP: Bill Stabert
Director of Sales & Marketing: Joe Viviano
Estimated Sales: $10-20 Million
Number Employees: 20-49

3034 **Conte's Pasta Company**
310 Wheat Rd
Vineland, NJ 08360 856-697-3400
Fax: 856-697-1757 800-211-6607
contespasta@comcast.net www.contespasta.com
Wheat and gluten free pasta, pizza, pierogi and more
Principal: Adelina Portillo
Marketing: Mike Conte
Estimated Sales: $140,000
Number Employees: 2

3035 **Contessa Food Products**
222 W 6th St Fl 8
San Pedro, CA 90731 310-832-8000
Fax: 310-832-8333 contessa@contessa.com
www.contessa.com
Manufacturer and importer of frozen shrimp, scallops, calamari, shrimp and chicken convenience meals and pineapple chunks
President/CEO: John Blazevich
Estimated Sales: $100-500 Million
Number Employees: 100-249
Brands:
Contessa
Islander
Shanghai

3036 **Conti Packing Company**
P.O.Box 23025
Rochester, NY 14692 585-424-2500
Fax: 585-424-2504
Manufacturer and importer of fresh and frozen meats including lamb, pork, beef, veal and sausage
President: Douglas Conti
Treasurer: Thomas Conti
Estimated Sales: $5-10 Million
Number Employees: 10-19

3037 **Contigroup Companies**
4110 Continental Dr
Oakwood, GA 30566-2800 770-538-2120
Fax: 770-538-2121 Information@Conti.com
www.waynefarmsllc.com
Poultry
President: Elton Maddox
Chairman/CEO: Paul Fribourg
VP/CFO: Kathy McManus
CEO: Paul Fribourg
Director Of Sales: Stan Haymaen
Number Employees: 10,000+
Type of Packaging: Bulk
Brands:
DUTCH QUALITY HOUSE
Wayne Farms

3038 **Continental Coffee Products Company**
235 N Norwood St
Houston, TX 77011-2311 713-928-6281
Fax: 713-924-9870 800-323-6178
www.saralee.com
Coffee, tea
President: Peter JW Roorda
Sales Manager: Scott Kolber
Plant Manager: Dan Hickman
Number Employees: 5-9

3039 **Continental Culture Specialists**
333 S Hope St
Los Angeles, CA 90071 818-240-7400
Fax: 818-243-3601 vasacont@aol.com
www.continentalyogurt.com
Processor of yogurt, kefir and lebni cheese and liquid acidophilus culture
President: Martha Frazier
Quality Control: M Josie Uy
Marketing Director: Martha Frazier
National Sales Manager: Gary Correll
Production Manager: Erroll McGowen
Estimated Sales: $50-100 Million
Number Employees: 50-99
Sq. footage: 22000
Type of Packaging: Consumer
Brands:
Continental
Continental Yogurt
Lebini-Kefer Cheese

3040 **Continental Custom Ingredients**
1170 Invicta Drive
Oakville, ON L6H 6G1
Canada 905-815-8158
Fax: 905-815-9194 rhames@cci-can.net
www.cci-can.net
Specializes in the design and application of stabilization, emulsification, and functional ingredient systems to impart the desired body and texture characteristics and self life stability to processed foods, beverage and dairyproducts.
Number Employees: 20-49
Type of Packaging: Private Label, Bulk
Brands:
AQUAMIN
DURAFRESH
FARGO

3041 **Continental Deli Foods**
1300 S Lake St
Cherokee, IA 51012 712-225-6529
Fax: 712-225-6513 www.tyson.com
Processor of meats including smoked, cured, pork, ham, beef, hot dogs and cold cuts
President: Jerry Menke
General Manager: Jerry Menke
Asst. Plant Manager: Mark Fassler
Estimated Sales: $100-500 Million
Number Employees: 500-999
Sq. footage: 175000
Parent Co: FoodBrands America
Type of Packaging: Consumer, Food Service, Private Label
Brands:
American Favorite
Black Forest
Fresh Cut
Wilson Continental D

3042 **Continental Food Products**
P.O.Box 540928
Flushing, NY 11354-0928 718-358-7894
Fax: 718-463-6580 www.betzios.com
Processor of frozen pizzas
President: Elias Betzios
Controller: Richard Betzios
VP: Paul Betzios
Estimated Sales: $20-50 Million
Number Employees: 50-99
Brands:
Betzios

3043 **(HQ)Continental Grain/ContiGroup Companies**
277 Park Ave
New York, NY 10172 212-207-5200
Fax: 212-207-2910 information@conti.com
www.contigroup.com
Processor and exporter of poultry, meat, grain, flour and feed.
Chairman/CEO: Paul Fribourg
EVP/CFO: Michael Zimmerman
Evp: Teresa McCaslin
EVP Human Resources: Teresa McCaslin
Estimated Sales: 1.14billion
Number Employees: 14,200
Type of Packaging: Bulk
Brands:
WAYNE FARMS

3044 **Continental Group**
21062 Brookhurst St # 203
Huntington Beach, CA 92646-7404 858-391-5670
Fax: 858-965-0260 norm_tcg@sbcglobal.net
Manufacturer of sardines, tuna, olive oils, balsamic vinegar, and pasta
Owner: Dean Beerbower

3045 **Continental Mills**
P.O.Box 88176
Seattle, WA 98138-2176 253-872-8400
Fax: 253-872-7954 www.continentalmills.com
Manufacturer and exporter of baking products including dry flour mixes. Continental Mills has acquired the Pillsbury foodservice small package dry mix business from Best Brands Corporation
President: John Heily
CFO: Michael Castle
Vice President: Bob Wallach
Research & Development: Dan Donahue
Quality Control: Christy Johnson
Marketing Director: Steve Donley
Sales Director: Steve Giuditta
Public Relations: Clyde Walker
Operations Manager: Mark Harris
Production Manager: Mike Meredith
Estimated Sales: $43.2 Million
Number Employees: 500-999
Sq. footage: 300000
Type of Packaging: Consumer, Food Service, Private Label, Bulk
Brands:
ALPINE
CLASSIC HEARTH
EAGLE MILLS
GHIRARDELLI
KRUSTEAZ
KRUSTEAZ CARBSIMPLE
SNOQUALMIE FALLS LODGE

3046 **Continental Sausage**
911 E 75th Ave
Denver, CO 80229 303-288-9787
Fax: 303-288-9789 www.continentalsausage.com
Meats, sausage
President: Eric Gutknecht
Vice President: Ursula Gutknecht
Purchasing Manager: Eric Gutknecht
Estimated Sales: $2.5-5 Million
Number Employees: 5-9

3047 **Continental Seasoning**
1700 Palisade Ave
Teaneck, NJ 7666 201-837-6111
Fax: 201-837-9248 800-631-1564
info@continentalseasoning.com
www.continentalseasoning.com
Processor, importer and exporter of sauces, spices, seasonings and food additives
President: Pete Federer
CFO: Jeffrey Bovit
Vice President: Edward Levine
Quality Control: Marty Haas
VP Production: Ann Davis
Plant Manager: Steve Wagner
Estimated Sales: $5 Million
Number Employees: 50
Sq. footage: 20000
Type of Packaging: Food Service, Private Label, Bulk

3048 **Continental Vitamin Company**
4510 S Boyle Ave
Vernon, CA 90058 323-581-0176
Fax: 323-589-6667 800-421-6175
ronald@cvc4health.com www.cvc4health.com
Vitamins
President: Ron Deckenfield
CEO: Hal Frank
Estimated Sales: $ 5 - 10 Million
Number Employees: 50-99
Brands:
Cvc Specialsties
Superior Source

3049 **Continental Yogurt**
1358 E Colorado Street
Glendale, CA 91205-1474 818-240-7400
Fax: 818-243-3601
Processor of yogurt
Sales Manager: Gary Correll
Purchasing Agent: Juan Garcia
Estimated Sales: $ 1 - 3 Million
Number Employees: 10-19
Type of Packaging: Food Service

3050 **Convenience Food Suppliers**
607 Ellis Road
Suite 52a
Durham, NC 27703-6008 919-596-9338
Fax: 919-596-9339 800-922-1586
cfspop@mindspring.com
Processor of popcorn; wholesaler/distributor of popcorn machinery and concession supplies; serving the food service market
Owner: Harold Pittman

Estimated Sales: Less than $500,000
Number Employees: 1-4
Sq. footage: 8500

3051 Conway Import Company
11051 Addison Ave
Franklin Park, IL 60131 847-455-5600
Fax: 847-455-5630 800-323-8801
conwaydressings@minspring.com
www.conwaydressings.com
Processor of oils, mayonaise, salad dressings, maple syrup, sauces and marinades.
President: Scott Heineman
VP: Gregg Haineman
VP Marketing: Robert Burns
VP Sales: Robert Burns
Estimated Sales: $50-100 Million
Number Employees: 50-99
Number of Products: 600
Type of Packaging: Food Service, Private Label, Bulk

3052 Cook Inlet Processing
909 W 9th Ave
Anchorage, AK 99501-3322 907-243-1166
Fax: 907-243-4231
VP Operations: Tim Blott
Estimated Sales: $ 1 - 3 Million
Number Employees: 1-4

3053 (HQ)Cook Inlet Processing
P.O.Box 8163
Nikiski, AK 99635-8163 907-776-8174
Fax: 907-776-5302 www.oceanbeauty.com
Processor and exporter of frozen seafood including crab, salmon, halibut, clams, etc
President: Mike Schupe
COO: Mel Morris
Accounts Payable: Norma Johnson
Controller, Plant Manager: Pat Hardina
Production Manager: Tuck Bonney
Plant Manager: Wayne Kvasinkoff
Estimated Sales: $20-50 Million
Number Employees: 100-249
Parent Co: Polar Equipment
Type of Packaging: Consumer, Food Service, Bulk
Brands:
Cook Inlet Processing

3054 Cook Natural Products
2109 Frederick St
Oakland, CA 94606-5317 510-534-2665
Fax: 510-534-2509 800-537-7589
brendan@cooknaturally.com
www.cooknaturally.com
Organic flour, grains, seeds, beans
Vice President: Jeffrey Barnes
Personnel Manager: Brendan McEntee
Vice President: Jeffrey Barnes
Estimated Sales: $12 Million
Number Employees: 10-19

3055 Cook Natural Products
2109 Frederick St
Oakland, CA 94606-5317 510-534-2665
Fax: 510-534-2509 800-537-7589
brendan@cooknaturally.com
www.cooknaturally.com
Organic grains
President/CEO: Brendan Mc Entee
Estimated Sales: $1-2.5 Million
Number Employees: 10-19

3056 Cook's Gourmet Foods
5821 Wilderness Ave
Riverside, CA 92504-1004 951-352-5700
Fax: 951-352-5710 www.triplehfoods.com
Co-packers of gourmet foods
President: Tom Harris Jr
Estimated Sales: $500,000-$1 Million
Number Employees: 50-99

3057 Cook-In-The-Kitchen
P.O.Box 961
White River Junction, VT 05001 802-333-4141
Fax: 802-333-4624 info@citk.com
www.cookinthekitchen.com
All natural pancake, bakery and soup mixes.
President: Mary Spata
VP/General Manager: Murray Burk
Estimated Sales: $1-2.5 Million
Number Employees: 3
Number of Products: 20
Type of Packaging: Consumer, Private Label

3058 Cooke Aguaculture
874 Main Street
Blacks Harbour, NB E5H-1E6
Canada 506-456-6600
Fax: 506-456-6652 nhalse@cookeaqua.com
www.cookeaqua.com/
Distributor of fresh and smoked salmon.
CEO: Glenn Cooke
CFO: Peter Buck
VP Marketing: Jean Lamontagne
VP Sales: Alan Craig
VP Public Relations/Communications: Neil Halse

Purchasing Director: Don Bourque
Number Employees: 20-49
Number of Brands: 3
Number of Products: 60
Sq. footage: 2500
Brands:
APPLEDORE
HORTON'S

3059 Cooke Tavern Ltd
4158 Penns Valley Rd
Spring Mills, PA 16875 814-422-7687
Fax: 814-422-8752 866-422-7687
gregw@cooketavernsoups.com
www.cooketavernsoups.com
Soups
President/Owner: Greg Williams
Number Employees: 5

3060 Cookie Cupboard Baking Corporation
12 Commerce Rd
Fairfield, NJ 7004 973-227-2800
Fax: 973-882-6998 800-217-2938
www.davidscookies.com
Baked goods
Owner: Ari Margulies
Vice President: Howard Freundlich
VP Sales: Ken Schiliro
Estimated Sales: $15 Million
Number Employees: 95
Brands:
DAVID'S COOKIES

3061 Cookie Kingdom
1201 E Walnut St
Oglesby, IL 61348 815-883-3331
Fax: 815-883-3332
Processor of baked goods
President: Cliff Sheppard
Director: Patty Smith
Estimated Sales: $13 Million
Number Employees: 100

3062 Cookie Specialties
482 N Milwaukee Ave
Wheeling, IL 60090-3067 847-537-3888
Fax: 847-537-6709 matt@mattscookies.com
www.mattscookies.com
Processor of cookies
President: Grant Pierce
VP: Matthew Pierce
Estimated Sales: $10-20 Million
Number Employees: 10-19
Type of Packaging: Consumer, Food Service, Private Label
Brands:
MATT'S COOKIES

3063 Cookie Tree Bakeries
P.O.Box 57888
Salt Lake City, UT 84157-0888 801-268-2253
Fax: 801-265-2727 800-998-0111
www.cookietree.com
Processor and exporter of frozen gourmet cookies and cookie dough; also, fat-free available
President: Greg Schenk
Purchasing: Wayne Davis
Estimated Sales: $20-50 Million
Number Employees: 1-4
Type of Packaging: Consumer, Food Service, Private Label, Bulk
Brands:
COOKIETREE BAKERIES

3064 Cookies Food Products
614 W 1st St
Wall Lake, IA 51466 712-664-2662
Fax: 712-664-2676 800-331-4995
www.cookiesbbq.com
Processor of barbecue and taco sauces
President: Speed Herrig
Purchasing Manager: Jeff Herrig
Estimated Sales: $10-20 Million
Number Employees: 10-19
Sq. footage: 61000
Type of Packaging: Consumer, Food Service
Brands:
COOKIES

3065 Cookietree Bakeries
P.O.Box 57888
Salt Lake City, UT 84157 801-268-2253
Fax: 801-265-2727 800-998-0111
cheryl@cookietree.com www.cookietree.com
Owner: Greg Schenk
VP Sales: Mike Dougherty
Estimated Sales: $ 20 - 50 Million
Number Employees: 50-99

3066 Cookiezen, LLC
Po Box 2519
Falls Church, VA 22042-0519 703-389-9274
Fax: 866-496-6034 lenglander@cookiezen.com
www.cookiesandcorks.com
Cookies
Marketing: Laura Englander

3067 Cookshack
2304 N Ash St
Ponca City, OK 74601 580-765-3669
Fax: 580-765-2223 800-423-0698
sales@cookshack.com www.cookshack.com
US Manufacturers of the World Famous Smart Smokers, Smokette, Fast Eddy's OVens Barbeque Sauces & Spices, Smoking Wood Accessories for Better Barbeque, Cookshack Smoked Foods Cookbooks & more
President: Brent Matthews
CEO: Stuart Powell
Finance/Marketing/Sales Manager: John Shiflet
VP: Edward Aguiar Jr
Marketing Coordinator: Cayley Armstrong
Production Manager: Jim Linnebur
Estimated Sales: $4 Million
Number Employees: 30
Number of Brands: 2
Number of Products: 1
Sq. footage: 11000
Type of Packaging: Consumer, Food Service, Private Label, Bulk
Brands:
Cookshack

3068 Cool
801 E Campbell Rd # 348
Richardson, TX 75081-1866 972-437-9352
Fax: 972-644-7231
Sodas and sports drinks
Manager: Dan C Cole
Estimated Sales: $500-1 Million appx.
Number Employees: 1-4
Brands:
Cool Natural Sodas
Cool Quencher Sports

3069 (HQ)Cool Brands International
4175 Veteran's Memorial Highway
3rd Floor
Ronkonkoma, NY 11779 631-737-9700
Fax: 631-737-9792 www.coolbrandsinc.com
Ice cream and ice cream novelties
President/CEO: David Kewer
General Manager: Antonio Brooks
Number Employees: 20-49
Parent Co: CoolBrands International

3070 Cool Mountain Beverages
1065 E Prairie Ave
Des Plaines, IL 60016 847-759-9330
Fax: 847-759-9332 www.coolmountain.com
Produces gourmet flavored sodas.
President: Bill Daker
Estimated Sales: $ 3 - 5 Million
Number Employees: 1-4
Brands:
COOL MOUNTAIN GOURMET SODA

3071 Coombs Vermont Gourmet
74 Cotton Mill Hl Unit A106
Brattleboro, VT 05301 802-257-8100
888-266-6271
info@maplesource.com www.maplesource.com

Processor, importer and exporter of pure maple syrup and sugar; also, organic and kosher varieties available
President: Arnold Coombs
Estimated Sales: $ .5 - 1 million
Number Employees: 1-4
Number of Brands: 3
Type of Packaging: Consumer, Food Service, Private Label, Bulk
Brands:
COOMBS FAMILY FARMS

3072 **Cooper Farms**
6793 Us Route 127
Van Wert, OH 45891-9601 419-238-4056
Fax: 419-238-1587 www.cooperfarms.com
Processor of fresh turkey products
Manager: Greg Cooper
Product Development Manager: Dale Siebeneck
Regional Sales Manager: Scott Habben
Human Resources Manager: Paula Flemming
Production Superintendent: Mike Parker
Plant Operations Manager: Greg Cooper
Purchasing Manager: Duaine Hampton
Estimated Sales: $10-20 Million
Number Employees: 100-249

3073 **Cooper Mountain Vineyards**
20100 SW Leonardo Ln
Beaverton, OR 97007 503-649-0027
Fax: 503-649-0702
sales@coopermountainwine.com
www.coopermountainwine.com
Wines
Owner: Robert Gross
Sales Director: Susan Baltus
Winemaker: Rich Cushman
Estimated Sales: $1-2.5 Million
Number Employees: 5-9
Type of Packaging: Private Label

3074 **Cooper Vineyards**
13372 Shannon Hill Rd
Louisa, VA 23093 540-894-5253
Fax: 804-285-8773 www.coopervineyards.com
Wine
Owner: Jaque Hogge
Estimated Sales: $ 1 - 3 Million
Number Employees: 1-4

3075 **Cooperative Elevator**
P.O.Box 619
Pigeon, MI 48755 989-453-4500
Fax: 989-453-3942 co-opinquiry@coopelev.com
www.coopelev.com
Processor of dried beans
President/CEO: Pat Anderson
Chairman: Kurt Ewald
Finance VP: Mike Wehner
VP: Barry Albrecht
Estimated Sales: $500,000-$1 Million
Number Employees: 1-4

3076 **Cooperative Elevator Company**
P.O.Box 619
Pigeon, MI 48755 989-453-4500
Fax: 989-453-3942 co-opinquiry@coopelev.com
www.coopelev.com
Processor and exporter of beans, wheat, barley, oats and corn
President/CEO: Pat Anderson
Purchasing Manager: Michelle Sting
Estimated Sales: $ 50 - 100 Million
Number Employees: 100-249
Type of Packaging: Bulk

3077 **Cooperstown Cookie Company**
P.O.Box 64
Cooperstown, NY 13326 888-269-7315
Fax: 607-547-2673 888-269-7315
goodies@cooperstowncookie.com
www.cooperstowncookie.com
all natural baseball cookies
President/Owner: Pati Grady

3078 **(HQ)Coors Brewing Company**
17735 W 32nd Ave
PO Box 4030
Golden, CO 80401 303-279-6565
Fax: 303-277-2805 800-642-6116
www.coors.com
Manufacturer and exporter of malt beverages, ale and beer including regular, light, seasonal and nonalcoholic. Principle subsidiary is Coors Brewing Company, the nation's third-largest brewer.
President/CEO: Peter Swinburn
CFO: Bill Waters
VP/CIO: John Crowther
Chief Marketing Officer: Andrew England
Estimated Sales: $900 Million
Number Employees: 2000
Parent Co: Molson Coors Brewing Company
Type of Packaging: Consumer
Other Locations:
Shenandoah Facility
Elkton VA
Sandlot Brewery
Denver CO
Coors Brewing Company
Canada
Coors Brewing Company
Puerto Rico
Coors Brewing Company
Carribean
Coors Brewing Company
United Kingdom
Coors Brewing Company
China
Coors Brewing Company
Japan
Brands:
BLUE MOON™
COORS LIGHT®
COORS NON-ALCOHOLIC®
COORS® BANQUET
EXTRA GOLD™LAGER
KEYSTONE®
KILLIAN'S® IRISH RED™
WINTERFEST
ZIMA®

3079 **Copper Hills Fruit Sales**
4337 N Golden State Boulevard
Suite 102
Fresno, CA 93722-3801 559-277-1970
Fax: 559-277-6971
Packers of peaches, plums, nectarines, apricots, pomegranates, and persimmons

3080 **Copper Tank Brewing Company**
504 Trinity Street
Austin, TX 78701-3714 512-854-9380
Fax: 512-478-1832
Processor of seasonal beer, ale, stout, lager and porter
President: Aaron Scharff
Purchasing: Patrick Bradshaw
Estimated Sales: $2.5-5 Million
Number Employees: 50-99
Type of Packaging: Food Service

3081 **Cora Italian Specialties**
9630 Joliet Rd
La Grange, IL 60525-4138
US 708-482-4660
800-969-2672
info@corainc.com www.corainc.com
Importer and exporter of espresso machinery, pasta cookers and panini grills. Midwest distributor of Monin syrups, Oregon chai, Guitiard and Ghirardelli chocolates, Mocafe, Jet tea etc
President: John Cora
Sales: Paul Rekstad
Estimated Sales: 1.80 Million
Number Employees: 13
Sq. footage: 15000
Type of Packaging: Food Service
Brands:
DANESI
DOLCE
GHIRARDELLI
GUITTARD
JET TEA
MOCAFE
MONIN
MUSETTI
NIKOLA'S BISCOTTI
NUMI TEA
OREGON CHAI
SOY DREAM
WHITE WAVE

3082 **Cora-Texas Manufacturing Company**
Po Box 280
White Castle, LA 70788 225-545-3679
Fax: 225-545-8360 www.coratexas.com
Processor of raw sugar and blackstrap molasses
President: Paul Buckley Kessler
Assistant Manager: Charles Schudmak
Vice President: Clayburn Dugas
Estimated Sales: $20-50 Million
Number Employees: 100-249
Type of Packaging: Bulk

3083 **Corbin Foods-Edibowls**
P.O.Box 28139
Santa Ana, CA 92799-8139 714-966-6695
Fax: 949-640-0279 800-695-5655
www.edibowls.com
Processor and exporter of edible bowls for salads, desserts and tarts; club packs available
Manager: R J Hill
Estimated Sales: $5-10 Million
Number Employees: 5-9
Sq. footage: 100000
Type of Packaging: Consumer, Food Service, Bulk
Brands:
EDIBOWL

3084 **Corby Distilleries**
193 Yonge Street
Toronto, ON M5B 1M8
Canada 416-369-1859
Fax: 416-369-9809 800-367-9079
corbyweb@adsw.com www.corby.ca
Processor and importer of whiskey, Scotch whiskey, Irish whiskey, bourbon, rum, gin, vodka, tequila, cognac and brandy.
President/CEO: Patrick O'Driscoll
VP/CFO: Thierry Pourchet
VP Marketing: Jeff Agdern
VP Sales: Andy Alexander
VP SP/Customer Service: Chris Chan
VP Production: Jim Stanski
Number Employees: 100-249
Number of Brands: 45
Parent Co: Allied Lyons
Type of Packaging: Consumer, Food Service
Brands:
BALLANTINE'S FINEST
BARCLAY'S
BEEFEATER DRY
BELVEDERE
CANADIAN CLUB
CHOPIN
COURVOISIER
D'EAUBONNE VSOP NAPOLEON
DE KUYPER GENEVA
GLENDRONACH
HORNITOS SAUZA
LAMB'S NAVY
LAMB'S PALM BREEZE
LAMB'S WHITE
LAPHROAIG
LEMON HART
MAKER'S MARK
MALIBU COCONUT RUM
POLAR ICE TASSEL
REVELSTOKE
ROYAL RESERVE
SAUZA COMMEMORATIVO
SAUZA EXTRA GOLD
SAUZA SILVER
SAUZA TRIADA
SCAPA SINGLE MALT
SILK TASSEL
SPECIAL OLD
STOLICHNAYA
STOLICHNAYA RAZBERI
STOLICHNAYA RED
STOLICHNAYA VANIL
TEACHER'S HIGHLAND CREAM
TRES GENERACIONES
TULLAMORE DEW
WISER'S DELUXE
WISER'S SPECIAL BLEND
WISER'S VERY OLD

3085 **Cordoba Foods LLC**
15912 Nw 48th Avenue
Hialeah, FL 33014-6410 786-925-9072
Fax: 815-366-9786 sales@gauchoranchfoods.com
www.gauchoranchfoods.com

Other condiments, BBQ sauce, ethnic sauces (soy, curry, etc.), grilling sauces, marinades, other sauces, seasonings and cooking enhancers, dessert toppings (i.e. fudge sauce, caramel sauce, whipped cream, etc.) other spreads &syrup.

3086 Cordon Bleu International

8383 Rue J Rene Ouimet
Anjou, QC H1J 2P8
Canada 514-352-3000
Fax: 514-352-3226

Processor and exporter of pickled food products, sauces, gravies, chicken broth, meat pates, beef and chicken entrees and red kidney beans in tomato sauce.

Director Advertising/Promotions: Michelle Guibord
Director Sales: Jacques LeGare
Purchasing: Kristen Gerard
Number Employees: 100-249
Parent Co: J-R Ouimet
Type of Packaging: Consumer, Private Label

3087 Corea Lobster Cooperative

191 Crowley Island Rd
Corea, ME 04624 207-963-7936
Fax: 207-963-5952

Lobster

President: Michael Hunt
Vice President: Gary Moore
Estimated Sales: $ 1 - 3 Million
Number Employees: 5-9

3088 (HQ)Corfu Foods

755 Thomas Dr
Bensenville, IL 60106-1624 630-595-2510
Fax: 630-595-3884 www.corfufoods.com

Processor and exporter of pita bread, honey mustard sauce and beef and chicken gyro products including cones, patties, deli kits, sauce and loaves; importer of cheese, olives and stuffed grape leaves.

President: Vasilios Memmos
VP: Sophie Maroulis
Purchasing Agent: Ron Fallot
Estimated Sales: $ 10 - 20 Million
Number Employees: 50-99
Sq. footage: 70000
Other Locations:
Corfu Foods
Long Island City NY
Brands:
CORFU
GYROS USA
OMEGA
TASTY

3089 Corfu Tasty Gyros

755 Thomas Dr
Bensenville, IL 60106 630-595-2510
Fax: 630-595-3884

Gyros

President: Vasilios Memmos
Estimated Sales: $ 10 - 20 Million
Number Employees: 50-99

3090 Corim International Coff

1116 Industrial Pkwy
Brick, NJ 08724 732-840-1670
Fax: 732-840-1608 800-942-4201

Coffee

President: Rame Teren
CEO: Sam Teren
Vice President: Effie Uzan
Estimated Sales: $1-2.5 Million
Number Employees: 20-49

3091 Corky's Bar-B-Q

5259 Poplar Ave
Memphis, TN 38119 901-685-9744
Fax: 901-685-1102 800-926-7597
pbqinfo@corkysbbq.com www.corkysbbq.com

Processor of frozen barbecue ribs, pork shoulders and beef brisket

President: Barry Pelts
CEO: Andrew Woodman
Principal: Don Pelts
Estimated Sales: $5-10 Million
Number Employees: 100-249
Type of Packaging: Consumer, Food Service

3092 Cormier Rice Milling Company

P.O.Box 152
De Witt, AR 72042 870-946-3561
Fax: 870-946-3029 www.cormierrice.com

Processor and exporter of long and medium grain, milled, brown and organic brown rice

Owner: Carol Cormier
Vice President: Julie Simpson
VP: J Ferguson
Estimated Sales: $10-20 Million
Number Employees: 20-49
Type of Packaging: Consumer, Food Service, Private Label, Bulk
Brands:
Lone Pine
Regal
Snow Goose

3093 Corn Poppers

PO Box 620156
San Diego, CA 92162-0156 858-231-2617
Fax: 858-231-2985 info@cornpoppers.com
www.cornpoppers.com

Processor of flavored, organic and plain popcorn.

President: Richard Kratze
CFO: Betty Melton
General Manager: Jose Alves
Number Employees: 20-49
Parent Co: Corn Poppers
Brands:
POPCORN DIPPERS

3094 (HQ)Corn Products International

5 Westbrook Corporate Ctr
Westchester, IL 60154 708-551-2600
Fax: 708-551-2700 800-443-2746
info@cornproducts.com www.cornproducts.com

Processor, importer and exporter of corn oils, starches, gluten and sweeteners including high fructose syrups, dextrose and meltodextrin.

Chairman, President & CEO: Ilene Gordon
VP & CFO: Cheryl Beebe
VP & President, North America Division: Jack Fortnum
Estimated Sales: $1.41 Billion
Number Employees: 10,000
Type of Packaging: Bulk
Other Locations:
Corn Products International
Etobicoke ON
Brands:
ABC CARRIER
BREWER'S CRYSTALS
BUFFALO
CERELOSE
ENZOSE
FIBERBOND
GLOBE
GLOBE PLUS
INVERTOSE HFCS
PROFERM
ROYAL
ROYAL-T
STABLEBOND
SUREBOND
ULTRABOND
UNIDEX

3095 Cornaby's LLC

421 S 200 E
Spanish Fork, UT 84660-2418 801-754-4968
Fax: 801-423-7838 janetstocks@cornabys.com
www.cornabys.com

Manufacturer of jams & jellies.

Marketing: Janet Stocks

3096 Cornell Beverages

105 Harrison Pl
Brooklyn, NY 11237 718-381-3000
Fax: 718-381-3001

Carbonated soft drinks

President/CEO: Allan Hoffman
Treasurer: Donna Hoffman
Purchasing: Jim Dehaan
Estimated Sales: $850,000
Number Employees: 10
Brands:
Cornell Beverages

3097 Cornfields, Inc.

3898 Sunset Avenue
Waukegan, IL 60087 847-263-7000
Fax: 847-263-7090 jbweiler@cornfieldsinc.com
www.cornfieldsinc.com

Chips, nuts, popcorn, pretzels, puffed snacks.

Marketing: Jb Weiler

3098 Corona College Heights Orange & Lemon Associates

8000 Lincoln Ave
Riverside, CA 92504 951-688-1811
Fax: 951-689-5115 www.cchcitrus.com

Processor and exporter of oranges, lemons and grapefruit.

President: John Demshki
Purchasing: Dale Stogner
Estimated Sales: $100-500 Million
Number Employees: 100-249
Type of Packaging: Consumer, Bulk

3099 Corrin Produce Sales

23667 E Dinuba Ave
Dinuba, CA 93618 559-596-0517
Fax: 559-638-8508 Sharonb@corrin.com
www.corrin.com

Grower and exporter of fresh fruit including peaches, plums, nectarines and table grapes; also, raisins

President: Harold Seitz
CFO: Robert Greiner
Manager: Lisa Macedo
Estimated Sales: $400,000
Number Employees: 5
Type of Packaging: Bulk

3100 Corsair Pepper Sauce

1110 42nd Avenue
Gulfport, MS 39501-2663 228-452-0311
Fax: 228-452-0152

Pickled fruits and vegetables, vegetable sauces and seasonings and salad dressings.

President: Martha Murphy
Estimated Sales: $120,000
Number Employees: 2

3101 Corsetti's Pasta Products

1001 N Evergreen Ave
Woodbury, NJ 08096-3557 856-853-0999
Fax: 856-853-7438 800-989-1188

Manufacturer of various pasta products such as lasagna and spaghetti.

Owner: Dan Pellegrino
Plant Manager: Michael Corsetti
Purchasing: Michael Corsetti
Estimated Sales: $2.5-5 Million
Number Employees: 5-9
Type of Packaging: Bulk

3102 Corte Provisions

574 Ferry Street
Newark, NJ 07105-4402 201-653-7246
Fax: 201-653-2271 leao51@aol.com
www.cortesausage.com

Processor of Spanish, Portuguese and Brazilian sausages and serrano-style hams.

Estimated Sales: $2 Million
Number Employees: 10-19
Number of Brands: 6
Number of Products: 20
Sq. footage: 15000
Parent Co: Seabrite Corporation
Type of Packaging: Consumer, Private Label, Bulk
Brands:
CORTE'S
EL BATURRO
EL RICO

3103 Corus Brands

14030 NE 145th St
Woodinville, WA 98072-6994 425-806-2600
Fax: 425-488-3460 info@corusbrands.com
www.corusbrands.com

Producers of various red, white and blush wines.

CEO: Andrew Browne
Estimated Sales: $270,000
Number Employees: 4
Brands:
ALDER RIDGE
BATTLE CREEK
SAWTOOTH
ZEFINA

3104 Cosa de Rio Foods

3701 W Magnolia Ave
Louisville, KY 40211-1635 502-772-2500
Fax: 502-772-7300 www.cdof.com

Manufactures tortilla products and flatbreads.

President: Ted Longacre
Director Operations: Richard Sawyer
Estimated Sales: $25-49.9 Million
Number Employees: 100-249

Type of Packaging: Private Label
Brands:
CHI-CHI'S

3105 **Cosco International**
1826 N Lorel Ave
Chicago, IL 60639-4376 773-889-1400
Fax: 773-889-0854 800-621-4549
www.sethnessgreenleaf.com
Manufacturer of flavors.
President: Patrick Carney
CFO: Joe Hughes
Purchasing Agent: Ken Ciukowski
Estimated Sales: $1-$2.5 Million
Number Employees: 20-49
Brands:
APPLE SIDRA
COSCO FLAVORS

3106 **Cosentino WineryVintage Grapevine, Inc.**
7415 St. Helena Hwy.
Yountville, CA 95476 707-944-1220
Fax: 707-944-1254 800-764-1220
finewines@cosentinowinery.com
www.cosentinowinery.com
Manufactures fine red and white wines.
President: Mitch Cosentino
CEO: Larry Soldinger
Marketing Director: Shawn Lutwalla
Public Relations: Julie Weinstock
Estimated Sales: $5-10 Million
Number Employees: 25
Type of Packaging: Private Label

3107 **Cosgrove Distributors**
120 S Greenwood St
Spring Valley, IL 61362 815-664-4121
Fax: 815-663-1433
Wholesaler/distributor of general line products; serving the food service market.
President: Nora Cosgrove
Purchasing Manager: Nora Cosgrove
Estimated Sales: $2.5-5 Million
Number Employees: 10-19

3108 **Cosmo's Food Products**
200 Callegari Dr
West Haven, CT 06516-6234 203-933-9323
Fax: 203-937-7283 800-933-6766
claudano@cosmosfoods.com
www.cosmosfoods.com
Processor, packer and importer of olives, artichokes, capers, peppers, marinated mushrooms and roasted peppers; also, sun-dried tomatoes, hot cherry peppers, pepperoncini and garlic.
President: Cosmo Laudano
VP: Lisa Laudano
Sales Manager: Mario Laudano
Production: Peter Merola
Purchasing: Cosmo Laudano
Estimated Sales: $5-10 Million
Number Employees: 20-49
Number of Products: 39
Sq. footage: 22500
Type of Packaging: Consumer, Food Service, Private Label, Bulk
Brands:
COSMO'S

3109 **Cosmopolitan Foods**
138 Essex Avenue
Glen Ridge, NJ 07028-2409 973-680-4560
Sauces such as BBQ, Worcestershire and Spaghetti
President: Nick Ten Velde
Purchasing Manager: Nick Ten Velde
Number Employees: 5-9

3110 **Costa Deano's Gourmet Foods**
PO Box 6367
Canton, OH 44706-0367 330-453-1555
Fax: 330-453-9766 800-337-2823
Processor and exporter of gourmet pasta sauces in glass jars
President: Dean Bacopoulos
VP: Bill Bacopoulos
Number Employees: 5-9
Sq. footage: 15000
Parent Co: Costa Deano's Enterprises
Type of Packaging: Consumer, Food Service, Private Label, Bulk
Brands:
Costa Deano's

3111 **Costa Macaroni Manufacturing**
PO Box 32308
Los Angeles, CA 90032-0308
Fax: 323-225-1667 800-433-7785
info@costapasta.com www.costapasta.com
Manufacturer of homemade various shapes and sizes of pastas
VP, Southwest Region: Stephen Zoccoli
General Sales Manager: Buzz Weisman
Estimated Sales: $5-10 Million
Number Employees: 20-49
Type of Packaging: Food Service, Bulk
Brands:
COSTA

3112 **Costa's Pasta**
2045 Attic Pkwy NW
Kennesaw, GA 30152-7610 770-514-8814
Fax: 770-514-9766 www.costaspasta.com
Fresh pasta
President: Mary Costa
CFO: Joe Costa
Vice President: Stephen Zoccoli
Sales Director: Stephen Saferite
Estimated Sales: $2.5-5 Million
Number Employees: 5-9
Brands:
Costa's Pasta

3113 **Costadeanos Gourmet Foods**
PO Box 6367
Canton, OH 44706-0367 330-453-1555
Fax: 330-493-9766
Gourmet foods
President: Dean Bacopoulos
Estimated Sales: $5-10 Million
Number Employees: 20-49
Sq. footage: 10
Type of Packaging: Private Label
Brands:
Costadeanos Gourmet

3114 **Cotswold Cottage Foods**
9820 W 60th Ave
Arvada, CO 80004 303-423-2987
Fax: 303-423-2987 800-208-1977
cotscotfds@aol.com
www.marthasuescookies.com
Scone mixes, gingerbread mixes, stuffing mixes, lemon curd, jams, and tea
President: Tricia Mackell
Estimated Sales: $300,000-500,000
Number Employees: 5-9
Type of Packaging: Consumer

3115 **Cott Beverage West**
4810 76th Avenue SE
Calgary, AB T2C 2V2
Canada 403-279-6677
Fax: 403-279-2260
Processor and exporter of nonalcoholic beverages
Sales Manager (Western Canada): Lou Pituello
General Manager: Mark Wiens
Number Employees: 100-249
Parent Co: GH Beverage
Type of Packaging: Consumer, Food Service
Brands:
Cott
RC
Sun Mountain

3116 **Cott Concentrates/RoyalCrown Cola International**
P.O.Box 1440
Columbus, GA 31902-1440 706-494-7500
Fax: 706-571-9189 800-652-5642
info@cott.com www.cott.com
Processor of soft drinks
Manager: Jamy Wilsord
Estimated Sales: $ 50 - 100 Million
Number Employees: 100-249
Parent Co: Cott Beverages
Type of Packaging: Consumer, Food Service

3117 **(HQ)Cott Coporation**
5519 W Idlewild Avenue
Tampa, FL 33634 813-313-1800
Fax: 813-881-1926 info@cott.com
www.cott.com
Manufacturer, importer and exporter of juice and drinks
CEO: Jerry Fowden
President, US Business Unit: Michael Gibbons
CFO: Neal Cravens
Chief Procurement Officer: William Reis
Estimated Sales: $1.8 Billion
Number Employees: 1,300
Type of Packaging: Consumer, Food Service, Private Label, Bulk
Other Locations:
Cliffstar Manufacturing Plant
East Freetown MA
Cliffstar Manufacturing Plant
Fontana CA
Cliffstar Manufacturing Plant
Fredonia NY
Cliffstar Manufacturing Plant
Greer SC
Cliffstar Manufacturing Plant
Joplin MO
Cliffstar Manufacturing Plant
N East PA
Cliffstar Manufacturing Plant
Walla Walla WA
Cliffstar Manufacturing Plant
Warrens WI
Brands:
Cliffstar
Golden Crown

3118 **Cottage Bakery**
1831 S Stockton St
Lodi, CA 95240-6302 209-333-8044
Fax: 209-333-7428 info@cottagebakery.com
www.cottagebakery.com
Bakery products
President: Terry Knutson
Estimated Sales: $20-50 Million
Number Employees: 500-999

3119 **Cottage Street Pasta**
167 S Main Street
Barre, VT 05641-4813 802-476-4024
pastajules@aol.com
Manufactures a variety of fresh pasta and ravioli.
Purchasing Agent: Karen Gordon
Estimated Sales: $300,000-500,000
Number Employees: 1-4

3120 **Cotton Baking Company**
4151 Viking Dr
Bossier City, LA 71111-7408 318-747-3168
Fax: 318-747-0118 800-777-1832
www.interstatebakeriescorp.com
Processor of baked products including bread
Manager: David Amos
Sales Manager: Slade Cooper
Estimated Sales: $20-50 Million
Number Employees: 20-49
Type of Packaging: Consumer
Brands:
Holsum Bread
Wonder Bread

3121 **Cottonwood Canyon Winery**
3940 Dominion Rd
Santa Maria, CA 93454-9678 805-937-8463
Fax: 805-937-8418 info@cottonwoodcanyon.com
www.cottonwoodcanyon.com
Wine
Owner/Winemaker: Norman Beko
VP: Stephen Beko
Estimated Sales: $1-2.5 Million
Number Employees: 5-9
Number of Products: 24
Brands:
Cottonwood Canyon

3122 **Couch's Country Style Sausages**
4750 Osborn Rd
Cleveland, OH 44128 216-823-2332
Fax: 216-663-3311
Processor of sausage including pork, beef and turkey
President: Ludie Couch
Manager: Stanley Redd
Estimated Sales: $500,000-$1 Million
Number Employees: 5-9
Sq. footage: 3500
Type of Packaging: Consumer, Bulk

3123 **Couch's Original Sauce**
5323 E Nettleton Ave
Jonesboro, AR 72401-6650 870-932-0710
Fax: 870-910-0619 800-264-7535
www.couchsbbq.com
Processor of barbecue sauce
Chairman: Beth Couch
General Manager: Sharon Spurlock
Estimated Sales: $ .5 - 1 million
Number Employees: 20-49
Sq. footage: 6200
Brands:
Couch's Original

3124 **Cougar Mountain Baking Company**
4224 24th Ave W
Seattle, WA 98199 206-467-5044
Fax: 206-467-0993
comments@cougar-mountain.com
www.cmbc.com
Producers of bakery products.
Owner: David Saulnier
Marketing/Sales: David Saulnier
Customer Service: Dana Pantley
Estimated Sales: $300,000-500,000
Number Employees: 5-9
Brands:
COUGAR MOUNTAIN

3125 **Country - Fed - Meats Company**
633 Roberts Drive
Riverdale, GA 30274-2913 770-991-5888
Fax: 770-991-0469 800-637-7559
Meat
CEO: Harry Peaden, Jr.

3126 **Country Bob's**
211 S Lincoln Blvd
Centralia, IL 62801 618-533-2375
Fax: 618-533-7828 800-373-2140
www.countrybobs.com
Producers of sauces and seasonings.
President: Terry Edson
Estimated Sales: $2.5-5 Million
Number Employees: 10-19

3127 **Country Butcher Shop**
524 E Water St
Palmyra, MO 63461 573-769-2257
Fax: 573-769-4652
Processor and distributor of lamb, beef and pork.
President: Edward Dent
Purchasing Agent: Edward Dent
Estimated Sales: $10-20 Million
Number Employees: 5-9
Type of Packaging: Private Label

3128 **Country Choice Naturals**
9531 W 78th St # 230
Eden Prairie, MN 55344-8000 952-829-8824
Fax: 952-833-2090
www.countrychoiceorganic.com
Manufacturer of organic hot cereals, cookies and cocoas.
President: Chuck Endersen
Number of Brands: 1
Number of Products: 35
Type of Packaging: Consumer
Brands:
COUNTRY CHOICE

3129 **Country Club Bakery**
1211 Country Club Rd
Fairmont, WV 26554 304-363-5690
Fax: 304-363-6099 pallotajcp2@aol.com
Processor of bread, sandwich rolls, hoagie buns and pepperoni rolls
Owner: Chris Pallotta
Owner: Chris Pallotta
Estimated Sales: $5-10 Million
Number Employees: 5-9
Type of Packaging: Consumer, Food Service

3130 **Country Clubs Famous Desserts**
83 Bustleton Pike
Langhorne, PA 19053-6465 215-322-0700
Fax: 215-322-1534 800-843-2253
Desserts
Owner: Brian Rothaus
VP Sales: Bruce Davidsen
Estimated Sales: $20-50 Million
Number Employees: 50-99

3131 **Country Cupboard**
P.O.Box 673
Virginia City, NV 89440-0673 775-847-7300
Fax: 775-847-7722 beanman01@aol.com
www.countrycupboard.com
Processor of dehydrated soups, pastas, rices, sauces, relish, jams, beans, sugar-free chocolates, cornbread, honey and salsa, among other products.
Owner: Beverly Cowan
Estimated Sales: $5-10 Million
Number Employees: 5-9

3132 **Country Delight Farms**
P.O.Box 25210
Nashville, TN 37202-5210 615-320-1440
Fax: 615-329-3017
Dairy products
Marketing Director: Jim Greaving
Public Relations: Royce McClintock
Operations Manager: Charles Hilton
Plant Manager: Rodney Hillis
Estimated Sales: $25-49.9 Million
Number Employees: 100-249
Brands:
Country Delight

3133 **Country Delite**
P.O.Box 25210
Nashville, TN 37202-5210 615-320-1440
Fax: 615-329-3017
Milk
Director: Suzie Lusk
Plant Manager: Rodney Hillis
Estimated Sales: $ 50 - 100 Million
Number Employees: 100-249
Parent Co: Suiza Dairy Group
Type of Packaging: Bulk
Brands:
Country Delite

3134 **Country Estate Pecans**
1625 E Sahuarita Rd
Sahuarita, AZ 85629-0007 520-625-8809
Fax: 520-629-0119 800-473-2267
sales@pecans.com www.pecans.com
Pecans, snacks
President: Liz Alexander
General Manager: DeWayne McCasland
Estimated Sales: $ 20 - 50 Million
Number Employees: 4
Parent Co: Fermers Investment
Type of Packaging: Private Label

3135 **Country Foods**
46835 Us Highway 93
Polson, MT 59860 406-883-4384
Fax: 406-883-3275 www.countrypasta.com
Manufacturers of pasta.
President: Fred Kellogg
Vice President: Linda Knutson
Marketing Director: Dan Johnson
Operations Manager: Gary Ivory
Estimated Sales: $2.5-5 Million
Number Employees: 20-49
Type of Packaging: Private Label
Brands:
COUNTRY PASTA

3136 **Country Fresh**
31770 Enterprise Dr
Livonia, MI 48150 734-261-7980
Fax: 734-261-2633 800-968-7980
Manufacturer of milk.
Manager: Jerry Shannon
Purchasing Agent: Bruce Evans
Estimated Sales: $100+ Million
Number Employees: 100-249
Parent Co: Suiza Dairy Group

3137 **Country Fresh**
2555 Buchanan Ave SW
Grand Rapids, MI 49548 616-243-0173
Fax: 616-954-2813 800-748-0480
www.deanfoods.com
Processor of dairy products including ice cream, yogurt, sour cream, cottage cheese and milk
SVP: Joe Risdon
Vice President: Pete Reynolds
Estimated Sales: $ 10 - 20 Million
Number Employees: 347
Parent Co: Suiza Dairy Group
Type of Packaging: Consumer, Food Service, Private Label
Brands:
Country Fresh

3138 **(HQ)Country Fresh Farms**
432 W 3440 S
Salt Lake City, UT 84115 801-263-6667
Fax: 801-269-9666 800-878-0099
www.bluechipgroup.net
Producers of whey drinks, dairy products and dry mixes.
President: George Moo
CFO: Mike Leonard
Estimated Sales: $5 Million
Number Employees: 23
Sq. footage: 10600
Type of Packaging: Consumer, Food Service, Private Label, Bulk
Brands:
COUNTRY FRESH FARMS
SWISS WHEY D'LITE

3139 **Country Fresh Food & Confections, Inc.**
405 Main Street
Po Box 604
Oliver Springs, TN 37840 865-435-2655
Fax: 865-435-1930 800-545-8782
info@countryfreshfood.com
www.countryfreshfood.com
Manufacturer of Country Fresh Fudge, regular & sugar-free, Pamela Ann Classic Confections, Jim Bean Fudge, Kahula Fudge, Papa Joe's Downhome Gourmet.
President: Edward Stockton
Estimated Sales: $1-2.5 Million
Number Employees: 20-49
Number of Brands: 6
Number of Products: 150
Sq. footage: 8000
Type of Packaging: Consumer, Food Service, Private Label, Bulk
Brands:
Country Fresh
Country Fresh Fudge
Papa Joe's Downhome

3140 **Country Fresh Golden Valley**
31770 Enterprise Dr
Livonia, MI 48150-1960 734-261-7980
Fax: 734-261-1049
Manufacturer of fluid and frozen milk
President: Jerry Shannon
Plant Manager: Ken Andrews
Estimated Sales: $50-100 Million
Number Employees: 100-249
Type of Packaging: Consumer, Food Service, Private Label, Bulk
Brands:
Burger
Country Fresh
Frost Bite
McDonald's

3141 **Country Fresh Mushrooms**
8990 Gap Newport Park
PO Box 489
Avondale, PA 19311 610-268-3033
Fax: 610-268-0479
info@countryfreshmushrooms.com
www.countryfreshmushrooms.com
Processor of mushrooms including exotic, fresh, processed, whole and sliced.
Chairman/CEO: Ed Leo
Purchasing Manager: Ed Sourney
Estimated Sales: $20-50 Million
Number Employees: 100-249
Sq. footage: 30750
Type of Packaging: Consumer, Food Service, Private Label, Bulk
Brands:
COUNTRY FRESH

3142 **Country Harbor Sea Farms**
71 Deming Point Rd
Larrys Riveror, NS B0H 1T0
Canada 902-358-2002
Fax: 902-387-2526
Processor and exporter of mussels
President: Bruce Hancock
Number Employees: 5-9
Type of Packaging: Bulk

3143 **Country Hearth Bread**
855 Scott St
Murfreesboro, TN 37129-2735 615-893-6041
Fax: 615-893-1463
Bread
Manager: Rick Hardesty
Manager: Ray Ping
Estimated Sales: $20-50 Million
Number Employees: 100-249

3144 **Country Home Bakers**
21100 S Western Avenue
Torrance, CA 90501-1700 310-533-6010
Fax: 310-328-2608 800-989-9534
www.countryhomebakers.com
Processor of bread, cookies and fruit pies
President: Judith Borck
G.M.: Jesse Rodriguez
Vice President: Doris Zelinsky
Research & Development: Bob Tetrault
Quality Control: George Rupp
Marketing Director: Katy Callahan
VP Operations: Kevin McDonough
Purchasing Manager: Dick Warren
Estimated Sales: $10-20 Million
Number Employees: 100-249
Parent Co: Country Home Bakers
Type of Packaging: Consumer, Food Service, Private Label, Bulk
Brands:
Jessie Lord
Readi Bake
Sanders

3145 **Country Home Bakers**
720 Metropolitan Pkwy SW
Atlanta, GA 30310 404-215-5540
Fax: 404-527-6690 800-241-6445
Processor of frozen dough including danish, doughnut, roll and cookie and frozen bread dough including jalapeno/cheese, salsa, spinach/mushroom/cheese, vegetable, focaccia, etc.; also, frozen baked and unbaked pies, frozen cakestoppings, ice cream and candy
President: Judith L Borck
Manager: Kevin McDonough
Senior VP: V Wolczek
COO: Doris Zelinsky
Regional Sales Manager: Jim Rasmussen
General Manager: Roy Lowery
Plant Manager: Mike Harvison
Estimated Sales: $20-50 Million
Number Employees: 100-249
Sq. footage: 80000
Parent Co: Borck's Country Home Bakery
Type of Packaging: Consumer, Food Service, Private Label, Bulk
Other Locations:
Country Home Bakers
Highland Park MI
Brands:
Chop Block Breads
Country Home Bakers
Jessie Lord, Inc.
Sanders
Warme Bakker

3146 **Country Home Creations**
P.O.Box 126
Goodrich, MI 48438 800-457-3477
Fax: 810-244-5348 800-457-3477
chcdips@countryhomecreations.com
www.countryhomecreations.com
Processor and exporter of mixes including cheesecake, cookie, dip and soup.
Owner: Shirley Kautman Jones
Estimated Sales: $-5 Million
Number Employees: 20-49
Sq. footage: 10000
Type of Packaging: Consumer, Private Label
Brands:
CAMP MIXES
CLASSIC COUNTRY
COUNTRY HOME CREATIONS
GINGER KIDS
MY MOM'S MIXES
PERFECT PARTY MIXES

3147 **Country Life**
101 Corporate Dr
Hauppauge, NY 11788 631-231-1031
Fax: 631-231-2331 800-645-5768
info@country-life.com www.country-life.com
Supplements and health beverages
CEO: Halbert Drexler
Estimated Sales: $ 10 - 20 Million
Number Employees: 100-249
Brands:
BIOCHEM
COUNTRY LIFE
IRON-TEK
LONG LIFE BEVERAGES
NATURAL PERSONAL CARE

3148 **Country Maid**
1919 S Kinnickinnic Ave
Milwaukee, WI 53204 414-383-3970
Fax: 414-383-9809 800-628-4354
www.countrymaid.com
Processor of refrigerated salads, entrees and desserts
President: Wayne Becker
CFO: Jordan Plotkin
Office Manager: Pat Plotkin
Estimated Sales: $6.7 Million
Number Employees: 55
Sq. footage: 40000
Type of Packaging: Consumer, Food Service, Private Label
Brands:
Country Maid

3149 **Country Pies**
2465 Alberni Hwy
Coombs, BC V0R 1M0
Canada 250-248-6415
Fax: 250-248-6415
Processor of frozen meat pies including pork, cornish, steak/kidney, steak/onion, steak/mushroom and chicken/vegetable; also, sausage rolls
President: Brian Forseth
Estimated Sales: $243,000
Number Employees: 6
Type of Packaging: Bulk
Brands:
Country Pies

3150 **Country Pure Foods**
681 W Waterloo Rd
Akron, OH 44314 330-753-2293
Fax: 330-745-7838 www.countrypurefoods.com
Manufacturer of juices
President: Raymond Lee
CEO: Tom Kolb
Quality Control: Susan Woods
Marketing Director: Joe Koch
Sales Director: Jon Hanley
Sr VP Operations: Paul Sukalich
Estimated Sales: I
Number Employees: 250-499
Type of Packaging: Consumer, Food Service, Private Label
Other Locations:
Ellington CT
Deland FL
Brands:
ARDMORE FARMS

3151 **Country Pure Foods**
58 West Rd
Ellington, CT 6029 860-872-8346
Fax: 860-875-6539 www.countrypurefoods.com
Manufacturer and exporter of fruit drinks, bottled spring water and juices including apple, orange, grape and pineapple
President/CEO: Ray Lee
Director: George Bean
Vice President: Jon Hanley
Director: Stuart Clink
Estimated Sales: $50-100 Million
Number Employees: 106
Sq. footage: 80000
Parent Co: Country Pure Foods
Type of Packaging: Consumer, Food Service, Private Label
Brands:
GLACIER VALLEY
NATURAL COUNTRY
SUNFLO
SUNNY LEA

3152 **(HQ)Country Pure Foods**
681 W Waterloo Rd
Akron, OH 44314 330-753-2293
Fax: 330-745-7838 877-995-8423
www.countrypurefoods.com
Processor of fruit juices, drinks and nectars for food service and retail
President: Ray Lee
CEO: Ricardo Alvarez
CFO: Tom Kolb
Vice President: Rick Conrad
Quality Control: Jeff Ross
Marketing Director: Joe Koch
Sales Director: Rick Conrad
Public Relations: Janet Dye
Operations Manager: Paul Sukalich
Plant Manager: Tim Hunter
Purchasing Manager: Dan Goric
Estimated Sales: I
Number Employees: 250-499
Number of Brands: 3
Number of Products: 500
Sq. footage: 111000
Type of Packaging: Consumer, Food Service, Private Label
Other Locations:
Country Pure Foods
Deland FL
Country Pure Foods
Ellington CT
Brands:
Ardmore Farms Grove
Glacier Valley
Natural Country

3153 **Country Smoked Meats**
PO Box 171
Bowling Green, OH 43402-0171 419-353-0783
Fax: 419-352-7330 800-321-4766
Processor and exporter of chunked, sliced and deli style Canadian bacon, smoked sausage, pork loins, hocks, turkey parts and ham, pepperoni, bratwurst, kielbasa, chorizos, egg and muffin sandwiches, fresh link sausage and freshboneless pork loins and ten
National Sales Manager: Bruce Schroeder
Estimated Sales: $2.5-5 Million
Number Employees: 20-49
Sq. footage: 21000
Type of Packaging: Consumer, Food Service, Private Label, Bulk

3154 **Country Village Meats**
401 N Pennsylvania St
Sublette, IL 61367 815-849-5532
Processor of beef, pork, lamb, veal, sausage, hot dogs, etc.; slaughtering services available
Owner: Edward Morrissey
Co-Owner: Edward Morrissey
Estimated Sales: $1-2.5 Million
Number Employees: 1-4
Type of Packaging: Consumer, Bulk

3155 **Counts Sausage Company**
222 Church St
Prosperity, SC 29127 803-364-2392
Fax: 803-364-1570
Processor and wholesaler/distributor of pork and beef products; serving the food service market
President: Jimmy Counts
VP: Larry Graham
Estimated Sales: $20-50 Million
Number Employees: 20-49
Type of Packaging: Consumer, Food Service, Bulk

3156 **County Gourmet Foods, LLC**
751 Chestnut Road
Sewickley, PA 15143-1143 412-741-8902
Fax: 412-741-9176 www.wolfganpucksoup.com
Gourmet foods
Quality Control: Thomas MacMurray, Ph.D.

3157 **Coupla Guys Foods**
401 N Racine Ave
Chicago, IL 60642 312-829-2332
Fax: 312-829-8866 ute@couplaguys.com
www.couplaguys.com
Manufacturer of pasta sauces including: sesame; arrabiata; puttanesca; tapenade; buoy base; marinara; and creme de la crimini sauce.
General Manager: Joe Rowley
Sales Manager: Ute Rowley
Sales Representative: Rob Ryan
Type of Packaging: Food Service

3158 **Coutts Specialty Foods**
1190 Liberty Square Rd
Boxborough, MA 01719 978-263-2952
Fax: 978-263-2953 800-919-2952
csf@couttsspecialtyfoods.com
www.couttsspecialtyfoods.com

Mother's Prize - sweet red pepper, hot sweet red pepper, corn, picclilli relishes, apple butter, and applesauce (with and with no sugar). No preservatives or fillers are added to any of our products. Mother's Pure Preserves - jamsjellies, and marmalades
President: Alison Coutts Chateawneuf
Estimated Sales: $ 3 - 5 Million
Number Employees: 2
Number of Brands: 2
Number of Products: 38
Type of Packaging: Consumer, Food Service
Brands:
MOTHER'S PRIZE
MOTHER'S PURE PRESERVES

3159 **Couture Farms**
P.O.Box 569
Kettleman City, CA 93239 559-945-2226
Fax: 559-945-2936 cfhuron@aol.com
Processor and importer of asparagus, pistachios and mixed melons
Co-Partner: Steve Couture
Co-Partner: Christina Couture
Estimated Sales: $50-100 Million
Number Employees: 20-49
Sq. footage: 30000
Type of Packaging: Consumer, Food Service, Private Label, Bulk

3160 **Couture's Maple Shop**
560 Vt Route 100
Westfield, VT 05874 802-744-2733
Fax: 802-744-6275 800-845-2733
jcouture@together.net
www.maplesyrupvermont.com
Maple syrup and candy
Co-Owner: Jacques Couture
Co-Owner: Pauline Couture
Estimated Sales: $ 1 - 3 Million
Number Employees: 1-4

3161 **Covered Bridge Potato Chip Company**
35 Alwright Ct
Waterville, NB E7P 0A5 506-375-2447
Fax: 506-375-2448
info@coveredbridgechips.com
www.coveredbridgechips.com
Old fashioned kettle style potato chips
Marketing Manager/Customer Relations: Krysten Scott
Production: Mike McCartney
Estimated Sales: $2 Million
Number Employees: 14

3162 **Cow Girl Creamery**
P.O.Box 594
Point Reyes Sta, CA 94956-0594 415-663-8153
Fax: 415-663-5418 www.cowgirlcreamery.com
Manufacturers of cheese.
President: Sue Conley
Estimated Sales: $500,000-$1 Million
Number Employees: 20-49
Type of Packaging: Private Label
Brands:
COWGIRL CREAMERY

3163 **Cow Palace Too**
1631 N Liberty Rd
Granger, WA 98932-9713 509-829-5777
Fax: 509-829-5495 cowpal@dolsenco.com
Processor of milk
Manager: Jeff Boivin
Estimated Sales: $20-50 Million
Number Employees: 50-99
Type of Packaging: Consumer, Food Service
Brands:
Dairy Gold

3164 **Cowart Seafood Corporation**
755 Lake Landing Dr
Lottsburg, VA 22511 804-529-6101
Fax: 804-529-7374
Manufacturer of seafood including fresh, frozen, and breaded oysters, frozen softshell crabs, and canned herring roe
President: Samuel Cowart
VP: Lake Cowart Jr
Estimated Sales: $10-20 Million
Number Employees: 50-99
Sq. footage: 10000
Type of Packaging: Food Service, Private Label
Brands:
CHESAPEAKE PRIDE
MANNINGS
SEA MIST

3165 **Cowboy Caviar**
169 Fairlawn Dr
Berkeley, CA 94708 510-841-0635
Fax: 510-594-8058 877-509-1796
cowboycaviar@earthlink.net
Processor of spreads and chunky marinara sauces
President: Gary Forbes
Estimated Sales: $1-2.5 Million
Number Employees: 1-4
Type of Packaging: Private Label

3166 **Cowboy Foods**
770 Canyon View Road
Bozeman, MT 59715-1610
US 406-587-5489
Fax: 406-522-9337 800-759-5489
hucklebuddy@hotmail.com
www.westernfoodtrails.com
Processor of natural barley without hulls; also, barbecue and bean sauces, bean soups, pancake, bread and baking mixes, flours, cereals and whole grains canning fruits and vegies,prepares flour,grain, and mill products.
Co-Ownert/President: Jean Clem
Co-Owner: Bud Clem
Estimated Sales: $ 1 - 3 Million
Number Employees: 2
Number of Products: 30
Sq. footage: 2800
Type of Packaging: Consumer, Food Service, Bulk
Brands:
Cowboy Foods

3167 **Cowgirl Chocolates**
824 Ford St
Moscow, ID 83843 208-882-4098
Fax: 208-882-0265 888-882-4098
cowgirl@moscow.com
www.cowgirlchocolates.com
Manufacturers of chocolate candies.
Manager: Marilyn Coates
Estimated Sales: $ .5 - 1 million
Number Employees: 5-9
Brands:
COWGIRL CHOCOLATES

3168 **Cowie Wine Cellars**
101 N Carbon City Rd
Paris, AR 72855-4630 479-963-3990
Fax: 479-963-3990
bettekay@cowiewinecellars.com
www.cowiewinecellars.com
Wines
President: Robert Cowie
Sales Room Manager: Katie Cowie
Estimated Sales: Less than $50,000
Number Employees: 1-4
Brands:
COWIE

3169 **Cozy Harbor Seafood**
P.O.Box 389
Portland, ME 04112-0389 207-879-2665
Fax: 207-879-2666 800-225-2586
jnorton@cozyharbor.com www.cozyharbor.com
Buys, processes and distributes premium quality seafood products
President/CEO: John Norton
Operations VP: Joseph Donovan Norton
Estimated Sales: $ .5 - 1 million
Number Employees: 100-249
Type of Packaging: Consumer, Food Service, Bulk

3170 **Cr. Manufacturing**
10240 Deer Park Rd
Waverly, NE 68462 402-786-2000
Fax: 402-786-2096 877-789-5844
info@crmfg.com www.crmfg.com
Manufacturer of plastic supplies and smallwares to the food service, food prep, bakery, restaurant, scoop and scoop accessories, specialty items, pourers and pourer accessories, bar supply and bar accessories markets
VP Operations: Daryl Chapelle
Marketing/Sales: Sheila Camprecht
Plant Manager: Bob Cooper
Estimated Sales: $20 Million
Number Employees: 100-249
Number of Brands: 27
Number of Products: 29
Sq. footage: 120000
Parent Co: PMC Group Companies
Type of Packaging: Food Service, Private Label, Bulk
Brands:
3-Cup Measurer
Betterway Pourers
CR Scoops
CR food baskets
Cake Comb
Crystal shooter tubes
Drip catchers
Econo pourer
Exacto-Pour tester
Ezy-Way pourer
Jigg-All
Jumbo Straws
Kover All dust cap
Lid-Off Pail Opener
Magic-Mesh
Marga-Ezy
Pizza slicer
Polar pitcher
Posi-Pour 2000 pourer
Posi-Pour pourer
Pour Mor
Pro-Flo pourer
Roxi rimming supplies
Roxi sugar and salt spices/flavors
Shakers prepackaged accessories
Shotskies gelatin mixes
Steakmarkers
Super Slicer
Whisky gate pourer

3171 **Crab Quarters**
2909 Eastern Blvd
Baltimore, MD 21220 410-686-2222
Fax: 410-686-0343
President: James Myrick
Estimated Sales: $ 1 - 3 Million
Number Employees: 20-49

3172 **Craby's Fish Market**
303 S Black Horse Pike
Blackwood, NJ 08012-2893 856-227-9743
Seafood
Manager: Stephen Palo
Estimated Sales: Less than $500,000
Number Employees: 1-4

3173 **Crain Ranch**
10660 Bryne Ave
Los Molinos, CA 96055 530-527-1077
Fax: 530-529-4143 crainranch@snowcrest.net
www.crainranch.com
Processor, grower and exporter of walnuts in the shell. Also packs for domestic markets
Partner: C Crain
Partner: W Crain
Estimated Sales: $300,000-500,000
Number Employees: 20-49
Sq. footage: 80000
Type of Packaging: Consumer, Private Label, Bulk
Brands:
Crain Ranch

3174 **Cranberry Isles Fisherman's Cooperative**
P.O.Box 258
Islesford, ME 04646 207-244-5438
Fax: 207-244-9479
Manager: Mark Neighman
Estimated Sales: $ .5 - 1 million
Number Employees: 1-4

3175 **Cranberry Sweets Company**
1005 Newmark Ave
Coos Bay, OR 97420 541-888-9824
Fax: 541-888-2824 cranberrysweets@att.net
www.cranberrysweetsandmore.com
Manufacturers of cranberries, jellies and candies.
Owner: Clayton Shaw
Estimated Sales: $1-2.5 Million
Number Employees: 20-49
Brands:
CRANBERRY SWEETS
OREGON BERRIES
SWEET BASICS

3176 **Crane & Crane**
P.O.Box 277
Brewster, WA 98812 509-689-3447
Fax: 509-689-2214 www.cranefamilyorchards.com
Grower and exporter of apples and pears
President: Bob Brammer
CFO/President: Bob Brammer
Secretary: Sam McKee
Estimated Sales: $100+ Million
Number Employees: 250-499
Type of Packaging: Consumer, Food Service, Private Label, Bulk
Brands:
Crane's Aqua Line
Crane's Blue Line
Crane's Gray Line
Crane's Maroon Line
Crane's Red Line

3177 **Crane's Pie Pantry Restaurant**
6054 124th Ave
Fennville, MI 49408-9440 269-561-2297
Fax: 269-561-5545 pies@cranespiepantry.com
www.cranespiepantry.com
Pies
Owner: Beckey Crane-Hagger
Owner: Lue Crane
Co-Owner: Lue Crane
Winemaker: Rob Crane
Estimated Sales: $500,000-$1 Million
Number Employees: 20-49

3178 **Crater Meat Packing Company**
2813 Biddle Rd
Medford, OR 97504 541-772-6966
Processor of meat products
Owner: James Cearley
Estimated Sales: Less than $100,000
Number Employees: 1-4
Type of Packaging: Consumer
Brands:
Crater's Meats

3179 **Crave Natural Foods**
104 Main St
Northampton, MA 01060-3160 413-587-7999
comments@craveorganic.com
www.craveorganic.com
Processor of nondairy whipped cream, dressings, ice cream and cheese sauce
Owner: Sally A Conway
Number Employees: 1-4
Sq. footage: 400
Type of Packaging: Consumer

3180 **Craven Crab Company**
PO Box 3321
New Bern, NC 28564-3321 252-637-3562
Fax: 252-637-3562
Crab
President: Gaston Fulcher
Brands:
Craven Crab

3181 **Crawford Sausage Company**
2310 S Pulaski Rd
Chicago, IL 60623 773-277-3095
Fax: 773-277-7749 866-653-2479
csjudy@crawfordsausage.com
www.crawfordsausage.com
Bratwursts, frankfurters, polish sausage, other linked sausage, slicing lunchmeats, fresh sausages, smoked meats and gift boxes.
President: Donald Kepka
Office Manager: Judy Zicha
Estimated Sales: $5-10 Million
Number Employees: 20-49
Type of Packaging: Consumer, Food Service, Bulk
Brands:
Daisy Brand Meat Products

3182 **Crazy Jerry's**
P.O.Box 891
Roswell, GA 30077-0891 770-993-0651
Fax: 770-993-8201 info@crazyjerrysinc.com
www.crazyjerrysinc.com
Processor of sauces, can mixed nuts, garlic mushrooms, maters in spicy vermouth, stuffed olives, can beef stew, soup mix and gumbo mix
President: Jerry Gualtieri
Estimated Sales: $1 Million
Number Employees: 1-4
Type of Packaging: Private Label
Brands:
Crazy Jerry's

3183 **Crazy Mary's**
321 138th Street S
Tacoma, WA 98444-4749 253-536-8690
bozenverry@aol.com
www.flavor2die4.com

3184 **CreAgri**
25565 Whitesell St
Hayward, CA 94545 510-732-6478
Fax: 510-732-6493 info@supremooil.com
www.creagri.com
Extra virgin olive oil
Founder/Chairman: Roberto Crea
Estimated Sales: $1 Million
Number Employees: 5-9
Type of Packaging: Consumer, Food Service, Bulk
Brands:
Integrale
Supremo

3185 **CreaFill Fibers Corporation**
10200 Worton Rd
Chestertown, MD 21620 410-810-0779
Fax: 410-810-0793 800-832-4662
www.creafill.com
Processor and exporter of powdered cellulose and pure vegetable fibers
President: Paolo Fezzi
Sales Associate: Sara Emgland
Estimated Sales: $5.5 Million
Number Employees: 29
Type of Packaging: Bulk
Brands:
QC FIBERS
SC FIBERS

3186 **Cream O'Weaver Dairy**
4282 W 1730 S
Salt Lake City, UT 84104-4805 801-973-9922
Fax: 801-977-5073 www.creamoweber.com
Processor of buttermilk and milk including whole, 1% and 2%; wholesaler/distributor of cottage cheese, yogurt, ice cream and butter
Marketing: Dave Gardner
Plant Manager: Walt Kohl
Estimated Sales: $50-99.9 Million
Number Employees: 100-249
Parent Co: Dean Foods Company
Type of Packaging: Consumer, Food Service

3187 **Cream of the West**
P.O.Box 2909
Harlowton, MT 59036 800-477-2383
800-477-2383
cotw@mtintouch.net www.creamofthewest.com
Company products line includes cereals, pancake mixes, jams and jellies, honey, coffee and gift baskets.
Manager: Freida Robertson
Estimated Sales: $1-2.5 Million
Number Employees: 1-4
Sq. footage: 6000
Type of Packaging: Consumer, Food Service, Bulk
Brands:
CREAM OF THE WEST

3188 **Creamland Dairies**
P.O.Box 25067
Albuquerque, NM 87125 505-247-0721
Fax: 505-246-9696
connie_holdren@deanfoods.com
www.creamland.com
Manufacturer of dairy products including ice cream, milk, cultured, cottage cheese, sour cream and dips.
CEO: Howard Miller
Public Relations: Connie Holdren
Number Employees: 20-49
Parent Co: Dean Foods Company
Type of Packaging: Consumer
Brands:
CREAMLAND
DEAN'S

3189 **Creative Confections**
945 Bermuda Dunes Pl
Northbrook, IL 60062-3125 608-455-1448
alicia@creativeconfections.net
www.creativeconfections.net
Processor of gourmet candy including chocolate and English toffee
President: Alicia Russell
Estimated Sales: $ 1 - 3 Million
Number Employees: 5-9
Type of Packaging: Consumer
Brands:
Creative Confections

3190 **Creative Flavors**
P.O.Box 23307
Chagrin Falls, OH 44023-0307 440-543-9881
Fax: 440-543-8707 800-848-9043
info@creativeflavorsinc.com
www.creativeflavorsinc.com
Flavors and ingredients for the dairy industry including cherries, flavors and core powders for novelty bars and sour cream dip bases
President: Michael Ramsey
Public Relations: Cindy Ramsey
Estimated Sales: $2.5-5 Million
Number Employees: 5-9

3191 **Creative Flavors & Specialties LLP**
991 E Linden Ave
Linden, NJ 7036 908-862-4678
Fax: 908-862-7458 creativeflavors@aol.com
Manufacturer of flavors for coffee, candy, fruit drinks, bagels, ice cream, ice tea, coffee syrups, snack seasonings, spices and much more. We also customize any flavors, spray drieds and blending
President: Esther Baita
CEO: Mike DiPierro
VP: Danielle Lau
Quality Control: Esther Baita
Production: Fredy Lau
Plant Manager: Fredy Lau
Estimated Sales: $100,000
Number Employees: 5
Number of Products: 5000
Sq. footage: 5000
Type of Packaging: Bulk

3192 **Creative Foods**
P.O.Box 368
Osceola, AR 72370 870-563-2601
Fax: 870-563-3824 800-643-0006
manderson@creativefoodsllc.com
www.creativefoodsllc.com
Margarine, cheese, salsa
President: Mart Massey
CFO: Jason Collard
Executive VP: Mike Anderson
Executive VP: Mike Anderson
VP Sales: Mike Anderson
Estimated Sales: $100+ Million
Number Employees: 100-249
Brands:
Creative Foods

3193 **Creative Foodworks**
1011 S Acme Rd
San Antonio, TX 78237-3218 210-212-4761
Fax: 210-212-4919
Manufacturer of private label condiments
President: Dorothea Garcia
CEO: Roqke Garcia, Jr.
Quality Control: Michael Billings
Operations Manager: Emilio Herrera
Plant Manager: Norman Diggec
Purchasing Manager: Chris Boynton
Estimated Sales: $5-10 Million
Number Employees: 10-19
Type of Packaging: Consumer, Food Service, Private Label, Bulk

3194 **Creative Seasonings**
34 Audubon Road
Wakefield, MA 01880-1203 617-246-1461
Fax: 617-246-5381 www.conagrafoods.com
Seasonings
President/CEO: Greg Heckman
CEO: Gary Rodkin

3195 **Creative Spices**
33436 Western Avenue
Union City, CA 94587-3202 510-471-4956
Fax: 510-471-9174
Bread and bakery products
President: Carmella Hagman
Treasurer: Virginia Holmes
VP: Donna Hagman
Estimated Sales: $10-24.9 Million
Number Employees: 20-49
Brands:
Creative Spices

3196 **Creekside Mushrooms**
1 Moonlight Dr
Worthington, PA 16262 724-297-5491
Fax: 724-297-5101
mailbox@creeksidemushrooms.com
www.creeksidemushrooms.com
Manufacturer of fresh mushrooms
President/Ceo: Roger Claypoole
VP Finance: Russell Hogue
VP: Bill Swanik
Estimated Sales: $99 Million
Number Employees: 500-999
Sq. footage: 375000
Type of Packaging: Consumer, Food Service, Private Label, Bulk
Brands:
MOONLIGHT MUSHROOMS

3197 **Creemore Springs Brewery**
139 Mill St
Creemore, ON L0M 1G0
Canada 705-466-2240
Fax: 705-466-3306 800-267-2240
thefolks@creemoresprings.com
www.creemoresprings.com
Processor of lager beer
President/CEO: Jason Moore
Estimated Sales: $6.9 Million
Number Employees: 90
Type of Packaging: Consumer, Food Service
Brands:
Creemore Springs Premium Lager
Creemore Springs Urbock

3198 **Creighton Brothers**
P.O.Box 220
Atwood, IN 46502 574-267-3101
Fax: 574-267-6446
info@creightonbrothersllc.com
www.creightonbrothersllc.com
Processor of fresh, frozen and hard cooked eggs
President: Ron Pruex
Quality Assurance: Tad Borchers
Sales Manager: Brian Hayward
Public Relations: Mindy Creighton
Plant Manager: Bill Kelly
Estimated Sales: $20,800,000
Number Employees: 10-19
Type of Packaging: Consumer, Food Service, Private Label, Bulk
Brands:
Good News Eggs
Grandpa's Choice

3199 **Creme Curls Bakery**
5292 Lawndale Ave
PO Box 276
Hudsonville, MI 49426 616-669-6230
Fax: 616-669-2468 800-466-1219
www.cremecurls.com
Processor of creme horns, eclairs and cream puffs, strudel and turnovers, and pie dough
President: A Bierling
CFO: Lee Deboer
Marketing Director: Gerald Veldkamp
VP Sales: Michael Burkett
President/Purchasing Agent: Gary Bierling
Estimated Sales: $11.7 Million
Number Employees: 140
Sq. footage: 66000
Type of Packaging: Consumer, Food Service, Private Label, Bulk
Brands:
Creme Curls

3200 **Creme D'Lite**
2366 Hill N Dale Dr
Irving, TX 75038-5619 972-255-7255
Processor of a frozen nondairy cream beverage
President: Don Allen
Estimated Sales: $99,000
Number Employees: 2
Sq. footage: 2500
Type of Packaging: Consumer, Food Service, Private Label, Bulk
Brands:
Creme D'Lite
Tropic D'Lite

3201 **(HQ)Creme Glacee Gelati**
8390 Le Creusot
Montreal, QC H1P 2A6
Canada 514-322-0111
Fax: 514-322-0250 888-322-0116
domenic@italgelati.com www.italgelati.com
Processor and exporter of kosher frozen desserts including gelato, sherbet, spumoni, ice cream cakes, cassata, granita and tartufo.
Estimated Sales: $1-3 Million
Number Employees: 20-49
Sq. footage: 13000
Type of Packaging: Consumer, Food Service, Private Label
Other Locations:
Creme Glacee Ital Gelati
Plattsburg NY
Brands:
ITAL GELATI
ITALIAN GELATO NOVELTIES
LA BELLA ITALIANA
TARTUFO

3202 **Cremer North America**
3202 Francis Hughes
Laval, QC H7L 5A7
Canada 450-629-2229
Fax: 450-629-4666 sales.na@cremer.com
www.cremer.com
President: Fred Cremer
Marketing: Dennis Hebert
CEO: Fred Cremer
Brands:
Cremer Cunter

3203 **Cremes Unlimited**
600 Holiday Plaza Dr Ste 520
Matteson, IL 60443 708-748-1336
Fax: 708-748-4985 800-227-3637
Non-dairy whipped toppings and icings
Manager: John Evans
Estimated Sales: $10-20 Million
Number Employees: 5-9
Brands:
Cremes

3204 **Creminelli Fine Meats, LLC**
310 Wright Brothers Drive
Salt Lake City, UT 84116 801-428-1820
Fax: 202-478-0434 scott@creminelli.com
www.creminelli.com
Organic/natural, cured meats i.e. prociutto/bacon, other meat/game/pate.

3205 **Creole Delicacies Pralines**
533 Saint Ann St
New Orleans, LA 70116-3318 504-523-6425
Fax: 504-288-0042 info@cookincajun.com
Manufacturer of pralines
President: Lisette Verlander
Estimated Sales: $2.5-5 Million
Number Employees: 28
Type of Packaging: Consumer
Brands:
Cookin' Cajun
Creole Delicacies

3206 **Creole Fermentation Industries**
7331 Ben Frederick Rd
Abbeville, LA 70510 337-898-9377
Fax: 337-898-9376
Processor of vinegar including white distilled; manufacturer of vinegar production equipment
President: Albert Steen
General Manager: Bill Tribados III
Plant Manager: Bill Tribaldos
Estimated Sales: $5-10 Million
Number Employees: 5-9
Type of Packaging: Bulk

3207 **Crepinicafe.Com**
101 Castleton Street
Pleasantville, NY 10570 914-533-6645
Fax: 914-206-4848 paula@crepinicafe.com
www.crepinicafe.com
Organic crepes
Production Manager: Mike McCartney
Estimated Sales: A
Number Employees: 1-4

3208 **Crescent City Crab Corporation**
PO Box 2668
New Orleans, LA 70176-2668 504-646-6645
Fax: 504-649-5064
Crabs
President: Gary Bauer

3209 **Crescent City Seafoods**
55 Holomua St
Hilo, HI 96720-5142 808-961-0877
Fax: 808-935-1603 www.hilofish.com
Seafood
President: Charles Umamoto
Estimated Sales: $ 20 - 50 Million
Number Employees: 20-49

3210 **Crescent Duck Farm**
10 Edagr Ave
Aquebogue, NY 11931 631-722-8700
Fax: 631-722-5324
Processor and exporter of frozen whole ducklings and parts
CEO/President/Vp: Douglas Corwin
Plant Manager: Arnold Tilton
Estimated Sales: $ 7 Million
Number Employees: 50-99
Type of Packaging: Consumer, Food Service
Brands:
Crescent
Peconic Bay
White Pekin

3211 **Crescent Ridge Dairy**
355 Bay Rd
Sharon, MA 02067 781-784-2740
Fax: 781-784-8446 800-660-2740
info@crescentridge.com www.crescentridge.com
Fluid milk
President: Mark Parrish
VP: Jim Carroll
Estimated Sales: $2.5-5 Million
Number Employees: 50-99
Type of Packaging: Private Label
Brands:
Crescent Ridge Dairy

3212 **Crescini Wines**
PO Box 216
Soquel, CA 95073-0216 831-462-1466
Wines
President: Richard Crescini
Co-Owner: Paula Crescini
Estimated Sales: $1-2.5 Million
Number Employees: 5-9
Sq. footage: 3
Type of Packaging: Private Label

3213 **Crest Foods Company**
502 Brown St
Ashton, IL 61006 815-453-7411
Fax: 815-453-2646 800-435-6972
www.crestfoods.com
Processor of food ingredients including emulsifying agents, proteins, caseinates, whey, stabilizers and flavors for dips, bases and seasonings; contract packaging available
President: Jeff Meiners
CEO: Shirley Reif
VP Quality Assurance: Marty Barclay
VP Corporate Sales: Steven Meiners
VP Manufacturing: Mike Meiners
Estimated Sales: $20-50 Million
Number Employees: 250-499
Type of Packaging: Consumer, Food Service, Private Label

3214 **Crest International Corporation**
P.O.Box 83309
San Diego, CA 92138-3309 619-296-4300
Fax: 619-296-3624 800-548-1232
service@crestinternational.net
www.crestinternational.com
Fresh or frozen fish and seafoods, fresh and frozen packaged seafood
Owner/President: Stephen Willis
Corporate Secretary: Lourdes Garber
Estimated Sales: $2 Million
Number Employees: 10
Type of Packaging: Food Service, Bulk

3215 **Crestar Crusts**
1104 Clinton Ave
Washington Ct Hs, OH 43160 740-335-4813
Fax: 740-335-3908 www.richelieufoods.com

Frozen pizza crusts
CFO: Mike Lauren
Controller: Dan Walsh
Manager: Roger Shackleford
Sales: Don Farrow
Plant Manager: Jason Yoakum
Estimated Sales: $20-50 Million
Number Employees: 400

3216 **Crestmont Enterprises**
1420 Crestmont Ave
Camden, NJ 8103 856-966-0700
Fax: 856-966-6137
Processor of flavors and extracts
President: Amy Baskin
VP: Joseph Shediack, Jr.
VP: Annette Rapaport
Estimated Sales: $ 5 - 10 Million
Number Employees: 10-19

3217 **Creuzebergers Meats**
3001 6th Avenue
Duncansville, PA 16635 814-695-3061
Meat processing
Owner: Sieglinde Creuzberger
Estimated Sales: Less than $500,000
Number Employees: 1-4

3218 **Crevettes Du Nord**
Cp 6380
Gaspe, QC G4X 2R8
Canada 418-368-1414
Fax: 418-368-1812 gesco@globetrotter.qc.ca
Processor and exporter of fresh and frozen shrimp
President: Gaetan Denis
Manager: Amedee La Pierre
Number Employees: 50-99
Type of Packaging: Bulk

3219 **Cribari Vineyards**
4180 W Alamos Ave Ste 108
Fresno, CA 93722 559-277-9000
Fax: 559-277-2420 800-277-9095
bulk@cribari.net www.cviwines.com

Processor and exporter of high quality California bulk wine

Presidnt/CEO/CFO: John Cribari
Sales: Ben Cribari
Estimated Sales: $730,000
Number Employees: 9
Number of Brands: 7
Type of Packaging: Bulk
Brands:
CVI BULK WINES

3220 **Crickle Company**
90 Genesis Pkwy
Thomasville, GA 31792 229-225-1902
Fax: 229-225-2116 800-237-8689
www.crickle.com
Brittle and popcorn
President/Owner: Harry Jones
VP: Jerry Hunter
Number Employees: 12

3221 **Cricklewood Soyfoods**
250 Sally Ann Furnace Road
Mertztown, PA 19539-9036 610-682-4109
Fax: 717-484-4789 cricklewood@aol.com
Processor of kosher vegetarian soy-based foods including burgers and low-fat three bean, organic soy and three grain tempeh, organic and GMO free foods
President: Renate Krummenoehl
Estimated Sales: $380,000
Number Employees: 4
Number of Products: 5
Sq. footage: 600
Type of Packaging: Consumer, Food Service, Bulk
Brands:
Cricklewood Soyfoods
Cricklewood Soyfoods

3222 **Criders Poultry**
1 Plant Avenue
Stillmore, GA 30464-0398 912-562-4435
Fax: 912-562-4168 800-342-3851
cpcorp@cridercorp.com www.cridercorp.com
Processor and exporter of fresh, frozen, canned and further processed chicken
Owner/CEO: William Crider Jr
CFO: Max Harrell
CEO: William A Crider
Research & Development: Phil Hudspeth
Quality Control: Stan Wallen
Operations: Lee Thompkins
Plant Manager: Kenneth Houghton
Purchasing: Ritchie Young
Estimated Sales: $ 20 - 50 Million
Number Employees: 400
Type of Packaging: Food Service, Private Label, Bulk
Brands:
CRIDER

3223 **Crillon Importers**
80 E State Rt 4 Ste 108
Paramus, NJ 7652 201-368-8878
Fax: 201-368-4450
support@crillonimporters.com
www.crillonimporters.com
Wines and liquors
Owner: Michel Roux
CEO: Michael Roux
Estimated Sales: $ 10 - 20 Million
Number Employees: 10-19
Brands:
ABSENTE
AGAVERO
AQUAVITS
DOUCE PROVENCE
ELISIR MP ROUX
HB PASTIS
MAGELLIN GIN
RHUM BARBANCOURT
RINQUINQUIN
TALAPA MEZCAL
UNICUM ZWACK

3224 **Crispy Bagel Company**
230 N Franklintown Rd
Baltimore, MD 21223 410-566-4102
Fax: 410-945-8783 800-522-7655
Processor of fresh and frozen bagels
President: John Paterakis
Estimated Sales: $6 Million
Number Employees: 79
Brands:
Crispy Bagel

3225 **Crispy Green Inc.**
144 Fairfield Rd
Fairfield, NJ 07004 973-679-4515
Fax: 973-755-0358 info@crispygreen.com
www.crispygreen.com
Freeze-dried fruits, including all natural and 100-calorie
President: Angela Liu
Estimated Sales: $680,000
Number Employees: 7

3226 **Cristom Vineyards**
6905 Spring Valley Rd NW
Salem, OR 97304 503-375-3068
Fax: 503-391-7057 www.cristomwines.com
Wines
Co-Owner: Paul Gerrie
Co-Owner: Eileen Gerrie
Estimated Sales: $2.5-5 Million
Number Employees: 10-19
Type of Packaging: Private Label

3227 **Critchfield Meats**
2285 Danforth Dr
Lexington, KY 40511-1087 859-255-6021
Fax: 859-281-1129 800-866-3287
orders@critchfieldmeats.com
www.critchfieldmeats.com
Meats
Owner: Larry Mc Millan
Secretary/Treasurer: Mike Critchfield
Estimated Sales: $ 50 - 100 Million
Number Employees: 20-49
Brands:
Critchfield Meats

3228 **Critelli Olive Oil**
2445 South Watney Way
Fairfield, CA 94533-6721 707-426-3400
Fax: 707-265-6827 800-865-4836
info@critelli.com www.critelli.com
Organic extra virgin olive oils and oils crushed with lemons or fresh garlic
Director Food Service: Mike Brossier Mike Brossier
President: Serafino Bianchi
Brands:
Critelli

3229 **Criterion Chocolates**
125 Lewis St
Eatontown, NJ 7724 732-542-7847
Fax: 732-542-0045 800-804-6060
criterion@criterionchocolates.com
www.criterionchocolates.com
Chocolates
President: George Karagias
VP: James Samaras
Marketing Director: Ron Boyadjian
Estimated Sales: $5-10 Million
Number Employees: 20-49
Brands:
Criterion

3230 **Criveller Group**
6935 Oakwood Drive
Niagara Falls, ON L2E 6S5
Canada 905-357-2930
Fax: 905-374-2930 888-849-2266
info@criveller.com www.criveller.com
Processor of ale and lager
President: Bruce McCubbin
Marketing Director: Matt Johnson
Manager: Barbara Criveller
Number Employees: 20-49
Sq. footage: 6000
Type of Packaging: Consumer, Food Service
Brands:
Eisbock
Gritstone
Honey Brown
Millstone
Niagara
Paleao

3231 **Crocetti Oakdale Packing**
378 Pleasant St
East Bridgewater, MA 02333-1349 508-587-0035
Fax: 508-587-8758
Packer of hamburger meat and sausage
President: Carl Crocetti
Marketing Director: Carl Crocetti
CFO: Carl Crocetti
Estimated Sales: $5-10 Million
Number Employees: 20-49
Type of Packaging: Consumer, Food Service, Bulk

3232 **Crockett-Stewart Honey Company**
1040 W Alameda Dr
Tempe, AZ 85282-3332 480-731-3936
Fax: 480-731-3938 bnipper@crocketthoney.com
www.crocketthoney.com
Processor and exporter of honey
President: Harold Nipper
Secretary: Linda Nipper
VP: Brian Nipper
Estimated Sales: $5-10 Million
Number Employees: 10-19
Sq. footage: 12000
Type of Packaging: Consumer, Food Service, Bulk
Brands:
Crockett's
Mrs. Crockett's

3233 **Croda**
300 Columbus Cir Ste A
Edison, NJ 8837 732-417-0800
Fax: 732-417-0804 www.croda.com
Super refined marine and plant oils, proteins, and peptides for nutraceuticals, functional foods and dietary supplements.
President: Kevin Gallagher
Marketing Head: Kavin Gallaghar

Estimated Sales: $20-50 Million
Number Employees: 20-49
Parent Co: Croda International P/C

3234 **Croft's Crackers**
504 14th Avenue
Monroe, WI 53566-1140 608-325-1223
Fax: 608-325-1289 crofts@mail.tds.net
Crackers, granola, cookies
President: John King
Public Relations: John or Kathy King
Estimated Sales: $500,000-$1 Million
Number Employees: 1-4

3235 **Crofton & Sons**
P.O.Box 698
Brandon, FL 33509 813-685-7745
Fax: 813-689-4535 800-878-7675
Processor of beef and pork smoked sausage, Italian sausage and smoked turkey links; also, full line of smoked meats
President/CEO: Kevin Crofton
Co-Owner: Noble Crofton
Estimated Sales: $8 Million
Number Employees: 20-49
Sq. footage: 40000
Type of Packaging: Consumer, Food Service, Private Label, Bulk
Brands:
Bean Brothers
Smokehouse Favorite
Uncle John's Pride

3236 **(HQ)Crompton Corporation**
1 American Ln
Greenwich, CT 06831-2560 203-552-2000
Fax: 203-552-2010 800-295-2392
www.cromptoncorp.com
Processor of chemical ingredients and food additives
CEO and President: Robert Wood
CEO: Robert Wood
CFO: Stephen Forsyth
Vice President: Stephen Forsyth
Global Market Manager: Bob Ruckle
Sales Director: Rick Beitel
Number Employees: 20-49
Other Locations:

3237 **Cronin Vineyards**
11 Old La Honda Road
Woodside, CA 94062-2604 650-851-1452
Fax: 650-851-5696
www.travelenvoy.com/wine/SantaCruz/Cronin-Vineyard
Wines
Prorietor: Duane Cronin
VP: Mora Cronin
Estimated Sales: $300,000
Number Employees: 1-4
Type of Packaging: Consumer
Brands:
Cizonin Vineyards
Portola Hills

3238 **Crooked River Brewing Company**
1101 Center St
Cleveland, OH 44113-2405 216-771-2337
Fax: 216-771-7990
Processor of beer, ale, stout, lager and porter
Owner: Stephen Danckers
CO-Owner: Stuart Sheridan Stuart Sheridan
General Manager: Stuart Sheridan
Estimated Sales: $5-9.9 Million
Number Employees: 10-19
Type of Packaging: Consumer, Food Service, Bulk
Brands:
Cool Mule
Crooked River Brewing
Lighthouse Gold

3239 **Crookes & Hanson**
PO Box 46033
Bedford, OH 44146-0033 216-426-1111
Fax: 216-426-1120 800-999-0263
Processor and exporter of English shortbread
President: Miles Small
Sales Manager: Jay Tener
Type of Packaging: Consumer, Food Service, Private Label, Bulk
Brands:
Crookes & Hanson

3240 **Crookston Bean**
1600 S Main St
Crookston, MN 56716 218-281-2567
Fax: 218-281-2567
Processor and exporter of dried edible beans
Owner: Bob Seaver
Manager: Dave Seaver
Estimated Sales: $10-20 Million
Number Employees: 1-4
Type of Packaging: Private Label, Bulk

3241 **Cropp Cooperative-Organic Valley**
One Organic Way
La Farge, WI 54639-0159 888-444-6455
Fax: 608-625-3025 888-444-6455
organic@organicvalley.com
www.organicvalley.com
Organic dairy, eggs, meat, produce
Estimated Sales: $30 Million
Number Employees: 100-249
Type of Packaging: Private Label

3242 **Crosby Molasses Company**
PO Box 2240
St John, NB E2L 3V4
Canada 506-634-7515
Fax: 506-634-1724 feedback@crosbys.com
www.crosbys.com
Processor of molasses, drink crystals, table syrup, pancake mix and iced tea; importer and exporter of molasses
President: James Crosby
General Manager: Lorne Goodman
Estimated Sales: $7.8 Million
Number Employees: 60
Type of Packaging: Consumer, Food Service, Private Label, Bulk
Brands:
Crosby

3243 **Crossroad Farms Dairy**
400 S Shortridge Rd
Indianapolis, IN 46219 317-229-7600
Fax: 317-357-6719 www.kroger.com
Dairy products
General Manager: George coark
Marketing Manager: Ralph Strope
CEO: George Clark
Production Manager: Mike Hanisch
Estimated Sales: $100-499.9 Million
Number Employees: 250-499
Brands:
Crossroad

3244 **Crowley Beverage Corporation**
526 Boston Post Road
Wayland, MA 01778-1835 508-358-7177
Fax: 978-358-0057 800-997-3337
Soft drinks
President/CEO: Hill Crowley
Chairman: Edward Crowley
Marketing Director: Jill Crowley
Estimated Sales: $3 Million
Number Employees: 10-19
Brands:
Razcal

3245 **Crowley Cheese**
14 Crowley Ln
Mount Holly, VT 5758 802-259-2340
Fax: 802-259-2347 800-683-2606
sales@crowleycheese.com
www.crowleycheese.com
Processor of cheese including colby, sage, pepper, smoked, dill, garlic and caraway
Manager: Cindy Dawley
Principal: Jill Jones
President: Galen Jones
Estimated Sales: $730,000
Number Employees: 5-9
Type of Packaging: Consumer, Food Service, Private Label, Bulk
Brands:
Crowley

3246 **(HQ)Crowley Foods**
93 Pennsylvania Ave
Binghamton, NY 13903 607-779-3289
Fax: 607-779-3440 800-637-0019
linda.farley@crowleyfoods.com
www.crowleyfoods.com
Manufactures and distributes a full line of dairy products, refrigerated beverages, frozen desserts, and specialty products.
President/CEO: John Kaneb
VP/CFO: Gail Glover
Consumer Affairs: Linda Farley
Corporate Comunications: Lynne Bohan
Chief Operating Officer: Joseph Cervantes
Estimated Sales: $2 Billion
Number Employees: 1,660
Number of Brands: 6
Sq. footage: 12000
Parent Co: HP Hood LLC
Type of Packaging: Consumer, Food Service, Private Label, Bulk
Other Locations:
Crowley Foods
Albany NY
Binghamton NY
Hatfield PA
Philadelphia PA
Arkport NY
Bristol VA
LaFargeville NY
Sodus NY
Walcott NY
Brands:
AXELROD
CROWLEY
HELUVA GOOD
MAGGIO CHEESE
PENN MAID DAIRY
ROSENBERGER'S DAIRY

3247 **Crown Candy Corporation**
P.O.Box 6273
Macon, GA 31208-6273 478-781-4911
Fax: 478-781-5649 800-241-3529
info@crowncandy.com www.crowncandy.com
Processor and exporter of confectionery products including brittles, chocolate, coconut, peanut and pecan candies and fudge.
CEO: James Weatherford
Estimated Sales: $10-24.9 Million
Number Employees: 100-249
Type of Packaging: Consumer, Private Label, Bulk
Brands:
DELIGHTS
ROYAL RECIPE

3248 **Crown City Brewery**
2100 N Anzac Ave
Compton, CA 90222 626-577-5548
Fax: 626-577-1529
Brewer of beer
Manager: Mike Hansen
Estimated Sales: $1-2.5 Million
Number Employees: 20-49
Type of Packaging: Private Label
Brands:
ARROYO AMBER ALE
BLACK BEAR STOUT
BLACK CLOUD STOUT
DOO DAH PALE ALE
FATHERCHRISTMAS WASSAIL
GOLD LABEL
MASTER'S TOUCH
MOUNT WILSON
MOUNT WILSON WHEAT BEER
OOM PAH PAH OKTOBERFEST
YORKSHIRE PORTER

3249 **Crown Pacific Fine Foods**
8809 S 190th St
Kent, WA 98031 425-251-8750
Fax: 425-251-8802 contact@cpff.net
www.cpff.net
Specialty foods
President: Tony Ataee
Estimated Sales: $20-50 Million
Number Employees: 20-49

3250 **(HQ)Crown Packing Company**
P.O.Box 247
Salinas, CA 93902 831-424-2067
Fax: 831-424-7812
Grower and packer of lettuce, celery and cauliflower; exporter of lettuce and celery
President: Chris Bunn
Sales Manager: Rob Steitz
Sales: Tonya Tempalski
Estimated Sales: $ 3 - 5 Million
Number Employees: 5-9
Type of Packaging: Consumer, Food Service, Private Label, Bulk

Brands:
Bunny

3251 **Crown Point**
P.O.Box 309
St John, IN 46373-0309 219-365-3200
Fax: 219-365-1944
Processor and exporter of canned and frozen products including tomato paste, vegetables, nuts, juice concentrates, flexible packaging and spices.
President: Kevin Gates
Estimated Sales: $10-20 Million
Number Employees: 5-9
Parent Co: Unaka Corporation
Type of Packaging: Consumer, Food Service, Private Label, Bulk
Brands:
Crown Point

3252 **Crown Prince**
P.O.Box 3568
City of Industry, CA 91744-0568 626-912-3700
Fax: 626-854-0350 800-255-5063
webmaster@crownprince.com
www.crownprince.com
Processors and packers of specialty canned seafood.
President: Robert Hoffman
Marketing Manager: Denise Hines
Sales Director: Gary Gruettner
Estimated Sales: $ 20 - 50 Million
Number Employees: 50-99
Number of Products: 3
Type of Packaging: Consumer, Private Label
Brands:
CROWN PRINCE NATURAL
CROWN PRINCE SEAFOOD
OCEAN PRINCE SEAFOOD

3253 **Crown Prince Naturals**
940 Mountain View Ave
Petaluma, CA 94952-4837
Fax: 707-766-8582 cpnatural@earthlink.net
www.crownprince.com
Family owned, canned seafood importer in business since 1948. Anchovies, tuna, salmon, sardines, crab, mackerel, oysters and clams.
CEO: Dustan Hoffman
CFO: Chris Bruno
Quality Control: Colette Tauzin
Marketing Director: Denise Hines
Sales Director: Gary Gruettner
Operations Manager: Jeanie Stobaugh
Number Employees: 40
Number of Brands: 4
Number of Products: 125
Type of Packaging: Consumer, Private Label
Brands:
Crown Prince

3254 **Crown Processing Company**
PO Box 1
Bellflower, CA 90707-0001 562-865-0293
Processor, importer and exporter of citrus rinds including graded, sliced, cooked and canned
President: John Bowen
Estimated Sales: $5-10 Million
Number Employees: 20-49
Sq. footage: 27000
Type of Packaging: Food Service
Brands:
Crown

3255 **Crown Regal Wine Cellars**
586 Montgomery St
Brooklyn, NY 11225 718-604-1430
Fax: 718-384-1336 ywine@hotmail.com
Wine and grape juice
Owner: Joseph Baycount
Estimated Sales: $2.5-5 Million
Number Employees: 5-9

3256 **Crown Valley Food Service**
P.O.Box 2101
Beaumont, CA 92223-1001 951-769-8786
Fax: 951-769-8788
President: Sheldon Zaritsky
CEO: Mike Cavanaugh
Estimated Sales: $ 1 - 3 Million
Number Employees: 10-19

3257 **Crum Creek Mills**
700 Old Marple Road
Springfield, PA 19064-1236 413-581-3501
Fax: 413-581-3501 888-607-3500
rich@crumcreek.com www.crumcreek.com
Soy-based pastas, breadsticks and soy powders
President: Dr Ara Yeramyan

3258 **Crumbs Bake Shop**
110 W 40th Street
Suite 2100
New York, NY 10018
877-278-6270
info@crumbs.com www.crumbs.com
Cupcakes
President: Jason Bauer
Owner/VP: Mia Bauer

3259 **Cruse Vineyards**
2883 Lakeshore Dr
Chester, SC 29706 803-377-3944
Wines
Owner: Kenneth Cruse
Owner: susan Cruse
Estimated Sales: $1-4.9 Million
Number Employees: 1-4
Brands:
Cruse Vineyards
Red Vines

3260 **Crusoe Seafood LLC**
9500 El Dorado Avenue
Sun Valley, CA 91352-1339 866-343-7629
Fax: 818-768-2366 jcohen@sugarfoods.com
www.crusoeseafood.com
Seafood.

3261 **Crustacean Foods**
5369 W Pico Blvd
Los Angeles, CA 90019-4037 323-460-4387
Fax: 323-933-4863 866-263-2625
info@anfamily.com www.anfamily.com
Manufacturer of gourmet sauces.
Owner: Elizabeth An
Estimated Sales: $300,000-500,000
Number Employees: 5-9

3262 **Crustaces de la Malbaie**
PO Box 6380
Gaspe, QC G4X 2R8
Canada 418-368-1414
Fax: 418-368-1812 gesco@globetrotter.qc.ca
Processor of live lobster
President: Gaetan Denis
Number Employees: 50-99
Type of Packaging: Bulk

3263 **Crusty Bakery, Inc.**
60 Broad Street
Suite 3502
New York, NY 10004-2356 646-356-0460
Fax: 646-349-2240 cyrili@crustybakery.com
www.crustybakery.com
Baked goods.

3264 **Crystal & Vigor Beverages**
174 Sanford Ave
Kearny, NJ 07032-5920 201-991-2342
Fax: 201-991-1882
Alcoholic and non-alcoholic beverages
Owner: Martinho Oliveira
Estimated Sales: $2.5-5 Million
Number Employees: 10-19
Type of Packaging: Private Label

3265 **(HQ)Crystal Cream & Butter Company**
8340 Belvedere Ave
Sacramento, CA 95826 916-447-6455
Fax: 916-381-0187 www.crystal-milk.com
President: Don Hanson
CEO: Donald Hansen
Quality Control: Gina Dezzani
Marketing: Kevin Nagle
Sales & Distribution: David Walker
Public Relations: Kim Patterson
Estimated Sales: $160 Million
Number Employees: 500-999
Type of Packaging: Consumer, Food Service, Private Label, Bulk
Other Locations:
Crystal Cream & Butter Co.
Sacramento CA

Brands:
Crystal

3266 **Crystal Farms**
P.O.Box 7101
Chestnut Mtn, GA 30502 770-967-6152
Fax: 770-967-7248 scotthordon@bellfouth.net
www.crystalfarmsga.com
Processor of eggs
President: Jim Brock
CEO: Ben Lancaster
Marketing Manager: Ban lancaster
Sales Manager: Jackie Jones
Estimated Sales: $50-100 Million
Number Employees: 20-49

3267 **Crystal Foods**
P.O.Box 4009
Brick, NJ 8723 732-477-0073
Fax: 732-477-0073
Processor and exporter of dehydrated flavors and beverage bases
President: Peter Kewitt
VP: Wendy Kewitt
Estimated Sales: $5-10 Million
Number Employees: 5-9
Sq. footage: 10000
Type of Packaging: Food Service, Private Label, Bulk
Brands:
Sun Country

3268 **Crystal Geyser Roxanne LLC**
6300 Pensacola Blvd
Pensacola, FL 32505-1999 850-476-8844
Fax: 850-476-4341 www.saturn.com
Processor, bottler and exporter of beer, ale, lager, stout and seasonal; also, natural and sparkling bottled spring water
Manager: Stan Williams
VP/General Manager: Ken Janowitz
Executive VP: Mark Wiggins
Controller: Jack Mayer
Plant Manager: Jim Sullivan
Purchasing Manager: Frank Benham
Estimated Sales: $5-10 Million
Number Employees: 50-99
Sq. footage: 45000
Type of Packaging: Consumer, Food Service
Brands:
CASTLE SPRINGS

3269 **Crystal Geyser Water Company**
501 Washington St
Calistoga, CA 94515 707-942-0500
Fax: 707-942-0647 800-443-9737
cgwconsumers@crystalgeyse.com
www.crystalgeyser.com
Bottler of natural beverages including spring water, sparkling mineral water, teas and juices.
President: Peter Gordon
Chairman: Peter Gordon
Plant Manager: Carmen Maib
Estimated Sales: $5-10 Million
Number Employees: 50-99
Brands:
Juice Squeeze
Tejava

3270 **Crystal Geyser Water Company**
55 Francisco St Ste 410
San Francisco, CA 94133 415-616-9590
Fax: 415-616-9595
customerservice@crystalgeyserasw.com
www.crystalgeyserwater.com
Bottler of natural beverages including spring water, sparkling mineral water, java tea and juices.
Manager: Karen Kimen
Estimated Sales: $5-10 Million
Number Employees: 10-19

3271 **(HQ)Crystal Lake**
P.O.Box 248
Decatur, AR 72722-0248 479-752-5100
800-382-4425
www.petersonfarms.com
Processor and exporter of chicken
Manager: Daryl Hopkins
Sr Director, Commodity Sales: Bruce Bayley
VP Human Resources: Janet Wilkerson
Sr VP, Development: Dennis Martin
Estimated Sales: $500,000-$1 Million
Number Employees: 5-9

Type of Packaging: Food Service, Private Label, Bulk
Other Locations:
Crystal Lake
North Kansas City MO
Brands:
Crystal Lake

3272 **Crystal Lake LLC**
6500 W Crystal Lake Rd
Warsaw, IN 46580-8986 574-858-2514
Fax: 574-858-9886 www.crystallakellc.net
Liquid, frozen and cooked egg products
CEO: Ron Truex
Sales: Brian Hayward
Plant Manager: Jason Nichols
Estimated Sales: $10-20 Million
Number Employees: 100-249
Type of Packaging: Food Service, Private Label, Bulk

3273 **Crystal Rock Spring Water Company**
1050 Buckingham Street
Watertown, CT 06795 860-443-5000
Fax: 860-443-6995 www.crystalrock.com
Processor of spring water; also, office coffee service available
Director: Cheryl Gustafson
Estimated Sales: $500,000-$1 Million
Number Employees: 1-4
Type of Packaging: Consumer

3274 **Crystal Seed Potato Company**
652 6th St
Crystal, ND 58222-4021 701-657-2143
Fax: 701-657-2366
Processor of seed potatoes
President: Bruce Otto
Partner: Robert Otto
Estimated Sales: $600,000
Number Employees: 1-4
Type of Packaging: Consumer
Brands:
Dr. Red Norland
Goldrush
Norchip
Red Lasoda
Shephody
Snowden

3275 **Crystal Springs**
1200 Britannia Road East
Mississauga, ON L4W 4T5
Canada 905-795-6500
Fax: 905-670-3628 800-822-5889
www.crystalsprings.ca
Bottled water
Marketing Manager: Jeff Smith
Retail Manager: Steve Bondmini
General Manager: Paul Elliot
Production Manager: Eric Chastain
Estimated Sales: $5-10 Million
Number Employees: 100-249
Type of Packaging: Private Label
Brands:
Crystal Springs
Value Glacier

3276 **Crystal Springs Water Company**
5331 NW 35th Ter
Fort Lauderdale, FL 33309-6372 954-484-0100
Fax: 954-733-7913 800-432-1321
customerservice@water.com
www.crystalspringswater.com
Bottler of drinking, distilled and spring water
Owner: David Cappadona
Estimated Sales: $20-50 Million
Number Employees: 100-249
Parent Co: Suntory Water Group
Brands:
Belmont Springs
Crystal Springs
Crystal Springs
Hinckley Springs
Kentwood Springs
Sierra Springs
Sparkletts

3277 **Crystal Star Herbal Nutrition**
1542 N Sanborn Rd
Salinas, CA 93905-4760 831-422-7500
Fax: 800-260-4349 info@crystalstar.com
www.crystalstar.com
Processor, importer and exporter of herbal extracts, capsules, teas, powdered drink mixes and sports nutrition products
Manager: Julie Lu
Founder: Linda Page PhD
VP Sales: Scott Seabaugh
VP Operations: Glenn Korando
Estimated Sales: Less than $500,000
Number Employees: 1-4
Sq. footage: 10000
Parent Co: Jones Products International
Type of Packaging: Consumer, Bulk

3278 **Crystal Water Company**
3866 Shader Rd
Orlando, FL 32808-3145 407-625-3523
Fax: 407-578-7790 800-444-7873
sales@crystalspringswater.com
www.crystalspringswater.com
Processor of bottled water
Owner/Operator: David Cappadona
Plant Manager: Larry Caldwell
Number Employees: 1-4
Parent Co: Suntory Water Group
Type of Packaging: Consumer, Food Service, Private Label, Bulk
Brands:
Crystal Springs

3279 **Cucina Antica Foods Corp**
333 N Bedford Rd, Ste 118
Mount Kisco, NY 10549 914-244-9700
Fax: 914-244-1794 877-728-2462
neil@cucina-antica.com www.cucina-antica.com
Manufacturer of Italian sauces
Owner: Neil Fusco
Estimated Sales: $5-10 Million
Number Employees: 5-9

3280 **Cudlin's Market**
8 Cox Rd
Newfield, NY 14867-9420 607-564-3443
Processor of meat products; also, slaughtering services available
Owner: Vince Distefano
Estimated Sales: Less than $500,000
Number Employees: 1-4
Type of Packaging: Consumer

3281 **Cugino's Gourmet Foods**
1000 Meyer Dr
Crystal Lake, IL 60014 815-455-7242
Fax: 815-455-1948 888-592-8446
dhochstatter@cuginos.com www.cuginos.com
Garlic bread spread, gourmet soups, pasta sauce, BBQ sauce and marinades
Owner: Daniel Hochstatter
Estimated Sales: $ 10 - 20 Million
Number Employees: 10-19

3282 **Cuisinary Fine Foods**
3301 Conflans Rd
Irving, TX 75061 972-790-2004
Fax: 214-559-2131 888-283-5303
cuisinary@aol.com
Gourmet chocolate cookies, chocolate and pretzel snacks, assorted gourmet coffees, white chocolate/liquer, toppings, bourbon-pecan
President: Sandra Goodloe
Type of Packaging: Consumer, Food Service, Private Label
Brands:
Creme and Chocolate
Dolce Praline
Twigs & Bark

3283 **Cuisine Perel**
1001 Canal Blvd Ste A
Richmond, CA 94804 510-232-0343
Fax: 510-232-0321 800-887-3735
info@cuisineperel.com www.cuisineperel.com
Processor of chocolate, salad dressings, flavored grapeseed oil, mayonnaise, pasta and barbecue sauces, dry pastas and mustard; private label available
Owner: Mark Birchall
Estimated Sales: $2.5-5 Million
Number Employees: 5-9
Sq. footage: 6000
Type of Packaging: Private Label

3284 **Cuisine Solutions**
2800 Eisenhower Ave Ste 450
Alexandria, VA 22314 703-270-2900
Fax: 703-750-1158 888-285-4679
www.cuisinesolutions.com
Manufacturers of prepared foods.
President/CEO: Stanislas Vilgrain
CFO: Ronald Zilkowski
COO: Felipe Hasselmann
Estimated Sales: $87 Million
Number Employees: 354
Sq. footage: 44000
Brands:
CUISINE SOLUTIONS
FIVE LEAF

3285 **Cuizina Food Company**
18744 142nd Ave NE
Woodinville, WA 98072-8523 425-486-7000
Fax: 425-486-1148 www.cuizina.com
Processor of sauces including alfredo, marinara, primavera and spaghetti; also, minestrone and croppino soup and pastas including frozen, filled, extruded and vegetable blends.
President: Ric Ferrera
Estimated Sales: $5 Million
Number Employees: 35
Sq. footage: 10000
Type of Packaging: Consumer, Food Service, Private Label, Bulk
Brands:
CUIZINA ITALIA

3286 **Culinaire**
1111 W Exposition Ave
Denver, CO 80223 303-592-9100
Fax: 303-592-7619 877-502-9100
admin@culinaire.com www.culinairefoods.com
Hand made gourmet hors d oeuvres and entrees. Custom production available
President: Leo Reiff
Number Employees: 50-99
Number of Brands: 2
Number of Products: 110+
Sq. footage: 10000
Type of Packaging: Consumer, Food Service, Private Label
Brands:
BISTRO FAIRE
CULINAIRE

3287 **Culinar Canada**
58 Av William-Dobell
Baie-Comeau, QC G4Z 1T7
Canada 418-296-4395
Fax: 418-296-4395
Processor of cakes
Number Employees: 500-999
Parent Co: Culinar Canada
Brands:
Frenzi

3288 **Culinary Farms, Inc.**
1244 E Beamer St
Woodland, CA 95776 916-375-3000
Fax: 916-375-3010 888-383-2767
info@culinaryfarms.com
www.culinaryfarms.com
Processors of dried tomatoes, tomato paste and mexican chile peppers.
President: Kirk Bewley
CFO: Bal Pattar
Estimated Sales: $5-10 Million
Number Employees: 10-19
Sq. footage: 6000
Type of Packaging: Bulk

3289 **Culinary Foods**
4201 S Ashland Ave
Chicago, IL 60609 773-650-1814
Fax: 773-650-4501 800-621-4049
Processor and exporter of prepared and frozen foods including chicken, turkey, veal, cornish hens, hors d'oeuvres, omelets, crepes, quiche and sauces
Owner/President: Wayne Butler
Sales/Marketing Executive: Rick Trainor
Purchasing Agent: Rick Trainor
Number Employees: 1,000-4,999
Parent Co: Tyson Foods
Brands:
Lady Aster

3290 **Culinary Masters Corporation**
69 Brandywine Trl
Suite 109
Alpharetta, GA 30005 770-667-1688
Fax: 770-667-1682 800-261-5261
holzer@culinarymasters.com
www.culinarymasters.com
Wholesaler/distributor and importer of specialty foods, baked goods, equipment and tools; serving the food service market; exporter of spices, blends and specialty equipment
Master Chef/President: Helmut Holzer
Controller: Beth Ann Jackson
Vice President: Sara Jane Holzer
Sales: Michelle Brayley
Estimated Sales: $ 3 - 5 Million
Number Employees: 5-9
Sq. footage: 4000
Type of Packaging: Food Service, Private Label
Brands:
Affiorato
DreiMeister
Ravifruit
Stubi
Symphony Pastries
Vincotto

3291 **Culinary Revolution**
1320 Inspiration Drive
La Jolla, CA 92037-6810 858-454-4390
Fax: 323-939-4844 chefakasha@aol.com
www.chefakasha.com
Organic and diet food
Owner: Harry Coplan

3292 **Culinary Standards Corporation**
P.O.Box 4547
Louisville, KY 40204-0547 502-587-8877
Fax: 502-587-0150 800-778-3434
www.culinarystandards.com
Manufacturer of frozen prepared foods including soups, entrees, barbecue and cooked meats, side dishes, vegetables, chilies, sauces & gravies, dips & spreads as well as Mexican foods.
President: Joe Stefanutti
Estimated Sales: $20-30 Million
Number Employees: 100-249
Sq. footage: 65000
Type of Packaging: Consumer, Food Service
Brands:
ALL AMERICAN SOUP COLLECTION
HALL'S
KENTUK

3293 **(HQ)Culligan Water Technologies**
9399 W Higgins Rd
Rosemont, IL 60018-6900 847-205-6000
Fax: 847-205-6030 1 8-6 7-5 02
feedback@culligan.com www.culligan.com
Water
President: Douglas Pertz
CFO/VP Finance: M E Salvati
Chairman: Ralph Hubley
Secretary: E A Christensen
Estimated Sales: $50-100 Million
Number Employees: 1,000-4,999
Brands:
Culligan

3294 **Culture Systems**
3224 N Home St
Mishawaka, IN 46545 574-258-0602
Fax: 574-258-1136 www.culturesystems.net
Processor, exporter and wholesaler/distributor of dairy ingredients; also, researcher for the food industry
President: Hyung Kim
Estimated Sales: $1-2.5 Million
Number Employees: 10-19
Sq. footage: 4000

3295 **Cultured Specialties**
P.O.Box 3248
Fullerton, CA 92834-3508 714-772-8861
Fax: 714-956-1478
Processor and exporter of milk, yogurt and cottage cheese
Manager: Rick Struble
Sales/Marketing Executive: Jim Duffy
Plant Manager: Ed Stewart
Purchasing Agent: Lorraine Coulter
Estimated Sales: $50-100 Million
Number Employees: 1-4
Parent Co: Morningstar-Avoset
Type of Packaging: Consumer, Food Service

3296 **Cultured Specialties**
P.O.Box 3248
Fullerton, CA 92834-3508 714-772-8861
Fax: 714-956-1478 www.deanfoods.com
Manager: Rick Struble
Operations Manager: Michael Buchanan
Estimated Sales: $ 50 - 100 Million
Number Employees: 100-249

3297 **Culver Duck**
P.O.Box 910
Middlebury, IN 46540-0910 574-825-9537
Fax: 574-825-2613 800-825-9225
info@culverduck.com www.culverduck.com
Processor and exporter of duck, chicken and sausage products.
President: Herbert R Culver
Estimated Sales: $20-50 Million
Number Employees: 100-249
Sq. footage: 30000
Type of Packaging: Food Service
Brands:
CULVER DUCK

3298 **Culver's Fish Farm**
1316 W Kansas Ave
Mc Pherson, KS 67460-6053 620-241-5200
Fax: 620-241-5202 800-241-5205
www.culverfishfarm.com
Fish
Owner: Brent Culver
Estimated Sales: $300,000-500,000
Number Employees: 5-9

3299 **Cumberland Dairy**
P.O.Box 308
Rosenhayn, NJ 08352 856-451-1300
Fax: 856-451-1332
ccatalana@cumberlanddairy.com
www.cumberlanddairy.com
Processor and exporter of ice cream mixes, juices, soy products and milk including whole, skim, 1% and 2%; processor of ice cream
President: Carmine Catalana
Sales Director: David Catalana
Director Operations: Frank Catalana
Estimated Sales: $20-50 Million
Number Employees: 65
Type of Packaging: Consumer, Food Service, Private Label, Bulk
Brands:
Cumberland Dairy

3300 **Cumberland Gap Provision Company**
S 23rd St
Middlesboro, KY 40965 606-248-3311
Fax: 606-248-6517 800-331-7154
www.johnmorrell.com
Processor of fresh smoked sausage and ham
President/CEO: Ray Mc Gregor
Vice President: Patrick Flanagan
Quality Control: Kim Treiter
Sales Director: Tim Kreiter
Purchasing Manager: Gary Evans
Estimated Sales: $20-50 Million
Number Employees: 320
Parent Co: Smithfield Foods
Type of Packaging: Consumer, Food Service, Private Label
Brands:
Cumberland Gap
Hickory Hills
Old Kentucky

3301 **Cumberland Packing Corporation**
2 Cumberland St
Brooklyn, NY 11205 718-222-3233
Fax: 718-858-6386 info@cpack.com
www.cpack.com
Processor and exporter of artificial sweeteners and butter flavor spreads
Chairman: Benjamin Eisenstadt
President: Marvin Eisenstadt
VP: Jeff Eisenstadt
Estimated Sales: $100-500 Million
Number Employees: 250-499
Type of Packaging: Consumer
Brands:
SWEET 'N LOW

3302 **Cumberland Pasta**
PO Box 238
Cumberland, MD 21501-0238 301-777-1270
Fax: 301-777-1330 800-572-7821
www.nevy.org
Macaroni and egg noodles
President: Robert Bratti
Plant Manager: Richard Crawford
Estimated Sales: $10-24.9 Million
Number Employees: 50-99
Brands:
American Eagle
Marco Polo

3303 **Cumberland Seafood Corporation**
40 Macondray St
Cumberland, RI 02864-8131 401-728-6088
Frozen fish
Owner: John Clairo
Estimated Sales: $5-9.9 Million
Number Employees: 1-4

3304 **Cummings Lobster Company**
5 Alewive Park Road
Kennebunk, ME 04043-6134 207-985-1677
Fax: 207-985-1686
Lobster
President: William Cummings
Estimated Sales: $1,400,000
Number Employees: 5

3305 **Cummings Studio Chocolates**
679 E 900 S
Salt Lake City, UT 84105-1101 801-328-4858
Fax: 801-328-4801 800-537-3957
candy@CummingsStudioChocolates.com
www.cummingsstudiochocolates.com
Processors of candy including chocolates
President: Marion Cummings
CEO: Marion Cumming
VP: Marion Cummings
Marketing Manager: Jolend Proter
Estimated Sales: $2.5-5 Million
Number Employees: 50-99
Sq. footage: 7000

3306 **Cuneo Cellars**
9360 SE Eola Hills Road
Amity, OR 97101-2416 503-835-2782
Wines
Partner: Gino Cuneo
Estimated Sales: Less than $500,000
Number Employees: 1-4

3307 **Cupid Candies**
7637 S Western Ave
Chicago, IL 60620 773-925-8191
Fax: 773-925-7736 www.cupidcandies.com
Processor of candy
President: John Stefanos
Estimated Sales: $3 Million
Number Employees: 40
Sq. footage: 7128
Type of Packaging: Consumer, Private Label

3308 **Cupoladua Oven**
PO Box 266
Wexford, PA 15090 412-592-5378
info@cupoladuaoven.com
www.cupoladuaoven.com
All natural baked goods, sweet treats and savory snacks.

3309 **(HQ)Cupper's Coffee Company**
331 5th Street S
Lethbridge, AB T1J 2B4
Canada 403-380-4555
Fax: 403-328-8004

Importer and exporter of coffee
President: Al Anctil
Number Employees: 20-49

3310 **Curly's Custom Meats**
P.O.Box 123
Jackson Center, OH 45334 937-596-6518
Fax: 937-596-6518
Meats
President: Larry Edwards
Estimated Sales: $2.5-5 Million
Number Employees: 1-4

3311 **Curly's Foods**
5201 Eden Avenue
Suite 265
Edina, MN 55436-2365 612-920-3400
Fax: 612-920-9889 800-722-1127
www.curlys.com
Processor of beef including roast, corned, barbecued and cooked and frozen ribs.
President: John Pauley
Senior VP: Ken Feinberg
Estimated Sales: $100-150 Million
Number Employees: 1000
Sq. footage: 100000
Parent Co: John Morrell/Smithfield Foods
Type of Packaging: Consumer, Food Service, Private Label, Bulk
Brands:
CURLY'S

3312 **Curran's Cheese Plant**
W8850 Davis Rd
Browntown, WI 53522-9741 608-966-3361
Fax: 608-966-3309
Cheese products
Owner: James Curran
Estimated Sales: $10-24.9 Million
Number Employees: 10-19
Brands:
Curran Cheese

3313 **Curry King Corporation**
34 W Prospect St
Waldwick, NJ 7463 201-652-6228
Fax: 201-447-3291 800-287-7987
curryusa@aol.com www.curryking.com
Processor and importer of curry, balti and tandoori sauce; also, mango chutney; exporter of curry sauce
President: Lall Kwatra
Vice President: Pamela Kwatra
Estimated Sales: Under $500,000
Number Employees: 3
Sq. footage: 2500
Type of Packaging: Food Service, Private Label, Bulk
Brands:
Curry King

3314 **Curtice Burns FoodsGlk Foods**
11 Clark St
Shortsville, NY 14548-9755 585-289-4414
Fax: 585-289-4280
Processor of canned fruits and vegetables
Cfo: Tom Palmer
Manager: Luke Plamondon
Estimated Sales: $ 1 - 3 Million
Number Employees: 40
Parent Co: Curtice Burns
Type of Packaging: Consumer, Food Service, Private Label

3315 **Curtis Packing Company**
P.O.Box 1470
Greensboro, NC 27402 336-275-7684
Fax: 336-275-1901
www.curtispackingcompany.com
Packer of meat products including frankfurters, bologna, bacon, ham, beef and fresh pork
President: Douglas Curtis
Secretary: Paul Hale Jr
Controller: Paul Hale
Sales Manager: Steve Henderson
Sales: John Curtis
Estimated Sales: $50-100 Million
Number Employees: 125
Type of Packaging: Consumer
Brands:
Beef Master
Curtis
IBP
Mbpxl
Monfort
Porter House

3316 **Cusack Wholesale Meat Company**
P.O.Box 25111
Oklahoma City, OK 73125-0111 405-232-2114
Fax: 405-232-2127 800-241-6328
cusack@cusackmeats.com
www.cusackmeats.com
Processor of beef, pork, lamb, veal and poultry
Owner: Donnie Cusack
General Manager: Al Cusack
Estimated Sales: $20-50 Million
Number Employees: 20-49
Type of Packaging: Food Service

3317 **Cusano's Baking Company**
2798 SW 32nd Ave
Hollywood, FL 33023 954-458-1010
Fax: 954-458-1052 sales@cusanosbakery.com
www.cusanosbakery.com
Italian bread and bakery products
Owner: Mike Greco
General Manager: Sal Grego
Office Manager: Stiffeny Novembre
Estimated Sales: $5-10 Million
Number Employees: 79
Brands:
Cusano's

3318 **Cushner Seafood**
4141 Amos Ave
Baltimore, MD 21215 410-358-5564
Fax: 410-358-5558
Fish & Seafood
Owner: Jack Deckelbaum
Estimated Sales: $1,600,000
Number Employees: 1-4

3319 **Custom Confections & More**
PO Box 62
Algonquin, IL 60102-0062 888-457-4676
Fax: 208-342-5996
stacey@customconfectionsandmore.com
www.customconfectionsandmore.com
Hard candy, lollipops
President: Lowell Fugal
Estimated Sales: $5-10 Million
Number Employees: 20-49

3320 **Custom Culinary**
2505 S Finley Road
Suite 100
Lombard, IL 60148 708-388-8883
Fax: 630-928-4899 800-621-8827
www.customculinary.com
Gravy mixes, bases and sauce & gravy concentrates
President: Herve De Le Vauvre
VP: Diane Zuroweste
Human Resources Director: Bob Ufferman
Estimated Sales: $53 Million
Number Employees: 80
Sq. footage: 90000
Type of Packaging: Food Service, Bulk
Brands:
GOLD LABEL
MASTER'S TOUCH
PANROAST

3321 **Custom Cuts**
2842 S 5th Ct
Bay View, WI 53207 414-483-0491
Fax: 888-888-3717 www.ccuts.com
Processor of pre-washed and cut lettuce, cabbage, onions, potatoes, melons, pineapples and watermelons
Owner: Brad Beckman
Director Sales: Andy Siegel
General Manager: Monty Vikse
Estimated Sales: $100-500 Million
Number Employees: 250-499
Type of Packaging: Food Service, Private Label

3322 **Custom Food Processors International**
450 Bailey Ave
New Hampton, IA 50659-1061 641-394-4802
Fax: 641-394-4735 www.bayvalleyfoods.com
Contract packager and exporter of spray dried products including nondairy creamer, powdered milk, mixes, etc
President: John Nicolaisen
Plant Manager: Bob Sanford
Estimated Sales: $ 5 - 10 Million
Number Employees: 50-99
Type of Packaging: Bulk

3323 **Custom Food Solutions**
2505 Data Dr
Louisville, KY 40299 502-671-6966
Fax: 502-671-6906 800-767-2993
www.customfoodsolutions.com
A USDA, FDA and AIB inspected food manufacturing facility specializing in custom batch, fresh ingredient production of soups, sauces, fillings and Sous Vide cooked proteins in flexible sized pouches.
Sales: Karen Reid
Number Employees: 30
Number of Products: 50
Sq. footage: 65000
Type of Packaging: Food Service

3324 **Custom House Coffee RoasJodyana Corporation**
18367 Ne 4th Ct
Miami, FL 33179-4531 305-651-0110
Fax: 305-651-4535 888-563-5282
roastabean@earthlink.net
Specialty coffees; including flavored coffees
President: Corey Colaciello
CEO: Joe Colaciello
Sales Director: Barbara Colaciello
Estimated Sales: $620,000
Number Employees: 5
Number of Brands: 115
Sq. footage: 3000
Type of Packaging: Food Service, Private Label, Bulk

3325 **Custom House Seafoods**
P.O.Box 7112
Portland, ME 04112 207-773-2778
Fax: 207-761-9458
Fish and seafood.
President: Craig Johnson
Estimated Sales: $820,000
Number Employees: 1-4

3326 **Custom Industries**
9807 S 40 Dr
St Louis, MO 63124-1103 314-787-2828
Fax: 314-787-2828 sales@cusombits.com
Confectionery bits for baking and cereal industries, chocolate dairy powders, ice cream inclusion and fruit drinks for dairies
CEO: Dale Musick
Estimated Sales: $ 20 - 50 Million
Number Employees: 100-249
Parent Co: Kerry Group
Type of Packaging: Bulk

3327 **Custom Ingredients**
1614 N Ih 35
New Braunfels, TX 78130 830-608-0915
Fax: 830-625-7914 800-457-8935
info@customingredients.com
www.customingredients.com
Ingredients, snacks, dips, bakery, sauces, tortilla
President: James Curry PhD
Marketing: D Ames
Operations: Grey Baker
Production: R Nahn
Estimated Sales: $2.5-5 Million
Number Employees: 20-49
Type of Packaging: Bulk

3328 **Custom-Pak Meats**
PO Box 5377
Knoxville, TN 37928-0377 865-687-0871
Fax: 865-688-3276
Packer of meat
President: C Hobbs
Executive VP: Christopher Satterfield
Number Employees: 42
Sq. footage: 24800
Type of Packaging: Food Service
Brands:
Nugget
Pocahontas

3329 **Cut Above Foods**
6100 Avenida Encinas
Carlsbad, CA 92009 760-931-6777
Fax: 760-931-5749

Processor and importer of raw and roasted garlic, shallots, ginger and IQF fire-roasted vegetables including onions, tomatoes, peppers, eggplant, squash, etc
Owner/President: Michael Crouse
COO: John Rosingana
National Sales: Keith Shelby
Estimated Sales: $20-50 Million
Number Employees: 20-49
Sq. footage: 12200
Type of Packaging: Consumer, Food Service, Private Label, Bulk
Brands:
A Cut Above

3330 **Cutie Pie Corporation**
443 W 400 N
Salt Lake City, UT 84103 801-533-9550
Fax: 801-355-8021 800-453-4575
www.horizonsnackfoods.com
Processor and exporter of frozen fruit snack pies
Principal: Bob Sharp
CFO: Lee Rucker
Director: Lee Wacker
Estimated Sales: Under $500,000
Number Employees: 5-9
Type of Packaging: Consumer, Food Service
Brands:
Cutie Pies

3331 **Cutler Egg Products**
496 Industrial Park Rd
Abbeville, AL 36310 334-585-2268
Fax: 334-585-2473 cutleregg@ala.net
www.cutleregg.com
Processor and exporter of dried, frozen, liquid and extended shelf life egg products
Manager: Jeff Cutler
VP: Harold Cutler
VP Manufacturing: Joel Cutler
Estimated Sales: $100-500 Million
Number Employees: 100-249
Parent Co: Cutler Dairy Products
Type of Packaging: Food Service, Bulk

3332 **Cutone Specialty Foods**
145 Market Street
Chelsea, MA 02150 617-889-1122
Fax: 617-884-3944
customerservice@cutonespecialtyfoods.com
www.cutonespecialtyfoods.com
Marinated and blanched mushrooms
President/Owner: Mario Cutone III

3333 **Cutrale Citrus Juices**
602 McKean St
Auburndale, FL 33823 863-965-5000
Fax: 863-965-5149 information@cutrale.com
www.cutrale.com
Manufacturer of grapefruit and orange juices
President: Hugh Thompson III
Estimated Sales: $150 Million
Number Employees: 250-499
Parent Co: Sucocitrico Cutrale Ltd
Type of Packaging: Consumer, Food Service, Private Label, Bulk

3334 **Cutrale Citrus Juices**
11 Cloud St
Leesburg, FL 34748 352-728-7800
Fax: 352-728-7840 information@cutrale.com
www.cutrale.com
Processor of pasteurized orange juice and concentrate
Operations Manager: Jim Fitzgerald
Plant Manager: Jose Zamperlini
Estimated Sales: $100-500 Million
Number Employees: 100-249
Type of Packaging: Consumer

3335 **Cuvaison Vineyard**
4550 Silverado Trl
Calistoga, CA 94515-9604 707-942-6266
Fax: 707-942-5732 www.cuvaison.com
Processor of red and white wines.
President: Jay Schuppert
Estimated Sales: $10-20 Million
Number Employees: 20-49
Type of Packaging: Consumer, Food Service

3336 **Cw Resources**
200 Myrtle St
New Britain, CT 06053 860-229-7700
Fax: 860-229-6847 rbuccilli@cwresources.org
www.cwresources.org
Processor of gourmet products including flavored vinegars and oils, salsas, sauces, jellies, baking mixes, dips/dip mixes, baked goods, rubs and salad dressings
Sr. VP: Robert Williams
VP Sales/Production: Alix Capsalors
Production: Bill Blonski
Estimated Sales: $33 Million
Number Employees: 150
Sq. footage: 100000
Type of Packaging: Consumer, Food Service, Private Label, Bulk
Brands:
B&B
Sumptuous ions

3337 **Cyanotech Corporation**
73-4460 Queen K Hwy Ste 102
Kailua Kona, HI 96740 808-326-1353
Fax: 808-329-4533 800-395-1353
info@cyanotech.com www.cyanotech.com
Cyanotech Corporation, the world's leader in microalgae technology, produces high-value natural products from microalgae, and is the world's largest commercial producer of natural astaxanthin from microalgae. Products include HawaiiamSpirulina Pacifica, a nutrient-rich dietary supplement; BioAstin, a natural astaxanthin, a powerful antioxidant with expanding applications as a human nutraceutical
Executive VP: Gerald R Cysewski
VP Sales/Marketing: Robert Capelli
Sales Manager: Jeane Vinson
Estimated Sales: F
Number Employees: 50-99
Number of Brands: 3
Number of Products: 2
Sq. footage: 653400
Parent Co: Cyanotech Corporation
Type of Packaging: Consumer, Private Label, Bulk
Brands:
BioAstin Natural Astaxanthin
Spirulina Hawaiian Spirulina

3338 **Cybros**
P.O.Box 851
Waukesha, WI 53187-0851 262-547-1821
Fax: 262-547-8946 800-876-2253
sales@cybrosinc.com www.cybrosinc.com
Manufacturer of fine breads, rolls, cookies and other products
Owner: Debbie Brooks
General Manager: Paul Geboy
Estimated Sales: $2.5-5 Million
Number Employees: 10-19
Sq. footage: 8000

3339 **Cyclone Enterprises**
146 Knobcrest Dr
Houston, TX 77060 281-872-0087
Fax: 281-872-7645 www.cyclone-ent.com
Processor and importer of Mexican food including hot sauce and peppers. Distributors of dry, canned, processed and frozen grocery items including juices, drinks, dairy products, meats, cheeses, deli products, specialty foods, herbsspices, candy and snac
President: Mark Mendenhall
CEO: Mark Mindenhall
VP Sales: Ronny Thomas
Customer Support: Dora Mendoza
General Information: Martha Gibbs
Purchasing: Ted Spafford
Estimated Sales: $2.5-5 Million
Number Employees: 100-249
Type of Packaging: Consumer, Food Service, Private Label

3340 **Cygnet Cellars**
PO Box 1956
Hollister, CA 95024-1956 831-637-7559
Wine
Partner: Jim Johnson
Estimated Sales: $500,000 appx.
Number Employees: 1-4
Brands:
Cygnet

3341 **Cypress Grove Chevre**
1330 Q St
Arcata, CA 95521 707-825-1100
Fax: 707-825-1101
bobo@cypressgrovechevre.com
www.cypressgrovechevre.com
Maker of goat's milk cheeses including Humboldt Fog, Bermuda Triangle, chevre, Fromage Blanc, cheddar, hub and ash coated chevre.
President: Mary Keehn
Estimated Sales: $1-5 Million
Number Employees: 20-49
Number of Brands: 2
Number of Products: 18
Sq. footage: 6000
Type of Packaging: Consumer, Food Service, Private Label, Bulk
Brands:
CYPRESS GROVE CHEVRE
CYPRESS GROVE CREAM

3342 **(HQ)Cyril's Bakery Company**
2890 W State Road 84
Unit 103
Fort Lauderdale, FL 33312 954-797-1272
Fax: 413-473-9708 800-929-7457
cyril@cyrils.com www.cyrils.com
Frozen bakery products including breads and pastries.
VP: Adam Weizer
Marketing: Kelly Wechsler
Public Relations: Shannon Campbell
Operations: Steve Tarrick
Estimated Sales: $15 Million
Number Employees: 18
Number of Brands: 1
Number of Products: 75
Type of Packaging: Consumer, Food Service

3343 **Czepiel Millers Dairy**
PO Box 277
Ludlow, MA 01056-0277 413-589-0828
Fax: 413-589-0828
Dairy
President: Stanly Czepiel

3344 **Czimer's Game & Sea Foods**
13136 W 159th St
Homer Glen, IL 60491 708-301-0500
Meat and fish
Owner: Richard Czimer Jr
Estimated Sales: $300,000
Number Employees: 1-4

3345 **D & D Foods**
3715 4th Ave
Columbus, GA 31904 706-322-4507
Fax: 706-327-4121 ddfoods@aol.com
www.ddfoods.com
Manufacturer of barbecue sauces, marinades and salad dressings; also, contract packaging available
President: Marlene Dodelin
CFO: Fred Dodelin
Estimated Sales: $3-5 Million
Number Employees: 5-9
Type of Packaging: Consumer, Food Service, Private Label, Bulk
Brands:
FOY'S B.B.Q. SAUCE

3346 **D Seafood**
2723 S Poplar Avenue
Chicago, IL 60608-5915 312-808-1086
Fax: 312-808-0869
Seafood
Owner: De Trinh

3347 **D Steengrafe & Company**
1726 Main St
Pleasant Valley, NY 12569 845-635-4067
Fax: 845-635-4239

Manufacturer and importer of beeswax, botanicals, kola nuts and nut powder, quassia chips, dried ginger and spices
VP: Margot Nordenholt
VP: Carl Schmidt
Estimated Sales: $5 Million
Number Employees: 1-4
Type of Packaging: Bulk

3348 **D Waybret & Sons Fisheries**
3 Clam Point
Shelburne, NS B0T 1W0
Canada 902-745-3477
Fax: 902-745-2112
Manufacturer and exporter of fresh and salted haddock, cod, halibut and hake; also, fresh lobster
President/Co-Owner: Dewey Waybret
Manager/Co-Owner: Cecil Waybret
Number Employees: 50
Type of Packaging: Bulk

3349 **D&A Foodservice**
PO Box 2762
Dartmouth, NS B2W 4R4
Canada 902-468-4715
Fax: 902-468-4715
Manufacturer of sandwiches, chicken wings, chicken wing sauces and prepared dinners
President/Owner: Pat McCluskey
VP: Gary Keigan
Number Employees: 9
Type of Packaging: Food Service
Brands:
DAVE'S
KOKOMO'S

3350 **D&M Seafood**
135 N King St # 2b
Honolulu, HI 96817-5084 808-531-0687
Fax: 808-531-4947 www.shrimphawaii.com
Seafood
Owner: Hansen Chong

3351 **D'Arrigo Brothers Company of California**
P.O.Box 850
Salinas, CA 93902-0850 831-424-3955
Fax: 831-424-3136 800-995-5939
promero@darrigo.com www.andyboy.com
Manufacturer of vegetables: broccoli, fennel, hearts of romaine, broccoli rabe, cauliflower and cactus pear.
Chairman: Andrew D'Arrigo
President: John D'Arrigo
Director Sales: Dave Martinez
EVP Operations: Margaret D'Arrigo-Martin
Estimated Sales: $79.9 Million
Number Employees: 1,000-4,999
Type of Packaging: Consumer, Bulk
Brands:
ANDY BOY
GREEN HEAD

3352 **D'Artagnan**
280 Wilson Ave
Newark, NJ 07105-3844 973-344-0565
Fax: 973-465-1870 800-327-8246
pattia@dartagnan.com www.dartagnan.com
Manufacturer of pates, game sausages, smoked items, ducks, meats, game birds, mushrooms and specialty products
President: Ariane Daguin
Marketing: Donna Brunnguell
Purchasing: Kris Kelleher
Estimated Sales: $30 Million
Number Employees: 100-249
Type of Packaging: Consumer, Food Service, Bulk

3353 **D'Oni Enterprises**
PO Box 962
San Juan Capistrano, CA 92693-0962949-240-3053
Fax: 949-240-3086 800-809-8298
info@gmbfoods.com www.d-oni.com
Sauces
President: Janis Dallessandro
Vice President: David Dallesandro
Shipping/Receiving: Linda Trudeau

3354 **D'Orazio Foods**
960 Creek Rd
Bellmawr, NJ 8031 856-931-1900
Fax: 856-931-1907 888-328-7287
web@dorazio.com www.dorazio.com
Manufacturer of all natural frozen pasta products.
President: Anthony D'Orazio
CFO: Michael Romano
VP Sales/Marketing: Terry D'Ozario
VP Operations/COO: Frank D'Orazio
VP Production: Anthony D'Orazio
Estimated Sales: $8.4 Million
Number Employees: 70
Sq. footage: 25000
Brands:
DORAZIO

3355 **D-Liteful Baking Company**
9012 NW 105 Way
Medley, FL 33178 305-883-6449
Fax: 305-883-8797 www.d-litefulbaking.com
Product line includes that of Heavenly Desserts featuring a variety of sugar free products such as cheesecakes and meringues available in vanilla, chocolate, cappuccino, strawberry and lemon flavors. Their Heavenly Harvest lineincludes sugar free baked products such as sesame and wheat crackers.
Founder: Jorge Guevara Sr
Type of Packaging: Food Service

3356 **D.D. Williamson & Company**
1901 Payne Street
Louisville, KY 40206 502-895-2438
Fax: 502-895-7381 800-227-2635
info@ddwmson.com www.caramel.com
Manufacturer and exporter of caramel coloring
President/COO: Alexander Nixon
Chairman/CEO: Ted Nixon
VP/CFO: Rob Houchens
VP/Chief People Officer: Elaine Gravatte
VP Global Sales/Marketing: G Campbell Barnum
Human Resources Manager: Barbara Evans
Plant Manager: Henry Ackerman
Estimated Sales: $5-10 Million
Number Employees: 63
Sq. footage: 30000
Type of Packaging: Consumer, Bulk
Other Locations:
DDW Support Center
Louisville KY
D.D. Williamson Ireland
Cork, Ireland
D.D. Williamson Ingredients
Shanghai, China
D.D. Williamson do Brazil
Manaus, Brazil
D.D. Williamson & Company
Louisville KY
Colormaker
Anaheim CA
D.D. Williamson
Matsapha, Swaziland
D.D. Williamson UK
Manchester UK
Brands:
WILLIAMSON'S

3357 **D.L. Geary Brewing**
38 Evergreen Dr
Portland, ME 4103 207-878-2337
Fax: 207-878-2388 www.gearybrewing.com
Manufacturer of beers
President: David Geary
Marketing: Kelly Lucas
Operations: Kelly Lucas
Estimated Sales: $2 Million
Number Employees: 20
Brands:
DL GEARY BREWING

3358 **DB Kenney Fisheries**
PO Box 1210
Westport, NS B0V 1H0
Canada 902-839-2023
Fax: 902-839-2070
dbkenney@dbkenneyfisheries.com
www.dbkenneyfisheries.com
Manufacturer and exporter of scallops, lobster, cod and haddock
President: Daniel Kenney Jr
Number Employees: 50-99
Type of Packaging: Bulk

3359 **DCI Cheese Company**
3018 Helsan Dr
Richfield, WI 53076 262-677-3407
Fax: 262-677-3806 kjury@dcicheeseco.com
www.dcicheeseco.com
imported cheeses, dips, spreads, hummus and other exotic and flavorful offerings
President: Timothy Omer
VP: Dominique Delugeau
Marketing: Katy Jury
Estimated Sales: $12.8 Million
Number Employees: 280

3360 **DCL**
628 Laumaka St
Honolulu, HI 96819 808-845-3834
Fax: 808-845-4901
Manufacturer of various fresh Hawaiian seafoods
President: Dennis Goto
Estimated Sales: $ 5 - 10 Million
Number Employees: 10-19

3361 **DD Williamson & Company**
1901 Payne Street
Louisville, KY 40206 502-895-2438
Fax: 502-895-7381 800-227-2635
info@ddwmson.com www.caramel.com
Manufacturer and exporter of caramel color
President: T H Nixon
Estimated Sales: $ 20 - 50 Million
Number Employees: 50-99
Parent Co: Williamson Group
Type of Packaging: Bulk

3362 **DE Wolfgang Candy Company**
50 E 4th Ave
York, PA 17404-2507 717-843-5536
Fax: 717-845-2881 800-248-4273
info@wolfgangcandy.com
www.wolfgangcandy.com
Manufacturer of confectionery products including chocolate and peanut brittle
Partner: Benjamin McGlaughlin
Managing Partner/Marketing: Mike Schmid
Managing Partner/Sales: Steve Schmid
Managing Partner: Brad McGlaughin
Managing Partner/Operations: Robert Wolfgang III
Managing Partner/Finance/Adminsitration: Benjamin McGlaughin
Estimated Sales: $20-50 Million
Number Employees: 100-249
Type of Packaging: Consumer

3363 **DEKO International**
4283 Shoreline Drive
Earth City, MO 63045 314-298-0910
Fax: 314-298-0081 dekointl@aol.com
www.dekointl.com
Manufacturer of food ingredients, seasoning and spices
President/CEO: Peter Guo
Vice President: Nung Kuo
Number Employees: 35

3364 **DF Stauffer Biscuit Company**
360 S Belmont St
York, PA 17403-2616 717-843-9016
Fax: 717-843-0592 800-673-2473
www.stauffers.net
Manufacturer of animal crakers, cookies and other snacks.
President: Marc Garrett
CFO: Carlous Sutton Jr
VP: Scott Stauffer
Quality Control: Janet Dunlap
Sales: Rodney Stauffer
Operations: Gary Shortt
Purchasing: Diane Toomey
Estimated Sales: $50-100 Million
Number Employees: 500-999
Parent Co: Meiji Seika
Type of Packaging: Consumer, Food Service, Private Label, Bulk
Other Locations:
DF Stauffer Biscuit Company
Blandon PA
DF Stauffer Biscuit Company
Cuba NY
DF Stauffer Biscuit Company
Santa Ana CA
Brands:
STAUFFERS
YORK FARMS

3365 **DG Yuengling & Son**
310 Mill Creek Avenue
Pottsville, PA 17901 570-622-0153
Fax: 570-622-4011 www.yuengling.com

Manufacturer of beer including ale, porter, lager and light
President & Owner: Dick Yuengling Jr Jr
Coo: David Casinelli
Estimated Sales: $50-100 Million
Number Employees: 100-249
Brands:
YUENGLING

3366 **DGZ Chocolates**
6909 Ashcroft Dr # 315
Houston, TX 77081-5819 713-777-3444
Fax: 713-777-9444 877-949-9444
www.dgzchocolates.com
Chocolates, caramel apples, popcorn covered in chocolate and caramel
Owner: Debbie Zissman
Purchasing: Deborah Zissman
Estimated Sales: $5-10 Million
Number Employees: 1-4
Brands:
APPLERAZZI
POPARAZZI
TOFFARASSI
TURTLERAZZI

3367 **DMH Ingredients**
1228 American Way
Libertyville, IL 60048 847-362-9977
Fax: 847-362-9988 www.dmhingredients.com
Confectionery, gums and stabilizers, cheese and dairy powders, fruit and vegetable products, powdered cellulose, savory flavors, flavor enhancers, sweet flavors, coffee, tea and botanicals, vitamins, amino acids and food chemicalsgrain products, meat aspartame
President: David Damlich
Purchasing: David Damlich
Estimated Sales: $5-10 Million
Number Employees: 5-9

3368 **DNE World Fruit Sales**
1900 Old Dixie Hwy
Fort Pierce, FL 34946-1423 772-465-1110
Fax: 772-465-1181 800-327-6676
www.dneworld.com
Grower, packer, marketer, and importer of citrus fruit including navel oranges, clementines, lemons and limes; exporter of grapefruit, oranges, tangerines and juice
President: Gregory Nelson
VP: David Mixon
Manager Fresh Juices: Robert Poyner
Estimated Sales: $20-50 Million
Number Employees: 100-249
Parent Co: Bernard Egan & Company
Type of Packaging: Consumer, Food Service, Private Label, Bulk
Brands:
INDIAN RIVER PRIDE
OCEAN SPRAY
PRIDE

3369 **DPI Dairy Fresh Products Company**
601 S Rockefeller Avenue
Ontario, CA 91761-7871 909-605-7300
Fax: 909-975-7259
Dairy products
President: James De Keyser
Purchasing: Cheryl Hopson
Estimated Sales: $5-10 Million
Number Employees: 5-9
Brands:
DPI DAIRY

3370 **(HQ)DS Waters of America**
5660 New Northside Dr NW
Suite 500
Atlanta, GA 30328 770-933-1400
Fax: 770-956-9495 800-728-5508
customerservice@water.com www.water.com
Manufacturer and distributor of bottled water
CEO: Dillon Schickli
President: Gilbert Gibson
VP/CIO: Bob Bramski
Communications Director: Elizabeth Webb
COO: Tom Harrington
Estimated Sales: $800 Million
Number Employees: 4800
Sq. footage: 80000
Parent Co: Suntory Water Group
Type of Packaging: Consumer, Food Service, Private Label, Bulk
Brands:
ALHAMBRA®
ATHENA®
BELMONT SPRINGS®
CRYSTAL SPRINGS®
HINCKLEY SPRINGS®
KENTWOOD SPRINGS®
MOUNT OLYMPUS WATER®
NURSERY® WATER
ROAST2COAST®
SIERRA SPRINGS®
SPARKLETTS®

3371 **DSM Food SpecialtiesPeptoPro**
45 Waterview Boulevard
Parsippany, NJ 07054-1298 951-461-1619
Fax: 951-461-1638 info.peptopro@dsm.com
www.peptopro.com
DSM Food Specialties is a producer of value-added ingredient solutions for the international food, feed and beverage industries.
President: A Wessels
Finance & Control: G Nieboer
Legal Affairs: R De Graaf
Research & Development: B Poldermans
QESH & M: J Van Lemmen
Strategy & Marketing Services: A Stikkers
National Account Manager: Reto Rieder
Human Resources: A Twigt
Demand & Supply Chain Management: T Brett
Estimated Sales: $5-10 Million
Number Employees: 70

3372 **DSM Food Specialties**
N89w14475 Patrita Dr
Menomonee Falls, WI 53051 262-255-7955
Fax: 262-255-7732 800-423-7906
Yeast extracts, flavor systems, inactive dry yeast, fermentation nutrients, beverage enzymes, wine yeasts, coagulants, starter cultures, starter media, preservation systems and antibiotic residue tests
Marketing: Jim Whitt

3373 **Da Vinci Gourmet**
7224 1st Ave S
Seattle, WA 98108 206-768-7401
Fax: 206-768-1855 800-640-6779
info@davincigourmet.com
www.davincigourmet.com
Manufacturers flavored syrups, gourmet sauces, and confections
Manager: Gary Sletten
Estimated Sales: $14 Million
Number Employees: 50-99
Number of Products: 120+
Sq. footage: 65000
Type of Packaging: Consumer, Food Service, Private Label, Bulk

3374 **Dabruzzi's Italian Foods**
417 2nd St
Hudson, WI 54016 715-386-3653
Fax: 715-549-5202
Manufacturer of ravioli, garlic butter bread and red and white sauces
Owner: Sharon Ellstrom
Manager: Nancy Cramer
Estimated Sales: $1-2.5 Million
Number Employees: 5-9

3375 **Dagoba Organic Chocolate**
14 E Chocolate Avenue
Hershey, PA 17033 717-534-4200
Fax: 717-534-5297 oracle@dagobachocolate.com
www.dagobachocolate.com
Organic chocolates
Founder: Frederick Schilling
Marketing: Gail Lang
Plant Manager: Doug Massey
Estimated Sales: $ 10 - 20 Million
Number Employees: 20-49

3376 **(HQ)Dahlgren & Company**
1220 Sunflower St
Crookston, MN 56716 218-281-2985
Fax: 218-281-6218 800-346-6050
cconsidine@sunflowerseed.com
www.sunflowerseed.com
Manufacturer and exporter of in-shell and kernel sunflower seeds, soynuts including roasted, salted and flavored. Custom roasting and packaging also available
President: Tim Egeland
Human Resources Director: Julie Oertwich
COO: Charles Considine
Operations Manager/Plant Manager: Ray Mitchell
Estimated Sales: $20.2 Million
Number Employees: 150
Sq. footage: 12000
Type of Packaging: Consumer, Food Service, Bulk
Other Locations:
Dahlgren & Company
Grace City ND
Dahlgren & Company
Fargo ND

3377 **Dahm's Foods**
5234 Brown Street
Skokie, IL 60077-3616 847-673-0653
Salad dressings, jellies and jams
President: Bruce Dahm
Estimated Sales: $150,000
Number Employees: 3
Brands:
DAHM'S

3378 **Daily Juice Products**
1 Daily Way
Verona, PA 15147 412-828-9020
Fax: 412-828-8876 800-245-2929
info@ambev.com www.ambev.com
Manufacturer of cocktail mixes including pina colada, strawberry colada, whiskey sour, strawberry daiquiri and juice concentrates; also, pancake syrup
President: Kevin McGahren-Clemens
Vice President: Michael Barlett
Research & Development: Jack Cornelius
VP Sales/Marketing: Paul Beranek
VP Operations: Keneth Janowitz
Director Engineering: Kevin Tappa
Estimated Sales: $50-100 Million
Number Employees: 550
Parent Co: Wessanen
Type of Packaging: Consumer, Food Service, Private Label, Bulk
Brands:
BIG JUICY

3379 **Daily Soup**
134 E 43rd St # 1
New York, NY 10017-4019 212-949-7687
Fax: 212-687-7839 888-393-7687
soup@dailysoup.com www.dailysoup.com
Fresh soups
Owner: Young Yoon
Executive Chef: Leslie Kaul
Estimated Sales: Less than $500,000
Number Employees: 10-19
Brands:
DAILY MADE

3380 **Daily's Premium Meats**
3535 S 500 W
Salt Lake City, UT 84115-4205 801-269-1998
Fax: 801-269-1409 800-328-7695
info@dailysmeats.com www.dailymeats.com
Manufacturer of a variety of premium meat products, including bacon, hams and breakfast sausages.
President: Russell Wilcox
Production Manager: Russ Wilcox
Estimated Sales: $100-500 Million
Number Employees: 250-499
Parent Co: Seaboard Foods
Type of Packaging: Consumer, Food Service
Brands:
DAILY FOODS

3381 **Dainty Confections**
725 Broadway Boulevard
Windsor, ON N9C 3W5 519-972-8888
Fax: 519-966-3298 800-268-0222
jones@dainty.ca www.daintyrice.com
Candy
President: Catherine Diehl
Marketing: Sherry Jones

3382 **Dairiconcepts**
3253 E. Chestnut Expressway
Springfield, MO 65802 417-829-3400
Fax: 417-829-3401 877-596-4374
dcinfo@dairiconcepts.com
www.dairiconcepts.com

Dairy powders and replacement systems, cheese powders and cheese concentrates, block and grated Italian cheeses.

3383 **Dairy Concepts**
7014 County Road Mm
Greenwood, WI 54437 715-267-5422
Fax: 715-267-5409 888-680-5400
Fresh/dry, grated and shredded parmesan cheese, romano cheese, asiago cheese. Retail, food service/ingredients
Quality Control: Loni Duell
Plant Manager: Scott Anderson
Estimated Sales: Under $500,000
Number Employees: 10
Type of Packaging: Consumer, Food Service, Private Label, Bulk

3384 **Dairy Farmers of America**
5001 Brittonfield Parkway
East Syracuse, NY 13057 315-431-1352
www.dfamilk.com
Manufacturer of milk and milk products
COO/Northeast Area: Brad Keating
Sq. footage: 24000
Parent Co: Dairy Farmers of America
Type of Packaging: Consumer, Food Service

3385 **Dairy Farmers of America**
1035 Medina Road
Suite 300
Medina, OH 44256 330-670-7800
www.dfamilk.com
Manufacturer of milk and milk products
COO/Mideast Area: Dennis Rodenbaugh
Plant Manager: Robert Gehlke
Parent Co: Dairy Farmers of America
Type of Packaging: Consumer

3386 **Dairy Farmers of America**
10411 Cogdill Road
Knoxville, TN 37932 865-218-8500
www.dfamilk.com
Manufacturer of milk and milk products
COO/Central & Southeast Areas: Randy McGinnis
Parent Co: Dairy Farmers of America
Type of Packaging: Bulk

3387 **Dairy Farmers of America**
1140 S 3200 W
Salt Lake City, UT 84104 801-977-3000
Fax: 801-977-3090 www.dfamilk.com
Cooperative of dairy processors
Manager: Sandy Whalen
Finance Executive: Richard Carroll
Sales Executive: Don Jensen
Estimated Sales: $ 10 - 20 Million
Number Employees: 35
Sq. footage: 32659
Type of Packaging: Consumer

3388 **(HQ)Dairy Farmers of America**
10220 N Ambassador Drive
Kansas City, MO 64153 816-801-6455
Fax: 816-801-6456 888-332-6455
webmail@dfamilk.com www.dfamilk.com
Milk and milk products
President/CEO: Rick Smith
VP/Business Integration: David Knecht
VP/Legal: Alex Bachelor
President/Global Dairy Products Group: Mark Korsmeyer
VP/Corporate Communications: Monica Massey
SVP/Supply Chain Services: John McDaniel
Media/Public Relations: Agnes Schaffer
VP/Sustainability & Public Affairs: David Darr
SVP/COO: Randy McGinnis
VP/Sales & Marketing: Lavonne Dietrick
SVP/Finance & Business Development: Pat Panko
Estimated Sales: $8 Billion
Number Employees: 3750
Type of Packaging: Private Label, Bulk
Brands:
DAIRY FARMERS

3389 **Dairy Farms of America**
925 State Route 18
New Wilmington, PA 16142-5023 724-946-8729
Fax: 724-946-2261 800-837-5214
www.dfamilk.com
Manufacturers of dairy products
President: Shawn Koddoura
Plant Manager: Tim Sallman
Estimated Sales: $ 50 - 100 Million
Number Employees: 250-499
Brands:
SAVOLDI CHEESE

3390 **Dairy Fresh**
2221 N Patterson Ave
Winston Salem, NC 27105 336-723-0311
Fax: 336-723-0353 800-446-5577
Milk, dairy products
President: Barney Meredith
Sales: Sam Garrett
Operations Manager: Robert Paxton
Plant Manager: Robert Paxton
Estimated Sales: I
Number Employees: 250-499
Parent Co: Suiza Dairy Group
Brands:
DAIRY FRESH

3391 **Dairy Fresh Corporation**
915 Tuscaloosa St
Greensboro, AL 36744 334-624-3041
Fax: 334-624-4889 800-239-5114
www.dairyfreshcorp.com
Manufacturer of dairy products including ice cream, milk, sour cream and dip
President: W E Burt
Estimated Sales: $7 Million
Number Employees: 39
Sq. footage: 3908
Type of Packaging: Consumer, Food Service, Bulk
Brands:
DAIRY FRESH
NESTLE

3392 **(HQ)Dairy Fresh Foods**
21405 Trolley Industrial Dr
Taylor, MI 48180 313-295-6300
Fax: 313-295-6950 jfarber@dairyfreshfoods.com
www.dairyfreshfoods.com
Manufacturer of beverages, cheeses, deli foods and frozen foods; importer of cheese and meats including corned beef and ham; exporter of cheese
President: Alan Must
Chairman: Mike Must
Truck Operator: Joel Must
Estimated Sales: $50-100 Million
Number Employees: 100-249
Sq. footage: 90000
Type of Packaging: Consumer, Food Service, Bulk
Brands:
BRITTNIA
DAIRY FRESH
DELI-FRESH
GOURMET
MARLA
OCEEN FRESH
PURE MAID

3393 **Dairy Group**
366 N Broadway Ste 410
Jericho, NY 11753 516-433-0080
Fax: 516-433-7657 ndorman@dairygroup.com
www.thedairygroup.com
Cheese
Owner: Ned Dorman
Estimated Sales: $1-3 Million
Number Employees: 1-4
Brands:
DAIRY GROUP

3394 **Dairy House**
150 Larkin Williams Ind Ct
Fenton, MO 63026 636-343-5444
Fax: 314-772-4280 www.dairyhouse.com
Manufacturer and suppliers of cocoa, chocolate dairy powders and beverage flavors.
President: Carl Fitzwater
Vice President: John Hutchinson
Estimated Sales: 4.6 Million
Number Employees: 30

3395 **Dairy King Milk Farms/Foodservice**

Whitter, CA 90606 818-243-6455
Fax: 818-243-2455 800-900-6455
www.dairyberries.com
Manufacturer of dairy products, frozen vegetables and dry goods; wholesaler/distributor of frozen foods, general merchandise, general line products, produce, meats and seafood; serving the food service market
VP: Joseph Goldstein
Number Employees: 50-99
Sq. footage: 10000
Type of Packaging: Consumer

3396 **Dairy Land**
2255 Gray Hwy
Macon, GA 31211-1058 478-742-6461
Fax: 478-745-3673 www.dairylandinc.com
Processor of citrus drinks and dairy products including ice cream
President: George Bush
VP: Sam Standard
Area Sales Manager: Harold Cross
Estimated Sales: $ 20 - 50 Million
Number Employees: 20-49
Parent Co: Atlanta Dairies
Type of Packaging: Consumer
Brands:
NEW ATLANTA
PARMALAT

3397 **Dairy Maid Dairy**
259 E 7th St
Frederick, MD 21701 301-695-0431
Fax: 301-695-0431 www.dairymaiddairy.com
Manufacturer of milk, sour cream, yogurt, buttermilk, juices and drinks
President/Co-Owner: Jody Vona
Co-Owner: James Vona
Controller: Clyde Faucheux
VP: Joseph Vona
Distribution Manager: Bill Fulmer
Production Supervisor: Robert Cullum
Plant Manager: Tony Vona
Office Manager: Cheryl Cowan
Estimated Sales: $20-50 Million
Number Employees: 100-249

3398 **Dairy Maid Ravioli Manufacturing Corporation**
216 Avenue U
Brooklyn, NY 11223 718-449-2620
Fax: 718-449-3206 dairymaid1@aol.com
www.dairymaidravioli.com
Manufacturer and distributor of pasta products including ravioli and tortellini
President/Co-Owner: Louis Ballarino
Co-Owner: Salvatore Ballarino
Vice President: Anthony Ballarino
Estimated Sales: $1-2.5 Million appx.
Number Employees: 5-9
Sq. footage: 11000
Type of Packaging: Consumer, Private Label, Bulk
Brands:
DAIRY MAID

3399 **Dairy Management**
10255 W Higgins Rd Ste 900
Rosemont, IL 60018 847-803-2000
Fax: 847-803-2077 800-248-8829
Amys@rosedmi.com
www.nationaldairycouncil.org
Manufacturer of bleaching compounds, chocolate, cultures, dairy powders, nonfat dry milk, milk, protiens, vegetable, sweetners
SVP Nutrition/Product Innovation: Greg Miller, PhD, FACN
CEO: Thomas P Gallagher
VP Nutrition Research: Doug DiRenzom, PhD, FACN
Brand Development Director: Jose Cubillos
Number Employees: 50-99
Parent Co: National Dairy Council

3400 **Dairy Queen of Georgia**
730 Dekalb Industrial Way
Decatur, GA 30033-5704 404-292-3553
Fax: 404-292-5535
Manufacturer of soft serve ice cream
Manager: Joe Denmark
VP: David Lyle
Plant Manager: Robert Crements
Estimated Sales: $500,000-$1 Million
Number Employees: 10-19
Parent Co: International Dairy Queen
Type of Packaging: Consumer

3401 **Dairy State Foods**
6035 N Baker Rd
Milwaukee, WI 53209 414-228-1240
Fax: 414-228-9747 800-435-4499
larry@dairystatefoods.com
www.dairystatefoods.com
Manufacturer and exporter of juvenile cookies and animal, oyster crackers, also contract packaging available
President: Lawrence Rabin
Estimated Sales: $1-2.5 Million
Number Employees: 20-49
Sq. footage: 40000
Type of Packaging: Consumer, Food Service, Private Label
Brands:
ALPHABET COOKIES
CIRCUS WAGON SPRINKLED ANIMAL CRACK
TOY BUS ANIMAL CRACKERS
WILD JUNGLE ANIMAL CRACKERS

3402 **(HQ)Dairy-Mix**
3020 46th Ave N
St Petersburg, FL 33714 727-525-6101
Fax: 727-522-0769 ecoryn@dairymix.com
Manufacturer and exporter of ice cream, ice milk and milk shake mixes, frozen dessert
President: Edward Coryn
Secretary: Ann Coryn
VP: John Coryn
Estimated Sales: $8 Million
Number Employees: 10-19
Type of Packaging: Food Service, Bulk

3403 **DairyAmerica**
4974 E Clinton Way Ste 121
Fresno, CA 93727 559-251-0992
Fax: 559-251-1078 800-722-3110
webmaster@dairyamerica.com
www.dairyamerica.com
Manufacturer and exporter of milk including low heat, medium heat, high heat, whole and dry buttermilk
President/SVP: Keith Gomes
Controller: Jean McAbee
CEO: Rich Lewis
Director Marketing: Doug White
COO: Richard Lewis
Estimated Sales: $1-2.5 Million
Number Employees: 20-49
Type of Packaging: Bulk
Brands:
DAIRYAMERICA

3404 **DairyChem Inc**
9120 Technology Lane
Fishers, IN 46038 317-849-8400
Fax: 317-849-8213 cservice@dairychem.com
www.dairychem.com
Manufacturer and exporter of natural dairy flavors including butter, cream, buttermilk, sour cream, cream cheese, cultured dairy, yogurt, milk, starter distillate and starter flavors.
Owner: Daniel Church
VP: Diana Church
Sales Manager: Travis McMahan
Operations Manager/Purchasing: Paul Hampton
Estimated Sales: $1 Million
Number Employees: 9
Sq. footage: 16700
Type of Packaging: Private Label, Bulk

3405 **Dairyfood USA Inc**
2819 County Road F
Blue Mounds, WI 53517 608-437-5598
Fax: 608-437-8850 800-236-3300
customerservice@dairyfoodusa.com
www.dairyfoodusa.com
cheeses, as well as candies, coffees, sausages and crackers
President/Owner: Daniel Culligan
Human Resources Manager: Teddy White
Purchasing: Vicki Mosure
Estimated Sales: $14.2 Million
Number Employees: 100

3406 **Dairyland Ice Cream Company**
487 Chancellor Ave
Irvington, NJ 7111 973-923-7625
Fax: 973-923-2557
Ice cream and frozen desserts
President: Arthur Anastasio
General Manager: Jim Kubeck
Estimated Sales: $800,000
Number Employees: 11
Type of Packaging: Private Label
Brands:
DAIRYLAND

3407 **(HQ)Dairymen's**
3068 W 106th Street
Cleveland, OH 44111-1899 216-671-2300
Fax: 216-671-1560
Dairy
President: Russell Dzurec
Estimated Sales: $50-100 Million
Number Employees: 250-499
Parent Co: Suiza Dairy Group

3408 **Dairytown Products Ltd**
49 Milk Board Road
Sussex, NB E4E 5L2
Canada 506-432-1950
Fax: 506-432-1940 800-561-5598
admin@dairytown.com www.dairytown.com
Manufacturer of butter and skim milk, whole milk and buttermilk powders
CEO: Derek Roberts
Quality Assurance: Wendy Palmer
VP Sales/Marketing: George MacPhee
Operations Manager: Lynn McLaughlin
Type of Packaging: Private Label

3409 **Daisy Brand**
12750 Merit Dr Ste 600
Dallas, TX 75251 972-726-0800
Fax: 972-726-0115 877-292-9830
www.daisybrand.com
Manufacturer and exporter of sour cream
President: David Sokolsky
Vice President: Tom Lambert
Information Systems Manager: Kevin Brown
Estimated Sales: $171 Million
Number Employees: 104
Type of Packaging: Consumer, Food Service, Private Label, Bulk
Brands:
DAISY LIGHT BRAND SOUR CREAM
DAISY NO FAT BRAND SOUR CREAM
DAISY REGULAR BRAND SOUR CREAM

3410 **(HQ)Dakota Brands Intl.nal**
2121 13th St NE
Jamestown, ND 58401 701-252-5073
Fax: 701-251-1047 800-844-5073
dearle@dakotabrands.com
www.dakotabrands.com
Manufacturer of bagels, rolls and frozen roll dough
President: Rex King
CEO: Donald Kerr
R&D/QA Manager: Colleen Miller
VP Operations: Darvin Becker
Estimated Sales: $2.5-5 Million
Number Employees: 45
Number of Products: 60
Sq. footage: 10500
Type of Packaging: Consumer, Food Service, Private Label, Bulk
Brands:
BAGELS
BAKEABLE
DAKOTA

3411 **Dakota Country Cheese**
2909 Twin City Dr
Mandan, ND 58554 701-663-0246
Fax: 701-663-9412 dakcoche@btigate.net
Manufacturer of cheese
President: Virgil Johnson
Secretary/Treasurer: Cindy Landenberger
Estimated Sales: $10-24.9 Million
Number Employees: 20-49
Sq. footage: 17000
Type of Packaging: Consumer
Other Locations:
Dakota Country Cheese - Plant
Mandan ND
Brands:
DAKOTA COUNTRY

3412 **Dakota Gourmet**
896 22nd Ave N
Wahpeton, ND 58075 701-642-3068
Fax: 701-642-9403 800-727-6663
info@dakotagourment.com
www.dakotagourmet.com
Manufacturer of roasted sunflower nuts, soynuts, and toasted corn
Manager: Lucy Spiekermeier
General Manager: Lucy Spiekermeier
Estimated Sales: $2.5-5 Million
Number Employees: 20-49
Sq. footage: 40000
Parent Co: Sonne
Type of Packaging: Consumer, Food Service, Private Label, Bulk
Brands:
GIANTS

3413 **Dakota Growers Pasta Company**
7300 36th Avenue North
New Hope, MN 55427 763-531-5360
Fax: 763-536-0100
ribrahim@dakotagrowers.com
www.dakotagrowers.com
Manufacturer of traditional and unique organinc and non-organic pastas.
President/Chief Executive Officer: Timothy Dodd

Chief Financial Officer: Edward Irion
Director, Research Development: Radwan Ibrahim
Estimated Sales: $100 Milion
Number Employees: 250
Type of Packaging: Consumer, Food Service, Private Label, Bulk
Brands:
DAKOTA GROWERS PASTA
PASTA SANITA
ZIA BRIOSA

3414 **Dakota Organic Products**
Po Box 815
500 19th Street Southwest
Watertown, SD 57201 605-884-1100
Fax: 605-884-1133 800-243-7264
hescoinc@hesco-inc.com www.hesco-inc.com
Processor and exporter of wheat, millet, durum, flour, sorghum meal, oat flour, flakes, triticale and rye flakes; organic forms available
President: Colleen Hestad
CEO: Bruce Hestad
VP: Rick Hanson
Quality Control: Michael Britt
Sales: Brad Hennrich
Plant Manager: Layne Glines
Purchasing: Travis Sitter
Estimated Sales: $ 50 - 100 Million
Number Employees: 20-49
Sq. footage: 15000
Parent Co: Hesco, Inc.
Type of Packaging: Bulk
Brands:
Enhanced Oat Fiber
Flaxgrain
Flaxmeal

3415 **Dakota Prairie Organic Flour Company**
500 North St W
Harvey, ND 58341 701-324-4330
Fax: 701-324-4334 www.dakota-prairie.com
Organic white & wheat flours, gluten free flour, bread, brownie, cake & cookie mixes.

3416 **Dakota Premium Foods**
100 Bridgepoint Curv Ste 249
South Saint Paul, MN 55075 651-552-8230
Fax: 651-552-2107
Manufacturer and exporter of beef
Manager: Pat Devitt
CEO: Thomas Rosen
COO: Greg Benedict
Plant Manager: Steve Cortinas
Estimated Sales: 169 Million
Number Employees: 5-9
Parent Co: Rosen Diversified
Type of Packaging: Consumer, Food Service, Private Label, Bulk

3417 **(HQ)Dale T. Smith & Sons Meat Packing Corporation**
12450 Pony Express Rd
Draper, UT 84020 801-571-3611
Fax: 801-571-3685 www.smithmeats.com

Manufacturer of beef, pork and lamb, packing service
President: Dale Smith
Vice President: Dennis Smith
Production Manager: Roger McNicol
Estimated Sales: $22 Million
Number Employees: 100
Type of Packaging: Consumer, Food Service

3418 **Dale and Thomas Popcorn**
1 Cedar Ln
Englewood, NJ 7631 201-645-4586
Fax: 201-645-4848 800-767-4444
info@daleanfthomaspopcorn.com
www.daleandthomaspopcorn.com
Flavored popcorn
Estimated Sales: $40.8 Million
Number Employees: 250

3419 **Daley Brothers ltd.**
215 Water Street, Suite 301
St John's, NL A1C 6C9
Canada 709-364-8844
Fax: 709-364-7216 sales@daleybrothers.com
www.daleybrothers.com
Manufacturer and exporter of fresh and frozen seafood
President: Terry Daley
CEO: Steve Hoskins
Sales Manager: Rosemary Buckingham
Number Employees: 20-49
Type of Packaging: Bulk

3420 **Dalla Valle Vineyards**
P.O.Box 329
Oakville, CA 94562-0329 707-944-2676
Fax: 707-944-8411 www.dallavallevineyards.com
Wines
President: Naoko Dalla Valle
Estimated Sales: $2.5-5 Million
Number Employees: 5-9
Type of Packaging: Private Label
Brands:
DALLA

3421 **Dallas City Packing**
3049 Morrell Ave
Dallas, TX 75203 214-948-3901
Fax: 214-942-2039
Manufacturer and exporter of boxed and carcass beef; also, cooked sausage products
President: Alan Rubin
Estimated Sales: $75 Million
Number Employees: 100-249
Type of Packaging: Food Service, Private Label

3422 **Dallas Dressed Beef**
1348 Conant St
Dallas, TX 75207 214-638-0142
Fax: 214-631-0765
Manufacturer of frozen meat patties including beef and pork
President: David Hampton
Chairman: Jack Hampton
Estimated Sales: $3 Million
Number Employees: 12
Type of Packaging: Consumer, Food Service

3423 **Dallis Brothers**
100-320 Atlantic Ave
Ozone Park, NY 11416 718-845-3010
Fax: 718-843-0178 800-424-4252
info@dallisbros.com www.dallisbros.com
Coffee and tea
President: Marcello Crescent
Sales: Jim Monahan
Operations Manager: Charles Bosworth
Estimated Sales: $20-50 Million
Number Employees: 20-49
Type of Packaging: Private Label
Brands:
DALLIS BROS. COFFEE

3424 **Dalton's Best Maid Products**
P.O.Box 1809
Fort Worth, TX 76101-1809 817-335-5494
Fax: 817-534-7117 800-447-3581
www.bestmaidproducts.com
Manufacturer of pickles, sauces, dressings and condiments.
President: Brian Dalton
Chairman: Gary Dalton
Marketing Director: Roger Fort
Estimated Sales: $50.4 Million
Number Employees: 100-249
Type of Packaging: Consumer
Brands:
DALTON'S

3425 **Dammann & Company**
20 Potash Rd
Oakland, NJ 07436-3100 201-337-3707
Fax: 201-337-0479
Wholesaler/distributor and importer of vanilla beans and products
President: Warren Gaffney
Vice President: Richard Reid
Director, Manufacturing/Operations: Richard Lee
Estimated Sales: $5-10 Million
Number Employees: 10-19

3426 **Damon Industries**
822 Packer Way
Sparks, NV 89431 775-331-3200
Fax: 775-331-3980 info@fruitful.com
www.fruitful.com
Manufacturer of shelf stable juice and beverage concentrates
President: Douglas Damon
Quality Control: Richard Johnson
Sales Manager: Larry Grant
Productions: Gary Messerli
Estimated Sales: $5-10 Million
Number Employees: 20-49
Brands:
FRUITFUL JUICE PRODUCTS
JUICE DIRECT

3427 **Damron Corporation**
4433 W Ohio St
Chicago, IL 60624 773-826-6000
Fax: 773-826-6004 800-333-1860
info@damrontea.com www.damroncorp.com
Tea
President/CEO: Ronald Damper
General Manager: Gina Gatta
Estimated Sales: $3 Million
Number Employees: 25
Type of Packaging: Bulk
Brands:
DAMRON
HARVEST DELIGHTA

3428 **Dan Carter**
3018 Helsan Drive
PO Box 282
Richfield, WI 53076-0282 26- 6-7 34
Fax: 26- 6-7 38 800-782-0741
www.dcicheeseco.com
Manufacturer of cheese
President: Timothy Omer
Estimated Sales: $500,000-$1 Million
Number Employees: 20-49
Brands:
DAN CARTER

3429 **Dan Tudor & Sons**
11081 Zachary Ave
Delano, CA 93215 661-792-2933
Fax: 661-792-6488
Packer and exporter of table grapes
Owner: John Buksa
Sales Manager: Anthony Buksa
Estimated Sales: $2.5-5 Million
Number Employees: 5-9
Type of Packaging: Consumer, Food Service, Bulk

3430 **Dan's Feed Bin**
806 Hammond Ave
Superior, WI 54880 715-394-6639
Fax: 715-394-5333
Manufacturer of flour
Owner: Dan Wicklund
Estimated Sales: $1-2.5 Million
Number Employees: 10-19

3431 **Dan's Prize**
226 Main St SW
Gainesville, GA 30501 770-503-1881
Fax: 770-503-7710 800-233-5845
Roast beef, full line deli meat
President/CEO: Joe Smith
Senior VP: James W Cavanaugh
VP Sales: Patrick Hutzel
Operations: Bob Uhlenkamp
Number Employees: 10-19
Parent Co: Hormel
Brands:
DAN'S PRIZE

3432 **Dan-D Foods Ltd**
11760 Machrina Way
Richmond, BC V7A-4VA
Canada 604-274-3263
Fax: 604-274-3268 info@dan-dpak.com
www.dan-d-pak.com
Fine food importer, manufacturer and distributor of cashews, dried fruits, rice crackers, snack foods, spices etc. from around the world.
Chairman/President/CEO/Founder: Dan On
Number Employees: 500
Type of Packaging: Food Service, Bulk

3433 **Dan-Dee Pretzel & Chip Company**
490 S Hamilton Rd
Columbus, OH 43213 614-322-0376
Fax: 216-341-9386 www.troyerfarms.com
Snack products
Manager: Gene Stiffler
Estimated Sales: $59,000
Number Employees: 2
Brands:
DAN DEE

3434 **Dancing Deer Baking Company**
65 Sprague Street
Building - west A
Boston, MA 02136 617-442-7300
Fax: 617-442-8118 888-699-3337
info@dancingdeer.com www.dancingdeer.com
Manufacturer of all natural cakes and cookies
President/CEO: Patricia Karter
CFO: James Tyson
Marketing: Duane Lefevre
Sales: Dave Lamlein
Production: Lissa McBurney
Estimated Sales: $59,000
Number Employees: 2
Number of Brands: 1
Number of Products: 25
Sq. footage: 14000
Type of Packaging: Consumer, Food Service, Private Label, Bulk

3435 **Dancing Paws**
8900 Eaton Avenue
Unit 1
Chatsworth, CA 91304 310-230-9898
Fax: 310-230-6777 888-644-7297
guidedog@dancingpaws.com
www.dancingpaws.com
Manufacturer of all natural dog and cat supplements that are human quality made
President: Werner Forster
COO: Buzz Truitt
Number Employees: 9
Brands:
COAT SHINE PREMIUM
DANCING PAWS
EDIBLE COAT CONDITIONER
HI-POTENCY JOINT RECOVERY
HOWLIN' GOURMET
HUMAN QUALITY MADE FOR PETS
JOINT MAINTENANCE
NATURAL FLEA EZE
SHAKE'N'ZYME

3436 **Dangold**
13843 78th Road
Flushing, NY 11367-3241 718-591-5286
Fax: 718-591-5193
Confectioneries and cookies
President/Public Relations: Daniel Gross
VP: Karen Gross
Number Employees: 5
Type of Packaging: Private Label

Brands:
DANGOLD

3437 **Daniel Weaver Company**
P.O.Box 508
Lebanon, PA 17042-0508 717-274-6100
Fax: 717-274-6103 800-932-8377
dweaverco@onemain.com www.godshalls.com
Beef, beef products
Manager: Jerry Landuyt
CFO: Toni Spangler
VP: Hugh Millen
Marketing: Hugh Miller
Estimated Sales: $10-20 Million
Number Employees: 20-49
Type of Packaging: Private Label
Brands:
BAUM'S SWEET BOLOGNA
WEAVER'S BEEF JERKY
WEAVER'S BEEF STICKS
WEAVER'S FAMOUS LEBANON BOLOGNA
WEAVER'S WOOD SMOKED BACON
WEAVER'S WOOD SMOKED HAMS

3438 **Daniel Webster Hearth N Kettle**
141 Falmouth Rd
Hyannis, MA 02601-2755 508-771-0040
Fax: 508-771-0883 888-774-5511
www.cataniahospitalitygroup.com
Fresh and frozen soups and chowders
President: Vincent J Catania
VP: Richard Catonia
Estimated Sales: $500,000-$1 Million
Number Employees: 500-999
Type of Packaging: Private Label
Brands:
CAPE COD CLAM CHOWDER
CAPE COD LOBSTER BISQUE
CAPE COD LOBSTER CHOWDER
LOBSTER CHOWDER
MINESTRONE

3439 **Daniel's Bagel & Baguette Corporation**
408 36th Avenue SE
Calgary, AB T2G 1W4
Canada 403-243-3207
danbagel@telusplanet.net
http://danielsbagel.foodpages.ca
Manufacturer of baked goods including specialty breads, bagels and pretzels
President: D Oppenheim
Estimated Sales: A
Number Employees: 6
Type of Packaging: Consumer, Food Service

3440 **Daniele Imports**
1150 University Ave # 8
Rochester, NY 14607-1694 585-244-3140
Fax: 585-461-2234 800-298-9410
info@eurocafeimports.com
www.eurocafeimports.com
Biscotti, chocolate, espresso, flavoring. Distributors of cafe and restaurant products
Owner: Barb Campbell
Public Relations: Danny Daniele
Estimated Sales: $1-2.5 Million
Number Employees: 5-9

3441 **Daniels Seafood Company**
Mill Landing Road
Wanchese, NC 27981 252-473-5779
Seafood
President: Mickey Daniels
Estimated Sales: $2.5-5 Million
Number Employees: 10-19
Brands:
DANIELS

3442 **Danisco USA**
4330 Drane Field Rd
Lakeland, FL 33811-1211 863-646-0165
Fax: 863-646-0991 usa.info@danisco.com
www.danisco.com
Manufacturer of natural fruit flavors
President: Kevin McCole
Vice President: Gil Escobar
Innovation Director: Robert Kryger
Director Operations: Paul Jones
Estimated Sales: $25-49.9 Million
Number Employees: 52

3443 **Danisco-Cultor**
430 Saw Mill River Rd
Ardsley, NY 10502-2605 914-674-6300
Fax: 914-674-6538 www.danisco.com
Ingredients for beverage products, including flavor enhancers, and functional botanicals, xylitol, industrial enzymes, sugar
President: Robert Mayer
CEO: Tom Knutzen
VP: Philippe Lavielle
Estimated Sales: $ 5 - 10 Million
Number Employees: 20-49

3444 **Danish Baking Company**
15215 Keswick St
Van Nuys, CA 91405-1014 818-786-1700
Fax: 818-786-3617
Manufacturer and exporter of fresh and frozen baked goods including brownies, muffins, pastries, fruit tortes, bread and cakes: individual portions available
President: Charlyn Jensen
Estimated Sales: $ 10 - 20 Million
Number Employees: 50-99
Sq. footage: 20000
Type of Packaging: Consumer, Food Service, Private Label, Bulk
Other Locations:
Brands:
BUBBLES BAKING CO.
GRANNY'S GOURMET GOODIES

3445 **Danish Creamery Association**
2000 N. Plaza Dr.
Visalia, CA 93291 559-625-2200
Fax: 559-625-5433 www.californiadairies.com
Creamery
Chairman: Tony Mendes
Vice Chairman: John Bidart
Executive VP: Jim Gomes
Plant Manager: Bob Ray
Estimated Sales: $2.38B
Number Employees: 100-249
Sq. footage: 135
Brands:
DANISH CREAMERY

3446 **Danish Maid Butter Company**
8512 S Commercial Ave
Chicago, IL 60617 773-731-8787
Fax: 773-731-9812
danishmaidbutter@hotmail.com
www.danishmaid.com
Manufacturer of dairy products including anhydrous milkfat, butter oil and regular and whipped butter; also, packaging services available
President: Susan Wagner
Plant Manager: Matthew Wagner
Estimated Sales: $5 Million
Number Employees: 10
Sq. footage: 18000
Type of Packaging: Consumer, Food Service, Private Label, Bulk

3447 **(HQ)Dankworth Packing Company**
1609 Eubank Ave
Ballinger, TX 76821 325-365-3552
Fax: 325-365-2367
Manufacturer of pork products including ham, bacon and sausage; also, barbecue meats and gift boxes available, packing services available
President: Michael Dankworth
Estimated Sales: $17 Million
Number Employees: 50-99
Type of Packaging: Consumer

3448 **Danner Salads**
P.O.Box 10585
Peoria, IL 61612-0585 309-691-0289
Fax: 309-691-5267 jenellesummas@yahoo.com
Manufacturer of prepared salads including potato
President: Jenelle Summers
VP Treasurer: Doreen Cunningham
Production Manager: Paula Riddle
Plant Manager: Chuck Summers
Estimated Sales: $ 3 Million
Number Employees: 20-49
Number of Products: 50
Type of Packaging: Food Service, Private Label, Bulk

3449 **Dannon Company**
1300 W Peter Smith St
Fort Worth, TX 76104 817-332-1264
Fax: 817-877-0854 800-211-6565
www.dannon.com
Manufacturer of yogurt
President/CEO: Juan Carlos Dalto
CFO: Tony Cicio
SVP Marketing: Andreas Ostermayr
Plant Manager: Mike Weidman
Estimated Sales: $100-500 Million
Number Employees: 250-499
Parent Co: Danone Group
Type of Packaging: Consumer, Food Service
Other Locations:
Dannon Plant
Minster OH
Dannon Plant
West Jordan UT
Brands:
DANNON

3450 **Dannon Company**
P.O.Box 122
Minster, OH 45865 419-628-3861
Fax: 419-628-4008 www.dannon.com
Manufacturer of yogurt
Manager: Didier Menu
CFO: Tony Cicio
VP R&D North America: Hans Leijtens
VP Quality Management: Todd Brown
SVP Marketing: Andreas Ostermayr
SVP Sales: Nick Krzyzaniak
VP Regulatory Affairs: Philipe Caradec
VP Manufacturing: Alain Foulgoc
VP Purchasing: Francois Blanckaert
Estimated Sales: $100-499.9 Million
Number Employees: 250-499
Parent Co: Groupe Danone
Other Locations:
Dannon Company
Minster OH
Dannon Company
Fort Worth TX
Dannon Company
West Jordan UT
Brands:
DANNON
DANONE

3451 **(HQ)Dannon Company**
100 Hillside Ave
White Plains, NY 10603 914-872-8400
Fax: 914-366-2805 877-326-6668
www.dannon.com
Manufacturer of yogurt products
President/CEO: Juan Carlos Dalto
CFO: Tony Cicio
CEO: Gustavo Valle
VP Quality Management: Todd Brown
Sales: Jim Murphy
Sr Director Public Relations: Michael Neuwirth
VP Purchasing: Francois Blankaert
Number Employees: 500-999
Parent Co: Dannon Groupe
Other Locations:
Dannon Company Plant
West Jordan UT
Dannon Company Plant
Fort Worth TX
Dannon Company Plant
Minster OH
Brands:
DANNON

3452 **Danny's Poultry**
2129 S Erie Hwy
Hamilton, OH 45011 513-737-7780
Fax: 513-868-7372
Poultry
Estimated Sales: $1-2.5 Million
Number Employees: 10-19
Brands:
DANNY'S

3453 **(HQ)Danone Waters**
10850 S Harlan Rd
French Camp, CA 95231-9600 209-982-5412
Fax: 626-585-8703 www.evian.com,
www.dannon.com

Manufacturer of bottled water
President: Thomas Kunz
CEO: William Holl
CFO: Dan Redfern
VP Marketing: Conrad Smits
Sales: Pascal Rigaud
Estimated Sales: $43,000
Number Employees: 1
Parent Co: Danone Group
Type of Packaging: Consumer
Brands:
ALHAMBRA
DANNON
EVIAN
SPARKLETTS

3454 **Danvers Bakery**
114 Water Street
Danvers, MA 01923-3751 978-774-9186
Breads, rolls, pastries, cakes
Estimated Sales: Less than $500,000
Number Employees: 5-9
Brands:
DANVERS

3455 **Daprano & Company**
Po Box 49228
Charlotte, NC 28277 704-927-0590
Fax: 704-927-0591 877-365-2337
sales@daprano.com www.daprano.com
Manufacturer of designer chocolates, bonbons, novelties, Italian cookies, biscotti, madeleines, shortbread
President: Angelo Daprano
Brands:
AMARETTI VIRGINIA
BONBON BARNIER
CAFFAREL
CANTATTI
FLAMIGNI
GATSBY'S/PIERRE KOENIG
JILA & JOLS
REINHARDT

3456 **Darby Plains Dairy**
9870 Us Highway 42 S
Plain City, OH 43064-9561 614-873-4574
Fax: 614-873-8304
Milk, dairy products
Owner: Derrick Yoder
Estimated Sales: $500,000-$1 Million
Number Employees: 10-19
Brands:
DARBY PLAINS

3457 **Dare Foods**
3750 N. Blackstock Rd.
Spartanburg, NC 29303 800-668-3273
Fax: 303-371-8185 cmollohan@darefoods.com
www.darefoods.com
Manufacturer of cookies and crackers
President: Carl Doerr
Plant Manager: Jeff Wilson

3458 **Dare Foods**
2481 Kingsway Drive
Kitchener, ON N2G 4G4
Canada 519-893-5500
Fax: 519-893-2644 800-265-8225
psinden@darefoods.com www.darefoods.com
Manufacturer and exporter of sweet biscuits, cookies and crackers; also, chocolate, regular and gummy candies
President: Lee Andrews
VP Bakery Marketing: Heather McTavish
SVP Sales: Gary MacLeod
VP Human Resources: David Lippert
Estimated Sales: $76 Million
Number Employees: 1400
Type of Packaging: Consumer, Food Service, Private Label, Bulk
Other Locations:
Dare Foods Ltd.
Milton ON
Brands:
BREMNER
BRETON
CABARET
DARE
GRISSOL
REALFRUIT GUMMI'S
SUNMAID
VIVANT

3459 **Dare Foods**
143 Tycos Drive
Toronto, ON M6B 1W6
Canada 416-878-0253
Fax: 416-787-0785 nvoutt@darefoods.com
Manufacturer and exporter of cookies, candies and crackers; also, ground cookie ingredients
National Sales Manager: Neil S Voutt
Number Employees: 60
Type of Packaging: Bulk

3460 **Dare Foods**
3750 N. Blackstock Rd.
Spartanburg, SC 29303 781-639-1808
Fax: 781-639-2286 1 8-0 6-8 32
mthompson@darefoods.com
www.darefoodsinc.com
Cookies and crackers
President: Graham Dare
VP/General Manager: Michael Thompson
Estimated Sales: $500,000-$1 Million
Number Employees: 1-4
Type of Packaging: Private Label
Brands:
BREALETINE COOKIES
BRENNER WAFERS
BRETON
COBRANT
DARE COOKIES
VINTA CRACKERS
VIVANT CRACKERS

3461 **Dare Foods Incorporated**
2481 Kingway Drive
PO Box 1058
Kitchener, ON N2C 1A6 519-893-5500
Fax: 519-893-2644 800-668-3273
akueneman@darefoods.com www.darefoods.com
Cookies, crackers, fine breads and candy
Number Employees: 1300

3462 **Daregal Gourmet**
100 Overlook Center
2nd Floor Suite 2014
Princeton, NJ 08540 609-375-2312
Fax: 609-375-2402 info@daregalgourmet.com
www.daregalgourmet.com
Frozen chopped herbs

3463 **Darifair Foods**
4131 Sunbeam Rd
Jacksonville, FL 32257 904-268-8999
Fax: 904-268-8666 info@darifair.com
www.darifair.com
Manufacturers of cultured dairy ice cream and dessert
President: Andrew Block
CFO: William Block
VP Business Development: Jeffrey Block
VP Marketing: Michele Block
VP Operations: Ed Stevens
Estimated Sales: $2.5-5 Million
Number Employees: 10-19
Type of Packaging: Private Label
Brands:
DAIRFAIR

3464 **Darigold**
1130 Rainier Ave S
Seattle, WA 98144 206-284-7220
Fax: 206-722-2569 800-333-6455
www.darigold.com
Milk, butter, sour cream, yogurt, cottage cheese, half & half/creamers/whipping cream and buttermilk
President/CEO: John Underwood
SVP Finance/CFO: John Wells
Sales Manager: Scott Campbell
SVP Operations: Jim Wegner
Plant Manager: Todd Aarons
Purchasing Agent: Ralph Goeckner
Estimated Sales: $2.1 Billion
Number Employees: 1,240
Sq. footage: 160000
Parent Co: Northwest Dairy Association
Type of Packaging: Consumer, Food Service, Private Label, Bulk
Brands:
Fred Meyer
Haggen
Safeway
Sysco Products
Western Family

3465 **Dark Mountain Winery and Brewery**
13605 E Benson Hwy
Vail, AZ 85641 520-762-5777
Fax: 520-762-5898
Wine and beer
President: H Clarke Romans
Estimated Sales: $1-2.5 Million
Number Employees: 1-4
Brands:
DARK MOUNTAIN

3466 **Dark Tickle Company**
PO Box 29
St Lunaire-Griquet, NL A0K 2X0
Canada 709-623-2354
Fax: 709-623-2354 darktickle@nf.sympatico.ca
www.darktickle.com
Manufacturer and exporter of wild berry jams, toppings, beverage concentrate, relish and vinegars
President: Stephen Knudsen
Number Employees: 6
Sq. footage: 2500
Type of Packaging: Consumer
Brands:
DARK TICKLE

3467 **Darling International**
P.O.Box 668
Bellevue, NE 68005 402-731-7600
Fax: 402-733-8460 www.darlingii.com
Manufacturer of edible oils; also, partially defatted chopped beef and beef tissue
General Manager: Mike Musgrave
Estimated Sales: $2.5-5 Million
Number Employees: 10-19
Parent Co: Darling Delaware

3468 **(HQ)Darling International**
1002 Belt Line Ave
Cleveland, OH 44109 216-651-9300
Fax: 216-651-5675 www.darlingii.com
Manufacturer of rendered grease
General Manager: Mike Musgrave
Plant Manager: Lori Horvath
Estimated Sales: $5-10 Million
Number Employees: 20-49

3469 **Das Foods**
2041 W Carroll Avenue
Chicago, IL 60612 312-224-8590
Fax: 800-861-1336 katie@dasfoods.com
www.dasfoods.com
Manufacture of gourmet salts, caramels, lollipops and other treats
President: Katie Das
Member: Dhurba Das
Estimated Sales: $500,000-1 Million
Number Employees: 1-4

3470 **Daume Winery**
300 S Lewis Rd
Camarillo, CA 93012-6619 805-484-0597
Fax: 805-484-0597 800-559-9922
Wines
President: John Daume
Estimated Sales: Less than $500,000
Number Employees: 1
Sq. footage: 2
Type of Packaging: Private Label
Brands:
DAUME

3471 **Dave Kingston Produce**
477 Shoup Ave # 207
Idaho Falls, ID 83402-3658 208-522-2365
Fax: 208-552-7488 800-888-7783
www.kingstonmarketing.com
Manufacturer, packager, shipper and exporter of produce including potatoes and onions
Owner: Dave Kingston
Contact: Jody Boline
Estimated Sales: $20-50 Million
Number Employees: 100-249
Brands:
AWESOME
RUSSETTS

3472 **Dave's Bakery**
1235 Main St
Honesdale, PA 18431-2062 570-253-1660
Manufacturer of baked goods including bread, cakes, cookies, rolls and pies
President: Edwin Day

Estimated Sales: $500,000-$1 Million
Number Employees: 10-19
Type of Packaging: Consumer

3473 **Dave's Gourmet**
2000 McKinnon Ave
Building 428, Suite 5
San Francisco, CA 94124 415-401-9100
Fax: 415-401-9107 800-758-0372
info@davesgourmet.com
www.davesgourmet.com
Manufacturer and exporter of hot sauce, mayonnaise, salsa, salad dressing, nuts, cheese and snacks
Owner: Dave Hirschcop
Estimated Sales: $3.5 Million
Number Employees: 7
Sq. footage: 20000
Type of Packaging: Consumer, Food Service, Private Label, Bulk
Brands:
BONSAL & LLOYD
GARLIC MASTERPIECE
INSANITY
JUMP UP & KISS ME
SOLES

3474 **Dave's Gourmet Albacore**
P.O.Box 2040
Kirkland, WA 98083 425-822-1891
800-454-8862
crew@davesalbacore.com
www.davesalbacore.com
Processor of salmon, albacore tuna, rainbow trout, oysters, dungeness crab, shrimp, pates and mousses
President: Thad Pound
Sales Manager: Lindsay Turner
Estimated Sales: $1000000
Number Employees: 1-4
Sq. footage: 10000
Type of Packaging: Consumer, Private Label, Bulk
Brands:
ALDER COVE

3475 **Dave's Hawaiian Ice Cream**
96-1361 Waihona St Ste 2
Pearl City, HI 96782 808-453-0500
Fax: 808-456-8078
www.daveshawaiianicecream.com
Manufacturer of ice cream including Hawaiian flavors available in pints; also, frozen yogurt, sherbet, ice cream pies and cakes
President, CEO: David Leong
Estimated Sales: $2.5-5 Million
Number Employees: 10-19
Sq. footage: 5000
Type of Packaging: Private Label, Bulk

3476 **David Berg & Company**
2501 N Damen Ave
Chicago, IL 60647 773-278-5195
Fax: 773-278-4759 info@davidberg.com
www.davidberg.com
Manufacturer of beef products including frankfurters, Polish sausage, bratwurst, knockwurst, pastrami, salami, beef sticks, corned beef and roast beef.
President: Jim Einsenberg
VP Sales: Craig Campbell
Estimated Sales: $100-500 Million
Number Employees: 250-499
Type of Packaging: Consumer, Food Service
Brands:
DAVID BERG

3477 **David Bradley Chocolatier**
92 North Main Street
Bldg 19
Windsor, NJ 08561 609-443-4747
Fax: 609-443-8762 877-289-7933
david@dbchocolate.com www.dbchocolate.com
Confectionery
President/CEO: Bob Hicks
Vice President: Marcy Hicks
Estimated Sales: $ 1 - 3 Million
Number Employees: 50-99
Type of Packaging: Private Label
Brands:
Gourmet Snack Bags
Sophisticated Chocol
Zany Pretzels

3478 **David Bruce Winery**
21439 Bear Creek Rd
Los Gatos, CA 95033 408-354-4214
Fax: 408-395-5478 800-397-9972
dbw@davidbrucewinery.com
www.davidbrucewinery.com
Wines
Owner: David Bruce
Director Sales/Marketing: Joe Kimbro
Director Vineyard Operations: Greg Stokes
Production Manager, Winemaker: Eric Glomski
Cellar Master, Winemaker: Mike Sones
Estimated Sales: $2.5-5 Million
Number Employees: 20-49
Type of Packaging: Private Label
Brands:
DAVID BRUCE

3479 **David Elliott Poultry Farms**
300 Breck St
Scranton, PA 18505 570-344-6348
Fax: 570-344-6349
Manufacturer and exporter of poultry
President: David Fink
VP: Moshe Fink
Estimated Sales: $ 10 - 20 Million
Number Employees: 50-99
Type of Packaging: Consumer

3480 **David Gollott Seafood**
PO Box 553
Biloxi, MS 39533-0553 228-374-2555
Fax: 228-374-2561
Refrigerated oysters, frozen shrimp
President: David Gollott, Sr.
Estimated Sales: $10-20 Million
Number Employees: 50-99
Brands:
DAVID'S BEST
GOLLOT

3481 **David Michael & Company**
10801 Decatur Rd
Philadelphia, PA 19154 215-632-3100
Fax: 215-637-3920 800-363-5286
dmflavor@dmflavors.com www.dmflavors.com
Manufacturer and exporter of flavors including beef extract replacement, savory, nut, fruit, vanilla extract and raisin juice concentrate; also, stabilizers
President: William B Rosskam Iii
President/COO: Skip Rosskam
EVP Operations: George Rosskam
Manager, Quality Systems and Safety: Barbara Willie
Estimated Sales: $100+ Million
Number Employees: 100-249
Number of Brands: 45
Number of Products: 26k
Sq. footage: 86000
Type of Packaging: Consumer, Private Label, Bulk
Brands:
BEEFMATE
COCOAMATE
DM CHOICE
DM OLE
FAIRWAY
GORILLA VANILLA
HONEYMATE
MICHAELOK
MICHTEX
PREMIER
RAISINMATE
SUPER SUPREME
SUPERVAN
SUPREME

3482 **David Mosner Meat Products**
E8 Hunts Point Co Op Mkt # E8
Bronx, NY 10474-7559 718-328-5600
Fax: 718-842-6693 info@davidmosner.com
www.davidmosner.com
Manufacturer and packer of veal and lamb
President: Michael Mosner
CEO: Philip Mosner
Sales/Production Manager: Benjamin Mosner
Directs Lamb Program: Larry Breth
Estimated Sales: $ 20 - 50 Million
Number Employees: 20-49
Type of Packaging: Consumer, Food Service, Private Label
Brands:
MVP

3483 **David Rio**
P.O.Box 885462
San Francisco, CA 94188 415-543-2733
Fax: 415-543-2749 800-454-9605
tessa.phosrithong@davidrio.com
www.davidrio.com
Chai and loose leaf teas
President: Scott Lowe
VP: Rio Miura
Marketing: Tessa Phosrithong
Sales: Laure Macanes
Estimated Sales: $2 Million
Number Employees: 10-19
Number of Brands: 2
Number of Products: 20
Sq. footage: 3150
Parent Co: David Rio San Francisco
Type of Packaging: Consumer, Food Service, Private Label, Bulk
Brands:
DAVID RIO CHAI

3484 **David's Cookies**
12 Commerce Rd
Fairfield, NJ 07004 973-227-2800
Fax: 973-882-6998 800-500-2800
luis@davidscookies.com
www.davidscookies.com
Manufacturers fresh and frozen cookie dough, scones, crumbcake rugulach, butter cookies, brownies and mini-muffins
President: Ari Margulies
Estimated Sales: $10-20 Million
Number Employees: 20-49
Sq. footage: 20000
Parent Co: Fairfield Gourmet Foods
Brands:
COOKIE CUPBOARD
DAVID'S COOKIES

3485 **David's Fish Market**
257 Davis St
Fall River, MA 02720 508-676-1221
Fax: 508-659-1223
Seafood
Owner: Maria Sardinha
Estimated Sales: $ 1 - 3 Million
Number Employees: 1-4

3486 **Davidson Meat Processing Plant**
6490 Corwin Ave
Waynesville, OH 45068 513-897-2971
Manufacturer of frozen meats including beef, pork and lamb
President: Adam Davidson
Estimated Sales: $1-2.5 Million
Number Employees: 1-4

3487 **Davidson Meat Products**
424 S 2nd Street
New Bedford, MA 02740-5749 508-999-6293
Fax: 508-991-4533
Manufacturer of frozen and fresh meat products including sausage, hamburger patties, frankfurters, kielbasa, salami, etc
Estimated Sales: $ 5 - 10 Million
Number Employees: 10-19
Type of Packaging: Consumer, Food Service
Brands:
DAVIDSON'S
MAC GREGOR

3488 **Davidson of Dundee**
28421 US Highway 27
Dundee, FL 33838 863-439-2284
Fax: 863-439-5049 800-294-2266
sales@davidsonofdundee.com
www.davidsonofdundee.com
Manufacturer of fresh citrus fruit including; oranges, ruby red grapefruits, all natural citrus candies, coconut patties, citrus marmalades, citrus jellies, butters and orange blossom honey. Gift baskets available
President: Glen Davidson
CEO: Susan Davidson
Estimated Sales: $6 Million
Number Employees: 100-249
Number of Brands: 1
Number of Products: 112
Sq. footage: 150000
Type of Packaging: Consumer, Private Label

3489 **Davidson's Organic Tea**
PO Box 11214
Reno, NV 89510 775-356-1690
Fax: 775-356-3713 800-882-5888
info@davidsonstea.com www.davidsonstea.com
Organic teas

3490 **Davidsons**
PO Box 11214
Reno, NV 89510-1214 775-356-1690
Fax: 775-356-3713 800-882-5888
tea@davidson.reno.nv.us
www.davidsonstea.com
Manufacturer, exporter and importer of teas, spices, and accessories for the specialty trade and retail use
Estimated Sales: $5-10 Million
Number Employees: 5-9
Sq. footage: 25000
Brands:
DAVIDSON'S INC

3491 **Davis Bakery & Delicatessen**
4572 Renaissance Pkwy Ste B
Cleveland, OH 44128 216-464-5599
Fax: 216-932-8282 www.davisbakery.net
Manufacturer of specialty baked goods including cakes, doughnuts and low-sodium
President: Joel Davis
VP Treasurer: Sheldon Davis
Supervisor Sales: Janice Davis
VP Deli Operations: Sam Perkul
Estimated Sales: $1-2.5 Million
Number Employees: 10-19
Brands:
KIDDIE KAKES
SODEX

3492 **Davis Bread & Desserts**
720 Olive Dr
Davis, CA 95616-4740 530-757-2700
Fax: 1 5-0 7-7 27 www.davisbreadanddesserts.com
Breads, rolls and desserts
Owner: Tom Kilbourn
Estimated Sales: $320,000
Number Employees: 10
Brands:
DAVIS BREAD

3493 **Davis Bynum Winery**
8075 Westside Rd.
Healdsburg, CA 95448-3445 866-442-7547
Fax: 707-433-0939 800-826-1073
info@davisbynum.com www.davisbynum.com
Wines
President: Lindley Bynum
GM: Susie Bynum
CFO: Susie Bynum
Purchasing: Hampton Bynum
Estimated Sales: $2.5-5 Million
Number Employees: 10-19
Number of Brands: 2
Type of Packaging: Private Label
Brands:
DAVIS BYNUM
RIVER BEND

3494 **Davis Cookie Company**
256 Baker St
Rimersburg, PA 16248 814-473-3125
Fax: 814-473-3042 sales@daviscookie.com
www.daviscookie.com
Cookies
President: Dana Davis
Owner: Dan Davis
Plant Manager: Bob Johnson
Estimated Sales: $7.6 Million
Number Employees: 64
Brands:
DAVIS COOKIE

3495 **Davis Custom Meat Processing**
206 W 1st
Overbrook, KS 66524 785-665-7713
Manufacturer of meat products and custom butchering
Owner: Aaron Higbie
Estimated Sales: $1-3 Million
Number Employees: 5-9
Type of Packaging: Consumer

3496 **Davis Food Company**
P.O.Box 16118
Plantation, FL 33318-6118 954-791-5868
Fax: 440-461-2261
ddwoskin@stadiummustard.com
www.stadiummustard.com
Mustard
President: Peggy D Davis
Estimated Sales: $1-2.5 Million
Number Employees: 1-4
Brands:
STADIUM MUSTARD

3497 **Davis Strait Fisheries**
71 McQuade Lake Crescent
Halifax, NS B3S 1C4
Canada 902-450-5115
Fax: 902-450-5006 admin@davisstrait.com
Manufacturer of northern shrimp, scallops, snowcraf, cod, haddock, pollock
President: Grant Stonehouse
Marketing Director: John Andrews
Manager: Grant Stonehouse
Estimated Sales: $32 Million
Number Employees: 82
Type of Packaging: Bulk
Brands:
DAVIS STRAIT FISHERIES LTD

3498 **Davis Street Fish Market**
P.O.Box 5173
Evanston, IL 60204-5173 847-869-3474
Fax: 847-869-6435
www.davisstreetfishmarket.com
Seafood
Manager: Matt Sherry
Estimated Sales: $ 3 - 5 Million
Number Employees: 50-99

3499 **Davisco Foods International**
11000 W 78th St # 210
Eden Prairie, MN 55344-8012 952-914-0400
Fax: 952-914-0887 800-757-7611
polly@daviscofoods.com
www.daviscofoods.com
Manufacturer of whey proteins
Manager: Dana Bellanger
CFO: Jim Ward
VP Finance/Business Administration: John Velgersdyk
Director Quality Assurance: Matt Davis
VP Sales/Marketing/Business Development: Pauline Olson
General Manager: Martin Davis
Estimated Sales: $10-20 Million
Number Employees: 20-49

3500 **Davisco International**
704 N Main St
Le Sueur, MN 56058-1403 507-665-8811
800-757-7611
info@daviscofoods.com www.daviscofoods.com
Manufacturer and exporter of spray dried dairy products including whey protein concentrate and isolate, lactose, sweet dairy whey and whey powder; custom processing and agglomeration available
Ceo: Mark Davis
CFO: Jim Ward
VP Finance/Business Administration: John Velgersdyk
Director Quality Assurance: Matt Davis
VP Sales/Marketing: Pauline Olson
General Manager: Martin Davis
Estimated Sales: $ 20 - 50 Million
Number Employees: 20-49
Brands:
BI-PRO
VERSA PRO

3501 **Dawes Hill Honey Company**
12 S State St
Po Box 429
Nunda, NY 14517 585-468-2535
Fax: 585-468-5995 888-800-8075
info@onceagainnutbutter.com
www.onceagainnutbutter.com
Manufacturer, exporter and importer of honey, royal jelly and fruit honey cream spread
Owner: Sandi Alexander
Comptroller: Sandra Alexander
Purchasing Agent: Lloyd Kirwan
Estimated Sales: $10-20 Million
Number Employees: 10-19
Sq. footage: 20000
Parent Co: Once Again Nut Butter
Type of Packaging: Consumer, Private Label, Bulk
Brands:
BEE SUPREME

3502 **Dawn Food Products**
6303 Kenjoy Dr
Louisville, KY 40214 502-361-8471
Fax: 502-368-9437 800-626-2542
louisville@dawnfoods.com
www.dawnfoods.com
Manufacturer of baking mixes, fillings, icings and frozen baked goods
Manager: David Lightheiser
CEO: Ron Jones
Executive VP: Miles Jones
Marketing: Frank Sliwinski
Product Manager: Sarah Jones
Estimated Sales: $1.4 Billion
Number Employees: 3150
Type of Packaging: Consumer, Food Service
Brands:
AMERICAN TRADITION
BAKERS' ADVANTAGE
C.K.'S GOURMET PRETZEL STRIPS
CHOC-O-LOTA FUDGE BASE
CHOCOLATE QUIK
CRATER CONE
CRATER CONE MIX
DAWN
DAWN/BAKER BOY
DAWN/BESCO
DELUX PANCAKE/WAFFLE MIX
DERBY SCONE MIX
DIP QUIK
DUTCHESS
EMPRESS
ENERGY BAR BASE CARROTS
ENGLISH MUFFIN MIX LORD BENCHLEY'S
EXTRA MOIST DEVILS'S FOOD CAKE MIX
FUL-O-FRUIT
GRISANTIS DEEP CRUST PIZZA
HARVEST DELIGHT
HERITAGE
HOMESTYLE BISCUIT
HONEYBUN
ICE'N BASE, CHOCOLATE
KING KORN
KOUNTRY KWIK
LIBERTY
LITTLE CEASAR'S SUGAR BLEND
LORD BENCHLEY
MAJESTIC
MASTER BLEND
O.J.
ORIGINATOR
PIZZA MIX, PAN STYLE
PRINCESS
REGENCY
SELECT
SELECT WHITE BUT-R CREME BASE
SOFT ROLL MIX
SPREAD N GLOSS
YOLAY

3503 **Dawn Food Products**
3701 Concord Rd
York, PA 17402-9101 717-840-0044
Fax: 717-840-9070 800-405-6282
www.dawnfoods.com
Manufacturer and exporter of cakes
Manager: John Duda
CEO: Ron Jones
Executive VP: Miles Jones
Product Manager: Sarah Jones
Estimated Sales: $1.4 Billion
Number Employees: 3150
Parent Co: Dawn Food Products
Type of Packaging: Consumer, Food Service, Private Label
Brands:
KNAUB'S

3504 **(HQ)Dawn Food Products**
3333 Sargent Rd
Jackson, MI 49201 517-789-4400
Fax: 517-789-4465 800-248-1144
web-admin@dawnfoods.com
www.dawnfoods.com

Doughnut, cake, brownie and other dry mixes, icings and fillings, frozen products
Chairman: Ron Jones
CEO: Carrie Jones-Barber
National Account Manager: Sam Barber
Co-Chairman: Miles Jones
Procurement: Aaron Jones
Supply & Demand Manager: Sam Jones
Estimated Sales: $1.4 Billion
Number Employees: 3150
Sq. footage: 95000
Type of Packaging: Consumer, Food Service

3505 **Dawn's Foods**
1530 La Dawn Dr
Portage, WI 53901-8823 608-742-2494
Fax: 608-742-1806 www.dawnsfoodsinc.com
Jellies
President: Greg Drewsen
Estimated Sales: $20-50 Million
Number Employees: 20-49
Brands:
DAWN'S FOODS

3506 **Day Spring Enterprises**
45 Benbro Dr
Cheektowaga, NY 14225-4805 716-685-4340
Fax: 716-685-0810 800-879-7677
info@rainbowpops.com www.rainbowpops.com
Manufacturer and exporter of hard candy and lollypops; also, seasonal items available
President: Roselyn Baran
Sales Manager: Jeff Baran
Plant Manager: George Sparks
Estimated Sales: $50,000
Number Employees: 1
Sq. footage: 16000
Type of Packaging: Consumer, Food Service, Private Label, Bulk
Brands:
RAINBOW POPS

3507 **Day's Bakery**
1235 N Main St
Honesdale, PA 18431 570-253-1660
Fax: 570-253-1462
Baked goods
President: Edwin Day
Estimated Sales: $500,000-$1 Million
Number Employees: 10-19
Number of Brands: 1
Number of Products: 25
Sq. footage: 2400
Brands:
DAY'S

3508 **Day's Crabmeat & Lobster**
1269 Route 1
Yarmouth, ME 04096 207-846-5871
Fax: 207-846-3423
Manufacturer and wholesaler/distributor of crabmeat and lobster
President/Owner: Sandy Thebeau
Number Employees: 1-4

3509 **Day-Lee Foods**
13055 E Molette Street
Santa Fe Springs, CA 90670 562-802-6800
Fax: 562-926-8630 800-329-5331
info@day-lee.com www.day-lee.com
Manufacturer of meats and poultry
President/CEO: Sumio Somura
Vice President: Kiyoshi Zobe
Marketing: Dan Van Gompel
VP Finance: Misako Ipavec
General Manager: Yasushi Yokozeki
Director Manufacturing: Toshiyuki Iho
Estimated Sales: $50-100 Million
Number Employees: 324
Parent Co: Nippon Meat Packers
Brands:
DAY-LEE FOODS

3510 **Daybreak Coffee Roasters**
2377 Main St Ste C
Glastonbury, CT 06033 860-657-4466
Fax: 860-633-6614 800-882-5282
freshcoffee@daybreakcoffee.com
www.daybreakcoffee.com
Coffee
President: Thomas Clarke
Sales: Cathy Reynolds
Estimated Sales: $500,000-$1 Million
Number Employees: 10-19
Brands:
DAYBREAK

3511 **Daybreak Foods**
609 6th St NE
Long Prairie, MN 56347 320-732-2966
Fax: 320-732-3690 www.daybreakfoods.com
Egg products
President: Robert Rehm
CEO: Brent Rehm
Finance Manager: Tom Bandevencer
Plant Manager: Steven Masia
Estimated Sales: $10 Million
Number Employees: 75
Type of Packaging: Bulk
Brands:
DAYBREAK FOODS

3512 **(HQ)Daybrook Fisheries**
P.O.Box 128
Empire, LA 70050 504-657-8400
Fax: 985-657-9916
Manufacturer of fish meal and fish oil
President: Gregory Holt
VP: Borden Wallace
Estimated Sales: $30 Million
Number Employees: 2
Type of Packaging: Bulk

3513 **Dayhoff**
802 N Belcher Road
Clearwater, FL 33765-2103 727-443-5544
Fax: 727-467-0272 800-354-3372
www.dayhoffinc.com
Candy
President/CEO: Uday Lele
Estimated Sales: $15 Million
Number Employees: 16
Brands:
CONNOISSEYR CHOCOLATES
CREAM SWIRLS
JUICEE GUMMEE
JUICEE JELLIE
JUST FRUITEE
JUST JUICEE

3514 **Dayhoff**
1947 Clarke Avenue
Pocomoke City, MD 21851 410-957-4301
Fax: 410-957-4171
Candy
President: Dave Lele
CFO: Aditi Lele
Sales: Marianne Pihl
Plant Manager: Kathy Karmine
Estimated Sales: $4 Million
Number Employees: 10-19
Sq. footage: 120
Type of Packaging: Private Label
Brands:
DAYHOFF

3515 **Daymar Select Fine Coffees**
460 Cypress Ln Ste B
El Cajon, CA 92020 619-444-1155
Fax: 619-444-1985 800-466-7590
daymarcoffee@pacbell.net
Manufacturer of chocolates, syrups, teas and coffees including flavored, organic, roast, ground, whole beans and instant
President: Roy Gallegos
Secretary: Diana Gallegos
Estimated Sales: $5-10 Million
Number Employees: 10-19
Type of Packaging: Consumer, Food Service, Private Label, Bulk
Brands:
CAFE EL MARINO

3516 **Dayton Nut Specialties**
919 N Main St
Dayton, OH 45405-4694 937-223-3225
Fax: 937-223-9456 800-548-1304
info@daytonnut.com
www.riverdalefinefoods.com
Confectionery and nuts
President: Stanley Maschino
VP: Kyle Maschino
Productions: Kurt Maschino
Estimated Sales: $10-20 Million
Number Employees: 20-49
Type of Packaging: Private Label
Brands:
CANDY FARM
FRIESINGER'S FINE CHOCOLATES
RIVERDALE

3517 **Dazbog Coffee Company**
1090 Yuma St
Denver, CO 80204-3838 303-892-9999
Fax: 303-893-9999 www.coffeeandtea.net
Manufacturer of coffee
President: Tony Yuffa
VP: Leo Yuffa
Estimated Sales: $5-10 Million
Number Employees: 10-19
Brands:
DAZBOG

3518 **De Bas Chocolate**
5877 E Brown Avenue
Fresno, CA 93727-1364 559-294-7638
Fax: 559-348-2289 888-461-1276
Candy and confectionery
President: Guy DeBas
Estimated Sales: $10-20 Million
Number Employees: 20-49
Brands:
DEBAS

3519 **De Bas Chocolatier**
5877 E Brown Avenue
Fresno, CA 93727-1364 559-294-7638
Fax: 559-348-2289 www.debas.com
Manufacturer of truffles, wine-filled biscotti and chocolate bars with fruits and nut meat
President: Guy De Bas
Estimated Sales: $10-20 Million
Number Employees: 20-49
Type of Packaging: Consumer
Brands:
DE BAS VINEYARD
INCOGNITO

3520 **De Beukelaer Corporation**
P.O.Box 1697
Madison, MS 39130-1697 601-856-7454
Fax: 601-856-1462 timsullivan@pirouline.com
www.pirouline.com
Manufacturer of cookies
Owner: Peter De Beukelaer
VP Sales: Joe Snyder
Plant Manager: Joe Couch
Estimated Sales: $50-100 Million
Number Employees: 100-249
Brands:
DE BEUKELAER

3521 **De Bruyn Produce Company**
P.O.Box 76
Zeeland, MI 49464-0076 956-262-6286
Fax: 956-262-8206 800-733-9177
debruyn@michcomm.com
www.debruynproduce.com
Manufacturer and exporter of onions and carrots
President: Robert De Bruyn
Manager: Jill Philip
Estimated Sales: $50-100 Million
Number Employees: 5-9
Type of Packaging: Consumer, Food Service
Brands:
CITATION
DEBCO
GOLD RIM
GULF

3522 **De Ciantis Ice Cream Company**
45 Quaker Ln
West Warwick, RI 2893 401-821-2440
Fax: 401-821-2440
Ice cream and frozen desserts
Owner: Stephen De Ciantis
Estimated Sales: $500,000-$1 Million
Number Employees: 10-19
Brands:
DE CIANTIS

3523 **De Cio Pasta Primo**
37801 Basin Road
Cave Creek, AZ 85331 480-488-4114
Fax: 480-488-8126 800-397-0770
Macaroni and spaghetti
Owner: Rebecca DeFalco
VP: Gary Ciminello
Estimated Sales: $500,000-$1 Million
Number Employees: 1-4
Brands:
DECIO PASTA

3524 **De Coty Coffee Company**
1920 Austin St
San Angelo, TX 76903 325-655-5607
Fax: 325-655-6837 800-588-8001
sales@decoty.com www.decotycoffee.com
Coffee, teas, spices, breading mix
President/CEO: Michael Agan
Sales Manager: Roger Gibbs
Director Operations: Ronnie Wallace
Productions: Eric Fischer
Estimated Sales: $1-2.5 Million
Number Employees: 20-49
Sq. footage: 34
Type of Packaging: Private Label
Brands:
DE COTY

3525 **De Lima Company**
7546 Morgan Rd
Suite 1
Liverpool, NY 13090-3502 315-457-3725
Fax: 315-457-3730 800-962-8864
info@delinacoffee.com www.delimacoffee.com
Coffee roasters
President: Stephen Zaremba
CEO: Paul De Lima
CEO: W J Drescher Jr
Marketing Manager: Wells Neale
Regional Sales Manager: Charles Miller
Plant Manager: Bill Neuman
Purchasing: Paul Michaud
Estimated Sales: $50-100 Million
Number Employees: 105
Type of Packaging: Private Label
Brands:
DE LIMA

3526 **De Loach Vineyards**
1791 Olivet Rd
Santa Rosa, CA 95401 707-526-9111
Fax: 707-526-4151 www.deloachvineyards.com
Wines
President: Michael DeLoach
VP: Christine DeLoach
Winemaker: Cecil DeLoach
Production Manager: Rob Cooper
Estimated Sales: $20-50 Million
Number Employees: 50-99
Brands:
DE LOACH

3527 **De Lorimier Winery**
2001 Highway 128
Geyserville, CA 95441 707-857-2000
Fax: 707-857-3262 800-546-7718
discover@delorimierwinery.com
www.delorimierwinery.com
Wines
President: Alfred De Lorimier
Marketing: John Woodward
Estimated Sales: $2.5-5 Million
Number Employees: 8
Number of Brands: 1
Number of Products: 10
Type of Packaging: Private Label
Brands:
DE LORIMEIR

3528 **De-Iorio's Frozen Dough**
2200 Bleecker St
Utica, NY 13501 315-732-7612
Fax: 315-732-7621 800-649-7612
www.deiorios.com
Frozen dough
President: Benjamin DeIorio
CEO: Nadine Benedict
Operations: Larry Evans
Manager: Donald King
Estimated Sales: $5-10 Million
Number Employees: 25
Number of Brands: 1
Number of Products: 87
Type of Packaging: Consumer, Food Service, Private Label
Other Locations:
De-Iorio's Frozen Dough
Utica NY
Brands:
DE-IORIO'S
MAMA DEIORIO

3529 **DeBenedetto Farms**
P.O.Box 9760
Fresno, CA 93794-9760 559-276-3447
Fax: 559-276-0797
Fresh figs
Owner: Maurice Debenedetto

3530 **DeChoix Specialty Foods**
5825 52nd Avenue
Woodside, NY 11377-7402 718-507-8080
Fax: 718-335-9150 800-332-4649
dechoix@dechoix.com
Specialty foods including chocolate, vegetables, imported cheeses, specialty meats, pate, caviar, smoked fish, oils and vinegars from Europe, Asian products and pastry and baking products.
President: Henry Kaplan
Parent Co: Amazon Coffee & Tea Company
Type of Packaging: Food Service, Bulk
Other Locations:
DeChoix Specialty Foods
San Francisco CA

3531 **DeFluri's Fine Chocolates**
130 N Queen Street
Martinsburg, VA 25401 304-264-3698
Fax: 304-264-3698 sales@defluris.com
www.defluris.com
truffles, nuts, crunches and chews, creams
President/Owner: Brenda Casabona
Estimated Sales: A
Number Employees: 5-9

3532 **DeFrancesco & Sons**
PO Box 605
Firebaugh, CA 93622 209-364-7000
Fax: 209-364-7001
Manufacturer and exporter of dehydrated onion, garlic and vegetable products
CEO/President: Mario DeFrancesco, Jr.
CFO: Tom Abert
COO: Frank DeFrancesco III
Estimated Sales: $100+ Million
Number Employees: 500-999
Sq. footage: 500000
Type of Packaging: Private Label, Bulk

3533 **DeLallo Italian Foods**
6390 Route 30
Jeannette, PA 15644-3193 724-523-6577
Fax: 724-853-0141 www.delallo.com
Olives, antipasti, sauces, pasta and oils & vinegars
Owner: Francis DeLallo
VP Marketing: Robert Lubic
Human Resources Director: Les Samila

3534 **DeLallo Italian Foods**
6390 Route 30
Jeannette, PA 15644
800-433-9100
www.delallo.com
Olives, antipasti, sauces, pasta, oils & vinegars
Owner: Francis DeLallo
VP Marketing: Robert Lubic
Type of Packaging: Consumer

3535 **(HQ)DeMedici Imports**
One Atalanta Plaza
Elizabeth, NJ 07206 908- 37- 096
Fax: 90- 3-2 09 info@demedici.com
www.demedici.com
Gourmet specialty foods
President: Paul Farber
Operations: Marilym O'Daniels
Estimated Sales: $5-10 Million
Number Employees: 5-9
Type of Packaging: Private Label
Brands:
COLONNA

3536 **DeSouza International**
P.O.Box 395
Beaumont, CA 92223-0395 951-849-5172
Fax: 951-849-1348 800-373-5171
info@desouzas.com www.desouzas.com
Manufacturer of solar-dried sea salt; also, chlorophyll liquid, tablets and capsules
President/CEO: Rosalie DeSouza
VP Operations: K Hill
Estimated Sales: $1-2.5 Million
Number Employees: 1-4
Sq. footage: 8000
Type of Packaging: Private Label

3537 **Dean & Deluca**
560 Broadway Frnt 2
New York, NY 10012 212-226-6800
Fax: 212-334-6183 800-221-7714
www.deandeluca.com
Gourmet foods
President: John Richards
CFO: Justin Seamonds
CEO: Mark Daley
Estimated Sales: $10-20 Million
Number Employees: 250-499
Brands:
DEAN & DELUCA

3538 **Dean Dairy Products**
1858 Oneida Ln
Sharpsville, PA 16150 724-962-7801
Fax: 724-962-8566 800-942-8096
www.deanfoods.com
Manufacturer of milk and fruit juices
CEO: Joseph Neubauer
Number Employees: 250-499
Parent Co: Dean Foods Company
Type of Packaging: Consumer, Food Service, Private Label
Brands:
DEAN

3539 **Dean Distributing Inc**
1215 Ontario Rd
Green Bay, WI 54311 920-469-6500
Fax: 920-469-6505
customerservice@deandist.com
www.abwslr.com/deandistributing/home
Manufacturer of beers and malt beverages.
President: Jim Dean
Chairman/CEO: Robert Dean
Marketing Director: Jim Gibbons
VP Sales: Ken Eggen
Team Leader: Denis Gillis
Team Leader: Pat Petasek
Team Leader: Wayne Wasurick
Team Leader: Mark Williquette
Estimated Sales: $700 Million
Number Employees: 100
Parent Co: Dean Foods Company
Type of Packaging: Consumer, Food Service, Private Label, Bulk
Other Locations:
Deans Specialty Foods
LaJunta CO
Deans Specialty Foods
New Hampton IA
Deans Specialty Foods
Chicago IL
Deans Specialty Foods
Dixon IL
Deans Specialty Foods
Pecatonica IL
Deans Specialty Foods
Plymouth IN
Deans Specialty Foods
Benton Harbor MI
Deans Specialty Foods
Waylan MI
Deans Specialty Foods
Faison NC
Deans Specialty Foods
Portland OR
Brands:
BACARDI SILVER
BUDWEISER
BUSCH
MICHELOB
O'DOUL'S

3540 **Dean Distributors**
1350 Bayshore Highway
Suite 400
Burlingame, CA 94010-1813 650-340-1754
Fax: 800-928-2090 800-792-0816
corporate@deandistributors.com
www.deandistributors.com
Manufacturer of specialty food products including sauces, kosher and Mexican soups and gravy bases, tenderizers and aid, consomme, smoke and cheese flavors, syrups, extracts and nutritional supplements
President: Ralph Schulz
Director Sales/Marketing: Mark Schulz
Estimated Sales: $15 Million
Number Employees: 5-9
Sq. footage: 70000
Parent Co: Dean Distributors
Type of Packaging: Food Service

Brands:
BERNARD FINE FOODS
DEAN
FLAVOR-GLOW

3541 **(HQ)Dean Foods Company**
2711 N Haskell Avenue
Suite 3400
Dallas, TX 75204 214-303-3400
Fax: 214-303-3499 800-431-9214
media@deanfoods.com www.deanfoods.com
Manufacturer and distributor of milk, dairy products, soy products, water, juices and drinks, ice cream and novelties, yogurt, cottage cheese, sour cream and dips.
Chairman/CEO: Gregg Engles
CEO/Alpro: Bernard P.J. Deryckere
EVP/CFO: Shaun Mara
SVP/General Counsel/Corp Secretary: Steven Kemps
EVP/Research & Development: Kelly Duffin-Maxwell
EVP/Chief Strategy Officer: Gregory McKelvey
Chief Commercial Officer: Christopher Silva
EVP/Human Resources: Tommy Zanetich
EVP/Chief Supply Chain Officer: Gregg Tanner
Estimated Sales: $12 Billion
Number Employees: 25000
Type of Packaging: Food Service
Brands:
ADOHR FARMS
ALTA DENA
BARBER'S
BERKELEY FARMS
BORDEN
BROUGHTON FOODS
BROWN'S DAIRY
CELTA
COUNTRY DELITE
COUNTRY FRESH
CREAMLAND
DAIRY
DAIRY EASE
DAIRY FRESH
DEAN'S
FOREMOST
FRIENDSHIP DAIRIES
GANDY'S
GARELICK FARMS
LAND O' LAKES
LEHIGH VALLEY DAIRY FARMS
LOUIS TRAUTH
MAYFIELD DAIRY FARMS
MCARTHUR DAIRY
MEADOW BROOK DAIRY
MEADOW GOLD
MEADOWN GOLD, HAWAII
MODEL DAIRY
OAK FARMS DAIRY
ORGANIC COW
PET DAIRY
PRICE'S CREAMERIES
PURITY DAIRIES
REITER DAIRY
ROBINSON DAIRY
SCHENKEL'S
SCHEPPS DAIRY
SILK SOYMILK
SUIZA
SWISS TEA
T.G. LEE DAIRY
TUSCAN DAIRY
ULTRA
VERIFINE
WENGERT'S DAIRY

3542 **Dean Milk Company**
4420 Bishop Ln
Louisville, KY 40218 502-451-9111
Fax: 502-459-7858 800-451-3326
www.deanfoods.com
Manufacturer of milk; wholesaler/distributor of cream, cottage cheese, butter and orange juice; serving the food service market.
Chairman/CEO: Gregg Engles
EVP/CAO/General Counsel & Corp Secretary: Michelle Goolsby
EVP/Chief Financial Officer: Jack Callahan
VP: Steve Gurley
SVP/Corporate Development: Ronald Klein
SVP/Chief Information Officer: Arthur Fino
SVP/Human Resources: Robert Dunn
Estimated Sales: $100+ Million
Number Employees: 100-249
Parent Co: Dean Foods Company
Type of Packaging: Consumer, Food Service, Private Label

3543 **Dean Sausage Company**
3750 Pleasant Valley Rd
Attalla, AL 35954 256-538-6082
Fax: 256-538-2584 800-228-0704
deansausage@deansausage.com
www.deansausage.com
Manufacturer of sausage.
President/Treasurer: Marsue Lancaster
Secretary: Jane Moore
Vice President: Garry Shirley
Marketing Director: Hugh Miller
Estimated Sales: $10-20 Million
Number Employees: 100-249
Sq. footage: 25000
Type of Packaging: Consumer, Food Service, Private Label
Brands:
DEAN'S COUNTRY
KENTUCKY FARM

3544 **Dearborn Sausage Company**
2450 Wyoming St
Dearborn, MI 48120 313-842-2375
Fax: 313-842-2640 866-900-4426
info@dearbornbrand.com
www.dearbornsausage.com
Sausage
President: Donald Kosch
Marketing Manager: Leo Tomoson
VP Sales/Marketing: Todd Meier
Estimated Sales: $10-20 Million
Number Employees: 20-49
Brands:
DEARBORN SAUSAGE

3545 **Deaver Vineyards**
12455 Steiner Rd
Plymouth, CA 95669 209-245-4099
Fax: 209-245-5250
deaverwinery@deavervineyard.com
www.deavervineyard.com
Wines
President/Marketing Manager: Ken Deaver
Purchasing: Ken Deaver
Estimated Sales: $2.5-5 Million
Number Employees: 10-19
Number of Brands: 19
Number of Products: 1
Type of Packaging: Private Label
Brands:
19
DEAVER VINEYARDS WINE

3546 **Deb-El Foods**
2 Papetti Plz
Elizabeth, NJ 07206-1421 908-351-0330
Fax: 908-351-0334 800-421-3447
mgrossman@debelfoods.com
www.debelfoods.com
Manufacturer of egg products
Owner/President/CEO: Elliot Gibber
Estimated Sales: $7.7 Million
Number Employees: 50-99
Brands:
JUST WHITES
SCRAMBLETTES

3547 **Debbie D's Jerky & Sausage**
2210 Main Ave N
Tillamook, OR 97141 503-842-2622
debbiedssausage@oregoncoast.com
www.debbiedssausage.com
Manufacturer of smoked beef jerky and sausage
President: Debbie Downie
Estimated Sales: $1-2.5 Million
Number Employees: 1-4
Type of Packaging: Consumer, Bulk
Brands:
DEBBIE D'S

3548 **Deborah's Kitchen Inc.**
147 King Street
Suite 406
Littleton, MA 01460 617-216-9908
Fax: 413-552-3259
deborah@deborahskitchen.com
www.deborahskitchen.com
Manufacturer of all natural, low-sugar spreadable fruit and relish.
Owner: Deborah Taylore
Type of Packaging: Food Service, Private Label

3549 **Debragga & Spitler**
826 Washington St
New York, NY 10014 212-924-1311
Fax: 212-206-8437 debragga@aol.com
www.debraggaandspitler.com
Manufacturer of beef, veal, lamb and pork; wholesaler/distributor of further processed beef, veal, lamb and pork; serving the food service market
President: Marc Sarrazin
Estimated Sales: $20-50 Million
Number Employees: 50-99
Type of Packaging: Food Service, Bulk
Brands:
NATURAL CERTIFIED ANGUS BEEF

3550 **Debrand Fine Chocolates**
10105 Auburn Park Drive
Fort Wayne, IN 46825 260-969-8335
Fax: 260-969-8334 cathy@debrand.com
www.debrand.com
Chocolate bars, chocolate truffles, full-line chocolate, other chocolate, toffee.
Marketing: Cathy Brand-Beere

3551 **Decadent Desserts**
831 10th Ave SW
Calgary, AB T2R 0B4
Canada 403-245-5535
www.decadentdesserts.ca
Manufacturer of cakes including cheese and wedding; also, pies and cookies
President: Pamela Fortier
Estimated Sales: B
Number Employees: 6
Type of Packaging: Consumer, Food Service

3552 **Decas Cranberry Products**
4 Old Forge Way Ste 1
Carver, MA 02330 508-866-8506
Fax: 508-291-1417 800-649-9811
paradise@decascranberry.com
www.decascranberry.com
All-natural cranberry and fruit products
President/CEO: John Decas
VP Sales: Nick Decas
Estimated Sales: $ 5 - 10 Million
Number Employees: 100

3553 **Decatur Dairy**
W1668 County Road F
Brodhead, WI 53520 608-897-8661
Fax: 608-897-4587 www.decaturdairy.com
Brick, muenster, farmer cheese, pavarti
President: Steven Stettler
Estimated Sales: $500,000-$1 Million
Number Employees: 10-19
Brands:
DECATUR DAIRY

3554 **Decker & Son Company**
1500 Arch St
Colorado Springs, CO 80904-4199 719-634-8311
Manufacturer of sausages: pork, Italian, mild, medium and hot; also, sausage patties: mild, medium and hot
Manager: Carrol Ellis
VP: Mary Decker
Plant Manager: Robert Lilley
Estimated Sales: $500,000-$1 Million
Number Employees: 5-9
Sq. footage: 4000
Type of Packaging: Food Service
Brands:
PIG-IN-THE-SACK

3555 **Decker Farms**
12475 SW River Rd
Hillsboro, OR 97123 503-628-1532
Fax: 503-628-3696 marvin@deckerfarm.com
www.deckerfarm.com
Manufacturer of frozen fruits including red and black raspberries and strawberries; also, frozen filberts and hazelnuts
President: Marvin Decker
Type of Packaging: Bulk
Brands:
DECKER FARMS FINEST

3556 **Decko Products**
2105 Superior St
Sandusky, OH 44870 419-626-5757
Fax: 419-626-3135 800-537-6143
shumphrey@decko.com www.decko.com
Manufacturer and exporter of edible cake and candy decorations and packaged rings, gels
President: F William Niggemyer
Marketing Director: Sara Humphrey
Estimated Sales: $10 Million
Number Employees: 100-249
Sq. footage: 35000
Type of Packaging: Private Label
Brands:
ROYAL ICING DECORATION

3557 **Deconna Ice Cream**
P.O.Box 39
Orange Lake, FL 32681 352-591-1530
Fax: 352-591-4418 800-824-8254
www.deconna.com
Manufacturers and distributors of ice cream
Owner: Vince Deconna
Sales: Jim Carpenter
Estimated Sales: $14 Million
Number Employees: 65
Type of Packaging: Bulk
Brands:
DECONNA

3558 **Decoty Coffee Company**
1920 Austin St
San Angelo, TX 76903-8704 325-655-5607
Fax: 325-655-6837 800-588-8001
eric@decoty.com www.decotycoffee.com
Manufacturer and importer of cappuccino, flavored and regular coffees, teas, etc
CEO/President: Michael Agan
Sales/Marketing: Bryan Baker
Operations: Ronnie Wallace
Estimated Sales: $20-50 Million
Number Employees: 20-49
Sq. footage: 50000
Type of Packaging: Food Service, Private Label, Bulk

3559 **Dee Bee's Feed**
2135 270th Street
Milford, IA 51351 712-262-4850
Fax: 712-262-8764
Oilseeds production (corn & soybean)
President: Denny Winterboer
Number Employees: 1-4
Parent Co: D Double U Inc

3560 **Dee Lite Bakery**
1930 Dillingham Blvd
Honolulu, HI 96819 808-847-5396
Fax: 808-842-7056 www.stghi.com
Breads, rolls, bakery products
Owner: Shigeru Shilohara
Estimated Sales: $10 Million
Number Employees: 84
Brands:
DEE LITE

3561 **(HQ)Dee's All Natural Baking Company**
PO Box 1262
Bettendorf, IA 52722 319-359-8500
Fax: 319-359-8901 800-358-8099
Manufacturer of frozen bakery products except bread
President: Diane Benge
VP Sales/Marketing: Lonny Benge
Brands:
DEE'S ALL

3562 **(HQ)Dee's Cheesecake Factory/Dee's Foodservice**
3300 Menaul Blvd NE
Albuquerque, NM 87107 505-884-1777
Fax: 505-884-2242
smager@deesfoodservice.com
www.deescheesecakefactory.com
Deli-style specialty sandwiches, soups, salads, famous desserts and more
Owner: Steven Mager
Sales Director: Devon Jones
Purchasing: Mike Abramovich
Estimated Sales: $200,000
Number Employees: 4
Number of Products: 4500
Sq. footage: 4161
Type of Packaging: Consumer, Food Service, Private Label
Other Locations:
Dee's Cheesecake Factory/Dee'
Albuquerque NM
Brands:
DEE'S CHEESECAKE FACTORY
DEE'S FAMOUS DESSERTS

3563 **Deen Meat Company**
813 E Northside Dr
Fort Worth, TX 76102 817-335-2257
Fax: 817-338-9256 800-333-3953
webmaster@deenmeat.com www.deenmeat.com
Meat
President: Danny Deen
VP Sales: Craig Deen
Production: Joe Cholopisa
Purchasing Manager: David Burns
Estimated Sales: $50-100 Million
Number Employees: 20-49
Brands:
DEEN
DOUBLE L

3564 **Deep Creek Custom Packing**
Mile 137 Sterling Highway
PO Box 39752
Ninilchik, AK 99639 907-567-3395
Fax: 907-567-3579 800-764-0078
dccp@ptialaska.net
www.deepcreekcustompacking.com
Manufacturer and exporter of Alaska smoked salmon, halibut, canned giftpacks, custom processing and gourmet seafood
CEO: Jeff Berger
Plant Manager: Chris Baobo
Estimated Sales: $7 Million
Number Employees: 40
Sq. footage: 12000

3565 **Deep Foods**
1090 Springfield Road
Union, NJ 07083 908-810-7500
Fax: 908-810-8482 www.deepfoods.com
Manufacturer of Indian foods such as snacks, frozen meals, ice creams and others.
President: Arvind Amin
VP Marketing: Archit Amin
Sales Director: Chintam Trivedi
Estimated Sales: $5-10 Million
Number Employees: 150
Sq. footage: 60000
Type of Packaging: Consumer, Food Service, Bulk
Other Locations:
Deep Foods
Mississagua, CANADA ON
Brands:
BABU'S POCKET SANDWICHES
BANSI
DEEP
DEEP DAIRY
GUJARATI
HOT MIX
HOT WOK
MIRCH MASALA
REENA'S
TANDOOR CHEF
UDUPI

3566 **Deep River Snacks**
PO Box 373
Old Lyme, CT 06371 860-434-7347
Fax: 860-434-7512 info@DeepRiverSnacks.com
www.deepriversnacks.com
chips and popcorn
President/Owner: Jim Goldberg
Estimated Sales: $2 Million
Number Employees: 6

3567 **Deep Rock Fontenelle Water Company**
4110 S 138th St
Omaha, NE 68506 402-330-9000
Fax: 402-330-9769 800-433-1303
www.deeprockwater.com
Manufacturer of bottled distilled and mineral water
General Manager: Tom Somers
Estimated Sales: $1-2.5 Million
Number Employees: 10-19
Sq. footage: 30000
Parent Co: Deep Rock Water Company
Type of Packaging: Consumer, Food Service, Private Label, Bulk
Brands:
DEEP ROCK FONTENELLE

3568 **(HQ)Deep Rock Water Company**
2640 California St
Denver, CO 80205 303-292-2020
Fax: 303-296-8812 800-695-2020
questions@deeprockwater.com
www.deeprockwater.com
Manufacturer of bottled spring, artesian and distilled water
President/CEO: Tom Schwein
CEO/Partner: Ron Frump
VP Sales & Marketing: Craig Dodd
Estimated Sales: $10-20 Million
Number Employees: 100-249
Type of Packaging: Consumer, Food Service
Brands:
DEEP ROCK

3569 **Deep Rock Water Company**
225 Thomas Ave N
Minneapolis, MN 55405-1098 612-374-2253
Fax: 612-374-2397 800-800-8986
info@deeprockwater.com
www.deeprockwater.com
Processor and bottler of water
Manager: John Monahan
General Manager: Craig Puhr
Estimated Sales: $10-20 Million
Number Employees: 100-249
Type of Packaging: Consumer, Food Service
Brands:
Glenwood-Inglewood

3570 **(HQ)Deep Sea Foods**
13050 N Wintzell Ave
Bayou La Batre, AL 36509-2110 251-824-7000
Fax: 251-824-2148
Manufacturer of frozen shrimp; warehouse providing freezer and cold storage of seafood and poultry
President: C Kraves
Number Employees: 5-9

3571 **(HQ)Deep South Products**
255 Jacksonville Hwy
Fitzgerald, GA 31750 229-423-1121
Fax: 229-424-9039
Manufacturer of carbonated beverages, ketchup, sauces, cooking oils, peanut butter, mayonnaise, jams, jellies, marmalades and preserves; importer of olives, olive oil and Greek peppers; exporter of carbonated beverages
President: James Kufeldt
CFO: Rick McCook
General Manager: Dale Williams
Quality Assurance Manager: Eric Fowler
Human Resources Manager: Becky Russell
Plant Manager: Jerome Thomas
Estimated Sales: $74 Million
Number Employees: 500
Sq. footage: 30000
Parent Co: Winn Dixie
Type of Packaging: Private Label
Brands:
ASTOR
CHEK
DEEP SOUTH
TROPICAL

3572 **(HQ)Deepsouth Packing Company**
3536 Lowerline Street
New Orleans, LA 70125-1004 504-488-4413
Fax: 504-488-4432
Seafood, seafood products
President: Eric Skrmetta
VP: Dennis Skrmetta
Number Employees: 20-49
Type of Packaging: Private Label
Brands:
DEEPSOUTH PACKING

3573 **Deer Creek Honey Farms**
551 E High St
London, OH 43140 740-852-0899
Fax: 740-852-4530 deercreekhoneyfarms.com
Manufacturer of kosher certified honey and molasses
Owner: Lee Dunham
Estimated Sales: $650,000
Number Employees: 8
Sq. footage: 22000

Type of Packaging: Consumer, Food Service, Private Label, Bulk
Brands:
DEER CREEK

3574 **Deer Meadow Vineyard**
199 Vintage Lane
Winchester, VA 22602-3247 540-877-1919
Fax: 540-877-1919 800-653-6632
info@dmeadow.com www.dmeadow.com
Wines
Owner: Charles Sarle
Owner: Jennifer Sarle
Estimated Sales: $220,000
Number Employees: 2
Type of Packaging: Private Label
Brands:
DEER MEADOW

3575 **Deer Mountain Berry Farms**
P.O.Box 257
Granite Falls, WA 98252-0257 360-691-7586
Manufacturer of preserves including strawberry, blackberry and raspberry
Owner: Barb Neal
Estimated Sales: $1-2.5 Million
Number Employees: 1-4
Type of Packaging: Consumer

3576 **Deer Park Winery**
14936 Malberg Road
Elk Creek, MO 65464-9610 707-963-5411
Wines
President: David Clark
Estimated Sales: $500,000-$1 Million
Number Employees: 1-4
Brands:
DEER PARK

3577 **Deer River Wild Rice**
E Highway 2
Deer River, MN 56636 218-246-2713
Fax: 218-246-8722
Manufacturer of wild rice
President: Judy Myers
VP: Rex Myers
Manager: Tim Blanchard
Estimated Sales: $5.7 Million
Number Employees: 55
Sq. footage: 8700
Type of Packaging: Consumer, Food Service, Bulk

3578 **Deerfield Bakery**
201 N Buffalo Grove Rd
Buffalo Grove, IL 60089-1748 847-520-0068
Fax: 847-520-0135 sheila@deerfieldbakery.com
www.deerfieldsbakery.com
Cakes and full service bakery
Owner: Kurt Schmitt
Estimated Sales: Less than $500,000
Number Employees: 100-249
Type of Packaging: Private Label
Brands:
DEERFIELD

3579 **Dehlinger Winery**
4101 Vine Hill Rd
Sebastopol, CA 95472 707-823-2378
Fax: 707-823-0918 www.dehlingerwinery.com
Wines
President: Tom Dehlinger
Estimated Sales: $2.5-5 Million
Number Employees: 10-19
Brands:
DEHLINGER

3580 **Dehydrates Inc.**
1251 Peninsula Blvd
Hewlett, NY 11557 516-295-3700
Fax: 516-295-3777 800-983-4443
dehydrates123@hotmail.com
www.dehydratesinc.com
Dehydrated fruits, vegetables and herbs
President: Steven Reich
Marketing: Gail Whiteford
Public Relations: Lori Zahler
Estimated Sales: $1.5 Million
Number Employees: 10
Sq. footage: 20000
Type of Packaging: Food Service, Private Label, Bulk
Brands:
DEHYDRATES

3581 **Dei Fratelli**
411 Lemoyne Road
Toledo, OH 43619 416-693-0531
Fax: 419-693-0744 800-837-1631
info@hirzel.com www.deifratelli.com
Salsas, tomatoes, tomato juice, pasta sauces
Research & Development: Karl Hirzel
Sq. footage: 250000
Type of Packaging: Consumer

3582 **Del Campo Baking Company**
PO Box 2510
Wilmington, DE 19805-0510 302-656-6676
Fax: 302-652-4678 www.delcampo.com
Manufacturer of fresh and frozen hearth baked bread and rolls.
President/CEO: John Del Campo
Purchasing: Tom Pacchioli
Estimated Sales: $20-50 Million
Number Employees: 100-249
Sq. footage: 42000

3583 **Del Mar Food Products Corporation**
1720 Beach Road
PO Box 891
Watsonville, CA 95077 831-722-3516
Fax: 831-722-7690 www.delmarfoods.com
Apricots, blackberries, peaches, strawberries, brussel sprouts, red bell peppers and spinach
President: P J Mecozzi
VP: Wayne Jordan
VP Quality Assurance: Scott Taylor
Human Resources Director: Emma Terras
Estimated Sales: $57 Million
Number Employees: 50
Brands:
DEL MAR

3584 **(HQ)Del Monte Fresh Produce**
241 Sevilla Ave
Suite 200
Coral Gables, FL 33134-6600 305-520-8400
Fax: 305-567-0320 800-950-3683
contact-us-executive-office@freshdelmonte.com
www.freshdelmonte.com
Manufacturer, marketers and distributor of high quality fresh and fresh-cut fruit and vegetables, as well as a producer and distributor of prepared fruit and vegetables.
Chairman/CEO: Mohammad Abu-Ghazeleh
President/COO: Hani El-Naffy
SVP/CFO: Richard Contreras
VP/Research & Development: Thomas Young PhD
SVP/North American Sales: Emanuel Lazopoulos
SVP/North American Operations: Paul Rice
VP/Shipping Operations: Helmuth Lutty
Estimated Sales: $3.5 Billion
Number Employees: 1050
Parent Co: Del Monte Foods
Type of Packaging: Consumer, Food Service, Bulk
Brands:
DE L'ORA
DEL MONTE
DEL MONTE GOLD
FRUITINI
GOLDEN RIPE
JUST JUICE
MISSION
ROSY
UTC

3585 **Del Monte Fresh Produce**
14 Stuart Dr
Kankakee, IL 60901 815-936-7400
Fax: 815-936-7409
contact-us-executive-office@freshdelmonte.com
www.freshdelmonte.com
Processor of fresh vegetables including lettuce, carrots, potatoes and onions; also, fruit.
Manager: John Mc Conaghy
President/Chief Operating Officer: Hani El-Naffy
EVP/Chief Financial Officer: John Inserra
SVP/General Counsel & Secretary: Bruce Jordan
VP/Research-Development Agricultural Svs: Thomas Young Ph.D
SVP/North American Sales & Product Mgmt: Emanuel Lazopoulos
VP/Human Resources: Marissa Tenazas
SVP/North American Operations: Paul Rice
Parent Co: Del Monte Fresh Produce Company
Type of Packaging: Consumer, Food Service

3586 **Del Rey Packing Company**
Po Box 160 Rey Ave
5287 So Del Ray Ave
Del Rey, CA 93616 559-888-2031
Fax: 559-888-2715
gchooljian@delreypacking.com
www.delreypacking.com
Manufacturer and exporter of raisins
President: Carl Chooljian
Treasurer/Secretary: Gerald Chooljian
Vice President: Kenneth Chooljian
Estimated Sales: $20-50 Million
Number Employees: 50-99
Type of Packaging: Consumer, Food Service, Private Label, Bulk
Brands:
DELUXE
REGENT

3587 **Del Rio Nut Company**
15391 Vinewood Ave
Livingston, CA 95334 209-394-7945
Fax: 209-394-7955 delrio@evansinet.com
www.delrionut.com
Manufacturer and exporter of all varieties of natural almonds
President: David Arakelian
Estimated Sales: $ 3 - 5 Million
Number Employees: 20-49
Sq. footage: 18000
Type of Packaging: Consumer, Food Service, Private Label, Bulk
Brands:
DEL RIO

3588 **Del Sol Food Company**
3015 S Blue Bell Rd
Brenham, TX 77833-5169 979-836-5978
Fax: 979-836-6953
info@briannassaladdressing.com
www.briannassaladdressing.com
Salad dressings
President: Jerry Brown
Director Sales/Marketing: Betty O'Connor
Estimated Sales: $6.1 Million
Number Employees: 50
Number of Brands: 1
Number of Products: 10
Sq. footage: 20000
Type of Packaging: Consumer, Food Service
Brands:
BRIANNAS

3589 **Del's Lemonade & Refreshments**
1260 Oaklawn Ave
Cranston, RI 2920 401-463-6190
Fax: 401-463-7931 www.dels.com
Lemonade
Owner: Bruce De Lucia
VP: Joe Padula
Estimated Sales: $3 Million
Number Employees: 20-49
Brands:
DEL'S
DEL'S ITALIAN ICES
DEL'S LEMONADE

3590 **Del's Pastry**
344 Bering Avenue
Etobicoke, ON M8Z 3A7
Canada 416-231-4383
Fax: 416-231-3254 www.delspastry.com
Manufacturer of muffins, turnovers, pies, tea biscuits, cakes and danish
President: Benno Mattes
Vice President: Tom Mattes
Estimated Sales: $9 Million
Number Employees: 170

3591 **Del's Seaway Shrimp & Oyster Company**
PO Box 648
Biloxi, MS 39533-0648 228-432-2604
Fax: 228-432-8919
Manufacturer of frozen shrimp
President: George Higginbotham
Executive VP: Paul Delcambre
Estimated Sales: $10-20 Million
Number Employees: 50-99
Type of Packaging: Consumer, Food Service
Brands:
SEAWAY

3592 **Del-Rey Tortilleria**
5201 W Grand Ave
Chicago, IL 60639 773-637-8900
Fax: 773-637-5195
Flour tortilla shells
President: Jeannette Toledo
Office Manager: Maria Toledo
Estimated Sales: $20-50 Million
Number Employees: 150
Brands:
DEL-RAY TORTILLERIA

3593 **DelGrosso Foods**
Old Route 220
Tipton, PA 16684 814-684-5880
Fax: 814-684-3943 800-521-5880
info@delgrossos.com www.delgrossos.com
Spaghetti sauce, pizza sauce, salsa, sloppy joe sauce and meatballs.
President: James DelGrosso
VP Global Sales/Marketing: Michael DelGrosso
VP Operations: Joseph DelGrosso
Number Employees: 68
Sq. footage: 135000
Type of Packaging: Consumer

3594 **Delallo Italian Foods**
6390 State Route 30
Jeannette, PA 15644-3188 724-523-5000
Fax: 724-523-0981 http://www.delallo.com
Olives
Manager: Eric Baker
Estimated Sales: $2.5-5 Million
Number Employees: 20-49
Brands:
DELALLO

3595 **Delancey Dessert Company**
573 Grand St
New York, NY 10002-4381 914-393-5209
Fax: 914-574-5270 800-254-5254
delancey@babka.com www.babka.com
Candy and confectionery
Owner: Zvia Levi
Estimated Sales: $1-2.5 Million
Number Employees: 1-4
Brands:
DELANCEY DESSERT

3596 **(HQ)Delano Growers Grape Products**
32351 Bassett Ave
Delano, CA 93215 661-725-3255
Fax: 661-725-0279
www.delanogrowersgrapeproducts.com
Manufacturer and exporter of white grape juice concentrate
President: Ray Cox
Sales: Luis Caratan
Production: Herold Nelson
Estimated Sales: $26.30 Million
Number Employees: 50-99
Type of Packaging: Bulk

3597 **Delavau LLC**
10101 Roosevelt Blvd
Philadelphia, PA 19154-2105 215-671-1400
Fax: 215-671-1401 sales@delavau.com
www.delavau.com
Contract manufacturer and packager for the pharmaceutical, food and nutritional industries
President/CEO: Steve Bryan
CFO: Christopher Meyer
VP: Al Farado
Director of Human Resources: Alma Dickerson
COO: Kevin Lang
Purchasing Manager: Linda Branch
Estimated Sales: $34 Million
Number Employees: 350
Sq. footage: 20000
Type of Packaging: Consumer, Bulk
Brands:
Herbal Capsules

3598 **Delectable Gourmet LLC**
1110 Route 109 # 1
Lindenhurst, NY 11757-1025 631-957-1350
Fax: 631-957-1013 800-696-1350
info@icebakers.com
www.intercountybakers.com
Pesto, cranberry sauce, and gourmet cranberry juice
President: Ted Heim Sr
Estimated Sales: $ 20 - 50 Million
Number Employees: 50-99

3599 **Delftree Farm**
234 Union St
North Adams, MA 01247-3522 413-664-4907
Fax: 413-664-4908 800-243-3742
Gourmet foods and vegetables
Manager: Lori Garvey
VP: Steve Rich
Estimated Sales: $2.5-5 Million
Number Employees: 20-49
Brands:
DELFTREE

3600 **Delgrosso Foods Inc.**
P.O. Box 337
Tipton, PA 16684 814-684-5880
Fax: 814-684-3943 800-521-5880
michaeld@delgrossofoods.com
www.delgrossofoods.com
Manufacturer and importer of traditional spaghetti sauce, pizza sauce, salsa, sloppy joe sauce, country garden spaghetti sauce and meatballs.
President: James Del Grosso
R&D: Sean Etters
Quality Control: Fredrick Del Grosso
Marketing: Michael Del Grosso
Sales Manager: Robert DelGrosso
Public Relations: Sean Albright
Manager: Joseph Del Grosso
Estimated Sales: $10-20 Million
Number Employees: 50-99
Sq. footage: 105000
Type of Packaging: Consumer, Food Service
Brands:
DEL GROSSO

3601 **Deli Express/EA Sween Company**
16101 W 78th St
Eden Prairie, MN 55344-5798 952-937-9440
Fax: 952-937-0186 800-328-8184
tsween@deliexpress.com www.deliexpress.com
Prepackaged individual sandwiches
President/CEO: Tom Sween
CFO: Dick Pearson
VP: Bill Bastian
R&D: Grant Nellis
VP Product Safety: Lavonne Kucera
Marketing: Cheryl Peterson
Production: Curt Karger
Plant Manager: Curt Karger
Purchasing: Janet Robling
Estimated Sales: $100-150 Thousand
Number Employees: 250-499
Parent Co: E.A. Sween Company
Type of Packaging: Consumer
Brands:
DELI EXPRESS
SENSIBLE CARBS

3602 **Delicae Gourmet**
1310 East Lake Dr
Tarpon Springs, FL 34688 727-942-2502
Fax: 727-942-1837 800-942-2502
sales@delicaegourmet.com
www.delicaegourmet.com
Bread topppers, slow cooker meals, spice rubs, mustards, relishes, chutneys, jams, jellies, spices, infused oils and vinegars.
Owner: Barbara Macaluso
CEO: Barbara Macaluso
CFO: Linda Parish
VP: Leonard Macaluso
R&D: Eugene Mann
Quality Control: James Parish
Marketing: Janice Strayer
Sales: Janice Strayer
Public Relations: Barbara Macaluso
Operations: James Parish
Production: Scott Shepard
Purchasing Director: Scott Shepard
Estimated Sales: $1,500,000
Number Employees: 10-19
Number of Brands: 1
Number of Products: 120
Sq. footage: 10000
Type of Packaging: Consumer, Food Service, Private Label, Bulk

3603 **(HQ)Delicato Vineyards**
455 Devlin Rd Ste 201
Napa, CA 94558 707-265-1700
Fax: 707-265-7837 877-824-3600
info@delicato.com www.delicato.com
Manufacturer and exporter of wine
President/CEO: Chris Indelicato
SVP Operations: Jay Indelicato
CFO: Don Allen
VP Marketing: Steve Morgan
VP National Sales: Charles Spelman
VP Human Resources: Lillian Bynum
Estimated Sales: $100-500 Million
Number Employees: 250-499
Sq. footage: 250000
Type of Packaging: Consumer, Food Service, Private Label, Bulk
Brands:
DELICATO

3604 **Delicious Desserts**
785 5th Ave
Brooklyn, NY 11232 718-680-1156
Fax: 718-369-6665 www.deldes.com
Manufacturer of Italian desserts including spumoni, tartufo, tortoni, tiramisu, cannolis and cakes; importer of fruit sorbet and Italian cakes
President: Joe Fusceo
Estimated Sales: $1-2.5 Million
Number Employees: 1-4
Sq. footage: 2000
Type of Packaging: Private Label

3605 **Delicious Popcorn Company**
P.O.Box 188
Waupaca, WI 54981-0188 715-258-7683
Fax: 715-258-1514 www.wisnack.com
Manufacturer of potato chips and popcorn; wholesaler/distributor of pretzels, tostados, tortillas, baked and fried corn curls, party snack mix, corn chips, raw popcorn and popping oil and gourmet popcorn products
President/Co-Owner: James Hollnbacher
CEO/Co-Owner: Jeff Hollnbacher
Marketing/Sales: Jeff Hollnbacher
Production Manager: James Hollnbacher
Purchasing Manager: James Hollnbacher
Estimated Sales: $2-5 Million
Number Employees: 10-19
Type of Packaging: Consumer, Food Service, Private Label, Bulk
Brands:
DE-LISH-US
WISNACK

3606 **Delicious Valley FrozenFoods**
1200 E Ridge Rd # 9
McAllen, TX 78503-1528 956-631-7177
Fax: 956-630-1757
Frozen foods
Manager: Sylvia Villarreal
Estimated Sales: $ .5 - 1 million
Number Employees: 1-4

3607 **Dell'Amore Enterprises**
948 Hercules Dr # 1
Colchester, VT 05446-5926 802-655-6264
Fax: 802-655-6262 800-962-6673
info@dellamore.com www.dellamore.com
All natural pasta sauces
President: Frank Dell'amore
VP: David Dell'Amore
Estimated Sales: $2.5-5 Million
Number Employees: 5-9
Type of Packaging: Private Label

3608 **Dellaco Classic Confections**
8002 352nd Ave
Burlington, WI 53105-8938 262-537-2656
Fax: 262-843-1634 dellaco@busynet.net
www.pamperedpetscatalog.com
Confections and nuts
Chairman: Cynthia Delligatti
President: Laura Delligatti
Sales/Marketing: Margaret Delligatti
Estimated Sales: $2.5-5 Million
Number Employees: 10-19

3609 **(HQ)Delmonico's Winery**
56 Beaver St
New York, NY 10004 212-509-1144
Fax: 212-509-3130
Manufacturer and exporter of sherry flavors
President/Winemaker: Gerald Della Monica
Estimated Sales: $3 Million
Number Employees: 1-4
Type of Packaging: Bulk

3610 **Delphos Poultry Products**
205 S Pierce St
Delphos, OH 45833 419-692-5816
Fax: 419-692-1606 simtom@1m3.com
Manufacturer of chicken products including marinated breasts, breaded, breast fillets, hot wings, wingettes and gizzards
President: Thomas Schimmoller
Estimated Sales: $1-2.5 Million
Number Employees: 10-19
Sq. footage: 7000
Type of Packaging: Consumer, Food Service, Private Label, Bulk
Brands:
VOLCANO WINGS

3611 **Delta BBQ Sauce Company**
6231 Pacific Ave # A2
Stockton, CA 95207-3700 209-472-9284
Fax: 209-472-9284 www.spfloraldesigns.com
Manufacturer of marinades and barbecue sauces
Owner: Katie Wendland
Estimated Sales: $300,000-$500,000
Number Employees: 1-4
Sq. footage: 1800
Type of Packaging: Consumer, Food Service
Brands:
DELTA
RIVERBOAT

3612 **Delta Catfish Products**
PO Box 99
Eudora, AR 71640-0099 870-355-4192
Fax: 714-778-0998
Catfish
President/CEO: Thomas Marshall

3613 **Delta Distributors**
610 Fisher Rd
Longview, TX 75604-5201 903-759-7151
Fax: 903-759-7845 800-945-1858
www.deltadist.com
Beverages, confectionery, canned foods, processed cheese, bakery, meat, seafood, dairy
President: Tom Corcoran
Product Manager: Mike Leahy
Number Employees: 50-99

3614 **Delta Food Products**
10557 114th Street NW
Edmonton, AB T5H 3J6
Canada 780-424-3636
Fax: 780-424-1536 deltafoods@shaw.ca
Manufacturer of frozen Chinese dim sum, fresh noodles, egg and spring rolls, microwaveable Oriental dinners and green onion cakes
President: Gordon Becker
Manager: Mei-ling Chan
Estimated Sales: $1.8 Million
Number Employees: 22
Sq. footage: 15000
Type of Packaging: Consumer, Food Service, Private Label
Brands:
DELTA FOODS
WOK MENU

3615 **Delta Pacific Seafoods**
6001 60th Avenue
Delta, BC V4K 4E2
Canada 604-946-5160
Fax: 604-946-5157 800-328-2547
customerservice@icicleseafoods.com
www.icicleseafoods.com
Processor of fresh and frozen salmon, hake, sardines, halibut
Director: Don Pollard
Estimated Sales: $8 Million
Number Employees: 20
Type of Packaging: Consumer, Food Service

3616 **Delta Packing Company of Lodi**
6021 E Kettleman Ln
Lodi, CA 95240 209-334-0811
Fax: 209-334-0811 mail@deltapacking.com
www.deltapacking.com
Packer/shipper of produce including cherries, onions, juice grapes, pears, asparagus and bell peppers
Manager: Paul Poutre
CEO: Jeff Rostomily
Sales Manager: Paul Poutre
Estimated Sales: $20-50 Million
Number Employees: 100-249
Type of Packaging: Consumer, Food Service, Private Label
Brands:
DELTA FRESH

3617 **Delta Pride Catfish**
1301 Industrial Pkwy
Indianola, MS 38751 662-887-5401
Fax: 662-887-5950 800-421-1045
walterh@deltapride.com www.deltapride.com
Manufacturer of farm-raised catfish and wholesaler/distributor of fresh and frozen farm raised catfish and hush puppies
President: Bill Osso
Owner: Adrian Percy
CEO: David Boswell
Estimated Sales: $30 Million
Number Employees: 450
Parent Co: Delta Pride Catfish

3618 **Delta Valley Farms**
1365 N Highway 6
Delta, UT 84624-7471 435-864-2725
Fax: 435-864-4823
Natural and processed cheese
President: Elwin Johnson
Estimated Sales: $5-10 Million
Number Employees: 5-9

3619 **Deluxe Ice Cream Company**
P.O.Box 12459
Salem, OR 97309-0459 503-581-4923
Fax: 503-370-8516 800-304-7172
www.deluxeicecream.com
Manufacturer of ice cream novelties
President: Bill McMillan
Controller: Norma Morlock
Plant Manager: Harry Price
Estimated Sales: $50-100 Million
Number Employees: 100-249
Type of Packaging: Consumer, Food Service, Private Label, Bulk

3620 **Demaria Seafood**
12544 Warwick Blvd
Newport News, VA 23606-2644 757-930-3474
Fax: 757-930-4847
Catfish, cod, flounder, haddock, halibut, mackerel, perch, salmon, shad, tuna, monkfish fillets, blue crabmeat, clams, shrimp
Owner: John De Maria
Estimated Sales: $500,000-$1 Million
Number Employees: 5-9
Brands:
DEMARIA SEAFOOD

3621 **Demeter Agro**
2802 5th Ave N
Lethbridge, AB T1H 0P1
Canada 403-329-4111
Fax: 403-329-4418 800-661-1450
demeter@agricoreunited.com
www.agricoreunited.com
Manufacturer and exporter of spices, herbs, spice seeds, bird seed complete, mustard seed, peas seed
President/Sales Manager: Walter Dyck
Export Sales/Marketing: M L Dyck
Unit Manager: Blair Roth
Estimated Sales: $20 - 50 Million
Number Employees: 35
Sq. footage: 60000
Parent Co: Agricore United
Other Locations:
Demeter Agro
Warner AB
Brands:
DEMETER AGRO
WARNER AB

3622 **Demitri's Bloody Mary Seasonings**
1705 S 93rd St # F1
Seattle, WA 98108-5150 206-764-6006
Fax: 206-764-3163 800-627-9649
www.demitris.com
Manufacturer of concentrated Bloody Mary Seasonings
President: Demitri Pallis
Estimated Sales: Under $300,000
Number Employees: 1-4
Sq. footage: 1200
Parent Co: Gourmet Mixes
Type of Packaging: Consumer, Food Service, Bulk
Brands:
DEMITRI'S BLOODY MARY SEASONINGS

3623 **Dempseys Restaurant**
50 E Washington St
Petaluma, CA 94952 707-765-9694
Fax: 707-762-1259 www.dempseys.com
Beer
President/CEO: Bernadette Burrell
CFO: Peter Burrell
Estimated Sales: $1-2.5 Million
Number Employees: 20-49
Sq. footage: 6000
Brands:
GOLDEN EAGLE ALE
RED ROOSTER ALE
SONOMA BREWING
UGLY DOG STOUT

3624 **(HQ)Denatale Vineyards**
11020 Eastside Road
Healdsburg, CA 95448-9487 707-431-8460
Fax: 707-431-8736 www.denatalevineyards.net
Wines
President: Ron DeNatale
Owner: Sandy De Natale
Estimated Sales: $98,000
Number Employees: 2

3625 **Deneen Company**
34 Uss Thresher Ln
Belen, NM 87002-8233 505-988-1515
Fax: 505-988-1300
Manufacturers and distributors for variety of food products ranging from salsa to orange juice
President: Greg Deneen
Estimated Sales: $5-10 Million
Number Employees: 20
Type of Packaging: Private Label

3626 **Deneen Foods**
33859 United Avenue
Santa Fe, NM 81001 50- 3-2 20
Fax: 50- 3-3 71 80- 8-6 46
info@santafeseasons.com
www.santafeseasons.com
Sauces
President: Greg Deneen
VP: Edith Deneen
Estimated Sales: $1-2.5 Million
Number Employees: 39009
Number of Brands: 3+
Number of Products: 5+
Sq. footage: 17000
Type of Packaging: Consumer, Food Service, Private Label, Bulk
Brands:
Coyote Cocina
Santa Fe Seasons

3627 **Dennco**
14350 S Saginaw Ave
Chicago, IL 60633 708-862-0070
Fax: 708-862-0097
Bakery products and bakery ingredients
President: Dennis Slomski
Vice President: Tricia Yakas
Estimated Sales: $10-20 Million
Number Employees: 15

3628 **Dennison Meat Locker**
P.O.Box 128
Dennison, MN 55018 507-645-8734
Manufacturer of frankfurters and sausage
Owner: Dori Gregory
Estimated Sales: $ 1 - 3 Million
Number Employees: 1-4
Type of Packaging: Consumer

3629 **Denomega Nutritional Oils**
6640 Gunpark Drive
Boulder, CO 88301 303-581-9000
Fax: 303-581-9005 www.denomega.com
Manufacturer of edible fats and oils, Omege-3
Owner: Jennifer Kibel
CEO: Thomas Grys

3630 **Denzer's Food Products**
PO Box 5632
Baltimore, MD 21210-0632 410-889-1500
Fax: 410-235-7032 jake@denzer.com
Conch chowder, crab soup, lima bean soup, peanut soup. Southeastern and US regional foods
President: Jacob Slagle
Estimated Sales: $1-3 Million
Number Employees: 1-4
Type of Packaging: Consumer

3631 **Deosen USA Inc**
1140 Stelton Road
Suite 205
Piscataway, NJ 08854 908-382-6518
Fax: 908-292-1165
lawrence.herbolsheimer@doesenusa.com
www.doesenusa.com
Xanthan gum
CEO: Lawrence Herbolsheimer

3632 **Depoe Bay Fish Company**
PO Box 1650
Newport, OR 97365-0121 541-265-8833
Fax: 541-265-2145 dbfc@newportnet.com
www.depoebayfish.com
Manufacturer fresh seafood including groundfish, shrimp, crab, salmon, whiting, herring, tuna and swordfish
President: Gerald Bates
VP: Mike Freels
Estimated Sales: $100-500 Million
Number Employees: 200
Sq. footage: 32000
Type of Packaging: Consumer, Food Service
Brands:
DEPOE BAY
PACIFIC TRAWLER

3633 **Deppeler Cheese Factory**
P.O.Box 788
Monroe, WI 53566 608-325-6311
Fax: 608-325-6935
Cheese and cheese products
Manager: Silvan Blum
Plant Manager: Silvan Blum
Estimated Sales: Less than $500,000
Number Employees: 5-9
Type of Packaging: Private Label

3634 **Derco Foods**
2670 W Shaw Ln
Fresno, CA 93711-2772 559-435-2664
Fax: 559-435-8520 leond@dercofoods.com
www.dercofoods.com
Manufacturer of dried fruits, nuts and specialty foods; importer of dried fruits, nuts, pineapple, mushrooms and canned fruit; exporter of dried and canned fruit, nuts, mushrooms, beans and popcorn
Owner: Leon Dermenjian
Estimated Sales: $20-50 Million
Number Employees: 10-19
Sq. footage: 6000
Brands:
DERCO

3635 **Derlea Foods**
1739 Orangebrook Court
Pickering, ON L1W 3G8
Canada 905-839-7212
Fax: 905-839-7217 888-430-7777
derlea@fympatico.ca www.derlea.com
Manufacturer of fresh garlic
President: Salvatore Geraci
Estimated Sales: $1.2 Million
Number Employees: 30
Type of Packaging: Consumer, Food Service, Private Label, Bulk

3636 **Deschutes Brewery**
901 Simpson Ave
Bend, OR 97702 541-385-8606
Fax: 541-383-4505 www.deschutesbrewery.com
Manufacturer of seasonal beer, ale, stout, lager and porter
President: Gary Fish
COO: Michael LaLonde
Estimated Sales: $44 Million
Number Employees: 70
Type of Packaging: Consumer, Food Service
Brands:
BLACK BUTTE
CASCADE ALE
MIRROR POND PALE ALE
OBSIDIAN STOUT

3637 **Deseret Dairy Products**
784 W 700 S
Salt Lake City, UT 84104 801-240-7350
Fax: 801-240-7352
Fluid milk
Manager: Bill Beane
Production Supervisor: Curtis Frame
Estimated Sales: $10-24.9 Million
Number Employees: 20-49

3638 **Desert King International**
3802 Main Street
Suite 10
Chula Vista, CA 91911-6248 619-427-7121
Fax: 619-427-9041 800-982-2235
rkramer@desertking.com
Manufacturer and exporter of quillaja and yucca extracts for root beer and oil flavors
President: Paul Hiley
VP: Joel Powers
Regional Sales Manager: Raymond Kramer
Estimated Sales: $3-5 Million
Number Employees: 65
Sq. footage: 15000
Type of Packaging: Private Label, Bulk
Brands:
FOAMATION

3639 **Desert Valley Date**
86740 Industrial Way
Coachella, CA 92236 760-398-0999
Fax: 760-398-1514 sales@desertvalleydate.com
www.desertvalleydate.com
Dates
President: George Kirkjan
Estimated Sales: $10-20 Million
Number Employees: 50-99

3640 **Designed Nutritional Products**
P.O.Box 1242
Orem, UT 84059-1242 801-224-4518
Fax: 801-434-8270
info@designednutritional.com
www.designednutritional.com
Manufacturer of dietary supplements including organic germanium, saw palmetto extracts, ascorbigen, melatonin and indole-3-carbinol; exporter of melatonin, gramine, bisindolylmethance and glycogen
President: David Parish
Marketing: Omar Filippelli
Purchasing Director: Craig Hansen
Estimated Sales: $10-20 Million
Number Employees: 5-9
Sq. footage: 5000
Type of Packaging: Bulk

3641 **Dessert Innovations**
25-B Enterprise Boulevard
Atlanta, GA 30336 404-691-5000
Fax: 404-691-5001 800-359-7351
sales@dessertinnovations.com
www.dessertinnovations.com
Industrial dessert manufacturer; barcakes, cupcakes, parfaits, layer cakes, and petit fours
President: Tony Ereddia
VP Finance/Operations: Rolf Schittli
General Manager: Tim Guidry
Production Manager: Ralph Ferdinand
Estimated Sales: $10-20 Million
Number Employees: 23
Sq. footage: 48000
Brands:
Classic Confections
Custom Up Cakes
Singel serving Sundae

3642 **Desserts On Us**
57 Belle Falor Court
Arcata, CA 95521 707-822-0160
Fax: 707-822-5908 desonus@aol.com
www.dessertsonus.com
Cookies.

3643 **Desserts by David Glass**
400 Chapel Road
Unit 2d Bissell Commons
South Windsor, CT 06074 860-462-7520
Fax: 860-242-4408 david@davidglass.com
www.davidglass.com
Manufacturer and exporter of desserts including chocolate truffle cake, cheesecake and chocolate mousse balls
President: David Glass
Estimated Sales: $10-20 Million
Number Employees: 20-49
Sq. footage: 10000
Type of Packaging: Consumer, Food Service
Brands:
DESSERTS BY DAVID GLASS

3644 **Desserts of Distinction**
5365 SE International Way
Milwaukie, OR 97222 503-654-8370
Fax: 503-654-1322 www.dessertsofdistinction.com
Manufacturer of baked goods including frozen cheesecake
Owner: Sue Sanders
Estimated Sales: $10-20 Million
Number Employees: 20-49
Type of Packaging: Food Service

3645 **Destileria Serralles Inc**
Num 1 Calle La Esperanza
Mercedita, PR 00715 787-840-1000
Fax: 787-840-1000 aleman@donq.com
www.donq.com
Manufacturer of rum, vodka, gin, cordials and wine; importer of scotch; exporter of rum; wholesaler/distributor of general merchandise
President/CEO: Felix Serralles, Jr.
VP Sales: Jose Higuera
Estimated Sales: $118 Million
Number Employees: 376
Sq. footage: 300000
Type of Packaging: Consumer, Private Label, Bulk

3646 **Destileria Tlacolula**
Av. 2 De Abril No 173
Tlacoulula De Matamoros, OA 70403
Mexico 951-562-1101
Fax: 951-562-1101 adalid.hc@gmail.com
www.ilegalmezcal.com
Alcoholic beverages.

3647 **Detroit Chili Company**
21400 Telegraph Rd
Southfield, MI 48033 248-440-5933
Fax: 248-440-5945 www.dtigroup.biz
Manufacturer of frozen chili
Owner: Tim Keros
Purchasing Agent: Terry Keros
Estimated Sales: $500,000-$1 Million
Number Employees: 10-19
Sq. footage: 5000
Type of Packaging: Consumer, Food Service

3648 **Detroit City Dairy**
21405 Trolley Indus Dr
Taylor, MI 48180-1811 313-295-6300
Fax: 313-295-6950
Dairy foods
President/Marketing: Alan Must
Estimated Sales: $46.9 Million
Number Employees: 190
Type of Packaging: Private Label

3649 **Deutsch Kase Haus**
11275 W 250 N
Middlebury, IN 46540 574-825-9511
Fax: 574-825-1102 www.babyswiss.com
Cheese
CEO: Richard Guggisber
CEO: Dick Bylsma
Plant Manager: David Gall
Estimated Sales: $20-50 Million
Number Employees: 50-99

3650 **Devansoy**
206 W 7th St
Carroll, IA 51401-2317 712-792-9665
Fax: 712-792-2712 800-747-8605
info@devansoy.com www.devansoy.com
Manufacturer and exporter of powdered and liquid soy milk and soy flours;. Organic and parve available
President: Elmer Schettler
VP/Sales & Mktg: Montgomery Kilburn
VP/Operations: Deb Wycoff
Estimated Sales: $510,000
Number Employees: 5
Number of Products: 8
Type of Packaging: Food Service, Private Label, Bulk
Brands:
ENZACT
SOY ROAST

3651 **Devault Foods**
P.O.Box 587
Devault, PA 19432-0587 610-644-2536
Fax: 610-644-2631 800-426-2874
devault@devaultfoods.com
www.devaultfoods.com

Manufacturer of fresh and frozen portion controlled ground beef, hamburgers, pre-cooked meat balls and Philadelphia-style sandwich steaks
President: Tom Fillippo
CFO: Carl Sorzano
Marketing Manager: Mark Pepe
VP Sales/Marketing: Gerry Mello
Estimated Sales: $ 50 - 100 Million
Number Employees: 100-249
Sq. footage: 114000
Parent Co: Devault Packing Company
Type of Packaging: Food Service, Private Label, Bulk
Brands:
MINUTE MENU
MRS DIFILLIPPO'S
STEAKWICH
STEAKWICH LITE

3652 **Devine Foods**
8 S Plum St
Media, PA 19063-3309 610-566-2400
888-338-4631
denise@devinefoods.com www.devinefoods.com
Beverages, frozen confections
President: Denise Devine
Operations: Jerome Renners
Estimated Sales: $ 5 - 10 Million
Number Employees: 5-9
Brands:
DEVINE NECTAR
FIBRYMID
FRUICE
SIMPLY DEVINE

3653 **Devlin Wine Cellars**
PO Box 728
Soquel, CA 95073-0728 831-476-7288
Fax: 831-479-9043 www.webwinery.com/devlin
Wines
President: Cheryl Devlin
Estimated Sales: Less than $500,000
Number Employees: 1-4
Type of Packaging: Private Label

3654 **Devro, Inc.**
785 Old Swamp Rd
Swansea, SC 29160-8387 803-796-9730
enquiries@devro-casings.com
www.devro.plc.uk
Manufacturer of casings for sausages, hams, salami, as well as other meat products.
Estimated Sales: 28.8 Million
Number Employees: 373

3655 **Dewey's Bakery**
100 Vinegar Hill Rd
Winston-Salem, NC 27104-5068 336-765-2095
Fax: 336-748-0501 800-274-2994
mike@deweys.com www.deweys.com
Bakery products
Owner/President: Guy Wilkerson
Estimated Sales: $57,000
Number Employees: 2

3656 **(HQ)Dewied International**
5010 East I H 10
San Antonio, TX 78219 210-661-6161
Fax: 210-662-6112 800-992-5600
hq@dewiedint.com www.dewied.com
Manufacturer, importer and exporter of natural and synthetic sausage casings specializing in hog, sheep and beef casings
President: Howard deWied
CEO: Howard W Dewied
VP Sales: George Burt
Estimated Sales: $10-20 Million
Number Employees: 50-99
Brands:
DEWIED

3657 **Dhidow Enterprises**
PO Box 285
Oxford, PA 19363-0285 610-932-7868
Fax: 509-753-0570 dhidow@brandywine.net
Manufacturer of nonvinegar based hot sauces
President: Dhidow Stephens
CEO: Paulette Colman
Estimated Sales: $300,000
Number Employees: 2
Type of Packaging: Consumer, Food Service, Bulk
Brands:
DHIDOW ENTERPRISE 150X
DHIDOW ENTERPRISE 20X
DHIDOW ENTERPRISE 50X
DHIDOW ENTERPRISE ZERO

3658 **Di Camillo Bakery**
811 Linwood Ave
Niagara Falls, NY 14305-2584 716-282-2341
Fax: 716-282-2596 800-634-4363
dicamillo@dicamillobakery.com
www.dicamillobakery.com
Cakes, biscuits, biscotti, cookies, crispbreads and flatbreads
President/CEO/CFO/Sales: David Di Camillo
VP Marketing: Michael Di Camillo
Estimated Sales: $20-50 Million
Number Employees: 50-99

3659 **Di Grazia Vineyards**
131 Tower Rd
Brookfield, CT 06804 203-775-1616
Fax: 203-775-3195 800-230-8853
wine@prodigy.net www.digrazia.com
Wine
Owner: Paul Di Grazia
VP: Paul DiGrazia
Sales: Matthew Guglielmo
Estimated Sales: $500,000-$1 Million
Number Employees: 1-4
Brands:
CONVETUAL FRANCISCAN FRIARS
DI GRAZIA VINEYARDS

3660 **Di Paolo Baking Company**
598 Plymouth Ave N
Rochester, NY 14608 585-232-3510
Fax: 585-423-5975
Breads, rolls and pastries
Owner: Genario Della Porta
CEO: Dominick P Massa
Estimated Sales: $10-20 Million

3661 **DiCarlo's Bakery**
1701 N Gaffey Street
San Pedro, CA 90731-1274 310-831-2524
Muffins and buns
Estimated Sales: $25-49.9 Million
Number Employees: 5-9

3662 **DiGregorio Food Products**
2232 Marconi Ave
St Louis, MO 63110-3114 314-776-1062
Fax: 314-776-3954 www.digregoriofoods.com
Manufacturer of sausage, meat balls and spaghetti sauce
President: Dora Di Gregorio
CEO: John DiGregorio
Estimated Sales: $ .5 - 1 million
Number Employees: 20-49
Sq. footage: 50000
Type of Packaging: Food Service, Private Label

3663 **(HQ)DiMare InternationalDmb Packing Corp**
82025 Avenue 44
Indio, CA 92201-2244 760-347-3336
Fax: 760-347-7981 www.dimareinc.com
Manufacturer, importer and exporter of lemons, oranges, grapefruit, dates, asparagus, grapes, green onions and mixed vegetables
Owner: Thomas Dimare
VP Government Relations: Dominic DiMare
General Sales Manager: Jim DiMare
General Manager: Thomas DiMare
Estimated Sales: $20-50 Million
Number Employees: 20
Sq. footage: 45000
Type of Packaging: Consumer, Food Service, Private Label, Bulk
Brands:
BERMUDA DUNES
DI-MARE GOLD LABEL
RANCHO PALM SPRINGS
SEA VIEW

3664 **DiPasquale's**
3700 Gough St
Baltimore, MD 21224-2539 410-276-6787
Fax: 410-276-0161 mustogusto@aol.com
www.depasquales.com
Distributor of fine Italian foods and specialties.
Owner: Joseph Di Pasquale
Estimated Sales: $20-50 Million
Number Employees: 20-49
Type of Packaging: Consumer, Food Service

3665 **Diageo Canada Inc.**
401 The West Mall
Suite 800
Toronto, ON M9C 5P8
Canada 416-626-2000
Fax: 416-626-2688 www.diageo.com
Processor and exporter of gin and wine
President/Board Member: John Kennedy
Board Member: Rick Fitzgerald
Board Member: Randy Dionisi
Parent Co: Grand Metropolitan
Type of Packaging: Consumer, Food Service

3666 **(HQ)Diageo United Distillers**
801 Main Avenue
Norwalk, CT 06851-1127 203-229-2100
Fax: 203-229-8901 media.comms@diageo.com
www.diageo.com
Alcoholic beverages
President: Ivan Menezes
CFO: Chris Davies
Chief Marketing and Innovation Officer: Peter McDonough
Estimated Sales: $1 Billion +
Number Employees: 8,000-9,000
Parent Co: Diageo
Brands:
BAILEY'S
BARTON & GUESTIER
BEAULIEU VINEYARD
BUSHMILLS
CAPTAIN MORGAN
CROWN ROYAL
CUERVO
GUINNESS
HARP
J&B
JOHNNIE WALKERS
KILKENNY
SMIRNOFF
SMITHWICK'S
STERLING VINEYARD
TANQUERAY

3667 **(HQ)Diamond Bakery Company**
756 Moowaa St
Honolulu, HI 96817 808-847-3551
Fax: 808-847-7482 info@diamondbakery.com
www.diamondbakery.com
Manufacturer and exporter of crackers and cookies, including all natural crackers.
President: Brent Kunimoto
CFO: George Price
Marketing Director: Maggie Li
Sales Director: Brian Oue
Estimated Sales: $ 20 - 50 Million
Number Employees: 48
Number of Products: 50+
Sq. footage: 50500
Type of Packaging: Consumer, Food Service, Private Label, Bulk
Brands:
DIAMOND BAKERY

3668 **Diamond Blueberry**
548 Pleasant Mills Rd
Hammonton, NJ 8037 609-561-3661
Fax: 609-567-4423
Manufacturer and packer of fresh and frozen blueberries
President: John Bertino
Sales: Tim Wetherbee
Estimated Sales: $500,000-$1 Million
Number Employees: 1-4
Brands:
DIAMOND

3669 **Diamond Creek Vineyards**
1500 Diamond Mountain Rd
Calistoga, CA 94515-9669 707-942-6926
Fax: 707-942-6936
www.diamondcreekvineyards.com
Wines
President: Al Brounstein
Estimated Sales: $2.5-5 Million
Number Employees: 5-9
Type of Packaging: Private Label

3670 **Diamond Crystal Brands**
3000 Tremont Road
Savannah, GA 31405 912-651-5112
Fax: 912-650-3500 800-654-5115
www.diamondcrystal.com

Manufacturer and exporter of low-sodium mixes including soup, milk shake, ice cream, sauce, sugar-free dessert and fruit drink; also, instant breakfast beverages, cookies, nutritional chocolate bars and portion packed condimentsincluding jelly, mustard, etc
President: Karl Kaiser
VP Finances: Dave Lewis
Estimated Sales: $100-500 Million
Number Employees: 1000
Sq. footage: 300000
Parent Co: Hormel Foods Corporation
Type of Packaging: Food Service, Private Label
Other Locations:
Diamond Crystal Specialty Foo
Aurora ON
Brands:
DIAMOND CRYSTAL
DIAMOND SHAKERS
DIET KIT
DIXIE CRYSTALS
HOLLY
IMPERIAL
MIGHTYSHAKES
PACKET
SINGLE SERV
SPLENDA
SPRECKLES

3671 **Diamond Foods**
11899 Exit 5 Pkwy
Fishers, IN 46037-7938 317-845-5534
Fax: 317-577-3588 www.goldenstream.com
Manufacturer, importer and wholesaler/distributor of dried fruit, seeds, fruit and nuts
President/CEO: Michael Mendes
Estimated Sales: $20-50 Million
Number Employees: 20-49
Type of Packaging: Consumer, Bulk

3672 **(HQ)Diamond Foods Inc**
1050 Diamond St
Stockton, CA 95205 209-467-6000
Fax: 209-467-6709 aburke@diamondfoods.com
www.diamondnuts.com
Manufacturer of walnuts, almonds, pecans, hazelnuts, pine nuts, Brazil nuts and raw Spanish peanuts.
President/CEO/Director: Michael Mendes
EVP/COO: Gary Ford
EVP/CFO: Seth Halio
VP General Counsel: Stephen Kim
VP Marketing: Andrew Burke
VP Investor Relations/Treasurer: Robert Philips
VP Corporate Affairs/Human Resources: Sam Keiper
Estimated Sales: $350 Million
Number Employees: 500-999
Type of Packaging: Food Service
Other Locations:
Diamond Foods Processing Plant
Stockton CA
Diamond Foods Processing Plant
Linden CA
Diamond Foods Processing Plant
Modesto CA
Diamond Foods Processing Plant
Lemont IL
Diamond Foods Processing Plant
Robertsdale AL
Brands:
DIAMOND

3673 **Diamond Fruit Growers**
P.O.Box 185
Odell, OR 97044 541-354-5300
Fax: 541-354-5394 MartinC@diamondfruit.com
www.diamondfruit.com
Cooperative grower, packer, shipper and exporter of apples, pears and cherries
President/GM: Ron Girardelli
VP Finance: David Garcia
VP Sales: Neil Galone
Operations Manager: Robert Wymore
Information Services Manager: Martin Cohen
Estimated Sales: $ 20 - 50 Million
Number Employees: 500-999
Type of Packaging: Bulk

3674 **Diamond Oaks Vineyard**
26700 Dutcher Creek Rd
Cloverdale, CA 95425-9749 707-894-3191
Wines
Owner: Ronald Brown
Estimated Sales: $60,000
Number Employees: 1

3675 **Diamond Seafood**
204 N Edgewood Avenue
Wood Dale, IL 60191-1610 630-787-1100
Fax: 630-787-1309
Seafood
President: Thomas Hannagan
Estimated Sales: $ 5 - 10 Million
Number Employees: 10-19

3676 **Diamond Water**
P.O.Box 1610
Hot Springs, AR 71902-1610 501-623-1251
Fax: 501-623-2648
Manufacturer of bottled spring water
Plant Manager: Brian Hinds
Estimated Sales: $5-10 Million
Number Employees: 10-19
Parent Co: Mountain Valley Water
Type of Packaging: Consumer

3677 **Diamond of California**
600 Montgomery St.
17th Floor
San Francisco, CA 94111-2702 415-912-3180
Fax: 925-251-3820 www.diamondfoods.com
Nuts
President: Michael Mendes
CEO: Michael Mendes
CFO: Seth Halio
VP: Mario Alioto
Sales: Frank Morgan
Public Relations Manager: Vicki Zeigler

3678 **Diana Fruit Company**
651 Mathew St
Santa Clara, CA 95050 408-727-9631
Fax: 408-727-9890 tklevay@dianafruit.com
www.dianafruit.com
Producer and supplier of high quality Maraschino Cherries.
President: Gene Acronico
VP Sales/Marketing: Thomas Klevay
Estimated Sales: $ 20 - 50 Million
Number Employees: 50-99
Parent Co: Gene Acronico Canners & Packing
Type of Packaging: Bulk

3679 **Diana Naturals**
707 Executive Blvd Ste E
Valley Cottage, NY 10989 845-268-5200
Fax: 845-268-4626
contact@diana-naturals-inc.com
www.diana-naturals.com
Ingredients
Manager: Karina Giusto
Parent Co: Diana Naturals

3680 **Diana's Specialty Foods**
2305 Aurora Dr
Pingree Grove, IL 60140-6442 847-683-1200
Fax: 847-683-1207 dsf@elnet.com
Maunfacturer of Vinegar, fancy gifts, Italian riviera and provencial bread dippers, grapeseed oils, miniature bread dipping oils, salsa, jams, jelly, mustard, herb mayonnaise, and olive oil
Manager: Mark Pagnoni
Estimated Sales: $12,000
Number Employees: 10-19
Sq. footage: 3000
Type of Packaging: Private Label

3681 **Dick & Casey's Gourmet Seafoods**
16372a Lower Harbor Rd
Harbor, OR 97415 541-469-9494
Fax: 541-469-0757 800-662-9494
inquire@gourmetseafood.com
www.gourmetseafood.com
Manufacturer of canned and frozen seafood including shrimp, lobster, crab meat, etc
Owner: Julie Tomlinson
Estimated Sales: $190,000
Number Employees: 2
Type of Packaging: Consumer, Food Service
Brands:
DICK & CASEY'S

3682 **(HQ)Dick Garber Company**
7900 SW 245h Street
Suite 202
Davie, FL 33324 954-236-0456
Fax: 954-236-0468 dgarber@garbersales.com
Cheese, meat, bakery specialties
President/CEO: Dick Garber
CFO: Rosalie Garber
Sales: Mark Finocchio
Estimated Sales: $5-10 Million
Number Employees: 5-9
Type of Packaging: Private Label

3683 **Dickinson Frozen Foods**
600 NW 21st St
Fruitland, ID 83619 208-452-5200
Fax: 208-452-5365
www.dickinsonfrozenfoods.com
Manufacturer of frozen onions and bell peppers
President: Paul Fox
Finance: Chuck White
VP Marketing: Charles Murphy
Sales/Marketing: Aaron Mann
VP Operations: Craig Culver
VP Production: Bob Pedracini
Plant Manager: Roger Ingebritsen
Estimated Sales: $100-500 Million
Number Employees: 100-249
Type of Packaging: Consumer, Food Service, Private Label
Brands:
DICKINSON FROZEN FOODS

3684 **Dickson's Pure Honey**
4331 Hatchery Road
San Angelo, TX 76903-1513 915-655-9233
Pure honey
President: Andrew Dickson
Estimated Sales: $1-2.5 Million appx.
Number Employees: 1
Brands:
DICKSON'S PURE HONEY

3685 **Dicola Seafood**
10754 S Western Ave
Chicago, IL 60643-3199 773-238-7071
Fax: 773-238-8337
Seafood
Owner: Robert Di Cola
Estimated Sales: $ 5 - 10 Million
Number Employees: 20-49

3686 **Didion Milling**
520 Hartwig Blvd
Johnson Creek, WI 53038 920-699-3633
Fax: 920-348-6203 jdillon@didionmilling.com
www.didionmilling.com
Dry corn miller, corn products
President: Dow Didion
Vice President: Dow Drachenberg
Sales: Jeff Dillon
Number Employees: 80

3687 **Diedrich Coffee**
28 Executive Park, Ste 200
Irvine, CA 92614 949-260-1600
Fax: 949-260-1610 800-354-5282
java@diedrich.com www.diedrich.com
Manufacturer of coffee
President/CEO: Sean McCarthy
Executive VP/CFO: Martin Lynch
Vice President: Dana King
Estimated Sales: $62 Million
Number Employees: 150
Parent Co: Green Mountain Coffee
Brands:
COFFEE PEOPLE
DIEDRICH COFFEE
GLORIA JEANS

3688 **Dieffenbach Potato Chips**
51 Host Rd
Womelsdorf, PA 19567-9421 610-589-2385
Fax: 610-589-2866 www.dieffenbachs.com
Potato chips
Owner: Elan Dieffenbach
Estimated Sales: $ 5 - 10 Million
Number Employees: 10-19

3689 **Diehl Food Ingredients**
136 Fox Run Dr
Defiance, OH 43512 419-782-5010
Fax: 419-783-4319 800-251-3033
diehl@bright.net www.diehlinc.com

Manufacturer and exporter of lactose free beverages, powdered fat, coffee creamers and whip topping bases.
President: Charles Nicolais
CFO: Darren Lane
CEO: Peter Diehl
Research & Development: Joan Hasselman
Quality Control: Kelly Roach
Marketing Director: Dennis Reid
Sales Director: Jim Holdrieth
Number Employees: 100-249
Parent Co: Diehl
Type of Packaging: Consumer, Food Service, Bulk
Brands:
CHOCOMITE
VITAMITE

3690 **Dietrich's Milk Products**
100 McKinley Ave
Reading, PA 19605 610-929-5736
800-526-6455
www.dietrichsmilk.com
Manufacturer and exporter of cream and powdered and condensed milk; contract drying services available for nondairy powders
President/CEO: Thomas Dietrich
CFO: Eric Borgity
Quality Assurance Manager: Susan Landis
Human Resources Manager: Patricia Miller
Plant Manager: Freeman Covert
Estimated Sales: $50-75 Million
Number Employees: 165
Sq. footage: 66000
Parent Co: Dairy Farmers of America
Type of Packaging: Bulk
Brands:
CHOCOLATE CRUMB POWDER

3691 **Dietz & Watson**
5701 Tacony Street
Philadelphia, PA 19135 215-831-9000
Fax: 215-831-8719 800-333-1974
www.dietzandwatson.com
Deli meats and artisan cheeses
President: Eni Dietz
President/CEO: John Dietz
CFO: Ann Shire
VP Sales/Marketing: Rich Wright
Human Resources Director: Judy Corcoran Smith
COO: Christopher Eni
Purchasing Manager: Steve Yingling
Estimated Sales: $50-100 Million
Number Employees: 900
Sq. footage: 180000
Type of Packaging: Consumer, Bulk
Brands:
DIETZ & WATSON

3692 **Difiore Pasta Company**
556 Franklin Ave
Hartford, CT 06114-3024 860-296-1077
Fax: 860-296-5635
Pasta
Owner: Louise Di Fiore
Estimated Sales: $1-2.5 Million
Number Employees: 5-9
Brands:
DIFIORE PASTA

3693 **(HQ)Diggs Packing Company**
1207 Rogers St
Columbia, MO 65201-4796 573-449-2995
Fax: 573-449-3163
Manufacturer of beef, ham, sausage, meat packing services, distributes fresh meat, provides slaughtering
Owner: Dale Diggs
Public Relations: Dan Reynolds
Estimated Sales: $14.10 Million
Number Employees: 20-49
Type of Packaging: Consumer

3694 **Dilettante Chocolates**
19016 72nd Ave S
Kent, WA 98032 206-709-0306
Fax: 206-709-0309 888-600-2462
patricksnider@dilettante.com
www.seattlegourmetfoods.com
Candy and confectionery
President: David Taylor
CEO: Brian Davenport
Director Sales/Marketing: Tom Davis
Sales Manager: Chris Ratliff
Production Manager: Brian Hubbard
Estimated Sales: $1-2.5 Million
Number Employees: 5-9

3695 **Dillanos Coffee Roasters**
1607 45th St E
Sumner, WA 98390 253-826-1807
Fax: 253-826-1827 800-234-5282
www.dillanos.com
Manufacturer and importer of coffee
President: David Heilbrunn
CFO: Rand Hill
Estimated Sales: $3 Million
Number Employees: 20
Type of Packaging: Food Service

3696 **Dillard's Bar-B-Q Sauce**
3921 Fayetteville St
Durham, NC 27713-1135 919-544-1587
Fax: 919-361-3410
Manufacturer of barbecue sauce
Co-Partner: Geneva Dillard
Co-Partner/General Manager: Wilma Dillard
Estimated Sales: Less than $500,000
Number Employees: 10-19
Type of Packaging: Consumer
Brands:
DILLARD'S

3697 **Dillman Farm**
4955 W State Road 45
Bloomington, IN 47403 812-825-5525
Fax: 812-825-4650 800-359-1362
dillman@dillmanfarm.com
www.dillmanfarm.com
Manufacturer of fruit butters, preserves, jellies, salsa, mustard, bbq, no preservatives, cane sugar or grape juice to sweeten products
President: Cary Dillman
Treassurer: Amy Dillman
Director of Sales: Jean Brook
Estimated Sales: $820,000
Number Employees: 8
Sq. footage: 15000
Brands:
DILLMAN FARM
DILLMAN'S ALL NATURAL

3698 **Dillon Candy Company**
19927 Us Highway 84 E
Boston, GA 31626 229-498-2051
Fax: 229-498-2201 800-382-8338
amy@dilloncandy.com www.dilloncandy.com
Manufacturer of candy including peanut and pecan log rolls, sand brittles, divinity, coated pecans, pralines and pecan puffs
Owner/President: Oscar Cook
Sales: Michele Tull
Estimated Sales: $10-20 Million
Number Employees: 20-49
Type of Packaging: Consumer

3699 **Dillon Dairy Company**
5512 Leetsdale Dr
Denver, CO 80246 303-388-1645
Fax: 303-388-0514
Milk, dairy products
Manager: William Weyhrich
Estimated Sales: $10-20 Million
Number Employees: 20-49

3700 **Dimitria Delights**
81 Creeper Hill Rd
North Grafton, MA 01536-1421 508-839-3035
Fax: 508-839-1685 800-763-1113
sales@dimitriadelights.com
www.dimitriadelights.com
Manufacturer of frozen baked and nonbaked desserts including spinach pies, puff pastries, fruit strudels, regular and filled danish and croissant dough
President/Production Manager: John Colorio
Vice President: Mary Colorio
Estimated Sales: $10-20 Million
Number Employees: 50-99
Sq. footage: 35000
Type of Packaging: Consumer, Food Service, Private Label
Brands:
MARY'S
PITA
STRUDELKINS

3701 **Dimock Dairy Products**
P.O.Box 26
Dimock, SD 57331 605-928-3833
Fax: 605-928-3390 dimockdairy@santel.net
www.dimockdairy.com
Manufacturer of cheese
GM: Roger Swemby
Manager: Mike Royston
Estimated Sales: $5-10 Million
Number Employees: 5-9
Sq. footage: 4500
Type of Packaging: Consumer

3702 **Dimond Tager Company Products**
2801 E Hillsborough Ave
Tampa, FL 33610-4410 813-238-3111
Fax: 813-238-3114
Manufacturer and wholesaler/distributor of produce
President: Raymond Charlton
Estimated Sales: $1.7 Million
Number Employees: 10
Sq. footage: 4000
Type of Packaging: Consumer, Food Service, Bulk

3703 **Dimpflmeier Bakery**
26-36 Advance Road
Toronto, ON M8Z 2T4
Canada 416-236-2701
Fax: 416-239-5370 800-268-2421
carolm@dimpflmeierbakery.com
www.dimpflmeierbakery.com
Manufacturer and exporter of German-style breads including rye, pumpernickel, sourdough and monastery; also, rolls and buns
President: Alfonse Dimpflmier
Number Employees: 170
Type of Packaging: Consumer, Food Service
Brands:
HOLZOFEN
KLOSTERBROT
MUENCHNER/STADTBROT

3704 **Dina's Organic Chocolate**
39 Smith Ave
Mt Kisco, NY 10549 914-242-0124
Fax: 914-242-5289 888-625-2008
dina@dinakhader.com www.dinakhader.com
Organic chocolate bars in four different flavors
President/Owner: Dina Khader

3705 **Dinkel's Bakery**
3329 N Lincoln Ave
Chicago, IL 60657 773-281-7300
Fax: 773-281-6169 800-822-8817
norm@dinkels.com www.dinkels.com
Manufacturer of baked goods including chocolate chip butter cookies, cakes, pecan fudge brownies and snacks; contract baking available
President: Norman Dinkel
Controller/Treasurer: Holly Dinkel
General Manager: Luke Karl
Human Resource Manager: J Norman
Estimated Sales: $870,000
Number Employees: 25
Sq. footage: 15000
Type of Packaging: Consumer, Food Service, Private Label, Bulk
Brands:
DINKEL'S
DINKEL'S FAMOUS STOLLEN
DINKEL'S SIP'N
DINKEL'S SOUTHERN DOUBLE

3706 **Dinner Bell Meat Product**
240 Angus Rd
Concord, VA 24538-3117
Fax: 434-847-6305
Manufacturer of sausage
President: Butch Anderson
Estimated Sales: $10-20 Million
Number Employees: 10-19
Type of Packaging: Consumer

3707 **Dino's Sausage & Meat Company**
722 Catherine St
Utica, NY 13501-1304 315-732-2661
Fax: 315-732-3094
Manufacturer of sausage and beef products; wholesaler/distributor of bacon, ham, pork, lamb, etc
President: Carmen Bossone

Estimated Sales: $10-20 Million
Number Employees: 10-19
Type of Packaging: Consumer
Brands:
DINO'S

3708 **Dino-Meat Company**
PO Box 95
White House, TN 37188-0095 615-643-1022
Fax: 615-643-1022 877-557-6493
dinomeatco@bellsouth.net www.dinomeat.com
Manufacturer of emu meat including steaks, ground, breakfast sausage, summer sausage, hot dogs, hot links, meat balls, snack sticks and jerky. Also emu oil and emu oil products
President: Neil Williams
Type of Packaging: Consumer, Food Service
Brands:
BACK COUNTRY EMU PRODUCTS
DINE-MEAT EMU PRODUCTS

3709 **Dion Herbs & Spices**
801 Montee St. Nicolas
St-Jerome, QC J7Y 4C7 450-569-8001
Fax: 450-569-0062 877-569-8001
gaston@alimentsgdion.com
www.alimentsgdion.com
Extracts, herbs, salt, spices, private label.
Marketing: Gaston Dion

3710 **Dip Seafood**
1870 Dauphin Island Pkwy
Mobile, AL 36605-3000 251-479-0123
Fax: 251-479-9869
Seafood
Owner: Trina Nguyen
Estimated Sales: $300,000-500,000
Number Employees: 1-4

3711 **Dipasa**
6600 East Fm 802
Brownsville, TX 78526-6953 956-831-5893
Fax: 956-831-5893 info@dipasausa@com
www.dipasausa.com
Manufacturer, importer and exporter of tahini and sesame seeds, raisins, oil, flour and candy; wholesaler/distributor of onion and cheese breadsticks, baked snacks, halvah and confectionery items, natural colors, oleoresins
Estimated Sales: $8 Million
Number Employees: 10-19
Number of Brands: 2
Number of Products: 10
Sq. footage: 20000
Parent Co: Dipasa De C.V.
Type of Packaging: Consumer, Food Service, Private Label, Bulk
Brands:
BILADI
BILADI TOHINA
DE CHAMPAQUE BAKERY SNACKS
DIPASA BILADI
DIPASA DE CHAMPAGNE
DIPASA USA
SESAMIN

3712 **Dippin' Dots**
5101 Charter Oak Dr
Paducah, KY 42001 270-443-8994
Fax: 270-443-8997 slaes@dippindots.com
www.dippindots.com
Ice cream, yogurt, flavored ices and sherbets
President: Curt Jones
CFO: Sheri Dikin
Director Sales: Tammy Wilson
Public Relations: Terry Reeves
Director Operations: Rick Noble
Estimated Sales: $20-50 Million
Number Employees: 165
Brands:
DIPPIN' DOTS

3713 **Dippy Foods**
10554 Progress Way Ste K
Cypress, CA 90630 714-816-0150
Fax: 714-816-0153 800-819-8551
erin@dippyfoods.com www.dippyfoods.com
Single-serving meals to schools and other institutional food servers
President: Jon Stevenson
VP: Erin Stevenson
Brands:
EARTH'S BEST
HAIN KIDZ
HEALTH VALLEY

3714 **Diricom**
Av Stim No 97-4
Lomas Del Chamizal
1 Seccion, MC 05129
Mexico 555-596-0898
Fax: 555-596-3144 edr@diricom.com.mx
www.ahuacatlan.mx
Oils.
Marketing: Eduardo Diaz Rivera

3715 **Discovery Foods**
2395 American Ave
Hayward, CA 94545 510-780-9238
Fax: 510-293-1830 www.lingling.com
Manufacturer of ethnic and frozen foods
President: Clarence Mou
Public Relations: Charlene Crosby
Estimated Sales: $ 20 - 50 Million
Number Employees: 100-249

3716 **Dismat Corporation**
336 N Westwood Ave
Toledo, OH 43607 419-531-8963
Fax: 419-531-8965 www.mckaysseasoning.com
Manufacturer and exporter of powdered soup mixes and seasonings
President: John Donofrio
Operations VP: Sandra Lee Jones
Estimated Sales: $1-$2 Million
Number Employees: 5-9
Number of Brands: 1
Number of Products: 3
Sq. footage: 12000
Type of Packaging: Consumer, Bulk
Brands:
MCKAY'S

3717 **Distant Lands Coffee Roaster**
11754 State Highway 64 W
Tyler, TX 75704 903-592-9771
Fax: 903-593-2699 800-346-5459
sales@dlcoffee.com www.dlcoffee.com
Roasters of organic, flavored and fair-trade coffees.
President: Bill McAlpin
Marketing: Kristin Jones
VP Sales: Todd Hughes
Estimated Sales: $5 Million
Number Employees: 50
Type of Packaging: Private Label, Bulk
Brands:
COUNTRY COFFEE

3718 **Distillata Company**
1608 E 24th St
Cleveland, OH 44114 216-771-2900
Fax: 216-771-1672 800-999-2906
ClevelandCustomerService@Distillata.com
www.distillata.com
Manufacturer and bottler of spring and distilled water
Owner: Kevin Schroeder
Office Manager: Kelly Stewart
Estimated Sales: $10-20 Million
Number Employees: 100-249
Type of Packaging: Consumer, Food Service, Private Label, Bulk
Brands:
DISTILLATA

3719 **Distribution Plus Incorporated (DPI)**
P.O.Box 5940
Mesa, AZ 85211-5940 480-969-9333
Fax: 480-461-3645 www.epicurean-foods.com
Distributor of imported and domestic specialty foods along with multi-unit and school foodservice
President: Chip Forster
Estimated Sales: $ 50 - 100 Million
Number Employees: 50-99

3720 **Diversified Avocado Products**
25950 Acero Street
Suite 360
Mission Viejo, CA 92691-7900 949-837-6464
Fax: 949-837-6464 800-879-2555
rflores@dapguacamole.com
www.dapguacamole.com
Manufacturer of frozen guacamole and fresh avocados
Account Executive: Alberto Castro
Director Sales/Marketing: Ray Flores
Estimated Sales: $500,000- 1 Million
Number Employees: 5-9
Sq. footage: 100000
Type of Packaging: Consumer, Food Service

3721 **(HQ)Diversified Foods**
3115 6th St
Metairie, LA 70002 504-831-6651
Fax: 504-831-8288 dfi@diversifiedfoods.com
www.diversifiedfoods.com
Manufacturer of ready-to-eat cereal, Cream of Coconut, Powder Drink Mixes, Powder Gelatins, Fruit Juice Concentrates, UHT Milk and Flavored Milk, Shelf Stable Milk, Aseptic UHT, Milk Products, Textured Vegetable Protein and many otherFood Service Products.
Co-President: Tab Damiens
Co-President: Michelle Damiens
Estimated Sales: $ 10 - 20 Million
Number Employees: 10-19
Type of Packaging: Food Service, Private Label, Bulk

3722 **Diversified Foods & Seasoning**
1012 S Harimaw Ct
Metairie, LA 70001 504-846-5090
Fax: 504-834-0395
diversifiedfoodsandseasonings.com
Manufacturer of frozen beans, gravy, sauce and soups; also, dry mixes, meat glazes and seasonings
Operations Manager: Conrad Howe
Estimated Sales: $20-50 Million
Number Employees: 100-249
Parent Co: A.L. Copeland
Type of Packaging: Food Service, Private Label
Brands:
CHIEF'S CREATIONS

3723 **Divine Chocolate**
418 7th St SE
Washington, DC 20003 202-332-8913
Fax: 202-332-8916
sales@divinechocolateusa.com
www.divinechocolateusa.com
Chocolate bars
Ceo: Erin Gorman
Marketing: Niki Lagos
Estimated Sales: $1 Million
Number Employees: 3

3724 **Divine Delights**
1250 Holm Rd
Petaluma, CA 94954-1106 707-559-7099
Fax: 707-559-7098 800-443-2836
divinedelights@sbcglobal.com
www.divinedelights.com
Premium petit fours and petite confections
President: Angelique Fry
Estimated Sales: $5-10 Million
Number Employees: 20-49
Type of Packaging: Private Label, Bulk
Brands:
CHECKERBITES
DIVINE DELIGHTS
MICE-A-FOURS
TRUFFLECOTS

3725 **Divine Foods**
Po Box 490
Elizabethtown, NC 28337-0490 910-862-2576
Fax: 910-862-2799 allienance@divinefoods.com
www.divinefoods.com
Functional (antioxidants), bread/bisucits, juice/cider, wine, salsa/dips, jams, jellies.
Marketing: Miller Taylor

3726 **Division Baking Corporation**
250 Dyckman St
New York, NY 10034-5354 212-567-4500
Fax: 212-942-7682 800-934-9238
Manufacturer of cheese cake
Owner: Robert Gruenebaum
Estimated Sales: $5-10 Million
Number Employees: 20-49

3727 **Divvies**
700 Oakridge Cmns
South Salem, NY 10590 914-533-0333
madetoshare@divvies.com
www.divvies.com

Dairy free, egg free, peanut free, tree nut free food snacks

3728 **Dixie Dairy Company**
1200 W 15th Ave
Gary, IN 46407 219-885-6101
Fax: 219-882-7533 www.dixiedairy.com
Manufacturer of milk, cream, eggs, cottage cheese and butter
President: Thomas Eskilson
Estimated Sales: $20-50 Million
Number Employees: 80
Type of Packaging: Consumer

3729 **Dixie Dew Products**
1360 Jamike Ave
Erlanger, KY 41018 859-283-1050
Fax: 859-282-3781 800-867-8548
info@dixiedewproducts.com
www.dixiedewproducts.com
Manufacturer of fruit glazes, dips, puddings, toppings, day blends and specialty sauces; contract processing and packaging available
CEO: Robert Carl
Quality Controll: Glen Delong
Estimated Sales: $2 Million
Number Employees: 20
Sq. footage: 40000
Type of Packaging: Consumer, Food Service, Private Label, Bulk
Brands:
CLASSIC TRADITIONS
HARRY'S CHOICE
HERITAGE FANCY FOODS

3730 **Dixie Egg Company**
5139 Edgewood Ct
Jacksonville, FL 32254 904-783-0950
Fax: 904-786-6227 800-394-3447
kjkeggs@aol.com www.dixieegg.com
Manufacturer and exporter of fresh shell eggs
President: Jacques Klempf
CEO: Edward Klempf
Controller: Paul Stevenson
Operations/General Manager: John Reece
Feed/Production Manager: Dennis Hughes
Number Employees: 250-499
Parent Co: Foodonics International
Type of Packaging: Consumer, Bulk

3731 **Dixie Rice**
600 Pasquiere St
Gueydan, LA 70542 337-536-9276
Fax: 337-536-5099
Rice
CHB: Harold Simmons
Number Employees: 8
Brands:
DIXIE

3732 **Dixie Trail Farms**
PO Box 4082
Wilmington, NC 28406-1082 800-665-3968
Fax: 800-765-7482 info@dixietrail.com
www.dixietrail.com
Grilling sauces and marinades

3733 **Dixie Usa**
15555 Fm 2920 Rd
Tomball, TX 77377 281-516-3535
Fax: 800-688-2507 800-233-3668
info@dixieusa.com www.dixiediner.com
Manufacturer of meat analogs, tofu, soy products and low carb products; exporter of soy
President: Brenda Oswalt
Chairman/CEO: Robert Beeley
EVP: Jim Oswalt
Estimated Sales: $5-10 Million
Number Employees: 20-49
Sq. footage: 30000
Type of Packaging: Consumer, Food Service, Private Label, Bulk
Brands:
BEEF NOT
CHICKEN NOT
DUTLETTES

3734 **Dixon Associates**
PO Box 1250
Mechanicsburg, PA 17055-1250 717-691-0800
Fax: 717-691-4153
Specialty dairy beverages
President: John Kober
Estimated Sales: $25-49.9 Million
Number Employees: 1-4

3735 **Dixon Canning Company**
P.O.Box 340
Dixon, CA 95620 707-678-4406
Fax: 707-441-3718
Manufacturer of canned tomato products including diced and paste
Plant Manager: Pete Imhoff
Estimated Sales: $50-100 Million
Number Employees: 250-499
Parent Co: Campbell Soup Company
Type of Packaging: Bulk

3736 **Dixon's Fisheries**
1807 N Main St
East Peoria, IL 61611 309-694-1457
Fax: 309-694-0539
Seafood
President: Robert Dixon
Estimated Sales: $ 20 - 50 Million
Number Employees: 50-99

3737 **Dizzy Pig Barbeque Company**
8763 Virginia Meadows Dr
Manassas, VA 20109 703-273-3580
Fax: 206-984-3736
chris.capell@dizzypigbbq.com
dizzypigbbq.com
Other condiments, rubs, spices, foodservice, gift packs.
Marketing: Chris Capell

3738 **Dmv Intl. Nutritionalional**
40196 State Highway 10
Delhi, NY 13753 607-746-0100
Fax: 607-746-2710 www.dmv-international.com
Manufacturer of food additives including hydrolized proteins, bioactive peptides and protein fractions
President: Steve Brown
CFO: Joost Schijndel
Estimated Sales: $50-100 Million
Number Employees: 120
Parent Co: DMV International
Brands:
AERION
ESPRION
GLUTAMINE
LACTOPEROXIDASE
LACTOVAL
PEPTIDE FM
PHARMATOSE
PRIMELLOSE
PRIMOJEL
RESPITOSE
TEXTRION

3739 **Dno**
4561 E 5th Ave Ste 3
Columbus, OH 43219 614-231-3601
Fax: 614-231-5032 800-686-2366
dno@core.com www.dnoinc.com
Manufacturer of pre-cut prepackaged fresh fruit and vegetables
Owner: Tony Dinovo
Vice President: Carol Dinovo
Sales Representative: Jim Davis
Sales Representative: Jim Fryer
Purchasing Manager: Tony DiNovo
Estimated Sales: $10-20 Million
Number Employees: 20-49
Sq. footage: 10000
Type of Packaging: Consumer, Food Service, Private Label, Bulk
Brands:
FRESH HEALTH
OLD FASHIONED CARAMEL APPLE

3740 **Dobake**
810 81st Ave
Oakland, CA 94621-2510 510-834-3134
Fax: 510-834-4408 800-834-3134
dobeinc@aol.com www.dobake.com
Gourmet and premium baked sweet goods.
Manager: David Shenson
VP Marketing/Sales: Jack Dellert
Number Employees: 100-249
Brands:
DOBAKE

3741 **Doc Miller's Fish & Seafood Company**
PO Box 426
Syracuse, IN 46567-0426 574-457-8469
Fax: 547-457-5887
Seafood
President: Gary Miller
Estimated Sales: $ 5 - 10 Million
Number Employees: 20-49

3742 **Dockside Market**
PO Box 1002
Key Largo, FL 33037 305-283-6678
Fax: 305-397-2389 800-813-2253
donna@docksidemarket.com
www.docksidemarket.com
Cakes, cookies, salsa, sauces, hot sauces, coffee & tea

3743 **Doctors Best**
197 Avenida La Pata # A
San Clemente, CA 92673-6307
Fax: 949-498-3952 800-333-6977
info@drbvitamins.com www.drbvitamins.com
Manufacturer of food supplements
President: Ken Halvorsrude
VP Operations: Ranate Halvorsrude
Estimated Sales: $1-2.5 Million
Number Employees: 10-19
Sq. footage: 5000

3744 **(HQ)Doerle Food Services**
113 Kol Drive
Broussard, LA 70518-3825 337-252-8551
Fax: 337-252-8558 www.doerlefoodservice.com
Manufacturer and distributor of fresh and frozen meats and poultry, a wide variety of beverages and chemical supplies, also includes seafood, gourmet foods, fresh produce, dry groceries, dairy products, disposables, small ware andtable top items, specialty healthcare products and janitorial supplies
President/CEO: Carolyn Doerle-Ray
Senior Vice President Food Services: Allen Boudreaux
Estimated Sales: $ 20 - 50 Million
Number Employees: 100-249
Other Locations:
Doerle Food Service
Shreveport LA

3745 **Dogfish Head Craft Brewery**
22 Nassau Commons
Lewes, DE 19958-1607 302-644-4660
Fax: 302-644-4140 888-834-3474
dogfish@dogfish.com www.dogfish.com
Manufacturer of beer
President: Sam Caglione
Estimated Sales: $10-20 Million
Number Employees: 10-19
Brands:
CHICORY STOUT
IMMORT ALE
INDIAN BROWN ALE
RAISON D'ETRE
SHELTER PALE ALE

3746 **Dogswell LLC**
1964 Westwood Boulevard
Suite 350
Los Angeles, CA 90025 310-651-5200
Fax: 877-327-3145 888-559-8833
info@dogswell.com www.dogswell.com
Functional (antioxidants), other lifestyle, pet food.
Marketing: Marco Giannini

3747 **Dogwood Brewing Company**
1222 Logan Cir NW
Atlanta, GA 30318 404-367-0500
Fax: 404-367-0505 www.dogbrewing.com
Manufacturer of ale and stout
President: Crawford Moran
Estimated Sales: $1-2.5 Million
Number Employees: 1-4
Type of Packaging: Consumer, Food Service
Brands:
DOGWOOD

3748 **Dohar Meats**
1979 W 25th St
Cleveland, OH 44113-3455 216-241-4197
Manufacturer of pork including sausage and deli meats
Owner: Angela Dohar
Manager: Mike Szucs

Estimated Sales: Less than $500,000
Number Employees: 1-4
Type of Packaging: Consumer, Bulk

3749 **Dohler Milne Aseptics**
804 Bennett Avenue
Prosser, WA 99350 509-786-2611
Fax: 630-797-2001 www.doehler-milne.com
Manufacturer of flavoring extracts and syrups
Controller: Joe Stoops
Estimated Sales: $1.2 Million
Number Employees: 15

3750 **Dol Cice' Gelato Company**
PO Box 343
Yardley, PA 19067 215-499-5661
Fax: 215-493-6348 Info@DolCice.com
www.dolcice.com
Manufacturer and wholesaler/distributor of Italian water ices
President: Laurence Dobelle
Type of Packaging: Food Service, Private Label

3751 **Dolce Nonna**
162-43 12th Avenue
Whitestone, NY 11357 718-767-3501
Fax: 718-767-3501 info@dolcenonnas.com
www.dolcenonnas.com
Marinated string beans, agri-dolce peppers and marinated eggplant
President/Owner: Gisella Civale

3752 **Dolci Gelati LLC**
5766 2nd St Ne
Washington, DC 20011-2524 202-257-5323
Fax: 202-526-8064 dolcigelati@gamil.com
www.dolcigelati.net
Frozen desserts, ice cream/sorbet, co-packing, private label.
Marketing: Gianluigi Dellaccio

3753 **Dold Foods**
2929 N Ohio St
Wichita, KS 67219 316-838-9101
Fax: 316-838-9053 www.hormel.com
Manufacturer of fresh and frozen ham and bacon
Manager: Terry W Hadden
Plant Manager: Mark Coffey
Number Employees: 250-499
Sq. footage: 100000
Parent Co: Hormel Foods Corporation
Type of Packaging: Consumer

3754 **(HQ)Dole & Bailey**
16 Conn St
Woburn, MA 1801 781-935-1234
Fax: 781-935-9085 www.doleandbailey.com
Meats, seafood, gourmet groceries
President: Nancy Matheson-Burns
CEO: Aileen Darragh
Marketing: Jennifer Hertig
COO: Scott Matheson
Estimated Sales: $25 Million
Number Employees: 120
Brands:
CHEF'S SIGNATURE

3755 **(HQ)Dole Food Company**
1 Dole Dr
Westlake Village, CA 91362 818-879-6600
Fax: 818-879-6615 www.dole.com
Manufacturer of more than 200 products, such as; fresh fruit, fresh vegetables and packaged foods
Chairman: David Murdock
President/CEO: David DeLorenzo
EVP/CFO: Joseph Tesoriero
Estimated Sales: $7.6 Billion
Number Employees: 75,800
Parent Co: Coastal Berry Company
Type of Packaging: Consumer, Food Service, Private Label, Bulk
Brands:
CAMEO
CINNARAISINS
COSMIC
DOLE
DOLE CAESAR SALAD
DOLE CANNED FRUIT
DOLE CLASSIC COLESLAW
DOLE DRIED FRUIT AND NUTS
DOLE FRESH CUT VEGETABLES
DOLE HERB RANCH
DOLE PINEAPPLE
DOLE RAISINS
DOLE SHREDDED RED CABBAGE
DOLEWHIP
FRUITBOWLS
FUN SHAPES
GREENER SELECTION
LUNCH FOR ONE
SEA CREATURES

3756 **Dole Fresh Vegetable Company**
32655 Camphora Rd
Soledad, CA 93960 831-678-5030
Fax: 831-678-5391 800-333-5454
www.dole.com
Manufacturer and grower of fresh broccoli, lettuce and salad mixes
Manager: Tony Stanton
Estimated Sales: $100+ Million
Number Employees: 1,000-4,999
Parent Co: Tropicana
Type of Packaging: Consumer, Food Service

3757 **Dole Fresh Vegetables**
2959 Salinas Hwy
Monterey, CA 93940 831-422-8871
Fax: 831-422-3627 www.dole.com
Fresh Vegetables
President/CEO: Lawrence Kern
VP: Rick Bravo
Plant Manager: Lenny Pelifian
Estimated Sales: $100-500 Million
Number Employees: 1,000-4,999
Parent Co: Dole Food Company
Type of Packaging: Food Service
Brands:
DOLE

3758 **Dole Nut Company**
P.O.Box 845
Orland, CA 95963-0845 530-865-5511
Fax: 530-865-7864 tmdduchenut.com
www.duchenut.com
Food and almond processing
Manager: John Wilson
Sales: Steve Spellman
Estimated Sales: $500,000-$1 Million
Number Employees: 20-49
Type of Packaging: Private Label
Brands:
T.M. DUCHE NUT

3759 **Dole Pond Maple Products**
PO Box 841
Jackman, ME 04945-0841 418-653-5322
Fax: 418-653-5322 jcpare@xplornet.com
www.dolepondmapleproducts.com
Manufacturer of maple syrup
President: Jean-Claude Pare
Number Employees: 1-4

3760 **Dolefam Corporation**
2821 N Vista Rd
Arlington Hts, IL 60004-2108 847-577-2122
Fax: 708-577-4244
Manufacturer of sauces, dips and dressings
Owner: Arlen Gould
Executive VP: Arlen Gould
Brands:
DOLEFAM

3761 **Dolisos America**
1710 Whitney Mesa Dr
Henderson, NV 89014-2055 702-871-7153
Fax: 702-871-9670 800-365-4767
dolisos@earthlink.net www.santeactiveusa.com
Homeopathic medicines.
President/CEO: Luc Clouatre

3762 **Dollar Food Manufacturing**
1410 Odlum Drive
Vancouver, BC V5L 4X7
Canada 604-253-1422
Fax: 604-253-2226
Manufacturer of salted and/or dried salmon, sausage cured, golden pork hock
Director: Kelly Chow
Number Employees: 35
Type of Packaging: Consumer, Food Service

3763 **Dolly Madison BakeryInterstate Brands Corporation**
3080 N National Rd
Columbus, IN 47201 812-376-7432
Fax: 812-378-4482 www.butternut.com
Manufacturer of cakes, pies, muffins, biscuits, rolls and bread
Manager: Pam Smith
General Manager: Don Dorr
Purchasing Agent: Keith Ritzline
Estimated Sales: $100+ Million
Number Employees: 1,000-4,999
Parent Co: Interstate Brands Corporation
Type of Packaging: Consumer, Food Service, Private Label, Bulk

3764 **Dolores Canning Company**
1020 N Eastern Ave
Los Angeles, CA 90063 323-263-9155
Fax: 323-269-4876 www.dolorescanning.com
Manufacturer of pickled pork products, chili bricks and specialty Mexican items
President: Steve Munoz
Marketing: David Munoz
Sales: Bert Munoz
Estimated Sales: $1 Million
Number Employees: 7
Type of Packaging: Consumer, Food Service, Private Label
Brands:
DOLORES

3765 **Dolphin Natural Chocolates**
1975 Woodview Avenue
Cambria, CA 93428-5168 805-927-7103
Fax: 831-722-0318 800-236-5744
hank@dolphinnatural.com
www.dolphinnatural.com
Manufacturer and exporter of sugar and dairy-free chocolates; also, chocolate dipped apricots, papaya and pineapple
Owner: Henry McKowen
Estimated Sales: $2.5-5 Million
Number Employees: 5-9
Sq. footage: 1000
Type of Packaging: Consumer
Brands:
DOLPHIN NATURAL

3766 **Dom's Sausage Company**
10 Riverside Park
Malden, MA 2148 781-324-6390
Fax: 781-322-6776 www.domsausage.com
Meats
President: Buddy Botticelli
Plant Manager: Angelo Botticelli
Estimated Sales: $15 Million
Number Employees: 40
Type of Packaging: Bulk
Brands:
DOM'S

3767 **Domaine Chandon**
1 California Dr
Yountville, CA 94599 707-944-2280
Fax: 707-944-1123 800-242-6366
info@chandon.com www.chandon.com
Sparkling and aperitif wines
President/CEO: John Wright
CFO: Dan Marotto
CEO: Malcolm Dunbar
Marketing: Allison Evanow
Public Relations: Sue Furdek
Engineer: Michael Morris
Estimated Sales: $20-50 Million
Number Employees: 250-499
Parent Co: LVMH Moet-Hennessy Louis Vitton
Type of Packaging: Consumer
Brands:
BLANC DE NOIRS
BRUT CLASSIC
CHARDONNAY
MT. VEEDER BLANC DE BLANCS
PINOT MEUNIER
PINOT NOIR
RESERVE BRUT
RESERVE BRUT ROSE
RICHE
VINTAGE

3768 **Domaine St. George Winery**
1141 Grant Ave
Healdsburg, CA 95448 707-433-5508
Fax: 707-433-5736 dswines@domstgeo.com
www.domainesaintgeorge.com
Wines
President: Somchai Likitprakong
Chairman: Yu Yee

Estimated Sales: $5-10 Million
Number Employees: 22
Type of Packaging: Private Label
Brands:
DOMAINE ST

3769 **Dominex**
P.O.Box 5069
St Augustine, FL 32085 904-810-2132
www.dominexeggplant.com
Manufacturer of eggplant cutlets and appetizers; including peeled, breaded, battered, deep fried and IQF. All natural fully cooked breaded in italian crumbs, eggplant appetizers and cutlets
President: John McGarvey
Director- Sales and Marketing: Miranda Chalke
Estimated Sales: 10-19
Number Employees: 50-99
Number of Brands: 10
Number of Products: 145
Type of Packaging: Food Service, Private Label, Bulk
Brands:
DOMINEX

3770 **Dominion Wine Cellars**
PO Box 1057
Culpeper, VA 22701-1057 540-825-8772
Fax: 540-829-0377
Wine
President: Wade D Sampson

3771 **Domino Foods**
One North Clematis Street
Suite 200
West Palm Beach, FL 33401-5551 561-366-5150
www.dominosugar.com
Fully integrated refiner of cane sugar. Product line includes liquid sugar, granulated sugar, brown and powdered sugar in addition to a full line of specialty ingredients that are sucrose based
President/CEO: Brian O'Malley
CFO: Gregory Smith
Vice President: Armando Tabernilla
Director Marketing/Sales: Kevin McElvanry
Senior Director: Gary Black
VP Production: Joseph Goodwin
Estimated Sales: $100+ Million
Number Employees: 25-100
Parent Co: Con Agra Foods
Type of Packaging: Consumer, Food Service, Private Label, Bulk
Brands:
DOMINO SUGAR

3772 **Domino Specialty Ingredients**
One North Clematis Street
Suite 200
West Palm Beach, FL 33401 561-366-5150
Fax: 561-366-5158 800-446-9763
www.dominospecialtyingredients.com
Brownulated brown sugars, icings sugars, molasses sugars, honey sugars, invert sugars, fondant sugars.
President: Richard Baker
Communications Director: Lynda Law
Estimated Sales: $100+ Million
Number Employees: 250-499
Brands:
C&H SUGAR
DOMINO SUGAR
FLORIDA CRYSTALS
REDPATH SUGAR

3773 **Domino Sugar Corporation**
1100 E Key Hwy
Baltimore, MD 21230 410-752-6150
Fax: 410-783-8612 www.dominosugar.com
Manufacturer of sugar including crystallized and granulated; also, honey, molasses and brown sugar
President: Richard Baker
Sales Manager: David Poust
Estimated Sales: $100+ Million
Number Employees: 250-499
Type of Packaging: Consumer, Private Label
Brands:
DOMINO
QUIK-FLO

3774 **Don Alfonso Foods**
7218 McNeil Drive
Austin, TX 78729-7980 512-335-2370
Fax: 512-335-0636 800-456-6100
Mexican food ingredients (prepared moles) dried chiles, spices and sauces
President: Jose Marmolejo
Brands:
DON ALFONSO

3775 **Don Francisco Coffee Traders**
PO Box 58271
Los Angeles, CA 90058-0271 800-697-5282
Fax: 804-385-5333 www.don-francisco.com
Gourmet coffee products
Brands:
DON FRANCISCO

3776 **Don Hilario Estate Coffee**
3003 W Harbor View Ave
Tampa, FL 33611 813-254-1900
Fax: 813-254-6030 800-799-1903
info@donhilario.com www.donhilario.com
Coffee
CEO/Marketing Director: Russell Versaggi
Estimated Sales: $2.5-5 Million
Number Employees: 1-4
Type of Packaging: Private Label
Brands:
DON HILARIO ESTATE COFFEE

3777 **Don Jose Foods**
4140 Oceanside Boulevard
159-315
Oceanside, CA 92056-6005 760-631-0243
Fax: 760-945-0651 www.donjosefoods.com
Fruit and juice beverages, chocolate drinks and assorted non-dairy items
President: Chuck Kuhlman
Vice President: Robby Kuhlman
Sales Manager: Enrique Ibarra
Parent Co: Paradise Valley Foods
Type of Packaging: Private Label
Brands:
CEREAL MATCH
CHOCO D' LITE
DON JOSE HORCHATA

3778 **Don Miguel Mexican Foods**
1501 W Orangewood Ave
Orange, CA 92868 714-634-8441
Fax: 714-978-3743 www.donmiguel.com
Manufacturer of frozen Mexican foods such as tacos, burritos, chimichangas and more
President/Owner: John Signorino
CFO: Michael Chaignot
EVP: Saralyn Brown
Quality Assurance Supervisor: Jose Cortez
Sales Director: Alan Anglemyer
Human Resource Manager: Jenny Ortiz- Asmis
Operations Executive: David Nieh
VP Manufacturing: Don Goglia
Purchasing Director: Shirley Lattis
Estimated Sales: $50-99.9 Million
Number Employees: 600
Number of Brands: 4
Number of Products: 100
Sq. footage: 80000
Type of Packaging: Consumer, Food Service, Bulk
Brands:
DON MIGUEL
EL CHARRITO
LEAN OLE
LUCCA
PINATA
XLNT

3779 **Don Sebastiani & Sons**
PO Box 1248
Sonoma, CA 95476 707-933-1704
Fax: 707-939-7115 hbast@donandsons.com
www.donandsons.com
Wine
President/Owner: Don Sebastiani
VP: Don Staaveren
VP Marketing: Robert Carroll
Sales Manager: Rusty Boddeker
President/COO: Mike Holden
Estimated Sales: $9.4 Million
Number Employees: 10

3780 **Don Tango Foods**
P.O.Box 3153
Sterling, VA 20167 703-406-8303
Fax: 703-406-8955 877-406-4064
btoruno@bellatlantic.net
www.dontangofoods.com
Chimichurri: Argentine grilling and marinade
Estimated Sales: Less than $500,000
Number Employees: 1-4

3781 **Don's Dock Seafood**
1220 E Northwest Hwy
Des Plaines, IL 60016-3352 847-827-1817
Fax: 847-827-1846 www.donsdockseafood.com
Manufacturer of fresh seafood
Co-Owner: Andy Johnson
Co-Owner: George Johnson
Co-Owner: Don Johnson
Estimated Sales: $ 3 - 5 Million
Number Employees: 10-19

3782 **Don's Food Products**
4461 Township Line Road
Schwenksville, PA 19473 888-321-3667
www.donssalads.com
Salads, cream cheeses, commodity salads, soups and desserts
President/Owner: Victor Skloff

3783 **Dona Yiya Foods**
Carr 125 Km 19 0 Interior St Ca
San Sebastian, PR 00685 787-896-4007
Fax: 787-280-1430 donyiyafoods@PRtC.net
www.donayiya.com
Manufacturer, exporter and importer of spices and seasonings including garlic in oil or water, soffritto, condiments and tropical candies
President: Javier Quinones
Plant Manager: Luis Denis
Estimated Sales: $3.1 Million
Number Employees: 12
Number of Brands: 2
Number of Products: 23
Sq. footage: 10000
Type of Packaging: Consumer, Food Service, Private Label, Bulk

3784 **Donald E. Hunter Meat Company**
4612 Turkey Rd
Hillsboro, OH 45133 937-466-2311
Manufacturer of beef
Owner: Donald Hunter
Estimated Sales: $1-2.5 Million
Number Employees: 1-4
Type of Packaging: Consumer

3785 **Donaldson's Finer Chocolates**
600 S State Road 39
Lebanon, IN 46052 765-482-3334
Fax: 765-482-7994 800-975-7236
www.donaldsonschocolates.com
Manufacturer of chocolates and candy
President: George Donaldson
Estimated Sales: $5-10 Million
Number Employees: 5-9
Type of Packaging: Consumer

3786 **Donatoni Winery**
10604 S La Cienega Boulevard
Inglewood, CA 90304-1115 310-645-5445
Fax: 310-645-5445
Wines
President/CEO: Mark Donatoni
Manager Sales: Tina Donatoni
Estimated Sales: Less than $500,000
Number Employees: 1-4
Brands:
DONATONI

3787 **Donells' Candies**
201 E 2nd St Ste 2
Casper, WY 82601 307-234-6283
Fax: 307-235-9119 877-461-2009
sales@donnellschocolates.com
www.donnellschocolates.com
Manufacturer of confectionery products including hand-dipped chocolates and fudge
Partner: Donald Stepp
President: Mike Stepp
Estimated Sales: $1-2.5 Million
Number Employees: 5-9
Type of Packaging: Consumer

3788 **Dong Kee Company**
2252 S Wentworth Ave
Chicago, IL 60616-2042 312-225-6340
Fax: 312-567-9119

Manufacturer of canned Chinese products including egg rolls, water chestnuts, bamboo shoots, mushrooms and fortune and almond cookies
Owner: Herman Wong
Estimated Sales: $500,000-$1 Million
Number Employees: 5-9
Type of Packaging: Consumer, Food Service

3789 **Donna & Company**
505 Orange Avenue
Cranford, NJ 07016-2047 908-272-4380
bob@shopdonna.com
www.shopdonna.com
Chocolate bars, chocolate truffles, full-line chocolate, other chocolate, toffee.
Marketing: Robert Koshinskie

3790 **Donsuemor Madeleines**
2080 N Loop Rd
Alameda, CA 94502 510-865-6406
Fax: 510-865-6947 888-420-4441
remember@donsuemor.com
www.donsuemor.com
Gourmet French madeleine cookies

3791 **Door Country Potato Chips**
3840 N Fratney St
Milwaukee, WI 53212-1341 414-964-1428
Fax: 414-964-1484 swsherbi@aol.com
Potato chips and pasta and contract packaging
Owner: Jamie Swisher
Number Employees: 1-4
Brands:
DOOR COUNTY POTATO CHIPS
STRENDGE PASTA

3792 **Door County Fish Market**
2831 Dundee Rd
Northbrook, IL 60062-2501 847-559-9229
Fax: 847-559-9273
Seafood
President: Steven Messner
Estimated Sales: $ .5 - 1 million
Number Employees: 1-4

3793 **Door-Peninsula Winery**
5806 State Highway 42
Sturgeon Bay, WI 54235-9767 920-743-7431
Fax: 920-743-5999 800-551-5049
DPW@DCwis.com www.dcwine.com
Wines
Owner: Bob Polman
VP: Robert Pollman
Marketing: Bob Pollman
Estimated Sales: $2.5-5 Million
Number Employees: 10-19
Sq. footage: 8
Type of Packaging: Private Label
Brands:
DOOR-PENINSULA

3794 **Doral International**
215-10 42nd Avenue
Bayside, NY 11361 718-224-7413
Fax: 718-224-7429 doral@doralgourmet.com
www.doralgourmet.com
Organic/natural, cakes/pastries. cookies, balsamic vinegar, full-line chocolate, gummies/jellies/pates de fruits, pasta (dry), other sauces, seasonings and cooking enhancers.
Marketing: Dora Lara Bonaccolta

3795 **(HQ)Dorchester Crab Company**
2076 Wingate Bishops Head Rd
Wingate, MD 21675 410-397-8103
Fax: 410-376-3179
Manufacturer of fresh and frozen seafood, shellfish including crabs and crab meat
Owner: Zach Seaman
Estimated Sales: $1.70 Million
Number Employees: 10-19
Type of Packaging: Consumer, Bulk

3796 **(HQ)Dorina/So-Good**
17400 Jefferson St
Union, IL 60180 815-923-2144
Fax: 815-923-2151
Manufacturer and exporter of shelf stable barbecue beef and pork; also, mustard, sauces, salsa, salad dressings, chip dips, olive salad and cheesespreads
President: Tim Young
CEO: Darwin Young
Estimated Sales: $.5-1 Million
Number Employees: 20-49
Sq. footage: 8000
Type of Packaging: Consumer, Food Service, Private Label, Bulk
Brands:
BAR-B-Q FIESTA
BAR-B-Q TREAT
CONEY ISLAND
DUFFY
FARM COUNTRY
OLD WEST BAR-B-Q DELIGHT
SO-GOOD BAR-B-Q DELIGHT
SO-GOOD PORK BAR-B-Q
SUPER
YOUNG'S BREADING

3797 **Dorothy Dawson Foods Products**
251 W Euclid Ave
Jackson, MI 49203-4101 517-788-9830
Fax: 517-788-7852 www.dawsonfoods.com
Manufacturer of all-natural, ready-to-use frozen soups, sauces, batters, breadings and mixes including soup, marinade and steak au jus; also, pizza products including sauces, mixes and seasoning blends
President: Phillip Dawson Sr
VP: David Elias
Estimated Sales: $ 10 - 20 Million
Number Employees: 20-49
Type of Packaging: Food Service, Private Label, Bulk
Brands:
EMILY'S GOURMET
FRESHDRY
KETTLE GOURMET
SIMON'S
STARTERS
ZIP

3798 **Dorothy Timberlake Candies**
2351 Eaton Rd
Madison, NH 03849 603-447-2221
Fax: 603-447-2221 faith@timberlakecandies.com
www.timberlakecandies.com
Hard candy and lollipops
President: William Timberlake
Estimated Sales: $1-2.5 Million
Number Employees: 1-4
Brands:
DOROTHY

3799 **Dorset Fisheries**
215 Water St
Suite 302
St Josephs, NL A1C 6C9
Canada 709-739-7147
Fax: 709-739-0586 dorsetfish@roadrunner.nf.net
Manufacturer and exporter of fresh lobster and cod
President: Derick Philpott
Estimated Sales: $5 Million
Number Employees: 30
Type of Packaging: Bulk

3800 **Doscher's Candies**
24 W Court St
Cincinnati, OH 45202-1062 513-381-8656
Fax: 513-381-8656
Manufacturer of candy including bars, canes and taffy products
President: Greg Clark Sr
VP: Harry J Doscher
Estimated Sales: $1-2.5 Million
Number Employees: 5-9
Sq. footage: 8400
Type of Packaging: Consumer
Brands:
FERNCH CHEW

3801 **Double B Distributors**
1031 W New Circle Rd
Lexington, KY 40511 859-255-8822
Fax: 859-233-1241
Manufacturer of meat snack foods
Owner: Bob Heim
Estimated Sales: $ 5 - 10 Million
Number Employees: 10-19

3802 **Double B Foods**
800 West Arbrook Blvd
Suite 200
Arlington, TX 76105 469-567-6000
Fax: 469-567-6021 800-679-0349
www.doubleb.com
Manufacturer of chicken, eggs, frankfurters and Mexican foods
President: Kevin Migdal
CFO: Ron Bowlin
Estimated Sales: $25-49.9 Million
Number Employees: 20-49

3803 **Double Play Foods**
500 E 77th Street
Apt 3525
New York, NY 10162-0011 212-682-4611
Fax: 212-570-4488 www.overloadcup.com
Peanut butter cups

3804 **Double Rainbow Gourmet Ice Creams**
275 S Van Ness Ave
San Francisco, CA 94103 415-861-5858
Fax: 415-861-5872 800-489-3580
www.doublerainbow.com
Manufacturers of ice cream and nondairy desserts
President: Steve Fink
Number Employees: 10-19

3805 **Double-Cola Company**
537 Market St # 100
Chattanooga, TN 37402-1229 423-267-5691
Fax: 423-267-0793 info@double-cola.com
www.double-cola.com
Soft drinks
President: Alnoor Dhanini
VP Sales/Marketing: Gilford Thomas
Production: Roy Chisenall
Estimated Sales: $5-10 Million
Number Employees: 5-9
Brands:
CHASER
DIET CHASER
DIET DOUBLE-COLA
DIET SKI
DOUBLE DRY GINGERALE
DOUBLE-COLA
DOUBLE-DRY MIXERS
JUMBO FLAVORS
SKI

3806 **Doug Hardy Company**
Mountainville Rd
Deer Isle, ME 04627 207-348-6604
Fax: 207-348-6100
Manufacturer of seafood
Owner: Doug Hardy
Estimated Sales: $ 3 - 5 Million
Number Employees: 5-9

3807 **Dough Works Company**
710 Oak Ln Stop 2
Horicon, WI 53032 920-485-4550
Fax: 920-485-4035 800-383-8808
info@doughworks.biz www.doughworks.biz
Manufacturer of frozen bakery products, organic cookies and bread/specialty distributor of food products and supply goods 80% of WI/Chicago
President: Robert Scott
VP: Kim Gassner
Sales: Robert Scott
Estimated Sales: $500,000-$1 Million
Number Employees: 11
Sq. footage: 32000

3808 **Dough-To-Go**
3535 De La Cruz Blvd
Santa Clara, CA 95054 408-727-4094
Fax: 408-727-4095 betsyl@doughtogo.com
www.dough-to-go.com
Manufacturer of frozen raw dough and cookies, scones and brownies
President: Elizabeth Sanders
Vice President: Rosel Witt
Estimated Sales: $2 Million
Number Employees: 15
Sq. footage: 10000
Type of Packaging: Food Service
Brands:
DOUGH-TO-GO
JANE DOUGH

3809 **Douglas Cross Enterprises**
2030 5th Ave
Seattle, WA 98121-2505 206-448-1193
Fax: 206-448-1979 richmond@tomdouglas.com
www.tomdouglas.com
BBQ Sauces
President: Tom Douglas

Estimated Sales: $5-10 Million
Number Employees: 10-19

3810 Doumak
2201 Touhy Ave
Elk Grove Vlg, IL 60007 847-437-2100
Fax: 847-437-1809 800-323-0318
www.doumak.com
Manufacturer of marshmallows
President: Barry Blum
VP Manufacturing: Barry Blum
Estimated Sales: $2.5-5 Million
Number Employees: 10-19
Sq. footage: 40000
Type of Packaging: Consumer, Food Service, Private Label
Brands:
FIRESIDE
WONDERFOOD

3811 Douwe Egberts
670 Lakeview Plaza Boulevard
Suite B
Worthington, OH 43085 614-436-6112
Fax: 888-886-1533 800-582-6617
sales@enjoybettercoffee.com
www.enjoybettercoffee.com
Coffee.
Marketing: Victor Borsukevich

3812 Dove Mushrooms
P.O.Box 340
Avondale, PA 19311-0340 610-268-3535
Fax: 610-268-3099 info@modernmush.com
www.modernmush.com
Manufacturer of fresh, canned and dried mushrooms
President: Chuck Ciarrocchi
Estimated Sales: $20-50 Million
Number Employees: 20-49
Sq. footage: 25000
Parent Co: Modern Mushroom Farms
Type of Packaging: Consumer, Food Service, Private Label, Bulk
Brands:
MODERN
SHER ROCKEE

3813 Dow Distribution
524 Ohohia St
Honolulu, HI 96819 808-836-3511
Fax: 808-833-3634
Fish and seafood
President: Craig Mitchell
Estimated Sales: $ 10 - 20 Million
Number Employees: 10-19

3814 Dowd & Rogers
1400 Kearns Blvd.
Park City, UT 84060260 916-451-6480
Fax: 800-767-8514 800-669-8877
info@dowdandrogers.com
www.dowdandrogers.com
Premium wheat free and gluten free products
President: Derek Dowd
Number of Brands: 2
Number of Products: 8
Type of Packaging: Consumer, Food Service, Private Label, Bulk
Brands:
DOWD AND ROGERS

3815 Down East Specialty Products/Cape Bald Packers
171 Virginia St
Portland, ME 04103-3943 207-878-9170
Fax: 207-878-9104 800-369-6327
cnally@capebaldpackers.com
www.capebaldpackers.com
Manufacturer of lobster, mussels, rock crab and red crab
Manager: Kathy Nally
Manager: Patrice Landry
Estimated Sales: $ 1 - 3 Million
Number Employees: 1-4
Parent Co: Cape Bald Packers
Type of Packaging: Private Label
Brands:
DOWNEAST

3816 Downeast Candies
P.O.Box 25
Boothbay Harbor, ME 04538 207-633-5178
decinc@dwi.net
Manufacturer of fudges and taffy
President: David Carmolli
VP: Elaine Miller
Production Manager: Rick Carmolli
Estimated Sales: $1-2.5 Million
Number Employees: 1-4
Type of Packaging: Consumer, Private Label, Bulk
Brands:
DOWNEAST CANDIES

3817 Downeast Coffee
259 East Avenue
Pawtucket, RI 02860-3801 401-724-6393
Fax: 401-724-0560 800-345-2007
jpeterman@downeastcoffee.com
http://www.downeastcoffee.com/
Coffee
President/CEO: William Kapos
CFO: Frank DeLuca
VP: James Peterman
Marketing: Mark Bishop
Plant Manager: Ron Yanko
Estimated Sales: $1-2.5 Million
Number Employees: 10-19
Type of Packaging: Private Label
Brands:
DOWNEAST

3818 Doyon & Doyon
68 Tycos Drive
Toronto, ON M6B 1V9
Canada 416-789-4391
Fax: 416-789-9112 888-851-3110
info@billybee.com www.mieldoyon.com
Manufacturer of beeswax and honey; exporter of honey; importer of pollen
President: Paul Doyon
CEO: David Sugarman
Number Employees: 15
Sq. footage: 15000
Type of Packaging: Consumer, Food Service, Bulk
Brands:
DOYON
PURE HONEY

3819 Dpi Specialty Foods, Inc
1007 Church Street
Suite 314
Evanston, IL 60201 503-692-0662
Fax: 847-492-8036
dpishow@dpispecialtyfoods.com
www.dpispecialtyfoods.com
Organic/natural, full-line, baked goods, full-line oils, full-line candy, full-line dairy and eggs, full-line frozen, full-line meat/game/pate, foodservice.
Marketing: Frank Patrick

3820 Dr McDougall's Right Foods
105 Associate Road
South San Francisco, CA 94080 650-583-4993
Fax: 650-583-6376 rits@sfspice.com
www.rightfoods.com
instant meal cups
President/Owner: John McDougall MD

3821 Dr Pepper/Seven Up
5301 Legacy Drive
Plano, TX 75024 97- 6-3 70
80- 6-6 58
www.dpsubg.com
Carbonated soft drinks and fountain syrup concentrate
President: Larry Young
Chairman: Wayne Sanders
CFO: Martin Ellen
Estimated Sales: $5 Billion
Number Employees: 100
Parent Co: Cadbury Schweppes PLC
Type of Packaging: Consumer, Food Service, Bulk
Brands:
7 UP
A&W
CANADA DRY
COUNTRY TIME
DEJA BLUE
DIET RITE
DR. PEPPER
HAWAIIAN PUNCH
HIRES ROOT BEER
RASING COW
RC COLA
RED FUSION
SCHEPPES
SLUSH PUPPIES
SQUIRT
SUNDROP
SUNKIST
VERNORS
WELCH'S
dnL

3822 Dr Pete's
2224 Gamble Rd
P.O. Box 24089
Savannah, GA 31403 912-233-3035
Fax: 912-233-0001 888-599-0047
info@dr-petes.com www.dr-petes.com
Manufacturer of sauces, marinades and dressings
CEO: Joel Coffee
Estimated Sales: $600,000
Number Employees: 5-9
Type of Packaging: Consumer, Food Service
Brands:
Dr. Pete's

3823 Dr. Christopher's Original Foods
155 W 2050 N
Spanish Fork, UT 84660 801-453-1406
Fax: 801-794-6801 800-453-1406
www.drchristopher.com
Manufacturer and exporter of supplements and herbal formulas
Sales/Marketing: Troy Fukumitsu
Estimated Sales: $20-50 Million
Number Employees: 20-49
Type of Packaging: Consumer, Private Label, Bulk

3824 Dr. Cookie
2112 6th Ave
Seattle, WA 98121-2513 206-389-9321
orderdesk@drcookie.com
www.drcookie.com
Cookies, breads, rolls
Manager: Steve Krendall
Estimated Sales: $1-5 Million appx.
Number Employees: 1-4
Brands:
DR COOKIE

3825 Dr. Frank's Vinifera Wine Cellar
9749 Middle Rd
Hammondsport, NY 14840 607-868-4884
Fax: 607-868-4888 800-320-0735
info@drfrankwines.com www.drfrankwines.com
Manufacturer and exporter of table wine and champagne
Chairman: Willie Frank
President: Fred Frank
Estimated Sales: $ 5 - 10 Million
Number Employees: 10-19
Type of Packaging: Consumer
Brands:
CHATEAU FRANK CHAMPAGNE CELLARS
DR. KONSTANTIN FRANK

3826 Dr. Konstantin Frank Vin
9749 Middle Rd
Hammondsport, NY 14840-9612 607-868-4884
Fax: 607-868-4888 800-320-0735
frankwines@aol.com www.drfrankwines.com
Wines and champagne. Founded by Dr. Konstantin Frank, pioneer grower of European wine grape varieties in Eastern United States.
President: Fredrick Frank
VP: Eric Volz
Estimated Sales: $5-9.9 Million
Number Employees: 10-19
Type of Packaging: Private Label
Brands:
DR KONSTANTIN FRANK
SALMON RUN

3827 Dr. Kracker
1100 Klein Rd
Plano, TX 75054 97- 63- 110
Fax: 972-633-1130 alan.konecny@drkracker.com
www.drkracker.com
organic flatbreads, snacker krackers, snack chips and snack flats.
President: Carsten Kruse
Sales/Marketing Director: George Eckrich
Estimated Sales: $1.1 Million
Number Employees: 21

3828 **Dr. Paul Lohmann Inc.**
1757-10 Veterans Memorial Hwy
Islandia, NY 11749 631-851-8810
Fax: 631-851-8815 service@lohmann-inc.com
www.lohmann-inc.com
Manufacturer of specialty mineral salts

3829 **Dr. Pepper/Seven-Up**
3131 Phillips Ave
Racine, WI 53403-3547 262-634-3369
Fax: 262-634-8870 800-696-5891
www.dpsu.com
Manufacturer of bottled beverages including soft drinks
Manager: Tom Andersen
Sales Manager: Brad Allbee
Estimated Sales: $12 Million
Number Employees: 1-4
Parent Co: Cadbury Schweppes & Carlyle Group
Brands:
7 UP
A&W
CANADA DRY
COUNTRY TIME
DEJA BLUE
DIET RITE
DR PEPPER
HAWAIIAN PUNCH
HIRES ROOT BEER
RAGING COW'S
RC COLA
RED FUSION
SCHWEPPES
SLUSH PUPPIE
SQUIRT
SUNDROP
SUNKIST
VERNORS
WELCHOS
dnL

3830 **Dr. Pete's**
2224 Gamble Rd
PO Box 24089
Savannah, GA 31403 912-233-3035
Fax: 912-233-0001 info@dr-petes.com
www.dr-petes.com
sauces, marinades, dressings, baking mixes
CEO: Joel Coffee
VP: Jan Coffee
Number Employees: 5

3831 **Dr. Praeger's Sensible Foods**
9 Boumar Pl
Elmwood Park, NJ 07407-2615 201-703-1300
Fax: 201-703-9333 877-PRA-GER
nurit@drpraegers.com www.drpraegers.com
Manufacturer of kosher natural frozen products such as veggie burgers, fish sticks and potato pancakes
President: Dr Peter Praeger
Director Sales/Marketing: Larry Praeger
Estimated Sales: $ 20 - 50 Million
Number Employees: 50-99
Type of Packaging: Food Service
Brands:
DR PRAEGER'S
UNGAR'S

3832 **Dr. Smoothie Brands**
1730 Raymer Avenue
Fullerton, CA 92833 714-449-9787
Fax: 714-449-9474 888-466-9941
info@drsmoothie.com www.drsmoothie.com or
www.cafeessentials.com
Dr. Smoothie Brands is a full line beverage company manufacturing shelf-stable , liquid natural fruit smoothies and powdered cocoa, mocha, latte, and chai blends. Manufactures nutritional blends ranging from raw, whole food nutritionbars to a full range of botanicals, including medically endorsed products like The Complete Meal, and Amino line.
Number of Brands: 6
Number of Products: 93
Type of Packaging: Consumer, Food Service

3833 **Dr. Tima Natural Products**
131 Groverton Pl
Los Angeles, CA 90077-3732 310-472-2181
Fax: 310-652-9884
Natural health products and soda
Owner: Potito Depaolis
VP: Mary Caronna
Estimated Sales: $2.5-5 Million
Number Employees: 5-9
Brands:
DR TIMA

3834 **Draco Natural Products**
539 Parrott Street
San Jose, CA 95112 408-287-7871
Fax: 408-287-8838 www.dracoherbs.com
Wholesales herbal extracts
CEO: Jerry Wu
Sales: Ed Schack
Estimated Sales: $3 Million
Number Employees: 20

3835 **Drader Manufacturing Industries**
5750-50 Street NW
Edmonton, AB T6B 2Z8
Canada 780-440-2231
Fax: 780-440-2244 800-661-4122
bakery@drader.com www.drader.com
Manufacturer of custom carriers, bread baskets, bakery trays, hand trucks, dollies and bakery shelving
President/General Manager: Gordon McTavish
Account Manager: Chris Gaucher
Sales Manager: Jeff McTavish
Manager: Glenn Eckert
Number Employees: 60
Sq. footage: 35000

3836 **Dragnet Fisheries**
4141 B St
Anchorage, AK 99503-5940 907-276-4551
Fax: 907-274-3617
Manufacturer of fresh and frozen herring, black cod, halibut and salmon
President: Jay Cherrier
Estimated Sales: Less than $500,000
Number Employees: 1-4
Type of Packaging: Consumer, Food Service
Brands:
DRAGNET

3837 **Dragoco**
300 North St
Teterboro, NJ 7608 973-256-3850
Fax: 973-256-8874 www.symrise.com
Manufacturer and exporter of natural and artificial concentrated food flavors
President: Klaus Stanzl
Estimated Sales: $50-100 Million
Number Employees: 1,000-4,999
Sq. footage: 250000
Parent Co: Dragoco
Brands:
EXTRAPONES
MICROSEAL
NEOROM

3838 **Dragunara LLC**
Po Box 1111
Palos Verdes Estate, CA 90274 310-618-8818
info@dragunara.com
www.dragunara.com
Other lifestyle, full-line condiments, BBQ sauce, ethnic sauces (soy, curry, etc.), full-line spices, marinades, other sauces, seasonings and cooking enhancers, rubs.

3839 **Drakes Brewing**
1933 Davis Street
Suite 177
San Leandro, CA 94577-1256 510-568-BREW
Fax: 510-568-9857 drinkdrakes@jbrfoods.com
www.drinkdrakes.com
Beer
Principal: Adolfo Carrera
CFO: Peter Rogers
Director Manufacturing: Roger Lind
Estimated Sales: $ 1-2.5 Million
Number Employees: 100
Brands:
AUTUMN FEST
BLOOD RED
CHOCOLATE MILK STOUT
DRAKES AMBER ALE
DRAKES BLOND ALE
DRAKES HEFE-WEIZEN
DRAKES IPA
EXPEDITION
HARVEST ALE BRITISH ESB
IMPERIAL IPA BLACK PILSNER
IMPERIAL IPA PILSNER
IMPERIAL STOUT
JOLLY ROGERS
SIR FRANCIS STOUT
ZATEC PILSNER

3840 **Drakes Fresh Pasta Company**
P.O.Box 5072
High Point, NC 27262 336-861-5454
Fax: 336-861-4823 www.drakesfreshpasta.com
Pasta products
President: Richard Drake
Vice President: Simone Drake
Sales: Ginger Edward
Estimated Sales: $5 Million
Number Employees: 50
Brands:
DRAKES FRESH

3841 **Drangle Foods**
300 S Riverside Dr
Gilman, WI 54433 715-447-8241
Fax: 715-447-8242
Flavored processed cheese
President: Tom Hand
Office Manager: Char Hand
Estimated Sales: $1 Million
Number Employees: 80
Sq. footage: 20
Type of Packaging: Private Label
Brands:
DRANGLE

3842 **Draper Valley Farms**
1000 Jason Lane
Mount Vernon, WA 98273-2490 425-793-4135
www.drapervalleyfarms.com
Free range chicken
President/Co-Owner: Jim Koplowitz
CEO/Co-Owner: Richard Koplowitz
VP: John Jefferson
VP: Jim Calhoun
Comptroller: Mel Call
Sales Manager: Larry Morris
Human Relations Manager: Colleen Helergson
Trucking Supervisor: Mark Anderson
Plant Manager: John Michalak
Estimated Sales: $74 Million
Number Employees: 200
Sq. footage: 32799
Type of Packaging: Consumer, Food Service

3843 **(HQ)Dream Confectioners**
540 Cedar Ln
Teaneck, NJ 07666-1742 201-836-9000
Fax: 201-836-9015
Manufacturer and exporter of pretzels
President: Joseph Podolski
Estimated Sales: $2.5-5 Million
Number Employees: 1-4
Type of Packaging: Consumer, Private Label, Bulk
Brands:
GREAT

3844 **Dream Foods International LLC**
1223 Wilshire Boulevard
Suite 355
Santa Monica, CA 90403 310-315-5739
Fax: 310-388-1322 info@dreamfoods.com
www.dreamfoods.com
Dairy-free, functional (antioxidants), gluten-free, kosher, organic/natural, USDA, juice/cider.
Marketing: Adriana Kahane

3845 **Dream Time**
1115 Thompson Avenue #5
Santa Cruz, CA 95062 831-464-6702
Fax: 831-464-6703 877-464-6702
info@dreamtimeinc.com
www.dreamtimeinc.com
Manufacturer of natural ingredient health products
Owner: Judy Day
Estimated Sales: $ 1 - 3 Million
Number Employees: 10-19

3846 **Dreamous Corporation**
2720 Monterey St Ste 401
Torrance, CA 90503 310-787-7002
Fax: 310-787-7276 800-251-7543
info@dremous.com www.dreamous.com
Manufacturer and distributor of all natural health supplements, homeopathic formula, and beauty products
Owner: Susan Negus
VP Product Development: Dr Howard Davis
Estimated Sales: $ 20 - 50 Million
Number Employees: 20-49

Type of Packaging: Private Label

3847 **Dresden Stollen Company**
7 Heathcote Drive
Albertson, NY 11507 516-746-5802
Fax: 516-746-5918 http://www.dresdenstollen.com
gourmet foods
President/Owner: Joan Greenfield
Estimated Sales: A
Number Employees: 1

3848 **Dressed in Style/ChaseChase Food Company**
1528 Emory Rd Ne
Atlanta, GA 30306-2409 404-377-3757
Fax: 404-872-3211 888-368-2698
chasefood@mindspring.com
www.chasefood.com
Salad dressings, sauces and marinades
President: Sue Chase
Estimated Sales: $150,000
Number Employees: 2
Brands:
DRESSED

3849 **(HQ)Dressel Collins Fish Company**
5131 S Director St
Seattle, WA 98118 206-725-0121
Fax: 206-725-1354
Manufacturer of canned and smoked salmon
President: Mike Bonney
Estimated Sales: $10 Million
Number Employees: 1-4
Type of Packaging: Consumer, Food Service

3850 **Drew's**
PO Box 8181
926 Vermont Rt. 103 South
Chester, VT 05143 800-228-2980
Fax: 413-367-9357 800-228-2980
chefdrew@chefdrew.com www.chefdrew.com
Hot sauces
President: Andrew Starkweather
CFO: Catherine Wescott
Marketing/Public Relations: Michelle Swedick
Plant Manager: Joe Brent
Estimated Sales: $ 1.5 Million
Number Employees: 11
Type of Packaging: Private Label

3851 **Drew's All Natural**
926 Vt Route 103 S
Chester, VT 05143 802-875-1184
Fax: 413-367-9357 800-228-2980
chefdrew@chefdrew.com www.chefdrew.com
All natural salad dressings and salsa, Certified Organic
President/CEO: Andrew Starkweather
Assistant Controller: Rob Feakes
Plant Manager: Joe Brent
Estimated Sales: $1.5 Million
Number Employees: 10-19
Type of Packaging: Consumer, Private Label
Brands:
DREW'S ALL NATURAL

3852 **Dreyer Sonoma**
161 Fox Hollow Rd
Woodside, CA 94062-3607 650-851-9448
Fax: 650-851-3268 jdreyer@dreyerwine.com
www.dreyerwine.com
Wines
Co-Owner: Walter Dreyer
Co-Owner: Bettina Dreyer
General Manager: Jonathan Dreyer
Estimated Sales: $2.5-5 Million
Number Employees: 5-9
Brands:
Dreyer Wine

3853 **(HQ)Dreyer's Grand Ice Cream**
5929 College Ave
Oakland, CA 94618 510-652-8187
Fax: 570-301-4538 877-437-3937
dsbailey@dreyers.com www.dreyers.com
Manufacturer of ice cream, packaged and novelties
President/CEO: Mike Mitchell
EVP/CFO: Steve Barbour
Research & Development: Donald Birnbaum
Director Consumer Communications: Dori Sera Bailey
Public Relations Premium Brands: Kim Goeller Johnson
Public Relations Super Premium Brands: Diane McIntyre
Estimated Sales: $1 Billion
Number Employees: 7500
Number of Brands: 5
Type of Packaging: Consumer, Food Service
Other Locations:
Dreyer's Grand Ice Cream
Fort Wayne IN
Brands:
DIBS
DREAMERY
DREAMERY BANANA SPLIT
DREAMERY BLACK RASPBERRY AVALANCHE
DREAMERY CARAMEL TOFFEE BAR HEAVEN
DREAMERY CASHEW PRALINE PARFAIT
DREAMERY CHERRY CHIP BA DA BING
DREAMERY CHOCOLATE ALMOND BAR
DREAMERY CHOCOLATE PEANUT BUTTER CH
DREAMERY CONEY ISLAND WAFFLE CONE
DREAMERY COOL MINT
DREAMERY DEEP DISH APPLE PIE
DREAMERY DULCE DE LECHE
DREAMERY GRANDMA'S COOKIE DOUGH
DREAMERY HARVEST PEACH
DREAMERY NEW YORK CHEESECAKE
DREAMERY NOTHING BUT CHCOLATE
DREAMERY NUTS ABOUT MALT
DREAMERY RASPBERRY BROWNIE ALA MODE
DREAMERY STRAWBERRY FIELDS
DREAMERY TIRAMISU
DREAMERY TRUFFLE EXPLOSION
DREAMERY VANILLA
EDY'S
GODIVA
M&M/MARS
STARBUCKS
WHOLE FRUIT

3854 **Dreymiller & Kray**
140 S State St
Hampshire, IL 60140 847-683-2271
Fax: 847-683-2272 www.dreymillerandkray.com
Packer/processor of sausage, ham and bacon
President: Ed Reiser
Estimated Sales: $500,000-$1 Million
Number Employees: 10-19
Type of Packaging: Consumer

3855 **Drier's Meats**
14 S Elm St
Three Oaks, MI 49128-1122 269-756-3101
Fax: 616-756-9285 info@driers.com
www.driers.com
Smoked meats
Owner: Carolyn Drier
Estimated Sales: Less than $500,000
Number Employees: 1-4
Brands:
DRIER MEATS

3856 **Driftwood Dairy**
10724 E Lower Azusa Road
El Monte, CA 91731-1390 626-444-9591
Fax: 626-448-7649 drifty@driftwooddairy.com
www.driftwooddairy.com
Manufacturer of dairy products
President: James Dolan
CEO: Mike Dolan
VP: Jeep Dolan
COO: Tom Dolan
Estimated Sales: $100+ Million
Number Employees: 150
Type of Packaging: Consumer, Food Service, Bulk

3857 **Driscoll Strawberry Associates**
345 Westridge Drive
Watsonville, CA 95077 831-763-5100
Fax: 831-724-4530 www.driscolls.com
Grower and exporter of fresh organic strawberries, raspberries, blackberries and blueberries
Owner/President: Myles Reiter
Chairman/President/CEO: J M Reiter
CFO: Brian McLaughlin
VP: Al Rodrigues
Head of Research & Development: Fred Cook
VP Marketing: Douglas Ronan
VP Human Resources: Steven Stein
Estimated Sales: $20-50 Million
Number Employees: 412
Sq. footage: 19932
Brands:
ASSOCIATES
DRISCOLL'S
DSA
ISLANDER

3858 **Drohan Company**
29 Preston St
Huntington, NY 11743 718-898-9672
Fax: 718-335-7815
Manufacturer of fresh and frozen poultry
President: John Howell
Estimated Sales: $10-20 Million
Number Employees: 10-19

3859 **Droubi's Imports**
7333 Hillcroft Street
Houston, TX 77081-6203 713-988-7138
Fax: 713-988-9506
Manufacturer, importer and wholesaler/distributor of tea and coffee
President: A Droubi
VP: Sharon Droubi
Estimated Sales: $1-2.5 Million
Number Employees: 20-49
Sq. footage: 12000
Parent Co: Droubi's Bakery & Delicatessen
Brands:
GOLD STAR

3860 **Drum Rock Specialty Company**
P.O.Box 7001
Warwick, RI 2887 401-737-5165
Fax: 401-737-5060 www.drumrockproducts.com
Manufacturer and exporter of fritter breading and batter mixes for vegetables, seafood and poultry; also, custom dry blending and mixing and private labeling services available
President: Stephen Hinger
Sales Manager: Paul Skorupa
Estimated Sales: $1-2.5 Million
Number Employees: 5-9
Type of Packaging: Food Service, Private Label, Bulk
Brands:
FIS-CHIC WONDER BATTER

3861 **Drusilla Seafood Packing & Processing Company**
3482 Drusilla Ln # D
Baton Rouge, LA 70809-1800 225-923-0896
Fax: 225-928-4936 800-364-8844
www.drusillaplace.com
Manufacturer and packer of seafood, spices, salad dressings and breading mixes
President: James Zito
Marketing Manager: Nancy Zito
Estimated Sales: $300,000-$500,000
Number Employees: 100-249
Sq. footage: 2500
Parent Co: Seafood Restaurant
Brands:
DRUSILLA

3862 **Dry Creek Vineyard**
3770 Lambert Bridge Rd
Healdsburg, CA 95448 707-433-1000
Fax: 707-433-5329 800-864-9463
dcv@drycreekvineyard.com www.dcgstore.com
Wines
Owner: Gina Gallo
VP: Don Wallace
VP Marketing: Kim Stare-Wallace
Estimated Sales: $10-20 Million
Number Employees: 10-19
Type of Packaging: Consumer, Food Service
Brands:
LATE HARVEST ZINFANDEL-LIMITED ED.
MERITAGE
REGATTA
SOLEIL-LATE HARVEST SAUVIGNON BLANC

3863 **Dryden & Palmer Company**
101 Erie Blvd
Canajoharie, NY 13317-1148
Fax: 203-488-8085 info@rockcandy.com
www.rockcandy.com
Rock candy
President: Stephen Besse
Estimated Sales: $10-20 Million
Number Employees: 20-49

3864 **Dryden Provision Company**
1016 E Washington St
Louisville, KY 40206 502-583-1777
Fax: 502-583-3006 www.drydenprovidin.com
Manufactuer of beef, meat products
President: John Dryden
Co-Owner: Janinne Agee
Estimated Sales: $3 Million
Number Employees: 13
Brands:
DRYDEN

3865 **Dubois Seafood**
204 Saint Peter St
Houma, LA 70363 985-876-2514
Fax: 985-851-6147
Seafood
President: Kerry Dubois
Estimated Sales: $ 1 - 3 Million
Number Employees: 5-9

3866 **Duck Pond Cellars**
P.O.Box 429
Dundee, OR 97115 503-538-3199
Fax: 503-538-3190 800-437-3213
duckpond@duckpondcellars.com
www.duckpondcellars.com
Wines
President: Doug Fries
CFO: Jo Ann Fries
Sales: Scott Jenkins
VP Operations: Lisa Jenkins
Estimated Sales: $1-2.5 Million
Number Employees: 10-19
Type of Packaging: Private Label
Brands:
DUCK POND CELLARS

3867 **Duckhorn Vineyards**
1000 Lodi Ln
St Helena, CA 94574-9713 707-963-7108
Fax: 707-963-7595 888-354-8885
welcome@duckhorn.com
www.duckhornvineyards.com
Wines
President: Daniel Duckhorn
VP Marketing/Sales: Margaret Duckhorn
Estimated Sales: $10-20 Million
Number Employees: 50-99
Brands:
DECOY
DUCKHORN VINEYARDS
GOLDENEYE
KING EIDER
PARADUXX

3868 **Ducktrap River Fish Farm**
57 Little River Dr
Belfast, ME 4915 207-338-6280
Fax: 207-338-6288 800-434-8727
smoked@ducktrap.com www.ducktrap.com
Manufacturer, importer and exporter of pate and smoked seafood including trout fillets, Atlantic salmon, peppered and herb mackerel, mussels, scallops and shrimp
CEO: Rafaeo Puga
Estimated Sales: $20-50 Million
Number Employees: 10-19
Sq. footage: 25000
Type of Packaging: Consumer, Food Service, Bulk
Brands:
DUCKTRAP
KENDALL BROOK
SPRUCE POINT
WINTER HARBOR

3869 **Duda Redifoods**
P.O.Box 620257
Oviedo, FL 32762-0257 407-365-2111
Fax: 407-365-2147 www.duda.com
Manufacturer of canned and frozen celery
Manager: Joseph Duda
Estimated Sales: $10-20 Million
Number Employees: 20-49
Parent Co: A. Duda & Sons
Type of Packaging: Consumer, Bulk

3870 **Dufflet Pastries**
166 Norseman Street
Toronto, ON M8Z ZR4
Canada 416-536-9640
Fax: 416-538-2366 heather@dufflet.com
www.duffletsweets.com
Manufacturer of cakes, tortes, pies, flan, tarts, brownies, cookies, etc
President: Daniele Bertrand
CEO: Dufflet Rosenberg
Marketing: Karin Jensen
Number Employees: 65
Number of Products: 100
Sq. footage: 10000
Type of Packaging: Consumer, Food Service

3871 **Dufour Pastry Kitchens**
251 Locust Ave
Bronx, NY 10454-2004 718-402-8800
Fax: 718-402-7002 800-439-1282
jon.vaughn@dufourpastrykitchens.com
www.dufourpastrykitchens.com
Manufacturer of frozen puff pastry products including hors d'oeuvres, doughs, snacks, lunch products, tart shells, etc
President: Judi Arnold
Vice President: Carla Krasner
Estimated Sales: $20-50 Million
Number Employees: 50
Sq. footage: 9600
Type of Packaging: Consumer, Food Service, Bulk
Brands:
DUFOUR PASTRY KITCHENS

3872 **Dugdale Beef Company**
4224 W 71st St
Indianapolis, IN 46268 317-291-9660
Fax: 317-298-7608
Manufacturer of meat products, and meat packager
President: Jean Deering
Estimated Sales: $ 20 - 50 Million
Number Employees: 20-49
Type of Packaging: Consumer

3873 **Duguay Fish Packers**
1062 Bas-Cap-Pele Ch
Cap-Pele, NB E4N 1K9
Canada 506-577-2287
Fax: 506-577-1995
Manufacturer of smoked herring fillets hand-cured, alewives pickled
Owner: Omer Duguay
Contact: Bobby Duguay
Estimated Sales: $2.7
Number Employees: 20
Type of Packaging: Food Service

3874 **(HQ)Duis Meat Processing**
1991 E 6th St
Concordia, KS 66901 785-243-7850
800-281-4295
duis@dustdevil.com
Manufacturer of fresh and frozen meat including sausages, buffalo and smoked meats
President: Toby Duis
Estimated Sales: $1-3 Million
Number Employees: 5-9
Sq. footage: 3200
Type of Packaging: Consumer, Food Service, Private Label, Bulk
Other Locations:
Duis Meat Processing
Salina KS

3875 **Dulce de Leche DelcampoProducts**
15908 NW 48th Ave
Hialeah, FL 33014 305-620-1444
Fax: 305-624-2728 877-472-9408
info@delcampoproducts.com
www.delcampoproducts.com
Manufacturer of dulce de leche, cholesterol-free white cheese, guava spread and filling
President: Carlos Ruiz DeLuque
Estimated Sales: $ 3 - 5 Million
Number Employees: 10-19
Type of Packaging: Consumer, Food Service, Private Label, Bulk
Brands:
DEL CAMPO

3876 **Dulcette Technologies**
2 Hicks Street
Lindenhurst, NY 11757 631-752-8700
Fax: 631-752-8117 sales@dulcettetech.com
www.dulcettetech.com
Manufacturer of sweeteners, nutraceuticals & antioxidants
Estimated Sales: $500,000-1 Million
Number Employees: 7

3877 **Duma Meats**
857 Randolph Rd
Mogadore, OH 44260 330-628-3438
Fax: 330-628-3438
www.dumameatsfarmmarket.com
Manufacturer of fresh and frozen beef, lamb and pork; slaughtering services available
President: David Duma Jr
Estimated Sales: $1-2.5 Million
Number Employees: 20-49
Type of Packaging: Consumer, Food Service, Bulk

3878 **Dummbee Gourmet Foods**
PO Box 70159
Albany, GA 31708-0159 229-435-4800
Fax: 229-420-4108 800-569-1657
Gourmet foods
President: Tammy Barber
Owner: Steve Barber
Estimated Sales: Under $500,000
Number Employees: 1
Brands:
DUMMBEE GOURMET

3879 **Dunbar Foods**
P.O.Box 519
Dunn, NC 28335 910-892-3175
Fax: 910-892-6311
Manufacturer of canned sweet potatoes and peppers
President: Stanley Dunbar
Managing Director: Ron Austin
Estimated Sales: $50-100 Million
Number Employees: 40
Parent Co: Moody Dunbar
Type of Packaging: Consumer, Food Service, Private Label

3880 **Duncan Peak Vineyards**
P.O.Box 358
Hopland, CA 95449 707-744-1129
Fax: 925-283-3632 wine@duncanpeak.com
www.duncanpeak.com
Wines
President: Hubert Lenczowski
Estimated Sales: Less than $500,000
Number Employees: 1-4
Type of Packaging: Private Label
Brands:
DUNCAN

3881 **Dundee Brandied Fruit Company**
P.O.Box 445
Dundee, OR 97115 503-537-2500
Fax: 503-538-8599 sadler@dundeefruit.com
Manufacturer of brandied fruit
Owner: Richard Sadler
Estimated Sales: Under $500,000
Number Employees: 5
Brands:
DUNDEE BRANDIED

3882 **Dundee Candy Shop**
2112 Bardstown Rd
Louisville, KY 40205 502-452-9266
Fax: 502-459-7981 VOLINDAHJ@aol.com
www.dundeecandy.com
Candy
Owner: Maria Moore
Estimated Sales: $1-2.5 Million
Number Employees: 5-9
Brands:
DUNDEE CANDY SHOP

3883 **Dundee Citrus Growers**
P.O.Box 1739
Dundee, FL 33838 863-439-1574
Fax: 863-439-1535 800-447-1574
info@dun-d.com www.dun-d.com
Manufacturer of all varieties of Florida citrus fruits including oranges, grapefruit, tangerines and red grapefruit
President: W.Lindsay Raley Jr.
EVP/CEO: Steve Callaham
VP Operations: Greg Dunnahoe

Estimated Sales: $58.9 Million
Number Employees: 500-999
Sq. footage: 125000
Type of Packaging: Consumer, Food Service
Brands:
DUN-D

3884 **Dundee International**
3 Center Plz # 440
Boston, MA 02108-2086 617-742-4000
Fax: 617-742-5000 www.oldrepublic.com
Manufacturer of fish and seafood
VP: Stephen Wilson

3885 **Dundee Wine Company**
P.O.Box 220
Dundee, OR 97115-0220 503-538-3922
Fax: 503-538-2055 888-427-4953
wine@argylewinery.com www.argylewinery.com
Wines
Administrator: Rob Daykin
Sales: Craig Eastman
Estimated Sales: $1-2.5 Million
Number Employees: 5-9
Type of Packaging: Private Label
Brands:
DUNDEE

3886 **Dunford Bakers**
509 W Spring St
Fayetteville, AR 72701-5056 479-521-3000
Fax: 479-521-3006 donuts@coastlink.com
www.flyingburritoco.com
Donuts, danish, muffins, cookies, cakes, pan breads, specialty breads, and bagels
Owner: Mike Rohrbach
VP/CEO: Gary Gottfredson
CFO: Stephen Ames
Production: Bevin Crowther
Plant Manager: Ronald Stevens
Estimated Sales: $10-20 Million
Number Employees: 100-249
Brands:
DUTCH DELIGHT
HARVEST HAVEN

3887 **Dunford Bakers Company**
8556 S 2940 W
West Jordan, UT 84088 801-304-0400
Fax: 801-304-0511 800-748-4335
donuts@dunfordbakers.com
www.dunfordbakers.com
Manufacturer of doughnuts
Manager: Coelen Williamson
Estimated Sales: $5-10 Million
Number Employees: 20-49
Type of Packaging: Consumer, Private Label, Bulk

3888 **Dunham's Lobster Pot**
60 Mt Blue Pond Rd
Avon, ME 04966-3301 207-639-2815
Fax: 207-639-2815 durhamsfish@tds.net
Manufacturer of fresh seafood including fish, clams, haddock, scallops, crab meat, mussels, oysters, shrimp, lobster and rib-eye steaks
Owner: Tom Philbrick
Estimated Sales: $300,000-500,000
Number Employees: 1-4
Type of Packaging: Food Service, Bulk

3889 **Dunham's Meats**
5999 E State Route 29
Urbana, OH 43078 937-653-6709
Fax: 937-834-2411
Manufacturer of meat products; also, slaughtering services available
Owner/VP: Barry Dunham
Estimated Sales: $1-2.5 Million
Number Employees: 5-9
Type of Packaging: Consumer, Bulk

3890 **Dunkin Brands Inc.**
130 Royall St
Canton, MA 02021 781-737-3000
Fax: 781-737-4000 800-458-7731
www.dunkinbrands.com
coffee and ice cream
Chairman: Jon Luther
CEO: Nigel Travis
CFO: Kate Lavelle
SVP/General Counsel: Richard Emmett
Chief Marketing Officer: John Costello
SVP Human Resources: Christine Deputy
Estimated Sales: K
Number Employees: 1,126
Type of Packaging: Food Service
Brands:
BASKIN ROBBINS
DUNKIN DONUTS

3891 **Dunn Vineyards**
805 White Cottage Rd N
Angwin, CA 94508 707-965-3642
Fax: 707-965-3805 www.dunnvineyards.com
Wines
Owner: Randall Dunn
Estimated Sales: $1-2.5 Million
Number Employees: 1-4
Brands:
DUNN

3892 **Duo Delights**
301 Broadway Drive
Sun Prairie, WI 53590 608-837-8535
Fax: 866-720-6109 800-843-1381
CustomerService@mille-lacs.com
www.mille-lacs.com
Confections
President: Jay Singer
Estimated Sales: $ 5 - 10 Million
Number Employees: 20-49

3893 **Duplin Wine Cellars**
P.O.Box 756
Rose Hill, NC 28458-0756 910-289-3888
Fax: 910-289-3094 800-774-9634
info@duplinwinery.com www.duplinwinery.com
Wines
Owner: David Fussell Jr
Marketing/Sales: Bill Hatcher
Estimated Sales: $5-10 Million
Number Employees: 20-49
Type of Packaging: Private Label
Brands:
DUPLIN

3894 **Dupont Cheese**
N10140 State Road 110
Marion, WI 54950 715-754-5424
Fax: 715-754-1313 800-895-2873
dupontcheese@yahoo.com
www.dupontcheeseinc.com
Manufacturer of cheese including colby, mini-horus and longhorn
President: Fred Laack
Estimated Sales: $10-20 Million
Number Employees: 20-49
Type of Packaging: Consumer

3895 **Durango Brewing**
3000 Main Ave
Durango, CO 81301-5951 970-247-3396
www.durangobrewing.com
Beer
Owner: Mark Harvey
Estimated Sales: $1-2.5 Million
Number Employees: 5-9
Brands:
DURANGO

3896 **Durey-Libby Edible Nuts**
100 Industrial Rd
Carlstadt, NJ 7072 201-939-2775
Fax: 201-939-0386 800-332-6887
info@dureylibby.com www.dureylibby.com
Custom roasting
President: Wnedy Dicker
CEO: Billy Dicker
Plant Manger: William Dicker
Estimated Sales: $1-2.5 Million
Number Employees: 20-49
Sq. footage: 30000
Type of Packaging: Bulk

3897 **Durham/Ellis Pecan Country Store**
308 S Houston St
Comanche, TX 76442-3237 325-356-5291
Fax: 325-356-3161 www.durhams.com
Manufacturer of pecans and other nuts
President: Oldie Dollins
Estimated Sales: $4 Million
Number Employees: 50-99

3898 **Durkee-Mower**
P.O.Box 470
Lynn, MA 01903 781-593-8007
Fax: 781-593-6410
customerservice@marshmallowfluff.com
www.marshmallowfluff.com
Manufacturer and exporter of marshmallow creme
President: Donald D Durkee
Vice President: George Murray
Treasurer: Jonathan Durkee
VP Sales: Dan Quirk
Factory Manager: Paul Walker
Estimated Sales: $ 5 - 10 Million
Number Employees: 20-49
Sq. footage: 35000
Type of Packaging: Consumer, Food Service
Brands:
MARSHMALLOW FLUFF

3899 **Durney Vineyards**
P.O.Box 999
Carmel Valley, CA 93924 831-659-6220
Fax: 831-659-6226 800-625-8466
info@hellerestate.com www.durneywines.com
Manufacturer and exporter of wine
General Manager: Rene Schober
Estimated Sales: $1-2.5 Million
Number Employees: 10-19
Type of Packaging: Consumer

3900 **Durrett Cheese Sales**
188 Volunteer Ct
Manchester, TN 37355-6492 931-723-3422
Fax: 931-723-3435 800-209-6792
greg@durrettcheese.com
www.durrettcheesesales.net
Manufacturer of cheeses specializing in slicing, chunking and cubing; serving delis, meat departments and food service operations
President: Bill Hemperly
Estimated Sales: Less than $500,000
Number Employees: 20-49
Type of Packaging: Consumer, Food Service

3901 **Dutch Ann Foods Company**
14 Moran Rd
Natchez, MS 39120 601-445-5566
Fax: 601-445-8738 sales@dutchann.com
Manufacturer of frozen pie crusts
President: William Jones Jr
Estimated Sales: $ 1 - 3 Million
Number Employees: 5-9
Type of Packaging: Consumer, Food Service, Private Label
Brands:
BEST WAY
DUTCH ANN

3902 **Dutch Farms Inc**
700 E 107th St
Chicago, IL 60628 773-660-0900
Fax: 773-660-1044 800-637-3447
lbultema@dutchfarms.com
www.dutchfarms.com
Manufacturer/processor of eggs, cheeses, dairy products, deli, bakery and meat items.
Chairman: Archie Boomsma
President: Brian Boomsma
Executive Officer: Bruce Boomsma
Administration/Customer Service: Linda Bultema
Customer Service Representative: Cindi Richardson
Number Employees: 100-249
Type of Packaging: Food Service

3903 **Dutch Girl Donuts**
19000 Woodward Ave
Detroit, MI 48203-1903 313-368-3020
Manufacturer of doughnuts
Owner: Jon Timmer
CEO: Gene Timmer
Estimated Sales: $300,000 appx.
Number Employees: 10-19

3904 **(HQ)Dutch Gold Honey, Inc.**
2220 Dutch Gold Dr
Lancaster, PA 17601 717-393-1716
Fax: 717-393-8687 800-338-0587
info@dutchgoldhoney.com
www.dutchgoldhoney.com

Manufacturer, exporter, importer and packer of honey and honey products.
President/CEO: Nancy Gamber Olcott
CEO: Nancy J Gamber
VP Sales/Marketing: Alan Ernst
VP Operations: Norman Randall
Estimated Sales: $20-50 Million
Number Employees: 20-49
Sq. footage: 100000
Type of Packaging: Consumer, Food Service, Private Label, Bulk
Other Locations:
Dutch Gold Honey
Littleton NH
Brands:
BLOSSOM HILL
DUTCH GOLD
HONEY IN THE ROUGH

3905 **Dutch Henry Winery**
4300 Silverado Trl
Calistoga, CA 94515 707-942-5771
Fax: 707-942-5512 888-224-5879
info@Dutchhenry www.dutchhenry.com
Wines
Owner: Scott Chafen
VP: Scott Chafen
Estimated Sales: $2.5-5 Million
Number Employees: 5-9
Type of Packaging: Private Label
Brands:
DUTCH HENRY

3906 **Dutch Kitchen Bakery**
12 John Fitch Hwy
Fitchburg, MA 01420-5902 978-345-1393
Fax: 978-345-6651
Breads, rolls, cakes and pastries
President: Joseph Raimo
Estimated Sales: $1-2.5 Million
Number Employees: 20-49
Brands:
DUTCH KITCHEN

3907 **Dutch Packing Company**
4115 NW 28th St
Miami, FL 33142 305-871-3640
Fax: 305-871-3668 dutchplayer@msn.com
Manufacturer of sausage
President: Guillermo Rodriguez
VP Sales: William Rodriguez
VP Production: Victor Rodriguez
Estimated Sales: Less than $500,000
Number Employees: 20-49
Type of Packaging: Consumer, Food Service
Brands:
GARCIA

3908 **Dutch Valley Veal**
One Dutch Valley Dr
Po Box 703
South Holland, IL 60473-0703 708-849-7990
Fax: 708-849-8094 800-832-8325
sales@dutchvalleyveal.com
www.dutchvalleyveal.com
Manufacturer and packer of meat including beef and pork
Coo: Bryan Scott
Vice President: Brian Oedzes
Estimated Sales: $ 20 - 50 Million
Number Employees: 50-99
Type of Packaging: Consumer
Brands:
Holly

3909 **Dutchess Bakery**
715 Bigley Ave
Charleston, WV 25302 304-346-4237
Manufacturer of cookies
Owner: Edward S Rada Iii Jr
Estimated Sales: $500,000-$1 Million
Number Employees: 5-9
Type of Packaging: Consumer

3910 **Dutchie Sales Corporation**
570 Carlisle St
Hanover, PA 17331-2163 717-632-9343
Fax: 717-632-4190 wege@supernet.com
www.wege.com
Pretzels
Manager: Carol Arentz
VP: Tony Laughman
Estimated Sales: $500-1 Million appx.
Number Employees: 50-99
Type of Packaging: Private Label
Brands:
DUTCHIE

3911 **Dutchland Frozen Foods**
205 Main St
Lester, IA 51242 712-478-4349
Fax: 712-478-4554 888-497-7243
info@dutchlandfrozenfoods.com
www.dutchlandfrozenfoods.com
butter pastry puffs

3912 **Dutterer's Home Food Service**
2700 Lord Baltimore Drive
Baltimore, MD 21244-2648 410-298-3663
Fax: 410-298-1625
Manufacturer of meats including frankfurters, pastrami, roast and corned beef and poultry products
President: Mark Mules
Estimated Sales: $ 10 - 20 Million
Number Employees: 10-19
Type of Packaging: Consumer, Private Label

3913 **Duval Bakery Products**
1733 Evergreen Ave
Jacksonville, FL 32206 904-354-7878
Fax: 904-354-7828
Manufacturer of stuffing and bread crumbs
Owner: Robert Gorsuch
Estimated Sales: $500,000-$1 Million
Number Employees: 5-9
Sq. footage: 6000
Type of Packaging: Food Service, Private Label, Bulk

3914 **Duxbury Mussel & Seafood Corporation**
8 Joseph St # B
Kingston, MA 02364-1122 781-585-5517
Fax: 781-585-2976
Seafood
President: Robert Marconi

3915 **Dwayne Keith Brooks Company**
6628 Fiesta Ln
Orangevale, CA 95662 916-988-1030
Fax: 916-988-4442 dkbrooksco@home.com
Manufacturer of school and institutional frozen foods
President: Dwayne Brooks
Estimated Sales: $500,000
Number Employees: 1-4
Sq. footage: 1800
Parent Co: SA Products Company
Type of Packaging: Food Service, Bulk

3916 **DynaPro International**
451 North Main
Kaysville, UT 84123 801-621-8224
Fax: 801-621-8258 800-877-1413
sales@dynaprointernational.com
www.dynaprointernational.com
Manufacturer and exporter of vitamins and herbal supplements
President: Rowene Visser
Accounting Director: Tammy Hair
Marketing Director: Gary Hoffman
Estimated Sales: $ 1 - 3 Million
Number Employees: 9
Sq. footage: 3900

3917 **Dynagel**
10 Wentworth Ave
Calumet City, IL 60409 708-891-8405
Fax: 708-891-8432 888-396-2435
dynagel@aol.com www.dynagel.com
Manufacturer and exporter of gelatin including hydrolyzed
Manager: Nicholas Liu
CEO: Chuck Markham
CFO: Rib Mayberry
Plant Manager: Conrad Heisner
Estimated Sales: $20-50 Million
Number Employees: 50-99
Sq. footage: 70000
Type of Packaging: Bulk
Brands:
SOL-U-PRO

3918 **Dynamic Coatings Inc**
5629 E Westover Ave
Fresno, CA 93727-1320
Fax: 559-225-4606 dycoatings@aol.com
www.dynamiccoatingsinc.net
Product and service line is concrete restoration and protective coating products for floors and walls applications of which include that of food processing plants, kitchens, wineries, dairies, bakeries and breweries.
Owner: Jose A Gonzales
IT/Webmaster: Dennis Stemper
Sales Representative: Jose Gonzalez

3919 **Dynamic Confections**
1050 S. 200 West
Salt Lake City, UT 84101 801-355-4422
Fax: 801-756-7791 800-288-8002
info@dynamicconfections.com
www.dynamicconfections.com
candy
CEO: Taz Murray
President: Keith Elliot

3920 **Dynamic Foods**
1001 E 33rd St
Lubbock, TX 79404 806-747-2777
Fax: 806-723-5680 jsullivan@dynamicfoods.com
www.furrs.net
Manufacturer of baked goods, cakes, muffins, cornbread, pies, cobblers, frozen dinner rolls, casseroles, side dishes, soups, sauces, glazes, mexican foods, breaded fish, bread sticks
President: Mike Blasdell
Controller: Todd Hill
Research & Development: Beth Tay
Quality Control: George Railsback
Sales Director: Justine Sullivan
Production Manager: Richard Hill
Purchasing Manager: Connie Carpenter
Estimated Sales: $50-100 Million
Number Employees: 100-249
Number of Products: 100+
Sq. footage: 225000
Type of Packaging: Food Service, Private Label
Brands:
DYNAMIC FOODS
PRIVATE LABEL

3921 **Dynamic Health Labs**
110 Bridge St # 2
Brooklyn, NY 11201-1575 718-858-0100
Fax: 718-392-9301 800-396-2214
information@dynamic-health.com
www.dynamichealth.com
Manufacturer of liquid diet supplements, certified kosher
President: Bruce Burwick
Estimated Sales: $ 3 - 5 Million
Number Employees: 20-49

3922 **Dynatabs**
1933 E 12th Street
Brooklyn, NY 11229-2703 718-376-4508
Fax: 718-376-6084 sales@dynatabs.com
www.dynatabs.com
Manufacturer of health, wellness, beauty products including oral edible strips, aloe vera drinking gel and passion punch.
CEO: Sarah Gani
CFO: Sarah Setton
Marketing: Harold Baum
Number Employees: 11
Parent Co: Baum International, Inc
Type of Packaging: Consumer, Private Label

3923 **(HQ)Dynic USA Corporation**
4750 NE Dawson Creek Dr
Hillsboro, OR 97124 503-693-1070
Fax: 503-648-1185 800-326-1249
cesar@dynic.com www.dynic.com
Manufactures complementary product lines to serve the needs of the labeling and printing industry
President: Shigeru Tamura
Sales Director: Cesar Santa
Estimated Sales: $ 5 - 10 Million
Number Employees: 50-99
Parent Co: Dynic Corporation
Other Locations:
Dynic UK Ltd
Cardiff, South Wales UK
Dynic Corporation
Minatoku, Tokyo, Japan HK
Brands:
CABIN AIR FILTERS
CETUS TEXTILE FABRICS
OLED DESICCANT
SIRIUS TTR

3924 **E U Blending Company**
1221 West Gila Bend Highway
Casa Grande, AZ 85222 520-374-2603
www.erifoods.com
Manufacture of dry blending, extrusion, milling, grinding and pouch packaging machines.
President: David Reisenbigler
Sq. footage: 200000
Parent Co: Erie Foods, Inc.

3925 **E&G Food**
5600 1st Ave # 4nb
Brooklyn, NY 11220-2550 718-680-1300
Fax: 718-680-2392 888-525-8855
Chicken, turkey
President: Meir Grunbaum
Plant Manager: Ignacio Quirch
Estimated Sales: $1-2.5 Million
Number Employees: 5-9

3926 **E&H Packing Company**
2453 Riopelle St
Detroit, MI 48207 313-567-8286
Fax: 313-567-8287
Manufacturer of beef
Owner/President: Robert Buzar
Treasurer: Bob Buzar
Estimated Sales: $1-2.5 Million
Number Employees: 5-9
Type of Packaging: Consumer, Food Service

3927 **(HQ)E&J Gallo Winery**
600 Yosemite Boulevard
Modesto, CA 95354-2760 209-341-3111
Fax: 209-341-8857 www.gallo.com
Manufacturer of wines, brandy and sparkling wine
Pres/Ceo: John De Luca
Co-Chairman, President, and CEO: Joseph Gallo
Co-Chairman: Robert Gallo
VP Operations: Steven Kidd
Estimated Sales: $3.6billion
Number Employees: 4,600
Type of Packaging: Consumer, Food Service
Other Locations:
E&J Gallo Winery
Mississauga ON
Brands:
ANAPAMU®
ANDRE®
BALLATORE®
BAREFOOT BUBBLY®
BAREFOOT® CELLARS
BARTLES & JAYMES®
BELLA SERA®
BLACK SWAN®
BOONE'S FARM®
BRIDLEWOOD® ESTATE WINERY
CARLO ROSSI®
CASK & CREAM®
CLARENDON HILLS
DANCING BULL®
DAVINCI
DON MUGUEL GASCON
E. & J.® VS BRANDY
E. & J.®VSOP BRANDY
ECCO DOMANI®
ESTATE
FREI BROTHERS®
FRUTEZIA®
GHOST PINES®
HORNSBY'S®
INDIGO HILLS®
LAS ROCAS®
LIBERTY CREEK®
LIVINGSTON CELLARS®
LOUIS M. MARTINI®
MACMURRAY RANCH®
MARCELINA®
MARTIN CODAX®
MASO CANALI®
MATTIE'S PERCH®
MCWILLIAM'S®
MIRASSOU®
NEW AMSTERDAM® GIN
PETER VELLA®
POLKA DOT®
RANCHO ZABACO®
RED BICYCLETTE®
RED ROCK WINERY®
REDWOOD CREEK®
RESERVE®
SEBEKA®
SINGLE VINEYARD
SONOMA
STARBOROUGH™
TISDALE VINEYARDS®
TURNING LEAF®
TURNING LEAF® SONOMA RESERVE
TWIN VALLEY®
WHITEHAVEN®
WILD VINES®
WILLIAM HILL ESTATE™
WYCLIFF® SPARKLING

3928 **E&J Gallo Winery**
5610 E Olive Ave
Fresno, CA 93727 559-458-2480
Fax: 559-453-2411 www.ejgallo.com
Manufacturer of white, red and pink wines
Plant Manager: Gary Schmidt
Purchasing: Sharon Kirby
Estimated Sales: $50-100 Million
Number Employees: 1-4
Type of Packaging: Consumer, Food Service

3929 **E&J Gallo Winery**
18000 River Rd
Livingston, CA 95334 209-394-6219
Fax: 209-394-4425 www.ejgallo.com
Manufacturer of wine
Manager: Thomas Green
Estimated Sales: $100-500 Million
Number Employees: 100-249
Type of Packaging: Consumer, Food Service

3930 **E&J Gallo Winery**
6685 Millcreek Dr
Units 1 & 2
Mississauga, ON L5N 5M5
Canada 905-819-9600
Fax: 905-602-9709
Manufacturer of brandy and wine
President: Joseph Gallo
Director Sales: Tim Maletich
Estimated Sales: $26 Million
Number Employees: 70
Type of Packaging: Consumer, Food Service

3931 **E-Fish-Ent Fish Company**
1941 Goodridge Road
Sooke, BC V0S 0C6
Canada 250-642-4007
Fax: 250-642-4057 www.e-fish-ent.ca
Manufacturer and exporter of smoked salmon in retort pouch; meat products in pouch, stews, chili, curry.
President: Bryan Mooney
VP: Linda Mooney
Estimated Sales: $552,000
Number Employees: 4
Sq. footage: 8000
Type of Packaging: Private Label

3932 **E. Gagnon & Fils**
405 Rte 102
St Therese-De-Gaspe, QC G0C 3B0
Canada 418-385-3011
Fax: 418-385-3021
Manufacturer and exporter of frozen snow crabs, crab
President: Roger Gagnon
Estimated Sales: $2.3 Million
Number Employees: 5
Type of Packaging: Food Service

3933 **E. Waldo Ward & Son Corporation**
273 E Highland Ave
Sierra Madre, CA 91024-2014 626-355-1218
Fax: 626-355-5292 800-355-9273
jelly@waldoward.com www.waldoward.com
Manufacturer and importer of gourmet foods including olives, preserves, jellies, marmalades, brandied fruits and sauces including meat, relish and seafood cocktail; exporter of marmalades. Services, private labeling and anufacturing tolarge and small companies. Also offers consulting services
President: Richard Ward
VP: Jeffrey Ward
Estimated Sales: $5 Million
Number Employees: 10-19
Number of Brands: 2
Number of Products: 150
Sq. footage: 10000
Type of Packaging: Consumer, Private Label
Brands:
E. WALDO WARD
SIERRA MADRE BRAND

3934 **E.C. Phillips & Son**
PO Box 8235
Ketchikan, AK 99901-3235 907-225-3121
Fax: 907-225-7249
Manufacturer of smoked Alaska salmon
President: Larry Elliott
Estimated Sales: $ 10 - 20 Million
Number Employees: 100-249
Type of Packaging: Consumer

3935 **E.D. Smith Foods Ltd**
944 Highway 8
Winona, ON L8E 5S3
Canada 905-643-1211
Fax: 905-643-3328 800-263-9246
inquiry@edsmith.com www.edsmith.com
Manufacturer and exporter of jams, ketchup, pie fillings, barbecue and pasta sauces, fruit toppings, salsas and syrups
President/CEO: Michael Burrows
VP Finance: David Smith
VP Operations: Dorothy Pethick
Estimated Sales: $120 Million
Number Employees: 250-490
Sq. footage: 400000
Parent Co: Imperial Capital Corporation
Type of Packaging: Consumer, Food Service, Private Label, Bulk
Brands:
E.D. SMITH
HABITANT
LEA & PERRINS

3936 **E.E. Mucke & Sons**
2326 Main St
Hartford, CT 6120 860-246-5609
Fax: 860-541-6403 800-726-5598
Manufacturer of meat products including sausage, kielbasa, frankfurters, salami and liverwurst
President: Ernest Mucke
Estimated Sales: $5-10 Million
Number Employees: 20-49
Type of Packaging: Consumer, Food Service, Private Label
Brands:
Circle M

3937 **E.F. Lane & Son**
P.O.Box 500
Colton, CA 92324 510-569-8980
Fax: 510-569-0240
Manufacturer and exporter of honey and peanut products
Manager: Phyllis Tut
Estimated Sales: $500,000-$1 Million
Number Employees: 1-4
Type of Packaging: Consumer, Food Service, Private Label, Bulk

3938 **E.J. Green & Company**
287 Main Street
Winterton, NL A0B 3MO
Canada 709-583-2670
Fax: 709-583-2804 ejgreen@nf.sympatico.ca
Manufacturer of sea urchins
President: Derek Green
Estimated Sales: $6.5 Million
Number Employees: 45
Type of Packaging: Food Service

3939 **E.M.D. Sales, Inc.**
2000 Washington Blvd
Baltimore, MD 21230 301-322-4503
Fax: 301-322-4504 emdsales@aol.com
www.emdsalesinc.com
Salsa/dips, olive oil, gummies/jellies/pates de fruit, pasta (dry), rice, soups/broths, ethnic sauces (soy, curry, etc.), spices.

3940 **E.W. Bowker Company**
581 New Lasbon
Pemberton, NJ 08068 609-894-9508
Fax: 609-894-2165 ewbowker@yahoo.com
Manufacturer of fresh cranberries and blueberries
President: Ernest Bowker
Vice President: Betty Minkus
Estimated Sales: 500,000-$1 Million
Number Employees: 5-9
Type of Packaging: Consumer, Food Service, Bulk

3941 **(HQ)E.W. Knauss & Son**
625 E Broad St
Quakertown, PA 18951-1713 215-536-4220
Fax: 215-536-1129 800-648-4220
sales@knaussfoods.com www.alderfermeats.com
Manufacturer of sliced dried beef products including beefsticks, beef jerky, hot sausage and pickled meat products.
President: Sherry Russell
Chairman: E William Knauss
VP Sales: Richard Harlan
Estimated Sales: $20-50 Million
Number Employees: 50-99
Sq. footage: 100000
Type of Packaging: Consumer, Food Service, Private Label, Bulk
Brands:
BEARDSLEY
BULL
CARSON
HANNAH
KNAUSS

3942 **EB Botanicals**
50 Church St
Montclair, NJ 07042-2772 973-655-9585
Fax: 973-696-7666 service@eccobella.com
www.eccobella.com
Botanicals
President: Sally Malagna

3943 **EFCO Products**
130 Smith St
Poughkeepsie, NY 12601 845-452-4715
Fax: 845-452-5607 800-284-3326
info@efcoproducts.com www.efcoproducts.com
Leading supplier of mixes, fruit and creme style fillings, jellies, jams and concentrated icing fruits to the baking industry.
President: Jack Effron
Executive VP: Ira Effron
Estimated Sales: $2.5-5 Million
Number Employees: 50-99

3944 **EMD Chemicals**
480 S Democrat Rd
Gibbstown, NJ 8027 856-224-0094
Fax: 914-592-9469 800-364-4535
www.emdchemicals.com
Manufacturer of food additives and preservatives including ascorbic acid, niacin, niacinamide, d-Bioton, etc.; also, vitamins, minerals, salts and nutraceuticals
President: Douglas Brown
Estimated Sales: $100+ Million
Number Employees: 100-249
Parent Co: K&A Merck
Type of Packaging: Bulk

3945 **EOS Estate Winery**
P.O.Box 1287
Paso Robles, CA 93447-1287 805-239-2562
Fax: 805-239-2317 800-349-9463
info@eosvintage.com www.eosvintage.com
Wines
President: Kerry Vix
CFO: Pati Withers
Marketing: Christopher Vix
Sales: Luis Cota
Public Relations: Denise McLean
Operations: Steve Felten
Production: Leslie Melendez
Plant Manager: Gary Cargill
Purchase Manager: Pat Withers
Estimated Sales: $1-2.5 Million
Number Employees: 5-9
Number of Brands: 4
Type of Packaging: Private Label
Brands:
ARUERO
CUPAGRANOLS
EOS
NOVELLA

3946 **EPI Breads**
1749 Tullie Cir NE
Atlanta, GA 30329-2305 404-325-1016
Fax: 404-325-0735 800-325-1014
bdoan@epibreads.com www.epibreads.com
Manufacturers of bread
Owner: Nick Mulliez
Estimated Sales: $100+ Million
Number Employees: 100-249
Parent Co: Lavoi Corporation
Brands:
EPI

3947 **ERBL**
2525 Commerce Way
Vista, CA 92081 760-599-6088
Fax: 760-599-6089 800-275-3725
support@coromega.com www.coromega.com
Omega-3 dietary supplements.
Manager: Suzanne Goodrich
Estimated Sales: $ 5 - 10 Million
Number Employees: 10-19

3948 **Eagle Agricultural Products**
PO Box 1451
Huntsville, AR 72740-1451 501-738-2203
Fax: 501-738-2203
Manufacturer of organic unbleached white, whole wheat, corn and rice flour, corn meal, white and brown basmati and long grain rice
Owner/CEO: Kathy Turner
Owner: Gary Turner
Estimated Sales: $1-4.9 Million
Number Employees: 1
Sq. footage: 10000
Type of Packaging: Private Label, Bulk
Brands:
Eagle Agricultural Products

3949 **(HQ)Eagle Coffee Company**
1019 Hillen St
Baltimore, MD 21202 410-752-1229
Fax: 410-528-0369 800-545-4015
info@eaglecoffee.com www.eaglecoffee.com
Manufacturer, importer and wholesaler/distributor of restaurant and gourmet coffees, coffee machines and grinders and coffee beans; serving the food service market
Owner: Nick Constantine
Vice President: Arthur Constantinides
Estimated Sales: $1-2.5 Million
Number Employees: 10-19
Sq. footage: 40000
Type of Packaging: Food Service, Private Label
Other Locations:
Eagle Coffee Co.
Baltimore MD

3950 **Eagle Crest Vineyards**
7107 Vineyard Rd
Conesus, NY 14435 585-346-2321
Fax: 585-346-2322
Wines
President: Michael Secretan
VP: Sarah Brown
Estimated Sales: $2.5-5 Million
Number Employees: 5-9

3951 **Eagle Family Foods**
1 Strawberry Ln
Orrville, OH 44667 614-501-4200
Fax: 330-684-6410 888-656-3245
corporate@effinc.com
www.eaglefamilyfoods.com
Sweetened condensed milk, citrus juices, lemonade concentrate, nondairy creamers
Co-CEO: Richard Smucker
Co-CEO: Tim Smucker
CEO: Craig A Steinke
Number Employees: 48
Brands:
BORDEN
CREMORA
EAGLE BRAND
KAVA
NONE SUCH
REALEMON
REALIME

3952 **Eagle Rock Food Company**
1225 12th St NW
Albuquerque, NM 87104 505-323-1183
eaglerock@abq.com
Meat
Owner: Mike Perea
Estimated Sales: $ 1 - 3 Million
Number Employees: 1-4

3953 **Eagle Seafood Producers**
56 N 3rd Street
Brooklyn, NY 11211-3925 718-963-0939
Fax: 718-963-1306 info@eagleseafood.com
www.eagleseafood.com
Manufacturer of fresh and frozen seafood
President: Mark Rudes
VP: Donald Draghi
Estimated Sales: $10-20 Million
Number Employees: 20-49
Type of Packaging: Food Service

3954 **Earth & Vine Provisions**
PO Box 1637
Loomis, CA 95650 916-434-8399
Fax: 916-434-8398 888-723-8463
customerservice@earthnvine.com
www.earthnvine.com
jams, sauces, beverage elixirs and dressings
President/Owner: Tressa Cooper
CEO: Ron Cooper
CFO: Ron Cooper
Number Employees: 10

3955 **Earth & Vine Provisions**
Po Box 1637
Loomis, CA 95650 916-434-8399
Fax: 916-434-8398 888-723-8463
tressac@earthvine.com www.earthnvine.com
Manufacturer of jams, cooking sauces, vinaigrettes, chutneys, relishes and dessert sauces
President: Tressa Cooper
Estimated Sales: $ 3 - 5 Million
Number Employees: 10-19

3956 **Earth Fire Products**
507 N East Ave
Viroqua, WI 54665-1412 608-735-4711
Manufacturer of organic food, miso
President: Robert Ribbens
Estimated Sales: $5-10 Million
Number Employees: 5-9

3957 **Earth Grains Baking Companies**
PO Box 756
Neenah, WI 54957-0756 800-323-7117
www.earthgrains.com
Manufacturer of bakery products including sweet rolls
Estimated Sales: $ 50 - 100 Million
Number Employees: 60
Parent Co: Sara Lee Bakery Group
Type of Packaging: Consumer

3958 **Earth Island Natural Foods**
P.O.Box 9400
Canoga Park, CA 91309-0400 818-725-2820
Fax: 818-725-2812 www.followyourheart.com
Manufacturer of prepared deli salads, vegetarian specialties, nondairy cheese alternative, meat analogues, egg-free mayonnaise and dressings
President/Co-Owner: Robert Goldberg
Co-Owner: Paul Lewin
Estimated Sales: $1-3 Million
Number Employees: 20-49
Sq. footage: 6000
Type of Packaging: Consumer, Food Service, Private Label, Bulk
Brands:
FOLLOW YOUR HEART
VEGENAISE

3959 **Earth Products**
2320 Cousteau Ct # 100
Vista, CA 92081-8363 760-494-2000
Fax: 760-494-2005 randersn@connectnet.com
Manufacturer of nutritional products, chia seed
President: Bob Andersen
CEO: Jeff Larsen
Estimated Sales: D
Number Employees: 50-99

3960 **Earth Science**
475 N Sheridan St
Corona, CA 92880 951-371-7565
Fax: 909-371-0509
Manufacturer of creams, lotions, AHA/BHA, Vitamin C products, shampoos, conditioners, styling aids, body care, liquid vitamins
President: Kristine Schoenauer
VP: Michael Rutledge
Contract Sales Manager: Diane Smart
Number Employees: 100-249
Sq. footage: 80000
Type of Packaging: Consumer, Bulk

3961 **Earth Song Whole Foods**
4880 San Juan Avenue
Suite 216
Fair Oaks, CA 95628-4719 916-332-1355
Fax: 916-332-1355 877-327-8476
julie@earthsongwholefoods.com
www.earthsongwholefoods.com
Vegan natural food products
Owner: Julie Rogers
Estimated Sales: $300,000-500,000
Number Employees: 1-4
Brands:
EARTH SONG WHOLE FOOD BARS
GRANDPA'S SECRET OMEGA-3 MUESLI

3962 **Earthen Vessels Herb Company**
PO Box 1375
Hockessin, DE 19707-5375 302-234-7667
Fax: 302-234-7667
Manufacturer of Seasonings, spices
President: Timothy Rodden
Estimated Sales: $500,000-$1 Million
Number Employees: 1-4

3963 **Earthrise Nutritionals**
2151 Michaelson Drive
Suite 258
Irvine, CA 92612 949-623-0980
Fax: 949-623-0990 800-949-7473
info@earthrise.com www.earthrise.com
Manufacturer of Spirulina based green food nutritional products
VP: Walter Rick
Number Employees: 65
Type of Packaging: Private Label

3964 **Easley Winery**
205 N College Ave
Indianapolis, IN 46202 317-636-4516
Fax: 317-974-0128 info@easleywinery.com
www.easleywinery.com
Manufacturer of table wine
President/Winemaker: Mark Easley
Estimated Sales: $2.6 Million
Number Employees: 25
Type of Packaging: Consumer, Food Service, Private Label, Bulk
Brands:
Cape Sandy Vineyards
Easley's

3965 **East Balt Bakery**
4701 E 50th Avenue
Denver, CO 80216-3106 303-377-5533
Fax: 303-388-0258
Manufacturer of buns and rolls
President: John Petenes

3966 **East Balt Bakery**
1108 Collins Dr
Kissimmee, FL 34741-4697 407-933-2222
Fax: 407-933-5367
Manufacturer and exporter of buns
Manager: Tim Weitfeldt
Plant Manager: Tim Weitfeldt
Estimated Sales: $50-100 Million
Number Employees: 50-99
Sq. footage: 45000
Type of Packaging: Food Service

3967 **(HQ)East Balt Commissary**
1801 W 31st Pl
Chicago, IL 60608 773-376-4444
Fax: 773-376-8137 www.eastbalt.com
Bread
President: John Petenes
Vice President: George Kezios
Plant Manager: George Guiness
Estimated Sales: $20-50 Million
Number Employees: 130
Type of Packaging: Private Label

3968 **East Beauregard Meat Processing Center**
5362 Highway 113
Deridder, LA 70634-8119 337-328-7171
Fax: 337-328-8132
Manufacturer of beef, pork, mutton, venison and goat meat; also, custom slaughtering available
Estimated Sales: $ 1 - 3 Million
Number Employees: 1-4
Type of Packaging: Private Label

3969 **East Coast Fresh Cuts Company**
8704 Bollman Pl
Savage, MD 20763 410-799-9900
Fax: 410-799-8000
mgeorge@eastcoastfreshcuts.com
www.eastcoastfreshcuts.com
Manufacturer of fresh cut vegetables including onions, peppers, carrots, celery, etc
President: John Phillip Muth
Sales: Tom Brown
Estimated Sales: $100+ Million
Number Employees: 250-499
Sq. footage: 30000
Parent Co: Coastal Sun Belt
Type of Packaging: Food Service, Private Label, Bulk

3970 **East Coast Olive Oil**
75 Wurz Avenue
Utica, NY 13502-2524 315-797-3151
Fax: 315-797-6981 gem-ecoo.com
Olive oil
President: Stephen Mandia
VP: Robert Mandia
Sales Manager: Tim Morrison
Operations: Roger Bateman
Plant Manager: Fran Mandia
Estimated Sales: $5-10 Million
Number Employees: 20-49

3971 **East Coast Seafood of Phoenix**
2311 E Jones Ave
Phoenix, AZ 85040 602-268-4591
Fax: 602-268-3988
Manufacturer of Seafood
Manager: Anwer Haider
Estimated Sales: $ 20 - 50 Million
Number Employees: 50-99

3972 **East Dayton Meat & Poultry**
1546 Keystone Ave
Dayton, OH 45403 937-253-6185
Fax: 937-253-1040 eastdaytonmeat@yahoo.com
www.eastdaytonmeat.com
Manufacturer of beef, pork and poultry
President: Kim Lakey
Estimated Sales: $ 20 - 50 Million
Number Employees: 10-19

3973 **East India Coffee & TeaCompany**
1731 Aviation Blvd
Lincoln, CA 95648-9317
Fax: 510-638-0760 800-829-1300
www.rogersfamilyco.com
Manufacturer of Coffee and teas
President: Jon Rogers
Sales Director: Mike Carlin
Operations Manager: Pete Rogers
Purchasing Manager: Tom Garber
Estimated Sales: $20-50 Million
Number Employees: 50-99
Type of Packaging: Private Label

3974 **East Indies Coffee & Tea Company**
7 Keystone Dr
Lebanon, PA 17042-9791 717-228-2000
Fax: 717-228-2540 800-220-2326
mstea@pa.online.com www.eastindies.com
Gourmet and flavored coffees and teas
President: Walter Progner
VP: Mim Enck
Estimated Sales: Less than $500,000
Number Employees: 5-9

3975 **East Kentucky Foods**
P.O.Box 33
Winchester, KY 40392 859-744-2218
Fax: 859-744-8511
Healthy snacks
President: Greg Ginter
Estimated Sales: $ 10 - 20 Million
Number Employees: 5-9

3976 **East Point Seafood Company**
P.O.Box 127
South Bend, WA 98586 360-875-5507
Fax: 360-875-5417 888-317-8459
info@eastpointseafood.com
www.eastpointseafood.com
Seafood
Owner: Joel Van Ornun
Estimated Sales: $ 1 - 3 Million
Number Employees: 5-9
Type of Packaging: Private Label

3977 **East Poultry Company**
2615 E 6th St
Austin, TX 78702-3900 512-476-5367
Fax: 512-476-5360 epoultry@att.net
www.eastpoultry.com
Poultry and eggs
President: Kenneth J Aune
Estimated Sales: $4.10 Million
Number Employees: 34
Sq. footage: 13500
Type of Packaging: Food Service, Bulk

3978 **East Shore Specialty Foods**
643 Cardinal Ln
Po Box 379
Hartland, WI 53029 262-367-8988
Fax: 262-367-9081 800-236-1069
customerservice@eastshorefoods.com
www.eastshorefoods.com
Manufacturer of gourmet mustards, pretzels, chocolate sauces
President: Jeri Mesching
CEO: Khristian Graves
Manager: Greg Seales
Marketing: Kristin Graves
Estimated Sales: $760,000
Number Employees: 15
Type of Packaging: Private Label

3979 **East Side Winery/Oak Ridge Vineyards**
6100 E Hwy 12 (Victor Rd)
Lodi, CA 95240 209-369-4758
Fax: 209-369-0202
eswinery@oakridgevineyards.com
www.oakridgewinery.com
Manufacturer of bottled wines
Owner: Rudy Maggio
Estimated Sales: $10-20 Million
Number Employees: 20-49
Type of Packaging: Consumer, Food Service, Private Label, Bulk

3980 **East Wind Nut Butters**
Hc 3 Box 3370
Tecumseh, MO 65760-9503 417-679-4682
Fax: 417-679-4684 www.eastwindnutbutters.com
Manufacturer of peanut and organic peanut butters; also, cashew and almond butters and tahini
Manager: Lena Berglund
Sales Director: Sam Lucas
Estimated Sales: $1-3 Million
Number Employees: 10-19
Sq. footage: 7000
Parent Co: East Wind Community
Type of Packaging: Consumer, Food Service, Private Label
Brands:
East Wind
East Wind Almond
East Wind Cashew
East Wind Organic Peanut Butter
East Wind Peanut
East Wind Tahini

3981 **Eastern Brewing Corporation**
P.O.Box 497
Hammonton, NJ 8037 609-561-2700
Fax: 609-561-9441
Beer
Estimated Sales: Less than $500,000
Number Employees: 1-4

3982 **(HQ)Eastern Fish Company**
300 Frank W Burr Blvd
Teaneck, NJ 7666 201-801-0800
Fax: 201-801-0802 800-526-9066
dkapar@easternfish.com www.easternfish.com
Manufacturer and importer of farm raised shrimp and other seafood, bay and sea scallops, lobster, king crab legs and claws, snow crab clusters, yellow fin tuna
President: Eric Bloom
CEO: William Bloom
VP: Lee Bloom
Estimated Sales: $200 Million
Number Employees: 10-19
Type of Packaging: Private Label
Other Locations:
Norwestern Sales Office
Kingston WA
Western Sales Office

Anaheim CA
Northeastern Sales Office
Gloucester MA
Southeastern Sales Office
South Springs FL
Brands:
SAIL

3983 **Eastern Food Industries**
2832 S County Trl
East Greenwich, RI 02818-1742 401-884-8798
Manufacturer of Pasta sauces
President: Henry Caniglia
VP/Treasurer: Stephen Caniglia
Purchasing Manager: Henry Caniglia
Estimated Sales: $5-10 Million
Number Employees: 5-9

3984 **Eastern Foods NaturallyFresh**
1000 Naturally Fresh Blvd
College Park, GA 30349-2909 404-765-9000
Fax: 404-765-9016 www.naturallyfresh.com
Salad dressings, dips and sauces
President: Robert Brooks
CEO: Jerry Greene
Plant Manager: Jerry Greene
Purchasing Agent: Cindi Mullis
Estimated Sales: $50-100 Million
Number Employees: 1-4

3985 **Eastern Sea Products**
11 Addison Avenue
Scoudouc, NB E4P 3N3
Canada 506-532-6111
Fax: 506-532-9111 800-565-6364
maurice@easternsea.ca www.easternsea.ca
Manufacturer and exporter of salted and smoked seafood: herring, mackerel, salmon
President: Maurice Allain
Operations: Donald Richard
Estimated Sales: $1.3 Million
Number Employees: 10
Number of Brands: 2
Number of Products: 10
Sq. footage: 12000
Type of Packaging: Consumer, Private Label
Brands:
Cape Royal
Seapro

3986 **Eastern Seafood Company**
1020 W Hubbard St
Chicago, IL 60642 312-243-2090
Fax: 312-243-9467
Seafood
President: Mario Falco
Estimated Sales: $ 3 - 5 Million
Number Employees: 5-9

3987 **Eastern Shore Seafood Products**
P.O.Box 38
Mappsville, VA 23407-0038 757-824-5651
Fax: 757-987-6543 800-466-8550
www.easternshoreseafood.com
Manufacturer and exporter of clams and clam products including juice, prepared, canned, frozen, whole, chopped, minced, etc
President: Rick Myers
Sales: Denise Chance
Sales: Scott James
Estimated Sales: $25-49.9 Million
Number Employees: 250-499
Parent Co: Eastern Shore Seafood Products
Type of Packaging: Consumer, Bulk

3988 **Eastern Shore Tea**
9 W Aylesbury Rd # T
Lutherville, MD 21093-4121 410-561-5079
Fax: 410-561-4816 800-823-1408
bct@baltcoffee.com www.easternshoretea.com
Manufacturer of tea including whole leaf and bagged
President: Stanley Constantine
CEO: Janice Burns
Estimated Sales: $5-9.9 Million
Number Employees: 5-9
Type of Packaging: Consumer
Brands:
Baltimore Tea

3989 **Eastern Tea Corporation**
1 Engelhard Drive
Monroe Township, NJ 08831-3722 609-860-1100
Fax: 609-860-1105 800-221-0865
Manufacturer, importer and exporter of packaged and loose tea; also, tea bags and tapioca
President: Paul Barbakoff
Vice President: Ira Barbakoff
VP of Manufacturing: Glenn Barbakoff
Estimated Sales: $5-10 Million
Number Employees: 50-99
Sq. footage: 90000
Type of Packaging: Consumer, Food Service, Private Label

3990 **Eastman Chemical Company**
P.O.Box 511
Kingsport, TN 37662 423-229-2000
Fax: 423-229-2145 800-327-8626
jstokes@eastman.com www.eastman.com
Chemical, fibers and plastics that are used in the packaging and health and wellness industries as well as many other industries.
President/CEO/Chairman: James Rogers
SVP/CFO: Curt Espeland
Chief Marketing Officer: Mark Costa
Estimated Sales: $5.8 Billion
Number Employees: 10,000
Brands:
Nutriene
Tenox

3991 **Eastrise Trading Corporation**
16025 Arrow Hwy Ste A
Baldwin Park, CA 91706-2063
Fax: 626-330-0205 teas@eastrise.com
www.eastriseteas.com
Manufacturer of Teas; certified organic
Owner: Stephen Chau
Estimated Sales: $1-2.5 Million
Number Employees: 5-9
Brands:
RARE TEAS

3992 **Eastside Deli Supply**
2601 W Main St
Lansing, MI 48917 517-485-4630
Fax: 517-485-7904 800-349-6694
www.eastsidedeli.com
Manufacturer of fresh prepared deli sandwiches and beef jerky
President: Jeffrey Jacobs
Manager: Kari Price
Estimated Sales: $7.5 Million
Number Employees: 50
Sq. footage: 2500
Type of Packaging: Food Service
Brands:
Eastside Deli
Fresh From the Deli
Tillamook Country Smoker

3993 **Eastside Seafood**
1248 Jeffersonville Rd
Macon, GA 31217 478-743-1888
Fax: 478-272-5800
Manufacturer of Seafood
Owner: Riccardo Del Mastro
Estimated Sales: $300,000-500,000
Number Employees: 1-4

3994 **Eat It Corporation**
52 39th Street
Brooklyn, NY 11232 718-768-7950
Fax: 718-832-0406 eatitcorp@aol.com

3995 **Eat Your Heart Out**
332 Bleecker St
New York, NY 10014-6492 212-989-8303
Fax: 212-691-8661
snackgirl@eatyourheartout.com
www.neighborhoodoffice.com
Freeze-dried fruit and vegetables sanck foods
Owner: Helen Lally
Estimated Sales: $ .5 - 1 million
Number Employees: 1-4
Number of Products: 5

3996 **Eatem Foods Company**
1829 Gallagher Dr
Vineland, NJ 08360 856-692-1663
Fax: 856-692-0847 800-683-2836
jrandazzi@eatemfoods.com
www.eatemfoods.com
Food base manufacturing; supplier of savory flavor systems, flavor concentrates, broth concentrates and seasoning bases.
Owner/CEO: Robert Buono
Product Development Manager: William Cawley
VP Sales/Marketing: James Gervato
Human Resources Executive: Mario Riviell
Production Manager: Darryl Latimore
Plant Manager: Jerry Santo
Estimated Sales: $170,000
Number Employees: 2
Sq. footage: 3229
Type of Packaging: Consumer, Food Service, Bulk
Brands:
Eatem

3997 **Eau Galle Cheese Factory Shop**
N6765 State Highway 25
Durand, WI 54736 715-283-4276
Fax: 715-283-0711 800-283-1085
info@eaugallecheese.com
www.eaugallecheese.com
Cheese
President: John Buhlman
Estimated Sales: $10-20 Million
Number Employees: 20-49

3998 **Eberhard Creamery**
235 Se Evergreen Ave
Redmond, OR 97756-2347 541-548-5181
Fax: 541-548-7009
Manufacturer of dairy products and frozen foods
President: John Eberhard
Vice President: Richard Eberhard
Plant Manager: Jack Eberhard
Estimated Sales: $10-24.9 Million
Number Employees: 40
Type of Packaging: Consumer, Food Service

3999 **Eberle Winery**
P.O.Box 2459
Paso Robles, CA 93447-2459 805-238-9607
Fax: 805-237-0344 sales@eberlewinery.com
www.eberlewinery.com
Wine
Owner: Gary Eberle
Estimated Sales: $5-10 Million
Number Employees: 20-49

4000 **Eberly Poultry**
1095 Mount Airy Rd
Stevens, PA 17578 717-336-6440
Fax: 717-336-6905 www.eberlypoultry.com
Poultry
President: Robert Eberly
Estimated Sales: $ 10 - 20 Million
Number Employees: 50-99

4001 **Ebro Foods**
1330 W 43rd St
Chicago, IL 60609 773-696-0150
Canned vegetables and sausage
Owner: Silvio Vega
Controller: Zenaida Abreu
Sales: Marta Jimenez
Production: Steve Abreu
Estimated Sales: $13.5 Million
Number Employees: 80

4002 **Echo Farms Puddings**
573 Chesterfield Rd
Hinsdale, NH 03451-2210 603-336-7706
Fax: 603-336-5964 866-488-3246
www.echofarmpuddings.com
Desserts, pudding
Owner: Robert Hodge
Estimated Sales: $ 10 - 20 Million
Number Employees: 10-19
Brands:
ECHO FARM PUDDING

4003 **Echo Lake Farm Produce Company**
33102 S Honey Lake Rd
Burlington, WI 53105 262-763-9551
Fax: 262-763-4593 c.bull@echoforeggs.com
www.echoforeggs.com
Frozen and liquid egg processing, pancakes, French toast, waffle, crepe and blintz manufacturing
Manager: Jerry Warntjes
VP: Jerry Warntjes
Sales Manager: Scott Hall
Operations: David Warntjes

Estimated Sales: $20-50 Million
Number Employees: 100-249
Type of Packaging: Consumer, Food Service, Private Label, Bulk

4004 **Echo Spring Dairy**
706 Oscar St
Eugene, OR 97402 541-342-1291
Fax: 541-342-8379
Manufacturer of dairy products
Manager: Mike Miller
Estimated Sales: $10-20 Million
Number Employees: 20-49
Parent Co: Darigold
Type of Packaging: Consumer, Food Service

4005 **Eckert Cold Storage**
905 Clough Rd
Escalon, CA 95320 209-838-4040
Fax: 209-838-4049 eckert@thevision.net
Manufacturer of IQF red, green and yellow bell and jalapeno peppers, cabbage leaves, diced cabbage, bok choy, kabocha and mangos
President: G P Thompson
VP: Craig West
VP Quality Control: Mark Thompson
Estimated Sales: $100+ Million
Number Employees: 250-499
Sq. footage: 100000
Type of Packaging: Bulk

4006 **(HQ)Eckhart Corporation**
7110 Redwood Blvd Ste A
Novato, CA 94945 415-892-3880
info@eckhartcorp.com
www.eckhartcorp.com
Manufacturer and exporter of vitamins, food supplements and diet aids
President: Deepak Chopra
Marketing/Sales: Ryan Friman
Purchasing: Kathleen McClendon
Estimated Sales: $500,000-1 Million
Number Employees: 8
Sq. footage: 160000
Type of Packaging: Consumer, Food Service, Private Label, Bulk
Brands:
Nature's Edge
Stay Well

4007 **Eckhart Seed Company**
P.O.Box 7176
Spreckels, CA 93962-7176 831-758-0925
Fax: 831-758-0388 baney12@aol.com
Manufacturer of dried beans
President: Andrew Smith
Secretary: Peter Eckhart
VP: Richard Eckhart
Estimated Sales: Less than $500,000
Number Employees: 10-19
Type of Packaging: Bulk

4008 **Eckroat Seed Company**
1106 N Martin Luther King Ave
Oklahoma City, OK 73117 405-427-2484
Fax: 405-427-7174 www.eckroatseed.com
Manufacturer, importer and exporter of mung beans
President: Robert Eckroat
VP: Don Eckroat
Estimated Sales: $5-10 Million
Number Employees: 10-19
Sq. footage: 100000
Type of Packaging: Consumer, Food Service, Private Label, Bulk
Brands:
Green Dragon

4009 **Eclat Chocolate**
24 South High Street
West Chester, PA 19382-3225 610-672-5206
info@eclatchocolate.com
www.eclatchocolate.com
Chocolate.

4010 **Eclectic Institute**
36350 Industrial Way
Sandy, OR 97055 503-668-4120
Fax: 503-668-3227
customerservice@eclecticherb.com
www.eclecticherb.com
Organic alcohol extracts, alcohol free glycerins and nutritional supplements.
Owner: Edward Alstat
Estimated Sales: $ 5 - 10 Million
Number Employees: 50-99

4011 **Eclipse Sports Supplements**
PO Box 460
Clarks Summit, PA 18411
Fax: 570-543-4827 866-898-0885
eclipsecec@excite.com www.eclipse2000.com
Sports supplements
Brands:
ECLIPSE2000

4012 **Eco Foods**
2905 W Main Street
St Charles, IL 60175-1020 630-443-1646
Fax: 630-377-2996 866-326-1646
www.ecobar.com
Manufacturer of energy snacks
Brands:
ECOBAR

4013 **Eco-Cuisine**
P.O.Box 19006
Boulder, CO 80308-2006 303-444-6634
Fax: 303-444-6647 ron@eco-cuisine.com
www.ecocycle.org
Manufacturer of vegetarian, organic and kosher mixes for bakery items and meat analogs, vegetarian broth powders, instant soy puddings, pancakes
Executive Director: Eric Lombardi
VP: Nancy Loving
Estimated Sales: $ 20 - 50 Million
Number Employees: 50-99
Number of Brands: 13
Number of Products: 25
Type of Packaging: Consumer, Food Service, Private Label, Bulk
Brands:
Eco-Cuisine

4014 **EcoNatural Solutions**
997 Dixon Rd
Boulder, CO 80302 303-527-1554
Fax: 303-527-3885 877-684-5159
customerservice@econaturals.com
www.stclaires.com
Manufacturer and exporter of organic sweets
CEO: Debra St Claire
Estimated Sales: $2.5-5 Million
Number Employees: 5-9
Type of Packaging: Consumer
Brands:
St. Claire

4015 **Ecom Agroindustrial Corporation Ltd**
17 State Street
23rd Floor
New York, NY 10004 212-248-1190
Fax: 212-248-1816 www.ecomtrading.com
Cocoa powder, cocoa butter, cocoa liquor, cocoa beans, coffee, oilseeds, grains, cotton
Vice President: Pablo Esteve
Research & Development: Nar Lin
Estimated Sales: $2 Billion
Number Employees: 1000
Type of Packaging: Consumer
Brands:
AMSA
ECOM COCOA

4016 **Ecom Manufacturing Corporation**
80 Telson Road
Markham, ON L3R 1E5
Canada 905-477-2441
Fax: 905-477-2511 dsoknacki@ecomcanada.com
www.ecomcanada.com
Manufacturer of natural colors and flavors including garlic, onion, rosemary, allspice, turmeric, jalapeno, cilantro and nutmeg extracts,capsicum,enhancers.
President: David Soknacki
Sales/Marketing: Kan Husband
Plant Manager: Hoody Minski
Estimated Sales: $203.25k
Number Employees: 5
Sq. footage: 40000
Type of Packaging: Bulk

4017 **Ed & Don's Candies**
4462 Malaai St
Honolulu, HI 96818 808-423-8200
Fax: 808-423-0550 www.oritz.com
Manufacturer of Chocolate candies
President: Julie Marcello
Director: Gale Sasagawa
Sales Manager: Gladys Ornellas
Estimated Sales: $5-10 Million
Number Employees: 100
Parent Co: Oritz Corporation
Type of Packaging: Private Label
Brands:
Ed & Don's Chocolate Macadamias
Ed & Don's Macadamia Brittles
Ed & Don's Macadamia Chews

4018 **Ed Kasilof's Seafoods**
P.O.Box 18
Kasilof, AK 99610-0018 907-262-7295
Fax: 907-262-1617 800-982-2377
eks@alaska.net www.kasilofseafoods.com
Seafood
President: James Trujillo
Estimated Sales: $ 5 - 10 Million
Number Employees: 10-19

4019 **(HQ)Ed Miniat**
16250 S. Vincennes Ave.
South Holland, IL 60473 708-589-2400
Fax: 708-589-2525 www.miniat.com
Frozen prepared meats
President: Ed Miniat
Executive VP: Michael Miniat
Sales Manager: Chuck Nalon
Production: David Jackson
Plant Manager: Neil Brodrick
Purchasing: Richard Krups
Estimated Sales: $ 5 - 10 Million
Number Employees: 20-49

4020 **Ed Miniat Inc.Headquarters/Cooked Meat Plant**
16250 S. Vincennes Ave
South Holland, IL 60473 708-589-2400
Fax: 708-589-2525 www.miniat.com
Processor of cooked beef and pork products; also, shortenings and oils
Owner/President: Dave Miniat
COO: Don Ervin
Sales/Marketing Executive: Chuck Nalon
Estimated Sales: $ 5 - 10 Million
Number Employees: 20-49
Type of Packaging: Bulk

4021 **Ed Oliveira Winery**
155 Center Street
Arcata, CA 95521-6056 707-822-3023
Manufacturer of Wines
President: Douglas Oliveira
Estimated Sales: $75,000
Number Employees: 1-4

4022 **Ed's Honey Company**
497 10th Ave SE
Dickinson, ND 58601 701-225-9223
Manufacturer of honey
Owner: Ed Fetch
Estimated Sales: $2.5-5 Million
Number Employees: 1-4
Type of Packaging: Consumer

4023 **Eda's Sugarfree Candies**
4900 N 20th St
Philadelphia, PA 19144-2402 215-324-3412
Fax: 215-324-3413 edasugarfree@msn.com
www.edasugarfree.com
Processor and exporter of sugar-free hard candies
President: Brian Berry
Vice President: Dan Harasewyah
Number of Brands: 1
Number of Products: 28
Sq. footage: 20000
Parent Co: Lehman Sugarfree Confectionery
Type of Packaging: Consumer, Food Service, Private Label, Bulk
Brands:
EDA SUGARFREE HARD CANDIES

4024 **Eddy's Bakery**
380 N Five Mile Rd
Boise, ID 83713-8959 208-377-8100
Fax: 208-322-7823
Manfuacturer of baked goods including bread and cakes
Sales Manager: Gary Davis

Estimated Sales: $ 3 - 5 Million
Number Employees: 1-4
Type of Packaging: Consumer

4025 Edelman Meats
P.O.Box 433
Antigo, WI 54409-0433 715-623-7686
Fax: 715-623-7688
Manufacturer of beef, pork, chicken, fish, etc
President: Joseph Edelman
Estimated Sales: $20-50 Million
Number Employees: 10-19
Type of Packaging: Food Service

4026 (HQ)Edelmann Provision Company
10000 Martins Way
Harrison, OH 45014-7594 513-881-5800
Fax: 513-881-5803 www.freshsausage.com
Manufacturer of fresh sausage
President: James Frondorf
Vice President: James Burke
Estimated Sales: $44.6 Million
Number Employees: 80

4027 Edelweiss Patisserie
56 Roland St # 200
Charlestown, MA 02129-1233 617-628-0225
Fax: 617-628-0882 rcebi@edelweisspastry.com
www.hbook.com
Manufacturer of baked goods including cakes, pastries, muffins, croissants, pullman and tea loaves, rustic breads, cookies, etc
Manager: Roger Sutton
Estimated Sales: $20-50 Million
Number Employees: 50-99
Type of Packaging: Food Service

4028 (HQ)Eden Foods Inc.
701 Tecumseh Rd
Clinton, MI 49236 517-456-7424
Fax: 517-456-6075 800-248-0320
info@edenfoods.com www.edenfoods.com
Manufacturer, importer and exporter of natural and organic foods including pasta, soymilk, green tea, beans, tomatoes, spaghetti sauce, etc
President/CEO: Michael Potter
CFO: Jay Hughes
Vice President: Jim Fox
Quality Control: Jon Solomon
VP Marketing & Sales: Sue Becker
VP Operations: William Swaney
Estimated Sales: $20-50 Million
Number Employees: 100-249
Type of Packaging: Food Service
Brands:
EDEN
EDEN ORGANIC
EDENBALANCE
EDENBLEND
EDENSOY
EDENSOY EXTRA

4029 Eden Organic Pasta Company
9104 Culver St
Detroit, MI 48213 313-921-2053
Fax: 313-921-0282 800-248-0320
info@edenfoods.com www.edenfoods.com
Manufacturer of organic and vegetable pastas
Manager: Steven Swaney
Vice President: Jim Fox
Chief Financial Officer: Jay Hughes
General Manager: Steve Swaney
Operations Manager: William Swaney
Estimated Sales: $2.5-5 Million
Number Employees: 10-19
Parent Co: Eden Foods
Type of Packaging: Food Service
Other Locations:
Eden Foods Plant
Detroit MI
Eden Foods Plant
Union City CA
Brands:
EDEN'S

4030 Eden Processing
100 East St
Poplar Grove, IL 61065 815-765-2000
Fax: 815-765-2777 www.edencherry.com
Manufacturer of bakers' and confectioners' supplies including maraschino cherries, sweetened coconut, mince meat pie fillings, orange, lemon, melon, grapefruit and citron peels, etc
President, CEO: Louis Tenore, Jr.
Marketing Director: Pam McDowell
Estimated Sales: $3.10 Million
Number Employees: 14
Sq. footage: 55000
Type of Packaging: Bulk
Brands:
True Blue

4031 Eden Vineyards Winery
19709 Little Ln
Alva, FL 33920 239-728-9463
info@edenwinery.com
www.edenwinery.com
Wines
President: Earl Kiser
Estimated Sales: $1-2.5 Million
Number Employees: 1-4

4032 Edgar A Weber & Company
549 Palwaukee Drive
Wheeling, IL 60090 847-215-1980
Fax: 847-215-2073 800-558-9078
info@weberflavors.com www.weberflavors.com
Manufacturer and exporter of flavoring extracts for wine, liquor, baked goods and ice cream
Owner/President/CEO: Andrew Plennert
CFO: James Doig
Marketing Manager: Roger Passaglia
Plant Manager: Mike Sciore
Estimated Sales: $3 Million
Number Employees: 20
Sq. footage: 5000
Brands:
Hy Van
Simply Natural
Simply Natural-Like

4033 Edge Labs
PO Box 33067
Trenton, NJ 08629-3067 732-617-1100
Fax: 732-536-9179 866-334-3522
info@edgelabsproducts.com www.edgelabs.com
Powdered drink dietary suuplements.
Marketing Manager: Cindy Filippone

4034 Edgewood Estate Winery
607 Airpark Road
Napa, CA 94558-6272 800-755-2374
Fax: 707-254-4920 sales@edgewoodestate.com
www.edgewoodestate.com
Wines
CEO: Jeff O'Neill
CFO: John Kelleher
Sales: Steve Lindsay
Purchasing: David Weckerle
Estimated Sales: $1-2.5 Million
Number Employees: 7
Number of Brands: 1
Number of Products: 14
Sq. footage: 70000
Parent Co: Golden State Vintners
Type of Packaging: Consumer, Private Label
Brands:
EDGEWOOD ESTATE

4035 (HQ)Edlong Dairy Flavors
225 Scott St
Elk Grove Village, IL 60007 847-439-9230
Fax: 847-439-0053 888-698-2783
info@edlong.com www.edlong.com
Concentrated Dairy flavors. Flavors are available in liquid, powder, emulsion, paste and spray-dried forms and a variety of solubilities. Specialties include cheese, butter, dairy, dairy brown and functional dairy flavors.
President: Laurie Smith
CEO: Eugene Rondenet
CFO: Harold Stover
Finance VP: Paul Simkus
R&D VP: Eric Johnson
Safety Manager: Lloyd Sapoa
Marketing/Sales VP: Paula Gallagher
Public Relations: David Booth
Purchasing: Cindy Johnson
Estimated Sales: $50-100 Million
Number Employees: 50-99
Sq. footage: 90000
Type of Packaging: Food Service, Private Label, Bulk
Other Locations:
Edlong Dairy Flavors
Suffolk
Edlong Dairy Flavors
United Kingdom
Edlong Dairy Flavors
Mexico City
Brands:
CAPSULONG
CHEOLONG
ED-VANCE
VISION

4036 Edmonds Chile Company
3236 Oregon Ave
St Louis, MO 63118-3004 314-772-1499
Fax: 314-664-7735
Manufacturer of sliced pork and gravy, sliced beef and gravy, beef au jus, vegetable soup, beef stew, meat sauce, beef chili, chili con carne, beef patties and tamales
President: Mark Adelman
Estimated Sales: $2.5-5 Million
Number Employees: 10-19
Type of Packaging: Consumer

4037 Edmonton Meat Packing Company
8310 Yellowhead Trail NW
Edmonton, AB T5B 1GS
Canada 780-474-2471
Fax: 780-479-6167 800-361-6328
Manufacturer and exporter of fresh and frozen beef, pork, lamb, veal, smoked meats, sausage and seafood
Plant Manager: Bruce Larson
Number Employees: 100-249
Type of Packaging: Consumer, Food Service, Bulk

4038 Edmonton Potato Growers
12220 170th St.
Edmonton, AB T5V 1L7
Canada 780-447-1860
Fax: 780-447-1899 admin@epg.ab.ca
www.epg.ab.ca
Manufacturer and exmporter of potatoes including table, seed and processed, onions
President: Wayne Groot
Sales: Darcy Olson
General Manager: Bob Jensen
Estimated Sales: F
Number Employees: 35
Type of Packaging: Consumer, Food Service, Bulk
Brands:
CANADA GOOSE

4039 Edmunds St. John
1331 Walnut St
Berkeley, CA 94709-1408 510-981-1510
Fax: 510-981-1610 www.edmundstjohn.com
Wine
President: Steve Edmunds
Estimated Sales: $1-2.5 Million
Number Employees: 1-4

4040 Edna Valley Vineyard
2585 Biddle Ranch Rd
San Luis Obispo, CA 93401 805-544-5855
Fax: 805-544-0112 info@ednavalley.com
www.ednavalley.com
Manufacturer of table wines including Chardonnay and Pinot Noir
President: William Hamilton
CEO: Tom Selfridge
Sales Manager: Robert Farber
Plant Manager: Randy Weaver
Estimated Sales: $5-10 Million
Number Employees: 45
Sq. footage: 60000
Parent Co: Chalone Company
Type of Packaging: Consumer, Food Service, Private Label
Brands:
Edna Valley
Videyards

4041 Edner Corporation
1200 Zephyr Ave
Hayward, CA 94544 510-441-8504
Fax: 510-441-9395

Manufacturer of breads (specialty), cakes, cookies, croissants (filled and unfilled), muffins, pastries, & scones (filled and unfilled)
President: Ed Kirschner
VP Technical Sales: Mark Aquilar
Estimated Sales: $10-20 Million
Number Employees: 10-19
Parent Co: Edner Corporation
Type of Packaging: Consumer, Food Service, Private Label, Bulk
Brands:
Edna Foods
Extreme
Huckleberry
Jonathan International Foods
La Patisserie
Warfarers

4042 **(HQ)Edom Laboratories**
100 E Jefryn Blvd # M
Deer Park, NY 11729-5729 631-586-2266
Fax: 631-586-2385 800-723-3366
www.edomlaboratories.com
Manufacturer, exporter and wholesaler/distributor of vitamins and dietary supplements
President: Arthur Pollack
Estimated Sales: $20-50 Million
Number Employees: 1-4
Type of Packaging: Consumer, Private Label, Bulk

4043 **Edward & Sons Trading Company**
P.O.Box 1326
Carpinteria, CA 93014 805-684-8500
Fax: 805-684-8220 alison@edwardsons.com
www.edwardandsons.com
Manufacturer, importer and exporter of natural, organic and specialty foods: condiments, confectionery products, crackers, vegetarian soup mixes, snack foods, canned organic vegetables, vegetarian bouillon cubes, cake decorationsorganic coconut milk
President: Joel Dee
Vice President: Alison Cox
Operations Manager: Dean Seicher
Estimated Sales: $ 5 - 10 Million
Number Employees: 10-19
Type of Packaging: Consumer, Food Service, Private Label
Brands:
EDWARD&SONS
HERITAGE SOUPS
LET'S DO
LET'S DO ORGANIC
NATIVE FOREST
ORGANIC COUNTRY
PREMIER JAPAN
RAINFOREST ORGANIC
TROY'S
WIZARDS

4044 **Edwards Baking Company**
1 Lemon Ln NE
Atlanta, GA 30307 404-377-0511
Fax: 404-378-2074 800-241-0559
www.edwardsbaking.com
Frozen dessert pies
Manager: Brian Schneider
Branch Manager: Mark Glennon
Operations Director: Joe Leonardo
Estimated Sales: $20-50 Million
Number Employees: 432
Parent Co: Schwan's

4045 **Edwards Mill**
P.O.Box 17
Point Lookout, MO 65726-0017 417-334-6411
Fax: 417-335-2618 800-222-0525
admiss4@cofo.edu www.cofo.edu
Manufacturer of whole grains that are blended into mixes; pancake, waffle, biscuit, muffin, fruitcakes, jams, jelly, preserves, apple butter
President: Jerry Davis

4046 **Edy'sDreyers Grand Ice Cream**
301 Round Hill Drive
Rockaway, NJ 07866-1224
Fax: 973-627-7005 800-362-7899
www.dryersinc.com
Manufacturer of ice cream cones and sandwiches, ice pops, fruit bars and frozen yogurt; serving retail grocery markets
Division Marketing Manager: Ellen Sparano
Division Manager (Northeast): Stan Fabian
Estimated Sales: $100-500 Million
Number Employees: 250-499
Parent Co: Dreyer's Grand Ice Cream
Type of Packaging: Consumer
Brands:
EDY'S

4047 **Edy's Grand Ice Cream**
601 Wall St
Glendale Heights, IL 60139 630-924-7755
Fax: 630-924-8336 888-377-3397
www.edys.com
Manufacturer and wholesaler/distributor of ice cream and frozen yogurt; serving the food service market
Finance Executive: Marshall Osterloh
Business Development Manager: Nick De Pinto
Sales/Marketing Executive: Patty SanFilippo
Regional Manager: Mike Olsen
Estimated Sales: $100-500 Million
Number Employees: 100-249
Parent Co: Dreyer's Grand Ice Cream
Type of Packaging: Consumer, Food Service

4048 **Edy's Grand Ice Cream**
3255 Meridian Pkwy
Weston, FL 33331 954-384-7133
Fax: 954-384-0815
Manufacturer of dairy products including ice cream and frozen yogurt; serving supermarket chains and restaurants
Manager: Gary Bruner
District Manager: Mark Servaes
Estimated Sales: $50-100 Million
Number Employees: 50-99
Sq. footage: 20000
Parent Co: Dreyer's Grand Ice Cream
Type of Packaging: Consumer, Food Service

4049 **Edy's Grand Ice Cream**
3426 N Wells St
Fort Wayne, IN 46808 260-483-3102
Fax: 260-482-4152 www.edys.com
Manufacturer of ice cream, sherbet and frozen yogurt
Manager: Wayne Clive
Estimated Sales: $50-100 Million
Parent Co: Dreyer's Grand Ice Cream
Type of Packaging: Consumer, Food Service

4050 **Efco Products**
130 Smith St
Poughkeepsie, NY 12601 845-452-4715
Fax: 845-452-5607 800-284-3326
service@efcoproducts.com
www.efcoproducts.com
Bakery mixes and ingredients, fruit and creme-style fillings, jellies, jams, and concentrated icing fruits
Chairman: Jack Effron
President: Ira Effron
Estimated Sales: $2.5-5 Million
Number Employees: 50-99

4051 **Effie's Homemade**
One Westinghouse Plaza
Hyde Park, MA 02136 617-364-9300
Fax: 617-364-9333 joan@effieshomemade.com
www.effieshomemade.com
all natural oatcakes and crispy corncakes
President/Owner: Joan MacIsaac

4052 **Egg Cream America**
633 Skokie Boulevard
Suite 200
Northbrook, IL 60062-2858 847-559-2703
Fax: 847-559-2709 getcreamed@aol.com
www.getcreamed.com
Dairy based carbonated beverages
Estimated Sales: $1-5 Million
Number Employees: 5-9

4053 **Egg Low Farms**
35 W State St
Sherburne, NY 13460 607-674-4653
Fax: 607-674-9216 www.egglowfarms.com
Fresh eggs including diced and scrambled. Also salad ready diced eggs and tray ready scrambled eggs; all fresh
President: Helen Dunckel
CEO: David Dunckel
Estimated Sales: $1-2.5 Million
Number Employees: 5-9
Sq. footage: 40000
Type of Packaging: Food Service, Private Label
Brands:
Egg Low Farms
The Unbeatable Eatable Egg

4054 **Egg Roll Fantasy**
PO Box 7895
Auburn, CA 95604-7895 530-887-9197
Fax: 530-887-9199
Manufacturer of gourmet egg rolls
President: Louie Buendia
VP: Robert DiMiceli
Estimated Sales: $500,000-$1 Million
Number Employees: 10
Number of Brands: 3
Number of Products: 20
Sq. footage: 4000
Type of Packaging: Consumer, Food Service, Private Label, Bulk

4055 **Eggland's Best Foods**
860 First Ave # 842
King of Prussia, PA 19406-4033 610-265-6500
Fax: 610-265-8380 888-922-3447
ataylor@eggland.com www.eggland.com
Manufacturer of Dairy, organic eggs
President/CEO: Charles Lanktree
Director Quality Assurance: Bart Slaugh PhD
Marketing Manager: Francis Kane
Estimated Sales: $10-20 Million
Number Employees: 10-19
Type of Packaging: Private Label
Brands:
Cage Free Organic
Eggland's Best
Eggs & More
Eggs To Go

4056 **Eggology**
6728 Eton Ave
Canoga Park, CA 91303 818-610-2222
Fax: 818-610-2223 information@eggology.com
www.eggology.com
Manufacturer of pure liquid egg whites
President: Brad Halpern
Estimated Sales: $ 5 - 10 Million
Number Employees: 20-49

4057 **Egon Binkert Meat Products**
8805 Philadelphia Rd
Baltimore, MD 21237-4310 410-687-5959
Fax: 410-687-5023
Manufacturer and distributor of German style lunch meats and sausages
Owner: Sonya Weber
Estimated Sales: $300,000-500,000
Number Employees: 1-4
Sq. footage: 2800

4058 **Egypt Star Bakery**
2225 Macarthur Rd
Whitehall, PA 18052 610-434-3762
Fax: 610-443-1915
Breads, rolls
President: Esther Erdossy
Estimated Sales: $500,000-$1 Million
Number Employees: 10-19

4059 **Ehmann Olive Company**
1800 Idora St
Oroville, CA 95966 530-533-3303
Fax: 530-534-8137
Manufacturer of green and black olives
Manager: George Hoag
Estimated Sales: $ 10 - 20 Million
Number Employees: 20
Parent Co: George DeLallo
Type of Packaging: Consumer, Food Service, Private Label
Brands:
Delallo
Ehmann

4060 **Ehresman Packing Company**
P.O.Box 403
Garden City, KS 67846 620-276-3791
Fax: 620-276-1916
Manufacturer of meat products; also, custom butchering available
Co-Owner: Mike Plankenhorn
Co-Owner: Velda Plankenhorn
Estimated Sales: $5-10 Million
Number Employees: 10-19
Type of Packaging: Consumer, Private Label

4061 **Eickman's Processing**
P.O.Box 118
Seward, IL 61077-0118 815-247-8451
Fax: 815-247-8463
Manufacturer of beef, pork, lamb and wild game
President: Mike Eickman
Estimated Sales: $2.5-5 Million
Number Employees: 20-49
Type of Packaging: Consumer, Food Service

4062 **Eidon Mineral Supplements**
12330 Stowe Dr
Poway, CA 92064-6802 858-668-0900
Fax: 858-668-3593 800-700-1169
questions@eidon.com www.eidon.com
Manufacturer of mineral supplements
Manager: Deborah Stewart
VP: Fred Elsner
Sales Director: Barbara G.
Production Manager: Cory Wagner
Plant Manager: Cory Wagner
Estimated Sales: $1 Million
Number Employees: 5-9
Number of Brands: 1
Number of Products: 30
Sq. footage: 11500
Type of Packaging: Consumer, Private Label, Bulk

4063 **Eight O'Clock Coffee Company**
155 Chestnut Ridge Road
Montvale, NJ 07645-0418 201-571-0300
Fax: 201-571-8719 800-299-2739
www.eightoclock.com
Supermarket coffee
CEO/President: Barbara Roth
Vice President: Liesel Bell
Marketing Director: Don Sommerville
Consumer Promotions Manager: Marion Milrod
Plant Manager: Pete Notard
Estimated Sales: $100-500 Million
Number Employees: 200
Sq. footage: 13000
Type of Packaging: Consumer
Brands:
BURGER KING
Caffè Ritazza
EIGHT O'CLOCK
Harry Ramsden's
Royale
Sbarro
Upper Crust

4064 **Eilenberger Bakery**
P.O.Box 710
Palestine, TX 75802-0710 903-729-2253
Fax: 903-723-2915 800-831-2544
sales@eilenbergerbakery.com
www.eilenberger.com
Manufacturer of gourmet cakes and brownies
President: Tresas Smith
Estimated Sales: $ 3 - 5 Million
Number Employees: 20-49

4065 **Eiserman Meats**
401 12 St SE
Slave Lake, AB T0G 2A3
Canada 780-849-5507
Fax: 780-849-6097 info@eisermanmeats.com
www.eisermanmeats.com
Manufacturer of fresh beef, pork, sausage and wild game; also, beef jerky; slaughtering services available
President/Co-Owner: Russell Eiserman
Co-Owner: Annellen Eiserman
Estimated Sales: A
Number Employees: 1-4
Type of Packaging: Consumer

4066 **El Aguila Food Products**
42 W Market St
Salinas, CA 93901-2653 831-422-3629
Fax: 831-422-3328 800-398-2929
www.elaguila.com
Manufacturer of corn and flour tortillas and other mexican food products
President: Russel Chisum
Estimated Sales: $50-100 Million
Number Employees: 50-99
Type of Packaging: Consumer, Food Service, Private Label, Bulk
Brands:
EL AGUILIA

4067 **El Brands**
267 Van Heusen Drive
Ozark, AL 36360-1054 334-445-2828
Fax: 334-352-7263
Manufacturer of peanuts
CEO: Ed Lindley
VP Sales/Marketing: Steve Ratliff

4068 **El Charro Mexican Food Industries**
1711 S Virginia Ave
Roswell, NM 88203-1829 575-622-8590
Fax: 575-622-8590 ectortilla@yahoo.com
Manufacturer and exporter of chili sauce and tortilla chips
Owner: Michael Trujillo
Owner: Mireya Trujillo
Estimated Sales: $5-10 Million
Number Employees: 10-19
Type of Packaging: Consumer, Food Service, Private Label, Bulk
Brands:
EL CHARRO
LA PABLANITA

4069 **El Charro Mexican Foods**
1711 S Virginia Ave
Roswell, NM 88203-1829 575-622-8590
Fax: 575-622-8590
Tortillas
President: Michael Trujillo
Estimated Sales: $500-1 Million appx.
Number Employees: 10-19
Type of Packaging: Private Label
Brands:
Don Jose's
Elcharro
Lapoblanita

4070 **El Dorado Coffee**
5675 49th St
Flushing, NY 11378-2012 718-418-4100
Fax: 718-418-4500 800-635-2566
info@eldoradocoffee.com
www.eldoradocoffee.com
Manufacturer and roaster of coffee
President: Segunda Martin
Vice President: John Canal
VP: Andres Martin
Estimated Sales: $20-50 Million
Number Employees: 20-49
Type of Packaging: Consumer, Food Service, Private Label
Brands:
EL DORADO COFFEE ROASTERS

4071 **El Grano De Oro**
1710 Francisco Blvd
Pacifica, CA 94044-2515 650-355-8417
Fax: 650-355-7705
Mexican Restaurant
Owner: Mauricio Garcia
Estimated Sales: $1-2.5 Million
Number Employees: 10-19

4072 **El Matador Foods**
7201 Bayway Dr
Baytown, TX 77520 281-424-4555
Fax: 281-838-1375
Manufacturer of Tortilla chips
Owner: Erick Ybarra
Estimated Sales: $5-10 Million
Number Employees: 5-9
Brands:
El Matador Tortilla Chip

4073 **El Molino Winery**
P.O.Box 306
Saint Helena, CA 94574 707-963-3632
Fax: 707-963-1647 info@elmolinowinery.com
www.elmolinowinery.com
Manufacturer of Wine
Sales/Marketing: Mimi Buttenheim
General Manager: Lily Oliver
Winemaker: Jon Berlin
Labelling/Foiling Wines: Altagracia Rincon
Estimated Sales: Less than $500,000
Number Employees: 1-4

4074 **El Paso Chile Company**
909 Texas Ave
El Paso, TX 79901-1524 915-544-3434
Fax: 915-544-7552 888-472-5727
info@alpasochile.com www.elpasochile.com
Manufacturer of Salsas, condiments, barbecue sauce, trail mixes, nuts, drink mixes, spices and fixings
Owner: William Parker
VP: Norma Kerr
Estimated Sales: $10-20 Million
Number Employees: 136
Type of Packaging: Private Label

4075 **El Paso Meat Company**
1523 Myrtle Ave
El Paso, TX 79901 915-838-8600
Fax: 915-533-3997
Manufacturer of fresh and frozen beef and pork; slaughtering services available
Owner: Francis Ramos
General Manager: Javier Garcia
Estimated Sales: $3-5 Million
Number Employees: 5-9
Type of Packaging: Consumer, Food Service

4076 **El Paso Winery**
742 Broadway
Ulster Park, NY 12487 845-331-0491
www.elpasowinery.com
Manufacturer of red, white and rose wines
Owner: Maryl Marino-Vogel
Co-Owner: Maryl Vogel
Operations Manager: Felipe Beltra
Estimated Sales: Less than $500,000
Number Employees: 1-4
Type of Packaging: Consumer, Food Service

4077 **El Perico Charro**
204 N 7th St
Garden City, KS 67846 620-275-6454
Manufacturer and retailers of Mexican foods, tortillas
President/CEO: Natividad Hernandez
Estimated Sales: $500,000-$1 Million
Number Employees: 1-4
Number of Products: 2
Type of Packaging: Consumer, Food Service

4078 **El Peto Products**
65 Saltsman Drive
Cambridge, ON N3H 4R7
Canada 519-650-4614
Fax: 519-650-5692 800-387-4064
info@elpeto.com www.elpeto.com
Manufacturer and exporter of wheat, gluten and milk-free products including baking mixes, breads, muffins, cakes, buns, pies, cookies, frozen doughs and batters, pastas, soups and specialty flours
President: Elisabeth Riesen
VP: Peter Riesen
Estimated Sales: $2 Million
Number Employees: 18
Number of Brands: 3
Sq. footage: 4500
Type of Packaging: Consumer, Food Service, Bulk
Brands:
El Peto

4079 **El Ranchito**
19422 SE Stark St
Portland, OR 97233 503-665-4919
Fax: 503-669-2503
Manufacturer of Mexican spices
Owner: Francisco Sanchez
VP Sales/Marketing: Paul Bradley
Estimated Sales: $ .5 - 1 million
Number Employees: 10-19
Type of Packaging: Consumer, Food Service

4080 **El Rancho Tortilla**
623 New Laredo Hwy
San Antonio, TX 78211 210-922-8411
Fax: 210-922-9159
Manufacturer of corn and flour tortillas, tostadas, taco shells and picante sauce
Owner: Ruben Martinez
Estimated Sales: $2.5-5 Million
Number Employees: 10-19
Type of Packaging: Consumer

4081 **El Segundo Bakery**
219 W Grand Avenue
El Segundo, CA 90245-3740 310-322-3422
Fax: 310-322-8760
Manufacturer of cakes, danish, bread, rolls, cookies, decorated cakes and wedding cakes
President: Arthur Miltenberger
VP: Lisa Miltenberger
Sales: Peter Miltenberger

Estimated Sales: $900,000
Number Employees: 10
Sq. footage: 45800
Type of Packaging: Consumer, Food Service

4082 **El Toro Food Products**
504 El Rio Street
Watsonville, CA 95076-3540 831-728-9266
Fax: 831-688-8766 oeltoro@pacbell.net
Manufacture of canned salsas varieties including sauces and vegetables
President: Richard Thomas
Estimated Sales: $5-10 Million
Number Employees: 5-9
Number of Brands: 6
Number of Products: 10
Sq. footage: 6000
Type of Packaging: Food Service, Private Label, Bulk

4083 **El-Milagro**
2759 S Kedzie Ave
Chicago, IL 60623
Fax: 773-650-4692 www.elmilagro.com
Manufacturer and exporter of Mexican foods including corn flour tortillas and tortilla chips
President: Raphael Lopez
VP Finance: Jerry Slowik
VP: Linda Lopez
Director Marketing: Jesus Lopez
Human Resources Director: Hortencia Conderon
Estimated Sales: $20-50 Million
Number Employees: 540
Sq. footage: 3000
Type of Packaging: Consumer, Food Service

4084 **El-Rey Foods**
6190 Bermuda Dr
Ferguson, MO 63135-3298 314-521-3113
Manufacturer and exporter of frozen foods including chili, tamales, roast and barbecued beef, taco meat and pork; also, barbecue sauce
Owner: Joseph Frisella
Estimated Sales: $10-20 Million
Number Employees: 5-9
Sq. footage: 2000
Type of Packaging: Consumer, Food Service
Brands:
Chef's Helper
Menu a La Carte

4085 **Elaine's Toffee Co.**
Po Box 38
Clayton, CA 94517 925-524-0000
Fax: 925-524-9000 800-883-3050
info@elainestoffee.com www.elainestoffee.com
Kosher, sugar-free, chocolate bars, other chcoolate, toffee, other snacksprivate label.
Marketing: Janet Long

4086 **Elan Chemical Company**
268 Doremus Ave
Newark, NJ 07105-4875 973-344-8014
Fax: 973-344-1948 sales@elan-chemical.com
www.elan-chemical.com
Manufacturer and exporter of organic kosher certified vanilla extract, flavoring and synthetic and natural aromatic chemicals
President: Jocelyn Manship
CEO: Ira Kapp
Estimated Sales: $20-50 Million
Number Employees: 50-99
Type of Packaging: Bulk

4087 **Elan Nutrition**
4490 44th St SE
Grand Rapids, MI 49512-4011 616-940-6000
Fax: 616-940-9971 www.elannutrition.com
Manufacturer of Nutritional products
President/CEO: David Finnigan
Accounts Manager: Pam Lauroff
CEO: Tom Olive
Sales: Lee Covert
Estimated Sales: $75-125 Million
Number Employees: 100-249
Sq. footage: 230000
Type of Packaging: Private Label

4088 **Elba Custom Meats**
405 Alabama Highway 203
Elba, AL 36323-4217 334-897-2007
Manufacturer of meat products
Owner: Billy F Hudson
General Manager: F Hudson

Estimated Sales: $ 1 - 3 Million
Number Employees: 1-4
Type of Packaging: Consumer

4089 **(HQ)Eldorado Artesian Springs**
P.O.Box 445
Eldorado Springs, CO 80025-0445 303-499-1316
Fax: 303-499-1339 info@eldoradosprings.com
www.eldoradosprings.com
Bottled water
President/CEO: Douglas Larson
VP Marketing: Jeremy Martin
VP Operations: Kevin Sipple
Estimated Sales: $5.3 Million
Number Employees: 50-99
Type of Packaging: Private Label
Brands:
Eldorado Natural Spring Water
Eldorado Spring Water

4090 **Eldorado Seafood Inc**
27 Cambridge St
Burlington, MA 01803 781-270-4290
Fax: 781-270-4242 800-416-5656
www.eldoradoseafood.com
Manufacturer of shrimp including breaded, cooked, peeled and deveined
President: Christinne Randazzo
VP: Laura Randazzo
Estimated Sales: $2.5-5 Million
Number Employees: 1-4
Type of Packaging: Consumer, Food Service, Private Label
Brands:
Eldorado
Max-Sea

4091 **Elegant Desserts**
275 Warren St
Lyndhurst, NJ 7071 201-933-0770
Fax: 201-933-7309 info@elegantdesserts.com
www.elegantdesserts.com
Manufacturer and wholesaler/distributor of pastries including tarts and miniature grand viennas
President: John Mazur
Estimated Sales: $2 Million
Number Employees: 20-49
Type of Packaging: Food Service, Private Label

4092 **Elegant Edibles**
3311 Mercer St
Houston, TX 77027-6019 713-522-2884
Fax: 713-522-1777 800-227-3226
info@elegantedibles.com
www.elegantedibles.com
All natural, gourmet confections, snacks, and recipe ready ingredients
Owner: Diane Dagostino
R&D: Francis Jacquinet
Operations: Lori Lake
Production: Amanda Stults
Plant Manager: Ana Olmedo
Estimated Sales: Less than $500,000
Number Employees: 5-9
Number of Brands: 8
Type of Packaging: Consumer, Food Service, Private Label, Bulk
Brands:
Mrs. Powell's Gourmet

4093 **Elena's**
2650 Paldan Dr
Auburn Hills, MI 48326 248-373-1100
Fax: 248-373-1120 800-723-5362
info@elenas.com www.elenas.com
Manufacturer and exporter of pasta, pasta sauce and pasta salad
President: Elena Houlihan
VP Operations: John Houlihan
Estimated Sales: $2.5-5 Million
Number Employees: 20-49
Parent Co: Houlihan's Culinary Traditions
Type of Packaging: Food Service, Private Label, Bulk
Brands:
Bella Mercato
Bruschetta

4094 **Elena's Food Specialties**
405 Allerton Ave
S San Francisco, CA 94080-4818 650-871-8700
Fax: 650-871-0502 800-376-5368
peter@elenasfoods.com www.elenasfoods.com
Manufacturer of frozen Mexican foods including enchiladas and burritos
President: Peter Sartorio
VP Product Development: Nathan Steck
R&D Manager: Mark Cooley
Eastern Regional Sales Manager: Alice Pager
Western Regional Sales Manager: Susan Turtletaub
Plant Manager: Manuel Lara
Office Manager: Crystal Snearing
Estimated Sales: $5-10 Million
Number Employees: 50-99
Type of Packaging: Consumer, Food Service

4095 **Eleni's Cookies**
75 9th Ave
New York, NY 10011-7006 212-255-6804
Fax: 212-255-8923 info@elenis.com
www.elenis.com
Cookies
Owner: Eleni Giamopulos
Estimated Sales: $300,000-500,000
Number Employees: 5-9

4096 **Elgin Dairy Foods**
3707 W Harrison St
Chicago, IL 60624-3622 773-722-7100
Fax: 773-722-3230 800-786-9900
www.elgindairy.com
Manufacturer of ice cream, frozen yogurt, dairy and nondairy whipped toppings, sour cream and dairy mixes
President: Edward Gignac
Marketing/Sales: James Gignac
Operations: John Hartline
Purchasing: Vanessa Jackson
Estimated Sales: $12 Million
Number Employees: 95
Sq. footage: 29000
Brands:
Flav'r Top
Freeze-Thaw

4097 **Eli's Bread**
1064 Madison Ave
New York, NY 10028 212-831-4800
Fax: 212-996-2611 866-354-3547
customerservice@elizabar.com
www.elizabar.com
Hearth-baked European-style breads, rolls, bagels and crisps based on traditional European recipes
Owner: Eli Zabar
Administrative Executive: Uzziah Phillips
Director Sales: Judah Zweiter
Estimated Sales: $ 5 - 10 Million
Number Employees: 100-249
Sq. footage: 15000

4098 **Eli's Cheesecake Company**
6701 W Forest Preserve Ave
Chicago, IL 60634-1405 773-736-3417
Fax: 773-736-1169 800-999-8300
sales@elicheesecake.com
www.elicheesecake.com
Manufacturer of frozen cakes including cheese and carrot
President: Marc Schulman
CEO: Jolene Worthington
CFO: Bob Monn
VP Sales: Pete Filippelli
R&D: Diana Moles
Marketing: Debbie Littmann
Public Relations: Maureen Schulman
Operations: Jolene Worthington
Purchasing: Jeff Anderson
Estimated Sales: $20-50 Million
Number Employees: 100-249
Sq. footage: 60000
Brands:
Eli's

4099 **Elite Bakery**
709 Atlantic Avenue
Rochester, NY 14609-7422 585-482-5857
Fax: 585-482-1740 877-791-7376
Manufacturer of baked goods
Sales: Kathy Ewart
Operations: Tom Quinn
Type of Packaging: Consumer, Food Service, Private Label, Bulk
Brands:
ELITE BAKERY

4100 Elite Industries
6800 Jericho Tpke
Suite 216w
Syosset, NY 11791-4488 516-682-0479
Fax: 516-921-0228 888-488-3458
laurel@eliteconfections.com
Manufacturer of confections
Type of Packaging: Private Label

4101 Elite Spice
7151 Montevideo Rd
Jessup, MD 20794 410-796-1900
Fax: 410-379-6933 800-232-3531
jbrandt@elitespice.com www.elitespice.com
Spice, seasoning, capsicum, oil & oleoresin, and dehydrated vegetable producer.
Owner/CEO: Isaac Samuel
CFO/Human Resources Director: Debbie Ingle
R&D Director: Leslie Krause
Quality Control Directory: Dave Anthony
Marketing Executive: Kathy Lyons
Sales Executive: Paul Kurpe
Operations Manager: Cathy Lion
VP/Plant Manager: George Mayer
Purchasing Manager: Margie Schneidman
Estimated Sales: $20-50 Million
Number Employees: 260
Sq. footage: 11000
Type of Packaging: Private Label

4102 Elk Cove Vineyards
27751 NW Olson Rd
Gaston, OR 97119 503-985-7760
Fax: 503-985-3525 877-355-2683
info@elkcove.com www.elkcove.com
Wines
President: Patricia Campbell
Sales Manager: Shirley Brooks
Estimated Sales: $5-10 Million
Number Employees: 10-19

4103 Elk Run Vineyards
15113 Liberty Rd
Mount Airy, MD 21771 410-775-5089
Fax: 410-875-2009 800-414-2513
elk_run@msn.com www.elkrun.com
Wines
President/Winemaker: Fred Wilson
Treasurer: Neil Bassford
Marketing Director: Carol Wilson
Estimated Sales: $1-2.5 Million
Number Employees: 1-4
Type of Packaging: Private Label
Brands:
ELK RUN

4104 Ellie's Country Delights
PO Box 1059
Wainscott, NY 11975 631-478-5200
Fax: 631-604-1076
sales@elliescountrydelights.com
www.elliescountrydelights.com
Ratatouille
President: Ellenka Baumrind

4105 Elliott Bay Baking Co.
8300 Military Road S
Seattle, WA 98108-3951 206-762-7690
Fax: 206-762-7679 paula@elliottbaybaking.com
Manufacturer of Biscotti bites, java mocha cookies, European tea biscuits
President: Paula Lukoff
Estimated Sales: $ 2.5-5 Million
Number Employees: 20-49
Brands:
Ii Biscotto Della Nonna
My Bubby's

4106 Elliott Seafood Company
53 Stevens Ln
Cushing, ME 04563 207-354-2533
Fax: 207-354-2533
Manufacturer of Seafood
President: Stan Elliott

4107 Ellis Coffee Company
2835 Bridge St
Philadelphia, PA 19137 215-537-9500
Fax: 215-534-5311 800-822-3984
www.elliscoffee.com
Coffee
President: Eugene Kestenbaum
Executive VP: Frank Parker
VP Sales/Marketing: James O'Ferrell
Estimated Sales: Less than $500,000
Number Employees: 5-9

4108 (HQ)Ellis Popcorn Company
101 Poplar St
Murray, KY 42071 270-753-5451
Fax: 270-753-7002 800-654-3358
mailto:epc@ellispopcorn.com
www.ellispopcorn.com
Manufacturer and exporter of yellow popcorn
President: Ann Kelly Ellis
Sales Manager: Dave Roberts
Fundraising Coordinator: John Youngerman
Field Supervisor: Gerald Ray
Director Customer Service: Frances Wyatt
Customer Service: Michael Sunderland
Estimated Sales: $500,000-$1 Million
Number Employees: 10-19
Type of Packaging: Consumer, Food Service, Private Label, Bulk
Brands:
BLUE RIBBON
CALLOWAY COUNTY'S BEST

4109 Ellison Bakery
P.O.Box 9087
Fort Wayne, IN 46899-9087 260-747-6136
Fax: 260-747-1954 800-711-8091
todd@ebakery.com www.ellisonbakery.com
Manufacturer of cookies, ice-cream sandwich wafers, crunch and inclusion products
Chairman: William Ellis
President: Robert Ellis
Executive VP: Richard Smith
Account Executive: David Barton
Plant Manager: David Barton
Estimated Sales: $20-50 Million
Number Employees: 50-99
Type of Packaging: Consumer, Food Service, Bulk
Brands:
ARCHWAY

4110 Ellison Milling Company
PO Box 400
Lethbridge, AB T1J 3Z2
Canada 403-328-6622
Fax: 403-327-3772 sales@ellisonmilling.com
www.ellisonmilling.com
Manufacturer and exporter of Durum Semolina, Hard and Soft Wheat Flours
President: Michael Greer
Quality Control: Paolo Santangelo
Marketing Director: Bob Grebinsky
Sales Director: Bob Grebinsky
General Manager: M Greer
Operations Manager: B McConnell
Production Manager: K Novakowski
Plant Manager: B McConnell
Purchasing Manager: B McConnell
Number Employees: 65
Parent Co: Parrish & Heimbecker
Type of Packaging: Food Service, Private Label, Bulk
Brands:
ALEBRTA
BAKER'S GOLD
DREAM
ELLISON'S
ROYAL PASTRY
U-BAKE

4111 Elliston Vineyards
463 Kilkare Rd
Sunol, CA 94586 925-862-2377
Fax: 925-862-0316 elliston@elliston.com
www.elliston.com
Wines
President: Donna Flavetta
VP: Mark Piche
Estimated Sales: $1-2.5 Million
Number Employees: 20-49
Type of Packaging: Private Label

4112 Ellsworth Cooperative Creamery
P.O.Box 610
Ellsworth, WI 54011 715-273-4311
Fax: 715-273-5318 info@eaugallecheese.com
Dairy cooperative that is a distributor or butter, cheese, whey powder, cheese curds and other dairy items.
Manager: Ken Mc Mahon
CEO/General Manager: Ken McMahon
Estimated Sales: $101,000,000
Number Employees: 50-99
Type of Packaging: Consumer, Private Label, Bulk
Brands:
Ellsworth Cheese Curds

4113 Ellsworth Foods
1510 Eastman Dr
Tifton, GA 31793 229-386-8448
Fax: 229-387-9749
Grocery products
Owner: Ken Ellsworth Jr
Estimated Sales: $ 10 - 20 Million
Number Employees: 20-49

4114 Ellsworth Locker
317 S Broadway St
Ellsworth, MN 56129 507-967-2544
Manufacturer of sausage, beef, pork and venison
Co-Owner/Treasurer: Brian Chapa
Co-Owner: Kathy Chapa
Estimated Sales: $1-2.5 Million
Number Employees: 5-9
Type of Packaging: Consumer

4115 Elm City Cheese Company
2240 State St
Hamden, CT 6517 203-865-5768
Fax: 203-865-8303
Manufacturer of grated parmesan cheese
President: Richard Weinstein
Vice President: Marge Weinstein
Estimated Sales: $1.4 Million
Number Employees: 10
Type of Packaging: Consumer

4116 Elmer Candy Corporation
401 N 5th St
Ponchatoula, LA 70454 985-386-6166
Fax: 985-386-6245 800-843-9537
www.elmerchocolate.com
Manufacturer and exporter of candy including chocolate, hard, lollypops, mints, taffy, holiday, etc.; also, nut sundae toppings
President/CEO: Robert Nelson
Controller/Secretary: Robert Barousse Jr.
VP Sales/Marketing: Roch Lemieux
Customer Development Manager: Mike Martin
Estimated Sales: $50-100 Million
Number Employees: 250-499
Type of Packaging: Consumer
Brands:
FIDDLERS
GOLD BRICK
HEAVENLY HASH
JUST NUTS
SMALL TALK CONVERSATION HEARTS
SWEET OCCASION

4117 Elmer's Fine Foods
P.O.Box 3117
New Orleans, LA 70177-3117 504-949-2716
Fax: 504-948-2537 a.elmer@worldnet.att.net
www.elmerscheewees.com
Manufacturer of snack foods including potato chips, popcorn and cheese curls
President: Allen Elmer
VP/CEO: Rob Nelson
Estimated Sales: $3-5 Million
Number Employees: 10-19
Type of Packaging: Consumer

4118 Elmwood Lockers
P.O.Box 603
Elmwood, IL 61529-0603 309-742-8929
Fax: 309-742-7071
Manufacturer of sausage jerky, beef sticks and bratwurst
Owner: John Powers
Estimated Sales: $500,000-$1 Million
Number Employees: 1-4
Type of Packaging: Consumer, Bulk
Brands:
J & J

4119 Elmwood Pastry
1136 New Britain Ave
West Hartford, CT 06110-2413 860-233-2029
Fax: 203-865-8303
Manufacturer of hard rolls, bread, doughnuts, cakes and cookies
President: Richard S Winalski Jr
Estimated Sales: $500,000-$1 Million
Number Employees: 10-19
Type of Packaging: Consumer

4120 **(HQ)Elore Enterprises**
7224 NW 25th Street
Miami, FL 33122-1701 305-477-1650
Fax: 305-477-2291 elore@bellsouth.net
www.chorizoquijote.com
Manufacturer of Spanish sausage
President: Joe Alanso
VP: Juan Alanso
Estimated Sales: $1-2.5 Million
Number Employees: 5-9
Type of Packaging: Consumer, Food Service

4121 **Elwell Farms**
1101 S. Grand Ave
Suite J
Santa Ana, CA 92705 714-546-9280
Fax: 714-546-6496 800-698-5855
www.elwellfarms.com
Manufacturer of poultry
Estimated Sales: $10-20 Million
Number Employees: 50-99
Type of Packaging: Consumer, Food Service

4122 **Elwha Fish**
801 Marine Dr
Port Angeles, WA 98363 360-457-3344
Fax: 360-457-1205 www.elwhafish.com
Manufacturer of smoked and vacuum-packed salmon including no salt salmon and albacore tuna.
Business Manager: Ed Bedford
General Manager: Ken Foster
Estimated Sales: $1 Million
Number Employees: 6
Type of Packaging: Consumer, Private Label, Bulk
Brands:
ELWHA
HEGG & HEGG
NORTHWEST

4123 **Elwood International**
89 Hudson St
Copiague, NY 11726-1505 631-842-6600
Fax: 631-842-6603 info@elwoodintl.com
www.elwoodintl.com
Manufacturer and exporter of regular and dietetic portion controlled condiments including dressings, jellies, mayonnaise, mustard, ketchup, peanut butter, table syrups, private label and contract packaging
President: Stuart Roll
Vice President: Richard Roll
Estimated Sales: $2.90 Million
Number Employees: 10-19
Number of Brands: 3
Number of Products: 40
Sq. footage: 23000
Type of Packaging: Consumer, Food Service, Private Label, Bulk
Brands:
Elwood
RENAISSANCE
Winston

4124 **Embasa FoodsMegaMex Foods, LLC**
4340 Eucalyptus Ave
Unit A
Chino, CA 91710-9705 909-631-2000
Fax: 909-631-2100 888-236-2272
www.embasa.com
Manufacturer and distributor of full line ,high quality Mexican food products: chiles, salsa and nopalitos.
President: Ted Gardner
Estimated Sales: $5-10 Million
Number Employees: 25
Parent Co: Authentic Specialty Foods
Brands:
EMBASA
LA GLORIA
PUEBLITO

4125 **Embassy Flavours Ltd.**
5 Intermodal Drive
Unit 1
Brampton, ON L6T 5V9
Canada 905-789-3200
Fax: 905-789-3201 800-334-3371
sales@embassyfoods.com
www.embassyflavours.com
Manufacturer and exporter of extracts, flavors, colors, essential oils, bases and mixes including cake, pastry and bread
President: Martino Brambilla
R&D: Anne Klingerman
National Sales/Marketing Manager: Mike Taras
Estimated Sales: $1.7 Million
Number Employees: 38
Sq. footage: 14400
Type of Packaging: Consumer, Food Service, Private Label, Bulk
Brands:
Batter-Moist
Elite
Embassy
Prairie Sun

4126 **Embassy Wine Company**
10615 Foster Avenue
Brooklyn, NY 11236-2211 718-272-0600
Fax: 718-272-7845 abe@embassywines.com
www.embassywines.com
Manufacturer, exporter and importer of kosher wines
President: William Max Bauer
VP: Eli Fink
Estimated Sales: $10-20 Million
Number Employees: 10-19

4127 **Embassy of Spain TradesCommission**
405 Lexington Ave
New York, NY 10174-0002 212-907-6481
Fax: 212-867-6055 newyork@mcx.es
www.spainbusines.com
Manufacturer of Spanish foods
President: M Sanse
VP: Jeffrey Shaw
Estimated Sales: Under $500,000
Number Employees: 20-49

4128 **Embria Health Science**
2105 SE Creekview Drive
Ankeny, IA 50021
Fax: 515-964-9004 877-362-7421
info@embriahealth.com www.embriahealth.com
Manufacturer of nutritional supplements
President: Paul Faganel
Owner: Greg Thornton
VP Finance: Dave Lusson
Regional Sales Rep: Naz Kalantari
Estimated Sales: $500,000-1 Million
Number Employees: 10-19

4129 **Emerald Performance Materials**
2020 Front Street
Cuyahoga Falls, OH 44221 330-916-6700
Fax: 330-916-6734
corporate@emeraldmaterials.com
www.emeraldmaterials.com
Manufacturer of foods additives and process aids; including dye & colors, preservatives and flavor ingredients
President/CEO: Thomas Holleran
VP/CFO: Candace Wagner
Number Employees: 500-999

4130 **Emerald Performance Materials**
2235 Langdon Farm Road
Cincinnati, OH 45237 513-841-3859
Fax: 513-841-3808
jenny.smith@emeraldmaterials.com
www.emeraldmaterials.com
Applications for the food and beverage industry.
President/CEO: Thomas Holleran
VP/CFO: Candace Wagner
Environmental/Safety Manager: Tracy Wright
Sales/Marketing Manager: Jenny Smith
VP Human Resourced: Thomas Nelson
Plant Manager: Doug Jackson

4131 **Emerald Valley Kitchen**
1528 Moffet Street
Salinas, CA 93905 831-536-62
Fax: 831-536-55 www.emeraldvalleykitchen.com
Fresh organic sauces
Owner: Mel Bankoff
Plant Manager: Ken Eldrich
Estimated Sales: $5-10 Million
Number Employees: 10-19
Type of Packaging: Private Label

EMERLING INTERNATIONAL FOODS, INC.

4132 **Emerling International Foods**
2381 Fillmore Ave
Suite 1
Buffalo, NY 14214-2197 716-833-7381
Fax: 716-833-7386 pemerling@emerfood.com
www.emerlinginternational.com

We supply food manufacturers and food service customers worldwide (since 1988) with bulk ingredients including: Fruits & Vegetables; Juice Concentrates; Herbs & Spices; Oils & Vinegars; Flavors & Colors; Honey & Molasses. We alsoproduce PURE MAPLE SYRUP.

President: J P Emerling
Sales: Peter Emerling
Public Relations: Jenn Burke
Estimated Sales: $10-20 Million
Number Employees: 20-49
Sq. footage: 250000

4133 **Emery Smith Fisheries Limited**
5309 Hwy 3
Shag Harbour, NS B0W 3B0
Canada 902-723-2115
Fax: 902-723-2372 emfish@klif.com
www.hazem@bar.auracom.com
Manufacturer and exporter of salt fish
President: Emery Smith
Estimated Sales: $12 Million
Number Employees: 25
Type of Packaging: Bulk

4134 **Emilio Guglielmo Winery**
1480 E Main Ave
Morgan Hill, CA 95037-3299 408-779-2145
Fax: 408-779-3166 info@guglielmowinery.com
www.guglielmowinery.com
Manufacturer and exporter of wines and vintner
Owner: George E Guglielmo
VP: Gene Guglielmo
VP Sales: Gary Guglielmo
Estimated Sales: $10-20 Million
Number Employees: 20-49
Type of Packaging: Consumer, Private Label, Bulk
Brands:
EMILE'S
GUFLIELMO RESERVE
GUGLIELMO
GUGLIELMO VINEYARD SELECTION

4135 **Emkay Trading Corporation**
P.O.Box 504
Elmsford, NY 10523 914-592-9000
Fax: 914-347-3616 emkay@iname.com
www.emkaytrading.org
Manufacturer and distributor of cheese including cream, bakers, neuchatel, lite, tvorog (Russian style soft cheese) and quark, also, bulk cream, custom fluid diary blends, bulk skim, sour cream, bulk cultured buttermilk and condensedskim milk
Owner: Howard Kravitz
Vice President: Ruth Kravitz
Estimated Sales: $8 Million
Number Employees: 30
Sq. footage: 200000
Type of Packaging: Consumer, Food Service, Private Label, Bulk
Brands:
Emkay

4136 **Emkay Trading Corporation**
P.O.Box 504
Elmsford, NY 10523 914-592-9000
Fax: 914-347-3616 www.emkaytrading.org
Gourmet cheese
Owner: Howard Kravitz
Estimated Sales: Less than $500,000
Number Employees: 1-4

4137 **Emmy's Candy from Belgium**
9816 Emerald Point Drive
Unit 3
Charlotte, NC 28278-6536 704-588-5445
Fax: 704-588-2729 emmy@emmyscandy.com
www.emmyscandy.com
Candies

4138 **Empire Beef & Redistribution**
171 Weidner Rd
Rochester, NY 14624 585-943-4012
Fax: 585-235-1776 800-462-6804
www.empirebeef.com
Manufacturer and exporter of fresh beef; wholesaler/distributor of fresh and frozen poultry, pork, lamb and veal
President/CEO: Steven Levine
Cfo: Bill Fehr
Vice President/Coo: Paul Meilinger
Estimated Sales: $100-500 Million
Number Employees: 100-249
Type of Packaging: Bulk

4139 **Empire Cheese**
4520 Haskell Road
Cuba, NY 14727 585-968-1552
Fax: 585-968-2660
glcinfo@greatlakescheese.com
www.greatlakescheese.com
Manufacturer mozzarella and provolone cheese
President: Hans Epprecht
CEO/President: Gary Vanic
VP Finance: Russell Mullins
VP Sales: John Sleggs
Human Resources Director: Betty Edwards
Manufacturing/Operations Director: Steve Scott
Plant Manager: Thomas Eastham
Purchasing Clerk: Shelley Williamson
Estimated Sales: $5-10 Million appx.
Number Employees: 175
Sq. footage: 100000
Parent Co: Great Lakes Cheese Company
Type of Packaging: Private Label
Other Locations:
Great Lakes Cheese of New York
Adams NY
Great Lakes Cheese of Utah
Fillmore UT
Great Lakes Cheese Company - HQ
Hiram OH
Great Lakes Cheese of La Crosse
La Crosse WI
Great Lakes Cheese of Wisconsin
Plymouth WI

4140 **Empire Foods**
2543 Lefferts Pl
Bellmore, NY 11710 516-679-1414
Fax: 516-679-1419
Manufacturer of cheese
President: Leonard Epstein
Estimated Sales: Less than $500,000
Number Employees: 1-4

4141 **Empire Kosher Foods**
Rr 5 Box 228
Mifflintown, PA 17059-9409 717-436-5921
Fax: 717-436-7070 800-367-4734
empire@acsworld.net www.empirekosher.com
Manufacturer of kosher poultry
President/CEO: Rob Van Naarden
CFO: Richard Berger
CEO: Rob Van Naarden
Rabbinic Administrator: Rabbi Israel Weiss
Director QA/Food Technology: Dr Stan Wallen
VP Sales/Marketing: Barry Rosenbaum
Director Human Resources: Jeff Brown
VP Operations: Cloyd Bowsman
Director Live Operations: Keith Flanders
Plant Manager: Mike Goguts
Director Pricing/Inventory Control: Deb Fitzpatrick
Estimated Sales: $50-100 Million
Number Employees: 1,000-4,999
Type of Packaging: Private Label
Brands:
EMPIRE KOSHER POULTRY PRODUCTS

4142 **Empire Spice Mills**
908 William Avenue
Winnipeg, NB R3E 0Z8
Canada 204-786-1594
Fax: 204-783-2847
Manufacturer and importer of flavoring extracts and whole ground and blended spices, herbs and seeds, seasonings
President: Don Ramage
Estimated Sales: $1-2.5 Million
Number Employees: 8
Sq. footage: 16000
Type of Packaging: Consumer, Food Service, Private Label, Bulk
Brands:
EMPIRE'S BEST

4143 **Empire SweetsOswego Growers and Shippers**
103 Gardenier Rd
Oswego, NY 13126-5741
Fax: 315-343-5371 www.empire-sweets.com/
Grows and distributes Empire Sweets Onions.
President: John Zappala
Vice President: Sam Zappala Jr
Vice President: Jim Zappala
Type of Packaging: Food Service

4144 **Empire Tea Services**
1965 St James Pl
Columbus, IN 47201 812-375-1937
Fax: 812-376-7382 800-790-0246
sales@empiretea.com www.empiretea.com
Importer of tea in tins, black tea, green tea, herb tea bulk tea, tea bags in wood boxes and various forms of packing
President: Lalith Guy Paranavitana
Estimated Sales: $200,000
Number Employees: 1-4
Number of Brands: 3
Number of Products: 27
Sq. footage: 2000
Type of Packaging: Consumer, Food Service, Private Label, Bulk
Brands:
GUY'S TEA
TEA TEMPTATIONS

4145 **Empresa La Famosa**
PO Box 51968
Toa Baja, PR 00950-1968 787-251-0060
Fax: 787-251-2270 www.empresalafamosa.com
Juice
VP Operations: Sandy Martin

4146 **(HQ)Empresas La Famosa/CocoLopez**
Km 12 1 865 Rr 866
Toa Baja, PR 00949 787-251-0060
Fax: 787-251-2270 mvillegas@coqui.net
www.empresaslafamosa.com
Manufacturer of fruit juices, coconut, cream & milk, beans and tomato willow
President: Jose Coripio
Plant Manager: Rosalia Prieto
Estimated Sales: $5.6 Million
Number Employees: 61
Brands:
COCO LOPEZ, USA

4147 **Empress Chocolate Company**
5518 Avenue N
Brooklyn, NY 11234 718-951-2251
Fax: 718-951-2254 800-793-3809
sales@empresschocolate.com
www.empresschocolate.com
Manufacturer and exporter of custom and stock molded chocolate novelties, cream filled chocolates, truffles and gift boxes
President: Ernie Grunhut
VP: Jack Grunhut
Estimated Sales: $5-10 Million
Number Employees: 20-49
Sq. footage: 20000
Parent Co: Ernex Corporation
Type of Packaging: Consumer, Private Label
Brands:
EMPRESS CHOCOLATES

4148 **En Garde Health Products**
P.O.Box 370097
Reseda, CA 91337-97
Fax: 818-786-4699 www.engardehealth.com
Health products
CEO: Roberta Gabor
Estimated Sales: $ 1 - 3 Million
Number Employees: 1-4

4149 **EnWave Corporation**
1066 W Hastings Street
Suite 2000
Vancouver, BC V6E 3X2
Canada 604-822-4425
Fax: 604-806-6112 tdurance@enwave.net
www.enwave.net
Dehydration of food, live or active bulk liquids, and sensitive pharmaceuticals.
President/Co-CEO: John McNicol
Chairman/Co-CEO: Tim Durance
CFO: Salvador Miranda
EVP Sales: Beenu Anand
Estimated Sales: $127 Million
Number Employees: 5
Sq. footage: 4736

4150 **Endangered Species Chocolate**
5846 W 73rd St
Indianapolis, IN 46278 317-387-4372
Fax: 317-844-4951 800-293-0160
info@chocolatebar.com www.chocolatebar.com
Processor of Gourmet Belgian chocolate, chocolate squares
CEO: Curt Meer
Director Finance: Carl Dodds
Operations: Bryan Fuller
Estimated Sales: $9 Million
Number Employees: 60
Brands:
BUG BITES
ENDANGERED SPECIES CHOCOLATE BARS

4151 **Endico Potatoes**
160 N MacQuesten Pkwy
Mount Vernon, NY 10550 914-664-1151
Fax: 914-664-9267 www.endicopotatoes.com
Frozen potato, vegetable, chicken and appetizer products.
CFO: Mike Edwards
Estimated Sales: $870,000
Number Employees: 15
Sq. footage: 10000
Type of Packaging: Consumer, Food Service

4152 **(HQ)Ener-G Foods**
P.O.Box 84487
Seattle, WA 98124 206-767-6660
Fax: 206-764-3398 800-331-5222
samiii@ener-g.com www.ener-g.com
Manufacturer and exporter of wheat and gluten-free bread, hamburger buns, cereals, cookies, pasta, mixes, etc.; also, dairy-free drinks and allergy-free foods; importer of gluten-free pasta and starches. Medical and diet foods, lowprotein foods for PKU a
President: Sam Wylde Iii
CEO: Sam Wylde III
Marketing/Sales: Jerry Colburn
Production Manager: Roger Traynor
Purchasing Manager: Sabina Melovie
Estimated Sales: $3 Milion
Number Employees: 20-49
Number of Brands: 2
Number of Products: 200
Sq. footage: 20000
Type of Packaging: Consumer, Food Service, Private Label
Brands:
ENER-G
OLD WORLD

4153 **(HQ)Energen Products**
14631 Best Ave
Norwalk, CA 90650-5258 562-926-5522
Fax: 562-921-0039 800-423-8837
www.theadlgroup.com
Manufacturer and exporter of vitamins, wheat germ oil and brewers' yeast
President: Joseph Bensler
Estimated Sales: $3 Million
Number Employees: 10-19
Number of Brands: 13
Number of Products: 250
Sq. footage: 75000
Type of Packaging: Food Service, Private Label
Brands:
AMERICAN DIETARY
REAL LIFE
THE PIERSON COMPANY
VEGETRATES

4154 **Energenetics International**
P.O.Box 845
Keokuk, IA 52632 217-453-2340
Fax: 217-453-6759 egi@adams.net
www.energeneticsusa.com
Manufacturer of corn-based protein
President: Sammy Pierce
Number Employees: 5-9

4155 **Energique**
201 Apple Blvd
Woodbine, IA 51579 712-647-2499
Fax: 712-647-2588 800-869-8078
jesse@energiqueherbal.com
www.energiqueherbal.com
Manufacturer of liquefied herbal extracts
President: Jesse Rettig
Estimated Sales: $ 3 - 5 Million
Number Employees: 10-19
Type of Packaging: Private Label, Bulk
Brands:
ENERGIQUE®

4156 **Energy Brands/Haute Source**
1720 Whitestone Expy
Flushing, NY 11357-3000 718-746-0087
Fax: 718-747-5900 800-746-0087
ebi@energybrands.com www.energybrands.com
Manufacturer of distilled water
President/CEO: J Darius Bikoff
CEO: Darius Bitkoff
Estimated Sales: Less than $500,000
Number Employees: 1-4
Type of Packaging: Consumer, Food Service
Brands:
FRUIT WATER
GLACEAU VITAMINWATER
GO-GO DRINKS
SMART WATER
SOY WATER
VITAMIN WATER

4157 **Energy Club**
12950 Pierce St
Pacoima, CA 91331 818-834-8222
Fax: 818-834-8218 800-688-6887
eclub@energyclub.com www.eclub.com
Hispanic snacks, candy, nuts, stoys, trail mix extra large packages, salty snacks, beef jerky, accessories and supplies
President: Arnold Zane
VP: Miron Aviv
National Sales Manager: Vincent Guiliano
Estimated Sales: $5-10 Million
Number Employees: 100-249
Number of Products: 300
Sq. footage: 50000
Type of Packaging: Consumer, Private Label

4158 **Enfield Farms**
1064 Birch Bay Lynden Rd
Lynden, WA 98264 360-354-3019
Fax: 360-354-0503 info@enfieldfarms.com
www.enfieldfarms.com
Manufacturer and packer of frozen red raspberries and blueberries
Owner: Marv Enfield
President: Adam Enfield
Human Resources/Finance Executive: Mike Haveman
Plant Manager: Andy Enfield
Estimated Sales: $50-100 Million
Number Employees: 16
Sq. footage: 4361
Type of Packaging: Food Service, Private Label, Bulk
Brands:
ENFIELD FARMS

4159 **Engel's Bakeries**
4709 14 Street NE
Bay 6
Calgary, AB T2E 6S4
Canada 403-250-9560
Fax: 403-250-5381 engelbak@telus.net
www.engelsbakeriesltd.ca
Manufacturer of baked and frozen ready-to-bake products including breads, pastries, sausage rolls, cakes, etc
President: Mithoo Gillani
R&D: Brian Hinton
Marketing/Sales: Ron Clappison
Sales Manager: Aaron Goss
Production Manager: Greg Zub
Purchasing: Danoz McKinnon
Estimated Sales: D
Number Employees: 50-99
Sq. footage: 16000
Type of Packaging: Food Service

4160 **English Bay Batter**
2241 Citygate Dr
Columbus, OH 43219-3564 614-471-9994
Manufacturer of frozen batter and baked goods
Manager: Dan Rudd
Estimated Sales: $ 5 - 10 Million
Number Employees: 5-9
Parent Co: English Bay Batter
Type of Packaging: Consumer, Food Service, Private Label, Bulk
Brands:
ENGLISH BATTER

4161 **Enjoy Foods International**
10601 Beech Ave
Fontana, CA 92337 909-823-2228
Fax: 909-355-1573 info@EnjoyBeefJerky.com
www.enjoybeefjerky.com
Manufacturer and exporter of beef and turkey jerky and meat snacks; exporter of steak kabobs
Chairman: Waleed Saab
VP: Saadi Kabab
Plant Manager: Dennis Quinzon
Estimated Sales: $6.3 Million
Number Employees: 40
Sq. footage: 10146
Type of Packaging: Consumer

4162 **Enjoy Life Foods**
3810 River Road
Schiller Park, IL 60176-2307 847-260-0300
888-503-6569
kklippenstein@enjoylifefoods.com
www.enjoylifefoods.com
Gluten-free cookies, snacks, granola and bagels.
President: Federico Meade
Founder/CEO: Scott Mandell
CFO: Bert Cohen
Senior Manager of R&D/Innovation: Lindsey Herman
Quality Assurance Director: Sandy Kasten
Chief Marketing Officer: Joel Warady
Senior Director of Sales: Patricia Marko
Operations Manager: Marvin Rea
Estimated Sales: $6 Million
Number Employees: 50
Sq. footage: 30000
Parent Co: Enjoy Life Natural Brands, LLC

4163 **Ennio International**
1005 N. Commons Drive
Aurora, IL 60504-4100 630-355-1655
Fax: 630-851-7744 info@enniousa.com
www.enniousa.com
Manufacturer and supplier of high quality netting and casings for the meat and poultry industries.
Director Of Sales: Ralph Schuster

4164 **Enon Valley Cheese Compay**
1671 State Route 351
Enon Valley, PA 16120-3435 724-336-5207
Fax: 724-336-1200
Manufacturer of Swiss cheese
Owner: Thomas Bussers
Estimated Sales: $5-9.9 Million
Number Employees: 1-4
Type of Packaging: Bulk

4165 **Enray, Inc**
4569 Las Politas Road
Suite D
Livermore, CA 94551 925-218-2205
Fax: 925-365-0587 info@enray.com
www.truroots.com
Full-line grains, cereal and pasta.
Marketing: Esha Ray

4166 **Enrico's/Ventre Packing**
6050 Court Street Rd
Syracuse, NY 13206-1711 315-463-2384
Fax: 315-463-5897 888-472-8237
enrico@enricos-ventre.com www.ventre.com
Sauces and salsas.
President: Marty Ventre
Manager Quality Control: Kurt Alpha
Eastern Regional Sales Manager: Rick Alesia
Estimated Sales: $ 10 - 20 Million
Number Employees: 10-19

4167 **Ensemble Beverages**
600 S Court Street
Suite 460
Montgomery, AL 36104-4106 334-324-7719
www.ensemblebeverage.com
Manufacturer, importer and exporter of beverages including carbonated, sports drinks, nutritional shakes, iced tea and powders
President: James Harris
CFO: Cornelius Blanding, Jr
Number Employees: 10-19

4168 **Enslin & Son Packing Company**
2500 Glendale Ave
Hattiesburg, MS 39401 601-582-9300
Fax: 601-544-2010 800-898-4687
www.enslin.com
Manufacturer, packer and wholesaler/distributor of sausage
President: August Enslin
Estimated Sales: $4 Million
Number Employees: 30
Sq. footage: 8000
Type of Packaging: Consumer, Private Label, Bulk
Brands:
BOWIE RIVER
COUNTRY MORNING
GLENDALE
HICKORY

4169 **(HQ)Enstrom Candies**
P.O.Box 1088
Grand Junction, CO 81502 970-242-1655
Fax: 970-245-7727 800-367-8766
candy@enstrom.com www.enstrom.com
Manufactures and sells confectionery products including almond toffee, chocolates, brittles and fudges
President: Douglas Simons
Secretary/Treasurer: Jamee Enstorm Simons
Estimated Sales: $7 Million
Number Employees: 100-249
Number of Brands: 1
Sq. footage: 19360
Parent Co: Enstrom Candies
Type of Packaging: Consumer
Other Locations:
Enstrom Candies
Denver CO
Brands:
DENVER CO
ENSTROM CANDIES

4170 **Entenmann's-Oroweat/BestFoods**
264 S Spruce Ave
South San Francisco, CA 94080 650-583-5828
Fax: 650-875-3140
Manufacturer of whole grain bread, pizza dough and frozen bagels.
Director Sales: Jack Neugebaurer
General Manager: Noel Corpus
General Manager: Thad Mikols
Estimated Sales: $50-100 Million
Number Employees: 250-499
Sq. footage: 100000
Parent Co: Unilever USA
Type of Packaging: Consumer, Food Service

4171 **Enterprise Foods**
5315 Tulane Dr SW Ste D
Atlanta, GA 30336 404-351-2251
Fax: 404-351-3969
Wholesale bakery ingredients and emulsifiers, dough conditioners, bromate replacers
President: Gerald Anderson
Estimated Sales: $1 Million
Number Employees: 10-19
Number of Brands: 1
Number of Products: 10
Sq. footage: 75000
Type of Packaging: Bulk

Brands:
ENTERPRISE
SIP
ZEELANCO

4172 **Enterprises Pates et Croutes**
14 Rue De Montgolfier
Boucherville, QC J4B 7Y4
Canada 450-655-7790
Fax: 450-655-8037 info@patesetcoutes.com
Manufacturer and exporter of frozen pie dough and shells; processor of baked muffins,bakery products,pastry products,and food product machinery.
President: Francine Benoit
Estimated Sales: 3.8 Million
Number Employees: 40
Type of Packaging: Consumer, Food Service

4173 **Entner-Stuart Premium Syrups**
1852 Fescue St SE
Albany, OR 97322-7075 541-812-8000
Fax: 541-812-8010 800-926-6886
info@enterstuartsyrups.com
www.allannbroscoffee.com
Tea and coffee syrups
President/CEO: Allan Stuart
Estimated Sales: $ 5 - 10 Million
Number Employees: 10-19

4174 **EnviroPAK Corporation**
4203 Shoreline Dr
Earth City, MO 63045 314-739-1202
Fax: 314-739-2422 sales@enviropak.com
www.enviropak.com
Manufacturer of pulp packaging for numerous industries including that of food and beverage.
President: John Wichlenski
Accounting Manager: Stacey Bealke
Design: Mike Lembeck
Vice President Sales & Marketing: Bill Noble
Sales & Marketing Administrator: Kim Bryant
Vice President Manufacturing: Rodney Heenan
Sq. footage: 20000

4175 **Enway/Northwood**
16940 SE 130th Avenue
Clackamas, OR 97015-8945 503-657-9334
Fax: 503-657-9346 www.enway.com
Potatoes
President: Neal Pearson
Sales Manager: William Miller
Plant Manager: Steven Gersch
Estimated Sales: $5-9.9 Million
Number Employees: 50-99
Brands:
ENWAY POTATOES

4176 **Enz Vineyards**
1781 Limekiln Rd
Hollister, CA 95023 831-637-3956
Fax: 831-637-9382
Manufacturer of Wine
President: Robert Enz
Estimated Sales: $500,000-$1 Million
Number Employees: 1-4

4177 **Enzymatic Therapy**
825 Challenger Dr
Green Bay, WI 54311 800-558-7372
Fax: 920-469-4400 800-783-2286
etmail@enzy.com www.enzy.com
Nutritional supplements
President/CEO: Randy Rose
CEO: Randy Rose
CFO: Mike Devereux
VP Scientific Affairs: Bob Doster
Quality Control: Bob Doster
SVP: Matt Schueller
Sales Director: Mike Devereux
Public Relations: Toni Weiss
Operations SVP: Cathy Stone
Production SVP: Cathy Stone
Plant Manager: Tom Krojewski
Purchasing Manager: Greg Kolarik
Estimated Sales: $ 50 - 100 Million
Number Employees: 250-499
Number of Products: 350
Type of Packaging: Consumer, Private Label

4178 **Enzyme Development Corporation**
360 W 31st St
New York, NY 10001-2833 212-736-1580
Fax: 212-279-0056
info@enzymedevelopment.com
www.enzymedevelopment.com
Manufacturer, importer and exporter of industrial and specialty enzymes
President: Phillip Nelson
Marketing/Sales: C Peter Moodie
Estimated Sales: $ 20 - 50 Million
Number Employees: 20-49
Type of Packaging: Bulk
Brands:
ASPERZYME
ENZECO
LIQUIPANOL
PANOL

4179 **Enzyme Formulations**
6421 Enterprise Ln
Madison, WI 53719 608-273-8100
Fax: 608-273-8111 800-614-4400
info@loomisenzymes.com
www.naturalenzymes.com
Supplements
President: Howard Loomis

4180 **Eola Hills Wine Cellars**
501 S Pacific Hwy W
Rickreall, OR 97371 503-623-2405
Fax: 503-623-0350 800-291-6730
www.eolahillswinery.com
Wines
President: Tom Huggins
CEO: Eric Rogers
CFO: Cherie Haines
Estimated Sales: $4 Million
Number Employees: 25

4181 **Eola Specialty Foods**
3213 Waconda Rd NE
Gervais, OR 97026-9709 503-390-1425
Fax: 503-390-9526
codybell@eolaspecialtyfoods.com
www.eolacherry.com
A food processor, manufacturer specialized in co-packing
President: Craig Bell
CFO: Paul Leipzig
Marketing Director: Cody Bell
VP Sales: Doug Zibell
Plant Manager: Monica Guzman
Estimated Sales: $65,000
Number Employees: 20-49
Parent Co: Bell Farms
Type of Packaging: Consumer, Food Service, Private Label, Bulk
Brands:
EOLA

4182 **Epi De France Bakery**
1757 Tullie Cir NE
Atlanta, GA 30329 404-325-1016
Fax: 404-325-0735 800-325-1014
info@epibreads.com www.epibreads.com
Manufacturer and exporter of fresh and frozen bread; importer of machinery
President: Nic Mulliez
Estimated Sales: $20-50 Million
Sq. footage: 42500
Type of Packaging: Consumer, Food Service, Private Label, Bulk
Brands:
Epi De France
Graines De Vie

4183 **EpicCure Princess of Yum**
PO Box 1202
San Luis Obispo, CA 93406-1202 805-466-3655
Fax: 805-466-3642 info@princessofyum.com
www.princessofyum.com
Manufactuter of Naturally flavored sugars

4184 **(HQ)Epicurean Butter**
9355 Elm Court
Federal Heights, CO 80260 720-261-8175
Fax: 303-254-5381 epicureanbutter@msn.com
ww.epicureanbutter.com
compound butters, both sweet and savory.
President/Owner: John Hubschman
VP: Janey Hubschman
Estimated Sales: $6.4 Million
Number Employees: 12

4185 **Equal Exchange**
50 United Dr
West Bridgewater, MA 02379 774-776-7400
Fax: 508-587-0088 kevans@equalexchange.coop
www.equalexchange.coop
Cooperative providing traded organic coffees
President: Rink Dickinson
Marketing: Bruce McKinnon
Sales: Mark Sweet
Director Operations: Mark Souza
Purchasing: Rob Everts
Estimated Sales: $20-50 Million
Number Employees: 50-99
Sq. footage: 10000
Type of Packaging: Bulk

4186 **Equinox Enterprises**
22040 Twp Road 520
Suite 101
Sherwood Park, AB T8E 1E7 780-922-5170
Fax: 780-922-4909 888-378-7364
Cereals, wheat, barley etc
Owner: Velma McKinney
Estimated Sales: $30 Million
Number Employees: 10-19
Type of Packaging: Private Label

4187 **Equity Group**
P.O.Box 1436
Reidsville, NC 27323-1436 336-342-6601
Fax: 336-349-2940
Manufacturer of chicken products including prepared, frozen, patties and nuggets
Manager: Tom Harris
Plant Manager: Kaylan Adams
Estimated Sales: $50-100 Million
Number Employees: 250-499
Parent Co: Keystone Food Corporation
Type of Packaging: Food Service

4188 **Erath Vineyards Winery**
9409 NE Worden Hill Rd
Dundee, OR 97115 503-538-3318
Fax: 503-538-1074 800-539-5463
info@erath.com www.erath.com
Wines
Owner/President: Dick Erath
Accounting Manager: Doug Moe
Marketing/Sales Manager: Steve Vuylsteke
Estimated Sales: $5-10 Million
Number Employees: 20-49
Number of Brands: 1
Number of Products: 1
Type of Packaging: Private Label, Bulk

4189 **(HQ)Erba Food Products**
2550 E New York Ave
Brooklyn, NY 11207-2323 718-272-7700
Fax: 718-272-7711 sales@haddar.com
Manufacturer, importer and exporter of kosher foods including vegetables, juices, coffee, spices, seasonings, baked goods, fruits, condiments, fish, nuts, oils, etc
Manager: Heeren Patel
VP of Marketing: Abraham Perkowski
Sales: Jen O'Connor
Number Employees: 10-19
Type of Packaging: Consumer, Food Service
Brands:
EMBASSY WINES
HADDAR

4190 **(HQ)Erie Foods International**
401 7th Ave
PO Box 648
Erie, IL 61250 309-659-2233
Fax: 309-659-2822 800-447-1887
glindsy@eriefoods.com www.eriefoods.com
Manufacturer and exporter of co-dried and concentrated milk proteins; also sodium, calcium, combination and acid-stable caseinates and dairy blends; importer of milk proteins
President/CEO: David Reisenbigler
CFO: Mark Delaney
Executive VP: Jim Klein
Research & Development: Craig Air
Quality Control: Jo Air
Marketing Director: Ryan Tranel
Operations Manager: Jim Jacoby
Production Manager: Jim Jacoby
Plant Manager: Jim Naftzgak
Purchasing Manager: Shawn Larson

Estimated Sales: $1-2.5 Million
Sq. footage: 30000
Parent Co: Erie Foods International Inc
Type of Packaging: Bulk
Other Locations:
Erie Foods International
Beenleigh QLD
Brands:
ECCO
ERIE
PRO-GIM

4191 **Erivan Dairy**
105 Allison Rd
Oreland, PA 19075 215-887-2009
Fax: 215-885-3679
Manufacturer of yogurt
President: Harry Fereshetian
Plant Manager: Paul Fereshetian
Estimated Sales: $1-2.5 Million
Number Employees: 20-49
Type of Packaging: Consumer

4192 **Errol Cajun Foods**
6801 Highway 1001
Belle Rose, LA 70341- 225-746-1002
Fax: 225-746-1004 errolscajunfoods.com
Manufacturer of stuffed and frozen jalapeno peppers and value added seafood products including crab and shrimp; also, seafood gumbo and shrimp etouffee and patties
Owner: Errol Perera
Estimated Sales: $2.5-5 Million
Number Employees: 5-9
Type of Packaging: Consumer, Food Service

4193 **Ervan Guttman Company**
8208 Blue Ash Rd
Cincinnati, OH 45236-1997 513-791-0767
Fax: 513-891-0559 800-203-9213
hguttman@fuse.net
theervanguttmancompany.com
Manufacturer and exporter of candy making equipment and supplies including release papers and flavorings
Owner: Harold Guttman
Estimated Sales: $500,000-1 Million
Number Employees: 1-4
Sq. footage: 1000
Type of Packaging: Bulk

4194 **Escalade**
37 West Shore Road
Huntington, NY 11743 631-659-3374
Fax: 631-659-3376 latitudeltd@aol.com
www.escalade-latitude.com
Ingredients and additives, including anti-oxidants, preservatives, sweeteners and minerals
President: Lourel Mandel
Estimated Sales: $500,000- 1 Million
Number Employees: 8

4195 **Escalade Ltd**
37 W Shore Road
Huntington, NY 11743 631-659-3374
Fax: 631-659-3376 latitudeltd@aol.com
www.escalade-latitude.com
Sweeteners, vitamins, antioxidants, preservatives
President: Dedi Avner
President/VP: Lourel Mandel
Estimated Sales: $830,000
Number Employees: 8
Sq. footage: 1500

4196 **Escalon Premier Brand**
1905 McHenry Ave
Escalon, CA 95320 209-838-7341
Fax: 209-838-6206 www.escalon.net
Manufacturer of canned tomatoes and tomato products including sauces
Controller: Steve Kelly
Human Resource Executive: Susan McCready
Product Manager: Dan Milazzo
Plant Manager: John Raggio
Purchasing Agent: Tom Muller
Number Employees: 100-249
Parent Co: Heinz USA
Type of Packaging: Consumer, Food Service
Brands:
6-in-1
BELL 'ORTO
BELLA ROSA
CHRISTINA'S ORGANIC
HENIZ
MAMA LINDA

4197 **Eschete's Seafood**
229 New Orleans Blvd
Houma, LA 70364-3345 985-872-4120
Fax: 504-851-6147
Seafood
Owner: John Eschete
Estimated Sales: $300,000-500,000
Number Employees: 1-4

4198 **(HQ)Esco Foods**
131 Russ St
San Francisco, CA 94103-4009 415-864-2147
Fax: 415-822-2969
Manufacturer of syrups, toppings, salad dressings, marinades, bbq sauce, flavors
President: Marc Bosschart
Estimated Sales: $2.5-5 Million
Number Employees: 15

4199 **Eskimo Candy**
2665 Wai Wai Pl
Kihei, HI 96753 808-879-5686
Fax: 808-874-0504 eskimo@maui.net
www.eskimocandy.com
Seafood and other fine foods.
President: Jeffrey Hansen
Estimated Sales: $ 10 - 20 Million
Number Employees: 20-49

4200 **(HQ)Esper Products DeLuxe**
2793 N Orange Blossom Trl
Kissimmee, FL 34744-1375 407-847-3726
800-268-0892
colleen1014@webtv.com
Jellies and preserves
President: Andrew McFarland
Estimated Sales: $2.5-5 Million
Number Employees: 5-9
Brands:
ESPER DELUXE

4201 **Espresso Vivace**
901 E Denny Way Ste 100
Seattle, WA 98122 206-860-2722
Fax: 206-860-1567 vivace@speakeasy.net
www.espressovivace.com
Coffee
President: David Schomer
Estimated Sales: $1-2.5 Million
Number Employees: 20-49

4202 **Espro Manufacturing**
2800 Ayers Avenue
Vernon, CA 90058 323-415-8544
Fax: 323-268-4060 jernster@expromfg.com
www.expromfg.com
Manufacturer and packager of food ingredients, including custom dry powder blends.

4203 **Essen Nutrition**
1414 Sherman Rd
Romeoville, IL 60446 630-739-6700
Fax: 630-739-6464 essen@essen-nutrition.com
www.essen-nutrition.com
Dietary and health foods
President: Madhavan Anirudhan
Vice President: Mike Holland
VP Operations: Tom Grandys
Estimated Sales: $4 Million
Number Employees: 20
Type of Packaging: Private Label

4204 **Essentia Water**
22833 Bthell Everett Hwy
Suite 220
Bothell, WA 98021 425-402-9555
www.essentiawater.com
Purifying drinking water
President: Ken Uptain
CFO: Keith Huetson
Estimated Sales: $2 Million
Number Employees: 1-4

4205 **Essential Flavors & Fragrances, Inc**
1521 Commerce St
Corona, CA 92880 951-737-3889
Fax: 951-737-4237 888-333-9935
www.essentialflavors.com
Manufacturer of drink based concentrates, flavorings, herbal extracts and body building formulas
President: Michael Gulan
Vice President: Richard Staley
Office Manager: Susan Wakeling
Estimated Sales: $630,000
Number Employees: 4
Type of Packaging: Bulk

4206 **Essential Nutrients**
PO Box 5183
Cerritos, CA 90703-5183 562-407-5457
Fax: 562-407-5458 800-767-8585
www.superkmh.com
Deal in nutrients
President: Randy Haringa
Vice President: Vicki Heringa
Estimated Sales: $58,000
Number Employees: 1-4
Type of Packaging: Private Label
Brands:
Super Kmh

4207 **Essential Products of America**
6710 Benjamin Road
Suite 700
Tampa, FL 33634-4314 813-886-9698
Fax: 813-886-9661 800-822-9698
info@aromatherapyproducts.info
www.aromatherapyproducts.info
Manufacturer, importer and exporter of essential oils
President: Michael Alexander
Sales Manager: Michael Alexander
Estimated Sales: $2.5-5 Million
Number Employees: 5
Sq. footage: 1200
Type of Packaging: Consumer, Private Label, Bulk
Brands:
WHOLE SPECTRUM

4208 **Essiac Canada International**
164 Richmond Rd
Ottawa, ON K1Z 6W2 613-729-9111
Fax: 613-729-9555 maloney@essiac-canada.com
www.essiaccanadainternational.com
Manufacturer and exporter of herbal dietary supplements
President: Terrence Maloney
Estimated Sales: $975,000
Number Employees: 6
Number of Brands: 2
Number of Products: 2
Parent Co: Essiac Canada International
Type of Packaging: Consumer, Food Service
Brands:
ESSIAC (EXTRACT)
ESSIAC (POWDER)

4209 **Esteem Products**
1800 136th Pl NE Ste 5
Bellevue, WA 98005 425-562-1281
Fax: 425-562-1284 800-255-7631
amy@esteemproducts.com
www.esteemproducts.com
Manufacturer, wholesaler/distributor and exporter of nutritional supplements and specialty vitamins. All combination formulas for consumer simplicity
CEO/President: John Sheaffer
VP: Linda Sheaffer
Marketing: Amy Braisford
Estimated Sales: $500,000-$1 Million
Number Employees: 5-9
Sq. footage: 5000
Brands:
ARTHO LIFE
CARDIO LIFE
ESTEEM PLUS
GOLDEN LIFE
IMMUNE LIFE
SUPER LIFE
TOTAL MAN
TOTAL WOMAN
TRIM & FIRM AM/PM

4210 **Esterlina Vineyard & Winery**
P.O.Box 2
Philo, CA 95466-0002 707-895-2920
Fax: 707-895-2972 info@esterlinavineyards.com
www.esterlinavineyards.com
Wines
President: Craig Sterling
CEO: Eric Sterling
Marketing Manager: Steve Sterling

Estimated Sales: Under $500,000
Number Employees: 5-9
Brands:
Esterlina

4211 **Esther Price Candies & Gifts**
269 N Main St
Dayton, OH 45410 937-433-2535
Fax: 937-253-6034 800-782-0326
www.estherprice.com
Chocolates
President: James Day
Manager: Barb Dressman
Estimated Sales: Under $500,000
Number Employees: 5-9
Type of Packaging: Consumer, Private Label

4212 **Ethical Naturals**
330 H Sir Francis Drake Blvd
San Anselmo, CA 94960 415-459-4454
info@ethicalnaturals.com
www.ethicalnaturals.com
Manufacturers natural ingredients and flavors
President: Cal Bewicke
Estimated Sales: Under $500,000
Number Employees: 1

4213 **Ethnic Edibles**
2186 5th Avenue
Apt 17a
New York, NY 10037-2720 718-320-0147
Fax: 718-320-0147 ethnicedibles@aol.com
www.ethnicedibles.com
Cookies and cookie cutters with African and Puerto Rico themes
President: Heather McCartney
Brands:
COQUI COOKIES
ETHNIC EDIBLES

4214 **Ethnic Gourmet Foods**
700 Old Fern Hill Rd
West Chester, PA 19380 610-692-7575
Fax: 610-719-6399
Manufacturer of frozen gourmet foods
Manager: Richard Alexander
Estimated Sales: $20 Million
Number Employees: 50-99
Parent Co: Heinz Frozen Foods Company

4215 **Etna Brewing Company**
P.O.Box 757
Etna, CA 96027 530-467-5277
Fax: 530-567-3083 www.etnabrew.com
Manufacturer of Beer
Owner: Dave Krell
Brewer: Luke Hurlimann
Estimated Sales: $500,000-$1 Million
Number Employees: 10-19
Brands:
DARK LAGER
ETNA ALE
ETNA BOCK
ETNA DOPPELBOCK
ETNA OKTOBERFEST
ETNA WEIZEN
EXPORT LAGER

4216 **(HQ)Ettlinger Corporation**
175 Olde Half Day Rd Ste 247
Lincolnshire, IL 60069 847-564-5020
Fax: 847-564-0802
Manufacturer of cereal grains, barley & wheat, reduced lactose whey
President: Edward Ettlinger
Estimated Sales: $1-2.5 Million
Number Employees: 5-9
Type of Packaging: Food Service, Bulk

4217 **Euphoria Chocolate Company**
4080 Stewart Rd
Eugene, OR 97402 541-344-4914
Fax: 541-344-5223 www.euphoriachocolate.com
Chocolate truffles, trail mix
President/CEO: Bob Bury
Estimated Sales: Less than $500,000
Number Employees: 1-4

4218 **Eureka Lockers**
P.O.Box 194
Eureka, IL 61530-0194 309-467-2731
Fax: 309-467-2731
Manufacturer of beef, pork and lamb
President: Scott Bittner
Estimated Sales: $500,000-$1 Million
Number Employees: 1-4
Type of Packaging: Consumer

4219 **Eureka Water Company**
729 S W Third Street
Oklahoma City, OK 73109 405-235-8474
Fax: 405-235-6344 800-310-8474
info@ozarkah2o.com www.ozarkah2o.com
Manufacturer of bottled water
President/CEO: Steve Raupe
Plant Manager: Robert DeShazo
Estimated Sales: $5-10 Million
Number Employees: 50-99
Type of Packaging: Consumer, Private Label, Bulk
Brands:
MOUNTAIN VALLEY
OZARKA
SHAMROCK

4220 **Euro Chocolate Fountain**
2647 Ariane Dr
San Diego, CA 92117-3422 858-270-9863
Fax: 858-270-6801 800-423-9303
info@eurochocolate.com
www.eurochocolatefountain.com
Bakery products, chocolate confections and specialty baking
Owner: Urs Huwyler
VP: Don Rein
Estimated Sales: Below $ 5 Million
Number Employees: 1-4
Brands:
Euro Chocolate

4221 **Euro Source Gourmet**
220 Little Falls Road
Unit 2
Cedar Grove, NJ 07009-1255 973-857-6000
Fax: 973-857-8862 tjvambass@aol.com
www.eurosourcegourmet.net
Gourmet foods
Owner: Thomas Calvaruso
Sales: Janka Delatte

4222 **EuroAm**
1302 S 293rd Place
Federal Way, WA 98003-3756 253-839-5240
Fax: 253-839-4171 888-839-2702
euroaminc1@aol.com www.scorpa.com
Coffee
President: Vito Rizzo
VP: Anita Goransson
Estimated Sales: $270,000
Number Employees: 2
Number of Brands: 10
Number of Products: 20
Sq. footage: 1800
Parent Co: Euro Am Imports

4223 **Eurobubblies**
13440 Ventura Blvd
Sherman Oaks, CA 91423 818-990-5510
800-273-0750
info@eurobubblies.com www.eurobubblies.com
Beverage and food products from Europe
President: Pascal Benichou
Estimated Sales: Under $500,000
Number Employees: 5-9
Type of Packaging: Consumer, Food Service, Private Label, Bulk
Brands:
BASILIC PISTOU
BEL NORMANDE - SPRITZERS
CLOS NORMAND
DUPONT D'ISIGNY - CANDIES
EAT NATURAL
EFFERVE
EUROBUBBLIES
EUROSUPREME
HARRGATE
HOBGOBLIN - BEER
JOKER - FRUIT JUICE
LORINA - LEMONADE
PAMPRYL
PRIMEL
SEASONING SALT
SIRACUSE
SPOONTY
ST PETER'S
TERRAFOOD
WYCHWOOD

4224 **Eurocaribe Packing Company**
P.O.Box 4435
Vega Baja, PR 694-4435
Fax: 787-752-8983 europak@coqui.net
Manufacturer of smoked meats
President: Jose Casanova
CFO: John Erickson
Purchasing: Hiram Morales
Estimated Sales: $10-20 Million
Number Employees: 100-249
Type of Packaging: Private Label, Bulk
Other Locations:
Zona Industrial
Carolina PR

4225 **Europa Foods**
400 Lyster Avenue
Saddle Brook, NJ 07663-5910 201-368-8929
Fax: 201-368-2065
Manufacturer of baked products, sauces, mustard
President: Larry LaPane
Estimated Sales: $5-10 Million
Number Employees: 10-19
Type of Packaging: Private Label
Brands:
Barral
China's Secret
DEA
Duke of Modena
Gawler Park
Haudecoeur
Louis Regis
Pyett
Saslins
Toastalettes
Valade
Viniberra
Viniberra

4226 **Europa Sports Products**
11401 Granite St Ste H
Charlotte, NC 28273 704-525-0792
Fax: 704-405-2025 800-447-4795
info@eurosports.com www.europasports.com
Sports foods
Owner: Eric Hillman
Estimated Sales: $ 50 - 100 Million
Number Employees: 50-99

4227 **European Bakers**
5055 S Royal Atlanta Dr
Tucker, GA 30084 770-723-6180
Fax: 770-939-6632
Manufacturer of baked goods including breads and buns
President: James Allen
Estimated Sales: $10-20 Million
Number Employees: 100-249
Sq. footage: 130000
Parent Co: Flowers Baking Company
Type of Packaging: Consumer

4228 **European Coffee**
1401 Berlin Rd
Cherry Hill, NJ 08034-1402 856-428-7202
Fax: 856-428-7262 www.melitta.com
Manufacturer of Coffee
President/CEO: H Radtke
VP: John Masters
Plant Manager: Vincent Tagliaferro
Estimated Sales: $5-10 Million
Number Employees: 20-49
Brands:
FRAC-PACKS

4229 **European Egg Noodle Manufacturing**
14815 Yellowhead Trail Nw
Edmonton, AB T5L 3C4
Canada 780-453-6767
Fax: 780-453-6769 pastatime@sprint.ca
Manufacturer of frozen pastas, sauces, sausages and pizzas
President/Sales: Fausto Chinellato
Operations: Dorothy Chinellato
Estimated Sales: $743,000
Number Employees: 5
Type of Packaging: Consumer
Brands:
BELLA FESTA
PASTA TIME

4230 **European Roasterie**
250 W Bradshaw St
Le Center, MN 56057-1121 507-357-2272
Fax: 507-357-4478 888-469-2233
sales@euroroast.comom www.euroroast.com
Coffee
President/CEO: Timothy Tulloch
Sales: Cindy Dorzinski
Operations: Thomas Dotray
Estimated Sales: $20-50 Million
Number Employees: 20-49
Type of Packaging: Private Label

4231 **European Style Bakery**
112 N Hamilton Drive
Unit 107
Beverly Hills, CA 90211-2279 818-368-6876
Manufacturer of blueberry filling, cakes and bakery items
President: Vladimir Landa
Estimated Sales: Less than $500,000
Number Employees: 5-9

4232 **Eva Gates Homemade Preserves**
456 Electric Ave
Bigfork, MT 59911 406-837-4356
Fax: 406-837-4376 800-682-4283
evagates@digisys.net www.evagates.com
Fruit preserves and fruit syrups
President: Gretchen Gates
Estimated Sales: $2.5-5 Million
Number Employees: 10-19
Type of Packaging: Private Label

4233 **Evan's Food Products**
4118 S Halsted St
Chicago, IL 60609-2612 773-254-7400
Fax: 773-254-7791 www.evansfood.com
Manufacturer of low carb snacks
President: Alex Silva
Number Employees: 100-249

4234 **Evans Bakery**
P.O.Box 284
Cozad, NE 69130-0284 308-784-2409
Fax: 308-784-3630 800-222-5641
e_bakery@cozadtel.net
Manufacturer of frozen breads, rolls, cakes, cookies, buns and bagels
Manager: Jerry Armagost
Estimated Sales: $10-20 Million
Number Employees: 50-99

4235 **Evans Creole Candy Company**
848 Decatur St
New Orleans, LA 70116 504-522-7111
Fax: 504-522-7113 800-637-6675
www.evanscreolecandy.com
Praline, chocolate candy and syrup
President: Hope Cuccia
Estimated Sales: $1-2.5 Million
Number Employees: 5-9
Type of Packaging: Bulk

4236 **Evans Food Products Company**
4118 S Halsted St
Chicago, IL 60609 773-254-7400
Fax: 773-254-7791 866-254-7400
sales@evansfood.com www.evansfood.com
Manufacturer and exporter of rendered pork rinds
Owner: Alex Silva
President: Jim Speakes
Operations Manager: Humberto Iniguez
Purchasing: Ed McKenna
Estimated Sales: $20-50 Million
Number Employees: 100
Sq. footage: 104000
Type of Packaging: Consumer

4237 **Evans Properties**
12833 Us Highway 301
Dade City, FL 33525-5812 352-567-5662
Fax: 352-567-3683
Frozen citrus juices
President: James Evans
Estimated Sales: $5-10 Million
Number Employees: 1-4

4238 **Evco Wholesale Foods**
309 Merchant St.
P.O.Box D
Emporia, KS 66801-7343 620-343-7000
Fax: 620-343-6375 support@evcofoods.com
www.evcofoods.com
Coffee, wholesale foods
President: Charles Evans
Estimated Sales: $20-50 Million
Number Employees: 50-99

4239 **Evensen Vineyards**
PO Box 127
Oakville, CA 94562-0127 707-944-2396
Wines
President: Richard Evensen

4240 **Ever Fresh Fruit Company**
35855 SE Kelso Rd
Boring, OR 97009 503-668-8026
Fax: 503-668-5823 800-239-8026
keithm@everfreshfruit.com
www.everfreshfruit.com
Processor of apples
Owner: Kurt Mc Knight
VP: LeAnn Miller
Estimated Sales: $10-20 Million
Number Employees: 50-99
Type of Packaging: Consumer, Food Service, Private Label
Brands:
NATURE'S QUEST

4241 **Everfresh Beverages**
6600 E 9 Mile Rd
Warren, MI 48091-2673 586-755-9500
Fax: 586-755-9587
everfreshmail@nationalbeverages.com
www.everfreshjuice.com
Manufacturer and exporter of soft drinks and fruit juices including orange and grape
President/CEO: Stan Sheridan
Telecommunications: Ray Laurinaitis
Operations: Dave Piontkowski
Plant Manager: Matt Filipovitch
Purchasing Director: Walter Koziara
Number Employees: 50-99
Sq. footage: 125000
Parent Co: National Beverages Corporation
Type of Packaging: Consumer, Private Label
Brands:
EVERFRESH
LACROIX

4242 **Everfresh Food Corporation**
501 Huron Blvd SE
Minneapolis, MN 55414 612-331-6393
Fax: 612-331-1172 george_edgar@yahoo.com
Manufacturer of chow mein noodles and vanilla including pure and imitation; importer of bamboo shoots and water chesnuts including whole and sliced
VP: Rita Sorsveen
Estimated Sales: $5-10 Million
Number Employees: 10-19
Type of Packaging: Consumer, Food Service, Private Label, Bulk
Brands:
CHINA BOY

4243 **Everglades Foods**
P.O.Box 595
Labelle, FL 33975 863-675-2221
Fax: 863-675-2289 800-689-2221
everglades92@aol.com
www.evergladeseasoning.com
Manufacturer of seasonings
President: Seth Howard
Estimated Sales: $1-2.5 Million
Number Employees: 5-9
Type of Packaging: Consumer, Food Service
Brands:
EVERGLADES
EVERGLADES HEAT
EVERGLADES ORIGINAL

4244 **Evergood Sausage Company**
1389 Underwood Ave
San Francisco, CA 94124-3308 415-822-4660
Fax: 415-822-1066 800-253-6733
salesinfo@evergoodfoods.com
www.evergoodfoods.com
Manufacturer of deli meats including corned beef, pastrami, and roast beef, skinless frankfurters, old world frankfurters and sausages.
President: Harlan Miller
Quality Control Manager: Christopher Ham
VP Sales/Marketing: Don Miller
Plant Manager: Richard Bower
Estimated Sales: $20-50 Million
Number Employees: 50-99
Type of Packaging: Consumer

4245 **Evergreen Juices**
Po Box 1 North York Stn Don Mills
Toronto, CA ON M3C 2R6 905-886-8090
877-915-8423
info@evergreenjuices.com
www.evergreenjuices.com
Juice
President: Don Mills
Treasurer: Robert MacIntosh

4246 **Evergreen Sweeteners, Inc**
600 Silks Run #1295
Hallandale Beach, FL 33009 305-931-1321
Fax: 954-458-5793 info@esweeteners.com
www.esweeteners.com

Evergreen Sweeteners is a full service sweetener distributor serving the entire Southeastern United States. From bulk liquid sweeteners to bagged sweeteners, Evergreen provides its customers with industry-leading service andunsurpassed quality.

President/CEO: Arthur Green
VP: Mark Gilden
Estimated Sales: $55 Million
Number Employees: 50+
Number of Products: 40
Sq. footage: 150000
Type of Packaging: Food Service, Bulk
Other Locations:
Evergreen Sweeteners
Atlanta GA
Evergreen Sweeteners
Sanford FL
Evergreen Sweeteners
Miami FL

4247 **Everson Spice Company**
P.O.Box 6097
Long Beach, CA 90806-0097 562-595-4785
Fax: 562-988-0219 800-421-3753
kenh@eversonspice.com www.eversonspice.com
Manufacturer of seasonings, dry rubs, stuffing mixes and marinades
Chairman: Tom Everson
President: Ken Hopkins
CEO: Kim Everson
Estimated Sales: $2.5-5 Million
Number Employees: 20-49
Type of Packaging: Food Service

4248 **Everything Yogurt**
1100 Pennsylvania Ave NW
Washington, DC 20004-2501 202-842-2990
Yogurt, salad products
Owner: January Kwak
Estimated Sales: Under $500,000
Number Employees: 20-49

4249 **Evesham Wood Vineyard &Winery**
2223 Cerise Ave NW
Salem, OR 97304 503-371-8478
Fax: 541-763-6015 eversham@open.org
www.convershamwood.com
Wines
President: Russell Raney
CFO: Mary Raney
Estimated Sales: Under $500,000
Number Employees: 1-4
Type of Packaging: Private Label

4250 **Eweberry Farms**
30377 Brownsville Rd
Brownsville, OR 97327 541-466-3470
eweberry@proaxis.com
www.eweberry.com
Manufacturer of gourmet jams and syrups
Owner: John Morrison

4251 **Ex Drinks**
1879 Whitney Mesa Dr
Henderson, NV 89014 702-949-6555
Fax: 702-949-6556 866-753-4929
hq@exdrinks.com www.exdrinks.com
Manufacturer of energy drinks and vitamin water
Headquarters Manager: Natasha Platin
Senior Director of Business Development: Clark Wright
Director of Strategic Planning: Kristen Hirtz
Marketing: Travis Arnesen
Estimated Sales: $500,000- 1 Million
Number Employees: 5-9

4252 **Excalibur Seasoning Company**
1800 Riverway Dr
Pekin, IL 61554 309-347-1221
Fax: 309-347-9086 800-444-2169
jay@excaliburseasoning.com
www.excaliburseasoning.com
Seasoning
President: Jay Hall
Estimated Sales: $ 5 - 10 Million
Number Employees: 50-99

4253 **Excel Corporation**
151 North Main
Wichita, KS 67202 316-832-7500
Fax: 316-291-2590 800-835-2837
www.excelmeats.com
Processor and packer of meat
President: William Buckner
CFO: Derek Kennedy
VP Sales/Marketing: Matthew Wineinger
Number Employees: 30,000

4254 **Exceldor Cooperative**
460 Rue Principale
St. Anselme, QC G0R 2N0
Canada 418-885-4451
Fax: 418-885-4271 877-320-8006
info@exceldor.com www.exceldor.ca
Manufacturer and exporter of fresh and frozen chicken
President: Jean-Pierre Dube
Operational Vice President: Eric Cadoret
Finance Vice President: Chrstian Jacques
Estimated Sales: $100-500 Million
Number Employees: 200
Type of Packaging: Consumer, Private Label, Bulk
Brands:
EXCELDOR EXPRESS

4255 **Excellent Coffee Company**
259 East Ave
Pawtucket, RI 2860 401-724-6393
Fax: 401-724-0560 800-345-2007
www.downeastcoffee.com
Coffee
President/CEO: William Kapos
CFO: Frank DeLuca
Marketing: Mark Bishop
Production Manager: Ron Yanku
Purchasing: Judy Hahn
Estimated Sales: $16 Million
Number Employees: 120
Type of Packaging: Private Label
Brands:
EXCELLENT COFFEE'S DOWNEAST
EXCELLENT COFFEE'S MICRO ROAST
EXCELLENT COFFEE'S OCEAN

4256 **(HQ)Excelline Foods**
20232 Sunburst St
Chatsworth, CA 91311-6218 818-701-7710
Fax: 818-701-5904 info@excellinefoods.com
www.excellinefoods.com
Manufacturer of frozen Mexican foods
Owner: Silvia Donhue
Estimated Sales: $25-49.9 Million
Number Employees: 50-99
Number of Brands: 1
Number of Products: 25
Type of Packaging: Consumer, Food Service, Private Label, Bulk
Brands:
EXCELLINE

4257 **Excelpro Manufacturing Corporation**
3760 E 26th Street
Los Angeles, CA 90023-4506 323-268-1918
Fax: 323-268-1993 pernsterjr@excelpro.com
Manufacturer of cheese and baking proteins including hydrolyzed proteins, sodium, calcium and potassium caseinates and blends
Chairman: John Ernster
President: Peter Ernster
Estimated Sales: $20-50 Million
Number Employees: 34
Sq. footage: 45000
Parent Co: Excelpro
Other Locations:
Excelpro Manufacturing Corp.
Wellsville UT

4258 **Excelsior Dairy**
458 Kekuanaoa Street
Hilo, HI 96720-4319 808-961-3608
Manufacturer of Milk, nectar, juice drinks

4259 **Excelso Coffee Company**
6700 Dawson Blvd Ste 3a
Norcross, GA 30093 770-449-8140
Fax: 770-448-6698 800-241-2138
www.excelso.com
Manufacturer of Coffee
President: Geoffrey Paul
Owner: Allen Shaw
Chairman: Charles Shaw
Sales Manager: Daniel Lane
Estimated Sales: $10-20 Million
Number Employees: 84

4260 **Exclusive Smoked Fish**
43 Mulock Avenue
Toronto, ON M6N 3C3
Canada 416-766-6007
Fax: 416-766-7313
Manufacturer and exporter of fresh and frozen smoked scallops and salmon
Number Employees: 5-9
Type of Packaging: Consumer, Food Service, Private Label, Bulk

4261 **Exeter Produce & Storage Company**
215 Thames Road West
Exeter, ON N0M 1S3
Canada 519-235-2180
Fax: 519-235-3515 800-881-4861
www.exterproduce.com
Manufacturer, importer and exporter of rutabagas, snap beans, bell peppers, cauliflower, cabbage, carrots, onions and potatoes
President: Leonard Veri
Director: James Veri
Director: Michael Veri
Estimated Sales: $21 Million
Number Employees: 50
Sq. footage: 55000
Type of Packaging: Bulk
Brands:
Huron Pride
Veri Fine

4262 **Expro Manufacturing**
2800 Ayers Avenue
Vernon, CA 90058 323-415-8544
Fax: 323-268-4060 jernster@expromfg.com
www.expromfg.com
Manufacturer and packager of food ingredients, including custom dry powder blends
President: Peter Ernster
CEO: Douglas Kantner
R&D: Greg Rowland
VP Sales: Michele Mullen
Purchasing: James Ernster
Number Employees: 20

4263 **Exquisita Tortillas**
700 W Chapin
Edinburg, TX 78541-2416 956-383-6712
Fax: 956-383-4226 questions@exquisita.com
www.exquisitatortillas.com
Manufacturer of corn and flour tortillas, chips, taco & challupa shells, pork skins
President: Humberto Rodriguez
Office Manager: Alicia Aleman
Estimated Sales: $100-500 Million
Number Employees: 175
Sq. footage: 46000
Brands:
EXQUISITA

4264 **Extracts Plus**
2460 Coral St
Vista, CA 92081-8430 760-597-0200
Fax: 760-597-0734 www.pluspharm.com
Manufacturer of herbs, gelatin and vegetarian capsules

4265 **Extracts and Ingredients Ltd**
One Gary Road
Union, NJ 07083-5527 908-688-9009
Fax: 908-688-9005 mbevilaque@morretec.com
www.morretec.com
Supplies botanical extracts, nutitive oils, certified organic products and special excipients
President: Leonard Glass
Quality Assurance Manager: Frimma Messer
Marketing Coordinator: Melissa Bevilaque
VP Sales/Marketing: David Fondots
VP Administration/Operations: Paul Caskey
Parent Co: Morre-Tec Industries, Inc

4266 **Extreme Creations**
4970 Windplay Dr Ste C5
El Dorado Hills, CA 95762 916-941-0444
Fax: 916-941-1777 usa@extremepops.com
www.extremepops.com
Manufacturer of jellied lollipops
Manager: Kamal Naim
Estimated Sales: $ .5 - 1 million
Number Employees: 1-4

4267 **Eyrie Vineyards**
935 E 10th St
Mcminnville, OR 97128 503-472-6315
Fax: 503-472-5124 www.eyrievineyards.com
Wines
President: David Lett
Vice President: Diana Lett
Estimated Sales: $5-10 Million
Number Employees: 20-49

4268 **Ezzo Sausage Company**
1415 Universal Rd
Columbus, OH 43207 614-445-8841
Fax: 614-445-8843 800-558-8841
www.ezzo.com
Sausage, pepperoni
President: Bill Ezzo
Number Employees: 10-19

4269 **F & A Dairy of California**
691 Inyo Ave
Newman, CA 95360 209-862-1732
Fax: 209-862-1043 800-554-6455
Manufacturer of cheddar, monterey jack, mozzarella, provolone, custom blends, shredded and diced cheeses
VP: Joe Gaglio
QC Manager: Glenn Lewis
General Manager: Joseph Smith
Estimated Sales: $50-100 Million
Number Employees: 100-249
Type of Packaging: Bulk

4270 **F & F Foods**
3501 W 48th Pl
Chicago, IL 60632 773-376-7432
Fax: 773-927-3906 800-621-0225
webmaster@fffoods.com www.fffoods.com
Manufacturer and exporter of vanilla, chocolate and strawberry cookie wafers, chewable vitamins and bagged hard candies, cough drops and mints; also, seasonal and vending varieties available
President: Dave Barnett
Manager Information Systems: Bill Cheevers
SVP Finance & Operations: Joe Nelson
Estimated Sales: $20-50 Million
Number Employees: 100-249
Sq. footage: 125000
Type of Packaging: Consumer, Private Label, Bulk
Brands:
Daily C
F&F Dietary Supplements
Fast Dry Zinc
Foxes Candy Mint Rolls
Polar Blast Breath Mints
Sen-Sen

Smith Brothers Cough Drops
SmokersGuard

4271 **F Gavina & Sons Inc.**
2700 Fruitland Ave
Vernon, CA 90058 323-582-0671
Fax: 323-581-1127 800-428-4627
sales@gavina.com www.gavina.com
whole bean coffee, ground coffee, espresso, teas, specialty drink mixes
President/Owner: Pedro Gavi□a
CEO: Jos, Gavi□a
VP: Leonor Gavi□a-Valls
Sales: Yolanda Sanchez
Estimated Sales: $88.1 Million
Number Employees: 295

4272 **F R LePage Bakeries**
P.O.Box 1900
Auburn, ME 04211-1900 207-783-9161
Fax: 207-784-4634
Manufacturer of bread, buns, rolls and bagels
Chairman: Albert LePage
President/CEO: Andrew Barowsky
CEO: Andrew P Barowsky
Estimated Sales: $300,000-500,000
Number Employees: 1-4

4273 **F&A Dairy Products**
P.O.Box 278
Dresser, WI 54009-0278 715-755-3485
Fax: 715-755-3480 mike@fadairy.com
www.fadairy.com
Manufacturer of cheese including mozzarella, provolone, romano and parmesan; importer of pecorino romano
President/Owner: Jeffrey Terranova
Controller: Clyde Loch
CFO: Jay Benusa
QC: Ralph Ramos
Sales: Chris Slavek
Sales: Renzo Sciortino
Human Resources: Carl Gutierrez
VP Wisconsin Operations: Mike Breault
VP New Mexico Operations: Bob Snyder
Estimated Sales: $10-24.9 Million
Number Employees: 50-99
Type of Packaging: Food Service
Other Locations:
F&A Dairy Products
Las Cruces NM
Brands:
F&A

4274 **F&M Brewery573054 Ontario Limited**
355 Elmira Rd N
Unit 135
Guelph, ON N1K 1S5
Canada 519-824-1194
Fax: 519-822-8201 877-316-2337
beer@fmbrewery.com www.fmbrewery.com
Manufacturer and exporter of beer, lager and cask condition ale
President: Frank Cerniuk
Brewmaster: Charles MacLean
Brewery Manager: Brian Reilly
Estimated Sales: $382,000
Number Employees: 5
Type of Packaging: Consumer, Food Service
Brands:
ERAMOSA HONEY WHEAT
F AND M SPECIAL DRAFT
MACLEANS CASK CONDITIONED
MACLEANS PALE
OAC GOLD
ROYAL CITY
SAINT ANDRE VIENNA
STONE HAMMER PILSNER

4275 **F&S Produce Company**
913 Bridgeton Ave
Rosenhayn, NJ 08352 856-453-0316
Fax: 856-453-0494 800-886-3316
www.freshcutproduce.com
Manufacturer of fresh, whole and pre-cut produce including peppers, onions, lettuce, carrots, spinach, cabbage, tomatoes and cucumbers; brine products including vegetables, cherry and bell peppers, onions and jalapenos; also, saladvegetable trays and fruit snacks
President: Sam Pipitone
Technical Services Director: Douglas Nicoll
VP Sales: Jason Landry
VP Operations: Sam Pipitone, III
Estimated Sales: $53 Million
Number Employees: 20-49
Type of Packaging: Consumer, Food Service, Private Label, Bulk

4276 **F&Y Enterprises**
1205 Karl Ct
Suite 115
Wauconda, IL 60084-1090 847-526-0620
Manufacturer and exporter of hickory smoked meat snacks including sausage sticks and beef jerky
President: Frank Vitek
VP: Bonnie Vitek
Estimated Sales: $2 Million
Number Employees: 40
Parent Co: F&Y Enterprises
Type of Packaging: Consumer, Food Service, Private Label
Brands:
TEXAS BRAND

4277 **F. Gavina & Sons**
2700 Fruitland Ave
Vernon, CA 90058 323-582-0671
Fax: 323-581-1127 sales@gavina.com
www.gavina.com
Manufacturer of coffee beans
President: Pedro Gavina
CFO: Jose Gavina
Vice President: Leonor Gavina-Valls
Controller: Lourdes Garcia
Estimated Sales: $55 Million
Number Employees: 295
Sq. footage: 220000
Type of Packaging: Consumer, Food Service, Private Label, Bulk
Brands:
CAFE GAVINA ESPRESSO
CAFE LA LLAVE ESPRESSO
DON FRANCISCO GOURMET COFFEE

4278 **F. Soderlund Company**
9240 Bonit Bch Rd SE Ste 1118
Bonita Springs, FL 34135 239-498-0600
Fax: 239-498-0606 soderlund@aol.com
Manufacturer of dairy products
Manager: Michael Cunningham
Estimated Sales: $2.5-5 Million
Number Employees: 1-4
Type of Packaging: Private Label

4279 **F.B. Purnell Sausage Company**
P.O.Box 366
Simpsonville, KY 40067-0366 502-722-5626
Fax: 502-722-5586 800-626-1512
info@itsgooo-od.com www.itsgooo-od.com
Manufacturer of sausages
President: Todd Purnell
Chairman/CEO: Allen Purnell Jr.
VP/Controller: Robert Scherrer
Estimated Sales: $39 Million
Number Employees: 250
Type of Packaging: Consumer, Food Service
Brands:
OLD FOLKS

4280 **F.X. Matt Brewing Company**
811 Edward St
Utica, NY 13502-4092 315-624-2400
Fax: 315-624-2452 800-690-3181
info@saranac.com www.saranac.com
Manufacturer, brewer and exporter of beer, ale, stout, lager and malt; also, soft drinks and juices
President: Nicholas Matt
Vice President: Fred Matt II
Public Relations: Marie McNamara
Operations Manager: Frank Vlossak
Plant Manager: Dave Campbell
Estimated Sales: $50-100 Million
Number Employees: 100-249
Sq. footage: 350000
Type of Packaging: Consumer, Food Service, Private Label, Bulk
Brands:
ADIRONDACK AMBER
AMERICAN PLSENER
BLACK AND TAN
BLACK FOREST
ENGLISH PALE ALE
LIGHT
MOUNTAIN BERRY
SARANAC DIET ROOT BEER
SARANAC GINGER BEER
SARANAC ORANGE CREAM
SARANAC ROOT BEER
TRADITIONAL LAGER

4281 **FB Washburn Candy Corporation**
137 Perkins Ave
Po Box 3277
Brockton, MA 02304-3277 508-588-0820
Fax: 508-588-2205 info@fbwashburgncandy.com
www.fbwashburncandy.com
Manufacturer and exporter of candy including hard, ribbon, rock, lollypops and Christmas novelties; available bagged, boxed and packaged for racks
President/Co-Owner: James Gilson
Treasurer/Co-Owner: Douglas Gilson
Sales: Robert Gilson
Estimated Sales: $5-10 Million
Number Employees: 50
Sq. footage: 150000
Type of Packaging: Consumer, Food Service, Private Label, Bulk
Brands:
BAY STATE
SEVIGNY
TRINITY
WALEECO
WASHBURN

4282 **FBC Industries**
500 Remington Rd Ste 300
Schaumburg, IL 60173 847-839-0880
Fax: 847-839-0884 888-322-4637
info@fbcindustries.com www.fbcindustries.com
Manufacturer of industrial ingredients including dipotassium phosphate, calcium chloride, sodium and potassuim citrates, lactates and benzoates used as buffering agents, emulsifers, firming agents, preservatives, antioxidantsflavorings, etc
President: Robert Bloom
VP: John Tramontana
Estimated Sales: $ 1 - 3 Million
Number Employees: 10-19
Type of Packaging: Bulk

4283 **FCC Coffee Packers**
8801 NW 15th Street
Doral, FL 33172-3027 305-591-1128
Fax: 305-591-1367 sales@fcccoffee.com
Coffee, instant coffee
President: Mike Ferrara
CFO: Alex Ramirez
VP: Ignacio Perez-Echeverria
Plant Manager: Jim Saenz
Estimated Sales: $2.5-5 Million
Number Employees: 20-49
Brands:
ROMA

4284 **FDP**
398 Tesconi Ct
Santa Rosa, CA 95401-4653 707-547-1776
Fax: 707-545-5270 sales@fdpusa.com
www.fdpusa.com
Manufacturer of dehydrated fruits and vegetables
President: Mark Martindill
Quality Control: Scott Klinger
Sales: Nancy Costa
Estimated Sales: $20-50 Million
Number Employees: 20-49
Parent Co: FDP GmbH
Brands:
SOUBRY INSTANT PASTA
TAURA URC

4285 **FINA LLC**
4700 Este Ave
Cicinnati, OH 45232 814-218-3439
www.fina-us.com
Manufactures shortenings and filling fats made from domestic oils
Member: Paul Angelico
Member: Irwin Heller
Number Employees: 20-49

4286 **FNI Group LLC**
188 Lake Street
Sherborn, MA 01770-1606 508-655-4175
Fax: 508-655-8816 fnigrouplc@attbi.com
www.essensmart.com
Manufacturer of all natural cookies that are cholesterol and lactose free
President/Founder: Josephine Ho
Estimated Sales: $200.00 K
Number Employees: 2
Brands:
ESSEN SMART GLUTEN FREE
ESSEN SMART SINGLE COOKIE 2
ESSEN SMART SINGLE COOKIE 3
ESSEN SMART SOY COOKIES

4287 **FONA International Inc.**
1900 Averill Rd
Geneva, IL 60134 630-578-8600
www.fona.com
Manufacturer of flavoring extract and syrup
President/CEO: Joseph Slawek
CFO: James Evanoff
Purchasing Manager: Debbie Fleming
Estimated Sales: $ 50 Million
Number Employees: 100-249

4288 **FSI/MFP**
720 W Barre Road
Archbold, OH 43502-9304 419-446-6528
Frozen hors d'oeuvres-shrimp, egg rolls, pizza rolls, seafood rolls, stuffed clams
Principal: Gene Welka
Finance Director: Dennis Seffernick
Estimated Sales: $100+ Million
Number Employees: 100-249
Brands:
CRYSTAL BAY
MATLAW'S

4289 **FW Bryce**
8 Pond Rd
Gloucester, MA 01930-1833 978-283-7080
Fax: 978-283-7647 fwbryce@fwbryce.com
www.fwbryce.com
Manufacturer of frozen seafood
Chairman: Carl Moores
President: Keith Moores
Financial Controller: Robert Caldwell
General Counsel: Ian Moores
Quality Assurance Manager: Justin Moores
Inventory Control Manager: Mary Murch
Director Sales: Glenn Hale
VP Sales: Joe Flammia
Logistics Manager: Frank Souza
Warehousing/Logistics: Ralph Pierce
Number Employees: 10-19
Sq. footage: 26000

4290 **FW Thurston**
P.O.Box 178
Bernard, ME 04612-0178 207-244-3320
Fax: 207-244-3320
Manufacturer of fresh lobster
Owner: Michael Radcliffe
Estimated Sales: $ 3 - 5 Million
Number Employees: 20-49

4291 **FW Witt & Company**
1106 S Bridge St
Yorkville, IL 60560-1765 630-553-6366
Fax: 630-553-6599 www.newlywedsfoods.com
Manufacturer of spices, seasonings and soy products
President: Dennis Baxter
Estimated Sales: $ 20 - 50 Million
Number Employees: 50-99
Type of Packaging: Consumer

4292 **Fabbri Sausage Manufacturing**
166 N Aberdeen St
Chicago, IL 60607 312-829-6363
Fax: 312-829-0396 info@fabbrisausage.com
www.fabbrisausage.com
Manufacturer of Italian meats and other pizza supplies including italian sausage, meatballs, italian roast beef, italian style gravy, italian chili.
President: Ray Fabbri
Estimated Sales: $2.5-5 Million
Number Employees: 20-49
Sq. footage: 25000
Type of Packaging: Consumer, Food Service, Private Label, Bulk

4293 **Fabe's Natural Gourmet**
1145 Arroyo Street
Suite B
San Francisco, CA 91340 818-838-6633
Manufacturer of Gourmet
President/Owner: Lorraine Fabes
Estimated Sales: $4 Million
Number Employees: 35

4294 **Faber Foods and Aeronautics**
1153 Evergreen Parkway
Suite M105
Evergreen, CO 80439-9501 800-237-3255
Fax: 303-670-0971 mariafaber@earthlink.net
Manufacturer of low-fat muesli cereal including strawberry/banana, cranberry/apricot, papaya/peach, blueberry/peach, raspberry/apple, etc.; also, custom blend cereals; exporter of extruded crisp rice, edible seeds, canned oats driedfruit raisins and nuts
President: Maria Faber
Estimated Sales: $300,000-500,000
Number Employees: 10-19
Sq. footage: 10000
Type of Packaging: Consumer, Food Service, Private Label, Bulk
Brands:
LOW FAT BODY MUESLIX

4295 **Fabio Imports**
6048 De La Rosa Ln
Oceanside, CA 92057-2101 760-726-7040
Fax: 760-726-5731
Italian specialties
President/Owner: Fabio Peraro
Estimated Sales: $1 Million
Number Employees: 35

4296 **Fabrique Delices**
1610 Delta Ct
Suite 1
Hayward, CA 94544 510-441-9500
Fax: 510-441-9700 info@fabriquedelices.com
www.fabriquedelices.com
Manufacturer of Foie gras, terrine, block and mousse, smoked meats, mousses
CEO: Marc Poinsignon
VP Sales: Sebastian Espinasse
Estimated Sales: $2.5-5 Million
Number Employees: 20-49

4297 **Facciola Meat**
48811 Warm Springs Blvd
Fremont, CA 94539 510-438-8600
Fax: 510-498-5922 www.facciola.com
Meat
President: Ray Nicholas
CFO: Robert Cruz
VP: Dennis Welsh
Plant Manager: Richard Ficker
Estimated Sales: $50-100 Million
Number Employees: 35
Parent Co: Sysco

4298 **Fage USA**
1 Opportunity Drive
Johnsontown Industrial Park
Johnsontown, NY 12095 518-762-5912
Fax: 518-762-5918 info@fageusa.com
www.fageusa.com
Greek yogurt and feta cheese
Manager: Antonios Maridakis
Estimated Sales: $ 5 - 10 Million
Number Employees: 5-9

4299 **Faidley Seafood**
203 N Paca St
Baltimore, MD 21201 410-727-4898
Fax: 410-837-6495 www.faidleyscrabcakes.com
Seafood
President: Nancy Devine
Estimated Sales: $ 3 - 5 Million
Number Employees: 10-19

4300 **Fair Oaks Farms**
7600 95th St
Pleasant Prairie, WI 53158 262-947-0320
Fax: 262-947-0348 www.fairoaksfarms.com
Manufacturer of cooked and uncooked pork, turkey and chicken sausage
President/CEO: Michael Thompson
Corporate Controller: Susan Kellogg
Operations Manager: Elizabeth Molton
Estimated Sales: $50-100 Million
Number Employees: 190

4301 **Fair Scones**
P.O.Box 177
Medina, WA 98039-0177 425-486-3334
Fax: 425-398-0301 800-588-9160
pgimness@conifer-inc.com
www.conifer-inc.com
Manufacturer of bean soup and chili mixes, bread, breakfast, dessert and beverage mixes
President: Michael Maher
Estimated Sales: $ 10 - 20 Million
Number Employees: 20-49

4302 **Fairbury Food Products**
601 2nd St
Fairbury, NE 68352 402-729-3379
Fax: 402-729-2437
www.westonpackagedmeats.com
Processor of bacon bits
President: Arden Schacht
Number Employees: 20-49
Parent Co: Fairbury Food
Type of Packaging: Food Service, Private Label

4303 **Fairchester Snacks Corporation**
100 Lafayette Ave
White Plains, NY 10603 914-761-2824
Salty biscuts
Owner: John Barisano
Estimated Sales: $300,000-500,000
Number Employees: 1-4

4304 **Fairfield Farm Kitchens**
P.O.Box 333
Tamworth, NH 3886-333 508-584-9300
Fax: 508-580-9910
www.fairfieldfarmkitchens.com
Manufacturer and custom packer of frozen soups, entrees, side dishes, sauces, gravies, layer, sheet and pound cakes, etc
President/CEO: Frank Carpenito
Estimated Sales: $20-50 Million
Number Employees: 100-249
Sq. footage: 170000
Brands:
BASIC AMERICAN FROZEN FOODS
FAIRFIELD FARM

4305 **Fairhaven Cooperative Flour Mill**
808 N Hill Blvd
Burlington, WA 98233-4640
Fax: 360-734-9947
Manufacturer and exporter of flour including whole grain, wheat, rye, corn, buckwheat, rice, etc
President: Bill Distler
Manager: Bill Distler
Estimated Sales: $1-2.5 Million
Number Employees: 1-4
Type of Packaging: Consumer, Bulk

4306 **Fairmont Foods of Minnesota**
905 E 4th St
Fairmont, MN 56031 507-238-9001
Fax: 507-238-9560 morris@fairmontfoods.com
www.fairmontfoods.com
Manufacturer of frozen entrees including beef, chicken, chili, pork, lasagna, burritos and soups
President/CEO: Larry McGuire
Director: William Bosshard
VP Operations: Jerry Nasalroad
Estimated Sales: $50-100 Million
Number Employees: 280

4307 **Fairmont Products**
15 S Kishacoquillas St
Belleville, PA 17004 717-935-2121
Fax: 717-935-5473
Manufacturer of cultured dairy products including cottage cheese, sour cream, ice cream mix and cream
Manager: John Lacombe
VP Sales: Peter Menard
Plant Manager: John Lacombe
Estimated Sales: $20-50 Million
Number Employees: 50-99
Parent Co: Dean Foods Company
Type of Packaging: Private Label

4308 **Fairmont Snacks Group**
6133 Rockside Rd
Suite 208
Independence, OH 44131-2244 216-573-2777
Fax: 216-642-0748
Peanuts and snack items
Estimated Sales: $10-20 Million
Number Employees: 20-49

4309 **Fairview Swiss Cheese**
1734 Perry Hwy
Fredonia, PA 16124 724-475-4154
Fax: 724-475-4777
Manufacturer of cheeses
President: Richard Koller
Estimated Sales: $2 Million
Number Employees: 10
Sq. footage: 20000
Parent Co: John Koller and Son, Inc
Type of Packaging: Consumer, Food Service, Private Label, Bulk

4310 **Fairwinds Gourmet Coffee**
1731 Aviation Blvd.
Lincoln, CA 95648 916-543-0493
Fax: 603-668-0888 1 8-0 8-9 13
khybsch@jbfroods.com
www.fairwindscoffee.com
Manufacturer of gourmet Coffee and tea
President: Kathy Hybsch
Estimated Sales: $2.5-5 Million
Number Employees: 1-4
Parent Co: JBR Gourmet Foods
Type of Packaging: Bulk
Brands:
EAST INDIA COFFEE AND TEA
FAIRWINDS COFFEE
ORGANIC COFFEE CO

4311 **Fairytale Brownies**
4610 E Cotton Ctr Blvd Ste 100
Phoenix, AZ 85040 800-324-7982
Fax: 602-489-5133 800-324-7982
julieg@brownies.com www.brownies.com
Brownies, cookies
Owner/President: Eileen Spitalny
Marketing: Julie Gaffney

4312 **Faith Dairy**
3509 72nd Street E
Tacoma, WA 98443-1210 253-531-3398
Fax: 253-539-4198
Manufacturer of ice cream
President/CEO: Sidney Mensonides
COO: John Mensonides
Estimated Sales: $5-10 Million
Number Employees: 10-19
Type of Packaging: Consumer

4313 **Falafel Republic**
10r Charles Street
Needham Heights, MA 02494 781-444-2790
Fax: 781-444-1420 nancy@originalrangoon.com
www.falafelrepublic.com
Dairy-free, gluten-free, vegetarian, helath, fitness and energy bars, other snacks, foodservice.
Marketing: Greg Bukuras

4314 **Falcon Rice Mill Inc**
600 S Avenue D
Po Box 771
Crowley, LA 70527-0771 337-783-3825
Fax: 337-783-1568 800-738-7423
charles@falconrice.com www.falconrice.com
Manufacturer and exporter of white and popcorn rice
President: Mona Trahan
CFO/Office Manager: Linda Thibodeaux
VP: Randy Falcon
General Manager: Tom Dew
Plant Manager: Russell Cormier
Estimated Sales: $20-50 Million
Number Employees: 20-49
Type of Packaging: Consumer, Food Service, Private Label, Bulk

4315 **Falcone's Cookieland**
1648 61st St
Brooklyn, NY 11204 718-236-4200
Fax: 718-259-6133
Manufacturer of regular and dietetic cookies; also, crackers, biscuits, breadsticks and flatbread
President: Carmine Falcone
Vice President: Angelo Falcone
Estimated Sales: $5-9.9 Million
Number Employees: 20-49
Type of Packaging: Consumer, Food Service, Private Label, Bulk
Brands:
FALCONE'S
FALCONE'S BAKED GOODS
FALCONE'S COOKIES
FALCONE'S FLATBREAD

4316 **Fall Creek Vineyards**
1402 San Antonio St Ste 200
Austin, TX 78701 512-476-4477
Fax: 512-476-6116 www.fcv.com
Wine
President: Ed Auler
VP: Chad Auler
Operations Manager: Roy Nobles
Estimated Sales: $ 3 - 5 Million
Number Employees: 5-9
Type of Packaging: Bulk

4317 **Fall River Wild Rice**
41577 Osprey Rd
Fall River Mills, CA 96028 530-336-5222
Fax: 530-336-5265 800-626-4366
info@frwr.com www.frwr.com
Manufacturer of wild rice
General Manager: Walt Oiler
Estimated Sales: $420,000
Number Employees: 4
Sq. footage: 14000
Brands:
FALL RIVER

4318 **(HQ)Falla Imports**
P.O.Box 1532
Greenville, ME 4441-1532 609-476-4106
Fax: 609-476-0412
Importers of coffee
President: Roderick Falla
Number Employees: 1-4

4319 **Fallwood Corp**
75 South Broadway, Ste 494
White Plains, NY 10601 914-304-4065
Fax: 914-304-4063 ana@fallwoodcorp.com
www.fallwoodcorp.com
Manufacturer and supplier of all natural nutraceutical ingredients and raw materials
Executive Director: Graciela Rocchia
Principal: Tom Gilkison
Sales Manager: Anne-Marie Rodriguez
Estimated Sales: Under $500,000
Number Employees: 4
Parent Co: Loboratorio Opoterapico Argentino

4320 **Fama Sales**
450 W 44th St
New York, NY 10036 212-757-9433
Fax: 212-765-4193 famasales@aol.com
www.famasales.com
Food products
President: Ugo Quazzo
Estimated Sales: $1-2.5 Million
Number Employees: 10-19

4321 **Famarco**
1381 Air Rail Ave
Virginia Beach, VA 23455 757-460-3573
Fax: 757-460-2621 info@famarco.com
www.famarco.com
Raw material importer and processor for spice, botanicals and craob
President: Bruce Martin
VP: Ken Hartfelder
Quality Control: Darrick Bargher
Marketing: Mark Herrick
Plant Manager: James O'Neil
Estimated Sales: $10 Million
Number Employees: 20-49
Sq. footage: 40000
Parent Co: B&K International
Type of Packaging: Private Label, Bulk
Brands:
Martin's Virginia Roast
Virginia Roast

4322 **Famco Automatic SausageLinkers**
P. O. Box 8647
Pittsburgh, PA 15221 412-241-6410
Fax: 412-242-8877 info@famcousa.com
www.famcousa.com
Manufacturer of linking machines for sausage and frankfurter production
President: Charles Allen
Vice President: R. Robert Allen
Sales: Dick Carson

4323 **Family Brand International**
P.O.Box 429
Lenoir City, TN 37771-0429 865-986-8005
Fax: 865-986-7171 www.fbico.com
Manufacturer of fresh and frozen pork products
President: John Wampler
CEO: Harry Wampler
VP: Tim Wampler
Marketing: Clay Jones
Plant Manager: Bob Epley
Estimated Sales: $20-50 Million
Number Employees: 100-249
Type of Packaging: Consumer, Food Service
Brands:
Cades Cove
Dinner Delight
Elm Hill
Frosty Morn
Houser
Jubilee
Sycamore

4324 **Family Sweets Candy Company**
1099 Pratt Boulevard
Elk Grove Village, IL 60007-5120 336-788-5068
Fax: 336-784-6708 800-334-1607
www.familysweets.com
Candy
President: LeRoy Mansson

4325 **Family Tradition Foods**
PO Box 869
Wheatley, ON N0P 2P0
Canada 519-825-4673
Fax: 519-825-3134 www.familytradition.com
Manufacturer and importer of frozen fruits and vegetables; exporter of canned corn and IQF vegetables
President/CEO: John Omstead
Number Employees: 100-249
Sq. footage: 321000
Type of Packaging: Consumer, Food Service
Other Locations:
Family Tradition Foods
Tecumseh, Ontario
Brands:
FAMILY TRADITIONS
JOHN O'S

4326 **Family Tree Farms**
41646 Road 62
Reedley, CA 93654 559-591-6280
Fax: 559-595-7795 www.familytreefarms.com
Manufacturer, packer, shipper, exporter, and distributor of fresh fruit
President: David Jackson
CFO: Dan Clenney
Quality Control: Mary Ortiz
Estimated Sales: $ 20 - 50 Million
Number Employees: 250-499
Brands:
EAT SMART
GREAT WHITES

4327 **Famous Chili**
1421 N 7th St
Fort Smith, AR 72901 479-782-0096
Fax: 501-782-6825 www.famouschili.com
Manufacturer of chili and salsa
President: David Korkames
Estimated Sales: $5-10 Million
Number Employees: 5-9
Sq. footage: 5000
Type of Packaging: Consumer, Food Service, Private Label
Brands:
FAMOUS
FOUR STAR
HEAT & SERVE
STAR

4328 **Famous Pacific Dessert Company**
2414 SW Andover Street
Building C
Seattle, WA 98106-1153 206-935-1999
Fax: 206-935-2535 800-666-1950
mherna9334@aol.com
www.greatfood.com/pacificdessert
Gourmet tortes, cheesecakes, brownies, dessert bars and shortbreads
President: Anthony Rayner
CFO: Michelle Hernandez
Plant Manager: Tina McLaughlin
Estimated Sales: $20-50 Million
Number Employees: 20-49
Sq. footage: 15
Type of Packaging: Private Label
Brands:
CHOCOLATE DECADENCE

CHOCOLATE THUNDER/WHITE LIGHTNING
ELEPHANT BAR
ESPRESSO DECADENCE
FAMOUS PACIFIC DESSERT COMPANY
GORILLA BAR
JUNGLE BARS
LINZER TORTE MONKEY BAR
RHINO BAR
RUBY SLIPPERS
ZEBRA BAR

4329 Famous Specialties Company
55 Saratoga Blvd Unit B
Island Park, NY 11558 516-889-9099
Fax: 516-889-9099 877-273-6999
craig@famousspecialties.com
www.famousspecialties.com
Manufacturer of raw prepared strudel dough
President: Craig Tropp
Estimated Sales: $2.5-5 Million
Number Employees: 1-4
Sq. footage: 2500
Brands:
BARNEY'S TOWN & COUNTRY
BEEF INTERNATIONAL
BLUE RIDGE FARMS
BRANDT
CAESAR'S
CREATIVE BAKERS
FANCY FOODS
FANCY'S FINEST
FANTASIA
GILDA
HEATH & HEATHER
HIGH MEADOWS
LEAVES
REDI PREP STRUDEL
SILVER LAKE
STAHL MEYER
SWEET STREET

4330 Fancy Farms Popcorn
P.O.Box 209
Bernie, MO 63822-0209 573-276-3315
Fax: 573-276-2287 800-833-8154
sales@fancyfarmpopcorn.com
www.fancyfarmpopcorn.com
Manufacturer of portion-packed popcorn
President: Chris Tanner
Sales: J Smith
Estimated Sales: $500,000-$1 Million
Number Employees: 5-9
Parent Co: St. Francis River Farming
Type of Packaging: Food Service, Bulk
Brands:
FANCY FARM

4331 Fancy Lebanese Bakery
2573 Agricola St
Halifax, NS B3K 4C4
Canada 902-429-0400
Fax: 902-429-0403
Manufacturer of pita bread and submarine sandwich buns
President: Mary Laba
Manager: Maura Fougere
Estimated Sales: $2.6 Million
Number Employees: 20
Type of Packaging: Consumer, Food Service, Private Label
Brands:
FANCY LEBANESE BAKERY
FLB

4332 Fancy's Candy's
5601 Twin Creeks Trl
Rougemont, NC 27572-8657 919-644-2573
Fax: 919-732-2070 888-403-2629
akeller@fancyscandys.com
www.fancyscandys.com
Toffee, milk chocolate, dark chocolate, hazelnuts, white chocolate, and pecans
Director: Anne Keller
Estimated Sales: $ 1 - 3 Million
Number Employees: 1-4

4333 (HQ)Fanestil Packing Company
1542 S Highway 99
Emporia, KS 66801 620-342-6354
Fax: 620-342-8190 www.fanestils.com
Manufacturer of sausage, ham and bacon
President: Scott Sanders
CEO: Dan Smoots
General Manager: Jan Smoots
Estimated Sales: $9 Million
Number Employees: 65
Type of Packaging: Consumer, Food Service
Brands:
FANESTIL

4334 Fannie May Fine Chocolat
2457 W North Ave
Melrose Park, IL 60160 630-653-3088
800-999-3629
questions@fanniemay.com www.fanniemay.com
Manufacturer of candy including chocolate, hard and gummies
President: Larry Small
Estimated Sales: Less than $500,000
Number Employees: 5-9
Parent Co: Fannie Mae Candies
Type of Packaging: Consumer
Brands:
CELEBRATED COLLECTION
FANNIE MAY CANDIES

4335 Fannie May/Fanny Farmer
8550 W Bryn Mawr Ave # 550
Chicago, IL 60631-3225 773-693-9100
800-333-3629
questions@archibaldcandy.com
www.fanniemay.com
Chocolates
President: Ted Shepherd
CEO: David Taiclet
Number Employees: 5-9
Parent Co: Archibald Candy Corporation

4336 Fanny Mason Farmstead Cheese
13 Boggy Meadow Ln
Walpole, NH 03608 603-756-3300
Fax: 603-756-9645 info@fannymasoncheese.com
www.fannymasoncheese.com
Cheese
Owner: Marcus Lovell-Smith
CEO: Scott Lyndecker
CFO: Sharlene Braldey
Plant Manager: Mark Whitney
Estimated Sales: $ .5 - 1 million
Number Employees: 5-9
Number of Products: 3
Type of Packaging: Private Label

4337 Fantasia
PO Box 1267
Sedalia, MO 65302-1267 660-827-1172
Fax: 660-827-3653
Frozen cakes
President: Robert Wright
VP Sales: Thad Bagnato
Plant Manager: Trent Wanamaker
Purchasing Agent: Mike Mallory
Estimated Sales: $10-20 Million
Number Employees: 147

4338 Fantastic Foods
580 Gateway Dr
Napa, CA 94558 707-254-3700
Fax: 707-259-0219 800-288-1089
jforaker@consorzio.com
www.fantasticfoods.com
Manufacturer of vegetarian convenience foods including soups and rice; importer of rice
Founder: Jim Rosen
Finance Executive: John Foraker
SVP: Mark Mortimer
Marketing Executive: Sarah Bird
VP Sales: Karen Borie
Human Resources Executive: Mark Wagner
VP Operations: Randy Hopkins
Estimated Sales: $20-50 Million
Number Employees: 30
Sq. footage: 150000
Type of Packaging: Consumer
Brands:
FANTASTIC
JUMPING BLACK BEANS
NATURE'S BURGER MIX
TABOULI SALAD MIX
TOFU BURGER MIX
TOFU SCRAMBLER MIX

4339 Fantasy Chocolates
2885 S Congress Ave Ste A
Delray Beach, FL 33445 561-276-9007
Fax: 561-265-0027 800-804-4962
fantasychocolate@aol.com
Manufacturer and exporter of chocolate novelties and gourmet pretzels including chocolate, keylime, chocolate pizza, caramel and chocolate apple
President: Becky Gardner
Products: Bill Gardner
Estimated Sales: $2.5-5 Million
Number Employees: 5-9
Type of Packaging: Consumer, Private Label, Bulk
Brands:
CHOCOLATE OREOS
CHOCOLATE PIZZA
FORBIDDEN FRUIT
KEYLIME GRAHAM CRACKERS
LOGO CHOCOLATES
NOVELTY CHOCOLATES
PARTY PRETZELS
PEANUT BUTTER DREAM

4340 Fantasy Cookie Company
12322 Gladstone Ave
Sylmar, CA 91342-5318 818-361-6901
Fax: 818-365-0040 800-354-4488
www.fantasycookie.com
Manufacturer of cookies including low fat, fruit juice sweetened and holiday; also, gingerbread houses
President/CEO: Joseph Semder
VP Sales: Richard Semder
Estimated Sales: $ 3 - 5 Million
Number Employees: 5-9
Type of Packaging: Private Label, Bulk

4341 Fantazzmo Fun Stuff
425 N Martingale Road
Suite 1680
Schaumburg, IL 60173-2214 847-413-1700
Fax: 847-413-1885 mikecavalier@fantazzmo.com
www.fantazzmo.com
Manufacturer of Novelty candy
VP Marketing: Deirdre Gonzalez
Brands:
CANDY WHISTLER
SLIDE POPS
SPORT TOTOE 'EMS
TOTE 'EMS
WONKA
WONKA PIXY STIX MIXERS
XTREME NERDS

4342 Fantini Baking Company
375 Washington St
Haverhill, MA 01832 978-912-7530
Fax: 978-373-6250 800-343-2110
Breads
President: Robert Fantini
VP: Joe Fantini
Estimated Sales: $1-2.5 Million
Number Employees: 100-249

4343 Fantis Foods
60 Triangle Blvd
Carlstadt, NJ 07072 201-933-6200
Fax: 201-933-8797 info@fantisfoods.com
www.fantisfoods.com
Olive oil, olives, cheese, seafood, gourmet, pasta, mineral water, cookies and baked goods, gyros, frozen pastries, herbs and spices, confectionary, bean and rice, drinks
President: George Makris
VP/CFO: Jerry Makris
VP/Manager: Steve Makris
Sales Executive/Sales Manager: Bill Paelekanos
Estimated Sales: $6 Million
Number Employees: 35
Sq. footage: 70000
Type of Packaging: Consumer

4344 Far Eastern Coconut Company
200 Corporate Plz Ste 201a
Islandia, NY 11749 631-851-8800
Fax: 631-851-7950 flakes350@aol.com
www.fareasterncoconut.com
Manufacturer and importer of desiccated and sweetened coconut
President: Mitchell Bauman
VP: Anthony Armen
Estimated Sales: $ 3 - 5 Million
Number Employees: 10
Sq. footage: 4000
Type of Packaging: Food Service, Bulk
Brands:
PALM FLAKE

4345 **Far Niente Winery**
1350 Acacia Dr
Oakville, CA 94562 707-944-2861
Fax: 707-944-2312 www.farniente.com
Wines
Owner: Beth Nickel
CFO: Laura Harwood
Estimated Sales: $10-20 Million
Number Employees: 50-99

4346 **Far West Rice Inc**
P.O.Box 370
Durham, CA 95938 530-891-1339
Fax: 530-891-0723 greg@greatrice.com
www.farwestrice.com
Mill, paakage and market rice for food service and retail demands.
President: C W Johnson
CEO: Greg Johnson
Research & Development: Steve Ross
Marketing Director: Greg Johnson
Operations Manager: Steve Ross
Estimated Sales: $10 Million
Number Employees: 20-49
Number of Brands: 10
Number of Products: 100
Type of Packaging: Consumer, Food Service, Private Label, Bulk
Brands:
CALROSE RICE
FUKUSUKE RICE
KOMACHI PREMIUM RICE
VALLEY SUN ORGANIC BROWN RICE

4347 **Farallon Fisheries**
207 S Maple Ave
South San Francisco, CA 94080 650-583-3474
Fax: 650-583-0137
Manufacturer of seafood
Manager: Juan De Alva
Contact: Aiden Coburn
Estimated Sales: $500,000-$1 Million
Number Employees: 10-19
Brands:
Farallon Foods

4348 **Farb's**
241 Pismo St
San Luis Obispo, CA 93401 805-543-1412
President: Phillip Farber
Vice President: Barbara Farber
Estimated Sales: $1.3 Million
Number Employees: 9

4349 **Farbest Foods**
4689 S 400w
Huntingburg, IN 47542 812-683-4200
Fax: 812-683-4226 www.farbestfoods.com
Manufacturer of turkey and turkey products
President: Charles La Rue
Plant Manager: Charlie LaRue
Purchasing Manager: S Jean Mikula
Estimated Sales: $82 Million
Number Employees: 500-999
Type of Packaging: Consumer, Food Service, Private Label, Bulk
Brands:
COUNTRY FESTIVAL
FARBEST FOODS
HERITAGE PRIDE

4350 **(HQ)Farbest-Tallman Foods Corporation**
160 Summit Ave Ste 2
Montvale, NJ 7645 201-573-4900
Fax: 201-573-0404 dwhobrey@farbest.com
www.farbest.com
Manufacturer of dairy and soy proteins, carbohydrate sytems, vitamins, and nutraceuticals
President: Daniel Meloro
Estimated Sales: $20-50 Million
Number Employees: 20-49
Type of Packaging: Bulk
Other Locations:
Farbest Brands
Louisville KY
Farbest Brands
Huntington Beach CA
Farbest Brands - Manufacturing
Plain City OH
Brands:
FARBEST

4351 **Farella-Park Vineyards**
2222 N 3rd Ave
Napa, CA 94558-3840 707-254-9489
www.farella.com
Wines
Owner: Frank Farella
Estimated Sales: $ 1 - 3 Million
Number Employees: 1-4

4352 **Farfelu Vineyards**
13058 Crest Hill Road
Flint Hill, VA 22627-1814 540-364-2930
Fax: 540-364-3930 c-info@farfeluwine.com
www.farfeluwine.com
Wines
Owner: C Raney
Estimated Sales: $500,000-$1 Million
Number Employees: 1-4

4353 **Fargo Packing & SausagecCompany**
307 Main Ave E
West Fargo, ND 58078 701-282-3211
Fax: 701-282-0325 800-342-4250
lmccleary@qualitymeats.com
www.qualitymeats.com
Manufacturer and packer of meat and meat products including ham, bacon and sausage
President: Dan Richard
CEO: Cary Wetzstein
Director of Purchasing: Lee McCleary
Estimated Sales: $20-50 Million
Number Employees: 20-49
Parent Co: Quality Boneless Beef Company
Type of Packaging: Consumer, Food Service

4354 **(HQ)Faribault Foods**
222 S 9th St Ste 3380
Minneapolis, MN 55402 612-333-6461
Fax: 612-342-2908 MKTG@faribaultfoods.com
www.faribaultfoods.com
Manufacturer of canned beans, chicken, chili, pasta, soups, stews and vegetables including peas, corn and green beans.
President: Reid V Mac Donald
EVP/CFO: Gary Kindseth
EVP Research/Engineering: Jim Nelson
EVP Sales/Marketing: Frank Lynch
VP Strategic Sourcing: Jim Montealegre
Director Human Resources: Amy Dellis
VP Manufacturing: Scott King
VP Purchasing/Contract Management: Andy Murray
Estimated Sales: $164 Million
Number Employees: 5-9
Type of Packaging: Consumer, Private Label
Other Locations:
Faribault Foods Distribution
Faribault MN
Faribault Foods Plant
Cokato MN
Brands:
BUTTER KERNEL
CHILLI MAN
FINEST
KUNERS
MRS GRIMES
PASTA SELECT
PRIDE
SEASIDE
SUN VISTA

4355 **(HQ)Faribault Foods**
222 S 9th St Ste 3380
Minneapolis, MN 55402 612-333-6461
Fax: 612-342-2908 www.faribaultfoods.com
Manufacturer and exporter of canned food products including dried beans, peas, corn and pasta
President: Reid V Mac Donald
CEO: Reid MacDonald
CFO: Mark Hentges
Exec VP/Treasurer: Gary Kindseth
Exec VP Marketing: Mike Peroutka
Exec VP Sales: Mike Peroutka
VP Operations: Mike Cureton
Production Superintendent: Brenda Probst
Plant Manager: Dave Cross
VP Purchasing/Contract Management: Andy Murray
Estimated Sales: $50-100 Million
Number Employees: 5-9
Type of Packaging: Consumer, Private Label
Other Locations:
Faribault Foods
Faribault MN
Faribault Foods - Mondovi Plant
Mondovi WI
Faribault Foods - Grimes Dist.
Grimes IA
Faribault Foods - Kuner's Dist.
Brighton CO
Faribault Foods - Cokato Plant
Cokato MN
Brands:
BUTTER KERNEL®
CHILLIMAN® CHILI
KUMER'S SOUTHWESTERN®
KUNER'S®
MRS. GRIMES®
PASTA SELECT®
PRIDE®
S&W BEANS®

4356 **Faribault Foods**
15403 Us Highway 12 SW
Cokato, MN 55321 320-286-2166
Fax: 320-286-5142 www.faribaultfoods.com
Manufacturer and exporter of canned corn and pasta products
President/CEO: Reid MacDonald
Vice President: Gary Kindseth
EVP Corporate Research/Engineering: Jim Nelson
Senior QA Manager: Jean Berger
Product Development Manager: Judene Smahal
Food Technologist Manager: Phyllis Nichols
HR Supervisor/Office Manager: Kathy Nowak
Maintenance Superintendent: Ray Youngkrantz
Production Manager: Tina Noyes
Plant Manager: Allen Anderson
Purchasing Coordinator: Terry Hauth
Estimated Sales: $ 50 - 100 Million
Number Employees: 100-249
Parent Co: Faribault Foods
Type of Packaging: Consumer

4357 **Faridault Food**
13512 Business Center Dr NW
Elk River, MN 55330-4612 763-241-7343
Fax: 763-241-7412 service@spftpacinc.com
www.fairbaultfoods.com
Flexible packaging
president: John Ambrose
Marketing Manager: chris Ambrose
Plant Manager: John Anderson
Brands:
Faridault

4358 **Farley Candy Company**
2945 W 31st St
Chicago, IL 60623-5104 773-254-0900
Fax: 773-254-0795 www.kelloggs.com
Chocolate candy
President: Williams Sampson
Sales: Keith Barton
Plant Manager: Larry Carroll
Estimated Sales: $50-99.9 Million
Number Employees: 100-249

4359 **Farley's & Sathers Candy Company**
P.O.Box 28
Round Lake, MN 56167 507-945-8181
Fax: 507-945-8343 800-533-0330
comments@farleysandsathers.com
www.farleysandsathers.com
Processor and exporter of candy including butterscotch, caramels, chocolate, jelly beans, hard, licorice, lollypops, mints, marshmallows, nougats, etc.
President: Dennis Nemeth
CEO: Liam Killeen
CFO: Tammy Koller
R&D: John Flanyak
Marketing: Matthew Fenton
Sales: Mike Sprinkle
Public Relations: Theresa Neuburger
Operations: Kevin McElvain
Estimated Sales: $600 Million
Parent Co: Farley's & Sathers Candy Company
Type of Packaging: Food Service, Private Label, Bulk
Brands:
ANDES CANDIES
AUTUMN LEAVES
BEAR PAKS
BEST OF BROCK
BLUE RASPBERRY
BRACH

BRACH'S CANDY
BRACH'S TDS
BUNNY PRINTS
BUNNY TAILS
BUTTERLETS
CANDY DISH
CHAMPS COLLEGE
CHATTANOOGA CHOO CHOO
CHRISTMAS CRITTERS
CHUBBY SANTA
COOL BLUE
CORDIALLY YOURS
DOUBLE DIPPERS
EASTER BUTTERCREME CRITTERS
EASTER HUNT CANDIES
EASTER JORDAN
EASTER PARADE
FRIGHT BITES
FRITOS
FRUIT BASKET
FRUIT SNACKERS
GUM DINGER
GUMMY SQUIRMS
HECTOR RABBIT
HIDE A PAKS
HIDE-A-WAY EGGS
KENTUCKY MINTS
LOVE
MEMORY
MINI-MONSTERS CANDY
MINT COOLERS
MINT PEARLS
MINTS JOTS
MY OWN BUNNY
NIK NAKS
NINJA TROLLS
NUBBINS
OLD FASHIONED
OLDE WORLD GOURMET GUMMIES
PERKY'S
POWER PLUS
PUCKER HUSTLE
PUTTERS
SANTA SNACKS
SASSY HEARTS
SCARY POPS
SCARY TARTS
SCHULER
SIZZLE HEART
SOUR BEASTIES GUM
SOUR SPOTS JELLY BIRD EGGS
SPARKLES
SPEARMINTLETS
SPECIAL TREASURES
SPERRY
SPRING BOUQUET
SQUIRMS
STARS
TARGETS
TREE TRIMMERS
VILLA CHERRIES
TARGETS
TREE TRIMMERS
VILLA CHERRIES
YUMMY GUMMY MUMMIES

4360 Farm 2 Market

P.O.Box 124
Roscoe, NY 12776 607-498-5448
Fax: 607-498-5275 800-663-4326
info@farm-2market.com
www.farm-2-market.com
Manufacturer of seafood including farm raised shrimp, freshwater prawns, scallops, crawfish and oysters; importer of Australian crawfish and freshwater prawns
President: Marshall Shnider
Estimated Sales: $3-5 Million
Number Employees: 10-19
Type of Packaging: Consumer, Food Service
Brands:
SWEET-WATER

4361 (HQ)Farm Boy Food Service

P.O.Box 996
Evansville, IN 47706-0996 812-425-5231
Fax: 812-428-8432 800-852-3976
www.farmboyfoodservice.com
Manufacturer of beef and pork; wholesaler/distributor of frozen, refrigerated and dry food products, meat, equipment and fixtures, etc.; serving the food service market
President/Co-Owner: Bob Bonenberger
VP/Co-Owner: Rich Bonenberger
Estimated Sales: $38 Million
Number Employees: 50-99
Type of Packaging: Consumer, Food Service, Private Label

4362 Farm Fresh Catfish Company

1616 Rice Mill Road
Hollandale, MS 38748 662-827-2204
Fax: 662-827-7348 800-647-8264
Manufacturer and exporter of fresh and frozen farmed raised catfish
President/CEO: Willard Fehr
Estimated Sales: $50-99.9 Million
Number Employees: 250-499
Type of Packaging: Consumer, Food Service, Private Label, Bulk
Brands:
FARM FRESH

4363 Farm Pak Products

7840 Old Bailey Hwy
Spring Hope, NC 27882-8393 252-459-3101
Fax: 252-459-9020 www.farmpak.com
Manufacturer and exporter of produce including sweet potatoes
Owner/President: Carson Barnes
Sales: Eddie Lee
Packhouse Manager: Frank Salinas
Estimated Sales: $20-50 Million
Number Employees: 50-99
Type of Packaging: Consumer, Bulk

4364 Farm Stores

18001 Old Cutler Rd, Ste 370
Palmetto Bay, FL 33157 305-255-5933
Fax: 305-513-4176 800-726-3276
www.farmstores.com
Ice cream and dairy products
President/CEO: Carlos Bared
VP Marketing: Manuel Portuondo
COO: Maurice Bared
Estimated Sales: $50-100 Million
Number Employees: 700

4365 Farm T Market Company

P.O.Box 727
Somerville, TN 38068-0727 901-465-2844
Fax: 901-465-6812
Produce
President: Frank Boswell
Estimated Sales: $ 1 - 3 Million
Number Employees: 10-19

4366 FarmGro Organic Foods

101-2445 13th Avenue
Regina, SK S4P 0W1
Canada 306-522-0092
Fax: 306-721-3130 info@farmgro-organic.com
Manufacturer of organic food
President: Bruce Johnson
CFO: Dennis Puff
Purchase Manager: Tim Beard

4367 FarmSoy Company

116 Second Road
Summertown, TN 38483 931-964-2411
barbara@farmsoy.com
www.farmsoy.com
Soymilk and tofu
President: Thomas Elliot
VP: Barbara Elliot
Estimated Sales: $50,000
Number Employees: 7
Sq. footage: 1200

4368 Farmacopia

23600 Big Basin Way
Saratoga, CA 95070-9755 831-335-8401
Fax: 831-335-5601 888-827-3623
roberta@sosbee.com www.farmacopia.com
Condiments, dressings and sauces
Owner: Bette Mermis
Vice President: John Mermis
Estimated Sales: $5-9.9 Million
Number Employees: 5
Brands:
Saveur

4369 Farmdale Creamery

1049 W Base Line St
San Bernardino, CA 92411 909-889-3002
Fax: 909-888-2541 www.farmdale.net
Creamery
Vice President: Vince Sibilio
Plant Manager: Norman Shotts
Estimated Sales: $10 Million
Number Employees: 70

4370 (HQ)Farmer Brothers Company

P.O.Box 2959
Torrance, CA 90509 310-787-5350
Fax: 310-787-5246 800-735-2878
info@farmerbroscousa.com
www.farmerbroscousa.com
Manufacturer of coffees, teas, beverage mixes and spices
Chairman/President/CEO: Guenter Berger
CFO/Treasurer: John Simmons
CEO: Roger M Laverty Iii
Estimated Sales: $193,600,000
Number Employees: 1,000-4,999
Type of Packaging: Food Service

4371 Farmers Co-operative Grain Company

P.O.Box 246
Kinde, MI 48445 989-874-4200
Fax: 989-874-5793 kindecoop@centurytel.net
www.kindecoop.com
Manufacturer of dried beans
President: Jeff Kreh
CEO: Dan Gottschalk
Estimated Sales: $10-20 Million
Number Employees: 20-49
Type of Packaging: Consumer

4372 Farmers Coop Creamery

700 N. Hwy 99W
McMinnville, OR 97128 503-472-2157
Fax: 503-472-3821 info@farmerscoop.org
www.farmerscoop.org
Manufacturer and exporter of butter and powdered milk
President: Dan Bansen
CEO/Secretary: Mike Anderson
CEO: Michael Anderson
Estimated Sales: $50-100 Million
Number Employees: 20-49
Type of Packaging: Consumer, Food Service, Bulk

4373 (HQ)Farmers Cooperative Dairy

PO Box 8118
Halifax, NS B3K 5Y6
Canada 902-835-3373
Fax: 902-835-1583 800-565-1945
customerservice@farmersdairy.ca
www.farmersdairy.ca
Manufacturer of dairy products including milk, yogurt, ice cream, cheese, sour cream, etc
CEO/President: Kenneth Peacock
Export Manager: Ron Burry
Estimated Sales: $100+ Million
Number Employees: 500-999
Type of Packaging: Consumer, Food Service, Private Label
Other Locations:

4374 Farmers Dairies

7321 N Loop Dr
El Paso, TX 79915 915-772-2736
Fax: 915-772-0907
Dairy products
Partner: Adalberto Navar
Partner: Miguel Navar
Office Manager: Monica Navar
Estimated Sales: $19 Million
Number Employees: 108

4375 Farmers Hen House

1956 520th St SW
Kalona, IA 52247-9173 319-683-2206
Fax: 319-683-2256
Manufacturer of eggs; commercial, organic and cage free
President: Mark Miller
Estimated Sales: $10-20 Million
Number Employees: 10-19
Brands:
FARMERS HEN HOUSE

4376 (HQ)Farmers Investment Company

1625 E Sahuarita Rd
Sahuarita, AZ 85629 520-625-8809
Fax: 520-791-2853

President: Elizabeth Alexander
Manager: Layne Brandt
Plant Manager: Albert Celaya
Estimated Sales: $20-50 Million
Number Employees: 20-49

4377 **Farmers Meat Market**
5213 50 St
Viking, AB T0B 4N0
Canada 780-336-3241
Fax: 780-336-0180
Processor of bologna, cured meats and wild game including deer, elk and moose, famous original viking wieners
President: Eugene Miskew
Sales: Shirley Miskewn
Purchasing Manager: Chris Ferguson
Estimated Sales: $150,000
Number Employees: 2
Type of Packaging: Private Label

4378 **Farmers Produce**
103 Melby Ave
Ashby, MN 56309 218-747-2749
Manufacturer of chicken
Owner: Paul Ellingson
Estimated Sales: $ 3 - 5 Million
Number Employees: 10-19
Type of Packaging: Consumer

4379 **Farmers Rice Milling Company**
P.O.Box 3704
Lake Charles, LA 70602-3704 337-433-5205
Fax: 337-433-1735 sales@FRMCO.com
www.frmco.com
Manufacturer and exporter of rice and rice bran
President: Jamie Warshaw
CFO: Gregory Mack
Vice President: Charles Miia
VP Sales: Charles Miia
Production Manager: Richard Deville
Estimated Sales: $50-100 Million
Number Employees: 50-99
Parent Co: Powell Group
Type of Packaging: Consumer, Food Service
Brands:
Cajun Pride Rice

4380 **Farmers Seafood Company**
P.O.Box 1225
Shreveport, LA 71163-1225 318-221-9957
Fax: 318-424-2029 800-874-0203
farmersseafood@aol.com
www.farmersseafood.com
Wholesaler/distributor of groceries, dairy products and seafood; serving the food service market
President: Alexander Mijalis
Estimated Sales: $5-10 Million
Number Employees: 50-99

4381 **Farmers' Rice Cooperative**
P.O.Box 15223
Sacramento, CA 95851 916-923-5100
Fax: 916-920-4295 800-326-2799
www.farmersrice.com
Domestic, international, institutional, bulk and packaged rice milling and marketing
President/CEO: Robert Sandrock
CFO/VP: James Dodson
Estimated Sales: $100-500 Million
Number Employees: 20-49

4382 **Farmington Food**
7419 W Franklin St
Forest Park, IL 60130 708-771-3600
Fax: 708-771-2643 800-609-3276
info@farmingtonfoods.com
www.farmingtonfoods.com
Manufacturer and wholesaler/distributor and packer of meat
President: Frank Dijohn
Estimated Sales: $50-100 Million
Number Employees: 100-249

4383 **Farmland Dairies**
520 Main Avenue
Wallington, NJ 07057 973-777-2500
Fax: 973-249-3849 888-727-6252
questions@farmlanddairies.com
www.farmlanddairies.com
Manufacturer of milk, ice cream, yogurt, juice and ice tea
President/CEO: Martin Margherio
VP Finance: Anthony Mayzun
Estimated Sales: $200+ Million
Number Employees: 500
Sq. footage: 150000
Parent Co: Groupo LALA/LALA National Dairy Group
Type of Packaging: Consumer, Food Service
Other Locations:
Farmland Dairies Facility
Wallington NJ
Farmland Dairies Facility
Newark NJ
Farmland Dairies Facility
Grand Rapids MI
Brands:
ALTANTA DAIRY
CLINTON'S
FARMLAND DAIRIES
FARMLAND DAIRIES SPECIAL REQUEST
SCHOOL MILK!
SKIM PLUS
SUNNYDALE FARMS
WELSH FARMS

4384 **Farmland Foods**
401 N Grant Rd
Carroll, IA 51401 712-792-1660
Fax: 712-792-1372 www.farmlandfoods.com
Manufacturer and canner of ham
Plant Manager: Jeff Bowden
Estimated Sales: $50-100 Million
Number Employees: 120
Parent Co: Farmland Industries
Type of Packaging: Consumer, Food Service, Private Label, Bulk
Brands:
FARMLAND

4385 **Farmland Foods**
800 Industrial Dr
Denison, IA 51442 712-263-5002
Fax: 712-263-7330 800-831-1812
rxcarlson@farmland.com
www.farmlandfoods.com
Manufacturer, exporter and packager of pork; also, slaughtering services available
Manager: Todd Gerken
Mannufacturing/Operations Director: Jim Schaben
Plant Manager: Jerry Behrens
Purchasing Manager: Larry Schwarte
Estimated Sales: $500 Million-$1 Billion
Number Employees: 900
Sq. footage: 382000
Parent Co: Farmland Industries
Type of Packaging: Consumer, Food Service

4386 **(HQ)Farmland Foods**
P.O.Box 20121
Kansas City, MO 64195 816-801-4300
Fax: 816-243-3343 888-327-6526
info@farmlandfoods.com
www.farmlandfoods.com
Manufacturer and exporter of fresh and frozen bacon, ham, hot dogs, deli & lunch meat and sausage.
Presidnt/COO: Michael Brown
CFO: Shelly Phalen
VP Human Resources: Mark Garrett
Estimated Sales: $1 Billion
Number Employees: 6,123
Type of Packaging: Consumer, Food Service, Private Label, Bulk
Other Locations:
Farmland Foods Plant
Monmouth IL
Farmland Foods Plant
Denison IA
Farmland Foods Plant
Wichita KS
Farmland Foods Plant
Springfield MA
Farmland Foods Plant
Crete NE
Farmland Foods Plant
New Riegel OH
Farmland Foods Plant
Carroll IA
Farmland Foods Plant
Salt Lake City UT
Brands:
CARANDO
FARMLAND
OHSE
ROEGELEIN

4387 **Farmland Foods**
401 N Grant Rd
Carroll, IA 51401 712-792-1660
Fax: 712-792-1372 www.farmlandfoods.com
Manufacturer of meats
VP: Tom Farner
Plant Manager: Jeff Bowden
Estimated Sales: $20-50 Million

4388 **Faroh Candies**
7223 Pearl Rd
Cleveland, OH 44130-4805 440-888-9866
Fax: 440-842-4013
Manufacturer of confectionery products including boxed chocolates, chocolate cherries and popcorn specialties.
Owner: George Faroh
Purchasing: Donna Parrot
Estimated Sales: $5-10 Million
Number Employees: 20-49
Type of Packaging: Consumer

4389 **Farr Candy Company**
250 S Boulevard
Idaho Falls, ID 83402 208-522-8215
Fax: 208-523-3307 www.farrcandy.com
Manufacturer of confectionery products including cherry cordials, peanut clusters and malo nuts; also, ice cream
President/Owner: Kevin Call
Estimated Sales: $ 3 - 5 Million
Number Employees: 10-19

4390 **Farrell Baking Company**
26 Stefanak Dr
West Middlesex, PA 16159-3138 724-342-7906
Bread and bakery products
President: Rick Vatavuk
Owner: Richard Vatavuk
Estimated Sales: $1-2.5 Million
Number Employees: 10-19
Brands:
Farrell Baking

4391 **Fast Fixin Foods**
1481 Us Highway 431
Boaz, AL 35957 256-593-7221
Fax: 256-593-7208
Manufacturer of fast foods
Owner: Ricky Ragsdale
Estimated Sales: $ 10 - 20 Million
Number Employees: 10-19

4392 **Fast Food Merchandisers**
2641 Meadowbrook Rd
Rocky Mount, NC ÿ27801-949 252-450-4000
Fax: 252-985-6605
Producers of prepared foods.
Estimated Sales: Under $500,000
Number Employees: 10-19

4393 **Fastachi**
598 Mount Auburn St
Watertown, MA 02472 617-924-8787
800-466-3022
info@fastachi.com www.fastachi.com
Produces candy, chocolate, dried fruits and nuts.
Estimated Sales: $300,000-500,000
Number Employees: 1-4

4394 **Fastachi**
598 Mount Auburn St
Watertown, MA 02472 617-924-8787
Fax: 617-924-8844 800-466-3022
souren@fastachi.com www.fastachi.com
Processor of almonds, cashews, pistachios, hazelnuts, peanuts and sunflower seeds; also, gift baskets available
President/CEO: Souren Etyenezian
Estimated Sales: Less than $500,000
Number Employees: 1-4
Brands:
Fastachi

4395 **(HQ)Fasweet Company**
P.O.Box 5000
Jonesboro, AR 72403 870-932-1562
Fax: 870-932-1114 www.fasweet.com
Manufacturer of sugar substitutes
President: Jake Morse
Estimated Sales: $5-10 Million
Number Employees: 5-9
Sq. footage: 10000
Parent Co: Morse Company

Type of Packaging: Consumer, Food Service
Brands:
Fasweet

4396 **Fat Witch Bakery**
75 Ninth Avenue
New York, NY 10011 212-807-1335
Fax: 212-807-7993 888-419-4824
patwitch@fatwitch.com www.fatwitch.com
Brownies

4397 **FatBoy Cookie Company**
18-01 River Road
Fair Lawn, NJ 07410 201-796-1000
Fax: 201-475-3501 888-328-2690
fatboycookies@aol.com
www.outrageouscookiedough.com
Cookie dough
President/Owner: Joel Ansh

4398 **Father Sam's Bakery**
105 Msgr Valente Dr
Buffalo, NY 14206 716-853-1071
Fax: 716-853-1062 800-521-6719
info@fathersams.com OR
dziolkowski@fathersams.com
www.fathersams.com
Manufactures regular and large pocket bread, mini pocket bread, and wraps.
Founder: Albert Sam
President: William Sam
Marketing: Dennis Ziolkowski
VP Sales: Glenn Povitz
Estimated Sales: $ 20 - 50 Million
Number Employees: 50-99
Type of Packaging: Food Service

4399 **Father Sam's Syrian Bread**
105 Monsignor Valente Dr
Buffalo, NY 14206-1815 716-853-1071
Fax: 716-853-1062 800-521-6719
info@fatherssams.com www.fathersams.com
Manufacturer of Syrian-style pocket bread, tortilla shells and thin-style pita bread
President: William Sam
Estimated Sales: $20-50 Million
Number Employees: 50-99
Sq. footage: 40000
Type of Packaging: Consumer, Food Service, Private Label
Brands:
FATHER SAM'S POCKET BREADS
FATHER SAM'S TORTILLAS
FATHER SAM'S WRAPS

4400 **Father's Country Hams**
P.O.Box 99
Bremen, KY 42325-0099 270-525-3554
Fax: 270-525-3333 www.fatherscountryhams.com
Ham, bacon, and smoked sausage
President: Charles Gatton Jr
Estimated Sales: $ .5 - 1 million
Number Employees: 5-9

4401 **Fauchon**
442 Park Ave
New York, NY 10022 212-308-5919
Fax: 212-605-0421 877-605-0130
Chocolate, tea, coffee, cookies, mustard, oil
Estimated Sales: Less than $500,000
Number Employees: 1-4

4402 **Favorite Foods**
6934 Greenwood Street
Burnaby, BC V5A 1X8
Canada 604-420-5100
Fax: 604-420-9116
Manufacturer and exporter of sauces including light and dark soy, oyster, teriyaki, marinade, barbecue, black bean, stir fry, Szechuan spicy hot and plum
President: Henry Lam
Number Employees: 10-19
Sq. footage: 35000
Type of Packaging: Consumer, Food Service, Private Label, Bulk
Brands:
Golden Dragon

4403 **Fayes Bakery Products**
216 E Business Us Highway 60
Dexter, MO 63841-1222 573-624-4920
Manufacturer of bakery products
Owner: Dale Parks
Estimated Sales: $ .5 - 1 million
Number Employees: 1-4

4404 **Faygo Beverages**
3579 Gratiot Ave
Detroit, MI 48207 313-925-1600
Fax: 313-571-7611 800-347-6591
www.faygo.com
Manufacturer of carbonated soft drinks
President: Stan Sheridan
CEO: Nick A Caporella
Number Employees: 500-999
Parent Co: National Beverage Company
Type of Packaging: Consumer, Private Label

4405 **Fayter Farms Produce**
69400 Jolon Rd
Bradley, CA 93426-9676 831-385-8515
Fax: 831-385-0833 fayterfarms@earthlink.net
Fresh herbicide pesticide-free Kiss of Burgundy globe artichokes.
President: Thomas Fayter
Estimated Sales: $300,000-500,000
Number Employees: 1-4
Type of Packaging: Private Label, Bulk
Other Locations:
Fayter Farms Produce
Bradley CA
Brands:
Globe Artichoke
Kiss of Burgundy

4406 **Fearn Natural Foods**
P.O.Box 248
Thiensville, WI 53092 262-242-2400
Fax: 262-242-2751 800-877-8935
modernfearn@aol.com www.modernfearn.com
Manufacturer and exporter of natural food products including baking, pancake and dehydrated soup mixes, soybean and rice flour, breakfast cereals, wheat germ and powdered milk
President: Gaylord Palermo
Estimated Sales: $ 10 - 20 Million
Number Employees: 20-49
Sq. footage: 70000
Parent Co: Modern Products
Type of Packaging: Consumer, Food Service, Private Label, Bulk
Brands:
FEARN®
GAYELORD HAUSER®

4407 **Fearnow Brothers**
994 Ocean Dr
Cape May, NJ 08204-5400 609-884-0440
Fax: 609-898-2409 fearnow@lov-stew.com
www.lov-stew.com
Canned foods
Controller: Larry Rossello
Estimated Sales: $5-9.9 Million
Number Employees: 100-249
Brands:
MRS. FEARNOW'S

4408 **Feaster Foods**
11808 W Center Rd
Omaha, NE 68144-4434 402-691-8800
Fax: 402-691-7920 800-228-6098
www.marioolive.com
Real bacon bits, sunflower kernels, imitation bacon bits
CEO: Dick Westin
Purchasing Manager: Scott Bailey
Estimated Sales: F
Number Employees: 20-49

4409 **Feature Foods**
15 Meteor Drive
Etobicoke, ON M9W 1A3
Canada 416-675-7350
Fax: 416-675-7428 info@featurefoods.com
www.featurefoods.com
Manufacturer and exporter of pickled eggs and herring; also, herb horseradish
Number Employees: 20-49
Type of Packaging: Consumer

4410 **Federal Pretzel Baking Company**
300 Eagle Court
Bridgeport, NJ 08014 215-467-0505
Fax: 215-467-3153 www.federalpretzel.biz
Manufacturer of soft pretzels
Owner: Florence Sciambi
Estimated Sales: $1-2.5 Million
Number Employees: 20-49
Type of Packaging: Consumer

4411 **Federal Pretzel Baking Company**
638 Federal Street
Philadelphia, PA 19147-4845 215-467-0505
Fax: 215-467-3153
Manufacturer of pretzels, cookies
President: Florence Sciambi
Plant Manager: Rich Bezila
Estimated Sales: $1-2.5 Million
Number Employees: 20-49
Brands:
Federal Pretzel

4412 **Federation of Southern Cooperatives**
2769 Church St
East Point, GA 30344 404-765-0991
Fax: 404-765-9178 fsc@mindspring.com
www.federation.coop
Manufacturer and exporter of fresh vegetables
Executive Director: Ralph Paige
Executive Director: Ralph Paige
Estimated Sales: $500,000-$1 Million
Number Employees: 20-49
Type of Packaging: Consumer, Bulk

4413 **Fee Brothers**
453 Portland Ave
Rochester, NY 14605 585-544-9530
Fax: 585-544-9530 800-961-3337
info@feebrothers.com www.feebrothers.com
Manufacturer and exporter of cocktail mixes including whiskey sour, daiquiri, margarita, pina colada, etc.; also, slush bases, bitters, nonalcoholic cordials, tea and juice concentrates, grenadine, coffee flavoring syrups, maraschinocherries, olives, cocktail
President: John Fee
CEO: Ellen Fee
Treasurer: Joe Fee
Estimated Sales: $1 Million
Number Employees: 5-9
Number of Brands: 1
Number of Products: 90
Sq. footage: 32000
Type of Packaging: Food Service, Private Label, Bulk
Brands:
Fee Brothers

4414 **Fehr Foods**
5425 N 1st St
Abilene, TX 79603 325-691-5425
Fax: 325-691-5471 www.fehrfoods.com
Manufacturer of Lil' Dutch Main Sandwich Center wirecut cookies
President/CEO: Steven Fehr
Controller: Bruce Foreman
Production: Harry Kessner
Estimated Sales: $29 Million
Number Employees: 200

4415 **Felbro Food Products**
5700 W Adams Blvd
Los Angeles, CA 90016 323-936-5266
Fax: 323-936-5946 800-335-2761
info@felbro.com www.felbrofoods.com
Manufacturer, importer and exporter of fountain syrups, sauces, soup, gravy and beverage bases, ice cream toppings, flavors, colors and extracts; also, custom formulations and private labeling available
President: Barton Feldmar
Operations Manager: John Pesce
Estimated Sales: $20-50 Million
Number Employees: 20-49
Sq. footage: 40000
Type of Packaging: Consumer, Food Service, Private Label, Bulk
Brands:
Coffee Express
Food Tone

4416 **Felix Custom Smoking**
17461 147th St SE Ste 2a
Monroe, WA 98272 425-485-2439
Fax: 425-485-2439
Manufacturer of smoked and vacuum-packed salmon, cod and halibut
Owner: Diane Zollinger
Estimated Sales: Less than $500,000
Number Employees: 5-9
Type of Packaging: Private Label

4417 **Felix Roma & Sons**
2 S Page Avenue
Endicott, NY 13760 607-748-3336
Fax: 607-748-3607 www.felixroma.com
Manufacturer of breads, rolls and pizza dough
President/CEO: Eugene Roma
VP: Barry Roma
VP/Sales Manager: Anthony Roma Jr
Office Manager: Mary Consentio
Bakery General Manager: James Wasley
VP/Frozen Foods Manager: Michael Roma
Production Manager: Brian Bertoni
Plant Manager: Eugene Roma Jr
Estimated Sales: $4.3 Million
Number Employees: 60
Sq. footage: 43000
Type of Packaging: Consumer, Food Service, Private Label, Bulk
Brands:
FELIX ROMA

4418 **Fenchem Enterprises**
5595 Daniels Street # F
Chino, CA 91710 909-627-5268
Fax: 909-627-3619 katyw@fenchem.com
www.fenchem.com
Manufactures natural ingredients for nutrition supplements and functional foods
President: Yanyan Zhu
Estimated Sales: 5-9

4419 **Fendall Ice Cream Company**
463 7th Ave
Salt Lake City, UT 84103 801-355-3583
Fax: 801-521-0133 gunter@fendalls.com
www.fendalls.com
Manufacturer and wholesaler/distributor of ice cream, sherbet, water ices, sorbets and frozen yogurt
Owner: Carol Radinger
Estimated Sales: $1-2.5 Million
Number Employees: 5-9
Type of Packaging: Consumer
Brands:
Cream of Weber
Fendall's

4420 **Fenestra Winery**
83 Vallecitos Rd
Livermore, CA 94550-9603 925-447-5246
Fax: 925-447-4655 800-789-9463
www.fenestrawinery.com
Wines
Owner: Lanny Replogle
Estimated Sales: $500,000-$1 Million
Number Employees: 1-4
Type of Packaging: Private Label
Brands:
FENESTRA WINERY

4421 **(HQ)Fenn Valley Vineyards**
6130 122nd Ave
Fennville, MI 49408-9457 269-561-2396
Fax: 269-561-2973 800-432-6265
winery@fennvalley.com www.fennvalley.com
Wines
President: Douglas Welsch
Estimated Sales: $500,000-$1 Million
Number Employees: 10-19

4422 **Fennimore Cheese**
1675 Lincoln Ave
Fennimore, WI 53809 608-822-6416
Fax: 608-822-6007 888-499-3778
igo@fennimorecheese.com www.fennimore.com
Manufacturer of cheese
Manager: Linda Parrish
Estimated Sales: $2.5-5 Million
Number Employees: 5-9
Type of Packaging: Consumer, Private Label, Bulk
Brands:
Bahl Baby

4423 **Fentimans North America**
2286 Holdom Avenuet
Burnaby, BC V5B 4Y5 877-326-3248
Fax: 877-326-3250 info@drinkfentimans.com
www.drinkfentimans.com
Botanically brewed beverages-natural sodas
President/Owner: Greg Warwick
Marketing: Craig James

4424 **Fenton & Lee Chocolatiers**
35 E 8th Avenue
Eugene, OR 97401-2906 541-343-7629
Fax: 541-343-6385 800-336-8661
www.fentonandlee.com
Chocolates and confections
President: Janele Smith
Estimated Sales: $2.5-5 Million
Number Employees: 5-9

4425 **Feridies/The Peanut Patch Inc.**
Po Box 186
28285 Mill Creek Drive
Courtland, VA 23837 757-653-9118
Fax: 757-653-9530 866-732-6883
tfries@feridies.com www.ferides.com/retailers
Gluten-free, kosher, organic/natural, other candy, hors d'oeuvres/appetizers, nuts, other snacks, gift packs.
Marketing: Jane Riddick-Fries

4426 **Ferko Meat Company**
P.O.Box 170966
Milwaukee, WI 53217 414-967-5500
Fax: 414-967-5515
Manufacturer of beef, chicken, veal, lamb and pork
President: Craig Nevins
Vice President: Ken Fischer
Purchasing Manager: Craig Nevins
Estimated Sales: $20-50 Million
Number Employees: 20-49
Sq. footage: 28000
Type of Packaging: Food Service

4427 **Ferme Ostreicole Dugas**
675 St-Pierre Blvd W
Caraquet, NB E1W 1A2
Canada 506-727-3226
Fax: 506-727-4950
Manufacturer of fresh oysters
President: Gaetan Dugas
Purchasing: Gaetan Dugas
Estimated Sales: $520,000
Number Employees: 6
Type of Packaging: Consumer, Food Service

4428 **Fernandez Chili Company**
8267 County Road 10 S
Alamosa, CO 81101-9176 719-589-6043
Fax: 719-587-0485
Manufacturer and importer of chili and taco sauces, spices and prepared chili mixes; also, Mexican corn products
President: Donald Fernandez
Estimated Sales: $5-10 Million
Number Employees: 5-9
Sq. footage: 15000
Type of Packaging: Consumer, Food Service, Bulk

4429 **Fernando C Pujals & Bros**
B St Cntro De Dist Amlia St
Guaynabo, PR 00968 787-792-3080
Fax: 787-792-8797
Manufacture of candy
President: Fernando Pujals
Estimated Sales: $ 24 Million
Number Employees: 80

4430 **Ferolito Vultaggio & Sons**
60 Crossways Park Dr W # 400
Woodbury, NY 11797-2003
Fax: 516-326-4988 800-832-3775
Manufacturer of beverages, general grocery
President: John Ferolito
CEO: Rick Adonailo
CEO/CFO: Richard Adonailo
CFO: Rick Adonailo
VP Corporate Communications: Francie Patton
Estimated Sales: $10-100 Million
Number Employees: 500-999
Type of Packaging: Private Label
Brands:
Arizona Iced Tea
Ferolito Vultaggio

4431 **Ferrante Winery & Ristorante**
5585 State Route 307
Geneva, OH 44041 440-466-6046
Fax: 440-466-7370 info@ferrantewinery.com
www.ferrantewinery.com
Manufacturer of wines
President: Peter Ferrante
VP: Nicholas Ferrante
General Manager: Mary Jo Ferrante
Estimated Sales: $10-20 Million
Number Employees: 20-49
Brands:
Ferrante

4432 **Ferrara Bakery & Cafe**
195 Grand St
New York, NY 10013 212-226-6150
Fax: 212-226-0667 information@ferraracafe.com
www.ferraracafe.com
Manufacturer and importer of confectionery products including candies, novelties, Italian and seasonal products; also, syrups, coffee and baked goods
Owner: Ernest Lepore
Owner/CEO: Peter Lepore
Estimated Sales: $5-10 Million
Number Employees: 100-249
Type of Packaging: Consumer, Private Label

4433 **Ferrara Pan Candy Company**
7301 W Harrison St
Forest Park, IL 60130 708-366-0500
Fax: 708-366-5921 800-323-1768
alana.ferrera@ferrarapan.com
www.ferrarapan.com
Manufacturer of candy including gummy, glazed nuts, sour balls, Valentine, jelly beans, licorice, hard candies, etc
President/COO: Salvatore Ferrara
CEO/Chairman: Nello Ferrara
CFO: Thomas Polke
VP International Sales: Louis Buffardi
Estimated Sales: $50-100 Million
Number Employees: 450
Type of Packaging: Consumer
Brands:
Atomic Fireball
Jaw Busters
Lemonheads
Original Boston Baked Beans
Red Hots
The Original Black Forest

4434 **Ferrara Winery**
1120 W 15th Ave
Escondido, CA 92025 760-745-7632
Manufacturer of wines
Owner: Gasper D Ferrara
CEO: Vera "Ferrara,"
Estimated Sales: $1-2.5 Million
Number Employees: 5-9
Brands:
Ferrara

4435 **Ferrari-Carano Vineyards& Winery**
8761 Dry Creek Rd
Healdsburg, CA 95448 707-433-6700
Fax: 707-431-1742 800-831-0381
info@ferrari-carano.com www.fcwinery.com
Manufacturer of wines
President: Don Carano
Director, Vineyard Operations: Steve Domenichelli
Co-Owner/Vice President: Rhonda Carano
Public Relations Director: Nancy Gilbert
Winemaker: George Bursick
Estimated Sales: $20-50 Million
Number Employees: 110
Type of Packaging: Private Label

4436 **Ferrero Usa**
600 Cottontail Ln
Somerset, NJ 08873 732-764-9300
Fax: 732-764-2700 800-337-7376
www.ferrerousa.com
Manufacturer of confectionery items including breath mints, chocolates, chocolate and hazelnut wafers and spread; also, chocolate espresso coffee
CEO: Michael Gilmore
VP Sales: Lawrance Fineburg
Estimated Sales: $10-20 Million
Number Employees: 100-249
Parent Co: Ferrero, SPA
Type of Packaging: Consumer
Brands:
MON CHERI
RAFFAELLO
ROCHER
SILVERS
TIC TAC

4437 **Ferrigno Vineyard & Winery**
17301 State Route B
St James, MO 65559-8583 573-265-7742
Manufacturer of wine
Owner: Richard Ferrigno
Estimated Sales: $500,000-$1 Million
Number Employees: 5-9

4438 **Ferrigno Vineyards & Win**
Rr 2 Box 2346
St James, MO 65559-8583 573-265-7742
ferrigno@fidnet.com
www.ferrignovineyards.com
Wines
President: Dick Ferrigno
Estimated Sales: $150,000
Number Employees: 3
Type of Packaging: Private Label
Brands:
Ferrigno

4439 **Ferris Organic Farm**
3565 Onondaga Rd
Eaton Rapids, MI 48827-9608 517-628-2506
Fax: 517-628-8257 800-628-8736
ferrisorganicfarm@excite.com
www.ferrisorganicfarm.com
Manufacturer, grower and exporter of organic beans including black, soy, black turtle and pinto; also, grains including wheat and barley; wholesaler/distributor of organic natural foods
Co-Owner: Richard Ferris
Estimated Sales: $1-2.5 Million
Number Employees: 1-4
Sq. footage: 7000
Type of Packaging: Bulk

4440 **(HQ)Ferris Stahl-Meyer Packing Corporation**
1560 Boone Ave
Bronx, NY 10460-5600 718-328-0059
Fax: 718-328-0729
Manufacturer of frankfurter and meat products
Ceo: Guillermo Gonzalez
Purchasing: Guillermo Gonzalez
Estimated Sales: $63.70 Million
Number Employees: 10-19
Number of Brands: 5
Number of Products: 50
Type of Packaging: Consumer, Food Service, Private Label, Bulk
Brands:
FERRIS
STAHLMEYER
SWEET MEADOW FARMS

4441 **Ferroclad Fishery**
Highway 17 N
Batchawana Bay, ON P0S 1A0
Canada 705-882-2295
Fax: 705-882-2297
Manufacturer, importer and exporter of herring, trout, whitefish and caviar
Owner: Gary Symons
Number Employees: 20-49
Parent Co: Presteve Foods Limited
Type of Packaging: Consumer, Food Service

4442 **Fess Parker Winery**
2963 Grand Ave
Los Olivos, CA 93441-0908 805-688-1545
Fax: 805-686-1130 800-446-2455
www.fessparker.com
Wines
Manager: Rosemary Williams
Estimated Sales: $110,000
Number Employees: 20-49
Sq. footage: 9
Type of Packaging: Private Label
Brands:
AMERICAN TRADITION RESERVE
PINOT NOIR SANTA BARBARA COUNTY
SANTA BARBARA COUNTY
SYRAH SANTA BARBARA COUNTY
VIOGNIER SANTA BARBARA COUNTY

4443 **Festida Food**
P.O.Box 326
Cedar Springs, MI 49319-0326 616-696-0400
Fax: 616-696-0496 www.festidafoods.com
Corn, tortilla chips and flour tortillas
President: Raul Vega
VP: Gloria Vega
Purchasing: Robert Robbins
Estimated Sales: $500,000-$1 Million
Number Employees: 20-49
Type of Packaging: Private Label

4444 **Festive Foods**
389 Edwin Dr Ste 100
Virginia Beach, VA 23462 757-490-9186
Fax: 757-490-9494
Manufacturer and exporter of sauces including spicy and extra spicy
President: Robert Buchanan
Purchasing: Robert Buchanan
Estimated Sales: $ .5 - 1 million
Number Employees: 1-4
Type of Packaging: Consumer
Brands:
BUFFALO BOB'S EVERYTHING SAUCE

4445 **Fiberstar**
713 St. Croix Street
River Falls, WI 54022 715-425-7550
Fax: 715-425-7572 www.fiberstar.net
Manufacturer of food ingredients and additives
CTO: Brock Lundberg
Number Employees: 10

4446 **Fibred-Maryland**
P.O.Box 3349
Cumberland, MD 21504-3349 301-724-6050
Fax: 301-722-7131 800-598-8894
dennis@fibred.com www.fibred.com
Manufacturer of soy fiber
Owner: Karen Ort
SVP/Director Sales: Rick Thayer
Estimated Sales: $10-20 Million
Number Employees: 20-49
Type of Packaging: Bulk
Brands:
F1-1 Soy Fibre

4447 **Ficklin Vineyards**
30246 Avenue 7 1/2
Madera, CA 93637 559-674-4598
www.ficklin.com
Wines
President: Peter Ficklin
Estimated Sales: $500,000-$1 Million
Number Employees: 1-4

4448 **Fidalgo Bay Coffee**
856 N Hill Blvd
Burlington, WA 98233 360-757-8818
Fax: 360-757-8810 800-310-5540
www.fidalgobaycoffee.com
Coffee
Owner: Gary Swoyer
CEO: David Evans
Purchasing: Gary Sawyer
Estimated Sales: $1-2.5 Million
Number Employees: 20-49

4449 **Fiddlers Green Farm**
16 Mayo St
Belfast, ME 04915 207-338-3872
Fax: 207-338-3872 800-729-7935
fiddlers@fiddlersgreenfarm.com
www.fiddlersgreenfarm.com
Manufacturer of organic and stone ground grains, flour and corn meal
Owner: Laine Alexander
Owner: Judy Ottmann
Vice President: Laine Alexander
Estimated Sales: Under $500,000
Number Employees: 1-4
Sq. footage: 300
Type of Packaging: Consumer, Food Service
Brands:
Belleweather
Bertha's
Bread & Biscuits
Fiddle Cakes
Fiddlers Green Farms
Islander's Choice
Oatbran & Brown Rice
Penobscot Porridge
Spice
Toasted Buckwheat

4450 **Field Stone Winery & Vineyard**
10075 Highway 128
Healdsburg, CA 95448 707-433-7266
Fax: 707-433-2231 800-544-7273
fieldstone1@earthlink.com
www.fieldstonewinery.com
Manufacturer of Wines
President: John Staten
CFO: Ben Staten
Vice President: Katrina Staten
Tasting Room Manager: Helen Weber
Public Relations: Roger Hull
Winemaker: Tom Milligan
Estimated Sales: $2.5-5 Million
Number Employees: 10-19

4451 **Field's**
100 Fields Row
Pauls Valley, OK 73075 405-238-7381
Fax: 405-238-5075 800-286-7501
www.fieldspies.com
Manufacturer of frozen pies including pecan, German chocolate and lemon chess
President: Chris Field
Purchasing Manager: Chris Field
Estimated Sales: $20-50 Million
Number Employees: 20-49
Sq. footage: 12500
Type of Packaging: Consumer, Food Service, Private Label, Bulk
Brands:
FIELD'S

4452 **Fieldale Farms**
1540 Monroe Dr
Gainesville, GA 30507 770-536-3899
Fax: 770-297-9261 800-241-5400
danwhite@fieldale.com www.fieldalefarms.com
Manufacturer of fresh chicken including whole and parts
Manager: Claude Sullens
CEO: Joe Hatfield Jr
VP/Director Sales/Marketing: Gus Arrendale
Estimated Sales: $100+ Million
Number Employees: 500-999
Parent Co: Fieldale Farms
Type of Packaging: Consumer, Food Service, Private Label, Bulk

4453 **(HQ)Fieldale Farms Corporation**
555 Broiler Blvd
Baldwin, GA 30511 706-778-5100
Fax: 706-776-3191 800-241-5400
donclick@fieldale.com www.fieldale.com
Manufacturer of fresh and frozen chicken
Chairman/CEO: Joe Hatfield
EVP/CFO: Thomas Hensley
Quality Assurance Manager: Corbett Kloster
EVP Sales/Marketing: Thomas Arrendale III
Human Resources Executive: Debbie Smith
EVP Operations: Joseph Hatfield
Product Manager: David Murray
Plant Manager: David Stevens
VP Purchasing: Donna Myers
Estimated Sales: $ 50 - 100 Million
Number Employees: 75
Sq. footage: 21000
Type of Packaging: Consumer, Food Service, Private Label, Bulk

4454 **(HQ)Fieldale Farms Corporation**
555 Broiler Blvd
Baldwin, GA 30511 706-778-5100
Fax: 706-776-3191 www.fieldale.com
Manufacturer of fresh and frozen poultry
Chairman: Joe Hatfield
CEO: Joe Hatfield
VP: Steven Collier
VP/CFO: Thomas Hensley
Director Sales/Marketing: Thomas Arrendale III
Estimated Sales: $470 Million
Number Employees: 1-4
Type of Packaging: Consumer, Food Service, Private Label, Bulk

4455 **(HQ)Fieldbrook Farms**
One Ice Cream Drive
PO Box 1318
Dunkirk, NY 14048 716-366-5400
Fax: 716-366-3588 800-333-0805
webmaster@fieldbrookfarms.com
www.fieldbrookfarms.com
Manufacturer and exporter of ice cream, frozen yogurt, sherbert & sorbet, sandwiches, IC/fudge bars, ice pops, juice and fruit bars, cones, cups, sorbet bars
President/CEO: Kenneth Johnson
Controller: Ron Odebralski
SVP Sales/Marketing: Jim Masood
Manager Operations: Kevin Grismore

Estimated Sales: $50-100 Million
Number Employees: 500-999
Sq. footage: 280000
Type of Packaging: Consumer, Food Service, Private Label, Bulk
Other Locations:
Fieldbrook Farms
Columbus GA
Brands:
DEERING
HOWARD JOHNSON
MY FAVORITE

4456 **Fieldbrook Valley Winery**
4241 Fieldbrook Rd
McKinleyville, CA 95519 707-839-4140
www.fieldbrookwinery.com
Manufacturer of Wines
President: Dr Robert Hodgson
COO: Judith Hodgson
Estimated Sales: $1-2.5 Million
Number Employees: 1-4

4457 **Fiera Foods**
50 Marmora Street
Toronto, ON M9M 2X5
Canada 416-744-1010
Fax: 416-746-8399 info@fierafoods.com
www.fierafoods.com
Manufacturer of frozen French pastries including croissants, danish and turnovers; also, muffin mixes
President: Boris Serebryany
Director: Alex Garber
Estimated Sales: $100 Million
Number Employees: 250-499
Sq. footage: 200000
Type of Packaging: Food Service

4458 **Fiesta Candy Company**
25 Old Dover Rd Unit I
Rochester, NH 03867 603-926-6053
Fax: 603-926-6628 800-285-9735
Manufacturer of Candy
President: Jose Mayoral
Estimated Sales: $ 5 - 10 Million
Number Employees: 5-9

4459 **Fiesta Canning Company**
8071 N Central Hwy
Mc Neal, AZ 85617 520-642-3376
Fax: 520-642-3271
Manufacturer of canned chili pepper paste
President: Gary Johnson
CFO: Bob Myers
VP: Stephen Johnson
Marketing: Ernie Jayme
Sales: Sharisse Johnson
Plant Manager: Bob Godfrey
Sq. footage: 10000
Brands:
Cochise Farms
Fiesta Del Sole
Macayo Mexican Foods

4460 **Fiesta Farms**
350 Commercial Ave
Nyssa, OR 97913 541-372-2248
Fax: 541-372-2474 fiesta@fmtc.com
Manufacturer and exporter of onions including red, yellow and white
President: Garry Bybee
Secretary: Tamara Bybee
VP: Marc Bybee
Estimated Sales: $ 10 - 20 Million
Number Employees: 20-49
Type of Packaging: Consumer, Food Service, Private Label, Bulk
Brands:
Bloombuilder
Bybee's
FF
Ru-Bee
Zoombees

4461 **Fiesta Gourmet of Tejas**
42 Oak Villa Road
Canyon Lake, TX 78133-3102 210-212-5233
Fax: 210-212-5240 800-585-8250
Manufacturer and exporter of Texas-made wines, chiles, salsas, sauces, jellies, oils, coffees and teas; custom-made gift baskets available
Owner: Maricela Smith
Estimated Sales: Less than $500,000
Number Employees: 1-4
Sq. footage: 2000
Parent Co: Fiesta Gourmet del Sol
Type of Packaging: Consumer, Food Service, Private Label
Brands:
FIESTA DEL SOL
POBLANOS
SERRANOS
TEJAS SIZZLE

4462 **Fiesta Mexican Foods**
979 G St
Brawley, CA 92227 760-344-3577
Fax: 760-344-3580
Tortillas
President: Raymond Armenta
Estimated Sales: $3 Million
Number Employees: 30

4463 **Fife Vineyards**
3620 Road B
Redwood Valley, CA 95470 707-485-0323
Fax: 707-485-0832 info@fifevineyards.com
www.fifevineyards.com
Wines
President: Dennis Fife
Estimated Sales: $2.5-5 Million
Number Employees: 5-9

4464 **Fife Vineyards**
3620 Road B
Redwood Valley, CA 95470 707-485-0323
Fax: 707-485-0832 info@fifevineyards.com
www.fifevineyards.com
Wine
President: Dennis Fife
Owner: Karen MacNeil
Co-Owner: Dennis Fife
Estimated Sales: $ 3 - 5 Million
Number Employees: 5-9
Type of Packaging: Bulk

4465 **Fig Garden Packing**
5545 W Dakota Ave
Fresno, CA 93722-9749 559-275-2191
Fax: 559-271-1332
Manufacturer, exporter and packer of dried and diced figs and fig paste including regular and crushed seed
President: Michael Jura
Sales Director: Bert Zigenman
Estimated Sales: $1.3 Million
Number Employees: 8
Sq. footage: 4823

4466 **Figamajigs**
133 White Oak Circle
Petaluma, CA 94952 707-992-0023
Fax: 707-581-1753 mel@figamajigs.com
www.figamajigs.com
all natural, gluten free, low fat, kosher fig bars and fig pieces covered in chocolate

4467 **Figaro Company**
3601 Executive Blvd
Mesquite, TX 75149 972-288-3587
Fax: 972-288-1887 dave@figaroco.com
www.figaroco.com
Manufacturer and exporter of hickory liquid smoke, mesquite liquid smoke, fajita marinade, brisket cooking sauce
Owner: J K Mc Kenney
CEO: Dave McCormack
Sales: Dave McCormack
Public Relations: Linda Willett
Operations: Anita Watson
Production: C Platero
Number Employees: 10-19
Number of Products: 6
Sq. footage: 21000
Type of Packaging: Consumer, Food Service, Private Label
Brands:
FIGARO

4468 **Figueroa Brothers**
1740 Hurd Drive
Irving, TX 75038-4324 214-351-9060
Fax: 214-351-9061 sales@melindas.com
www.figbros.com
Marketing: Greg Figueroa

4469 **Figuerola Laboratories**
P.O.Box 1569
Santa Ynez, CA 93460 805-688-6626
Fax: 805-688-8099 800-219-1147
customerservice@figuerola-labs.com
www.figuerola-laboratories.com
Manufacturer of dietary supplements
President: Rossana Figuerola
Executive Marketing Director: Antonio Figuerola
Brands:
Figuerola

4470 **Fiji Ginger Company**
2801 Ocean Park Boulevard
Suite 232
Santa Monica, CA 90405-2905 310-452-0878
Fax: 310-452-7977 info@fijiginger.com
www.fijiginger.com
Manufacturer of Ginger products

4471 **Fiji Water Company**
11444 W. Olympic Blvd., 2nd Floor
Los Angeles, CA 90064 310-312-2850
Fax: 310-312-2828 877-426-3454
info@fijiwater.com www.fijiwater.com
Natural artesian water known for its signature soft, smooth taste and well-balanced mineral content including a high level of silica, a youth-preserving antioxidant
President: John Cochran
CFO: Kim Katzenberger
Brands:
FIJI

4472 **Fiji Water LLC**
11444 W Olympic Blvd Ste 210
Los Angeles, CA 90064 310-312-2850
Fax: 310-312-2828 888-426-3454
info@fijiwater.com www.fijiwater.com
Manufacturer of bottled water
President: John Edward Cochran
CEO: Doug Carlson
Parent Co: Roll International Corporation
Brands:
FIJI

4473 **Filippo Berio Brand**
9 Polito Ave Fl 10
Lyndhurst, NJ 7071 201-525-2900
Fax: 201-525-0805 www.filippoberio.com
Manufacturer of Olive oil
President: Thomas Mueller
Estimated Sales: $10-20 Million
Number Employees: 22
Brands:
Casale Degli Ulivi
Centanni
FILIPPO BERIO EXTRA
FILIPPO BERIO EXTRA
FILIPPO BERIO EXTRA
FILIPPO BERIO EXTRA
FILIPPO BERIO GREEN/ Farmhouse
Fattoria Dell'ulivo
Filippo Berio
Filippo Berio Olive
Francesconi
Sagri
Tiger Brand

4474 **Fillmore Piru Citrus Association**
P.O.Box 350
Piru, CA 93040 805-521-1781
Fax: 805-521-0990 800-524-8787
www.fillmorepirucitrus.com
Manuafacturer, packer and exporter of oranges
President: Thomas Hardison
Corporate Secretary/Treasurer: Lois Yates
VP: Brian Edmonds
Office Manager: Phillis Sigoviano
Estimated Sales: $ 20 - 50 Million
Number Employees: 20-49
Type of Packaging: Consumer, Food Service
Brands:
AIRSHIP
BELLE OF PIRU
CUPID
CYCLE
DESIRABLE
GLIDER
HOME OF RAMONA
MANSION
ORIOLE
WEAVER

4475 **Fillo Factory**
P.O.Box 155
Dumont, NJ 7628 201-439-1036
Fax: 201-385-0012 800-653-4556
ronrex@bellatlantic.net www.fillofactory.com
Manufacturer of gourmet appetizers, baklava, strudel, pastries and fillo dough; importer of dough
President: Ron Rexroth
VP Sales: Tony Falletta
Estimated Sales: $1-3 Million
Number Employees: 10-19
Sq. footage: 12000
Type of Packaging: Consumer, Food Service, Private Label, Bulk
Brands:
Fillo Factory

4476 **Filsinger Vineyards & Winery**
32374 Corte Palacio
Temecula, CA 92592 951-302-6363
Fax: 909-302-6650 www.filsingerwinery.com
Wines
President: William Filsinger
Estimated Sales: $500-1 Million appx.
Number Employees: 5-9

4477 **Filtration Solutions Inc**
4361 Charlotte Hwy Ste 301
Clover, SC 29710 803-831-8379
Fax: 803-831-8476 803-831-8476
sales@filtrationsolutions.com
www.filtrationsolutions.com
Filtration products and systems.
President: Billie Wells
Office Manager: Tamara Hartman
Engineernig Consultant: Larry Seitz
Sales Representative: April Sadler
Sales Representative: Pete Dawes
Customer Service Representative: Robbie Putnam

4478 **Finchville Farms**
5157 Taylorsville Rd
Finchville, KY 40022-6771 502-834-7952
Fax: 502-834-7095 www.finchvillefarms.com
Manuafacturer of country ham
Dir: Nathan Arvin
Estimated Sales: $1 Million
Number Employees: 14
Type of Packaging: Consumer

4479 **Fine Choice Foods**
23111 Fraserwood Way
Richmond, BC V6V 1B3
Canada 604-522-3110
Fax: 604-278-4938 info@finechoicefoods.com
www.finechoicefoods.com
Manufacturer of dim sum, frozen Chinese entrees and egg rolls
President: Charles Lui
Operations Manager: Christina Lui
Estimated Sales: $5.9 Million
Number Employees: 45
Sq. footage: 10000
Type of Packaging: Consumer, Food Service, Private Label, Bulk

4480 **Fine Dried Foods International**
2553 Mission St Ste A
Santa Cruz, CA 95060 831-426-1413
Fax: 831-426-0870 awesomefruit@yahoo.com
Natural and organic tropical dried fruits
President: Rusty Brown
Estimated Sales: $2.5-5 Million
Number Employees: 1-4
Type of Packaging: Private Label
Brands:
True Fruit

4481 **Fine Foods International**
9907 Baptist Church Rd
St Louis, MO 63123-4903 314-842-4473
Fax: 314-843-8846 ffinylp@aol.com
Tea and coffee industry bags (brick packs), coffee and cappuccino mixes
Manager: Carole Garnett
VP: Keith Sheller
Operations: Carole Garnett
Estimated Sales: Less than $500,000
Number Employees: 1-4
Type of Packaging: Bulk

4482 **Fine Foods Northwest**
12736 35th Ave NE
Seattle, WA 98125-4508 206-361-7960
Fax: 206-361-7985 800-862-3965
info@mochamax.com www.mochamax.com
Manufacturer of Chocolate covered dried strawberries, chocolate peanut butter pretzels, chocolate covered espresso beans, nuts, fruits, coffee and chocolate covered nuts
Estimated Sales: $1-2.5 Million
Number Employees: 1-4
Brands:
MOCHA MAGIC
MOCHA MARBLES

4483 **Fine Line Seafood**
4 Terry Dr # 14
Newtown, PA 18940-1838 215-860-1144
Fax: 215-598-7235
Manufacturer of Seafood
President: Herbert Young
Estimated Sales: $5-10 Million
Number Employees: 1-4

4484 **(HQ)Fineberg Packing Company**
P.O.Box 80432
Memphis, TN 38108 901-458-2622
Fax: 901-458-7449
richard@finebergpacking.com
www.finebergpacking.com
Manufacturer of meat products: boloney, hot dogs, bacon, smoked hams, packing services available
President: Richard Freudenberg
Estimated Sales: $13.8 Million
Number Employees: 50-99

4485 **Finer Foods**
3100 W 36th St
Chicago, IL 60632 773-579-3870
Fax: 773-890-1115
Manufacturer of frozen foods
President: James Fitzgerald
Estimated Sales: $ 10 - 20 Million
Number Employees: 50-99

4486 **Finestkind Fish Market**
855 Us Route 1
York, ME 03909-5835 207-363-5000
Fax: 207-363-2664 800-288-8154
info@finestkindlobster.com
www.finestkindlobster.com
Manufacturer and Wholesaler full service seafood company.
Owner: Michael Goslin
Estimated Sales: $ 2.2 Million
Number Employees: 5

4487 **Finger Lakes Coffee Roasters**
6081 State Route 96
Farmington, NY 14425-1062 585-742-6218
Fax: 585-742-6211 800-420-6154
mail@fingerlakescoffee.com
www.fingerlakescoffee.com
Manufacturer of fresh roasted coffee
Manager: Kierna McGhan
VP: Robert Cowdery
Estimated Sales: Less than $500,000
Number Employees: 10-19
Sq. footage: 1100
Brands:
CANANDAIGUA BLEND
LAKE BLEND
SENECA BLEND

4488 **Finkemeier Bakery**
3103 Strong Avenue
Kansas City, KS 66106-2113 913-831-3103
Manufacturer of Bakery products
President: Bill Crum
Estimated Sales: $500,000 appx.
Number Employees: 5-9

4489 **(HQ)Finlandia Cheese**
2001 Us Highway 46 Ste 303
Parsippany, NJ 7054 973-316-6699
Fax: 973-316-6609 www.finlandiacheese.com
www.finlandiacheese.com
Cheese, dairy
President: Christopher Franco
CEO: Chet Brandes
Operations: John Sottile
Estimated Sales: $5-10 Million
Number Employees: 20
Brands:
FINLANDIA LAPPI
FINLANDIA NATURALS
FINLANDIA SWISS
HEAVENLY LIGHT
MUENSTER
SANDWICH NATURALS

4490 **Finlay Tea Solutions**
163 Madison Ave Ste 7
Morristown, NJ 7960 973-539-8030
Fax: 973-538-8366 tea@finlayusa.com
www.finlayusa.com
Tea extracts.
Owner: Herb Finlay
CFO: Jim Klucharits
Quality Control: Joe Stout
Marketing Director: E Fernando
Sales Director: L Malkin
Manager Tea Extract Sales: Gary Vorsheim
Estimated Sales: $ 10-20 Million
Number Employees: 1-4
Type of Packaging: Bulk

4491 **Fiore Winery**
3026 Whiteford Rd
Pylesville, MD 21132 410-879-4007
Fax: 410-879-4926 fiore@verison.net
www.fiorewinery.com
Wines
President: Michael Fiore
VP: Erich Fiore
Estimated Sales: $1-2.5 Million
Number Employees: 5-9

4492 **Fiori-Bruna Pasta Products**
5395 NW 165th St Ste 103
Hialeah, FL 33014 305-621-0074
Fax: 305-621-4997 fiori.bruna@worldnet.att.net
www.fioribrunapasta.com
Manufacturer and exporter of frozen cheese tortellini, ravioli, cavatelli and potato gnocchi; also, dry egg fettuccine and linguine
President: Jose Yimin
VP Sales/Co-Founder: Cesare Bruna
Estimated Sales: $2.5-5 Million
Number Employees: 10-19
Sq. footage: 10000
Type of Packaging: Consumer, Food Service, Private Label, Bulk
Brands:
Fiori-Bruna

4493 **Fiorucci Foods**
1800 Ruffin Mill Rd
Colonial Heights, VA 23834 804-520-7775
Fax: 804-520-7180 800-524-7775
www.fioruccifoods.com
Manufacturer and exporter of Italian speciality meats including prosciutto, salami, regional specialty meats, pre-sliced, diced, small salamis, pepperoni, balsamic vinegar
President/CEO: Claudio Colmignoli
CFO: Chris Maze
Quality Assurance Manager: Richard Wilson
VP Sales/Marketing: Keith Amrhein
Human Resources Manager: Carey Tillett
VP Operations: Oliviero Colmignoli
Plant Manager: Mark Bragalone
Purchasing Manager: Jennifer Erdelyi
Estimated Sales: $10-20 Million
Number Employees: 175
Sq. footage: 140000
Parent Co: Cesare Fiorucci
Type of Packaging: Consumer, Food Service, Private Label, Bulk
Brands:
Colosseum
Fiorucci

4494 **Firefly Fandango**
3217 33rd Avenue S
Seattle, WA 98144-6901 206-760-3700
Fax: 206-721-0909
fireflyfandango@earthlink.com
Chocolate and cookies
Estimated Sales: $300,000-500,000
Number Employees: 5-9

4495 **Firelands Wine Company**
917 Bardshar Rd
Sandusky, OH 44870 419-625-5474
Fax: 419-625-4887 800-548-9463
info@firelandswinery.com
www.firelandswinery.com
Wines
Manager: Claudio Salvador
Office Manager: Vicky Rogers
Estimated Sales: $5-10 Million
Number Employees: 15
Parent Co: Paramount Distillers

4496 **Fireside Kitchen**
3430 Prescott Street
Halifax, NS B3K 4Y4
Canada 902-454-7387
Fax: 902-453-0275 info@prescottgroup.ca
www.prescottgroup.ca
Manufacturer of natural jams, marmalades, cranberry sauce, cookies, muffins and fruit cakes; also, available in gift packs
Executive Director: Susan Slaunwhite
Sales Coordinator: Cindy Kingwell
Production Supervisor: Karen Walters
Brands:
FIRESIDE KITCHEN

4497 **Firestone Packing Company**
P.O.Box 61928
Vancouver, WA 98666 360-695-9484
Fax: 360-695-0040 sales@firestonepacking.com
Wine
President: Stanley Firestone
Estimated Sales: $2.5-5 Million
Number Employees: 100-249

4498 **Firestone Vineyard**
P.O.Box 244
Los Olivos, CA 93441-0244 805-688-3940
Fax: 805-686-1256 info@firestonewine.com
www.firestonevineyard.com
Wines
President: Adam Firestone
Controller: Heather McCollum
National Sales Director: Steve Mann
Estimated Sales: $10-20 Million
Number Employees: 20-49
Brands:
CABERNET SAUVIGNON
CHARDONNAY
GEWURZTRAMINER
MERLOT
RIESLING
SAUVIGNON BLANC
SYRAH
ZINFANDEL

4499 **Fireworks Popcorn Company**
P.O.Box 215
Belgium, WI 53004 262-285-4800
Fax: 262-285-4820 877-668-4800
kathy@popcornlovers.com
www.popcornlovers.com
Manufacturer of gourmet popcorn in fourteen varieties, and carmel corn in six different types
President: Rick Hercules
Sales: Don Sothman
Operations: Kaye Croatt
Purchasing Director: Rick Hercules
Estimated Sales: $1 Million
Number Employees: 10-19
Number of Brands: 4
Number of Products: 60
Sq. footage: 20000
Type of Packaging: Consumer, Food Service, Private Label, Bulk
Brands:
Settler's Popcorn

4500 **Firmenich**
250 Plainsboro Rd
Plainsboro, NJ 8536 609-452-1000
Fax: 609-452-6077 800-452-1090
www.firmenich.com
Manufacturer of flavors and fragrances
CEO: Patrick Firmenich
Purchasing Director: Linda Campbell
Estimated Sales: $500 Million +
Number Employees: 5,680
Other Locations:
Firmenich Chemical Plant
Newark NJ
Fermenich Citrus Center
Safety Harbor FL

4501 **First Choice Ingredients**
N112 W19528 Mequon Rd
Germantown, WI 53022 262-251-4322
Fax: 262-251-3881 mooren@fcingredients.com
www.fcingredients.com
Food flavor and ingredients manufacturers; including cheese powders & pasts, dairy powders, meat flavors, savory flavors, bakery flavors, and beverage liquids & powders
President: Jim Pekar
EVP: Roger Mullins
Sales Manager: Natalie Moore
Estimated Sales: $3 Million
Number Employees: 20

4502 **(HQ)First Colony Coffee & Tea Company**
204 W 22nd Street
Po Box 11005
Norfolk, VA 23517 757-622-2224
Fax: 757-623-2391 800-446-8555
sales@firstcolonycoffeeinc.com
www.firstcolonycoffee.com
Processor, importer and exporter of teas and coffees including varietal, blends and flavored
President/CEO: Miguel Abisambra
Marketing Director: Julie Anderson
National Sales Manager: Joyce Jordan
Human Resources Director: Marie Anastacio
Production Manager: Justin Goodman
Plant Manager: Bruce Grembowtiz
Estimated Sales: $13 Million
Number Employees: 80
Sq. footage: 47000
Type of Packaging: Consumer, Food Service, Private Label, Bulk
Brands:
BENCHELEY
CAROLAN'S
FIRST COLONY
FRANGELICO
GHIRARDELLI
JACK DANIEL'S
SOUTHERN COMFORT

4503 **First Colony Winery**
1650 Harris Creek Rd
Charlottesville, VA 22902 434-979-7105
Fax: 434-293-2054 877-979-7105
info@firstcolonywinery.com
www.firstcolonywinery.com
Wine
Owner: Randolph Mc Elroy
Estimated Sales: $ 3 - 5 Million
Number Employees: 5-9

4504 **First District Association**
101 S Swift Ave
Litchfield, MN 55355 320-693-3236
Fax: 320-693-6243 1stdist@hutchtel.net
www.firstdistrict.com
Manufacturer of dairy products including lactose blends and mixes, specialty cheeses, cream, wheys, whey protein concentrates and milk powders; exporter of lactose, whey protein concentrates and dairy calcium
President: Clint Fall
Quality Control/Lab Manager: Kevin Hagen
Plant Manager: Doug Anderson
Human Resources/Purchasing Manager: Dean Grabow
Estimated Sales: $267 Million
Number Employees: 100-249
Sq. footage: 180000
Brands:
Fieldgate

4505 **First Food International**
333 Cantor Ave
Linden, NJ 07036 908-862-5558
Fax: 908-474-1119 info@redflowerltd.com
www.redflowerltd.com
Oilseed production (coconut, peanut, soybean and sunflower)
President: Tony Chiang
Estimated Sales: 1-2.5 Million
Number Employees: 7

4506 **First Foods Company**
P.O.Box 560029
Dallas, TX 75356-0029 214-637-0214
Fax: 214-905-0605
Manufacturer of gelatins for desserts, salads, etc
President: Burke Hogan
Estimated Sales: $ 5 - 10 Million
Number Employees: 20-49
Type of Packaging: Consumer, Food Service, Private Label, Bulk

4507 **First Oriental Market**
2774 E Ponce De Leon Ave
Decatur, GA 30030 404-377-6950
Fax: 404-377-7505
Tilapia, flounder, catfish, mackerel, oriental food items
Owner: Diane Bounngaseng
Estimated Sales: $ 5 - 10 Million
Number Employees: 5-9

4508 **First Original Texas Chili Company**
P.O.Box 4281
Fort Worth, TX 76164-0281 817-626-0983
Fax: 817-626-9105 sales@texaschilicompany.cm
www.texaschili.com
Manufacturer of frozen chili con carne, chili sauce and beef taco filling
President: Danny Owens
Estimated Sales: $5-10 Million
Number Employees: 5-9
Type of Packaging: Consumer, Food Service, Private Label
Brands:
Our Famous Texas Chili
Sloppy Joe
Tex-O-Gold
Texas One Step

4509 **First Roasters of Central Florida**
863 N Highway 17/92
Longwood, FL 32750-3167 407-699-6364
Fax: 407-699-6301
Manufacturer of Coffee
Manager: Leomild Lamascus
Estimated Sales: $2.5-5 Million
Number Employees: 1-4
Brands:
First Roasters of Central Florida

4510 **(HQ)First Spice Mixing Company**
33-33 Greenpoint Ave
Long Island City, NY 11101-2084 718-361-2556
Fax: 718-361-2515 800-221-1105
info@firstspice.com www.firstspice.com
Manufacturer, importer and exporter of seasonings, binders and curing compounds; also, textured vegetable protein, hydrolyzed dairy products, nonfat dry milk, curing ingredients, phosphate compounds, MSG-flavor boosters and spices
President: Peter Epstein
Vice President: Vickie Miller
Research & Development: Marcy Epstein
Estimated Sales: $ 5 - 10 Million
Number Employees: 10-19
Other Locations:
First Spice Mixing Company
San Francisco CA
Brands:
Albunate
Flavolin
Flavor 86
Savorlok
Texite
Tietolin
Vegolin Hvp
Vita-Curaid
Vitaphos

4511 **First Spice Mixing Company**
3333 Greenpoint Ave
Long Island City, NY 11101-2084 718-361-2556
Fax: 718-361-2515 800-221-1105
info@firstspice.com www.firstspice.com

Manufacturer and exporter of food ingredients including seasonings, spices, soy products, antioxidants, flavor enhancers, etc.; wholesaler/distributor of gelatin, garlic and marinades; also, custom packaging and product developmentservices available.
President: Peter Epstein
VP: Vicki Miller
R&D: Marcy Epstein
Marketing: Wendy Epstein
VP: Elizabeth Miller
Plant Manager: Glenn Davis
Estimated Sales: $5+ Million
Sq. footage: 50000
Parent Co: First Spice Mixing Company
Type of Packaging: Food Service, Private Label, Bulk
Other Locations:
San Francisco CA
Toronto, Canada
Brands:
ALBUNATE
FLAVOLIN
FLAVOR 86
SAVORLOK
TEXITE
TIETOLIN
VEGOLIN HVP
VITA-CURAID
VITAPHOS

4512 **Firth Maple Products**
22418 Firth Rd
Spartansburg, PA 16434 814-654-7265
Fax: 814-654-7265 www.firthmapleproducts.com
Maple syrup
President: Troy Firth
Estimated Sales: $720,000
Number Employees: 11

4513 **Fischer & Wieser Specialty Foods, Inc.**
411 S Lincoln St
Fredericksburg, TX 78624 830-997-7194
Fax: 830-997-0455 800-880-8526
info@jelly.com www.jelly.com
Manufacturer of jams, jellies, preserves, marmalades, mustard, sauces, salsa, syrup, honey and snacks
President/CEO: Case Fischer
Purchasing: Jenny Wieser
Estimated Sales: $1-3 Million
Number Employees: 100-249
Type of Packaging: Consumer, Food Service, Private Label
Brands:
FISCHER & WIESER
MOM'S
OLD CHISHOLM TRAIL

4514 **Fischer Honey Company**
2001 N Poplar St
North Little Rock, AR 72114 501-758-1123
Fax: 501-758-8601
Manufacturer of honey including table, creamed and bakers
President: Joe Callaway
Vice President: Ellen Callaway
Estimated Sales: $5-10 Million
Number Employees: 5-9
Sq. footage: 25000
Type of Packaging: Consumer, Food Service, Private Label, Bulk

4515 **Fischer Meats**
85 Front St N
Issaquah, WA 98027 425-392-3131
Fax: 425-392-0168
Manufacturer of meat
Owner: Chris Chiechi
Estimated Sales: Less than $500,000
Number Employees: 1-4
Type of Packaging: Consumer, Food Service

4516 **Fish Breeders of Idaho**
10215 W. Emerald Street,Suite #160
Boise, ID 83704 208-947-3678
Fax: 208-837-6254 888-414-8818
fpi@cyberhighway.net
http://www.cyberhighway.net
Manufacturer and exporter of fresh and frozen farm-raised trout, catfish, tilapia, sturgeon and alligator
Owner/President: Leo Ray
Estimated Sales: $5-10 Million
Number Employees: 20-49
Parent Co: Fish Processors
Type of Packaging: Consumer, Food Service
Brands:
Pride of Idaho

4517 **Fish Brothers**
P.O.Box 416
Blue Lake, CA 95525-0416 707-668-9700
Fax: 707-668-9701 800-244-0583
fishbro@fishbrothers.com
www.fishbrothers.com
Manufacturer of smoked fish including, salmon, nova lox and albacore
Owner: Scott Bradshaw
Estimated Sales: $500,000-1 Million
Number Employees: 1-4
Sq. footage: 2500
Type of Packaging: Consumer, Food Service, Private Label, Bulk
Brands:
Fish Brothers

4518 **Fish Express**
3343 Kuhio Hwy # 10
Lihue, HI 96766 808-245-9918
Fax: 808-246-9188
Seafood
President: David Wada
Estimated Sales: $ 3 - 5 Million
Number Employees: 10-19

4519 **Fish Hopper**
700 Cannery Row Ste O
Monterey, CA 93940 831-372-2406
Fax: 831-372-2026 www.fishhopper.com
Manufacturer of canned clam chowder
Owner: Sabu Shake
CEO: Sabu Shake Jr
Estimated Sales: $2.5-5 Million
Number Employees: 50-99
Type of Packaging: Private Label

4520 **Fish King Processors**
710 Squalicum Way
Bellingham, WA 98225 360-733-9090
Fax: 360-733-9152
Processor of smoked salmon
CEO: Terrill Beck
Estimated Sales: $ 10 - 20 Million
Number Employees: 20-49
Parent Co: Unisea Foods
Type of Packaging: Consumer, Food Service
Brands:
Pride of Alaska
Salmon Bay

4521 **Fish Market**
1406 West Chestnut Street
Louisville, KY 40203-1776 502-587-7474
Fax: 502-587-7503
Seafood
President: Steven Smith
Estimated Sales: $10 Million

4522 **Fish Processors**
18374 Highway 30
Hagerman, ID 83332 208-837-6114
Fax: 208-837-6254
Manufacturer of frozen fish and seaford, Rainbow trout, channel catfish
President: Leo Ray
Vice President: Tod Ray
Treasurer: Judith Ray
Estimated Sales: $5-10 Million
Number Employees: 25
Brands:
Pride of Idaho

4523 **FishKing**
722 N Glendale Ave
Glendale, CA 91206 818-244-2161
www.fishkingseafood.com
Processor of seafood including breaded and IQF scallops, shrimp and calamari
President: Tom Furuckawa
Number Employees: 125
Type of Packaging: Consumer, Food Service

4524 **Fisher Honey Company**
1 Belle Ave # 21
Lewistown, PA 17044-2433 717-242-4373
Fax: 717-242-3978
fisherhoney@fisherhoney.com
www.fisherhoney.com
Manufacturer and exporter of honey, beeswax, beekeepers supplies, containers, glass, metal and plastic
President: W Dyson Fisher
Plant Supervisor: Scott Fisher
Estimated Sales: $1-2 Million
Number Employees: 1-4
Sq. footage: 20000
Type of Packaging: Consumer, Food Service, Private Label, Bulk
Brands:
Fisher Honey
Stewarts Honey

4525 **Fisher Rex Sandwiches**
1519 Brookside Dr
Raleigh, NC 27604 919-901-0739
Fax: 919-832-4865
Manufacturer of sandwiches, pastries and snack foods
VP: Tom Fisher
Estimated Sales: $40 Million
Number Employees: 99
Type of Packaging: Consumer

4526 **Fisher Ridge Wine Company**
529 Sheridan Cir
Charleston, WV 25314 304-342-8702
Wines
Owner: Wilson Ward
Estimated Sales: $1-2.5 Million
Number Employees: 1-4

4527 **Fisher Vineyards**
6200 Saint Helena Rd
Santa Rosa, CA 95404 707-539-7511
Fax: 707-539-3601 info@fishervineyards.com
www.fishervineyards.com
Wines
President: Fred Fisher
Vice President: Juelle Fisher
Sales/Marketing/Public Relations: Whitney Fisher
Estimated Sales: $500,000
Number Employees: 5
Type of Packaging: Private Label

4528 **Fisher's Popcorn**
Po Box 3130, B301
Ocean City, MD 21843-3130 302-539-8833
Fax: 302-539-2160 888-436-6388
ben@fishers-popcorn.com
www.fishers-popcorn.com
Other candy, popcorn.
Marketing: Ben Bauer

4529 **Fisher's Popcorn**
200 S Atlantic Ave
Ocean City, MD 21842 410-289-1399
Fax: 410-289-1720 888-395-0335
fishers@dmv.com www.fisherspopcorn.com
Caramel-coated popcorn
Owner: Donald Fisher
Number Employees: 50-99

4530 **Fisherman's Market International**
607 Bedford Highway
Halifax, NS B3M 2L6
Canada 902-445-3474
Fax: 902-443-5561 monte@fmii.com
www.fmii.com
Manufacturer of live lobster and fresh or frozen seafood
President: Fred Greene
Director International Marketing: Gino Nadalini
Sales: J R Ewing
General Manager: Monte Snow
Plant Administrator: Bill Murphy

Estimated Sales: $20+ Million
Number Employees: 150
Sq. footage: 20000
Type of Packaging: Consumer, Food Service, Private Label

4531 **Fisherman's Reef ShrimpCompany**
P.O.Box 26006
Beaumont, TX 77720-6006 409-842-9528
Fax: 409-842-6905
Manufacturer of frozen domestic shrimp
President: Vikki Jones
Sales: Trudy Verdine
Number Employees: 100-249
Parent Co: Farmer Boys Catfish International
Type of Packaging: Food Service, Private Label
Brands:
Fisherman's Reef

4532 **Fishermens Net**
849 Forest Ave
Portland, ME 04103-4162 207-772-3565
Fax: 207-828-1726
Seafood
Owner: Benjamin Lindner
Estimated Sales: $6 Million
Number Employees: 5-9

4533 **(HQ)Fishery Products International**
18 Electronics Ave
Danvers, MA 01923 978-750-5000
Fax: 978-777-6849 800-374-4700
www.fpil.com
Manufacturer and importer of fresh and frozen seafood including shrimp, crab, cod, flounder, perch, pollack, tilapia and salmon
President: Kevin Murphy
CEO: Derrick Rowe
Executive: Bill Dimento
Research & Development: Bob Saville
Quality Control: William DiMento
Marketing Director: Dave Jermain
Estimated Sales: $100-500 Million
Number Employees: 1-4
Sq. footage: 105000
Parent Co: Fishery Products International
Type of Packaging: Consumer, Food Service
Other Locations:
Fishery Products
Seattle WA
Brands:
BLATIN REDFISH
CARIBOU
FPI
LUXURY
MIRABEL
SEA CUISINE
SEA NUGGETS
SEA STRIPS
SEAFOOD ELITE
SHOREGRILL
SIMPLE SERV
TREASURE ISLE

4534 **Fishery Products International**
2001 Western Ave # 300
Seattle, WA 98121-2164 206-782-9979
Fax: 206-782-0209 800-374-4770
webmaster@fisheryproducts.com
www.fisheryproducts.com
Manufacturer of fresh and frozen seafood
Manager: Grimes Williams
Estimated Sales: $5-10 Million appx.
Number Employees: 10-19
Number of Brands: 8
Parent Co: Fisher Products International
Brands:
Acadian Supreme
FPI
Luxury
Margaritaville
Mirabel
Sea Cuisine
Tiki Island
Upper Crust

4535 **Fishhawk Fisheries**
P.O.Box 715
Astoria, OR 97103 503-325-5252
Fax: 503-325-8786 www.fishhawkfisheries.com
Manufacturer of crab, shrimp, canned fish, salmon, sturgeon, shad, smelt, halibut and black cod
President: Steve Fick
Director: Carol Fratt
Estimated Sales: $1 Million
Number Employees: 10
Sq. footage: 6000
Type of Packaging: Bulk
Brands:
Fishhawk

4536 **Fishking**
PO Box 1068
Bayou La Batre, AL 36509-1068 251-824-2118
Fax: 334-824-7181
Manufacturer of Seafood
President/CEO: Eugene Laurendeau
Estimated Sales: $20-50 Million
Number Employees: 100-249

4537 **Fishland Market**
117 Ahui Street
C
Honolulu, HI 96813-5545 808-523-6902
Fax: 808-523-6905
Manufacturer of Aku, ahi, a'u, bottomfish, reef fish, Kona crab, white crab, Hawaiian crab
President: Paul Nishimoto

4538 **Fishmarket Seafoods**
1406 W Chestnut St
Louisville, KY 40203 502-587-7474
Fax: 502-587-7503
Manufacturer of frozen seafood
President: Steven Smith
Estimated Sales: $5-10 Million
Number Employees: 5-9
Sq. footage: 7000
Type of Packaging: Consumer, Food Service, Private Label
Brands:
Fishmarket Seafoods

4539 **Fitzkee's Candies**
2352 S Queen St
York, PA 17402-4997 717-741-1031
Fax: 717-741-5176
Manufacturer of assorted chocolates
President: Robert Fitzkee
Estimated Sales: $2.5-5 Million
Number Employees: 10-19
Type of Packaging: Consumer

4540 **Fitzpatrick Winery & Lodge**
7740 Fairplay Rd
Somerset, CA 95684 530-620-3248
Fax: 530-620-6838 800-245-9166
brian@fitzpatrickwinery.com
www.fitzpatrickwinery.com
Wines
President: Brian Fitzpatrick
VP: Diana Fitzpatrick
Estimated Sales: $500,000-$1 Million
Number Employees: 1-4
Brands:
Fitzpatrick

4541 **Five Ponds Farm**
1933 E Mill Rd
Lineville, AL 36266 256-396-5217
Fax: 256-386-5899
Fruits and vegetables
President: Edward Donlon

4542 **Five Star Food Base Company**
865 Pierce Butler Rte
St Paul, MN 55104-3073 651-488-2300
Fax: 651-488-2094 800-505-7827
cjoyce@fivestarfood.com www.fivestarfood.com
Soup bases and blended seasonings
President: Sid Larson
Estimated Sales: $5-10 Million
Number Employees: 10-19

4543 **Fizz-O Water Company**
809 N Lewis Ave
Tulsa, OK 74110 918-834-3691
Fax: 918-832-0899 www.fizzowater.com
Bottler and wholesaler/distributor of spring, drinking and distilled water
President: Harry R Doerner
Owner: Hency Doerner
CFO: Rick Doerner
Plant Manager: Rick Malkey
Estimated Sales: $1-3 Million
Number Employees: 20-49
Number of Brands: 4
Sq. footage: 10000
Type of Packaging: Consumer
Brands:
DOUBLEPURE DISTILLED
MOUNTAIN VALLEY
OZARKA
SPRING HOUSE

4544 **Fizzle Flat Farm**
18773 E 1600th Avenue
Yale, IL 62481-2215 618-793-2060
Fax: 618-793-2060
Manufacturer of organic popcorn and food grade certified organic grains including white, yellow and blue corn, wheat, soybeans, buckwheat
Owner: Marvin Manges
Estimated Sales: $1-3 Million
Number Employees: 2
Sq. footage: 8750
Type of Packaging: Bulk
Brands:
Fizzle Flat Farm

4545 **Fizzy Lizzy**
265 Lafayette St
Suite D20
New York, NY 10012 212-966-3232
Fax: 212-966-6621 800-203-9336
love@fizzylizzy.com
whole fruit juice and sparkling water.
President: Aaron Morrill
VP: Amy Drown
Estimated Sales: $1.1 Million
Number Employees: 5

4546 **Fjord Pacific Marine Industries**
2400 Simpson Road
Richmond, BC V6X 2P9
Canada 604-270-3393
Fax: 604-270-3826 jbomhof@fjordpacific.com
Manufacturer and exporter of pickled herring, smoked salmon and salmon and halibut portions and steaks
President: Grant Keays
Sales Manager: John Bomhof
General Manager: Don Pollard
Estimated Sales: $12 Million
Number Employees: 75
Sq. footage: 10000
Type of Packaging: Consumer, Food Service, Private Label
Brands:
Dutch Boy
Fjord

4547 **Flagship Atlanta Dairy**
P.O.Box 3790
Belleview, FL 34421-3790
Fax: 404-581-9650 800-224-0669
Manufacturer of orange juice, citrus punch, teas, fruit juice drinks, milk, half and half, cream, yogurt and ice cream including novelties; importer of pasta, sauces and filled cookies
Plant Manager: Rudy Terrizzi
Estimated Sales: $14.7 Million
Number Employees: 220
Sq. footage: 78000
Type of Packaging: Consumer, Food Service, Private Label
Brands:
PARAMLAT/NEW ATLANTA DAIRIES
PARMALAT/FARM BEST

4548 **Flagstaff Brewing Company**
16 E Route 66
Flagstaff, AZ 86001-5792 928-773-1442
Fax: 928-773-7772 www.flagbrew.com
Beer
Owner: Jeff Thorsett
Estimated Sales: $10-20 Million
Number Employees: 20-49
Brands:
AGASSIZ AMBER
BITTERROOT EXTRA SPECIAL BITTER
BLACKBIRD PORTER
BUBBAGANOUJ IPA
GREAT GOLDEN ALE
SASQUATCH STOUT
THREE-PIN PALE ALE

4549 **Flaherty**
9047 Terminal Ave
Skokie, IL 60077 847-966-1005
Fax: 847-966-1072
Manufacturer of mustard
Owner: Catherine Flaharty
Finance Manager: Deirdre Flaherty
General Manager: Bridget Flaherty
Estimated Sales: $5-10 Million
Number Employees: 10-19

4550 **Flamin' Red's Woodfired**
Robinson Hill Rd
Pawlet, VT 05761 802-325-3641
Fax: 802-325-3641 woodfire@vermontel.net
Pizza crusts made with organic flour
Owner: Carson Lake
Estimated Sales: $300,000-500,000
Number Employees: 1-4

4551 **(HQ)Flamm Pickle & Packing Company**
4502 Hipps Hollow Rd
Eau Claire, MI 49111 269-461-6916
Fax: 269-461-6166
Manufacturer of pickle relish
President/General Manager: Gina Flamm
Estimated Sales: $4.20 Million
Number Employees: 10-19
Sq. footage: 30000
Type of Packaging: Food Service, Bulk
Brands:
Flamm's

4552 **Flamous Brands**
312 Agostino Rd.
San Gabriel, CA 91776 626-551-3201
Fax: 626-551-3088 www.flamousbrands.com
vegetarian chips and dips

4553 **(HQ)Flanders Provision Company**
P.O.Box 720
Waycross, GA 31502-0720 912-283-5191
Fax: 912-283-6228 info@flandersprovisions.com
Manufacturer, distributor and packager of beef patties
President/CEO: Huey Dubberly
CEO: Chris Huff
Sales: Hollis Yarn
Estimated Sales: $36.80 Million
Number Employees: 100-249

4554 **Flanigan Farms**
9522 Jefferson Blvd
Culver City, CA 90232-2918 310-836-8437
Fax: 310-838-0743 800-525-0228
nuts@flaniganfarms.com
www.flaniganfarms.com
Manufacturer and exporter of nut mixes and dried organic persimmons
President: Patsy Flanigan
Operations: C Flanigan
Estimated Sales: $3 Million
Number Employees: 10-19
Number of Products: 42
Sq. footage: 12000
Type of Packaging: Consumer, Food Service, Private Label
Brands:
Nuts 'n' Fruit
Nuts 'n' Things

4555 **Flannery Seafood Company**
3445 California St
San Francisco, CA 94118-1836 415-346-1303
Fax: 415-346-1304 cohan@earthlink.net
Manufacturer of fresh swordfish, tuna and exotic seafoods
President/CEO: Walker Flannery
Plant Manager: Alex Guerrero
Estimated Sales: $10-20 Million
Number Employees: 10-19
Type of Packaging: Private Label

4556 **Flathau's Fine Foods**
211 Greenwood Place
Hattiesburg, MS 39402 601-582-9629
Fax: 601-544-2333 888-263-1299
info@flathausfinefoods.com
www.flathausfinefoods.com
Flavored shortbread cookies covered with powdered sugar

4557 **Flaum Appetizing**
288 Scholes St
Brooklyn, NY 11206 718-821-1970
Fax: 718-821-9051 www.flaum.com
Manufacturer of sour pickles, sauerkraut, pickled herring, cole slaw, lox spreads and potato, whitefish, tuna and eggplant salads
President: Morris Grunhut
Production Manager: Salomon Benatar
Estimated Sales: Less than $500,000
Number Employees: 10-19
Sq. footage: 25000
Parent Co: M&M Food Products
Type of Packaging: Consumer, Food Service, Private Label, Bulk

4558 **Flavex Protein Ingredients**
25 Commerce Dr
Suite 130
Cranford, NJ 07016-3605 908-709-4045
Fax: 908-709-9221 800-851-1052
info@arnhemgroup.com www.arnhemgroup.com
Owner: Michael J Bonner
CEO: Michael Bonner
Estimated Sales: $ 3 - 5 Million
Number Employees: 1-4

4559 **(HQ)Flavor & Fragrance Specialties**
3 Industrial Ave
Mahwah, NJ 07430 201-825-2025
Fax: 201-825-4785 800-998-4337
customer.service@ffs.com www.ffs.com
Manufacturer of flavor concentrates and fragrance extracts
President: Michael Bloom
Executive Vice President: Steve Vanata
VP Sales: William Palmer
Estimated Sales: $2.5-5 Million
Number Employees: 20-49
Sq. footage: 40000
Type of Packaging: Bulk
Brands:
Ammonia Guard
E.O.C.
High Impact

4560 **(HQ)Flavor & Fragrance Specialties**
300 Corporate Dr
Mahwah, NJ 07430 201-825-2025
Fax: 201-828-9449 800-998-4337
customer.service@ffs.com www.ffs.com
Manufacturer and exporter of flavors and flavoring agents; also, fragrances
President/CEO: Michael Bloom
Owner/VP: Steve Vanata
Quality Control Director: Amy Bourreasu
VP Marketing: Jeffrey Nichols
Sales/Marketing Director: Robert Frantzen
Production Manager: Gary Dausch
Plant Manager: Jeffery Wichman
Estimated Sales: $28 Million
Number Employees: 100
Sq. footage: 45000
Type of Packaging: Bulk
Other Locations:
Flavor & Fragrance Specialties
Baltimore MD
Brands:
AMMONIA GUARD
EFS ENHANCED FLAVOR SYSTEMS
ENHANCER 21
EOC ENVIRONMENTAL ODOR CONTROL
HIGH IMPACT

4561 **Flavor Consortium**
2017 Camfield Avenue
Los Angeles, CA 90040-1501 323-724-1010
Fax: 323-724-3183
Manufactures flavors extracts, syrups and related products
Estimated Sales: $5-10 Million
Number Employees: 10-19

4562 **Flavor Dynamics**
640 Montrose Ave
South Plainfield, NJ 7080 908-822-8855
Fax: 908-822-8547 888-271-8424
customercare@flavordynamics.com
www.flavordynamics.com
Food and beverage flavors
President: Dolf Rovira
Owner/VP: Marilyn Rovira
Quality Control Director: Joseph Callari
Sales Director: Colleen Roberts
Plant Manager: Ken Warren
Purchasing: Kristi Callari
Estimated Sales: $2.6 Million
Number Employees: 24
Sq. footage: 29000
Type of Packaging: Food Service, Private Label, Bulk
Other Locations:
Flavor Dynamics
Glenview IL
Flavor Dynamics
Corona Del Mar CA
Flavor Dynamics
Cape Charles VA

4563 **Flavor House**
9516 Commerce Way
Adelanto, CA 92301 760-246-9131
Fax: 909-599-3517
Manufacturer and exporter of flavor concentrates including meat, poultry and seafood; also, hydrolyzed vegetable proteins and liquid and dry soy sauce
President/Manager: Richard Staley
Estimated Sales: $4 Million
Number Employees: 40
Sq. footage: 42000
Type of Packaging: Bulk

4564 **Flavor Right Foods Group**
2200 Cardigan Ave
Columbus, OH 43215-1092 614-488-2536
Fax: 614-488-0307 888-464-3734
info@flavorright.com www.instantwhip.com
Dessert and pastry toppings and icings, frozen dessert mixes.
President: Doug Smith
Estimated Sales: $ 5 - 10 Million
Number Employees: 10-19
Brands:
FESTEJOS
WHIP N ICE
WHIP N TOP

4565 **(HQ)Flavor Sciences**
652 Nuway Circle
Lenior, NC 28645 828-758-2525
Fax: 828-758-2424 800-535-2867
information@flavorscience.com
www.flavorsciences.com
Manufacturer of natural and artificial flavors and essential oils; exporter of natural and artificial flavors and extracts
President: Roger Kiley
Executive VP: Joyce Kiley
Sales Manager: Scott Derrick
Estimated Sales: $ 3 - 5 Million
Number Employees: 5-9

4566 **Flavor Specialties**
790 E Harrison St
Corona, CA 92879 951-734-6620
Fax: 951-734-4214 flavspec@earthlink.net
www.flavorspecialties.com
Liquid and dry ingredients and flavors including natural beverage flavors-mango, guava, tropical, kiwi strawberry; botanical bases for carbonated and noncarbonated beverages; herbal tea and green tea beverage base blends
President: Bob Dayton
Estimated Sales: $20-50 Million
Number Employees: 20-49

4567 **Flavor Systems Intl.**
10139 Commerce Park Dr
Cincinnati, OH 45246 513-870-4900
Fax: 513-870-4909 800-498-2783
info@flavorsystems.com
www.flavorsystems.com
Manufacturer and exporter of custom flavorings and specialty food systems
President: William Wasz
Owner: Bob Bahoshy
VP: William Baker
R&D: Angie Lantman
Quality Control: Alan Baker
Plant Manager: Rick Messinger
Purchasing: Roger Sage
Estimated Sales: $20 Million
Number Employees: 55
Sq. footage: 25000

Type of Packaging: Bulk

4568 **Flavorbank Company**
6372 E Broadway Blvd
Tucson, AZ 85710-3538 520-747-5431
Fax: 520-790-9469 800-835-7603
spices@flavorbank.com www.flavorbank.com
Manufacturer of Spices and seasonings
Owner: Jennifer English
Public Relations: Jan Jorden
Operations: Jackie Brooks
Production: James Husser
Plant Manager: Ramona Flores
Estimated Sales: $1-2.5 Million
Number Employees: 1-4
Type of Packaging: Private Label
Brands:
DANIEL ORR
FLAVORBANK

4569 **Flavorchem**
1525 Brook Dr
Downers Grove, IL 60515 630-932-8100
Fax: 630-932-4626 800-435-8867
info@flavorchem.com www.flavorchem.com
Manufacturer and exporter of flavorings and food colorings; processor of pure vanilla extract; importer of fine chemicals and essential oils
President: Ken Malinowski
EVP: Gary Wyshel
VP Sales/Marketing: Phillip Sprovieri
Human Resources Manager: Connie Sprovieri
Plant Manager: David Russo
President/Purchasing Manager: Salvatore Sprovieri
Estimated Sales: $20-50 Million
Number Employees: 125
Sq. footage: 170000
Type of Packaging: Consumer, Food Service, Private Label, Bulk
Brands:
Spicery Shoppe Natural

4570 **Flavorganics**
268 Doremus Ave
Newark, NJ 07105-4875 973-344-8014
Fax: 973-344-1948 jason@flavorganics.com
www.flavorganics.comm
Manufacturer and exporter of organic extracts including vanilla, almond, peppermint, lemon and orange
President: Jocelyn Manship
Estimated Sales: $ 20 - 50 Million
Number Employees: 50-99
Parent Co: Elan
Type of Packaging: Private Label, Bulk
Brands:
Flavorganics
Kogee

4571 **(HQ)Flavormatic Industries**
230 All Angels Hill Rd
Wappingers Falls, NY 12590
Fax: 845-297-2881 sales@flavormatic.com
www.flavormatic.com
Manufacturer, importer and exporter of flavors, fragrances and essential oils
President: Judith Back
Executive VP: Ronald Black
Estimated Sales: $2.5 Million
Number Employees: 20-49
Sq. footage: 21000
Type of Packaging: Bulk
Other Locations:

4572 **Flavors**
250 W Side Mall # 217
Edwardsville, PA 18704-3106 570-287-8642
Fax: 717-284-2892
Flavors
President: Bruce Gutterman
Estimated Sales: $1-2.5 Million
Number Employees: 1-4

4573 **Flavors from Florida**
203 Bartow Municipal Arprt
Bartow, FL 33830 863-533-0408
Fax: 863-533-9478 www.flavorsfromflorida.com
Manufactures Ice cream, sherbert, drink base flavoring, flavoring extracts and syrups
President: Robert K Prendes
General Manager/Contact: Mike Benewiat
Estimated Sales: $25-50 Million
Number Employees: 20-49

4574 **Flavors of Hawaii**
945 Waimanu St
Honolulu, HI 96814 808-597-1727
Fax: 808-597-1728
Coconut syrup, guava syrup, cocopine syrup
President: Alexander Lee
Vice President: Violet Mau
Estimated Sales: $650,000
Number Employees: 5
Brands:
Hawaii

4575 **Flavors of North America**
1900 Averill Rd
Geneva, IL 60134-1601 630-578-8600
Fax: 630-578-8601 800-308-3662
info@fona.com www.fonaflavors.com
Flavors, creation and manufacture of confection flavors, beverage flavors, cereal flavors, snack flavors, bakery flavors, dessert flavors, dairy flavors and flavors for use in functional food, prepared food and animal foodindustries.creates and manufactures a full line of quality flavors for the food, beverage, pharmaceutical and nutraceutical industries
President: Robert Allen
CEO: Joseph J Slawek
R&D: Sue Johnson
Quality Control: Carol Lund
Marketing: Tracy Bergfeld
Sales: TJ Widuch
Purchasing: Terry Emmel
Estimated Sales: $50-100 Million
Number Employees: 100-249

4576 **Flavors of the Heartland**
204 2nd St
Rocheport, MO 65279 573-698-2063
800-269-3210
Manufacturer of Gourmet foods
Manager: Roger Pilkinton
Estimated Sales: Less than $500,000
Number Employees: 1-4
Brands:
Flavors of the Heartland

4577 **Flavouressence Products**
1-6750 Davand Drive
Mississauga, ON L5T 2L8
Canada 905-795-0318
Fax: 905-795-0317 866-209-7778
info@flavouressence.com
www.flavouressence.com
Manufacturer of beverage syrups, juices, bar mixes and slush; exporter of juices, bar mixes and beverage syrups
President/CEO: Mark Weber
CFO: Brain Ferry
Marketing: Bob Graham
Sales: Jolene Davies
Plant Manager: David Milner
Estimated Sales: $5 Million
Number Employees: 5-9
Sq. footage: 10500
Type of Packaging: Food Service, Private Label, Bulk

4578 **Flavours Inc**
24855 Corbit Pl Ste B
Yorba Linda, CA 92887 714-692-2950
Fax: 951-520-1151 gmichaud@flavoursinc.com
www.flavoursinc.com/
Products and services includes that of: development of dietary supplements, nutraceutical enhanced products, and low/high acid shelf stable beverages; flavor development and manufacturing; spun matrix micro-encapsulation technology;aseptic dosing of vitamins, flavors, nutraceutical/herbal extracts; and PET/HDPE filling for clinical trials and market testing.
Director of Aseptic Packaging: Geramy Michaud

4579 **FlavtekGeneva Flavors Inc.**
3330 Millington Rd
Beloit, WI 53511 323-588-5880
Fax: 323-588-0178 800-562-5880
flavtek@flavtek.com
Manufacturer of flavors, oils, extracts and emulsions to the dairy, beverage, wine, bakery and confectionery industries.
President: Cary Chow
VP: Dan Yang
Estimated Sales: $2.5-5 Million
Number Employees: 10-24
Parent Co: Geneva Flavors
Type of Packaging: Private Label, Bulk
Brands:
Flavtek, Inc.

4580 **Flavurence Corporation**
1916 S Tubeway Ave
Commerce, CA 90040 323-727-1957
Fax: 323-728-8380 800-717-1957
www.flavurence.com
Manufacturer and exporter of flavors
Manager: Chris Long
Estimated Sales: $25 Million
Number Employees: 5-9
Sq. footage: 60000
Type of Packaging: Private Label, Bulk

4581 **Fleet Fisheries**
20 Blackmer St
New Bedford, MA 02744 508-996-3742
Fax: 508-996-3785
Manufacturer and wholesale of scallops
Owner: Lars Jerud
Estimated Sales: $ 5 - 10 Million
Number Employees: 10-19

4582 **Fleischer's Bagels**
1688 N Wayneport Rd
Macedon, NY 14502 315-986-9999
Fax: 315-986-7200 marc@fleischersbagels.com
www.fleischersbagels.com
Manufacturer and exporter of fresh, frozen and refrigerated bagels
President: Robert Drago
SVP Operations/CFO: Keith Bleier
Quality Assurance Manager: George Sparks
VP Sales/Marketing: Robert Pim
Human Resources Manager: Dwight Kreuter
Production Manager: Mike O'Hara
Estimated Sales: $6 Million
Number Employees: 135
Sq. footage: 42685
Type of Packaging: Consumer, Food Service, Private Label, Bulk
Brands:
Fleischer's

4583 **Fleischmann's Vinegar**
12604 Hiddencreek Way
Suite A
Cerritos, CA 90703-2137
Canada 562-483-4600
Fax: 562-483-4644 800-443-1067
http://www.fleischmannsvinegar.com
Manufacturer of vinegar
President: Daniel Muth
CEO: Ken Simril
Number Employees: 1-4
Parent Co: Burns Philp Foods
Type of Packaging: Consumer, Food Service, Private Label, Bulk
Brands:
Allens
Fleischann's
Spice Islands

4584 **Fleischmann's Yeast**
1350 Timberlk Mnr Pkwy Ste 550
Chesterfield, MO 63017 636-349-8800
Fax: 636-349-8825 800-247-7473
consumerinfo@bpna.com www.breadworld.com
Manufacturer and exporter of active and inactive yeasts, vinegars, leaveners and mold inhibitors; also, technical consulting for bakeries available
President: Andrew Armstrong
VP: Brian Thronquist
Marketing Manager: Keith Dierberg
Sales Manager: Rick Mercuri
Operations Manager: Terry Strang
VP Industrial Production: Rex Mercuri
Plant Manager: Bob Williams
Estimated Sales: $50-100 Million
Number Employees: 1,000-4,999
Parent Co: Burns Philp Foods
Type of Packaging: Food Service, Bulk

4585 **Fleischmanns Vinegar**
12604 Hiddencreek Way # A
Cerritos, CA 90703-2137 562-483-4600
Fax: 562-483-4644 800-443-1067
sales@fvinegar.com
www.FleischmannsVinegar.com

Leading manufacturer and marketer of industrial vinegar in North America. We offer a full line of standard and specialty vinegars and cooking wines
CEO: Daniel Muth
CFO: Larry McKeown
CEO: Ken Simril
R&D/Quality Control: Sylvain Norton
Public Relations: Daniel Muth
Type of Packaging: Bulk
Brands:
FLEISCHMANNS VINEGAR
FLEISHCMANNS COOKING WINE

4586 **Fletcher's Fine Foods**
502 Boundary Blvd
Algona, WA 98001-6503
Canada 253-735-0800
Manufacturer and exporter of pork and by-products
President/CEO: Fred Knoedler
President: Michael Lattifi
Number Employees: 95
Parent Co: Fletcher's Fine Foods
Type of Packaging: Food Service, Bulk
Brands:
Fletcher's
Goodlife

4587 **Fleur De Lait Foods**
150 W Jackson St
New Holland, PA 17557 717-355-8500
Fax: 717-355-8561 www.alouettecheese.com
Cheese manufacturer
President: James Williams
Manager: Shoua Yang
Manager: Sue Groff
Estimated Sales: $20-50 Million
Number Employees: 250-499

4588 **Fleurchem**
33 Sprague Ave
Middletown, NY 10940-5128 845-341-2100
Fax: 845-341-2121 info@fleurchem.com
www.fleurchem.com
Manufacturer, importer and exporter of natural and synthetic flavoring agents and fragrances including acidulants, anethole, citronellal, eucalyptol, furfural, geraniol, heptanal, methyl actetate, etc
CEO: George Gluck
CFO: Sara Gluck
VP: Rochele Gluck
Quality Control: Brian Merdler
VP Marketing: Jack Snicolo
Operations Manager: Louis Mercun
Production Manager: Larry Costa
Purchasing Manager: Angie Roman
Estimated Sales: $10-20 Million
Number Employees: 10-19
Sq. footage: 200000
Type of Packaging: Private Label, Bulk

4589 **Fliinko**
PO Box 80102
South Dartmouth, MA 02748-0102 508-996-9609
Fax: 508-990-1281
President: Ingrid Flynn
Marketing: Thomas Flynn
Estimated Sales: $1-22.5 Million
Number Employees: 1-4
Type of Packaging: Private Label
Brands:
Nectarade

4590 **Flint Hills Foods**
P.O.Box 253
Alma, KS 66401
Fax: 785-765-2294
Manufacturer of cooked and portion controlled steaks
President: Bernie Hansen
Estimated Sales: $50 Million
Number Employees: 50-99
Sq. footage: 50000
Type of Packaging: Consumer, Food Service
Brands:
FLINT HILLS

4591 **Flippin-Seaman**
5529 Crabtree Falls Hwy
Tyro, VA 22976-3103 434-277-5828
Fax: 434-277-9057 info@flippin-seaman.com
www.flippin-seaman.com
Growers, packer and shippers of fine fruit.
Owner: Bill Flippin
Owner: Richard Seaman
Estimated Sales: $10-20 Million
Number Employees: 20-49
Brands:
Seaman Orchard
Silver Creek

4592 **Flora**
805 E Badger Rd
PO Box 73
Lynden, WA 98264
Fax: 888-354-8138 800-446-2110
www.florahealth.com
Digestive enzymes, herbal extracts, herbal teas, herbal tonics, nutritional oils, nutritional supplements, organic chocolates, probiotics and whole foods.
President: Thomas Greither
Marketing Manager: Gabriel Lightfriend
Estimated Sales: $10-20 Million
Number Employees: 50-99
Type of Packaging: Consumer
Brands:
Flor-Essence
Flora

4593 **(HQ)Flora Manufacturing & Distributing**
7400 Fraser Park Drive
Burnaby, BC V5J 5B9
Canada 604-436-6000
Fax: 604-436-6060 888-436-6697
bonnie@florahealth.com www.florahealth.com
Manufacturer of natural health products, herbal remedies
President/CEO: Thomas Greither
Quality Control: Summer Sit
Marketing: Guru Simran Khalsa
Sales: Amber Davies
Public Relations Coordinator: Jasmin Tamdoo
Estimated Sales: $22 Million
Number Employees: 180
Sq. footage: 40000
Brands:
FLORA

4594 **Flora Springs Wine Company**
1978 Zinfandel Ln
Saint Helena, CA 94574 707-963-5711
Fax: 707-963-7518 info@florasprings.com
www.florasprings.com
Wines
President: John Komes
Finance: Ronette Aiello
Estimated Sales: $1.8 Million
Number Employees: 19

4595 **Florence Macaroni Manufacturing**
5701 S San Pedro St
Los Angeles, CA 90011-5321 323-232-7269
Fax: 323-232-7143
Manufacturer of macaroni products
President: Roy Pier-Dominici
Merchandising Manger: Joseph Esposito
Plant Manager: Matt Koch
Estimated Sales: $1-2.5 Million
Number Employees: 1-4
Sq. footage: 20000
Type of Packaging: Consumer, Food Service

4596 **Florence Macaroni Manufacturing**
4334 W Chicago Ave
Chicago, IL 60651-3422 773-252-6113
Fax: 773-252-7085 800-647-2782
florencemacaroni@aol.com
Manufacturer of macaroni products including regular/orangic semolina and whole wheat
President: Roy Dominici
Sales Manager: Gino Riccardi
Plant Manager: Thomas Benhke
Estimated Sales: $3.3 Million
Number Employees: 25
Type of Packaging: Consumer, Food Service, Private Label, Bulk

4597 **Florence Pasta & Cheese**
115 W College Drive
Marshall, MN 56258-1747 800-533-5290
Fax: 507-537-8159 info@foodpros.com
www.foodpros.com
Manufacturer of frozen pasta and dehydrated cheese
President: Alfred Schwan
Parent Co: Schwann's Sales
Type of Packaging: Consumer, Food Service, Bulk

4598 **Florentyna's Fresh Pasta Factory**
1864 E 22nd St
Vernon, CA 90058 213-742-9374
Fax: 310-677-2782 800-747-2782
jascha@freshpasta.com www.freshpasta.com
Manufacturer of fresh and fresh frozen pasta products for the food service industry
Manager: Jascha Smuloviez
Estimated Sales: $1-4.9 Million
Number Employees: 20-49
Number of Products: 60
Type of Packaging: Food Service, Private Label, Bulk

4599 **Florida Bottling**
1035 NW 21st Ter
Miami, FL 33127 305-324-5932
Fax: 305-325-9573 info@floridabottling.com
www.floridabottling.com
Manufacturer and exporter of glass-packed fruit juices
President: Vivian Calzadilla
CEO: R Fuhrman
VP, Sales: Joseph Letiz
Estimated Sales: $7 Million
Number Employees: 50
Type of Packaging: Consumer, Food Service, Bulk
Brands:
Coconut Grove
Lakewood
Rainberry
Summer Song

4600 **Florida Brewery**
202 Gandy Rd
Auburndale, FL 33823 863-965-1825
Fax: 863-967-6965
info@thefloridabreweryinc.com
www.floridabreweryinc.com
Beer
President: Ramon Campos
Controller: Julie Williams
Operations: Erich Schalk
Estimated Sales: $3 Million
Number Employees: 27
Sq. footage: 62
Type of Packaging: Private Label

4601 **Florida Carib Fishery**
1301 NW 89th Ct
Doral, FL 33172-3034 305-696-2896
Fax: 305-547-2772
Manufacturer of frozen prepared, whole fresh and fillet seafood including conch meats, kingfish steaks, mullet roe, cooked whole lobsters and lobster tails
Estimated Sales: $1-2.5 Million
Number Employees: 1-4
Parent Co: Beaver Street Fisheries
Type of Packaging: Consumer, Food Service, Private Label

4602 **Florida Citrus**
Po Box 9010
Bartow, FL 33831-9010 863-537-3999
Fax: 877-352-2487 john@citrusbarn.com
www.floridajuice.com
Manufacturer of fruit cocktails, juice and syrup. Product categories are vegetables, canned fruits and fresh fruits
President: John Roberts
VP: Scott Stallard
Estimated Sales: $5-10 Million
Number Employees: 10-19
Type of Packaging: Consumer

4603 **Florida Crystals**
P.O.Box 4671
West Palm Beach, FL 33402 561-366-5100
Fax: 561-366-5158 877-835-2828
heather_forbes@floridacrystals.com
www.floridacrystals.com
Sugar cane and rice, including premium white rice, sem-chi rice, organic foods
President: Jose Fanjul
CEO: Alfonso Fanjul
CFO: Luis Fernandez
Estimated Sales: $ 5 - 10 Million
Number Employees: 20-49

Brands:
FLORIDA CRYSTALS
SEMI-CHI

4604 **Florida Deli Pickle**
200 NW 20th Avenue
Fort Lauderdale, FL 33311-8724 954-463-0222
Fax: 954-463-5992
Manufacturer of pickles, relishes and pickled products; wholesaler/distributor of meats, cheese, poultry, salads and frozen foods
President: George Bell
Type of Packaging: Consumer, Food Service, Private Label, Bulk

4605 **Florida Distillers Company**
530 N Dakota Ave
Lake Alfred, FL 33850 863-956-3477
Fax: 863-956-3979 oyu@todhunter.com
www.todhunter.com
Alcoholic and nonalcoholic beverages
President/CEO: Terry Karr
CFO: Troy Edwards
Executive VP: Ron Call
Sales Director: Dennis Mitchell
Production: Lee Stewart
Plant Manager: Bob Miller
Purchasing: Frank Dieling
Estimated Sales: $100-499.9 Million
Number Employees: 250-499
Type of Packaging: Private Label
Brands:
Albertsons
Bacardi
Cruzan
Jacquins
Porfidio
Ron Matusalem
Seagrams

4606 **(HQ)Florida Food Products**
2231 W County Road 44 Ste 1
Eustis, FL 32726 352-357-4141
Fax: 352-483-3192 800-874-2331
contact@floridafood.com www.floridafood.com
Vegetable juice concentrates, aloe vera gel, fruit juice powders, vegetable juice powders
President: Jerry Brown
Vice President: Tom Brown
Research & Development: Scott Ruppe
VP Operations & Manufacturing: Charles Hamrick
Plant Manager: Keith Burt
Purchasing Manager: James Arnett
Estimated Sales: $15-20 Million
Number Employees: 50
Sq. footage: 100000
Other Locations:
Florida Food Products
Sabila
Brands:
FLORIDA FOOD PRODUCTS
VEG CON BEET
VEG CON CARROT
VEG CON CELERY

4607 **Florida Fruit Juices**
7001 W 62nd St
Chicago, IL 60638-3924 773-586-6200
Fax: 773-586-6651
Manufacturer of fruit juices including apple, grape, orange, grapefruit, pineapple, etc
President: Donald Franko Sr
CEO: Don Franko
VP: Don Franko, Jr.
Estimated Sales: $ 5 - 10 Million
Number Employees: 20-49
Type of Packaging: Consumer, Food Service, Private Label

4608 **Florida Juice Products**
PO Box 3628
Lakeland, FL 33802-3628 863-802-4040
Fax: 863-686-3649
Manufacturer of Orange and grapefruit juice
President: Ronald Grigsby
Estimated Sales: $50-99.9 Million
Number Employees: 5-9

4609 **Florida Key West**
5470 Division Dr
Fort Myers, FL 33905 239-694-8787
Fax: 239-694-0402 juice@florida-juice.com
www.florida-juice.com
Lemon and key lime juices
President: Earl Tanner
VP: Sandra Tanner
Estimated Sales: $1-2.5 Million
Number Employees: 5-9
Type of Packaging: Consumer, Food Service, Private Label, Bulk
Brands:
Florida Key West

4610 **Florida Natural Flavors**
P.O.Box 181125
Casselberry, FL 32718 407-834-5979
Fax: 407-834-6333 800-872-5979
info@floridanaturalflavors.com
www.floridanaturalflavors.com
Manufacturer, exporter and importer of juice and beverage concentrates including carbonated, noncarbonated and frozen products
President: David Erdman
Vice President: Gary Erdman
Manager: Leonard Combs
Estimated Sales: $4 Million
Number Employees: 35
Parent Co: Florida Natural Flavors
Type of Packaging: Private Label
Brands:
DIET RITE
Davy's Mix
Juicemaster
MISTIC ICED TEA
NEHI FLAVORS
Polynesian Pleasure
R-Own Cola
STEWART'S
Tropical Pleasure

4611 **Florida Shortening Corporation**
3200 NW 125th St Stop 4
Miami, FL 33167 305-691-2992
Fax: 305-691-2997 flshortening@aol.com
Manufacturer, importer and exporter of shortenings, margarines, oils, puff paste, pan releases and spices including garlic; packaging services available
President: Calvin Theobald
Sales Director: Gerald Delmonico
Estimated Sales: $2.5-5 Million
Number Employees: 1-4
Number of Brands: 20
Number of Products: 9
Sq. footage: 20000
Type of Packaging: Food Service, Private Label, Bulk

4612 **Florida Veal Processors**
6712 State Road 674
Wimauma, FL 33598 813-634-5545
Fax: 813-633-1405
Manufacturer of fresh and frozen veal
Co-Owner: Richard Nusman
Co-Owner: Max Nusman
Estimated Sales: $5.70 Million
Number Employees: 20
Type of Packaging: Consumer, Food Service

4613 **Florida's Natural Growers**
20205 Us Highway 27 North
Lake Wales, FL 33853 863-676-1411
Fax: 863-676-1640 888-657-6600
www.floridasnatural.com
Manufacturer, canner and exporter of frozen fruit juices, concentrates and blends including grapefruit, orange, lemonade, lime, apple and grape; also, frozen sections
Owner/President: Frank Hunt
CEO: Steve Caruso
CFO: William Hendry
VP Sales/Marketing: Walt Lincer
Estimated Sales: $100+ Million
Number Employees: 800
Parent Co: Citrus World
Type of Packaging: Consumer, Food Service, Private Label
Brands:
ADAMS
BIG TEX
BLUEBIRD
DONALD DUCK
FLORIDA'S NATURAL
LAKE WALES

4614 **Floron Food Services**
2545 96th Street
Edmonton, AB T6N 1E3
Canada 780-438-9300
Fax: 780-438-9200 info@floron.com
www.floron.com
Manufacturer of mozzarella and cheddar cheese, manufacturer of private label pasta sauce, full line distribution
President: Greg Lamorie
VP: Stephen Robbins
Estimated Sales: $20 Million
Number Employees: 40
Sq. footage: 20000
Type of Packaging: Consumer, Food Service

4615 **Flower Essence Services**
P.O.Box 1769
Nevada City, CA 95959-1769 530-265-0258
Fax: 530-265-6467 800-548-0075
info@fesflowers.com www.fesflowers.com
Manufactuer of flower essences
Owner: Richard Katz
Estimated Sales: $ 1 - 3 Million
Number Employees: 10-19

4616 **(HQ)Flowers Foods Bakeries**
1919 Flowers Cir
Thomasville, GA 31757-1137 229-226-9110
Fax: 229-225-3806 www.flowersfoods.com
Breads, bins, rolls, snack cakes and pastries
President: Allen Shiver
Chairman/CEO: George Deese
EVP/CFO: R Steve Kinsey
EVP: Stephen Avera
SVP/Chief Information Officer: Vyto Razminas
SVP/Sales & Marketing: H Mark Courtney
EVP/Corporate Relations: Marta Jones Turner
EVP/COO: Gene Lord
EVP/Supply Chain: Michael Beaty
Estimated Sales: $2.6 Billion
Number Employees: 8800
Sq. footage: 29000
Type of Packaging: Consumer, Food Service, Private Label, Bulk
Other Locations:
Atlanta GA
El Paso TX
Fort Smith AK
Goldsboro NC
Houston TX
Lafayette LA
New Orleans LA
Pine Bluff AR
San Antonio TX
Brands:
AUNT HATTIE'S
BLUEBIRD
BUNNY
BUTTERKRUST
CAPTAIN JOHN DERST'S
COBBLESTONE MILL
EUROPEAN BAKERS
EVANGELINE MAID
HOLSUM
MARY JANE
MARY JANE & FRIENDS
MI CASA
MRS. FRESHLEY'S
NATURE'S OWN
SUNBEAM
TASTYCAKE
WHITEWHEAT

4617 **Flying Dog Brewery**
4607 Wedgewood Blvd
Frederick, MD 21703 301-694-7899
Fax: 301-694-2971 www.flyingdogales.com
Manufacturer of seasonal beer, ale, stout and porter
President/CEO: Jim Caruso
CFO: Kelly McElroy
VP Plant Operations: Mark Matovich
Estimated Sales: $20-50 Million
Number Employees: 20-49
Type of Packaging: Consumer, Food Service
Brands:
Flying Dog
Railyard

4618 **Flying Seafood Incorporated**
73-4776 Kanalani St # 8
Kailua Kona, HI 96740-2625 808-326-7708
Fax: 808-329-3669 www.hilofish.com
Manufacturer of fresh, frozen seafood
Owner: Kerry Umamoto

Estimated Sales: $ 5 - 10 Million
Number Employees: 10-19

4619 Flynn Vineyards Winery
2200 N Pacific Hwy W
Rickreall, OR 97371-9774 503-623-8683
Fax: 503-623-0908 888-427-4953
www.flynnvineyards.com
Wines
President: Howard Rossbach
Estimated Sales: $5-10 Million
Number Employees: 5-9
Type of Packaging: Private Label

4620 Fm Brown Sons
797 Commerce St
Reading, PA 19608 610-678-3353
Fax: 610-678-6640 800-345-3344
www.fmbrown.com
Small animal food
Manager: Marianne Egolf
VP Marketing: Sue Brown
Manager: Harvey Brown
Estimated Sales: $10-20 Million
Number Employees: 14

4621 (HQ)Fmali Herb
831 Almar Avenue
Santa Cruz, CA 95060-5899 831-423-7913
Fax: 831-429-5173 sales@fmali.com
Manufacturer and contract packager of ginseng, hibiscus flowers, orange and lemon peels, herbal, green and black teas and chamomile; importer of ginseng, royal jelly and panax extractum; exporter of herbal teas and orange and lemonpeels
President/Co-Founder: Ben Zaricor
Executive VP/Co-Founder: Louise Veninga
Estimated Sales: $14.0 Million
Number Employees: 50-99
Sq. footage: 42000
Type of Packaging: Consumer, Food Service, Private Label, Bulk
Brands:
FAMLI
GOOD EARTH
WILDCRAFT

4622 Foell Packing Company
PO Box 4595
Naperville, IL 60567-4595 919-776-0592
Fax: 919-774-1627 info@foellpacking.com
www.foellpacking.com
Manufacturer and exporter of canned meats including tripe, Vienna sausage and pork brains; also, contract packaging available
President: D Johnson
Vice President: T O'Shea
Estimated Sales: $5-10 Million
Number Employees: 20-49
Sq. footage: 36000
Type of Packaging: Consumer, Private Label
Brands:
Beverly
Rose

4623 Fogo Island CooperativeSociety
85 Harbour Dr
Seldom Come By, NL A0G 3Z0
Canada 709-627-3452
Fax: 709-627-3495
Manufacturer and exporter of live and frozen crabs
President: Roy Freake
General Manager: Keith Watts
Estimated Sales: $1.4 Million
Number Employees: 10
Type of Packaging: Consumer, Food Service, Bulk

4624 Fold-Pak East, Inc.
33 Powell Dr
Hazleton, PA 18201 570-454-0433
Fax: 570-454-0456 800-486-0490
east@gsdpackaging.com
www.gsdpackaging.com
Wire handled square paper food containers, round cup style closeable food and soup containers, square closeable paper food containers (microwaveable, carry out and storage capable)
Manager: Charlie Mattson
Marketing Director: Wes Gentles
Sales Director: Jim Keitges
Corporate Credit Manager: William Moon
Plant Manager: Lee King
Number Employees: 5,000-9,999
Number of Brands: 16
Number of Products: 66
Sq. footage: 104000
Parent Co: Rock-Tenn Company
Type of Packaging: Consumer, Food Service, Private Label

4625 Foley Estates Vineyards& Winery
6121 E Highway 246
Lompoc, CA 93436 805-737-6222
Fax: 805-737-6923 info@foleywines.com
www.foleywines.com
Wines
President: Robert Lidquist II
Marketing Manager: Lisa Schaeffer
Sales: Mike Keonig
Production Manager: Norm Yost
Estimated Sales: $2.5-5 Million
Number Employees: 10-19
Type of Packaging: Private Label

4626 Foley's Candies
12671 No 5 Road
Richmond, BC V7A 4E9
Canada 604-274-2131
Fax: 604-275-1682 888-236-5397
info@foleyscandies.com
www.foleyscandies.com
Manufacturer of chocolate and confectionery products including wafers, blocks, chips, almond barks, squares, mints, yogurt covered almonds, raisins, peanuts and coffee beans
Number Employees: 20-49
Type of Packaging: Private Label, Bulk

4627 Folgers Coffee Company
1 Strawberry Lane
Orrville, OH 44667-0280 513-983-1100
Fax: 513-983-4905 877-693-6543
www.folgers.com
Manufacturer of roasted, ground, regular and decaffeinated coffee. Also, Folgers is the licensed manufacturer and distributor of Dunkin' Donuts retail coffee brand.
Executive Chairman/Co-CEO: Richard Smucker
Chairman/Co-CEO: Tim Smucker
VP: Diana Ferguson
Estimated Sales: $5 Billion
Number Employees: 1,200
Parent Co: J.M Smucker Company
Type of Packaging: Consumer
Brands:
FOLGERS

4628 Folie a Deux Winery
7481 St. Helena Highway
Oakville, CA 94562 707-944-2565
Fax: 707-944-0250 1 8-0 5-5 64
adinfo@folieadeux.com www.folieadeux.com
Wines
Manager: Paul Scholfield
CEO: Richard Peterson
CFO: George Schofield
Marketing: Cardace Guridi
Public Relations: David Foster
Operations: Carla Clift
Production: Alejandro Pantoja
Purchasing: Marc Norwood
Number Employees: 10-19
Number of Brands: 3
Type of Packaging: Consumer
Brands:
Fantaisie
Folie a Deux
La Grande Folie
La Petite Folie

4629 Folklore Foods
9 N B St
Toppenish, WA 98948 509-865-4772
Fax: 509-865-7363 www.folklorefoods.com
Manufacturer and exporter of espresso syrups and granita concentrate
President/CEO: Daniel Hanson
VP: Chris Hanson
Estimated Sales: $690,000
Number Employees: 5
Sq. footage: 11000
Type of Packaging: Consumer, Food Service, Private Label
Brands:
Folklore
Folklore Cream Soda
Folklore Gourmet Syrups
Folklore Sasaparilla
Folklore Sparkling Beverages

4630 Follmer Development/Americana
840 Tourmaline Dr
Newbury Park, CA 91320 805-498-4531
Fax: 805-376-2404 800-499-4668
www.follmerdevelopment.com
Vegetable oil cooking sprays
CEO: Kit Follmer
Vice President: Garrett Follmer
Marketing: David McKenzie
Estimated Sales: $9 Million
Number Employees: 41
Type of Packaging: Consumer, Food Service, Private Label

4631 Foltz Coffee Tea & Spice Company
7733 Edinburgh Street
New Orleans, LA 70125-1505 504-486-1545
Fax: 504-486-1545
Coffee and tea
President: George Foltz
Estimated Sales: $2.5-5 Million
Number Employees: 10-19

4632 Fontaine Sante Foods IncFountain Of Health
450 Deslauriers
Montreal, QC H4N 1V8 514-956-7730
Fax: 514-956-7734 jfcollette@fontainesante.com
www.fontainesante.com
Health foods.
Marketing: Sami Damnati

4633 Fontana Flavors
2342 Fulton Street
Janesville, WI 53546 608-754-9668
Fax: 608-754-0803 www.fontanaflavors.com
Flavors manufacturer for seafood, meats, prepared foods and vegetarian products
President: Peter Krug
Estimated Sales: $4 Million
Number Employees: 14

4634 Fontana's Casa De La Pasta
115 Grant Avenue
Vandergrift, PA 15690-1229 724-567-2782
Fax: 724-567-1429
Dried pasta and ravioli
President: William Fontana
Estimated Sales: $5-9.9 Million
Number Employees: 1-4
Sq. footage: 4
Type of Packaging: Private Label

4635 Fontanini Italian Meats& Sausages
8751 W 50th Street
McCook, IL 60525 773-890-0600
Fax: 773-890-1680 800-331-6328
webinfo@fontanini.com www.fontanini.com
Manufacturer of meatballs, breakfast items, pizza toppings, beef
President: Joann Fontanini
Account Executive: Rita Rufo
Controller Midwest: Eric Divelbiss
Director QC: Anthony Pavel
General Manager: Charles Brown
Regional Manager: Jim Doherty
West Coast Regional Manager: Gene Borgomainero
Director Operations: Mike Catania
Estimated Sales: $46 Million
Number Employees: 260
Sq. footage: 240000
Parent Co: Capitol Wholesale Meats Company
Type of Packaging: Consumer, Food Service
Brands:
MAMA RANNE

4636 Fontazzi/Metrovox Snacks
612 N. Eckhoff St
Orange, CA 92868 323-771-3221
Fax: 714-634-4424 800-428-0522
metrovox@aol.com www.giftbasketsupplies.com
Popcorn, pretzels, snack mixes, gift packs, gift boxes, sourdough truffles
President: Paul Voxrand
Estimated Sales: $300,000-500,000
Number Employees: 1-4

4637 **Fonterra USA**
9525 Bryn Mawr Ave
Suite 700
Chicago, IL 60018 847-928-1872
Fax: 847-274-4740
dorothy.muszynska@fonterra.com
www.fonterra-northamerica.com
Manufactures dairy ingredients
President: Jerry Stritzke
VP Finance: Kim Wallace
Vice President: Stuart Burgdoerfer
Estimated Sales: $1 Billion +
Number Employees: 45

4638 **Food & Paper Supply**
7247 S South Chicago Ave
Chicago, IL 60619 773-752-0700
Fax: 773-752-0747
President: Bruce Goldberg
Estimated Sales: $ 10 - 20 Million
Number Employees: 50-99

4639 **Food & Vine**
68 Coombs St Ste I-2
Napa, CA 94559 707-251-3900
Fax: 707-251-3939 info@grapeseedoil.com
www.grapeseedoil.com
Manufacturer of grapeseed oil
President: Valentin Humer
VP/Public Relations: Nanette Humer
Estimated Sales: $620,000
Number Employees: 1-4
Sq. footage: 1000
Type of Packaging: Consumer, Food Service, Private Label, Bulk
Brands:
Salute Sante
Salute Sante! Grape Oil

4640 **Food & Vine**
68 Coombs St Ste I-2
Napa, CA 94559 707-251-3900
www.grapeseedoil.com
Grapeseed oil
President: Valentin Humer

4641 **Food City Pickle Company**
2501 N Damen Ave
Chicago, IL 60647
Fax: 616-781-3422
Manufacturer of sweet relish, dill relish, whole dill pickles, dill slices, sweet pickles, pepperoncini and peppers including hot and mild banana
President: Ron DeRuiter
Estimated Sales: $2.5-5 Million
Number Employees: 5-9
Sq. footage: 22000
Type of Packaging: Consumer, Food Service, Private Label, Bulk
Brands:
King's Choice

4642 **Food City USA**
4752 W 60th Ave Unit A
Arvada, CO 80003 303-321-4447
Fax: 303-428-4143
information@grandmaspasta.com
Manufacturer of fresh and frozen pre-cooked pasta including wide egg noodles, linguini, fettuccine and angel hair
Owner: Moni Piz-Wilson
Estimated Sales: $ 3 - 5 Million
Number Employees: 5-9
Parent Co: Grandma's Pasta Products
Type of Packaging: Consumer, Food Service
Brands:
Grandma's

4643 **Food Concentrate Corporation**
921 NW 72nd St
Oklahoma City, OK 73116 405-840-5633
Fax: 405-843-6832
Manufacturer of barbecue sauce concentrate and muffin and seasoning mixes
President: Walter Seideman
Estimated Sales: $2.5-5 Million
Number Employees: 1-4
Sq. footage: 4000
Type of Packaging: Consumer, Food Service, Private Label
Brands:
Food Concentrate Corp.
Oat-N-Bran
Uncle Walter's

4644 **Food Factory**
875 Waimanu St Ste 535
Honolulu, HI 96813 808-593-2633
Fax: 808-591-2943
Frozen foods
President: David Phillips
Estimated Sales: $300,000-500,000
Number Employees: 5-9

4645 **Food Ingredients**
2425 Alft Ln
Elgin, IL 60124-7864 847-683-0001
Fax: 847-683-0007 800-500-7676
leonardra@aol.com
Manufacturer of Dairy and flavor products, colloids, cereal and legumes, fats and oils, sweeteners, process enrichment aids, surficatants, peanut butter and fruit flakes
President: Robert Leonard
Estimated Sales: $5-10 Million
Number Employees: 1-4
Sq. footage: 7000

4646 **Food Ingredients Solutions**
300 Corporate Dr
Blauvelt, NY 10913-1144 845-353-8501
Fax: 212-541-9087 jgreaves@foodcolor.com
www.foodcolor.com
Manufacturer and distributor of Ingredients for barbeque sauces, spices, seasonings, colors, flavors, gums
President/CEO/CFO: Jeff Greaves
Estimated Sales: $6 Million
Number Employees: 1-4
Number of Brands: 2
Number of Products: 80
Type of Packaging: Food Service, Private Label, Bulk
Other Locations:
Food Ingredients Solutions
Signal Hill CA
Brands:
Grill-In-A-Bottle
Safrante

4647 **Food Masters**
300 W Broad St
Griffin, GA 30223 770-227-0330
Fax: 770-228-4281 888-715-4394
sales@foodmasters.com www.foodmasters.com
Mesquite BBQ sauce, Caesar, cucumber dressing and dip, sea sauce, honey mustard, dill delight, vinaigrette, poppy seed
President: Pradeep Kumarhia
Estimated Sales: $1-2.5 Million
Number Employees: 5-9

4648 **Food Mill**
3033 Macarthur Blvd
Oakland, CA 94602-3299 510-482-3848
Fax: 510-482-0344 www.foodmillonline.com
Manufacturer of nut butter, cookies and breads
President/Co-Owner: Kirk Watkins
Treasurer/Co-Owner: Arthur Watkins
Estimated Sales: $1-2.5 Million
Number Employees: 20-49
Sq. footage: 12000
Type of Packaging: Consumer, Bulk
Brands:
Food Mill

4649 **Food Processor of New Mexico**
PO Box 3672
Albuquerque, NM 87190-3672 505-881-4921
Fax: 505-797-2505 877-634-3772
fpnm@comcast.net
www.foodprocessorsofnm.com
Manufacturer of bar-b-que sauces, green chile, red chile, habanero
Co-Owner: Phillip Clark
Co-Owner: Wanda Clark

4650 **Food Products Corporation**
3121 E Washington St
Phoenix, AZ 85034 602-273-7139
Fax: 602-275-9429
Manufacturer of Mexican foods including flour and corn tortillas, tortilla chips and masa
CEO: David Brennan
Plant Manager: Joaquin Amaro
Estimated Sales: $5-10 Million
Number Employees: 50-99
Sq. footage: 40000
Parent Co: Sparta Foods
Type of Packaging: Consumer, Food Service, Private Label, Bulk
Brands:
ARIZONA

4651 **(HQ)Food Reserves**
P.O.Box 88
Concordia, MO 64020-0088 660-463-2158
Fax: 660-463-2159 800-944-1511
info@goodforyouamerica.com
www.goodforyouamerica.com
Manufacturer and exporter of emergency and survival food tablets and canned freeze-dried foods; importer of bulk ingredients and freeze-dried foods
Manager: Deborah Collins
Manager: Landy Coldwell
Estimated Sales: $ 3 - 5 Million
Number Employees: 5-9
Sq. footage: 10000
Type of Packaging: Consumer, Private Label, Bulk
Other Locations:
Food Reserves - Laboratory
Kansas City MO
Food Reserves
Syracuse NY
Brands:
FOOD RESERVES
STOREHOUSE FOODS

4652 **(HQ)Food Reserves/Good ForYou America**
P.O.Box 88
Concordia, MO 64020-0088 660-463-2158
Fax: 660-463-2159 800-944-1511
info@FoodReserves.com
www.goodforyouamerica.com
Processor, importer and exporter of natural snack foods
Manager: Deborah Collins
General Manager: Jennifer Winklebauer
Estimated Sales: $ 3 - 5 Million
Number Employees: 5-9
Sq. footage: 10000
Type of Packaging: Consumer, Private Label, Bulk
Brands:
Good For You America
The Original Food Tab

4653 **Food Sciences Corporation**
821 E Gate Dr
Mount Laurel, NJ 8054 856-778-8080
Fax: 856-778-4192 800-320-7928
www.foodsciences.com
Manufacturer of Nutritional shakes, puddings; protein snack bars, chips; soups, pastas, hot beverages, other nutritional food supplements
Owner: Robert Schwartz
Estimated Sales: $ 10 - 20 Million
Number Employees: 50-99

4654 **Food Should Taste Good**
117 Kendrick St
Suite 550
Needham Heights, MA 02494 781-455-8500
Fax: 781-455-8550
james@foodshouldtastegood.com
www.foodshouldtastegood.com
Flavored tortilla chips
CEO: Peter Lascoe
CFO: Bob Craig
Marketing: James Borteck
Estimated Sales: $5 Million
Number Employees: 8

4655 **Food Source**
2200 Redbud Blvd
Mc Kinney, TX 75069 972-548-9001
Fax: 972-542-0884 www.foodsourcelp.com
Manufacturer of frozen custom-made lasagna, manicotti, cannelloni and ravioli; also, soups and sauces
President: Richard Riccardi
Executive VP: Anita Riccardi
VP: Carmine Riccardi
Estimated Sales: $20-50 Million
Number Employees: 50-99

4656 **Food Source Company**
1335 Fewster Drive
Mississauga, ON L4W 1A2
Canada 905-625-8404
Fax: 905-238-9160

Manufacturer, exporter and importer of salad dressings, sauces and fat-free mayonnaise
President: Ralph Murray
Estimated Sales: $2 Million
Number Employees: 18
Sq. footage: 20000
Type of Packaging: Consumer, Food Service, Private Label

4657 Food Specialties
1727 Expo Ln
Indianapolis, IN 46214 317-271-0862
Fax: 317-634-8482
Manufacturer of salad dressing, mayonnaise, prepared mustard and barbecue sauce
President: John Bradshaw
Estimated Sales: $.5-1 Million
Number Employees: 5-9
Sq. footage: 20000
Type of Packaging: Food Service, Private Label, Bulk
Brands:
Ambassador
Tasty Rich

4658 Food Specialties Company
12 Sunnybrook Dr
Cincinnati, OH 45237 513-761-1242
Fax: 513-821-3733
Manufacturer of mayonnaise, tartar sauce, salad dressings, salsa and sandwich spreads
Owner: Susan Rollman
VP/GM: Stuart Schulman
Plant Manager: Ron Simmons
Estimated Sales: $5-10 Million
Number Employees: 10-19
Sq. footage: 35000
Type of Packaging: Consumer, Food Service, Private Label, Bulk
Brands:
Caddy
Lady Rose

4659 Food for Life Baking Company
P.O.Box 1434
Corona, CA 92878-1434 951-279-5090
Fax: 951-279-1784 www.foodforlife.com
Baked goods including sprouted grain breads
President: Jim Torres
CEO: Larry Cappetto
VP: Charlie Torres
Estimated Sales: $10-20 Million
Number Employees: 50-99

4660 Food of Our Own Design
1988 Springfield Ave
Maplewood, NJ 7040 973-762-0985
Fax: 973-762-7895
www.foodofourowndesign.com,
www.maplewoodonline.com
Manufacturer of cakes, pastries, brownies and crunch bars
Owner: Timothy Quickel
VP Sales/Operations: Tisha Jackson
Estimated Sales: $10-20 Million
Number Employees: 10-19
Sq. footage: 4000

4661 FoodMatch Inc
575 Eight Avenue
Fl 23
New York, NY 10018 212-244-5050
Fax: 212-334-5042 800-350-3411
info@foodmatch.com www.foodmatch.com
Olives, fig spreads and dolmas
President/Owner: Philip Meldrum
President: Phil Meldrum
Estimated Sales: $2.5 Million
Number Employees: 23

4662 FoodScience of Vermont
20 New England Dr
Essex Junction, VT 05452-2896 802-878-5508
Fax: 802-878-0549 800-874-9444
info@foodscienceofvermont.com
www.foodsciencecorp.com
Manufacturer and exporter of vitamin supplements, joint and immune support supplements and specialty nutritional formulas
President: Dom Orlandi
CEO: Dale Metz
CFO: Tricia Wunsch
QC: Mary Helrich
Sales/Marketing: Mark Ducharme
Operations: Sarah Oliveira
Estimated Sales: $300,000-500,000
Number Employees: 1-4
Parent Co: FoodScience Corporation
Brands:
AANGAMIK DMG
CHITOLEAN
DISCOVERY
HERB ALCHEMY

4663 Foodbrands America
840 Research Pkwy
Oklahoma City, OK 73104-3616 405-290-4000
Fax: 405-879-5325 www.labcorp.com
Manufacturer of kosher and breaded and battered appetizers, gourmet hors d'oeuvres, pastries, soups, sauces, lasagna, burritos, pizza toppings and crusts, snacks, side dishes and meat products including boneless ham, bologna, salamifrankfurters, sausage, etc
President: Richard Bond
CEO: Richard Bond
CFO: Wade Miquelon
VP: William Lovette
Plant Manager: Bert Kock
Purchasing Agent: Randy Allison
Number Employees: 50-99
Parent Co: IBP
Type of Packaging: Consumer, Food Service, Private Label, Bulk
Other Locations:
Foodbrands America
Buffalo NY

4664 Foodmark
180 Linden St Ste 7b
Wellesley, MA 2482 781-237-7088
Fax: 781-237-7455 ggavris@foodmark.com
www.foodmark.com
Broker of dairy/deli products, frozen foods, groceries, meat products and private label items. Also product development and marketing services for ice cream novelties and pizza available
Partner: George Gavris
Partner: Rob Simmons
Partner: Lee Gavris
Estimated Sales: $10-20 Million
Number Employees: 10-19

4665 Fool Proof Gourmet Products
PO Box 2442
Grapevine, TX 76099-2442 817-329-1839
Fax: 817-329-1819
chefmark@foolproof-foods.com
www.foolproof-foods.com
Manufacturer and exporter of gourmet seasonings, spices, sauces, etc
President: Mark Pierce
VP: Jeff Covington
Estimated Sales: $1-3 Million
Number Employees: 5-9
Sq. footage: 10000
Parent Co: Coulton Associates
Type of Packaging: Consumer, Food Service
Brands:
Fool Proof Gourmet

4666 (HQ)Foothills Creamery
4235-16th Street SE
Calgary, AB T2G 3S2
Canada 403-263-7725
Fax: 403-237-5051 800-661-4909
www.foothillscreamery.com
President: Don Bayrack
Vice President: Barry Northfield
Sales Manager: Randy Wagner
Estimated Sales: $24 Million
Number Employees: 700
Number of Brands: 3
Number of Products: 24
Type of Packaging: Consumer, Food Service, Private Label, Bulk
Brands:
Jersey Supreme
Lone Pine Country
Rocky Mountain

4667 Foothills Creamery
4235 16th Street SE
Calgary, AB T2G 352
Canada 403-263-7725
Fax: 403-237-5051 800-661-4909
foothills.cream@cadvision.com
www.foothillscreamery.com
Manufacturer of ice cream, butter and ice cream cones
President: Don Bayrack
Estimated Sales: G
Number Employees: 50-99
Type of Packaging: Consumer
Brands:
Foothills
Unique Cones

4668 Foppiano Vineyard
12707 Old Redwood Hwy
Healdsburg, CA 95448-9241 707-433-7272
Fax: 707-433-0565 louis@foppiano.com
www.foppiano.com
Manufacturer and exporter of wines
President: Louis Foppiano
Winemaker: Bill Regan
Estimated Sales: $ 10 - 20 Million
Number Employees: 20-49
Type of Packaging: Consumer
Brands:
FOPPIANO
FOX MOUNTAIN
RIVERSIDE

4669 Forakers Joy Orchard
3696 Hamlin Road
Malaga, WA 98828-9759 509-663-6097
FRUITS

4670 Foran Spice Company
7616 S 6th St
Oak Creek, WI 53154 414-764-1220
Fax: 414-764-8803 800-558-6030
foran@foranspice.com www.foranspice.com
Manufacturer of re-cleaned and sterilized spices, custom engineered seasonings, and value-added food products
President: Patty Goto
CFO: Andy Gitter
Vice President: Joy Hauser
Engineer: Alan Goto
Estimated Sales: $19 Million
Number Employees: 128
Sq. footage: 71000
Type of Packaging: Food Service, Private Label, Bulk

4671 Forbes Candies
1300 Taylor Farm Road
Virginia Beach, VA 23452 757-468-6602
Fax: 757-486-0646 800-626-5898
www.forbescandies.com
Manufacturer of confectionery products including salt water taffy, fudge, assorted brittle, and peanuts.
President: William Lawton
Sales Manager: Lynn Watson
Estimated Sales: $5-10 Million
Number Employees: 20-49
Type of Packaging: Consumer

4672 Forbes Chocolate
800 Ken Mar Industrial Parkway
Broadview Hgts, OH 44147 440-838-4400
Fax: 440-838-4438 800-433-1090
orders@forbeschocolate.com
http://forbeschocolate.com/
Chocolate
President: Keith Geringer
VP: Douglas Geringer
Estimated Sales: $1.4 Million
Number Employees: 13

4673 Forbes Chocolates
800 Ken Mar Industrial Parkway
Broadview Heights, OH 44147
Fax: 440-838-4438 800-433-1090
sales@forbeschocolate.com
www.forbeschocolate.com
Manufacturer and exporter of cocoa and flavor powders for dairies. Chocolate ,mocha, strawberry, vanilla, orange cream, root beer, banana, mango and others
President/Owner: Keith Geringer
Quality Control: Ellon Waters
Marketing/Sales: Rick Stunek

Estimated Sales: $1.4 Million
Number Employees: 13
Sq. footage: 17000
Type of Packaging: Bulk

4674 **Ford Gum & Machine Company**
18 Newton Ave
Akron, NY 14001 716-542-4561
Fax: 847-542-4610 800-225-5535
www.fordgum.com
Manufacturer and exporter of value added gums and sour balls; also, vending machines
President: George Stege
Finance Manager: Luela Lo
R&D Director: K Clark
SVP Sales/Marketing: Steven Greene
Production Manager: Jim Monteleone
Purchasing: Jill Rosenberg
Estimated Sales: $20 Million
Number Employees: 120
Sq. footage: 125000
Parent Co: Ford Gum
Type of Packaging: Consumer, Food Service, Private Label, Bulk
Brands:
CAROUSEL
CHUNK A CHEW
YOWSER!!

4675 **Ford's Fancy Fruit**
1109 Agriculture St
Raleigh, NC 27603-2373 919-833-9621
Fax: 919-821-5781 800-446-0947
sales@bonesuckin.com www.bonesuckin.com
Manufacturer of Sauces, mustards, salsa and nuts
Vice President: Connie Ford
VP: Patrick Ford
Estimated Sales: $11.6 Million
Number Employees: 60
Type of Packaging: Private Label
Brands:
Big Chunks Salsa
Blessing's Mustard
Bone Suckin' Sauce
Ford's Foods
Hiccuppin' Hot Sauce
J. Berrie Brown Wine Nuts
We're Talking Serious Salsa

4676 **Ford's Foods, Inc.**
1109 Agriculture Street
Raleigh, NC 27603 919-833-7647
Fax: 919-821-5781 800-446-0947
patford@bonesuckin.com www.bonesuckin.com
Gluten-free, kosher, organic/natural, mustards, salsa/dips, BBQ sauce, grilling sauces, rubs.
Marketing: Sandi Ford

4677 **Fords Gourmet Foods**
1109 Agriculture Street
Raleigh, NC 27603 919-833-7647
Fax: 919-821-5781 800-446-0947
patford@bonesuckin.com www.bonesuckin.com
Sauces, marinades, mustards, and nuts
President/Owner: Phil Ford

4678 **Foreign Candy Company**
1 Foreign Candy Dr
Hull, IA 51239-7499 712-439-1496
Fax: 712-439-1434 800-831-8541
jc.reichter@foreigncandy.com
www.foreigncandy.com
Distributors of confectionery
CEO: Peter DeYager
CEO: Peter Deyager
VP Marketing: Art Zito
VP Sales: Jim Finelli
Estimated Sales: $5-10 Million
Number Employees: 50-99
Type of Packaging: Private Label
Brands:
MEGA WARHEADS
RIPS TOLL

4679 **Foreign Domestic Chemicals Corporation**
3 Post Road
Oakland, NJ 07436 201-651-9700
Fax: 201-651-9703
Manufactures ingredients and additives
President: Heinrich Dieseldorff
Estimated Sales: $500,000-1 Million
Number Employees: 1-4

4680 **Foremost Farms**
220 St Paul Street
Preston, MN 55965 507-765-3831
www.foremostfarms.com
Manufacturer of dry blends, specialty whey protein concentrate, condensed skim milk, buttermilk and nonfat dry milk
Plant Manager: Jon Ebner
Plant Manager: Jon Ebner
Number Employees: 35
Parent Co: Foremost Farms USA
Type of Packaging: Food Service, Private Label, Bulk
Brands:
Golden Guernsey Dairy Products
Morning Glory Products

4681 **Foremost Farms**
2294 Randall Road
Athens, WI 54411 715-257-7015
www.foremostfarms.com
Manufacturer of mozzarella, provalone, asadero, condensed whey protein and permeate
Manager: Robert Voss
Quality Assurance Manager: Jerry LaBelle
General Manager: Bob Voss
Plant Manager: Robert Voss
Purchasing Manager: Donald Storhoff
Number Employees: 64
Sq. footage: 60000
Parent Co: Foremost Farms USA
Type of Packaging: Consumer, Food Service, Private Label

4682 **Foremost Farms**
100 N Main Street
Clayton, WI 54004 715-948-2166
www.foremostfarms.com
Manufacturer of provolone, mozzarella, condensed permeate and condensed whey protein concentrate
Plant Manager: Andrew VanHeuklom
Plant Manager: Eric Van Der Huevel
Number Employees: 63
Parent Co: Foremost Farms USA
Type of Packaging: Consumer, Food Service, Private Label

4683 **(HQ)Foremost Farms**
E 10889 Penny Lane
Baraboo, WI 53913-8115 608-355-8700
Fax: 608-356-5458 800-362-9196
linda.strachan@foremostfarms.com
www.foremostfarms.com
Manufacturer of cheese, butter and a host of value-added whey ingredients. Also supply bulk fluid milk to handlers.
President: David Fuhrmann
VP Finance/CFO: Michael Doyle
VP Member Services & Milk Marketing: Joseph Weis
VP Marketing: Douglas Wilke
VP HR/Safety/Communications: Michael McDonald
VP Manufacturing: Michael Pronschinske
Plant Manager: Terry Sutton
Estimated Sales: $1.4 Billion
Number Employees: 1100
Type of Packaging: Food Service, Bulk
Other Locations:
Foremost Farms USA Coop.
Plover WI
Brands:
Foremost Farms
Natural Choice

4684 **Foremost Farms**
W 3286 Highway F
Chilton, WI 53014 920-849-9339
www.foremostfarms.com
Manufacturer of mozzarella, provolone, string cheese, whey protein concentrate, permeate, condensed skim milk and cream
Plant Manager: Steve Rukamp
Plant Manager: Tom Matthews
Number Employees: 58
Parent Co: Foremost Farms USA
Type of Packaging: Bulk

4685 **Foremost Farms**
487 Highway 128
Wilson, WI 54027 715-772-4211
www.foremostfarms.com
Manufacturer of mozzarella, condensed whey, condensed whey protein concentrate and condensed permeate
Plant Manager: Andrew VanHeuklom
Plant Manager: Bruce Snitker
Number Employees: 31
Parent Co: Foremost Farms USA
Type of Packaging: Bulk

4686 **Foremost Farms**
W12215 County Road FF
Alma Center, WI 54611-8409 715-964-7411
Fax: 715-964-1122 www.foremostfarms.com
Manufacturer of mozzarella cheese and condensed whey
Plant Manager: Gordon Kleba
Number Employees: 53
Parent Co: Foremost Farms USA
Type of Packaging: Bulk

4687 **Foremost Farms**
10202 Foremost Drive
PO Box 98
Rothschild, WI 54474 715-359-0534
www.foremostfarms.com
Producer of lactose powder
Plant Manager: Patrick Merrick
Plant Manager: Ed Fallon
Number Employees: 78
Parent Co: Foremost Farms USA
Type of Packaging: Bulk

4688 **Foremost Farms**
932 N Madison Street
Lancaster, WI 53813 608-723-7381
www.foremostfarms.com
Manufacturer of milled cheddar, milled marbled cheddar, condensed whey, condensed whey protein concentrate and condensed permeate
Plant Manager: Tom Mathews
Plant Manager: Dan Williams
Number Employees: 60
Parent Co: Foremost Farms USA
Type of Packaging: Bulk

4689 **Foremost Farms**
1511 East 4th Street
Marshfield, WI 54449 715-384-5616
www.foremostfarms.com
Manufacturer of cheddar cheese, farmers cheese, colby, monterey jack and condensed whey
Plant Manager: David Schmidt
Number Employees: 48
Parent Co: Foremost Farms USA
Type of Packaging: Bulk

4690 **Foremost Farms**
S1856 County Road U
Cochrane, WI 54622 608-626-2121
www.foremostfarms.com
Manufacturer of cheddar, monterey jack, colby jack, mozzarella, muenster, condensed whey, condensed permeate and condensed whey protein concentrate
Plant Manager: Jim Potter
Plant Manager: Kelton Greenway
Number Employees: 55
Parent Co: Foremost Farms USA
Type of Packaging: Consumer, Food Service, Private Label, Bulk

4691 **Foremost Farms**
501 S Pine Street
Reedsburg, WI 53959 608-524-2351
www.foremostfarms.com
Manufacturer of butter, condensed skim milk, sweet cream and condensed buttermilk
Plant Manager: Dan Belk
Number Employees: 49
Parent Co: Foremost Farms USA
Type of Packaging: Bulk

4692 **Foremost Farms**
427 E Wisconsin Street
Sparta, WI 54656 608-269-3126
www.foremostfarms.com
Manufacturer of whole milk powder, bulk fluid milk, condensed skim milk, buttermilk powder, nonfat dry mil, organic nonfat dry milk, cultured skim milk powder, condensed whole milk, whey protein concentrate powder and cream
Plant Manager: Scott Overfelt
Plant Manager: Scott Oberfelt
Number Employees: 42
Parent Co: Foremost Farms USA

Type of Packaging: Bulk

4693 **Foremost Farms**
684 S Church St
Richland Center, WI 53581 608-647-2186
Fax: 608-647-2955 www.foremostfarms.com
Manufacturer of mozzarella, condensed whey, whole whey powder, whey protein concentrate and permeate
Plant Manager: Daniel Williams
Plant Manager: Dan Williams
Number Employees: 121

4694 **Forest Packing Company**
P.O.Box D
Forest, MS 39074-0558 601-469-3321
Fax: 601-469-4251
Poultry
President: William Haralson
Estimated Sales: $25-49.9 Million
Number Employees: 100-249

4695 **Forge Mountain Foods**
1215 Greenville Hwy
Hendersonville, NC 28792 828-692-9470
Fax: 828-692-6135 800-823-6743
pbrim@forgemountain.com
www.forgemountain.com
Specialty foods company with over 250 varieties of old timey food products; jams and jellies, pickles and relishes and more
President: Brian Pawling
VP Sales/Marketing: Paul Brim
Estimated Sales: $500,000-$1 Million
Number Employees: 5-9
Number of Products: 250+
Brands:
FORGE MOUNTAIN

4696 **Foris Vineyards**
654 Kendall Rd
Cave Junction, OR 97523 541-592-3752
Fax: 541-592-4424 foris@foriswine.com
www.foriswine.com
Wines
President: Ted Gerber
Estimated Sales: $2.5-5 Million
Number Employees: 10-19
Number of Brands: 10
Type of Packaging: Private Label

4697 **Forkless Gourmet Inc**
10 S Riverside Plz
Chicago, IL 60606-3728 312-474-5746
Fax: 312-474-6127 www.forklessgourmet.com/
Manufacturers forkless bun meals available in several varieties including: chicken sesame teriyaki; thai style chicken; beef & broccoli; pork & vegetables with Five Fortune BBQ Sauce; kung pao shrimp (spicy); vegetarian feast withtofu & edamame; chipotle chicken (spicy); margarita chicken; beef asada; pork & vegetable with Ancho Honey BBQ Sauce, and black bean adobo.
Bun Meal Pioneer: Gregory Stahl
Bun Meal Pioneer: Christopher Scott
Bun Meal Pioneer: Katie Torres
Bun Meal Pioneer: Steven Spiegel
Bun Meal Pioneer: Susan Schneider
Type of Packaging: Food Service

4698 **Forman Vineyards**
P.O.Box 343
St Helena, CA 94574-0343 707-963-3900
Fax: 707-963-5384 www.formanvineyard.com
Wines
President: Rick Forman
Estimated Sales: Under $500,000
Number Employees: 5-9

4699 **Formax/Provisur Technologies**
9150 W 191st Street
Mokena, IL 60448 708-479-3500
Fax: 708-479-3598 info@provisur.com
www.provisur.com
Food processing equipment: forming machines, multi-loaf slicers and automatic transport equipment
Number Employees: 250-499

4700 **Formost Friedman Company**
152 Frankel Boulevard
Merrick, NY 11566-4033 516-378-4919
Fax: 516-379-8301
General grocery
President: William MacMelville
Estimated Sales: $1-2.5 Million
Number Employees: 1-4

4701 **Fort Boise Produce Company**
103 Main St
Nyssa, OR 97913 541-372-5174
Fax: 541-372-3326
Packed onions
President: Thomas Stephens
Estimated Sales: $1-2.5 Million
Number Employees: 50-99

4702 **Fort Garry Brewing Company**
130 Lowson Crescent
Winnipeg, NB R3P 2H8
Canada 204-487-3678
Fax: 204-487-0839 info@fortgarry.com
www.fortgarry.com
Manufacturer of beer
President/CEO: Doug Saville
CFO: Denis Chabbert
Marketing: Wayne Vanlandeghem
Sales: Orest Horechko
Estimated Sales: B
Number Employees: 23
Number of Brands: 13
Number of Products: 1
Sq. footage: 25000
Type of Packaging: Private Label, Bulk

4703 **Forte Stromboli Company**
3129 S 13th Street
Philadelphia, PA 19148-5234 215-463-6336
Fax: 215-463-8616
Manufacturer of frozen stromboli
President: Ronald Conti
Estimated Sales: $ 5 - 10 Million
Number Employees: 5-9
Type of Packaging: Consumer, Food Service

4704 **Fortella Fortune Cookies**
214 W 26th St
Chicago, IL 60616 312-567-9000
Fax: 312-567-9119
Manufacturer of fortune, almond and specialty cookies
Owner: Herman Wong
Company Manager: Brenda Wong
Estimated Sales: $1-2.5 Million
Number Employees: 10-19
Type of Packaging: Consumer, Food Service

4705 **Fortenberry Ice Company**
3128 Fortenberry Rd
Kodak, TN 37764 865-933-2568
Fax: 865-933-2568
Manufacturer of ice
Owner: Jeff Fortenberry
Estimated Sales: $1-2.5 Million
Number Employees: 5-9
Type of Packaging: Consumer
Other Locations:
Fortenberry Ice Company
Kodak TN

4706 **Fortino Winery**
4525 Hecker Pass Rd
Gilroy, CA 95020 408-842-3305
Fax: 408-842-8636 888-617-6606
gino@fortinowinery.com
www.fortinowinery.com
Wines
Owner: Gino Fortino
Vice President: Terri Fortino
Estimated Sales: $900,000
Number Employees: 10

4707 **(HQ)Fortitech**
2105 Technology Dr
Schenectady, NY 12308 518-372-5155
Fax: 518-372-5599 800-950-5156
info@fortitech.com www.fortitech.com
Manufacturer and exporter of vitamin and mineral pre mixes
President: Walt Borisenok
CFO: Brian Wilcox
Research & Development: Ram Chaudhari
Communications Manager: Patrick Morris
VP Sales: Sam Sylvestky
Production Manager: Ed Webster
Purchasing Manager: Tom Morba
Estimated Sales: $100 Million
Number Employees: 137
Sq. footage: 100000
Type of Packaging: Food Service
Other Locations:
Fortitech
Europe
Fortitech
South America
Fortitech
Mexico

4708 **Fortitude Brands LLC**
6925 Almansa Street
Coral Gables, FL 33146-3809 305-661-8198
Fax: 305-662-4977 fstanzl@aol.com
www.fortitudebrands.com
Manufacturer and importer of exotic and natural tropical food products
CEO: Franco Stanzione
CFO: Juan Serna
Marketing: Robert Hunt
Sales: Bob Ottmar
Public Relations: Renee Morales
Estimated Sales: $400,000
Number Employees: 21
Number of Brands: 5
Number of Products: 14
Type of Packaging: Consumer
Brands:
CASABE RAINFOREST CRACKERS
ISABO HEARTS OF PALM
SAMAI

4709 **Fortress Systems LLC**
2132 S 156th Cir
Omaha, NE 68130-2503 402-333-3532
Fax: 402-333-3536 888-331-6601
info@8-ballnutrition.com
www.8-ballnutrition.com
Manufacturer of dietary supplements
CEO: Mike Carnazzo
VP R&D: Joseph Carnazzo BS, RPh
Consultant: Dr Martha Garcia, PharmD
Consultant: Dr Brian Sakurada, PharmD
Number Employees: 1-4
Parent Co: FSI Nutrition

4710 **Fortuna Cellars**
2124 Fortuna Court
Davis, CA 95616-0603 530-756-6686
Wines
President: Gerald Bowes

4711 **Fortunate Cookie**
PO Box 1386
Stowe, VT 05672-1386 802-888-5706
Fax: 802-888-5563 866-266-5337
portico@stowevt.net
www.thefortunatecookie.com
Specialty cookies/gift baskets made from scratch and to order signature offering: fortune cookies in 4 sizes and 19 flavors
President: Portia Arthur
CEO: Portia Arthur
Type of Packaging: Consumer

4712 **Fortune Brands**
300 Tower Pkwy
Lincolnshire, IL 60069 847-484-4529
Fax: 847-541-5750 www.accobrands.com
Manufacturer of liquor
Chairman/CEO: Norman Wesley
CEO: Robert J Keller
Estimated Sales: $160 Million
Number Employees: 5,000-9,999
Parent Co: Jim Beam Brands Worldwide
Type of Packaging: Consumer, Food Service, Private Label
Other Locations:
Fortune Brands
Fairhaven MA
Brands:
ABSOLUT VODKA
AFTER SHOCK
ALBERTA SPRINGS
BAKER'S
BANFF ICE
BOOKER'S
CALVERT
CANYON ROAD
CHINACO TEQUILA
COURVOISIER
DALMORE
DALMORE SCOTCH
DE PON FELIPE
DEKUYPER
DISTILLERS MASTERPIECE
EL TESCERO

GEYSER PEAK
GILBEY'S
JIM BEAM
KAMCHATKA
KESSLER
KNOB CREEK
LEROUX
LORD CALVERT
OLD CROW
OLD GRAND DAD
OLD OVERHOLT
RONRICO
SOURZ
TAGLE RIDGE
VOX
WILD HORSE
WINDSOR
WOLFSCHMIDT

4713 **Fortune Cookie Factory**
261 12th St
Oakland, CA 94607 510-832-5552
Fax: 510-832-2565
Fortune cookies
President: Andrew Wong
Estimated Sales: $2.5-5 Million
Number Employees: 5-9

4714 **Fortune Seas**
42 Rogers Street
Gloucester, MA 01930-5000 978-281-6666
Fax: 978-281-8519 fseas@aol.com
Seafood
President/CEO: Donald Short
VP Sales: Charles Bencal
Brands:
FORTUNE'S CATCH
OCEAN DELI

4715 **Fortunes International Teas**
11 Tunnel Way
Mc Kees Rocks, PA 15136 412-771-7767
Fax: 412-771-2122 800-551-8327
teaman3000@cs.com www.fortunescoffee.com
Black, green and herbal teas
Owner: Richard Cefola Sr
VP Marketing: Michael Brunk
Estimated Sales: $500,000-$1 Million
Number Employees: 1-4
Type of Packaging: Private Label
Brands:
Commonwealth
Fortunes
London Herb & Spice
Ridgways

4716 **Forty Second Street Bagel Cafe**
1726 W 9th St
Upland, CA 91786-5603 909-949-7334
Fax: 909-949-0721
Manufacturer of Bagels and rolls
Owner: Robert Hall
Estimated Sales: $ 3 - 5 Million
Number Employees: 5-9

4717 **Fosselman's Ice Cream Company**
1824 W Main St
Alhambra, CA 91801 626-282-6533
Fax: 626-282-0246 info@fosselmans.com
www.fosselmans.com
Ice cream, sherbet
President: F Fosselman
VP: Christian Fossleman
Estimated Sales: $2.5-5 Million
Number Employees: 10-19
Type of Packaging: Consumer, Bulk

4718 **Fossil Farms**
81 Fulton St
Boonton, NJ 7005 201-651-1190
Fax: 201-651-1191 sales@fossilfarms.com
www.fossilfarms.com
Farm raised game and all natural meats
CEO/Co-Owner: Lance Appelbaum
Sales Manager: Sturgess Spanos
COO/Co-Owner: Todd Appelbaum
Warehouse Manager: Jose Rivera
Estimated Sales: $1.1 Million
Number Employees: 7

4719 **Foster Family Farm**
90 Foster St
South Windsor, CT 06074 860-648-9366
www.fosterfarms.com
Manufacturer and exporter of pickled asparagus and beans
President: Chris Foster
Co-Owner: Teresa Robertson
Estimated Sales: $10-20 Million
Number Employees: 50-99

4720 **Foster Farms**
232 Industrial Park Dr N
Demopolis, AL 36732 334-289-5082
Fax: 334-289-1774 www.fosterfarms.com
Packing
Estimated Sales: $ 3 - 5 Million
Number Employees: 5-9

4721 **(HQ)Foster Farms**
1000 Davis St
Livingston, CA 95334
US 209-394-7901
Fax: 209-394-6342 800-255-7227
comments@fosterfarms.com
www.fosterfarms.com
Manufacturer and exporter of chicken and turkey products including frankfurters and corn dogs
CEO: Ron Foster
SVP/CFO: John Landis
Svp Marketing: Bob Wangerien
Plant Manager: Mark Silvas
Estimated Sales: $2.20billion
Number Employees: 10,500
Sq. footage: 25000
Type of Packaging: Consumer, Food Service, Private Label, Bulk
Other Locations:
Foster Farms
Porterville CA
Brands:
FIRCREST FARMS
FOSTER FARMS
FOSTER FARMS DAIRY PRODUCTS
FOSTER FARMS DELI MEAT
FOSTER FARMS POULTRY
VALCHRIS FARMS

4722 **Foster Farms**
232 Industrial Park Dr N
Demopolis, AL 36732 334-289-5082
Fax: 334-289-1774 800-255-7227
www.fosterfarms.com
Manufacturer of meat products including sausage; wholesaler/distributor of corn dogs
President/CEO: Ron Foster
Estimated Sales: $500,000-$1 Million
Number Employees: 5-9
Type of Packaging: Consumer

4723 **Foster Farms**
P.O.Box 8
Creswell, OR 97426-0008 541-895-2161
Fax: 541-895-2166 www.fosterfarms.com
Manufacturer of fresh and frozen chicken and turkey
President: Mike Avalos
Estimated Sales: $25-49.9 Million
Number Employees: 100-249
Parent Co: Foster Farms
Type of Packaging: Consumer, Food Service
Brands:
FOSTER FARM

4724 **Foster Farms**
855 NW 8th Street
Corvallis, OR 97330-6210 541-754-6211
Fax: 541-757-0276 800-255-7227
www.fosterfarms.com
Manufacturer and exporter of chicken products including frankfurters
Estimated Sales: $50-100 Million
Number Employees: 50-99
Parent Co: Foster Farms
Type of Packaging: Consumer, Food Service, Private Label, Bulk

4725 **Foster Farms Dairy**
415 Kansas Ave
Modesto, CA 95351 209-576-2300
Fax: 209-576-2397
mzanos@fosterdairyfarms.com
www.fosterfarms.com
Manufacturer and exporter of cottage cheese, yogurt, sour and heavy cream, milk, butter, ice cream, milk powder and juice
President/CEO: Jeff Foster
CFO: Tom Van Autreve
Estimated Sales: $10-20 Million
Number Employees: 400
Parent Co: Foster Farms
Type of Packaging: Consumer, Food Service, Bulk

4726 **Foster Farms Dairy**
3380 W Ashlan Ave
Fresno, CA 93722-4448 559-244-2200
Fax: 559-244-2003 800-241-0008
www.fosterfarmsdairy.com
Manufacturer of milk
Owner/President: Ron Foster
Sales Manager: Dennis Roberts
Plant Manager: Dennis Bettencourt
Estimated Sales: $50-100 Million
Number Employees: 1-4
Type of Packaging: Consumer, Food Service, Private Label, Bulk
Brands:
KNUDSEN

4727 **(HQ)Foulds**
520 E Church St
Libertyville, IL 60048 847-362-3062
Fax: 847-362-6658 www.fouldspasta.com
Macaroni, spaghetti and egg noodles
Owner: Chris Bradley
VP: Joseph Bradley
Director: Marge Simpson
Sales: Lowell Wilkins
Maintenance Manager: Jon Zemanek
Estimated Sales: $6 Million
Number Employees: 49
Brands:
KABOODLES
NO YOLKS EGG NOODLES
WACKY MAC

4728 **Fountain Products**
1308 Arlington Cir
Hanover Park, IL 60133 630-443-1113
Fax: 630-443-1344
Manufacturer of equipment
President: Paul Lamb
Inside Sales: Sue Bellecomo
Sales Representative: PJ Lamb
Estimated Sales: $ 1 - 3 Million
Number Employees: 1-4
Brands:
Dynamic
Leer
SSP

4729 **Fountain Shakes/MS Foods**
13508 Orchard Road
Minnetonka, MN 55305 952-988-6940
Fax: 952-988-6941 astone2454@aol.com
www.fountainshake.com
Fountain shake in six flavors: chocolate malt, cappuccino, strawberry, vanilla, banana and chocolate
President: Alan B Stone
Marketing: Lou Ann Stone
Public Relations: Melanie Stone
Parent Co: MS Foods
Type of Packaging: Consumer, Bulk
Brands:
FOUNTAIN SHAKE

4730 **(HQ)Fountain Valley Foods**
1420 Aviation Way
Colorado Springs, CO 80916 719-573-6012
Fax: 303-695-0284
mark@fountainvalleyfoods.com
www.fountainvalleyfoods.com
Processor of salsa, ketchup, bean dip and specialty chili products; Importer/Distributor of cheese sauce, jalapeno peppers, banana peppers, chipotle peppers, green chile.
President: James Loyacono
Estimated Sales: $4.9 Million
Number Employees: 4
Sq. footage: 10000
Type of Packaging: Consumer, Food Service, Private Label, Bulk
Other Locations:
Den-Mar Products
Trinidad CO
Brands:
LONE TREE FARM
NACHO GRANDE

4731 **Fountainhead Water Company**
3280 Green Pointe Parkway
Suite 300
Norcross, GA 30092-6656 864-944-1993
Fax: 864-944-0001 www.fountainheadwater.com
Bottled water
President: Kevin McClanahan
VP: Mark Rehl
Production: Gene Wells
Estimated Sales: $10-15 Million
Number Employees: 50-99
Number of Brands: 1
Brands:
FOUNTAINHEAD BOTTLED WATER

4732 **Four Chimneys Farm Winery Trust**
211 Hall Rd
Himrod, NY 14842-9783 607-243-7502
Fax: 607-243-8156
info@fourchimneysorganicwine.com
www.fourchimneysorganicwines.com
Manufacturer of organically grown grape juice, wine, cooking wine and vinegar
Owner: Scott Smith
Sales Manager: W Daniel
Estimated Sales: Less than $500,000
Number Employees: 5-9
Type of Packaging: Consumer, Bulk

4733 **Four Percent Company**
16145 Hamilton Ave
Highland Park, MI 48203-2615 313-345-5880
Fax: 313-345-8686 singerextract@msn.com
www.singerextract.com
Flavors
President: Harold Samhat
Estimated Sales: $500,000-$1 Million
Number Employees: 1-4
Type of Packaging: Food Service, Private Label
Brands:
SEELY

4734 **Four Seasons Produce, Inc**
400 Wabash Road
PO Box 788
Ephrata, PA 17522-0788 717-721-2800
Fax: 717-721-2597 800-422-8384
www.fsproduce.com
Fruits and vegetables
President/CEO: Ron Carkoski
VP Finance: Loretta Radanovic
VP/General Manager: Rob Kurtz
Quality Manager: Daniel Oloro
National Sales Manager: Stan Paluszewski
Number Employees: 423
Sq. footage: 261000

4735 **Four Sisters Winery**
783 County Road 519
Belvidere, NJ 7823 908-475-3671
Fax: 908-475-3555 matty@goes.com
www.matarazzo.com
Wines
President: Robert Matarazzo
Production: Valerie Tishuk
Estimated Sales: $1-2.5 Million
Number Employees: 5-9
Type of Packaging: Private Label

4736 **Fowler Packing Company**
8570 S Cedar Ave
Fresno, CA 93725 559-834-5911
Fax: 559-834-5272 www.fowlerpacking.com
Manufacturer of peaches, nectarines, plums, apricots, grapes and pomegranates
Owner: Dennis Parnagian
Estimated Sales: $ 20 - 50 Million
Number Employees: 50-99

4737 **Fox Deluxe Foods**
370 N Morgan St
Chicago, IL 60607 312-421-3737
Fax: 312-421-8067
Wholesale frozen meats
Owner: Sam Samano
Estimated Sales: $ 50 - 100 Million
Number Employees: 50-99

4738 **Fox Hollow Farm**
10 Old Lyme Rd
Hanover, NH 03755 603-643-6002
Fax: 603-643-2540
Manufacturer sweet and spicy mustard sauce used as a glaze, marinade and a mustard on meat, fish, chicken and sandwiches
President: Phyllis Fox
Estimated Sales: $500,000-$1 Million
Number Employees: 1-4
Type of Packaging: Consumer
Brands:
FOX HOLLOW FARM MUSTARD
FOX-MORE THAN A MUSTARD

4739 **Fox IV Technologies**
6011 Enterprise Dr
Export, PA 15632 724-387-3500
Fax: 724-387-3516 foxiv@foxiv.com
www.foxiv.com
President/CEO: Rick Fox
Estimated Sales: $ 10 - 20 Million
Number Employees: 20-49

4740 **Fox Meadow Farm**
1439 Clover Mill Road
Chester Springs, PA 19425-1108 610-827-9731
Wines
President: Harry Mandell, Jr.
Estimated Sales: $500,000 appx.
Number Employees: 1-4

4741 **Fox Meadow Farm of Vermont**
135 N Main St # 5
Rutland, VT 05701-3238 802-775-5460
Fax: 802-773-2242 888-754-4204
hoermann@mt-mainsfield.com
www.vtgrocers.org
Dry seasoning and herb blends, dry mixes
President: James Harrison
Estimated Sales: $300,000-500,000
Number Employees: 1-4

4742 **Fox Run Vineyards**
670 State Route 14
Penn Yan, NY 14527 315-536-4616
Fax: 315-536-1383 800-636-9786
info@foxrunvineyards.com
www.foxrunvineyards.com
Wines
President: Mike Lally
Vice President: Brooks Hale
Vice President: Andy Hale
Estimated Sales: $1.6 Million
Number Employees: 30
Sq. footage: 6

4743 **Fox Vineyards Winery**
225 Highway 11 S
Social Circle, GA 30025-5003 770-787-5402
Fax: 770-787-5402
Wines
President: John Fuchs
Estimated Sales: $1-2.5 Million
Number Employees: 1-4

4744 **Fox's Fine Foods**
303 Broadway St Ste 106
Laguna Beach, CA 92651 949-497-8910
Fax: 949-497-1763 888-522-3697
foxsfine@aol.com www.foxfinefoods.com
Pestos, relishes, condiments, soups
President: Kim Fox
Estimated Sales: Under $500,000
Number Employees: 5-9
Type of Packaging: Private Label

4745 **Foxen Vineyard**
7200 Foxen Canyon Rd
Santa Maria, CA 93454 805-937-4251
Fax: 805-937-0415 www.foxenvineyard.com
Wines
President: Richard Dore
Estimated Sales: $1-2.5 Million
Number Employees: 5-9

4746 **Foxtail Foods**
6880 Fairfield Business Center Drive
Fairfield, OH 45014-5476
Fax: 513-881-7910 800-487-2253
www.foxtailfoods.com
Pies, cookies, muffin batter, mixes and syrups and specialty products
President: Lonnie Howard
VP: Matt Daniel
Quality Control Manager: Doug Snedden
VP Sales/Marketing: Athos Rostan
Purchasing Agent: Rich Frysinger
Estimated Sales: $10-20 Million
Number Employees: 130
Sq. footage: 59685
Parent Co: Perkins
Type of Packaging: Consumer, Food Service, Private Label, Bulk
Other Locations:
Foxtail Foods - Corporate
Memphis
Foxtail Foods - Corporate
Tennesse
Foxtail Foods - R&D
Cincinnati
Brands:
FOXTAIL

4747 **Frair & Grimes**
PO Box 3647
Kent, WA 98089-0210 206-935-0134
Fax: 206-935-7937 sales@frairandgrimes.com
www.frairandgrimes.com
Manufacturer of teas including darjeeling, black, green, oolong, fruit blends, flavored, etc
Owner: Timothy Frair
Number Employees: 1-4

4748 **Fralinger's**
1325 Boardwalk # 1
Atlantic City, NJ 08401-7287 609-345-2177
Fax: 609-344-0758 800-938-2339
sales@fralingers.com www.seashoretaffy.com
Taffy and candy
Manager: Barbara Brennan
VP: Arthur Gager
VP Marketing/Sales: Lisa Glaser
Operations: Susan Saraceni
Estimated Sales: $500,000-$1 Million
Number Employees: 5-9
Type of Packaging: Private Label

4749 **Fran's Chocolates**
1300 East Pike St
Seattle, WA 98122 206-322-0233
Fax: 203-322-0452 800-422-3726
orders@franschocolates.com
www.franschocolates.com
Chocolates
President/Owner: Fran Bigelow
Marketing: Adriana Bigelow
Estimated Sales: $5 Million
Number Employees: 30

4750 **Fran's Healthy Helpings**
840 Hinckley Road
Suite 128
Burlingame, CA 94010-1505 650-652-5772
Fax: 650-652-5773
Health foods
President: Fran Lent
VP Operations: Ada Chang
Estimated Sales: $1-2.5 Million
Number Employees: 5-9
Brands:
FRAN'S HEALTHY HELPINGS

4751 **(HQ)France Croissant**
227 W 40th St
New York, NY 10018-1513 212-888-1210
Fax: 212-719-5940
Manufacturer of frozen muffin doughs and baked goods including croissants, danishes, puff pastries and breads
Owner: Fanny Paderganana
Number Employees: 10-19
Type of Packaging: Private Label, Bulk

4752 **France Delices**
5065 Rue Ontario E
Montreal, QC H1V 3V2
Canada 514-259-2291
Fax: 514-259-1788 800-663-1365
information@francedelices.com
Manufacturer and exporter of cakes including fresh, frozen and gourmet
President: Colette Durot
VP: Laurent Durot
Estimated Sales: $13million
Number Employees: 190
Sq. footage: 50000
Type of Packaging: Consumer, Food Service

4753 **Franciscan Oakville Estates**
P.O.Box 407
Rutherford, CA 94573-0407 707-963-7111
Fax: 707-963-7867 800-529-9463
www.franciscan.com
Manufacturer of Wines, liquors, mixers
President: Jean-Michael Valette
Director Public Relations: Lisa Supple
Senior Winemaker: Larry Levin
Production: Bill Skowronski
Plant Manager: Lee Isola
Estimated Sales: $10-20 Million
Number Employees: 100-249
Parent Co: Constellation Brands

4754 **Franciscan Vineyards**
1178 Galleron Rd at Hwy 29
St. Helena, CA 94574 707-963-3830
Fax: 707-963-7867 800-529-9463
info@franciscan.com www.franciscan.com
Manufacturer and exporter of fine wines
President/CEO: John Wright
General Manager/ Director Winemaking: Janey Myers
Winemaker: Jay Turnipseed
Estimated Sales: $ 50 - 100 Million
Number Employees: 100-249
Number of Brands: 7
Parent Co: Canandaigua Wine Company
Type of Packaging: Consumer
Brands:
ESTANCIA
FRANCISCAN OAKVILLE ESTATE
MT VEEDER
QUINTESSA
SIMI RAVENSWOOD
VERAMONTE

4755 **Franco's Cocktail Mixes**
121 SW 5th Ct
Pompano Beach, FL 33060 954-782-7491
Fax: 954-786-9253 800-782-4508
Francocktl@aol.com
www.francoscocktailmixes.com
Manufacturer and exporter of liquid and dry cocktail mixes; also, colored margarita salt and colored rimming sugars
President: Brenda Franco
Quality Controll: Guy Haret
Public Relations: Laura Schnell
Estimated Sales: $10-24.9 Million
Number Employees: 10-19
Number of Brands: 12
Number of Products: 100+
Sq. footage: 25000
Type of Packaging: Food Service, Private Label
Brands:
CROWN'S PRIDE
FLORIDA STRAITS RUM RUNNER
FLORIDA'S GOLD COCKTAIL
FLORIDA's PRIDE
FRANCO'S MARGARITA SALT SOMBRERO
JOSE CUERVO MARGARITA SALT SOMBRERO
PAT O'BRIEN'S
SAUZA MARGARITA SALT WITH JUICER
TOUT FINI COCKTAIL MIXES

4756 **Frank & Dean's CocktailMixes**
1395 Coronet Avenue
Pasadena, CA 91107-1639 626-351-4272
Fax: 909-596-4640
Bloody Mary, margarita, pina colada, mai tai, strawberry margarita, lime juice and grenadine
President: Frank Abbadessa
CFO: John Kennick
VP: Dean Carbone
Number Employees: 1-4
Type of Packaging: Private Label
Brands:
FRANK & DEAN'S COCKTAIL MIXES

4757 **Frank Capurro & Son**
2250 Highway 1
Moss Landing, CA 95039 831-728-3904
Fax: 831-728-0241 info@capurromkt.com
www.capurromkt.com
Manufacturer, packer and exporter of produce including parsley, radishes, endive, escarole, spinach, collards, kale, brussels sprouts, Italian squash, beets, bell peppers, etc
Partner: Kris Capurro
Partner: John Manfre
Controller: Lavelle Brown
Director Marketing: Rick Osterhues
Sales Manager: Steve Timsak
General Manager: Frank Capurro
Production Manager: Gary Bertone
Facilities Manager: Robert Bertone
Estimated Sales: $20-50 Million
Number Employees: 100-249
Type of Packaging: Consumer, Food Service, Bulk
Brands:
TOPLESS

4758 **Frank Family Vineyard**
1091 Larkmead Ln
Calistoga, CA 94515 707-942-0859
Fax: 707-942-2581
www.frankfamilyvineyards.com
Wines
Owner: Richard Frank
Director Marketing/Sales: Emily Kaufman
Estimated Sales: $ 10 - 20 Million
Number Employees: 20-49
Type of Packaging: Private Label

4759 **Frank Korinek & Company**
4828 W 25th St
Cicero, IL 60804-3432 773-242-1917
Fax: 773-242-1917
Pastry fillings, fruit pie filling, donut mixes
President: George Korinek
Estimated Sales: $1-2.5 Million
Number Employees: 5-9
Brands:
BOHEMIAN MAID
KORINEK

4760 **Frank Mattes & Sons Reliable Seafood**
2327 Edwards Lane
Bel Air, MD 21015-5001 410-879-5444
Fax: 410-734-6061
Seafood

4761 **Frank Pagano Company**
1527 S State Street
Lockport, IL 60441-3550 815-838-0303
Fax: 815-723-9861
Manufacturer of quality meats
President/CEO: Mary Pagano

4762 **Frank Wardynski & Sons**
336 Peckham St
Buffalo, NY 14206 716-854-6083
Fax: 716-854-4887 info@wardynski.com
www.wardynski.com
Smoked polish sausage, italian sausage, natural casing wieners, tender casing weiners, skinless weiners, knockwurst, bologna, cooked salami, liver sausage, kiska, blood tongue, sweet or sour head cheese.
Chairman/President: Raymond Wardynski
Estimated Sales: $ 5 - 10 Million
Number Employees: 20-49
Sq. footage: 35000

4763 **Frank's Foods**
1141 W Kawailani St
Hilo, HI 96720-3299 808-959-9121
Fax: 808-959-1330 franksfd@interpac.net
Manufacturer and packer of meat products
President: Michael Frenz
Estimated Sales: $5-10 Million
Number Employees: 5-9
Type of Packaging: Consumer

4764 **Frank-Lin Distillers**
650 Lenfest Rd
San Jose, CA 95133 408-259-8900
Fax: 408-258-9527 production@frank-lin.com
www.frank-lin.com
Alcoholic beverages
President: Frank Lin
Sales/Marketing: Michael Maestri
Estimated Sales: $ 3 - 5 Million
Number Employees: 1-4
Type of Packaging: Bulk

4765 **Frankford Candy & Chocolate Company**
9300 Ashton Rd
Philadelphia, PA 19114 215-735-5200
Fax: 215-735-0721 800-523-9090
www.frankfordcandy.com
Processor of solid, hollow chocolate molded novelities and nonchocolate candies for Christmas, Easter, Halloween and Valentine's Day
CEO: Stu Selarnik
Vice President: Harry Hoffman
VP Marketing: Kurt Dungan
VP Operations: Nathan Hoffman
Estimated Sales: $20-50 Million
Number Employees: 300
Sq. footage: 65000
Type of Packaging: Bulk
Brands:
BARBIE
BEATRIX POTTER
BRACH
FRANKFORD
HOT WHEELS
NICKELODEON
PETER PAN
PETER RABBIT
POWER PUFF GIRLS
ROCKET POWER
RUGRATS
SCOOBY DOO
SIMPSONS
SPONGE BOB SQUARE PANTS
THE GRINCH WHO STOLE CHRISTMAS

4766 **Frankfort Cheese**
F1705 County Rd N
Edgar, WI 54426-9648 715-352-2345
Fax: 715-352-2346
Cheese
President: Dennis Telschow
Estimated Sales: Less than $500,000
Number Employees: 5-9

4767 **Franklin Baking Company**
500 W Grantham Street
Goldsboro, NC 27530 919-735-0344
Fax: 919-705-2029 800-248-7494
Manufacturer of baked goods including breads, bisuits and rolls
President: Tom Buffkin
Sales Director: John Roam
Human Resource Director: Beverly Ham
Operations Manager/SVP R&D: William Pearman
Estimated Sales: $50-100 Million
Number Employees: 700
Sq. footage: 200000
Type of Packaging: Consumer
Brands:
BLUEBIRD
BUNNY
COBBLESTONE MILL
MARY JANE
NATURE'S OWN
ROMAN MEAL
SUNBEAM

4768 **Franklin Baking Company**
2004 N Queen Street
Kinston, NC 28501-1621 252-527-1155
Fax: 252-527-9871 800-248-7494
Bakery items
President: Eugene Franklin
Production: Randy Brock
Estimated Sales: $10-24.9 Million
Number Employees: 100-249

4769 **Franklin Farms**
931 Rout 32
North Franklin, CT 06254-0018 860-642-3019
Fax: 860-642-3024 800-204-1503
judy@franklinfarms.com
www.franklinfarms.com
Manufacturer of organic mushrooms
President: Wilhelm Meya
Estimated Sales: $100+ Million
Number Employees: 600
Sq. footage: 400000
Brands:
VEGGIBALLS
VEGGIBURGER
VEGGIDOGS
VEGGINUGGETS

4770 **Franklin Foods**
P.O.Box 486
Enosburg Falls, VT 05450-0486 802-933-4338
Fax: 802-933-2300 800-933-6114
info@franklinfoods.com www.franklinfoods.com
Manufacturer of baker's cheese, regular and flavored cream cheese, salsa and cream cheese dips
President/CEO: Jon Gutknecht
Sales Director: Steve Barrows
Plant Manager: John Ovitt
Estimated Sales: $25-49.9 Million
Number Employees: 100-249
Sq. footage: 43000
Type of Packaging: Consumer, Food Service, Private Label, Bulk
Brands:
ALL SEASON'S KITCHENS
BRUEGGERS
HAHN'S
LOMBARDI'S ITALIAN CLASSICS
VERMONT GOURMET

4771 **Franklin Hill Vineyards**
7833 Franklin Hill Rd
Bangor, PA 18013 610-588-8708
Fax: 610-588-8158 888-887-2839
franklinhill@enter.net
www.franklinhillvineyards.com
Wines
Owner: Elaine Pivinski
Estimated Sales: $2.5-5 Million
Number Employees: 5-9
Type of Packaging: Private Label

4772 **Frankly Natural Bakers**
7740 Formula Pl
San Diego, CA 92121 858-536-5910
Fax: 858-536-5911 800-727-7229
mail@franklynatural.com
www.franklynatural.com
Manufacturer of brownies, cookies, energy bars, etc
Owner: Jerry Sarnow
Estimated Sales: $3-5 Million
Number Employees: 10-19
Number of Brands: 3
Number of Products: 26
Sq. footage: 10000
Type of Packaging: Consumer, Private Label, Bulk
Brands:
98% FAT-FREE
AMAZINGLY TASTY
BEACH
COAST
FRANKLY NATURAL3
FRANKLY ORGANIC
RICE CRUNCHIES
VEGAN DECADENCE

4773 **Franz Family Bakeries**
315 NE 10th Ave
Portland, OR 97232 503-731-5670
Fax: 503-731-5680 http://franzbakery.com
Bakery products
CEO: Bob Albers
President/COO: Marc Albers
CFO: Jerry Boness
VP Human Resources: Forrest Clayton
Systems Manager: Jonathan Dolp
Divisional Vice President: Kim Nisbet
Corporate Controller: Keith VanEmmerik
VP Sales Operations: Todd Cornwell
VP Purchasing: Ken Waltos
Estimated Sales: $100+ Million
Number Employees: 2000

4774 **Franzia Winery**
17000 E State Highway 120
Ripon, CA 95366 209-599-4111
Fax: 209-599-5892 info@franzia.com
www.franzia.com
Manufacturer of wines
Plant Manager: Lou Dambrosio
Estimated Sales: $460,000
Number Employees: 4
Sq. footage: 3087
Type of Packaging: Consumer, Food Service, Private Label

4775 **Fratelli Perata**
1595 Arbor Road
Paso Robles, CA 93446-9669 805-238-2809
Fax: 805-238-2809 www.fratelliperata.com
Wines
Owner: Gene Perata
Estimated Sales: Under $500,000
Number Employees: 1-4

4776 **Fratello Coffee Roasters**
4021 9th Street SE
Calgary, AB T2G 3C7
Canada 403-265-2112
Fax: 403-263-3255 800-465-7227
info@fratellocoffee.com www.fratellocoffee.com
Processor of gourmet coffee
President: Henry Kutarna
VP: Jason Prefontaine
Marketing Director: David Selley
Estimated Sales: E
Number Employees: 20-49
Type of Packaging: Consumer, Food Service
Brands:
Fratello

4777 **Frazier Nut Farms**
10830 Yosemite Blvd
Waterford, CA 95386 209-522-1406
Fax: 209-874-9638 fraznut@aol.com
Manufacturer and exporter of nuts including shelled and in-shell English walnuts and shelled almonds
President: Jim Frazier
VP: Steve Slacks
Estimated Sales: $2.5-5 Million
Number Employees: 100-249
Type of Packaging: Bulk
Brands:
FRAZIER'S FINEST

4778 **Fred Meyer Bakery**
16253 SE 122nd Ave
Clackamas, OR 97015-9136 503-650-2000
Fax: 503-650-2128 www.fredmeyer.com
Bread and bakery products
Manager: Warren Ali
Estimated Sales: $10-24.9 Million
Number Employees: 100-249

4779 **Fred Usinger**
1030 N Old World 3rd St
Milwaukee, WI 53203-1300 414-276-9105
Fax: 414-291-5277 800-558-9998
allenw@usinger.com www.usinger.com
Sausages
President: Frederick Usinger IV
VP Marketing/Sales: John Gabe
Estimated Sales: $20-50 Million
Number Employees: 1-4
Brands:
SAUSAGE A LA CARTE

4780 **(HQ)Freda Quality Meats**
1007 W Oregon Ave
Philadelphia, PA 19148-4420 215-755-1899
Fax: 215-336-1353 800-443-7332
jimfreda@aol.com www.fredatech.com/home
Manufacturer and wholesaler/distributor of deli items including proscuitto, salami, pepperoni, soppras ata, panchetta, cappicola, frozen pork chops, butter, pickles, vinegar, relish, peppers, meat balls, steaks, mozzarella sticksbuffalo wings, etc
President: James Giuffrida
Account Manager: Charles Sedlack
Plant Manager: Matthew Oorsaro
Estimated Sales: $300,000-500,000
Number Employees: 1-4
Parent Co: Freda

4781 **Frederick Brewing Company**
4607 Wedgewood Blvd
Frederick, MD 21703 301-694-7899
Fax: 301-694-2971 888-258-7434
www.frederickbrewing.com
Manufacturer and exporter of beer, ale, stout, lager and porter
CEO: David Snyder
CEO: Eric Warner
VP Marketing: Julie Stolzer
VP Sales: Kirk Larimore
VP Operations: John Niziolek
Estimated Sales: 1-2.5 Million
Number Employees: 20-49
Sq. footage: 57000
Type of Packaging: Private Label
Brands:
BLUE RIDGE
BRIMSTONE
HEMPEN
WILD GOOSE

4782 **Frederick Wildman & Sons**
307 E 53rd St. #3
New York, NY 10022 212-355-0700
Fax: 212-355-4719 800-733-9463
info@frederickwildman.com
www.frederickwildman.com
Manufacturer and importer of wines
President: Richard Cacciato
CFO: Rocco Lombardo
Senior VP: Vincenzo Marino
Marketing Director: Roger Bohmrich
Sales Director: Peter Ascher
Public Relations: Odila Gaier-Noel
VP/Director Operations: Joseph Losardo
Estimated Sales: $20-50 Million
Number Employees: 50-99
Brands:
KANONKOP
POL ROGER

4783 **Fredericksburg Herb Farm**
405 Whitney St
Fredericksburg, TX 78624 830-997-8615
Fax: 830-997-5069 800-259-4372
info@fredericksburgherbfarm.com
www.fredericksburgherbfarm.com
Gourmet herbs and vinegars
Owner: Bill Varney
Estimated Sales: $1-2.5 Million
Number Employees: 20-49

4784 **Fredericksburg Lockers/OPA's Smoke**
P.O.Box 487
Fredericksburg, TX 78624-0487 830-997-3358
Fax: 830-997-9916 800-543-6750
comments@opassmokedmeats.net
www.opassmokedmeats.net
Manufacturer of smoked and fresh sausage, ham, jerky and poultry products.
President: Helen Wahl
Controller: Ken Wahl
COO: Michael Schandua
Estimated Sales: $ 20 - 50 Million
Number Employees: 50-99
Type of Packaging: Consumer, Food Service
Brands:
OPA'S

4785 **Freed, Teller & Freed**
436 N Canal Street
Suite 2
South San Francisco, CA 94080-4668650-589-8500
Fax: 650-589-0711 800-370-7371
info@freedscoffeetea.com freedscoffeetea.com
Manufacturer of tea, coffee, preserves, condiments and sugars
President: Augi Tethiera
Estimated Sales: $570,000
Number Employees: 7
Number of Brands: 10
Number of Products: 275
Type of Packaging: Consumer, Private Label, Bulk
Brands:
DEPENDABLE
FREED'S
FREED, TELLER & FREDD

4786 **Freeda Vitamins**
4725 34th St Fl 3
Long Island City, NY 11101 718-433-4344
Fax: 718-433-4373 800-777-3737
info@freedavitamins.com
www.freedavitamins.com
Manufacturer and exporter of kosher yeast-free vitamins and supplements including garlic
President/CEO: P Zimmerman
VP: S Zimmerman
R&D: Eliyahu Zimmerman
Production Manager: R Zimmerman
Estimated Sales: $2.5 Million
Number Employees: 10-19
Number of Brands: 1
Number of Products: 200
Sq. footage: 9150
Type of Packaging: Consumer
Brands:
FREEDA

4787 **Freedman's Bakery**
803 Main St
Belmar, NJ 7719 732-681-2334
Fax: 732-681-1269

Bakery items
President: Herb Freedman
VP: Mark Freedman
Estimated Sales: $500,000-$1 Million
Number Employees: 100-249

4788 **Freedom Gourmet Sauce**
278 Cathy Jo Drive
Nashville, TN 37211-3840 615-333-9063
hello@freedomsauces.com
www.freedomsauce.com
Gormet sauces

4789 **Freeland Bean & Grain**
1000 E Washington Rd
PO Box 515
Freeland, MI 48623 989-695-9131
Fax: 989-695-5241 800-447-9131
freeland.i@att.net
www.freelandbeanandgrain.com
Manufacturer and exporter of dried beans and grains
Owner/President: John Hupfer
VP: Elenor Hupfer
Estimated Sales: $3.8 Million
Number Employees: 5-9
Type of Packaging: Bulk

4790 **Freeman Industries**
100 Marbledale Rd
Tuckahoe, NY 10707 914-961-2100
Fax: 914-961-5793 800-666-6454
freeman@lanline.com www.freemanllc.com
Manufacturer of dairy vitamin concentrates and zein. Importer and exporter of dried fruits and vegetables, pectin, herbal extracts and natural colors. Processor of citrus bioflavonoids and rice bran and rice bran derivates
President/CEO: Joel G Freeman
VP: Paul Freeman
Estimated Sales: $1-3 Million
Number Employees: 10-19
Sq. footage: 5000
Type of Packaging: Bulk
Brands:
A/D/F
D' SOL

4791 **Freemark Abbey Winery**
3022 St. Helena Highway North
Helena, CA 94574 800-963-9698
Fax: 707-963-7633 800-963-9698
wineinfo@freemarkabbey.com
www.freemarkabbey.com
Manufacturer and exporter of wines including cabernet sauvignon, chardonnay and johannisberg riesling
Estimated Sales: $5-9.9 Million
Number Employees: 20-49
Type of Packaging: Food Service
Brands:
FREEMARK ABBEY

4792 **Freestone Pickle Company**
610 N Center St
Bangor, MI 49013 269-427-7702
Fax: 269-427-5542 877-874-2553
freestonepickles@freestonepickles.com
www.freestonepickles.com
Manufacturer of pickles, relish and pickled peppers and cauliflower
President/CEO: Michael Hescott
Estimated Sales: $10-20 Million
Number Employees: 20-49
Type of Packaging: Consumer, Food Service, Private Label, Bulk
Brands:
FREESTONE
HOLIDAY ROYAL
PARTETIME

4793 **Freeze-Dry Foods**
111 West Avenue
Albion, NY 14411 905-844-1471
Fax: 905-844-8140 www.freeze-dry.com
Processor of freeze dried ingredients specializing in meat, seafood and protein items
President: Karen Richardson
Estimated Sales: $4.5 Million
Number Employees: 40
Type of Packaging: Consumer

4794 **Freeze-Dry Ingredients**
5440 St Charles Road
Suite 201
Berkeley, IL 60163 708-544-1880
Fax: 708-544-4117 info@fdiusa.net
www.fdiusa.net
Canned and frozen foods; uses freeze-drying to preserve herbs, fruits, vegetables, spices, meat, pasta and fish
President: Joseph Lucas
National Sales Manager: Barbara Laffey
Estimated Sales: $1.3 Million
Number Employees: 10
Parent Co: Groneweg Group
Type of Packaging: Consumer

4795 **Freeze-Dry Products**
398 Tesconi Ct
Santa Rosa, CA 95401 707-547-1776
Fax: 707-545-5270 sales@fdpusa.com
www.fdpusa.com
Industrial ingredients, dehydrated and freeze dried vegetables, freeze dried fruit, dairy and meat products
President: Alan Anger
VP: Mark Martindill
Estimated Sales: $20-50 Million
Number Employees: 20-49

4796 **Freezer Queen Foods**
975 Fuhrmann Blvd
Buffalo, NY 14203 716-826-7000
Fax: 716-824-4258 800-828-8383
info@freezerqueen.com
www.freezerqueenfoods.com
Manufacturer and contract packager of prepared frozen entrees; salisbury steak, chicken nuggets, veal, pot roast, stew, meat balls, sliced turkey, sliced beef, meat loaf, chicken and turkey croquettes, lasagna, rigatoni, vegetable andpasta dishes
Manager: Matt Kwasek
Director Finance: Michael Bradley
Research & Development Manager: Karen Centofani
Marketing Director: Jerry Brozowski
Transportation Services: Bob Lewandowski
Plant Manager: William Rouse
Purchasing Manager: Sharon Piehlei
Estimated Sales: $100-500 Million
Number Employees: 250-499
Sq. footage: 58000
Parent Co: Home Market Foods
Type of Packaging: Consumer, Food Service, Private Label, Bulk
Brands:
FREEZER QUEEN

4797 **Freezer Queen Foods**
975 Fuhrmann Blvd
Buffalo, NY 14203 716-826-7000
Fax: 716-824-4258 800-828-8383
info@freezerqueenfoods.com
www.freezerqueenfoods.com
Manufacturer of pulled and diced poultry, all white meat, natural proportion (white and dark), pulled dark/white and all dark; canned poultry; chunk white chicken, white and dark chicken and premium chunk white turkey
President: Matthew W Kwasek
Vice President/CFO: Wesley Atamain
Research & Development Manager: Karen Centofanti
Traffic Manager, Freight Services: Bob Lewandowski
Plant Manager: William Rouse
Purchasing Manager: Sharon Piehler
Estimated Sales: $20-50 Million
Number Employees: 250-499
Sq. footage: 58000
Type of Packaging: Consumer, Food Service, Private Label, Bulk
Brands:
Valley Fresh

4798 **(HQ)Freixenet**
P.O.Box 1949
Sonoma, CA 95476-1949 707-996-4981
Fax: 707-996-0720 info@freixenetusa.com
www.freixenetusa.com
Manufacturer and importer of Spanish champagnes and wines; also, processor of California wines
President: Juan Furne
Executive VP: Eva Bertran
VP Marketing: David Brown
VP Sales: Peter Zilocchi
Estimated Sales: $75 Million
Number Employees: 50-99
Type of Packaging: Consumer
Brands:
CASTELLBLANCH
FREIXENET SPANISH WINES
FREIXENET WINES
GLORIA FERRER
HENRI ABELE
RENE BARBIER
SEGURA VIUDAS

4799 **Fremont Authentic Brands**
802 N Front St
Fremont, OH 43420 419-334-8995
Fax: 419-334-8120
katie.smith@fremontcompany.com
www.fremontcompany.com
Manufacturer of tomatoes, sauerkraut, salsa and barbecue sauces
President: Richard Smith
CFO: Bill Armstrong
VP Sales: Chuck Merrill
Estimated Sales: $52 Million
Number Employees: 160
Type of Packaging: Consumer, Food Service, Private Label
Brands:
FRANKS
HIAWATHA
MILFORD
SNOW FLOSS
WATOUGA

4800 **Fremont Beef Company**
960 Schneider St
Fremont, NE 68026 402-727-7200
Fax: 402-727-0907 www.fremontbeef.com
Meats
President: Les Leech
Vice President: Jim Pomrenke
Director, Marketing and Sales: Laun Hinkle
Estimated Sales: $20-50 Million
Number Employees: 110

4801 **Fremont Special Brands**
802 N Front Street
Fremont, OH 43420 419-334-8995
Fax: 419-334-8120 sales@sauerkraut.com
www.fremontcompany.com
Tomato based sauces, sauerkraut, ketchup and bbq

4802 **French Baking**
429 Soundview Ave
Stratford, CT 06615 203-378-7381
Fax: 203-378-7253
Bakery products
Estimated Sales: $1-2.5 Million
Number Employees: 10-19

4803 **French Creek Seafood**
1097 Lee Road
Parksville, BC V9P 2E1
Canada 250-248-7100
Fax: 250-248-7197 seafood@nanaimo.ark.com
Manufacturer and exporter of fresh and frozen seafood
President: Gordon McLean
Production Manager: Brad McLean
Estimated Sales: $6 Million
Number Employees: 15
Type of Packaging: Bulk

4804 **French Gourmet**
500 Kuwili St
Honolulu, HI 96817-5355 808-524-4000
Fax: 808-528-0329 linda@frenchgourmet.com
www.frenchgourmet.com
Manufacturer of frozen dough, croissants, danish, puff pastry, breads, and muffin, cookie batters
President: Patrick Novak
VP: Linda Coffman
Estimated Sales: $10-20 Million
Number Employees: 20-49
Number of Brands: 1
Number of Products: 57
Sq. footage: 50000

Type of Packaging: Food Service, Private Label, Bulk

4805 **French Market Foods**
3935 Ryan St
Lake Charles, LA 70605 337-477-9296
Fax: 337-477-9140 purchasing@fmfoods.com
www.fmfoods.com
Processor of shrimp, frozen and fresh
Manager: Larry Avery
Estimated Sales: $5-9.9 Million
Number Employees: 20-49

4806 **French Meadow Bakery**
1000 Apollo Road
Eagan, MN 55121 651-286-7861
Fax: 651-454-3327 877-669-3278
bread@frenchmeadow.com
www.frenchmeadow.com
Organic and all-natural products including yeast-free, vegan, sprouted grain, gluten-free and Kosher Parve options.
Owner: Steve Shapiro
VP: Steven Shapiro
Plant Manager: Michael Simon
Purchasing: Debra Gordon
Estimated Sales: $5-9.9 Million
Number Employees: 20-49
Number of Brands: 4
Number of Products: 32
Sq. footage: 24000
Type of Packaging: Consumer, Food Service, Private Label, Bulk
Other Locations:
French Meadow Bakery
Auburn WA
Brands:
HEALTHSEED
HEALTHY HEMP
MENS BREAD
WOMENS BREAD

4807 **French Patisserie**
1090 Palmetto Ave
Pacifica, CA 94044 650-738-4990
Fax: 650-738-4995 800-300-2253
fpatis@frenchpatisserie.com
www.frenchpatisserie.com
Frozen cakes, tarts, and dessert sauces
President: Marta Spasic
Estimated Sales: $5-10 Million
Number Employees: 20-49

4808 **French Quarter Seafood**
2933 Paris Road
Chalmette, LA 70043-3346 504-277-1679
Fax: 504-277-1679
Seafood
Owner: Philippe Despointes

4809 **French and Brawn**
1 Elm St
Camden, ME 04843 207-236-3361
Fax: 207-236-4880 mail@frenchandbrawn.com
www.frenchandbrawn.com
Manufacturer of choice meats, lobsters, soups and sandwiches
President: Todd Anderson
Estimated Sales: $ 5 - 10 Million
Number Employees: 20-49

4810 **French's Coffee**
1400 Central Rd
Walnut Creek, CA 94596-3794 925-978-6105
Coffee
Owner: Chet Parker
Estimated Sales: Under $500,000
Number Employees: 1-4

4811 **French's Flavor Ingredients**
4343 E Mustard Way
Springfield, MO 65803-7139 417-837-1865
Fax: 417-837-1801 800-437-3624
jim.ciaccio@rb.com
www.frenchsflavoringredients.com
Manufacturer of mustard and sauces including barbecue and hot sauce; fried onions and potato sticks
Technical Sales: Rhonda McRae
Estimated Sales: $100+ Million
Number Employees: 250-499
Parent Co: Reckitt & Benckiser
Type of Packaging: Consumer, Food Service, Private Label, Bulk
Brands:
CATTLEMEN'S
FRANK'S
FRENCH'S
REDHOT

4812 **Fresca Mex. Foods**
11193 W Emerald St
Boise, ID 83713 208-376-6922
Fax: 208-375-2330 www.frescamex.com
Flour, corn tortillas and flavored wraps
President: Andrew Savin
VP: Richard Kay
Sales: Heather Granahan
Operations: Jim Anderson
Estimated Sales: $16 Million
Number Employees: 130
Number of Brands: 1
Number of Products: 60
Type of Packaging: Food Service, Private Label

4813 **(HQ)Fresh Dairy Direct/Morningstar**
2711 North Haskell Ave
Suite 3400
Dallas, TX 75204
800-395-7004
www.deanfoods.com
Processor and exporter of fresh and frozen nondairy and dairy coffee creamers, frozen nondairy whipped toppings and frozen cakes including cheese, mousse, ice cream and frozen yogurt; also, pancake and waffle batters
President: Miguel Calado
Chairman/CEO: Gregg Engles
Executive VP/Chief Financial Officer: Barry Fromberg
Estimated Sales: K
Number Employees: 10,000+
Sq. footage: 120000
Parent Co: Dean Foods
Type of Packaging: Consumer, Private Label
Other Locations:
Morning Star Foods
Santa Fe Springs CA
Brands:
Affair
Frostin Pride
Jakada
Mocha Mix
Pastry Pride
Signature Flavors By Mocha Mix
Topping Pride

4814 **Fresh Express**
950 E Blanco Road
Salinas, CA 93901
800-242-5472
webmaster@chiquita.com
www.freshexpress.com
Manfuacturer of ready made salads, carrots and coleslaw and salad kits.
Manager: Stuart Wilcox
CEO: Steve Taylor
VP Operations: Brian Hill
Estimated Sales: $72 Million
Number Employees: 500-999
Parent Co: Chiquita Brands
Brands:
Fresh Express

4815 **Fresh Farm**
7255 Sheridan Boulevard
Arvada, CO 80003-3301 303-429-1536
Fax: 303-429-1252
Estimated Sales: $2.5-5 Million
Number Employees: 10-19

4816 **Fresh Fish**
2700 Avenue D
Birmingham, AL 35218-2139 205-252-0344
Fax: 205-252-3432
Seafood
President: George Drakos
VP: George Sarris

4817 **Fresh Frozen Foods**
1814 Washington St
PO Box 215
Jefferson, GA 30549 706-367-9851
Fax: 706-367-4646 800-277-9851
wecare@freshfrozenfoods.com
www.freshfrozenfoods.com
Manufacturer of frozen fruits and vegetables, also biscuits.
Founder/Managing Member: Billy Griffin Sr
Managing Member: Billy Griffin Jr
Plant Manager: Victoria Martinez
Estimated Sales: $40 Million
Number Employees: 120
Sq. footage: 5600

4818 **Fresh Hemp Foods**
15.2166 Notre Dame Avenue
Winnipeg, NB R3H 0K1
Canada 800-665-4367
Fax: 204-956-5984 www.freshhempfoods.com
Hemp food products
President/CEO: Mike Fata
Type of Packaging: Bulk

4819 **Fresh Island Fish Company**
312 Alamaha St Ste F
Kahului, HI 96732 808-871-1111
Fax: 808-871-6818 www.freshislandfish.com
Seafood
President: Mike Lee
Estimated Sales: $ 10 - 20 Million
Number Employees: 20-49

4820 **Fresh Juice Company**
280 Wilson Avenue
Newark, NJ 07105-3844 973-465-7100
Fax: 973-465-7170
Manufacturer and exporter of fresh and fresh-frozen juices including citrus and blended
Estimated Sales: $ 20 - 50 Million
Number Employees: 20-49
Parent Co: Saratoga Beverage
Type of Packaging: Consumer, Food Service
Brands:
Florida Pik't
Fresh Pik't
Just Pik't

4821 **Fresh Mark**
1600 Harmont Ave NE
Canton, OH 44705 330-430-5686
Fax: 330-430-7660 800-860-6777
www.freshmark.com
Bacon, ham, weiners, deli and luncheon meats, dry sausage and other specialty meat items.
President/COO: Harry Valentino
Chairman/CEO: Neil Genshaft
Administrative VP/CFO: David Cochenour
Plant Manager: Rick Hawley
Estimated Sales: $500 Million-$1 Billion
Number Employees: 500-999
Parent Co: Superiors Brand Meats
Type of Packaging: Consumer, Food Service, Private Label

4822 **Fresh Market Pasta Company**
43 Exchange Street
Portland, ME 04101-5009 207-773-7146
Fax: 207-871-7156
Manufacturer of Pasta, noodles of all kinds, including ginger and squid's ink
President: Alex Gingrich
Estimated Sales: $500,000-$1 Million
Number Employees: 10-19

4823 **Fresh Pack Seafood**
PO Box 1008
Waldoboro, ME 04572-1008 207-832-7720
Fax: 207-832-7795
Manufacturer of fresh seafood
President: Frank Minio
VP/General Manager: Roger Greene

4824 **Fresh Roast Systems**
456 Lindbergh Avenue
Livermore, CA 94551-9552 925-456-2270
info@freshroastsystems.com
www.frestroastsystems.com
Coffee roaster
President: Roger Allington
Number Employees: 5-9
Type of Packaging: Private Label

4825 **Fresh Roasted Almond Company**
24536 Gibson
Warren, MI 48089 877-478-6887
sales@freshroastedalmond.com
www.freshroastedalmondco.com

Manufacturer of dry roasted, sweetened and flavored kosher nut confections including almonds, pecans, cashews, peanuts and walnuts flavored in cinnamon, honey, maple, vanilla, cherry and spices
President: Dan Levy
Estimated Sales: $1-3 Million
Number Employees: 10-19
Sq. footage: 4500
Type of Packaging: Consumer, Private Label, Bulk
Brands:
KARS
RITTER

4826 **Fresh Samantha**
84 Industrial Park Road
Saco, ME 04072-1840 207-284-0011
Fax: 207-284-8331 800-658-4635
www.freshsamantha.com
Manufacturer of fresh juice
CEO: Doug Levin
Estimated Sales: Less than $500,000
Number Employees: 1-4
Type of Packaging: Consumer
Brands:
FRESH SAMANTHA

4827 **Fresh Seafood Distributors**
9910 Milton Jones Rd
Daphne, AL 36526 251-626-1106
Fax: 251-626-1109
Seafood
President: Steve Miller
Estimated Sales: $ 3 - 5 Million
Number Employees: 5-9

4828 **Fresh Start Bakeries**
649 S 7th Ave
City of Industry, CA 91746-3174 626-961-2525
Fax: 626-330-9890 www.freshstartbakeries.com
Manufacturer of buns and English muffins
President: Craig Olsen
Plant Manager: Bob Mitchell
Estimated Sales: $5-10 Million
Number Employees: 100-249
Parent Co: Fresh Start Bakeries
Type of Packaging: Consumer, Food Service

4829 **Fresh Start Bakeries**
920 Shaw Rd
Stockton, CA 95215 209-462-3601
Fax: 209-462-3618 www.freshstartbakeries.com
Manufacturer of hamburger buns, hot dog buns, rolls, English muffins
Manager: Scott Parker
Quality Assurance Manager: Virginia Taylor
Plant Manager: Brent Minardi
Estimated Sales: $ 10 - 20 Million
Number Employees: 50
Sq. footage: 18376
Parent Co: Fresh Start Bakeries
Type of Packaging: Food Service
Other Locations:
Fresh Start Bakeries
Brea CA
Fresh Start Bakeries
City of Industry CA
Fresh Start Bakeries
Waipahu HI
Best Harvest Bakeries
Kansas City KA
Tennessee Bun Company
Dickson TN
Nashville Bun Company
Nashville TN
Galasso's Bakery
Mira Loma CA

4830 **(HQ)Fresh Start Bakeries**
P.O.Box 9939
Brea, CA 92822-1939 714-256-8900
Fax: 714-256-8916 www.freshstartbakeries.com
Manufacutrer of baked goods including hamburger buns and English muffins
President: Craig Olson
Senior VP/CMO: Mike Ward
VP Engineer: Clyde Kawamoto
Estimated Sales: $50-100 Million
Number Employees: 20-49
Sq. footage: 60000
Parent Co: Fresh Start Bakeries
Type of Packaging: Food Service

4831 **Fresh Tofu, Inc**
1101 Harrison Street
Allentown, PA 18103 610-433-4711
Fax: 610-433-5611 info@freshtofu.com
www.freshtofu.com
Organic tofu and other soyfood products.
Owner/President: Gary Abramowitz
Estimated Sales: $2 Million
Number Employees: 20
Sq. footage: 18000

4832 **Freshco**
7929 SW Jack James Drive
Stuart, FL 34997-7243 772-595-0070
Fax: 772-595-9522 888-373-7426
www.indianriverjuice.com
Manufacturer of bottled orange and grapefruit juice
President: J Patrick Shirard
CEO: Clifford Burg
Estimated Sales: $13.80 Million
Number Employees: 82
Type of Packaging: Consumer, Food Service, Private Label
Brands:
INDIAN RIVER SELECT

4833 **Freshwater Farms of Ohio**
2624 N Us Highway 68
Urbana, OH 43078 937-652-3701
Fax: 937-652-3481 800-634-7434
www.fwfarms.com
Owner: Dave Smith
Estimated Sales: $1-2.5 Million
Number Employees: 10-19

4834 **Freshwater Fish Market**
8542 126th Avenue NW
Edmonton, AB T5B 1G9
Canada 780-495-5103
Fax: 780-495-5384 800-345-3113
edmonton@freshwaterfish.com
www.freshwaterfish.com
Manufacturer of freshwater fish, whitefish and northern pike
President: Tom Dunn
Sales Manager: Doug Clayton
Type of Packaging: Consumer, Food Service

4835 **Freund Baking Company**
611 Sonora Ave
Glendale, CA 91201 818-502-1400
Fax: 818-502-1338 www.freundbaking.com
Bread and bakery products
President: James Freund
Estimated Sales: $100+ Million
Number Employees: 100-249

4836 **Frey Vineyards**
14000 Tomki Rd
Redwood Valley, CA 95470-6135 707-485-5177
Fax: 707-485-7875 800-760-3739
info@freywine.com www.freywine.com
Wines
President: Paul Frey
VP: Jonathan Frey
VP Marketing/Sales: Katrina Frey
Estimated Sales: $5-10 Million
Number Employees: 10-19
Type of Packaging: Private Label

4837 **Frick Winery**
23072 Walling Road
Geyserville, CA 95441 707-857-1980
Fax: 707-857-1980 frick@frickwinery.com
www.frickwinery.com
Winery; Alcoholic beverages
Owner: Bill Frick
Estimated Sales: $500,000
Number Employees: 3

4838 **Fricks Meat Products**
360 M E Frick Drive
Washington, MO 63090-1050 636-239-3313
Fax: 636-239-2200 800-241-2209
frickmeats@frickmeats.com
www.frickmeats.com
Manufacturer of cured and smoked meats including sausage and ham
Sales Director: David King
Estimated Sales: $10-20 Million
Number Employees: 50-99

4839 **Fried Provisions Company**
P.O.Box F
Evans City, PA 16033-0310 724-538-3160
Fax: 724-538-3262
Manufacturer of cheese, luncheon meats, chopped ham, poultry and sausage
President: James Deily
Sales Manager: Tim Deily
Estimated Sales: $1.40 Million
Number Employees: 1-4
Parent Co: Fort Pitt Brand Meats
Type of Packaging: Consumer, Food Service, Private Label, Bulk
Brands:
Fort Pitt
Harmony

4840 **Frieda's**
4465 Corporate Center Dr
Los Alamitos, CA 90720 714-826-6100
Fax: 714-816-0277 800-421-9477
mail@friedas.com www.friedas.com
Exotic fruits and vegetables
President/CEO: Karen Caplan
Chairman: Frieda Caplan
VP: Jackie Caplan Wiggins
Estimated Sales: $18.5 Million
Number Employees: 80

4841 **Friendly Ice Cream Corporation**
1855 Boston Rd
Wilbraham, MA 01095 413-543-3240
Fax: 413-773-1447 800-966-9970
www.friendlys.com
Manufacturer of ice cream including low-fat and sugar-free; also, frozen yogurt
President/CEO: Ned Lidvall
CFO: Steve Sanchioni
SVP Marketing: Lawrence Rusinko
SVP Company Operations: John Bowie
Estimated Sales: $575 Million
Number Employees: 12,787
Type of Packaging: Consumer, Food Service, Private Label, Bulk
Brands:
FRIENDLY ICE CREAM

4842 **(HQ)Friendship Dairies**
2711 N Haskell Ave Ste 3400
Dallas, TX 75204 516-719-4000
Fax: 516-719-3866
myfriends@friendshipdairies.com
www.friendshipdairies.com
Manufacturer of all natural cultured dairy products such as; cottage cheese, sour cream, buttermilk and yogurt and cheese
President: Joe Murgolo
VP: Douglas Gerbosi
Marketing Manager: Marc Silverstein
VP Sales: Bob Grasso
Estimated Sales: $6.7 Million
Number Employees: 20-49
Type of Packaging: Consumer, Food Service, Private Label, Bulk
Brands:
FRIENDSHIP
METCO
SOUR TREAT

4843 **Friendship Dairies**
6701 County Road 20
Friendship, NY 14739 585-973-3031
Fax: 585-973-2401 www.friendshipdairies.com
Manufacturer of dairy products including cottage cheese and whey and whey powders including acid and neutralized; also, calcium lactate powder and sodium lactate
President: David Buteyan
Plant Manager: Greg Knapp
Estimated Sales: $50-100 Million
Number Employees: 100-249
Parent Co: Friendship Dairies
Type of Packaging: Consumer, Food Service

4844 **Friendship International**
12 Merrill Drive
Rockland, ME 04841-2142 207-273-4621
Fax: 207-236-6103 waaddman@hotmail.com
Manufacturer and exporter of live sea urchins
President: Jim Wadsworth

4845 **FrieslandCampina Domo**
61 South Paramus Road
Suite 422 201-655-7786
Fax: 201-655-7786 www.domo.nl
Manufacturer of ingredients and additives; whey and milk products
Parent Co: FrieslandCampina Domo EMEA

4846 **Frio Foods**
8600 Wurzbach Road
Suite 500
San Antonio, TX 78240-4331 210-278-4525
Fax: 210-278-1094
Processes frozen foods
President: Ron Trine
Brands:
FRIO

4847 **Frionor U.S.A.**
P.O.Box 2087
New Bedford, MA 02741-2087 508-997-0031
Fax: 508-991-6432 800-343-8046
www.americanprideseafoods.com
Cod, haddock, pollock, salmon, whiting, great silver smelt, fishsticks
President: John Cummings
Director Sales: Bob Bruno
Estimated Sales: $50-100 Million
Number Employees: 100-249
Sq. footage: 210000
Brands:
ARCTIC CAPE
BAYSIDE
BISTRO
BUNCH O'CRUNCH
FRIONER
NORTH CAPE
OCEAN CUTS

4848 **Frisco Baking Company**
621 W Avenue 26
Los Angeles, CA 90065 323-225-6111
Fax: 323-225-3554
Baked goods
President: James Pricco
Estimated Sales: $100-500 Million
Number Employees: 100-249

4849 **Frisinger Cellars**
2275 Dry Creek Rd
Napa, CA 94558 707-255-3749
Fax: 707-963-7867 www.francisanico.com
Wines
President: Raymond Reyes
Estimated Sales: Under $500,000
Number Employees: 1-4
Parent Co: Consolation Brand

4850 **(HQ)Frito-Lay**
PO Box 660634
Dallas, TX 75266-0634 972-334-7000
Fax: 214-331-7005 800-352-4477
beth.struckell@fritolay.com www.fritolay.com
Manufacturer and exporter of potato, tortilla and corn chips, pretzels, popcorn, peanuts and cookies.
President/CEO: Al Carey
SVP/Chief Customer Officer: Randy Whaley
CFO: George Legge
SVP/General Counsel: Marc Kesselman
Group VP R&D: Mike Zbuchalski
SVP/Strategy & Business Innovation: Daniel Naor
SVP/CMO: Anindita Mukherjee
SVP/GM Central Business Unit: Randy Melville
SVP Human Resources: Michele Thatcher
SVP/Operations: Leslie Starr Keating
SVP/CIO: Jaime Montemayor
SVP/GM South Business Unit: Vivek Sankaran
SVP/GM North Business Unit: Dave Scalera
Estimated Sales: $13 Billion
Number Employees: 40,000
Sq. footage: 550000
Parent Co: PepsiCo Inc
Type of Packaging: Consumer, Food Service
Brands:
100 CALORIE MINI BITES
BAKED!
BAKEN-ETS®
CHEETOS®
CRACKER JACK®)
CRACKERS
DORITOS®
EL ISLENO®
FRITO-LAY® DIPS
FRITO-LAY® NUTS AND SEEDS
FRITOS®
FRITOS® DIPS
FUNYUNS®
GAMESA®
GRANDMA'S®
LAY'S®
LAY'S® DIPS
MATADOR
MAUI STYLE®
MISS VICKIE'S®
MUNCHIES®
MUNCHOS®
NATURAL
NUT HARVEST®
QUAKER®
ROLD GOLD®
RUFFLES®
SABRITONES®
SMARTFOOD® POPCORN
SMARTFOOD® POPCORN CLUSTERS
SPITZ®
STACY'S®
SUNCHIPS®
TOSTITOS®
TOSTITOS® DIPS AND SALSAS
TRUENORTH®

4851 **Frog City Cheese**
PO Box 94
106 Messer Hill Road
Plymouth Notch, VT 05056 802-672-3650
Fax: 802-672-1629 frogcity@vermontel.net
Manufacturer of granular curd (whole milk) cheese
Co-Owner: Jackie McCuin
Co-Owner: Tom Gilbert
Estimated Sales: $3-5 Million
Number Employees: 10-19
Type of Packaging: Consumer

4852 **Frog Ranch Foods**
5 S High St
Glouster, OH 45732 740-767-3705
Fax: 740-767-4658 800-742-2488
info@frogranch.com www.frogranch.com
Traditional style salsas, pickles, peppers, tortilla chips
President: Craig Cornett
Estimated Sales: $2.5-5 Million
Number Employees: 1-4
Type of Packaging: Private Label

4853 **Frog's Leap Winery**
P.O.Box 189
Rutherford, CA 94573-0189 707-963-4704
Fax: 707-963-0242 800-959-4704
greenmailbox@frogsleap.com
www.frogsleap.com
Wines
President: John Williams
Estimated Sales: $5-10 Million
Number Employees: 20-49
Brands:
CABERNET SAUVIGNON
CHARDONNAY
MERLOT
SAUVIGNON BLANC
ZINFANDEL

4854 **Frolic Candy Company**
20 Central Avenue
Farmingdale, NY 11735-6906 516-756-2255
President: L Hirshheimer
Estimated Sales: $2.5-5 Million
Number Employees: 5-9

4855 **From Oregon**
2787 Olympic Street
Suite 4
Springfield, OR 97477-7809 541-747-4222
Fax: 541-747-5456
Jams, marmalades and berries
President: Bonnie Koenig
Estimated Sales: $1-4.9 Million
Number Employees: 1-4

4856 **Froma-Dar**
378 rue Principale
St. Boniface, QC G0X 2L0
Canada 819-535-3946
Fax: 819-535-7010
Manufacturer of dairy products including cheddar, curd and partly skim cheeses
President: Michel Veillette
Number Employees: 50-99
Sq. footage: 20000
Type of Packaging: Consumer, Food Service, Private Label, Bulk
Brands:
DES COTEAUX
FROMA-DAR
JUNEAU

4857 **Frontenac Point Vineyard**
9501 State Route 89
Trumansburg, NY 14886 607-387-9619
contactus@frontenacpoint.com
www.frontenacpoint.com
Wines
Estimated Sales: Under $500,000
Number Employees: 1-4

4858 **Frontera Foods**
449 N Clark St
Suite 205
Chicago, IL 60654 312-595-1624
Fax: 312-595-1625 800-509-4441
gkeller@fronterafoods.com
www.fronterakitchens.com
Processor of tortilla chips, sauces, spices, salsas, nut mixes, and drink mixes
President: Manuel Valdes
Founder/Owner: Rick Bayless
Vice President: Jean Bronson
Marketing: Greg Keller
Estimated Sales: $5-10 Million
Number Employees: 12
Type of Packaging: Food Service
Brands:
FRONTERA FOODS
SALPICA

4859 **Frontier Beef Company**
PO Box 927
Huntingdon Valley, PA 19006-0927 215-663-2120
Beef
President: Bill Hardimon

4860 **Frontier Commodities**
8255 Country Club Road W
Byron, MN 55920-4201 507-775-2174
Fax: 507-775-7049 soybn@aol.com
www.puregrain.net/frontier/frontier.htm
Manufacturer of a wide of variety of grains
Partner: Randy Brown

4861 **(HQ)Frontier Cooperative Herbs**
2990 Wilderness Place
Boulder, CO 80301-2388 303-449-8137
Fax: 800-717-4372 800-669-3275
customercare@frontiercoop.com
www.frontiercoop.com
Herbs and spices packaging
President: Rick Stewart
Marketing: Clint Landis
Sales: Tony Bedard
Production: Lana Miller
Plant Manager: Tony Bedard
Estimated Sales: Less than $500,000
Number Employees: 1-4

4862 **Frontier Ingredients**
3021 78th St
PO Box 299
Norway, IA 52318 319-227-7996
Fax: 800-717-4372 800-669-3275
customercare@frontiercoop.com
www.frontiercoop.com
Organic spices
CEO: Tony Bedard

4863 **Frontier Natural Co-op**
PO Box 299
Norway, IA 52318-0299 303-449-8137
Fax: 303-449-8139 bob.fan@frontiercoop.com
www.frontier.coop.com
Certified organic coffee
VP: Adam Strauss
Sales: Bob Fan
Purchasing: Rob Stephen
Type of Packaging: Private Label
Brands:
FRONTIER ORGANIC COFFEE
JOE BEAN ORGANIC COFFEE

4864 **Frontier Soups**
895 Northpoint Blvd
Waukegan, IL 60085 847-688-1200
Fax: 847-688-1206 800-300-7867
info@frontiersoups.com www.frontiersoups.com
Manufacturer of dried soup and pasta salad mixes
President: Trisha Anderson
Production: Eva Dantoja
Estimated Sales: $2.5-5 Million
Number Employees: 10-19
Sq. footage: 8000
Type of Packaging: Consumer
Brands:
FRONTIER
HEARTY ORIGINALS
HOMEMADE IN MINUTES
I'LL BRING THE SALADD
ILLINOIS PRAIRIE
MINNESOTA HEARTLAND
NEW LINE HOMEMADE
WISCONSIN LAKESHORE

4865 **Frookie**
2070 Maple Street
Des Plaines, IL 60018-3019 847-699-3200
Fax: 847-699-3201
Cookies.
President: Phil Roos

4866 **Frostbite**
4117 Fitch Rd
Toledo, OH 43613-4007 419-473-9621
Fax: 419-473-3183 800-968-7711
bob_strayer@deanfoods.com
www.deanfoods.com
Manufacturer and exporter of frozen dessert novelties including yogurt, ice cream and water ices; also, baked goods for ice cream novelties
Plant Manager: Randy Bevier
Estimated Sales: $20-50 Million
Number Employees: 250-499
Sq. footage: 100000
Parent Co: Suiza Dairy Group
Type of Packaging: Consumer, Food Service, Private Label
Brands:
CHILLY THINGS
FROSTBITE
YOPLAIT

4867 **Frostproof Sunkist Groves**
P.O.Box 1098
Fort Meade, FL 33841-1098 863-635-4873
Fax: 863-635-3447 www.frostproofgroves.com
Citrus fruits and juices
Owner: John Stephens
Estimated Sales: $ 1 - 3 Million
Number Employees: 1-4

4868 **Frozen Specialties**
P.O.Box 410
Archbold, OH 43502 419-445-9015
Fax: 419-445-9465
Manufacturer of frozen pizza bites, sandwiches, egg rolls and stuffed clams
Chairman/President/CEO: Eugene Welka
CFO: Ken Dippman
VP Operations: Ron Zaleski
Plant Manager: Brian Replogle
Purchasing Manager: Jeff Miller
Estimated Sales: $102 Million
Number Employees: 100-249
Type of Packaging: Consumer, Private Label
Brands:
FOX DELUXE
G&W
MR P'S
NATLANS
PIZZA BITES

4869 **Frozfruit Corporation**
14805 S San Pedro Street
Gardena, CA 90248-2030 310-217-1034
Fax: 310-715-6943
Manufacturer and exporter of frozen ice cream novelties and fruit bars
President: Tom Guinan
Estimated Sales: $500,000-$1 Million
Number Employees: 5-9
Sq. footage: 75000
Type of Packaging: Consumer, Food Service, Private Label, Bulk
Brands:
FROZFRUIT
FROZFRUIT ALL NATURAL FRUIT BARS
SUMMER NATURALS

4870 **(HQ)Frozsun Foods**
701 W Kimberly
Suite 210
Placentia, CA 92870 714-630-6292
Fax: 714-630-0920 dyvanovi@frozsun.com
www.frozsun.com
Manufacturer, exporter and importer of frozen strawberries and purees
President: Doug Circle
CFO: Tim Graven
Estimated Sales: $10-20 Million
Number Employees: 250-499
Sq. footage: 500000
Type of Packaging: Consumer, Food Service, Private Label, Bulk
Other Locations:
Frozsun Foods
Oxnard CA
Brands:
FROZSUN

4871 **(HQ)Fruit Acres**
33309 County Road 1
La Crescent, MN 55947 507-895-4750
Fax: 507-895-8353 rpyates@acegroup.cc
Manufacturer of Apples
Manager: Ralph Yates
Secretary: Ralph Yates
Estimated Sales: $.5-1 Million
Number Employees: 1-4
Sq. footage: 4000
Brands:
King

4872 **Fruit Acres Farm Marketand U-Pick**
2559 Friday Rd
Coloma, MI 49038-9712 269-468-5076
peaches@parrett.net
www.fruitacresfarms.com
230 acre fruit farm growing sweet cherries, apples, sweet corn and peaches. Also sells gourmet jams, jellies, honey, sauces, pickles and country gifts.
Co-Owner: Annette Bjorge
Co-Owner: Randy Bjorge
Estimated Sales: $ 5 - 10 Million
Number Employees: 10-19

4873 **Fruit Belt Foods**
P.O.Box 81
Lawrence, MI 49064-0081 269-674-3939
Fax: 269-674-8354 office@fruitbeltfoods.com
www.fruitbeltfoods.com
Manufacturer, wholesaler/distributor of fruits and vegetables such as; asparagus, red tart cherries and strawberries
President: David Frank
Vice President: Warren Frank
Marketing/Sales: Jim Armstrong
Estimated Sales: $5-9.9 Million
Number Employees: 20-49
Type of Packaging: Food Service, Private Label, Bulk
Brands:
Fruit Belt
Solar

4874 **Fruit D'Or Inc**
604 Saint-Louis Ouest
Notre-Dame De Lourdes, QC G0S 1T0 819-385-1126
Fax: 819-715-0058 simon@fruit-dor.ca
www.fruit-dor.ca
Juice/cider, frozen vegetables, canned or preserved vegetables/fruit, dried fruit.
Marketing: Simon Dessureault

4875 **Fruit Fillings**
2531 E Edgar Ave
Fresno, CA 93706-5410 559-237-4715
Fax: 559-237-0728 www.fruitfillings.com
Pie and pastry filling, fruit glazes, pectin based jams, fresh California fruit
President: Stephen Norcross
Estimated Sales: $2.5-5 Million
Number Employees: 20-49

4876 **Fruit Growers MarketingAssociation**
112 N Bridge St
Newcomerstown, OH 43832 740-498-8366
Fax: 740-498-8367 800-466-5171
fruitgrow@tusco.net www.web.tusco.net
Cooperative group supplying apples and apple cider
Manager: Bill Dodd
Sales: Lorrie Jurin
General Manager: David Gress
Assistant Manager: Peggy Caudill
Estimated Sales: $ 3 - 5 Million
Number Employees: 1-4
Sq. footage: 1200
Type of Packaging: Consumer, Private Label, Bulk
Brands:
AUTUMN PRIDE
GROWERS PRIDE
ORCHARD GEM

4877 **Fruit a Freeze**
12919 Leyva St
Norwalk, CA 90650 562-407-2881
Fax: 562-407-2889 www.fruitafreeze.com
Frozen fruit products
President/CEO: David Stein
Estimated Sales: $5-10 Million
Number Employees: 20-49

4878 **Fruit of the Land Products**
1 Promenade Circle
Po Box 977
Thornhill, ON L4J 8G7 905-761-9611
Fax: 905-761-9617 877-311-5267
info@fruitoftheland.com
www.fruitoftheland.com
Kosher, olive oil, honey, jams, jellies, preserves, foodservice, private label.
Marketing: Michael Kurtz

4879 **Fruitcrown Products Corporation**
250 Adams Blvd
Farmingdale, NY 11735 631-694-5800
Fax: 631-694-6467 800-441-3210
info@fruitcrown.com www.fruitcrown.com
Aseptic fruit flavors and bases for beverage, dairy and baking industries
President: Robert Jagenburg
Number Employees: 50-99
Type of Packaging: Bulk
Brands:
ASP
EXQUIZITA
FRUITCROWN
HUNTINGCASTLE

4880 **Fruithill**
6501 NE Highway 240
Yamhill, OR 97148-8507 503-662-3926
Fax: 503-662-4270 fruithilee@worldnet.att.net
www.fruithill.yamhillbusiness.com
Manufacturer of frozen cherries, plums and fruit purees
President: Lee W Schrepel
EVP/Sales: Lee Schrepel
Estimated Sales: $10-20 Million
Number Employees: 50-99
Type of Packaging: Food Service, Private Label

4881 **(HQ)FrutStix Company**
1525 State St # 203
Santa Barbara, CA 93101-6512 805-965-1656
Fax: 805-963-8288 info@frutstix.com
www.frutstix.com
Manufacturer of fresh frozen fruit bars, fudge bars
Owner: William Mc Kinley
Operations Assistant: Lynne Burton
Estimated Sales: $ 5 - 10 Million
Number Employees: 5-9
Type of Packaging: Food Service, Private Label
Other Locations:
FrutStix - Manufacturing Plant
San Diego CA

4882 **Frutarom Meer Corporation**
9500 Railroad Ave
North Bergen, NJ 07047-1422 201-861-9500
Fax: 201-861-8711 800-526-7147
info@us.frutarom.com www.frutarom.com

Manufacturer, exporter and importer of botanicals, extracts, gums, stabilizers, oleoresins, natural colors, enzymes and hydrocolloids
President: Rafi Friedman
VP R&D: Tom Gluckson
Executive VP Marketing/Development: Clayton Bridges
Estimated Sales: $20-50 Million
Number Employees: 100-249
Sq. footage: 100000
Parent Co: Frutarom
Type of Packaging: Bulk
Brands:
MERECOL
MERETEC
MEREZAN
STAMERE

4883 **Frutech International**
180 South Lake Ave, Ste 335
Pasadena, CA 91010 626-844-0200
Fax: 626-844-0202 info.mx@frutech.com
www.frutech.com
Citrus oil production
Treasurer: Gene Adams
VP Finance: Pat Breyer
Estimated Sales: $500,000
Number Employees: 6
Parent Co: Frutech International Corporation

4884 **Fry Foods**
P.O.Box 837
Tiffin, OH 44883 419-448-0831
Fax: 419-448-8363 800-626-2294
sales@fryfoods.com www.fryfoods.com
Manufacturer and importer of frozen and breaded appetizers such as; onion rings, cheese sticks, mushrooms, jalapeno, zucchini sticks and cauliflower
President: Norman Fry
VP: David Fry
Estimated Sales: $20-50 Million
Number Employees: 50
Sq. footage: 45000
Type of Packaging: Food Service
Brands:
FRY FOODS

4885 **Fry Krisp Food Products**
3360 Spring Arbor Rd
Jackson, MI 49203 517-784-8531
Fax: 517-784-6585 frykrisp@tds.net
www.frykrisp.com
manufacturer of batter mixes for poultry and seafood, funnel cake, corn dogs and onion ring for fairs, and breakfst items such as pancakes, cornbread, biscuit mix and distributor of yellow corn grits.
President: Richard Neuenfeldt
VP: Richard Nuenfeldt
Estimated Sales: $2.5-5 Million
Number Employees: 10
Number of Brands: 2
Number of Products: 15
Sq. footage: 8000
Type of Packaging: Consumer, Food Service, Private Label, Bulk
Brands:
FRY KRISP
FRY KRISP BATTER MIXES
OVEN KRISP COATING MIXES

4886 **Fudge Farms**
204 N Red Bud Trl
Buchanan, MI 49107-1366 269-695-2008
800-874-0261
goldenfarmcandies@goldenfarmcandies.com
www.goldenfarmcandies.com
Manufacturer of confectionery products including hard and soft, sugar-free, salt-free, caramels, nougats, taffy, fruit chews, coffee, boxed chocolates, candy bars, and sugar-free lollipops
President: Kenneth Harrington
Estimated Sales: $2-2.5 Million
Number Employees: 20-49
Sq. footage: 21500
Brands:
GOLDEN FARM CANDIES

4887 **Fudge Fatale**
11950 Ventura Blvd.
Suite 3
Studio City, CA 91604 310-287-0600
Fax: 949-240-3086 800-809-8298
sales@fudgefatale.com www.fudgefatale.com
Manufacturer of fudge
President: Alexander Black
Sales: Rich Pariseau
Estimated Sales: $ 3 - 5 Million
Number Employees: 5-9

4888 **Fuji Foods**
6206 Corporate Park Dr
Browns Summit, NC 27214 336-375-3111
Fax: 336-375-3663
information@fujifoodsusa.com
www.fujifoodsusa.com
Manufacturer of chicken, pork and beef broths including concentrated pastes and powders; also, savory flavors, soup bases; and spray dried flavor powders; spray drying services available
President: Maria Keating
CFO: Timm Phillips
General Manager: Aki Kajiya
Research & Development: Dr Ben Cheng
Quality Control: Pat Pittman
President/Top Marketing Executive: Yahushi Muranaka
VP Operations: Michael Russell
Plant Manager: Jarrett Pearman
Purchasing Director: Dan Dechant
Estimated Sales: $20-50 Million
Number Employees: 40
Sq. footage: 20000
Parent Co: Fuji Foods Corporation
Type of Packaging: Food Service, Bulk

4889 **Fuji Foods**
4340 Glencoe St
Denver, CO 80216-4508 303-377-3738
Fax: 303-377-9397 sales@fujifoodsus.com
www.fujifoodsus.com
Manufacturer and exporter of frozen, boxed, sliced and marinated beef and pork; importer of beef slicers
President/CEO: Maria Keating
Human Resources: Eva Walz
Estimated Sales: $10-20 Million
Number Employees: 50-99
Number of Products: 50
Type of Packaging: Food Service
Brands:
Fuji Food

4890 **Fuji Health Science**
3 Terri Lane # 12
Burlington, NJ 08016 609-386-3030
Fax: 609-386-3033
contact@fujihealthscience.com
www.fujihealthscience.com
Markets and manufacturers natural specialty food ingredient, AstaReal astaxanthin, a powerful anti-oxidant
President/Owner: Joe Kuncewitch
Estimated Sales: Under $500,000
Number Employees: 10

4891 **Fuji Vegetable Oil**
1 Barker Ave Ste 290
White Plains, NY 10601 914-761-7900
Fax: 914-761-7919 fvonyk@aol.com
Vegetable and other oil
Manager: Andre Cormeau
Quality Control: Thomas McBrayer
Estimated Sales: $2.5-5 Million
Number Employees: 5-9

4892 **Fujiya**
454 Waiakamilo Rd
Honolulu, HI 96817 808-845-2921
www.fujiyahawaii.com
Manufacturer of Japanese cookies including moliti, tea cakes and nut
VP: Junko Iwata
Estimated Sales: $2.5-5 Million
Number Employees: 10-19
Type of Packaging: Consumer, Food Service

4893 **Ful-Flav-R Foods**
P.O.Box 82
Alamo, CA 94507 925-838-0300
Fax: 925-838-0310
customerservice@ffrfoods.com
www.fulflavr.com
Manufacturer of Premium Ground Garlic, Minced Garlic (in oil & water), Ground and Minced Ginger, Ground Roasted Garlic, Ground Onion, diced Sweet Bell Peppers, Ground and Diced Jalepeno's, Fire Roasted Anaheim chili's, GroundChili-Garlic Blends and other unique custom formulated blends. All of our products are pasteurized and pH controlled.
President: Joseph Farrell
Chief Operations Officer: Glen Farrell
Director Sales/Marketing: Steve Linzmeyer
Plant Manager: John Small
Estimated Sales: $1-2.5 Million
Number Employees: 5-9
Type of Packaging: Food Service, Bulk
Brands:
Ful-Flav-R

4894 **Fulcher's Point Pride Seafood**
101 South Ave
Oriental, NC 28571 252-249-0123
Fax: 252-249-2337 www.bluecrabusa.net
Manufacturer of seafood
President: Chris Fulcher
Owner: G Fulcher
Vice President: Deborah Fulcher
Purchasing: Ralph Bard
Estimated Sales: $4 Million
Number Employees: 47
Type of Packaging: Consumer, Food Service, Bulk

4895 **Fulgenzi Foods**
2100 S Illini Rd
Leland Grove, IL 62704-4366 217-787-7495
Fax: 217-787-7495
Pizza and pasta
President: Danielle Fulgenzi
Estimated Sales: Under $500,000
Number Employees: 1-4

4896 **Full Sail Brewing Company**
506 Columbia St
Hood River, OR 97031 541-386-2281
Fax: 541-386-7316 fullsail@fullsailbrewing.com
www.fullsailbrewing.com
Brewing
CEO: Irene Firmat
CFO: Chris Firmat
Marketing/Sales: Bob Lauron
Estimated Sales: $20-50 Million
Number Employees: 50
Brands:
FULL SAIL ALES AND LAGERS

4897 **(HQ)Full Service Beverage Company**
2900 S Hydraulic St
Wichita, KS 67216-2403 316-524-3201
Fax: 316-529-1608 800-540-0001
Manufacturer and importer of soft drinks and bottled water
Manager: Jerry Mc Broom
Estimated Sales: $20-50 Million
Number Employees: 100-249
Type of Packaging: Consumer, Food Service
Other Locations:
Full Service Beverage Co.
Denver CO
Brands:
7-UP
CRYSTAL LITE
DIET-RITE
EVIAN
SNAPPLE

4898 **Fulton Provision Company**
16123 NE Airport Way
Portland, OR 97230 503-254-3000
Fax: 503-408-5640 800-333-6328
www.fultonprovision.com
Manufacturer of meats
CEO: Carl F Walther
Sales Contact: Tom Semke
Estimated Sales: $20-50 Million
Number Employees: 50-99
Parent Co: Sysco

4899 **Fumoir Grizzly**
159 Rue D'Amsterdam
St-Augustin-De-Desmaures, QC G3A 2V5
Canada 418-878-8941
Fax: 418-878-8942 info@grizzly.qc.ca
www.grizzly.qc.ca

Manufacturer and exporter of smoked salmon, trout, halibut
President: Pierre Fontaine
VP/Partner/Sales: Bernard Ruby
Quality Control Inspector/R&D: Michele Tessier
Sales Representative - Quebec: Normand Richard
Production Supervisor: Johanne Laroche
Estimated Sales: $6.3 Million
Number Employees: 37
Type of Packaging: Consumer, Food Service, Private Label, Bulk

4900 **Fun City Popcorn**
3211 Sunrise Ave
Las Vegas, NV 89101 702-367-2676
Fax: 702-876-1099 800-423-1710
Manufacturer of caramel, cheese and butter popcorn; manufacturer of popcorn processing machinery
President/CEO: Richard Falk
CFO: Maryann Talavera
Estimated Sales: $1-3 Million
Number Employees: 5-9
Sq. footage: 20000
Type of Packaging: Consumer, Food Service, Private Label, Bulk

4901 **Fun Factory**
6223 W Forest Home Ave
Milwaukee, WI 53220 414-543-5887
Fax: 414-543-7850 877-894-6767
Gum, candy
President: Mike Dunlap
Brands:
FACE TWISTERS SOUR BUBBLE GUM

4902 **Fun Foods**
99 Murray Hill Pkwy # D
East Rutherford, NJ 07073-2143 201-896-4949
Fax: 201-896-4911 800-507-2782
funfoodspasta@yahoo.com
Manufacturer and exporter of bi- and tri-colored holiday shaped gourmet pasta including Christmas trees, hearts, bunnies, stars and stripes, Jack O'Lanterns, star of David, angels, etc
President: Sharon Nicklas
Estimated Sales: $5-10 Million
Number Employees: 5-9
Sq. footage: 4000
Type of Packaging: Consumer, Food Service, Private Label, Bulk
Brands:
ALL-AMERICAN SPORTS PASTA
BUNNY PASTA
FUNFOODS HOLIDAY PASTA
FUNFOODS PREMIUM
HARVEST PASTA
HOLIDAY PASTA
I LOVE PASTA
LUCKY PASTA
PASTA DELLA FESTA
PATRIOTIC PASTA
STAR OF DAVID PASTA

4903 **Fun Foods**
99 Murray Hill Pkwy # D
East Rutherford, NJ 07073-2143 201-896-4949
Fax: 201-896-4911 800-507-2782
funfoodspasta@yahoo.com
Custom-shaped pastas
President: Sharon Nicklas
Estimated Sales: $5-10 Million
Number Employees: 5-9
Type of Packaging: Private Label
Brands:
PASTA DELLA FESTA

4904 **Functional Foods**
15765 Sturgeon St
Roseville, MI 48066 586-445-0550
Fax: 586-445-1118 877-372-0550
www.smartchocolate.com
Chocolate
President/CEO: Thomas Morley, Jr
Brands:
SMARTCHOCOLATES

4905 **Functional Foods**
470 Us Highway 9
Englishtown, NJ 7726 732-972-2232
Fax: 732-536-9179 800-442-9524
yshah5462@aol.com
www.functionalfoodscorp.com
Manufacturer of microcrystalline and hydroxypropyl cellulose, cellulose and psyllium fiber, gum arabic and guar, cellulose and vegetable gums
Marketing Manager: Alpa Nanavati
Manufacturing Manager: Yogi Shah
Estimated Sales: $2.5-5 Million
Number Employees: 20-49

4906 **Functional Products LLC**
1179 Atlantic Blvd
Atlantic Beach, FL 32233 904-249-8074
Fax: 904-249-8467 800-628-5908
sales@functional-products.com
www.functional-products.com
Vitamins and food supplements.
Owner: Dirk Mueggenburg
CEO: Dirk Mueggenburg
Sales: Laura Lambs
Estimated Sales: $ 1 - 3 Million
Number Employees: 1-4

4907 **Fungi Perfecti**
P.O.Box 7634
Olympia, WA 98507-7634 360-426-9292
Fax: 360-426-9377 800-780-9126
www.fungi.com
Gourmet and medicinal mushrooms.
Owner: Paul Stamets
Estimated Sales: $ 3 - 5 Million
Number Employees: 20-49

4908 **FungusAmongUs Inc**
2210 Lake Avenue
Po Box 352
Snohomish, WA 98290 360-568-3403
Fax: 360-563-2663
shrooms@fungusamongus.com
www.fungusamongus.com
Gourmet organic mushrooms

4909 **Funkandy Corporation**
1180 Olympic Drive
Suite 206
Corona, CA 92881-3393 909-371-6282
Fax: 909-371-6291 866-386-2263
Candy
Brands:
ALIEN EX-TREME
TONGUE ROLLER LOLLIPOP
TUBE-A-GOO

4910 **Funkychunky Inc.**
7452 W 78th St
Edina, MN 55439 952-938-6663
Fax: 952-938-2294 888-473-8659
tore@funkychunkyinc.com
www.funkychunkyinc.com
Chocolate covered pretzels, chocolate popcorn, caramel corn and bars
Marketing: Tore Villberg

4911 **FunniBonz**
3 Lake View Court
West Windsor, NJ 08850
Fax: 609-845-1806 877-300-2669
info@funnibonz.com www.funnibonz.com
BBQ sauces, rubs and marinades
President/Owner: Jim Barbour
CEO: Ryan Marrone

4912 **(HQ)Furmano Foods**
P.O.Box 500
Northumberland, PA 17857-0500 570-473-3516
Fax: 570-473-7367 877-877-6032
www.furmanos.com
Manufacturer of canned pizza sauce and tomatoes including pureed, crushed, stewed and whole peeled
President/CEO: Dave Geise
VP Sales/Marketing: Robert Vanderhook
Estimated Sales: $ 20 - 50 Million
Number Employees: 500-999
Type of Packaging: Consumer, Food Service
Brands:
FURMANO'S

4913 **Furmano's Foods**
PO Box 500
Northumberland, PA 17857 877-877-6032
Fax: 570-473-7367 www.furmanos.com
Tomatoes, beans and vegetables
President/CEO: David Geise
VP Sales/Marketin: Bob Vanderhook
VP Human Resources: Kermit Kohl
Number Employees: 250
Sq. footage: 600000
Type of Packaging: Consumer

4914 **Furukawa Potato Chip Factory**
P.O.Box 1129
Captain Cook, HI 96704-1129 808-323-3785
Fax: 808- 32-3 37
Potato chips and snack foods
Owner: Jerome Furukawa
Estimated Sales: $ 1 - 3 Million
Number Employees: 1-4

4915 **Fusion Gourmet**
14824 S Main St
Gardena, CA 90248 310-532-8938
Fax: 310-532-8991 cindygee@world.att.net
www.fusiongourmet.com
Specializes in authentically prepared, fines quality and all-natural cooking sauces, marinades, and dips from Southeast Asia
President: Annie Chu
Marketing: Sandra Liaw
Estimated Sales: $ 3 - 5 Million
Number Employees: 1-4
Brands:
ABC
BALI'S BEST
FATAL ATTRACTION
PEARL EMPRESS
SWEET SEDUCTION

4916 **Future Bakery & Cafe**
106 N Queen Street
Etobicoke, ON M8Z 2E2
Canada 416-231-1491
Fax: 416-231-1879
Manufacturer of specialty and artisan breads, European pastries and cheesecakes
President: Borys Wrzesnewskyj
Estimated Sales: $2.5-5 Million
Number Employees: 50-99
Sq. footage: 22000
Type of Packaging: Consumer
Brands:
FUTURE BAKERY

4917 **FutureCeuticals**
300 West 6th Street
Momence, IL 60954 815-472-3100
Fax: 815-472-3850 888-472-3545
Sales@futureceuticals.com
www.jopling.co.uk/ingredients/frame_future.html
Primary processor of nutraceuticals, functional foods and cosmetic ingredients. Processing capabilities include: fermentation, refining, IQF freezing, freeze drying, drum drying, air drying, spray drying, vacuum evaporationextraction, synthesis, milling, grinding and blending.
President: Edward Van Drunen
Director New Business Development Europe: Zheko Kounev Ph.D
Vice President Business Development: John Hunter
Vice President Research & Development: Zbigniew Pietrzkowski Ph.D
Director Quality Control: Boris Nemzer Ph.D
FutureCeuticals Technical Sales: Kit Kats
Sq. footage: 6000000

4918 **Futurebiotics**
70 Commerce Dr
Hauppauge, NY 11788-3936 631-273-6300
Fax: 631-273-1165 800-645-1721
info@futurebiotics.com www.futurebiotics.com
Manufacturer and distributor of natural health food supplements and vitamins
Owner: Saisul Kibria
Marketing Director: Ed Keenan
Public Relations: Ed Keenan
Director Operations: Wendy L Kauffman
Estimated Sales: $10-20 Million
Number Employees: 5-9
Type of Packaging: Consumer, Private Label, Bulk
Brands:
VITAL K

4919 **Fuzz East Coast**
140 Sylvan Avenue
3rd Floor
Englewood Cliffs, NJ 07632 866-438-3893
Fax: 201-461-1091 info@fuzebev.com
www.drinkfuze.com/

Manufacturers a variety of Fuze Health Infusions drinks including green tea and fruit juice flavored beverages.
Co-Founder: Lance Collins
Co-Founder: Joe Rosamilia
Co-Founder: Bruce Lewin
Co-Founder: Paula Grant
Type of Packaging: Food Service

4920 **Fuzzy's Wholesale Bar-B-Q**
408 W End Blvd
Madison, NC 27025 336-548-2283
Fax: 336-548-2272
Frozen pork barbecue, brunswick stew, gourmet chicken pot pies, home replacement meals.
President: Fred Nelson
Estimated Sales: Less than $500,000
Number Employees: 1-4

4921 **G Banis Company And Services, Inc.**
2711 Centerville Road
Suite 400
Wilmington, DE 19808 617-516-9092
info@banistradition.com
Olive oil, dried fruit, olives, pickles & pickled vegetables, sun-dried tomatoes, foodservice, private label.
Marketing: George Banis

4922 **G Cefalu & Brothers**
P.O.Box 946
Jessup, MD 20794-0946 410-799-3414
Fax: 410-799-8694 jessup29@aol.com
Processor/repacker of tomatoes and all types of produce.
Owner: John Cefalu
Estimated Sales: $10-20 Million
Number Employees: 20-49
Type of Packaging: Consumer, Food Service, Bulk

4923 **G Di Lullo & Sons**
1004 Edgewater Ave
Westville, NJ 08093-1246 856-456-3700
Fax: 856-456-7161
Manufacturer and exporter of canned foods including chili con carne, beef cubes, meatballs in sauce, meatballs, in gravy and also, sauces including spaghetti, Creole, parmigiana, etc.; importer of canned and frozen meat
Owner: Ugo Di Lullo
Estimated Sales: $620,000
Number Employees: 10
Number of Products: 25
Sq. footage: 15000
Type of Packaging: Food Service

4924 **G S Robins & Company**
126 Choteau Avenue
Saint Louis, MO 63102 314-621-5155
Fax: 314-621-1216 800-777-5155
info@gsrobins.com www.gsrobins.com
Supplier for hundreds of specialty chemical products and services that meet your chemical needs.
President: G Stephen Robins
Sales: Doug Kutz
Estimated Sales: $50-100 Million
Number Employees: 20-49

4925 **G Scaccianoce & Company**
1165 Burnett Pl
Bronx, NY 10474-5716 718-991-4462
Fax: 718-991-0154
Processor and exporter of confectionery items including Jordan almonds, French mints and licorice
President: Donald Beck
Estimated Sales: $2.5-5 Million
Number Employees: 5-9
Type of Packaging: Consumer, Food Service, Private Label, Bulk

4926 **G&F Manufacturing Company**
5555 W 109th St
Oak Lawn, IL 60453-5070 708-424-4170
Fax: 708-424-4922 866-865-1591
www.gandf.com
Designing and manufacturing high quality chemical resistant, durable and rugged Stainless steel products such as steel tanks, filling machines, piston filters, cappers, and labeling.
President: Ron Bais
Purchasing Manager: Ron Bais
Number Employees: 10-19
Sq. footage: 15000
Type of Packaging: Food Service

4927 **G&G Foods**
322 Bellevue Ave
Santa Rosa, CA 95407 707-542-6300
Fax: 707-542-6370 www.gandgfoods.com
Strive to produce restaurant quality, convenient, entertaining and snacking products which include specialty and fat-free cheese spreads, gourmet cheese, hummus and dips
President: Rich Goldberg
Operations: David Blair
Estimated Sales: $100-500 Million
Number Employees: 100-249
Type of Packaging: Consumer
Brands:
GOLDY'S
LA TORTA
MEZA

4928 **G&G Marketing**
315 Dunes Blvd Apt 1003
Naples, FL 34110 239-593-4564
Fax: 239-593-0937 gary@athenamelons.com
www.athenamelons.com
Growers, exporters, and distributors of melons, and other fresh fruits and vegetables

4929 **G&G Sheep Farm**
11406 Boston Road
Boston, KY 40107-8602 502-833-4863
Processor of lamb
Estimated Sales: Under $300,000
Number Employees: 1-4
Type of Packaging: Consumer

4930 **G&J Land and Marine Food Distributors**
506 Front St
Morgan City, LA 70380 985-385-2620
Fax: 985-385-3614 800-256-9187
www.gjfood.com
Full service food distributor dedicated to providing an extensive grocery and janitorial product line to the offshore oil and gas, commercial shipping and restaurant industry.
President: Mike Lind
VP/Sales: Mike Lind
Operations: Adam Mayon
Purchasing: Jarrod Leonard
Estimated Sales: $ 10 - 20 Million
Number Employees: 100-249

4931 **G&J Pepsi-Cola Bottlers**
9435 Waterstone Blvd, Ste. 390
Cicinnati, OH 43249-8205 513-785-6060
Fax: 513-683-9467 www.pbg.com
Processor of regular, diet and caffeine-free soft drinks
President/Vice Chairman: Thomas R Gross
Chairman: Stanley Kaplan
COO: Timothy Hardig
Estimated Sales: $50-100 Million
Number Employees: 250-499
Type of Packaging: Consumer, Food Service

4932 **G&R Food Sales**
5736 W Loma Lane
Glendale, AZ 85302-5938 602-939-7337
Fax: 602-939-7337
Partner: Juanita Linder
Partner: Fridolin Linder

4933 **G&W Packing Company**
822 W Exchange Ave
Chicago, IL 60609-2507 773-847-5400
Fax: 773-847-3364 tschicagosteak@aol.com
www.chicagosteaks.com
Meat packaging
President, CEO, Treasurer: Tom Summers
CEO, Principal: Thomas Campbell
Vice President: Rick Allison
Estimated Sales: $ 5.50 Million
Number Employees: 20-49

4934 **G. L. Mezzetta**
105 Mezzetta Ct
American Canyon, CA 94503 707-648-1050
Fax: 707-648-1060 consumerinfo@mezzetta.com
www.mezzetta.com
Leading manufacturer of imported and domestic peppers, roasted peppers, fancy stuffed olives, green and specialty olives, imported olive oil and capers, pickled vegetables, cocktail and appetizer specialties, assorted gourmetspecialties.
President: Jeff Mezzetta
Senior VP: Thomas Rickard Jr
Midwest Sales Manager: Tony Guidio
Sales Manager: Paul Kastl
Food Technologist: Shea Rosen
Estimated Sales: $20-50 Million
Number Employees: 100-249
Type of Packaging: Consumer, Food Service, Private Label
Brands:
KONA COAST
MEZZETTA
TULELAKE

4935 **G. M. Allen & Son**
P.O.Box 454
Orland, ME 04472 207-469-7060
Fax: 207-469-7060
www.gmallenwildblueberries.com
Processing of frozen wild blueberries.
President/CEO: Wayne Allen
VP Operations: Kermit Allen
Estimated Sales: $2 Million
Number Employees: 7

4936 **G.E.F. Gourmet Foods Inc**
35584 County Road 8
Mountain Lake, MN 56159-2106 507-427-2631
Fax: 507-427-2631 800-692-6762
greatsnack@frontiernet.net www.gladcorn.com/
Manufactures Glad Corn A-maizing Corn Snacks.
Founder/Co-Owner: Stan Friesen
Founder/Co-Owner: Gladys Friesen
Type of Packaging: Food Service

4937 **G.L. Mezzetta Inc**
105 Mezzetta Ct
American Canyon, CA 94503 707-648-1050
Fax: 707-648-1060 info@mezzetta.com
www.mezzetta.com
Glass-packed peppers and olives
President/Owner: Ronald Mezzetta
Estimated Sales: $12.3 Million
Number Employees: 80

4938 **G.S. Dunn Limited**
80 Park Street N
Hamilton, ON L8R 2M9 905-522-0833
Fax: 905-522-4423 info@gsdunn.com
www.gsdunn.com
Manufacturer of dry mustard products
President: Don Henry
Estimated Sales: $4.3 Million
Number Employees: 30

4939 **G.S. Gelato and Desserts, Inc.**
1785 Fim Boulevard
Fort Walton Beach, FL 32547 850-243-5455
Fax: 850-243-5443 sfaroni@gsgelato.com
www.gsgelato.com
Dairy-free, gluten-free, organic/natural, frozen desserts, full-line frozen, ice cream/sorbet, foodservice, private label.
Marketing: Simona Faroni

4940 **GB Ratto & Company International**
821 Washington St
Oakland, CA 94607-4089 510-832-6503
Fax: 510-836-2250 800-325-3483
Full line of imported Italian foods and ingredients. Olives, oils and spices - a 'specialty food emporium'.
Owner: Elena Voiron
General Manager: Susan Nelson
Estimated Sales: $2.5-5 Million
Number Employees: 5-9

4941 **GCI Nutrients (USA)**
1163 Chess Dr # H
Foster City, CA 94404-1119 650-697-4700
Fax: 650-697-6300 walter@gcinutrients.com
www.gcinutrients.com

Processor, importer and exporter of vitamins and supplements including beta carotene, essential fatty acids, herbal products, botanical extracts, food supplements, bulk ingredients, premium raw materials for nutritional and beverageindustries with over 33 years of experience
President: Richard Merriam
CFO: Jennifer Evich
R&D: William Forgach
Marketing Director: Walter Rick
Production: Mike Cronin
Plant Manager: Mike Crowin
Purchasing Manager: Derek Cronin
Estimated Sales: $10 Million
Number Employees: 10-19
Number of Brands: 10
Number of Products: 300
Sq. footage: 10000
Brands:
ABG
CM - 22
ELEUTHEROGEN
GAMMA - E
GE - OXY 132
LIPO - SERINE
OLIVIR
OXI - GAMMA
OXI - GRAPE

4942 **(HQ)GE Barbour**
165 Stewart Avenue
Sussex, NB E4E 3H1
Canada 506-432-2300
Fax: 506-432-2323 www.barbours.ca
Processor of food colors and mustards; importer of teas, coffees, spices, cheeses, food colors, extracts, syrups and mustards
President: Grant Brenan
VP: Sylvia MacVey
Marketing: Don Macleod
Number Employees: 100-249
Type of Packaging: Consumer, Food Service, Private Label
Other Locations:
G.E. Barbour
St. John NB
Brands:
BARBOURS
KING COLE

4943 **GE Hawthorn Meat Company**
164 Guy Hawthorn Ln
Hot Springs, AR 71901 501-623-8111
Manufacturer of fresh pork and beef; also, slaughtering services available
President: Richard Hawthorn
Estimated Sales: $1-3 Million
Number Employees: 1-4
Sq. footage: 250000
Type of Packaging: Consumer

4944 **GEM Berry Products**
804 Airport Way
Sandpoint, ID 83864 208-263-7503
Fax: 208-263-3247 800-426-0498
gamberry92@hotmail.com
Processor and exporter of spreads, jams and syrups including raspberry and huckleberry; berry filled chocolates, berry barbecue sauce and many other berry products.
President: Jack O' Brien
CFO: Betty Menser
Marketing: Harry Menser
Production: Elizabeth O Brien
Estimated Sales: $50,000-100,000
Number Employees: 1-4
Sq. footage: 2500
Type of Packaging: Food Service, Bulk
Brands:
GEM BERRY
LITEHOUSE
TASTE THE BEAUTY OF NORTH IDAHO
TASTE THE BEAUTY OF THE ROCKIES

4945 **GEM Cultures**
30301 Sherwood Rd
Fort Bragg, CA 95437-6100 707-964-2922
www.gemcultures.com
Manufacturer and exporter of shelf stable starters for cultured vegeterian foods including tempeh, miso, shoyu, natto, sourdough, nonyogurt and dairy cultures; importer of koji and natto starters
Owner: Betty Stechmeyer
Public Relations: Gordon McBride
Estimated Sales: $70,000
Number Employees: 1
Sq. footage: 1000
Type of Packaging: Private Label
Brands:
GEM

4946 **GFA Brands**
115 W Century Rd Ste 260
Paramus, NJ 7652 201-568-9300
Fax: 201-568-6374 pdray@gfabrands.com
www.smartbalance.com
Manufacturer of cheese, margarine, mayonnaise, cereals, salad dressings, pickles and oils
President: Robert Harris
CEO: Steve Hughes
Estimated Sales: $1-3 Million
Number Employees: 10-19
Type of Packaging: Consumer
Brands:
GFA
H-O
MRS FANINGS
SPIN BLEND

4947 **GFF**
145 Willow Ave
City of Industry, CA 91746 323-846-2700
Fax: 323-726-0934 wjperry@girardsdressing.com
www.girardsdressing.com
Salad dressings, marinades, sauces and mayonnaise
President/Co-CEO: William Perry
CEO: Farrell Hursch
CFO: Tim Schoenbaum
Research & Development: Jeff Stalley
Marketing: Ron Caplan
Maintenance Manager: Dan Roope
Estimated Sales: $14 Million
Number Employees: 90
Number of Brands: 3
Number of Products: 175
Sq. footage: 20000
Type of Packaging: Food Service, Private Label, Bulk
Brands:
CHEFS IDEAL
GIRARDS
STATE FARM

4948 **(HQ)GFI Premium Foods**
2815 Blaisdell Ave
Minneapolis, MN 55408-2312 612-872-6262
Fax: 612-870-4955 800-669-8996
customerservice@gfiamerica.com
www.gfipremiumfoods.com
Processors beef, poultry, and pork for its food service and institutional customers
President: Robert Goldberger
VP Sales: Joe Goldberger
Estimated Sales: $100+ Million
Number Employees: 250-499
Type of Packaging: Consumer, Food Service, Private Label, Bulk
Other Locations:
GFI Premium Foods
Rapid City SD
Brands:
SMART MEAT STEAKS & HAMBURGERS
THE NATURAL

4949 **GH Bent Company**
7 Pleasant St
Milton, MA 02186 617-698-5945
Fax: 617-696-7730 info@bentscookiefactory.com
www.bentscookiefactory.com
Processor of cookies, brownies and crackers.
Owner: Eugene Pierotti
CEO: Eugene Pierotti
VP: James Pierotti
Sales: Eugene Pierotti, Sr
Estimated Sales: $500,000-$1 Million
Number Employees: 10-19
Sq. footage: 20000
Type of Packaging: Food Service
Brands:
BENT'S

4950 **GH Ford Tea Company**
Po Box 683
Shokangers Falls, NY 12481 845-834-2068
Fax: 845-296-0375 info@ghfordtea.com
www.ghfordtea.com
Processor, importer and exporter of whole leaf teas in tea ball packaging. Offers 30 to 50 blends and flavors utilizing original blending formulas and all natural flavoring.
President: Keith Capolino
Estimated Sales: $2.5-5 Million
Number Employees: 5-9
Type of Packaging: Consumer, Food Service, Private Label, Bulk
Brands:
G.H. Ford

4951 **GH Leidenheimer BakingCompany**
1501 Simon Bolivar Ave
New Orleans, LA 70113-2399 504-525-1575
Fax: 504-525-1596 800-259-9099
info@leidenheimer.com www.leidenheimer.com
Have a full line of breads that meet every foodservice needs. Established since 1896
President: Robert J Whann Iv III
Estimated Sales: $10-20 Million
Number Employees: 50-99

4952 **GINCO International**
Ste C
725 Cochran St
Simi Valley, CA 93065-1974 805-520-2592
800-284-2598
sales@gincointernational.com
www.ginsengcompany.com
The choice of nine different types of ginseng. We hand select and pure-grind our products.
President: Gary Raskin
Vice President: Linda Raskin
Director Marketing: Rick Seibert
Estimated Sales: $ 1 - 3 Million
Number Employees: 10-19

4953 **GJ Shortall**
107 Clyde Avenue
Mount Pearl, NL A1N 4R9
Canada 709-747-0655
Fax: 709-747-2223
Processor, exporter and wholesaler/distributor of dried and frozen squid, capelin, herring and mackerel
President: Steven Shortall
Estimated Sales: $3 Million
Number Employees: 10
Type of Packaging: Bulk

4954 **GKI Foods**
7926 Lochlin Road
Brighton, MI 48116 248-486-0055
Fax: 248-486-9135 chuck@gkifoods.com
www.gkifoods.com
Manufacturer of milk chocolate, sugar free chocolate, yogurt and cards products, panned and enrobed, bulk or packaged. Also produces custom granola (all natural, highly nutritional, low in fat and fat free), trail mixes, etc. Customformulation. Aid certified, GMP and HACCP accreditation.
President: Sue Wilts
General Manager: Jim Frazier
Number Employees: 20-49
Sq. footage: 30000
Type of Packaging: Consumer, Private Label, Bulk

4955 **GLG Life Tech Corporation**
1050 West Pender Street
Suite 2168
Vancouver, BC V6E 3S7
Canada 604-669-2602
Fax: 604-662-8858 info@glglifetech.com
www.glglifetech.com
Supplier of Stevia, which is a natural, zero calorie sweetening additive used in the food and beverage industries.
President/Vice Chairman: Brian Palmieri
Chairman & CEO: Dr. Luke Zhang
Vice President, Marketing: James Kempland
Vice President, Sales: Jack Tokarczyk

4956 **GLG Life Tech Corporation**
999 Canada Place
Suite 519 World Trade Centre
Vancouver, BC V6C 3E1 604-641-1368
Fax: 604-844-2830 info@glglifetech.com
www.glglifetech.com
Manufacturers all-natural sweetener, stevia extract
President: Brian Palmieri
CEO: Luke Zhang

Estimated Sales: $58 Million
Number Employees: 50-99

4957 GMB Specialty Foods

P.O.Box 962
San Juan Cpstrno, CA 92693-0962 949-240-3053
Fax: 949-240-3086 800-809-8098
info@gmbfoods.com
Quaility foods for the gourmet industry.
President: Greg Bloom
Marketing Director: Helen Bloom
Estimated Sales: $1 Million
Number Employees: 5-9
Type of Packaging: Private Label
Brands:
BASITAN'S
EDELWEISS DRESSINGS
NORMAN BISHOP
SALLIE'S
SCOTTSDALE MUSTARD CO

4958 GMF Corporation

54 Commercial Street
Gloucester, MA 01930-5025 978-283-0479
Fax: 978-283-8738

4959 GMI Products

2525 Davie Road
Suite 330
Plantation, FL 33317-7403 305-474-9608
Fax: 954-474-0989 800-999-9373
Gelatin and flavors

4960 (HQ)GMI Products/Originates

1301 Sawgrass Corporate Pkwy
Sunrise, FL 33323-2813 954-233-3300
Fax: 954-233-3301 800-999-9373
info@gmi-originates.com
www.natures-products.com
Manufacturer and supplier of raw materials specializing in gelatin, flavors, active pharmaceuticals, botanicals and pharmaceutical additives. Providing import/export services, warehousing and freight forwarding to and from the UnitedStates and worldwide
President: Jose Minski
Number Employees: 100-249
Type of Packaging: Private Label, Bulk
Brands:
CURT GEORGI FLAVORS & FRAGRANCES
GMI GELATIN
HEALTH ASSURE

4961 GMP Laboratories

2931 E La Jolla St
Anaheim, CA 92806-1306 714-630-2467
Fax: 714-237-1374 info@gmplabs.com
www.gmplabs.com
Leading contract manufacturer of high quality vitamins and nutritional supplements. Our laboratories can assist you in formulating, manufacturing, packaging your products while always maintaining absolute confidentiality.
President/CEO: Suhail Ishaq
Estimated Sales: $ 20 - 50 Million
Number Employees: 50-99

4962 GNS Foods/Pacific Gold

2109 E Division St
Arlington, TX 76011-7817 817-795-4671
Fax: 817-795-4673 carissa@gnsfoods.com
www.gnsfoods.com
Processor of raw and roasted nuts, packaged pecan candy and dried fruits including raisins, mango, pineapple, apple, banana chips, apricots and mixed; wholesaler/distributor of specialty foods; serving the food service market
President: Kim Peacock
Marketing: Carissa Mark
Estimated Sales: $5-10 Million
Number Employees: 20-49
Sq. footage: 12596
Type of Packaging: Consumer, Food Service, Private Label, Bulk
Brands:
GROVE ON THE GO
GROVE, JR
PECAN STREET SWEETS
THE GROVE

4963 GNS Spices

766 Trotter Ct
Walnut, CA 91789-1277 909-594-9505
Fax: 909-594-5455
Processor and exporter of red savina and orange habanero peppers including pods, flakes and ground
President: Frank Garcia Jr
VP: Mary Garcia
Operations Manager: Frank Garcia Sr
Estimated Sales: $150,000
Number Employees: 2
Type of Packaging: Bulk

4964 GNT USA

203 Redwood Shores Pkwy
Redwood City, CA 94065-1198 650-596-0900
Fax: 650-596-0911 info@gntusa.com
www.gntusa.com
Manufacturer of colouring foodstuffs, natural colours and phytochemicals.
Managing Director: Paul Collins
Managing Director: Stefan Hake
Managing Director: Wolfgang Quehl
Managing Director: Peter Van De Riet
Senior Food Scientist: Rachael Rothman

4965 GPI USA LLC.

931 Hill Street
Athens, GA 30606 706-850-7826
Fax: 706-850-7827 www.gumproducts.com
www.gumproducts.com
Specialize in carageenan used for stabilization and as an additive for both dairy products and in the red meat and poultry industries.

4966 GS Dunn & Company

80 Park Street N
Hamilton, ON L8R 2M9
Canada 905-522-0833
Fax: 905-522-4423 info@gsdunn.com
www.gsdunn.com
Global supplier and manufacturer of dry mustard products
President: Ron Kramer
Director Technical Services: Nancy Post
Estimated Sales: $5 Million
Number Employees: 20-49
Sq. footage: 35000
Type of Packaging: Food Service, Private Label, Bulk

4967 GS-AFI

238 Saint Nicholas Avenue
South Plainfield, NJ 07080-1810 908-753-9100
Fax: 908-753-9635 800-345-4342
dhiller@gsafi.com www.gsafi.com
Specialty premixes, spices and seasonings
President: David Hiller
Contact: Dagmar Hiller
Number Employees: 250-499

4968 GSB & Associates

3115 Cobb International Blvd
Kennesaw, GA 30152-4354 770-424-1886
Fax: 770-422-1732 877-472-2776
sales@gsbflavorcreators.com
www.gsbflavorcreators.com
To provide the flavor industry with new innovative flavor creations that never been tasted before. Our products include natural, natural and artifical, artificial, water or oil soluble, liquid and spray dried flavors. Flavors areKosher Certified. We also offer a line of Certified Organic Flavors.
President: Eugene Buday
Estimated Sales: $5-10 Million
Number Employees: 10-19
Type of Packaging: Bulk

4969 GTC Nutrition Company

23567 Genesee Village Rd
Golden, CO 80401-5719
Fax: 303-216-2477 800-522-4682
generalinfo@gtcnutrition.com
www.gtcnutrition.com
A leading provider of high-quality, science based nutritional ingredients for today's healthy lifestyles. Proudly takes a multi-disciplinary approach to it's business by offering customer support that reaches beyond standard needs.Areas of expertise include scientific and technical counsel, marketing and brand development, applications innovation, logistics and regulatory support and customer service.
CEO: Patrick Smith
Marketing: Trina O'Brien
Estimated Sales: $5-10 Million
Number Employees: 20-49

4970 GWB Foods Corporation

PO Box 228
Brooklyn, NY 11204-0228 718-686-6611
Fax: 718-686-6161 877-977-7610
www.gwbfoods.com
Processor, exporter, importer and wholesaler/distributor of specialty and frozen foods including cookies, candies, crackers, rice cakes, vegetables in jars, bottled water, pickles and pimiento peppers
President: Joshua Weinstein
Export Manager: S Williams
Sales Manager: Jack Yhumns
Estimated Sales: $2.5-5 Million
Number Employees: 10-19
Sq. footage: 40000
Parent Co: President Baking Company
Type of Packaging: Consumer, Food Service, Private Label, Bulk
Brands:
Presidor

4971 GYMA IQF

PO Box 113
Stroudsburg, PA 18360-0113 570-422-6311
Fax: 570-422-6301 888-496-2872
gjgyma@pnpa.net
Processor, importer and exporter of IQF herbs, garlic, mushrooms, leeks, asparagus, string beans, etc
VP Industrial Sales: Pierre Hellivan
Sales Manager Technical: Ghislaine Joly
Estimated Sales: $5-10 Million
Number Employees: 10-19
Parent Co: GYMA Group
Type of Packaging: Bulk
Brands:
Gyma

4972 Gabilas Knishes

120 S 8th St
Brooklyn, NY 11211
Fax: 718-384-8621
Processor and exporter of frozen knishes
President: Gloria Gabay
Partner: Sophie Levy
Controller: Linda Ghignone
Estimated Sales: $1-2.5 Million
Number Employees: 20-49
Type of Packaging: Consumer
Brands:
KING OF POTATO PIES

4973 Gabriele Macaroni Company

P.O.Box 90564
City of Industry, CA 91715 626-964-2324
Fax: 626-912-1058 sales@gabrielepasta.com
www.gabrielepasta.com
Manufactures macaroni, egg noodles, whole wheat pasta, flavored and organic pasta.
President: Ann Fusano
VP: Victor Fusano
Estimated Sales: $5-10 Million
Number Employees: 10-19
Sq. footage: 20000
Type of Packaging: Consumer, Private Label, Bulk
Brands:
GABRIELE
HEALTH BEST
HEALTH VALLEY
PURE & SIMPLE
TRADER JOE'S

4974 Gad Cheese Company

2401 County Road C
Medford, WI 54451-9009 715-748-4273
Fax: 715-748-4299
Processor of cheddar cheese, cheese curds, monterey jack, specialty cheese and more than 30 varieties. Retail outlet and an observation window.
President: Bruce Albrecht
VP: Diane Albrecht
Estimated Sales: $500,000-$1 Million
Number Employees: 10-19
Type of Packaging: Consumer, Food Service, Private Label, Bulk

4975 Gadot Biochemical Industries

1440 Hicks Rd Ste C
Rolling Meadows, IL 60008 847-259-1809
Fax: 847-259-6984 888-424-1424
gadot@jstewartandcompany.com
www.gadotbio.com

Gadot is a producer of citric acid, sodium citrate, potassium citrates, fumaric acid, calcium citrate, magnesium citrate, zinc citrate, tri calcium phosphate, and mono potassium phosphate
President: Jim Stewart
Estimated Sales: $5-10 Million
Number Employees: 5-9
Parent Co: Haifa Bay
Type of Packaging: Bulk

4976 **Gadoua Bakery**
150 Industrial Boulevard
Napierville, QC J0J 1L0
Canada 450-245-3326
Fax: 450-245-7609
Processor and exporter of bread and buns
President/CEO: Benoit Gregoire
Estimated Sales: $40-60 Million
Number Employees: 550
Sq. footage: 150000
Type of Packaging: Food Service
Brands:
GADOUA

4977 **Gadsden Coffee/Caffe**
P.O.Box 460
Arivaca, AZ 85601-0460 520-398-3251
Fax: 520-398-2001 888-514-5282
roaster@gadsdencoffee.com
www.gadsdencoffee.com
Specialty coffees
President: Tom Shook
Estimated Sales: $2.5-5 Million
Number Employees: 10-19

4978 **Gaf Seelig**
5905 52nd Ave
Woodside, NY 11377 718-899-5000
Fax: 718-803-1198 info@gafseeling.com
www.gafseelig.com
Distributor of fine baked foods to restaurants, hotels, hospitals and cooperative businesses.
President: Rodney Seelig
Estimated Sales: $5-10 Million
Number Employees: 100-249
Type of Packaging: Private Label

4979 **Gai's Northwest Bakeries**
P.O.Box 24327
Seattle, WA 98124-0327 206-322-0931
Fax: 206-726-7533
Bread rolls, buns
Manager: Barry Ware
Estimated Sales: Under $500,000
Number Employees: 1,000-4,999

4980 **Gaia Herbs**
101 Gaia Herbs Rd
Brevard, NC 28712 828-884-4242
Fax: 800-717-1722 800-831-7780
info@gaiaherbs.com www.gaiaherbs.com
Organic processor of herbal extracts. Plant specific methods for extraction are used to assure that we obtain the highest yields from the plant with disturbing the plant's natural chemical profile. We are one of the few herbal extractcompanies in the world that controls production from seed selection and plant horticulture, through every phase of extraction, concentration and testing, to the product that you can rely upon to deliver theraputic results.
President: James Sebastain
Finance Executive/Plant Manager: Ric Scalzo
VP: Daniel Vickers
Quality Control Director: Jim Grant
VP Marketing: Ann Buchman
VP Sales: Angela Guerrant
Human Resources Manager: Cynthia Chandler
Purchasing: Kate Daigle
Estimated Sales: $11.5 Million
Number Employees: 90
Sq. footage: 30000
Brands:
ECHINACEA
ECHINACEA/GOLDENSEAL SUPREME
GINSENG EXTRACT

4981 **Gainey Vineyard**
3950 E Highway 246
Santa Ynez, CA 93460 805-688-0558
Fax: 805-688-5864 www.gaineyvineyard.com
To create wines of uncompromising quality with optimum flavor and aromatic components that reflect the unique characteristics of the vineyards from which they come. Our varieties consist of Bordeaux varieties, Pinot Nois, Chardonnayand Syrah.
President: Daniel Gainey
Estimated Sales: $5-10 Million
Number Employees: 10-19

4982 **Gaiser's European StyleProvisions**
2019 Morris Ave
Union, NJ 7083 908-686-3421
Fax: 908-686-7131
Processor, exporter and wholesaler/distributor of sausage, liverwurst and smoked ham
Owner: Efem Rablov
Estimated Sales: $500,000-$1 Million
Number Employees: 10-19
Brands:
GAISER'S

4983 **Galante Vineyards**
18181 Cachagua Rd
Carmel Valley, CA 93924 831-659-7620
Fax: 831-624-3200 800-425-2683
wine@galantevineyards.com
www.galantevineyards.com
Recognized as one of the premier Cabernet Sauvignon producers in Monterey county in all of California.
President: Jack Galante
Purchasing: Jack Galante
Estimated Sales: Less than $500,000
Number Employees: 1-4
Type of Packaging: Private Label
Brands:
BLACKJACK PASTURE CABERNET
GALANTE WINES
RANCHO GALANTE CABERNET
RED ROSE HILL CABERNET

4984 **Galassos Bakery**
10820 San Sevaine Way
Mira Loma, CA 91752-1116 951-360-1211
Fax: 951-360-0427 webmaster@galassos.com
www.galassos.com
Manufacturer of sourdough, french, specialty and sliced breads, hot dog and hamburger buns and assorted rolls
President: John Galasso
VP: John Roundtree
Plant Manager: Armando Ramirez
Estimated Sales: $100+ Million
Number Employees: 100-249
Sq. footage: 110000
Type of Packaging: Consumer, Food Service, Private Label, Bulk
Brands:
GALASSO

4985 **Galaxy Dairy Products, Incorporated**
700 Lake St # E
Ramsey, NJ 07446-1246 201-818-2030
Fax: 201-818-1969 galxdairy@aol.com
Import and export dairy products.
President: Thomas Phiebig
VP: Carole Phiebig
Estimated Sales: $30 Million+
Number Employees: 5-9
Type of Packaging: Private Label

4986 **Galaxy Desserts**
1100 Marina Way S
Suite D
Richmond, CA 94804 510-439-3160
Fax: 415-439-3170 800-225-3523
sales@galaxydesserts.com
www.galaxydesserts.com
Worldwide leader in individual gourmet desserts producing the finest individual mousse cakes, tarts and cheesecakes
President/CEO: Paul Levitan
Sales/Marketing: Lisa Weaver
Estimated Sales: $20-50 Million
Number Employees: 200
Sq. footage: 20000
Type of Packaging: Consumer, Food Service
Brands:
GALAXY DESSERTS

4987 **Galaxy Nutritional Foods**
66 Whitecap Dr
North Kingstown, RI 2852
Fax: 407-855-7485 800-441-9419
www.galaxyfoods.com
Leading producer of healthy diary products such as soy based dairy, low-fat, and cholestral-free. Category leader in both supermarkets and health food stores.
President: Angelo Morini
CEO: Michael Broll
CFO: Salvatore Furnari
CEO: Michael E Broll
Operations: Thomas Perno
Estimated Sales: $50-100 Million
Number Employees: 20-49
Brands:
FORMGG
GALAXY NUTRITIONAL FOODS
LITE BAKERY
NATURE'S ALTERNATIVE
SOYCO
SOYMAGE
VEGGIE
VEGGIE CAFE
VEGGIE LITE BAKERY
WHOLESOME VALLEY

4988 **Galco Food Products**
3691 Weston Rd
Toronto, ON M9L 1W4
Canada 416-743-9671
Processor and exporter of fresh and frozen chicken including whole and parts
Number Employees: 250-499
Type of Packaging: Consumer, Food Service, Private Label, Bulk

4989 **Galena Canning Company**
106 S Main Street
Galena, IL 61036 815-777-2882
Fax: 773-477-5627 info@galenacanning.com
www.galenacanning.com
Specialties in salsas, pasta sauce, BBQ sauces, chili, relishes, pickles, hot sauces, mustard, jams and jellies, fruit butter, syrups, toppings, flavored oils and vinegar.
Owner: Ivo Puidak
Estimated Sales: $ 1 - 3 Million
Number Employees: 10-19

4990 **Galena Cellars Winery**
P.O.Box 207
Galena, IL 61036 815-777-3330
Fax: 815-777-3335 800-397-9463
wine@galenacellars.com www.galenacellars.com
Producers, bottles and cellars a variety of wines using grapes, juice and fruit from across the US. Classic dry wines such as Chardonay, Cabernot Sauvignon, White Zinfandel, semi-dry and semi-sweet wines, selection of fruit wines anddessert ports.
Owner/President: Scott Lawlor
VP: Karen Lawlor
Estimated Sales: $1.8 Million
Number Employees: 20-49
Number of Products: 32
Type of Packaging: Consumer, Bulk
Brands:
GALENA CELLARS

4991 **Galilean Seafoods**
P.O.Box 1140
Bristol, RI 02809-0903 401-253-3030
Fax: 401-253-9207 galileansf@aol.com
www.galileanseafoods.com
Largest and most respected hand shucked clam supplier in the country. Frozen and refrigerated clams, hard shell clams, scallops, conch, and mussels and a full line of hand shucked breaded clam items.
President: Mark Montopoli
Estimated Sales: $10-20 Million
Number Employees: 50-99
Brands:
GALILEAN
KING CONCH
PURE BRAND PRODUCTS

4992 **Gallands Institutional Foodservice**
P.O.Box 3007
Bakersfield, CA 93385-3007 661-631-5505
Fax: 661-631-5513

Distributors of a full service food line, exceptions produce and meat.
President: Joan Galland
CFO: Leonard Galland
Estimated Sales: $ 3 - 5 Million
Number Employees: 10-19

4993 **Galleano Winery**
4231 Wineville Ave
Mira Loma, CA 91752 951-685-5376
Fax: 951-360-9180 info@galleanowinery.com
www.galleanowinery.com
Processor of wines and wine grapes
President/CEO: Donald Galleano
EVP: Charlene Galleano
Human Resources Director: Debbie Kreinbring
Estimated Sales: $810 Million
Number Employees: 8
Sq. footage: 90000
Type of Packaging: Consumer, Private Label, Bulk
Brands:
GALLEANO
GREEN VALLEY

4994 **(HQ)Galliker Dairy**
P.O.Box 159
Johnstown, PA 15907-0159 814-266-8702
Fax: 814-266-4619 800-477-6455
info@gallikers.com www.gallikers.com
Processor and distributor of milk, ice cream, orange juice and iced tea.
Chairman: Louis Gilliker III
President: Charles Price
CEO: Mark Duray
Estimated Sales: $86,100,000
Number Employees: 250-499
Brands:
GALLIKER'S
POTOMAC FARMS
QUALITY CHEKD
SLIM 'N' TRIM

4995 **Galloway Company**
601 S Commercial St
Neenah, WI 54956 920-722-7741
Fax: 920-722-1927 800-722-8903
info@gallowaycompany.com
www.gallowaycompany.com
Processor of sweetened condensed milk and candy and frozen dessert mixes. Also custom industrial ingredients and beverage bases
President: Doug Dietrich
CEO: Timothy Galloway
VP Sales/Marketing: Ted Galloway
Sales Manager: Pat Galloway
Estimated Sales: $20-50 Million
Number Employees: 20-49
Type of Packaging: Food Service, Private Label, Bulk
Brands:
GOLDEN CREST

4996 **Galluccio Estate Vineyards**
PO Box 1269
Cutchogue, NY 11935-0885 631-734-7089
Fax: 631-734-7114 info@gallucciowineries.com
www.gristinawines.com
Wines such as Chardonney, Mirlot and Cabernet Sauvignon
Owner: Vince Galluccio
Estimated Sales: $2.5-5 Million
Number Employees: 10-19

4997 **Gallup Sales Company**
530 E Historic Highway 66
Gallup, NM 87301 505-863-5241
Fax: 505-863-4219
Distributors of beer and wine.
President: Reed Ferrari
Estimated Sales: $1-2.5 Million
Number Employees: 10-19

4998 **Gama Products**
11725 NW 100th Rd Ste 3
Medley, FL 33178 305-883-1200
Fax: 305-883-0741 info@gamaproducts.com
www.gamaproducts.com
Processor, importer and exporter of oils including corn, soy, canola, vegetable, rice bran and cottonseed.
President: Alberto Abrante
CFO: Marilia Roure
General Manager: Jose Abrante
Estimated Sales: $1.6 Million
Number Employees: 12
Parent Co: ARA Group
Type of Packaging: Private Label
Brands:
BEKAL
REAL

4999 **Gamay Flavors**
2770 S 171st St
New Berlin, WI 53151-3510 262-785-5104
Fax: 262-789-5149 888-345-4560
dawnm@gamayflavors.com
www.gamayflavors.com
Supplier to the food industry with products such as heat stable cheese flavorings, complete flavor systems and thermostable fillings. Gamay flavors include enzyme modified cheeses, natural cheese flavors, lipolyzed butter oils andcreams, natural butter and cream flavors, starter distillate replacers, liquid flavors, sweet flavors, savory flavors, and food colors. Flavors and colors are manufactured in New Berlin, Wisconsin and shipped throughout the world.
President: Dr. Aly Gamay
Operations: Randy Cook
Estimated Sales: $1-5 Million
Number Employees: 5-9
Parent Co: Gamay Flavors

5000 **(HQ)Gambino's**
2308 Piedmont St
Kenner, LA 70062-7960 504-712-0809
Fax: 504-466-1507 www.gambinos.com
Distribution of confections, specialty cakes, Italian cookies and pastries, internet specialties, Mardi Gras packages, Doberge cakes and King Cake packaging. Every cake is baked fresh daily and we now ship overnight.
Owner: Sam Scelfo
Estimated Sales: $300,000-500,000
Number Employees: 1-4

5001 **(HQ)Gambrinus Company**
14800 San Pedro Ave
San Antonio, TX 78232-3785 210-490-9128
Fax: 210-490-9984 www.gambrinusco.com
Best known as importer of the Grupo Modelo brand portfilio for the eastern US. Also imports Moosehead Lag from Canada. Includes more than 300 corporate, sales, distribution, brewing and support personnel and markets five brandportfolios throughout the US and Caribbean. Modelo brands include Corona Extra and the fast growing Corona Light, Modelo Especial, Negra Modelo and Pacifico Clara.
President/CEO: Carlos Alvarez
CFO: James Bolz
Estimated Sales: Under $500,000
Number Employees: 50-99
Brands:
KOSMOS LAGER
LORUNITA EXTRA
MODELO ESPECIAL
NEGRA MODELO
PACIFICO CLARA
SHINER BOCK
SHINER PREMIUM

5002 **Ganong Acosta Head Office West**
One Chocolate Drive
New Brunswick, BC E3L 2X5
Canada 50- 46- 560
Fax: 506- 46- 561 888-270-8222
feedback@ganong.com www.ganong.com
Acosta branch office of Ganong Bros. Ltd., a chocolate/confectionery company that processes and exports a varity of products including bagged candy, boxed chocolate and fruit snacks, varieties of which include milk caramel, chocolatetruffles, peanut butter cups, double dipped cherries and the original chicken bones candies.
President: David Ganong
Chief Financial Officer: Doug Gaudett
VP/Chief Information Officer: Marc Lefebvre
VP/Business Development: Danay Branscombe
VP/Marketing & Sales: Greg Fash
VP/Sales United States Region: Terry Arthurs
Chief Operating Officer: David Pigott
Logistics Manager: Harold Ryan
Industrial/Custom Products/Private Label: Bryana Ganong
Number Employees: 250-499
Type of Packaging: Consumer, Private Label, Bulk

5003 **Ganong Atlantic Sales Division**
500 St. George Street
Moncton, NB E1C 1Y3
Canada 506-389-7898
Fax: 506-854-5826 888-270-8222
feedback@ganong.com www.ganong.com
Sales division office of Ganong Bros. Ltd., a chocolate/confectionery company that processes and exports a varity of products including bagged candy, boxed chocolate and fruit snacks, varieties of which include milk caramel, chocolatetruffles, peanut butter cups, double dipped cherries and the original chicken bones candies.
President: David Ganong
Chief Financial Officer: Doug Gaudett
VP/Chief Information Officer: Marc Lefebvre
VP/Business Development: Danay Branscombe
VP/Marketing & Sales: Greg Fash
VP/Sales United States Region: Terry Arthurs
Chief Operating Officer: David Pigott
Logistics Manager: Harold Ryan
Industrial/Custom Products/Private Label: Bryana Ganong
Number Employees: 250-499
Type of Packaging: Consumer, Private Label, Bulk

5004 **(HQ)Ganong Bros LimitedCorporate Office**
One Chocolate Drive
St. Stephen, NB E3L 2X5
Canada 506-465-5600
Fax: 506-465-5610 888-426-6647
feedback@ganong.com www.ganong.com
Processor and exporter of confectionery products including bagged candy, boxed chocolate and fruit snacks. Many old fashion varieties such as rich milk caramel, sinful chaocolate truffles, peanut butter cups, delicious double dippedcherries and the one and only chicken bones.
Chairman: David Ganong
President/CEO: Doug Ettinger
CFO/Treasurer: Doug Gaudett
VP/Business Development: Dana Branscombe
VP Marketing/Quality Assurance: Bryana Ganong

VP Sales: Terry Arthurs
Human Resources Director: Sherri Deveau Gibbs
COO: David Pigott
VP Manufacturing: Jeff Purcell
Plant Manager: Rob Snow
Estimated Sales: $32 Million
Number Employees: 325
Type of Packaging: Consumer, Private Label, Bulk
Brands:
BETWEEN FRIENDS PROMOTIONAL CANDY
DELECTO CHOCOLATES
FUN FRUITS FRUIT SNACKS-SUNKIST
GANONG CHICKEN BONES
GANONG CHOCOLATES
GANONG FRUITFULL
GANONG SUGAR CONFECTIONS
PAL-O-MINE CHOCOLATE BARS
SUNKIST FLAVOUR BURSTS
SUNKIST FRUIT FIRST FRUIT SNACKS
TIFFANY BAGGED CANDY
WILDFRUIT FRUIT SNACKS

5005 **Ganong Ontario and National Sales Division**
2000 Argentia Road
Mississauga, ON L5N 1P7
Canada 905-766-2244
Fax: 289- 29- 000 888-270-8222
feedback@ganong.com www.ganong.com
Ontario and National Sales Division branch office of Ganong Bros. Ltd., a chocolate/confectionery company that processes and exports a varity of products including bagged candy, boxed chocolate and fruit snacks, varieties of whichinclude milk caramel, chocolate truffles, peanut butter cups, double dipped cherries and the original chicken bones candies.
President: David Ganong
Chief Financial Officer: Doug Gaudett
VP/Chief Information Officer: Marc Lefebvre
VP/Business Development: Danay Branscombe
VP/Marketing & Sales: Greg Fash
VP/Sales United States Region: Terry Arthurs
Chief Operating Officer: David Pigott
Logistics Manager: Harold Ryan
Industrial/Custom Products/Private Label: Bryana Ganong
Number Employees: 250-499

Type of Packaging: Consumer, Private Label, Bulk

5006 **Ganong USA Division**
8170 Corporate Park Dr # 137
Cincinnati, OH 45242-3306 513-489-8439
Fax: 513-489-2728 888-270-8222
feedback@ganong.com www.ganong.com
United States regional division branch office of Ganong Bros. Ltd., a chocolate/confectionery company that processes and exports a varity of products including bagged candy, boxed chocolate and fruit snacks, varieties of which includemilk caramel, chocolate truffles, peanut butter cups, double dipped cherries and the original chicken bones candies.
President: David Ganong
Chief Financial Officer: Doug Gaudett
VP: Terry Arthurs
VP/Business Development: Danay Branscombe
VP/Marketing & Sales: Greg Fash
VP/Sales United States Region: Terry Arthurs
Chief Operating Officer: David Pigott
Logistics Manager: Harold Ryan
Industrial/Custom Products/Private Label: Bryana Ganong
Number Employees: 250-499
Type of Packaging: Consumer, Private Label, Bulk

5007 **Ganong Western Canada Division**
1400-1500 West Georgia Street
Vancouver, BC V6G 2Z6
Canada 604-688-6772
Fax: 604-688-7723 888-270-8222
feedback@ganong.com www.ganong.com
Vancouver/Western Canada Division branch office of Ganong Bros. Ltd., a chocolate/confectionery company that processes and exports a varity of products including bagged candy, boxed chocolate and fruit snacks, varieties of whichinclude milk caramel, chocolate truffles, peanut butter cups, double dipped cherries and the original chicken bones candies.
President: David Ganong
Chief Financial Officer: Doug Gaudett
VP/Chief Information Officer: Marc Lefebvre
VP/Business Development: Danay Branscombe
VP/Marketing & Sales: Greg Fash
VP/Sales United States Region: Terry Arthurs
Chief Operating Officer: David Pigott
Logistics Manager: Harold Ryan
Industrial/Custom Products/Private Label: Bryana Ganong
Number Employees: 250-499
Type of Packaging: Consumer, Private Label, Bulk

5008 **Garber Farms**
3405 Descannes Hwy
Iota, LA 70543 337-824-6328
Fax: 337-824-2676 800-824-2284
www.garbergifts.com
Processor and exporter of long grain white rice and yams
General Partner: Walter Garber
Sales/Marketing Partner: Wayne Garber
Production Manager: Earl Garber
Estimated Sales: $1-2.5 Million
Number Employees: 10-19
Sq. footage: 100000
Type of Packaging: Consumer, Food Service, Private Label, Bulk
Brands:
CREOLE CLASSIC
CREOLE DELIGHTS
CREOLE ROSE
LOUISIANA MINI

5009 **Garber Ice Cream Company**
P.O.Box 3265
Winchester, VA 22604-2465 540-662-5422
Fax: 540-722-5088 800-662-5422
Manufacturing of ice cream and frozen desserts and yogurt.
President: David Garber
Estimated Sales: $5-10 Million
Number Employees: 50-99
Type of Packaging: Consumer, Private Label

5010 **Garcias Mexican Foods**
2920 Old Norcross Road
Duluth, GA 30096-4952 770-638-0881
Fax: 770-638-1485
Mexican cuisine at its best.
Estimated Sales: $5-10 Million
Number Employees: 20-49

5011 **(HQ)Garcoa**
26135 Mureau Rd Ste 100
Calabasas, CA 91302 818-225-0375
Fax: 818-225-9251 800-831-4247
www.garcoa.com
Processor and exporter of vitamins and supplements. Manufacturer skin care, hair care, powder, oral care. Private label/contract
President: Gregory Rubin
VP/Sales: Terry Williams
Estimated Sales: $ 10 - 20 Million
Number Employees: 10-19
Sq. footage: 750000
Type of Packaging: Consumer, Private Label
Brands:
CLEAN N' NATURAL
NATURE'S BEAUTY
NATURE'S GLORY
VITAMIN CLASSICS

5012 **Garden & Valley Isle Seafood**
225 N Nimitz Hwy Unit 3
Honolulu, HI 96817 808-524-4847
Fax: 808-528-5590 800-689-2733
info@gvisfd.com www.gvisfd.com
Processor of ahi, sashimi, swordfish and snapper; importer and exporter of fresh seafood; wholesaler/distributor of smoked fish and general merchandise
President: Robert Fram
CFO: Richard Jenks
Vice President: David Marabella
Operations: Cliff Yamauchi
Estimated Sales: $13.5 Million
Number Employees: 36
Sq. footage: 9000
Type of Packaging: Bulk

5013 **(HQ)Garden Complements**
920 Cable Rd
Kansas City, MO 64116-4244 816-421-1090
Fax: 816-421-4220 800-966-1091
gardcomp@sprintmail.com www.sauceman.com
Processor of sauces including barbecue, Mexican, Italian and Asian marinades, salsas, salad dressing, gourmet products
President: Don Blackman
Marketing Director: Jim Pirotte
Estimated Sales: $1-2.5 Million
Number Employees: 5-9
Sq. footage: 15000
Type of Packaging: Consumer, Food Service, Private Label, Bulk
Brands:
AMIGO
AUSSIE
AUSSIE SAUCE
BEST CHOICE
CAMPFIRE
GAETANO'S
HERITAGE
OLD SOUTHERN
PRIMO

5014 **Garden Fresh Salsa**
1505 Bonner St
Ferndale, MI 48220 248-336-8486
Fax: 248-336-8487 866-725-7239
info@gardenfreshsalsa.com
www.gardenfreshsalsa.com
Family owned fresh made salsa company.
Owner/President: Jack Aronson
Estimated Sales: $ 5 - 10 Million
Number Employees: 10-19

5015 **Garden Protein International**
200-12751 Vulcan Way
Richmond, BC V6V 3C8 604-278-7300
Fax: 604-278-8238 877-305-6777
www.gardein.com
Manufacturer of frozen and fresh meals
President: Yves Potvin
Vice President: Ihab Leheta
VP Sales: Richard Bauman
Estimated Sales: $3 Million
Number Employees: 20-49
Type of Packaging: Food Service

5016 **Garden Row Foods**
10929 Franklin Ave # N
Franklin Park, IL 60131-1430 847-455-2200
Fax: 847-455-9100 800-555-9798
hotfood@xnet.com
Manufacturer and distribuor of hot sauces and other products, including Endorphin Rush, Pyromania, Brutal Bajan and 350 more products.
Owner: Gary Poppins
Estimated Sales: $2.5-5 Million
Number Employees: 10-19
Type of Packaging: Consumer, Food Service, Bulk
Brands:
BRUTAL BAJAN
ENDORPHIN
MONGO
PYROMANIA

5017 **Garden Row Foods**
411 Stone Drive
St Charles, IL 60174-3301 800-555-9798
Fax: 847-455-9110 800-505-9999
gardenrowfoods@eathot.com
Manufacturer and distributor of hot sauces and other products, including Engorphin Rush, Pyromania, Brutal Bajan, and 350 more products.
President: George Kosten
Number of Products: 15
Sq. footage: 2500
Parent Co: Garden Row Foods
Brands:
CARIBBEAN MARKETPLACE
GREAT GRUB RUBS
TROPICAL CHILE CO

5018 **(HQ)Garden Spot Distributors**
191 Commerce Dr
New Holland, PA 17557 717-354-4936
Fax: 717-354-4934 800-829-5100
info@gardenspotsfinest.com
www.gardenspotdist.com
Natural, organic and specialty foods. Whole grain flours, beans, raw nuts and dried fruits; frozen foods; cereals and granola; breads and baked goods; snack foods; free-range and natural meats and seafood; special-dietary foods andprepared meals including more than 400 gluten free products
President: John Clough
Marketing Coordinator: Amanda Byrd
Sales Director: Jean O'Donnell
General Manager/Operations Director: Brad Crull

Purchasing Manager: Mark Drury
Estimated Sales: $8 Million
Number Employees: 20-49
Number of Brands: 100+
Sq. footage: 20000
Type of Packaging: Consumer, Private Label, Bulk
Other Locations:
Garden Spot Distributors
Sulphur Springs AR

5019 **Garden Valley Foods**
850 Garden Valley Cir
Sutherlin, OR 97479-9860 541-459-9565
Fax: 541-459-1865 gvc@rosenet.net
Dehydrated vegetables: peas, lentils and legumes
Owner: Mark M Sterner
Estimated Sales: $2.5-5 Million
Number Employees: 10-19

5020 **Garden of the Gods Seasonings**
2028 W Cucharras St
Colorado Springs, CO 80904 719-473-5181
Fax: 719-577-4896 877-229-1548
godsseasonings@aol.com
www.godsseasonings.com
A multi-faceted gourmet company. A unique blend of seasonings and spices, plus a variety of fresh and frozen specialty foods.
President: Sandy Vanderstoup
Estimated Sales: Less than $500,000
Number Employees: 5-9

5021 **Gardenburger**
P.O.Box 160427
Clearfield, UT 84016-0427 801-773-8855
Fax: 801-773-1955 www.whfoodsco.com
Frozen veggie patties
President: Scott Wallace
Marketing: Mary Dillon
Plant Manager: David Samuelson
Estimated Sales: $25-49.9 Million
Number Employees: 5-9
Type of Packaging: Private Label, Bulk
Brands:
ALMOND CHEESE
GARDENBURGER
GARDENDOG

GARDENMEXI
GARDENSAUSAGE
GARDENSTEAK
GARDENVEGAN
GARDENVEGGIE
WHITE ALMOND BEVERAGE

5022 **Gardner Pie Company**
191 Logan Pkwy
Akron, OH 44319 330-245-2030
Fax: 330-245-2036 www.gardnerpie.com
Manufacturer of frozen pies
Owner: Robert Goff
CEO: Tom Gardner
Estimated Sales: $3-5 Million
Number Employees: 50-99
Sq. footage: 18000
Type of Packaging: Consumer, Food Service, Private Label

5023 **Gardner's Gourmet**
45450 Industrial Pl # 3
Fremont, CA 94538-6474 510-490-6106
Fax: 510-490-4563 800-676-8558
info@greatdrink.com www.greatdrink.com
Processor and exporter of frosted caffe ghiaccio, granitas, iced cappuccino and smoothie mixes, our original fruit ices, concentrates, frozen cocktails, fruit purees and flavoring syrups.
Owner: Beverly Fritz
Estimated Sales: $ 3 - 5 Million
Number Employees: 1-4
Brands:
GHIACCIO
X-TREME FREEZE

5024 **Gardners Candies**
2600 Adams Avenue
PO Box E
Tyrone, PA 16686 814-684-3925
Fax: 814-684-3928 800-242-2639
info@gardnerscandies.com
www.gardnerscandies.com
Original peanut butter meltaways®, boxed chocolates, pretzels and popcorn, brittle and roasted nuts, sugar free
Manager: Kristin Barrett
Estimated Sales: $25-49.9 Million
Number Employees: 11
Sq. footage: 6708
Type of Packaging: Consumer

5025 **Gardunos Mexican Food**
180 E 6th St
Pomona, CA 91766-3301 909-469-6611
Mexican foods
Owner: Martha Santiago
Estimated Sales: $10-100 Million
Number Employees: 1-4

5026 **Garelick Farms**
626 Lynnway
Lynn, MA 01905 781-599-1300
Fax: 781-599-7810 800-487-8700
www.deanfoods.com
Processor of milk, ice cream and juice
President: Arthur Pappathanasi
VP: Phillip Drexler
Estimated Sales: $100+ Million
Number Employees: 500-999
Parent Co: Suiza Dairy Group
Type of Packaging: Consumer, Food Service, Private Label, Bulk

5027 **(HQ)Garelick Farms**
1199 W Central St
Franklin, MA 02038 508-528-9000
Fax: 508-520-0307 800-343-4982
http://www.garelickfarms.com
Processor of milk, juice, spring water, cider and egg-nog
President: Marty Devine
Sales/Marketing: Chris Keyes
Purchasing: Steve Stewart
Number Employees: 1,000-4,999
Parent Co: Suiza Dairy Group
Type of Packaging: Consumer, Food Service
Other Locations:
Garelick Farms 508 473-0550
Mendon MA
Garelick Farms 800 343-4982
Franklin MA
Garelick Farms 800 648-0135
Burlington NJ
Brands:
ALL NATURAL
GARELICK

5028 **Garelick Farms**
504 3rd Ave Ext
Rensselaer, NY 12144 518-283-0820
Fax: 518-283-9524 www.deanfoods.com
Produces milk, chocolate milk and orange juice
VP: Chris Inzerello
Sales: Rich Gold
Plant Manager: Charles Smith
Estimated Sales: $300,000-500,000
Number Employees: 1-4
Parent Co: Suiza Dairy Group

5029 **Garlic Company**
18602 Zerker Rd
Bakersfield, CA 93314 661-393-4212
Fax: 661-393-9340 www.thegarliccompany.com
Peeled and process garlic and jalapenos to the foodservice
Marketing: Tiffany Lane
Sales: Bob Lords
Plant Manager: John Merkle
Estimated Sales: $ 50 - 100 Million
Number Employees: 100-249

5030 **Garlic Festival Foods**
P.O. Box 2309
Hollister, CA 95024 831-638-9556
Fax: 831-638-9556 888-427-5423
custserv@garlicfestival.com
www.garlicfestival.com
Processor of garlic seasoning, sauce, mustard and dressing
President: Caryl Simpson
Estimated Sales: $500,000-$1 Million
Number Employees: 5-9
Sq. footage: 10300
Parent Co: Randan Corporation
Type of Packaging: Consumer, Bulk
Brands:
GARLI GARNI
GARLIC FESTIVAL
GOURMET GOLD

5031 **Garlic Survival Company**
1094 Revere Avenue
Suite A1
San Francisco, CA 94124 415-822-7112
Fax: 415-822-6224 garlicsurv@aol.com
Garlic sauces, spices and gift packs
President: Greg Bloom
Vice President: Carl Donato
Estimated Sales: Under $500,000
Number Employees: 5
Brands:
GARLIC SURVIVAL

5032 **Garlic Valley Farms Inc**
624 Ruberta Ave
Glendale, CA 91201-2335 818-247-9600
Fax: 818-247-9828 800-424-7990
anderson@garlicvalleyfarms.com
www.garlicvalleyfarms.com
Processor, importer and exporter of liquid garlic products including juices and purees
President: William Anderson
CFO: Sonja Anderson
R&D: Bill Brock
Estimated Sales: $1.2 Million
Number Employees: 5-9
Number of Products: 2
Sq. footage: 15000
Type of Packaging: Consumer
Brands:
GARLIC JUICES

5033 **Garon Industries**
2294 County Road Db
Mosinee, WI 54455 715-693-0558
Fax: 715-693-1594 info@garonfoods.com
wwwgaronfoods.com
Manufactures peppers including jalapenos, habaneros and bell, vegetables, herbs and fruits.
President: Gary Griesbach
Estimated Sales: Under $500,000
Number Employees: 1-4
Number of Brands: 1
Type of Packaging: Bulk
Brands:
EL GUSTO

5034 **Garratt & Gunn**
3565 Airway Dr
Santa Rosa, CA 95403-1605 707-578-8192
Fax: 707-578-5221
Health foods
Owner: Duncan Garrett
Estimated Sales: Under $500,000
Number Employees: 1-4

5035 **Garrett Popcorn Shops**
676 N Saint Clair St Ste 1940
Chicago, IL 60611 312-944-4730
Fax: 312-280-9611 888-476-7267
www.garrettpopcorn.com
Several varieties of popcorn caramel crisp, cheese corn, cashew caramel crisp, macadamia caramel crisp
President: Karen Galaba
Estimated Sales: $300,000-500,000
Number Employees: 1-4
Type of Packaging: Bulk

5036 **Garry Packing**
11272 E Central Ave
PO Box 249
Del Rey, CA 93616 559-888-2126
Fax: 559-888-2848 800-248-2126
info@garrypacking.com www.garrypacking.com
Dried fruit and nuts, gift packing (trays, baskets, crates), gift components
VP/Sales Manager: James Garry
VP/COO: Jessie Garry
Estimated Sales: $1.2 Million
Number Employees: 8
Sq. footage: 100000
Type of Packaging: Consumer
Brands:
GARRY'S
GARRY'S DRIED FRUIT & NUTS

5037 **Gartner Studios**
220 East Myrtle Street
Stillwater, MN 55082 888-522-9722
duffsales@gartnerstudios.com
www.duff.com
Cakes, pastries.
Marketing: Steve Griffith

5038 **Garuda International**
180 West Chestnut Street
Exeter, CA 93221 559-594-4380
Fax: 559-594-4689 garudainfo@garudaint.com
www.garudaint.com
Manufactures ingredients derived from natural sources
President: John Matkin
Owner: Roger Matkin
Estimated Sales: $1.8 Million
Number Employees: 9

5039 **Garuda International**
P.O.Box 44380
Lemon Cove, CA 93244 559-594-4380
Fax: 559-594-4689 garudainfo@garudaint.com
www.garudaint.com
We have specialized in the development, manufacturing and the marketing of ingredients derived from natural sources for more than 23 years. Our products provide a variety of nutraceutical benefits to foods, beverages, dietarysupplements and cosmeceuticals. A well known and globally recognized for the pioneering and development of natural milk calcium in the United States. Garuda manufactures the COWCIUM® Natural Milk Calcium and the equally recognizedLesstanol®.
President/CEO: J Roger Matkin
Marketing/Sales: Bassam Faress
Estimated Sales: $500,000-$1 Million
Number Employees: 5-9
Sq. footage: 15000
Type of Packaging: Private Label, Bulk
Brands:
COWCIUM
LESSTANOL
MILCAL
MILCAL-FG
MILCAL-TG
MOO-CALCIUM
OCTACOSANOL GF
VEGe-COAT

5040 Gary Farrell Wines
PO Box 342
Santa Rosa, CA 95402-0342 707-433-6616
Fax: 707-433-9060 http://garyfarrellwines.com
Producer of a 1982 Russian River Valley Pinot Noir. Also produces premium Chardonnay, Merlot, Cabernet Sauvignon and Zinfandel.
President: Gary Farrell

5041 Gary's Frozen Foods
2311 109th St
Lubbock, TX 79423-7256 806-745-1933
Fax: 806-745-3141
Manufacturer of barbecue beef, frozen smoked beef brisket, corn dogs and super dogs
President: Buddy Tidwell
Estimated Sales: Under $500,000
Number Employees: 1
Type of Packaging: Consumer, Food Service

5042 Gaskill Seafood
124 Spencer Street
Bayboro, NC 28515 252-745-4211
Fax: 252-745-3170
Fish and shrimp
President: Clifton Gaskill
Estimated Sales: $500,000-$1 Million
Number Employees: 1-4

5043 Gaslamp Popcorn Company
330 Heron Ln
Riverside, CA 92507 951-684-6767
Fax: 619-671-5858 877-237-8276
customer.service@gaslamppopcorn.com
http://www.gaslamppopcorn.com
Popcorn and kettle corn
Senior VP: Hap Eliott
Estimated Sales: $ 1 - 3 Million
Number Employees: 10-19

5044 Gaspar's Sausage Company
384 Faunce Corner Rd
North Dartmouth, MA 02747-1257 508-998-2012
Fax: 508-998-2015 800-542-2038
gaspars@linguica.com www.linguica.com
Portugese sausage, linguica, chourico, turkey linguica and chourico, andouille, kielbasa, salapicao, chourizos and morcela
President: Charles Gaspar
Sales Director: Randy Gaspar
Plant Manager: Charles Gaspar
Estimated Sales: $6 Million
Number Employees: 47
Sq. footage: 34000
Type of Packaging: Consumer, Food Service, Private Label

5045 Gaston Dupre
1000 Italian Way
Suite 200
Excelsior Springs, MO 64024-8016 817-629-6275
Fax: 816-502-6722 mrsleepers@aipc.com
www.mrsleeperspasta.com
Wheat products - pasta
President: Terri Webb McMillin
Co-owner: Michelle Muscat
Estimated Sales: $10-20 Million
Number Employees: 20-49
Brands:
Eddie's
Michelle's

5046 Gateway Food Products Company
P.O.Box 278
Dupo, IL 62239 618-286-4844
Fax: 618-286-6706 877-220-1963
traines@gatewayfoodproducts.com
www.gatewayfoodproducts.com
Processor of syrups, vegetable oils and shortenings; exporter of corn syrup; wholesaler/distributor of general line items; also shortening flakes, popcorn oils and butter toppings
President: John Crosley
Vice President: Carroll Crosley
Quality Control: Jeremy Gray
Marketing Director: Teresa Raines
Sales Director: Teresa Raines
Operations Manager: Jeremy Gray
Production Manager: Jim Raines
Plant Manager: Jim Raines
Purchasing Manager: John Crosley
Estimated Sales: $10-20 Million
Number Employees: 10-19
Number of Products: 9
Sq. footage: 25000
Type of Packaging: Food Service, Private Label, Bulk
Brands:
DU CROSE
DU GLAZE
DU SWEET
GATEWAY - DU BAKE

5047 Gator Hammock
P.O.Box 360
Felda, FL 33930-0360 863-675-0687
Fax: 863-675-4938 800-664-2867
hotgator@iline.com www.gatorsauce.com
Manufacturer of hot and spicy sauces, dressings, mustard, cabbage, pickles, and jam. Contains no MSG - only natural ingredients.
President: Buddy Taylor
VP: David Romano, PE
Purchasing: Judy Stewart
Estimated Sales: Less than $500,000
Number Employees: 1-4
Type of Packaging: Private Label

5048 Gaucho Foods
2516 Main Avenue
Fayetteville, IL 62258 877-677-2282
Fax: 618-677-2210 mscinc@aol.com
www.gauchofoods.com
Processor of beef including frozen, barbecue, Southern-brand in barbecue sauce and regular gravy and Italian style and gravy; also, spaghetti sauce with meat
President: Jack Lachmann
Estimated Sales: $5-9.9 Million
Number Employees: 15
Sq. footage: 6000
Type of Packaging: Consumer, Food Service, Private Label, Bulk
Brands:
GAUCHO

5049 Gaudet & Ouellette
Gd Stn Main
Cap-Pele, NB E4N 2A5
Canada 506-577-4016
Fax: 506-577-4006
Processor and exporter of smoked herring
President: Normand Ouellette
Estimated Sales: $5 Million
Number Employees: 30
Type of Packaging: Bulk

5050 Gay & Robinson
P.O.Box 156
Kaumakani, HI 96747 808-335-3133
Fax: 808-335-6424 gnr@gayandrobinson.com
Sugar and condiments
President: E Alan Kennett
VP: Bruce Robinson
Estimated Sales: $20-50 Million
Number Employees: 250-499

5051 Gay's Wild Maine Blueberries
PO Box 100
Old Town, ME 04468 207-570-3535
Fax: 207-581-3499 wildblueberries@gwi.net
www.wildblueberries.com
Blueberry
President: Paul Gay

5052 Gayle's Sweet 'N Sassy Foods
269 S Beverly Dr # 472
Beverly Hills, CA 90212-3851 310-246-1792
Fax: 310-246-1794 sassybbq@aol.com
www.gaylesbbq.com
Processor of barbecue sauce
Owner: Gayle Gannes
Estimated Sales: Under $500,000
Number Employees: 5-9

5053 Gazin's
PO Box 19221
New Orleans, LA 70179-0221 504- 48-2 03
Fax: 504- 48-8 62 800-262-6410
gazins@aol.com www.gazins.com
Gumbo roux
Owner: Kary Le Fleur
Brands:
Kary's Gumbo Roux

5054 Gearharts Fine Chocolates, Inc.
416 W Main Street C
Charlottesville, VA 22903-5557 434-972-9100
Fax: 434-972-9104
info@gearhartschocolates.com
www.gearhartschocolates.com
Chocolate.
Marketing: William Hamilton

5055 Gecko Gary's
PO Box 15185
Scottsdale, AZ 85267-5185 602-765-3756
Fax: 602-765-3450 877-994-3256
gary@geckogarys.com www.geckogarys.com
Co-Owner: Gary Soultanian
Co-Owner: Cindy Soultanian

5056 Geeef America
19550 S Dominguez Hills Dr
Compton, CA 90220 310-609-2940
Fax: 310-944-9476
Gum, candy
President: Stanley Park
Brands:
BUBBLE POP
CHOCO POP
IMAGE LOLLIPOP CANDY
MAGIC POP

5057 Geetha's Gourmet of India
1589 Imperial Road
Las Cruces, NM 88011-4805 505-522-5740
Fax: 505-522-0930 800-274-0475
Processor and exporter of natural Indian pastas, sauces, marinades, chutneys, salsas, curries, lentil soup and tempura mixes, basmati rice pilaf, spiced tea, garam masala and honey sticks
President: Geetha Pai
Estimated Sales: Under $500,000
Number Employees: 5-9
Sq. footage: 4000
Type of Packaging: Consumer, Food Service
Brands:
FIESTA OLE
GEETHA'S GOURMET OF INDIA

5058 Gehl Foods, Inc.
N116 W 15970 Main Street
PO Box 1004
Germantown, WI 53022-0038 262-251-8570
Fax: 262-251-9597 800-521-2873
help@gehls.com www.gehls.com
Beverages, savory sauces, wholesome puddings, chips and jalapenos.
President: Andrew Gehl
CEO: Katherine Gehl
VP: Michael Stewart
VP Marketing: John Slawny
VP Sales: Tracy Propst
Human Resources Manager: Keri Cannestra
VP Operations: John Shaughnessy
Purchasing: Ken St Clair
Number Employees: 220
Sq. footage: 633000

5059 Gehl Guernsey Farms
P.O.Box 1004
Germantown, WI 53022-8204 262-251-8570
Fax: 262-251-8744 800-434-5713
www.gehls.com
Processor of canned puddings, cheese sauces, condensed milk, nutritional drinks and iced cappuccino
President: John Gehl
National Sales Manager: Tracy Propst
VP Operations: John Shaugnessy
Estimated Sales: $20-50 Million
Number Employees: 100-249
Sq. footage: 60000
Type of Packaging: Food Service
Brands:
GEHL MAINSTREAM CAFE
GEHL'S GOURMET

5060 Gel Spice Company, Inc
48 Hook Rd
Bayonne, NJ 7002 201-339-0700
Fax: 201-339-0024 800-922-0230
jacob@gelspice.com www.gelspice.com
A full line of bulk, food service and retail spices, seeds and bakery ingredients.
President: Andre Engle
Vice President: Jacob Engel
Marketing Director: Sherman Engel
Purchasing Manager: Gershon Engel

Number Employees: 100-249
Sq. footage: 250000
Type of Packaging: Consumer, Food Service, Private Label, Bulk

5061 **Gelati Celesti**
612 Meyer Ln Ste 2
Redondo Beach, CA 90278 310-372-2593
Fax: 310-798-0043 800-550-7550
www.gelaticelesti.com
Processor of gelati, sorbets and gelato truffles
President: Steve Edmonds
Estimated Sales: $2.5-5 Million
Number Employees: 10-19
Type of Packaging: Consumer, Food Service, Private Label, Bulk
Brands:
GELATI CELESTI

5062 **Gelato Fresco**
60 Tycos Drive
Toronto, ON M6B 1V9
Canada 416-785-5415
Fax: 416-781-3133 www.gelatofresco.com
Processor of natural ice cream, sorbet and tartufo
President: Hart Melvin
Estimated Sales: $1.3 Million
Number Employees: 5
Sq. footage: 10000
Type of Packaging: Consumer, Food Service
Brands:
GELATO FRESCO

5063 **Gelato Giuliana LLC**
240 Sargent Drive
110 Terminal Plaza
New Haven, CT 06511 203-772-0607
Fax: 203-772-0612 gelatogiuliana@sbcglobal.net
www.gelatogiuliana.com
gelatos and flavored gelatos
President/Owner: Giuliana Maravalle

5064 **Gelita USA**
2445 Port Neal Industrial Road
Sergeant Bluff, IA 51054 712-943-5516
Fax: 712-943-3372 service.na@gelita.com
www.gelita.com
Research, manufacture and marketing of high-quality gelatines
President: Jorg Siebert
VP Finance: Robert Mayberry
VP Manufacturing: Tom Kennan
Estimated Sales: $ 50-100 Million
Number Employees: 250
Sq. footage: 450000
Brands:
Gelita

5065 **(HQ)Gelita/Kind & Knox Gelatine**
2445 Port Neal Rd
Sergeant Bluff, IA 51054-7728 712-943-5516
Fax: 712-943-3372 service.na@gelita.com
www.gelita.com
Processor of gelatine.
President: Jorg Siebert
Pre-Sec-Treas/Vp Finanace: Rob Mayberry
VP Communications: Michael Teppner
Research & Development: Dr J Michael Dunn
National Sales/Marketing Manager: John Harty
Sales Director: George Riejenfeld
Number Employees: 250
Brands:
GELITA

5066 **Gelnex Gelatins**
1615 Northern Blvd
Suite 101
Manhasset, NY 11030 516-869-1623
Fax: 516-869-1057 fchaluppe@gelnex.com
www.gelnex.com
Manufacturer of high quality gelatins
President: Alessandro Luize
CEO: Ross Priebbenow
Executive VP: Felipe Chaluppe
Estimated Sales: $500,000-1 Million
Number Employees: 4

5067 **Gelsinger Food Products**
2209 Honolulu Ave
Montrose, CA 91020-1616 818-248-7811
Fax: 818-957-2545
Frozen and refrigerated beef, game meats, lamb, pork, veal, smoked meats, poultry, cured meats, cooked meats
President: Ron Gelsinger
Sales/Marketing Manager: Kirk Gelsinger
Estimated Sales: $2.5-5 Million
Number Employees: 20-49

5068 **(HQ)Gem Berry Products**
804 Airport Way
Sandpoint, ID 83864 208-263-7503
Fax: 208-263-3247 800-426-0498
gemberry92@hotmail.com
Jams, jellies, syrups, gift packs
President: Jack O' Brien
Sales Director: Harry Menser
Production Manager: Elizabeth O'Brien
Estimated Sales: $500,000-$1 Million
Number Employees: 1-4
Type of Packaging: Private Label

5069 **Gem Meat Packing Company**
515 E 45th St
Boise, ID 83714 208-375-9424
Fax: 208-375-1568 gempackonline@live.com
www.gempackonline.com
Processor and packer of beef, pork and sausages including kitchen cured and smoked; slaughtering services available
Owner: Brent Compton
Estimated Sales: $ 7 Million
Number Employees: 20-49

5070 **Gemini Food Industries**
25 Trolley Crossing Rd
Charlton, MA 01507 508-248-2730
Processor and importer of frozen foods including marinated, breaded and battered chicken, par-baked and full-baked goods, cooked and sliced beef, boil-bag sauces and soups and glazed, breaded and battered seafood; importer of baby backribs, riblets, etc
President: Warren Kenniston
Chairman/CEO: Robert Gibson
Estimated Sales: $500,000-999,999
Number Employees: 10-19
Sq. footage: 7500
Type of Packaging: Consumer, Food Service, Private Label, Bulk

5071 **Genarom International**
6 Santa Fe Way
Cranbury, NJ 08512-3288 609-409-6200
Fax: 609-409-6500 www.conagrafoods.com
Processor and exporter of marinades, sauces and flavors including beef, chicken, turkey, pork, ham, cheese, seafood and creams
President: Bob Gallatine
Co-Founder/Chairman: Werner Hiller
Number Employees: 20-49
Sq. footage: 30000
Type of Packaging: Food Service, Bulk
Brands:
DOHLAR
GENAROM

5072 **Gene & Boots Candies**
2939 Pittsburgh Rd
Perryopolis, PA 15473 724-736-8959
800-864-4222
customerservice@geneandboots.com
www.geneandboots.com
Chocolates and old fashion ice cream
President: Bob Ferguson
Estimated Sales: $5-9.9 Million
Number Employees: 4
Sq. footage: 4098
Type of Packaging: Consumer

5073 **Gene Belk Fruit Packers**
10380 Alder Ave
Bloomington, CA 92316 909-877-1819
Fax: 909-877-2460
Fruit and vegetable by-products
Manager: Curtis Belk
Estimated Sales: $20-50 Million
Number Employees: 20-49

5074 **Gene's Citrus Ranch**
7672 15th St E
Sarasota, FL 34243-3213
Fax: 941-723-3620 888-723-2006
www.citrusranch.com
Grower of oranges and grapefruit; processor of fresh orange and grapefruit juice
President: Gene Mixon
Estimated Sales: $10-20 Million
Number Employees: 10-19
Type of Packaging: Consumer, Food Service

5075 **Genencor International**
2600 Kennedy Dr
Beloit, WI 53511 608-365-1112
Fax: 608-365-4526 www.genencor.com
Manufacturer and exporter of carbohydrate enzymes for wet milling, baking, brewing, etc
Chairman/CEO: Robert Mayer
President: Thomas Pekich
SVP Technology: Michael Arbige PhD
SVP Global Supply: Carol Beth Cobb
Estimated Sales: $ 10 - 20 Million
Number Employees: 10-19
Parent Co: Danisco Company
Type of Packaging: Bulk
Brands:
G-ZYME

5076 **General Henry Biscuit Company**
300 Bakery Blvd
Du Quoin, IL 62832-4414 618-542-6222
Fax: 618-542-5099
Biscuits, breads, rolls
Plant Manager: Steven Scaff
Estimated Sales: $ 50 - 100 Million
Number Employees: 100-249

5077 **General Mills**
704 W Washington St
West Chicago, IL 60185 630-231-1140
Fax: 630-231-6968 800-248-7310
www.generalmills.com
Branch division manufacturers cereals, foods preparations and pasta products.
Chairman/Chief Executive Officer: Stephen Sanger
President/Chief Operating Officer: Kendall Powell
Vice Chairman/Chief Financial Officer: James Lawrence
SVP/General Counsel & Governance: Siri Marshall
SVP/Strategic Technology Development: Rory Delaney
SVP/External Relations: Christina Shea
SVP/Human Resources & Corporate Services: Michael Peel
Parent Co: General Mills Inc
Type of Packaging: Food Service

5078 **(HQ)General Mills**
P.O.Box 1113
Minneapolis, MN 55440 763-764-7600
Fax: 763-764-7384 800-248-7310
www.generalmills.com
Manufacturer and exporter of ready-to-eat breakfast cereals, dry packaged dessert, main meal and side dish mixes, fruit and grain snacks, microwave popcorn, flour, baking mixes, refrigerated and soft-frozen yogurt, food serviceproducts and bakery flours.
President/Ceo: Kendall Powell
EVP/CFO: Donal Mulligan
VP: Jon Nudi
SVP/Chief Marketing Officer: Mark Addicks
SVP Retail Sales: Shawn O'Grady
SVP/Global Human Resources: Michael Davis
Financial Operations: Keith Woodward
Estimated Sales: $3.65 Billion
Number Employees: 33,000
Type of Packaging: Consumer, Food Service
Other Locations:
General Mills
Covington GA
General Mills
Chelsea MA
General Mills
Swedesboro NJ
General Mills
Chanhassen MN
Brands:
BETTY CROCKER
BIG G CEREALS
BIG T BURGERS
BISQUICK
BUGLES
CASCADIAN FARM
CHEERIOS
CHEX

CINNAMON TOAST CRUNCH
DIABLITOS UNDERWOOD
FIBER ONE
FRESCARINI
FRUIT SNACKS
GARDETTO'S
GOLD MEDAL
GREEN GIANT
HAAGEN-DAZS
HAMBURGER HELPER
JUS-ROL
KIX
KNACK & BACK
LA SALTENA
LARABAR
LATINA
LUCKY CHARMS
MACARONI GRILL
MONSTERS
MUIR GLEN
NATURE VALLEY
OLD EL PASO
PILLSBURY
PILLSBURY ATTA
PROGRESSO
TOTAL
TOTINO'S/JENO'S
TRIX
V.PEARL
WANCHAI FERRY
WHEATIES
YOPLAIT

5079 General Mills
300 Reliance Ave
Federalsburg, MD 21632 410-754-5000
Fax: 410-479-3980 www.generalmills.com
Manufacturer of specialty crumbs and croutons
Chairman/CEO: Stephen Sanger
President/COO: Kendall Powell
Vice Chairman/CFO: James Lawrence
EVP/CTO Worldwide Ops & Technology: Randy Darcy
EVP/Worldwide Health/New Business Dvlpmt: Y Marc Belton
EVP/Worldwide Sales/Channel Development: Jeffrey Rotsch
EVP/COO International: Christopher O'Leary
EVP/COO US Retail: Ian Friendly
Estimated Sales: $50-100 Million
Number Employees: 500-999
Parent Co: General Mills
Type of Packaging: Food Service, Bulk

5080 General Spice
238 Saint Nicholas Avenue
South Plainfield, NJ 07080-1810 908-753-9100
Fax: 908-753-9635 800-345-7742
khillerl@crfc.com
Food development, fire roasted, sauteed and roasted vegetable bases, Kosher meat flavors and bases, glazes and marinades
President: Werner Hiller
Co-Owner: Dagmar Hiller Laramie
Number Employees: 10-19
Type of Packaging: Bulk

5081 General Taste Bakery
5830 Triangle Dr
Commerce, CA 90040-3637 323-888-2170
Estimated Sales: Less than $500,000
Number Employees: 1-4

5082 Generation Farms
1109 NE McKinney St
Rice, TX 75155 903-326-4263
Fax: 903-326-6511 generationfarms@pflash.com
www.generationfarms.com
Grower of fresh culinary herbs and edible flowers
President: Ethan Milkes
Estimated Sales: $ 5 - 10 Million
Type of Packaging: Food Service, Private Label, Bulk

5083 Generation Foods Too
20969 Ventura Blvd
Woodland Hills, CA 91364-2305 818-887-5858
Fax: 626-331-0040
Candy
Owner: David Ginsberg
VP: Steffani Corri-Dolivo
Director Of Sales: Scott Corri
Estimated Sales: $ 10 - 20 Million
Number Employees: 20-49
Brands:
MOUTH FOAMING GUMBALLS
SHAVING CREAM CANDY FUN FOAM
SOUR LIQUID CANDY
SOUR POWDER CANDY

5084 Generation Tea
6 Sydell Ln
Spring Valley, NY 10977 845-352-1216
Fax: 845-352-2973 866-742-5668
contact@generationtea.com
www.generationtea.com
Manufacturer of premium whole leaf chinese tea - contains no additives or preservatives
President/Co-Owner: Michael Sanft
Co-Owner: Marci Sanft
Estimated Sales: $300,000-500,000
Number Employees: 1-4

5085 (HQ)Genesee Farms
33 S Main St
Oakfield, NY 14125 585-948-9418
President: Alvin Scrogen
Manager: Pam Morre
Estimated Sales: $10-20 Million
Number Employees: 100-249
Sq. footage: 18
Type of Packaging: Private Label

5086 Genesis Research Corporation
918 Sherwood Drive
Lake Bluff, IL 60044-2204 847-810-3416
Fax: 847-234-5545 888-225-2201
www.genesisresearchonline.com
CEO: Mark Nottoli
Marketing Director: Bill Froese
Purchasing Manager: Ernie Hughes
Type of Packaging: Private Label, Bulk

5087 Geneva Foods
119 Commerce Way, Ste B
Sanford, FL 32771 407-323-5518
Fax: 407-323-4394 800-240-2326
www.lysanders.com
Dried beans, soups, marinades, dip mixes and seasoning blends
President: Tom Vandermar
Senior Partner: Gary Clark
Partner: Angie Fontes
Estimated Sales: $10-20 Million
Number Employees: 14

5088 (HQ)Geneva Ingredients
413 Moravian Valley Rd
Waunakee, WI 53597 608-849-9440
Fax: 608-850-3762 800-828-5924
www.mastertaste.com
Processor and exporter of flavors including butter, fish, meat, pork, poultry, seafood and vegetable
President: Warren Meyer
VP Technical Service: Jay Wickeham
Estimated Sales: $20-50 Million
Number Employees: 20-49
Type of Packaging: Bulk
Other Locations:
Geneva Ingredients
Union NJ

5089 Geni
1250 Conner St # 201
Noblesville, IN 46060-2900 317-219-0355
Fax: 317-776-3750 888-656-4364
info@geniherbs.com www.geniherbs.com
Boswellia Serrata Extract
Owner/President/CEo: Ajay Patel
Research & Development: Dr Lal Hingorani
Marketing Director: Sonya Bucklew
Sales Director: Nipen Lavingia
Estimated Sales: $ .5 - 1 million
Number Employees: 10-19
Number of Brands: 2
Number of Products: 30
Brands:
WOKVEL

5090 GeniSoy
100 W 5th Street
Suite 700
Tulsa, OK 74103 918-728-8702
Fax: 918-728-2850 800-228-4656
contactgenisoy@genisoy.com www.genisoy.com
Bars, shakes and powders and snacks made from soy.
CFO: Scott Simon
VP Sales/Marketing: Jan Grywczynski
Human Resources: Alice Kirk
Type of Packaging: Consumer

5091 Genisoy Food Company
100 W 5th Street
Suite 700
Tulsa, OK 74103 866-606-3829
888-437-4769
Contactgenisoy@genisoy.com www.genisoy.com
Mission is to provide convenient, delicious and affordable soy products that make it easy to incorporate the benefits of soy in the average person's everyday diet. Products include bars, shakes, powders, soy nuts, trail mixes, soycrisps, potato soy crisps and low carb bars.
Founder/President: Paul Wenner
CFO: Scott Simon
Type of Packaging: Food Service

5092 Genisoy Products Company
100 W. 5th Street,Suite 700
Suite C
Tulsa, OK 74103 800-228-4656
Fax: 707-399-2518 800-228-4656
info@mloproducts.com www.mloproducts.com
Mission is to provide convenient, delicious and affordable soy products that make it easy to incorporate the benefits of soy in the average person's everday diet. Products include bars, shakes, powders, soy nuts, trail mixes, soycrisps, potato soy crisps and low carb bars.
President/CEO: Doug Williamson
CFO: Al Larson
Director Of Marketing: Sharon Jacobson
VP Sales/Marketing: Duke Field
Estimated Sales: $ .5 - 1 million
Number Employees: 350
Brands:
GENISOY SOY PRODUCTS
MLO SPORTS NUTRITION

5093 Gentile Brothers Company
10310 Julian Dr
Cincinnati, OH 45215-1131 513-531-6000
Fax: 513-771-5569 800-877-7954
www.gentilebros.com
Serving and processor of quality produce to the retail chains and foodservice distributors around the world
President/COO: Ed Sabin
CEO: Glen Bryant
West Virginia Sales Director: Ernie Coe
Director Marketing: Tom Rettig
VP Sales/Logistics: Dave Schirman
Sales/Product Manager: Chris Deier
Specialist/Banana/Pineapple: Jim Flehmer
Type of Packaging: Consumer

5094 Gentilini's Italian Products
55415 Lazy River Dr
Sunriver, OR 97707-2539 541-593-5053
Fax: 541-593-5609 pasta@teleport.com
www.gentilinis.com
Processor of fresh pastas including egg and gluten-free, fettucine, angel hair, linguine, seafood and herb and vegetable stuffed, cheese free pesto, fresh tomato sauce; also, sauces including pesto, marinara and alfredo; gift basketsavailable
Owner: Wesley Vinc Acker
Co-Owner: Becky Gentilini
Estimated Sales: $5-10 Million
Number Employees: 1-4
Sq. footage: 5000

5095 Gentle Ben's Brewing Company
P.O.Box 3458
Tucson, AZ 85722 520-624-4177
Fax: 520-884-9776 www.gentlebens.com
Manufacturing of beer and ale
President: Dennis Arnold
Estimated Sales: $1-2.5 Million
Number Employees: 50-99
Type of Packaging: Private Label
Brands:
Copperhead Pale Ale
Gentle Ben Winter Brau
Nolan Porter
Red Cat Amber
Taylor Jane's Raspberry Ale
Tucson Blonde

5096 **Gentry's Poultry Company**
262 Speigner Rd
Ward, SC 29166 803-254-8724
Fax: 864-445-2331 800-926-2161
Processor of poultry
President: Wesley Gentry Jr Jr
VP: Wesley Gentry III III
Estimated Sales: $ 5 - 10 Million
Number Employees: 5-9
Type of Packaging: Consumer, Food Service

5097 **Geon Technologies**
35 Melanie Ln
Whippany, NJ 07981-1638 973-929-3700
Fax: 973-889-4340 800-467-3041
support@trimspa.com www.trimspa.com
Nutritional Supplements
President: Alex Goen
Public Relations Specialist: Chrissy Kulig
Estimated Sales: $ 20 - 50 Million
Number Employees: 100-249
Brands:
TrimSpa
Winsuel

5098 **George A Dickel & Company**
Po Box 1448
Tullahoma, TN 37388
888-342-5352
www.dickel.com
Processor of whiskey
Master Distiller: John Lunn
Plant Manager: Jennings Backus
Estimated Sales: $10-20 Million
Number Employees: 20-49
Parent Co: Guiness PLC
Type of Packaging: Consumer

5099 **George A Jeffreys & Company**
504 Roanoke St
Salem, VA 24153-3552 540-389-8220
Fax: 540-387-7418 www.novozymes.com
Manufacturer and exporter of enzymes
Manager: Doug Acksel
Estimated Sales: $5-10 Million
Number Employees: 10-19
Sq. footage: 50000

5100 **George Braun Oyster Company**
30840 Main Rd
Cutchogue, NY 11935 631-734-7770
Fax: 631-734-7462
Processor and distributor of oysters
Estimated Sales: $2.5-5 Million
Number Employees: 20-49

5101 **George Chiala Farms**
15500 Hill Rd
Morgan Hill, CA 95037-9516 408-778-0562
Fax: 408-779-4034 georgejr@gcfarm-inc.com
www.gcfarmsinc.com
Processor of tomatillos, garlic and peppers including jalapeno, chile, bell, habanero, kosher, organic, etc
President: George Chiala
CFO: Alan Chiala
Marketing/Sales: George Chiala, Jr
Sales Director: Don Hall
Plant Manager: Pat Connelly
Estimated Sales: $20-50 Million
Number Employees: 100-249
Number of Products: 300
Sq. footage: 40000
Type of Packaging: Food Service, Bulk

5102 **George E De Lallo Company**
6390 State Route 30
Jeannette, PA 15644 724-523-5000
Fax: 724-523-0198 800-307-0198
delallo@delallo.com www.delallo.com
Importer and packer of Italian foods including pasta, sauces, grocery products, olives, oils, etc
President: Francis De Lallo
Purchasing Agent: J Panichella
Estimated Sales: $500,000-$1 Million
Number Employees: 5-9
Type of Packaging: Consumer

5103 **George F Brocke & Sons**
P.O.Box 159
Kendrick, ID 83537 208-289-4231
Fax: 208-289-4242
Garbanzo beans, rapeseed
President: George Brocke
General Manager: Dean Brocke
Estimated Sales: $10-20 Million
Number Employees: 20-49

5104 **George H Hathaway Coffee Company**
6210 S Archer Rd
Summit Argo, IL 60501 708-458-7668
Fax: 708-458-7668
Coffee
President: B Gordon

5105 **George H Leidenheimer Baking**
1501 Simon Bolivar Ave
New Orleans, LA 70113-2399 504-525-1575
Fax: 504-525-1596 800-259-9099
www.leidenheimer.com
Bread, rolls
President: Robert J Whann Iv III
Estimated Sales: $10-20 Million
Number Employees: 50-99

5106 **George L. Wells Meat Company**
982 North Delaware Avenue
Philadelphia, PA 19123 215-627-3903
Fax: 215-922-7648 800-523-1730
www.wellsmeats.com
Processor of beef, pork, veal, seafood, frozen vegetables, frozen desserts, butter, eggs and processed chicken
President/Owner: James Conboy
VP Sales/Marketing: Shawn Padgett
Estimated Sales: $100-500 Million
Number Employees: 50-99

5107 **George Noroian**
1133 N Wheeler Ridge Rd
Arvin, CA 93203-9777 661-858-2457
Fax: 661-858-2656
Processor of canned peaches including white nectar, Elberta and organic; also, frozen peach puree and canned and frozen orange slices
Proprietor: George Noroian
Estimated Sales: $1-2.5 Million
Number Employees: 5-9
Sq. footage: 100000

5108 **George Richter Farm**
4512 70th Ave E
Fife, WA 98424 253-922-5649
Fax: 253-926-0621
Grower, processor and exporter of fresh and frozen raspberries, blackberries, tayberries and nectarberries; also, currants and rhubarb
President: George Richter
Estimated Sales: $100+ Million
Number Employees: 10-19
Number of Brands: 1
Sq. footage: 6000
Type of Packaging: Consumer, Food Service
Brands:
RICHTERS

5109 **George Robberecht Seafood**
440 McGuires Wharf Rd
Montross, VA 22520 804-472-3556
Fax: 804-472-4800
Processor and exporter of live blue crab, soft-shell crab, oyster meats, eel, croaker, spot, and striped bass.
President/CEO: Maurice Bosse
Estimated Sales: $2.5-5 Million
Number Employees: 1-4

5110 **George W Saulpaugh & Sons**
1790 Route 9
Germantown, NY 12526 518-537-6500
Fax: 518-537-5555
Processor and exporter of apples, pears, grapes and prunes
President: Alan Saulpaugh
VP: David Jones
Estimated Sales: $10-20 Million
Number Employees: 20-49
Type of Packaging: Consumer, Food Service, Bulk
Brands:
CLERMONT

5111 **George's**
P.O.Box G
Springdale, AR 72765 479-927-7500
Fax: 479-927-7525 877-855-3447
jlossing@george'sinc.com
Frozen chickens whole raw, chicken parts, chicken prepared
President: Monty Henderson
CEO: Gary George
Executive VP: Otto Jech
Field Operations Manager: Fred Edwards
Plant Manager: Pat Mareth
Estimated Sales: $50-100 Million
Number Employees: 50-99
Type of Packaging: Private Label
Brands:
GEORGE'S
TASTE O'SPRIING

5112 **Georges Chicken**
19992 Senedo Rd
Edinburg, VA 22824-3172 540-984-4121
Fax: 540-984-8360 866-444-2449
Manufacturer and exporter of fresh and frozen turkey and chicken including whole, without giblets, livers, legs, leg quarters, pieces and hot dogs
President: Robert Kenney
Contact: Gary Richman
Estimated Sales: $100+ Million
Number Employees: 1,000-4,999
Sq. footage: 130000
Parent Co: Rocco
Type of Packaging: Consumer, Food Service, Bulk

5113 **(HQ)Georgetown Farm**
P.O.Box 106
Free Union, VA 22940 434-973-6761
Fax: 434-973-7715 888-328-5326
info@georgetownfarm.com www.eatlean.com
Processor of piedmontese beef and bison meat including sausage and jerky products
Production: Craig Gibson
Plant Manager: Matt Albert
Estimated Sales: $3-5 Million
Number Employees: 5-9
Brands:
GEORGETOWN FARM BISON
GEORGETOWN FARM PIEDMONTESE

5114 **Georgetown Fisherman's Co-Op**
79 Moores Tpke
Georgetown, ME 04548 207-371-2950
Fax: 207-371-2907
Seafood
Manager: Mohamed Khan
Estimated Sales: $ .5 - 1 million
Number Employees: 1-4

5115 **Georgia Fruit Cake Company**
5 S Duval St
Claxton, GA 30417-2027 912-739-2683
Fax: 912-739-3419
www.georgiafruitcakecompany.com
Processor and exporter of canned fruit cakes
President: Ira S Womble Jr
CEO: Ira Womble Jr
Estimated Sales: $5-10 Million
Number Employees: 5-9
Number of Brands: 2
Number of Products: 2
Sq. footage: 10000
Type of Packaging: Consumer
Brands:
GEORGIA
GEORGIA FRUIT CAKE

5116 **Georgia Nut Company**
7500 Linder Ave
Skokie, IL 60077 847-324-3635
Fax: 847-674-1173 800-621-1264
www.georgianut.com
Processor of nut meats and candies including malted milk balls, chocolate raisins, double dip peanuts and coated pretzels
CEO: Rick Drehobl
VP Sales & Marketing: Rick Lytle
Sales Manager: Steve Coryea
Estimated Sales: $20-50 Million
Number Employees: 100-249
Type of Packaging: Private Label
Brands:
DRIZZLS!
GEORGIA'S
MALT TEENIES
SPECKLS!
TEENIES

5117 **Georgia Nut Ingredients**
7500 Linder Ave
Skokie, IL 60077-3270 847-324-3600
Fax: 847-674-1173 877-674-2993
sgi@solofoods.com www.georgianuts.com
Processor of fruit and nut fillings, European pastry fillings, marshmallow creme, toffees, malt balls, brittles, etc
President: Tom Musso
Marketing Manager: Alet Schneider
R & D: Carol Anderson
CEO: Richard A Drehobl
CFO: Rick Trehobl
CFO: Arends Jack
Estimated Sales: $ 20-50 Million
Number Employees: 100-249
Sq. footage: 2000
Parent Co: Georgia Nut Company
Type of Packaging: Bulk
Brands:
Georgia's
Solo

5118 **Georgia Seafood Wholesale**
5634 New Peachtree Rd
Chamblee, GA 30341 770-936-0483
Fax: 770-936-9332
Scallops, frozen seafood, shrimp
Owner: Jack Wong
Estimated Sales: $ 3 - 5 Million
Number Employees: 5-9

5119 **Georgia Spice Company**
3600 Atlanta Industrial Parkway
Atlanta, GA 30331 404-696-6200
Fax: 404-696-4546 800-453-9997
gaspice@aol.com
Processor, importer and exporter of blended spices and seasonings for snacks, poultry and meat; also, custom blending and kosher available
Owner/CEO/Plant Manager: Selma Shapiro
R&D Director: Brian Lusty
Human Resources Director: S Lafosse
Manufacturing Director: Bob Kupinsky
Estimated Sales: $5 Million
Number Employees: 19
Sq. footage: 39000
Type of Packaging: Food Service, Private Label, Bulk

5120 **Georgia Sun**
50 Amlajack Blvd
Newnan, GA 30265 770-251-2500
Processor and importer of beverage bases and juice concentrates
President: Walter Loesche
Estimated Sales: Less than $500,000
Number Employees: 1-4
Sq. footage: 40000
Type of Packaging: Consumer, Food Service, Private Label, Bulk
Brands:
Georgia Sun

5121 **Georgia Vegetable Company**
P.O.Box 2037
Tifton, GA 31793-2037 229-386-2374
Fax: 229-386-2500
georgiavegetable@surfsouth.com
Processor of produce including snap beans, pole beans, cabbage, corn, cucumbers, eggplant, peppers, squash, etc
President: Billy Thomas
Co-Owner: Rebecca Kilby
Co-Owner: Shay Briggs
Estimated Sales: $5-10 Million
Number Employees: 10-19
Type of Packaging: Consumer, Bulk

5122 **Georgia Winery**
6469 Battlefield Pkwy
Ringgold, GA 30736 706-937-2177
info@georgiawines.com
www.georgiawines.com
Winery - red wines such as: concord, blackberry, raspberry, roses and blushes and white wines
President: Martha Prouty
Estimated Sales: $5-10 Million
Number Employees: 15

5123 **Georis Winery**
4 Pilot Rd
Carmel Valley, CA 93924 831-659-1050
Fax: 831-659-1054 info@georiswine.com
www.georiswine.com
Grows, producers and bottles only the finest Merlot and Cabernet Sauvignon wines.
President: Walter Georis
Purchasing: Sylvia Georis
Estimated Sales: $500,000-$1 Million
Number Employees: 5-9
Type of Packaging: Private Label
Brands:
ESTATE CABERNET SAUVIGNON
ESTATE MERLOT

5124 **Gerard's French Bakery**
4226 County Road 22
Longmont, CO 80504-9403 303-772-4710
Fax: 303-581-0212 gerard@aol.com
Processor of focaccia, sourdough, baked and par-baked breads, croissants and hamburger buns
President: Gerry Watson
VP Operations: Gary Hoerner
Estimated Sales: $20-50 Million
Number Employees: 100-249
Parent Co: Mountain View Harvest Cooperative
Type of Packaging: Food Service, Private Label
Brands:
GERARD'S FRENCH BAKERY
MOUNTAINVIEW HARVEST BAKERY

5125 **Gerawan Farming**
15749 E Ventura Ave
Sanger, CA 93657 559-787-8780
Fax: 559-787-8798 primasales@gerawan.com
www.gerawan.com
Grower and exporter of grapes and tree fruit
President: Dan Gerawan
Sales Manager: Karen Osborn
Estimated Sales: $100-500 Million
Number Employees: 50-99
Type of Packaging: Bulk
Brands:
PRIMA

5126 **(HQ)Gerber Products Company**
200 Kimball Dr
Parsippany, NJ 7054 973-503-8000
Fax: 973-503-8450 800-443-7237
www.novartis.com
More than 350 Gerber and NUK branded products. Processor and importer of banana flakes, essence and nonhomogenized frozen banana purees and concentrates. Aseptic, organic, kosher and homogenized available. ISD-9002 certified, HACCPmonitored
President/CEO: Frank Palantoni
CFO: Kurt Furger
CEO: Larry Allgaire
VP R&D/Quality Control: Jan Relford
Marketing Director: David Yates
Public Relations: Terry Boylan
Number Employees: 100-249
Parent Co: Novartis Consumer Health
Type of Packaging: Food Service, Bulk
Brands:
GERBER 1ST FOODS
GERBER 2ND FOODS
GERBER 3RD FODOS
GERBER GRADUATES

5127 **Gerber Products Company**
26 Lote
Carolina, PR 00984 787-769-7745
Baby foods
Parent Co: Gerber Products Company

5128 **Gerbers Poultry**
P.O.Box 206
Kidron, OH 44636-0206 330-857-2731
Fax: 330-857-1841 800-362-7381
mgerber@gerbers.com www.gerbers.com
Processor of poultry
President: D Michael Gerber
Controller: John Metzger CPA
VP Sales/Distribution: Timothy Gerber
Estimated Sales: $20-50 Million
Number Employees: 250-499

5129 **Gerhard's Napa Valley Sausage**
910 Enterprise Way
Napa, CA 94558-6209 707-252-4116
Fax: 707-252-0879 gnvs@jps.net
www.gerhardsausage.com
Processor of gourmet sausage
Owner: Gerhard Twele
Estimated Sales: $10-20 Million
Number Employees: 50-99
Sq. footage: 27000
Type of Packaging: Consumer

5130 **Gerhart Coffee Company**
224 Wohlsen Way
Lancaster, PA 17603 717-397-8788
Fax: 717-397-3677 800-536-4310
sales@gerhartcoffee.com
www.gerhartcoffee.com
Processor of coffee that is available in decaf, flavored and blended. Food service available to: hotels, coffee houses, fund raisers, schools and colleges, bagel shops, grocery stores, gift shops, etc.
Owner/President: Charles Braungard
Representative: Donald Platt
Representative: Darrel Burns
Representative: Peter Bard
Estimated Sales: $1-2.5 Million
Number Employees: 1-4
Sq. footage: 4200

5131 **Gerhart Coffee Company**
224 Wohlsen Way
Lancaster, PA 17603 717-397-8788
Fax: 717-397-3677 800-536-4310
www.gerhartcoffee.com
Coffee
President: Charles Braungard
Sales Director: Charles Braungard
Estimated Sales: $1-2.5 Million
Number Employees: 1-4
Type of Packaging: Private Label

5132 **Gerkens CacaoWilbur Chocolate Company**
20 N Broad Street
Lititz, PA 17543-1005 717-626-3450
Fax: 717-626-3488 800-233-0139
gerkenscocao@cargill.com
www.gerkenscocoa.com
Manufacturer of chocolate
President: William Shaughnessy
Parent Co: Cargill Incorporated

5133 **Germack Pistachio Company**
2140 Wilkins St
Detroit, MI 48207 313-393-2000
Fax: 313-393-0636 800-872-4006
questions@germack.com www.germack.com
Processor and importer of dried fruit, chocolate and nuts including cashews, filberts, peanuts and pistachios
Owner: Frank Germack
Estimated Sales: $1-2.5 Million
Number Employees: 20-49
Type of Packaging: Consumer, Food Service

5134 **Germain-Robin**
P.O.Box 1059
Ukiah, CA 95482 707-462-0314
Fax: 707-462-8885 800-782-8145
alambic@pacific.net www.germain-robin.com
Distiller and exporter of brandy. Marketing of specialty spirits
President: Ansley J Coale Jr
Estimated Sales: $1-2.5 Million
Number Employees: 10-19
Sq. footage: 20000
Type of Packaging: Consumer, Private Label

5135 **Germain-Robin/Alambic**
P.O.Box 175
Ukiah, CA 95482-0175 707-462-0314
Fax: 707-462-8885
Distilled spirits
President: Ansley J Coale Jr
Co-Founder: Hubert Germain-Robin
Estimated Sales: $1-2.5 Million
Number Employees: 1-4
Type of Packaging: Private Label

5136 **German Bakery at Village Corner**
6655 James B Rivers Dr
Stone Mountain, GA 30083-2232 770-498-0329
Fax: 770-498-9863 866-476-6443
germanrestaurant@aol.com
www.germanrestaurant.com
Full line of bakery products, breads and rolls
Owner: Hilde Friese
Co-Owner: Clause Friese

Estimated Sales: $ 1 - 3 Million
Number Employees: 10-19
Brands:
Bailey's Irish Cream

5137 **German Village Products**
P.O.Box 417
Wauseon, OH 43567-0417 419-335-1515
Fax: 419-337-0514
Processor and exporter of dried pasta
Estimated Sales: $10-20 Million
Number Employees: 20-49
Sq. footage: 80000
Parent Co: Campbell Soup Company
Type of Packaging: Bulk

5138 **Germanton Winery**
3530 Nc 8 and 65 Hwy
Germanton, NC 27019 336-969-2075
Fax: 336-969-6559 800-322-2894
sales@germantongallery.com
www.germantongallery.com
Wine list consists of chardonnay, seyval blanc, white zinfandel, vermillion, merlot, niagara, and sweet red wines.
President: David Simpson
Treasurer: Judy Simpson
Estimated Sales: Less than $500,000
Number Employees: 1-4

5139 **Gertrude & Bronner's Magic Alpsnack**
P.O.Box 28
Escondido, CA 92033-0028 760-743-2211
Fax: 760-745-6675 allone@drbronner.com
www.drbronner.com
Manufacturer of energy snack bars that contain hemp nut
President: David Bronner
VP: Ralph Bronner
Estimated Sales: $ 1 - 3 Million
Number Employees: 1-4
Type of Packaging: Consumer
Brands:
Dr. Bronner's

5140 **Gertrude Hawk Chocolates**
9 Keystone Industrial Park
Dunmore, PA 18512 570-342-7556
Fax: 570-342-0266 800-706-6275
jkenny@markave.com
www.markavenuechocolates.com
Milk chocolate, dark chocolate, nno-chocolate confections, sugar-free chocolates and white chocolate
President: David Hawk
CFO/VP: Steven Arling
VP Sales/Marketing: Christopher Cuneo
Human Resources Director: David Garton
VP Operations/Producstion/Manufacturing: Steve Liddic
Purchasing Manager: Sandra Koch

5141 **Gertrude Hawk Chocolates**
9 Keystone Industrial Park
Dunmore, PA 18512 570-342-7556
Fax: 570-342-0261 800-822-2032
webmaster@gertrudehawk.com
www.gertrudehawkchocolates.com
Processor of chocolates including truffles, molds and bulk chocolates, sugar-free chocolates
President: Bob Parkins
Chairman: Ethan Hawk
CIO: Bruce Cottle
Estimated Sales: $20-50 Million
Number Employees: 300

5142 **Gertrude Hawk Ingredients**
9 Keystone Park
Dunmore, PA 18512
800-822-2032
info@gertrudehawk.com
http://www.gertrudehawkchocolates.com/ingredients
Chocolate confections for bakery and frozen desserts
President: David Hawk
Chairman: Ethan Hawk

5143 **Gesco ENR**
Cp 830
Gaspe, QC G4X 6H4
Canada 418-368-1414
Fax: 418-368-1812 gesco@globetrotter.qc.ca
Processor and exporter of fresh and frozen shrimp
President: Gaetan Denis
Number Employees: 20-49
Type of Packaging: Consumer, Food Service, Private Label, Bulk

5144 **Getchell Brothers**
1 Union St
Brewer, ME 04412 207-989-7335
Fax: 207-989-7810 800-949-4423
Wines
President: Willard Farnham
Estimated Sales: $2.5-5 Million
Number Employees: 20-49

5145 **Geyser Peak Winery**
22281 Chianti Road
PO Box 25
Geyserville, CA 95441 707-857-2500
Fax: 707-857-3545 800-255-9463
tastingroom@geyserpeakwinery.com
www.geyserpeakwinery.org
Processor and exporter of table wines
Manager: Lisa Flohr
VP/Winemaker: Daryl Groom
Public Relations: Tim McDonald
Production Manager: Paul White
Estimated Sales: $20-50 Million
Number Employees: 45
Sq. footage: 10746
Parent Co: Jim Beam Brands Worldwide
Brands:
CANYON ROAD
GEYSER PEAK
VENEZIA

5146 **Ghirardelli Chocolate Company**
1111 139th Avenue
San Leandro, CA 94578-2631 800-877-9338
Fax: 510-297-2649 www.ghirardelli.com
Processor of confections and chocolate baking products including chips, bars and powders; also, hot beverages
Sr. VP Sales: Andrew Nestler
VP Sales: Mark Greenhall
Number Employees: 150
Type of Packaging: Food Service

5147 **Ghirardelli Chocolate Company**
1111 139th Ave
San Leandro, CA 94578 510-483-6970
Fax: 510-297-2649 800-877-9338
www.ghirardelli.com
Manufacturer of chocolate and cocoa
President/CEO: Fabrizio Parini
CFO: Jurgen Auerbach
VP Sales/Marketing: Marty Thompson
Estimated Sales: $100-500 Million
Number Employees: 250-499
Type of Packaging: Private Label
Brands:
GHIRARDELLI

5148 **Ghirardelli Ranch**
496 Pepper Rd
Petaluma, CA 94952 707-795-7616
Grower of fresh produce including zucchini, leeks, lettuce and beets
Co-Owner: Dorothy Ghirardelli
Co-Owner: Gildo Ghirardelli
Number Employees: 10-19
Type of Packaging: Consumer, Bulk
Brands:
GHIRARDELLI RANCH

5149 **Ghyslain Chocolatier**
350 W Deerfield Rd
Union City, IN 47390 765-964-7905
Fax: 765-964-9138 866-449-7524
ghyslain@pop.skyenet.net www.ghyslain.com
Artisan chocolates
President: Ghyslain Maurais
Estimated Sales: $2.5-5 Million
Number Employees: 10-19

5150 **Gia Michael's Confections, Inc.**
318 Meacham Avenue
Elmont, NY 11003-3214 516-354-3905
Fax: 516-328-3311 hia@giamichaels.com
www.giamichaels.com
Ckae decorations, full-line chocolate, candy decorations, chewing gum, full-line candy, hard candy, popcorn, pretzels.
Marketing: Nicky Juliano

5151 **Gia Russa**
65 Coitsville Hubbard Rd
Coitsville, OH 44505 330-743-6050
Fax: 330-743-0739 800-527-8772
customers@giarussa.com www.giarussa.com
pasta and sauces

5152 **Giacorelli Imports**
20423 State Road 7
Boca Raton, FL 33498-6797 561-451-1415
Fax: 561-451-1618 giacorelli@aol.com
All-natural, sparkling fruit juice imported from Italy
President: Thomas Spirelli
Estimated Sales: $2 Million
Number Employees: 5-9
Brands:
GIACOBAZZI JUICE SPA
PEACH-STRAWBERRY-RASPBERRY-SPARKLE
RED & WHITE GRAPE JUICE
TANGERINE SPARKLING BEVERAGE

5153 **Giambri's Quality Sweets**
26 Brand Ave
Clementon, NJ 08021-4211 856-783-1099
Fax: 856-783-6377 866-238-0169
dave@giambris.com www.giambris.com
Hard candies, creamy fudge and chocolates
President/Owner: David Giambri
VP: Josephine Giambri
Number Employees: 6

5154 **Giant Food**
10515 Greenbelt Rd
Lanham, MD 20706 301-666-1180
Fax: 301-618-4967 888-469-4426
www.giantfood.com
Processor of baked products including bread, rolls, cakes, pies, sweetgoods, doughnuts and cookies
Manager: Tarjani Shah
Executive VP/General Manager: Bill Holmes
VP Quality Control: David Richman
Public Relations: Barry Scher
Manufacturing Director: Walter Auman
Number Employees: 5,000-9,999
Type of Packaging: Consumer

5155 **Giasi Winery**
4194 State Route 14
Rock Stream, NY 14878-9612 607-535-7785
Wines
Estimated Sales: $300,000-500,000
Number Employees: 1-4

5156 **Gibbon Packing**
P.O.Box 730
Gibbon, NE 68840 308-468-5771
Fax: 308-468-5262
Manufacturer of boneless beef and offal products
President: Wesley Hodge
Estimated Sales: $100-500 Million
Number Employees: 250-499
Parent Co: IBP
Type of Packaging: Consumer

5157 **Gibbons Bee Farm**
314 Quinnmoor Dr
Ballwin, MO 63011 636-394-5395
Fax: 636-256-0303 877-736-8607
info@gibbonsbeefarm.com
www.gibbonsbeefarm.com
Processor of honey, salad dressing and honey mustard
Owner: Sharon Gibbons
Sales Manager: John Gibbons
Estimated Sales: $ 1 - 3 Million
Number Employees: 1-4
Type of Packaging: Consumer
Brands:
GIBBONS

5158 **Gibbsville Cheese Company**
W2663 County Road Oo
Sheboygan Falls, WI 53085 920-564-3242
Fax: 920-564-6129 sales@gibbsvillecheese.com
www.gibbsvillecheese.com
Manufacturer of fine cheddar, colby, montery jack, and two-tone (montery and colby) cheeses
Owner: Phillip Van Tatenhove
Estimated Sales: $1-2.5 Million
Number Employees: 10-19
Sq. footage: 5000
Type of Packaging: Consumer

5159 **Gibson Wine Company**
1720 Academy Ave
Sanger, CA 93657 559-875-2505
Fax: 559-875-4761
Processor and exporter of table wines
President/VP: Jack Constance
CFO: Robert Tusan
General Manager: Kim Spruance
Human Resource Manager: Lynn Higginson
Estimated Sales: $20-50 Million
Number Employees: 25
Sq. footage: 2000
Parent Co: Bronco Wine Company
Type of Packaging: Consumer, Private Label, Bulk
Brands:
GIBSON VINEYARDS

5160 **Gibsonburg Canning Company**
401 S Gibson St
Gibsonburg, OH 43431-1306 419-637-2221
Fax: 419-637-2003
Canned whole tomatoes, diced tomatoes, stewed tomatoes, no salt added tomatoes, Italian style stewed tomatoes
President: Jerry Schuett
Estimated Sales: $1-2.5 Million
Number Employees: 5-9
Brands:
J & J

5161 **Gielow Pickles**
5260 Lakeshore Rd
Lexington, MI 48450 810-359-7680
Fax: 810-359-2408 www.gielowpickles.com
Manufacturer, importer and exporter of pickles, sweet relish
President: Douglas Gielow
VP Sales: Craig Gielow
Sales Representative: Sue Burgess
Order/Receiving: Lisa Disser
Assistant Plant Manager: Dennis Coker
Purchasing: Doug Gielow
Estimated Sales: $10-20 Million
Number Employees: 20-49
Sq. footage: 30000
Type of Packaging: Food Service, Private Label
Brands:
COOL CRISP

5162 **Gifford's Dairy**
25 Hathaway St
Skowhegan, ME 04976 207-474-9821
Fax: 207-474-6120 giffords@kynd.com
www.giffordsicecream.com
Processor of ice cream and sugar-free and nonfat yogurt
President: Roger Gifford
Treasurer: John Gifford
Estimated Sales: $ 10 - 20 Million
Number Employees: 20-49
Type of Packaging: Consumer, Food Service
Brands:
GIFFORD'S

5163 **Gifford's Ice Cream & Candy Co**
8810 Brookville Rd
Silver Spring, MA 20910
800-708-1938
info@giffords.com www.giffords.com
Ice cream and candy
President/CEO: Marcelo Ramagem
VP: Neal Lieberman
Number Employees: 5

5164 **Gift Basket Supply World**
815 Haines Street
Jacksonville, FL 32206-6050 904-353-6278
Fax: 904-633-8764 800-786-4438
www.gbswimports.com
Gourmet foods
Estimated Sales: $2.5-5 Million
Number Employees: 5-9

5165 **Gil's Gourmet Gallery**
577 Ortiz Ave
Sand City, CA 93955 831-394-3305
Fax: 831-394-9144 800-438-7480
gil@gilsgourmet.com www.gilsgourmet.com
Condiments, salsa, pasta sauce, olives
President: Gil Tortolani
VP: Dylan Tortolani
Marketing Manager: Dave Elgin
Estimated Sales: $1-2.5 Million
Number Employees: 5-9

Type of Packaging: Private Label, Bulk

5166 **Gilardi Foods**
1085 Fairington Dr
Sidney, OH 45365 937-498-4511
Fax: 937-497-8786
Processor of frozen and refrigerated foods including pizza, lasagna and submarine sandwiches
President: Bill Mackin
Plant Manager: Ken Baptist
Estimated Sales: $100+ Million
Number Employees: 250-499
Type of Packaging: Consumer, Food Service, Private Label, Bulk
Brands:
GILARDI
MA MA ROSA
OLD ITALIAN
OUR DELI
SPANKY'S

5167 **Gilda Industries**
P.O.Box 133355
Hialeah, FL 33013 305-887-8286
Fax: 305-888-4064 www.gildaindustries.com
Crackers
President/Owner: Juan Blazquez
Director: Carmen Blazquez
Estimated Sales: $12 Million
Number Employees: 97
Type of Packaging: Private Label

5168 **Gile Cheese Company**
116 N Main St
Cuba City, WI 53807-1538 608-744-3456
Fax: 608-744-3457 www.gilecheese.com
Cheese, cheese products
Co-Ower/President: John Gile
Co-Owner: Diane Gile
Marketing: Tim Gile
Estimated Sales: $2.5-5 Million
Number Employees: 1-4

5169 **Gilette Foods**
751 Rahway Ave
Union, NJ 7083 908-688-0500
Fax: 908-688-0012
Supplier and importer of juices and concentrates
Manager: Luis Rodriguez
Estimated Sales: $10-20 Million
Number Employees: 10-19

5170 **Gill's Onions**
1051 Pacific Ave
Oxnard, CA 93030 805-240-1983
Fax: 805-271-1932 800-348-2255
www.gillsonions.com
Processor of onions
President: Steve Gill
Director Sales and Marketing: Nelia Alamo
Estimated Sales: $3.5 Million
Number Employees: 55
Sq. footage: 80000
Type of Packaging: Food Service, Bulk

5171 **Gilleshammer Thiele Farms**
P.O.Box 261
Saint Thomas, ND 58276 701-257-6634
Agriculture farming, vegetables, meats
President: Orville Gilleshammer
Estimated Sales: $1-2.5 Million
Number Employees: 5-9

5172 **(HQ)Gilliam Candy Brands**
PO Box 1060
Paducah, KY 42002-1060 270-443-6532
Fax: 270-442-1922 800-445-3008
jwyatt@gilliamcandybrands.com
www.gilliamcandybrands.com
Processor and exporter of candy, including hard, mints taffy sticks and brittles, lollypopa, and sugar-free candy.
President: Brian Duwe
CEO: Bill Lacy
VP Sales: Jeff Wyatt
Estimated Sales: $10-20 Million
Number Employees: 50-99
Sq. footage: 30000
Type of Packaging: Consumer, Food Service, Private Label, Bulk
Other Locations:
Gilliam Candy Brands
Edwardsville KS
Brands:
GILLIAM CANDY
KITS & BB BATS
SLO POKE
SOPHIE MAE BRITTLE

5173 **Gillies Coffee Company**
150 19th St
Brooklyn, NY 11226 718-499-7766
Fax: 718-499-7771 800-344-5526
info@gilliescoffee.com www.gilliescoffee.com
Processor, importer, exporter and wholesaler/distributor of roasted specialty coffees and blended specialty teas; exporter of roasted coffee
President: Schoelt Donald
Estimated Sales: $3.4 Million
Number Employees: 25
Sq. footage: 14000
Type of Packaging: Food Service, Private Label, Bulk
Brands:
BROOKLYN JAVA
GILLIES
LONG ISLAND ICED TEA

5174 **Gills Onions**
1051 Pacific Avenue
Oxnard, CA 93030 805-240-1983
Fax: 805-240-1932 800-348-2255
www.gillsonions.com
Onion and onion products
Food Safety/Quality Assurance Director: Nivia Santiago
Sales/Marketing Director: Nelia Alamo
Plant Manager: Fernando Luna
Pakcaging Purchasing Manager: Stacy Mann
Estimated Sales: $3.3 Million
Number Employees: 55
Sq. footage: 6443
Type of Packaging: Consumer, Food Service

5175 **Gilly's Hot Vanilla**
P.O.Box 1991
Lenox, MA 1240 413-637-1515
Fax: 413-637-1515
Processor of hot vanilla drink mixes
Owner: Joanne Deutch
Production Manager: Carl Deutch
Estimated Sales: Under $500,000
Number Employees: 1-4
Type of Packaging: Consumer, Food Service, Bulk
Brands:
GILLY'S HOT VANILLA

5176 **Gilmore's Seafoods**
131 Court St
Bath, ME 04530-2054 207-443-5231
Fax: 207-386-3271 800-849-9667
gilmore@gilmoreseafood.com
www.gilmoreseafood.com
Seafood
Co-Owner: Kevin Gilmore
Co-Owner: Ben Gilmore
Estimated Sales: $300,000-500,000
Number Employees: 1-4

5177 **(HQ)Gilroy Foods**
1350 Pacheco Pass
Gilroy, CA 95020-9559 408-846-7817
Fax: 408-846-3523 800-921-7502
customerservice@gilroyfoods.com
www.gilroyfoodsandflavors.com
Fresh, dehydrated, frozen or pureed garlic and onion, flavor systems and seasonings.
Branch Manager: Randall Stuewe
Director Specialty Sales: Cathy Katavich
Purchasing Manager: Dan Hager
Estimated Sales: $1 Billion+
Number Employees: 2,400
Parent Co: Olam International
Type of Packaging: Food Service, Private Label, Bulk
Brands:
AIRE FREEZ DRIED
CERTIFIED ORGANIC
DEHYDROFROZEN
DIAL-A-HEAT
ENDURACOLOR
GARDENFROST
GILROY FRESH
PUFF DRIED
QUICK COOK
REDI-MADE/HI-FLAVOR

5178 **Gilster Mary Lee/JasperFoods**
311 W Mercer St
Jasper, MO 64755-9345 417-394-2567
Fax: 417-394-3003 800-777-2168
www.gilstermarylee.com
Processes raw popcorn and packages both poly and microwave popcorn.
President/CEO: Donald Welge
CFO: Michael Welge
VP Technical Sales: Tom Welge
Plant Manager: Jim Cook
Estimated Sales: $300,000-500,000
Number Employees: 1-4
Sq. footage: 60000
Type of Packaging: Consumer, Food Service, Private Label, Bulk
Brands:
Ozark
Pop 'n Snak
Wyman's Wild Blueberries
Wyman's Wild Raspberries

5179 **(HQ)Gilster-Mary Lee Corporation**
1037 State St
Chester, IL 62233 618-826-2361
Fax: 618-826-2973 800-851-5371
webmaster@gilstermarylee.com
www.gilstermarylee.com
Manufacturer and exporter of baking mixes, ready-to-eat and hot breakfast cereals, macaroni and cheese, chocolate, pasta, instant potatoes, microwaveable popcorn, dinner mixes, hot cocoa mix, instant cocoa mix, sugar-sweetened drinkmixes, specialty potatoes, and stuffing mixes
President/CEO: Donald Welge
CFO: Michael Welge
Estimated Sales: $100-500 Million
Number Employees: 1,000-4,999
Sq. footage: 165000
Type of Packaging: Consumer, Food Service, Private Label, Bulk
Brands:
DUFF'S
HOSPITALITY
PY-O-MY

5180 **Gilt Edge Flour Mills**
1090 W 1200 N
Richmond, UT 84333 435-258-2425
Fax: 435-258-2428
customerservice@giltedgeflour.com
www.giltedgeflour.com
Processor of flour
President: Keith Giusto
Vice President: Evan Perry
Operations Manager: Dave Baker
Estimated Sales: $14 Million
Number Employees: 88
Type of Packaging: Consumer, Food Service, Private Label, Bulk
Brands:
GILT EDGE

5181 **Gimbal's Fine Candies**
250 Hillside Blvd
S San Francisco, CA 94080-1644 650-588-4844
Fax: 650-588-0150 800-344-6225
info@gimbals.net www.gimbalscandy.com
Processor of licorice, confectionery products, fruit slices and candy including sour balls, jelly beans and seasonal
President/CEO: Lance Gimbal
VP Sales/Marketing: Estle Kominowski
Purchasing: Ward Sims
Estimated Sales: $5-10 Million
Number Employees: 20-49
Number of Brands: 1
Number of Products: 100
Sq. footage: 30000
Type of Packaging: Consumer, Bulk
Brands:
JELLY BEAN
KLEERGUM
LOWCOOM
SOFT CHEWS
TAFFY DELIGHT
TAFFY LITE
ULTIMATE

5182 **Ginco International**
725 Cochran St # C
Simi Valley, CA 93065-1974 805-520-7500
Fax: 805-520-7509 800-423-5176
ginseng@ginsengcompany.com
www.ginsengcompany.com
Processor, importer and exporter of ginseng products
President: Gary Raskin
Estimated Sales: $ 1 - 3 Million
Number Employees: 10-19
Sq. footage: 15000

5183 **Gindi Gourmet**
1845 Range Street
Boulder, CO 80301-2745 303-473-9177
Fax: 303-473-9158
Gourmet foods

5184 **Ginger People®**
215 Reindollar Avenue
Marina, CA 93933 831-582-2494
Fax: 831-582-2495 800-551-5284
info@gingerpeople.com www.gingerpeople.com
Over 80 ginger products and receipes. Crystallized ginger made in Australia to premium fresh Hawaiian ginger. The spice has endless versatility and impressive medical properties.
President: Bruce Leeson
VP: Diana Cumberland
Estimated Sales: $9 Million
Number Employees: 18
Parent Co: Royal Pacific Foods

5185 **Gingerhaus, LLC**
7486 North Shore Rd
Norfolk, VA 23505 757-348-4274
Fax: 888-712-4493 lee@gingerhaus.com
www.gingerhaus.com
Cakes/pastries, cookies, ther bakes goods, baking mixes, cake decorations, other baking mixes and ingredients, candy decorations, cooking implements/housewares.
Marketing: Lee Walker Shepherd

5186 **Gingras Vinegar**
1132 Grand Caroline
Rougemont, QC J0L 1M0 514-293-4591
dgare@pomdial.com
www.pomdial.com
Variety of vinegars

5187 **Gingro Corp**
5103 Main Street
Manchester Center, VT 05255 802-362-0836
Fax: 802-362-0741 candeleros@gmail.com
www.candeleros.net
Ethnic cuisine and all-natural, gourmet sauces, salsas and snacks

5188 **Ginkgoton**
1225 W 190th Street
Suite 225
Gardena, CA 90248-4322 310-538-8383
Fax: 310-538-8651 shelle@ ginkgoton.com
President: Seung Choi
Estimated Sales: $2.5-5 Million
Number Employees: 1-4

5189 **Ginseng America**
PO Box 246
Roxbury, NY 12474-0246 607-326-3123
Ginseng products
President: Steven Roth

5190 **Ginseng Up Corporation**
24 Link Drive
Rockleigh, NJ 07647 201-660-8081
Fax: 201-660-8082 mling10@aol.com
www.ginsengup.com
Processor and exporter of natural soft drinks; contract packaging and tunnel pasteurization available
President: Sang Han
Estimated Sales: $ 3 - 5 Million
Number Employees: 1-4
Parent Co: One Up
Type of Packaging: Consumer
Brands:
COLD/HOT PACK TUNNEL PASTERIZED
FLAVOR
GINSENG UP

5191 **Giorgio Foods**
P.O.Box 96
Temple, PA 19560 610-926-2139
Fax: 610-926-7012 800-220-2139
lbortz@giorgiofoods.com
www.giorgiofoods.com
Manufacturer and exporter of fresh and frozen mushrooms and frozen breaded cheese sticks, pierogies, breaded pierogies, portabella burgers, and veggie burgers
President: John Majewski
CFO: Mike Butto
Sr. Customer Service Coordinator: LuAnn Bortz
VP Sales/Marketing: Brian Threlfall
Regional Sales Manager: Lisa Hemker
Estimated Sales: $100-500 Million
Number Employees: 250-499
Type of Packaging: Consumer, Food Service, Private Label, Bulk
Brands:
BRANDYWINE
DUTCH COUNTRY
GIORGIO
PENNSYLVANIA

5192 **Giovanni Food Company**
6050 Court Street Road
Syracuse, NY 13206 315-457-2373
www.giovannifoods.com
Pasta sauce, pizza sauce, salsa, bruschetta, barbeque sauce and juice.
Estimated Sales: $300,000
Number Employees: 5
Brands:
DEMENT'S
HARVEST TRADITIONS
JOSE PEDRO
LUIGI GIOVANNI
TUSCAN TRADITIONS

5193 **Giovanni Food Company, Inc**
4645 Crossroads Park Drive
Liverpool, NY 13088-3515 315-457-2373
Fax: 315-457-2837 myotti@giovannifoods.com
www.giovannifoods.com
Spaghetti sauce
President: L John DeMent
Vice President: Louis DeMent
Marketing: Mollie Yotti
Production Manager: Jim Doyen
Plant Manager: Rick Latimer
Estimated Sales: $ 20 - 50 Million
Number Employees: 20-49
Type of Packaging: Private Label
Brands:
DIMENTO
LUIGI GIOVANNI
MARIA ANGELINA

5194 **Giovanni's Appetizing Food Products**
P.O.Box 26
Richmond, MI 48062 586-727-9355
Fax: 586-727-3433 INFO@GIOAPP.COM
www.gioapp.com
Processor, canner and exporter of gourmet foods including antipasto, pickled mushrooms, chopped chicken liver and pates: meat, fish and poultry; also, fish pastes: anchovy, lobster, shrimp and smoked salmon; importer of saltedanchovies.
President: Philip Ricossa
Secretary/Treasurer: Elvira Ricossa
Estimated Sales: $2.5-5 Million
Number Employees: 10-19
Sq. footage: 16000
Type of Packaging: Consumer, Food Service
Brands:
CHAMPAGNE DELIGHT
GIOVANNI'S

5195 **Girard Spring Water**
1100 Mineral Spring Ave
North Providence, RI 2904 401-725-7298
Fax: 401-725-7913 800-477-9287
Manufacturer of spring water and water coolers
President: John Ponton
Estimated Sales: $500,000-$1 Million
Number Employees: 5-9
Sq. footage: 2500
Type of Packaging: Consumer, Private Label, Bulk

5196 **Girard Winery/Rudd Estates**
P.O.Box 105
Oakville, CA 94562-0105 707-944-8577
Fax: 707-944-2823 www.ruddwines.com
Processor and exporter of wines
Owner: Leslie Rudd
Director Sales/Winery Director: Kenny Koda
Director of Hospitality: Mark Sherwood
Estimated Sales: $5-10 Million
Number Employees: 20-49
Brands:
GIRARD

5197 **Girard's Food Service Dressings**
145 Willow Avenue
City of Industry, CA 91746-2047 323-724-2519
Fax: 323-726-0934 888-327-8442
sales@girardsdressings.com
www.girardsdressings.com
Processor and exporter of mayonnaise, salad dressings, sauces and marinades
Chairman/Co-CEO: Jack Tucey
President/Co-CEO: William Perry
Controller: Tim Schoenbaum
Quality Control/R&D Manager: Jeff Stalley
Marketing/Sales Coordinator: Dottie Dinkheller
Sales Manager Deli/Airline Retail Sales: Steve Shapiro
Plant Manager: Dennis Tyler
Purchasing/Logistics Manager: Walt Richmond
Estimated Sales: $24 Million
Number Employees: 60
Number of Brands: 3
Number of Products: 175
Sq. footage: 25000
Parent Co: T Marzetti Company
Type of Packaging: Consumer, Food Service, Bulk
Brands:
GIRARD'S

5198 **Girardet Wine Cellars**
895 Reston Rd
Roseburg, OR 97471 541-679-7252
Fax: 541-679-9502 genuine@girardetwine.com
www.girardetwine.com
Collection of wines such as: Baco Noir, Pinot Noir, Cabernet Sauvignon, Riesling and Grande Rouge
President: Philippe Girardet
CEO: Bonnie Girardet
Winemaker/General Manager: Marc Girardet
Estimated Sales: Under $500,000
Number Employees: 5
Type of Packaging: Private Label

5199 **Giulia Specialty Food**
10 Dell Glen Ave Ste 4
Lodi, NJ 7644 973-478-3111
Fax: 973-478-1133
giuliaspecialty@worldnet.att.net
Mineral water, balsamic vinegar, olive oil, coffee, Easter eggs, rice
VP: Carmelo Lamonto
Estimated Sales: $2.5-5 Million
Number Employees: 1-4
Brands:
BASSO
LASANTA MARIA
MAKO
PASTA MALTAGLIATI

5200 **Giulianos' Specialty Foods**
12132 Knott Street
Garden Grove, CA 92841 714-895-9661
Fax: 714-373-6872 www.giulianopeppers.com
Pickled peppers and vegetables
Estimated Sales: $3.3 Million
Number Employees: 20
Sq. footage: 40000
Type of Packaging: Consumer, Food Service

5201 **Giumarra Companies**
3646 Avenue 416
Reedley, CA 93654-9111 559-897-5060
Fax: 559-897-8363 eblaylock@giumarra.com
www.giumarra.com
Grapes, stonefruit, berries, apples/pears, tomatoes, vegetables, avocados, emlons and kiwi
Estimated Sales: $ 3 - 5 Million
Number Employees: 5-9
Brands:
ARRA GIUMARRA VINEYARDS
ARRAcado
BAUZA EXPORT
CARLSBAD
DAVID DEL CURTO S.A.
FRESH
FRUIT KING
GRAPE KING GIUMARRA VINEYARDS
LTD PERFECT PICK
LTD TREE RIPENED FRUIT
LUVYA
NATURE'S PARTNER
SOUTH HILLS
STA TERESA
YUMMY FRUIT COMPANY

5202 **Giumarra Companies**
15651 Old Milky Way
Escondido, CA 92027-7104 760-480-8502
Fax: 760-489-1870 www.giumarra.com
Processor, exporter and importer of avocados
Manager: Tom Vaughn
VP: John Corsaro
Sales Manager: Bruce Dowhan
Estimated Sales: $10-20 Million
Number Employees: 50-99
Sq. footage: 22000
Parent Co: Giumarra Brothers Fruit Company
Type of Packaging: Bulk
Other Locations:
Giumarra Brothers
Los Angeles CA
Brands:
ARRACADO

5203 **Giumarra Vineyards**
P.O.Box 1969
Bakersfield, CA 93303 661-395-7000
Fax: 661-395-7195 www.giumarra.com
Processor and exporter of grape concentrate and juice; co-packer of water, juices, wines, beers, distilled spirits cocktails, ciders and teas
President: John Giumarra
Estimated Sales: $100 Million
Number Employees: 1,000-4,999
Sq. footage: 600000

5204 **Giusto's Specialty Foods**
344 Littlefield Ave
S San Francisco, CA 94080-6103 650-873-6566
Fax: 650-873-2826 leslie@giustos.com
www.giustos.com
General grocery
President: Fred Giusto
Secretary/Treasurer: Albert Giusto
Estimated Sales: $10-20 Million
Number Employees: 20-49

5205 **Givaudan Flavors**
110 E 69th St
Cincinnati, OH 45216-2008 513-948-3428
Fax: 513-948-4338 www.givaudan.com
Flavors, extracts
Brands:
Givaudan

5206 **(HQ)Givaudan Flavors**
1199 Edison Drive 1-2
Cincinnati, OH 45126 513-948-8000
Fax: 513-948-3214 www.givaudan.com
Manufacturer and exporter of flavors, fruit drinks, ice cream/yogurt flavors, cocoa, flavored base powders for milk, yogurt, fruit, sherbet bases, egg nog bases, nondairy drinks and vitamins to fortify milk; importer of cocoa
President/CEO: Michael Davis
SVP: Robert Eilerman
VP: Bob Antenucci
Estimated Sales: $100 Million
Number Employees: 2700
Brands:
CHOCOLATE DELIGHT
DINOSAUR
GOLDEN
GOLDEN DELIGHT
GRAND PRIX
LEMONADE STAND
MOO-MANIA
SKIM SELECT
VITA-RITE

5207 **Givaudan Flavors**
580 Tollgate Road
Suite A
Elgin, IL 60123 847-608-6200
Fax: 847-608-6201 www.givaudan.com
Manufacturer, exporter and importer of flavors and extracts
Parent Co: Givaudan Flavors
Type of Packaging: Bulk
Brands:
ALDEMAX
ASEPTILOK
FLAV-O-LOK
PRIME
REDD
SUGARONE

5208 **Givaudan Flavors**
245 Merry Lane
East Hanover, NJ 07936 973-386-9800
Fax: 973-428-6312 www.givaudan.com
Flavor enhancers
Purchasing Manager: Kurt Scaturro
Parent Co: Givaudan Flavors

5209 **Glacial Ridge Foods**
24350 Joy Road
Suite 9
Redford, MI 48239-1265 612-239-2215
Fax: 313-535-4466
Country grown multi-grain chips, pop-lite popcorn and multi-grain pretzels
President: Mark Shirkey
National Sales Manager: Roger Spagnola
Estimated Sales: $500,000 appx.
Number Employees: 1-4
Brands:
COUNTRY GROWN FOODS

5210 **Glacier Bay Seafood & Meat Company**
1900 W 31st Street
B-21
Lawrence, KS 66046-5505 785-832-2650
Fax: 785-832-1192
Seafood, meat
Owner: Chris McCue

5211 **Glacier Fish Company**
1200 Westlake Ave N Ste 900
Seattle, WA 98109 206-298-1200
Fax: 206-298-4750 info@glacierfish.com
www.glacierfish.com
Processor of frozen surimi, halibut roe and Alaskan cod, pollack and salmon; also, frozen king, dungeness and snow crabs; exporter of cod, pollack and surimi
President: Jeff Hendricks
Owner/CEO: Erik Breivik
CFO: Robert Wood
CEO: Merle Knapp
Estimated Sales: $20 Million
Number Employees: 250
Type of Packaging: Food Service, Bulk
Brands:
GLACIER FREEZE

5212 **Glacier Foods**
1117 K St
Sanger, CA 93657-3200 559-875-3354
Fax: 559-875-3179
Processor, importer, domestic and exporter of frozen and fresh fruit and vegetables
Owner: Jack Mulvaney
Plant Manager: Alvin McAvoy
Assistant Plant Manager: Sheila Young
Estimated Sales: $ 10 - 20 Million
Number Employees: 50-99
Sq. footage: 748260
Parent Co: JR Wood
Type of Packaging: Consumer, Food Service, Private Label, Bulk

5213 **Gladder's Gourmet Cookies**
1403 Industrial Blvd
Lockhart, TX 78644-3701 512-398-1970
Fax: 512-398-6323 888-398-4523
gladders.com www.gladders.com
Processor of frozen raw cookie dough, ready-to-bake brownies and thaw and serve cookies and brownies
Owner: Dusty Baker
Marketing Director: Susan Glader
VP Sales/Marketing: Dave Foreman
Director Operations: Kevin Cobb
General Manager: Mark Brown
Estimated Sales: $1-2.5 Million
Number Employees: 20-49
Sq. footage: 40000

Type of Packaging: Food Service
Brands:
GLADDER'S GOURMET COOKIE

5214 **Gladstone Candies**
7480 Brookpark Road
Cleveland, OH 44129 216-472-0206
Fax: 216-274-9200 888-729-1960
www.groovycandies.com
Processor of candy including lollypops, black anise, red-hot cinnamon and molded Christmas, Easter, Halloween and Valentine holiday candies.
President: Ed Kitchen
Chairman: Bert Hiddie
Estimated Sales: $5-9.9 Million
Number Employees: 20-49
Number of Brands: 1
Number of Products: 25
Sq. footage: 10000
Type of Packaging: Consumer, Private Label, Bulk
Brands:
GLADSTONE CANDIES

5215 **Gladstone Food ProductsCompany**
P.O.Box 28010
Kansas City, MO 64188 816-436-1255
Fax: 816-436-1255
Mexican foods
President: Joe Catalano
Estimated Sales: $1-2.5 Million appx.
Number Employees: 1-4

5216 **(HQ)Glanbia Foods**
1373 Fillmore St
Twin Falls, ID 83301 208-733-7555
Fax: 208-733-9222 800-427-9477
custserv@glanbiausa.com www.glanbia.com
Manufacturer of cheese including natural, barrel, cheddar, Swiss and Monterey jack; also, processor and exporter of whey protein concentrate and lactose
President/CEO: Jeff Williams
Director Cheese Sales/Marketing: Dave Snyder
Estimated Sales: $20-50 Million
Number Employees: 20-49
Parent Co: Glanbia PLC
Type of Packaging: Consumer, Food Service, Private Label, Bulk
Brands:
PROVON

5217 **Glanbia Foods**
1373 Fillmore St
Twin Falls, ID 83301 208-733-7555
Fax: 208-733-9222 custsrv@glanbiausa.com
www.glanbia.com
Natural and processed cheese
President: Jeff Williams
Sales Manager: Steve Singer
VP of Production: William Hanson
Cheese Technology Director: Dave Perry
Mktg Services Mgr: Tammy Hasse-mcguir
Operations Manager: Bjorn Sorensen
Plant Manager: Tim Opper
Maintenance Manager: Dick Bawser
Estimated Sales: $20-50 Million
Number Employees: 65
Brands:
Glanbia Foods

5218 **Glanbia Nutritionals**
523 6th Street
Monroe, WI 53566 608-329-2800
Fax: 608-329-2828 nutrition@glanbiausa.com
www.glanbiausa.com
Manufacturers nutritional ingredients for healthy beverages, nutrition bars, processed foods and supplements
President: Jerry O'Dea
CEO: Kevin Toland
CFO: Alan Morris
Number Employees: 25

5219 **Glanbia Nutritionals**
523 6th St
Monroe, WI 53566 608-329-2800
Fax: 608-329-2828 800-336-2183
nutrition@glanbiausa.com
www.glanbianutritionals.com
Provide innovative, science-based nutritional solutions. A leader in production of natural whey protein isolates, whey protein concentrates, whey fractions, heat-stable whey proteins, protein blends, milk proteins, lactose and dairycalcium. They also offer flax seed products and vitamins and minerals.
President: Jerry O'Dea
CEO: Kevin Toland
CFO: Alan Morris
VP: Robert Beausire
R&D: Eric Bastian
Quality Control: Mary Pierson
Marketing Manager: Eric Borchardt
Operations: Carl Garcia
Number Employees: 50-99
Number of Brands: 12
Number of Products: 7
Parent Co: Glandia Ingredients, PLC
Type of Packaging: Consumer, Private Label, Bulk
Brands:
AVONLAC™
BARFLEX®
BARGAIN™
BARPRO™
CFM®
PROLIBRA®
PROVON®
SALIBRA®
SOLMIKO MILK PRODUCTS
THERMAX®
TRI-FX®
TRUCAL®

5220 **Glasco Locker Plant**
119 N Railroad Ave
Glasco, KS 67445 785-568-2364
Processor of beef, pork and lamb; also, slaughtering and curing available
Owner: Kelly L Cool
Estimated Sales: $1-2.5 Million
Number Employees: 5-9
Type of Packaging: Consumer

5221 **Glatech Productions**
325 2nd St
Lakewood, NJ 8701 732-364-8700
Fax: 732-886-2131 glatech@gmail.com
www.koshergelatin.com
Producers of kolatin kosher gelatin and Elyon confectionery products
VP: Moshe Eider
Type of Packaging: Consumer, Bulk

5222 **Glazier Packing Company**
3140 State Route 11
Malone, NY 12953 518-483-4990
Fax: 518-483-8300 www.glazierhotdog.com
Processor of sausage and frankfurters; wholesaler/food service wholesaler distributor and importer of meat products; serving the food service market
President/Owner: John Glazier
Vice President: Shawn Glazier
General Manager: Lynn Raymond
Estimated Sales: $10-11 Million
Number Employees: 20-49
Sq. footage: 30000
Type of Packaging: Consumer, Food Service
Brands:
TAST-T
TAST-T TENDER

5223 **Glazier Packing Company**
7170 Us Highway 11
Potsdam, NY 13676 315-265-2500
Fax: 315-265-2502
Processor of sausage; wholesaler/distributor of fresh and frozen foods; serving the food service market
Manager: John Glazier
Estimated Sales: $5-10 Million
Number Employees: 20
Sq. footage: 25000
Type of Packaging: Consumer, Food Service, Bulk

5224 **Glcc Company**
PO Box 329
Paw Paw, MI 49079 269-657-3167
Fax: 269-657-4552 glcc@triton.net
www.glccflavors.com
Processor of flavors, juice concentrates and blends; custom repackaging available
President: Johnathan Davis
Quality Assurance Manager: Nicole Charron
Sales Executive: Thomas Manion
VP Operations/Plant Manager: Fred Jeffers
Estimated Sales: $2.5 Million
Number Employees: 20
Sq. footage: 35000
Type of Packaging: Bulk

5225 **Glee Gum**
305 Dudley Street
Providence, RI 02907 401-351-6415
Fax: 401-272-1204 info@gleegum.com
www.gleegum.com
Chewing gum and candy making kits

5226 **Glen Rose Meat Company**
4561 Loma Vista Ave
Vernon, CA 90058 323-589-3393
Fax: 323-589-3712
Grocery items
CEO: Glen Rose
Estimated Sales: $10-20 Million
Number Employees: 20-49
Brands:
Glen Rose Meat

5227 **Glen Summit Springs Water Company**
P.O.Box 129
Mountain Top, PA 18707 570-474-5861
Fax: 570-474-9840 800-621-7596
www.glensummitspringswater.com
Processor of bottled spring water
Manager: Kevin Duffy
Estimated Sales: $2.5-5 Million
Number Employees: 20-49

5228 **Glen's Packing Company**
P.O.Box 244
Hallettsville, TX 77964 361-798-2601
Fax: 361-798-1201 800-368-2333
Manfuacturer of fresh meats, special cuts - quarters and halves, pork and beef sausage, slaughtering available
President: Harold Dolezal
VP: Glen Jr Dolezal
Estimated Sales: $5-10 Million
Number Employees: 10-19
Type of Packaging: Consumer

5229 **Glencourt**
1205 Hillview Ln
Napa, CA 94558-9789 707-944-4444
Fax: 925-944-4009 www.omnibrands.com
Processor and exporter of beverages, dairy products, baked goods, sauces, preserves, frozen concentrates, juices, peanut butter, mayonnaise, spices and natural cheeses
Owner: Susie Hasenpusch
VP Sales: David Maco
Sales Manager: Dave Hackney
Sales Manager: Dennis Drennon
Export Sales Manager: Joanne Goh
Sales Development Analyst: Christopher Hartig
Export Sales Specialist: Joyce Stump
Number Employees: 1-4
Parent Co: Safeway Stores
Type of Packaging: Private Label

5230 **Glendora Quiche Company**
210 W Arrow Hwy Ste O
San Dimas, CA 91773 909-394-1777
Fax: 909-394-1780
Processor of gourmet quiche including lorraine, broccoli, green chile, spinach and mushroom
Owner: Todd Bilef
Estimated Sales: $ 1 - 3 Million
Number Employees: 1-4
Sq. footage: 3000
Parent Co: Kovar Companies
Type of Packaging: Consumer, Food Service, Private Label, Bulk
Brands:
Glendora Quiche Co.

5231 **Glenmark Food Processors**
4545 S Racine Ave
Chicago, IL 60609-3371 773-927-4800
Fax: 773-847-2946 800-621-0117

Processor and exporter of frozen steak and veal, canned and frozen stews and beef patties
Manager: Todd Ryan
VP: Bob Martin
Director Operations: John Dobias
Estimated Sales: $5-10 Million
Number Employees: 20-49
Parent Co: OSI Industries
Type of Packaging: Consumer, Food Service, Private Label, Bulk
Brands:
Great Grilsby

5232 **Glenmark Industries**
4545 S Racine Ave
Chicago, IL 60609-3371 773-927-4800
Fax: 773-847-2946
Processor of ground beef patties, pork chopettes, ribettes and sausage, meatloaf, meatballs and breaded beef and poultry products
President: Dave Van Kampen
Chif Information Officer: Teresa Kaiser
Purchasing Manager: Dominic Pinto
Estimated Sales: $50-100 Million
Number Employees: 250-499
Brands:
Blazer
Glenmark
Glenmark

5233 **Glenn Sales Company**
6425 Pow Fy Rd NW Ste 120
Atlanta, GA 30339 770-952-9292
Fax: 770-988-9325
Seafood, Whiting, Sea Trout, Flounder, Croaker, Pollock
President: Bruce Pearlman
Estimated Sales: $1,600,000
Number Employees: 5-9

5234 **Glennys**
371 S Main St
Freeport, NY 11520-5114 516-377-1400
Fax: 516-377-9046 888-864-1243
www.glennys.com
Processor of natural snacks including soy veggie nuts and snack, soy crisps, animal cookies, vitamin C lollypops, hard candies, carob coated bee pollen, spirulina and ginseng, and moist'n chewy bars
Manager: Rhonda Talbot
Estimated Sales: $5-10 Million
Number Employees: 20-49
Type of Packaging: Consumer, Food Service
Brands:
Glenny's

5235 **Glenoaks Food**
11030 Randall St
Sun Valley, CA 91352 818-768-9091
Fax: 818-767-0742 info@glenoaksfood.com
www.glenoaksfood.com
All natural meat snacks without preservatives or MSG. beef, turkey, buffalo, venison and ostrich jerky in 18 flavors
Owner: John J Fallon Jr
Estimated Sales: $ 1 - 3 Million
Number Employees: 1-4
Sq. footage: 26000
Type of Packaging: Consumer, Private Label, Bulk
Brands:
J.C. RIVERS GOURMET JERKY

5236 **Glenora Wine Cellars**
5435 State Route 14
Dundee, NY 14837 607-243-5511
Fax: 607-243-5514 800-243-5513
info@glenora.com www.glenora.com
Processor of sparkling and table wines - premium New York State wines including, Brut Sparkling, Chardonnay, Riesling, Merlot, Cabernet Sauvignon, Cayuga and Seyval
Principal: Gene Pierce
Principal: Ed Dalrymple
Principal: Scott Welliver
Director Marketing: Gail Fink
Winemaker: Steve diFrancesco
Estimated Sales: $5-10 Million
Number Employees: 10-19
Sq. footage: 17500
Type of Packaging: Consumer, Food Service, Private Label
Brands:
FINGER LAKES
GLENORA
PEACH ORCHARD FARMS
TRESTLE CREEK

5237 **Glier's Meats**
533 Goetta Pl
Covington, KY 41011 859-291-1800
Fax: 859-291-1846 800-446-3882
www.goetta.com
Processor of German breakfast sausage - contains pork, beef and steel-cut (pinhad oats) and seasonings.
President: Daniel Glier
Director Marketing: Mark Balasa
Plant Manager: Tom Rabe
Estimated Sales: $2.2 Million
Number Employees: 10-19
Sq. footage: 12000
Type of Packaging: Food Service, Private Label
Brands:
Glier's

5238 **Global Bakeries**
13336 Paxton St
Pacoima, CA 91331 818-896-0525
Fax: 818-896-3237 www.globalbakeriesinc.com
Manufacturer of baked goods including bagels, croissants, pita breads, rolls and pitochips.
President: Albert Boyajian
Owner: Eric Boyajian
VP Finance: Nick Hamalian
Estimated Sales: $10 Million
Number Employees: 60
Number of Products: 5
Sq. footage: 40000
Type of Packaging: Consumer, Food Service, Private Label, Bulk

5239 **Global Beverage Company**
PO Box 25107
Rochester, NY 14625-2834 585-381-3560
Fax: 585-381-4025 webmaster@wetplanet.com
www.wetplanet.com
Carbonated soft drinks, ice teas, fruit juices, energy drinks and bottled water
President: Cj Rapp
Number Employees: 20-49

5240 **(HQ)Global Botanical**
545 Welham Road
Barrie, ON L4N 8Z6
Canada 705-733-2117
Fax: 705-733-2391 info@globalbotanical.com
www.globalbotanical.com
Processor, wholesaler/distributor, importer and exporter of herbs, spices, oils, etc., also; custom formulation available
President: Sandra Thuna
Office Manager: Therese White
General Manager: Joel Thuna
Number Employees: 12
Sq. footage: 20000
Type of Packaging: Private Label, Bulk
Brands:
Excalibur
Global Botanical
Kidz
Naturalvalves
Pure-Li Natural

5241 **Global Citrus Resources**
1835 Stonecrest Ct
Lakeland, FL 33813 863-647-9020
Fax: 863-683-0267
sales@globalcitrusresources.com
www.globalcitrusresources.com
Processor and exporter of frozen juice concentrates
President: David Alpin
CFO: Richard Reichler
VP Sales/Marketing: Joe Hart
Production Manager: David Tegreene
Estimated Sales: $20-50 Million
Number Employees: 5-9

5242 **Global Egg Corporation**
283 Horner Ave
Etobicoke, ON M8Z 4Y4
Canada 416-231-2309
Fax: 416-231-8991 abk@globalegg.com
Processor of whole, cooked, liquid, frozen and pelletized eggs; also, salt and sugar egg yolks; exporter of frozen egg whites and whole eggs
CEO: Aaron Kwinter
Estimated Sales: $13 Million
Number Employees: 70
Sq. footage: 25000
Type of Packaging: Food Service, Bulk
Brands:
Egg King
Global

5243 **Global Express Gourmet**
315 Edelweiss Drive
Bozeman, MT 59718-3928 406-587-5571
Fax: 406-582-0614 www.eprovisions.com
Gourmet foods
Marketing/Sales: Cameron Haag

5244 **Global Food Industries**
307 Circle Dr
Townville, SC 29689 864-287-1212
Fax: 864-287-1335 800-225-4152
info@globalfoodindustries.com
www.globalsoyfood.com
Processor of dairy, industrial ingredients, dehydrated foods, beverages, halal, and vegetarian foods
President: Neal Pfeiffer
Vice President: Paulette Harary
Office Manager: Sandra Sanoh
Number Employees: 5-9
Number of Brands: 1
Number of Products: 30
Type of Packaging: Food Service, Bulk
Brands:
Global Food

5245 **Global Health Laboratories**
9500 New Horizons Blvd
Amityville, NY 11701 631-777-2134
Fax: 631-777-3348
Processor and exporter of health products including nutritional drinks, energy bars, food and nutritional supplements, vitamins, herbs and weight loss products
Administrator: Susan Mc Guckian
Sales Director: James Gibbons
Type of Packaging: Consumer, Private Label
Brands:
Herb Actives
Nature's Plus
Source of Life
Spirutein
Thermo Tropic

5246 **(HQ)Global Marketing Associates**
1901 N Roselle Road
Schaumburg, IL 60195-3176 847-397-2350
Fax: 847-397-2354
Processor of fruit juices, dry drink mixes and macaroni and cheese dinners; exporter of nonalcoholic beverages, confectionery products, ingredients, ketchup, mustard and salad dressings
Owner: James Biesinger
Estimated Sales: $1-2.5 Million
Number Employees: 1-4
Type of Packaging: Consumer, Private Label, Bulk
Brands:
Suncoast

5247 **Global Nutrition Research Corporation**
3120 S Potter Dr
Tempe, AZ 85282 602-454-2248
Fax: 602-454-2249 shannon@gnrc.us
Provide a comprehensive database of herbal supplements, health products, and herbal companies available on the internet. We are not only an information provider, but also an herbal and alternative medicine community site.
President: Ken Ardisson
Sales Contact: Shannon Purcell
Estimated Sales: $ 20 - 50 Million
Number Employees: 20-49

5248 **Global Organics**
339 Massachusetts Ave
Arlington, MA 02474 781-648-8844
Fax: 781-648-0774
amy.dinsmore@global-organics.com
www.global-organics.com
Supplier of certified organic ingredients
President: Dave Alexander
Vice President: Roland Hoch
Strategic Account Manager: Brian Banks
Sales and Marketing Coordinator: Amy Dinsmore
Estimated Sales: Under $500,000
Number Employees: 5-9

5249 **Global Preservatives**
P.O.Box 3023
Lake Charles, LA 70602 337-491-0816
Fax: 337-433-5253 800-256-2253
www.globalpreservatives.com
Manufactures Food Processing aids and preservatives for meats, produce and the bakery industry.
President: William Woodward
R&D: Damon Thibodeaux
Operations Director: Tim Vaughan
Plant Manager: Bryan Hymel
Estimated Sales: $2.5 -$5 Million
Number Employees: 1-4
Sq. footage: 20000

5250 **Global Trading**
6571 Altura Blvd Ste 200
Buena Park, CA 90620
Fax: 864-234-5815 www.globaltrading.net
Processor and exporter of frozen fruits and purees
President: Arthur Price
Accounting: Karen Gray
Inventory Control: Joyce Lambert
Information Technology: Kevin Martin
Sales Manager: Terry Miller
Office Manager: Karen Berry
FDA/Customs Coordinator: Denise Roof
Production Coordinator: Jeanice Messick
Transportation: Pam Torres
Purchasing: Beanie Lee
Estimated Sales: $2.5-5 Million
Number Employees: 5-9
Type of Packaging: Consumer, Bulk

5251 **GlobeTrends**
11 the Esplanade
Morris Plains, NJ 07950-1360 973-984-7444
Fax: 973-984-7422 800-416-8327
info@globetrends.com www.globetrends.com
Importer and distributor of Taylors of Harrogate teas from England, Harrisons and Crosfield teas. Also imports Granja San Francisco, Spain's #1 selling honey. We ship throughout the US
President: Al Sharif
Marketing/Public Relations: Cheryl Templeton
Estimated Sales: $500,000-$1 Million
Number Employees: 1-4
Type of Packaging: Private Label
Brands:
British Honey Company
Taylors of Harrogate

5252 **Globus Coffee**
426 Plandome Rd
Manhasset, NY 11030 631-390-2233
Fax: 516-364-4558
Coffee traders
Owner: Kurt Kappeli
CFO: Salvatore Errico
Manager: Ronald Levy
Estimated Sales: $820,000
Number Employees: 6

5253 **Gloria Ferrer Champagne**
P.O.Box 1427
Sonoma, CA 95476-1427 707-996-7256
Fax: 707-996-0720 info@gloriaferrer.com
www.gloriaferrer.com
Most honored and accaimed sparkling wines
President: Juan Furne
EVP: Eva Bertran
VP/Winemaker: Bob Iantosca
VP/Vineyard Manager: Mike Crumly
VP Marketing/Advertising: David Brown
Estimated Sales: $20-50 Million
Number Employees: 50-99
Brands:
Freixenet Spanish Wines
Freixenet Wines

5254 **Gloria Jean's Gourmet Coffees**
17691 Mitchell N
Irvine, CA 92614-6827 949-589-5040
Fax: 949-589-5041 877-320-5282
customerservice@gloriajeans.com
www.gloriajeans.com
Gourmet flavored coffees, varietals and blends, tea and hot chocolate
CEO: Neil Gill
VP Marketing: Diane Hays-Hoag
Franchising Manager: Shereen Rai
Communications Manager: Diane Hays-Hoag
Customer Service: Patti Graves
Estimated Sales: $100-500 Million
Number Employees: 5000
Parent Co: Diedrich Coffee

5255 **Gloria Winery & Vineyard**
1648 E 8th St N
Springfield, MO 65802 417-926-6263
Wines
President: William Toben
Estimated Sales: $500,000-$1 Million
Number Employees: 1-4

5256 **Gloria's Gourmet**
36 Carver Street
New Britain, CT 06053-1302 860-225-9196
Fax: 860-224-2602 gloria306870@aol.com
Dip and spread mixes, herbs and spices

5257 **Glory Foods**
901 Oak St
Columbus, OH 43205 614-252-2042
Fax: 614-252-2043 www.gloryfoods.com
Fresh and frozen vegetables, fresh - cut vegetables, and gluten - free products
President: Jacqueline Neal
Founder: Iris Cooper
Founder/Plant Manager: Dan Charna
Founder: Garth Henley
Controller: Julie Eikenberry
Estimated Sales: $3.5 Million
Number Employees: 25
Type of Packaging: Food Service, Bulk

5258 **Glorybee Foods**
P.O.Box 2744
Eugene, OR 97402 541-689-0913
Fax: 541-689-9692 800-456-7923
info@glorybeefoods.com www.glorybee.com
Natural foods and sweeteners
President: Richard Turanski
Quality Control: Gary Powell
Marketing: Michele Lukowski
Sales: Greg Wilson
Operations: Alan Turanski
Estimated Sales: $2.5-5 Million
Number Employees: 50-99
Sq. footage: 30000
Type of Packaging: Food Service, Bulk

5259 **Glorybee Natural Sweeteners**
PO Box 2744
Eugene, OR 97402-0277 800-456-7923
Fax: 541-607-8803 800-456-7923
sales@glorybee.com www.glorybee.com
Process retail natural sweeteners-both organic and commercial. Manufactures all natural honeystix
President: Richard Turanski
Marketing Director: Rae Jean Wilson
Plant Manager: Ron Okonski
Estimated Sales: $50-99.9 Million
Number Employees: 50-99
Sq. footage: 16
Type of Packaging: Private Label
Brands:
Aunt Patty's Natural Sweetners
Glorybee Foods Honeystix
Glorybee Herbal Honey
Glorybee Honey

5260 **Glover's Ice Cream**
705 W Clinton St
Frankfort, IN 46041 765-654-6712
Fax: 765-654-7977 800-686-5163
Manufacturer of ice cream, frozen yogurt and frozen novelties
President: Steve Glover
Estimated Sales: $3-5 Million
Number Employees: 5-9
Sq. footage: 6000
Type of Packaging: Consumer, Private Label

5261 **Glucona America**
114 E Conde Street
Janesville, WI 53546-3054 608-752-0449
Fax: 608-752-7643 cfields@glucona.com
www.glucona.com
Processor and importer of gluconates including ferrous, magnesium, potassium, sodium and zinc; also, calcium supplements and glucono-delta lactone (GDL); exporter of glucono-delta lactone
Development Manager: Charles King
Marketing Manager: Scott Wellington
General Manager: Sean Trac
Estimated Sales: $20-50 Million
Number Employees: 20-49
Parent Co: Avebe
Type of Packaging: Food Service
Brands:
Gluconal

5262 **Glue Dots International**
5515 S Westridge Dr
New Berlin, WI 53151 262-814-8500
Fax: 262-814-8505 888-688-7131
info@gluedots.com www.gluedots.com
Providing adhesive solutions to people, businesses and industries worldwide. Packaging/product assembly, printing and bindery, direct mail/sales promotion, gift baskets, balloon decorating, candlemaking, greeting cards, customproducts, kids and school, scrapbooking and rubber stamping and many more.
Manager: John Downs
Marketing/Communications Manager: Jennie Staghano
Estimated Sales: $ 10 - 20 Million
Number Employees: 10-19
Type of Packaging: Consumer, Bulk

5263 **Glunz Family Winery & Cellars**
888 E Belvidere Rd Ste 107
Grayslake, IL 60030 847-548-9463
Fax: 847-548-8038 winetogo@gfwc.com
www.gfwc.com
Our wines consist of white, red, Chardonnay, White Zinfandel, Merlot, Port, fruit wines (rasberry, black currant) and hertiage wines such as: May Wine, Sangria, and Glogg
Owner: Matthew Glunz
VP/Winemaker: Joe Glunz Jr
Cellarmaster: Cipriano Luvieanos
Estimated Sales: $1-2.5 Million
Number Employees: 1-4

5264 **Glutenus Minimus, LLC**
697 Belmont Street
Belmont, MA 02478-4401 617-484-3550
Dairy-free, gluten-free, nut-free, other lifestyle, baking mixes.

5265 **(HQ)Glutino**
2055 Boul Dagenais Quest
Laval, QC H7L 5V1
Canada
Fax: 450-629-4781 800-363-3438
info@glutino.com www.glutino.com
Manufacturer and distributor specializing in gluten free products. Our mission is provide a healthy lifestyle to all those with Celiac Disease and those who follow a gluten-free/wheat-free diet.
President: Steven Singer
EVP: David Miller

5266 **Go Lightly Candy**
35 Hillside Avenue
Hillside, NJ 07205-1833 973-926-2300
Fax: 973-926-4440 800-524-1304
info@hillsidecandy.com www.hillsidecandy.com
Manufacturer of Sugar free candy and 100% natural candy
President: Ted Cohen
Marketing/Export Sales: Sandy Gencarelli
Estimated Sales: $ 5 - 10 Million
Number Employees: 40
Type of Packaging: Consumer, Food Service, Private Label, Bulk
Brands:
GOLIGHTLY SUGAR FREE CANDY
SHAKEN COUNTRY MEADOWS SWEETS

5267 **Go-Rachel.com**
8120 Penn Avenue S
Minneapolis, MN 55431-1358 952-884-2305
Fax: 952-884-2307
Potato chips

5268 **Godiva Chocolatier**
355 Lexington Ave Fl 16
New York, NY 10017 212-984-5900
Fax: 212-984-5901 800-946-3482
www.godiva.com

Manufacturer of chocolates, coffee, biscuits and biscotti
President: Archie Van Beuren
CEO: James A Goldman
VP Marketing: Michael Simon
National Sales: Scott Jones
Global Senior Manager: Parmela Smith
Number Employees: 10,000 +
Brands:
GODIVA
GODIVA CHOCOLATE

5269 **Godiva Chocolatier**
355 Lexington Ave Fl 16
New York, NY 10017 212-984-5900
Fax: 212-984-5901 800-946-3482
letters@godiva.com www.godiva.com
Manufacturer of chocolate candy including boxed and covered cherries, ice-cream, liqueur and coffee
President, Worldwide: James Goldman
SVP: Paul Amorello
VP Marketing/Merchandising: Michael Simon
Director PR/Promotions: Erica Lapidus
Master Chocolatier: Thierry Muret
Number Employees: 10,000+
Parent Co: Campbell Soup
Type of Packaging: Consumer
Brands:
Godiva
Godiva Chocolate

5270 **Godshall's Quality Meats**
675 Mill Rd
Telford, PA 18969-2411 215-256-8867
Fax: 215-256-4965 888-463-7425
www.godshalls.com
Processor and wholesaler/distributor of poultry, beef, pork, lamb and veal; serving the food service industry
President/Ceo: Matthew Teller
VP: Floyd Kratz
Estimated Sales: $300,000-500,000
Number Employees: 150
Sq. footage: 12000
Type of Packaging: Food Service

5271 **Godwin Produce Company**
P.O.Box 163
Dunn, NC 28335 910-892-4171
Fax: 910-892-2232 godwinproduce@aol.com
www.sweettater.com
Manufacturer of produce including sweet potatoes, watermelons and cantaloupes
Owner: Anthony Godwin
Owner: David Godwin
Office Manager: Susan Moore
Estimated Sales: $5-10 Million
Number Employees: 5-9
Sq. footage: 85000
Type of Packaging: Consumer, Food Service, Private Label, Bulk
Brands:
Dunn's Best
Godwin
Godwin Produce
Godwin's Blue Ribbon
Sweet Carolina

5272 **Goebbert's Home Grown Vegetables**
40 W Higgins Road
South Barrington, IL 60010-9319 847-428-6727
Fax: 847-428-6850
Processor/grower of vegetables including tomatoes, sweet corn, peppers, cabbage, eggplant, broccoli, pumpkins and squash
Owner: J.H. Goebbert
Estimated Sales: $1-2.5 Million
Number Employees: 10-19

5273 **Goedens Fish Market**
529 University Avenue
Madison, WI 53703-1909 608-256-1991
Seafood

5274 **Goetze's Candy Company**
3900 E Monument St
Baltimore, MD 21205 410-342-2010
Fax: 410-522-7681 800-638-1456
office@goetzecandy.com www.goetzecandy.com
Manufacturer and exporter of caramel creams, chocolate cow tales, strawberri cream candy
President: Randle Goetze
CEO: Spaulding Goetze
VP Administration: Mitchell Goetze
VP Sales: Marty Thompson
Estimated Sales: $20-50 Million
Number Employees: 50-99
Type of Packaging: Consumer, Food Service, Bulk
Brands:
GOETZE'S

5275 **Goglanian Bakeries**
3710 S Susan St
Suite 175
Santa Ana, CA 92704 714-444-3500
Fax: 714-444-3800 info@goglanian.com
www.goglanian.com
Pizza crust, thin crust, wraps, focaccia, pita bread, bread sticks, flat bread and frozen dough.
President: George Goglanian
CEO/General Manager: Alex Goglanian
CFO: Mark Johnson
Senior Director R&D: Edward Nashawaty
Sales/Marketing Executive: Eric Porat
Senior Director Human Resources: Linda Orienza-Gerard
Operations Director: Stan Shaffer
Plant Manager: Javier Avila
Purchasing Manager: Hratch Doctorian
Estimated Sales: $5-10 Million
Number Employees: 400
Sq. footage: 71500
Type of Packaging: Consumer, Food Service, Private Label

5276 **Gold Coast Baking Company**
1590 E Saint Gertrude Pl
Santa Ana, CA 92705 714-545-2253
Fax: 714-751-2253
mflaherty@goldcoastbakery.com
www.goldcoastbakery.com
Bread and bakery products
Manager: Rick Lamb
CFO: Mike Flaherty
Manager: Mike Martinez
Estimated Sales: $100-500 Million
Number Employees: 100-249

5277 **Gold Coast Ingredients**
2429 Yates Ave
Commerce, CA 90040 323-724-8935
Fax: 323-724-9354 800-352-8673
info@goldcoastinc.com www.goldcoastinc.com
A wholesale manufacturer of flavors and colors
CEO: Chuck Brasher
Vice President: Laurie Goddard
Estimated Sales: $12 Million
Number Employees: 53
Type of Packaging: Private Label, Bulk

5278 **Gold Crust Baking Company, Inc.**
501 E Monroe Avenue
Alexandria, VA 22301-1626 703-549-0420
Fax: 703-549-0416 nausika@goldcrust.com
www.goldcrust.com
Bakery goods

5279 **Gold Cup Farms**
242 James St
Clayton, NY 13624 315-686-2480
Fax: 315-686-4701 800-752-1341
support@riverratcheese.com
www.riverratcheese.com
Distributor NYS Cheese, Adirondack Sausage
President: Richard Brown
CFO: Barb Leeson
VP: Cindy Major
Marketing/Sales: Dick Brown
Estimated Sales: $2,500,000
Number Employees: 10-19
Type of Packaging: Consumer, Food Service, Private Label, Bulk
Brands:
Adirondack Cheese
Gold Cup
Ny State River Rat Cheese

5280 **Gold Dollar Products**
6073 Mt Moriah Rd Ext Ste 12
Suite 12
Memphis, TN 38115 901-326-6027
Fax: 901-948-0309 800-971-8964
golddoll@bellsouth.net
Vinegar, mustard, hot sauce, lemon juice, bottled water
Owner: Sondra Abraham
VP, Consultant: Herbert Abraham
VP Marketing: George Abraham
Estimated Sales: $2.5-5 Million
Number Employees: 1-4
Brands:
Gold Dollar
Gold Dollar Lemon
Gold Dollar/Monedade'oro

5281 **Gold Medal Bakery**
21 Penn St
Fall River, MA 02724 508-679-8958
Fax: 508-674-6090 800-642-7568
www.goldmedalbakery.com
Processor of bread and rolls.
President: Roland Le Comte
VP of Marketing: Peggy Cavalo
VP Sales: Carl Culotta
Estimated Sales: $50-100 Million
Number Employees: 250-499
Type of Packaging: Private Label
Brands:
Holsum

5282 **Gold Medal Baking Company**
901 N 3rd St
Philadelphia, PA 19123 215-627-4787
Fax: 215-925-0179 www.goldmedalbakery.com
Processor of bread, cakes, rolls, muffins, etc
Owner: Stan Silverman
Marketing Director: Stan Silverman
Estimated Sales: $1-2.5 Million
Number Employees: 20-49
Type of Packaging: Consumer, Food Service
Brands:
Gold Medal Baking

5283 **Gold Mine Natural FoodCompany**
7805 Arjons Drive
Suite B
San Diego, CA 92126-4368 858-537-9830
Fax: 858-695-0811 800-475-3663
sales@goldminenaturalfoods.com
www.goldminenaturalfoods.com

5284 **Gold Pure Foods Products Company**
1 Brooklyn Rd
Hempstead, NY 11550-6619 516-483-5600
Fax: 516-483-5798 800-422-4681
www.goldshorseradish.com
Processor and exporter of kosher salad dressings, horseradish, sauces, mustard, salsa, borscht, schav and vinegar; importer of horseradish roots, dried peaches and dried apricots
President: Steven Gold
VP: Herbert Gold
VP Sales: Marc Gold
Estimated Sales: $5-10 Million
Number Employees: 50-99
Sq. footage: 100000
Type of Packaging: Consumer, Food Service, Private Label, Bulk
Brands:
Baker
Baker's
Dip N' Joy
Gold's
Nathan's
Old World
Uncle Dave's

5285 **Gold Seal Fruit Bouquet**
6301 W Bluemound Rd
Milwaukee, WI 53213-4146 414-259-9552
Fax: 414-258-9377 800-558-5558
fruitranchgifts@hotmail.com
www.fruitranch.com
Processor of fruit gift baskets. Wholesaler of baskets and supplies
Owner: Tanya Gearheart
Estimated Sales: $1 Million
Number Employees: 5-9
Sq. footage: 10000
Type of Packaging: Consumer, Private Label, Bulk

5286 **Gold Standard Baking**
3700 S Kedzie Ave
Chicago, IL 60632 773-523-2333
Fax: 773-523-7381 800-648-7904
www.gsbaking.com

Processor of fully and partially baked bakery products including breads, pizza crusts, croissants, etc.
President: Yianny Caparos
VP: Joe Chiodo
VP Business Development: Charles Chiodo
Estimated Sales: $2.5-5 Million
Number Employees: 5-9
Sq. footage: 50000
Type of Packaging: Consumer, Food Service, Private Label, Bulk
Brands:
Croissant De Paris
Gold Standard

5287 **Gold Star Chocolate**
250 Lorraine Street
Brooklyn, NY 11231-3806 718-330-0187
Fax: 718-330-0534
Dkatz@goldstarchocolate.com
www.goldstarchocolate.com
Chocolate
VP: Doron Katz
Brands:
CANTALOU
CAXTON
CEMOI
COPPELLA
ELGORRIAGA
FOULLON
FRANKONIA
MR
PELLETIER
PHOSCAO
PUPIER
SAINT SIFFREIN

5288 **Gold Star Coffee Company**
51 Bridge St # A
Salem, MA 01970-4198 978-744-2672
Fax: 978-744-8238 888-505-5233
Coffee
President: David Desimone
Estimated Sales: $10-20 Million
Number Employees: 10-19
Type of Packaging: Private Label

5289 **Gold Star Dairy**
6901 Interstate 30
Little Rock, AR 72209 501-565-6125
Fax: 501-568-5245
Milk & milk products
Estimated Sales: $10-20 Million
Number Employees: 10-19

5290 **Gold Star Sausage Company**
2800 Walnut St
Denver, CO 80205 303-295-6400
Fax: 303-294-0495 800-258-7229
rick@goldstarsausage.com
www.goldstarsausage.com
Processor of smoked ribs, hot dogs, and sausage products
CEO: Phil Pisciotta
Vice President: Bob Sanner
Plant Manager: Ed Telgenhoff
Estimated Sales: $22,600,000
Number Employees: 50-99
Sq. footage: 50000
Type of Packaging: Consumer, Food Service, Private Label, Bulk
Brands:
Gold Star
Old Timer

5291 **Gold Star Seafood**
2300 W 41st St
Chicago, IL 60609-2214 773-376-8080
Fax: 773-376-9879 Vang@goldstarseafood.com
goldstarseafood.com
Seafood
President: Van Giragosian
Estimated Sales: $ 10 - 20 Million
Number Employees: 10-19

5292 **Gold Star Smoked Fish**
570 Smith St
Brooklyn, NY 11231 718-522-1545
Fax: 718-260-9194 intl@goldstarco.com
www.goldstarco.com
Smoked fish and specialty foods from 20 European countries
President: Robert Pinkow
Estimated Sales: $ 10 - 20 Million
Number Employees: 20-49
Brands:
Cuetara
Denmark: Officer
Germany: Wessergold
Gerolsteiner
Gold Star
Hargita
Heine's
Iceland: Armant
Latvia: Unda
Poland: Solidarnosc
Teaports
Ukraine: Chumak, Nektar

5293 **Gold Sweet Company**
331 Old Ice House Road
Po Box 247
Lake Wales, FL 33859 863-676-0963
Fax: 863-676-0968 www.goldsweetco.com
Packer of honey for health food distributors and the bakery industry
Owner/Manager: Richard Phillips
Estimated Sales: $500,000-$1 Million
Number Employees: 1-4
Sq. footage: 3000
Type of Packaging: Consumer, Food Service, Bulk

5294 **Gold'n Plump Poultry**
P.O.Box 1106
St Cloud, MN 56302-1106 320-251-3570
Fax: 320-240-6250 800-328-2838
www.goldenplump.com
Processor and exporter of poultry including pre-packaged, roasters, parts and whole
VP Finance: Steve Jurek
Operations Manager: Kerri Schramel
Estimated Sales: $50-100 Million
Number Employees: 50-99
Parent Co: JFC International
Type of Packaging: Consumer, Food Service, Bulk
Brands:
Gold'n Plump

5295 **Goldcoast Salads**
3565 Plover Ave
Naples, FL 34117 239-304-0710
Fax: 239-304-2156 pradno@goldcoastsalads.com
www.goldcoastsalads.com
Maine lobster, blue crab and smoked salmon spreads
President: Peter Radno Jr
Plant Manager: Ruben Valenzuela

5296 **Golden Alaska Seafoods**
2200 6th Ave Ste 707
Seattle, WA 98121 206-441-1990
Fax: 206-441-8112 www.goldenalaska.com
Frozen seafood
President: Lou Fleming
CFO: Randy Adamson
Sales Manager: Markna Franklyn
Estimated Sales: $1-2.5 Million
Number Employees: 5-9

5297 **Golden Apples Candy Company**
P.O.Box 735
Southport, CT 06890 203-336-9188
Fax: 203-336-9538 800-776-0393
sales@goldenapplesinc.com
www.goldenapplesinc.com
Processor and exporter of confectionery items including hard, bagged, packaged for racks, sugar-free and all natural lollypops; also, sugar-free, all natural, homeopathic and cough pops; importer of hard candy
President: Arthur Baltimore
Vice President: Margaret Baltimore
Sales Director: David Baltimore
Estimated Sales: $500,000-$1 Million
Number Employees: 1-4
Type of Packaging: Consumer, Bulk
Brands:
7 Calorie Candy
Golden Apples 7 Calorie Candy
Kid's Choice Cough Pops
Mother Natures Health Pops
People Drops
Peoplepops

5298 **Golden Bounty Food Processors**
7410 Scout Ave
Bell Gardens, CA 90201-4932 562-806-1100
Fax: 562-806-2047 www.certi-fresh.com
President: Salvatore Galletti
CEO: Paul Demoss
CEO: Nino Palma
Estimated Sales: $ 3 - 5 Million
Number Employees: 1-4

5299 **Golden Boys Pies of SanDiego**
2667 Camino Del Rio S
San Diego, CA 92108-3707 619-293-7400
Fax: 619-293-3009 800-746-0280
Pies, breads
Estimated Sales: $10-20 Million
Number Employees: 10-19
Type of Packaging: Private Label

5300 **Golden Brands**
2520 Seventh Street Road
Louisville, KY 40208 502-636-3712
Fax: 502-636-3904 800-622-3055
jasong@gfgb.com www.gfgb.com
Manufacturer and exporter of shortenings including flaked, creamy liquid and votated; also, soybean and cottonseed oils; as well as identity preserved oils for GMO-free market. Sell to industrial baking industry and food service
President/CEO: Timothy Helson
Director Business Development: Jason Glaser
Director Sales/Customer Service: Brent Campbell

VP Technical Sales: Bob Delaney
VP Production: Sam Marrillia
Estimated Sales: $100 Million
Number Employees: 150
Sq. footage: 250000
Type of Packaging: Food Service, Bulk
Brands:
Golden Brands
Golden Foods

5301 **Golden Brown Bakery**
421 Phoenix St
South Haven, MI 49090 269-637-3418
Fax: 269-637-7822 www.goldenbrownbakery.com
Full service retail bakery and cafe with wholesale capabilities
Owner: David Braschi
Estimated Sales: $1-1.5 Million
Number Employees: 45
Type of Packaging: Consumer, Food Service, Private Label, Bulk

5302 **Golden Cheese Company of California**
1138 W Rincon St
Corona, CA 92880 951-493-4700
Fax: 951-493-4749
Manufacturer of natural, processed and imitation cheese and flavoring syrup
President: David Simon
Estimated Sales: $100+ Million
Number Employees: 250-499
Type of Packaging: Consumer, Food Service, Bulk

5303 **Golden Cheese of California**
1138 W Rincon St
Corona, CA 92880 951-493-4700
Fax: 951-493-4749 800-842-0264
Manufacturer of milk, cottage cheese, butter, sweet and sour cream, orange juice and yogurt
President: Dave Simon
Plant Controller: Richard Pluimer
VP International Sales: Gabriel Sevilla
Sales/Marketing: Doug Moore
Customer Service Manager: Christine Merritt
Plant Manager: Dermot O'Brien
Estimated Sales: $ 1 - 3 Million
Number Employees: 10-19
Sq. footage: 420000
Parent Co: Dairy Farmers of America
Type of Packaging: Consumer, Food Service
Brands:
GOLDEN CHEESE

5304 **Golden City Brewery**
920 12th St
Golden, CO 80401-1181 303-279-8092
Fax: 303-279-8092
Beer
President: Jennie Sturdavant
Director Manufacturing: Charles Sturdevant
Estimated Sales: $5-9.9 Million
Number Employees: 1-4
Type of Packaging: Private Label

5305 **Golden Creek Vineyard**
4480 Wallace Road
Santa Rosa, CA 95404-1433 707-538-2350
Wines
President: Ladi Danielik
Estimated Sales: Less than $500,000
Number Employees: 1-4
Type of Packaging: Private Label

5306 **Golden Drop**
1306 N San Fernando Rd
Los Angeles, CA 90065 323-225-9161
Fax: 323-225-9163
Beverages
President: Arthur Papazyan
Estimated Sales: $730,000
Number Employees: 10

5307 **Golden Eagle Olive Products**
P.O.Box 390
Porterville, CA 93258-0390 559-784-3468
Fax: 559-784-2186
Processor of virgin, extra virgin and pure olive oil
Owner: Jerry Padula
Assistant Manager: Traci Padula
Estimated Sales: $5-10 Million
Number Employees: 1-4
Sq. footage: 10000
Type of Packaging: Consumer
Brands:
Golden Eagle

5308 **Golden Eagle Syrup Manufacturing Company**
205 1st Ave SE
Fayette, AL 35555 205-932-5294
Fax: 205-932-5296 info@goldeneaglesyrup.com
www.goldeneaglesyrup.com
Manufacturer of syrups including table, waffle and pancake
Co-Owner/President: Trent Mobley
Co-Owner/Plant Manager: Vic Herren
Office Manager: Martha Kimbrell
Estimated Sales: $2.5-5 Million
Number Employees: 5-9
Type of Packaging: Consumer, Food Service, Bulk

5309 **Golden Edibles LLC**
10396 W State Road 84
Suite 103
Davie, FL 33324 866-779-7781
Fax: 973-807-1637 nicole@goldenedibles.com
www.goldenedibles.com
Cookies, other chocolates, frozen desserts, other snacks, popcorn, pretzels, gift packs, private label.

5310 **Golden Eye Seafood**
17640 Clarke Rd
Piney Point, MD 20674 301-994-2274
Fax: 301-994-9960
Processor and wholesaler/distributor of seafood including live and cooked blue crabs, oysters and soft shelled
President: Robert Lumpkins
Estimated Sales: $1.2 Million
Number Employees: 6

5311 **Golden Flake Snack Food**
1 Golden Flake Dr
Birmingham, AL 35205 800-239-2447
Fax: 205-458-7335 www.goldenflake.com
Snacks
President/CEO: Mark McCutcheon
Estimated Sales: I
Number Employees: 500-999
Brands:
GOLDEN FLAKE

5312 **(HQ)Golden Flake Snack Foods**
1 Golden Flake Dr
Birmingham, AL 35205 800-239-2447
Fax: 205-458-7335 www.goldenflake.com
Snacks-salted
President: Mark McCutcheon
Quality Control: Joe Elliott
Marketing Director: June Strauss
Sales Director: Randy Bates
Operations Manager: Dave Jones
Production Manager: Neil Hunt
Purchasing Manager: Jeff Clemmons
Estimated Sales: $110 Million
Number Employees: 500-999
Number of Brands: 4
Sq. footage: 350000
Type of Packaging: Consumer, Food Service, Bulk
Other Locations:
Golden Flake Manufacturing Plant
Ocala FL
Golden Flake Manufacturing Plant
Birmingham AL

5313 **(HQ)Golden Flake Snack Foods**
3031 W Silver Springs Blvd
Ocala, FL 34475 352-351-2277
Fax: 352-351-3197 800-239-2447
www.goldenflake.com
Processor of potato and tortilla chips
President/CEO: Mark W McCutcheon
VP/CFO: Mark Mccutcheon
CFO: Patty Townsend
Vice President: Randy Bates
Sales Director: Randy Bates
Production Manager: Larry Wood
Plant Manager: John Wagner
Estimated Sales: $20-50 Million
Number Employees: 20-49
Type of Packaging: Consumer, Private Label
Brands:
Golden Flake

5314 **Golden Fluff Popcorn Company**
118 Monmouth Ave
Lakewood, NJ 08701-3347 732-367-5448
Fax: 732-367-1028 goldenfluff@aol.com
www.goldenfluff.com
Pre-popped popcorn, potato sticks, microwave popcorn, tortilla chips, toppings, nuts & dried fruits, elyon marshmallow and dontil sugar free chewing gum.
President: Ephraim Schwinder
Estimated Sales: Less than $500,000
Number Employees: 10-19
Type of Packaging: Consumer, Bulk
Brands:
Dontil
Elyon
Golden Fluff

5315 **Golden Foods**
5743 Smithway St # 305
Commerce, CA 90040-1549 323-721-1882
Fax: 323-721-4526 800-350-2462
gsfoods@gowebway.com
Processor of confectionery products, cake and pie fillings, syrups, dessert toppings, frozen edible coatings and low-fat fudge variegates
President: Jonathan Freed
CEO: Kit Phillips
CFO: Ezekiel Freed
VP: Rose Freed
Purchasing Manager: Kit Phillips
Estimated Sales: $1-2.5 Million
Number Employees: 5-9
Sq. footage: 8000
Type of Packaging: Bulk
Brands:
Gelite
Pectose-Standard

5316 **Golden Gate Foods**
1618 W Commerce St
Dallas, TX 75208 214-747-2223
Fax: 214-760-7611
Processor of chow mein, egg rolls, egg and pork sausage rolls, egg and cheese rolls, noodles, wontons, stir fry rice, sesame oil, soy sauce, dim sum and pot stickers
President: Buck Jung
CEO: Helen Jung
CFO: Lai Chun Jung
Estimated Sales: $2.5-5 Million
Number Employees: 20-49
Number of Products: 10
Sq. footage: 13000
Type of Packaging: Consumer, Food Service, Private Label, Bulk
Brands:
Golden Gate

5317 **Golden Glow Cookie Company**
1844 Givan Ave
Bronx, NY 10469 718-379-6223
Fax: 718-379-4417 ggcookies@aol.com
www.goldenglowcookie.com
Processor of cookies, cakes and Italian pastries
President: Rose Florio
VP Sales: Sal Florio
VP Production: Joan Florio
Estimated Sales: $2.5-5 Million
Number Employees: 10-19
Brands:
Mama Rose

5318 **Golden Grain**
4576 Willow Rd
Pleasanton, CA 94588-2715 925-734-8800
Fax: 925-416-7065 www.pepsico.com
Dry pasta
President: Mark Shapiro
VP: Jim Richard
Estimated Sales: $100-500 Million
Number Employees: 100-249
Brands:
Golden Grain
Mission
Pasta Roni

5319 **Golden Grain Company**
7700 W 71st St
Bridgeview, IL 60455 708-458-7020
Fax: 708-458-7023 www.goldengrainpasta.com
Processor of pasta and rice products
Principal: Stewart Seaton
Comptroller: Dan Arcury
Plant Manager: Dave Corazzi
Estimated Sales: $100-500 Million
Number Employees: 250-499
Sq. footage: 7000
Parent Co: Quaker Oats Company
Type of Packaging: Consumer, Food Service, Private Label

5320 **Golden Gulf Coast Packing Company**
642 Bayview Ave
Biloxi, MS 39530-2307 228-374-6121
Fax: 228-374-0599
Processor and exporter of frozen and breaded shrimp
President/Owner: Richard Gollott
Estimated Sales: $ 10 - 20 Million
Number Employees: 50-99
Sq. footage: 8000

5321 **Golden Harvest Pecans**
348 Vereen Bell Road
Cairo, GA 39828-4910
US 229-377-5617
Fax: 229-762-3335 800-597-0968
gharvest@rose.net
Processor, co-packer and exporter of certified organic pecans, gift baskets and southern delicacies,preserves,cookies,jellies.
President/CEO: J Van Ponder
Estimated Sales: $250,000
Number Employees: 2
Sq. footage: 3109
Type of Packaging: Consumer, Food Service, Private Label, Bulk

5322 **Golden Heritage Food**
P.O.Box 97
Latty, OH 45855-0097 419-399-5786
Fax: 419-399-4924 888-233-6446
info@ghfllc.com www.ghfllc.com
Premium honey
president: dwight Stoller
CEO: Brent Barkman
Estimated Sales: Below $ 5 Million
Number Employees: 20-49
Brands:
Busy Bee

5323 **Golden Heritage Foods**
120 Santa Fe St
Hillsboro, KS 67063-9688 620-947-3173
800-530-5827
info@ghfllc.com www.ghfllc.com
Processor and packager of honey and flavored honey spreads
CEO: Dwight Stoller
CFO: Doug Weinbrenner
Estimated Sales: $20 - 50 Million
Number Employees: 20-49
Sq. footage: 23000
Type of Packaging: Consumer, Food Service, Private Label, Bulk

5324 **Golden Kernel Pecan Company**
PO Box 613
Cameron, SC 29030 803-823-2311
Fax: 803-823-2080 800-845-2448
info@goldenkernel.com www.goldenkernel.com

Pecans and nuts, fruit cakes, candies and hams
President: David K Summers Jr
VP/Treasurer: J Williams Summers
Marketing Director: Bill Summers
Operations Manager: Jerry Fogle
Estimated Sales: $50 Million
Number Employees: 20-49
Sq. footage: 17100
Type of Packaging: Consumer, Private Label, Bulk
Brands:
GOLDEN KERNEL

5325 **Golden Locker Cooperative**
P.O.Box 279
Golden, IL 62339-0279 217-696-4456
Processor of beef and pork
Manager: Rick Huntley
Estimated Sales: $2.5-5 Million
Number Employees: 5-9
Type of Packaging: Consumer, Bulk

5326 **Golden Malted**
4101 William Richardson Drive
South Bend, IN 46628 574-247-2270
Fax: 574-247-2280 800-253-0590
retail@goldenmalted.com
www.goldenmalted.com
pancake and waffle flour

5327 **Golden Moon Tea**
Ste 204
1043 Sterling Rd
Herndon, VA 20170-3842 425-820-2000
Fax: 425-821-9700 877-327-5473
service@goldenmoontea.com
www.goldenmoontea.com
Specialty tea and fine chocolates, tea accessories
President: Cynthia Knotts
Number of Products: 30
Type of Packaging: Consumer, Food Service, Private Label, Bulk
Brands:
Golden Moon Tea

5328 **Golden Peanut Company**
P.O.Box 488
Ashburn, GA 31714 229-567-3311
Fax: 229-567-2006 www.goldenpeanut.com
Processor and exporter of shelled peanuts
VP: K McRee
Plant Manager: Bill Leverette
Estimated Sales: $ 5 - 10 Million
Number Employees: 100-249
Parent Co: Gold Kist Poultry
Type of Packaging: Bulk

5329 **Golden Peanut Company**
100 N Point Ctr E Ste 400
Alpharetta, GA 30022 770-752-8160
Fax: 770-752-8306 www.goldenpeanut.com
Sheller and processor of peanuts and peanut products. Raw shelled and inshell peanuts, peanut flours, peanut extracts, roasted aromatic and refined various peanut oils, and peanut seed.
President/CEO: James Dorsett
CFO: Fritz Holzgrefe
Plant Manager: Craig Smith
Regional Procurement Manager: Milton Smith
Estimated Sales: $500 Million-$1 Billion
Number Employees: 1000
Type of Packaging: Consumer

5330 **Golden Peanut Company**
P.O.Box 279
Aulander, NC 27805 252-345-1661
Fax: 252-345-1991 www.goldenpeanut.com
Processor and exporter of peanuts
President: John Monahan
Plant Manager: Merle Yates
Estimated Sales: $5-10 Million
Number Employees: 150
Parent Co: Golden Peanut
Type of Packaging: Consumer

5331 **Golden Peanut Company**
100 N Point Ctr E Ste 400
Alpharetta, GA 30022 770-752-8160
Fax: 770-752-8306 www.goldenpeanut.com
Sheller and processor of peanuts and peanuts products including raw shelled and inshell peanuts, peanut flours, peanut extracts, roasted aromatic and refined various peanut oils and peanut seed.
President/CEO: James Dorsett
CFO: Fritz Holzgrefe
VP International Sales: Alex Izmirlian
Estimated Sales: $500 Million+
Number Employees: 1000
Type of Packaging: Bulk

5332 **Golden Peanuts Company**
100 N Point Ctr E # 400
Alpharetta, GA 30022-8262 770-752-8205
Fax: 770-752-8306 www.goldenpeanut.com
Sheller and processor of peanuts and peanut products. Golden's primary product lines include raw shelled and inshell peanuts, peanut flour, various peanut oils, and peanut seed.
President/CEO: Jimmy Dorsett
CFO: Fritz Holzgrefe
VP Sales: Bill Grant
Estimated Sales: $500,000-$1 Million
Number Employees: 50
Type of Packaging: Private Label

5333 **Golden Platter Foods**
37 Tompkins Point Rd
Newark, NJ 07114 973-242-0290
Fax: 973-242-5892 scott@goldenplatter.com
www.goldenplatter.com
Processor and exporter of poultry products including frozen nuggets, patties and parts and turkey sausages; also, Halal meats
President: Scott Bennett
CEO: Eli Bennett
Estimated Sales: $6.5 Million
Number Employees: 50
Type of Packaging: Consumer, Food Service

5334 **Golden River Fruit Company**
505 66th Ave SW
Vero Beach, FL 32968 772-562-8610
Grower and shipper of grapefruit
CEO: George Lamberth
VP: David Milwood
General Manager/Purchasing Director: Fred Antwerp
Estimated Sales: $2 Million
Number Employees: 25
Sq. footage: 6737
Type of Packaging: Bulk
Brands:
Bland Farms
Golden Eagle
Golden One
Golden River
Golden Sun
National Gold
National One
Sundance

5335 **Golden Rod Broilers**
2352 County Road 719
Cullman, AL 35055 256-734-0941
Fax: 256-739-4024
Manufacturer and exporter of poultry
President: Forrest Ingram
VP: Wynona Cooley
Estimated Sales: $50-100 Million
Number Employees: 500-999
Parent Co: Ingram Farms
Type of Packaging: Consumer, Food Service, Private Label, Bulk

5336 **Golden Specialty Foods**
14605 Best Ave
Norwalk, CA 90650 562-802-2537
Fax: 562-926-4491
Processor of canned dips, salad dressings, sauces, Mexican seasonings, chicken and beef bases, etc.; exporter of salsa and chili con carne
President: Phil Pisciotta
CEO: James Kim
Quality Assurance Director: Javed Atcha
Operations Manager: Wayne Lam
Estimated Sales: $3.5 Million
Number Employees: 25
Sq. footage: 31000
Type of Packaging: Consumer, Food Service, Private Label, Bulk

5337 **Golden State Citrus Packers**
P.O.Box 697
Woodlake, CA 93286 559-564-3351
Fax: 559-564-3865 vcpg@vcpg.com
www.vcpg.com
Golden State Citrus Packers is a licensed commercial shipper of citrus products for Sunkist Growers, Inc.
General Manager: Cliff St Martin
Assistant Manager: John Clower
Plant Manager: Raul Gamez
Parent Co: Visalia Citrus Packing Group
Type of Packaging: Food Service

5338 **(HQ)Golden State Foods**
18301 Von Karman Avenue
Suite 1100
Irvine, CA 92612-1009 949-252-2000
Fax: 949-252-2080
gsfinfo@goldenstatefoods.com
www.goldenstatefoods.com
Sauces, dressings, syrups, jams/jellies and toppings, cooked beef, taco meat, chili and burrito fillings, produce, rolls and buns, elongated buns, and mini roll.
Chairman/President/CEO: Mark Wetterau
Vice Chairman: Michael Waitukaitis
Estimated Sales: $4 Billion
Number Employees: 4000
Sq. footage: 27000
Other Locations:
Golden State Foods
Sixth of October City

5339 **Golden State Vintners**
38558 Road 128
Cutler, CA 93615 559-528-3033
Fax: 559-528-2627 www.gsvwine.com
Processor and exporter of wine, grape juice and brandy.
President/CEO: Jeffrey O'Neill
Vice President: Jon Powell
CFO: David Johnson
Plant Manager: Ted Miller
Estimated Sales: $5-10 Million
Number Employees: 20-49
Type of Packaging: Consumer, Food Service, Private Label, Bulk
Brands:
BOUNTY
EDGEWOOD
LE BLANC
MONTHAVEN
SUMMERFIELD

5340 **Golden Temple**
1616 Preuss Rd
Los Angeles, CA 90035-4212 310-275-9891
Fax: 310-275-2923 http://www.peacecereal.com
Natural foods, organic teas, natural and organic cereals, body care products and herbal supplements.
President/Owner: Gurudhan Khalsa
International Sales Administrator: Sarib Khalsa
Estimated Sales: $ 1 - 3 Million
Number Employees: 16

5341 **(HQ)Golden Temple**
950 International Way
Springfield, OR 97477-1081
Fax: 541-461-2191 800-964-4832
cs2006@kiit.com www.yogitea.com
Processor and exporter of natural products including low-fat granola cereals and muesli, herbal tea blends and confectionery products; importer of herbs and spices
President: Sopurkh Khalsa
CEO: Kartar Khalsa
Director R&D: Gura Hari Shigh Khalsa
Sales Manager: Grundhan Khalsa
Estimated Sales: $500,000- 1 Million
Number Employees: 100-249
Sq. footage: 100000
Parent Co: Yogi Tea
Type of Packaging: Consumer, Food Service, Private Label, Bulk
Other Locations:
Golden Temple
Seattle WA
Brands:
Ancient Healing Formulas
Golden Temple
Herb Technology
Rain Forest

Sweet Home Farm
Yogi Tea

5342 **Golden Temple, Sunshine& Yogi Tea**
1616 Preuss Rd
Los Angeles, CA 90035-4212 310-275-9891
Fax: 310-275-2923 800-225-3623
www.goldentemple.com
Natural foods and health products and Yogi Tea
President: Yogi Bhajan
National Sales Manager: Gurudhan Singh Khalsa
Estimated Sales: $ 1 - 3 Million
Number Employees: 20-49
Brands:
Yogi Tea

5343 **Golden Town Apple Products**
170 5th Avenue
Rougemont, QC J0L 1M0
Canada 519-599-6300
Fax: 519-599-2103
keithc@goldentownapples.com
www.goldentownapples.com
Specializing in apple processing, especially apple peeling and apple-juice production. Leading producer in Ontario
President: Thomas Kritsch
Business Manager: Gerry Williams
Technical Director: Doug Johnson
Office Administrator: Darlene Gardner
Maintenance/Engineering Manager: Ron McQuarrie
Juice Production Coordinator: Jennifer Rear
Plant Manager: Bryan Lowe
GM/Purchasing/Sales: Keith Cummings
Number Employees: 20-49
Sq. footage: 40000
Parent Co: A. Lassonde, Inc
Type of Packaging: Consumer, Bulk

5344 **Golden Valley Dairy Products**
1025 E Bardsley Ave
Tulare, CA 93274-5752 559-687-1188
Fax: 559-685-6551 webamster@gvdairy.com
www.saputo.com
Processor of cheese
Manager: Mike Kothbauer
CEO: John Prince
Estimated Sales: $500,000-$1 Million
Number Employees: 5-9
Parent Co: DCCA
Type of Packaging: Consumer
Brands:
Ben & Jerry
Breyers
Haagen Dazs
Klondike

5345 **Golden Valley Foods**
Po Box 1800
31632 Marshall Road
Abbotsford, BC V2S 7G3
Canada 604-855-7431
Fax: 604-855-7439 888-299-8855
gvfoods@goldenvalley.com
www.goldenvalley.com
Egg production through grading, wholesaling, and distribution of eggs
President: Ken Funk
Manager/Controller: Marion Juhasz
Quality Assurance/Plant Manager: Frank Curtis
Manager/Food Service Division: John Funk
Director Sales/Marketing: Bryan Piazza
Manager Human Resources: Carol Wayner
General Manager: Walt Puetz
VP Operations: Ralph Paine
Estimated Sales: $90 Million
Number Employees: 150
Type of Packaging: Consumer, Food Service, Private Label
Brands:
FRASER VALLEY
GOLDEN VALLEY FOODS

5346 **Golden Valley Seed**
202 E Main Street
El Centro, CA 92243 760-337-3100
Fax: 760-337-3135 info@goldenvalleyseed.com
www.goldenvalleyseed.com
Developer, producer and marketer of vegetable seeds.
President: Nassif Burkhuch
CFO/Secretary: Clark Sarchet
VP: Irene Davila
Warehouse Supervisor: Miguel Izarraras
Estimated Sales: $2.7 Million
Number Employees: 12
Sq. footage: 12000
Type of Packaging: Bulk
Brands:
AMERICAN SEED
GOLDEN VALLEY SEED
NEUMAN SEED
SEED EXPORT
SUN VALLEY SELECT SEED

5347 **Golden Walnut SpecialtyFoods**
3200 16th St
Zion, IL 60099-1416 847-731-3200
Fax: 847-731-6433 800-843-3645
sales@goldenwalnut.com
www.goldenwalnut.com
Processor of specialty food products including cookies, cakes, cheesecakes, shortbread and candy; exporter of cookies
President: Mark Sigel
Estimated Sales: $5-10 Million
Number Employees: 20-49
Parent Co: EMAC International
Type of Packaging: Consumer, Private Label, Bulk
Brands:
Almond Ingot
Amelia's Sugar Free Shoppe
Buckley's
Golden Walnut
Ingot
Monica's
Razzlenuts
Sideboard Sweets & Savories
Thimble

5348 **Golden West Fruit Company**
2151 Saybrook Ave
Commerce, CA 90040 323-726-9419
Fax: 323-726-9504 www.goldenwestfruit.com
Processes fruits, toppings, syrups, fillings & bottled fruit & beverages.
President: Donald Campolo
Estimated Sales: $280,000
Number Employees: 1-4
Sq. footage: 20000
Type of Packaging: Private Label, Bulk

5349 **Golden West Nuts**
1555 Warren Rd
Ripon, CA 95366 209-599-6193
Fax: 209-599-6013 steve@goldenwestnuts.com
www.goldenwestnuts.com
Golden West Nuts, Inc. is a grower, processor and shipper of California almonds. We offer natural and blanched forms of whole, sliced, slivered and diced almonds. We are also one of the largest shippers of inshell almonds. For almondapplication ideas and recent nutritional research on the health benefits of almonds, visit the all about almonds section of our web site at www.goldenwestnuts.com. Contact Steve Gikas at (209)-599-6193 or at steve@goldenwestnuts.com forinformation
President: Jon Hoff
CEO: Steve Gikas
Estimated Sales: $ 20 - 50 Million
Number Employees: 100-249
Type of Packaging: Bulk

5350 **Golden West Nuts**
1555 Warren Rd
Ripon, CA 95366 209-599-6193
Fax: 209-599-6013 sales@goldenwestnuts.com
www.goldenwestnuts.com
Manufacturer of California almonds.
President: Jon Hoff
VP/CFO: Jonathan Hoff
Production Supervisor: Marcelino Martinez
Plant Manager: Miguel Fernandez
Estimated Sales: $60 Million
Number Employees: 60
Sq. footage: 21000
Type of Packaging: Bulk
Brands:
Golden West

5351 **Golden West Specialty Foods**
300 Industrial Way
Brisbane, CA 94005 650-553-9327
Fax: 415-657-0110 800-584-4481
info@gwsfoods.com www.gwsfoods.com
Gourmet foods, sauces, cookies, shortbread, pesto sauce, cocktail sauce, BBQ sauce, marinades, dressings and chocolate poker chips.
President: Lawrence Ames
Estimated Sales: $2-4 Million
Type of Packaging: Consumer, Food Service, Private Label, Bulk

5352 **Golden Whisk**
P.O.Box 2131
South San Francisco, CA 94083 650-952-7677
Fax: 650-952-9004 800-660-5222
laregina@goldenwhisk.com'
www.goldenwhisk.com
Processor, exporter and wholesaler/distributor of olive oil, pasta, vinegar, specialty sauces and condiments including Asian, south-western and Mexican; serving the retail and food service markets
President/CEO: Elinor Hill-Courtney
Executive VP: A Courtney
Marketing Director: Julie Hutchinson
Purchasing Manager: Elinor Hill-Courtney
Estimated Sales: $500,000-$1 Million
Number Employees: 5-10
Sq. footage: 10000
Type of Packaging: Consumer, Food Service, Private Label, Bulk
Brands:
A.J's Frisco B-B-Q
Albear's Apri-Dijon
Alla Primavera
Aloha Gold
Arti-Garlico
Basically Basil
Canzone Del Mare
Cucina Della Regina
Earl Grey Vinaigre Det
Expressly Oriental
Formaglio
Garlirosti
Golden Whisk
Honeyed Ginger
Jazzy Garlic Jazz
La Regina's Balsamic
Lala's Bar & Grill
Marinara Mia
Porcini Toscanini
Really Garlicky
Red Raspberry Razzle
Salsa Di Marco Polo
Smokey Lap-Souchang Vinaigre Det
Star of Siam
Vinegar Paradiso
Vinegar Siam
Vinegar Tropicana
Wokin'n Tossin'
Zesta Italiana
Zia Maria's Verde

5353 **Goldenberg Candy Company**
7701 State Rd
Philadelphia, PA 19136-3405 215-335-4500
Fax: 215-335-4510 800-727-2439
info@goldenbergcandy.com
www.peanutchews.com
Manufacturer and exporter of candy including coated bars, and miniatures with syrup and peanuts, Halloween, fund raising, etc
VP: Mindy Goldenberg
Estimated Sales: $20-50 Million
Number Employees: 100-249
Sq. footage: 100000
Type of Packaging: Consumer, Food Service, Bulk
Brands:
Chew-Ets
Peanut Chews

5354 **Goldenrod Dairy Foods/U C Milk Company**
234 N Scott St
Madisonville, KY 42431-2067 270-821-7221
Fax: 270-821-7292 800-462-2354
www.goldenroddairy.com
Milk and dairy products
General Manager: Tony Mayes
Sales Manager: Mark Miller
Human Resource Manager: Steve Shoots
Plant Manager: Aaron Johnson

Estimated Sales: $ 50 - 100 Million
Number Employees: 155
Parent Co: National Dairy
Type of Packaging: Bulk

5355 **Goldilocks Bakeshop**
3569 Callan Blvd
South San Francisco, CA 94080 925-681-1888
www.giustos.com
Flour and other grains
Owner: Albert Giusto
Estimated Sales: $5-10 Million
Number Employees: 20-49

5356 **Golding Farms Foods**
6061 Gun Club Rd
Winston Salem, NC 27103 336-766-6161
Fax: 336-766-3131
information@goldingfarmsfood.com
www.goldingfarmsfoods.com
Processor and private label co-packer of condiments and sauces including barbecue, steak, cocktail, salad dressing, tartar and salsa; also, honey, molasses and relishes including chow chow and onion
President/Owner: Tony Golding
EVP: Ron Foster Jr
Technical Director: Daniel Sortwell
Director Sales: Tom Clayton
Operations Manager: Preston Myers
Production Manager: Lawrence Logan
Estimated Sales: 2.5-5 Million
Number Employees: 50-99
Number of Products: 150
Sq. footage: 40000
Type of Packaging: Consumer, Food Service, Private Label, Bulk
Brands:
Golding
Golding Farms
Golding Gourmand
Mrs. Campbells
Naturally Healthy
Old Laredo

5357 **Goldrush Sourdough**
491 W San Carlos Street
San Jose, CA 95110-2632 408-288-4090
Fax: 408-286-1503 christine@commissary.com
www.mccornbread.com
Distribution of cornbread
President: Henry Down
Marketing Director: Barry Johnson
Purchasing Manager: Preston Myers
Estimated Sales: $2.5-5 Million
Number Employees: 10-19

5358 **Goldwater's Food's Of Arizona**
Salsa Express
PO Box 9846
Fredericksburg, TX 78624
Fax: 830-990-9481 800-488-4932
goldwaters@goldwaters.com
www.goldwaters.com
Processor of fruit salsa and bean dips, barbecue sauces and chili
President: Carolyn Ross
Estimated Sales: $1-2.5 Million
Number Employees: 1-4
Type of Packaging: Consumer
Brands:
Goldwater's
Goldwater's Taste of the Southwest

5359 **Golf Mill Chocolate Factory**
332 Golf Mill Ctr
Niles, IL 60714 847-635-1107
Fax: 847-390-1737
Processor of chocolate candy
Owner: Ella Faybysh
CEO: Lela Faybysh
Estimated Sales: $ 1-2.5 Million
Number Employees: 5-9
Type of Packaging: Consumer

5360 **Goll's Bakery**
234 N Washington St
Havre De Grace, MD 21078 410-939-4321
Fax: 410-939-2556 www.grollsbakery.com
Family owned german style bakery, breads, wedding cakes, birthday cakes, cookies baked fresh every day.
Owner: Robert K Goll Jr
Estimated Sales: Less than $500,000
Number Employees: 5-9

5361 **Gollott Brothers Seafood Company**
555 Bayview Ave
Biloxi, MS 39530-2418 228-432-7865
Fax: 228-435-3820
Processor and importer of fresh shrimp and oysters
President: Larry Gollott Jr
Estimated Sales: $20-50 Million
Number Employees: 50-99
Type of Packaging: Consumer

5362 **Gonard Foods**
3915 Edmonton Trail NE
Unit 7
Calgary, AB T2E 6T1
Canada 403-277-0991
Fax: 403-277-0664
Processor of frozen entrees, meat patties, chicken products, veal cutlets, fresh entrees, packaged sandwiches, red and deli meats
President/Owner: Munir Lakha
Estimated Sales: $975,000
Number Employees: 3

5363 **Gondwanaland**
1599 Camino De La Tierra
Corrales, NM 87048 505-899-2843
Fax: 505-890-5315 larry@gondwanaland1.com
www.gondwanaland1.com
Processor of gourmet coffee including organic, arabican, Columbian, Costa Rican, Indonesian, Mexican, Ethiopian and Tanzanian
Owner: Larry Ward

5364 **(HQ)Gonnella Baking Company**
2006 W Erie St
Chicago, IL 60612 312-733-2020
Fax: 312-733-7056 www.gonnella.com
Frozen bread and baked goods
President: Nicholas Marcucci
Vice President: Tom Marcucci
Research & Development: Karen Fusaro
VP Sales: Paul Gonnella
Human Resources: Kathleen Heinzman
Estimated Sales: $10-20 Million
Number Employees: 60

5365 **Gonnella Frozen Products**
1117 Wiley Rd
Schaumburg, IL 60173-4337 847-884-8829
Fax: 847-884-9469 www.gonnella.com
Frozen dough products
President: Ken Gonnella
Treasurer: George Mancucci
Sales: Ronald Lucchesi
Human Resources/Safety Manager: James Mazukelli
Plant Manager: Kent Beernink
Estimated Sales: $20-50 Million
Number Employees: 250-499
Type of Packaging: Consumer, Food Service, Private Label, Bulk

5366 **Good 'N Natural**
2100 Smithtown Ave
Ronkonkoma, NY 11779 800-544-0095
800-544-0095
questions@goodnnatural.com
www.goodnnatural.com
Processor of vitamins and supplements

5367 **(HQ)Good Earth® Teas**
831 Almar Avenue
Santa Cruz, CA 95060-5804 831-423-7913
Fax: 831-429-5173 888-625-8227
sales@goodearthteas.com
www.goodearthteas.com
Processor of highest quality standards and great tasting flavors of teas such as: green, chai, red, black, herbal, black and medicinal to name a few.
President: Jeffrey Freeman
CEO: Louise Zaricor
VP Marketing: Clive Rowlandson
VP Sales: Randall Duarte
Manufacturing/Operations Director: Arn Parker
Estimated Sales: $13.8 Billion
Number Employees: 70
Sq. footage: 41000
Parent Co: Tetley US Holdings Limited
Type of Packaging: Private Label
Brands:
China Collection Teas
Energy Supplements
Functional Teas
Good Earth Teas
Herbal Teas

5368 **Good Food**
4960 Horseshoe Pike
Honey Brook, PA 19344 610-273-3776
Fax: 610-273-2087 800-327-4406
goodfood@goldenbarrel.com
www.goldenbarrel.com
Molasses, syrups, shoofly pie and funnel cake mixes; vegetable, cotton seed, coconut, peanut, corn, olive, canola and blended cooking oils
President: Larry Martin
CEO: Ean Johnson
Estimated Sales: $20-50 Million
Number Employees: 100-249

5369 **Good Fortunes & Edible Art**
6754 Eton Ave
Canoga Park, CA 91303-2813 818-595-1555
Fax: 818-595-1550 800-644-9474
order@goodfortunes.com
www.corporatecandyworks.com
Gourmet dipped fortune cookies, classical-sized dipped and decorated fortune cookies, sourdough pretzels sticks dipped in chocolate, Bavarian pretzels dipped
Owner: Karen Staitman
Brands:
A Dose of Good Fortunes
Candy Art
Cookie Art
Fractured Fortunes
Good Fortunes
Pretzel Twisters
Pretzel Wands
Sugar Art

5370 **Good Harbor Fillet Company**
21 Great Republic Dr
Gloucester, MA 01930 978-675-9100
Fax: 978-675-9190 www.goodharborfillet.com
Specializes in the manufacture and distribution of a complete line of made-to-order, processed seafood products, as well as a variety of innovative specialty items.
President: William Stride
Chief Financial Officer: Mike Joyce
Northeast Regional Manager: Ned Hawkins
Southeast Regional Manager: Dave Galloway
Quality Control Manager: Alan Pothier
VP Sales/Marketing: Annette Chalmers
West Coast Sales Manager: Joel Bortz
Chief Operating Officer: Dave Nelson
Purchasing Manager: Alan Gilbert
Number Employees: 50-99
Type of Packaging: Consumer, Food Service

5371 **Good Harbor Vineyards**
34 S Manitou Trl
Lake Leelanau, MI 49653-9589 231-256-7165
Fax: 231-256-7378 winery@goodharbor.com
www.goodharbor.com
Wines: White Riesling, Chardonnay, Fishtown White, Trillium®, Pinot Grigio, Manitou, and specialty wines.
Winemaker/Owner: Bruce Simpson
Associate: Richard Flores
Associate: Rocky Flores
Retail Sales/Owner: Debbie Simpson
Operations: William Schaub
Operations: Gary Schaub
Assistant Winemaker: David Hooper
Growing/Management Workforce: Ovidio Chapa
Estimated Sales: Under $500,000
Number Employees: 1-4
Type of Packaging: Private Label

5372 **Good Health Natural Foods**
81 Scudder Avenue
Northport, NY 11768-2966 631-261-2111
Fax: 631-261-2147
francois@goodhealthnaturalfoods.com
Olive oil, potato chips, popcorn, pretzels, candy, apple chips crackers and cookies
Estimated Sales: $ 3 - 5 Million
Number Employees: 5-9

5373 **Good Health Natural Foods**
81 Scudder Avenue
Northport, NY 11768-2966 631-261-2111
Fax: 631-261-2147 info@e-goodhealth.com
www.goodhealthnaturalfoods.com

Good health natural snacks and energy-well high protein snacks with soy, south of France natural body care. Organic olive oil potato chips, popcorn, pretzels, natural candy, apple chips and crackers.
President: Francois Bogrand
Estimated Sales: $2.5-5 Million
Number Employees: 1-4

5374 **(HQ)Good Humor Breyers Ice Cream Company**
2271 Hutson Road
Green Bay, WI 54303-4712 920-499-5151
Fax: 920-497-6523 www.breyers.com
Processor and exporter of ice cream and novelties
President: Eric Walsh
VP Finance: Pete Allcox
VP: Mark Freeman
VP Sales: Joe Culligan
VP Human Resources: Mark Freeman
Estimated Sales: $1.1 Billion
Number Employees: 240
Parent Co: Unilever
Type of Packaging: Consumer, Food Service, Private Label, Bulk
Brands:
Breyers
Good Humor
Klondike
Popsicle

5375 **Good Old Dad Food Products**
185 Industrial Court B
Sault Ste. Marie, ON P6B 5Z9
Canada 705-253-7426
Fax: 705-949-0871 800-267-7426
godfoods@shaw.ca
Processor of frozen and snack pasta, etc
President: Enrico Palarchio
Vice President: Richard Palarchio
Number Employees: 10-19
Sq. footage: 11000
Type of Packaging: Consumer, Food Service
Brands:
Rico's

5376 **Good Old Days Foods**
3300 S Polk St
Little Rock, AR 72204 501-565-1257
Fax: 501-562-7439 www.goodolddaysfoods.com
Processor of frozen fruit cobblers, corn bread dressing, bread pudding, sweet potato casserole, pecan cobbler. Old fashioned, farm kitchen foods.
Chairman/CEO: Carroll Elder
CFO: Jim Fletcher
VP: Pam Paladino
Sales Director: Doyle Rice
VP Manufacturing/Operations: Robert Cochran
Estimated Sales: $10-20 Million
Number Employees: 80
Sq. footage: 42780
Type of Packaging: Consumer, Food Service, Private Label

5377 **Good Star Foods**
9310 Prototype Dr
Reno, NV 89521 775-851-2442
Fax: 775-851-7436 nans@qualitycrisp.com
www.qualitycrisp.com
Processor and contract packager of crisped grains, protein crisps, extruded cereals and fat-free extruded cereal snacks; also, contract product development available
President: Hans Bohner
Estimated Sales: $ 1 - 3 Million
Number Employees: 5-9
Sq. footage: 11000
Type of Packaging: Bulk

5378 **Good Wives, Inc.**
330 Ballardville Street
Wilmington, MA 01902 781-596-0070
Fax: 781-596-1131 800-521-8160
customer.service@goodwives.com
www.goodwives.com
Manufacturer of frozen hors d'oeuvres, pastries, tortilla wraps, and flatbreads
President: Chris Collias
CFO: Bruce Robertson
Marketing: Sandra Gamble
Plant Manager: John Reardon III
Estimated Sales: Under $500,000
Number Employees: 100-249
Sq. footage: 10000

Type of Packaging: Consumer, Food Service, Private Label

5379 **Good-O-Beverages Company**
1801 Boone Ave
Bronx, NY 10460 718-328-6400
Fax: 718-328-7002 info@good-o.com
www.good-o.com
Processor, bottler and exporter of flavored soft drinksjuices, teas and energy drinks.
Owner: Richard Hahn
Plant Manager: Irving Mendelson
Estimated Sales: $10-20 Million
Number Employees: 40
Sq. footage: 53000
Type of Packaging: Consumer
Brands:
Coco Rico
Kola Champagne
Red Pop
West Indian Kola

5380 **GoodMark Foods**
536 Fairfield Avenue
Stamford, CT 06902-7525 919-790-9940
Fax: 919-790-6537 www.slimjim.com
Snacks
Trade Marketing: Jeff Seccombe
Brands:
ANDY CAPP'S
PEMMICAN
PENROSE
SLIM JIM

5381 **Goodart Candy**
P.O.Box 901
Lubbock, TX 79408-0901 806-747-2600
Fax: 806-747-8330
Manufacturer of peanut patties and peanut brittle
President: Ron Harbuck
VP: Ron Harbuck
Estimated Sales: $500,000-$1 Million
Number Employees: 10-19
Sq. footage: 12500
Type of Packaging: Private Label, Bulk
Brands:
Goodart's

5382 **Goodheart Brand Specialty Foods**
11122 Nacogdoches Rd
San Antonio, TX 78217-2314 210-637-1963
Fax: 210-637-1391 888-466-3992
tkennedy@goodheart.com www.goodheart.com
Processor and exporter of quail, venison, bison, wild boar, pheasant and Argentinian all-natural beef; importer of Argentinian beef
Owner: Amalia Palmaz
Director Sales: Chef Tim Kennedy
Plant Manager: Demetrio Molales
Estimated Sales: $5-10 Million
Number Employees: 50-99
Sq. footage: 15000
Parent Co: Bluebonnet Company
Type of Packaging: Consumer, Food Service
Brands:
Goodheart

5383 **Goodman Manufacturing Company**
P.O.Box 294
Carthage, MO 64836 417-358-3231
Fax: 417-358-3231 www.goodmansvanilla.com
Processor of flavoring extracts including vanilla
President: Mike Kimrey
Estimated Sales: $2.5-5 Million
Number Employees: 1-4

5384 **Goodnature Products**
3860 California Rd
Orchard Park, NY 14127 716-855-3325
Fax: 716-855-3328 800-875-3381
sales@goodnature.com www.goodnature.com
Manufacturer and exporter of food and juice processing equipment
President: Dale Wettlaufer
Marketing: Angela Dedlin
Operations: Diane Massett
Estimated Sales: $3.5 Million
Number Employees: 27
Number of Brands: 1
Number of Products: 21
Brands:
CMP PASTEURIZER
JUICE-IT
MAXIMIZER
SQUEEZEBOX
X-1

5385 **Goodson Brothers Coffee**
138 Sherlake Ln
Knoxville, TN 37922 865-531-8022
Fax: 865-691-8578 sales@goodsonbrothers.com
www.goodsonbrothers.com
Coffee and tea products
President: Jeff Goodson
Estimated Sales: $1.2 Million
Number Employees: 25

5386 **Goodwives Hors D'Oeuvres**
330 Ballardvale Street
Wilmington, MA 01887 781-596-0070
Fax: 781-596-1331 800-521-8160
customer.service@goodwives.com
www.goodwives.com
Hors d'oeuvres such as flatbreads, wontons, tortilla wraps and crisps, puff pastry, profiteroles, skewers & kabobs, chicken tenders, seafood, specialty, fillo products, mini quiche & tartlets, southwest specialties, spring rollsbreakfast items, plated appetizers and entrees.

5387 **Goose Island Brewing**
1800 N Clybourn Ave Ste B
Chicago, IL 60614 312-915-0071
Fax: 312-915-0788 info@gooseisland.com
www.gooseisland.com
Processor of beer, ale, stout, lager and porter. Many specialities such as Oatmeal Stout, Kelgubbin Red Ale, (Irish style red ale), and craft sodas
Manager: Rob England
Brewmaster: Greg Hall
General Manager: Tim Lane
Estimated Sales: $2.5-5 Million
Number Employees: 50-99
Sq. footage: 37000
Type of Packaging: Consumer, Food Service
Brands:
Hey Nut
Honkers
IPA
Oatmeal

5388 **Goosecross Cellars**
1119 State Ln
Yountville, CA 94599 707-944-1986
Fax: 707-944-9551 800-276-9210
webmaster@goosecross.com
www.goosecross.com
Specialize in limited production Chardonnay, Viognier, Chenin Blanc, Merlot, Syrah, Zinfandel, Cabernet, Pinot Noir and a very special blend of Sangiovese and Cabernet we call Amerital.
President/CEO: David Topper
Vice President/Winemaker: Geoff Gorsuch
Hospitality/Public Relations: Colleen Topper
Business Development/Distribution: Pamela Topper
Estimated Sales: $2.5-5 Million
Number Employees: 10-19
Type of Packaging: Private Label
Brands:
Aeros
Bernard Pradel Cabernet
Goosecreek
Goosecross
Goosecross Cabernet
Goosecross Chardonnay
Goosecross Chardonnay Winemaker
Goosecross Eros
Goosecross Goosecreek
Goosecross Mountain Cabernet
Goosecross Sauvignon Blanc
Goosecross Syrah
Goosecross Zinfandel

5389 **Gopicnic**
4011 N Ravenswood Avenue
Suite 12
Chicago, IL 60613-3696 773-328-2490
Fax: 773-345-0734
carolyn.wiesemann@gopicnic.com
www.gopicnic.com
Gluten-free, organic/natural, vegetarian, meals,cured meats i.e. prosciutto/bacon, tuna, other snacks.
Marketing: Carolyn Wiesemann

5390 **Gorant Candies**
8264 East Market Street
Warren, OH 44484 330-856-5043
Fax: 330-726-0325 800-572-4139
kris.stephens@amgreetings.com
www.gorantcandiesofwarren.com
Processor of chocolate-coated candies
Estimated Sales: $50-99.9 Million
Number Employees: 500-999
Sq. footage: 60000
Parent Co: American Greetings
Type of Packaging: Consumer, Private Label
Brands:
GORANT & YUM YUM CHOCOLATES

5391 **Gordon Biersch Brewing Company**
33 E San Fernando St
San Jose, CA 95113-2508 408-294-6785
Fax: 408-294-4052 info@gbrestaurants.com
www.gordonbiersch.com
Beer
Manager: Sean McKennan
Marketing Director: Mike curtis
CFO: Larry Nally
Vice President: Dean Biersch
CEO: Allin Strikli
Sales Director: Mark Blecher
Operations Manager: Eddie Sipple
Estimated Sales: $2.5-5 Million
Number Employees: 100-249
Brands:
Gordon Biersch Blonde Black
Gordon Biersch Golde
Gordon Biersch Marzen
Gordon Biersch Pilsner
Maibock Hefeweizen
Winter Block

5392 **Gordon Food Service**
1410 Gordon Food Service Drive
Plant City, FL 33562 813-703-6500
www.gfs.com
Distributor of food, beverages, and supply items to the food service industry
Parent Co: Gordon Food Service

5393 **Gorman Fisheries**
PO Box 10
Conception Bay, NL A1X 2E2
Canada 709-229-6536
Fax: 709-229-6864
Processor and exporter of fresh and frozen mackerel, herring, squid, tuna, lumpfish roe, capelin and live and frozen lobster
President: Patrick Gorman
Number Employees: 100-249
Type of Packaging: Consumer, Food Service, Private Label, Bulk

5394 **Gormly's Orchard**
150 Dorset Street
Pmb 200
South Burlington, VT 05403 802-879-5297
Fax: 802-876-3001 800-639-7604
info@gormlys.com www.gormlys.com
Processor of pancake and scone mixes, jellies, preserves, mustards, barbecue sauce and spiced apple cider concentrate
President: Bill Gormly
Estimated Sales: $500,000 appx.
Number Employees: 5-9
Sq. footage: 9500
Type of Packaging: Consumer, Food Service, Private Label

5395 **Gorton's Seafood**
128 Rogers St
Gloucester, MA 01930-5005 978-283-3000
Fax: 978-281-7949 www.gortons.com
Processor, importer and exporter of frozen seafood including clams, fish cakes, flounder, breaded sticks and fillets, restaurant-style entrees, whiting, shrimp, sole, crabs, lobster, scallops, etc.; also, batter
Manager: Karen Carter
CEO: Steve Warhover
Director Marketing: Mark Lamothe
Plant Manager: John Gates
Purchasing Manager: Lisa Webb
Number Employees: 500-999
Parent Co: Unilever USA
Type of Packaging: Consumer, Food Service
Other Locations:
Gorton's Seafood
Cleveland OH
Brands:
Batters & Breaders
Blue Water
Gorton's
Gorton's Frozen Entrees
Matlaws
Specialty

5396 **Goshen Dairy Company**
3110 Oldtown Valley Rd SW
New Philadelphia, OH 44663-7932 330-339-1959
Fax: 330-339-2252
Milk, ice cream and butter
President: Jerry Bichsel
VP/General Manager: Chris Bichsel
Estimated Sales: $5-9.9 Million
Number Employees: 20-49
Type of Packaging: Private Label

5397 **(HQ)Gossner Food**
1051 North 1000 West
Logan, UT 84321-6852 435-713-6100
Fax: 435-713-6200 800-944-0454
cheese@gossner.com www.gossner.com
Processor and exporter of cheese and aseptic-packaged milk
President/CEO: Dolores Wheeler
Vice President: Greg Rowley
Marketing Director: James Liddle
UHT Plant Manager: Kelly Luthi
Cheese Plant Manager: Dave Larsen
Estimated Sales: $20-50 Million
Number Employees: 250-499
Type of Packaging: Consumer, Food Service, Private Label, Bulk
Brands:
Fridge Free

5398 **Gotliebs Guacamole**
PO Box 1036
Sharon, CT 06069-1036 860-364-0842
Guacamole
President: Richard Gotlieb
VP Marketing: Leslie MacKenzie
Production Manager: Laura Mars
Estimated Sales: $500,000-$1 Million
Number Employees: 5-9
Brands:
Gotliebs

5399 **Gould's Maple Sugarhouse**
Mohawk Trl
Shelburne Falls, MA 01370 413-625-6170
info@goulds-sugarhouse.com
www.goulds-sugarhouse.com
Processor of pure maple syrup and also a selection of pies
Owner/President: Edgar Gould
Owner/President: Helen Gould
Estimated Sales: $1-2.5 Million
Number Employees: 5-9

5400 **Gouldsboro Enterprises**
14 Factory Rd
Gouldsboro, ME 04607-4222 207-963-2203
Fax: 212-925-1913
Lobster
President, Owner: Leonard Bishko
Vice President: Joseph Boyd
Estimated Sales: $300,000-500,000
Number Employees: 1-4

5401 **Gourmantra Foods**
95 Silver Rose Crescent
Markham, ON L6C 1W6
Canada 416-225-6711
Fax: 416-225-6711 info@gourmanta.com
www.gourmantra.com
Spices
CEO: Rachna Prasad
VP R&D: Rekha Prasad
COO: Mona Prasad
Number Employees: 5

5402 **Gourme' Mist**
10880 Wiles Rd
Coral Springs, FL 33076 954-608-6858
Fax: 954-252-2247 866-502-8472
info@gourmemist.com www.gourmemist.com
oil and vinegar misters
President/CoFounder: Paige Simona

5403 **Gourmedas Inc**
2661 Boulevard du Versant Nord
Quebec, QC G1V 1A3
Canada 418-210-3703
Fax: 418-948-4083 info@gourmedas.com
www.gourmedas.com
Chocolate
President/CEO: Christoph Klein
Director of Operations: Giordano Perini

5404 **Gourmet Baker**
4190 Lougheed Highway
Suite 502
Burnaby, BC V5C 6A8
Canada 604-298-2652
Fax: 604-296-1001 800-663-1972
bchomatt@multifoods.com
www.gourmetbaker.com
Manufacturer and marketer of baked and unbaked desserts and breakfast pastries to the in-store bakery and foodservice channels
VP/General Manager: John Gebbie
Estimated Sales: $81 Million
Number Employees: 625
Number of Brands: 2
Parent Co: Robin Hood Multifoods
Type of Packaging: Consumer, Food Service, Private Label
Brands:
Fantasia
Gourmet Baker

5405 **Gourmet Basics**
67 35th Street
Suite 3
Brooklyn, NY 11232-2200 718-509-9366
Fax: 866-900-7833 jbenz@gourmetbasics.com
www.gourmetbasics.com
Organic/natural, chips, puffed snacks.

5406 **Gourmet Central**
47 Industrial Park
Romney, WV 26757 304-822-6047
Fax: 304-822-3148 800-984-3722
gourmetcentral@usa.net www.chefharv.com
Jams, jellies, sauces, dressings, toppings, salsa
Owner/President: Christy Christie
Estimated Sales: $1.4 Million
Number Employees: 19
Number of Products: 200+
Sq. footage: 20000
Type of Packaging: Consumer, Food Service, Private Label, Bulk

5407 **Gourmet Concepts International**
2855 Rolling Pin Lane
Suwanee, GA 30024-7218 770-491-2100
Fax: 770-326-6157 800-241-4166
www.hartmutgourmet.com
Desserts

Estimated Sales: $50-100 Million
Number Employees: 100-249
Sq. footage: 66
Type of Packaging: Private Label

5408 **Gourmet Conveniences Ltd**
457 Bantam Road
Litchfield, CT 06759 860-567-3529
Fax: 860-631-1012 866-793-3801
sales@sweetsunshine.com
www.sweetsunshine.com
Sauces
Founder/CEO: Paul Sarris
Number Employees: 4

5409 **Gourmet Croissant**
948 3rd Ave
Brooklyn, NY 11232 718-499-4911
Fax: 718-499-6394
Processor of fresh and frozen baked goods including croissants, danish, yogurt muffins and loaves
Co-Owner: Dino Alatsas
Co-Owner: Teddy Alatsas
Estimated Sales: Less than $500,000
Number Employees: 1-4
Sq. footage: 8000

5410 **Gourmet Food Mall**
2400 Veteren's Boulevard
Suite 484
Kenner, LA 70062 504-733-2400
Fax: 504-733-0939 800-903-7553
info@gourmetfoodmall.com
www.gourmetfoodmall.com
Search engine for gourmet and speciality foods including pasta, olive oil and spices
Founder: Andrew Restivo
Estimated Sales: $ 1 - 3 Million
Number Employees: 10-19

5411 **(HQ)Gourmet Foods**
2910 E Harcourt St
Compton, CA 90221 310-632-3300
Fax: 310-632-0303 sales@gourmetfoodsinc.com
www.gourmetfoodsinc.com
Processor of hors d'oeuvres and banquet items
President: Heinz Naef
Estimated Sales: $5-10 Million
Number Employees: 100-249

5412 **Gourmet Foods Market**
5107 Kingston Pike
Knoxville, TN 37919-5152 865-584-8739
Fax: 865-584-5661
www.shopgourmetsmarket.com
Gourmet and specialty foods
President: Eric Nelson
CEO: Eric Nelson
Estimated Sales: $1-2.5 Million
Number Employees: 20-49
Brands:
Gourmet Foods Market

5413 **Gourmet House**
301 Tower Street NW
Clearbrook, MN 56634 218-776-2100
Fax: 218-776-3119 www.gourmethouserice.com
Rice
Marketing Manager/Sales Executive: Julie Wraa
Operations/Branch Manager: Steve Wraa
Number Employees: 60
Sq. footage: 14432
Parent Co: Riviana Foods
Type of Packaging: Consumer, Private Label

5414 **Gourmet Kitchen, Inc.**
1238 Corlies Avenue
Neptune, NJ 07753 732-775-5222
Fax: 732-775-5225 800-492-3663
kgrossman@gourmetkitcheninc.com
www.gourmetkitcheninc.com
Hors d'ooeuvres/appetizers, foodservice.
Marketing: Kathleen Grossman

5415 **Gourmet Mondiale**
6865 Route 132
Ste-Catherine, QC J5C 1B6 450-638-6380
Fax: 450-638-7049
nino.piazza@mostimondiale.com
www.gourmetmondiale.com
Wine, olive oil, balsamic vinegar.
Marketing: Nino Piazza

5416 **Gourmet Organics**
44 Greenwood Ln
Waynesville, NC 28786-7123 828-452-7700
Fax: 828-452-7832 serenahd@earthlink.net
www.serenas.com
Frozen bakery products
President: Serena Dossenko
Marketing Director: Barry Dossenko
Estimated Sales: $1-2.5 Million
Number Employees: 1-4
Type of Packaging: Private Label

5417 **Gourmet Products**
PO Box 387
Thomaston, CT 06787-0387 860-283-5147
Fax: 860-283-6912
Sauces, mustards, relishes, salsas
Owner: A Yurgelun
Marketing Director: W Yurgelun
VP Operations: David Yurgelun
Production Manager: T Del Gadio
Purchasing Manager: T Curnell
Number Employees: 10-19
Sq. footage: 12000
Type of Packaging: Consumer, Private Label, Bulk
Brands:
GOURMET PRODUCTS
NEW CLASSICS
NEW ENGLAND

5418 **Gourmet Treats**
1860 W 220th St # 445
Torrance, CA 90501-3679 310-212-6975
Fax: 310-212-0709 800-444-9549
inquiry@gourmettreats.com
www.gourmettreat.com
Processor of gourmet regular and fat-free cakes and cookies
President: Shaffin Jinnah
Estimated Sales: Less than $500,000
Number Employees: 1-4
Sq. footage: 3000
Type of Packaging: Consumer, Private Label
Brands:
Gourmet Lite
Gourmet Treats

5419 **Gourmet Village**
539 Village Rd
Morin Heights, QC J0R 1H0 450-226-7377
Fax: 450-226-8329 800-668-2314
sales@gourmetduvillage.com
www.gourmetduvillage.com
gourmet dips, coffee, tea and cool drinks, desserts, hot chocolate and festive drinks
President/Owner: Mike Tott
VP North American Sales: Drew Bunn
VP Product Development: Linda Tott

5420 **Gourmet's Finest**
704 Garden Station Rd
Avondale, PA 19311 610-268-6910
Fax: 610-268-2298 info@gourmetsfinest.com
www.gourmetsfinest.com
Fresh and processed mushrooms, mushroom salads, and marinades
Owner: Richard Pia
Type of Packaging: Food Service, Private Label

5421 **Gourmet's Secret**
5304 Roseville Rd # F
North Highlands, CA 95660-5049 916-334-6161
Fax: 916-334-6161 gourmetsec@aol.com
www.thegourmetsecret.com
Beer-based marinade and sauce packaged in German beer bottles, herb and fruit-flavored vinegars and flavor-infused grapeseed oil bottled in European glass bottles
Partner: Rita Nelson
Estimated Sales: $100,000
Number Employees: 1-4
Brands:
Bachelor's Brew
Java Jelly

5422 **Gourmets Fresh Pasta**
950 N Fair Oaks Ave
Pasadena, CA 91103-3009 626-798-0841
Fax: 626-798-3591 mayagjian@aol.com
www.gourmetpasta.com
Processor of refrigerated, frozen and precooked pasta - sold to restaurantsand markets throughout the US
President/CEO: Michael Yagjian
Estimated Sales: $2.5-5 Million
Number Employees: 20-49
Sq. footage: 30000
Type of Packaging: Consumer, Food Service, Private Label, Bulk
Brands:
California Cuisine
Gourmet Fresh

5423 **Gouw Quality Onions**
5801-54 Avenue
Taber, AB T1G 1X4
Canada 403-223-1440
Fax: 403-223-2036
onions@gouwqualityonions.com
www.gouwqualityonions.com
Grower, importer and packer of onions, radish and red beets
Chairman: Casey Gouw, Sr.
Sales Manager/Controller: Casey Gouw
Warehouse/Plant Operations: Ken Gouw
Farm Manager: Kyle Gouw
Estimated Sales: D
Number Employees: 20-49
Type of Packaging: Consumer

5424 **Govadinas Fitness Foods**
2651 Ariane Drive
San Diego, CA 92117-3422 858-270-0691
Fax: 858-270-0696 800-900-0108
blissbar@earthlink.net www.govindabars.com
Manufacturer of health food bars and natural snacks
President: Larry Gatpandan
CEO: Larry Gatpandan
Accountant: Alberto Hael
VP: Zenaida Gatpandan
Marketing: Michael Pugliese
Sales: Lisa Gatpandan
Production: Jose Marquez
Purchasing: Nila Morrill
Estimated Sales: $3 Million
Number Employees: 20-49
Number of Products: 25
Sq. footage: 5000
Type of Packaging: Private Label
Brands:
BLISS BAR
HEMP BAR
PRALINE PACK
RAW POWER

5425 **Govatos**
800 Market St
Wilmington, DE 19801 302-652-5252
Fax: 302-652-3418 888-799-5252
GVTSCANDY@AOL.COM
www.govatoschocolates.com
High quality assortment of homemade chocolates
President: Richard Govatos Jr
Estimated Sales: $1-2.5 Million
Number Employees: 10-19
Type of Packaging: Consumer

5426 **(HQ)Goya Foods**
100 Seaview Dr
Secaucus, NJ 7094 201-348-4900
Fax: 201-348-6609 info@goya.com
www.goya.com
Beans, rice, regional specialities, condiments, beverages, pantry, frozen foods and reduced sodium and organic.
President: Robert Unanue
VP Finance: Miguel Lugo
EVP: Peter Unanue
VP General Counsel: Carlo Ortiz
VP Logistics: Rebecca Rodriguez-Llerena
VP Sales/Marketing: Conrad Colon
Public Relations Director: Rafael Toro
Estimated Sales: $1.3 Billion
Number Employees: 3,000
Type of Packaging: Consumer, Food Service
Brands:
Goya Beans
Goya Beverages
Goya Caribbean Specialties
Goya Central American Specialties
Goya Condiments
Goya Foods
Goya Frozen
Goya Mexican
Goya Refrigerated
Goya Rices
Goya South American Specialties
Goya Tropical Fruit Blast Drink
Sazon

5427 **Goya Foods of Florida**
1900 NW 92nd Avenue
Miami, FL 33172 305-592-3150
Fax: 305-591-8019 info@goya.com
www.goyafoods.com
Wholesaler/distributor of Hispanic and Latin foods including olive oil, olives, beans, rice, fish preserves, canned meats, frozen foods, etc.
President: Mary Unanue
Controller: Raul Zabala
VP: Uben Chavez
Human Resource Manager: Maria Banos
Purchasing Director: Luis Olarte
Estimated Sales: $ 20 - 50 Million
Number Employees: 100
Sq. footage: 26541
Parent Co: Goya Foods

5428 **Goya de Puerto Rico**
PO Box 601467
Bayamon, PR 00960-6067 787-740-4900
Fax: 787-740-5040

Manufacturer, distribution and office for Goya Foods
President: Frank Unanue
Parent Co: Goya Foods

5429 **Goya of Great Lakes NewYYork**
P.O.Box 152
Angola, NY 14006-0152 716-549-0076
Fax: 716-549-7259 www.goya.com
Packer and canner of dry besns including pink, pinto, black, small white and red, cannellini, kidney, butter, roman and Great Northern
President: Robert Drago
Marketing Director: Rubin Montalvo
CFO: John Saccammano
VP Sales/Purchasing: Greg Drago
Estimated Sales: $ 50 - 100 Million
Number Employees: 50-99
Number of Brands: 1
Number of Products: 18
Parent Co: Goya Foods
Type of Packaging: Consumer
Brands:
Goya

5430 **Grabill Country Meats**
13211 West St
Grabill, IN 46741 260-627-3691
Fax: 219-627-2106 866-333-6328
grabillmeats@aol.com www.grabillmeats.com
Processor of canned beef, pork, chicken, and turkey products containing no preservatives or additives and no water added
President: Patrick Fonner
Secretary/Treasurer: Dennis Fonner
Estimated Sales: $5-10 Million
Number Employees: 10-19
Type of Packaging: Consumer

5431 **Grace Baking Company**
3200 Regatta Blvd Ste G
Richmond, CA 94804 510-231-7200
Fax: 510-231-7210 gracebaking@mapleleaf.ca
www.gracebaking.com
Manufacturer of baked goods including breads; desserts; morning pastries, and focaccia.
Founder/Co-Owner: Glenn Mitchell
Co-Owner: Cindy Mitchell
Public Relations and Marketing: Fred Doar
Plant Manager: Mike Cassie
Parent Co: Maple Leaf Foods Inc
Type of Packaging: Food Service

5432 **Grace Foods International**
39-36 32nd Street #1
Astoria, NY 11106 718-433-4789
Fax: 718-433-0384 www.gracefoods.com
Beverages, canned meats and fish, chips, coconut products, jams and jellies, ready mixes, rice combos, sauces and condiments, spices and seasoning, teas and veggie meals.

5433 **Grace Tea Company**
14-A Craig Road
Acton, MA 01720 978-635-9500
Fax: 978-635-9701 gracerarctea@aol.com
www.gracetea.com
Exporter, importer, blender and packer of gourmet loose orthodox teas
President: Marguerita Sanders
VP: Richard Verdery
Operations Director: Richard Sanders
Estimated Sales: $48,000
Number Employees: 1
Number of Brands: 1
Number of Products: 20
Sq. footage: 2000
Brands:
CHINA YUNNAN SILVER TIP CHOICE
CONNOISSEUR MASTER BLEND
DARJCELING SUPERB 6000
DEMITASSE AFTER DINNER TEA
EARL GREY SUPERIOR MIXTURE
FLOWERY JASMINE-BEFORE THE RAIN
FORMOSA OOLONG CHAMPAGNE OF TEA
GUN POWDER PEARL PINHEAD GREEN TEA
LAPSANG SOUCHONG SMOKY #1 BLEND
MOUNTAIN-GROWN FANCY CEYLON
OWNER'S BLEND PREMIUM CONGOU
PURE ASSAM IRISH BREAKFAST
RUSSIAN CARAVAN ORIGINAL CHINA
WINEY KEEMUN ENGLISH BREAKFAST

5434 **Graceland Fruit**
1123 Main St
Frankfort, MI 49635 231-352-7181
Fax: 231-352-4881 800-352-7181
gracelandinfo@gracelandfruit.com
www.gracelandfruit.com
Infused dried fruits, and vegetables, Fridg-N-Fresh™vegetables, and Soft-N-Frozen™fruit products
President/CEO: Donald W Nugent
CFO: Troy Terwilliger
CEO: Donald Negent
VP R&D: Nirmal Sinha
Procurement Manager: Ken Fitzhugh
Marketing/Public Relations: Suzi Mills
National Sales Manager: Derek Klein
VP Operations: Douglas Pumstead
Director Engineering: Bob Donnan
Manager/Grower/Processor Relations: Ben Evans
Estimated Sales: $40 Million
Number Employees: 100-249
Number of Brands: 1
Number of Products: 50
Type of Packaging: Food Service, Private Label, Bulk
Brands:
GRACELAND FRUIT

5435 **Graceland Fruit Inc**
1123 Main St
Frankfort, MI 49635 231-352-7181
Fax: 231-352-4711 800-352-7181
cwalrad@wildveggiesus.com
www.wildveggieus.com
Fruit and vegetable products
President: Donald Nugent
CFO: Troy Terwilliger
VP R&D: Nirmal Sinha
Sales/Marketing Manager: Suzi Mills
National Sales Manager: Derek Klein
COO: Steve Nugent
Estimated Sales: $63.8
Number Employees: 70

5436 **Gracious Gourmet**
PO Box 218
Bridgewater, CT 06752 860-350-1213
Fax: 860-350-1214
info@thegraciousgourmet.com
www.thegraciousgourmet.com
Chutneys, glazes, pestos, spreads and tapenades

5437 **Graf Creamery**
N4051 Creamery Rd
Bonduel, WI 54107-8441
Fax: 715-758-8020 Jimb@ezwebtech.com
Processor of butter and condensed and powdered buttermilk
President/CEO: James Bleick
Plant Manager: Dale Hodmiewicz
Purchasing Director: Jay Winter
Estimated Sales: $10-24.9 Million
Number Employees: 50-99
Sq. footage: 56000
Type of Packaging: Private Label, Bulk
Brands:
CLOVERDALE
GOLD MEDAL
GOLDEN GLOW

5438 **Graffam Brothers Lobster Company**
211 Union Street
Rockport, ME 04856 207-236-3396
Fax: 207-236-2569 800-535-5358
sales@lobsterstogo.com www.lobsterstogo.com
Distributor of fresh Maine lobsters and clams, cooked lobster meat and frozen lobster tails.
President/Co-Owner: James Graffam

5439 **Grafton Village Cheese**
Po Box 87
Grafton, VT 05146 802-246-2221
Fax: 802-843-2210 800-472-3866
info@graftonvillagecheese.com
www.graftonvillagecheese.com
Processor of cheddar cheese
President: Stephan Morse
VP Marketing: Peter Mohn
Media Contact: Melissa Gullotti
Cheesemaker: Kevin Bush
Cheesemaker: Scott Fletcher
Plant Manager: Brian Joslyn
Estimated Sales: $1-2.5 Million
Number Employees: 20-49
Parent Co: Windham Foundation
Type of Packaging: Consumer, Food Service, Private Label, Bulk
Brands:
Classic Reserve
Classic Reserve Ext Sharp Cheddar
Grafton Gold
Grafton Gold-Ext Aged Cheddar

5440 **Graham & Rollins**
19 Rudd Ln
Hampton, VA 23669 757-723-3831
Fax: 757-722-3762 800-272-2728
johnny@grahamandrollins.com
www.grahamandrollins.com
Processors of bluecrab (live and steamed), soft-shell crab and crabmeat, fresh, pasteurized and frozen cakes and bites
President: John Graham Sr
VP: Johnny Graham Jr
Estimated Sales: $1-2.5 Million
Number Employees: 100-249

5441 **Graham Cheese Corporation**
Hwy 57 N
Elnoragton, IN 47529 812-692-5237
Fax: 812-692-5650 800-472-9178
www.grahamcheese.com
Cheese blocks, longhorns, pieces and spreads; including colby, cheddar, pepper, calico cheeses and cheese gifts
President: Ura Miller
Plant Manager: Jerry Sims
Estimated Sales: $2 Million
Number Employees: 20
Type of Packaging: Consumer, Food Service, Private Label, Bulk

5442 **Graham Chemical Corporation**
1250 S Grove Avenue
Suite 206
Barrington, IL 60010 847-304-4400
Fax: 847-304-8752 info@grahamchemical.com
www.grahamchemical.com
Specialty chemical intermediates, surfactants, and performance additives.
Owner/Human Resources Executive: Brad Graham
Sales/Marketing Manager: Terri Kent
Estimated Sales: $1 Million
Number Employees: 6
Sq. footage: 2000

5443 **Graham Fisheries**
13890 Shell Belt Rd
Bayou La Batre, AL 36509 251-824-2890
Fax: 251-824-7370 shrimp1951@aol.com
Processor of seafood -shrimp
Owner: Darrell Graham
Estimated Sales: $ .5 - 1 million
Number Employees: 1-4

5444 **Grain Bin Bakers**
P.O.Box 1296
Carmel, CA 93921-1296 831-624-3883
Fax: 831-624-1459 www.allsaintscarmel.org
Religious Leader: Richard Matters
Estimated Sales: Under $500,000
Number Employees: 5-9

5445 **(HQ)Grain Millers**
9531 W 78th St Ste 400
Eden Prairie, MN 55344 952-829-8821
Fax: 952-829-8819 800-232-6287
info@grainmillers.com www.grainmillers.com
Manufacturer of specialty grain products and organic grain products such as oats, wheat, barley, rye and corn
President: Steven Eilertson
SVP: Rick Schwein
Sales/Marketing Manager: Kris Nelson
Estimated Sales: $ 20 - 50 Million
Number Employees: 20-49
Type of Packaging: Food Service, Private Label, Bulk
Brands:
GRAIN MILLERS

5446 **Grain Millers Eugene**
315 Madison St
Eugene, OR 97402-5034 541-687-8000
Fax: 541-343-7820 800-443-8972
info@grainmillers.com www.grainmillers.com
Manufacturer of flour and other grain mill products
President, West Coast Operations: Christian Kongsore
Logistics Manager: Lorna Yarbourgh
QA Manager: Mark Kruk
VP Product Development: Robert Serrano
VP Sales/Marketing: Darren Schubert
VP Operations: Keith Horton
Mix Plant Manager: Dick Green
Plant Manager: Tony Selby
VP Purchasing: Perry Anderson
Estimated Sales: $20-50 Million
Number Employees: 50-99

5447 **Grain Place Foods**
1904 N Highway 14
Marquette, NE 68854 888-714-7246
Fax: 402-854-2566 davegpf@hamilton.net
www.grainplacefoods.com
Processor of grains, cereals
President: David Vetter
Estimated Sales: $1-2.5 Million
Number Employees: 10-19
Type of Packaging: Consumer, Private Label, Bulk
Brands:
Grain Place

5448 **Grain Process Enterprises Ltd.**
105 Commander Boulevard
Scarborough, ON M1S 3M7
Canada 416-291-3226
Fax: 416-291-2159 800-387-5292
gbjr@grainprocess.com
Processor of stone ground hard and soft wheat flours, granola cereals, grain, bread and muffin mixes, cereal blends, etc.; exporter of granolas and flours
President: George Birinyi Sr
Number Employees: 20-49
Sq. footage: 75000
Type of Packaging: Consumer, Private Label, Bulk
Brands:
Brimley Stone
Grain-Pro
Happy Home
Millbrook

5449 **Grain Processing Corporation**
1600 Oregon Street
Muscatine, IA 52761 563-264-4265
Fax: 913-851-0414 www.grainprocessing.com
corn-based products for food, alcohol and pharmaceutical
President: John Thorpe
CEO: Gage Kent
VP Finance/Controller: Carter Van Hemert
SVP Research & Development: Frank Barresi
VP Marketing: Ron Schroder
SVP Sales/Marketing: Ralph Wilkinson
SVP Operations: Ron Zitzow
Number Employees: 656
Sq. footage: 100000
Parent Co: Muscatine Foods Corporation

5450 **Grain Processing Corporation**
1600 Oregon St
Muscatine, IA 52761 563-264-4727
Fax: 563-264-4289 800-448-4472
sales@grainprocessing.com
www.grainprocessing.com
Manufacturer and worldwide marketer of corn-based products.
President: Doyle Tubandt
CEO: Gage Kent
VP: Brian Tompoles
R&D: Frank Barresi
Quality Control: Rani Thomas
Marketing/Public Relations: Diane Rieke
Sales: Chad Christensen
Operations: Ron Zitzow
Purchasing: Brian Hasser
Number Employees: 1-4
Brands:
INCOSITY
INSTANT PURE-COTE
MALTRIN
MALTRIN QD
PURE-BIND
PURE-COTE
PURE-DENT
PURE-GEL

5451 **Grain-Free JK Gourmet**
303 Joicey Blvd
Toronto, ON M5M 2V8
Canada 416-782-0045
Fax: 416-785-0686 800-608-0465
info@jkgourmet.com www.jkgourmet.com
All-natural, preservative-free granola, biscotti, almond flour and muffin loaves.
President/Owner: Jodi Bager
Number Employees: 3

5452 **Grainaissance**
1580 62nd St
Emeryville, CA 94608 510-547-7256
Fax: 510-547-0526 800-472-4697
amazake@grainaissance.com
www.grainaissance.com
Food processing, producing 2 brown rice products, Mochi-bake and serve rice popover, Amazake-healthy rice shake. Both refrigerated.
President: Tony Plotkin
Estimated Sales: $1.4 Million
Number Employees: 11
Type of Packaging: Consumer
Brands:
Amazake
Grainaissance
Mochi

5453 **(HQ)Graminex**
95 Midland Rd
Saginaw, MI 48638 989-797-5502
Fax: 989-799-0020 877-472-6469
graminex@graminex.co www.graminex.com
Exclusive, original grower, harvester, processor and manufacturer and distributor of flower pollen extract and fabales - Red Clover Extract - other extracts include lactose, gluten and talc free
President: Cynthia May
Estimated Sales: $ 3 - 5 Million
Number Employees: 1-4

5454 **Grand Avenue Chocolates**
1021 Detroit Avenue
Concord, CA 94518
Fax: 925-682-1900 877-934-1800
info@grandavenuechocolates.com
www.grandavenuechocolates.com
Manufactures chocolate covered grahams, french cream truffles, crisp chashew thin brittles, bite sized cookies and the original unbelievable apple covered with carmel, chocolate and nuts
Owner: Rachel Dunn
Estimated Sales: $10-20 Million
Number Employees: 10-19
Type of Packaging: Private Label
Brands:
Ebird's
Grand Avenue

5455 **Grand Rapids Brewing Company**
3689 28th St SE
Grand Rapids, MI 49512 616-285-5970
Fax: 616-285-5923 grbc17@aol.com
www.michiganmenu.com
Processor of beer, ale, stout and lager
Manager: Terry Mundwiler
Chef: Kim Chase
Manager: Missy Kroll
Manager: Dan Mast
Brewer: John Svoboda
General Manager: Terry Mundwiler
Estimated Sales: $2.5-5 Million
Number Employees: 100-249
Type of Packaging: Consumer

5456 **Grand Teton Brewing**
430 Old Jackson Hwy
Victor, ID 83455 208-787-9000
Fax: 208-787-4114 888-899-1656
beermail@GrandTetonBrewing.com
www.grandtetonbrewing.com
Processor of pale, amber and wheat beer; also, ale, stout and porter, as well as soda.
President/CEO: Charlie Otto
VP: Ernie Otto
Estimated Sales: $ 5-10 Million
Number Employees: 10-19
Type of Packaging: Consumer, Food Service
Brands:
Grand Teton Brewing
Teton

5457 **Grand View Winery**
P.O.Box 91
East Calais, VT 05667 802-456-7012
Fax: 802-456-7012 info@grandviewwinery.com
www.grandviewwinery.com
Wines: Rhubarb, Foch, Seyval, Riesling, Montmorency Cherry, Pear Wine, Blueberry Apple, Dandelion Wine, Raspberry Infusion, Blueberry Wine, Elderberry Wine, Mac Jack Hard Cider
Winemaker/Owner: Phil Tonks
Estimated Sales: $ 3 - 5 Million
Number Employees: 5-9

5458 **Grande Cheese Company**
P.O.Box 67
Brownsville, WI 53006 920-583-3122
Fax: 920-269-7124 800-678-3122
elio.camilotto@grande.com www.grande.com
Manufactures Mozzarella and FIOR-di-LATTE Fresh Mozzarella, and whey products
President: Wayne Matzke
VP Marketing/Sales: Elio Camilotto Jr
Estimated Sales: $20-50 Million
Number Employees: 5-9
Type of Packaging: Consumer, Food Service

5459 **Grande Custom Ingredients Group**
Dairy Rd
Brownsville, WI 53006-0067 920-269-7200
Fax: 920-269-7124 800-678-3122
gcig@grande.com www.grande.com
Processor and exporter of specialty whey products and lactose
CEO: Wayne Matzke
CEO: Wayne Matzke
R&D: Michelle Ludtke
Marketing Director: Stephen Dott
Operations: Mike Nelson
Purchasing Director: Kevin Hampton
Estimated Sales: $25 Million
Number Employees: 5-9
Sq. footage: 10000
Parent Co: Grande Cheese Company
Type of Packaging: Bulk
Brands:
Grande Bravo Whey Protein
Grande Gusto Natural Flavor
Grande Ultra Nutritional Whey Prot.

5460 **Grande River Vineyards**
787 Elberta Ave
Palisade, CO 81526 970-464-5867
Fax: 970-464-5427 800-264-7696
info@www.granderiverwines.com
www.granderiverwines.com
Wines- consisting of Sauvgnon Blanc, Meritage white, barrel select Chardonnay, Merlot, Syrah and Desert Blend and many more selections
Founder/Owner/Winemaker: Stephen Smith
Vineyard Manager: Jim Mayrose
Manager: Javanne Pergola
Estimated Sales: $660,000
Number Employees: 12
Type of Packaging: Private Label
Brands:
Grande River Vineyards
Grande River Vineyards Everyday
Grande River Vineyards Meritage

5461 **Grande Tortilla Factory**
914 N Grande Ave
Tucson, AZ 85745 520-622-8338
Processor of flour and corn tortillas; also, tamales including green, corn and beef
President: Frank Pesqueira Jr
Estimated Sales: $200,000
Number Employees: 5-9
Type of Packaging: Consumer

5462 **Grandma Beth's Cookies**
1221 Toluca Avenue
Alliance, NE 69301-2447 308-762-8433
Fax: 308-762-6165 cookie@premaonline.com
Old fashioned homemade cookies
Owner: Beth Fetcher
Estimated Sales: $500,000-$1 Million
Number Employees: 1-4
Type of Packaging: Private Label

5463 **Grandma Brown's BeansInc**
P.O.Box 230
Mexico, NY 13114-0230 315-963-7221
Fax: 315-963-4072
grandmabrownsbeans@verizon.net
Manufacturer of baked beans, saucepan beans, bean soup and split pea soup under the Grandma Brown's brand.
President: Sandra Brown
Estimated Sales: $2.5-3 Million
Number of Products: 4
Sq. footage: 36000
Type of Packaging: Consumer, Food Service
Brands:
GRANDMA BROWN'S

5464 **Grandma Hoerner's Foods**
31862 Thompson Rd
Alma, KS 66401 785-765-2300
Fax: 785-765-2303 hoerner@kansas.net
www.grandmahoerners.com
Organic reduced sugar preserves, pie fillings, fruit butters, hamburger relish and red pepper jelly
President/Owner: Duane McCoy
VP: Regina McCoy
Estimated Sales: $7.9 Million
Number Employees: 40

5465 **Grandma Pat's Products**
PO Box 158
Albin, WY 82050-0158 307-631-0801
Fax: 307-673-5765 waypal@daltontel.net
Soup and chili-bean mixes, popcorn, and winter wheat
Co-Owner: Pat Palm
Co-Owner: Chuck Palm

5466 **Grandma's Recipe Ruglactch**
409 W 15th Street
New York, NY 10011-7006 212-627-2775
Fax: 212-463-8670
Bread and bakery related products
President: Patricia Alessi
Estimated Sales: $920,000
Number Employees: 18
Type of Packaging: Private Label

5467 **Grandpa Po's Nutra Nuts**
4528 E Washington Blvd
Commerce, CA 90040 323-260-7457
Fax: 888-812-4234 gocorny@nutranuts.com
www.nutranuts.com
Crunchy organic popcorn with snack with soybeans.
President: Mark Porro
CFO: Michael Porro
Estimated Sales: $200,000
Number Employees: 5
Sq. footage: 3300

5468 **Grandpops Lollipops**
2600 Burlington St # A
Kansas City, MO 64116-3019 816-421-5282
Fax: 816-421-5599 800-255-7873
Lollipops and candy
President: Josh Sitzer
Estimated Sales: Under $500,000
Number Employees: 5-9
Brands:
Grandpops Lollipops

5469 **Granello Bakery**
5045 W Mardon Ave
Las Vegas, NV 89139 702-361-0311
Fax: 702-361-0415 orders@granellobakery.com
www.granellobakery.com
Specialty baked goods such as breads, pastry, cake, tarts, cookies and bar cookies.
Owner: Laurie Steed
Estimated Sales: $ 20 - 50 Million
Number Employees: 100-249

5470 **Granite Springs Winery**
5050 Granite Springs Winery Rd
Somerset, CA 95684 530-620-6395
Fax: 530-620-4884 800-638-6041
latcham@directcon.net www.latcham.com
Wines consisting of: Zinfandels, Chardonnay, Sauvignon Blanc, Merlot, Syrahplus Port and many other varieties.
President: Jon Latcham
Winemaker: Craig Boyd
Estimated Sales: $1-2.5 Million
Number Employees: 5-9

5471 **Granite State Potato Chip Company**
227 N Broadway
Salem, NH 03079 603-898-2171
Fax: 603-894-5158
Proccesor of snack foods including nuts, popcorn and potato chips
President/CEO: William Croft
General Manager: Buddy Croft
Estimated Sales: $1-2.5 Million
Number Employees: 1-4
Type of Packaging: Consumer, Food Service
Brands:
Granite State Potato Chip

5472 **Granny Annie Jams**
Old School Street
South Londonderry, VT 05155 802-824-6625
Fax: 802-824-6625
Jams flavors include: strawberry rhubarb, strawberry blueberry, raspberry, raspberry blueberry, orange rhubarb and pear apple honey

5473 **Granny Blossom Specialty Foods**
Route 30
Wells, VT 05774 802-645-0507
Fax: 802-645-0860 gblossom@sover.net
www.grannyblossomsspecialtyfoods.com
Producers specialty foods such as: fruit salsas, traditional salas, relishes, Bloody Mary mix, apple cider BBQ sauce, picked garlic, dilly beans and spices. Manufactured in West Pawlet and shipped nationwide.
Owner: Bob Kopp
Owner: Doris Kopp

5474 **Granny Roddy's LLC**
4226 Holborn Avenue
Annandale, VA 22003 703-503-3431
customerservice@graanyroddys.net
www.grannyroddys.net
Baking mixes, full-line baking mixes and ingredients, other baking mixes and ingredients, foodservice, gift packs, private label.
Marketing: Joanne Buto

5475 **Granny's Best Strawberry Products**
PO Box 9
Victoria, ON L7C 3L6
Canada 519-426-0705
Fax: 519-428-0211
Processor of frozen strawberry puree
President: Gary Cooper
Type of Packaging: Private Label

5476 **Granny's Kitchens**
178 Industrial Park Drive
Frankfort, NY 13340-4798 315-735-5000
Fax: 315-735-3200
Frozen doughnuts
President: Alan Rosenblum
VP: Barry Thaler
Estimated Sales: $10-20 Million
Number Employees: 100-249

5477 **Granowska's**
175 Roncesvalles Avenue
Toronto, ON M6R 2L3
Canada 416-533-7755
Fax: 416-533-3261
Manufacturer of baked goods including specialty mousse cakes, cheesecakes, poppy seed cakes, fruit flans, butter cream cakes, whipped cream cakes, cookies and doughnuts
President: Elizabeth Klodas
Estimated Sales: $813,000
Number Employees: 15
Sq. footage: 3500
Brands:
Granowska's

5478 **Grant & Janet Brians**
743 Shore Rd
Hollister, CA 95023-9427 831-637-8497
bob@ihollister.com
www.heirloom-organic.com
Organic vegetables
President: Grant Brians
Estimated Sales: $ .5 - 1 million
Number Employees: 5-9

5479 **Grant Park Packing**
842 W Lake St
Chicago, IL 60607 312-421-4096
Fax: 312-421-1484 vince@grantparkpacking.com
www.grantparkpacking.com
Pork, beef, poultry, sausage and italian sausage
President/Manager: Joe Maffei
General Manager/Partner: Vince Maffei
Estimated Sales: $10 Million
Number Employees: 45
Sq. footage: 17500
Type of Packaging: Consumer

5480 **Grantstone Supermarket**
8 W Grant Rd
Tucson, AZ 85705 520-628-7445
Fax: 520-628-1259
Specializes in Chinese, Japanese, Korean, Thai and Vietnamese products wholesale and retail. Fresh Chinese fruit and produce.
President: Janet Hom
Estimated Sales: $ 3 - 5 Million
Number Employees: 20-49

5481 **Granville Gates & Sons**
60 Fish Plant Rd
Hubbards, NS B0J 1T0
Canada 902-228-2559
Fax: 902-228-2368 ed.granville@nssympatico.ca
Processor and exporter of dried and salted seafood
General Manager: Gary Harnish
Office Manager: Norma Young
Plant Manager: Ed Grant
Estimated Sales: 5,000,000 - 9,999,999
Number Employees: 32
Type of Packaging: Bulk

5482 **Grapevine Trading Company**
738 Wilson St
Santa Rosa, CA 95401 707-576-3950
Fax: 707-576-3945 800-469-6478
sanvan@grapevinetrading.com
www.grapevinetrading.com
Manufacturer of mustards, fruit and balsamic vinegars, olive oils, tapenades, wild mushrooms, chile peppers, pine nuts, dried tomatoes, polenta mixes, vanilla extract
President: Sandra Voorhis
Estimated Sales: $1.3 Million
Number Employees: 10
Brands:
California Harvest
Gourmet Fare
Grapevine Trading Co.
Wine Gift Packaging

5483 **Graseby Goring Kerr**
642 Blackhawk Drive
Westmont, IL 60559-1116 416-438-9711
Fax: 416-438-2340

5484 **Grassland Dairy Products**
N8790 Fairground Ave
Greenwood, WI 54437 715-267-6182
Fax: 715-267-6044 800-428-8837
email@grassland.com www.grassland.com
Processor and exporter of anhydrous milk fat and butter including whipped, salted, unsalted and oil
President/Owner: Dallas Wuethrich
Vice President: Trevor Wuethrich
VP/Director Sales/Marketing: Jill Cornman
Director Operations: Laverne Gregorich
Estimated Sales: $50-100 Million
Number Employees: 100-249
Sq. footage: 70000
Type of Packaging: Consumer, Food Service, Private Label, Bulk
Brands:
Fall Creek
Grassland

5485 **Grasso Foods**
P.O.Box 127
Swedesboro, NJ 8085-127
Fax: 856-467-5474
Processor of frozen fruit and vegetables
President: Joseph Grasso
Plant Manager: Tony Verchio
Estimated Sales: $25-49.9 Million
Number Employees: 100-249
Type of Packaging: Consumer, Food Service, Private Label, Bulk

5486 **Grating Pacific/Ross Technology Corporation**
3651 Sausalito St
Los Alamitos, CA 90720-2436 562-598-4314
Fax: 562-598-2740 800-321-4314
sales@gratingpacific.com
www.gratingpacific.com
President: Ron Robertson
Estimated Sales: $ 20 - 30 Million
Number Employees: 50-99

5487 **Graves Mountain Lodge Inc.**
Route 670
Syria, VA 22743 540-923-4747
Fax: 540-923-4312
cannery@gravesmountain.com
www.gravesmountain.com
Processor of pepper and cucumber relish, fruit preserves, jellies, chutney, apple butter and apple sauce
President: James Graves
VP: James Graves
Plant Manager: Gail Ford
Estimated Sales: $300,000- $500,000
Number Employees: 8
Number of Brands: 1
Sq. footage: 10000
Parent Co: Graves Mountain Lodge
Type of Packaging: Consumer, Private Label
Brands:
Colonial Williamsburg
Graves Mountain

5488 **(HQ)Gravymaster, Inc.**
101 Erie Blvd
Canajoharie, NY 13317-1148 518-533-4218
Fax: 888-673-2451 800-839-8938
info@richardsonbrands.com www.gravy.com
Processor of sauces including seasoning and browning
President: Stephen Besse
Consultant: John Mills Jr.
Sales Coordinator: MaryLou Sweet
Promotional Products Representative: Laurie Bluitt
Supply Chain Manager: Rebecca Woodruff
Estimated Sales: $10-20 Million
Number Employees: 20-49
Parent Co: Founders Equity
Type of Packaging: Consumer, Food Service
Brands:
Gravy Master
Gravymaster

5489 **(HQ)Gray & Company**
P.O.Box 218
Forest Grove, OR 97116 503-357-3141
Fax: 503-359-0719 800-551-6009
fruitsales@cherryman.com www.cherryman.com
Processor and exporter of maraschino cherries, glazed fruit and chocoate cherry cordials.
President: James G Reynolds
Chief Executive Officer: Jim Reynolds Sr.
Vice President Sales/Marketing: Josh Reynolds
Estimated Sales: H
Number Employees: 500-999
Brands:
QUEEN ANNE CORDIAL CHERRIES
QUEEN ANNE JUBILEES

5490 **Gray & Company**
2331 23rd Avenue
PO Box 218
Forest Grove, OR 97116 503-357-3141
Fax: 503-359-0719 sales@cherryman.com
cherryman.com
Processor and exporter of maraschino cherries, glace fruit and chocolate cherry cordials
Chairman: James Reynolds
CFO: Jeffrey Grimm
Marketing Director: Josh Reynolds
Senior VP Sales: Bob Vugar
Operations Manager: Judd Marlatt
Director Manufacturing: J Marlatt
Plant Manager: P Lieber
Estimated Sales: H
Number Employees: 500-999
Type of Packaging: Consumer, Food Service, Private Label, Bulk
Brands:
Cherryman
Pennant
Queen Anne
Towie
White Swan

5491 **Gray Brewing Company**
2424 W Court St
Janesville, WI 53548 608-752-3552
Fax: 608-752-0821 www.graybrewing.com
Processor of beer, ale, stout and porter
Co-Owner: Fred Gray
Sales: Robert Gray
Estimated Sales: Under $500,000
Number Employees: 5-9
Type of Packaging: Consumer, Food Service

5492 **Grays Ice Cream**
16 East Rd
Tiverton, RI 2878 401-624-4500
Fax: 401-624-4500 www.graysicecream.com
Homemade ice cream, frozen desserts
President: Marilyn Dennis
Estimated Sales: $580,000-1 Million
Number Employees: 20

5493 **Graysmarsh Farm**
6187 Woodcock Rd
Sequim, WA 98382 800-683-4367
Fax: 360-683-6509 800-683-4367
grysmrsh@olypen.com www.graysmarsh.com
Processor of barley, jams, jellies, marmalades and processed raspberries. U-pick rasberries, strawberries, loganberries, blueberries and have fields of lavender.
General Manager: Arturo Flores
Production: Susan Trapp
Estimated Sales: $ 20 - 50 Million
Number Employees: 20-49
Type of Packaging: Consumer, Food Service, Bulk

5494 **Great American Appetizers**
216 8th St N
Nampa, ID 83687 208-465-5111
Fax: 208-465-5059 800-282-4834
marco@appetizer.com www.appetizer.com
Processor and exporter of frozen, battered and breaded appetizers including vegetables, onion rings and cheese sticks; and other specialty appetizers; New Betty Crocker frozen homestyle mashed potatoes, mashed sweet potatoes andgourmet twice baked potatoes.
President: Ellen Meyer
Marketing/Sales Coordinator: Debbie Lindley
VP Retail Sales: Frank Benso
COO: Marco Meyer
Purchasing Director: Tammy Mika
Estimated Sales: $26.6 Million
Number Employees: 375
Number of Products: 100
Sq. footage: 60000
Parent Co: Westin Foods
Type of Packaging: Consumer, Food Service, Private Label, Bulk
Brands:
Big Red
Brew House
Questias
Wahoo! Appetizers

5495 **Great American BarbecueCompany**
1078 Highway 90
Weimar, TX 78962-4402 510-865-3133
catering@greatbbq.com
www.greatbbq.com
Frozen and refrigerated beef prepared, chicken prepared
Owner: Dave Mann
Owner: Dan Ferreira
VP Sales: Troy Gall
Brands:
Great American Barbecue

5496 **(HQ)Great American Dessert**
5842 Maurice Ave
Flushing, NY 11378 718-894-3494
Fax: 718-894-6105 www.juniorscheesecake.com
Processor of gourmet desserts including cakes, pies, tortes, rugulach and brownies, also cookies, petit fours, dried fruit, babkas, hammentaschen and puff pasteries.
Owner: Michael Goodwin
Public Relations: Theresa Kramer
Purchasing: Grace Pavlak
Estimated Sales: $1-5 Million
Number Employees: 20-49
Type of Packaging: Private Label
Brands:
Granny Cheescakes
Rode Lee

5497 **Great American Foods Commissary**
7566 Us Highway 259 N
Ore City, TX 75683-5639 903-968-8630
Fax: 903-968-4376 www.davidbeards.com
Process foods including, catfish, tomato relish, hot sauce and hushpuppies
President: David Beard
Purchasing: Terry Simpler
Estimated Sales: $20-50 Million
Number Employees: 20-49
Brands:
David Beards
David Beards Texas Style

5498 **Great American Popcorn Works of Pennsylvania**
336 W Broad St
Telford, PA 18969 215-721-0414
Fax: 215-721-6082 800-542-2676
info@popcornworks.com
www.popcornworks.com
Gift tinsfilled with gourmet popcorn, bags of all natural and flavored popcorns, jars of kernels, and toppings
Manager: Alice Barnes
Vice President: Jack Egner
Sales Director: Rob Rosen
Public Relations: Giselle Wetzel
Estimated Sales: Less than $500,000
Number Employees: 1-4
Number of Products: 65
Sq. footage: 6000
Type of Packaging: Consumer, Food Service, Private Label, Bulk

5499 **Great American Seafood Company**
2900 Ayers Avenue
Los Angeles, CA 90058 323-262-8222
contact@greatamericanseafood.com
www.greatamericanseafood.com
Great American Seafood is a premier provider of quality seafood to America.
Estimated Sales: $300,000-500,000
Number Employees: 5-9

5500 **Great American Smokehouse & Seafood Company**
15657 Highway 101 S
Brookings, OR 97415 541-469-6903
Fax: 541-469-9692 800-828-3474
nancy@smokehouse-salmon.com
www.smokesalmon.com
Seafood
Owner: Lee D Myers Sr
Co-Owner: Nancy Myers
Co-Owner: Lee Myers Jr
Estimated Sales: $500,000-$1 Million
Number Employees: 10-19

5501 **Great Atlantic Trading Company**
563 Seaside Rd SW
Ocean Isle Beach, NC 28469 910-575-7979
Fax: 910-575-7978 888-268-8780
info@caviarstar.com www.caviarstar.com
Fresh and frozen seafood, American and imported caviar
President: Dana Leavitt
Estimated Sales: $3.2 Million
Number Employees: 1-4
Sq. footage: 5000

5502 **Great Cakes**
8956 Ellis Avenue
Los Angeles, CA 90034-3302 310-287-0228
Fax: 310-202-8305
Cakes, breads, rolls
President: Pamela Freedman
Estimated Sales: $5-10 Million appx.
Number Employees: 10-19

5503 **Great Circles**
P.O.Box 495
Bellows Falls, VT 05101-0495 802-463-2111
Fax: 802-463-2110 877-877-2120
gcircles@sover.net http://www.sover.net

Health foods
President: Dwane Kurisu
CEO: Rich Kendall
Estimated Sales: $2.5-5 Million
Number Employees: 1-4

5504 **Great Divide Brewing Company**
2201 Arapahoe St
Denver, CO 80205 303-296-9460
Fax: 303-296-9464 info@greatdivide.com
www.greatdivide.com
Processor of beer and ale
President/Brewmaster: Brian Dunn
Vice President: Tara Dunn
Vice President Operations: Mason Thomas
Estimated Sales: $5-10 Million
Number Employees: 10-19
Brands:
Arapahoe
Bee Sting
Denver
Hibernation
Saint Brigid's
WIT
Whitewater
Wild Raspberry

5505 **Great Earth Chemical**
7007 SW Cardinal Lane, Ste 135
Portland, OR 97224 608-752-7417
Fax: 608-752-7418 kruszkadr@gmail.com
www.greatearthchemical.com
Manufacturer of food additives, nutritional supplements, vitamins and preservatives
Director of Sales: Daniel Kruszka
Number Employees: 20
Parent Co: North American World Trade Group

5506 **Great Eastern Sun**
92 McIntosh Rd
Asheville, NC 28806-1406 828-665-7790
Fax: 828-667-8051 800-334-5809
weborders@great-eastern-sun.com
www.great-eastern-sun.com
Manufacturer and importer Asian organic and natural foods including miso, green and black teas, dressings, sweeteners, noodles, sea vegetables, etc
Owner: Berry Evans
Finance: Brett Martin
Sales Manager: Mary Griffin
VP Operations/Purchaser: Jan Paige
Assistant Production Manager: Wendy Young
Warehouse/Shipping: Joe Putnam
Estimated Sales: $ 5 - 10 Million
Number Employees: 20-49
Brands:
Emerald Cove Sea Vegetables
Emperor's Kitchen
Haiku Teas
Miso Master Miso
One World Teas
Organic Planet Asian Pastas

5507 **Great Expectations Confectionery Gourmet Foods**
1911 W Warren Boulevard
Chicago, IL 60612 773-525-4865
Fax: 773-281-5506
Candy and confections
President: John Prescott
Estimated Sales: $110,000
Number Employees: 2
Type of Packaging: Consumer, Private Label
Brands:
Great Expectations

5508 **Great Garlic Foods**
709 5th Ave
Bradley Beach, NJ 7720 732-775-3311
Fax: 732-774-9386
Garlic spreads, pesto sauces, chopped garlic in oil, chopped garlic in water
Owner: Joe De Santis
Estimated Sales: $ 1 - 3 Million
Number Employees: 5-9
Type of Packaging: Consumer, Food Service, Private Label, Bulk

5509 **Great Glacier Salmon**
PO Box 1137
Prince Rupert, BC V8J 4H6
Canada 250-627-4955
Fax: 250-627-7945 greatglacier@hotmail.com
www.wildsalmon.ca
Small specialty fisherman owned salmon processor
Accounting: Mary Allen
General Manager: Robert Gould
Estimated Sales: $250,000 To 1,000,000
Number Employees: 20-49
Number of Brands: 2
Sq. footage: 3200
Type of Packaging: Private Label, Bulk
Brands:
GLACIER CAVIAR
GLACIER SALMON

5510 **Great Grains Milling Company**
105 Four Buttes Railroad Ave W
Scobey, MT 59263 406-783-5581
organic@greatgrainsmilling.com
www.greatgrainsmilling.com
Processor of stone ground and whole organic hard red spring wheat flour and bran, cracked wheat cereal, pancake and waffle mix.
President: Alvin Rustebakke
Estimated Sales: $500,000-$1 Million
Number Employees: 1-4
Sq. footage: 800
Type of Packaging: Consumer, Food Service, Private Label

5511 **Great Hill Dairy**
160 Delano Rd
Marion, MA 02738 508-748-2208
Fax: 508-748-2282 888-748-2208
info@greathillblue.com www.greathillblue.com
Manufacturer of gourmet quality raw milk non-homogenized aged Blue cheese in 6 lbs wheels and 1.5 lb wedges wrapped in foil
President: Tim Stone
President: Nancy Weaver
Estimated Sales: $500,000-$1 Million
Number Employees: 1-4
Brands:
Great Hill Blue

5512 **Great Lakes Brewing**
30 Queen Elizabeth Boulevard
Etobicoke, ON M8Z 1L8
Canada 416-255-4510
Fax: 416-255-4907 800-463-5435
info@greatlakesbeer.com
www.greatlakesbeer.com
Premium Canadian malt and choice German hops are used in brewing of Golden Horseshoe Premium lager which contains no additives or preservatives.
Vice President: Peter Bulut Jr
Number Employees: 20-49
Type of Packaging: Consumer, Food Service

5513 **Great Lakes Brewing Company**
2516 Market Ave
Cleveland, OH 44113 216-771-4404
Fax: 216-771-4466 info@greatlakesbrewing.com
www.greatlakesbrewing.com
Processor of beer, ale, stout, lager and porter
Manager: Elenore Walters
CFO: Kevin Cawneen
Estimated Sales: $3 Million
Number Employees: 85
Type of Packaging: Consumer, Food Service
Brands:
Burning River
Edmond Fitzgerald

5514 **(HQ)Great Lakes Cheese Company**
P.O.Box 1806
Hiram, OH 44234 440-834-1002
Fax: 440-834-1002
glcinfo@greatlakescheese.com
www.greatlakescheese.com
Manufacturer and supplier of high quality cheese products
President/CEO: Gary Vanic
CFO: Russell Mullins
VP Sales/Marketing: Bill Andrews
Estimated Sales: $2.2 Billion
Number Employees: 1,700
Type of Packaging: Private Label

5515 **Great Lakes Cheese of NY**
23 Phelps St
Adams, NY 13605 315-232-4511
Fax: 315-232-4055
glcinfo@greatlakescheese.com
www.greatlakescheese.com
Manufacturer and packer of natural and processed bulk, shredded and sliced cheeses.
CEO: Gary Vanic
VP: John Epprecht
Quality Control Manager: Bob Mann
Plant Manager: John Jennings
Purchasing Director: Lloyd Caird
Estimated Sales: $50-100 Million
Number Employees: 79
Sq. footage: 88000
Parent Co: Great Lakes Cheese Company
Type of Packaging: Consumer, Private Label

5516 **Great Lakes Foods**
101 Brockley Drive
Hamilton, ON L8E 3C4
Canada 905-560-4223
Fax: 905-560-5540
Processor of canned mushrooms, fruit and vegetable canning, pickling and drying
President: Tom Ireland
Vice President: Johanne Ubbels
Estimated Sales: $1-2.5 Million
Number Employees: 10-19
Parent Co: Ubbelea Farms
Type of Packaging: Consumer, Food Service, Private Label
Brands:
Chateau
Riviera

5517 **Great Lakes Kraut Company**
P.O.Box 217
Bear Creek, WI 54922 715-752-4105
Fax: 715-752-3432
Manufacturer and exporter of canned, bagged and glass packed sauerkraut and pickled asparagus; also, bulk cabbage
Owner: Ryan Downs
VP of Sales: Ryan Downs
Estimated Sales: $2.5-5 Million
Number Employees: 20-49
Type of Packaging: Consumer, Food Service, Private Label, Bulk
Brands:
Flanagan
Pixie Pak
Symco

5518 **(HQ)Great Lakes Kraut Company**
11 Clark Street
Shortsville, NY 14548 585-289-4414
Fax: 585-289-4280 www.greatlakeskraut.com
Sauerkraut, cabbage products
President: David Flanagan
Controller: Shane Sieracki
Plant Manager: Mark Mette
Estimated Sales: $10-20 Million
Number Employees: 100-249
Type of Packaging: Bulk

5519 **Great Lakes Packing Company**
6556 Quarterline Rd
Kewadin, MI 49648 231-264-5561
Fax: 231-264-5594
Processor of frozen cherries
President: Norman Veliquette
Vice President: Dean Veliquette
Manager: Trudy Cullimore
Estimated Sales: $1.7 Million
Number Employees: 20
Type of Packaging: Consumer, Private Label
Brands:
Great Lakes

5520 **Great Lakes Products**
2540 Ridge Road
Highland Park, IL 60035-1606 847-406-3076
Fax: 847-406-3077
President: Joe Schuetz

5521 **Great Lakes Tea & SpiceCompany**
6610 Western Ave
PO Box 661
Glen Arbor, MI 49636 231-334-6747
Fax: 231-326-2333 877-645-9363
contact@glteaandspice.com
www.glteaandspice.com
loose teas, flowering teas and spices
President/Owner: Chris Sack

5522 **Great Northern Baking Company**
443 Hoover St NE
Minneapolis, MN 55413 612-331-1043
Fax: 612-331-1052
Daniel@GreatNorthernBaking.com
www.greatnorthernbaking.com
Muffins, cakes, cookie bars and pretzels
President: Fred Johnson
Estimated Sales: $ 5-9.9 Million
Number Employees: 50-99
Brands:
Mrs Feldman's Desserts

5523 **Great Northern Brewing Company**
2 Central Ave
Whitefish, MT 59937 406-863-1000
Fax: 406-863-1001 joe@greatnorthernbrewing
www.greatnorthernbrewing.com
Processor of beer and lager
Owner: Dennis Konopatzke
Accounts Management/Retail Sales: Pam Barberis

Tasting Room/Customer Service: Jessica Stanhope
Production Manager: Dan Rasmussen
Estimated Sales: $2.5-5 Million
Number Employees: 1-4
Parent Co: McKenzie River Partners
Type of Packaging: Consumer, Food Service
Brands:
Black
Premium
Whitefish
Wild Huckleberry

5524 **Great Northern Maple Products**
331 Rue Principale
Saint Honor, De Shenley, QC G0M 1V0
Canada 418-485-7777
Fax: 418-485-6185
info@greatnorthernmaple.com
www.greatnorthernmaple.com
Supply organic made maple and fruit syrups to distributors, supermarkets, importers and manufacturers
Director General: Gary Coppola
International Marketing Manager: Luc Tardiff

5525 **Great Northern Products**
PO Box 7622
Warwick, RI 02887 401-490-4590
Fax: 401-490-5595 info@northernproducts.com
www.northernproducts.com
Processor of Natural Scallops, Cold Water Shrimp, Farmed Atlantic Salmon, Snow Crab Products
President: George Nolan
VP: David Sussman
Marketing Director: Tom Lucia
Human Resources Coordinator: Chery; Healy
VP/Operations Manager: Elaine Weygand
Estimated Sales: $220,000
Number Employees: 10-19
Number of Brands: 4
Number of Products: 40
Sq. footage: 2208
Brands:
Commonwealth
Fruits De Mer
Langlois
Sabana
Sealicious
Simmonds

5526 **Great Pacific Seafoods**
4201 Old Intl Airport Rd
Anchorage, AK 99502 907-248-7966
Fax: 907-248-8190
Processor of fresh and frozen salmon
Manager: Roger Stiles
Estimated Sales: $10-20 Million
Number Employees: 50-99
Type of Packaging: Consumer, Food Service
Brands:
Great Pacific

5527 **Great Plains Seafood**
6360 Carter Street
Shawnee, KS 66203-3600 913-262-6060
Fax: 913-393-0238
Quality seafood products.
President: Doug Hensley
Estimated Sales: $ 20 - 50 Million
Number Employees: 20-49

5528 **(HQ)Great Recipes Company**
P.O.Box 647
Beaverton, OR 97075 503-590-1108
Fax: 800-585-2331 800-273-2331
contactus@great-recipes.com
www.great-recipes.com
Processor of bread, cookie, cake, brownie and muffin mixes; custom mixes available such as beer bread
President: Mark Bonebrake
Estimated Sales: $1-2.5 Million
Number Employees: 1-4
Type of Packaging: Private Label
Brands:
FIRENZA
Great Recipes

5529 **(HQ)Great River Milling**
P.O.Box 185
Fountain City, WI 54629-0185 608-687-9580
Fax: 608-687-3014
rhaverson@greatrivermilling.com
www.greatrivermilling.com
Supplier of certified organic grains, flour and mixes
Owner: Rick Halverson
Customer Service: Nadine Bayer
Estimated Sales: $300,000-500,000
Number Employees: 1-4
Type of Packaging: Bulk

5530 **Great Spice Company**
12101 Moya Blvd
Reno, NV 89506-2600
Fax: 760-744-0401 800-730-3575
jslatic@greatspice.com www.greatspice.com
Processor and exporter of dehydrated and fresh herbs such as: Dill, Basil, Italian Parsley, Greek Oregano, Marjoram and many other culinary herbs.
President: Jay Fishman
Inventory Manager: Steve Addison
Quality Manager: Ja Attaphongse
VP Sales: Jim Slatic
Founder/VP Operations: Jerry Tenenberg
Operations Manager: Dan Sullivan
Shipping Manager: Michael Tenenberg
Global Purchasing Coordinator: Rommina Chavarria
Estimated Sales: $ 3 - 5 Million
Number Employees: 20-49
Type of Packaging: Food Service, Private Label, Bulk

5531 **Great Valley Mills**
P.O.Box 220
Barto, PA 19504 610-754-7800
Fax: 610-754-6490 800-688-6455
gvm1710@pdt.net www.greatvalleymills.com
Stone ground flour, pancake, muffin, bread and specialty dry food mixes.
Owner: Steve Kantoor
Estimated Sales: $690,000
Number Employees: 5-9
Sq. footage: 15000
Type of Packaging: Consumer, Food Service, Private Label
Brands:
1710
Covered Bridge Mills
Flip It
Great Valley Mills
Great Valley Mixes

5532 **Great West of Hawaii**
1165 Hopaka Street
Suite B
Honolulu, HI 96814 808-593-9981
Fax: 808-593-2805
Wholesaler/distributor of frozen food, general line products, provisions/meats and seafood; serving the food service market
President: Robert Henry
Estimated Sales: $10-20 Million
Number Employees: 10
Sq. footage: 15000

5533 **Great Western Brewing Company**
519 Second Avenue N
Saskatoon, SK S7K 2C6
Canada 306-653-4653
Fax: 306-653-2166 800-764-4492
info@greatwesternbrewing.com
www.greatwesternbrewing.com
A malt beverage company with an overriding commitment to quality. Processor of beer, lager and stout.
President/CEO: Ron Waldman
Brewmaster: Garry Johnston
Number Employees: 50-99
Type of Packaging: Consumer, Food Service

5534 **(HQ)Great Western Juice Company**
16153 Libby Rd
Maple Heights, OH 44137 216-475-5770
Fax: 216-475-5772 800-321-9180
suegwjuice@sbcglobal.net
www.greatwesternjuice.com
Manufacturer and exporter of fruit juices, beverages syrups and cocktail mixes
President: Bill Overton
VP: William Overton
Estimated Sales: $2.5-5 Million
Number Employees: 20-49
Sq. footage: 50000
Type of Packaging: Food Service, Private Label

5535 **Great Western Juice Company**
16153 Libby Rd
Maple Heights, OH 44137 216-475-5770
Fax: 216-475-5772 800-321-9180
gwjuice@sbcglobal.net
www.greatwesternjuice.com
Manufacturer of concentrated beverage syrups, cocktail mixes, frosted cocktails, teas, lemonades and energy drinks.
President: Jack Golberg
VP: Bill Overton
Marketing/Sales: Phil Leroy
Public Relations: Connie Rice
Operations Manager: John Stevens
Plant Manager: John Taziros
Purchasing Manager: Bill Overton Jr.
Estimated Sales: $1.6 Million
Number Employees: 18
Sq. footage: 30000
Parent Co: Great Western
Type of Packaging: Food Service, Private Label
Brands:
ICE & EASY
PERFECTION
SUNNY MORNING

5536 **Great Western Malting Company**
P.O.Box 1529
Vancouver, WA 98668-1529 360-693-3661
Fax: 360-696-8354 877-770-7055
mblackmore@conagramalt.com
Processor and exporter of processed malt including brewers', distillers' and wheat
Finance Executive: Steve Rosvold
Contact: Marla Blackmore
Estimated Sales: $50-100 Million
Number Employees: 50-99
Parent Co: ConAgra Foods
Type of Packaging: Bulk

5537 **Great Western Products Company**
1001 Echols St
Bismarck, MO 63624 573-734-2210
Fax: 573-734-6454
Processor and exporter of popcorn, popping corn oil, cotton candy, sno-cone syrup, candy apple coatings, funnel cakes, waffle cones, corn dog mix, etc.; manufacturer of concession equipment including corn poppers
Manager: Marvin Scott
Estimated Sales: $500,000-$1 Million
Number Employees: 5-9
Type of Packaging: Consumer, Food Service, Private Label, Bulk

5538 **Great Western Products Company**
2047 E 1350 North Rd
Assumption, IL 62510 217-226-3241
Fax: 217-226-3569
Processor and exporter of popcorn, popping corn oil, cotton candy, sno-cone syrup, candy apple coatings, funnel cakes, waffle cones, corn dog mix, etc.
General Manager: Mike Calcara
Estimated Sales: $10-20 Million
Number Employees: 40
Type of Packaging: Consumer, Food Service, Private Label, Bulk

5539 **Great Western Tortilla**
P.O.Box 16346
Denver, CO 80216-0346 303-298-0705
Fax: 303-298-0216 info@tortilla-chips.com
www.tortilla-chips.com
Tortilla chips, nuts, salsa, hot sauces and snack mix
Director Sales/Marketing: John Amerman
Estimated Sales: $10-20 Million
Number Employees: 50-99

5540 **(HQ)Greater Omaha Packing Company**
3001 L St
Omaha, NE 68107 402-731-1700
Fax: 402-731-8020 info@greateromaha.com
www.greateromaha.com
Processor and exporter of boxed beef
President/CEO: Henry Davis
Executive Vice President: Angelo Fili
Vice President Technical Resources: Kathleen Krantz
Vice President Sales/Marketing: Roy Wiggs
Cattle Procurement Manager: Joe Goergen
Estimated Sales: $100+ Million
Number Employees: 500-999
Sq. footage: 200000
Type of Packaging: Consumer, Food Service, Private Label, Bulk

5541 **Greaves Jams & Marmalades**
PO Box 26
Niagara-on-the-Lake, ON L0S 1J0
Canada 905-468-3608
Fax: 905-468-0071 800-515-9939
greaves@greavesjams.com
www.greavesjams.com
Processor of all natural jams, jellies, marmalades and condiments; exporter of portion controlled jams, marmalades and honey - 100% pure, no preservatives, no additives, no pectin -
Preident: Lloyd Redekopp
Vice President: Angela Redekopp
Production Manager: Rudy Doerwald
Estimated Sales: $1.4 Million
Number Employees: 15
Number of Products: 1
Sq. footage: 10000
Type of Packaging: Consumer, Private Label
Brands:
Greaves

5542 **Grebe's Bakery & Delicatessen**
5132 W Lincoln Ave
Milwaukee, WI 53219-1684 414-543-7000
Fax: 414-543-8863 800-356-9377
Manufacturer of bread, rolls, doughnuts and cakes.
Manager: Joan Janczak
Estimated Sales: $10-20 Million
Number Employees: 100-249
Sq. footage: 31000
Type of Packaging: Consumer, Bulk
Brands:
GREBE'S

5543 **Grecian Delight Foods**
1201 Tonne Rd
Elk Grove Village, IL 60007 847-364-1010
Fax: 847-364-1077 800-621-4387
www.greciandelight.com
Processor of ethnic frozen baked goods, meat products, pita bread, gyros, Greek entrees and desserts
Owner/Human Resources & Sales Manager: Peter Parthenis
VP/CFO: Bill Pierreakeas
Research/Development Manager: John Matchuk
Quality Control Manager: Mary Funteas
Marketing Director: Deme Katsulis
VP Operations: Tom Valnoha
Purchasing Director: George Georganas
Estimated Sales: $50-100 Million
Number Employees: 180
Sq. footage: 200000
Type of Packaging: Consumer, Food Service, Private Label
Brands:
Athenian
Chicago Style
Pita Folds

5544 **Greek Gourmet Limited**
38 Miller Avenue PMB 510
Mill Valley, CA 94941 415-480-8050
Fax: 617-833-6056
Importer of chocolate, rolled wafers, olives, olive oil, salad dressings, preserves, peppers, spreads, teas, spices, coffee
President: George Nassopoulos
Vice President: Diane Nassopoulos
Sales Director: James Contis
Production Manager: P Margaritidis
Estimated Sales: $2.5-5 Million
Number Employees: 5-9
Number of Brands: 4
Number of Products: 35
Sq. footage: 10000
Type of Packaging: Consumer, Food Service, Private Label, Bulk
Brands:
7 Day Round
Bolero
Chelsea
Greek Gourmet
Santorina

5545 **Greeley Elevator Company**
700 6th St
Greeley, CO 80631 970-352-2575
Fax: 970-352-6390 greecal@aol.com
Processor of dried beans
Owner: Matt Geib
General Manager: Matthew Geib
Estimated Sales: $1-2.5 Million
Number Employees: 5-9
Type of Packaging: Consumer, Food Service, Bulk

5546 **Green Bay Cheese Company**
P.O.Box 11766
13190 Velp Ave
Green Bay, WI 54313-8040 920-434-3233
Fax: 920-434-3262 jayw@greenbaycheese.com
www.greenbaycheese.com
Cheese (cutting, shredding and packaging)
President: Thomas Vorpahl
Manager: Michael Smith
Manager: Charles Lefebre
Manager: Forest Kentworthy
Human Resources Director: Jean Pautz
National Sales Manager: Jay Wistenberg
Plant Manager: Dean Zaretzke
Estimated Sales: $20-50 Million
Number Employees: 100-249
Parent Co: DCI Cheese Company

5547 **Green County Foods**
1112 7th Ave
Monroe, WI 53566 608-328-8800
Fax: 608-328-8648 800-233-3564
greencity@tds.net www.greencountyfoods.com
Petitfours, tortes-bite-sized desserts-contract bakery, fudge, gingerbread
President: Gene Curran
Sales: Wally Wagner
Public Relations: Jim Mason
Operations: Sharee Marzolf
Estimated Sales: $2.5-5 Million
Number Employees: 10-19
Parent Co: Swiss Colony
Type of Packaging: Consumer, Food Service, Private Label, Bulk
Brands:
Richly Deserved
Sweet Treasures

5548 **Green Foods Corporation**
320 Graves Ave
Oxnard, CA 93030 805-983-7470
Fax: 805-983-8843 800-777-4430
gfc@greenfoods.com www.greenfoods.com
Processor, importer and exporter of health foods including barley and vegetable juice powders, green magma, wheat germ extracts, etc
President: Takahiko Amano
Technical Service Manager: Bob Terry PhD
Office Manager: Deborah Pollack
Estimated Sales: $10-20 Million
Number Employees: 10-19
Sq. footage: 9800
Type of Packaging: Consumer
Brands:
Green Essence

5549 **Green Garden Food Products**
5851 S 194th St
Kent, WA 98032 253-395-4460
Fax: 253-395-0408 800-304-1033
info@ggfoods.com www.ggfoods.com
Processor of salad dressings, sauces, marinades, dips, salsas, mayonnaise
President: Mark Hockman
Director Technical Services: Kyle Anderson
Estimated Sales: $25,000,000
Number Employees: 50-99
Type of Packaging: Consumer, Food Service

5550 **Green Gold Group**
13905 Stettin Dr
Marathon, WI 54448 715-842-8546
Fax: 715-842-4614 888-533-7288
Processor, wholesaler/distributor and exporter of ginseng, herbs, whole roots, prong, fiber, capsules, tablets and extracts
Owner: Sam Chen
CEO: Phouangmala Chen
Estimated Sales: $ 1 - 3 Million
Number Employees: 10-19
Sq. footage: 7200
Type of Packaging: Consumer, Bulk

5551 **Green Grown Products Inc**
13600 Marina Pointe Dr
Suite 315
Marina Del Ray, CA 90292 310-828-1686
Fax: 310-822-6440
ggpsales@greengrownproducts.com
greengrownproducts.com
Processor and importer of herbs, royal jelly, propolis, bee pollen, chia and sesame seeds, apricot kernels and turbinado sugar; exporter of herbs, propolis, bee pollen and royal jelly
President: Hal Neiman
CEO: Teri Bernardi
Estimated Sales: $2 Million
Number Employees: 1-4
Sq. footage: 8000
Parent Co: Earth Commodities
Type of Packaging: Private Label, Bulk

5552 **Green House**
PO Box 497
San Luis Rey, CA 92068-0497 760-439-6515
Fax: 760-439-4163
Fresh herbs
President: Megan Williams
Estimated Sales: $1-2.5 Million
Number Employees: 20-49

5553 **Green House Fine Herbs**
PO Box 231069
Encinitas, CA 92023-1069 760-942-5371
Processor of fresh and dehydrated herbs including mint, edible flowers, basil, chives and dill; also, industrial blends available
New Bus.: Mike Murphy
Number Employees: 250-499
Sq. footage: 40000
Type of Packaging: Consumer, Food Service, Private Label, Bulk
Brands:
Green House
Herb Farm

5554 **Green Mountain Chocolates**
835 W Central St Ste 1
Franklin, MA 02038 508-520-7160
Fax: 508-520-7161
info@greenmountainchocolate.com
www.greenmountainchocolate.com
Chocolate candies (Petite Truffles, Chocolate Covered Potato Chips, Butter Crunch, Desssert Truffles, Turtles, Bark)
Manager: Karen Tyler
Estimated Sales: $2.5-5 Million
Number Employees: 1-4
Brands:
GREEN MOUNTAIN CHOCOLATE TRUFFLE

5555 **Green Mountain Cidery**
153 Pond Ln
Middlebury, VT 05753-1190 802-388-0700
Fax: 802-388-0600 gmbinfo@gmbeverage.com
www.woodchuck.com
Processor of hard cider (Woodchuck Draft Cider, Strongbow, Woodpecker, Cider Jack)
President: Joseph Cerniglia
VP: Dan Rowell
Director Marketing: Alan MacDonald
General Manager: Rob Hyman
Estimated Sales: $2.5-5 Millioin
Number Employees: 20-49
Sq. footage: 50

Type of Packaging: Private Label
Brands:
WOODCHUCK DRAFT CIDER

5556 **Green Mountain Coffee Roasters**
33 Coffee Ln
Waterbury, VT 5676 802-244-5621
Fax: 802-244-5436 800-545-2326
www.greenmountaincoffee.com
Coffee roaster
President/CEO: Lawrence Blanford
CFO/VP/Treasurer: Frances Rathke
VP/CIO: James Prevo
VP Environmental Affairs: Paul Comey
VP Corporate Social Responsibility: Mike Dupee
Chief Operating Officer: Scott McCreary
Estimated Sales: $1 Billion
Number Employees: 500-999
Number of Brands: 1
Number of Products: 85
Sq. footage: 300000
Type of Packaging: Consumer, Food Service, Bulk
Brands:
GREEN MOUNTAIN COFFEE

5557 **Green Mountain Gringo**
P.O.Box 4329
Winston Salem, NC 27115
Fax: 802-875-3140 gmgringo@sover.net
www.greenmountaingringo.com
Manufacturer of salsa, hot, medium, and mild

5558 **Green Mountain Gringo**
P.O.Box 4329
Winston Salem, NC 27115
Fax: 336-661-1901
info@greenmountaingringo.com
www.greenmountaingringo.com
Manufacturer of salsa,(hot, medium, mild) roasted garlic, roasted Chile peppers and tortilla strips - all homemade.
President: Ralph Garner
VP: Ann Garner Riddle
Estimated Sales: $3.5 Million
Number Employees: 10-19
Parent Co: TW Garner Food Company
Type of Packaging: Private Label

5559 **Green Options**
17 Paul Dr # 104
San Rafael, CA 94903-2043 415-526-1450
Fax: 415-526-1453 888-473-3667
info@vegiedeli.com www.greenoptions.net
Health foods, Vegi-Deli®, Vegi-Deli®Slices, Vegi-Jerky™, Vegi-Deli® Quick Stick
Manager: Michael Madden
Sales Manager: Jill Koperweis
Estimated Sales: $ 1 - 3 Million
Number Employees: 9

5560 **Green River Chocolates**
49 Sunset Ct
Hinesburg, VT 05461 802-482-6727
info@grchocolates.com
www.grchocolates.com
Vermont maple syrup. chocolates, (and sugar free), chocolate sauce, fresh butter corn syrup, crepes and pancake mixes, ice cream and pepper sauces
Estimated Sales: $ 1 - 3 Million
Number Employees: 5-9

5561 **Green Spot Packaging**
100 S Cambridge Ave
Claremont, CA 91711 909-625-8771
Fax: 909-621-4634 800-456-3210
Processor, importer and exporter of juices, juice concentrates, drinks, flavors and fragrances; aseptic packaging services available
CEO: Mike Staudt
Plant Manager: Roy Cooley
Estimated Sales: $6.5 Million
Number Employees: 20-49
Sq. footage: 100000
Type of Packaging: Consumer, Food Service, Private Label, Bulk
Brands:
Action Ade
Apple Delight
Apple Royal
Awesome Orange
Black Cherry Royal
Citrus Royal
Galactic Grape
Good Buddies
Green Spot
Peach Royal
Superstar Strawberry
Tropical Royal

5562 **Green Turtle Bay Vitamin Company**
P.O.Box 642
Summit, NJ 7902 908-277-2240
Fax: 908-273-9116 800-887-8535
mail@energywave.com www.energywave.com
Processor and exporter of vitamin supplement formulas including herbal antioxidants, oils and herbs
President: Karen Horbatt
CEO: Gloria Mckenna
Quality Control: Monica Harris
Marketing: Michele Murphy
Estimated Sales: $600,000
Number Employees: 5
Number of Brands: 8
Number of Products: 8
Type of Packaging: Consumer
Brands:
Diabetiks
Maple Melts
Powermate
Powersleep
Powervites
Primrose Oile
Signal 369
Sunnie

5563 **Green Turtle Cannery & Seafood**
PO Box 585
81219 Overseas Hwy
Islamorada, FL 33036 305-664-9595
Fax: 305-664-9564
Manhattan clam chowder, New England clam chowder, turtle chowder, turtle consumme, conch chowder, New England fish chowder, key lime pie filling
Jr.: Henry Rosenthal
Estimated Sales: $1-2.5 Million
Number Employees: 20-49
Brands:
Sid and Roxie's

5564 **(HQ)Green Valley Apples of California**
14322 Di Giorgio Rd
Arvin, CA 93203-9519 661-854-4436
Fax: 661-854-0810 grnvby@lightseed.com
www.greenvalleypackers.com
Apples: sliced, diced, concentrates
Owner: Bruce Goren
General Manager: Jim Carlisle
Estimated Sales: $ 20 - 50 Million
Number Employees: 50-99
Type of Packaging: Private Label

5565 **Green Valley Foods**
P.O.Box 456
Tranquility, NJ 07879-0456 908-852-8300
Fax: 908-852-0021 800-853-8399
Importer and wholesaler/distributor of cheese, meats, pates, cookies, crackers, breads, jams, jellies, preserves, soups, snack foods, pasta and confections; custom packer of domestic and imported cheeses
President: Philip Stites
Estimated Sales: $2,100,000
Number Employees: 5-9
Sq. footage: 60000

5566 **Green Valley Pecan Company**
1525 W Sahuarita Rd
Sahuarita, AZ 85629 520-791-2880
Fax: 520-629-0119 800-533-5269
bcaris@greenvalleypecan.com
www.greenvalleypecan.com
Pecans
President: Richard Walden
CFO: Heather Triana
R&D Manager: John Lamonica
Director Sales/Marketing: Bruce Caris
Plant Manager: Brenda Lara
Estimated Sales: $20-50 Million
Number Employees: 200
Sq. footage: 4000
Parent Co: Farmers Investment Company
Type of Packaging: Consumer, Bulk
Brands:
GREEN VALLEY PECANS

5567 **Greenberg Cheese Company**
245 Berkshire Ave
Le Canada, CA 91011-4017 818-949-0323
Fax: 213-617-1188 800-301-4507
Cheese, cheese products
President/CEO: Michael Greenberg
Director of Administration: Dick Holly
CFO: Merilyn Greenberg
Vice President: Douglas Smith
Operations Manager: Michael Burns
Estimated Sales: $30 Million
Number Employees: 1
Number of Products: 300
Sq. footage: 20000
Parent Co: Dairy Commodities Corporation
Type of Packaging: Food Service, Bulk

5568 **Greene Brothers Specialty Coffee Roaster**
313 High Street
Hackettstown, NJ 07840-1908 908-979-0022
info@greenesbeans.com
http://www.greenesbeans.com/
Processor of regular, flavored and decaffeinated whole bean coffees, espresso and loose tea
Co-President: David Greene
Co-Presidemt: Brian Greene
Estimated Sales: $ 1 - 3 Million
Number Employees: 10-19
Sq. footage: 1500

5569 **Greenfield Mills**
7560 N 1050 E
Howe, IN 46746 260-367-2394
customerservice@newrinkelflour.com
http://www.newrinkelflour.com/
Processor of wheat and buckwheat flour; also, pancake mixes, Certified Organic whole wheat and white soft wheat flour
President: Howard Rinkel
Vice President: Joyce Rinkel
Secretary/Treasurer: Helen Rinkel
Estimated Sales: $300,000-500,000
Number Employees: 1-4
Sq. footage: 8000
Type of Packaging: Consumer, Food Service
Brands:
New Rinkel

5570 **Greenfield Noodle & Specialty Company**
600 Custer St
Detroit, MI 48202 313-873-2212
Fax: 313-873-0515
Processor of sheeted noodles; wholesaler/distributor of specialty and kosher foods
President: Kenneth Michaels
VP: Mary Michaels
Estimated Sales: $1.3 Million
Number Employees: 12
Sq. footage: 13000
Type of Packaging: Consumer, Food Service, Private Label, Bulk
Brands:
Greenfield
Mrs. Asien

5571 **Greenfield Wine Company**
205 Jim Oswalt Way Ste B
Vallejo, CA 94503-9695 707-552-5199
Fax: 707-963-8537
Wines
Owner: Tony Cartlidge
VP/Partner: Robert Babbe
Vice President: Elijah Selby
Marketing Manager: Dan Waggerman
General Manager: Tony Cartlidge
Estimated Sales: $10-24.9 Million
Number Employees: 48

5572 **Greenhills Irish Bakery**
780 Adams Street
Dorchester, MA 02124 617-825-8187
Fax: 617-698-0335 cquinn3k@comcast.net
www.greenhillsbakery.com
Bakery products; Irish brown bread and soda bread, scones, cakes, pastries
Co-Owner: Dermot Quinn
Co-Owner: Cindy Quinn
Estimated Sales: $10-20 Million
Number Employees: 10-19

5573 **Greens Today®**
91 Commercial St # 2
Plainview, NY 11803-2409 516-576-1665
Fax: 516-576-1662 800-473-3641
www.greenstoday.com
Processor and exporter of powdered nutritional supplements
President: Ellen Piernick
Estimated Sales: $ 1 - 3 Million
Number Employees: 5-9
Parent Co: Nature's Answer, Inc.
Type of Packaging: Bulk
Brands:
Greens Today
The Organic Frog

5574 **Greenwell Farms**
345 Popcorn Rd
Morganfield, KY 42437 270-389-3289
Fax: 270-389-3307 greenwellfarms@prodig.net
www.greenwellfarms.com
Processor of coffee, chocolate covered coffee beans, chocolate covered macadamia nuts, hawaiian chocolate bars, sugar, honey
Owner/President: Tom Greenwell
CEO: Jennifer Greenwell
Estimated Sales: $1-2.5 Million
Number Employees: 10-19
Type of Packaging: Consumer, Food Service, Private Label, Bulk
Brands:
GREENWELL FARMS

5575 **Greenwood Associates**
600 Central Ave Ste 240
Highland Park, IL 60035 847-579-5500
Fax: 847-579-5501
info@greenwoodassociates.com
www.greenwoodassociates.com
Processor, distributor and re-packer of fruit concentrates and purees including lemon, grape, apple, berry, lime, grapefruit, peach, apricot, tropical, cherry, tangerine and pineapple. All to custom specs
President: Ron Kaplan
Estimated Sales: $5-10 Million
Number Employees: 50-99
Sq. footage: 1000
Type of Packaging: Bulk

5576 **Greenwood Ice Cream Company**
4829 Peachtree Rd
Atlanta, GA 30341 770-455-6166
Fax: 770-455-4152 www.greenwoodicecream.com
Ice cream, frozen desserts
President: Mitchell Williams
Director: Robert Street
Director: Tony Yen
Estimated Sales: $4 Million
Number Employees: 30
Brands:
Greenwood

5577 **Greenwood Ridge Vineyards**
5501 Highway 128
Philo, CA 95466 707-895-2002
Fax: 707-895-2001
everybody@greenwoodridge.com
www.greenwoodridge.com
Wines consisting of White Riesling, Cabernet, Sauvignon, Merlot and Pinot Noir
Owner: Allan Green
Estimated Sales: $1-2.5 Million
Number Employees: 5-9

5578 **Greg's Lobster Company**
136 Factory Road
Harwich Port, MA 02645-1675 508-432-8080
Fax: 508-432-2203
Lobster
President: Leslie Sykes
Estimated Sales: $ 2.75 Million
Number Employees: 20

5579 **Gregerson's Foods**
P.O.Box 1460
Gadsden, AL 35902-1460 256-549-0644
Fax: 256-549-1435 clubgreg@aol.com
Supermarket chain
President: Greg Gregerson
CEO: Peter V Gregerson Jr
Estimated Sales: G
Number Employees: 100-249

5580 **Gregg Candy & Nut Company**
4715 Woodhill Drive
Munhall, PA 15120-3537 412-461-0301
Candy

5581 **Gregory's Box'd Beverages**
247 Rome Street
Newark, NJ 07105 973-465-1113
Fax: 973-465-7307 tracy@gregorysboxdbev.com
www.gregorysboxdbev.com
Processor of portion controlled frozen juices including apple, grapefruit, cranberry and orange
President: Edward Gregory
Vice President: Daniel Gregory
Marketing: Tracy Benz
Estimated Sales: $20-50 Million
Number Employees: 50-99
Type of Packaging: Consumer, Food Service, Private Label, Bulk
Brands:
Draft Cider
Woodchuck

5582 **Gregory's Foods**
1301 Trapp Rd
Eagan, MN 55121-1247 651-454-0277
Fax: 651-454-2254 800-231-4734
ghelland@mn.mediaone.net
www.gregorysfoods.com
Processor of frozen baked goods, mixes and bases; wholesaler/distributor of bakery ingredients and supplies; serving the food service market
President: Greg Helland
Quality Control: Tom Hoebbel
Sales/Marketing: Randy Clemons
Estimated Sales: $5.7 Million
Number Employees: 40
Sq. footage: 22000
Type of Packaging: Food Service, Private Label, Bulk

5583 **Gregory-Robinson Speas**
4647 Bronze Way
Dallas, TX 75236-2009 214-352-1761
Fax: 214-339-7245
Processor of vinegar including white distilled, cider and wine
Plant Manager: Palmer Mamola
Estimated Sales: $$10-20 Million
Number Employees: 20-49
Parent Co: Speaco Foods
Type of Packaging: Consumer, Food Service, Private Label, Bulk

5584 **Grennan Meats**
Maple Avenue
Rochelle, IL 61068 815-562-5565
Fax: 815-562-7262
Meat products
President: John Grennan
Estimated Sales: $1 Million
Number Employees: 5-9

5585 **Gress Poultry**
992 N South Rd
Scranton, PA 18504-1412 570-561-0150
Fax: 570-314-1299
Processor and exporter of frozen chicken parts: legs, wings, breasts, thighs and drumsticks
President: Edward Gress
VP/General Manager: Keith Gress
VP Marketing: Glenn Gress
Estimated Sales: $5-10 Million
Number Employees: 20-49
Type of Packaging: Food Service, Bulk

5586 **Grey Eagle Distributors**
2340 Millpark Dr
Maryland Heights, MO 63043 314-429-9100
Fax: 314-429-9137 www.greyeagle.com
Anheuser-Busch and Budweiser products
President: Steven Nolan
CEO: David Stokes
CFO: Jerry Jasiek
Director Sales/Marketing: James Bannes
VP Operations: Neil Komadoski
Estimated Sales: $110 Million
Number Employees: 220
Brands:
Hy-5
Sports Drinks

5587 **Grey Owl Foods**
510 11th St S.E.
Grand Rapids, MN 55744 218-327-2281
Fax: 218-327-2283 800-527-0172
Processor and exporter of wild rice and gourmet rice blends; specializing in lake harvested Canadian jumbo wild rice
Director Sales/Marketing: Jim McCool
Estimated Sales: $10-20 Million
Number Employees: 10-19
Sq. footage: 6000
Parent Co: SIAP Marketing Company
Type of Packaging: Consumer, Food Service, Bulk

5588 **Greyston Bakery**
104 Alexander St
Yonkers, NY 10701 914-375-1510
Fax: 914-375-1514 800-289-2253
info@greystonbakery.com
www.greystonbakery.com
Cakes, tarts, brownies and other baked goods
President/CEO: Julius Walls, Jr.
Estimated Sales: $20-50 Million
Number Employees: 130
Type of Packaging: Consumer, Food Service

5589 **Griffin Food Company**
111 S Cherokee St
Muskogee, OK 74403 918-687-6311
Fax: 918-687-3579 800-580-6311
griffin@ok.azalea.net www.griffinfoods.com
Contract packager and wholesaler/distributor of sauces, vegetables and condiments including jams and syrups; serving the food service, retail and private label markets
President: John Griffin
Vice President: David Needham
VP Sales/Marketing: Sam Ramos
Director Midwest Sales: D C Smith
Director Southeast Region Sales: Wayne Fuller
Estimated Sales: $10-20 Million
Number Employees: 50-99
Sq. footage: 216099
Type of Packaging: Consumer, Food Service, Private Label, Bulk
Brands:
CHEROKEE MAID
DELTA
GRIFFIN
LUCKY DUTCH
OLD SANTA FE
OLDE FARM
PRIZE TAKER

5590 **(HQ)Griffin Industries**
4221 Alexandria Pike
Cold Spring, KY 41076 859-781-2010
Fax: 859-572-2575 sales@griffinind.com
www.griffinind.com
Manufacturer of meat products including chicken and bone meal produces exotic animal feed.
Chairman: John Griffin
CEO: Robert Griffin
CFO: Anthony Griffin
Sales: David Walker
Purchasing: Joe Harris
Estimated Sales: $1.5 Billion
Number Employees: 1,800
Parent Co: Darling International Inc.
Type of Packaging: Private Label, Bulk
Brands:
BAKERY FEEDS
BIO G-3000
NATURE SAFE
VERSAGEN

5591 **Griffin Industries**
11313 SE 52nd Ave
Starke, FL 32091 904-964-8083
Fax: 904-964-8483 sales@griffinind.com
www.griffinind.com
Processor of meat and poultry meal; also, tallow rendering
President: Dennis Griffin
Estimated Sales: $20-50 Million
Number Employees: 50-99

5592 **Griffin Seafood**
P.O.Box 640
Golden Meadow, LA 70357-0640 985-396-2453
Fax: 985-396-2459
Seafood
Owner: Archie Dantin

Estimated Sales: Under $500,000
Number Employees: 5-9

5593 **Griffith Laboratories**
1 Griffith Center
Alsip, IL 60803
Canada 708-371-0900
Fax: 708-389-4055 800-346-9494
contactsalesna@griffithlabs.com
www.griffithlaboratories.com
Processor of binders, bread crumbs and croutons, breading, meat flavors, batters, seasonings, spices and stuffing; also, agricultural and regular analytical, custom sterilization and packaging services available
President: David Morrison
Vice President Technical: Ken Darley
Number Employees: 325
Parent Co: Griffith Laboratories
Type of Packaging: Food Service, Bulk
Brands:
Imperial
Krusto
Robust

5594 **(HQ)Griffith Laboratories Worldwide**
1 Griffith Ctr
Alsip, IL 60803 708-371-0900
Fax: 708-389-4055 800-346-4743
sandersen@griffithlabs.com
www.griffithlabs.com
Processor of food ingredient mixes including gravy, breading, salad dressings, batter, sauces, soups, spices, etc.; also, flavors
Chairman: Dean Griffith
Worldwide President/CEO: Herve de la Vauvre
Executive Vice President/CFO: Joe Maslick
CEO: Herve De La Vauvre
Chief Chemist: Dr Lloyd Hall
Senior Director Marketing: Christine Carr
Vice President National Sales: Mike Kregor
Associate Communications Manager: Susan Andersen
Estimated Sales: $ 150 - 200 Million
Number Employees: 1,000-4,999
Type of Packaging: Food Service, Private Label, Bulk

5595 **Grimaud Farms**
1320 S Aurora St # A
Stockton, CA 95206-1616 209-466-3200
Fax: 209-466-8910 800-466-9955
grimaud@grimaud.com www.grimaud.com
Processor and exporter of muscovy ducks and guinea fowl
President: Rheal Cayer
Accounting Manager: Ciba Williams
Vice President Sales: Jim Galle
Customer Service: Cecile Halverson
Live Production: Diego Davalos
Estimated Sales: $50-100 Million
Number Employees: 100-249
Sq. footage: 25000
Parent Co: Groupe Grimaud
Type of Packaging: Consumer, Food Service, Private Label, Bulk
Brands:
Grimaud Farms
Grimaud Farms Muscovy Ducks
Sonoma Foie-Gras

5596 **Grimm's Fine Food**
2355 52nd Ave Se
Bay 1
Calgary, AB T2C 4X7
Canada 780-415-4331
Fax: 780-477-5287 877-577-5220
georgemccorry@grimmsfood.com
www.grimmsfinefoods.com
Processor and exporter of processed meats and sausages
President: Rick Grimm
Plant Manager: George McCorry
Number Employees: 50-99
Parent Co: Fletcher's Fine Foods
Type of Packaging: Consumer, Food Service, Private Label, Bulk
Brands:
Deli Flavor
Fletchers

5597 **Grimm's Locker Service**
P.O.Box 4524
Sherwood, OH 43556-0524 419-899-2655
Fax: 419-899-2655
Canned meat and poultry
Owner: Michael Oskey
Estimated Sales: Below $ 5 Million
Number Employees: 1-4

5598 **(HQ)Grimmway Farms**
PO Box 81498
Bakersfield, CA 93380 661-854-6230
Fax: 661-854-6999 800-301-3101
pverderber@grimmway.com
www.grimmway.com
Processor of carrots and organic produce
President: Jeff Merge
CFO: Steve Barnes
Vice President: Jeff Huckaby
Sales Manager: Paul Verderber
Estimated Sales: $7 Million
Number Employees: 4,000
Type of Packaging: Consumer, Food Service
Other Locations:
Grimmway Farms
Bakersfield CA
Brands:
Grimmway

5599 **Grimmway Frozen Foods**
P.O.Box 81498
830 Sycamore Rd
Arvin, CA 93203-2132 661-854-2132
Fax: 661-845-9745 www.grimmway.com
Frozen green beans, carrots, celery, red bell peppers, whole or sliced potatoes, vegetables for soup or stew
Manager: Fred Rappleye
Executive VP: Michael Davis
Number Employees: 400
Type of Packaging: Private Label
Brands:
Grimmway

5600 **Grindle Point Lobster Company**
RR 1
Box 4690
Lincolnville, ME 04849 207-763-4142
Fax: 207-763-3861
Lobster
Owner: David Aho

5601 **Grippo's Food Products**
6750 Colerain Ave
Cincinnati, OH 45239 513-923-1900
Fax: 513-923-3645 info@grippos.com
www.grippopotatochips.com
Manufacturer of potato chips, pretzels, dips, hot and spicy and low carb snacks.
President: Ralph Pagel II
VP: Nancy Schreiber
Purchasing: Ralph Pagel
Estimated Sales: $7.2 Million
Number Employees: 50
Sq. footage: 33000
Type of Packaging: Consumer

5602 **Groeb Farms**
P.O.Box 269
Onsted, MI 49265-0269 517-467-2065
Fax: 517-467-2840 groeb@groebfarms.com
www.groebfarms.com
Processor, importer and exporter of honey, honey powder, mustard, peanut butter, molasses, molasses powder and fresh salsa
Owner: Ernest Groeb
VP/COO: Troy Groeb
Estimated Sales: $80 Million
Number Employees: 50-99
Type of Packaging: Consumer, Food Service, Private Label, Bulk
Brands:
GOURMET JOSE
GROEB FARMS

5603 **Groezinger Provisions**
1200 7th Ave
Neptune, NJ 07753-5190 732-775-3220
Fax: 732-775-3223 800-927-9473
informationrequest@alexianpate.com
www.alexianpate.com
Processor of pates, mousses and specialty meats
President: Laurie Groezinger
Estimated Sales: $10-20 Million
Number Employees: 10-19

5604 **Groff Meats**
33 N Market St
Elizabethtown, PA 17022 717-367-1246
Fax: 717-367-1952 www.groffsmeats.com
Retail and wholesale beef, pork, poultry, deli items and specialty foods.
President: John Groff
VP: Virginia Groff
Estimated Sales: $4 Million
Number Employees: 40
Sq. footage: 4500
Type of Packaging: Consumer, Food Service, Private Label

5605 **Grossinger's Home Bakery**
244 W 54th St
New York, NY 10019-5515 212-362-8672
Fax: 212-362-8627 800-479-6996
hrgrsin@aol.com
Ice cream cakes
Owner: Herb Grossingers
Estimated Sales: $140,000
Number Employees: 5-9
Brands:
Bombe Glaze

5606 **Grosso Foods**
P.O.Box 127
Swedesboro, NJ 8085-127
Fax: 856-467-5762
Frozen peppers (green bell, red bell, mixed red and green, yellow bell)
President: Joseph Grasso
Estimated Sales: $ 50 - 100 Million
Number Employees: 100-249

5607 **Grote & Weigel**
76 Granby St
Bloomfield, CT 6002 860-242-8528
Fax: 860-242-4162
customerservice@groteandweigel.com
www.groteandweigel.com
Processor of low sodium processed meats including frankfurters, kielbasa, hams, ham steaks and specialty sausages
Owner: Mike Grenier
Vice President: John Shieding
Estimated Sales: $ 5 - 10 Million
Number Employees: 60
Sq. footage: 15000
Brands:
CLEARFIELD
GROTE & WEIGEL
JERSEY BOARDWALK
MARCELLO
MEINEL
RILEY'S BEEF SAUSAGE
TEXAN WIENER

5608 **Grote Bakery**
9285 Princeton Glendale Rd
Hamilton, OH 45011-8952 513-874-7436
Fax: 513-874-5299
Bread, rolls and cakes
President: Joseph Grote
Sales Manager: Robert Grote
Plant Manager: Tony Grote
Estimated Sales: $5-10 Million
Number Employees: 5-9

5609 **Groth Vineyards & Winery**
P.O.Box 390
Oakville, CA 94562 707-944-0290
Fax: 707-944-8932 info@grothwines.com
www.grothwines.com
Wines such as Cabernet Sauvignon, Chardonnay, Sauvignon Blanc
President: Dennis Groth
CFO: Carl Ebbeson
Vice President: Judith Groth
Marketing Director: Suzanne Groth
Finance Manager: Dawn Selanders
Winemaker: Michael Weis
Estimated Sales: $1.2 Million
Number Employees: 20
Type of Packaging: Private Label

5610 **Grounds for Thought**
133 W Wooster St
Bowling Green, OH 43402 419-354-2326
Fax: 419-354-7512 www.groundsforthought.com
Processor of fresh roasted gourmet coffees including Arabica blends
Owner: Kelly Wicks

Estimated Sales: Under $500,000
Number Employees: 1-4
Sq. footage: 3000
Type of Packaging: Consumer, Food Service, Private Label, Bulk
Brands:
BLACK SWAMP
BLUEGRASS
GROUNDS FOR THOUGHT
JOHN Z'S BIG CITY

5611 **(HQ)Groupe Paul Masson**
110-50, Rue De La Barre
Longueuil, QC J4K 5G2
Canada 514-878-3050
Fax: 450-651-5453
Processor of beverages including wines, ciders, coolers and aperitifs; importer of wines and coolers; exporter of coolers
President: Jean Denis Cote
VP Marketing Development: Alain Lecours
Number Employees: 100-249
Type of Packaging: Consumer
Brands:
Aperossimo
Bau Maniere
Castelet
De Lescot
Dubleuet
El Condor
Foret Noire
L'Ombrelle
Nobella
Pica
Robert De Serbie
Valentino

5612 **Grouse Hunt Farms**
458 Fairview St
Tamaqua, PA 18252 570-467-2850
Fax: 570-467-2850
Processor of dressings, relishes, mustards, sauces, seasonings, jellies, preserves, butters, fruits, horseradish, etc
President: Paul Zukovich
Estimated Sales: $1 Million
Number Employees: 10-19
Number of Brands: 2
Number of Products: 108
Sq. footage: 20000
Type of Packaging: Private Label
Brands:
Grouse Hunt Farms
Pennsylvania Dutch Foods
Wos-Wit

5613 **Grove Fresh Distributors**
7553 S South Chicago Avenue
Chicago, IL 60619-2604 773-288-2065
Fax: 773-288-2065
President: Cecil Troy

5614 **Grow Company**
55 Railroad Ave
Ridgefield, NJ 7657 201-941-8777
Fax: 201-342-9127 growco@aol.us
www.growco.us
Processor and exporter of vitamins, minerals and flavors
President: Andrew Szalay
VP: Massoud Avanaghi
Estimated Sales: $1-2.5 Million
Number Employees: 10-19
Sq. footage: 45600
Brands:
Re-Natured

5615 **Grow-Pac**
2220 SW Lafollett Rd
Cornelius, OR 97113 503-357-9691
Fax: 503-357-2155
Frozen blackberries, blueberries, strawberries, marionberries
President: Lloyd Duyck
Co-owner: Geraldine Duyck
Estimated Sales: Under $500,000
Number Employees: 5
Brands:
Grow-Pac

5616 **Grower Shipper Potato Company**
P.O.Box 432
Monte Vista, CO 81144 719-852-3569
Fax: 719-852-5917
Processor and exporter of potatoes
Manager: Mark Lounsbury
Vice President: Ron Heersink
Manager: Ken Shepherd
Estimated Sales: $10-20 Million
Number Employees: 20-49
Sq. footage: 40000
Type of Packaging: Consumer, Food Service, Bulk
Brands:
Big Ram
Colorado Gold
Diamond
Jackpot

5617 **(HQ)Growers Cooperative Grape Juice Company**
112 N Portage St
Westfield, NY 14787-1054 716-326-3161
Fax: 716-326-6566 growersb@cecomet.net
www.concordgrapejuice.com
Processor and exporter of grape juice and juice concentrate
President: Steve Baran
Quality Assurance Manager: Jim Gillespie
General Manager: David Momberger
Plant Manager: Todd Donato
Estimated Sales: $5-10 Million
Number Employees: 20-49
Type of Packaging: Bulk

5618 **Growth Products**
1638 Taylor Avenue
Racine, WI 53403-2120 262-637-9287
President: Allen Buhler

5619 **Gruet Winery**
8400 Pan American Fwy NE
Albuquerque, NM 87113-1832 505-821-0055
Fax: 505-857-0066 888-897-9463
nathalie@gruetwinery.com
www.gruetwinery.com
Wines: Brut, Blanc, Rose, Demi-sec, Gruet Grande Reserve, Gruet Chardonnay, Pinot Noir
President/Winemaker: Laurent Gruet
Vice President: Farid Himeur
Estimated Sales: $1-2.5 Million
Number Employees: 5-9
Type of Packaging: Private Label
Brands:
Domaine St. Vincent
Gruet Winery

5620 **GuS Grown-up Soda**
424 E 57th St
Suite 3C
New York, NY 10022 212-355-7454
Fax: 212-208-4444 info@drinkgus.com
www.drinkgus.com
sodas made with real juice and real flavor extracts
President/Owner: Steve Hersh

5621 **Guapo Spices Company**
6200 E Slauson Avenue
Los Angeles, CA 90040-3012 213-322-8900
Fax: 213-627-0601
Seasonings, spices

Estimated Sales: $2.5-5 Million
Number Employees: 20-49
Type of Packaging: Private Label

5622 **Guayaki Sustainable Rainforest Products**
6782 Sebastopol Ave
Sebastopol, CA 95472-3861 707-823-3442
Fax: 707-824-6607 888-482-9254
info@guayaki.com www.guayaki.com
Organic rainforest herbs
Co-Founder: Alex Pryer
Co-Founder: David Karr
Chief Executive Officer: Chris Mann
CEO: Chris Mann
Sales Manager: Eileen McHale
Vice President Operations: Richard Bruehl
Estimated Sales: $3 Million
Number Employees: 10-19
Number of Brands: 1
Number of Products: 13
Sq. footage: 15000
Type of Packaging: Consumer, Food Service, Bulk
Brands:
ORGANIC GUAYAKI YERBA MATE

5623 **Guerra Nut Shelling Company**
P.O.Box 1117
Hollister, CA 95024 831-637-4471
Fax: 831-637-1358 info@guerranut.com
www.guerranut.com
Processor and exporter of walnuts including shelled
President: Anthony Guerra
Vice President: Irene Camarena
Estimated Sales: $5-10 Million
Number Employees: 50-99
Sq. footage: 50000
Type of Packaging: Bulk
Brands:
Cal Best
Hillcrest

5624 **Guers Dairy**
P.O.Box 513
Pottsville, PA 17901-0513 570-277-6611
Fax: 570-277-0135
Milk and milk products
President: Daniel Guers
Treasurer: William Yaag
VP: Edward Guers
Purchasing Manager: Dwight Manbeck
Estimated Sales: $10-20 Million
Number Employees: 50-99

5625 **Guggisberg Cheese**
5060 State Route 557
Millersburg, OH 44654 330-893-2500
Fax: 330-893-3240 800-262-2505
info@babyswiss.com www.babyswiss.com
Processor of cheese including premium and baby swiss, lucerne, black wax cheddar, aged yellow cheddar, amish butter cheese, colby cheeses, smoked cheeses and hot pepper cheeses.
President: Richard Guggisberg
Human Resources Manager: Trae Kropf
Estimated Sales: $20-50 Million
Number Employees: 50
Sq. footage: 10000
Type of Packaging: Consumer, Food Service, Bulk
Brands:
AMISH FARM
GUGGISBERG
ORIGINAL BABY

5626 **Guida's Milk & Ice Cream**
433 Park Street
New Britain, CT 06051 860-224-2404
Fax: 860-612-3386 800-832-8929
www.supercow.com
Processor of dairy products which includes milk, ice cream, orange juice, drinks and water
Chairman: Al Guida
President/CEO: Mike Guida
EVP/CFO: Michael Young
SVP Sales & Marketing: James Guida
Director Plant Operations: Wesley Sliwinski
Director Transportation: David Drezek
Director Plant Operations: Wesley Sliwinski
Estimated Sales: $149 Million
Number Employees: 300
Number of Brands: 75
Sq. footage: 75000
Type of Packaging: Consumer, Food Service, Private Label
Brands:
GUIDA'S

5627 **Guido's International Foods**
1669 La Cresta Dr
Pasadena, CA 91103-1260 626-296-1427
Fax: 626-296-0306 877-994-8436
guidoserious@earthlink.net
www.guidoseriousbbq.com
Manufacturer all-purpose spicy-seasonings and roots, BBQ sauce and hot sauce
President: Guido Meindl
Estimated Sales: $20,000
Number Employees: 2
Number of Brands: 7
Type of Packaging: Consumer, Food Service, Private Label, Bulk
Brands:
GUIDO'S SERIOUS

5628 **Guidry's Catfish**
1093 Henderson Hwy
Breaux Bridge, LA 70517 337-228-7546
Fax: 337-228-7544

Processor of fresh catfish
Owner: Bobby Jules
Administrative Executive: Sandra Robertson
Operations: Sandra Guidry-Robertson
Estimated Sales: $ 10 - 20 Million
Number Employees: 100-249

5629 **Guilliams Winery**
3851 Spring Mountain Rd
St Helena, CA 94574-9678 707-963-9059
Fax: 707-963-9059
Family owned business - wines consisting of: Cabernet Sauvignon, Merlot and Cab Franc
President: John Guilliams
Estimated Sales: Less than $500,000
Number Employees: 1-4

5630 **Guiltless GourmetThe Manischewitz Company**
One Harmon Plaza
10th Floor
Secaucus, NJ 07094 201-553-1100
www.guiltlessgourmet.com
Processor and exporter of natural, low-fat baked snacks including tortilla and potato chips; also, non-fat dips and salsas
President: Michael Shaw
VP Finance: Bart Glaser
VP Sales/Marketing: Robert Greenberg
Number Employees: 20-49
Type of Packaging: Consumer, Food Service, Private Label, Bulk
Brands:
Guiltless Gourmet

5631 **Guiltless Gourmet®**
One Harmon Plaza
Tenth Floor
Secaucus, NJ 07094 512-389-0770
Fax: 512-443-5052 www.guiltlessgourmet.com
dessert bowls, sandwich wraps, chips and dips, potato crisp, tortilla chips, salsa and bean dip, hummus
President/CEO: Michael Schall
VP Marketing, RAB Food Group: David Rossi
Estimated Sales: $ .5 - 1 million
Number Employees: 1-4
Parent Co: R.A.B. Food Group, LLC
Brands:
GUILTLESS GOURMET

5632 **Guinness-Bass Import Company**
6 Landmark Square
Stamford, CT 06901-2704 203-323-3311
Fax: 203-359-7209 800-521-1591
guinness@consumer-care.net www.guiness.com
Processor and importer of beer and stout
President: Tim Kelly
Chief Information Officer: Lynda Gutman
Vice President Operations: Colin Funnell
Number Employees: 50-99
Parent Co: Guiness PLC
Type of Packaging: Consumer
Brands:
Asahi
Bass Ale
Furstenberg
Guinness Stout
Harp Lager
Kaliber

5633 **Guittard Chocolate Company**
10 Guittard Rd
Po Box 4308
Burlingame, CA 94010
Fax: 650-692-2761 800-468-2462
sales@guittard.com www.guittard.com
Manufactures chocolate and pastel coatings, cocoa cookie drops, chocolate liqueurs and bulk and bitter white cocoa
President/CEO: Gary Guittard
Director Sales/Marketing: Mark Spini
Estimated Sales: $20-50 Million
Number Employees: 100-249
Brands:
Chocolate Products
Dick Servaes
Melt-N-Mold
Smooth-N-Melty

5634 **Gulf Atlantic Freezers**
PO Box 2493
Gretna, LA 70054-2493 504-392-3590
Fax: 504-392-3443
Frozen seafood

5635 **Gulf Central Seafood**
PO Box 373
Biloxi, MS 39533-0373 228-436-6346
Fax: 228-374-1207
Custom seafood, fresh, live and frozen shrimp
President: Rock Sekul
Estimated Sales: $2.5-5 Million
Number Employees: 20-49
Brands:
Gulf Central
Gulf Star
Treasure Bay

5636 **Gulf City Marine Supply**
14090 Shell Belt Rd
Bayou La Batre, AL 36509 251-824-2516
Fax: 251-824-7980
Processor of seafood including shrimp, oysters and stuffed flounder
President: Charles Graham
Estimated Sales: $500,000-$1 Million
Number Employees: 5-9
Parent Co: Gulf City Seafood

5637 **Gulf Crown Seafood**
809 S Railroad St
Delcambre, LA 70528 337-685-4724
Fax: 337-685-4241
Peeled shrimp, shell-on shrimp
President: John Floyd
Manager: Bonnie Richard
Sales: Crystal Marcaux
Estimated Sales: $7 Million
Number Employees: 75
Brands:
Gulf Crown

5638 **(HQ)Gulf Food Products Company**
509 Commerce Pt
New Orleans, LA 70123 504-733-1516
Fax: 504-733-1517 roberthoy@worldnet.att.net
Wholesaler/distributor, importer and exporter of seafood; serving the food service market
Owner: Albert Lin
Estimated Sales: Less than $500,000
Number Employees: 1-4
Sq. footage: 4000

5639 **(HQ)Gulf Island Shrimp & Seafood**
3935 Ryan Street
Lake Charles, LA 70605 337-477-9296
Fax: 337-477-9140 888-626-7264
info@gulfislandshrimp.com
http://www.fmfoods.com
Shrimp processing plant
Contact: Steve Loga
Estimated Sales: $ 20 - 50 Million
Number Employees: 85

5640 **Gulf Marine & Industrial Supplies**
5501 Jefferson Hwy # 116
New Orleans, LA 70123-4237 504-525-6252
Fax: 504-525-4761 800-886-6252
service@gulfmarine.net www.gulfmarine.net
Wholesaler/distributor of seafood, pork, beef, poultry, canned and frozen foods, fresh vegetables, beer, wine and general merchandise
Owner: Steve Cotsoradis
Marketing: Dimitris Karmoukos
Estimated Sales: $30-50 Million
Number Employees: 175
Sq. footage: 250000
Type of Packaging: Food Service

5641 **Gulf Marine Products Company**
501 Louisiana St
Westwego, LA 70094-4141 504-436-2682
Fax: 504-436-1585
sales@gulfmarineproducts.com
www.lapack.com/index.htm
Gulf Marine is a processor of domestic and imported shrimp, crawfish tail meat and whole-cooked crawfish. Additional products include tilapia, redfish, imitation crab meat, salmon, grouper, frog legs, squid, mussels, and clams.
President: David Lai

5642 **Gulf Packing Company**
618 Commerce St
San Benito, TX 78586 956-399-2631
Fax: 956-399-2675
Processor/packer, exporter and wholesaler/distributor of meat including heifer calf and packaged meats
President: Charlie Booth
VP: Carlos Selainais
Quality Control Manager: Fred Frausto
Manager: Ace Delacerta
Mngr: Frank Esquivel
Estimated Sales: $10-20 Million
Number Employees: 50-99
Type of Packaging: Consumer
Brands:
Quality Minded

5643 **Gulf Pecan Company**
6522 Highway 90
Gulf Shores, AL 36542-8279 251-943-4320
Salted and roasted nuts and seeds
President: Danny Fritz
Estimated Sales: $5-9.9 Million
Number Employees: 3

5644 **Gulf Pride Enterprises**
P.O.Box 355
Biloxi, MS 39533-0355 228-432-2488
Fax: 228-374-7411 888-689-0560
Processor, importer and exporter of fresh frozen shrimp: peeled, shell-on headless, peeled & deveined. White, Grey, Neutral
President: Janet Seymour
Vice President: Wally Gollott
Estimated Sales: $ 10 Million - $50 Million
Number Employees: 50-99
Type of Packaging: Consumer, Private Label
Brands:
Captain Pierre
Gulf Pride
Magnolia Bay

5645 **Gulf Shrimp, Inc.**
P.O.Box 2490
Fort Myers Beach, FL 33932 239-463-8788
Fax: 239-463-3550
Shrimp
Owner: Dennis Henderson
Manager: Dan Schribner
Estimated Sales: $2.5-5 Million
Number Employees: 20-49

5646 **Gulf States Canners**
1006 Industrial Park Dr
Clinton, MS 39056-3298 601-924-0511
Fax: 601-924-7746
Processor of canned soft drinks
Manager: Randy Lee
Manager: Randy Lee
Estimated Sales: $50-100 Million
Number Employees: 50-99
Type of Packaging: Consumer, Food Service

5647 **Gulf Stream Crab Company**
13871 Shell Belt Rd
Bayou La Batre, AL 36509 251-824-4717
Fax: 251-824-7416
Crabs
President: Bryan Cumbie
Estimated Sales: $ .5 - 1 million
Number Employees: 1-4

5648 **Gum Technology Corporation**
509 W Wetmore Rd
Tucson, AZ 85705-1521 520-888-5500
Fax: 520-888-5585 800-369-4867
info@gumtech.com www.gumtech.com
Processor, importer and exporter of vegetable gums and stabilizers
President/CEO: Allen Freed
R&D/Laboratory Director: Aida Prenzno
VP/Sales: Joshua Brooks
Estimated Sales: $ 5 - 10 Million
Number Employees: 5-9
Sq. footage: 3000
Type of Packaging: Bulk
Brands:
COYOTE
COYOTE STAR

5649 Gumix International
2160 N Central Rd # 202
Fort Lee, NJ 07024-7547 201-947-6300
Fax: 201-947-9265 800-248-6492
info@gumix.com www.gumtragacanth.com
Processor and exporter of natural water-soluble gums including karaya, gum ghatti, carageenan, tragacanth, arabic (acacia), guar, locust bean, agar agar and xanthan.
President: Sean Katir
Estimated Sales: $2.5-5 Million
Number Employees: 1-4

5650 Gumpert's Canada
2500 Tedlo Street
Mississauga, ON L5A 4A9
Canada 905-279-2600
Fax: 905-279-2797 800-387-9324
info@gumpert.com www.gumpert.com
Toppings, puddings, flavors & extracts, glazes, icings, cake bases, powder fillings, creme pie fillings, fruit pie fillings, and bavarians
President: George Johnson
R&D/QA Manager: Erica Tulloch
Estimated Sales: $5 Million
Number Employees: 40
Number of Products: 200
Sq. footage: 53000
Type of Packaging: Bulk
Brands:
Gumpert's

5651 Gumtech International
246 E Watkins St
Phoenix, AZ 85004-2926 602-252-7425
www.gum-tech.com
Processor of chewing gum
CEO/President: Gary Kehoe
R&D Engineer: Stephen Roman
Estimated Sales: $ 5 - 10 Million
Number Employees: 5-9

5652 Gundlach Bundschu Winery
2000 Denmark St
Sonoma, CA 95476 707-938-5277
Fax: 707-938-9460 info@gumbun.com
www.gunbun.com
Wines consisting of: Chardonnay, Pinot Nois, Merlot, Zinfandel, Red Bearitage, Mountain Cuvee
President: Jeff Bundschu
Winemaker: Keith Emerson
Director of Viticulture: Jim Bundschu
Estimated Sales: $1-2.5 Million
Number Employees: 5-9
Number of Brands: 3

5653 Gunnoe Farms-Sausage & Salad Company
2115 Oakridge Dr
Charleston, WV 25311 304-343-7686
Fax: 304-343-4748 gunnoefarm@aol.com
Manufacturer of meat including sausage
President: Glenn Gunnoe
Manager: Joy Gunnoe
Vice President: Joy Gunnoe
Estimated Sales: $15 Million
Number Employees: 20-49
Type of Packaging: Consumer

5654 Gunther's Gourmet
Po Box 18215
Richmond, VA 23226 804-240-1796
Fax: 804-747-4813
chefmike@gunthersgourmet.com
www.gunthersgourmet.com
Salad dressing, salsa/dips, grilling sauces, marinades.
Marketing: Mike Lampros

5655 Guptill's Farms
PO Box 129
Machias, ME 04654-0129 207-255-8536
Fax: 207-255-6176

5656 Gurley's Foods
1118 Highway 12 E
Willmar, MN 56201 320-235-0600
Fax: 320-235-0659 800-426-7845
www.gurleysfoods.com
Bakery foods, snacks, candy, gum, general groceries
President: Mike Mickelson
Estimated Sales: $ 20 - 50 Million
Number Employees: 50-99
Brands:
GURLEY'S CANDY
GURLEY'S GOLDEN RECIPE NUTS
GURLEY'S NATURES HARVEST
ROCKY MOUNTAIN

5657 Gustafsons Dairy
4169 County Road 15a
Green Cove Springs, FL 32043 904-284-3750
Fax: 904-284-5570 hmiller@gustafsonsdairy.com
www.gustafsonsdairy.com
Manufacturer of dairy products
President: Randy Peck Jr.
Plant Manager: David Plumley
Estimated Sales: $21.7 Million
Number Employees: 250-499
Type of Packaging: Consumer

5658 Gutheinz Meats
520 Cedar Ave
Scranton, PA 18505 570-344-1191
Fax: 570-344-1193
Processor of prepared meat products
President: Alan Leach
Estimated Sales: $2.5-5 Million
Number Employees: 5-9
Type of Packaging: Consumer

5659 Guttenplan's Frozen Dough
100 Highway 36
Middletown, NJ 07748
Fax: 732-495-2415 888-422-4357
info@guttenplan.com www.guttenplan.com
Frozen rolls, bread, dough and bagels, sweet goods
Owner/President: Jack Guttenplan
Estimated Sales: $10-25 Million
Number Employees: 50-99
Number of Products: 7
Sq. footage: 70000
Type of Packaging: Private Label

5660 Guy's Food
405 S Leonard Street
Liberty, MO 64068-2520 816-781-6700
Fax: 816-792-9546 800-821-2405
www.guyssnacks.com
Snacks
President: Ron Hirasawa
CEO: John Morris
CFO: Thomas Price
VP of Sales: Reid Bennett
Operations Manager: Thomas Anderson
Plant Manager: George Flughum
Number Employees: 500-999
Type of Packaging: Private Label
Brands:
Guy's

5661 Guylian USA Inc.
560 Sylvan Ave
Englewood Cliffs, NJ 07632 201-871-4144
Fax: 201-871-3632 800-803-4123
seashells@guylian.us www.guylian.be
Confectionery imports
President/CEO: Leslie Coopersmith
Marketing: Greg Rosendahl
Estimated Sales: $360,000
Number Employees: 1-4
Type of Packaging: Private Label
Brands:
Guylian

5662 Gwaltney Food ServiceGwanltney+Smithfeild Ltd
601 N Church St.
Smithfield, VA 23430-1221
US 757-357-3131
Fax: 757-357-1568 www.gwaltney.com
Processor and exporter of fresh and frozen pork and pork products HOT DOGS,hams,bologna,bacon.
CEO: Joseph Luter
VP: Joe Bailey
National Account Manager: Fred Bailey
Number Employees: 3,000
Parent Co: Smithfield Foods
Type of Packaging: Consumer, Food Service, Private Label, Bulk
Brands:
Gwaltney

5663 Gwaltney of Smithfield
P.O.Box 489
Smithfield, VA 23431-0489 757-357-3131
Fax: 757-357-1576 800-888-7521
www.gwaltneyfoods.com
Processor and exporter of fresh and processed meat products including ham, bacon, frankfurters and sausage
CEO: Clarry Pope
VP Marketing: Bob Darrell
VP Sales: Ron Marsh
VP Operations: Rob Bogaard
Number Employees: 1,000-4,999
Parent Co: Smithfield Foods
Type of Packaging: Consumer, Food Service, Private Label
Brands:
Gwaltney

5664 Gwaltney of Smithfield
2175 Elmhurst Ln
Portsmouth, VA 23701 757-465-0666
Fax: 757-465-1745
Processor of frankfurters, lunch meats and sausage
President: Timothy A Seely
VP: Daniel G Stevens's
Plant Manager: Jim Honnoll
Estimated Sales: $100-500 Million
Number Employees: 250-499
Parent Co: Smithfield Foods
Type of Packaging: Consumer, Private Label
Brands:
Gwaltney of Smithfield

5665 Gwinn's Foods
6190 Bermuda Dr
St Louis, MO 63135-3264 314-521-8792
Fax: 314-521-8792
Beef, beef products, hot tamales
Owner: Joseph Frisella
Estimated Sales: $1-2.5 Million
Number Employees: 5-9

5666 Gyma
115 Seven Bridge Road
East Stroudsburg, PA 18301-9100 570-422-6311
An IQF, frozen food company

5667 H B Taylor Company
4830 S Christiana Ave
Chicago, IL 60632 773-254-4805
Fax: 773-254-4563 www.hbtaylor.com
Flavors, colors and food essentials.
Owner/Human Resources Executive: Saul Juskaitis
Research & Development Director: Joy Souders
Quality Control Manager: Larry King
Operations Manager: Edward Juskaitis
Purchasing Manager: Mary Power
Estimated Sales: $3 Million
Number Employees: 10-19
Sq. footage: 25000
Type of Packaging: Private Label, Bulk
Brands:
Cocoa Replacers
Dark Roast
Golden Roast
Hyskor
Lipo Butter
Liquimul Black
Mahogany Black
Sesa-Krunch
Sesame Seed

5668 H Cantin
1910 Av Du Sanctuaire
Beauport, QC G1E 3L2
Canada 418-663-3523
Fax: 418-663-0717 800-463-5268
cantinh@microtec.ca
Processor of jams, pie fillings, pudding mixes, maple syrup, soup bases, bakery products and candies; importer of frozen fruit; exporter of marshmallow cones and caramels
President/General Manager: Leonce Tremblay
Number Employees: 50-99
Sq. footage: 60000
Parent Co: Bon Bons Associates
Type of Packaging: Consumer, Food Service, Private Label, Bulk

5669 **H Coturri & Sons Winery**
6725 Enterprise Rd
Glen Ellen, CA 95442 707-525-9126
Fax: 707-542-8039 866-268-8774
www.coturriwinery.com
Producers of red and white wines.
Manager: Tony Coturri
Marketing Director: Harry Coturo
Operations Manager: Tony Coturri
Estimated Sales: $500,000-$1 Million
Number Employees: 1-4

5670 **H E Williams Candy Company**
1230 Perry St
Chesapeake, VA 23324-1334 757-545-9311
Candy
Owner: Lillie Williams
Estimated Sales: $220,000
Number Employees: 5-9

5671 **H H Dobbins**
99 West Ave
Lyndonville, NY 14098 585-765-2271
Fax: 585-765-9710 877-362-2467
hhdobbins@wnyapples.com
www.wnyapples.com
Processor and exporter of produce including apples, cabbage, pears and prunes; also, apple packers
Owner/President: Howard Dobbins
Estimated Sales: $ 3 - 5 Million
Number Employees: 20-49
Type of Packaging: Consumer, Food Service, Bulk
Brands:
Old Dobbin

5672 **H R Nicholson Company**
6320 Oakleaf Ave
Baltimore, MD 21215 410-580-0975
Fax: 410-764-9125 800-638-3514
410-764-2323@yahoo.com
www.hrnicholson.com
Canned fruit juice concentrates and beverage bases
President: Bob Nicholson
Regional Manager Mid-Atlantic: Scott Thompson
Estimated Sales: $25-50 Million
Number Employees: 20-49

5673 **H&A Canada, Inc.**
1160 Tapscott Road
Toronto, ON M1X 1E9
Canada 416-412-9518
Fax: 416-293-9066 sales@hacanada.com
www.hacanada.com
Flavor enhancers, preservatives, sweeteners, food gums/hdrocolloids, shrink bags and casings.

5674 **H&B Packing Company**
P.O.Box 2344
Waco, TX 76703 254-752-2506
Fax: 254-752-1451
Processor of summer, hot and smoked link sausage
President: Jake K Bauer
Vice President: David Bauer
Estimated Sales: $20-50 Million
Number Employees: 50-99

5675 **H&H Bagels**
2239 Broadway at 80th Street
New York, NY 10024-0607 212-595-8000
Fax: 212-799-6765 800-692-2435
www.hhbagels.com
Processor, exporter and wholesaler/distributor of fresh and frozen bagels; serving the food service market
President: Helmer Toro
Estimated Sales: $20-50 Million
Number Employees: 20-49
Sq. footage: 20000
Type of Packaging: Food Service
Brands:
H&H BAGELS

5676 **H&H Fisheries Limited**
100 Government Wharf Rd
Eastern Passage, NS B3G 1M8
Canada 902-465-6330
Fax: 902-465-2572 rhartlen@hhseafood.com
www.fishbasket.com
Processor and exporter of fresh/frozen whole fish, fresh fillets, salt fish, shellfish and lobster. Products include: Lobster, Halibut, Cod, Haddock, Pollock, Cusk, Catfish, Mackerel, Herring, Crab-Snow, Shark, Swordfish, Tuna andAltantic Salmon
Contact: Regionald Hartlen
Estimated Sales: $13.8 Million
Number Employees: 30
Type of Packaging: Consumer, Food Service, Private Label, Bulk

5677 **H&H Foods**
P.O.Box 358
Mercedes, TX 78570-0358 956-565-6363
Fax: 956-565-0228 800-365-4632
www.hhfoods.com
Fully integrated meat company that produces raw as well as fully cooked products.
Owner: Libo Hinojosa
CEO: Andrew Guerra
CFO: Onder Ari
Sales Director: Ruben Hinojosa Jr
Operations Manager: Frederick Garcia
Production Manager: Libo Hinojosa Jr
Estimated Sales: $50-100 Million
Number Employees: 250-499
Type of Packaging: Food Service, Private Label, Bulk

5678 **H&H Products Company**
6600 Magnolia Homes Rd
Orlando, FL 32810 407-299-5410
Fax: 407-298-6966
customerservice@hartleysbrand.com
www.hartleysbrand.com
Manufacturer of juices, drink bases, liquid teas and syrups including fountain, fruit, pancake and waffle
President: Morris Hartley
Secretary: Betty Hartly
Estimated Sales: $6 Million
Number Employees: 20-49
Sq. footage: 40000
Type of Packaging: Food Service, Private Label
Brands:
Bloody Mary Juice Burst
Citrus Punch Sugar-Free
Flavor Burst Liquid Citrus Tea
Flavor Burst Liquid Sweet Tea
Flavor Burst Liquid Unsweet Tea
Flavorburst
Hartley's
Juiceburst
Lemon/Lime Thristaway
Neutral Slush
Orange Thirstaway

5679 **H&K Packers Company**
420 Turenne Street
Winnipeg, NB R2J 3W8
Canada 204-233-2354
Fax: 204-235-1258 hkpack@mb.sympatico.ca
Processor and exporter of pork and beef
President: Albert Kelly
Production Manager: Jake Penner
Plant Manager: Andy Van Patter
Number Employees: 20-49
Sq. footage: 10000
Type of Packaging: Bulk
Brands:
H&K Packers
Kings Choice

5680 **H&K Products-Pappy's Sassafras Teas**
10246 Road P
Columbus Grove, OH 45830
Fax: 419-659-5110 877-659-5110
pappy@q1.net www.sassafrastea.com
Sassafras tea, green tea, raspberry tea and tea concentrate
President: Sandra Nordhaus
VP: Don Nordhaus
Marketing/Sales: Jeff Nordhaus
Production/VP: Jeff Nordhaus
Estimated Sales: $360,000
Number Employees: 5
Number of Brands: 1
Number of Products: 2
Sq. footage: 15000
Type of Packaging: Consumer, Food Service, Private Label, Bulk
Brands:
Pappy's

5681 **H&R Florasynth**
300 North St
Teterboro, NJ 7608 201-288-3200
Fax: 973-467-3514
www.ajtsc.com/hr_Florasynth.htm
Flavors, fragrances and aroma chemicals
Number Employees: 250-499

5682 **H&S Edible Products Corporation**
119 Fulton Lane
Mount Vernon, NY 10550-4697 914-664-4041
Fax: 914-664-8304 800-253-3364
info@hsbreadcrumbs.com
www.hsbreadcrumbs.com
Dry bread crumbs, nuts
President: Mari Rowan
Vice President: Peter Rowan
Marketing Director: P Rowan, Jr.
Estimated Sales: $2 Million
Number Employees: 20-49
Number of Products: 1
Sq. footage: 13000
Type of Packaging: Food Service, Private Label, Bulk
Brands:
H&S Bread Crumbs

5683 **H&W Foods**
2029 Lauwiliwili St
Kapolei, HI 96707 808-682-8300
Fax: 808-841-8687 shawn@hwfoodservice.com
www.hwfoodservice.com
Stock and distribute over 5,500 plus items of refrigerated, frozen and dry products - an in-house line of raw and cooked meat products
Owner: Bill Loose
Chief Executive Officer: Bill Loose
Chief Financial Officer: Jeff Sakamoto
IT Manager: Shelle Andrade
Estimated Sales: $ 5 - 10 Million
Number Employees: 5-9
Sq. footage: 90000

5684 **H. & S Bakery**
601 S Caroline St
Baltimore, MD 21231 410-276-7254
Fax: 410-522-5200 800-959-7655
www.hsbakery.com
Bread and baked goods; fresh and frozen
President: John Paterakis
Vice President: William Paterakis
Director Sales: Charlie Alves
Estimated Sales: $50-100 Million
Number Employees: 340

5685 **H. Fox & Company**
416 Thatford Ave
Brooklyn, NY 11212 718-385-4600
Fax: 718-345-4283 www.foxs-u-bet.com
Processor and exporter of chocolate and fruit flavored syrups; processor of imitation pancake and dietetic syrups, sundae toppings and juice mixes - been in existance for 100+ years
President: David Fox
Estimated Sales: $10-20 Million
Number Employees: 20-49
Sq. footage: 36000
Type of Packaging: Food Service
Brands:
FOX
Fox's U-Bet
No-Cal

5686 **H. Gass Seafood**
38945 Jacqueline Street
Hollywood, MD 20636 301-373-6882
Fax: 301-884-8350
Processor of fresh oysters and crabs
Owner: James Payne
Number Employees: 10-19
Sq. footage: 1000

5687 **(HQ)H. Interdonati**
P.O.Box 262
Cold Spring Harbor, NY 11724 631-367-6611
Fax: 631-367-6626 800-367-6617
flavorplus@aol.com
Manufacturer, importer and exporter of ingredients including tartaric acid, chlorophyll, inositol, natural furanone, gamma deca lactone, bioflavonoids, menthol, fructose, sodium and calcium saccharin
President: Robert Interdonati
Sales Manager: Andrew Interdonati
Estimated Sales: $3 Million
Number Employees: 1-4
Sq. footage: 1000
Brands:
Alnose

5688 **H. Meyer Dairy Company**
415 John St
Cincinnati, OH 45215 513-948-8811
Fax: 513-948-8837 800-347-6455
www.meyerdairy.com
Fluid dairy products (milk and juice drinks) other dairy products such as eggs, cheese and yogurt.
CEO: Mike Meyer
Sales Manager: Mike Osborne
Number Employees: 250-499
Sq. footage: 60000
Parent Co: Dean Foods Company
Type of Packaging: Food Service

5689 **H. Nagel & Son Company**
2428 Central Pkwy
Cincinnati, OH 45214 513-665-4550
Fax: 513-665-4570
Processor and exporter of flour and flour based mixes including whole wheat, graham, cake and pastry
President: William Nagel
CEO: Mike Norris
CFO: Brian Mitchell
Estimated Sales: $ 20 - 50 Million
Number Employees: 20-49
Type of Packaging: Food Service, Private Label, Bulk
Brands:
Gilt Edge

5690 **H. Naraghi Farms**
20001 McHenry Ave
Escalon, CA 95320 209-577-5777
Fax: 209-838-3299
Processor and exporter of grapes, peaches, apples, walnuts, pistachios and almonds
Owner/President: H Naraghi
Manager: Isidro Vaca
Number Employees: 20-49

5691 **H. Reisman Corporation**
P.O.Box 759
Orange, NJ 7051 973-677-9200
Fax: 973-882-0323 lcullen@us.lycored.com
Processor, exporter and importer of vitamins including natural carotenoid products and standardized herbal extracts - supplier of saccharin, mannitol, quinine hydrochloride, vitamin food chemicals, cyclamates, luten, soy proteinsolvable products and many more
Owner/President: Frank Molinaro
Estimated Sales: $5-10 Million
Number Employees: 20-49
Sq. footage: 100000
Parent Co: LycoRed Company
Type of Packaging: Bulk
Brands:
Bionova
Floraglow
Lycomato
Phyto Foods

5692 **H.B. Dawe**
PO Box 100
Cupids, NL A0A 2B0
Canada 709-528-4347
Fax: 709-528-3463
Processor and exporter of fresh, frozen, salted and cooked groundfish and shellfish
General Manager: Philip Hillyard
Number Employees: 100-249
Type of Packaging: Consumer, Food Service, Private Label, Bulk

5693 **H.B. Taylor**
4830 S Christiana Avenue
Chicago, IL 60632 773-254-4805
Fax: 773-254-4563 www.hbtaylor.com
Custom color, flavor and ingredient manufacturer
Owner: Saul Juskaitis
R & D Director: Joy Souders
Quality Control Manager: Larry King
Purchasing Manager: Mary Power
Estimated Sales: $3 Million
Number Employees: 19

5694 **H.B. Trading**
10 Taft Road
Totowa, NJ 07512-1006 973-812-1022
Fax: 973-812-2191 nico@nideco.com
www.nideco.com
Manufacturer and distributor of cookies and candies
Brands:
BRENT & SAM's
CAPE COD CRANBERRY C
COW-TOWN and RANCHER's

5695 **H.C. Berger Brewery**
1900 E Lincoln Avenue
Fort Collins, CO 80524-2750 970-493-9044
Fax: 970-493-4508 info@hcberger.com
www.hcberger.com
Brewer of beer, ale and lager
President: Peter Davidoff
Estimated Sales: $5-10 Million
Number Employees: 5-9
Type of Packaging: Consumer, Food Service

5696 **H.C. Brill Company**
1912 Montreal Rd
Tucker, GA 30084 678-937-0267
Fax: 770-939-2934 800-241-8526
contactbrill@hcbrill.com www.hcbrill.com
Processor and exporter of icings, fillings, frozen cake/muffin batters, whipped toppings and cookie dough
CEO: Bret Weaver
National Sales Manager: Keith Appling
Estimated Sales: $100-500 Million
Number Employees: 250-499
Parent Co: Carpro
Type of Packaging: Food Service

5697 **(HQ)H.E. Butt Grocery Company**
P.O.Box 839999
San Antonio, TX 78283-3999 210-938-8000
Fax: 210-938-8169 800-432-3113
customer.relations@heb.com www.heb.com
Processor of ice cream, cottage cheese, milk, cookies, chips and yogurt
President/Chief Operating Officer: James Clingman
CEO/Chairman: Charles Butt
CEO: Charles C Butt
Director Public Affairs: Greg Flores
Plant Manager: John Elia
Purchasing Agent: Gary Sullivan
Estimated Sales: $20-50 Million
Number Employees: 10,000+
Type of Packaging: Consumer

5698 **(HQ)H.J. Heinz Company**
1 PPG Place
Suite 3100
Pittsburgh, PA 15222-5448 412-456-5700
Fax: 412-456-6128 800-872-2229
www.heinz.com
Manufacturer of beans, cheese pouches/condiments, dry soup mixes, frozen appetizers, entrees, soups and sauces, ketchup, pasta and pasta sauce, peanut butter and jelly, pickles, relishes and vinegar. Also, frozen foods and babyfood.
Chairman/President/CEO: William Johnson
EVP/CFO: Art Winkleback
EVP/General Counsel: Ted Bobby
VP Corporate Affairs: Michael Mullen
EVP/CEO Heinz North America: C Scott O'Hara
SVP Chief Supply Chain Officer: Robert Ostryniec
Estimated Sales: $10.5 Billion
Number Employees: 30,000
Type of Packaging: Consumer, Food Service
Other Locations:
Heinz Factory
Atlanta GA
Heinz Factory
Cedar Rapids IA
Heinz Factory
Chatsworth CA
Heinz Factory
Dallas TX
Heinz Factory
Escalon CA
Heinz Factory
Fremont OH
Heinz Factory
Holland MI
Heinz Factory
Irvine CA
Heinz Factory
Jacksonville FL
Heinz Factory
King of Prussia PA
Heinz Factory
LeCentre MN
Heinz Factory
Mason OH
Heinz Factory
Muscatine IA
Brands:
BAGEL BITES
BOSTON MARKET
CHEF FRANCISCO
CLASSICO
DELIMEX
HEINZ
LEA & PERRINS
ORE-IDA
T.G.I. FRIDAYS
WEIGHT WATCHERS SMART ONES

5699 **(HQ)H.K. Canning**
130 N Garden St
Ventura, CA 93001 805-652-1392
hkcanning@earthlink.net
Processor, exporter and contract packager of canned and dry beans, soup and mushrooms; also, kosher approved
President: Henry Knaust
CFO: Richard Hanson
Vice-President: Carol Knaust
Estimated Sales: $4 Million
Number Employees: 40
Type of Packaging: Consumer, Food Service, Private Label, Bulk
Brands:
Freshman
Henry's Kettle
Knaust Beans
Meridian Foods
Norteno
Sea Valley
Seaside

5700 **H.R. Nicholson Company**
6320 Oakleaf Ave
Baltimore, MD 21215 410-764-2323
Fax: 410-764-9125 800-638-3514
oakleaf@erols.com www.hrnicholson.com
Processor, importer and exporter of fruit juice and tea concentrates, ready-to-serve juices and flavor bases
President: H Robert Nicholson
Secretary/Treasurer: Su Shaffer
VP Sales/Marketing: Bob Homewood
Number Employees: 35
Sq. footage: 38000
Type of Packaging: Consumer, Food Service
Brands:
Bombay Gold 100
Nicholson's Bestea
Nicholson's Bottlers
Nicholson's Chok-Nick

5701 **H3O**
PO Box 482
Beckley, WV 25802-0482 304-256-0436
Fax: 304-256-0520 888-436-9287
www.click-into.com/h30/contactus
Bottled water
President: Jamison Humphrey
Estimated Sales: Under $500,000
Number Employees: 1-4
Brands:
H3O

5702 **HB Taylor Company**
4830 S Christiana Ave
Chicago, IL 60632 773-254-4805
Fax: 773-254-4563 sjukaitis@hbtaylor.com
www.hbtaylor.com
Manufacturing and exporter of flavorings, colors and food essentials, FDA approved, natural, artificial, vanilla, chocolate, fruit, citrus, and nut, dairy products, butter, cheese and cheese flavors and cream, coffee creamers, powdersroasted sesame seed, dairy flavors, liquids, emulsions, spray dried, custom products, custom blending/packaging
Owner: Saul Juskaitis
Sales Manager: Peggy Drabek
Plant Manager: Edward Juskaitis
Estimated Sales: $ 5 - 10 Million
Number Employees: 10-19
Type of Packaging: Bulk

5703 **HC Brill Company**
1912 Montreal Rd
Tucker, GA 30084 770-938-3823
Fax: 770-939-2934 800-241-8526
contactbrill@hcbrill.com www.hcbrill.com

Ingredients and mixes; bulk supplier
President: Cefo Grteor
CEO: Bret Weaver
Estimated Sales: $5-10 Million
Number Employees: 50-99
Brands:
Brill's

5704 **HFI Foods**
17515 Northeast 6th Court
Redmond, WA 98074 425-883-1320
Fax: 425-861-8341
Processor of fresh and frozen surimi products, frozen entrees, frozen mousse desserts and pasta salads; exporter of frozen mousse desserts
President: Byron Kuroishi
CFO: Yoshinari Kuroishi
Vice President: Christina Gaimaytan
Quality Control: Jenel Lee
Marketing Director: Gwen McLellan
Sales Director: Nori Ishiwari
Public Relations: Cindy Fuller-Stephens
Production Manager: Kazue Yamada
Plant Manager: Kazuo Yamada
Purchasing Manager: Cindy Fuller-Stephens
Estimated Sales: $12 Million
Number Employees: 50-99
Sq. footage: 40000
Parent Co: JMS
Type of Packaging: Consumer
Brands:
Fitness First
Kibun
King Core
King Cove
Seastix

5705 **HMC Marketing Group**
13138 S Bethel Ave
Kingsburg, CA 93631-9216 559-897-1009
Fax: 559-897-1610 hmcinfo@hmcmarketing.com
www.hmcmarketing.com
Peaches, nectarines, persimmons, pomegranates, apricots, plums, grapes, satsumes, navels, valencias and vegetables
Owner: Harold Mc Clarty
Estimated Sales: $ 20 - 50 Million
Number Employees: 10-19

5706 **(HQ)HP Hood**
6 Kimball Lane
Lynnfield, MA 01940 617-887-3000
Fax: 617-887-8484 800-343-6592
www.hphood.com
Produces a variety of branded, private label, licensed and franchise products including milk, culture foods, citrus, estended shelf-life dairy, frozen desserts, non-dairy and specialty drinks
Chairman/President/CEO: John Kaneb
Chief Financial Officer: Gary Kaneb
Vice President: Jeffery Kaneb
SVP R&D/Engineering/Procurement: Mike Suever
Executive Vice President Sales: James Walsh
VP Public Relations/Government Affairs: Lynne Bohan
Senior Vice President Operations: H Scott Blake
Estimated Sales: $2 Billion
Number Employees: 3000
Type of Packaging: Consumer, Food Service, Private Label
Other Locations:
HP Hood
Agawab MA
HP Hood
Barre VT
HP Hood
Oneida NY
HP Hood
Portland ME
HP Hood
Suffield CT
HP Hood
Vernon NY
HP Hood
Winchester VA
Brands:
AXELROD
BRIGHAM'S
CALORIE COUNTDOWN
CARNATION
COFFEE-MATE
CROWLEY
HELUVA GOOD
HENDRIE'S
HOOD
HORIZON
LACTAID
LAND O' LAKES
MAGGIO
NESQUIK
ORGANIC COW
PEAK TREASURES
PENN MAID
ROSENBERGER'S
SHAKE-UPS
SIMPLY CHOCOLATE
SIMPLY SMART
STIX
STRASSEL'S
SUNNY MEADOW
ULTIMATE VANILLA BEAN

5707 **HP Schmid**
231 Sansome St # 300
San Francisco, CA 94104-2322 415-765-5925
Fax: 415-765-5922 organic@hpschmid.com
www.hpschmid.com
Specializing in edible seeds: sesame, sunflower, poppy and caraway; dry peas, beans and lentils; dried fruits, nuts and organic products - dehydrated garlic and onions
President/International Sales: Hans Schmid
Sales North America: Analucia Melendez
Sales Organics: Marinda Thomas
Customer Service: Whitney Weaver
Estimated Sales: $20-50 Million
Number Employees: 5-9

5708 **HSR Associates**
18829 Paseo Nuevo Drive
Tarzana, CA 91356 818-757-7152
Fax: 818-757-7141 sales@hsrassociates.net
www.hsrassociates.net
Salad dressing, frozen baked goods, frozen desserts, full-line frozen, hors d'oeuvres/appetizers, ready meals/pizza/soup, jams, preserves.
Marketing: Steven Goodman

5709 **HV Food Products Company**
1221 Broadway
Oakland, CA 94612-1837 510-271-7000
800-537-2823
www.hiddenvalley.com
Processor of Hidden Valley Ranch products, salad dressings, dressing mixes, dips, and salad toppings
VP: George C Roeth
VP Marketing: George Roeth
Manager: John White
Estimated Sales: $100-500 Million
Number Employees: 100-249
Parent Co: Clorox Company
Brands:
HIDDEN VALLEY RANCH

5710 **HVJ International**
2609 N Spring Dr
Spring, TX 77373 281-288-8560
Fax: 281-288-9000 877-730-3663
info@hvj-international.com
Olives, pickled vegetables, sauces, salsas, condiments, pasta sauces, dressings, olive oil, hot sauces
President/CEO: Hank Van Joslin
Operations Manager: Jake Jalufka
Estimated Sales: $5-10 Million
Number Employees: 5-9
Number of Brands: 8
Number of Products: 240
Type of Packaging: Consumer, Food Service, Bulk
Brands:
0007
Cartagena
Fiorevante
HVJ
Joslin
Occasions
Peppers of the World
Rainforest
Spicy Jones

5711 **Haas Baking Company**
9769 Reavis Park Dr
St Louis, MO 63123-5315 314-631-6100
Fax: 314-631-3464 800-325-3171
joseph@haasbaking.com www.haasbaking.com
Processor of frozen doughnuts, fat free pastry, danish, coffee cake
President: Joseph Haas
Estimated Sales: $ 20 - 50 Million
Number Employees: 100-249
Type of Packaging: Consumer, Food Service

5712 **Haas Coffee Group**
1110 Brickell Avenue
Suite 400
Miami, FL 33131 305-371-7473
Fax: 305-418-7384 info@haasgroup.com
www.haasgroup.com
Leading independent grower, processor, marketer and merchant of coffee - ground, instant and coffee extract. Also a leading independent processor and marketer of soft commodities and frozen foods which include meats (beef and pork)and poultry.
Contact: Michael Dibbs
Estimated Sales: $10-100 Million
Number Employees: 5-9

5713 **Habby Habanero's Food Products**
6475 Ferber Road
Jacksonville, FL 32277-1513 904-333-9758
mail@habbys.net
http://www.habbys.net/
Fire and brimstone barbecue sauces
Contact: Malcolm Quincy
Contact: Jerry Quincy

5714 **Habersham Winery**
7025 S Main St
Helen, GA 30545 770-983-1973
Fax: 706-878-8466 info@habershamwinery.com
www.habershamwinery.com
Collection of wines such as: Creekstone Wines, Habersham Estate Wines and Southern Harvest Wines
Manager: Steve Gibson
Winemaker: Andrew Beatty
Operations Manager: Russell Jones
General Manager: Steve Gibson
Vineyard Manager: Terri Haney
Estimated Sales: $2.5-5 Million
Number Employees: 10-19
Type of Packaging: Private Label
Brands:
Creekstone
Habersham Estates
Southern Harvest

5715 **Haby's Alsatian Bakery**
207 Us Highway 90 E
Castroville, TX 78009 830-931-2118
Fax: 830-931-2194
Processor of cookies, pies, cakes, apple fritters, strudels, stollens, bread and coffeecakes.
President: Sammy Tschirhart
VP/Secretary/Treasurer: Yvonne Tschirhart
Estimated Sales: $500,000-$1 Million
Number Employees: 10-19
Sq. footage: 5400
Type of Packaging: Consumer

5716 **Hach Co.**
P.O.Box 608
P.O. Box 389
Loveland, CO 80539 970-669-3050
800-227-4224
info@hach.com www.hach.com
manufacturer of oxygen sensors and water analysis products for the beverage and water bottling industries. Also manufactures, designs, and distributes test kits for testing the quality of water in food industry applications.

5717 **Hacienda De Paco**
9564 Sidney Hayes Rd
Orlando, FL 32824 407-859-5417
Fax: 407-850-9317
Processor of Mexican foods including tortillas, tamales and burritos
President: Richard Dubler
Estimated Sales: $20-50 Million
Number Employees: 20-49
Type of Packaging: Food Service
Brands:
Hacienda

5718 **Hadley Date Gardens**
83555 Airport Blvd
Thermal, CA 92274-9341 760-399-5191
Fax: 760-399-1311 sdougherty@hadleys.com
www.hadleys.com

Processor and exporter of whole, pitted and diced dates and date products
President: John Keck
CEO: Albert Keck
CFO: Melinda Dougherty
Marketing Director: Sean Dougherty, Sr.
Estimated Sales: $25 Million
Number Employees: 50-99
Sq. footage: 12000
Parent Co: Haldeys
Type of Packaging: Consumer, Food Service, Private Label, Bulk
Brands:
Hadley Date Gardens

5719 **Hafner USA**
4609 Lewis Rd
Stone Mountain, GA 30083 678-406-0101
Fax: 678-406-9222 888-725-4605
pieshells@hafner.com www.hafner.com
Pastry shells, cream puffs, puff pastries, cake kits, savory shells and 17 Kosher desserts
President: Xavier M De Goursac
Marketing: Maria Dziebakowski
Estimated Sales: $5-10 Million
Number Employees: 5-9

5720 **Hafner Vineyard**
4280 Pine Flat Rd
Healdsburg, CA 95448 707-433-4606
Fax: 707-433-1240 info@hafnervineyard.com
www.hafnervineyard.com
Estate wines
Partner/Owner: Richard Hafner
Partner: Julianne Farrell
Partner: Elizabeth Hafner
Managing Partner: Scott Hafner
Winemaker: Sarah Hafner
Estimated Sales: $2.5 Million
Number Employees: 10
Type of Packaging: Private Label
Brands:
Hafner

5721 **Hagelin & Company**
200 Meister Ave
Branchburg, NJ 8876 908-707-4400
Fax: 908-707-4408 800-229-2112
flavors@hagelin.com www.hagelin.com
Processor and exporter of flavors, extracts, vanilla and beverage bases including health drink containing antioxidants
President: Craig Hagelin
VP Operations: Barry Fielding
Estimated Sales: $20-50 Million
Number Employees: 80
Sq. footage: 26000
Brands:
Isotonic
Rebound

5722 **Hagensborg Chocolates LTD.**
3686 Bonneville Place
Unit #103
Burnaby, BC V3N 4T6
Canada 604-215-0234
Fax: 604-215-0235 877-554-7763
sales@hagensborg.com www.hagensborg.com
Exporter and importer of canned pate, chocolate and confectionery items, olive oils, sherry vinegar; also, exporter of smoked salmon fillets
President: Shelley Miller
Marketing: Shelley Wallace
Estimated Sales: $10-20 Million
Number Employees: 10-19
Sq. footage: 15000
Type of Packaging: Consumer, Food Service, Private Label
Brands:
HAGENSBORG MELTAWAYS TRUFFLES
KISS ME FROG TRUFFLES
TRUFFLES TO GO

5723 **Hagerty Foods**
987 N Enterprise St
Suite J
Orange, CA 92867 714-628-1230
Processor and contract packager of condiments, relishes, salad dressings, pasta sauces, salsas, BBQ sauce and hot sauces
President: Francisco Esquivel
Estimated Sales: $220,000
Number Employees: 3
Sq. footage: 10000
Type of Packaging: Consumer, Food Service, Private Label
Brands:
Hagerty Foods
La Napa
Winemaker's Choice

5724 **Hahn & Company**
601 Montgomery St # 840
San Francisco, CA 94111-2611 415-394-6512
Fax: 415-861-7400 www.hahncap.com
Owner: Elaine Hahn
Estimated Sales: $5-10 Million
Number Employees: 5-9

5725 **Hahn Brothers**
Po Box 395
Westminster, MD 21157 410-848-4200
Fax: 410-848-1247 800-227-7675
wholesale@hahnsofwestminster.com
www.hahnsofwestminster.com
Processor of varieties of pork products and cooked beef and corn beef
Owner: Ed Ladzinski
Vice President/Production Manager: Barbara Brown
Sq. footage: 23000
Type of Packaging: Consumer, Food Service, Private Label

5726 **Hahn Estates and Smith &Hook**
P.O.Box C
37700 Foothill Road
Soledad, CA 93960 866-925-7994
Fax: 831-678-0557
tastingroom@hahnestates.com
www.hahnestates.com
Estate Wines
Owner: William Leigon
President: William Leigon
Marketing/Public Relations: Sandy Martini-Coero

Winemaker: Adam LaZarre
Estimated Sales: $7.5 Million
Number Employees: 50-99
Sq. footage: 30
Type of Packaging: Private Label
Brands:
Smith & Hook Winery

5727 **Hahn's Old Fashioned Cake Company**
75 Allen Boulevard
Farmingdale, NY 11735 631-249-3456
Fax: 631-249-3492 hofcc@optonline.net
www.crumbcake.net
Processor of coffee cake
Co-Owner: Andrew Hahn
Co-Owner: Regina Hahn
Chief Operating Officer: Andrew Hahn
Estimated Sales: $2.5-5 Million
Number Employees: 20-49
Type of Packaging: Consumer, Food Service

5728 **Haight-Brown Vineyard**
29 Chestnut Hill Rd
Litchfield, CT 06759-4101 860-567-4045
Fax: 860-567-1766 800-577-9463
haightvineyard@aol.com
www.haightvineyards.com
Wines: Chardonnay, Merlot, Riesling, Covertside White, Barely Blush, Picnic Red, and an old New England tradition Honey Nut Apple.
Manager: Sal Cimino
Co-Partner: Amy Brown
Cellar Master: Salvatore Cimino
Estimated Sales: $2.5-5 Million
Number Employees: 5-9
Brands:
Haight Vineyard Wines

5729 **Haile Resources**
2650 Freewood Dr
Dallas, TX 75220 214-357-1471
Fax: 214-357-9381 800-357-1471
www.haileresources.com
Food and beverage ingredients
President: Howard Haile
Vice President: Elaine Haile
Estimated Sales: $500,000
Number Employees: 6
Type of Packaging: Private Label

5730 **Hain Celestial Canada**
1638 Derwent Way
Delta, BC V3M 6R9
Canada 604-525-1345
Fax: 604-525-2555 866-983-7834
yvc@yvesveggie.com www.arrowheadfoods.com
Processor of vegetarian foods including tofu hot dogs, garden patties and veggie dogs
President: Beena Goldenberg
Chief Executive Officer: Philippe Woitrin
Managing Director: David Arrow
Director Marketing: Janice Harada
Estimated Sales: $126 Million
Number Employees: 181
Number of Brands: 1
Number of Products: 30
Parent Co: Hain Celestial Group
Type of Packaging: Consumer, Food Service, Private Label, Bulk
Brands:
CASBAH
EARTHS BEST
GARDEN OF EATEN
GOOD SLICE
HAIN
HEALTH VALLEY
PRIMA VEGGIE
TERRA

5731 **(HQ)Hain Celestial Group**
58 S Service Rd
Melville, NY 11747 631-730-2200
Fax: 631-730-2550 800-434-4246
www.hain-celestial.com
Manufacturer and exporter of natural and specialty soy beverages, snacks, canned goods, baked products and cereals. The company signed an agreement and plan of merger with Spectrum Organics Products in California
Chairman/President/CEO: Irwin Simon
EVP/CFO/Treasurer/Secretary: Ira Lamel
EVP/President Grocery & Snacks: John Carroll
Chief Marketing Officer Grocery & Snacks: Maureen Putman
VP Operations Grocery & Snacks: James Meiers
Estimated Sales: $1-2.5 Million
Number Employees: 1,000-4,999
Brands:
Agrain & Agrain
Alba Foods
Apple Corns
Arrowhead Crunch
Arrowhead Mills
Bear Mush
Bits'o Barley
Boston Popcorn
Breadshop
Hains Celestial
Natural Gourmet
Nature O's
Nature Puffs
QBR
Rice & Shine
Seitan Quick Mix
Simpler Life
Terra Chips

5732 **Haines City Citrus Growers Association**
P.O.Box 337
Haines City, FL 33845 863-422-4924
Fax: 863-421-4754 800-422-4245
www.hilltopcitrus.com
Grower of citrus fruits including oranges, grapefruits, tangerines, etc
President: Bob Turner
Finance Executive: Rod Hamric
Director Field Operations: Charles Counter
Packing House Manager: John Soles
Estimated Sales: $10-20 Million
Number Employees: 250-499
Parent Co: Citrus World

5733 **Hains Celestial Group**
58 S Service Rd # 250
Melville, NY 11747-2338 631-730-2200
Fax: 631-730-2550 877-612-4246
info@acirca.com www.hain-celestial.com

Processor of certified organic foods and beverages including soups, salsas, sauces and juices
President/CEO: Irwin Simon
General Manager: Maurene Putman
CFO: William Urich
VP, Sales: Terence Dalton
Consultant: William Russell
Estimated Sales: C
Number Employees: 1,000-4,999
Brands:
Fruitti Di Bosco
Millina's Finest
Moutain Sun
Walnut Acres

5734 **Hair Fitness**
203 Argonne Ave
203
Long Beach, CA 90803 562-438-4247
888-348-4247
hairfitness@lycos.com
www.healthandbodyfitness.com
Designed not only for body fitness but hair fitness benefits - supplements plus hair conditioners -
Founder/President: Jeannie Maxon
Estimated Sales: $300,000-500,000
Number Employees: 1-4

5735 **Hair of the Dog BrewingCompany**
61 SE Yamhill St
Portland, OR 97214-2134
Fax: 503-235-8743 www.hairofthedog.com
German style beer
President/Founder: Alan Sprints
Brewer: Pat Savage
Estimated Sales: $500,000-$1 Million
Number Employees: 1-4

5736 **Halal Transactions**
P.O.Box 4546
Omaha, NE 68104 402-572-6120
Fax: 402-572-4020 halal2eat@hotmail.com
Processing and certification of Halal meat-beef, lamb, goat and poultry. Brokerage of Halal meats.
President: Ahmad Absy
CEO: Dr. Ahmad Al-Absy
Estimated Sales: $ .5 - 1 Million
Number Employees: 10-19
Brands:
All Halal

5737 **Halben Food Manufacturing Company**
4553 Gustine Ave
Saint Louis, MO 63116-3433 314-832-1906
Fax: 314-932-7566 800-888-4855
Processor of mixes including beverage, sauce, gravy, dressing and dessert; also, sauces, mayonnaise and dressings
President: Bob Baker
Vice President: Louis Cohen
Vice President: Richard Allen
Vice President: Stanley Allen
Sales Director: Joel Allen
Estimated Sales: $20-50 Million
Number Employees: 100-249
Sq. footage: 100000
Parent Co: Allen Foods
Type of Packaging: Food Service

5738 **Haldin International**
3 Reuten Dr
Closter, NJ 7624 201-784-0044
Fax: 201-784-2180 haldinus@haldin-natural.com
www.haldin-natural.com
Began as importer of Indonesian vanilla beans and now has a wide range of products including essential oil to meet the flavor and fragrance industry. Items such as: betel peper liquid extract, citronella oil, and eurycoma longifaliapowder extract
Manager: Khelly Boon
Founder/Chief Executive Officer: Ali Haliman
Estimated Sales: $ 5 - 10 Million
Number Employees: 1-4
Sq. footage: 12000
Parent Co: Pt. Haldin Pacific Semesta
Type of Packaging: Bulk
Other Locations:
Haldin International
Cikarang, Bekasi

5739 **Hale & Hearty Soups**
75 Ninth Avenue
New York, NY 10011 646-214-5700
www.haleandhearty.com
All fresh and homemade ingredients for our chowders, chicken vegetable with noodles soup and delicious roast beef sandwiches with shaved parmesan.
President: Simon Jacobs
Chief Executive Officer: Simon Jacobs
Co-Owner: Jonathan Schnipper
Marketing: Chance Negri
Estimated Sales: $5-10 Million
Number Employees: 5-9

5740 **Hale Indian River Groves**
P.O.Box 700217
Wabasso, FL 32970-0217 772-581-9915
Fax: 772-226-3503 800-562-4502
customerservice@halegroves.com
http://www.halegroves.com/
Processor of oranges, grapefruit, tangerines and fruit juice; manufacturer of fruit gift baskets
President: Stephen Hale III
VP: Fred Kuester
Estimated Sales: $20-50 Million
Number Employees: 50-99
Type of Packaging: Consumer, Bulk

5741 **Hale's Ales**
4301 Leary Way NW
Seattle, WA 98107-4538 206-706-1544
Fax: 360-706-1572 pub@halesbrewery.com
www.halesales.com
Beers such as: Hales cream, Wee Heavy Winter Ale, Irish style Nut Brown ale, O'Brien Harvest Ale, Pale American, Hales Dublin Style Stout and German Style Kolsch Ale
President/Founder: Michael Hale
Marketing Manager: Barbara Dollarhide
Chief Operating Officer: David Metzger
General Manager: Pat Foote
Estimated Sales: $20-50 Million
Number Employees: 50-99
Brands:
Hale's Celebration Porter
Hale's Pale American Ale
Hale's Special Bitter
Moss Bay Extra Ale
Moss Bay Stout

5742 **Half Moon Bay Trading Company**
Po Box 330718
Atlantic Beach, FL 32233 904-246-9493
Fax: 904-246-9442 888-447-2823
info@halfmoonbaytrading.com
www.halfmoonbaytrading.com
Purveyors of fine imported condiments including hot pepper sauces, mixers, salsas and glaze toppings.
President: Robin Shephard
CFO: Jeff Hite
VP: Tom Nuijens
Marketing: Tom Nuijens
Sales: Tom Nuijens
Public Relations: Tina Kicklighter
Operations Manager: Regina Story
Estimated Sales: Under $1 Million
Number Employees: 5-9
Number of Brands: 5
Number of Products: 21
Sq. footage: 10000
Type of Packaging: Consumer, Food Service, Private Label
Brands:
BEESTING
CARIBBEAN CONDIMENTS
IGUANA
SWEETSTING
TAMARINDO BAY

5743 **Half Moon Fruit & Produce Company**
203 Court St
Woodland, CA 95695 530-662-1727
Fax: 530-662-6072
Grower and packer of prunes, plums, melon
President: B E Giovannetti
Operations Manager: Richard Monford
Estimated Sales: $10-20 Million
Number Employees: 5-9
Brands:
Buster
Melo-Glow
Morning Cheer
Valley King

5744 **Haliburton International Corporation**
2539 East Philadelphia St
Ontario, CA 91761 909-428-8507
Fax: 909-428-8521 877-980-4295
info@haliburton.net www.haliburton.net
Processor and importer of fire roasted vegetables including peppers, tomatoes, tomatillos, onions, garlic, shallots, squash, zucchini
Owner: Ian Schenkel
Contact: Desiree Mettille-Schenkel
Technical Contact: Joseph Antonio
Estimated Sales: $10-20 Million
Number Employees: 50-99
Type of Packaging: Food Service, Bulk

5745 **Halifax Group**
3264 McCall Dr
Doraville, GA 30340-3306 770-452-8828
Fax: 770-457-4546 info@oakhillfarms.com
www.oakhillfarms.com
Gourmet sauces, dressings, salsa, condiments and beverages
Estimated Sales: $ 5 - 10 Million
Number Employees: 10-19
Brands:
Hill Farms
Redneck Gourmet
Scorned Woman
Southern Sensations
Wild Man

5746 **Hall Brothers Meats**
27040 Cook Rd
Cleveland, OH 44138-1111 440-235-3262
Fax: 440-235-6696 www.hallsqualitymeats.com
Processor of fresh and frozen beef, pork, poultry, lamb and seafood
President: Richard Hall
Estimated Sales: $ 10 - 20 Million
Number Employees: 5-9
Type of Packaging: Consumer, Food Service, Bulk

5747 **Hall Grain Company**
101 W Railroad Ave
Akron, CO 80720 970-345-2206
Fax: 970-345-6680
Processor of grains such as: millet, milo, safflower, sunflower and wheat
Manager: Tim Mayes
Controller: Kevin Hall
VP: Pat Hall
Estimated Sales: $10-20 Million
Number Employees: 50-99

5748 **Halladays Harvest Barn**
6 Webb Ter
Bellows Falls, VT 05101-3157 802-463-3331
Fax: 802-460-1132 halladay@sover.net
www.halladays.com
Seasonings, dips, cheesecake mixes, dry soup mixes, garlic oil, and vinegars - products are all natural - contain no msg and many contain no salt -
Co-Owner: Rich Govotski
Co-Owner: Kathleen Govotski
Estimated Sales: $ 1 - 3 Million
Number Employees: 5-9

5749 **Hallcrest Vineyards**
379 Felton Empire Rd
Felton, CA 95018-9167 831-335-4441
Fax: 831-335-4450 info@hallcrestvineyards.com
www.hallcrestvineyards.com
Wines: Perez Estates Chardonnay, Andersen Cabernet/Merlot, Ciardella Pinot Noir, Belle Farms Pinot Noir
Co-Owner/President: John Schumacher
Lab Director: Paul Bouswa
Sales Manager: Will Warto
Co-Owner/Public Relations: Lorraine Schumacher
Cellar Master: Giovanni Jovel
Estimated Sales: $2.5-5 Million
Number Employees: 10-19
Type of Packaging: Private Label
Brands:
Hallcrest Vineyards
The Organic Wine Work
Vinatopia

5750 **Hallman International**
2935 Saint Xavier Street
Louisville, KY 40212-1936 502-778-0459
Fax: 502-778-0435

President: James Smith
CFO: Jay Broder
Sales Director: David Wallace
Plant Manager: Clarence Philpott
Estimated Sales: $10-20 Million
Number Employees: 20-49
Sq. footage: 20
Type of Packaging: Private Label

5751 **Hallmark Fisheries**
P.O.Box 5390
Charleston, OR 97420-0606 541-888-3253
Fax: 541-888-6814 info@hallmarkfisheries.com
www.hallmarkfisheries.com
Processor of fresh, frozen and canned seafood including crab meat, shrimp, tuna and boxed fillets
Inventory Specialist: Blair Samuelson
QC/HACCP Supervisor: Crystal Adams
Sales Manager: Judi Houston
General Manager: Jack Emmons
Production/Plant Manager: Scott Adams
Plant Manager: Scott Adams
Estimated Sales: $20-50 Million
Number Employees: 100-249
Parent Co: California Shellfish
Type of Packaging: Consumer, Food Service, Private Label, Bulk
Brands:
Hallmark
Peacock
Point St. George

5752 **Halsted Packing House**
445 N Halsted St
Chicago, IL 60642 312-421-4511
Fax: 312-421-4511
Processor of lamb, pork and goat meat
Co-Owner: William Davos
Co-Owner: Ann Davos
Estimated Sales: Less than $500,000
Number Employees: 1-4
Sq. footage: 6400
Type of Packaging: Consumer, Food Service

5753 **Ham I Am**
5505 Longview St
Dallas, TX 75206 972-447-0440
Fax: 972-447-0460 800-742-6426
www.hamiam.com
Pork products, quail, duck, turkey, Texas BBQ, desserts, breakfast ideas, homemade tamales, hors d'oeuvres, and party foods
President: Sharon Meehan
Estimated Sales: Under $500,000
Number Employees: 1-4
Type of Packaging: Private Label, Bulk

5754 **Hama Hama Oyster®Company**
301 N Webb Rd
Lilliwaup, WA 98555 360-877-6938
Fax: 360-877-6942 888-877-5844
Seafood: Oysters, Manila clams, native Little Neck Clams and Geoducks
Owner: David Robins
Sales, Wholesale: Adam James
Estimated Sales: $500,000-$1 Million
Number Employees: 1-4
Type of Packaging: Private Label, Bulk

5755 **Hamburg Industries**
218 Pine St
Hamburg, PA 19526 610-562-3031
Fax: 610-562-0209 800-321-6256
sales@hamburgindustries.com
www.hamburgindustries.com
Manufacturer and importer of brooms, brushes, mops and handles
President/CEO/Marketing: Richard Stiller
CFO: Donna Ladd
VP: William Bast
Quality Control: Donald Banres
Sales: John Stevens
Operations: Donald Barnes
Plant Manager: Patty Frankenfield
Number Employees: 28
Sq. footage: 65000
Type of Packaging: Consumer, Private Label, Bulk

5756 **Hamilos Brothers Inspected Meats**
1117 Greenwood St
Madison, IL 62060 618-451-7877
Fax: 618-876-3732
Processor of beef, pork, poultry and fresh and frozen fish; wholesaler/distributor of canned goods, paper products and pre-packaged meat
Owner: Mike Skinner
Owner: Jeff Skinner
Estimated Sales: $500,000-$1 Million
Number Employees: 5-9
Type of Packaging: Consumer

5757 **Hamm's Custom Meats**
307 W Louisiana
McKinney, TX 75069 972-562-7511
http://www.hammsmeats.com/
Honey Glazed Spiral-Cut Ham, Choice USDA Steaks cut to order, Bacon, Chili, Cheese, Smoked Brisket and Ribs, Honey Glazed Smoked Ribs.
Owner: Ken Uselton
Estimated Sales: $ .5 - 1 million
Number Employees: 1-4
Type of Packaging: Consumer, Food Service, Bulk

5758 **Hammer Corporation**
3765 Atlanta Industrial Dr NW
Suite A
Atlanta, GA 30331-1031 404-505-7332
Fax: 404-696-4003 800-621-1954
www.tootarts.com
Processor and exporter of fat and calorie-free coffee, tea, cappuccino, soft drink and water flavors
President: Armand Hammer
VP Sales: Al Silva
Estimated Sales: $20-50 Million
Number Employees: 50-99
Brands:
TPP TARTS KIDS KANDY

5759 **Hammond Pretzel Bakery**
716 S West End Ave
Lancaster, PA 17603-5050 717-392-7532
Fax: 717-392-8085 info@hammondpretzels.com
www.hammondpretzels.com
Processor of handmade pretzels and chocolate pretzels
President: Thomas Nicklaus
General Manager: Brian Nicklaus
Estimated Sales: $ 10 - 20 Million
Number Employees: 10-19
Type of Packaging: Consumer
Brands:
Hammond's

5760 **Hammond's Candies**
5735 Washington Street
Denver, CO 80216 303-333-5588
Fax: 303-333-5622 888-226-3999
www.hammondscandies.com
Chocolates and traditional hard candy and confections
Owner: Bob List
CIO: Ross Chism
Marketing: Andrew Whisler
Manager: Karlyn Pulst
Master Candymaker: Ralph Nafziger
Estimated Sales: $850,000
Number Employees: 10

5761 **Hammons Meat Sales**
P.O.Box 40638
Bakersfield, CA 93384-0638 661-831-9541
Fax: 661-831-2656
Processor of fresh beef, lamb, pork and seafood - some items are frozen
Owner/President: Craig Hammons
Estimated Sales: $ 50 - 100 Million
Number Employees: 20-49

5762 **Hammons Products Company**
P.O.Box 140
Stockton, MO 65785 417-276-5121
Fax: 417-276-5187 888-429-6887
bwsalesdave@u-n-i.net www.black-walnuts.com
Processor and exporter of shelled black walnuts
President: Brian Hammons
VP Sales: David Steinmuller
Estimated Sales: $10-20 Million
Number Employees: 100-249
Sq. footage: 229000
Type of Packaging: Consumer, Food Service, Bulk
Brands:
Hammons

5763 **Hampton Associates & Sons**
12728 Dogwood Hills Lane
Fairfax, VA 22033-3244 703-968-5847
jamcola@hotmail.com
Soft drinks
CEO/Chairman: Hampton Brown III
Estimated Sales: Under $500,000
Number Employees: 1-4
Type of Packaging: Consumer, Food Service
Brands:
Bahama Berry
Bahama Black Cherry
Bahama Blue Creme
Bahama Grape
Bahama Kiwi Strawberry
Bahama Orange Mango
Bahama Pink Lemonade
Bahama Punch
Bahama Strawberry
Deep Purple
Diet Clear Jazz
Falcon Orange Soda
Jazz Cola
Rustler Root Beer

5764 **Hampton Chutney Company**
P.O.Box 1050
Amagansett, NY 11930
Fax: 631-267-6169 hamptonchutney@verizon.net
www.hamptonchutney.com
Fresh chutneys including mango chutney, cilantro chutney, tomato chutney, curry chutney, pumpkin chutney and peanut chutney, continental, seafood and southIndian foods
Owner: Gary Mac Gurn
Co-Owner: Isabel MacGurn
Chef: Patty Gentry
Estimated Sales: Less than $500,000
Number Employees: 5-9

5765 **Hampton Farms**
PO Box 149
Severn, NC 27877-0149
Fax: 757-654-0994 800-313-2748
companystore@hamptonfarms.com
www.hamptonfarms.com
Premier roaster and marketer of in-shell peanuts and peanut products
VP Sales/Marketing: Thomas Nolan
Operations: Dan Hutton
Estimated Sales: $25 Million
Number Employees: 100-249
Parent Co: Meherrin Chemical
Type of Packaging: Private Label, Bulk
Brands:
Hamptom Farms

5766 **Hampton HouseJ.D. Sweid Ltd**
7542 Gilley Ave
Burnaby, BC V5J 4X5
Canada 604-430-1173
Fax: 604-432-9184 800-665-4355
www.jdsweid.com
Processor and exporter of poultry and meat products including chicken strips, nuggets, burgers and flavored boneless and skinless breasts; also, barbecued baby back ribs, vegetarian patties and falafel
President: Blair Shier
Director Sales/Marketing: Hari Aroon
General Manager: Don Davidson
Estimated Sales: $64 Million
Number Employees: 300
Sq. footage: 55000
Parent Co: J.D. Sweid
Type of Packaging: Consumer, Food Service, Private Label, Bulk
Brands:
Hampton House
Sensations

5767 **Hanan Products Company**
196 Miller Pl
Hicksville, NY 11801 516-938-1000
Fax: 516-938-1925 info@hananproducts.com
www.hananproducts.com
Processor and exporter of kosher non-dairy creamer, sour dressings, whipped toppings, icings, fillings, and specialty desserts
President: Frank Hanan
Estimated Sales: $2.5-5 Million
Number Employees: 20-49
Type of Packaging: Consumer, Food Service

5768 **Hancock Lobster GourmetCompany**
46 Park Drive
Topsham, ME 04086 207-725-1855
Fax: 207-725-1856 800-266-1700
service@hancockgourmetlobster.com
www.hancockgourmetlobster.com
frozen lobster, shrimp and crab dishes

5769 **Hancock Peanut Company**
P.O.Box 100
Courtland, VA 23837 757-653-9351
Fax: 757-653-2147
Processor and exporter of peanuts - cooked and raw -
President: J Matthew Pope
VP Sales: Robert Pope
Contact: Melissa Rose
Number Employees: 50-99
Type of Packaging: Consumer, Food Service

5770 **Hancock's Old Fashioned**
1716 Academy Road Ext
Franklinville, NC 27248-8093 336-824-2145
Fax: 336-824-2312
Processor of country ham and dry cure pork bellies
President: Wilburt Hancock
VP: Shirley Hancock
Plant Manager: Lloyd Newman
Estimated Sales: $64,000
Number Employees: 65
Parent Co: Gwaltney of Smithfield

5771 **Hand Made With Love Inc.**
2234 N Federal Hwy #459
Boca Raton, FL 33431-7706 561-400-7444
Fax: 561-392-2204 denzykatz@aol.com
www.oldeestate.com
Marketing: Denise Katz

5772 **Handley Cellars**
3151 Highway 128
Philo, CA 95466 707-895-3876
Fax: 707-895-2603 800-733-3151
info@handleycellars.com
www.handleycellars.com
Collection of wines such as: Zinfandel, Pinot Gris, Ranch House Red, Water Tower White, Chardonnay, Dry Creek Valley
President/Winemaker: Milla Handley
National Sales Manager: Andrea Lederle
Retail Sales: Ellen Springwater
Assistant Winemaker: Kristen Barnhisel
Estimated Sales: $5-10 Million
Number Employees: 10-19
Type of Packaging: Private Label

5773 **Handy International**
700 E Main St
Salisbury, MD 21804-5037 410-912-2000
Fax: 410-912-0097 800-426-3977
www.handycrab.com
Processor and exporter of frozen seafood including soft shell crabs, crab and salmon cakes and stuffed crabs
President: Carol Haltaman
Estimated Sales: $8000000
Number Employees: 100-249
Type of Packaging: Consumer, Food Service
Brands:
Handy

5774 **(HQ)Handy Pax**
53 York Ave
Randolph, MA 02368 781-963-8300
Processor and wholesaler/distributor of snack foods including crackers with peanut butter, cheese, pretzel sticks, brownies and cookies
President: Jay Sussman
Sales Manager: David Sussman
Number Employees: 10-19
Type of Packaging: Consumer, Private Label

5775 **Hangzhou Sanhe Food Company**
20536 Carrey Rd
Walnut, CA 91789-2459 909-869-6016
Fax: 909-869-6015 aili28@hotmail.com
www.hzsanhe.com
Food additives
Owner: Duan Zong
Marketing Director: Alili Chen
Brands:
Hangzhou Sanhe

5776 **Hangzhou Sanhe USA**
20536 Carrey Road
Walnut, CA 909-869-6016
Fax: 909-869-6015 www.sanheinc.com
Food ingredients, additives and preservatives
President: Alli Chen
Parent Co: Sanhe Enterprise

5777 **Hank's Beverage Company**
4625 E Street Rd
Feastervl Trvs, PA 19053-6630 215-396-2809
Fax: 215-396-8077 800-289-4722
info@hanksbeverages.com
www.hanksbeverages.net
Diversified line of classic old fashioned gourmet flavors such as: Root Beer, Diet Root beer, Orange Cream, Vanilla Cream and Black Cherry. Specialty flavors as Birch Beer, Highland Berry;, Citrus and Fruit Punch
Manager: Jennifer Brady
Estimated Sales: $ 5 - 10 Million
Number Employees: 5-9

5778 **Hanmi**
5447 N Wolcott Ave
Chicago, IL 60640 773-271-0730
Fax: 773-271-1756 http://www.hanmi.com
Oriental and Korean foods
Owner: Young Kim
Contact: Sung Sohn
CFO: Michael Winiarski
Vice President: John Kim
Estimated Sales: $ 10 - 20 Million
Number Employees: 10-19

5779 **Hanna's Honey**
4760 Thorman Ave Ne
Salem, OR 97303-4644 503-393-2945
Fax: 503-393-2945
Small business: We package and wholesale gourmet Oregon honey. We also carry honey sticks-flavored colored honey in straws
President: Jean Hunter
CEO: Claude Hunter
Estimated Sales: $100,000
Number Employees: 2
Type of Packaging: Consumer
Brands:
Hanna's

5780 **Hanover Foods Corp**
PO Box 334
Hanover, PA 17331 717-632-6000
Fax: 717-637-2890 www.hanoverfoods.com
Processor and exporter of freeze-dried vegetables, poultry, meats, dairy products and ice
Chairman/President/CEO: John Warehime
EVP/CFO: Gary Knisely
VP Quality Assurance/R&D: Tim Mechler
Marketing Director: Tim Vance
Human Resources Director: Patty Townsend
Manufacturing Supervisor: Roy Bollinger
Purchasing Director: Rick Ramage
Estimated Sales: $20-50 Million
Number Employees: 2205
Sq. footage: 5161
Type of Packaging: Consumer, Bulk

5781 **(HQ)Hanover Foods Corporation**
P.O.Box 334
Hanover, PA 17331 717-632-6000
Fax: 717-637-2890 www.hanoverfoods.com
Processor and importer of canned, frozen, freeze-dried and fresh vegetables, beans, mushrooms, potato chips, pretzels, juices, sauces, salads, entrees, soups, desserts, etc.; also, spaghetti and meat balls in tomato sauce
President/CEO: John Warehime
Executive Vice President/CFO: Gary Knisely
VP: Dave Still
Research & Development: Tim Mechler
Advertising/Marketing: Jerry Neidigh
Retail Sales: Dan Schuchart
Foodservice Sales: Kathy Shaffer
Private Label Sales: Donna Bowser
Senior Vice President Purchasing: Alan Young
Estimated Sales: $20-50 Million
Number Employees: 2205
Sq. footage: 5161
Type of Packaging: Consumer, Private Label, Bulk
Brands:
Alcosa
Aunt Kitty's
Bickel's
Casa Maid
Clayton Farms
Dawn Glo
Dutch Farms
Farmer Girl
Gibbs
Hanover
Hanover Farms
Lk Burman
Maryland Chef
Mitchell's
Myers
O & C
Phillips
Round the Clock
Spring Glen
Spring Glen Fresh Foods
Sunnyside
Sunwise
Super Fine
Superfine
Vegetable Cocktail

5782 **Hanover Potato Products**
60 Black Rock Rd
Hanover, PA 17331 717-632-0700
Fax: 717-632-0756
Processor and wholesaler/distributor of fresh potato products including fries, whole and diced; serving the food service market
President: Kenneth Ruhlman
Estimated Sales: $250,000
Number Employees: 4
Sq. footage: 8700
Type of Packaging: Food Service

5783 **Hans Kissle Company**
9 Creek Brook Dr
Haverhill, MA 01832 978-372-2504
Fax: 978-556-4612 info@hanskissle.com
www.hanskissle.com
Refrigerated salads - traditional, protein, contemporary and heart healthy, quiches, stuffings and desserts
President/CEO: Steven Zenlea
National Sales Manager: Kymberley Feldman
Regional Sales Manager: Ken Boyle
Vice President Operations: Mary Connolly
Plant Technical Director: Robin Beane
Estimated Sales: $20-50 Million
Number Employees: 5-9
Sq. footage: 112000
Type of Packaging: Private Label

5784 **Hansel 'N Gretel**
7936 Cooper Ave
Flushing, NY 11385-7593 718-326-0041
Fax: 718-326-2069 healthydeli@healthydeli.com
www.healthydeli.com
Processor of meats including cold cuts and sausage and ham
President: Milton Rattner
CEO: Milton Rattner
CFO: Steve Rosbash
Vice President: Wayne Williamson
COO: Ron Walsen
Public Relations: Dawn Rattner
Operations Manager: James Rowe
Plant Engineer: John Krauss
Plant Manager: John Dinisi
Estimated Sales: $20-50 Million
Number Employees: 100-249
Type of Packaging: Consumer, Bulk
Brands:
Healthy Deli

5785 **Hansen Beverage**
550 Monica Cir Ste 201
Corona, CA 92880 951-739-6200
Fax: 951-739-6210 800-426-7367
www.hansens.com
Natural juices, sodas, teas, energy drinks
Vice Chairman/President: Hilton Schlosberg
Chairman/CEO: Rodney Sacks
CEO: Rodney C Sacks
Marketing: Tim Hansen
SVP/National Sales Manager: Michael Schott
Estimated Sales: $10-20 Million
Number Employees: 250-499
Brands:
Equator Products Teas
Hansen Apple Juice
Hansen Fruit Juice B
Hansen Lemonades

Hansen Smoothies
Hansen Sodas
Hansen Spring Water
Hansen Tea
Hansen's Healthy Ant
Hansen's Healthy Imm
Hansen's Healthy Int
Hansen's Healthy Vit
Hansen's Healthy Vit
Lost Five-0
Lost Perfect 10
Monster Energy Khaos

5786 **Hansen Caviar Company**
P.O.Box 677
Lake Katrine, NY 12449-677
Fax: 845-331-8075 800-735-0441
hcaviar@aol.com www.hansencaviar.com
Caviar (Russian and American), foie gras, truffles, smoked fish and other specialty food products
President: Michael Hansen-Sturm
Estimated Sales: $500,000-$1 Million
Number Employees: 1-4
Type of Packaging: Private Label
Brands:
Hansen
Hansen-Norge
St. Etienne

5787 **Hansen Packing Meat Company**
807 State Highway 16
Jerseyville, IL 62052-2813 618-498-3714
Fax: 618-498-5507
info@hansenpackingmeats.com
http://www.hansenpackingmeats.com/
Processor of meat
President: Ron Hansen
Customs Processor/Logistics Operations: Todd Pearse
Customs Processor/Logistics Operations: Jim Woelfel
Marketing/Sales Manager: Ryan Hansen
Retail Manager/Daily Operations: Shon Kennedy
Manager Administrative Operations: Terrie Perry
Lead Meat Processor: Mike Pearse
Livestock Consultant/Cattle Buyer: Ronnie Hansen
Driver Wholesale Orders: Dan Monroe
Estimated Sales: $ 3 - 5 Million
Number Employees: 5-9
Type of Packaging: Bulk
Brands:
Hansen

5788 **Hansen's Juices**
935 W 8th St
Azusa, CA 91702-2246
US 626-812-6022
Fax: 626-334-6439 800-426-7367
www.nakedjuice.com
Processor and exporter of fresh citrus and blended juices including strawberry, lemon and apple,soda natural soda,diet soda ,green teas,junior juice,junior water,smoothie,java monster.
CEO/President: Jeff Heavirland
Telecommunications: Paul Lingenfelder
Estimated Sales: $1.4 Billion
Number Employees: 100-249
Parent Co: Fresh Juice Company
Type of Packaging: Consumer, Food Service

5789 **Hansen's Natural**
1031 Rosecrans Ave # 104
Fullerton, CA 92833-1946 714-870-0310
Fax: 909-739-6210 www.cdchealth.com
Number Employees: 250-499

5790 **Hansmann's Mills**
336 Court Street
Binghamton, NY 13904-1653 607-722-1372
Baking mixes, cakes, pastries and pies, pancakes and waffles
President: George Slilaty
VP: Eileen Lawyer
VP: Bob Wright JR
Owner: Robin Fellows
Estimated Sales: $5-10 Million
Number Employees: 75

5791 **Hanson Thompson Honey Farms**
P.O.Box 129
Redfield, SD 57469 605-472-0474
Processor of honey
President: Bruce Hanson
Co-Owner: Adrian Thompson
Estimated Sales: Under $500,000
Number Employees: 1-4

5792 **Hanzell Vineyards**
18596 Lomita Ave
Sonoma, CA 95476 707-996-3860
Fax: 707-996-3862 maildesk@hanzell.com
www.hanzell.com
Wines: Chardonnay, Pinot Noir and many others
Proprietor: Alexander de Byre
President: Jean Arnold Sessions
Consulting Winemaker: Bob Sessions
National Sales Manager: Armen Khatchaturian
General Manager/Winemaker: Michael Terrien
Estimated Sales: $5-9.9 Million
Number Employees: 5-9

5793 **Hapag-Lloyd America**
245 Townpark Dr NW Ste 300
Kennesaw, GA 30144 678-355-5025
Fax: 678-801-8464 888-851-4083
www.hapag-lloyd.com
International transportation, cold storage, box cars
Senior VP: James I Newsome
Director Sales: Stuart Sandlin
Director Operations: John Palmer
Number Employees: 100-249

5794 **Happy & Healthy Products**
1600 S Dixie Hwy Ste 200
Boca Raton, FL 33432 561-367-0739
Fax: 561-368-5267 behappy@fruitfull.com
www.fruitfull.com
Committed to producing and supplying the highest quality frozen fruit bars and other products such as decadent dips, frozen dessert bars, fruit smoothies, and healthy snacks that promote a happy and healthy life-syle.
President: Linda Kamm
General Manager: Rosemary Harris
Marketing Director: Tabitha Locke
Customer Service Manager: Susan Scotts
Public Relations: Mary Galinat
Operations Manager: Len Murray
Estimated Sales: $4 Million
Number Employees: 20-49
Number of Brands: 5
Type of Packaging: Consumer, Food Service, Private Label, Bulk
Brands:
BE HAPPY 'N HEALTHY SNACKS
FRUITFULL
HAPPY INDULGENCE
HAPPY INDULGENCE DELADENT DIPS

5795 **Happy Acres Packing Company**
PO Box 444
Petal, MS 39465-0444 601-584-8301
Sausage
President: Helen Jernigan
Estimated Sales: $500-1 Million appx.
Number Employees: 1-4

5796 **Happy Egg Dealers**
3204 E 7th Ave
Tampa, FL 33605-4302 813-248-2362
Fax: 813-247-1754
Processor and exporter of eggs
Owner: Frank Selph Sr
Estimated Sales: $ 10 - 20 Million
Number Employees: 10-19
Type of Packaging: Consumer, Bulk
Brands:
Belle Mead

5797 **Happy Goat**
1 Frederick Court
Menlo Park, CA 94025-2241 650-922-8667
Fax: 415-762-5282
michael@happygoatcaramel.com
www.happygoatcaramel.com
Caramels, dessert toppings (i.e. fudge sauce, caramel sauce, whipped cream, etc.)
Marketing: Michael Winnike

5798 **Happy Herberts Food Company**
444 Washington Boulevard
Apt 2524
Jersey City, NJ 07310 201-386-0984
Fax: 201-386-0984 800-764-2779
info@happyherberts.com
www.happyherberts.com
Snacks
Owner: Gary Plutchok
Estimated Sales: $500,000-$1 Million
Number Employees: 1-4
Brands:
Happy Herberts

5799 **Happy Hive**
4476 Tulane St
Dearborn Heights, MI 48125 313-562-3707
Fax: 313-562-3707
Candy/confectionery
Owner: Stanley Kozlowicz
Estimated Sales: Less than $100,000
Number Employees: 1-4
Type of Packaging: Consumer, Food Service, Bulk
Brands:
Happy Hive

5800 **Happy Refrigerated Services**
900 Turk Hill Rd
Fairport, NY 14450-8747 585-388-0080
Fax: 585-388-0185
Ice
President: David Blind
Estimated Sales: $2.5-5 Million
Number Employees: 20-49

5801 **Happy's Potato Chip Company**
3900 Chandler Dr NE
Minneapolis, MN 55421 612-781-3121
Fax: 612-781-3125
Processor and exporter of snack foods including potato chips, popcorn, tostados and cheese puffs
President: Steve Aanenson
Plant Manager: Finn Henrikssen
Estimated Sales: $5 Million
Number Employees: 50
Sq. footage: 46000
Parent Co: Old Dutch Foods
Type of Packaging: Consumer, Food Service

5802 **Harbar Corporation**
320 Turnpike St
Canton, MA 02021 781-828-0848
Fax: 781-828-0849 800-881-7040
www.harbar.com
Processor of fresh tortillas including white corn, blue corn, white flour, wholewheat and flavored flour
Owner: Ezequiel Montmayor
Estimated Sales: $3 Million
Number Employees: 50-99
Sq. footage: 40000
Type of Packaging: Consumer, Food Service, Private Label, Bulk
Brands:
Harbar's
It's a Wrap
La Sabrosa
Maria & Ricardo's Tortilla Factory
Real Chip
Wrappy

5803 **Harbison Wholesale Meats**
2115 County Road
Suite 401
Cullman, AL 35057 256-739-5105
Fax: 256-739-8123
Meat
Proprietor: Gary Harbison

5804 **Harbor Fish Market**
9 Custom House Wharf
Portland, ME 4101 207-775-0251
Fax: 207-879-0611 info@harborfish.com
www.harborfish.com
Cephalopods, lobster, fish, frozen products, shellfish
President: Benjamin Alfiero
Owner/VP: Michael Alfiero
Estimated Sales: $6.2 Million
Number Employees: 30
Sq. footage: 8029

5805 **Harbor Food Sales & Services**
PO Box 21
Alameda, CA 94501-0321 360-405-0677
Fax: 360-405-0752

5806 **Harbor Lobster**
Shag Harbor
Lower Wood Harbor, NS B0W 3B0
Canada 902-723-2500
Fax: 902-723-2568
Processor and exporter of live lobster and salted groundfish
President: Wayne Banks
Number Employees: 5-9
Type of Packaging: Bulk

5807 **Harbor Seafood**
969 Lakeville Rd
New Hyde Park, NY 11040 516-775-2400
Fax: 516-775-2407 800-645-2211
www.harborseafood.com
Processor and importer of seafood
President/CEO: Pete Cardone
CFO: Bill Kienke
Sales/Marketing/Purchasing Director: Enrique Oyaga
Human Resources Manager: Dill Jienke
Estimated Sales: $50-100 Million
Number Employees: 29
Sq. footage: 5000

5808 **Harbor Spice Company**
100 Industry Ln
Forest Hill, MD 21050 410-893-9500
Fax: 410-893-9502 www.harborspice.com
Spices
Manager: Dan Sanchuck
Estimated Sales: $1-2.5 Million
Number Employees: 10-19

5809 **Harbor Sweets**
85 Leavitt St
Palmer Cove
Salem, MA 01970 978-745-7648
Fax: 978-741-7811 800-234-4887
dougs@harborsweets.com
www.harborsweets.com
Processor of gift chocolates including wedding favors, perennial sweets, classics, dark horse collection, hunt collection, sweet treats, easter and spring gifts, custom chocolates and sugar-free
Owner: Phyllis Le Blanc
Estimated Sales: $50-100 Million
Number Employees: 100-249
Brands:
DARK HORSE CHOCOLATES
MARBLEHEAD MINTS
PERENNIAL SWEETS
SWEET SHELLS
SWEET SLOOPS
TOPIARY TOFFEE

5810 **Harbor Winery**
610 Harbor Blvd
West Sacramento, CA 95691 916-371-6776
Wines
Owner: Charles Myers
Estimated Sales: Less than $100,000
Number Employees: 1-4
Brands:
Harbor

5811 **Hard-E Foods**
3228 N Broadway
Saint Louis, MO 63147 314-533-2211
Fax: 314-533-2656 www.hardefoods.com
Processor of hard cooked and deviled egg products; also, fresh cut vegetables
President/CEO: Judy Rutz
Plant Manager: Larry Rutz
Estimated Sales: $2 Million
Number Employees: 20-49
Sq. footage: 50000
Type of Packaging: Consumer, Food Service, Private Label
Brands:
Hard-E Foods

5812 **Hardin's Bakery**
546 15th St
Tuscaloosa, AL 35401 205-752-6431
Fax: 205-752-1780
Processor of baked goods including breads, buns and rolls.
Partner: Charles A Hardin
Estimated Sales: $ .5 - 1 million
Number Employees: 1-4
Parent Co: Flowers Baking Company
Type of Packaging: Consumer

5813 **Hardscrabble Enterprises**
PO Box 1124
Franklin, WV 26807-1124 304-358-2921
Processor and wholesaler/distributor of American dried shiitake mushrooms and maitake mushrooms
President: Paul Goland
Estimated Sales: Under $500,000
Number Employees: 1-4
Sq. footage: 3500
Type of Packaging: Consumer, Food Service, Bulk
Brands:
American Shiitake
Hen-Of-The-Woods

5814 **Hardy Farms Peanuts**
Rr 2 Box 2120
Hawkinsville, GA 31036-8945 478-783-3044
Fax: 478-783-0606 888-368-6887
info@hardyfarmspeanuts.com
www.hardyfarmspeanuts.com
Processor of fresh green and boiled peanuts
President: Alex Hardy
Estimated Sales: $1 Million
Number Employees: 10-19
Number of Brands: 1
Number of Products: 3
Sq. footage: 100000
Type of Packaging: Consumer, Food Service, Bulk

5815 **Harford Glen Water**
331 Creamery Rd
Harford, NY 13784 607-844-8351
Fax: 607-844-8351 866-844-8351
edsjet@yahoo.com www.deeprockaqua.com
Company is a supplier of natural spring water.
President/CEO: Edmund McHale
CFO/VP: Lura McHale
Number Employees: 6
Number of Brands: 2
Number of Products: 5
Sq. footage: 6000
Type of Packaging: Food Service, Private Label

5816 **Hari Om Farms**
8416 Shelbyville Hwy
Eagleville, TN 37060-9603 615-368-7778
Fax: 615-368-7650 kkpaul@h20farms.ne
www.h20farms.com
Processor of herbs and lettuce
Manager: Pedro Lopez
Estimated Sales: $1-2.5 Million
Number Employees: 1-4
Sq. footage: 60000
Type of Packaging: Consumer, Food Service, Bulk
Brands:
H2O
Hari Om Farms

5817 **Haribo of America**
1825 Woodlawn Drive
Suite 204
Baltimore, MD 21207 410-265-8890
Fax: 410-265-8898 800-638-2327
info@us.haribo.com www.haribo.com
Processor of Gummi and licorice candy products
President: Christian Jegen
Marketing: Margie Walter
Vice President Plant Operations: Ryan Schader
Estimated Sales: $5-10 Million
Number Employees: 10-19
Type of Packaging: Private Label
Brands:
HARIBO

5818 **Haring's Pride Catfish**
681 Pete Haring Rd
Wisner, LA 71378 318-724-6133
Fax: 318-724-6138 800-467-3474
info@haringspridecatfish.com
www.haringspridecatfish.com
Frozen and refrigerated catfish, catfish fillets, catfish nuggets, catfish strips, catfish tidbits, breaded catfish products
President/Owner: Carl Haring
Estimated Sales: $100-500 Million
Number Employees: 250-499

5819 **(HQ)Harker's Distribution**
801 6th St SW
Le Mars, IA 51031 712-546-8171
Fax: 712-536-3159 800-798-7700
www.harkers.com
Wholesaler/distributor of frozen foods, meats, center-of-the-plate foods, poultry and seafood; serving the food service market
President: Ron Geiger
CEO: Jim Harker
Sr. VP Sales/Marketing: Stan Dickman
Purchasing Agent: Kevin Regan
Number Employees: 100-249
Other Locations:
Harker's Distribution
Denver CO

5820 **Harlan Bakeries**
7597 E US Highway 36
Avon, IN 46123 317-272-3600
Fax: 317-272-1110 info@harlanbakeries.com
www.harlanbakeries.com
Processor and importer of bagels including fresh, frozen, fully baked, partially baked and raw dough; also, breads, bialys, bagel sticks, muffins, cakes, cookies, pies.
President: Hugh P Harlan
Executive Vice President: Doug R Harlan
Director Research/Development: Keith Lockwood

EVP Sales/Marketing: Joseph Latouf
Vice President Operations: Michael L Hulsebos
Estimated Sales: $100-500 Million
Number Employees: 250-499
Sq. footage: 150000
Brands:
Bagel King
Bigger Better
Giant Gourmet
Harlan Bakeries
World's Best

5821 **Harlin Fruit Company**
602 N 17th St
Monett, MO 65708 417-235-7370
Fax: 417-235-7316
Fresh fruits and vegetables
Owner: Jerry Sutton
President: Dennis Hughes
Estimated Sales: $1-2.5 Million
Number Employees: 10-19
Type of Packaging: Consumer, Bulk
Brands:
Harlin Fruit

5822 **Harlon's L.A. Fish, LLC**
P.O.Box 486
Kenner, LA 70063-0486 504-467-3809
Fax: 504-466-1503
Seafood
Owner: Harlon Pearce
Estimated Sales: $ 10 - 20 Million
Number Employees: 20-49

5823 **Harlow House Company**
PO Box 12018
Atlanta, GA 30355 404-325-1270
Fax: 678-560-8355 sales@harlowhouse.com
Confectionery
President: David Swain
Estimated Sales: Less than $500,000
Number Employees: 4
Type of Packaging: Consumer, Bulk

5824 **Harmon's Original Clam Cakes**
P.O.Box 1113
Kennebunkport, ME 04046-1113 207-967-4100
Fax: 207-967-1008
steve@harmonsclamcakes.com
www.harmonsclamcakes.com
Clam Cakes
Owner: Steven Liautaud

5825 **Harmony Cellars**
3255 Harmony Valley Rd
Harmony, CA 93435 805-927-1625
Fax: 805-927-0256 800-432-9239
www.harmonycellars.net
Wines consisting of white, red, and blush
Co-Owner/Winemaker: Charles Mulligan
Co-Owner/Business Manager: Kim Mulligan
Estimated Sales: $500,000-$1 Million
Number Employees: 5-9

Brands:
Harmony Cellars

5826 **Harmony Foods Corporation**
11899 Exit 5 Pkwy
Fishers, IN 46037-7938 317-567-2700
gummy@harmonyfoods.com
www.harmonyfoods.com
Processor and exporter of gummys, jelly beans, gels, yogurt, chocolate confections and sugar-free and natural candies; also, dried fruit, banana chips and snack and trail mixes
Cfo: Dennis Barrow
Vice President: Dennis Daniels
Estimated Sales: $1-2.5 Million
Number Employees: 100-249
Sq. footage: 200000
Type of Packaging: Consumer, Food Service, Private Label, Bulk
Brands:
Bold Beans
Harmony Snacks
Planet Harmony

5827 **Harmony Foods Corporation**
11899 Exit Five Parkway
Fishers, IN 46037-7938 317-567-2700
Fax: 317-577-3588 800-837-2855
info@harmonyfoods.com
www.harmonyfoods.com
Nourish healthy lifestyles by providing delicious and better snacks made with the highest quality wholesome ingredients. Such items are trail mixes, dried fruits, nuts and seeds, sweet snacks and sugar-free specialty sweets andorganic snacks
Cfo: Dennis Barrow
Vice President: Dennis Daniels
Estimated Sales: $90,000
Number Employees: 2
Sq. footage: 125000

5828 **Harner Farms**
2191 W Whitehall Road
State College, PA 16801-2332 814-237-7919
Fax: 814-238-8349
Processor of produce including apples, cherries, plums and vegetables
Owner: Daniel Harner
Estimated Sales: $220,000
Number Employees: 4
Type of Packaging: Consumer, Food Service

5829 **Harney & Sons Fine Teas**
5723 Route 22
Millerton, NY 12546 518-789-2100
Fax: 518-789-2100 800-832-8463
richina@harneyteas.com www.harney.com
Processor, importer and exporter of teas including black, green, fruit, iced and herbal
President: John Harney
Marketing: Justin Panzer
Sales: Michael Harney
Manager: Paul Harney
Purchasing: Elvira Cardenos
Estimated Sales: $2.5-5 Million
Number Employees: 5-9
Sq. footage: 12000
Type of Packaging: Consumer, Food Service, Private Label, Bulk
Brands:
Harney & Sons

5830 **Harold Food Company**
11949 Steele Creek Road
Charlotte, NC 28273 704-588-8061
Fax: 704-588-4636
Processor of frozen fruit cobblers, salads, spreads, chili and barbecue products; wholesaler/distributor of dry, paper, frozen, fresh and refrigerated products; serving the food service market
President: Susan Yandle
Marketing Director: Tom Taylor
General Manager: Butch Summey
Estimated Sales: $20-50 Million
Number Employees: 50-99
Sq. footage: 46500
Type of Packaging: Food Service, Private Label, Bulk
Brands:
Harold Food Co.

5831 **Harold L. King & Company**
1420 Stafford St Ste 3
Redwood City, CA 94063 650-368-2233
Fax: 650-368-3547 888-368-2233
kingcoffee@aol.com
Green coffee
President: Robert King
Secretary/Treasurer: John King
Vice President: Tim Kallok
Estimated Sales: $25 Million
Number Employees: 5-9
Type of Packaging: Consumer

5832 **Harold M. Lincoln Company**
2130 Madison Ave Ste 101
Toledo, OH 43604 419-255-1200
Fax: 419-259-5631 800-345-4911
hmlincoln@aol.com
Broker of confectionery and dairy/deli products, frozen foods, general merchandise, groceries, etc. Marketing, sales planning and promotional tracking services available
President: David Lincoln
VP/Account Manager: J Lincoln
Chairman: H Lincoln
Estimated Sales: $20-50 Million
Number Employees: 5-9
Sq. footage: 7000

5833 **Harper Seafood Company**
1348 White Point Rd
Kinsale, VA 22488 804-472-3310
Fax: 804-472-2682
Processor of refrigerated oysters
President: Robert Harper
Estimated Sales: $10-20 Million
Number Employees: 10-19
Type of Packaging: Consumer, Food Service
Brands:
Harper Seafood

5834 **Harper's Country Hams**
2955 Us Highway 51 N
Clinton, KY 42031 270-653-2081
Fax: 270-653-2409 888-427-7377
info@hamtastic.com www.hamtastic.com
Country ham
President: Gary Harper
Treasurer: Doris Harper
Vice President: Brian Harper
Plant Manager: John Mcauliffe
Purchasing Manager: Brant Dublin
Estimated Sales: $20-50 Million
Number Employees: 100-249

5835 **Harper's Seafood**
526 W Jackson St
Thomasville, GA 31792-5903 229-226-7525
Fax: 229-228-6446
Seafood
President: Wayne Harper
Estimated Sales: $ 3 - 5 Million
Number Employees: 10-19

5836 **Harpersfield Vineyard**
6387 N River Rd W
Geneva, OH 44041 440-466-4739
info2@harpersfield.com
www.harpersfield.com
Wines
Manager: Adolf Ribic
Co-Owner: Wesley Gerlosky
Estimated Sales: $1-4.9 Million
Number Employees: 1-4
Type of Packaging: Private Label

5837 **Harpo's**
477 Kapahulu Avenue
Honolulu, HI 96815 808-735-6456
Fax: 808-735-6456 alohaharpos@hawaii.rr.com
www.harposdressings.com
Processor of gourmet salad dressings, marinades, and pizza
Manager: Ingrid Larsson
Number Employees: 1-4

5838 **Harpoon Brewery**
306 Northern Ave Ste 2
Boston, MA 02210-2367 617-574-9551
Fax: 617-482-9361 800-427-7666
akeyser@harpoonbrewery.com
www.harpoonbrewery.com
Beer
Owner: Patricia Michaels
Co-Founder/President: Daniel Kenary
Manager: Richard Doyle
Manager: Rodney Depoter
Estimated Sales: $10-100 Million
Number Employees: 50-99
Brands:
Harpoon
Pickwick
U.F.O.

5839 **Harrington's In Vermont**
210 Main Rd
Richmond, VT 05477 802-434-7500
Fax: 802-434-3166 info@harringtonham.com
www.harringtonham.com
Smoked meats, cheese, maple syrup, seafood, sweets & snacks, condiments and cakes and pastries
Owner/Chairman: Peter Klinkenberg
Director: John Balczuk
CFO: R Klinkenberg
Marketing: Carol Wiseley
Estimated Sales: $20-50 Million
Number Employees: 10

5840 **Harris Baking Company**
P.O.Box 129
Rogers, AR 72757 479-636-3313
Fax: 479-631-3895
Processor of baked products including bread and buns.
Manager: Josh Carosh
Estimated Sales: $100-500 Million
Number Employees: 100-249
Sq. footage: 70000
Type of Packaging: Consumer
Brands:
Best Choice
IGA
Ozark
Tender Crust

5841 **Harris Farms**
Rr 1 Box 400
Coalinga, CA 93210 559-935-0703
Fax: 559-884-2253 800-742-1955
info@harrisfarms.com www.harrisfarms.com
Processor of tomatoes, onions, melons, almonds, bell peppers and garlic
President: John Harris
Senior VP: Donald Devine
Estimated Sales: $5-10 Million
Number Employees: 100-249
Type of Packaging: Consumer, Food Service, Private Label, Bulk
Brands:
Harris Farms
Harris Fresh
Harris Ranch

5842 **Harris Freeman & Company**
3110 E Miraloma Ave
Anaheim, CA 92806-1906 714-765-1190
Fax: 714-765-1199 800-275-2378
www.harrisfreeman.com
Distributor and importer of spices, teas and coffee
Owner/President: Anil Shah
Owner: Chirayu Borooah
Vice President: Al Paruthi
Estimated Sales: 20-50 Million
Number Employees: 20-49

5843 **Harris Moran Seed Company**
PO Box 4938
Modesto, CA 95352 209-579-7333
Fax: 209-527-5312 www.harrismoran.com
Processor and exporter of vegetable seeds (bean, cabbage, cauliflower, sweet corn, cucumber, lettuce, melon, pepper, pumpkin, radish, squash, tomoato and watermelon)
President/COO: Matthew Johnston
VP Research: Jeff McElroy
Marketing Director: Bernie Hamel
US/Canada Sales Director: Dan Bailey
Purchasing Agent: Maxine Corbett
Estimated Sales: $ 10 - 20 Million
Number Employees: 250
Parent Co: Groupe Limagrain
Brands:
Niagra Seed

5844 **Harris Ranch Beef Company**
P.O.Box 220
Selma, CA 93662 559-896-3081
Fax: 559-896-3095 800-742-1955
www.harrisranchbeef.com
Processor, packer and exporter of fresh beef products
Corporate Chairman/Owner: John Harris
CEO: Dave Wood
CEO: Dave Wood
Research & Development Manager: Bruce Hurley

QA/Food Safety Director: Dr. Patrick Mies
Vice President Marketing: Brad Caudill
Director International Sales: Doug Fariss
Estimated Sales: $100-500 Million
Number Employees: 500-999
Sq. footage: 160000
Type of Packaging: Consumer, Food Service, Private Label, Bulk
Brands:
Harris Ranch

5845 **Harrisburg Dairies**
P.O.Box 2001
Harrisburg, PA 17105-2001 717-233-8701
Fax: 717-231-4584 800-692-7429
sales@harrisburgdairies.com
www.harrisburgdairies.com
Processor of frozen orange juice, spring water and milk including regular and chocolate
President: Fred Dewey
CEO: Fred B Dewey Jr
Operations Manager: Matthew Zehring
Plant Manager: Ralph Watts
Estimated Sales: $50-100 Million
Number Employees: 100-249
Type of Packaging: Consumer
Brands:
Harrisburg Dairies

5846 **Harrison Napa Valley**
1443 Silverado Trail
Saint Helena, CA 94574 707-963-8762
Fax: 707-963-8762 www.whwines.com
Wines
Owner/Winemaker: Lyndsey Harrison
Manager: Rob Monaghan
Estimated Sales: Less than $500,000
Number Employees: 1-4
Type of Packaging: Private Label
Brands:
Harrison

5847 **Harrison Poultry**
107 Star St W
Bethlehem, GA 30620 770-867-9105
Fax: 770-867-0999
Manufacturer, hatcher, of fresh whole birds and parts; exporter of frozen poultry parts
Owner: Patsy Harrison
Controller: Greg Finch
Estimated Sales: $50-100 Million
Number Employees: 500-999
Sq. footage: 150000
Type of Packaging: Consumer, Food Service, Private Label, Bulk
Brands:
HARRISON GOLDEN GOODNESS
PRIDE OF GEORGIA

5848 **Harry & David**
P.O.Box 712
Medford, OR 97501 541-864-2121
Fax: 541-864-2194 877-322-1200
www.harryanddavid.com
Producer of fruit, frozen gourmet truffles, beef steaks, ham, turkey, cakes, cheesecake, cookies and cinnamon rolls
President/CEO: Bill Williams
EVP Sales/Marketing: Cathy Fultineer
EVP Operations: Peter Kratz
Number Employees: 1,000-4,999
Parent Co: Bear Creek Corporation
Type of Packaging: Consumer, Food Service
Brands:
Harry & David

5849 **Harry H. Park Company**
3539 W Lawrence Avenue
Chicago, IL 60625-5627 773-478-4424
Fax: 773-478-2313
Owner: Harry Park

5850 **Harry London Candies Inc**
5353 Lauby Rd
North Canton, OH 44720 330-494-0833
Fax: 330-499-6902 800-321-0444
eds@fanniemaybrands.com
www.harrylondon.com
Processor of chocolates, and truffles
President: Terry Mitchell
Chief Executive Officer: Rex Mason
Chief Financial Officer: Matthew Anderson
Vice President Business Development: Bob Happel
Estimated Sales: $50-100 Million
Number Employees: 100-249
Brands:
HARRY LONDON CHOCOLATES
HEARTLAND CHOCOLATES

5851 **Harry's Cafe**
3621 Vt Route 103 S
Mount Holly, VT 05758 802-259-2996
eat@harryscafe.com
www.harryscafe.com
Manufacturer of sauces - also restaurant -
Owner/Chef: Trip Pearce
Estimated Sales: $300,000-500,000
Number Employees: 5-9

5852 **Hart Winery**
P.O.Box 956
Temecula, CA 92593 951-676-6300
Fax: 951-676-6300 877-638-8788
hartwinery@speedband.com
www.thehartfamilywinery.com
Manufacturer of wines
Owner/Winemaker: Joe Hart
Owner/CEO: Nancy Hart
Winemaker: Bill Hart
Estimated Sales: $1-2.5 Million
Number Employees: 1-4
Sq. footage: 3
Type of Packaging: Private Label
Brands:
Hart Winery

5853 **Harten Corporation**
18 Commerce Rd Ste H
Fairfield, NJ 7004 973-808-9488
Fax: 973-808-3966 866-642-7836
Supplier of herbal extracts, botanicals, powders, and nutritional supplements for the health food industry.

5854 **Hartford City Foam Packaging & Converting**
P.O.Box D
Hartford City, IN 47348-0151 765-348-2500
Fax: 765-348-1635 www.hartfordcityfoam.com
Processor of aseptic canned diced and whole tomatoes and canned tomato paste; also, sauces including pizza, marinara, salsa, picante and tomato; importer of aseptic canned tomato paste
President/CEO: John Jackson
CEO: Russell Mitchel
Estimated Sales: $10-24.9 Million
Number Employees: 50-99
Sq. footage: 220000
Type of Packaging: Consumer, Food Service, Private Label, Bulk
Brands:
Mama Rizzo

5855 **Hartford Family Winery**
8075 Martinelli Rd
Forestville, CA 95436 707-887-1756
Fax: 707-887-7158 800-588-0234
hartford.winery@hartfordwines.com
www.hartfordwines.com
Wines specializing in Pinot Noir, Chardonnay, and Old-Vine Zinfandel
Manager: Jeff Mangahas
Co-Owner: Jennifer Hartford
Events Manager: Melissa Cook
Estimated Sales: $ 5 - 10 Million
Number Employees: 10-19
Brands:
HARTFORD
HARTFORD COURT

5856 **Hartford Provision Company**
P.O.Box 1228
625 Nutmeg Rd N
South Windsor, CT 06074-2440 860-583-3908
Fax: 860-583-6570 www.hpcss.com
President: Barry Pearson
CEO: Barry Pearson
Director: Mike Fauth
Marketing Manager: Ken Annini
Estimated Sales: $50-100 Million
Number Employees: 130
Brands:
Heinz

5857 **Harting's Bakery**
P.O.Box 220
Bowmansville, PA 17507-0220 717-445-5644
Fax: 717-445-4818
www.hartingscountrymaidbky.com
Doughnuts and buns
President/CEO: Jocelyn Heft
COO: Thomas Lester
Plant Manager: William Burkhart
Estimated Sales: $1-2.5 Million
Number Employees: 20-49

5858 **Hartley's Potato Chip Company**
2157 Back Maitland Rd
Lewistown, PA 17044 717-248-0526
Fax: 717-248-3512
hartleyspotatochips@gmail.com
www.hartleyspotatochips.com
Processor and packager of potato chips, pretzels, cheese curls
President: Carl Hartley
VP: Daniel Hartley
Estimated Sales: $1 Million
Number Employees: 12
Sq. footage: 6871
Type of Packaging: Consumer, Food Service

5859 **Hartog Rahal Foods**
529 5th Ave
New York, NY 10017-4608 212-687-2000
Fax: 212-687-2659 info@hartogfoods.com
www.hartogfoods.net
Fruit juice concentrates, fruit purees, frozen fruits and flavoring ingredients
President: Jack Hartog Jr
VP: Randy Loewis
Estimated Sales: $ 10 - 20 Million
Number Employees: 20-49
Parent Co: Hartog Rahal Foods

5860 **Hartselle Frozen Foods**
PO Box 544
Hartselle, AL 35640-0544 256-773-7261
Fax: 709-722-1116
Frozen meats
President: Billy Wiley
Secretary/Treasurer: Sam Wiley
Vice President: Danny Wiley

5861 **Hartsville Oil Mill**
311 Washington St
Darlington, SC 29532-4755 843-393-2855
Fax: 843-395-2690
Oils
President/ Owner: Edgar Lawton
Estimated Sales: $20-50 Million
Number Employees: 50-99

5862 **Hartville Kitchen**
1015 Edison St NW Ste 1
Hartville, OH 44632 330-877-9353
Fax: 330-877-2101 www.hartvillekitchen.com
Dressings, light dressings
President: Vernon Sommers
VP: Vernon Sommers Jr.
Estimated Sales: $5-10 Million
Number Employees: 250-499

5863 **Hartville Locker**
P.O.Box 7
Hartville, OH 44632-0007 330-877-9547
Beef processing
Owner: Young
Estimated Sales: $2.5-5 Million
Number Employees: 1-4

5864 **Harvard Seafood Company**
PO Box 208
Grand Bay, AL 36541-0208 251-865-0558
Fax: 251-865-2187

Seafood

5865 **Harvest 2000**
683 New York Drive
Pomona, CA 91768-3313 909-622-8039
Fax: 909-622-9789
Oriental dry mixes
President: Howard Goh
Public Relations: Grace Law
Estimated Sales: $1-2.5 Million
Number Employees: 5-9

5866 **Harvest Bakery**
84 Farmington Ave
Bristol, CT 06010 860-589-8800
Fax: 860-583-4693
Processor of bread and pastries
President: Martin Hurwitz
Estimated Sales: $1-2.5 Million appx.
Number Employees: 20-49
Type of Packaging: Consumer
Brands:
Harvest Bakery

5867 **(HQ)Harvest Day Bakery**
6565 Knott Avenue
Buena Park, CA 90620-8100 714-739-6318
Fax: 714-739-6626
Baked goods

5868 **Harvest Direct**
P.O.Box 50906
Knoxville, TN 37950 865-539-6305
Fax: 865-523-3372 800-838-2727
monty@harvestdirect.com
www.harvestdirect.com
Meat and milk alternatives
President: Roger Kilburn
Marketing Director: Monty Kilburn
Manager Wholesale Division: Mary Ellen Kilburn
Estimated Sales: $500,000-$1 Million
Number Employees: 5-9
Type of Packaging: Private Label
Brands:
Protflan
Solait
Veggie Ribs

5869 **Harvest Food Products Company**
1381 Franquette Ave Ste B1
Concord, CA 94520 925-676-8208
Processor and importer of pot stickers, egg rolls, wontons, barbecue pork buns and tempura shrimp
President: Danny Kha
Estimated Sales: $ 10 - 20 Million
Number Employees: 50-99
Sq. footage: 17000
Type of Packaging: Consumer, Food Service, Private Label, Bulk
Brands:
Harvest Foods

5870 **Harvest Innovations**
1210 North 14th Street
Indianola, IA 50125 515-962-5063
info@harvest-innovations.com
www.harvest-innovations.com
Manufacturer of natural ingredients such as legumes, soy & multigrain flours, cereal grains and oilseeds for the food industry.
Director Of Research: Dr. Noel Rudie
Product Development & Quality Assurance: Regena Butler
Director Food Technology: Dr. Wilmot Wijeratne

5871 **Harvest States Processing & Refining**
2020 S Riverfront Dr
Mankato, MN 56001 507-625-7911
Fax: 507-345-2254 800-525-6237
daveschosthet@chsinc.com www.chsinc.com
Soybean crushing and refined soybean meal, soybean flour, refined oils
President: Jim Graham
VP Manufacturing: James Amlie
Estimated Sales: $500 Million to $1 Billion
Number Employees: 100
Brands:
Teneric

5872 **Harvest Time Foods**
3857 Emma Cannon Rd
Ayden, NC 28513-7413 252-746-6675
Fax: 252-746-3160 impressions10@earthlink.net
www.annesdumplings.com
Processor of frozen dumplings
President: Bryan Grimes
VP: Wendy Grimes
Estimated Sales: $5-9.9 Million
Number Employees: 20-49
Sq. footage: 17000
Type of Packaging: Consumer, Food Service
Brands:
Anne's Chicken Base
Anne's Dumpling Squares
Anne's Dumpling Strips
Anne's Flat Dumplings
Anne's Old Fashioned
Anne's Pot Pie Squares
Mac's Dumplings

5873 **Harvest Valley Bakery**
348 N 30th Rd
La Salle, IL 61301 815-224-9030
Fax: 815-224-9033
Cookies, brownies, and bar cookies. Offers diet and kosher foods
President: Nancy Norton
Estimated Sales: $10-20 Million
Number Employees: 20-49
Sq. footage: 24000
Type of Packaging: Food Service, Private Label, Bulk

5874 **Harvest-Pac Products**
22131 Bloomfield Rd
Chatham, ON N7M 5J6
Canada 519-436-0446
Fax: 519-436-0319 sales@harvestpac.com
www.harvestpac.com
Processor of canned pumpkin, dark red kidney beans, chick peas and crushed and pureed tomatoes; also, pizza sauce, tomato juice
President: Dan O'Neill
Operations Manager: Roger Sterling
Type of Packaging: Food Service, Private Label
Brands:
Harvest-Pac
Mom's Choice

5875 **Harvin Choice Meats**
P.O.Box 939
Sumter, SC 29151-0939 803-775-9367
Fax: 803-775-9369 www.harvinmeats.com
Meats
Owner: S A Harvin Jr
Estimated Sales: $20-50 Million
Number Employees: 50-99

5876 **Has Beans Coffee & Tea Company**
1011 S Mount Shasta Blvd
Mount Shasta, CA 96067 530-926-3602
Fax: 530-926-6503 800-427-2326
coffeeorders@hasbeans.com www.hasbeans.com
Coffee roasting, wholesale coffee and tea
Owner: Anne Rivera
Estimated Sales: $10-20 Million
Number Employees: 10-19
Type of Packaging: Private Label

5877 **Hastings Cooperative Creamery**
1701 Vermillion St
Hastings, MN 55033 651-437-9414
Fax: 651-437-3547
Processor of milk
Manager: John Cook
General Manager: John Cook
Estimated Sales: $ 20 - 50 Million
Number Employees: 20-49
Type of Packaging: Consumer, Private Label

5878 **Hastings Meat Supply**
202 W 12th St
Hastings, NE 68901-3967 402-463-9857
Fax: 402-463-7181
Processor of meat
Owner: Gary Deal
Director: Jeff Andreasen
Estimated Sales: $ 1 - 3 Million
Number Employees: 1-4
Type of Packaging: Consumer, Food Service, Bulk

5879 **Hatch Chile Company**
2003 S Commercial Drive
Brunswick, GA 31525 972-459-2520
Chiles, chile powder and dip mix
Marketing: David Gregory

5880 **(HQ)Hatfield Quality Meats**
P.O.Box 902
Hatfield, PA 19440 215-368-2500
Fax: 215-368-3018 800-523-5291
www.hqm.com
Processor and exporter of fresh and frozen pork products including ham, sausage and frankfurters
Chairman: Philip Clemens
Sr VP: Kenneth Clemens
HR Director: David Kolesky
Estimated Sales: $100-500 Million
Number Employees: 1,000-4,999
Type of Packaging: Consumer, Food Service, Private Label
Other Locations:
Hatfield Quality Meats
Chester PA
Brands:
Beaver Falls
Butcher Wagon
CVF
Chef Pleaser
Gold Ribbon
Hatfield
Medford
Olde Philadelphia
Prima Porta
Tender Plus

5881 **Haug North America**
Units 14 & 15
Mississauga, ON L4W 2S7
Canada 905-206-9701
Fax: 905-206-0859 800-714-8331
haug@pathcom.com www.haug-static.com
President: Toby Wagener
Estimated Sales: Below $ 5 Million
Number Employees: 4

5882 **Haug Quality Equipment**
18443 Technology Dr
Morgan Hill, CA 95037-2822 408-465-8160
Fax: 408-842-1265 sales@haugquality.com
www.haugquality.com
President: Brian Haug
Estimated Sales: $ 1 - 3 Million
Number Employees: 5-9
Brands:
Haug

5883 **Haus Barhyte**
P.O.Box 1499
Pendleton, OR 97801-0950 541-276-0259
Fax: 503-691-8918 800-407-9241
chris@mustardpeople.com
www.mustardpeople.com
Processor, importer and exporter of gourmet and yellow mustards; private labeling and co-packing available
Owner: Susan Barhyte
Secretary/Treasurer: Irene Barhyte
Director Sales Marketing: Chris Barhyte
Estimated Sales: $2.5-5 Million
Number Employees: 5-9
Brands:
Aviator Ale Micro Brew Mustards
Food and Wine
Food and Wine Mustards
Haus Barhyte Mustard
Williamette Valley Mustard

5884 **Hausbeck Pickle Company**
1626 Hess Ave.
Saginaw, MI 48601 989-754-3797
Fax: 989-754-3855 866-754-4721
tim@hausbeck.com www.hausbeck.com
Processor and exporter of relish and pickles including dill, kosher, sweet, fresh pack kosher and hamburger sliced dill
President: John Hausbeck
Vice President: Jim Hausbeck
Treasurer: Richard Hausbeck
Sales Manager: John Schnepf
Estimated Sales: $5-10 Million
Number Employees: 10-19
Sq. footage: 30000
Type of Packaging: Consumer, Food Service

5885 **Hauser Chocolate**
59 Tom Harvey Rd
Westerly, RI 02891-3685 401-596-8866
Fax: 401-596-0020 888-599-8231
hauser@hauserchocolates.com
www.hauserchocolates.com
Chocolate manufacturer
Owner: Ruedi Hauser Sr Jr
Vice President Research/Development: Ruedi Hauser Sr
Estimated Sales: $2.5-5 Million
Number Employees: 10-19

5886 **Hauser Chocolates**
59 Tom Harvey Road
Westerly, RI 02891 401-596-8866
Fax: 401-596-0020 800-289-8783
hausero@hauserchocolates.com
www.hauserchocolates.com
Processor and exporter of assorted chocolates including Swiss style truffles
President: Rudi Hauser Jr
Estimated Sales: $2.5-5 Million
Number Employees: 5-9
Type of Packaging: Consumer

5887 **Hausman Foods**
P.O.Box 2422
Corpus Christi, TX 78403-2422 361-883-5521
Fax: 361-883-1003 800-364-5521
info@samhausman.com www.samhausman.com
Processor and exporter of fresh and frozen beef
President/CEO: Steve R McClure, Sr.
CEO: Steve R McClure Sr
Operations Manager: Jerry Simpson
Estimated Sales: $ 50-100 Million
Number Employees: 100-249
Type of Packaging: Consumer, Food Service, Bulk

5888 **Havana's Limited**
4420 Coquina Avenue
Titusville, FL 32780-6552 321-267-0513
Fax: 321-267-5340 havanasltd@aol.com
www.acebandito.com
Producing gourmet products of the highest quality with no additives - hot sauces, dry rubs and seasonings and BBQ sauces - use only whole fresh vegetables and high quality dry spices
President/CEO: Mark Webber
Vice President: Bruce Webber
Number of Brands: 1
Number of Products: 10
Sq. footage: 5000
Type of Packaging: Consumer, Food Service, Private Label, Bulk
Brands:
ACE BANDITO

5889 **Haven's Candies**
87 County Rd
Westbrook, ME 04092 207-772-1557
Fax: 207-775-0086 800-639-6309
havens@havenscandies.com
www.havenscandies.com
Processor of chocolates, fudge, salt water taffy, cooked nuts and candy canes; custom chocolate molding available
Owner: Andy Charles
Marketing Director: Krista Viola
Production Manager: Arthur Dillon
Estimated Sales: $1-2.5 Million
Number Employees: 20-49
Sq. footage: 8000
Type of Packaging: Consumer, Private Label, Bulk

5890 **Havi Food Services Worldwide**
227 South Blvd
Oak Park, IL 60302-4711 708-445-1700
Fax: 630-351-9479
Breads, rolls, baked goods
President: Jeff Somers
CEO: Jeff Somers
Number Employees: 50-99

5891 **(HQ)Havoc Maker Products**
121 Old Sachems Head Rd
Guilford, CT 06437 203-453-4943
Fax: 203-453-4943 800-681-3909
havoc@snet.net www.havocmaker.com
Processor of hot sauce, salsa, chili and hot sauce mixes, black bean dip, popcorn and bottled spices
Owner: Ernest Neri
Number Employees: 1-4
Sq. footage: 500
Type of Packaging: Food Service, Private Label, Bulk
Other Locations:
Havoc Maker Products
Old Lyme CT
Brands:
Havoc Maker

5892 **Hawaii Candy**
2928 Ualena St Ste 4
Honolulu, HI 96819 808-836-8955
Fax: 808-839-4040 info@hawaiicandy.com
www.hawaiicandy.com
Processor and exporter of confectionery items, snacks, puff rice cakes, coconut balls and fortune cookies
President: Keith Ohta
Secretary: Richard Ohta
Estimated Sales: $5-10 Million
Number Employees: 20-49
Sq. footage: 11000
Type of Packaging: Consumer, Food Service, Private Label, Bulk
Brands:
Hawaiian Island Crisp
Hawaiian Island Crisp Cookies

5893 **Hawaii Coffee Company**
1555 Kalani St
Honolulu, HI 96817 808-847-3600
Fax: 800-972-0777 800-338-8353
webinfo@hicoffee.com www.hicoffeeco.com
Processor of Kona coffee
President: Jim Wayman
Vice President Sales, Foodservice: Jim Lenhart
VP Sales, Retail/Military/Int'l: Sharon Zambo-Fan
Estimated Sales: $28,000,000
Number Employees: 100-249
Parent Co: C. Brewer & Company

5894 **Hawaii Coffee Company**
1555 Kalani St
Honolulu, HI 96817 800-338-8353
Fax: 808-847-3434 800-338-8353
lion@lioncoffee.com www.lioncoffee.com
A leader in premium delicious blends of Hawaiian coffees from Kona and the surrounding islands and delicious Hawaiian Island teas.
President: Jim Wayman
Marketing Coordinator: Tom Tsuhako
Vice President/Sales: James Lenhart
Vice President/Sales -Retail, Military: Sharon Zambo-Fan
Wholesale US/International Customers: Kevin Chang
Mailorder/Catalog Request/Online Orders: Eriko Fong
Estimated Sales: $9 Million
Number Employees: 100-249
Number of Brands: 4
Parent Co: Paradise Beverages
Brands:
Hawaii Coffee Company
Lion Coffee
Royal Kona Coffee
Tiger Tea

5895 **Hawaii International Seafood**
P.O.Box 30486
Honolulu, HI 96820-0486 808-839-5010
Fax: 808-833-0712 www.cryofresh.com
Fish and seafood
President: Bill Kowalski
Estimated Sales: $2,000,000
Number Employees: 5-9

5896 **Hawaii Star Bakery**
944 Akepo Ln Ste 3
Honolulu, HI 96817 808-841-3602
Fax: 808-842-7941
Processor of French, sourdough and rye bread, English muffins and rolls
Owner: Liane Small
Estimated Sales: $10-20 Million
Number Employees: 20-49
Type of Packaging: Consumer, Food Service

5897 **Hawaiian Bagel**
753 Halekauwila Street
Honolulu, HI 96813-5318 808-596-0638
Fax: 808-593-2434 hibagel@gte.net
Bagels and breads
President: Steve Gelson
Estimated Sales: $5-9.9 Million
Number Employees: 20-49
Parent Co: Fch Enterprises, Inc.

5898 **Hawaiian Candies & Nuts**
707 Waiakamilo Rd
Honolulu, HI 96817 808-841-3344
Fax: 808-841-2551 hcn@iav.com
Chocolate-covered macadamia nuts
President: Patrick Arakaki
Controller: Kenneth Arakaki
VP: Neal Arakaki
Estimated Sales: $5-10 Million
Number Employees: 20-49

5899 **Hawaiian Fruit Specialties**
P.O.Box 637
2-2741 Kaumualii Hwy
Kalaheo, HI 96741-8346 808-332-9333
Fax: 808-332-7650
customerservice@kukuibrand.com
www.kukuibrand.com
Tropical fruit mustard, sauces, mango chutney, jams/preserves, guava jelly, tropical fruit marmalade, fruit syrup
Owner: Jeanne Toulon
Chief Executive Officer: George Morvis Jr
CEO: Greg Shredder
Consultant: Fay Tateishi
Estimated Sales: $2.5-5 Million
Number Employees: 8

5900 **(HQ)Hawaiian Host**
500 Alakawa St Rm 111
Honolulu, HI 96817 808-848-0500
Fax: 808-845-7466 888-529-4678
info@hawaiianhost.com www.hawaiianhost.com
Created the chocolate covered Macadamia nut, premium chocolates, specialty chocolates, gift baskets, tea, cofee and cookies
President/CEO: Keith Sakamato
CEO: Dennis Teranishi
Vice President Sales: Tad Teraizumi
Estimated Sales: $20-50 Million
Number Employees: 100-249

5901 **Hawaiian Housewares**
P.O.Box 820
Aiea, HI 96701-0820 808-453-8000
Fax: 808-456-5043
Owner: Diana Allen
Estimated Sales: $ 50 - 100 Million
Number Employees: 50-99

5902 **Hawaiian Isles Kona Coffee Co**
2864 Mokumoa St
Honolulu, HI 96819 808-833-2244
Fax: 808-833-6328 www.hawaiianisles.com
Coffee
President: Sidney Boulware
Estimated Sales: $50-100 Million
Number Employees: 50-99

5903 **Hawaiian King Candies**
550 Paiea St # 501
Honolulu, HI 96819-1837 808-833-0041
Fax: 808-839-7141 800-570-1902
dniiro@lava.net
Manufacturer of Foil-Bagged Macadamia Nuts, Macadamia Nut Chocolates, Macadamia Nut Cookies
President: David Niiro
Estimated Sales: $10-24.9 Million
Number Employees: 50-99
Type of Packaging: Consumer, Food Service, Private Label
Brands:
AMERICA
ENJOYING LAS VEGAS
ENJOYING SAN FRANCISCO
FAVORITES OF HAWAII
HAWAIIAN DELIGHT
HAWAIIAN JOYS
HAWAIIAN KING
HAWAIIAN MAJESTY
NEW YORK CLUB
PASSPORT
SAN FRANCISCO BAY TRADERS
THAT'S HOLLYWOOD
USA

5904 **Hawaiian Natural Water Company**
98-746 Kuahao Pl Ste F
Pearl City, HI 96782 808-483-0520
Fax: 808-483-0536 hisprings@aol.com
www.hawaiianspring.com
Bottled spring water
President/CEO: Marcus Bender
CFO: Willard D Irwin
CFO: David Leaha
CEO: Tom Van Dixhorn
Executive VP Marketing: Ray Riss
Operations Manager: Tony Persson
Number Employees: 5-9
Type of Packaging: Private Label
Brands:
Hawaiian Natural Water

5905 **Hawaiian Salrose Teas**
500 Alakawa St # 111
Honolulu, HI 96817-4576 808-848-0500
Fax: 808-845-7466 www.hawaiianhost.com
Chocolate candies
President: Dick Hollier
CEO: Dennis Teranishi
Public Relations: Harvey Hahn
Estimated Sales: $20-50 Million
Number Employees: 100-249

5906 **Hawaiian Sun Products**
259 Sand Island Access Rd
Honolulu, HI 96819 808-845-3211
Fax: 808-842-0532 mailorder@hawnsun.com
www.hawaiiansunproducts.com
Processes and cans tropical fruit juices; manufactures macadamia nut candy
President: Burt K Okura
Estimated Sales: $20-50 Million
Number Employees: 50-99
Brands:
Hawaiian Sun
Pokka

5907 **Hawk Pacific Freight**
PO Box 4080
Napa, CA 94558-0407 707-259-0266
Fax: 707-259-0120
General Manager: Patrick Minehan
Estimated Sales: Under $500,000
Number Employees: 20-49

5908 **(HQ)Hawkhaven Greenhouse International**
W9554 Blackhawk Ct.
Wautoma, WI 54982 920-540-3536
Fax: 920-787-4295 800-745-4295
verdegrass@gmail.com www.hawkhaven.com
Processor of certified organic fresh cut wheat grass and fresh frozen organic wheat grass juice; exporter of fresh-frozen certified organic wheat grass and juice
President/Owner: Timothy Paegelow
Estimated Sales: Under $300,000
Number Employees: 1-4
Sq. footage: 5000
Type of Packaging: Consumer
Brands:
Grower's Pack
Hawkhaven
Verdegrass

5909 **Hawkins Farms**
PO Box 1
Pennfield, NB E5H 2M1
Canada 506-755-6241
Fax: 506-755-6241

5910 **Hawkins Inc**
3100 E Hennepin Ave
Minneapolis, MN 55413 612-617-8572
Fax: 612-331-5304 800-328-5460
fritz.wagner@hawkinsinc.com
www.hawkinsinc.com
Food ingredients; including phosphates, sodium lactate and custom blends
President: Patrick Hawkins
VP Operations: Mark Beyer
Estimated Sales: $297 Million
Number Employees: 120

5911 **Hawthorne Valley Farm**
327 County Route 21c
Ghent, NY 12075 518-672-5808
Fax: 518-672-4887 www.vspcamp.com
400 acre biodynamic® farm
Executive Director: Nick Franceschelli
Farm Tours: Rachel Schneider
Estimated Sales: $2.5-5 Million
Number Employees: 10-19
Type of Packaging: Private Label
Brands:
Hawthorne Valley Farm

5912 **Hayashibara Intl. Inc.**
390 Interlocken Cres Ste 680
Broomfield, CO 80021 303-650-4590
Fax: 303-650-9860
ahashino@hayashibara-intl.com
www.hayashibara-intl.com
Carbohydrate-based ingredients; including specialty sugars
Director- North America: Tomonari Mozumi
VP: Alan Richards
Sales: Akihiro Hashino
Number Employees: 10
Type of Packaging: Bulk

5913 **Haydel's Bakery**
4037 Jefferson Hwy
Jefferson, LA 70121 504-837-0190
Fax: 504-837-5512 800-442-1342
www.haydelbakery.com
Mardi Gras cakes, other gourmet cakes and pastries
Owner: David Haydel
Estimated Sales: $1-2.5 Million
Number Employees: 20-49

5914 **Haydenergy Health**
200 W 58th St Apt 1b
New York, NY 10019-1478
Fax: 212-246-9344 800-255-1660
www.naura.com
Processor of health food products including vitamins and energy shakes
President: Naura Hayden
Vice President: Nancy Leonard
Estimated Sales: $2.5-5 Million
Number Employees: 1-4
Number of Brands: 1
Number of Products: 3
Sq. footage: 4000
Type of Packaging: Consumer
Brands:
DYNAMITE ENERGY SHAKE
DYNAMITE VITES

5915 **Haypress Gourmet Pasta**
7f Hoover Avenue
Haverstraw, NY 10927-1024 845-947-4580
Fax: 845-947-2147
Pasta
General Manager: Nicholas DiNapoli
Estimated Sales: $5-10 Million
Number Employees: 5-9

5916 **Hazel Creek Orchards**
227 Smiling Apple Dr
Mt Airy, GA 30563-2714 706-754-4899
Fax: 706-754-1524
Processor of apples and apple juice; also, cider including apple, cherry, peach, raspberry and blueberry
Owner: Horace Yearwood
Estimated Sales: $1-2.5 Million
Number Employees: 1-4
Sq. footage: 8400
Type of Packaging: Consumer, Bulk
Brands:
Hazel Creek

5917 **Hazelnut Growers of Oregon**
401 N 26th Ave
Cornelius, OR 97113-8510 503-648-4176
Fax: 503-648-9515 nutsales@hazelnut.com
www.hazelnut.com
Processor, roaster and exporter of hazelnuts
Chairman: Jeff Koenig
President: Compton Lansdale
CFO: Osmond Hyde
Quality Control: Don Marshall
VP Marketing: Troy Johnson
Sales Director: Bob Hoffman
VP Operations: Dick Vanderschuere
Plant Manager: Ken Guinn
Purchasing Manager: Mike Sook
Estimated Sales: $32 Million
Number Employees: 60
Type of Packaging: Consumer, Bulk
Brands:
Oregan Orchard

5918 **Hazelwood Farms Bakery**
155 Balta Dr
Rochester, NY 14623-3142 585-424-1240
Fax: 585-424-1286 www.pillsbury.com
Processor of frozen pies
President: Peter Statt
Plant Manager: Rich Sychterz
Estimated Sales: $ 20 - 50 Million
Number Employees: 50-99
Parent Co: Pillsbury Company
Type of Packaging: Consumer, Food Service

5919 **(HQ)Hazle Park Packing Co**
260 Washington Ave
West Hazleton, PA 18202 570-455-7571
Fax: 570-455-6030 800-238-4331
www.hazlepark.com
hot dogs, hams, cooked salami, bologna, kielbasa, olive loaf, sausages, smoked pork loins and more.
CEO: Gary Kreisel
Estimated Sales: $6 Million
Number Employees: 40
Sq. footage: 30000
Type of Packaging: Consumer, Food Service, Private Label, Bulk
Brands:
HAZLE

5920 **Hazlitt's 1852 Vineyard**
P.O.Box 53
Hector, NY 14841-0053 607-546-9463
Fax: 607-546-5712 888-750-0494
info@hazlitt1852.com www.hazlitt1852.com
Producers of red and white wines.
VP: D Hazlitt
Estimated Sales: $5-10 Million
Number Employees: 10-19
Number of Brands: 2
Brands:
HAZLITT

5921 **Hazy Grove Nuts**
PO Box 2354
Lake Oswego, OR 97035-0601 503-670-8344
Fax: 503-968-2111 800-574-6887
lobbok7@gte.net www.hazygrove.com
Processors of hazelnuts.
President: Karen Lobb
Number Employees: 1-4
Type of Packaging: Private Label

5922 **Head Country Food Products**
P.O.Box 2324
Ponca City, OK 74602 580-762-1227
Fax: 580-765-8867 888-762-1227
chead@poncacity.net www.headcountry.com
Manufacturer of BBQ sauces, seasonings and salsas
President: Danny Head
Marketing: Carey Head
Estimated Sales: $5-10 Million
Number Employees: 10-19
Number of Brands: 1
Number of Products: 6
Type of Packaging: Consumer, Food Service, Private Label, Bulk
Brands:
HEAD COUNTRY

5923 **Healing Light**
PO Box 613
Germantown, NY 12526 518-537-7000
Fax: 518-537-8003 877-307-4372
info@thehealinglight.com
www.thehealinglight.com

5924 **Health & Nutrition Systems International**
6615 Boyntn Bch Blvd # 117
Boynton Beach, FL 33437-3526 561-433-0733
Fax: 888-478-8467 info@hnsglobal.com
www.hnsglobal.com
Designed to help you with your individual diet goals, whether that is to lose weight or stop gaining. Our products include Original Carb Cutter, Carb Cutter Phase 2, Carb Cuttler A&B, Fat Cutter and Eat Less -
President: Christopher Tisi
Controller: Al Dugan
Marketing Director: Steven Sarafian
Marketing Assistant: Lindsay Garveyff
Product Development/Sales: Jamie Heithoff
Human Resources/Director Operations: Mona Lalia
Graphic Design: Derek Lopez
Graphic Design: Cathy Card
Shipping/Receiving: Tonya Davis
Number Employees: 10-19

5925 **Health Concerns**
8001 Capwell Dr
Oakland, CA 94621 510-639-0280
Fax: 510-639-9140 800-233-9355
info@healthconcerns.com
www.healthconcerns.com
Processor and exporter of Chinese herbs, medicinal mushrooms and energy tonics.
President: Andrew Gaeddert
Estimated Sales: $3-5 Million
Number Employees: 5-9
Sq. footage: 6000
Type of Packaging: Consumer
Brands:
HEALTH CONCERNS

5926 **Health Plus**
13837 Magnolia Ave
Chino, CA 91710 909-627-9393
Fax: 909-591-7659 800-822-6225
www.healthplusinc.com
Importer and exporter of psyllium and nutritional herbs, tablets and capsules.
President: Rita Mediratta
Estimated Sales: $1-2.5 Million
Number Employees: 20-49
Sq. footage: 17000
Type of Packaging: Bulk
Brands:
ADRENAL CLEANSE
ASTAZANTHIN
AZ-ONE
BLOOD CLEANSE
BRAIN VITA
COLON CLEANSE
ENER JET
FIREBALL FAT BURNER
HEART CLEANSE
JOINT CLEANSE
KIDNEY CLEANSE
LIVER CLEANSE
ORA-PLUS
PAT'S PSYLLIUM SLIM
PROSTATE CLEANSE
SHELLY'S HAIR CARE
SUPER FAT BURNER

5927 **Health Products Corporation**
1060 Nepperhan Ave
Yonkers, NY 10703 914-423-2900
Fax: 914-963-6001 zurion2@aol.com
www.hpc7.com
Importer and exporter of psyllium and nutritional herbs, tablets and capsules; contract packager of blending and filling powders
President: J Lewin
Vice President: K Linnington
Estimated Sales: $ 50 - 100 Million
Number Employees: 50-99
Sq. footage: 45000
Parent Co: Health Products Corporation
Brands:
Aspi-Cor
Khg-7
Lactalins
Malpotane
Tick Stop

5928 **Health Valley Company**
16100 Foothill Boulevard
Irwindale, CA 91706 626-334-3241
Fax: 626-334-0220 800-334-3204
Processor and exporter of natural foods including cookies, cereal bars, tarts, crackers, granola bars, cereals, chilis, soups, snacks, corn puffs and canned vegetarian entrees
President: Ben Brecher
CFO/Sr VP: Diane Beardsley
Number Employees: 250-499
Parent Co: Intrepid Food Holdings
Type of Packaging: Consumer, Food Service, Private Label, Bulk
Brands:
Health Valley

5929 **Health from the Sun/ArkoPharma**
1 Clock Tower
Suite 100
Maynard, MA 01754 781-276-0505
Fax: 781-276-7335 800-447-2229
mkradjian@nutracorp.com
www.healthfromthesun.com
Brands:
LEAN FOR LESS

5930 **Health is Wealth Foods**
217 Prosser Ave
Williamstown, NJ 08094-8600 856-728-1998
Fax: 856-629-0378
customerservice@healthiswealthfoods.com
www.healthiswealthfoods.com
Processor of boxed, frozen and all natural egg rolls, spring rolls, appetizers, beef and chicken hot dogs, pot stickers and chicken including grilled cutlets, nuggets, patties and tenders. Also vegeterian and vegan items.
President: Val Vasilief
Vice President: Jerry Colt
Estimated Sales: $ 5 - 10 Million
Number Employees: 5-9
Sq. footage: 10000
Type of Packaging: Food Service, Private Label
Brands:
HEALTH IS WEALTH

5931 **Health-Tech**
950 Third Avenue
New York, NY 10022 212-755-9300
Fax: 212-755-9305 877-673-9777
customercare@sweetbreath.com
www.sweetbreath.com
Breath fresheners, energy strips, vitamin strips and cough and cold strips instant energy for your body and mind
Founder/President: Jeffrey Hirschman
National Account Manager: David Hirschman
Vice President Marketing: Roger Mascall
Brands:
ICE CHEWS
ICE CHIPS
ICE CHUNKS
SWEET BREATH XTREME INTENSE BREATH

5932 **HealthBest**
133 Mata Way # 101
San Marcos, CA 92069-2937 760-752-5230
Fax: 760-752-1322 www.globalkaizen.com
Processor, importer and exporter of natural and organic beans, dried fruits, snack foods, grains, herbs, spices, seasonings, nuts, seeds, bee pollen, pasta, sugar-free candy, etc
President: Jamie Hickerson
President: Laurence Hickerson
Estimated Sales: $3 Million
Number Employees: 20-49
Number of Brands: 2
Number of Products: 300
Sq. footage: 40000
Parent Co: Nature's Best
Type of Packaging: Consumer, Private Label, Bulk
Brands:
Healthbest

5933 **Healthco Canada Enterprises**
PO Box 8249
Victoria, BC V8W 3R9
Canada 250-382-8384
Fax: 250-868-2195 877-468-2875
jb-rebar@shaw.ca www.healthcocanada.com
Manufactures organic nutrition bars.

5934 **Healthmate Products**
1510 Old Deerfield Rd Ste 103
Highland Park, IL 60035 847-579-1051
Fax: 847-579-1059 800-584-8642
tburke@healthmateproducts.com
www.healthmateproducts.com
VP: Tim Burke
Estimated Sales: $1 Million
Number Employees: 1-4
Type of Packaging: Consumer, Food Service

5935 **Healthwave**
PO Box 4614
Santa Barbara, CA 93140-4614 805-899-4240
Fax: 805-899-1113 info@aromapatches.com
www.aromapatches.com
President/CEO: Art Williams

5936 **Healthy Beverage**
329B S Main Street
Doylestown, PA 18901 215-321-8330
Fax: 215-321-8335 800-295-1388
info@steaz.com www.steaz.com
Manufacturer of green tea, iced tea, energy drinks, energy shots and zero calorie iced and green teas.
Owner: Eric Schnell
VP Marketing: Lee Brody
COO: Jim Depietro
Estimated Sales: $1-2.5 Million
Number Employees: 5-9

5937 **Healthy Grain Foods**
4125 Yorkshire Ln
Northbrook, IL 60062 847-272-5576
Fax: 847-272-5576 www.healthygrainfoods.com
Research and development of frozen food products. Cereal breakfast foods.
President: Harold Zukerman
Estimated Sales: $1-2.5 Million
Number Employees: 5-9

5938 **Healthy Oven**
62 Grand Street
Croton on Hudson, NY 10520-2519 914-271-5458
Fax: 914-271-9279 healthyovn@aol.com
www.low-fat.com
President: Sarah Phillips
Estimated Sales: Under $500,000
Number Employees: 1-4
Brands:
Healthy Oven

5939 **Healthy Times**
14861 Pomerado Rd
Suite 104
Poway, CA 92064 858-513-1550
Fax: 858-513-1533 htbaby@healthytimes.com
www.healthytimes.com
President: Rondi K Prescott
Estimated Sales: $5-10 Million appx.
Number Employees: 5-9

5940 **Healthy'N Fit Nutritionals**
435 Yorktown Rd
Croton on Hudson, NY 10520-3703 914-271-6040
Fax: 914-271-6042 800-338-5200
healthynfit@aol.com www.behealthynfit.com
Processor of vitamins, minerals and food supplements; importer of herbs, nutraceuticals, ascorbic acid and nutritional raw materials; exporter of food and dietary supplements
President: Robert J Sepe
VP/CFO: Irene Sepe
Public Relations: Denise O'Neill
Estimated Sales: $7 Million appx.
Number Employees: 10-19
Number of Products: 1000
Sq. footage: 40000
Type of Packaging: Consumer, Food Service, Private Label, Bulk
Brands:
DOCTOR'S NUTRICEUTICALS
HEALTHY'N FIT NUTRITIONALS

5941 **Heart Foods Company**
2235 E 38th St
Minneapolis, MN 55407 612-724-5266
Fax: 612-724-5516 800-229-3663
www.heartfoods.com

Processor of encapsulated herbal and high potency cayenne formulas.
Estimated Sales: $1-2.5 Million
Number Employees: 1-4
Number of Brands: 1
Number of Products: 13
Sq. footage: 2500
Type of Packaging: Consumer

5942 **Heart to Heart Foods**
P.O.Box 6096
Logan, UT 84341-6096 435-753-9602
Fax: 435-753-9605
Ice cream products
Owner: Craig Earl
Estimated Sales: $2.5-5 Million
Number Employees: 10-19

5943 **Hearthstone Whole GrainBakery**
4717 Meadow Lane
Bozeman, MT 59715-9631 406-586-1227
Fax: 406-586-1227 800-757-7919
Bakery
President: Gwen Phillips
Manager: Mavis Mason

5944 **Heartland Brewery**
35 Union Sq W Frnt 1
New York, NY 10003 212-645-3400
Fax: 212-645-8306 www.heartlandbrewery.com
Processor of ale, beer and lager
President: John Bloostein
CEO: John Bloostein
Marketing Director: Bonnie Bernier
Estimated Sales: $2.5-5 Million
Number Employees: 50-99
Type of Packaging: Consumer, Food Service
Brands:
Heartland

5945 **Heartland Farms**
1241 N Wells Street
Fort Wayne, IN 46808-2791 888-757-7423
Fax: 888-757-7423 888-747-7423
mail@spiceintel.com www.spiceintel.com
Bread mixes, mesquite and barbecue sauces, and smoke powder

5946 **Heartland Fields**
4401 Westown Pkwy Ste 225
West Des Moines, IA 50266 515-225-1166
Fax: 515-225-1177 www.heartlandfields.com
Manufacturers of prepared soy meals and snacks.
Owner: John Schillinger
Estimated Sales: $ 5 - 10 Million
Number Employees: 5-9
Type of Packaging: Consumer

5947 **Heartland Fields, Llc**
4401 Westown Pkwy Ste 225
West Des Moines, IA 50266 515-225-1166
Fax: 515-225-1177 866-769-7200
heartland@heartlandfields.com
www.heartlandfields.com
Manufacturer and exporter of soybeans
President/Founder/CEO: John Schillinger PhD
Marketing/Sales Director: Karen Labenz
Estimated Sales: $10-20 Million
Number Employees: 100-249
Parent Co: Monsanto
Type of Packaging: Consumer, Bulk
Brands:
DEKALB

5948 **Heartland Flax**
PO Box 777
Valley City, ND 58072
Fax: 701-845-2276 866-599-3529
info@rcmflax.com www.rcmflax.com
Manufacturer of flax ingredients

5949 **Heartland Food Products**
1900 W 47th Pl Ste 302
Mission, KS 66205 913-831-4446
Fax: 913-831-4004
patkearney@heartlandfoodproducts.com
www.heartlandfoodproducts.com
Processor and wholesaler/distributor of waffle and pancake mixes for the institutional food market
President: Bill Steeb
Founder: Mary Steeb
Estimated Sales: Less than $500,000
Number Employees: 10-19
Type of Packaging: Bulk
Brands:
Bascoms Paprika
Bascoms Tapioca

5950 **Heartland Gourmet LLC**
1700 Cushman Dr
Lincoln, NE 68512-1238 402-423-1234
Fax: 402-423-4586 800-222-3276
susan.heartlandgourmet@gmail.com
www.heartlandgourmet.com
Processor and exporter of organic grain mixes
President: Susan Zink
Marketing: Mark Zink
Estimated Sales: $2.3 Million
Number Employees: 20-49
Brands:
Wanda's

5951 **Heartland Gourmet Popcorn**
131 Martin Lane
Elk Grove Village, IL 60007-1309 847-593-6471
Fax: 262-743-1848 866-945-5346
customerservice@heartlandpopcorn.com
www.heartlandpopcorn.com
Packaged gourmet popcorn kernels, packaged organic popcorn kernels, all natural seasonings, canola oil and sea salt, private label popcorn poppers and caramelized popcorn bags
President: Gary Petersen
VP: Brent Petersen
Estimated Sales: $1-2 Million
Number Employees: 9
Number of Brands: 2
Number of Products: 19
Sq. footage: 10000
Parent Co: Leasetronix
Type of Packaging: Consumer, Food Service
Other Locations:
Heartland Gourmet Popcorn
Elkhorn WI
Brands:
HEARTLAND FARMS
HEARTLAND GOURMET

5952 **Heartland Gourmet Popcorn**
1760 Cottage Dr
Lake Geneva, WI 53147-4851
Fax: 262-743-1848 866-489-4676
customerservice@heartlandpopcorn.com
http://www.heartlandpopcorn.com
Packaged gourmet popcorn kernels, packaged organic popcorn kernels, all natural seasonings, canola oil and sea salt; private label popcorn poppers and caramelized popcorn bags.
Founder/President: Gary Petersen
Vice President: Brent Petersen
Estimated Sales: $1-2 Million
Number Employees: 5-9
Number of Brands: 2
Number of Products: 19
Sq. footage: 10000
Parent Co: Leusetronix
Type of Packaging: Consumer, Private Label
Other Locations:
Heartland Gourmet Popcorn
Elkhorn WI

5953 **Heartland Mill**
124 N. Hwy 167
Marienthal, KS 67863 620-379-4472
Fax: 620-379-4459 info@heartlandmill.com
www.heartlandmill.com
Manufacturer of organic flours, grains and flakes
President: Larry Decker
Vice President: Mark Nightengale
Estimated Sales: $3.7 Million
Number Employees: 20-49
Type of Packaging: Bulk

5954 **Heartland Mill**
Rt 1 Box 2
Marienthal, KS 67863 620-379-4472
Fax: 620-379-4459 800-232-8533
info@heartlandmill.com www.heartlandmill.com
Grower, marketer, processor, importer and exporter of organic grains, flour, oat products and sunflower seeds. Organic and Kosher certified.
President: Larry Decker
VP: Mark Nightengale
Sales Executive: Carl Rosenlund
Estimated Sales: $3.7 Million
Number Employees: 29
Sq. footage: 14000
Type of Packaging: Food Service, Private Label, Bulk
Brands:
HEARTLAND MILL

5955 **Heartland Vineyards**
24945 Detroit Rd # G
Cleveland, OH 44145-2554 440-871-0701
jwdover@aol.com
www.heartlandvineyards.com
Wines
Owner: Jerome M Welliver
Estimated Sales: $500-1 Million appx.
Number Employees: 1-4

5956 **Heartline Foods**
830 Post Road E
Westport, CT 06880-5222 203-222-0381
Fax: 203-226-6445
Processor of paprika, beans, noodles, sauces, seasonings, pasta, soups and tapiocas.
Estimated Sales: $ .5 - 1 million
Number Employees: 1-4
Brands:
CHINA BOWL
DINNY ROBB
SINATRA
WYE RIVER

5957 **Heaven Hill Distilleries**
1064 Loretto Rd
Bardstown, KY 40004 502-348-3921
Fax: 502-348-0162 www.heaven-hill.com
Manufacturer and distiller of spirits including bourbon, brandy, gin, whiskey, vodka, liqueurs and rum.
President: Max Shapira
Director Marketing: Kate Latts
Corporate Communications Manager: Josh Hafer
Master Distiller: Parker Beam
Master Distiller: Craig Beam
Estimated Sales: $100+ Million
Number Employees: 250-499
Type of Packaging: Consumer, Private Label, Bulk
Brands:
ANSAC COGNAC
ARANDAS
BURNETT'S CITRUS VODKA
BURNETT'S GIN
BURNETT'S ORANGE VODKA
BURNETT'S RASPBERRY VODKA
BURNETT'S VANILLA VODKA
BURNETT'S VODKA
CHRISTIAN BROTHERS
CLUNY
COPA DE ORO
CORONET VSQ BRANDY
DU BOUCHETT
DUBONNET
EL CONQUISTADOR
ELIJAH CRAIG
EVAN WILLIAMS
EVAN WILLIAMS EGG NOG
FIGHTING COCK
GLEN SALEN
HENRY MCKENNA
HPNOTIQ
ISLE OF JURA
KILBEGGAN
LAZZARONI
O'MARA'S IRISH COUNTRY CREAM
OLD FITZGERALD
RON LLAVE
TWO FINGERS
TYRCONNELL
WHALER'S

5958 **Heaven Scent Natural Foods**
2516 California Ave
Santa Monica, CA 90403 310-829-9050
Fax: 310-829-6745 info@heavenscent-foods.com
www.heavenscent.com
Processor of croutons, breadcrumbs, breadsticks and cookies including seasonal, butter, natural, wheat-free, fat-free and special dietary baked without refined sugar; also, gingerbread houses and cookies. We also do private label
President: Tom Mosk
Estimated Sales: $2 Million approx.
Number Employees: 1-4
Sq. footage: 40000
Type of Packaging: Private Label
Brands:
HEAVEN SCENT WINDMILL COOKIES
Heaven Scent
Heaven Scent Butter Cookies
Heaven Scent Croutons

Heaven Scent Fat Free Cookies
Heaven Scent Natural Foods

5959 **Heavenly Hemp Foods**
PO Box 1794
Nederland, CO 80466-1794 303-938-0195
Fax: 303-443-1869 888-328-4367
bhc@hempfoods.com www.hempfoods.com
Health foods
President: David Almquist
Marketing Director: Tom White
Operations Manager: Kathleen Chippi
Number Employees: 1
Brands:
Heavenly Hemp Blue Tortillas
Heavenly Hemp Garlic
Heavenly Hemp Spicy

5960 **Heavenscent Edibles**
402 E 90th Street
New York, NY 10128-5119 212-369-0310
Fax: 212-369-0310
Brownies and holiday cookies

5961 **Hebert Candies**
575 Hartford Tpke
Shrewsbury, MA 1545 508-845-8051
Fax: 508-842-3065 866-432-3781
www.hebertcandies.com
Processor of Kosher chocolate candies and confectionery products
CEO: Tom O'Rourke
CFO: Jeff Goodman
CEO: Tom O'Rourke
Purchasing Manager: Bob Kerekon
Estimated Sales: $10-20 Million
Number Employees: 50-99
Sq. footage: 50000
Type of Packaging: Consumer

5962 **Heck Cellars**
15401 Bear Mountain Winery Rd
Arvin, CA 93203 661-854-6120
Fax: 661-854-2876
Processor and exporter of table wine, wine coolers and brandy; also, juices and bottled water
Owner: Gary Heck
Plant Manager: Tim Holt
Estimated Sales: $10-20 Million
Number Employees: 20-49
Sq. footage: 600000
Parent Co: F. Korbel & Brothers
Type of Packaging: Private Label, Bulk

5963 **Hecker Pass Winery**
4605 Hecker Pass Rd
Gilroy, CA 95020 408-842-8755
Fax: 408-842-9799 carlo@heckerpasswinery.com
www.heckerpasswinery.com
Wines
Owner/President: Mario Fortino
VP/Operations/Marketing: Carlo Fortino
Owner: Frances Fortino
Estimated Sales: $500,000-$1 Million
Number Employees: 1-4
Type of Packaging: Private Label
Brands:
Hecker Pass

5964 **Hedgehaven Specialty Foods**
P.O.Box 719
Ilwaco, WA 98624 360-642-4700
Fax: 360-642-3014 inforequest@hedgehaven.com
www.hedgehaven.com
Manufacturer of cookies, shortbread and bakery goods.
President: Linda Hedge
Estimated Sales: $5-9.9 Million
Number Employees: 5-9

5965 **Heffy's BBQ Company**
Kansas City, MO 66117 816-200-2271
Fax: 816-366-3920 mike.farag@heffys.com
www.heffys.com
BBQ sauce, grilling sauces, other sauces, seasonings and cooking enhancers, rubs, spices.
Marketing: Mike Farag

5966 **Hega Food Products**
6 Santa Fe Way
Cranbury, NJ 08512-3288 609-409-6200
Fax: 609-409-6500 800-345-7742
www.conagrafoods.com
President: Greg Heckman
Estimated Sales: $10-20 Million
Number Employees: 20-49
Brands:
Butterball
Crunch N Munch

5967 **Hegy's South Hills Vineyard & Winery**
PO Box 727
Twin Falls, ID 83303-0727 208-599-0074
Fax: 208-734-6369
Wines
Owner/Vineyard Manager: Frank Hegy
Estimated Sales: Under $500,000
Number Employees: 1-4
Brands:
South Hills

5968 **Heidi's Gourmet Desserts**
1651 Montreal Cir
Tucker, GA 30084 770-449-4900
Fax: 770-326-6157 800-241-4166
Processor and exporter of frozen custom desserts including cheesecakes, multi-layer tortes, brownies a la mode and special occasion cakes; also, cheesecake batter.
President: Larry Obertfell
Operations Director: Brian Schendider
Estimated Sales: $10-20 Million
Number Employees: 100-249
Sq. footage: 67000
Type of Packaging: Consumer, Food Service, Private Label
Other Locations:
Heidi's Gourmet
Atlanta GA
Heidi's Gourmet
Sun Valley CA
Heidi's Gourmet
Salt Lake City UT

5969 **Heineman's Winery**
P.O.Box 300
Put In Bay, OH 43456-0300 419-285-2811
Fax: 419-285-3412 info@HeinemansWinery.com
http://www.heinemanswinery.com/
Manufacturer of fruit juices and wine.
President/Winemaker: Ed Heineman
Vice President: Louis Heineman
Assistant Manager: Michael Bianichi
Estimated Sales: $500,000-$1 Million
Number Employees: 1-4
Parent Co: Heineman Beverage
Other Locations:
Heineman Distributing
Port Clinton OH
Brands:
CATAWBA GRAPE JUICE
HEINEMAN'S

5970 **Heinemann's Bakeries**
223 E Northwest Hwy
Palatine, IL 60067 847-358-3501
Fax: 773-523-7985 feedback@heinemanns.com
www.heinmanns.com
Manufacturer of cakes, cookies, Danish, brownies, muffins and breads.
President: Vincent Graham
CFO: Andrew Geryol
Sales: John Termine
Purchasing: Paul Krug
Estimated Sales: $25 Million
Number Employees: 250
Number of Brands: 1
Number of Products: 150
Type of Packaging: Consumer, Food Service, Private Label, Bulk
Brands:
HEINEMANN'S

5971 **Heiner's Bakery**
1300 Adams Ave
Huntington, WV 25702 304-523-8411
Fax: 304-525-9268 800-776-8411
www.heinersbakery.com
Processor of breads, rolls and buns.
Sales Manager: Greg Bryant
Plant Manager: Charles Heiner
Estimated Sales: $20-50 Million
Number Employees: 500
Sq. footage: 130000
Parent Co: Sara Lee Food & Beverage

5972 **Heini's Cheese Company**
6005 County Road 77
Millersburg, OH 44654 330-893-2131
Fax: 330-893-2079 800-253-6636
info@heinis.com www.heinis.com
Processor of yogurt cultured and natural cheeses
Owner/President: Peter Dauwalder
Marketing Director: Bob Walker
Finance/Sales Executive: Lisa Troyer
Plant Manager: Bob Troyer
Purchasing Manager: Mark Schlabach
Estimated Sales: $6.2 Million
Number Employees: 50
Sq. footage: 80000
Type of Packaging: Consumer, Bulk
Brands:
AMISH VALLEY FARMS
HEINI'S BRAND CHEESE

5973 **Heinke Industrial Park**
5365 Clark Rd
Paradise, CA 95969-6392 530-877-1059
Beef, beef products
President: David Heinke
Estimated Sales: $500,000-$1 Million
Number Employees: 2

5974 **Heinkel's Packing Company**
2005 N 22nd St
Decatur, IL 62526 217-428-4401
Fax: 217-428-4403 800-594-2738
Processor of smoked meats including ham, bacon, pork, turkey and smoked sausages; also, lunch meats and fresh sausage available; wholesaler/distributor of boxed beef and pork; serving the food service market. Venison processing
President: Miles Wright
CFO: Neal Wright
Vice President: Dennis Heinkel
Estimated Sales: $5-9.9 Million
Number Employees: 10-19
Type of Packaging: Consumer, Food Service, Bulk
Brands:
Heinkel's

5975 **Heino's German-Style Wholesale Bakery**
3951 Arnold Avenue
Naples, FL 34104-3358 941-643-3911
Baked goods
Estimated Sales: $5-10 Million
Number Employees: 5-9

5976 **Heintz & Weber Company**
150 Reading St
Buffalo, NY 14220 716-852-7171
Fax: 716-852-7173 info@webersmustard.com
www.webersmustard.com
Processor of condiments including horseradish, hot garlic and jalapeno mustard, dill pickle and hot green tomato piccalilli relish, and hot texan sandwich auce.
President: Steven Desmond
Executive VP: Suzanne Desmond
CEO: Steven Desmond
Estimated Sales: $5-10 Million
Number Employees: 5-9
Sq. footage: 24000
Type of Packaging: Consumer, Bulk
Brands:
Weber's Horseradish Mustard
Weber's Hot Garlic M
Weber's Hot Piocacic
Weber's Spicy Dill Pickles
Weber's Sweet Pickle

5977 **Heinz Company of Canada**
90 Shepherd Avenue East
Suite 400
North York, ON M2M 7K5
Canada 416-226-5757
Fax: 416-226-5064 877-574-3469
Processor and exporter of beans, ketchup, mustard, mayonnaise, relish, salad, salad dressing, olives, pickles, sandwich spreads, sauces, tomato products, tuna, vinegar, soups, stews, croutons, canned pasta and frozen entrees
President/Ceo: Peter Luik
Cfo: Bruna Gambino
Vice President: Steve Oakes
Number Employees: 100-249
Parent Co: H.J. Heinz Company
Type of Packaging: Consumer, Food Service, Private Label

Other Locations:
H.J. Heinz Co. of Canada Ltd.
Wheatley ON

5978 **Heinz Portion Control**
7325 Snider Rd
Mason, OH 45040-9193 513-398-0400
Fax: 513-459-5300 800-547-8924
sales@portionpac.com
www.heinzportioncontrol.com
Manufacturer and exporter of portion control sugar, pepper, salt, ketchup, mustard, sauces, dressings, jams, jellies, syrup, preserves, mayonnaise and artificial sweeteners
Managing Director: Arthur Jack III
General Manager, Finance: Susan Al
Executive: Glenn Corbin
GM Administration/Finance/MIS: Susan Al
GM Business Development/Marketing: Bob Ripp
National Sales Manager: Ralph Saltsgaver
General Manager, Operations: Michael Nolan
Estimated Sales: $356.20 Million
Number Employees: 1700
Sq. footage: 130000
Parent Co: H J Heinz USA
Type of Packaging: Food Service, Private Label
Other Locations:
Portion Pac
Stone Mountain GA
Brands:
CHATSWORTH
MADEIRA FARMS
PITCH'R PAK
SALSA DEL SOL
SQUEEZERS
SWEET PLEASERS GOURMET
SWEET PORTION
TASTE PLEASERS GOURMET

5979 **Heise's Wausau Farms**
2805 Valley View Rd
Wausau, WI 54403-8799 715-675-3584
Fax: 715-675-3256 800-764-1010
heisewausaufarms@yahoo.com
Processor and exporter of cultivated Wisconsin ginseng and bottled bee pollen capsules
President/Owner: Lyn Heise
Estimated Sales: $1-2 Million
Sq. footage: 4000
Brands:
Heise's
Jar-Lu

5980 **Heisler Food Enterprises**
5760 Broadway
A
Bronx, NY 10463-4143 718-543-0855
Fax: 718-543-2498
Kosher baked goods
President: Judith Heisler
Treasurer: Richard Heisler
Estimated Sales: $5-9.9 Million
Number Employees: 20-49

5981 **Heitz Wine Cellar**
500 Taplin Rd
Saint Helena, CA 94574 707-963-3542
Fax: 707-963-7454 www.heitzcellar.com
Processor and exporter of wine
President/COO: Kathleen Heitz Myers
Winemaker: David Heitz
COO: Kathleen Heitz-Myers
Estimated Sales: $5-10 Million
Number Employees: 10-19
Sq. footage: 6242
Type of Packaging: Consumer
Brands:
Heitz

5982 **Heitzman Bakery**
3800 Shepherdsville Rd
Louisville, KY 40218 502-452-1891
Fax: 502-452-6789 linda@heitzmanbakery.net
www.heitzmanbakery.net
Processor of donuts, cookies, brownies, desert cakes, custom decorated ckaes and wedding cakes. Also provides deli trays.
President: Paul Osting
Manager: Nancy Kasey
Estimated Sales: $500,000-$1 Million
Number Employees: 5-9
Type of Packaging: Consumer, Food Service
Brands:
Springerlies

5983 **Hela Spice Company**
119 Franklin St
Uxbridge, ON L9P 1N6 905-852-5100
Fax: 905-852-1113 877-435-2649
www.helacanada.com
Manufactures custom blends, spice mixtures and seasoning blends for the meat and bakery industry
President: Walter Knecht
Estimated Sales: $7 Million
Number Employees: 40

5984 **Helen Grace Chocolates**
3303 Mlk Jr Blvd
Lynwood, CA 90262 310-638-8400
Fax: 310-605-0704 800-367-4240
orders@helengrace.com www.helengrace.com
Chocolate candy
Partner: Robert Worth
Partner: David Worth
VP: Mike Harrigian
Estimated Sales: $5-10 Million
Number Employees: 20-49
Type of Packaging: Consumer
Brands:
Helen Grace

5985 **Helena View/Johnston Vineyard**
3500 Highway 128
Calistoga, CA 94515-9715 707-942-4956
Fax: 707-942-4956 info@helenaview.com
www.helenaview.com
Wines
VP: Charles Johnston
Manager Public Relations: Sarah Marie Johnston
VP Administration: Charles Johnston
Brands:
Helena View
Moon Mountain

5986 **Helens Pure Foods**
301 Ryers Ave
Cheltenham, PA 19012 215-379-6433
Vegetarian dips, salads and sandwiches
President: Richard Goldberg
Estimated Sales: $5-9.9 Million
Number Employees: 5-9

5987 **Hell on the Red**
13716 E Sm 273
Telephone, TX 75488 903-664-2573
Fax: 903-664-2301 hellonthered@gcsco.net
www.hellontheredinc.com
Pickled fruits and vegetables, vegetable sauces and seasonings, & salad dressings. Manufacturer of picante sauce hot mustard cheese dip and barbecue sauce
President: Thomas Baugh
Vice President: Patricia Baugh
Estimated Sales: $575,395
Number Employees: 8
Type of Packaging: Consumer, Private Label
Brands:
Hell on the Red

5988 **Heller Brothers PackingcCorporation**
288 9th Street
Winter Garden, FL 34787 407-656-2124
Fax: 407-656-1751 ptanner@hellerbros.com
www.hellerbros.com
Processor and exporter of citrus fruits including grapefruit, tangelos, tangerines and oranges
Owner/President: Harvey Heller
Owner/CEO: Harry Falk
General Manager: Billy Howard
VP Sales/Marketing: Rob Brath
Human Resources/Finance Executive: Jeff McKinney
VP/Operations Executive: Don Barwick
Estimated Sales: $3 Million
Number Employees: 56
Sq. footage: 500000
Type of Packaging: Consumer

5989 **(HQ)Heller Seasonings**
150 S Wacker Dr Ste 3200
Chicago, IL 60606 312-546-6800
Fax: 312-346-3140 800-323-2726
Seasonings
VP Finance: Allen Marshall
CEO: John Heller
President: Roger Maehler
VP Finance: Allen Marshall

Estimated Sales: $ 5 - 10 Million
Number Employees: 5-9

5990 **Hells Canyon Winery**
18835 Symms Rd
Caldwell, ID 83607 208-454-3300
800-318-7873
hellwine@yahoo.com
www.hellscanyonwinery.org
Wines
Owner: Steve Robertson
Vineyard Manager: Stephen Robertson
Estimated Sales: Less than $500,000
Number Employees: 1-4
Brands:
Hells Canyon

5991 **Helm New York**
1110 Centennial Avenue
Piscataway, NJ 08854 732-981-1160
Fax: 732-981-0965 info@helmnewyork.com
www.helmnewyork.com
Manufacturer of ingredients, additives and flavors
President: Philipp Mangold
CFO: Bill Van Fossen
Senior Vice President: Arun Manalkar
Number Employees: 20
Parent Co: Helm AG

5992 **Helms Candy Company**
P.O.Box 607
Bristol, VA 24203-0607 276-669-2612
Fax: 276-669-0150 www.helmscandy.com
Various candies and lollipops as well as pharmaceuticals such as cough drops and medicated lollipops
President: George Helms III
CEO: Helen Helms
VP Candy Division: Buzz Helms
VP Pharmaceutical Division: Mark Helms
Accounting Department: Deborah Smith
Estimated Sales: $5-10 Million
Number Employees: 10-19
Sq. footage: 65000
Brands:
Cool-E-Pops
Happy Day Pops
Helms
Hot-C-Pops
Hot-N-Coldpops
Mint Lumps
Mint Puffs
Thank You Pops
Virginia Beauty
Zippy Pop

5993 **Helmuth Country Bakery**
6706 W Mills Ave
Hutchinson, KS 67501 620-567-2301
Fax: 620-567-2036 800-567-6360
info@helmuthfoods.com
www.helmuthfoods.com
Processor of cookies, candies, noodles and cotton candy
Owner: Jim Rein
VP: Katie Helmuth
Estimated Sales: $1-4.9 Million
Number Employees: 5-9
Sq. footage: 3000
Type of Packaging: Consumer, Food Service
Brands:
Cortland Manor
Hatties
Helmuth

5994 **Helshiron Fisheries**
6 Old Factory Round Turn Road
Grand Manan, NB E5G 2J4
Canada 506-662-3111
Fax: 506-662-3786 lobfish@nbnet.nb.ca
Processor of salted cod, pollack and hake; also, fresh sea urchins, lobster and scallops
President: Ronald Benson
Marketing Director: Morton Benson
VP: Morton Benson
Estimated Sales: $1.5 Million
Number Employees: 9
Type of Packaging: Bulk
Brands:
Helshiron

5995 **Heluva Good Cheese**
P.O.Box 410
Sodus, NY 14551 315-483-6971
Fax: 315-483-9927 hgcl@heluvagood.com
www.heluvagood.com
Processor of naturally aged cheese, dips, horseradish, cocktail sauce, and mustard
Owner/President: Martin Margherio
Vice President: John Boylean
COO: Bob Fratangelo
Marketing Director: Neil Giudice
Sales Director: John Snedeker
Operations: Robert Fratangelo
Plant Manager: Steve De Mass
Purchasing Manager: Claudia Putman
Estimated Sales: $20-50 Million
Number Employees: 100-249
Sq. footage: 42000
Parent Co: Wessanen
Type of Packaging: Consumer, Food Service, Private Label, Bulk
Brands:
Heluva Good Cheese

5996 **Hemisphere Associated**
7 High St #200
Huntington, NY 11743-3417 631-673-3840
Fax: 631-673-3870
Processor, importer and exporter of apple, cherry, grape, cranberry and strawberry fruit juice concentrates; also, mustard oil and mustard oil blends
President: Dolores Mayoka
Estimated Sales: $870,000
Number Employees: 1-4
Sq. footage: 10000
Type of Packaging: Bulk

5997 **HempNut**
1286 Winter Solstice Avenue
Henderson, NV 89014-8869 707-576-7050
Fax: 707-579-0940 steve@thehempnut.com
www.thehempnut.com
Tastes like sunflower seeds, looks like sesame seeds and can be used in any recipe. High-quality protein, most nutritious plant food available and very high in vitamins
Founder/President: Richard Rose

5998 **Hena Coffee**
660 Berriman St
Brooklyn, NY 11208-5304 718-272-8237
Fax: 718-272-8391 www.henacoffee.com
Manufacturer of iced coffee, iced tea mix and liquid concentrates.
President: Scott Tauber
Estimated Sales: $ 5 - 10 Million
Number Employees: 5-9
Type of Packaging: Food Service, Private Label

5999 **Henderson's Gardens**
Box 214
Berwyn, AB T0M 0E0
Canada 780-338-2128
Fax: 780-338-2128
Processor and packer of corn, cucumbers, potatoes, tomatoes, cabbage, peas, beans and peppers
President: Robert Henderson
Marketing Director: Robert Henderson
Manager: Bob Henderson
Manager: Bob Henderson
Number Employees: 5-9
Type of Packaging: Consumer, Food Service
Brands:
Pride of Peace Vegetables

6000 **Hendon & David**
PO Box 836
Millbrook, NY 12545-0836 845-677-9696
Fax: 845-677-9699 hendonco@aol.com
Macadamia nuts, cranberry grand marnier, exotic meat sauces, honeys, latin specialties, relishes, mustards
Owner: Helen Hendon
Brands:
Bushman's Best Mazavaroo
Clove Valley Farms
Hendon

6001 **Hendricks Apiaries**
4001 S Elati Street
Englewood, CO 80110-4555 303-789-3209
www.coloradosunshinehoney.com
Processor of specialty clover, alfalfa and knapweed honey
President: Paul Hendricks
Co-Owner: Linda Hendricks
Estimated Sales: Under $500,000
Number Employees: 1-4
Sq. footage: 3400
Type of Packaging: Consumer, Food Service, Private Label, Bulk
Brands:
Colorado Sunshine Honey

6002 **Henggeler Packing Company**
P.O.Box 313
Fruitland, ID 83619 208-452-4212
Fax: 208-452-5416
Processor, exporter and packer of apples, plums and prunes
President: Gerald Henggeler
Vice President: Anthony Henggeler
Estimated Sales: $4 Million
Number Employees: 12
Type of Packaging: Consumer, Bulk
Brands:
Fortress
Fruitland

6003 **Henkel Corporation**
5051 Estecreek Road
Cincinnati, OH 45232-1447 513-482-3000
Fax: 513-482-5513 800-543-7370
Processor and exporter of fatty acids and alcohol, glycerine, plasticizers, methyl esters and other chemicals
Sr Marketing Manager: Steve Kennedy
Marketing Manager: Jeff Mahaffey
Marketing Manager: Chris Scheider
Number Employees: 500-999
Parent Co: Henkel Corporation

6004 **Henkel Corporation**
5325 9th Ave
Countryside, IL 60525 708-579-1123
Fax: 708-579-6150 800-328-6199
holgerbecker@henkel-americas.com
Processor, importer and exporter of food ingredients including natural antioxidants, bread and baking additives and whipped topping concentrates
Manager Food Ingredients: Holger Becker
Estimated Sales: $2.5-5 Million
Number Employees: 20-49
Sq. footage: 10000
Parent Co: Henkel Corporation
Brands:
Covi-Ox
Delios
Lamegin
Lamequick
Nutrilife
Spongolit

6005 **Henning's Cheese**
20201 Ucker Point Creek Rd
Kiel, WI 53042-4299 920-894-3032
Fax: 920-894-3022 kay@henningscheese.com
www.henningcheese.com
Processor of cheese including cheddar, colby, colby jack and mozzarella
President: Kay Henning
Estimated Sales: $10-20 Million
Number Employees: 10-19
Type of Packaging: Consumer, Food Service, Private Label, Bulk
Brands:
Henning's

6006 **Henningsen Foods**
14334 Industrial Rd
Omaha, NE 68144 402-330-2500
Fax: 402-330-0875 dianet@henningsenfoods.com
www.henningsenfoods.com
Processor of dried meats and eggs, and contract dehydration
CFO: Gary Schaften
Vice President: Gary Lorimor
Research/Development: John Toney
Research/Development: Karen Moss
National Sales Manager: Mike McGuire
Sales/Marketing Associate: Sarah Hortz
Customer Service Coordinator: Diane Torpy
Estimated Sales: $5-10 Million
Number Employees: 500
Type of Packaging: Food Service, Private Label, Bulk

6007 **Henningsen Foods**
2700 Westchester Ave # 311
Purchase, NY 10577-2554 914-701-4020
Fax: 914-701-4050 www.henningsenfoods.com
Processor of cheese, eggs, poultry and dehydrated foods
Manager: Daves Splendour
Owner: Victor Henningsen Jr
CEO: Michael Cruger
Marketing Director: John Wankewicz
Manager: Earl Bals
Estimated Sales: $5-10 Million
Number Employees: 100-249
Parent Co: Henningsen Foods
Type of Packaging: Private Label, Bulk

6008 **Henningsen Foods**
2700 Westchester Ave # 311
Purchase, NY 10577-2554 914-701-4020
Fax: 914-701-4050 johnw@henningsenfoods.com
www.henningsenfoods.com
A manufacturer of frozen and dehydrated egg products for use in baking, mayonnaise, salad dressing, pasta and confectionary applications. Products include; egg whites, egg yolk, whole egg and egg blends. Henningsen also manufacturesdehydrated meat products for use in soups, side dishes, gravies and sauces. Meat products includes; chicken, turkey, beef, veal, pork and seafood. Custom manufacturing is also done for various protein and carbohydrate products
CEO: Michael Cruger
Vice President International Sales: Kit Henningsen
Sales Manager: Jamie Conetta
Vice President Operations: Mike Cruger
Estimated Sales: $50-100 Million
Number Employees: 100-249
Number of Products: 80
Type of Packaging: Bulk

6009 **Henry & Henry**
3765 Walden Ave
Lancaster, NY 14086 716-685-4000
Fax: 716-685-0160 800-828-7130
elarson@henryandhenry.com
www.henryandhenry.com
Bakery ingredients, soda fountain toppings and syrups
President: Richard Gahlin
Estimated Sales: $50-100 Million
Number Employees: 100-249

6010 **Henry Broch & Company/APK, Inc.**
704 Florsheim Dr
Libertyville, IL 60048-5002 847-816-6225
Fax: 847-816-6238 sales@hbroch.com
www.hbroch.com
An industrial food brokerage representing natural food ingredients processors around the world. Henry Broch & Company markets more than 400 products - and more than 1,000 varieties of those products —including spray-dried, dehydratedand freeze dried vegetables, fruit concentrates and purees, spice oleoresins, spices and air-dried herbs, IQF herbs and onions, and mint and other herb extracts.
President: Jim Antonetti
Marketing Director: Jim Kuzma
VP: Jim Kuzman
Sales: JoAnne Stefanick
Director: Greg Antonetti
Estimated Sales: $1-2.5 Million
Number Employees: 5-9
Brands:
Henry Broch

6011 **Henry Davis Company**
3405 W 15th Ave
Gary, IN 46404-1964 219-949-8555
Fax: 219-949-9764
President: Henry Davis
Estimated Sales: $ 1 - 3 Million
Number Employees: 20-49

6012 **Henry Estate Winery**
687 Hubbard Creek Rd
Umpqua, OR 97486 800-782-2686
Fax: 541-459-5146 800-782-2686
winery@henryestate.com www.henryestate.com

Wines: Pinot Noir, Chardonnay, Gewurztraminer and White Riesling
President/Owner: Calvin Scott Henry III
Export Sales: Doyle Hinman
Public Relations Manager: Syndi Henry Beavers
Winemaker/Operations Manager: Calvin Scott Henry IV
Estimated Sales: $5-10 Million
Number Employees: 10-19
Brands:
HENRY ESTATE

6013 **Henry H. Misner Ltd.**
469 Norfolk St. N
Simcoe, ON N3Y 3P8
Canada 519-426-5546
Fax: 519-583-1529 hhmfoods.com
Processor of frozen shellfish and groundfish
President: Donald Misner
CFO: Nancy Misner
Marketing Director: Donald Misner
General Manager: Donald Misner
Number Employees: 20-49
Type of Packaging: Consumer, Food Service

6014 **Henry Hill & Company**
5 Financial Plz
Napa, CA 94558-3082 707-224-6565
Fax: 707-257-2990 bhill@billhill.com
Wines
Partner: William Hill
Estimated Sales: $1.5 Million
Number Employees: 20-49
Brands:
Broken Rock Cellars

6015 **Henry J Meat Specialties**
4460 W Armitage Ave
Chicago, IL 60639-3574 773-227-5400
Fax: 773-227-0414 800-242-1314
www.henryjmeats.com
Processor of sliced pastrami and corned, roast and Italian beef
President/CEO: Forrest Krisco
Vice President: James Dragatsis
Estimated Sales: $ 5 - 10 Million
Number Employees: 10-19

6016 **Henry J's Hashtime**
4460 W Armitage Ave
Chicago, IL 60639-3574 773-227-5400
Fax: 773-227-0414 800-242-1313
www.henryjmeats.com
Prepared meats
President: Henry Juracic
Plant Manager: Forest Krisco
Estimated Sales: $5-10 Million
Number Employees: 10-19

6017 **Herb Bee's Products**
210 Mallard Drive
Colchester, VT 05446-7013 802-864-7387
sierrassong@aol.com
Jam, jelly, relish, quick breads, cheese spreads, and vinegars
Owner: Rhonda Tebeau

6018 **Herb Connection**
188 S Main St
Springville, UT 84663-1849 801-489-4254
Fax: 801-489-8341
www.drchristophersherbshop.com
Food supplements manufacturer, private label items, herbs and health foods
President: David Christopher
Vice President: Ruth Christopher Bacalla
Production Manager: James Webster
Purchasing Manager: Josh Bruni
Estimated Sales: $ 1 - 3 Million
Number Employees: 5-9
Sq. footage: 7500
Type of Packaging: Private Label

6019 **Herb Patch of Vermont**
30 Industrial Drive
Bellows Falls, VT 05101-3122 802-463-1400
Fax: 802-463-1911 800-282-4372
Manufacturer of all natural cocoas, dessert beverages, dips, teas and herb blends; exporter of cocoa
Owner: John Molsis
Estimated Sales: Less than $500,000
Number Employees: 1-4
Sq. footage: 6500
Brands:
Country Cow
Country Cow Cocoa
Cowpuccino Toppers

6020 **Herb Pharm**
P.O.Box 116
Williams, OR 97544 541-488-4595
Fax: 541-846-6112 800-348-4372
info@herb-pharm.com www.herb-pharm.com
Health supplements and personal care products
Founder/Co-Owner: Ed Smith
Co-Owner: Sara Katz
Number Employees: 50-99

6021 **Herb Society of America**
9019 Kirtland Chardon Rd
Willoughby, OH 44094 440-256-0514
Fax: 440-256-0541 herbs@herbsociety.org
www.herbsociety.org
Seasonings, spices
Executive Director: Katrinka Morgan
Administrative Assistant: Nancy Walczak
Office Administrator: Michelle Milks
Horticulturist: Robin Siktberg
Librarian: Michele Meyers
Estimated Sales: $500,000-$1 Million
Number Employees: 5-9
Type of Packaging: Private Label
Brands:
Herb Society of America

6022 **Herb Tea Company**
P.O.Box 1962
Oxnard, CA 93032-1962 805-486-6477
Fax: 805-385-3216
Tea
Religious Leader: Robert Cox
Sales Coordinator: Robert Lessin
Plant Manager: William Ashwell
Estimated Sales: $ 2.5-5 Million
Number Employees: 10-19
Type of Packaging: Consumer, Private Label

6023 **Herb's Specialty Foods**
112 Schoolhouse Road
Mount Holly, NJ 08060 609-267-0276
Fax: 609-261-1949 800-486-0276
email@kaptainsketch.com
www.kaptainsketch.com
Processor of frozen value-added poultry and seafood
President: Nash Cohen
Estimated Sales: $10-20 Million
Number Employees: 20-49
Type of Packaging: Consumer, Food Service, Private Label
Brands:
Herb's Five Star
Kaptain's Ketch
Westhampton Farms

6024 **HerbaSway Laboratories**
P.O.Box 6098
Wallingford, CT 06492-0089 203-269-6991
Fax: 203-269-9703 800-672-7322
herbs@herbasway.com www.herbasway.com
Manufacturer of liquid dietary health supplements
Owner: Franklin St John
Founder/Owner: Lorraine St. John
Estimated Sales: $ 10 - 20 Million
Number Employees: 20-49

6025 **Herbal Coffee International**
120 28th Avenue S
Jacksonville Beach, FL 32250-6014 904-259-6350
800-743-8774
coffeephd@aol.com www.herbalcoffee.com
Processor of herbal coffees
Number Employees: 5-9

6026 **Herbal Magic**
P.O.Box 70
Forest Knolls, CA 94933 415-488-9488
Fax: 415-488-1057 melren@aol.com
www.herbalmagic.com
Herbs for colds, flu, immune system, feminine needs, herbs for children, St. John's Wort, parasite kit and femopause
Founder/Master Herbalist: Renee Ponder
Estimated Sales: $300,000-500,000
Number Employees: 1-4

6027 **Herbal Products & Development**
P.O.Box 1084
Aptos, CA 95001 831-688-8706
info@centralcoastnutrition.com
www.centralcoastnutrition.com
Processor and exporter of high energy food concentrates, digestive enzymes,antioxidants, probiotics, tinctures, oils and liquid vitamins and minerals
President: Paul Gaylon
Number Employees: 1-4
Sq. footage: 1200
Type of Packaging: Consumer, Private Label
Brands:
Liquid Life Essential Day & Night
Liver Restore
Plant Power
Power Plus
Pro Plus
Supreme 7

6028 **Herbal Water**
PO Box 800
Narberth, PA 19072 610-668-4000
Fax: 610-642-4082 nerdosy@herbalwater.com
www.herbalwater.com
organic naturally enhanced flavored water.
President/Owner: Albert Cahana

6029 **Herbalist & Alchemist**
51 S Wandling Ave
Washington, NJ 07882-2192 908-689-9020
Fax: 908-689-9071 herbalist@nac.net
www.herbalist-alchemist.com
Herbal products: Osteo Herb Capsules, Throat Spray, Herbal Formulas, Alcohol Free Formulas, Tea Blends, Solid Extracts, Herbal Ointments, Astral Tea Remedies, Single Extracts, Chinese Bulk Herbs, Ceremonial Herbs, Herbal Oils, and 5LUNG RE-LEAF™Formulas.
President: David Winston
Estimated Sales: $ 1 - 3 Million
Number Employees: 10-19

6030 **Herbco International**
16661 W Snoqualmie River Rd NE
Duvall, WA 98019 425-788-7903
Fax: 425-844-9114 herbco@msn.com
www.herbco.net
Owner: Ted Andrews
Estimated Sales: $ 5 - 10 Million
Number Employees: 50-99

6031 **Herbs Seafood**
112 Schoolhouse Road
Mount Holly, NJ 08060-3774 609-267-0276
Fax: 609-261-1949 800-486-0276
Prepared fish and poultry
President: Nash Cohen
Owner: Nash Cohen
VP Sales: Gary Cannard
Sales Manager: Richard Applebam
Plant Manager: William Byrne
Estimated Sales: $10-20 Million
Number Employees: 2
Type of Packaging: Private Label
Brands:
Herbs Seafood

6032 **Herbs from China**
1601 S State Street
Chicago, IL 60616-1478 312-886-2066
Fax: 312-945-1111 866-823-4372
service@herbsfromchina.com
www.herbsfromchina.com
Chinese herbs
Cheif Executive Officer: Thomas Lowrance
CFO/Health Care Consultant: Cynthia Lowrance RN, BS, MBA
Nutritionist/Sport Medicine Consultant: James Hicks PhD, MD
Estimated Sales: $ 20 - 50 Million
Number Employees: 20-49

6033 **Herbs, Etc.**
1345 Cerrillos Rd
Santa Fe, NM 87505 505-982-1265
Fax: 505-984-9197 888-433-1212
retail@herbsetc.com www.herbsetc.com
Manufacturer of bulk herbs, herbal remedies, supplements and essential oils.
Manager: B Siebel
Estimated Sales: $ .5 - 1 million
Number Employees: 5-9

6034 **Herbs, Etc.**
1345 Cerrillos Rd
Santa Fe, NM 87505 505-982-1265
Fax: 505-984-9197 888-694-3727
www.herbsetc.com
Processor and exporter of liquid herbal extracts, and fast acting softgel herbal medicines.
Manager: B Siebel
Estimated Sales: $2.5-5 Million
Number Employees: 20-49
Sq. footage: 7000
Type of Packaging: Consumer
Brands:
Allertonic
Deep Chi Builder
Deep Sleep
Depiezac
Echinacea Triple Source
Herbs, Etc.
Kidalin
Lung Tonic
Lymphatonic
Singers Saving Grace

6035 **Heringer Meats**
16 W 7th St
Covington, KY 41011 859-291-2000
Fax: 859-291-0052 www.heringermeats.com
Processor of fresh and frozen meat including pork, beef, veal and lamb
President: Ray Niemeyer
Vice President: Robert Hoeweller
Estimated Sales: $2.3 Million
Number Employees: 11
Type of Packaging: Consumer, Food Service
Brands:
Kahns
Plue Grass
Sara Lee

6036 **Heritage Cheese House**
PO Box 376
Heuvelton, NY 13654-0376 315-344-2216
Fax: 315-344-2260
www.northcountrysidecybermall.com/heritage.htm
l
Producers of cheese, honey, bologna, cheese curd and maple syrup.
Estimated Sales: Less than $500,000
Number Employees: 1-4

6037 **Heritage Dairy Stores**
P.O.Box 158
Thorofare, NJ 8086
Fax: 856-845-8392 www.heritages.com
Milk, dairy products
President: Harold R Heritage
Number Employees: 500-999

6038 **Heritage Family Specialty Foods**
901 Santerre Dr
Grand Prairie, TX 75050 972-660-6511
Fax: 972-249-0028 800-648-2837
don.barnes@hfsfoods.com www.hfsfoods.com
Sauces, salsa, soups, salad dressings.
President: Daniel Brackeen
VP: Cheryl Brackeen
CFO: Cheryl Brackeen
Vice President: Johnny Lee Stanley
Marketing: Don Barnes
Production Manager: Fred Bertschi
Estimated Sales: $20-50 Million
Number Employees: 20-49
Type of Packaging: Food Service, Private Label
Brands:
Heritage Chipotle Roasted Salsa
Heritage Fresh Salsa
Heritage Garlic Mayo

6039 **Heritage Fancy Foods Marketing**
PO Box 18310
Erlanger, KY 41018-0310 859-282-3782
Fax: 859-282-3781
Gourmet foods
President: Robert Carl
Brands:
Heritage Fancy Foods

6040 **Heritage Farms Dairy**
1100 New Salem Rd
Murfreesboro, TN 37129 615-895-2790
Fax: 615-895-0570 www.kroger.com
Processor of fresh apple and orange juices; also, dairy products including cottage cheese, milk and yogurt
Manager: Bill Crabtree
General Manager: Bill McCarthy
General Manager: Robert Allard
Number Employees: 100-249
Parent Co: Kroger Company
Type of Packaging: Consumer, Private Label, Bulk
Brands:
Kroger

6041 **Heritage Foods**
14515 124th Avenue
Edmonton, AB T5L 3B2
Canada 780-454-7383
Fax: 780-454-2685 cheemo@cheemo.com
www.cheemo.com
Processor of frozen cabbage rolls and pierogies.
Type of Packaging: Consumer, Food Service, Private Label
Brands:
CHEEMO

6042 **Heritage Foods**
PO Box 630
Holicong, PA 18928-0630 215-244-0900
Fax: 215-244-6122
Gefilte fish

6043 **Heritage Northwest**
625 W 7th St
Juneau, AK 99801-1803 907-586-1088
Fax: 907-586-4446 info@heritagecoffee.com
www.heritagecoffee.com
Fair-trade, environmentally friendly coffees roasted to order.
Estimated Sales: $1-2.5 Million
Number Employees: 20-49
Brands:
BLACK WOLF BLEND
HERITAGE COFFEE

6044 **Heritage Salmon**
P.O.Box 263
Eastport, ME 04631 207-853-6081
Fax: 207-853-6056 www.heritagesalmon.com
Salmon
President: Glen Cooke
Marketing: Aian Craig
Number Employees: 100-249
Number of Products: 60
Brands:
Heritage Salmon

6045 **Heritage Salmon Company**
100-12051 Horseshoe Way
Richmond, BC V7A 4V4
Canada 604-277-3093
Fax: 604-275-8614 heritagesalmon.com
Processor and exporter of fresh Atlantic salmon
President: Ken Hirtle
CFO: Rob Reisen
Type of Packaging: Bulk

6046 **Heritage Shortbread**
35 Hunter Rd
Suite F
Hilton Head Island, SC 29926 843-342-7268
Fax: 888-744-6697 info@heritageshortbread.com
www.heritageshortbread.com
shortbread cookies
President/Owner: Thomas Cole

6047 **Heritage Store**
314 Laskin Rd
Virginia Beach, VA 23451-3020 757-428-0100
Fax: 757-428-3632 800-862-2923
heritage@caycecures.com www.caycecures.com
Processor and exporter of essential oils, health foods, food supplements, vitamins, herbal teas, massage oils, castor oil, oral care products, herbal tonics and supplements
Cfo: Jean Baviera
Marketing Director: David Riblet
Estimated Sales: $9 Million
Number Employees: 90
Sq. footage: 6000
Type of Packaging: Consumer, Private Label, Bulk

6048 **Heritage Tymes/Pancake House**
159 Dixon Road
3121
Spearsville, LA 71277-3547 806-765-8566
Fax: 806-765-8507
Processor and exporter of sweet potato pancake, muffin and waffle mixes
Co-Owner/President: Scott Johnson
Co-Owner/VP: Jane Johnson
Co-Owner/VP: Jason Johnson
Number Employees: 20-49
Sq. footage: 4000
Type of Packaging: Consumer, Food Service, Private Label, Bulk
Brands:
Jane's

6049 **Heritage Wine Cellars**
12162 E Main Rd
North East, PA 16428 814-725-8015
Fax: 814-725-8654 800-747-0083
bostwick@erie.net www.heritagewine.biz
Wine
VP: Matthew Bostwick
CEO: Robert Bostwick
President: Josh Bostwick
General Manager: Bob Bostwick
Estimated Sales: $2.5-5 Million
Number Employees: 5-9
Brands:
Heritage

6050 **Herkimer Foods**
P.O.Box 310
Herkimer, NY 13350 315-895-7832
Fax: 315-895-4664 herkimer@cnymail.com
www.herkimerfoods.com
Manufacturer of cheese, spreads, dips, fudge, nuts, gelatine and jello snacks
President/Director Marketing: Michael Basloe
Estimated Sales: $ 3 - 5 Million
Number Employees: 20-49
Type of Packaging: Consumer, Food Service, Private Label, Bulk
Brands:
HERKIMER
IDA MAE

6051 **Herkimer Foods**
P.O.Box 310
Herkimer, NY 13350 315-895-7832
Fax: 315-895-4664 www.herkimerfoods.com
Dairy foods
President: Michael Basloe
VP: Robert Basloe
Estimated Sales: $ 3 - 5 Million
Number Employees: 20-49

6052 **Herlocher Foods**
415 E Calder Way
State College, PA 16801 814-237-0134
Fax: 814-237-1893 800-437-5624
info@herlocherfoods.com
www.herlocherfoods.com
Processor of dipping mustard and salsa, including licensed Penn State novelty dipping mustard.
President: Neil Herlocher
Estimated Sales: $1-2.5 Million
Number Employees: 5-9
Brands:
HERLOCHER'S DIPPING MUSTARD

6053 **Herman Falter Packing Company**
384 Greenlawn Ave
Columbus, OH 43223 614-444-1141
Fax: 614-445-3915 800-325-6328
info@faltersmeats.com www.faltersmeats.com
Processor of meat
President: James Falter
General Sales Manager: Charles Honeycutt
Estimated Sales: $ 10 - 20 Million
Number Employees: 100

6054 **Herman's Bakery Coffee Shop**
130 Main St S
Cambridge, MN 55008-1621 763-689-1515
Fax: 763-689-9642
Bakery products
President: Herman Oestreich
Estimated Sales: $1-2.5 Million
Number Employees: 20-49

6055 **Hermann J. Wiemer Vineyard**
P.O.Box 38
Dundee, NY 14837-0038 607-243-7971
Fax: 607-243-7983 800-371-7971
wines@wiemer.com www.wiemer.com
Wines
Manager: Fred Merwarth
Estimated Sales: $5-10 Million
Number Employees: 10-19
Brands:
Hermann J. Wiemer

6056 **Hermann Laue Spice Company**
119 Franklin Street
Uxbridge, ON L9P 1J5
Canada 905-852-5100
Fax: 905-852-1113 hela@helacanada.com
www.helacanada.ca
Processor, importer and exporter of custom blended spices, sodium erythorbate, carrageenan, potassium sorbate, ascorbic acid and sodium ascorbate for the meat and poultry industries; also, technical assistance available
President: Walter Knecht
Number Employees: 35
Sq. footage: 57000
Parent Co: Laue, Herman, GmbH
Type of Packaging: Food Service
Brands:
HELA

6057 **Hermann Pickle Farm**
P.O.Box 347
Garrettsville, OH 44231-0347 330-527-2696
Fax: 330-527-2327 800-245-2696
Processor of dill and kosher pickles, dill tomatoes and peppers
President/CEO: Larry Hermann
Treasurer: Ruth Hermann
Vice President: Don Hermann
Estimated Sales: $10-20 Million
Number Employees: 20-49
Type of Packaging: Consumer, Bulk
Brands:
Hermann Pickle

6058 **Hermann Wiemer Vineyards**
3962 Rt 14
Dundee, NY 14837-0038 607-243-7971
Fax: 607-243-7983 800-371-7971
wines@wiemer.com www.wiemer.com
Vinter of vinifera wines; also, grafted grape vines.
Manager: Fred Merwarth
Estimated Sales: $ 5 - 10 Million
Number Employees: 10-19
Type of Packaging: Consumer
Brands:
HERMANN J WIEMER

6059 **Hermannhof Winery**
104 Industrial Dr
Hermann, MO 65041-9650 573-486-5959
Fax: 573-486-3415 800-393-0100
hermannhofinfo@hermannhof.com
www.hermannhof.com
Producers of red and white wines and champagne.
Manager: Stacy Wright
President: James Dierberg
CFO: Kim Leroy
Estimated Sales: $10-20 Million
Number Employees: 12

6060 **Hermany Farms**
2338 Hermany Avenue
Room 1
Bronx, NY 10473-1130 718-823-2989
Fax: 718-828-8110
Dairy products
President: Robert Marrow
Manager: Philip Carloson
Vice President: Sam Katz
Director Engineering: Mark Butler
Plant Manager: Phil Carlson
Estimated Sales: $2.5-5 Million
Number Employees: 50-99
Type of Packaging: Private Label
Brands:
American DG
Hermany

6061 **Hernan**
1525 South Main Street
Suite 400
Del Rio, TX 78840 646-263-3598
ihernandez@hernanllc.com
www.hernanllc.com
Hot chocolate, chocolate truffles, other chocolate, cooking implements/housewares.
Marketing: Isela Hernandez

6062 **Hero of America**
100 Hero Drive
Amsterdam, NY 12010 877-437-6526
Fax: 314-655-2201 herousa@herousa.com
www.heroamerica.com
Fruit spreads, nectars and swiss potatoes
SVP: Tim Kennedy
VP/Chief Sales Officer: Joe Gordon
Estimated Sales: $260,000
Number Employees: 5
Sq. footage: 4583
Type of Packaging: Consumer

6063 **Herold's Salad, Inc**
17512 Miles Ave
Cleveland, OH 44128-3481 216-991-7500
Fax: 216-991-9565 800-427-2523
www.heroldssalads.com
Processor of potato and pasta salads, side dish vegetables and desserts
President/Owner: Cathy Herold
Quality Control: Stephanie Hunt
Marketing: Greg Johns
Sales Manager: Todd Kaminoski
Plant Manager: Walt Doughty
Estimated Sales: $2 Million
Number Employees: 25
Sq. footage: 18000
Type of Packaging: Consumer, Food Service, Private Label, Bulk

6064 **Heron Hill Winery**
9301 County Route 76
Hammondsport, NY 14840 607-868-4241
Fax: 607-868-3435 800-441-4241
www.heronhill.com
Producers of red and white wines and champagne.
Owner: John Ingle
Estimated Sales: $5-10 Million
Number Employees: 20-49
Type of Packaging: Private Label

6065 **Heronwood Farm**
PO Box 1555
Kent, WA 98035-1555 877-203-5908
Fax: 253-520-0282
Jams, jellies, fruit butters
President: Jeannie Hertel
Type of Packaging: Private Label
Brands:
Heronwood Farm 100% Pure Honey
Heronwood Farm Apple Butter
Heronwood Farm Apricot Jam
Heronwood Farm Apricot Jam
Heronwood Farm Blackberry Jelly
Heronwood Farm Blackberry Syrup
Heronwood Farm Blueberry Jam
Heronwood Farm Blueberry Syrup
Heronwood Farm Cherry Jam
Heronwood Farm Cranberry-Raspberry
Heronwood Farm Jennifer Plum Jam
Heronwood Farm Orange Marmalade
Heronwood Farm Peach Butter
Heronwood Farm Peach Jam
Heronwood Farm Pear Butter
Heronwood Farm Pear Jam
Heronwood Farm Raspberry Jam
Heronwood Farm Rhubarb Jelly
Heronwood Farm Ruby Salmon Jelly
Heronwood Farm Slug Butter
Heronwood Farm Strawberry Jam
Salmonberry

6066 **Herr Foods**
476 E 7th St
Chillicothe, OH 45601 740-773-8282
Fax: 740-775-8286 800-523-8468
www.herrfoods.com
Snack foods, potato chips, pretzels, tortilla chips, cheese curls, popcorn, crackers, nuts, pork rinds, onion rings and meat sticks.
VP: Scott Carmean
Branch Manager: Dale Garrison
Plant Manager: Mike Cook
Estimated Sales: $ 20 - 50 Million
Number Employees: 40
Sq. footage: 1000
Type of Packaging: Consumer

6067 **(HQ)Herr's Foods**
20 Herr Dr
Nottingham, PA 19362 610-932-9462
Fax: 610-932-2137 800-344-3777
www.herrfoods.com
Processor of snack foods including potato chips, pretzels, popcorn, cheese curls, onion rings and corn, nacho and tortilla chips; also, kosher products available
Founder: James Herr
Chairman/CEO: J M Herr
President/Director: Ed Herr
Vice President Finance: Gerry Kluis
Vice President Sales/Marketing: Richard White
Vice President Manufacturing: Harold Blank
Estimated Sales: $100-500 Million
Number Employees: 1,000-4,999
Type of Packaging: Consumer
Brands:
Herr's

6068 **Herrell's Ice Cream**
8 Old South St
Northampton, MA 01060 413-586-9700
Fax: 413-584-5320 www.herrells.com
Manufacturers of ice cream.
CEO: Stephen Herrell
Number Employees: 20-49

6069 **Herring Brothers**
PO Box 526
Dover Foxcroft, ME 04426 207-876-2631
Fax: 207-876-2631 herringbros@hotmail.com
www.herringbrothersmeats.com
Processor and wholesaler/distributor of meats
Owner: Andrea Gilbert
Owner: Thomas Gilbert
Owner: Trey Gilbert
Owner: Ellie Patterson
Estimated Sales: $5-10 Million
Number Employees: 5-9
Type of Packaging: Consumer, Private Label

6070 **Hershey**
2350 Matheson Boulevard E
Mississauga, ON L4W 5E9
Canada 905-602-9200
Fax: 905-602-8766 800-468-1714
cdnheadoffice@hersheys.com
www.hersheys.com
Processor of chocolate products including candy, chips, drinks and syrups; also, candy including mints, toffee, hard, licorice and chocolate covered almonds.
Chairman/President/CEO Corporate Office: Richard Lenny
VP/International Business Development: Bryan Crittenden
VP/International Commmerical Marketing: Richard Andrews
VP/Chief Information Officer: George Davis
Number Employees: 150
Parent Co: Hershey Company
Type of Packaging: Consumer

6071 **Hershey Canada Inc**
5750 Explorer Drive
Suite 500
Mississauga, ON L4W 0B1
Canada 902-469-2470
Fax: 902-469-7169 800-468-1714
www.hersheycanada.com OR www.hersheys.com
Manufactures, distributes and sells confectionery, snack, refreshment and grocery products in Canada.
Chairman/President/CEO Corporate Office: Richard Lenny
VP/Global Strategy Business Intelligence: Robert Goodpaster
VP/International Business Development: Bryan Crittenden
VP/International Commerical Marketing: Richard Andrews
VP/Chief Information Officer: George Davis
Number Employees: 650
Parent Co: Hershey Company
Type of Packaging: Consumer
Brands:
CHIPITS
EAT-MORE

GLOSETTE
HERSHEY'S
JOLLY RANCHER
OH HENRY!
REESE
TWIZZLER

6072 **Hershey Chocolate & Confectionery Division**
6130 Stoneridge Mall Rd # 140
Pleasanton, CA 94588-3770 925-460-0359
Fax: 925-937-4139 www.hersheys.com
Processor of chocolate candy including bars
Chairman/President/CEO: Richard Lenny
VP/Finance & Planning: Humberto Alfonso
VP/International Business Development: Bryan Crittenden
VP/Quality & Regulatory Compliance: Donald Mastrorocco Jr
VP/International Marketing: Richard Andrews
VP/Global Strategy Business Intelligence: Robert Goodpaster
VP/Chief Information Officer: George Davis
EVP/Chief Operating Officer: David West
Estimated Sales: $10-20 Million
Number Employees: 50-99
Parent Co: Hershey Company
Type of Packaging: Consumer

6073 **Hershey Company**
100 Crystal a Dr
Hershey, PA 17033 717-534-4200
Fax: 717-534-6760 800-468-1714
www.hersheys.com
Chocolate and chocolate candies
President/CEO: David West
SVP/CFO: Humberto Alfonso
SVP/General Council & Secretary: Burton Snyder

VP Global R&D: C Daniel Azzara
SVP/Global Chief Marketing Officer: Michele Buck
SVP/Chief People Officer: Charlene Binder
SVP Global Operations: Terence O'Day
Estimated Sales: $5.3 Billion
Number Employees: 13,000
Type of Packaging: Consumer, Food Service, Private Label, Bulk
Other Locations:
Hershey Foods Corp.
Lake Forest IL
Brands:
HERSHEY'S
ICE BREAKERS
JOLY RANCHER
KISSES
KIT KAT
REESE'S
SNACK
TWIZZLERS

6074 **Hershey Company**
14 E Chocolate Ave
Hershey, PA 17033 717-534-4200
Fax: 717-534-6324 800-468-1714
PR@hersheys.com www.hersheys.com
Cocoa, baking chips, baking chocolate, syrups, pourable peanut butter
President: David West
Marketing Director: Thomas K Hernquist
CFO: David J West
Parent Co: Hershey Foods Corporation
Brands:
Heath
Hershey's
Reese's

6075 **(HQ)Hershey Corporation**
P.O.Box 810
Hershey, PA 17033 717-534-6799
Fax: 717-534-6550 800-468-1714
Info@HersheyPA.com www.hersheys.com
Manufacturer of chocolate and sugar confectionery products. hershey kisses,reese's, york pep patties,chocolate syrup, ounds,almond joy ice cream toppings, cookies,snacknuts,twizzlers.
President/CEO: David West
SVP/Chief Financial Officer: Humberto Alfonso
SVP/General Counsel: Burton Snyder
VP/Global Research and Development: C Daniel Azzara
SVP/Global Chief Marketing Officer: Michele Buck
SVP/Global Operations: Terence O'Day
Estimated Sales: $5.67Billion
Number Employees: 12,000
Parent Co: Milton Hershey School
Type of Packaging: Consumer, Food Service, Private Label
Brands:
HERSHEY'S COOKIES & CREME
HERSHEY'S EXTRA CREAMY CHOCOLATE
HERSHEY'S MILK CHOCOLATE
HERSHEY'S MILK CHOCOLATE W/ALMONDS
HERSHEY'S SPECIAL DARK CHOCOLATE
HERSHEY'S SPECIAL DARK W/ALMONDS
ICE BREAKERS ALPINE SPLASH
ICE BREAKERS CINNAMON
ICE BREAKERS CITRUS FREEZE
ICE BREAKERS COOL MINT
ICE BREAKERS SPEARMINT
JOLLY RANCHER DOUBLE BLASTS
JOLLY RANCHER GUMMIES CANDY
JOLLY RANCHER JELLY BEANS
JOLLY RANCHER LOLLIPOPS
JOLLY RANCHER SOFT & CHEWY
JOLLY RANCHER SOUR BLASTS
JOLLY RANCHERS
KISSES
KISSES CHERRY CORDIAL
KISSES FILLED w/CARAMEL
KISSES HUGS
KISSES SPECIAL DARK
KISSES w/ALMOND
REESE'S BROWNIE
REESE'S CRISPY CRUNCHY
REESE'S EGG
REESE'S HEART
REESE'S PB & MILK CHOCOLATE BIG CUP
REESE'S PB & WHITE CHOCOLATE
REESE'S PB & WHITE CHOCOLATE BIG CU
REESE'S PEANUT BUTTER & MILK CHOC
REESE'S PUMPKIN
REESE'S SELECT CLUSTERS
REESE'S SNACK BARZ
REESE'S TREE
TWIZZLERS CHERRY
TWIZZLERS CHOCOLATE
TWIZZLERS LICORICE
TWIZZLERS STRAWBERRY

6076 **Hershey Creamery Company**
301 S Cameron St
Harrisburg, PA 17101 717-238-8134
Fax: 717-233-7195 888-240-1905
info@hersheyicecream.com
www.hersheyicecream.com
Processor of ice cream
Chairman/President/CEO: Richard Lenny
VP/Finance & Planning: Humberto Alfonso
CEO: George H Holder
VP/International Business Development: Bryan Crittenden
VP/Quality & Regulatory Compliance: Donald Mastrorocco Jr
VP/International Marketing: Richard Andrews
VP/Chief Information Officer: George Davis
EVP/Chief Operating Officer: David West
Estimated Sales: $50-100 Million
Number Employees: 100-249
Parent Co: Hershey Company
Type of Packaging: Consumer, Food Service, Bulk
Brands:
Hershey

6077 **Hershey International**
2700 S Commerce Parkway
Weston, FL 33331-3628 954-385-2600
Fax: 954-385-2625 exports@hersheys.com
www.thehersheycompany.com
Processor and exporter of chocolate and nonchocolate confectionery products, cookies, biscuits and ice cream.
Chairman/President/CEO: Richard Lenny
VP/Finance & Planning: Humberto Alfonso
VP/Global Strategy Business Intelligence: Robert Goodpaster
VP/International Business Development: Bryan Crittenden
VP/Quality & Regulatory Compliance: Donald Mastrorocco Jr
VP/Chief Information Officer: George Davis
EVP/Chief Operating Officer: David West
Number Employees: 1-4
Parent Co: Hershey Company
Type of Packaging: Consumer, Food Service, Bulk

6078 **Hershey Pasta Group**
2521 S Floyd Street
Louisville, KY 40209-1809 502-637-2563
Fax: 502-637-6328 800-468-1714
www.hersheys.com
Egg noodles, macaroni, spaghetti and crisp rice
Chairman/President/CEO: Richard H Lenny
CEO: Richard Lenny
VP/Finance & Planning: David West
Vice President: Marcella K Arline
VP/International Business Development: Bryan Crittenden
VP/Quality & Regulatory Compliance: Donald Mastrorocco Jr
VP/International Marketing: Richard Andrews
VP/Chief Information Officer: George Davis
EVP/Chief Operating Officer: David West
Estimated Sales: $25-50 Million
Number Employees: 100-249
Parent Co: Hershey Company
Brands:
Almond Joy
Hershey's
Jolly Rancher
Kit Kat

6079 **Hess Collection Winery**
4411 Redwood Rd
Napa, CA 94558 707-255-1144
Fax: 707-253-1682 877-707-4377
info@hesscollection.com
www.hesscollection.com
Wines
President: Clement Firko
Owner: Donald Hess
CEO: Max Leinhard
VP Director Winemaking: Dave Guffy
Winemaker: Julie Murrell
Estimated Sales: $10-100 Million
Number Employees: 50-99
Type of Packaging: Private Label
Brands:
ARTEZIN
HESS COLLECTION
HESS ESTATE
HESS SELECT

6080 **Heterochemical Corporation**
111 E Hawthorne Ave
Valley Stream, NY 11580-6319 516-561-8225
Fax: 516-561-8413
Processor and exporter of vitamin K products
President: Lynne Galler
VP: Raymond Berruti
Estimated Sales: $990,000
Number Employees: 10
Sq. footage: 20000

6081 **Hetty Fair Foods Company**
51 N Gates Avenue
Buffalo, NY 14218-1029 716-876-4345
Fax: 716-876-7455
Vegetables
President: Thomas Amabile
Estimated Sales: $1-2.5 Million
Number Employees: 6
Number of Brands: 1
Number of Products: 4
Type of Packaging: Consumer, Food Service, Private Label, Bulk

6082 **Hey Brothers Ice Cream**
8297 S Main Street
Dixon, IL 61021-9408 815-288-4242
Ice cream

6083 **Heyerly Bakery**
107 N Jefferson St
Ossian, IN 46777 260-622-4196
Processor of baked goods including cookies
Owner: Ron Heyerly
Estimated Sales: $500,000-$1 Million
Number Employees: 10-19
Type of Packaging: Consumer

6084 **Hi Ball Energy**
1862 Union Street
San Francisco, CA 94123 415-420-4801
Fax: 415-931-1096 info@hiballer.com
www.hiballer.com

naturally flavored sparkling energy water and sparkling energy waters.
Founder/President: Todd Berardi
Director of Sales: Dan Craytor
Sales Director: Dan Craytor

6085 **Hi Point Industries**
4767 E 49th St
Vernon, CA 90058-2703 323-589-7211
Fax: 323-589-8270 800-959-7292
www.goldenovaleggs.com
Processor of egg products including whole fresh, liquid and frozen; also, whites, frozen salted and sugared yolks, substitute blends and powders; also, salted and sweet butter
President: Fred Alejo
Estimated Sales: $5 Million
Number Employees: 40
Sq. footage: 45000
Type of Packaging: Food Service, Bulk
Brands:
Amatex
X-Mix

6086 **Hi-Country Corona**
P.O.Box 338
Selah, WA 98942 951-272-2600
Fax: 909-272-8438 hicountrycorona@aol.com
Processor and exporter of fruit juices and concentrates including orange, grapefruit, lemon and lime; also essential oils. Packer of juice and juice drinks in Hot-Fill PET, 46 ounce cans, aluminum cans and HDPE bottles
Industrial Sales: Norman Saldana
Sales Director: Cindy Henry
Plant Manager: Jolene Crosby
Estimated Sales: $10-20 Million
Number Employees: 50-99
Sq. footage: 161913
Type of Packaging: Consumer, Food Service, Private Label, Bulk
Brands:
Cal-Glory
Citra-Gold

6087 **Hi-Country Foods Corporation**
P.O.Box 338
Selah, WA 98942 509-697-7292
Fax: 509-697-3498 hcfoods@hcfoods.com
www.yakamajuice1855.com
Processor of fruit juice concentrates, apple and fruit juices, bottled water, teas and new age beverages; exporter of apple and fruit juices
President/Owner: Otis Harlan
CFO: Richard Johnson
CEO: Pat Kelly
Quality Control: Judy Groves
VP/Operations/Marketing: Patrick Kelly
Estimated Sales: $10-20 Million
Number Employees: 50-99
Sq. footage: 75000
Type of Packaging: Food Service, Private Label, Bulk
Brands:
Hi-Country
Wenatchee Valley

6088 **Hi-Country Snack Food**
P.O.Box 159
Lincoln, MT 59639-0159 406-362-4203
Fax: 406-362-4275 800-433-3916
mt@hicountry.com www.hicountry.com
Processor of high energy bars
President: James Johnson
CEO: James Johnson
Sales Manager: Randy Wagoner
Estimated Sales: $ 20 - 50 Million
Number Employees: 50-99
Parent Co: Hi Country Snack Foods
Type of Packaging: Consumer, Private Label
Brands:
High Country
Trekbarr

6089 **Hi-Seas of Dulac**
8345 Shrimpers Row
Dulac, LA 70353 985-563-7155
Fax: 985-563-2536
Shrimp
Owner: Eric Authamant
Estimated Sales: $ 5 - 10 Million
Number Employees: 10-19

6090 **HiBix Corporation**
5860 W Las Positas Blvd
Suite 21
Pleasanton, CA 94588 925-225-0800
Fax: 925-225-0700 jdee@hibixcorp.com
www.oobabeverage.com
all natural, refreshingly clean, sparkling beverage that infuses the pure extracts of the incredible hibiscus flower into every bottle.
President/CEO: John-David Enright
SMO: Janet DiGiovanna
VP Sales: James Curley

6091 **(HQ)Hialeah Products Company**
2207 Hayes St
Hollywood, FL 33020 954-923-3379
Fax: 954-923-4010 800-923-3379
richnuts@aol.com www.newurbanfarms.com
Packer of nuts, dried fruits, candy and snacks; wholesaler/distributor and exporter of dried fruits, pecans, Brazil nuts, almonds, walnuts, cashews, pistachios, peanuts, gourmet snack mixes and spicy snack mixes; all kosher; servingthe food service market
President: Richard Lesser
CEO: Kathy Lesser
Research & Development: Noah Lesser
Estimated Sales: $5-10 Million
Number Employees: 24
Number of Brands: 2
Number of Products: 200+
Sq. footage: 15000
Type of Packaging: Consumer, Food Service, Private Label, Bulk
Brands:
OH NUTS

6092 **Hibiscus Aloha Corporation**
826 Queen St # 200
Honolulu, HI 96813-5286 808-591-8826
President: Elvira Lo
Estimated Sales: $ 1 - 3 Million
Number Employees: 5-9

6093 **Hickey Foods**
P.O.Box 2312
Sun Valley, ID 83353 208-788-9033
Fax: 208-788-8879
Manufacturer of vacuum-packed smoked trout
President: Thomas M Hickey
Estimated Sales: $ 1 - 3 Million
Number Employees: 5-9

6094 **Hickory Baked Food**
3221 Commerce Ct
Castle Rock, CO 80109-9458 303-688-2633
Fax: 303-688-8431
Manufacturer of smoked and cured poultry and meats.
President: Robert Anderson
Purchasing Manager: Robert Anderson
Estimated Sales: $500,000-$1 Million
Number Employees: 1-4
Sq. footage: 6000
Parent Co: Hickory Baked Food
Type of Packaging: Consumer, Food Service, Private Label, Bulk
Brands:
HICKORY BAKED
HIGH VALLEY FARM

6095 **Hickory Farms**
P.O.Box 219
Maumee, OH 43537 419-893-7611
Fax: 419-893-0164 www.hickoryfarms.com
Manufacturer of beef, cheese, fruit, desserts, nuts, seafood and more
President/CEO: John Langdon
VP: James O'Neill
Estimated Sales: $16.3 Million
Number Employees: 500-999
Type of Packaging: Consumer, Food Service, Bulk

6096 **Hickory Harvest Foods**
90 Logan Parkway
Akron, OH 44319 330-644-6887
Fax: 330-644-2501 askus2@hickoryharvest.com
www.hickoryharvest.com
Processor and importer of nuts and dried fruits; wholesaler/distributor of speciality candy
President: George Swiatkowski
Estimated Sales: $20-50 Million
Number Employees: 20-49
Sq. footage: 25000
Type of Packaging: Consumer, Food Service, Private Label, Bulk

6097 **Hidden Mountain Ranch Winery**
2740 Hidden Mountain Rd
Paso Robles, CA 93446-8712 805-226-9907
Fax: 805-238-4997
Wine
Owner: Richard Gumerman
Estimated Sales: $1-2.5 Million
Number Employees: 5-9

6098 **Hidden Villa Ranch**
310 N Harbor Blvd Ste 205
Fullerton, CA 92832 714-680-3447
Fax: 714-680-3380 800-326-3220
info@hiddenvilla.com www.hiddenvilla.com
Manufacturer of Cheese and cheese products, liquid eggs
Founder/President: Timothy Luberski
Senior Vice President: Michael Sencer
Vice President, Pinehill Division: Robert Kelly
Estimated Sales: $50-100 Million
Number Employees: 100-249
Brands:
Arizona Ranch Fresh
California Ranch Fresh
California Sunshine Dairy Pproducts
Hidden Villa Ranch
Horizon Orangic

6099 **Hig-Country Corona**
P.O.Box 698
Selah, WA 98942-0698 509-697-7950
Fax: 909-272-8438 hccorona@hcfoodf.com
www.hcfoods.com
Fruit and vegetable beverage bases
Owner: Leo Hogue
Estimated Sales: $10-20 Million
Number Employees: 1-4

6100 **Higa Meat and Pork Market Limited**
225 N Nimitz Hwy Unit 2
Honolulu, HI 96817 808-531-3591
Fax: 808-521-4951
Wholesale fresh meat; market meat
President: Marshall Higa
Estimated Sales: $ 50 - 100 Million
Number Employees: 20-49

6101 **Higgins Seafood**
2798 Jean Lafitte Blvd
Lafitte, LA 70067 504-689-3577
Processor of frozen seafood including crabs and oysters
President: Denny Higgins
Estimated Sales: $300,000-500,000
Number Employees: 1-4
Type of Packaging: Consumer

6102 **High Coffee Corporation**
9601 Katy Freeway
Houston, TX 77024-1342 713-465-2230
Fax: 713-465-5751 hi-co@msn.com
President: Antonio Pinero
Manager: Marcello Frau
Estimated Sales: Less than $500,000
Number Employees: 1-4

6103 **High Country Elevators**
P.O.Box 597
Dove Creek, CO 81324 970-677-2251
Fax: 970-677-2461 akmbr@yahoo.com
Processor of dried beans
Manager: Bruce Riddel
Estimated Sales: Less than $500,000
Number Employees: 1-4
Type of Packaging: Consumer, Food Service, Bulk

6104 **High Country Gourmet**
225 Mountain Way Drive
Orem, UT 84058-5121 801-426-4383
Fax: 801-426-4385 hictrygrmt@aol.com
Procesor of dehydrated soup mixes
President: Rod Meldrum
Type of Packaging: Consumer, Food Service, Private Label, Bulk
Brands:
HIGH COUNTRY GOURMET

6105 **High Country Snack Foods**
P.O.Box 159
Lincoln, MT 59639-0159 406-362-4203
Fax: 406-362-4275 800-433-3916
customerservice@highcountrymail.com
www.hicountry.com
Processor of beef jerky
President: James Johnson
Estimated Sales: $20 - 50 Million
Number Employees: 50-99
Type of Packaging: Consumer, Food Service

6106 **High Falls Brewing**
445 Saint Paul St
Rochester, NY 14605 585-546-1030
Fax: 585-546-8928 www.highfalls.com
Manufacturer of beer and ale
President: Johnhen Henderson
CEO: Tom Hubbard
CEO: Norman Snyder
Vice President/Marketing: David Boggs
Sales: Donald Cotter
Brew Master: David Schlosser
Purchasing Manager: James Barber
Estimated Sales: $100-499.9 Million
Number Employees: 100-249
Type of Packaging: Consumer, Food Service
Brands:
12 HORSE
GENESEE BEER
GENESEE LAGER
GENESEE RED BEER
GENNY CREAM ALE
GENNY ICE
GENNY LIGHT BEER
GENNY NON-ALCOHOLIC
GOLDEN ANNIVERSARY
HONEY BROWN LAGER
JW DUNDEE'S HONEY BROWN LAGER
JW DUNDEE'S HONEY LIGHT
MICHAEL SHEA'S BLACK & TAN
MICHAEL SHEA'S IRISH AMBER
SHEA'S BLACK & TAN
TW DUNDEES CLASSIC LAGER

6107 **High Falls Brewing Company**
445 Saint Paul St
Rochester, NY 14605 585-546-1030
Fax: 585-546-8928 800-729-4366
consumeraffairs@genbrew.com
www.highfalls.com
Manufacturer of beer
President/CEO: Tom Hubbard
CEO: Norman Snyder
Brewmaster: Dave Schlosser
Estimated Sales: $100-500 Million
Number Employees: 250-499
Type of Packaging: Consumer, Food Service
Brands:
GENESEE
GENNY LIGHT
JW DUNDEE'S
KOCH'S
MICHAEL SHEA'S

6108 **(HQ)High Liner Foods Inc**
100 Battery Point Road
PO Box 910
Lunenburg, NS B0J 2C0
Canada 902-634-9475
Fax: 902-634-4785 info@highlinerfoods.com
www.highlinerfoods.com
Manufacturer of fresh and frozen cod, haddock, sole, perch, cured roe, pollack, halibut, grenadier and salmon; also, kippers, cheese bites and pasta
President/CEO: Henry Demone
President/COO Canadian Operations: Mark Marino
President/COO High Liner Foods USA: Keith Decker
EVP/CFO/Secretary: Kelly Nelson FCA
VP/Procurement: Paul Snow
VP/Human Resources: Joanne Brown CRHP
Estimated Sales: CAN $600 Million
Number Employees: 1100
Type of Packaging: Consumer, Food Service, Private Label, Bulk
Other Locations:
High Liner Foods
Secaucus NJ
Brands:
40 FATHOMS
FISHER BOY
FLORESTA
GINA ITALIAN VILLAGE
HIGH LINER
SEA FRESH

6109 **High Liner Foods USA**
18 Electronics Ave
Danvers, MA 01923-1011 603-431-6865
Fax: 603-430-9205 888-860-3664
feedback@highlinerfoodsusa.com
www.highlinerfoodsusa.com
Seafood products
President/COO: Keith A Decker
Estimated Sales: $ 10-100 Million
Number Employees: 100-249
Parent Co: High Liner Foods
Type of Packaging: Consumer, Private Label
Brands:
FISHER BOY
FISHERY PRODUCTS INTERNATIONAL
SEA CUISINE

6110 **High Ridge Foods LLC**
424 Ridgeway
White Plains, NY 10605-4208 914-761-2900
Fax: 914-761-2901 alzerez@mindspring.com
Cultured dairy products, sugars, flowers, cheese, etc
President: Nestor Alzerez
Sales Manager: Nestor Alzerez, Jr
Estimated Sales: $2.5 Million
Number Employees: 1-4
Type of Packaging: Private Label, Bulk

6111 **High Rise Coffee Roasters**
2421 W Cucharras St
Colorado Springs, CO 80904 719-633-1833
Fax: 719-471-4815
Coffee
President: Toby Anderson
Estimated Sales: $1-2.5 Million
Number Employees: 1-4

6112 **High Road Craft Ice Cream, Inc.**
2241 Perimeter Park Drive
Suite 7
Atlanta, GA 30341-1309 678-701-7623
sales@highroadcraft.com
www.highroadcraft.com
Frozen desserts, ice cream/sorbet
Marketing: Hunter Thornton

6113 **High Sea Foods**
188a Main Street N
Glovertown, NL A0G 2L0
Canada 709-533-2626
Fax: 709-533-2627
Processor of frozen eel, catelin, herring, salmon, smelt, sea urchin, lobster and whelk; also, fresh lobster
President: Emerson Oram
VP: Cory Oram
Number Employees: 20-49
Type of Packaging: Bulk

6114 **High Tide Seafoods**
P.O.Box 2141
Port Angeles, WA 98362 360-452-8488
Fax: 360-452-6710
Processor of fresh and frozen salmon
Owner: Jim Shefler
President: Ernest Vail
Estimated Sales: $2.5 Million
Number Employees: 30
Type of Packaging: Consumer, Food Service
Brands:
HIGH TIDE SEAFOODS

6115 **High Valley Farm**
3221 Commerce Court
Castle Rock, CO 80109-9458 303-634-2944
Fax: 303-688-8431
Sausages and other processed meats
President: Robert Anderson
Plant Manager: Kenneth Trapp
Estimated Sales: $10-20 Million
Number Employees: 20-49

6116 **High's Dairies**
10630 Riggs Hill Rd
Jessup, MD 20794-9450 301-776-7727
Fax: 301-776-2440
Dairy products
President: Jack Sherman

6117 **Highland Dairies**
P.O.Box 2199
Wichita, KS 67201-2199 316-267-4221
Fax: 316-267-1050 800-336-0765
www.hilanddairy.com
Milk, dairy products
Manager: Jerald Grey
President: Gary Aggus
Marketing Director: Ted Barlows
Number Employees: 100-249
Brands:
Highland
Old Chester

6118 **Highland Fisheries**
PO Box 459
Glace Bay, NS B1A 6C9
Canada 902-849-6016
Fax: 902-849-7794
Processor and exporter of fresh and frozen finfish
Plant Manager: Greg Mitchelitis
Number Employees: 100-249
Type of Packaging: Bulk

6119 **Highland Laboratories**
PO Box 199
Mount Angel, OR 97362 503-845-9223
Fax: 503-845-6364 888-717-4917
answers@highlandvitamins.com
www.highlandvitamins.com
Processor of vitamins, minerals and protein powders
Owner/President: Kenneth Scott
CEO: Candy Scott
CFO/Human Resources: Jolyn Rothgery
Quality & Compliance Manager: John Mills
Sales Manager: Brian Taschereau
COO: Michael Carlson
Manufacturing Supervisor: Vadim Osipovich
Purchasing Manager: Michelle Brumer
Estimated Sales: $5.4 Million
Number Employees: 41
Sq. footage: 30000
Type of Packaging: Private Label

6120 **Highland Manor Winery**
2965 S York Hwy
Jamestown, TN 38556 931-879-9519
Fax: 931-879-2907 www.highlandmanorwinery.net
Wine
Co-Owner: Butch Campbell
Co-Owner: Gertie Campbell
Estimated Sales: $2.5-5 Million
Number Employees: 5-9

6121 **Highland Sugarworks, Inc**
49 Parker Road
Wilson Industrial Park, Po Box 58
Websterville, VT 05678 615-274-3959
Fax: 802-479-1737 800-452-4012
jclose@highlandsugarworks.com
www.highlandsugarworks.com
Pure maple syrup and pancake mixes including apple cinnamon,buttermilk and blueberry; also, gift packs available
President: Jim Mac Isaac
Sales/Marketing: Jim Close
Operations: Deb Frimodig
Estimated Sales: $500,000-$1 Million
Number Employees: 10-19
Sq. footage: 15000
Type of Packaging: Consumer, Food Service, Private Label, Bulk
Brands:
HIGHLAND SUGARWORKS

6122 **Highlandville Packing**
P.O.Box 190
Highlandville, MO 65669 417-443-3365
Fax: 417-443-3365 sales@hillbillymeats.com
www.goatworld.com
Processor of meat products
Owner: Neva Smith
Estimated Sales: $1-2.5 Million
Number Employees: 1-4

6123 **Hightower's Packing**
1713 Highway 518
Minden, LA 71055 318-377-5459
Fax: 318-377-5408
Processor of meat products
President: Marvin Hightower
Estimated Sales: $2.5-5 Million
Number Employees: 10-19
Type of Packaging: Consumer, Bulk

6124 **Highwood Distillers**
PO Box 5693
High River, AB T1V 1M7
Canada 403-652-3202
Fax: 403-652-4227 hrplant@telus.net
www.highwood-distillers.com
Processor and exporter of whiskey, vodka, rums, liqueurs and tequila; also, pre-mixers
President/Sales: Barry Wilde
Chairman/CEO: W Miller
Number Employees: 20-49
Sq. footage: 30000
Type of Packaging: Consumer, Private Label
Brands:
BUCCANEER
CHINA WHITE
COLITA
HIGHWOOD
MARUSHKA
OLD MEXICO
TRIPLE SEC
WHITE LIGHTNING

6125 **Hiland Dairy Foods Company**
PO Box 118
Highway D
Kaiser, MO 65047 573-248-3974
Fax: 573-348-1760 www.hilanddairy.com
Milk

6126 **Hiland Dairy Foods Company**
105 South Alma
Nevada, MO 64772 417-667-8814
www.hilanddairy.com
Milk

6127 **Hiland Dairy Foods Company**
3000 Commerce Drive
Rolla, MO 65401-9338 573-364-3700
www.hilanddairy.com
Milk

6128 **Hiland Dairy Foods Company**
463 NE Highway 13
Warrensburg, MO 64093 660-747-6722
www.hilanddairy.com
Milk

6129 **Hiland Dairy Foods Company**
PO Box 721
West Plains, MO 65775 417-256-6117
www.hilanddairy.com
Milk

6130 **Hiland Dairy Foods Company**
266 Claremont Drive
Branson, MO 65616 417-334-0090
www.hilanddairy.com
Manufacturer of dairy products including; ice cream, milk, butter, cheese, yogurt, dips, juice and to-go dairy drinks
Parent Co: Prairie Farms Dairy/Dairy Farmers of America
Type of Packaging: Consumer, Food Service
Brands:
HILAND DAIRY

6131 **(HQ)Hiland Dairy Foods Company**
PO Box 2270
Springfield, MO 65801-2270 417-862-9311
Fax: 316-267-1050 www.hilanddairy.com
Processor of milk, juice, fruit-flavored drinks, lemonade, water, ice cream, creams/half and half, lactose-free milk, butter, cottage cheese, cheese, shredded cheese, yogurt, sour cream, dips, to-go drinks, egg substitute and eggnog.
Manager: Jerald Grey
Estimated Sales: $20-50 Million
Number Employees: 100-249
Type of Packaging: Consumer, Food Service

6132 **Hiland Dairy Foods Company**
601 Maiden Lane
Joplin, MO 64801 417-623-2272
www.hilanddairy.com
Milk
Manager: Jerald Grey
Sales Director: Larry Powers
Plant Manager: Jeff Zielke
Type of Packaging: Bulk
Brands:
Hiland

6133 **Hill Nutritional Products**
1950 Old Cuthbert Road
Suite M
Cherry Hill, NJ 08034-1439 856-857-0811
hillherbal@aol.com
www.hillherbal.com

6134 **Hill Top Berry Farm & Winery**
2800 Berry Hill Rd
Nellysford, VA 22958 434-361-1266
Fax: 434-361-1266 hilltop1@intelos.net
www.hilltopberrywine.com
Wine
Owner: Marlyn Allen
Estimated Sales: $ 3 - 5 Million
Number Employees: 5-9

6135 **Hill of Beans Coffee Roasters**
3438 W 43rd St
Los Angeles, CA 90008-4906 323-291-2160
Fax: 213-665-7769 888-527-6278
Coffee Roasters
Owner: Leo Hill
Estimated Sales: $5-10 Million appx.
Number Employees: 5-9

6136 **Hillandale Llc**
Us Highway 41 North
Lake City, FL 32055 386-397-1300
Fax: 386-397-1130 www.hillandalefarms.com
Supplier of shell eggs to supermarkets, foodservice operators, restaurants, and food processors.
President: Gary Bethel
Vice President: Steve Vendemia
Estimated Sales: $10-20 Million
Number Employees: 100-249
Type of Packaging: Consumer, Food Service

6137 **Hillard Bloom Packing Co**
2601 Ogden Ave
Port Norris, NJ 8349 856-785-0120
Fax: 856-785-2341
www.hillardbloomshellfish.com
Processor of fresh and frozen clams and oysters
President: Hillard Bloom
VP: Todd Reeves
Human Resource Manager: Barbara Huggins
Estimated Sales: $7600000
Number Employees: 9
Sq. footage: 5000
Parent Co: Tallmadge Brothers

6138 **Hillbilly Smokehouse**
1801 S 8th St
Rogers, AR 72756 479-636-1927
Fax: 479-636-4590 hillbilly@ipa.net
www.hillbillysmokehouse.com
Manufacturer of smoked ham, bacon, sausage, turkey, chicken, pork and beef
President: Tom Baumgartner
Vice President: Drew Baumgartner
Estimated Sales: $1 Million
Number Employees: 10
Number of Brands: 1
Number of Products: 20
Sq. footage: 5000
Type of Packaging: Consumer

6139 **Hillcrest Orchard**
101 Autumn Ter
Lake Placid, FL 33852-6275 865-397-5273
Fax: 865-397-5273 ftpresto@tnni.net
Processor of apple butter and jellies including apple, peach, plum and grape; grape juice; grower of fresh apples and grapes
Co-Owner: Frank Preston
Co-Owner: Twylia Preston
Estimated Sales: Under $100,000
Number Employees: 1-4
Number of Brands: 1
Number of Products: 15
Sq. footage: 92000
Type of Packaging: Consumer, Food Service, Bulk
Brands:
HILLCREST ORCHARD

6140 **Hillcrest Vineyard**
240 Vineyard Ln
Roseburg, OR 97471 541-673-3709
finewine@sorcum.com
Wines
Manager: Della Terra
Owner: Richard Sommer
Estimated Sales: $1-2.5 Million
Number Employees: 1-4

6141 **Hiller Cranberries**
131 Hiller Rd
Rochester, MA 02770 508-763-5257
Fax: 508-763-3204
Quince concentrate, currant concentrate, crabapple concentrate, fruit puree/pulp, noncitrus fruit juices
Owner: Robert Hiller
Owner: Robert Hiller III
Estimated Sales: $5-10 Million
Number Employees: 1-4

6142 **Hillestad Pharmaceuticals**
178 Us Highway 51 N
Woodruff, WI 54568-9501 715-358-2113
Fax: 715-358-7812 800-535-7742
info@hillestadlabs.com www.hillestadlabs.com
Manufacturer and exporter of nutritional products
Marketing: Dan Hillestad
Estimated Sales: $10-20 Million
Number Employees: 10-19
Type of Packaging: Consumer, Private Label

6143 **Hilliard Corporation**
100 W 4th St
Elmira, NY 14901 607-733-7121
Fax: 607-737-1108 hilliard@hilliardcorp.com
www.hilliardcorp.com
The Hilliard Corporation products offer a broad line of motion control products, oil filtration and reclaiming equipment, starters for industrial gas, diesel engines and gas turbines, and plate and frame filter presses used in the foodand beverage industry.
President: Paul Webb
CEO: Nelson Mooers Van Den
CEO: Nelson Mooers Van Den Blink
Regional Sales Manager: Gerry Lachut
Estimated Sales: $ 50 - 75 Million
Number Employees: 500-999

6144 **Hillman Shrimp & OysterCompany**
10700 Hillman Drive
Dickinson, TX 77539 281-339-1506
Fax: 281-339-1509 800-582-4416
info@hillmanoysters.com
www.hillmanoysters.com
Processor of IQF half shell, whole frozen, breaded oysters, oyster meats and half shell clams.
President: Clifford Hillman
VP Marketing: Chris Hillman
Marketing Director: Tricia Roberts
Sales: Dale Rymer
Public Relations: Wendy Taylor
COO: Steve Taylor
Estimated Sales: $15 Million
Number Employees: 290
Number of Brands: 1
Number of Products: 12
Sq. footage: 14930
Type of Packaging: Consumer, Food Service, Bulk
Brands:
HILLMAN

6145 **Hillsboro Coffee Company**
4416 N Hubert Avenue
Tampa, FL 33614-7649 813-877-2126
Fax: 813-879-0524
Custom coffee
President: Neil McTague
VP Sales: John Sakkis
Estimated Sales: $5-10 Million
Number Employees: 8

6146 **Hillside Candy**
35 Hillside Ave
Hillside, NJ 07205 973-926-2300
Fax: 973-926-4440 800-524-1304
sales@hillsidecandy.com
www.townshipofhillside.org
Manufactures Sugar-free confections
Manager: David Klurman
CFO: Ray La Conte
VP Marketing & Exports: Susan Rosenthal Jay
Estimated Sales: $2.5-5 Million
Number Employees: 10-19
Number of Brands: 3
Type of Packaging: Consumer, Private Label
Brands:
BLUE BIRD TOFFE
GOLIGHTLY SUGAR FREE
SHAKER COUNTRY MEADOWSWEETS

6147 **Hillside Dairy**
W11299 Broek Rd
Stanley, WI 54768-8215 715-644-2275
Fax: 715-644-0720
Cheese
Owner: Randy La Grander
Estimated Sales: $1-2.5 Million
Number Employees: 20-49

6148 **Hillside Lane Farm**
160 Hillside Ln
Randolph, VT 05060 802-728-0070
Fax: 802-728-0071 info@hillsidelane.com
www.hillsidelane.com
Organic maple pancake & baking mixes, infused vinegars, body syrups
President: Cathy Bacon
Estimated Sales: $ 1 - 3 Million
Number Employees: 1-4
Number of Brands: 4
Number of Products: 17
Type of Packaging: Consumer, Food Service, Private Label, Bulk

6149 **Hillson Nut Company**
P.O.Box 602038
Cleveland, OH 44102 216-961-4477
Fax: 216-961-4480 800-333-2818
nuts@hillsonnut.com www.hillsonnut.com
Roasted, raw salted nuts and peanut butter
President: Richard Hillson
Vice President: Troy Sawvel
Estimated Sales: $500,000-$1 Million
Number Employees: 10-19

6150 **Hilltop Herb Farm & Restaurant**
235 Chain O Lakes Resort
Cleveland, TX 77327 832-397-4020
Fax: 281-592-6288 info@hilltopherbfarm.com
www.hilltopherbfarm.com
Processor of jams, jellies, pickles and relishes
Owner: James Smith
Executive Chef: Jim Condra
Number of Brands: 1
Number of Products: 100
Parent Co: Chain-O-Lakes Resort
Type of Packaging: Private Label
Brands:
HILL TOP FARM

6151 **Hilltop Meat Company**
27630 Us 29 North
Andalusia, AL 36421 334-388-2393
Fax: 334-388-2394 800-781-0053
www.hilltopmeatcompany.com
Processor of meat products
President: William Green
Estimated Sales: $1-2.5 Million
Number Employees: 5-9
Type of Packaging: Consumer

6152 **Hilltown Whole Food Company**
445 Berkshire Trl
Cummington, MA 01026-9610 413-634-5677
Fax: 413-634-5409
Cereal, granola
President: Robert Berenson
Number Employees: 5-9
Type of Packaging: Private Label
Brands:
MY DAD'S CEREAL

6153 **Hilmar Cheese Company**
PO Box 910
Hilmar, CA 95324 209-667-6076
Fax: 209-634-1408 800-577-5772
info@hilmarcheese.com www.hilmarcheese.com
Manufacturer of Cheddar, Monterey Jack, Colby, Colby Jack, flavored Jacks, Mozzarella and Hispanic cheeses for use in food service, ingredients, retail and the restaurant/fast food trade.
President/CEO: John Jeter
CFO: Donald Hicks
VP Sales/Marketing: Phil Robnett
VP Human Resources: Nancy Goss
COO: Ted Dykzeul
VP Purchasing: Gordon Larum
Estimated Sales: $100-500 Million
Number Employees: 1000
Type of Packaging: Consumer, Food Service, Private Label
Brands:
Gina Marie Cream Cheese

6154 **Hilmar Ingredients**
9001 Lander Avenue
Hilmar, CA 95324 209-667-6076
Fax: 209-656-1184 info@hilmaringredients.com
www.hilmaringredients.com
Manufacturer of cheese and whey products
President: Art De Rooy
CEO: John Jeter
CFO: Jay Hicks
Number Employees: 600

6155 **Hilo Fish Company**
55 Holomua St Ste A
Hilo, HI 96720 808-961-0877
Fax: 808-935-1603 www.hilofish.com
President: Charles Umamoto
Estimated Sales: $ 20 - 50 Million
Number Employees: 20-49

6156 **Himalaya**
10440 Westoffice Dr
Houston, TX 77042-5309 713-863-1622
Fax: 713-863-1686 800-869-4640
healthcare@himalayausa.com
www.himalaya-proselect.com
President/CEO: Nabeel Manal
CEO: Nabeel Manal
National Sales Manager: Connie Deans
Estimated Sales: $ 5 - 10 Million
Number Employees: 20-49

6157 **Himalayan Heritage**
N5821 Fairway Dr
Fredonia, WI 53021-9742 262-692-9500
Fax: 262-692-6387 888-414-9500
colin@himalayanheriatge.com
www.blueskymassage.com
Processor, importer and exporter of herbal dietary supplements
Co-Owner: Blair Lewis
Co_Owner: Karen Lewis
Estimated Sales: $ 1 - 3 Million
Number Employees: 10-19
Type of Packaging: Consumer, Food Service, Private Label, Bulk
Brands:
ATTNETION SPAN
ERJUV-POWDER
FIVE FORCES OF NATURE
IMMUNO FORCE
JOYFUL MIND

6158 **Hinckley Springs Water Company**
6055 S Harlem Ave
Chicago, IL 60638-3985 773-586-8600
Fax: 773-586-8613 www.water.com
Bottled water
President/CEO: George Schmitt
CFO: Chet Matykiewicz
VP: Mike Garrity
Director, Corporate Communications: Debbie Lawrence
Estimated Sales: $500,000-$1 Million
Number Employees: 50-99
Sq. footage: 1500
Parent Co: DS Waters
Type of Packaging: Consumer, Food Service, Bulk
Brands:
ALHAMBRA®
BELMONT SPRINGS®
CRYSTAL SPRINGS®
HINCKLEY SPRINGS®
KENTWOOD SPRINGS®
NURSERY® WATER
SIERRA SPRINGS®
SPARKLETTS®

6159 **Hingham Shellfish**
25 Eldridge Ct
Hingham, MA 02043 781-749-1374
Fax: 405-631-8473
President/Treasure: Myrle Derbyshire
Estimated Sales: $ .5 - 1 million
Number Employees: 1-4

6160 **Hinojosa Bros Wholesale**
P.O.Box 901
Roma, TX 78584 956-849-2386
Fax: 956-849-2386 800-554-4119
Candy and confectionary.
Owner: Antonio Hinojosa
Estimated Sales: $600,000
Number Employees: 1-4
Brands:
HINOJOSAS BROTHERS PORL CRACKLINGS

6161 **Hint**
2124 Union Street
Suite D
San Francisco, CA 94123 415-513-4050
Fax: 415-276-1786 info@drinkhint.com
www.drinkhint.com
naturally flavored water
CEO/Founder: Kara Goldin

6162 **Hint Mint**
2432 East 8th St
Los Angeles, CA 90021 213-622-6468
Fax: 213-622-1780 800-991-6468
info@hintmint.com www.hintmint.com
Breathmints and peppermint
Owner: Cooper Bates
Marketing: Wendy Campbell
Estimated Sales: $ .5 - 1 million
Number Employees: 5-9
Brands:
HINT MINT

6163 **Hinzerling Winery**
1520 Sheridan Ave
Prosser, WA 99350 509-786-2163
Fax: 509-786-2163 800-722-6702
info@hinzerling.com www.hinzerling.com
Wine, vinegar
President/Winemaker: Michael Wallace
Cellarmaster: Stan Kelly
Estimated Sales: $1-2.5 Million
Number Employees: 1-4
Type of Packaging: Private Label
Brands:
HINZERLING
WALLACE

6164 **Hipard International**
Km 36 Carretera Jacona - Los Reyes
Tinguindin, MC 59995
Mexico
hipinternacional@hotmail.com
www.hipardinternacional.com.mx
Salsa/dips, other vegetables/fruit.
Marketing: Victor Hugo Pardo Delgado

6165 **Hiram Walker & Sons**
P.O.Box 2409
Fort Smith, AR 72902 479-646-6100
Fax: 479-646-2626
www.canadianclubwhiskey.com
Manufacturer and importer of gin, tequila, vodka, whiskey and liqueurs; exporter of liqueurs and tequila
President: W S Walker Sr
Plant Manager: Brian Hastings
Estimated Sales: $10-20 Million
Number Employees: 20-49
Parent Co: Allied Domecq
Type of Packaging: Consumer
Brands:
BALLATINES
BEEFEATER
CANADIAN CLUB
CORVOISIER
IRISH MIST
KAHLUA
MAKER'S MARK
MALIBU
MIDORI
SAUZA
STOLICHNAYA

6166 **(HQ)Hiram Walker & SonsLimited**
2072 Riverside Drive E
Windsor, ON N8Y 1A7
Canada 519-254-5171
Fax: 519-971-5732 www.hiramwalker.com
Processor and exporter of blended whiskey, gin, scotch, vodka, rum, liqueurs, etc schnapps flavors include...peah,peppermint,blackberry,pumpkin spice,melon,triple sec blend, there are 43 alltogether.
President: Con Constandis
VP Operations: Jim Stanski
Estimated Sales: $199.43million
Number Employees: 500
Parent Co: Allied Domecq
Type of Packaging: Consumer, Food Service

Brands:
BALLANTINE'S
BEEFEATER
CANADIAN CLUB
COURVOISIER
IRISH MIST
KAHLUA
MAKER'S MARK
MALIBU
MIDORI
SAUZA
STOLICHNAYA

6167 Hirsch Brothers & Company
1838 S Shore Drive
Holland, MI 49423-4343 616-335-5806
Fruits and vegetables.
President: L Hirsch
Estimated Sales: $500-1 Million appx.
Number Employees: 1-4

6168 (HQ)Hirzel Canning Company &Farms
411 Lemoyne Rd
Northwood, OH 43619 419-693-0531
Fax: 419-693-4859 info@hirzel.com
www.hirzel.com
Manufacturer and exporter of canned tomatoes and tomato products, sauerkraut, sauces, salsa, tomato juice, tomato soup and more
President/CEO: Karl Hirzel Jr
Vice President: William Hirzel
Quality Control: Karl Hirzel
Retail Sales Manager: Steve Hirzel
Estimated Sales: $20-50 Million
Number Employees: 50-99
Number of Brands: 4
Number of Products: 30
Sq. footage: 500000
Type of Packaging: Consumer, Food Service, Private Label, Bulk
Brands:
Dei Fratelli
Silver Fleece
Starcross

6169 His Catch Value Added Products
PO Box 770
Homer, AK 99603-0770 800-215-7110
Fax: 907-235-1040 stuart@xyz.net
www.hiscatch.com
Processing plant, catch & process salmon and halibut as well as a variety of other fish and shellfish
President: Douglas Stuart
Vice President: Alexander Stuart IV

6170 Hiscock Enterprises
Keating Road
PO Box 40
Brigus, NL A0A 1K0
Canada 709-528-4577
Fax: 709-528-4575
Processor of frozen wild berries
President: David Hiscock
Director: Charles Hiscock
Vice President: Graham Hiscock
Estimated Sales: $1-2.5 Million
Number Employees: 5-9
Sq. footage: 15000

6171 Hitz Cheese Company
519 E Linwood Road
Linwood, MI 48634-9706 517-697-5932
Chesse
President: Dolores Hitz
Estimated Sales: $500,000 appx.
Number Employees: 1-4

6172 Hobarama Corporation
400 NW 26th St
Miami, FL 33127-4120 305-531-9708
Fax: 305-531-9709 880-439-2295
www.bawls.com
Manufacturer of beverages
President: Hobart Buppert
Senior VP: Christina Staalstrom
Estimated Sales: $2.5-5 Million
Number Employees: 10-19
Type of Packaging: Bulk

6173 Hobe Laboratories
6479 S Ash Ave
Tempe, AZ 85283 480-413-1950
Fax: 480-413-2005 800-528-4482
hobelabs@aol.com www.hobelabs.com
Processor and exporter of weight loss and herbal teas
President: William Robertson
Marketing Director: Brenda Martin
Operations Manager: Peter Samuell
Estimated Sales: $1.4 Million
Number Employees: 12
Sq. footage: 6985
Type of Packaging: Consumer, Private Label
Brands:
SLIM
THERMO SLIM
ULTRA SLIM

6174 Hodgson Mill Inc.
1100 Stevens Ave
Effingham, IL 62401 217-347-0105
Fax: 217-347-0198 800-525-0177
martin@hodgsonmill.com
www.hodgsonmill.com
All natural and organic foods-flours, cereals, baking mixes, whole wheat pastas, gluten free pastas, gluten free mixes, baking ingredients-producers and manufacturers of whole grain foods. Co-packing for private label available
President: Robert Goldstein
Executive VP Sales/Marketing: Paul Kirby
Estimated Sales: $25-30 Million
Sq. footage: 120000
Brands:
DON'S CHUCK WAGON
HODGSON MILL
KENTUCKY KERNEL
PASTAMANIA
VIDALIA SWEET

6175 Hoechst Food Ingredients
PO Box 3053
Edison, NJ 08818-3053 800-344-5807
Manufacturer of artificial sweeteners
Parent Co: Hoechst Celanese Corporation
Brands:
SUNETT

6176 Hoff's Bakery
1 Brainard Ave
Medford, MA 02155 781-396-8384
Fax: 781-396-7918 888-871-5100
www.hoffsbakery.com
cakes and tortes, cheesecakes, pies and tarts, 1/2 sheet tray, individual desserts, and trifle cups
President/Owner: Vincent Frattura
Estimated Sales: $1.5 Million
Number Employees: 20

6177 Hoff's United Foods
P.O.Box 145
Brownsville, WI 53006 920-583-3734
Smoked sausage, bacon
Owner: Dorothy Hoff
Marketing: Tim Hoff
Estimated Sales: $1-2.5 Million
Number Employees: 10-19
Type of Packaging: Private Label, Bulk

6178 Hoffman Aseptic Packaging Company
PO Box 225
Hoffman, MN 56339-0225 320-986-2084
Fax: 320-986-2087 hapcoalx@rea-alp.com
Aseptic-packed sauces and puddings
President: Tom Ashley
Estimated Sales: $20-50 Million
Number Employees: 50-99

6179 Hoffman Sausage Company
2111 Kindel Ave
Cincinnati, OH 45214 513-621-4160
Fax: 513-621-7205 hoffmannsausage@aol.com
Processor of sausage and luncheon meats
Owner/President: Howard Tallen
Estimated Sales: $5-10Million
Number Employees: 20-49
Type of Packaging: Consumer, Bulk

6180 Hofmann Sausage Company
6196 Eastern Ave
Syracuse, NY 13211 315-437-7257
Fax: 315-437-2391 800-724-8410
sales@hofmannsausage.com
www.hofmannsausage.com
hot dogs, coneys, sausages and German mustard.
President: Rusty Flook
Estimated Sales: $4 Million
Number Employees: 26
Number of Brands: 15
Number of Products: 75
Sq. footage: 12500
Type of Packaging: Consumer, Food Service, Bulk
Brands:
GERMAN
SANPPY'S

6181 Hog Haus Brewing Company
430 W Dickson St
Fayetteville, AR 72701 479-521-2739
Fax: 479-442-0077 hops@ozarkbrew.com
www.hoghaus.com
Processor of seasonal beer, ale, stout, lager and porter
President: Kari Larson
VP: Julie Sill
Managing Director: Kari Larson
Estimated Sales: Below $ 5 Million
Number Employees: 50-99
Type of Packaging: Consumer, Food Service
Brands:
HogHaus
Ploughman's Pils
WoodStock Wheat

6182 Hogtown Brewing Company
2351 Royal Windsor Drive
Unit 6
Mississauga, ON L5J 4S7
Canada 905-855-9065
Fax: 905-822-0990 hogman@infinity.net
www.hogtownbeer.com
Processor of beer; also, bottling services available
President: Maria Lopez
General Manager: Peter Lazaro
Number Employees: 5-9
Type of Packaging: Consumer, Food Service

6183 Hogtowne B-B-Q Sauce Company
1712 W University Ave
Gainesville, FL 32603-1839 352-375-6969
Fax: 352-373-6969 www.saltydogsaloon.com
Wholesaler/distributor of hot sauces, BBQ sauces, marinades and other specialty food products
Manager: Keith Singleton
Vice President: Pam Taylor-Kinard
Estimated Sales: $500,000-$1 Million
Number Employees: 20-49
Sq. footage: 2000
Parent Co: Original Alan's Cubana
Type of Packaging: Consumer, Food Service, Private Label, Bulk
Brands:
CAROLINA STYLE B-B-Q-SAUCE
HOGTOWNE
KINARD'S MARINADE
PRIME STEAK SAUCE

6184 Holey Moses Cheesecake
115 Francis S Gabreski Airport
Westhampton Beach, NY 11978 631-288-8088
Fax: 631-288-0551 800-225-2253
www.holeymosescheesecake.com
Processor of cheesecake
President: Christopher Weber
Estimated Sales: Less than $500,000
Number Employees: 1-4

6185 Holistic Products Corporation
10 W Forest Avenue
Englewood, NJ 07631-4020 201-569-1188
Fax: 201-569-3224 800-221-0308
Processor, wholesaler/distributor and importer of health food products including propolis lozenges
President: Arnold Gans
VP Sales: Myra Gans
Number Employees: 10-19
Sq. footage: 8000
Parent Co: MNI Group

6186 **Holland American International Specialties**
10343 Artesia Blvd
Bellflower, CA 90706 562-925-6914
Fax: 562-925-4507 sales@dutchmall.com
www.1dutchmall.com
European and domestic specialty gourmet foods.
Manager: Maria Cervantes
Estimated Sales: $ .5 - 1 million
Number Employees: 1-4

6187 **Holland Sweeteners N A**
1640 Powers Ferry Rd #11-260
Merietta, GA 30067
US 770-956-8443
Fax: 770-956-7102
Processor of aspartame,sugar manufacturers.
President: Ken Dooley
CEO: Barbara Durrance
Estimated Sales: $210.00k
Number Employees: 5-9
Sq. footage: 3200
Parent Co: Holland Sweeteners N.A.
Type of Packaging: Bulk

6188 **Hollman Foods**
5423 N Wayne Ave
Chicago, IL 60640 308-468-5635
Fax: 308-468-6141 888-926-2879
info@hollmans.com www.hollmans.com
Processor of barbecue sauce, seasonings, spices, smoked turkey, breading mixes, gourmet jellies and fruit butters; also, gift box items, dip mixes, and honey
Owner: Byron Holl
CEO: Judith Holl
Estimated Sales: $ 3 - 5 Million
Number Employees: 5-9
Number of Brands: 2
Number of Products: 30
Sq. footage: 3000
Type of Packaging: Consumer, Food Service, Private Label
Brands:
EDEN FARMS
HOLLMANS

6189 **Hollow Road Farms**
271 Hollow Rd
Stuyvesant, NY 12173 518-758-7214
Fax: 518-758-1899
Yogurt.
President: Joan Snyder
Estimated Sales: $500,000-$1 Million
Number Employees: 5-9

6190 **Holly Hill Locker Company**
P.O.Box 355
Holly Hill, SC 29059 803-496-3611
Manufactuer of beef and pork
Owner: L Kenneth Folse Jr
Estimated Sales: Less than $500,000
Number Employees: 1-4
Type of Packaging: Consumer, Bulk

6191 **Holly's Oatmeal**
241 Northside Drive
19 Calhoun Street
Torrington, CT 06790 860-618-0090
Fax: 860-618-3008 hdimauro@optonline.net
www.hollysoatmeal.com

6192 **Holmes Cheese Company**
9444 State Route 39
Millersburg, OH 44654-9733 330-674-6451
Fax: 330-674-6673
Manufacturer of cheese and whey
President/CEO: Robert Ramseyer
VP: Walter Ramseyer
Estimated Sales: $4 Million
Number Employees: 25
Sq. footage: 42000
Type of Packaging: Consumer, Food Service, Private Label, Bulk

6193 **Holmes Foods**
603 W Central Ave
Nixon, TX 78140 830-582-1970
Fax: 830-582-1090
Poultry
President: Phillip A Morris
General Manager: Phillip Morris
Estimated Sales: $20-50 Million
Number Employees: 100-249

6194 **(HQ)Holsum Bakery**
P.O.Box 6690
Phoenix, AZ 85005 602-252-2351
Fax: 602-252-6505 800-755-8167
www.holsumaz.com
Manufacturer of breads and rolls
Owner: L Edward Eisele Jr
Estimated Sales: $20-50 Million
Number Employees: 500-999
Other Locations:
Holsum Manufacturing Plant
Tempe AZ
Holsum Manufacturing Plant
Tolleson AZ
Brands:
Aunt Hattie's
Aunt Hattie's Quality Breads
Bar S
Holsum
LeFrancias
Roman Meal
Smart Kids

6195 **Holsum Bakery**
20.1 Carretera 2
Toa Baja, PR 00949 787-798-8282
Fax: 787-251-2060
Processor of baked goods
President: Ramon Calderon
VP: Julio Vigoreaux
Estimated Sales: $100 Million
Number Employees: 5,000-9,999
Type of Packaging: Consumer, Food Service, Private Label, Bulk

6196 **Holsum Bakery**
P.O.Box 11468
Fort Wayne, IN 46858-1468 260-456-2130
Fax: 260-745-1404
Processor of bread including white, rye, whole wheat, low-fat, etc
President: Wayne Davidson
VP Sales: Frank Kerr
Number Employees: 100-249
Parent Co: Lewis Brothers Bakeries
Type of Packaging: Consumer, Food Service

6197 **Holsum Bread**
5120 8th Ave
Kenosha, WI 53140 262-637-6544
Fax: 262-658-0029
Baked goods
President: Edward Eisele, Jr
Estimated Sales: $10-20 Million
Number Employees: 20-49

6198 **Holt's Bakery**
101 Sellers St
Douglas, GA 31533-4607 912-384-2202
Fax: 912-384-7467
Baked goods, pastries, cookies
Owner: Howard Holt
CEO/Manager: Cecil Holt, Jr
Purchasing Agent: Paul Spivey
Estimated Sales: $1-2.5 Million
Number Employees: 20-49

6199 **Holten Meats**
1682 Sauget Business Blvd
Sauget, IL 62206-1454 618-337-8400
Fax: 618-337-3292 800-851-4684
info@holtenmeat.com www.holtenmeat.com
Processor of frozen beef, pork and veal patties
President: Mike Holten
Chairman/Chief Executive Officer: Jim Holten
COO: R Scott Hudspeth
Estimated Sales: $32 Million
Number Employees: 200
Sq. footage: 50000
Type of Packaging: Food Service
Brands:
EXTRA VALUE
HOLTEN

6200 **Holton Food Products Company**
500 W Burlington Ave
La Grange, IL 60525 708-352-5599
Fax: 708-352-3788
Processor of ingredients for frozen pies, cakes and cookies including egg whites and stabilizers
President: Ross Holton
CEO: Paul Holton
Executive VP: John Holton
Estimated Sales: $2.5-5 Million
Number Employees: 10-19
Type of Packaging: Bulk

6201 **Holton Meat Processing**
701 Arizona Ave
Holton, KS 66436 785-364-2331
Processor of beef
Owner: Ben Hartley
Estimated Sales: $ 1 - 3 Million
Number Employees: 1-4
Type of Packaging: Consumer

6202 **Holy Mole**
PO Box 203128
Austin, TX 78720-3128 512-310-8453
Fax: 512-671-4766 877-310-8453
info@holymole.comm
www.holymole.com/index2.ivnu
Manufacturer of salsa available in several flavors including hot red salsa, fire roasted habanero; gift packs available.
President: Pat Jones
Estimated Sales: $300,000-500,000
Number Employees: 1-4

6203 **Homarus**
476 Armour Circle NE
Atlanta, GA 30324-4002 404-877-1988
Fax: 404-877-1999 www.smoked.salmon.com
Processor and exporter of smoked salmon, nova, lox, sturgeon, trout, tuna loins, scallops, shrimp, mussels and whitefish; also, custom-cured salmon
Co-Owner/President: Peter Heineman
CEO: Chris Harvey
VP Sales: Thomas Marshall
Type of Packaging: Consumer, Food Service
Brands:
HOMARUS
RIVERBANK

6204 **Hombres Foods**
102 Cedar Ln
Cedar Creek, TX 78612 512-303-4558
Fax: 515-303-4558 877-446-6273
Sales@HombresFoods.com
www.hombresfoods.com/start.html
Specializes in gourmet salsas, chili and cornbread fixins, dip mixes, soup, brownie mixes and BBQ seasonings.
President: Dennis Willms
Estimated Sales: $ .5 - 1 million
Number Employees: 1-4

6205 **Home Baked Group**
1084 S Rogers Cir
Boca Raton, FL 33487-2815 561-995-0767
Fax: 561-995-0294 www.homebaked.com
Fat-free and low-fat brownies, sugar-free baked goods
Estimated Sales: $1-4.9 Million
Number Employees: 5-9

6206 **Home Bakery**
304 S 2nd St # Main
Laramie, WY 82070-3648 307-742-2721
Fax: 307-745-3346
Manufacturer of baked goods and chocolate
President: Kim Campbell
Estimated Sales: $500,000-$1 Million
Number Employees: 10-19
Type of Packaging: Food Service

6207 **Home Baking Company**
900 16th St N
Birmingham, AL 35203 205-252-1161
Fax: 205-323-7610 www.flowersfoods.com
Manufacturer and exporter of hamburger buns
President: Carter Wood
Estimated Sales: $10-20 Million
Number Employees: 100-249
Sq. footage: 65000
Parent Co: Flowers Baking Company
Type of Packaging: Consumer

6208 **Home Delivery Food Service**
PO Box 215
Jefferson, GA 30549-0215 706-367-9551
Fax: 706-367-4646
Frozen foods, meats and chicken
President: William Griffin, Sr.

6209 **Home Made Brand Foods Company**
2 Opportunity Way
Newburyport, MA 1950 978-462-3663
Fax: 978-462-7117
Processor of deli and meat salads, chilled entrees, quiche, pot pies, soups, stews, chowders, dips, spreads and desserts
President: Richard Walthers
CEO: John Palmieri
VP Operations: Dayne Wayhl
Estimated Sales: $20-50 Million
Number Employees: 50-99

6210 **Home Maid Bakery**
1005 Lower Main St
Wailuku, HI 96793 808-244-4150
Fax: 808-242-8458 info@homemaidbakery.com
www.homemaidbakery.com
Bakery products
President: Jeremy Kozuki
Sales Director: Leighton Saito
Purchasing Manager: Steven Tarnoff
Estimated Sales: $4-5 Million
Number Employees: 50-99
Number of Brands: 1
Number of Products: 100+
Type of Packaging: Consumer, Private Label

6211 **Home Market Foods**
140 Morgan Dr # 100
Norwood, MA 02062-5013 781-948-1500
Fax: 781-702-6171 info@homemarketfoods.com
www.homemarketfoods.com
Cooked steak, cooked meatballs, sausage, Italian sausage, cooked sausage
President: Wesley Atamian
Manager: Andy Stone
VP: Steve Smith
Director Sales: Dana Geremonte
VP Sales: Mike Wieirmiller
Estimated Sales: $ 1 - 3 Million
Number Employees: 150
Brands:
CHEF'S CHOICE

6212 **Home Roast Coffee**
25126 State Road 54
Lutz, FL 33559 813-949-0807
Fax: 813-948-6998
Coffee
Owner/President: Marvis Wood
Estimated Sales: $500,000-$1 Million
Number Employees: 1-4

6213 **Home Run Inn Frozen Foods**
1300 Internationale Pkwy
Woodridge, IL 60517-4928 630-783-9696
Fax: 630-783-0069 800-636-9696
gyarka@homeruninn.com www.homeruninn.com
Processor of frozen pizza including original thin crust and deep dish varieties.
President/CEO: Joseph Perrino
Marketing Director: Gina Bolger
Operations: Dan Costello
Estimated Sales: $10-24.9 Million
Number Employees: 50-99
Type of Packaging: Consumer, Food Service, Private Label
Brands:
HOME RUN INN

6214 **Home Style Bakery**
924 N 7th St
Grand Junction, CO 81501 970-243-1233
Processor of baked goods
President: Jan Wilke
Estimated Sales: $1-2.5 Million
Number Employees: 10-19
Sq. footage: 2000
Type of Packaging: Consumer, Food Service

6215 **Homegrown Naturals**
564 Gateway Dr
Napa, CA 94558 707-254-3700
Fax: 707-259-0219 800-288-1089
erciborgstrom@fantasticfoods.com
www.homegrownnaturalfoods.com
Manufacturer of natural foods products
Chief Executive Officer: John Foraker
CEO: John Foraker
VP Research/Development: Bob Kaake
Brand Team: Kathryn Keslosky
Web Marketing Manager: Mark Berger
Human Resources Manager: Amy Barberi
Consumer Relations Associate: Corrie Aldous
Consumer Relations Manager: Sherrie Crespin
Number Employees: 20-49
Brands:
Annie's

6216 **Homemade By Dorothy**
5150 N Montecito Pl
Boise, ID 83704 208-375-3720
dorothys@micron.net
http://dorothys.cc/
Jellies, syrups, toppings, pancake and baking mixes, soups, beverages, candy, gift crates and baskets, seasonal and holiday products.
President/Owner: Dorothy Baumhoff
Estimated Sales: $1-2.5 Million
Number Employees: 1-4

6217 **Homer's Ice Cream**
1237 Green Bay Rd
Wilmette, IL 60091-1699 847-251-0477
Fax: 847-251-0495 www.homersicecream.com
Processor of ice cream and sorbet
Owner: Dean Poulos
Marketing Director: Tean Poulous
VP: John Poulos
CEO: Stephen Poulous
Estimated Sales: $10-20 Million
Number Employees: 20-49
Sq. footage: 8000
Type of Packaging: Consumer, Food Service, Private Label, Bulk

6218 **Homer's Wharf Seafood Company**
43 Blackmer St
New Bedford, MA 02744-2613 508-997-0766
Fax: 508-999-9666
Processor of fish
Manager: Bruce Fontes
General Manager: Bruce Fontes
Estimated Sales: $10-20 Million
Number Employees: 50-99
Type of Packaging: Consumer

6219 **Homes Packaging Company**
PO Box 29
Millersburg, OH 44654-0029 330-674-2520
Fax: 330-674-5451 800-401-2529
Clay pot baked goods, baking mixes
Public Relations: Bruce Cameron
Estimated Sales: $1-2.5 Million
Number Employees: 1-4
Type of Packaging: Private Label

6220 **(HQ)Homestead Baking Company**
145 N Broadway
Rumford, RI 02916 401-434-0551
Fax: 401-438-0542 800-556-7216
pvican@homesteadbaking.com
www.homesteadbaking.com
Breads, rolls, hard rolls, english muffins
President: Peter Vican
VP: Bill Vican
Sales Manager: Vinny Palmiotti
Estimated Sales: $7 Million
Number Employees: 95
Sq. footage: 40000
Type of Packaging: Food Service, Private Label, Bulk
Brands:
MATTHEWS ALL NATURAL
MRS KAVANAGH'S
NEW ENGLAND PREMIUM

6221 **Homestead Dairies**
41 Churchill Avenue
Massena, NY 13662-1630 315-769-2456
Fax: 315-769-8975
Dairy
President: Robert Squires
Estimated Sales: $10-100 Million
Number Employees: 1-4

6222 **Homestead Fine Foods**
315 S Maple Ave
Suite 106
S San Francisco, CA 94080-6307 650-615-0750
Fax: 650-615-0764 www.homesteadpasta.com
Processor of fresh and frozen lasagna, ravioli, gnocchi and tortellini; also, mushroom and meat sauces
President: Terry Hall
Estimated Sales: $ .5 - 1 million
Number Employees: 10-19
Type of Packaging: Consumer, Food Service, Private Label
Brands:
HOMESTEAD

6223 **Homestead Mills**
221 N River St
Cook, MN 55723 218-666-5233
Fax: 218-666-5236 800-652-5233
aho.uslink.net www.homesteadmills.com
Processor and exporter of grain and wild rice, hot cereal and pancake mixes; also, corn and rye meal and flour including whole wheat, cracked wheat, rye, barley and buckwheat. Also backpacker meals
Owner/President: Keith Aho
Owner/Vice President: Carol Aho
Plant Manager: Anita Reinke
Estimated Sales: $1 Million
Number Employees: 5-9
Number of Brands: 2
Number of Products: 27
Sq. footage: 13000
Type of Packaging: Consumer, Food Service, Private Label, Bulk
Brands:
COUNTRY BLEND CEREAL
HOMESTEAD MILLS
NOPRTHERN LITES PANCAKES
POTATO PANCAKE MIX
SOUTH OF THE BORDER CHILI
SPECIALTY FLOUR
UNCLE WAYNES FISH BATTER

6224 **Homestead Ravioli Company**
315 S Maple Ave
South San Francisco, CA 94080 650-615-0750
Fax: 650-615-0764 www.homesteadpasta.com
Italian frozen specialties
President: Terry Hall
Estimated Sales: $5-9.9 Million
Number Employees: 10-19

6225 **Homestyle Bread**
3305 E Broadway Rd
Phoenix, AZ 85040-2829 602-268-0677
Fax: 602-276-1468
Bread and bakery products
President: James Boots
Vice President: Robert Schurman
Estimated Sales: $5-9.9 Million
Number Employees: 20-49

6226 **Homestyle Foods Company**
5163 Edwin St
Hamtramck, MI 48212-3388 313-874-3250
Fax: 313-874-1026 www.homestylefoods.com
Processor and exporter of fresh salads including macaroni, potato and cole slaw.
President: Mike Kadian
Estimated Sales: $10-20 Million
Number Employees: 20-49
Type of Packaging: Private Label, Bulk

6227 **Homewood Winery**
23120 Burndale Rd
Sonoma, CA 95476 707-996-6353
Fax: 707-996-6935 www.homewoodwinery.com
Wines
President/Vineyard Manager: David Homewood
Estimated Sales: Under $500,000
Number Employees: 1-4
Type of Packaging: Private Label

6228 **Honest Tea**
4827 Bethesda Ave
Bethesda, MD 20814
Fax: 301-652-3556 800-865-4736
sethandbarry@honesttea.com
www.honesttea.com

Processor of organic bottled ice tea with wholeleaf bags
President/CEO: Seth Goldman
CFO: Jonathan Clark
VP of Sales: Melanie Knitzer
Estimated Sales: $10-20 Million
Number Employees: 10-19
Type of Packaging: Bulk

6229 **Honey Acres**
P.O.Box 46
PO Box 346
Ashippun, WI 53003-46
Fax: 920-474-4018 800-558-7745
sales@honeyacres.com www.honeyacres.com
Processor and exporter of honey and honey products including fruit bars and mustard
President/CEO: Eugene Brueggeman
National Sales Director: Kathy Sedan
Estimated Sales: $5-9.9 Million
Number Employees: 30
Number of Products: 50
Sq. footage: 36000
Type of Packaging: Consumer, Food Service, Private Label, Bulk
Brands:
1852
HI HONEY
HONEY ACRES

6230 **Honey Baked Ham Company**
12170 Mason Montgomery Rd
Cincinnati, OH 45249 513-583-8792
Fax: 513-583-4190 www.honeybaked.com
Baked hams, turkey, frozen desserts and party trays
President/CEO: Craig Kurz
Estimated Sales: $5-10 Million
Number Employees: 20-49
Brands:
HONEY BAKED HAM

6231 **Honey Bar/Creme de la Creme**
335 Albany Avenue
Kingston, NY 12401 845-331-4643
Fax: 845-331-4576 rvezina@delacreme.com
www.delacreme.com/
Owner: Roger Vezina

6232 **Honey Bear Fruit Basket**
6321 Washington St # N
Denver, CO 80216-1100 303-297-3390
Fax: 303-297-3393 888-330-2327
info@honeybearbasket.com
www.honeybearbaskets.com
Fine wine jelly, sauce, scone mix, lemon curd
Owner: Carol Kincler
General Manager: Linda Wenz
Estimated Sales: $500,000-$1 Million
Number Employees: 1-4
Brands:
Penelope's

6233 **Honey Bee Company**
865 N Main St
Alpharetta, GA 30009-8371 770-753-8057
Fax: 770-612-0815 800-572-8838
joejmarcou@aol.com
www.honeybakedonline.com
Processor of flavored honey
Manager: Ray Grant
Estimated Sales: $2.5-5 Million
Number Employees: 1-4
Type of Packaging: Private Label, Bulk

6234 **Honey Butter Products Company**
103 S Heintzelman St
Manheim, PA 17545 717-665-9323
Fax: 717-665-4422 downeyshoneybutter.com
Processor of bread spread: honey, butter and cinnamon blend
Owner: Kevin Sadd
Estimated Sales: $1 Million
Number Employees: 7
Sq. footage: 10000
Type of Packaging: Consumer, Food Service
Brands:
DOWNEY'S

6235 **Honey Cell**
850 Union Avenue
PO Box 5187
Bridgeport, CT 06610-0187 203-925-1818
Fax: 203-367-5266 cellpak@aol.com
www.valleycontainer.com/honey
Manufacturer of packaging pallets, corrugated pallets, void fillers, corner protection, runners, dunnage, and separator pads.
Sales Manager: Bruce Padden
Sales Representative: Richard Jackson
Estimated Sales: $ 20-50 Million
Number Employees: 20-50
Sq. footage: 40000
Parent Co: Valley Containers
Type of Packaging: Consumer

6236 **Honey Hut Ice Cream**
4674 State Rd
Cleveland, OH 44109 216-749-7077
Fax: 216-661-1883 HoneyHut@Adelphia.net
www.honeyhuticecream.com/
Ice cream, frozen desserts
President/Owner: Frank Page
Estimated Sales: Less than $500,000
Number Employees: 10-19

6237 **Honey Ridge Farms**
12310 NE 245th Ave
Brush Prairie, WA 98606 360-256-0086
Fax: 360-883-2679 info@honeyridgefarms.com
www.honeyridgefarms.com
gourmet honey, honey cremes, balsamic honey vinegar, honey sauces
Owner: Leeanne Goetz

6238 **Honey Rose Baking Company**
4107 La Portalada Dr
Carlsbad, CA 92010-2805
Fax: 760-722-5203
Cookies, pies and tarts
President: Terry Cooper
Estimated Sales: $5-9.9 Million
Number Employees: 10-19
Type of Packaging: Private Label

6239 **Honey Wafer Baking Company**
13952 Kildare Ave
Crestwood, IL 60445 708-388-9010
Fax: 708-388-9680 800-261-2984
honeywafer@yahoo.com
www.anisihoneywafer.com
Manufacturer of gourmet honey wafers, all naturally made in the European style
Owner/President: Tony Lewandowski
Vice President: Adrienne Lewandowski
Estimated Sales: Under $500,000
Number Employees: 5
Type of Packaging: Consumer
Brands:
Anisi

6240 **Honey World**
P.O.Box 459
Parker, SD 57053-0459 605-297-4188
Fax: 605-297-4118 candles@iw.net
Processor of whipped honey, and flavored honey
President: Glen Wollman
Estimated Sales: $5-10 Million
Number Employees: 1-4
Type of Packaging: Private Label, Bulk

6241 **HoneyRun Winery**
2309 Park Ave
Chico, CA 95928 530-345-6405
Fax: 530-894-6639 honeyrun@honeyrun.com
www.honeyrun.com
Wine in a variety of flavors including blackberry, cherry, elderberry, and cranberry.
President: John Hasle
VP: Amy Hasle
Estimated Sales: $ .5 - 1 million
Number Employees: 1-4

6242 **Honeybake Farms**
5051 Speaker Rd
Kansas City, KS 66106 913-371-7777
Fax: 913-371-7799 www.chefspride.com
Processor of fresh and frozen sandwiches; also, salads, desserts and gourmet cinnamon rolls
President/CEO/Owner: Neil Sloman
Estimated Sales: $5-10 Million
Sq. footage: 50000
Type of Packaging: Consumer, Private Label
Brands:
HONEYBAKE FARMS

6243 **Honeydrop Foods**
PO Box 6428
Bridgewater, NJ 08807-0428 908-203-1577
Fax: 908-203-9063
comments@honeydropfoods.com OR
funlayo@honeydropfoods.com
www.honeydropfoods.com
Authentic African Foods
President: Jide Adedeji
Marketing/Sales/Product Information: Yvonne Adedeji
Brands:
OBE SAUCE
OBE SAUCE MIX

6244 **Honeypot Treats**
642 Hillsboro Road
Camden, NY 13316-4411 315-245-2415
Fax: 315-245-3000 800-223-1024
Honey
President/CEO: Dan Russell

6245 **Honeyville Grain**
11600 Dayton Dr
Rancho Cucamonga, CA 91730 909-980-9500
Fax: 909-980-6503 888-810-3212
info@honeyvillegrain.com
www.honeyvillegrain.com
Processor of bakery mixes, soy and corn products, dry milk, whey powder, flour and rolled oats; wholesaler/distributor of ingredients including flour, corn meal, edible oils, salt, etc.; exporter of beverages, corn, flour, etc.
VP: John C Hadfield
Quality Assurance Manager: Jose Parra
VP Marketing/Sales: John Hadfield
Human Resources Manager: Jacob Walters
VP Operations: Richard Larsen
General Manager: Tyler Christensen
Assistant Mix Plant: Natalia Espinoza
Purchasing: Brian Davis
Estimated Sales: $3-5 Million
Number Employees: 1-4
Sq. footage: 25000
Type of Packaging: Food Service, Bulk

6246 **Honeyville Grain**
635 Billy Mitchell Rd # A
Salt Lake City, UT 84116-2980 801-972-2168
Fax: 801-972-8412 infoslc@honeyvillegrain.com
www.honeyvillegrain.com
Processor of bakery mixes, soy and corn products, dry milk, whey powder, flour and rolled oats; wholesaler/distributor of ingredients including flour, corn meal, edible oils, salt, etc.; exporter of beverages, corn, flour, etc.
President: Bruce Merrell
VP Finance: Robert Anderson
Executive VP: Trevor Christensen
Director Marketing/Sales: Don Mann
Sales Manager: Craig Dunford
Assistant Operations Manager: Garth Rollins
Estimated Sales: $ 10 - 20 Million
Number Employees: 10-19
Sq. footage: 60000
Parent Co: Honeyville Grain
Type of Packaging: Consumer, Food Service, Private Label, Bulk

6247 **Honeywood Winery**
1350 Hines St SE
Salem, OR 97302-2521 503-362-4111
Fax: 503-362-4112 800-726-4101
info@honeywoodwinery.com
www.honeywoodwinery.com
Processor and exporter of specialty wines including pinot gris, pinot noir, chardonnay, cranberry, peach, fruit, etc.
President: Paul Gallick
VP: Marlene K Gallick
Estimated Sales: $1 Million+
Number Employees: 5-9
Number of Brands: 5
Number of Products: 45
Sq. footage: 22000
Type of Packaging: Private Label
Brands:
HONEYMAN & WOOD
HONEYWOOD GRANDE
HONEYWOOD NORTH AMERICAN GRAPE
HONEYWOOD PREMIUM

6248 **Hong Kong Market Company**
2425 S Wallace St
Chicago, IL 60616-1855 312-791-9111
Fax: 312-791-1324
Processor of bean sprouts, snow peas and other Chinese vegetables
President: Gloria Lam
VP: Thomas Lam
Estimated Sales: $1-2.5 Million
Number Employees: 10-19
Type of Packaging: Consumer, Food Service, Private Label, Bulk

6249 **Hong Kong Noodle Company**
2350 S Wentworth Ave
Chicago, IL 60616 312-842-0480
Fax: 312-842-7069 ron@hongkongnoodle.com
www.hongkongnoodle.com
Manufactures dry egg, plain or water noodles
Manager: Glenn Jung
Vice President/Co-Owner: Harry Chung
Estimated Sales: $2.5-5 Million
Number Employees: 20-49
Type of Packaging: Food Service

6250 **Hong Kong Supermarket**
4166 Buford Hwy NE
Atlanta, GA 30345-1081 404-325-3999
Fax: 404-325-3311
Oriental food items, ethnic foods, full line seafood
Owner: Ly Tieu
Estimated Sales: $ 10 - 20 Million
Number Employees: 50-99

6251 **Hong Tou Noodle Company**
7059 N Figueroa St
Los Angeles, CA 90042 323-256-3843
Noodles
Owner: Peter Kwong
General Manager: Peter Kong
Estimated Sales: $500,000-$1 Million
Number Employees: 1-4

6252 **Hongar Farm Gourmet Foods**
2121 Tucker Industrial Rd
Tucker, GA 30084 770-938-9884
Fax: 770-938-8964 888-296-7191
info@hongarfarms.com www.hongarfarms.com
Gourmet seasoned oils and vinegars, marinades, bread dippers, and specialty items.
President: Joe Oxman
Estimated Sales: $1-2.5 Million
Number Employees: 5-9
Brands:
HONGAR FARMS

6253 **HongryHawg Products**
16414 Chris Rd
Prairieville, LA 70769 225-622-4011
Fax: 225-622-0546 888-772-4294
answers@cajunsauce.com
www.hongryhawg.com OR www.cajunsauce.com
Hot sauce, barbecue sauce, jambalaya mix, cajun seasoning and gift boxes.
Owner: Hiram Davis
Estimated Sales: $ 5 - 10 Million
Number Employees: 5-9

6254 **Honickman Affiliates**
8275 N Crescent Blvd
Pennsauken, NJ 08110-1435 856-665-6200
Fax: 856-661-4684 800-573-7745
Processor, canner and bottler of soft drinks
Chairman: Harold Honickman
CEO: Jeffrey Honickman
CFO: Walt Wilkinson
Business Development Manager: Larry Linder
Production Manager: Phil Forte
Estimated Sales: $ 10 - 20 Million
Number Employees: 20-49
Parent Co: PepsiCo North America
Type of Packaging: Consumer, Food Service
Brands:
Cadbury Schweppes
Coors
Pepsi-Cola
Snapple
South Beach

6255 **Honig Vineyard and Winery**
P.O.Box 406
Rutherford, CA 94573-0406 707-963-5618
Fax: 707-963-5639 800-929-2217
www.honigwine.com
Wines, including: Sauvignon Blanc, Rutherford Sauvignon Blanc, Cabernet Sauvignon, Bartolucci Vineyard Cabernet, Late Harvest Sauvignon Blanc.
President: Michael Honig
CFO: Tony Benedetti
Marketing Director: Regina Weinstein
Estimated Sales: $5-9.9 Million
Number Employees: 5-9
Type of Packaging: Private Label

6256 **Honolulu Fish & SeafoodCompany**
3109 Koapaka St
Honolulu, HI 96819-1998 808-833-1123
Fax: 808-836-1045 www.honolulufish.com
Offers more than 14 species of sashimi grade fish to restaurants around the world.
President/CEO: Wayne Samiere

6257 **Honso USA**
P.O.Box 6729
Chandler, AZ 85246 602-377-8787
Fax: 480-377-6649 888-461-5808
info@honso.com www.HonsoUSA.com
Manufacturer of Chinese herbal products.
President: Dan Wen
Estimated Sales: $300,000-500,000
Number Employees: 1-4

6258 **Hood River Coffee Company**
1310 Tucker Rd
Hood River, OR 97031 541-386-3908
Fax: 541-386-3998 800-336-2954
customerservice@hoodrivercoffeeco.com
www.hoodrivercoffeeco.com
Coffee available in several varieties including: African, American, Indonesian, Organic, Dark Roast, Espresso, Decaffeinated; also organic teas, gifts and gear.
Owner: Mark Hudon
Number Employees: 1-4

6259 **Hood River Distillers**
660 Riverside Dr
Hood River, OR 97031 541-386-1588
Fax: 541-386-2520 HRDsales@HRDspirits.com
www.hrdspirits.com
Hood River Distillers creates, produces, imports and distributes 15 brands of spirits ranging from value to premium products: whisky, rum, gin, vodka, schnapps, Irish cream whiskey, scotch and liqueurs.
President/CEO: Ronald Dodge
CFO: Gary Goatcher
VP/General Manager: Lynda Webber
Marketing Manager: Tia Bledsoe
VP Sales: Erik Svenson
Public Relations/Media: Olga Haley
Estimated Sales: $ 50 - 100 Million
Number Employees: 46
Number of Brands: 7
Number of Products: 46
Sq. footage: 53000
Brands:
BROKER'S GIN
HRD
KICKERS IRISH CREAM
MONARCH
PENDELTON WHISKEY
ULLR SCHNAPPS
YAZI GINGER VODKA

6260 **Hood River Vineyards and Winery**
4693 Westwood Dr
Hood River, OR 97031 541-386-3772
Fax: 541-386-5880 hoodriverwines@gorge.net
http://hoodrivervineyards.us/home/
Produces a variety of table and dessert wines including: Chardonnay, Pinot Noir, Zinfandel, Cabernet Sauvignon, Merlot, Riesling, Black Muscat, Zinfandel Port, Marionberry, and Black Cherry.
President: Bernie Lerch
VP: Anne Lerch
Estimated Sales: $1-2.5 Million
Number Employees: 1-4

6261 **Hoodsport Winery**
23501 N Us Highway 101
Hoodsport, WA 98548 253-396-9463
Fax: 253-877-9508 800-580-9894
wine@hoodsport.com www.hoodsport.com
Produces a variety of wines; also offers gourmet coffee and chocolate wine truffles.
President: Peggy Patterson
Estimated Sales: $5-10 Million
Number Employees: 10-19
Type of Packaging: Private Label
Brands:
HOODSPORT

6262 **Hoody Corporation**
8344 Pateywoods Rd
Newark, MD 21841-2012 410-632-1766
VP Sales/Marketing: Darryl Hamilton
VP Operations: Sid Harvey
Estimated Sales: Under $500,000
Number Employees: 5-9

6263 **Hook's Cheese Company**
320 Commerce St
Mineral Point, WI 53565 608-987-3259
Fax: 608-987-2658
Monterey jack, cheddar and colby cheese
President: Tony Hook
Estimated Sales: $1-2.5 Million
Number Employees: 1-4

6264 **Hoonah Cold Storage**
P.O.Box 470
Hoonah, AK 99829 907-945-3264
Fax: 907-945-3441
Manager: Terrence Barry

6265 **(HQ)Hoopeston Foods**
101 W Burnsville Pkwy Ste 107
Burnsville, MN 55337 952-854-0903
Fax: 952-854-6874
choerning@hoopestonfoods.com
http://hfinc3.qwestoffice.net/
Full line of canned dry beans, chili, stews, soups, sauces, tamales, meats in a variety of sizes.
President: Eric Newman
CEO: Tad Ballentyne
SVP/CFO/CAO: Corey Hoerning
CEO: Tad Ballantyne
VP Sales/Marketing: Tony Trenkle
Estimated Sales: $ 5 - 10 Million
Number Employees: 5-9
Type of Packaging: Food Service, Private Label
Brands:
NATURE'S GOLD
TIO FRANCO

6266 **Hoople Country Kitchens**
714 N 5th St
Rockport, IN 47635 812-649-2351
Fax: 812-649-2836
Processor of pork sausage, prepared salads, corn meal mush and horseradish
President: David Caskey
Treasurer: Franklin Caskey
VP: Denise Caskey
Estimated Sales: $5-10 Million
Number Employees: 20-49
Type of Packaging: Consumer

6267 **Hop Growers of America**
P.O.Box 1207
Moxee, WA 98936 509-248-7043
Fax: 509-457-8561 info@usahops.org
www.usahops.org
Hop Growers of America represents and promotes the interests of U.S. growers both domestically and internationally. As the national organization, HGA provides support, coordination and communication to growers, brewers and the worldhop industry in areas of common interest, including; marketing statistics, promotion, education and research.
Administrator: Ann George
Public Relations: Michelle Palacios
Number Employees: 1-4

6268 **Hop Kee**
2425 S Wallace St
Chicago, IL 60616-1855 312-791-9111
Fax: 312-791-1324
http://www.orientaldelicacies.com
President: Thomas Lamb
Estimated Sales: $ 8 Million

6269 **Hop Kiln Winery**
6050 Westside Rd
Healdsburg, CA 95448-8318 707-433-6491
Fax: 707-433-8162 info@hopkilnwinery.com
www.hopkilnwinery.com

Producer of a variety of wines including: Rushin' River Red, Thousand Flowers, Zinfandel, Sauvignon Blanc, and Big Red. Also offers mustards, vinegars, pestos, oils, vinaigrettes, and dessert sauces.
President: David Di Loreto
Plant Manager: Erich Bradley
Estimated Sales: $5-9.9 Million
Number Employees: 10-19
Brands:
CHARDONNAY BARREL SELECT
LATE HARVEST ZINFANDEL
MARTY GRIFFIN BIG RED
PRIMIVITO ZINFANDEL
SONOMA COUNTY ZINFANDEL
THOUSAND FLOWERS
VALDIGUIE

6270 **Hope Creamery**
P.O.Box 42
Hope, MN 56046 507-451-2029
Manufacturer of butter
President/Owner: Victor Mrotz
Operations: Gene Kruckeberg
Estimated Sales: $300,000-$500,000
Number Employees: 1-4
Sq. footage: 4000
Type of Packaging: Consumer, Bulk
Brands:
HOPE

6271 **Hopkins Food Service**
272 Oak Hill Road
Cairo, GA 39828-6119 229-872-3214
Fax: 229-872-3216
Estimated Sales: $ 1 - 3 Million
Number Employees: 5-9

6272 **Hopkins Inn**
22 Hopkins Rd
Warren, CT 06777 860-868-7295
Fax: 860-868-7464 www.thehopkinsinn.com
Gourmet salad dressings
President: Beth Schober
Estimated Sales: $1-2.5 Million
Number Employees: 20-49
Brands:
HOPKINS INN CAESAR DRESSING
HOPKINS INN HOUSE DRESSING

6273 **Hopkins Vineyard**
25 Hopkins Rd
Warren, CT 06777 860-868-7954
Fax: 860-868-1768 info@hopkinsvineyard.com
www.hopkinsvineyard.com
Wine
President: Hilary Hopkins
Estimated Sales: $1-2.5 Million
Number Employees: 5-9
Type of Packaging: Private Label
Brands:
HIGHLAND ESTATES
HOPKINS VINEYARD CABERNET FRANC
HOPKINS VINEYARD CHARDONNAY
HOPKINS VINEYARD HARD CIDER
HOPKINS VINEYARD HIGHLAND ESTATES
HOPKINS VINEYARD ROSE
HOPKINS VINEYARD SACHEM'S PICNIc
HOPKINS VINEYARD SPARKLING WINE
HOPKINS VINEYARD VIDAL BLANC
HOPKINS WESTWIND

6274 **Hops Extract Corporation of America**
305 N 2nd Ave
Yakima, WA 98902 509-248-1530
Fax: 509-457-1639 sales@hopsteiner.com
www.hopsteiner.com
Processor of hops.
Manager: Dave Dunmham
Operations: Paul Signorotti
Estimated Sales: $20-50 Million
Number Employees: 20-49
Parent Co: S. S. Steiner, Inc.

6275 **Hopson**
PO Box 38
Ottumwa, IA 52501-0038 515-682-8164
Fax: 515-682-3123
President: Rodney Hopson

6276 **Hopunion LLC**
203 Division St
Yakima, WA 98902 509-453-4792
Fax: 509-453-1551 800-952-4873
hops@hopunion.com www.hopunion.com
Processor and exporter of hops and hops products
President: Dennis Bakos
President/CEO: Don Bryant
General Manager: Ralph Olson
Sales Executive: Ralph Woodall
Plant Manager: Tracy McCorkle
Estimated Sales: $ 10 - 20 Million
Number Employees: 20
Sq. footage: 20000
Type of Packaging: Bulk

6277 **Horizon Organic**
12002 Airporkway
Broomfield, CO 80021 303-635-4000
888-494-3020
www.horizonorganic.com
Milk, buttery products
President: Mike Ferry
Estimated Sales: Less than $500,000
Number Employees: 1-4
Brands:
Organic Cow

6278 **Horizon Organic Dairy**
12002 Airport Way
Bloomfield, CO 80021
888-494-3020
info@horizonorganic.com
www.horizonorganic.com
Processor of organic dairy products including milk, yogurt, sour cream, cottage cheese, cream cheese, cheese, butter and dry milk
Public Relations: Jarod Ballentine
VP Operations: Jule Taylor
Estimated Sales: $20-50 Million
Number Employees: 50-99
Type of Packaging: Consumer

6279 **Horizon Poultry**
92 Cartwright Avenue
Toronto, ON M6A 1V2
Canada 519-364-3200
Fax: 519-364-4692 cphilipp@schneiderfoods.ca
www.schneiderfoods.ca/
Hatchery and processor of chickens; importer of eggs
Quality Assurance: Cynthia Philippe MD
Number Employees: 165
Parent Co: J.M. Schneider
Type of Packaging: Consumer, Food Service, Private Label, Bulk

6280 **Horizon Winery**
PO Box 191
Santa Rosa, CA 95402-0191 707-544-2961
Wines
President: Paul Gardner

6281 **Horlacher's Fine Meats**
30 W 700 N
Logan, UT 84321-3214 435-752-1287
Processor of fresh and frozen ham, beef jerky and roast beef
Owner: Betty Horlacher
Estimated Sales: $5-10 Million appx.
Number Employees: 1-4
Sq. footage: 8000
Type of Packaging: Consumer, Bulk

6282 **Hormel Foods Corporation**
P.O.Box 69
Fremont, NE 68026 402-721-2300
Fax: 402-721-0445 rrheisinger@hormel.com
www.hormel.com
Processor of canned and smoked meats, sausage, ham, bacon and hot dogs; slaughtering services available.
Manager: Mark Coffey
Executive Vice President: Ronald Fielding
SVP/Chief Financial Officer: Jody Feragen
VP/Finance & Treasurer: Roland Gentzler
Corporate Media Information: Julie Craven
Corporate Brand Informtation: Joan Hanson
General Manager: Bruce Schweitzer
Operations Manager: Randy R Heisinger
Estimated Sales: $100+ Million
Number Employees: 1,000-4,999
Parent Co: Hormel Foods Corporation
Type of Packaging: Consumer

6283 **Hormel Foods Corporation**
1118 Highway 18 E
Algona, IA 50511 515-295-8777
Fax: 515-295-2470 www.hormel.com
Processor of pepperoni
Manager: Pete Von Ruden
VP/Finance & Treasurer: Roland Gentzler
SVP/Chief Financial Officer: Johy Feragen
SVP/General Counsel: James Cavanaugh
Corporate Media Information: Julie Craven
Corporate Brand Information: Joan Hanson
Manager: Peter Von Ruden
Estimated Sales: $100-500 Million
Number Employees: 100-249
Parent Co: Hormel Foods Corporation
Type of Packaging: Consumer

6284 **(HQ)Hormel Foods Corporation**
501 16th Ave NE
Austin, MN 55912 507-437-5395
Fax: 507-437-5129 800-523-4635
www.hormelfoods.com
Processor of soups, entrees, desserts, broths, puddings, sauces and meats including ham, sausage, bacon, turkey, pre-packaged chicken and deli items.
Chairman/President/CEO: Jeffrey Ettinger
EVP/Corporate Strategy: Ronald Fielding
SVP/CFO: Jody Feragen
EVP/Refigerated Products: Steven Binder
Group VP/Hormel Foods International: Richard Bross
Group VP/Foodservice: Thomas Day
Group VP/Grocery Products: James Splinter
Group VP/Specialty Foods: Michael Tolbert
Group Vp/Consumer Products Sales: Larry Vorpahl
SVP/Supply Chain: William Snyder
VP/Corporate Innovation: Deanna Brady
VP/Corporate Communications: Julie Craven
VP/Operations, Grocery Products: Michael Devine
Estimated Sales: $7 Billion
Number Employees: 10,000+
Type of Packaging: Consumer, Food Service, Private Label
Brands:
CHI-CHI'S
DI LUSSO
DINTY MOORE
FARMER JOHN
HERB-OX
HERDEZ
HORMEL
HORMEL NATURAL CHOICE
JENNIE-O
LLOYD'S BARBEQUE
MEGAMEX
NOT-SO-SLOPPY-JOE
SAAG'S SAUSAGES
SPAM
STAGG CHILI
VALLEY FRESH
WORLD FOOD

6285 **Hormel Foods Corporation**
3075 Southwestern Blvd Ste 210
Orchard Park, NY 14127 716-675-7700
Fax: 716-675-7700 www.hormel.com
Processor of fresh, frozen and canned meats, soups, shelf-stable prepared entrees, pre-packaged chicken, Oriental sauces, bouillon, olive oils, deli items and Mexican, Indian and Mediterranean foods.
Manager: Jennifer Johnson
Estimated Sales: $5-10 Million
Number Employees: 5-9
Parent Co: Hormel Foods Corporation
Type of Packaging: Consumer, Food Service

6286 **Hormel Foods Corporation**
10550 New York Ave Ste A1
Des Moines, IA 50322 515-276-8872
Fax: 515-276-2641 www.hormel.com
Processor of fresh and frozen ingredients, meats, soups, entrees, desserts, pre-packaged chicken, Oriental sauces, deli items and Mexican foods
Manager: Steve Anderson
Estimated Sales: $10-20 Million
Number Employees: 13
Parent Co: Hormel Foods Corporation
Type of Packaging: Consumer, Food Service

6287 **Hormel Foods Corporation**
6760 Alexander Bell Dr Ste 240
Columbia, MD 21046 410-290-1916
Fax: 410-290-1855 www.hormel.com
Processor of fresh and frozen meat, pre-packaged chicken, Asian sauces and Mexican and deli items
Owner: Geo Hormel
Manager: Tom Martin
Estimated Sales: $20-50 Million
Number Employees: 10-19
Parent Co: Hormel Foods Corporation
Type of Packaging: Consumer, Food Service

6288 **Hormel Foods Corporation**
65 Germantown Ct Ste 226
Cordova, TN 38018 901-753-4282
Fax: 901-753-2762 www.hormel.com
Processor of fresh and frozen ingredients, meats, soups, entrees, prepackaged chicken, Mexican foods, Oriental sauces and deli items
Principle: Linda Ray
Manager: Bob Sack
Manager: Matt King
Estimated Sales: $10-20 Million
Number Employees: 10-19
Parent Co: Hormel Foods Corporation
Type of Packaging: Consumer, Food Service

6289 **Hormel Foods Corporation**
5000 Hopyard Rd Ste 440
Pleasanton, CA 94588 925-734-9555
Fax: 925-734-9888 www.hormel.com
Processor of meats, entrees, pre-packaged chicken, Oriental sauces and deli items
Business Manager: Gary Prince
Estimated Sales: $20-50 Million
Number Employees: 20-49
Parent Co: Hormel Foods Corporation
Type of Packaging: Consumer, Food Service

6290 **Hormel Foods Corporation**
4222 E Thomas Rd Ste 340
Phoenix, AZ 85018 602-230-2400
Fax: 602-230-2405 www.hormel.com
Processor of fresh and frozen ingredients, meats, soups, entrees, desserts, pre-packaged chicken, Mexican foods, Oriental sauces and deli items
Manager: Patrick McDonald
Estimated Sales: $5-10 Million
Number Employees: 5-9
Parent Co: Hormel Foods Corporation
Type of Packaging: Consumer, Food Service

6291 **Hormel Foods Corporation**
100 Corporate Dr Ste 202
Lebanon, NJ 8833 908-236-7009
Fax: 908-236-7767 www.hormel.com
Processor of fresh and frozen ingredients, meats, soups, entrees, desserts, pre-packaged chicken, deli items and sauces
Director: John Campion
Manager: Kent Kreuer
Sales Manager: Steve Jensen
Estimated Sales: $20-50 Million
Number Employees: 30
Parent Co: Hormel Foods Corporation
Type of Packaging: Consumer, Food Service

6292 **Hormel Foods Corporation**
4055 Executive Park Dr Ste 300
Cincinnati, OH 45241 513-563-0211
Fax: 513-563-5054 www.hormel.com
Processor of fresh and frozen ingredients, meats, soups, entrees, desserts, pre-packaged chicken, Asian sauces and Mexican and deli items
Director of Administration: Ted Lawson
Sales Executive: Jim Tupy
Estimated Sales: $20-50 Million
Number Employees: 20-49
Parent Co: Hormel Foods Corporation
Type of Packaging: Consumer, Food Service

6293 **Hormel Foods Corporation**
4601 Hollow Tree Dr Ste 107
Arlington, TX 76018 817-465-4735
Fax: 817-468-4011 www.hormel.com
Processor and importer of fresh, frozen and canned ingredients, meats, soups, entrees, chicken, turkey, Asian sauces and Mexican and deli items
District Manager: Lynn Egner
Manager: Robert Joyner
Estimated Sales: $20-50 Million
Number Employees: 10
Parent Co: Hormel Foods Corporation
Type of Packaging: Consumer, Food Service

6294 **Hormel Foods Corporation**
651 Holiday Dr Ste 110
Pittsburgh, PA 15220 412-921-7036
Fax: 412-921-7018 www.hormel.com
Processor of ingredients, meats, soups, entrees, desserts, pre-packaged chicken, Asian sauces and deli items
Manager: Dick Gaffney
Manager: Jeff Baker
Sales Representative: Timothy Meek
Estimated Sales: $10-20 Million
Number Employees: 10
Parent Co: Hormel Foods Corporation
Type of Packaging: Consumer, Food Service

6295 **Hormel Foods Corporation**
901 N Lake Destiny Rd Ste 101
Maitland, FL 32751 407-660-1433
Fax: 407-660-1990 www.hormel.com
Processor of ham, bacon, beef, pork, frankfurters and sausage
District Manager: Greg Worley
Manager: Marti Harrison
Estimated Sales: $20-50 Million
Number Employees: 13
Parent Co: Hormel Foods Corporation
Type of Packaging: Consumer, Food Service

6296 **Hormel Foods Corporation**
500 Franklin Vllg Dr Ste 205
Franklin, MA 02038 508-541-7101
Fax: 508-541-7278 www.hormel.com
Processor of fresh and frozen ingredients, meats, entrees, pre-packaged chicken, deli items and sauces including Asian, Mediterranean, Greek and Indian; also, fresh and canned soups.
Manager: Paul Gillis
Estimated Sales: $20-50 Million
Number Employees: 20
Parent Co: Hormel Foods Corporation
Type of Packaging: Consumer, Food Service

6297 **Hormel Foods Corporation**
501 16th Ave NE
Austin, MN 55912 507-437-5395
Fax: 507-437-5129 carapelli@worldfood.com
www.hormel.com
Olive and grape seed oils, vinegars in addition to pre-packaged Carapelli Pasta and Sauce mixes.
Chairman/President/CEO: Richard Sommese
CEO: Jeffrey M Ettinger
SVP/General Counsel: James Cavanaugh
Corporate Brand Information: Joan Hanson
Corporate Media Information: Julie Craven
Estimated Sales: $500,000-$1 Million
Number Employees: 10,000+
Parent Co: Hormel Foods Corporation

6298 **Hormel Foods Ethnic Specialty Sales**
1 Hormel Place
Austina, MN 55912
Fax: 507-434-6509 800-533-2000
kakreuer@hormel.com www.hormelfoods.com
Processor of fresh and frozen ingredients, meats, soups, entrees, prepackaged chicken, Mexican foods, Oriental sauces and deli items
Marketing: Kent Kreuer
Estimated Sales: $10-20 Million
Number Employees: 10-19
Parent Co: Hormel Foods Corporation
Type of Packaging: Consumer, Food Service

6299 **Hornell Brewing Company**
5 Dakota Dr
New Hyde Park, NY 11042-1109 516-812-0300
Fax: 516-326-4988
President: John Ferolito
Estimated Sales: F
Number Employees: 500-999

6300 **Horner International**
5304 Emerson Drive
Raleigh, NC 27609 919-787-3112
Fax: 919-787-4272 sales@hornerintl.com
www.hornerinternational.com
Supplier of natural exracts and flavors
Parent Co: Horner International

6301 **Horriea 2000 Food Industries**
P.O.Box 975
Reynolds, GA 31076-0975
Canada 478-847-4186
Fax: 478-847-4464 gafruit@pstel.net
www.taylororchards.com
Owner: Jeff Wainwright
VP Marketing: Hassan El Findi
Production Manager: Mohamed El Findi
Estimated Sales: $11 Million
Number Employees: 10-19
Number of Products: 38
Type of Packaging: Private Label

6302 **Horst Alaskan Seafood**
2315 Industrial Blvd
Juneau, AK 99801-8534 907-790-4300
Fax: 907-790-5534 877-518-4300
horsts@gci.net www.horstsalaskanseafood.com
Processor of fresh and frozen seafood (vacuum packed)
President: Horst Schramm
Estimated Sales: Less than $500,000
Number Employees: 1-4
Type of Packaging: Consumer

6303 **Horstmann Mix & Cream**
3011 12th St
Long Island City, NY 11102 718-932-4735
Fax: 718-932-4794
Dairy
President: William Horstmann
Estimated Sales: $2.5-5 Million
Number Employees: 5-9

6304 **Horton Cellars Winery**
6399 Spotswood Trl
Gordonsville, VA 22942 540-832-7440
Fax: 540-832-7187 800-829-4633
vawinee@aol.com www.hbwine.com
Wine
President: Dennis Horton
Estimated Sales: $ 5 - 10 Million
Number Employees: 10-19

6305 **Horton Fruit Company**
4701 Jennings Ln
Louisville, KY 40218 502-969-1371
Fax: 502-964-1515 800-626-2245
www.hortonfruit.com
Re-packer of tomatoes and onions and a processor of spinach, kale, coleslaw, bananas, avocados, pineapples and caramel apples.
Chairman/CEO: Albert Horton
President/COO: Jackson Woodward
Treasurer: Steve Edelen
Vice President: Bill Benoit
Sales/Procurement: Tom Smith
Transportation Manager: Bobby Harlow
Estimated Sales: $50-100 Million
Number Employees: 250-499
Type of Packaging: Consumer, Food Service

6306 **Hosemen & Roche Vitamins & Fine Chemicals**
340 Kingsland Street
Building 787
Nutley, NJ 07110-1199 973-235-5000
Fax: 973-235-7605 800-526-6367
www.roche.com
Processor of bulk vitamins, carotenoids and citric acids for food manufacturing
President: Dr Franz B Humer
Estimated Sales: Less than $500,000
Number Employees: 1-4
Parent Co: Hoffman-La Roche
Type of Packaging: Bulk
Brands:
Roche

6307 **Hosford & Wood Fresh Seafood Providers**
2545 E 7th Street
Tucson, AZ 85716-4701 520-795-1920
Fax: 520-795-1010
Seafood
President: Anita Wood
Secretary: Bruce Hosford

6308 **Hosmer Mountain Bottling**
217 Mountain St
Willimantic, CT 06226 860-423-1555
Fax: 860-423-2207 800-763-2445
www.hosmersoda.com/index.php
Soft drinks
President/CEO: Andrew Potvin
VP Marketing Manager: Bill Potvin
Estimated Sales: $2.5-5 Million
Number Employees: 5-9
Type of Packaging: Private Label
Brands:
HOSMER MOUNTAIN SOFT DRINKS

6309 **Hospitality Mints**
213 Candy Ln
Boone, NC 28607 828-264-3045
Fax: 828-264-6933 800-334-5181
mints@boone.net www.hospitalitymints.com
Processor of mints; also, sugar-free breath mints; kosher available
President: Alan Peterson
Sales: Kathi Guy
Estimated Sales: $ 3 - 5 Million
Number Employees: 50-99
Sq. footage: 65000
Type of Packaging: Food Service

6310 **Hospitality Mints LLC**
213 Candy Ln
Boone, NC 28607 828-264-3045
Fax: 828-264-6933 800-334-5181
mints@hospitalitymints.com
www.hospitalitymints.com
Processor and exporter of dessert mint candies; custom printed packaging available
President/CEO: Allen Peterson
COO: Ira Wagner
Vice President: Walter Kaudelka
Estimated Sales: $500,000-$1 Million
Number Employees: 100-249
Sq. footage: 63000
Type of Packaging: Consumer, Food Service, Private Label, Bulk
Brands:
Hospitality

6311 **Hostess Brands**
6031 Connection Dr
Irving, TX 75039 972-532-4500
Fax: 972-892-7694 www.hostessbrands.com
Manufacturer of bread and other baked goods
CEO: Brian Driscoll
EVP/CFO: John Stewart
EVP Operations: Gary Wandschneider
Estimated Sales: Over $2 Billion
Number Employees: 10,000 +
Type of Packaging: Bulk

6312 **Hostess Brands**
1 East Armour Blvd
Kansas City, MO 64111 816-502-4000
Fax: 816-502-4126 www.hostessbrands.com
Processor of baked goods including bread, cakes, doughnuts, pies, buns and rolls.
Type of Packaging: Consumer, Food Service, Private Label
Brands:
Banama
Braun's
Buttercup
Butternut
Colombo Bread Bakery
Delmaid
Delmar
Devil Dogs
Diclaro
Dolly Madison
Dolly Madison Cakes
Drake's
Drake's Cakes
Eddy's
Holsum
Hostess
Merita
Millbrook
Mrs. Cubbison's
Nissen
Nu-Maid
Old Country
Parisian
Rainbo
Ring Dings
Roman Meal
San Francisco French Bread
Satin Gold
Sunmaid
Supreme
Sweetheart
Sweetheart Bread
Toscana
Weber's
Wonder
Wonder Bread
Yodels

6313 **(HQ)Hostess Brands**
6031 Connection Drive
Irving, TX 75039 972-532-4500
Fax: 972-892-7694 www.hostessbrands.com
Processor of breads and sweet snacks
CEO: Brian Driscoll
SVP/Chief Customer Officer: John Akeson
EVP/CFO: John Stewart
SVP/Information Technology: Steve Birgfield
EVP/Human Resources: David Loeser
EVP/Chief Marketing Officer: Richard Seban
EVP/Operations: Gary Wandschneider
Plant Manager: Jim Hutton
Purchasing Agent: Melinda Wilsey
Estimated Sales: $2.7 Billion
Number Employees: 20,000
Sq. footage: 25000
Type of Packaging: Consumer, Food Service, Private Label
Brands:
BEEFSTEAK
BREAD DU JOUR
BUTTERNUT
DING DONGS
DOLLY MADISON
DONETTES
DRAKE'S
HO HO'S
HOME PRIDE
HOSTESS
J.J. NISSEN
MERITA
MILLBROOK
NATURE'S PRIDE
SNO BALLS
SWEETHEART
TWINKIES
WONDER

6314 **Hostess Frito-Lay Company**
261 13th Ave Ne
Swift Current, SK S9H 2V8
Canada 306-773-9621
Processor of snack foods including potato, corn and tortilla chips, cheese twists and popcorn
Technical Manager: Alain Bedard
Plant Manager: Dean Bordner
Number Employees: 250-499
Parent Co: Pepsico
Type of Packaging: Consumer

6315 **Hot Licks Hot Sauces**
2820 Via Orange Way
Spring Valley, CA 91978-1742 619-232-6444
Fax: 619-660-7429 888-766-6468
hotlicks@juno.com www.2hotlicks.com
Hot sauces, salsas, mustards, condiments, snacks, mixes and seasonings, bbq sauces, marinades, and gifts.
Estimated Sales: Less than $500,000
Number Employees: 1-4
Brands:
AMAZON PEPPER PRODUCTS
CALIFORNIA JUST CHILE!
DEATH VALLEY HABANERO
HOT! HOT! HOT!
OTTIMO
PEPE'S SAUCE
RING OF FIRE

6316 **Hot Potato Distributor**
1133 W Randolph St
Chicago, IL 60607 312-243-0640
Fax: 312-243-0659
President: Irwin Brottman
VP: Wayne Newman
VP Operations: Bill Ferkaluk
Estimated Sales: $ 20 - 50 Million
Number Employees: 20-49

6317 **Hot Springs Packing Company**
220 Weston Rd
Hot Springs, AR 71914 501-767-3673
Fax: 501-767-9715 800-535-0449
hspc@hotspringspacking.com
www.hotspringspacking.com
Processor and exporter of polish sausage, andouille sausage, smoked sausage, hot links, pork and beef franks, knockwurst, deli meats and hams
President/CEO: John Stubblefield
Estimated Sales: $4.3 Million
Number Employees: 35
Type of Packaging: Consumer, Food Service

6318 **Hot Wachula's**
P.O.Box 2376
Lakeland, FL 33806-2376
Fax: 863-665-0358 877-883-8700
www.hotwachulas.com
Gourmet dips and sauces, marinades
President: Matt Barber
Estimated Sales: $1 Million
Number Employees: 5-9
Brands:
HOT WACHULA'S GOURMET DIPS & SAUCES

6319 **Houdini**
4225 N Palm St
Fullerton, CA 92835 714-525-0325
Fax: 714-996-9605 rritts@houdini.com
www.houdiniinc.com
Manufacturer, importer and exporter of food and wine; manufacturer of gift baskets
President: Timothy Dean
Estimated Sales: $ 500,000 - $ 1 Million
Number Employees: 50-99
Brands:
CALIFORNIA PANTRY
WINE COUNTRY

6320 **Houlton Farms Dairy**
25 Commonwealth Ave
Houlton, ME 04730 207-532-3170
Fax: 207-532-3613
Milk processing
President: Leonard Lincoln
Estimated Sales: $5-10 Million
Number Employees: 10-19

6321 **House Autry Mills**
7000 Us Highway 301 S
Four Oaks, NC 27524 919-963-6200
Fax: 910-594-0739 800-849-0802
info@house-autry.com www.house-autry.com
Baking mixes including breaders, coating mixes, hushpuppy mixes, biscuit and cornbread mixes, corn meal.
President: Roger Mortenson
Estimated Sales: $10-20 Million
Number Employees: 20-49
Type of Packaging: Private Label

6322 **House Foods America Corporation**
7351 Orangewood Ave
Garden Grove, CA 92841-1411 714-901-4350
Fax: 714-901-4235 www.house-foods.com
Processor of tofu and tofu products; importer of curry, spices, ramen noodles and tea.
President: Gerald Shirasaka
Estimated Sales: $100-$500 Million
Number Employees: 100-249
Sq. footage: 221600
Parent Co: House Foods Corporation, Japan (HFC)
Brands:
HINOICHI
HOUSE FOODS

6323 **House of Coffee Beans**
2348 Bissonnet St
Houston, TX 77005 713-524-0057
Fax: 713-795-5410 800-422-1799
contact@houseofcoffeebeans.com
www.houseofcoffeebeans.com
Processor of gourmet coffees including dark roasted and espresso, decaffeinated, flavored, and blended coffee.
Owner: Roger Farber
Estimated Sales: Less than $500,000
Number Employees: 1-4
Sq. footage: 14000
Type of Packaging: Consumer, Food Service, Private Label, Bulk

6324 **House of Flavors**
110 N William St
Ludington, MI 49431 231-845-7369
Fax: 231-845-7371 800-930-7740
flavors@houseofflavors.com
www.houseofflavors.com
Processor and exporter of kosher ice cream and frozen novelties
Owner: Robert Neil
Number Employees: 20-49
Type of Packaging: Consumer, Food Service

6325 **House of Raeford Farms**
520 E Central Ave
Raeford, NC 28376 910-875-5161
Fax: 910-844-3306 800-888-7539
rhonda.murphy@houseofraeford.com
www.houseofraeford.com
Manufacturer and exporter of poultry
Chairman: E Marvin Johnson
Vice Chairman/CEO: Bob Johnson
President/COO: Don Taber
CEO: Chris Chavis
Commodity/Export Manager: Harold Brock
Director Marketing: Rhonda Murphy
VP Sales/Marketing: Brenda Branch
Sales Manager: Tonya Smith
Estimated Sales: $100 Million
Number Employees: 1,000-4,999
Type of Packaging: Food Service
Other Locations:
Further Processing Plant/Distrib.
Raeford NC
Chicken Processing Plant
Arcadia LA
Columbia Farms Chicken Processing
Columbia SC
Breaded Chicken & Turkey Products
Hemingway SC
Columbia Farms Chicken Plant
Greenville SC
Brands:
COLUMBIA FARMS

6326 **(HQ)House of Raeford Farms**
520 E Central Ave
Raeford, NC 28376 910-875-5161
Fax: 910-875-8300 800-888-7539
raefrdtrky@aol.com www.houseofraeford.com
Manufacturer and exporter of turkey and chicken products
President/COO: Don Tabor
Chairman: E Marvin Johnson
Vice Chairman/CEO: Bob Johnson
VP: Steve Dunn
Sales Manager: Tonya Smith
Marketing Director: Rhonda Murphy
VP Sales/Marketing: Brenda Branch
Commodity/Export Manager: Harold Brock
Complex Manager: Greg Steenblock
VP National Accounts: Steve Dunn
Plant Manager: Sherwood Locklear
Estimated Sales: $100-500 Million
Number Employees: 1,000-4,999
Type of Packaging: Consumer, Food Service, Private Label, Bulk
Brands:
HOUSE OF RAEFORD

6327 **House of Spices**
12740 Willets Point Blvd
Flushing, NY 11368 718-507-4900
Fax: 718-507-4683
customerservice@hosindia.com
www.hosindia.com
daals, beans, nuts, spices, edible oils, flours, pickels, pastes, chutneys, frozen vegetables and frozen meals.
President/Owner: Gordhandas Soni
CFO: Chetan Soni
VP: Krishnakumar Soni
Estimated Sales: $28 Million
Number Employees: 65

6328 **House of Spices India**
12740 Willets Point Blvd
Flushing, NY 11368-1506 718-507-4900
Fax: 718-507-4798
customerservice@hosindia.com
www.hosindia.com
Processor of pickles, condiment pastes, chutney, snack foods, candy, ice cream and frozen foods; importer of Indian-Pakistani basmati rice, lentils, spices, oils and nuts; exporter of pickles, condiments and spices.
President: G Soni
Manager: Raj Udeshi
Estimated Sales: $5-10 Millio
Number Employees: 50-99
Number of Brands: 25
Number of Products: 2000
Sq. footage: 300000
Type of Packaging: Consumer, Food Service, Private Label, Bulk
Brands:
A-1
GITZ
JANTA
LAXMI
MAAZA
MAGGIE
NESTLE
PARLE
ROOHAFZA
SHAMIANA
VICCO-ZANDVADILD

6329 **House of Spices India**
4030 Bluebonnet Dr
Stafford, TX 77477 281-313-5224
Fax: 281-494-5963
customerservice@hosindia.com
www.houseofspices.com
Processor of pickles, condiment pastes, chutney, snack foods, candy, ice cream and frozen foods; importer of Indian-Pakistani basmati rice, lentils, spices, oils and nuts; exporter of pickles, condiments and spices.
Manager: Anu Goshavi
CEO: Kumar Soni
Parent Co: House of Spices
Type of Packaging: Consumer, Food Service, Private Label, Bulk

6330 **House of Spices India**
13821 Struikman Rd
Cerritos, CA 90703 562-407-0711
Fax: 562-407-0712
customerservice@hosindia.com
www.hosindia.com/contact.html
Processor of pickles, condiment pastes, chutney, snack foods, candy, ice cream and frozen foods; importer of Indian-Pakistani basmati rice, lentils, spices, oils and nuts; exporter of pickles, condiments and spices.
President: G Soni
CEO: Kumar Soni
Parent Co: House of Spices
Type of Packaging: Consumer, Food Service, Private Label, Bulk

6331 **House of Spices India**
2411 United Ln
Elk Grove Vlg, IL 60007-6818 847-595-2929
Fax: 847-595-9595
customerservice@hosindia.com
www.hosindia.com/contact.html
Processor of pickles, condiment pastes, chutney, snack foods, candy, ice cream and frozen foods; importer of Indian-Pakistani basmati rice, lentils, spices, oils and nuts; exporter of pickles, condiments and spices.
Manager: Subhash Majmudar
CEO: Kumar Soni
Parent Co: House of Spices
Type of Packaging: Consumer, Food Service, Private Label, Bulk

6332 **House of Spices India**
7908 Fernham Ln
Forestville, MD 20747-4517 301-420-1088
Fax: 301-967-7001
customerservice@hosindia.com
www.hosindia.com
Processor of pickles, condiment pastes, chutney, snack foods, candy, ice cream and frozen foods; importer of Indian-Pakistani basmati rice, lentils, spices, oils and nuts; exporter of pickles, condiments and spices.
Manager: Gunvant Pabari
CEO: Kumar Soni
Parent Co: House of Spices
Type of Packaging: Consumer, Food Service, Private Label, Bulk

6333 **House of Spices India**
25377 Huntwood Ave
Hayward, CA 94544-2212 510-732-8014
Fax: 510-732-7829
customerservice@hosindia.com
www.hosindia.com/contact.html
Processor of pickles, condiment pastes, chutney, snack foods, candy, ice cream and frozen foods; importer of Indian-Pakistani basmati rice, lentils, spices, oils and nuts; exporter of pickles, condiments and spices.
Manager: Dushyant Jani
CEO: Kumar Soni
Parent Co: House of Spices
Type of Packaging: Consumer, Food Service, Private Label, Bulk

6334 **House of Spices India**
3445 Bartlett Boulevard
Orlando, FL 32811 407-841-4608
Fax: 407-841-4611
customerservice@hosindia.com
www.hosindia.com
Processor of pickles, condiment pastes, chutney, snack foods, candy, ice cream and frozen foods; importer of Indian-Pakistani basmati rice, lentils, spices, oils and nuts; exporter of pickles, condiments and spices.
President: G Soni
CEO: Kumar Soni
Parent Co: House of Spices
Type of Packaging: Consumer, Food Service, Private Label, Bulk

6335 **House of Spices India**
4140 Blue Rdg Ind Pkwy
Norcross, GA 30071 770-263-0202
Fax: 770-797-9669
customerservice@hosindia.com
www.hosindia.com/contact.html
Processor of pickles, condiment pastes, chutney, snack foods, candy, ice cream and frozen foods; importer of Indian-Pakistani basmati rice, lentils, spices, oils and nuts; exporter of pickles, condiments and spices.
Manager: Piyusha Zope
CEO: Kumar Soni
Parent Co: House of Spices
Type of Packaging: Consumer, Food Service, Private Label, Bulk

6336 **House of Spices India**
243 Stafford St
Worcester, MA 01603-1168 508-757-6555
Fax: 508-757-6554
customerservice@hosindia.com
www.hosindia.com
Processor of pickles, condiment pastes, chutney, snack foods, candy, ice cream and frozen foods; importer of Indian-Pakistani basmati rice, lentils, spices, oils and nuts; exporter of pickles, condiments and spices.
Manager: Sejeal Vora
CEO: Kumar Soni
Parent Co: House of Spices
Type of Packaging: Consumer, Food Service, Private Label, Bulk

6337 **House of Thaller**
1600 Harris Rd
Knoxville, TN 37924 865-689-5893
Fax: 865-689-7132 800-462-3365
sales@houseofthaller.com
www.houseofthaller.com
Sandwich spreads, seafood salads, pasta salads, salad mixes and dessert salads.
Finance Executive/HR Manager: Stephanie Cooper
R&D Director: Beth Ann Disney
Marketing Manager/Sales Executive: John Thaller

Production Manager: Wes Curnutt
Purchasing Agent: Katherine Reed
Estimated Sales: $8 Million
Number Employees: 40
Sq. footage: 8000
Type of Packaging: Consumer, Food Service, Private Label, Bulk

6338 **House of Tsang**
2345 3rd St
San Francisco, CA 94107-3108 415-282-9952
Fax: 415-243-0157 lgmarconi@hormel.com
www.worldfood.com OR
www.hormelfoods.com/brands/worldFood/houseof tsang.as
Processor of Asian sauces, marinades, oils, vegetables and sauce combinations.
Owner: David Haase
Estimated Sales: $1 Million
Parent Co: Hormel Foods International Corporation

6339 **House of Webster**
1013 North Second Street
Po Box 1988
Rogers, AR 72756 479-636-4640
Fax: 479-636-2974 800-369-4641
www.houseofwebster.com
Processor of apple butter, jelly, salsa, barbecue sauce and preserves, ice cream toppings, ham, bacon and sausage, candy and cheese, pancake mix and assorted gifts.
Owner: Dale Webster
Chairman/President: John Griffin
Marketing Manager: David Tankersley
Estimated Sales: $6.7 Million
Number Employees: 65
Sq. footage: 98000
Type of Packaging: Consumer, Private Label
Brands:
WEBSTER'S

6340 **House-Autry Mills**
Po Box 460
Four Oaks, NC 27524 919-963-6200
Fax: 919-963-6458 800-849-0802
info@house-autry.com www.house-autry.com
Processor of flour based dairy mixes and corn meal
President: Roger Mortenson
Chief Financial Officer: Tim Johns
Vice President: Ken Gilbert
Number Employees: 20-49
Sq. footage: 45000
Type of Packaging: Consumer, Food Service
Other Locations:
House-Autry Mills
Four Oaks NC
Brands:
GOLDEN EAGLE
HOUSE AUTRY
THOMPSON'S

6341 **Houser Meats**
Rr 2 Box 180b
Rushville, IL 62681 217-322-4994
Fax: 217-322-4994 www.housermeats.com
Processor of beef, pork, lamb and venison
Partner: Douglas Houser
Partner: Terri Houser
Estimated Sales: $500,000-$1 Million
Number Employees: 5-9
Sq. footage: 2500
Type of Packaging: Bulk

6342 **Houston Calco**
2400 Dallas St
Houston, TX 77003 713-236-8668
Fax: 713-236-1920 kent@hypercon.com
Bean sprouts, egg rolls, wontons and tofu.
Owner: Alice Chang
Estimated Sales: $5-10 Million
Number Employees: 20-49
Type of Packaging: Private Label
Brands:
CALCO

6343 **Houston Harvest**
3501 Mount Prospect Rd
Franklin Park, IL 60131-1305 847-957-9191
Fax: 847-616-8886 800-548-5896
www.houstonharvestgifts.com
Manufacturer, importer and exporter of gourmet popcorn and candy gifts packaged in ceramics, wooden baskets and tins
Ceo/Executive Chairman: Gay Burke
Executive Vice President: Kenneth Olendzki
VP Sales: Ron Gerstung
Estimated Sales: $50-100 Million
Number Employees: 100-249
Sq. footage: 1000000

6344 **Houston Tea & Beverage**
1700 Wirt Rd
Houston, TX 77055 713-956-6751
Fax: 713-956-6751 800-585-4549
wms@pdq.net
Processor and importer of blended and flavored teas
President: Linda Williams
Estimated Sales: Less than $500,000
Number Employees: 1-4
Sq. footage: 8500
Type of Packaging: Private Label

6345 **Howard Foods**
P.O.Box 2072
Danvers, MA 01923 978-774-6207
Fax: 978-777-2384 howardfoods@verizon.net
www.howardfoods.com
Howard's products include: sweet pepper relish, hot pepper relish, green tomato piccalilli, ham glaze, sugar free syrup, garlic and onion seasoning juices, chopped and minced garlic in various sizes.
Estimated Sales: $ 1 - 3 Million
Number Employees: 5-9
Brands:
HOWARD'S

6346 **Howard Turner & Son**
1659 Route 1 Highway 7
Marie Joseph, NS B0J 2G0
Canada 902-347-2616
Fax: 902-347-2714
Processor and exporter of fresh and frozen lobster and groundfish
President: Randy Turner
Type of Packaging: Bulk

6347 **Howjax**
PO Box 246063
Pembroke Pines, FL 33024-0117 954-441-2491
Fax: 954-962-7258 info@howjax.com
www.howjax.com
Gourmet condiments, and Caribean style chutney

6348 **Howson & Howson Limited**
40605 Walton Rd
Blyth, ON N0M 1H0
Canada 519-523-9624
Fax: 519-523-9814 800-663-3653
howson@howsonandhowson.ca
www.howsonandhowson.ca
Durum flour milling
President: Jim Howson
VP: Jeff Howson
R&D/Plant Manager: Doug Howson
Marketing: Dan Greyerbighl
Operations/Purchasing: Jeff Howson
Estimated Sales: $30 Million
Number Employees: 35
Type of Packaging: Bulk

6349 **Hoyt's Honey Farm**
11711 Interstate 10 E
Baytown, TX 77523 281-576-5383
Fax: 281-576-2191 hoyts@imsday.com
www.hoytshoney.com
Processor and importer of honey
President: Gordon Brown
Estimated Sales: $5-10 Million
Number Employees: 5-9
Sq. footage: 7500
Type of Packaging: Consumer, Food Service, Private Label, Bulk
Brands:
HOYT'S PURE HONEY
HOYTS

6350 **Hsin Tung Yang Foods Co.**
405 S Airport Blvd
S San Francisco, CA 94080-6909 650-589-6789
Fax: 650-589-3157 info@htyusa.com
www.htyusa.com
Manufacturer and canner of Asian meat products including beef jerky, pork jerky, sausage and ham
President: Kailen Mai
Director Manufacturing: Pin Chong
Estimated Sales: $ 10 - 20 Million
Number Employees: 50-99

6351 **Hsu's Ginseng Enterprises**
P.O.Box 509
Wausau, WI 54402-0509 715-675-2325
Fax: 715-675-3175 800-826-1577
info@hsuginseng.com www.hsuginseng.com
Processor and exporter of ginseng products, royal jelly, bee pollen, astragalus, dong quai and goldenseal
President: Paul Hsu
Vice President: Sharon Hsu
Estimated Sales: $5-10 Million
Number Employees: 50-99
Brands:
ROOT TO HEALTH

6352 **Hubbard Meat Company**
500 N Birdwell Ln
Big Spring, TX 79720 432-267-7781
Processor of meats
Owner: T Hubbard
Estimated Sales: $1-2.5 Million
Number Employees: 1-4

6353 **Hubbard Peanut Company**
P.O.Box 94
Sedley, VA 23878 757-562-4081
Fax: 757-562-2741 800-889-7688
hubs@hubspeanuts.com www.hubspeanuts.com
Processor and exporter of cocktail peanuts
President: Lynne Rabil
Plant Manager: David Benton
Estimated Sales: $10-24.9 Million
Number Employees: 10-19
Sq. footage: 30000
Type of Packaging: Consumer, Food Service, Private Label

6354 **Huber's Orchard Winery**
19816 Huber Rd
Borden, IN 47106 812-923-9813
Fax: 812-923-3013 800-345-9463
info@huberwinery.com www.huberwinery.com
Produces a variety of Wines in addition to offering numerous fruits and vegtables at their farmer's market, including: strawberries, raspberries, blueberries, black raspberries, and blackberries. Homegrown summer vegetables includecorn, green beans, tomatoes, peppers, broccoli, and cauliflower.
President: Ted Huber
VP: Greg Huber
Estimated Sales: $5-10 Million
Number Employees: 20-49

6355 **Huck's Seafood**
508 Cynwood Dr # D
Easton, MD 21601-3892 410-770-9211
Fax: 410-763-8811
Processor of crabs, oysters and clams; wholesaler/distributor of fish including rock, perch, blue, spot and flounder; serving the food service market
Owner/President: James Ford, Jr
Orders: Amber Ford
Estimated Sales: $ .5 - 1 million
Number Employees: 1-4
Sq. footage: 2500
Type of Packaging: Consumer, Food Service, Bulk
Brands:
HUCK'S

6356 **Huckleberry Patch**
P.O.Box 1
Hungry Horse, MT 59919-0001 406-387-5000
Fax: 406-387-4444 800-527-7340
info@huckleberrypatch.com
www.huckleberrypatch.com
Wildberry jellies, syrups, jams, preserves
Manager: Laurie Carpy
Estimated Sales: $5-10 Million
Number Employees: 10-19

6357 **Hudson Valley Fruit Juice**
33 White St
Highland, NY 12528 845-691-8061
Fax: 845-691-9056
Fruit and vegetable juices and vinegar
President: Vincent Nemeth
Estimated Sales: $1-2.5 Million
Number Employees: 1-4

6358 **Hudson Valley Homestead**
102 Sheldon Ln
Craryville, NY 12521 518-851-7336
Fax: 518-851-7553
sales@hudsonvalleyhomestead.com
www.hudsonvalleyhomestead.com
Gourmet foods including vinegars, mustards, salad dressings, sauces, spreads, oils, and jams.
President: John King

Estimated Sales: Less than $500,000
Number Employees: 1-4
Type of Packaging: Private Label
Brands:
BASHWHACBER'S MUSTARD
BLOW HARD MUSTARD
HUDSON VALLEY HOMESTEAD

6359 **Hudsonville Creamery & Ice Cream**
345 E 48th St Ste B
Holland, MI 49423 616-546-4005
Fax: 616-546-4020
hello@hudsonvilleicecream.com
www.hudsonvilleicecream.com
Processor of regular and low-fat ice cream, frozen yogurt and sherbet
Owner: Dennis Ellens
VP Marketing & Sales: Jon Vanderwoude
Estimated Sales: $12 Million
Number Employees: 28
Number of Brands: 2
Type of Packaging: Consumer, Bulk
Brands:
HUDSONVILLE ICE CREAM

6360 **Hue's Seafood**
105 S 14th Street
Baton Rouge, LA 70802-4753 225-383-0809
Fax: 225-383-0809
Seafood
President: Tu Nguyen

6361 **Hughes Company Inc**
1200 W James St
Columbus, WI 53925 920-623-2000
Fax: 920-623-4098 Hughes@Powerweb.net
www.hughescompany.biz
Manufacturer of machinery for the food processing industry including air cleaners; bins; rotary blanchers and cookers; rotary coolers; bulk unloading feeders; fillers; graders; inspection tables, etc.
President: Todd Belz
Sales Engineer: Dave Olson

6362 **Hughes Springs Frozen Food Center**
P.O.Box 206
Hughes Springs, TX 75656 903-639-2941
Meat packer
Owner: Alvin Dannelley
Estimated Sales: $1-2.5 Million
Number Employees: 1-4
Type of Packaging: Consumer

6363 **Hughson Meat Company**
407 S Guadalupe St
San Marcos, TX 78666 512-392-3368
Fax: 512-392-4190 877-462-6328
http://www.hughson-meat.com/retail
Manufacturer of meat products; slaughtering also available
Owner: Marvin Rutkowski
Estimated Sales: $3-5 Million
Number Employees: 5-9
Type of Packaging: Consumer

6364 **Hughson Nut Company**
1825 Verduga Rd
Hughson, CA 95326 209-883-0403
Fax: 209-883-2973 info@hughsonnut.com
www.hughsonnut.com
Almond nuts diced, sliced, slivered, milled, blanched and dry toasted
President: Martin Pohl
Estimated Sales: $2.5-5 Million
Number Employees: 10-19
Number of Brands: 1
Sq. footage: 75000
Type of Packaging: Consumer, Private Label, Bulk

6365 **Huisken Meat Center**
245 Industrial Blvd
Sauk Rapids, MN 56379 320-259-0305
Fax: 320-240-0654 info@huiskenmeats.com
www.huiskenmeats.com
Manufacturer and packer of meats and meat snacks
President: James Hanson
Estimated Sales: $15.3 Million
Number Employees: 80
Parent Co: Branding Iron Holding Company
Type of Packaging: Consumer, Private Label
Brands:
BESURE
HUISKEN
RG'S

6366 **Hulman & Company**
P.O.Box 150
Terre Haute, IN 47808-0150 812-232-9446
Fax: 812-478-7181
bakingpowder@brickyard.com
www.clabbergirl.com
Processor and exporter of regular and double-acting baking powder
President: Anton Hulman George
CEO: Tony George
Estimated Sales: $20-50 Million
Number Employees: 1,000-4,999
Parent Co: Clabber Girl Corporation

6367 **Humble Cremery**
572 Highway 1
Fortuna, CA 95540-9711 323-269-9481
Fax: 323-261-7555 800-697-9925
www.humboldtcreamery.com
Processor of ice cream
Plant Manager: Dale Killen
Sales Manager: Don Baker
Plant Manager: Kevin Creviston
Estimated Sales: $ 20 - 50 Million
Number Employees: 50-99
Parent Co: West Farm Foods
Type of Packaging: Consumer, Food Service, Private Label
Brands:
Humble

6368 **Humboldt Creamery Association**
572 State Highway 1
Fortuna, CA 95540 707-725-6182
Fax: 707-725-6186
info@humboldtcreamery.comm
www.humboldtcreamery.com
Processor and exporter of ice cream and milk including specialty powders, whole, skim, 1% and 2%
CEO: Len Mayer
CFO: Ralph Titus
Operations Manager: Mike Callihan
Estimated Sales: $50-100 Million
Number Employees: 115
Type of Packaging: Consumer, Food Service, Bulk

6369 **Humboldt Sausage Company**
1515 15th St N
Humboldt, IA 50548-1017 515-332-4121
Fax: 515-332-2629
Manufacturer of sausage and salami; exporter of hard and Genoa salami and pepperoni
Founder/General Manager: Roger Lawson
Plant Manager: Gary Pearson
Estimated Sales: $25 Million
Number Employees: 50-99
Sq. footage: 45000
Parent Co: SMG
Type of Packaging: Consumer, Food Service, Private Label, Bulk
Brands:
AQUILA D'ORA
BEIRMEISTER
BUON GIORNO
GRATIFICA
LIGURIA

6370 **Humbolt Brewing Company**
856 10th Street
Arcata, CA 95521-6232 707-826-1734
Fax: 707-826-2045 www.humbrews.com/
Processor of beer, ale and lager
President: Mario Celotto
Number Employees: 50-99
Type of Packaging: Consumer, Food Service, Bulk
Brands:
GOLD NECTAR
RED NECTAR

6371 **Humco**
7400 Alumax Rd
Texarkana, TX 75501-0282 903-334-6200
Fax: 903-334-6300 www.humco.com
Processor and exporter of OTC liquid and powder herbal supplements
CEO/Presidnet: Greg Pulido
CEO: Greg Pulido
CFO: Steve Woolf
Vice President: Susan Hickey
VP Quality/Regulatory Affairs: Steve Bryant
VP Sales: Alan Fyke
Estimated Sales: $10-20 Million
Number Employees: 100-249

6372 **Hume Specialties**
291 Pleasant St
Chester, VT 05143-9351 802-875-3117
Fax: 802-875-3140
www.greenmountaingringo.com
Processor of salsa and tortilla chips and strips
President: Christine Hume
Executive VP/Production Manager: Dave Hume
Estimated Sales: $2.5-5 Million
Number Employees: 20-49
Sq. footage: 7000
Type of Packaging: Consumer
Brands:
GREEN MOUNTAIN GRINGO

6373 **Humeniuk's Meat Cutting**
PO Box 11
Ranfurly, AB T0B 3T0
Canada 780-658-2381
Processor of fresh and frozen beef and pork; also, wild game including deer
President: Nector Humeniuk
Owner/Manager: Gerald Humeniuk
Secretary: Oksana Humeniuk
Number Employees: 10-19
Sq. footage: 80000
Type of Packaging: Consumer, Food Service, Private Label, Bulk
Brands:
GRANNY'S

6374 **Hummel Brothers**
180 Sargent Dr
New Haven, CT 6511 203-787-4113
Fax: 203-498-1755 800-828-8978
www.hummelbros.com
Manufacturer of cold cuts, frankfurters and sausage
President: William Hummel
Vice President: Robert Hummel
Estimated Sales: $8 Million
Number Employees: 50
Sq. footage: 47000
Type of Packaging: Consumer, Private Label
Brands:
HUMMEL MEATS

6375 **Hummingbird Kitchens**
P.O.Box 1286
Whitehouse, TX 75791 903-839-6244
800-921-9470
wfaulkner@cox-internet.com
www.hummingbirdkitchens.com
Processor of gourmet food mixes including bread, soup, dip, salad dressing, tea, jambalaya, spice, seasoning and rice. Including American, Southwestern, and Tex-mex style foods
President: Janet Faulkner
CEO: William Faulkner
Estimated Sales: $1-2.5 Million
Number Employees: 5-9
Number of Products: 51
Type of Packaging: Consumer, Private Label, Bulk

6376 **Humphrey Blue Ribbon Meats**
1821 S 15th St
Springfield, IL 62703-3298 217-544-7445
Fax: 217-544-7518 800-747-6328
Processor of specialty sausage and hams
President: T Humphrey
Chairman: E Humphrey
Estimated Sales: $10-20 Million
Number Employees: 10-19
Sq. footage: 14600

6377 **Humphrey Company**
20810 Miles Pkwy
Cleveland, OH 44128-5508 216-662-6629
Fax: 216-662-6619 800-486-3739
humphreycompany@ameritech.net
www.humphreycompany.com
Premium white popcorn
Owner: Dudley Humphrey
VP: Betsy Humphrey
Estimated Sales: $500,000-$1 Million
Number Employees: 10-19
Number of Brands: 1
Number of Products: 10
Sq. footage: 11000
Type of Packaging: Consumer, Private Label

6378 **Humpty Dumpty Snack Foods**
88 Pleasant Hill Road
Scarborough, ME 04074-8719 207-883-8422
Fax: 207-885-0773 877-228-2273
consumercare@olddutchfoods.com
www.humptydumpty.com
Snacks
President: Steve Aanenson
Brands:
HUMPTY DUMPTY

6379 **Humpty Dumpty Snack Foods**
2100 Rue Norman
Lachine, QC H8S 1B1
Canada 514-367-3521
Fax: 514-639-5419 800-361-6440
reception@humptydumpty.com
www.olddutchfoods.ca
Processor of snack foods including kettle-style potato chips, popcorn, tortilla chips and extruded corn products
President: David Murphy
CFO: Lois Norris
Vice President: Lynda Murray
Marketing Director: Linda Murray
Director Sales: Gerard Pacull
Parent Co: Small Fry Snack Foods
Type of Packaging: Consumer, Food Service, Private Label
Brands:
Humpty Dumpty
Krunchers
Mexitos

6380 **Hung's Noodle House**
25-1410 40th Avenue NE
Calgary, AB T2E 6L1
Canada 403-250-1663
Fax: 403-291-0632
Processor of noodles including rice
President: Ricky Chung
Production: Cindy Chung
Parent Co: Hung Kee Holdings Company
Brands:
HUNG'S NOODLE HOUSE

6381 **Hungerford J Smith Company**
1500 N Central Ave
Humboldt, TN 38343-1798 731-784-3461
Fax: 731-784-2124 www.conagrafoodservice.com
Processor of ice cream toppings, syrups, coatings and shake base mixes.
Estimated Sales: $10-20 Million
Number Employees: 50-99
Parent Co: ConAgra Foods
Type of Packaging: Consumer, Private Label

6382 **Hungry Sultan**
14 Rancho Cir
Lake Forest, CA 92630-8325 949-215-0000
Fax: 949-215-0965 info@HungrySultan.com
www.hungrysultan.com
Mediterranean snack products
President: Fouad El-Abd
Public Relations: Darren El-Abd
Estimated Sales: Less than $500,000
Number Employees: 10-19

6383 **Hunt Brothers Cooperative**
P.O.Box 631
Lake Wales, FL 33859-0631 863-676-9471
Fax: 863-676-8362
Processor of citrus fruits including grapefruits, limes, oranges and tangerines
President: Frank Hunt Iii III
Estimated Sales: $20-50 Million
Number Employees: 250-499
Type of Packaging: Consumer, Food Service, Bulk
Brands:
SEALD SWEET
TREASURE PAK

6384 **Hunt Country Foods**
P.O.Box 876
Middleburg, VA 20118 540-364-2622
Fax: 540-364-3112 best.of.luck@starpower.net
www.send-best-of-luck.com
Proceesor of specialty cookies, cakes, chocolates
Owner: Maggi Castelloe
Estimated Sales: Less than $500,000
Number Employees: 5-9
Brands:
BEST OF LUCK
BEST OF LUCK HORSESHOE CHOCOLATES
HORSESHOE CAKE
HORSESHOES AND NAILS

6385 **Hunt Country Vineyards**
4021 Italy Hill Rd
Branchport, NY 14418 800-946-3289
Fax: 315-595-2835 800-946-3289
info@HuntWines.com www.huntwines.com
Processor and exporter of wines including red, white, table, late harvest, ice, wine, sherry, port
President: Joyce Hunt
CEO: Arthur Hunt
Marketing/Sales Manager: James Alsina
Operations Manager: David Mortensen
Estimated Sales: $500,000-$1 Million
Number Employees: 20-49
Sq. footage: 8000
Type of Packaging: Consumer, Private Label
Brands:
Fingerlakes Wine Cellars
Foxy Lady
Hunt Country Vineyards

6386 **Hunt-Wesson Food Service Company**
PO Box 25309
Rochester, NY 14625-0309 949-437-1000
866-484-8676
www.hunt-wesson.com
Frozen and prepared entrees, pasta, vegetables and sauces
President: Jeff Wayne
Number Employees: 500-999
Parent Co: ConAgra
Brands:
KNOTT'S BERRY FARM
LA CHOY
ROSARITA

6387 **Hunt-Wesson Foods**
2239 Edgewood Avenue S
Minneapolis, MN 55426-2822 612-544-2761
Fax: 612-525-9274 www.hwfoods.com
Ice cream toppings and cones
President: Edward Snell
Estimated Sales: $25-49.9 Million
Number Employees: 100-249
Parent Co: ConAgra Foods

6388 **Hunter Farms**
1900 N Main St
High Point, NC 27262-2132 336-822-2300
Fax: 336-882-2341 800-446-8035
email@hunterfarms.net www.hunterfarms.com
Processor of dairy products including milk, ice cream, frozen yogurt and sour cream
VP: Dwight Moore
Sales Development: Karin Cavanaugh
Director Sales: Bob Cooke
General Manager: Dwight Moore
Estimated Sales: $10-24.9 Million
Number Employees: 50-99
Parent Co: Harris Teeter
Type of Packaging: Consumer

6389 **Hunter Food Inc**
3700 E Melville Way
Anaheim, CA 92806 714-666-1888
Fax: 714-666-1222 www.hunterfood.com
Poultry processing plant specializing in various types of chicken breast, leg, thigh, and portion products.
Owner: Ricky Lee
CEO: Hsin Jung Le
Estimated Sales: $ 20 - 50 Million
Number Employees: 100-249

6390 **Huppen Bakery**
8721 Santa Monica Boulevard
Suite 201
Los Angeles, CA 90069-4507 323-656-7501
Fax: 323-656-1090
verticalsales@worldnet.att.net
Processor of swiss chocolates and wafer rolls
President: Urs Brauchli
Type of Packaging: Consumer, Bulk

6391 **Hurd Orchards**
17260 Ridge Rd
Holley, NY 14470 585-638-8838
Fax: 585-638-5175 market@hurdorchards.com
www.hurdorchards.com
Processor of preserves, vinegars, brandied fruit, pickles, chili sauce, jams, marmalades, canned fruit and dried fruit
Owner: Susan Machamer
VP: Amy Machamer
Estimated Sales: $ .5 - 1 million
Number Employees: 1-4

6392 **Hurd Orchards**
17260 Ridge Rd
Route 104
Holley, NY 14470 585-638-8838
Fax: 585-638-5175 amachame@rochester.rr.com
www.hurdorchards.com
Preserves, vinegars, brandied fruit, pickles, chili sauce, jams, marmalades, conserves, canned and dried fruit
Owner: Susan Machamer
Owner: Amy Macharmer
Estimated Sales: $ .5 - 1 million
Number Employees: 1-4

6393 **(HQ)Husch Vineyards**
4400 Highway 128
Philo, CA 95466-9476 707-895-3216
Fax: 707-895-2068 800-554-8724
www.huschvineyards.com
Produces a variety of wines including: Sauvignon Blanc, Pinot Noir, Cabernet Sauvignon, Chardonnay, Muscat Canelli, and Syrah.
President: Zach Robinson
VP: Amanda Robinson Holstine
Operations Manager: Al White
Production Manager: Brad Holstine
Estimated Sales: $2.5-5 Million
Number Employees: 5-9

6394 **Huse's Country Meats**
3697 State Highway 171
Malone, TX 76660 254-533-2205
Fax: 254-533-2498 mcarpent@internetwork.net
Processor of smoked beef and pork sausage
Owner: Randy Huse
Estimated Sales: $5-10 Million
Number Employees: 10-19

6395 **Husman Snack Food Company**
1621 Moore Street
Cincinnati, OH 45210 859-282-7490
Fax: 513-562-2646 www.birdseyefoods.com
Manufacturer of potato and tortilla chips
President/CEO: David Ray
Quality Assurance Manager: John Barlage
Plant Manager: Leroy Pennekamp
Number Employees: 100-249
Sq. footage: 70000
Parent Co: Birds Eye Foods
Type of Packaging: Consumer, Private Label, Bulk
Brands:
HUSMAN'S

6396 **Huval Baking Company**
P.O.Box 2339
Lafayette, LA 70502-2339 337-232-1611
Processor of baked goods including bread, buns and rolls
Comptroller: Kerry Schexnayder
VP: Ronald Harison
Estimated Sales: Less than $500,000
Number Employees: 5-9
Parent Co: Flowers Baking Company
Type of Packaging: Consumer

6397 **Hybco USA**
363 S Mission Rd
Los Angeles, CA 90033 323-269-3111
Fax: 323-269-3130 sales@hybco.com
www.hybco.com
Products include oils (soy, cottonseed, vegetable, corn, canola, peanut, and shortenings); long grain rice and long grain rice flour.
President: David Kashani
Estimated Sales: $2.5-5 Million
Number Employees: 10-19

6398 **Hyde & Hyde**
300 El Sobrante Rd.
Corona, CA 92879 951-817-2300
Fax: 951-270-3526 sales@hydeandhyde.com
www.hydeandhyde.com
Condiments for the fresh-cut produce industry. Also offers custom packaging and co-packaging.
President: Timothy Hyde
Number Employees: 100-249

Type of Packaging: Consumer

6399 **Hyde Candy Company**
1916 E Mercer Street
Seattle, WA 98112-4029 206-322-5743
Candy manufacturer
President: Alfred Hyde

6400 **Hydroblend**
1801 N Elder St
Nampa, ID 83687 208-467-7441
Fax: 208-467-2220
customerservice@hydroblendinc.com
www.hydroblendinc.com
Crispy and crunchy coating for potatoes, appetizers, fish, chicken and vegetbles
President: Mike Guthrie
CEO: Bill Cyr
VP Sales/Marketing: Randy Hobert
R&D: Henning Melvej
Quality Control: Joshua Bevan
Customer Service: Gay Tisdale
Purchasing Director: Matt Haines
Estimated Sales: $ 10 - 20 Million
Number Employees: 100-249
Sq. footage: 110000
Type of Packaging: Bulk
Brands:
HB Batters
HB Breadings

6401 **Hye Cuisine**
4730 S Highland Ave
Del Rey, CA 93616 559-834-3000
Fax: 559-834-5882 hyecuisine@aol.com
Processor of specialty marinated vegetables and stuffed grape leaves; exporter of grape leaves
President: Raffi Santikian
Secretary: Hilda Santikian
Estimated Sales: $1 Million
Number Employees: 10
Sq. footage: 8000
Type of Packaging: Food Service, Private Label

6402 **Hye Quality Bakery**
2222 Santa Clara St
Fresno, CA 93721 559-445-1511
Fax: 559-445-1540 877-445-1778
info@hyequalitybakery.com
www.hyequalitybakery.com
Processor of cracker breads, gourmet crackers and soft cracker bread.
President: Sammy Ganimian
Estimated Sales: $10-20 Million
Number Employees: 10-19
Brands:
HYE DELITES
HYE ROLLER

6403 **Hygeia Dairy Company**
525 Beaumont Ave
McAllen, TX 78501 956-686-0511
Fax: 956-630-6747
Manufacturer of dairy products including ice cream, ices, sherbets, chocolate milk, buttermilk, milk and cream; also, ice cream and ice milk mixes
Manager: Jimmy Wallace
General Manager: Jimmy Wallace
Estimated Sales: $3-5 Million
Number Employees: 50-99
Parent Co: Deans Foods
Type of Packaging: Consumer, Food Service

6404 **Hygeia Dairy Company**
5330 Ayers St
Corpus Christi, TX 78415-2104 361-854-4561
Fax: 361-854-7267 www.deanfoods.com
Processor and exporter of regular and chocolate milk and orange juice
Manager: Scott Mc Clarren
VP: Doug Purl
Human Resources Director: Robin Somsngyi
Estimated Sales: $20-50 Million
Number Employees: 45
Sq. footage: 34002
Parent Co: Hygeia Dairy Company
Type of Packaging: Consumer, Food Service, Private Label, Bulk
Brands:
HYGEIA
SUPER GOOD

6405 **Hygrade Ocean Products**
P.O.Box 6918
New Bedford, MA 02742-6918 508-993-5700
Fax: 508-991-5133 soaked@aol.com
Processor of fresh and frozen scallops including bay and sea and fillets including flounder, cod, yellow tail and haddock; importer of cod fish and scallops; exporter of scallops
Owner: Carmine Romano
CFO: Linda Wisnewski
Estimated Sales: $10-20 Million
Number Employees: 20-49
Sq. footage: 28000
Type of Packaging: Consumer, Food Service, Private Label, Bulk
Brands:
DING GUA GUA
HYDRADE
OLD CAPE HARBOR
TEDDY'S

6406 **I & K Distributors**
P.O.Box 369
Delphos, OH 45833 419-692-6911
Fax: 419-695-7585 800-869-6337
custserv@ikdist.com www.ikdist.com
Manufacturer of frozen pizza
President/CEO: Robert Fishbein
Director Business Development: Tom Baker
Director Human Resources: Jason Leffel
Estimated Sales: $347.5 Million
Number Employees: 250-499
Parent Co: Countryside Foods, LLC
Type of Packaging: Consumer
Brands:
BERNEA FARMS
MICHIGAN
RENOS
YODER

6407 **I Heart Olive Oil**
1513 Se 2nd Court
Ft Lauderdale, FL 33301-3937 954-607-1539
Fax: 954-761-1166
beth.haralson@iheartoliveoil.com
www.iheartoliveoil.com
Olive oil, balsamic vinegar, full-line vinegar, other vinegar, sherry vinegar.
Marketing: Beth Haralson

6408 **I Rice & Company**
11576 Roosevelt Blvd.
Philadelphia, PA 19116 215-673-7423
Fax: 215-673-2616 800-232-6022
sales@iriceco.com www.iriceco.com
Processor and exporter of syrups, flavorings, sundae toppings, fudge, bakery fillings and stabilizers
President: Steve Kuhl
Estimated Sales: $20-50 Million
Number Employees: 20-49
Number of Brands: 3
Number of Products: 1000
Sq. footage: 85000
Type of Packaging: Food Service, Private Label, Bulk
Brands:
RICE'S PRODUCTS

6409 **I. Deveau Fisheries**
Po Box 577
Barrington Passage, NS B0W 2J0
Canada 902-769-0333
Fax: 902-645-2211 ideveau.com
Processor and exporter of fresh haddock and herring roe; also, live lobster
President: Berton German
Number Employees: 5-9
Type of Packaging: Bulk

6410 **I. Epstein & Sons**
8 Joanna Court
East Brunswick, NJ 08816-2108 800-237-5320
Fax: 732-432-3928

6411 **IBC Holsum**
PO Box 100435
Atlanta, GA 30384-0435 305-888-3441
Fax: 561-464-6931 800-465-7861
Processor of baked goods including bread, rolls, muffins and croissants
President: Edward Eisele
Marketing Manager: Scott Currie
Estimated Sales: $50-100 Million
Number Employees: 250-499
Parent Co: IBC
Type of Packaging: Consumer, Food Service

6412 **ICL Performance Products**
622 Emerson Road
Suite 500
St. Louis, MO 63141
800-244-6169
www.icl-perfproductslp.com
Manufactures food-grade phosphoric acid, phosphate salts and food additives
President/CEO: Charles Weidhas
VP Finance: Paul Schlessman
VP Operations: Terry Zerr
Number Employees: 500-999
Parent Co: ICL Holdings

6413 **IFM**
20 West 20th Street
Suite 303
New York, NY 10011 212-229-1633
Fax: 212-898-9024 franck@ifm-usa.com
www.ifm-usa.com
cookies (butter, chocolate and fruit), mushrooms, truffles, wildberries, mustards, mayonnaises, sauces and salad dressings
Marketing: Frank Foulloy

6414 **IFive Brands**
P.O.Box 9134
Seattle, WA 98109-0134 206-783-2498
Fax: 206-789-1016 800-882-5615
adam@peppermints.com www.peppermints.com
Fat-free and sugar free mints
Owner: Brett Canfield
Estimated Sales: $ 3 - 5 Million
Number Employees: 1-4
Brands:
PENGUIN

6415 **II Sisters**
850 Airport St Ste 9
Moss Beach, CA 94038 650-728-5613
Fax: 650-728-5611 800-282-7058
summin_t@yahoo.com
Seasoned oils, herbal vinegars
President/Owner: Sudi Taleghani
CFO: Simmin Taleghani
Estimated Sales: $1-2.5 Million
Number Employees: 5-9
Brands:
II Sisters
Ii Sisters
Sorrell Flavours

6416 **IL HWA American Corporation**
16 Plum
Worcester, MA 01604 973-759-1996
Fax: 973-450-0562 800-446-7364
support@ilhwaamerica.com
www.ilhwaamerica.com
Processor, importer, exporter and wholesaler/distributor of Korean ginseng
President: Sang Kil Han
Warehouse Manager: Edner Louis
Estimated Sales: $2.5-5 Million
Number Employees: 1-4
Brands:
Il Hwa

6417 **IMAC**
1702 N Sooner Rd
Oklahoma City, OK 73141-1222 405-424-8794
Fax: 405-424-4822 888-878-7827
Processor of dried foods including citrus, rice, grain, milk and cheese; also, anti-caking agents, flavor extenders, soy milk and cheese cultures
President: Jim Baird
Mananager: Ed Price
Manager: Alvin Thompson
Plant Manager: Bill Armstrong
Estimated Sales: $ 3 - 5 Million
Number Employees: 20-49
Sq. footage: 80000
Parent Co: ADFAC
Type of Packaging: Private Label, Bulk

6418 **IMC-Agrico Company**
7250 La 44
Convent, LA 70723-2418 225-562-3501
Fax: 225-562-2797 www.mosaicco.com

Manufacturer of phosphoric acid
General Manager: Robert Dennis
Estimated Sales: $ 50 - 100 Million
Number Employees: 250-499
Parent Co: Freeport Minerals Company

6419 **IMEX Enterprises**
110 Gerstley Rd
Hatboro, PA 19040 215-672-2887
Fax: 215-672-9552 info@imexEnterprises.com
www.imexenterprises.com
Pepper, salt, nutmeg mills and coffee grinders, SS cookware, SS gadgets, SS serving ware, copper molds
President: Norbert Hein
Estimated Sales: $10-20 Million
Number Employees: 20-49
Brands:
Ultima
Zassenhaus

6420 **IMO Foods**
9-10 Ragged Lake Boulevard
Halifax, NS B3S 1C2
Canada 902-450-5060
Fax: 902-450-5061 fancyfoods@yahoo.com
www.websight.ns.ca/imo
Processor and exporter of canned fish including herring, mackerel, sardines, skinless/boneless salmon and herring roe; manufacturer of aluminum cans, lids, etc
President: Sidney Hughes
Executive VP/General Manager: Phillip Le Blanc
Director Marketing: David Jollimore
Number Employees: 100-249
Parent Co: IMO Foods
Type of Packaging: Consumer, Food Service, Private Label
Other Locations:
Brands:
Golden Treasure
Kersen
West Island

6421 **IMS Food Service**
1-2 Corporate Dr #136
Shelton, CT 06484-6208
US 203-929-2254
Fax: 203-926-0916 800-235-7072
Processor of fine specialty teas including bags and loose,they are food brokers.
President/Owner: Arnold D'Angelo
VP: Thomas O'Hara
Sales Executive: Scott Ricci
Estimated Sales: $ 5 - 10 Million
Number Employees: 33
Parent Co: International Marketing Systems
Type of Packaging: Consumer, Food Service

6422 **INCA Kola Golden Kola**
215 W 64th St
New York, NY 10065-6662 212-688-1895
rincakola@aol.com
www.incakola-usa.com
Processor and exporter of soft drinks
Principal: Louis Jardines
Estimated Sales: $2.5-5 Million
Number Employees: 5-9
Type of Packaging: Consumer, Food Service, Private Label
Brands:
Golden Kola
Inca Kola

6423 **IOE Atlanta**
P.O.Box 267
Galena, MD 21635-0267 410-755-6300
Fax: 410-755-6367
Shellfish, sushi
Manager: Denise Ford
Chairman: Charles Cully Jr.
CFO: Denise For
Number Employees: 10-19

6424 **(HQ)ISE America, Inc.**
P.O.Box 267
Galena, MD 21635-0267 410-755-6300
Fax: 410-755-6367 www.iseamerica.com
Processor of fresh eggs
Chairman: Hikonobu Ise
VP/COO: Gregg Clanton
Estimated Sales: $100-500 Million
Number Employees: 250-499
Type of Packaging: Consumer, Food Service

6425 **ISE Newberry**
P.O.Box 7582
Newberry, SC 29108-0752 803-276-5803
Fax: 803-276-4468 www.iseamerica.com
Processor and exporter of eggs
Parent Co: Ise America
Type of Packaging: Consumer, Food Service, Private Label, Bulk
Brands:
NEWBERRY
SOUTHERN BREAKFAST

6426 **ISF Trading**
P.O.Box 772
Portland, ME 04104-0772 207-879-1575
Fax: 207-761-5877 isfco@aol.com
www.seaurchinmaine.com
Manufacturer of Fresh Sea Urchin Roe, Live Sea Urchin, Dry Sea Urchin Shell, Live Lobster, Live Rock Crab, Live Whelk, Fresh Atlantic Salmon, Frozen Salmon Roe, Fresh Marine Shrimp, Fresh Pine Tree Mushroom.
Founder: Atchan Tamaki
Office Manager: Lan Gao
Estimated Sales: $ 50 - 100 Million
Number Employees: 10-19

6427 **ITW Dynatec**
31 Volunteer Dr
Hendersonville, TN 37075-3156 615-824-3634
Fax: 615-264-5248 dynatec@itwdynatec.com
www.itwdynatec.com
President: Zent Myer
CFO: Doug Betew
CFO: Doug Detew
R & D: Marie McLain
Number Employees: 100-249

6428 **IVC American Vitamin**
500 Halls Mill Rd
Freehold, NJ 07728-8811 732-308-3000
Fax: 732-761-2878 800-666-8482
www.invernessmedical.com
Processor and exporter of vitamin supplements, herbal products and antioxidants
Manager: Barb McCleer
Number Employees: 250-499
Type of Packaging: Consumer

6429 **Ians Natural Foods**
360 Merrimack Street
Building 9, Suite 320
Lawrence, MA 01843 781-284-1999
Fax: 97- 98- 060 800-543-6637
customerservice@iansnaturalfoods.com
www.iansnaturalfoods.com
Only all natural, antibiotic and hormone free line of beef, poultry and specialty french fry prepared foods in a retail packaged format. Allergen Free fish stick and chicken nuggets, funfoods, appetizers, breakfast, desserts, friesand entrees.
Manager: Terrence Dalton
VP Marketing: Jeff Canner

6430 **(HQ)Iberia Sugar Coop**
P.O.Box 12040
New Iberia, LA 70562 337-367-2230
Fax: 337-365-0030 iberiasugar@aol.com
www.iberiasugar.com
Manufacturer of raw cane sugar and blackstrap molasses
President: Ronald Gonsoulin
Estimated Sales: $23 Million
Number Employees: 65
Sq. footage: 90000
Type of Packaging: Bulk

6431 **Icco Cheese Company**
1 Olympic Dr
Orangeburg, NY 10962 845-398-9800
Fax: 845-398-1669 johna@iccocheese.com
www.iccocheese.com
Processor, importer and exporter of grated parmesan cheese in shaker canisters and glass pet containers; processor and exporter of bread crumbs
President: Joseph Angiolillo
Vice President: John Angiolillo
Vice President: John Angiolillo
Estimated Sales: $10-15 Million
Number Employees: 50-99
Type of Packaging: Consumer, Food Service, Private Label, Bulk
Brands:
America's Choice
American Beauty
Berkley & Jensen
D'Agostino
Dominick's
Food Club
Giant
Icco Brand
Luigi Vitelli
Pastene
PathMark
Price Chopper
Reggano
Ronzoni
San Giorgio
Shop Rite
Splendido
Weis

6432 **Ice Cream & Yogurt Club**
1580 High Ridge Rd
Boynton Beach, FL 33426-8724 561-731-3331
Fax: 561-731-0311 info@icecreamclub.com
www.icecreamclub.com
Processor of ice cream, yogurt, ice cream cones, toppings and syrups; also, soft serve machines available
Co-President: Marie Lawson
CEO: Richard Draper
Estimated Sales: D
Number Employees: 20-49
Type of Packaging: Consumer, Food Service, Private Label, Bulk

6433 **Ice Cream Specialties**
P.O.Box 440307
Saint Louis, MO 63144 314-962-2550
Fax: 314-962-1990 www.northstarfrozentreats.com
Processor of ice cream including novelties, bars, cups and pops
President: John Kroll
Marketing Intern: Chris McQueen
Plant Manager: Mary Luebbert
Estimated Sales: $50-100 Million
Number Employees: 100-249
Sq. footage: 250000
Parent Co: Prairie Farms Dairy
Type of Packaging: Consumer

6434 **Ice Cream Specialties**
P.O.Box 679
Lafayette, IN 47902-0679 765-474-2989
Fax: 765-474-6150 cotegolf@dwi.com
Processor of novelty ice cream including cones, sandwiches and cups
President: Robert Theissen
CEO: Roger Capps
Sales: Tom Gueltzow
Production: John Fitz Simons
Plant Manager: Robert Thiessen
Estimated Sales: $20-50 Million
Number Employees: 100-249
Parent Co: Prairie Farms Dairy
Type of Packaging: Consumer

6435 **Ice House**
PO Box 430133
Big Pine Key, FL 33043-0133 305-872-1215
Owner: R Lucas

6436 **Ice Land Corporation**
5777 Baum Blvd
Pittsburgh, PA 15206-3745 412-441-9512
Fax: 412-441-9517 catchup@bellatlantic.net
Processor and exporter of plain and kosher frozen pizza; also, Italian specialties including pasta
President: Daniel Paskoff
COO: Tonald Paskoff
Estimated Sales: $2.5-5 Million
Number Employees: 5-9
Type of Packaging: Consumer, Food Service, Private Label, Bulk
Brands:
Cholov Yisrael
Tambellini

6437 **Icelandic Milk and SkyrCorporation**
135 W 26th Street
2nd Floor
New York, NY 10001 212-966-6950
Fax: 646-536-8159 info@skyr.com
www.skyr.com
icelandic-style yogurt
CEO: Vicky Hilmarsson

Number Employees: 4

6438 **Icelandic USA**
190 Enterprise Dr
Newport News, VA 23603 757-820-4000
Fax: 757-888-6250 http://www.icelandic.com/
Fish and seafood
President/CEO: Evar Agnarsson
Executive Vice President: Daniel Murphy
VP Finance/Administration: Michael Thome
VP Supply Chain: Rick Barnhardt
VP Foodservice Distribution/Services: Robert Mizek
VP Marketing: Tom Sherman
VP Human Resources: Christine Searles
VP Manufacturing: Steve Bloodgood
Estimated Sales: $25-49.9 Million
Number Employees: 250-499
Sq. footage: 170000
Parent Co: Icelandic Group HF
Type of Packaging: Consumer, Food Service, Private Label
Other Locations:
Icelandic Processing Plant
Cambridge MD
Icelandic Processing Plant
Newport News VA
Brands:
ICELANDIC
SAMBAND

6439 **(HQ)Icicle Seafoods**
4019 21st Ave W
Seattle, WA 98199 206-282-0988
Fax: 206-282-7222
customerservice@icicleseafoods.com
www.icicleseafoods.com
Manufacturer and exporter of fresh and frozen cod, pollock, halibut, sablefish, herring, herring roe, salmon, salmon roe, crabs, and surimi based products
President/CEO: Don Giles
Sr Executive Vice President, Asia: Larry Hill
CFO: Brenda Morris
National Sales Manager: Rick Speed
National Fresh Sales Manager: Mark Callaghan
Director Canned Sales: John Boynton
VP Frozen Sales: Mark Sandvik
Estimated Sales: $400 Million
Number Employees: 500
Sq. footage: 8000
Type of Packaging: Consumer, Food Service, Private Label, Bulk

6440 **Icy Bird**
1151 Jim Hennessee Road
Sparta, TN 38583-1115 931-738-3557
Processor of citrus juices and frozen juice bars including grape, cherry/apple and orange
President: William Norvell
Number Employees: 1-4
Parent Co: M&B Products

6441 **Idaho Beverages**
2108 1st Ave N
Lewiston, ID 83501-1699 208-743-6535
Fax: 208-746-2273
Beverages
President: Gary Parsio
Estimated Sales: $5-10 Million
Number Employees: 10-19

6442 **Idaho Candy Company**
412 S 8th St
Boise, ID 83702 208-342-5505
Fax: 208-384-5310 800-898-6986
info@idahospud.com www.idahospud.com
Processor of vending, boxed and bagged candy including bars, butter toffee, mints, marshmallows, hard, jelly beans, brittles, chocolate, Valentine, glazed nuts, etc
Chairman: John Wagers
President: Dave Wagers
Estimated Sales: $10-20 Million
Number Employees: 20-49
Sq. footage: 28000
Type of Packaging: Consumer, Food Service, Bulk
Brands:
IDAHO SPUD
OLD FAITHFUL
OWYHEE

6443 **Idaho Milk Products**
2249 S. Tiger Drive
Jerome, ID 83338 208-644-2882
Fax: 208-644-2899 www.idahomilkproducts.com
Supplier of milk cream derivatives, milk protein concentrate and milk permeate used in the cheese, yogurt and dairy food industries.

6444 **Idaho Pacific Corporation**
P.O.Box 478
Ririe, ID 83443-0478 208-538-6971
Fax: 208-538-5082 800-238-5503
ipc@idahopacific.com www.idahopacific.com
Manufacturer and exporter of dehydrated potato flakes, granules, agglomerates, and flour.
CEO: Dick Nickel
CFO: Baden Burt
Executive VP/COO: Wally Browning
R&D: Jennifer Weekes
Quality Control: Jennifer Weekes
VP/Sales & Marketing: Jon Schodde
VP/Operations: Todd Sutton
Plant Manager: Steve McLean
Purchasing: Brian Hart
Estimated Sales: $40-50 Million
Number Employees: 100-249
Parent Co: AgraWest Foods
Type of Packaging: Food Service, Private Label, Bulk
Brands:
Idaho-Pacific

6445 **Idaho Supreme Potatoes**
614 E 800 N
Firth, ID 83236 208-346-6841
Fax: 208-346-4104 info@idahosupreme.com
www.idahosupreme.com
Supplier of slices, diced, and shredded potatoes.
President/General Manager: Wade Chapman
CFO: Steve Prescott
VP: Art Polson
Estimated Sales: $ 37.60 Million
Number Employees: 250-499
Sq. footage: 100000
Type of Packaging: Consumer, Private Label
Brands:
Idaho Supreme

6446 **Idaho Trout Company**
P.O.Box 72
Buhl, ID 83316 208-326-5430
Fax: 208-543-8476 866-878-7688
rainbowtrout@idahotrout.com
www.idahotrout.com
Processor and exporter of rainbow and golden trout
Manager: Harold Johnson
Vice President: Gregory Kaslo
Sales/Shipping: Janie Higgins
General Manager: Harold Johnson
Estimated Sales: $10-25 Million
Number Employees: 50-99
Type of Packaging: Food Service, Private Label, Bulk
Brands:
Cold River
Idaho's Best
Rainbow Springs

6447 **Idaho-Frank Associates**
391 Taylor Blvd # 180
Pleasant Hill, CA 94523-2282 925-609-8458
Fax: 925-609-9318 info@idahofrank.com
www.idahofrank.com
Dehydrated potato granules, flakes, slices, dices, frozen dices and flour
President: Mark Lyons
Estimated Sales: $5-10 Million
Number Employees: 1-4
Type of Packaging: Food Service, Private Label, Bulk

6448 **Idahoan**
P.O.Box 130
Lewisville, ID 83431-0130 208-754-4686
Fax: 208-754-8188 800-635-6100
ifp.talk@idahoan.com www.idahoan.com
Processor of dehydrated mashed potatoes
President/CEO: Gale Clement
Controller: Rod Roberts
CEO: Gordon Lewis
Research & Development: Dena Shatila
Quality Control: Cal McCombes
Marketing Director: Drew Facer
Public Relations: Drew Forcer
COO: Norman Hart
Plant Manager: Gene Christiansen
Estimated Sales: $ 50 - 100 Million
Number Employees: 250-499
Type of Packaging: Consumer, Food Service
Brands:
Idahoan
Loaded Baked
Mashed Potatoes
Roasted Garlic

6449 **(HQ)Idahoan Foods**
P.O.Box 130
Lewisville, ID 83431 208-754-4686
Fax: 208-754-0094 800-635-6100
www.idahoanfoods.com
Manufacturer of dehydrated potato products for retail and foodservice, as well as potato ingredients, and frozen fruits and vegetables. J.R. Simplot markets and distributes Idaho Fresh-Pack potato products under the Idahoan brand.
Chairman: J R Simplot
President: Bill Whitacre
VP Sales: Boyd Blair
Sales Manager: Val Lambert
Estimated Sales: $98.7 Million
Number Employees: 700
Type of Packaging: Consumer, Food Service, Bulk
Other Locations:
Simplot Potato Processing
Aberdeen ID
Simplot Potato Processing
Caldwell ID
Simplot Potato Processing
Grand Forks ND
Simplot Potato Processing
Moses Lake WA
Simplot Potato Processing
Nampa ID
Simplot Potato Processing
Othello WA
Simplot Vegetable Processing
Pasco WA
Simplot Vegetable Processing
West Memphis AK
Simplot Fertilizer Plant
Brandon, Manitoba
Simplot Fertilizer Plant
Helm CA
Simplot Fertilizer Plant
Lathrop CA
Simplot Fertilizer Plant
Pocatello ID
Simplot Fertilizer Plant
Portland OR

6450 **Idahoan Foods, LLC**
529 N 3500 E
PO Box 130
Lewisville, ID 83431 208-754-4686
Fax: 208-754-8188 800-635-6100
ifp.talk@idahoan.com www.idahoan.com
Manufacturer of dehydrated potato products such as; instant mashed potatoes, hash browns, scalloped, au gratin as well as potato ingredients like flakes, shreds and slices
President/CEO: Gordon Lewis
CFO: Kerry Buck
VP Sales/Marketing: Drew Facer
Human Resources Director: Richard Nelson
VP Manufacturing: Sam Huffman
Estimated Sales: $74.5 Million
Number Employees: 361
Type of Packaging: Food Service, Private Label
Brands:
IDAHOAN

6451 **Ideal American**
PO Box 70
Holland, IN 47541-0070 812-424-3351
Fax: 812-423-9809
Processor of milk including whole fat-free, low and reduced-fat and chocolate
Plant Manager: Tim McAllister
Estimated Sales: $20-50 Million
Number Employees: 50-99
Parent Co: Prairie Farms Dairy
Type of Packaging: Consumer, Food Service

6452 **Ideal Dairy**
490 S Main St
Richfield, UT 84701 435-896-5061
Fax: 435-896-1909 idealdairy1@yahoo.com
www.theidealdairy.com
Processor of dairy products including milk, cream and ice cream
Owner: Kristie Sorsen
Estimated Sales: $10-20 Million
Number Employees: 20-49
Sq. footage: 2500
Type of Packaging: Consumer, Food Service

6453 **Ideal Distributing Company**
23800 7th Place W
Bothell, WA 98021-8508 425-488-6121
Fax: 425-488-8159
Tea, coffee
Principal: John Erdman
Co-Ownr: Cathy Erdman

6454 **Ideal Snacks**
89 Mill St
Liberty, NY 12754 845-292-7000
Fax: 845-292-3100 www.idealsnacks.com
Snacks
President: Zeke Alenick
Director of Operations: LJ Goldstock
Estimated Sales: $ 3 - 5 Million
Number Employees: 100-249

6455 **Iguana Tom's**
44477 Parkmeadow Dr
Fremont, CA 94539-6581 704-847-5923
Fax: 704-847-4857 888-827-2572
iguanatom@carolina.rr.com
www.iguanatoms.com
Co-Owner: Ellen Siegler
President: Tom Siegler
Brands:
Iguana Tom's

6456 **Il Gelato**
2451 46th Street
Astoria, NY 11103-1007 718-937-3033
Fax: 718-786-5543 800-899-9299
Processor of baked goods, gelato and individual desserts
President: Dimitri Pauli
Estimated Sales: $142,000
Number Employees: 30

6457 **Il Giardino Bakery**
2859 N Harlem Ave
Chicago, IL 60707-1638 773-889-2388
Fax: 773-889-5990 www.ilgiardinobakery.com
Processor of cannoli shells, mini pasteries, butter cookies and cakes
Owner: Maria Ventrella
Estimated Sales: Less than $500,000
Number Employees: 10-19
Type of Packaging: Consumer
Brands:
Giardino

6458 **Il Tiramisu**
64 E Merrick Road
Suite G1
Valley Stream, NY 11580-5946
US 516-599-1010
Fax: 516-599-6540 www.iltiramisu.com
Exporter and processor of Italian desserts including chocolate mousse, tiramisu, gelato, tartufo, tortoni and spumoni; importer of Italian cakes and pasta
Owner/President: Aldo Antonoacci
Estimated Sales: $500.000k
Number Employees: 154

6459 **Il Vicino Pizzeria**
136 E 2nd St
Salida, CO 81201-2115 719-539-5219
Fax: 719-539-2918
Processor of beer, ale and stout
Owner: Kathie Younghans
Estimated Sales: $1-2.5 Million
Number Employees: 20-49
Parent Co: Il Vicino Holding Company
Type of Packaging: Consumer, Food Service
Brands:
Web Mountain

6460 **Illes Seasonings & Flavors**
2200 Luna Rd Ste 120
Carrollton, TX 75006 214-631-8499
Fax: 214-689-1381 800-683-4553
customerserv@illesseasonings.com
www.illesfood.com
Manufacturer and exporter of sauce bases, seasonings, flavors and worcestershire products
Chairman/CEO: Rick Illes
VP Administration: Linda Mullin
Estimated Sales: $20-50 Million
Number Employees: 1-4
Type of Packaging: Consumer, Food Service, Private Label

6461 **Iltaco Food Products**
1378 W Hubbard Street
Chicago, IL 60642
Fax: 312-421-0774 800-244-8935
www.iltaco.com
Processor of frozen pizza, pizza puffs, pasta with marinara sauce, burritos, tamales and taco puffs
Owner/Vice President: Rebecca Shabaz
Estimated Sales: $10-20 Million
Number Employees: 50-99
Type of Packaging: Consumer, Food Service, Private Label
Brands:
Iltaco

6462 **Imaex Trading**
5405 Buford Highway
Suite 350
Norcross, GA 30071-3982 770-825-0848
Fax: 770-825-0166
President: Seng Angkawijana

6463 **Image Development**
PO Box 150028
San Rafael, CA 94915-0028 415-626-0485
Fax: 415-255-7597
Estimated Sales: Less than $500,000
Number Employees: 1-4

6464 **Imagine Foods**
58 S Service Rd
Melville, NY 11747-2344 631-730-2200
Fax: 631-730-2550 800-333-6339
questions@imagine.com www.imaginefoods.com
Processor of kosher beverages, drink mixes, ice cream and frozen novelties
President: Irwin Simon
CFO/EVP: Ira Lamel
COO: James Meiers
Estimated Sales: $20-50 Million
Number Employees: 130
Type of Packaging: Consumer, Food Service
Brands:
IMAGINE NATURAL
POWER DREAM
RICE DREAM SUPREME
SOY DREAM

6465 **Imaginings 3**
6401 W Gross Point Rd
Niles, IL 60714 847-647-1370
Fax: 847-647-0633 www.flixcandy.com
President: Sidney Diamond
VP Sales: Jeff Grossman
Estimated Sales: $ 5 - 10 Million
Number Employees: 20-49

6466 **Immaculate Baking Company**
333 North Avenue
Wakefield, MA 01880 828-696-1655
Fax: 828-696-1663 888-826-6567
info@immaculatebaking.com
www.immaculatebaking.com
cookies
President/Owner: Scott Blackwell

6467 **Immaculate Consumption**
PO Box 299
Flat Rock, NC 28731-0299 828-696-1655
Fax: 828-696-1663 888-826-6567
info@immaculateconsumption.com
www.immamculatecomsumption.com
Processor of bakes goods, cookies, scones, biscotti, and mojos
President/CEO: Scott Blackwell
Vice President: Caroline Blackwell
VP Sales: Don Porter
Estimated Sales: Under $1 Million
Number Employees: 10-19
Number of Brands: 1
Number of Products: 29
Sq. footage: 10000
Type of Packaging: Consumer, Food Service, Private Label
Brands:
IMMACULATE CONSUMPTION

6468 **Immediate Gratification**
1840 41st Avenue
Suite 102-199
Capitola, CA 95010-2513 831-457-9602
Fax: 831-457-9602
Owner: Andra Rudolph
Estimated Sales: Under $500,000
Number Employees: 1-4

6469 **ImmuDyne**
7453 Empire Dr Ste 300
Florence, KY 41042 859-746-3909
Fax: 859-746-8772 888-246-6839
sales@immudyne.com www.immudyne.com
Processor and exporter of beta glucan dietary natural supplements - helping our wold eat better, live healthier and look younger
VP: Alfred Munoz
Investor: Mark McLaughlin
Number Employees: 1-4
Type of Packaging: Consumer, Food Service, Bulk

6470 **Impact Confections**
10822 W Toller Dr
Suite 350
Littleton, CO 80127 303-626-2222
Fax: 877-771-7677 info@impactconfections.com
www.impactconfections.com
Processor of confectionery products including gourmet, seasonal, custom made and novelty lollypops
Founder/President: Brad Baker
Director Marketing: Steve Moskowitz
Estimated Sales: $25-49.9 Million
Number Employees: 20-49
Number of Products: 40
Type of Packaging: Consumer
Brands:
ALIEN POP
ALIEN POPPIN' POPS
CAROUSEL POP
COLOR BLASTER
GLOW POP
HAPPY HEART LOLLIPOPS
HOPPIN' POPS
LILLIDAY POPS
LOLLIPOP PAINT SHOP
POP-A-BEAR
SOCCER POPS

6471 **Impact Nutrition**
1155 S Havana Street
Suite 11-392
Aurora, CO 80012-4019 720-374-7111
www.impactnutrition.com
Contract packager of vitamins, minerals, herbal and nutritional supplements, sports nutrition products, capsules, tablets and powders - true innovator in the field of nutritional supplements and sports nutrition
President: Patrick Frazier
General Manager: Julene Frazier
Estimated Sales: $10-20 Million
Number Employees: 20-49
Sq. footage: 15000

6472 **Imperia Foods**
40 New Dutch Ln
Fairfield, NJ 07004-2514 973-227-0030
Fax: 908-756-6076 800-526-7333
General grocery
President: Ira Weissman
Estimated Sales: $2.5-5 Million
Number Employees: 9
Sq. footage: 37
Type of Packaging: Private Label

6473 **(HQ)Imperial Flavors Beverage Company**
6300 W Douglas Ave
Milwaukee, WI 53218 414-536-7788
Fax: 414-536-7730 info@imperialflavors.com
www.imperialflavors.com
Processor of bag-in-box juice and soda concentrates including soda water; also, juice products for soft-serve machines
President: Jack Pettigrew

Estimated Sales: $10-20 Million
Number Employees: 10-19
Sq. footage: 12000
Type of Packaging: Consumer, Food Service, Private Label, Bulk
Brands:
CAPTAIN JACK'S
FRUIT N' JUICE
JUICE PLUS
JUICY ORANGE
MILWAUKEE SELTZER COMPANY
TROPICS

6474 **Imperial Food Supply**
4800 North St
Baton Rouge, LA 70806-3497 225-924-4222
Fax: 225-924-3362
Owner/President: Michael Divincenti, Jr.

6475 **Imperial Foods**
5014 39th St
Long Island City, NY 11104-4508 718-784-3400
Fax: 718-361-7993 www.imperialfoods.com
Processor and wholesaler/distributor of dairy products including Armenian string, Naboulsi, Akawi and Syrian cheeses, yogurt and kefir spread
General Manager: Charles Mkhitarian
Estimated Sales: $2.5-5 Million
Number Employees: 10-19
Sq. footage: 4000
Brands:
GREENFIELD
VICTOR'S

6476 **Imperial Nougat Company**
12035 Slauson Ave Ste C
Santa Fe Springs, CA 90670 562-693-8423
Fax: 562-945-8852
Candy
President: Al Maghsoudi
Estimated Sales: $2.5-5 Million
Number Employees: 5-9

6477 **Imperial Salmon House**
1632 Franklin Street
Vancouver, BC V5L 1P4
Canada 604-251-1114
Fax: 604-251-3177 smokedsalmon@sprint.ca
Processor and exporter of smoked salmon
President: Robert Blair
Number Employees: 5-9
Type of Packaging: Consumer, Food Service, Bulk

6478 **Imperial Sensus**
PO Box 9
Sugar Land, TX 77487-0009 281-490-9522
Fax: 281-490-9615 pgalvin@imperialsensus.com
www.isullc.com
Processor, importer and exporter of inulin, a natural extract from chicory uses include as a texture modifier, flavor masking and gut health benefits
VP Sales/Marketing: Sally Brain
VP of Technical Affairs: Bryan Tungland
Parent Co: Imperial Sugar Company
Type of Packaging: Food Service, Bulk
Brands:
Frutafit
Nutralin

6479 **(HQ)Imperial Sugar Company**
8016 Highway 90A
PO Box 9
Sugar Land, TX 77487-0009 281-491-9181
Fax: 281-490-9530 800-727-8427
Consumers@ImperialSugar.com
www.imperialsugar.com
Sugar
President/CEO: John Sheptor
SVP/CFO: H P Mechler
SVP/Secretary/General Counsel: Louis Bolognini
Director/Enviromental, Safety & Health: Wayne Maksylewich
VP/Technology: Brian Harrison
SVP/Commodities Mgmt & Sales: Patrick Henneberry
VP/Sales Planning & Supply Chain: George Muller
VP/Manufacturing: Raylene Carter
VP Manufacturing/Engineering: Ralph Clements
Estimated Sales: $900 Million
Number Employees: 500-999
Brands:
DIXIE CRYSTALS
IMPERIAL SUGAR
REDI-MEASURE
STEVIACANE

6480 **Imperial Sugar Company**
201 Oxnard Drive
PO Box 4225
Port Wentworth, GA 31407
800-727-8427
www.imperialsugar.com
Processor and marketer of refined sugar to grocery customers, food manufacturers and food service distributors.
Sq. footage: 1000000
Parent Co: Imperial Sugar Company
Type of Packaging: Consumer, Food Service, Private Label, Bulk
Other Locations:
Cane Operations
Gramercy LA
Cane Operations
Savannah GA
Brands:
DIXIE CRYSTAL®
HOLLY®
IMPERIAL PURE SUGAR CANE®

6481 **Imperial Sugar Company**
1230 Firth Avenue
Gramercy, LA 77052
800-727-8427
Producer of sugar
Parent Co: Imperial Sugar Company
Type of Packaging: Consumer, Food Service, Private Label, Bulk

6482 **Imprint Plus**
21320 Gordon Way
Unit 260
Richmond, BC V6W 1J8
Canada 604-278-7147
Fax: 604-278-7149 800-563-2464
sales@imprintplus.com www.imprintplus.com
Imprint Plus is a designer, manufacturer and worldwide distributor of name badges, name badge systems, and accessories
President: Ellen Flanders
CEO: Marla Kott
Marketing Director: Chuck Beebe
Sales Director: Phil Coles
Operations Manager: Kristin MacMillian
Number Employees: 65

6483 **Impromtu Gourmet**
141 Wooster Street
Apt 7d
New York, NY 10012-3199 212-475-4640
Fax: 212-475-5794
ychi@impromptugourmet.com
www.impromptugourmet.com
Fresh gourmet foods
Founder/CEO: Max Polaner

6484 **Imsco Technology**
40 Bayfield Drive
North Andover, MA 01845-6016 978-689-2080
Fax: 978-689-2585
Chairman/CEO: Timothy Keating
Estimated Sales: $500,000-$1 Million
Number Employees: 5-9

6485 **Imus Ranch Foods**
16 West Ave
Darien, CT 06820-4401 505-892-0883
Processor of tortilla chips, salsa and coffee
President: Fred Imus
Cfo: John Imus
Estimated Sales: $200,000
Number Employees: 2
Type of Packaging: Consumer, Food Service
Brands:
FRED IMUS SOUTHWEST
FRED IMUS TURQUOISE
IMUS BROTHERS COFFEE

6486 **Inca Kola/Golden Kola**
215 E 64th Street
New York, NY 10021-6662 212-688-1895
Fax: 212-688-1895 973-688-0970
Processor of beverages.
President: Rodolfo Salas
Estimated Sales: $5-10 Million appx.
Number Employees: 1-4

6487 **Increda-Meal**
PO Box 30
Cato, NY 13033-0030 315-626-2111
Fax: 315-626-2777
Nutrition bars
Estimated Sales: $10-20 Million
Number Employees: 50-99

6488 **Incredible Cheesecake Company**
3161 Adams Ave
San Diego, CA 92116 619-563-9722
Fax: 619-563-1022 www.incrediblecheesecake.net
Processor of frozen cheesecakes
Co-Owner/President: Michelle Satren
Co-Owner/VP: Scott Satren
Estimated Sales: $1-2.5 Million
Number Employees: 10-19
Sq. footage: 3500

6489 **(HQ)Indel Food Products**
11415 Cedar Oak Dr
El Paso, TX 79936 915-590-5914
Fax: 915-590-5913 800-472-0159
customerservice@indelfoods.com
www.indelfoods.com
Red, green, mixed and roasted peppers and pimentos, jalapenos, green chiles, cherry and banana peppers. (Food service, private label, bulk)
Owner: Gustavo Deandar
Estimated Sales: $2.5-5 Million
Number Employees: 1-4
Sq. footage: 20000
Type of Packaging: Food Service, Private Label, Bulk
Other Locations:
Indel Food Products
Delicias, Chihuahua
Brands:
DEL SOL

6490 **Indel Food Products**
11415 Cedar Oak Dr
El Paso, TX 79936 915-590-5914
Fax: 915-590-5913 800-472-0159
indl@dzn.com www.indeofoods.com
Processor and exporter of canned hot, jalapeno nacho, whole jalapeno peppers:also, green and red salsa
President: Gustavo Deandar
Estimated Sales: $2.5-5 Million
Number Employees: 1-4
Parent Co: Agroindustrias Deandar
Type of Packaging: Consumer, Food Service, Private Label, Bulk
Brands:
DEL SOL

6491 **Indena USA**
811 1st Ave # 218
Seattle, WA 98104-1434 206-340-6140
Fax: 206-340-0863 greg@indenausa.com
www.indena.com
Processor of herbal extracts
President: Ezio Bombardelli
CEO: Dario Bonacorsi
VP: Greg Ris
VP Sales: Greg Ris
Estimated Sales: $1-2.5 Million
Number Employees: 1-4
Parent Co: Indena S.p.A.
Type of Packaging: Bulk

6492 **Independent Bakers Association**
1223 Potomac St NW
Washington, DC 20007-3212 202-333-8190
Fax: 202-337-3809
npyle@independentbaker.com
www.independentbaker.org
Baked goods
President: Robert Pyle
VP Sales: Nicholas Pyle

6493 **Independent Dairy**
126 N Telegraph Rd
Monroe, MI 48162 734-241-6016
Fax: 734-241-1251
Ice cream
President: Michael Cheney
Estimated Sales: $5-9.9 Million
Number Employees: 50-99

6494 **(HQ)Independent Food Processors Company**
311 N 4th Street
Suite 204
Yakima, WA 98901 509-457-6487
Fax: 509-457-7983 800-476-5398
glewis@indfoodpro.com www.indfoodpro.com
Canner and exporter of apples, apple sauce, cherries and pears
President: Peter Plath
Director/Sales & New Business Dev.: Doug Hearron
Retail & Foodservice Sales Manager: Bill Notley
Plant Manager: Mike Trader
Estimated Sales: $ 5 - 10 Million
Number Employees: 250
Type of Packaging: Consumer, Food Service, Private Label
Other Locations:
Independent Food Processors C
Sunnyside WA

6495 **Independent Food Processors**
1525 S 4th Street
Sunnyside, WA 98944 509-837-3806
Fax: 509-837-3573
Manufacturer and exporter of canned fruit including apples, pears and cherries
President: Peter Plath
Plant Manager: Mike Trader
Parent Co: Independent Food Processing
Type of Packaging: Private Label

6496 **Independent Master Casing Company**
904111 Dice Road
Santa Fe Springs, CA 90670 562-946-1913
Fax: 562-946-1913 800-635-9518
President: Manil Whig
Vice President: Frank Drozdowski
Estimated Sales: $2.5-5 Million
Number Employees: 10-19

6497 **Independent Meat Company**
P.O.Box Ee
Twin Falls, ID 83303 208-733-0980
Fax: 208-734-9702 info@salmoncreekfarms.com
www.independentmeat.com
Processor and packer of meat and sausage
President/CEO: Patrick Florence
Vice President: Mike McBride
Estimated Sales: $43 Million
Number Employees: 238
Type of Packaging: Consumer

6498 **Independent Packers Corporation**
2001 W Garfield St Ste C102
Seattle, WA 98119 206-285-6000
Fax: 206-285-9236
Custom processor and packer of fresh and frozen seafood including crab, cod, halibut, salmon and tuna
President/CEO: Bill Manning
Estimated Sales: $3-5 Million
Number Employees: 100-249
Sq. footage: 30000
Type of Packaging: Food Service, Private Label

6499 **Indi-Bel**
1842 Highway 82 W
Indianola, MS 38751 662-887-1226
Fax: 662-887-5630
Jams, jellies and spreads
President: Lester Myers
Vice President: Julian Allen
Estimated Sales: $14 Million
Number Employees: 65

6500 **India Tree Gourmet Spices & Specialties**
5309 Shilshole Ave NW
Suite 150
Seattle, WA 98107 206-270-0293
Fax: 206-282-0587 800-369-4848
india@indiatree.com www.indiatree.com
purveyor of sugar, spices and other fine food products from around the world
President/Owner: Gretchen Gorren
Number Employees: 10

6501 **(HQ)India's Rasoa**
25 N Euclid Ave
St Louis, MO 63108-1445 314-361-6911
Fax: 314-727-8331 harinder@rasoi.com
www.rasoi.com
Indian specialties
President: Harinder Singh
Estimated Sales: Less than $500,000
Number Employees: 5-9

6502 **Indian Bay Frozen Foods**
PO Box 160
Centreville, NL A0G 4P0
Canada 709-678-2844
Fax: 709-678-2447 ackermans@ibffinc.com
www.ibffinc.com
Processor and exporter of blueberries, lingonberries, jams and pie fillings; also, fish including capelin
President: Calvin Ackerman
Estimated Sales: 2.5-5 Million
Number Employees: 20-49
Sq. footage: 10000
Type of Packaging: Consumer, Private Label, Bulk
Brands:
ACKERMAN'S WILD

6503 **Indian Foods Company**
7575 Golden Valley Rd # 135
Minneapolis, MN 55427-4570 763-593-3000
Fax: 763-593-3003 kmehta@gotindia.com
www.sccnet.com
Processor of Indian naam pizzas
Owner: Erik Phorsell
Estimated Sales: $300,000-500,000
Number Employees: 1-4
Brands:
ASHOKA

6504 **Indian Harvest**
P.O.Box 910
Colusa, CA 95932-0910 530-458-8512
Fax: 530-458-8344 800-294-2433
www.indianharvest.com
Processor and exporter of rice, grain and bean products, soup and chili mixes, seasonings and pasta; importer of rice
Plant Manager: Don Kuiken
Estimated Sales: $5-10 Million
Number Employees: 20-49
Type of Packaging: Food Service, Private Label

6505 **Indian Harvest Specialitifoods**
P.O.Box 428
Bemidji, MN 56619-0428 218-751-8500
Fax: 218-751-8519 800-346-7032
www.indianharvest.com
Processor of heirloom beans and specialty rice blends and grains including red, wheat, wild, brown, white and basmati
Manager: Jenni Hillman
VP: John DeVos
Sales Manager: Joe Bofferding
Corporate Chef: Michael Holleman
Estimated Sales: $20-50 Million
Number Employees: 20-49
Type of Packaging: Consumer, Food Service, Private Label, Bulk
Brands:
GUEST CHEF
INDIAN HARVEST

6506 **Indian Hollow Farms**
15321 Us Hwy 14
Richland Center, WI 53581 608-536-3499
800-236-3944
Processor of apples and apple cider
Owner: John Symons
Estimated Sales: $1-2.5 Million
Number Employees: 5-9
Sq. footage: 100000
Type of Packaging: Consumer, Food Service, Private Label, Bulk
Brands:
COUNTRY ROAD
IDDIAN HOLLOW

6507 **Indian Ridge Shrimp Company**
120 Doctor Hugh St Martin Dr
Chauvin, LA 70344 985-594-3361
Fax: 985-594-2168 594-5869(985)
www.triple-t-shrimp.com
Processor, importer and exporter of frozen shrimp
Owner: Andrew Blanchard
COO: Richard Fakier
Sales Manager: Daniel Babin
Estimated Sales: $2.5-5 Million
Number Employees: 50-99
Sq. footage: 25000
Type of Packaging: Consumer, Food Service
Brands:
PEARL

6508 **Indian River Foods**
3798 Selvitz Rd
Fort Pierce, FL 34981 772-462-2222
Fax: 561-462-2224
Processor and exporter of frozen orange and grapefruit juices and concentrates; importer of orange, grape and apple concentrates
Sales Manager: Doug Burlan
Manager (Materials): Bruce Gowan
Plant Manager: Larry Gray
Number Employees: 100-249
Sq. footage: 150000
Parent Co: Becker Holding Corporation
Type of Packaging: Food Service, Private Label, Bulk

6509 **Indian Rock Produce**
P.O.Box 428
Perkasie, PA 18944-0428 215-536-9600
Fax: 215-529-9448 800-882-0512
Grower of organically grown vegetables and fruits including asparagus, beets, broccoli, cabbage, carrots, cauliflower, corn, eggplant, lettuce, onions, squash, tomatoes, etc
Co-Owner: Lu Ann Buehrer
Co-Owner: Albert Buehrer
Sales Contact: Bill Neely
Estimated Sales: $50-100 Million
Number Employees: 5-9
Type of Packaging: Consumer, Food Service, Bulk

6510 **Indian Rock Vineyards**
1154 Pennsylvania Gulch Rd
Murphys, CA 95247 209-728-8514
www.indianrockvineyards.com
Wines
President: Boyd Thompson
Estimated Sales: $ 3 - 5 Million
Number Employees: 5-9

6511 **Indian Springs Fresh Poultry**
217 Hawkeye Ct
Columbus, OH 43235-1489 614-443-7473
Processor of poultry
President: Lindy O Brien
Office Manager: Dick Neblette
Estimated Sales: $500,000-$1 Million
Number Employees: 1-4

6512 **Indian Springs Vineyards**
330 Broad Street
Nevada City, CA 95959-2405 530-478-1068
Fax: 530-478-0903
Wines
President: David McCord
Production Manager: Julie Holmes
Estimated Sales: Under $500,000
Number Employees: 8
Type of Packaging: Private Label

6513 **Indian Valley Meats**
Hc 52 Box 8809
Indian, AK 99540-9604 907-653-7511
Fax: 907-653-7694 ivm@alaska.net
www.indianvalleymeats.com
Processor of poultry, venison and fish including halibut and salmon; exporter of smoked fish and meats including sausage
President: Douglas Drum
Plant Manager: Renia Drum
Estimated Sales: $2.5-5 Million
Number Employees: 10-19
Sq. footage: 17000

6514 **Indiana Botanic Gardens**
3401 W 37th Ave
Hobart, IN 46342 219-947-4040
Fax: 219-947-4148 www.botanicchoice.com

Processor of herbal products and vitamins
President: Tim Cleland
VP Marketing: Brian Minoge
Sales Executive: Pauline Cleland
Operations Director: Cathy Bilderback
Purchasing: Greg Villaroman
Estimated Sales: $25 Million
Number Employees: 157
Sq. footage: 50000

6515 **Indiana Grain Company**
1700 Beason St
Baltimore, MD 21230-5347 410-685-6410
Fax: 410-685-0233 www.silopoint.com
Grain and flour
President: Patrick Turner
Number Employees: 20-49
Type of Packaging: Bulk

6516 **Indiana Sugar**
745 McClintock Dr
Burr Ridge, IL 60527-0880 630-986-9150
Fax: 630-986-1030
Processor of sugar
President: John Yonover
CEO/Treasurer: Ronald Yonover
VP: James O'Connell
Estimated Sales: $5-10 Million
Number Employees: 10-19

6517 **Indianola Pecan House**
1013 Highway 82 E
Indianola, MS 38751 662-887-5420
Fax: 662-887-2906 800-541-6252
pecan@pecanhouse.com www.pecanhouse.com
President/Owner: Wheeler Timbs III
Estimated Sales: $5.1 Million
Number Employees: 28

6518 **Indianola Pecan House, Inc./Wheeler's Gourmet Pecans**
Po Box 367
1013 Highway 82 East
Indianola, MS 38751 662-887-5420
Fax: 662-887-2906 800-541-6252
pecan@pecanhouse.com www.pecanhouse.com
Processor of gourmet pecans, cookies and candies
President: Timmy Timbs
Vice-President: Wheeler Timbs
Estimated Sales: $2.5-5 Million
Number Employees: 5-9
Number of Brands: 1
Number of Products: 30

6519 **Indigo Coffee Roasters**
660 Riverside Dr
Florence, MA 01062 413-586-4537
Fax: 413-586-0019 800-447-5450
info@indigocoffee.com www.indigocoffee.com
Artisan roaster of specialty coffees, organic coffee, fair trade coffee; custom roasting available
President: Lourdes Tallet
Number Employees: 5-9
Sq. footage: 1000
Type of Packaging: Consumer, Food Service, Private Label, Bulk
Brands:
INDIGO

6520 **Indo Med**
38 Millers Ln
New Hyde Park, NY 11040-4939 516-437-8390
Fax: 516-488-5117
Owner: Dan Wesler
Estimated Sales: $ 5 - 10 Million
Number Employees: 20-49

6521 **Indochina Tea Company**
8569 Wonderland Ave
Los Angeles, CA 90046-1463 323-650-8020
Fax: 323-650-8022
Indochina tea
President/CEO: Gabriella Karsch
Estimated Sales: Under $500,000
Number Employees: 1-4

6522 **Industria Lechera de Puerto Rico**
PO Box 360454
198 Ave Carlos Chardon
San Juan, PR 00918-1700 787-753-0974
Fax: 787-758-1126
Cheese and milk
President: Jose Benitez
Marketing Director: Jos, Passalacqua
Estimated Sales: $10-100 Million
Number Employees: 20-49
Type of Packaging: Private Label, Bulk

6523 **Industrial ConstructionServices Inc**
215 15th St S
Saint James, MN 56081 507-375-4633
Fax: 507-375-7513 800-795-8315
cbrown@icsmn.com www.icsmn.com
Design and construction of contamination controlled environments, services of which include biocontainment laboratories, clean rooms, antimicrobial atmospheres for pharmaceutical, bio-medical, and nutraceutical development, and sanitaryenvironments for food and beverage processing and manufacturing.
President: Clint Brown
Sales Representative: Josh Brown

6524 **Industrial Products**
24 N Clinton St
Defiance, OH 43512-1807 419-782-5010
Fax: 419-783-4319 800-251-3033
diehl@bright.net www.diehlinc.com
Evaporated milk, nondairy coffee creamer, whipped toppings, powdered shortening and dairy products
President: John Diehl
Estimated Sales: $50-100 Million
Number Employees: 100-249

6525 **Ineeka Inc**
2023 W Carroll Ave Ste C263
Chicago, IL 60612 312-733-8327
Fax: 312-277-2555 sg@ineeka.co
www.ineeka.com
organic teas
Number Employees: 5

6526 **InfraReady Products Ltd.**
1438 Fletcher Road
Saskatoon, SK S7M 5T2
Canada 306-242-4950
Fax: 306-242-4213 800-510-1828
info@infrareadyproducts.com
www.infrareadyproducts.com
cereal grains, oilseeds, pulses, ancient grains, and blends
President: Mark Pickard
Estimated Sales: $4.5 Million
Number Employees: 25
Sq. footage: 19763

6527 **Ingleby Farms**
123 N Main Street
Dublin, PA 18917-2107 215-249-1118
Fax: 215-249-3722 877-728-7277
carin@peppersauces.com
www.peppersauces.com
Chilies, hot sauce and specialty foods
President: Carin Froehlich
Vice President: Dietrich Froehlich
Plant Manager: Hans Froehlich
Estimated Sales: $1-2.5 Million
Number Employees: 1-4
Type of Packaging: Private Label

6528 **Ingleside Plantation Winery**
5870 Leedstown Rd
Colonial Beach, VA 22443 804-224-7111
Fax: 804-224-8573
Wine
Owner: Douglas Flemer
Director Sales: Doug Weaver
Estimated Sales: $20-50 Million
Number Employees: 10-19

6529 **Ingomar Packing Company**
PO Box 1448
Los Banos, CA 93635 209-826-9494
Fax: 209-854-6292 staff@ingomarpacking.com
www.ingomarpacking.com
Processor of diced tomatoes and tomato paste
President: Greg Pruett
Quality Control: Matt Bianchi
Estimated Sales: $20-50 Million
Number Employees: 251
Sq. footage: 10000
Type of Packaging: Bulk

6530 **Ingredient Innovations**
313 NW North Shore Dr
Kansas City, MO 64151 816-587-1426
Fax: 816-587-4167
Roxanne@IngredientInnovations.com
www.ingredientinnovations.com
Processor of natural dairy, chemical and fruit flavors, cultures, probiotics and soy food ingredients
President: Roxanne Armstrong
Estimated Sales: $ 1 - 3 Million
Number Employees: 1-4

6531 **Ingredient Specialties**
180 West Chestnut St
Exeter, CA 93221 559-594-4380
Fax: 559-594-4689
bfaress@ingredientspecialties.com
www.ingredientspecialties.com
Distributor of food and industrial ingredients; specializes in artificial sweetners
Director of Marketing and Sales: Bassam Faress
Estimated Sales: $1-2.5 Million
Number Employees: 9

6532 **Ingredients Corporationoof America**
1270 Warford St
Memphis, TN 38108-3421 901-458-5003
Fax: 901-525-4425 888-242-2669
ica@memphi.net www.memphi.net
Manufacturer and packer of dried beans and spice
President: Damon Arney
Estimated Sales: $1 Million
Number Employees: 1-4
Sq. footage: 5500
Brands:
Barzi

6533 **Ingredients Unlimited**
PO Box 3146
Bell Gardens, CA 90202-3146 562-806-7560
Fax: 562-806-7562 info@ingunl.com
www.ingunl.com
President: Kathryn Hicks
Estimated Sales: $ 5 - 10 Million
Number Employees: 20-49
Type of Packaging: Private Label

6534 **Ingredients, Inc.**
1130 W Lake Cook Rd
Suite 320
Buffalo Grove, IL 60089-1976 847-419-9595
Fax: 847-419-9547 sales@ingredientsinc.com
www.ingredientsinc.com
Supplies specialty ingredients to the food/beverage, nutraceutical and pharmaceutical industries in North America.
President: James Stewart
Estimated Sales: $ 5-10 Million
Number Employees: 5-9
Parent Co: J. Stewart & Company
Type of Packaging: Bulk

6535 **Ingretec**
1500 Lehman St
Lebanon, PA 17046 717-273-1360
Fax: 717-273-1364 ingretec@poonline.com
Food ingredients, cheese flavors, cheese products, spice blends, savory flavors, and dairy flavors
President: Philippe Jallon
Quality Control: Annabel Ries
Operations Manager: Valerie Jalloy
Estimated Sales: $5 Million
Number Employees: 5-9
Number of Products: 50
Sq. footage: 30000
Type of Packaging: Food Service, Bulk

6536 **Initiative Foods**
1117 K Street
Sanger, CA 93657 559-875-3354
Fax: 559-875-1879 www.initfoods.com
Organic baby food
President/Marketing Director: John Ypma
VP: Jim Schneider
Plant Manager: Richard Aguirre
Estimated Sales: $830,000
Number Employees: 6
Sq. footage: 4985
Type of Packaging: Consumer

6537 **Inko's White Iced Tea**
205 Jackson St
Englewood, NJ 07631
866-747-4656
www.healthywhitetea.com
flavored white iced tea
President/Owner: Andy Schamisso

6538 **Inland Empire Foods**
5425 Wilson St
Riverside, CA 92509 951-682-8222
Fax: 951-682-6275 888-452-3267
janelle@inlandempirefoods.com
Precooked vegetables: beans, peas and lentils
President: Mark Sterner
Estimated Sales: $20-50 Million
Number Employees: 20-49

6539 **Inland Fresh Seafood Corporation**
122 Menlo Drive
Atlanta, GA 30318 404-350-5850
Fax: 404-350-5870
Seafood
President/CEO: Joel Knox
Purchasing Manager: Bill Demond
Number Employees: 100-249

6540 **Inland Northwest Dairies**
P.O.Box 7310
Spokane, WA 99207-0310 509-489-8600
Fax: 509-482-3402 www.dairygold.com
Processor of dairy products including buttermilk, half and half, milk, eggnog and sour cream
President: Jerrald Barsten
Plant Manager: Bruce Senn
Estimated Sales: $20-50 Million
Number Employees: 50-99
Type of Packaging: Consumer, Food Service, Private Label
Brands:
Albertson
Broadview Dairy
Janet Leigh

6541 **Inland Products**
545 N Main St
Carthage, MO 64836 417-358-4048
Fax: 417-358-7196
Animal and marine fats and oils
Vice President: Jack Sweeny
Estimated Sales: $10-20 Million
Number Employees: 20-49

6542 **Inland Seafood**
P.O.Box 172
Milbridge, ME 04658 207-546-7591
Fax: 207-546-3334 www.inlandseafood.com
Seafood
Manager: Billy Thinney
VP: Bill Demmond
Estimated Sales: $ 1 - 3 Million
Number Employees: 10-19

6543 **Inmark**
PO Box 43309
Atlanta, GA 30336-0309 404-267-2020
Fax: 404-267-2021
Packaging supplies, plastic food containers
President: Brian Murphy
Vice President: James Curlee
Estimated Sales: $ 20 - 50 Million
Number Employees: 50-99

6544 **Inn Foods**
310 Walker St
Watsonville, CA 95076 831-724-2026
Fax: 831-728-5708 mrandle@innfoods.com
www.innfoods.com
Frozen vegetables, fruits french fries, blends, potatoes, custom blends
President: Mike Randle
Owner: Arnold Hummel
Human Resources Manager: Matt Haas
Operations Executive: Nenita Victory
Estimated Sales: $50-100 Million
Number Employees: 50
Sq. footage: 10000
Type of Packaging: Consumer, Food Service
Brands:
Freidel's Finest
Gold Premium
The Inn
Valley Pokt

6545 **Inn Maid Food**
PO Box 1972
Lenox, MA 01240-4972 413-637-2732
Fax: 413-499-3839 inmaidfood@aol.com
Processor of natural foods including multi-grain cereal, granola, sunflower seeds, trail mix, multi-grain pancake and waffle mix and sugar-free fruit syrups
President: Jane Peters
Estimated Sales: $1-2.5 Million appx.
Number Employees: 1-4
Sq. footage: 2000
Type of Packaging: Consumer, Food Service, Private Label, Bulk
Brands:
Berrylicious
Colonial Jacks
New Granola

6546 **Inniskillin Wines**
1499 Line 3
Niagra Parway
Niagara-On-The-Lake, ON L0S 1J0
Canada 905-468-2187
Fax: 905-468-5355 888-466-4754
inniskil@inniskillin.com www.inniskillin.com
Processor, exporter and importer of wines including ice, red, white, dessert and limited editions
President: Donald Ziraldo
VP: Karl Kaiser
Estimated Sales: $650,000
Number Employees: 20
Sq. footage: 16000
Type of Packaging: Consumer, Food Service
Brands:
Inniskillin

6547 **Innophos**
259 Prospect Plains Rd, Bldg 2
Cranbury, NJ 08512 609-495-2495
Fax: 609-860-0138
joseph.golowski@innophos.com
www.innophos.com
Producer of specialty grade phosphate products
CEO: Randolph Gress
CFO: Neil Salmon
Vice President: Joseph Golowski
Estimated Sales: $667 Million
Number Employees: 700

6548 **Innova Flavors**
2505 S Finley Rd
Lombard, IL 60148 630-928-4813
Fax: 630-928-4830 jma@innovaflavors.com
www.innovaflavors.com
Meat flavor manufacturer
General Manager: Enrique Medina
Senior Food Scientist: Jennifer Ma
Estimated Sales: $680,000
Number Employees: 30
Parent Co: Griffith Laboratories

6549 **Innovative Fishery Products**
3569 1 Hwy
Belliveau Cove, NS B0W 1J0
Canada 902-837-5163
Fax: 902-837-5165
Processor and exporter of fresh, frozen and salted clams, scallops, groundfish and lobster
President: Mark Blinn
VP: Victor (Allan) McGuire
Number Employees: 20-49
Sq. footage: 16000
Type of Packaging: Bulk

6550 **Innovative Food Solutions LLC**
4516 Kenny Road
Suite 320
Columbus, OH 43220-3711 614-326-1421
Fax: 614-326-1443 800-884-3314
jliebrec@columbus.rr.com
www.innovativefoodsolutions.com
Innovative Food Solutions LLC is a food industry R&D consulting firm ready to assist you to quickly launch new food products and manufacturing processes, new food industry ingredients, perform technical troubleshooting and produceprototype samples for trade shows and market research studies. Areas of experience include organic, natural and nutraceutical/functional food products, including aseptic and retort liquids, and spray dried powders.
President: Jeff Liebrecht
R&D: Jeff Liebrecht

6551 **Innovative Health Products**
6950 Bryan Dairy Rd
Largo, FL 33777 727-544-8866
Fax: 727-544-4386 800-654-2347
victoriat@onlineihp.com www.onlineihp.com
Innovative Health Products, Inc. is a turn-key, contract manufacturer of cosmeceutical, nutraceutical and pharmaceutical products. IHP produces tablets, capsules, powders, liquids, creams, lotions and gels. Our services range fromformulation to fulfillment.
President: Dr Sekharam Kotha
Estimated Sales: $ 5 - 10 Million
Number Employees: 5-9
Sq. footage: 100000

6552 **Innovative Health Products**
6950 Bryan Dairy Rd
Largo, FL 33777 727-544-8866
Fax: 727-544-4386 800-654-2347
victoriat@onlineihp.com www.onlineihp.com
Contract manufacturer of nutraceuticals, cosmeceuticals, and pharmaceuticals. Produces tablets, capsules, powders, liquids, creams, lotions and gels.
President: Kotha Sekharam
CEO: Mihir Taneja
Falcone: Carol Dore
R&D: Colen Lanke
Quality Control: Jose Vasquez
VP Sales/Marketing: Victoria Travers
Operations: Steve Kovalik
Production/Plant Manager: Steve Kovalik
Plant Manager: Liz Gifford
Purchasing: Terry Crocket
Estimated Sales: $ 20 - 50 Million
Number Employees: 100
Sq. footage: 100000
Parent Co: Geopharma
Type of Packaging: Private Label, Bulk

6553 **Innovative Ingredients**
11620 Reisterstown Road
830
Reisterstown, MD 21136-3702 888-403-2907
Fax: 435-655-8276
randy@innovativeingredients.com
www.innovativeingredients.com
Processor of dairy ingredients for prepared foods, dairy products, baked goods, beverages, dips, sports drinks and snacks. Custom formulations-color and flavor solutions
Brands:
California Sunshine
Doc's
Yonkers

6554 **Inny's Wholesale**
1068 Puuwai St
Honolulu, HI 96819-4330 808-841-3172
Fax: 808-841-1410
President: Stanley Lum
Estimated Sales: $ 3 - 5 Million
Number Employees: 1-4

6555 **(HQ)Inovatech USA**
8400 St-Laurent Boulevard
Montreal, QC H2P 2M6
Canada 360-527-1919
Fax: 360-527-1881 800-367-3447
info@inovatech.com www.inovatech.com
Produces whey protein isolates, concentrates and modified milk ingredients in our leading edge ulta-filtration facilities; produces high quality egg white proteins; and continually works to identified and refine new technology to meetthe needs of our customers
President: Philip Vanderpol
General Manager Bio-Products: Stephen Smith
Research & Development: Jerry Middleton
Quality Control: Dr. Peter Bertram
Operations Manager: Mike Vanderpol
Estimated Sales: $ 5 - 10 Million
Number Employees: 10-19
Type of Packaging: Bulk
Brands:
ALPHAPRO 34
INPRO 80
INPRO 90

6556 **Inshore Fisheries**
PO Box 118
Middle West Pubnico, NS B0W 2M0
Canada 902-762-2522
Fax: 902-762-3464 inshore@inshore.ca
www.inshore.ca

Processor and exporter of fresh and frozen catfish, pollack, perch, haddock, cod, flounder and ground fish
President: Claude d'Entremont
Number Employees: 50-99
Type of Packaging: Consumer, Food Service

6557 **Instant Products of America**
835 S Mapleton Street
Columbus, IN 47201-7359 812-372-9100
Fax: 812-372-9132
Processor, importer and exporter of instant beverages, dry mixes, syrups, toppings and ready-to-drink beverages
President: Rolf Walendy
Vice President: George Moon
Plant Manager: Mike Brannan
Estimated Sales: $10-24.9 Million
Number Employees: 50
Sq. footage: 35000
Parent Co: Kruger Gmbh & Company
Type of Packaging: Consumer, Food Service, Private Label, Bulk
Brands:
Impress
Kruger

6558 **Instantwhip Foods**
1031 Hot Wells Blvd
San Antonio, TX 78223 210-333-2717
Fax: 210-333-0717 800-544-9447
www.instantwhip.com
Processor of dairy and nondairy coffee creamer, sour and whipped cream, salad dressing, etc.; processor and exporter of bakery toppings
President: Lindal Hardwick
Quality Control: Mylissa Rios
Plant Manager: Dene Smith
Estimated Sales: $20-50 Million
Number Employees: 20-49
Sq. footage: 30000
Parent Co: Instantwhip Foods
Type of Packaging: Food Service, Private Label, Bulk

6559 **Instantwhip: Arizona**
2517 E Chambers St
Phoenix, AZ 85040 602-232-2570
Fax: 602-232-2569 800-454-7878
info@instantwhip.com www.instantwhip.com
Processor and exporter of nondairy portion packaged creamers, half and half, ready-to-whip dessert toppings and sour dressing
VP: Kyle Tillman
VP Operations: Douglas Smith
Estimated Sales: $10-20 Million
Number Employees: 20-49
Sq. footage: 22000
Parent Co: Instantwhip Foods
Type of Packaging: Food Service, Private Label, Bulk

6560 **Instantwhip: Chicago**
1535 N Cicero Ave
Chicago, IL 60651 773-235-5588
Fax: 773-235-0578 800-933-2500
info@instantwhip.com www.instantwhip.com
Distributor of dairy and nondairy toppings, dairy products, egss, baked goods and desserts.
General Manager: Jim Ring
VP: Tom Michaelides
Estimated Sales: $10-20 Million
Number Employees: 15
Sq. footage: 20837
Parent Co: Instant Whip
Type of Packaging: Private Label, Bulk
Brands:
Instantwhip

6561 **Instantwhip: Florida**
3803 E Columbus Dr
Tampa, FL 33605-3220 813-621-3233
Fax: 813-626-1516 www.instantwhipflorida.com
Processor and exporter of dairy products including dessert toppings; also, salad dressings
President: William Tiller
Estimated Sales: $10-20 Million
Number Employees: 50-99
Parent Co: Tiller Foods
Type of Packaging: Consumer

6562 **Institut Rosell/Lallemand**
8480 St Laurent Boulevard
Montreal, QC H2P 2M6
Canada 514-381-5631
Fax: 514-383-4493 800-452-4364
americas-hn@lallemand.com
www.lallemand.com
Well researched, high quality yeast - cultures are fermented before being high density concentrated and granulated. Yeasts are then fluid bed-dried and bacteria are freeze-dried. Certified yeast for many of the wine countries aroundthe world.
Sales Director: Aldo Fuoco

6563 **(HQ)Integrated Therapeutics**
3 Monroe Pkwy
Lake Oswego, OR 97035-1486 503-697-8697
Fax: 503-582-0467 800-648-4755
info@tyler-inz.com
Manufacturer, exporter and wholesaler/distributor of dietary supplements and medical nutritionals; also, specialty nutritional products for patients with end stage renal disease
President: Steve Libernan
General Manager: Reagen Miles
Technical Director: Corey Resnick
Number Employees: 250-499
Sq. footage: 44000
Other Locations:
Vitaline Formulas
Oakdale CA
Brands:
Biotin Forte
Carni-Vite
Phos-Ex
Total Formula

6564 **Inter-American Products**
1015 Vine St
Cincinnati, OH 45202-1108 513-762-4900
Fax: 513-762-4565 800-645-2233
edi@inter-americanfoods.com
www.interamericanproducts.com
Supplier of gelatins and puddings, nuts, powdered beverages, natural processed cheese, tea, extracts, peanut butter, coffee, soy sauce, steak and Worcestershire sauce, coconut, syrup, salad dressing, mayonnaise, preserves, jellies andbeverages.
Senior Marketing Manager: Jeff Pahl
Technical Director: Terry Shamblin
Estimated Sales: Under $500,000
Number Employees: 5-9
Parent Co: Kroger Company

6565 **Inter-Continental Imports Company**
149 Louis St
Newington, CT 06111 860-665-1101
Fax: 860-665-1085 800-424-4422
gitalia@grande-italia.com www.icaffe.com
Coffee roaster
President/CEO: Vincent Saccuzzo
Office Manager: Lucy Pluchino
Purchasing Manager: Vincent Saccuzzo
Estimated Sales: $5-10 Million
Number Employees: 5-9
Type of Packaging: Private Label
Brands:
Grande Italia
Miscela Bar
Miscela Napoli

6566 **Inter-Ocean Seafood Traders**
1200 Industrial Rd Ste 12
San Carlos, CA 94070 650-508-0691
Fax: 650-595-1261
Seafood
President: John Chen
Treasurer: Jeanne Chen
Vice President: Grace Chai
Estimated Sales: $25,000,000
Number Employees: 5-9

6567 **Inter-State Cider & Vinegar Company**
101 N Warwick Ave
Baltimore, MD 21223 410-947-1529
Fax: 410-947-7585 www.interstatevinegar.com
Worcestershire & steak sauce, sour beef mix; bottled & herbal vinegar
President: Jeanne Lanciotti
VP: Richard Lanciotti, Jr.
Estimated Sales: $1-2.5 Million
Number Employees: 5-9
Sq. footage: 15000
Type of Packaging: Consumer, Food Service, Private Label, Bulk
Brands:
Casa Vina
Log Cabin

6568 **InterHealth**
5451 Industrial Way
Benicia, CA 94510-1010 707-751-2800
Fax: 707-751-2801 800-783-4636
info@interhealthusa.com
www.interhealthusa.com
Processor, importer and exporter of specialty nutritional and botanical ingredients including niacin bound chromium, zinc monomethionine, grape seed and green tea extracts and garcinia cambogia
President: William Ceroy
CEO: Paul Dijkstra
Vice President: Debasis Bagchi
Marketing Cordinator: Cindy Reilly
VP Sales/Marketing: Michael Hogge
Operations Manager: Massood Moshrefi
Estimated Sales: $ 10 - 20 Million
Number Employees: 20-49
Type of Packaging: Private Label
Brands:
ALLER-7
CHROMEMATE
L-OPTIZINC
OPTIBERRY
PROTYKIN
SUPER CITRIMAX
UC II
ZMA

6569 **Interbake Foods**
1122 Lincoln St
Green Bay, WI 54303 920-497-7669
Fax: 888-497-1893 804-576-3459
www.norse.com
Ice cream cones
Plant Manager: Steven Krotz
Estimated Sales: $ 5 - 10 Million
Number Employees: 5-9
Type of Packaging: Private Label

6570 **Interbake Foods Corporate Office**
2821 Emerywood Pkwy # 210
Richmond, VA 23294-3726 804-755-7107
Fax: 804-755-7173 inquiries@interbake.com
www.interbake.com
Manufacturer of crackers and cookies
President/CEO: Ray Baxter
SVP/CFO: Donald Niemeyer
Number Employees: 1,000-4,999
Type of Packaging: Consumer, Food Service, Private Label, Bulk

6571 **Intercafe**
Av. Japon 5 Manzana I
Parque Industrial, "Oaxaca 2000"
Magdelena Apasco, OA 68090
Mexico 951-521-6011
Fax: 951-521-6012 mcuevas@blason.com.mx
www.cafeblason.com.mx
Kosher, coffee.
Marketing: Marcela Alicia Cuevas Leon

6572 **Intercorp Excelle Foods**
90 Sheppard Avenue East
Suite 400
North York, ON M2N 7K5
Canada 416-226-5757
Fax: 416-226-7544
Processor of refrigerated and shelf stable sauces, marinades, dips and dressings
President: Peter Luik
Treasurer: David Sharpe
Estimated Sales: Under $500,000
Number Employees: 1-4
Sq. footage: 85000
Parent Co: Heinz Canada
Type of Packaging: Consumer, Food Service
Brands:
EXCELLE
RENEE'S GOURMET

6573 **Interfood Ingredients**
60 Hickory Drive
Waltham, MA 02451 781-370-9983
Fax: 781-370-9997 info@interfoodinc.com
www.interfoodingredients.com
Supplier of dairy ingredients
President: Ferry Veen
Vice President: Jack Engels
Estimated Sales: $235 Million
Number Employees: 18
Parent Co: Interfood Holding

6574 **Interfrost**
349 W Commercial St
East Rochester, NY 14445-2407 585-381-0320
Fax: 585-381-1052 www.interfrost.com
Processor and importer of frozen fruits and vegetables
VP/General Manager: Thomas Crandall
Estimated Sales: $5-10 Million
Number Employees: 5-9
Parent Co: Cobi Foods

6575 **Intergum North America**
1365 Westgate Center Dr
Winston Salem, NC 27103-2980 336-760-5420
Fax: 336-760-5434

6576 **Interhealth Nutraceuticals**
5451 Industrial Way
Benicia, CA 94510 707-751-2800
Fax: 707-751-2801 800-783-4636
info@interhealthusa.com
www.interhealthusa.com
Nutraceuticals
President: William Ceroy
Executive VP: Gary Troxel
Purchasing: Joe Mies
Estimated Sales: $ 10 - 20 Million
Number Employees: 20-49

6577 **(HQ)Interior Alaska Fish Processors**
P.O.Box 81522
2400 Davis Rd
Fairbanks, AK 99701 907-456-3885
Fax: 907-456-3889 800-478-3885
www.alaskasbest.com
Salmon and salmon products
Owner: Kade Mendelowitz
CEO/President: Virgil Humphenour
COO: Janet McCormick
Vice President: Marie Mitchell
Marketing Director: Shelbie Umphenour
Estimated Sales: $2.5-5 Million
Number Employees: 21
Type of Packaging: Private Label, Bulk

6578 **Intermex Products**
1375 Avenue S Ste 300
Grand Prairie, TX 75050 972-660-2071
Fax: 972-660-5941 j.lacy@intermexproducts.com
www.intermexproducts.com
Mexican dishes and sauces
President: David Hagli
CFO: Susen Hurt
CEO: Carlos Lorenzo
Plant Manager: Gonzalo Branch
Estimated Sales: $ 10-20 Million
Number Employees: 20-49

6579 **Intermountain Canola Cargill**
2300 N Yellowstone Hwy
Idaho Falls, ID 83401-1662 208-522-4113
Fax: 208-522-0794 800-822-6652
Processor of specialty canola oils
President: Erwin Kelm
Finance Executive: Joann Wages
General Manager: Ernie Unger
Manager: R Covington
Estimated Sales: $10-20 Million
Number Employees: 10-19
Parent Co: Cargill Foods
Type of Packaging: Consumer, Food Service, Bulk

6580 **Internacional De Productos Y Semillas**
Andres Guajardo 340
Parque Industrial, Apodaca 1
Apodaca, NL 66670
Mexico 811-160-0700
Fax: 811-160-0600 ljgarcia@winnuts.com.mx
www.winnuts.com.mx
Other candy, Full-line snacks.
Marketing: Liliana Garcia

6581 **International Bakers Services**
1902 N Sheridan Ave
South Bend, IN 46628-1592 574-287-7111
Fax: 574-287-7161 800-345-7175
ibsflavors@aol.com
www.internationalbakers.com
Manufacturer of kosher certified flavors and flavor blends for the baking industry. Also manufacturers liquid and dry flavors, natural, and natural/artificial.
President/CEO: William Busse
Sales Contact: Christopher Lee
Estimated Sales: $10-20 Million
Number Employees: 20-49

6582 **International Baking Company**
5200 S Alameda St
Vernon, CA 90058 323-583-9841
Fax: 323-588-3652
Processor of fresh bread, rolls and sweet goods
Owner/President: Simon Mani
VP: Dan Smith
Purchasing Director: Sam Abekian
Estimated Sales: $100+ Million
Number Employees: 250-499
Parent Co: Sara Lee Corporation
Type of Packaging: Consumer, Food Service, Private Label

6583 **International Bar-B-Que**
PO Box 5
Unionville, IN 47468-0005 812-988-6150
Fax: 812-988-7039 ibbq12762@aol.com
Barbaque

6584 **International Brownie**
602 Middle St
East Weymouth, MA 02189 781-340-1588
Fax: 781-331-1900 800-230-1588
info@internationalbrownie.com
www.internationalbrownie.com
Processor of gourmet brownies including sugar-free; mail order available
President: Cindy Rice
Estimated Sales: Less than $500,000
Number Employees: 1-4
Sq. footage: 1500
Brands:
INTERNATIONAL BROWNIE

6585 **International Casein Corporation**
111 Great Neck Rd
Great Neck, NY 11021-5402 516-466-4363
Fax: 516-466-4365
Processor and wholesaler/distributor of casein
President: Marvin Match
Number Employees: 5-9

6586 **(HQ)International Casing Group**
4420 S Wolcott Avenue
Chicago, IL 60609-3159 773-376-9200
Fax: 773-376-9292 800-825-5151
sales@casings.com www.casings.com
Processor, importer and exporter of natural beef, pork and lamb casings
President/CEO: Paul Lankveld
General Manager: Tom Sanecki
Estimated Sales: $ 50 - 100 Million
Number Employees: 120
Sq. footage: 40000
Type of Packaging: Food Service
Other Locations:
Tyrone GA
Sante Fe Springs CA
Montreal, Canada

6587 **(HQ)International Casings Group, Inc**
4420 S Wolcott Ave
Chicago, IL 60609 773-376-9200
Fax: 773-376-9292 800-825-5151
sales@casings.com www.casings.com
Processor and exporter of natural sausage casings
President/CEO/Plant Manager: Paul Lankveld
CFO: Bryan Schultz
VP: Eric Svendsen
Operations Manager: Jim Wilt
VP Manufacture/General Manager: Tom Sanecki
Estimated Sales: $10-20 Million
Number Employees: 120
Sq. footage: 52000
Type of Packaging: Food Service
Brands:
NATURE'S BEST

6588 **International Casings Group**
12207 Los Nietos Rd Ste F
Santa Fe Springs, CA 90670 562-946-2100
Fax: 562-946-1913 800-635-9518
www.casings.com
Processor, importer and exporter of natural sausage casings including sheep, hog and beef
Manager: Peter Jimenez
Estimated Sales: $1-2.5 Million
Number Employees: 5-9
Sq. footage: 5200
Parent Co: International Casings Group
Brands:
REDI-2-STUF

6589 **International Cheese Company**
67 Mulock Avenue
Toronto, ON M6N 3C5
Canada 416-769-3547
Fax: 416-769-7153
Processor of Italian cheese
President: M Pelosi
Number Employees: 10-19
Sq. footage: 9999
Type of Packaging: Consumer, Food Service

6590 **International Chemical**
PO Box 188
Milltown, NJ 08850-0188 732-238-5160
Fax: 732-238-5970 800-914-2436
95263@msn.com www.intl-chem.com
Processor, importer and exporter of acids including ascorbic, citric, sorbic and tartaric; also, sodium citrate, sodium ascorbate and vanillin
President: Jimmy Hsu
Number Employees: 20-49
Sq. footage: 50000
Type of Packaging: Private Label, Bulk
Brands:
ICI

6591 **International Coconut Corporation**
225 W Grand St
Elizabeth, NJ 7202 908-289-1555
Fax: 908-289-1556
sales@internationalcoconut.com
www.internationalcoconut.com
Processor, wholesaler/distributor, importer and exporter of coconut including sweetened, desiccated and toasted
Owner: A Kaye
Vice President: Richard Kesselhaut
Estimated Sales: $2.5-5 Million
Number Employees: 5-9
Sq. footage: 11500
Type of Packaging: Consumer, Food Service, Private Label, Bulk
Brands:
SNO-TOP

6592 **International Coffee Corporation**
300 Magazine St
New Orleans, LA 70130 504-586-8700
Fax: 504-523-3301 intocof@worldnet.att.net
www.iccnola.com
Coffee traders and brokers
President: William Madary II
VP: Matthew Madary
Estimated Sales: $1-2.5 Million
Number Employees: 10-19

6593 **International Cuisine**
164 S Us Highway 17
East Palatka, FL 32131-4024 904-325-0002
Fax: 904-325-6600
Oriental frozen foods

6594 **International Dairy Ingredients**
625 Commerce Drive
Wapakoneta, OH 45895 419-738-4060
Fax: 419-738-4426
b.leclercq@idi-ingredients.com
www.idi-ingredients.com
Manufacturers dairy ingredients
CEO: Alain Thibault
General Manager: Benot Leclercq
Number Employees: 50-99
Parent Co: Coop Laitiere Artois Flandre

6595 International Dehydrated Foods
3801 E. Sunshine Street
Springfield, MO 65809 417-881-7820
Fax: 417-881-7274 800-641-6509
www.idf.com
Powdered chicken broth
President: Kurt Hellweg
SVP and CFO: Paul Fry
Estimated Sales: $ 20 - 50 Million
Number Employees: 10
Type of Packaging: Food Service, Bulk

6596 International Dehydrated Foods
3801 E Sunshine Street
Springfield, MO 658809 417-881-7820
Fax: 417-881-7274 800-525-7435
customerservice@idf.com www.idf.com
Manufactures further processed meat and poultry ingredients, which are available in fresh, frozen, concentrated and powdered forms.
President: Kurt Hellweg
SVP/CFO: Paul Fry
R&D Director: Roger Drake
VP Sales/Marketing: Robert Hoopingarner
VP Human Resources: Dan Beeman
SVP/COO: Mike Gerke
VP Manufacturing: Mike Scabarozi
Purchasing Manager: Dennis Scholl
Estimated Sales: $76 Million
Number Employees: 130
Sq. footage: 6973
Type of Packaging: Bulk
Brands:
IDF

6597 International Delicacies
1485 Park Avenue
Emeryville, CA 94608-3559 510-428-9364
Fax: 510-428-2457 Intl_delicacies@msn.com
Olive oils, pasta, bastoncini, cookies, panettone, pickles, balsamic vinegar, honey, infused oils, mustard, dolma, dried figs, fruit preserves, artichokes
VP Sales/Marketing: Maxx Sherman
Brands:
AMIR
ANNA'S
AUDISIO & LORI
LOOZA
PAN DUCALE
RUBINO & VERO
VICENZI

6598 International Diverse Foods
189 Spence Ln
Nashville, TN 37210 615-889-8345
Fax: 615-231-5983 www.diversefoods.com
General grocery
President: Philip Francis
CFO: Drew Nethery
Marketing: Connie Brown
Research Director: Rebecca Carothers
Estimated Sales: $10-100 Million
Number Employees: 250-499

6599 International Enterprises
PO Box 158
Herring Neck, NL A0G 2R0
Canada 709-628-7406
Fax: 709-628-7875
Processor and exporter of fresh cultivated mussels
President: Wayne Fudge
Estimated Sales: $975,000
Number Employees: 7
Type of Packaging: Consumer, Food Service, Bulk

6600 International EquipmentInternational Equipment And Supplies
El Pasaje 75
Arecibo, PR 00612 787-879-3151
Fax: 787-879-1569 intequi@xsn.net
Processor of baked goods including bread, rolls and pastries; wholesaler/distributor and importer of restaurant supplies including bakers' equipment and supplies; serving the food service market
President: Juan Guzman
Estimated Sales: $200.000
Number Employees: 3
Type of Packaging: Consumer, Food Service

6601 International Farmers Market
PO Box 81226
Chamblee, GA 30366-1226 770-455-1777
Fax: 770-451-7474
www.internationalfarmersmarket.com
Dairy, meats, seafood, general grocery items, poultry, blue crab, catfish, clams

6602 International Fiber Corporation
50 Bridge St
North Tonawanda, NY 14120-6895 716-693-4040
Fax: 716-693-3528 888-698-1936
info@ifcfiber.com www.ifcfiber.com
Executive VP: Brian Finn
Executive VP: Jit Ang
CEO: Dan Muth
VP Industrial Sales: Steve Godin
Estimated Sales: $ 20 - 50 Million
Number Employees: 50-99
Brands:
Alpha-Cel
FloAm
Keycel
NutraFiber
QualFlo
SolkaFloc

6603 International Fiber Corporation
50 Bridge St
North Tonawanda, NY 14120-6895 716-693-4040
Fax: 716-693-3528 888-698-1936
info@ifcfiber.com www.ifcfiber.com
A leading manufacturer of dietry fiber.
President/CEO: Dan Muth
Executive VP: Mike Bailey
R&D: Jit Ang
Exec VP of Operations: Brian Finn
Purchasing Manager: Steve Couladis
Number Employees: 100-249
Number of Brands: 10+
Type of Packaging: Bulk
Brands:
Justfiber

6604 International Flavors & Fragrances
3005 International Blvd
Augusta, GA 30906 706-796-2800
Fax: 706-560-3640 iffusaflavors@iff.com
Ingredients manufacturer
Parent Co: International Flavors & Frangrances

6605 International Flavors & Fragrances
1620 West Crosby
Carrolton, TX 75006-6656 972-245-2117
Fax: 972-242-2966 iffusaflavors@iff.com
www.iff.com
Flavors manufacturer
Parent Co: International Flavors & Fragrances

6606 International Flavors & Fragrances
600 Highway 36
Hazlet, NJ 07730 732-264-4500
Fax: 732-335-2551 iffusaflavors@iff.com
www.iff.com
Fragrance manufacturer
Parent Co: International Flavors & Fragrances

6607 International Flavors & Fragrances
2051 North Lane Avenue
Jacksonville, FL 32254 904-783-2180
Fax: 904-695-4616 iffusaflavors@iff.com
www.iff.com
Ingredients Manufacturer
Parent Co: International Flavors & Fragrances

6608 International Flavors & Fragrances
1515 State Highway #36
Union Beach, NJ 07735 732-264-4500
Fax: 732-335-2591 iffusaflavors@iff.com
www.iff.com
Flavors and fragrance manufacturer
Parent Co: International Flavors & Fragrances

6609 (HQ)International Flavors &Fragrances
521 W 57th St
New York, NY 10019 212-765-5500
Fax: 212-708-7132 iff.information@iff.com
www.iff.com
Manufacturer of flavors and fragrances used in a wide variety of consumer products, from fine fragrances to toiletries, to soaps, detergents, and other household products, as well as food and beverage products
Chairman/CEO: Doug Tough
EVP/CFO: Kevin Berryman
Marketing Director: Sharon Maes
VP Global Corporate Communications: Gail Belmuth
EVP Global Operations: D Wayne Howard
Purchasing Director: Gladys Gabriel
Estimated Sales: $2.3 Billion
Number Employees: 5,400
Type of Packaging: Bulk

6610 International Flavors & Fragrances
150 Docks Corner Road
PO Box 439
Dayton, NJ 08810-0439 732-329-4600
Fax: 732-274-6550 iffusafragrances@iff.com
www.iff.com
Food flavorings, fragrances, ingredients
Parent Co: International Flavors & Fragrances
Type of Packaging: Bulk

6611 International Food
N114w18937 Clinton Dr
Germantown, WI 53022-3009 262-251-9230
Fax: 414-255-8810 800-558-8696
pat.eckert@ifoodsolutions.com
www.ifoodsolutions.com
Seasonings
Estimated Sales: $20-50 Million
Number Employees: 100-249

6612 International Food Packers Corporation
4693 SW 71st Ave
Miami, FL 33155 305-669-1662
Fax: 305-669-1447
Processor, importer and exporter of canned corned beef, frozen cooked beef and beef cuts; importer of canned fish and rice
President: Richard Spradling
Estimated Sales: $2.5-5 Million
Number Employees: 5-9
Sq. footage: 6000

6613 International Food Products Corporation
165 E Prarie Ave
Saint Louis, MO 63147-2924 314-421-6151
Processor of salad dressings, sauces, syrups and condiments
President: Bill Holtgrieve
CEO: Fred Brown
Sales Manager: Ed Carle
Director Operations: Bob Bullock
COO: Clayton Brown
Warehouse Manager: Kirk Greer
VP Purchasing: John Hany
Estimated Sales: $10-100 Million
Number Employees: 7
Type of Packaging: Consumer, Food Service
Brands:
IFP

6614 International Food Solutions
N114w18937 Clinton Dr
Germantown, WI 53022-3009
US 262-251-9230
Fax: 909-737-1953 www.ifoodsolutions.com
Processor and exporter of flavors for sauces, seasonings, bases and spices
President: George Zabrycki
Sales Manager: Carol Mayer
Estimated Sales: $20-50 Million
Number Employees: 1-4
Parent Co: Bestfoods

6615 International Food Technologies
PO Box 5555
Evansville, IN 47716-5555 812-853-9432
Fax: 812-853-3157 ift@evansville.net
www.internationalfoodtech.com

Processor and exporter of Powdered Dessert and Beverage mixes including; ice cream mixes (hard pack and soft serve), Low carbohydrate dessert products, frozen yogurt, granita, cappuccino (hot and cold), smoothie mixes, smoothieproteins, chai and lemonade. Custom, private label, food service
President: Joseph Greif
Number Employees: 10-19
Sq. footage: 10000
Type of Packaging: Food Service, Private Label, Bulk
Brands:
CAPPUCCINO FREEZE
JOE'S LOW-CARB
POWER BOOSTS

6616 **International Food Trade**

Amherst, NS B4H 3Y4
Canada 902-667-3013
Fax: 902-667-0350
Processor and exporter of IQF wild blueberries
President: Chris Gaklis
Estimated Sales: $1.95 Million
Number Employees: 15
Parent Co: International Food Trade
Brands:
BLUE BOY
CHRISTY CROPS

6617 **International FoodcraftCorporation**
1601 E Linden Ave
Linden, NJ 07036-1508 908-862-8810
Fax: 908-862-8825 800-875-9393
info@intlfoodcraft.com www.intlfoodcraft.com
Manufacturer and exporter of anti-stick lubricants, release agents and food color concentrates for the food, confectionery, cosmetic and pharmaceutical industries
President/Owner: David Dukes
Technical Director: Ted Palumbo
Estimated Sales: $2 Million
Number Employees: 20
Type of Packaging: Bulk
Brands:
COLOREZE
CONFECTO
EEZ-OUT
PANO

6618 **International Foods & Confections**
6590 Shiloh Rd E
Alpharetta, GA 30005-2260 770-887-0201
Gourmet delicacies
Estimated Sales: $ 10 - 20 Million
Number Employees: 10-19

6619 **International Glace**
1616 East Lyons Avenue
Spokane, WA 99217 760-731-3220
Fax: 760-731-3221 800-884-5041
alan@internationalglace.com
www.internationalglace.com
Importer of ginger, brewers' yeast spread and glace fruits including apricots, orange slices and peels, pineapple, peaches, pears, figs and kiwifruit
Manager: Marilyn Guest
Vice President: Bill Davids
Sales Director: Alan Sipole
Estimated Sales: $1-2.5 Million
Number Employees: 1-4
Type of Packaging: Consumer, Bulk

6620 **International Glatt Kosher**
5600 1st Ave Ste 19
Brooklyn, NY 11220 718-630-5555
Fax: 718-921-1542
Kosher foods
President: Leib Chaimovitz
Estimated Sales: Less than $500,000
Number Employees: 1-4

6621 **International Harvest**
606 Franklin Ave
Mt Vernon, NY 10550-4518 914-699-5600
Fax: 718-279-0623
Dry foods company
President: Robert M Sterling

6622 **International Home Foods**
1633 Littleton Rd
Parsippany, NJ 07054 973-359-9920
Fax: 973-254-5473 www.intlhomefoods.com
Processor and exporter of canned beans, peas, apples, pasta, chicken, tomato paste and chili; also, mustard, instant hot cereal, nonstick cooking spray and glazed popcorn
Chairman/CEO: C Dean Metropoulos
SVP/CFO: Craig Steeneck
President/COO: Lawrence Hathaway
Sales/Marketing Executive: Mike Larney
Number Employees: 100
Parent Co: ConAgra Foods
Type of Packaging: Consumer
Brands:
Bumble Bee
Campfire
Campfire Marshmallows
Captain Jac
Chef Boyardee
Chef Boyardee Pastas
Clover Leaf
Crunch 'n Munch
Crunch'n'munch Glazed Popcorn
Dennison
Dennison's
Fireside
Franklin Crunch 'n' Munch
Golden Touch
Gulden's
Iron Kettle
Jiffy Pop
Libby's
Louis Kemp
Luck's
Luck's Beans
Maypo
Orleans
PAM
Pam Cooking Spray
Paramount
Ranch Style
Ranch Style Brand Beans
Ro*Tel
Royal Reef
Seafest
Swiftwater
Tuxedo
Western Gold
Wheatena

6623 **International Leisure Activities**
107 Tremont City Rd
Springfield, OH 45502-9506 937-399-0783
Fax: 937-399-0784 800-782-7448
www.ilaproducts.com
Distributor of chocolate
President: George Keriazes
Estimated Sales: $500,000-$1 Million
Number Employees: 5-9
Type of Packaging: Private Label

6624 **International Malting Company**
3830 W Grant St
Milwaukee, WI 53215 414-671-1166
Fax: 414-671-1385 info@imc-world.com
www.imc-world.com
Processor and exporter of malt
President: Steve Furcich
COO: Dale West
Estimated Sales: $100+ Million
Number Employees: 100-249
Parent Co: Lesaffre International Corporation
Type of Packaging: Bulk

6625 **International Meat Company**
7107 W Grand Ave
Chicago, IL 60707 773-622-1400
Fax: 773-622-6829
www.internationalmeatcompany.com
Processor of meat products including fresh beef, pork, poultry and veal
President: Joseph Bomprezzi
Estimated Sales: $5-10 Million
Number Employees: 10-19
Type of Packaging: Food Service

6626 **(HQ)International Multifoods Corporation**
1 Strawberry Lane
Suite 3000
Orrville, OH 44667-1241 330-682-3000
Fax: 330-684-3062 800-664-2942
Manufacturer, wholesaler/distributor, and exporter of dessert and baking products, baking mixes and frozen products to the food service industry in North America. Manufacturer and marketer of consumer foods in Canada
President/COO: Dan Swander
CEO: Gary Costley
SVP Finance/CFO: John Byom
Public Relations: Jill Schmidt
Estimated Sales: $2.5 Billion
Number Employees: 1,450
Parent Co: JM Smucker Company
Type of Packaging: Consumer, Food Service, Private Label, Bulk
Other Locations:
International Multifoods
Windsor CT
Brands:
FANTASIA

6627 **International Noodle Company**
32811 Groveland St
Madison Heights, MI 48071-1330 248-583-2479
Fax: 248-583-3004
Chinese noodle, egg roll wrapper, pasta, perogi wrapper
President: Robert Ip
Estimated Sales: $1-2.5 Million
Number Employees: 5-9

6628 **International Oceanic Enterprises of Alabama**
9225 Seafood House Rd
Bayou La Batre, AL 36509 251-824-4193
Fax: 251-824-7687 800-816-1832
Processor of IQF shrimp and crab
President: Jens Sunde
Vice President: Clinton Jones
Estimated Sales: $20-50 Million
Number Employees: 20-49
Type of Packaging: Private Label, Bulk
Brands:
GOLDEN GULF
LITTLE BAY
MASTERMARINE

6629 **International Seafood Distributors**
P.O.Box 1130
Hayes, VA 23072-1130 804-642-1417
Fax: 804-642-1009
sales@internationalseafood.com
www.internationalseafood.com
Processor of frozen squid; processor and exporter of frozen scallops, dogfish, monkfish, conch meat, croaker and crabs; importer of frozen scallops, pollack, crawfish, frogs' legs and shrimp
President: Thomas Fass
Estimated Sales: $50-100 Million
Number Employees: 20-49
Sq. footage: 30000
Type of Packaging: Food Service, Private Label, Bulk
Brands:
Delicate Seas
Ocean Classic

6630 **International Seafoods of Chicago**
1133 W Lake St
Chicago, IL 60607-1618 312-243-2330
Fax: 312-243-1923
Seafood
President: Inkie Hong
Estimated Sales: $1,800,000
Number Employees: 5-9

6631 **International Seafoods of Alaska**
P.O.Box 2997
Kodiak, AK 99615-2997 907-486-4768
Fax: 907-486-4885
Prepared fresh or frozen fish and seafoods
Administrator: Ted Kishimoto
Estimated Sales: $4,200,000
Number Employees: 5-9
Type of Packaging: Consumer, Food Service, Private Label
Brands:
Internation Seafood of Alaska
Kodiak Seafood

6632 **International Service Group**
4080 McGinnis Fry Rd Ste 1403
Alpharetta, GA 30005 770-518-0988
Fax: 770-518-0299

Processor and exporter of peanuts, popcorn
President: John Kopec
Estimated Sales: $ 3 - 5 Million
Number Employees: 1-4
Type of Packaging: Consumer, Private Label, Bulk

6633 **(HQ)International SpecialtySupply**
820 E 20th St
Cookeville, TN 38501-1451 931-526-1106
Fax: 931-526-8338 bob@sproutnet.com
www.sproutnet.com
Manufacturer and exporter of commercial sprouting systems; grower and exporter of fresh alfalfa and bean sprouts. Also carry beansprouts, sunflower, cabbage, broccoli, onion, clover and pea sprouts
Owner: Robert Rust
Estimated Sales: $ 5 - 10 Million
Number Employees: 20-49
Sq. footage: 105000
Type of Packaging: Consumer, Food Service, Private Label, Bulk
Brands:
Rota Tech
Sentrex
Track I
Wetlite

6634 **International Tea Importers**
8551 Loch Lomond Dr
Pico Rivera, CA 90660 562-801-9600
Fax: 323-722-6368 tealand@msn.com
www.teavendor.com
Tea
Owner: DeVan Shah
Estimated Sales: $2.5-5 Million
Number Employees: 1-4

6635 **International Trade Impa**
30 Gordon Ave
Lawrenceville, NJ 08648-1033 609-987-0550
Fax: 609-987-0252 800-223-5484
info@iTitropicals.com www.ititropicals.com
Tropical juices
Owner: Gerrit Van Manen
Estimated Sales: $2.5-5 Million
Number Employees: 5-9
Brands:
iTitropicals

6636 **International Trademarks**
149 Leroy Avenue
Darien, CT 06820-3413 203-656-4046
Fax: 203-655-1690
Import broker of soft drinks. Also marketing, importing and sales consultation
President: Nicholas Ord
VP: Stewart Warner

6637 **International Trading Company**
300 Portwall Street
Houston, TX 77029-1336 713-224-5901
Fax: 713-678-1718
Importer of gourmet foods including Danish hams, cheeses, snails and pate
Sales Manager: Lenny Yassie

6638 **International Yogurt Company**
5858 NE 87th Ave
Portland, OR 97220 503-257-0210
Fax: 503-256-3976 800-962-7326
info@yocream.com www.yocream.com
Frozen dessert, snacks and beverages
Marketing Director: Suzanne Gardner
Sales Director: Tyler Bargas
Estimated Sales: $ .5 - 1 million
Number Employees: 5-9
Type of Packaging: Consumer, Food Service, Private Label, Bulk
Brands:
Sorbet By Yo Cream
The Yogurt Stand
Yo Cream
Yo Cream Smoothies

6639 **Internatural Foods**
1455 Broad Street
Bloomfield, NJ 07003 973-338-1499
Fax: 973-338-1485 800-225-1449
info@internaturalfoods.com
www.internaturalfoods.com
Organic and natural products; hot and cold cereal, pastas, crisp breads, soups, salad dressings and balsamic vinegar, chocolate and wafers
President: Peter Leiendecker
VP: Linda Palame
Estimated Sales: $1-2.5 Million
Number Employees: 1-4
Type of Packaging: Private Label
Brands:
Bio-Familia
Bisca
Blanchard & Blanchard
Cafix
Clipper
DaVinci
DrSoy
Eddie's
Helwa
Kavli
McCann'S
Monari Federzoni
Mount Hagen
Mrs Leeper's
Pero
Pritikin
Ryvita
Vivani

6640 **Interstate Seed Company**
304 Center St
West Fargo, ND 58078 701-282-7338
Fax: 701-281-1888 800-437-4120
info@interstateseed.com
www.interstateseed.com
Processor of soybean seeds
President: Bruce Hovland
Marketing Coordinator: Gerri Leach
Sales Director: Bill Webber
Operations Manager: Vic Nordstrom
Estimated Sales: $2.5-5 Million
Number Employees: 20-49

6641 **Intervest Trading Company Inc.**
5435 Spring Garden Road
Halifax, NS B3J 1G1
Canada 902-425-2018
Fax: 902-420-0763 info@intervest.ca
Processor and exporter of fresh and frozen groundfish and shellfish
President: Jeff Whitman
Number Employees: 1,000-4,999
Type of Packaging: Bulk

6642 **Inventure Foods**
5415 E High Street
Suite 350
Phoenix, AZ 85054 623-932-6200
Fax: 602-522-2690 www.inventurefoods.com
Snack foods
President/CEO: Terry McDaniel
CFO: Steve Weinberger
SVP Sales/Marketing: Rick Suchenski
Human Resources Director: Kirk Roles
VP Operations: Alex Rembert
Estimated Sales: $134 Million
Number Employees: 389
Type of Packaging: Consumer
Brands:
BOB'S TEXAS STYLE
BOULDER CANYON NATURAL FOODS
BRAIDS PRETZELS
BURGER KING
JAMBA
POORE BROTHERS
RADER FARMS
T.G.I. FRIDAY'S
TATO SKINS

6643 **Inventure Foods**
5415 E High Street
Suite 350
Phoenix, AZ 85054 623-932-6200
Fax: 602-522-2690
steve.weinberger@inventurefoods.com
www.inventurefoods.com
Manufacturer of potato chips, snacks and pretzels.
CEO: Terry McCaniel
CFO: Steve Weinberger
SVP/Sales & Marketing: Rick Suchenski
Estimated Sales: $134 Million
Type of Packaging: Consumer, Private Label
Brands:
BOB'S TEXAS STYLE
BOULDER CANYON
BURGER KING
JAMBA
POORE BROTHERS
RADER FARMS
TATO SKINS
TGI FRIDAY'S

6644 **Inverness Dairy**
1631 Woiderski Rd
Cheboygan, MI 49721 231-627-4655
Fax: 231-627-4655
Milk and butter
President: David Woiderski
Estimated Sales: $5-10 Million
Number Employees: 20-49

6645 **Iowa Ham Canning**
812 3rd St NW
Independence, IA 50644 319-334-7134
Fax: 319-334-7259
Processor of ham and turkey
President: Brooks Burkhart
Quality Control: Brian Hayek
Estimated Sales: $ 50 - 100 Million
Number Employees: 100-249
Type of Packaging: Private Label

6646 **Iowa Quality Meats**
2075 NW 92nd Ct
Clive, IA 50325-5458 515-225-6868
Fax: 515-225-2677 800-677-6868
Processor and exporter of portion-control and roast-ready pork products; also, custom processing available
Manager: Craig Raecker
National Account Sales: David Mercer
Purchasing Agent: Matt George
General Manager: Pat Watkins
Estimated Sales: $50-100 Million
Number Employees: 100-249
Sq. footage: 25000
Type of Packaging: Consumer, Food Service, Private Label
Brands:
Iowa Quality Meats

6647 **Ipswich Bay Seafoods**
19 Longmeadow Drive
Ipswich, MA 01938-1174 978-356-9292
Fax: 978-356-7979
Seafood
President: Louis Malaquias
Estimated Sales: $ 330.00 K
Number Employees: 2

6648 **Ipswich Maritime Product Company**
43 Avery St
Ipswich, MA 01938 978-356-9866
Fax: 978-356-9894 www.ipswichmaritime.com
Seafood
President: Peter Maistrellis
Estimated Sales: $ 10 - 20 Million
Number Employees: 10-19

6649 **Ipswich Shellfish Company**
8 Hayward St
Ipswich, MA 01938 978-356-6800
Fax: 978-356-9235 www.ipswichfishmarket.com
Shellfish and shellfish products
Manager: Zina Smith
Estimated Sales: $50-100 Million
Number Employees: 5-9

6650 **Ira Higdon Grocery Company**
150 IGA Way
Cairo, GA 39828 229-377-1272
Fax: 229-377-8756 www.irahigdongc.com
Wholesaler/distributor of general line products
President: Larry Higdon
VP/Operations Manager: Nathan Higdon
VP Sales: Bruce Bining
Estimated Sales: $113 Million
Number Employees: 100
Sq. footage: 170000

6651 **Ira Middleswarth & Son**
250 Furnace Rd
Middleburg, PA 17842 570-837-1431
Fax: 570-837-1731 toddhestor@hotmail.com
Potato Chips
President: Robert Middleswarth
Estimated Sales: $20-50 Million
Number Employees: 50-99

Type of Packaging: Private Label

6652 **Irani & Company**
PO Box 29297
7961 W Twilight Dr
Fairland, IN 46126-9521 317-862-1257
Fax: 317-894-4478
Teas
Managing Director: Katrina Donohue
Partner: S Irrani

6653 **Iron Horse Products**
5109 W 48th St
Edina, MN 55436-1533 952-920-7722
Fax: 952-920-7722
Bottle and can soft drinks and carbonated waters
President: John Justice
Estimated Sales: $750,000
Number Employees: 1-4
Type of Packaging: Consumer, Food Service
Brands:
IRON HORSE

6654 **Iron Horse Ranch & Vineyard**
9786 Ross Station Rd
Sebastopol, CA 95472 707-887-1507
Fax: 707-887-1337 info@ironhorsevineyards.com
www.ironhorsevineyards.com
Wines
Co-Founder: Barry Sterling
CEO: Joy E Sterling
Vineyard Manager: Forrest Tancer
Co-Founder: Audrey Sterling
Manager: Laurence Sterling
Marketing Director: Joy Anne Sterling
Estimated Sales: $10-20 Million
Number Employees: 40
Type of Packaging: Private Label

6655 **Ironstone Vineyards**
1894 6 Mile Rd
Murphys, CA 95247 209-728-1251
Fax: 209-728-1275 kautz@goldrush.com
www.ironstonevineyards.com
Wines, brandies, grappa, port
President: Stephen Kautz
Controller: Lynn Gentry
Sales Director: Bob Reider
Public Relations: Jo Diaz
Operations Manager: John Kautz
Bottling Foreman: John McVarish
Estimated Sales: $50-100 Million
Number Employees: 100-249
Type of Packaging: Private Label
Brands:
Angels Creek
Creekside
Delta Bay

6656 **Irresistible Cookie Jar**
PO Box 3230
Hayden Lake, ID 83835-3230 208-664-1261
Fax: 208-667-1347
service@irresistiblecookiejar.com
www.irresistablecookiejar.com
Cookie and muffin mixes, cookie cutters and decorations
President: Wanda Hall
Estimated Sales: $300,000-500,000
Number Employees: 10
Brands:
Boyds' Kissa Bearhugs
Mimi's Muffins
Susan Winget

6657 **Irving R. Boody & Company**
11 Penn Plz
Suite 310
New York, NY 10001-2006 212-947-8300
Fax: 212-947-8301 info@boody.com
www.boody.com
Processor, exporter and importer of oils including cod liver, fish, essential and edible
Owner: Irving R Boody
Ceo/President: Anthony Scocco
Vice President: Joyce Leong
Estimated Sales: $50-100 Million
Number Employees: 6

6658 **Isaar Cheese**
N9310 Isaar Road
Seymour, WI 54165-9423 920-833-6190
Cheese products
Estimated Sales: $500,000 appx.
Number Employees: 5-9

6659 **Isabel's Country Mustard**
1213c Old Highway 63 N
Columbia, MO 65201-6319 573-441-9188
Fax: 573-442-4736 877-441-9188
Mustard and other condiments
President: Susan Stalcupgray
Estimated Sales: $1-2.5 Million
Number Employees: 1-4

6660 **Isabella's Healthy Bakery**
170 Muffin Ln
Cuyahoga Falls, OH 44223-3358 330-929-0000
Fax: 330-920-8329 800-476-6328
mramcharran@isabellashealthybakery.com
www.mainstreetmuffins.com
Supplier of healthy baked goods including muffins, cookies & cakes. Specializing in sugar free, no sugar added, fat free and whole grain categories. All products are certified kosher and packaged for retail.
CEO: Steve Marks
CEO: Harvey Nelson
President: Monica Curtis
Quality Control: Angela Stoughton
Marketing: Joe Schaefer
Sales/Marketing: Manorma Ramcharran
Plant Manager/Operations: Mike Braun
Production: Tommie Smith
Production: Bryan Smith
Purchasing Director: Jim Braun
Estimated Sales: $15 Million
Number Employees: 100-249
Number of Brands: 1
Number of Products: 39
Sq. footage: 65000
Parent Co: Feature Foods dba Main Street Gourmet
Type of Packaging: Consumer, Private Label, Bulk
Brands:
Isabella's

6661 **Isadore A. Rapasadi & Son**
P.O.Box 66
Canastota, NY 13032 315-697-2216
Fax: 315-697-3300 www.rapasadi.com
X
Izzy: Rapasadi President
CEO: Rapasadi CEO
Sales: Rapasadi Sales Manager
Estimated Sales: Grower, packer and exporter of onions an
Number Employees: $10-20 Million
Sq. footage: 60000
Type of Packaging: Bulk
Brands:
Raps Blue Ribbon
Stars & Stripes

6662 **Isernio Sausage Company**
5600 7th Ave S
Seattle, WA 98108 206-762-6207
Fax: 206-762-5259 888-495-8674
info@isernio.com www.isernio.com
Processor and exporter of pork, beef and lamb sausage
President: Frank Isernio
Estimated Sales: $2.5-5 Million
Number Employees: 20-49
Type of Packaging: Consumer, Food Service

6663 **Island Farms Dairies Cooperative Association**
2220 Dowler Place
Po Box 38
Victoria, BC V8W 2M1
Canada 250-360-5200
Fax: 250-360-5220 info@islandfarms.com
www.islandfarms.com
Processor and wholesaler/distributor of a full range of dairy products
President: George Aylard
CEO: David McMillan
CFO: Eric Erikson
Quality Control: Sam Arora
Marketing: Jona De Jesus
Sales: Art Paulo
Operations: Greg Martin
Plant Manager: Al Snedden
Purchasing Director: Steve Wainwright
Number Employees: 250-499
Number of Products: 500
Type of Packaging: Consumer, Food Service, Private Label, Bulk

6664 **Island Lobster**
PO Box 258
Matinicus, ME 04851-0258 207-366-3937
Fax: 207-366-3380
Lobster
Owner: Marc Ames

6665 **Island Marine Products**
PO Box 40
Clarks Harbour, NS B0W 1P0
Canada 902-745-2222
Fax: 902-745-3247
Processor and exporter of haddock, lobster and lobster meat and tuna
President: Cyril Swim
Estimated Sales: $10-20 Million
Number Employees: 20-49
Type of Packaging: Food Service, Bulk

6666 **Island Oasis Frozen Cocktail Company**
P.O.Box 769
141 Norfolk St.
Walpole, MA 02081-0769 508-660-1176
Fax: 508-660-1435 800-777-4752
vponline@mail.islandoasis.com
www.islandoasis.com
Processor and exporter of premium all-natural nonalcoholic beverage mixes; manufacturer and exporter of ice shavers and blenders
President: J Michael Herbert
President/: Anthony Batlaglia
Research & Development: Bill Flynn
Marketing Director: Larry Painter
VP of Sales/Marketing: Michael Walsh
Public Relations: Andrea Scavuzzo
VP of Production: Joseph Cunnane
Estimated Sales: $20-50 Million
Number Employees: 230
Number of Products: 16
Sq. footage: 25000
Brands:
SB-3X

6667 **Island Princess**
2846 Ualena St
Honolulu, HI 96819-1943 808-839-5222
Fax: 808-836-2019 866-872-8601
info@islandprincesshawaii.com
www.islandprincesshawaii.com
Manufacturer of specialty macadomia nut products, luscious chocolates and unique gourmet coffees - caramel popcorn, chocolate coffee beans and macadomia nuts.
President: Michael Purdy
VP: Owen Purdy
Estimated Sales: $8 Million
Number Employees: 50-99
Number of Brands: 10
Number of Products: 100
Sq. footage: 12000
Type of Packaging: Consumer, Food Service, Private Label, Bulk
Brands:
HAWAIIAN PRINCESS SMOKE
ISLAND PRINCESS

6668 **Island Scallops**
5552 Island Highway W
Qualicum Beach, BC V9K 2C8
Canada 250-757-9811
Fax: 250-757-8370
islandscallops@bcsupernet.com
www.islandscallops.com
Processor of fresh and frozen scallops; also, marine research hatchery
President/CEO: Robert Saunders
R&D: Barb Bunting
Processing Manager: Lorraine Hopps
Estimated Sales: $1 Million
Number Employees: 10
Type of Packaging: Consumer, Food Service

6669 **Island Seafood**
32 Brook Rd
Eliot, ME 03903 207-439-8508
Fax: 207-439-6609
Seafood
Owner: Randy Townsend
Estimated Sales: $ 3 - 5 Million
Number Employees: 20-49

6670 **Island Seafoods**
317 Shelikof St
Kodiak, AK 99615 907-486-8575
Fax: 907-486-3007 800-355-8575
islandseafood@gci.net www.islandseafoods.com
Seafood such as king crab, halibut, salmon, scallops, prawns, smoked salmon, rockfish and cod
Owner: Frank Tulcich
Estimated Sales: $ 5 - 10 Million
Number Employees: 20-49

6671 **Island Spices**
15270 SW 15th Street
Miami, FL 33194 786-208-2066
Fax: 732-775-6840
lawrence_shadeed@hotmail.com
www.islandspice.com
Dry spices and sauces
Owner: Andre Schwab

6672 **Island Spring**
P.O.Box 747
Vashon, WA 98070 206-463-9848
Fax: 206-463-5670 lakeskie@wolfenet.com
www.islandspring.com
Processor of organic soy and tofu products
President: W M Luke Lukoskie
R&D: Suni Kim Lukoskie
Estimated Sales: $2.5-5 Million
Number Employees: 10-19
Sq. footage: 4000
Type of Packaging: Consumer, Food Service, Private Label, Bulk
Brands:
Island Spring

6673 **Island Sweetwater Beverage Company**
825 Lafayette Road
Bryn Mawr, PA 19010-1816 610-525-7444
Fax: 610-525-7502 www.peacemountain.com
Processor, exporter and importer of soft drinks, bottled waters, energy drinks; exporter of beer
President: Michael Salaman
Sq. footage: 10000
Parent Co: A/S Beverage Marketing
Type of Packaging: Private Label
Brands:
4th of July Cola
Absolutenergy
Activin Energy
Beverly Hills
Citrimax
Citrimax - French Diet Cola
French Paradox
Island Sweetwater
Jazz
Kiwi Kola
Nicola
Rebound
Sangria Cola
Santa-Claus
Slender
Stampede

6674 **Island Treasures Gourmet**
9413 Center Point Lane
Manassas, VA 20110 703-590-7900
Fax: 703-590-8796 kcraigcgc@yahoo.com

6675 **Island Treasures Gourmet**
Po Box 6806
Woodsbridge, VA 22195 703-590-7900
Fax: 703-590-8796 kcraigcgc@yahoo.com

6676 **Island Treasures MusselProcessing**
PO Box 10
Little Bay, NL A0J 1J0
Canada 709-267-3146
Fax: 709-267-3149
Processor and exporter of fresh mussels
Co-Owner: Edward Sheppard
Co-Owner: Denyse Sheppard
Number Employees: 10-19
Type of Packaging: Consumer, Food Service, Bulk

6677 **Island of the Moon Apiaries**
17560 Company Road
85-B
Esparto, CA 95627 530-787-3993
Fax: 530-787-3993
Bee pollen, honey
President: Jerry Kaplan
Estimated Sales: $2.5-5 Million
Number Employees: 1-4

6678 **Issimo Food Group**
PO Box 1991
La Jolla, CA 92038-1991 619-260-1900
Fax: 619-260-8400 sales@issimo.com
www.issimo.com
White and dark chocolate specialty candies and desserts
President/Owner: Willing Howard
Sales Manager: Kathleen Hornbacher
Estimated Sales: $1-2.5 Million
Number Employees: 20-49
Brands:
Chef Howard's Williecake
Ecco!
Issimo Celebrations!
Issimo's Creme Br–L,
Lilycake

6679 **It's It Ice Cream Company**
865 Burlway Rd
Burlingame, CA 94010 650-347-2122
Fax: 650-347-2703 800-345-1928
comments@itsiticecream.com
www.itsiticecream.com
Processor of ice cream novelties
President: Charles Shamieh
Sales Executive: Charles Shamieh
Production Manager: Peter Zaru
Plant Manager: Alex McDow
Estimated Sales: $4 Million
Number Employees: 30
Sq. footage: 17000
Brands:
It's It

6680 **Italia Foods**
2365 Hammond Drive
Schaumburg, IL 60173 847-397-4479
Fax: 847-397-6817 800-747-1109
italiainc@aol.com www.italiafoods.com
Processor of frozen pasta and sauces
President: Filippo Carabetta
Chairman: Arsenio Carabetta
EVP: Maria Carabetta
Estimated Sales: $3.3 Million
Number Employees: 26
Sq. footage: 6000
Brands:
Italia
Mama Lina

6681 **Italian Bakery**
205 1st St S
Virginia, MN 55792 218-741-3464
Fax: 218-741-2531 www.potica.com
Processor of fresh pies
President: Joseph Prebonich
Estimated Sales: $1-2.5 Million
Number Employees: 20-49
Type of Packaging: Consumer

6682 **Italian Baking Company**
4028 Windsor Rd
Youngstown, OH 44512 330-782-1358
Fax: 330-788-9044
Processor of baked products including pizza
Owner/CEO: Greg Deniro
CEO: Heidi Deniro
Estimated Sales: $1-2.5 Million
Number Employees: 20-49

6683 **Italian Baking Company**
10644 97th Street NW
Edmonton, AB T5H 2L6
Canada 780-424-4830
Fax: 780-425-6577
Processor of Italian-style bread, cakes, pies, muffins and rolls
President/Owner: Antonio Frattin
Marketing Director: Frank Debenz
CFO: Tony Frattin
Number Employees: 10-19
Type of Packaging: Consumer, Food Service

6684 **Italian Connection**
55 W Shore Ave # B
Dumont, NJ 7628 201-385-2226
Fax: 201-385-9026
Italian specialty foods
Owner: John Stracquadanio
Estimated Sales: $1-2.5 Million
Number Employees: 1-4

6685 **Italian Foods**
606 Ridgewood Avenue
Holly Hill, FL 32117-3618 904-255-5200
Italian foods

6686 **Italian Foods Corporation**
7330 Chapel Hill Rd
Suite 102
Raleigh, NC 27607 919-341-0605
Fax: 510-868-4522 888-516-7262
sales@italianfoods.com www.italianfoods.com
pasta, sauces, spreads & toppings, oil & vinegar, rice, risotto, gnocchi, snacks, grilled vegetables, pasta express
President/Owner: Elena Lapiana
Sales: Francesca Lapiana
Operations: Kirk Newcross

6687 **Italian Gourmet Foods Canada**
809 1st Avenue NE
Calgary, AB T2E 0C2
Canada 403-263-6996
Fax: 403-266-6061
Processor of fresh pasta
President: Peter Bellusci
Type of Packaging: Consumer, Food Service
Brands:
The Perfect Pasta

6688 **Italian Peoples Bakery**
31 Scotch Rd
Ewing, NJ 8628 609-771-1369
Fax: 609-771-1369
Baked goods
Manager: Sandy Elmer
Secretary/Treasurer: Carmen Guagliardo
Estimated Sales: $ .5 - 1 million
Number Employees: 100-249
Parent Co: Italian Peoples Bakery

6689 **Italian Products USA Inc**
29 Walnut Avenue
Clark, NJ 07066 201-770-9130
Fax: 201-770-1551 info@italian-products.it
www.italian-products.com
Kosher, coffee, water, olive oil, balsamic vinegar, full-line chocolate, cheese, mushrooms/truffles.
Marketing: Cecilia Ercolino

6690 **Italian Rose Garlic Products**
1380 W 15th St Ste A
West Palm Beach, FL 33404 561-863-5556
Fax: 561-863-1462 800-338-8899
irg@italian-rose.com www.italian-rose.com
Processor of garlic powder and sauces, gourmet garlic, roasted garlic products, toppings, dips, sauces and gifts
President: Ken Berger
VP: Aurthor Conlan
Marketing Director: Aurthor Conlan
Estimated Sales: $30 Million
Number Employees: 100
Type of Packaging: Consumer, Food Service, Private Label
Brands:
Italian Rose

6691 **Italian Specialty Foods**
5600 7th Avenue S
Seattle, WA 98108-2644 206-322-5790
Italian foods
President: Jerry Mascio
Estimated Sales: $50-100 Million
Number Employees: 50-99

6692 **Italian Village Ravioli& Pasta Products**
P.O.Box 839
Portsmouth, NH 03802-0839 603-431-6865
Fax: 603-430-9205
italianvillage@highlinerfoods.com
www.highlinerfoods.com
Processor of frozen ravioli, cavatelli and gnocchi
President: Keith A Decker
VP, Procurement: Paul W Snow
VP: Dave Johnson
VP Human Resources: Mario G Patenaude

Estimated Sales: $ 50 - 100 Million
Number Employees: 100-249
Parent Co: High Liner Foods
Type of Packaging: Consumer, Food Service, Private Label
Brands:
Gina Italian Village

6693 **Itarca**
1864 E 22nd St
Los Angeles, CA 90058 310-419-6433
Fax: 310-677-2782 800-747-2782
www.florentyna.com
Processor of fresh and frozen Italian pasta including ravioli, tortellini, cavatelli, potato and cheese gnocchi, cannelloni and lasagna
President: Yvonne Smulovitz
Manager: Jascha Smulovitz
Estimated Sales: $1.60 Million
Number Employees: 17

6694 **Itella Foods**
1729 E 21st Street
Los Angeles, CA 90058 213-765-0967
Fax: 213-745-3009
General grocery
Owner: Salveatore Gallatti
Vice President: Frank Brigulio
Estimated Sales: $20-50 Million
Number Employees: 100-249

6695 **(HQ)Ito Cariani Sausage Company**
3190 Corporate Pl
Hayward, CA 94545-3916 510-887-0882
Fax: 510-387-8323
Manufacturer and exporter of meat products including sausage, wine-flavored dry salami, roast and smoked beef, headcheese, pepperoni and bologna
President: Tony Nakashima
VP Finance: Allen Shiroma
Executive VP/General Manager: Ken Kamata
VP Sales: Al Lera
Estimated Sales: $10-20 Million
Number Employees: 50-99
Sq. footage: 85000
Type of Packaging: Consumer, Food Service, Private Label, Bulk
Other Locations:
Ito Cariani Sausage Co.
Nishinomiya
Brands:
Cariani Italian Dry Salami
Cariani Italian Specialty Loaves

6696 **Itoen**
125 Puuhale Rd
Honolulu, HI 96819-4992 808-847-4477
Fax: 808-841-4384 www.itoen-usa.com
Processor of fruit juice, sports drinks, iced tea and coffee, canned teas and frozen concentrates; also, Oriental noodles and soup bases
President: Shigeyuki Utsugi
Marketing Director: Alan Pollock
Estimated Sales: $20-50 Million
Number Employees: 50-99
Type of Packaging: Consumer, Food Service
Brands:
Aloha Maid
Itoen

6697 **Ittella Foods**
2050 Long Beach Avenue
Los Angeles, CA 90058-1022 213-746-6201
Fax: 213-745-3009
Pinto beans, tomato sauce, sauces, imitation crab salad, salsa, guacamole
President: Sam Galetti
VP Sales: Peter Roddy
Production Manager: Jose Reveles
Brands:
De La Casa
Del Rancho
El Pueblo

6698 **Ittels Meats**
P.O.Box 676
Howard Lake, MN 55349-0676 320-543-2285
Fax: 320-543-2285
Manufacturer of beef jerky and summer sausage
Owner: Don Schwartz
Estimated Sales: $1-3 Million
Number Employees: 1-4

Type of Packaging: Consumer, Food Service, Private Label, Bulk

6699 **Ivanhoe Cheese Inc**
11301 Hwy 62 Rr 5
Madoc, ON K0K 2K0
Canada 613-473-4269
Fax: 613-473-5016 ivanhoecheese@sympatico.ca
www.ivanhoecheese.com
Manufacturer, processor, importer and exporter of natural, process and cold pack cheeses including cheddar, swiss and parmesan; also, cheese sauces
President: Bruce Kingston
Vice President: Larry Hook
Sales: Paul McKinlay
Plant Manager: Chris Spencer
Estimated Sales: $16.5 Million
Number Employees: 80
Type of Packaging: Consumer, Food Service, Private Label, Bulk
Brands:
Ivanhoe
Ivanhoe Classics
Ivanhoe Fresh

6700 **Iversen Baking Company**
PO Box 28
Bedminster, PA 18910 215-636-5904
Fax: 215-575-5076
Cookies
President: David Collins
Estimated Sales: Under $500,000
Number Employees: 1-4

6701 **Iveta Gourmet**
2125 Delaware Ave Ste F
Santa Cruz, CA 95060 831-423-5149
Fax: 831-423-5169 iveta@iveta.com
www.iveta.com
Natural scones, muffins and savory biscuit mixes. Imports jams, curds and clotted cream to serve with them.
Owner: John Bilanko
Co-Owner: Yvette Bilanko
Estimated Sales: $2.5-5 Million
Number Employees: 5-9
Brands:
Iveta Gourmet

6702 **Ivy Cottage Scone Mixes**
530 Fremont Ln
S Pasadena, CA 91030 626-441-2761
Fax: 626-441-9657
Prepared mixes for scones
President: Elaine Osmond

6703 **Ivy Foods**
3851 E. Thunderhill Place
Phoenix, AZ 85044-6679 480-626-2025
Fax: 480-704-4116 877-223-5459
support@nutribase.com www.nutribase.com
Manufacturer of wheat based meat substitutes including chicken, sausage and burger analogs
President: Mira Blue Machlis
Estimated Sales: $2.5-5 Million
Number Employees: 1-4
Sq. footage: 12000
Brands:
Meat of Wheat

6704 **Ivydaro**
PO Box 369
Putney, VT 05346-0369 802-387-5597
ivydaro@sover.net
Foiled wraped chocolate apples

6705 **Iwamoto Natto Factory**
143 Hana Hwy # C
Paia, HI 96779 808-579-9933
Fax: 808-579-9933
Natto and noodles
Owner: Robert Yamashita
Estimated Sales: $110,000
Number Employees: 1-4
Type of Packaging: Consumer, Food Service

6706 **J & B Seafood**
9301 Faith St
Coden, AL 36523-3057 251-824-4512
Fax: 251-824-1260
Seafood
President: Raymond Barbour
Estimated Sales: $7.7 Million
Number Employees: 50-99

6707 **J & M Foods**
9100 Frazier Pike Road
Po Box 250080
Little Rock, AR 72206 501-663-1991
Fax: 501-663-2822 800-264-2278
sales@jm-foods.com www.jm-foods.com
Processor of flavored straws.
President: Jamie Parham
VP: Scott Thibault
Director Sales/Marketing: Greg Parham
Production Manager: Jeff Stockman
Estimated Sales: $ 10-20 Million
Number Employees: 20-49
Type of Packaging: Private Label

6708 **J Bernard Seafood & Processing**
P.O.Box 623
Cottonport, LA 71327-0623 318-876-3885
Fax: 318-876-2925
Seafood
President: James Bernard
Estimated Sales: $3.2 Million
Number Employees: 10-19

6709 **J Freirich Food Products**
4601 5th St
Long Island City, NY 11101-5311 718-361-9111
800-221-1315
sales@freirich.com www.freirich.com
Marinated beef, corned beef, roast beef, pastrami, rib roasts, pot roasts, prok
President/CEO: Paul Bardinas
VP Finance/CFO: Doug Sokolowski
VP Sales/Marketing: Phil Percoco
VP Operations/COO: Dennis Arrasmith
Estimated Sales: $25 Million
Number Employees: 10-19
Sq. footage: 35000
Type of Packaging: Consumer, Food Service
Brands:
Freirich Porkette
Regal Chef

6710 **J G Townsend Jr & Company**
P.O.Box 430
Georgetown, DE 19947 302-856-2525
Fax: 302-855-0922
Processor of frozen vegetables including beans and peas
President: Paul Townsend
VP: John Townsend IV
Plant Manager: Soloman Henry
Estimated Sales: $ 2.5-5 Million
Number Employees: 20-49
Type of Packaging: Consumer, Food Service
Brands:
Country Fair
Townsend

6711 **J J Gandy's Pies**
3725 Alt 19 Ste A
Palm Harbor, FL 34683 727-938-7437
Fax: 727-938-7437
Bakery items
President: Gay Schmidt
Estimated Sales: Less than $100,000
Number Employees: 1-4
Type of Packaging: Food Service

6712 **J M Clayton Company**
108 Commerce St
Cambridge, MD 21613 410-228-1661
Fax: 410-221-0216 800-652-6931
jmclayton@shorenet.net www.jmclayton.com
Processor of Chesapeake Bay blue crabs including whole and steamed; also, custom packaging in fresh pasteurized and frozen containers available
President: John C Brooks Jr
CEO: William Brooks
Estimated Sales: $3000000
Number Employees: 100-249
Sq. footage: 29000
Type of Packaging: Consumer, Food Service, Private Label, Bulk
Brands:
EPICURE

6713 **J Vineyards & Winery**
11447 Old Redwood Hwy
Healdsburg, CA 95448 707-431-5400
Fax: 707-431-5410 800-885-9463
winefolk@jwine.com www.jwine.com

Wines
Marketing Director: Judy Jordan
CEO: Bruce Lundquist
CEO: Judy Jordan
CFO: Bruce Lundquist
Public Relations: Robin Oden
Winemaker: Lisa Kashin
Estimated Sales: $ 5-9.9 Million
Number Employees: 50-99
Type of Packaging: Private Label
Brands:
J Nicole Vineyard Pinot Noir
J Russian River Vall
J Sparkling Wine

6714 **J W Allen Company**
555 Allendale Dr
Wheeling, IL 60090-2638 847-459-5400
Fax: 847-459-0314 marksr@ameritech.net
www.richs.com
Baked goods
President/CEO: William Allen Jr
CFO: Ron Vantz
VP Sales: Allan Foster
Director Marketing: Jerry Widdick
General Manager: J Joy
General Manager-Cereal Mix Division: Don Colson
Plant Manager: Rene Marcos
Purchasing Manager: Dorothy Wood-Johnson
Estimated Sales: $ 50-100 Million
Number Employees: 100-249
Type of Packaging: Private Label

6715 **J&B Sausage Company**
P.O.Box 7
Waelder, TX 78959-0007 830-788-7511
Fax: 830-788-7279 contact@jbfoods.com
www.jbfoods.com
Processor and exporter of smoked sausage, bacon, ham and jerky; also, barbecued meat
President: Danny Janecka
CEO: Ron Bushaw
Estimated Sales: $42040000
Number Employees: 250-499
Type of Packaging: Consumer, Food Service, Private Label, Bulk
Brands:
J Bar B Foods
Singletree Farms
Texas Smokehouse

6716 **J&G Cheese Company**
847 Colony Way
Columbus, OH 43235-1755 614-436-1070
Fax: 614-436-9683
Cheese
Marketing Director: David Holmberg

6717 **J&G Poultry**
P.O.Box 2414
Gainesville, GA 30503-2414 770-536-5540
Fax: 770-531-0829
Poultry
Manager: Bob Gregory
Estimated Sales: $ 10 - 20 Million
Number Employees: 10-19

6718 **J&J Produce Company**
105 Frederick St
Hattiesburg, MS 39401 601-582-1512
Fax: 601-582-1515
Processor of produce
President: Joseph R Forte
Co-Owner: Joe Forte
Vice President: Richard Nause
Estimated Sales: $ 5 - 10 Million
Number Employees: 10-19

6719 **J&J Snack Foods Corporation**
6000 Central Hwy
Pennsauken, NJ 8109 856-665-9533
Fax: 856-663-8002 webmaster@jjsnack.com
www.jjsnack.com
Manufacturer and exporter of various nutritional snack foods and beverages.
Chairman/President/CEO: Gerald Shreiber
CFO/VP/Secretary/Treasurer: Dennis Moore
COO/Sr VP: Robert Radano
SVP Marketing: Michael Karaban
Estimated Sales: $ 100 + Million
Number Employees: 1,000-4,999
Type of Packaging: Food Service, Private Label
Brands:
BARQ'S
CAMDEN CREEK
CHILL
ICEE
LUIGI'S
MAMA TISH'S
MINUTE MAID
MRS GOODCOOKIE
PRETZEL FILLERS
SHAPE UPS
SUPERPRETZEL
THE FUNNEL CAKE FACTORY
TIO PEPE'S

6720 **J&J Snack Foods Corporation**
5353 S Downey Rd
Vernon, CA 90058 323-581-1681
Fax: 323-583-4732 800-486-7622
www.jjsnack.com
Processor and exporter of health food cookies including fruit filled, fruit juice sweetened, wheat-free, dairy-free and fat-free as well as soft pretzels and cookie doughs for food service
Manager: Mark Slakter
R&D: Joyce Berham
Vice President: Robert Radano
Marketing Director: Michael Karabon
Sales Director: Steve Taylor
Estimated Sales: $353187000
Number Employees: 250-499
Sq. footage: 150000
Parent Co: J&J Snack Foods Company
Type of Packaging: Consumer, Food Service, Private Label, Bulk
Brands:
BAKERS BEST
BAVARIAN
CHURROS
DUTCHIE
FROSTAR
FUNNEL CAKE
ICEE
LUIGI'S
MAMA TISH'S
MR. TWISTER
MRS. GOODCOOKIE
PRETZEL COOKIE
PRETZEL FILLERS
SHAPE-UPS
SUPERJUICE
SUPERPRETZEL
TIO PEPE'S

6721 **(HQ)J&J Snack Foods Corporation**
6000 Central Hwy
Pennsauken, NJ 08109 856-665-9533
Fax: 856-663-8002 800-486-9533
webmaster@jjsnack.com www.jjsnack.com
Manufacturer, marketer, and distributor of various nutritional snack foods and beverages
Chairman/President/CEO: Gerald Shreiber
SVP/CFO: Dennis Moore
VP R&D/Quality Assurance: Kathleen Wong
SVP Sales/Marketing: Robert Pape
VP Human Resources: Harry Fronjian
SVP/COO: Robert Radano
Plant Manager: Jack Manderbaugh
Purchasing: Jessica Kimley
Estimated Sales: $697 Million
Number Employees: 2700
Sq. footage: 70000
Type of Packaging: Food Service, Private Label
Brands:
ARCTIC BLAST
DUTCHIE
FROSTAR
ICEE
LUIGI'S
MR. IWISTER
MRS. GOODCOOKIE
PRETZEL FILLERS
SHAPE-UPS
SUPERJUICE
SUPERPRETZEL
TANGO WHIP
TIO PEPE'S

6722 **J&J Wall Baking Company**
8800 Fruitridge Rd
Sacramento, CA 95826 916-381-1410
Fax: 916-381-6008 www.jjwallbaking.com
Processor of frozen bread and rolls
President: Janet Wall
Estimated Sales: $ 20 - 50 Million
Number Employees: 20-49
Type of Packaging: Consumer

6723 **J&J Wholesale**
2925 Industrial St
Junction City, KS 66441-8519 785-238-4721
Fax: 785-762-6869
President: Dan Coffey
Plant Manager: Dirk Francis
Estimated Sales: $ 20 - 50 Million
Number Employees: 20-49

6724 **J&K Ingredients**
160 E 5th St
Paterson, NJ 7524 973-340-8700
Fax: 973-340-4994 jkfoods1@aol.com
www.jkingredients.com
Bakery flavorings, extracts and mold inhibitors
President: Paul W Kinney
Estimated Sales: $ 10-25 Million
Number Employees: 20-30
Brands:
Bred-Mate
Sausville's

6725 **J&L Grain Processing**
12456 Addison Ave
Riceville, IA 50466 641-985-4255
Fax: 641-985-4256 800-244-9211
jlgiain@omnitelcon.com
Processing of grain
President/CEO: Joel Yorgey
Estimated Sales: Below $ 5 Million
Number Employees: 5-9

6726 **J&L Seafood**
P.O.Box 272
Bayou La Batre, AL 36509-0272 251-824-2371
Fax: 251-824-2371
Seafood
President: Joshua Alderman
Estimated Sales: $ 3 - 5 Million
Number Employees: 10-19

6727 **J&M Industries**
300 Ponchatoula Pkwy
Ponchatoula, LA 70454 985-386-6000
Fax: 985-386-9066 800-989-1002
www.jm-ind.com
President: Rene Gaudet
Plant Manager: Al Bourgeois
Estimated Sales: $ 20 - 50 Million
Number Employees: 100-249

6728 **J&M Meats**
PO Box 370
Warburg, AB T0C 2T0
Canada 780-848-7598
Fax: 780-848-7532 midge@telusplanet.net
www.jandmmeats.com
Processor and exporter of fresh and frozen pork
President: J McCullough
Administrator Quality Control: Kevin McCullough
Sales Manager: Nannette McCullough
Number Employees: 22
Sq. footage: 18000
Type of Packaging: Consumer, Food Service, Bulk

6729 **J&R Fisheries**
PO Box 3302
Seward, AK 99664-3302 907-224-5584
Fax: 907-224-5572
Seafood
Estimated Sales: $300,000-500,000
Number Employees: 1-4

6730 **J&R Foods**
307 Morris Ave
Long Branch, NJ 07740 732-229-4020
Fax: 732-229-0111
Processor of half shell mussels and marinara sauce with mussels
President: Rocco F Raimondi III
Estimated Sales: $1 Million
Number Employees: 10-19
Type of Packaging: Consumer, Food Service

6731 **J-N-D Company**
11424 Tweedsmuir Run
Fort Wayne, IN 46814-8217 260-459-6206
Fax: 219-485-9242
President: Dennis Thomas
Manager: Peggy Baughman
Estimated Sales: $ 5-10 Million
Number Employees: 6

6732 **J. Crow Company**
P.O.Box 172
New Ipswich, NH 03071-0172 603-878-1965
Fax: 603-878-1965 800-878-1965
jcrow@jcrow.mv.com www.jcrow.com
Processor of herbs, spices, essential and fragrance oils and teas
Owner: Jeff Krouk
Estimated Sales: Less than $500,000
Number Employees: 1-4
Sq. footage: 50000
Type of Packaging: Consumer
Brands:
J. Crow's

6733 **J. Dickerson**
2914 Commerce Sq S
Birmingham, AL 35210 205-956-0881
President: Jerry Dickerson
CEO: Charlene Dickerson
Number Employees: 12

6734 **J. Filippi Winery**
12467 Baseline Rd
Etiwanda, CA 91739 909-899-5755
Fax: 909-899-9196 jfilippiwinery@aol.com
www.josephfilippiwinery.com
Wine
President: Joseph Filippi
CEO: Joseph Filippi
Marketing Director: Gino Filippi
Estimated Sales: $ 10-20 Million
Number Employees: 20-49
Brands:
J. Filippi

6735 **J. Frasinetti & Sons**
PO Box 292368
7395 Frasinetti RD
Sacramento, CA 95828 916-383-2444
Fax: 916-383-5825 www.frasinetti.com
Wine

6736 **J. Fritz Winery**
24691 Dutcher Creek Rd
Cloverdale, CA 95425 707-894-3389
Fax: 707-894-4781 info@fritzwinery.com
www.fritzwinery.com
Wines
President: Clayton Fritz
Winemaker: Christina Pallmann
Estimated Sales: $ 2.5-5 Million
Number Employees: 10-19
Brands:
Fritz

6737 **J. G. Van Holten & Son**
703 W Madison St
Waterloo, WI 53594 920-478-2144
Fax: 920-478-2316 800-256-0619
info@vanholtenpickles.com
www.vanholtenpickles.com
Processor and exporter of pre-packaged pickles and relish
President: James D Byrnes
VP and General Manager: Steve Byrnes
VP of Sales: Stef Espiritu
Estimated Sales: $7000000
Number Employees: 50-99
Type of Packaging: Consumer, Private Label, Bulk
Brands:
BIG PAPA
GARLIC GUS
HOT MAMA
LIL' PEPE
VAN HOLTEN

6738 **J. Hoelting Produce**
P.O.Box 2260
Decatur, IL 62524-2260 217-429-7774
Fax: 217-429-8129
Produce
President: Bob Tipsword
Estimated Sales: $ 20 - 50 Million
Number Employees: 20-49

6739 **J. K Marley's Llc**
7703 La Montee Dr
Unit C
Rockford, IL 61103-7739
Fax: 800-717-5043 www.bigpapasbarbecue.com
BBQ sauce
Number Employees: 5
Type of Packaging: Consumer

6740 **J. Matassini & Sons Fish Company**
2008 N Garcia Ave
Tampa, FL 33602 813-229-0829
Fax: 813-229-7327
Processor of fresh and frozen seafood including catfish, trout, lobsters, oysters, crabs, scallops, breaded shrimp and crab cakes
President: Pasquale Matassini
Estimated Sales: $ 1 - 3 Million
Number Employees: 5-9
Type of Packaging: Consumer, Food Service
Brands:
Matassini Seafoods

6741 **J. Moniz Company**
91 Wordell St
Fall River, MA 02721 508-674-8451
Fax: 508-673-6464
Seafood
President/Treasurer/Clerk: John Moniz
Estimated Sales: $1,000,000
Number Employees: 5-9

6742 **J. Rettenmaier**
16369 Us Highway 131 S
Schoolcraft, MI 49087-9150 269-679-2340
Fax: 269-679-2364 877-243-4661
info@jrsusa.com www.jrusa.com
Fiber products: cellulose, wheat, oat, apple, orange, tomato for bakery, cereal, snack food, pasta and diet beverage markets
Manager: Gerhard Goss
Estimated Sales: $ 10 - 20 Million
Number Employees: 50-99

6743 **J. Stonestreet & Sons Vineyard**
PO Box 46
Healdsburg, CA 95448-0046 707-473-3307
Fax: 707-433-9469 800-723-6336
www.stonestreetwines.com
Wines
President: Jess Jackson
Sales Manager: Mick Unti
Estimated Sales: $ 2.5-5 Million
Number Employees: 10
Brands:
Alexander Valley
Christopher's
Legacy Red Wine

6744 **J. Turner Seafoods**
4 Smith St
Gloucester, MA 01930-2710 978-281-8535
Fax: 978-281-1710
Seafood
Estimated Sales: $2,000,000
Number Employees: 5-9

6745 **J. Weil & Company**
5907 Clinton St
Boise, ID 83704-9304 208-377-0590
Fax: 208-378-1682 800-755-3885
www.jweil.com
Food service distributor
President: Bill Tippetts
Estimated Sales: $ 5 - 10 Million
Number Employees: 20-49

6746 **J.A.M.B. Low Carb Distributor**
4100 N Powerline Road
Suite W3
Pompano Beach, FL 33073-3065 954-917-9881
Fax: 954-917-2590 800-708-6738
mike@jambco.com www.jambco.com
Low carb and sugar free foods.
CEO: Alan Beyda

6747 **J.B. Peel Coffee Roasters**
7582 N Broadway
Red Hook, NY 12571-1469 845-758-1792
Fax: 845-758-1814 800-231-7372
jbpeel@citlink.net www.jbpeelcoffee.com
Gourmet coffee
President: Gil Klein
VP: Pat Klein
Estimated Sales: Less than $500,000
Number Employees: 10,000+
Number of Products: 200
Type of Packaging: Consumer, Private Label, Bulk

6748 **J.B. Sons**
564 Mile Square Rd
Yonkers, NY 10701-6333 914-963-5192
Fax: 914-963-5192
Processor of ricotta cheese, hand-made mozzarella cheese and pasta including ravioli, manicotti, stuffed shells, cavatelli and gnocchi
President: Joseph L Brunetto Jr
Sales: Steven Brunetto
Estimated Sales: $ 5 - 10 Million
Number Employees: 5-9
Sq. footage: 3000
Type of Packaging: Consumer, Food Service, Private Label, Bulk

6749 **J.C. Watson Company**
P.O.Box 300
Parma, ID 83660 208-722-5141
Fax: 208-722-6646 nancy@soobrand.com
www.soobrand.com
Processor and exporter of produce including onions, apples, potatoes and plums
Manager: Kent Sutherland
Sales Manager: Nancy Carter
Transportation Manager: Melanie Steinhaus
Number Employees: 5-9
Type of Packaging: Consumer, Food Service
Brands:
SOO

6750 **J.D. Mullen Company**
211 S Main St
Palestine, IL 62451 618-586-2727
Fax: 618-586-2718 mullins11@verizon.net
www.mullensdressing.com
Processor of Imitation French, French, Creamy Italian and Special Salad Dressings, as well as BBQ Sauce and Ham's Delight.
President: Jeff Shaner
CFO/Quality Control: Jeff Shaner
Estimated Sales: $300,000-500,000
Number Employees: 5-9
Sq. footage: 7500
Type of Packaging: Consumer, Food Service
Brands:
Mullen's

6751 **J.F.C. International**
1925 N Norcross Tucker Rd
Norcross, GA 30071-3411 770-448-0070
Fax: 770-263-9790 www.jfc.com
Manager: Shoso Ota
Estimated Sales: $ 20 - 50 Million
Number Employees: 20-49

6752 **J.G. British Imports**
15302 21st Ave E
Bradenton, FL 34212-8121 941-745-1474
Fax: 941-926-1701 888-965-1700
info@ratherjolly.com
www.sarasotamilitaryacademy.com
Tea
President: David Grace
CEO: Grace Sern
Manager: Felisa Choi
Estimated Sales: $100,000
Number Employees: 2
Type of Packaging: Private Label
Brands:
Rather Jolly Tea

6753 **J.H. Verbridge & Son**
6700 Lake Ave
Williamson, NY 14589 315-589-2366
Fax: 315-589-7478
Processor of frozen cherries, pineapples and strawberries
President: Robert Verbridge
Executive VP: Gerald Verbridge
Plant Manager: Lloyd Verbridge
Estimated Sales: $1 Million
Number Employees: 20-49
Type of Packaging: Consumer, Food Service
Brands:
Big V

6754 **J.M. Schneider**
254 Rue Principale
Saint Anselme, QC G0R 2N0
Canada 418-885-4474
Fax: 418-885-9408 www.schneiders.ca
Processor of beef and pork
Plant Manager: Narie Claude Lamontadne
Plant Manager: Cal Petraszko
Number Employees: 100-249
Parent Co: J.M. Schneider
Type of Packaging: Consumer, Food Service
Brands:
Schneider

6755 **J.M. Smucker**
340 Old Bay Ln
Havre De Grace, MD 21078 410-939-1403
Fax: 410-939-6263 www.jmsmucker.com
Fruit juices
General Manager: Doug Arington
Branch Manager: Dan Hastings
Estimated Sales: $ 20 - 50 Million
Number Employees: 44
Parent Co: Smucker

6756 **(HQ)J.M. Smucker Company**
1 Strawberry Ln
Orrville, OH 44667 330-682-3000
Fax: 330-684-6410 888-550-9555
www.smuckers.com
Fruit spreads, retail packaged coffee, peanut butter, shortening and oils, ice cream toppings, sweetened condensed milk, and health and natural foods beverages
President/COO: Vincent Byrd
Executive Chairman/Co-CEO: Richard Smucker
VP/Chief Financial Officer: Mark Belgya
SVP Chief Administrative Officer: Barry Dunaway
President/Foodservice & Natural Foods: Steven Oakland
VP/Chief Information Officer: Andrew Platt
VP/Marketing Communications: Christopher Resweber
VP/U.S. Grocery Sales: James Brown
VP & General Manager/Natural Foods: Julia Sabin
SVP/Logistics & Operations Support: Dennis Armstrong
President/U.S. Retail Consumer Foods: Paul Smucker Wagstaff
Estimated Sales: $4.6 Billion
Number Employees: 4,000
Sq. footage: 130000
Type of Packaging: Consumer, Food Service
Brands:
ADAMS
CRISCO
CROSSE & BLACKWELL
DICKINSON'S
DUNKIN DONUTS
DUTCH GIRL
EAGLE BRAND
FOLGERS
HUNGRY JACK
JIF
KAVA
KNOTT'S BERRY FARM
LAURA SCUDDER'S
MAGNOLIA
MARHTA WHITE
MARY ELLEN
MILLSTONE
NATURAL BREW
NATURE'S PEAK
NONE SUCH
PET
PILLSBURY
R.W. KNUDSEN FAMILY
R.W. KNUDSEN FAMILY
SANTA CRUZ ORGANIC
SMUCKER'S
WHITE LILY

6757 **J.M. Smucker Company**
P.O.Box 608
Grandview, WA 98930-0608 509-882-1530
Fax: 509-882-2212 www.smuckers.com
Processor of grape juice concentrate
Manager: Randy Hecker
Plant Manager: Randy Hecker
Estimated Sales: $ 5 - 10 Million
Number Employees: 20-49
Sq. footage: 12000
Parent Co: J.M. Smucker Company
Type of Packaging: Bulk

6758 **J.N. Bech**
214 Dexter St
Elk Rapids, MI 49629 231-264-5080
Fax: 231-264-5107 800-232-4583
sales@themustardwithauthority.com
www.themustardwithauthority.com
Processor of gourmet water-cooled stone ground mustards and barbecue glazes including additive/preservative and fat-free
President: John Bech
Office Manager: Lynn Haveman
Estimated Sales: $600000
Number Employees: 7
Type of Packaging: Consumer, Food Service, Private Label
Brands:
Bech

6759 **J.P. Green Milling Company**
P.O.Box 187
Mocksville, NC 27028 336-751-2126
Fax: 336-751-1349
Processor of grits, feed, flour and corn meal
President: Ralph Naylor
Estimated Sales: $ 5 - 10 Million
Number Employees: 10-19

6760 **J.P. Shellfish**
P.O.Box 666
Eliot, ME 03903-0666 207-439-6018
Fax: 207-439-7794
Seafood
President: John Price
Estimated Sales: $ 10 - 20 Million
Number Employees: 20-49

6761 **J.P. Sunrise Bakery**
14728 119th Avenue NW
Edmonton, AB T5L 2P2
Canada 780-454-5797
Fax: 780-452-7696 office@sunrise-bakery.com
www.sunrisebakery.com
Processor of baked goods including nanaimo bars and tarts; exporter of cinnamon buns
President: Gary Huising
Director: Tony Bron
Director: Hank Renzenbrink
Number Employees: 80
Sq. footage: 30000
Type of Packaging: Consumer, Food Service

6762 **J.R. Fish Company**
PO Box 774
Wrangell, AK 99929-0774 907-874-2399
Fax: 907-874-2398
Seafood
President: Janell Privett
Secretary/Treasurer: William Privett

6763 **J.R. Poultry**
2924 Maus Road
Fults, IL 62244-1506 618-476-7342
Fax: 706-777-8690
Poultry

6764 **J.R. Short Canadian Mills**
54 Harding Boulevard
Toronto, ON M4G 2B5
Canada 416-421-3463
Fax: 416-421-2876 a.norris@jrshort.com
Processor and exporter of confectioners corn flakes, corn meal, stablized wheat bran, wheat germ and corn germ
Vice President: Alexa Norris
Parent Co: J.R. Short Milling Company

6765 **(HQ)J.R. Short Milling Company**
1580 Grinnell Rd
Kankakee, IL 60901 815-937-5201
Fax: 815-937-3981 800-544-8734
info@shortmill.com www.shortmill.com
Manufacturer and exporter of corn grits, meal, flour, brewer's flakes, heat stabilized fours and snack pellets; also corn germ for flavor.
President/CEO: John Luikart
President/VP: Raleigh Wilkinson
Estimated Sales: $25 Million
Number Employees: 100-249
Type of Packaging: Private Label, Bulk
Other Locations:
Short, J.R., Milling Co.
Kankakee IL
Brands:
CERATEX
SNO-FLUF
SUNLITE
WYTASE

6766 **J.R. Short Milling Company**
1580 Grinnell Rd
Kankakee, IL 60901 815-937-5201
Fax: 815-937-3981 800-457-3547
judih@shortmill.com www.shortmail.com
Snack foodss, bakery dough improvers
General Manager: Dennis Bunck
Sales: Judy Hunter
Research & Development: Raleigh Wilkinson
Quality Control: Richard Cochran
Sales Director: Bruce Dunlap
Operations Manager: Dennis Bunck
Purchasing Manager: Don Pitzer
Estimated Sales: $ 50-100 Million
Number Employees: 100-249
Brands:
Sunlite

6767 **(HQ)J.R. Simplot Company**
999 W Main Street
Suite 1300
Boise, ID 83702 208-336-2110
Fax: 208-389-7515 jrs_info@simplot.com
www.simplot.com
Processes potatoes, grains and vegetables to produce fresh and frozen bulk, private label, and consumer products. supplies mcdonalds and bk and wendys with their fries.
President & CEO: Bill Whitacre
Chairman: Scott Simplot
SVP Finance/CFO: Annette Elg
President, Food Group: Kevin Storms
Manager Of Marketing: Kristi Smith
VP Sales, Food Group: Steve Patterson
Public Relations: David Cuoio
Purchasing: John Glerum
Estimated Sales: $4.5 Billion
Number Employees: 10,000
Type of Packaging: Consumer, Food Service, Private Label
Other Locations:
J.R. Simplot Potato Processing
Aberdeen ID
J.R. Simplot Potato Processing
Caldwell ID
J.R. Simplot Potato Processing
Grand Forks ND
J.R. Simplot Potato Processing
Moses Lake WA
J.R. Simplot Potato Processing
Nampa ID
J.R. Simplot Potato Processing
Othello WA
J.R. Simplot Vegetable Processing
West Memphis AR
Brands:
CHEF'S CHOICE
CONQUEST®
CULINARY SELECT™
DEHYDROFROZEN
FIESTA
FREEZERFRIDGE®
GLORI FRI®
GRAND VALLEY®
HARVEST SUPREME™
IDAHOAN®
INFINITY®
JR BUFFALO®
KRUNCHIE WEDGES®
MARINER®
MEGACRUNCH®
NATURALCRISP®
OLD FASHIONED WAY®
PANCAKE PODS®
PAYETTE FARMS®
PLATE-PERFECT®
QUICKMASH®
RECIPE QUICK®
ROASTWORKS®
SAVORY
SEASONEDCRISP®
SELECT RECIPE®
SIMPLOT®
SIMPLOT® CULINARY FRESH™
SKINCREDIBLES®
SKINCREDIBLES® PLUS

SOUR CREAM & CHIVE
SPUDSTERS®
SUN CROP®
TASTEE SPUD™
TATER PALS®
TOP CAT®
TRADITIONAL
TRUE RECIPE®
ULTRA CLEAR®
UPSIDES®
WONDER FRY

6768 **J.R. Simplot Company**
PO Box 27
Boise, ID 83707 208-336-2110
Fax: 208-389-7515 jrs_info@simplot.com
www.simplot.com
Processor of frozen vegetables and French fried potatoes; also fruits and vegetables
Parent Co: J.R. Simplot Company
Brands:
Simplot

6769 **J.R. Simplot Company**
3630 Gateway Dr
Grand Forks, ND 58203 701-746-6431
Fax: 701-780-7882 jrs_info@simplot.com
www.simplot.com
Avocado products, instant mashed potatoes, frozen potatoes, fruits, roasted products, sweet potato products, and vegetables
Parent Co: J.R. Simplot Company
Type of Packaging: Consumer, Food Service, Bulk

6770 **J.R.'s Seafood**
9908 Southwest Highway
Oak Lawn, IL 60453 708-422-4555
Fax: 914-624-0329
Seafood
President: Frank Cestro
Estimated Sales: $ 1 - 3 Million
Number Employees: 5-9

6771 **J.S. McMillan Fisheries**
12 Orwell St
North Vancouver, BC V7J 2G1
Canada 604-981-4000
Fax: 604-981-4001 sparkhill@jsm.bc.ca
www.bcseafoodonline.com
Processor of canned salmon and ground fish
President: Steve Parkhill
VP Sales: Guy Dean
Number Employees: 250-499
Parent Co: J.S. McMillan
Type of Packaging: Consumer, Food Service
Brands:
Hywave
J.S. McMillan
Pinnacle
Snow Cod

6772 **J.S. McMillan Fisheries**
2199 Commissioner Street
Vancouver, BC V5L 1A9
Canada 604-255-5191
Fax: 604-255-4600
Processor of canned salmon and frozen halibut
President: Tarry Mcmillan
Brands:
J.S. McMillan Fisheries

6773 **J.T. Pappy's Sauce**
1909 1/4 N Las Palmas Avenue
Los Angeles, CA 90068-3270 323-969-9605
Fax: 323-969-9659 saucecentral@aol.com
www.jtpappys.com
Manufacturer, sales and marketing of sauces and marinades
Number Employees: 8
Number of Brands: 1
Number of Products: 12
Type of Packaging: Consumer, Food Service, Private Label

6774 **J.T. Ward Meats & Provisions**
4561 Loma Vista Avenue
Vernon, CA 90058-2601 323-585-9935
Processor of meats
Estimated Sales: $ 2.5-5 Million
Number Employees: 1-4

6775 **J.T.R.**
Hc 32
Box 189
Sebasco Estates, ME 04565 207-389-1819
Fax: 207-389-1819

6776 **J.W. Haywood & Sons Dairy**
1744 W Burnett Ave
Louisville, KY 40210-1740 502-774-2311
Processor of ice cream
Owner: Charles Haywood
Estimated Sales: $300,000-500,000
Number Employees: 5-9
Type of Packaging: Consumer, Food Service

6777 **J.W. Raye & Company**
83 Washington St
Eastport, ME 4631 207-853-4451
Fax: 207-853-2937 800-853-1903
mustards@rayesmustard.com
www.rayesmustard.com
Processor of natural stone ground mustard and mustard sauces
Owner: Karen Raye
General Manager: Nancy Raye
Estimated Sales: $ 5 - 10 Million
Number Employees: 5-9
Type of Packaging: Consumer, Food Service, Bulk

6778 **J.W. Raye & Company**
PO Box 2
Mira Loma, CA 91752-0002 909-428-8630
Fax: 909-428-6264
Mustard flavors
General Manager: Nancy Raye
Estimated Sales: $5-10 Million
Number Employees: 5

6779 **J.W. Treuth & Sons**
328 Oella Ave
Baltimore, MD 21228 410-465-4650
Fax: 410-465-4867 info@jwtreuth.com
www.jwtreuth.com
Processor of meat products
President: Vernon L Treuth Jr Jr
Estimated Sales: $28.1 Million
Number Employees: 50-99
Type of Packaging: Consumer, Food Service

6780 **JBS Natural Products**
5 Jacquelyn Lane
Suite A
Dallas, PA 18612-9107 800-565-6207
Fax: 570-255-2501 jbs@naturalquit.com
www.naturalquit.com
Supplier of natural smoking cessation program and other natural products for your health.
Vice President: Bill Schechter

6781 **JBS Packing Company**
P.O.Box 399
Port Arthur, TX 77641 409-982-3216
Fax: 409-982-3549 jimistring@aol.com
Processor of fresh and frozen shrimp
Officer: Trey Pearson
Plant Manager: Jimmy Stringfellow
Estimated Sales: $20-50 Million
Number Employees: 40
Type of Packaging: Consumer, Food Service
Brands:
Lucky Seas
Sea Market

6782 **JC World Foods**
310 Johnson Avenue
Brooklyn, NY 11206-2801 347-386-1130
Fax: 718-628-7400
Canned soups
Estimated Sales: $ 5-9.9 Million
Number Employees: 8

6783 **JC'S Natural Bakery**
1701 Naranca Avenue
El Cajon, CA 92019-1065 619-239-4043
Bakery products
President: Joe Lewis
Estimated Sales: Below $ 5 Million
Number Employees: 3

6784 **JC's Midnite Salsa**
PO Box 89451
Tucson, AZ 85752-9451 520-574-3993
Fax: 520-572-1151 800-817-2572
jc@jcsmidnitesalsa.com
www.jcsmidnitesalsa.com
Salsa
Estimated Sales: $300,000-500,000
Number Employees: 1-4

6785 **JE Bergeron & Sons**
7 Rue St John Baptiste
Bromptonville, QC J0B 1H0
Canada 819-846-2761
Fax: 819-846-6217 800-567-2798
jebergeron@faltec.net www.nuvel.ca
Processor and exporter of shortening and margarine including soya, canola, vegetable, etc
President: Philippe Bergeron
Secretary: Berengere Bergeron
VP: Danielle Bergeron
Number Employees: 20-49
Sq. footage: 30000
Parent Co: Margarine Thibault
Type of Packaging: Consumer, Food Service, Private Label, Bulk
Brands:
BANQUET
BERGERON
CANOLEAN
CHEF GASTON
G BLANCHET
REXPO
SILVER
TRADITION
WONDER

6786 **JEJ Food Company**
7608 Fullerton Road
Springfield, VA 22153 703-455-0155
Fax: 703-451-8917

6787 **JES Foods**
4703 Broadway Ave
Cleveland, OH 44127 216-883-8987
Fax: 216-883-8984 info@jesfoods.com
www.jesfoods.com
Processor of produce including carrots, onions, celery, peppers and melons
President: Elaine R Freed
Estimated Sales: $ 5 - 10 Million
Number Employees: 10-19

6788 **JF Braun & Sons Inc.**
P.O.Box 6061
Elizabeth, NJ 7207 516-997-2200
Fax: 516-997-2478 800-997-7177
steve@jfbny.com www.jfbny.com
Imported dried fruits and nuts
President: Stephen O'Mara
Number Employees: 20-49
Brands:
J.F. Braun

6789 **JF Clarke Corporation**
173 Franklin Ave
Franklin Square, NY 11010-1441 516-328-8333
Fax: 516-328-8346 800-229-7474
jclarke@jfclarke.com www.jfclarke.com
Frozen shrimp and seafood
President: James Clarke
Estimated Sales: $ 5-10 Million
Number Employees: 5-9
Type of Packaging: Food Service
Brands:
Amazonas
Avila
Bee Gee
Fresh Cargo
Yutaka

6790 **JFC International Inc.**
7101 East Slauson Ave
Commerce, CA 90040 323-721-6100
Fax: 323-721-6133 nsugisaw@jfc.com
www.jfc.com
Processor of fortune cookies
Manager: Koichi Inagaki
Marketing: Nori Sugisawa
Estimated Sales: $2.5-5 Million
Number Employees: 10-19
Parent Co: JFC International
Type of Packaging: Consumer, Food Service

6791 **JFG Coffee Co**
3434 Mynatt Ave
Knoxville, TN 37919 865-546-2120
Fax: 865-524-8725
Coffee; coffee beans; peanut butter oil
VP Sales: Ken Christopher

6792 **JJ's Tamales & Barbacoa**
1611 Culebra Rd
San Antonio, TX 78201-5914 210-737-1300
Fax: 210-733-8133
Mexican foods
Manager: Gilbert Aparipio
Manager: M Rodriguez
Estimated Sales: Under $500,000
Number Employees: 1-4

6793 **JK SucraLose Inc**
98a Mayfield Ave
Edison, NJ 8837-3821
Fax: 732-512-0188 jkusa@jksucralose.com
www.jksucralose.com
sweetners, sucralose
President/Owner: Hugh Zhang
VP: Florey Ye
Marketing: Elvis Arce
Sales: Shawn Miller
Public Relations: Lynn Cruzado
Estimated Sales: $25 Million
Number Employees: 219
Number of Brands: 1
Number of Products: 1
Sq. footage: 135000

6794 **JLH European Trading**
1179 Howard Street
San Francisco, CA 94103-3925 415-626-3672
Fax: 415-626-3673
Confectionery, candy novelties, chocolate and non-chocolate candy.
President: Jean-Luc Hoffer
Estimated Sales: Under $500,000
Number Employees: 1-4

6795 **JM All Purpose Seasoning**
PO Box 22162
Lincoln, NE 68542-2162 402-421-8326
whollow@navix.net
www.jmaps.com
Processor of seasonings herbs and spices for fish, chicken and beef
Owner: James Meeks
Number Employees: 1-4

6796 **JM Swank Company**
395 Herky St
North Liberty, IA 52317
Fax: 402-516-0585 800-593-6375
bill.burgeson@conagrafoods.com
www.jmswank.com
Food ingredients for the dairy, beverage, meat, bakery, snack, confection, ethnic and prepared food industries
Vice President: James Strubell
Sales: Ron Pardekooper
Number Employees: 155
Parent Co: ConAgra

6797 **JMAC Trading, Inc.**
369 Van Ness Way
Suite 707
Torrance, CA 90501 310-781-9734
Fax: 310-212-6768 877-566-4569
mizuhashi@crystalnoodle.com
www.crystalnoodle.com
instant noodle soup
President/CEO: Masaki Mizuhashi

6798 **JMH International**
394 Williamstowne
Suite C
Delafield, WI 53018-2322 262-646-7460
Fax: 435-645-9109 888-741-4564
info@jmhpremium.com www.jmhpremium.com
Processor of premium flavor base; soup, sauce, flavor bases
President: Kirk Mellecker
Sales Director: Michael Norman
Estimated Sales: $500,000-$1 Million
Number Employees: 1-4
Type of Packaging: Consumer, Food Service, Bulk
Brands:
Jmh Premium

6799 **JMP Bakery Company**
P.O.Box 120307
Brooklyn, NY 11212-0307 718-272-5400
Fax: 718-272-5427
Processor of baked goods including Italian breads, egg twists, Kaiser breads, bagels, etc
President: Chris Palagonia
Plant Manager: Richard Palagonia
Estimated Sales: $12 Million
Number Employees: 250-499
Sq. footage: 100000
Brands:
Italian Bread Products
Kaiser Rolls
Palagonia
Stuhmer's

6800 **JMS Specialty Foods**
126 Jefferson St
Ripon, WI 54971 920-745-6100
Fax: 920-745-6150 800-535-5437
Processor of bottled fruit, peanut butter, barbacue and meat sauces, dessert toppings, maple syrup, jams, jellies, preserves and condiments
Marketing Manager: Carrie Hogan
General Manager: Ken Miller
Plant Manager: Tim Carr
Number Employees: 100-249
Sq. footage: 120000
Parent Co: J.M. Smucker Company
Type of Packaging: Consumer, Food Service, Private Label

6801 **JR Carlson Laboratories**
15 W College Dr
Arlington Hts, IL 60004-1985 847-255-1600
Fax: 847-255-1605 888-234-5656
carlson@carlsonlabs.com www.carlsonlabs.com
Processor, importer and exporter of vitamins, minerals, food supplements, omega three fish oil capsules, liquid cod liver oil, amino acids and anti-oxidant formulas
President/CEO: J Carlson
CFO: Trish Lange
VP: Susan Carlson
R&D: Carilyn Anderson
Quality Control: Dolores Rokos
Marketing: Kirsten Carlson
Sales: Vicki Accardi
Public Relations: Toni Edwards
VP Pharmaceuticals: S Carlson
Production: Robert Meyer
Plant Manager: Robert Meyer
Purchasing Director: Lindy Eck
Estimated Sales: $ 50 - 100 Million
Number Employees: 100-249
Number of Brands: 40
Number of Products: 275
Sq. footage: 40000
Type of Packaging: Consumer, Private Label
Brands:
Aces
Carlson
E-Gems
Key-E
Niacin-Time
Super-1-Daily

6802 **JR Laboratories**
Smith Hill Rd
Honesdale, PA 18431 570-253-5826
www.jrlaboratories.com/
Processor of Chinese herbal products and fluids
President: Jainie Minogue
Estimated Sales: $300,000-500,000
Number Employees: 1-4

6803 **JR Wood/Big Valley**
P.O.Box 545
Atwater, CA 95301-0545 209-358-5643
Fax: 209-358-6351
Processor and exporter of frozen fruits including apricots, berries, peaches, importer of pineapples, mangos, blackberries, raspberries and melons
Chairman: Ann Wood
President/CEO: Grey Costley
CFO: Tim Nelson
VP: Jerry Widick
VP, Marketing: Denise Rohm
VP, Sales: Bob Barnhouse
Estimated Sales: $300,000-500,000
Number Employees: 1-4
Sq. footage: 1000000
Type of Packaging: Consumer, Food Service, Private Label, Bulk
Brands:
Big Valley
Flavorland

6804 **(HQ)JRL**
2321 Industrial Way
Vineland, NJ 08360 856-690-9000
Fax: 856-690-0700 info@luccacoldstorage.com
www.luccacoldstorage.com
Buy and sell blueberries and peaches fresh pack
President: Joseph Lucca
Estimated Sales: Below $ 5 Million
Number Employees: 4

6805 **JSL Foods**
3550 Pasadena Ave
Los Angeles, CA 90031-1946 323-223-2484
Fax: 323-223-9882 800-745-3236
wnielsen@jslfoods.com www.jslfoods.com
Processor of chilled and frozen pre-cooked noodles; also, nutritional/power bars and cookies
President: Tieji Kawana
EVP: Koji Kawana
CFO: Jerry Chung
Vice President: Terri Kishimoto
R & D: Swee Seet
Quality Control: Rhaun Turner
Estimated Sales: $ 100-500 Million
Number Employees: 180
Sq. footage: 100000
Type of Packaging: Food Service, Private Label, Bulk
Brands:
Amber Farms
Fortune
Stir fryNoodels

6806 **JTM Food Group**
200 Sales Ave
Harrison, OH 45030 513-367-4900
Fax: 513-367-1132 800-626-2308
comments@jtmfoodgroup.com
www.jtmfoodgroup.com
Processor of beef patties, buns, bread sticks, dinner rolls, French bread pizza, spaghetti and meatballs, chili, taco and barbecue sauce
President: Anthony Maas
CFO: Bill Meier
VP Sales: Jack Maas
VP Plant Operations: Joseph Maas
Estimated Sales: 100 Million
Number Employees: 250-499
Sq. footage: 120000
Type of Packaging: Consumer, Food Service
Brands:
CHEF VITO PASTA MEALS
Cincy Style
J.T.M. Food Group
Texas Jack's Tex-Mex
VITO'S BAKERY

6807 **Ja-Ca Seafood Products**
3 Center Plaza
Boston, MA 02108-2003 978-281-8848
Fax: 978-281-2247
Seafood
President: Kenichi Kawauchi

6808 **Jack & Jill Ice Cream Company**
101 Commerce Dr
Moorestown, NJ 08057-4212 856-813-2300
Fax: 856-813-2303 sv@jackjillicecream.com
www.jackjillicecream.com
Processor and exporter of ice cream and frozen yogurt; wholesaler/distributor of cakes and fancy desserts
President: Jay Schwartz
Marketing Director: Shawn Brady
VP Sales: John Corral
General Manager: Ken Schwartz
Number Employees: 500-999
Type of Packaging: Consumer, Food Service

6809 **Jack Brown Produce**
8035 Fruit Ridge Ave NW
Sparta, MI 49345 616-887-9568
Fax: 616-887-9765 800-348-0834
john@jackbrownproduce.com
www.jackbrownproduce.com

Processor and exporter of produce
President: John Schaefer Jr
Chairman/VP: Philip Succop
VP Sales: Mitch Brinks
Operations Manager: Pat Chase
Estimated Sales: $6.5 Million
Number Employees: 50
Sq. footage: 500000
Type of Packaging: Consumer, Food Service, Private Label, Bulk
Brands:
Apple Ridge
Peach Ridge

6810 **Jack Daniel's Distillery**
280 Lynchburg Hwy
Lynchburg, TN 37352 931-759-4221
Fax: 931-327-1551 www.jackdaniels.com
Processor and exporter of whiskey
President: W L Lyons Brown
Manager-Accounting: James Ramsey
Manager (Lynchburg Promotions): Roger Brashears
VP/Director Operations: William Roof
Estimated Sales: J
Number Employees: 300
Parent Co: Brown-Forman Corporation
Type of Packaging: Consumer
Brands:
JACK DANIEL'S

6811 **Jack Link Snack Foods**
P.O.Box 397
Minong, WI 54859-0397 715-466-2234
Fax: 715-466-5151 www.linksnacks.com
Beef products
CEO: Jack Link
President: Troy Link
CFO: John Hermeier
Estimated Sales: $ 50-100 Million
Number Employees: 100-249
Brands:
Jack Link's Beef Jerky

6812 **Jack Miller's Food Products**
646 Jack Miller Rd
Ville Platte, LA 70586 337-363-1541
Fax: 337-363-4784 800-646-1541
jackmiller@jackmillers.com
www.jackmillers.com
Cajun barbecue and cocktail sauces
President/CEO: Kermit Miller
Estimated Sales: Below $ 5 Million
Number Employees: 5-9
Sq. footage: 7000
Type of Packaging: Food Service, Bulk
Brands:
Jack Miller

6813 **Jack's Bean Company**
402 N Interocean Ave
Holyoke, CO 80734 970-854-3656
Fax: 970-854-3707 800-274-3702
Processor of beans and popcorn
General Manager: Steve Brown
Human Resources Manager: Henry Moore
Manufacturing/Operations Director: Rick Daniel
Estimated Sales: $10.3 Million
Number Employees: 20
Sq. footage: 55000
Parent Co: ConAgra Foods
Type of Packaging: Consumer, Food Service, Private Label, Bulk

6814 **Jack's Lobsters**
Limited Oyster Pond
Musquodoboit Harbor, NS B0J 1P0
Canada 902-889-2771
Fax: 902-889-2720
Processor and exporter of fresh and frozen lobsters
President: Joseph Goyetche
Type of Packaging: Consumer, Food Service

6815 **Jack's Wholesale Meat Company**
719 S Pearl St
Trenton, TX 75490-3111 903-989-2293
Processor of beef and pork
President: Ricky Glasscock
Estimated Sales: $ 3 - 5 Million
Number Employees: 5-9
Type of Packaging: Consumer

6816 **Jackson Brothers Food Locker**
121 S Avenue H
Post, TX 79356-3330 806-495-3245
Fax: 806-495-3741
Processor of beef, pork and deer meat; slaughtering services also available
Owner: Joe Rodriguez
Partner: Anna Wilson
Estimated Sales: $ 3 - 5 Million
Number Employees: 5-9
Type of Packaging: Consumer

6817 **Jackson Frozen Food Center**
13 W 6th Ave
Hutchinson, KS 67501 620-662-4465
Manufacturer of meat products
Owner: Michael Jackson
Estimated Sales: $10-20 Million
Number Employees: 5-9
Type of Packaging: Consumer, Bulk

6818 **Jackson Ice Cream Company**
400 Yuma St
Denver, CO 80204 303-534-2454
Fax: 303-534-7648
Processor of frozen dairy desserts, low calorie ice cream and frozen yogurt
Plant Manager: M Day
Number Employees: 100-249
Parent Co: Dillon Corporation
Type of Packaging: Consumer, Food Service, Private Label
Other Locations:
Jackson Ice Cream Co.
Hutchinson KS

6819 **Jackson Milk & Ice CreamCompany**
2600 E 4th Avenue
Hutchinson, KS 67501-1902 620-663-1244
Processor of dairy products including milk, ice cream and novelties; also, orange juice and bottled water
Number Employees: 20-49
Parent Co: Kroger Company
Type of Packaging: Consumer, Food Service, Private Label, Bulk

6820 **Jackson Valley Vineyards**
4851 Buena Vista Road
Ione, CA 95640-9625 209-274-4721
Wines
Vineyard Manager: John Bree
Estimated Sales: $ 100-250 Million
Number Employees: 20

6821 **Jacob & Sons Wholesale Meats**
P.O.Box 217
Martins Ferry, OH 43935-0217 740-633-3091
Fax: 740-633-3106 www.jacobandsonsmeat.com
Manufacturer of fresh and frozen beef, pork and poultry
Owner: Michael Jacob
Estimated Sales: $2.5 Million
Number Employees: 10-19
Type of Packaging: Consumer, Food Service, Bulk

6822 **Jacob & Sons Wholesale Meats**
306 Center St
Martins Ferry, OH 43935-1793 740-633-3091
Fax: 740-633-3106 chops070@aol.com
www.jacobandsonsmeat.com
Wholesale meats
President: Michael Jacob
Estimated Sales: $1.60 Million
Number Employees: 12

6823 **Jacobs Meats**
8127 N State Route 66
Defiance, OH 43512-6724 419-782-7831
Fax: 419-782-8128 www.jacobsmeats.com
Manufacturer of beef, pork and poultry
President: Paul Stork
Estimated Sales: $1-3 Million
Number Employees: 10-19
Type of Packaging: Consumer, Food Service, Private Label, Bulk

6824 **Jacobs, Malcolm, & Burtt**
2001 Jerrold Ave
San Francisco, CA 94124 415-285-0400
Fax: 415-285-2056
Processor of produce including asparagus and melons
Owner: Leo Rolandeli
Estimated Sales: $54486391
Number Employees: 20-49
Type of Packaging: Consumer, Food Service, Bulk

6825 **Jacobsmuhlen's Meats**
1415 NW Susbauer Rd
Cornelius, OR 97113 503-359-0479
Fax: 503-359-0479 larry@jacobsmuhlens.com
www.jacobsmuhlens.com
Manufacturer of pork and beef
Owner: Harry Jacobsmuhlen
Estimated Sales: $15 Million
Number Employees: 5-9
Type of Packaging: Consumer

6826 **Jacques' Bakery**
27122b Paseo Espada
San Juan Capistrano, CA 92675-5706949-496-5322
Fax: 949-496-2941
Bakery products

6827 **Jaeger Bakery**
918 W Somers St
Milwaukee, WI 53205 414-263-1700
Cookies
COO: William Metzler
Sales Manager: Randy Johnson
Estimated Sales: $ 100-500 Million
Number Employees: 250-499

6828 **Jager Foods**
613 Birch St S
Sauk Centre, MN 56378-1534 320-491-7249
Fax: 320-732-4047 800-358-7251
Dried soup mixes
President: Pete Jager
Owner: Pete Jager
Number Employees: 2
Brands:
Jager
Shitake Mushroom Soup Mixes (4)

6829 **Jaguar Yerba Company**
P.O.Box 1192
Ashland, OR 97520-0040 541-482-7745
Fax: 541-482-6780 800-839-0775
ecoteas@ecoteas.com www.yerbamate.com
Yerba mate teas
Owner: Stefan Schachter
Co-Founder: Brendan Girardi
Partner: Joe Chermesino
Estimated Sales: $ 3 - 5 Million
Number Employees: 1-4

6830 **Jagulana Herbal Products**
P.O.Box 45
Badger, CA 93603 559-337-2188
Fax: 559-337-2354 www.gynostemma.com
Dedicated to researching, developing and marketing jiaogulan and jiaogulan-based herbal products of the highest quality
President: Chris Gleen
Research: Michael Blumert
Technical Assistant: Chris Glenn
Estimated Sales: $ 1 - 3 Million
Number Employees: 1-4

6831 **Jain Ltd**
1819 Walcutt Road
Suite I
Columbus, OH 43228 614-850-9400
Fax: 614-850-8600
Producer of dehydrated onion and vegetables, fruit purees, puree concentrates and clarified juices
President: Anil Jain
CEO: Narinder Gupta
Executive Vice President: Murali Ramanathan
Number Employees: 81

6832 **Jaindl's Turkey Farms**
3150 Coffeetown Rd
Orefield, PA 18069 610-395-3333
Fax: 610-395-8608 800-475-6654
jaindl2@aol.com www.jaindl.com
Processor of turkey
Owner/President: David Jaindl
Controller: Pat Seng
Sales/Marketing: Alice Brown
General Manager: David Jaindl

Estimated Sales: $ 20 - 50 Million
Number Employees: 110
Sq. footage: 6000
Type of Packaging: Consumer, Food Service, Private Label, Bulk
Brands:
Grand Champion

6833 **Jakeman's Maple ProductsAuvergne Farms Limited**
454414 Trillium Line
Beachville, ON N0J 1A0
Canada 519-539-1366
Fax: 519-421-2469 800-382-9795
bob@themaplestore.com
www.themaplestore.com
Processor and exporter of maple syrup, sugar, candy and yogurt, coffee, tea and cookies
President: Robert Jakeman
CFO: Jane Henderson
Quality Control: Melissa Martin
Sales: Mary Jakeman
Production: Heather Crane
Estimated Sales: $1 Million
Number Employees: 11
Number of Brands: 1
Number of Products: 78
Sq. footage: 6620
Parent Co: Auvergne Farms
Type of Packaging: Consumer, Food Service, Private Label, Bulk

6834 **Jakes Brothers Country Meats**
6089 Clarksville Pike
Joelton, TN 37080 615-876-2911
Cured meats
Owner: Johny Jakes
Estimated Sales: $ 1-2.5 Million
Number Employees: 1-4

6835 **Jalapeno Foods Company**
1215 W Imperial Highway
Suite 205
Brea, CA 92821-3735 714-521-9900
Fax: 714-521-9940 800-863-9198
ralbanol@aol.com/snavares@aol.com
http://www.aol.com/snavares
Condiments, ethnic foods
President: Arturo Pimiento
Sales Manager: Sabrina Navares
Estimated Sales: $ 5-10 Million
Number Employees: 20
Type of Packaging: Private Label
Brands:
Mi Mexico

6836 **(HQ)Jalapeno Foods Company**
1450 Lake Robbins Drive
Suite 350
The Woodlands, TX 77380-3252 281-363-4585
Fax: 281-364-8452 800-896-2318
www.jalapenofoods.com
Processor, importer, exporter and packager of red and green Mexican salsas, chipotle and chile peppers, shelf-stable guacamole and jalapenos including whole, nacho, sliced and diced
CEO: Carlos Gosselin
Vice President: Sue Doolittle
Estimated Sales: $ 5 - 10 Million
Number Employees: 5-9
Sq. footage: 60000
Type of Packaging: Consumer, Food Service, Private Label, Bulk
Brands:
Jake & Amos
Mi Mexico

6837 **Jamae Natural Foods**
PO Box 481096
5958 W Pico Blvd
Los Angeles, CA 90035-2658 323-937-3670
Fax: 323-937-0849 800-343-0052
crystal@jamae.com www.jamae.com
Cookies, soy nut crunch bars
President: Crystal You
Estimated Sales: $300,000
Number Employees: 3
Type of Packaging: Private Label
Brands:
Health Cookie
Soynut Crunch Bar
Soynuts

6838 **Jamaica John**
9140 Belden Ave
Franklin Park, IL 60131-3506 847-451-1730
Fax: 847-451-1590 sales@jamaicajohn.com
www.jamaicajohn.com
Manufacture, package and distribute liquid and sauce food products
President: John Capozzoli
Quality Control: John Capozzoli Jr
Estimated Sales: $ 5-10 Million
Number Employees: 10-19

6839 **Jamaican Gourmet CoffeeCompany**
250 South 18th st
Philadelphia, PA 19129
800-261-2859
sales@coffeeforless.com
www.jamaicancoffeeco.com
Coffee, tea
President: Lloyd Parchment
Estimated Sales: Below $ 5 Million
Number Employees: 20
Sq. footage: 13800

6840 **James Candy Company**
1519 Boardwalk
Atlantic City, NJ 08401-7012 609-344-1519
Fax: 609-344-0246 800-938-2339
www.seashoretaffy.com
Processor of confectionery products including salt-water taffy, lollypops, fudge and macaroons
President: Frank Glaser
EVP Sales/Marketing: Lisa Glaser Whitley
VP Operations: Susan Saraceni
Estimated Sales: $2 Million
Number Employees: 50-99
Type of Packaging: Consumer, Bulk
Brands:
James Chocolate Seal Taffy
James Cream Mints
James Salt Water Taffy
Mumsey

6841 **James Cowan & Sons**
20 Temple St
Worcester, MA 01604 508-753-3259
Processor and wholesaler/distributor of groceries, dairy products, equipment and fixtures, fresh and frozen fish, poultry and meat; serving the food service market
Vice President: Anne Sibson
Comptroller: Debra Ross
Number Employees: 10-19
Sq. footage: 9600
Type of Packaging: Food Service

6842 **James Frasinetti & Sons**
PO Box 292368
7395 Frasinetti Rd
Sacramento, CA 95828-3718 916-383-2444
Fax: 916-383-5825 www.frasinetti.com
Wines
Partner: Howard Frasinetti
Partner: Gary Frasinetti
Estimated Sales: $ 2.5-5 Million
Number Employees: 36

6843 **James J. Derba Company**
206 Commonwealth Avenue
Apt 9
Boston, MA 02116-2558 617-884-6700
Fax: 617-884-6764 800-732-3848
www.prime-steaks.com
Manufacturer of portion control premium steaks, poultry and gourmet food
President: Paul Derba
Estimated Sales: $115 Million
Number Employees: 40
Sq. footage: 20000
Type of Packaging: Food Service

6844 **James L. Mood Fisheries**
130 Falls Point Rd
Lower Woods Harbour, NS B0W 2E0
Canada 902-723-2360
Fax: 902-723-2880 info@moodfisheries.com
www.moodfisheries.com
Processor and exporter of fresh seafood including tuna, lobster, swordfish and groundfish
President: Corey Mood
Vice President: Almond Mood
Manager: Almond Mood

Estimated Sales: $674,000
Number Employees: 10
Type of Packaging: Consumer, Food Service, Private Label, Bulk

6845 **James Skinner Company**
4657 G St
Omaha, NE 68117-1410 402-734-1672
Fax: 402-734-0516 800-358-7428
www.skinnerbaking.com
Processor and exporter of frozen baked goods including danish, pastries, muffins, cinnamon rolls and coffee cakes
President: James Skinner
VP Marketing: Doug Dinnin
VP Sales: Doug Dinnin
VP Operations: Audie Keaton
Plant Manager: Tom Urzendowski
Estimated Sales: $7.6 Million
Number Employees: 100-249
Sq. footage: 75000
Type of Packaging: Consumer, Food Service, Private Label, Bulk
Brands:
Skinner Bakery

6846 **Jamieson Laboratories**
4025 Rhodes Dr
Windosr, ON N8W 5B5
Canada 519-974-8482
Fax: 519-974-4742 www.jamiesonvitamins.com
Manufacturer, importer and exporter of kefir, yogurt, cod liver oil, vitamins, mineral supplements, water purifying systems and filters
President/Ceo: Vic Neufeld
Owner: Eric Margolis
Estimated Sales: $42 Million
Number Employees: 450
Sq. footage: 40000
Parent Co: Jamieson Pharmacal
Type of Packaging: Consumer
Brands:
Super Vita Vim

6847 **Janca's Jojoba Oil & Seed Company**
456 E Juanita Avenue
Suite 7
Mesa, AZ 85204-6538 480-497-9494
Fax: 480-629-5870 custsvc@jancas.com
www.jancas.com
Processor and exporter of vegetable oils and waxes, rice bran oil and jojoba oil, butter, waxes and herbs; also, essential oils and fragrances
President: Tom Janca
Executive Vice President: David Janca
VP Marketing: David Murphy
Sales Manager: Jennifer Hathaway
Sales Manager: Matt Drapcho
Production Manager: Mike Green
Purchasing Manager: Sam Flaherty
Estimated Sales: $ 1 - 3 Million
Number Employees: 1-4
Sq. footage: 2000
Type of Packaging: Private Label, Bulk
Brands:
Janca's

6848 **Jane Specialty Foods**
PO Box 19057
Green Bay, WI 54307-9057 920-497-7131
Fax: 920-497-4604 800-558-4700
Pickles and pickle relish
Plant Manager: Dave Schindler
Estimated Sales: Under $500,000
Number Employees: 250-499
Type of Packaging: Private Label

6849 **Janes Family Foods**
3340 Orlando Drive
Mississauga, ON L4V 1C7
Canada 905-673-7145
Fax: 905-677-0607 800-565-2637
Processor of frozen breaded and battered seafood, poultry, vegetable and cheese products
Plant Manager: Pat Palmer
Estimated Sales: $19 Million
Number Employees: 100
Sq. footage: 100000
Type of Packaging: Consumer, Food Service, Private Label, Bulk
Brands:
Crisp & Delicious
Golden Gate

J&J Gourmet
Janes Family Favourites

6850 **Janet's Own Home Sweet Home**
1101 Dalton Ln
Austin, TX 78742 512-385-4708
President: Janet Morgan
Estimated Sales: Under $500,000
Number Employees: 1-4

6851 **Janowski's Hamburgers**
15 S Long Beach Rd
Rockville Centre, NY 11570 516-764-9591
Fax: 516-764-1908
www.janowskishamburgers.com
Butcher quality meats and Weber products
Owner: Bill Vogelsberg
Estimated Sales: $ 10-20 Million
Number Employees: 5-9

6852 **Jarchem Industries**
414 Wilson Ave
Newark, NJ 7105 973-578-4560
Fax: 973-344-5743 info@jarchem.com
www.jarchem.com
Processor, importer and exporter of calcium chloride, acetic acid, sodium diacetate and sodium benzoate
CEO: Arnold Stern
Mngr.: Howard Honing
Estimated Sales: $ .5 - 1 million
Number Employees: 1-4

6853 **Jardine Foods**
1 Chisholm Trl
Buda, TX 78610 512-295-4600
Fax: 512-295-3020 800-544-1880
bwillcox@jardinefoods.com
www.jardinefoods.com
Ketchup, chilies, sauces, dips, salsa, BBQ sauce, jelly
Manager: Scott Bolding
VP Sales/Mearketing: Garth Gardner
VP of Operations: Scott Jackson
Director: Craig Lieberman
Director: Brad Wallace
Estimated Sales: $ 5-10 Million
Number Employees: 100-249
Number of Brands: 20
Number of Products: 200
Type of Packaging: Consumer, Food Service, Private Label, Bulk
Brands:
D.J. JARDINE

6854 **Jardine Organic Ranch Co**
910 Nacimiento Lake Dr
Paso Robles, CA 93446-8713 805-238-2365
Fax: 805-239-4334 866-833-5050
order@jardineranch.com www.jardineranch.com
Processor and exporter; gift baskets of nuts
Owner: Bill Jardine
Owner: Mary Jardine
Manager: Duane Jardine
Estimated Sales: Less than $500,000
Number Employees: 1-4
Type of Packaging: Consumer, Food Service, Bulk

6855 **Jarrow Industries**
12246 Hawkins St
Santa Fe Springs, CA 90670 562-906-1919
Fax: 562-906-1979 info@jiimfg.com
www.jiimfg.com
Manufacturing and packaging of the highest quality and clean vitamins and supplements for their customers.
President/CEO: Silva Hari
Estimated Sales: $ 50 - 100 Million
Number Employees: 20-49

6856 **Jasmine & Bread**
4478 Howe Hill Rd
South Royalton, VT 05068 802-763-7115
Fax: 802-763-7115
Processor of condiments
Owner: Sherrie Maurer
Estimated Sales: $500,000-$1 Million
Number Employees: 1-4
Type of Packaging: Private Label, Bulk

6857 **Jasmine Vineyards**
33319 Pond Road
Delano, CA 93215 661-792-2141
Fax: 661-792-6365 jvine@jasminevineyards.com
www.jasminevineyards.com
Processor, packer and exporter of grapes
President/CFO: George Zaninovich
Chairman/CEO: Martin Zaninovich
VP: Jon Zaninovich
Estimated Sales: $35 Million
Number Employees: 20
Sq. footage: 2500
Type of Packaging: Consumer, Food Service, Bulk
Brands:
HAVREN
JASVINE
MEV
VINMAR

6858 **Jason & Son Specialty Foods**
2590 Mercantile Dr Ste A
Rancho Cordova, CA 95742 916-635-9590
Fax: 916-635-9711 800-810-9093
info@jasonson.com www.jasonson.com
Processor of enrobed, panned and specialty packed confectionery items including trail mixes, nut clusters and raisins; also, sugar-free products available
President: William Jason
VP: Margaret Jason
General Manager: Richard Antti
Estimated Sales: $1255895
Number Employees: 15
Type of Packaging: Consumer, Food Service, Private Label, Bulk
Brands:
Jason & Son

6859 **Jason Pharmaceuticals**
11445 Cronhill Dr
Owings Mills, MD 21117 410-581-2080
Fax: 410-581-8070 800-638-7867
www.medibix.com
Dietetic products
President: John Hereford
CEO: William Vitale
Managing Director: William Vitale
Number Employees: 100-249
Brands:
Jason Pharmaceuticals

6860 **Jasper Products LLC**
3877 E 27th St
Joplin, MO 64804 417-206-2099
Fax: 417-206-3434 877-769-7367
info@jasperproducts.com
www.jasperproducts.com
Soy products
President: Ken Haubein
Estimated Sales: $ 50 - 100 Million
Number Employees: 250-499

6861 **Jasper Wyman & Son**
P.O.Box 100
Milbridge, ME 04658 207-546-3381
Fax: 207-546-2074 800-341-1758
jwyman@wymans.com www.wymans.com
Processor of frozen, canned, dried and fresh wild blueberries, raspberries and cranberries; exporter of IQF wild blueberries
President: Edward Flanagan
Director International Sales: J Kim Higgins
Estimated Sales: $ 1 - 3 Million
Number Employees: 5-9

6862 **Jasper Wyman & Son Canada**
41 Mcewen Road
Morell, PE C0A 1S0
Canada 902-961-5610
Fax: 902-961-5610
General Manger: Reg Trainor

6863 **Java Cabana**
P.O.Box 520845
Miami, FL 33152-0845 305-592-7302
Fax: 305-592-9471 jc@javacabana.com
www.javacabana.com
Produces a variety of coffee products - whole beans and ground in addition to instant; iced tea mixes; decaf; expresso; cappucciono; demitasse sets; expresso machines.
Owner: Jose Souto
Marketing Director: Beatriz Vescovacci
Estimated Sales: $2.5-5 Million
Number Employees: 20-49

Type of Packaging: Food Service, Private Label

6864 **Java Jungle**
208 W Main Street
Visalia, CA 93291-6265 559-732-5282
Fax: 559-732-5282
Coffee
President: Cruz Ann Borges
Estimated Sales: $410,000
Number Employees: 10

6865 **Java Sun Coffee Roasters**
35 Atlantic Ave
Marblehead, MA 01945 781-631-7788
Coffee
Owner: Cheryl Burka
Estimated Sales: $500,000-$1 Million
Number Employees: 10-19

6866 **Java-Gourmet/Keuka LakeCoffee Roaster**
2792 Route 54A
Penn Yan, NY 14527 315-536-7843
888-478-2739
susan@java-gourmet.com
www.java-gourmet.com
coffee, rubs, sauces and marinades, a brine mix, a dessert topper, a finishing salt, and a chocolate and espresso bean candy.
President/Owner: Susan Atkisson

6867 **Javalution Coffee Company**
2485 E Sunrise Blvd Ste 201a
Fort Lauderdale, FL 33304 954-568-1747
Fax: 954-568-0854 877-528-2348
customerservice@javalution.com
www.javalution.com/index.php
Producer of Latin American gourmet arabica blend coffee products including diet plus; energy plus; gourmet diet plus, and single serve gourmet coffee.
President: Scott Pumper
CEO: Tony Sanzari
Chief Science Officer: Jose Antonio
Type of Packaging: Food Service

6868 **Jaxsons Ice Cream**
130 SW 1st Ave
Dania, FL 33004 954-922-7650
Fax: 954-922-8293 jaxsons@bellsouth.net
www.jaxsonsicecream.com
Ice cream, frozen desserts
Owner: Monroe Udell
Estimated Sales: $ 1-2.5 Million
Number Employees: 20-49
Brands:
Jaxsons

6869 **Jay & Boots Meats**
6458 MCFALL LANE
Knoxville, TN 37918 423-922-3213
Fax: 865-922-8095
Meat
President: Jay Willard
Vice President: Shannon Willard
Operations Manager: Nancy Anderson
Brands:
Jay & Boots Meats

6870 **Jay Poultry Corporation**
1010 Haddonfield Berlin # 402
Voorhees, NJ 08043-3514 856-435-0900
Fax: 856-435-3019 info@oakvalleyfarms.com
www.oakvalleyfarms.com
Poultry
President: Leo Rubin
Co-Owner: Joseph Milgrim
Estimated Sales: $ 5-10 Million
Number Employees: 5 to 9
Brands:
Oak Valley Farms

6871 **Jay Shah Foods**
1121 Meyerside Drive
Mississauga, ON L5T 1J6
Canada 905-696-0172
Fax: 905-696-0174
Processor of East Indian specialty snack foods and chutneys
President: Jayant Shah
Sales/Marketing Manager: Jay Shah
Purchasing Manager: Shushi Shah
Estimated Sales: $1 Million
Number Employees: 6
Sq. footage: 10000

6872 **Jay's Foods**
825 E 99th Street
Chicago, IL 60628-1590 773-731-8400
Fax: 773-933-2100 800-621-6152
www.jayfoods.com
Potato chips, prok rinds, pretzels, potato sticks, corn chips
President/CEO: Joe Shanklind
President: Scott Shipman
CFO: William Luegers Jr
VP Sales/Marketing: John Plys
Estimated Sales: $78 Million
Number Employees: 850
Parent Co: Snyder's od Hanover
Type of Packaging: Consumer

6873 **Jayone Foods, Inc/G. East Co., LTD**
7212 Alondra Boulevard
Paramount, CA 90723 562-633-7400
Fax: 562-633-7474 khchoi21@jayone.com
www.jayone.com
Gluten-free, sugar-free, tea, juice/cider, full-line condiments, yogurt, ethnic sauces (soy,curry,etc.), other snacks.
Marketing: Seung Hoon Lee

6874 **Jazz Fine Foods**
5065 Ontario E Street
Montreal, QC H1V 3V2
Canada 514-255-0110
Fax: 514-259-1788 laurent.durot@videotrona.ca

6875 **Jazzie J. Enterprises**
PO Box 2748
Grapevine, TX 76099-2748 817-481-3421
Fax: 817-421-5383
President: Janet Williams

6876 **(HQ)Jbs Packerland Inc**
1330 Lime Kiln Rd
Green Bay, WI 54311-6044
Fax: 920-468-7140 www.packerland.com
Meat packing and non-local trucking.
President & CEO: Richard V Vesta
CFO: Craig Liegel
Estimated Sales: $290 Million
Number Employees: 1000
Type of Packaging: Food Service, Bulk
Other Locations:
Packerland-Green Bay
Green Bay WI
Packerland-Plainwell
Plainwell MI
Moyer Packing Company
Souderton PA
Sun Land Beef Company
Tolleson AZ
Brands:
Grand River Ranch
Showcase Supreme

6877 **Jcw Tawes & Son**
206 S 10th St
Crisfield, MD 21817 410-968-1288
Fax: 410-968-1289
Processor of seafood including fresh and pasteurized blue crabs and hard shell crabs
Manager: Norman Tyler
Estimated Sales: $ 5 - 10 Million
Number Employees: 20-49
Type of Packaging: Consumer, Food Service, Private Label

6878 **Jecky's Best**
26450 Summit Cir
Santa Clarita, CA 91350-2991 661-259-1313
Fax: 661-259-5855 888-532-5972
info@jabfoods.com www.jabfoods.com
Frozen dough and unbaked goods
President: Jecky Bicer
VP: Eitay Bicer
VP: Areila Bicer
Estimated Sales: $ 5-10 Million
Number Employees: 20-49
Type of Packaging: Private Label
Brands:
Jecky's Best

6879 **Jed's Maple Products**
475 Carter Road
Westfield, VT 05874-9719 802-744-2095
Fax: 802-744-2095 866-478-7388
wheeler@jedsample.com www.jedsample.com
Maple syrup, candy, cream, lollipops salad dressings, and sauces
Co-Owner: Stephen Wheeler
Co-Owner: Amy Wheeler

6880 **Jedwards International**
39 Broad St
Quincy, MA 02169-4689 617-472-9300
Fax: 617-472-9359 info@jedwardsinc.com
www.codliveroil.com
Jedwards International, Inc. is a supplier of Specialty oils to the Food, Dietary Supplement, and Cosmetic industries in North America. Jedwards International, Inc. is a leading supplier of the omega-3 fatty acids: EPA and DHA, thepurest Cod Liver Oil and the finest GLA and omega-3 rich Seed oils.
President: Christos Iorio
Estimated Sales: $1,200,000
Number Employees: 5-9

6881 **Jefferson Packing Company**
765 Marlene Drive
Gretna, LA 70056-7639 504-366-4451
Fax: 504-366-9382
President: William Marciante

6882 **Jefferson Vineyards**
1353 Thomas Jefferson Pkwy
Charlottesville, VA 22902 434-977-3042
Fax: 434-977-5459 800-272-3042
info@jeffersonvineyards.com
www.jeffersonvineyards.com
Wine
Manager: Chad Zakaib
Winemaker/Vineyard Manager: Frantz Ventre
Estimated Sales: $ 5 - 10 Million
Number Employees: 10-19

6883 **Jel-Sert Company**
P.O.Box 261
West Chicago, IL 60186 630-231-7590
Fax: 630-231-3993 800-323-2592
www.jelsert.com
Manufacturer and exporter of powdered drink mixes, juices and novelty frozen ice pops.
Chairman: Charles Wegner IV
CEO: Gary Ricco
CFO: Tony D'Anna
Sales Manager: Vincent Morgan
Estimated Sales: $175 Million
Number Employees: 250-499
Sq. footage: 500000
Type of Packaging: Food Service
Brands:
FLA-VOR-AID
FLA-VOR-ICE
POP-ICE

6884 **Jelks Coffee Roasters**
P.O.Box 8667
Shreveport, LA 71148-8667 318-636-6391
Fax: 318-635-1384 info@jelkscoffee.com
www.jelks-coffee.com
Processor of regular, decaffeinated and flavored coffee including banana hazelnut, chocolate cheesecake, pumpkin spice, vanilla almond, orange creamsicle, victorian caramel, etc
President: Harvey Jelks
Estimated Sales: $ 2.5-5 Million
Number Employees: 5-9
Brands:
Toddy

6885 **(HQ)Jelly Belly Candy Company**
One Jelly Belly Lane
Fairfield, CA 94533 707-428-2800
Fax: 707-428-2863 800-522-3267
specialtysales@jellybelly.com
www.jellybelly.com
Processor and exporter of candy including bagged, cremes, jelly beans, candy corn, gums, jellies, Halloween, Valentine, Christmas, Easter, etc.
CEO: Herman Rowland
Director Of Marketing: John Harrington
Estimated Sales: $100+ Million
Number Employees: 250-499
Number of Brands: 2
Number of Products: 150
Type of Packaging: Consumer, Private Label
Brands:
GOELITZ
JELLY BELLY

6886 **(HQ)Jelly Belly Candy Company**
1 Jelly Belly Lane
Fairfield, CA 94533 707-428-2800
Fax: 707-428-2863 800-522-3267
www.jellybelly.com
The Jelly Belly Candy Co. makes more than 100 mouthwatering candies, including such delights as chocolates, gummies, sour candies, and confections for all seasons.
Chairman/Chief Executive Officer: Herman Rowland Sr
President/Chief Operations Officer: Robert Simpson
Founder of Company: Gustav Goelitz
Vice President Business Development: Ryan Schader
Vice President Plant Operations: Mike Bianco
Estimated Sales: $50-100 Million
Number Employees: 250-499
Type of Packaging: Consumer, Bulk
Brands:
Dutch
Goelitz Confections
Jelly Belly
Pet Rat
Pet Tarantula

6887 **Jemm Wholesale Meat Company**
4649 W Armitage Ave
Chicago, IL 60639-3405 773-523-8161
Fax: 773-523-8890
information@jemmburger.com
www.jemmburger.com
Processor of frozen portion controlled steaks and ground beef items including patties
President: Daniel Goldman
VP: Thomas Nacht
Plant Manager: Dominic Pinto
Estimated Sales: $14,100,000
Number Employees: 20-49
Type of Packaging: Consumer, Food Service
Brands:
Seasoned Delux

6888 **Jenkins Foods**
14245 Birwood St
Detroit, MI 48238 313-834-0800
Fax: 313-834-0443 800-800-3286
sandy@unclerays.com www.unclerays.com
Snack foods
President: Raymond Jenkins
Marketing Director: Dennis BaPra
CFO: Sandra Subotich
CFO: Sandra Jenkins
General Manager: James Coomes
Estimated Sales: $ 20-30 Million
Number Employees: 100-249
Brands:
Unclerays

6889 **Jennie-O Turkey Store**
P.O.Box 778
Willmar, MN 56201 320-235-6080
Fax: 320-231-7100 turkeyinfo@j-ots.com
www.jennie-oturkeystore.com
Processor and exporter of turkey products
President: Michael Tolbert
CEO: Jerry Jerome
CFO: Dwight York
VP Marketing: Bob Tegt
Sales Director: Jime Splinter
Public Relations: Dave Suheke
Operations Manager: Bob Wood
Purchasing Agent: Larry Hammond
Number Employees: 5,000-9,999
Parent Co: Hormel Foods Corporation
Type of Packaging: Consumer, Food Service

6890 **Jenny's Country Kitchen**
438 Main St S
Dover, MN 55929 507-932-3035
Fax: 507-932-4777 800-357-3497
info@jennyscountrykitchen.com
www.jennyscountrykitchen.com
Cocoa and coffee products
President: Jenny Wood
CEO: Dan Wood
VP: Dan Wood
Marketing Manager: Dan Wood
Estimated Sales: Below $ 5 Million
Number Employees: 10
Brands:
Jenny's Country Kitchen

6891 Jenport International Distributors
Suite 107
Coquitlam, BC V3K 6H1
Canada 604-464-9888
Fax: 604-464-8388
Processor, importer and exporter of frozen foods including fruit and seafood; also, polyethylene bags
President: Dato Tan
Estimated Sales: Below $5 Million
Number Employees: 10
Brands:
Deep Cove
Sea Pearl
Sun King
Tuff 'n' Tidy

6892 Jensen Luhr & Sons
P.O.Box 297
Hood River, OR 97031-0065 541-386-3811
Fax: 541-386-4917 info@luhrjensen.com
www.luhrjensen.com
Processor of sausage and brine mixes and seasonings and spices; also, sausage making kits, electric smokers and wood flavor fuels
President: Philip Jensen
Customer Service: Linda Gordon
Estimated Sales: $10-20 Million
Number Employees: 250-499
Sq. footage: 50000

6893 Jensen Meat Company
2525 Birch St
Vista, CA 92081 760-727-6700
Fax: 760-727-8598 gebbley@jensenmeat.com
www.jensenmeat.com
Processor and exporter of ground beef
President: Robert Jensen
VP: Shirley Jenson
General Manager: Ken Duhram
Estimated Sales: $26.9 Million
Number Employees: 100-249
Type of Packaging: Consumer, Food Service, Private Label, Bulk

6894 Jensen Seafood Packing Company
9584 Grand Caillou Rd
Dulac, LA 70353
Fax: 985-563-4858
Fish and seafood
President: Ken Trinh
Estimated Sales: $ 3 - 5 Million
Number Employees: 5-9

6895 Jensen's Old Fashioned Smokehouse
10520 Greenwood Ave N
Seattle, WA 98133-8721 206-364-5569
Fax: 206-364-0880
sales@jensenssmokehouse.com
www.jensenssmokehouse.com
Processor of smoked seafood
President: Michael Jensen
Estimated Sales: Below $ 5 Million
Number Employees: 5-9
Type of Packaging: Consumer, Food Service
Brands:
Wild Keta Salmon
Wild Keta Salmon
Wild Red King Salmon
Wild White King Salmon

6896 Jer's Handmade Chocolates
Po Box 801
Solana Beach, CA 92075 858-792-2287
Fax: 858-792-4196 800-540-7265
info@jers.com www.jers.com
gourmet chocolate peanut butter bars, chocolate covered peanut brittle bites
President/Owner: Jerry Swain

6897 Jer-Mar Foods
PO Box 1114
Windsor, ON N9A 6P8
Canada 519-256-3474
Fax: 519-258-4455
Processor and exporter of fresh and frozen fish including perch, pickerel and whitefish
President: Mark Goldhar
Type of Packaging: Consumer, Food Service, Private Label, Bulk

6898 Jerabek's New Bohemian Coffee House
63 Winifred St W
Saint Paul, MN 55107 651-228-1245
Fax: 651-228-3011 www.jerabeks.com
Baked goods, coffees, collectables
Manager: Russell Sprangler
Estimated Sales: $500,000 appx.
Number Employees: 10-19

6899 Jerbeau Chocolate
1080 Avenida Acaso
Camarillo, CA 93012-8725 805-484-4686
Fax: 805-484-2477 800-755-3723
mary_decker@jerbeau.com www.jerbeau.com
Chocolates
President: Katalin Coburn
Estimated Sales: $ 10-24.9 Million
Number Employees: 33

6900 (HQ)Jeremiah's Pick Coffee Company
1495 Evans Ave
San Francisco, CA 94124 415-206-9900
Fax: 415-206-9542 800-537-3642
office@jeremiahspick.com
www.jeremiahspick.com
Roasted gourmet coffee
President: Jeremiah Pick
Operations Manager: Jay Meltesen
Estimated Sales: Below $ 5 Million
Number Employees: 20-49
Sq. footage: 14000
Type of Packaging: Consumer, Food Service, Private Label, Bulk
Brands:
Cafe Pick
Chocatal
Jeremiah's Pick

6901 Jerrell Packaging
802 Labarge Dr
Bessemer, AL 35022-8320 205-426-8930
Fax: 205-426-8989 john@jerrellpackaging.com
www.jerrellpackaging.com
Popcorn
President: John Lyon
Estimated Sales: Below $ 5 Million
Number Employees: 10-19

6902 Jerry's Nut House
2101 Humboldt St
Denver, CO 80205-5327 303-861-2262
Fax: 303-861-1214 888-214-0747
Products include raw, roasted and salted inshell; raw redskins, raw blanched, roasted snack peanuts, honey coated/roasted, granules, hot & spicy seasoned; chocolate covered, peanut bars/squares.
President: Claude Julia
Vice President: Wendy Julia
General Manager: Jim Ohrt
Estimated Sales: $2600000
Number Employees: 10-19
Sq. footage: 20000
Type of Packaging: Consumer, Food Service, Private Label, Bulk
Brands:
Jerry's
Jerry's Caramel Corn
Jerry's Cheese Corn
Jerry's Popcorn
Jerry's Snack Packs

6903 Jersey Fruit CooperativeAssociation
800 Ellis Mill Rd # B
Glassboro, NJ 08028-0885 856-863-9100
Fax: 856-863-9490 sales@jerseyfruit.com
www.jerseyfruit.com
Bluberries, peaches, nectarines, and cranberries.
President: Louis Deeugenio
Director of Sales: Francisco Allende
Estimated Sales: $ 10-20 Million
Number Employees: 20-49
Type of Packaging: Food Service

6904 Jersey Juice
186 Stanton Mountain Road
Lebanon, NJ 08833-3103 609-406-0500
Processor of fruit juice concentrates
Manager: Chuck Gandle
VP Sales: Chuck Gandle
VP Operations: David Montes
Number Employees: 20-49
Sq. footage: 24000
Type of Packaging: Food Service, Private Label, Bulk

6905 Jersey Pride
PO Box 10796
211 Livingston Ave
New Brunswick, NJ 08901-2931 732-214-2965
Fax: 406-585-0035
President: Laura Pople
Estimated Sales: $500,000-$1 Million
Number Employees: 2

6906 Jerusalem House
2425 W 18th Ave
Eugene, OR 97402 541-485-1012
Fax: 541-687-6853
Mideastern natural refrigerated foods: hummus, baba ghannouj, tabbouleh, tihini, baklava, spinich & artichoke dips and salads.
President: Simon Oueis
Estimated Sales: Less than $500,000
Number Employees: 1-4

6907 Jeryl's Jems
43 Eagle Lane
Tappan, NY 10983-1810 201-236-8372
Fax: 845-359-7386 info@jerylsjems.com
www.jerylsjems.com
Cake truffles, cookies, brownies
President: Jeryl Kipnis Kronish

6908 Jess Jones Farms
6496 Jones Ln
Dixon, CA 95620 707-678-3839
Fax: 707-678-3898
Processor, packer and exporter of popcorn
President: Jess Jones
CEO: Mary Ellen Jones
Estimated Sales: $700,000
Number Employees: 1-4
Sq. footage: 10000
Type of Packaging: Consumer, Bulk
Brands:
CALIFORNIA GOLDEN POP
CUSTOMER'S BAGS
JESS JONES FARMS

6909 (HQ)Jesse's Best
1201 Progress Road
Suffolk, VA 23434-2145 757-489-8383
Fax: 757-489-8382 dapeck@supremeonline.com
www.jessesbest.com
Processor of fresh and frozen meats including beef, pork and veal
President: Dave Peck
Manager: Tim Reeves
Number Employees: 10-19
Type of Packaging: Consumer, Food Service, Private Label
Other Locations:
Jesse's Best
Suffolk VA
Brands:
Jesse's Best

6910 Jesses Fine Meats
100 Washburn Rd
Cherokee, IA 51012 712-225-3637
Fax: 712-225-6113
www.advancefoodcompany.com
Manufacturer of meat specialty items including beef, pork and chicken
President/CEO: Larry Schlichting
President: Greg Allen
Plant Manager: Paul Beermann
Estimated Sales: $8.5 Million
Number Employees: 50-99
Sq. footage: 13000
Type of Packaging: Consumer, Food Service, Private Label
Brands:
FARMLAND
FOOD MASTER
QUIK TO FIX
SYSCO

6911 Jessie's Ilwaco Fish Company
117 Howerton Way SE
Ilwaco, WA 98624 360-642-3773
Fax: 360-642-3362 pierrem@ilwacofish.com

Processor, importer and exporter of fresh and frozen fish fillets, shrimp, salmon, perch, sturgeon, tuna, whiting, sardines, smelt, and Dungeness crab
Owner: Pierre Marchand
VP: Doug Ross
Marketing: George Alexander
Production: Phil Marchand
Estimated Sales: $20-40 Million
Number Employees: 100-249
Sq. footage: 25000
Type of Packaging: Consumer, Food Service, Private Label, Bulk
Brands:
Custom Lable
Seaside

6912 **Jet's Le Frois Foods Corporation**
56 High St
Brockport, NY 14420-2058 585-637-5003
Fax: 585-637-2855
Barbeque sauces and vinegars
Owner: Duncan Tsay
Estimated Sales: $ 5-10 Million
Number Employees: 5-9
Type of Packaging: Private Label

6913 **Jewel Bakery**
1955 W North Ave
Melrose Park, IL 60160-1131 708-531-6000
Fax: 708-343-9450
Breads
CEO: Stephen Bowater
Number Employees: 100-249

6914 **Jewel Date Company**
56474 Us Highway 111
Thermal, CA 92274 760-399-4474
Fax: 760-399-4476 jeweldate@aol.com
www.jeweldate.com
Processor and exporter of natural and organic pecans, dates, raisins, nuts and dried fruits
President: Gregory Raumin
Estimated Sales: $1300000
Number Employees: 20-49
Parent Co: Covalda
Type of Packaging: Consumer

6915 **Jianlibao America**
420 5th Avenue
26th Floor
New York, NY 10018-2729 212-354-8898
Fax: 212-354-8838 800-526-1688
sales@orientalfoodmaster.com www.janlibo.com
Beverages, Oriental foodstuffs
President: Qishu Lin
Estimated Sales: $ 3 Million
Number Employees: 20

6916 **Jillipepper**
P.O.Box 7546
Albuquerque, NM 87194-7546 505-344-2804
Fax: 505-344-6633 jilli@jillipepper.com
www.jillipepper.com
Salsas, sauces, dips
President: Jill Levin
VP: Lowell Levin
Production Manager: Martin Dobyns
Estimated Sales: $ 1 - 3 Million
Number Employees: 1-4
Type of Packaging: Private Label

6917 **Jim Foley Company**
1121 Chestnut Hill Cir SW
Marietta, GA 30064-4652 770-427-0999
Fax: 770-427-5102
Seafood
President: Jim Foley

6918 **Jim's Cheese Pantry**
410 Portland Rd
Waterloo, WI 53594 920-478-3571
Fax: 920-478-2320 800-345-3571
retail@jimscheesepantry.com
www.jimscheesepantry.com
Processor of cheese sculptures and wholesaler/distributor of jams, jellies and crackers; serving the food service market
President: James Peschel
VP: Judy Peschel
Estimated Sales: $9.5 Million
Number Employees: 50
Sq. footage: 25000
Type of Packaging: Consumer, Food Service

6919 **Jimbo's Jumbos**
P.O.Box 465
Edenton, NC 27932 252-482-2193
Fax: 252-482-7857 800-334-4771
www.jimbosjumbos.com
Snacks and peanuts, custom formulation is available
Manager: Hal Burns
Number Employees: 100-249
Type of Packaging: Private Label

6920 **Jimmy Dean Foods**
PO Box 25111
Cincinnati, OH 45225-0111 513-281-9104
Fax: 901-758-6709 800-925-3326
www.jimmydean.com
Breakfast sandwiches and sausage
President: Jerry Laner
VP Procurement: Jim Morey
Executive VP Retail Sales: Wes Jackson
Estimated Sales: $300,000-500,000
Number Employees: 1-4
Parent Co: Sara Lee
Type of Packaging: Consumer, Food Service, Private Label, Bulk
Brands:
FRESH TASTE FAST!
JIMMY DEAN

6921 **Jimmy's Chiles**
16336 67th Ct
Tinley Park, IL 60477-1706 708-532-2650
Fax: 847-685-4099
Chilie peppers and other vegetables
Owner: James Doyle
Number Employees: 1

6922 **Jimmy's Cookies**
18-01 River Rd
Fair Lawn, NJ 07410 201-797-8900
Fax: 201-797-2090 info@jimmycookies.net
www.jimmyscookies.net
Cookies
President/Owner: Michael Pisani
CEO: Howard Hirsch
CFO: Debbie Kinzley
Estimated Sales: $15-20 Million
Number Employees: 50+
Sq. footage: 40000
Type of Packaging: Consumer, Food Service, Private Label, Bulk

6923 **Jimtown Store**
6706 Highway 128
Healdsburg, CA 95448 707-433-1212
Fax: 707-433-1252 jimtown@jimtown.com
www.jimtown.com
Vegetable spreads
President: Carrie Brown
Marketing Director: Haley Callahan
Catering: Susan Schmid
Estimated Sales: Less than $500,000
Number Employees: 10-19
Brands:
Chickpea Chipotle
Fig & Olive Tapenade
SPICY OLIVE

6924 **Jitney Jungle Stores ofAmerica**
1770 Ellis Ave
Ste. 200
Jackson, MS 39204 601-965-8600
Fax: 601-965-8171 800-647-2364
Processor and exporter of poultry products
President: Ronald Johnson
CFO: Greg Presley
Number Employees: 250-499

6925 **Jo Mar Laboratories**
583 Division St # B
Campbell, CA 95008-6915 408-374-5920
Fax: 408-374-5922 800-538-4545
info@jomarlabs.com www.jomarlabs.com
Wholesaler/distributor and exporter of health products including packaged amino acids and food supplements; also, contract packaging available
President: Joanne Brown
Estimated Sales: $ 1 - 3 Million
Number Employees: 10-19
Sq. footage: 3500
Parent Co: Jo Mar Labs
Type of Packaging: Consumer, Private Label

6926 **Jo Mints**
2101 E Coast Highway
Suite 250
Corona Del Mar, CA 92625-1928 310-401-1894
Fax: 310-388-5647 877-566-4687
tom@jomints.com www.jomints.com
Marketing: Tom Knutson
Sales: Tom Knutson
Public Relations: Ashley Talbott
Number Employees: 3
Number of Brands: 2
Number of Products: 3
Brands:
JO CITRUS
JOMINTS
M60 ENERGY MINTS

6927 **Jo's Candies**
2530 W 237th Street
Torrance, CA 90505 310-257-0260
Fax: 310-257-0266 800-770-1946
sales@joscandies.com www.jos-candies.com
chocolate graham crackers, s'mores, coco jo's, peppermint crunch, english toffee bars, chocolaty toffee corn, peanut butter meltaways, handmade meltaways, handmade turtles, buttery toffee corn, toffee nuggets, peanut brittle, englishtoffee, chocolate gift tower, marshmallow squares, lemon breeze

6928 **Jo's Candies**
2560 W 237th St
Torrance, CA 90505-5217 310-257-0260
Fax: 310-257-0266 800-770-1946
sales@joscandies.com www.joscandies.com
Manufacturer of gourmet chocolates, English toffee, chocolate graham crackers, caramels, chocolate covered peppermints, smores and toffee caramel corn.
President: Tom King
Controller: Grant Philders
Plant Manager: Dave Good
Estimated Sales: Below $ 5 Million
Number Employees: 5-9
Type of Packaging: Private Label, Bulk
Brands:
Chocolate Covered Graham Crackers
Dr. Peter's Peppermint Crunch
Jo's Candies
Jo's Original

6929 **Jodar Vineyard & Winery**
2393 Gravel Road
Placerville, CA 95667 530-621-0324
Fax: 530-621-0324 jodarwinery@foothill.net
www.jodarwinery.com
Manufacturer of wines
President: Vaughn Jodar
Partner: Byron Joder
Partner: Sherril Jodar
Estimated Sales: $500,000-$1 Million
Number Employees: 4
Brands:
Jodar

6930 **Jodie's Kitchen**
6349 82nd Ave N
Pinellas Park, FL 33781
Fax: 727-934-9967 800-728-3704
info@jodieskitchen.com www.jodieskitchen.com
Processor of gourmet herb and spice blends, private label for dry mixes
President: Nobert Moore
VP: Vickey Auge
Estimated Sales: $300,000-500,000
Number Employees: 1-4
Sq. footage: 2400
Type of Packaging: Consumer, Private Label, Bulk
Brands:
Country Classic
Dip-Idy-Dill
Galloping Garlic
Garlic Galore
Magically Mexican
Obviously Onion

6931 **Jodie's Kitchen**
6349 82nd Ave N.
Pinellas Park, FL 33781 727-939-3444
Fax: 727-939-3444 800-728-3704
admin@jodieskitchen.com
www.jodieskitchen.com
Food spice blends, dip mixes
President: Norbert Moore
Marketing Director: Norbert Moore

Estimated Sales: $ 5-9.9 Million
Number Employees: 5-9
Brands:
Dipidy Dill
Simply Spinach

6932 **Jody Maroni's Sausage Kingdom**
P.O.Box 1487
Burbank, CA 91507-1487
Fax: 310-822-0065 www.jodymaroni.com
Processor of sausages
Owner: Jordan Monkarsh
VP Marketing: Richard Leivenberg
Number Employees: 50-99
Type of Packaging: Consumer, Food Service
Brands:
Jody Maroni

6933 **Jody's Gourmet Popcorn**
205 Laskin Rd
Virginia Beach, VA 23451 757-425-5639
Fax: 757-425-0059 866-797-5639
danny@jodyspopcorn.com
www.jodyspopcorn.com
flavored popcorn and flavored fudge

6934 **Joe Corbis' Wholesale Pizza**
1430 Desoto Rd
Baltimore, MD 21230-1202 410-525-3810
Fax: 410-525-0531 888-526-7247
baltimore@joecorbi.com www.joecorbi.com
Pizza
President: Rocco Violi
CEO: Victor Corbi
Estimated Sales: $ 10-20 Million
Number Employees: 20-49
Brands:
Joe Corbi's

6935 **Joe Fazio's Bakery**
1717 Sublette Ave
St Louis, MO 63110-1926 314-645-6239
Fax: 314-645-2410 fazioinfo@faziosbakery.com
www.faziosbakery.com
Bakery products
President: Charles Fazio
Estimated Sales: Below $ 5 Million
Number Employees: 100-249
Brands:
Fazio's

6936 **Joe Fazio's Famous Italian**
1008 Bullitt St
Charleston, WV 25301 304-344-3071
http://www.fazios.net
Italian foods, seafoods, steaks, sandwiches
President: Joe Fazio
Owner: Joe Fazio
Quality Control: Nell Fazio
Marketing Manager: Joe Fazio
Manager: Nell Fazio
Estimated Sales: Below $ 5 Million
Number Employees: 20-49
Brands:
Fazio's

6937 **Joe Hutson Foods**
8331 Sanlando Avenue
Jacksonville, FL 32211-5135 904-731-9065
Fax: 904-731-9066 keithhutson@juno.com
Processor and exporter of spicy salsas and steak, hot and cocktail sauces; also, gift baskets
President: Teresa Foster
CEO: Keith Hutson
Chairman Board: Joe Hutson
Number Employees: 1-4
Sq. footage: 1200
Parent Co: Joe Hutson Foods
Brands:
Put Me Hot

6938 **Joe Patti Seafood Company**
P.O.Box 12567
Pensacola, FL 32591 850-432-3315
Fax: 850-435-7843 800-500-9929
www.joepattis.com
Seafood, seafood products
President: Frank Patti
Marketing Director: Maria Walker
Estimated Sales: $ 20-50 Million
Number Employees: 100-249

6939 **Joe's Vegetables**
PO Box 2494
Hollister, CA 95024-2494 831-636-3224
Fax: 831-636-3226 joesveg@aol.com
Vegetables
President: Joe Herbert
VP: Catherine Herbert
Estimated Sales: Below $ 5 Million
Number Employees: 5
Type of Packaging: Private Label
Brands:
Organic Convenience

6940 **Joel & Diane Laperyhouse Company**
7241 Shoreline Drive
Chauvin, LA 70344-2425 504-594-9744
Fax: 504-594-9744

6941 **Joel Harvey Distributing**
8800 Ditmas Ave
Brooklyn, NY 11236 718-629-2690
Fax: 718-629-2172 sales@joelharvey.com
www.joelharvey.com
Chocolate, cookies, crackers, jellies and juices
President: Mark Statfeld
Estimated Sales: $ 1-2.5 Million
Number Employees: 10-19
Brands:
Ferrara
Guylian
Hero
Hershey
Kedem
Perugina
Venus

6942 **Joelle's Choice Specialty Foods LLC**
1829 Highway 1
Fairfield, IA 52566 641-472-2414
Fax: 641-472-3774 800-880-2779
sales@joelleschoice.com
http://joelleschoice.com
Manufacturer of shelf stable soy puddings; soymilks; rapid culture soy yogurts; gourmet gelatos and sorbets; gourmet soy-brat hybrids; soy-sausage brat hybrids, and soy-burger hybrids.
President: Larry Sutton
Type of Packaging: Food Service

6943 **Joey Oysters**
P.O.Box 904
Amite, LA 70422-0904 985-748-7140
Fax: 985-748-8300 800-748-1525
oyster@i-55.com
Processor of oysters
President: Vito Caronna
VP: Frank Boudreaux
Estimated Sales: $ 20 - 50 Million
Number Employees: 100-249
Type of Packaging: Consumer, Food Service, Bulk
Brands:
Louisiana

6944 **Joey's Fine Foods**
135 Manchester Pl
Newark, NJ 7104 973-482-1400
Fax: 973-482-1597 sales@joeysfinefoods.com
www.joeysfinefoods.com
Processor and wholesaler/distributor of mixes and baked goods
President: Aaron Aihini
VP Sales: Anthony Romano
Estimated Sales: $5.5 Million
Number Employees: 40
Sq. footage: 42000
Type of Packaging: Consumer, Food Service, Private Label, Bulk
Brands:
Cottage Bake
Joey's
New Englander

6945 **Jogue Inc**
One Vanilla Lane
Northville, MI 48167 248-349-1500
Fax: 248-349-1505 800-521-3888
info@jogue.com www.jogue.com
Manufacturer of flavoring extracts, essential oils, food colors, ice cream toppings, juices and syrups
President/Owner: Dattu Sastry
Technical Sales Manager: Gary Holtquist
Estimated Sales: $10-20 Million
Number Employees: 20-49
Type of Packaging: Food Service, Private Label, Bulk
Other Locations:
Jogue
Detroit MI
Western Syrup Company
Santa Fe Springs CA
High Mountain Manufacturing Company
Salt Lake City UT
Brands:
GOLD LABEL

6946 **Johanna Foods**
P.O.Box 272
Flemington, NJ 08822 908-788-2200
Fax: 908-788-2331 800-727-6700
www.johannafoods.com
Manufacturer of yogurt and chilled, aseptic juices and drinks
President/CEO: Robert Facchina
VP Marketing: Melinda Champion
VP Human Resources: Don Griffin
Estimated Sales: $97.5 Million
Number Employees: 500-999
Type of Packaging: Consumer, Food Service, Private Label, Bulk
Brands:
LA YOGURT
SABOR LATINO
SSIPS
TREERIPE

6947 **Johlin Century Winery**
3935 Corduroy Rd
Oregon, OH 43616 419-693-6288
Fax: 419-693-6429
Wines
President/Owner: Richard Johlin
Sales Director: Rich Johlin
Estimated Sales: $500,000-$1 Million
Number Employees: 1-4
Type of Packaging: Private Label

6948 **John A. Vassilaros & Son**
2905 120th St
Flushing, NY 11354 718-886-4140
Fax: 718-463-5037 sales@vassilaroscoffee.com
www.vassilaroscoffee.com
Coffee and tea
President: John Vassilaros
Director: Ann Vassilaros
Estimated Sales: $ 10-20 Million
Number Employees: 20-49
Type of Packaging: Private Label

6949 **John B Sanfilippo & Son**
16435 Ih 35 N
Selma, TX 78154-1200 210-651-5300
Fax: 210-651-6244 800-423-6546
jasperjr@jbssinc.com www.jbssinc.com
Manufaturer of shelled nuts including walnuts, pecans, almonds, cashews and peanuts; packaged in cellophane, jars, cans and bulk
Chairman/CEO: Mathias A Valentine
SVP/Secretary: Michael Valentine
Plant Manager: Ruben Roecker
Estimated Sales: $520 Million
Number Employees: 500-999
Type of Packaging: Consumer, Food Service, Private Label, Bulk
Other Locations:
John B. Filippo & Son
Bainbridge GA
John B. Filippo & Son
Garysburg NC
John B. Filippo & Son
Gustine CA
John B. Filippo & Son
Walnut CA
Brands:
EVON'S
FISHER
FLAVOR TREE
SUNSHINE COUNTRY
TEX PRIDE

6950 **John B Sanfilippo & Son**
1703 N Randall Rd
Elgin, IL 60123 847-289-1800
Fax: 847-289-1843 www.fishernuts.com

Processor, marketer and distributor of nut based snacking solutions
CEO: Jeffrey Sanfilippo
CFO: Michael Valentine
Sales: James Baker
SVP Human Resources: Tom Fordonski
Manager: Bill Schwann
Estimated Sales: $ 520 Million
Number Employees: 90
Parent Co: John B. Sanfilippo & Son
Type of Packaging: Consumer, Bulk
Brands:
Evon's
Fisher
Flavor Tree
Sunshine
Texas

6951 **(HQ)John B Sanfilippo & Son**
1703 N Randall Rd
Elgin, IL 60123 847-289-1800
Fax: 847-289-1843 ebulkfoods@jbssinc.com
www.jbssinc.com
Nutmeats, snack foods
Chairman/ Chief Executive Officer: Jasper Sanfilippo
EVP/Finance and Chief Financial Officer: Michael Valentine
Research & Development: Russell Tietz
Controller: Herbert Marros
EVP/Sales and Marketing: Jeffrey Sanfilippo
EVP Operations: Jasper Brian Sanfilippo
Production Manager: Mark Bardon
Plant Manager: Jerry Needham
Purchasing Manager: Paul Rabe
Estimated Sales: $520 Million
Number Employees: 1,000-4,999
Number of Brands: 4
Type of Packaging: Consumer, Food Service, Private Label, Bulk
Brands:
Evon's
Fisher
Flavor Tree
Sunshine
Texas Pride
VANDERMINT
WHALER'S RUM

6952 **John B Sanfilippo & Son**
8060 Nc Highway 46
Garysburg, NC 27831 252-536-5111
Fax: 252-536-5587
Runner and Virginia type peanuts
Manager: Barry Smith
Estimated Sales: $520 Million
Number Employees: 50-99
Parent Co: John B. Sanfilippo & Son

6953 **John B Sanfilippo & Sons**
16435 Ih 35 N
Selma, TX 78154-1200 210-651-5300
Fax: 210-651-6244 800-423-6546
ebulkfoods@jbssinc.com www.jbssinc.com
Pecans, almonds, walnuts, sunflowers, pistachios, peanuts, pine nuts, macadamias, brazil nuts, cashews, hazelnuts and mixed nuts
President: Michael Valentine
Plant Manager: Ruben Roecker
Estimated Sales: $ 20 - 50 Million
Number Employees: 500-999
Brands:
Evon's
Fisher
Flavor Tree
Sunshine Country

6954 **John B. Sanfilippo & Son**
29241 Cottonwood Rd
Gustine, CA 95322 209-854-2455
Fax: 209-854-3135 800-218-3077
ebulkfoods@jbssinc.com www.jbssinc.com
Processor and exporter of almonds and walnuts
President: Sid Cortez
Vice President: Jasper Sanfilippo
Export Sales Manager: Kim Sziraki
Estimated Sales: $20-50 Million
Number Employees: 400
Parent Co: John B. Sanfilippo & Son
Type of Packaging: Bulk

6955 **John B. Wright Fish Company**
427 Main St
Gloucester, MA 01930 978-283-4205
Fax: 978-281-5944
Seafood
President: Brian Wright
Estimated Sales: $ 5 - 10 Million
Number Employees: 5-9

6956 **John C. Meier Juice Company**
6955 Plainfield Rd
Cincinnati, OH 45236-3733 513-891-2900
Fax: 513-891-6370 800-346-2941
info@meierswinecellars.com
www.meierswinecellars.com
Juice, jams, jellies
President: John Lucia
CEO: Bob szabo
Chairman: Robert Gottesman
Marketing Director: Lyn Lubin
Estimated Sales: $ 5-10 Million
Number Employees: 20-49
Brands:
Breckenridge Farm Sparkling Juices
Meier's
Meier's Sparkling Ju

6957 **John Conti Coffee Company**
4406 Ole Brickyard Cir
Louisville, KY 40218 502-499-8600
Fax: 502-499-2944 800-928-5282
www.johnconti.com
Coffee
President: John Conti
VP Coffee Services: Tami Conti
Human Resources: Debbie Redmon
Operations Director: Mark Nethery
Estimated Sales: Under $500,000
Number Employees: 100-249

6958 **John Copes Food Products**
759 Long Road
Manheim, PA 17545-8613 717-367-5142
Fax: 717-367-7317 800-745-8211
larry@copefoods.com www.copefoods.com
Processor of canned corn and frozen vegetables
President: Larry Jones
VP/Sales and Marketing: Steve Davis
CFO/Treasurer: Don Long
Controller: Stephen Gaukler
Estimated Sales: $ 30-50 Million
Number Employees: 130
Type of Packaging: Consumer, Private Label
Brands:
Copes
Dutch Delight

6959 **John Garner Meats**
2365 N Rudy Road
Van Buren, AR 72956-8702 479-474-6894
Fax: 479-474-6897 800-543-5473
Processor of portion controlled pork, poultry and beef including ground and frozen patties
President: Dewayne Garner
President: T D Garner
Marketing Director: Ralph Farrar
Sales Director: Gary Scott
Public Relations: Steve Fow
Operations Manager: Rusty Underwood
Production Manager: Rusty Polk
Estimated Sales: $5 Million
Number Employees: 30
Sq. footage: 10000
Type of Packaging: Food Service, Private Label, Bulk

6960 **John Gust Foods & Products Corporation**
1350 Paramount Pkwy
Batavia, IL 60510-1461 630-879-8700
Fax: 630-879-8708 800-756-5886
sales@northern-pines.com
www.northern-pines.com
Processor of pancake, waffle and muffin mixes; also, pancake and sugar-free syrups
President: Gus Koutselas
Estimated Sales: $1 Million
Number Employees: 5-9
Type of Packaging: Consumer, Food Service, Private Label, Bulk
Brands:
Northern Pines Gourmet

6961 **John Hofmeister & Son**
2386 S Blue Island Ave
Chicago, IL 60608 773-847-0700
Fax: 773-847-6707 800-923-4267
ehofmeis@hofhaus.com www.hofhaus.com
Processor of smoked and boiled hams both boneless and semi boneless and smoked turkeys.
President/VP: Mark Rataj
Marketing Manager: Matt Hofmeister
Human Resources Manager: Bob Bukala
Production: Chris Chin
Estimated Sales: $32,000
Number Employees: 60
Sq. footage: 60000
Type of Packaging: Consumer, Food Service, Private Label
Brands:
Hofmeister Haus

6962 **(HQ)John I. Haas**
5185 Macarthur Blvd NW Ste 300
Washington, DC 20016 202-777-4800
Fax: 202-777-4895 www.barthhaasgroup.com
Processor, importer and exporter of hops and hop aroma extract and oils
President: Henry Von Eichel
Vice President: Kyle Lambert
Managing Partner: Stephen Barth
Estimated Sales: $ 10-20 Million
Number Employees: 20
Type of Packaging: Food Service, Private Label, Bulk
Other Locations:
Haas, John I.
Yuen Long, N.T.
Brands:
Aromahop
Beta Stab
Hepahop Gold
Isahop
Lacto Stab
Redihop
Tetrahop Gold

6963 **John J. Nissen Baking Company**
34 Abbott St
Brewer, ME 4412 207-989-7654
Fax: 207-989-7654 contact@twinkies.com
www.interstatebakeriescorp.com
Processor of baked goods including bread, pastries, cakes and rolls
President: Michael D Kafoure
CEO: Antonio C Alvarez II
CFO: Ronald B Hutchison
Estimated Sales: $ 10 - 20 Million
Number Employees: 20-49
Brands:
Hostess
Wonder Bread

6964 **(HQ)John J. Nissen Baking Company**
2406 Cranberry Hwy
Wareham, MA 02571-1043 508-295-2337
Fax: 508-295-6230
Processor of breads including white, whole wheat and rye
President: Michael Kafoure
Estimated Sales: $ 5 - 10 Million
Number Employees: 5-9

6965 **John Kelly Chocolates**
1506 North Sierra Bonita Avenue
Los Angeles, CA 90046 323-851-3269
Fax: 323-851-1789 800-609-4243
wholesale@johnkellychocolates.com
www.johnkellychocolates.com
chocolates
Marketing: John Nelson

6966 **John Koller & Sons**
1734 Perry Hwy
Fredonia, PA 16124-2720 724-475-4154
Fax: 724-475-4777 rkoller54@aol.com
Manufacturer of cheese
President: Richard Koller
Estimated Sales: $ 10-20 Million
Number Employees: 10-19
Parent Co: Fairview Swiss Chesse
Brands:
Fairview Swiss Cheese

6967 **(HQ)John Morrell & Company**
805 E Kemper Rd
Cincinnati, OH 45246 712-279-7360
Fax: 513-346-7556 www.johnmorrell.com
Smoked sausage, hams, off the bone lunchmeats. bacon, hot dogs, off the bone quarter hams, cocktail smokies, ham cuts and lunchmeat.
President/CEO: Joseph Sebring
EVP Sales/Marketing: John Pauley
VP Human Resources: Gary Junso
Estimated Sales: $1+ Billion
Number Employees: 6,565
Type of Packaging: Consumer, Food Service, Private Label
Other Locations:
JM Sioux Falls Plant
Sioux Falls SD
JM Sioux City Plant
Sioux City SD
JM Springdale Plant
Cincinnati OH
JM Great Bend Plant
Great Bend KS
Brands:
Dinner bell
E-Z-Cut
Farmers Hickory
Hunter
Iowa Quality
John Morrell
Kretschmar
Peytons
Rath Black Hawk
Rodeo
Shenson
Tobin's First Prize

6968 **John Morrell & Company**
805 E Kemper Rd
Cincinnati, OH 45246 712-279-7360
Fax: 712-279-7351 www.johnmorrell.com
Smoked sausage, hams, off the bone lunchmeat, bacon, hot dogs, off the bone quarter hams, cocktail smokies, ham cuts, lunchmeat.
Manufacturing/Operations Director: Craig Schmidt
Manager: Carol Dermit
Estimated Sales: Over $ 1 Billion
Number Employees: 150
Parent Co: Smithfield Foods
Type of Packaging: Consumer, Food Service

6969 **John Morrell & Company**
805 E Kemper Rd
Cincinnati, OH 45246 712-279-7360
Fax: 605-330-3162 800-345-0743
www.johnmorrell.com
Processor and exporter of fresh and frozen pork and sausage products
President: Joe Sebring
General Manager: Steve Crim
Manager Human Resources: Buth Anderson
Purchasing Agent: Ben Flottman
Estimated Sales: Over $ 1 Billion
Number Employees: 1,000-4,999
Parent Co: Smithfield Companies
Type of Packaging: Consumer, Private Label, Bulk

6970 **(HQ)John Morrell & Company**
805 E Kemper Rd
Cincinnati, OH 45246 712-279-7360
Fax: 513-346-7556 www.johnmorrell.com
Smoked sausage, hams, off the bone lunchmeat, bacon, hot dogs, off the bone quarter hams, cocktail smokies, ham cuts, lunchmeat
Presdient/CEO: Joseph Sebring
EVP Sales/Marketing: John Pauley
VP Human Resources: Gary Junso
Estimated Sales: Over $1 Billion
Number Employees: 6,565
Parent Co: Smithfield Companies
Type of Packaging: Food Service, Private Label
Other Locations:
Sioux Falls SD
Sioux City IA
Des Moines IA
Great Bend KS
San Jose CA
Middlesboro KY
Brands:
ARMOUR AND ERICKSON
CURLY'S
DINNER BELL
E Z CUT
HUNTER
JOHN MORRELL
KRETSCHMAR
MOHAWK
PEYTON'S
RATH BLACK HAWK
RODEO
TOBIN'S FIRST PRIZE

6971 **(HQ)John Morrell & Company**
805 E Kemper Rd
Cincinnati, OH 45246 712-279-7360
Fax: 513-346-7556 800-445-2013
jweiler@johnmorrell.com www.johnmorrell.com
Smoked sausage, hams, off the bone lunchmeat, bacon, hot dogs, off the bone quarter hams, cocktail smokies, ham cuts, lunchmeat
President/CEO: Joseph Sebring
EVP Sales/Marketing: John Pauley
VP Human Resources: Gary Junso
Estimated Sales: $2 Billion
Number Employees: 6,565
Type of Packaging: Consumer, Food Service, Private Label
Brands:
CURLY'S
DINNER BELL
E Z CUT
HUNTER
JOHN MORRELL
KRETSCHMAR
MOHAWK
PEYTON'S
RATH BLACK HAWK
RODEO
TOBIN'S FIRST PRIZE

6972 **John N Wright Jr**
402 Railroad Ave
Federalsburg, MD 21632 410-754-9044
Fax: 410-754-9045
Processor of canned tomatoes
President: Mary Harding
Estimated Sales: $100,000
Number Employees: 1-4

6973 **John Paton**
73 E State St
Doylestown, PA 18901 215-348-7050
Fax: 215-348-8147
www.goldenblossomhoney.com
Honey
President/Chairperson: Jill Paton
Estimated Sales: $860,000
Number Employees: 5-9

6974 **John R. Daily**
P.O.Box 16007
Missoula, MT 59808 406-721-7007
Fax: 406-721-1540 wwilcox@dailybacon.com
www.seaboardfoods.com
Manufacturer of meat including bacon
President: Mark Wilson
Sr. Vice President: Sig Skarland
CEO: A Wilcox
Estimated Sales: $30 Million
Number Employees: 50-99
Brands:
BIG SKY
HONEY CURED
PEPPERED

6975 **John R. Morreale**
216 N Peoria St
Chicago, IL 60607 312-421-3664
Fax: 312-421-6995 morrealemeat@aol.com
Processor and wholesaler/distributor of beef and pork
Owner: John Lucachoni
VP: Mike Magrini
VP Operations: Steve Hurckes
Estimated Sales: $25,000,000
Number Employees: 50-99
Number of Products: 1
Sq. footage: 100000
Type of Packaging: Bulk

6976 **John Volpi & Company**
5263 Northrup Ave
St Louis, MO 63110 314-772-8550
Fax: 314-772-0411 800-288-3439
www.volpifoods.com
Processor of Italian meat products including salami, dry cured coppa, mortadella, prosciutto ham, etc
President: Lorenza Pasetti
National Sales Manager: Christine Illuminato
General Manager: Lorenza Pasetti
Estimated Sales: $ 20 - 50 Million
Number Employees: 100-249
Type of Packaging: Consumer, Food Service, Private Label, Bulk
Brands:
Volpi Foods

6977 **John Wm. Macy's Cheesesticks**
80 Kipp Ave
Elmwood Park, NJ 07407-1036 201-791-8036
Fax: 201-797-5068 800-643-0573
timmacy@cheesesticks.com
www.cheesesticks.com
Processor of cheesesticks, cheesecrisps and bread sticks
CEO: John Macy
VP/Sales Manager: Tim Macy
Marketing: Julia D'Arcy
Estimated Sales: $8 Million
Number Employees: 60
Sq. footage: 45000
Type of Packaging: Consumer, Food Service, Private Label, Bulk
Brands:
John Wm. Macy's Cheesecrips
John Wm. Macy's Cheesesticks
John Wm. Macy's Sweetsticks

6978 **Johnny Harris Famous Barbecue Sauce**
2801 Wicklow St
Savannah, GA 31404 912-354-8828
Fax: 912-354-6567
Processor of barbecue sauce
President: Phillip Donaldson
CFO: Yvonne Donaldson
VP: Norman Heidt
Estimated Sales: $ 5 - 10 Million
Number Employees: 5-9
Sq. footage: 3000
Type of Packaging: Consumer

6979 **Johns Cove Fisheries**
RR 3
Yarmouth, NS B5A 4B1
Canada 902-742-8691
Fax: 902-742-3574 sales@johnscove.com
www.johnscove.com
Processor and exporter of live lobster and herring roe and scallops
President: Don Cunningham
Number Employees: 60
Type of Packaging: Consumer, Food Service, Bulk

6980 **Johnson Brothers Produce Company**
Highway 44 E
Whitakers, NC 27891-0730 252-437-2111
Fax: 252-437-2121 hbjfarms@coastalnet.com
Processor of sweet potatoes
President: Hursel Johnson
VP: Lou Johnson
Estimated Sales: $ 10 - 20 Million
Number Employees: 20-49
Type of Packaging: Bulk
Brands:
Norma Lou

6981 **Johnson Canning Company**
300 Warehouse Ave
Sunnyside, WA 98944-1310 509-837-4188
Fax: 509-839-3243 www.princesspickled.com
Processor of canned maraschino cherries and pickled vegetables
Manager: Pete Krause
CEO: George Jhonson
Marketing Director: George Jhonson
Manager: Gary Stonemetz
Manager: Pete Krause
Estimated Sales: $ 5 - 10 Million
Number Employees: 20-49
Parent Co: Johnson Canning Company
Type of Packaging: Consumer, Food Service, Private Label
Brands:
Princess
Sunnyside

6982 **Johnson Concentrates**
310 E Edison Ave
Sunnyside, WA 98944 509-837-4600
Fax: 509-837-5151
info@johnsonconcentrates.com
www.johnsonconcentrates.com
Processor, importer and exporter of fruit purees and concentrates
Owner: Gorge Johnson
CFO: Nyle Farmer
VP: David Watkins
General Manager: James Gauley
Estimated Sales: $3 Million
Number Employees: 30
Sq. footage: 40000
Type of Packaging: Bulk
Brands:
Johnson Concentrates

6983 **Johnson Estate Wines**
P.O.Box 52
Westfield, NY 14787-0052 716-326-2191
Fax: 716-326-2131 800-374-6569
jwinery@cecomet.net www.johnsonwinery.com
Processor of wine
President: Frederick Johnson
Marketing Contact: Bob Dahl
Operations Manager: Mark Lancaster
Estimated Sales: $ 3 - 5 Million
Number Employees: 5-9
Sq. footage: 15000
Type of Packaging: Consumer

6984 **Johnson Fruit Company**
336 Blaine Ave
Sunnyside, WA 98944 509-837-4600
Fax: 509-837-5151
info@johnsonconcentrates.com
www.johnsonconcentrates.com
Manufacturer and exporter of maraschino and dark sweet cherries, IQF asparagus and pickled vegetables including beans, peas, carrots, bell peppers, asparagus and dried tomatoes in oil
President: Gary Johnson
Estimated Sales: $ 10 - 20 Million
Number Employees: 20-49
Sq. footage: 20000
Type of Packaging: Consumer, Food Service, Private Label, Bulk

6985 **Johnson Sea Products**
P.O.Box 665
Coden, AL 36523 251-824-2693
Fax: 251-824-7808
Seafood
Principal: Sean Johnson
Human Resources: Bridget Sprinkle
Estimated Sales: $100+ Million
Number Employees: 100-249

6986 **Johnson's Alexander Valley Wines**
8333 Highway 128
Healdsburg, CA 95448-9639 707-433-2319
Fax: 707-433-5302 800-888-5532
johnsons@funvacation.net
www.funvacation.net/johnsons.html
Wines
Owner/President: Ellen Johnson
CEO: Ellen Johnson
Marketing Director: Ellen Johnson
Estimated Sales: Below $ 5 Million
Number Employees: 1-4
Type of Packaging: Private Label
Brands:
Diamond Springs

6987 **(HQ)Johnson's Food Products**
1 Mt Vernon St
Dorchester, MA 02125-1604 617-265-3400
Fax: 617-265-1099
Processor of bakers' and confectioners' supplies including mixes, bases, flavorings and whipped toppings
President: Chris Anton
VP: Peter Anton
Estimated Sales: $ 5 - 10 Million
Number Employees: 10-19
Sq. footage: 20000
Type of Packaging: Consumer, Food Service, Bulk

6988 **Johnson's Real Ice Cream**
2728 E Main St
Columbus, OH 43209 614-231-0014
Fax: 614-231-5450
jim@johnsonsrealicecream.com
www.johnsonsrealicecream.com
Processor of ice cream and sherbet
President: Jim Wilcoxon
Estimated Sales: $380000
Number Employees: 10-19
Sq. footage: 2400
Type of Packaging: Consumer, Food Service

6989 **Johnson's Wholesale Meats**
161 N Sixth St
Opelousas, LA 70570 337-948-4444
Fax: 337-948-4495
Meat packer
Manager: David Comoeuax
Sales Manager: Billy Baque
Estimated Sales: $ 1 - 3 Million
Number Employees: 5-9
Type of Packaging: Consumer, Bulk

6990 **Johnson, Nash, & Sons Farms**
Hwy 117 North
Rose Hill, NC 28458 910-289-3113
Fax: 910-289-2644 800-682-6843
Manufacturer of fresh poultry and eggs
President/Coo: Don Taber
Chairman: E. Marvin Johnson
Vice Chairman/Ceo: Robert Johnson
Estimated Sales: $567.8 Million
Number Employees: 5-9
Type of Packaging: Consumer, Food Service, Bulk
Brands:
HOUSE OF RAEFORD

6991 **Johnsonville Food Company**
Po Box 906
Sheboygan Falls, WI 53085 920-459-6800
Fax: 920-459-7824 888-556-2728
www.johnsonville.com
Processor of sausage
Type of Packaging: Consumer
Brands:
Hot'n Zesty Links
Johnsonville Bratwur
Johnsonville Country
Sage'n Pepper
Table Two Entree

6992 **Johnston County Hams**
P.O.Box 489
204 N. Bright Leaf Boulevard
Smithfield, NC 27577 919-934-8054
Fax: 919-934-1091 800-543-4267
rufus@countrycuredhams.com
www.countrycuredhams.com
Hams, bacon and turkey
Cure Master: Rufus Brown
Estimated Sales: Below $ 5 Million
Number Employees: 10-19

6993 **Johnston Farms**
P.O.Box 65
Edison, CA 93220 661-366-3201
Fax: 661-366-6534 www.johnstonfarms.com
Packer, exporter and wholesaler/distributor of navel oranges, peppers and potatoes
President: Don Johnston
Co-Prtnr.: Gerald Johnston
Plant Manager: Steve Stacker
Number Employees: 250-499

6994 **Johnston's Home Style Products**
PO Box 1737
Charlottetown, PE C1A 7N4
Canada 902-629-1300
Fax: 902-368-1776
Processor of canned wild cranberry sauce, beef stew and chicken parts and stew
President: Harris Johnston
Type of Packaging: Food Service, Private Label

6995 **Johnston's Winery**
5140 Bliss Rd
Ballston Spa, NY 12020 518-882-6310
Fax: 518-882-5551
Manufacturer of wine
President: Kurt Johnston
Estimated Sales: Less than $500,000
Number Employees: 1-4
Brands:
Johnston's Winery

6996 **Jolina Foods**
10516 Route 116
Hinesburg, VT 05461-8500 802-434-2185
Fax: 802-434-2784
Executive Director: Bob Barton
Estimated Sales: $ 1-2.5 Million appx.
Number Employees: 20

6997 **Jon Donaire Pastry**
9420 Sorensen Ave
Santa Fe Springs, CA 90670 562-941-1856
Fax: 562-946-3781 877-366-2473
JDdesserts@rich.com www.jondonaire.net
Cheese cake mousse
Dessert Specialist: Lisa Tanner
Estimated Sales: $ 30 Million
Number Employees: 100-249
Brands:
Jon Donaire

6998 **Jonathan Lord Corporation**
87 Carlough Rd Unit A
Bohemia, NY 11716 631-563-4445
Fax: 631-563-8505 800-814-7517
jlcorp@optonline.net www.jonathanlord.com
Bakery Products
Owner: Kathy Dancik
Sales Director: William Kentrup
Estimated Sales: Below $ 5 Million
Number Employees: 10-19
Type of Packaging: Consumer, Food Service, Private Label, Bulk

6999 **Jonathan's Sprouts**
384 Vaughan Hill Rd
Rochester, MA 02770 508-763-2577
Fax: 508-763-3316 bob@jonathansorganic.com
www.jonathansorganic.com
Manufacturer of alfalfa sprouts, mung bean sprouts, citrus fruits and vegetables. Certified packer and shipper of organic produce
Owner/President: Robert Sanderson
Owner/President: Barbara Sanderson
CEO: John Musser
Sales Director: Cathy Rounseville
Estimated Sales: $4 Million
Number Employees: 20-49
Sq. footage: 15000
Type of Packaging: Consumer
Brands:
Jonathan's Organics
Jonathan's Sprouts

7000 **Jones Brewing Company**
P.O.Box 746
Smithton, PA 15479-0746 724-872-6626
Fax: 724-872-6538 800-237-2337
info@stoneysbeer.com www.stoneysbeer.com
Processor and exporter of beers, lagers, nonalcoholic beers and other malt beverages in kegs, cans and bottles
President: Sandra Podlucky
Vice President: Sandra Podlucky
Inventory Control: Joyce Winkler
Production Manager: John Lonesky
Estimated Sales: $1.1 Million
Number Employees: 5-9
Type of Packaging: Consumer, Private Label
Brands:
Equire
Eureka
Stoney's
Stoney's Black & Tan
Stoney's Harvest Gold
Stoney's Light
Stoney's Non-Alcoholic Brew

7001 **(HQ)Jones Dairy Farm**
800 Jones Ave
Fort Atkinson, WI 53538 920-563-2431
Fax: 920-563-6801 800-563-1004
jdfxprt@idcnet.com www.jonesdairyfarm.com
Manufacturer, packer and exporter sausage, bacon and ham products, maple syrup
President/CEO: Philip Jones
VP Finance: Loren Gray
SVP Sales/Marketing: Richard Lowry
Operations Manager: Roger Borchardt
Natl. Food Service Accounts Manager: Richard Klippstein

Estimated Sales: $58 Million
Number Employees: 250-499
Type of Packaging: Consumer, Food Service, Bulk
Brands:
JONES SAUSAGEST
RALPH & PAULA ADAMS SCRAPPLE

7002 **Jones Packing Company**
22701 Oak Grove Rd
Harvard, IL 60033 815-943-4488
Processor of beef, lamb, pork and goat
Owner: Ray Jones
Estimated Sales: $4 Million
Number Employees: 10-19
Type of Packaging: Consumer, Food Service, Private Label

7003 **Jones Potato Chip Company**
823 Bowman St
Mansfield, OH 44903-4107
Fax: 419-529-6789 800-466-9424
chips@joneschips.com www.joneschips.com
Processor of potato chips
President: Robert Jones
Director Sales: Don Markov
Office Manager: Jim Ford
Production Manager: Roy Kehl
Estimated Sales: $6 Million
Number Employees: 20-49
Type of Packaging: Consumer, Food Service, Private Label
Brands:
Jones
Thomasson's
Thomasson's Potato Chips

7004 **Jones Produce**
903 a St SE
Quincy, WA 98848 509-787-3537
Fax: 509-787-1275 merchant@jonesproduce.com
Vegetables, fuits
Owner: Jack Jones
Estimated Sales: $ 20 - 50 Million
Number Employees: 20-49

7005 **Jones Soda Company**
234 9th Ave N
Seattle, WA 98109 206-624-3357
Fax: 206-624-6857 800-656-6050
www.jonessoda.com
Soda
President/CEO: William Meissner
Chairman: Richard Eiswirth
CFO: Michael O'Brien
VP Operations: Eric Chastain
Estimated Sales: $20-50 Million
Number Employees: 50-99
Type of Packaging: Consumer
Brands:
BERRY WHITE
BETTY
DAVE
PURPLE CARROT

7006 **Jones Soda Vancouver**
1501 Haro Street
Suite 1007
Vancouver, BC V6G 1G4
Canada 604-682-3013
Fax: 604-270-6421 800-656-6050
www.jonessoda.com
Soda
Director: Peter Van Stolk
Estimated Sales: $414.63K
Number Employees: 4

7007 **Jonny Almond Nut Company**
G4254 Fenton Road
Flint, MI 48507-3614 810-767-6886
Fax: 810-767-6889 rich@jonnyalmond.com
www.jonnyalmond.com
Nuts, other snacks, pocorn.
Marketing: Rich Krafsur

7008 **Joray Candy**
1258 Prospect Avenue
Brooklyn, NY 11218 718-871-6300
Fax: 718-871-6300 joraycandy@msn.com
www.joraycandy.com
Kosher, gummies/jellies/pates de fruits, other candy, other snacks, dries fruit.
Marketing: Ray Shalhoub

7009 **Jordahl Meats**
25585 State Highway 13
Manchester, MN 56007 507-826-3418
Processor of meat products including lamb, beef, pork, veal, etc
Owner: Brian Jordahl
Estimated Sales: $520,000
Number Employees: 1-4
Type of Packaging: Consumer, Food Service, Private Label, Bulk

7010 **Josef Aaron Syrup Company**
16541 Redmond Way
Suite 206
Redmond, WA 98052-4492 425-820-7221
Fax: 425-702-9292
Tea and coffee flavors, syrups
President: Judy Toller
Number Employees: 5-9

7011 **Joseph Adams Corporation**
P.O.Box 583
Valley City, OH 44280 330-225-9135
Fax: 330-225-9105
Processor and exporter of oleoresins, essential oils, natural flavors and colors from spices and botanicals
President: Patrick Adams
Estimated Sales: $3 Million
Number Employees: 10-19

7012 **Joseph Bertman Foods**
P.O.Box 6562
Cleveland, OH 44101-1562 216-431-4460
Fax: 216-561-2232
Mustard, horseradish
President: Pat Mazoh
Estimated Sales: $ 1 - 3 Million
Number Employees: 1-4
Brands:
Bertman Raddish Sauce
Joe Bertman's Ballpark Mustard
Mustard
Original

7013 **Joseph D Teachey Produce**
1307 N Norwood St
Wallace, NC 28466-0965 910-285-4502
Fax: 910-285-5491
Processor of sweet potatoes including Jewel, Beauregard and Hernandez
Owner: Joseph Teachey
Estimated Sales: $ 10-20 Million
Number Employees: 20-49
Brands:
Mary Jo's Blueberries
Mary Jo's Fancy

7014 **Joseph Filippi Winery**
12467 Base Line Rd.
Rancho Cucamonga, CA 91739-9522 909-899-5755
Fax: 909-899-9196 jfilippiwinery@aol.com
www.josephfilippiwinery.com
A variety of wines including: Cabarnet, Cinq Vignobles, Alicante Bouschet,Ruby-Ruby Port, Angelica Elena, Syrah and Zinfandel.
President: Joseph P Filippi
Vice President: Jared Fillippi
VP Sales/Marketing: Gino Filippi
Estimated Sales: Below $ 5 Million
Number Employees: 22
Number of Brands: 2
Number of Products: 25
Type of Packaging: Private Label
Other Locations:
Joseph Filippi Winery
Guasti-Ontario, Canada
Brands:
Guasti Altar Wines
Joseph Filippi

7015 **Joseph Foodservice**
P.O.Box 1187
Valdosta, GA 31603-1187 229-242-0867
Fax: 912-242-8877 800-333-2261
info@jfs.com www.ijconnect.com
Wholesaler/distributor of general line products; serving the food service market
Manager: Casey Kinker
CEO: Luis Quintero
VP Purchasing: Bobby Joseph
Estimated Sales: $30 Million
Number Employees: 20-49
Sq. footage: 150000
Parent Co: IJ Company

7016 **Joseph Gallo Farms**
10561 State Highway 140
PO Box 775
Atwater, CA 95301 209-394-7984
Fax: 209-394-2392 jgfinfo@josephfarms.com
www.josephfarms.com
Processor of cheese
Plant Manager: Mike Gallo
CEO: Michael Gallo
Estimated Sales: Over $ 1 Billion
Number Employees: 250-499
Type of Packaging: Consumer, Food Service
Brands:
Joseph Farms Cheese

7017 **Joseph J. White**
1 Pasadena Rd
Browns Mills, NJ 08015-7113 609-893-2332
Fax: 609-893-2316
Processor of cranberries
President: Joe Darlington
Chairman Board: Thomas Darlington
Estimated Sales: $500,000-$1 Million
Number Employees: 10-19
Type of Packaging: Bulk

7018 **Joseph Kirschner & Company**
193 Riverside Dr
Augusta, ME 04330 207-623-3544
Fax: 207-623-1557
Processor of meats
President: Marco Desalle
Manager: Daniel Poulin
Estimated Sales: $200,000
Number Employees: 2

7019 **Joseph Phelps Vineyards**
200 Taplin Rd
Saint Helena, CA 94574 707-967-9153
Fax: 707-963-4831 www.napavalleysearch.com
Processor and exporter of wines
President: Tom Shelton
Estimated Sales: $100+ Million
Number Employees: 250-499
Type of Packaging: Consumer
Brands:
Innisfree
Myers Winery

7020 **Joseph Sanders**
P.O.Box 128
Custer, MI 49405-0128 231-757-4768
Fax: 231-757-4786 800-968-5035
www.sandersmeats.com
Processor of beef and pork products; also, slaughtering services available
Owner: Dale Sanders
Estimated Sales: $ 5 - 10 Million
Number Employees: 10-19
Type of Packaging: Consumer

7021 **Joseph Schmidt Confections**
100 Crystal a Dr
Hershey, PA 17033-9524
Fax: 415-626-7991 866-237-0152
customercare@jsc.com
www.josephschmidtconfections.com
Processor of Chocolate truffles and chocolate novelties
President: Charles Huggins
CFO: Jeff Smith
CEO: Joseph Scmidt
VP Marketing: Ellen Meuse
Production Manager: Richard Chaeniot
Estimated Sales: $ 5-10 Million
Number Employees: 100-249
Brands:
Chocolate Slicks

7022 **Joseph's Gourmet Pasta & Sauces**
133 Hale St
Haverhill, MA 01830-3969 978-521-1718
Fax: 978-374-7917 800-863-8998
josephsgourmetpasta.com
Processor of gourmet filled and cut pastas including ravioli, triangoli, agnolotti, tortelloni, tortellini, gnocchi and angel hair
President: Joseph Faro
Marketing: David Robinson
Operations: Tom Bean
Estimated Sales: $ 50 - 100 Million
Number Employees: 100-249

7023 Joseph's Lite Cookies
3700 J St SE
Deming, NM 88030 575-546-2839
Fax: 575-546-6951
customerservice@jospehslitecookies.com
www.josephslitecookies.com
Sugar free cookies, fat free cookies, brownies, syrups and more.
President: Joseph Semprevivo
Estimated Sales: $ 5-10 Million
Number Employees: 20-49
Sq. footage: 52000
Type of Packaging: Consumer

7024 Joseph's Pasta Company
262 Primrose Street
Haverhill, MA 01830 978-521-1718
Fax: 978-374-7917 888-327-2782
josephsgourmetpasta.com
Manufacturers of fresh and frozen pasta, filled ravioli, pesto and sauces
Owner: Joseph Faro
Vice President: David Gillen
Estimated Sales: $ 51 Million
Number Employees: 175

7025 Josh & John's Ice Cream
111 E Pikes Peak Ave
Colorado Springs, CO 80903-1803 719-632-0299
Fax: 719-632-2833 800-530-2855
joshjohn1@earthlink.com
www.joshandjohns.com
Processor of ice cream products
President/CEO/CFO: John Krakauer
Estimated Sales: $300,000-500,000
Number Employees: 100-249
Brands:
Josh & John's Ice Cream

7026 Josh Early Candies
4640 W Tilghman St
Allentown, PA 18104 610-395-4321
Fax: 610-398-8502
Candy and confections
Marketing: Barry Bobil
Public Relations: Lisa Medero
Estimated Sales: Below $ 5 Million
Number Employees: 10

7027 Jost Chemical
8150 Lackland
Saint Louis, MO 63114 314-428-4300
Fax: 314-428-4366 www.jostchemical.com
Manfucaturer high purity chemical ingredients for food and nutritional markets
President/Owner: Jerry Jost
CFO: Jeff Lenger
Vice President: Keith Wunderli
Estimated Sales: $15.5 Million
Number Employees: 105

7028 Josuma Coffee Corporation
P.O.Box 1115
Menlo Park, CA 94026 650-366-5453
Fax: 650-366-5464 info@josuma.com
www.josuma.com
Coffee
President: Joseph John
Vice President: Urmila John
Estimated Sales: Under $300,000
Number Employees: 1-4
Type of Packaging: Private Label
Brands:
Espresso Blend
Green Coffee
Malabar Gorld Premium
Monsooned Malabar

7029 Jou Jou's Pita Bakery
166 W Valley Ave
Birmingham, AL 35209-3620 205-945-6001
Fax: 205-945-6021 www.pita.net
Processor of plain and wheat pita bread
Owner; President: Naji Constantine
Estimated Sales: Less than $500,000
Number Employees: 10-19
Sq. footage: 6000
Brands:
Pito

7030 Joullian Vineyards
20300 Cachagua Rd
Carmel Valley, CA 93924 831-659-2800
Fax: 831-659-2802 877-659-2800
Wines
Manager: Raymond E Watson Iii
Owner: Jeannette Joullian Sias
VP: Raymond Watson III
CFO: Robert Fain
General Manager/Winemaker: Ridge Watson
Estimated Sales: $ 2.5-5 Million
Number Employees: 5-9
Brands:
Joullian Vineyards

7031 Joy Cone Company
3435 Lamor Rd
Hermitage, PA 16148 724-962-5747
Fax: 724-962-3470 800-242-2663
joycone@joycone.com www.joycone.com
Processor and exporter of ice cream cones
President: Joseph George
CFO: Scott Kaomanek
Quality Control: Sharon George
Director Food Service/Sales: Juergen Kloo
Estimated Sales: $ 100-500 Million
Number Employees: 250-499
Brands:
Joy
Scoopy

7032 Joy's Specialty Foods
300 N Willow St
Mancos, CO 81328 970-533-1500
Fax: 970-533-2011 800-831-5697
joy@joysfoods.com www.joysfoods.com
Gourmet specialty foods that include salas and hot sauces, marinades and grilling sauces, chile jams and seasonings and dips
President: Joy Kyzer
Vice President: Dave Kyzer
Estimated Sales: $300,000-500,000
Number Employees: 5
Type of Packaging: Consumer, Bulk
Brands:
Joy's

7033 Joyce Food Products
Boumar Place
Elmwood Park, NJ 07407 201-791-4300
Fax: 201-791-0324
Dry baked goods
President: Howard Freundlich
Controller: Rhoda Sallay
VP: Victor Ostreicher
Operations Manager: Anthony Benzinger
Purchasing Manager: Art Hersh
Estimated Sales: $ 20-50 Million
Number Employees: 200
Type of Packaging: Private Label

7034 Joyva Corporation
53 Varick Ave
Brooklyn, NY 11237 718-497-0170
Fax: 718-366-8504 richard@joyva.com
www.joyva.com
Processor of confectionery products including bagged, bars, boxes chocolate, fund raising, gums, jellies, Halloween, hard, marshmallows, packaged for racks, theatre packaging and vending
President: Milton Radutzky
Director: Richard Radutzky
Vice President: Harry Radutzky
Estimated Sales: $10-20 Million
Number Employees: 75
Type of Packaging: Consumer

7035 Juanita's Foods
P.O.Box 847
Wilmington, CA 90748-0847 310-834-5339
Fax: 310-834-5064
customerservice@juanitasfoods.com
www.juanitasfoods.com
Processor and exporter of Mexican foods including soups, hot sauce, hominy and ready-to-serve mole
President: George Delatorre
CEO: Aaron De Latorre
Sales Director: Bill Sneen
Operations Manager: Mark De La Torre
General Manager: Gina Harpur
Plant Manager: Frank Andrade
Purchasing Manager: Leo Medina
Estimated Sales: $41500000
Number Employees: 100-249
Type of Packaging: Consumer, Food Service, Private Label, Bulk
Brands:
Juanita's
Pico Pica
Tia Anita

7036 Jubelt Variety Bakeries
216 W Main St
Mount Olive, IL 62069 217-999-5231
Fax: 217-999-2613
Processor of cakes, breads, doughnuts and cookies
President: Lance Jubelt
Estimated Sales: $1,200,000
Number Employees: 35
Number of Brands: 2
Sq. footage: 8000
Type of Packaging: Food Service, Bulk

7037 Jubilations
1536 Gardner Blvd Ste 7
Columbus, MS 39702 662-328-9210
Fax: 662-329-1558 cheesecakes@jubilations.com
www.jubilations.com
Cheesecakes.
President: Tamara Craddock
Sales/Marketing: George Purnell
Purchasing Manager: Ed Griffith
Estimated Sales: $984807
Number Employees: 5-9
Sq. footage: 6000
Type of Packaging: Consumer, Food Service, Private Label
Brands:
Jubilations

7038 Jubilee Foods
Rt 140 & Rt 15
Emmitsburg, MD 21727 301-447-6688
patrick@jubileefoods.com
www.jubileeseafood.com
Processor of fresh and frozen shrimp
President: Charles Walton Kraver
Vice President: Frank Kawana
Quality Control: Mike Williams
Plant Manager: Charles Kraver
Estimated Sales: Below $ 5 Million
Number Employees: 15
Brands:
Buyer Label
Jubilee
Southern Supreme

7039 Jubilee Gourmet Creations
PO Box 6305-0318
Manchester, NH 03108 603-625-0654
Fax: 603-625-0654
Processor of brandied cherries, peaches and berries
President: Joyce Davis
Type of Packaging: Consumer, Food Service, Bulk

7040 Jubilee-Sedgefield Salads
PO Box 29114
Greensboro, NC 27429-9114 336-288-6646
Fax: 336-545-1880
Manufacturers of salami and sausages
President: Jerry McMasters
Estimated Sales: $ 50-100 Million
Number Employees: 100

7041 Judicial Flavors
11400 Atwood Road
Auburn, CA 95603-9017 530-885-1298
Fax: 530-888-0311 shyster@judicialflavor.com
www.judicialflavors.com
Products include hot sauces, barbecue sauces, coffe, dressings, fruit sauces, marinades, mustards, nuts, oils, salsa, spices & rubs
Estimated Sales: $ 1 - 3 Million
Number Employees: 5-9

7042 Judith Ann
1 Schuster Road
Falmouth, ME 04105-2531 207-871-0551
Fax: 207-871-0167

7043 Judson-Atkinson Candies
P.O.Box 200669
San Antonio, TX 78220 210-359-8380
Fax: 210-359-8392 800-962-3984
customerservice@judsonatkinsoncandies.com
www.judsonatkinsoncandies.com

Processor of confectionery products including hard candies, taffy, marshmallow candies, mints, jellies, jelly beans, seasonal candy products and assorted bagged goods; importer of gum, gummies and mints
President/CEO/Chairman: Basil Atkinson Jr
VP Finance: Rachel Espinosa
VP Sales/Marketing: Doyle Huntsman
Estimated Sales: $100 Million
Number Employees: 100-249
Sq. footage: 123000
Type of Packaging: Consumer, Food Service, Private Label, Bulk
Brands:
Chewy Pralines
Sours-Soft Centers

7044 **Judy's Cream Caramels**
19995 SW Chapman Rd
Sherwood, OR 97140 503-625-7161
Fax: 503-625-1602
Processor and exporter of cream caramels
Owner: Debbie Judy
Number Employees: 5-9
Type of Packaging: Consumer

7045 **Judyth's Mountain**
1737 Lorenzen Dr
San Jose, CA 95124 408-264-3330
Fax: 408-269-7979
President: Jerry Johnson
Estimated Sales: $ 5-10 Million
Number Employees: 20

7046 **Juice Bowl Products**
2090 Bartow Rd
Lakeland, FL 33801 863-665-5515
Fax: 863-667-7116 www.juicebowl.com
Juices and juice drinks
CEO: Paul Grady
VP Operations: Terry Simmers
VP: Carl Anderson
Quality Control: Rey Dedmon
Director Marketing/Sales: Kim Grady Brock
Plant Manager: Carl Anderson
Estimated Sales: $12 Million
Number Employees: 100-249
Brands:
JB

7047 **Juice Guys**
45 Dunster Street
Cambridge, MA 02138-5908 508-228-4464
Fax: 781-868-5490 800-896-8667
www.juiceguys.com
Processor of juice, juice products and cocktails, iced tea and nutraceuticals
President: Mark Hellendrung
National Sales Manager: Ken Traenkle
Estimated Sales: $20-50 Million
Number Employees: 50-99

7048 **Juice Mart**
6758 Julie Ln
West Hills, CA 91307 818-992-4442
Fax: 818-992-4479 877-888-1011
juice@juicemart.com www.juicemart.com
Juice concentrates and nutripaks. Design and set-up of juice bars.
President: Linda Renaud
Estimated Sales: $500,000-$1 Million
Number Employees: 1-4

7049 **Juice Tyme**
4401 S Oakley Ave
Chicago, IL 60609 773-579-1291
Fax: 773-579-1251 800-236-5823
juicetyme@aol.com www.juicetyme.com
Juices
President: Philip L Scott
CFO: Thomas Martens
Executive VP: Michael Schmidt
Estimated Sales: Below $ 5 Million
Number Employees: 20-49

7050 **Juicy Whip**
1668 Curtiss Ct
La Verne, CA 91750 909-392-7500
Fax: 626-814-8016 www.juicywhip.com
Manufacturer of Hispanic bottled and bag-in-the-box concentrates.
President/CEO: Gus Stratton
Purchasing: Craig Allen
Estimated Sales: $4 Million
Number Employees: 25
Sq. footage: 22000
Brands:
Juicy Whip

7051 **Julian's Recipe, LLC**
Po Box 323
Montgomery, NY 12549-0323 888-640-8880
Fax: 888-645-8030
rosa.jacquez@juliansrecipe.com
www.juliansrecipe.com
Marketing: Alex Dzieduszycki

7052 **Julie Anne's**
10634 San Palatina Street
Las Vegas, NV 89141 702-767-4765
julie@julieannes.com
www.julieannes.com
Organic/natural, vegetarian, breakfast cereals, granola, other snacks.
Marketing: Julie Hession

7053 **Julius Sturgis Pretzel House**
219 E Main St
Lititz, PA 17543 717-626-4354
Fax: 717-627-2682 info@sturgispretzel.com
www.sturgispretzel.com
Pretzels
Manager: Aerin Sturgis
Co-Owner: Clyde Tshudy
Co-Owner: Barbara Ann Tshudy
Estimated Sales: Under $ 1 Million
Number Employees: 10-19

7054 **Jungbunzlauer**
7 Wells Ave Ste 15
Newton, MA 02459 617-969-0900
Fax: 617-964-2921 800-828-0062
info@jungbunzlauer-inc.com
www.jungbunzlauer.com
Processor and wholesaler/distributor of acidulants, gums, potassium, sodium, caffeine, etc
President: George Mieling
CEO: Jack Doyle
Technical Service Manager: Tom West
Estimated Sales: $3300000
Number Employees: 16
Type of Packaging: Bulk

7055 **Junior's Cheesecake**
58-42 Maurice Avenue
PO Box 780-208
Maspeth, NY 11378 718-852-5257
Fax: 718-260-9849 800-458-6467
info@juniorscheesecake.com
www.juniorscheesecake.com
traditional plain cheesecake, as well as flavored cheesecake

7056 **Juniper Valley Farms**
15504 Liberty Ave
Jamaica, NY 11433-1000 718-291-3333
Fax: 718-291-0560
President: Ken Schlossberg
Estimated Sales: $ 5-10 Million
Number Employees: 20-49

7057 **Juno Chef's**
1 6 1/2 Station Rd
Goshen, NY 10924-6723 845-294-5400
Processor of frozen breakfast foods, macaroni and cheese and pasta with tomato sauce
President: Julius Spessot
General Manager: Vilma Falcon
Estimated Sales: $6-10 Million
Number Employees: 50-99
Sq. footage: 25000
Type of Packaging: Food Service

7058 **Junuis Food Products**
800 E Northwest Hwy # 510
Palatine, IL 60074-6511 847-359-4300
Fax: 847-359-4364
Processor and packer of frozen and fresh horseradish
President: John Russell
Estimated Sales: Less than $500,000
Number Employees: 1-4
Type of Packaging: Consumer, Food Service

7059 **Jurgielewicz Duck Farm**
P.O.Box 68
Moriches, NY 11955 631-878-2000
Fax: 631-878-4281 800-543-8257
Processor of frozen ducklings including free range long island duckling, kosher and parts
Owner: Benjamin Jurgielewicz
Partner: Tom Jurgielewicz
Office Manager: Amy Grimminger
Estimated Sales: $860,000
Number Employees: 10
Type of Packaging: Consumer, Food Service
Brands:
South Shore
South Side
Twin Lake

7060 **(HQ)Jus-Made**
9761 Clifford Dr Ste 100
Dallas, TX 75220 972-241-5544
Fax: 972-241-3399 800-969-3746
info@jus-made.com www.jus-made.com
Processor of bar mixes, fruit juices and drinks, fruit granitas, coffee granitas and smoothies; also sells beverage equipment.
President: Gene Barfield
VP Sales: Jim Tanner
Operations Manager: Mike Sayre
Estimated Sales: $ 1 - 3 Million
Number Employees: 50-99
Sq. footage: 3500
Type of Packaging: Consumer, Food Service, Private Label, Bulk
Other Locations:
Jus-Made
Houston TX
Brands:
Floria Julep
Orogold

7061 **Just Born**
1300 Stefko Blvd
Bethlehem, PA 18017 610-867-7568
Fax: 610-867-9931 800-445-5787
www.justborn.com
Manufacturer of confectionery products including boxed and bagged, chewy candy, holiday novelties, jelly beans and marshmallow products
Co-CEO: Ross Born
Co-CEO: David Shaffer
President/COO: David Yale
Estimated Sales: $ 20 - 50 Million
Number Employees: 250-499
Type of Packaging: Consumer
Brands:
Hot Tamales
Marshmellow Peeps
Mike and Ike
Peanut Chews
Teenee Beanee
Zours

7062 **Just Delicious Gourmet Foods**
PO Box 2747
Seal Beach, CA 90740-1747 949-215-5341
Fax: 714-870-0332 800-871-6085
www.justdelicious.net
Processor of dry soup, bread and dip mixes; exporter of dry soup mixes
President: Diana Ferguson
Estimated Sales: $500,000
Number Employees: 5-9
Sq. footage: 10000
Type of Packaging: Consumer, Food Service, Bulk
Brands:
Just Delicious

7063 **Just Desserts**
1970 Carroll Avenue
San Francisco, CA 94124-2511 415-602-9245
Fax: 415-468-4811 Mareya@justdesserts.com
http://www.justdesserts.com/
Specialty cakes, pastries, cookies
President: Elliot Hoffman
Controller: Shyam Kataruka
Marketing Manager: Mareya Ibrahim
Director Retail: John Grubb
Operations Manager: David Parker
Estimated Sales: $ .5 - 1 million
Number Employees: 100-249
Type of Packaging: Private Label

7064 **Just Off Melrose**
1196 Montalvo Way
Palm Springs, CA 92262 714-533-4566
Fax: 714-533-4567 800-743-4109
inforequest@justoffmelrose.com
www.justoffmelrose.com

Manufacturer of crisps, croutons, chips, biscotti and gourmet snacks.
President: Brandon Tesmer
Sales Rep: Ryan Niesen
Estimated Sales: Below $ 5 Million
Number Employees: 40
Brands:
Just Chips
Just Crisps
Just Croutons

7065 **Just Off Melrose, Inc.**
1196 Montalvo Way
Palm Springs, CA 92262 760-320-7414
Fax: 760-327-0331 800-743-4103
inforequest@justoffmelrose.com
www.justoffmelrose.com
Bread and baked goods
President: David Parker
Chairman: Robert Penner
CFO: David Parker
Marketing: Jeremy Flores
Estimated Sales: $ 10-20 Million
Number Employees: 50-99

7066 **Just Tomatoes Company**
P.O.Box 807
Westley, CA 95387-0807 209-894-5371
Fax: 209-894-3146 800-537-1985
info@justtomatoes.com www.justtomatoes.com
Processor of dried fruits and vegetables including tomatoes, red and green bell peppers, corn, peas, carrots, apples, persimmons, blueberries, mango, cherries, raspberries, etc.; also, mixed fruit and vegetable trail mix, crunchyraisins and dry roasted soy nuts. Food theme greeting cards, cookbooks
Co-Owner: Karen Cox
Co-Owner: Bill Cox
Estimated Sales: $ 50 - 100 Million
Number Employees: 50-99
Sq. footage: 7000
Type of Packaging: Consumer, Food Service, Private Label, Bulk
Brands:
Hot Just Veggies
Just Apples
Just Bell Peppers
Just Blackberries
Just Blueberries
Just Carrots
Just Cherries
Just Corn
Just Crunch Onions
Just Crunchy
Just Fruit Munchies
Just Fruit Snacks
Just Green Onions
Just Mango
Just Peas
Just Persimmon
Just Persimmons
Just Pineapple
Just Raisins
Just Raspberries
Just Roasted Garlic
Just Soy Nuts
Just Strawberries
Just Tomatoes
Just Veggies
Tomato Press

7067 **Just the Berries**
350 S Figueroa Street
Suite 562
Los Angeles, CA 90071 213-613-9807
Fax: 213-613-9847 www.justtheberries.com
Manufacturers and wholesales New Zealand Cassis ingredients, including: dried fruits, extracts, antioxidants, vitamins, minerals, etc
President: Eddie Shiojima
Sales Manager: Travis Kiro
Estimated Sales: $800,000
Number Employees: 8

7068 **Justin Lloyd Premium Tea Company**
1111 E Watson Center Road
Carson, CA 90745-4217 310-834-4000
Fax: 310-834-0300
Brands:
Flavors & Fusions
Herbals
Traditional

7069 **Justin Winery & Vineyard**
11680 Chimney Rock Rd
Paso Robles, CA 93446-9792 805-238-6932
Fax: 805-238-7382 800-726-0049
info@justinwine.com www.justinwine.com
Wines
President: Justin Baldwin
VP/Director Sales/Marketing: Rich Richardson
VP/Director Finance/Human Resources: Cheryl Wieczorek
Sales Manager: Paul Sowerby
Estimated Sales: $ 2.5-5 Million
Number Employees: 20-49
Type of Packaging: Private Label
Brands:
Justin

7070 **Justin's Nut Butter**
2438 30th Street
Boulder, CO 80301 303-449-9559
Fax: 303-442-0881
comments@justinsnutbutter.com
www.justinsnutbutter.com
flavored nut butters
President/Owner: Justin Gold
Sales/Marketing: Lance Gentry
Operations: Skip Latimer

7071 **(HQ)Jyoti Cruisine IndiaGourmail Inc**
816 Newtown Rd
Berwyn, PA 19312-2200 610-296-4620
Fax: 610-889-0492 jyoti@jyotifoods.com
www.jyotifoods.com
Processor and exporter of Indian foods including vegetables, soups, bean products, frozen vegetarian meals and sauces
President: Jyoti Gupta
VP: Vijai Gupta
Number Employees: 5
Type of Packaging: Consumer, Food Service, Private Label
Brands:
INDIA HOUSE
JYOTI

7072 **Jyoti Cuisine India**
816 Newtown Rd
Berwyn, PA 19312 610-296-4620
Fax: 610-889-0492 jyoti@jyotifoods.com
www.jyotifoods.com
Sauces (masala, rogan josh, saffron cream), Indian foods, chhole, matar paneer, sambar karhi, saag, dal, basmati rice
VP: Vijay Gupta
President: Jyoti Gupta
Estimated Sales: $300,000-500,000
Number Employees: 10-19
Brands:
Jyoti

7073 **K Horton Specialty Foods**
28 Monument Sq
Portland, ME 04101-6447 207-228-2056
Fax: 207-228-2059 Kris@KHortonFoods.com
www.khortonfoods.com
Specialty cheeses, olives, dried cured meats and meat pates, smoked seafood.
President: Kris Horton

7074 **K&B Company**
P.O.Box 100
601 S. Main
Schulenburg, TX 78956-0100 979-743-4422
Fax: 979-743-4422 www.primeproductsinc.net
President: Elgin Kristinik
Estimated Sales: $ 50-100 Million
Number Employees: 100-249

7075 **K&F Select Fine Coffees**
2801 SE 14th Ave
Portland, OR 97202 503-234-7788
Fax: 503-231-9827 800-558-7788
sandyj@kfcoffee.com kfcoffee.com
Wholesaler/distributor of coffee products from around the world, torami syrups and sauces, taza rica cocoas, powdered drink mixes, liquid fruit smoothie products, and allied coffee products
President: Don Dominguez
Director Sales/Marketing: Sandy Jumonville
Sales: Steve O Brien
Estimated Sales: $3228000
Number Employees: 10-19
Type of Packaging: Consumer, Food Service, Private Label, Bulk
Brands:
K&F
TAZA RICA MEXICAN SPICED COCOA

7076 **K&K Gourmet Meats**
300 Washington St
Leetsdale, PA 15056 724-266-8400
Fax: 724-266-8402
Processor of frozen philly and chicken philly steaks; also, frozen chicken
Owner: Art Kotz
Number Employees: 10-19
Type of Packaging: Consumer, Food Service

7077 **K&K Laboratories**
3305 Tyler St
Carlsbad, CA 92008 760-434-6044
Fax: 760-720-9888 knklabspacball.net
kklabs.com
Formulator and technical services of vitamin tablets, hard-shell capsules and powders.
President: Alex Kononchuk
Estimated Sales: $3500000
Number Employees: 20-49
Type of Packaging: Private Label, Bulk

7078 **K&N Fisheries**
130 Seal Point Rd Rr 1
Upper Port La Tour, NS B0W 3N0
Canada 902-768-2478
Fax: 902-768-2385
Processor and exporter of fresh and salted fish including cod, haddock and pollack
Owner/Manager: Kirk Nickerson
Vice President: Gregory Nickerson
Plant Manager: Gregory Nickerson
Estimated Sales: $2.3 Million
Number Employees: 17
Type of Packaging: Bulk

7079 **K&R Pretzel Bakery**
1700 Flesher Ave
Dayton, OH 45420 937-299-2231
Pretzels
President: Ralph Glaze
Estimated Sales: $500,000-$1 Million
Number Employees: 1-4

7080 **K&S Bakery Products**
10637 172nd Street NW
Edmonton, AB T5S 1P1
Canada 780-481-8155
Fax: 780-481-8441 ksbakery@telus.net
Processor of muffins, cakes, scones, dry mixes, doughs, batters and spreads
President: Eric Kettner
VP/Manager: Ruth Snider
VP: Ruth Snider
Manager: Earle Snider
Estimated Sales: A
Number Employees: 1-4
Type of Packaging: Consumer, Food Service
Brands:
Cakes
Jumbo Muffins
K&S
Scones

7081 **K&S Riddle**
5701 White Street
Buzzards Bay, MA 02542-1411 508-563-7333

7082 **K.B. Hall Ranch**
11999 Ojai Santa Paula Road
Ojai, CA 93023-8323 805-646-4512
Manager: Thomas Hall

7083 **K.B. Specialty Foods**
1225 N Broadway St
Greensburg, IN 47240 812-663-8184
Fax: 812-663-5680 ncortolillo@kroger.com
www.kroger.com
Bakery items
Manager: Nick Cortolillo
Operation Manager: Rod Taylor
Production Manager: Nick Cortolillo
Purchasing Manager: R Stutes
Estimated Sales: $ 100-500 Million
Number Employees: 250-499

7084 **K.L. Keller Imports**
230 Madison St
Oakland, CA 94607 510-839-7890
Fax: 510-839-7895 klkeller@ix.netcom.com
www.klkellerimports.com
Distributors of fine foods
Owner: Kitty Keller

7085 **K.S.M. Seafood Corporation**
PO Box 3057
Baton Rouge, LA 70821-3057 225-383-1517
Fax: 225-387-6641
Seafood
President: Bo Wallenhom
Estimated Sales: $ 10 - 20 Million
Number Employees: 50-99

7086 **KB Electronics Inc**
12095 NW 39th St
Coral Springs, FL 33065 954-346-4900
Fax: 954-346-3377 info@kbelectronics.com
www.kbelectronics.com
KB Electronics manufactures a variety of AC Drives, DC Drives, Fan Speed Controls, DC-DC Low Voltage Battery Controls and RFI/EMI Filters and Signals.
CFO: Fred Mush
CEO: Gilbert Knauer
Marketing Director: Gilbert Kanver
National Sales Manager: Richard Fritts
Plant Manager: Jason Morgan
Purchasing Manager: Omar Blackwood
Estimated Sales: $20-50 Million
Number Employees: 100-249
Number of Brands: 60
Sq. footage: 27000

7087 **KC Innovations**
2900 W 43rd Avenue
Kansas City, KS 66103-3129 816-506-9023
nina@kc-innovations.com
www.kcclassicgourmetfoods.com
Salsa/dips, co-packing, private label.
Marketing: Nina Ward

7088 **KDK Inc**
1128 E 12400 S
Draper, UT 84020-9628 801-571-3506
Processor of milk including skim, whole, 1% and 2%
Number Employees: 20-49
Sq. footage: 28000
Type of Packaging: Consumer, Food Service, Private Label, Bulk
Brands:
Dairy Rich
Golden Dairy

7089 **KHS-Bartelt**
5501 N Washington Blvd
Sarasota, FL 34243 941-359-4000
Fax: 941-359-4086 800-829-9980
mschroeder@barteltinc.com
www.barteltinc.com
Bakery, confectionery, biscuit/cracker, pharmaceutical products
President: Reno N Cruz
Marketing Manager: Samantha Bishop
Executive: Paul Rosile
Customer Service Manager: Michael Schroeder
Estimated Sales: $ 10-25 Million
Number Employees: 50-99
Brands:
Bartlett

7090 **KMC Citrus Enterprises**
P.O.Box 1819
Winter Haven, FL 33882 352-821-3666
Fax: 352-821-1400
Processor of fresh and frozen orange puree and dried citrus
President: Maristela Ferrari
VP: Keith Bowen
Estimated Sales: $ 1 - 3 Million
Number Employees: 10-19
Type of Packaging: Consumer, Bulk
Brands:
KMC Citrus

7091 **KP USA Trading**
500 S Anderson Street
Los Angeles, CA 90033-4222 323-881-9871
Fax: 323-268-3669
Processor, wholesaler/distributor and exporter of soybean, corn, cottonseed, sesame and other vegetable oils; importer of oriental foods including jasmine, sweet rice, noodles, rice stick and candy
VP: Jerry Wong
Manager: Joe Beatly
Manager: Nancy Wong
Number Employees: 10-19
Sq. footage: 25000
Type of Packaging: Consumer, Food Service, Private Label, Bulk
Brands:
King Products
Mama

7092 **KT's Kitchens**
1065 E Walnut Street
Suite C
Carson, CA 90746-1384 310-764-0850
Fax: 310-764-0855 ktaggares@ktskitchens.com
www.ktskitchens.com
Frozen pizza and refrigerated salad dressings
President: Kathy Taggares
VP: Sheryl Schneider
Vice President: David Fortney
Quality Control: Mario Ayon
Sales Manager: Steve Redmond
Operations Manager: Joan Paris
Purchasing Manager: Curt Ramsey
Estimated Sales: 32 Million
Number Employees: 100-249
Sq. footage: 120000
Type of Packaging: Private Label
Brands:
BOB'S BIG BOY
KT'S KITCHENS

7093 **KTI-Keene Technology**
14357 Commercial Pkwy
South Beloit, IL 61080-2621 815-624-8989
Fax: 815-624-4223 info@keenetech.com
www.keenetech.com
Manufacturer of automatic zero speed splicers, matrix iturret rewinders, web tension controls, infeeds, unwind/rewind stands and related web handling equipment.
President: John Keene
Sales Manager: Darrel Spors
Plant Manager: Bill Carpenter
Estimated Sales: $5-10 Million
Number Employees: 50-99
Sq. footage: 65000

7094 **Kabco**
2000 New Horizons Blvd
Amityville, NY 11701-1137 631-842-3600
Fax: 631-842-6002 skibria@aol.com
www.kabcopharm.com
Processor and exporter of vitamins and dietary supplements
Chairman: Abu Kabir
Director Purchasing: Rezaur Rahman Yousuf
Estimated Sales: $ 20 - 50 Million
Number Employees: 100-249
Sq. footage: 30000
Type of Packaging: Private Label

7095 **Kabob's**
5423 N Lake Dr
Lake City, GA 30260-3534 404-361-6283
Fax: 404-361-8008 800-732-9484
jherrera@kabobs.com www.kabobs.com
Processor of hors d'oeuvres including mini-beef Wellingtons, spanakopita and coconut chicken
Founder/Chairman: Terry Hunt
President/Ceo: Steve Law
Vice President/Cfo: D.Scott Barnett
Vice President/Coo: Bill Rosenhoover
Quality Control: Lisa Moris
R & D: Nilson Haynes
VP Sales/Marketing: Steve Law
Regional Sales Manager: Dan Grant
Purchasing: Ric Consuegra
Estimated Sales: $ 75-100 Million
Number Employees: 100-249
Type of Packaging: Food Service
Brands:
Kabob's

7096 **Kachemak Bay Seafood**
PO Box 4004
4470 Homer Spit Rd
Homer, AK 99603-8003 907-235-2799
Fax: 907-235-2799

Various fishes and other seafoods
Estimated Sales: Less than $500,000
Number Employees: 5

7097 **Kaffe Magnum Opus**
412 S Wade Blvd Ste 2
Millville, NJ 08332-3534 856-327-9975
Fax: 856-794-8900 800-652-5282
support@Icafe.com www.icafe.com
Regular, flavored and decaffeinated coffee
President: Robert Johnson
CEO: Robert Kraeuter
VP: Cathy Johnson
Estimated Sales: $500,000-$1 Million
Number Employees: 5-9
Brands:
Coffee Time
Kaffe Magnum Opus

7098 **(HQ)Kagome**
333 Johnson Rd
Los Banos, CA 93635 209-826-8850
Fax: 209-826-8858 www.kagomeusa.com
Canned fruit, fruit beverages and sauces
President: Wataru Kise
CFO: Hiroshi Mori
R&D Manager: Kristi Tallerico
Quality Assurance Director: Bob Craner
VP Sales/Marketing: Joseph Flannigan
VP Manufacturing/Operations: Luis De Oliveira
Production Manager: Jaime Sandoval
Purchasing Director: April Garza
Estimated Sales: $ 50 - 100 Million
Number Employees: 1942
Brands:
Kagome

7099 **Kahiki Foods**
1100 Morrison Rd.
Gahanna, OH 43230 614-322-3180
Fax: 614-751-0039 888-436-2500
President: Allan Hoover
VP Finance: Frederick Niebauer
VP Logistics: Mark Novak
Plant Manager: Andy Chan
Estimated Sales: $ 2.5-5 Million
Number Employees: 100

7100 **Kahns Bakery Company**
4130 Rio Bravo St # B
El Paso, TX 79902-1002 915-533-8433
Fax: 915-534-0043
Bakery
Estimated Sales: Under $500,000
Number Employees: 1-4

7101 **Kaiser Pickles**
500 York St
Cincinnati, OH 45214 513-621-2053
Fax: 513-455-8284 888-291-0608
customerservice@kaiserpickles.com
www.kaiserpickles.com
Pickle and pepper products
President: Ted G Kaiser
Estimated Sales: $ 10 - 20 Million
Number Employees: 16
Sq. footage: 12308
Type of Packaging: Consumer, Food Service, Private Label, Bulk

7102 **Kajun Kettle Foods**
698 Saint George Ave
New Orleans, LA 70121 504-733-8800
Fax: 504-736-0517 mdavidson@kajunkettle.com
www.kajunkettle.com
Processor of sauces, gumbo and corn shrimp soup
President: Pierre Hilzim
VP: Monica Davidson
Estimated Sales: Below $ 5 Million
Number Employees: 20-49
Sq. footage: 86000
Type of Packaging: Consumer, Food Service, Private Label, Bulk

Brands:
Crawfish Monica

7103 **(HQ)Kake Tribal Corporation**
P.O.Box 263
374 Keku Rd
Kake, AK 99830-0263 907-785-3221
Fax: 907-785-4107
Seafood and seafood products
Owner: Steve Malin
CEO: Sam Jackson
Estimated Sales: $2.4 Million
Number Employees: 20
Brands:
fuel

7104 **Kaladi Brothers**
6921 Brayton Dr Ste 201
Anchorage, AK 99507-5601
Fax: 907-344-5935 sales@kaladi.com
www.kaladi.com
Coffee
President: Tim Gravel
Estimated Sales: $ 2.5-5 Million
Number Employees: 20-49

7105 **Kalama Chemical**
1296 Third Street, N.W.
Kalama, WA 98625 360-673-2550
Fax: 360-673-3564 800-223-0035
kalama@emeraldmaterials.com
www.emeraldmaterials.com/epm/kalama
Manufacturer and exporter of specialty chemicals including benzaldehyde, cinnamic aldehyde, benzyl benzoate, benzyl alcohol, benzylacetate, potassium benzoate, benzoic acid and sodium benzoate
President: James Hamberick
VP Marketing: Jim Harris
VP Engineering: Jarl Opgrande
Number Employees: 175
Parent Co: Emerald Performance Materials

7106 **Kalamar Seafoods**
2490 W 78th Street
Hialeah, FL 33016-2762 305-822-5586
Fax: 305-557-4418
rvazquez@kalamarseafood.com
www.kalamarseafood.com
Frozen seafoods
President: Roberto R Vazquez
Controller: Carl Johnson
Vice President: Barbara Vazquez
Estimated Sales: $ 10-20 Million
Number Employees: 20-50
Number of Products: 500
Type of Packaging: Private Label

7107 **Kalamazoo Brewing Company**
8938 Krum Ave
Galesburg, MI 49053 269-382-2338
Fax: 269-382-3820 fredb@bellsbeer.com
www.bellsbeer.com
Processor of ale and stout
President: Larry Bell
VP: Angie Bell
Estimated Sales: $ 5-10 Million
Number Employees: 50-99
Type of Packaging: Consumer, Food Service
Brands:
Bell's Amber Ale
Bell's Best Brown Ale
Bell's Kalamazoo Stout
Bell's Oberon Ale
Bell's Pale Ale
Bell's Porter
Third Coast Beer
Two Hearted Ale

7108 **Kalamazoo Creamery**
706 Lake Street
Kalamazoo, MI 49001-2201 616-343-2558
Fax: 616-343-1620
Dairy products
President: william Steers
CEO: William Steers
Brands:
Kalamazoo

7109 **Kalashian Packing Company**
1850 S Parallel Avenue
Fresno, CA 93702-4137 559-237-4287
Fax: 559-237-4280
Figs, fig paste
President: Richard Kalashian
Controller: Deborah Fries
Vice President: Jerry Floratos
VP Sales/Marketing: Ron Garabedian

7110 **Kalin Cellars**
61 Galli Dr Ste G
Novato, CA 94949 415-883-3543
Fax: 415-883-3543 sales@kalincellars.com
www.kalincellars.com
Wines
President: Terrance Leighton
Secretary: Frances Leighton
CFO: Frances Leighton
Estimated Sales: Under $500,000
Number Employees: 1-4
Brands:
Kalin Cellars

7111 **Kalle Usa Inc.**
5750 Centerpoint Ct Ste B
Gurnee, IL 60031 847-775-0781
Fax: 847-775-0782 www.kalle.de
Manufacuturer of sausage casings. Also manufacture sponge cloths that can be used to wipe up large spills.
Sales Manager: John Lample
Brands:
PULLULAN
SUNMALT
TREHALOSE

7112 **Kalman Floor Company**
1202 Bergen Pkwy # 110
Evergreen, CO 80439-9559 303-674-2290
Fax: 303-674-1238 866-266-7146
Karl.Johnson@kalmanfloor.com
www.kalmanfloor.com
Manufacturer of seamless industrial concrete floors suitable for the food and beverage industries.
President: Donald Ytterberg
Sales Engineer: Karl Johnson

7113 **Kalsec**
P.O.Box 50511
Kalamazoo, MI 49005-0511 269-349-9711
Fax: 269-349-9055 info@kalsec.com
www.kalsec.com
Processor and exporter of natural flavors, colors, extracts, spice oleoresins and essential oils
President: George Todd
Treasurer: Don Baird
Research & Development: Don Berdahl
Marketing Director: Bill Goodrich
VP Sales: Gary Hainrihar
Plant Manager: Harry Todd
Purchasing Manager: Walt Bower
Estimated Sales: $ 3 - 5 Million
Number Employees: 5-9
Parent Co: Kalamazoo Holdings
Type of Packaging: Food Service, Bulk
Brands:
Aquaresin Spices
Aquaresins
Durabrite
Durabrite Colors
Duralox
Duralox Blends
Herbalox
Herbalox Seasonings
Hexahydrolone
Hexalone
Hop Oil
Hoppy Drops
Hydraisolone
Hydrolone
Isolone
Kalsec
Kettle Aroma Extract
Strolone
Tetrahydrolone
Tetralone
Vegetone
Vegetone Colors

7114 **Kalustyan Corporation**
855 Rahway Ave
Union, NJ 07083-6633 908-688-6111
Fax: 908-688-4415 info@kalustyan.com
www.kalustyans.com
Manufacturer, importer and exporter of herbs, spices, rice, nuts, dried fruits, beans, seeds, oils, etc
President: John Bas
Estimated Sales: $3 Million
Number Employees: 20-49
Sq. footage: 100000
Type of Packaging: Food Service, Bulk

7115 **Kalva Corporation**
P.O.Box 215
Gurnee, IL 60031 847-336-1200
Fax: 847-336-0712 800-525-8220
info@kalvacorp.com www.kalvacorp.com
Manufacturer of cone dips; chocolate, caramel and butterscotch toppings, hot fudge, syrups, variegates and ice cream bases; fruited shake bases and syrups; dry ice cream mix; caramel for candy manufacturers, bakeries and ice creammanufacturers
President: Robert Semred
VP: Allen Ballerini
VP Sales/Marketing: Allen Ballerini
Estimated Sales: $ 2.5-5 Million
Number Employees: 10-19
Sq. footage: 30000
Brands:
Kalva

7116 **Kamish Food Products**
5846 N Kolmar Ave
Chicago, IL 60646-5806 773-725-6959
Fax: 773-267-0400
Processor and exporter of baking mixes, chocolate products, jams, jellies and dehydrated fruit nuggets
President: Ted Kamish
VP: Ronald Kamish
Estimated Sales: $5000000
Number Employees: 20-49
Type of Packaging: Food Service, Private Label, Bulk

7117 **Kamloops Brewing Co**
965 McGill Place
Kamloops, BC V2C 6N9
Canada 250-851-2543
Fax: 250-851-9953 info@kbbeer.com
www.kbbeer.com
Beer
President: David Beardsell
CFO: George Tetreau
Sales/Marketing: Brian Keast
General Manager: Eric Spence
Estimated Sales: $2.5 Million
Number Employees: 10-19
Number of Brands: 18
Number of Products: 18
Sq. footage: 10000
Type of Packaging: Consumer, Food Service
Brands:
ALBINO RHINO ALE
BLACK BEAR ALE
BROWN BEAR ALE
BROWN ISLAND BITTER
HEMP CREAM ALE
JOW STIFF'S SPIKED ROOTBEER
POLAR BEAR ALE
RETHINK BEER

7118 **Kammeh International Trade Co**
2002 N Austin Ave
Chicago, IL 60639 312-804-0800
Fax: 773-804-0804 800-252-6634
President: Reza Rezai
CEO: Morris Rezai
Marketing Director: Elham Jazab
Sales Director: Shon Barnette
Operations Manager: Alexander Rezai
Production Manager: Mike Simkhim
Plant Manager: Athena Uslander
Purchasing Manager: Charles Uslander
Estimated Sales: $ 6.8 Million
Number Employees: 32
Sq. footage: 12
Type of Packaging: Private Label
Brands:
Athena's Brownies
Athena's Cookies
Floryn
Isadora
Ixima
Pure Breath
Regal
Silverland
Tokyo

7119 **Kan-Pac**
1016 S Summit St
Arkansas City, KS 67005-3339 620-442-6820
Fax: 620-442-6867
Juices, creamers, dairy, ice creams
VP: Steven Soza
President: Dennis Cohlmai
Estimated Sales: $ 10-20 Million
Number Employees: 50-99

7120 **Kanai Tofu Factory**
515 Ward Ave Ste B
Honolulu, HI 96814 808-591-8205
Fax: 808-591-8225
Prepared foods and soybean products
Owner: Richard Kanada
President: Mark Kaneda
Quality Control: Mark Kaneda
Sales Manager: Mark Kaneda
Estimated Sales: Below $ 5 Million
Number Employees: 20-49
Brands:
Kanai Tofu

7121 **Kandia's Fine Teas**
PO Box 797
Lewiston, ME 04243-0797 207-782-6300
Fax: 207-225-2513 kandiasteas@cs.com
www.kandiasteas.com
Herbal teas
Estimated Sales: $ 1-2.5 Million
Number Employees: 1-4

7122 **Kang's Seafood**
3000 S Shields Ave
Chicago, IL 60616-2630 312-225-2250
Fax: 312-225-6495 800-269-8425
srhea42781@aol.com www.kangsseafood.com
Seafood
Owner: Steve Rhee
CEO: Seokjuh Rhea
CFO: Sunok Rhea
Estimated Sales: $5 Million
Number Employees: 5-9
Sq. footage: 15000
Type of Packaging: Food Service

7123 **Kangaroo Brands**
7620 N 81st St
Milwaukee, WI 53223-3836 414-355-9696
Fax: 414-355-4295 800-798-0857
sales@kangaroobrands.com
www.kangaroobrands.com
Bread, pita bread, flat bread, pocket bread, wraps
President: John Kashou
Treasurer: Bill Podewils
VP: George Kashou
Marketing: Salem Kashou
VP Sales: Phillip Gass
Operations Manager: Kristina A Kashou
Plant Manager: John Kashou
Purchasing/Human Resources: Kristina Kashou
Estimated Sales: $ 5-10 Million
Number Employees: 50-99
Number of Brands: 1
Number of Products: 3
Type of Packaging: Private Label

7124 **(HQ)Kantner Group**
P.O.Box 157
Wapakoneta, OH 45895-0157 419-738-4060
Fax: 419-738-4426 www.kantnergroup.com
Kantner Group includes Kantner Ingredients, Blue Valley Foods and Chianti Cheese. Kantner Ingredients (formerly Euro Proteins) is a manufacturer and distributor of dairy proteins and a custom/contract dry blender. Blue Valley Foods isa manufacturer of pi
President: Doug Kantner
General Manager: John Sadowsky
CFO: Mike Koon
Quality Control: Joe Chayka
Sales/Operations: Pam Jeffery
Sales: Jack Salemi
Purchasing: Paul Sharp
Purchasing: Mark Howell
Estimated Sales: $ 3 - 5 Million
Number Employees: 20-49
Type of Packaging: Food Service, Private Label, Bulk
Other Locations:
Kantner Ingredients
Wapakoneta OH
Blue Valley Foods
Hebron NE
Chianti Cheese of New Jersey
Pemberton NJ
Brands:
Chianti Cheese

7125 **Kapaa Bakery**
PO Box 688
Kapaa, HI 96746-0688 808-822-4541
Baked goods
President: Paul Nishijo
Estimated Sales: $500,000 appx.
Number Employees: 5-9

7126 **Kapaa Poi Factory**
1181 Kainahola Rd
Kapaa, HI 96746 808-822-5426
Processor of poi, tofu and kulolo
President: Kenneth Fujinaga
Estimated Sales: $500000
Number Employees: 1-4
Type of Packaging: Consumer

7127 **Kaplan & Zubrin**
P.O.Box 1006
Camden, NJ 8101 856-964-1083
Fax: 856-964-0510 800-334-0002
kz.pickles@verizon.net www.kzpickles.com
Institutional and private brand packers of pickled products including pickles, condiments, relishes or peppers.
President: Ronald Kaplan
Estimated Sales: $4773872
Number Employees: 20-49
Sq. footage: 72000
Type of Packaging: Food Service
Brands:
Garden State
K&Z
Shupak

7128 **Kapono Sales**
2688 Kilihau Bay H
Honolulu, HI 96823 808-839-2714
Fax: 808-833-5444
President: Cal Odo

7129 **Kara Chocolates**
575 E University Pkwy # B43
Orem, UT 84097-7567 801-224-9515
Fax: 801-224-9588 800-284-5272
info@giftbasketsuppliers.com
www.giftbasketsuppliers.com
Chocolate candies
Manager: Susan Boren
Manager: Steve Peterson
Estimated Sales: $ 5-10 Million
Number Employees: 20-49
Brands:
Kara

7130 **Karabetian Import And Export, Inc.**
2450 Crystal Street
Los Angeles, CA 90039 323-664-8956
Fax: 323-664-8958 karabetian@aol.com

7131 **Karam Elsaha Baking Company**
102 Fairgrounds Dr
Manlius, NY 13104
Fax: 315-682-2781
Processor of pita bread including white, wheat, onion and cinnamon raisin; also, prepared pitas including spinach turnovers, lentil, meat, pizza, apple, cherry, blueberry and raspberry
Manager: Shawn Ryan
Marketing Director: Kay Dara
Number Employees: 10-19
Sq. footage: 5000
Type of Packaging: Consumer, Food Service, Private Label
Brands:
Elsaha
Elsaha Cinnamon Raisin
Elsaha Wheat Pita

7132 **Karen's Fabulous Biscotti**
50 Main St
White Plains, NY 10606-1901 914-682-2165
Fax: 914-328-4276 karen@biscotti-co.com
www.biscotti-co.com
Processor of bulk and wrapped shelf stable biscotti and gourmet cookies
President: Gary Spirer
Marketing Director: Jerry O'Donnell
Sales Director: Debbie Rittberg
General Manager: Jerry O'Donnell
Number Employees: 10-19
Sq. footage: 9000
Type of Packaging: Consumer, Bulk
Brands:
Alex & Dani's Biscotti
Karen's Fabulous Biscotti

7133 **Karen's Wine Country Cafe**
P.O.Box 447
3266 Hwy 82
Sonoita, AZ 85637-0447 520-455-5282
Fax: 520-455-0075 800-453-5650
President: Jennifer Wyrick
CEO: Jarde Wyrick
Estimated Sales: Less than $500,000
Number Employees: 5-9
Type of Packaging: Private Label

7134 **Kargher Corporation**
3131 Sandstone Dr
Hatfield, PA 19440 215-822-1186
Fax: 215-822-9666 800-355-1247
dlkcsk@aol.com
Chocolate chips, chocolate products, chocolate nonpareils, confectionary coated pretzels
President: Douglas Kargher
CEO: Douglas Kargher
Estimated Sales: $ 5-10 Million
Number Employees: 20-49
Type of Packaging: Consumer, Food Service, Private Label, Bulk
Brands:
Kargher Chocolate Chips
Kargher Milk Chocolate Chips
Kargher White Chocolate Chips

7135 **Kari-Out Company**
399 Knollwood Rd Ste 309
White Plains, NY 10603 914-580-3200
Fax: 914-580-3248 800-433-8799
info@kariout.com www.kariout.com
Manufacturer and importer of sauces including hot, mustard, soy and duck/sweet and sour; also, cooking sherry, ketchup, vinegar and food colors
President: Howard Epstein
Sales Manager: David Chan
Estimated Sales: $ 50 - 100 Million
Number Employees: 100-249
Sq. footage: 40000
Parent Co: Perk-Up
Brands:
China Pack
Chinese-Lady
Kari-Out

7136 **Karl Bissinger French Confections**
32 Maryland Plz
St Louis, MO 63108-1526 314-367-9750
Fax: 314-534-2419 800-325-8881
orders@bissingers.com www.bissingers.com
Processor and exporter of chocolate candy solids, covered cream centers, covered cherries and nuts, covered pretzels and half dipped oranges
Manager: Cindy Abrewczynski
Estimated Sales: $6000000
Number Employees: 5-9
Type of Packaging: Consumer, Bulk

7137 **Karl Ehmer**
6335 Fresh Pond Rd
Flushing, NY 11385-2623 718-456-8100
Fax: 718-456-2270 800-487-5275
info@karlehmer.com www.karlehmer.com
Sausages and deli and smoked meats.
President: Mark Hanssler
Quality Control: Gary Durante
Production Manager/VP: Allen Hanssler
Marketing Director: Will Osanitsch
Purchasing Manager: Daniel Durante
Estimated Sales: $ 5-10 Million
Number Employees: 20-49
Brands:
KARL EHMER

7138 **Karl Strauss Breweries**
5985 Santa Fe St
San Diego, CA 92109-1623 858-273-2739
Fax: 858-581-5691 www.karlstrauss.com

Brewer and importer of beer, amber lager and pale ale
Owner: Karl Strauss
CFO: Matthew Rattner
Marketing Director: Brian Bolten
Sales: Paul Timm
Operations: Grant Gotteshon
Production: Paul Segura
Estimated Sales: $ .5 - 1 million
Number Employees: 10-19
Number of Brands: 25
Number of Products: 2
Sq. footage: 22000
Parent Co: Associated Micro Breweries
Brands:
DOWNTOWN AFTER DARK
ENDLESS SUMMER GOLD
Karl Strauss
RED TROLLEY ALE
STARGAZER
WINDANSEA WHEAT

7139 **Karla's Smokehouse**
P.O.Box 537
Rockaway Beach, OR 97136-0537 503-355-2362
Smoke fish
Owner: Karla Steinhauser
Estimated Sales: Less than $500,000
Number Employees: 1-4

7140 **Karlin Foods Corporation**
1845 Oak St Ste 19
Northfield, IL 60093 847-441-8330
Fax: 847-441-8640 karlin@karlinfoods.com
www.karlinfoods.com
Dry food products: dehydrated soup mixes
President: Mitchell Karlin
Estimated Sales: $ 10-20 Million
Number Employees: 10-19

7141 **Karlsburger Foods**
3236 Chelsea Rd W
Monticello, MN 55362 763-295-2273
Fax: 763-323-1745 800-383-6549
www.karlsburger.com
Processor of soup, sauce and gravy bases; also, seasonings
President: Michael Maher
Estimated Sales: Below $ 5 Million
Number Employees: 10-19
Type of Packaging: Food Service
Brands:
Karlsburger

7142 **Karly Wines**
11076 Bell Rd
Plymouth, CA 95669 209-245-3922
Fax: 209-245-4874 karly@karlywines.com
www.karlywines.com
Manufacturer of wine
Co-Owner: Karly Cobb
Co-Owner: Lawrence Cobb
Estimated Sales: Under $500,000
Number Employees: 1-4
Brands:
Karnival Pink Lemonade
Plastic Fruit Drink

7143 **Karn Meats**
931 Taylor Ave
Columbus, OH 43219 614-252-3712
Fax: 614-252-8273 800-221-9585
ckarn@karnmeats.com www.karnmeats.com
Fresh vacuumed packed patties and IQF ground beef patties, also cooked ground beef crumbles
VP Operations: Michael Furr
Production Supervisor: Tony Furr
Plant Manager: Richard Karn
Estimated Sales: $10 Million
Number Employees: 50
Sq. footage: 50000
Type of Packaging: Food Service, Private Label, Bulk

7144 **Karoun Dairies**
9027 Glenoaks Blvd
Sun Valley, CA 91352 818-767-7000
Fax: 818-767-7024 contact@karouncheese.com
www.karouncheese.com
Specialty cheeses in the Mediterranean style
President: Anto Baghdassarian
Marketing: Rostom Baghdassarian
Estimated Sales: $ 10-20 Million
Number Employees: 20-30
Brands:
Karoun Dairies

7145 **Karp's**
6 Mazel Way
Georgetown, MA 01833
US 800-373-5277
Processor and exporter of frozen muffin batters and pre-baked breakfast desserts
Sales Manager: Mark Ake
Number Employees: 10-19
Type of Packaging: Consumer, Food Service
Brands:
Karp's
Scoop-N-Bake

7146 **Karpa Trading**
PO Box 3877
Alhambra, CA 91803-0877 626-448-2223
Fax: 626-448-2221
President: Ashley Tsao
General Manager: Joseph Chu

7147 **Karsh's Bakery**
5555 N 7th St Ste 116
Phoenix, AZ 85014 602-264-4874
Fax: 602-264-7986 gloria@karshsbakery.com
www.karshsbakery.com
Bread and bakery products
President: Wayne Kindig
Marketing Director: Gloria Gardner
Estimated Sales: Below $ 5 Million
Number Employees: 20-49
Brands:
AJ's Fine Foods
Don & Charlies
Miracle Mile
Park Central Delis

7148 **Kasel Engineering**
5911 Wolf Creek Pike
Dayton, OH 45426 937-854-8875
Fax: 937-854-8875 don@kaselengineering.com
www.kaselengineering.com
Bacon equipment, slicing machines and scales.
Owner: Donald Kasel
Estimated Sales: A
Number Employees: 8

7149 **Kashi Company**
P.O.Box 8557
La Jolla, CA 92038 858-274-8870
Fax: 858-274-8894 info@kashi.com
www.kashi.com
Processor and exporter of multi-grain products including dry cereal, pilaf and specialty mixes
President: Philip Tauber
Co-founder: Gayle Tauber
Product Manager: Karen Moyer
Marketing Director: Greg Fleishman
Estimated Sales: $5-10 Million
Number Employees: 20-49
Type of Packaging: Food Service, Private Label
Brands:
Golean Slimming Systems
Kashi
Kashi Medley
Kashi Products

7150 **Kashi Company**
P.O.Box 8557
La Jolla, CA 92038 858-274-8870
Fax: 858-274-8894 info@kashi.com
www.kashi.com
Ready to eat cereals
General Manager: David Denholm
Marketing Director: David Desoza
CFO: David Garner
CFO: David Carmor
Estimated Sales: $ 5-10 Million
Number Employees: 20-49
Brands:
Kashi

7151 **Kasilof Fish Company**
1930 Merrill Creek Pkwy Ste B
Everett, WA 98203 360-658-7552
Fax: 360-653-3560 800-322-7552
www.ilovesalmon.com
Processor of smoked salmon and smoked seafood
President: Drew Ellison
Finance Manager: Julie Lorig
VP Sales & Marketing: Patti Moore
Estimated Sales: $2.5 Million
Number Employees: 25
Parent Co: Trident Seafoods
Type of Packaging: Consumer, Food Service, Private Label, Bulk
Brands:
Eagle RIVER Brand
Kasilof Fish

7152 **Kastner's Pastry Shop &Grocery**
9467 Harding Ave
Surfside, FL 33154-2803 305-866-6993
Pastry
Owner: Philip Cohen
Estimated Sales: Less than $500,000
Number Employees: 5-9

7153 **Kate Latter Candy Company**
937 Decatur St,
New Orleans, LA 70116 504-525-5359
Fax: 504-828-0045 800-825-5359
klcandy@bellsouth.net
www.katelattercandy.com
New Orleans pralines, Southern candies, Cajun and Creole food products
President: Pam Randazza
CEO: Pam Randazza
Marketing Director: Pam Randazza
Estimated Sales: Below $ 5 Million
Number Employees: 12
Brands:
Chef Hans
Kate Latters Chocolates

7154 **Kate's Vineyard**
5211 Big Ranch Rd
Napa, CA 94558-1004 707-255-2644
Fax: 707-966-2813 info@katesvineyard.com
www.katesvineyard.com
Wine
President: William Bryant
VP: Sally Bryant
Marketing VP: Kate Bryant
Estimated Sales: Below $ 5 Million
Number Employees: 1-4
Brands:
Kate's
Sedna

7155 **Kateri Foods**
5415 Opportunity Court
Hopkins, MN 55343 952-933-9732
Fax: 952-933-9942 800-330-8351
pgknight@katerifoods.com
www.katerifoods.com
Gluten-free, other chocolate, other candy, nuts, popcorn, gift packs, private label.
Marketing: Patrick Knight

7156 **Kathryn Kennedy Winery**
13180 Pierce Rd
Saratoga, CA 95070-4212 408-867-4170
Fax: 408-867-9463
cabernet@KathrynKennedyWinery.com
www.kathrynkennedywinery.com
Manufacturer of wine
President/Winegrower: Marty Mathis
Estimated Sales: Below $ 5 Million
Number Employees: 1-4
Brands:
Kathryn Kennedy

7157 **Kathy's Gourmet Specialties**
PO Box 1058
Mendocino, CA 95460-1058 707-937-1383
Fax: 707-937-1383 info@kathysgourmet.com
www.kathysgourmet.com
Specialty sauces, mustards and condiments.
Owner: Shelley Pittman
Estimated Sales: $ 81.00 K
Number Employees: 2
Number of Products: 8
Type of Packaging: Consumer, Food Service, Private Label, Bulk
Brands:
KATHY'S GOURMET SPECIALTIES

7158 **Katie's Korner**
1105 Tibbetts Wick Rd
Girard, OH 44420-1137 330-539-4140
Fax: 330-534-1412 kkinfo@zoominternet.net
www.katiesicecream.com

Homemade ice cream and yogurt
Owner/President: Katherine Martin
Secretary/Treasurer: Keith Martin
Estimated Sales: Less than $500,000
Number Employees: 1-4

7159 **Katrina's Tartufo**
585 Bicycle Path
Port Jeffrsn Sta, NY 11776-3431 631-476-0863
Fax: 631-331-1269 800-480-8836
Processor of ice cream
Owner: Rob Dineon
Estimated Sales: Less than $500,000
Number Employees: 10-19
Sq. footage: 3000

7160 **Katy's Smokehouse**
P.O.Box 621
Trinidad, CA 95570-0621 707-677-0151
Fax: 707-677-9328
service@katyssmokehouse.com
www.katyssmokehouse.com
Processor of smoked fish including salmon, sturgeon, albacore, shark, swordfish and halibut
President: Robert Lake
CEO: Judy Lake
Estimated Sales: $500,000-$1 Million
Number Employees: 1-4
Type of Packaging: Consumer, Food Service
Brands:
Katy's Smokehouse

7161 **(HQ)Kauai Coffee Company**
P.O.Box 530
Kalaheo, HI 96741 808-335-5497
Fax: 808-335-0036 800-545-8605
greensales@kauaicoffee.com
www.kauaicoffee.com
Coffee, green and roasted
Manager: Donn Soares
Manager: Donn Soares
VP/General Manager: Frank Kiger
Marketing Manager: Annette Burton
Public Relations: Joan Morita
Estimated Sales: $ 10-100 Million
Number Employees: 5-9
Type of Packaging: Private Label
Brands:
Kauai Coffee

7162 **Kauai Kookie Kompany**
P.O.Box 68
Eleele, HI 96705 808-335-5003
Fax: 808-335-5186 800-361-1126
cookie@aloha.net www.kauaikookie.com
Cookies and dressings
Marketing: Ruth R Hashisaka
Director Sales/Marketing: Ruth Hashisaka
Plant Manager: Ellen Albarado
Estimated Sales: $1 Million
Number Employees: 20-49
Number of Brands: 2
Brands:
Hawaiian Hula Dressing
Kauai Kookie

7163 **(HQ)Kauai Organic Farms**
4301 N Waiakalua St
Kilauea, HI 96754 808-651-1777
Fax: 808-826-6809 phil@kauaiorganicfarms.com
www.kauaiorganicfarms.com
Growers of certified organic hawaiian yellow ginger. Fresh ginger in season. Ginger puree. Ginger juice.
Owner/President: Phil Green
Quality Control: Phil Green
Marketing: Phil Green
Sales: Phil Green
Public Relations: Linda Green
Estimated Sales: $ .5 - 1 million
Number Employees: 5
Number of Products: 4
Sq. footage: 2000
Type of Packaging: Bulk

7164 **Kauai Producers**
3185 Oihana St
Lihue, HI 96766 808-245-4044
Fax: 808-245-9061 kauai@hvcb.org
www.kauaivisitorsbureau.org
Wholesaler/distributor of produce and dairy, frozen, dry and refrigerated products
President: Scott Nonaka
Vice President: Pearl Nonaka
Marketing Manager: Merle Nonaka
Estimated Sales: $4.5 Million
Number Employees: 23

7165 **Kauffman Turkey Farms**
P.O.Box 205
Waterman, IL 60556-0205 815-264-3470
Fax: 815-264-7820 hoka@indianvalley.com
www.hokaturkeys.com
Processor of turkey
President: Robert Kauffman
General Manager: Tom Klopsentein
Estimated Sales: $1618790
Number Employees: 5-9
Type of Packaging: Consumer, Bulk
Brands:
Ho-Ka

7166 **Kaufman Ingredients**
P.O.Box 5609
Vernon Hills, IL 60061-5609 847-573-0844
Fax: 847-573-0945
Flour, wheat and grain
Owner: Michael Kaufman
Estimated Sales: $500,000-$1 Million
Number Employees: 1-4

7167 **Kaurina's, LLC**
2750 Northaven Road
Suite 302
Dallas, TX 75229-7072 972-888-9990
Fax: 972-888-9991 aman@kaurinas.com
www.kaurinas.com

7168 **Kava King**
123 N Orchard Street
Suite 4a
Ormond Beach, FL 32174-9514 386-673-7566
Fax: 386-671-9500 888-670-5282
info@kavaking.com www.kavaking.com
Instant Kava drink mixes
VP: William Darby
Marketing Director: Jared White
Sales: Richard Bahmann
Estimated Sales: $300,000-500,000
Number Employees: 1-4
Type of Packaging: Consumer
Brands:
Kava King Beverage Mixes
Kava King Chocolates

7169 **Kay Foods Company**
1352 Division St
Detroit, MI 48207-2604 313-393-1100
Fax: 313-393-1083
Processor of deli salads including potato, macaroni and coleslaw; also, gourmet candies including peanut brittles and clusters
President: Stuart Siegel
Vice President: Mark Kisel
Estimated Sales: $2 Million
Number Employees: 10
Sq. footage: 20000
Type of Packaging: Consumer, Food Service, Private Label
Brands:
Kay Foods

7170 **Kayem Foods**
75 Arlington St
Chelsea, MA 02150-2365 617-889-1600
Fax: 617-889-5931 800-426-6100
consumer.support@kayem.com
www.kayemfoods.com
Manufacturer and distributor of deli products and also hot dogs, traditional italian sausages, deli meats, and fresh gourmet chicken sausage.
Chairman: Ray Monkiewicz
President/CEO: Ralph Smith
Marketing: Matt Monkiewicz
VP Operations: Ed Blanchette
VP Manufacturing: Peter Monkiewicz
Estimated Sales: $135 Million
Number Employees: 250-499
Sq. footage: 200000
Type of Packaging: Consumer, Food Service, Private Label, Bulk
Other Locations:
Genoa Sausage Company
Woburn MA
Brands:
Al Fresco Chicken Sausage
Genoa Sausage
Kayem Bratwurship
Kayem Old Tyme Hot Dogs
McKenzie of Vermont
Meisterchef
Schonland's Original Recipe
Triple M Spiral Hams

7171 **Keebler Company**
545 Lomante Rd
Battlecreek, MI 49014 630-956-9742
www.keebler.com
Manufacturer of baked goods including biscuits, cookies and crackers
President: David McKay
Human Resource Manager: Monica Dunlap
Operations Manager: Mike Williams
Production Manager: Mike Jones
Plant Engineer: David Sitton
Estimated Sales: $622 Million
Number Employees: 400
Sq. footage: 325000
Parent Co: Kellogg Company
Type of Packaging: Consumer

7172 **Keebler Company**
P.O.Box 3423
Battle Creek, MI 49016 269-961-2000
Fax: 419-332-1598 800-962-1413
media.hotline@kellogg.com www.kelloggs.com
Processor of cheese and whey products
CEO: Carlos Gutierrez
Board Member: Claudio X Gonzalez
Managing Director: Benjamin S Carson
Plant Manager: John Chambers
Number Employees: 20-49
Sq. footage: 25000
Parent Co: Kellogg Company
Type of Packaging: Bulk
Brands:
Austin Crackers
Carr's Cookies
Carr's Crackers
Cheez-It Crackers
Famous Amos Cookies
Kellogg
Murray Sugar Free Cookies

7173 **Keebler Company**
7 Brick Plant Rd
Suite A
South River, NJ 08882-1145 732-613-4381
www.keebler.com
Processor and exporter of cookies, crackers and biscuits
Manager: Frank Brzynski
Manager: Peter Dydensborg
Plant Manager: Joe Henry
Number Employees: 3
Parent Co: Kellogg Company
Type of Packaging: Consumer, Food Service, Private Label, Bulk
Brands:
Sunshine

7174 **Keenan Farms**
P.O.Box 99
Avenal, CA 93204 559-945-1400
Fax: 559-945-1414 keenan@keenanpistachio.com
www.keenanpistachio.com
Pistachios
President: Robert Keenan
VP: Charles Keenan
Estimated Sales: Below $ 5 Million
Number Employees: 100-249
Brands:
Keenan Farms

7175 **Keeter's Meat Company**
P.O.Box 41
Tulia, TX 79088 806-995-3413
800-456-5019
Manufacturer of meat products
Owner: Jerry Keeter
Owner: Kati Keeter
Estimated Sales: $3 Million
Number Employees: 1-4
Type of Packaging: Consumer

7176 **Kehr's Kandy Kitchen**
3533 W Lisbon Ave
Milwaukee, WI 53208 414-344-4305
Fax: 414-933-2985 Paul@kehrs.com
http://www.kehrs.com
Candy
Owner: Paul Martinka

Estimated Sales: Less than $500,000
Number Employees: 5-9
Brands:
Kehr's Kandy

7177 **Kelatron Corporation**
1675 W 2750 S
Ogden, UT 84401 801-394-4558
Fax: 801-394-4559 biomin@kleatroncorp.com
www.kelatroncorp.com
Bioactive mineral nutrients
President: Robert Wilkins
Vice President of Technical Services: Brent Hagen
Plant Manager: Venus Hall
Estimated Sales: $ 20 - 50 Million
Number Employees: 50-99

7178 **Kelble Brothers**
9111 Reiger Rd
Berlin Heights, OH 44814 419-588-2015
Fax: 419-588-3116 800-247-2333
Processor of beef and lamb
President/Treasurer: Richard Palmer
VP: William Fox
Purchasing Agent: Rose Austin
Estimated Sales: $4 Million
Number Employees: 17
Sq. footage: 12000
Type of Packaging: Consumer, Food Service, Bulk

7179 **Kelchner's Horseradish**
161 S Main St
Dublin, PA 18917 215-249-3439
Fax: 215-249-1931
Manufacturer of prepared horseradish, tartar sauce, cocktail sauce, horseradish mustard and horseradish with beets
President: John Slaymaker
Chairman of the Board: Walter Slaymaker
Production Manager: Richard Rankin
Estimated Sales: $4700000
Number Employees: 10-19
Sq. footage: 10000
Type of Packaging: Consumer, Food Service
Brands:
Kelchner's

7180 **Kellbran Candies & Snacks**
PO Box 266
2196 E Market St
Akron, OH 44312 330-794-1448
Fax: 330-794-1448
Snack foods
Owner: Jim Buck

7181 **Keller's Bakery**
1012 Jefferson St
Lafayette, LA 70501 337-235-1568
Fax: 337-235-8817
Manufacturer of baked products
President: Kenneth Keller
Estimated Sales: $1-3 Million
Number Employees: 10-19

7182 **(HQ)Keller's Creamery**
855 Maple Ave
Harleysville, PA 19438 215-256-8871
Fax: 215-859-4001 800-535-5371
www.kellerscreamery.com
Manufacturer of butter, butter oil, powdered milk, cream cheese, cheese products, heavy cream
President/CEO/Managing Partner: Frank Otis
CFO/VP Administration: Mark Stinson
VP: Larry Weaver
Marketing Director: Joe Fallon
VP Sales/Customer Satisfaction: Larry Weaver
Estimated Sales: $250 Million
Number Employees: 50-99
Sq. footage: 100000
Type of Packaging: Consumer, Food Service, Private Label, Bulk
Other Locations:
Keller's Creamery - Production
Winnsboro TX
Brands:
BORDEN
BREAKSTONES
FALFURRIAS
HOTEL BAR
KELLER'S
MID-AMERICA FARMS
PLUGRA
SCULPTURES

7183 **Keller's Creamery**
855 Maple Ave
Harleysville, PA 19438 215-256-8871
Fax: 215-859-4001 800-535-5371
sales@kellerscreamery.com
www.kellerscreamery.com
Processor of regular and unsalted butter
President: Mark Korsneyer
Marketing Director: Joe Sallon
CFO: Mark Stinson
VP: Larry Weaver
Quality Control: Brent Nyce
Sales/Marketing Executive: Larry Weaver
Estimated Sales: $ 300 Million
Number Employees: 50-99
Parent Co: Keller's Cremery LLC
Brands:
Breakstone's
Keller's
Plugra

7184 **Kelley Bean Company**
P.O.Box 638
Torrington, WY 82240 307-532-2131
Fax: 307-532-4293 www.kelleybean.com
Processor of dried beans
Manager: Jerry Notman
Manager: Dan Smith
Estimated Sales: $ 5 - 10 Million
Number Employees: 10-19
Type of Packaging: Consumer, Food Service, Bulk
Brands:
Buffalo

7185 **Kelley Bean Company**
P.O.Box 2488
Scottsbluff, NE 69363 308-635-6438
Fax: 308-635-7345 kkelley@kelleybean.com
www.kelleybean.com
Manufacturer and exporter of dry beans and seeds
President: Robert Kelley
CFO: Lee Glenn
VP: Lee Glenn
Estimated Sales: $ 50 - 100 Million
Number Employees: 20-49
Type of Packaging: Consumer, Food Service, Bulk
Brands:
BROWN'S BEST

7186 **(HQ)Kelley Bean Company**
P.O.Box 2488
Scottsbluff, NE 69363 308-635-6438
Fax: 308-635-7345 www.kelleybean.com
Processor and exporter of dried beans including Great Northern and pinto
President: Robert Kelley
CEO: Gary Kelley
Sales Manager: Stephen Snyder
Estimated Sales: $500,000-$1 Million
Number Employees: 5-9
Sq. footage: 100000
Type of Packaging: Consumer, Food Service, Private Label, Bulk

7187 **Kelley Foods of Alabama**
1697 Lower Curtis Rd
Elba, AL 36323 334-897-5761
Fax: 334-897-2712 eddiek@kelleyfoods.com
www.kelleyfoods.com
Processor of sausage; wholesaler/distributor of meats, dairy items, frozen foods, equipment and fixturers, paper products, poultry, spices and catfish; serving the food service market
President: Edwin Kelley
CEO: Eddie Kelley
Controller: Alex Mount
Vice President: J Kelley
VP Marketing: C Kelley
VP Operations: Dwight Kelley
Estimated Sales: $ 10 - 20 Million
Number Employees: 100-249
Type of Packaging: Food Service
Brands:
Bryan
Excel
Hormel
Kelley's

7188 **Kelley Meats**
8937 Beckwith Rd
Taberg, NY 13471 315-337-4272
Fax: 315-337-4272
Processor of beef, pork, veal, bacon, smoked ham and sausage; also, custom slaughtering
President: Dean Kelley
CEO: Dean Kelley
Estimated Sales: $120,000
Number Employees: 1-4
Type of Packaging: Consumer

7189 **Kelley's Katch Caviar**
210 Washington St
Savannah, TN 38372 731-925-7360
Fax: 731-925-5631 888-681-8565
americasfinest@kellyskatch.com
www.kelleyskatch.com
Manufacturer of all-natural American paddlefish caviar and sturgeon caviar.
Owner: Vickie Kelley
Estimated Sales: Less than $500,000
Number Employees: 1-4

7190 **Kelley's Katch Caviar**
210 Washington St
Savannah, TN 38372 731-925-7360
Fax: 731-925-5631 888-681-8565
americasfinest@kelleyskatch.com
www.kelleyskatch.com
caviar

7191 **Kelley's Katch Caviar**
210 Wahington Street
Savannah, TN 38372 731-925-7360
Fax: 731-925-5631 888-681-8565
office@kelleyskatch.com www.kelleyskatch.com

7192 **Kelleys Island Wine Company**
P.O.Box 747
Kelleys Is, OH 43438 419-746-2678
bretlynn@cros.net
www.kelleysislandwine.com
Wines
President: Kirt Zettler
Owner: Toby Zettler
Estimated Sales: $ 5-9.9 Million
Number Employees: 5-9
Brands:
Coyote White
Inscription White
Long Sweet Red
Sunset Pink

7193 **Kellogg Canada Inc**
5350 Creekbank Road
Mississauga, ON L4W 5S1
Canada 905-290-5200
Fax: 905-290-5388 888-876-3750
diane.bellissimo@kellogg.com www.kelloggs.ca/
Processor of breakfast foods including cereals, natural grain waffles and toaster tarts.
President/Ceo: John Bryant
Cfo: Ronald Dissinger
Vp Quality: Maragret Bath
Cmo: Mark Baynes
Public Relations/Media: Diane Bellissimo
Estimated Sales: $1.2 Billion
Number Employees: 850
Parent Co: Kellogg Company
Type of Packaging: Consumer

7194 **Kellogg Company**
2168 Frisco Ave
Memphis, TN 38114 901-743-0052
Fax: 901-745-9882
paulina.ruiz-lang@kellogg.com
www.kellogg.com
Processor and exporter of breakfast cereals.
Quality Control Manager: Melissa Dunham
Corporate Affairs Manager: Paulina Ruiz-Lang
Personnel Assistant: Cindy Taylor
General Manager: Tim Blair
Plant Manager: Jim Ambrose
Purchasing Agent: Robin Milligan
Estimated Sales: $500 Million to $1 Billion
Number Employees: 750
Parent Co: Kellogg Company
Type of Packaging: Consumer
Brands:
ALL-BRAN®
AUSTIN®
BEAR NAKED®
CHEEZ-IT®
CHIPS DELUXE®
CLUB®
EGGO®
FAMOUS AMOS®

GARDENBURGER®
KASHI®
KEEBLER®
KELLOGG'S®
MINI-WHEATS®
MORNINGSTAR FARM®
MURRAY®
NUTRI-GRAIN®
POP-TARTS®
RICE KRISPIES®
SANDIES®
SPECIAL K®
STRETCH ISLAND(190

7195 **Kellogg Company**
P.O.Box 3866
Omaha, NE 68103 402-331-7717
Fax: 402-593-2688 rheylan@kellogg-fcu.org OR paulina.ruiz-lang@kellogg.com
www.kellogg.com
Manufacturer of breakfast cereals.
President/CEO: Roger B Hylen
VP Lending: Linda Bohac
Corporate Affairs Manager: Paulina Ruiz-Lang
Plant Manager: Virgil Thomas
Estimated Sales: $ .5 - 1 million
Number Employees: 500-999
Parent Co: Kellogg Company
Type of Packaging: Consumer, Bulk

7196 **Kellogg Company**
322 S Egg Harbor Rd
Hammonton, NJ 8037 609-567-2300
Fax: 609-567-4948
investor.relations@kellogg.com OR paulina.ruiz-lang@kellogg.com
www.kellogg.com
Processor of frozen waffles.
Chairman/CEO: James Jenness
President/COO: A D David Mackay
Executive VP: John A Bryant
Corporate Affairs Manager: Paulina Ruiz-Lang
Plant Manager: Patrick Taylor
Estimated Sales: $ 50 - 100 Million
Number Employees: 100-249
Parent Co: Kellogg Company
Type of Packaging: Consumer
Brands:
Kellogg's

7197 **Kellogg Food Away From Home**
545 Lamont Road
Elmhurst, IL 60126 630-956-9645
Fax: 630-833-6880 877-511-5777
susan.danner@kellogg.com
www.kelloggsfoodawayfromhome.com
Ready-To-Eat Cereal; Crackers; Grab 'N Go Snacks; Cones, Pie Crusts, & Crushed Cookies; Cookies; Waffles & Veggie Products.
Operations Manager: Frank Costanza
Number Employees: 160
Parent Co: Kellogg Company
Type of Packaging: Food Service

7198 **(HQ)Kelly Flour Company**
1208 N Swift Rd
Addison, IL 60101-6104 630-678-5300
Fax: 630-678-5311 info@foodblends.com
www.oxydry.com
Dry milk replacers and dry egg extenders
Manager: Dan Hoberg
Executive VP: Donald Kelly, Jr.
Plant Manager: Samuel Vergara
Estimated Sales: $ 3-5 Million
Number Employees: 20-49
Sq. footage: 15
Type of Packaging: Food Service, Private Label
Brands:
Chickadee Products
Hi-Bak
Kel-Yolk
Thel-Egg

7199 **Kelly Foods**
513 Airways Blvd
Jackson, TN 38301 731-424-2255
info@kellyfoods.com
www.kellyfoods.com
Processor of canned meat products including hash, chili, beef stew, corned beef, tamales, etc.; importer of corned beef
President: Ann Koch
VP Operations: Mark Koch
Plant Manager: Bob James
Purchasing Manager: Mike Rushing
Estimated Sales: $5700000
Number Employees: 50
Sq. footage: 65000
Type of Packaging: Consumer
Brands:
Hypower
Kelly

7200 **Kelly Gourmet Foods**
2095 Jerrold Ave Ste 218
San Francisco, CA 94124 415-648-9200
Fax: 415-648-6164 edkelly@kellyfds.com
www.kellygourmetfoods.com
Processor and exporter of cooked, smoked and raw chicken, sausage, roasters and chicken including whole, parts, boneless, skinless, breast and legs
President: Rina Kelly
VP: Chris Kelly
Sales Director: Ed Kelly
Estimated Sales: Less than $500,000
Number Employees: 1-4
Type of Packaging: Consumer, Food Service, Bulk
Brands:
Fulton Organic Free Range Chicken
Fulton Valley Farms
Sierra Sausage Co.

7201 **Kelly Kornbeef Company**
3531 N Elston Ave
Chicago, IL 60618-5687 773-588-2882
Fax: 773-588-0810
Processor of beef hot dogs and deli foods including corned beef and pastrami
President: Marvin Eisenberg
Estimated Sales: $510000
Number Employees: 20-49
Parent Co: Eisenberg Sausage Company
Brands:
Eisenberg
Kelly

7202 **Kelly Packing Company**
P.O.Box 27
Torrington, WY 82240-0027 307-532-2210
Fax: 307-532-8482
Manufacturer of meat products including beef, pork and lamb; also, smoked turkey and honey ham available
President: David K Kelly
Estimated Sales: $4 Million
Number Employees: 5-9
Type of Packaging: Consumer
Brands:
KELLY

7203 **Kelly's Candies**
9250 Highland Rd
Pittsburgh, PA 15237 412-795-8922
Fax: 412-573-0044 800-523-3051
kellyscandies@comcast.net
www.kellycandies.com
Processor of homemade fudge and chocolate candies
Owner: Gina Broderick
Estimated Sales: $ .5 - 1 million
Number Employees: 5-9
Type of Packaging: Consumer, Private Label, Bulk
Brands:
Kelly's

7204 **Kelly-Eisenberg GourmetDeli Products**
3531 N Elston Ave
Chicago, IL 60618-5687 773-588-2882
Fax: 773-588-0810 sales@kellyeisenberg.com
www.kellyeisenberg.com
Corned beef, hot dogs, roast beef, pastrami, Polish sausage
President: Marvin Eisenberg
CEO: Marvin Eisenberg
VP: Cliff Eisenberg
VP: Howard Eisenberg
Marketing Director: Marvin Eisenberg
Operations Manager: Greg Timm
Estimated Sales: Below $ 5 Million
Number Employees: 20-49
Type of Packaging: Private Label
Brands:
Eisenberg Beef Hot Dogs
Eisenberg Corned Bee
Eisenberg Pastrami
Kelly Corned Beef

7205 **Kelsen, Inc.**
40 Marcus Drive
Suite 101
Melville, NY 11747 631-694-8080
Fax: 631-694-8085 888-253-5736
gq@kelsen.com www.cookies.dk
Danish butter cookies
President: Lars Norgaard
Marketing: Gilbert Quiles Jr
Estimated Sales: $ 5 - 10 Million
Number Employees: 5-9
Number of Brands: 4
Brands:
Bisca
Karenvolf
Kjeldsens
Royal Dansk

7206 **Kelson Creek Winery**
19919 Shenandoah School Rd
Plymouth, CA 95669 209-245-4700
Fax: 209-245-4707
sales@kelsoncreekwinery.com
www.kelsoncreekwinery.com
Manufacturer of wine; Formerly Sonora Winery and Port Works
Manager: April Ysmael
CEO: Tim Tado
Estimated Sales: $500,000-$1 Million
Number Employees: 1-4
Type of Packaging: Private Label
Brands:
Kelson Creek

7207 **Kemach Food ProductsCorporation**
9920 Farragut Rd
Brooklyn, NY 11236 718-272-5655
Fax: 718-272-6226 888-453-6224
s.salzman@kemach.com www.kemach.com
Company provides drink mixes, soup mixes, cookies, crackers, flour, cereals, kosher, pasta, noodles, breadsticks, flatbread, candy, chocolates, health food, natural foods, chocolate syrup, juices, pasta sauces, ices, cones, etc
President: Samuel Salzman
CFO: Aaron Daum
VP: Nik Salzman
Estimated Sales: $2.5-5 Million
Number Employees: 15
Sq. footage: 15000
Type of Packaging: Consumer, Food Service, Private Label, Bulk
Brands:
A'Guania
Kemach
Matzo Meal
Mekach

7208 **Kemin Health**
600 E Court Ave Ste A
Des Moines, IA 50309 515-248-4000
Fax: 515-248-4051 888-248-5040
info@kemin.com www.kemin.com
Vitamin and supplement ingredients, natural preservatives, FloraGLO lutein, natural antioxidant preservatives
President: Rodney Ausich
VP: Charles Brice
Marketing Director: Andy Martin
Sales Manager: Linda Fullmer
Customer Service: Lori Barker
Number Employees: 10-19
Brands:
FloraGlo
Myco CURB
Naturox
Oro GLO
PALASURANCE
Paradigmox
Roseen
Satise
ZeniPRO

7209 **Kemper Bakery Systems**
3 Enterprise Dr Ste 108
Shelton, CT 06484 203-929-6530
Fax: 203-929-7089 pat@kemperusa.com
www.kemperusa.com
Manufacturer of bakery equipment
President: Patricia Kennedy
VP Marketing/Mixer Product Manager: Shawna Goldfarb
Estimated Sales: $5 Million
Number Employees: 5-9

7210 **Kemps**
W55 N 155 McKinley Boulevard
Cedarburg, WI 53012 262-377-5040
Fax: 262-377-9532 r.kraus@kemps.com
Processor of flavored fruit drinks and dairy products including milk, cream and half and half
VP/General Manager: Tom Hall
VP: Robert Mathison
Sales Manager: Roger Kraus
Operations Manager: Roger Domask
Manufacturing Director: Robert Godfrey
Plant Manager: Jeff Slaasted
Estimated Sales: $ 50 - 100 Million
Number Employees: 120
Sq. footage: 70000
Parent Co: Marigold Foods
Type of Packaging: Consumer, Food Service, Private Label, Bulk

7211 **Kemps**
1270 Energy Ln
Saint Paul, MN 55108 651-379-6500
800-322-9566
kempscrd@kemps.com www.kemps.com
Products include frozen novelties, frozen yogurt, ice cream, sherbert, milk and cultured products and juices.
President: Jim Green
CEO: Jim Green
Distribution Manager: Roger Kraus
Estimated Sales: $ 1-2.5 Million
Number Employees: 5-9

7212 **Ken's Foods**
1 Dangelo Dr
Marlborough, MA 01752 508-229-1100
Fax: 508-485-6882 800-633-5800
service@kensfoods.com www.kensfoods.com
Manufacturer of salad dressings, mayonnaise and sauces
Owner: Dorothy H Keene
CEO: Andy Crowley
Estimated Sales: 100+ Million
Number Employees: 1-4
Other Locations:
Ken's Plant Facility
McDonough GA
Ken's Plant Facility
Las Vegas NV

7213 **Kenai Custom Seafoods**
PO Box 1649
Kenai, AK 99611-1649 907-283-9109
Fax: 907-283-6475
Seafood
Proprietor: James Hill

7214 **Kenai Packers**
PO Box 31179
Seattle, WA 98103-1179 206-433-6917
Salmon
President: Hisashi Sugiyama
Estimated Sales: $ 10-100 Million
Number Employees: 20

7215 **Kencraft**
119 East 200
North Alpine, UT 84004 801-756-6916
Fax: 801-756-7791 800-377-4368
sales@kencraftcandy.com
www.kencraftcandy.com
Manufacturer of Candy and other confectionery products
President: David Taiclet
CEO: David Taiclet
VP Sales: Frank Trinnaman
Estimated Sales: $ 100-500 Million
Number Employees: 200
Number of Brands: 12
Sq. footage: 95000
Parent Co: Alpine Confections
Brands:
BUBBLEGUM BUDDIES
CANDY CLIMBERS
CHOCO PALS
CHUMMY CHUMS
CIRCUS STICKS
KENCRAFT CLASSICS
KOOKIE KAKES
LIL' LOLLIES
LOLLIPALS
PUPPET PALS
TWIST POPS
TWISTIX

7216 **Kendall Citrus Corporation**
PO Box 157
Goulds, FL 33170 305-258-1628
Fax: 305-258-2445
Citrus juice, oils, flavors, orange, grapefruit, lemon, lime
Estimated Sales: $ 10-25 Million
Number Employees: 30

7217 **(HQ)Kendall-Jackson Wine**
P.O.Box 1900
Windsor, CA 95492-1900 707-544-4000
Fax: 707-569-0105 800-544-4413
kjwines@kj.com www.kj.com
Wines
Chairman of the Board: Jesse Jackson Jr
President: John Grant
CFO: Alfred Rossow, Jr. Jr
CEO: Lewis Platt
Executive VP Finance/Administration: John Bridendall
Sales Director: Bob Roux
Public Relations: Jim Caudill
Operations Manager: Chuck Shea
Winemaster: Randy Ullom
Estimated Sales: $ 50-100 Million
Number Employees: 100-249
Type of Packaging: Private Label
Brands:
Kendall-Jackson College
Kendall-Jackson Grand Reserve
Kendall-Jackson Great Estates
Kendall-Jackson Vitner's Reserve
Stuature

7218 **Kendrick Gourmet Products**
302 Brown Ave
Columbus, GA 31903-1253 706-687-0161
Fax: 706-682-1528 800-356-1858
info.kendrick@columbusgourmet.com
www.columbusgourmet.com
Pecan candies/cakes/brownies
President: Bryan Stone
Vice President: Liz Kendrick
Manager: Stacey Chambers
Sales Manager: Robbing Carr
Estimated Sales: $ 5-9.9 Million
Number Employees: 10-19
Sq. footage: 60000
Parent Co: Columbus Gourmet

7219 **Kenko International**
6984 Bandini Blvd
Los Angeles, CA 90040 323-721-8300
Fax: 323-721-9600 ronu@kenko-intl.com
www.kenkoco.com
Manufactures sweeteners, food acidulants, antioxidants, preservatives and other food chemicals
President: Satomi Tsuchibi
Estimated Sales: $2.7 Million
Number Employees: 15

7220 **Kenlake Foods**
300 N Lp Miller St
Murray, KY 42071 270-762-5100
Fax: 270-759-1919 800-632-6900
tcolson@kroger.com www.kroger.com
Processor of hot chocolate mixes, breakfast drinks, instant teas and oatmeal; also, canned nuts
Manager: Bob Beuhler
Number Employees: 10,000+
Parent Co: Kroger Company
Type of Packaging: Consumer, Private Label
Brands:
Kenlake Foods

7221 **Kennebec Fruit Company**
2 Main St
Lisbon Falls, ME 04252 207-353-8173
Moxie; yellow gentian based soft drink
Owner: Frank Anicetti II
Estimated Sales: Less than $500,000
Number Employees: 1-4

7222 **Kennedy Gourmet**
9087 Knight Rd
Houston, TX 77054 713-795-5500
Fax: 713-795-5534 800-882-6253
info@kennedygourmet.com
www.kennedygourmet.com
Manufacturer of gourmet candy and foods
President: J Read Boles III
Plant Manager: Sandy Lewis
Purchasing Manager: Sue Williams
Estimated Sales: Below $ 5 Million
Number Employees: 50
Sq. footage: 40
Type of Packaging: Private Label
Brands:
Brazos Legends
Choc-Quitos
Chocolate Covered Pretzels
Chocolate Flavored Coffee Spoons
Chocolate Fortune Cookies
Graham Dunks
Gram Dunks
Nostalgic Creations
Sir George Fudge
Stirring Sticks
Tea Sickles
Which Ends

7223 **Kennesaw Fruit & Juice**
1300 SW 1st Ct
Pompano Beach, FL 33069-3204 954-782-9800
Fax: 954-784-1222 800-949-0371
www.kennesawfruitandjuice.com
Processor of citrus juices including orange, grapefruit, lemonade, etc.; also, cored and chunked pineapple, fresh orange and grapefruit slices and fruit salad available
President: Len Roseberg
V.P./Prtnr.: Ed Zukerman
Estimated Sales: $ 3 - 5 Million
Number Employees: 20-49
Sq. footage: 38000
Type of Packaging: Consumer, Food Service

7224 **Kenny's Candy Company**
P.O.Box 269
Perham, MN 56573 218-346-2340
Fax: 218-346-2343 800-782-5152
www.klnenterprises.com
Licorice
President: Kenneth Nelson
CFO: Mike Holper
VP: Shane Kangas
National Sales Manager: Shane Kangas
Estimated Sales: $ 20-50 Million
Number Employees: 100-249
Sq. footage: 52000
Brands:
JUICY TWISTS
KENNY'S

7225 **(HQ)Kenosha Beef International**
P.O.Box 639
Kenosha, WI 53141 262-859-2272
Fax: 262-859-2078 800-541-1685
bwinfo@bwfoods.com www.bwfoods.com
Processor of meat products including frozen boxed beef patties
Purchasing: Don Wirch
CEO: Charles Vignieri
Number Employees: 500-999
Type of Packaging: Consumer, Food Service
Brands:
K-Pack

7226 **Kent Foods**
P.O.Box 658
Gonzales, TX 78629-0658 830-672-7993
Fax: 830-672-7223
Manufacturer of frozen and liquid egg products
President: Daw Lu
Estimated Sales: $1-3 Million
Number Employees: 20-49
Sq. footage: 15000
Type of Packaging: Food Service, Bulk
Brands:
KENT FOODS

7227 **Kent Meats**
703 Leonard St NW
Grand Rapids, MI 49504-4236 616-459-4595
Fax: 616-459-5802 800-748-0141
www.kentqualityfoods.com
Makes sausages
President: Charles Soet Jr
Estimated Sales: $ 10-100 Million
Number Employees: 100-249

7228 **Kent Quality Foods**
703 Leonard St NW
Grand Rapids, MI 49504 616-459-4595
Fax: 616-459-5802 800-748-0141
info@kentqualityfoods.com
www.kentqualityfoods.com
Manufacturer and packer of meat products including skinless frankfurters and sausages
President: Charles Soet Jr
Estimated Sales: $30 Million
Number Employees: 100-249
Type of Packaging: Consumer, Food Service, Private Label, Bulk

7229 **Kent's Wharf**
31 Steamboat Hl
Swans Island, ME 04685 207-526-4186
Fax: 207-526-4291
Seafood
Owner: David Niquette
Estimated Sales: $300,000-500,000
Number Employees: 1-4

7230 **Kentucky Beer Cheese**
P.O.Box 206
Nicholasville, KY 40340 859-887-1645
Fax: 859-885-3555
kentuckybeercheese@alltel.net
www.kentuckybeercheese.com
Processor and wholesaler/distributor of cheese spread and dip including hot, garlic and beer flavored
Owner: Diane Evans
Estimated Sales: $500,000-$1 Million
Number Employees: 1-4
Sq. footage: 1000
Parent Co: Evans Gourmet Foods, LLC
Type of Packaging: Consumer, Food Service
Brands:
Kentucky Beer Cheese

7231 **Kentucky Bourbon**
P.O.Box 16
Westport, KY 40077-0016 502-222-6154
Fax: 502-222-1848 866-472-7797
tracy@bourbonQ.com www.bourbonQ.com
Gourmet sauces & spices
President: Shane Best
Estimated Sales: $300,000-500,000
Number Employees: 10-19
Brands:
BEAR CLAW
CULTURED RED NECK T-SHIRTS
FIGHTING COCK
KENTUCKY BOURBONQ
LADY IN RED
MOONSHINE MADNESS
PAPPY'S BEST PREMIMUM MARINADE
PAPPY'S XXX WHITE LIGHTININ
SAUCE FOR SISSIES
SHRIMP BUTLER
SMOKY MOUNTAIN TRAIL RUB

7232 **Kenwood Vineyards**
P.O.Box 447
Kenwood, CA 95452 707-833-5891
Fax: 707-833-1146 info@kenwoodvineyards.com
www.kenwoodvineyards.com
Processor and exporter of Sonoma county table wines
Manager: Alan Jensen
Sales/Marketing: Paul Young
Public Relations: Margie Healy
Winemaker: Mike Lee
Number Employees: 50-99
Sq. footage: 50000
Parent Co: Korbel Champagne
Type of Packaging: Consumer
Brands:
Kenwood Vineyards

7233 **Kerala Curry**
2277 Otis Johnson Road
Pittsboro, NC 27312 919-545-9401
Fax: 919-545-9402 rolls@keralacurry.com
www.keralacurry.com
Gluten-free, organic/natural, USDA, chutney/relish, hors d'oeuvres/appetizers, ready meals/pizza/soup, ethnic sauces (soy, curry, etc.), foodservice.
Marketing: Rollo Varkey

7234 **Kern Meat Distributing**
Rr 2 Box 339
Brooksville, KY 41004 606-756-2255
Fax: 606-756-2114
Meat
President: Ed Kern
Estimated Sales: $ 10 - 20 Million
Number Employees: 20-49

7235 **Kern Ridge Growers**
25429 Barbara Street
Arvin, CA 93203-0455 661-854-3141
Fax: 661-854-7229 scott@kernridge.com
www.kernridge.com
Carrots, also packs and ships bell and chile peppers and Sunkist Navel Oranges.
CFO: Walter Wurtman
Sales Executive: Andrew Bianchi
General Manager/Human Resource Manager: Robert Giragosian
COO: Zak Karlan
Estimated Sales: $36 Million
Number Employees: 50
Sq. footage: 53000
Type of Packaging: Consumer, Bulk
Brands:
Kern Ridge
Morn'n Fresh

7236 **Kernel Fabyan's GourmetPopcorn**
3722 Illinois Avenue
St Charles, IL 60174-2421 630-485-4680
Fax: 630-513-0396 847-483-1377
eddien@kernelfabyans.com
www.kernelfabyans.com
Popcorn
Marketing: Eddie Nusinow

7237 **Kernel Season's LLC**
2401 E Devon Ave
Elk Grove Village, IL 60007 773-292-4567
Fax: 773-326-0869 866-328-7672
info@kernelseasons.com
www.kernelseasons.com
Manufacturer of popcorn seasonings, machines and accessories.
Founder/Owner/President/CEO: Brian Taylor
Marketing: Jean Doyle

7238 **Kerr Brothers**
956 Islington Avenue
Toronto, ON M8Z 4P6
Canada 416-252-7341
Fax: 416-252-6054 www.kerrs.com
Manufacturer and exporter of confectionery products
Pres.: R Patterson

7239 **Kerr Concentrates**
2340 Hyacinth St NE
Salem, OR 97301 503-378-0493
Fax: 503-378-1123 800-910-5377
info@kerrconcentrates.com
www.kerrconcentrates.com
Processor of frozen fruit and vegetable juice concentrates, purees and puree concentrates
President: Andy Stormant
CFO: David Gatti
Sales: Michael Roth
Research & Development: Mike January
Quality Control: Sam Grubb
Sales Director: Mike Roth
VP of Operations: Micheal Coughlin
Plant Manager: Bart Hoopman
Purchasing: Jerry Mink
Estimated Sales: $ 5 - 10 Million
Number Employees: 50-99
Sq. footage: 48000
Parent Co: International Flavors & Fragrances
Type of Packaging: Bulk
Other Locations:
Kerr Concentrates Div.
Woodburn OR

7240 **Kerr Jellies**
PO Box 599
Dana, NC 28724-0599 828-685-8381
Fax: 828-685-8381 877-685-8381
Jellies
President: Kathy Thompson
Estimated Sales: $ 5-10 Million
Number Employees: 5-9

7241 **Kerrobert Bakery**
PO Box 454
Kerrobert, SK S0L 1R0
Canada 306-834-2461
Processor of bagel, bread, buns, pastries, doughnuts and muffins
President: Eileen Mackay
Number Employees: 1-4
Sq. footage: 2000
Type of Packaging: Consumer, Food Service, Bulk
Brands:
Kerrobert Bakery

7242 **Kerry Ingredients**
1640 W 1st St
Blue Earth, MN 56013 507-526-7575
Fax: 507-526-5026 www.kerryingredients.com
Manufacturer of particulates, inclusions, toppings, and half products for bars, cereals, fillings, ice creams, snacks and bakery products
President/CEO: Verle Grove
Plant Engineer: Todd Gackstetter
Estimated Sales: $20-50 Million
Number Employees: 230
Number of Brands: 2
Number of Products: 45
Sq. footage: 130000
Parent Co: Kerry Group
Type of Packaging: Consumer, Food Service, Private Label, Bulk
Brands:
NUCHEWS
PROTI-OATS

7243 **Kerry Ingredients & Flavours**
3330 Millington Road
Beloit, WI 53511 608-362-1651
Fax: 608-363-1490 800-248-7310
sales@kerryingredients.com www.kerry.com
Processor of ingredients and flavorings
CEO: Stan McCarthy
CFO: Brian Mehigan
Marketing Director: Jim Andrews
Sales Director: Verle Grove
Director of Corporate Affairs: Frank Hayes
Operations Manager: Michael Leahy
Purchasing Manager: Daryl Adei
Estimated Sales: $6 Billion
Number Employees: 1,000-4,999
Parent Co: Kerry Group Plc
Brands:
Baker's Aid
DCA
Golden Dipt
Modern Maid

7244 **Kerry Sweets Ingredients**
P.O.Box 427
Gridley, IL 61744-0427 309-747-3534
Fax: 309-747-2485 gregu@ringgerfoods.com
www.kerrygroup.com
Processor of cookie pieces and rice crisps for cereals, including soy crispies and flakes. Private labeling available
Manager: Marc Johnson
Eastern Sales Manager: Greg Umland
Research & Development: Jonathan Baner
Estimated Sales: $ 10-20 Million
Number Employees: 50-99
Sq. footage: 70000
Type of Packaging: Food Service, Private Label
Brands:
Kerry Sweets

7245 **Kershenstine Beef Jerky**
550 Industrial Park Rd
Eupora, MS 39744 662-258-2049
Fax: 662-258-2002
Processor and exporter of beef jerky
President: Timothy Kershenstine
Estimated Sales: $710000
Number Employees: 5-9
Type of Packaging: Consumer

7246 **Kess Industries Inc**
130 37th St NE
Auburn, WA 98002 253-735-5700
Fax: 253-735-2851 800-578-5564
ray@kessind.com www.kessind.com
Kess Industries produces an extensive array of standard and custom equipment for accumulating, chilling, coating, depositing, distributing, drying, dumping, metering, pasteurizing, transferring, washing and weighing products. Allequipment designs are acc
President: K Jell Fogelgren
Sales and Estimating: Ray Cassingham
Estimated Sales: Below $5 Million
Number Employees: 10-19
Sq. footage: 12000

7247 **Kessler Foods, Inc**
1201 Hummel Ave
Lemoyne, PA 17043 717-763-7162
Fax: 717-763-4982 info@kesslerfoods.com
www.kesslerfoods.com
Smoked and fresh meats, sausage products, ham, bacon and deli items.
President/CEO: Bob Kessler Jr Jr
CFO: Lee Fake
Quality Control: Glen Sansom
Sales Director: Bob Kessler Jr
Operations/Production/Plant Manager: Richard Caramaga
Estimated Sales: $ 20 - 50 Million
Number Employees: 40
Number of Brands: 4
Number of Products: 600
Sq. footage: 39000
Type of Packaging: Consumer, Food Service, Private Label, Bulk
Brands:
KESSLER'S
NITTANY LION FRANKS
PRIMAL SCREAM
SUSQUEHANNA VALLEY

7248 **(HQ)Keto Foods**
56 Park Pl
Suite 2
Neptune, NJ 7753 732-922-0009
Fax: 732-643-6677 email@keto.com
www.keto.com
Processor of diet coffee, tea and creamer. Manufacturing and developmnet of largest line of low carbohydrate foods and snacks
President: Arnie Bey
Quality Control: Allan Nargolies
VP Corporation Counsel: Dan Majollo
Sales/Marketing Executive: Arnie Bey
Purchasing Agent: Megan Holman
Estimated Sales: $ 2.5-5 Million
Number Employees: 30
Sq. footage: 30000
Type of Packaging: Consumer, Food Service, Bulk
Brands:
Slim Diez

7249 **Ketters Meat Market & Locker Plant**
118 W Main Ave
Frazee, MN 56544 218-334-2351
Manufacturer of beef, pork, turtle and deer
President: Kenneth Ketter
Estimated Sales: $1-3 Million
Number Employees: 5-9
Type of Packaging: Consumer, Food Service

7250 **Kettle Cooked Food**
7401 Will Rogers Blvd
Fort Worth, TX 76140-6019 817-615-4500
Fax: 817-551-1578 www.kprfoods.com
Producers and packages custom soups, sauces and side dishes
President: John Tyson
Plant Manager: Greg Irby
Estimated Sales: $ 50-100 Million
Number Employees: 100-249
Parent Co: Tyson Foods
Type of Packaging: Food Service, Private Label
Brands:
Tyson

7251 **Kettle Cuisine**
270 2nd St
Chelsea, MA 02150-1802 617-884-1219
Fax: 617-884-1341 877-302-7687
sales@kettlecuisine.com www.kettlecuisine.com
Processor of fresh soups and chowders
President: Jerry Shafir
Marketing: Brian McGinnis
Estimated Sales: $ 20 - 50 Million
Number Employees: 100-249
Type of Packaging: Consumer, Food Service

7252 **Kettle Foods**
P.O.Box 664
Salem, OR 97308-0664 503-364-0399
Fax: 503-371-1447 kettlejohn@aol.com
www.kettlefoods.com
Processor of Kettle brand hand cooked potato chips; krinkle cut potato chips; pretzel chips; pita chips; tortilla chips; nut butters; and nuts, nut mixes and trail mixes.
President: Tim Fallon
Vice President Finance: Michael Bays
Kettle Foods Ambassador: Jim Green
Chief Flavor Architect: Carolyn Richards
Consumer Affairs: Janet Wilson
Vice President Sales: Greg Intlekofer
Public Relations: Jan Maxwell Muir
Vice President Operations: Jim McMullen
Vice President Human Resources: Bret Hughes
Estimated Sales: $ 50 - 100 Million
Number Employees: 500-999

7253 **Kettle Foods**
P.O.Box 664
Salem, OR 97308-0664 503-364-0399
Fax: 503-371-1447 www.kettlefoods.com
Processor of potato and tortilla chips, nuts, nut butters and popcorn
President: Tim Fallon
VP Marketing: Michelle Peterman
Estimated Sales: $170 Million
Number Employees: 100-249

7254 **Kettle Master**
497 Farmers Market Rd
Hillsville, VA 24343-5106 276-728-7571
sales@kettlemaster.com
www.kettlemaster.com
Manufacturer of jellies, jams, salsa and sauces
Manager: Rex Horton
Marketing Sales Director: Ben Web
Operations Manager: Fred Jones
Number Employees: 5-9
Type of Packaging: Consumer, Private Label
Other Locations:
Chesapeake Bay Gourmet
Baltimore MD

7255 **Kettle Valley FruitsSunOpta Inc**
14014 Highway 97 N
Summerland, BC V0H 1Z0
Canada 250-494-0335
Fax: 250-494-0334 888-297-6944
sales@kettlevalley.net www.kettlevalley.net
Processor, importer and exporter of fruit-based snacks and energy bars
President: John Boot
Number Employees: 55
Sq. footage: 30000
Type of Packaging: Consumer, Food Service, Private Label, Bulk

7256 **Keurig, Inc**
55 Walkers Brook Drive
Reading, MA 01867 781-928-0162
www.keurig.com
Single cup coffee and brewers. Also tea, hot cocoa and iced beverages.
President: Michelle Stacy
VP Finance: John Heller
VP/General Counsel: Mike Degnan
Director of Research: Karl Winkler
Director of Quality: William Hartman
Director of Retal Marketing: Lori Anderson
VP Manufacturing/Operations: Dick Sweeney
Number Employees: 185
Type of Packaging: Consumer

7257 **Kevton Gourmet Tea**
385 Fm 416
Streetman, TX 75859-3024 903-389-2905
Fax: 903-389-5607 888-538-8668
kevtoen@kevtoenteatyme.com
www.kevtoenteatyme.com
Honey, flavored mixes, sour cream, tea, cocoa
President: Tanya Miller
CEO: Tanya Miller
Marketing Director: Tanya Miller
Brands:
Bee My Honey
Good Stuff Cocoa
Not Just Jam
Tea Tyme Cookies
countrymixes
joy
tease

7258 **Key Colony/Red Parrot Juices**
4424 Prescott Ave
Lyons, IL 60534 708-442-2007
Fax: 708-447-0188 800-424-0868
Processor of bag-in-box juices
President: James Behrens
Estimated Sales: Below $ 5 Million
Number Employees: 5-9
Type of Packaging: Food Service
Brands:
Red Parrot

7259 **Key Essentials**
30322 Esperanza Ste 400
Rancho Santa Margarita, CA 92688 949-635-1000
Fax: 949-636-1001 hhaget@keyessentials.com
www.keyessentials.com
Beverage flavors, bakery flavors, candy flavors, beverage product development, coffee and tea flavors
Chairman: Thomas H Quinn
CEO: Hector Haget
Estimated Sales: $ 10-20 Million
Number Employees: 50-99

7260 **Key III Candies**
4211 Earth Dr
Fort Wayne, IN 46809 260-747-7514
Fax: 260-747-9898 800-752-2382
Processor of milk chocolate candies including cream peanut clusters, caramels and pretzels covered in chocolate or confectionery coatings
Manager: Gary Yarger
V.P./Co-Ownr.: Richard Dickmeyer
Estimated Sales: $ 3 - 5 Million
Number Employees: 10-19
Sq. footage: 10000
Type of Packaging: Consumer, Bulk
Brands:
Key Iii

7261 **Key Ingredients**
802 S 16th Street
Harrisburg, PA 17104-2601 717-233-0451
Fax: 717-238-4017 800-227-4448
Cheese products, spaghetti sauce, dressings, prepared meals

7262 **Key Largo Fisheries**
1313 Ocean Bay Drive
Key Largo, FL 33037
800-432-4358
www.keylargofisheries.com
Crab, lobster, shrimp, fish and other products.
Owner/President: Tom Hill
Finance Manager: Rick Hill
Estimated Sales: $10 Million
Number Employees: 35
Sq. footage: 3000
Type of Packaging: Consumer, Food Service, Private Label

7263 **Key Lime**
5200 Highlands Parkway SE
Smyrna, GA 30082-5163 770-333-0840
Fax: 770-436-4280
Processor and exporter of key lime pies, pie filling, sorbet and novelty desserts
President: Kenneth Burts
Plt. Mgr.: K Michael Miller
Quality Control: Slorence Clay
Estimated Sales: $ 5-10 Million
Number Employees: 20-50
Sq. footage: 12000
Type of Packaging: Food Service, Private Label
Brands:
Kenny's
Kenny's Island Style
Kenny's Key Lime Crunch

7264 **Key West Key Lime Pie CoLLc**
225 Key Deer Blvd
Big Pine Key, FL 33043 305-872-7400
Fax: 305-872-7600 877-882-7437
kwklpco@bwisk.net keywestkeylimepieco.com

Distribute/sell key lime products to food establishments
President: James Brush
Vice President: Alison Sloat
Estimated Sales: $400,000
Number Employees: 5-9
Number of Brands: 4
Number of Products: 100+
Sq. footage: 1200
Type of Packaging: Consumer, Food Service, Private Label
Brands:
KEY LIME PIE SLICES DIPPED IN CHOCO
KEY LIME PIES ASSORTED FLAVORS
PACKAGE BULK KEY LIME FILLING

7265 **Keynes Brothers**
1 W Front St
Logan, OH 43138 740-385-6824
Fax: 740-385-9076
Soft and whole wheat flour milling
President: William Keynes
Quality Control: Jeff Brown
Estimated Sales: $ 20-30 Million
Number Employees: 50-99

7266 **Keyser Brothers**
1146 Honest Point Rd
Lottsburg, VA 22511 804-529-6837
Fax: 804-529-5144 rkeyser@skyelink.com
Processor of fresh and frozen seafood including crabs and pasteurized crab meat
President/CEO: R Calvin Keyser
Executive VP: Norman Keyser
Estimated Sales: $350,000
Number Employees: 20-25
Number of Brands: 1
Sq. footage: 17500
Type of Packaging: Private Label
Brands:
Potomac River
Potomac River Brand

7267 **Keystone Coffee Company**
2230 Will Wool Dr
San Jose, CA 95112-2605 408-998-2221
Fax: 408-998-5021 sales@keystonecoffe.com
www.keystonecoffee.com
Processor and exporter of gourmet coffee
President: Tim Wright
Estimated Sales: $3000000
Number Employees: 10-19
Brands:
Keystone

7268 **Keystone Food Products**
3767 Hecktown Road
Easton, PA 18045-0888 610-258-0888
Fax: 610-250-0721 800-523-9426
Key_Contact@Keystonefoods.com
www.keystonefoods.com
Processor of snack foods including pretzels, cheese twists, popcorn, pork skins and corn and tortilla chips
President/VP Sales & Marketing: Eduardo Gonzalez
Estimated Sales: $21 Million
Number Employees: 150
Sq. footage: 131000
Type of Packaging: Consumer, Food Service, Private Label, Bulk
Brands:
BEST BUY
KEYSTONE
PRIZE

7269 **Keystone Foods**
P.O.Box 369
Camilla, GA 31730-0369 229-336-5211
Fax: 229-336-1818 www.keystonefoods.com
Processor of fresh and frozen chicken
Manager: Clay Banks
Estimated Sales: $750,000
Number Employees: 10-19
Parent Co: Keystone Food Corporation
Type of Packaging: Consumer, Bulk

7270 **Keystone Foods Corporation**
300 Barr Harbor Dr Ste 600
West Conshohocken, PA 19428 610-667-6700
Fax: 610-667-1460
key.contact@keystonefoods.com
www.keystonefoods.com
Processor and exporter of beef hamburgers and chicken
Chairman: Herbert Lotman
Pres.: Gerome Dean
CFO: John Coggins
CEO: Jerry Dean
President: Jerry Dean
Number Employees: 50-99
Type of Packaging: Bulk
Brands:
Keystone Foods

7271 **Keystone Foods Corporation**
6767 Old Madison Pike NW Ste 500
Huntsville, AL 35806 256-964-1000
Fax: 256-533-4870 800-327-6701
key.contact@keystonefoods.com
www.keystonefoods.com
Manufactures and supplies beef, poultry, fish, pork products and custom distribution services to the food industry
Manager: Wendy Parker
VP: Jerry Wilson
Estimated Sales: $ 600 Million
Number Employees: 80
Type of Packaging: Food Service

7272 **Keystone Pretzel Bakery**
124 W Airport Rd
Lititz, PA 17543 717-560-1882
Fax: 717-560-2241 888-572-4500
sales@keystonepretzels.com
www.keystonepretzels.com
Manufacturer of pretzels
President: George Phillips
Estimated Sales: $12 Million
Number Employees: 20-49
Type of Packaging: Consumer, Food Service, Bulk

7273 **Khalsa International Trading**
1616 Preuss Rd
Los Angeles, CA 90035-4212 310-275-9891
Fax: 310-275-2923
customerservice@yogitea.com
www.goldentemple.com
Medicinal teas, packaged cereal, bulk granolas
President: Sopurkh K Khalsa
Vice President: Sada Sat Kalsa
VP Marketing: Parampal Singh
Public Relations: Jagat Joti Khalsa
Operations Manager: Ajeet Khalsa
Estimated Sales: $ 20-50 Million
Number Employees: 20-49
Type of Packaging: Private Label
Brands:
Ancient Healing Formula
Golden Temple
Peace Cereal
Sunshine Spa
Wha Guru Chews
Yogi Tea

7274 **Khatsa & Company**
PO Box 50754
13805 Main St
Bellevue, WA 98005-3733 425-649-5508
Fax: 425-649-0774 888-542-8728
info@khatsa.com www.khatsa.com
President: Dachs Kyaping
Vice President: Nanang Nornang
Public Relations: Dachen Kyaping
Estimated Sales: $500,000-$1 Million
Number Employees: 1-4
Brands:
Khatsa
Liberate Your Senses
Urban Nomad Food

7275 **Kibun Foods**
2101 4th Ave # 1240
Seattle, WA 98121-2323 206-467-6287
Fax: 206-467-6612 kibun@aloha.com
Beer
President: Tadahiko Mitsui
Estimated Sales: $7,500,000
Number Employees: 5-9

7276 **Kicking Horse Coffee**
491 Arrow Rd
Invermere, BC V0A 1K2 888-287-5282
Fax: 250-342-4450 mia@kickinghorsecoffee.com
www.kickinghorsecoffee.com
Coffee.
Marketing: Elana Rosenfeld

7277 **Kid's Kookie Company**
1000 Calle Negocio
San Clemente, CA 92673-6205 949-661-7880
Fax: 949-498-5496 800-350-7577
info@kidscookies.com www.kidscookies.com
Processor of holiday, theme, decorated, specialty shaped and pre-baked cookies
Owner: Dennis Sellers
VP: Gay Sellers
Estimated Sales: $ 5 - 10 Million
Number Employees: 5-9
Type of Packaging: Food Service
Brands:
Kids Cookie

7278 **Kid's Pantry**
215 NE Hillcrest Drive
Grants Pass, OR 97526-3593 541-476-8812
Fax: 541-476-8812 800-452-9551
President: Pat Enos
Estimated Sales: Under $500,000
Number Employees: 1-4

7279 **Kids Cooking Club**
1261 Missouri St
San Diego, CA 92109 858-539-2620
Fax: 858-539-2010 kidscook@kidscook.com
www.kidscook.com
Cooking projects for kids including pizza, pretzel kits and other make, bake and decorate kits
Number Employees: 1-4

7280 **Kidsmania**
12332 Bell Ranch Dr
Santa Fe Springs, CA 90670 562-946-8822
Fax: 562-946-8802 sales@candynovelties.com
www.candynovelties.com
Candy toys and novelties
Owner: Foreman Lam
Estimated Sales: $300,000-500,000
Number Employees: 1-4
Number of Products: 100

7281 **Kiefer Company**
1406 W Chestnut St
Louisville, KY 40203 502-587-7474
Fax: 502-587-7503
Processor of meat
Owner: Steve Smith
Estimated Sales: $3000000
Number Employees: 20-49

7282 **(HQ)Kikkoman International**
P.O.Box 420784
San Francisco, CA 94142 415-956-7750
Fax: 415-956-7760 dac@kikkoman.com
www.kikkoman-usa.com
Manufacturer of soy-based flavor enhancers and sauces including soy and teriyaki
Chairman: Yuzaburo Mogi
Sales/Marketing Manager: Shigeru Nemoto
Estimated Sales: $110 Million
Number Employees: 100-249
Number of Brands: 1
Type of Packaging: Consumer, Food Service, Bulk
Other Locations:
Kikkoman Production Facility
Walworth WI
Kikkoman Production Facility
Folsom CA
Brands:
Kikkoman

7283 **(HQ)Kikkoman International**
P.O.Box 420784
San Francisco, CA 94142 415-956-7750
Fax: 415-956-7760 www.kikkoman-usa.com
Processor and exporter of soy and teriyaki sauces
President: H Takamatsu
Executive VP: B Nelson
Estimated Sales: $ 3 - 5 Million
Number Employees: 100-249
Parent Co: Kikkoman Corporation
Type of Packaging: Consumer, Food Service
Other Locations:
Kikkoman Production Facility
Walworth WI
Kikkoman Production Facility
Folsom CA
Brands:
Kikkoman

7284 **Kikkoman International**
17330 Preston Rd
Suite104D
Dallas, TX 75252 972-267-4207
Fax: 972-267-4206 www.kikkoman-usa.com
Manufacturer of liquid and dehydrated soy sauces, teriyaki sauce, specialty sauces, natural flavor enhancers, and gravinol.
Exec. V.P.: H Takamatsu
V.P.: B Nelson
Estimated Sales: $ 5 - 10 Million
Number Employees: 5-9
Parent Co: Kikkoman Corporation
Type of Packaging: Consumer, Food Service

7285 **Kikkoman International**
2 Mid America Plz Ste 1022
Oakbrook Terrace, IL 60181 630-954-1244
Fax: 630-954-1309 www.kikkoman-usa.com
Manufacturer of liquid and dehydrated soy sauces, teriyaki sauce, specialty sauces, natural flavor enhancers, and gravinol.
Manager: Tom Gufler
V.P.: B Nelson
Estimated Sales: $ 3 - 5 Million
Number Employees: 5-9
Parent Co: Kikkoman Corporation
Type of Packaging: Consumer, Food Service

7286 **Kikkoman International**
1979 Lakeside Pkwy Ste 930
Tucker, GA 30084 770-496-0605
Fax: 770-496-0918 www.kikkoman.com
Processor and exporter of soy and teriyaki sauces
Manager: Earl Haraguchi
V.P.: B Nelson
Number Employees: 100-249
Parent Co: Kikkoman Corporation
Type of Packaging: Consumer, Food Service

7287 **Kilauea Agronomics**
PO Box 80
Kilauea, HI 96754-0080 808-828-1761
Fax: 808-828-1880
Estimated Sales: $ 20 - 50 Million
Number Employees: 50-99

7288 **Kilgus Meats**
3346 W Laskey Rd
Toledo, OH 43623 419-472-9721
Processor of sausage including wieners, bratwurst and bologna; also, lunch meats
President: Erich Schiehlen
General Manager: Till Ballongo
Estimated Sales: $540,000
Number Employees: 7
Sq. footage: 1200
Type of Packaging: Consumer, Food Service, Bulk

7289 **Kilwons Foods**
326 May Ave
Santa Cruz, CA 95060-4109 831-426-9670
Fax: 831-426-2720 kilwonsfoods@hotmail.com
www.kilwonsfoods.com
Manufactures sauce, gravy, dressing & dip mixes
Owner: Kilwon Poveromo
Estimated Sales: Under $500,000
Number Employees: 5-9
Brands:
Kilwons Foods

7290 **Kim & Scott's Gourmet Pretzels**
2107 West Carroll Ave
Chicago, IL 60612 312-243-9971
800-578-9478
cust-serv@kimandscotts.com
www.kimandscotts.com
Manufacturer of soft pretzels and other baked goods
President/Owner: Kimberly Oster-Holstein
CEO/Owner: Scott Holstein
CFO: Maura Finn
Estimated Sales: $10 Million
Number Employees: 50-99

7291 **Kim and Scott's GourmetPretzels**
2107 W Carroll Avenue
Chicago, IL 60612
800-578-9478
cust-serv@kimandscotts.com
www.kimandscotts.com
Classic pretzels, stuffed pretzels, gluten-free pretzels and stuffed bagels.

7292 **Kimball Enterprise International**
3129 S Hacienda Heights Boulevard
Suite 410
Hacienda Heights, CA 91745 213-276-8898
Fax: 213-947-1888 sales@garlicpeeler.com
www.garlicpeeler.com
Processor and exporter of roasted, peeled and chopped garlic, peeled and chopped shallots and garlic juice
President: Jimmy Tani
Estimated Sales: $ 2 Million
Number Employees: 20
Sq. footage: 15000
Type of Packaging: Consumer, Food Service, Private Label, Bulk
Brands:
Kimball

7293 **Kimes Cider Mill**
P.O.Box 419
Bendersville, PA 17306-0419 717-677-7539
Fax: 717-677-7151 kimescid@cvn.net
www.kimescidermill.com
Processor of apple butter and cider
Partner: Rick Kime
Prtnr.: Randy Kimes
Estimated Sales: Below $ 5 Million
Number Employees: 10-19
Type of Packaging: Consumer
Brands:
Kimes

7294 **Kimmie Candy Company**
525 Reactor Way
Reno, NV 89502 775-284-9200
Fax: 775-284-9206 888-532-1325
info@kimmiecandy.com www.kimmycandy.com
A manufacturer of quality panned candies. Located in Reno NV, we specialize in colorfull candy shells over chocolate or not centers. Branded products include sunbursts and choco rocks and corn bitz
President/CEO: Joseph Dutra
VP Sales/Marketing: Bernie Leas
Public Relations: Tina Norberg
Operations: John Dutra
Production: Ooln Jung
Estimated Sales: $ 1-5 Million
Number Employees: 20
Sq. footage: 20000
Type of Packaging: Consumer, Food Service, Private Label, Bulk
Brands:
Baby Dino Eggs
Choco Rocks
Kandy Kookies
Peanut Crunchers
Raisin Royales
Sunbursts

7295 **Kimson Chemicals**
24 Crescent Street
Waltham, MA 02453-4358 781-893-6878
Fax: 781-893-6881
Sodium citrate, ascorbic acid, sodium benzoate, citric acid, ammonium bicarbonate, potassium sorbate
Estimated Sales: Below $ 5 Million
Number Employees: 7

7296 **Kind Snacks**
P.O.Box 1393
Old Chelsea Station
New York, NY 10113-1393 212-616-3006
Fax: 212-616-3005 800-732-2321
mariana@kindsnacks.com www.kindsnacks.com
Functional (antioxidants), kosher, organic/natural, other lifestyle, vegetarian, gluten-free, health, fitness and energy bars.
Marketing: Mariana Rittenhouse

7297 **King & Prince Seafood Corporation**
P.O.Box 899
Brunswick, GA 31521-0899 912-265-5155
Fax: 912-264-4812 800-841-0205
sales@kpseafood.com www.kpseafood.com
Processor of shrimp including breaded, boil-in-bag, stuffed, battered, cooked, steamed, IQF scampi and steaks; also, lobster tails and stuffed fish; importer of frozen shrimp
President: Robert Brubaker
CEO: Russell Mentzer
Marketing Executive/ EVP: Russ Mentzer
Operations Director: Tom Sublett
Purchasing Manager: Howard Browning
Estimated Sales: $ 50 - 100 Million
Number Employees: 500-999
Sq. footage: 133747
Brands:
Flying Jib
Golden Shore
Gulf Stream
King & Prince

7298 **King 888 Company**
PO BOX 51360
Sparks, NV 89436 800-785-3674
Fax: 800-785-3674 info@king888.com
www.king888.com
Manufacturers an energy drink that is available in Silver Label (citrus blend flavor), Original Gold (ginger/lemon flavor) and Authentic Cola (natural cola flavor).
Sales Representative: Gary Larson
Type of Packaging: Food Service

7299 **King Arthur Flour**
135 Us Route 5 S
Norwich, VT 05055 802-649-3881
Fax: 802-649-3323 bakers@kingauthurflour.com
www.kingarthurflour.com
Manufacturer of flour
President/CEO: Steve Voigt
Estimated Sales: $45 Million
Number Employees: 100-249
Number of Brands: 1
Sq. footage: 16600

7300 **King B Meat Snacks**
P.O.Box 397
Minong, WI 54859-0397 715-466-2234
Fax: 715-466-5151 800-346-6896
info@linksnacks.com www.linksnacks.com
Manufacturer and exporter of jerky and meat snacks
President: Troy Link
CEO: John Link
CFO: John Hermeier
Estimated Sales: $10-20 Million
Number Employees: 250-499
Type of Packaging: Consumer, Food Service, Private Label, Bulk
Brands:
B. King
Taylor Country Farms

7301 **(HQ)King Brewing Company**
1350 Gateway Blvd # A8
Fairfield, CA 94533-6905 707-428-4503
Fax: 707-864-2232
Wines
Owner: Tom King
Operations Manager: Robert Egelhoff
Estimated Sales: Under $500,000
Number Employees: 1-4
Sq. footage: 18
Type of Packaging: Private Label

7302 **King Cole Ducks Limited**
PO Box 185
Aurora, ON L4G 3H3
Canada 905-836-9461
Fax: 905-836-4440 800-363-3825
rgrant@kingcoleducks.com
www.kingcoleducks.com
Processor and exporter of fresh and frozen duck including parts, smoked, boneless breast, peppered, fully cooked, etc
President: James Murby
VP: Robert Murby
Sq. footage: 1000
Type of Packaging: Consumer, Food Service, Private Label, Bulk
Brands:
King Cole

7303 **King David's All NaturalFood**
129 Marshall St Ste 1
Syracuse, NY 13210 315-471-5000
Fax: 315-471-1310

Gourmet foods
President: Milad Hatem
VP: Madeo Hatem
Estimated Sales: Below $ 5 Million
Number Employees: 1-4

7304 **King Estate Winery**
80854 Territorial Hwy
Eugene, OR 97405 541-942-9874
Fax: 541-942-9867 800-884-4441
info@kingestate.com www.kingestate.com
Wines
CEO: Ed King
Director Sales: Steve Thomson
CFO: Doyal Eubank
Estimated Sales: Less than $500,000
Number Employees: 20-49
Brands:
Oregon

7305 **King Food Service**
94-272 Pupuole St
Waipahu, HI 96797-2329 808-671-5464
Fax: 808-676-8888
Supplier of food products to hotels and restaurant. Cold storage leasing.
President: Dana H Y Chun
CEO: Bill Hughes
Assistant Controller: Lisa Tomihama
Estimated Sales: $ 24-34 Million
Number Employees: 50 to 99
Sq. footage: 38000

7306 **King Food Service**
7810 42nd St W
Rock Island, IL 61201-7319 309-787-4488
Fax: 309-787-4501
sales11@kingfoodservice.com
www.kingfoodservice.com
Providing superior service, quality & pricing since 1945. Specialists in seafood, poultry & meat, distributor, importer, broker and processor.
President/CEO: Mike Cutkomp
Marketing Director: Chef Albert Ames
Sales Director: Matt Cutkomp
Operations Manager/Purchasing: Rick White
Estimated Sales: $24 Million
Number Employees: 10-19
Number of Products: 1500

7307 **King Henry's Inc.**
29124 Hancock Parkway
Valencia, CA 91355-1066 661-295-5566
Fax: 661-295-5099 henry@kinghenrys.com
Organic/natural, other chocolate, gummies/jellies/pates de fruit, nuts, other snacks, pretzels, dried fruit.
Marketing: Joseph DeFelice

7308 **King Juice**
851 W Grange Ave
Milwaukee, WI 53221 414-482-0303
Fax: 414-482-0719 inquiries@kingjuice.com
www.kingjuice.com
Juices
President: Tim Kezman
Estimated Sales: $500,000-$1 Million
Number Employees: 20-49
Brands:
Calypso
King Juice
Villa Quenchers

7309 **King Kat**
RR 2
Box 185
Carlisle, AR 72024-8607 870-854-8187
Fax: 209-464-8135

7310 **King Kelly Marmalade Company**
P.O.Box 1
Bellflower, CA 90707 562-865-0291
Fax: 562-865-9318
Manufacturer of jams, jellies and orange marmalade
President: John Bowen
Estimated Sales: $ 5 - 10 Million
Number Employees: 20-49
Sq. footage: 25000
Type of Packaging: Consumer, Food Service, Private Label
Brands:
KING KELLY

7311 **King Kold**
1920 Swarthmore Ave. Suite 1
Lakewood, NJ 08701 732-730-2157
Fax: 732-730-9913 info@kingkold.com
www.kingkold.com
Beef, potato pancakes, vegetable pancakes, maztoh balls
CEO: Michael K Hahn
Founder: Jacob Harmatz
Estimated Sales: $ 5-10 Million
Number Employees: 50-99
Brands:
Ratner's

7312 **King Kold Meats**
331-333 N Main Street
Englewood, OH 45322 937-836-2731
Fax: 937-836-5919 800-836-2797
dougsmith@woh.rr.com www.kingkoldinc.com
Fresh and frozen meat products and entrees.
President: Doug Smith
Distributor Sales: Mike DeFrancis
Estimated Sales: $ 10 - 20 Million
Number Employees: 20-49
Number of Brands: 3
Number of Products: 125
Sq. footage: 10000
Type of Packaging: Consumer, Food Service, Private Label, Bulk
Brands:
EVELYN SPRAGUE
HEARTH & KETTLE
KINGKOLD

7313 **King Meat**
4215 Exchange Ave
Los Angeles, CA 90058 323-582-7401
Fax: 323-582-1813
Processor, exporter and importer of beef
President: Raymond Rosenthal
VP: Michael Hughes
Sales Manager: Tony Santare
Human Resources Director: Sylvia Valdepena
Operations Manager: Andrew Lofquist
Estimated Sales: $ 50 - 100 Million
Number Employees: 200
Sq. footage: 100000
Type of Packaging: Food Service

7314 **King Milling Company**
115 S Broadway St
Lowell, MI 49331 616-897-9264
Fax: 616-897-4350 jcantrell@kingflour.com
www.kingflour.com
Manufacturer of wheat and white flour
President: Brian Doyle
VP: Steve Doyle
SVP: James Doyle
Estimated Sales: $ 20 - 50 Million
Number Employees: 20-49
Type of Packaging: Food Service, Bulk
Brands:
Kimco
Pathfinder
Pure Gold
Sincerity
Super Kleaned Wheat

7315 **King Neptune**
21 Bay St
Winslow, ME 04901-7045 207-872-5015
Fax: 415-485-6921
Owner: Jeannine Hendsbee
Estimated Sales: $300,000-500,000
Number Employees: 1-4

7316 **King Nut Company**
31900 Solon Rd
Solon, OH 44139 440-248-8484
Fax: 440-248-0153 800-860-5464
customer@kingnut.com www.kingnut.com
Manufacturer of snack mixes, chocolates, nuts and tropical fruit tins; exporter of salted nuts
President: Martin Kanan
VP Sales/Marketing: Matthew Kanan
Product Development: Debra Smith
Plant Operations: James Dedario
Estimated Sales: $35 Million
Number Employees: 100-249
Sq. footage: 50000
Parent Co: Kanan Enterprises/King Nut
Type of Packaging: Consumer, Food Service, Private Label, Bulk
Brands:
Blossom
Kelling-Kernel Fresh
Peterson's

7317 **King Nut Company**
31900 Solon Rd
Solon, OH 44139 440-248-8484
Fax: 440-248-0153 800-860-5464
info@kingnut.com www.kingnut.com
Manufacturer and packager of nuts and snacks including; roasted/salted nuts, roasted no salt nuts, raw nuts, snacks, dried fruit, chocolates, candy
President/CEO: Martin Kanan
Chairman: Michael Kanan
SVP Finance/Administration: Joseph Valenza
VP Quality Assurance/Product Development: Debra Smith
EVP Sales/Marketing: Matthew Kanan
VP Manufacturing/Plant Operations: James DeDario
Estimated Sales: $35 Million
Number Employees: 185
Sq. footage: 200000
Type of Packaging: Consumer, Food Service, Private Label, Bulk
Brands:
KINGS
SUMMER HARVEST BRANDS

7318 **King Soopers Bakery**
PO Box 5567
Denver, CO 80217 303-778-3128
Fax: 303-871-9260 877-415-4647
www.kingsoopers.com
Manufacturer of bread and pastries
President: Russ Dispense
Plant Manager: Dave Higgins
Estimated Sales: $100 Million
Number Employees: 250-499
Parent Co: Kroger

7319 **King's Cupboard**
P.O.Box 27
Red Lodge, MT 59068-0027 406-446-3060
Fax: 406-446-3070 800-962-6555
sales@kingscupboard.com
www.kingscupboard.com
All natural dessert sauces and hot chocolate mixes
Owner: Richard Poore
Estimated Sales: $ 5 - 10 Million
Number Employees: 50-99
Type of Packaging: Consumer, Food Service, Private Label, Bulk
Brands:
Beartooth Kitchens

7320 **King's Hawaiian**
19161 Harborgate Way
Torrance, CA 90501-1316 310-533-3250
Fax: 310-533-8732 800-800-5461
consumer@kingshawaiian.com
www.kingshawaiian.com
Hawaiian sweet bread and rolls
CEO: Mark Taira
CEO: Mark Tiara
Estimated Sales: $ 10-20 Million
Number Employees: 250-499
Sq. footage: 150000
Brands:
King's Hawaiian

7321 **Kingchem**
5 Pearl Ct
Allendale, NJ 07401-1656 201-825-9988
Fax: 201-825-9148 800-211-4330
p.sivolella@kingchem.com www.kingchem.com
Processor of herbal supplements
Manager: Carmine Covino
VP: Austin Bishop
Marketing Manager: Frank Fortuna
Director/Sales: Patrick Sivolella
Director Of Purchasing: Lillian Wu
Estimated Sales: $ 10-20 Million
Number Employees: 10-19
Sq. footage: 2500
Brands:
Kingchem

7322 **Kingfish**
7400 New Lagrange Rd # 405
Louisville, KY 40222-4870 502-339-0565
Fax: 502-339-0230
http://www.kingfishrestaurants.com

Director of HR: Laura Vance
CEO: Kyle Noltmeyer
Estimated Sales: $10,000,000
Number Employees: 5-9

7323 **Kingly Heirs**
PO Box 283
Elkhart, IN 46515 574-596-3763
Fax: 527-296-1188 info@kinglyheirs.com
www.kinglyheirs.com/
Manufacturer and distributor of gourmet cake mixes.
Founder/Owner/President: Kingly Heirs

7324 **Kings Canyon Corrin**
1750 S Buttonwillow Avenue
Reedley, CA 93654-4400 559-638-3571
Fax: 559-638-6326 sales@kccfruit.com
www.kccfruit.com
Peaches, apricots and other fruits
President: Steve Kenfield
VP Sales: Fred Berry

7325 **Kings Command Foods**
7622 S 188th St
Kent, WA 98032 425-251-6788
Fax: 425-251-0523 800-247-3138
info@kingscommand.com
www.kingscommand.com
Portion controlled, pre-cooked and ready-to-eat beef, chicken, pork and veal products.
President: Ron Baer
GM/CFO: Van Kramer
Quality Assurance Manager: Jerry Clark
VP Sales: Chuck Nyman
Human Resources Manager: Angela Nelson
VP Operations: Mark Wallace
Product Development Manager: Angelina Boland
Plant Manager: Ryan Small
Estimated Sales: $29900000
Number Employees: 120
Sq. footage: 24000
Type of Packaging: Consumer, Food Service

7326 **Kings Delight**
2075 Industrial Dr
Gainesville, GA 30504 770-536-5177
Fax: 770-531-1603 www.kingsdelight.com
Processor of processed poultry
CEO: Rick Morris
CFO: Lee Turner
SVP: Stan Hayman
Estimated Sales: $47 Million
Number Employees: 837

7327 **Kings Delight**
2063 Memorial Park Dr
Gainesville, GA 30504 770-536-5177
Fax: 770-531-1603 www.kingsdelight.com
Processor of processed poultry including chargrilled nuggets, hot wings, boneless skinless breast filets, breaded chicken rings and fries, breaded fritters, tenders, breakfast patties, etc
President: Rick Morris
CFO: Lee Turner
SVP: Stan Hayman
Estimated Sales: $47 Million
Number Employees: 837

7328 **Kings Processing**
14 Freeman St
Middleton, NS B0S 1P0
Canada 902-825-2188
Fax: 902-825-2180
Processor of fresh salads and vegetables
President: Bruce Rand
Vice President: Arthur Woolaver
Estimated Sales: $6.9 Million
Number Employees: 50
Type of Packaging: Consumer, Food Service

7329 **Kingsburg Apple Sale**
10363 Davis Ave
Kingsburg, CA 93631 559-897-5132
Fax: 559-897-4532 sales@kingsburgapple.com
www.kingsburgapple.com
Apples, Asian pears, peaches, nectarines, persimmons, pluots
President: John Hein
Estimated Sales: $100+ Million
Number Employees: 100-249

7330 **Kingsbury Country Market**
5001 S Us 35
Kingsbury, IN 46345 219-393-3016
Processor of beef, hog, rabbit, ostrich and lamb; custom butchering available
Pres.: Jerry Winter
Secy./Treas.: Sandra Winter
Number Employees: 5-9
Brands:
Butcher Boy

7331 **Kingsville Fisherman's Company**
PO Box 37
Kingsville, ON N9Y 2E8
Canada 519-733-6534
Fax: 519-733-6959
Processor and exporter of fresh and frozen perch and pickerel
Sls. Mgr.: John Murray
Pres.: Carl Fraser
Number Employees: 50-99
Type of Packaging: Bulk

7332 **Kinnikinnick Foods**
10940-120 Street
Edmonton, AB T5H 3P7
Canada 780-424-2900
Fax: 780-421-0456 877-503-4466
info@kinnikinnick.com www.kinnikinnick.com
Manufacturer of gluten free bakery products
President: Ted Wolf
CEO: Jerry Bigam
CFO: Lynne Bigam
VP: Jay Bigam
Estimated Sales: E
Number Employees: 60
Number of Products: 120
Sq. footage: 30000
Type of Packaging: Consumer, Food Service
Brands:
Kinnikinnick Foods, Inc.

7333 **Kintetsu World Express**
1 Jericho Plz Ste 100
Sutie 326
Jericho, NY 11753 516-933-7100
800-275-4045
www.kweusa.com
Manager: Yasuo Tanaka

7334 **Kiolbassa Provision Company**
1325 S Brazos St
San Antonio, TX 78207 210-226-8127
Fax: 210-226-7464 800-456-5465
link@kiolbassa.com www.kiolbassa.com
Manufacturer of sausage products including smoked, polish and jalapeno flavored sausage and Mexican style chorizo
President: Michael Kiolbassa
CEO: Robert Kiolbassa
Vice President: Sandra Kiolbassa
Secretary/Treasurer: Barbara Kiolbassa
Estimated Sales: $21 Million
Number Employees: 115
Type of Packaging: Consumer

7335 **Kiona Vineyards Winery**
44612 N Sunset Rd
Benton City, WA 99320 509-588-6716
Fax: 509-588-3219 info@kionawine.com
www.kionawine.com
Wines and wine grapes
Owner: John Williams
Owner: Ann Williams
Manager/Winemaker: Scott Williams
Estimated Sales: Below $ 5 Million
Number Employees: 5-9
Number of Brands: 1
Number of Products: 16
Type of Packaging: Private Label
Brands:
Kiona

7336 **Kirby & Holloway Provisions**
966 Jackson Ditch Rd
Harrington, DE 19952 302-398-3705
Fax: 302-398-4088 800-995-4729
www.kirbyandhollowayinc.com
Processor of sausage and scrapple; wholesaler/distributor of meat and cheese products
President: Russell Kirby
Owner: Rudy Kirby
General Manager: Bill Moore
Estimated Sales: $7 Million
Number Employees: 50
Type of Packaging: Consumer, Food Service, Private Label, Bulk

7337 **Kirigin Cellars**
11550 Watsonville Rd
Gilroy, CA 95020 408-847-8827
Fax: 408-847-3820 folks@kirigincellars.com
www.kirigincellars.com
Manufacturer of wines
Manager: Allen Kreutzer
Winemaker: Allen Kreutzer
Estimated Sales: Below $5 Million
Number Employees: 1-4
Brands:
Kirigin Cellars

7338 **Kiska Farms**
P.O.Box 4707
Pasco, WA 99302 509-547-7765
Fax: 509-547-7746 kathy@kiskafarms.com
www.kiskafarms.com
Potatos
Co-Owner: Kathy Blasdel
Co-Owner: Judy Johnston

7339 **Kistler Vineyards**
4707 Vine Hill Rd
Sebastopol, CA 95472 707-823-5603
Fax: 707-823-6709 abc@kistlerwine.com
www.kistlerwine.com
Wines
President: Stephen Kistler
CEO: Stephen Kistler
Estimated Sales: $ 20-50 Million
Number Employees: 50-99
Brands:
Durell Vineyard
Dutton Ranch
Hyde Vineyard
McCrea Vineyard
Sonoma Coast

7340 **Kitch'n Cook'd Potato Chip Company**
1703 W Beverley St
Staunton, VA 24401 540-886-4473
Fax: 540-886-0558 800-752-1535
kitncook@ntelos.net www.kitchncookd.com
Processor of potato chips
President: George Raymond Curry
Estimated Sales: $1100000
Number Employees: 10-19
Type of Packaging: Consumer

7341 **Kitchen Basics**
6940 S Edgerton Rd Unit 1
Brecksville, OH 44141 440-838-1344
Fax: 440-838-5841 info@kitchenbasics.net
www.kitchenbasics.net
cooking stocks

7342 **Kitchen Kettle Foods**
3529 Old Philadelphia Pike
PO Box 380
Intercourse, PA 17534 717-768-8261
Fax: 717-768-3614 800-732-3538
info@continentalinn.com
www.kitchenkettle.com
Manufacturer of jams, jellies and relishes
President: Michael Burnley
CEO: Pat Burnley
VP: Joanne Ladley
Estimated Sales: $ 50 - 100 Million
Number Employees: 100-249

7343 **Kitchen Pride Mushroom Farms**
1034 County Road 348
Gonzales, TX 78629-2774 830-540-4517
Fax: 830-540-4556 sales@kitchenpride.com
www.kitchenpridemushrooms.com
Grower of mushrooms
President: Greg McLain
Ceo: Darrell McLain
Estimated Sales: $3 Million
Number Employees: 100
Sq. footage: 100000
Type of Packaging: Consumer, Food Service, Private Label, Bulk
Brands:
Kitchen Pride Farms

7344 **Kitchen Products**
18 Rackliffe Street
Gloucester, MA 01930-4151 978-283-1384
President: William O'Connor
Estimated Sales: $ 1-2.5 Million
Number Employees: 5

7345 **Kitchen Table Bakers**
41 Princeton Drive
Syosset, NY 11973 516-931-5113
Fax: 516-932-5467 800-486-4582
info@kitchentablebakers.com
www.kitchentablebakers.com
gourmet, wheat, gluten and sugar free wafer crisps
President/Owner: Barry Novick

7346 **Kitchens Seafood**
1001 E Baker St
Plant City, FL 33563-3700 813-750-1888
Fax: 813-750-1889 800-327-0132
sales@kitchensseafood.com
www.kitchensseafood.com
Manufacturer, packer and importer of frozen seafood including lobster, crab, shrimp, shrimp meat and langostinos
President: Dan La Fleur
Estimated Sales: $51 Million
Number Employees: 1-4
Type of Packaging: Consumer, Food Service, Private Label, Bulk
Other Locations:
Kitchens Seafood - Production
Jacksonville FL

7347 **Kittery Lobster Company**
21 Ranger Dr
Kittery, ME 03904 207-439-6035
Fax: 207-763-3861
Lobster
Owner: Hugh Reynolds
Estimated Sales: $1 Million
Number Employees: 5-9

7348 **(HQ)Kittling Ridge Estate Wines & Spirits**
297 S Service Road
Grimsby, ON L3M 1Y6
Canada 905-945-9225
Fax: 905-945-4330 www.kittlingridge.com
Processor and exporter of alcoholic beverages including liqueurs, whiskey, rum, vodka, brandy, bitters, wines, icewine and ready-to-drink cocktails
V.P. Finance: Peter Kosacky
V.P. Sales: Tim Burrows
CEO/President: John Hall
Estimated Sales: $20-50 Million
Number Employees: 100-249
Brands:
Canadian
Kingsgate

7349 **Kittridge & FredricksonFine Coffees**
2801 SE 14th Ave
Portland, OR 97202-2203 503-234-7788
Fax: 503-231-9827 800-558-7788
info@kfcoffee.com www.kfcoffee.com
Coffees
President: Don Dominguez
Founder: Bud Dominguez
Estimated Sales: $ 10 - 20 Million
Number Employees: 10-19
Brands:
K&F

7350 **Kitts Meat Processing**
P.O.Box 8
Dedham, IA 51440-0008 712-683-5622
Processor of bologna
Partner: David Kitt
Partner: Shawn Kitt
Estimated Sales: $190,000
Number Employees: 5-9

7351 **Kitty Clover Snacktime Company**
6916 N 97th Cir
Omaha, NE 68122-3037 402-342-7342
Potato chips and snack foods

7352 **Klaire Laboratories**
10439 Double R Boulevard
Reno, NV 89521-8905
Fax: 775-850-8810 888-488-2488
www.klaire.com
Processor and exporter of allergen-free nutritional supplements
President: Cary Fereuson
Number Employees: 20-49
Parent Co: Kek Industries
Brands:
VITAL LIFE

7353 **Klamath River Barbeque**
PO Box 711
Montague, CA 96064 530-459-5629
Fax: 530-459-3612 klamathbbq@aol.com
Wholesale and retail consumer products, foodservice products, private labeling, co-packing, PFR, cannery license, pH controlled processing.
Owner: Kendra Gill
Vice President: Francis Gill
Plant Manager: Linda Oliver
Estimated Sales: $30,000
Number of Products: 7
Sq. footage: 2000
Type of Packaging: Consumer, Food Service, Private Label
Other Locations:
Klamath River Barbeque
Yreka CA
Brands:
Klamuth River BBQ
Nucci's Restaurant
Pat's Pimentos
RWB Mt Ranch Foods
Wildfire Foods

7354 **Klein Foods**
P.O.Box 656
Marshall, MN 56258 507-532-3127
Fax: 507-537-1940 800-657-0174
honey@starpioint.net
Honey and honey products
President: Stephen Klein
Estimated Sales: $5-9.9 Million
Number Employees: 5-9
Type of Packaging: Private Label

7355 **Klein Pickle Company**
4118 W Whitton Ave
Phoenix, AZ 85019 602-269-2072
Fax: 602-269-2069
Pickles and condiments
Owner: Byron Arnold
Estimated Sales: $ 1-2.5 Million
Number Employees: 20-49

7356 **Klein's Kosher Pickles**
4118 W Whitton Ave
Phoenix, AZ 85019-3625 602-269-2072
Fax: 602-269-2069 sales@kleinpickles.com
www.kleinpickleco.com
Processor of kosher pickles
President: Byron Arnold
VP: Mark Arnold
Estimated Sales: $ 1-2.5 Million
Number Employees: 20-49
Sq. footage: 300000
Type of Packaging: Consumer, Food Service
Brands:
Mrs. Klein's

7357 **Kleinpeter Farms Dairy**
14444 Airline Hwy
Baton Rouge, LA 70817 225-753-2121
Fax: 225-752-8964 www.kleinpeterdairy.com
Milk, cream, cottage cheese
President: Jeff Kleinpeter
CEO: D Kleinpeter
Estimated Sales: $ 20-30 Million
Number Employees: 100-249

7358 **Klement Sausage Company**
207 E Lincoln Ave
Milwaukee, WI 53207 414-744-2330
Fax: 414-744-2438 800-553-6368
tomajack@klements.com www.klements.com
Sausage and beef products
President: James T Klement
Co-President: Roger Klement
Vice President: Tim Gibbons
Director: Dan Lipke
Plant Manager: Bryan DuCharme
Estimated Sales: $ 50-75 Million
Number Employees: 100-249
Sq. footage: 220000

7359 **Klemme Cooperative Grainery**
122 W Main Street
Klemme, IA 50449-9053 641-444-4262
Plant Manager: Darryl Schweers
Estimated Sales: $ 2.5-5 Million
Number Employees: 20

7360 **Klingshirn Winery**
33050 Webber Rd
Avon Lake, OH 44012 440-933-6666
Fax: 440-933-7896
contactus@klingshirnwine.com
www.klingshirnwine.com
Wines
President: Allan Klingshirn
Director Manufacturing: Lee Kingshirn
Estimated Sales: Below $ 5 Million
Number Employees: 5-9
Brands:
Klingshirn Winery

7361 **Klinke Brothers Ice Cream Company**
2450 Scaper St
Memphis, TN 38114 901-743-8250
Fax: 901-743-8254
Processor of ice cream and frozen yogurt
President: John Klinke
Vice President: Russell Klinke
Estimated Sales: $ 20 - 50 Million
Number Employees: 50-99
Type of Packaging: Consumer, Food Service
Brands:
Angel Food

7362 **Klomar Ship Supply Company**
2200 Perimeter Rd
Mobile, AL 36615 251-471-1153
Transportation company providing ocean transport
Owner: Mike Kloumassis

7363 **Klondike Cheese**
W7839 State Road 81
Monroe, WI 53566-9179
Fax: 608-325-3027 ron@klondikecheese.com
www.klondikecheese.com
Processor of cheese
President: Ron Bulholzer
Marketing Director: Ron Buholzer
Estimated Sales: $ 10 - 20 Million
Number Employees: 20-49
Type of Packaging: Consumer, Private Label

7364 **Klondike Cheese Factory**
W7839 State Road 81
Monroe, WI 53566 608-325-3021
Fax: 608-325-3027 ron@klondikecheese.com
www.klondikecheese.com
Manufacturer of cheese
President: Dave Bulholzer
EVP: Steven Buholzer
Manager: Ryan Buholzer
Estimated Sales: $51 Million
Number Employees: 75

7365 **Kloss Manufacturing Company**
7566 Morris Ct Ste 310
Allentown, PA 18106 610-391-3820
Fax: 610-391-3830 800-445-7100
questions@klossfunfood.com
www.klossfunfood.com
Processor and exporter of flavoring extracts for Italian ices and slushes; also, concession equipment and supplies, fountain syrups, popcorn, cotton candy, nachos and waffles; wholesaler/distributor serving the food service market
President: Richard C Kloss
Vice President: Stephen Kloss
Estimated Sales: $ 3 - 5 Million
Number Employees: 10-19
Sq. footage: 30000
Type of Packaging: Food Service, Private Label, Bulk
Brands:
Kloss

7366 **(HQ)Klosterman Baking Company**
4760 Paddock Rd
Cincinnati, OH 45229 513-242-1004
Fax: 513-242-3151
comments@klostermanbakery.com
www.klostermanbakery.com

Breads, buns, hoagies and rolls.
President: Kenneth Klosterman Jr
CFO: John Kronenberger
EVP: Dennis Wiltshire
Marketing Manager: Tom Franz
Sales Director: Mike Braun
Human Resources Manager: Tim McCoy
Head of Manufacturing & Operations: Todd Crow

Purchasing Manager: Larry Wright
Estimated Sales: $47900000
Number Employees: 630
Type of Packaging: Consumer, Food Service

7367 **Klosterman Baking Company**
508 W Main St
Springfield, OH 45504 937-322-7658
Fax: 937-322-6733 www.klostermanbakery.com
Processor of bread
Chairman of the Board: Kenneth Klosterman
President: Chip Klosterman
Plant Manager: John Tucker
Estimated Sales: $47900000
Number Employees: 100-249
Parent Co: Klosterman Baking Company
Type of Packaging: Consumer, Food Service

7368 **Kluge Estate Winery & Vineyard**
100 Grand Cru Dr
Charlottesville, VA 22902-7763 434-977-3895
Fax: 434-977-0606 info@klugeestate.com
www.klugeestateonline.com
Wines
President: Patricia Kluge
COO: John Beckman
Vineyard Manager: Tom Child
Estimated Sales: $ 3 - 5 Million
Number Employees: 5-9

7369 **Knapp Vineyards**
2770 Ernsberger Rd
Romulus, NY 14541-9757 607-869-9271
Fax: 607-869-3212 800-869-9271
winery@knappwine.com www.knappwine.com
Wines
Owner: Gene Pierce
Vice President: Susanna Knapp
Estimated Sales: Below $ 5 Million
Number Employees: 20-49
Type of Packaging: Private Label
Brands:
Knapp

7370 **Knappen Milling Company**
110 S Water St
Augusta, MI 49012 269-731-4141
Fax: 269-731-5441 800-562-7736
wheat@knappen.com www.knappenmilling.com
Manufacturer of soft wheat, cereal bran, wheat and flour
President: Charles Knappen III
CFO: Darrell Roese
CEO: C B Knappen Iii
Sales Director: Todd Wright
Plant Manager: John Shouse
Number Employees: 20-49
Type of Packaging: Private Label, Bulk
Brands:
100% FLAKED WHEAT
ARBUTUS FLOUR
HEAVY BRAN
SATIN WHITE FLOUR
SOTAC

7371 **Knese Enterprise**
P.O.Box 20475
27 Huron Rd
Bellerose, NY 11426 516-354-9004
Fax: 516-354-9004 bradstasteofny@aol.com
Spicy gourmet mustard, kettle potato chips, pretzels and pretzel dip
President: Brad Knese
VP: Nancy Knese
Estimated Sales: $ 1 - 3 Million
Number Employees: 5-9
Type of Packaging: Consumer
Brands:
Brad's Pretzel Dip
Kettle Chips
Pretzels

7372 **(HQ)Knight Seed Company**
12550 W Frontage Road
Suite 203
Burnsville, MN 55337-2402 952-894-8080
Fax: 952-894-8095 800-328-2999
ksc@knightseed.com www.knightseed.com
Processor, importer and exporter of soybeans, dried beans, peas and buckwheat; exporter of lentils
President/CEO: Dave Dornacker
Manager: Jeff Pricco
VP: Tom Kennelly
Marketing: Tim Kukowski
Sales: Dan Dahlquist
Estimated Sales: $ 3 - 5 Million
Number Employees: 16
Sq. footage: 3000
Other Locations:
Knight Seed Co.
Vanscoy SK
Brands:
KNIGHT
KSC
LEGACY

7373 **(HQ)Knights Appleden Fruit**
RR 3
Colborne, ON K0K 1S0
Canada 905-349-2521
Fax: 905-349-3129
Processor, importer and exporter of apples
Pres.: Roger Knight
Estimated Sales: 1-2.5 Million
Number Employees: 20-49

7374 **Knipschildt ChocolatierLLC**
12 South Main Street
Norwalk, CT 06854 203-838-3131
Fax: 203-838-3137 amanda@knipschildt.com
www.knipschildt.com
chocolates
President/Owner: Fritz Knipschildt
Marketing: Amanda Ciaszki

7375 **Knott's Berry Farm Foods**
200 Boysenberry Lane
Placentia, CA 92870-6422 714-579-2400
Fax: 714-579-2490 800-289-9927
info@knottsberryfarmfoods.com
www.knottsberryfarmfoods.com
Processor of jams, jellies and preserves; also, pancake and fruit syrups, spaghetti sauces, salad dressings, specialty foods and gift packs
President/CEO/Chairman: Bruce Rohde
EVP/CFO: Frank Sklarsky
Senior VP Corporate Affairs/CCO: Michael Fernandez
Senior VP/Controller: John Gehring
Number Employees: 100-249
Sq. footage: 250000
Parent Co: ConAgra Grocery Products
Type of Packaging: Consumer, Food Service

7376 **Knotts Whlse. Foods**
125 N Blakemore St
Paris, TN 38242 731-642-1961
Fax: 731-644-1962 joshknott@knottsfoods.com
www.knottsfoods.com
Processor of refrigerated sandwiches and sandwich spreads; wholesaler/distributor of specialty foods; rack jobber services available
President: Jerry Knott
VP Operations: Josh Knott
VP Sales: BJ Knott
Estimated Sales: $5000000
Number Employees: 20-49
Sq. footage: 60000
Brands:
Knott's
Knott's Meat Snacks
Knott's Novelty Candy
Knott's Salads

7377 **(HQ)Knouse Foods Coop**
800 Peach Glen Road - Idaville Road
Peach Glen, PA 17375-0001 717-677-8181
Fax: 717-677-7069 sriley@pg.knouse.com
www.knouse.com
Manufacturer and exporter of apple products, pie fillings, juices, cider and vinegar; also, cheese sauces and puddings available
President/CEO: Ken Guise
CFO: Thomas DeNisco
VP/Technical Services: Robert Binkley
Marketing Manager: Ken Millage
Manager Special Markets: Rick Esser
Estimated Sales: $229 Million
Number Employees: 415
Sq. footage: 557450
Type of Packaging: Consumer, Food Service, Private Label, Bulk
Brands:
APPLE TIME
COBBLER
LINCOLN
LUCKY LEAF
MUSSLEMAN'S
SPEAS FARM

7378 **Knouse Foods Coop**
815 S Kalamazoo St
Paw Paw, MI 49079-0249 269-657-5524
Fax: 269-657-7512 www.knouse.com
Manufacturer and exporter of processed apple, cherry and other fruit products including sauces, pie fillings, juices, cider and vinegar
Manager: Bill Jensen
Dir. of Private Label: Lee Esser
Number Employees: 110
Parent Co: Knouse Foods Cooperative
Type of Packaging: Consumer, Food Service, Bulk

7379 **Knouse Foods Coop**
421 East Grant Street
Chambersburg, PA 17201-1675 717-263-9177
Fax: 717-263-6262 www.knouse.com
Processor of canned and jarred apples and apple sauce
President: Kenneth E Guise Jr
Plant Manager: Chet Amick
Number Employees: 180
Parent Co: Knouse Foods Cooperative
Type of Packaging: Consumer

7380 **Knouse Foods Coop**
1505 Orrtanna Rd
Box 3008
Orrtanna, PA 17353-0308 717-642-8291
Fax: 717-642-5096 www.knouse.com
Processor of canned and jarred apples and apple sauce
Manager: Greg Monn
Plant Manager: Mike Binkley
Number Employees: 240
Parent Co: Knouse Foods Cooperative
Type of Packaging: Consumer

7381 **Knox Mountain Farm**
RR 1
Franklin, NH 03235 603-934-9826
800-943-2822
President: Cynthia Huber
Estimated Sales: $ 2.5-5 Million
Number Employees: 5

7382 **Knoxage Water Company**
227 9th Avenue
San Diego, CA 92101-7403 619-234-3333
Fax: 858-530-2529
Water
Manager: Hank Adair
President: Doug Reed
Director Manufacturing: Robert Wagner
Estimated Sales: $ 1-2.5 Million appx.
Number Employees: 18

7383 **Knudsen's Candy**
25067 Viking Street
Hayward, CA 94545-2703 800-736-6887
Fax: 510-293-6890 anyone@knudsens.com
www.knudsens.com
Dessert toppings, caramel topping, wrapped caramels, boxed chocolates all homemade ice cream and candy
President: Gary Love
CEO: Gary Love
Sales Director: Gina Quiriconi
Estimated Sales: $2.5-5 Million
Number Employees: 10-19
Sq. footage: 20000

Brands:
Gramms Bep's Gourmet Ffoods
Grand Finale

7384 **Koa Trading Company**
2975 Aukele St
Lihue, HI 96766 808-245-6961
Fax: 808-245-8036 info@koatradingcoinc.com
www.koatradingcoinc.com
Food and beverage products.
President: Peter Yukimura
Estimated Sales: $300,000-500,000
Number Employees: 1-4

7385 **Koala Moa Char Broiled Chicken**
755 N. Nimitz Hwy
Honolulu, HI 96817 808-523-6701
Fax: 808-671-3527 koalamoa@inix.com
www.koala-moa.com
Broiled chicken
President: Gerald Shimabukuro
VP: Kristana Speach
Estimated Sales: $ 1-2.5 Million
Number Employees: 5-9
Sq. footage: 7

7386 **Kobricks Coffee Company**
693 Luis Munoz Marin Boulevard
Jersey City, NJ 07310-1225 201-656-6313
Fax: 201-656-3665 800-562-3662
info@kobricks.com www.kobricks.com
Italian espresso and other coffees
President: Lee Kobrick
Co-Owner: Steve Kobrick
Estimated Sales: $ 10-24.9 Million
Number Employees: 30-50
Brands:
Kobricks Coffee Company
La San Marco
Leodoro Espresso Com
Shearer
Tazo Teas
Torani Italian Syrup

7387 **Koch Food**
P.O.Box 749
Chattanooga, TN 37401-0749 423-266-0351
Fax: 423-266-8833 dannuc@kochfoods.com
www.kochfoods.com
Processor of poultry
Manager: Don Davis
Estimated Sales: $ 50 - 100 Million
Number Employees: 250-499
Parent Co: Koch Foods
Type of Packaging: Consumer

7388 **(HQ)Koch Foods**
1300 Higgins Rd # 100
Park Ridge, IL 60068-5766 847-384-5940
Fax: 847-384-5961 800-837-2778
www.kochfoods.com
Manufacturer and exporter of frozen, portion control and specialty chicken; also turkey cranberry burgers.
CFO: Mark Kaminsky
CEO: Joseph C Grendys
Estimated Sales: $1 Million
Number Employees: 20-49
Type of Packaging: Consumer, Food Service
Other Locations:
Koch Foods Export Office
Gainesville GA
Koch Foods Sales Office
Morton MS
Brands:
Bc Rogers

7389 **Koch Foods**
P.O.Box 603
Morristown, TN 37815 423-586-3668
Fax: 423-586-5710 www.kochfoods.com
Fresh and frozen poultry products
President: Joe Grundy
Safety Manager: Barry Harkey
Human Resources Director: Lee Markem
Purchasing Agent: Mark Wimer
Estimated Sales: $60000000
Number Employees: 5-9
Sq. footage: 45000
Type of Packaging: Consumer, Food Service, Private Label, Bulk

7390 **Koch Foods**
1835 Kerr St
Chattanooga, TN 37408 423-266-0351
Fax: 423-266-8833 dannuc@kochfoods.com
www.kochfoods.com
Manufacturer and exporter of fresh, raw and frozen chicken
Manager: Nick Strange
Communications Director: Todd Womack
General Manager: R Pendergraft
Manager: Nick Nuckolls
Estimated Sales: $1 Billion
Number Employees: 250-499
Parent Co: Koch Poultry
Type of Packaging: Food Service

7391 **Koch Poultry**
4404 W Berteau Ave
Chicago, IL 60641 773-286-4343
Fax: 773-286-8952 800-837-2778
www.kochfoods.com
Processor of fresh and frozen chicken breasts
President, Koch Meats: Joe Grendys
Plant Manager: Jim Dunbar
Estimated Sales: $ 20-50 Million
Number Employees: 100-249
Type of Packaging: Consumer, Food Service

7392 **Koda Farms**
P.O.Box 10
South Dos Palos, CA 93665-0010 209-392-2191
Fax: 209-392-6558 info@kodafarms.com
www.kodafarms.com
Processor of rice and rice flour
President: Edward K Koda
Estimated Sales: $ 50 - 100 Million
Number Employees: 100-249
Type of Packaging: Consumer
Brands:
Blue Star Mockiko
Diamond K
Kokuho Rose
Sho Chiku Bai

7393 **Kodiak Salmon Packers**
PO Box 38
Larsen Bay, AK 99624-0038 907-847-2250
Fax: 907-847-2244
Processor of frozen and canned wild Alaskan salmon
President: Alan Beardsley
Executive VP: Van Johnson
Plant Manager: Grant Mirick
Estimated Sales: $750000

7394 **Koegel Meats**
3400 W Bristol Rd
Flint, MI 48507 810-238-3685
Fax: 810-238-2467 questions@koegelmeats.com
www.koegelmeats.com
Processor and packer of sausage, natural casing and long frankfurters, bratwurst, bockwurst and smoked specialties
President: John Koegel
CEO: Albert Koegel
Vice President: Kathryn Koegel
Sales Director: Tom Lakies
Operations Manager: Jim Lay
Estimated Sales: $21840933
Number Employees: 50-99
Number of Products: 35
Sq. footage: 100000
Type of Packaging: Consumer, Food Service

7395 **Koepplinger Bakery**
535 Griswold Street
Suite 2600
Detroit, MI 48226-3687 248-967-2020
Fax: 248-967-0722
Breads and rolls
President: John Mather
Estimated Sales: $ 10-24.9 Million
Number Employees: 100-150

7396 **Koeze Company**
2555 Burlingame Ave SW
Wyoming, MI 49509-2237 616-724-2620
Fax: 616-243-5430 800-555-3909
bdekker@koeze.com www.koeze.com
Processor of nut candies including peanut, tree nuts, and candy
President: Scott Koeze
CEO: Jeff Koeze
Marketing: Beth Dekker
Sales Director: Tom Lakos
Purchasing Manager: John Feenstra
Estimated Sales: $9672287
Number Employees: 20-49
Sq. footage: 80000
Type of Packaging: Consumer, Bulk

7397 **Koffee Kup Bakery**
436 Riverside Ave
Burlington, VT 05401 802-863-2696
Fax: 802-860-0116 c52345arol@aol.com
www.koffeekupbakery.biz
Bread and doughnuts
President: Ronald Roberge Sr
CEO: Andrew Mathews
Quality Control: Tom Beauregard
Vice President: Carol Roberge
CFO: Eddie Matthews
VP: James Kokinos
General Manager: Mattson Davis
Purchasing Manager: Steve Hebert
Estimated Sales: $ 10-20 Million
Number Employees: 50-99
Type of Packaging: Private Label
Brands:
Koffee Kup

7398 **Koha Food**
500 Alakawa St # 104
Honolulu, HI 96817-4576 808-845-4232
Fax: 808-841-5398
Oriental foods
President: Paul Kim
Estimated Sales: $ 5 - 10 Million
Number Employees: 20-49

7399 **Kohana Coffee**
1221 S Mopac Expressway
Suite 100
Austin, TX 78746 512-904-1174
Fax: 512-532-0581 info@kohanacoffee.com
www.kohanacoffee.com
Manufacturer and wholesaler of coffee, decaff and cold brew coffee
Owner: Victoria Lynden
Sales: Nate Creasey
Operations: Piper Jones
Estimated Sales: Under $500,000
Number Employees: 2

7400 **Kohinoor Foods**
40 Northfield Avenue
Edison, NJ 08837 732-868-4400
Fax: 732-868-3143 888-440-7423
info@kohinoorfoods.com
www.kohinoorfoods.com
Rice
CEO: Ganesh Skandan
Marketing: Rajan Kapoor
Estimated Sales: $ 2.5-5 Million
Number Employees: 10-19
Brands:
Kohinoor
Satman Overseas

7401 **Kohler Mix Specialties**
4041 Highway 61 N
White Bear Lake, MN 55110 651-426-1633
Fax: 651-426-7876 www.deanfoods.com
Processor of dairy products including ice cream mixes, ice milk, shakes, etc
Director National Sales: Mark Johnson
VP Procurement: Lee Groehler
Plant Manager: Matt Mensink
Estimated Sales: $100+ Million
Number Employees: 100-249
Parent Co: Michael Foods
Type of Packaging: Consumer, Food Service

7402 **Kohler Mix Specialties**
100 Milk Ln
Newington, CT 06111-2242 860-666-1511
Fax: 860-667-9274 fabbri@michaelfoods.com
www.michaelfoods.com
Processor of soft serve ice cream and shake mix
President: Gregg Ostrander
Plt. Mgr.: Peter Fabbri
Plant Manager: John Lacombe

Estimated Sales: $ 50 - 100 Million
Number Employees: 50-99
Parent Co: Michael Foods
Type of Packaging: Food Service

7403 **Kokinos Purity Ice CreamCompany**
806 S Grand St
Monroe, LA 71201-8412 318-322-2930
Processor of ice cream
President: Harry Kokinos
Vice President: Mary Kokinos
Number Employees: 10-19
Type of Packaging: Consumer, Food Service

7404 **Kokopelli's Kitchen**
9116 N Cave Creek Rd
Phoenix, AZ 85020 602-943-8882
Fax: 602-943-8740 888-943-9802
kokopellis@mindspring.com
www.kokopelliskitchen.com
Manufacturer of wide array of gourmet Southwest dry-mixes: bread, muffins, pancakes, bean and soups, rice dishes, salad dressings, salsas, enchilada sauce and cocoas
President: Cheryl Joseph
Estimated Sales: $ .5 - 1 million
Number Employees: 1-4
Number of Products: 45
Sq. footage: 3000
Parent Co: Kokopelli's Kitchen
Type of Packaging: Consumer, Bulk
Brands:
KOKOPELLI'S KITCHEN

7405 **Kolatin Real Kosher Gelatin**
325 Second Street
Lakewood, NJ 08701 732-364-8700
Fax: 732-370-0877 info@koshergelatin.com
www.koshergelatin.com
Supplier of real kosher gelatin used in confectionary products, meats, pates and as a thickener and emulsifier in soups, gravies and sauces.
Parent Co: Glatech Productions

7406 **(HQ)Kolb-Lena Cheese Company**
3990 N Sunnyside Rd
Lena, IL 61048-9613 815-369-4577
Fax: 815-369-4914
Manufacturer of cheese including camembert, baby and bay Swiss, brie, feta and soft; also, gourmet foods
Manager: Tom Dahmen
Estimated Sales: $35.7 Million
Number Employees: 50-99
Parent Co: BC USA
Type of Packaging: Consumer, Food Service
Brands:
DELICO

7407 **Kollar Cookies**
PO Box 502
10 3rd Ave
Long Branch, NJ 07740-6503 732-229-3364
Fax: 732-750-1960 ibn@home.com
www.kollarcookies.com
Cookies
Owner: Pam Kimble
Estimated Sales: $ 1-2.5 Million
Number Employees: 5
Brands:
Kollar

7408 **Kombucha King International**
PO Box 44203
Phoenix, AZ 85064-4203 602-263-0792
Fax: 602-263-0792 800-896-9676
President: John Gutowski

7409 **Kombucha Wonder Drink**
P.O.Box 4244
Portland, OR 97208 503-224-7331
Fax: 503-224-2295 877-224-7331
info@teaports.com www.wonderdrink.com
Tea and herbal infusions
Founder/Owner: Steve Lee
CEO: Craig Decker
Research & Development: Koei Kudo
Marketing Director: Koei Kudo
Sales Director: Todd Hager
Estimated Sales: $650,000
Number Employees: 5-9
Type of Packaging: Private Label
Brands:
Empire
Teaports

7410 **Kona Brewing**
75-5629 Kuakini Hwy Ste X
Kailua Kona, HI 96740 808-334-2739
Fax: 808-329-8869 808-334-2739
pub@konabrewingco.com
www.konabrewingco.com
Beer
President: Mattson Davis
CFO: Keith Kinsey
Quality Control: Rich Tucciarone
Marketing Director: Steve Cole
Estimated Sales: $ 30-50 Million
Number Employees: 50-99
Type of Packaging: Private Label
Brands:
Kona Brewing

7411 **Kona Coffee Council**
P.O.Box 9002
Kealakekua, HI 96750-9002 808-323-2911
inquiries@kona-coffee-council.com
www.kona-coffee-council.com
Coffee
Manager: Barry Gitelson
VP: Bob Foerster
Estimated Sales: $ .5 - 1 million
Number Employees: 1-4

7412 **Kona Cold Lobsters Ltd**
73-4460 Queen K Hwy Ste 103
Kailua Kona, HI 96740 808-329-4332
Fax: 808-326-2882
Lobsters
President: Joseph Wilson
Estimated Sales: Less than $300,000
Number Employees: 5-9

7413 **Kona Kava Coffee Company**
PO Box 168
Philo, CA 95466-0168 707-985-3913
Fax: 707-895-3913
Coffee
Owner: Jonathan O Bergin
Estimated Sales: Under $500,000
Number Employees: 1-4

7414 **Kona Premium Coffee Company**
75 Keke St
Keauhou, HI 96739 808-322-9550
Fax: 808-322-9275 888-322-9550
info@konapremium.com
www.konapremium.com
Commercial and retail coffee
Owner: Robert Millslagle
CFO: Jeff Woode
Director of Sales: James Lenhart
VP Operations: Peter Donovan
Estimated Sales: $ 20-50 Million
Number Employees: 20-49
Type of Packaging: Private Label
Brands:
Kona Coffee
Royal Konaccino

7415 **Konetzkos Market**
P.O.Box 341
Browerville, MN 56438-0341 320-594-2915
Processor of smoked meat and sausage
Owner: Jim Becker
Estimated Sales: Less than $500,000
Number Employees: 1-4
Type of Packaging: Consumer

7416 **Konica Minolta SensingAmericas**
101 Williams Drive
Ramsey, NY 07446 201-785-2413
Fax: 201-785-2482
Manufacturer of food ingredients
President: Hal Yamazaki
Vice President: Grant Hume
Number Employees: 35

7417 **Konto's Foods**
P.O.Box 628
Paterson, NJ 07544-0628 973-278-2800
Fax: 973-278-7943 info@kontos.com
www.kontos.com
Manufacturer of hand stretched flat bread and Kontos fillo dough and fillo products.
Founder/President: Evripides Kontos
Vice President/Director of Sales: Steve Kontos
Estimated Sales: $ 50-100 Million
Number Employees: 50-99
Sq. footage: 65000
Type of Packaging: Food Service
Brands:
Konto's

7418 **Kookaburra Liquorice Co**
14497 Fryelands Blvd SE
Monroe, WA 98272-2941
Fax: 360-805-6859 sales@kookaburrapacific.com
www.kookaburrapacific.com
licorice
President/Owner: Donald Cook
CEO: Bradley Cook
Number Employees: 5

7419 **Kool Ice & Seafood Company**
110 Washington St
Cambridge, MD 21613 410-228-2300
Fax: 410-228-1027
www.freshmarylandseafood.com
Seafood
Owner: Dave Nickerson
Estimated Sales: $ 5 - 10 Million
Number Employees: 20-49

7420 **Kopali Organics**
8101 Biscayne Blvd
#609
Miami, FL 33138-4668 305-751-7341
Fax: 305-751-7344 www.kopaliorganics.com
organic foods
COO: Norman Brooks

7421 **(HQ)Kopper's Chocolate**
39 Clarkson St
New York, NY 10014-3605 212-243-0220
Fax: 212-243-3316 800-325-0026
keechon@kopperschocolate.com
www.kopperschocolate.com
Processor, importer and exporter of confectionery items including chocolate covered espresso beans, chocolate covered gummy bears and Danish mint lentils.
President: Jeffrey Alexander
Estimated Sales: $7800000
Number Employees: 1-4

7422 **Koppert Cress USA**
3000 Marcus Ave
Ste 3w4
New Hyde Park, NY 11042-1009 516-437-5700
Fax: 516-437-5703 info.usa@koppertcress.com
www.koppertcress.com
micro-vegetables
Member: Janny Hendrikse

7423 **Korbs Baking Company**
540 Pawtucket Avenue
Pawtucket, RI 02860-6098 401-726-4422
Fax: 401-726-4446
Baked goods
President: Edmund Korb
Estimated Sales: $ 1-2.5 Million
Number Employees: 50

7424 **Kornfections**
14516 Lee Rd # C
Chantilly, VA 20151-1638 703-378-0009
Fax: 703-817-9560 800-469-8886
kornfections@verizon.net
www.kornfections.com
Gourmet popcorn and confections.
President: Gerald Lerner
Vice President: Helen Lerner
Marketing/Public Relations: Jerry Lerner
Estimated Sales: $ 3 - 5 Million
Number Employees: 6
Number of Brands: 1
Number of Products: 22
Sq. footage: 2400
Type of Packaging: Consumer, Food Service, Private Label, Bulk

7425 **Korte Meat Processors**
810 Deal St
Highland, IL 62249 618-654-3813
Fax: 618-654-8207

Processor of beef and pork
Owner: Dave Korte
Estimated Sales: $ 3 - 5 Million
Number Employees: 5-9
Type of Packaging: Consumer, Bulk

7426 **Koryo Winery Company**
13719 Alma Ave
Gardena, CA 90249 310-532-9616
Fax: 310-532-3240
Wines
President: Sarah Kym
Operations Manager: Roy Kym
Estimated Sales: Less than $500,000
Number Employees: 20-49
Type of Packaging: Private Label
Brands:
Dong Dong Joo Rice Wine
Mackoly Rice Wine
Sochu Distilled Rice

7427 **Kosher French Baguettes**
683 McDonald Ave
Brooklyn, NY 11218 718-633-4994
Baguettes
Owner: Paul Gima
Estimated Sales: $300,000-500,000
Number Employees: 5-9

7428 **Kossar's Bialystoker Kuchen Bakery**
367 Grand St
New York, NY 10002-3951 212-473-4810
Fax: 212-253-2146 877-424-2597
kossarsmail@kossarsbialys.com
www.kossarsbialys.com
Bakery products
Owner: Danny Cohen
Owner: Danny Cohen
Estimated Sales: $500,000-$1 Million
Number Employees: 10-19
Brands:
Bialy
Kashruth

7429 **Kosto Food Products Company**
1325 N Old Rand Rd
Wauconda, IL 60084 847-487-2600
Fax: 847-487-2654 www.kostofoods.com
Processor and exporter of salad dressings, food colorings, pudding and ice cream mixes; importer of colorants, stabilizers, ice cream mixes, drink crystals, meat extenders and puddings
President: Donald F Colby
CEO: Steve Colby
Sales Director: Richard Gray
Estimated Sales: $1300000
Number Employees: 10-19
Type of Packaging: Consumer, Food Service, Private Label, Bulk
Brands:
Dari Pride
Food Pak
Freezerta
Kosto
Mack's
Mrs Slaby's
Slushade

7430 **Kotarides Baking Company of Virginia**
117 E 16th St
Norfolk, VA 23510-2629 757-625-0301
Fax: 757-622-1260
Processor of bread and rolls
President: Christopher Kotarides Sr
Vice President: John Kotarides
Estimated Sales: $ 10 - 20 Million
Number Employees: 450
Brands:
GOLDEN GRAIN
MARY JANE
NATURAL GRAIN

7431 **Kowalski Sausage Company**
2270 Holbrook St
Hamtramck, MI 48212 313-873-8200
Fax: 313-873-4220 800-482-2400
www.kowality.com
Processor and packer of sausage
President: Michael Kowalski
Estimated Sales: $32800000
Number Employees: 100-249
Number of Products: 75
Type of Packaging: Consumer, Food Service

7432 **Koyo Foods**
2410 Santa Clara Street
Richmond, CA 94804-5622 510-527-7066
Fax: 510-527-0178
Rice cakes

7433 **Kozlowski Farms**
5566 Hwy 116
Forestville, CA 95436 707-887-1587
Fax: 707-887-9650 800-473-2767
koz@kozlowskifarms.com
www.kozlowskifarms.com
Manufacturer of natural and specialty food products, including: 100% fruit spreads, jams, mustards, preserves, chutneys, jellys, fruit butters, dessert sauces, steak and BBQ sauces, fruit vinegar, salad dressings and chipotle sauces.CCOF apples an Pinot Noir grapes are farmed on the property. Visitors are also welcomed to visit the farm and try fresh, homemade fruit tarts, pies and cookies from the bakery. Most products certified Kosher.
President: Carmen Kozlowski
CEO: Perry Kozlowski
CFO: Cindy Kozlowski-Hayworth
VP: Carol Kozlowski-Every
Estimated Sales: $1,000,000
Number Employees: 20-49
Number of Brands: 1
Number of Products: 90
Sq. footage: 20000
Type of Packaging: Consumer, Private Label
Brands:
Kozlowski Farms
Sonoma County Classics

7434 **Kozy Shack**
83 Ludy St
Hicksville, NY 11801 516-870-3000
Fax: 516-870-3001 www.kozyshack.com
Manufacturer and exporter of ready-to-eat puddings including rice, tapioca, chocolate, vanilla, banana; also, flan
Chairpman: Vincent Gruppuso
President/CEO: Lenny Pippin
Marketing Manager: Diana Gruppuso
VP Business Development: John Rooney
Estimated Sales: $100 Million
Number Employees: 250-499
Sq. footage: 70000
Type of Packaging: Consumer, Food Service, Bulk
Brands:
KOZY SHACK

7435 **Kraemer's Wisconsin Cheese**
1173 N 4th St
Watertown, WI 53098-3201 920-261-6363
Fax: 920-261-9606 800-236-8033
kwcheese@kraemercheese.com
www.kraemercheese.com
Cheese
President: Richard Kraemer
Estimated Sales: Below $ 5 Million
Number Employees: 5-9

7436 **(HQ)Kraft Canada Headquarters**
Po Box/Cp 1200
Don Mills, ON M3C 3J5
Canada 416-441-5000
Fax: 416-441-5328 888-572-3806
www.kraftcanada.com/
Manufacturer and distribution of grocery products; canned fruits and vegetables, canned soups, pickles, jam, baking products, seasonings and dressings, cookies and crackers.
President Kraft Canada: Fred Schaeffer
CEO: Wynn Willard
CFO: Angela Holtham
VP & General Manager: Dino Bianco
Manager Export Sales/Marketing: Larry Inglis
Associate Director Corporate Affairs: Lynne Galia
Estimated Sales: $50 Million
Number Employees: 7100
Parent Co: Kraft Foods
Type of Packaging: Consumer, Food Service

7437 **(HQ)Kraft Canada Lake ShoreBakery**
P.O. Box/C.P. 1200
Don Mills, ON M3C 3J5
Canada 416-503-6000
Fax: 406-503-6100 888-572-3806
www.kraftcanada.com/
Manufacturer and distribution of bakery products.
President Kraft Canada: Fred Schaeffer
CEO: Wynn Willard
CFO: Angela Holtham
VP General Manager: Dino Bianco
Manager Export Sales/Marketing: Larry Inglis
Associate Director Corporate Affairs: Lynne Galia
Number Employees: 500-999
Parent Co: Kraft Foods
Type of Packaging: Consumer, Food Service

7438 **(HQ)Kraft Canada Nabisco Division**
10 Park Lawn Road
Toronto, ON M8Y 3H8
Canada 416-253-3200
Fax: 416-253-3210 www.kraftcanada.com/
Manufacturer and distributor of Nabisco brand products including cookies and crackers.
President Kraft Canada: Fred Schaeffer
CEO: Wynn Willard
CFO: Angela Holtham
Manager Export Sales/Marketing: Larry Inglis
Associate Director Corporate Affairs: Lynne Galia
Number Employees: 500-999
Parent Co: Kraft Foods
Type of Packaging: Consumer, Food Service

7439 **Kraft Foods**
1400 Murphy Ave SW
Atlanta, GA 30310 404-756-6000
Fax: 404-756-6027 www.kraftfoodscompany.com
Manufacturer of baked goods including biscuits, cookies and crackers.
Parent Co: Kraft Foods
Type of Packaging: Consumer
Brands:
Breakstones
Breyers
Country Time
Crystal Light
Handi Snacks
Jack's Pizza
Jell-O
Kraft Cooking
Krafts Food
Minute Rice
Post Healthy Classics
Stove Top

7440 **Kraft Foods**
P.O.Box 300
Albany, MN 56307 320-845-2131
Fax: 320-845-2402 www.kraftfoodscompany.com
Manufacturer of cheese powders
Parent Co: Kraft Foods
Type of Packaging: Consumer

7441 **Kraft Foods**
2035 E Bennett St
Springfield, MO 65804 417-881-2701
Fax: 417-881-2139 www.kraftfoods.com
Manufacturer of natural and processed cheese, cream cheese, macaroni and cheese and pasta.
Parent Co: Kraft Foods
Type of Packaging: Consumer
Brands:
A1 STEAK SAUCE
ALTOIDS
BAKER'S
BREAKSTONE'S COTTAGE CHEESE
BREYER'S YOGURT
COUNTRY TIME
CRYSTAL LIGHT
DIGIORNO RISING CRUST
GENERAL FOOD INTERNATIONAL COFFEE
GRAPE NUTS
HANDI-SNACKS
HOP ABOARD
JACK'S PIZZA
JACOBS
JELL-O
KNOX
KOOL-AID

KRAFT CHEESE
KRAFT MACARONI AND CHEESE
LUNCHABLES
MAXWELL HOUSE
MILLKA
MINUTE RICE
MIRACLE WHIP
OREO
OSCAR MAYER
PHILADELPHIA
PLANTERS PEANUTS
POLLY-O TRATTORIA
POST HEALTHY CLASSIC
SHAKE 'N BAKE
STOVE TOP
TERRY'S
TOBLERONE
UNEEDA BISCUITS
VELVEETA

7442 **Kraft Foods**
2340 Forest Ln
Garland, TX 75042 972-272-7511
Fax: 972-485-7706 www.kraftfoodscompany.com
Manufacturer of barbecue sauce, salad dressing, mayonnaise and mustard.
Parent Co: Kraft Foods
Type of Packaging: Consumer

7443 **Kraft Foods**
261 Delaware St
Walton, NY 13856 607-865-7131
Fax: 607-865-5830 www.kraftfoodscompany.com
Manufacturer of cultured products including sour cream, cottage cheese and flavored dips.
Parent Co: Kraft Foods
Type of Packaging: Consumer

7444 **Kraft Foods**
7352 Industrial Blvd
Allentown, PA 18106 610-398-0311
Fax: 610-366-6560 www.kraftfoodscompany.com
Manufacturer and exporter of cheese and salad dressing.
Parent Co: Kraft Foods
Type of Packaging: Consumer, Food Service, Private Label, Bulk

7445 **(HQ)Kraft Foods**
3 Lakes Dr
Northfield, IL 60093 847-646-2000
Fax: 847-646-6005 800-323-0768
gec@kraft.com www.kraftfoodscompany.com
Manufacturer of mayonnaise, cheeses, sauces, snacks, meats, cereals, etc.
Chairman/CEO: Irene Rosenfeld
EVP/President, Kraft Foods North America: W Anthony Vernon
EVP/CFO: David Brearton
EVP/President, Developing Markets: Sanjay Khosla
EVP/Research Development & Quality: Jean Spence
EVP/Strategy: Sam Orvit
EVP/Chief Category & Marketing Officer: Mary Beth West
EVP/Global Human Resources: Karen May
EVP/President, Kraft Foods Europe: Michael Clarke
Estimated Sales: $49 Billion
Number Employees: 127,000
Sq. footage: 10000
Type of Packaging: Consumer, Food Service
Brands:
A.1
ATHENOS
BACK TO NATURE
BAKER'S
BALANCE
BALANCE CARBWELL
BARNUM'S ANIMALS
BOCA
BREAKSTONE'S
CAPRI SUN
CHEESE NIPS
CHEEZ WIZ
COOL WHIP
CORN NUTS
COUNTRY TIME
CREAM OF WHEAT
CRYSTAL LIGHT
DIGIORO
GENERAL FOODS INTERNATIONAL
GEVALIA
GOOD SEASONS
GREY POUPON
HANDI-SNACKS
HONEY MAID
JACK'S
JELL-0
JET-PUFFED
KNOX GELATINE
KNUDSEN
KOOL-AID SLUSHIES
KRAFT
KRAFT DELI DELUXE
LIGHT N' LIVELY
LOUIS RICH
LUNCHABLES
MINUTE
MIRACLE WHIP
NEWTONS
NUTTER BUTTER
OSCAR MAYER
POLLY-O
POST
RITZ
SANKA
STELLA D'ORO
SURE-JELL
TEDDY GRAHAMS
TOMBSTONE
TRISCUIT
VELVEETA
WHEAT THINS
WHOLE GRAIN CHIPS AHOY!
WHOLE GRAIN FIG NEWTONS
WHOLE GRAIN WHEAT THINS
YUBAN

7446 **Kraft Foods**
100 Deforest Ave
East Hanover, NJ 7936 973-503-2000
Fax: 201-794-4997 www.kraftfoodscompany.com
Processor of cookies and crackers.
Parent Co: Kraft Foods
Type of Packaging: Consumer, Food Service
Brands:
Nabisco

7447 **Kramarczuk Sausage Company**
215 E Hennepin Ave
Minneapolis, MN 55414 612-379-3018
Fax: 612-379-7693 www.kramarczuk.com
Sausages
President: Orest Kramarczuk
Estimated Sales: $500,000-$1 Million
Number Employees: 20-49

7448 **Kramer Vineyards**
26830 NW Olson Rd
Gaston, OR 97119 503-662-4545
Fax: 503-662-4033 800-619-4637
info@kramerwine.com www.kramerwine.com
Wines
President/CEO/Winemaker: Trudy Kramer
CEO: Kramer
VP/Secretary/Vineyard Manager: Keith Kramer
Marketing VP: Trudy Kramer
Estimated Sales: Less than $500,000
Number Employees: 5-9
Brands:
Kramer

7449 **Kraus & Company**
3136 Martin Rd
Commerce Township, MI 48390 248-960-7555
Fax: 248-960-7221 800-662-5871
info@krausecompany.com
www.krauscompany.com
Flavors, extracts, food colors, fruit preps, variegating sauces, toppings
Co-Founder/President: Gerry Kraus
Co-Founder/CEO: Eva Kraus
CFO: Saad Alhir
Estimated Sales: $1-$2 Million
Number Employees: 5-9
Type of Packaging: Food Service, Bulk

7450 **(HQ)Kreamo Bakers**
1910 Lincoln Way W
South Bend, IN 46628 574-234-0188
Fax: 574-287-1839 www.alphabaking.com
Manufacturer of bread and buns
President: Larry Mitchell
VP: Barbara Boyer
Estimated Sales: $7 Million
Number Employees: 10-19
Type of Packaging: Consumer, Food Service

7451 **Krema Nut Company**
1000 Goodale Blvd
Columbus, OH 43212-3889 614-299-4131
Fax: 614-299-1636 800-222-4132
nuts@krema.com www.krema.com
Processor of peanut butter and nuts including cashews
President: Mike Giunta
Estimated Sales: Less than $500,000
Number Employees: 5-9
Type of Packaging: Consumer, Food Service, Private Label
Other Locations:
Krema Nut Company
Columbus OH
Brands:
Krema

7452 **Kretschmar**
71 Curlew Drive
Don Mills, ON M3A 2P8
Canada 416-441-1100
Fax: 416-441-3386 800-561-4532
info@kretschmar.com www.kretschmar.com
Pork, beef, poultry, chubs and sticks, hot dogs and franks, luncheon meat, sausages, pate and coils
President: Gerhart Huber
Number Employees: 200
Type of Packaging: Private Label
Brands:
Karl Kramer
Kretschmar
Royal
Superior

7453 **Krier Foods**
520 Wolf Road
Random Lake, WI 53075 920-994-2469
Fax: 414-355-5577
Processor of beverages including juice and soda
Chairman of the Board: B Bruce Krier
Executive VP: Thoma Bretza
Purchasing Director: Steve Ihrcke
Estimated Sales: $740,000
Number Employees: 8
Sq. footage: 4114
Type of Packaging: Consumer
Brands:
Fruitland
Jolly Good

7454 **Krinos Foods**
12477 Calle Real
Santa Barbara, CA 93117 805-562-1456
Fax: 805-562-1464 800-624-4896
info@sbolive.com www.sbolive.com
Importer, distributor and manufacturer of Greek specialty foods.
Owner: Eric Moscahlaidis
VP Sales/Marketing: Paul Vertullo
Estimated Sales: $30400000
Number Employees: 100
Sq. footage: 125000
Type of Packaging: Consumer, Food Service, Bulk
Brands:
APOLLO
ATHENS
ATTIKI
FLORINA
HAITOGLOU
HERMES
HORIO
MACEDONIAN
MELISSA
MEVGAL
MINERVA
MYTHOS
SARANTIS
STELLA
VLAHA
YIOTIS
ZANAE

7455 **Krispy Bakery**
532 E Lakewood Road
West Palm Beach, FL 33405-2912 561-585-5504
Baked goods
Executive V.P.: Brian Wilson
Estimated Sales: Under $500,000
Number Employees: 100-249

7456 **Krispy Kernels**
2620 Rue Watt
Sainte Foy, QC G1P 3T5
Canada 418-658-1515
Fax: 418-657-5971 877-791-9986
info@krispykernals.com www.krispykernels.com
Peanuts, popcorn, candy and dried fruits and nuts
Owner: Denis Jalbert
CEO: Pierce Rivard
Quality Control: Stephen Jackson
Marketing Director: Renee Maude Jalbert
Sales Director: Stephane Gravel
Plant Manager: Jacques Bieion
Purchasing Manager: Marc Parent
Sq. footage: 100000
Brands:
KRISPY KERNELS

7457 **Krispy Kreme Doughnut Company**
370 Knollwood St Ste 500
Winston Salem, NC 27103 336-725-2981
Fax: 336-733-3896 800-457-4779
customer@krispy/creme.com
www.krispykreme.com
Bakery products and coffee
Chairman/President: Scott Livengood
CFO: Michael Phalen
CEO: James H Morgan
Quality Control: Betty Anders
Buyer: Carol Craig
Manufacturing Services Director: Gene Fockman
Plant Manager: Stanley Lowry
Purchasing: Phil Hendrix
Estimated Sales: $670 Million
Number Employees: 1,000-4,999

7458 **Kristian Regale**
14 Birkmose Park Ln
Hudson, WI 54016-2286
US 715-386-8388
Fax: 715-386-9295 info@kristianregale.com
www.kristianregale.com
Manufacturer and Importer of Swedish nonalcoholic apple and pear sparkling ciders,there are six flavors including the following, ap-ple,peach.pear,poegranate-apple,lingonberry-ap-ple,black currant.
Owner: Nancy Bieraugel
CHR/CEO: Ed Doherty
CFO: Dave Baldwin
Evp: Bob Gillespie
Estimated Sales: $3.4 Million
Number Employees: 7
Type of Packaging: Consumer, Food Service
Brands:
Kristian Regale

7459 **Kristin Hill Winery**
3330 SE Amity Dayton Hwy
Amity, OR 97101 503-835-4012
Fax: 503-835-4012
Wine
Owner: Eric Aberag
Co-Owner: Eric Aberg
Estimated Sales: Under $300,000
Number Employees: 1-4
Type of Packaging: Private Label
Brands:
Kristin Hill

7460 **Kristy Kremarie**
1218 Memorial Pkwy NW
Huntsville, AL 35801-5940 256-536-7475
Fax: 256-536-7474 gkheath@mindspring.com
www.krispykreme.com
Doughnuts
Manager: Perry Harris
Estimated Sales: $ 5-9.9 Million
Number Employees: 50-99

7461 **Kroger Anderson Bakery**
433 Sayre St
Anderson, SC 29624 864-226-9135
Fax: 864-224-6531 www.kroger.com
Processor of bakery products; wholesaler/distributor of general line products and baked goods
Manager: Gerald Spieth
Sls. Mgr.: Jerry Iven
Quality Control: Larry Skagts
Estimated Sales: $100+ Million
Number Employees: 100-249
Parent Co: Kroger Company

7462 **(HQ)Kroger Company**
1014 Vine St
Cincinnati, OH 45202 513-762-4000
Fax: 513-762-1160 800-576-4377
www.kroger.com
Grocery
President/COO/Director: W Rodney McMullen
Chairman/CEO: David Dillion
SVP/CFO: J Michael Schlotman
Senior VP: Don McGeorge
Manager Bakery Operations: John Masa
Estimated Sales: $76.7 Billion
Number Employees: 334,000
Brands:
Springdale Beverages
Turkey Hill
Wawa

7463 **Krohn Dairy Products**
N2915 County Road Ab
Luxemburg, WI 54217-7713 920-845-2901
Fax: 920-845-5466 danl@tregafoods.com
www.tregafoods.com
Processor of Italian cheeses including mozzarella and provolone.
President: Doug Simon
VP: Mike Sipple
Estimated Sales: $ 20 - 50 Million
Number Employees: 50-99
Type of Packaging: Consumer

7464 **Kronos Products**
1 Sexton Dr
Glendale Heights, IL 60139 773-847-2250
Fax: 773-847-2376 800-621-0099
info@kronos.com www.kronos.com
Greek specialties, frozen
President/CEO: Mike Austin
Chairman of the Board: Joel Jacks
Controller: Margreth Chreiber
VP: Costello Bartiz
VP Operations: George Baumgarten
Estimated Sales: $ 25-49.9 Million
Number Employees: 250-499
Brands:
Kronos

7465 **Kruger Foods**
18362 E Highway 4
Stockton, CA 95215-9433 209-941-8518
hanskr@aol.com
www.krugerfoods.com
Processor and exporter of condiments including rel-ish, pickles and sauerkraut
President: Dennis Kruger
VP: Hans Kruger
Plant Manager: Eric Kruger
Estimated Sales: $22000000
Number Employees: 100
Type of Packaging: Consumer

7466 **Krugers**
2366 7th St W
St Paul, MN 55116-2825 651-699-1356
Fax: 651-699-9577
Processor of produce
President: William Kruger
Estimated Sales: $3600000
Number Employees: 20-49

7467 **Krupka's Blueberries**
2647 68th St
Fennville, MI 49408 269-857-4278
Fax: 269-857-4278
Processor of blueberries
Partner: Harold Krupka
Partner: Carmen Krupka
Sales Manager: Connie Krupka
Estimated Sales: $3 Million
Number Employees: 50-99
Type of Packaging: Consumer, Bulk

7468 **Kruse & Son**
P.O.Box 945
Monrovia, CA 91017-0945 626-358-4536
Fax: 626-303-7349
Processor of meats
President: Dave Kruse
Estimated Sales: $3200000
Number Employees: 100-249
Type of Packaging: Consumer, Food Service

7469 **Kruse Meat Products**
2100 Kruse Loop
Alexander, AR 72002 501-316-2100
Fax: 501-316-1046
Processor of meat products
President: Jeanne Hutchinson
Estimated Sales: $1.8 Million
Number Employees: 15
Type of Packaging: Consumer

7470 **Kubisch Sausage Company**
50400 Rizzo Dr
Shelby Twp, MI 48315-3275 586-566-4661
Fax: 586-566-8661
Sausage and other prepared meats
Owner: Vasilj Markovich
Estimated Sales: Less than $300,000
Number Employees: 1-4

7471 **Kubla Khan Food Company**
3369 SE Raymond Street
Portland, OR 97202-4360 503-234-7494
Fax: 503-234-7716
Frozen fruits and vegetables
President: Percy Loy
Estimated Sales: $470,000
Number Employees: 5
Type of Packaging: Food Service, Bulk
Brands:
KUBLA KHAN

7472 **Kuhlmann's Market Gardens & Greenhouses**
RR 6
Edmonton, AB T5B 4K3
Canada 780-475-7500
Fax: 780-472-9923
Processor, exporter and packer of cabbage, carrots, broccoli, peas and potatoes
Pres.: Dietrich Kuhlmann
Estimated Sales: C
Number Employees: 20-49
Type of Packaging: Consumer, Food Service

7473 **Kulana Foods**
590 W Kawailani St Apt J
Hilo, HI 96720 808-959-9144
Fax: 808-959-8484
Beef and pork slaughtering and processing
President: Brady Yagi
Estimated Sales: Below $ 5 Million
Number Employees: 10-19
Type of Packaging: Private Label
Brands:
Fresh Aland Beef and Pork
Kulana Foods

7474 **Kunde Estate Winery**
P.O.Box 639
Kenwood, CA 95452 707-833-5501
Fax: 707-833-2204 wineinfo@kunde.com
www.kunde.com
Wines
President: Don Chase
CFO: Jim Meredith
Marketing Director: Marcia Kunde Mickelson
Operations Manager: Bill Kunde
Estimated Sales: $ 30-50 Million
Number Employees: 50-99
Type of Packaging: Private Label
Brands:
Estate Cabernet Sauvignon
Estate Chardonnay
Estate Merlot
Estate Syrah
Estate Viognier
Estate Zinfandel (Ce

7475 **Kunzler & Company**
652 Manor Street
Lancaster, PA 17604-4747 717-299-6301
Fax: 717-390-2170 888-586-9537
customerservice@kunzler.com
www.kunzler.com
Manufacturer of meat products: bacon, bologna, ham, hot dogs, scrapple, steaks, luncheon meats
President/CEO: Chris Kunzler III
VP: Phil Loht
Director Marketing: Rob Kunzler
Director Sales: Tom McCarty
VP/Manufacturing: John Kunzler
Estimated Sales: $100 Million
Number Employees: 500
Sq. footage: 130000

Type of Packaging: Consumer, Food Service, Private Label, Bulk
Brands:
KUNZLER PRIVATE LABEL

7476 **Kupris Home Bakery**
23 Williams Road
Bolton, CT 06043-7235 860-649-4746
Household Bakery
Owner: Jeris Kupris
Number Employees: 1 to 5

7477 **Kurtz Produce**
5894 8th Line
Ariss, ON N0B 1B0
Canada 519-824-3279
Fax: 519-824-4299 kpi@on.aibn.com
Grower and exporter of agricultural products and bottled drinking water.
Pres.: Wilf Kurtz
CEO: Brad Kurtz
VP: Brad Kurtz
Sales: Mike Wilson
Plant Manager: Darren Hedges
Number Employees: 18
Number of Brands: 3
Brands:
Bethune
Black Cat
Superior

7478 **Kusha Inc.**
1211 Mcgaw Ave
Irvine, CA 92614-5536 949-930-1400
Fax: 949-250-1520 800-550-7423
jerry@kusharice.comm www.kusharice.com
Rice, basmati, jasmine, tea, grape seed oil, cheese
Vice President: Jerry Taylor
Estimated Sales: Under $500,000
Number Employees: 30
Type of Packaging: Consumer, Food Service, Private Label, Bulk
Brands:
Nasim
Pari
Royal

7479 **Kusmi Tea**
26 W 23rd Street
6th Floor
New York, NY 10010 646-346-1756
Fax: 646-624-2893 info.us@kusmitea.com
www.us.kusmitea.com
Kosher, other lifestyle, full-line hot beverages, tea, foodservice.
Marketing: Lauriane Penfornis

7480 **Kutik's Honey Farm**
285 Lyon Brook Road
Norwich, NY 13815-3420 607-336-4105
Fax: 607-895-6298 www.kutikshoney.com
Processor of portion packed honey and honey sticks; also, custom gift packs available
Owner/President: Charles Kutik
Owner: Caryn Kutik
Estimated Sales: $500,000-1 Million
Number Employees: 1-4
Sq. footage: 4685
Type of Packaging: Consumer, Food Service, Private Label, Bulk
Brands:
Kutik's Honey

7481 **Kutztown Bologna Company**
1500 Oregon Rd # 100
Leola, PA 17540-9753 717-556-0901
Fax: 717-560-0680 800-723-8824
info@kutztownbologna.com
www.actionvideoinc.com
Processor of frozen beef and pork products
President: Gordon Harrower
VP: Gary Landuy
Estimated Sales: $670000
Number Employees: 1-4
Type of Packaging: Consumer, Private Label
Brands:
Kutztown

7482 **Kwikpak Fisheries**
1016 W 6th Avenue
Suite 301
Anchorage, AK 99501-1963 206-443-1565
Fax: 206-443-1912 800-509-3332
ruthc@ydfda.org www.kwikpakfisheries.com
Smoked seafood.
Marketing: Ruth Carter

7483 **Kyger Bakery Products**
3825 State Road 38 E
Lafayette, IN 47905-5212 765-447-1252
Fax: 765-447-7989 info@harlanbakeries.com
www.kygerbakeries.com
Processor of frozen desserts including cream and meringue pies and angel food and sheet cakes; also, retail and institutional packaging available
President: Joseph Latoufe
Vice President: Doug Harlan
Type of Packaging: Consumer
Brands:
Kyger

7484 **Kyler Seafood**
2 Washburn St
New Bedford, MA 2740 508-999-5631
Fax: 508-991-4664 888-859-5377
info@kylerseafood.com www.kylerseafood.com
Processor of fresh and frozen cod and flounder
Owner: Jeff Manfelt
EVP: Billy Arruda
Manager: Don Viera
Estimated Sales: $14 Million
Number Employees: 100
Type of Packaging: Private Label

7485 **Kyong Hae Kim Company**
2330 Kalakaua Ave # 85
Honolulu, HI 96815-5001 808-926-8720
Fax: 808-841-2178
Owner: Kyong Kim

7486 **Kyowa Hakko**
767 3rd Ave # 9
New York, NY 10017-9023 212-715-0572
Fax: 212-421-1283 sullivan@kyowa-usa.com
www.kyowa-usa.com
Manufacturer of amino, nuclei and organic acids; exporter of food ingredients
President: Michinobu Inouc
CEO: Mike Inoue
Sales: Neil Sullivan
Estimated Sales: $ 20-50 Million
Number Employees: 10-19
Parent Co: Kyowa Hakko Kogyo Company
Brands:
Gmp
Imp
Wmp Kyowa

7487 **L & S Packing Company**
101 Central Ave
Farmingdale, NY 11735 631-845-1717
Fax: 631-420-7309 877-879-6453
www.paesana.com
Manufacturer of olives
President: Louis Scaramelli
Estimated Sales: $ 3 - 5 Million
Number Employees: 20-49

7488 **L C Good Candy Company**
1825 E Tremont St
Allentown, PA 18109-1615 610-432-3290
Fax: 610-432-7455
Candy and confections
President: Roland R Mink Jr
Estimated Sales: Below $200,000
Number Employees: 1-4

7489 **L K Bowman & Company**
P.O.Box 80
Nottingham, PA 19362-0080 610-932-2240
Fax: 610-932-4186 800-853-1919
lkbowman@hanoverfoods.com
www.hanoverfoods.com
Manufacturer of mushrooms
President: Robert Shelton
Estimated Sales: $10-20 Million
Number Employees: 20-49
Sq. footage: 18139
Parent Co: Hanover Foods Corporation
Type of Packaging: Food Service, Private Label, Bulk
Brands:
GARDEN PATH
MOTHER EARTH
NOTTINGHAM

7490 **L&C Fisheries**
French River
Kensington, PE C0B 1M0
Canada 902-886-2770
Fax: 902-886-3003
calvin@greengablesmussels.com
www.greengablesmussels.com
Processor and exporter of fresh mussels, oysters and fresh and frozen lobsters
Owner: Calvin Jollimore
Number Employees: 10-19
Type of Packaging: Consumer, Food Service

7491 **(HQ)L&H Packing Company**
P.O.Box 831368
San Antonio, TX 78283-1368 210-532-3241
Fax: 210-532-9819 sales@lhpacking.net
www.lhpacking.com
Processor of cooked meats, sauces, gravies, patties, fajitas, etc.
President/CEO: Kenneth Leonard
CFO: Terry Black
COO/VP Sales: Neal Leonard
Estimated Sales: $100+ Million
Number Employees: 300
Type of Packaging: Consumer, Food Service, Private Label, Bulk
Brands:
SURLEAN

7492 **(HQ)L&L Packing Company**
527 W 41st St
Chicago, IL 60609 773-285-5400
Fax: 773-285-0366 800-628-6328
info@worldsbeststeak.com
www.worldsbeststeak.com
Prime and choice aged beef, pork, veal and lamb
President: Alan Lezak
Sales Manager: Phil Lombardi
Estimated Sales: $24000000
Number Employees: 20-49
Type of Packaging: Private Label

7493 **L&M Bakery**
203 S Union St
Lawrence, MA 01843 978-687-7346
Fax: 978-682-4397 www.lm-bakery.com
Processor of fruit squares, nut bread, regular and sour cream coffee cakes and macaroons
Owner: Paul La Plante
VP: Johanne La Plante
Sales Director: Rick Fermoyle
Plant Manager: Andy Stoehrer
Estimated Sales: $ 10 - 20 Million
Number Employees: 10-19
Sq. footage: 10000
Type of Packaging: Consumer, Food Service
Brands:
L & M Bakery

7494 **L&M Evans**
P.O.Box 81997
Conyers, GA 30013-9428 770-918-8727
Fax: 847-647-1509
Seafood, clams, fish, fillets
President: L W Bill Evans
Estimated Sales: $300,000-500,000
Number Employees: 1-4

7495 **L&M Frosted Food Lockers**
P.O.Box 199
Belt, MT 59412 406-277-3522
Fax: 406-277-3522
Processor of meat and fish
Owner: Steve Serquina
Partner: Jerry Wojtala
Estimated Sales: $200,000+
Number Employees: 1-4
Type of Packaging: Consumer, Food Service

7496 **L&M Slaughtering**
903 Mill Rd
Georgetown, IL 61846-6341 217-662-6841
abitor@aol.com
Processor of beef, veal, lamb and pork; slaughtering sevices available
Owner: Todd Green
Estimated Sales: $ 1 - 3 Million
Number Employees: 1-4
Type of Packaging: Consumer

7497 **(HQ)L&S Packing Company**
101 Central Ave
Farmingdale, NY 11735 631-845-1717
Fax: 631-420-7309 800-286-6487
sales@paesana.com www.paesana.com
Importer of gourmet condiments such as olives, capers, pickles, cocktail onions, mushrooms, etc.; serving food service, industrial and private label markets. Also, high quality authentic pasta sauces and Chinese sauces, see our ad onthe back cover of Vol
President: Louis Scaramelli III
Estimated Sales: $ 3 - 5 Million
Number Employees: 20-49
Type of Packaging: Consumer, Food Service, Private Label, Bulk
Other Locations:
L&S Packing Co.
Flushing NY
Brands:
Mi-Kee
Paesana
Table Joy

7498 **L'Esprit de Campagne**
P.O.Box 3130
Winchester, VA 22604 540-955-1014
Fax: 540-955-1018 800-692-8008
lespritfods@hotmail.com
www.lespritdecampagne.com
Dried tomatoes, apples, cherries, blueberries, cranberries
President: Joy Lokey
CEO: Carey Lokey
Estimated Sales: Below $ 5 Million
Number Employees: 50-99
Brands:
L'Esprit

7499 **L. Craelius & Company**
370 N Morgan St
Chicago, IL 60607-1321 312-666-7100
Fax: 312-666-9747
President: Lawrence Craelius
Estimated Sales: $ 20 - 50 Million
Number Employees: 20-49

7500 **L. Craven & Sons**
1600 N 25th Ave Ste B
Melrose Park, IL 60160 708-343-0500
Fax: 708-343-6674 800-453-4303
closeouts@lcraven.com www.lcraven.com
Wholesaler/distributor of closeout items including candy, groceries and snack foods; all quantities and packaging bought and sold
President: Barry Craven
Vice President: Jack Craven
Estimated Sales: $32 Million
Number Employees: 35
Sq. footage: 35000

7501 **L. East Poultry Company**
P.O.Box 6499
Austin, TX 78762-6499 512-476-5367
Fax: 512-476-5360 epoultry@att.net
www.eastpoultry.com
Poultry
President: Ken Aune
Estimated Sales: Below $ 5 Million
Number Employees: 20-49

7502 **L. Isaacson**
800 W Fulton Market
Chicago, IL 60607-1375 312-421-2444
Fax: 312-421-2736
President: Ben Willner
Estimated Sales: $ 5 - 10 Million
Number Employees: 20-49

7503 **L. Mawby Vineyards**
4519 S Elm Valley Rd
Suttons Bay, MI 49682 231-271-3522
Fax: 231-271-2927 larry@lmawby.com
www.lmawby.com
Wines
President: Lawrence Mawby
Estimated Sales: $500,000-$1 Million
Number Employees: 1-4
Brands:
L.Mawby
M.Lawrence

7504 **L.F. Lambert Spawn Company**
1507 Valley Rd
Coatesville, PA 19320-2726 610-384-5031
Fax: 610-384-0390 lambert@lambertspawn.com
www.lambertspawn.com
Processor and exporter of mushroom spawns
President: Hugh McIntyre
General Manager: Joseph Mascrangelo
Estimated Sales: $3300000
Number Employees: 100-249

7505 **L.H. Hayward & Company**
P.O.Box 23751
New Orleans, LA 70183-0751 504-733-8480
Fax: 504-733-8155 info@camelliabeans.com
www.lhhco.com
Packaging of beans
President: Ken Hayward
CO-Owner: Rick Hayward
Estimated Sales: $ 5-10 Million
Number Employees: 20-49
Type of Packaging: Private Label
Brands:
Camellia

7506 **L.H. Rodriguez Wholesale Seafood**
3541 S 12th Ave
Tucson, AZ 85713-5914 520-623-1931
Fax: 520-623-0737
Seafood
President: Levi Rodriguez
Treasurer: Albert Rodriguez
Vice President: Joe Rodriguez
Estimated Sales: $ 3 - 5 Million
Number Employees: 5-9

7507 **L.I. Cauliflower Association**
139 Marcy Ave
Riverhead, NY 11901-3099 631-727-2212
Fax: 631-727-4295 www.licauliflower.com
Manufacturer of cauliflower
President/CEO: Carl Key
Estimated Sales: $5-10 Million
Number Employees: 10-19

7508 **L.K. Bowman Company**
P.O.Box 334
Hanover, PA 17331 717-632-6000
Fax: 71- 6-7 28 800-853-1919
ikbowman@hanoverfoods.com
www.hanoverfoods.com
Processor and exporter of canned, frozen, fresh, freeze-dried, and refrigerated mushrooms
President: Robert Shelton
Vice President: C Jack Shelton
Quality Control: Jennifer Brickley
Sales Director: Paul Bozzone
Plant Manager: Charles Reed
Estimated Sales: $ 10 - 20 Million
Number Employees: 20-49
Parent Co: Hanover Foods Corporation
Type of Packaging: Food Service, Private Label, Bulk
Brands:
Garden Path
Nottingham
Wayside

7509 **L.L. Curley Packing Company**
551 Lafayette St
Colonial Beach, VA 22443 804-224-7544
Fax: 804-224-7035
President: Lloyd L Curley Jr
Estimated Sales: $ 1-2.5 Million
Number Employees: 5-9

7510 **L.P.B. LLC**
Po Box 8344
Richmond, VA 23226-0344 804-385-4700
Fax: 804-622-6891 tokie@tokiesbrownies.com
www.tokiesbrownies.com

7511 **LA Dreyfus**
3775 Park Avenue
Edison, NJ 08820-2595 732-549-1600
Fax: 732-549-1685 ddiaz@ladreyfus.com
www.ladreyfus.com
Chewing gum base
Estimated Sales: $ 15 - 20 Million
Number Employees: 100-250
Sq. footage: 500000

7512 **LA Lifestyle NutritionalProducts**
2230 Cape Cod Way
Santa Ana, CA 92703-3582 714-835-6367
Fax: 714-835-4948 800-387-4786
customerservice@lalifestyle.com
www.lalifestyle.com
Processor and wholesaler/distributor of teas and herbal products
Owner: Patricia J Logsdon
Estimated Sales: $ 10 - 20 Million
Type of Packaging: Consumer

7513 **LA Wholesale Produce Market**
1601 E Olympic Blvd
Los Angeles, CA 90021-1936 213-622-8905
Fax: 213-622-7075 888-454-6887
webinfo@lanuthouse.com www.lanuthouse.com
Manufacturer, importer and exporter of tree nuts and peanuts; also, processor of peanut butter and manufactured and coated materials
President: Pat Nakahara
Estimated Sales: $ 3 - 5 Million
Number Employees: 5-9
Sq. footage: 22000
Parent Co: Morven Partners
Type of Packaging: Consumer, Food Service, Private Label, Bulk

7514 **LBA**
18842 13th Pl S
Seatac, WA 98148-2342 206-241-9343
Fax: 206-433-2844 800-522-1185
gsimeon@lba-inc.com www.lba-inc.com
Frozen dough, thaw and serve pastries
President/Owner: Michael Robert
Vice President: Randal Chicoine
Estimated Sales: $ 5-10 Million
Number Employees: 20-49
Type of Packaging: Private Label
Brands:
French Does
LBA

7515 **LD Foods**
PO Box 1990
Annapolis, MD 21404-1990 410-216-9300
Fax: 410-216-9900
CEO: James Loftis, Jr.

7516 **LEF McLean Brothers International**
PO Box 128
Wheatley, ON N0P 2P0
Canada 519-825-4656
Fax: 519-825-7374
Processor and exporter of fresh and frozen lake fish and seafood
President: Robert Ricci
VP Business Development: Danny Ricci
Type of Packaging: Consumer, Food Service, Private Label, Bulk

7517 **LFI**
271 Us Highway 46 Ste C101
Fairfield, NJ 7004 973-882-0550
Fax: 973-882-0554 lfiinc@aol.com
Imported foods
President: Antonio Lisanti
Marketing Director: Danielle Iannacconi
Public Relations: Carol Lisanti
Estimated Sales: Below $ 5 Million
Number Employees: 5-9
Type of Packaging: Private Label
Brands:
Antonia
Casa Primo

7518 **LK Bowman**
P.O.Box 80
Nottingham, PA 19362-0080 610-932-2240
Fax: 610-932-4186 800-853-1919
lkbowman@hanoverfoods.com
www.hanoverfoods.com
Mushrooms
President: Robert Shelton
Estimated Sales: $ 10-20 Million
Number Employees: 20-49

7519 **LLJ's Sea Products**
P.O.Box 296
Round Pond, ME 04564-0296 207-529-4224
Fax: 207-529-4223
Canned and cured fish and seafood.
Owner: Stephen J Brackett

Estimated Sales: $3,000,000
Number Employees: 5-9

7520 **LPI**
3400 W 35th St
Chicago, IL 60632-3399 773-254-7200
Fax: 773-254-8546 www.lapreferida.com
Distributors of Mexican food
Owner: Richard Steinbarth
Estimated Sales: $ 50-100 Million
Number Employees: 1-4
Type of Packaging: Private Label, Bulk

7521 **LPO/ LaDolc**
4953 W 135th St
Overland Park, KS 66224-6901 913-681-7757
Fax: 913-681-7757
President: Leslie Oliver

7522 **LSK Smoked Turkey Products**
1575 Bronx River Ave
Bronx, NY 10460 718-792-1300
Fax: 718-792-8883 www.smokedmeat.com
Smoked turkey products
President: Dan Salmon
CEO: Owen Grossblatt
Plant Manager: John Garvin
Estimated Sales: $ 9 Million
Number Employees: 10-19
Brands:
LSK

7523 **(HQ)LUXCO**
5050 Kemper Ave
St Louis, MO 63139-1106 314-772-2626
Fax: 314-772-6021 info@luxco.com
www.luxco.com
Manufacturer, bottler, importer and exporter of quality distilled spirits and wines
President/CEO: Donn Lux
VP: David Bratcher
VP Finance/CFO: Steve Soucy
R&D/Quality Manager: John Rempe
VP Sales/Marketing: Dan Streepy
VP Operations: David Bratcher
Production Scheduler: Heather Sokol
Warehouse Manager: Jeff Presson
Purchasing Manager: Daniel Jennings
Estimated Sales: $23.8 Million
Number Employees: 165
Sq. footage: 200000
Type of Packaging: Private Label
Brands:
ADMIRAL NELSONS
ARROW CORDIALS
BARBELLA
BOUCHERON
CAFFE' LOLITA
DOS TIRANOS
EVERCLEAR
EZRA BROOKS
INFERNO
JAKOB DENNER
JUAREZ
MARGARITAVILLE
PEARL
PURPLE PASSION
REBEL YELL
ROMERO AMARETTO
SAINT BRENDAN'S
SALVADOR'S
TEQUILA EL MAYOR RESERVE
TVARSCKI
YAGO SANT GRIA

7524 **LVO Manufacturing**
P.O.Box 188
Rock Rapids, IA 51246-0188 712-472-3734
Fax: 712-472-2203 marilyn_lvo@yahoo.com
www.lvomfg.com
President: Marilyn Mammenga
CFO: Lambert Benno
Estimated Sales: $ 5 - 10 Million
Number Employees: 20-49

7525 **LWC Brands Inc**
151 Regal Row
Dallas, TX 75247 214-630-9101
Fax: 214-630-7360 800-552-8006
orders@ladywaltons.com www.lwcbrands.com
cookies
President/Owner: Mary Alizon-Walton
Estimated Sales: $2.3 Million
Number Employees: 20

7526 **La Abra Farm & Winery**
1362 Fortunes Cove Ln
Lovingston, VA 22949 434-263-5392
Fax: 434-263-8540
Wines
President: Albert C Weed Ii II
Estimated Sales: Less than $200,000
Number Employees: 1-4

7527 **La Bonita Ole Inc**
5804 E Columbus Dr
Tampa, FL 33619 813-319-2252
Fax: 813-319-2263 800-522-6648
martha@tamxicos.com www.tamxicos.com
Manufacturer of tortillas (Tamxicos and Wrapitz).
Founder/Owner/President/CEO: Tammy Young
Executive Administrator: Melanie Bodiford
Director of IT: Gary Macri
VP Operations: Dave Waters

7528 **La Boulangerie**
7740 Formula Pl
San Diego, CA 92121 858-578-4040
Fax: 858-536-5911
Baked goods
Owner: Gerald Sarnoo
Estimated Sales: Below $ 5 Million
Number Employees: 10-19
Brands:
La Boulangerie

7529 **La Brasserie McAuslan Brewing**
4850 Rue St Ambroise
Montreal, QC H4C 3N8
Canada 514-939-3060
Fax: 514-939-6136
Processor and exporter of beer and ale including stout
President: Peter McAuslan
Estimated Sales: E
Number Employees: 100-249
Type of Packaging: Consumer, Food Service

7530 **La Brea Bakery**
15963 Strathern Street
Van Nuys, CA 91406 818-742-4242
Fax: 818-742-4276 info@labreabakery.com
www.labreabakery.com
Processor of bread and rolls; also, par-baked and frozen available
CEO: John Yamin
EVP/Sales: Rick Anderson
SVP/Operations: Ger Crosbie
Estimated Sales: $100+ Million
Number Employees: 1200
Sq. footage: 65000
Parent Co: ARYZTA

7531 **La Buena Mexican Foods Products**
P.O.Box 26626
Tucson, AZ 85726-6626 520-624-1796
Fax: 520-624-1846
Manufacturer of Mexican food products including corn and flour tortillas, tamales and taco and tostado shells
Owner: Carlos Portillo
Estimated Sales: $5-10 Million
Number Employees: 20-49
Type of Packaging: Consumer

7532 **La Buena Vida Vineyards**
416 E College St
Grapevine, TX 76051 817-481-9463
Fax: 817-421-3635 lbv@labuenavida.com
www.labuenavida.com
Wines
Manager: Adam Artho
Marketing Director: Camille McBee
Estimated Sales: $ 2.5-5 Million
Number Employees: 5-9
Number of Products: 15
Brands:
La Buena Vida Vineyards

7533 **La Caboose Specialties**
145 S Budd St
Sunset, LA 70584 337-662-5401
Fax: 337-662-5813
Canned fruits, vegetables, preserves, jams and jellies
Owner: Margaret Brinkhaus
Estimated Sales: Under $100,000
Number Employees: 1-4
Type of Packaging: Consumer
Brands:
La Caboose

7534 **La Canasta Mexican FoodProducts**
3101 West Jackson Street
Phoenix, AZ 85009 602-269-7721
Fax: 602-269-7725 855-269-7721
www.la-canasta.com
Flour and corn tortillas, chips, hot sauce and salsa fresca
Owner: Carmen Abril
CEO: Roger Kelling
CFO: Chance Eaton
Quality Control: Jesus Gonzalez
Sales Director: Hector Quijada
Public Relations: Diane Hamel
Operations Manager: Jesus Castaneda
Plant Manager: Manny Hernandez
Purchasing Manager: Linda Rios
Estimated Sales: $100+ Million
Number Employees: 130
Sq. footage: 12000
Type of Packaging: Food Service, Private Label
Brands:
LA CANASTA
MY NANA'S

7535 **La Casita's Home Style Mexican Food**
100 Lacasita Drive
Holts Summit, MO 65043 573-896-8306
Fax: 573-896-8309
Tortilla chips
Estimated Sales: $ 5-9.9 Million
Number Employees: 6

7536 **La Chapalita**
316 N Ford Blvd
Los Angeles, CA 90022-1121
Fax: 323-221-2162 lachapalita@earthlink.net
www.lachapalita.com
Tortillas, Mexican food
Owner: Luis Moya
Estimated Sales: Below $ 5 Million
Number Employees: 20-49

7537 **La Chiquita Tortilla Manufacturing**
3451 Atlanta Industrial Parkway
Atlanta, GA 30331 404-351-9822
Fax: 404-351-4446 800-486-3942
custserv@lctortilla.com
www.lachiquitatortilla.com
Flour and corn tortillas, hand cut chips and wraps and flavored tortillas
Owner/President/CEO: Marcelino Solis
EVP/General Manager: Adam Oliaro
Marketing Manager: Jose Solis
Plant Manager: Henry Sanchez
Estimated Sales: $10.7 Million
Number Employees: 90
Sq. footage: 11000
Type of Packaging: Food Service
Brands:
La Chiquita
Provecho

7538 **La Chiripada Winery**
P.O.Box 191
Dixon, NM 87527 505-579-4437
Fax: 505-579-4437 800-528-7801
info@lachiripada.com www.lachiripada.com
Wine
Owner/President: Michael Johnson
VP: Michael Johnson
Tasting Room Manager: Minna Santos
Estimated Sales: Below $ 5 Million
Number Employees: 20-49
Brands:
La Chiripada

7539 **La Cigale Bakery**
PO Box 540223
Opa Locka, FL 33054-0223 305-688-7868
Fax: 305-688-1004 800-333-8578
Processor and exporter of French desserts, breads and pastries
Owner/President: Serge Bonvallot
Sales/Marketing Manager: Serge Bonvallot
Number Employees: 1-4
Parent Co: JSK Trading Corporation

Brands:
La Cigale Bakery
La Tarte De Saint-Tropez

7540 **La Colonial/Robles Brothers**
1700 Rogers Ave
San Jose, CA 95112-1107 408-436-5551
Fax: 408-441-0430 www.lacolonial.com
Flour tortillas
President: George Robles
CEO: George Robles
Marketing Director: George Robles
Estimated Sales: Below $ 5 Million
Number Employees: 20-49

7541 **La Cookie**
5700 Savoy Dr
Houston, TX 77036 713-784-2722
Fax: 713-784-3415
Processor of frozen cookie, muffin and brownie dough
Manager: Brian Fung
Estimated Sales: $300,000-500,000
Number Employees: 10-19
Sq. footage: 10000
Parent Co: Pilsner Group
Type of Packaging: Food Service
Brands:
Neal's

7542 **La Cookie**
5700 Savoy Dr
Houston, TX 77036 713-784-2722
Fax: 713-784-3415
Baked goods
Manager: Brian Fung
Vice President: Victor Young
Estimated Sales: $ 1-2.5 Million
Number Employees: 1-4

7543 **La Costa Coffee Roasting**
6965 El Camino Real Ste 208
Carlsbad, CA 92009 760-438-8160
Fax: 760-438-5314
Coffee
President: Doug Novak
Estimated Sales: $ 10-20 Million
Number Employees: 10-19

7544 **La Crema Coffee Company**
9848 Crescent Park Dr
West Chester, OH 45069 513-779-6278
Fax: 513-779-1908
melissa@lacremacoffeecompany.com
www.lacremacoffeecompany.com
coffee and tea
President/Owner: Melissa Flohn
Operations Manager: Cheryl Windhorst

7545 **La Ferme Martinette**
1728 Chemin Martineau
Coaticook, QC J1A 2S5 819-849-7089
Fax: 819-849-4042
martinet@lefermemartinette.com
Maple syrup.
Marketing: Lisa Nadeau

7546 **La Flor Spices**
25 Hoffman Avenue
Hauppaugue, NY 11788-4717 631-885-9601
Fax: 631-851-9606 www.laflor.com
Manufacturer, importer, exporter and contract packager of spices, herbs, blends, seasonings and ground peppers
President: Ruben La Torre Sr
VP: Dan La Torre
Sales/Distribution Manager: Ruben La Torre Jr
Estimated Sales: $5 Million
Number Employees: 45
Sq. footage: 31000
Type of Packaging: Private Label

7547 **La Flor Spices Company**
25 Hoffman Ave
Hauppauge, NY 11788-4717 631-851-9601
Fax: 631-851-9606 www.laflor.com
Spices
President: Reuben Latorre
Estimated Sales: $7.4 Million
Number Employees: 20-49
Type of Packaging: Consumer, Food Service, Bulk
Brands:
La Flor

7548 **La Font Shrimp Company**
PO Box 697
Golden Meadow, LA 70357-0697 504-475-5138
Fax: 504-475-5138
Manufacturers and suppliers of shrimps and seafoods
President/CEO: Daniel Lafont
Estimated Sales: $ 20-50 Million
Number Employees: 50

7549 **La Francaise Bakery**
111 Northwest Ave
Melrose Park, IL 60164-1603 708-562-0100
Fax: 708-498-2305 800-654-7220
jimv@lafrancaise.com www.chefsolutions.com
Processor of croissants, cinnamon rolls, bagels and danish; also, unbaked frozen croissants and cookie batter
COO: Jim Vadevoulis
Vice President: Russell Doll
Manager: Roberto Carillo
Estimated Sales: $ 20 - 50 Million
Number Employees: 250-499
Type of Packaging: Food Service, Private Label, Bulk
Brands:
Spoon-N-Bake

7550 **La Fronteriza**
6142 American Rd
Toledo, OH 43612-3902 419-729-4070
Fax: 419-729-9661 800-897-1772
www.tiarosa.com
Processor of corn and flour tortillas and tortilla chips
Manager: Jerry Stump
Estimated Sales: $ 20 - 50 Million
Number Employees: 50-99
Parent Co: Bimar Foods
Type of Packaging: Private Label
Brands:
La Fronteriza

7551 **La Have Seafoods**
3371 Hwy 331
La Have, NS B0R 1C0
Canada 902-688-2773
Fax: 902-688-2766
Processor and exporter of fresh and salted fish including pollack, cod, haddock and scallops
President: Dave Himmelman
Estimated Sales: $6.2 Million
Number Employees: 45
Type of Packaging: Bulk

7552 **La Jota Vineyard Company**
1102 Las Posadas Rd
Angwin, CA 94508 707-965-3020
Fax: 707-965-0324 877-222-0292
info@lajotawines.com
www.lajotavineyardco.com
Wines
Manager: Ed Farver
VP: Joan Smith
Sales Manager: John Smith
Estimated Sales: Below $ 5 Million
Number Employees: 10-19

7553 **La Maison Le Grand**
935 Chemin Principal
St-Joseph-du-Lac, QC J0N 1M0
Canada 450-623-3000
info@maisonlegrand.com
www.maisonlegrand.com
Pesto, savory tapenades and aromatic sauces
Owner: Bernard Le Grand

7554 **La Mexicana**
2703 S Kedzie Ave
Chicago, IL 60623-4735 773-247-5443
Fax: 773-247-9004 www.lamexicanawraps.com
Processor of tortillas and corn chips
President: Rudolph Guerrero
Estimated Sales: $4600000
Number Employees: 20-49
Type of Packaging: Consumer

7555 **La Mexicana**
10020 14th Ave SW
Seattle, WA 98146-3703 206-763-1488
Fax: 206-768-1050 info@lamexicana.com
www.lamexicana.com
Mexican foods
President: Keith Bloxham
General Manager: William Fry
Estimated Sales: Below $ 5 Million
Number Employees: 50-99
Type of Packaging: Private Label
Brands:
Habero
La Mexicana
Souena

7556 **La Mexicana Tortilla Factory**
715 Skyline Dr
Duncanville, TX 75116-3923 214-943-7770
Fax: 505-842-0317
email@lamexicanatortilla.com
Manufacturer of tortillas
President: Ricardo Garza
Estimated Sales: $ 50 - 100 Million
Number Employees: 35
Sq. footage: 1500
Type of Packaging: Consumer

7557 **La Mexicana Tortilla Factory**
236 a St
Hayward, CA 94541-4946 510-889-8225
Fax: 510-889-1080
Processor of corn tortillas
President: Jesus Villarreal
Estimated Sales: $ 20 - 50 Million
Number Employees: 20-49

7558 **La Moderna**
Leandro Valle N 404
Col Centro, TL 50070
Mexico
robertofl@juno.com
www.lamoderna.com.mx
Cookies, flour, pasta (dry), soups/broths.
Marketing: Robert Flegnann

7559 **La Monegasque**
2200 Fletcher Ave
Suite 5
Fort Lee, NJ 07024-5016 201-585-8834
Fax: 201-585-8575
Seafood, seafood products
Owner: Alain Cruanes
Treasurer: Sergio Bonfiglio
Number Employees: 4

7560 **La Monita Mexican Food**
2200 E 7th St # B
Austin, TX 78702-3570 512-524-4294
Fax: 713-692-8217
Mexican food
Estimated Sales: $500,000-$1 Million
Number Employees: 1-4

7561 **La Morena**
Av. Virgen De La Caridad Lote 20 Al 27
Ciudad Industrial Xicohtencatl 2
Huamantla, TL 90500
Mexico 222-211-0515
Fax: 222-237-2700 rromo@grupo.com.mx
www.lamorena.com.mx
Mayo/ketchup, salsa/dips, beans, spices, canned of preserved vegetables/fruit.
Marketing: Roberto Romo Michaud

7562 **La Nova Wings**
371 W Ferry St
Buffalo, NY 14213-1947 716-881-3355
Fax: 716-881-3366 800-652-6682
wingman@ianova.com www.lanova.com
Processor of frozen chicken wings and tenders
President/CEO: Joseph Todaro Jr
Sales, Eastern: Ben Lamonte
Sales (Midwest): Sam Pantano
Sales (Western): Joe Pettruzzella
Estimated Sales: $4.1 Million
Number Employees: 15
Type of Packaging: Consumer, Food Service
Brands:
La Nova

7563 **La Panzanella**
18475 Olympic Ave S
Tukwila, WA 98188 206-903-0500
Fax: 206-903-0698
croccantini@lapanzanella.com
www.lapanzanella.com
herb infused rustic crackers
Marketing: Antonio Galati
Estimated Sales: $2.7 Million
Number Employees: 25

7564 **La Parisienne Bakery**
7945 Wellingford Dr
Manassas, VA 20109 703-369-2890
Fax: 301-770-0975 800-727-4790
bonjour@laparisienne.com
www.laparisienne.com
Bakery items
CEO and President: Mark Salman
CFO: Robert Greenblatt
Vice President: George Jermstad
Operations Manager: Glenn Price
Production Manager: Tony Richa
Estimated Sales: $ 20-50 Million
Number Employees: 100-249
Type of Packaging: Private Label
Brands:
Bonjour La Parisienne
Loafin' Around Organ
Planet Bagels

7565 **La Pasta, Inc.**
2727 Pittman Drive
Silver Spring, MD 20910 301-588-1111
Fax: 301-588-7243 alexis@lapastainc.com
www.lapastainc.com

7566 **La Patisserie**
1317 W McKinley St
Phoenix, AZ 85007-2366 602-254-5868
Fax: 602-253-7430
Bakery products
Owner: Eduardo Teixidor
President: Ed Teixidor
Estimated Sales: Below $ 5 Million
Number Employees: 20-49
Type of Packaging: Private Label
Brands:
La Patisserie

7567 **La Paz Products**
P.O.Box 459
Brea, CA 92822-0459 714-990-0982
Fax: 714-990-2246 info@lapazproducts.com
www.lapazproducts.com
Processor of cocktail mixes
President: Larry Casey
Estimated Sales: $ 10 - 20 Million
Number Employees: 10-19
Type of Packaging: Consumer, Food Service

7568 **La Piccolina**
1075 N Hills Drive
Decatur, GA 30033-4220
US 406-636-1909
Fax: 404-296-2008 800-626-1624
piccola@lapiccolina.com www.lapiccolina.com
Processor and exporter of breadsticks, dips, biscotti, gourmet coffee, cranberry pecan bread, pasta, pasta sauces, olive oil, etc.; manufacturer of biscotti and breadsticksmanufacturers of food preparations.
President: Olympia Manning
VP: Denise Walsh-Bandini
National Sales Manager: Denise Walsh-Bandini
Estimated Sales: $270000k
Number Employees: 5
Sq. footage: 3600

7569 **La Reina**
316 N Ford Blvd
Los Angeles, CA 90022-1121 323-268-2791
Fax: 323-265-4295
sales@lareinafamilybrands.com
www.lareinafamilybrands.com
Processor of flour tortillas
President: Ricardo Robles
CEO: Mauro Robles
VP: Walt Boudreaux
Operations: Francisco Arellano
Purchasing: Luis Farfan
Estimated Sales: $16000000
Number Employees: 1-4
Type of Packaging: Consumer, Food Service, Private Label
Brands:
LA REINA

7570 **La Reina**
P.O.Box 1349
Monterey, CA 93942-1349 831-372-4003
Owner: Riccardo Giuliano
Estimated Sales: $ 20-50 Million
Number Employees: 50-99

7571 **La Rocca Vineyards**
P.O.Box 541
Forest Ranch, CA 95942 530-899-9463
Fax: 530-894-7268 800-808-9463
wine@laroccavineyards.com
www.laroccavineyards.com
Wines
President/CEO: Philip La Rocca
Marketing Director: Phaedre LaRocco Morril
Estimated Sales: Under $500,000
Number Employees: 5-9
Brands:
La Rocca Vineyards

7572 **(HQ)La Rochelle Winery**
5443 Tesla Rd
Livermore, CA 94550 925-243-6442
Fax: 408-270-5881 888-647-7768
smirassou@lrwine.com www.lrwine.com
Processor of vintaged varietal wine
Manager: Janice Fisher
Partner: James Mirassou
Partner: Peter Mirassou
Public Relations: Dave Muret
Sq. footage: 120000
Other Locations:
Mirassou Vineyards
Los Gatos CA
Brands:
Mirassou

7573 **La Romagnola**
2215 Tradeport Drive
Orlando, FL 32824-7005 407-856-4343
Fax: 407-856-7555 800-843-8359
Processor of fettucine, spaghetti, linguine, angel hair pasta, pasta sheets, tortelloni, ravioli, triangoli and gnocchi; also, noodles including tomato, spinach, black and egg
Ceo: Andreas Rieder
Estimated Sales: $190,000
Number Employees: 3
Sq. footage: 34000
Brands:
La Romagnola
Le Patron

7574 **La Rosa**
1480 W Bernard Drive
Addison, IL 60101-4334 630-916-9552
Fax: 630-916-9561
Gourmet baked goods
President: Joe Verzillo
Estimated Sales: Less than $500,000
Number Employees: 5-9

7575 **La Spiga D'Oro Fresh Pasta Co**
75 Pelican Way
Suite J
Pacifica, CA 94901 650-359-9526
Fax: 650-359-0654 800-847-2782
sales@lapigadoro.com www.laspigadoro.com
Gourmet fresh and frozen pasta.
President: Robert Clifford
Estimated Sales: Below $ 5 Million
Number Employees: 10
Brands:
La Spiga Doro

7576 **La Superior Food Products**
4307 Merriam Dr
Shawnee Mission, KS 66203 913-432-4933
Fax: 913-432-0121 www.lasuperiorfood.com
Nacho chips, taco shells, flour tortillas, corn tortillas
President: George Young
CFO: Larry O'Brian
R & D: Gordan Grahm
Estimated Sales: $ 2.5-5 Million
Number Employees: 20-49
Type of Packaging: Private Label, Bulk
Brands:
La Superior

7577 **La Tang Cuisine Manufacturing**
3824 Artdale St
Houston, TX 77063-5246 713-780-4876
Fax: 713-780-4296
Manufacturer of Asian foods including egg rolls, wonton, crab rangoon, spring roll and burritos.
President: Virginia Limbo
CEO: Joey Limbo
Estimated Sales: $250,000-$1 Million
Number Employees: 20-49
Number of Brands: 2
Number of Products: 5
Sq. footage: 10000
Type of Packaging: Food Service, Private Label, Bulk
Brands:
LA TANG
LA VIDA

7578 **La Tapatia Tortilleria**
104 E Belmont Ave
Fresno, CA 93701-1403 559-441-1030
Fax: 559-441-1712 800-219-7329
customerservice@latapatiaca.org
www.tortillas4u.com
Corn and flour tortillas
Owner/President: Helen Chavez-Hansen
SVP: John Hansen
Controller: Jose Angulo
Export Director: Dan Soleno
Regional Sales Manager: Dennis Walsh
Regional Sales Manager: Vickie Maravel
Sales & Marketing: Linda Ghilarducci
Estimated Sales: $25 Million
Number Employees: 170
Type of Packaging: Private Label
Brands:
Tapatia Tortilleria

7579 **La Tempesta**
439 Littlefield Ave
S San Francisco, CA 94080-6106
US 650-873-8944
Fax: 650-873-1190 800-762-8330
ltwebinfo@latempesta.com www.latempesta.com
Biscotti candy and confectionary products
President: Robert Sharp
CFO: Lee Rucker
VP Marketing: Karen Hunt
Sales/Marketing: Sonia Azar
Public Relations: Jeff Miller
Plant Manager: Sonia Azar
Estimated Sales: $9000000
Number Employees: 60
Type of Packaging: Consumer
Brands:
Amore Bianco
Biscotti Toscani
Panforte

7580 **La Tolteca Foods**
720 W 8th St
Pueblo, CO 81003 719-543-5733
Fax: 719-543-2128 www.latoltecafoods.com
Processor of fresh and frozen tortillas
Owner: Tom Carpenter
Estimated Sales: $1700000
Number Employees: 20-49
Sq. footage: 50000
Type of Packaging: Consumer, Food Service, Private Label
Brands:
MEXICAN BEAR

7581 **La Tortilla Factory**
3300 Westwind Blvd
Santa Rosa, CA 95403 707-586-4000
Fax: 707-586-4017 800-446-1516
info@latortillafactory.com
www.latortillafactory.com
Processor and exporter of corn and flour tortillas and healthy and delicious wraps; wholesaler/distributor of Mexican food products including tortilla chips and masa (locally only)
President: Carlos Tamayo
Owner/President/VP Sales/Marketing: William Tamayo
CFO: Stan Mead
R&D Manager: Luz Ana Osbun
Executive Director Sales/Marketing: Jan Remak
Human Resources Manager: Jonna Green
COO/VP/Plant Manager: Sam Tamayo
Estimated Sales: $8000000
Number Employees: 100
Sq. footage: 13660
Type of Packaging: Consumer, Food Service, Private Label, Bulk
Brands:
La Tortilla Factory
Wrap Arounds
Wrappers

7582 **La Tourangelle**
1145 Harbour Way S
Richmond, CA 94804 510-970-9960
Fax: 510-970-9964 866-688-6457
contact@latourangelle.com
www.latourangelle.com
Oils
Marketing: Matthieu Kohlmeyer
Number Employees: 12

7583 **La Vans Coffee Company**
158 2nd St
Bordentown, NJ 8505 609-298-0688
Coffees
Manager: Kostas Halkiadakis
Estimated Sales: Less than $500,000
Number Employees: 1-4

7584 **La Vencedora Products**
3322 Fowler St
Los Angeles, CA 90063 323-269-7273
Fax: 323-269-8775 800-327-2572
Processor of fresh salsa, tortilla chips, black bean and garlic and jalapeno
President: Gregg Victor
CEO: Richard Victor
Estimated Sales: $500,000-1 Million
Number Employees: 5-9
Sq. footage: 8000
Type of Packaging: Consumer, Food Service, Private Label, Bulk
Brands:
El Rancho
El Rancho Bean Chips
El Rancho Salsa Fresca
El Rancho Tortilla Chips
Pocos

7585 **La Victoria Foods**
9200 Whitmore
Rosemead, CA 91770 626-312-2925
Fax: 626-280-4416 800-523-4635
questions@lavicclub.com www.lavictoria.com
Manufacturer of salsa, taco sauce, enchilada sauce, chiles and peppers
President: R Tanklage
CEO: R Tanklage
VP: Jon Tanklage
Estimated Sales: $5-$10 Million
Number Employees: 5-9
Type of Packaging: Private Label
Brands:
La Victoria
La Victoria Salsa Su

7586 **La Vigne Enterprises**
PO Box 2890
Fallbrook, CA 92088-2890 760-723-9997
Fax: 760-728-2710 www.lavignefruits.com
Gourmet processor of exotic organically grown fruits. Gained from a single organic source in California, top varietal fruits are pureed using state-of-the-art equipment. Packaged frozen in 2 lb. or 28 lb. pails. Also, dried fruits andgourmet condiments.
President: Helene Beck
Number of Products: 10
Type of Packaging: Food Service, Private Label
Brands:
LA VIGNS

7587 **La Vina Winery**
4201 Highway 28
Anthony, NM 88021 575-882-7632
Fax: 575-882-7632 stark@lavinawinery.com
www.lavinawinery.com
Wine
Owner/President: Ken Stark
Co-Owner/CEO: Denise Stark
Estimated Sales: Below $ 5 Million
Number Employees: 1-4
Brands:
La Vina

7588 **LaCrosse Milling Company**
P.O.Box 86
Cochrane, WI 54622-0086 608-248-2222
Fax: 608-248-2221 800-441-5411
jbackus@lacrossemilling.com
www.lacrossemilling.com
Processor of oatmeal and rolled oat flakes; exporter of milled oat products
President: Dan Ward
Sales: Glenn Hartzell
Plant Manager: Bill Brueger
Estimated Sales: $ 10 - 20 Million
Number Employees: 50-99
Number of Products: 50
Type of Packaging: Food Service, Private Label, Bulk
Brands:
DIAMOND

7589 **LaGrander Hillside Dairy**
W11299 Broek Rd
Stanley, WI 54768-8215 715-644-2275
Fax: 715-644-0720
Processor of cheese and dairy products
Owner: Randy La Grander
Estimated Sales: $3500000
Number Employees: 20-49
Type of Packaging: Consumer

7590 **LaMonde Wild Flavors**
500 S Jefferson St
Placentia, CA 92870-6617 714-993-7700
Fax: 714-342-3610 www.wildflavors.com
Natural food, pharmaceutical and cosmetic coloring blends
Estimated Sales: $ 1-5 Million
Number Employees: 1-4

7591 **LaMonica Fine Foods**
P.O. Box 309
Millville, NJ 08332-0309 856-825-8111
Fax: 856-825-9354 info@lamonicafinefoods.com
www.lamonicafinefoods.com
A processor of surf clams and ocean clams from US certified waters. Serving the fresh, canned and frozen markets, we produce a complete line of clam products.
Owner: Danny La Vecchia
CFO: Jack Pipala
VP Operations: Michael LaVecchia
Estimated Sales: $50-100 Million
Number Employees: 20-49
Sq. footage: 90000
Type of Packaging: Consumer, Food Service, Private Label, Bulk
Brands:
CAPE MAY
LAMONICA
MARYLAND HOUSE
OCEAN CHEF

7592 **LaRosa's Bakery**
79 E. Newman Springs Road
Shrewsbury, NJ 07702-4038 732-842-4324
Fax: 732-842-8029 800-527-6722
www.ecannoli.com
Processor of cannolis, cannoli cream, gourmet butter, cookies and biscotti
President: Sal Larosa
VP: Peter LaRosa
Sales Manager: George Delaney
Estimated Sales: $ 1 - 3 Million
Number Employees: 10-19
Type of Packaging: Consumer, Food Service, Bulk

7593 **LaRosa's Bakery**
79 E Newman Springs Road
Shrewsbury, NJ 07702-4038 732-842-4921
Fax: 732-842-8029 800-527-6722
www.ecannoli.com
Cannoli, cannoli cream, biscotti, cookies
Owner/President: Sal La Rosa, Jr.
Owner/VP: Peter La Rosa
Estimated Sales: $1.3 Million
Number Employees: 30
Brands:
Larosa's Famous Biscotti
Larosa's Famous Cannoli
Larosa's Famous Cookies

7594 **Laack Brothers Cheese Company**
7050 Morrison Rd
Greenleaf, WI 54126 920-864-2815
Fax: 920-864-2867 800-589-5127
Processor of cold pack cheese spreads and cream cheese spreads; also, shredded mozzarella and cheddar cheeses; wholesaler/distributor of cheeses; serving the food service market; and retail grocery markets
President: Jeff Laack
VP: Mark Laack
Estimated Sales: $ 10 - 20 Million
Number Employees: 10-19
Sq. footage: 25000
Type of Packaging: Consumer, Food Service, Private Label, Bulk
Brands:
Laack's Finest

7595 **(HQ)Labatt Breweries**
207 Qeen's Quay West
Suite 299
Toronto, ON M5J 2T3
Canada 416-361-5050
Fax: 416-361-5200 800-268-2337
www.labatt.com
Processor and exporter of beer
President: Marcio Froes
VP/General Counsel: Susan Rabkin
Estimated Sales: $100-500 Million
Number Employees: 100-249
Parent Co: Interbrew Company
Type of Packaging: Consumer, Food Service
Brands:
BLEUE DRY
BLEUE LEGERE
BLUE STAR
BOOMERANG
BOOMERANG
BUD LIGHT
BUDWEISER
CARLSBERG
CLUB
JOHN LABATT CLASSIC
KOKANEE
KOKANEE GOLD
KOKANEE LIGHT
KOOTENAY BLACK LAGER
KOOTENAY MOUNTAIN ALE
KOOTENAY PALE ALE
KOOTENAY TRUE ALE
LABATT 50
LABATT BLUE
LABATT GENUINE DARFT
LABATT ICE
LABATT LIGHT
LUCKY LAGER
WILDCAT
WILDCAT STRONG

7596 **Labatt Breweries**
4415 Calgary Trail N
Edmonton, AB T6H 5R7
Canada 780-436-6060
Fax: 780-436-3656 800-268-2997
www.labatt.com
Processor of domestic beer
President: Jeff Clark
Marketing Manager: Lori Owen Turner
Sales Manager: Trent Carroll
Brewery Manager: Alann Fernandes
Number Employees: 100-249
Parent Co: Interbrew Company
Type of Packaging: Consumer, Food Service
Brands:
Bohemia
Carta Blanca
Dos Equis
John Labatt Classic
Labatt 50
Labatt Bleue Dry
Labatt Blue
Labatt Blue Light
Labatt Crystal
Labatt Extra Dry
Labatt Genuine Draft
Sol

7597 **Labatt Breweries**
50 Resources Road
Etobicoke, ON M9N 3N7
Canada 416-248-0751
Fax: 519-667-7304 800-268-2337
dale.hill@labatt.com www.labatt.com

Processor of beer, ale, stout and lager
President: Carlos Britol
VP, Supply Chain: Charles Oliver
Public Affairs Director: Bob Chant
Plant Manager: Steve Kawai
Number Employees: 500-999
Parent Co: Labatt Breweries
Type of Packaging: Consumer, Food Service
Brands:
Bed Lies
Bed Wiser
Belle-Vue Kriek
Blue Light
Classic
Coconies
Hoegaarden
Kittis
Leffe Blonde
Stella Artois

7598 **Labatt Breweries**
PO Box 5050
London, ON N6A 4M3
Canada 519-663-5050
Fax: 519-667-7304 www.labatt.com
Processor and exporter of beer, stout, ale and lager
Manager: Les Sparling
Number Employees: 500-999
Type of Packaging: Consumer, Food Service

7599 **Labatt Brewing Company**
1220 Erikson Street
Creston, BC V0B 1G3
Canada 250-428-9344
Fax: 250-428-3433 www.labatt.com
Processor and exporter of brewed beer and ale
Manager: Murray Oswald
Brewmaster: Scott Stokes
Number Employees: 104
Parent Co: Labatt Breweries
Type of Packaging: Consumer
Brands:
Kokanee
Kootenay True

7600 **Lacas Coffee Company**
7950 National Hwy # A
Pennsauken, NJ 8110 856-910-8662
Fax: 856-910-8671 800-220-1133
info@lacascoffee.com www.lacas.com
Coffee
President: John Vastardis
Treasurer: Michael Vlahos
R & D: Tony Cigounis
Estimated Sales: $ 10-20 Million
Number Employees: 20-49

7601 **Lacassagne's**
495 North 49th Street
Baton Rouge, LA 70806-3453 225-218-0237
Wholesale food distributor
President: Louis Lacassagne III
Vice President: Herbert Lacassagne
Number Employees: 20

7602 **Lacey Milling Company**
P.O.Box 1193
Hanford, CA 93232-1193 559-584-6634
Fax: 559-584-9165
Manufacturer of flour
Owner: Scott Lindrum
Plant Manager: Steve Verschelden
Estimated Sales: $ 10 - 20 Million
Number Employees: 10-19
Type of Packaging: Bulk
Brands:
CALIFORNIA SPECIAL
LACEY

7603 **(HQ)Lactalis Deli**
950 Third Avenue
22nd Floor
New York, NY 10022 212-758-6666
Fax: 212-758-7383 888-766-3353
cheese@lactalis-usa.com www.lactalis-usa.com
Processor, exporter and importer of cheeses including brie, Swiss, roquefort, feta, edam, gouda, mozzarella, ricotta, shredded, fontina, asiago, grated, parmesan and romano, as well as snack and spreadable cheese.
President: Frederick Bouisset
VP Sales: Paul Peterson
Estimated Sales: $85000
Number Employees: 765
Sq. footage: 1500
Parent Co: Lactalis American Group
Type of Packaging: Consumer, Food Service, Private Label, Bulk
Other Locations:
Belmont Plant & Distribution Center
Belmont WI
Merrill Plant
Merrill WI
Brands:
Bridel
Martin-Collet
Mozzarella Fresca
Pere
Precious
President
Rondele
Societe

7604 **Lactalis IngredientsSouth Park Plant & Distribution Center**
2375 South Park Avenue
Buffalo, NY 14220
www.liusa.com
Produces whey products, milk powders, caseins, industrial butters, nutritional and formulated products.
Number Employees: 500
Parent Co: Lactalis USA
Type of Packaging: Food Service, Bulk

7605 **Lactalis USABelmont Plant & Distribution Center**
218 South Park Street
Belmont, WI 53510-9639 608-762-5173
www.liusa.com
Produces whey products, milk powders, caseins, industrial butters, nutritional and formulated products.
CEO: Erick Boutry
VP & Manager: Lenny Bass
Estimated Sales: $37.5 Million
Number Employees: 150
Parent Co: Lactalis USA
Type of Packaging: Food Service, Bulk

7606 **Lactalis USAMerrill Plant**
8100 Wighway K South
Merrill, WI 54452 715-675-3326
Fax: 715-536-3028 888-766-3353
www.liusa.com
Manufactures cheeses and cheese products.
Parent Co: Lactalis USA
Type of Packaging: Consumer, Food Service

7607 **Lacto Milk Products Corporation**
Johanna Farms Rd
Flemington, NJ 08822-0272 908-788-2200
Fax: 908-788-2737
Processor of yogurt and juices
General Manager: Edward Steward
Estimated Sales: $100+ Million
Number Employees: 500-999
Parent Co: Johanna Farms
Type of Packaging: Consumer, Private Label, Bulk

7608 **Lad's Smokehouse Catering**
3731 School St
Needville, TX 77461 979-793-6210
Fax: 979-793-4220 info@ladssmokehouse.com
www.ladssmokehouse.com
Processor of sausage
President: Robert Case
Estimated Sales: $ 1 - 3 Million
Number Employees: 1-4
Type of Packaging: Consumer
Brands:
Lad's

7609 **Ladish Malting**
N5355 Junction Rd
Jefferson, WI 53549 920-674-3730
Fax: 920-674-8570 www.cargill.com
Malt
President: Sergio Barroso
Estimated Sales: $ 50 - 100 Million
Number Employees: 50-99

7610 **Ladoga Frozen Food & Retail Meat**
P.O.Box 262
Ladoga, IN 47954-0262 765-942-2225
Processor of frozen meat including beef and pork; wholesaler/distributor of fruit and vegetables
President: Harold Lowe
Number Employees: 1-4
Type of Packaging: Consumer, Food Service

7611 **Ladson Homemade Pasta Company**
3334 W Wilshire Drive
Suite 33
Phoenix, AZ 85009-1455 480-353-0874
Fax: 480-661-1156
Macaroni, spaghetti
President: Gary Capra
Estimated Sales: $ 1-4.9 Million
Number Employees: 3

7612 **Lady Gale Seafood**
101 Charenton Rd
Baldwin, LA 70514-0058 337-923-2060
Fax: 337-923-6909
Processor of fresh and frozen shrimp
Owner: Wayne Stevens
CFO: Jessica Burns
Estimated Sales: Below $ 5 Million
Number Employees: 4-10
Type of Packaging: Consumer, Food Service

7613 **Lady Walton's Cookies**
151 Regal Row # 118
Dallas, TX 75247-5609 214-630-9101
Fax: 214-630-9101 800-552-8006
ladywalton@ladywalton.com
www.ladywalton.com
Owner: Susan Walton
CEO: Walton Alizon
Estimated Sales: $ 1 - 3 Million
Number Employees: 20

7614 **Lady Walton's and Bronco Bob's Cowboy Brand Specialty Foods**
151 Regal Row # 118
Dallas, TX 75247-5609 214-630-9101
Fax: 214-630-9101 800-552-8006
ladywalton@ladywalton.com
www.ladywalton.com
Chipotle sauces
Owner: Susan Walton
Estimated Sales: $ 1 - 3 Million
Number Employees: 20-49
Brands:
Bronco Bob's

7615 **Laetitia Vineyard**
453 Laetitia Vineyard Dr
Arroyo Grande, CA 93420-9701 805-481-1772
Fax: 805-481-6920 888-809-8463
info@laetitiawine.com www.laetitiawine.com
Wine
Manager: Eric Hickey
Sales: Mark Newman
Operations: Dave Hickey
Production: Eric Hickey
Estimated Sales: Below $ 5 Million
Number Employees: 5-9
Brands:
Avila
Barnwood
Laetitia

7616 **Lafayette Brewing Company**
622 Main St
Lafayette, IN 47901 765-742-2591
Fax: 765-742-3443
mail@lafayettebrewingco.com
www.lafayettebrewingco.com
Processor of ale
President: Greg Emig
Brewer: Chris Johnson
Quality Control: Nancy Emig
Estimated Sales: Below $ 5 Million
Number Employees: 20-49
Type of Packaging: Consumer, Food Service

7617 **Lafitte Frozen Foods Corporation**
5165 Caroline St
Lafitte, LA 70067 504-689-2041
Fax: 504-689-3270
Fresh and frozen shrimp processor.
President: Paul Poon
Estimated Sales: $8.5 Million
Number Employees: 50-99

7618 **Lafleur Dairy Products**
617 Hill St
New Orleans, LA 70121-1000 504-729-3330
Fax: 504-461-8655

Processor of milk and yogurt
President: Cedric Lafleur
VP: Tommy Baker
CFO: Monica Sosta
Estimated Sales: Below $ 5 Million
Number Employees: 40
Parent Co: Borden
Type of Packaging: Consumer, Food Service, Bulk
Brands:
Borden

7619 **Lafollette Vineyard & Winery**
64 Harlingen Rd
Belle Mead, NJ 8502 908-359-5018
Fax: 908-874-7884
Wines
Owner: Miriam Summerskill
Estimated Sales: $68,000
Number Employees: 1
Type of Packaging: Private Label
Brands:
La Follette

7620 **Lafourche Sugar Corporation**
141 Leighton Quarters Rd
Thibodaux, LA 70301 985-447-3210
Fax: 985-447-8728 GN.Lafourche@charter.net
Manufacturer of sugar and blackstrap molasses
President/CEO: Greg Nolan
Estimated Sales: $1-3 Million
Number Employees: 5-9
Type of Packaging: Consumer

7621 **Lago Tortillas International**
1700 E 4th St
Austin, TX 78702-4427 512-476-0945
Fax: 512-476-4931 800-369-9017
www.ellago.net
Tortillas
Manager: Luis Centeno
Estimated Sales: $ 5-10 Million appx.
Number Employees: 100-249

7622 **Lagomarcino's**
1422 5th Ave
Moline, IL 61265-1334 309-764-1814
Fax: 309-736-5423 lagos@netexpress.net
www.lagomarcinos.com
Ice cream and confections
President: Tom Lagomarcino
Estimated Sales: $ 1-2.5 Million
Number Employees: 10-19
Brands:
Lagomarcino's

7623 **Lagorio Enterprises**
2771 E French Camp Rd
Manteca, CA 95336-9689 209-982-5691
Fax: 209-982-0235 mail@lagorio.com
www.lagorio.com
Grower, packer and exporter of fresh tomatoes
President: Ed Beckman
Estimated Sales: $ 5 - 10 Million
Number Employees: 100-249
Sq. footage: 158943
Brands:
Ace-Hi

7624 **Laguna Beach Brewing Company**
422 S Coast Hwy
Laguna Beach, CA 92651 949-494-2739
Fax: 949-497-0659
Processor of ale, stout, lager and porter
President: Ross Bartlett
Number Employees: 30-50
Type of Packaging: Consumer, Food Service, Private Label, Bulk
Brands:
Diver's Hole Dunkelweizen
Festival Light Ale
Greeter's Pale Ale
Laguna Beach Blinde
Main Beach Brown
Renaissance Red
Salt Kriek Cherry Be
Thousand Steps Stout
Victoria E.S.B.
Wipe Out

7625 **Laguna Cookie & DessertCompany**
4041 W Garry Ave
Santa Ana, CA 92704-6315 714-546-6855
Fax: 714-556-2491 800-673-2473
Cookies and Deserts
President: Mark McPeak
Estimated Sales: $ 20-50 Million
Number Employees: 250-499

7626 **Lahaha Tea Company**
9108 Huntington Dr
Apt D
San Gabriel, CA 91775-1323 626-215-6960
lahahatea@yahoo.com

7627 **Laird & Company**
3638 Laird Ln
North Garden, VA 22959 434-296-6058
Fax: 434-296-0071 877-438-5247
sales@lairdandcompany.com
www.lairdandcompany.com
Processor of apple products, wines, spirits, imported olive oils and balsamic vinegar
President: Larrie Laird
General Manager: Lester Clements
Estimated Sales: $10-20 Million
Number Employees: 1-4
Parent Co: Laird & Company
Type of Packaging: Consumer
Brands:
Captains
Virginia Fruit

7628 **Laird & Company**
1 Laird Rd
Scobeyville, NJ 07724 732-542-0312
Fax: 732-542-2244 877-438-5247
sales@lairdandcompany.com
www.lairdandcompany.com
Processor and exporter of apple brandy, bourbon, vodka, gin, blended whiskey and other spirits; importer of wine and bulk alcoholic beverages; also, contract bottling available
President/CEO: Larrie Laird
EVP/CFO: John Laird IV
VP Sales/Marketing: Tom Alberico
VP Public Relations/Advertising: Lisa Laird Dunn
VP Production: Janice Custer
Plant Manager: Ray Murdock
Estimated Sales: $47 Million
Number Employees: 56
Sq. footage: 155000
Type of Packaging: Private Label, Bulk
Brands:
Apple Jack
Bankers Club
Barrister
Five Star
Kasser
Laird
Villa Masa

7629 **Lake Arrowhead**
P.O.Box 11
Twin Peaks, CA 92391-0011 909-337-9228
Fax: 909-336-1548 877-237-8528
info@lakearrowhead.net www.lakearrowhead.net
President: Larry Luciano
Chairman: Richard Teachout
CFO: Grant Mayne
Number Employees: 5-9
Brands:
Lake Arrowhead

7630 **Lake Champlain Chocolates**
750 Pine St
Burlington, VT 5401 802-864-1807
Fax: 802-864-1806 800-465-5909
sales@lakechamplainchocolates.com
Specialty chocolate candies
President/Founder: James Lampman
Sales Manager: Allyson Meyers
Estimated Sales: Less than $500,000
Number Employees: 80
Sq. footage: 24000
Type of Packaging: Consumer, Food Service, Private Label, Bulk
Brands:
FIVE STAR BARS
ORIGINAL CHOCOLATES OF VERMONT

7631 **Lake Charles Poultry**
2808 Fruge St
Lake Charles, LA 70615 337-433-6818
Fax: 318-433-7855
President: Danny Bellard
Estimated Sales: $ 5 - 10 Million
Number Employees: 5-9

7632 **Lake City Foods**
5185 General Road
Mississauga, ON L4W 2K4
Canada 905-625-8244
Fax: 905-625-8244
Processor and exporter of drink mixes, jelly powders, soup bases and mixes, army rations, nondairy coffee creamers and camping and trail foods
Proprietor: Eyal Adda
Number Employees: 10-19
Parent Co: Eden Manufacturing Company
Type of Packaging: Consumer, Food Service, Private Label, Bulk
Brands:
Anytime
Camp Rite
Gibbons
Quickset

7633 **Lake Country Foods**
132 S Concord Rd
Oconomowoc, WI 53066 262-567-5521
Fax: 262-567-5714 mthomas5@execpc.com
www.lcfoods.com
Processor of malted milk, malt extract, dry blended foods, etc
Owner: David Erdman
CFO: John Waltenberry
Vice President: Phillip Vanderhyden
VP Sales: Myron Jones
Estimated Sales: $25 Million
Number Employees: 95
Sq. footage: 150000

7634 **Lake Erie Frozen Foods Company**
1830 Orange Rd
Ashland, OH 44805 419-289-9204
Fax: 419-281-7624 800-766-8501
mbuckingham@leffco.net www.leffco.net
Manufacturer of breaded cheese and vegetables
President: William Buckingham
Estimated Sales: $2.4 Million
Number Employees: 20-49
Type of Packaging: Consumer, Food Service, Private Label

7635 **Lake Helen Sprout Farm**
145 W Michigan Avenue
Lake Helen, FL 32744-2935 386-228-2871
Processor, packer and wholesaler/distributor of sprouts
Assistant Manager: N Hazen
Number Employees: 5-9
Sq. footage: 6000
Type of Packaging: Food Service, Private Label, Bulk
Brands:
Lake Helen Sprout Farm

7636 **Lake Packing Company**
755 Lake Landing Dr
Lottsburg, VA 22511 804-529-6101
Fax: 804-529-7374 lapco@sylvaninfo.net
Processor of frozen oysters and canned tomatoes, tomato juice and hominy
President: Sameul Lake Cowart
Estimated Sales: Under $ 1 Million
Number Employees: 20-49
Parent Co: Cowart Seafood
Type of Packaging: Consumer, Food Service, Private Label

7637 **Lake Shore Frozen Foods**
10307 Hall Ave
Lake City, PA 16423 814-774-3131
Fax: 814-774-3136 877-774-3668
www.lakeshorefrozenfood.com
Frozen donuts, pie shells, unfinished donuts, waffles
Chairman: Bruce MacLeod
CEO: Nat Burnside
Estimated Sales: $ 10-20 Million
Number Employees: 50-99

7638 **Lake Sonoma Winery**
340 Healdsburg Ave
Healdsburg, CA 95448-4106 707-473-2999
Fax: 707-431-8356 877-850-9463
info@lswinery.com www.lakesonomawinery.net

Wines
President: Gary Heck
CEO: Gary Heck
President: David Ready
Sales: Pat Paulson
Marketing Director: Gary Heck
Estimated Sales: $1-$2.5 Million
Number Employees: 5
Brands:
LAKE SONOMA WINERY

7639 **Lake St. George Brewing**
RR 1
Box 2505
Liberty, ME 04949 207-589-4690
WINES
President: Marilyn Beer
Estimated Sales: Under $500,000
Number Employees: 1-4

7640 **Lake States Yeast**
428 W Davenport Street
Rhinelander, WI 54501-3325 715-369-4949
Fax: 715-369-4034 vbond@wausaupaper.com
Manufacturer and exporter of yeasts including inactive dried, torula, autolyzed, formulated and specialty grades that inlcudes smoked, roasted, and grill flavors.
President/Manager: Antoine Chagnon
Sales Director: Vernon Bond
Operations Manager: Stuart Bacon
Production Manager: Rick Bishop
Plant Manager: Linda Fox
Number Employees: 26
Parent Co: Rhinelander Paper Company
Type of Packaging: Private Label, Bulk
Brands:
Lake States

7641 **Lake Titus Brewery**
Hc 1
Box 58b
Malone, NY 12953 518-483-2337
Brewers
Owner: Fred Ruvola
Estimated Sales: $500,000-$1 Million
Number Employees: 20-49

7642 **Lakefront Brewery**
1872 N Commerce St
Milwaukee, WI 53212 414-372-8800
Fax: 414-372-4400 info@lakefrontbrewery.com
www.lakefrontbrewery.com
Processor of beer
Owner: Russ Davis
Marketing Director: Orlando Segura
Estimated Sales: Below $ 5 Million
Number Employees: 5-9
Type of Packaging: Private Label
Brands:
River West Stein

7643 **Lakeport Brewing Corporation**
180 Henri Dunant St
Moncton, NB E1E 1E6
Canada 905-523-4200
Fax: 905-523-6564 800-268-2337
www.lakeportbrewing.ca
Processor and exporter of beer, ale, lager and stout
President: Teresa Cascioli
Sales/Marketing Executive: Ian McDonald
Estimated Sales: F
Number Employees: 200
Type of Packaging: Consumer, Food Service
Brands:
BRAVA
LAKEPORT HONEY LAGER
LAKEPORT ICE
LAKEPORT LIGHT
LAKEPORT PILSENER
LAKEPORT STRONG
MONGOOSE
STEELER LAGER
WEE WILLY

7644 **Lakeridge Winery & Vineyards**
19239 Us Highway 27
Clermont, FL 34715 352-394-8627
Fax: 352-394-7490 800-768-9463
lakeridgew@aol.com www.lakeridgewinery.com
Wines
President: Geary Cox
Estimated Sales: $ 10-20 Million
Number Employees: 20-49
Brands:
Lakeridge

7645 **Lakeshore Winery**
5132 State Route 89
Romulus, NY 14541-9779 315-549-7075
Fax: 315-549-7102 info@lakeshorewinery.com
www.lakeshorewinery.com
Farm winery
President/CEO/CFO: John Bachman
Estimated Sales: $ 5-9.9 Million
Number Employees: 2
Brands:
Lakeshore

7646 **Lakeside Foods**
1055 W Broadway
Plainview, MN 55964 507-534-3141
Fax: 507-534-3005 www.lakesidefoods.com
Manufacturer and exporter of frozen and canned vegetables including corn, peas and lima beans; also, meat
Manager: Bill Arendt
VP Human Resources: Tom Reilly
Director Operations: Jim Schwarzhoff
General Manager: Bill Arendt
Estimated Sales: $100 Million
Number Employees: 20-49
Type of Packaging: Consumer
Other Locations:
Lakeside Foods - Manufacturing
Manitowoc WI
Lakeside Foods - Manufacturing
Belgium WI
Lakeside Foods - Manufacturing
Random Lake WI
Lakeside Foods - Manufacturing
Reedsburg WI
Lakeside Foods - Manufacturing
Seymour WI
Lakeside Foods - Manufacturing
Plainview MN
Lakeside Foods - Manufacturing
Brooten MN
Lakeside Foods - Manufacturing
Owatoona MN
Lakeside Foods - Manufacturing
New Richmond WI
Lakeside Foods - Manufacturing
Eden WI
Lakeside Foods - Distribution
Manitowoc WI
Lakeside Foods - Distribution
Plainview MN
Lakeside Foods - Distribution
Belgium WI
Brands:
EUREKA
HOBBY
LAKESIDE

7647 **(HQ)Lakeside Foods**
808 Hamilton Street
Manitowoc, WI 54220 920-684-3356
Fax: 920-686-4033 jkautzer@lakesidefoods.com
www.lakesidefoods.com
Canned vegetables, frozen vegetables, canned meats, organic vegetables and meal starters
President/COO: David Yanda
CEO/Chairman: J. Douglas Quick
Human Resources VP: Thomas Reilly
Processed Food Sales SVP: Jeff Lund
Operations VP: Jim Schwarzhoff
Estimated Sales: $200 Million
Number Employees: 1700
Sq. footage: 28000
Type of Packaging: Consumer, Food Service, Private Label
Other Locations:
Lakeside Foods Processing Plant
Manitowoc WI
Lakeside Foods Processing Plant
Belgium WI
Lakeside Foods Processing Plant
Random Lake WI
Lakeside Foods Processing Plant
Reedsburg WI
Lakeside Foods Processing Plant
Seymour WI
Lakeside Foods Processing Plant
Planview MN
Lakeside Foods Processing Plant
Brooten MN
Lakeside Foods Processing Plant
New Richmond WI
Lakeside Foods Processing Plant
Eden WI
Lakeside Foods Processing Plant
Owatonna MN
Brands:
Festal
Read
Tendersweet

7648 **Lakeside Foods**
530 E Wisconsin St
Seymour, WI 54165 920-833-2371
Fax: 920-833-7504 www.lakesidefoods.com
Processor of canned vegetables including peas, carrots, beets, corn, etc
General Manager: John Silmer
Marketing Manager: James Farley
Estimated Sales: $ 10 - 20 Million
Number Employees: 20-49
Sq. footage: 170000
Parent Co: Lakeside Foods
Type of Packaging: Consumer, Food Service, Private Label, Bulk

7649 **Lakeside Foods**
P.O.Box 430
Brooten, MN 56316 320-346-2900
Fax: 320-346-2903 www.lakesidefoods.com
Processor of frozen vegetables including corn, peas and lima beans
Plant Manager: Jeff Griep
Operations Manager: Paul Baumert
Estimated Sales: $ 20-50 Million
Number Employees: 60
Sq. footage: 65000
Parent Co: Lakeside Foods
Type of Packaging: Bulk

7650 **Lakeside Foods**
457 Canal St
Mondovi, WI 54755 715-926-5075
Fax: 715-926-5076 www.lakesidefoods.com
Manufacturer of canned and frozen vegetables, canned dry beans, jellies and preserves, frozen and shelf stable meals, canned meats and stew
President/CEO: Doug Quick
SVP Processed Food Sales: Jeff Lund
SVP Operations: Dan Cavanaugh
Purchasing: Gary Sabelko
Estimated Sales: $20-50 Million
Number Employees: 100-249
Type of Packaging: Private Label
Other Locations:
Lakeside Foods - HQ
Manitowoc WI

7651 **Lakeside Mills**
P.O.Box 230
Rutherfordton, NC 28139-0230 828-286-4866
Fax: 828-287-3361 sales@lakesidemills.com
www.lakesidemills.com
Processor of corn meal, hush puppy mix and breadings; importer of peppers and spices
VP: Aaron King
Number Employees: 10-19
Parent Co: Lakeside Mills
Type of Packaging: Consumer, Food Service, Private Label, Bulk
Brands:
Blue Ribbon
Kings Old Fashion

7652 **Lakeside Packing Company**
667 County Road #50
Harrow, ON N0R 1G0
Canada 519-738-2314
Fax: 519-738-3684 info@lakesidepacking.com
www.lakesidepacking.com
Pickles, peppers, relish, salsa, tomatoes
President/Board Member: Donald Woodbridge
VP/Board Member: Alan Woodbridge
Estimated Sales: $813,000
Number Employees: 20
Type of Packaging: Consumer, Food Service

7653 **Lakespring Winery**
2055 Hoffman Lane
Yountville, CA 94599 707-944-2475
Wines
President: Frank Battat

7654 **Lakeview Bakery**
6449 Crowchild Trail SW
Calgary, AB T2E 5R7
Canada 403-246-6127
Fax: 403-246-6609 info@organicbaking.com
members.shaw.ca/organicbaking/

Processor of bread, buns and pastries
President: Maureen Hinton
Sales/Distribution: David Hinton
Number Employees: 5-9
Type of Packaging: Consumer, Food Service

7655 **Lakeview Farms**
P.O.Box 98
Delphos, OH 45833 419-695-9925
Fax: 419-695-9900 800-755-9925
lvfsales@lakeviewfarms.com
www.lakeviewfarms.com
Sour cream, mousse, cheesecake, fruit gelatins, sour cream dip, soy oil dips, imitation sour cream
President: Gene Graves
CEO: Mardy Garlack
VP Sales: Joh Kopilchack
Estimated Sales: $ 30-50 Million
Number Employees: 100-249
Type of Packaging: Bulk
Brands:
Lakeview Farms
Merkt's
Merkt's Bristol Gold
Owl's Nest Cheese
Real Desserts
Winky Foods

7656 **Lakewood Juices**
P.O.Box 420708
Miami, FL 33242 305-324-5932
Fax: 305-325-9573
newberry@floridabottling.com
www.lakewoodjuices.com
Fruit juices
Manager: Lee Wilson
Sales Manager: Holly Newberry
Estimated Sales: $ 20 - 50 Million
Number Employees: 20-49
Parent Co: Florida Bottling

7657 **Lakewood Vineyards**
4024 State Route 14
Watkins Glen, NY 14891 607-535-9252
Fax: 607-535-6656
wines@lakewoodvineyards.com
www.lakewoodvineyards.com
Wines
President: Charles Stamp
Estimated Sales: $ 2.5-5 Million
Number Employees: 5-9
Brands:
Lakewood Vineyards
Mystic Mead

7658 **Lallemand**
PO Box 5512
Petaluma, CA 94955-5512 707-795-1468
Fax: 661-835-4990 800-423-6625
info@lallemand.com www.lallemand.com
Wine industry yeasts
Director: William Pursley
Brands:
Enoferm
Fermaid
Lalvin
Uvaferm

7659 **Lallemand Inc**
1620 Rue Prefontaine
Montreal, QC H1W 2N8
Canada 514-522-2133
Fax: 514-522-2884 www.lallemand.com
Manufacturer and exporter of food and dairy microbial cultures, lactobacilli and bifidobacteria; also, custom formulations available
President: Jean Chagnon
Vice President: Francois Leblanc
Estimated Sales: $10-20 Million
Number Employees: 50-99
Sq. footage: 50000
Parent Co: Placements Lallemand Inc
Type of Packaging: Consumer, Private Label, Bulk
Brands:
Ferlac
Gastro-Ad
Polylacton
Probiotic-2000
Rosell
Rosellac
Standard Formulation
Vitanat

7660 **Lallemand/American Yeast**
47-00 Northern Boulevard
L.I.C., NY 11101 773-267-2223
Fax: 773-267-4508 gedwards@lallemand.com
www.lallemand.comcurves
Yeast
President: Joanie joans
Estimated Sales: $300,000-500,000
Number Employees: 5-9

7661 **Lallemand/American Yeast**
1417 Jeffrey Dr
Addison, IL 60101-4331 630-932-1290
Fax: 630-932-1291 mlegel@lallemand.com
www.lallemand.com
Baking enzymes, baking ingredients, dough conditioners, such as bromate replacers, chocolate, cocoa, eggs, nuts, oils, oxidizers, raisins, spices, sweetners, yeast foods, yeast (fresh & dry), starter cultures, baking powder, moldinhibitors
President: Gary Edwards
VP: Merna Legel
Quality Control: Mike Hudson
Sales: Steven Marinella
Estimated Sales: Below $ 5 Million
Number Employees: 20-49
Parent Co: Lallemand, Inc.
Type of Packaging: Food Service, Bulk
Brands:
American Yeast
Eagle
Essential
Fermaid
Lallemand

7662 **Lam's Foods Inc**
9723 218th Street
Queens, NY 11429 718-271-0476
andrew@lamsnacks.com
www.lamsnacks.com
Plantain and yuca chips in different flavors.
President: Andrew Lam
VP: Trevor Lam
Sales/Marketing: Melissa Gaviria
Estimated Sales: $520,000
Number Employees: 6
Sq. footage: 4800

7663 **Lamagna Cheese Company**
1 Lamagna Dr
Verona, PA 15147 412-828-6112
Fax: 412-828-6782 info@lamagnacheese.com
www.lamagnacheese.com
Ricotta, feta, shredded mozzarella
President: Rudolph Lamagna
Estimated Sales: $ 10-20 Million
Number Employees: 10-19
Brands:
Lamagana

7664 **Lamb-Weston**
P.O.Box 705
Hermiston, OR 97838 541-567-2211
Fax: 541-567-2211 800-766-7783
brian.hersch@lambweston.com
www.lambweston.com
Manufacturer and exporter of frozen French and shoestring fries
Branch Manager: Horst Ellendt
Estimated Sales: $742 Million
Number Employees: 50
Parent Co: ConAgra Foods
Type of Packaging: Consumer, Food Service, Bulk
Brands:
GENERATION 7 FRIES
LAMB'S SUPREME
LW PRIVATE RESERVE
STEALTH FRIES
TIME SAVOR

7665 **Lamb-Weston**
8701 W Gage Blvd
Kennewick, WA 99336-1034 509-735-4651
Fax: 509-736-0448 800-766-7783
www.lambweston.com
Manufacturer of potato products: French fries (Shoestrings, Twister, CrissCut, Curley QQQ's, seasoned, wedge, crinkle, etc.), mashed, hash browns, chopped and formed products, etc. Also, pizza and snack pockets and fruit turnovers.Foodservice, institutional and retail
President/Ceo: Jeffery Delapp
Chairman/Director: Richard Porter
Vice President: Steve Rummel
Number Employees: 5,000-9,999
Parent Co: ConAgra Foods
Type of Packaging: Consumer, Food Service, Private Label
Brands:
Crisscut
Curley Qqq's
Munchers
Twister

7666 **Lamb-Weston**
103 Depot St
Weston, OR 97886-5020 541-566-3511
Fax: 541-566-2053 800-766-7783
lwinfo@conagrafoods.com
www.lambweston.com
Processor of frozen fruit turnovers and pizza pockets. Specialty potato products.
CFO: Dawnet E Stewart
Plant Manager: Jeff Brasch
Estimated Sales: $ 50 - 100 Million
Number Employees: 100-249
Parent Co: ConAgra Foods
Type of Packaging: Consumer, Food Service, Private Label, Bulk
Brands:
Generation 7 Fries
LW Private Reserve
Lamb's Supreme
Stealth
TimeSavor

7667 **Lambent Technologies**
7247 Central Park Ave
Skokie, IL 60076 847-675-3951
Fax: 847-675-3013 800-432-7187
lambent@petrofirm.com www.petrofirm.com
Manufacturer and exporter of nonionic emulsifiers including polysorbates, sorbitan esters and glycerol esters; also, silicone and nonsilicone antifoams and defoamers
President: Michael Hayes
Marketing Manager: Randy Cobb
Sales Manager: Kevin Hrebenar
Estimated Sales: $9800000
Number Employees: 55
Sq. footage: 10000
Parent Co: Petroferm
Brands:
Lambent

7668 **Lambert Bridge Winery**
4085 W Dry Creek Rd
Healdsburg, CA 95448 707-431-9600
Fax: 707-433-3215 800-975-0555
wines@lambertbridge.com
www.lambertbridge.com
WINE
President: Patricia Chambers
Winemaker: Jill Davis
Estimated Sales: $1.1 Million
Number Employees: 10-19
Type of Packaging: Private Label
Brands:
Lambert Bridge Winery

7669 **Lamesa Cotton Oil Mill**
PO Box 2710
Chandler, AZ 85244-2710 806-872-2166
Fax: 806-872-8880
Processor of cottonseed hull and cottonseed oil
Number Employees: 20-49
Parent Co: Chickasha Cotton Oil Company

7670 **Lamex Foods**
8500 Normandale Ste 1150
Bloomington, MN 55437 952-844-0585
Fax: 952-844-0083 usa@lamex-foods.com
www.lamexfoods.com
Manufacture of food items
Estimated Sales: $ 50-100 Million
Number Employees: 50
Parent Co: Lamex Foods

7671 **Lamm Food Service**
P.O.Box 2957
Lafayette, LA 70502-2957 337-896-0331
Fax: 337-896-9213 800-223-7752
kthibodeaux@glacoxmail.com
http://lammfoodservice.com
Owner: J D Lively
Estimated Sales: $ 50 - 100 Million
Number Employees: 50-99

7672 **Lammes Candies Since 1885**
P.O.Box 1885
Austin, TX 78767-1885 512-310-2223
Fax: 512-238-2019 800-252-1885
www.lammes.com
Candy
Manager: Crystal Bertrand
VP: Bryan Teich
Estimated Sales: $ 5 - 10 Million
Number Employees: 10-19
Number of Products: 1000
Brands:
CASHEW CRITTERS
CHOC-ADILLOS
LONGHORNS
PEANUT PAWS
TEXAS CHEWIE PECAN PRALINE

7673 **Lamonaca Bakery**
304 7th St
Windber, PA 15963 814-467-4909
Processor of bread products and pizza shells
President: Mary La Monaca
Estimated Sales: $ 5 - 10 Million
Number Employees: 10-19
Type of Packaging: Consumer, Food Service

7674 **Lamoreaux Landing Wine Cellar**
9224 State Route 414
Lodi, NY 14860 607-582-6011
Fax: 607-582-6010 llwc@capital.net
www.lamoreauxwine.com
Wines
Owner: Mark Wagner
Retail Sales Manager: Susan Whitaker
Estimated Sales: $ 5-10 Million
Number Employees: 10-19
Type of Packaging: Private Label

7675 **Lampost Meats**
805 Shawver Drive
Grimes, IA 50111-1118 515-288-6111
Fax: 515-288-5727 sglksl@aol.com
www.lampostmeats.com
Processor of pork and beef offals
President: Stanley Lammers
Number Employees: 2
Parent Co: Walking S Farms

7676 **Lanaetex Products Incorporated**
151 3rd St
Elizabeth, NJ 07206 908-351-9700
Fax: 908-351-8753
Processor and exporter of food grade waxes
President: Mike Gutowski
Estimated Sales: $ 10 - 20 Million
Number Employees: 10-19

7677 **Lancaster County Winery**
799 Rawlinsville Rd
Willow Street, PA 17584 717-464-3555
www.lancastercountywinery.com
Wines
President: Suzanne Dickel
Estimated Sales: Below $ 5 Million
Number Employees: 5-9

7678 **Lancaster Packing Company**
P.O.Box 7595
Lancaster, PA 17604-7595 717-397-9727
Fax: 717-397-7744 www.jakeandamos.com
Processor of Pennsylvania Dutch-style pickles, preserves, relishes, syrups, pickled vegetables and fruits, chow chow and fruit butters packed in glass canning jars
President: David Doolittle
CEO: Sue Doolittle
Estimated Sales: $ 5 - 10 Million
Number Employees: 5-9
Sq. footage: 10000
Type of Packaging: Consumer, Private Label
Brands:
Jake & Amos

7679 **Lance Private Brands**
8600 South Boulevard
Charlotte, NC 28273 704-557-8313
Fax: 704-556-5781 888-722-1163
orderfulfillment@lance.com
www.brentandsams.com
Kosher, organic/natural, cookies, private label.
Marketing: Drew Snyder

7680 **(HQ)Lanco**
350 Wireless Blvd Ste 200
Hauppauge, NY 11788 631-231-2300
Fax: 631-231-2731 800-938-4500
sales@lancopromo.com www.lancopromo.com
Processor of chocolate candy including squares, circles and triangles
President: Brian Landow
Number Employees: 175
Type of Packaging: Consumer, Food Service

7681 **Land O Lakes Milk**
1200 W Russell St
Sioux Falls, SD 57104 605-330-9526
Fax: 605-336-7206 www.landolakesinc.com
Manufacturer of beverages including milk, juice, etc.; wholesaler/distributor of frozen food and dairy products
Chairman/CEO: Gregg Engles
Executive: Steve Sneer
General Manager: Dana Loseke
Estimated Sales: $36 Million
Number Employees: 100-249
Parent Co: Dean Foods Company
Type of Packaging: Consumer

7682 **(HQ)Land O'Frost**
16850 Chicago Ave
PO Box 670
Lansing, IL 60438-0670 708-474-7100
Fax: 708-474-9329 800-323-3308
www.landofrost.com
Manufacturer and importer of lunch and deli meats such as; beef, chicken, turkey, ham and meat ingredients
President: Charles Niementowski
Chairman/CEO: Donna Van Eekeren
CFO: George Smolar
VP Operations: William Marion
Estimated Sales: $100+ Million
Number Employees: 900
Sq. footage: 100000
Type of Packaging: Consumer, Food Service, Private Label
Brands:
DAGWOOD
LAND O'FROST
PREMIUM
TASTE ESCAPES

7683 **Land O'Frost**
911 Hastings Ave
Searcy, AR 72143 501-268-2473
Fax: 501-268-0357 800-643-5654
www.landofrost.com
Processor and importer of ham, beef, chicken and turkey; also, pre-sliced luncheon meats, pre-portioned julienne meat strips and diced meats
Sq. footage: 263000
Parent Co: Land O'Frost
Type of Packaging: Consumer, Food Service, Private Label, Bulk
Brands:
Perfect-O-Portion
Salad Toppers
Sandwich Shop

7684 **Land O'Lakes**
306 Park St
Spencer, WI 54479 715-659-2311
Fax: 715-659-5990 www.landolakes.com
Processor and exporter of processed, sliced, dried and loaf cheese.
President/CEO: Chris Policinski
Chairman: Pete Kappelman
SVP/CFO: Dan Knutson
VP/General Counsel: Peter Janzen
VP/Strategy & Business Development: Barry Wolfish
EVP/Land O'Lakes Purina Feed: Fernando Palacios
EVP/COO Dairy Foods Value-Added: Steve Dunphy
EVP/COO Dairy Foods Industrial: Alan Pierson
VP/Public Affairs: Jim Fife
VP/Human Resources: Karen Grabow
Plant Manager: Dennis Thomas
Purchasing Agent: Deanne Luepke
Estimated Sales: $100+ Million
Number Employees: 250-499
Parent Co: Land O'Lakes
Type of Packaging: Consumer, Food Service, Private Label, Bulk

7685 **Land O'Lakes**
927 8th St
Kiel, WI 53042 920-894-2204
Fax: 920-894-2956 www.landolakes.com
Processor of cheese
President/CEO: Chris Policinski
Chairman: Pete Kappelman
SVP/CFO: Dan Knutson
VP/Strategy & Business Development: Barry Wolfish
VP/General Counsel: Peter Janzen
EVP Land O'Lakes Purina Feed: Fernando Palacios
EVP/COO Dairy Foods Industrial: Alan Pierson
EVP/COO Dairy Foods Value-Added: Steve Dunphy
VP/Public Affairs: Jim Fife
VP/Human Resources: Karen Grabow
Plant Manager: Kevin Schwartz
Estimated Sales: $ 50 - 100 Million
Number Employees: 50-99
Parent Co: Land O'Lakes
Type of Packaging: Consumer
Brands:
Land O Lakes

7686 **Land O'Lakes**
405 Park Dr
Carlisle, PA 17015 717-486-7000
Fax: 717-486-3730 www.landolakes.com
Processor of dry milk, buttermilk, butter and condensed products.
President/CEO: Chris Policinski
Chairman: Pete Kappelman
SVP/CFO: Dan Knutson
VP/General Counsel: Peter Janzen
VP/Strategy & Business Development: Barry Wolfish
EVP/COO Dairy Foods Value-Added: Steve Dunphy
EVP/COO Dairy Foods Industrial: Alan Pierson
EVP/Land O'Lakes Purina Feed: Fernando Palacios
VP/Public Affairs: Jim Fife
VP/Human Resources: Karen Grabow
Plant Manager: Alan Vanderneut
Estimated Sales: $100+ Million
Number Employees: 100-249
Parent Co: Land O'Lakes

7687 **Land O'Lakes**
2001 Mogadore Rd
Kent, OH 44240 330-678-1578
Fax: 330-678-2950 800-328-9680
www.landolakesinc.com
Processor of regular and light butter, margarine and spreads.
Chairman: Dan Knutson
CEO: Christopher Policinski
VP/Strategy & Business Development: Barry Wolfish
EVP/Land O'Lakes Purina Feed: Fernando Palacios
EVP/COO Dairy Foods Value-Added: Steve Dunphy
VP/Public Affairs: Jim Fife
VP/Human Resources: Karen Grabow
Plant Manager: Steve Schafer
Number Employees: 100-249
Sq. footage: 85000
Parent Co: Land O'Lakes
Type of Packaging: Food Service, Private Label

7688 **Land O'Lakes Procurement**
1200 W Russell St
Sioux Falls, SD 57104 605-330-9526
Fax: 605-336-7206 www.landolakesinc.com
Non-fermented uncultured & unflavored milk & cream Products.
President/CEO: Chris Policinski
Chairman: Pete Kappelman
SVP/CFO: Dan Knutson
Executive: Steve Sneer
VP/Strategy & Business Development: Barry Wolfish
EVP/Land O'Lakes Purina Feed: Fernando Palacios
EVP/COO Dairy Foods Value-Added: Steve Dunphy
EVP/COO Dairy Foods Industrial: Alan Pierson
VP/Public Affairs: Jim Fife
VP/Human Resources: Karen Grabow

Estimated Sales: $300,000
Number Employees: 5-9
Parent Co: Land O'Lakes
Type of Packaging: Consumer, Food Service
Brands:
Land O'Lakes

7689 **(HQ)Land O'Lakes, Inc.**
4001 Lexington Ave N
Arden Hills, MN 55126-2998
Fax: 651-481-2000 800-328-9680
www.landolakesinc.com
Manufacturer of Milk and dairy products including whey blends, butter, margarine, cheese, milk powders, whey powder, whey protein concentrate, whey protein isolate and deproteinized whey powder.
President/CEO: Christopher Policinsky
SVP/Chief Financial Officer: Dan Knutson
SVP/General Counsel: Peter Janzen
VP/International: Carol Kitchen
EVP & COO, Retail Foods: Steve Dunphy
SVP/Corporate Marketing & Communications: Barry Wolfish
SVP/Business Dev. & Gov't Relations: Karen Grabow
SVP/Member & Public Affairs: Jim Fife
SVP/Human Resoures: Loren Heeringa
EVP/COO, Dairy Foods Industrial: Jerry Kaminski
Estimated Sales: $11.15 Billion
Number Employees: 9,000
Number of Products: 300+
Type of Packaging: Consumer, Food Service, Private Label, Bulk
Other Locations:
Land O'Lakes
Gustine CA
Brands:
4-QUART
BETTY CROCKER POP SECRET POPCORN
CAV QUR D
CHEDDEASE
CO-JACK
DAIRY BELT
DOWNTOWN CAFE ICED CAPPUCINO
GOLDEN VELVET
LA CHEDDA
LAND O'LAKES ALL NATURAL FARM EGGS
LAND O'LAKES BUTTER
LAND O'LAKES BUTTERSCOTCH CANDY
LAND O'LAKES CAPPUCINO CLASSICS
LAND O'LAKES CHEESE
LAND O'LAKES COCOA CLASSICS
LAND O'LAKES DAIRY CASE CHEESE
LAND O'LAKES DELI CHEESE
LAND O'LAKES FLAVORED BUTTER
LAND O'LAKES INTERNATIONAL PASTAS
LAND O'LAKES MACARONI AND CHEESE
LAND O'LAKES MARGARINE, SPREADS
LAND O'LAKES SOUR CREAM
LAND O'LAKES ULTRA CREAMY BUTTER
NATURALLY SLENDER
NEW HOLSTEIN
NEW YORKER
NORTHVIEW
PRIMO

7690 **Land-O-Sun Dairies**
610 E State St
O Fallon, IL 62269 314-436-6820
Fax: 618-628-3309 www.deanfoods.com
Processor of fluid milk and cottage cheese
Manager: Bill Schaefer
Operations Manager: Chuck McQuaig
Estimated Sales: $ 10 - 20 Million
Number Employees: 50-99
Parent Co: Suiza Foods
Type of Packaging: Consumer, Food Service, Bulk

7691 **(HQ)Land-o-Sun**
2900 Bristol Hwy
Johnson City, TN 37601-1502 423-283-5700
Fax: 423-283-5716 800-283-5765
www.suizafoods.com
Manufacturer of PET and Flav-O-Rich dairy brands
President: Rick Fehr
CEO: Loreen White
Executive: Rod Barnett
Sales Director: Fred Myette
Number Employees: 50-99
Parent Co: Suiza Dairy Group
Type of Packaging: Consumer
Other Locations:
PET 828 322-3730
Hickory NC
PET 423 245-5154
Kingsport TN
PET 618 632-6381
O'Fallon IL
PET 757 397-2387
Portsmouth VA
PET 864 576-6280
Spartansburg SC
Flav-O-Rich 606 878-7301
London KY
Flav-O-Rich 540 669-5161
Bristol VA
Brands:
FLAV-O-RICH
PET

7692 **Landies Candies Company**
2495 Main St Ste 350
Buffalo, NY 14214 716-834-8212
Fax: 716-833-9113 800-955-2634
larrys@landiescandies.com
www.trulysugarfree.com
Processor of boxed chocolates including pecan, peanut, cashew, no sugar, cherry cordials and nut clusters; also, divinity, toffee, taffy, fondant mints, dipped pretzels, peppermint kisses, caramels, truffles and pecan praline desserttopping
President: Larry Szrama
CEO: David Tiech
Vice President: Bryan Tiech
Director Sales: Barbera Kelly
Plant Manager: John Davis
Estimated Sales: $1670977
Number Employees: 10-19
Type of Packaging: Consumer, Private Label, Bulk
Brands:
Cashew Critters
Choc Adillos
Choc'adillos
Longhorns
Texas Chewie

7693 **Landis Meat Company**
787 California Rd
Quakertown, PA 18951 215-536-2150
Fax: 215-538-2409 800-421-1565
dwalls@landismeat.net www.landismeat.net
Processed meat
President: David Landis
VP: Roland Felix
Vice President: Mark Landis
Quality Control: Robin Moyer
Plant Manager: Wally Huhn
Estimated Sales: $ 10-20 Million
Number Employees: 50-100

7694 **Landis Peanut Butter**
641 E Cherry Ln
Souderton, PA 18964-1236 215-723-9366
www
Peanut butter
Owner: Raymond Landis
Estimated Sales: $500-1 Million appx.
Number Employees: 1-4

7695 **Landlocked Seafoods**
219 E 3rd St
Carroll, IA 51401 712-792-9599
Fax: 712-792-9599
mebner@landlockedseafood.com
Seafood
President: Michael Ebner

7696 **Landmark Vineyards**
101 Adobe Canyon Rd
Kenwood, CA 95452 707-833-0053
Fax: 707-833-1164 800- 45- 636
info@landmarkwine.com
www.landmarkwine.com
Wines
Owner/CFO: Michael Colhoun
Winemaker: Eric Stern
Public Relations: Mary Colhoun
Estimated Sales: $ 5-10 Million
Number Employees: 10-19
Brands:
Landmark Damaris Chardonnay
Landmark Grand Detou
Landmark Kastania Pi
Landmark Overlook Ch

7697 **Landolfi Food Products**
302 Cummings Ave
Trenton, NJ 08611 609-392-1830
Fax: 609-396-6581 landolfis@gmail.com
www.landolfifoods.com
Frozen pasta, garlic bread and pizza dough
President: Jack Fu
Sales Director: Lori Landolfi
Director Manufacturing: Paul Melovich
Estimated Sales: $2 Million
Number Employees: 16
Sq. footage: 10000
Type of Packaging: Consumer, Food Service, Private Label, Bulk

7698 **Landreth Wild Rice**
2320 Industrial Blvd
Norman, OK 73069-8518 405-360-2333
Fax: 405-360-6644 800-333-3533
Processor and exporter of wild rice
Principal: George Landreth
Estimated Sales: $110,000
Number Employees: 2
Type of Packaging: Consumer, Food Service, Private Label

7699 **Landrin USA**
18201 Collins Ave Apt 502
Suite 1200
Sunny Isles Beach, FL 33160-5112
Fax: 302-250-4396 info@landrinusa.com
www.landrinusa.com
Confectionery products
CEO: Stan Kissele
Estimated Sales: $3 Million
Number Employees: 10

7700 **Landry Armand Company**
P.O.Box 623
Cottonport, LA 71327-0623 318-876-2716
Fax: 318-876-2490
Owner: James Bernard

7701 **Landry's Pepper Company**
1606 Cypress Island Hwy
Saint Martinville, LA 70582 337-394-6097
Fax: 337-394-7629 landry6097@aol.com
Hot sauces
President: Lamar Bertrand
VP: Toby Bertrand
Estimated Sales: $500,000
Number Employees: 3
Sq. footage: 30000
Type of Packaging: Consumer, Food Service, Private Label, Bulk
Brands:
Cajun Gourmet Magic
Landry's
Premium

7702 **Landshire**
727 N 1st St
Saint Louis, MO 63102-2501 618-398-8122
Fax: 618-398-7627 800-468-3354
sales@landshire.com www.landshire.com
Processor of deli foods including sandwiches; also, coffee and snack foods
Chairman: Joseph Trover
President: Dale Musick
CFO: Mark Wilcutt
Estimated Sales: $22.7 Million
Number Employees: 250-499
Type of Packaging: Consumer, Food Service, Private Label
Brands:
Deli Maid
Landshire

7703 **Lane Packing Company**
50 Lane Rd
Fort Valley, GA 31030 478-825-3362
Fax: 478-825-0015 www.lanepacking.com
Packer of peaches and pecans
President: Duke Lane Jr
Sales Manager: Bobby Lane
Estimated Sales: $100+ Million
Number Employees: 100-249
Type of Packaging: Bulk
Brands:
Diamond D

7704 **Lane's Dairy**
310 N Concepcion St
El Paso, TX 79905-1605 915-772-6700
Fax: 915-772-3097 hjlane3541@aol.com
Manufacturer and exporter of milk and canned and bottled fruit juice
President: John Lane
Owner: Hilda Lane
Production Manager: Chris Lane
Estimated Sales: $2 Million
Number Employees: 20-49
Sq. footage: 15000
Type of Packaging: Consumer
Brands:
LANES DAIRY

7705 **Laney Family Honey Company**
25725 New Rd
North Liberty, IN 46554-9379 574-656-8701
Fax: 574-656-8603 info@laneyhoney.com
www.laneyhoney.com
Honey, nuts/honey from America's heartland
President: Dave Laney
Co-Owner: Kay Laney
Estimated Sales: Below $ 500,000
Number Employees: 10-19
Type of Packaging: Consumer
Brands:
Apple Blossom
Autumn Wildflower
Basswood
Blueberry Blossom
Buckwheat
Clover
Cranberry Blossom
Michigan Star Thistle
Orange Blossom
Spring Blossom
Wild Blackberry
Wildflower

7706 **Lang Creek Brewery**
655 Lang Creek Rd
Marion, MT 59925 406-858-2200
Fax: 406-858-2499 info@langcreekbrewery.com
www.langcreekbrewery.com
Beer and ale
Owner/Brewmaster: John Campbell
Estimated Sales: $ 2.5-5 Million
Number Employees: 5-9
Number of Brands: 1
Number of Products: 8
Brands:
Tri-Motor
Windsock

7707 **Lang Naturals**
20 Silva Ln
Newport, RI 02842 401-848-7700
Fax: 401-848-7701
customer.service@langnaturals.com
www.langnaturals.com
Nutritional supplements, beverages, bars and functional foods.
Owner: Dave Lang
Vice President: Bruce Lang
Estimated Sales: $10-20 Million
Number Employees: 20-49
Number of Products: 250
Type of Packaging: Consumer, Food Service, Private Label, Bulk
Brands:
Enerjuice
Mr. Spice
Tangy Bang

7708 **Lange Winery**
18380 NE Buena Vista Dr
Dundee, OR 97115 503-538-6476
Fax: 503-538-1938 don@langewinery.com
www.langewinery.com
Wines
Owner: Don Lange
Owner/CEO: Wendy Lange
Winemaker: Don Lange
Winemaker: Jesse Lange
General Manager: Jesse Lange
Estimated Sales: $680,000
Number Employees: 5-9
Brands:
Lange Winery

7709 **Langer Juice Company**
16195 Stephens St
City of Industry, CA 91745-1718 626-336-3100
Fax: 626-961-2021 bruce@langers.com
www.langers.com
Processor of juices
President: Nathan Langer
CEO: Bruce Langer
National Sales Manager: Tom Bottiaux
Estimated Sales: $160 Million
Number Employees: 200
Sq. footage: 140000
Type of Packaging: Consumer, Food Service, Private Label
Brands:
Dole
Langers Juice
Packers Pride
Tropicana

7710 **Langer Juice Company**
16195 Stephens St
City of Industry, CA 91745-1718 626-336-1666
Fax: 626-961-2021 bruce@langers.com
www.langers.com
Bottled and canned fruit juices, soft drinks
President: Nathan Langer
VP: Bruce Langer
Vice President: David Langer
National Sales Manager: Tom Bottiaux
Estimated Sales: $30-$50 Million
Number Employees: 20-49
Sq. footage: 140000
Brands:
Langers

7711 **Langtry Estate & Vineyards**
21000 Butts Canyon Rd
Middletown, CA 95461-9606 707-987-9127
Fax: 707-987-9351
tastingroom@langtryestate.com
www.langtryestate.com
Wines: Chardonnay, Petite Sirah, Cabernet Sauvignon, Sauvignon Blanc, Merlot, Pinot Grigio
Manager: Michael Pryor
Vice President/Winemaker: Bob Broman
Director Marketing: Karen Melander-Magoon
National Sales Manager: Greg Brolin
Estimated Sales: $20-50 Million
Number Employees: 1
Sq. footage: 72000
Brands:
Domaine Breton
Guenoc
Langtry

7712 **Lanthier Bakery**
PO Box 640
Alexandria, ON K0C 1A0
Canada 613-525-4981
Fax: 613-525-2818
Processor of bread and rolls
President/CEO: Marc Lanthier
Type of Packaging: Consumer, Food Service
Brands:
Lanthier

7713 **Lantic Sugar**
4026 Rue Notre-Dame E
Montreal, QC H1W 2K3
Canada 514-527-8686
Fax: 514-527-1401 info@lantic.ca
www.lantic.ca
Processor of sugar including liquid, bulk, soft, icing, granulated, coarse, medium, instant, etc
President: Edward Makin
Number Employees: 400
Type of Packaging: Consumer, Food Service, Bulk
Brands:
Lantic

7714 **Lapasta**
2727 Pittman Dr
Silver Spring, MD 20910-1807 301-588-1111
Fax: 301-588-7243 info_lapasta@verizon.net
www.lapastainc.com
Manufacture fresh, frozen, and shelf-life pasta
President: Alexis Konownitzine
Estimated Sales: $ 5 - 10 Million
Number Employees: 10-19

7715 **Larabar**
PO Box 18932
Denver, CO 80218 720-942-1155
Fax: 720-941-1158 800-543-2147
info@larabar.com www.larabar.com
All natural bars

7716 **Laredo Mexican Foods**
1616 Woodside Ave
Fort Wayne, IN 46816-3942 260-447-2576
Fax: 219-447-2577 800-252-7336
http://www.laredomexicanfoods.com
Processor and wholesaler/distributor of Mexican food products including salsa, tortillas and tortilla chips; serving the food service market
President: Benito Trevino
General Manager: Raul Trevino
VP: Reynol Trevino
Number Employees: 5-9
Parent Co: Tregar
Type of Packaging: Consumer, Food Service, Private Label, Bulk
Brands:
Don Pedro

7717 **Lark Fine Foods**
8 Scot's Way
Essex, MA 01929 978-768-0012
Fax: 978-890-7135 mamccormick@gmail.com
www.larkfinefoods.com
Cookies, crackers.
Marketing: Mary Ann McCormick

7718 **Larkin**
47-55 27th Street
Long Island City, NY 11101 718-937-2007
Fax: 718-937-3250 www.larkin.com
Chocolate bars, butter, cheese, other dairy and eggs, yogurt, honey, pickles & pickled vegetables, accesories/supplies i.e. picinic baskets.
Marketing: Adam Moskowitz

7719 **Laronga Bakery**
599 Somerville Ave
Somerville, MA 02143 617-625-8600
Fax: 617-625-1853 tcono@hotmail.com
www.larongabakery.com
Bakery products
President: Michael Ronga
Owner: Louis Ronga
Estimated Sales: $ 20-50 Million
Number Employees: 50-99
Brands:
La Ronga Bakery

7720 **Larry J. Williams Company**
2686 Savannah Hwy
Jesup, GA 31545-5511 912-427-7729
Fax: 912-427-0611
Shrimp, crab, oysters, scallps, flounder, etc.
President: Larry Williams
Estimated Sales: $ 1 - 3 Million
Number Employees: 20-49

7721 **Larry Matthews Company**
P.O.Box 60
Dennysville, ME 04628-0060 207-726-0609
Fax: 207-726-9571
Owner: Larry Matthews
Estimated Sales: $ 1 - 3 Million
Number Employees: 1-4

7722 **Larry Towns Company**
1601 W Douglas Ave
Wichita, KS 67213-4022 316-265-3474
Fax: 316-262-7770
Owner: Larry Towns
Estimated Sales: $300,000-500,000
Number Employees: 10-19

7723 **Larry's Beans Inc**
1509 Gavin St
Raleigh, NC 27608 919-828-1234
Fax: 919-833-4567 www.larrysbeans.com
wholesale coffee roaster
President/CEO: Larry Larson
CFO: Brad Lienhart
VP: Kevin Bobal
Marketing: Kyley Schmidt
Sales: Erik Iverson
Plant Manager: Neal England
Estimated Sales: $3.0 Million
Number Employees: 16

7724 **Larry's Sausage Corporation**
P.O.Box 4
Fayetteville, NC 28302-0004 910-483-5148
Fax: 910-483-2526
Processor of sausage
President: Sheila Abe
Estimated Sales: $ 5 - 10 Million
Number Employees: 20-49
Type of Packaging: Consumer

7725 **Larry's Vineyards & Winery**
3001 Furbeck Road
Altamont, NY 12009 518-355-7365
v1945p@juno.com
Wine
President/Owner: Larry Brooks
Estimated Sales: Under $500,000
Number Employees: 1-4
Brands:
Larry's Vineyards

7726 **Larsen Farms**
2650 N 2374 E
Hamer, ID 83425-0188 208-662-5501
Fax: 208-374-5497 lfsales@larsenfarms.com
www.larsenfarms.com
Dehydrated, prepared potatoes
President: Blaine Larsen
VP/Information Technology: Dave Ward
Director/Sales & Marketing: Lynn Ruffell
Estimated Sales: $100-500 Million
Number Employees: 300
Sq. footage: 125000

7727 **Larsen Packers**
326 W Main Street
Burwick, NS B0P 1E0
Canada 902-538-8060
Fax: 902-538-8694
Processor and exporter of bologna, salami, pepperoni and pork including fresh, cooked, bacon, ham, sausage and wieners; slaughtering services available; importer of fresh pork
President: Richard Young
Estimated Sales: $50-100 Million
Number Employees: 500-999
Sq. footage: 150000
Type of Packaging: Consumer, Food Service, Private Label, Bulk
Brands:
Brandywine
Farmland
Fine Old Tradition
Fireside
Larsen
Light N' Low
Simons
Trimcut

7728 **Larsen of Idaho**
P.O.Box 188
Hamer, ID 83425-0188 208-662-5501
Fax: 208-662-5568 800-767-6104
lfsales@larsenfarms.com www.larsenfarms.com
Processor and exporter of dehydrated potato products including flaked, sliced, diced and shredded; also, fresh potatoes available
President: Blaine Larsen
Estimated Sales: $ 10 - 20 Million
Number Employees: 20-49
Type of Packaging: Consumer, Food Service, Bulk

7729 **Larson Potato**
7147 137th Ave NE
Park River, ND 58270 701-284-6437
Fax: 701-284-6580
Processor of produce including potatoes
President: Gene Larson
Estimated Sales: $350,000
Number Employees: 1-4
Type of Packaging: Consumer

7730 **Lartigue Seafood**
25802 Chamberlain Drive
Daphne, AL 36526-6083 251-625-6202
President: Paul Lartigue Jr
Vice President: Paul Lartigue III
Number Employees: 5

7731 **Larue Pope Company**
2713 Abundance Street
New Orleans, LA 70122-5803 504-948-2234
Fax: 732-270-3033
Variety of prepared foods for restaurants.
Owner: Larue Pope

7732 **(HQ)Las Cruces Foods**
P.O.Box 98
Mesilla Park, NM 88047 575-526-2352
Fax: 575-523-5271
Processor of Mexican products including tortillas and taco shells
President: David Grijalva
VP: Miguel Grisalva
Estimated Sales: $461369
Number Employees: 10-19
Other Locations:
Las Cruces Foods
Albuquerque NM

7733 **Laska Stuff**
132 Griggs Street
Rochester, MI 48307-1414 248-652-8473
Specialty and organic food.
President: Steve Sparks

7734 **Lassen Foods**
5154 Hollister Ave
Santa Barbara, CA 93111-2526 805-683-7696
Fax: 805-683-7627 www.lassens.com
Health food store
Owner: Peter Lassen
Estimated Sales: Under $500,000
Number Employees: 10-19
Sq. footage: 5000
Parent Co: Lassen Foods
Type of Packaging: Consumer, Food Service, Private Label, Bulk
Brands:
Lassen

7735 **Latah Creek Wine Cellars**
13030 E Indiana Ave
Spokane Valley, WA 99216 509-926-0164
Fax: 509-926-0710 mconway@latahcreek.com
www.latahcreek.com
Wines
President: Mike Conway
VP: Ellena Conway
Estimated Sales: $340,000
Number Employees: 1-4
Type of Packaging: Private Label

7736 **Latcham Vineyards**
P.O.Box 80
Mt Aukum, CA 95656-0080 530-620-6642
Fax: 530-620-5578 800-750-5591
latcham@directcon.net www.latcham.com
Wines
President: Frank Latcham
Winemaker: Craig Boyd
Sales Manager: Margaret Latcham
Estimated Sales: $500,000-$1 Million
Number Employees: 10-19
Brands:
Barbera
Port

7737 **Late July Organic Snacks**
3166 Main St
Barnstable, MA 2630 508-362-5859
Fax: 508-362-5868 salesinfo@latejuly.com
www.latejuly.com
Organic snacks
President/Owner: Nicole Dawes
Marketing: Darby Ziruk

7738 **Latitude**
37 West Shore Road
Huntington, NY 11743 631-659-3374
Fax: 631-659-3376 latitudeltd@aol.com
www.escalade-latitude.com
Food ingredients manufacturer; including: sweeteners, vitamins, antioxidants and preservatives
Director: Laurel Eastman
Office Manager: Elissa Farrugia

7739 **Latonia Bakery**
3612 Decoursey Ave
Covington, KY 41015-1438 859-491-8855
Fax: 859-431-4169
Baked goods
President: Bernie Holmer
Estimated Sales: Under $500,000
Number Employees: 5-9

7740 **Latteria Soresina**
35 Meadow Street #306
Brooklyn, NY 11206-1710 347-725-4096
Fax: 718-678-9520 jpbricca@thefoodsolution.net
www.latteriasoresina.it

7741 **Laura Chenel's Chevre**
22085 Carneros Vineyard Way
Sonoma, CA 95476 707-996-4477
Fax: 707-996-1816
Goat cheese
Manager: John Van Dyke
Estimated Sales: $ 10-20 Million
Number Employees: 20-49
Brands:
Laura Chenel's

7742 **Laura Paige Candy Company**
13 Jeanne Drive
Newburgh, NY 12550-1702 845-566-4209
Fax: 845-566-4766 sales@laurapaige.com
www.marshalls.com
Processor of lollipops including hand painted seasonal and regular assortment
President: Elissa Koenig
Chairman: Dr. Louis Korngold
Vice President: Tracey Chalupa
Estimated Sales: Less than $500,000
Number Employees: 30
Sq. footage: 8000
Type of Packaging: Consumer, Food Service

7743 **Laura's French Baking Company**
6721 S Alameda St
Los Angeles, CA 90001-2123 323-585-5144
Fax: 323-585-0591 888-353-5144
sales@labakery.com www.labakery.com
Processor of bread, croissants, danish, cakes and pastries
President: Sterling Kim
Estimated Sales: Below $ 5 Million
Number Employees: 20-49
Type of Packaging: Food Service
Brands:
Laura's

7744 **Laurel Glen Vineyard**
P.O.Box 1419
Glen Ellen, CA 95442-1419 707-526-3914
Fax: 707-526-9801 denise@laurelglen.com
www.laurelglen.com
Wines
Proprietor: Patrick Campbell
Winemaker: Patrick Campbell
Estimated Sales: $ 4 Million
Number Employees: 5-9
Number of Brands: 5
Type of Packaging: Private Label

7745 **Laurel Hill Foods**
39 Franklin McKay Road
Attleboro, MA 02703 877-759-8141
Fax: 508-226-7060 sales@laurelhillfoods.com
www.laurelhillfoods.com
Chips, Full-line snacks, other snacks.
Marketing: Jen Huntley-Corbin

7746 **Laurent Meat Market**
528 Avenue A
Marrero, LA 70072-2117 504-341-1771
Fax: 504-341-0299
Processor and meat packer of fresh and smoked sausages, hogshead cheese, andouille, hamburger and hot patties
Owner: Layton Laurent Sr
Estimated Sales: $500000
Number Employees: 1-4
Type of Packaging: Consumer, Food Service, Bulk

7747 **Lava Cap Winery**
2221 Fruitridge Rd
Placerville, CA 95667 530-621-0175
Fax: 530-621-4399 lavacap@calweb.com
www.lavacap.com
Wines
President: David Jones
General Manager: Jeanne Jones
National Sales Director: Bill Johnston
Tour Coordinator: Julia Rosenkrantz
Winemaker: Thomas Jones
Vineyard Manager: Charles Jones
Estimated Sales: Below $ 5 Million
Number Employees: 10-19
Number of Brands: 1

Number of Products: 1
Sq. footage: 24000
Type of Packaging: Private Label

7748 Lavash Corporation
2835 Newell St
Los Angeles, CA 90039 323-663-5249
Fax: 323-663-8062
aminassi@westernfiltercor.com
Processor of flatbread
Manager: Edmund Hartounian
Director Marketing: Arthur Minassian
National Sales Manager: Adam Cardenas
Cust./Technical Support Manager: Lori Akian
Estimated Sales: Below $ 5 Million
Number Employees: 10-19
Brands:
Wrap'n Roll

7749 Lavazza Premium Coffee Corporation
3 Park Ave Fl 35
New York, NY 10016 212-725-8800
Fax: 212-725-9475 800-466-3287
info@lavazzausa.com www.lavazzausa.com
Lavazza coffees
General Manager: Ennio Ranaboldo
Founder: Luigi Lavazza
Estimated Sales: Below $ 5 Million
Number Employees: 20-49
Brands:
Lavazza

7750 Lawler Foods
P.O.Box 2558
Humble, TX 77347 281-540-3321
Fax: 281-446-3806 desserts@lawlers.com
www.lawlers.com
Processor of frozen cheesecakes, pies, brownies and sheetcakes
President: Bill Lawler
CEO: Carol Lawler
Estimated Sales: $10-20 Million
Number Employees: 160
Sq. footage: 110000
Type of Packaging: Consumer, Food Service, Private Label, Bulk

7751 Lawrence Foods
2200 Lunt Ave
Elk Grove Village, IL 60007 847-437-2400
Fax: 847-437-2567 800-323-7848
info@lawrencefoods.com
www.lawrencefoods.com
Processor of bakers' and confectioners' supplies including fruit and cream fillings, icings, glazes, preserves and jellies; available in cans, pails and flexible pouches
President/COO: Marc Lawrence
CFO: Floyd Andrew
Quality Control Director: Darrell Patt
Marketing Manager: Brooke Lawrence
VP Sales: Mark Labar
Human Resource Manager: Erica Moser
Manufacturing Director: Casey Bouton
Purchasing Manager: Michelle English
Estimated Sales: $15 Million
Number Employees: 98
Sq. footage: 200000
Type of Packaging: Food Service, Private Label, Bulk
Brands:
Lawrence

7752 Lawrences Delights
3126 Oakcliff Industrial St
Doraville, GA 30340-2902 770-451-7774
Fax: 770-451-7623 800-568-0021
aboulos@lawrencedelights.com
www.lddelights.us
Processor and exporter of baked goods including nondairy and sugar-free walnut baklava, chocolate pecan logs and cashew lady fingers
President: Emile Bseibess
Estimated Sales: $ 3 - 5 Million
Number Employees: 10-19
Sq. footage: 5000
Parent Co: Le Liban
Type of Packaging: Food Service, Private Label, Bulk
Brands:
Lawrence's Delights

7753 Lawry's Foods
222 E Huntington Drive
Monrovia, CA 91016-8006 626-930-8870
Fax: 626-930-8851 800-595-8917
bote@usmpagency.com www.lawrys.com
Processor of prepared gravy and sauce mixes, marinades, seasoned salt and pepper, lemon pepper, garlic spread, etc
President: Thomas Fueling
COO: John Heil
Director Marketing: Joe Scaccia
Estimated Sales: $ 20 - 50 Million
Number Employees: 20-49
Parent Co: Unilever USA
Type of Packaging: Consumer
Brands:
Adolph's Food Seasoning
Lawry's Chicken Saute Sauce
Lawry's Seasonings and Spices
Tio Sancho Mexican Foods

7754 Lax & Mandel Bakery
14439 Cedar Rd
Cleveland, OH 44121-3309 216-382-8877
Fax: 216-382-8875 kosher@laxandmandel.com
www.laxandmandel.com
Cakes, pastries
Co-Owner: Sheldon Weiser
Co-Owner: Helen Weiser
Co-Owner: Jeffrey Weiser
Estimated Sales: $500,000-$1 Million
Number Employees: 3

7755 Laxson Provision Company
264 W Lachapelle
San Antonio, TX 78204-1853 210-226-8397
Fax: 210-226-0537
President: Gary Laxson
Estimated Sales: $ 20-50 Million
Number Employees: 20-49

7756 Lay Packing Company
3515 Neal Dr
Knoxville, TN 37918-5255 865-922-4320
Fax: 865-922-4321
Processor of beef, pork, lamb and veal
Owner: F L Lay
Estimated Sales: $ 1 - 3 Million
Number Employees: 10-19
Parent Co: Lay Packing Company
Type of Packaging: Consumer, Food Service, Private Label, Bulk

7757 Lay's Fine Foods
622 East Jackson Ave.
Knoxville, TN 37902 865-522-1147
Fax: 865-522-9575 800-251-9636
www.laysmarket.com
Processed meat products
President: Joe Lay
Sales Manager: Ferril Maddox
Estimated Sales: $ 20-50 Million
Number Employees: 275
Sq. footage: 175
Type of Packaging: Private Label, Bulk

7758 Laymon Candy Company
276 Commercial Rd
San Bernardino, CA 92408 909-825-4408
Fax: 909-825-4693
Processor of candy including brittles, fudge, chocolate creams, chews, nut clusters and taffy. Distributor for thirty-two large candy manufacturers
Owner: Paul T Applen
VP/Owner: Paul Applen
Marketing: Linda Laymon-Applen
Estimated Sales: $ 5 - 10 Million
Number Employees: 20-49
Number of Brands: 2028
Number of Products: 122
Sq. footage: 43000
Brands:
Laymon's

7759 Lazy Creek Vineyard
4741 Highway 128
Philo, CA 95466 888-529-9275
Fax: 707-895-3623 chandler@lazycreek.com
www.lazycreekvineyards.com
Estate wines
President: Josh Chandler
VP Marketing: Mary Beth Chandler
Estimated Sales: $ 5-10 Million
Number Employees: 10-19
Brands:
Lazy Creek Vineyards

7760 Lazzaroni USA
299 Market St # 160
Saddle Brook, NJ 07663-5312 201-368-1240
Fax: 201-368-1262
Manufacturer and distributor of chocolates and cookies
President: Stefano Tombetti
Executive VP: Kathy Ecoffey

7761 Le Bleu Corporation
3134 Cornatzer Rd
Advance, NC 27006 336-998-2894
Fax: 336-998-4167 800-854-4471
info@lebleu.com www.lebleu.com
Manufacturer and distributor of bottled water
President/CEO: Jerry Smith
Owner/Finance/HR & Sales Executive: Andy Scotchie
Public Relations Director: Debbie Pullen
Plant Manager: Ed Hauser
Estimated Sales: $17700000
Number Employees: 115
Sq. footage: 150000
Type of Packaging: Consumer
Brands:
Le Bleu Bottled Water
Nascar Bottled Water

7762 Le Boeuf & Associates
PO Box 932
North Falmouth, MA 02556-0932 78- 4-9 76
Fax: 508-884-2040 800-444-5666
nmleboeuf@msn.com
Wines
President: Normand LeBoeuf
VP: Christopher LeBoeuf
CFO: Chris LeBoeuf
VP: Steve LeBoeuf
VP Marketing: Chris Le Boeuf
Operations Manager: Louise Setterlund
Estimated Sales: $ 20-30 Million
Number Employees: 10
Type of Packaging: Private Label
Brands:
Emerald Bay

7763 Le Caramel
8047 El Capitan Dr
La Mesa, CA 91942-5515 619-562-0713
Fax: 619-562-1604 kugner@le-caramel.com
www.le-caramel.com
Caramels, dessert toppings (i.e. fudge sauce, caramel sauce, whipped cream, etc.).
Marketing: Christine Kugener

7764 Le Chic French Bakery
1043 Washington Ave
Miami Beach, FL 33139 305-673-5522
Fax: 305-673-5522
Bakery products including baguettes, buttery croissants, danishes; as well as European style cakes, pies, tarts and pastries
President: Medardo Sanchez
Estimated Sales: $ 2.5-5 Million
Number Employees: 5-9

7765 Le Frois Foods Corporation
56 High St
Brockport, NY 14420-2058 585-637-5003
Fax: 585-637-2855
Vinegar
President: Duncan Tsay
Estimated Sales: Under $500,000
Number Employees: 5-9

7766 Le Grand Confectionary,Inc.
4527 Harlin Drive
Sacramento, CA 95826 888-361-2125
Fax: 916-361-2150
customerservice@legrandtruffles.com
www.legrandtruffles.com
Other lifestyle, chocolate truffles, other chocolate, other candy, gift pakcs.
Marketing: Jack Shaw

7767 Le Notre, Alain & MarieBaker
7070 Allensby St
Houston, TX 77022-4322 713-692-0077
Fax: 713-692-7399 800-536-6873
lenotre@wt.net www.ciaml.com

Processor, importer and exporter of frozen strudel, muffins, cakes, cookies, danish, etc
Owner: Alain Lenotre
VP: Marie Le Notre
Estimated Sales: $2 Million
Number Employees: 25
Sq. footage: 30000
Type of Packaging: Private Label

7768 **Le Pique-Nique**
3871 Piedmont Avenue
Oakland, CA 94611-5378 800-400-6454
Fax: 510-339-7141 www.thomasnet.com
Processor of sausage including chicken, turkey, chicken/apple, cranberries, orange, maple syrup, etc
President: Dennis Donegan
Estimated Sales: Under $500,000
Number Employees: 1-4
Type of Packaging: Consumer, Food Service
Brands:
Calypso Caribbean
Tandoori
Thai Chicken

7769 **(HQ)Le Sueur Cheese**
719 N Main St
Le Sueur, MN 56058 507-665-3353
Fax: 507-665-2820 800-757-7611
info@daviscofoods.com www.daviscofoods.com
Manufacturer and exporter of variety of cheese including low-fat, no-fat, enzyme-modified cheeses and other customer specified varieties
President: Mark Davis
VP: Marty Davis
VP: Mitch Davis
VP: Jon Davis
Estimated Sales: $112 Million
Number Employees: 100-249
Other Locations:
Le Sueur Cheese Plant
Jerome ID

7770 **LeHigh Valley Dairies**
880 Allentown Rd
Lansdale, PA 19446 215-855-8205
Fax: 215-855-9834
www.lehighvalleydairyfarms.com
Processor of milk, cream and juice
Executive Director: James Macri
Sales/Marketing Executive: Frank Mariello
VP Operations: Jim Macrey
Number Employees: 100-249
Parent Co: Suiza Dairy Group
Type of Packaging: Consumer, Food Service

7771 **LePage Bakeries**
P.O.Box 1900
11 Adamian Dr
Auburn, ME 04210-8304 207-783-9161
Fax: 1 2-7 7-3 33 lbck@lepagebakeries.com
www.barowskys.com
Manufacturer of bread, donuts and english muffins
President: Andrew Barowsky
Chairman: Albert Lepage
VP Marketing: Regis Lepage
Estimated Sales: $300,000-500,000
Number Employees: 40
Brands:
Bakers' Select
Barowsky's
Country Kitchen

7772 **LeRaysville Cheese**
Rr 2 Box 71a
Le Raysville, PA 18829-9621 570-744-2554
Fax: 570-744-1050 800-595-5196
Cheese
President: James Amory
Estimated Sales: Less than $500,000
Number Employees: 5-9
Type of Packaging: Private Label

7773 **Lea & Perrins**
15-01 Pollitt Dr
Fair Lawn, NJ 07410 201-791-1600
Fax: 201-791-8945 800-289-5797
lpinfo@danone.com www.leaperrins.com
Manufacturer of sauces and condiments
President/CEO: Ralph Abrams
Estimated Sales: $24 Million
Number Employees: 100-249
Parent Co: Danone Group
Type of Packaging: Consumer, Food Service
Brands:
HP
LEA & PERRINS SAUCES

7774 **Leach Farms**
W1102 Buttercup Ct
Berlin, WI 54923 920-361-1880
Fax: 920-361-4474 www.leachfarms.com
Processor of fresh and frozen spinach, and celery
President: Thomas Leach
CFO: Bill Zander
Marketing Manager: Marybeth Yonke
Estimated Sales: $620,000
Number Employees: 8
Sq. footage: 10000
Type of Packaging: Food Service, Private Label

7775 **Leach Farms Inc.**
W1102 Buttercup Ct
Berlin, WI 54923-8327 920-361-1880
Fax: 920-361-4474 leachfarms.com
Processor of fresh and IQF celery
President: Thomas Leach
CFO: John Zander
Sales Manager: Steve Wahlgreen
Plant Manager: Brian Thiel
Estimated Sales: $ 30-50 Million
Number Employees: 100-249
Sq. footage: 10000
Type of Packaging: Bulk

7776 **Leader Candies**
132 Harrison Place
Brooklyn, NY 11237-1522 718-366-6900
Fax: 718-417-1723
Processor and exporter of candies including hard, caramels, jelly beans, novelties, lollypops, filled, fundraising, hard toffee, starch jellies, bagged and nonchocolate; also, nonfrozen freeze pops available
President: Howard Kastin
Sales: Helen Garfield
VP Manufacturing: Malcom Kastin
Number Employees: 155
Sq. footage: 80000
Type of Packaging: Consumer, Food Service, Private Label, Bulk
Brands:
Beaver Pop
Freez-A-Pops
Kastin's
Leader
Lolly Lo's

7777 **Leahy Orchards**
1772 Route 209
Franklin Centre, QC J0S 1E0
Canada 450-827-2544
Fax: 450-827-2470 800-667-7380
doug@applesnax.com www.applesnax.com
Processor of apple sauce in cans, jars and portion packs; also, pie filling
President/CEO: Michael Leahy
CEO: Beahy
VP Finance/Administration: Guylaine Yelle
VP Sales/Marketing/R&D: Doug Anderson
Purchasing Director: Philip Seguin
Number Employees: 50-99
Type of Packaging: Consumer
Brands:
Apple Snax

7778 **Leams**
906 Texas Court
Hutchinson, KS 67502-5136 316-662-4287
Fax: 620-662-4287
Sweet and savory flavors
President: Alice Grigrest
Number Employees: 1-4

7779 **Leatex Chemical Company**
2722 N Hancock St
Philadelphia, PA 19133 215-739-2000
Fax: 215-739-5910
Manufacturer of sulphonated castor oils
President: Kevin Mc Chesney
VP Marketing: L Kevin McChesney
Estimated Sales: $5000000
Number Employees: 10-19

7780 **Leavenworth Coffee Roast**
10171 Chumstick Hwy Ste B
Leavenworth, WA 98826 509-548-1428
Fax: 509-548-4251 800-246-2761
java@alpinecoffeeroasters.com
www.alpinecoffeeroasters.com
Processor of coffee including 25 blends
President: Dale Harrison
VP: Veronica Harrison
Estimated Sales: $ 1-2.5 Million
Number Employees: 10-19
Type of Packaging: Consumer, Food Service
Brands:
Chatter Creek

7781 **Leaves Pure Teas**
7435 E Tierra Buena Ln
Scottsdale, AZ 85260 480-998-8807
Fax: 650-583-1163 800-242-8807
teas@leaves.com www.leaves.com
Teas
President & Chief Operations Officer: Rommie Flammer
Co Founder, Co Chairman, Co CEO: Dan Schweiker
Operations Manager: Jeff Morris
Number Employees: 5-9
Type of Packaging: Private Label
Brands:
Leaves Pure Tea

7782 **(HQ)Leavitt Corporation**
100 Santilli Hwy
Everett, MA 02149 617-389-2600
Fax: 617-387-9085 contact@teddie.com
www.teddie.com
Processor and exporter of peanut butter and salted and unsalted cashews and peanuts; importer of raw cashews
President/CEO: James Hintlian
Executive VP: Mark Hintlian
Quality Control: Christopher Hayes
Operations Manager: Joseph Saraceno
Production Manager: Jack Skamarakas
Purchasing Manager: Frank Ciampa
Estimated Sales: $10-24.9 Million
Number Employees: 50-99
Type of Packaging: Consumer, Food Service, Private Label, Bulk
Brands:
Americana
River Queen
River-Queen
Teddie

7783 **Lebanon Cheese Company**
3 Railroad Ave
Lebanon, NJ 8833 908-236-2611
Fax: 908-236-6870 jglotito@blast.net
Cheese
President: Joe Lotito
Estimated Sales: $3 Million
Number Employees: 5-9
Brands:
Lebanon Cheese

7784 **Lebermuth Company**
P.O.Box 4103
South Bend, IN 46634 574-259-7000
Fax: 574-258-7450 800-648-1123
info@lebermuth.com www.lebermuth.com
A world-class fragrance and flavor company that empowers our passionate and creative team to provide quality and innovative products using expertise and technology, which enhances and strengthens our partners' brand identity.
President: Robert Brown
CEO: Irvin Brown
Vice President: Alan Brown
VP Marketing/Public Relations: Alan Brown
Production Manager: Mike Ryan
Plant Manager: Robert Hall
Purchasing Manager: Jim Gates
Estimated Sales: $12500000
Number Employees: 50
Sq. footage: 45000
Type of Packaging: Bulk

7785 **Lebermuth Company**
P.O.Box 4103
South Bend, IN 46634 574-259-7000
Fax: 574-258-7450 800-648-1123
lbrown@lebermuth.com www.labermuth.com

Peppermint processing, fragrances and flavors
Chairman: Irvin Brown
President: Rob Brown
Vice President: Robert Brown
VP Administration: Alan Brown
Estimated Sales: $ 5-10 Million
Number Employees: 50
Brands:
The Lebermuth

7786 **Leblanc Seafood**
PO Box 509
Lafitte, LA 70067-0509 504-689-2631
Fax: 504-689-4303
Seafood

7787 **Lecoq Cuisine Corp**
35 Union Avenue
Bridgeport, CT 06607 203-334-1010
Fax: 203-334-1800 croissant@lecoqcuisine.com
www.lecoqcuisine.com
Cakes/pastries, frozen desserts, full-line frozen, hors d'oeuvres/appetizers, other frozen, puffed snacks.
Marketing: Eric Lecoq

7788 **Ledonne Brothers Bakery**
143 Chestnut St
Roseto, PA 18013 610-588-0423
cbath@epix.net
Processor of breads: anchiove, French, Italian, sweet and Viennese, also; tomato pies
Co-Owner: Robert Bath
Co-Owner: Connie Bath
Estimated Sales: Less than $500,000
Number Employees: 1-4
Type of Packaging: Consumer

7789 **Lee Andersons's CovaldaDates**
51392 Harrison Street
Coachella, CA 92236-1563 760-398-3441
Marketing Manager: Ann Jolly
Estimated Sales: Under $500,000
Number Employees: 1-4

7790 **Lee Kum Kee**
3056 Whitestone Expy
Flushing, NY 11354-1966 718-353-3826
Fax: 718-821-2989 800-346-7562
www.lkk.com
Processor, importer and exporter of condiments and sauces including chili
General Manager: Gary Cheung
Estimated Sales: $190,000
Number Employees: 3
Sq. footage: 20000
Parent Co: Lee Kum Kee Company
Type of Packaging: Consumer, Food Service, Private Label, Bulk
Brands:
Lee Kum Kee
Panda

7791 **(HQ)Lee Kum Kee**
14455 Don Julian Rd
City of Industry, CA 91746-3102 626-709-1888
Fax: 626-709-1899 800-654-5082
customer_service@lkk.com www.lkk.com
Asian condiments and cooking sauces
President: Alan Chang
Marketing Manager: Betty Tsang
Estimated Sales: $ 10-20 Million
Number Employees: 50-99
Type of Packaging: Private Label
Brands:
Choy Sun
Full House
Kum Chun Brand
Lee Kum Kee
Lee Kum Kee Premium
Panda Brand

7792 **Lee Seed Company**
2242 Iowa 182 Ave
Inwood, IA 51240 712-753-4403
Fax: 712-753-4542 800-736-6530
info@soynuts.com www.soynuts.com
Roasted soynuts in 16 flavors
Co-Owner: Paul Lee
Co-Owner: Joyce Lee
Marketing Director: Scott Lee
Estimated Sales: $ 3 - 5 Million
Number Employees: 10-19
Type of Packaging: Consumer, Private Label, Bulk
Brands:
Super Soynuts

7793 **Lee's Century Farms**
81356 Lower Dry Creek Road
Milton Freewater, OR 97862-7323 541-938-6532
Fax: 541-938-0705
President: Deborah Lee
VP Sales/Marketing: John Lee
Estimated Sales: Less than $500,000
Number Employees: 1-4
Brands:
Lee's

7794 **Lee's Food Products**
1233 Queen Street E
Toronto, ON M4L 1C2
Canada 416-465-2407
Processor of canned soy sauce and Chinese vegetables including bamboo shoots, water chestnuts and mushrooms; importer of mushrooms, instant noodles and mini corn
President: Marilyn Wong
Secretary/Treasurer: L Wong
Type of Packaging: Consumer, Food Service

7795 **Lee's Ice Cream**
11431 Cronhill Dr # C
Owings Mills, MD 21117-2269 410-581-0234
Fax: 410-581-7044 888-669-5337
info@leesicecream.com www.leesicecream.com
Makers of premium gourmet ice cream products available in a variety of flavors.
Founder: Leon Garfield
Co-Founder: Jaques Rubin
Co-Founder: Steven Rubin
CEO: Steve Rubin
Number Employees: 100-249

7796 **Leech Lake Reservation**
115 6th St NE
Cass Lake, MN 56633 218-335-8200
Fax: 218-335-8309
Processor of natural lake and river wild rice
Manager: Cheryl Dunn
Number Employees: 1-4
Brands:
Leech Lake

7797 **Leech Lake Wild Rice**
51664 County Road 137
Deer River, MN 56636 218-246-2746
Fax: 218-246-2748 877-246-0620
llwrice@paulbunyan.net
www.leechlakewildricecompany.com
Wild rice
Prime Manager: George Donnell
CFO: Mike Ziemer
Quality Control: Christine Cummings
R & D: Steve Mortinson
Public Relations: Don June
Production Manager: George Donnell
Estimated Sales: Below $ 5 Million
Number Employees: 5
Type of Packaging: Private Label
Brands:
Leech Lake Wild Rice

7798 **Leelanau Fruit Company**
2900 S West Bay Shore Dr
Suttons Bay, MI 49682 231-271-3514
Fax: 231-271-4367 info@leelanaufruit.com
www.leelanaufruit.com
Processer and exporter of frozen and brined cherries and strawberries
President: Glen Lacross
General Manager: Allen Steimel
Estimated Sales: $ 1 - 3 Million
Number Employees: 100-249
Type of Packaging: Consumer, Food Service, Private Label, Bulk

7799 **Leelanau Wine Cellars**
P.O.Box 68
Omena, MI 49674 231-386-5201
Fax: 231-386-9797 800-782-8128
lisa@leelanaucellars.com
www.leelanaucellars.com
Wines
Manager: Tony Lenyth
General Manager: Bob Jacobson
Estimated Sales: $ 5-10 Million
Number Employees: 10-19
Brands:
Leelanau

7800 **Lees Sausage Company**
1054 Neeses Hwy
Orangeburg, SC 29115-8606 803-534-5517
Fax: 803-531-2809
Manufacturer of sausage, liver pudding, BBQ meat and sauce, chili, and BBQ hash
President: Walter Lee Jr
Estimated Sales: $18 Million
Number Employees: 20-49
Type of Packaging: Consumer, Private Label

7801 **Leeward Resources**
401 E Pratt Street
Suite 354
Baltimore, MD 21202-3117 410-837-9003
Fax: 410-837-7527 bbrown@leeward.com
www.leeward.com
Spices, herbal extracts, botantials, essential oils, fruit juices
President: William Brown
Estimated Sales: $ 3.5 Million
Number Employees: 3

7802 **Leeward Winery**
2511 Victoria Ave
Oxnard, CA 93035-2931 805-656-5054
Fax: 805-656-5092
Processor and exporter of table wines
President: Charles Brigham
Co-Owner: Chuck Gardner
Estimated Sales: $260,000
Number Employees: 4
Sq. footage: 8500
Type of Packaging: Consumer, Food Service
Brands:
Leeward

7803 **Lef Bleuges Marinor Incorporated**
1015 Rg Double
St-Felicien, QC G8K 2M1
Canada 418-679-4577
Fax: 418-679-9602
Processor of frozen blueberries - exports worldwide
President: Jeanne-Pierre Senneville

7804 **Lefse House**
5014 48th Street
Camrose, AB T4V 1M1
Canada 780-672-7555
Fax: 780-608-2377 info@theLefseHouse.ca
www.thelefsehouse.ca
Processor of Scandinavian all natural baked goods including potato lefse, flatbread and specialty items
President/CFO: Bernell Odegard
Purchasing Manager: Helen Lien
Estimated Sales: Under $300,000
Number Employees: 5-9
Sq. footage: 1600
Type of Packaging: Consumer, Food Service
Brands:
Lefse House

7805 **Left Hand Brewing Company**
1265 Boston Ave
Longmont, CO 80501 303-772-0258
Fax: 303-772-9572
brewer@lefthandbrewing.com
www.lefthandbrewing.com
Processor and wholesaler/distributor of English style ale, stout and porter; also, German style lager and weiss beer
President: Jon Wallace
Quality Control: Andy Brown
Marketing/Sales/Public Relations: Chris Lennert
Operations Manager: Joe Schiraldi
Estimated Sales: Below $ 5 Million
Number Employees: 20-49
Sq. footage: 13000
Type of Packaging: Food Service, Bulk
Brands:
Deep Cover Brown
Imperial
Juju Ginger
Left Hand Black Jack
Sawtooth
Tabernash

7806 **Lefty Spices**
2062 Crain Highway
Waldorf, MD 20601-3147 301-885-1817
Fax: 240-607-6721 walternashjr@leftyspices.ocm
www.leftyspices.com
Flour, full-line baking mixes and ingredients, other meat/game/pate, BBQ sauce, other sauces, seasonings and cooking enhancers, rubs, spices.
Marketing: Walter Nash Jr

7807 **Legend Brewing Company**
321 W 7th St
Richmond, VA 23224 804-232-8871
Fax: 804-231-3417 www.legendbrewing.com
Processor of beer, ale, stout and lager
President: Thomas E Martin
Brewmaster: Brad Mortensen
Estimated Sales: Below $ 5 Million
Number Employees: 20-49
Type of Packaging: Consumer, Food Service
Brands:
Brown Ale
Legand Brown
Legand Pilsner
Porter

7808 **Legumes Plus**
PO Box 380
Fairfield, WA 99012-0380 509-283-2347
Fax: 509-283-2314 800-845-1349
Processor and exporter of soup mixes including lentil and split pea; also, chili
President: Judy Hahner
Marketing Director: Jan Moore
Plant Manager: Gial Ohosen
Number Employees: 5-9
Sq. footage: 8600
Type of Packaging: Consumer, Food Service, Private Label, Bulk
Brands:
Legumes Plus
Lentils of the Palouse

7809 **Lehi Roller Mills**
833 E Main St
Lehi, UT 84043 801-768-4401
Fax: 801-768-4557 800-660-4346
sdejohn@lehirollermills.com
www.lehirollermill.com
Processor of flour, feed and meal; also, mills
President: Sherm Robinson
COO: Brock Knight
CFO: Kevin David
Estimated Sales: $20-50 Million
Number Employees: 20-49
Type of Packaging: Private Label
Brands:
Peacock
Turkey

7810 **Lehi Valley Trading Company**
4955 E McKellips Rd
Mesa, AZ 85215 480-684-1402
Fax: 480-461-1804 info@lehivalley.com
www.lehivalley.com
beans, candy, dried fruit, granola, ice cream mix-ins, nuts and seeds, popcorn and nuggets, snack items and trail mix
President/Owner: Lewis Freeman
Estimated Sales: $7.7 Million
Number Employees: 50

7811 **Lehr Brothers**
12901 Packing House Road
Edison, CA 93220 661-366-3244
Fax: 661-366-1449 spudron1@aol.com
Processor and exporter of potatoes
President: Ronald Lehr
VP: Ronald Lehr Jr
Estimated Sales: $17155306
Number Employees: 50
Sq. footage: 22500
Type of Packaging: Bulk

7812 **Leiby's Premium Ice Cream**
116 Mountain Rd
Tamaqua, PA 18252 570-668-2399
Fax: 570-668-6065 877-453-4297
sales.leibys@earthlink.net
www.leibysicecream.com
Processor of ice cream including mixes
President: Keith Zimmerman
VP/Secretary: William Parks
Estimated Sales: $ 5 - 10 Million
Number Employees: 10-19
Sq. footage: 30000
Type of Packaging: Consumer, Bulk

7813 **Leidenfrost Vineyards**
P.O.Box 221
Hector, NY 14841
Wines
Owner: John Leidenfrost
Estimated Sales: $340,000
Number Employees: 4
Brands:
Leidenfrost Vineyards

7814 **Leidenheimer Baking Company**
1501 Simon Bolivar Ave
New Orleans, LA 70113 504-525-1575
Fax: 504-525-1596 info@leidenheimer.com
www.leidenheimer.com
Manufacturer of fresh and frozen New Orleans style French breads and rolls
President: Robert J Whann Iv III
Plant Manager: Terry Park
Estimated Sales: $20 Million
Number Employees: 50-99
Sq. footage: 40000
Type of Packaging: Consumer, Food Service

7815 **Leidy's**
266 W Cherry Ln
Souderton, PA 18964 215-723-4606
Fax: 215-721-2003 800-222-2319
dans@leidys.com www.leidys.com
Pork processing
President: Andrew Leidy
Co-Owner: Terry Leidy
CFO: Scott Schanzembach
Quality Control: John Capra
Sales Manager: Duane Zoscin
Plant Engineer: Denny Gehman
VP Production: Andy Leidy
Estimated Sales: $ 20-50 Million
Number Employees: 100-249
Type of Packaging: Consumer, Bulk
Brands:
Leidy's

7816 **Leigh Olivers**
PO Box 8346
Tyler, TX 75711 903-245-9183
Fax: 903-421-1669
customerservice@leigholivers.com
www.leigholivers.com
Dips/salsa and cheeses
CEO: Leigh Vickery
VP: Ron Vickery

7817 **(HQ)Leighton's Honey**
1203 W Commerce Ave
Haines City, FL 33844 863-422-1773
Fax: 863-421-2299 www.leightonshoney.com
Manufacturer and packer of honey
President: Harry Posey
VP: Janet McCord
Estimated Sales: $22 Million
Number Employees: 10-19
Type of Packaging: Consumer, Food Service, Private Label, Bulk
Brands:
LEIGHTON'S
ORANGE BLOSSOM SPECIAL

7818 **Leiner Davis Gelatin**
366 N Broadway
Jericho, NY 11753-2025 516-942-4940
Fax: 516-822-4044
cheryl.michaels@pbleiner.com
www.gelatin.com
Processor, exporter and importer of food grade gelatin including kosher; also, technical service available
NAFTA Sales Manager: Cheryl Michaels
Estimated Sales: $ 5 - 10 Million
Number Employees: 5-9
Brands:
Leiner Davis

7819 **Leiner Health Products**
901 E 233rd St
Carson, CA 90745 310-835-8400
Fax: 310-952-7760 info@leiner.com
www.leiner.com
Manufacturer of vitamins
President: Gale Bansussen
CEO: Bob Kaminski
CEO: Robert R Reynolds
Manager Sales/Marketing: Tom Bovich
Number Employees: 500-999
Brands:
Beneflex
Bumble Bee
Cardio Discovery
LiquiMax
Natural Life
Omega Care
Pharmacist Formula

7820 **Leininkugel Brewing Company**
124 E. Elm Street
PO Box 337
Chippewa Falls, WI 54729-1318 88- 53- 643
Fax: 715-723-7158 www.leinie.com
Alcoholic malt beverages, beer
President: Bill Leinenkugel
CFO: Dave Kahn
VP Marketing: Richard Leininkugel
Point-of-Sale Manager: John Leininkugel
Operations Manager: Pete Dawson
Estimated Sales: $ 5-10 Million
Number Employees: 50-99
Brands:
Amber Light
Berry Weiss
Honey Weiss
Leinenkugel Original
Light
Northwoods
Oktoberfest
Red

7821 **Leisure Time Ice & Spring Water**
P.O.Box 168
4496 State Route 42
Kiamesha Lake, NY 12751 845-794-7040
Fax: 845-794-0016 800-443-1412
http://www.leisuretimespringwater.com
Bottled water
President: Harold Reynolds
Co-President: Bruce Reynolds
Controller: Michael Spear
Estimated Sales: $ 10-20 Million
Number Employees: 100-249

7822 **Lemate of New England**
11 Perry Dr
Suite C
Foxboro, MA 02035-1047 508-543-9035
Processor of sweetened cocktail mixes and flavored syrups
President: Kevin Christman
VP: Marianne Christman
Number Employees: 7
Type of Packaging: Consumer, Food Service, Private Label, Bulk

7823 **Lemke Cheese Company**
101 Devoe St
Wausau, WI 54403-3228 715-842-3214
Fax: 715-842-4452 www.greatlakescheese.com
Cheese
COO: Randy Lewis
President Administration: Daniel E Zagzebski
Treasurer: Daniel Zagzebski
Estimated Sales: Below $ 5 Million
Number Employees: 100-249
Brands:
Great Lakes

7824 **Lemke Wholesale**
1727 W Poplar Street
Rogers, AR 72758-4146 501-636-3288
Fax: 501-751-4671
Variety of food products.
President: Ron Lemke

7825 **Lemmes Company**
7 Alice Street
Coventry, RI 02816-7300 401-821-2575
Spaghetti sauce, grated cheese, BBQ sauce, relish, jam, mustard
President: Michael Lemme
Estimated Sales: $ 2.5-5 Million
Number Employees: 1

7826 **Lemon Creek Winery**
533 E Lemon Creek Rd
Berrien Springs, MI 49103-9714 269-471-1321
Fax: 616-471-1322 info@lemoncreekwinery.com
www.lemoncreekwinery.com
Wines
President: Tim Lemon
Estimated Sales: $1.8 Million
Number Employees: 20-49
Brands:
Lemon Creek Winery

7827 **Lemon-X Corporation**
168 Railroad St
Huntington Station, NY 11746 631-424-2850
Fax: 631-424-2852 800-220-1061
customerservice@lemon-x.com
www.lemon-x.com
Juices and cocktail mixes
President: James Grassi
Sales Manager: Steve Bogdanos
Purchasing Manager: Stacy Robertson
Estimated Sales: $ 20-50 Million
Number Employees: 100-249
Type of Packaging: Consumer, Food Service, Private Label, Bulk
Brands:
Growers Fancy Juice Concentrates
Lemon-X Cocktail Mixes

7828 **Len Libby's Candy Shop**
419 Us Route 1
Scarborough, ME 04074-9705 207-883-4897
Fax: 207-885-5824 lenlibby@lenlibby.com
www.lenlibby.com
Chocolates and candies
Manager: Shirley Morneault
Vice President: Maureen Hemond
Estimated Sales: $500,000-$1 Million
Number Employees: 10-19

7829 **Lena Maid Meats**
500 W Main St
Lena, IL 61048 815-369-4522
Fax: 815-369-2075 www.lenamaidmeats.com
Processor of beef, pork, lamb and venison
Manager: Kevin Koning
Secretary/Treasurer: Suzanne McGiveron
Estimated Sales: $500000
Number Employees: 10-19
Type of Packaging: Bulk
Brands:
Lena Maid

7830 **Lenchner Bakery**
50 Drumlin Cir Suite 1
Concord, ON L4K 3G1
Canada 905-738-8811
Fax: 905-738-3822
Processor and exporter of kosher frozen entrees and dessert pastries including chocolate, almond, cheese, apple, blueberry, cherry, prune, lemon, spinach feta cheese, potato onion, etc.; also, bagels; private labeling available
President: Zeev Lenchner
Estimated Sales: $1-2.5 Million
Number Employees: 20-49
Sq. footage: 10000
Parent Co: Lechner's
Type of Packaging: Consumer, Food Service, Private Label, Bulk
Brands:
Boueka
Rrrogala

7831 **Lender's Bagel Bakery**
3801 Dewitt Ave
Mattoon, IL 61938 217-235-3181
Fax: 217-258-3205
Frozen and refrigertaed bagels.
Quality Control: Mary Young
Plant Manager: Brad Sam
Estimated Sales: $100+ Million
Number Employees: 250-499
Parent Co: Aurora Foods
Type of Packaging: Consumer, Food Service, Private Label, Bulk

7832 **Lendy's**
1581 General Booth Blvd # 101
Virginia Beach, VA 23454-5106 757-491-3511
Fax: 757-491-8821 lendus@series200.com
www.lendys.com
Processor of sauces including buffalo wing, habanero hot and barbecue
Owner: Kent Von Fecht
Estimated Sales: Less than $500,000
Number Employees: 10-19
Sq. footage: 1250
Type of Packaging: Consumer, Food Service, Private Label, Bulk
Brands:
Buckman's Best
Buckman's Best Snack

7833 **Lengacher's Cheese House**
5015 Lincoln Highway
Kinzers, PA 17535-9709 717-355-6490
Cheese
President: Arthur Lengacher
Estimated Sales: $500,000 appx.
Number Employees: 1-4

7834 **Lengerich Meats**
P.O.Box 411
Zanesville, IN 46799 260-638-4123
Processor of beef, pork and lunch meats
Owner: Jim Stephen
Sales Manager: Debbie Woods
Estimated Sales: $670000
Number Employees: 5-9
Type of Packaging: Consumer, Food Service

7835 **Lennox Farm**

Shelburne, ON L0N 1S6
Canada 519-925-6444
Fax: 519-925-3285 lennoxfarms@huronatio.net
Processor of fresh and frozen rhubarb
President: William French
Estimated Sales: $1.4 Million
Number Employees: 12
Type of Packaging: Consumer, Food Service
Brands:
Lennox

7836 **Lenny's Bee Productions**
403 Wittenberg Road
Bearsville, NY 12409-5635 845-679-4514
lennybee@ulster.net
Processor of smoked trout, bee pollen and honey products
President: Lenny Busciguo
Marketing Manager: Leonardo Busciglio
Vice President: Lynn Duvall
Type of Packaging: Consumer, Food Service, Private Label
Brands:
Lenny's Bee Productions

7837 **Lenox-Martell**
89 Heath St
Jamaica Plain, MA 02130 617-442-7777
Fax: 617-522-9455 www.lenoxmartell.com
CEO: James Lerner
Sales Director: Howard Segal
Estimated Sales: $ 20 - 50 Million
Number Employees: 20-49

7838 **Lenox-Martell**
89 Heath St
Boston, MA 02130 617-442-7777
Fax: 617-522-9455 www.lenoxmartell.com
Processor of colas and juices; wholesaler/distributor of refrigerators and ice and soda machines; serving the food service market; also, installation and maintenance of draft beer systems available
CEO/Sales Executive: Jim Lerner
VP Finance: David Nitishin
VP Marketing: John Dixon
Operations Director: Rick Freitas
Estimated Sales: $8 Million
Number Employees: 82
Sq. footage: 30000

7839 **Lenson Coffee & Tea Company**
PO Box 1103
Pleasantville, NJ 08232-6103 609-646-3003
Fax: 609-646-8606
Processor of coffee; wholesaler/distributor of tea; serving the food service market
Owner: Jimmie Anderson
Estimated Sales: $ 5-10 Million
Number Employees: 20-49
Type of Packaging: Consumer, Food Service, Private Label

7840 **Leo G. Atkinson Fisheries**
89 Daniel Head Road
South Side
Clarks Harbor, NS B0W 1P0
Canada 902-745-3047
Fax: 902-745-1245
Processor and exporter of fresh, frozen and salted seafood including haddock, cod, halibut and lobster
President: Leo Atkinson
Estimated Sales: $9.9 Million
Number Employees: 20
Type of Packaging: Consumer, Food Service, Private Label, Bulk

7841 **Leo G. Fraboni Sausage Company**
1202 13th Ave E
Hibbing, MN 55746-1218 218-263-5074
Fax: 218-263-5074 sales@frabonis.com
www.frabonis.com
Processor of smoked Polish sausages and frozen beef patties
President: Mark Thune
VP: Wayne Thune
Plant Manager: Don Johnson
Estimated Sales: $ .5 - 1 million
Number Employees: 5-9
Type of Packaging: Consumer, Private Label, Bulk

7842 **Leo's Bakery**
1179 Ocean St
Marshfield, MA 02050 781-837-3300
Fax: 781-837-8949
Bakery products
President: Robert Gagnon
Estimated Sales: $500,000-$1 Million
Number Employees: 10-19

7843 **Leon's Bakery**
1000 Universal Dr N
North Haven, CT 06473-3151 203-234-0115
Fax: 203-234-7620 800-223-6844
www.pennantfoods.com
Processor of frozen dough; exporter of wheat and white rolls
President: Luis Alpizar
CEO: John Ruth
CFO: Eric Olson
Sales Manager: Terry Ginn
Plant Manager: Fred Macey
Estimated Sales: $ 5 - 10 Million
Number Employees: 5-9
Sq. footage: 75000
Type of Packaging: Food Service, Private Label, Bulk

7844 **Leon's Texas Cuisine**
P.O.Box 1850
Mc Kinney, TX 75070 972-529-5050
Fax: 972-529-2244 scott@texascuisine.com
www.texascuisine.com
Producer of corny dogs and stuffed jalapenos
Owner: Bob Clements
VP Human Resources: Cindy Stephens
Director Sales: Scott Elwonger
SVP Operations: John Vroman
Estimated Sales: $500,000-$1 Million
Number Employees: 100-249
Brands:
Leon's Texas Cuisine

7845 **Leona Meat Plant**
P.O.Box 156
Troy, PA 16947 570-297-3574
Fax: 570-297-3562 www.leonameatplant.com
Processor of meat including ham, bacon and sausage
President: Charles Debach Ii
Estimated Sales: $1200000
Number Employees: 5-9
Type of Packaging: Consumer

7846 **Leonard Fountain Specialties**
4225 Nancy St
Detroit, MI 48212 313-891-4141
Fax: 313-892-9200 sales@leonardssyrups.com
www.leonardssyrups.com
Syrups, juices, frozen cocktails
Owner: Leonard Bugajewski
CFO: Maria Cintron
Marketing Director: Leroy Goodall
Production Manager: Tom Niconcher
Plant Manager: John Bamford
Estimated Sales: $ 5-10 Million
Number Employees: 100-249
Sq. footage: 75

Type of Packaging: Food Service, Private Label
Brands:
Bar-Pak
Bulk Co2
Frosty Pak
Lemon Twist
Orange Mist
Polar Pak
Quali-Tea
Thrifty Pak
Tropical Mist

7847 **Leonard Mountain Trading**
P.O.Box 67
Leonard, OK 74043 918-366-2800
Fax: 918-366-2800 fred@leonardmountin.com
www.leonardmountain.com
Fruit & Veggie Dips, Pasta Salads, Peanuts, Dirty Drink Mixes, Olives and Pickled Vegetables
President: Debbie Berckefeldt
Sales Manager: Fred Berckefeldt
Estimated Sales: $ 10-20 Million
Number Employees: 10
Brands:
Boot Scootin'
Leonard Mountain
Mama Leone's

7848 **Leonas Foods**
Manzana Center Highway 76
Chimayo, NM 87522 505-351-4660
Fax: 505-351-2189 www.leonas.com
Flour, corn tortillas and tamales
President: Roy Trujillo
Owner: Lila Salazar
Estimated Sales: $10-24.9 Million
Number Employees: 20-49

7849 **Leone Provision Company**
916 SE 14th Avenue
Cape Coral, FL 33990-3020 239-458-0013
Fax: 239-574-6707
Importer of Italian meats including meat balls and sausages; also, andouille and Polish sausage
President: Armando Leone
Estimated Sales: $290,000
Number Employees: 3
Type of Packaging: Consumer, Food Service

7850 **Leonetti Cellar**
1875 Foothills Ln
Walla Walla, WA 99362 509-525-1428
Fax: 509-525-4006 www.leonetticellar.com
Wines
President: Gary Figgins
VP Operations: Chris Figgins
Marketing: Nancy Figgins
Vineyard Manager: Jason Magnaghi
Estimated Sales: $500,000-$1 Million
Number Employees: 5-9
Brands:
Leonetti Cellar

7851 **Leonetti's Frozen Food**
5935 Woodland Ave
Philadelphia, PA 19143 215-729-4200
Fax: 215-729-7581 leonettifrozenfo@aol.com
www.leonettisfrozenfoods.com
Processor of frozen stromboli and calzones
President: Richard Di Pietro
Plant Manager: Leroy Douglas
Estimated Sales: $1500000
Number Employees: 20-49
Sq. footage: 33000
Type of Packaging: Consumer, Food Service, Private Label, Bulk
Brands:
Leonetti's

7852 **Lep Profit International**
1950 Spectrum Cir SE
Marietta, GA 30067-8479 770-951-8100
Fax: 770-952-8122

7853 **Lepage Bakeries**
Country Kitchen Plaza
PO Box 1900
Auburn, ME 04211-1900 207-783-9161
lbck@lepagebakeries.com
www.lepagebakeries.com
Processor of bread, rolls, English muffins and donuts
President/CEO: Andrew Barowsky
Chairman: Albert Lepage
VP: Thomas Mato
Human Resources Director: Betty Bartos
Estimated Sales: $5-10 Million
Number Employees: 525
Type of Packaging: Consumer

7854 **(HQ)Leprino Foods Company**
1830 W 38th Ave
Denver, CO 80211 303-480-2600
Fax: 303-480-2605 800-537-7466
cheese@leprinofoods.com
www.leprinofoods.com
Manufacturer of cheese and an exporter of whey products
President: Larry Jensen
SVP Administration/CFO: Ron Klump
SVP QA/R&D: Richard Barz
SVP Sales/Marketing: Robert Boynton
SVP Production Operations: Tom Haggerty
Estimated Sales: $21.2 Billion
Number Employees: 2500
Type of Packaging: Food Service, Bulk
Other Locations:
Leprino Foods
Allendale MI
Leprino Foods
Fort Morgan CO
Leprino Foods
Ravenna NE
Leprino Foods
Remus MI
Leprino Foods
Roswell NM
Leprino Foods
Waverly NY
Brands:
Le-Pro
Quality-Locked

7855 **Leroux Creek Foods**
9754 3100 Rd
Hotchkiss, CO 81419-6114 970-872-2256
Fax: 970-872-2250 877-970-5670
info@lerouxcreek.com www.lerouxcreek.com
Processor of organic apple sauce and fruit puree.
President: Edward Tuft
Quality Control: Wende Michael
Marketing: Sarah Tuft
Operations: Amy Sanders
Plant Manager: Arturo Mendoza
Purchasing: Edward Tuft
Estimated Sales: $1500000
Number Employees: 20-49
Number of Products: 14
Type of Packaging: Consumer, Private Label
Brands:
Leroux Creek

7856 **Leroy Hill Coffee Company**
3278 Halls Mill Rd
PO Drawer 6210
Mobile, AL 36660-9219 251-476-1234
Fax: 251-476-1296 800-866-5282
goodtasteiseverything@leroyhillcoffee.com
www.leroyhillcoffee.com
Processor and wholesaler/distributor of coffee and tea; wholesaler/distributor of general merchandise; serving the food service market
President: Debra Hill
CFO: Travis Goodloe
Sales Manager: Greg King
Operations Manager: Dan Buckley
Estimated Sales: $18000000
Number Employees: 130
Sq. footage: 60000
Type of Packaging: Consumer, Food Service

7857 **Leroy Hill Coffee Company**
3278 Halls Mill Rd
Mobile, AL 36606 251-476-1234
Fax: 251-476-1296 800-866-5282
goodtasteiseverything@leroyhillcoffee.com
www.leroyhillcoffee.com
Coffee
President: Leroy Hill
Production Manager: Dan Buckley
Estimated Sales: $ 15-20 Million
Number Employees: 100-249
Type of Packaging: Private Label
Brands:
Leroy Hill

7858 **(HQ)Leroy Smith & Sons Inc**
P.O.Box 716
Vero Beach, FL 32961-0716 772-567-3421
Fax: 772-567-8428 www.leroysmith.com
Manufacturer and exporter of citrus fruit including grapefruit and oranges
President: Elson R Smith Jr
Vice President: Trey Smith
Estimated Sales: $38 Million
Number Employees: 250-499
Type of Packaging: Consumer
Brands:
GOLDEN MAGIC
ISLAND FRUIT
MAGIC RIVER
MYSTIC RIVER

7859 **Lerro Candy Company**
601 Columbia Ave
Darby, PA 19023 610-461-8886
sales@lerrocandyco.com
http://www.lerrocandyco.com
Processor of confectionery products including chocolate cherries
Owner/Manager: John Lerro
Estimated Sales: $$2.5-5 Million
Number Employees: 10-19
Type of Packaging: Consumer

7860 **Les Aliments Livabec Foods**
95 Rang St Louis Rr 2
Sherrington, QC J0L 2N0
Canada 450-454-7971
Fax: 450-454-9100
Processor and exporter of marinated mixed and roasted vegetables and mushrooms in oil; processor of antipasto calabrese, basil and sun-dried tomato pesto; importer of sun-dried tomatoes
President: Lino Cimagila
VP: Lino Cimaglia, Jr.
Estimated Sales: $2 Million
Number Employees: 5
Sq. footage: 20000
Brands:
Livabec
Livia

7861 **Les Aliments Ramico Foods**
8245 Rue Le Creusot
St. Leonard, QC HIP 2A2
Canada 514-329-1844
Fax: 514-329-5096
Processor, canner and exporter of beans, soups, sauces, chicken and meat with beans
VP: Galal Matta
Number Employees: 10-19
Sq. footage: 12000
Type of Packaging: Private Label

7862 **Les Bourgeois Vineyards**
12847 W Highway Bb
Rocheport, MO 65279 573-698-2300
Fax: 573-698-2170 info@missouriwine.com
www.missouriwine.com
Wines
CEO: Curtis Bourgeois
Marketing Director: Laura Royse
Office Manager: Sue Good
Estimated Sales: Below $ 5 Million
Number Employees: 50-99
Type of Packaging: Private Label
Brands:
Les Bourgeois

7863 **Les Brasseurs Du Nord**
875 Michele Bohec Boulevard
Blainville, QC J7C 5J6
Canada 450-979-8400
Fax: 450-979-3733 800-378-3733
info@boreale.com www.boreale.com
Processor and distributor of beer, ale and stout
President: Bernard Morin
Marketing Manager: Bernard Morin
Vice President: Laura Urtinowski
CEO: Daniel Lampron
Estimated Sales: $ 5-10 Million
Number Employees: 50-100
Sq. footage: 35000
Type of Packaging: Consumer, Food Service
Brands:
BER Boreale

7864 **Les Brasseurs GMT**
5585 De La Rouche
Montreal, QC H2J 3K3
Canada 514-274-4941
Fax: 514-274-6138 888-253-8330
info@brasseursrj.com www.brasseursrj.com
Processor of beer, ale, lager and stout
Manager: Alain Hudon
Partner: Brasserie Le Cheval Blanc
Pioneer: Les Brasseurs GMT
Estimated Sales: E
Number Employees: 100-249
Type of Packaging: Consumer, Food Service
Brands:
Belle Gueule

7865 **Les Chocolats Vadeboncoeur**
8350 Parkway D'Anjou
Montreal, QC H1K 4S3
Canada 514-493-8504
Fax: 514-483-3956 800-276-8504
www.chocolatvadeboncoeur.com/eng/index.html
Chocolate

7866 **Les Industries Bernard Et Fils**
104 Rue Industrielle Du Boise
Saint Victor, QC G0M 2B0
Canada 418-588-3590
Fax: 418-588-6836
Processor and exporter of pure maple syrup
President: Yves Bernard
Estimated Sales: $4.4 Million
Number Employees: 35
Type of Packaging: Consumer, Food Service, Private Label, Bulk

7867 **Les Mouts De P.O.M.**
169 Rang 2
Sain-Francois-Xavier, QC J0B 2V0 819-845-5555
Fax: 819-845-2555 guy@lesmoutsdepom.com
www.lemoutsdepom.com
Other hot beverages, tea, juice/cider, non-alcoholic beverages, other cold non-carbonated beverages, RTD - ready to drink (coffee, tea, concentrates, powders), water, soft drinks.
Marketing: Guy Bergeron

7868 **Les Palais Des Thes**
1001 Ave Of The Americas
Suite 1117
New York, NY 10018 917-515-2887
Fax: 212-813-2883
wholesale@us.palaisdesthes.com
www.palaisdesthes.com
Functional (antioxidants), vegetarian, tea, soft drinks.
Marketing: Cyrille Bessiere

7869 **Les Salaisons Brochu**
183 Route Du President-Kennedy
St. Henri De Levis, QC G0R 3E0
Canada 418-882-2282
Fax: 418-882-5212 a.lafleur@videotron.ca
Processor of fresh and frozen pork
Contact: Laurent Brochu
Number Employees: 250-499
Type of Packaging: Consumer, Food Service, Private Label

7870 **Les Trois Petits Cochons**
4223 1st Avenue
2nd Floor
Brooklyn, NY 11232 212-219-1230
Fax: 212-941-9726 800-537-7283
info@3pigs.com www.3pigs.com
Processor of natural pates and mousses: meat, poultry, game, vegetable and seafood; also, garlic sausage; importer of cornichons, cepes and petits toasts
President: Alain Sinturel
Marketing Director: Valentine Colin
Sales Director: Maha Freij
Estimated Sales: 6.3 Million
Number Employees: 40
Number of Brands: 2
Type of Packaging: Consumer, Food Service
Brands:
Coeur De France
Les Trois Petits Cochons

7871 **Les Trois Petits Cochons 3 Little Pigs**
4223 1st Ave Fl 2
Brooklyn, NY 11232 212-219-1230
Fax: 212-941-9726 davidh@3pigs.com
www.3pigs.com
Manufacturer of pates, mini terrines, mousses, vegetable and seafood terrines, charouterie and pork free products.
President: Alain Sinturel
Manager: Michael Tuccillo
Accounting Manager: Teressa Chikout
Sales Manager: Maha Freij
Estimated Sales: $20-50 Million
Number Employees: 12

7872 **Les Viandes Or-Fil**
2080 Rue Monterey
Laval, QC H7L 3S3
Canada 450-687-5664
Fax: 450-687-2733
Processor and exporter of fresh and frozen pork
President: Antonio Filice
Vice President: Bernard Paquette
Estimated Sales: $15 Million
Number Employees: 50
Type of Packaging: Bulk

7873 **Les Viandes du Breton**
150 Ch Des Raymond
Riviere-Du-Lup,, QC G5R 5X8
Canada 418-863-6711
Fax: 418-863-6767 cbreton@quebectel.com
www.dubreton.com
Processor of fresh and frozen pork; exporter of hams, spare ribs, bellies, etc
President: Vincent Breton
Sales Manager: Gaetan Gauvin
Estimated Sales: $169 Million
Number Employees: 540
Parent Co: Bose Corporation
Type of Packaging: Consumer, Food Service, Private Label, Bulk
Brands:
Dubreton Natural

7874 **Lesaffre Yeast Corporation**
777 E Wisconsin Ave # 11
Milwaukee, WI 53202-5302 414-271-6755
Fax: 414-347-4795 mail@lesaffre.com
www.sensient-technologies.com
Yeast
CEO: Kenneth P Manning
Estimated Sales: $ 20 - 50 Million
Number Employees: 1,000-4,999

7875 **Lesley Elizabeth**
877 Whitney Dr
Lapeer, MI 48446 810-664-8192
Fax: 810-667-7287 800-684-3300
sales@lesleyelizabeth.com
www.lesleyelizabeth.com
Gourmet sauces, oils, vinegarettes, pestos and crisps
President: Lesley Mc Cowen
Marketing: Gary Bates
Estimated Sales: $ 1-5 Million
Number Employees: 10-19
Type of Packaging: Private Label
Brands:
Lesley Elizabeth
Lesley Elizabeth's Crisps
Lesley Elizabeth's Dipping Oils
Lesley Elizabeth's Dips
Lesley Elizabeth's Pesto
Lesley Elizabeth's Vinegarettes
Lesley Marinara

7876 **Lesley Stowe Fine FoodsLTD.**
#100-13955 Bridgeport Rd
Richmond, BC V6V 1J6 604-731-3663
www.lesleystowe.com
Crackers.
Marketing: Margaret Aro

7877 **Leslie Leger & Sons**
34 Chemin De La Cote
Trois-Ruisseaux, NB E4N 2V7
Canada 506-577-4730
Fax: 506-577-4960 http://www.leslieandsons.com
Processor and exporter of smoked herring and brined alewife
President: Leslie Leger
Estimated Sales: $4.8 Million
Number Employees: 35
Type of Packaging: Bulk

7878 **LesserEvil Snacks**
P.O.Box 4098
Greenwich, CT 06831-401
Fax: 914-779-3099 www.lesserevil.com
all natural snacks
Number Employees: 8

7879 **Let Them Eat Cake**
3805 S West Shore Blvd Ste B
Tampa, FL 33611 813-837-6888
Fax: 813-831-6741
admin@chocolateismycrayon.com
www.chocolateismycrayon.com
Processor of custom mini pastries
President/CEO: Michael Baugh
Marketing Manager: Michael Baugh
Estimated Sales: Less than $500,000
Number Employees: 1-4

7880 **Let's Serve**
3 Plattsburgh Ave
Plattsburgh, NY 12901
Fax: 518-293-7119 letsserve@aol.com
Processor of apple butter, apple sauce, peach preserves, jams and fruit spreads
Owner: Donald Papson
Co-Owner: Vivian Papson
Estimated Sales: Under $300,000
Number Employees: 400
Sq. footage: 400
Brands:
Adirondack Orchard
Heritage Sauces
Thank the Trees

7881 **Let's Serve**
3 Plattsburgh Ave
Plattsburgh, NY 12901
Fax: 518-293-7119 letsserve@aol.com
Applesauce, butter, honey cream, jam
President: Don Papson
CEO: Don Papson
Vice President: Vivian Papson
Type of Packaging: Private Label
Brands:
Let's Serve

7882 **Letraw Manufacturing Company**
200 Quaker Rd Ste 2
Rockford, IL 61104 815-987-9670
Fax: 815-987-9830 rwartell@letraw.com
www.letraw.com
Manufacture cleaning products
President: Lane Wartell
Vice President: Ralph Wartell
Estimated Sales: Less than $500,000
Number Employees: 5-9
Type of Packaging: Bulk
Brands:
Letraw

7883 **Letterman Enterprises Inc.**
109 Fairfield Dr
State College, PA 16801-8248 814-574-4339
Fax: 814-466-6820 david@lettermaninc.com
www.feeltheflavors.com
Ethnic sauces (soy, curry, etc.), grilling sauces, marinades, other sauces, seasonings and cooking enhancers, foodservice.
Marketing: David Letterman

7884 **Level Valley Creamery**
4350 Hurricane Creek Blvd
Antioch, TN 37013 615-641-1027
Fax: 615-641-7038 800-251-1292
www.schreiber.com
Processor of dairy products including butter and cream cheese; also, milk including condensed, sweetened condensed, nonfat dry, whole powder and 28 1/2% fat; exporter of anhydrous milk fat
President: Ronald Povinelli
CFO: Dick Rosenbalm
VP: David Moss
Maintenance Engineer: Henry Lorenz
Plant Manager: Bill Merrick
Estimated Sales: $32000000
Number Employees: 50-99
Sq. footage: 85000
Parent Co: Level Valley Creamery
Type of Packaging: Consumer, Food Service, Private Label, Bulk

Brands:
Country Squire
Level Valley
Swift's Brook

7885 **Level Valley Creamery**
807 Pleasant Valley Rd
West Bend, WI 53095 262-675-6533
Fax: 262-675-2827 800-558-1707
contact@levelvalley.com www.levelvalley.com
Butter and butter oil, cream cheese, anhydrous milk and cream
President: Alexander J Costigan
Estimated Sales: $ 100-500 Million
Number Employees: 200-250

7886 **Levonian Brothers**
P.O.Box 629
Troy, NY 12181-0629 518-274-3610
Fax: 518-274-0098 chrispkeller@yahoo.com
www.2eatcab.com
Manufacturer and exporter of meat products including cooked and raw corn beef, pastrami, cooked and smoked hams, roast beef, natural casing frankfurters and sausages including Polish, pork and Italian
President: Robert Nazarian
Plant Manager: George Lindemann
Estimated Sales: $20-50 Million
Number Employees: 50-99
Type of Packaging: Consumer, Food Service

7887 **Lewes Dairy**
660 Pilottown Rd
Lewes, DE 19958 302-645-6281
Fax: 302-645-6290 www.lewesdairy.com
Processor of dairy products
President: Archie Brittingham
Vice President: Walter Brittingham
Estimated Sales: $2.3 Million
Number Employees: 22
Type of Packaging: Consumer

7888 **Lewis Bakeries**
200 Albert Street
London, ON N6A 1M1
Canada 519-434-5252
Fax: 519-434-6277
Processor of baked goods including bread, rolls and pastries
Board Member: Mike Juma
Estimated Sales: $2.8 Million
Number Employees: 75

7889 **Lewis Brothers Bakeries**
2972 S Old Decker Road
Vincennes, IN 47951-7603 812-886-6533
www.lewisbakeries.net
Processor of bread and buns
General Manager: Carl Finfrock
Plant Manager: Dan Seyer
Type of Packaging: Consumer, Food Service
Brands:
BUNNY
BUTTERNUT
CINNABON
GATEWAY
HARTFORD FARMS
HEALTHY LIFE
HOLSUM
LEWIS
POTATO BREAD
ROMAN MEAL
SUN-MAID
SUNBEAM

7890 **(HQ)Lewis Brothers Bakeries**
500 N Fulton Ave
Evansville, IN 47710-1597 812-425-4642
Fax: 812-425-7609 www.lewisbakeries.net
Manufacturer of low-fat, low-carbohydrate breads. Products include whole grain and white breads, buns and several sugar free varieties.
President: R J Lewis Jr
CEO: R J Lewis Jr
VP Finance: Rodger Lesh
VP Sales: Harry Lincoln
Buyer: Carol Stratman
Estimated Sales: $ 240 Million
Number Employees: 2100
Type of Packaging: Consumer, Food Service
Brands:
BUNNY BREAD
GATEWAY
HARTFORD FARMS
HEALTHY LIFE
INDIANA SPUD POTATO BREAD
LEWIS

7891 **Lewis Brothers Bakeries**
855 Scott St
Murfreesboro, TN 37129 615-893-6041
Fax: 615-893-1463 www.lewisbakeries.net
Processor of bread
Manager: Rick Hardesty Jr
General Production Manager: Kenneth Burkhart
General Manager: Rick Hardesty
Parent Co: Lewis Brothers Bakeries
Type of Packaging: Consumer, Food Service

7892 **Lewis Cellars**
4101 Big Ranch Rd
Napa, CA 94558 70- 2-5 34
Fax: 70- 2-5 34 wine@lewiscellars.com
www.lewiscellars.com
Wines
President: Randy Lewis
CEO: John Lewis
CFO: Debbie Lewis
Estimated Sales: Below $ 500,000
Number Employees: 1

7893 **Lewis Laboratories International**
49 Richmondville Ave # 118
Westport, CT 06880-2053 203-226-7343
Fax: 203-454-0329 800-243-6020
customerservice@lewis-labs.com
www.lewis-labs.com
Nutritional suppliments
President: Diana Lewis
Estimated Sales: $500,000-$1 Million
Number Employees: 5-9
Brands:
Brewer's
Fabulous Fiber
Famous Original Formula Staminex
Lewis Labs RDA
Super Fabulous Fiber
Weigh Down

7894 **Lewis Packing Company**
17480 Shelley Ave
Sandy, OR 97055-8055 503-668-8122
Owner: Kris Jones
Estimated Sales: Under $500,000
Number Employees: 1-4

7895 **Lewis Sausage Corporation**
P.O.Box 280
Burgaw, NC 28425 910-259-2642
Fax: 910-259-9881
Manufacturer of smoked and mild sausage
President: Edgar Hardy
Manager: Bruce Sure
Estimated Sales: $3 Million
Number Employees: 25
Type of Packaging: Consumer

7896 **Lewis-Vincennes Bakery**
2792 S Old Decker Rd
Vincennes, IN 47591-7603 812-886-6533
Fax: 812-886-6921
Processor of baked goods
President: Jack Louis
Plant Manager: Dan Seyer
Estimated Sales: $ 20 - 50 Million
Number Employees: 100-249
Parent Co: Lewis-Vincennes Bakery
Type of Packaging: Consumer, Food Service, Private Label, Bulk

7897 **Lexington Coffee & Tea Company**
2571 Regency Rd
Lexington, KY 40503-2920 859-277-1102
Fax: 859-277-6490
Coffee and tea
Owner: Terri Wood
Estimated Sales: $ 5-10 Million
Number Employees: 5-9
Brands:
Lexington Coffee Tea

7898 **Li'l Guy Foods**
3631 Ne Kimball Dr
Kansas City, MO 64161 816-241-2000
Fax: 816-241-2025 800-886-8226
LilGuyFoods@lilguyfoods.com
www.lilguyfoods.com
Manufacturer of Mexican foods including corn tortillas, flour tortillas, flavored tortilla wraps, taco shells, tortilla chips, spices, taco sauce and salsa picante, cheeses and chorizo and chicharones.
President: David Sloan
CFO/Director of Sales: Christina Sloan
VP: Edward Sloan
Sales Manager: Allen Carriere
Office Manager/Customer Service: Jennifer Hart
Plant Manager: Edward Sloan
Estimated Sales: $2000000
Number Employees: 20-49
Sq. footage: 30000
Parent Co: Sloan Acquisition Corporation
Type of Packaging: Consumer, Food Service
Brands:
Li'l Guy
V&V Supremo Cheeses & Meats

7899 **Liberty Dairy**
530 N River St
Evart, MI 49631 231-734-5592
Fax: 231-734-3880 800-632-5552
www.deanfoods.com
Processor of juice and milk
VP Sales/Marketing: Scott Jacobs
Plant Manager: Gordon Willis
Estimated Sales: $100+ Million
Number Employees: 100-249
Parent Co: Dean Foods Company
Type of Packaging: Consumer, Food Service, Private Label

7900 **Liberty Enterprises**
PO Box 5250
Stateline, NV 89449-5250 775-588-3656
Fax: 775-588-7366 800-723-3690
jpensec@harland.net
www.libertysite.com/harland
President/CEO: Timothy C Tuff
Estimated Sales: Under $500,000
Number Employees: 1-4
Brands:
Altafi
Cavion Plus
Mydas

7901 **Liberty Natural Products**
20949 S Harris Road
Oregon City, OR 97045 503-631-4488
Fax: 503-631-2424 800-289-8427
jim@libertynatural.com www.libertynatural.com
Processor and exporter of gourmet breath fresheners, natural flavors and oils; processor of vitamins; importer of essential oils and botanical extracts; wholesaler/distributor of gourmet breath fresheners
President/CEO: Jim Dierking
Sales Manager: Tabor Helton
Operations Manager: Shane Reaney
Purchasing Manager: Michelle Falls
Estimated Sales: $1-2.5 Million
Number Employees: 20-49
Sq. footage: 17000
Type of Packaging: Consumer, Bulk
Brands:
MAX
Natural Gourmet Flavor Oil
TIB

7902 **Liberty Orchards Company**
117 Mission Ave
Cashmere, WA 98815 509-782-2191
Fax: 509-782-1487 800-888-5696
service@libertyorchards.com
www.libertyorchards.com
Processor and exporter of confectionery products including chocolate, holiday and boxed nonchocolate candy
President: Greg Taylor
VP Marketing & Sales: Michael Rainey Sr
Estimated Sales: $12377000
Number Employees: 50-99
Type of Packaging: Consumer, Food Service
Brands:
APLETS
COTLETS
FRUIT CHOCOLATES
FRUIT DELIGHTS
FRUIT FESTIVES
FRUIT PARFAITS
FRUIT SOFTEES
GRAPELETS
HAWAIIAN FESTIVES

7903 **(HQ)Liberty Richter**
400 Lyster Ave
Saddle Brook, NJ 07663 201-291-8749
Fax: 201-368-3575 lr@mediaetc.com
www.libertyrichter.com
Processor and importer of caviar, mustard, cookies, crackers, olives, breakfast cereals, pasta, rice, anchovies, sardines and dried fruits
President: Lawrence J Lapare
Marketing Director: John Affer
Operations Manager: Kathie Gibbs Forkouski
Estimated Sales: $ 5 - 10 Million
Number Employees: 5-9
Type of Packaging: Consumer
Brands:
Agnesi
Amore
Apollinaris
Arnott's
Arriba
Balanced
Better Than Milk
Chatfield's
Cookie Lovers
Debel
Delacre
Downey's Original
Fazer
Fini
Fre
Harmony Farms
Honeycup
International Collection
Kame
Kitchens of India
Kozlowski Farms
London Fruit & Herb Company
Mazzetti
Melinda's
Mi-Del
Perfect Cup
Rademaker
Sacla
Sapori
Sesmark
Steaz Sparkling Green Tea
Swan Gardens
Tofu Rella
Vegan Rella
Vermont Village Cannery

7904 **Liberty Vegetable Oil Company**
15306 Carmenita Rd
Santa Fe Springs, CA 90670 562-921-3567
Fax: 562-802-3476
liberty@libertyvegetableoil.com
www.libertyvegetableoil.com
Vegetable oils
President: Irwin Field
VP: Edward Field
Controller: Warren Parr
Executive VP: C Adams
Sales Manager: Ronald Field
Estimated Sales: $ 50 - 100 Million
Number Employees: 50-99
Brands:
Lvo

7905 **Lieber Chocolate & FoodProducts**
142 44th St
Brooklyn, NY 11232 718-499-0888
Fax: 718-499-5636
Chocolates
President: Mark Moskowitz
Estimated Sales: $ 20-50 Million
Number Employees: 20
Brands:
Lieber

7906 **Life Extension Foods**
P.O.Box 407198
1100 W Coml Blvd Ste 100
Fort Lauderdale, FL 33309 954-966-4886
Fax: 954-761-9199 800-678-8989
customerservice@lifeextension.com www.lef.org
Owner: William Faloon
Director Nutrition: Ross Pelton
Director, Place for Achieving Total He: Eric R Braverman
Estimated Sales: F
Number Employees: 100
Brands:
Life Extension Mixo

7907 **Life Force Winery**
1055 Saddle Ridge Road
Moscow, ID 83843-8774 208-882-9158
Fax: 208-882-9158 garric@turbonet.com
Honey wine
President: Garrick Kruse
Estimated Sales: $5-9.9 Million
Number Employees: 8
Brands:
Life Force

7908 **Life International**
8889 Pelican Bay Boulevard
Suite 301
Naples, FL 34108-7501 239-592-9788
Fax: 941-592-9787 efgonzalez@prodigy.com
Estimated Sales: Less than $500,000
Number Employees: 5-9

7909 **LifeSpice Ingredients**
300 Cherry Lane
Palm Beach, FL 33480 561-844-6334
Fax: 561-844-6335 www.lifespiceingredients.com
Supplier of spice blends and flavor systems.

7910 **LifeTime Nutritional Specialties**
1967 N Glassell St
Orange, CA 92865-4320 714-634-9340
Fax: 714-634-9340
lifetimevitamins@sbcglobal.net
www.lifetimevitamins.com
Vitamins
President: Tom Pinkowski
Vice President of Sales/Marketing: Tom Pinkowski

7911 **Lifeforce Labs LLC**
920 Britt Ct
Altamonte Spgs, FL 32701-2080 407-830-0009
Fax: 407-830-0039 info@lifeforce-labs.com
www.lifeforce-labs.com
Manufacturer of protein based nutritional drinks.
Managing Partner: Bruce Svetz
Managing Partner: John Sericka

7912 **Lifeline Food Company**
426 Orange Ave
Sand City, CA 93955-3569 831-899-5040
Fax: 831-899-0285 www.lifetimecheese.com
Dairy and cheese
President: Jone Chappell
CFO: Greg Chappell
Estimated Sales: Below $ 5 Million
Number Employees: 5-9
Number of Brands: 2
Type of Packaging: Private Label
Brands:
Dairytime
ENERGY BARS
Lifetime
Lifetime Fat Free Cheese
Lifetime Lactose/Fat Free Cheese
Lifetime Low Fat Cheese
Lifetime Low Fat Rice Cheese
SOY CHEESE

7913 **Lifestar Millennium**
PO Box 3837
Sedona, AZ 86340 925-202-4302
Fax: 970-422-4739 877-422-4739
lsmail@lifestar.com www.lifestar.com
Processor and exporter of natural nutritional supplements; importer of grapeseed oil
President: J Bentley
Estimated Sales: $300,000-500,000
Number Employees: 1-4
Type of Packaging: Consumer, Food Service
Brands:
Living Food Concentrates
Multiplex

7914 **Lifeway Foods Inc**
6431 W Oakton St
Morton Grove, IL 60053-2727
Fax: 847-967-6558 877-281-3874
info@lifeway.net www.lifeway.net
Processor and exporter of dairy products including drinkable yogurt, kefir and cheese.
President/CEO: Julie Smolyansky
Founder of Lifeway Foods: Mike Smolyansky
Estimated Sales: $ 4 Million
Number Employees: 100-249
Sq. footage: 60000
Type of Packaging: Consumer
Brands:
BASICS PLUS
FARMER'S CHEESE
KEFIR
KEFIR STARTER
LA FRUTA
SOY TREAT
SWEET KISS

7915 **Lifewise Ingredients**
350 Telser Rd
Lake Zurich, IL 60047-6701 847-550-8270
Fax: 847-550-8272 info@lifewise1.com
www.lifewise1.com
Processor and exporter of health food ingredients including monosodium glutamate replacements, fat replacers, flavor enhancers, flavor maskers
Founder: Richard Share
Sales Director: Richard Share
Lab Manager: Millie Galey
General Manager: Carol Bender
Purchasing Manager: Carol Bender
Estimated Sales: Below $ 5 Million
Number Employees: 5-9
Sq. footage: 3500
Brands:
Bitzels
Lifewise Ingredients
Potentiator Plus
simply rich

7916 **Light Rock Beverage Company**
9 Balmforth Ave
Danbury, CT 06810 203-743-3410
Fax: 203-792-7909
Bottled water, other beverages
President: George Antous
Vice President: Fred Antous
General Manager: Thomas Antous
Estimated Sales: Below $ 5 Million
Number Employees: 18
Brands:
Light Rock

7917 **Light Vision Confections**
1776 Mentor Avenue
Cincinnati, OH 45212-3554 513-351-9444
Fax: 253-981-0758 sales@lightvision.com
www.lightvision.com
Processor of holographic confectionery items including lollypops, hard candy and chocolate
President: Eric Begleiter
CEO: Mike Wodke
CFO: Paul Graham
Estimated Sales: Below $ 5 Million
Number Employees: 20-30
Type of Packaging: Food Service, Private Label
Brands:
HOLOPOP
PopArt

7918 **Lightlife Foods**
153 Industrial Blvd
Turners Falls, MA 01376 413-863-0252
Fax: 413-774-9080 800-274-6001
www.lightlife.com
Processor and exporter of soy-based products like chili, sausages, deli meats, ground meat, tempeh, chicken, burgers and bacon
President: Patricia Collins
General Manager: Darcy Zbinovec
R&D: Ron Desautels
Human Resources Director: Bobby Riley
Product Manager: Dean Kuhlka
Estimated Sales: $ 20 - 50 Million
Number Employees: 150
Sq. footage: 80000
Parent Co: ConAgra Foods
Brands:
GIMME LEAN
LIGHT BURGERS
ORGANIC FLAX TEMPEH
ORGANIC GARDEN VEGGIE TEMPEH
ORGANIC SMOKY TEMPEH STRIPS
ORGANIC SOY TEMPEH
ORGANIC THREE GRAIN TEMPEH
ORGANIC WILD RICE TEMPEH
SMART BACON
SMART BBQ
SMART CHILI
SMART CUTLETS
SMART DELI
SMART DOGS
SMART GROUND

SMART LINKS
SMART SAUSAGE
SMART TENDERS
SMART WINGS
TOFU PUPS

7919 **Lily of the Desert**
1887 Geesling Rd
Denton, TX 76208 940-566-9914
Fax: 940-566-9915 800-229-5459
custserv@lilyofthedesert.com
www.lilyofthedesert.com
Processor and exporter of certified organic aloe vera beverages and dietary supplements
President: Don Lovelace
Estimated Sales: $ 1 - 3 Million
Number Employees: 10-19
Type of Packaging: Consumer, Food Service, Private Label, Bulk
Brands:
Lily of the Desert

7920 **Lilydale Foods**
7727-127 Avenue
Edmonton, AB T5C 1R9
Canada 780-448-0990
Fax: 780-473-0020 800-661-5341
contactus@lilydale.com www.lilydale.com
Processor and exporter of fresh and frozen meats, poultry, sausages and sandwiches; also, further processed poultry products including fully cooked, par cooked, breaded and unbreaded
President: Ed Rodenburg
Purchasing Agent: Gerry Doyle
Estimated Sales: $788 Million
Number Employees: 2,700
Sq. footage: 80000
Parent Co: Lilydale Cooperative
Type of Packaging: Consumer, Food Service, Bulk
Brands:
Country Fair
Lilydale
Royal Fancy

7921 **Limited Edition**
3106 N Big Spring St Ste 101
Midland, TX 79705 432-686-2008
Fax: 432-686-2035
Processor of flavored honey butter, dip mixes, jalapenos, pickles and vegetables
Owner: Beverly Vaughan
Controller: Ann Wimberly
Estimated Sales: $300-500,000
Number Employees: 1-4
Sq. footage: 10000
Type of Packaging: Consumer, Food Service, Private Label, Bulk
Brands:
Limited Edition Presents
Udderly Delightful

7922 **Limoneria Company**
1141 Cummings Rd
Santa Paula, CA 93060-9709 805-525-5541
Fax: 805-525-8761 info@limoneira.com
www.limoneira.com
Packinghouse for Sunkist Growers, Inc. citrus fruit.
President/CEO: Harold Edwards
VP/Finance & Administration: Don Delmatoff
Senior Vice President: Alex Teague
Business Development Manager: David McCoy
Marketing Director: John Chamberlain
Director Packing & Sales: Tomas Gonzales
Director Information Systems: Eric Tovias
Agritourism Operations Manager: Ryan Nasalroad
Estimated Sales: G
Type of Packaging: Food Service

7923 **Limpert Brothers**
PO Box 1480
Vineland, NJ 8362
Fax: 856-794-8968 800-691-1353
general_info@limpertbrothers.com
www.limpertbrothers.com
Processor, importer and exporter of marshmallow fluff, hot fudge, cherries, butterscotch, carmel, and other toppings, flavors and ingredients.
President: Pearl Giordano
R&D: Jim Behringer
Quality Control: Donna Phrampus
Estimated Sales: $1 Million
Number Employees: 24
Number of Brands: 1
Number of Products: 400
Sq. footage: 70000
Type of Packaging: Food Service, Bulk
Brands:
LIMPERT BROTHERS

7924 **Limur Winery**
945 Green Street
5
San Francisco, CA 94133-3601 415-781-8691
Fax: 415-781-6303
Wines
Vineyard Manager: Doug Wight
Estimated Sales: $500,000-$1 Million
Number Employees: 1-4

7925 **Lin Court Vineyards**
1711 Alamo Pintado Rd
Solvang, CA 93463-9712 805-688-8554
Fax: 805-688-9327 info@lincourtwines.com
www.lincourtwines.com
Processor of red and white wines
General Manager: Alan Phillips
Number Employees: 5-9
Sq. footage: 4000
Parent Co: Folly Estates
Type of Packaging: Consumer
Brands:
Lin Court Vineyards

7926 **Lincoln Mills**
352 W Side Avenue
Jersey City, NJ 07305-1135 201-433-0070
President: Jane Jasper
Estimated Sales: Below $ 5 Million
Number Employees: 4

7927 **Lincoln Snacks Company**
30 Buxton Farm Rd
Stamford, CT 06905-1224 203-329-4545
Fax: 203-329-4555 800-872-7622
www.demets.com
Processor of popcorn snacks
President/CEO: Hendrick Hartong
CFO: Joanne Prier
CEO: David Clarke
Estimated Sales: $ 3 - 5 Million
Number Employees: 5-9
Type of Packaging: Consumer
Brands:
Fiddle Faddle
Golden Gourmet Nuts
Poppycock

7928 **Linda's Gourmet Latkes**
PO Box 491413
Los Angeles, CA 90049 818-453-8690
Fax: 818-453-8679 888-452-8537
info@lindasgourmetlatkes.com
www.lindasgourmetlatkes.com
latkes
President/Owner: Linda Hausberg

7929 **Linda's Lollies Company**
54 W 21st St
Suite 607
New York, NY 10010 212-447-6740
Fax: 212-447-1350 800-347-1545
info@lindaslollies.com www.lindaslollies.com
Processor and exporter of gourmet lollypops and confectionery gifts
President: Linda Harkavy
Sales & Marketing: Tammy Demone
Customer Services: Connie Atticella
Estimated Sales: $1500000
Number Employees: 1-4
Type of Packaging: Consumer, Food Service, Bulk
Brands:
Linda's Little Lollies
Linda's Lollies

7930 **Lindemann Produce**
1111 G Street
Los Banos, CA 93635-3762 209-826-2442
Fax: 209-826-0787
Exporter and processor of melons including cantaloupes and honeydews
General Manager: George Meek
Parent Co: Lindemann Farms
Type of Packaging: Bulk

7931 **Linden Beverage Company**
4675 John Marshall Hwy
Linden, VA 22642 540-635-2118
Fax: 540-636-4470
customerservice@alpenglow.net
www.alpenglow.net
Processor and exporter of sparkling cider
President: Ben R Lacy Iii III
Manager: Richard Wadkins
Sales Manager: Debra Hunter
Estimated Sales: $944344
Number Employees: 20-49
Sq. footage: 25000
Type of Packaging: Consumer
Brands:
Alpenglow

7932 **Linden Cheese Factory**
P.O.Box 439
Linden, WI 53553 608-623-2531
Fax: 608-623-2567 800-660-5051
Monterey jack, cheddar, colby, longhorn cheese
President: David Schroeder
Estimated Sales: $ 5-10 Million
Number Employees: 15

7933 **Linden Cookies**
25 Brenner Dr
Congers, NY 10920 845-268-5050
Fax: 845-268-5055 800-660-5051
info@lindencookies.com
www.lindencookies.com
Cookies and crackers
President: Paul Sturz
VP Sales: John Kraemer
Operation Manager: Paul Sturz
Estimated Sales: $ 10-20 Million
Number Employees: 20-49
Brands:
Linden's Originals

7934 **Lindner Bison**
27060 Victoria Lane
Apt 111
Valencia, CA 91355-5139 866-247-8753
Fax: 661-254-0224 klindner@bisurkey.com
www.bisurkey.com
Processor of bison/turkey burgers
President: Kathy Lindner
COO: Ken Lindner
Number Employees: 1-4
Brands:
Bison
Bisurkey

7935 **Lindsay Farms**
10 Georgia Road SW
Cave Spring, GA 30124-2031 706-777-9797
Fax: 706-777-0007
Gourmet food
Owner: Pam Beard
Estimated Sales: Less than $100,000
Number Employees: 1
Type of Packaging: Private Label
Brands:
Lindsay Farms

7936 **Lindsay's Tea**
380 Swift Ave # 13
S San Francisco, CA 94080-6232 650-952-5446
Fax: 650-871-4845 800-624-7031
www.mouncanostoul.com
Coffee
Manager: Melanie Mountanos
Estimated Sales: $ 20 - 50 Million
Number Employees: 20-49
Brands:
Lindsay's Tea

7937 **Lindt & Sprungli**
PO Box 276
1 Fine Chocolate Pl
Stratham, NH 03885-2577 603-778-8100
Fax: 603-778-3102 800-338-0839
info@lindt.com www.lindt.com
Chocolate
Estimated Sales: $ 30-50 Million
Number Employees: 650
Brands:
American Classics
Lindor Truffles
Lindt Chocolate

7938 **Linette Quality Chocolates**
P.O.Box 212
Womelsdorf, PA 19567 610-589-4526
Fax: 610-589-2706 nutcrckr@ralcorp.com
www.nutcrackerbrands.com/linette
Candy and confections
VP Finance: Natalie Denette
President/CEO: Lars Norgaard
VP: James P Linette
Sales Manager: Patti King
Estimated Sales: $ 20-50 Million
Number Employees: 100-249
Brands:
Linette

7939 **Linette Quality Chocolates**
P.O.Box 212
Womelsdorf, PA 19567 610-589-4526
Fax: 610-589-2706 www.ralcorp.com
Chocolate candy
President: Bill Gatto
VP: James P Linette
Marketing Director: Maurice Archambault
Sales: Ronald Buch
Estimated Sales: $ 25-49.9 Million
Number Employees: 100-249
Brands:
Linette

7940 **Lingle Brothers Coffee**
6500 Garfield Ave
Bell Gardens, CA 90201-1897 562-927-3317
Fax: 562-928-1505
Coffee
President: Earl Lingle
Estimated Sales: $ 10-20 Million
Number Employees: 20-49

7941 **Link Snacks**
1 Snack Food Ln
Minong, WI 54859 715-466-2234
Fax: 715-466-5151 800-346-6896
www.linksnacks.com
Snacks
President/CEO: Jack Link
Executive VP Marketing: Troy Link
Executive VP Sales: Jay Link
Estimated Sales: $100+ Million
Number Employees: 250-499
Brands:
JACK LINK'S
PICKLED PETE
TOMAHAWK

7942 **Linkmark International**
60 Richards Avenue
Paxton, MA 01612-1148 508-753-2797
Fax: 508-752-7476
Diet Foods
Chairman: George Abernathy
Estimated Sales: $290 K
Number Employees: 3

7943 **Lins International**
1601 S Federal Street
Chicago, IL 60616-1229 773-523-4478
Fax: 773-523-3829
President: Su Ju Hsu

7944 **Lion Brewery**
700 N Pennsylvania Ave
Wilkes Barre, PA 18705 570-823-8801
Fax: 570-823-6686 800-233-8327
info@lionbrewery.com www.lionbrewery.com
Processor of ale, porter, lager and alcoholic and nonalcoholic malt beverages
President/COO: Cliff Risell
CEO: Ronald Hammond
VP/CFO: Debbie Dennis
VP Sales/Marketing: Tom Farina
Public Relations/Marketing: Shelly Pheiff
Operations Director/Brewmaster: Leo Orlandini
Purchasing: Ray Buchman
Estimated Sales: $37349000
Number Employees: 135
Sq. footage: 2000
Type of Packaging: Consumer, Bulk
Brands:
1857
Brewery Hill Black & Tan
Brewery Hill Centennial
Brewery Hill Cherry Wheat
Brewery Hill Pale
Brewery Hill Raspberry
Liebotschauer
Steg Maier
Stegmaier

7945 **Lion Brewery**
700 N Pennsylvania Ave
Wilkes Barre, PA 18705 570-823-8801
Fax: 570-823-6686 800-233-8327
lorlandini@lionbrewery.com
www.lionbrewery.com
Beer
President: Cliff Risell
CEO: Ronald Hammond
CFO: Patrick Belardi
Controller: Debbie Dennis
Estimated Sales: $30 Million
Number Employees: 125
Type of Packaging: Private Label
Brands:
Brewery Hill Black & Tan
Brewery Hill Centennial
Brewery Hill Cherry Wheat
Brewery Hill Pale
Brewery Hill Rasberry
Liebotschauer
Steg Maier

7946 **Lion Raisins**
9500 S De Wolf Ave
Selma, CA 93662 559-834-6677
Fax: 559-834-6622 blion@lionraisins.com
www.lionraisins.com
Grower and processor of California raisins and raisin products
President/CEO: Al Lion
CFO: Susan Keller
Operations Manager: Dan Lion
Estimated Sales: $70000000
Number Employees: 400
Sq. footage: 13000
Type of Packaging: Consumer, Food Service, Private Label, Bulk
Brands:
CALIFORNIA GROWN
LION
SUNSHINE CALIFORNIA

7947 **Lionel Hitchen Essitional Oils**
1867 Porter Lake Drive
Sarasota, FL 34240 941-379-1400
Fax: 941-379-1433 lhitchenusa@aol.com
www.lheo.co.uk
Manufacturer of natural flavors and oils
President: Alison Barnes
General Manager: Suzy Nolan
Estimated Sales: $700,000
Number Employees: 8

7948 **Lioni Latticini, Inc.**
555 Lehigh Avenue
Union, NJ 07083 908-686-6061
Fax: 908-686-3449 info@lionimozzarella.com
www.lionimozzarella.com
Fresh whole milk mozzarella products
Owner: Michael Virga
Owner/VP: Salvatore Salzarulo
Marketing: Guiseppe (Sal) Salzarulo
Sales Manager: Michelina Salzarulo
Operations Director: Guiseppe (Sal) Salarulo
Production Supervisor: Salvatore Salzarulo
Plant Supervisor: Salvatore Salzarulo
Estimated Sales: $5,700,000
Number Employees: 1-4

7949 **Liono Latticini**
555 Lehigh Ave
Union, NJ 07083 908-686-6061
Fax: 908-686-3449 info@lionimozzarella.com
www.lionimozzarella.com
fresh mozzarella products
Estimated Sales: $1.9 Million
Number Employees: 39

7950 **Lipid Nutrition**
24708 W Durkee Road
Channahan, IL 60410 815-730-5208
Fax: 815-730-5202 info@lipidnutrition.com
www.lipidnutrition.com
Manufacturer natural lipid ingredients

7951 **Lipsey Mountain Spring Water**
P.O.Box 1246
Norcross, GA 30091-1246 770-449-0001
Fax: 770-242-7601 sales@lipseywater.com
www.lipseywater.com
Bottled water
President: Joseph Lipsey Iii III
Estimated Sales: $ 1-2.5 Million
Number Employees: 20-49

7952 **Lisa Shively's Kitchen Helpers, LLC**
802 Clarkway Ave
Po Box 2123
Eden, NC 27288 336-623-7511
Fax: 336-623-7511
Gluten-free, organic/natural, meals, hot chocolate, other soups, stews, beans, rubs, spices, cookbooks.
Marketing: Lisa Shively

7953 **Lisanatti Foods**
1815 Red Soils Court
Oregon City, OR 97045 503-652-1988
Fax: 503-653-1979 866-864-3922
lisanattifoods.com
vegetarian cheese alternatives
National Sales/Marketing: Teresa Lisac
Production Manager: Andy Ingersoll

7954 **Lisanatti FoodsP.J. Lisac & Associates, Inc**
1815 Red Soils Ct
Oregon City, OR 97045-4139 503-652-1988
Fax: 503-653-1979 866-864-3922
www.lisanatti.com
Processor of cheese analogs including soy satin
President: Philip J Lisac
Estimated Sales: $ 5-10 Million
Number Employees: 10-19
Type of Packaging: Consumer, Food Service
Brands:
Lisanatti
Soy-Sation

7955 **Lisbon Sausage Company**
433 S 2nd St
New Bedford, MA 02740-5764 508-993-7645
Fax: 508-994-0453
Portuguese sausage
President: Antonio Rodrigues
Vice President: Joan Sparrow
Estimated Sales: Below $ 5 Million
Number Employees: 5-9

7956 **Lisbon Seafood Company**
1428 S Main St
Fall River, MA 02724 508-672-3617
Fax: 508-672-4698
Seafood
Owner: Victor Da Silva
Estimated Sales: $ 1 - 3 Million
Number Employees: 10-19

7957 **Litehouse**
1109 N Ella Ave
Sandpoint, ID 83864 208-263-7569
Fax: 208-263-7821 vbrady@litehouseinc.com
www.litehousefoods.com
Processor of portion controlled refrigerated dressings and dips
President: Douglas Hawkins
CEO: Edward Hawkins Jr
Estimated Sales: $50-100 Million
Number Employees: 370
Type of Packaging: Food Service

7958 **Litehouse Foods**
1109 N Ella Ave
Sandpoint, ID 83864 208-263-7569
Fax: 208-263-7821 800-669-3169
rlowther@litehouseinc.com
www.litehousefoods.com
Processor and importer of salad dressings, sauces, mustards, dips and horseradish; exporter of salad dressings
President: Douglas Hawkins
CEO: Edward Hawkins Jr
VP Operations: Doug Hawkins
Purchasing Manager: Amy Van Sickle
Estimated Sales: $133 Million
Number Employees: 370

Sq. footage: 80000
Parent Co: Meyer Horseradish Company
Type of Packaging: Consumer, Food Service, Private Label, Bulk
Brands:
Chad's
Chadalee Farms
Meyer

7959 **Little Amana Winery**
4400 i St
Amana, IA 52203 319-668-9664
Fax: 319-668-2853
Wine
Owner: Bob Zuber
Brands:
Ackerman
Breezy Hills
Jasper
Little Swan Lake
Park Farm
Sugar Grove
Summerset
Village

7960 **Little Angel Foods**
530 N BEACH ST
Daytona Beach, FL 32114-2245 904-257-3040
Fax: 904-257-1727
Cheesecakes
President: Jim Omeara
Estimated Sales: $ 10-20 Million
Number Employees: 20

7961 **Little Crow Foods**
P.O.Box 1038
Warsaw, IN 46581-1038 574-267-7141
Fax: 574-267-2370 800-288-2769
customerservice@littlecrowfoods.com
www.littlecrowfoods.com
Manufacturer and contract packager of dry blended products including flour, pancake mixes and breakfast cereals; exporter of flour, cereals and seasoned coating mixes
President: Dennis Fuller
EVP: Kimberly Fuller
VP Operations: Ron Shipley
Estimated Sales: $8 Million
Number Employees: 50-99
Sq. footage: 90000
Type of Packaging: Consumer, Food Service, Private Label, Bulk
Brands:
MIRACLE MAIZE

7962 **Little Dutch Boy Bakeries**
12349 S 970 E
Draper, UT 84020 801-571-3800
Fax: 801-571-3802
Processor of cookies including shortbread, chocolate chip, coconut, sugar, oatmeal, spice and fudge
President: Frank Bakker
VP: Robert Bakker
Estimated Sales: $20-50 Million
Number Employees: 50-99
Type of Packaging: Consumer, Private Label
Brands:
Little Dutch Boy Bakeries

7963 **Little Freddy's**
22151 Us Highway 19 N
Clearwater, FL 33765-2365 727-791-1118
Fax: 727-791-4092 littlefreddys@aol.com
CEO/CFO: Fred Lewis
Estimated Sales: $1-4.9 Million
Number Employees: 5-9
Type of Packaging: Private Label

7964 **Little Hills Winery**
710 S Main St
Saint Charles, MO 63301 636-946-6637
Fax: 636-724-1121 877-584-4557
restaurant@little-hills.com www.little-hills.com
Wines
Co-Owner: David Campbell
Co-Owner: Tammy Campbell
Estimated Sales: $8.5 Million
Number Employees: 50-99

7965 **Little I**
815 3rd Street
Blaine, WA 98230 360-332-3258
Fax: 360-332-3279 sales@littlei.com
www.littlei.com
mints and gums

7966 **Little Lady Foods**
2323 Pratt Blvd
Elk Grove Vlg, IL 60007 847-806-1440
Fax: 847-806-0026 800-439-1440
info@llf.com www.littleladyfoods.com
Customer food creator and manufacturer of premium pizzas, gourmet sandwiches, wraps, paninis grab-n-go items, breakfast items and desserts
President: John Geocaris
CEO: Dan Scales
VP Sales & Marketing: Peter Cokinos
VP Operations: Chris Celeslie
VP Procurement: Bruno Del Rio
Estimated Sales: $350,000,000
Number Employees: 400+
Sq. footage: 50000
Brands:
Bravissimo!
Connie's Pizza
Little Lady
Primerro
Tenaro

7967 **Little Miss. Muffin**
4014 N Rockwell St
Chicago, IL 60618 773-463-6328
Fax: 773-463-7101 800-456-9328
info@littlemissmuffin.com
www.littlemissmuffin.com
Processor of fresh and frozen cakes and pastries
Owner: Staci Minic Mintz
Estimated Sales: $1.8 Million
Number Employees: 40
Type of Packaging: Consumer, Food Service
Brands:
Little Miss Muffin
Wide Shoulders Bakin

7968 **Little Rhody Brand Frankfurts**
5 Day St
Johnston, RI 2919 401-831-0815
sales@littlerhodyhotdogs.com
www.littlerhodyhotdogs.com
Manufacturer of sausage, frankfurters, meat products and fast foods
President: Edward Robalisky
Estimated Sales: $3 Million
Number Employees: 1-4
Sq. footage: 10000
Type of Packaging: Consumer, Food Service
Brands:
LITTLE RHODY BRAND

7969 **Little River Lobster Company**
P.O.Box 507
East Boothbay, ME 04544-0507 207-633-2648
Fax: 604-276-8371
Whole fish/seafood
President: Mike Dalton
Estimated Sales: $810,000
Number Employees: 1-4

7970 **Little River Seafood**
440 Rock Town Rd
Reedville, VA 22539 804-453-3670
Fax: 804-453-5421 kelly@littleriverseafood.com
www.littleriverseafood.com
Processor of quality crab products.
President: J Gregory Lewis
Marketing Executive: Kelly Minor
Estimated Sales: $10026306
Number Employees: 20-49
Type of Packaging: Consumer, Food Service, Private Label, Bulk
Brands:
Little River Seafood

7971 **Live A Little Gourmet Foods**
37330 Cedar Boulevard
Suite H
Newark, CA 94560-4157 510-744-3683
Fax: 510-744-3684 888-744-2300
info@livealittle.com www.livealittle.com
Fresh salads dressings and croutons
Owner: Virginia Davis
Estimated Sales: $ 1 - 3 Million
Number Employees: 1-4
Number of Brands: 2
Brands:
Live a Little Dressings
Perfect Croutons

7972 **Live Food Products**
P.O.Box 7
Santa Barbara, CA 93102 805-968-1020
Fax: 805-968-1001 800-446-1990
info@bragg.com www.bragg.com
Processor of liquid aminos and organic apple cider vinegar and extra-virgin olive oil
Manager: Sandi Enriquez
Controller: Sandy Gooch
Estimated Sales: $ 5 - 10 Million
Number Employees: 20-49
Brands:
Bragg

7973 **Live Oaks Winery**
3875 Hecker Pass Road
Gilroy, CA 95020 408-842-2401
Wines
President: Richard Blocher
Estimated Sales: $500-1 Million appx.
Number Employees: 20-49

7974 **Livermore Falls Baking Company**
49 Gilbert St
Livermore Falls, ME 04254 207-897-3442
Fax: 207-897-6381
Processor of baked goods including rolls and pizza crusts
President: Anthony Maxwell
Estimated Sales: $990000
Number Employees: 5-9

7975 **Livermore Valley Cellars**
1193 Ava St
Livermore, CA 94550 925-454-9463
Fax: 925-454-9463 info@lvcwines.com
www.lvcwines.com
Producer of wine
President: Chris Lagiss
CEO: Tim Sauer
Marketing Director: Tim Sauer
Estimated Sales: $1-2.5 Million
Number Employees: 1-4
Brands:
LVC

7976 **Living Farms**
352 3rd Street E
Tracy, MN 56175-1527 507-629-3517
Fax: 507-629-4258
Food products
Owner: Ardell Anderson
Vice President/CEO: Janet Anderson
Director of Administration: Lori Dardis
Estimated Sales: Under $500,000
Number Employees: 3

7977 **Living Harvest Foods**
PO Box 4407
Portland, OR 97208 503-274-0755
888-690-3958
customerservice@livingharvest.com
www.livingharvest.com
Non dairy hemp milk, ice cream bars, ice cream, hemp protein powder, hemp oil
President/CEO: Hans Faster
CFO/COO: Catherine Hearn
Marketing Manager: Christina Volgyesi
Estimated Sales: $5 Million
Number Employees: 10
Sq. footage: 3200

7978 **Livingston Farmers Association**
641 6th Street
Livingston, CA 95334 209-394-7941
Fax: 209-394-7952
Processor and exporter of sweet potatoes, peaches and almonds
President: Steve Moler
CEO: Jim Snyder
Sales Director: Raul Aguilas
Estimated Sales: $6 Million
Number Employees: 45
Sq. footage: 23800
Brands:
Yamato Colony

7979 **Livingston Moffett Winery**
1895 Cabernet Ln
Saint Helena, CA 94574 707-963-2120
Fax: 707-963-9385 800-788-0370
info@livingstonwines.com
www.livingstonwines.com

Winery
President: Diane Livingston
Production Manager: Mark Moffett
Estimated Sales: Below $ 5 Million
Number Employees: 4
Brands:
Gemstone Vineyard
Moffett
Stanley's
Starrey's ion
Syrah

7980 Livingston's Bull Bay Seafood
P.O.Box 70
Mc Clellanville, SC 29458-0070 843-887-3519
Fax: 843-887-3989
Shrimp and oysters
Co-Owner/President: Bull Livingston
Co-Owner/CEO: Kathy Livingston
Estimated Sales: $1 Million
Number Employees: 5-9

7981 Llano Estacado Winery
P.O.Box 3487
Lubbock, TX 79452-3487 806-745-2258
Fax: 806-748-1674 800-634-3854
info@llanowine.com www.llanowine.com
Wine
President: Mark Hyman
CFO: Mary McGill
Vice President: James Morris
Operations Manager: Greg Bruni
Estimated Sales: Below $ 5 Million
Number Employees: 20-49
Type of Packaging: Private Label

7982 Lloyd's
P.O.Box 2727
Berwyn, PA 19312-0270 610-293-0516
Fax: 610-293-0689 lloydsofpa@aol.com
www.lloydspa.com
Frozen dessert mixes
President: Barry Jones
Marketing/Sales: Andy Jones
Purchasing Manager: Betty Clark
Estimated Sales: $ 5-10 Million
Number Employees: 1-4
Number of Brands: 1
Number of Products: 20
Type of Packaging: Food Service, Private Label, Bulk

7983 Lloyd's Barbeque Company
1455 Mendota Heights Rd
Eagan, MN 55120 651-688-6000
Fax: 651-681-1430 www.lloydsbbq.com
Barbeque sauce
President: Stuart Applebaum
President: Lloyd Sigel
Executive VP: Franz Hofmeister
Plant Manager: Jack Goldbach
Estimated Sales: I
Number Employees: 250-499

7984 Loafin' Around
555 Eastview Dr
Madison, AL 35758-7824 301-570-4513
Fax: 301-216-1575 loafin@erols.com
Breads
President: Blake Daniel
Estimated Sales: $62 K
Number Employees: 1

7985 Lobster Gram International
4664 N Lowell Ave
Chicago, IL 60630 773-777-8315
Fax: 773-777-5546 800-548-3562
www.livelob.com
Lobster
President: Daniel Zawacki
Estimated Sales: $ 1 - 3 Million
Number Employees: 10-19

7986 Lobsters Alive Company
3200 N Richmond Rd
Johnsburg, IL 60051 708-562-7837
Fax: 815-344-4479
Wholesaler/distributor of lobster tank supplies and parts; also, sales and service of new and reconditioned lobster tanks available; design consultant specializing in large holding systems
General Manager: Joann Baureis
Equipment Specialist: Dennis Baureis

Estimated Sales: $500,000-$1 Million
Number Employees: 1-4
Sq. footage: 2000

7987 Local Tofu
PO Box 333
Nyack, NY 10960-0333 845-727-6393
Processor of tofu, soy milk, tofu salads, herbal spreads and vegetarian burgers
President: Sam Weinreb
Estimated Sales: Under $500,000
Number Employees: 1-4
Type of Packaging: Consumer
Brands:
Tofu

7988 Lochhead Manufacturing Company
527 Axminister Dr
Fenton, MO 63026 636-326-1222
Fax: 636-326-4447 888-776-2088
sales@lochheadvanilla.com
www.lochheadvanilla.com
Processor and exporter of vanilla extracts including pure, natural and artificial blends.
Member/Owner: John Lochhead
Member: George Lochhead
Estimated Sales: $ 10 - 20 Million
Number Employees: 10-19
Type of Packaging: Consumer, Private Label, Bulk

7989 (HQ)Lochhead Manufacturing Company
527 Axminister Dr
Fenton, MO 63026 636-326-1222
888-776-2088
www.lochheadvanilla.com
Produces a variety of vanilla extracts and flavorings available in several blends including both natural and artificial in addition to whole vanilla beans and powders.
President/Co-Owner: George Lochhead
Co-Owner: John Lochhead
Estimated Sales: $ 5 - 10 Million
Number Employees: 5-9
Brands:
Lochhead Vanilla

7990 Lockcoffee
6 Kilmer Road
Larchmont, NY 10538-2636 914-273-7838
Fax: 212-827-0945
Coffee
President: B Brown Lock
Estimated Sales: Under $500,000
Number Employees: 1-4

7991 Lockwood Vineyards
9777 Blue Larkspur Ln # 102
Monterey, CA 93940-6554 831-642-9200
Fax: 831-644-7829 lockwoodoaks@inreach.com
www.lockwoodvineyard.com
Wines
Owner: Paul Toeppen
Estimated Sales: $ 2.5-5 Million
Number Employees: 5-9
Type of Packaging: Private Label

7992 Locus Foods
237 Stanford Parkway
Findlay, OH 45840-1733 41- 4-3 49
Fax: 419-425-0656
President: Tom Klevay
Estimated Sales: Under $500,000
Number Employees: 1-4

7993 Locustdale Meat Packing
P.O.Box 15
Locustdale, PA 17945 570-875-1270
Processor of sausage, kielbasa, ring bologna and roast chicken and turkey
Owner: Jack Holderman
Estimated Sales: $ 1 - 3 Million
Number Employees: 1-4

7994 Loders Croklaan
24708 W Durkee Rd
Channahon, IL 60410 815-730-5200
Fax: 815-730-5202 800-621-4710
fats.lc@croklaan.com www.croklaan.com

Processor of fats, oils, flavored flakes, emulsifiers, dietary fiber and encapsulates, shortenings
President: Julian Veicht
Marketing Manager: Mary Thomas
Sales: Manuel Laborde
Communications: Ed McIntosh
Estimated Sales: $100+ Million
Number Employees: 100-249
Number of Brands: 25
Parent Co: Loders Croklaan

7995 Lodi Canning Company
307 Nestles St
Lodi, WI 53555 608-592-4236
Fax: 608-592-4742 bob@lodicanning.com
Manufacturer of canned peas and creamed corn
President: Bob Goeres
Estimated Sales: $2-5 Million
Number Employees: 100-249
Type of Packaging: Private Label
Brands:
DAY BY DAY
IDOL
LODI'S

7996 Lodi Nut Company
1230 S Fairmont Ave
Lodi, CA 95240 209-334-2081
Fax: 209-369-6815 800-234-6887
lodinut@inreach.com www.lodinut.com
Processor of black walnut kernels and nut factory gourmet nuts; also, custom processor and co-packer of English walnut, almond and macadamia kernels
President/Sales & Marketing Director: Kelvin Suess
Executive VP: Virgil Suess
Controller/Human Resources Director: Rocky Suess
Plant Manager: Reuben Rodriguez
Estimated Sales: $7,001,000
Number Employees: 75
Sq. footage: 40000
Type of Packaging: Consumer, Food Service, Private Label, Bulk

7997 Loew Vineyards
14001 Liberty Rd
Mount Airy, MD 21771 301-831-5464
Fax: 301-831-5464 loew@loewvineyard.net
www.loewvineyards.net
Wines
President: William Loew
Estimated Sales: $800,000
Number Employees: 1-4

7998 Loffredo Produce
500 46th St
Rock Island, IL 61201 309-786-0969
Fax: 309-786-0660 800-397-2096
lbeener@loffredo.com www.loffredo.com
Manager: Jerry Moore
Branch Manager: Jerry Moore
Sales: Dave Dalton
Estimated Sales: $ 5-10 Million appx.
Number Employees: 50-99
Parent Co: Lofredo Fresh Produce

7999 Loftshouse Foods
215 N 700 W
A
Ogden, UT 84404-1342 801-317-1480
Fax: 801-392-3015 800-877-7055
investorrelations@ralcorp.com www.ralcorp.com
President: Kevin J Hunt
CEO: David Skarie
Brands:
Bakery Chef
Bremner
Carriage House
Nutcracker Brands
Ralston Foods

8000 Log 5 Corporation
4 Glenberry Court
Phoenix, MD 21131 410-329-9580
Fax: 443-705-0223 jdekker@log5.com
www.log5.com
Food ingredients; pasteurization process
President: Joost De Koomen
Vice President: Jochem Dekker

8001 **Log House Foods**
700 Berkshire Ln N
Plymouth, MN 55441 763-546-8395
Fax: 763-546-7339 info@loghousefoods.com
www.loghousefoods.com
Processor of twice-baked cinnamon toast and biscotti, flaked coconut, European-style melting creams for dipping and coating desserts, chocolate chips, candy coatings, etc.
President: Alan Kasdan
VP Operations: Josh Kasdan
Estimated Sales: $17000000
Number Employees: 20-49
Type of Packaging: Consumer, Food Service, Private Label
Brands:
Bella Crema
Jacobsen's Toast
Log House
Log House Candiquik
Plymouth Pantry

8002 **(HQ)Loggins Meat Company**
P.O.Box 7369
Tyler, TX 75711 903-595-1011
Fax: 903-595-6847 800-527-8610
logginsinc@aol.com www.loggins-meat.com
Manufacturer of pre-portioned beef, pork and chicken items as well as a complete line of ground and breaded products
President: Bobby Loggins
VP Sales/Marketing: George Skinner
Estimated Sales: $ 50 - 100 Million
Number Employees: 250-499
Sq. footage: 75000
Type of Packaging: Consumer, Food Service, Private Label, Bulk
Brands:
Flavor-Best
Grill Sensations
Loggins Legends
Loggins Meat Co.

8003 **Lohr Winery**
1000 Lenzen Ave
San Jose, CA 95126-2739 408-288-5057
Fax: 408-993-2276 sjwinecenter@jlohr.com
www.jlohr.com
Wines
President: Jerome J Lohr
VP: Jeff Sunquist
Marketing Director: Mark Dirickson
Plant Manager: Dave Mezynski
Estimated Sales: $ 30-50 Million
Number Employees: 50-99
Type of Packaging: Private Label

8004 **Lola Savannah**
1701 Commerce St # 1a
Houston, TX 77002-2244 713-222-9800
Fax: 713-222-9802 888-663-9166
lola@lolasavannah.com www.lolasavannah.com
Roasted coffee and tea
Owner: Duke Furgh
Vice President: Michael Spencer
Operations Manager: Hank Segelke
Estimated Sales: Less than $500,000
Number Employees: 5-9
Type of Packaging: Consumer, Food Service, Private Label, Bulk

8005 **Lolonis Winery**
1930 Tice Valley Blvd
Walnut Creek, CA 94595-2203 925-938-8066
Fax: 925-938-8069 sls.mrkting@lolonis.com
www.lolonis.com
Wines
President: Petros Lolonis
Estimated Sales: $600,000
Number Employees: 5-9
Brands:
Ladybug White Old Vines

8006 **(HQ)Lombardi Brothers Meat Packers**
4720 Tejon Street
Denver, CO 80211-1257 303-458-7441
Fax: 303-458-7444 800-421-4412
Manufacturer of beef, pork, lamb and veal; importer of wild game; wholesaler/distributor of frozen pastas and desserts, soups, health foods, meats and smoked salmon and trout; serving the food service market
President/Owner: Irwin Fishman
VP: George Lombardi
Director Operations: Doug Wax
General Manager: Mike Walters
Estimated Sales: $30 Million
Number Employees: 60
Sq. footage: 30000
Type of Packaging: Food Service
Other Locations:
Lombardi Brothers Meat
Fridley MN
Lombardi Brothers Meat
Le Mars IA

8007 **Lombardi's Bakery**
177 E Main St
Torrington, CT 06790-5432 860-489-4766
Fax: 860-489-4766
Baked goods
President: Carmen Lombardi
Estimated Sales: Less than $500,000
Number Employees: 1-4
Brands:
Lombardi's

8008 **Lombardi's Seafood**
7491 Brokerage Dr
Orlando, FL 32809 407-859-1015
Fax: 407-240-2562 800-879-8411
quality@lombardis.com www.lombardis.com
Processor, importer and wholesaler/distributor of fresh and frozen seafood; serving the food service market
Owner: Vince Lomabardi
VP: Vince Lombardi
Supervisor: Mike Lombardi
Estimated Sales: $10-20 Million
Number Employees: 100-249
Type of Packaging: Food Service

8009 **Lone Elm Sales**
N9695 Van Dyne Rd
Van Dyne, WI 54979 920-688-2338
Fax: 920-688-5233 800-950-8275
www.loneelm.com
Wholesale distributors
President: Glen Dedow
Vice President: Matthew Dedow
Estimated Sales: Below $ 5 Million
Number Employees: 20-49
Type of Packaging: Private Label
Brands:
Lone Elm

8010 **Lone Pine Enterprises**
P.O.Box 416
Carlisle, AR 72024 870-552-3217
Processor and exporter rice and soybeans
Owner/President: Carl Garrich
Estimated Sales: $200,000
Number Employees: 1-4
Type of Packaging: Consumer, Food Service, Bulk

8011 **Lone Star Bakery**
106 W Liberty St
Round Rock, TX 78664 512-255-3629
Fax: 512-255-6405 info@roundrockdonuts.com
www.roundrockdonuts.com
Processor and exporter of pre-baked and frozen buttermilk biscuits, muffins, cinnamon rolls, brownies, sheet cakes, fruit cobblers,pie shells, pecan and fruit pie,and portioned cookie and dough
Owner: Dale Cohrs
VP: Bill Scott
Sales: Rick Perrett
Operations: Damon Smith
Plant Manager: Fred Alexander
Purchasing: Clint Scott
Estimated Sales: $450000
Number Employees: 10-19
Sq. footage: 150000
Type of Packaging: Food Service, Private Label, Bulk
Brands:
Lone Star

8012 **Lone Star Beef Jerky Company**
2314 Colgate St
Lubbock, TX 79415 806-762-8833
Fax: 806-762-8835
Manufacturer of beef jerky and brisket
President: Don Shobert
Estimated Sales: $200000
Number Employees: 1-4
Type of Packaging: Consumer, Food Service

8013 **Lone Star Consolidated Foods**
1727 N Beckley Ave
Dallas, TX 75203 214-946-2185
Fax: 214-946-2286 800-658-5637
sales@lonestarfunfoods.com
www.lonestarfunfoods.com
Processor of frozen baked goods including pastries, sweet rolls and yeast raised and cake doughnuts; also, hush puppies
President: Jim Rader
CEO: Dolores Burdine
Sales/Marketing Executive: Dick Melby
Purchasing Agent: T Griffith
Estimated Sales: $ 20 - 50 Million
Number Employees: 100-249
Sq. footage: 50000000
Parent Co: Burdine Companies
Type of Packaging: Consumer, Food Service

8014 **Lone Star Food Products**
1727 N Beckley Ave
Dallas, TX 75203-1007 214-946-2185
Fax: 214-946-2286 www.lonestarfunfoods.com
President: Kathy Burdine
Director Marketing: Joe Cabbeneseh
Controller: Bobbie Burgess
CEO: Dolores Burdine
Sales Manager: Dick Melby
Estimated Sales: $ 20 - 50 Million
Number Employees: 100-249
Brands:
Lone Star

8015 **Lone Wolf Brewing**
403 Main Street
Carbondale, CO 81623-2068 970-963-9757
Beer
Owner: Patricia Cross
Brewmaster: Donald Wolfe
Estimated Sales: Under $500,000
Number Employees: 1-4

8016 **(HQ)Long Beach Seafoods**
825 W 16th St
Long Beach, CA 90813 562-435-5357
Fax: 714-590-0408 honcho2@aol.com
www.longbeachseafood.com
Processor and exporter of fresh and frozen fish including halibut, salmon, sea bass and swordfish
President: Tony Delucia
Vice President: Antonio de Lucia
Director Manufacturing: Robert Stillwell
Plant Manager: Tony de Lucia
Estimated Sales: $ 20 - 50 Million
Number Employees: 20-49
Sq. footage: 29000
Type of Packaging: Consumer, Food Service, Private Label, Bulk
Other Locations:
Long Beach Seafoods
Del Mar CA
Brands:
Fan-Sea
Stars Pride
Stilwell's

8017 **Long Expected Coffee Company**
960 Nepperhan Ave
Yonkers, NY 10703
Fax: 914-969-8248
Coffee
Manager: Dean Peialteos
Estimated Sales: Below $ 5 Million
Number Employees: 20-49

8018 **Long Food Industries**
709 Rock Beauty Road
Fripp Island, SC 29920-7344 843-838-3205
Fax: 843-838-3918 longfood@isle.net
www.longfoodindustries.com
Shrimp, cooked/diced chicken, clam (meat and broth), beef (diced/cooked), lobster, fish and pork
President: Leon Long
Estimated Sales: $ 10-20 Million
Number Employees: 1
Type of Packaging: Food Service

8019 Long Grove ConfectioneryCompany
333 Lexington Dr
Buffalo Grove, IL 60089 847-459-3100
Fax: 847-459-4871 800-373-3102
linda_gadas@longgrove.com
www.longgrove.com
Processor of confectionery items including chocolates, molded chocolate, apples, novelties, custom molded logos and holiday boxes.
President: John Mangel II
Vice President: David Mangel
Marketing: Linda Gadas
Estimated Sales: $5-10 Million
Number Employees: 50-99
Sq. footage: 25000
Type of Packaging: Consumer, Food Service, Private Label, Bulk
Brands:
Chicago Mints
Long Grove Confections
Myrties
Myrtles
Ultimate Apple

8020 Long Trail Brewing Company
P.O.Box 168
Bridgewater Corners, VT 05035 802-672-5011
Fax: 802-672-5012 itales@longtrail.com
www.longtrail.com
Brewers
President: Andy Pherson
Director Manufacturing: Thomas O'Brien
Purchasing Manager: Mathew Quinian
Estimated Sales: $ 10-20 Million
Number Employees: 20-49
Brands:
Double Bag
Harvest
Hibernator
India Pale Ale
Long Trail Ale

8021 Long Vineyards
1535 Sage Canyon Rd
St Helena, CA 94574-9628 707-963-2496
Fax: 707-963-5016 bob@longvineyards.com
www.longvineyards.com
Wines
Co-Owner/President: Robert Long
Co-Owner: Zelma Long
Marketing/PR Director: Pat Perini Long
Winemaking Operations Director: Sandi Belcher
Estimated Sales: $500,000-$1 Million
Number Employees: 1-4
Brands:
Johannisberg Riesling
Sangiovese

8022 Longacres Modern Dairy
P.O.Box 69
Barto, PA 19504 610-845-7551
Fax: 610-845-2041 www.longacresicecream.com
Dairy
President: Daniel T Longacre Jr
VP: Newton T Longacre
Treasurer: Kathryn Longacre
CFO: Timoty T Longacre
Plant Engineer: Daniel Longacre
Estimated Sales: Below $ 5 Million
Number Employees: 20-49
Brands:
Longacre

8023 Longbottom Coffee & Tea
4893 NW 235th Ave
Hillsboro, OR 97124 503-648-1271
Fax: 503-681-0944 800-288-1271
info@longbottomcoffee.com
www.longbottomcoffee.com
Processor and importer of specialty coffees including certified organics, espresso, flavored, regionals and blends; wholesaler/distributor of espresso machines and fine teas
President: Michael Baccellieri
Marketing Director: Lisa Walker
Sales Director: Gabrielle Paeson
Manufacturing/Operations Director: Tom Brandon
Estimated Sales: $8 Million
Number Employees: 50
Sq. footage: 28000
Type of Packaging: Consumer, Food Service, Private Label, Bulk

8024 Longford-Hamilton Company
17885 SW Tualatin Valley Hwy
Beaverton, OR 97006 503-642-5661
Fax: 503-649-1321 oldmill566@aol.com
oldmillrum.com
Imported specialty foods and up-scale confectionery products
President: Malarkey Wall
Sales Director: Jan Rudolph
Estimated Sales: Below $ 5 Million
Number Employees: 1-4
Number of Brands: 1
Number of Products: 20
Type of Packaging: Consumer
Brands:
Old Mill Brand

8025 Longleaf Plantation
P.O.Box 511
Lumberton, MS 39455-0511 601-794-6001
Fax: 601-794-5052 800-421-7370
longleaf@c-gate.net www.longleafplantation.net
Manufacturers of pecans
President: Warren Hood Jr
Estimated Sales: $ 5-10 Million
Number Employees: 20-49
Brands:
Longleaf Plantation

8026 Longmeadow
20 Williams St
Longmeadow, MA 01106-1950 413-565-4153
Fax: 413-565-4112 http://www.longmeadow.org
Specialty sauces
Manager: Mark Denver
General Manager: Suzie Barton
Estimated Sales: $ 2.5-5 Million
Number Employees: 5-9

8027 Longmeadow Foods
PO Box 1405
Gray, ME 04039-1405 207-529-5879
Fax: 207-529-5813 800-255-8401
jlmeadow@midcoast.com www.fancyfare.com
Gourmet foods
Estimated Sales: $ 2.5-5 Million
Number Employees: 5-9
Brands:
Blackburn's
Death By Chocolate
Downeast Pasta
Kandia
Maine Marinades
Maine Mountain Morni
Nomad Apiaries
Oyster Creek Mushroo
Pemberton's Dessert
Porcupine Island
Raye
Spruce Mountain Blub
Spruce Mountain Blub

8028 Longmont Foods
150 Main St
Longmont, CO 80501 303-776-6611
Fax: 303-776-4965 www.longmontarts.com
Processor of fresh and frozen turkey and turkey frankfurters
Owner: Brad Long
Operations Manager: Miguel Ramirez
Estimated Sales: $100+ Million
Number Employees: 1,000-4,999
Parent Co: ConAgra Foods
Type of Packaging: Consumer, Food Service, Private Label

8029 Longo Coffee & Tea
201 Bleecker St
New York, NY 10012-1446 212-477-5421
Fax: 212-979-2303 www.portorico.com
Coffee and tea
President: Peter Longo
Estimated Sales: $ 5-10 Million
Number Employees: 36

8030 Longo's Bakery
138 W 21st St
Hazleton, PA 18201 570-454-5825
Fax: 570-454-6246
Breads, rolls, pizza shells
Estimated Sales: $500,000-$1 Million
Number Employees: 10-19

8031 Longview Meat & Merchandise Ltd
PO Box 173
Longview, AB T0L 1H0
Canada 403-558-3706
Fax: 403-558-3708 866-355-3759
lbj@longviewjerky.com
www.longviewjerky.com
Processor of beef jerky, wholesaler of bavarian style sausage and pepperonis
President/Owner: Peter Lawson
Plant Manager: Jacky Lau
Estimated Sales: $1 Million
Number Employees: 12
Sq. footage: 6500
Type of Packaging: Consumer, Food Service, Private Label, Bulk

8032 Lonz Winery
1965 Fox Road Middle Bass Is
Middle Bass, OH 43446 419-285-5411
Wines
Estimated Sales: Under $500,000
Number Employees: 20-49

8033 Look Lobster
P.O.Box 504
Jonesport, ME 04649-0504 207-497-2353
Fax: 207-497-5559
Lobster
President: Bert Sid Look Iii
Vice President: Priscilla Look
Estimated Sales: $ .5 - 1 million
Number Employees: 1-4

8034 (HQ)Look's Gourmet Food Company
P.O.Box 450
East Machias, ME 04630-450
Fax: 207-259-3343 800-962-6258
office@amlook.com
www.looksgourmetfood.com
Manufacturer of canned clams, crabs, crab meat and lobster, lobster and clam bisque, seafood spreads/dips and clam chowder
President: Michael Cote
President: Jeffrey Look
Estimated Sales: $2.5-5 Million
Number Employees: 10-19
Type of Packaging: Consumer, Food Service, Private Label
Brands:
Atlantic
Bar Harbor
CAP'N JOHN

8035 Lopez Foods
9500 NW 4th St
Oklahoma City, OK 73127 405-789-7500
Fax: 405-499-0114
consumerinfo@lopezfoods.com
www.lopezfoods.com
President: Etuardo Sanchez
CFO: Jim English
Plant Manager: Richard Lane
Senior VP: Frank McKee
CFO: Jim English
Quality Control: Keven Nanke
Marketing Director: David Kovirik
Estimated Sales: $ 100-500 Million
Number Employees: 500-999
Brands:
Carneco Foods
Lopez Foods

8036 LorAnn Oils Inc
4518 Aurelius Rd
Lansing, MI 48910 517-882-0215
Fax: 571-822-0807 888-456-7266
customercare@lorannoils.com
www.lorannoils.com
candy oils and flavorings, vanilla extract, food colorings, specialty ingredients, supplies
President/Owner: John Grettenberger Sr
VP: Carl Thalen
Estimated Sales: $4.4 Million
Number Employees: 17

8037 Lora Brody Products
91 Edgewater Dr
Waltham, MA 02453-2405 617-928-1005
Fax: 617-558-5383 blanche007@aol.com
www.lorabrody.com

Bread dough enhancer
President: Lora Brody
Estimated Sales: $160 K
Number Employees: 2
Brands:
Dough Relaxer
Lora Brody Bread Dou
Sourdough Bread Enha

8038 **Lorann Oils**
4518 Aurelius Road
Lansing, MI 48910 517-882-0215
Fax: 517-882-0507 800-862-8620
customercare@lorannoils.com
www.lorannoils.com
Processor of coffee flavors, cocoa butter, flavoring oils, vanilla extracts, food colorings, fountain syrups, candy making molds and supplies, industrial ingredients, etc
Manager: John Grettenberger
CEO: Carl Thelen
VP: Carl Thalen
Marketing: Troy Sprague
Estimated Sales: $2.6 Million
Number Employees: 17
Sq. footage: 15000
Type of Packaging: Consumer, Food Service, Bulk
Brands:
Lorann Gourmet
Lorann International

8039 **Lords Sausage & CountryhHam**
P.O.Box 1000
Dexter, GA 31019 478-875-3101
Fax: 478-875-3039 800-342-6002
Manufacturer of fresh and smoked pork sausage and cured country ham
President: Wayne Lord
VP: Britt Lord
Estimated Sales: $10-20 Million
Number Employees: 20-49
Sq. footage: 20000
Type of Packaging: Consumer, Food Service, Private Label, Bulk
Brands:
LORD'S

8040 **Loretta's Authentic Pralines**
1100 N Peters St Ste 17
New Orleans, LA 70116 504-529-6170
Fax: 504-945-5912 loretta.pralines@att.net
www.lorettapralines.com
Pralines and confections
Owner: Loretta Harrison
Estimated Sales: $ 1-2.5 Million
Number Employees: 10-19

8041 **Loriva Culinary OilsWorldpantry.Com, Inc**
1192 Illinois Street
San Francisco, CA 94107 415-401-0080
Fax: 415-401-0087 866-972-6879
info@nspiredfoods.com www.worldpantry.com
Processor and exporter of specialty oils including roasted, infused and toasted sesame, peanut, safflower, walnut, garlic, olive, avocado, hazelnut, macadamia, etc.; also, kosher varieties available
President: Patrick Lee
CEO: David Miller
Consumer Relations: Liz Scatena
Number Employees: 10-19
Parent Co: NSpired Natural Foods
Type of Packaging: Consumer, Food Service, Private Label, Bulk
Brands:
Loriva
Loriva Jazz Roasted Oils
Loriva Supreme Flavored Oils
Loriva Supreme Oils

8042 **Los Altos Food Products**
15130 Nelson Ave
City of Industry, CA 91744-4334 626-330-6555
Fax: 626-330-6755 info@losaltos.com
www.losaltosfoods.com
Processor and exporter of Mexican and Swiss cheese
President: Raul Andrade
CFO: Alin Andrag
Director Sales/Marketing: Bill Finicle
Estimated Sales: $ 50-100 Million
Number Employees: 100-249
Type of Packaging: Consumer, Food Service

8043 **Los Amigos Tortilla Manufacturing**
251 Armour Dr NE
Atlanta, GA 30324-3979 404-876-8153
Fax: 404-876-8102 800-969-8226
ruben@losamigos.com www.losamigos.com
Corn and flour tortillas and chips
President: Zoila Rodriguez
General Manager: Ruben Rodriguez
Plant Supervisor: Carlos Perez
Estimated Sales: Below $ 5 Million
Number Employees: 50-99

8044 **(HQ)Los Angeles Nut House Brands**
1601 E Olympic Blvd
Los Angeles, CA 90021-1936 213-481-0134
Fax: 213-481-0084
Nuts
Executive Director: Azuka Uzoh
Sales Director: Terry McClean
Purchasing Manager: Jon Anderson
Estimated Sales: $ .5 - 1 million
Number Employees: 6
Type of Packaging: Private Label

8045 **Los Angeles Smoking & Curing Company**
1100 West Ewing Street
Seattle, WA 98119 213-628-1246
Fax: 213-614-8857
ron.christianson@oceanbeauty.com
http://www.oceanbeauty.com
Herring, kippers, lox, roe, cod, mackerel, salmon, shad, caviar and whitefish
President: Howard Klein
VP Sales/Marketing: Richard Schaeffer
Number Employees: 100-249
Parent Co: Ocean Beauty
Type of Packaging: Consumer, Food Service
Brands:
Kodikook
Lascco

8046 **Los Arcos Tortillas**
2912 N Commerce St
North Las Vegas, NV 89030-3945 702-399-3300
Fax: 702-399-2507 www.tortillasinc.com
Tortillas
Owner: Gus Gutierrez
Partner: Jose Gutierrez
Owner: Salvo Gutierrez
Estimated Sales: $ 2.5-5 Million
Number Employees: 20-49

8047 **Los Chileros de Nuevo Mexico**
PO Box 6215
Santa Fe, NM 87502 505-768-1100
Fax: 505-242-7513 888-EAT-CHIL
www.loschileros.com
chiles, corn products, salsa, rubs and mixes
Estimated Sales: $1 Million
Number Employees: 12

8048 **Los Gatos Brewing Company**
130 N Santa Cruz Ave Ste G
Los Gatos, CA 95030 408-395-9929
Fax: 408-395-2769 dine@lgbrewingco.com
www.lgbrewingco.com
Restaurant and brewing center
Owner: Andy Pavicich Jr
Director Manufacturing: Jeff Alexander
General Manager: Randall Bertho
Estimated Sales: $ 2.5-5 Million
Number Employees: 100-249
Brands:
Hefeweizen
Los Gatos Lager
Nut Brown Ale

8049 **Los Gatos Tomato Products**
PO Box 429
Huron, CA 93234 559-945-2700
Fax: 559-945-2661 cwoolf@losgatostomato.com
www.losgatostomato.com
Processor of tomato concentrates
President: Chris Woolf
Quality Control: Brandon Clement
Marketing Executive: Ann Delaware
Sales Manager: David Bodine
Plant Manager: Ray Medeiros
Purchasing Agent: Pat Bronson

Estimated Sales: $50 Million
Number Employees: 20
Sq. footage: 35000
Type of Packaging: Bulk

8050 **Los Olivos Vintners**
P.O.Box 636
Los Olivos, CA 93441-0636 805-688-9665
Fax: 805-686-1690 800-824-8584
Wines
President: Arthur White
Estimated Sales: $ 1-2.5 Million
Number Employees: 5-9
Type of Packaging: Private Label
Brands:
Los Olivos Vintners

8051 **Los Pericos Food Products**
2814 Whittier Blvd
Los Angeles, CA 90023-1527 323-269-5816
Fax: 323-269-1983 sales@lospericosfood.com
www.lospericosfood.com
Mexican tostada shells
Partner: Marcelino Ortega
Owner: Guadalupe Ortega
Partner: Luis Ortega
Estimated Sales: $3.9 Million
Number Employees: 46
Brands:
Tostada

8052 **Lost Coast Brewery**
617 4th St
Eureka, CA 95501-1013 707-445-4480
Fax: 707-445-4483 brewbarb@northcoast.com
www.lostcoast.com
Beer
President: Barbara Groom
Sales Director: Briar Bush
Plant Manager: Bill Estles
Estimated Sales: $ 20-50 Million
Number Employees: 50-99
Type of Packaging: Private Label
Brands:
8-Ball Stout
Alleycat Amber
Downtown Brown Ale
Lost Coast Ale
Raspberry Brown Ale
Winter Brown Ale

8053 **Lost Hills Winery**
3125 E Orange Street
Acampo, CA 95220 209-369-2746
Fax: 209-369-2746
Wines
President: Douglas Charboneau

8054 **Lost Mountain Winery**
2958 Lost Mountain Rd
Sequim, WA 98382 360-683-5229
Fax: 360-683-7572 888-683-5229
wine@lostmountain.com www.lostmountain.com
Wine
Co-Owner/Winemaker: Steve Conca
Co-Owner/Winemaker: Sue Conca
Estimated Sales: Less than $500,000
Number Employees: 1-4
Brands:
Lost Mountain Winery

8055 **Lost Trail Root Beer Com**
PO Box 670
Louisburg, KS 66053-0670 913-837-5202
Fax: 913-837-5762 800-748-7765
lcmill@micoks.net www.louisburgcidermill.com
Processor, wholesaler/distributor and exporter of apple cider and root beer; also, apple butter
President/Owner: Tom Schierman
Estimated Sales: $500,000-$1 Million
Number Employees: 5-9
Sq. footage: 10000
Type of Packaging: Consumer, Private Label
Brands:
LOST TRAIL
LOUISBURG

8056 **Losurdo Creamery**
34 Union St
Heuvelton, NY 13654 315-344-2444
Fax: 315-344-2362 www.losurdofoods.com

Processor of Italian cheeses including washed curd, provolone, mozzarella and ricotta; importer of pecorino romano cheese
President: Michael Losurdo, Sr.
VP Sales: Mark Losurdo
Plant Manager: William Muir
Number Employees: 50-99
Sq. footage: 150000
Parent Co: Losurdo Foods
Type of Packaging: Consumer, Food Service, Private Label
Brands:
Angustus
Bel-Capri

8057 **(HQ)Losurdo Creamery**
20 Owens Rd
Hackensack, NJ 07601-3297 201-343-6680
Fax: 201-343-8078 800-245-6787
info@losurdofoods.com www.losurdofoods.com
Processor of kosher ricotta cheese
President: Michael Losurdo Sr
Marketing Head: Dincenva Tulibutz
VP: Mark Losurdo
Estimated Sales: $ 20 - 50 Million
Number Employees: 100-249
Type of Packaging: Consumer, Food Service
Other Locations:
Losurdo Creamery
Heuvelton NY
Brands:
Losurdo

8058 **Losurdo Foods**
20 Owens Rd
Hackensack, NJ 07601-3297 201-343-6680
888-567-8736
marc@losurdofoods.com
www.losurdofoods.com
Providing transportation for cheeses
President: Michael Losurdo Sr
VP Marketing: Marc Losurdo
Number Employees: 10-19

8059 **Lotsa Pasta**
1762 Garnet Ave
San Diego, CA 92109 858-581-6777
Fax: 858-581-6783 chef@yumm.com
www.lotsapasta.com
Pasta
President: Carol Blomstrom
Estimated Sales: Below $ 5 Million
Number Employees: 20-49
Brands:
Lotsa Pasta

8060 **Lotte USA**
5243 Wayne Rd
Battle Creek, MI 49037 269-963-6664
Fax: 269-963-6695 lotteusa-inc@yahoo.com
www.lotteusainc.com
Processor of cream-filled cookies, throat drops and chewing gum
President: T Kaneko
Marketing Manager: Julie Fanning
Sales Manager: Frank Deleo
Operations Manager: Dick Thomason
Purchasing Manager: Ron Parsons
Estimated Sales: $15000000
Number Employees: 20-49
Type of Packaging: Consumer, Food Service
Brands:
FULL BLAST GUM
KOALA NO MARCH COOKIE

8061 **Lotus Bakery**
3336 Industrial Dr
Santa Rosa, CA 95403 707-526-1520
Fax: 415-526-6377 800-875-6887
sales@lotusbakery.com www.lotusbakery.com
Bread, cookies and energy bars
Owner: Mark Menning
Estimated Sales: $400,000
Number Employees: 10-19
Type of Packaging: Private Label
Brands:
Spirulina Bee Bar
Spirulina Trail Bar

8062 **Lotus Brands**
P.O.Box 1008
Silver Lake, WI 53170-1008 262-889-8561
Fax: 262-889-8591 800-824-6396
lotusbrands@lotuspress.com
www.lotusbrands.com
Sells natural products, including teas and herbal supplements
President: Santosh Krinsky
Estimated Sales: $ 1-2.5 Million
Number Employees: 50-99
Number of Brands: 16
Number of Products: 1000
Sq. footage: 38000
Type of Packaging: Consumer, Private Label, Bulk
Brands:
Ancient Secrets
Blue Pearl Incense
Dragon Eggs
Eco-DenT
Fuchs Tooth Brushes
Life Tree Products
Light Mountain
Nature's Alchemy
Neem Aura
Nirvana
Paul Penders
Rainforest Remedies
Sai Baba Nag Champa
Smile Brite
Tifert Aromatherapy
Yakshi Fragrances

8063 **Lotus Foods**
5210 Wall Avenue
Richmond, CA 94804 510-525-3137
Fax: 510-525-4226 info@lotusfoods.com
www.lotusfoods.com
Rice products
President/Partner: Kenneth Lee
CEO: Caryl Levine
Partner/VP: Caryl Levine
Marketing Director: Caryl Levine
Estimated Sales: $170,000
Number Employees: 3
Type of Packaging: Consumer, Food Service, Bulk
Brands:
A World of Rice
Bhutanese Red Rice
Cal Riso
Kaipen
Kalijira
Lowell Farms Organic

8064 **Lotus Manufacturing Company**
529 San Pedro Avenue
San Antonio, TX 78212-5057 210-223-1421
Fax: 21- 22- 273
President: Germino Trevino
Estimated Sales: $ 1-2.5 Million appx.
Number Employees: 1

8065 **Lou Ana Foods**
715 N Railroad Ave
Opelousas, LA 70570-6561 337-948-6561
Fax: 337-942-6239 800-723-3652
louanainfo@venturafoods.com www.louana.com
Edible oils
CEO: William Minor
VP: Don Gulley
Estimated Sales: $ 100-500 Million
Number Employees: 100-249
Parent Co: Ventura Foods
Type of Packaging: Consumer

8066 **Lou Pizzo Produce**
9660 NW 67th Pl
Parkland, FL 33076 954-941-8830
Fax: 954-941-8870
Produce
President: Louis Pizzo
VP: Angelina Pizzo
Estimated Sales: Below $ 5 Million
Number Employees: 1-4
Brands:
Lou Pizzo

8067 **Lou-Retta's Custom Chocolates**
3764 Harlem Rd
Buffalo, NY 14215 716-833-7111
Fax: 716-689-8113 chocolate@louretta.com
www.lourettas.com
Chocolate laced popcorn, chocolate pretzel nuggets dusted with gold dust and flavored with fresh ground coffee
President: Loretta Kaminsky
VP Marketing: Ellen Bradbury
Estimated Sales: Below $ 5 Million
Number Employees: 15
Type of Packaging: Private Label
Brands:
Buffalo Gold
Espresso Gold

8068 **Lougheed Fisheries**
539 2nd Avenue E
Owen Sound, ON N4K 2G5
Canada 519-376-1586
Fax: 519-376-1589
Processor of fresh and frozen fish and seafood
President: Greg Lougheed
Number Employees: 10-19
Type of Packaging: Bulk

8069 **Louis Dreyfus Citrus**
355 9th St
Winter Garden, FL 34787 407-656-1000
Fax: 407-656-1229 800-549-4272
www.ldcitrusfl.com
Processor of frozen fruit juice concentrates, citrus oils, pulp and purees
General Manager: Rick Tomlin
Sales Manager (Bulk): Kenneth Kelly
District Sales Manager: Robert Toadvine
Estimated Sales: $ 50 - 100 Million
Number Employees: 250-499
Type of Packaging: Consumer, Food Service, Private Label, Bulk
Brands:
Sunshine State
Whole Sun
Winter Gold

8070 **Louis Dreyfus Corporation**
20 Westport Rd
Wilton, CT 06897-4549 203-761-2000
Fax: 203-761-2275 drh-paris@louisdreyfus.fr
www.louisdreyfus.com
Processor and exporter of long grain milled and brewers' rice, rice bran, beans, wheat, soybeans, etc
VP Board of Directors: Pierre Louis-dreyfus
VP Board of Directors: Jean Louis-Dreyus
CFO: Len Federico
CEO: William C Reed
VP Board of Directors: Bernard Baldensperger
VP Board of Directors: Claude Boquin
Sr. Executive: Lorraine Bouvier
Sr. Executive: Patrice De Camaret
Sr. Executive: Aurelio A.P.Cidade
Sr. Executive: Peter Griffin
Sr. Executive: Philippe Louis-Dreyfus
Sr. Executive: Robert Louis-Dreyfus
Number Employees: 500-999
Parent Co: Louis Dreyfus Corporation
Type of Packaging: Food Service, Private Label, Bulk
Brands:
Delta Rose
Missouri's Finest
Showboat

8071 **Louis Dreyfus Corporation - Coffee Division**
40 Danbury Rd
Wilton, CT 06897-4406 203-761-2000
Fax: 203-761-2275 ldwltsugar@louisdreyfus.com
www.louisdreyfus.com
Coffee
General Manager: Bernard Baldensperger
President: Gerard Louis Dreyfus
CEO: William C Reed
Sr VP Finance: Leopold Dreyfus
Estimated Sales: $7.83 Billion
Number Employees: 200

8072 **Louis J. Rheb Candy Company**
3352 Wilkens Ave
Baltimore, MD 21229 410-644-4321
Fax: 410-646-0327 800-514-8293
www.rhebscandy.com
Manufacturer of chocolate candy
President: Edwin Harger
Estimated Sales: $5-10 Million
Number Employees: 20-49
Type of Packaging: Consumer

8073 **Louis Kemp Seafood Company**
1348 Highway 10 S
Motley, MN 56466 218-352-6600
Fax: 218-352-6609 800-325-4732
www.tridentseafoods.com
Processor and exporter of frozen and refrigerated surimi and seafood products
Quality Control: Suzie Burtels
VP: Mike Robinson
Production Manager: Jim Johnson
Purchasing Manager: Bob Storry
Number Employees: 250-499
Sq. footage: 110000
Parent Co: Bumble Bee Seafoods
Type of Packaging: Food Service, Private Label
Brands:
Captain Jac
Louis Kemp
Pacific Mate
Seafest

8074 **Louis Kemp Seafood Company**
2001 Butterfield Road
Downers Grove, IL 60515-1050 218-624-3636
Fax: 218-624-4791
President: Louis Kemp
COO: Greg Moore
Manager: Jim Olson
Estimated Sales: $ 20-50 Million
Number Employees: 100-249

8075 **Louis M. Martini**
254 South St. Helena Highway
St. Helena, CA 94575 707-963-2736
Fax: 707-963-8750 866-549-2582
www.louismartini.com
Wines
President: Carolyn Martini
Sales Director: Bob Matheny
VP Operations/Winemaker: Michael Martini
Plant Manager: Michael Mullen
Estimated Sales: $100 million +
Number Employees: 100-249
Type of Packaging: Consumer

8076 **Louis Maull Company**
219 N Market St
Saint Louis, MO 63102 314-241-8410
Fax: 314-241-9840 info@maull.com
www.maull.com
Processor of sauces including barbeque, worcestershire and steak
President: Louis T Maull Iv
Estimated Sales: $ 5-10 Million
Number Employees: 10-19
Brands:
Maull's Barbecue Sauce

8077 **Louis Severino Pasta**
110 Haddon Ave
Collingswood, NJ 08108 856-854-7666
Fax: 856-854-6098
Pasta
President: Peter Severino
VP/Partner: Louis Servino
Estimated Sales: Below $ 5 Million
Number Employees: 20-49

8078 **Louis Sherry**
3537 W North Avenue
Chicago, IL 60647-4808 773-486-8243
Fax: 773-486-1620
Ice cream and frozen desserts
Director Operations: Israel Gonzalez

8079 **Louis Swiss Pastry**
400 Aabc
Aspen, CO 81611-2545 970-925-8592
Fax: 970-925-1269 karse@packlab.com
Bread and bakery products
Owner: Felix Tornare
Owner: Karse Simon
Estimated Sales: $10-20 Million
Number Employees: 10-19

8080 **Louis Trauth Dairy**
P.O.Box 721770
Newport, KY 41072 859-431-7553
Fax: 859-431-0349 800-544-6455
info@trauthdairy.com www.trauthdairy.com
Processor of orange juice, spring and distilled water and cultured dairy products including cottage cheese, ice cream and nonfat and low-fat sour cream
Senior VP: Gary Sparks
Sales Manager Milk Division: Dan Smith
Operations VP: Steve Trauth
Estimated Sales: $100000000
Number Employees: 250-499
Sq. footage: 100000
Parent Co: Suiza Foods
Type of Packaging: Consumer, Food Service, Private Label, Bulk
Brands:
Jersey Farms
Louis Trauth

8081 **Louisa Food Products**
1918 Switzer Ave
Saint Louis, MO 63136 314-868-3000
Fax: 314-868-3014
Processor of frozen Italian foods including ravioli, cannelloni, tortellini and sauces
Owner/President: Thomas Baldetti
Sales Executive: Rob Foskett
Estimated Sales: $ 50 - 100 Million
Number Employees: 50-99
Type of Packaging: Consumer, Food Service, Private Label, Bulk
Brands:
Louisa Pastas

8082 **Louisburg Cider Mill**
14730 Highway K68
Louisburg, KS 66053-8223 913-837-5202
Fax: 913-837-5762 800-748-7765
info@louisburgcidermill.com
www.louisburgcidermill.com
Cider, beverages and a variety of gift items
President: Shelly Schierman
Vice President: Tom Schierman
Estimated Sales: $1-2.5 Million
Number Employees: 10-19
Type of Packaging: Private Label
Brands:
Lost Trail Root Beer
Louisburg Cider
Louisburg Farms

8083 **Louise Metafora Company**
600 Pleasant St
Watertown, MA 02472 61- 39- 191
Fax: 61- 39- 063
President: John Greeley
Estimated Sales: $ 1-2.5 Million
Number Employees: 1
Brands:
Espresso Gold

8084 **Louise's**
1700 Isaac Shelby Drive
Shelbyville, KY 40065-9172 502-633-9700
Fax: 502-633-3543
Fat free potato chips and crisps
Quality Assurance Manager: John Lindle
Estimated Sales: $ 5-9.9 Million
Number Employees: 40

8085 **Louisiana Coca-Cola Bottling Company**
5601 Citrus Blvd
Harahan, LA 70123-5508 504-818-7000
Fax: 504-826-7212 800-362-6996
Processor of soft drinks
Manager: Jay Ard
Number Employees: 500-999
Parent Co: Coca-Cola Enterprises
Type of Packaging: Consumer, Food Service, Bulk

8086 **Louisiana Crawfish Company**
140 Russell Cemetery Rd
Natchitoches, LA 71457 318-379-0539
Fax: 318-379-2816

8087 **Louisiana Fish Fry Products**
5267 Plank Rd
Baton Rouge, LA 70805-2730 225-356-2905
Fax: 225-356-8867 800-356-2905
info@louisianafishfry.com
www.louisianafishfry.com
Cajun food mixes, breadings, seasonings and sauces
Owner/President: Cliff Pizzolato
Owner: Anthony Pizzolato
VP: Joseph Pizzolato
Owner: Anthony Pizzolato
Estimated Sales: $ 10-20 Million
Number Employees: 18
Brands:
Louisiana Fish Fry
Tony's Seafood

8088 **Louisiana Fresh Express**
18120 Old Covington Highway
Suite B
Hammond, LA 70403-0652 985-542-1256
Fax: 985-898-5993
President: Mark Malkemus

8089 **Louisiana Gourmet Enterprises**
574 Belle Terre Blvd
La Place, LA 70068 985-783-2446
Fax: 985-783-6079
Processor of Cajun/Creole sauces, gumbo, piquante, seasonings and mixes including rice, dinner, cake and frosting
President: Nancy Wilson
Number Employees: 5-9
Type of Packaging: Consumer, Private Label, Bulk
Brands:
Lemon Velvet
Mam Papaul's
Mama Papaul's
Mardi Gras King
Red Velvet

8090 **Louisiana Oyster Processors**
10557 Cherry Hill Ave
Baton Rouge, LA 70816 225-291-6923
Fax: 626-571-0613
Processor of fresh oysters
Owner: Chester Williams
Estimated Sales: $ 5-10 Million
Number Employees: 10-19
Type of Packaging: Consumer, Food Service

8091 **Louisiana Packing Company**
501 Louisiana St
Westwego, LA 70094 504-436-2682
Fax: 504-436-1585 800-666-1293
lapack@iamerica.net www.lapack.com
Processor, importer and exporter of shrimp including breaded, cooked and IQF
President: David Lai
CEO: John Mao
Plant Manager: David Lai
Estimated Sales: $500,000-$1 Million
Number Employees: 1-4
Sq. footage: 33000
Type of Packaging: Consumer, Food Service, Private Label, Bulk
Brands:
Bayou Segnette
Fresh Sea Taste
Sea Ray
White Premium

8092 **Louisiana Premium Seafoods**
P.O.Box 68
Palmetto, LA 71358 337-623-4232
Fax: 337-623-5852 800-222-4017
info@louisianaseafood.com
www.louisianaseafood.com
Frozen alligator meat, blue crabmeat, crawfish meat, cooked crawfish
President/CEO: Gregory Benhard
CFO: Jorge Benhard
Executive Marketing Assistant: Kathy Johnson
Estimated Sales: $ 50-100 Million
Number Employees: 50-99
Brands:
Louisiana Premium Seafoods

8093 **Louisiana Pride Seafood**
2021 Lakeshore Drive Suite 300
New Orleans, LA 70122 504-286-8736
Fax: 504-286-8738
http://www.louisianaseafood.com
Seafood
President: Anthony Lama

8094 **Louisiana Rice Company**
PO Box 705
17299 Highway 99
Welsh, LA 70591-0705 337-734-4362
Rice
Co-Owner: Paul Guillory
Co-Owner: Anne Guillory
Estimated Sales: $110 K
Number Employees: 2

8095 **Louisiana Royal Seafood**
1031 Frank Wyatt Road
Henderson, LA 70517-7714 318-228-2988
Fax: 337-228-2472
Fresh or frozen packaged fish (seafoods)
President: Alvin Folse
Estimated Sales: $ 10-20 Million
Number Employees: 50-99

8096 **Louisiana Royal Seafoods**
1031 Frank Wyatt Road
Breaux Bridge, LA 70517-7714 318-228-7506
Fax: 318-228-2472
Seafood
President: Alvin Folse

8097 **Louisiana Seafood Exchange**
2021 Lakeshore Drive Suite 300
New Orleans, LA 70122 504-283-9393
Fax: 504-283-9468
http://www.louisianaseafood.com
Processor and exporter of seafood including bass, garfish, catfish, trout, amberjack, crab, shark and snapper
President: Thomas Lusco
Director Sales: Robert Walker
Estimated Sales: $ 20-50 Million
Number Employees: 50-99
Type of Packaging: Consumer, Food Service, Private Label, Bulk

8098 **Louisiana Shrimp & Packing Company**
2021 Lakeshore Drive Suite 300
New Orleans, LA 70122 504-286-8736
Fax: 504-286-8738
http://www.louisianaseafood.com
Shrimp
President: Gerard Thomassie
Executive Director: Ewell Smith

8099 **Louisiana Sugar Cane Cooperative**
6092 Resweber Hwy
Saint Martinville, LA 70582 337-394-3255
Fax: 337-394-3787 info@LASUCA.com
www.lasuca.com
Processor of sugar
President: Mike Melancon
Secretary: John Melancon
Estimated Sales: $ 20 - 50 Million
Number Employees: 50-99
Type of Packaging: Consumer

8100 **Louisiana Sugar Cane Cooperation**
6092 Resweber Hwy
Saint Martinville, LA 70582 337-394-3255
Fax: 337-394-3787 info@lasuca.com
www.lasuca.com
Processor of sugar and blackstrap molasses
President: Micheal Melancon
Secretary: John Melancon
Estimated Sales: $ 20 - 50 Million
Number Employees: 50-99
Type of Packaging: Consumer

8101 **(HQ)Lounsbury Foods**
11 Wiltshire Avenue
Toronto, ON M6N 2V7
Canada 416-656-6330
Fax: 416-656-6803 lounsbury@lounsbury.ca
Processor of vinegar, beet relish, mustard and sauces including regular and extra hot horseradish, seafood cocktail, mint, tartar, hot and barbecue
General Manager: Gil Marks
VP: Tim Higgins
VP: David Higgins
Type of Packaging: Consumer, Food Service, Private Label, Bulk
Brands:
Cedarvale

8102 **Lov-It Creamery**
P.O.Box 19010
Green Bay, WI 54307-9010 920-437-7601
Fax: 920-437-1617 800-344-0333
www.schreiberfoods.com
Processor and exporter of butter and butter and margarine blends; also, cream cheese
Chairman: Larry Ferguson
President/CEO: Mike Haddad
VP Finance/CFO: Matt Mueller
Estimated Sales: $3.8 Million
Number Employees: 5,000-9,999
Sq. footage: 181000
Parent Co: Schreiber Foods
Type of Packaging: Consumer, Food Service, Private Label, Bulk
Brands:
Buttercup
Lov-It
Lov-It Butter
Lov-It Butter Blends
Lov-It Butterup
Lov-It Cream Cheese
Lov-It Margarine
Lov-It Mascarpone
Lov-It Neufchatel Cheese
Lov-It Salted Butter
Lov-It Sour Cream
Lov-It Unsalted Butter
Lov-It Wisconsin Blend
Seymour
Wisconsin Blend

8103 **Love & Quiches Desserts**
178 Hanse Ave
Freeport, NY 11520 516-623-8800
Fax: 516-623-8817 800-525-5251
saxelrod@loveandquiches.com
www.loveandquiches.com
Processor of frozen layer cakes, mousses, tarts, pies, cheesecakes and quiches; exporter of cakes, cheesecakes and brownies
President: Susan Axelrod
CEO: Andrew Axelrod
R&D: Michael Goldstien
Executive VP: Karen Sullivan
Marketing Director: Karen Grossman
Director PR/Buisness Development: Joan A Wapner
Info Systems Manager: Douglas Mendoza
Production: Olga Thorsell
Plant Manager: Mike Mazzola
Purchasing: Bonnie Warstdt
Estimated Sales: $ 50 - 100 Million
Number Employees: 250-499
Sq. footage: 65000
Brands:
Deep Dish Tiramisu Classico Tray
Susan's Sweet Talk
Sweet Singles

8104 **Love Creek Orchards**
P.O.Box 1401
Medina, TX 78055-1401 830-589-2588
Fax: 830-589-2880 800-449-0882
adamsapples@lovecreekorchards.com
www.lovecreekorchards.com
Grower of apples; processor of apple cider, jams, jellies, butter, sauce and gourmet flavored coffee
Owner: Baxter Adams
Estimated Sales: $3-5 Million
Number Employees: 20-49
Sq. footage: 2000
Type of Packaging: Consumer, Food Service, Private Label, Bulk
Brands:
Apple Strudel Coffee Beans
Love Creek Orchards

8105 **Love and Quiches Desserts**
178 Hanse Ave
Freeport, NY 11520 516-623-8800
Fax: 516-623-8817 mgahn@loveandquiches.com
www.loveandquiches.com
Desserts and cakes manufacturer
CEO: Irwin Axelrod
Estimated Sales: $ 50 - 100 Million
Number Employees: 250-499
Type of Packaging: Food Service

8106 **Love'n Herbs**
70 Deerwood Lane
Apt 8
Waterbury, CT 06704-1665 203-756-4932
Fax: 203-756-4932 lovenherbs@aol.com
Distributors of all natural salad dressings and marinades that contain Canola oil, vineger, herbs and spices. No salt, no sugar, no MSG or preservatives. Also pure canola oil
President: Maria Klanko
Treasurer: Donald Klanko
VP: Peter Klanko
Estimated Sales: Under $300,000
Number Employees: 1-4
Sq. footage: 1000
Parent Co: DaSilva-Klanko
Type of Packaging: Consumer
Brands:
All Natural Herbal
Love'n Herbs

8107 **Love's Bakery**
P.O.Box 294
911 Middle St
Honolulu, HI 96819-2317 808-235-5171
Fax: 808-841-2646 888-455-6837
loveshi@gte.net
Breads
Manager: Donna Ajimine
CEO/President: Michael Walters
Chairman of the Board: Masahide Hosokai
General Sales Manager: Kevin Takaesu
Production Manager: Larry Lopes
Purchasing Manager: Clifford Goya
Estimated Sales: $ 18 Million
Number Employees: 310

8108 **Lovin' Oven**
1072 Harvey Point Road
Suite 115
Hertford, NC 27944 252-426-3003
Fax: 252-482-5000 888-775-0099
carol@lovin-oven.com www.lovin-oven.com
Homemade gingerbread cookies
Owner: Carol Hammer
Estimated Sales: Less than $500,000
Number Employees: 5-9

8109 **Low Country Produce**
1919 Trask Parkway
Lobeco, SC 29931 800-935-2792
Fax: 800-985-0405 800-935-2792
info@lowcountryproduce.com
www.lowcountryproduce.com
pickles, chutneys & relishes, soups & sauces, salsas & dips, jellies & preserves
Estimated Sales: A
Number Employees: 1-4

8110 **Lowell Farms**
4 N Washington St
El Campo, TX 77437 979-543-4950
Fax: 979-541-5655 888-484-9213
lowellfm@swbell.net www.lowellfarms.com
Processor of organic jasmine rice
Owner: Linda Raun
VP: Linda Raun
Estimated Sales: Below $ 5 Million
Number Employees: 5-9
Type of Packaging: Consumer, Bulk
Brands:
Lowell Farms

8111 **Lowell Packing Company**
P.O.Box 220
Fitzgerald, GA 31750 229-423-2052
Fax: 229-423-6601 800-342-0313
sales@lowellpacking.com
www.lowellpacking.com
Manufacturer of pork; slaughtering services available
President: Morris Downing
VP: Scott Downing
Estimated Sales: $20 Million
Number Employees: 100-249
Sq. footage: 48000
Type of Packaging: Consumer, Food Service
Brands:
COLONY CITY
GEORGIA STAR
LOWELL

8112 **(HQ)Lowell Provision Company**
23 Aiken Ave
Lowell, MA 01850 978-454-5603
www.lowellprovisionco.com
Processor of beef, pork, lamb, chicken and veal
President: Peter Doyle
VP: Dennis Doyle
Purchasing Manager: Dennis Doyle
Estimated Sales: $ 20 - 50 Million
Number Employees: 10-19
Sq. footage: 6000
Type of Packaging: Consumer, Food Service, Private Label, Bulk
Other Locations:
Lowell Provision Company
Chelmsford MA

Brands:
Doyle's
Lowell Provision

8113 **Lowell-Paul Dairy**
14332 County Road 64
Greeley, CO 80631-9317 970-353-0278
Fax: 970-353-0338
Fluid milk, cream and related products
President: Margaret Paul
Estimated Sales: $ 5-10 Million
Number Employees: 20-49

8114 **Lower Foods**
700 S Highway 91
Richmond, UT 84333 435-258-2449
Fax: 435-258-5177 larry@llranch.com
www.llranch.com
Processor of roast beef, pastrami, corned beef, etc
President: Larry Lower
VP: Allan Lower
Sales: Charles Johnson
Plant Manager: Mike Mortensen
Estimated Sales: $100+ Million
Number Employees: 20-49
Type of Packaging: Consumer

8115 **Lowery's Home Made Candies**
6255 W Kilgore Ave
Muncie, IN 47304-4794 765-288-7300
Fax: 765-747-9662 800-541-3340
customerservice@loweryscandies.com
www.loweryscandies.com
Manufacturer of confectionery including caramel, taffy, chocolate, chocolate covered nuts and chocolate covered cherries
President: Michael Brown
Owner: Thelma Brown
Owner: Donald Brown
Estimated Sales: $7 Million
Number Employees: 20-49
Type of Packaging: Consumer

8116 **Lowery's Premium Roast Coffee**
P.O.Box 1858
Snohomish, WA 98291-1858 360-668-4545
Fax: 360-863-9742 800-767-1783
jzimm@loweryscoffee.com
www.loweryscoffee.com
Coffee, wholesale and custom roasters, espresso machines, espresso accessories
President: Donald Lowery
CFO: Jeanette Zimmerman
Marketing: Mike Lowery
Roast/Operations Manager: Jerry Lowery
Estimated Sales: Below $ 5 Million
Number Employees: 20-49
Number of Brands: 2
Number of Products: 100
Sq. footage: 5000
Type of Packaging: Private Label
Brands:
Lowery's Coffee
Pasano's Syrups

8117 **Lowland Seafood**
569 Kelly Watson Rd
Lowland, NC 28552 252-745-3751
Fax: 252-745-5040
Processor of fish, shrimp, crabs and scallops
President: Carol Potter
Estimated Sales: $1500000
Number Employees: 25
Type of Packaging: Consumer, Food Service, Bulk

8118 **Lt Blender's Frozen Concoctions**
1202 Post Office St
Galveston, TX 77550-5041 409-765-5666
Fax: 409-966-1581 info@ltblender.com
www.ltblender.com
Manufacturer of frozen concoction drinks in a bag. Flavors include: margarita; strawberry daiquiri; pina colada; mudslide; hurricane; mojito; peach bellini wine freezer; sangria wine freezer; strawberry wine freezer; and margaritawine freezer.
Founder/President: Ralph McMorris
Vice President Marketing: Scott Treadaway

8119 **Luban International**
9900 NW 25th St
Doral, FL 33172 305-629-8730
Fax: 305-629-8740 www.fans-usa.com
Cereals
Owner: Luis Banegas

8120 **Lubbers Dairy**
RR 3
Pella, IA 50219 515-628-4284
Dairy
President: Andy Lubber

8121 **Lubbock Cotton Oil Company**
2300 E 50th St
Lubbock, TX 79404-4128 806-763-4371
Fax: 806-744-1235
Processor of cottonseed oils
Plant Manager: Frank Sherman
Estimated Sales: $ 50 - 100 Million
Number Employees: 50-99
Parent Co: Archer Daniels Midland Company

8122 **Lubriplate Lubricants**
129 Lockwood St
Newark, NJ 7105 973-589-9150
Fax: 973-589-4432 800-733-4755
richardm@lubriplate.com www.lubriplate.com
Manufacturer and exporter of food grade lubricating oils and grease
President: Richard Mc Cluskey
VP/General Manager: Jim Girard
Number Employees: 100-249
Parent Co: Fisk Brothers

8123 **Lucas Meyer**
765 E Pythian Ave
Decatur, IL 62526-2412 217-875-3660
Fax: 217-877-5046 800-769-3660
lecithin@midwest.net www.lucasmeyer.com
Processor of lecithin and soy flour
President: Peter Rohde
VP: Scott Hagerman
Director Sales/Marketing: Scott Hagerman
Sales Manager: Jack Chenault
Estimated Sales: $600000
Number Employees: 10-19

8124 **Lucas Vineyards**
3862 County Road 150
Interlaken, NY 14847-9653 607-532-4825
Fax: 607-532-8580 800-682-9463
info@lucasvineyards.com
www.lucasvineyards.com
Processor of wines
President: Ruth Lucas
Marketing Director: Stephanie Lucas
Plant Manager: Ruthie Lucas
Estimated Sales: $ 5 - 10 Million
Number Employees: 10-19
Type of Packaging: Consumer, Food Service
Brands:
Lucas

8125 **Lucas Winery**
18196 N Davis Rd
Lodi, CA 95242 209-368-2006
Fax: 209-368-4900 www.lucaswinery.com
Fine wines
Owner: David Lucas
Estimated Sales: Less than $500,000
Number Employees: 1-4
Type of Packaging: Private Label
Brands:
Lucas

8126 **Lucas World**
5709 Springfield Avenue
Laredo, TX 78041-3282 528-625-1000
Fax: 528-625-1099 888-675-8227
www.lucasworld.com
President: Euzondo Alejandro
CEO: Martinez Alejandro
COO: Hugo Martinez
Research & Development: Maru Valdez
Sales Director: Juan Pablo Gonzalez
Parent Co: Lucas World
Brands:
Acidito Lucas
Chorreada
Crazy Hair
Gusano Lucas
Limon Lucas
Muecas
Pelucas
Skwinkles

8127 **Lucerne Foods**
1020 64th Ave, NE
Calgary, AB T2E 7V8
Canada 403-790-3500
Fax: 403-730-3888
Processor of bread and rolls
Number Employees: 100-249

8128 **Lucerne Foods**
5115-57th Street
Taber, AB T1G 1X1
Canada 403-223-3546
Fax: 403-223-2804
Processor of aseptically-packaged juices and drinks; also, spices
Plant Manager: Loreen Sernowski
Parent Co: Canada Safeway
Type of Packaging: Consumer
Brands:
Edwards
Generic
Town House

8129 **Lucerne Foods**
131 22nd Street N
Lethbridge, AB T1H 3R6
Canada 403-328-5501
Fax: 403-327-4737
Processor, exporter and importer of frozen vegetables and juice concentrates
Manager: David Jensen
Superintendent: Ed Uyesugi
Production: Vaughn Caldwell
Number Employees: 100-249
Parent Co: Canada Safeway
Type of Packaging: Consumer, Food Service, Private Label, Bulk
Brands:
Party Pride
Safeway
Scotch Bay
Sunny Dawn
Town House

8130 **Lucero Olive Oil**
2120 Loleta Avenue
2120 Loleta Avenue
Corning, CA 96021 916-625-4360
Fax: 530-824-1243 877-330-2190
mail@lucerooliveoil.com
www.lucerooliveoil.com
Olive oils

8131 **Lucia's Pizza Company**
10989 Gravois Industrial Ct
Saint Louis, MO 63128 314-843-2553
Fax: 314-843-3576
Processor and wholesaler/distributor of frozen pizza
President: Darrell Long
Estimated Sales: $1600000
Number Employees: 20-49
Sq. footage: 25000
Type of Packaging: Consumer, Private Label
Brands:
Lucia's

8132 **Lucich Farms**
P.O.Box 1266
Delano, CA 93216 661-725-4550
Fax: 661-725-5283 lucich@lightspeed.net
www.grapegift.com
Processor and exporter of table grapes
President: Dave Clyde
CFO: Daril Bishop
VP/Marketing: David Clyde
Sales: Bob Schultz
VP Operations: Mike Ahumada
Controller: Ben Miramontes
Purchasing Manager: Steve Lackey
Estimated Sales: $100+ Million
Number Employees: 100-249
Type of Packaging: Consumer, Bulk
Brands:
Sall-N-Ann

8133 **Lucile's Creole Foods**
2124 14th St
Boulder, CO 80302-4804 303-442-4743
Fax: 303-939-9848 www.luciles.com
Gourmet Creole foods
Owner: Fletcher Richards
Estimated Sales: $500,000-$1 Million
Number Employees: 20-49
Type of Packaging: Private Label

8134 **Lucile's Famous Creole Seasonings**
2124 14th St
Boulder, CO 80302-4804 303-442-4743
Fax: 303-939-9848 800-727-3653
info@luciles.com www.luciles.com
Processor of Creole seasonings and French roast blend coffee
President: Fletcher Richards III
Sales Manager: Jennifer Fowler
Estimated Sales: $500,000-$1 Million
Number Employees: 20-49
Sq. footage: 4000
Type of Packaging: Consumer, Food Service, Bulk
Brands:
Lucile's

8135 **Lucille Farm Products**
150 River Road
Montville, NJ 07045 973-334-6030
Fax: 973-402-6361
lucillefarms@lucille-farms.com
www.lucille-farms.com
Processor and exporter of cheese including mozzarella, provolone and feta
CEO: Alfonso Falivene
EVP Quality Control: Gennaro Falivene
VP Sales/Marketing: David McCarthy
Sales Director: David Braff
Operations Manager: Jerry Falivene
Production Manager: Jim Johnson
Estimated Sales: $36691000
Number Employees: 2
Sq. footage: 1434
Brands:
Monte Carlo Premium Mozerella
Mozi Rue Cholesterol Free
Tasty-Lite Cheese Fat Free/Premium

8136 **Lucille's Own Make Candies**
156 Route 72 E
Manahawkin, NJ 08050-3597 609-597-7300
Fax: 609-597-7393 800-426-9168
jeismann@aol.com www.lucillescandies.com
Candy and confections
President: Nathaniel Eismann
VP Sales: Janice Eismann
Estimated Sales: $500,000-$1 Million
Number Employees: 5-9

8137 **Lucini Italia Company**
601 22nd Street
San Francisco, CA 94107 866-972-6879
Fax: 415-401-0087 888-558-2464
renee@lucini.com www.lucini.com
Extra virgin olive oil
President: Renee Frigo
Estimated Sales: Less than $500,000
Number Employees: 5-9

8138 **Lucks Food Decorating Company**
3003 S Pine St
Tacoma, WA 98409 253-383-4815
Fax: 253-383-0071 800-426-9778
info@lucks.com www.lucks.com
Processor and exporter of cake decorations and food colorings; exporter of flavoring extracts
President: Rick Ellison
CFO: Carl Lucks
R&D/Quality Assurance Manager: Megan Leifson
Marketing Manager: Heather Sisson
SVP Operations: Dan Elliott
Purchasing Manager: Leigh Goodier
Estimated Sales: $28100000
Number Employees: 50
Sq. footage: 21748
Parent Co: Lucks Company
Type of Packaging: Food Service
Brands:
Decons
Edible Image
Lucks
Lucks Roses

8139 **Lucks Food Decorating Company**
3003 S Pine St
Tacoma, WA 98409 253-383-4815
Fax: 206-674-7250 info@lucks.com
www.lucks.com
Processor of popcorn, canned apples, chicken, vegetables, collard greens and beans
President: Rick Ellison
VP: Darius Luck
Sr. VP Operations: Frank Valdez
Plant Manager: Darius Luck
Number Employees: 100-249
Sq. footage: 198000
Parent Co: International Home Foods
Type of Packaging: Consumer, Private Label

8140 **Lucky Seafood Corporation**
6203 Jonesboro Road
Morrow, GA 30260-1723 770-960-9889
Fax: 770-968-9400
Seafood
President: David Ng

8141 **Lucky You**
3167 Commercial Street
San Diego, CA 92113 619-450-6700
Fax: 619-450-6701 customerservice@yldinc.com
www.yldinc.com
Other Chocolate, other candy.
Marketing: Deborah Roberts

8142 **Lucy's Sweet Surrender**
12516 Buckeye Rd
Cleveland, OH 44120 216-752-0828
Fax: 216-767-0735 mislkel@aol.com
www.lucyssweetsurrender.com
Hungarian pastries and custom European baked goods; including hungarian
President: Michael Feigenbaum
Estimated Sales: $250,000
Number Employees: 5-9

8143 **Lucys Foods**
408 Longs Rd
Latrobe, PA 15650 724-539-1430
Fax: 724-532-0525 nzappone@aol.com
www.zapsausage.com
Frozen Italian Foods, pasta and sausage
President: Nicholas Zappone
Estimated Sales: $6 Million
Number Employees: 1-4
Type of Packaging: Consumer
Brands:
DELGROSSO
DENUNZIO
LOTITO
RIZZO'S
ROSIE'S

8144 **Ludfords**
8707 Utica Ave
Rancho Cucamonga, CA 91730 909-948-0797
Fax: 909-948-0597 ludfords@earthlink.com
Processor, importer and exporter of fresh, frozen and canned fruit juices including orange, apple, grape, etc
President: Paul Ludford
Estimated Sales: Below $ 5 Million
Number Employees: 10-19
Sq. footage: 20000
Type of Packaging: Consumer, Food Service, Private Label
Brands:
Ludford's

8145 **Ludo LLC**
5325 Naiman Pkwy Ste G
Solon, OH 44139 440-542-6000
Fax: 440-542-9555 www.ludocandytoys.com
Candy
Manager: Stephanie Holmes
Estimated Sales: $300,000-500,000
Number Employees: 1-4
Brands:
BUBBLE CANDY

8146 **Ludwick's Frozen Donuts**
3217 3 Mile Rd NW
Grand Rapids, MI 49534-1223
US 616-453-6880
Fax: 616-453-1930 800-366-8816
info@kneadinthedough.com
Processor of frozen doughnuts, fresh cookies, and seafoam candy frozen pastries.pies,cakes.
President: Thomas Ludwick
CEO: Jack Brown
DIRECTOR Of SALES: Jim Glupker
Estimated Sales: $ 5 - 10 Million
Number Employees: 19
Type of Packaging: Consumer, Food Service, Private Label, Bulk
Brands:
Kneadin The Dough

8147 **Ludwig Dairy**
1270 Mark St
Dixon, IL 60007-6708 815-284-7791
Fax: 815-284-7704
Cheese
President: Mirekge Gebaka
Assistant Plant Manager: Duane Hadaway
VP Manufacturing: Mario Jedwabrik
Maintenance Manager: Rich Majewiski
Plant Manager: Michael Imel/ Ed Tomasziewicz
Estimated Sales: $410 K
Number Employees: 5
Type of Packaging: Private Label

8148 **Ludwig Fish & Produce Company**
711 Washington St
La Porte, IN 46350 219-362-2608
Fax: 219-325-8311
Wholesaler/distributor of frozen food, general line products, produce, provisions/meats and seafood; serving the food service market
President: Harold Robinson
Estimated Sales: $3800000
Number Employees: 20-49

8149 **Ludwigshof Winery**
22684 Ne Highway K4
Eskridge, KS 66423-9153 785-449-2498
Fax: 785-449-2498
Winery
President: Vernon Robinson
Estimated Sales: A
Number Employees: 2

8150 **Lukas Confections**
231 W College Ave
York, PA 17401-2103 717-843-0921
Fax: 717-854-9743 sales@warrellcorp.com
www.classiccaramel.com
Processor and exporter of sugarless and regular caramel toffee, taffy nougat and caramel including liquid; also salt water taffy and nutraceuticals
President/CEO: Robert Lukas
CFO: G Mark Zelinski CPA
Operations Manager: Joseph Stuck
Estimated Sales: $4 Million
Number Employees: 50
Number of Brands: 4
Number of Products: 110
Sq. footage: 52000
Type of Packaging: Consumer, Private Label, Bulk
Brands:
Caramel Milk Roll
Classic
Dark Fruit Chews
Dorks
Flipsticks

8151 **Lumar Lobster Corporatio**
297 Burnside Ave
Lawrence, NY 11559 516-371-0083
Processor of live lobster
President: Stanley Jassem
Estimated Sales: Less than $500,000
Number Employees: 1-4
Type of Packaging: Food Service

8152 **Luna's Tortillas**
8524 Harry Hines Blvd
Dallas, TX 75235 214-747-2661
Fax: 214-747-5862
Processor of Mexican food products including corn tortillas, flour tortillas, tostadas, taco shells, nacho chips, tamales, hot sauce, pico de gallo, beans, chorizo, masa and hojas.
President: Francisco Luna
Sales/Marketing Executive: Fernando Luna
Purchasing Agent: J Luna
Estimated Sales: $1200000
Number Employees: 10-19
Sq. footage: 10000
Type of Packaging: Consumer, Food Service
Brands:
Luna's

8153 **Lund's Fisheries**
P.O.Box 830
Cape May, NJ 08204-0830 609-884-7600
Fax: 609-884-0664 info@lundsfish.com
www.lundsfish.com
Processor and exporter of frozen cod, flounder, mackerel, squid, sturgeon, tuna, herring and shad
President: Jeffery Reichle
Sales: Dennis Dowe
Operations: Darren Dowe
Purchasing Manager: Henry Buchianico
Estimated Sales: $21900000
Number Employees: 250-499
Type of Packaging: Consumer, Food Service

8154 **Lundberg Family Farm**
P.O.Box 369
Richvale, CA 95974-0369 530-882-4551
Fax: 530-882-4500 tkluger@lundberg.com
www.lundberg.com
Processor of rice and rice products including cereal, flour, dinners, cakes and mixes; also, organic rice
President: Harlan Lundenberg
CEO: Grant Lundberg
VP Sales/Marketing: Tim O'Donnell
Regional Sales Manager: Dirk Burgon
Estimated Sales: $73,000
Number Employees: 1
Type of Packaging: Consumer, Food Service, Private Label, Bulk
Brands:
Evergood
Lundberg

8155 **Lupi**
1801 Bush Street
Baltimore, MD 21230-2044 410-752-3370
President: Lupi Domil

8156 **Lupi Marchigiano Bakery**
169 Washington Ave
New Haven, CT 06519 203-562-9491
Fax: 203-562-5456
Baked goods
President: Pete Lupi
Estimated Sales: Below $ 5 Million
Number Employees: 20-49

8157 **Lusitania Bakery**
PO Box 319
Blandon, PA 19510-0319 610-926-1311
Processor of cakes, danish and gourmet muffins
Chairman/CEO: Samuel Chudnovsky
Number Employees: 20-49
Sq. footage: 50000
Type of Packaging: Consumer, Private Label
Brands:
Dutch Kettle Foods
Old Dutch Bakery

8158 **Lusty Lobster**
10 Portland Fish Pier # A
Portland, ME 04101-4620 207-773-2829
Fax: 207-774-3956
Lobster
President: Doug Douty
Estimated Sales: $ 10 - 20 Million
Number Employees: 10-19

8159 **(HQ)Luv Yu Bakery**
3410 Bashford Avenue Ct Ste 1
Louisville, KY 40218 502-451-4511
Fax: 502-451-5510 luvyubrand@aol.com
www.luvyu.com
Chocolate-dipped, buffet and organic cookies, unique snacks, rice crackers and shrimp chips
President: Abel Yu
Vice President: Serena Yu
Sq. footage: 25000

8160 **Luxembourg Cheese Factory**
12495 N Pleasant Hill Rd
Orangeville, IL 61060 815-789-4227
Fax: 815-789-4434 www.tateandlyle.com
Processor of sodium, calcium and potassium caseinates, milk protein hydrolyzate and hydrolyzed vegetable proteins
President: Mike Ernster
Plant Manager: Frank Furgal
Number Employees: 10-19
Sq. footage: 15000

8161 **Luxor California ExportsCorporation**
3659 India Street
2nd Floor
San Diego, CA 92103-4767 619-692-9330
Fax: 619-692-4292
Supplier and exporter of agricultural commodities closeouts including dry beans, grains, oils, yeast, dry milk, butter, etc
President: Kamil Kafaji
Estimated Sales: $1000000
Number Employees: 5
Type of Packaging: Bulk

8162 **Luyties Pharmacal Company**
4200 Laclede Avenue
Saint Louis, MO 63108 314-533-9600
Fax: 314-535-9600 800-325-8080
luytiesstl@aol.com
Processor and exporter of vitamins and homeopathic products
Director Marketing: Michael Smith
Number Employees: 50-99
Parent Co: Manola Company
Brands:
Luyties

8163 **Lyle's Seafoods**
PO Box 547
Ocean Park, WA 98640-0547 36- 6-5 41
Fax: 360-665-4666
Canned salmon, smoked salmon, sturgeon, clams, oysters, crab, oyster products
Owner: Kim Lobry
Brands:
Shoalwater Bay

8164 **Lyman Jenkins**
PO Box 53
Jericho Center, VT 05465-0053 802-899-3056
Fax: 802-899-3056 800-528-7021
Manufacturer of food products
President: Lyman Jenkins

8165 **Lynard Company**
15 Maple Tree Ave
Stamford, CT 06906 203-323-0231
Fax: 203-973-0545
snacks and candy
President/Owner: Lillian Flaster
VP: Howard Flaster

8166 **Lynard Company**
15 Maple Tree Ave
Stamford, CT 06906 203-323-0231
Fax: 203-323-0231 lynardco@aol.com
Chocolates, candies, pretzels, nuts, popcorn, cookies, dried fruits, honey package designing
President: Lillian Flaster
Estimated Sales: Less than $200,000
Number Employees: 5-9

8167 **Lynch Foods**
72 Railside Road
North York, ON M3A 1A3
Canada 416-449-5464
Fax: 416-449-9165 info@lynchfoods.com
www.lynchfoods.ca
Dessert Toppings, Chocolate Syrup, Corn Syrup, Mincemeat, Condiment sauces, Asian sauces, Marinades as well as Hot Drink and Iced Tea mixes.
President/Board Member: Scott Lynch
Chairman: Walker Lynch
VP Marketing: Peter Henderson
VP Sales: Scott Lynch
Estimated Sales: $16 Million
Number Employees: 140
Sq. footage: 120000
Type of Packaging: Consumer, Food Service, Private Label, Bulk

8168 **Lynch Supply**
15551 W 109th St
Lenexa, KS 66219-1307 913-492-8500
Fax: 913-492-8532 info@fieldmaster.com
www.fieldmaster.com
Manufacturer and exporter of pressure cookers, smokers and roaster ovens; also, seasoning for meat and chicken
President: David Lynch
Estimated Sales: $ 1 - 2.5 Million
Number Employees: 1-4

8169 **Lynden Meat Company**
1936 Front St
Lynden, WA 98264 360-354-2449
Fax: 360-354-7687
Meat packer; custom slaughtering and packing services available
Owner: Rick Biesheuvel
Estimated Sales: $ 3 - 5 Million
Number Employees: 5-9
Type of Packaging: Consumer

8170 **Lynfred Winery**
15 S Roselle Rd
Roselle, IL 60172 630-529-9463
Fax: 630-529-4971 888-298-9463
info@lynfredwinery.com
www.lynfredwinery.com
Wines
President: Fred Koehler
CEO: Fred Koehler
CFO: Diane Schramer
Vice President: Valerie Koehler
Sales Manager: Valerie Anderson
Public Relations Officer: Christina Anderson
Estimated Sales: $ 10-20 Million
Number Employees: 20-49
Number of Products: 50
Sq. footage: 24000
Type of Packaging: Private Label
Brands:
LYNFRED

8171 **Lynn Dairy**
W1929 Us Highway 10
Granton, WI 54436 715-238-7129
Fax: 715-238-7130 lynndairy@tds.net
www.lynndairy.com
Makers of cheese
President: William Schwantes
Marketing Director: Rick Beilke
Estimated Sales: $ 5-10 Million
Number Employees: 100-249
Type of Packaging: Bulk
Brands:
Lynn Dairy
Lynn Protiens

8172 **Lynn Springs Water LLC**
4325 1st Ave # 562
Tucker, GA 30084-4498 770-572-5928
trthomas@tjafg.com
freewebs.com/xtanaina
Water
President: Tandrias Thomas
CEO: Jocelyn Facen
CFO: Al Thomas
Vice President: Derrick Smith
Estimated Sales: $1-2 Million
Number Employees: 20-49
Number of Brands: 1
Number of Products: 1
Sq. footage: 6000
Type of Packaging: Bulk

8173 **Lyo-San**
PO Box 598
Lachute, QC J8H 4G4
Canada 450-562-8525
Fax: 450-562-1433
Manufacturer and exporter of freeze-dried yogurt cultures and bifido-bacteria; custom freeze-drying available
President/Owner: Celine St-Pierre
Number Employees: 10-19
Sq. footage: 45000
Type of Packaging: Consumer, Food Service, Private Label, Bulk
Brands:
Yogourmet

8174 **Lyoferm & Vivolac Cultures**
3862 E Washington St
Indianapolis, IN 46201-4470 317-356-8460
vivolac@iquest.net
www.iquest.net
Processor of cultures including dairy, meat and bakery starter, freeze dried/lyophilized and food fermentation; exporter of freeze dried cultures
President/Vice President: Ethel Sing
Vice President: Edmond Sing
Estimated Sales: $2 Million
Number Employees: 23

Brands:
Lyoferm
Vivolac

8175 **(HQ)Lyons-Magnus**
3158 E Hamilton Ave
Fresno, CA 93702 559-268-5966
Fax: 559-233-8249 www.lyonsmagnus.com
Manufacturer and marketer of dessert toppings/sauces, chocolate syrups, hot fudges, fruit fillings, preserves, syrups, juices, and beverages
President: Robert Smittcamp
SVP National Sales: Brad Kirk
Operations Manager: Keith Brantley
Estimated Sales: $100+ Million
Number Employees: 250-499
Sq. footage: 380000
Type of Packaging: Food Service, Private Label, Bulk
Other Locations:
Lyons-Magnus Plant Facility
Walton KY

8176 **M & M Label Company**
380 Pearl Street
Malden, MA 02148-6607 781-321-2737
Fax: 781-322-9065 mjm@mmlabel.com
www.mmlabel.com
Packaging.
President: Michael McCourt
Estimated Sales: $1.2 Million
Number Employees: 18

8177 **M K Meat Processing Plant**
P.O.Box 317
Burton, TX 77835-0317 979-289-4022
Fax: 978-989-4001
Manufacturer of beef, pork and sausage
Owner: Jerry Schultz
Estimated Sales: $2.5 Million
Number Employees: 1-4
Type of Packaging: Consumer, Bulk

8178 **M&B Fruit Juice Company**
955 Home Ave
Akron, OH 44310 330-253-7465
Fax: 330-253-8401
Processor of fruit drink concentrates including orange, lemonade, pink lemonade, grape, cherry, lime, loganberry, iced tea and punch; also, vanilla and strawberry syrups
President: James Stone
Estimated Sales: $ 1 - 3 Million
Number Employees: 5-9
Sq. footage: 10000
Type of Packaging: Consumer, Food Service, Private Label, Bulk
Brands:
Magic-Mix
Party Punch
Super-Mix
Trim-Lite
WIZ

8179 **M&CP Farms**
3986 County Road Nn
Orland, CA 95963 530-865-9810
Fax: 530-865-9793 greatolives@greatolives.com
www.greatolives.com
Products include olive spreads, mixes, cured olives,olive oil, stuffed olives, in addition to spicy beans, and sweet/sour pickles.
President: Maurice Penna
Secretary/Treasurer: Cynthia Penna
Estimated Sales: Below $ 5 Million
Number Employees: 5-9
Sq. footage: 15000
Parent Co: D. Beccaris
Type of Packaging: Consumer, Food Service, Private Label, Bulk
Brands:
Loam Ridge
M&Cp Farms

8180 **M&G Honey Farms**
411 S 1st St
Bushton, KS 67427 620-562-3643
Honey and honey products

8181 **M&I Seafood Manufacturers**
8805 Kelso Dr
Essex, MD 21221-3112 410-780-0444
Fax: 410-780-3167
Processor and exporter of frozen seafood crab cakes, crab balls, mushroom caps stuffed with crab imperial, flunder fillets stuffed with crab imperial, breaded fantailed shrimp, fish cakes, flounder fillets, I.Q.F. gulf shrimpshrimpura, shrimp sticks, crab imperial in natural shell, crab meat stuffing, seafood soups and chowders, frozen and pasteurized crab meat
President: Steve Cohen
Controller: Mark Stachlorlwski
Vice President: Ron Kauffman
General Manager: Steve Cohen
Estimated Sales: $ 20 - 50 Million
Number Employees: 100-249
Sq. footage: 50000
Type of Packaging: Consumer, Food Service, Private Label, Bulk
Brands:
Chesapeake Bay
Chesapeake Bay Gourmet

8182 **M&L Gourmet Ice Cream**
2524 E Monument St
Baltimore, MD 21205-2539 410-276-4880
Fax: 410-525-8320
Processor and exporter of kosher ice cream
Owner: Chris Napfel
Estimated Sales: Less than $500,000
Number Employees: 1-4
Type of Packaging: Consumer, Food Service

8183 **M&L Ventures**
1471 W Commerce Ct
Tucson, AZ 85746-6016 520-884-8232
Fax: 520-770-9649 info@meritfoods.net
www.meritfoods.net
Products include produce and groceries, eggs and cheese, deli meats and salad dressings.
President: Matt Sadowsky
Secretary/Treasurer: Lynn Sadowsky
Manager: Bob Richter
Manager: Paul Rosthenhausler

8184 **M&M Fisheries**
PO Box 190
Shelburne, NS B0W 2E0
Canada 902-723-2390
Fax: 902-723-2967
mm.fisheries@ns.sympatico.ca
Processor and exporter of fresh and frozen haddock, cod, pollack, red fish and silver hake
President: Gary Goreham
Manager Sales: Glenn Maxwell
Number Employees: 60
Sq. footage: 14000
Type of Packaging: Consumer
Brands:
M&M Fisheries
Novie Fresh

8185 **M&M Food Distributors/Oriental Pride**
3322 Virginia Beach Blvd
Virginia Beach, VA 23452-5608 757-499-5676
Fax: 757-499-0807
Ethnic foods
President: Joan Mallen

8186 **M&M Industries Inc**
316 Corporate Place
Chattanooga, TN 37419 423-821-3302
Fax: 423-821-9017 800-331-5305
cstone@mmcontainer.com
www.mmcontainer.com/
Manufacturer of Life Latch plastic pails suitable for a variety of purposes including the food industry. Uses include livestock feed and grains; pet food storage; seeds; vitamin supplements, etc.
VP: Glenn H Morris Jr
Regional Accounts Manager: Rae Green
Regional Accounts Manager: Cindy Stone
Regional Accounts Manager: Tiffany King
Regional Accounts Manager: Janet Rogers
Estimated Sales: $10-25 Million
Number Employees: 25

8187 **M&M Shrimp Company**
408 Lee Street
Biloxi, MS 39530-2455 228-435-4915
Fax: 228-435-3821
Processor of frozen shrimp
Number Employees: 20-49
Type of Packaging: Consumer, Food Service, Private Label
Brands:
Captain Joey
M&M
Suarez

8188 **M&R Company**
33 E Tokay St
Lodi, CA 95240 209-369-4760
Fax: 209-369-7943
Grower, packer and exporter of fruits and vegetables including bell peppers, asparagus, eggplant, beans, cherries, grapes, apples and pears as well as grape juice
President: Donald Reynolds
Vice President: Don Reynolds
Manager Marketing: Craig Lusk
Sales Director: Andy Foccaci
Estimated Sales: $ 50 - 100 Million
Number Employees: 50-99
Sq. footage: 100000
Type of Packaging: Consumer
Brands:
Four Aces
M&R

8189 **M&S Tomato Repacking Company**
1026 Bay St
Springfield, MA 01109-2427 413-737-1308
Fax: 413-736-6433
Packer of tomatoes
President: Simone Severino
Treasurer: Laurie Chruscieo
Estimated Sales: $4 Million
Number Employees: 22
Type of Packaging: Consumer

8190 **M-CAP Technologies**
3521 Silverside Rd
Wilmington, DE 19810-4900 302-695-5329
Fax: 302-695-5350 jdoncheck@lakefield.net
Processor and exporter of industrial ingredients including bromate replacers, additives and preservatives; also, temperature release vitamins and minerals
President: Ernie Porta
VP Technology: James Doncheck
Number Employees: 5
Parent Co: DuPont Chemical
Brands:
Baker's Label

8191 **M-G**
201 E Post Road
Weimar, TX 78962 979-725-8584
Fax: 979-725-9428 800-460-8581
Processor of egg products; wholesaler/distributor of poultry products, frozen foods and seafood; serving the food service market
President: Alvin Mueller
Vice President: Wilbert Heger
Manager: Bobby Wick
Estimated Sales: $ 20 - 50 Million
Number Employees: 35
Sq. footage: 10000
Type of Packaging: Food Service
Brands:
Mighty Good

8192 **M. & B. Products**
8601 Harney Rd
Tampa, FL 33637 813-988-2211
Fax: 813-980-6596 800-899-7255
rocky@mbproducts.com www.mbproducts.com
Processor of juice including orange, apple, orange/pineapple, grape, etc.; also, milk, milkshakes and frozen fruit juice bars
President: Dale McClellan
CFO: Howard Hutchinson
Estimated Sales: $ 10 - 20 Million
Number Employees: 95
Type of Packaging: Consumer

8193 **M. Brown & Sons**
114 N Center St
Bremen, IN 46506 574-546-4942
Fax: 574-258-7468 800-258-7450
info@lebermuth.com www.lebermuth.com
Botanicals, herbs, and essential oils
President: Larry Brown
Chairman: Irvin Brown
VP: Alan Brown
VP: Robert Brown

Estimated Sales: $ 10-15 Million
Number Employees: 20-49
Parent Co: Lebermuth Company
Type of Packaging: Bulk

8194 **M. Licht & Son**
P.O.Box 507
Knoxville, TN 37901 865-523-5593
Fax: 865-523-0270 smncs@ix.netcom.com
www.smsweetener.com
Processor and exporter of liquid artificial sweeteners
President: Richard M Licht
VP: Karen McGuire
Estimated Sales: $ 5 - 10 Million
Number Employees: 5-9
Sq. footage: 3200
Type of Packaging: Food Service
Brands:
Smoky Mountain

8195 **M. Marion & Company**
422 Larkfield Center
Suite 2553
Santa Rosa, CA 95403-1408 707-836-0551
Wine
President: M Dennis Marion
Estimated Sales: $500,000-$1 Million
Number Employees: 1-4

8196 **M.A. Gedney**
P.O.Box 8
Chaska, MN 55318 952-448-2612
Fax: 952-448-1790 info@gedneypickle.com
www.gedneypickle.com
Processor of condiments, barbecue sauces, vinegars, syrups, pickles, relishes, sauerkraut, salsa, salad dressing, mayonnaise, mustard, etc.; importer of cucumbers
President/CEO: Chuck Weil
VP Sales/Marketing: Ted Forbes
Operations Manager: Thomas Hitch
Estimated Sales: $33000000
Number Employees: 100-249
Type of Packaging: Consumer, Food Service, Private Label, Bulk
Brands:
Devil's Fire
Gedney
Geraldo's
Hiawatha
Max's
Minnesaurus Dill Picklodon
Northland
Northwoods
Pep Fest
State Fair

8197 **M.A. Hatt & Sons**
405 Hwy 324
Lunenburg, NS B0J 2C0
Canada 902-634-8407
Fax: 902-634-8407
Processor of sauerkraut
President: Ralph Hatt
VP: Gladys Hatt
Number Employees: 5-9
Type of Packaging: Consumer, Food Service, Bulk
Brands:
Tan Cook

8198 **M.A. Johnson Frozen Foods**
1912 E Monroe Pike
Marion, IN 46953-2610 76- 66- 802
Fax: 76- 66- 666
Frozen foods
President: S Allen Johnson
Estimated Sales: $ 5-10 Million appx.
Number Employees: 10

8199 **M.A. Patout & Son**
3512 J Patout Burns Rd
Jeanerette, LA 70544 337-276-4592
Fax: 337-276-4247 www.mapatout.com
Processor of sugar cane
President: William Patout III
CEO: Craig P Caillier
Estimated Sales: $156451778
Number Employees: 100-249
Type of Packaging: Bulk

8200 **M.E. Swing Company**
612 S Pickett St # D
Alexandria, VA 22304-4620 703-370-5050
Fax: 703-370-7286 800-485-4019
darren@swingscoffee.com
www.swingscoffee.com
Processor of roasted coffee
Owner: Mark Woarmuth
Executive Vice President: Dwayne Walker
VP Marketing: Dwayne Walker
Director of Operations: Darren Dimisa
Estimated Sales: Less than $500,000
Number Employees: 5-9
Sq. footage: 3000
Type of Packaging: Consumer, Food Service, Bulk

8201 **M.H. Greenebaum**
64 Campbell Avenue
Airmont, NY 10901-6407 973-538-9200
Fax: 973-538-3599
Cheese, cheese products
President: Rasmus Andersen
Estimated Sales: $ 10-20 Million
Number Employees: 5-9

8202 **M.J. Kellner Company**
5700 International Pkwy
Springfield, IL 62711 217-483-1770
Fax: 217-483-1771 mjk@mjkellner.com
www.mjkellner.com
Wholesaler/distributor of groceries, meats, produce, frozen foods, baked goods, equipment and fixtures, general merchandise and seafood; serving the food service market
President: Bill Kellner
CFO: S David Rikas
CEO: Chad Nassif
Sales Development Manager: Gary Kelley
Estimated Sales: $ 50 - 100 Million
Number Employees: 50-99

8203 **M.M. Bake Shop**
444 N 6th Avenue
Laurel, MS 39440-3969 601-428-5153
Bread, rolls
President: Ethel Stewart
Estimated Sales: Less than $500,000
Number Employees: 5-9

8204 **M.S. Walker**
20 3rd Ave
Somerville, MA 02143 617-776-6700
Fax: 617-776-5808 www.mswalker.com
Processor and importer of brandy, liqueurs, wines and spirits
President: Harvey Allen
CEO: Richard Sandler
Estimated Sales: $ 1 - 3 Million
Number Employees: 100-249

8205 **M.S. Walker**
20 3rd Ave
Somerville, MA 02143 617-776-6700
Fax: 617-776-5808 info@mswalker.com
www.mswalker.com
A wholesale distributor of wines, spirits and cigars, in addition to manufacturing their own brands of spirit products.
CEO: Richard Sandler
Estimated Sales: $ 1-2.5 Million
Number Employees: 100-249

8206 **M/S Smears**
490 Old U.S. Highway 74
P.O. Box 467
Chadbourn, NC 28431-0467 910-654-5163
Fax: 910-654-4734 www.sweetpotatoes.com
Pies
CEO: George Wooten
CFO: Stuart Hill

8207 **(HQ)MAFCO Worldwide Corporation**
300 Jefferson St
Camden, NJ 08104 856-964-8840
Fax: 856-964-6029
magnasweet@mafcolicorice.com
www.mafcolicorice.com
Processor and exporter of food ingredients including licorice extracts, flavoring agents and enhancers
President: Steven Taub
Marketing/Sales: Jeff Robinson
Estimated Sales: $36 Million
Number Employees: 230
Type of Packaging: Bulk
Brands:
Mafco Magnasweet

8208 **MAK Enterprises**
37315 26th Street E
Palmdale, CA 93550-6414 661-272-1867
mtaylor1@netport.com
makenterprisesllc.com
Processor of salsa and hot sauces
President/Owner: Mike Klumpp
CEO: Mark Taylor
CFO: Renee Taylor
Underground Operations Mgr: Doug Nestle
Number Employees: 20-49
Brands:
Hell's Furry Fire Hot Sauce
The Salsa Addiction

8209 **MAS Sales**
11225 W Grand Ave
Northlake, IL 60164-1036 847-451-0005
Fax: 847-451-6563 800-615-6951
pastafactoryusa@juno.com
Frozen spaghetti sauce, lasagna, macaroni, ravioli, spaghetti no meat, spaghetti with meat, manicotti, stuffed shells, tortellini, cannelloni pasta. A full line of fresh frozen string pasta's, frozen extruded shapes, frozen tortellinitortelloni, ravioli, stuffed and regualar gnocchi entrees and frozen sauces
President: Michael Sica
VP: Irene Sica
Quality Control: Jodeph Sica
Marketing: Tom Lichon
Sales: Tom Lichon
Estimated Sales: $ 20 - 50 Million
Number Employees: 50 to 99
Number of Brands: 1
Number of Products: 1000
Sq. footage: 16000
Type of Packaging: Consumer, Food Service, Private Label, Bulk
Brands:
Pasta Factory

8210 **MB Candies**
Alternate Route 250
Bridgeport, IL 62417 618-945-7778
888-MBC-ANDY
makinbatch@hotmail.com www.makinbatch.com
Manufacturer of quality hard candy including sugar free varities.
Estimated Sales: $ 1-5 Million
Number Employees: 5-9

8211 **(HQ)MBM Corporation**
P.O.Box 800
Rocky Mount, NC 27802 252-985-7200
Fax: 252-985-7241 www.mbmfoodservice.com
Processor and exporter of custom cut pork
President: Jerry Wordsworth
Business Development Director: Dennis Parent
Agent: Mitch Brantley
Estimated Sales: $100+ Million
Number Employees: 500-999
Type of Packaging: Consumer, Food Service
Other Locations:
MBM Corp.
Fort Worth TX

8212 **ME Franks**
175 Strafford Ave # 230
Wayne, PA 19087-3333 610-989-9688
Fax: 610-989-8989 www.mefranks.com
M.E. Franks specializes in manufactured milk products such as: non-fat dry milk, whole milk powder, whey powder, whey protein concentrates, functional milk fractions, lactose, buttermilk powder, anhydrous milk fat, cheese, whole milkpowder, casien and caseinates.
President: Don Street
Estimated Sales: $ 10-25 Million
Number Employees: 5-9

8213 **MEYENBERG Goat Milk Products**
PO Box 934
Turlock, CA 95381-0934 209-634-2731
Fax: 209-668-4977 800-891-4628
info@meyenberg.com www.meyenberg.com

Processor and exporter of goat's milk including evaporated, powdered, and fresh, butter, and goat cheese.
President: Robert Jackson
COO/Marketing: Tracy Plante-Darrimon
Plant Manager: Frank Fillman
Estimated Sales: $18-20 Million
Number Employees: 50
Number of Products: 25
Type of Packaging: Consumer, Bulk
Brands:
MEYENBERG
PROFESSIONAL PREFERENCE

8214 **MFI Food Canada**
70 Irene Street
Winnipeg, MB R3T 4E1 204-477-1830
Fax: 204-475-7740 www.michaelfoods.com
Manufacturer of egg products
President: J. Hugh Wiebe
Director: Gregg Ostrander
Estimated Sales: $37 Million
Number Employees: 200

8215 **MG Fisheries**
PO Box 909
Grand Manan, NB E5G 4M1
Canada 506-662-3471
Fax: 506-662-3779
Products include sea urchin, scallops, shark, monkfish, flounder, pollock-dried, cod-dried, pollock-salted, hake-dried, hake-salted, lobster-live, and cod-salted.
President: Morris Green
Number Employees: 10-19
Type of Packaging: Consumer, Food Service

8216 **MGP**
100 Commercial St., Cray Business Plz
P.O. Box 130
Atchinson, KS 66002-0130 913-367-1480
Fax: 913-367-0192 www.mgpingredients.com
www.mgpingredients.com
Supplier of dry powders used as binders in chicken patties, meat, and vegetarian burgers.
President, CEO: Tim Newkirk

8217 **MIC Foods**
8701 SW 137th Avenue
306-308
Miami, FL 33183-4078 786-507-0540
Fax: 786-507-0545 800-788-9335
info@micfood.com www.micfood.com/
Processor and importer of frozen plaintains, yuca, cassava and frozen fruit products.
President: Alfredo Lardizabal
Sales VP: Maria Krogh
Estimated Sales: $ 5 - 10 Million
Number Employees: 5-9
Brands:
Big Banana
Costa Clara
Tio Jorge

8218 **MJ Barleyhoppers**
621 21st St
Lewiston, ID 83501-3285 208-746-5300
Fax: 208-799-1000 mjbarleyhoppers@msn.com
www.redlionlewiston.com
Processor of ale, stout and lager
Principal: Lee Duncan
Estimated Sales: $230,000
Number Employees: 7
Parent Co: Impact Restaurants
Type of Packaging: Consumer, Food Service
Brands:
Oktoberfest

8219 **MKE Enterprises LTD**
375 5th Avenue
New York, NY 10016-3323 212-447-0051
Fax: 212-447-0068 mkegroupltd@gmail.com

8220 **MLO/GeniSoy Products Company**
100 W. 5h Street
Suite 700
Tulas, OK 74103 866-606-3829
Fax: 918-278-2850 info@genisoy.com
www.genisoy.com
Powdered beverage mixes, protein bars, sports nutrition products and soy protein bars
President: Tim Bruer
Marketing: Rich Martin
Plant Manager: Jeff Amlin
Estimated Sales: $ .5 - 1 million
Number Employees: 1-4

8221 **MNH Erickson Ranch**
3916 County Road Mm
Orland, CA 95963-9702 530-865-9587
Fax: 530-865-8637
Co-Owner: Heidi Erickson
Co-Owner: Merritt Erickson

8222 **MO Air International**
183 Madison Avenue
Suite 1202
New York, NY 10016 212-792-9400
Fax: 212-490-1763 800-247-3131
reservation@moair.com www.moair-usa.com
Manager: Sherry Kawabe

8223 **MPK Sonama Corporation**
21707 8th Street E #100
Sonoma, CA 95476-9781 707-996-3931
Fax: 707-996-3999 ginger@mpksonoma.com
www.mpksonoma.com
Sauces, dressings, specialty foods
President: Charles Boles
Plant Manager: Todd Pimentel
Estimated Sales: $ 5-10 Million
Number Employees: 15
Type of Packaging: Private Label

8224 **MPK Sonoma Company**
21684 8th St E Ste 100
Sonoma, CA 95476 707-996-3931
Fax: 707-996-3999
Frozen garlic and ginger, dressings, sauces, dessert toppings, specialty products
President: Charles Boles
Estimated Sales: $ 5 - 10 Million
Number Employees: 5-9
Brands:
Charles Premium
Marinpak

8225 **MSRF, Inc.**
2501 N Elston Ave
Chicago, IL 60647 773-227-1115
Fax: 773-227-2031 snejman@msrf.com
www.msrf.com
Gourmet food gifts
President: David Reich
Marketing: Scott Nejman
Estimated Sales: $10-15 Million
Number Employees: 10-19
Brands:
MSRF

8226 **MYNTZ!**
19016 72nd Ave S.
Kent, WA 98032 425-656-9076
Fax: 425-656-8059 800-800-9490
www.seattlegourmetfoods.com www.myntz.com
MYNTZ! is a confection company that manufactures, packages and distributes up-scale consumer breath mints in a variety of flavors that include vanillamyntblast sugar-free, tropical fruit and orchard fruit.
President/CEO: David Parker
National Sales Director: Robert Kingsley
Customer Service: Diana Klein
Number Employees: 50-99
Brands:
DROPZ
MYNTZ! BREATH MINTS
MYNTZ! INSTASTRIPZ
MYNTZ! LIP BALM
SQYNTZ! SUPERSOURZ

8227 **Maat Nutritionals**
1875 Century Park E
6th Floor
Los Angeles, CA 90067-2501 310-407-8608
Fax: 310-407-8618 888-818-6228
info@e-maat.com www.e-maat.com
Dietary supplements, vitamins and minerals
President: Rick Mandell

8228 **Mac's Donut Shop**
P.O.Box 1172
Aliquippa, PA 15001 724-375-6776
Fax: 724-378-2961
Processor of baked goods including doughnuts, cakes, pastries, cookies, muffins, brownies, etc
Owner: Twila Mc Kittrick
VP: Twila McKittrick
Estimated Sales: $1100000
Number Employees: 20-49
Type of Packaging: Consumer

8229 **Mac's Farms Sausage Company**
P.O.Box 190
Newton Grove, NC 28366 910-594-0095
Fax: 910-594-1812 macfarms@intrstar.net
Sausage, air dried medium and hot, fresh link, fresh patty
Owner: Scott Mc Lamb
CEO: Scott McLamb
Estimated Sales: $700,000
Number Employees: 5-9
Type of Packaging: Bulk
Brands:
Double D
Mac's

8230 **Mac's Meats Wholesale**
1761 W Hadley Ave
Las Cruces, NM 88005-4122 575-524-2751
Fax: 575-526-3826
Processor of meat including pork and beef
President: Al Guerrero
Estimated Sales: $ 10 - 20 Million
Number Employees: 5-9
Type of Packaging: Consumer, Food Service

8231 **Mac's Oysters**
414 Emerton Rd
Fanny Bay, BC V0R 1W0
Canada 250-335-2233
Fax: 250-335-2065 gordy@macsoysters.com
www.macsoysters.com
Processor of clams and fresh shucked oysters
Managing Director: Gordon McLellan
General Managaer: Sally Kew
Number Employees: 50-99
Type of Packaging: Consumer, Food Service, Private Label, Bulk

8232 **Mac's Snacks**
615 N Great Southwest Pkwy
Arlington, TX 76011 817-640-5626
Fax: 817-649-7832 sales@evansfoods.com
www.macssnacks.com
Pork skins and cracklings
VP: Jim Speake
Operations Manager: Brad Bothe
Estimated Sales: $ 10-20 Million
Number Employees: 20-49
Parent Co: Evans Food Products
Type of Packaging: Private Label, Bulk

8233 **MacEwan's Meats**
9620 Elbow Drive SW
Calgary, AB T2V 1M2
Canada 403-228-9999
Fax: 403-228-9999
Processor of meat pies including chicken, steak and scotch
President: John Hopkins
VP: Lynne Hopkins
Marketing Director: John Hopkins
Director: John Hopkins
Number Employees: 1-4
Sq. footage: 1500
Type of Packaging: Consumer, Food Service, Bulk
Brands:
MacEwan's

8234 **MacFarlane Pheasants**
2821 S Us Highway 51
Janesville, WI 53546-8945 608-757-7881
Fax: 608-757-7884 877-269-8957
info@pheasant.com www.pheasant.com
Producer of high quality, young, pheasants; available fresh, frozen, smoked as whole birds or cut down sized products.
Owner: Bill Mac Farlane
CFO: Brad Lillie
Sales: Mary Jo Bergs
Shipping Manager: David Lennox
Plant Manager: Bryan Carter
Estimated Sales: $ 1 - 3 Million
Sq. footage: 5000
Type of Packaging: Food Service

8235 **MacFarms of Hawaii**
89-406 Mamalahoa Hwy
Captain Cook, HI 96704-8941 808-328-2435
Fax: 808-328-8081 sales@macfarms.com
www.macfarms.com

Processor and exporter of chocolate covered macadamia nuts and macadamia nut cookies
President: Jeff Gilbrech
VP Sales: Brian Loader
Manager: Rick Vigden
Estimated Sales: $ 20 - 50 Million
Number Employees: 100-249
Parent Co: Blue Diamond Growers
Type of Packaging: Consumer, Private Label, Bulk
Brands:
Macfarms of Hawaii

8236 **MacGregors Meat & Seafood**
265 Garyray Drive
Toronto, ON M9L 1P2
Canada 416-749-5951
Fax: 416-740-3230 888-383-3663
graham@macgregors.com www.macgregors.com
Processor of poultry, seafood and meat products; importer of beef and seafood
CEO: D MacGregor
Controller/Treasurer: Ed de Vries
Number Employees: 180
Sq. footage: 46000
Brands:
Macgregors
Steak King

8237 **MacKay's Cochrane Ice Cream**
PO Box 250
220 1st St W
Cochrane, AB T4C 1A5
Canada 403-932-2455
Fax: 403-932-2455
generalinfo@mackaysicecream.com
www.mackaysicecream.com
Processor of ice cream, frozen yogurt, sherbet and sorbet
Manager: Robyn MacKay
Production Manager: Rhona Mackay
Estimated Sales: B
Number Employees: 1-4
Type of Packaging: Consumer, Food Service
Brands:
Mackay's

8238 **MacKinlay Teas**
1289 Waterways Dr
Ann Arbor, MI 48108-2783 734-846-0966
Fax: 734-747-9193 sales@mackinlay.com
www.mackinlay.com
Processor of teas; private label packaging is available to selected customers.
President: Davinder Singh
Estimated Sales: $2.9 Million
Number Employees: 1-4
Type of Packaging: Private Label
Brands:
MacKinlay Tea's
Queen Jasmine
White Tiger Rice
Wild Blend Rice

8239 **MacKnight Smoked Foods**
550 NE 185th St
Miami, FL 33179-4513 305-655-0332
Fax: 305-655-2278 sales@macknight.com
www.macknight.com
Processor and importer of smoked and fresh fish
President: Jonathan Brown
General Manager: Alex McMorran
Estimated Sales: $ 10 - 20 Million
Number Employees: 20-49
Sq. footage: 10000
Type of Packaging: Consumer, Food Service, Private Label, Bulk

8240 **Macabee Foods**
250 West Nyack Road
West Nyack, NY 10994 845-623-1300
Fax: 845-623-7649 www.macabeefoods.com
Processor of kosher frozen pizza
President: Marvin Kochansky
VP: Jeffery Schmelzer
Number Employees: 5-9
Sq. footage: 4000
Type of Packaging: Consumer, Food Service, Private Label
Brands:
Macabee

8241 **Macco Organiques**
100 Rue Mc Arthur
Valleyfield, QC J6S 4M5
Canada 450-371-1066
Fax: 450-371-5519 macco@macco.ca
www.macco.ca
Processor and exporter of food preservatives including: calcium acetate; calcium chloride dihy; calcium propionate; potassium acetate; potassium benzoate; sodium acetate anh; sodium benzoate; sodium diacetate; and sodium propionate.
President: Robert Brscoe
VP: Jacques Rochon
Logistics Manager: Simon Rinella
Sales Manager: Simon Rinella
Estimated Sales: 9.27 Million
Number Employees: 60

8242 **Machias Bay Seafood**
503 Kennebec Rd
Machias, ME 04654 207-255-8671
Fax: 207-255-8243
Seafood
Owner: Randy Ramsdell
Estimated Sales: $ 1 - 3 Million
Number Employees: 1-4

8243 **Mack's Homemade Ice Cream**
2695 S Queen St
York, PA 17402 717-741-2027
Fax: 717-747-0065 www.macksicecream.com
Processor of ice cream
President: Walter Bloss
Estimated Sales: $ 1 - 3 Million
Number Employees: 20-49
Type of Packaging: Consumer

8244 **Mackie Intl.**
719 Palmyrita Ave
Riverside, CA 92507-1811 323-722-0772
Fax: 323-722-0681 800-733-9762
www.mackieinternational.net
Processor of ice pops, fruit flavored drinks and jellies
President: Ernesto Dacay
Finance Executive; Manager: Carmel Canete
Estimated Sales: 10-19
Number Employees: 50-99
Sq. footage: 60000
Type of Packaging: Private Label, Bulk
Brands:
Berry Cool
Snowtime

8245 **Macrie Brothers**
750 S 1st Rd
Hammonton, NJ 08037-8407 609-561-6822
Fax: 609-561-6296 bluebuck@bellatlantic.net
www.blueblueberries.com
Blueberries
Owner: Paul Macrie Iii
CEO: Paul Macrie III
Superviser: Al Macrie
Operations: Nicholas Macrie
Production: Michael Macrie
Estimated Sales: Below $ 5 Million
Number Employees: 5
Sq. footage: 30000
Type of Packaging: Consumer, Food Service, Private Label, Bulk
Brands:
Blue Buck

8246 **Mad Chef Enterprise**
PO Box 321
Mentor, OH 44061-0321 440-951-0846
Fax: 440-269-2387 800-951-2433
info@madchef.com www.madchef.com
Products include sauces, seasonings, rubs. Additional products include aprons, grilling mitts, basting brushes, grill lighters, spatulas, grilling baskets, salt & pepper mills, skewers, and mugs.
President: Michael D'Amico

8247 **Mad River Farm**
540 Bayside Rd
Arcata, CA 95521 707-822-0248
Fax: 707-822-4441 calnorth@humboldt1.com
www.mad-river-farm.com
Mad River Farms produces gourmet food products such as sunshine marmalade, lemon marmalade, plum orange jam with brandied raisins and wild huckleberry jam.
Owner: Marika Mrick
Vice President: Steven Ulrich
Estimated Sales: Below $ 5 Million
Number Employees: 1-4
Number of Brands: 1
Number of Products: 25
Sq. footage: 1000
Type of Packaging: Consumer, Food Service, Private Label, Bulk
Brands:
Mad River Farm

8248 **Mad Will's Food Company**
2043 Airpark Ct Ste 30
Auburn, CA 95602 530-823-8527
Fax: 530-823-1756 888-275-9455
orders@madwills.com www.madwills.com
Manufacturer of barbecue sauces, salsas, salad dressings, mustards, marinades, marinara sauces, hot sauces, other sauces and specialty food sauces; private label and contract packaging
President: Kim Sullivan
Marketing Director: Tim Sullivan
Operations Manager: Roy Ballard
VP Purchasing: Vanessa Johnson
Estimated Sales: $2700000
Number Employees: 20
Number of Products: 70
Sq. footage: 21168
Type of Packaging: Private Label

8249 **Mada'n Kosher Foods**
128 SW 3rd Ave
Dania, FL 33004 954-925-0077
Fax: 954-921-8739 info@madankosher.com
www.madankosher.com
Processor of frozen kosher foods including beef, fish and poultry
President: Samuel Weiss
VP: Richard Marsico
Director Operations: Richard Anthony
Estimated Sales: $210000
Number Employees: 10-19
Sq. footage: 3500
Parent Co: Mada'n Corporation
Type of Packaging: Consumer, Food Service

8250 **Made Rite Foods**
2229 Sunnybrook Dr
Burlington, NC 27215 336-229-5728
Fax: 336-545-1880
Processor of salads and sandwiches
President: Jerry McMasters
Plant Manager: Alan Harder
Number Employees: 100-249
Parent Co: Made Rite Foods
Type of Packaging: Consumer, Food Service, Private Label, Bulk
Brands:
Made Rite
Sedgefield

8251 **Made in Nature**
2500 S Fowler Ave
Fresno, CA 93725 559-445-8601
Fax: 559-445-8601 800-906-7426
info@sonomawestholdings.com
www.madeinnature.com
Organic dried fruits and vegetables
President: Gary Hess
Marketing Manager: Ren Lawrence
Operations: Kimberly Musgrove
Estimated Sales: $ 2.5-5 Million
Number Employees: 10
Brands:
Made In Nature

8252 **Made-Rite Sandwich Company**
P.O.Box 27
Ooltewah, TN 37363 423-238-5492
Fax: 423-238-5844 800-343-1327
info@GreatAmericanDeli.com
www.greatamericandeli.com
Products include sandwiches, cakes, Hot 2 Go sandwiches, burritos, pocket sandwiches and rollergrill products.
President: Earl R Sullivan
VP: Steven Corley
Plant Manager: Nelson Shiver

Estimated Sales: $ 10-20 Million
Number Employees: 100-249
Parent Co: Great American Deli

8253 **Madera Enterprises**
32565 Avenue 9
Madera, CA 93636 559-431-1444
Fax: 559-674-8214 800-507-9555
maderaent@aol.com
Processor and exporter of custom fruit juice concentrates and purees including grape, apple, strawberry, plum, prune, date, raisin, pomegranate, etc.; also, dried fruits and vinaigrettes
President: Susan Nury
Marketing: Rosanna Andrews-White
Estimated Sales: $ 3 - 5 Million
Number Employees: 5-9
Type of Packaging: Bulk
Brands:
Mina
Zary

8254 **(HQ)Madhava Honey**
14300 E I-25 Frontage Road
Longmont, CO 80504 970-535-4269
Fax: 303-823-5755 800-530-2900
info@madhavahoney.com
www.madhavasweeteners.com
Colorado and Rocky Mountain Honey products
Principal: Larry Lane
Plant Foreman: Harry Hasty
Estimated Sales: $710,000
Number Employees: 12
Sq. footage: 4487
Type of Packaging: Consumer, Food Service, Private Label, Bulk
Other Locations:
Madhava Honey
Parachute CO
Brands:
AGAVE NECTAR
AMBROSIA HONEY
MOUNTAIN GOLD HONEY

8255 **Madhouse Munchies**
382 Hercules Dr Ste 3
Colchester, VT 05446 802-655-6662
Fax: 802-655-7711
info@madhousemunchies.com
www.madhousemunchies.com
Low-fat, hand-cooked potato chips
President: J Ehlen
Sales/Marketing Associate: Eric Bleckner
Estimated Sales: $ 740000
Number Employees: 10
Brands:
Madhouse Munchies

8256 **Madison Dairy Produce Company**
1018 E Washington Ave
Madison, WI 53703-2939 608-256-5561
Fax: 608-256-0985 gstein@maddairy.com
Processor of butter and margarine
Manager: Bob Gettel
VP: Chuck Steinhauer
VP Sales: Gary Steinhauer
Estimated Sales: $32400000
Number Employees: 50-99
Type of Packaging: Consumer, Food Service, Private Label
Brands:
Creamery Blend
Deerfield
Lady Lee
Red Rose
Roundys

8257 **Madison Foods**
238 Chester St
Saint Paul, MN 55107 651-265-8212
Fax: 651-297-6286
Processor of butter substitutes; also, contract packager of retail and food service sauces
President: Steve Anderson
Estimated Sales: $ .5 - 1 million
Number Employees: 1-4
Type of Packaging: Consumer, Food Service, Private Label, Bulk
Brands:
Better

8258 **Madison Vineyard**
Hc 72 Box 490
Ribera, NM 87560-9706 575-421-8028
Fax: 575-421-8028 www.madison-winery.com
Wines
Owner: Bill Madison
Partner: Elise Madison
Director: Shirley Flint
Owner: Elise Madison
Estimated Sales: $190 K
Number Employees: 3

8259 **Madonna Estate Mont St John**
5400 Old Sonoma Rd
Napa, CA 94559-9708 707-255-8864
Fax: 707-257-2778 mail@madonnaestate.com
www.madonnaestate.com
Wines include Chardonnay, Pinot Noir, Due Ragazze, Pinot Noir Riserva, Merlot, Cabernet Sauvignon.
President: Andrea Bartolucci
Marketing: Ron Arata
Public Relations: Brette Bartolucci
Vineyard Manager: Andrea Bartolucci
Estimated Sales: $ 2.5-5 Million
Number Employees: 5-9
Brands:
Madonna Estate Mont St John
Poppy Hill

8260 **Madrange**
85 Division Avenue
Millington, NJ 07946-1316 908-647-6485
Fax: 908-646-8305 mkessler@charter.net
www.fromartharie.com/
Products include cooked hams, goat cheese, dips, butter, and pates/mousse.
President: Ron Schinbeckler
Vice President: Richard Kessler
Number Employees: 10-19
Type of Packaging: Private Label, Bulk

8261 **Madrona Specialty Foods**
18475 Olympic Avenue South
Tukwila, WA 98188 425-814-2500
Fax: 425-823-2345 csr@elegantgourmet.com
www.elegantgourmet.com
Manufacturer of chocolate almond toffee, chcolate shapes, caramels, holiday candies, cookies, and hot cocoa
Principal: Paul Pigott
Marketing: Erin Cammarano
Estimated Sales: $3.4 Million
Number Employees: 24
Type of Packaging: Private Label, Bulk
Brands:
Elegant Sweets
Hannah's Delishts
Kingsley's Caramels

8262 **Madrona Vineyards**
PO Box 454
2560 High Hill Road
Camino, CA 95709-0454 530-644-5948
Fax: 530-644-7517
winery@madronavineyards.com
www.madronavineyards.com
Products include white wines, red wines, reserve wines and dessert wines.
President: Richard Bush
Estimated Sales: Below $ 5 Million
Number Employees: 20
Type of Packaging: Consumer

8263 **Madys Company**
1555 Yosemite Ave
San Francisco, CA 94124-3268 415-822-2227
Fax: 415-822-3673 support@madys.com
www.madys.com
Processor, importer, exporter and wholesaler/distributor of herbal, medicinal and regular teas; also, vitamins, ginseng root, etc
Owner: Sandy Su Wing
General Manager: Marian Hong
Number Employees: 10-19
Sq. footage: 3400
Parent Co: Azeta Brands
Type of Packaging: Consumer, Food Service, Private Label, Bulk
Brands:
Butterfly
Evergreen
Madys
Weiloss

8264 **Maebo Noodle Factory**
711 W Kawailani St
Hilo, HI 96720-3155 808-959-8763
Fax: 808-959-4404 877-663-8667
sales@one-ton.com www.one-ton.com
Processor of Chinese foods including noodles, wonton chips and saimin
President/Manager: Blane Maebo
VP: Rachel Maebo
Estimated Sales: $550000
Number Employees: 10-19
Type of Packaging: Consumer, Bulk
Brands:
Maebo Noodle Factory, Inc.

8265 **Mafco Natural Products**
4400 Williamsburg Ave
Richmond, VA 23231 804-222-1600
Fax: 804-226-6325
Manufacturer of herbal powders and teas; also recently added a line of fruit teas.
President: Steven Taub
Customer Service: Phyllis Grigg
Estimated Sales: $8200000
Number Employees: 10-19

8266 **Mafco Worldwide Corporation**
300 Jefferson St
Camden, NJ 8104 856-964-8840
Fax: 856-964-6029
magnasweet@mafcolicorice.com
www.mafcolicorice.com
Manufacturers of licorice
CEO: Stephen Taub
Sales Manager: Jeffrey Robinson
Number Employees: 100-249

8267 **Maggie Gin's**
127 10th Avenue
San Francisco, CA 94118-1126 415-221-6080
Fax: 415-221-1197 mgin@aol.com
www.goldenwestsf.com
Sauces, marinades
Number Employees: 1-4
Parent Co: Golden West Specialty Foods
Type of Packaging: Private Label
Brands:
Chinese Chicken Salad Dressing
Thai Sauce
Traditional Stir Fry Sauce

8268 **Maggie Lyon Chocolatiers**
6000 Peach Ind Blvd Ste B
Norcross, GA 30071 770-446-1299
Fax: 770-446-2191 800-969-3500
sales@maggielyon.com
www.sweetinnovations.com
Products include gourmet chocolates, truffles, toffee, caramels, bark and nut clusters, toffee, special occassion and gift baskets, easter selections, bulk chocolates, and promotional products.
President: Jeffery Pollack
Cfo: Linda Pollack
VP: Michael Pollack
Estimated Sales: $1.8 Million
Number Employees: 15
Type of Packaging: Private Label
Brands:
CONNIE'S HANDMADE TOFFEE

8269 **Maggie's Salsa**
1303 Turley Rd
Charleston, WV 25314 304-550-5460
Fax: 304-881-0289 maggie@maggiesalsa.com
www.maggiessalsa.com
salsa
President/Owner: Maggie Cook

8270 **Maggiora Baking Company**
1900 Garden Tract Road
Richmond, CA 94801-1219 510-235-0274
Fax: 510-235-2427 info@maggiorabaking.com
www.maggiorabaking.com
Products include sourdoughs, french breads, focaccia, bread sticks, pesto dinner roll clusters, garlic rounds, Hawaiian bread/dinner rolls, Greek rings, egg bread and dinner rolls, and various specialty breads.
President: Dennis Maggiora
Sales Director: Robert Maggiora
General Manager: Don Maggiora
Estimated Sales: $ 5-10 Million
Number Employees: 75

8271 **Magic Gumball International**
9310 Mason Ave
Chatsworth, CA 91311 818-716-1888
Fax: 818-341-4234 800-576-2020
info@magicgumball.com
www.magicgumball.com
Candy
Owner: Guy Hart
VP: Guy Hart
Estimated Sales: $ 5 - 10 Million
Number Employees: 50-99

8272 **Magic Ice Products**
1326 Ethan Ave
Cincinnati, OH 45225
800-776-7923
magiciceproducts@gmail.com
www.magiciceproducts.com
Processor and exporter of gourmet coffee flavor, slush and ice syrups; importer of shave ice machines and equipment
President: Shirley Weist
Estimated Sales: C
Number Employees: 5-9
Type of Packaging: Consumer, Food Service, Private Label
Brands:
Flavor Magic
Magic Ice

8273 **Magic Seasoning Blends**
720 Distributors Row
Po Box 23342
New Orleans, LA 70183 504-731-3578
Fax: 504-731-3576 800-457-2857
jmcmbride@chefpaul.com www.chefpaul.com
Dry spices, rubs, bottled sauces and marinades.
Owner: Paul Prudhomme
President/CEO: Shawn McBride
CFO: Paula LaCour
R&D Director: Sean O'Meara
VP Sales/Marketing: John McBride
Human Resources Director: Naomi Roundtree
Operations Director: Jeff Hanson
Manufacturing Director: David Hickey
Purchasing Director: Patricia Cantrelle
Estimated Sales: $9.6 Million
Number Employees: 85
Number of Brands: 3
Number of Products: 29
Sq. footage: 130000
Type of Packaging: Consumer, Food Service, Private Label, Bulk
Brands:
BARBECUE MAGIC
BLACKENED REDFISH MAGIC
BLACKENED STEAK MAGIC
BREADING MAGIC
GRAVY & GUMBO MAGIC
MAGIC PEPPER SAUCE
MAGIC SAUCE & MARINADES
MEAT MAGIC
PIZZA & PASTA MAGIC
PORK & VEAL MAGIC
POULTRY MAGIC
SALMON MAGIC
SEAFOOD MAGIC
SHRIMP MAGIC
SWEETFREE MAGIC
VEGETABLE MAGIC

8274 **Magic Valley Fresh Frozen**
2100 Trophy Dr
McAllen, TX 78504 956-618-1251
Fax: 956-994-8948
Frozen butter beans, carrots, greens, okra, onions, southern peas
Manager: Ben Bellarrel
Operations Manager: George Calhoon
Estimated Sales: $100+ Million
Number Employees: 100-249

8275 **Magic Valley Growers**
PO Box 850
Wendell, ID 83355-0850 208-536-6693
Fax: 208-536-6695
onions@magicvalleygrowers.com
www.magicvalleygrowers.com
Grower and packer of specialty onions including pearl, boiler, peeled pearl and sets; exporter of pearl and boiler onions
President: Robert Reitveld
VP: James Kelly
Estimated Sales: $1.1 Million
Number Employees: 20
Sq. footage: 53100
Type of Packaging: Consumer, Private Label, Bulk
Brands:
Dutch Boiler
Dutch Girl
Top Hat

8276 **Magic Valley Quality Milk Producers**
1756 S Buchanan St
Jerome, ID 83338 208-324-7519
Fax: 208-324-7554 mvqmp@lightcom.net
Cooperative selling raw milk to food processors
General Manager: Alan Stutzman
Estimated Sales: $ .5 - 1 million
Number Employees: 1-4

8277 **Magna Foods Corporation**
16010 Phoenix Drive
City of Industry, CA 91745-1623 626-336-7500
Fax: 626-336-3999 800-995-4394
magnafoods@aol.com
Processor and exporter of confectionery, candy, cookies, crackers and cocoa products
President: Yogi Atmadja
VP: Peter Surjadinata
Estimated Sales: $1500000
Number Employees: 25
Sq. footage: 5000
Parent Co: IBIS
Brands:
Coffeego
Danisa
Roma Marie

8278 **Magnanini Winery**
172 Strawridge Rd
Wallkill, NY 12589-3905 845-895-2767
Fax: 845-895-9458 www.magwine.com
Wines
Owner: Richard Magnanini
CEO: Galba Magnanini
Estimated Sales: $500,000-$1 Million
Number Employees: 1-4
Type of Packaging: Private Label

8279 **Magnetic Springs Water Company**
1917 Joyce Ave
Columbus, OH 43219-1029 614-421-1780
Fax: 614-421-1681 800-572-2990
www.magneticsprings.com
Processor of drinking, distilled, spring, artesian and infant water
President: Jeff Allison
Plant Manager: Tim VanSickle
Estimated Sales: $11900000
Number Employees: 50-99
Sq. footage: 100000
Type of Packaging: Consumer, Food Service, Private Label, Bulk
Brands:
Magnetic Springs

8280 **Magnificent Muffin Corporation**
64 Toledo St
Farmingdale, NY 11735-6628 631-454-8022
Fax: 631-454-8574
Muffins and baked goods
President: John Schreckinger
Estimated Sales: Below $150,000
Number Employees: 1-4
Type of Packaging: Consumer, Bulk

8281 **Magnolia Beef Company**
P.O.Box 220
Elizabeth, NJ 07201 908-352-9412
Fax: 908-352-1576
Processor of beef, veal, lamb and pork
Owner: Manny Dasilva
Estimated Sales: $6300000
Number Employees: 25
Type of Packaging: Food Service, Bulk

8282 **Magnolia Citrus Association**
1014 E Teapot Dome Ave
Porterville, CA 93257 559-784-4455
Fax: 559-781-9182
Processor, packer and exporter of Valencia and navel oranges
Manager: Dominick Arcure
Manager: Larry Fultz
Sales: Dominick Arcure
Estimated Sales: $ 10 - 20 Million
Number Employees: 20-49
Type of Packaging: Private Label, Bulk
Brands:
Magnolia
Malta
Memory

8283 **Magnolia Meats**
1904 Kings Hwy
Shreveport, LA 71103 318-221-2814
Processor of beef, pork and chicken
President: E Dean
Estimated Sales: $ 3 - 5 Million
Number Employees: 5-9
Type of Packaging: Consumer, Food Service, Bulk

8284 **(HQ)Magnotta Winery Corporation**
271 Chrislea Road
Vaughan, ON L4L 8N6
Canada 905-738-9463
Fax: 905-738-5551 800-461-9463
mailbox@magnotta.com www.magnotta.com
Manufacturer, retailer, and exporter of beer, spirits and juice for home winemaking
President/Ceo: Rossana Magnotta
Cfo: Fulvio De Angelis
Estimated Sales: $23 Million
Number Employees: 107
Sq. footage: 60000
Type of Packaging: Consumer
Other Locations:
Magnotta Winery Corp.
Scarborough ON
Brands:
Magnotta

8285 **Magnum Coffee Roastery**
1 Java Blvd
Nunica, MI 49448 616-837-0333
Fax: 616-837-0777 888-937-5282
sales@magnumcoffee.com
www.magnumcoffee.com
Provides a full range of coffee roasting and quality packaging services.
President: Kevin Kihnke
General Manager: Nick Andres
Estimated Sales: $ 2.5-5 Million
Number Employees: 40
Type of Packaging: Private Label
Brands:
Island Trader
Magnum Exotic

8286 **Magrabar Chemical Corp**
6100 Madison Ct
Morton Grove, IL 60053 847-965-7550
Fax: 847-965-7553 www.magrabar.com
Manufactures additives, release agents and viscosity modifiers
President: Susan Jenkins
Vice President: Dale Roy
Estimated Sales: $3.4 Million
Number Employees: 20

8287 **Mah Chena Company**
1416 W Ohio St
Chicago, IL 60642-7156 312-226-5100
Fax: 312-277-7170
Chinese frozen foods
President: Heather Shadur
Sales Manager: Jeffrey Hoffman
Plant Manager: Willis Yee
Number Employees: 10-19

8288 **Mahantongo Game Farms**
559 Flying Eagle Rd
Dalmatia, PA 17017 570-758-6284
Processor and exporter of game birds including pheasants and partridges
President: Lynn Laudenslager
Estimated Sales: $360000
Number Employees: 20-49

8289 **Maharishi Ayurveda Products International**
104 N Main St
Fairfield, IA 52556 641-472-6274
Fax: 719-260-7400 800-255-8332
questions@mapi.com www.mapi.com
Processor and importer of herbs and herbal products including teas, supplements and seasonings
President: Prakash Srivastava
Senior VP: Steven Barthe
Marketing Director: Russ Guest
Public Relations: Marsha Bonne
Operations Manager: Kevin Olson
Plant Manager: Kishore Nareundkar
Estimated Sales: $280000
Number Employees: 50-99
Number of Brands: 4
Number of Products: 600
Sq. footage: 47000
Type of Packaging: Consumer
Brands:
Ayurveda
Clarified Butter
Maharishi
Yata, Pilta, Kapha Teas

8290 **Maher Marketing Services**
1616 Corporate Ct # 140
Irving, TX 75038-2209 972-751-7700
Fax: 972-751-7777 mmaher@mahermark.com
www.mahermark.com
Products include imported and domestic cheeses, dairy products, frozen entrees, specialty snacks, crackers and cookies.
President: Dan Vines
CEO: Mike Maher
CFO: Anne Maher
Marketing Manager: April Tieken
Estimated Sales: $ 5-10 Million appx.
Number Employees: 5-9
Type of Packaging: Bulk

8291 **Mahoning Swiss Cheese Cooperative**
24062 Route 954 Highway N
Smicksburg, PA 16256-3428 814-257-8884
Fax: 724-286-9259
Cheese and butter
President: John Schablach
Plant Manager: Ralph Juart
Estimated Sales: Below $ 1 Million
Number Employees: 10

8292 **Maid-Rite Steak Company**
PO 105 Keystone Industrial Park
PO Box 509
Dunmore, PA 18512 570-343-4748
Fax: 570-969-2878 800-233-4259
customerservice@maidritesteak.com
www.maidritesteak.com
Manufacturer and supplier of fine quality, portioned controlled meat products, including quick frozen beef, ground beef, pork, veal, and lamb products.
President: Donald Bernstein
Controller: Alfred Jordano
R&D Director/Quality Control Manager: Kurt Sorenson
VP Marketing: Elaine Herzog
VP Sales: Mark Golden
Human Resources Director: Ashley Matechak
Operations Manager: John Mekilo
Plant Manager: Bruce Palevac
Estimated Sales: $41,500,000
Number Employees: 255
Sq. footage: 115000
Type of Packaging: Consumer, Food Service, Private Label, Bulk
Brands:
Chef Italia
Maid-Rite
Minit Chef
Polarized

8293 **Main Squeeze**
28 S 9th St
Columbia, MO 65201 573-817-5616
goodfood@main-squeeze.com
www.main-squeeze.com
Juice concentrates and bar mixes
Owner: Leigh Lockhart
Estimated Sales: $500,000-$1 Million
Number Employees: 5-9

8294 **Main Street Brewery**
1203 Main Street
Cincinnati, OH 45202-6326 513-665-4678
Processor of beer, ale and stout, including Woody's American Wheat, Main Street Pale Ale, Abigail's Amber and Steamboat Stout.
President: Vince Bryant
Number Employees: 50-99
Type of Packaging: Consumer, Food Service

8295 **Main Street Custom Foods**
170 Muffin Ln
Cuyahoga Falls, OH 44223-3358 330-929-0000
Fax: 330-920-8329 800-533-6246
snatoli@mainstreetgourmet.com
www.mainstreetmuffins.com
Manufacturer of custom and proprietary products including frozen dough, batter, and thaw and serve products. Will create new recipe for your application or match an existing recipe while packaging the product to meet your needs.
President/CEO: Steven Marks
President/CEO: Harvey Nelson
Quality Control: Angela Stoughton
Marketing: Joe Schaefer
Sales: Keith Kropp
Operations: Mike Braun
Production: Tommie Smith
Production: Bryan Smith
Purchasing Director: Jim Braun
Estimated Sales: $15 Million
Number Employees: 100-249
Number of Products: Cust
Sq. footage: 65000
Parent Co: Feature Foods dba Main Street Gourmet
Type of Packaging: Consumer, Food Service, Private Label, Bulk

8296 **(HQ)Main Street Gourmet**
170 Muffin Lane
Cuyahoga Falls, OH 44223 330-929-0000
Fax: 330-920-8329 800-533-6246
snatoli@mainstreetgourmet.com
www.mainstreetmuffins.com
Manufacturer of gourmet frozen bakery items including an extensive selection of muffins and muffin batter, cookies, brownies and bars, granola, loaf cakes, cakes and baked goods, toppings.
President/CEO: Steven Marks
President/CEO: Harvey Nelson
Quality Control: Angela Stoughton
Marketing: Joe Schaefer
Sales: Keith Kropp
Plant Manager/Operations: Mike Braun
Production: Tommie Smith
Production: Bryan Smith
Purchasing Director: Jim Braun
Estimated Sales: $15 Million
Number Employees: 100-249
Number of Brands: 6
Number of Products: 158
Sq. footage: 65000
Type of Packaging: Consumer, Food Service, Private Label, Bulk
Other Locations:
Brands:
Cambritt Cookies
Isabella's Extraordinary Muffins
Main Street Muffins
More Than Moist Muffins
The Softer Biscotti
Wild Fudge Brownies

8297 **Main Street Gourmet Fundraising**
170 Muffin Ln
Cuyahoga Falls, OH 44223 330-929-0000
Fax: 330-920-8329 800-533-6246
snatoli@mainstreetgourmet.com
www.mainstreetmuffins.com
Manufacturer of muffin batter, cookie dough, strudel, cinnamon rolls and brownies packaged for sale in the fund raising industry.
President/CEO: Steven Marks
President/CEO: Harvey Nelson
Quality Control: Angela Stoughton
Marketing: Joe Schaefer
Sales: Harvey Nelson
Plant Manager/Operations: Mike Braun
Production: Tommie Smith
Production: Bryan Smith
Purchasing Director: Jim Braun
Estimated Sales: $15 Million
Number Employees: 100-249
Number of Products: 10
Sq. footage: 65000
Parent Co: Feature Foods dba Main Street Gourmet
Type of Packaging: Consumer

8298 **Main Street Ingredients**
2340 Enterprise Avenue
La Crosse, WI 54603-1713 608-781-2345
Fax: 608-781-4667 800-359-2345
info@mainstreetingredients.com
www.mainstreetingredients.com
Processor of hydrocolloids, stabilizers, and dairy ingredients including whey proteins, milk proteins, and milk powders serving the dairy, bakery and nutrition industries; also a private-label contract manufacturer
President: Bill Schmitz
VP/Sales: Aaron Macha
Director of Sales: Mike Homewood
VP/Operations: Rudy Rott
Estimated Sales: $100+ Million
Number Employees: 50-99
Parent Co: Agropur
Brands:
Cornerstone
Keystone

8299 **Main Street Muffins**
170 Muffin Ln
Cuyahoga Falls, OH 44223-3358 330-929-0000
Fax: 330-920-8329 800-533-6246
snatoli@mainstreetgourmet.com
www.mainstreetmuffins.com
Manufacturer of gourmet muffins available in both frozen batter and thaw and serve formats. Muffin batters are all natural, preservative free and kosher with an extensive selection that includes fat free, low fat and whole grain. Thawand serve are available in bulk-packaged format.
President/CEO: Steven Marks
President/CEO: Harvey Nelson
Quality Control: Angela Stoughton
Marketing: Joe Schaefer
Sales: Keith Kropp
Plant Manager/Operations: Mike Braun
Production: Tommie Smith
Production: Bryan Smith
Purchasing Director: Jim Braun
Estimated Sales: $15 Million
Number Employees: 100-249
Number of Brands: 2
Number of Products: 50
Sq. footage: 65000
Parent Co: Feature Foods dba Main Street Gourmet
Type of Packaging: Food Service, Private Label, Bulk
Brands:
Main Street Muffins
More Than Moist Muffins

8300 **Main Street's Cambritt Cookies**
170 Muffin Ln
Cuyahoga Falls, OH 44223-3358 330-929-0000
Fax: 330-920-8329 800-533-6246
snatoli@mainstreetgourmet.com
www.mainstreetmuffins.com
Manufacturer of frozen gourmet cookie dough in various pre-portioned sizes. The Classic line features all of the standards while the Decadent line is loaded with huge premiums, has great eye-appeal and a variety of unique flavorcombinations.
President/CEO: Steven Marks
President/CEO: Harvey Nelson
Quality Control: Angela Stoughton
Marketing: Joe Schaefer
Sales: Keith Kropp
Plant Manager/Operations: Mike Braun
Production: Tommie Smith
Production: Bryan Smith
Purchasing Director: Jim Braun
Estimated Sales: $15 Million
Number Employees: 100-249
Number of Brands: 1
Number of Products: 45
Sq. footage: 65000
Parent Co: Feature Foods dba Main Street Gourmet
Type of Packaging: Food Service, Private Label, Bulk
Brands:
Cambritt Cookies

8301 **Maine Coast Nordic**
133 Smalls Point Rd
Mahiasport, ME 04655-3231 207-255-6714

Processor of fresh salmon
President: Glen Cooke
VP: William Groom
Estimated Sales: $760,000
Number Employees: 10
Parent Co: Nordic Enterprises
Type of Packaging: Bulk

8302 **Maine Coast Sea Vegetables**
3 George's Pond Rd
Franklin, ME 04634 207-565-2907
Fax: 207-565-2144 info@seaveg.com
www.seaveg.com
Processor of edible seaweed products including candies, sea vegetables, seasonings, chips and pickles; wholesaler/distributor of seaweed including whole and ground
President: Shepard Erhart
General Manager: Carl Karush
Operations Manager: Mary Ellen Lasell
Production Manager: Hannah Russell
Estimated Sales: $2 Million
Number Employees: 20
Number of Products: 40
Sq. footage: 9000
Type of Packaging: Consumer, Bulk
Brands:
Maine Coast Crunch
Maine Coast Sea Vegetables
Sea Cakes
Sea Chips
Sea Seasonings
Sea Vegetables
Wild Crafted Food From the Gulf Of

8303 **Maine Lobster Outlet**
360 Us Route 1
York, ME 03909 207-363-9899
Fax: 207-363-0613 tea6977aol.com
www.mainelobsteroutlet.com
Lobster
President: Gregory Tsairis
Estimated Sales: $ 1 - 3 Million
Number Employees: 5-9

8304 **Maine Mahogony Shellfish**
8 Johnson Ln
Addison, ME 04606 207-483-2865
Fax: 207-483-4389 www.mahogany.qpg.com/
Wholesale and retail products include lobster, clams, crab, halibut, mussels, and a wide variety of shellfish.
Manager: Robert Johnson

8305 **Maine Seaweed Company**
P.O.Box 57
Steuben, ME 04680 207-546-2875
Fax: 207-546-2875 www.alcasoft.com/seaweed/
Processor of dried seaweed which includes a wide variety of Atlantic seaweeds such as kelp, laminaria, longicruris, alaria, alaria esculenta, digitata, palmaria palmata and fucus vesiculosis.
President: Larch Hanson
Type of Packaging: Consumer

8306 **Maine Wild Blueberry Company**
P.O.Box 128
Cherryfield, ME 04622-0128 207-546-7573
Fax: 207-546-2713 800-243-4005
www.cherryfieldfoods.com
Processor and exporter of canned, dehydrated and frozen wild blueberries
Chairman of the Board: John Bragg
Treasurer: Geoff Baldwin
Estimated Sales: $27 Million
Number Employees: 20-49
Sq. footage: 100000
Brands:
Maine Wild

8307 **Maine Wild Blueberry Company**
P.O.Box 128
Cherryfield, ME 04622-0128 207-255-8364
Fax: 207-255-8341 800-243-4005
Frozen, canned and dried fruits
CEO: Regner Kemps
President: John Pragg
COO: Jeff Vose
Sales Manager: Tom Rush
Operations Manager: Earl Wagner
Operations Manager: Ragner Kemp
Plant Manager: Jeff Vose
Estimated Sales: $ 20-50 Million
Number Employees: 155

Type of Packaging: Private Label
Brands:
Blue Berry

8308 **Maison Le Grand**
935 Chemin Principal
St Joseph du Lac, QC J0N 1M0
Canada 450-623-3000
Fax: 450-623-2300 info@maisonlegrand.com
www.maisonlegrand.com
cold-processed sauces (pestos, tapenades, aromatic sauces)

8309 **Maisons Marques & Domaines USA**
383 4th St Ste 400
Oakland, CA 94607 510-286-2000
Fax: 510-286-2010 www.mmdusa.net
Maisons, Marques & Domaines is a marketer of family-owned, prestigious producers from the world's great wine regions. Some of the wineries represented by MMD are owned by the House of Louis Roederer, including Porto Ramos-PintoChampagne Deutz, Delas Freres and the Bordeaux properties of Chateau de Pez and also Chateau Haut-Beausejour.
President/CEO: Gregory Ballogh
CFO: Guillaune Fomilleron
CEO: Gregory Balogh
Manager: Heidi Donaldson
Estimated Sales: $ 5-10 Million
Number Employees: 20-49
Brands:
Champagne Deutz
Chateau De Pez
Chateau Haut-Beausejour
Delas Freres
Ramos-Pinto

8310 **Maitake Products**
1 Madison St
East Rutherford, NJ 7073 973-470-0010
Fax: 973-773-9717 800-747-7418
customerservice@maitake.com
www.maitake.com
Processor and exporter of nutritional mushroom supplements and teas
Owner/President/CEO: Mike Shirota
VP: Joe Carroll
R&D: Dr. Cun Shuang
VP Marketing: Donna Noonan
Production: Masashi Ohara
Estimated Sales: $ 3 - 5 Million
Number Employees: 10-19
Number of Brands: 2
Number of Products: 24
Sq. footage: 4500
Type of Packaging: Consumer, Food Service, Private Label, Bulk
Other Locations:
Maitake Products
Ridgefield Park NJ
Brands:
Grifron
Grifron D-Fraction
Grifron Mushroom Emperors
Grifron Prost Mate
Mai Green Tea
Mai Tonic Tea
Mushroom Wisdom

8311 **Maitake Products**
1 Madison St
East Rutherford, NJ 7073 973-470-0010
Fax: 973-773-9717 800-747-7418
customerservice@maitake.com
www.maitake.com
Dietary supplements from medicinal mushrooms
President: Mike Shirota
VP: Joe Carroll
Estimated Sales: $ 2.5-5 Million
Number Employees: 10-19
Number of Products: 26
Type of Packaging: Private Label
Brands:
Grifron
Grifron D-Fraction
Grifron Mushroom Emp
Maigreen Tea
Maitonic Tea

8312 **Majestic Coffee & Tea**
2027 San Carlos Ave
San Carlos, CA 94070 650-591-5678
bobgard@gardfoods.com
Coffee, tea
President: Bob Gard
Estimated Sales: Less than $400,000
Number Employees: 1-4
Brands:
Majestic Coffee and Tea

8313 **Majestic Distilling Company**
2200 Monumental Rd
Baltimore, MD 21227 410-242-0200
Fax: 410-247-7831
lschuman@majesticdistilling.com
www.majesticdistilling.com
Processor and exporter of alcoholic beverages including brandy, scotch, tequila, gin, etc.; importer of brandy, scotch, tequila, whiskey and Canadian rum. Also importing a line of premium spirits
President/General Manager: Lee Schuman
Marketing Manager: Corky Graff
VP National Sales: Corky Graff
Estimated Sales: $ 20 - 50 Million
Number Employees: 20-49
Number of Brands: 8
Number of Products: 15
Sq. footage: 45000
Brands:
BLACK WATCH
CANADIAN LEAF
ODESSE
OLD SETTER
PORT ROYAL
RED BULL
RED BULL VODKA
RIKALOFF
SHAKESPEARE VODKA
TREVELERS CLUB
ZELKO

8314 **Majestic Flex Pac**
3337 Grapevine Street
Mira Loma, CA 91752 951-361-0247
Fax: 951-361-0260 sales@majesticflexpac.com
www.majesticflexpac.com/
Majestic Flex PAC is a manufacturer and supplier of shrink sleeves, pouches, laminations, and custom bags to numerous industries including that of food and beverage, dairy, bakery and snack, candy and confection.
President: Leonardo Gutierrez
Type of Packaging: Consumer

8315 **Majestic Foods**
22 High St Ste 2
Huntington, NY 11743 631-424-9444
Fax: 631-424-5874 www.majesticfoods.com
Fruit concentrates, blends, essences and purees, canned fruits and vegetables, frozen fruits, dried fruits, nuts, vegetables and natural colors
Branch Manager: Ted Farynick
Estimated Sales: $ 20-50 Million
Number Employees: 10-19

8316 **Makers Mark Distillery**
3350 Burk Spring Rd
Loretto, KY 40037 270-865-2881
Fax: 270-865-2196 www.makersmark.com
Processor and exporter of whiskey
President: Bill Samuels Jr
Master Distiller: David Pickerell
COO: Rob Samuels
Estimated Sales: $50-100 Million
Number Employees: 50-99
Parent Co: Hiram Walker & Sons
Type of Packaging: Consumer
Brands:
Makers Mark

8317 **Makers Mark Distillery**
3350 Burk Spring Rd
Loretto, KY 40037 270-865-2881
Fax: 270-865-2196 www.makersmark.com
Processor and exporter of whiskey
President: Bill Samuels Jr
CEO: Bill Samuels Jr
Estimated Sales: $24300000
Number Employees: 10-19
Parent Co: Hiram Walker & Sons
Type of Packaging: Consumer
Brands:
Makers Mark

8318 **Malabar Formulas**
28537 Nuevo Valley Dr
Nuevo, CA 92567 909-866-3678
Processor of milk digestants and activated enzyme concentrate
Owner: Shirley Partito

8319 **Malcolm Meat Company**
2657 Tracy Rd
Northwood, OH 43619 419-666-6145
Fax: 419-666-2619 800-822-6328
Meat
President: Jerry R Pasquale
President: Jeff Savage
Estimated Sales: $ 20-50 Million
Number Employees: 100-249

8320 **Malibu Beach Beverage**
885 Woodstock Rd
Roswell, GA 30075-2277 770-998-7204
877-825-0655
info@malibubev.com www.malibubev.com
Manufacturer of nutritional fruit flavored drinks including malibu mango; sunset strawberry; redondo raspberry; oceanside orange; beach peach; and tropical tea.
Chief Financial Officer: William Wager
Vice President Corporate Development: Jeff Glattstein Sr
Chief Operations Officer: Patrick Doran

8321 **Malie Kai Hawaiian Chocolates**
PO Box 1146
Honolulu, HI 96807 808-599-8600
Fax: 808-599-8600 info@maliekai.com
www.maliekai.com
chocolate bars
President/Owner: Nathan Sato

8322 **Mallet & Company**
P.O.Box 474
Carnegie, PA 15106 412-276-9000
Fax: 412-276-9002 800-245-2757
sales@malletoil.com www.malletoil.com
Manufacturer and exporter of oils, ingredients and custom food processing equipment
President: Robert Mallet
EVP: Aaron Mallet
Estimated Sales: $100-500 Million
Number Employees: 50-99
Number of Brands: 10
Number of Products: 70
Sq. footage: 110000
Type of Packaging: Consumer, Food Service, Private Label
Brands:
EVERITE
FRY WELL
FRY'N GOLD
HIFLEX
KAKE MATE
MELLO GOLD
PAN & GRIDDLE GOLD
PIC 77
PRIME FRY
SATIN DONUT FRY
SATIN FRY
SATIN GLO
SATIN PLUS
SPARKLE
SUNNY GOLD
SUNSHINE
THRIFTEE GOLD
TOUCH O'GOLD
VEGALUBE

8323 **Mallorie's Dairy**
11039 Hazelgreen Rd NE
Silverton, OR 97381 503-873-5346
Fax: 503-873-2278 www.malloriesdairy.com
Processed milk products include nonfat milk, 1% lowfat milk, 2% reduced fat milk, and vitamin D milk.
President: Richard Mallorie
Operations Manager: Terri Mallorie Kilgus
Estimated Sales: $ 10-20 Million
Number Employees: 50-99

8324 **Maloney Seafood Corporation**
350 Copeland St
Quincy, MA 02169 617-472-1004
Fax: 617-472-7722 800-566-2837
info@maloneyseafood.com
www.maloneyseafood.com
Importers of seafood
President: Thomas Maloney
Estimated Sales: $ 10-20 Million
Number Employees: 5-9

8325 **Malt Products Corporation**
88 Market St
Saddle Brook, NJ 7663 201-845-0209
Fax: 201-845-9209 800-526-0180
Info@maltproducts.com www.maltproducts.com
Manufacturer of malt, molasses, natural sweeteners. We are the largest producer of pure, high quality malts and molasses, liquids and powders, with precisely the characteristics needed for a wide variety of applications. We specializein prompt and professional service
Manager: John Johannson
VP Sales/Marketing: Joe Hickenbottom
Number Employees: 10-19
Type of Packaging: Bulk

8326 **Malt-Diastase Company**
141 Lanza Ave
Bldg 31
Garfield, NJ 07026-3539 973-772-2103
Fax: 973-772-0623 800-772-0416
Processor and exporter of flavoring extracts and syrups
President: Art Levy
Estimated Sales: $ 10 - 20 Million
Number Employees: 10-19
Type of Packaging: Food Service, Bulk

8327 **Malt-O-Meal Company**
701 5th St W
Northfield, MN 55057 507-645-6681
Fax: 612-339-5710 www.malt-o-meal.com
Manufacturer and exporter of hot wheat cereal and ready-to-eat cereals
CEO: Chris Neugent
CFO: John Gappa
Sales Manager: Mike Allen
Estimated Sales: $500 Million
Number Employees: 1400
Type of Packaging: Consumer, Food Service, Private Label, Bulk
Brands:
MALT-O-MEAL

8328 **Malt-O-Meal Company**
701 5th St W
Northfield, MN 55057 507-645-6681
Fax: 612-339-5710 800-743-3029
www.malt-o-meal.com
Cereal and grain products
President: John Lettmann
CEO: John Lettmann
CEO: Christopher Neugent
Estimated Sales: $450,000,000
Number Employees: 1,000-4,999
Brands:
Cheerios
Malt-O-Meal Original's
Scooter's
Topso

8329 **Mama Amy's Quality Foods**
5715 Coopers Avenue
Mississauga, ON L4Z 2C7
Canada 905-456-0056
Fax: 905-456-1536
Processor and exporter of pizza and broccoli and cheese sticks, calzones, jambalaya, etc
Sales/Marketing Director: Aldon Reed
Number Employees: 30
Sq. footage: 7000
Type of Packaging: Consumer, Food Service, Private Label, Bulk
Brands:
Mama Amy's

8330 **Mama Del's Macacroni**
420 Main St
East Haven, CT 06512-2838 203-469-6255
Fax: 203-469-6255
Homemade pasta
Owner: Edward Cole
Estimated Sales: Less than $200,000
Number Employees: 1-4
Type of Packaging: Consumer, Food Service, Bulk
Brands:
Mama Del's

8331 **Mama Lee's Gourmet Hot Chocolate**
9 Music Sq S
157
Nashville, TN 37203-3211 888-626-2533
Fax: 615-226-5763 1 8-8 m-male
claycoc@attglobal.com www.mamalees.com
Hot chocolate, cappucino, gourmetfoods, desserts
President: Rod Atkins
Production Manager: Wanda Jones
Plant Manager: Richard Allen
Estimated Sales: Under $500,000
Number Employees: 1-4
Type of Packaging: Private Label
Brands:
Mama Lee's Cocoa
Mama Lee's Coffee

8332 **Mama Lil's Peppers**
832 14th Avenue
Seattle, WA 98122 206-322-8824
Fax: 206-726-8372 mamalils@zipcon.net
www.mamalils.com
peppers in oil
President/Owner: Howard Lev

8333 **Mama Maria's Tortillas**
125 W 7200 S
Midvale, UT 84047-1011 801-566-5150
Fax: 801-566-7116 mamamarias@mtcon.net
Tortillas and tamales
President: Norbert Martinez
VP: Kenny Martinez
Estimated Sales: Below $ 5 Million
Number Employees: 20

8334 **Mama Mary's**
PO Box 1003
Fairforest, SC 29336-1003 864-595-6262
Fax: 864-576-5972 info@mamamarys.com
www.mamamarys.com
Pizza crusts, refrigerated pancakes, packaged pepperoni slices and pizza sauces.
Founder/President: Thomas Baliker
CEO: W McFall Pearce
Marketing Director: Peggy McKinney
VP Retail Sales: Vernon Gay
Human Resource Manager: Dawn Nix
Operations Manager: Mark Dion
Production Manager: Mike Benson
Purchasing Manager: Kimberly Witt
Estimated Sales: $51 Million
Number Employees: 204
Sq. footage: 50000

8335 **Mama Mucci's Pasta**
7676 Ronda Dr
Canton, MI 48187-2430 734-453-4555
Fax: 734-453-1722 info@mamamuccispasta.com
www.mamamuccispasta.com
Fresh, dry and frozen filled pastas
President: Vince Mucci
Estimated Sales: $10-20 Million
Number Employees: 10-19
Brands:
Mama Mucci

8336 **Mama Rap's & Winery**
P.O.Box 247
Gilroy, CA 95021-0247 408-842-5649
Fax: 408-842-8353 800-842-6262
djciv@garlic.com www.rapazziniwinery.com
Wine
Owner: Charles Larson
Estimated Sales: $ 1-2.5 Million
Number Employees: 5-9

8337 **Mama Rose's Gourmet Foods**
3434 W Earll Dr # 104
Phoenix, AZ 85017-5284 602-477-8333
Fax: 602-477-8338 877-325-4477
tonya@mamarosefoods.com
www.mamarosefoods.com
Sixteen years producing gourmet packaged foods ie.. salsa, hot sauce ,jams, jellies, marinara and pizza sauce, pickled olives, prickly pear products, importing italian pasta and olive oil. Private label and co-packaging specialists
President: Tonya Greenfield
VP: Al Greenfield
Sales/Marketing Manager: Al Greenfield
Estimated Sales: $5-9.9 Million
Number Employees: 6

Brands:
Mama Rose's

8338 Mama Rosie's Ravioli Company
10 Dorrance St
Charlestown, MA 02129-1027 617-242-4300
Fax: 617-242-4208 888-246-4300
Frozen pastas
President: Anthony Sardo
CEO: Nicholas Sardo
CFO: Nicholas Sardo
Marketing Director: Bryan Mtnulty
VP Sales: Charles Sardo
Plant Manager: Vicente Tagliamonte
Estimated Sales: $ 5-10 Million
Number Employees: 50-99
Brands:
Mama Rosie's

8339 Mama Tish's Italian Specialties
4800 S Central Avenue
Chicago, IL 60638-1500 708-929-2023
Fax: 708-458-0027
Italian ice cream and frozen desserts
President/CEO: M Rudasil
Marketing Director: M Wenzell
VP Sales: Fergal Mulchrone
Director Manufacturing: M Wenzell
Plant Manager: I Bidiman
Estimated Sales: $ 5-10 Million
Number Employees: 5

8340 Mama Vida
9631 Liberty Rd
Suite N
Randallstown, MD 21133-2434 410-521-0742
Fax: 410-521-0785 877-521-0742
nila@mamavida.com www.mamavida.com
Vegetarian chili, eggplant spread, dressings, mustard, sauces, soups, black bean dip, marinade, salsas, tapenades
President: Albert Mechali
President: Albert Toto
Director: Miki Mechali
Quality Control: Heidi Czakny
Marketing: Nila Mechali
Estimated Sales: $1 Million
Number Employees: 7
Number of Brands: 30
Number of Products: 18
Type of Packaging: Consumer, Food Service, Private Label, Bulk
Brands:
TOTO'S GOURMET PRODUCTS

8341 Mamma Lina Ravioli Company
6491 Weathers Pl
San Diego, CA 92121-2935 858-535-0620
Fax: 858-535-5993
Processor of pasta products including ravioli and frozen lasagna
President: Chick Massullo
Estimated Sales: Less than $500,000
Number Employees: 10-19
Type of Packaging: Consumer, Food Service

8342 Mamma Lombardi's All Natural Sauces
877 Main Street
Holbrook, NY 11741 631-471-6609
infovilla@villalombardis.com
www.mammalombardisauces.com
sauces

8343 Mamma Says
49 Lincoln Road
Butler, NJ 07405-1801 973-283-4463
Fax: 973-283-2799 877-283-6282
sharyn@mammasays.com www.mammasays.com
Gourmet biscotti in almond pistachio and chocolate macademia
VP: Jason Cohen
Brands:
Mamma Says

8344 Manchac Seafood Market
131 Bait Alley
Ponchatoula, LA 70454 985-370-7070
Fax: 985-386-2762
Seafood
President: Duke Robin

8345 Manchac Trading Company
38091 Hope Villa Drive
Prairieville, LA 70769-3850 225-677-8026
Fax: 225-673-1876
Estimated Sales: $ 3 - 5 Million
Number Employees: 1-4

8346 Manchester Farms
8126 Garners Ferry Rd
Columbia, SC 29209 803-783-9024
Fax: 803-227-3103 800-845-0421
customerservice@manchesterfarms.com
www.manchesterfarms.com
Quail and bacon wrapped chicken
VP: Janet Odom
Total Quality Manager: Liz Benson
Director of Operations: Michael Davis
Plant Manager: Jennifer Alexander
Estimated Sales: $6300000
Number Employees: 15
Sq. footage: 22000
Type of Packaging: Consumer, Food Service, Private Label
Brands:
Manchester Farms

8347 Mancini Packing Company
P.O.Box 157
Zolfo Springs, FL 33890 863-735-2000
Fax: 863-735-1172 rmancini@mancinifoods.com
www.mancinifoods.com
Manufacturer of peppers and olive oil
Chairman/President: Frank Mancini
VP: Alan Mancini
Estimated Sales: $11 Million
Number Employees: 100-249
Type of Packaging: Consumer, Food Service, Private Label, Bulk
Brands:
MANCINI

8348 Mancuso Cheese Company
612 Mills Rd
Joliet, IL 60433 815-722-2475
Fax: 815-722-1302 pfalbo@mancusocheese.com
www.mancusocheese.com
Processor of cheese including ricotta, mozzarella, etc.; exporter of pizza supplies; importer of pasta, olive oil, olives and anchovies; wholesaler/distributor of frozen foods, produce, meats, baked goods, general merchandise, etc.
President: Dominic Mancuso
VP: Philip Falbo
President/Sales Executive: Michael Berta
Estimated Sales: $6 Million
Number Employees: 19
Sq. footage: 20000
Type of Packaging: Consumer, Food Service, Bulk
Brands:
Mancuso

8349 (HQ)Manda Fine Meats
P.O.Box 3374
Baton Rouge, LA 70821-3374 225-344-7636
Fax: 225-344-7647 www.mandafinemeats.com
Processor of beef, ham and sausage
President: Tommy Yarborough
Sales Director: Steve Yarboruth
Estimated Sales: $ 20 - 50 Million
Number Employees: 100-249
Type of Packaging: Consumer, Food Service, Private Label, Bulk

8350 Mandarin Noodle Manufacturing Company
3715d Edmonton Trail Ne
Calgary, AB T2E 3P3
Canada 403-265-1383
Fax: 403-264-3038
Processor of rice and wonton noodles, rice rolls and wonton and egg roll wraps
President: Hang Trinh
Estimated Sales: $1.7 Million
Number Employees: 20
Type of Packaging: Consumer, Food Service

8351 Mandarin Soy Sauce
4 Sands Station Rd
Middletown, NY 10940 845-343-1505
Fax: 845-343-0731 info@wanjashan.com
www.wanjashan.com
Manufacturer of soy sauce, asian sauce, rice and vinegar
President: Michael Wu
VP: Mike Shapiro
Estimated Sales: $16500000
Number Employees: 25
Sq. footage: 85000
Brands:
Wan Ja Shan

8352 Mandarin Soy Sauce
4 Sands Station Rd
Middletown, NY 10940 845-343-1505
Fax: 845-343-0731 info@wanjashan.com
www.wanjashan.com
Manufacturer of naturally brewed soy sauce, regular, lite, clear, nonpreservative, stir-fry, tamari, teriyaki, hoisin and dry soy powder
President: Michael Wu
Estimated Sales: $ 5 - 10 Million
Number Employees: 20-49
Brands:
Wan Ja Shan

8353 Manderfield Home Bakery
811 Plank Rd
Menasha, WI 54952-2923 920-725-7794
Fax: 920-725-7958 www.manderfieldsbakery.com
Bakery products
President: Jerry Manderfield
Estimated Sales: $ 1-2.5 Million
Number Employees: 20-49

8354 Mandoo
16 Humphrey St
Englewood, NJ 7631-3445 201-568-9337
Fax: 201-568-9426 mandoo_inc@msn.com
Processor of dumplings
President: Kyo Lee
Estimated Sales: $ 2.5-5 Million
Number Employees: 10
Type of Packaging: Consumer, Food Service, Bulk
Brands:
Mandoo

8355 Mane Inc.
999 Tech Dr
Milford, OH 45150-9535 513-248-9876
Fax: 513-248-8808 requests@mane.com
www.mane.com
Manufacturer of flavors and seasoning blend
President: Jean Mane
President: Michell Mane
Executive Vice President: Kent Hunter
Estimated Sales: 20-50 Million
Number Employees: 50-99
Sq. footage: 65000

8356 Manfred Vierthaler Winery
17136 Highway 410 E
Sumner, WA 98390 360-863-633
Fax: 253-863-1633
Wines
Number Employees: 10-19

8357 Manger Packing Company
124 S Franklintown Rd
Baltimore, MD 21223 410-233-0126
Fax: 410-362-8065 800-227-9262
Manufacturer and packer of meat including pork, beef, chicken, lamb, veal and smoked ham; exporter of beef sausage
President: Alvin S Manger
Estimated Sales: $9 Million
Number Employees: 10-19
Type of Packaging: Consumer, Bulk

8358 Mangia Inc.
23166 Los Alisos Blvd #228
Mission Viejo, CA 92691 949-581-1274
Fax: 949-581-2906 866-462-6442
info@mangiainc.com www.mangiainc.com
Canned San Marzano tomato products, originally produced in Italy, with no preservatives or added salt
President: Matt Maslowski
Manager: Morgan Patterson
VP: Bob Maruca
Estimated Sales: $1.3 Million
Number Employees: 12
Number of Brands: 1
Number of Products: 7
Type of Packaging: Consumer, Food Service

Other Locations:
Conditalia
Nocera Superiore, Italy
Brands:
Carmelia

8359 **Manhattan Beach BrewingCompany**
124 Manhattan Beach Blvd
Manhattan Beach, CA 90266 310-798-2744
Fax: 310-798-0365
www.manhattanbeachbrewingcompany.com
Coffee
President: David Zislis
Director Manufacturing: Karol Kmeto
Estimated Sales: $ 1-2.5 Million
Number Employees: 20-49
Brands:
Dominator Wheat
Rat Beach Red
Strand Amber

8360 **Manhattan Chocolates**
186 E 22nd St
Bayonne, NJ 07002-5005 201-339-6886
Fax: 201-339-6760
www.manhattanchocolates.com
Products include premium, deluxe chocolates, jelly rings, truffles, holidayassortments, and a variety of sugar-free products that include chocolate covered nuts and truffles.
President: David Herzog
Estimated Sales: $ 10-20 Million
Number Employees: 20-49
Type of Packaging: Private Label, Bulk

8361 **Manhattan Coffee Company**
4333 Green Ash Dr
Earth City, MO 63045-1207 314-731-2500
Fax: 314-731-1938 800-926-3333
www.saralee.com
Processor and wholesaler/distributor of coffee
Manager: Carol Johnson
Sales Manager: C Wolf
General Manager: T Allen

8362 **Manhattan Special Bottling Corporation**
342 Manhattan Ave
Brooklyn, NY 11211 718-388-4144
Fax: 718-384-0244
comments@manhattanspecial.com
www.manhattanspecial.com
Pure Espresso, sodas and iced coffee drinks
President: Aurora Passaro
Estimated Sales: $ 2.5-5 Million
Number Employees: 5-9

8363 **Manhattan Wholesale MeatCompany**
P.O.Box 885
Manhattan, KS 66505-0885 785-776-9203
Fax: 785-776-5940
Wholesaler/distributor of meats; serving the food service market
President: Stephen D Saroff
Estimated Sales: $ 5 - 10 Million
Number Employees: 20-49

8364 **Manildra Milling Corporation**
4210 Shawnee Msn Pkwy Ste 312a
Fairway, KS 66205 913-362-0777
Fax: 913-362-0052 800-323-8435
info@manildrausa.com www.manildrausa.com
Processor, exporter and importer of wheat gluten; processor of wheat starch
President: Gerry Degnan
VP Sales/Marketing: Jay Piester
Number Employees: 10-19
Parent Co: Manildra Group
Type of Packaging: Bulk
Brands:
Gembond
Gemstar

8365 **Manitok Food & Gifts**
PO Box 97
Callaway, MN 56521-0097 218-375-3425
Fax: 218-375-4765 800-726-1863
Products include handmade jewelry, dolls, quilts, birch bark baskets, canoes, trays, corporate gift baskets filled with hand-harvested and handmade food products, wild rice, berry jellies and syrups.
Estimated Sales: $ 5-9.9 Million
Number Employees: 4

8366 **Manley Meats**
302 S 400 E
Decatur, IN 46733 260-592-7313
Fax: 260-592-6731
manleymeats@adamwells.com
www.manleymeats.com
Processor of canned and frozen beef, pork and chicken
President: Roger Manley
Vice President: Ronald Manley
Estimated Sales: $ 10-20 Million
Number Employees: 20-49
Type of Packaging: Consumer, Food Service

8367 **Mann Packing**
P.O.Box 690
Salinas, CA 93902-0690 831-422-7405
Fax: 831-422-1131 www.broccoli.com
Processor of produce including mixed vegetables and broccoli; also, broccoli with microwaveable cheese sauce
President: Joe Nucci
CEO: Mike Jarrod
Sales Director: Ron Fuqua
VP Retail Sales: Craig Enos
Estimated Sales: $30500000
Number Employees: 250-499
Type of Packaging: Consumer, Food Service, Bulk
Brands:
Broccoli Wokly
Sugar Valley
Sunny Shores
Sunny Shores Broccoli Wokly

8368 **Mann's International Meat Specialties**
9097 F St
Omaha, NE 68127 402-339-7000
Fax: 402-339-1579 800-228-2170
Packer and exporter of precooked roast beef, pastrami, corned beef, smoked meats, frozen prepared soups, entrees, Mexican foods and home meal replacements
President: Ivan Streit
VP: Linda Mann
VP Marketing: John Shipp
Plant Manager: Bruce Hamilton
Estimated Sales: $11200000
Number Employees: 50-99
Brands:
El Hombre Hambre
Gourmet International
Mann's International

8369 **Mannhardt Inc**
511 Broadway St
Sheboygan Falls, WI 53085-1500 920-467-1027
Fax: 773-625-5639 mannhardt1@aol.com
mannhardtice.com
Manufacturer of ice storage dispensers and bagging equipment
President: John Williams
Sales: Lori Justinger
Number Employees: 10-19

8370 **Manns Sausage Company**
125 N Main Street
Suite 500 #109
Blacksburg, VA 24060 540-605-0867
Fax: 540-953-0032 info@mannssausage.com
www.mannssausage.com
Sausages

8371 **Mansmith Enterprises**
P.O.Box 247
San Jn Bautista, CA 95045-0247 831-623-4981
Fax: 831-623-2150 800-626-7648
info@mansmith.com www.mansmith.com
Seasonings and spices
President: Jon Mansmith
CEO: Juanita Mansmith
CFO: John Mansmith
VP: Jon Mansmith
Estimated Sales: $237,000
Number Employees: 1-4
Type of Packaging: Private Label

8372 **Mansmith's Barbecue**
P.O.Box 247
San Jn Bautista, CA 95045-0247 831-623-4981
Fax: 831-623-2150 800-626-7648
info@mansmith.com www.mansmith.com
Processor of barbecue products including sauces, seasonings, pastes and grilling spices
Owner/President: Jon Mansmith
Owner/Secretary/Treasurer: Juanita Mansmith
Estimated Sales: Less than $250,000
Number Employees: 1-4
Parent Co: Mansmith Enterprises
Type of Packaging: Consumer, Food Service, Private Label
Brands:
Mansmith's Gourmet

8373 **Mantrose-Haeuser Company**
1175 Post Rd E
Westport, CT 06880-5431 203-454-1800
Fax: 203-227-0558 800-344-4229
Michelle.Frame@Mantrose.com
www.mantrose.com
Edible coatings and glazes
President: William Barrie
CFO: Sue Orouree
Quality Control: Mark Crossman
Product Manager: Michelle Frame
Plant Manager: John George
Estimated Sales: $ 10-20 Million
Number Employees: 100-249
Type of Packaging: Private Label
Brands:
Certicoat
Certicoat Polishes
Certified Gum Coats & Glazes
Certified Shellacs
Certiseal
Confectioners Glaze Thinner
Crystalac
Crystalac Polishing Glazes
Nature Seal
Sparkled Glow

8374 **Manuel's Mexican-American Fine Foods**
2007 S 300 W
Salt Lake City, UT 84115-1808 801-484-1431
Fax: 801-484-1440 800-748-5072
Broker of tortilla chips, taco shells, corn tortilla, tostada shells and pre-cut tortillas
President: Orlando Torres
VP: Mike Torres
VP/Sales Exec: Paul Torres
VP Sales: Paul Torres
Estimated Sales: Below $ 5 Million
Number Employees: 40
Type of Packaging: Consumer, Food Service, Private Label, Bulk

8375 **Manuel's Odessa Tortillaand Tamale Factory**
1915 E 2nd St
Odessa, TX 79761 432-332-6676
Fax: 915-332-6699
Manufacturer of tortillas, canned tamales and tortilla chips
President: Manuel Gonzalez
Estimated Sales: $10-20 Million
Number Employees: 10-19

8376 **Manzana Products Company**
P.O.Box 209
Sebastopol, CA 95473-0209 707-823-5313
Fax: 707-823-5218 manzanaca@aol.com
Manufacturer of applesauce, apple juice, apple cider and apple cider vinegar.
President: Suzanne C Kaido
Estimated Sales: $ 50 - 100 Million
Number Employees: 100-249
Type of Packaging: Consumer, Private Label, Bulk
Brands:
North Coast

8377 **Manzanita Ranch**
4470 Highway 78
Julian, CA 92036-9624 760-765-0102
Grower of apples; processor of fruit juices including apple, grape, cherry and raspberry
Manager: Jeff Cox
Estimated Sales: $ 3 - 5 Million
Number Employees: 5-9

8378 **Maola Milk & Ice Cream Company**
305 Avenue C
New Bern, NC 28563 252-514-2792
www.mdvamilk.com
Processes and packages fluid milk, ice cream, ice cream novelties, juice and other drinks for consumers
Division Head: Robert Green
Estimated Sales: $50-100 Million
Number Employees: 200
Type of Packaging: Consumer, Food Service, Private Label, Bulk

8379 **(HQ)Maola Milk & Ice Cream Company**
411 E 5th North Street
H
Summerville, SC 29483-5109 803-871-6311
Fax: 843-395-1808
Dairy products
President/CEO: Kenneth Reesman
Controller: Richard Ruffi
General Manager: Jim Green

8380 **Maple Acres**
13900 Campbell Rd
Kewadin, MI 49648 231-264-9265
Fax: 231-264-8532
Processor of pure Northern Michigan maple syrup in 1/2 pint to one gallon jugs; private label available
CEO: Chris Luchenbill
President: Leta Luchenbill
Sq. footage: 6000
Type of Packaging: Consumer, Food Service, Private Label, Bulk
Brands:
Maple Acres

8381 **Maple Donuts**
3455 E Market St
York, PA 17402 717-757-7826
Fax: 717-755-8725 800-627-5348
charliemaple@aol.com www.mapledonuts.com
Donuts, yeast raised; cake stye, fresh or frozen; pie shells, deep or shallow, organic all products, kosher, tran fat free
President: Charles Burnside
CEO: Nat Burnside
VP/General Manager: Ralph Wooten
R&D: Jose Rios
Quality Control: Ann Moates
Marketing/Sales: Damian Burnside
Publice Relations: Charles Burnside
Operations: Luke Burnside
Production: John Loucks
Plant Manager: Dan Haines
Purchasing: Tammy Howard
Estimated Sales: $40-50 Million
Number Employees: 310
Sq. footage: 80000
Parent Co: Maple Donuts LLC

8382 **Maple Grove Farms of Vermont**
1052 Portland St
St Johnsbury, VT 05819 802-748-5141
Fax: 802-748-9647 800-525-2540
maple@maplegrove.com www.maplegrove.com
Pure maple syrup, fruit flavored syrups, sugar free syrup, specialty salad dressings, pancake & waffle mixes, gluten free products, maple candies & spreads.
VP: Robert Cantwell
Quality Control: Danny Johnson
Plant Manager: Mark Bigelow
Estimated Sales: $70,000,000
Number Employees: 85
Parent Co: B&G Foods
Type of Packaging: Consumer, Food Service, Private Label, Bulk
Brands:
Cozy Cottage
Maple Grove Farms of Vermont
Up Country Naturals
Vermont Sugar Free

8383 **Maple Hill Farms**
12 Burr Rd
Bloomfield, CT 06002 860-242-9689
Fax: 860-243-2490 800-842-7304
www.mhfct.com
Dairy products
President: William Miller
Marketing Director: Scott Miller
Estimated Sales: $ 5 - 10 Million
Number Employees: 20-49

8384 **Maple Hollow**
W1887 Robinson Dr
Merrill, WI 54452 715-536-7251
www.maplehollowsyrup.com
Processor of maple syrup and sugar; wholesaler/distibutor of maple syrup processing machinery
Owner: Joe Polak
Vice President: Barbara Polak
Estimated Sales: $1 Million
Number Employees: 10
Number of Brands: 5
Number of Products: 4
Sq. footage: 10000
Type of Packaging: Consumer, Private Label
Brands:
Forest Country
Maple Gardens
Maple Hollow

8385 **Maple Island**
2497 7th Ave E Ste 105
Saint Paul, MN 55109 651-773-1000
Fax: 651-773-2155 800-369-1022
info@maple-island.com www.maple-island.com
Processor and packager of quality food powders; agglomerate, blend and package into pouches and canisters
President: Greg Johnson
Executive VP: Ronald Zirbel
Director Marketing/Sales: Jim Kelleher
Plant Manager: Robin Amundson
Estimated Sales: $28675000
Number Employees: 10-19
Type of Packaging: Consumer, Food Service, Private Label, Bulk
Brands:
Bounce
Diet Freeze
Maple Island
Shakequik

8386 **Maple Leaf Bakery**
P.O. Box 55021
Montreal, Qu H3G 2W5 416-926-2000
Fax: 416-926-2018 ÿ1 -00 -68 3
slotthm@mapleleaf.ca www.mapleleaf.ca
Bakery products
President/CEO: Michael McCain
Corporate Director: Robert Stewart
Chairman: G. Wallace McCain,O.C.
Estimated Sales: $ 2.5-5 Million
Number Employees: 30-50
Brands:
California Goldminer
Eurofresh
Home Fresh
Maple Leaf

8387 **Maple Leaf Cheesemakers**
P.O.Box 974
New Glarus, WI 53574-0974 608-527-2000
Fax: 608-527-3050 mapleleaf1@tds.net
www.mapleleafcheeseandchocolatehaus.com
Processor and exporter of cheese including Monterey jack and gouda
Owner: Barbara Kummerfeldt
Estimated Sales: $500,000-$1 Million
Number Employees: 20-49
Type of Packaging: Consumer, Food Service, Private Label, Bulk
Brands:
Maple Leaf

8388 **Maple Leaf Consumer Foods**
7840 Madison Ave # 135
Fair Oaks, CA 95628-3591 916-967-1633
Fax: 916-967-1690 800-999-7603
www.mapleleaf.com
Processor of ham and bacon
General Manager: Charles Brougher
Estimated Sales: $ 5 - 10 Million
Number Employees: 10-19
Parent Co: Maple Leaf Foods
Type of Packaging: Consumer, Food Service, Private Label, Bulk

8389 **(HQ)Maple Leaf Farms**
Po Box 308
Milford, IN 46542 574-658-4121
Fax: 574-658-2246 800-384-2812
cturk@mapleleaffarms.com
www.mapleleaffarms.com
Produces duck products, supplying retail and food service markets worldwide. Also produces chicken patties, strips, nuggets and gourmet entrees.
Owners & Co-Presidents: John & Scott Tucker
Owner & Chairman of the Board: Terry Tucker
VP Finance: Scott Reinholt
Vice President: Bob Salegna
Food R&D: Kent Thrasher
Quality Assurance: Rick Prins
VP Sales & Marketing: Eric Errig
VP Operations: Don Ratliff
VP Live Production: Mike Turk
Plant Managers: Lee Allen Don Crandall
Purchasing Managers: Ron Buhr Ronda Morgan
Estimated Sales: $50 Million
Number Employees: 455
Type of Packaging: Consumer, Food Service, Private Label, Bulk
Brands:
C&D
C&D
Chef Tang
ECH
FCH
Gold Label
Maple Leaf

8390 **Maple Leaf Farms**
PO Box 507
Franksville, WI 53126-0507 262-878-1234
Fax: 262-878-3432 rrosdil@mapleleaffarms.com
www.mapleleaffarms.com
Processor and exporter of fresh and frozen duck
Co-President: Scott Tucker
CEO: Terry Tucker
Co-President: John Tucker
Plant Manager: Ray Olfzewski
Purchasing Agent: Sharon Ermi
Estimated Sales: $ 50 - 100 Million
Number Employees: 100-249
Parent Co: Maple Leaf Foods
Type of Packaging: Consumer, Food Service, Private Label

8391 **Maple Leaf Foods**
1 Warman Drive
Winnipeg, NB R2J 4E5
Canada 204-231-4114
Fax: 204-231-2944 800-564-6253
www.mapleleaf.com
Processor of pork
President: Michael H McCain
CEO: Michael H McCain
CFO: Michael H Vels
Plant Manager: Jeff Parsons
Number Employees: 250-499
Parent Co: Schneider's Dairy
Type of Packaging: Food Service
Brands:
Burns
California Goldminer
Hygrade
Maison-Cousin
Nutriwhip
Shopsy's
Tenderflake

8392 **Maple Leaf Foods & Scheider Foods**
6505 Trans Canada Highway
Saint Laurent, QC H4T 1S3
Canada 514-748-1469
Fax: 514-748-1630 800-567-1890
consumer@schneiderfoods.ca
www.schneiders.ca
Processor of beef and pork
President: Michael Mc cain
Sales Manager: Andre des Lauriers
Number Employees: 20-49
Parent Co: J.M. Schneider
Type of Packaging: Consumer, Food Service
Brands:
Schneider's Frozen Meats
Schneiders Egg Stuffs
Schneiders Hot Stuffs
Schneiders Lean Stuffs

8393 **(HQ)Maple Leaf Foods International**
5160 Yonge St
Suite 300
North York, ON M2N 6L9
Canada 416-480-8900
Fax: 416-480-8950 montgogm@mapleleaf.ca
www.mapleleaf.ca
Processor, importer and exporter of fresh and frozen meat, seafood, dairy products, produce, potato products and specialty grains
President: Michael Detlefsen
Senior VP/Corporate Secretary: Rocco Cappuccitti
Executive VP/Chief Strategy Officer: Douglas Dodds
Chief Information Officer: Patrick Ressa
Chief Financial Officer: Michael Vels
Estimated Sales: $6,365,000
Number Employees: 23,000
Sq. footage: 10500
Type of Packaging: Consumer, Food Service, Private Label, Bulk
Other Locations:
Maple Leaf Foods Internationa
Chatham NJ
Brands:
BITTNER'S
CALIFORNIA GOLDMINER
DEMPSTER'S
HOT & CRUSTY
HUDRAGE
MAISON COUSIN
MAPLE LEAF
MEDALLION NATURALLY
NATURE'S GOURMET
OLIVIERI
PRIME NATURALLY
PRIME TURKEY
READY CRISP
SHOPSY'S
SLO-ROAST DELI
TENDER FLAKE
TOP DOGS

8394 **Maple Leaf Meats**
PO Box 55021
Motreal, QC H3G 2W5
Canada 204-233-2421
Fax: 204-233-5413 800-268-3708
investorrelations@mapleleaf.com
www.mapleleaf.com
Processor of meat products
Director Corporate: James F Hankinson
President: Chaviva M Hosek
Controller: John Main
CEO: Chaviva M Hosek
Number Employees: 400
Sq. footage: 259000
Parent Co: Maple Leaf Foods
Type of Packaging: Consumer, Food Service, Private Label, Bulk
Brands:
Maple Leaf
Royale

8395 **Maple Leaf Pork**
PO Box 55021
Montreal, QC H3G 2W5
Canada
800-268-3708
ingrams@mapleleaf.ca www.mapleleaf.ca
Processor and exporter of pork
President: M McCain
CEO: Michael McCain
Director Finance: Michael Vels
VP/General Manager: Wayne Johnson
VP Sales/Marketing: J Moore
Number Employees: 1000
Parent Co: Maple Leaf Foods
Type of Packaging: Consumer, Food Service

8396 **Maple Leaf Pork**
4141 1st Avenue
Lethbridge, AB T1J 4P8
Canada 403-328-1756
Fax: 403-327-9821 info@mapleleaf.ca
www.mapleleaf.ca
Processor and exporter of fresh and frozen pork including carcass, boxed and by-products
President: Michael McCain
Sales: Wilf Fiebich
General Manager: Ralph Miller
Plant Manager: Dave Wood
Number Employees: 100-249
Parent Co: Maple Leaf Foods
Type of Packaging: Consumer, Bulk

8397 **Maple Leaf Potatoes**
2720 2a Avenue N
Lethbridge, AB T1H 5B4
Canada 403-380-9900
Fax: 403-328-5262 800-268-3708
info@mapleleaf.ca www.mapleleaf.ca
Processor of Frozen French fries
General Manager: Lee Gleim
Production Manager: Joe Thom
Parent Co: Maple Leaf Foods
Type of Packaging: Consumer, Food Service
Brands:
Snowcap
York

8398 **Maple Products**
1500 Rue De Pacifique
Sherbrooke, QC J1H 2G7
Canada 819-569-5161
Fax: 819-569-5168
Processor and exporter of maple syrup and sugar; also, kosher grades available
Production Manager: Ghislain Pare
Number Employees: 10-19
Parent Co: Citadelle
Type of Packaging: Food Service, Bulk
Brands:
Pride of Canada

8399 **Maple Ridge Farms**
RR 3 Suite 6, Compartment 4
Prince Albert, SK S6V 5R1
Canada 306-922-8056
Fax: 306-922-6189 mapleridge@sk.sympatico.ca
www.mapleridge.com
Processor for the production and extraction of essential oils and their fractions. Including caraway seed, cilantro (coriander foliage), dill seed and foliage. One hundred tons annually. Serving the bio-organic industry and ingredientmanufacturers
President: Martin Gareau

8400 **Maplebrook Farm**
Po Box 966
Bennington, VT 05201-8005 802-440-9950
Fax: 802-440-9956 meri@maplebrookvt.com
www.maplebrookvt.com
Cheese.
Marketing: Meri Spicer

8401 **Mapled Nut Company**
P.O.Box 116
Montgomery, VT 05470 802-326-4661
Fax: 802-326-3111 800-726-4661
nuts@maplenut.com www.maplenut.com
Gourmet maple sugar cashews, almonds, pecans and walnuts
Owner: Marsha Phillips
Estimated Sales: $ .5 - 1 million
Number Employees: 1-4

8402 **(HQ)Maplehurst Bakeries**
50 Maplehurst Dr
Brownsburg, IN 46112 317-858-9000
Fax: 317-858-9001
jbaumann@maplehurstbakeries.com
www.maplehurstbakeries.com
Bread and other bakery products except cookies and crackers
President: Paul Duriacher
CFO: Joseph Latouf
CEO: Dave Winiger
Plant Manager: Tom Nummerdor
Estimated Sales: $ 50-100 Million
Number Employees: 250-499
Type of Packaging: Food Service, Private Label, Bulk
Brands:
Arnie's Bagelicious
Petrofsky's

8403 **Maplehurst Bakeries**
62 Adamson Industrial Blvd
Carrollton, GA 30117 770-832-1111
Fax: 770-834-5589 800-482-4810
mnorred@maplehurstbakeries.com
www.maplehurstbakeries.com
Products include cakes, donuts, cookies, bagels, rolls, breads, pies, danish, cinnamon rolls and crackers.
President: Paul Durlacher
CFO: Revin Whitlock
Vice President: Dave Winiger
Operations Manager: Tom Nummendor
Plant Controller: Paul Allen
Estimated Sales: $ 50 Million
Number Employees: 100-249
Number of Products: 200
Parent Co: Maplehurst Bakeries
Type of Packaging: Food Service

8404 **Mar-Jac Poultry**
1020 Aviation Blvd
Gainesville, GA 30501 770-531-5000
Fax: 770-531-5015 800-226-0561
info@marjacpoultry.com
www.marjacpoultry.com
Manufacturer and exporter of fresh and frozen chicken
CEO: Jamal Al-Barzinji
VP Finance: Mahoud Mohamed
VP: Donald Bull
VP Poultry Operations: Pete Martin
Estimated Sales: $262 Million
Number Employees: 1200
Sq. footage: 300000
Type of Packaging: Food Service, Private Label
Brands:
M-J
MAR-JAC BRANDS

8405 **Mar-K Anchor Bar Hot Sauces**
1047 Main Street
PO Box 66
Buffalo, NY 14209-0066 71- 8-6 89
Fax: 86- 2-8 96 sales@buffalowings.com
www.buffalowings.com
Produces buffalo wings, a variety of sauces, and gift novelty items.
Owner/President: Ivano Toscani
Estimated Sales: Below $ 5 Million
Number Employees: 6
Brands:
Frank & Teressa's Original Anchor
Frank & Teressa's Wing Sauce

8406 **Mar-Key Foods**
P.O.Box 603
Vidalia, GA 30475 912-537-4204
Fax: 912-537-2542 info@markeyfoods.com
www.markeyfoods.com
Processor of soft drink concentrates, pre-sweetened drink mixes and freeze pops
President: Louie Powell
Secretary: Diane Collins
Estimated Sales: $110000
Number Employees: 20-49
Type of Packaging: Consumer, Food Service, Bulk
Brands:
Jolly Aid
Jolly Pops

8407 **Mar-Lees Seafood**
10 N Front St
New Bedford, MA 02740 508-991-6026
Fax: 508-990-3468 800-836-0975
info@marlees.com www.marlees.com
Seafoods
President: John A Lees
CEO: John Lees
CEO: John Lees Jr
VP Marketing/Sales: Jamie Dwyer
VP Operations: Dan Canavan
Estimated Sales: $ 20-50 Million
Number Employees: 50-99

8408 **(HQ)Maramor Chocolates**
1855 E 17th Ave
Columbus, OH 43219 614-291-2244
Fax: 614-291-0966 800-843-7722
orders@maramor.com www.maramor.com
Processor and exporter of kosher boxed chocolates, chocolate covered bagel chips and mints; packaged for racks and fund raising purposes; contract manufacturing available
President: Michael Ryan
Sales: Scott Sher
Estimated Sales: $1,600,000
Number Employees: 20-49
Sq. footage: 30000
Type of Packaging: Consumer, Private Label, Bulk

Brands:
Maramor

8409 **(HQ)Marantha Natural Foods**
1192 Illinois Street
San Francisco, CA 94107 415-401-0080
Fax: 415-401-0087 866-972-6879
info@worldpantry.com www.worldpantry.com
Processor of organic and regular nut and seed butters, trail mixes and dry roasted nuts and seeds; importer of cashews and sesame seeds; exporter of organic and regular nut and seed butters and trail mixes
President: Patrick Lee
CEO: David Miller
Estimated Sales: $ 10 - 20 Million
Number Employees: 20-49
Sq. footage: 14000
Type of Packaging: Consumer, Food Service, Private Label, Bulk
Other Locations:
Marantha Natural Foods
San Leandro CA
Brands:
Marantha
Nuttin' Butter

8410 **Marathon Cheese**
P.O.Box 185
Marathon, WI 54448 715-352-3391
Fax: 715-443-3843 www.mcheese.com
Custom packager of cheese
President: Dan Zastoupil
Chairman/CEO: John Skoug
SVP Finance: Gary Peterson
Estimated Sales: $ 500 Million-$ 1 Billion
Number Employees: 2,000
Type of Packaging: Consumer, Food Service, Private Label, Bulk

8411 **Marathon Cheese Corporation**
500 E Parker Dr
Booneville, MS 38829 662-728-6266
Fax: 662-728-6267 cbateman@mcheese.com
www.mcheese.com
Manufacturer of cheeses including Swiss, cheddar, blue and mozzarella
President: Robert Buchberger
Manager: Steve Banas
Plant Manager: Lisa Trace
Estimated Sales: $10-20 Million
Number Employees: 80
Type of Packaging: Private Label

8412 **Marathon Enterprises**
9 Smith St
Englewood, NJ 07631 201-935-3330
Fax: 201-935-5693 800-722-7388
info@sabrett.com www.sabrett.com
Manufacturer of meats including franfurters, hot sausage, kielbasa, salami, pastrami, corned beef, garlic rings and hamburgers; also condiments such as barbecue onions, mustard, relish, sauerkraut
President/CEO: Boyd Adelman
Chairman/Assistant VP: Gregory Papalexis
VP: Vicki Venturni
VP Sales/Marketing Executive: Mark Rosen
Human Resources Manager: Bruce Dalessio
Plant Manager: Herb Tetens
Estimated Sales: $60 Million
Number Employees: 100
Sq. footage: 4500
Type of Packaging: Consumer, Food Service, Private Label, Bulk
Brands:
Concure
Golde
House O'Weenies

8413 **Marathon Packing Corporation**
1000 Montague St
San Leandro, CA 94577 510-895-2000
Fax: 510-895-2022
Cooking oils and shortening
President: Nelson Chu
Estimated Sales: $10-20 Million
Number Employees: 10-19

8414 **Marburger Farm Dairy**
1506 Mars Evans City Rd
Evans City, PA 16033 724-538-4800
Fax: 724-538-3250 800-331-1295
http://www.marburgerdairy.com
Bottled milk and dairy products
President: James Marburger
Quality Control: Bronge Janzki
Plant Manager: Garrie Wearing
Estimated Sales: $ 10-20 Million
Number Employees: 50-99
Type of Packaging: Private Label

8415 **Marburger Foods**
3311 S State Road 19
Peru, IN 46970 765-472-1139
Fax: 765-689-5414 info@modernfoods.net
www.modernfoods.net
Processor and exporter of specialty bacon products including pre-cooked slices and pieces; also, condiments, sauces, relishes and frozen condensed soup
President: John Marburger
VP Marketing: Paul Marburger
Plant Manager: Mike Correll
Purchasing Manager: Steve Wheeler
Estimated Sales: $61900000
Number Employees: 5-9
Sq. footage: 270000
Parent Co: Armour/Swift-Eckrich
Type of Packaging: Consumer, Food Service, Private Label, Bulk
Brands:
DWIGHT YOAKAM'S BAKERFIELD BSICUITS

8416 **Marcel et Henri Charcuterie Francaise**
415 Browning Way
South San Francisco, CA 94080 650-871-4230
Fax: 650-871-5948 800-227-6436
marcelethenri@sbcglobal.net
www.marcelethenri.com
Processor of French pate and sausage.
President: Henri Lapuyade
Estimated Sales: $3 Million
Number Employees: 10-19
Number of Brands: 1
Number of Products: 50
Sq. footage: 15000
Type of Packaging: Consumer, Food Service, Bulk
Brands:
Marcel Et Henri

8417 **Marcetti Frozen Pasta**
803 8th St SW
Altoona, IA 50009-2306 515-967-4254
Fax: 515-967-4147 auntui@auntui.com
www.marzetti.com
Processor of frozen precooked pasta and dumpling products.
VP: Mike Warren
Point of Sale Manager: Jan Larson
Public Relations: Suzanne Woodyard
Operations Manager: Terry Warren
Production Manager: Chris Carpp
Plant Manager: Neil Pitman
Purchasing Manager: Ron Mathis
Estimated Sales: F
Number Employees: 100-249
Sq. footage: 100000
Type of Packaging: Consumer, Food Service, Private Label, Bulk
Brands:
Aunt Vi's
Warren

8418 **Marche Tramsatlantique**
4709 Rue St Denis
Montreal, QC H2J 2L5
Canada 514-287-3530
Processor and exporter of fresh and frozen salmon, eel, mackerel, hake, trout and sturgeon; importer of caviar
President: Bruno Marie
Number Employees: 5-9
Type of Packaging: Food Service

8419 **Marcho Farms Veal**
176 Orchard Ln
Harleysville, PA 19438-1681 215-721-7131
Fax: 215-721-9719 ltufft@marchofarms.com
Grower and packer of milk fed veal. Processing primal, fresh cuts, portion control, precooked meatballs, meat loaf, bacon and philly steaks
President: Wayne A Marcho

8420 **Marconi Italian Specialty Foods**
710 W Grand Ave
Chicago, IL 60654-5574 312-421-0485
Fax: 312-421-1286 sales@marconi-foods.com
www.marconi-foods.com
Manufacturers a variety of specialty Italian foods including cheeses; coffees; salad dressings; meats; olive oils; pasta; salads; sauces; seafoods; spices, and vinegars.
President: Robert Johnson
President/CEO/Co-Owner: Robert Johnson
Co-Owner: Sue Formusa
Estimated Sales: $ 5 - 10 Million
Number Employees: 5-9
Parent Co: V Formusa Company

8421 **Marcus Dairy**
3 Sugar Hollow Rd
Danbury, CT 06810 203-748-9427
Fax: 203-791-2759 800-243-2511
smarcus@marcusdairy.com
www.marcusdairy.com
Processor of dairy products including butter, cottage cheese, cream, sour cream, eggs and milk; also, orange juice
Manager: Fred Sescza
Vice President: Jeffrey Marcus
General Manager: Randy Peck
General Manager: William Fitchett
Estimated Sales: $ 20 - 50 Million
Number Employees: 20-49
Type of Packaging: Consumer, Food Service, Private Label, Bulk
Brands:
Marcus
Sun Fresh

8422 **Mardale Specialty Foods**
1120 Glen Rock Avenue
Waukegan, IL 60085-5458 847-336-4777
Fax: 847-336-5030
Processor of portion controlled condiments including salad dressing, syrup, jam and mayonnaise
President: Ronald Tarantino
Plant Manager: Jim Streiff
Number Employees: 20-49
Type of Packaging: Food Service

8423 **Marder Trawling Inc**
57 Hassey St
New Bedford, MA 02740 508-991-3200
Fax: 508-990-2901 800-499-3219
sales@marderbrands.com www.scallopguys.com
Produces a variety of seafood products including sea scallops, bay scallops, shrimp and scallops bar-b-skewers.
President: Brian Marder
Sales Director: Carlos Santaella

8424 **Mardi Gras**
150 Bloomfield Ave
Verona, NJ 7044 973-857-3777
Fax: 973-857-8884 contact@mardigrasfoods.com
www.mardigrasfoods.com
Gourmet fresh and frozen foods
Manager: Maria Carrozza
VP: Kim Newman
Estimated Sales: Below $ 5 Million
Number Employees: 10-19
Sq. footage: 2400
Type of Packaging: Consumer

8425 **Mareblu Naturals**
1150 N Red Gum Street C
Anaheim, CA 92806-2541
Fax: 714-238-1246 christyg@mbnaturals.com
www.mbnaturals.com
healthy and natural nuts, healthy and natural nuts with a tasty crunch
President/Owner: Michael Kim
Marketing: Christy Garcia
Estimated Sales: $2.7 Million
Number Employees: 40

8426 **Margarita Man**
10818 Gulfdale St
San Antonio, TX 78216 210-979-7191
Fax: 210-979-0718 800-950-8149
margman@idworld.net
www.margaritamansa.com
Processor of frozen drink mixes; wholesaler/distributor of frozen beverage machines
President: Chris Murphy
Plant Manager: Steve Snyder

Estimated Sales: $1 Million
Number Employees: 5-9
Number of Brands: 1
Number of Products: 15
Sq. footage: 2500
Brands:
Go Bananas
Go Mango
Just Add Tequila
Razzmatazzberry
The Margarita Man

8427 **Mari's New York**
115 4th Ave Apt 8a
Suite C5
New York, NY 10003-4909
Fax: 615-622-0281 support@marisny.com
www.marisny.com
brownies

8428 **Maria and Son Italian Products**
4201 Hereford St
Saint Louis, MO 63109 314-481-9009
Fax: 314-481-9109 866-481-9009
Frozen Italian pastas and sauces
President: John Ard
Estimated Sales: $5-10 Million
Number Employees: 10-19
Brands:
Maria & Son
Tita's

8429 **Mariani Nut Company**
P.O.Box 809
Winters, CA 95694-0809 530-662-3311
Fax: 530-795-2681 JohnA@marianinut.com
www.marianinut.com
Processor and exporter of walnuts and almonds
Partner: Jack Mariani
Partner: Dennis Mariani
Partner: Martin Mariani
Estimated Sales: $ 50 - 100 Million
Number Employees: 250-499
Type of Packaging: Consumer, Bulk

8430 **Mariani Packing Company**
500 Crocker Dr
Vacaville, CA 95688 707-452-2800
Fax: 707-452-2973 800-672-8655
productinfo@marianipacking.com
www.mariani.com
Manufacturer of fresh dried fruit including; plums, apricots, cranberries, apples, raisins and sun-dried tomatoes
President: George Sousa Jr
Chairman/CEO: Mark Mariani
EVP: Craig Mackley
Marketing Director: Lisa Goshgarian
Public Relations Director: Patti Sousa
Facilities/Operations Manager: Robert Miller
Production Manager: Andrew Kennedy
Purchasing: Richard Becker
Estimated Sales: $110 Million
Number Employees: 350
Sq. footage: 10773
Type of Packaging: Consumer, Private Label, Bulk
Brands:
MARIANI

8431 **Marich Confectionery Company**
2101 Bert Dr
Hollister, CA 95023-2562 831-634-4700
Fax: 831-634-4705 800-624-7055
sales@marich.com www.marich.com
Processor of candy including chocolate cherries, apricots, blueberries, strawberries and nut mixes; also, mints, toffee and maltballs.
President: Bradley Van Dam
Executive VP/COO: Troy van Dam
VP Marketing/Sales: Michelle van Dam
Sales Manager: Ellen Filberman
Plant Manager: Victor Moreno
Estimated Sales: Below $ 5 Million
Number Employees: 20-49
Type of Packaging: Consumer
Brands:
Holland Mints
Marich
Wallabeans

8432 **Maridee's Country Kitchen Cakes**
PO Box 247
Lindsay, OK 73052-0247 800-798-7730
Fax: 405-756-2702 mdcakes@hotmail.com
www.marideescakes.com
Cakes
Co-Owner: Marilou Munn
Co-Owner: Dee Stout

8433 **Marie Brizard Wines & Spirits**
849 Zinfandel Lane
St. Helena, CA 94574 800-878-1123
Fax: 415-979-0305 info@boisset.com
www.boissetamerica.com
Processor, importer and exporter of alcoholic beverages including vodka, bourbon, tequila, scotch, brandy, cognac, schnapps, gin, rum, cordials, wines and champagne
VP/Director Marketing: Michael Avitable
VP/Director Sales: Robert Bermudez
Director Operations: Hubert Surville
Number Employees: 20-49
Sq. footage: 6500
Parent Co: Marie Brizard Wines & Spirits USA
Brands:
Marie Brizard

8434 **Marie Callender's Gourmet Products/Goldrush Products**
491 San Carlos Street
San Jose, CA 95110-2632 408-288-4090
Fax: 408-279-3742 800-729-5428
comments@mccornbread.com
www.mccornbread.com
Processor of kosher sourdough baking mixes including pancake, biscuit, cornbread, nine-grain and wholewheat bread, etc
President: Henry Down Jr
Number Employees: 20-49
Parent Co: International Commissary Corporation
Type of Packaging: Consumer, Private Label, Bulk
Brands:
Goldrush

8435 **Marie F**
123 Denison Street
Markham, ON L3R 1B5
Canada 905-475-0093
Fax: 905-475-0038 800-365-4464
fmarie@ca.inter.net
Manufacturer of beef, butcher supplies and sausage and sheep casings; importer of sausage casings, butcher suppliers and cures; exporter of sausage casings
President: Sandra Marie Rundle
Plant Manager: Alaister Sears
Estimated Sales: $4 Million
Number Employees: 25
Sq. footage: 15000
Type of Packaging: Food Service

8436 **Marie's Candies**
P.O.Box 766
West Liberty, OH 43357-0766 937-465-3061
Fax: 937-465-3336 866-465-5781
info@mariescandies.com
www.mariescandies.com
Processor of candy including turkins, peanut brittle, toffee, butter creams, peppermint chews and melt-aways
President: Jay King
Co-Owner: Kathy King
Estimated Sales: $1,200,000
Number Employees: 20-49
Type of Packaging: Consumer

8437 **Marie's Quality Foods**
Po Box 1105
Brea, CA 92822
800-339-1051
www.maries.com
Salad dressing
President: Richard D Orr
VP Sales/Marketing: Richard Orr
Operations Manager: Drew Orr
Number Employees: 20-49
Sq. footage: 100000
Type of Packaging: Consumer, Food Service, Private Label

8438 **Marie's Refrigerated Dressings**
201 Armory Dr
Thornton, IL 60476-1044 708-877-5150
Fax: 708-877-1312 800-441-3321
www.maries.com
Processor of salad dressings
Plant Manager: Dorothy Munao
Purchasing Agent: Mike Rhein
Estimated Sales: $ 10 - 20 Million
Number Employees: 20-49
Parent Co: Dean Foods Company
Type of Packaging: Consumer, Food Service

8439 **Marietta Cellars**
22295 Chianti Rd
Geyservill, CA 95441 707-433-2747
Fax: 707-857-4910 www.mariettacellars.com
Producer of wines the list of which includes Angeli Cuvee, Petit Sirah, Cabernet Sauvignon and Zinfandel.
President/CEO: Chris Bilbro
Office Manager: Suzie Buchignani
Bookkeeper: Judy Summary
Marketing Manager: Jake Bilbro
Facilities Manager: Sarah Herrerra
Cellar/Bottling Manager: Roman Cisneros
Estimated Sales: $1.5 Million
Number Employees: 15

8440 **Marika's Kitchen**
106 Old Route 1
Hancock, ME 04640-3448 207-422-2300
Fax: 207-422-2300 800-694-9400
Processor of almond and walnut baklava and Greek biscota
Owner: Gloria Day
Vice President: Michael Savoy
Number Employees: 1-4
Sq. footage: 2500
Type of Packaging: Food Service, Bulk

8441 **Marimar Torres Estate**
11400 Graton Rd
Sebastopol, CA 95472 707-823-4365
Fax: 707-823-4496 info189@marimarestate.com
www.marimarestate.com
Wines
Proprietor/Winegrower: Marimar Torres
National Sales Manager: Kyle Ray
Cellar Master: Tony Britton
Vineyard Manager: Venutra Albor
Estimated Sales: $850,000
Number Employees: 10
Type of Packaging: Private Label
Brands:
Marimar Torres Estate

8442 **Marin Brewing Company**
1809 Larkspur Landing Cir
Larkspur, CA 94939 415-461-4677
Fax: 415-461-4688 brendan@moylans.com
www.marinbrewing.com
Beer
General Partner: Brendan Moylan
Sales Manager: Curtis Cassidy
Brewmaster: Arne Johnson
Estimated Sales: Below $ 5 Million
Number Employees: 50-99
Brands:
Albion Amber Ale
Marin Weiss
Miwok Weizen Bock
Mt. Tom Pale Ale
Old Dipsea Barley Wine
Point Reyes Porter
Raspberry Trail Ale
San Quentin's Breakout Stout

8443 **Marin Food Specialties**
P.O.Box 609
Byron, CA 94514-0609 925-634-6126
Fax: 925-634-4647
Processor, importer and exporter of specialty foods including cookies, fig and fruit bars, pasta, trail mixes, marinated vegetables, almond butter, spices and candy; gift baskets available
President: Joseph Brucia
VP: Fred Vuylsteke
Estimated Sales: $ 1 - 3 Million
Number Employees: 50-99
Sq. footage: 30000
Type of Packaging: Consumer, Private Label, Bulk

Brands:
Marin
Spanky's

8444 **Marin French Cheese Company**
7500 Red Hill Rd
Petaluma, CA 94952 707-762-6001
Fax: 707-762-0430 800-292-6001
maxx@marinfrenchcheese.com
www.marinfrenchcheese.com
Manufacturer of cheeses including camembert cheese, breakfast cheese, brie cheese, schloss cheese and specialty flavored bries; also gift boxes available.
Owner: Jim Boyce
Finance Manager: Candice Millhouse
Marketing: Maxx Sherman
Estimated Sales: $1.6 Million
Number Employees: 10
Type of Packaging: Consumer, Bulk
Brands:
Rouge Et Noir

8445 **Marina Foods**
117 Sw 1st St
Dania, FL 33004-3630 954-929-9047
Fax: 954-925-7833 marinafoods@netzero.com
www.marinafoods.com
Packers of edible oils and related products
CFO: Mike Inisinon
President: Mike Finos
Estimated Sales: $100 K
Number Employees: 2
Type of Packaging: Private Label, Bulk

8446 **Marine MacHines**
3 Strawberry Hill Road
Bar Harbor, ME 04609-1206 207-288-0107
Fax: 207-288-0462 www.acadia.net/marmac/
Company manufactures sea urchin procesing technology and equipment.
President: Mickey Kestner

8447 **Mariner Neptune Fish & Seafood Company**
472 Dufferin Avenue
Winnipeg, NB R2W 2X6
Canada 204-589-5341
Fax: 204-582-8135 800-668-8862
info@marinerneptune.com
www.marinerneptune.com
Distributor of fish, seafood and protein food products
President: John Alexander
VP: Russell Page
Marketing: Evan Page
Sales: Doug Chandler
Plant Manager: Chris Juerson
Purchasing Director: Evan Page
Estimated Sales: $16 Million
Number Employees: 42
Number of Products: 2000
Type of Packaging: Consumer, Food Service
Brands:
King Neptune
Mariner-Neptune

8448 **Mariner Seafoods**
150 Central St
Montague, PE C0A 1R0
Canada 902-838-2481
Fax: 902-838-3735
Processor of fresh and frozen cod, hake, flounder, lobster and crab
President: Mark Bonnell
Manager: Mark Bonnell
Estimated Sales: $33 Million
Number Employees: 235
Type of Packaging: Consumer, Food Service, Private Label, Bulk
Brands:
Mariner Seafoods

8449 **Mario's Gelati**
88 E 1st Avenue
Vancouver, BC V5T 1A1
Canada 604-879-9411
Fax: 604-879-0435 info@mariosgelati.com
www.mariosgelati.com
Processor, importer and exporter of ice cream
President: Mario Loscerbo
Vice President: Chris Loscerbo
Estimated Sales: $5.4 Million
Number Employees: 30
Sq. footage: 30000
Brands:
Mario's Gelati

8450 **Marion's Smart Delights**
4201 Wilson Boulevard #110-156
Arlington, VA 22203-1859 703-593-3450
marion@smartdelights.com
www.marionssmartdelights.com
Dairy-free, gluten-free, kosher, nut-free, organic/natural, vegetarian, baking mixes and ingredients.
Marketing: Marion Braswell, PhD

8451 **Marion-Kay Spices**
1351 W Us Highway 50
Brownstown, IN 47220-9530 812-358-3000
Fax: 812-358-3400 800-627-7423
www.marionkay.com
Processor of spice blends and extracts
President: John Reid
CEO: Kordell Reid
Estimated Sales: $2500000
Number Employees: 10-19
Type of Packaging: Consumer, Food Service, Bulk
Brands:
Claudia Sanders
Cream of Vanilla
The House of Flavors

8452 **Maris Candy**
2266 S Blue Island Ave
Chicago, IL 60608-4345 773-254-3351
Fax: 773-254-3581 mariscandy@msm.com
www.mariscandies.com
Processor of Mexican-style coconut candy
President/CEO: Raul Hernandez
VP/CEO: Maris Elena
VP of Retail: Raul Hernandez Jr.
VP of General Market: Maria Hernandez
VP of Wholesale: Rodrigo Hernandez
Estimated Sales: Below $ 5 Million
Number Employees: 1-4
Type of Packaging: Consumer

8453 **Maritime Pacific Brewing Company**
P.O.Box 17812
1111 Nw Ballard Way
Seattle, WA 98107-4639 206-782-6181
Fax: 206-782-0718 marpacbrew@aol.com
maritimebrewery.citsearch.com/
Micro-brewery
President: George Hancock
Estimated Sales: Below $ 5 Million
Number Employees: 19
Number of Brands: s

8454 **Marjie's Plantain Foods, Inc.**
Po Box 1211
New York, NY 10002 908-627-5627
Fax: 718-383-3337
info@marjiesplantainfoods.com
www.marjiesplantainfoods.com
Gluten-free, other lifestyle, vegetarian, frozen baked goods, other snacks.
Marketing: Majorie Gaston

8455 **Marjon Specialty Foods,Inc**
3508 Sydney Road
Plant City, FL 33567 813-752-3482
Fax: 813-754-4974
www.marjonspecialtyfoods.com
Sprouts (bean, alfalfa and others), salad dressings, fresh ginger stir-fry sauce, Tofu, Tofu Crumbles Vegetarian Hamburger, Grilled Tofu and other soy items.
Co-Founder/President: John Miller
VP: Marcia Miller
Director of R&D: Jim Martin
Human Resources Manager: Joe Miller
Operations Manager: Martha Clingenpeel
Director of Sales/Purchasing: Lisa Minnes
Estimated Sales: $11 Million
Number Employees: 90
Sq. footage: 21000

8456 **Mark West Vineyards**
7010 Trenton Healdsburg Road
Forestville, CA 95436-9639 707-544-4813
Fax: 707-837-7103 www.markwestwines.com
Wine

8457 **Mark-Lynn Foods**
1090 Pacific Ave
Bremen, GA 30110 770-537-5813
Fax: 770-537-0613 800-327-0162
contact@mark-lynn.com www.hormelfood.com
Contract packagers for dry products
President: Edward Dickinson
VP Operations: Joe Hoffer
Estimated Sales: $35656094
Number Employees: 100-249

8458 **Market Day Corporation**
555 W Pierce Rd Ste 200
Itasca, IL 60143 630-285-1470
Fax: 630-285-3340 877-632-7753
chairweb@marketday.com www.marketday.com
Market Day Corporation is a a Fund Raising Food Cooperative that supports educational institutions in their fundraising drives by providing a wide selection of high quality foods. Their year-round program offers parents and neighborsthe opportunity to buy restaurant quality food products through a school or related organization each month while contributing a portion of every purchase to their child's school.
President: Gregory Butler
CEO: Bill Sivak
Number Employees: 100-249

8459 **Market Fare Foods**
2512 E Magnolia St
Phoenix, AZ 85034-6908 888-669-6420
Fax: 801-363-6154 www.mffoods.com
Processor of pre-frozen and fresh sandwiches
President: Al Carfora
CFO: Barry Brooks
Vice President: Paul Miller
Sales Director: Paul Miller
Production Manager: Darrell Vannier
General Manager: Dave Nicklaw
Purchasing Manager: Bob Parker
Estimated Sales: $85 Million
Number Employees: 5-9
Number of Brands: 3
Number of Products: 2
Parent Co: MarketFare Foods
Type of Packaging: Consumer, Private Label
Brands:
Deli Pride
Marketfare Allstars
Select Allstars
Takeouts

8460 **Market Fare Foods**
3637 Scarlet Oak Boulevard
Saint Louis, MO 63122-6605 636-225-8808
Fax: 636-825-4514 888-669-6420
customerservice@marketfarefoods.com
Muffins, brownies, cakes, sandwiches, etc
President: Al Carsora
Marketing Director: Toni Belcher
CFO: Barry Brooks
Estimated Sales: $10 to 20 million
Number Employees: 50
Brands:
Phoenix

8461 **Market Fisheries**
7129 S State St
Chicago, IL 60619 773-483-3233
Fax: 773-483-0724
Seafood
President: Haim Brody
Estimated Sales: $ 3 - 5 Million
Number Employees: 10-19

8462 **Market Square Food Company**
1630 Old Deerfield Rd
Highland Park, IL 60035-3027 847-831-2228
Fax: 847-831-3533 800-232-2299
www.marketsquarefood.com
Specialty food gift items
Founder: James Lockhart
Founder: David Lockhart
Estimated Sales: $ 2.5-5 Million
Number Employees: 5-9
Brands:
Market Square's
Twistabout

8463 **Marketing & Sales Essentials**
701 Harrison Avenue
Blaine, WA 98230-9997 604-626-0881
Fax: 954-452-5141 877-915-5191
m_s_e@bellsouth.net
Manufaturer of gummy candies
President: Herbert Mederer
Number Employees: 6
Type of Packaging: Consumer, Food Service
Brands:
EFRUTTI

8464 **Markham Vineyards**
2812 Saint Helena Hwy N
Saint Helena, CA 94574 707-963-5292
Fax: 707-963-4616
admin@markhamvineyards.com
www.markhamvineyards.com
Processor and exporter of wines
President: Bryan Del Bondio
General Manager: Kathryn Fowler
Estimated Sales: $ 5 - 10 Million
Number Employees: 20-49

8465 **Markko Vineyard**
4500 S Ridge Rd W
Conneaut, OH 44030 440-593-3197
Fax: 440-599-7022 800-252-3197
markko@suite224.net
www.markko.com/mkwinery.html
Wines
President/ Winemaker: Arnie Esterer
Owner: Tim Hubbard
Estimated Sales: $500,000-$1 Million
Number Employees: 1-4

8466 **Marks Meat**
10290 S Mulino Rd
Canby, OR 97013-9797 503-266-2048
Processor of beef, pork and lamb; custom slaughtering services available
President: Kristie Akin
Estimated Sales: $110000
Number Employees: 5-9
Type of Packaging: Consumer

8467 **Marley Orchards Corporation**
2820 River Rd
Yakima, WA 98902 509-248-5231
Fax: 509-248-7358
Processor of produce including apples
Chief Financial Officer: Stanley Bostrom
President/Sales & Marketing Staff: William Gammie
Sales Representative: Tony Bishop
Estimated Sales: $2.8 Million
Number Employees: 75
Type of Packaging: Consumer, Food Service, Bulk

8468 **Marlow Candy & Nut Company**
65 Honeck St
Englewood, NJ 7631 201-569-7606
Fax: 201-569-9533 rickyl@marlowcandy.net
Candy and nuts
President: Eric Lowenthal
R & D: Aiden Kirk
Estimated Sales: $ 10-20 Million
Number Employees: 30

8469 **Marlow Wine Cellars**
Highway 41a-64
Monteagle, TN 37356 931-924-2120
Fax: 931-924-2587
Wines
President: Joe Marlow
Sales Manager: Gena Stevens
Estimated Sales: $ 1-2.5 Million
Number Employees: 1-4

8470 **Marnap Industries**
225 French St
Buffalo, NY 14211 716-897-1220
Fax: 716-897-1306
dnapora@marnap.comaol.com
www.marnap.com
Processor and exporter of essential oils, spice blends, seasonings, flavor compounds and oleoresins; importer of essential oils and oleoresins
President: Dennis J Napora
VP: Kevin Martin
Sales: Joanne Evans
Production: J Cogley
Estimated Sales: $ 3 - 5 Million
Number Employees: 5-9
Number of Products: 100+
Sq. footage: 12000
Type of Packaging: Bulk
Brands:
Marnap-Trap

8471 **Marquez Brothers International**
612 W 5th St
Hanford, CA 93230 559-584-8000
Fax: 559-584-8008
www.marquezbrothers.com/main
www.marquezbrothers.com
Processor of gelatin, sweet and sour cream, Mexican cheese and liquid yogurt
CEO: Gustave Marquez
VP: Juan Marquez
Plant Manager: Juan Luis De La Torre
Estimated Sales: Less than $500,000
Number Employees: 100-249
Parent Co: Marquez Brothers International
Type of Packaging: Consumer, Food Service

8472 **Marrese Cheese Company**
N10149 City Trk Ay
Lomira, WI 53048 920-269-4288
Cheese

8473 **Marroquin Organic International**
303 Potero Street
Suite 18
Santa Cruz, CA 95060 831-423-3442
Fax: 831-423-3432 www.marroquin-organics.com
Manufacturer of organic and non-GMO ingredients
President: Grace Marroquin
Vice President: Mark Nelson
Organic Ingredient Specialist: Helen Hudson
Estimated Sales: $4-5 Million
Number Employees: 5-9

8474 **(HQ)Mars, Inc.**
6885 Elm St
Mc Lean, VA 22101-6031 703-821-4900
Fax: 703-448-9678 www.mars.com
Chocolate, wrigley gum and confections, food, drinks
President/CEO: Paul Michaels
EVP/CFO: Olivier Goudet
VP/General Counsel: Alberto Mora
VP Supply/R&D/Procurement: Richard Ware
VP/Personnel & Organization: Aileen Richards
VP/Corporate Affairs: David Kamentzky
President/Chocolate: Grant Reid
Presdident/Wrigley Gum & Confections: Martin Radvan
President/Food: Poul Weihrauch
President/Mars Drinks: Andrew Clarke
Estimated Sales: $30 Billion
Number Employees: 65000
Type of Packaging: Consumer, Bulk
Brands:
3 MUSKETEERS
5 ACIDITO
ABOU SIOUF RICE
ACIDITO
AIRWAVES
ALTOIDS
AMICELLI
AQUADROPS
BALISTON
BANJO
BIG LEAGUE CHEW
BOMVASO
BOUNTY
CASTELLARI
CELEBRATIONS
COMBOS
CREME SAVERS
DOLMIO
DOUBLEMINT
DOVE
EBLY
ECLIPSE
EXTRA
FLING
FLYTE
GALAXY
GALAXY FLUTE
GENERATION MAX
GUSANO
HUBBA BUBBA
KANTONG
KUDOS
LIFE-SAVERS
LOCKETS
M&M'S
MALTESERS
MARS
MARS DELIGHT
MASTERFOODS
MILKY WAY
MILKY WAY CRISPY ROLLS
MUNCH
MY DOVE
MY M&M'S
NO NAME
ORBIT
RARIS
REVELS
RONDO
ROYCO
SEEDS OF CHANGE
SKITTLES
SNICKERS
STARBURST
SUZI WAN
SWINKLES
TOPIC
TRACKER
TUNES
TWIX
TWIX TOPIX
UNCLE BEN'S
WINTERFRESH
WORLD OF GRAINS
WRIGLEY'S BIG RED
WRIGLEY'S FREEDENT
WRIGLEY'S JUICY FRUIT
WRIGLEY'S BIG RED
WRIGLEY'S FREEDENT
WRIGLEY'S JUICY FRUIT
WRIGLEY'S SPEARMINT

8475 **Marsa Specialty Products**
5511 Long Beach Ave
Vernon, CA 90058 323-587-2288
Fax: 323-587-6729 800-628-0500
marsa@earthlink.net
www.marsaspecialtyproducts.com
Processor of dietetic products including syrups and ketchup
President: Helga Hanlein
Secretary/Treasurer: Allen Brown
Sales Director: James Hanelin
Operations Manager: Allen Brown
Estimated Sales: $1 Million
Number Employees: 10-19
Type of Packaging: Food Service

8476 **(HQ)Marsan Foods**
106 Thermos Road
Toronto, ON M1L 4W2
Canada 416-755-9262
Fax: 416-755-6790 sean@marsanfoods.com
www.marsanfoods.com
Processor and exporter of single-series frozen entries and bowls, family size entries, control and private label. Processor and exporter of specialty meal components for healthcare settings
President: James Jewett
Director Sales/Marketing: Sean Lippay
Number Employees: 100
Number of Products: 160
Sq. footage: 75000
Type of Packaging: Consumer, Food Service, Private Label
Brands:
Balanced Cuisine
Puree Marsan

8477 **Marshakk Smoked Fish Company**
6980 75th St
Flushing, NY 11379-2531 718-326-2170
Fax: 718-384-6661
Specialty foods
President: Marie Cook
Vice President: Gary Cook
Sales Director: Sean Cook
Estimated Sales: $ 10-24.9 Million
Number Employees: 50-99
Type of Packaging: Private Label
Brands:
Almondina
Aunt Jenny's
Babcock
Boone Maman
Bovril
Breadshop
Brianna's

Carapelli
Carr's
Celestial
Coco Pazzo
Colavita
Consorzio
Dececco
Del Verde
Dell Amore's
Delouis
Dessvilie
Dickinson
Droste
Dutch Gold
Eden
El Paso
Finncrisp
French Market
Green Mountain
Grielle
Guiltless Gourmet
Hero
Highland Sugar Vermont
Holgrain
Illy
Knorr
Konriko
La Marne Champ
La Posada
La Preferida
Langnese
Lindt
Maille
Marmite
McCann's
Melba
Melitta
Monnini
New York Flatbread
Old Monk
Poell
Pommery
Pritikin
Qugg
Rao's
Romanoff
Spice Hunter
Spice Island
St. Dalfour
Sunbrand
Texmati
Timpone's
Tip Tree
Tropical Bee
Twinings

8478 **Marshall Biscuits**
100 Jacintoport Blvd
Saraland, AL 36571-3304 251-679-6226
Fax: 251-679-6227 harris@marshallbiscuits.com
www.marshallbiscuits.com
Manufacturer of biscuits including buttermilk, homestyle, brown 'n serve and country style; also, dinner rolls
President/CEO: Harris Morrissette
Estimated Sales: $95.5 Million
Number Employees: 50-99
Type of Packaging: Consumer, Food Service, Private Label
Brands:
MARSHALL'S

8479 **Marshall Durbin Companies**
1301 James Street
Hattiesburg, MS 39401 601-544-3141
www.marshalldurbin.com
Poultry
Parent Co: Marshall Durbin Companies
Type of Packaging: Food Service

8480 **Marshall Durbin Companies**
3301 3rd Avenue
Jasper, AL 35502 205-387-1441
www.marshalldurbin.com
Poultry
Parent Co: Marshall Durbin Companies
Type of Packaging: Food Service, Bulk

8481 **(HQ)Marshall Durbin Companies**
2830 Commerce Blvd
Birmingham, AL 35210
Fax: 205-380-3251 800-768-2456
sales@marshalldurbin.com
www.marshalldurbin.com
Chicken eggs, chicken hatchery, raising, slaughtering and processing of chickens, wholesale poultry.
President: Melissa Durbin
VP/Finance: Mark Jeter
VP: John Perri
VP/Sales: Brian Roberts
Plant Manager: Robert Poe
Estimated Sales: $ 100-250 Million
Number Employees: 1900
Sq. footage: 49000

8482 **Marshall Durbin Companies**
1421 Robinwood Circle
Tarrant, AL 35217 205-841-7315
www.marshalldurbin.com
Manager: John Davies
Plant Manager: Alan Butler
Parent Co: Marshall Durbin Companies

8483 **Marshall Durbin Companies**
650 Ford Avenue
Jackson, MS 39209 601-969-1248
www.marshalldurbin.com
Chicken eggs, chicken hatchery, raising, slaughtering and procesing of chickens, wholesale poultry.
Manager: James Faison
Parent Co: Marshall Durbin Companies
Other Locations:
Irondale AL

8484 **Marshall Egg Products**
Rural Route 5
Po Box 1250
Seymour, IN 47274 812-497-2557
Fax: 812-497-3311 www.roseacre.com
Processor of eggs
President: Lois Rust
Plant Manager: Nick Cary
Estimated Sales: $ 5 - 10 Million
Number Employees: 1,000-4,999
Parent Co: Rose Acre Farms
Type of Packaging: Food Service, Bulk

8485 **Marshall Smoked Fish Company**
1111 NW 159th Dr
Miami, FL 33169-5807 305-625-5112
Fax: 305-625-5528 info@seaspecialities.com
www.seaspecialities.com
Smoked fish
Manager: Ron Alexander
President/CEO: Harvey Oxenburg
Controller: Arthur Hom
COO: Michael Metzkes
COO: Jack Karson
Manager: Ken Kosierowski
Estimated Sales: $ 50-75 Million
Number Employees: 325

8486 **Marshall's Biscuit Company**
100 Jacintoport Blvd
Saraland, AL 36571-3304 251-679-6226
Fax: 251-679-6227 800-368-9811
harris@marshallbiscuits.com
http://www.marshallbiscuits.com
Breads, rolls
President: A Robert Outlaw Jr
CEO: Harris V Morrissette
Estimated Sales: $ 10-20 Million
Number Employees: 50-99

8487 **Marshallville Packing Company**
P.O.Box 276
Marshallville, OH 44645 330-855-2871
Processor of beef, pork including sausage, luncheon meats, poultry and cheese
President: Frank Tucker
Assistant Manager: John Tucker
Estimated Sales: $3000000
Number Employees: 20-49
Sq. footage: 27000
Type of Packaging: Consumer, Food Service, Bulk

8488 **(HQ)Marshmallow Cone Company**
5141 Fischer Place
Cincinnati, OH 45217-1157 513-641-2345
Fax: 513-641-2557 800-641-8551
customerserv@marshmallowcone.com
www.marshmallowcone.com
Manufacturer and exporter of marshmallow filled ice cream cones and cups and candy
President: John B Arbino
Estimated Sales: $ 10 - 20 Million
Number Employees: 20-49
Sq. footage: 42000
Type of Packaging: Consumer, Food Service, Private Label, Bulk
Brands:
MARPRO

8489 **Marshmallow Products**
5141 Fischer Ave
Cincinnati, OH 45217-1157 513-641-2345
Fax: 513-641-2557 800-641-8551
customerserv@marshmallowcone.com
www.marshmallowcone.com
Marshmallow-filled ice cream cones and specialty candies
President: Dan Runk
Vice President: Pamela Arbino
Estimated Sales: $ 5-9.9 Million
Number Employees: 20-49
Brands:
Marpro

8490 **Marsyl**
308 16th Street
Cody, WY 82414-3214 307-527-6277
Confectionery
Brands:
Birthday Control Pills Candy
Confectionary Expres
Control Pills Candy
Eatable Greetables
Grouch Control Pills
Marsyl Candy
Over the Hill Pills
Passion Control Pill
Spaced Out Candy

8491 **Marten's Country Kitchen**
PO Box 428
Port Byron, NY 13140-0428 315-776-8821
Fax: 315-776-8201
Potatoes
Estimated Sales: $ 5 - 10 Million
Number Employees: 20-49
Sq. footage: 12500
Type of Packaging: Consumer, Food Service, Private Label, Bulk

8492 **Martha Olson's Great Foods**
P.O.Box 66
Sutter Creek, CA 95685-0066 209-234-5935
Fax: 209-223-7071 800-973-3966
Customercare@marthasallnatural.com
www.marthasallnatural.com
Processor of all natural baking mixes including pancake, muffin, waffle, bread, cake and scone; also, chocolate sauce
Owner: Martha Olson
CEO: Margaret Brown
Marketing/National Accounts: Roylene Brown
Production Manager: Harvey Archer
Estimated Sales: $ 2.5-5 Million
Number Employees: 1-4
Brands:
Martha's All Natural
Martha's All Natural Baking Mixes

8493 **Martha's Garden**
475 Horner Avenue
Toronto, ON M8W 4X7
Canada 416-251-6112
Fax: 416-251-8443 866-773-2887
qvs@marthasgarden.com
www.marthasgarden.com
Processor of fresh onions, cabbage, lettuce, celery, broccoli, cucumbers, carrots, cauliflower, tomatoes, zucchini, eggplant, etc
President: Gus Arrigo, Jr.
Quality Assurance Manager: Jefery Musumi
Sales Manager: Richard Sabourin
Number Employees: 20-49

8494 **Martin & Weyrich Winery**
P.O.Box 1330
Templeton, CA 93465 805-239-1640
Fax: 805-238-0887 sales@martinweyrich.com
www.martinweyrich.com

This winery produces a wide selection including Pinot Grigio, Moscato Allegro, Nebbiolo, Nebbiolo Vecchio, Insieme, Zinfandel La Primitiva, Cabernet Etrusco, Vin Santo, in addition to having a fine coffee selection includingcappuccino, espresso, latte and mochas.
Manager: Katie Stemper
Marketing Director: Larry Persinger
Production Manager: Craig Reed
Purchasing Manager: Cynthia Reed
Estimated Sales: $ 5-10 Million
Number Employees: 20-49
Sq. footage: 6

8495 **Martin Brothers Distributing Company**
406 Viking Rd
Cedar Falls, IA 50613 319-266-1775
Fax: 319-277-1238 srathbun@martinsnet.com
www.martinnet.com
Wholesaler/distributor of baked goods, dairy items, frozen food, groceries, meat, produce, seafood, janitorial supplies, equipment, etc.; serving the food service market; also, nutritional services, menu consulting, layout and designavailable
President: John Martin
Manager Marketing/Merchandising: Diane Chandler
Director Sales/Marketing: Doug Coen
Estimated Sales: $120000000
Number Employees: 250-499
Sq. footage: 86000

8496 **Martin Brothers SeafoodcCompany**
258 Sala Ave
Westwego, LA 70094 504-341-2251
Fax: 504-341-2251
Processor of frozen crabmeat and gumbo crabs
President: William Martin
Owner: Donna Martin
Estimated Sales: $5-9.9 Million
Number Employees: 1-4
Type of Packaging: Consumer, Food Service, Bulk

8497 **Martin Coffee Company**
1633 Marshall St
Jacksonville, FL 32206 904-355-9661
Fax: 904-355-9673 info@martincoffee.com
www.martincoffee.com
Manufacturer of coffee
President/Founder: Amy B Martin
VP: Harold Johnson
VP Sales/Marketing: Ben Johnson
Estimated Sales: $15 Million
Number Employees: 10-19
Type of Packaging: Consumer, Food Service, Private Label
Brands:
MARTIN

8498 **Martin Farms**
313 Magnolia Ave
Patterson, CA 95363 209-892-8653
Fax: 209-892-2652 877-838-7369
info@martinfarms.com www.martinfarms.net
Processor of sliced, diced and halved sun-dried tomatoes; available in bags and oil
Owner: Joseph Martin
Estimated Sales: Less than $500,000
Number Employees: 1-4

8499 **Martin Rosol's**
45 Grove St
New Britain, CT 6053 860-223-2707
Fax: 860-229-6690 orders@martinrosols.com
www.martinrosols.com
Processor of cold cuts, hot dogs and kielbasa
President: Robert Rosol
CEO: Eugene Rosol
Vice President: Sarah Rosol
Estimated Sales: $2 Million
Number Employees: 25
Type of Packaging: Consumer, Private Label

8500 **Martin Seafood Company**
7901 Oceano Ave Ste 46
Jessup, MD 20794 410-799-5822
Fax: 410-799-3545 info@martinseafoodco.com
www.martinseafoodco.com
Processor of frozen breaded seafood products; wholesaler/distributor of raw frozen seafood products; serving the food service market
Owner: Billy Martin
Secretary: Shawn Isaac
Estimated Sales: $3000000
Number Employees: 20-49
Sq. footage: 25000
Type of Packaging: Consumer, Food Service

8501 **Martin's Famous Pastry Shoppe, Inc**
1000 Potato Roll Lane
Chambersburg, PA 17201 717-263-9580
Fax: 717-263-6687 800-548-1200
www.mfps.com
Potato bread, rolls and stuffing; potato chips, pretzels, cheese puffys, popcorn and dips
President/CEO: James Martin
VP Finance: Ronald Gipe
SVP Research & Development: Ray Alleman
Chief Marketing Officer: Dennis Wenrick
Human Resources Manager: Aisah Eden
Estimated Sales: $20-50 Million
Number Employees: 464
Sq. footage: 39000
Parent Co: Consolidated Biscuit Company
Type of Packaging: Consumer, Food Service, Private Label
Brands:
Mr. C'S
Mr. G'S
Nibble With Gibble's

8502 **Martin's Potato Chips**
5847 Lincoln Hwy W
Thomasville, PA 17364 717-792-3565
Fax: 717-792-4906 800-272-4477
www.martinschips.com
Manufacturer of potato chips, popcorn and distributor of pretzels.
President/CEO: Kenneth Potter
CEO: Kevin Potter
VP Finance: C Fitz
Quality Control Director: Doug Branstetter
Marketing Director: David Potter
Sales Manager: Mike Biase
Human Resources Director: Susan Wernsdorfer
Operations Executive: Neal Rohrbough
Estimated Sales: $34 Million
Number Employees: 200
Sq. footage: 78000
Type of Packaging: Consumer, Food Service, Bulk

8503 **Martini & Prati Wines**
2191 Laguna Rd
Santa Rosa, CA 95401-3799 707-823-2404
Fax: 707-829-6151 info@martiniprati.com
www.martinraywinery.com
Processor of wines
Manager: Wendi Hawn
VP: Thomas Martini
Estimated Sales: $ 10 - 20 Million
Number Employees: 20-49
Sq. footage: 120000
Type of Packaging: Consumer
Brands:
Fountain Grove
Martini & Prati

8504 **Martino's Bakery**
335 N Victory Blvd
Burbank, CA 91502 818-842-0715
Fax: 818-842-5111 www.martinosbakery.com
Breads, cakes and related products
Owner: Mario Corradi
CEO: Andy Horvatch
Controller: Kathy Prince
Purchasing Agent: Diana Wang
Estimated Sales: Less than $500,000
Number Employees: 5-9

8505 **Marubeni America Corporation**
375 Lexington Ave
New York, NY 10017 212-450-0563
Fax: 212-450-0733 gendi-s@marubeni-usa.com
www.marubeni-usa.com
Oilseeds production (canola, rapeseed and soybean)
President: Koichi Mochizuki
Manager: Sherif Gendi
Estimated Sales: 1 Billion +
Number Employees: 100-249
Parent Co: Marubeni

8506 **Maruchan**
15800 Laguna Canyon Rd
Irvine, CA 92618 949-789-2300
Fax: 949-789-2350 maropoulos@worldnet.att.net
Processor and exporter of Oriental foods including wonton soup and instant ramen noodles
President: Kiyoshi Fukagawa
Estimated Sales: $33200000
Number Employees: 250-499
Parent Co: Toyo Suisan Kaisha
Type of Packaging: Consumer

8507 **Marukai Corporation**
1740 W Artesia Blvd # 114
Gardena, CA 90248-3238 310-660-6300
Fax: 310-660-6301 info@marukai.com
www.marukai.com
Manufacturer, importer and exporter of Japanese products
President: Hidejiro Matsu
Estimated Sales: $41 Million
Number Employees: 100-249
Parent Co: Marukai Corporation
Other Locations:
Marukai Corporation
Honolulu HI

8508 **Marukan Vinegar (U.S.A.) Inc.**
7755 Monroe St
Paramount, CA 90723 562-630-6060
Fax: 562-229-1107 anoble@marukan-usa.com
www.marukan-usa.com
Marukan Vinegar has been brewing natural rice vinegars since 1649. Using only selected rice, the vinegar is naturally matured by the traditional method and spends over a month brewing for a richer, more fully developed flavor.
President: Masahito Kikumoto
CEO: Junichi Oyama
VP Sales/Marketing: Jon Tanklage
Sales/Marketing: Tom McReynolds
Operations: Tosh Zamoto
Production: Toru Saito
Production: Michitsugu Ogawa
Estimated Sales: $7-10 Million
Number Employees: 20-49
Sq. footage: 15000
Parent Co: Marukan Vinegar Co, Ltd
Type of Packaging: Consumer, Food Service, Private Label, Bulk
Brands:
Marukan

8509 **Marukome USA Inc.**
17132 Pullman Street
Irvine, CA 92614 949-863-0110
Fax: 949-863-9813 mnagano@marukomeusa.com
www.marukomeusa.com
Miso manufacturer
President: Shigeru Sharasaka
Secretary: Tetsuhiko Iijima
Marketing: (Fred) Teruo Yamanaka
Number Employees: 17

8510 **Marva Maid Dairy**
5500 Chestnut Ave
Newport News, VA 23605 757-245-3857
Fax: 757-928-2449 800-544-4439
www.marvamaid.com
Manufacturer and exporter of cottage cheese, whipped sour cream, whole and low-fat milk and milk by-products; also, apple, grapefruit and orange juice
Manager: Danny Lovell
Sales Manager: Ed Boyd
Director Fluid Milk Operations: Bruce Manson
Plant Manager: Rick Meier
Estimated Sales: $397 Million
Number Employees: 1-4
Parent Co: Maryland & Virginia Milk Producers Association
Type of Packaging: Consumer
Brands:
HARVEST FRESH
MARVA MAID
SLENDO

8511 **Marwood Sales**
6400 Glenwood St Ste 308
Mission, KS 66202 913-722-1534
Fax: 913-262-9132
Dairy products
President: Mark Woodard

Estimated Sales: $8.2 Million
Number Employees: 1-4
Brands:
Marwood

8512 **Marx Brothers**
3100 2nd Ave S
Birmingham, AL 35233 205-251-3139
Fax: 205-324-6322 800-633-6376
www.marxbrothersinc.com
Manufacturer of sweetened coconut
President: Edgar Marx Jr
Estimated Sales: $3 Million
Number Employees: 20-49
Type of Packaging: Consumer, Food Service, Private Label, Bulk

8513 **Mary Ann's Baking Company**
8371 Carbide Ct
Sacramento, CA 95828-5636 916-681-7444
Fax: 916-681-7470 www.maryannsbaking.com
Processor of danish and pastries
President: George Demas
General Manager: Bob Burzinski
Plant Manager: Don Lavelle
Estimated Sales: $ 10 - 20 Million
Number Employees: 100-249
Type of Packaging: Consumer

8514 **Mary Of Pudding Hill**
201 E I-30
Greenville, TX 75402 903-455-2651
Fax: 903-455-4522

8515 **Mary Sue Candies**
1786 Union Ave
Baltimore, MD 21211-1417 410-467-9338
Fax: 410-467-1649 info@naroncandy.com
www.marysue.com
Chocolate and soft candy
President: William G Buppert
CFO: Mike Wiss
R & D: Mark Berman
Estimated Sales: $ 5-10 Million
Number Employees: 5-9

8516 **Mary of Puddin Hill**
P.O.Box 241
Greenville, TX 75403-0241 903-455-6931
Fax: 903-455-4522 800-545-8889
www.puddinhill.com
Processor of pecan fruit cakes and chocolate candy
Owner: Ken Bain
CEO: Ron Massey
Plant Manager: Jerry Davis
Estimated Sales: $1300000
Number Employees: 50-99
Type of Packaging: Private Label

8517 **Mary's Gone Crackers**
PO Box 965
Gridley, CA 95948 530-846-5100
Fax: 530-846-5500 888-258-1250
info@marysgonecrackers.com
www.marysgonecrackers.com
wheat free and gluten free baked goods
President: Dale Rodrigues
Vice President: Michael Quinn
Marketing: Mary Waldner
VP of Sales: Mike Quinn
Estimated Sales: $6.8 Million
Number Employees: 57

8518 **Maryland & Virginia Milk Producers Cooperative**
1985 Isaac Newton Square W
Reston, VA 20190 703-742-4250
Fax: 703-742-7459 jbryant@mdvamilk.com
www.mdvamilk.com
Processor of milk
Chairman/President: Steve Graybeal
CEO: Jay Brant
CFO: Jorge Gonzalez
First VP: Dwyane Myers
Sales Executive: Michael Curtis
Operations Manager: Craig Gentry
Estimated Sales: $1.2 Billion
Number Employees: 550
Sq. footage: 20600
Type of Packaging: Consumer

8519 **Maryland & Virginia Milk Cooperative Association**
1985 Isaac Newton Square West
Reston, VA 20190-5094 703-742-6800
Fax: 703-742-7459 jbryant@mdvamilk.com
www.mdvamilk.com
Milk and dairy products
Manager: David Blake
Manager: William King
Estimated Sales: $ 20-50 Million
Number Employees: 20-49
Brands:
Laurel

8520 **Maryland Fresh Tomato Company**
7460 Conowingo Avenue
Building B
Jessup, MD 20794-9361 410-799-5050
Fax: 410-799-1816
Tomatos and vegetables
Estimated Sales: $ 3 - 5 Million
Number Employees: 5-9

8521 **Marzipan Specialties**
1513 Meridian St
Nashville, TN 37207 615-226-4800
Fax: 615-226-4882 marizapan@isdn.net
www.marzipanspecialties.com
Processor of marzipan candy
Owner: Karl Schoenperger
Estimated Sales: Below $ 5 Million
Number Employees: 5-9
Type of Packaging: Consumer

8522 **Masala Chai Company**
P.O.Box 8375
Santa Cruz, CA 95061-8375 831-475-8881
Fax: 831-475-5967 masala@masalachaico.com
www.masalachaico.com
Processor and importer of chai teas including bottled and ready- to-drink, Indian spiced, regular, decaf and energy tonics
Co-Owner: Raphael Reuben
Co-Owner: Susan Beardsley
Estimated Sales: $240000
Number Employees: 1-4
Sq. footage: 1500
Type of Packaging: Consumer, Food Service, Private Label, Bulk
Brands:
Aphroteasiac Chai
Masala Chai

8523 **Mason County Fruit Packers Cooperative**
3958 W Chauvez Rd # 1
Ludington, MI 49431-8200 231-845-6248
Fax: 231-843-9453 doylefenner@yahoo.com
Processor of frozen cherries and apples, canned apple juice and sauce, peaches and plums
President: Roy Hackert
CEO: Doyle Fenner
Plant Manager: Joe Bates
Estimated Sales: $82800000
Number Employees: 100-249
Sq. footage: 1000000
Type of Packaging: Consumer, Bulk

8524 **Masson Cheese Corporation**
6180 Alcoa Ave
Vernon, CA 90058 323-583-1251
Fax: 323-585-8765 800-637-7262
sales@massoncheese.com
www.massoncheese.com
Natural and processed cheese
President: Morris Farinella
Marketing Director: Jean Hendrix
Estimated Sales: $ 10-20 Million
Number Employees: 50-99

8525 **Mastantuono Winery**
2720 Oakview Rd
Templeton, CA 93465-8798 805-238-0676
Fax: 805-238-9257
info@mastantuonowinery.com
www.mastantuonowinery.com
Wine
Owner: Pasquale Mastantuono
Operations Manager: Pasquale Mastantuono
Estimated Sales: Below $ 5 Million
Number Employees: 5-9
Brands:
Mastantuono Wines

8526 **Master Brew**
3550 Woodhead Drive
Northbrook, IL 60062 847-564-3600
Fax: 847-564-2317 cs@masterbrew.com
www.masterbrew.com
Coffee and tea
President: Ronald Weber
CEO: Joseph Weber
Estimated Sales: $9 Million
Number Employees: 120

8527 **Master Mix**
181 W Orangethorpe Avenue
Placentia, CA 92870-6931 714-524-1698
Fax: 714-524-8540
Processor and exporter of powdered mixes including soft serve, shake and yogurt; also, syrups, toppings, water soluable ginseng extract and drink bases
President: Pat Lagraffe
VP: Jim LaGraffe
Estimated Sales: $ 1 - 3 Million
Number Employees: 1-4
Sq. footage: 5000
Type of Packaging: Consumer, Food Service, Private Label, Bulk
Brands:
Chalet Gourmet
Dairy's Pride
Master Mix

8528 **Master Peace Food Imports**
PO Box 36
Pleasantville, NY 10570-0036 914-769-7148
Fax: 914-769-8944
Health and dietetic foods
President: John Peace, Jr.
Secretary: Jolaine Dow Peace
Estimated Sales: Under $500,000
Number Employees: 1-4
Brands:
Airborne

8529 **Masterfoods USA**
800 High St
Hackettstown, NJ 7840 908-852-1000
Fax: 908-850-2734 www.m-ms.com
Candy
Senior VP: Mike Tolkowsky
Number Employees: 5,000-9,999
Brands:
3 MUSKETEERS
DOVE CHOCOLATE
KUDOS
M&M'S
MILKY WAY
SKITTLES
SNICKERS
STARBURST
TWIX BRAND

8530 **Masters Gallery Foods**
P.O.Box 170
Plymouth, WI 53073 920-893-8431
Fax: 920-893-6075 800-236-8431
dmacphee@mastersgalleryfoods.com
www.mastersgalleryfoods.com
Cheese
President: Christopher Gentine
CFO: Catherine Schwartz
CEO: Jeff Giffin
Senior VP Marketing: Bob Wilson
Estimated Sales: $ 5-10 Million
Number Employees: 20-49

8531 **Masterson Company**
4023 W National Ave
Milwaukee, WI 53215 414-647-1132
Fax: 414-647-1170
contact@mastersoncompany.com
www.mastersoncompany.com
Premium fudge and caramel toppings, fruit toppings, shake bases, fountain syrups, marshmallow creme toppings, ice cream cone dips and coatings.
President: Mike Masterson
CEO: Joe Masterson
VP: Susan Hough
VP Sales: David Erickson
Human Resources Manager: Deborah Libert
General Manager: Nancy Albro
Plant Manager: Steve Burr

Estimated Sales: $33 Million
Number Employees: 200
Sq. footage: 380000
Type of Packaging: Food Service, Bulk
Brands:
Masterson

8532 **Mat Roland Seafood Company**
1674 Park Ter E
Atlantic Beach, FL 32233 904-246-9443
Fax: 904-241-0645
Processor of fish and shrimp
President: Brad Roland
Estimated Sales: $2300000
Number Employees: 10
Type of Packaging: Consumer, Food Service, Bulk
Brands:
Roland Star

8533 **Matador Processors**
P.O.Box 2200
Blanchard, OK 73010 405-485-3567
Fax: 405-485-2597 800-847-0797
matador@matadorprocessors.com
www.matadorprocessors.com
Processor of frozen foods including chile rellenos (stuffed peppers), stuffed jalapenos and breaded hors d'oeuvres including cheese bites, mushrooms, desserts, etc.; exporter of chile rellenos, stuffed jalapenos and mozzarellasticks
President: Betty Wood
CFO: Richard Clark
VP: Ron W Diggs
R&D: Debbie Funderburk
Sales: Richard Clark
Operations: Ron W Diggs
Plant Manager: Debbie Funderburk
Estimated Sales: $3000000
Number Employees: 50-99
Sq. footage: 27000
Type of Packaging: Food Service, Private Label
Brands:
Clif's
Matador

8534 **Matangos Candies**
S 15th & Catherine St
Harrisburg, PA 17101 717-234-0882
www.matangoscandies.com
Processor of candy and other confectionery products
Owner/President: Peter Matangos
Estimated Sales: $100,000
Number Employees: 1-4
Type of Packaging: Consumer
Brands:
Matangoes

8535 **Matanuska Maid Dairy**
814 W Northern Lights Blvd
Anchorage, AK 99503-3713 907-561-5223
Fax: 907-563-7492 info@matmaid.com
www.matmaid.com
Fluid milk, orange juice and related products
President: Joe Van Treeck
Sales Manager: Glenn Soby
Sales Manager: Linda Bowers
Plant Manager: Gary Nelson
Estimated Sales: $ 10-20 Million
Number Employees: 20-49
Brands:
Matanuska Maid

8536 **Matanzas Creek Winery**
6097 Bennett Valley Rd
Santa Rosa, CA 95404 707-528-6464
Fax: 707-571-0156 800-500-6464
info@matanzascreek.com
www.matanzascreek.com
Wines the selection of which includes the Sonoma County Series: Merlot, Chardonnay, Sauvignon Blanc, Cabernet Sauvignon and Syrah. Limited Production Series wines include 2002 Bennett Valley Merlot and 2001 Jackson Park Merlot.
General Manager: Patrick Connelly
Vice President: William MacIver
Marketing Director: Peter Kay
Winemaker: Susan Reed
Director Operations: Tad Sanders
Estimated Sales: $ 10-20 Million
Number Employees: 20-49
Sq. footage: 20
Type of Packaging: Private Label
Brands:
Journey
Matanzas Creek Winery

8537 **Mathews Packing Company**
950 Ramirez Rd
Marysville, CA 95901 530-743-1077
Fax: 530-742-6625
Dried prunes, pitted prunes, rice
Owner: Ed Mathews
VP/Marketing: Mark Mathews
Estimated Sales: $1-$2.5 Million
Number Employees: 5-9
Type of Packaging: Private Label

8538 **Matilija Water Company**
164 W Park Row Ave
Ventura, CA 93001 805-643-4675
Fax: 805-643-3825 www.getpurewater.com
Processor of bottled water; also, wholesaler/distributor of water purification systems; serving the food service market
President: Dom Schakleford
Estimated Sales: $ 1 - 3 Million
Number Employees: 10-19
Type of Packaging: Consumer, Food Service

8539 **Matouk International USAInc**
3801 North University Drive #320
Sunrise, FL 33351 954-742-2204
Fax: 954-742-2533 matoukusa@aol.com
Chutney/relish, full-line condiments, other condiments, other soups, stews, beans, BBQ sauce, ethnic sauces (soy, curry, etc.), herbs.
Manager: Riad Boulos
Marketing: Linda Chow-Quan
Estimated Sales: $100,000
Number Employees: 2

8540 **Matrix Health Products**
9316 Wheatlands Road
Santee, CA 92071-5644 619-448-7550
Fax: 619-448-2995 888-736-5609
info@earthsbounty.com www.matrixhealth.com
Manufacturer, importer and exporter of nutritional and herbal supplements including tablets, liquids, powders and capsules - also kosher & organic products. Teas, coffee & vanilla and nonjuice
President: Steven Kravitz
Number Employees: 10-19
Type of Packaging: Consumer, Private Label, Bulk
Brands:
Colloidal Silver
Dhea
Earth's Bounty
Melatonin
Meno-Select
Noni
Oxy-Caps
Oxy-Cleanse
Oxy-Max
Oxy-Mist
Prosta-Forte
Woman's Select

8541 **Matson Fruit Company**
201 N Railroad Ave
Selah, WA 98942 509-697-7100
Fax: 509-697-8168
daryl.matson@matsonfruit.com
www.matsonfruit.com
Processor and exporter of apples and pears
President: Rod Matson
Manager: Daryl Matson
Estimated Sales: $ 50 - 100 Million
Number Employees: 100-249
Type of Packaging: Consumer, Food Service

8542 **Matson Vineyards**
10584 Arapaho Dr
Redding, CA 96003 530-222-2833
ommatson@snowcrest.com
www.matsonvineyards.com
Wines
President: Oscar Matson
Analyst /Marketing Manager: Kdiko Goto
Winemaker: Roger Matson
Estimated Sales: Under $500,000
Number Employees: 1-4

8543 **Matthews 1812 House**
P.O.Box 15
Cornwall Bridge, CT 06754 860-672-0149
Fax: 860-672-1812 800-662-1812
info@matthews1812house.com
www.matthews1812house.com
Processor of all-natural cakes including apple crumb torte, brandied apricot, chocolate raspberry liqueur, chocolate rum, country spice, fruit and nut, fudge brownie torte, lemon rum, cookies, bar cookies, chocolate explosionbrownies
President: Deanna Matthews
Corporate Secretary: Blaine Matthews
Manager: Cheryl Cass
Estimated Sales: $1 Million
Number Employees: 10-19
Sq. footage: 2000
Type of Packaging: Consumer, Food Service, Private Label
Brands:
Matthews 1812 House

8544 **Matthiesen's Deer & Custom Processing**
3357 252nd St
De Witt, IA 52742 563-659-8409
Processor of meat products including, beef, lamb, venison, pork and mettwurst
President: Sandy Matthiesen
Estimated Sales: $500,000-$1 Million
Number Employees: 1-4
Type of Packaging: Consumer

8545 **Mattingly Foods of Louisville**
2055 Nelson Miller Parkway
Louisville, KY 40223 502-253-2000
www.mattinglyfoodslouisville.com
Offers the highest quality, center-of-the-plate prime choice steaks.
Division President: Edward Merry
Number Employees: 50
Parent Co: Mattingly Foods
Type of Packaging: Food Service

8546 **Mattus Lowfat Ice Cream**
PO Box 311
Glen Cove, NY 11542-0311 ÿ90- 56- 522
Fax: 718-472-2066 info@mattus.com
Ice cream
President: Denis Hurley
CFO: Anthony Rugel
VP: Keven Hurley
General Manager: Joe Lippolis
Estimated Sales: Below $ 5 Million
Number Employees: 20-49

8547 **Maui Bagel**
200 Dairy Rd
Kahului, HI 96732-2978 808-270-7561
Fax: 808-270-7919 www.mauicounty.gov
Bread, rolls, bagels, dounuts, sandwiches
Manager: Jeff Murray
Number Employees: 250-499

8548 **Maui Coffee Roasters**
444 Hana Hwy Ste B
Kahului, HI 96732 808-877-2877
Fax: 808-871-2684 800-645-2877
info@hawaiiancoffee.com
www.hawaiiancoffee.com
Roasted coffee
President: Nick Matichyn
CFO: Mike Vaki
Marketing Manager: Cark Musto
VP Sales: Mike Okazaki
Purchasing Manager: Nicky Matichyn
Estimated Sales: $ 1-2.5 Million
Number Employees: 10-19
Type of Packaging: Private Label, Bulk

8549 **Maui Pineapple Company**
P.O.Box 187
Kahului, HI 96733-6687 808-877-3351
Fax: 808-871-0953 info@mauipineapple.com
www.mauiland.com
Processor and exporter of whole fresh, canned and fresh-cut pineapple; also, pineapple juice and concentrates
President: David Cole
CEO: David Cole
CEO: Robert I Webber
Executive VP Marketing/Sales: James McCann
Estimated Sales: $168666000
Number Employees: 500-999

Type of Packaging: Consumer, Food Service, Private Label, Bulk
Brands:
Hawaiian Gold
King of Hawaii

8550 Maui Pineapple Company
1800 Sutter Street
Suite 850
Concord, CA 94520-2528 925-798-0240
Fax: 925-798-0253
Processor, packer and exporter of pineapple, frozen pineapple juice and pineapple juice concentrate; importer of fresh and processed tropical fruits
Manager: Kerry Born
Marketing Manager: Jim Duffy
Estimated Sales: $ 10 - 20 Million
Number Employees: 800
Parent Co: Maui Land & Pineapple Company
Type of Packaging: Consumer, Food Service, Private Label, Bulk
Brands:
Hawaiian Gold

8551 Maui Potato Chips
295 Lalo St
Kahului, HI 96732-2915 808-877-3652
Fax: 808-877-3652
Processor of potato chips
President: Mark Kobayashi
Estimated Sales: $150000
Number Employees: 1-4
Type of Packaging: Consumer
Brands:
Original Maui Kitch'n Cook'd

8552 Mauna Loa Macadamia NutCorporation
16-701 Macadamia Rd
Keaau, HI 96749-8020 808-982-6562
Fax: 808-966-8410 800-832-9993
info@maunaloa.com www.maunaloa.ocm
Macadamia nuts and various products made with macadamia nuts including chocolates, cookies and oils.
Manager: Darrell Askey
Plant Manager: Charlie Young
Estimated Sales: $ 50-100 Million
Number Employees: 250-499

8553 Maurice Carrie Winery
34225 Rancho California Rd
Temecula, CA 92591-5054 951-676-1711
Fax: 951-676-8397 800-716-1711
info@mauricecarriewinery.com
www.mauricecarriewinery.com
Wines
Owner: Budd VanRoekel
Owner: Maurice VanRoekel
Sales: Jana Prais
Accounting Manager: LaDawn Allen
Winemaker: Gus Vizgirda
Type of Packaging: Consumer

8554 Maurice French Pastries
4949 W Napoleon Ave
Metairie, LA 70001-2249 504-455-0830
Fax: 504-885-1527 888-285-8261
sales@mauricefrenchpastries.com
www.mauricefrenchpastries.com
Mardi Gras cakes
Owner: John Luc
Estimated Sales: $ 2.5-5 Million
Number Employees: 50-99
Brands:
Maurice French Pastries

8555 Maurice Lenell Cooky Company
53 W Jackson Blvd Ste 1050
Chicago, IL 60604 708-456-6500
Fax: 708-456-6552 800-323-1760
www.mauricelenell.com
Manufacturer of specialty cookies
President/Co-Owner: Sonny Cohen
Co-Owner: Terry Cohen
Estimated Sales: $ 50 - 100 Million
Number Employees: 100-249
Type of Packaging: Consumer, Food Service, Private Label, Bulk

8556 Maurice's Gourmet Barbeque
PO Box 6847
West Columbia, SC 29170 800-628-7423
Fax: 803-791-8707 800-628-7423
mail@mauricesbbq.com www.mauricesbbq.com
Pork, barbeque hams and barbeque products
President: L Bessinger
Founder: Maurice Bessinger
Estimated Sales: Less than $500,000
Number Employees: 10-19
Brands:
Maurice's

8557 Maxfield Candy
1050 S 200 W
Salt Lake City, UT 84101 801-355-5321
Fax: 801-355-5546 800-288-8002
info@maxfieldcandy.com
www.maxfieldcandy.com
Manufacturer of boxed chocolates, nut logs, cream sticks, holiday novelties, salt water taffy, cordial cherries, mint sandwiches, etc.; exporter of boxed chocolates
President: Taz Murray
Estimated Sales: $ 5 - 10 Million
Number Employees: 5-9
Sq. footage: 106000
Parent Co: Alpine Confections
Type of Packaging: Consumer
Brands:
MAXFIELD

8558 (HQ)Maxim's Import Corporation
2719 NW 24th Street
Miami, FL 33142-7005 305-633-2167
Fax: 305-638-1348 800-331-6652
Processor, importer and exporter of shrimp; processor of packaged fish; exporter of frozen chicken, duck, turkey, pork and beef; wholesaler/distributor of shrimp, pork, beef, poultry, fish, produce and frozen, specialty and healthfoods
President: Luis Chi
CEO: Jeo Chi
Estimated Sales: $4100000
Number Employees: 22
Sq. footage: 35000
Type of Packaging: Bulk
Other Locations:
Maxim's Import Corp.
Salvador
Brands:
Airex
Alpromar
Caribe
De La Marca
Fish House
Flodi Pesca
Golden Star
Golfo Mar
Gulf Garden
Inter Ocean
Ocean Pac
Pacific Pride
Pesaca
Stefan Mar

8559 Maxin Marketing Corporation
92 Argonaut, Suite #170
Aliso Viejo, CA 92656-5318 949-362-1177
Fax: 949-362-0449 info@realsnacks.com
www.realsnacks.com
Snack foods
President: Terry Kroll
Estimated Sales: Less than $500,000
Number Employees: 1-4
Number of Brands: 2
Number of Products: 10
Type of Packaging: Consumer, Private Label, Bulk
Brands:
Health Creation Caramel Pretzels
Health Creation Onion Pretzels
Pocket Pretzels

8560 Maxwell's Gourmet Food
3208 Wellington Ct # L
Raleigh, NC 27615-4121 919-878-4321
Fax: 919-878-4325 800-952-6887
info@maxwellsgourmet.com
www.maxwellsgourmet.com
Peanuts, peanut brittle, chocolate dipped peanut brittle, pecans, chocolate-dipped pecans, pecan brittle, chocolate dipped pecan brittle, cashews
Owner: Paxton Kemps
CEO: Don Kempf
CFO: Shelia Kempf
Director Of Marketing: David Chapman
Director of Sales: Amy Kempf
Production Manager: Ana Arrendondo
Estimated Sales: $500,000-$1 Million
Number Employees: 5-9
Brands:
Maxwell's Extraordinary

8561 Maya Kaimal Fine IndianFoods
PO Box 700
Rhinebeck, NY 12572 845-876-8200
Fax: 845-876-8212 info@mayakaimal.com
www.mayakaimal.com
simmer sauces and spicy ketchup
President/Owner: Maya Kaimal

8562 Mayacamas Fine Foods
824 Princeton Dr
Sonoma, CA 95476-4154
Fax: 707-996-4501 800-826-9621
info@mayacamasfinefoods.com
www.mayacamasfinefoods.com
Processor and exporter of dehydrated soups, salad dressings, pasta sauces, gravies and seasonings
President: Vicki Ranzau
VP: Walter Rahrau
Estimated Sales: $2,400,000
Number Employees: 1-4
Sq. footage: 18000
Type of Packaging: Consumer, Food Service, Private Label

8563 Mayacamas Vineyards
1155 Lokoya Rd
Napa, CA 94558 707-224-4030
Fax: 707-224-3979 mayacama@napanet.net
www.mayacamas.com
Processor and exporter of wines including cabernet sauvignon, chardonnay, sauvignon blanc and pinot noir
President: Robert Travers
Marketing Director: Trina Vaught
Estimated Sales: $88000
Number Employees: 10-19
Brands:
Mayacamas Vineyards

8564 Mayer Brothers
3300 Transit Rd
West Seneca, NY 14224-2525 716-668-1787
Fax: 716-668-2437 800-696-2937
www.mayerbrothers.com
Processor of bottled spring water, apple cider and juices including orange, grapefruit, grape and apple; also, concentrates including fruit punch, orange, grape, iced tea and lemonade
President: John Mayer
VP: Earl Mayer
VP/General Manager: Jim Dickinson
Director of Marketing: Jim Kalec
Plant Superintendent: Kent Wakefield
Plant Manager: John Mayer
Purchasing Manager: Mike Gancasz
Estimated Sales: $100+ Million
Number Employees: 100-249
Sq. footage: 45000
Type of Packaging: Consumer, Food Service, Private Label, Bulk
Brands:
Mayer Bros.

8565 Mayer's Cider Mill
P.O.Box 347
Webster, NY 14580-347
Fax: 585-671-5269 800-543-0043
www.mayerscidermill.com
Processor of cider, apples and apple pies; also, beer, grape juice and wine-making supplies
Owner: David N Bower
Estimated Sales: Less than $500,000
Number Employees: 10-19
Parent Co: Mayer's Cider Mill
Type of Packaging: Consumer, Bulk

8566 Mayfair Sales
1100 Military Rd
Buffalo, NY 14217 716-877-0800
Fax: 716-877-0385 800-248-2881

Candy, gum, snacks
Director Of Marketing: Chris Tzetzo
Plant Manager: Steve Tzetzo
Estimated Sales: $ 50 - 100 Million
Number Employees: 100-249
Type of Packaging: Private Label, Bulk

8567 **Mayfield Dairy Farms**
P.O.Box 310
Athens, TN 37371-0310 423-744-9509
Fax: 423-745-9118 800-362-9546
rob-mayfield@deanfoods.com
www.mayfielddairy.com
Manufacturer of dairy products such as; ice cream, sherbert, cottage cheese, dip, sour cream, milk, whip cream and juices
President: C S Mayfield Jr
Number Employees: 500-999
Parent Co: Dean Foods
Type of Packaging: Consumer, Food Service
Other Locations:
Braselton GA

8568 **Mayfield Farms**
4810 Mayfield Rd
Caledon, ON L7C 0Z4
Canada 905-846-0506
Fax: 905-846-1650
Processor of apple products including processed slices, dices, dumplings, fibre powder and juice
Owner: Ken Speirs
Number Employees: 5-9
Type of Packaging: Consumer, Food Service

8569 **Mayorga Coffee**
15151 Southlawn Lane
Rockville, MD 20850 301-315-8093
Fax: 301-315-8094 877-526-3322
info@mayorgacoffee.com
www.mayorgacoffee.com
Coffee
President: Martin Mayorga
VP Finance/Administration: Lorena Herrada
VP Sales/Marketing: Jennifer Rogers
Human Resources Coordinator: Nattakan Sa-Nguanpuak
Operations Director: Roger Fransen
Estimated Sales: $8.4 Million
Number Employees: 65
Sq. footage: 12000

8570 **Maysville Milling Company**
P.O.Box 716
Maysville, NC 28555 910-743-3481
Manufacturer of feed and cornmeal
President: Edward Trott Sr
Estimated Sales: $2 Million
Number Employees: 7
Brands:
MAYCO

8571 **Maytag Dairy Farms**
2282 E 8th St N
Newton, IA 50208 641-792-1133
Fax: 641-792-1567 800-247-2458
www.maytagblue.com
Processor of cheeses including blue, cheddar, Swiss, edam, brick and cold pack
President: Myrna Ver Ploeg
VP Operations/Production Manager: Jim Stevens
Plant Supervisor: Robert Wrdzinski
Estimated Sales: $4669423
Number Employees: 20-49
Type of Packaging: Consumer

8572 **Mayway Corporation**
1338 Mandela Pkwy
Oakland, CA 94607 510-208-3113
Fax: 510-208-3069 800-262-9929
info@mayway.com www.mayway.com
Herbal health foods
President/CEO: Yvonne Lau
Estimated Sales: Below $ 5 Million
Number Employees: 20-49

8573 **Maywood International Sales**
PO Box 9292
Sante Fe, NM 87504 505-982-2700
Fax: 505-982-9780
www.maywoodinternational.com
Oilseed manufacturer
Sales: Jacques Brazy
Sales: Peter Connick

8574 **Mazelle's Cheesecakes Concoctions Creations**
PO Box 59345
9016 Garland Rd.
Dallas, TX 75218
US 214-328-9102
Fax: 214-328-5202 sales@mazelles.com
www.mazelles.com
Processor of cheesecakes and cheesecake petit fours vanilla,chocolate decadence,raspberry cassis,chocolate marble,turtle-praline chocolate chip,pumpkin,strawberries nad cream,keylime margarita,amaretto.and dessert bars.
CEO: Gina Roidopoulos
Estimated Sales: $ 3 - 5 Million
Number Employees: 10-19
Type of Packaging: Consumer, Food Service
Brands:
Mazelle's

8575 **Mazzetta Company**
1990 Saint Johns Ave Ste 100
Highland Park, IL 60035 847-433-1150
Fax: 847-433-8973 seamazz@mazzetta.com
www.mazzetta.com
The SeaMazz product line includes a wide variety of seafood and fish such as orange roughy fillets, whiting fillets, greenshell mussels, raw and cooked shrimp, lobster tails, Chilean sea bass fillets, squid and crab meat.
President: Thomas Mazzetta
Estimated Sales: $ 1 - 3 Million
Number Employees: 10-19

8576 **Mazzocco Vineyards**
P.O.Box 486
Healdsburg, CA 95448 707-433-9035
Fax: 707-431-2369 vino@mazzocco.com
www.mazzocco.com
Wines
President: Thomas Mazzocco
Sales/Marketing Manager: Ned Carton
Winemaker: Antoine Favero
Estimated Sales: $ 1-2.5 Million
Number Employees: 5-9

8577 **Mazzoli Coffee**
6812 15th Avenue
Brooklyn, NY 11219-6309 718-259-6194
Fax: 718-234-0928 info@mazzolicoffee.com
www.mazzolicoffee.com
Coffee
Estimated Sales: $ 5 - 10 Million
Number Employees: 5-9

8578 **(HQ)McAnally Enterprises**
32710 Reservoir Rd
Lakeview, CA 92567 951-928-1935
Fax: 951-928-1947 800-726-2002
Processor and exporter of cartoned, frozen and liquid eggs and egg products
President: Carlton Lofgren
Rep. (S.W.): Glenn Lemley
Vice President: Don Brown
Marketing Director: John Klien
Operations Manager: Tom McAnally
Production Manager: Don Brown
Number Employees: 100-249
Sq. footage: 20000
Type of Packaging: Food Service
Other Locations:
McAnally Enterprises
Phoenix AZ

8579 **McArthur Dairy**
240 NE 71st St
Miami, FL 33138 305-795-7700
Fax: 305-576-9203 www.mcarthurdairy.com
Manufacturer of grape and prune juice and dairy products including buttermilk, regular, chocolate, low-fat and skim milk
VP: Brad Abell
Estimated Sales: $50-100 Million
Number Employees: 250-499
Type of Packaging: Consumer, Food Service, Private Label, Bulk

8580 **McArthur Dairy**
6851 Ne 2nd Ave
Miami, FL 33138 305-795-7700
Fax: 305-576-9203 877-803-6565
www.deanfoods.com
Processor of orange juice, milk, cottage cheese and ice cream
Director: Nelson Ortiz
Vice President: James Hoover
Estimated Sales: $ 20-50 Million
Number Employees: 37
Parent Co: Dean Foods Company
Type of Packaging: Consumer, Food Service

8581 **McArthur Dairy**
3579 Work Dr
Fort Myers, FL 33916-7535 239-334-1114
Fax: 239-334-1791 www.mcarthurdairy.com
Dairy products
Manager: Ray Scribner
Estimated Sales: $ 5-10 Million
Number Employees: 20-49
Brands:
McArthur Dairy

8582 **McCadam Cheese Company**
P.O.Box 900
Chateaugay, NY 12920-0900 518-497-6644
Fax: 518-497-3297 info@mccadam.com
www.mccadam.com
Processor of a variety of cheeses including aged and waxed cheddars; flavored and reduced fat cheddars; muenster cheese; monterey jack cheese, and extra sharp cheddar cheese in addition to smoked cheeses.
Chairman: Carl Peterson
Chief Executive Officer: Paul Johnston
EVP/Finance & Administration: Margaret Bertolino
SVP/Information Services: Ralph Viscomi
SVP/Economics & Legislative Affairs: Robert Wellington
Director Interational Sales: Peter Gutierrez
Communications Director: Douglas DiMento
EVP/Chief Operating Officer: Richard Wellington
Plant Manager: Ron Davis
Estimated Sales: $ 10 - 20 Million
Number Employees: 100-249
Parent Co: Agri-Mark Inc

8583 **(HQ)McCain Foods Canada**
Brookfield Place
181 Bay Street, Suite 3600
Toronto, ON M5J 2T3
Canada 416-955-1700
866-622-2461
www.mccain.com
Processor of frozen foods including beans, broccoli, brussels sprouts, cauliflower, corn, French fried potatoes, prepared dinners and pizza; also, beverage concentrates.
President/CEO: Dirk Van de Put
Chief Financial Officer: David Sanchez
Chief Science & Technology Officer: Theo Lioutas
Chief Strategy & Business Dev. Officer: Karen Basian
Chief Communications Officer: Susan Rogers
Chief Supply Chain Officer: Rick Ciccone
Chief Human Resources Officer: Janice Wismer
Estimated Sales: CAN $6 Billion
Number Employees: 20000
Type of Packaging: Consumer, Food Service

8584 **McCain Foods USA**
1620 N 8th Street
PO Box 680
Colton, CA 92324
800-938-7799
www.mccainusa.com
Processor of frozen vegetables including cauliflower, okra, onions, peppers, potatoes, sweet potatoes and squash; also, frozen onion rings and apple products.
Parent Co: McCain Foods USA
Type of Packaging: Consumer, Food Service

8585 **McCain Foods USA**
319 Richardson Rd
PO Box 159
Easton, ME 04740-4056 207-488-2561
Fax: 207-488-2829 800-938-7799
www.mccainusa.com
Processor and exporter of frozen French fries, potato puffs and hash browns
Parent Co: McCain Foods USA
Type of Packaging: Consumer, Food Service, Private Label, Bulk

8586 **(HQ)McCain Foods USA**
2275 Cabot Dr
Lisle, IL 60532-3653 630-955-0400
800-938-7799
webmaster@mccainusa.com
www.mccainusa.com
Processor of frozen potato products including French fries, slices, dices, formed and private label brands. Also manufacturer of breaded and battered appetizers
Regional President/McCain Foods USA: Frank Van Schaayk
Corporate Communications: Dierdre Dickerson
Purchasing Director: Gary Plant
Estimated Sales: J
Number Employees: 4300
Parent Co: McCain Foods
Brands:
ANCHOR
BEER BUTTERED KING RINGS
BREADED PRETZARELLA STIX
BREW CITY
ELLIO'S
FRYER SAVER
GOLDEN CRISP
MCCAIN
MOORE'S
MOZZALUNA
MOZZAMIA
OLIVENOS
ORE-IDA
POPPERS
PRIMASANO CUBES
PROVAGO WHEELS
QUESO TRIANGOS
SANTA FE
SPICY TORTILLA JUMPIN JACKS
SUN STIX
WRAPPETIZERS

8587 **McCain Foods USA**
11 Gregg Street
Lodi, NJ 07644
800-938-7799
www.mccainusa.com
Manufacturer of frozen foods; french fries and other potato products, vegetables, desserts, pizzas, juices and beverages, oven meals, entrees and appetizers.
Brands:
Flavour Last
Mc Cain

8588 **McCain Foods USA**
801 Rockwell Ave
Fort Atkinson, WI 53538-2458 920-563-6625
Fax: 920-563-1394 800-938-7799
www.mccain.com
Frozen specialties
Manager: Steve Prater

8589 **McCain Foods USA**
555 N Hickory Farm Lane
Appleton, WI 54914 920-734-0672
Fax: 920-997-7609 800-938-7799
www.mccainusa.com
Manufacturers a variety of snack foods including cheese, onion, vegetable, stuffed olives, specialty snacks and pizza.
Parent Co: McCain Foods USA
Type of Packaging: Consumer, Food Service, Private Label, Bulk

8590 **McCain Foods USA**
100 Lee Street
Othello, WA 99344
800-938-7799
www.mccainusa.com
Distribution center for manufacturer that provides a wide range of potato products, beverages, juices, pizzas and desserts.
Parent Co: McCain Foods USA
Type of Packaging: Consumer, Food Service

8591 **McCain Foods USA**
100 West Coleman Street
Rice Lake, WI 54868
800-938-7799
www.mccainusa.com
Distribution center for manufacturer that provides a wide range of potato products, beverages, juices, pizzas and desserts.
Parent Co: McCain Foods USA
Type of Packaging: Consumer, Food Service

8592 **McCain Foods USA**
Highway 54 West & 110 Street
PO Box 10
Plover, WI 54467-0010 715-421-3400
Fax: 715-421-7617 800-938-7799
www.mccainusa.com
Distribution center for manufacturer that provides a wide range of potato products, beverages, juices, pizzas and desserts.
Parent Co: McCain Foods USA
Type of Packaging: Consumer, Food Service

8593 **McCain Foods USA**
218 W Highway 30
Burley, ID 83318-5002 208-678-9431
Fax: 208-678-6722 800-938-7799
www.mccainusa.com
Distribution center for manufacturer that provides a wide range of potato products, beverages, juices, pizzas and desserts.
President/CEO McCain Foods Limited: Dale Morrison
CEO/Mccain Foods USA: Frank Van Schaayk
Human Resources: Linda Langer
Vice President/Innovation: Charles Gitkin
Vice President/Marketing: Patrick Davis
Vice President Sales: Mike Sullivan
Purchasing Director: Gary Plant
Parent Co: McCain Foods USA
Type of Packaging: Consumer, Food Service

8594 **McCain Foods USA**
2629 N Broadwell Ave
Grand Island, NE 68803-2166 308-382-7770
Fax: 308-389-4481 800-938-7799
www.mccainusa.com
Distribution center for manufacturer that provides a wide range of potato products, beverages, juices, pizzas and desserts.
Parent Co: McCain Foods USA
Type of Packaging: Consumer, Food Service

8595 **McCall Farms**
6615 S Irby St
Effingham, SC 29541-3577 843-662-2223
Fax: 843-665-5234 800-277-2012
wswink@mccallfarms.com
www.mccallfarms.com
Processor of canned garbanzo, green and lima beans, collard greens, kale, spinach, okra, tomatoes, corn, peas, squash, succotash and peanuts
President: Henry Swink
Regional Sales Manager: Woody Swink
Sales Manager: David Wold
Director Engineering: Jerry Gulledge
Estimated Sales: $ 5-10 Million
Number Employees: 100-249
Type of Packaging: Consumer, Food Service
Brands:
Canned Southern Vegetables
Lord Chesterfield
Margret Holmes

8596 **McCartney Produce Company**
P.O.Box 219
Paris, TN 38242-219
Fax: 270-443-5943 800-522-2791
Fruit and vegetables
Manager: Jim Pierce
Manager: Jim Pierce
Estimated Sales: $ 10-20 Million
Number Employees: 5-9

8597 **McClancy Seasoning Company**
One Spice Road
Fort Mill, SC 29707 803-548-2366
Fax: 803-548-2379 800-843-1968
info@mcclancy.com www.mcclancy.com
Processor and exporter of spices, seasonings and dry food mixes including salad dressing, dips, breadings, batters, gravies, soups, sauces and meat marinades, snack food seasonings, nut and pretzel coatings, whole and ground spices;custom blending available.
President: F Reid Wilkerson Iii III
Director: Charlie Czagas
VP: Allen Davis
VP Sales: Chuck Wiley
Estimated Sales: $21188697
Number Employees: 100-249
Type of Packaging: Consumer, Food Service, Private Label, Bulk

8598 **McCleary**
239 Oak Grove Ave
South Beloit, IL 61080 815-389-3053
Fax: 815-389-9842 800-523-8644
mcclearyshr@mcclearys.com
www.mcclearys.com
Manufacturer and exporter of snack foods including tortilla chips, potato chips, corn chips, cheese curls, pretzels, party mix, caramel corn, popcorn, hulless popcorn, hot snacks and sweet snacks.
Founder: Eugene McCleary
President: Pat McCleary
VP/General Manager: Jerry Stokely
VP/Sales & Marketing: Randy Morrow
Estimated Sales: $ 50 - 100 Million
Number Employees: 100-249
Sq. footage: 65000
Type of Packaging: Consumer, Food Service, Private Label
Brands:
Cheese Twisters
Corn Chips Ahh's
Fire Ballz
MAC'S Copper Kettle
McCleary's
Pajeda's
Potato Blasts
Pretzel O's Pretzels

8599 **(HQ)McCleskey Mills**
P.O.Box 98
197 Rhodes St
Smithville, GA 31787-0098 229-846-2003
Fax: 229-846-4805 mcmills@surfsouth.com
www.mccleskymills.com
Manufacturer and exporter of shelled peanuts
President: Keith Chandler
Chairman/Ceo: Jerry Chandler
Estimated Sales: $210 Million
Number Employees: 50-99
Type of Packaging: Consumer, Bulk

8600 **McClure's Pickles LLC**
330 E Maple 20
Suite Q
Troy, MI 38083 245-837-9323
Fax: 866-796-9679 bob@mcclurespickles.com
www.mcclurespickles.com

8601 **McConnell's Fine Ice Cream**
815 E Canon Perdido St
Santa Barbara, CA 93103-3007 805-963-2958
Fax: 805-965-3764
jimboyoung@mcconnells.com
www.mcconnells.com
Processor and exporter of ice cream
Owner: Jimmy Young
VP: Jimmy Young
Estimated Sales: Below $ 5 Million
Number Employees: 5-9
Type of Packaging: Consumer, Food Service

8602 **(HQ)McCormick & Company**
18 Loveton Circle
Sparks, MD 21152 410-771-7301
Fax: 410-771-7462 800-632-5847
webmaster@mccormick.com
www.mccormick.com
Manufacture, markets and distributes spices, herbs, seasonings, specialty foods and flavors
Chairman/President/CEO: Alan Wilson
EVP/CFO: Gordon Stetz
VP/General Counsel: W Geoffrey Carpenter
President/McCormick International: Lawrence Kurzius
VP Human Relations: Cecile Perich
President/Industrial Foods Americas: Charles Langmead
Estimated Sales: $3.3 Billion
Number Employees: 7,500
Type of Packaging: Private Label, Bulk
Brands:
Armanino Farms
Arte De Dulce
Bag N' Season
Bag'n Season
Bits
Daregal
El Toro
Garden Fare
Golden Dipt
La Grille
McCormick
McCormick Foods & Spices

Mojave
Old Bay
Produce Partners
Quick Classic Sauces
Salad's Dips
Sierra
Spice Cargo
Supherb Farms
Zebbie's

8603 McCormick Distilling Company
1 Mc Cormick Ln
Weston, MO 64098-9558 816-640-2276
Fax: 816-640-3082 888-640-3082
www.mccormickdistilling.com
Alcoholic beverages
President: James Zargo
Vice Chairman: Mike Griesser
VP Sales: Donald Hammond
Estimated Sales: $ 20-50 Million
Number Employees: 100-249
Type of Packaging: Consumer, Private Label
Brands:
McCormick

8604 McCormick Industrial Flavor Solutions
18 Loveton Circle
Sparks, MD 21152-6000 410-771-7301
Fax: 410-527-8289 800-632-5847
www.mccormickflavor.com
McCormick Flavors supplies natural, natural and artificial, and artificial flavors for industrial formulation needs. Products are available in a variety of forms, including liquid, paste, and powder; coatings and condiments; flavors;spices and herbs; and seasonings.
Chairman, President & CEO: Alan Wilson
EVP & CFO: Gordon Stetz
VP, Human Relations: Cecile Perich
Parent Co: McCormick & Company Inc
Type of Packaging: Consumer, Food Service, Bulk
Brands:
CHEEZ-ALL FLAVORS
FLAVORCELL
FLAVORSPICE FRUIT AND SWEET
SAVORY SELECT FLAVORS

8605 McCormick SupHerb Farms
P.O.Box 610
Turlock, CA 95381-0610 209-633-3600
Fax: 209-633-3644 800-787-4372
custserv@supherbfarms.com
www.supherbfarms.com
Processors and marketers of culinary herbs and specialty products the selection of which includes fresh, frozen and freeze-dried varieties.
President: Mike Brem
EVP/Strategic Planning & CFO: Francis Contino
SVP/General Counsel & Secretary: Robert Skelton
VP/Human Relations: Cecile Perich
Parent Co: McCormick & Company Inc

8606 McCoy Matt Frontier International
362 Capistrano Avenue
Pismo Beach, CA 93449-1907 805-773-2994
Fax: 805-773-0378
President: Mat McCoy
Estimated Sales: Under $500,000
Number Employees: 1-4

8607 McCutcheon's Apple Products
13 S Wisner St
Frederick, MD 21701-5625 301-662-3261
Fax: 301-663-6217 800-888-7537
mrjelly@mccutcheons.com
www.mccutcheons.com
Products include apple juice, apple cider, fruit butters, preserves, jellies, juice sweetened fruit spreads, salad dressings, relishes, hot sauces and more.
President: Robert J Mc Cutcheon III
VP Sales: Vanessa Smith
Estimated Sales: $ 10 - 20 Million
Number Employees: 20-49
Sq. footage: 63000
Type of Packaging: Consumer, Private Label
Brands:
McCutcheons

8608 McDaniel Fruit Company
P.O.Box 2588
Fallbrook, CA 92088-2588 760-728-8438
Fax: 760-728-4898 camcdan@sbsglobal.net
www.mcdanielavocado.com
Processor, importer and exporter of avocados
Owner: Kay Ahrend
VP Sales/Marketing: Rankin McDaniel
General Sales Manager: Laurie Johnson
Secretary: Larry McDaniel
Estimated Sales: $9300000
Number Employees: 20-49
Sq. footage: 10000
Type of Packaging: Consumer, Food Service, Private Label, Bulk
Brands:
Linda-Vista

8609 McDowell Fine Meats 2
1719 E McDowell Rd
Phoenix, AZ 85006-3035 602-254-6022
Fax: 602-257-0296
Owner: Matthew Drass
Estimated Sales: $ .5 - 1 million
Number Employees: 1-4

8610 McDowell Valley Vineyards & Cellars
P.O.Box 449
Hopland, CA 95449-0449 707-744-1774
Fax: 707-744-1826
mcdowell@mcdowellsyrah.com
www.mcdowellsyrah.com
Wine
CEO: Bill Crawford
CEO: Gary Leonard
VP: Gary Leonard
Sales Director: Bernadette Byrne
Winemaker/Winegrower: William Crawford
Estimated Sales: $ 1-2.5 Million
Number Employees: 5-9
Brands:
McDowell

8611 McDuffies Bakery
9920 Main St
PO Box 427
Clarence, NY 14031-2043 716-759-8510
Fax: 716-759-6082 800-875-1598
info@mcduffies.com www.mcduffies.com
Shortbread cookies and biscotti
President: Dave Thomas
VP: Brian Thomas
Operations: Duston Peace
Estimated Sales: $2 Million
Number Employees: 20
Sq. footage: 10000
Type of Packaging: Food Service, Private Label

8612 McFadden Farm
16000 Powerhouse Rd
Potter Valley, CA 95469-8771
US 707-743-1122
Fax: 707-743-1126 800-544-8230
mcfaddenfarm@pacific.net
www.mcfaddenfarm.com
Processor and exporter of organic herbs including garlic braids and wild rice
Owner: Eugene Mc Fadden
Estimated Sales: $1.5 Million
Number Employees: 50
Sq. footage: 1000
Type of Packaging: Consumer, Food Service, Bulk

8613 McFarland Foods
PO Box 460
Riverton, UT 84065-0460 209-869-6611
Processor and exporter of chicken bacon and ground chicken and turkey; exporter of chicken bacon
President: Gary McFarland
Purchasing Manager: Mike Walker
Number Employees: 20-49
Sq. footage: 13000
Type of Packaging: Consumer, Food Service, Private Label, Bulk
Brands:
Ol' McFarlands

8614 McFarland Foods
PO Box 460
Riverton, UT 84065-0460 801-254-5009
Fax: 801-254-0432 800-441-9596
info@dsi1968.com www.mcfarlandsfoods.com
Chicken and turkey products
President: Stephen Mcfarland
CFO: Barbara McFarland
Quality Control: Justin McFarland
Sales Director: Thomas Mathias
Number Employees: 20-49
Number of Brands: 1
Number of Products: 25
Sq. footage: 12000
Type of Packaging: Consumer, Food Service, Private Label, Bulk

8615 McFarling Foods
333 W 14th St
Indianapolis, IN 46202 317-635-2633
Fax: 317-687-6844 www.mcfarling.com
Wholesaler/distributor of groceries, provisions/meats, frozen foods, produce and seafood; serving the food service market
Chairman of the Board: Donald McFarling
Vice President: R McFarling
VP Sales: G Clay
Purchasing Manager: Leonard McFarling
Estimated Sales: $78000000
Number Employees: 100-249
Sq. footage: 104000

8616 McGrath's Frozen Foods
1 Elizabeth Pl
Streator, IL 61364-1192 815-672-2654
Fax: 815-672-3474
Frozen food
Owner: Kevin Gaede
Estimated Sales: $ .5 - 1 million
Number Employees: 1-4

8617 McGraw Seafood
3113 Main St
Tracadie Sheila, NB E1X 1G5
Canada 506-395-3374
Fax: 506-395-2821
Processor of fresh and frozen crab, scallops, cod, smelt, mackerel, herring and lobster
General Manager: Paul Boudreau
CEO: Paul Boudreau
Marketing Director: Paul Boudreau
Number Employees: 100-249
Type of Packaging: Consumer, Food Service, Private Label, Bulk
Brands:
Mc Graw

8618 (HQ)McGregor Vineyard Winery
5503 Dutch St
Dundee, NY 14837-9746 607-292-3999
Fax: 607-292-6929 800-272-0192
info@mcgregorwinery.com
www.mcgregorwinery.com
Processor of premium vinifera wines including chardonnay, pinot noir, riesling and gewurztraminer
Owner: John Mc Gregor
Estimated Sales: $ 5 - 10 Million
Number Employees: 10-19
Type of Packaging: Consumer, Food Service

8619 McHenry Vineyard
330 11th Street
Davis, CA 95616-2010 530-756-3202
Fax: 530-756-3202 lmchenry@dcn.davis.ca.us
Wines
Partner: Henry McHenry
Partner: Linda McHenry
Operations Manager: Henry McHenry
Vineyard Manager: Linda McHenry
Estimated Sales: $45 k
Number Employees: 2
Type of Packaging: Private Label

8620 McIlhenny Company
Hwy 329
Avery Island, LA 70130-6037
US 504-523-7370
Fax: 504-596-6444 800-634-9599
WhatsCooking@TABASCO.com
www.tabasco.com
Processor of hot pepper flavors and ingredients
President: Paul Mc Ilhenny
CFO: Michael Terrell
Director Marketing: Billy Boswell
Estimated Sales: $5-10 Million
Number Employees: 200
Sq. footage: 100880
Parent Co: McIlhenny's Son Corporation
Type of Packaging: Bulk

Brands:
TABASCO® brand Chipotle Pepper Sauc
TABASCO® brand Garlic
Tabasco® Green Sauce Miniatures
Tabasco® Original Red Miniatures
Tabasco® brand Garlic Pepper Sauce
Tabasco® brand Habanero Pepper Sauc
Tabasco® brand Pepper Sauce
• TABASCO® Bloody Mary Mix – Extra

8621 **McIntosh's Ohio Valley Wines**
2033 Bethel New Hope Rd
Bethel, OH 45106-9691 937-379-1159
Fax: 973-379-1962
Wine
President: Edward Covert
Estimated Sales: $ 1-2.5 Million
Number Employees: 1-4

8622 **McJak Candy Company LLC**
1087 Branch Rd
Medina, OH 44256 330-722-3531
Fax: 330-723-4793 800-424-2942
ljohns@mcjakcandy.com www.mcjakcandy.com
Produces fudge and lollipops
President: Larry Johns
Estimated Sales: $ 3 - 5 Million
Number Employees: 10-19
Number of Products: 20
Type of Packaging: Consumer, Private Label, Bulk

8623 **(HQ)McKee Foods Corporation**
10260 McKee Road
PO Box 750
Collegedale, TN 37315-0750 423-238-7111
Fax: 423-238-7101 mail@littledebbie.com
www.mckeefoods.com
Manufacturer of cookies, crackers, snack and granola bars, snack cakes and cereal
President/CEO: Mike McKee
VP/CFO: Barry Patterson
Evp: Debbie McKee-Fowler
Communications/Public Relations Manager: Mike Gloekler
Estimated Sales: 1.20 Billion
Number Employees: 6000
Type of Packaging: Consumer, Food Service, Private Label
Other Locations:
McKee Foods
Gentry AR
Stuarts Draft VA
Kingman AZ
Chattanooga TN
Brands:
FIELDSTONE™ BAKERY
HEARTLAND®
LITTLE DEBBIE®
SUNBELT®

8624 **McKenna Brothers**
PO Box 70
Cardigan, PE C0A 1G0
Canada 902-583-2951
Fax: 902-583-2891
mckenna.bros@pei.sympatico.ca
www.mckennabrothers.co.uk
Processor and exporter of potato seeds and potatoes
Director: Peter McKenna
Director: Shawn McKenna
Director: Kevin McKenna
Number Employees: 20
Sq. footage: 30000
Type of Packaging: Consumer
Brands:
PEI

8625 **McKenzie of Vermont**
160 Flynn Ave
Burlington, VT 05401-5401 802-864-4585
Fax: 802-651-7335
www.mckenziecountryclassics.com
Processor, packer and wholesaler/distributor of sausage and smoked meat products
President: Ray Monkiewicz
VP Finance and Controller: Arliene Torre
CEO: Ray Mankiewiecz
Estimated Sales: $ 20 - 50 Million
Number Employees: 10-19
Sq. footage: 25000
Type of Packaging: Consumer, Food Service

8626 **McKinlay Vineyards**
7120 NE Earlwood Road
Newberg, OR 97132-7010 503-625-2534
Fax: 503-625-2534
Wines
Estimated Sales: $67,000
Number Employees: 1

8627 **McKnight Milling Company**
15 Cross 138
Hickory Ridge, AR 72347-9268 870-697-2504
Fax: 870-697-2525
Basmati rice
Owner: Deloss Mc Knight
Plant Manager: Walter Pierce
Estimated Sales: $2500000
Number Employees: 1-4
Sq. footage: 5760
Type of Packaging: Consumer, Food Service, Private Label, Bulk
Brands:
Cache River

8628 **McLane Foods**
2512 E Magnolia St
Phoenix, AZ 85034-6908 602-275-5509
www.allstars.marketfarefoods.com/contact.htm
Processor and exporter of frozen sandwiches, burritos and hot dog sauce
President: Al Carfora
Controller: Nolin Shaw
CFO: Todd Monsen
Estimated Sales: $ 5 - 10 Million
Number Employees: 5-9
Parent Co: Market Fair
Type of Packaging: Food Service, Private Label
Brands:
Casa Buena
Colonial
Deli Shoppe
Sanditos
Smileys
Sonritos

8629 **McLane's Meats**
5710 56 Ave
Wetaskiwin, AB T9A 2Y9
Canada 780-352-4321
Fax: 780-352-8522
www.shop-alberta.com/wetaskiwin/mclanes-meats.htm
Processor of beef and pork sausage and wild game including deer, elk and moose; custom slaughtering services available
Owner: Robin McLane
Estimated Sales: C
Number Employees: 10-19
Type of Packaging: Private Label

8630 **McLaughlin Oil Company**
3750 E Livingston Ave
Columbus, OH 43227-2246 614-231-2518
Fax: 614-231-7431 www.mcglaughlinoil.com
Oils, flavored and pure
Owner: Steve Theodor
Estimated Sales: $ 5-10 Million
Number Employees: 10-19
Brands:
Petrol

8631 **McLaughlin Seafood**
728 Main St
Bangor, ME 04401-6810 207-942-7811
Fax: 207-947-9176 800-222-9107
kim@mclaughlinseafood.com
www.mclaughlinseafood.com
Products include seafood in addition to cookbooks, clothing and kitchenware.
Owner: Reid Mc Laughlin
Estimated Sales: $300,000-500,000
Number Employees: 1-4

8632 **McLemore's Abattoir**
1912 Center Dr
Vidalia, GA 30474-9317 912-537-4476
Processor of beef and pork
Owner: Gene Mc Lemore
Estimated Sales: $1300000
Number Employees: 10-19
Type of Packaging: Consumer

8633 **McNasby's Seafood Market**
723 2nd Street
Annapolis, MD 21403-3323 410-295-9022
Fax: 410-280-3707
Seafood

8634 **McNeil Nutritionals**
7050 Camp Hill Rd
Fort Washington, PA 19034 215-273-7000
Fax: 908-874-1120 www.splenda.com
Manufacturer of artificial sweetners
President: Peter Luther
Vice President: Sheila Bergey
Estimated Sales: $10-20 Million
Parent Co: Johnson & Johnson

8635 **McNeil Specialty Products Company**
PO Box 2400
501 George St.
New Brunswick, NJ 08903-2400
US 732-524-3799
Fax: 732-524-3303
artifical sweetners.such as sucralose.
President: Stephen Fanning
Director Sales (North America): Jim Thornton
Director International Sales: Joseph Zannoni
Estimated Sales: $10-25million
Number Employees: 20-49
Parent Co: Johnson & Johnson

8636 **McNeill's Brewery**
90 Elliot St
Brattleboro, VT 05301-3269 802-254-2553
Fax: 802-257-1167 www.mcneillsbrewery.com
Processor of beer, ale, stout, lager and porter
Owner: Holiday Mc Neill
Estimated Sales: Below $ 5 Million
Number Employees: 10-19
Type of Packaging: Consumer, Food Service
Brands:
Bucksnort Barleywine
McNeill's Alle Tage
McNeill's Champ Ale
McNeill's Duck's Bre
McNeill's Extra Spec
McNeill's Firehouse
McNeill's Imperial S
McNeill's Kolsch
McNeill's Oatmeal St
McNeill's Old Ringwo
McNeill's Pulman's P
McNeill's Ruby Ale
McNeill's Ruby Ale
McNeill's Summer IPA
McNeill's Wassail
McNeill's Yukon Gold
Slopbucket Brown

8637 **(HQ)McRedmond Brothers**
P.O.Box 100902
Nashville, TN 37224 615-361-8997
Fax: 615-361-5645
Processor of meat and blood meal
Owner: Stephen Mc Redmond
VP: Ellen Kade
Estimated Sales: $570000
Number Employees: 5-9
Type of Packaging: Consumer, Bulk

8638 **McSteven's, Inc**
5600 NE 88th St
Vancouver, WA 98665 360-944-5788
Fax: 360-944-1302 800-547-2803
sales@mcstevens.com www.mcstevens.com
Processor of beverage mixes including white chocolate, regular and sugar-free cocoa, lemonade, cappuccino, chai, and apple cider; exporter of cocoa mixes
Owner: Brent Houston
VP Marketing: Dave Demsky
VP Operations: Brent Huston
Estimated Sales: $500,000-$1 Million
Number Employees: 20-49
Type of Packaging: Consumer, Food Service, Private Label, Bulk

8639 **McTavish Company**
10234 NE Glisan St
Portland, OR 97220-4061 503-253-9394
Fax: 503-254-6616 800-256-9844
info@mctavish.biz
www.mctavishshortbread.com/

Processor of shortbread cookies
Co-Owner: Denise Pratt
Co-Owner: Bill Pratt
Estimated Sales: Less than $500,000
Number Employees: 10-19
Type of Packaging: Consumer, Food Service, Bulk
Brands:
McTavish

8640 **McIlhenny Company**
601 Poydras St # 1815
New Orleans, LA 70130-6028 504-523-7370
Fax: 504-596-6444 whatscooking@tabasco.com
www.tabasco.com
Manufacturer and exporter of hot, jalapeno and pepper sauces; also, Bloody Mary cocktail mixes
President: Paul Mc Ilhenny
CFO: Michael Terrell
VP Corporate Marketing: Martin Manion
Estimated Sales: $ 5 - 10 Million
Number Employees: 5-9
Sq. footage: 170300
Type of Packaging: Consumer, Food Service, Private Label, Bulk
Brands:
Tabasco

8641 **Mclure's Honey & Maple Products**
46 N Littleton Rd
Littleton, NH 03561-3814 603-444-6246
Fax: 603-444-6659 info@mclures.com
www.mclures.com
Processor of pure honey and maple syrup
Manager: Gordon Hartford
Number Employees: 20-49
Parent Co: Dutch Gold Honey

8642 **Mead Containboard**
1100 Circle 75 Parkway SE
Suite 500
Atlanta, GA 30339-3079 770-952-7455
Fax: 770-644-2384
Packaging supplies, corrugated boxes
President: Mike Snowball

8643 **Mead Containerboard**
100 SW South Avenue
Blue Springs, MO 64014-3034 501-782-6091
Fax: 501-783-6003

8644 **Mead Johnson Nutritional**
725 E Main Ave
Zeeland, MI 49464 616-748-7100
Fax: 616-748-7133 www.meadjohnson.com
Processor of evaporated milk
Estimated Sales: $ 10 - 20 Million
Number Employees: 10-19
Parent Co: Bristol-Myers Squibb Company
Type of Packaging: Consumer

8645 **Mead Johnson PediatricsNutritional Group**
2400 W Lloyd Expy
Evansville, IN 47712 812-429-5000
Fax: 812-429-7714 www.meadjohnson.com
nutritional brands and products for infants and children
President/CEO: Stephen Golsby
SVP/CFO: Peter Leemputte
VP/Controller: Stanley Burhans
SVP Global R&D: Dirk Hondmann
SVP Human Resources: Lynn Clark
Estimated Sales: K
Number Employees: 6000
Parent Co: Bristol-Myers Squibb Company
Type of Packaging: Consumer
Brands:
Boost
Enfamil
Lactofree
Nutramigen
Pregestimil
Prosobee

8646 **Meadow Brook Dairy**
2365 Buffalo Rd
Erie, PA 16510 814-899-3191
Fax: 814-899-9152 800-352-4010
www.meadowbrookdairy.com
Processor of milk including whole, skim, 1% and 2%
Marketing Director: Marty Schwartz
VP Sales/Marketing: Joseph Martin
Plant Manager: Rhett Flanders
Number Employees: 100-249
Parent Co: Dean Foods Company
Type of Packaging: Consumer, Food Service
Brands:
FlavorTight
Milk Chugs
Swiss Premium Drinks

8647 **Meadow Gold Dairies**
925 Cedar Street
Honolulu, HI 96814 808-949-6161
Fax: 808-944-5901 800-362-8531
joni_marcello@deanfoods.com
www.meadowgold.com
Processor of cottage cheese, yogurt, sour cream, buttermilk, milk, ice cream, ice cream novelties and juices including orange, guava, passion fruit, etc
President/General Manager: Glen Muranaka
Parent Co: Southern Foods Group
Type of Packaging: Consumer, Food Service

8648 **Meadow Gold Dairies**
1325 W Oxford Avenue
Englewood, CO 80110
Fax: 303-789-1718 800-525-3289
randy_kaufman@deanfoods.com
www.meadowgold.com
Distributors-dairy products including butter, ice cream, milk, cheese and yogurt
Parent Co: Southern Foods Group
Type of Packaging: Consumer, Bulk

8649 **Meadow Gold Dairies**
215 N Denver
Tulsa, OK 74103 918-587-2471
Fax: 918-582-4605 800-742-7349
dan_monroe@deanfoods.com
www.meadowgold.com
Processor of milk, cottage cheese, juice and ice cream mix
General Manager: Bob Lake
Sales/Marketing Executive: Bill Witt
Plant Manager: Bill Fralick
Purchasing Agent: Rick Rodney
Sq. footage: 85000
Parent Co: Southern Foods Group
Type of Packaging: Consumer, Food Service, Private Label, Bulk

8650 **(HQ)Meadow Gold Dairies**
1301 W Bannock St
Boise, ID 83707 208-343-3671
Fax: 208-345-7697 soverton@meadowgold.com
www.meadowgold.com
Processor of dairy products including milk, sour cream, cottage cheese, cream cheese, yogurt, butter solid & quarters, flavored ice cream, flavored sherbert and fruit drinks.
General Manager: Ralph Hallquist
Quality Control: Steve Overton
Sales: Craig Lund
Production: Chris Cappl
Estimated Sales: $100+ Million
Number Employees: 100-249
Parent Co: Southern Foods Group
Type of Packaging: Consumer, Food Service, Private Label, Bulk
Brands:
MEADOW GOLD
PRIVATE LABELS
TAMPICO
VIVA

8651 **Meadow Gold Dairies**
850 South State
Orem, UT 84058 801-225-3660
Fax: 801-224-9205 matt_evan@deanfoods.com
www.meadowgold.com
Fluid milk, cream, sour cream and related products
Parent Co: Southern Foods Group
Brands:
Meadow Gold
Viva

8652 **Meadowbrook Farm**
2338 Hermany Avenue
Bronx, NY 10473-1198 718-828-6400
Fax: 718-828-8110
Dairy products
Manager: Phil Carlson
Estimated Sales: $ 2.5-5 Million
Number Employees: 50-99
Brands:
Meadowbrook

8653 **Meadows Country Products**
811 Scotch Valley Road
Hollidaysburg, PA 16648-9693 814-693-9714
Fax: 814-693-4625 888-499-1001
jim@meadowscountryproducts.com
www.meadowscountryproducts.com
Refrigerated desserts, deli salads
President: James Meadows
Owner: Margie Meadows
Secretary/Treasurer: Margie Meadows
Quality Assurance/Plant Manger: Todd Hill
General Manager: Jon Thayer
Sales Manager: Norm Tucker
Office Manager: Eileen Snyder
Operations Manager: Jeff Meadows
Purchasing Director: Mike Ricker
Estimated Sales: Below $ 5 Million
Number Employees: 15
Number of Brands: 1
Number of Products: 60
Sq. footage: 12000
Type of Packaging: Food Service, Private Label, Bulk
Brands:
MEADOWS COUNTRY PRODUCTS

8654 **Meadowvale**
109 Beaver St
Yorkville, IL 60560 630-553-0202
Fax: 630-553-0262 800-953-0201
Wlsn75@aol.com www.meadowvale-inc.com
Processor of ice cream, shake and soft serve mixes
President: Steve Steinwart
Sales Executive: Jason Leslie
Plant Manager: Thomas Schuch
Estimated Sales: $3 Million
Number Employees: 20
Sq. footage: 15000
Type of Packaging: Consumer
Brands:
Dairy Queen

8655 **Meal Mart**
5620 59th St
Maspeth, NY 11378 718-894-2000
Fax: 718-326-4642 800-245-5620
www.mealmart.com
Processor of kosher fresh and frozen meat products, entrees and deli meats; private label and co-packing services available
President: Mendel Weinstock
Vice President: Marcus Bergman
Manager: Shlomo Halberstam
Research & Development: Udi Basis
Purchasing Manager: Zeer Weinstock
Estimated Sales: $ 10-20 Million
Number Employees: 25
Sq. footage: 150000
Parent Co: Alle Processing
Type of Packaging: Consumer, Food Service, Private Label, Bulk
Brands:
Meal Mart
Mou Cuisine
New York Kosher Deli

8656 **Meat & Fish Fellas**
5036 N 54th Ave Ste 7
Glendale, AZ 85301 623-931-6190
Fax: 623-931-2960
Meat and seafood
Partner: J Tarbell
Partner: Marty Menter
Partner: Inyol Kim
Estimated Sales: $ 3 - 5 Million
Number Employees: 20-49

8657 **Meat Center**
3035 Fm 822
Edna, TX 77957 361-782-3776
Meat packer
Owner: Eli Salinas
Estimated Sales: $ .5 - 1 million
Number Employees: 5-9
Type of Packaging: Consumer, Bulk

8658 **Meat Corral Company**
3695 Thompson Bridge Rd
Gainesville, GA 30506 770-536-9188
Fax: 918-622-8003
Meats
President: Richard Webb
Estimated Sales: $ 3 - 5 Million
Number Employees: 5-9

8659 **Meat-O-Mat Corporation**
592 Pacific St Ste B
Brooklyn, NY 11217 718-965-7250
Fax: 718-832-1027
Processor and exporter of frozen portion control meats including hamburger, beef, breaded chicken, breaded veal, turkey and ostrich patties; also, full line of Hispanic products including beef patties, taco products and soffrito
President: Ronald Fatato
General Manager: Tony Quaranta
VP: Louis Fatato
VP Sales/Director Marketing: Freddy Refino
Estimated Sales: $ 20 - 50 Million
Number Employees: 10-19
Type of Packaging: Consumer, Food Service, Bulk

8660 **Meatco Sales**
5315 54th Street
Mirror, AB T0B 3L0
Canada 403-788-2292
Fax: 403-788-2294 www.meatcosales.com
Processor of fresh and frozen beef, pork, wild game and sausage
Manager: Chris Pfisterer
Manager: Steven Pfisterer
Owner: Herman Pfisterer
Number Employees: 1-4
Type of Packaging: Consumer, Food Service, Private Label, Bulk

8661 **Meating Place**
185 Grant St
Buffalo, NY 14213 716-885-3623
Fax: 716-885-6328 www.meatingplace.com
Processor of meat products including pork sausage and beef patties
President: Vincent Lorigo
Estimated Sales: $4000000
Number Employees: 20-49
Type of Packaging: Consumer, Food Service

8662 **Meatland Packers**
3326 15th Avenue SW
Medicine Hat, AB T1B 3W5
Canada 403-528-4321
Fax: 403-529-5986
Processor of fresh and frozen beef, pork, lamb and wild game including elk, moose and deer
President: Frank Noel
Type of Packaging: Consumer, Food Service, Private Label, Bulk

8663 **Medallion Foods**
3636 Medallion Ave
Newport, AR 72112 870-523-3500
Fax: 870-523-4417 www.medallion-foods.com
Manufacturer of tortilla chips, cheese puffs and extruded corn snacks
President: Rusty Karschner
Number Employees: 100-249
Parent Co: Ralcorp Holdings
Type of Packaging: Consumer

8664 **Medallion Intl.**
233 W Parkway
Pompton Plains, NJ 7444 973-616-3401
Fax: 973-616-3405
Manufacturer of Flavors: natural and artificial;edible and essential oils
President: Michael Boudjouk
Director Sales/Marketing: Paula Boudjouk
Plant Manager: Gwen Kenyon
Estimated Sales: $2 Million
Number Employees: 15
Type of Packaging: Consumer, Food Service, Private Label, Bulk

8665 **Medeiros Farms**
P.O. Box 102
Kalaheo, HI 96741 808-332-8211
Fax: 808-332-8211
Processor of poultry, eggs, beef and sausage
President: Bernard M Medeiros
VP/Secretary: Natalie Silve
Estimated Sales: $ 10 - 20 Million
Number Employees: 10-19
Type of Packaging: Consumer

8666 **Meditalia**
P.O.Box 1393
New York, NY 10113-1393 212-616-3006
Fax: 212-616-3005 info@peaceworks.net
www.peaceworks.net
Dairy and egg-free jarred sauces
Founder/CEO: Daniel Lubetzky
VP/New Product Development & Marketing: Sasha Hare
VP/Sales: Rami Leshem
VP/Operations: Doris Rivera

8667 **Mediterranean Delights**
P.O.Box 214
Contoocook, NH 03229-214
Fax: 802-869-3559 800-347-5850
info@mediterraneandelights.com
www.mediterraneandelights.com
All natural and certified organic manufacturer of hummus, dips, mediterranean fruit spreads and salads.
President: Joan Day
CEO: Joan Day
Vice President: Nicole Day
Quality Control: David Taclof
Sales: Deanna Wilbur
Plant Manager: David Taclof
Estimated Sales: $ 5 - 10 Million
Number Employees: 20-49
Number of Brands: 4
Number of Products: 33

8668 **Mediterranean Gyros Products**
1102 38th Ave
Long Island City, NY 11101 718-786-3399
Fax: 718-786-8518
Wholesaler/distributor of Greek specialty items; processor of pita bread
President: Vasilios Memmos
Estimated Sales: $9000000
Number Employees: 20-49

8669 **Mediterranean Pita Bakery**
9006 132 Avenue NW
Edmonton, AB T5E 0Y2
Canada 780-476-6666
Processor of pita bread
Manager: Ahmed Hagar
Number Employees: 5-9
Type of Packaging: Consumer, Food Service

8670 **Meduri Farms Inc.**
P.O.Box 636
Dallas, OR 97338 503-623-0308
Fax: 503-623-0726 mzobel@diversifiedfood.com
www.medurifarms.com
Processor, importer and exporter of dried cherries, blueberries and strawberries; also, infused cherries with raspberry juice
President: Joe Meduri
Sales: Mike Zobel
Estimated Sales: $36 Million
Number Employees: 500
Parent Co: Meduri Farms
Type of Packaging: Food Service, Private Label, Bulk
Brands:
Razzcherries

8671 **Meeker Vineyard**
5377 Dry Creek Rd
Healdsburg, CA 95448 707-431-2148
Fax: 707-431-2549 charlie@meekerwine.com
www.meekerwine.com
Wines the selection of which includes Chardonnay, Dry Rose, Zinfandel, Petite Sirah, Cabernet Sauvignon and Merlot, in addition to others.
President: Charles Meeker
VP Marketing/Operations: John Burtner
Estimated Sales: Less than $500,000
Number Employees: 1-4

8672 **Meelunie America**
26105 Orchard Lake Rd Ste 210
Farmington Hills, MI 48334 248-473-2100
Fax: 248-473-2114 info@meelunie-america.com
www.meelunie.com
Starch products: potatos, corn and wheat
Owner: William Lauer
Estimated Sales: $ 3 - 5 Million
Number Employees: 1-4

8673 **Mega Pro International**
251 Hilton Dr Ste 100
St George, UT 84770 435-673-1001
Fax: 435-673-1007 800-541-9469
info@mega-pro.com www.mega-pro.com
Processor, importer and exporter of nutritional supplements including vitamins for weight gain and loss
President: Dave Smith
Estimated Sales: $1800000
Number Employees: 20-49

8674 **Mehaffie Pies**
3013 Linden Ave
Dayton, OH 45410 937-253-1163
Fax: 937-254-4977
Processor of cheesecake, fresh and frozen pies
President: Robert Columbus
Co-Owner: Jim Columbus
Sales: Mark Berry
Estimated Sales: $500,000-$1 Million
Number Employees: 1-4
Sq. footage: 4000
Type of Packaging: Consumer, Food Service, Private Label, Bulk

8675 **Mei Shun Tofu Products Company**
523 W 26th St
Chicago, IL 60616 312-842-7000
Fax: 312-791-9429
Canner and exporter of tofu
Owner: Yim Sung
Estimated Sales: Less than $500,000
Number Employees: 5-9
Type of Packaging: Consumer, Food Service, Private Label, Bulk

8676 **Meier's Wine Cellars**
6955 Plainfield Rd
Cincinnati, OH 45236 513-891-2900
Fax: 513-891-6370 800-346-2941
info@meierswinecellars.com
www.meierswinecellars.com
Processor of fruit juices and wine
President: Edward Moulton
VP: Jack Lucia
Marketing Director: Lynn Lubin
Estimated Sales: $69500000
Number Employees: 20-49
Parent Co: Paramount Distillers
Type of Packaging: Consumer

8677 **Meiji**
360 S Belmont Street
York, PA 17404
kvlanzy@stauffers.net
www.stauffers.net

8678 **Meister Cheese Company**
960 E Nebraska St
Muscoda, WI 53573 608-739-3134
Fax: 608-739-4348 800-634-7837
grandpa@meistercheese.com
www.meistercheese.com
Cheese
President: Scott Meister
Partner: Vicki Thingbold
Partner: Dan Meister
Sales/Marketing: Dan Meister
Estimated Sales: $ 5-10 Million
Number Employees: 20-49
Type of Packaging: Private Label

8679 **(HQ)Mel-O-Cream Donuts International**
5456 International Pkwy
Springfield, IL 62711 217-483-7272
Fax: 217-483-7744 www.mel-o-cream.com
Donuts, both frozen pre-formed dough and frozen pre-fried
President: Kelly A Grant Jr
CFO: Andrew Williams
VP: Andy Williams
Research & Development: Jim Eck, Jr.
Sales Director: Charlie Lumsdon
Operations Manager: David Waltrip
Production Manager: Dan Alewelt
Estimated Sales: $ 10-20 Million
Number Employees: 50-99
Number of Brands: 1

Number of Products: 200+
Sq. footage: 65000
Type of Packaging: Food Service, Bulk
Brands:
Mel-O-Cream

8680 **Melchers Flavors of America**
5600 W Raymond Street
Indianapolis, IN 46241-4343 513-858-6300
Fax: 513-858-3110 800-235-2867
sales@melchersflavors.com
www.melchersflavors.com
Food flavorings; including kosher, extracts, syrups and drink mixes
President: Hellmuth Starnitzkey
COO/VP: Wolfgang Boehmer
Purchasing Agent: Claudia Slaughter
Purchasing Manager: Kellie Hall
Estimated Sales: $ 5-9.9 Million
Number Employees: 20
Type of Packaging: Food Service, Bulk

8681 **Mele-Koi Farms**
P.O.Box 2987
Newport Beach, CA 92659 949-660-9000
Fax: 949-660-9000
Manufacturer and exporter of powdered tropical drink mixes
Owner: Lloyd L Aubert Jr Jr
Estimated Sales: $400,000
Number Employees: 1-4
Number of Brands: 1
Number of Products: 1
Type of Packaging: Consumer
Brands:
MELE-KOI HAWAIIAN COCONUT SNOW

8682 **Meleddy Cherry Plant**
1952 Shiloh Rd
Sturgeon Bay, WI 54235 920-743-2858
Frozen red tart cherries
President: Melvin Selvick
VP: Eddy Selvick
Estimated Sales: $ 5-10 Million
Number Employees: 20-49

8683 **Melissa's**
Po Box 21127
Los Angeles, CA 90021 323-588-0151
Fax: 323-588-9774 800-588-0151
hotline@melissas.com www.melissas.com
Fruits and vegetables
President/CEO: Joe Hernandez
CFO: Bill Schneider
Marketing: Lori Hirai
Plant Manager: Mike Stephens
Estimated Sales: $ 10-100 Million
Number Employees: 100-249
Sq. footage: 100000
Brands:
Don Enrique
Jo San
Melissas

8684 **Melitta**
13925 58th St N
Clearwater, FL 33760-3721 727-535-2111
Fax: 727-535-7376
consumerrelations@melitta.com
www.melitta.com
Processor, importer and exporter of coffee; also, coffee machines and filters
CEO: Marty Miller
CFO: Fred Lueck
CEO: Marty Miller
Marketing: Chris Hillman
Sales: Ed Mitchell
Public Relations: Donna Gray
Operations: Jeff Bridges
Plant Manager: Matthias Bloedorn
Estimated Sales: $ 50 - 100 Million
Number Employees: 100-249
Parent Co: Melitta North America
Type of Packaging: Consumer, Food Service
Brands:
Melitta

8685 **Mello's North End Manufacturings**
63 N Court St
Fall River, MA 02720-2755 508-673-2320
Fax: 508-675-0893 800-673-2320
info@melloschourico.com www.mellos.net
Processor and exporter of sausage patties, links and pork
Owner: Eduardo Rego
Sales Manager: Diane Rego
Estimated Sales: $500,000-$1 Million
Number Employees: 1-4
Type of Packaging: Consumer, Food Service, Bulk

8686 **Melville Candy Company**
70 Finnell Dr
Unit 16
Weymouth, MA 2188 781-331-2005
Fax: 800-466-0516 jmelville8878@aol.com
www.melvillecandycompany.com
gourmet hard candy lollipops
President/Owner: Gary Melville
CFO: Debra Katz
Marketing: Joe Melville
Manufacturing Staff: Liz Mazzilli
Number Employees: 22

8687 **Memba**
729 Loomis Trail Rd
Lynden, WA 98264-9111 360-354-7708
Fax: 360-354-3906 monte@maberrys.com
www.maberrys.com
Processor of fresh and frozen blueberries, strawberries and raspberries
President: Curt Maberry
Estimated Sales: $ 2.5-5 Million
Number Employees: 20-49
Type of Packaging: Private Label, Bulk

8688 **Mememe Inc**
1470 Birchmont Road
Toronto, ON M1P 2G1 416-972-0973
Fax: 416-972-9592 marcy@marcys.tv
www.marcys.tv
Organic/natural, other baked goods, other condiments, pudding.
Marketing: Marcy Mihalcheon

8689 **Mendocino Brewing Company**
1601 Airport Rd
Ukiah, CA 95482 707-463-2087
Fax: 797-744-1910 questions@mendobrew.com
www.mendobrew.com
Processor of beer, stout, ale and lager
President: Yashpal Singha
CFO: Jerome Merchant
CEO: Vijay Mallya
Marketing Director: Michael Lovett
Estimated Sales: $4300000
Number Employees: 50-99
Sq. footage: 65000
Type of Packaging: Consumer, Food Service
Brands:
Black Hawk
Blackhawk Stout
Blue Heron
Blue Heron Pale Ale
Eye of the Hawk
Eye of the Hawk Select Ale
Peregrine Golden
Peregrine Pale Ale
Red Tail
Red Tail Ale
Springtide Ale
Yuletide Porter

8690 **Mendocino Mustard**
1260 N Main St Ste 11
Fort Bragg, CA 95437 707-964-2250
Fax: 707-964-0525 800-964-2270
info@mendocinomustard.com
mendocinomustard.com
Processor of specialty mustards including hot/sweet and spicy seeded with ale. Foods available in fat-free and sodium-free
President: Devora Rossman
Production Manager: Kathy Silva
Estimated Sales: $255000
Number Employees: 1-4
Number of Brands: 1
Number of Products: 2
Sq. footage: 1600
Type of Packaging: Consumer, Food Service
Brands:
Mendocino
Seeds & Suds

8691 **Menemsha Fish Market**
P.O.Box 406
Chilmark, MA 02535 508-645-2282
Fax: 508-645-9783
www.menemshafishmarket.com
Processor of fresh and prepared seafood; fish, crabs, scallops and shellfish
Owner: Stanley Larsen
Estimated Sales: $300,000-500,000
Number Employees: 1-4
Type of Packaging: Consumer, Food Service, Private Label, Bulk
Brands:
Menemsha Bites
Poole's

8692 **Menghini Winery**
P.O.Box 1359
Julian, CA 92036 760-765-2072
Fax: 760-765-2072
Wines
President: Michael Menghini
Estimated Sales: Less than $300,000
Number Employees: 1-4
Type of Packaging: Private Label
Brands:
Menghini

8693 **Mennel Milling Company**
P.O.Box 806
Fostoria, OH 44830 419-435-8151
Fax: 419-436-5150 800-688-8151
info@mennel.com www.mennel.com
Processor of flour used in cake mixes, cookies, snack crackers, breadings, batters, gravies, soups, ice cream cones, pretzels and oriental noodles.
President: Donald Mennel
Vice President: Lyle Lahman
CFO: Mark Hall
Quality Control: Jan Levenhagen
VP Sales: Michael Kraus
Operations/Quality Control: Robert Reid
Plant Manager: Joel Hoffa
Estimated Sales: Below $ 5 Million
Number Employees: 100-249
Type of Packaging: Bulk

8694 **(HQ)Mennel Milling Company**
P.O.Box 806
Fostoria, OH 44830 419-435-8151
Fax: 419-436-5150 info@mennel.com
www.mennel.com
Manufacturer of milling soft, hard, spring and specialty wheat flours
President/CEO: Donald Mennel
Plant Manager: Frank Herbes
Estimated Sales: $24 Million
Number Employees: 100-249
Type of Packaging: Consumer, Private Label, Bulk

8695 **Mennel Milling Company**
128 W Crocker Street
Fostoria, OH 44830 419-435-8151
Fax: 419-435-8737 mmiller@mennel.com
www.mennel.com
Processor of flour including soft wheat, pastry and cake
VP: Rick Longbrake
VP R&D/Quality Assurance: C J Lin
Quality Assurance Manager: Jim Schuh
VP Marketing: Bill Cartwright
VP Sales: Dave Braun
Operations Executive: Jan Levenhagen
Plant Manager: Scott Flick
Estimated Sales: $5000000
Number Employees: 200
Sq. footage: 5000
Type of Packaging: Bulk

8696 **Mental Process**
1075 Zonolite Road NE
Atlanta, GA 30306-2013 404-875-7440
Processor and exporter of dry roasted pumpkin seed snacks
President: Scott Bradford
Estimated Sales: Under $500,000
Number Employees: 1-4
Type of Packaging: Consumer, Food Service, Private Label
Brands:
Pumpkorn

8697 **Meramec Vineyards**
600 State Route B
Saint James, MO 65559 573-265-7847
Fax: 573-265-3453 877-216-9463
mervine@fignet.com
www.meramecvineyards.com
Processor of natural grape juice
President: P Meagher
Estimated Sales: $ 3 - 5 Million
Number Employees: 5-9
Type of Packaging: Consumer, Food Service
Brands:
Meramec

8698 **Merbs Candies**
4000 S Grand Blvd
Saint Louis, MO 63118 314-832-7117
Fax: 314-832-0146 www.merbscandy.com
Processor of candy including chocolates and novelties.
President: Terry Bearden
Estimated Sales: $500,000-$1 Million
Number Employees: 10-19
Type of Packaging: Consumer

8699 **Mercado Latino**
245 Baldwin Park Blvd
City of Industry, CA 91746 626-333-6862
Fax: 626-333-5080
Processor of cookies, beans, candy, coconut milk, canned seafood, hominy, corn oil, chile peppers, sauces, spices, charcoal briquettes, brooms and cleaners; importer and exporter of chiles, spices and sauces; wholesaler/distributor ofMexican specialty foods
President: Graciliano Rodriguez
CFO: Jorge Rodriguez
VP/General Manager: Al Mena
Sr. VP/Marketing: Richard Rodriguez
Estimated Sales: $123600000
Number Employees: 100-249
Sq. footage: 225
Brands:
Brillasol
Faraon
Milpas
Ola Blanca
Payaso
Siesta
Sol-Mex
Sun Sun

8700 **Mercantile Food Company**
PO Box S
Philmont, NY 12565 518-672-0190
Fax: 518-672-0198 info@mercantilefood.com
Orgainic foods
President and CEO: Michael Marcolla
CFO/R&D/VP Operations: John Whitmer
VP Marketing: Brian Andrew
Estimated Sales: $ 10-100 Million
Number Employees: 10
Type of Packaging: Private Label
Brands:
American Prairie

8701 **Mercer Foods**
1836 Lapham Drive
Modesto, CA 95354 209-529-0150
Fax: 209-526-3406 dnoland@mercerfoods.com
www.mercerfoods.com
Manufacturers freeze-dried fruit and vegetable ingredients
Vice President: Parmela Denney
General Manager: Otto Werner
Estimated Sales: $10 Million
Number Employees: 75

8702 **Mercer Processing**
1836 Lapham Dr
Modesto, CA 95354 209-529-0150
Fax: 209-526-3406 dnoland@mercerfoods.com
www.mercerfoods.com
Dehydrated fruits, vegetables, soups, shrimp and crab
President: David Noland
Estimated Sales: $ 50 - 100 Million
Number Employees: 50-99
Brands:
Mercer

8703 **Mercer's Dairy**
13584 NYS Rt 12
Boonville, NY 13309 315-942-2611
Fax: 315-942-5315 866-637-2377
mercersdairy@gmail.com
www.mercersdairy.com
Gluten-free, kosher, organic/natural, wine, yogurt, ice cream/sorbet, co-packing, private label.
Marketing: Dalton Givens

8704 **Merci Spring Water**
11570 Rock Island Ct
Maryland Heights, MO 63043-3522 314-872-9323
Fax: 314-872-9544
Processor and exporter of water including spring, purified and distilled; also, concentrated juices
President: Don Schneeberger
Estimated Sales: Under $500,000
Number Employees: 1-4
Sq. footage: 22500

8705 **Mercon Coffee Corporation**
2 Hudson Pl
Hoboken, NJ 07030-5594 201-418-9400
Fax: 201-418-0306 info@merconcoffee.com
www.merconcoffee.com
Green coffee
President: Andy Enderlin
President: Andreas Enderlin
CFO/Treasurer: Salvador Rodriguez
Sales Manager: Richard Etkin
Number Employees: 20-49
Brands:
Mercon

8706 **Mercury Brewing Company**
23 Hayward St
Ipswich, MA 01938 978-356-3329
Fax: 450-973-1957
brewing@mercurybrewing.com
www.mercurybrewing.com
Manufacture of soda and beer
President: Robert Martin
Estimated Sales: Below $ 5 Million
Number Employees: 10-19
Type of Packaging: Consumer, Food Service
Brands:
Blueberry Ale
Ipswich Ale
Stone Cat Ale

8707 **Meredith & Meredith**
2343 Farm Creek Rd
Toddville, MD 21672 410-397-8151
Fax: 410-397-8130
Frozen soft shell crabs, refrigerated blue crabmeat, oysters
President: Jennings Tolley
VP: Morgan Tolley
Estimated Sales: Below $ 5 Million
Number Employees: 20-49
Type of Packaging: Consumer
Brands:
Meredith's

8708 **Meredyth Vineyard**
RR 628
Route 626
Middleburg, VA 20118 540-687-6277
Fax: 540-687-6288 www.meredythvineyards.com
Wine
Partner: Archie Smith

8709 **Meridian Beverage Company**
2255 Button Gwinnett Dr
Atlanta, GA 30340 770-248-9315
Fax: 770-263-6960 800-728-1481
slovinger@meridianclear.com
www.meridianclear.com
Processor of naturally flavored noncarbonated spring water beverages
President: Steve Lovinger
Convenience Store Manager: Ralph Grasso
Sales Manager: Marilyn Hunter
Number Employees: 20-49

8710 **Meridian Nut Growers**
1625 Shaw Ave
Clovis, CA 93611-4089 559-458-7272
Fax: 559-458-7270 jzion@meridiannut.com
www.meridiannut.com
Grower owned sales and marketing company supporting growers, processors, and buyers of California almonds, pistachios, walnuts, prunes, and raisins as well as South African macadamia nuts. In addition, they handle a full line ofvarious dried fruit and nut products from origins around the world.
Manager: Jim Zion
Grower Relations/Sales Coordinator: Cecilia Kjar
Sales Director: Stacy Dovali
Managing Director: Jim Zion
Accounting Manager: Julie Sawyer
Estimated Sales: $500,000-$1 Million
Number Employees: 20-49
Type of Packaging: Food Service, Private Label, Bulk
Brands:
A&P Growers

8711 **Meridian Trading**
1136 Pearl St Ste 201
Boulder, CO 80302 303-442-8683
Fax: 303-442-8684 meridiantc@qwest.net
www.meridiantrading.com
Herbal products
President: David Black
Estimated Sales: $ 5 Million
Number Employees: 1-4

8712 **Meridian Vineyards**
P.O.Box 3289
7000 E Highway 46
Paso Robles, CA 93446-7390 805-237-6000
Fax: 805-239-5715
inquiries@meridianvineyards.com
http://www.chateaustjean.com
Wines the selection of which includes Chardonnay Santa Barbara, Sauvignon Blanc, Merlot California, Pinot Noir, Cabernet Sauvignon Blanc, Meridian Shiraz-Cabernet and Cabernet-Merlot.
President: Walter Klenz
Finance Manager: Lisa Cruz
Finance Executive: Lisa Kruse
Marketing Manager: Cath Jager
Estimated Sales: $ 20-50 Million
Number Employees: 120
Type of Packaging: Private Label, Bulk

8713 **Merisant**
33 N Dearborn Street
Suite 200
Chicago, IL 60602 312-840-6000
Fax: 312-840-5541 www.merisant.com
Artifical sweeteners
President/CEO: Paul Block
CFO: Julie Wool
VP/General Counsel/Secretary: Jonathan Cole
Quality Assurance Manager: Lonnie Morgan
VP Human Resources: Vivian Glover
VP/COO: Richard Mewborn
Number Employees: 437
Sq. footage: 26300
Type of Packaging: Consumer, Food Service
Brands:
CANDEREL
EQUAL
PURE VIA

8714 **Merkel McDonald**
6301 E Stassney Ln # 7-100
Austin, TX 78744-3087 512-385-8822
Fax: 512-385-8985 800-356-0229
www.otisspunkmeyer.com
Processor of IQF gourmet cookie dough and thaw/serve cookies and brownies
CEO: Dave Merkel
President: Jeff McDonald
Partner/Sales: Steve Vincent
Marketing Director: Rachel Flesher
Estimated Sales: $ 20 - 50 Million
Number Employees: 50-99
Brands:
Chippery

8715 **Merkley & Sons Packing**
3994 W 180n
Jasper, IN 47546 812-482-7020
Fax: 812-482-7033
Manufacturer of meat products including beef and pork
President/CEO: James Merkley
Treasurer: Selma Merkley
VP: David Merkley
Estimated Sales: $10-20 Million
Number Employees: 20-49

Type of Packaging: Consumer, Bulk

8716 **Merkts Cheese Company**
P.O.Box 188
Bristol, WI 53104-0188 262-857-2316
Fax: 262-857-2276 sales@merktscheese.com
www.lakeviewfarms.com
Processor of cheese including spreads, pasteurized, processed and cold-pack
President/CEO Lake View Farms: Eugene Graves
VP: Pat Denor
General Manager: Pat Denor
Sales Manager: John Kopilchack
Purchasing Agent: Gary Nies
Estimated Sales: $$20-50 Million
Number Employees: 20-49
Sq. footage: 72000
Parent Co: Bel/Kaukauna USA
Type of Packaging: Consumer, Food Service, Private Label, Bulk
Brands:
Country Classic
Merkts
Owl's Nest

8717 **Merlin Candies**
5635 Powell St
Harahan, LA 70123 504-733-5553
Fax: 504-733-5536 800-899-1549
www.merlincandies.com
Processor, importer and exporter of confectionery products including custom molded and sugar-free chocolates, seasonal candies and chocolate trolls
President: Jean La Hoste
VP: Mary Crowley
Estimated Sales: $1000000
Number Employees: 5-9
Type of Packaging: Consumer, Food Service, Private Label
Brands:
Merlin's

8718 **Merlino Italian Baking Company**
771 Valley St Ste 100
Seattle, WA 98109 206-284-0744
Fax: 206-284-0915 800-207-2997
info@merlinobaking.com
www.merlinobaking.com
Italian bakery goods, specialty cookies, soy products, organic products, health foods, etc
President: Greg Merlino
Vice President: Basel Nassar
Marketing: Margaret Domer
Sales: Greg Merlino
Operations/Production/Purchasing: Basel Nassar
Plant Manager: Aurelio Coria
Estimated Sales: $ 3 Million
Number Employees: 20-49
Number of Brands: 3
Number of Products: 50
Sq. footage: 10000
Type of Packaging: Consumer, Food Service, Private Label
Brands:
MERLINO SIGNATURE BRANDS

8719 **Merlinos**
1330 Elm Ave
Canon City, CO 81212-4499 719-275-5558
Fax: 719-275-8980 www.den-air.com
Processor of fruit juices including cider-apple, cherry, apple-strawberry, blackberry, red raspberry and grape
President: Michael A Merlino
Estimated Sales: $1127516
Number Employees: 50-99
Type of Packaging: Consumer, Food Service, Private Label, Bulk

8720 **Mermaid Spice Corporation**
5702 Corporation Cir
Fort Myers, FL 33905 239-693-1986
Fax: 239-693-2099 mermaid@cyberstreet.com
www.angelpasta.com
Processor and importer of herbs, spices, seasonings, salt substitutes, rices, soup bases and salad dressings; exporter of spices and soup bases; also, custom blending available
General Manager: Mike Asaad
Estimated Sales: $1-3 Million
Number Employees: 1-4
Sq. footage: 18000
Type of Packaging: Food Service
Brands:
Mermaid Spice

8721 **Merrill Seafood Center**
6213 Merrill Rd
Jacksonville, FL 32277 904-744-3132
Seafood
President: Agostinho Arco
Estimated Sales: $500,000-$1 Million
Number Employees: 1-4

8722 **Merrill's Blueberry Farms**
P.O.Box 149
Ellsworth, ME 04605-0149 207-667-9750
Fax: 207-667-4052 800-711-6551
merrblue@merrillwildblueberries.com
www.merrillwildblueberries.com
Processor, exporter and importer of IQF wild blueberries
President: Delmont Merrill
Vice President: Richard Merrill
Marketing Director: Del Merrill
Plant Manager: Richard Merrill
Estimated Sales: $ 1 - 3 Million
Number Employees: 10-19
Number of Brands: 1
Number of Products: 1
Sq. footage: 50000
Type of Packaging: Private Label, Bulk
Brands:
MERRILL'S

8723 **Merrill's Meat Company**
P.O.Box 717
Encampment, WY 82325-0717 307-327-5345
Meat
President: Robert Merrill
Estimated Sales: $500,000-$1 Million
Number Employees: 1-4

8724 **Merrimack Valley Apiaries**
96 Dudley Rd
Billerica, MA 01821 978-667-5380
Fax: 978-318-0881
cardbee@mvabeepunchers.com
www.mvabeepunchers.com
honey
President/Owner: Andrew Card Jr
Number Employees: 6

8725 **Merritt Estate Wines**
2264 King Rd
Forestville, NY 14062-9703 716-965-4800
Fax: 716-965-4800 888-965-4800
nywines@merrittestatewinery.com
www.merrittestatewinery.com
Processor and exporter of table wines including red, white, rose, dry, sweet and sparkling
President: William T Merritt
Special Events: Jason Merritt
Estimated Sales: $$1-2.5 Million
Number Employees: 1-4
Sq. footage: 7000
Type of Packaging: Consumer, Food Service, Private Label
Brands:
Merritt

8726 **Merritt Pecan Company**
P.O.Box 28
Weston, GA 31832 229-828-6610
Fax: 229-828-2061 800-762-9152
Processor and exporter of shelled and in-shell pecans
President: John Merritt
President: Richard Merritt
Estimated Sales: $2000000
Number Employees: 20-49
Sq. footage: 27000
Type of Packaging: Consumer, Bulk
Brands:
Merritt Pecan Co.

8727 **Merryvale Vineyards**
1000 Main St
Saint Helena, CA 94574 707-963-2225
Fax: 707-963-1949 800-326-6069
info@merryvale.com www.merryvale.com
Wines
President: Jack Schlatter
CFO: Glenn Ochsner
Public Relations: Jean De Luca
Director Winemaking: Stephen Test
Estimated Sales: $ 10-20 Million
Number Employees: 50-99
Brands:
Merryvale

8728 **Mersey Seafoods**
26 Bristol Avenue
Liverpool, NS B0T 1K0
Canada 902-354-3467
Fax: 902-354-2319
Processor and exporter of fresh and frozen cod, flounder, haddock, halibut, herring, mackerel, perch, salted pollack and shrimp
President: William Murphy
Estimated Sales: $17 Million
Number Employees: 120
Type of Packaging: Consumer, Food Service

8729 **Mertz Sausage Company**
619 Cupples Rd
San Antonio, TX 78237 210-433-3263
Fax: 210-433-3218
Processor of smoked, fresh and Italian sausage; also, Mexican chorizo
President: Alejandro Pena
Estimated Sales: $250,000-$290,000
Number Employees: 1-4
Type of Packaging: Consumer
Brands:
Mertz Sausage

8730 **Mesa Cold Storage**
9602 W Buckeye Rd
Tolleson, AZ 85353-9101 623-478-9392
dcouryjr@mesacold.com
http://www.mesacold.com/
Warehouse providing coooler, freezer and dry storage; wholesaler/distributor of groceries; transportation firm providing local, long and short haul trucking
Owner: Dan Courey
Number Employees: 10-19
Sq. footage: 50000

8731 **Messina Hof Wine Cellars & Vineyards**
4545 Old Reliance Rd
Bryan, TX 77808 979-778-9463
Fax: 979-778-1729 800-736-9463
winemaker@messinahof.com
www.messinahof.com
Wines
President: Paul Bonarrigo
Co-Owner: Merrill Bonarrigo
Marketing Director: Steve Wiley
Public Relations: Julie Diefenthal
Estimated Sales: $ 10-20 Million
Number Employees: 20-49
Type of Packaging: Private Label, Bulk

8732 **Metabolic Nutrition**
10450 W McNab Rd
Tamarac, FL 33321
800-626-1022
info@metabolicnutrition.com
www.metabolicnutrition.com
Processor and exporter of general and sports nutritional supplements
President/CEO: Murray Cohen
VP Marketing/CFO: Brian Cohen
VP/Sales: Jay Cohen
Estimated Sales: $1-2.5 Million
Number Employees: 5-9
Number of Products: 15
Sq. footage: 14000
Type of Packaging: Private Label
Brands:
ADVANTAGE
CGP
HYDRAVAX
PROTIZYME
SYNEDREX
TAG

8733 **Metafoods, LLC**
2970 Clairmont Rd NE Ste 510
Atlanta, GA 30329 404-843-2400
Fax: 404-843-1119 info@metafoods.llc.net
www.metafoodsllc.net
Frozen foods, beef, pork, poultry, frozen seafood, canned goods
President: Joe Wright
CFO: Patricia Smith

Estimated Sales: $ 5 - 10 Million
Number Employees: 20-49

8734 **Metagenics, Inc.**
100 Avenida La Pata
San Clemente, CA 92673-6304 949-366-0818
Fax: 949-366-0853 800-621-6070
www.metagenics.com
Processor of vitamins, supplements and sports nutrition products
Chairman: Jeffrey Katke
CEO: Fred Howard
Estimated Sales: $100-500 Million
Number Employees: 100-249
Brands:
Ethical Nutrients
Metagenics
Unipro

8735 **(HQ)Metarom Corporation**
11 School Street
Newport, VT 05855 802-334-0117
Fax: 514-375-7953 888-882-5555
accuil@metarom.fr
Processor of natural and artificial flavors and colors; natural extracts
President: Andre Bilodeau
General Manager: Pierre Miclette
CFO: Fernande Dubois
Vice President: John Murphy
Quality Control: Alain Gauther
Estimated Sales: Less than $500,000
Number Employees: 1-4
Parent Co: Metarom Canada
Other Locations:
Metarom Corporation
Granby PQ

8736 **Metompkin Bay Oyster Company**
P.O.Box 671
Crisfield, MD 21817 410-968-0662
Fax: 410-968-0670 metbay@intercom.net
www.metompkinseafood.com
Fresh and frozen seafood
President: Casey Todd
Co-Owner: Mike Todd
Executive VP: Michael Todd
Estimated Sales: $ 5-10 Million
Number Employees: 100-249
Type of Packaging: Private Label

8737 **Metro Mint**
PO Box 885462
San Francisco, CA 94188 415-979-0781
Fax: 415-543-2749 info@metromint.com
www.metromint.com
pure water, real mint, no sweeteners
President/Owner: Rio Miura

8738 **Metropolis Sambeve Specialty Foods**
522 Essex St
Lawrence, MA 01840 978-683-2873
Fax: 978-683-6636 bensmfc@verizon.net
www.metropolisfineconfections.com
Gourmet hard candies, fruit jellies, roasted nuts, chocolates and taffy
Estimated Sales: $ 3 - 5 Million
Number Employees: 5-9
Brands:
Taffy Smooches

8739 **Metropolitan Bakery**
262 South 19th Street
Philadelphia, PA 19103 215-545-6655
877-412-7323
wsborn@gmail.com
www.metropolitanbakery.com
breads
President/Owner: Jim Lily
President: Wendy Born

8740 **Metropolitan Baking Company**
8579 Lumpkin St
Hamtramck, MI 48212 313-875-7246
Fax: 313-875-7792 www.metropolitanbaking.com
Bread
Manager: Mike Zrimec
Chairman of the Board: George Kordas
Vice President: Jean Kordas
Estimated Sales: $ 10-20 Million
Number Employees: 50-99
Brands:
Metropolitan

8741 **Metropolitan Sausage Manufacturing Company**
2908 Alexander Cres
Flossmoor, IL 60422-1704 708-331-3232
Fax: 708-798-2929
Meat and sausage
President: Willard Payne
Estimated Sales: $ 1-2.5 Million
Number Employees: 1-4

8742 **Metropolitan Tea Company**
41 Butterick Road
Toronto, ON M8W 4W4 416-588-0089
Fax: 416-588-7040 800-388-0351
sales@metrotea.com www.metrotea.com
Products include bagged teas, loose teas, gift boxes, tea pots and mugs, tea presses, tea infusers, spoons and squeezers.

8743 **Metz Baking Company**
1402 N 8th Street
Pekin, IL 61554-2103 309-347-7315
www.saralee.com
Manufacturer of baked goods
CEO: Richard Noll
General Sales Manager: Tom Hicks
Estimated Sales: $200,000
Number Employees: 8
Parent Co: Sara Lee Corporation
Type of Packaging: Bulk
Brands:
BIMBO
EARTHGRAINS
IRONKIDS
RAINBO
Rainbo
SARA LEE

8744 **Metzer Farms**
26000 Old Stage Rd
Gonzales, CA 93926 831-679-2355
Fax: 831-679-2711 800-424-7755
metzinfo@metzerfarms.com
www.metzerfarms.com
Processor of Asian duck egg products including incubated, salted and fresh; also, whole Chinese geese
President: John Metzer
Estimated Sales: $ 3 - 5 Million
Number Employees: 10-19
Number of Products: 45
Sq. footage: 31000
Type of Packaging: Consumer, Private Label
Brands:
Balut Sa Puti

8745 **Metzger Popcorn Company**
24197 Road U20
Delphos, OH 45833 419-692-2494
Fax: 419-692-0890 800-819-6072
mail@metzgerpopcorn.com
www.metzgerpopcorn.com
Processor and exporter of popcorn
President: Robert Metzger
Co-Owner: Marilyn Metzger
Production Manager: Todd Gable
Estimated Sales: $860000
Number Employees: 1-4
Sq. footage: 10000
Type of Packaging: Consumer, Food Service, Private Label, Bulk
Brands:
Indian Creek
Mello-Krisp
Metzger Popcorn Co.

8746 **Metzger Specialty Brands**
250 W 57th St
Suite 1005
New York, NY 10107 212-957-0055
Fax: 212-957-0918 info@tillenfarms.com
www.tillenfarms.com
asparagus (spicy and white), crunchy carrots, dilly beans, hot and spicy beans, maraschino cherries, snappers (snap peas), sweet bells (bell peppers), sunnysides (tomatoes), v-packed green beans
President/Owner: Tim Metzger
Human Resources Manager: Tony Palacios
Warehouse Manager: Robert Stuckey
Estimated Sales: $2 Million
Number Employees: 2

8747 **Mex. Accent**
16675 W Glendale Dr
New Berlin, WI 53151 262-784-4422
Fax: 262-784-5810 www.mexicanaccent.com
Processor and exporter of flour and corn tortillas; processor of tortilla chips; private labeling available
President: Mike Maglio
Estimated Sales: $13 Million
Number Employees: 150
Sq. footage: 120000
Type of Packaging: Consumer, Food Service, Private Label, Bulk
Brands:
MANNY'S
MEXICAN ACCENT
RIO REAL

8748 **MexAmerica Foods**
1037 Trout Run Rd
St Marys, PA 15857-3124 814-781-1447
Fax: 814-834-9042
wecare@mexamericafoods.com
www.mexamericafoods.com
Processor of tortillas including flour, whole wheat and corn; also, tortilla chips including white, yellow, blue and red
President: Gerald B Riddle
Marketing/Sales: Michael Renaud
Operations Manager: Tom Kornacki
Purchasing Manager: Thom Hoffman
Estimated Sales: $5000000
Number Employees: 20-49
Number of Brands: 3-4
Number of Products: 1
Sq. footage: 20000
Type of Packaging: Consumer, Food Service, Private Label, Bulk
Brands:
Mexamerica

8749 **Mexbest/Apoyos Y Servicios A La Comercialization Agroprecuaria**
1911 Pennsylvania Ave NW
Washington, DC 20006 202-728-1729
fgracia@gmail.com

8750 **Mexi-Frost Specialties Company**
37 Grand Avenue
Brooklyn, NY 11205-1309 718-625-3324
Fax: 718-852-8699
Processor and exporter of frozen West Indian, Mexican, Caribbean, Chinese and Italian foods including chicken, meat pies, tamales, burritos, egg rolls, etc
President: Gonzalo Armendariz Jr
VP: Gonzalo Armendariz, Jr.
VP Sales: Mark Armendariz
Plant Manager: Gonzaol Armendariz, Jr.
Estimated Sales: $ 5 - 10 Million
Number Employees: 20-49
Type of Packaging: Consumer, Food Service, Private Label, Bulk
Brands:
Gonzo's Little Big Meat
La Jolla
La Joya
Mexi-Frost

8751 **Mexi-Snax**
1790 W Cortland Ct. # B
Addison, IL 60101-4208 630-628-0211
www.mexisnax.com
Processor and exporter of regular and fat-free baked tortilla chips
President: Frank Schy
COO: Jerry Schy
Sales Manager: Jelli Meyer
Estimated Sales: $20-50 Million
Number Employees: 20-49
Sq. footage: 35000
Type of Packaging: Private Label
Brands:
Bake-Stos Tortilla Chips
Mexi-Snax Tortilla Chips

8752 **Mexisnax Corporation**
6860 El Paso Dr
El Paso, TX 79905-3336 915-779-5709
Fax: 915-779-4559
Processor of taco shells, tostada chips and flour and corn tortillas; also, salsa including jalapeno, red chile and chile con queso
President: Armando Viescas
General Manager: Enrique Galindo
Office Manager: Elvira Martinez

Estimated Sales: $ 5 - 10 Million
Number Employees: 20-49
Sq. footage: 6000
Type of Packaging: Consumer, Private Label
Brands:
Las Cruces

8753 **Mexnutri**
Nino Artillero 450 Int 1
San Luis Potosi, SLP 78290
MEX 444-841-5625
Fax: 444-841-5787
alejandro.rostro@mexnutri.com
www.mexnutri.com
Manufacturer of dehydrated ingredients and additives; including organic ingredients, seasonings, spices and dried vegetables
General Manager: Alejandro Rostro
Number Employees: 10-19

8754 **Meyer Brothers Dairy**
5130 Industrial St Ste 400
Maple Plain, MN 55359 952-473-7343
Fax: 952-473-8522
CustomerService@MeyerBrosDairy.com
www.meyerbrosdairy.com
Products include milk, breakfast items, yogurt, pizza, meat, juices, eggs and bacon, coffee, bottled water, appetizers, produce and vegetables, butter and margarine, cheese and bakery items.
Manager: Jim Otis
Quality Control Manager: Tom Janas
Estimated Sales: $ 2.5-5 Million
Number Employees: 20-49

8755 **(HQ)Meyer's Bakeries**
2700 E 3rd Street
Hope, AR 71802-0687 870-777-9031
Fax: 870-777-9769 800-643-1542
www.meyersbakeries.com
Processor of fresh and frozen baked goods including bread, bagels, rolls, English muffins and waffles
President: Gerald Hanna
General Manager: Mike Kraft
Operations: Rick Ledbetter
Estimated Sales: $51800000
Number Employees: 500-999
Type of Packaging: Consumer, Food Service, Private Label, Bulk
Brands:
De Wafelbakkers Janssen & Meyer

8756 **Meyer's Bakeries**
10491 W Battaglia Dr
Casa Grande, AZ 85293-7715 520-466-5491
Fax: 520-466-5996 800-528-5770
http://www.meyersbakeries.com
Processor of English muffins
Manager: Eric Robinson
Plant Manager: Frank Benefiel
Estimated Sales: $ 10 - 20 Million
Number Employees: 50-99
Sq. footage: 80000
Parent Co: Meyers Bakeries
Type of Packaging: Food Service, Private Label, Bulk

8757 **Mezza**
222 E Wisconsin Avenue
Suite 300
Lake Forest, IL 60045-1723 847-735-2516
Fax: 415-727-4471 888-206-6054
sales@emezza.com
Suppliers to the finest kitchens in America with a worldwide selection of gourmet pantry items
Type of Packaging: Food Service, Private Label

8758 **Mgp Ingredients, Inc.**
P.O.Box 130
Atchison, KS 66002 309-353-3990
Fax: 913-367-0192 800-255-0302
www.mgpingredients.com
Process starches and specialty wheat proteins for food and non-food applications.
President/CEO: Tim Newkirk
Number Employees: 195

8759 **Mh Zeigler & Sons**
1513 N Broad St
Lansdale, PA 19446 215-855-5161
Fax: 215-855-4548 www.zeiglers.com
Processor of apple cider, lemonades, teas, juices and spices
President: Art Dalzereit
CFO: Timothy Zeigler
Estimated Sales: $$20-50 Million
Number Employees: 50-99
Type of Packaging: Consumer, Food Service, Private Label, Bulk
Brands:
Zeigler's

8760 **Mi Mama's Tortilla Factory**
828 S 17th St
Omaha, NE 68108 402-345-2099
Fax: 402-345-1059 www.mimamas.com
Tortillas
General Manager: Paul Sharrar
Estimated Sales: $ 10-20 Million
Number Employees: 20-49

8761 **Mi Ranchito Foods**
P.O.Box 159
Bayard, NM 88023-0159 575-537-3868
Manufacturer of frozen tamales; also, tortillas, chili and chili con carne
President: Joe Ramirez
Estimated Sales: $17 Million
Number Employees: 5-9
Type of Packaging: Consumer, Food Service, Private Label, Bulk
Brands:
MI RANCHITO

8762 **Mia Products**
P.O.Box 377
Scranton, PA 18501 570-457-7431
Fax: 570-457-0915
Processor of frozen juice bars
General Manager: T Cousins
President: Gerald Shriber
VP: Ernest Fogle
Number Employees: 50-99
Parent Co: J&J Snack Foods Company
Type of Packaging: Food Service
Brands:
Mia

8763 **Miami Beef Company**
4870 NW 157th St
Hialeah, FL 33014 305-621-3252
Fax: 305-620-4562 info@miamibeef.com
www.miamibeef.com
Angus, steaks, hamburgers, meat, beef, chicken, lamb, pork, sausage, roast beef, veal, prime rib, patties, stew, sirlion, tenderloim, soy, ground beef, breaded, cooked, hoagie, palomolla, pepper, salisbury, t-bone, sliced sandwichsirloin, skirt steak, cubed steak, filet mignon
President: Michael Young
Head Sales: Barry Dean
Plant Manager: Russ Milina
Estimated Sales: $10800000
Number Employees: 50-99
Type of Packaging: Consumer, Food Service, Private Label, Bulk
Brands:
Miami Beef

8764 **Miami Crab Corporation**
10815 NW 33 Street
Miami, FL 33172 305-470- 150
Fax: 305-470- 150 800-269-8395
mail@miamicrab.com www.miamicrab.com
Crabmeat products
Estimated Sales: $ 5 - 10 Million
Number Employees: 5-9
Type of Packaging: Consumer, Food Service
Brands:
Flamingo
Jackpot
Windy Shoal

8765 **(HQ)Miami Purveyors**
7350 NW 8th St
Miami, FL 33126 305-262-6170
Fax: 305-262-6174
Manuafacturer and exporter of frozen foods including beef, pork, ham, poultry, seafood, fruits and vegetables
Owner: Rick Rothenberg
Marketing Manager: Andy Kleinberg
Estimated Sales: $14.1 Million
Number Employees: 50-99
Type of Packaging: Food Service

8766 **Micalizzi Italian Ice**
712 Madison Ave
Bridgeport, CT 06606 203-366-2353
JAYICE712@aol.com
www.micalizzis.com
Italian ice and ice cream
Co-Owner: Lucille Piccirillo
Co-Owner: Jay Piccirillo
Estimated Sales: $500,000-$1 Million
Number Employees: 1-4
Type of Packaging: Consumer, Food Service, Bulk

8767 **Miceli Dairy Products Company**
2721 E 90th St
Cleveland, OH 44104 216-791-6222
800-551-7196
mstorath@miceli-dairy.com
www.miceli-dairy.com
Processor of Italian cheeses
General Manager: John Pinjuh
EVP: John Miceli Jr
Marketing Manager: Maria Miceli
VP Sales: Charles Surace
Human Resources Director: Joseph Lograsso
Operations Executive: Douglas Trent
Plant Manager: James Salamon
Estimated Sales: $ 20 - 50 Million
Number Employees: 190
Sq. footage: 25000

8768 **Michael Angelo's Gourmet Foods**
200 Michael Angelo Way
Austin, TX 78728-1200 512-218-3500
Fax: 512-218-3600 877-482-5426
customerservice@michaelangelos.com
www.michaelangelos.com
Premier line of packaged Italian cuisine including italian entrees, lasagnas, stuffed pasta, snacks and appetizers, protein dishe
Owner/CEO: Michael Angelo Renna
President: Everett Carmody
CFO: Jason Dell
VP Retail/Food Service: Joe Keip
Marketing: Joe Kent
Estimated Sales: $100+ Million
Number Employees: 400
Number of Brands: 1
Number of Products: 100
Sq. footage: 132000
Type of Packaging: Consumer, Food Service, Bulk
Brands:
MICHAEL ANGELO'S

8769 **Michael D's Cookies & Cakes**
11 N Edgelawn Dr # 1
Aurora, IL 60506-4362 630-892-2525
Fax: 630-892-2556
Cookies
President: Calvin Gooch
Estimated Sales: Less than $500,000
Number Employees: 5-9
Brands:
Amazon Basin Brownie
Conservationist Chip
Lonesome George Chip
Okavango Chip
Savannah Chip
Stonewall Grant's

8770 **(HQ)Michael Foods, Inc.**
301 Carlson Pkwy Ste 400
Minnetonka, MN 55305 952-258-4000
Fax: 952-258-4911 www.michaelfoods.com
Processor and exporter of frozen and liquid egg products and microwaveable hash brown potato products.
President/CEO: James Dwyer
SVP and CFO: Mark Westphal
SVP Operations and Supply Chain: Thomas Jagiela
Estimated Sales: $1.8 Billion
Number Employees: 3,790
Parent Co: Thomas H Lee Partners
Type of Packaging: Consumer, Food Service, Private Label, Bulk
Other Locations:
Michael Foods
Minneapolis MN
Brands:
ABBOSTFORD FARMS
ALL DAY CAFE
ALL WHITES
BETTER 'N EGGS
CRYSTAL FARMS

DINER'S CHOICE
NORTHERN STAR
PAPETTI'S
SIMPLY POTATOES

8771 **Michael Granese & Company**
640 E Main Street
Norristown, PA 19401-5123 610-272-5099
Fax: 610-272-1995 elio.camilotto@grande.com
Processor of Italian cheeses including ricotta, mozzarella, scamorza and cream twist
President: John Carfagno Jr
Estimated Sales: $2900000
Number Employees: 10
Sq. footage: 4000
Type of Packaging: Consumer, Bulk
Brands:
Michael Granese Co.

8772 **Michael's Cookies**
10635 Scripps Ranch Blvd # D
San Diego, CA 92131-1087 858-578-0888
Fax: 858-578-3086 800-822-5384
info@michaelscookies.com
www.michaelscookies.com
Processor and exporter of frozen pre-portioned cookie doughs. Sells nationwide in the US
Manager: Scott Summeril
CFO: Scott Summeril
Estimated Sales: $ 20 - 50 Million
Number Employees: 20-49
Number of Brands: 1
Number of Products: 1
Sq. footage: 30000
Type of Packaging: Food Service, Private Label, Bulk
Brands:
Bonzers

8773 **Michael's Finer Meats &Seafoods**
P.O.Box 182700
Columbus, OH 43218 614-527-4900
Fax: 614-527-4520 800-282-0518
info@michaelsmeats.com
www.michaelsmeats.com
Processor and wholesaler/distributor of meat including beef, pork, lamb, veal and wild game
President: Jonathan (John) Bloch
CFO: Betsy Teater
VP: Victor Foreman
Estimated Sales: $100+ Million
Number Employees: 100-249
Sq. footage: 65000
Type of Packaging: Consumer, Food Service, Bulk

8774 **Michael's Naturopathic**
6003 Randolph Blvd
San Antonio, TX 78233-5719 210-661-8311
Fax: 210-661-8048 800-525-9643
staff@michaelshealth.com
www.michaelshealth.com
Processor of vitamins, minerals and herbal supplements
President: Michael Schwartz
Managing Director: Karen Trabucco
Estimated Sales: $5100000
Number Employees: 20-49
Sq. footage: 13000
Brands:
Michael's Health Products

8775 **Michael's Of Brooklyn**
2929 Avenue R
Brooklyn, NY 11229 718-998-7851
Fax: 718-645-9406 michaelsrest2929@aol.com
www.michaelsofbrooklyn.com

8776 **Michael's Provision Company**
317 Lindsey St
Fall River, MA 02720 508-672-0982
Fax: 508-672-1307
Processor of meat products including Portuguese sausage
President: Ronald Miranda
Owner: Joseph Miranda
Estimated Sales: $ 3 - 5 Million
Number Employees: 5-9
Type of Packaging: Consumer, Food Service, Bulk

8777 **Michaelene's Gourmet Granola**
7415 Deer Forest Ct
Clarkston, MI 48348 248-625-0156
Fax: 248-625-8521
michaelenes@gourmetgranola.com
www.gourmetgranola.com
Processor of granola
President: Michaelene Hearn
Estimated Sales: Below $ 5 Million
Number Employees: 5-9
Type of Packaging: Bulk
Brands:
Michaelene's Gourmet
Michaelene's Gourmet Granola
Michaelene's Granola

8778 **Michel's Bakery**
5698 Rising Sun Ave
Philadelphia, PA 19120-1698 215-725-3900
Fax: 215-745-1058 info@michelsbakery.com
www.michelsbakery.com
Danish pastry, muffins, cakes, brownies and pies
President: Jon Liss
Sales Manager: Carl Mauser
CFO: Bill Wagner
CEO: Joseph Liss
Quality Control: Jan Brownlee
Purchasing Manager: Flo Collington
Estimated Sales: $ 20-30 Million
Number Employees: 100-249
Type of Packaging: Private Label
Brands:
Michele's Family Bakery
Muffin Tops
Rittenhouse Food

8779 **Michel's Magnifique**
35 E 9th St Apt 4
New York, NY 10003 212-431-1070
Processor of pates, mousses and sausage including saucisson
President: Ken Blanchette
Operations Manager: Allan Moss
Number Employees: 5-9
Type of Packaging: Consumer, Food Service

8780 **Michel-Schlumberger**
4155 Wine Creek Rd
Healdsburg, CA 95448 707-433-7427
Fax: 707-433-0444 800-447-3060
winebench@aol.com
www.michelschlumberger.com
Wine
President: Jacques Schlumberger
CEO: Jerry Craven
President: Jacques Schlumberger
General Manager: Gary Brown
Public Relations: Joy Henderson
VP Operations/Production: Fred Payne
Estimated Sales: Below $ 5 Million
Number Employees: 20-49
Type of Packaging: Private Label
Brands:
25 Imports From France
Domaine Michel
Michel-Schlumberger

8781 **Michele's Chocolate Truffles**
14704 SE 82nd Dr
Clackamas, OR 97015-9607 503-656-0220
Fax: 503-656-0440 800-656-7112
truffles@micheles.com www.micheles.com
Processor of gourmet hand dipped chocolate truffles, chews, nut clusters, cordials, toffee and caramel
Owner: Todd Davis
Estimated Sales: $ 3 - 5 Million
Number Employees: 5-9
Number of Brands: 1
Number of Products: 50
Sq. footage: 2500
Type of Packaging: Consumer, Food Service, Private Label, Bulk
Brands:
MICHELE'S CHOCOLATE TRUFFLES
VICKI'S ROCKY ROAD

8782 **Michele's Family Bakery**
2731 S Queen St
York, PA 17403-9703 717-741-2027
Fax: 717-747-0065 www.macksicecream.com
Ice cream
Owner: Walt Bloss
Manager: Bill Lenick
Estimated Sales: $ 5-9.9 Million
Number Employees: 20-49

8783 **Michele's Foods**
16117 Lasalle Street
South Holland, IL 60473 708-331-7316
Fax: 708-331-7480 info@michelefoods.com
www.michelefoods.com
Processor of honey-based syrups
Owner: Michele Wierzgac
VP: Paul Walk
Estimated Sales: $1000000
Number Employees: 10-19
Sq. footage: 100
Type of Packaging: Consumer, Food Service
Brands:
Michele's Honey Creme

8784 **Michele's Original Gourmet Tofu Products**
PO Box 28903
Philadelphia, PA 19151-0903 215-922-2588
Fax: 215-474-8636
Health foods and sauces
Proprietor: Michael D'Ambrosio
Estimated Sales: $500,000-$1 Million
Number Employees: 1-4
Brands:
Caesar Dressing
Humus Tahini
Tofu Tahini

8785 **Michelle Chocolatiers**
122 N Tejon Street
Colorado Springs, CO 80903-1406 719-633-5089
Fax: 719-633-8970 888-447-3654
customerservice@michellecandies.com
www.michellecandies.com
Processor, importer and exporter of ice creams and candy including chocolates and gold coins
VP: Jim Michopoulos
Estimated Sales: $ 5-10 Million
Number Employees: 20-49
Type of Packaging: Consumer, Private Label
Brands:
Gremlin
Michelle

8786 **(HQ)Michigan Ag Commodities**
216 Eastman
Breckenridge, MI 48615 989-842-3104
Fax: 989-842-3108 800-472-4629
pfrasco@bwcoop.com www.michag.com
Manfuacturer and exporter of dried beans including navy, bush cranberry, black, pinto and adzuki
President: David Geers
Marketing Manager - Bean: Patrick Frasco
Estimated Sales: $50-100 Million
Number Employees: 100-249
Sq. footage: 100000
Type of Packaging: Food Service, Private Label, Bulk
Brands:
B&W

8787 **Michigan Celery Promotion Cooperative**
5009 40th Ave
Hudsonville, MI 49426 616-669-1250
Fax: 616-669-2890 dfrens@iserv.net
www.michigancelery.com
Processor of fresh celery including sliced and diced
General Manager: Duane Frens
Estimated Sales: $ 1 - 3 Million
Number Employees: 20-49
Type of Packaging: Bulk

8788 **Michigan Dairy**
29601 Industrial Rd
Livonia, MI 48150 734-367-5390
Fax: 734-367-5391
Processor of dairy products including pasteurized milk, ice cream, yogurt, cottage cheese and sour cream
Manager: Jack Housley
Plant Manager: Art Shank
Number Employees: 250-499
Parent Co: Kroger Company
Type of Packaging: Consumer

8789 **Michigan Dessert Corporation**
10750 Capital St
Oak Park, MI 48237-3134 248-544-4574
Fax: 248-544-4384 800-328-8632
sales@midasfoods.com www.midasfoods.com
Specializes in the development and production of sweet dry mix items. All of our products are dry blend and either pouch packed for restaurant chains or bulk packed for our food processing partners.
President: Richard Elias
Sr VP Sales/Marketing: Gary Freeman
Estimated Sales: $7 Million
Number Employees: 20-49
Sq. footage: 45000
Parent Co: Midas Foods India
Type of Packaging: Consumer, Food Service, Private Label, Bulk
Brands:
American Savory
Michigan Dessert
Sin Fill

8790 **Michigan Farm Cheese Dairy**
4295 E Millerton Rd
Fountain, MI 49410 231-462-3301
Fax: 231-462-3805 cheese@andrulischeese.com
www.andrulischeese.com
Processor of cheese including feta and farmer
President: Lu Andrulis
Marketing Director: Amanda Andrulis-Preston
Production Manager: Jim Stankowski
Estimated Sales: $1000000
Number Employees: 10-19
Type of Packaging: Consumer
Brands:
Farmers

8791 **Michigan Freeze Pack**
P.O.Box 30
Hart, MI 49420 231-873-2175
Fax: 231-873-3025 www.michiganfreezepack.com
Processor and exporter of asparagus, zucchini squash, celery, broccoli, peppers, carrots and eggplant
President: Gary Dennert
VP Sales/Finance: John Ritche
Production Manager: Ronald Clark
Estimated Sales: $1 Million
Number Employees: 10
Sq. footage: 100000
Type of Packaging: Food Service, Bulk

8792 **Michigan Milk ProducersAssociation**
431 W Williams St
Ovid, MI 48866 989-834-2221
Fax: 989-834-2486 Burkhardt@mimilk.com
www.mimilk.com
Milk products include standardized milks, condensed wholemilk, condensed skim milk, sweet condensed milks, instant nonfat dry milk, dried buttermilk, sweet cream butter, standarized cream, ice cream mixes, nonfat dry milk and driedwhole milk.
President: Eleood Kirkpatric
Quality Control Manager: Mike Watt
Member Relations/Public Affairs: Sheila Burkhardt
Operations Manager: Pete O'Connell
Buyer: Elwood Kirkpatrick
Estimated Sales: $ 20-50 Million
Number Employees: 50-99

8793 **Michigan Sugar Company**
2600 S Euclid Avenue
Bay City, MI 48706 989-686-0161
Fax: 989-671-3695 info@michigansugar.com
www.michigansugar.com
Processor of sweeteners including granulated beet sugar and molasses, dried beet pulp
President/CEO: Mark Flegenheimer
Chairman: Thomas Zimmer
Vice Chairman: Richard Maurer
VP/Administration: James Ruhlman
VP/Marketing: Jerry Coleman
VP/Sales: Barry Brown
VP/Commodities & Procurement: Paul Pfenninger
VP/Operations: Herbert Wilson
Number Employees: 20-49
Parent Co: Savannah Foods & Industries
Type of Packaging: Consumer, Food Service, Private Label, Bulk

8794 **Michigan Sugar Company**
2600 S Euclid Avenue
Bay City, MI 48706 989-686-0161
Fax: 989-671-3695 www.michigansugar.com
Manufacturer of beet sugar
Chairman: Thomas Zimmer
Secretary: Wayne Hecht
Treasurer: Chris Grekowicz
President/CEO: Mark Flegenheimer
VP Marketing: Jerry Coleman
VP Operations: Herbert Wilson
Number Employees: 450
Type of Packaging: Consumer, Food Service, Private Label, Bulk
Other Locations:
Michigan Sugar Factory
Bay City MI
Michigan Sugar Factory
Caro MI
Michigan Sugar Factory
Croswell MI
Michigan Sugar Factory
Sebewaing MI
Brands:
Big Chief
PIONEER

8795 **MicroSoy Corporation**
300 E Microsoy Drive
Jefferson, IA 50129 515-386-2100
Fax: 515-386-3287 info@microsoyflakes.com
www.microsoyflakes.com
MicroSoy Flakes
CFO: Mike Mumma
Estimated Sales: $3.5 Million
Number Employees: 15
Sq. footage: 28800

8796 **Microsoy Corporation**
300 Microsoy Dr
Jefferson, IA 50129 515-386-2100
Fax: 515-386-3287 www.microsoyflakes.com
Processor and exporter of microsoy flakes used in soy milk, tofu and other soy based foods
President/CEO: Terry Tanaka
CFO: Mike Mumma
Estimated Sales: $3.5 Million
Number Employees: 15
Sq. footage: 28800
Parent Co: Mycal Corporation
Type of Packaging: Bulk
Brands:
Microsoy Flakes

8797 **Mid Atlantic Vegetable Shortening Company**
125 Sanford Ave
Kearny, NJ 07032-5918 201-467-0200
Fax: 201-991-0765 800-966-1645
jhulihan@midatlanticveg.com
www.midatlanticveg.com
Manufactures a wide variety of shortenings, oils, margarines, pan releases, zero trans fat shortening and margarines, and specialty products such as lecithin, garlic spread and spice products. All products are manufactured under Koshersupervision
President: Calvin Theobald
CEO: Perry Theobald
VP Sales/Marketing: James Hulihan
Estimated Sales: $ 5-10 Million
Number Employees: 20-49

8798 **Mid States Dairy**
6040 N Lindbergh Blvd
Hazelwood, MO 63042-2804 314-731-1150
Fax: 314-731-1198 express@schnucks.com
www.schnucks.com
Processor of milk, buttermilk, yogurt, cheese, cottage cheese, ice cream, eggnog, sour cream dips, etc
Estimated Sales: $ 20 - 50 Million
Number Employees: 100-249

8799 **Mid-Atlantic Foods**
8978 Glebe Park Dr
Easton, MD 21601-7004 410-822-7500
Fax: 410-822-1266 800-922-4688
sales@seaclam.com www.seaclam.com
Processor and exporter of canned and frozen clams and seafood chowders, sauces and soups; also, clam juice
President: Bob Brennan
CEO: Steve Gordon
Marketing Director: Brian Shea
Estimated Sales: $20 Million
Number Employees: 5-9
Sq. footage: 33000
Type of Packaging: Consumer, Food Service, Private Label
Brands:
Gordon's Chesapeake Classics
Mid-Atlantic
Pot O' Gold
Tucker's Cove
Worcester

8800 **Mid-Eastern Molasses Company**
PO Box 100
Oceanport, NJ 07757-0100 732-462-1868
Fax: 732-431-0006
Bulk molasses

8801 **Mid-Georgia Processing Company**
425 3rd Street Ext
Vienna, GA 31092-1502 229-268-6496
Fax: 229-268-2618
Peanut oil, cake and meal
Manager: James Tinsley
Plant Manager: Dennis Billings
Estimated Sales: $ 20-50 Million
Number Employees: 56

8802 **Mid-Kansas Cooperative**
P.O.Box D
Moundridge, KS 67107-0582 620-345-6328
Fax: 620-345-6330 800-864-4428
webmaster@mkcoop.com www.mkcoop.com
Cooperative offering grains
President: Dave Christianson
Estimated Sales: Less than $500,000
Number Employees: 20-49

8803 **Mid-Pacific Hawaii Fishery**
Old Airport Road
Hilo, HI 96720 808-935-6110
Fax: 808-961-6859
Processor and exporter of fresh tuna, marlin and shark
Owner: John Romero
Estimated Sales: $ 2.5-5 Million
Number Employees: 7
Type of Packaging: Consumer, Food Service
Brands:
Mid Pacific

8804 **Mid-South Fish Company**
P.O.Box 185
Aubrey, AR 72311 870-295-5600
Fax: 870-295-3559
Owner: A L Jolly Jr
Estimated Sales: $ .5 - 1 million
Number Employees: 1-4

8805 **Mid-States Dairy Company**
P.O. Box 46928
St. Louis, MO 63146-6928 314-994-4400
Fax: 314-692-6193 800-264-4400
www.schnucks.com
Ice cream, milk, yoghurt, cottage cheese, sour cream, orange juice, specialty Alaskan Classics ice cream
Marketing Manager: Weiny Wedel
President: Sach Sphnuck
CEO: Scott C Schnuck
Owner: Sach Sphnuck
Operations Manager: John Sprangler
Estimated Sales: $ 20-50 Million
Number Employees: 10,000+
Number of Products: 450

8806 **Mid-Valley Nut Company**
2065 Geer Rd
Hughson, CA 95326-9614 209-883-4491
Fax: 209-883-2435 info@midvalleynut.com
www.midvalleynut.com
Processor and importer of walnuts
President: John Casazza
Estimated Sales: $4600000
Number Employees: 100-249
Type of Packaging: Consumer, Private Label, Bulk

8807 **Midamar Corporation**
P.O.Box 218
Cedar Rapids, IA 52406 319-362-3711
Fax: 319-362-4111 800-362-3711
www.midamar.com

Halal approved food products includes crescent chicken, ethnic sauces, beef, lamb, shawarma, turkey and pizzas.
President: Bill Aossey
Estimated Sales: $ 20 - 50 Million
Number Employees: 50-99

8808 **Middlefield Cheese House**
15815 Nauvoo Rd
Middlefield, OH 44062 440-632-5228
Fax: 440-632-5604 800-327-9477
shop@middlefieldcheese.com
www.middlefieldcheese.com
Swiss cheese, cheese spreads, apple butters and jams, maple syrup and malpe popcorn, beef sticks, summer sausage, beef jerky
President: Ann Rothenbuhler
Plant Manager: Steve Ilg
Estimated Sales: $130,000
Number Employees: 2
Sq. footage: 2000
Type of Packaging: Bulk
Brands:
Middlefield

8809 **Middleswarth Potato Chips**
181 E State St
Wilkes Barre, PA 18704-1011 570-288-2447
Fax: 570-288-1381 toddhestor@hotmail.com
Processor of potato chips including regular, barbecue, waffle style, sour cream and onion and salt and vinegar
President: Bob Middleswarth
Estimated Sales: $ 50 - 100 Million
Number Employees: 50-99
Type of Packaging: Consumer, Food Service, Bulk

8810 **Midland Bean Company**
P.O.Box 118
Cahone, CO 81320 970-562-4235
Fax: 970-677-2219
Manufacturer and wholesaler/distributor of pinto beans
President/Co-Owner: Rod Tanner
Manager: Jack Tanner
Estimated Sales: $20 Million
Number Employees: 1-4
Type of Packaging: Consumer

8811 **Midstate Mills**
P.O.Box 350
Newton, NC 28658 828-464-1611
Fax: 828-465-5139 800-222-1032
sales@midstatemills.com
www.midstatemills.com
Processor of flour, corn meal, biscuit flour and baking mixes
President: Boyd Drum
Vice President: Steve Arndt
Sales Manager: Don Floyd
Sales Director: Berry Coldwell
VP Operations: Brevard Arndt
Purchasing Manager: Kenny Anderson
Estimated Sales: $27100000
Number Employees: 100-249
Type of Packaging: Consumer, Food Service, Private Label, Bulk
Brands:
Redimix
Southern Biscuit
Tenda Bake

8812 **Midstates Dairy**
6040 N Lindbergh Blvd
Hazelwood, MO 63042-2804 314-731-1150
Fax: 314-731-1198
Ice cream, milk, yogurt, cottage cheese, sour cream, orange juice, specialty Alaskan Classics ice cream
President: Tim Mueller
Manager: Dale Parsons
Plant Manager: John Spangler
Estimated Sales: $ 20-50 Million
Number Employees: 100-249
Brands:
Schnucks

8813 **Midway Meats**
1721 Airport Rd
Centralia, WA 98531 360-736-5257
Fax: 360-330-2913
Manufacturer and packer of beef and pork
Manager: Denise Hinckley
Estimated Sales: $10-20 Million
Number Employees: 10-19

8814 **Midwest Blueberry Farms**
13720 Tyler St
Holland, MI 49424-9418 616-399-2133
Fax: 616-399-2133
Blueberries
Owner: Richard Keil
Estimated Sales: Under $300,000
Number Employees: 5-9
Brands:
Midwest Blueberry Farms

8815 **Midwest Foods**
3100 West 36th Street
Chicago, IL 60632 773-927-8870
Fax: 773-927-8718 www.midwestfoods.com
Processor of canned spaghetti dinners and stew including beef, chicken and meatball
Number Employees: 200
Parent Co: Owatonna Canning Company
Type of Packaging: Food Service, Private Label

8816 **Midwest Frozen Foods, Inc.**
2185 Leeward Ln
Hanover Park, IL 60133-6026 630-784-0123
Fax: 630-784-0424 866-784-0123
sales@frozenvegetables.com
Midwest Frozen Foods provides in house and private label frozen fruits and vegetables to the retail, food services and industrial manufacturing sectors.
President: Zafar Iqbal
VP: Athar Siddiq
Operations: Rob Linchesky
Production: Jose Manjarrez
Estimated Sales: $5 Million
Number Employees: 18
Number of Brands: 2
Number of Products: 100+
Sq. footage: 20000
Type of Packaging: Food Service, Private Label, Bulk

8817 **Midwest Seafood**
5500 Emerson Way
Suite A
Indianapolis, IN 46226-1477 317-466-1027
Fax: 317-466-1033
Estimated Sales: $ 1 - 3 Million
Number Employees: 5-9

8818 **Midwest/Northern**
3105 Columbia Ave NE
Minneapolis, MN 55418-1896 612-781-6596
Fax: 612-781-6728 800-328-5502
midwestnut@qwest.net
www.midwestnorthernnut.com
Processor of snack foods including salty and trail mixes and roasted and raw seeds including pumpkin and sunflower; also, confections
President: Laure Rockman
Plant Manager: Tim Fischer
Estimated Sales: $3000000
Number Employees: 20-49
Sq. footage: 40000
Type of Packaging: Consumer, Food Service, Private Label, Bulk
Brands:
Aristo Snacks
Dijon Crunch
Fun Foods
Giant Cashews
Hokey Pokey
Midwest

8819 **Miesse Candies**
60 N Queen St
Lancaster, PA 17603 717-397-9415
Fax: 717-392-6142 info@miessecandy.com
www.miessecandies.com
Hard, soft and chocolate candy
Owner: Ryan Dowd
Estimated Sales: Below $ 5 Million
Number Employees: 20-49

8820 **Mighty Leaf Tea**
136 Mitchell Blvd
San Rafael, CA 94903 415-491-2650
Fax: 415-331-1862 laurala@mightyleaf.com
www.mightyleaf.com
Whole-leaf tea blends
CEO: Gary Shinner
Estimated Sales: Below $ 5 Million
Number Employees: 5-9

8821 **Mighty Soy, Inc**
1227 S Eastern Ave
Los Angeles, CA 90022 323-266-6969
www.mightysoy.com
Soy milk
President: Maung Myint
VP/Secretary: Gin Lee
Estimated Sales: $486,000
Number Employees: 14
Sq. footage: 8000

8822 **Mignardise**
1963 Patrick Farrar
Suite 200
Chambly, QC J3L 4N7 450-447-0777
mignardise@bellnet.ca
www.mignardise.ca
Cakes/pastries, cookies.
Marketing: Joan Cartier

8823 **Miguel's Stowe Away**
17 Town Farm Ln
Stowe, VT 05672 802-253-8900
Fax: 802-253-3946 800-448-6517
mexicanfoods@miguels.com www.miguels.com
Processor and exporter of Mexican food products including salsa cruda, blue and white corn tortilla chips, red chili sauce, flavored salsa and smoked jalapeno
President: Christopher Pierson
Regional Sales Manager: Tim Couture
Estimated Sales: $ 3 - 5 Million
Number Employees: 1-4
Sq. footage: 5000
Type of Packaging: Consumer, Food Service, Bulk
Brands:
Miguel's

8824 **Mikawaya Bakery**
5563 Alcoa Ave
Vernon, CA 90058-3730
Fax: 213-625-0943 Sales@mikawayausa.com
www.mikawayausa.com
Japanese pastries and ice cream
President: Frances Hashimoto
CFO: Joel Friedman
Estimated Sales: $ 5-10 Million
Number Employees: 20-49
Type of Packaging: Private Label
Brands:
Mikawaya
Mochi Ice Cream

8825 **Mike & Jean's Berry Farm**
16402 Jungquist Rd
Mount Vernon, WA 98273 360-424-7220
Fax: 360-424-7225 mjberry@fidalgo.net
www.mikeandjeans.com
Processor of fresh cauliflower, strawberries and raspberries; also, frozen strawberries and raspberries
Owner: Michael Youngquist
Co-Owner: Jeanne Youngquist
Estimated Sales: $ 20-50 Million
Number Employees: 100-249
Type of Packaging: Food Service, Private Label

8826 **Mike and Lou's HandmadePizza**
1340 'B' Columbia Drive
Hershey, PA 17003 717-298-6175
Fax: 717-441-3787 info@BakedatHome.com
www.mikeandlous.com
Pizza, sandwiches and salads.
Co-Owner: Mike Schumeth
Co-Owner: Lou Schumeth
Type of Packaging: Food Service

8827 **Mike's Meats**
106 W Main Street
Eitzen, MN 55931-7759 507-495-3336
Processor of meat products including ham, sausage and dried beef; slaughtering services available
Owner: Mike Hartley
Estimated Sales: $140,000
Number Employees: 4
Type of Packaging: Consumer

8828 **Mike-Sell's Potato ChipCompany**
P.O.Box 115
Dayton, OH 45404 937-228-9400
Fax: 937-461-5707 800-853-9437
info@mike-sells.com www.mike-sells.com

Mike-Sell's Potato Chips include original, groovy, old fashiioned, reduced fat, and assorted flavors including barbecue, cheddar and sour cream, sour cream, green onion, salt and vinegar and smoked bacon. Additional products includepretzels, regular and cheese puffcorn, cheese curls, corn chips, tortilla chips, pork rinds and salsa dip.
President: Leslie C Mapp
CFO: Larry Pounds
CEO: David Ray
Quality Control: Troy Lyons
VP Sales & Marketing: L Nat Chandler
Plant Manager: Frank de Moss
Estimated Sales: $ 50-100 Million
Number Employees: 250-499
Parent Co: Mike-Sell's
Type of Packaging: Consumer, Food Service

8829 **Miko Meat**
230 Kekuanaoa Street
Hilo, HI 96720-6427 808-935-0841
Fax: 808-935-2781
Sausages and hot dogs
President: Ernest Matsumura
General Manager: Matt Asano
Estimated Sales: $ 620 K
Number Employees: 5-9

8830 **Milan Provision Company**
10815 Roosevelt Ave
Flushing, NY 11368 718-899-7678
Fax: 718-335-3354
Manufacturer of Mexican meat
Owner: Salvatore Laurita
Estimated Sales: $1-3 Million
Number Employees: 10-19
Type of Packaging: Consumer, Food Service, Private Label, Bulk

8831 **Milan Salami Company**
1155 67th St
Oakland, CA 94608 510-654-7055
Fax: 510-654-7257
Processor of Italian dry salami and loaf products; also, sausage and pepperoni
Owner: George Ramsey
Sales: Steven Ramsey
Plant Manager: Greg Ramsey
Estimated Sales: $ 50 - 100 Million
Number Employees: 10-19
Sq. footage: 12000
Type of Packaging: Consumer, Food Service, Private Label, Bulk

8832 **Miland Seafood**
2527 Perdido Street
New Orleans, LA 70119 504-821-4500
Fax: 504-821-4540 888-821-1916
marketing@inlandseafood.com
www.inlandseafood.com
Seafood
President: Eric Sussman
Estimated Sales: $ 10 - 20 Million
Number Employees: 20-49

8833 **Milani Gourmet**
2150 N 15th Avenue
Melrose Park, IL 60160-1410 708-216-0704
Fax: 708-216-0709 800-333-0003
www.milanifoods.com
Seasonings, salad dressings, sugar replacements, salt substitutes and base mixes
Manager of Milani Foods: Linda Fortino
Number Employees: 1-4
Parent Co: Precision Foods
Type of Packaging: Food Service, Bulk
Brands:
Bakers Joy
Charcol-It
Milani
Molly McButter
Mrs Dash Salt Free Seasoning
Sugartwin

8834 **Milano Baking Company**
433 S Chicago St
Joliet, IL 60436 815-727-4872
Fax: 815-727-3116 milano@uti.com
www.milanobakery.com
Italian bread and rolls
President: Mario Debenedetti
Estimated Sales: $ 50-100 Million
Number Employees: 55

8835 **Milano Winery**
14594 S Highway 101
Hopland, CA 95449 707-744-1396
Fax: 707-744-1138 800-564-2582
wines@milanowinery.com
www.milanowinery.com
Wines including Cabernet Sauvignon, Petit Verdot, Carignane, Syrah, Petite Syrah and Merlot.
President: Edward Starr
Vice President: Deanna Starr
Estimated Sales: Below $ 5 Million
Number Employees: 1-4
Number of Brands: 1
Number of Products: 10
Brands:
Milano Family Winery

8836 **Milat Vineyards**
1091 Saint Helena Hwy S
St Helena, CA 94574-2268 707-963-0758
Fax: 707-963-0168 info@milat.com
www.milat.com
Wines including Chenin Blanc, Chardonnay, Merlot, Cabernet Sauvignon, Zinfandel, Zivio and dessert wines.
Owner: Michael Milat
Estimated Sales: $ 1-2.5 Million
Number Employees: 1-4
Brands:
Milat Vineyards

8837 **Mild Bill's Spices**
PO Box 142
Bulverde, TX 78163 830-980-4124
sales@mildbills
http://www.mildbills.com/
Processor and exporter of chili powder, seasoning blends and barbecue spices, salsa, relish
Owner: Bill Dees
Co-Owner: Tamara Dees
Type of Packaging: Consumer, Food Service
Brands:
Big Bruce's Gunpowder Chili
Fire Marshall's Cajun

8838 **(HQ)Miles J H & Company**
902 Southampton Ave
Norfolk, VA 23510-1016 757-622-9264
Fax: 757-622-9261 thorp@exportla.com
Processor and exporter of frozen oysters and clams
President: Roy Parker
Director: Jyoti Mukerji
Sales Director: R Miles
Plant Manager: Roy Parker
Purchasing Manager: Ed Miles
Estimated Sales: $18534237
Number Employees: 50-99
Number of Brands: 1
Number of Products: 4
Sq. footage: 70000
Type of Packaging: Food Service, Private Label, Bulk

8839 **Milfico Foods**
1350 Greenleaf Ave
Elk Grove Vlg, IL 60007 847-427-0491
Fax: 847-427-0498 milficofoods@msn.com
Frozen catfish, cod, flounder, halibut, perch, pollock, salmon, tuna, whiting, orange roughy, sole, red snapper, grouper, swordfish, mahi mahi, tilapia, pike, lobster tails, oysters, scallops, shrimp, crab, mussells
President: Ira Gitlin
Estimated Sales: $ 5-10 Million
Number Employees: 20-49
Type of Packaging: Consumer, Food Service, Private Label

8840 **Miline Fruit Products**
P.O.Box 111
Prosser, WA 99350-0111 509-786-2611
Fax: 509-786-1724 jharris@milnefruit.com
www.milnefruit.com
Fruit concentrates
President: Randy Hageman
CEO: Dave Wyckoff
Director of Sales/Marketing: John J Schroeder
Number Employees: 50-99

8841 **Milk Specialties Company**
260 S Washington St
Carpentersville, IL 60110 847-426-3411
Fax: 847-426-4121 800-323-4274
msc@milkspecialties.com
www.msccompany.com
Processor of dairy and fat ingredients including hi-fats and calf milk replacers
President and COO: Bill Harrington
CFO: Michael Drennan
CEO: Trevor Tomkins
Estimated Sales: $35 Million
Number Employees: 20-49

8842 **Milk Specialties Global**
10125 Crosstown Circle
Ste 129
Eden Praire, MN 55344 952-942-7310
Fax: 952-942-7611 www.msccompany.com
Manufacturer of milk products
COO: Dave Lenzmeier
Director of Research: Ramon Gonzalez
Director of Supply Chain: Paul Lombard
Number Employees: 20-49
Parent Co: Milk Specialties Company

8843 **Milky Whey**
910 Brooks St Ste 203
Missoula, MT 59801 406-542-7373
Fax: 406-542-7377 800-379-6455
dairy@themilkywhey.com
www.themilkywhey.com
Domestic and international wholesaler/distributor of all whey proteins and dry dairy ingredients including nonfat dry milk, whole milk, whey powder, butter, buttermilk powder, caseinates, lactose, nondairy creamers, whey proteinconcentrates and isolates, and cheese powders. Custom and private label blends are available upon request. Please mention this directory when calling
President: Curt Pijanowski
Sales Director: Amy Shay
Operations Manager: Anita Turnbaugh
Reception: Tony Cavanaugh
Estimated Sales: $1200000
Number Employees: 5-9
Type of Packaging: Consumer, Private Label, Bulk

8844 **Mill Cove Lobster Pound**
PO Box 280
Boothbay Harbor, ME 04538-0280 207-633-3340
Fax: 207-633-7206
Processor and wholesaler/distributor of seafood including lobster, shrimp, frozen cod, ocean perch, pollack, clams and oysters
President: Jeffery Lewis
Estimated Sales: $4-$5 Million
Number Employees: 10-19
Type of Packaging: Consumer

8845 **Mill Creek Vineyards**
P.O.Box 758
Healdsburg, CA 95448 707-431-2121
Fax: 707-431-1714 877-349-2121
brian@mcvonline.com
www.millcreekwinery.com
Wines
Proprietor: William Kreck
General Manager: Yvonne Kreck
Winemaker: Jeremy Kreck
Wholesale Sales: John Miller
Tasting Room: Bruce Thomas
Bookkeeper: Julie Ricetti
IT: Brian Kreck
Estimated Sales: Below $ 5 Million
Number Employees: 10-19
Type of Packaging: Private Label
Brands:
Felta Springs
Mill Creek Vineyards
Reflections

8846 **Millbrook Vineyard and Winery**
26 Wing Rd
Millbrook, NY 12545-5017 845-677-8383
Fax: 845-677-6186 800-662-9463
millbrookwinery@millwine.com
www.millbrookwine.com

Wines the selection of which includes - White Wines: Pinot Grigio, Gewurztraminer, Tocai Friulano, Chardonnay and Castle Hill Chardonnay; Red Wines: Grand Reserve Pinot Noir, Merlot, Hunt Country Red, Cabernet Franc and Pinot NoirProprietor's Special Reserve.
Owner: John Dyson
CFO: Eric Grans
General Manager/Sales Manager: Gary Goddard
Estimated Sales: $ 5-10 Million
Number Employees: 10-19
Type of Packaging: Private Label
Brands:
Millbrook

8847 **Mille Lacs Gourmet Foods**
P.O.Box 8919
Madison, WI 53590 608-837-8535
Fax: 608-825-6463 800-843-1381
wjones@millelacs.com www.millelacs.com
Processor of gourmet cheeses and chocolates
President: Jay Singer
VP: John Manzer
President: Jay Singer
Sales Director: David Sandorn
Estimated Sales: $ 5 - 10 Million
Number Employees: 20-49
Brands:
Degeneve
Heart of Wisconsin
Mille Lacs

8848 **Mille Lacs MP Company**
P.O.Box 8919
Madison, WI 53708 608-837-8535
Fax: 608-825-6463 800-843-1381
dsanborn@mille-lacs.com www.mille-lacs.com
Manufacturer and exporter of specialty foods, chocolates, cheeses and gift baskets
President: Jay Singer
National Broker Manager: David Sanborn
National Sales Manager: Randy Krause
Estimated Sales: $ 5 - 10 Million
Number Employees: 20-49
Sq. footage: 750000
Parent Co: Wisconsin Cheeseman
Type of Packaging: Consumer, Bulk

8849 **Mille Lacs Wild Rice Corporation**
P.O.Box 200
Aitkin, MN 56431 218-927-2740
Fax: 218-927-6124 800-626-3809
info@canoewildrice.com
www.canoewildrice.com
Processor and exporter of kosher wild rice; importer of natural hot breakfast cereals for distribution to wholesalers/distributors
President: Chris Ratuski
Estimated Sales: $2500000
Number Employees: 20-49
Parent Co: Shoal Lake Wild Rice
Type of Packaging: Consumer, Food Service, Private Label, Bulk
Brands:
Canoe
Oh Canada

8850 **Millen Fish**
P.O.Box 864
Millen, GA 30442-864 478-982-4988
Fax: 912-982-1746
Fish and fish products
President: David McMillian
Estimated Sales: $ 3 - 5 Million
Number Employees: 10-19

8851 **Millennium Specialty Chemicals**
601 Crestwood St
Jacksonville, FL 32208 904-768-5800
Fax: 904-768-2200 800-231-6728
Processor and exporter of synthetic essential oils, flavors and fragrances
President: George Robbins
VP Materials Management: D Michael Gurkin
VP Sales/Marketing: Michael Wimberly
Estimated Sales: $100+ Million
Number Employees: 100-249
Parent Co: Hanson Industries
Type of Packaging: Bulk
Brands:
Arbanex
Arbanol
Glidmints
Zestoral

8852 **Millennium Specialty Chemicals**
601 Crestwood St
Jacksonville, FL 32208 904-768-5800
Fax: 904-768-2200 800-231-6728
www.millenniumchem.com
Aroma organic chemicals, flavors and fragrances
Estimated Sales: $100+ Million
Number Employees: 100-249

8853 **(HQ)Miller Brewing Company**
4000 West State Street
Milwaukee, WI 53208-3175 414-933-1846
Fax: 414-931-2818 www.millerbrewing.com
Processor and exporter of beer including light, ice, nonalcoholic, lager, ale and malt liquor.
President/CEO: Norman Adami
SVP/General Counsel & Secretary: Mike Jones
SVP/Finance: Gavin Hattersley
SVP/Miller International: Doug Brodman
SVP/Strategy & Planning: Kevin Self
EVP/Chief Marketing Officer: Randy Ransom
EVP/Sales & Distribution: Tom Cardella
SVP/Communication & Government Relations: Nehl Horton
COO: Michael Evans
SVP/Human Resources: Denise Smith
Estimated Sales: $300 Million
Number Employees: 800
Parent Co: SABMiller
Type of Packaging: Consumer, Food Service
Brands:
FOSTER'S LAGER
FOSTER'S SPECIAL BITTER
HAMM'S
HAMM'S DRAFT
HAMM'S SPECIAL LIGHT
HENRY WEINHARD'S BLUE BOAR PALE ALE
HENRY WEINHARD'S CLASSIC DARK
HENRY WEINHARD'S HEFEWEIZEN
HENRY WEINHARD'S NW TRAIL BLOND LAG
HENRY WEINHARD'S PRIVATE RESERVE
HENRY WEINHARD'S SUMMER WHEAT
ICE HOUSE 5.5
ICEHOUSE 5.0
ICHE HOUSE LIGHT
LEINENKUGEL'S APPLE SPICE
LEINENKUGEL'S BERRY WEISS
LEINENKUGEL'S BIG BUTT DOPPELBOCK
LEINENKUGEL'S CREAMY DARK
LEINENKUGEL'S HONEY WEISS
LEINENKUGEL'S LIGHT
LEINENKUGEL'S OKTOBERFEST
LEINENKUGEL'S ORIGINAL
LEINENKUGEL'S RED LAGER
LEINENKUGEL'S SUNSET WHEAT
MAGNUM MALT LIQUOR
MICKEY'S ICE
MICKEY'S MALT LIQUOR
MILLER GENUINE DRAFT
MILLER GENUINE DRAFT LIGHT
MILLER HIGH LIFE
MILLER HIGH LIFE LIGHT
MILLER LITE
MILWAUKEE'S BEST
MILWAUKEE'S BEST ICE
MILWAUKEE'S BEST LIGHT
OLD ENGLISH 800 MALT LIQUOR
OLDE ENGLISH HG800
OLDE ENGLISH HG800 7.5
PERONI NASTRO AZZURRO
PILSNER URQUELL
RED DOG
SHARP'S NON-ALCOHOLIC BREW
SHEAF STOUT
SOUTHPAW LIGHT
SPARKS
SPARKS LIGHT
SPARKS PLUS 6%
SPARKS PLUS 7%
STEEL RESERVE HIGH GRAVITY
STEEL RESERVE HIGH GRAVITY 6.0
STEEL RESERVE TRIPLE EXPORT 8.1%
STEEL SIX

8854 **Miller Brothers PackingcCompany**
P.O.Box 337
Sylvester, GA 31791 229-776-2014
Fax: 229-776-4728
Manufacturer of beef, sausage, pork, lamb and ostrich including emu and rhea; slaughtering services available
President/Co-Owner: Otis Miller Sr
VP/Co-Owner: Dan Miller
Estimated Sales: $5-10 Million
Number Employees: 10-19
Type of Packaging: Food Service, Bulk
Brands:
DAEAB
GOLD NUGGET

8855 **Miller Johnson Seafood**
4310 Heron Bay Loop Road S
Coden, AL 36523-3714 251-873-4444
Fax: 252-729-1427
Seafood

8856 **Miller's Cheese Corp**
196 28th Street
Brooklyn, NY 11232 718-965-1840
Fax: 718-965-0979
Processor of kosher cheese
Owner: Meyer Thurm
Marketing Director: Yudi Sherer
Sales: Sruly Sherer
Estimated Sales: $5 Million
Number Employees: 1-4
Type of Packaging: Consumer

8857 **Miller's Country Hams**
7110 Highway 190
Dresden, TN 38225-2276 731-364-3940
Fax: 731-364-5338 800-622-0606
millersham@crunet.com http://www.crunet.com
Country ham
President: Jan Frick
Quality Control: Mark Mash
Vice President: Mark Mash
CFO: Sharon Burress
Production Manager: Linda Burcham
Plant Manager: Barry King
Estimated Sales: $ 5-10 Million
Number Employees: 20-49
Brands:
Miller's Country Ham

8858 **(HQ)Miller's Honey Company**
125 E Laurel St
Colton, CA 92324 909-825-1722
Fax: 909-825-5932 mail@millershoney.com
www.millershoney.com
Manufacturer and exporter of honey
President: Steve Smith
GM: Richard Barrett
Estimated Sales: $ 5 - 10 Million
Number Employees: 20-49
Type of Packaging: Consumer, Food Service, Private Label, Bulk
Brands:
MILLERS

8859 **Miller's Honey Company**
PO Box 500
Colton, CA 92324 909-825-1722
Fax: 909-825-5932 mail@millershoney.com
www.millershoney.com
Manufacturer and exporter of honey and beeswax
President: Steve Smith
President/CEO: George Murdock
VP/General Manager: Steven Smith
Sales Manager: Merrill Paxman
Human Resources Manager: Roxanna Mielke
Estimated Sales: $29 Million
Number Employees: 34
Sq. footage: 33000
Type of Packaging: Consumer, Food Service, Private Label, Bulk
Brands:
Honey Valley
Millers
Rita Miller
Superior

8860 **Miller's Meat Market**
1524 S Main St
Red Bud, IL 62278 618-282-3334
Fax: 618-282-7799 millermeatman@yahoo.com
www.redbudchamber.com
Processor of fresh and cured meats including beef, pork, elk, buffalo, sausage, etc.; also, slaughtering services available
Owner: Kevin Miller

Estimated Sales: $300,000-500,000
Number Employees: 5-9
Sq. footage: 5000
Type of Packaging: Consumer, Food Service, Private Label

8861 MillerCoors
405 Cordele Rd
Albany, GA 31705-2109 229-420-5191
Fax: 229-420-5250 www.millercorrs.com
Processor of beer including light, lager, ice, nonalcoholic and malt liquor
Number Employees: 600
Parent Co: MillerCoors
Type of Packaging: Consumer
Brands:
COORS
COORS LIGHT
EXTRA GOLD LAGER
HAMM'S
HAMM'S GOLDEN DRAFT
HAMM'S SPECIAL LIGHT
ICEHOUSE
KEYSTONE ICE
KEYSTONE LIGHT
KEYSTONE PREMIUM
MAGNUM MALT LIQUOR
MICKEY'S
MICKEY'S ICE
MILLER CHILL
MILLER GENUINCE DRAFT 64
MILLER GENUINE DRAFT
MILLER HIGH LIFE
MILLER HIGH LIFE LIGHT
MILLER LITE
MILWAUKEE'S BEST ICE
MILWAUKEE'S BEST LIGHT
MILWAUKEE'S BEST PREMIUM
OLD ENGLISH 800 7.5
OLD ENGLISH HIGH GRAVITY 800
OLDE ENGLISH 800
RED DOG
SOUTHPAW LIGHT
STEEL RESERVE HIGH GRAVITY
STEEL RESERVE TRIPLE EXPORT 8.1%
STEEL SIX

8862 MillerCoors
863 E Meadow Rd
Eden, NC 27289-3327 336-627-2100
www.millercoors.com
Processor of beer including light, lager, ice, nonalcoholic and malt liquor
Manager: Janice Wangard
Operations Manager: Jerry Grubb
Parent Co: MillerCoors
Type of Packaging: Consumer
Brands:
Miller

8863 MillerCoors
5135 S Eastside Highway
Elkton, VA 22827
www.millercoors.com
Processor of beer including light, ice, nonalcoholic, lager and malt liquor
Sales/Marketing Executive: Chris Lierman
Sales Manager: Mike Rhodey
Sales Administration: Karen Loss
Parent Co: MillerCoors
Type of Packaging: Consumer, Food Service

8864 MillerCoors
2525 Wayne Madison Rd
Trenton, OH 45067-9799 513-579-8503
Fax: 513-621-8219 800-944-5483
www.millercoors.com
Processor of beer including light, ice, nonalcoholic, lager and malt liquor
Manager: Dennis B Puffer
CEO: Norman Adami
General Manager Sales: Grant Doster
Parent Co: MillerCoors
Type of Packaging: Consumer, Food Service

8865 MillerCoors
15801 East First St
Irwindale, CA 91706-2069
www.millercoors.com
Processor of beer including light, ice, nonalcoholic, lager and malt liquor
Parent Co: MillerCoors
Type of Packaging: Consumer, Food Service
Brands:
Miller
Miller Lite
Rusty's

8866 MillerCoors
7001 South Fwy
Fort Worth, TX 76134-4099 817-551-3300
Fax: 817-551-3322 800-645-5376
www.millercoors.com
Processor of beer including ice, light, lager, non-alcoholic and malt liquor
General Manager: Jeff Colbert
Sales/Marketing Executive: Shaun Brown
Plant Manager: Jack Jackson
Parent Co: MillerCoors
Type of Packaging: Consumer, Food Service

8867 MillerCoors
1515 North 10th Street
Milwaukee, WI 53205
www.millercoors.com
Processor of beer including ice, light, lager, nonalcoholic and malt liquor
Parent Co: MillerCoors
Type of Packaging: Consumer, Food Service
Brands:
Miller

8868 (HQ)MillerCoors
250 S Wacker
Suite 800
Chicago, IL 60606 312-496-2700
800-645-5376
www.millercoors.com
Processor of beer including light, lager, ice, nonalcoholic and malt liquor
CEO: Tom Long
EVP/CFO: Gavin Hattersley
Chief Legal Officer: Karen Ripley
Chief Human Resources Officer: Chris Kozina
Chief Responsibility & Ethics Officer: N Cornell Boggs III
EVP/Chief Marketing Officer: Andrew England
Chief Information Officer: Karen Alber
Chief Communications Officer: Nehl Horton
President/Sales & Distribution: Ed McBrien
EVP/Chief Integrated Supply Chain Offc: Fernando Palacios
Estimated Sales: $7 Billion
Number Employees: 9000
Parent Co: SABMiller/Molson Coors
Type of Packaging: Consumer
Brands:
AGUUILA
BLUE MOON BELGIAN WHITE
COORS BANQUET
COORS LIGHT
COORS NON-ALCHOLIC
CRISTAL
CUSQUENA
EXTRA GOLD LAGER
FOSTER'S
GEORGE KILLIAN'S IRISH RED
HAMM'S
HENRY WEINHARD'S PRIVATE RESERVE
ICEHOUSE
KEYSTONE LIGHT
LEINENKUGEL'S SUNSET WHEAT
MAGNUM MALT LIQUOR
MGD 64
MICKEY'S
MILLER CHILL
MILLER GENUINE DRAFT
MILLER HIGH LIFE
MILLER LITE
MILWAUKEE'S BEST LIGHT
MOLSON CANADIAN
OLD ENGLISH 800
PERONI NASTRO AZZURRO
PILSNER URQUELL
RED DOG
SHARP'S
SOUTHPAW LIGHT
SPARKS
STEEL RESERVE HIGH GRAVITY
TYSKIE

8869 Millers Blue Ribbon Beef
410 N 200 W
Hyrum, UT 84319-1024 435-245-6456
Fax: 435-245-6634 800-873-0939
www.eamiller.com
Manufacturer of flavors, flavors enhancers, extracts, hydrolyzed proteins and substitutes
President: Ted Miller
Marketing/Sales: Bruce Miller
Personnel Manager: Paul Barnard
Feeder Cattle Procurement: Alan Summers
Cattle Feeding Opportunities: Bryan Summers
Miller Brothers Trucking: Reed Baldwin
Estimated Sales: $ 50 - 100 Million
Number Employees: 250-499

8870 Millers Ice Cream
1918 Center Street
Houston, TX 77007-6105 713-861-3138
Processor of ice cream including novelties, pies, cakes, sandwiches and popsicles
Owner: Dianne Haren
Estimated Sales: $560000
Number Employees: 4
Type of Packaging: Consumer, Food Service, Private Label, Bulk

8871 Millflow Spice Corporation
60 Davids Drive
Hauppauge, NY 11788 631-884-7422
Fax: 631-231-5500 866-227-8355
info@millflowspicecorp.com
www.millflowspicecorp.com
Processor, importer and exporter of food colors, flavoring extracts, spices, seasonings and sauces including pesto, worcestershire, soy, barbecue, hot and smoke
President: Zane Moses
Estimated Sales: $2,600,000
Number Employees: 21
Parent Co: Regal Extract Company
Type of Packaging: Consumer, Food Service, Private Label, Bulk
Brands:
Bonton
Growers Company
Millflow
Regal

8872 Milliaire Winery
276 Main St
Murphys, CA 95247 209-728-1658
Fax: 209-736-1915 wines@milliairewinery.com
www.milliairewinery.com
Wines
Manager: Jana Nadler
Estimated Sales: $160,000
Number Employees: 1-4
Brands:
Milliaire Winery

8873 Millie's Pierogi
129 Broadway
Chicopee Falls, MA 01020 413-594-4991
800-743-7641
ann@milliespierogi.com
www.milliespierogi.com
Processor of fully cooked pierogies including cabbage, potato and cheese, cheese, prune and blueberry.
President: Ann Kerigan
Estimated Sales: Less than $500,000
Number Employees: 5-9
Brands:
Millie's Pierogi

8874 Milligan & Higgins
100 Maple Ave
Johnstown, NY 12095-1041 518-762-4638
Fax: 518-762-7039 milligan@superior.net
www.milligan1868.com
Manufacturer, importer and exporter of kosher edible and technical gelatins; protein factory providing gelatin blending and analytical and microbiological laboratories available
President: Lee Kornbluh
Technical Director: Jacob Utzig
Estimated Sales: $20-50 Million
Number Employees: 20-49
Parent Co: Hudson Industries Corporation
Type of Packaging: Bulk

8875 Milling Sausage Company
629 S 10th St
Milwaukee, WI 53204 414-645-2677
Fax: 414-645-2679
Processor of sausage and frankfurters
Owner: Matt Miklick
Number Employees: 5-9

Type of Packaging: Bulk

8876 **Millrose Brewing Company**
45 S Barrington Rd
South Barrington, IL 60010-9508 847-382-7673
Fax: 847-382-7693 800-464-5576
manager@millroserestaurant.com
www.millroserestaurant.com
Beer
Manager: Lisa Scoville
COO: Mike Sheridan
Director Manufacturing: Thomas Sweeney
Estimated Sales: $ 5-10 Million
Number Employees: 100-249

8877 **Mills**
375 W Market St
Salinas, CA 93901 831-757-1611
Fax: 831-424-9475 info@millsfamilyfarms.com
www.millsfamilyfarms.com
Grower and exporter of produce including celery, broccoli, cabbage, lettuce, cauliflower and whole leaf and mixed vegetables
Owner: Roger Mills
VP/General Manager: Ed Little
Estimated Sales: $ 20 - 50 Million
Number Employees: 20-49

8878 **Mills Brothers International**
16000 Christensen Rd # 300
Tukwila, WA 98188-2967 206-575-3000
Fax: 206-957-1362 edmills@ghfoods.com
/www.ghfoods.com
Processor, exporter and wholesaler/distributor of specialty and organic grains, dried peas, dried beans, lentils, millet rice and corn products including popcorn kernels, flour, grits, meal and starch; serving the food servicemarket
President: Eric Mills
Estimated Sales: $36306000
Number Employees: 50-99
Sq. footage: 26000
Type of Packaging: Consumer, Food Service, Private Label, Bulk
Brands:
Cascade
Mills Brothers International

8879 **Mills Coffee Roasting Company**
1058 Broad St
Providence, RI 2905 401-781-7860
Fax: 401-781-7978 888-781-5282
info@millscoffee.com www.millscoffee.com
Coffee
President: Susan Mills
Plant Manager: Mike Candy
Estimated Sales: Below $ 5 Million
Number Employees: 5-9
Type of Packaging: Private Label

8880 **Mills Seafood ltd.**
5 Mills Street
Bouctouche, NB E4S 3S3
Canada 506-743-2444
Fax: 506-743-8497 millsseafood.ca
Seafood processor
Owner: Steven Mills
Owner: Marie Allain
Vice President: Marie Allain
Quality Control: George Robichaud
Marketing Manager: Steven Mills
Marketing: Marie Allain
Plant Manager: Laurie Allain
Number Employees: 50-99
Type of Packaging: Food Service

8881 **Millstream Brewing**
835 48th Ave
Amana, IA 52203 319-622-3672
Fax: 319-622-6516
brewery@millstreambrewing.com
www.millstreambrewing.com
Processor of beers, ales and lagers
Owner: Chris Priebe
Estimated Sales: Below $ 5 Million
Number Employees: 10-19
Type of Packaging: Consumer, Food Service
Brands:
Millstream

8882 **Milmar Food Group**
1 6 1/2 Station Rd
Goshen, NY 10924 845-294-5400
Fax: 845-294-6687 www.milmarfoodgroup.com
Manufacturer of wide variety of value added, OU kosher endorsed, frozen foods including: breakfast selections, vegetarian, chicken, burrito, and pre-plated meal products
President: Martin Hoffman
EVP: Dov Peikes
Marketing Director: Rita O'Connor CMC
Director: Judah Koolyk
Purchasing: Barry Werk
Estimated Sales: $30 Million
Number Employees: 250
Number of Brands: 3
Number of Products: 100
Sq. footage: 60000
Type of Packaging: Consumer, Food Service, Private Label, Bulk
Brands:
MRS. VEGGIES
NO FORKS REQUIRED
SPRING VALLEY

8883 **Milne Fruit Products**
804 Bennett Aveune
P.O. Box 111
Prosser, WA 99350 509-786-2611
Fax: 509-786-4915 selkins@milnefruit.com
www.milnefruit.com
Processes fruit juice, fruit juice concentrates, purees, custom blends and nutritional ingredients. Flavors include concord grape, strawberry, cranberry, raspberry, blueberry and cherry and others
President: Randy Hageman
General Manager: Randall Hageman
Research & Development: Eric Johnson
Quality Control: Eric Johnson
National Sales Manager: Shannon Elkins
Sales Director: Ryan Callaway
Number Employees: 50
Parent Co: Ocean Spray Cranberries
Type of Packaging: Bulk

8884 **Milner Milling**
P.O.Box 2247
Chattanooga, TN 37409 423-265-2313
Fax: 770-358-0120
Flour and grain
Chairman: Vernon Grizzard Jr
Estimated Sales: $11,100,000
Number Employees: 20-49

8885 **Milnot Company**
P.O.Box J
Neosho, MO 64850-0560 417-776-2243
Fax: 417-776-2763 800-877-6455
www.milnot.com
Processor of butter, vegetable oil and evaporated milk
President: Craig Steinke
CFO: Alain Souligny
Estimated Sales: $ 50 - 100 Million
Number Employees: 50-99
Parent Co: Milnot Company

8886 **Milnot Company**
120 W Saint John Street
Litchfield, IL 62056-2169 217-324-2146
800-877-6455
www.milnot.com
Dairy products.
President: Christoph Rudolph
Number Employees: 20-49
Parent Co: Milnot Company
Type of Packaging: Consumer, Private Label, Bulk

8887 **(HQ)Milnot Company**
100 S 4th Street
Suite 1010
Saint Louis, MO 63102-1823 314-436-7667
Fax: 314-436-7679 888-656-3245
www.milnot.com
Dairy products, baby food, etc
President: Scott Meader
CFO: Alain Souligny
Senior VP Sales: Sal Stazonne
Purchasing Manager: John Witte
Estimated Sales: I
Number Employees: 250-499
Number of Brands: 3
Type of Packaging: Consumer, Private Label
Brands:
Beech-Nut Baby Food
Dairy Sweet
Milnot
Sunshine

8888 **Milo's Whole World Gourmet**
94 Columbus Rd
Athens, OH 45701 740-589-6456
Fax: 740-594-9151 866-589-6456
info@miloswholeworld.com
www.miloswholeworld.com
pasta sauces and salad dressings
President/Owner: Jonathan Milo
Wholesale Sales Manager: Maryjane Burch
Production: Jason Cogar

8889 **Milone Brothers Coffee**
P.O.Box 4367
Modesto, CA 95352-4367 209-526-0865
Fax: 209-526-1652 800-974-8500
mbc@milone.com www.milone.com
Fresh roasted whole bean highest grade coffees. Custom blending/roasting, espresso and coffee machine experts
Partner: Joseph Milone
Estimated Sales: $1,000,000
Number Employees: 5-9
Sq. footage: 3000
Type of Packaging: Food Service, Bulk
Brands:
Milone Brothers

8890 **Milos**
125 W 55th St Frnt 3
New York, NY 10019 212-245-7400
Fax: 212-245-4828 www.milos.ca
Frozen potato cakes
Owner: Costas Spiliadis
Estimated Sales: $ 2.5-5 Million
Number Employees: 10-19

8891 **Milroy Canning Company**
P.O.Box 125
Milroy, IN 46156 765-629-2221
Fax: 765-629-2645 milroy@comsys.net
Processor of canned tomatoes
President: Robert Tobian
Vice President: Morris Tobian
Estimated Sales: $ 10 - 20 Million
Number Employees: 20-49
Type of Packaging: Consumer

8892 **Milsolv Corporation**
P.O.Box 444
Butler, WI 53007-0444 262-252-3550
Fax: 262-252-5250 800-558-8501
allmilw@milsolv.com www.milsolv.com
Beverages, confectionery, canned foods, processed cheese, bakery, meat, seafood, dairy
Chairman: Ed mills
CEO: Ed Mills
Sales: Mark Hartung
Brands:
Milsolv

8893 **Milton A. Klein Company**
PO Box 363
New York, NY 10021-0006 516-829-3400
Fax: 516-829-3427 800-221-0248
allen@miltonklein.com www.miltonklein.com
President: Irene Klein
VP: Allen Klein
Number Employees: 10-19
Sq. footage: 6800

8894 **Milwhite**
5487 Padre Island Hwy
Brownsville, TX 78521 956-547-1970
Fax: 956-547-1999 www.milwhite.com
Manufacturer and importer of clay, talcs, calcium carbonate, barium sulfate, attapulgite, bentonite and other nonmetallic minerals; exporter of aflatoxin binders
President: Mike Hughes III
VP Operations: Mike Hughes
Estimated Sales: $ 20 - 50 Million
Number Employees: 20-49
Type of Packaging: Private Label, Bulk
Brands:
Blanca
Gel B
Milsorb
Super Gel B
TDM

8895 **Mimac Glaze**
271 Glidden Road
Unit 17
Brampton, ON L6W 1H9
Canada 905-457-7737
Fax: 905-457-9828 877-990-9975
dave@mimacglaze.com www.168.144.59.68
Processor of icing stabilizers and ready-to-use icings
President: W David Miles
Secretary/Treasurer: Marion Miles
Production Manager: Werner Barduhn
Estimated Sales: $975,000
Number Employees: 6
Sq. footage: 6600
Type of Packaging: Consumer, Food Service
Brands:
Paragon
Supreme

8896 **Mims Meat Company**
12634 East Fwy
Houston, TX 77015-5614 713-453-0151
Fax: 713-453-6714
Manufacturers and Distributors of Beef Patties and Steaks
President: Art Innis
Marketing Manager: Phillip Cash
Plant Manager: Dan Mims
Estimated Sales: $4.9 Million
Number Employees: 50

8897 **Min Tong Herbs**
318 7th St
Oakland, CA 94607 510-873-8677
Fax: 510-873-8671 800-562-5777
mintongherbs@hotmail.com
www.mintongherbs.com
Processor and importer of Chinese herbal extracts
President: Charles Chang
Vice President: Susan Chang
Sales: Tiffany Zhon
Estimated Sales: $500,000-$1 Million
Number Employees: 5-9
Number of Brands: 1
Type of Packaging: Consumer, Private Label, Bulk
Brands:
Min Tong

8898 **Mincing Overseas Spice Company**
10 Tower Rd
Dayton, NJ 8810 732-355-9944
Fax: 732-555-9964 mail@mincing.com
www.mincing.com
Importers, processor of spices, seeds and aromatic herbs
President: Manoj Rupaerlia
CFO: K Jobanputra
Quality Controol: Nagy Beskal
Sales: Dorothy Hollomay
Plant Manager: Charles Armgnti
Purchasing: H Ruparelia
Estimated Sales: $ .5 - 1 million
Number Employees: 1-4
Sq. footage: 50000
Parent Co: Mincing Trading Corporation

8899 **Mine & Mommy's Cookies**
2510 south 7th
Abilene, TX 79605 325-721-1958
Fax: 915-928-1067 cccookie@prodigy.net
mineandmommys.com
Processor and exporter of prepared flour mixes and doughs
Co-Owner: Monty Tittle
Co-Owner: Marilyn Tittle
Estimated Sales: $1-$2.5 Million
Number Employees: 1-4
Brands:
Mine & Mommy's

8900 **Mineral & Pigment Solutions**
1000 Coolidge St
South Plainfield, NJ 7080 908-561-6100
Fax: 908-757-3488 800-732-0562
customerservice@wcdinc.com www.wcdinc.com
Manufacturer of high quality minerals, colors, chemicals and additives for the food and pharmaceutical industries
President: Theodore Hubbard
Estimated Sales: $ 50-100 Million
Number Employees: 50-99

8901 **Minerva Cheese Factory**
P.O.Box 60
Minerva, OH 44657 330-868-4196
Fax: 330-868-7947 info@cheesehere.com
www.cheesehere.com
Processor of dairy products including butter, whey and cheese; also, gift boxes available
Owner: Phillip Muller
VP: Adam Muller
Estimated Sales: $6 Million
Number Employees: 40
Type of Packaging: Consumer, Food Service, Private Label, Bulk

8902 **Minerva Dairy**
430 Radloff Ave
Minerva, OH 44657 330-868-4196
Fax: 330-868-7947 info@minervacheese.com
www.cheesehere.com
Butter, colby and cheddar cheese
President: Phil Mueller
CEO: Adam Mueller
Plant Manager: Dave Saling
Treasurer: Polly Mueller
Marketing Director: Venae Banner
Estimated Sales: $ 25-49.9 Million
Number Employees: 20-49
Brands:
Amish Gourmet
Minerva
Oldworld

8903 **Mingo Bay Beverages**
721 Seaboard Street
Myrtle Beach, SC 29577-6520 843-448-5320
Fax: 843-448-4162 mingomoe@aol.com
www.iwebtech.com/mingobay
Processor and exporter of coffee, tea and fruit bases, mixes and concentrates
President: Larry Moses
Estimated Sales: $ 1-5 Million
Number Employees: 8
Sq. footage: 80000
Type of Packaging: Consumer, Food Service, Private Label, Bulk
Brands:
Mingo Bay Beverages

8904 **Mingo River Pecan Company**
P.O. Box 2030
Florence, SC 29503 843-662-2452
Fax: 843-664-2338 800-440-6442
tcoker@youngplantations.com
www.mingoriverpecans.com
Flavored pecans
Executive Director: Chenen Harvey
Estimated Sales: $ 20 - 50 Million
Number Employees: 100-249

8905 **Minh Food CorporationSchwan's Food Company**
1251 Scarborough Ln
Pasadena, TX 77506 713-740-7200
Fax: 713-740-7205 800-344-7655
Processor of frozen Asian foods
Manager: Cole Lewis
CEO: Ron Minist
Executive VP: Mike Minist
Number Employees: 10-19
Parent Co: Schwann's Sales
Type of Packaging: Consumer, Food Service, Private Label

8906 **Mini Pops, Inc**
208 Tosca Drive
Stoughton, MA 02072 781-436-5864
Fax: 781-533-9033 info@minipopsinc.com
www.myminipops.com
Flavored gluten free, organic, popped sorghum snack

8907 **(HQ)Minn-Dak Farmers Cooperative**
7525 Red River Rd
Wahpeton, ND 58075 701-642-8411
Fax: 701-642-6814 www.mdf.coop
Beet sugar manufacturer.
President/CEO: David H Roche
Executive VP/CFO: Steven M. Caspers
Plant Manager: Brent Muehlberg
Purchasing: John Nyquist
Estimated Sales: $198,900,000
Number Employees: 500-999
Type of Packaging: Bulk
Other Locations:
Minn-Dak Farmers Coop.
Wahpeton ND

8908 **Minn-Dak Growers Ltd.**
PO Box 13276
Grand Forks, ND 58208 701-746-7453
Fax: 701-780-9050 info@minndak.com
www.minndak.com
buckwheat, mustard, safflower and sunflower
Owner/President/General Manager: Harris Peterson
Principal/CFO: Mona Kozojed
R&D Director: Mohammad Badaruddin
Public Relations Director: Jaci Peau
Manufacturing Supervisor: Bruce Sondreal
Estimated Sales: $11 Million
Number Employees: 32
Number of Brands: 3
Number of Products: 9
Sq. footage: 60000
Type of Packaging: Consumer, Food Service, Bulk
Brands:
MDGL
MDM
MINN - DAK

8909 **Minn-Dak Yeast Company**
18175 Red River Rd W
Wahpeton, ND 58075 701-642-3300
Fax: 701-642-1908 csavoy@minndak.coop
www.dakotayeast.com
Processor of fresh bakers' yeast
EVP: Scott Miller
Plant Manager: Richard Ames
Purchasing Director: John Nyquist
Estimated Sales: $9.5 Million
Number Employees: 20-49
Sq. footage: 22000
Parent Co: Minn-Dak Farmers Cooperative
Brands:
Dakota Yeast

8910 **Minnehaha Spring Water Company**
1906 E 40th Street
Cleveland, OH 44103-3557 216-431-0243
Processor of bottled natural spring water
President: Michael Wright
Number Employees: 20-49
Type of Packaging: Consumer, Food Service, Private Label, Bulk

8911 **Minnesota Dehydrated Vegetables**
P.O.Box 245
Fosston, MN 56542 218-435-1997
Fax: 218-435-6770 info@mdvcorp.com
www.mdvcorp.com
Processor and importer of dehydrated carrots and potatoes; broker of industrial ingredients; serving processors and wholesalers/distributors
Sales: Karla Holm
Plant Manager: Jim Noyes
Estimated Sales: $ 5-10 Million
Number Employees: 60-100
Type of Packaging: Food Service, Bulk

8912 **Minnesota Dehydrated Vegetables**
P.O.Box 245
Fosston, MN 56542 218-435-1997
Fax: 218-435-6770 www.mdvcorp.com

Dehydrated vegetables
Manager: Jim Noise
Marketing Director: Jam Moyes
CFO: Jim Noyes
CFO: Jordy Alson
Estimated Sales: $ 5-10 Million
Number Employees: 50-99
Brands:
Minnesota Dehydrated Vegetables

8913 **Minnesota Specialty Crops**
P.O.Box 320
McGregor, MN 55760-0320 218-768-4917
Fax: 218-768-4413 800-328-6731
minnesotawild@citlink.com
Processor of wild berry syrups, jams, jellies and sauces, maple syrup, honey and whipped honey; also, wild rice pancake mix and organic wild, cultivated long grain and broken wild rice
President: Jack Erckenbrack
General Manager: Lori Gordon
Estimated Sales: $700000
Number Employees: 1-4
Sq. footage: 3200
Type of Packaging: Consumer, Food Service, Private Label, Bulk
Brands:
Minnesota Wild

8914 **Minnestalgia**
PO Box 860033
McGregor, MN 55760-0320 218-768-4917
Fax: 218-768-4413 800-328-6731
minnestalgia@citlink.net www.minnestalgia.com
Wines, soup and pancake mixes, berry and maple syrups, honeys, gift baskets and more!
President: Jay Erckenbrack
Estimated Sales: $ 1 - 3 Million
Number Employees: 1-4

8915 **Mino Corporation**
5406 Sheridan St
Davenport, IA 52806-2260 563-388-4770
Fax: 563-388-4772
President: Jeffrey Melchert
Estimated Sales: $ 10 - 20 Million
Number Employees: 10-19

8916 **Minor Fisheries**
176 West Street
Port Colborne, ON L3K 4E2
Canada 905-834-9232
Fax: 905-834-5662 minfish@itcanada.com
Processor of whole, dressed, filleted, fresh and frozen fresh water fish including yellow perch, yellow pickerel, white perch, whitefish, smelt, rock bass, silver bass and lingcod
President: Rod Minor
Director: Dan Minor
Estimated Sales: $2.8 Million
Number Employees: 7
Sq. footage: 2100
Type of Packaging: Consumer, Bulk

8917 **Minter Weisman Company**
1035 Nathan Ln N
Minneapolis, MN 55441-5002 952-545-3706
Fax: 612-545-0938 800-742-5655
mmanske@minter-weisman.com
www.minter-weisman.com
Candy
President: Paul Siegel
CEO: Jim Thompson
Number Employees: 100-249
Brands:
Camel
Hersey's
Marlboro

8918 **Minterbrook Oyster Company**
P.O.Box 432
Gig Harbor, WA 98335-0432 253-857-5251
Fax: 253-857-5521
Info@MinterbrookOysterCo.com
www.minterbrookoyster.com
Processor and exporter of fresh and frozen oysters, Manila clams and mussels
President: Harold E Wiksten
Sales Manager: Mike Paul
Estimated Sales: $8600000
Number Employees: 50-99
Sq. footage: 70
Type of Packaging: Consumer, Food Service, Private Label
Brands:
Minterbrook

8919 **(HQ)Minute Maid Company**
Po Box 17349
Atlanta, GA 30301 713-888-5000
Fax: 713-888-5959 800-438-2653
www.minutemaid.com
World's leading marketer of premium fruit juices and drinks. Processor of chilled, aseptic and frozen concentrated juices, punches and ades including orange, grape, grapefruit, tangerine, lemon, lime, etc.; also, citrus oils
CEO: E Neville Isdell
COO: Donald Knauss
Senior VP: Mike St John
Public Relations: Ray Crockett
Number Employees: 500-999
Parent Co: Coca-Cola Company
Type of Packaging: Consumer, Food Service
Other Locations:
Minute Maid
Dinuba CA
Apopka FL
Northampton MA
Paw Paw MI
Waco TX
Petersborough ON
Mississauga ON
Brands:
Andifruit
Bacardi Mixes
Bibo
Bright & Early
Cappy
Fruitopia
Hi-C
Juices To Go
Kapo
Minute Maid
Nectar Andina
Odwalla
Odwalla
Samantha
Simply Orange
Sunfill

8920 **Minute Maid Company**
427 San Christopher Dr
Dunedin, FL 34698 727-733-2121
Fax: 727-733-0212 800-237-0159
www.minutemaid.com / www.cocacola.com
Manufacturer of fruit juice and punch
Chairman/CEO, Coca-Cola: E Neville Isdell
EVP/CFO, Coca-Cola: Gary Fayard
Estimated Sales: $100+ Million
Number Employees: 100-249
Sq. footage: 400000
Parent Co: Coca-Cola Bottling Company
Type of Packaging: Food Service
Brands:
MINUTE MAID

8921 **Minute Maid Company**
2150 Town Square Pl # 400
Sugar Land, TX 77479-1278 281-302-4317
Fax: 713-888-5393 www.minutemaid.com
Manufacturer of orange, grapefruit and apple juices
President: Mike John
Number Employees: 100-249
Parent Co: Coca-Cola Bottling Company
Type of Packaging: Consumer

8922 **Minute Maid Company**
6900 Lougheed Way
Bombay, BC V6B 4G4
Canada 416-756-8100
Fax: 416-756-8147 800-438-2653
www.cocacola.com
Processor of fresh and frozen orange juice
CEO: Dan McCue
COO: E Neville Isdell
CFO: Gary Fayard
Vice President: Lisa Lowe
Number Employees: 50-99
Parent Co: Coca-Cola Bottling Company
Type of Packaging: Consumer, Food Service
Brands:
Coca Cola

8923 **Mira International Foods**
1200 Tices Ln Ste 203
East Brunswick, NJ 8816 732-846-5410
Fax: 732-613-7206 800-818-6472
mirasales@attglobal.net www.miramango.com
Tropical nectars
President: Ramses Awadalla
CEO: Mark Awadalla
Vice President: Pancy Awadalla
Marketing Director: Mariam Gandour
Sales Director: Joseph Awadalla
Public Relations: Mark Awadalla
Estimated Sales: $ 5-10 Million
Number Employees: 5-9
Sq. footage: 24000
Type of Packaging: Private Label
Brands:
Mira Mango Nectar

8924 **Miramar Fruit Trading Company**
2300 Nw 92nd Ave
Doral, FL 33172-4814 305-883-4774
Fax: 305-883-4773 miramarfruit.4t.com
Canned guava pulp, mango pulp, grated coconut, papaya chunks, guava shells, orange shells, pina colada mix, black beans, green pigeon peas
President: Carlos Unanue
Manager: Maria Miguel
Estimated Sales: $ 2.5-5 Million
Number Employees: 11
Brands:
Ancel

8925 **Miramar Pickles & Food Products**
200 NW 20th Ave
Fort Lauderdale, FL 33311-8724 954-351-8030
Fax: 954-462-6862 gr4pickles@aol.com
Sauerkraut, pickles, pickled tomatoes
President: George Bell
Quality Control: Daniel Singer
R & D: Micheal Hirschkorn
Estimated Sales: $ 50-75 Million
Number Employees: 10-19
Brands:
Miramar
Mrs. Nickles

8926 **Mirasco**
900 Circle 75 Pkwy SE Ste 200
Atlanta, GA 30339 770-956-1945
Fax: 770-956-0308 atlanta@mirasco.com
www.mirasco.com
Supplier of meats, poultry and seafood
President: Latif Rizk
Estimated Sales: $4.5 Million
Number Employees: 10-19
Type of Packaging: Food Service, Private Label, Bulk

8927 **Mirror Polishing & Plating Company Inc**
346 Huntingdon Ave
Waterbury, CT 06708 203-574-5400
Fax: 203-597-9448 chromerolls@mpp.net
www.mpp.net
Chromium roll fabricating and surface finishing company that provides rebuilding, grinding, plating and finishing services for all web processing applications used in the manufacturing of plastic sheet & film, paper, non-woven fabricsand food processing industries.
President: Gary Nalband
Vice President Sales & Marketing: Rimas Kozica

8928 **Miscoe Springs**
89 Northbridge Rd
Mendon, MA 1756 508-473-0550
Fax: 508-473-3971
Processor of bottled spring water
President: Alan Bernon
Managing Director: Mike Rossi
Vice President: Phil Drexler
Estimated Sales: $ 10-20 Million
Number Employees: 20
Parent Co: Miscoe Springs
Type of Packaging: Consumer, Food Service, Private Label
Brands:
Miscoe Springs

8929 **Mishawaka Brewing Company**
408 W Cleveland Rd
Granger, IN 46530 574-256-9993
misbrew@aol.com
www.mishawakabrewingcompany.com

Processor of seasonal beer, ale, stout, lager and porter
Owner: Thomas R Schmidt
CEO: Tom Scmidt
Marketing Director: Tom Scmidt
Estimated Sales: $ 1-2.5 Million
Number Employees: 20-49
Type of Packaging: Consumer, Food Service
Brands:
Four Horsemen

8930 **Mishler Packing Company**
5680 W 100 N
Lagrange, IN 46761 260-768-4156
Fax: 260-768-4354
Manufacturer of meat including beef, pork, cold and luncheon meats
President: Mike Monson
Secretary/Treasurer: Michael Monson
Estimated Sales: $20 Million
Number Employees: 20-49
Type of Packaging: Consumer

8931 **Miss Ginny's Orginal Vermont Pickle Works**
655 N Main Street
Northfield, VT 05663-6829
Bhutan 802-485-3057
Fax: 802-485-3057
Pickles

8932 **Miss Jenny's Pickles**
6104 Old Orchard Road
Kernersville, NC 27284-3296 336-978-0041
jenny@missjennyspickles.com
www.missjennyspickles.com

8933 **Miss Meringue**
1709 La Costa Meadows Dr
San Marcos, CA 92078 760-471-4978
Fax: 760-712-7814 800-561-6516
info@missmeringue.com
www.jacquesgourmet.com
Meringues and cookies
Owner: Roland D'Abel
CFO: Rick Lamb
Quality Control: Rom William
Estimated Sales: $ 5-10 Million
Number Employees: 100-249
Brands:
Miss Meringue
Splenda®

8934 **Miss Scarlett's**
P.O.Box 6729
Chandler, AZ 85246-6729 650-340-9600
Fax: 650-340-9680 800-345-6734
www.missscarlett.com
Marinated and pickled fruits, olives and vegetables; mushrooms, artichokes, asparagus, eggplant, baby corn, grren beans, carrots, Brussel sprouts, snow peas, snap peas, zucchini pickles, sweet baby onions, pickled garlic, cocktialtomatoes, baby okra, cap
Co-Owner: Peggy Luper
Co-Owner: Ralph Luper
Estimated Sales: $2.5-$5 Million
Number Employees: 4
Type of Packaging: Private Label
Brands:
Miss Scarlett

8935 **Miss Sophia's Old WorldKits & Gingerbread**
1401 Elm St
Dallas, TX 75202-2952 214-741-6800
Fax: 214-741-6807 877-446-4373
plumcreative@att.net www.misssophia.com
Gingerbread and candy winter village kits
Owner: Jason Osterberger
Brands:
Miss Sophia's Gingerbread

8936 **Mission Foods**
401 Gateway Dr
Goldsboro, NC 27534 919-778-7889
Fax: 919-751-2398
Refrigerated flavor tortillas
Principal: Gabriel Gutierrez
Manager: Brenda McIntosh
Plant Manager: Raymond Bigil
Estimated Sales: Under $500,000
Number Employees: 6
Parent Co: Mission Foods

8937 **(HQ)Mission Foods**
1159 Cottonwood Lane
Irving, TX 75038 469-232-5000
Fax: 972-232-5176 800-424-7862
www.missionfoods.com
Mexican foods including flour and corn tortillas, wraps, tortilla chips, taco shells and tostados, and chicharrones and pork cracklins.
President/CEO: Joel Suarez
CFO: Raul Pelaez Cano
Quality Control: Lucy Gonzalvez
Chief Marketing Officer: Sylvia Hernandez Benitez
VP Sales: Asmia Syed
Estimated Sales: $1.7 Billion
Number Employees: 6,610
Parent Co: GRUMA S.A.B de C.V.
Type of Packaging: Consumer, Food Service, Private Label, Bulk
Brands:
Diago's
Diane's
Guerrero
Mission

8938 **Mission Foodservice**
PO Box 2008
Oldsmar, FL 34677-7008 800-443-7994
Fax: 800-272-5207 mission@answers-sys.com
www.missionfoodsfsc.com
Manufacturer and exporter of Mexican foods including flour and corn tortillas, tortilla chips, pastries, taco and tostada shells
SVP/GM: Robert Smith
Marketing Director: Robin Tobor
VP Sales: Tom Daley
Number Employees: 1,000-4,999
Sq. footage: 420000
Type of Packaging: Consumer, Food Service, Private Label, Bulk
Brands:
Diago
Dianes
Guerrero
Marias
Mission

8939 **Mission Mountain Winery**
P.O.Box 100
Dayton, MT 59914-0100 406-849-5524
Fax: 406-849-5524 mmwinery@mountainsky.us
www.missionmountainwinery.com
Wines
President: Thomas Campbell Sr
Estimated Sales: $690,000
Number Employees: 10-19
Brands:
Mission Mountain

8940 **Mission Pharmacal Company**
P.O.Box 786099
San Antonio, TX 78278 210-696-8400
Fax: 210-696-6010 800-292-7364
www.missionpharmacal.com
Processor of vitamins and nutritional supplements
President: Neil Walsdorf Jr
CFO: Thomas Dooley
COO: Max Martin
Estimated Sales: $75 Million
Number Employees: 65
Type of Packaging: Consumer
Brands:
Calcet
Calcet Plus
Citracal
Compete
Fosfree
Iromin
Mission Prenatal

8941 **Mission San Juan Juices**
32565-B Golden Lantern
#282
Dana Point, CA 92629 949-495-7929
Fax: 949-495-8015 xtremebeverages@cox.net
www.xtremebeverages.com
Manufacturer and Marketer of 100% juices and smoothies in single-serve and mult-serve containers
President: William Quinley
VP: James Moffitt
Estimated Sales: $5 Million
Number Employees: 4
Number of Brands: 3
Number of Products: 20
Type of Packaging: Consumer, Food Service, Private Label
Brands:
Apple Brand Juices
Fruit Ole Smoothies
Mission San Juan Juices

8942 **Mission Valley Foods**
193 Falcon Crest Road
Middlebury, CT 06762-1526 203-573-0652
Fax: 203-574-5853
General grocery
President: Martin Smith
CFO: Marcia Tejeda
Marketing Director: Linda Ghignone
Public Relations: Janet Williams
Production Manager: David Yurselen
Estimated Sales: $300,000-500,000
Number Employees: 1-4
Type of Packaging: Private Label
Brands:
Brickenridge
Chef Martin

8943 **Mississippi Bakery**
834 Jefferson St
Burlington, IA 52601-5432 319-752-6315
Fax: 319-752-6233
Processor of bread and sweet goods
Director of Operations: Robert Brookhart
Estimated Sales: $ 20 - 50 Million
Number Employees: 50-99

8944 **Mississippi Blending Company**
121 Royal Rd
Keokuk, IA 52632 319-524-1235
Fax: 319-524-9889 800-758-4080
www.alliedstarch.com
Processor and wholesaler/distributor of baking powder, yeast foods, dusting starches. Custom blending, packaging, private labeling and tolling services available
President: Randy Schmelzel III
Executive VP: John Hicks
VP Operations: John Hicks
Estimated Sales: $ 20 - 50 Million
Number Employees: 20-49
Sq. footage: 28000
Parent Co: Allied Starch & Chemical
Brands:
Bakers Cream

8945 **Mississippi Cheese StrawFactory**
342s Mound Street
Yazoo City, MS 39194 662-746-7171
Fax: 662-746-7162 800-530-7496
info@mscheesestraws.com
www.mscheesestraws.com
Processor of specialty foods including cheese, lemon, and chopped pecan and cinnamon straws and Mississippi mud puppies, cookies, chocolate chip, oatmeal, pecan
President: Hunter Yerger
VP: Robbie Yerger
Estimated Sales: $2.5 Million
Number Employees: 15
Sq. footage: 10000
Type of Packaging: Consumer
Brands:
Mississippi Cheese Straws
Mississippi Mud Pupp
Original Lemon Straw

8946 **Missouri Winery Warehouse Outlet**
Old Us Highway 66
Cuba, MO 65453 573-885-2168
Wines
COO: Sherri Kloppe
Estimated Sales: $5-9.9 Million
Number Employees: 1-4

8947 **Mister Bee Potato Chip Company**
P.O.Box 1645
Parkersburg, WV 26102-1645 304-428-6133
Fax: 304-428-1291 doug.klein@misterbee.com
www.misterbee.com
Manufacturer of potato chips
President: John Klein
Marketing: John Roth
Sales: Steve Parson
Plant Manager: Marie Licot
Estimated Sales: $ 20 - 50 Million
Type of Packaging: Consumer, Food Service, Bulk

Brands:
MISTER BEE

8948 **Mister Cookie Face**
1989 Rutgers University Blvd
Lakewood, NJ 08701-4538 732-370-5533
Fax: 732-370-4015 brandy@cookieface.com
www.cookieface.com
Processor of novelty ice cream
Manager: Al Clark
Executive VP: Tammy Shaw
Estimated Sales: $12188199
Number Employees: 100-249
Sq. footage: 40000
Type of Packaging: Consumer, Private Label, Bulk
Brands:
Mr. Cookie Face

8949 **Mister Fish**
7211 Rolling Mill Rd
Baltimore, MD 21224-2033 410-288-2722
Fax: 410-288-4757
Seafood
Owner: Frank Petilo
Estimated Sales: $ 1 - 3 Million
Number Employees: 20-49

8950 **Mister Snacks**
PO Box 988
500 Creekside Drive
Amherst, NY 14228 716-691-1500
Fax: 716-210-1010 800-333-6393
sales@mistersnacks.com www.mistersnacks.com
Manufacturer of snacks, trail mixes, yogurt, candy and chocolate coated items
VP: Stephen Stern
President: Micheal Stern
Plant Manager: Ed Lilly
Estimated Sales: $ 10-20 Million
Number Employees: 30
Sq. footage: 14
Type of Packaging: Private Label
Brands:
Stone Mountain Snacks
Sunbird Snacks

8951 **Mister Spear**
2900 E Harding Way
Stockton, CA 95205 209-464-5365
Fax: 209-464-3846 800-677-7327
misterspear@misterspear.com
www.misterspear.com
Processor and packager of shiitake mushrooms, artichokes, asparagus, avocados, sugar snap peas, tomatoes, bi-color corn, bing cherries, Fuji apples, etc
President: Chip Arnett Jr
Estimated Sales: $500,000
Number Employees: 5-9
Type of Packaging: Consumer, Food Service
Brands:
MSI
Mister Spear

8952 **Misty**
6235 Havelock Ave
Lincoln, NE 68507-1279 402-466-8424
Fax: 402-466-7222 www.mistyslincoln.com
Processor of all-purpose seasonings and Bloody Mary mix
Owner: Lisa McMeen
Sales Representative: Dave Walbrecht
Director Operations: Brian Tones
Estimated Sales: $3800000
Number Employees: 10-19
Type of Packaging: Consumer, Food Service

8953 **Misty Islands Seafoods**
4000 W 50th Avenue
Suite 4
Anchorage, AK 99502-1039 907-248-6678
Fax: 907-279-6228
Seafood
Manager: Robert Melovidov
Manager: Richard Tremaine
Estimated Sales: $ 3 - 5 Million
Number Employees: 5-9

8954 **Mitake Trading International**
1011 Base Line Road
La Verne, CA 91750-2406 909-596-1981
Fax: 909-596-8231
Squash
President: Mike Amakasu
Estimated Sales: $ 5-10 Million
Number Employees: 5-9

8955 **Mitch Chocolate**
300 Spagnoli Rd
Melville, NY 11747-3507 631-777-2400
Fax: 631-777-1449 www.misschocolate.com
Processor of hard candy lollypops; wholesaler/distributor of salt water taffy and fundraising boxed chocolates; also, re-packing and private labeling available
President: Lawrence Hirsihheimer
VP Operations: Martin Bloomfield
Estimated Sales: $ 3 - 5 Million
Number Employees: 5-9
Sq. footage: 4000
Type of Packaging: Consumer, Private Label
Brands:
Frolic

8956 **Mitchel Dairies**
1591 E 233rd Street
Bronx, NY 10466-3336 718-324-6261
Fax: 1 7-8 9-4 61
Dairy products
President: Philip Tulotta
Co-Owner: Christine Tulotta
Treasurer: Linda Tulotta
Estimated Sales: $110 K
Number Employees: 1

8957 **(HQ)Mitchell Foods**
80 Mitchell Foods Ln
Barbourville, KY 40906 606-545-6677
Fax: 606-546-4190 888-202-9745
sales@mitchellfoods.com
www.mitchellfoods.com
Processor of fresh marinated boneless pork chops, rib eyes, chicken breast, meat loaf and barbecue products; also, chili and beer cheese
President: Luanne Mitchell
Owner: Jim Mitchell
VP Quality Control: Greg Mitchell
Estimated Sales: $ 1 - 3 Million
Number Employees: 5-9
Sq. footage: 15000
Type of Packaging: Consumer, Food Service, Private Label, Bulk
Other Locations:
Mitchell Foods
Lexington KY
Brands:
Mitchell Foods

8958 **Mitchum Potato Chips**
P.O.Box 36639
Charlotte, NC 28236 704-372-6744
Fax: 704-339-0066 jwilson@msn.com
Manufacturer of potato chips
President: John Wilson
Marketing Director: Henry Pully
COO: Tommy Thompson
Estimated Sales: $ 10-20 Million
Number Employees: 1-4
Type of Packaging: Bulk
Brands:
MDI
Mitchum Rices
Savealot
Tiggly Wiggly
Ukrop

8959 **Mitsubishi Chemical America**
1 N Lexington Ave
White Plains, NY 10601 914-286-3600
Fax: 914-761-0108 webapid@m-chem.com
www.mitsubishichemical.com
Processor of bacteriostatic emulsifiers; also, calcium suspension, confectionery including chocolate, low-fat spreads, dairy product analogs and fruit coatings
President: Hiro Tanaka
Sales: Takazumi Kanekiyo
Number Employees: 1,000-4,999
Parent Co: Mitsubishi Chemical Coorporation
Type of Packaging: Bulk
Brands:
RYOTO SUGAR ESTER

8960 **(HQ)Mitsubishi InternationalCorporation**
333 S Hope St # 2500
Los Angeles, CA 90071-1407 213-620-8652
Fax: 213-687-2993
Various food commodities
Manager: Osamu Takada
Estimated Sales: $ 7 Million
Number Employees: 10-19

8961 **(HQ)Mitsubishi InternationalCorporation**
520 Madison Avenue
Floor 18
New York, NY 10022-4327 212-759-5605
Fax: 212-605-1810 800-442-6266
inquire@mitsubishicorp.com www.micusa.com
Food commodities: coffee, cocoa, dairy products, fruits, vegetables and frozen juice concentrates. Food ingredients, enzymes, emulsifiers, baking agents.
President: James Brumm
CFO: Yasuyuki Sugiura
Executive VP/COO: Yoshihiko Kawamura
Sales/Purchasing Representative: Patrick Welch
Number Employees: 250-499
Other Locations:
Seattle WA

8962 **Mitsui Foods**
35 Maple St
Norwood, NJ 07648-2003 201-750-0500
Fax: 201-750-0150 800-777-2322
www.mitsui-foods.com
Food Service suppliers
President: Dennis Newnham
Estimated Sales: $ 20- 50 Million
Number Employees: 50-99

8963 **Mix Industries**
22332 Piccadilly Court
Apt 1a
Richton Park, IL 60471-2028 708-339-6692
BarbaraMix@prodigy.net
Manufacturer of Herbal Colon cleanser
President: Barbara Mix
Number Employees: 6

8964 **Mix-A-Lota Stuff LLC**
4828 N Kings Hwy
Fort Pierce, FL 34951 772-468-4688
brendassauces@aol.com
Sauce
President: Brenda Chinn

8965 **Mixerz All Natural Cocktail Mixers**
100 Cummings Center
Suite 220B
Beverly, MA 01915 978-922-6497
info@mixerz.com
www.mixerz.com
all natural cocktail mixers
Marketing: Christina Pesente

8966 **Mixes By Danielle**
615 Pelvedere Street
Warren, OH 44483 330-856-5190
Fax: 330-856-3386 800-537-6499
Urban spices
President: Trissa McClerry

8967 **Mixon Fruit Farms**
2712 26th Ave E
Bradenton, FL 34208-7427 941-748-5829
Fax: 941-748-1085 800-608-2525
info@mixon.com www.mixon.com
Manufacturer, packer and exporter of citrus fruits, vegetables, fudge, honey, jellies, marmalades and spreads, salsa, dips, pickles and nuts
President: William Mixon Jr
Estimated Sales: $ 50 - 100 Million
Number Employees: 50-99
Sq. footage: 90000
Brands:
MIXON

8968 **Miyako Oriental Foods**
4287 Puente Ave
Baldwin Park, CA 91706 626-962-9633
Fax: 626-814-4569 877-788-6476
joearai@coldmountainmiso.com
www.coldmountainmiso.com
Miso in different flavors and colors. Used in making sauces, soups, marinades, dressings, dips and main dishes.
VP: Teruo Shimizu
Marketing/Sales/Quality Assurance Mgr: Joe Arai

Estimated Sales: $3000000
Number Employees: 10-19
Sq. footage: 18000
Type of Packaging: Consumer, Food Service, Private Label, Bulk
Brands:
COLD MOUNTAIN
KANEMASA
YAMAIZUMI
YAMAJIRUSHI

8969 **Miyasaka Brewery**
575 Anton Blvd
Suite 300
Costa Mesa, CA 92626 714-623-2163
Fax: 714-432-6441
s.iwasaki@miyasaka-jozo.com
www.miyasaka-jozo.com
Sake produced with Miso; beverage, alcohol
President: Naotaka Miyasaka
Parent Co: Miyasaka Brewery

8970 **Miyasaka Foods Company**
471 W Lambert Road
Suite 107
Brea, CA 92821
Fax: 714-442-9923 www.miyasaka-jozo.com
Miso products
Sales Associate: Greg Wang

8971 **Mizkam Americas**
2400 Nicholson Ave
Kansas City, MO 64120-1672 816-483-1700
Fax: 816-483-7448
carolyn-moss@nakanofoods.com
www.mizkam.com
Processor of vinegar and condiments including mustard and hot sauce
Executive VP: Clarice Moore
Marketing Director: Tom Matthews
Operations Manager: Mike Cole
Plant Manager: Wayne Towe
Purchasing Manager: Phyllis Conover
Estimated Sales: $ 10 - 20 Million
Number Employees: 20-49
Type of Packaging: Consumer, Food Service, Private Label, Bulk
Brands:
Cushing
Lincoln
Ozark
Rogers
Speas
Springdale

8972 **Mizkan Americas**
1661 Feehanville Dr # 300
Mt Prospect, IL 60056-6031 847-590-0059
Fax: 847-590-0405 800-323-4358
www.mizkanamericas.com
Manufacturer of Specialty Vinegars, Cooking Wines, Mustards, Asian Sauces and Dressings, and other liquid condiments.
President: Craig Smith
Purchasing Manager: Bill Lehman
Estimated Sales: $32,300,000
Number Employees: 50-99
Brands:
Barengo
Four Monks
Mizkan
Nokano

8973 **Mo Hotta-Mo Betta**
1209 Us Highway 80 E
Pooler, GA 31322-9544 912-748-6111
www.mohotta.com
Processor and exporter of hot sauces
President/Ceo: James Kelly
Estimated Sales: $110,000
Number Employees: 6
Type of Packaging: Consumer, Food Service
Brands:
Hot Sauce For Cool Kids
Mo Hotta - Mo Betta

8974 **Mobile Bay Seafood**
11801 Old Shipyard Rd
Coden, AL 36523 251-973-0410
Fax: 706-538-6850
Seafood

8975 **Mobile Processing**
P.O.Box 501187 Mobile Al 36605
2201 Perimeter Rd Ste A
Mobile, AL 36615-1130
US 251-438-6944
Fax: 251-438-6948
Processor of fresh and frozen seafood including shrimp
Owner/PRESIDENT: James Higdon
Market MANAGER: James Higdon
Estimated Sales: $2000000
Number Employees: 25-100

8976 **Moceri South Western**
4909 Pacific Hwy
San Diego, CA 92110-4005 619-297-7900
Fax: 619-297-8900
Beverages and bottling
President: Grace Moceri
Estimated Sales: $ 10 - 20 Million
Number Employees: 10-19
Type of Packaging: Private Label

8977 **Model Dairy**
P.O.Box 3017
Reno, NV 89505 775-788-7900
Fax: 775-788-7951 800-433-2030
Processor and wholesaler/distributor of a full line of dairy products including ice cream
Manager: Jim Breslin
Controller: Peggy Baker
VP/General Manager: Jim Breslin
Number Employees: 100-249
Sq. footage: 50000
Parent Co: Suiza Dairy Group
Type of Packaging: Food Service

8978 **Model Diary**
P.O. Box 961447
El Paso, TX 79996 775-788-7900
Fax: 775-788-7940 1 8-0 3-5 70
www.deanfoods.com
Milk
CEO: Gregg L. Engles
Estimated Sales: $ 50-75 Million
Number Employees: 324

8979 **Modena Fine Foods**
158 River Road
Clifton, NJ 07014 201-842-8900
Fax: 201-842-9001 info@modenafinefoods.com
www.modenafinefoods.com
Balsamic products, including balsimic vinegar, specialty wine vinegars, and balsimic condiemnts
President: Fred Mortadi
Estimated Sales: $720,000
Number Employees: 5

8980 **Modern Baked Products**
301 Locust Ave
Oakdale, NY 11769 631-589-7300
Fax: 631-589-7383 877-727-2253
www.modernbakedprod.com
Processor of bagels and specialty breads
Owner: James Turco
President: James Turco
Sales Manager (Frozens): John Esposito
Estimated Sales: $100+ Million
Number Employees: 100-249
Type of Packaging: Food Service, Private Label
Brands:
Modern Baked Products

8981 **Modern Day Masala, LLC**
Po Box 682374
Marietta, GA 30068-0040 866-611-3757
Fax: 866-611-1596
ksharma@moderndaymasala.com
www.moderndaymasala.com
Gluten-free, organic/natural, USDA, full-line spices, spices, foodservice, private label.
Marketing: Kristin Sharma

8982 **Modern Italian Bakery of West Babylon**
301 Locust Ave
Oakdale, NY 11769-1652 631-589-7300
Fax: 631-589-7383 www.modernbakedprod.com
Italian baked goods
President: James Turco
Estimated Sales: $ 10-20 Million
Number Employees: 100-249

8983 **Modern Macaroni Company**
1708 Mary St
Honolulu, HI 96819 808-845-6841
Fax: 808-845-6841
Processor of dry oriental noodles, shrimp flakes and soybean flour; wholesaler/distributor of groceries serving the food service market
Manager: Loraine Okumura
Estimated Sales: $900,000-$1 Million
Number Employees: 10-19
Sq. footage: 2400
Type of Packaging: Consumer, Food Service
Brands:
Hula

8984 **Modern Mushroom Farms**
PO Box 340
Avondale, PA 19311 610-268-3535
Fax: 610-268-3099 info@modernmush.com
www.modernmush.com
Mushrooms, white, portabella, exotic, stuffed, dried, marinated
CFO: Ben Lazar
Director of Quality: Fran Kamp
VP Marketing/Director of Sales: Greg Sagan
Head of Human Resources: Serranno Lugo
COO: Jack Ruitenhuiur
Purchasing Director: Ray Ortiz
Estimated Sales: $25000000
Number Employees: 500
Sq. footage: 375000
Type of Packaging: Consumer, Food Service, Bulk
Brands:
Dove
Modern
Sherrockee Farms

8985 **Modern Packaging**
3245 N Berkeley Lake Rd NW
Duluth, GA 30096 770-622-1500
Fax: 770-814-0046
www.modernpackaginginc.com
Contract packager of condiments and liquid food items; warehouse providing dry, cooler and humidity-controlled storage of foodstuffs, liquid packaging products and seasonal sales items; also, pick and pack and rail siding available
President: Herb Sodel
VP: Nancy Sodel
Estimated Sales: $3.6 Million
Number Employees: 50-99
Sq. footage: 100000

8986 **Modern Products/Fearn Natural Foods**
6425 W Executive Dr
Mequon, WI 53092-4478 262-242-2400
Fax: 262-242-2751 800-877-8935
Seasonings, spices, bake mixes, natural products and soy products
President: Anthony Palermo
Director Sales/Marketing: Gaylord Palermo
Estimated Sales: Below $ 5 Million
Number Employees: 25
Number of Products: 200
Sq. footage: 100000
Type of Packaging: Consumer, Food Service
Brands:
Classique Fare
Rearn Naturefresh
Spice Garden
Spike
Swiss Kriss
Vegeful
Vegit

8987 **Modern Tea Packers**
P.O.Box 370708
Brooklyn, NY 11237-0708 718-417-1060
Fax: 718-417-6405
Tea and tea bags
Owner: Julius Medwin
CEO: Julius Neumann
Estimated Sales: $5-9.9 Million
Number Employees: 20-49

8988 **Moderncuts**
6425 W Executive Dr
Mequon, WI 53092-4482 262-242-2400
Fax: 262-242-2751 modernfearn@aol.com
www.modernfearn.com
Spices and seasonings
Chairman: Anthony Palermo
Marketing Director: Michille Tal

Estimated Sales: Below $ 5 Million
Number Employees: 20-49
Sq. footage: 125
Type of Packaging: Private Label
Brands:
Fearn
Spice Garden

8989 **Modesto WholeSoy**
PO Box 1277
Ceres, CA 95301 209-523-5119
Fax: 209-523-5519
frank@modestowholesoyco.com
www.modestowholesoyco.com
Produces the highest quality liquid soybase for use in soymilk, yogurt, smoothies, ice cream and other dairy-like products.
CEO: Ken Norquist
CFO: Henry Gloasser
Plant Manager: Frank Gasca
Estimated Sales: $290,000
Number Employees: 3
Sq. footage: 3834

8990 **Modoc Orchard Company**
3050 S Pacific Highway
Medford, OR 97501-8723 541-535-1437
Processor and packer of fresh fruit
Owner: Don Joseph
Number Employees: 100-249
Type of Packaging: Private Label
Brands:
Modoc
Mopac

8991 **Moet Hennessy USA**
85 10th Ave Fl 2
New York, NY 10011 212-888-7575
Fax: 212-251-8388 www.mhusa.com/
Wines and spirits.
President/CEO: Mark Cornelle
Estimated Sales: $ 500 Million-$ 1 Billion
Number Employees: 50-99
Parent Co: United Distillers & Vintners North AmericaMA
IL
FL
GA
TX
CA
Brands:
10 CANE
ARDBEG
BELVEDERE
CAPE MENTELLE VINEYARDS
CAPEZZANA
CHANDON
CHATEAU CHEVAL BLANC
CHATEAU D'YQUEM
CHATEAU DE SANCERRE
CHATEAU LA NERTHE
CHEVAL DES ANDES
CHOPIN
CLOUDY BAY VINEYARDS
DOM PERIGNON
ESPERTO
GLENMORANGIE
GRAND MARNIER
GREEN POINT
HENNESSY
KRUG
LAPOSTOLLE
LIVIO FELLUGA
MOET & CHANDON
MONSANTO
NAVAN
NEWTON VINEYARD
NUMANTHIA
RUINART
TERRAZAS DE LOS ANDES
VEUVE CLICQUOT

8992 **Mogen David Wine Corporation**
85 Bourne St
Westfield, NY 14787 716-326-3151
Fax: 716-326-4442
Processor and exporter of kosher and nonkosher wines including white, rose and red
Director Of Winery Operations: Don Beebe
Estimated Sales: $ 20 - 50 Million
Number Employees: 50-99
Parent Co: Wine Group/Franzia Wine
Type of Packaging: Consumer

8993 **Mohawk Distilled Products**
11900 Biscayne Boulevard
North Miami, FL 33181-2743 305-892-3460
Fax: 305-892-3460
Rum
President/CEO: Marshall Berowitz
CEO: Hubert Surville
Estimated Sales: $ 2.5-5 Million
Number Employees: 1-4
Brands:
MOHAWK

8994 **Mohn's Fisheries**
1144 Great River Rd
Harpers Ferry, IA 52146-7565 563-586-2269
Fax: 563-423-1579
Seafood
Owner: Diane Mohn
Estimated Sales: $300,000-500,000
Number Employees: 1-4

8995 **Mojave Foods Corporation**
6200 E Slauson Ave
Commerce, CA 90040 323-890-8900
Fax: 323-890-0910 www.mccormick.com
Manufacturer and exporter of Mexican foods including dried chile peppers, produce batter mixes, garlic products, seasonings and spices
President: Joseph Nibali
General Manager: Joseph Nibali
Estimated Sales: $36 Million
Number Employees: 250-499
Sq. footage: 100000
Parent Co: McCormick & Company
Type of Packaging: Consumer, Food Service, Private Label, Bulk

8996 **(HQ)Mojave Foods Corporation**
6200 E Slauson Ave
Commerce, CA 90040 323-890-8900
Fax: 323-890-0910 infoteam@elguapo.com
www.mccormick.com
Manufacturer, importer of dried and dehydrated foods, packages spice, dry chilies, corn husks, garlic and produce blends
President: Joseph Nibali
Marketing Director: Richard Adlai
Estimated Sales: $23.7 Million
Number Employees: 250-499
Sq. footage: 25000
Brands:
Camino Real
El Guapo
El Primero
El Rey
El Royal
Sol Maduro
Somberro
Sunripe

8997 **Mojave Foods Corporation**
6200 E Slauson Ave
Commerce, CA 90040 323-890-8900
Fax: 323-890-0910 800-995-8906
Spices, dry chilies and corn products
President: Joseph Nibali
CFO: Jeffrey Glaser
VP: Joseph Ross
Marketing Director: Joseph Ross
Public Relations: Joseph Ross
Estimated Sales: $ 25-49.9 Million
Number Employees: 250-499
Type of Packaging: Private Label

8998 **Moka D'Oro Coffee**
470 Smith St
Farmingdale, NY 11735-1105 718-387-1563
Fax: 718-387-1563 877-665-2367
info@mokadoro.com www.mokadoro.com
Processor and exporter of espresso, Colombian coffee and mineral water; wholesaler/distributor and importer of espresso machines; serving the food service market
President: Judith Ruggiero
VP: Michael Ruggiero
Sales Executive: Ana Espunola
Estimated Sales: 10-20 Million
Number Employees: 20-49
Type of Packaging: Consumer, Food Service
Brands:
Galvania
Nepi

8999 **Molbert Brothers Poultry & Egg Company**
415 Avenue D
Lake Charles, LA 70615-6883 337-439-2579
Fax: 337-439-2579
Poultry

9000 **Moledina Commodities**
5501 Muirfield Ct
Flower Mound, TX 75022 817-490-1101
Fax: 817-490-1105 mohamed@moledina.com
www.moledina.com
President: Mohamed Moledina
VP: Fidahusein R Moledina
Brands:
Moledina

9001 **Molinaro's Fine ItalianFoods**
50-2345 Stanfield Road
Mississauga, ON L4Y 3Y3
Canada 905-275-7400
Fax: 905-275-6701 800-268-4959
info@molinarosfinefoods.com
www.molinardosfinefoods.com
Processor, importer and exporter of pizza, fresh and frozen pizza shells, fresh pasta, flatbread, focaccia, pasta sauce, fresh and frozen pasta entrees, meat, vegetable and cheese lasagna, panzerottis and calzones
President: Vince Molinaro
CEO: Gino Molinaro
Sales/Marketing: Catherine Pyman
Purchasing Manager: Frank Molinaro
Number Employees: 140
Sq. footage: 76000
Type of Packaging: Consumer, Food Service, Private Label, Bulk
Brands:
FAMOSA
MOLINARO'S
SUPREMO

9002 **Molson Coors Brewing Company**
1225 17th Street
Suite 3200
Denver, CO 80202 303-927-2337
Fax: 303-277-5415 800-642-6116
consumers@coors.com www.molsoncoors.com
Manufacturer of beer
President/CEO: Peter Swinburn
President/Molson Coors International: Kandy Anand
Global Chief Financial Officer: Stewart Glendinning
Global Chief People Officer: Ralph Hargrow
Global Chief Supply Chain Officer: Gregory Wade
Global Chief Legal Officer: Samuel Walker
Estimated Sales: $3 Billion
Number Employees: 14,540
Type of Packaging: Consumer
Brands:
ASPEN EDGE
BLACK ICE
BLUE MOON
COORS LIGHT
COORS NON-ALCOHOLIC BEER
COORS ORIGINAL
EXTRA GOLD LAGER
KEYSTONE ICE
KEYSTONE LIGHT
KEYSTONE PREMIUM
KILLIAN'S
RICHARD'S RED ALE
ZIMA
ZIMA CITRUS
ZIMA XXX

9003 **Molto Italian Foods**
4005 Atlantic Avenue
Wildwood, NJ 08260-4730 609-522-5444
Fax: 609-522-5444
Italian foods
Jr."""": Joseph Scrocca
Estimated Sales: $ .5 - 1 million
Number Employees: 1-4

9004 **Mom 'N Pops**
834 Brooks St
New Windsor, NY 12553 845-567-0640
Fax: 845-567-0652 866-368-6767
info@momnpops.com www.momnpops.com

Manufacturers of candy and lollipops
President: Barbara Regenbaum
Sales Director: Stacy Zagon
Estimated Sales: $ 10-20 Million
Number Employees: 20-49
Type of Packaging: Private Label
Brands:
Absolutely Zbest Sweets
Mom 'n Pops

9005 **Mom's Bakery**
5585 Westfield Dr SW
Atlanta, GA 30336-2680 404-344-4189
Fax: 404-969-1144 info@momsbakery.com
www.momsbakery.com
Manufacturer of buttermilk and yeast raised biscuits
President: Kristi Kay
VP: Daniel Kay
Estimated Sales: $12 Million
Number Employees: 100-249
Sq. footage: 75000
Type of Packaging: Food Service, Bulk

9006 **Mom's Barbeque Sauce**
591 Treeside Drive
Stow, OH 44224-1111 330-929-7290
Seasonings, sauces
President: Peggy Parson
Vice President: R Parson
Number Employees: 1-4
Brands:
Mom's Barbeque Sauce

9007 **Mom's Famous**
145 NW 20th St
Boca Raton, FL 33431 561-750-1903
Fax: 561-750-4105 www.momsfamous.com
Baked goods
President: Tony Danesh
Estimated Sales: $575,000
Number Employees: 10-19
Brands:
Mom's Famous

9008 **Mom's Food Company**
1308 Potrero Avenue
South El Monte, CA 91733-3013 626-444-4115
Fax: 626-444-2793 800-969-6667
Processor of pre-baked buttermilk biscuits, cornbread products and dinner rolls
President: Sam Keith
Estimated Sales: $1100000
Number Employees: 23
Sq. footage: 12000
Type of Packaging: Consumer, Food Service, Private Label, Bulk
Brands:
Mom's

9009 **Mom's Gourmet, LLC**
17594 Walnut Trail
Chagrin Falls, OH 44023-6428 440-564-9702
skoepke@momsgourmet.net
www.momsgourmet.net
Dairy-free, gluten-free, lactose-free, organic/natural, sugar-free, vegetarian, full-line spices, rubs.
Marketing: Sally Koepke

9010 **Momence Packing Company**
334 W North St
Momence, IL 60954 815-472-6485
Fax: 815-472-2459
Processor of frozen sausage
President: Patrick Garinger
Estimated Sales: Below $ 5 Million
Number Employees: 250-499
Type of Packaging: Consumer, Private Label

9011 **Mon Ami Champagne Company**
3845 E Wine Cellar Rd
Port Clinton, OH 43452-3704 419-797-4445
Fax: 419-797-9078 800-777-4266
info@monamiwinery.com
www.monamiwinery.com
Champagne
Owner: John Kronberg
Estimated Sales: $500,000-$1 Million
Number Employees: 20-49
Brands:
Mon Ami

9012 **Mon Cuisine**
5620 59th St
Flushing, NY 11378-2314 718-894-2000
Fax: 718-326-4642 877-666-8348
mon@alleprocessing.com
www.alleprocessing.com
Manufacturer of kosher vegetarian and vegan entrees and IQF products including cutlets, burgers, steaks, meat balls, pasta, nuggets and stuffed cabbage. Packaged in CPET microwaveable/oven safe trays. Private label and co-packingavailable
Owner: Sruly Weinstock
Co-Owner: Sam Hollander
Vice President: Shlomi Pilo
Research & Development: Udi Basis
Plant Manager: Iran Talavera
Purchasing Manager: Zeer Weinstock
Estimated Sales: $ 20 - 50 Million
Number Employees: 50-99
Sq. footage: 150000
Parent Co: Alle Processing
Type of Packaging: Consumer, Food Service, Private Label, Bulk
Brands:
Mon Cuisine Vegetarian
The Natural Choice

9013 **Mona Lisa Food Products**
224 Thompson St #181
Hendersonville, NC 28792 828-685-2443
Fax: 828-685-8692 800-982-2546
jclark@mlfpi.com www.mlfpi.com
Manufacturer of gourmet chocolate products using fine European chocolate.
Owner: Peter Thom
Marketing: Jason Clark
Sales Director: Cecilia Bass
Estimated Sales: $ 20 - 50 Million
Number Employees: 20-49
Number of Products: 50
Sq. footage: 32000

9014 **Mona Lisa® Chocolatier**
Pob 1632/100426
Arlington, VA 22210 703-524-8888
Fax: 732-203-1690 866-662-5475
sales@monalisachocolate.com
www.monalisachocolate.com
Gourmet chocolates, hard chewable candies and gums. All Mona Lisa®
President/CEO/COB/Dir Int'l Development: James Sarkesian
VP/Gen Corporate Council/Treasurer/CFO: Sean Kidd Esq
General Corporate Council/Board/R&D: Martin Pedata Esq
R&D/QC: James Sarkesian
Quality Control: Martin Pedata
VP/Int'l Sales/Marketing Communications: Scott Bricker
Operations/R&D/QC/Production/Plant Mgr: Ken Mushinskie
Production: James Sankesian
Plant Manager: James Sankesian
Purchasing Director: Sean Kidd Esq
Estimated Sales: $500,000
Number Employees: 1-2
Number of Brands: 1
Number of Products: 22
Sq. footage: 45000
Type of Packaging: Consumer, Private Label
Brands:
CHOCOLATES/MONA LISA®
CHOCOLATIER/MONA LISA®
MONA LISA®

9015 **Monaco Baking Company**
14700 Marquardt Ave
Santa Fe Springs, CA 90670 562-404-5028
Fax: 562-229-0963 800-569-4640
info@monacobaking.com
www.monacobaking.com
Manufacturer of gingerbread and shorthbread cookies, shortbread and gingerbread cookie mixes.
Marketing: Oralia Lala Avalos
Sales/Marketing: Philip Moreau
Estimated Sales: $ 20 - 50 Million
Number Employees: 20-49

9016 **Monarch Beverage Company**
1123 Zonolite Rd NE Ste 10
Atlanta, GA 30306 404-262-4040
Fax: 404-262-4001 800-241-3732
info@monarchbeverages.com
www.monarchbeverages.com
Manufacturer and exporter of concentrates including sports and energy drinks, healthy fruit beverages, enhanced waters, ready-to-drink beverages, ready-to-drink coffees and soft drinks
COO: Kevin McClanahan
CEO: Jacques Bombal
VP Sales: Bill Lowler
Business & Procedure Manager: Amy Whitehead
Estimated Sales: $3.2 Million
Number Employees: 20-49
Type of Packaging: Bulk
Brands:
ACUTE FRUIT™
AMERICAN COLA®
COMOTION™
KICKAPOO JOY JUICE®
NTRINSIC™
PLANET COLA®
REAKTOR®
RUSH! ENERGY™

9017 **Monarch Seafoods**
515 Kalihi St
Honolulu, HI 96819 808-841-7877
Fax: 808-847-3930
Seafood and seafood products
President: Thomas Mukaigawa
Estimated Sales: $ .5 - 1 million
Number Employees: 10-19

9018 **Monastery Bakery At HolyCross Abbey**
901 Cool Spring Lane
Berryville, VA 22611-2700 540-955-9440
Fax: 540-955-4006 monasterybakery@aol.com
www.monasteryfruitcake.org
Other baked goods, chocolate truffles, other chocolate, honey.
Marketing: Ernie Polanskas

9019 **Mondial Foods Company**
P.O.Box 75036
Los Angeles, CA 90075-0036 213-383-3531
Processor and exporter of pineapple and other tropical juices
President: Ben Gattegno
Estimated Sales: $210000
Number Employees: 20-49
Type of Packaging: Food Service, Bulk

9020 **Mondiv/Division of Lassonde Inc**
3810 Alfred Laliberte
Boisbriand, QC J7H 1P8 450-979-0717
Fax: 450-979-0279 infomondiv@mondiv.com
www.mondiv.vom
tapenades, bruschetta, glass jar gravy, specialty sauces and dips, glass jar soups and stews, meat-based pasta sauce, pasta sauce (non-meat), organic pasta sauces, organic glass jar soups, glass jar (ready-to-serve)meals, pestos andchutneys
President/Owner: Vito Monopoli

9021 **Money's Mushrooms**
#800-1500 W Georgia Street
Vancouver, BC V6G 2Z6
Canada 604-669-3741
Fax: 604-669-9732 800-669-7992
info@moneys.com www.calbur.com
Processor, grower and exporter of canned and pickled mushrooms
President: Keith Potter
CFO: Cliff Lillicrop
VP Sales/Marketing: Dean Fleming
Number Employees: 900
Type of Packaging: Consumer, Food Service, Private Label, Bulk
Brands:
Moneys

9022 **Monin**
2100 Range Rd
Clearwater, FL 33765 727-461-3033
Fax: 727-461-3303 800-966-5225
monin-usa@monin.com www.monin.com
Processor and exporter of syrups.
President: Olivier Monin
CEO: Bill Lombardo

Estimated Sales: $14 Million
Sq. footage: 32200
Parent Co: George Monin S.A.
Type of Packaging: Consumer, Food Service, Private Label, Bulk
Brands:
Monin

9023 **Monini North America, Inc**
37 North Ave
Suite 201
Norwalk, CT 6851 203-750-0531
Fax: 203-750-0661 info@monini.us
www.monini.us
Oils
Chairman: Marco Petrini
Estimated Sales: Less than $200,000
Number Employees: 1-4
Type of Packaging: Private Label
Brands:
Amabile Umbro
GranFruttato
Ii Monello
Il Poggiolo
Monini

9024 **Monk's Bread**
P.O.Box 611
Victor, NY 14564-0611 585-243-0660
Fax: 585-243-4816
Bread

9025 **Monogramme Confections**
10630 Midwest Industrial Blvd
St Louis, MO 63132-1221 314-427-4099
Fax: 314-427-6646 888- 56- 409
www.ficoninc.com
Confectioneries
Owner: Charlie Hirschi
Estimated Sales: $ 1-2.5 Million
Number Employees: 5-9

9026 **Monroe Cheese Corporation**
PO Box 260
110 N Pratt Rd
Monticello, WI 53570 608-325-5161
Fax: 608-325-5168
Cheese
President: David Rufenacht
Manager: William Stuart
Marketing Director: Dan Pickett
Estimated Sales: $ 50-100 Million
Number Employees: 110

9027 **Monsanto**
800 N Lindbergh Blvd
St Louis, MO 63167-0001 314-694-1000
Fax: 314-694-3057 www.monsanto.com
Produce leading seed brands in large-acre crops like corn, cotton, wheat and oilseed (soybeans and canola), as well as small-acre crops like vegetables.
Chairman/President/CEO: Hugh Grant
EVP/Chief Commercial Officer: Brett Begemann
SVP/CFO: Pierre Coduroux
EVP/Chief Technology Officer: Robert Fraley
VP/Treasurer: Tom Hartley
EVP/Human Resources: Steven Mizell
SVP/Global Strategy: Kerry Preete
EVP/Sustainability & Corp. Affairs: Gerald Steiner
SVP/Chief of Staff & Community Relations: Janet Holloway
VP/Global Vegetable & Asia Commercial: Consuelo Madere
VP/Controller: Nicole Ringenberg
Estimated Sales: $11 Billion
Number Employees: 21000
Brands:
ACCELERON
ASGROW
DE RUITER SEEDS
DEKALB
DELTAPINE
GENUITY
PRESCRIPTIVE AG SERVICES
ROUNDUP AGRICULTURAL HERBICIDE
ROUNDUP READY
SEMINIS
VISTIVE
WESTBRED WHEAT AND BARLEY VARIETIES
YIELDGARD AND YIELDGARD VT

9028 **Monster Cone**
8500 Delmeade
Montreal, QC H4T 1L6
Canada 541-636-2022
Fax: 514-342-0346 800-542-9801
info@monstercone.com www.monstercone.com
Processor and exporter of waffle bowls and cones including plain and chocolate dipped
President: Daniel Mardinger
Number Employees: 50-99
Sq. footage: 20000
Type of Packaging: Consumer, Food Service, Private Label, Bulk
Brands:
MONSTER CONE

9029 **Mont Blanc Gourmet**
2925 E Colfax Ave
Denver, CO 80206 303-755-1100
Fax: 303-283-1100 800-877-3811
info@montblancgourmet.com
www.montblancgourmet.com
Processor of chocolate syrup, cocoa powders, chai mixes, cappuccino, mocha mixes, and powdered hot cocoa mix. Flavoring: chocolate, white chocolate, caramel, kahlua
President: Michael Szyliowicz
CEO: Irene Szyliowicz
Estimated Sales: $1-$3 Million
Number Employees: 8
Brands:
Mont Blanc Chocolate Syrups
Mont Blanc Gourmet H

9030 **Montage Foods**
885 Providence Rd
Scranton, PA 18508-2558 570-347-2400
Fax: 570-347-4123 800-521-8325
www.advance-food.com
Processor of portion-controlled and frozen veal and lamb
President: Marv Herman
Quality Control Manager: Debra Webber
Operations Manager: Murray Glick
Estimated Sales: $ 50-100 Million
Number Employees: 100-249
Parent Co: Advance Food Compnay Enid, OK
Type of Packaging: Consumer, Food Service, Private Label
Brands:
It's the Veal Thing

9031 **Montana Bakery**
26 Market Street
Stamford, CT 06902-5834 203-969-7700
Fax: 203-969-7440
Baked goods
President: Gary Zaretsky
Vice President: Scott Kulkin
Estimated Sales: $ 5-10 Million
Number Employees: 50

9032 **(HQ)Montana Coffee Traders**
5810 Us Highway 93 S
Whitefish, MT 59937 406-862-7633
Fax: 406-862-7680 800-345-5282
traders@coffeetraders.com
www.coffeetraders.com
Fresh roasted coffee
Owner: R C Beal
Estimated Sales: $ 20-50 Million
Number Employees: 50-99

9033 **Montana Flour & Grain**
P.O.Box 517
Fort Benton, MT 59442-0517 406-622-5436
Fax: 406-622-5439 info@montanaflour.com
www.montanaflour.com
Manufactures flour and other grain mill products specializing in organic flours
President: Andre Giles
Estimated Sales: Below $ 5 Million
Number Employees: 10-19
Number of Brands: 3
Number of Products: 15
Type of Packaging: Food Service, Private Label, Bulk

9034 **Montana Legacy Premium Ostrich Products**
2105 Central Avenue
Suite 100
Billings, MT 59102-4776 406-656-6444
Fax: 406-656-5077 ostrich@wtp.net
Ostrich products
Owner: David Casagrande
Manager: Clay Watson
Public Relations: Connie Hayes
Estimated Sales: Under $500,000
Number Employees: 5-9

9035 **Montana Mountain SmokedFish**
10 Elkhorn View Dr
Montana City, MT 59634 800-649-2959
Fax: 406-449-4755 800-649-2959
smkfishqueen@aol.com
www.mysmokedfish.com
Processor of smoked salmon, sockeye salmon, keta salmon, rainbow trout, halibut and salmon spread. All natural, no preservatives
President: Kim Waltee
Estimated Sales: Less than $500,000
Number Employees: 1-4
Type of Packaging: Private Label

9036 **Montana Naturals**
1400 Kearns Blvd
Park City, UT 84060-6725
800-672-8349
sales@mtnaturals.com www.mtnaturals.com
Processor and exporter of dietary supplements
General Manager: Sterling Gabbitas
Number Employees: 50-99
Sq. footage: 26000
Parent Co: HealthRite
Type of Packaging: Consumer, Private Label
Other Locations:
Montana Naturals by HealthRit
Arlee MT
Brands:
Pure Energy

9037 **Montana Ranch Brand**
PO Box 2036
Billings, MT 59103 406-294-2333
Fax: 406-294-2336 www.montanaranchbrand.com
natural piedmontese beef, ranch beef, pioneer pork, prairie lamb, and heritage bison
President/Owner: Ralph Peterson
Number Employees: 3

9038 **Montana Soup Company**
PO Box 971
4132 Lake Helena Dr
Helena, MT 59602-9543 406-862-7686
Fax: 406-862-7686 800-862-7687
Soup and soup ingredients
President: Ann Nickerson
Estimated Sales: $150 K
Number Employees: 2

9039 **Montana Specialty Mills**
300 3rd Ave S
Great Falls, MT 59405 406-761-2338
Fax: 406-761-7926
gordon@mtspecialtymills.com
www.mtspecialtymills.com
Primary agricultural processor providing contracting, origination, storage and processing of grain and oilseed-based products to secondary food manufacturers
President: Steve Chambers
Merchandising Manager: Gordon Svenby
Operations: Robert Bender
Estimated Sales: Below $ 5 Million
Number Employees: 20-49
Sq. footage: 20000

9040 **Montana Tea & Spice Trading**
PO Box 8082
Missoula, MT 59807 406-721-4882
Fax: 406-543-1126 montanatea@msn.com
www.montanatea.com
Tea and herbal tea blending, spice blending. Wholesale, retial and mail order
Owner: Bruce Lee
Estimated Sales: $750,000
Number Employees: 7
Number of Brands: 2
Number of Products: 300+
Sq. footage: 4000

9041 **Montchevre-Betin, Inc**
4030 Palos Verdes Drive North
Suite 201
Rolling Hills Estates, CA 90274 310-541-3520
Fax: 310-541-0376 arnaud@montchevre.com
www.montchevre.com

Goat cheese
Owner: Arnaud Solandt
Estimated Sales: $ 1 - 3 Million
Number Employees: 5-9

9042 **Monte Cristo Trading**
14 Harwood Ct
Scarsdale, NY 10583-4121 914-725-8025
Fax: 914-725-0869
General grocery
President: Anton Derosa
Estimated Sales: $530,000
Number Employees: 1-4
Type of Packaging: Consumer, Food Service, Bulk

9043 **Monte Vista Farming Company**
5043 N Montpelier Rd
Denair, CA 95316 209-874-1866
Fax: 209-874-2024
sales@montevistafarming.com
www.montevistafarming.com
Processor and exporter of almonds
Owner: Jim Crecelius
CFO: Bob McClain
VP Sales: Dan Whisenhunt
Operations Manager: Renee Crozier
Estimated Sales: $1.3 Million
Number Employees: 25
Sq. footage: 2000

9044 **Montebello Brands**
1919 Willow Spring Rd
Baltimore, MD 21222 410-282-8800
Fax: 410-282-8809
Processor and exporter of whiskey
President: Leo Conte
Estimated Sales: $24 Million
Number Employees: 20-49
Type of Packaging: Consumer, Food Service

9045 **Montebello Kitchens**
PO Box 610
Gordonsville, VA 22942 800-743-7687
Fax: 270-209-1371 www.montebellokitchens.com
Spices and rubs, dressing and marinades, sauces, virginia peanuts, coups and milled grains.
Founder: Steven Lynch

9046 **Montelle Winery**
P.O.Box 147
Augusta, MO 63332 636-228-4464
Fax: 636-228-4754 888-595-9463
mervine@fednet.com www.montelle.com
In the late 1960s and early 1970s, a few pioneering souls began to refurbish the old vineyards and winery buildings of Missouri's premier wine-growing regions. One of these pioneers was Clayton Byers, who founded Montelle Vineyards in1970.
Owner: Tony Kooyumjian
Founder: Clayton Byers
Estimated Sales: $ 1-2.5 Million
Number Employees: 1-4
Number of Products: 15

9047 **Montello**
6106 E 32nd Pl Ste 100
Tulsa, OK 74135 918-665-1170
Fax: 918-665-1480 800-331-4628
oncall@montelloinc.com www.montelloinc.com
Importer and distributor of emulsifiers and gums
President: Allen Johnson
VP: Leo Wooldridge
Estimated Sales: $6 Million
Number Employees: 5

9048 **Monterey Fish Company**
950 S Sanborn Rd
Salinas, CA 93901 831-771-9221
Fax: 831-775-0156 mntyfish@redshift.com
www.montereyfishcompany.com
Processor of canned and frozen herring, anchovies, herring roe, mackerel, sardines and squid
President: Carmelo J Trinqali
VP: Sal Trinquali
VP Operations: Anthony Trinqali
Plant Manager: Joseph Tringali
Estimated Sales: $1-$2.5 Million
Number Employees: 1-4
Type of Packaging: Consumer, Food Service, Private Label
Brands:
Bono
Seawave

9049 **Monterey Mushrooms**
260 Westgate Dr
Watsonville, CA 95076 831-763-5300
Fax: 831-763-0700
custserv@mushroomcanning.com
www.montereymushrooms.com
Manufacturer and exporter of canned, frozen and refrigerated mushroom stems/pieces, slices and buttons
Division Manager: Chris De Gruchy
CEO: Shah Kazmi
Sales Manager: George Temple
Estimated Sales: $100 Million
Number Employees: 1,000-4,999
Sq. footage: 23000
Type of Packaging: Consumer, Food Service, Private Label, Bulk
Other Locations:
Multi Site Fresh Operation Farms
Orlando FL
Multi Site Fresh Operation Farms
Princeton IL
Multi Site Fresh Operation Farms
Royal Oaks CA
Multi Site Fresh Operation Farms
Las Lomas CA
Multi Site Fresh Operation Farms
Morgan Hill CA
Multi Site Fresh Operation Farms
San Miguel, Mexico
Multi Site Fresh Operation Farms
Vancouver, BC Canada
Multi Site Fresh Operation Farms
Arroyo Grande CA
Multi Site Fresh Operation Farms
Madisonville TX
Multi Site Fresh Operation Farms
Loudon TX
Multi Site Fresh Operation Farms
Temple PA
Monterey Processing Facility
Bonne Terre MO
Monterey Product Development
Royal Oaks CA
Brands:
CLEAN N READY
MT LAUREL

9050 **(HQ)Monterey Mushrooms**
260 Westgate Dr
Watsonville, CA 95076 831-763-5300
Fax: 831-763-0700 800-333-6874
www.montereymushrooms.com
Processor and packer of fresh, frozen and canned mushrooms including shiitake, enoki and oyster
President/CEO: Shah Kazemi
CFO: Ray Selle
CEO: Shah Kazmi
VP Marketing: Joe Cadwell
Estimated Sales: I
Number Employees: 1,000-4,999
Type of Packaging: Food Service
Brands:
Wild Pack

9051 **Monterey Mushrooms**
2 Hazel St
Bonne Terre, MO 63628 573-358-3381
Fax: 573-358-2209 800-333-6874
corpmarketing@montmush.com
www.montereymushrooms.com
Processor of small and medium mushrooms including canned, glass-packed, marinated, stemmed, pieced, whole and sliced
Controller: Stephanie Carron
Quality Control Director: Kevin Andres
Director of Sales: Becky Hays
Operations Executive: Kent Hall
Plant Manager: Carl Bennett
Estimated Sales: $7900000
Number Employees: 50
Sq. footage: 25318
Parent Co: Monterey Mushrooms

9052 **Monterey Mushrooms Inc.**
1108 Beaumont Ave
Temple, PA 19560 610-929-1961
Fax: 610-929-3288 800-763-0700
corpmarketing@montmush.com
www.montereymushrooms.com
Processed mushrooms
Manager: Bruce Debuc
Vice President: Joe Caldwell
VP Sales: Jim Burt
Plant Manager: Terry Schadler
Estimated Sales: $ 2.5-5 Million
Number Employees: 100-249
Brands:
Baby Bella
Clean N Readyo

9053 **Monterey Vineyard**
800 S Alta St
Gonzales, CA 93926 831-675-4000
Fax: 831-675-4019
Wines
General Manager/President: Ken Greene
Operations Manager: Ken Greene
Winemaker: Chris Mallar
Production Manager: Noel Vofter
Estimated Sales: Less than $500,000
Number Employees: 5-9

9054 **Monterrey Products Company**
803 S Zarzamora St
San Antonio, TX 78207 210-435-2872
Fax: 210-435-2877 www.monterreyproducts.com
Manufacturer of Mexican products including mole sauce, candy, spices, chili powder and dry chili mixes
President/Owner: Ernesto De Los Santos
Vice President: Sylvia De Los Santos
Estimated Sales: $2 Million
Number Employees: 10
Type of Packaging: Consumer, Food Service

9055 **Monterrey Products Company**
803 S Zarzamora St
San Antonio, TX 78207 210-435-2872
Fax: 210-435-2877 800-872-1652
www.monterreyproducts.com
Spices, salsa and praline candies
President: Ernest De Los Santos
Estimated Sales: Below $ 5 Million
Number Employees: 10-19
Brands:
Monterrey

9056 **Monterrey Provisions**
5235 Lovelock St
San Diego, CA 92110-4012 619-294-2222
Fax: 619-294-2220 800-201-1600
information@monprov.com www.monprov.com
Cheese
President: Dick Herrman
Estimated Sales: $ 50-100 Million
Number Employees: 50-99
Brands:
Dietz & Watson
Farmland
Jennie-O
Poorebrothers
Schrieber

9057 **Montevina Winery**
20680 Shenandoah School Rd
Plymouth, CA 95669 209-245-6942
Fax: 209-245-6617 cmkenna@tfewines.com
www.montevina.com
Wine
CEO: Louis Trinchero
VP: Jeff Meyers
Estimated Sales: $ 2.5-5 Million
Number Employees: 10-19

9058 **Monticello Canning Company**
126 Sunset Dr
Crossville, TN 38555 931-484-3696
Fax: 931-484-2095
Manufacturer of canned vegetables including sweet red and green peppers, pimientos, etc
President: Earl Dean
Estimated Sales: $ 3 - 5 Million
Number Employees: 5-10
Type of Packaging: Consumer, Food Service, Private Label, Bulk
Brands:
Betty Ann

9059 **Monticello Canning Company**
126 Sunset Dr
Crossville, TN 38555 931-484-3696
Fax: 931-484-2095
Peppers, pimentos
President: Earl Dean
COO: Greg Barnwell
Estimated Sales: Below $ 5 Million
Number Employees: 20

9060 **Monticello Cellars**
4242 Big Ranch Rd
Napa, CA 94558 707-253-2802
Fax: 707-253-1019
Wine@CorleyFamilyNapaValley.com
www.corleyfamilynapavalley.com
Processor of wine and champagne
President: Kevin Corley
Chairman: Jay Corley
Marketing: Stephen Corley
Sales: Stephen Corley
Estimated Sales: $1,300,000
Number Employees: 10-19
Type of Packaging: Consumer

9061 **Montione's Biscotti & Baked Goods**
215 South Worcester St
Norton, MA 02766 508-285-4777
Fax: 508-285-4465 800-559-1010
info@montionesbiscotti.com
www.montionesbiscotti.com
Baked goods, biscotti
President: Mary Montione
CFO: Dan Mahoney
Estimated Sales: $1 Million
Number Employees: 5-9
Type of Packaging: Private Label

9062 **Montmorenci Vineyards**
2989 Charleston Hwy
Aiken, SC 29801 803-649-4870
Fax: 803-642-1834 vinonut@aol.com
www.montmorencivineyards.com
Wine
Owner/Winemaker: Robert Scott
Owner: Elaine Scott
General Manager: Stephanie Scott
Operation Manager: Elaine Scott
Estimated Sales: $500,000-$1 Million
Number Employees: 1-4
Type of Packaging: Private Label
Brands:
Blanc du Bois
Chambourcin
De Caradeuc White
Melody
Savannah White
Vin Eclipser

9063 **Montreal Chop Suey Company**
2100 Moreau Street
Montreal, QC H1W 2M3
Canada 514-522-3134
Fax: 514-522-8074
Processor of Chinese food products including fresh bean and alfalfa sprouts, egg roll and wonton paste, fresh fried noodles and canned bean sprouts
President: Bill Lee
Vice President: David Lee
VP: Robert Lee
Sales Director: John Zielinski
Production Manager: Marc Comtols
Number Employees: 30
Sq. footage: 46000
Type of Packaging: Consumer, Bulk
Brands:
MONTREAL CHOP SUEY

9064 **Monument Dairy Farms**
2107 James Road
Weybridge, VT 05753-9525 802-545-2119
Fax: 802-545-2117
Milk products
Co-Owner: Jon Rooney
Co-Owner: James Rooney
Estimated Sales: $ 10-24.9 Million
Number Employees: 30
Brands:
Monument Dairy Farms

9065 **Monument Farms**
2107 James Rd
Middlebury, VT 05753-9525 802-545-2119
Fax: 802-545-2117
Milk processor
Manager: Millicent Rooney
President: Robert James
Plant Manager: Jonathan Rooney
Estimated Sales: Below $ 5 Million
Number Employees: 33
Type of Packaging: Private Label

9066 **Moo & Oink**
7158 S Stony Island Ave
Chicago, IL 60649 773-493-7100
Fax: 773-493-2042 info@moo-oink.com
www.moo-oink.com
Processor of ready to cook chitterlings, beef and pork hot links; importer of spare ribs.
President: Morton Levy
Vice President: Barry Lezak
Sales Representative: Harvey Lezak
Sales Representative: Wayne McGill
Facilities Manager: Catherine Taylor
Estimated Sales: $ 20 - 50 Million
Number Employees: 50-99
Sq. footage: 20000

9067 **Moo Chocolate/Organic Children's Chocolate LLC**
Po Box 271
Cos Cob, CT 06807-0271 203-561-8864
Fax: 203-869-7040 jackie@moochocolates.com
www.moochocolates.com
Gluten-free, kosher, organic/natural, chocolate bars.
Marketing: Jackie Eckholm

9068 **(HQ)Moody Dunbar**
P.O. Box 6048
Johnson City, TN 37602-6048 423-952-0100
Fax: 423-952-0289 800-251-8202
esimerly@moodydunbar.com
www.moodydunbar.com
America's leading manufacturer of bell peppers, flame-roasted peppers and pimientos. From 2 oz. jars to 10# cans and 55 gallon drums, Moody Dunbar offers green, red, and yellow bell peppers in a variety of cuts and styles. Also aleading manufacturer of sweet potatoes and yams.
President/CEO: Stanley Dunbar
CFO: Christy Dunbar
Vice President: Ed Simerly
R&D/Quality Control: Dave Adkins
Marketing: Ed Simerly
Sales: Terri Sams
Public Relations: Tony Treadway
Plant Manager: Ron Austin
Estimated Sales: $ 10 - 20 Million
Type of Packaging: Consumer, Food Service
Other Locations:
Saticoy Foods
Santa Paula CA
Brands:
Dromedary
Dunbars
O-Sage
Sunshine

9069 **Moody Dunbar**
3202 Highway 107
Chuckey, TN 37641 423-257-4712
Fax: 423-952-0289 800-251-8202
Peppers, pimientos
Owner: Stanley Dunbar
President: Ed Simerly
Quality Control: Diva Ajins
R & D: Dawan Dunbar
VP Sales: Ed Simerly
Estimated Sales: $ 10-20 Million
Number Employees: 1-4
Brands:
Cal-Sun
Cannon
Dixie
Dunbars
Nature's Pride

9070 **Moon Enterprises**
11720 Voyageur Way
Suite 2
Richmond, BC V6X 3G9
Canada 604-270-0088
Fax: 604-270-8988 thomasleemoon@fido.ca
Processor and exporter of live lobsters, crabs, oysters and geoduck clams, prawn
President: Thomas Lee
Quality Control: Thomas Lee
Plant Manager: Thomas Lee
Estimated Sales: $3 Million
Number Employees: 8
Type of Packaging: Private Label

9071 **Moon Shine Trading Company**
1250 Harter Ave # A
Woodland, CA 95776-6106 530-668-0660
Fax: 530-668-6061 800-678-1226
mstco@moonshinetrading.com
www.moonshinetrading.com
Processor and exporter of gourmet chocolate and vanilla nut butters cremes, honey and honey products including fruit spreads and honey straws, bee pollen, bees wax, royal jelly and propolis; also, gift packs
Owner: Ishai Zeldner
Co-Owner: Ishai Zeldner
Estimated Sales: $ 3 - 5 Million
Number Employees: 1-4
Sq. footage: 4000
Type of Packaging: Consumer, Food Service, Private Label, Bulk
Brands:
Chocolate & Vanilla Nut Spread
Gourmet Butters & Spreads
Gourmet Honey Collection
Honey Fruit Spreads
Honey In the Straw

9072 **Moon's Seafood Company**
2513 Woodfield Cir
Melbourne, FL 32904-6657 321-872-0431
Fax: 321-872-0434 800-526-5624
info@moonseafood.com www.moonseafood.com
Shrimp, scallops, clams and crabs
President: Jay Moon
Vice President: Rick Madrigal
Estimated Sales: $ 1 - 3 Million
Number Employees: 1-4
Brands:
Moon's Seafood

9073 **MoonLight Kitchen**
199 Harriet Ct
Newark, DE 19711-5453 302-266-0558
Fax: 302-266-7810
General grocery
Manager: Tony Haan
Public Relations: D Lynn Sinclair
Estimated Sales: Under $500,000
Number Employees: 5-9

9074 **Mooney Farms**
1220 Fortress St
Chico, CA 95973 530-899-2661
Fax: 530-899-7746 mooneyfarm@aol.com
www.mooneyfarms.com
Processor and exporter of sun dried tomatoes, pesto, BBQ marinade and tomatoe sauces.
Partner/Sales: Mary Ellen Mooney
Partner/Production: Stephen Mooney
Estimated Sales: $27.5 Million
Number Employees: 50
Sq. footage: 100000
Type of Packaging: Consumer, Food Service, Private Label, Bulk
Brands:
Bella Sun Luci
Summer's Choice

9075 **Moonlight Brewing Company**
2218 Laughlin Road
PO Box 6
Windsor, CA 95492-8213 707-528-2537
moonlightguy@comcast.net
www.moonlightbrewing.com
Manufacturer of beer
President: Brian Hunt
Estimated Sales: $1-3 Million
Number Employees: 1-4
Brands:
Death and Taxes Black Beer
Full Moon Light Ale
Moonlight Pale Lager
Santa's Tipple
Twist of Fate Bitter Ale

9076 **Moonlite Bar Bq Inn**
2840 W Parrish Ave
Owensboro, KY 42301 270-684-8143
Fax: 270-684-8105 800-322-8989
pbosley@moonlite.com www.moonlite.com
Processor of barbecue meats including mutton, pork and beef; also, bean soup, sauces and chili
President: Fred Bosley
VP: Ken Bosley
Marketing Director: Pat Bosley
Estimated Sales: $3 Million
Number Employees: 120

Number of Brands: 1
Number of Products: 48
Type of Packaging: Private Label
Brands:
Moonlite Bbq Inn

9077 **Moore's Candies**
3004 Pinewood Ave
Baltimore, MD 21214 410-426-2705
Fax: 410-426-7073
www.moorescandiesmaryland.com
Manufacturer of handcrafted chocolates and candy including truffles, almond crunch, chocolate-covered potato chips and pretzels, holiday and wedding chocolate items and specialty items
Co-Owner: Jim Heyl Jr
Co-Owner: Lois Heyl
VP: Dana Heyl
Estimated Sales: $3 Million
Number Employees: 5-9
Sq. footage: 1250
Type of Packaging: Consumer, Food Service, Private Label, Bulk
Brands:
MOORES

9078 **Mooresville Ice Cream Company**
172 N Broad St
Mooresville, NC 28115 704-664-5456
Fax: 704-663-7829
Manufacturer of ice cream and novelties including chocolate covered bars, ice cream sandwiches, etc.
President: Gene Millsaps
Estimated Sales: $5-10 Million
Number Employees: 10-19
Type of Packaging: Consumer, Food Service, Bulk
Brands:
BIG SCOOP
DELUXE

9079 **Moorhead & Company**
PO Box 1799
Rocklin, CA 95677 818-787-2510
Fax: 916-624-1604 800-322-6325
www.mooragar.com
Manufacturer and importer of stabilizers including agar
President: Deborah Nichols
Sales/Marketing: Brenda Franklin
Estimated Sales: $180000
Number Employees: 3
Type of Packaging: Bulk
Brands:
Agarich
Agarloid
Agarmoor

9080 **Moosehead Breweries Ltd.**
89 Main Street W
St. John, NB E2M 3H2
Canada 506-635-7000
Fax: 506-635-7029 877-888-2337
consumerinquiries@moosehead.ca
www.moosehead.ca
Processor and exporter of beer
President: Andrew Oland
Exec Chairman: Derek Oland
VP Production: Peter Hennebarry
Purchasing Agent: Richard Osetchook
Number Employees: 5-9
Type of Packaging: Consumer, Food Service
Brands:
MOOSEHEAD LAGER

9081 **Moosewood Hollow LLC**
37 Industrial Park Drive
Morrisville, VT 05661 802-479-7999
Fax: 802-888-5909 800-828-2376
sales@vermontmaplesugarcompany.com
www.moosewoodhollow.com
Infused mayple syrup & oat biscotti
President: Claudia Clark
Estimated Sales: $ 1 - 3 Million
Number Employees: 1-4
Type of Packaging: Consumer

9082 **Mootz Candy**
P.O.Box 495
Pottsville, PA 17901-495
Fax: 570-622-1933 mootzweb@dsnow.com
www.mootzcandies.com
Processor of confectionery products including chocolate coated creams, caramels and nuts, chocolate and chocolate chunks
President: Ned Buckley
General Manager: Janes Haas
Estimated Sales: $ 3 - 5 Million
Number Employees: 10-19
Type of Packaging: Consumer, Private Label

9083 **Morabito Baking Company**
757 Kohn Street
Norristown, PA 19401 610-275-5419
Fax: 610-275-0358 800-525-7747
www.morabito.com
Sourdough breads and Spoletti rolls
General Manager: Mike Morabito III
Marketing Manager: Joanna Morabito
Sales Director: Marc Knox
Human Resources Director: Cassandra Morabito
Estimated Sales: $10 Million
Number Employees: 130
Sq. footage: 70000
Type of Packaging: Consumer, Food Service, Private Label, Bulk
Brands:
MORABITO

9084 **Moran Coffee Company**
P.O.Box 355
Dublin, OH 43017-0355 614-889-2500
Fax: 614-889-6500
Coffee
President: Thomas Moran
Estimated Sales: $ 5-10 Million
Number Employees: 1-4

9085 **Moravian Cookies Shop**
224 S Cherry St
Winston Salem, NC 27101-5231 336-924-1278
Fax: 336-924-9470 800-274-2994
sales@salembaking.com
www.moraviancookie.com
Cookies and baked goods
President/Owner: Dewey Wilkerson
Operations Manager: Vincent Pellegrino
Estimated Sales: $ 2.30 Million
Number Employees: 25

9086 **More Than Gourmet**
929 Home Ave
Akron, OH 44310 330-762-6652
Fax: 330-762-4832 800-860-9385
info@morethangourmet.com
www.morethangourmet.com
French sauces and stocks.
President/Owner: Bill Finnegan
CEO: Bradley Sacks
VP: Harvey Leff
Estimated Sales: $1.6 Million
Number Employees: 24

9087 **More Than Gourmet**
929 Home Ave
Akron, OH 44310 330-762-6652
Fax: 330-762-4832 800-860-9385
info@morethangourmet.com
www.morethangourmet.com
Processor of stocks and sauces
Owner: Brad Sacks
CFO: Scott Bonnette
Marketing: Todd Hohman
Estimated Sales: $500,000-$1 Million
Number Employees: 20-49
Type of Packaging: Consumer, Food Service
Brands:
Demi-Glace Veal Gold
Glace De Poulet Gold
Veggie Glace Gold

9088 **Morehouse Foods**
760 Epperson Dr
City of Industry, CA 91748-1336 626-854-1655
Fax: 626-854-1656 info@morehousefoods.com
www.morehousefoods.com
Processor, importer and exporter of mustard, horseradish and vinegar
President: David Latter
Estimated Sales: $ 20 - 50 Million
Number Employees: 50-99
Sq. footage: 80000
Type of Packaging: Consumer, Food Service, Private Label, Bulk
Brands:
Chalif
El Rey
Morehouse
Redwood Empire
Rhinegeld

9089 **Moresco Vineyards**
16865 E Gawne Road
Stockton, CA 95215-9646 209-467-3081
Wine
General Manager: Mark Moresco

9090 **Moretti's Poultry**
2124 Tremont Ctr
Columbus, OH 43221-3110 614-486-2333
Fax: 614-486-2333 www.morettisofarlington.com
Processor of fresh chicken and turkey
Owner: Tim Moretti
Estimated Sales: $ 1 - 3 Million
Number Employees: 20-49
Type of Packaging: Food Service, Bulk

9091 **Morey's Seafood Intl.ional**
1218 Highway 10 S
Motley, MN 56466 218-352-6345
Fax: 218-352-6523 www.moreys.com
Processor, importer and exporter of fresh and frozen fish including marinated salmon, marinated tilapia and marinated smoked fish as well as many other specialty products.
President: Lynn Geroard
Principal;VP Operations: Bob Thiede
CFO: Gary Ziolkowski
VP/COO: Loren Morey
Marketing Director: Michelle Pape
Sales Director: Brian Augustin
Plant Manager: Patti Zahler
Purchasing Manager: Greg Frank
Estimated Sales: $ 20 - 50 Million
Number Employees: 50-99
Sq. footage: 52000
Parent Co: Morey's Seafood International
Brands:
Morey's

9092 **Morgan Food**
90 W Morgan St
Austin, IN 47102-1741 812-794-1170
Fax: 812-794-1211 888-430-1780
mfi-web@morganfoods.com
www.morganfoods.com
Manufacturer and exporter of canned foods including condensed soups, baked and refried beans, gravies, condiments and sauces
Chairman/CEO: John Morgan
VP/CFO: Daniel Slattery
VP Marketing: Paul McCaig
Estimated Sales: $50-100 Million
Number Employees: 250-499
Type of Packaging: Consumer, Food Service, Private Label
Brands:
American Beauty
Royal Gem
Scott Country

9093 **Morgan Mill**
P.O.Box 525
Cherokee, NC 28719-0525 828-497-9227
Fax: 828-497-4330
Rainbow trout
Owner: Dale Owen
Estimated Sales: Less than $200,000
Number Employees: 1-4

9094 **Morgan Specialties**
1800 S Main St
Paris, IL 61944 217-465-8577
Fax: 217-463-2844
Lipid-based ingredients
Estimated Sales: $ 10-20 Million
Number Employees: 50-99

9095 **Morgan Winery**
590 Brunken Ave Ste C
Salinas, CA 93901 831-751-7777
Fax: 831-751-7780 www.morganwinery.com
Processor and exporter of wine including chardonnay and sauvignon blanc
President: Daniel Lee
Estimated Sales: $850000
Number Employees: 5-9

9096 **Morinaga Nutritional Foods**
2441 W 205th St Ste C102
Torrance, CA 90501 310-787-0200
Fax: 310-787-2727 info@morinu.com
www.morinu.com
Processor of aseptically packaged shelf-stable tofu, soy soups, soy smoothies
President: Yasuo Kumoda
Executive VP: Kingi Aoyana
Marketing Director: Susan Bucher
Director Sales: Avis Noble
Estimated Sales: $ 3 - 5 Million
Number Employees: 10-19
Sq. footage: 5000
Parent Co: Morinaga Milk Company
Type of Packaging: Consumer, Food Service, Private Label
Other Locations:
Morinaga Nutritional Foods
Tualatin OR
Brands:
Mori-Nu

9097 **Morning Glory/Formost Farms**
E10889 Penny Lane
Baraboo, WI 53913-8115 608-355-8700
Fax: 920-336-7165 800-362-9196
commdept@foremostfarms.com
www.foremostfarms.com
Processor of dairy products including fresh sour cream, milk; wholesaler/distributor of ice cream; serving the food service market
President/CEO: David Fuhrmann
General Manager: Jeff Koehler
Manager of Marketing/Sales: Donald Hoff
Manager: Don Mosher
Manager: Wally Heil
Number Employees: 100-249
Number of Products: 10
Parent Co: Foremost Farms USA
Type of Packaging: Consumer, Food Service, Private Label, Bulk
Brands:
Golden Guernsey
Morning Glory

9098 **Morning Star Coffee**
207 Carter Dr Ste E
West Chester, PA 19382 610-701-7022
Fax: 610-701-7032 888-854-2233
robin.mars@morningstarcoffee.us
www.morningstarcoffee.us
Coffee roasting
President: Charles Streitwieser
Estimated Sales: $450,000
Number Employees: 5-9
Type of Packaging: Private Label, Bulk
Brands:
Morning Star
Numit

9099 **Morning Star Foods**
8 Joanna Court
East Brunswick, NJ 08816-2108 800-237-5320
Fax: 732-432-3928
Manufacturer and marketer of consumer packaged goods
President/CEO: Herman Graffinder
CFO: Craig Miller
Sr. VP Marketing: Toby Purdy
Sr. VP Operations: Samuel Hillin
Parent Co: Dean Foods Company
Type of Packaging: Private Label, Bulk

9100 **Morning Star Foods**
2036 S Hardy Drive
Tempe, AZ 85282-1211 480-966-0080
Fax: 480-966-9456
Aseptic coffee creamers
President: Tom Ernesto
Plant Manager: Ernesto Martinez
Estimated Sales: $ 20-50 Million
Number Employees: 50-99

9101 **Morning Star Packing Company**
13448 Volta Rd
Los Banos, CA 93635 209-826-8000
Fax: 209-826-8266 kgashaw@morningstarco.com
www.morningstarco.com
Tomatoes and tomato paste
President: Chris Rufer
Quality Control: Tony Manuel
Executive: Ernie Sanchez
Purchasing Agent: Manuel Gonzales
Estimated Sales: $ 50-100 Million
Number Employees: 100-249

9102 **Morningland Dairy CheeseCompany**
6248 County Road 2980
Mountain View, MO 65548 417-469-3817
Fax: 417-469-5086
Processor of gourmet health and raw milk cheeses
President: James Reiners
Estimated Sales: $ 3 - 5 Million
Number Employees: 5-9
Type of Packaging: Consumer, Food Service, Private Label, Bulk
Brands:
Morningland Dairy
Ozark Hills

9103 **Moroni Feed Company**
Po Box 228
West Liberty, IA 52776-0228 435-436-8221
Fax: 435-436-8101 800-453-5327
norbest@norbest.com
www.norbest.com/a_moroni_feed.cfm
Processor of fresh and frozen turkeys
President: David Bailey
Estimated Sales: $ 125 Million +
Number Employees: 850
Type of Packaging: Private Label
Brands:
Norbest

9104 **Morr-Ad Foodservice**
920 Eha St
Wailuku, HI 96793-1426 808-877-2017
Fax: 808-270-9545
Purchasing Manager: Charles Nessel
Number Employees: 20-49

9105 **Morre-Tec Industries**
1 Gary Rd
Union, NJ 07083-5527 908-688-9009
Fax: 908-688-9005 sales@morretec.com
www.morretec.com
Manufacturer, importer and exporter of magnesium chloride, food grade and potassium bromate; importer and wholesaler/distributor of low sodium substitutes and licorice, spray, dried and powder
President: Leonard Glass
Marketing Director: Michael Fuchs
Operations Manager: Norm Cantoe
Estimated Sales: $ 10 - 20 Million
Number Employees: 10-19
Number of Products: 150
Sq. footage: 25000
Type of Packaging: Consumer, Bulk

9106 **Morris J. Golombeck**
960 Franklin Ave
Brooklyn, NY 11225 718-284-3505
Fax: 718-693-1941 golspice@aol.com
www.golombeckspice.com
Processor, importer and exporter of herbs and spices including basil, cassia, cayenne, garlic, ginger, paprika, etc
President: Hyman Golombeck
Vice President: Sheldon Golombeck
Estimated Sales: $ 5 - 10 Million
Number Employees: 10-19
Sq. footage: 120000
Type of Packaging: Bulk

9107 **(HQ)Morris National**
760 N McKeever Avenue
Azusa, CA 91702-2349 626-385-2000
Fax: 626-969-8670 www.specialtimegifts.com
Importer of specialty foods including gourmet cookies; processor of truffle-filled chocolates and hard candies; importer of specialty foods including gourmet cookies, candies, chocolates, preserves and teas
President/Ceo: Gerald Morris
Ceo: Sean Issell
VP Operations: Coaute Douesson
Estimated Sales: $21 Million
Number Employees: 330
Sq. footage: 145000
Type of Packaging: Consumer
Brands:
McKeever & Danlee
Very Special Chocolates

9108 **Morrison Farms**
85824 519th Ave
Clearwater, NE 68726 402-887-5335
Fax: 402-887-4709
morrison@nebraskapopcorn.com
www.morrisonfarms.com
High quality popcorn and dry, edible bean products
President: Frank Morrison
Estimated Sales: $300,000-500,000
Number Employees: 1-4

9109 **Morrison Lamothe**
5240 Finch Avenue East
Unit 2
Toronto, ON M1S 5A2
Canada 416-291-6762
Fax: 416-291-5046 877-677-6533
headofice@morrisonlamothe.com
www.morrisonlamothe.com
Manufacturer of frozen prepared entrees, dinners and pot pies including beef, chicken, salisbury steak, macaroni and cheese, cabbage rolls, pasta, etc
Vice President: Ross Sythes
President And Ceo: J.M. Pigott
Estimated Sales: $45 Million
Number Employees: 75
Sq. footage: 38000
Parent Co: Morrison Lamothe
Type of Packaging: Consumer, Private Label
Brands:
CLIFFSIDE
HOLIDAY FARMS
PUB PIES
SAVARIN

9110 **Morrison Meat Packers**
738 NW 72nd St
Miami, FL 33150 305-836-4461
Fax: 305-836-2750 800-330-4267
gilda@morrisonmeat.com
www.morrisonmeat.com
Processor of ham
Owner: Eduardo Rodriguez
Estimated Sales: $ 20 - 50 Million
Number Employees: 50-99
Type of Packaging: Consumer

9111 **Morrison Meat Pies**
3403 S 1400 W # C
West Valley, UT 84119-4050 801-977-0181
Fax: 801-977-0448 sales@morrisonmeatpies.com
www.morrisonmeatpies.com
Processor of meat pies and frozen meat pie crust
Owner: Eugene Tafoya
Estimated Sales: $ 3 - 5 Million
Number Employees: 1-4
Type of Packaging: Consumer

9112 **Morrison Milling Company**
319 E Prairie St
Denton, TX 76201 940-387-6111
Fax: 940-566-5992 800-580-5487
humanresources@morrisonmilling.com
www.morrisonmilling.com
Flour, processed corn, cornmeal, frosting mixes, soups, and gravies
President: Clifton Shoemaker
Chairman: Harry Crumpacker
Treasurer: Rudy Moreno
CEO: Cliff Shoemake
Quality Control: Kenny Newton
Operations Manager: Roger Biete
Purchasing Manager: David Hopkins
Estimated Sales: $ 20-50 Million
Number Employees: 100-249
Type of Packaging: Private Label
Brands:
Morrison Brand

9113 **Morrisons Pastries/TurfCheesecake**
47 Halstead Avenue
Suite 204
Harrison, NY 10528-4142 914-835-6629
Fax: 914-835-6793 ÿÿ -00 -21 8
turfcc.com@aol.com www.turfcc.com
Cheesecake, yogurt and baked goods
Brands:
Baby Watson
Grandpa Morrisons
New York's Turf

9114 **Morse's Sauerkraut**
3856 Washington Rd
Waldoboro, ME 04572 207-832-5569
Fax: 207-832-2297 866-832-5569
morses@midcoast.com
www.morsessauerkraut.com
Processor of salsa, beet relish, pickled beets and sauerkraut
Owner: David Swetnam
Estimated Sales: Below $ 5 Million
Number Employees: 10-19
Type of Packaging: Consumer, Food Service
Brands:
Morse's

9115 **Mortillaro Lobster Company**
65 Commercial St
Gloucester, MA 01930-5047 978-282-4621
Fax: 978-281-0579
Lobster
President: Vincent Mortillaro
Estimated Sales: $ 5 - 10 Million
Number Employees: 20-49

9116 **Mortimer's Fine Foods**
5341 John Lucas Drive
Burlington, ON L7L 6A8
Canada 905-336-0000
Fax: 905-336-0909 mortimer@lara.on.ca
www.mortimers.com
Processor and exporter of frozen beef, prepared and vegetarian entrees and meat pies
VP Sales: Karim Talakshi
Type of Packaging: Consumer, Food Service, Private Label, Bulk
Brands:
Mortimer Fine Foods

9117 **Morton & Bassett Spices**
84 Galli Dr
Novato, CA 94949 415-883-8530
Fax: 415-883-0813 866-972-6879
candymfs@verizon.net www.mortonbassett.com
Spices and seasonings
President: Morton Gothelf
Estimated Sales: Below $ 5 Million
Number Employees: 10-19
Number of Products: 70
Brands:
M B Spices

9118 **(HQ)Morton Salt**
123 N Wacker Dr Fl 24
Chicago, IL 60606 312-807-2000
Fax: 312-807-2929 800-789-7258
www.mortonsalt.com
Manufacturer of salts, salt substitutes and seasonings; also, salt shakers and water conditioning salt
President: Walter Becky
CEO: Mark Roberts
CFO: Andy Kotlarz
VP Sales/Marketing: Wayne Carney
Estimated Sales: $500 Million
Number Employees: 2900
Parent Co: Rohn and Haas Company
Type of Packaging: Consumer, Food Service, Private Label, Bulk
Brands:
Morton
Star Flake

9119 **Morton Salt Company**
123 N Wacker Dr Fl 24
Chicago, IL 60606 312-807-2000
Fax: 312-807-2949 www.mortonsalt.com
Processor and exporter of salt including food grade and rock
President: Walter W Becky
CEO: Mark Roberts
CFO: Andy Kotlarz
Quality Control: Jim Bazar
Sales: W Lopez
Operations: Jay Tangeman
Production: Bryce Lewis
Plant Manager: Charles Young
Purchasing: Gary Newman
Estimated Sales: 600,000,000
Number Employees: 2900
Parent Co: Rohm & Haas
Type of Packaging: Consumer, Food Service, Private Label, Bulk

9120 **Mosby Winery**
9496 Santa Rosa Rd
Buellton, CA 93427 805-688-2415
Fax: 805-686-4288 mosbywines@yahoo.com
mosbywines.com
Wines, California and Italian varietals
Estimated Sales: $ 2.5-5 Million
Number Employees: 4
Type of Packaging: Private Label

9121 **(HQ)Moscahlades Brothers**
30 N Moore St
New York, NY 10013 212-226-5410
Fax: 212-219-8486 g.moscahlades@earthlink.net
Manufacturer and importer of tomatoes, olives, olive oil and cheeses
President: Nick Moscahlades
Estimated Sales: $ 5 - 10 Million
Number Employees: 5-9
Type of Packaging: Consumer

9122 **Mosher Products**
4318 Hayes Ave
Cheyenne, WY 82001-2349 307-632-1492
Fax: 307-632-1492 info@wheatandgrain.com
www.mosherproducts.com
Organic grain
President: Leonard O Mosher
Estimated Sales: Below $ 5 Million
Number Employees: 16
Sq. footage: 60000
Other Locations:
Bushnell NE
Brands:
Mosher Products

9123 **Moss Creek Winery**
6015 Steele Canyon Rd
Napa, CA 94558 707-252-1295
Fax: 707-254-9327 info@mosscreekwinery.com
www.mosscreekwinery.com
Wines
Owner: Ann Moskowite
Owner: George Moskowite
Winemaker: Nils Venge
Estimated Sales: Less than $500,000
Number Employees: 1-4
Brands:
Moss Creek

9124 **Mossholder's Farm Cheese Factory**
4017 N Richmond Street
Appleton, WI 54913-9704 920-734-7575
lalomo@athenet.net
www.mossholdercheese.homestead.com
Cheese
Co-Owner: Larry Mossholder
Co-Owner: Lois Mossholder
Estimated Sales: Less than $500,000
Number Employees: 1-4

9125 **Mosti Mondiale/Gourmet Mondiale**
6865 Route 132
Ste-Catherine, QC J5C 1B6 450-638-6380
Fax: 450-638-7049
nino.piazza@mostimondiale.com
www.gourmetmondiale.com
Wine, olive oil, balsamic vinegar.
Marketing: Nino Piazza

9126 **Mother Earth Enterprises**
15 Irving Place
New York, NY 10003-2316 212-777-1250
Fax: 212-614-8132 866-436-7688
denis@hempnut.com www.hempnut.com
Wholesaler/distributor of hempnuts; hemp oil, meal and flour; and toasted, sterilized and roasted grain hemp (seed). Highly adaptable for baking and cooking needs
President: Denis Cicero
Type of Packaging: Food Service

9127 **Mother Murphy's Labs**
PO Box 16846
Greensboro, NC 27416-0846 800-849-1277
Fax: 336-273-2615 800-849-1277
info@mothermurphys.com
www.mothermurphys.com
Processor of food flavorings and beverage flavors
President: David Murphy
CEO: Bob Murphy
VP Finance: Tim Hansen
VP: Bruce Murphy
Directing Lab Manager: Patricia Stressler
Quality Control: Don Jarrell
Marketing/Public Relations: Devon Edmonson
Sales: David Wilhoit
Operations: Robin Conner
Production Manager: Guna Diggs
Plant Manager: Mike Harrison
Purchasing Manager: Nellie Brown
Estimated Sales: $25-35 Million
Number Employees: 86
Number of Products: 500
Sq. footage: 210000
Type of Packaging: Private Label, Bulk

9128 **Mother Nature's Goodies**
13378 California St
Yucaipa, CA 92399 909-795-6018
Fax: 909-795-0748
Processor of granola, seven grain bread, frozen pies and candy sundrops
President: Albert G Goude
Manager: Ronn Neish
CFO: Learner Guode
Estimated Sales: $ 3 - 5 Million
Number Employees: 20-49
Sq. footage: 8000
Type of Packaging: Private Label
Brands:
Mother Nature's Goodies

9129 **Mother Parker's Tea & Coffee**
2530 Stanfield Road
Mississauga, ON L4Y 1S4
Canada 905-279-9100
Fax: 905-279-9821 800-387-9398
www.mother-parkers.com
Processor and exporter of ground and whole bean coffees and teas including orange pekoe, regular, decaffeinated, black and herbal; importer of green coffee and teas
Co-CEO: Michael Higgins
Co-CEO: Paul Higgins, Jr.
Sr. VP/Finance/Administration: Brian Goard
Vice President: Chris Bklecki
Number Employees: 280
Type of Packaging: Consumer, Food Service, Private Label, Bulk
Brands:
Blue Ribbon
Higgins & Burke
Mother Parkers

9130 **Mother Shucker's Original Cocktail Sauce**
900 Gregg Street, 1A
Columbia, SC 29201-3913 803-261-3802
Fax: 803-779-3444
mothershuckersauce@gmail.com
www.mothershuckersauce.com
Other condiments, other sauces, seasonings and cooking enhancers.
Marketing: Mary Sparrow

9131 **Mother Teresa's**
700 W Plantation Dr
Clute, TX 77531-5248 979-265-7429
Fax: 979-297-0932 888-265-7429
motTfinefoods@cs.com www.italian-food.us
Vegetables, sauces and dressings
Owner: Teresa Polimano
Estimated Sales: Less than $500,000
Number Employees: 5-9
Brands:
MOTHER TERESA'S FINE FOODS

9132 **Mother's Kitchen**
499 Veterans Dr
Burlington, NJ 8016 609-589-3026
Fax: 609-386-5329 800-566-8437
smiller@motherskitchen.com
www.motherskitchen.com
Baked goods
President: Donald Butte
CFO: George Lasher
VP Marketing: Steve Shaw
Marketing Director: Vince Mannese
Plant Manager: Andy Cetrone

Estimated Sales: $ 10-20 Million
Number Employees: 100-249
Sq. footage: 105
Type of Packaging: Private Label
Brands:
Baby Watson
Country Club
Creative Bakers
Julf Cheesecake
Mother's Kitchen

9133 **Motherland International Inc**
8822 Flower Road
Suite 202
Rancho Cucamonga, CA 91730 909-596-8882
Fax: 909-596-8870 800-590-5407
source@motherlandusa.com
www.motherlandusa.com
Processor and exporter of herbs and vitamins in powder and extract forms used in nutritional supplements; contract manufacturing available
President: Jackson Wen
Marketing: Michael Pinson
Estimated Sales: $ 1 - 3 Million
Number Employees: 20-49
Sq. footage: 25000
Parent Co: Motherland International
Type of Packaging: Consumer, Food Service, Private Label, Bulk

9134 **Mothers Kitchen Inc**
499 Veterans Dr
Burlington, NJ 8016 609-589-3026
Fax: 609-386-5329 www.motherskitchen.com
Processor of kosher frozen baked goods including breads, cakes and pies
President: Donald Butte
Executive Sales Manager: Luca D'Aiuto
Plant Manager: Gene Finnigan
Estimated Sales: $16400000
Number Employees: 100-249
Sq. footage: 32000
Type of Packaging: Food Service
Brands:
Baby Watson Cheesecake

9135 **Mothers Mountain Mustard**
2 Mustard Hollow Way
Falmouth, ME 04105 207-781-4658
Fax: 207-781-2121 800-440-9891
sales@mothersmountain.com
www.mothersmountain.com
Mustard, horseradish, ketchup, dill, chili sauce, creamy horseradish sauce and hot pepper sauce. Just added - jams and jellies!
President: Carrol Tanner
CFO: Dennis Proctor
Co-Owner: Carol Tanner
Estimated Sales: Below $ 5 Million
Number Employees: 6

9136 **(HQ)Motivatit Seafoods**
412 Palm Ave
Houma, LA 70364 985-868-7191
Fax: 985-868-7472 msi1@cajunnet.com
www.motivatit.com
Fresh and frozen seafood
Owner: Michael Boisin
Director Manufacturing: Wayne DeHart
Purchasing Agent: Elgin Voisin
Estimated Sales: $ 20-50 Million
Number Employees: 100-249
Brands:
Wine Island Oysters

9137 **Mott's**
900 King St.
Rye Brook, NY 10573
US 914-612-4000
Fax: 914-612-4100 800-426-4891
consumer_relations@dpsu.com www.motts.com
Manufacturer of apple products that include apple sauce and apple juice
President/CEO: Larry Young
CFO: Martin Ellen
EVP: David Thomas Ph.D
EVP: James Trebilock
Sr. Product Manager: Amanda Vaughn
Estimated Sales: $ 60 Million
Number Employees: 100-249
Parent Co: Cadbury Schweppes
Type of Packaging: Consumer, Food Service
Brands:
Mistic
Mistic Carafes
Re Engerize

9138 **(HQ)Mott's**
55 Hunter Ln
Elmsford, NY 10523-1334
Fax: 914-612-4100
www.cadburyschweppes.com/en
Manufacturer of applesauce, cooking wine, cocktail mixes, fruit drinks, lime juice, apple juice, tomato-clam cocktail, fruit drinks, apple juice, tomato-clam cocktail, molasses
President/Sales: Michael McGrath
CFO: Dave Gerics
CEO: Jack Belsito
Estimated Sales: $300,000-500,000
Number Employees: 1-4
Parent Co: Cadbury Schweppes PLC
Type of Packaging: Consumer, Food Service, Bulk
Brands:
CLAMATO
GRANDMA'S MOLASSES
HAWAIIAN PUNCH
HOLLAND HOUSE
IBC
MAUNA LA'I
MOTT'S
MOTT'S FRUITSATIONS
MR & MRS T
REALEMON
REALLIME
ROSE'S
YPP-HOO

9139 **Motz Poultry**
2050 Sportys Drive
Batavia, OH 45103-8704 513-732-1381
Poultry, poultry products
President: Matt Motz
Estimated Sales: $ 2.5-5 Million
Number Employees: 20-49

9140 **Mound City Shelled Nut Company**
7831 Olive Blvd
St Louis, MO 63130-2039 314-725-9040
Fax: 314-725-9044 800-647-6887
sales@moundcity.com www.nutsgifts.com
Chocolate candy, nut meats, shelled nuts, peanuts
President: Byron Smyrniotis
Vice President: Stacy Smyrniotis
Estimated Sales: $1.8 Million
Number Employees: 10-19
Type of Packaging: Private Label
Brands:
Jordan Almonds

9141 **Mount Baker Vineyards**
4298 Mt Baker Hwy
Everson, WA 98247 360-592-2300
Fax: 360-592-2526 800-441-8263
www
Wines
President: Randy Finley
Manager: Philippe Renaud
Founder: Al Stratton
Estimated Sales: $ 10 - 20 Million
Number Employees: 20-49
Brands:
Mount Baker Vineyards

9142 **Mount Baker Vineyards**
4298 Mt Baker Hwy
Everson, WA 98247 360-592-2300
Fax: 360-592-2526
Wine
Owner: Randy Finley
Estimated Sales: $ 5-10 Million
Number Employees: 20-49
Brands:
Mount Baker Vineyards

9143 **Mount Bethel Winery**
5014 Mount Bethel Dr
Altus, AR 72821 479-468-2444
Fax: 479-468-2444 www.mountbethel.com
Wines
Owner: Eugene Post
Estimated Sales: $300,000
Number Employees: 5-9

9144 **(HQ)Mount Capra Cheese**
279 SW 9th St
Chehalis, WA 98532 360-748-4224
Fax: 360-748-3099 800-574-1961
www.mtcapra.com
Processor and exporter of dehydrated powder whey product and cheese including cheddar, feta and raw goat milk with no salt
Owner: Frank Stout
General Manager/Marketing Incharge: Arny Davis
Estimated Sales: $$1-2.5 Million
Number Employees: 10-19
Sq. footage: 5000
Other Locations:
Mount Capra Cheese
Chehalis WA

9145 **Mount Claire Spring Water**
160 Perkins St
Torrington, CT 06790-6846 860-489-3804
Fax: 860-496-9425 888-525-2473
Water and soft drink
Owner/CEO: Timothy Flynn
Estimated Sales: $500,000-$1 Million
Number Employees: 5-9

9146 **Mount Eden Vineyards**
22020 Mount Eden Rd
Saratoga, CA 95070-9729 408-867-5832
Fax: 408-867-4329 info@mounteden.com
www.mounteden.com
Wines
President: Jeffrey Patterson
Office Manager: Andrea Kyle
CEO: Neil Hagen
Business Manager: Eleanor Davis Patterson
Estimated Sales: Below $ 5 Million
Number Employees: 5-9
Type of Packaging: Private Label
Brands:
Mount Eden Vineyards

9147 **Mount Hope Estate Winery**
2775 Lebanon Road
Manheim, PA 17545-8711 717-665-7021
Fax: 717-664-3466 eduinfo@parenfaire.com
http://mounthopeshop.parenfaire.com
Wine
President/CEO: Charles Romito
VP: Barbara Lacek
Marketing: Barbara Lacek
Brands:
Mazza Vineyards

9148 **Mount Olive Pickle Company**
P.O.Box 609
Mount Olive, NC 28365 919-658-2535
Fax: 919-658-6296 800-672-5041
mrcrisp@mtolivepickles.com
www.mtolivepickles.com
Manufacturer of pickles, relishes and peppers
President: William Bryan
Human Resources Manager: Chris Martin
Community Relations: Lynn Williams
Estimated Sales: $100+ Million
Number Employees: 500-999
Sq. footage: 970000
Brands:
Mt. Olive

9149 **Mount Olympus Waters**
P.O.Box 25426
Salt Lake City, UT 84125-0426 801-974-5000
Fax: 801-973-0110 800-628-6056
lynn@mowi.com www.mowi.com
Manufacturer and supplier of bottler spring water, cups, water coolers and coffee brewers
Owner: William Bailey
VP/GM: John Andrew
Sales Manager: Dave Albistion
VP Operations: Larry Mulanex
Estimated Sales: $ 5 - 10 Million
Number Employees: 50-99
Type of Packaging: Consumer, Food Service, Private Label, Bulk
Brands:
Handi-Tap

9150 **Mount Palomar Winery**
33820 Rancho California Rd
Temecula, CA 92591 951-676-5047
Fax: 951-694-5688 800-854-5177
info@mountpalomar.com
www.mountpalomar.com
Wines
President: Peter Poole
CFO: Beth Raines
Public Relations: Ami Sansweet
Director Manufacturing: Etienne Cowper
Estimated Sales: $ 20-50 Million
Number Employees: 50-99
Brands:
Castelletto
Mount Palomar
Rey Sol

9151 **Mount Pleasant Winery**
5634 High St
Augusta, MO 63332 636-482-9463
Fax: 636-228-4426 800-467-9463
mailto@mountpleasant.com
www.mountpleasant.com
Wines
President: Phillip Dressel
Estimated Sales: Below $ 5 Million
Number Employees: 20-49

9152 **Mount Rose Ravioli & Macaroni Company**
157 Gazza Blvd
Farmingdale, NY 11735
Fax: 631-694-2101
Frozen ravioli and tortellini
President/CEO: Santo Minuto
Treasurer: Anthony Minuto, Sr.
Vice President: Thomas Minuto
Director Manufacturing: Anthony Minuto
Estimated Sales: $ 20-50 Million
Number Employees: 20-49

9153 **Mountain City Coffee Roasters**
P.O.Box 1058
Enka, NC 28728-1058 828-667-0869
Fax: 828-667-0869 888-730-0869
roastmaster@mountaincity.com
www.mountaincity.com
Coffee
Owner: Randall Sluder
Co-Owner/President: Debra Furr Sluder
Estimated Sales: $1-$2.5 Million
Number Employees: 1-4
Type of Packaging: Consumer, Bulk
Brands:
Mountain City

9154 **Mountain City Meat Company**
5905 E 42nd Ave
Denver, CO 80216 303-320-1116
Fax: 303-320-0449 800-937-8325
sales@mountaincitymeat.com
www.mountaincitymeat.com
Manufacturer of fresh, frozen and smoked meat including beef, pork, veal and lamb, portion controlled packaging
President/Co-Owner: Patrick Boyer
VP/Co-Owner: Anna Boyer
VP: Ralph Torres
Estimated Sales: $64.2 Million
Number Employees: 250-499
Type of Packaging: Consumer, Food Service

9155 **Mountain Cove Vineyards& Winegarden**
1362 Fortunes Cove Ln
Lovingston, VA 22949-2226 434-263-5392
Fax: 434-263-8540 aweed1@juno.com
www.mountaincovevineyards.com
Wines
President: Albert C Weed Ii
Estimated Sales: $ 1 - 3 Million
Number Employees: 1-4

9156 **Mountain Crest Brewing SRL LLC**
1208 14th Ave
Monroe, WI 53566-2055 608-325-3191
Fax: 608-325-3198 www.berghoffbeer.com
Processor and exporter of beer and malt liquor in kegs, bottles and cans; energy drinks and Blumer's Sodas
President/Plant Manager: Gary Olson
CEO: Harry Cumberbatch
Director of Brewing/Quality Control: Kris Kalav
Production Manager: Dick Tschanz
Estimated Sales: $10 Million
Number Employees: 50-99
Brands:
Berghoff Family
Blumer's Root Beer
Braumeister
Braumeister Light
Huber
Huber Bock
Wisi Club

9157 **Mountain Fire Foods**
2850 Main Road
Huntington, VT 05462-9608 802-434-2685
Fax: 802-434-2685 karylk@adelphia.net
Marinades and ketchup
Owner: Karyl Kent

9158 **Mountain High Yogurt**
Po Box 9452
Minneapolis, MN 55440 303-761-2210
Fax: 303-789-1718
mountainhigh@mountainhigh.net
www.mountainhighyoghurt.com
Processor of original and honey style yogurt
President: Greg Bngles
Plant Manager: Ralph Lee
Number Employees: 20-49
Parent Co: Borden
Type of Packaging: Consumer, Food Service, Private Label
Brands:
Mountain High

9159 **Mountain Lake SpecialtyIngredients Company**
PO Box 3100
Omaha, NE 68103-0100 402-595-7463
Fax: 402-595-5884 sgrisamo@conagra.com
Processor and exporter of food texturizing ingredients and natural grain based flavors; contract packaging available
General Manager: Stephen Grisamore
Plant Manager: Douglas Tenkley
Number Employees: 5-9
Brands:
Trimchoice

9160 **Mountain Roastery Coffee Company**
1908 Dove Street
Port Huron, MI 48060-6768 416-256-2727
Fax: 416-256-5622
Coffee, tea
Director: Eric Shabshore
Estimated Sales: Under $500,000
Number Employees: 5-9

9161 **Mountain States Pecan**
3801 W Country Club Rd
Roswell, NM 88201 575-623-2216
Fax: 505-625-0126 mspstore@pecan.com
www.pecan.com
Grower and processor of pecans; gift tins available
Owner: Bruce Haley
Operations Manager: Reba Haley
Estimated Sales: $2.5-5 Million
Number Employees: 5-9

9162 **(HQ)Mountain States Rosen**
355 Food Center Drive
Bld. C-16
Bronx, NY 10474-7000 718-842-4447
Fax: 718-617-4096 800-872-5262
info@rosenlamb.com www.usalamb.com
Processor and wholesaler/distributor of lamb and veal; serving the food service market
President/CEO: Bruce Rosen
Human Resources: Al Montanino
VP Marketing: Buddy Cooper
Estimated Sales: I
Number Employees: 50-99
Type of Packaging: Food Service
Other Locations:
Brands:
CEDAR SPRINGS LAMB
CEDAR SPRINGS NATURAL VEAL
SHEPHERD'S PRIDE

9163 **Mountain Sun Brewery**
1535 Pearl St
Boulder, CO 80302-5408 303-546-0886
Fax: 303-413-1312 www.mountainsunpub.com
Beer
Owner: Kevin Daly
Estimated Sales: $500,000-$1 Million
Number Employees: 20-49
Brands:
Colorado Kind Ale
Quinn's Golden Ale
Thunderhead Stout

9164 **Mountain Sun Organic & Natural Juices**
4600 Sleepytime Dr.
Boulder, CO 80301 970-882-2283
Fax: 970-882-2270 1 8-0 4-4 42
mountainsun@mountainsun.com
www.mountainsun.com
Natural and organic juices
Owner: William Russel
Estimated Sales: $ 20-50 Million
Number Employees: 50-99
Brands:
Apple Hill
Mountain Sun

9165 **Mountain Valley Poultry**
P.O.Box 6967
Springdale, AR 72766-6967 479-751-7266
Fax: 479-751-0506 chix@cox-internet.com
Processor of further processed poultry products including de-boned, cooked, etc
Owner: Don Walker
Owner: Don Walker
Estimated Sales: $ .5 - 1 million
Number Employees: 1-4

9166 **Mountain Valley ProductsInc**
P.O.Box 246
Sunnyside, WA 98944-0246 509-837-8084
Fax: 509-837-3481 www.valleyprocessing.com
Processor and exporter of fruit juice concentrates including apple and grape; also, apple juice
Owner: Mary Ann Bliesner
Maintenance Supervisor: Mark Mulford
Production/Personnel: David Perez
Estimated Sales: $1150000
Number Employees: 20-49
Sq. footage: 45000
Type of Packaging: Bulk

9167 **(HQ)Mountain Valley Spring Company**
150 Central Avenue
Hot Springs, AR 71901-3528 501-624-1635
Fax: 501-623-5135 800-643-1501
tcranor@mountainvalleyspring.com
www.mountainvalleyspring.com
We provide our water under Mountain Valley, Clear Mountain, Diamond, and private brands. In April 2004 we announced the purchase of the assets of Mountain Valley Spring Company. The combined companies will operate under the famousMountain Valley Spring Company name. Mountain Valley Spring Water was established in 1871 and has remained America's premium choice for spring water for 133 years. For more information please visit www.mountainvalleyspring.com
President: Breck Speed
CFO: Brad Fredrge
VP: Jack Henderson
Quality Control: Joe Russellprice
R & D: Asley Tillaway
Marketing: Jim Karrh
Sales: Philip Tappan
Public Relations: Jim Karrh
Operations: Chris Feree
Production: Chris Feree
Plant Manager: Brian Hinds
Estimated Sales: $ 10-20 Million
Number Employees: 100-249
Type of Packaging: Consumer, Food Service, Private Label
Brands:
Carolina Mountain Spring Water
Diamond Spring Water
Mountain Valley Spring Water

9168 **Mountain View Fruit Sales**
4275 Avenue 416
Reedley, CA 93654 559-637-9933
Fax: 559-637-9733
rataide@mountainviewfruit.com
www.mountainviewfruit.com
Necatrines, peaches and plums
President: Randy Ataide
Sales Manager: Mike Thurlow

9169 **Mountainbrook of Vermont**
P.O.Box 39
Jeffersonville, VT 05464 802-644-1988
Fax: 802-644-6795 lisa@mountainbrookvt.vom
www.mountainbrookvt.com
Dipping oils, fruit spreads, dressings, packaged dry mixes, mustards, and gift packs.
Owner: Lisa Bryan
Estimated Sales: $ 1 - 3 Million
Number Employees: 1-4
Type of Packaging: Consumer

9170 **Mountainside Farms Dairy**
304 Teichman Road
Roxbury, NY 12474 607-326-3320
Fax: 607-326-7838
Milk
Estimated Sales: $ 10-24.9 Million
Number Employees: 50-99

9171 **(HQ)Mountaire Corporation**
PO Box 1320
Millsboro, DE 19966 302-934-1100
877-887-1490
www.mountaire.com
Poultry
Chairman/CEO: Ronald Cameron
CFO/Secretary: Alan Duncan
EVP/President Mountaire Feeds: DeAnn Landreth
Estimated Sales: $900 Million
Number Employees: 6000
Brands:
Mountaire

9172 **Moutanos Brothers Coffee Company**
380 Swift Ave # 13
S San Francisco, CA 94080-6232 650-952-5446
Fax: 650-871-4845 800-624-7031
info@mountanosbros.com
www.mountanosbros.com
Coffee
President: Michael Mountanos
Estimated Sales: Less than $500,000
Number Employees: 20-49
Brands:
Lindsay's Teas
Shade Grown Organic
Straight Coffees

9173 **Movie Breads Food**
225 Industrial Blouevard
Chateauguay, QC J6J 4Z2
Canada 450-692-7606
Fax: 450-692-1810 trmblaykein05@hotmail.com
Grocery
Brands:
SHEI BRAND
TRADEWINDS

9174 **Moweaqua Packing**
601 N Main St
Moweaqua, IL 62550-3695 217-768-4714
Processor of beef and pork
Owner: Terry Yoder
Co-Owner: Don Baker
Estimated Sales: $160000
Number Employees: 1-4
Type of Packaging: Consumer

9175 **Moyer Packing Company**
249 Allentown Rd
Souderton, PA 18964 215-723-5555
Fax: 215-723-5294 800-967-8325
Manufacturer and packer of boxed and ground beef. Also an exporter of fresh and frozen boxed beef and offals.
President/CEO: Lee Delp
VP Marketing: Bruce Blanton
VP Sales: Bruce Blanton
Estimated Sales: $ .5 Billion
Number Employees: 1,600
Parent Co: Smithfield Foods
Type of Packaging: Consumer, Private Label, Bulk

9176 **Moyer Packing Company**
P.O.Box 64395
Souderton, PA 18964 215-723-5555
Fax: 215-723-5294 800-967-8325
publicrelations@mopac.com www.mopac.com
Manufacturer and packer of boxed and ground beef; exporter of fresh and frozen boxed beef and offals. Also provides grease recycling bins and services to restaurants
President/CEO: Lee Delp
VP Marketing/Sales: Bruce Blanton
Estimated Sales: $.5 Billion
Number Employees: 1600+
Sq. footage: 85000
Parent Co: Smithfield Foods
Type of Packaging: Consumer, Private Label, Bulk
Brands:
MOPAC

9177 **Mozzarella Company**
2944 Elm Street
Dallas, TX 75226 214-741-4072
Fax: 214-741-4076 800-798-2954
info@mozzco.com www.mozzco.com
Cow, goat milk and cheeses such as mozzarella, bocconcini, ricotta, mascarpone, mascarpone tortas, queso fresco and blanco, queso oaxaca, scamorza, crescenza, cream cheese, fresh goat cheese, caciotta, montasio and feta
President: Paula Lambert
Estimated Sales: Below $ 5 Million
Number Employees: 10-19
Type of Packaging: Consumer, Food Service
Brands:
Mozzarella Company

9178 **Mozzarella FrescaTipton Plant**
615 North North Burnett
Tipton, CA 93272 559-752-4823
cheese@lactalis.us
www.mozzarellafresca.com
Processor and exporter of cheese including mozzarella, mascarpone and ricotta.
President: Andrew Branagh
Branch Manager: Richard Roughton
Number Employees: 140
Sq. footage: 55000
Parent Co: Lactalis USA
Type of Packaging: Consumer, Food Service
Other Locations:
Tipton Plant
Tipton CA
Brands:
MOZZARELL FRESCA

9179 **Mozzarella FrescaCorporate & Commercial Headquarters**
1800 Gateway Blvd
Suite 100
Concord, CA 94520 925-887-9600
Fax: 925-887-9607 800-572-6818
cheese@lactalis.us www.mozzarellafresca.com
Processor and exporter of cheese including mozzarella, mascarpone and ricotta.
President: Andrew Branagh
Estimated Sales: $62.6 Million
Number Employees: 220
Sq. footage: 55000
Parent Co: Lactalis USA
Type of Packaging: Consumer, Food Service
Brands:
MOZZARELLA FRESCA

9180 **Mozzicato De Pasquale Bakery Pastry**
329 Franklin Ave
Hartford, CT 06114 860-296-0426
Fax: 860-296-8129 info@mozzicatobakery.com
www.mozzicatobakery.com
Bread, pizza, cakes, cookies and ice cream
Owner: Gisella Mozzicato
President: Luigi Mozzicato
COO: Gina Mozzicato
Estimated Sales: Less than $500,000
Number Employees: 20-49

9181 **Mozzicato Depasquale Bakery & Pastry Shop**
329 Franklin Ave
Hartford, CT 06114-1890 860-296-0426
Fax: 860-296-8129 info@mozzicatobakery.com
www.mozzicatobakery.com
Manufacturer of baked goods such as; breads, cakes, cookies, gelato, pastries and wedding cakes
Owner: Luigi Mozzicato
Estimated Sales: $ 1 - 3 Million
Number Employees: 20-49

9182 **Mr Jay's Tamales & Chili**
11200 Alameda St
Lynwood, CA 90262 310-537-3932
Fax: 310-537-3938
Processor of chili and tamales
President/CEO: Pat Lang
Estimated Sales: Less than $500,000
Number Employees: 1-4
Type of Packaging: Consumer
Brands:
Chicken Link
Chilly

9183 **Mr. Brown's Bar-B-Que**
10249 Northeast Clackamas Street
Portland, OR 97220 503-274-0966
Fax: 503-230-9298
Barbeque sauce
Estimated Sales: Under $500,000
Number Employees: 5-9

9184 **Mr. Dell Foods**
300 W Major St
Kearney, MO 64060 816-628-4644
Fax: 816-628-4633 mrdells@mrdells.com
www.mrdells.com
Various styles of hash browns, shredded potatoes, O'Brien potatoes, and souther style potatoes.
President: Kurt Johnsen
VP: Kurt Johnsen
Marketing/Sales Director: Tom Sherrer
Operations Manager: Rick Wilkins
Plant Manager: John Duncan
Estimated Sales: $8445651
Number Employees: 20-49
Sq. footage: 40000
Type of Packaging: Consumer, Food Service, Bulk
Brands:
Mr. Dell's I.Q.F. Country Potatoes
Mr. Dell's I.Q.F. Hash Browns
Mr. Dell's I.Q.F. Herb & Garlic
Mr. Dell's I.Q.F. Santa Fe

9185 **Mr. Espresso**
696 3rd St
Oakland, CA 94607 510-287-5200
Fax: 510-287-5204 info@mrespresso.com
www.mrespresso.com
Organic coffee
President: Carlo Di Ruocco
CFO: M Di Ruocco
CEO: Marie Francoise
Sales Director: Laura Zambrano
Public Relations: Robert Hunt
Operations Manager: Michael Clarke
Production Manager: John Di Ruocco
Plant Manager: Richard Ocampo
Estimated Sales: $ 10-20 Million
Number Employees: 20-49
Brands:
Faema
Mr. Espresso

9186 **Mr. Pickle**
44 Brooklyn Terminal Market
Brooklyn, NY 11236
Fax: 718-763-0503 www.mrpickleinc.com
Pickles
Owner: Alan Neiheis
Owner: Alan Neihaus
Treasurer: Alan Neihaus
Vice President: Scott Wiseman
Estimated Sales: Below $ 5 Million
Number Employees: 50-99

9187 **(HQ)Mrs Baird's Bakery**
14401 Statler Blvd
Fort Worth, TX 76155-2861 817-864-2500
Fax: 817-864-2753 www.mrsbairds.com
Manufacturer of bread, buns, donuts, cinnamon rolls, honey buns, applie pie and chocolate cup cakes
President: Reynaldo Reyna
Number Employees: 20-49
Type of Packaging: Consumer, Food Service, Private Label, Bulk
Other Locations:
Mrs Baird's Bakeries

Abilene TX
Mrs Baird's Bakeries
Fort Worth TX
Mrs Baird's Bakeries
Lubbock TX
Mrs Baird's Bakeries
Waco TX
Mrs Baird's Bakeries
Houston TX
Mrs Baird's Bakeries
San Antonio TX
Brands:
BAIRD'S
BIMBO
ENTENMANN'S
MARINELA
OROWEAT
THOMAS'
TIA ROSA

9188 **Mrs May's Naturals**
860 E 238th Street
Carson, CA 90745-6212 310-830-3130
Fax: 310-830-3045 877-677-6297
info@mrsmays.com www.mrsmays.com
vegan, non-GMO, cholesterol free, dairy free, wheat free, gluten free, 0 trans fat and contain no artificial colors or flavors, nut crunches and bars
President/Owner: Augustine Kim
Estimated Sales: $18 Million
Number Employees: 6

9189 **Mrs. Annie's Peanut Patch**
1019 B St
Floresville, TX 78114-1947 830-393-7845
Fax: 830-393-9605 mrsanniespeanut@aol.com
www.mrsanniespeanutpatch.com
Processor of home-made peanut brittle, jalapeno peanut brittle, pecan brittle, peanut patties, pecan chewies, pecan pralines, flavored peanuts, all natural peanut butter and raw peanuts
President: Mariano Sanchez
VP: Mary Ann Sanchez
Estimated Sales: $ 1 - 3 Million
Number Employees: 5-9

9190 **Mrs. Auld's Gourmet Foods**
572 Reactor Way Ste B4
Reno, NV 89502 775-856-3350
Fax: 775-856-3351 800-322-8537
john@mrs-aulds.com www.mrs-aulds.com
Processor, importer and exporter of gourmet foods including brandied cherries, sweet and spicy pickles, marmalades, preserves, pancake, scone and soda bread mix, salsa, pasta sauce and bean, red corn and barbeque chips, chili sausepesto sauce, chestnuts
President/CEO: Evelyn Auld
Sales Manager: Teresa West
Estimated Sales: $ 1 - 3 Million
Number Employees: 5-9
Sq. footage: 3000

9191 **Mrs. Baird's Bakeries**
7301 South Freeway
Fort Worth, TX 76134 817-293-6230
Fax: 817-615-3090 info@mrsbaird.com
www.mrsbairds.com
Bread and other bakery products except cookies and crackers.
President: Juan Muldoon Barrena
Estimated Sales: $300 Million
Number Employees: 5,000-9,999
Parent Co: Bimbo Bakeries USA
Type of Packaging: Consumer, Food Service
Brands:
Mrs. Baird

9192 **Mrs. Baird's Bakeries**
2701 Palm St
Abilene, TX 79605 325-692-3141
Fax: 325-692-7326 www.mrsbairds.com
Processor of buns, rolls, bread and pies
General Manager: Joe Dangelmaier
Plant Manager: Clarke Flowers
Estimated Sales: $20-50 Million
Number Employees: 100-249
Type of Packaging: Consumer, Food Service, Private Label

9193 **Mrs. Baird's Bakeries**
225 S 17th St
Waco, TX 76701 254-750-2500
Fax: 254-750-2599 www.mrsbairds.com
Processor of white bread and buns including hamburger and hot dog
Manager: Wesley Steel
Plant Manager: Raymond Kupak
Estimated Sales: $20-50 Million
Number Employees: 20-49
Parent Co: Mrs. Baird's Bakeries
Type of Packaging: Consumer, Food Service, Private Label, Bulk

9194 **Mrs. Clark's Foods**
740 SE Dalbey Dr
Ankeny, IA 50021 515-964-8100
Fax: 515-964-8397 800-736-5674
info@mrsclarks.com www.mrsclarks.com

Juices, salad dressings and sauces.

Senior VP of Sales & Marketing: Paul Burmeister
Marketing: Linda Keairns
Director Sales: Pete Knudsen
Director Purchasing: Gary Lukins
Number Employees: 100-249
Number of Brands: 1
Parent Co: Agri Industries
Type of Packaging: Food Service, Private Label
Other Locations:
Alljuice Company
Hendersonville NC
Brands:
Mrs. Clark's

9195 **Mrs. Denson's Cookie Company**
120 Brush St
Ukiah, CA 95482 707-462-2272
Fax: 707-462-2283 800-219-3199
info@mrsdensonscookies.com
www.mrsdensonscookies.com
Processor and exporter of fruit juice and honey sweetened cookies including energy, reduced fat, fat-free, vegan and organic
President/Owner: Mike Bielenberg
Vice President: Desi Ringor
Number Employees: 50-99
Sq. footage: 25000
Type of Packaging: Consumer, Food Service, Private Label, Bulk
Brands:
Monster Cookies
Mrs. Denson's
Total Fit

9196 **Mrs. Dog's Products**
PO Box 6872
Grand Rapids, MI 49516-6872 616-454-2677
Fax: 616-774-0193 800-2Mr-Dog
mrsdogs@mrsdogs.com www.mrsdogs.com
Processor and exporter of gourmet mustard, Jamaican jerk marinade and habanero pepper sauces; also, shelled green chile pistachio nuts
Owner: Julie Curtis Applegate
Estimated Sales: Less than $500,000
Number Employees: 1-4
Type of Packaging: Consumer
Brands:
Mrs. Dog's

9197 **(HQ)Mrs. Fields' Original Cookies**
2855 E Cottonwood Pkwy
Suite 400
Salt Lake City, UT 84121-7050 801-736-5600
Fax: 801-736-5970 800-266-5437
srusso@mrsfields.com www.mrsfields.com
Cookies and baked goods
Co-CEO: John Lauck
Co-CEO: Michael Ward
CFO: Gregory Barber
Estimated Sales: $60 Million
Number Employees: 200
Brands:
Mrs. Field's Original Cookies
Pretzel Maker
TCBY

9198 **Mrs. Fisher's**
1231 Fulton Ave
Rockford, IL 61103-4025 815-964-9114
Fax: 815-964-3880 info@mrsfisherschips.com
www.mrsfisherschips.com
Processor of potato chips including barbecue and sour cream and onion
Owner: Peter J Di Venti
VP: Chuck Diventi
Estimated Sales: $780000
Number Employees: 10-19
Sq. footage: 10000
Type of Packaging: Consumer
Brands:
Mrs. Fisher
Vita-Sealed

9199 **Mrs. Fly's Bakery**
608 W Main St
Collegeville, PA 19426-1925 610-489-7288
Fax: 610-489-7488
Bakery products
President: Richard Landis
Estimated Sales: $ 1-2.5 Million
Number Employees: 1-4

9200 **Mrs. Grissom's Salad**
2500 Bransford Ave
Nashville, TN 37204-2810 615-255-4137
Fax: 615-251-9763 800-255-0571
customerservice@mrsgrissoms.com
www.mrsgrissoms.com
Processor of prepared salad
President: Grace G Grissom
CEO: Kenneth Funger
Plant Manager: Jack McGhee
Estimated Sales: $3100000
Number Employees: 50-99
Sq. footage: 40000
Type of Packaging: Consumer

9201 **(HQ)Mrs. Kavanagh's EnglishMuffins**
145 N Broadway
Rumford, RI 02916-2801 401-434-0551
Fax: 401-438-0542 800-556-7216
www.homesteadbaking.com
Processor of breads, rolls and English muffins
President: Peter Vican
VP: Bill Vican
Sales Manager: Vinny Palmiotti
Estimated Sales: $ 20 - 50 Million
Number Employees: 50-99
Sq. footage: 40000
Type of Packaging: Food Service, Private Label, Bulk
Brands:
Matthew's All Natural
Mrs. Kavanagh's

9202 **Mrs. Leeper's Pasta**
1000 Italian Way
Excelsior Springs, MO 64024 816-502-6000
Fax: 816-502-6722 800-848-5266
www.mrsleeperspasta.com
Processor of flavored dry pasta including shapes, fettucine, angel hair, wheat-free, gluten-free, bulk, organic, kosher and private label
President: Michelle Muscat
VP/Director,Sales and Marketing: Ed Muscat
Number Employees: 700
Number of Brands: 6
Type of Packaging: Consumer, Food Service, Private Label, Bulk
Brands:
Eddie's Spaghetti Organic
Fortune Macaroni
Michelle's Organic
Mrs Leeper's Wheat/Gluten Free

9203 **Mrs. London's Confections**
1 Salem St # 1
Swampscott, MA 01907-1314 781-595-8140
Fax: 781-595-9141
infochoc@chocolatebydesign.com
www.chocolatebydesign.com
Confectionery
Owner: Hope Zabar

Estimated Sales: $500,000-$1 Million
Number Employees: 20-49
Type of Packaging: Private Label
Brands:
Chocolate By Design

9204 **Mrs. Malibu Foods**
23852 Pacific Coast Highway
Suite 372
Malibu, CA 90265-4876 310-589-2777
Fax: 310-589-9898 800-677-6254
MrsMalibu@aol.com www.mrsmalibu.com
Food
President/Owner: Debra Root
Estimated Sales: $500,000-$1 Million
Number Employees: 5-9
Type of Packaging: Private Label
Brands:
Mrs Malibu

9205 **Mrs. Mazzula's Food Products**
240 Carter Dr
Edison, NJ 08817-2097 732-248-0555
Fax: 732-248-0442 info@mazzula.com
www.mazzula.com
Sun dried tomatoes, zucchini, salsa, peppers
President: Christopher Lotito
President: Christopher Lotito
Estimated Sales: Less than $500,000
Number Employees: 20-49
Type of Packaging: Bulk

9206 **Mrs. McGarrigle's Fine Foods**
311 St Lawrence Street
PO Box 163
Merrickville, ON K0G 1N0
Canada 613-269-3752
Fax: 613-269-2736 877-768-7827
info@mustard.ca www.mustard.ca
gourmet mustards, chutneys, preserves and seasonings
Owner: Janet Campbell

9207 **Mrs. Miller's Homeade Noodles**
110 Crawford Street
Fredericksburg, OH 44627 330-695-2393
Fax: 330-695-6900 800-227-4487
jim@mrsmillersnoodles.com
www.mrsmillersnoodles.com
Dairy-free, kosher, organic/natural, pasta (dry).
Marketing: Jim Gray

9208 **Mrs. Prindable's Handmade Confections**
6300 Gross Point Rd
Niles, IL 60714 847-588-2900
Fax: 847-588-0392 888-215-1100
customerservice@mrsprindables.com
www.mrsprindables.com
Handmade confections. Gourmet Caramel apples with a variety of toppings
Owner: Stuart Sorkin
Marketing: Jenny Cueva
Estimated Sales: $10-20 Million
Number Employees: 100-249

9209 **Mrs. Prindable's Handmade Confections**
6300 Gross Point Road
Niles, IL 60714 847-588-2900
Fax: 847-588-0392 888-215-1100
customerservice@mrsprindables.com
www.mrsprindables.com
gourmet caramel apples

9210 **Mrs. Rio's Corn Products**
215 W Avenue N
San Angelo, TX 76903-8434 325-653-5640
Fax: 325-657-0825 www.mrsrios.earthlink.net
Flour and corn tortillas
President: Armando Martinez
Estimated Sales: $ 20-50 Million
Number Employees: 20-49

9211 **Mrs. Smith's Bakeries**
7101 Asheville Hwy
Spartanburg, SC 29303-1870 864-503-9588
Fax: 864-503-0219 800-756-4746
sales@mrssmiths.com www.mrssmiths.com
Processor of baked goods including cakes and convenience products
President: David Stanaland
Director Human Resources: Jesse Hobby
Estimated Sales: $ 50 - 100 Million
Number Employees: 250-499
Parent Co: Mrs. Smiths Bakeries
Type of Packaging: Consumer
Brands:
Deep Dish Blueberry
Deep Dish Cherry Crumb
Moose Tracks
No Sugar Added Apple

9212 **Mrs. Stratton's Salads**
P.O.Box 190187
Birmingham, AL 35219 205-940-9640
Fax: 205-940-9650 www.mrsstrattons.com
Processor of fresh salads including pimiento, potato, cole slaw, chicken and tuna
Owner/CFO/Chairman: John Bradford
President: R Vance Fulkerson
Director: Martha Bradford
Estimated Sales: $19 Million
Number Employees: 125
Type of Packaging: Consumer, Food Service, Private Label
Brands:
Mrs. Stratton

9213 **Mrs. Sullivan's Pies**
256 Preston St
Jackson, TN 38301-4967 731-427-2101
Fax: 731-422-1045 sales@mrssullivans.com
www.mrssullivans.com
Brownies and pies including coconut, chocolate and pecan
Operations/Maufacturing Director: Melvin Coope
Estimated Sales: $ 10 - 20 Million
Number Employees: 20
Sq. footage: 12000
Type of Packaging: Consumer
Brands:
Mrs. Sullivan's

9214 **Mrs. Ts Pierogies**
600 E Centre St
Shenandoah, PA 17976 570-462-2745
Fax: 570-462-1392 800-233-3170
www.pierogies.com
Processor of low-fat pierogies
President: Tom Twardzik
Vice President: Tim Twardzik
IT Manager: Ted Twardzik Jr
VP Marketing: Gary Loverman
VP Sales: Ron Suchecki
Estimated Sales: $10-20 Million
Number Employees: 100-249
Type of Packaging: Consumer, Food Service
Brands:
Mrs. T'S

9215 **Mrs. Weinstein's Toffee**
1316 Industrial Road
Mount Pleasant, TX 75455-2614 805-965-0422
Fax: 805-965-8123 www.sweetshopusa.com
Processor of toffee covered milk or dark chocolate with almond, hazelnuts, pistachios or pecans
President: Bryan Webb
Estimated Sales: $1.5 Million
Number Employees: 110
Parent Co: Sweet Shop Candies
Brands:
Toffolos

9216 **Mrs. Willman's Baking**
3732 Canada Way
Burnaby, BC V5G 1G4
Canada 604-434-0027
Fax: 403-250-8706 http://www.mrswillmans.com
Processor of sandwiches, doughnuts, pastries and sausage rolls
CEO: Winston Haffat
President: Eric Olsen
Parent Co: Beaumont Select Corporation
Type of Packaging: Consumer, Food Service
Brands:
ABM
Coral Food
Golden Crust
Prestige

9217 **Mt View Bakery**
P.O.Box 102
Mountain View, HI 96771-0102 808-968-6353
Processor of bread, cookies, pies, doughnuts, rolls, muffins, etc.
Owner: Russell Sueda
Estimated Sales: Less than $500,000
Number Employees: 5-9
Type of Packaging: Consumer
Brands:
Mt. View Bakery

9218 **Mt. Konocti Growers**
P.O.Box 365
Kelseyville, CA 95451 707-279-4213
Fax: 707-279-2251 mkg.annette@mchsi.com
Grower, packer and exporter of bartlett pears
Manager: Robert Gayaldo
Number Employees: 5-9
Sq. footage: 85000
Type of Packaging: Bulk
Brands:
Lady of the Lake
Lake Cove
Mt. Konocti

9219 **Mt. Nittany Vineyard**
300 Houser Rd
Centre Hall, PA 16828 814-466-6373
Fax: 814-466-3066 sales@mtnittanywinery.com
www.mtnittanywinery.com
Wines
President: Joe Carroll
VP: Betty Carroll
Estimated Sales: $ 1-2.5 Million
Number Employees: 5-9
Brands:
Mount Nittany

9220 **Mt. Olive Pickle Company**
P.O.Box 609
One Cucumber Boulevard
Mt Olive, NC 28365-0609 919-658-2535
Fax: 919-658-6296 800-672-5041
pdenlinger@mtolivepickles.com
www.mtolivepickles.com
Pickles
President/CEO: Bill Bryan
Chairman: E Pope
Sr."""": Robert Frye
Powell: Ken
Plant Manager: Production Manager Vic
Estimated Sales: $ 5-10 Million
Number Employees: 500-999
Brands:
Dill Pickles
Little Sister
Majestic
Mt. Olive
No Sugar Added Products
Pepper and Specialty Products
Relishes and Salad Cubes
Sweet Pickles

9221 **Mt. Olympus Specialty Foods**
1601 Military Road
Buffalo, NY 14217-1205 716-874-0771
Fax: 716-839-4006
info@mtolympusgreeksalad.com
www.mtolympusgreeksalad.com
Processor and exporter of meat, poultry and fish marinades, Greek salad dressings, pasta sauces and appetizers, gourmet foods, salsa, hot sauce and seasonings
CEO/President: George Bechakas
Executive VP: Nick Bechakas
Estimated Sales: $ 1 - 3 Million
Number Employees: 20-49

9222 **Mt. Vikos, Inc.**
313 Iron Horse Way
Providence, RI 02908 888-534-0246
Fax: 866-402-7371 info@mtvikos.com
www.mtvikos.com
Crackers, other baked goods, other condiments, cheese.
Marketing: Sheree Cardoos

9223 **Mucky Duck Mustard Company**
1505 Bonner St
Ferndale, MI 48220-1973 248-544-4610
Fax: 248-544-4610 zilkod@aol.com
Processor of gourmet marinades, salad dressings, mustard, ketchup, and BBQ sauces
President: Dave Zilko
Estimated Sales: Less than $500,000
Number Employees: 1-4
Type of Packaging: Consumer, Food Service
Brands:
American Connoisseur Gourmet

American Moir's
American Mucky Duck
American Special Edition
Mucky Duck

9224 **Muir Glen Organic Tomato**
424 N 7th Street
Sacramento, CA 95814-0210 916-557-0900
Fax: 916-557-0903
Tomato products
President: Bill Russell
Estimated Sales: $ 2.5-5 Million
Number Employees: 10

9225 **Muir-Roberts Company**
951 South 3600 West
Salt Lake City, UT 84104 801-908-6091
Fax: 801-908-6176 800-564-0949
Packer and exporter of potatoes, onions and frozen ready-to-process cherries; wholesaler/distributor of fresh fruits and vegetables; serving the food service market in the Salt Lake City metropolitan area
President: Phil Muir
Cfo/Vice President: Chuck Madsen
Estimated Sales: $16638274
Number Employees: 70
Sq. footage: 200000
Type of Packaging: Food Service, Private Label, Bulk
Brands:
Big M

9226 **Muirhead Canning Company**
5267 Mill Creek Rd
The Dalles, OR 97058 541-298-1660
Fax: 541-298-4158 info@muirheadcanning.com
www.muirheadcanning.com
Manufacturer of canned fruits including apricots, cherries, peaches, pears and plums
Co-Owner: James Barrett Jr
Co-Owner: Dawn Barrett
President: Russell Loughmiller
Estimated Sales: $5-10 Million
Number Employees: 20
Sq. footage: 12000
Type of Packaging: Consumer
Brands:
HOODCREST

9227 **Muirhead of Ringoes, NJ, Inc.**
43 Highway 202
Ringoes, NJ 08551 908-782-7803
Fax: 908-788-4221 800-782-7803
information@muirheadfoods.com
www.muirheadfoods.com
Specialty foods
President: Edward Simpson
Vice President: Doris Simpson
Marketing Director: Barbara Simpson
Estimated Sales: $500,000 appx.
Number Employees: 5-9
Number of Brands: 1
Number of Products: 25
Sq. footage: 1500
Type of Packaging: Consumer
Brands:
Dragon's Breath
Hazel's
Muirhead

9228 **Muller-Pinehurst Dairy C**
P.O.Box 299
Rockford, IL 61105-0299 815-968-0441
Fax: 815-961-1625
Manufacturer of dairy products
President: Neal Rosinsky
Estimated Sales: Less than $500,000
Number Employees: 100-249
Parent Co: Prairie Farms Dairy
Type of Packaging: Consumer

9229 **Mulligan Sales**
P.O.Box 90008
14314 Lomitas Ave
City of Industry, CA 91746-3016 626-968-9621
Fax: 626-369-8452 mulligansales@yahoo.com
Dairy products
President: Jeff Mulligan
Estimated Sales: $ 17 Million
Number Employees: 23

9230 **Mullins Food Products**
2200 S 25th Ave
Broadview, IL 60155 708-344-3224
Fax: 708-344-0153 info@sminty.com
www.mullinsfood.com
Processor of sauces, condiments and salad dressings
President: Jeanne Gannon
CFO: Joan Mullins
Vice President: William Mullins
Marketing Director: Judy Lucas
Sales Director: Shannon Smith
Public Relations: Tom Mullins
COO: Michael Mullins
Plant Manager: Michael Mazur
Purchasing Manager: Ray Johnson
Estimated Sales: $105 Million
Number Employees: 350
Sq. footage: 325000
Type of Packaging: Consumer, Food Service, Private Label

9231 **Multi Foods**
19606 NE San Rafael St
Portland, OR 97230-7449 503-666-8998
Fax: 503-661-1698 800-666-8998
www.vistar.com
Pizza products
President: Louis Kirchem
Estimated Sales: $ 50 - 100 Million
Number Employees: 50-99

9232 **Multi Marques**
4650 Rue Notre-Dame O
Montreal, QC H4C 1S6
Canada 514-934-1866
Fax: 514-934-1866
Manufacturer and distributor of bread, rolls, fruit cake and sponge cake
Regional Plant Director: Francine Henderson
Estimated Sales: $300 Million
Number Employees: 100-249
Parent Co: Canada Bread
Type of Packaging: Consumer, Food Service
Brands:
BON MATIN
CUISINE NATURE
DIANA
DURVIAGE
GAILURON
MAISON COUSIN
PETITE DONCEUR
POM

9233 **(HQ)Multiflex Company**
18 Utter Ave
Hawthorne, NJ 07506-2127 973-636-9700
marzipanco@aol.com
www.marzipan.com
Processor and exporter of confectionery items including marzipan, icing decorations, edible Easter eggs, chocolate dessert cups, chocolate liqueur cups, lollypops, sugar decorations and decorated chocolate covered sandwich cookies
President: Rita Keller
Vice President: Rozie Keller
VP Sales: Royce Keller
Estimated Sales: $120,000
Number Employees: 2
Sq. footage: 7500
Type of Packaging: Food Service, Private Label, Bulk
Brands:
Biermann
Crescent Confections
Keller's
Panorama Easter Eggs
Swissart
Ultra Dark Rondo Kosher

9234 **Multnomah Brewing**
1603 SE Pardee Street
Portland, OR 97202 503-236-3106
Beer
President: Jeff Hendryx
Estimated Sales: Under $500,000
Number Employees: 5-9

9235 **Mung Dynasty**
2200 Mary St
Pittsburgh, PA 15203-2160 412-381-1350
Grow, pack, ship sprouts; wholesaler/distributor of Oriental foods, specialty products
Owner: Chris Wahlberg
Estimated Sales: $1-2.5 Million
Number Employees: 1-4
Sq. footage: 5000
Brands:
Mori-Nu Tofu
Mung Dynasty

9236 **Munroe Dairy**
P.O.Box 14287
East Providence, RI 02914-0287 401-438-4450
Fax: 401-438-0035 info@abmunroedairy.com
www.cowtruck.com
Fluid milk
President: Robert Armstrong
Plant Manager: John Sherman
Estimated Sales: $ 10-20 Million
Number Employees: 50-99
Brands:
Munroe Dairy

9237 **Munsee Meats**
P.O.Box 2843
1701 W Kilgore Ave
Muncie, IN 47304-4924 765-288-3645
Fax: 765-282-8076
Beef, beef products
President: Steve Henderixson
CEO: Jeanie Bates
President: Rosalyn Selvey
Estimated Sales: $2.73 Million
Number Employees: 24
Brands:
Munsee Meats

9238 **Munson's Chocolates**
174 Hop River Rd
Bolton, CT 6043 860-649-4332
Fax: 860-649-7209 888-686-7667
munsons@munsonschocolates.com
www.munsonschocolates.com
Processor of chocolate candy
President: Robert Munson
CEO: Karen Munson
Estimated Sales: $10-20 Million
Number Employees: 100-249
Sq. footage: 35000
Type of Packaging: Consumer, Food Service, Private Label, Bulk
Brands:
Munson's

9239 **Muntons Ingredients**
2018 156th Ave NE, Ste 230
Bellevue, WA 98007 425-372-3082
terry.mcneill@muntons.com
www.muntons.com
Manufacture of grain malts and related ingredients
Sales: Terry McNeill
Parent Co: Muntons Malt

9240 **Muqui Coffee Company**
3398 Grossmont Drive
San Jose, CA 95132-3010 408-929-4405
Fax: 408-929-4505
Coffee
President: Clyde McMorrow

9241 **Murakami Farms**
1431 SE 1st St
Ontario, OR 97914 541-889-3131
Fax: 541-889-2933 800-421-8814
Packer and exporter of dry fresh yellow, red and white onions
President: Grant Kitamura
VP: David Murakami
General Manager: Grant Ktamma
Plant Manager: Paul Hopper
Estimated Sales: $2.5 Million
Number Employees: 25
Sq. footage: 3000
Type of Packaging: Consumer, Food Service, Private Label

9242 **Murdock Farm Dairy**
62 Elmwood Rd
Winchendon, MA 01475 978-297-0143
Dairy products
Estimated Sales: $500,000-$1 Million
Number Employees: 1-4

9243 **Murphy Goode Estate Winery**
20 Matheson St
Healdsburg, CA 95448-4121 707-431-7644
Fax: 707-431-8640
general@murphygoodewinery.com
www.murphygoodewinery.com
A wide selection of wines including chardonay, cabernet sauvignon, merlot, pinot noir, and zinfandel.
Manager: Lorri Emmerich
R & D: Lorri Emmerich
Vice President: David Ready
Plant Manager: Lorri Emmerach
Estimated Sales: $ 10-20 Million
Number Employees: 10-19
Number of Brands: 2
Type of Packaging: Private Label
Brands:
Goode & Ready
Murphy Goode

9244 **Murphy House**
108 S Bickett Blvd
Louisburg, NC 27549-2467 919-496-6054
Fax: 919-496-5097
Processor of deli meats and cheeses
President: John Sledge III
Estimated Sales: $ 1 - 3 Million
Number Employees: 20-49
Type of Packaging: Consumer, Food Service, Bulk

9245 **(HQ)Murray Biscuit Company**
4751 Best Rd Ste 140
Atlanta, GA 30337 678-366-7000
Fax: 678-366-7004 800-745-5582
www.murrayfoods.com
Manufacturer of cookies, crackers and fig bars
President/CEO: Jerry Cavitt
Controller: Bryon Russell
Marketing Director: Scott Chapman
Estimated Sales: $450 Million
Number Employees: 1300
Parent Co: Kellogg Company
Type of Packaging: Consumer, Food Service, Private Label
Brands:
BECKY KAY
BISHOP
FAMOUS AMOS
GREG'S
JACK'S
JACKSON'S
MURRAY
OLD NEW ENGLAND
PLANTATION
SUNNY

9246 **Murray Cider Company Inc**
103 Murray Farm Rd
Roanoke, VA 24019 540-977-9000
Fax: 540-977-1336 info@murraycider.com
www.murraycider.com
Processor of apple juice and cider, also cherry-flavored apple cider
President: Robert Murray
VP: Joe Murray
Estimated Sales: $100,000
Number Employees: 18
Sq. footage: 60000
Type of Packaging: Consumer, Food Service, Private Label, Bulk
Brands:
Murray's

9247 **Murrays Chicken**
5190 Main Street
South Fallsburg, NY 12779 845-436-5001
Fax: 845-436-5001 800-770-6347
info@murryschicken.com
www.murrayschicken.com
All-natural chicken burgers and marinated chicken breasts
President/Owner: Murray Bresky
VP Operations: Dean Koplik
Number Employees: 250-499
Brands:
Nature's Kitchen

9248 **Muruchan**
15800 Laguna Canyon Rd
Irvine, CA 92618-3103 949-789-2300
Fax: 949-789-2350 www.maruchan.com
Instant noodles
President: Kiyoshi Fukagawa
Sales Director: Dean Maropoulos
Estimated Sales: $ 100-500 Million
Number Employees: 600
Brands:
INSTANT LUNCH
MARUCHAN
YAKISOBA

9249 **Murvest Fine Foods**
5390 NW 12th Ave
Fort Lauderdale, FL 33309-3153 954-772-6440
Fax: 954-772-7728 murvest@msn.com
www.murvestfoods.com
Pate's and sausages
President: John Murphy
Estimated Sales: Below $ 5 Million
Number Employees: 10-19
Brands:
Murvest

9250 **Musco Family Olive Company**
17950 Via Nicolo
Tracy, CA 95377
800-523-9828
consumerrelations@olives.com www.olives.com
Olives and olive oil
President/General Manager: Felix Musco
CEO: Nicholas Musco
SVP Sales/Corporate Development: Bill McFarland
Human Resources/Operations Director: Janet Edwards
Plant Manager: Ben Hall
Number Employees: 180
Sq. footage: 700000
Type of Packaging: Consumer, Food Service

9251 **Musco Olive Products**
17950 Via Nicolo
Tracy, CA 95377 209-836-4600
Fax: 209-836-0518 800-523-9828
sales@muscoolive.com www.olives.com
Processor and exporter of canned olives including California stuffed green, Sicilian-style, black ripe and deli, and specialty olives and frozen ripe olives
President: Nicholas Musco
Vice President: Felix Musco
Quality Control: Ben Hall
Marketing Director: Yauna Throne
Sales Director: Fred Ghelardi
Public Relations: Janet Mitchell
Production/Plant Manager: Mike Splitstone
Number Employees: 250-499
Number of Brands: 7
Type of Packaging: Consumer, Food Service, Private Label
Brands:
Black Pearls
Bravo
Early California
Green Pearls
Mediterranean Pearls
Musco

9252 **Musco Olive Products**
P.O.Box 368
Orland, CA 95963-0368 530-865-4111
Fax: 530-865-5204 www.olive.com
Processor and exporter of pickled mixed vegetables and olives including Spanish and ripe
President: Dennis Burreson
Sales Manager: Felix Musco
Plant Manager: Dennis Burreson
Estimated Sales: $ 20 - 50 Million
Number Employees: 50-99
Type of Packaging: Consumer, Food Service, Private Label, Bulk

9253 **Mushroom Company**
902 Woods Rd
Cambridge, MD 21613-9470 410-221-8971
Fax: 410-221-8952
custserv@themushroomcompany.com
www.themushroomcompany.com
Canned, refrigerated, froze, organic, Kosher, seasoned, sauteed and sauced.
President/CEO: Dennis Newhard
Controller: Debbie Timmons
Quality Assurance Manager: Terry Myers
National Sales Manager: Ruth Newhard
Operations Executive: Mike Bayline
Estimated Sales: $20 Million
Number Employees: 70
Sq. footage: 150000
Type of Packaging: Consumer, Food Service, Private Label, Bulk
Brands:
MGA
Mother Earth
Mushroom Canning Company
Snocap

9254 **(HQ)Music Mountain Water Company**
PO Box 2252
Birmingham, AL 35246
Fax: 318-221-6650 800-349-6555
info@musicmountain.com
www.musicmountain.com
Manufacturer of bottled spring water
President: Marcus Wren III
Estimated Sales: $ 1-3 Million
Number Employees: 20
Other Locations:
Music Mountain Spring Water
Alexandria VA
Music Mountain Spring Water
Monroe VA
Music Mountain Spring Water
Lake Charles VA
Music Mountain Spring Water
Ruston VA
Music Mountain Spring Water
Lafayette VA
Music Mountain Spring Water
Natchitoches VA
Music Mountain Spring Water
Austin TX
Music Mountain Spring Water
Tyler TX
Music Mountain Spring Water
Longview TX
Music Mountain Spring Water
Marshall TX
Music Mountain Spring Water
Alto TX
Music Mountain Spring Water
Crockett TX
Music Mountain Spring Water
Glenwood AR

9255 **Musicon Deer Farm**
385 Scotchtown Rd
Goshen, NY 10924 845-294-6378
Fax: 516-239-8915 norman@koshervenison.com
www.koshervenison.com
Glatt kosher and venison
President: Norman Schlaff
Estimated Sales: $500,000-$1 Million
Number Employees: 1-4
Type of Packaging: Private Label

9256 **Mustard Seed**
203 Sanders Road
Central, SC 29630-9349 864-639-1083
877-621-2591
sheltoncj@aol.com
Processor of natural, organic, vegetarian, whole grain, high fiber, gourmet, heart healthy burger and protein replacement mixes, burger n' a bag
Owner: Jane Shelton
Brands:
Burgers N'A Bag

9257 **Mutchler's Dakota Gold Mustard**
511 W Jackson Blvd.
Spearfish, SD 57783 605-642-8166
Fax: 605-642-0708 mustard@blackhills.com
http://blackhills.com
Mustard
President: Kelly Hitson
CEO: Betty Lenners

9258 **Muth Candies**
630 E Market St
Louisville, KY 40202-1117 502-585-2952
Fax: 502-582-2639 www.muthscandy.com
Processor of candy including chocolate, caramel and peanut brittle
President: Martha Vories
Assistant Manager: Kimberly Bennett
Estimated Sales: Under $500,000
Number Employees: 10-19
Type of Packaging: Consumer
Brands:
Kentucky Tavern

Mojeska's
Muth's Kentucky

9259 **Mutiflex Company**
455 Braen Ave
Wyckoff, NJ 07481-2949 201-447-3888
Fax: 201-447-1455 marzipanco@aol.com
http://marzipancandies.com/
Marzipan and other candies
President: Royce Keller
Estimated Sales: $ 2.5-5 Million
Number Employees: 20-49

9260 **Mutual Fish Company**
2335 Rainier Ave S
Seattle, WA 98144 206-322-4368
Fax: 206-328-5889 www.mutualfish.com
Retail/wholesale seafood market that specializes in the freshest and liveliest seafood, custom seafood products as well as a complete line of Asian groceries.
President: Dick Yoshimura
Sales Director: Kevin Yoshimura
Estimated Sales: $1500000
Number Employees: 20-49
Sq. footage: 15000
Brands:
Three Fish

9261 **Mutual Flavors**
2558 Country Bend Drive
South Jordan, UT 84095-9441 801-231-1354
Fax: 888-343-2922 888-343-2922
sales@mutualflavors.com
www.mutualflavors.com
Exotic tropical flavors and other flavorings
VP: Maureen Glumit
President: James Mungar
VP Sales: Bill Stephens
Account Executive: Jode Hyman
Estimated Sales: $ 10-20 Million
Number Employees: 10-19
Brands:
Mutual Flavors

9262 **Mutual Trading Company**
431 Crocker St
Los Angeles, CA 90013 213-626-9458
Fax: 213-626-5130 www.lamtc.com
Ethnic foods
President: Noritoshi Kanai
Estimated Sales: $ 50-100 Million
Number Employees: 100-249
Brands:
Miyako
Mizken
My Pizza Raviolis
My Turkey Meatballs
Pizza Pasta, Please
Takara

9263 **My Bagel Chips**
66 E Walnut Street
Long Beach, NY 11561-3516 516-889-0732
Bagel and bagel products
President: Gerald Golden
Sales Manager: G Golden

9264 **My Boy's Baking LLC**
1466 Hampton Rd
Allentown, 3A 18104-2018 610-759-4552
Fax: 610-759-4525 robert@myboysbaking.com
www.myboysbaking.com
biscotti, cookies and rugelach
Marketing: Robert Levine

9265 **My Brother's Salsa**
Po Box 8095
Fayetteville, AR 72703 479-271-9404
Fax: 479-271-9401 helen@mybrotherssalsa.com
www.mybrotherssalsa.com

9266 **My Daddy's Cheesecake**
P.O.Box 9
Cape Girardeau, MO 63702-0009 573-335-6660
Fax: 573-335-8258 800-735-6765
sales@mydaddyscheesecake.com
www.mydaddyscheesecake.com
Processor and exporter of confectionery items, cheesecakes, desserts, wedding and birthday cakes and gourmet cookies
Owner: Kevin Stanfield
Estimated Sales: Less than $500,000
Number Employees: 5-9
Sq. footage: 2500
Type of Packaging: Consumer, Food Service, Private Label
Brands:
Cookie Wedgies
My Daddy's Cheesecake

9267 **My Favorite Jerky**
2000 5th Street
Apt C
Boulder, CO 80302-4948 303-444-2846
Fax: 303-444-9049 www.myfavoritejerky.com
Beef jerky
President: James David
Brands:
MY FAVORITE JERKY

9268 **My Grandma's Coffee Cakee of New England**
1636 Hyde Park Ave
Boston, MA 02136 617-364-9900
Fax: 617-364-0505 800-847-2636
customerservice@mygrandma.com
www.mygrandma.com
Manufacturers coffeecakes in a variety of flavors including Granny Smith Apple, Golden Raspberry, Cappuccino, New England Blueberry, Chocolate, Banana Walnut and Cape Cod Cranberry
President: Robert Katz
Marketing VP: Bruce Mills
Sales Manager: Gail Molino
VP Operations: Will Weeks
Estimated Sales: $ 5-6 Million
Number Employees: 20-49
Sq. footage: 8900
Brands:
My Grandma's of New England

9269 **My Grandma's of New England®**
1636 Hyde Park Ave
Hyde Park, MA 02136-2458 617-364-9900
Fax: 617-364-0505 800-847-2636
customerservice@mygrandma.com
www.mygrandma.com
Wide variety of homemade gourmet coffee cakes
Owner: Robert Katz
Corporate Account Manager: Joann Keeley
EVP: Dave Katz
Estimated Sales: $ 3 - 5 Million
Number Employees: 20-49

9270 **My Own Meals, Inc.**
P.O.Box 334
5410 W Roosevelt Rd
Chicago, IL 60644-1478 773-378-6505
Fax: 773-378-6416 sales@halalcertified.com
www.halalcertified.com
Manufacturer of certified, halal and dhabiha halal meals, rations and food products
President: Mary Jackson
CEO: Mary Anne Jackson
Manager: Robert Barnes
Estimated Sales: $ .5 - 1 million
Number Employees: 5
Type of Packaging: Private Label
Brands:
J&M

9271 **My Sister's Caramels**
325 Alabama St
Redlands, CA 92373-8031 909-792-6242
Fax: 909-798-7294
Processor of gourmet caramels including vanilla, chocolate, praline, peanut butter, holiday mix and raspberry
Estimated Sales: $ 5 - 10 Million
Number Employees: 5-9
Type of Packaging: Private Label, Bulk
Brands:
My Sister's Caramels

9272 **Myers Frozen Food Provisions**
405 W Dorsey St
Saint Paul, IN 47272 765-525-6304
Fax: 765-525-9635 info.myers@aol.com
Frozen foods
President: Tony Myers
Sales Manager: Dan Gindling
Production Manager: Mike Myers
Estimated Sales: $ 3 - 5 Million
Number Employees: 5-9
Brands:
Myers Frozen Food

9273 **Myron's Fine Foods**
One River Street
Renovators Supply
Millers Falls, MA 01349 413-659-0247
Fax: 413-659-0249 800-730-2820
myrons@chefmyrons.com www.chefmyrons.com
Processor of natural and kosher cooking sauces including tsukeyaki, soy sauce, szechuan, teriyaki, yakitori, ponzu, wild game and fish
President: Myron Becker
CFO: Lisa Richardson
Vice President: Kathy Becker
Production Manager: Steve Gambino
Plant Manager: Dawn Kennaway
Estimated Sales: Below $ 5 Million
Number Employees: 5-9
Number of Products: 9
Type of Packaging: Consumer, Food Service, Private Label, Bulk
Brands:
Chef Myron's Original #1 Yakitori
Chef Myron's Ponzu
Chef Myron's Premium
Chef Myron's Tsukeya
Myron's 20 Gauge Wil

9274 **Mystic Coffee Roasters**
8 Steamboat Wharf
Mystic, CT 06355 860-536-2999
Coffee, tea
President/Treasurer: Bruce Carpenter
Estimated Sales: $410,000
Number Employees: 10-19

9275 **Mystic Lake Dairy**
24200 NE 14th Street
Sammamish, WA 98074-3506 425-868-2029
Fax: 425-868-0553
Yogurt, bread, muffins and international line of food
President: Gary Wallace
CEO: Nellie Wallace
Estimated Sales: $500,000
Number Employees: 1 to 5
Brands:
Mystic Lake Dairy

9276 **N.A. Boullon**
3280 Glasco Drive
Cumming, GA 30041-8742 770-889-2356
Manufacuter of Grouper, Mahi - Mahi, Snapper, Sea Bass, Clams, Flounder
Owner: Bert Boullion

9277 **N.B.J. Enterprises**
2521 Hillcrest Rd # E
Mobile, AL 36695-3198 251-661-2122
Fax: 251-661-6198
Seafood
Owner: Toni Gulsby
Estimated Sales: $ 1 - 3 Million
Number Employees: 10-19

9278 **N.K. Hurst Company**
P.O.Box 985
Indianapolis, IN 46206-0985 317-634-6425
Fax: 317-638-1396 info@nkhurst.com
www.hambeens.com
Processor of dried beans
President: Needham R Hurst
Estimated Sales: $ 20 - 50 Million
Number Employees: 50-99
Type of Packaging: Consumer, Food Service, Bulk

9279 **N.Y.K. Line (North America)**
377 E Butterfield Rd
Lombard, IL 60148-5615 630-435-7800
Fax: 630-435-3110 888-695-7447
http://www2.nykline.com/
Estimated Sales: $ .5 - 1 million
Number Employees: 5-9

9280 **NAR**
75 Hawthorne Village Road
Nashua, NH 03062 603-888-5420
Fax: 603-888-5419 bahar@nargourmet.com
www.nargourmet.com
Organic/natural, other condiments, olive oil, other vinegar, spices, canned or preserved vegetables/fruit, dried fruit, gift packs.
Marketing: Bahar Ayasli

9281 **(HQ)NBTY**
2100 Smithtown Ave
Ronkonkoma, NY 11779 631-567-9500
Fax: 631-567-7148 800-920-6090
www.nbty.com
Manufacturer, marketer and distributor of nutritional supplements
President/CFO: Harvey Kamil
/CEO: Jeffery Nagel
Pres And Cfo Contact Num 631-200-2020: Harvey Kamil
SVP Marketing: James Flaherty
SVP Operations/Corporate Secretary: Hans Lindgren
Estimated Sales: $2.6 Billion
Number Employees: 14,400
Sq. footage: 1200000
Parent Co: Alphetbet Holdings
Type of Packaging: Consumer, Private Label, Bulk

9282 **NC Mountain Water**
PO Box 73
Marion, NC 28752-0073 828-756-4090
Fax: 828-756-4220 800-220-4718
ncwater@wnclink.com
www.wnclink.com/~ncwater1
Manufacturers of bottled water
President: Don Freeman
Estimated Sales: $ 1 - 3 Million
Number Employees: 10-19
Type of Packaging: Private Label, Bulk
Brands:
Natural Mountain Water

9283 **ND Labs Inc**
202 Merrick Rd
Lynbrook, NY 11563 516-504-0292
Fax: 516-504-0289 888-263-5227
sales@ndlabs.com www.ndlabs.com
Processor of nutritional supplements and foods, including fiber and soy products, soy proteins, high-fiber cookies, vegetarian entrees, etc
President: Diane Altos
Vice President: Beth Beller
Marketing/Sales: Michael Allen
Public Relations: Sherry Shah
Estimated Sales: $2500000
Number Employees: 1-4
Number of Brands: 10
Type of Packaging: Consumer, Food Service, Private Label, Bulk
Brands:
Fiber 7
Fiber Supreme
Life Savy
Nana Flakes
Soy-Liccous Meals
Soypro

9284 **(HQ)NORPAC Foods**
930 West Washington Street
Stayton, OR 97383 503-769-2101
www.norpac.com
Frozen vegetables, fruits and juices.
President/CEO: George Smith
CFO: Jack Sebastian
VP Operations: Mark Croeni
Estimated Sales: $400 Million
Number Employees: 4000
Type of Packaging: Consumer, Food Service, Private Label, Bulk
Other Locations:
NORPAC Foods
Salem OR
Brands:
FLAV-R-PAC
NORPAC
PASTA PERFECT
SANTIAM
SOUP SUPREME
WESTPAC

9285 **NORPAC Foods**
4350 SW Galewood St
Lake Oswego, OR 97035 503-635-9311
800-733-9311
www.norpac.com
Manufacturer of frozen vegetables, berry, fruit and juice products
Parent Co: NORPAC Foods
Type of Packaging: Consumer, Food Service, Private Label, Bulk
Brands:
FLAV-R-PAC
NORPAC
SOUP SUPREME
WEST-PAC

9286 **NOW Foods**
395 Glen Ellyn Rd
Bloomingdale, IL 60108 630-545-9098
Fax: 630-790-8019 888-669-3663
www.nowfoods.com
Manufacturer of health foods and supplements
Owner: Elwood Richard
Director Sales: Dan Richard

9287 **NPC Dehydrators**
11761 Highway 770 E
Eden, NC 27288 336-635-5190
Fax: 336-635-5193 npcmmorales@aol.com
www.npcbrewersyeast.com
Dry brewers yeast
President: R Dean Fullmer
Executive: Max Selty
Sales Director: Mike Morales
Public Relations: Charles Setlif
Plant Manager: Mike Morales
Estimated Sales: $ 5-10 Million
Number Employees: 30
Type of Packaging: Private Label
Brands:
Sonic Dried Yeast

9288 **NPC Dehydrators**
P.O.Box B
Payette, ID 83661-0017 208-642-4471
Fax: 208-642-4473 npcinc@earthlink.net
www.npcbrewersyeast.com
Dry brewers yeast
Manager: Vicki Swank
Estimated Sales: Less than $500,000
Number Employees: 1-4

9289 **NSpired Natural Foods**
58 S Service Rd
Melville, NY 11747-4625 631-845-4689
Fax: 510-686-0126 info@nspiredfoods.com
www.nspiredfoods.com
Manufacturer of Natural and organic foods
Executive Chairman: Charlie Lynch
President: Patrick Lee
CFO: Randy Sieve
Quality Assurance Manager: Fred Tabacchi
VP Marketing: Robin Robinson
VP Sales: Marty Hagge
Customer Service Manager: Liz Scatena
VP Operations, Ashland: Jeff Williams
Number Employees: 100-249
Brands:
AH!LASKA
CLOUD NINE
COOL FRUITS
LORIVA
MARANATHA
PUMPKORN
SKINNY
SUNSPIRE
TROPICAL SOURCE

9290 **NSpired Natural Foods**
4600 Sleepytime Dr
Boulder, CO 80301 631-845-4689
Fax: 510-686-0126 800-434-4246
www.sunspire.com
Processor and exporter of all natural carob and chocolate products including baking chips, coated nuts and raisins, English toffee and organic candies
Chairman: Charles Lynch
Ceo: Gordon Chapple
Cfo: Randy Sieve
VP Sales: Tom Tuggle
Director Operations: Tom Miner
Estimated Sales: $35 Million
Number Employees: 200
Sq. footage: 20000
Parent Co: Green Leaf Natural Foods
Type of Packaging: Consumer, Food Service, Private Label, Bulk
Brands:
Crystal
Fruitsource Confections
Sundrops
Sunspire
Sunspire Organics
Sweets-To-Go

9291 **NSpired Natural Foods**
58 S Service Rd
Suite 250
Melville, NY 11747-2342 541-488-2747
Fax: 925-228-4747 www.nspiredfoods.com
Processor of organic iced teas, cocoa and chocolate syrup; exporter of organic chocolate syrup and cocoas
Ceo: Gordon Chapple
Vice President: Paul Valhos
Estimated Sales: Less than $500,000
Number Employees: 66
Type of Packaging: Consumer, Food Service, Bulk
Brands:
Ah!Laska

9292 **NTC Marketing Inc**
5680 Main St
Williamsville, NY 14221 716-884-3345
Fax: 716-884-4680 800-333-1637
info@ntcmarketing.com www.ntcmarketing.com
Processor and importer of canned products including pineapples, pineapple juice, tropical fruits, tropical fruit mix, mandarin orange
Owner/Principal: Michael Derose
Human Resource Executive: Sue Godzala
Estimated Sales: $3.3 Million
Number Employees: 30
Sq. footage: 10000
Type of Packaging: Consumer, Food Service, Private Label, Bulk
Brands:
Libby's
P/L
Queen's Pride

9293 **NYSCO Products LLC**
P.O.Box 725
Bronx, NY 10473 718-792-9000
Fax: 718-792-7732 Chuck@NYSCO.com
www.nysco.com
NYSCO Products LLC designs and manufactures custom and stock displays.
Owner: Barry Kramer
Senior Vice President: Chuck Levin

9294 **Nabisco**
7 Campus Dr
Parsippany, NJ 07054-0311 973-682-5000
Fax: 973-503-2153 www.nabisco.com
Processor of baked goods including cookies and crackers
President/CEO: James Kilts Jr.
EVP/CFO: James Healey
EVP/CIO: Doreen Wright
Plant Manager: Larry Campbell
Purchasing Manager: Mike Swift
Estimated Sales: H
Number Employees: 500-999
Parent Co: Kraft Foods
Type of Packaging: Consumer, Food Service
Brands:
100 CALORIE PACKS
ARROWROOT
BARNUM'S ANIMALS CRACKERS
CAMEO
CHIPS AHOY!
CHOCOSTIX
EASY CHEESE
FLAVOR ORIGINALS
GINGER SNAPS
HONEY MAID
KRAFT CHEESE NIPS
KRAFT HANDI-SNACKS
MALLOMARS
MIXERS
NEWTONS
NILLA WAFERS
NUTTER BUTTER
OREO
PREMIUM
RITZ
RITZ BITS SANDWICHES
SNACKWELLS
TEDDY GRAHAM
TOASTED CHIPS
TRISCUIT
WHEAT THINS
WHEATSWORTH
ZWIEBACK

9295 **Nacan Products**
60 West Drive
Brampton, ON L6T 4W7
Canada 905-454-4466
Fax: 905-454-5207 info@nacan.com
www.nacan.com
Processor of modified starches derived from corn, waxy maize and tapioca
President: Roland Sirois
Vice-Chairman: Jim Grieve
Business Director: Bill Ruderman
Executive VP: John Morrell
Parent Co: National Starch & Chemical Company
Brands:
Nacan

9296 **Nafziger Ice Cream Company**
515 Industrial Drive
#100
Napoleon, OH 43545 419-592-1112
Fax: 419-592-4069
Ice cream, frozen desserts
Owner: Dale Nafziger
Estimated Sales: $5-10 Million
Number Employees: 10-19

9297 **Nagasako Fish**
800 Eha St Ste 11
Wailuku, HI 96793 808-242-4073
Fax: 808-244-7020
Seafood
Owner: Darryl Flinton
Estimated Sales: $ 5 - 10 Million
Number Employees: 10-19

9298 **Nagel Veal**
1411 E Base Line St
San Bernardino, CA 92410-4113 909-383-7075
Fax: 909-383-7079
Processor of veal, lamb and beef
President: Mike Lemler
Estimated Sales: $ 10-20 Million
Number Employees: 50-99

9299 **Nagel's Beverages Company**
8925 Birch Lane
East Nampa, ID 83706-1287 208-475-1250
Fax: 208-475-1274 www.nagelbev.com
Manufacturer of beverages
President/CEO: Ann Matthews
Estimated Sales: $44.8 Million
Number Employees: 105
Type of Packaging: Consumer, Food Service
Brands:
PEPSI-COLA

9300 **Najila's**
PO Box 74
Binghamton, NY 13905-0074 607-722-4287
Fax: 607-773-9012 cookies@najila's.com
Manufacturer of gourmet cookies
President/CEO: Najla Aswad
Type of Packaging: Food Service, Bulk
Brands:
NAJLA GONE CHUNKY

9301 **Najla's**
8007 Vine Crest Avenue
Suite 3
Louisville, KY 40222 502-412-4420
Fax: 502-412-4421 877-962-5527
cookies@najlas.com www.najlas.com
Kosher, cookies, toffee, frozen bars, nuts, gift packs.
Marketing: Najla Aswad

9302 **Naked Mountain Vineyard& Winery**
2747 Leeds Manor Rd
Markham, VA 22643-1715 540-364-1609
nakedmountain@yahoo.com
www.nakedmtn.com
Wines
Co-Owner: Phoebe Harper
Co-Owner: Bob Harper
Marketing/Sales Manager: Drew Hauser
Assistant Winemaker: Don Oldham
Office Manager: Darlene Call
Estimated Sales: Below $ 5 Million
Number Employees: 1-4
Type of Packaging: Private Label
Brands:
Naked Mountain

9303 **Naleway Foods**
233 Hutchings Street
Winnipeg, MB R2X 2R4
Canada 204-633-6535
Fax: 204-694-4310 800-665-7448
whalley@naleway.com www.naleway.com
Processor and exporter of frozen foods including pierogies and panzarotti
Sales: W Halley
Number Employees: 100-249
Type of Packaging: Consumer, Food Service

9304 **Nalle Winery**
2385 Dry Creek Rd
Healdsburg, CA 95448 707-433-1040
Fax: 707-433-6062 doug@nallewinery.com
www.nallewinery.com
Wines
Owner: Lee Nalle
Winemaker: Doug Nalle
Winemaker: Andrew Nalle
Number Employees: 1-4
Number of Brands: 1
Brands:
Nalle

9305 **Naman's Meat Company**
P.O.Box 88012
Mobile, AL 36608 251-633-2700
Fax: 251-633-2749
Meats
President: Christopher Naman
Estimated Sales: $ 20 - 50 Million
Number Employees: 10-19

9306 **Nan Sea Enterprises of Wisconsin**
900 Gale St
Waukesha, WI 53186-2515 262-542-8841
Fax: 262-542-4356 www.nanseaofwisc.com
Manufacturer and distributor of fresh frozen king, dungeness, golden and snow crab; also, lobster and lobster claws
President: Eric Muehl
VP: Robert Nell
Estimated Sales: $ 10-20 Million
Number Employees: 5-9
Type of Packaging: Food Service, Private Label

9307 **Nana Mae's Organics**
PO Box 2298
708 Gravenstein hwy north #174
Sebastopol, CA 95472 707-829-7359
Fax: 707-829-7356 appleman@nanamae.com
nanamae.com
Organic apple juice and sauce and vinegar and honey
Owner: Paul Kolling
R&D: Paul Kolling
Marketing: Paul Kolling
Sales: Kendra Kolling
Public Relations: Kendra Kolling
Estimated Sales: $1,000,000
Number Employees: 15
Number of Brands: 1
Number of Products: 15
Sq. footage: 264000
Type of Packaging: Consumer, Food Service, Private Label, Bulk

9308 **Nanci's Frozen Yogurt**
1754 N 48th St # 104
Mesa, AZ 85205-3303 480-834-4290
Fax: 480-834-4271 800-788-0808
info@nancis.com www.nancis.com
Soft serve dessert mixes including frozen yogurt, fruit freezer sorbet, non-dairy soft serve, no sugar added mixes, smoothie base mixes, granita mixes and more than 90 flavors
President/CEO: John Wudel
Spokesperson: Nanci Wudel
Estimated Sales: $ 1 - 3 Million
Number Employees: 10-19
Type of Packaging: Food Service, Bulk
Brands:
Nanci's

9309 **Nancy's Candy**
2684 Jeb Stuart Highway
Po Box 860
Meadows Of Dan, VA 24120 276-952-2112
Fax: 276-952-1042 800-328-3834
nancyscandy@embarqmail.com
www.nancyscandycompany.com
Fudge, chocolates, nut brittles and more
Marketing: Nancy Galli

9310 **Nancy's Pies**
3915 9th St
Rock Island, IL 61201-6721 309-732-4026
Fax: 309-793-0183 800-480-0055
sflorence@nancyspies.com www.nancyspies.com
Manufacturer of sugar free and no sugar added desserts for diabetics
President: Scott Florence
Quality Control: Susan Stoefen
Marketing Manager: Felicia Carlson
Sales & Marketing: Roseanna Knowles
Human Resource Manager: Richard Harper
Manager: Rudy Quick
Estimated Sales: $140 K
Number Employees: 6
Number of Brands: 1
Number of Products: 15
Sq. footage: 60000
Type of Packaging: Bulk

9311 **Nancy's Shellfish**
91 Falmouth Rd
Falmouth, ME 04105-1841 207-774-3411
Fax: 207-780-0044
Shellfish, seafood
President: Joe Scola
Estimated Sales: $1.4 Million
Number Employees: 5-9

9312 **Nancy's Specialty Foods**
6500 Overlake Pl
Newark, CA 94560 510-494-1100
Fax: 510-494-1140 nsf@nancys.com
www.nancys.com
Processor and exporter of frozen appetizers, entrees and desserts.
President: Bob Kroll
CFO: Adam Ferris
Marketing/Communications Director: Diane DiMartini
VP Sales: R L Booth
VP Operations: David Joiner
Plant Manager: Rick Shepherd
Estimated Sales: $19800000
Number Employees: 325
Sq. footage: 86000
Type of Packaging: Consumer, Food Service, Private Label, Bulk
Brands:
Nancy's

9313 **Nanka Seimen Company**
3030 Leonis Blvd
Vernon, CA 90058 323-585-9967
Fax: 323-585-9969
Processor of Japanese-style and egg noodles, chow mein, wontons, egg rolls and gyoza skins
President: Shoi Chi Sayano
VP: Toshiaki Yoshida
Estimated Sales: $ 5 - 10 Million
Number Employees: 18
Sq. footage: 20000
Type of Packaging: Consumer, Food Service
Brands:
Golden Dragon
Nanka Udon

9314 **Nantucket Nectars**
55 Hunter Ln
Elmsford, NY 10523-1334
Fax: 617-868-5490 lorianne@juiceguys.com
www.juiceguys.com
Juices
President: Mark Hellendrung
Chairman: Tom Scott
VP Marketing: Chris Pasta
Public Relations Director: Amy Hornyak
Estimated Sales: $ 20-50 Million
Number Employees: 50-99
Parent Co: Cadbury Schweppes PLC
Type of Packaging: Private Label

9315 **Nantucket Off-Shore Seasoning**
PO Box 1437
Nantucket, MA 02554-1437 508-994-1300
Fax: 508-257-4533
nantucketseasonings@mediaone.net

BBQ sauce, stuffing blends, BBQ glaze, BBQ marinade

9316 **Nantucket Pasta Company, Inc.**
20 Young's Way
Nantucket, MA 02584-2272 508-494-5209
liliana@nantucketpastagoddess.com
www.nantucketpastagoddess.com
Pasta (fresh).
Marketing: Liliana Dougan

9317 **Nantucket Tea Traders**
P.O.Box 179
Nantucket, MA 02554-0179 508-325-0203
Fax: 508-325-0203
Tea
President: Judy Kales
Sales: Paul Kales
Estimated Sales: $120,000
Number Employees: 1
Brands:
Nantucket Tea Trader

9318 **Nantucket Vineyards**
P.O.Box 2700
Nantucket, MA 02584 508-228-9235
Fax: 508-325-5209 jay@ciscobrewers.com
www.ciscobrewers.com
Wine
Owner: Randy Hudson
Founder/Co-Owner: Dean Long
Estimated Sales: $5-9.9 Million
Number Employees: 1-4
Type of Packaging: Private Label
Brands:
Nantucket Vineyard

9319 **Nantze Springs**
P.O.Box 1273
Dothan, AL 36302-1273 334-794-4218
Fax: 334-712-2899 800-239-7873
cindy@nantzesprings.com
www.nantzesprings.com
Water
President: Malone Garrett
Estimated Sales: $3-5 Million
Number Employees: 50-99
Brands:
Nantze Springs

9320 **Napa Cellars**
7830-40 St. Helena Hwy
Oakville, CA 94562 707-944-8669
Fax: 707-944-9749 800-848-9630
moreinfo@napawineco.com
www.napawineco.com
Wines
Manager: Dean Slattery
Winemaker: Rob Lawson
General Manager: Sheldon Parker
Estimated Sales: $1,600,000
Number Employees: 5-9
Type of Packaging: Private Label
Brands:
Napa Wine

9321 **Napa Creek Winery**
1001 Silverado Trl S
Saint Helena, CA 94574-9693 707- 25- 946
Wines

9322 **Napa Valley Kitchens**
564 Gateway Dr
Napa, CA 94558-7517 707-254-3700
Fax: 707-259-0219 contactus@consorzio.com
www.consorzio.com
Manufacturer and exporter of flavored oils, marinades, and dressings
Chairman: John Foraker
Cfo: Dale Eagle
Marketing Director: Sarah Bird
Sales Director: Terry Dudley
Production Manager: Mark Osborne
Estimated Sales: $10 Million
Number Employees: 75
Type of Packaging: Consumer
Brands:
Consorzio
Napa Valley Mustard Co.

9323 **Napa Valley Port Cellars**
736 California Blvd
Napa, CA 94559 707-257-7777
Fax: 707-257-1497
Wines
President: Shawn Denkler
CEO: M Thomas Lemasters
Estimated Sales: $500-1 Million appx.
Number Employees: 10-19

9324 **Napa Wine Company**
P.O.Box 434
Oakville, CA 94562 707-944-1710
Fax: 707-944-9749 800-848-9630
tastingroom@napawineco.com
www.napawineco.com
Wines
Managing Partner: Andrew Hoxsey
General Manager: Sheldon Parker
Winemaker: Rob Lawson
Estimated Sales: Under $500,000
Number Employees: 20-49
Type of Packaging: Consumer, Private Label

9325 **Napa Wine Company**
P.O.Box 434
Oakville, CA 94562 707-944-1710
Fax: 707-944-9749 800-848-9630
retail@napawineco.com www.napawineco.com
Custom crush wine production
Owner: Andrew Hoxsey
Managing Partner: Andrew Hoxse
General Manager: Sheldon Parker
Estimated Sales: Below $ 5 Million
Number Employees: 20-49
Brands:
Napa Wine Company

9326 **Napoleon Locker**
P.O.Box 38
Napoleon, IN 47034-0038 812-852-4333
Processor of beef and pork; slaughtering services available
Owner: Matt Brancamp
Co-Owner: Kimberly Brancamp
Estimated Sales: $ .5 - 1 million
Number Employees: 10-19
Type of Packaging: Private Label

9327 **Napoli Pasta Manufacturers**
9719 S Dixie Hwy # 8
Miami, FL 33156-2834 305-666-1942
Fax: 305-254-6139 npmgroup@aol.com
www.worldtrade.org/afb/companies
Pasta products
Owner: Gene Napoli
Plant Manager: Patricia Matuk
Estimated Sales: $5-9.9 Million
Number Employees: 1-4

9328 **Nardi Bakery & Deli**
12 Connecticut Boulevard
East Hartford, CT 06108-3007 860-289-5458
Fax: 860-289-9012 http://www.nardibakery.com
Bread and rolls
President: Charles Nardi
Estimated Sales: $ 5-9.9 Million
Number Employees: 17

9329 **Nardone Brothers BakingCompany**
420 New Commerce Blvd
Hanover Township, PA 18706 570-823-0141
Fax: 570-823-2581 800-822-5320
vjn1@att.net www.nardonebros.com
Manufacturer of pizza
President: Vince Nardone
CFO: Louis Nardone
VP: Frank Nardone
Manufacturing/Operations Director: Mario Nardone
Estimated Sales: $24.4 Million
Number Employees: 159
Sq. footage: 10000
Type of Packaging: Consumer
Brands:
NARDONE BROS.
VINCENZO'S

9330 **Naron Mary Sue Candy Company**
1786 Union Ave
Baltimore, MD 21211-1417 410-467-9338
Fax: 410-467-1649 800-662-2639
Manufacturer and importer of gourmet chocolate candy
President: Bill Buppert
VP Production: Mark Berman
Estimated Sales: $10 Million
Number Employees: 5-9
Sq. footage: 68000
Type of Packaging: Consumer, Private Label, Bulk

9331 **Nash Finch Company**
P.O.Box 490
Statesboro, GA 30459-0490 912-681-4580
Fax: 912-681-1817 www.nashfinch.com
Manager: Preston Benson
Estimated Sales: $ 50 - 100 Million
Number Employees: 50-99

9332 **Nash Produce Company**
6160 S Nc Highway 58
Nashville, NC 27856 252-443-6011
Fax: 252-443-6746 800-334-3032
www.nashproduce.com
Processor of sweet potatoes and cucumbers
President: Thomas Joyner
Sales and Marketing: Charles Edwards
VP Operations: Richard Joyner
Estimated Sales: $1.5 Million
Number Employees: 50
Brands:
Nash Produce

9333 **Nashoba Valley Winery**
92 Wattaquadock Hill Rd
Bolton, MA 01740 978-779-5521
Fax: 978-779-5523 nashoba.winery@gte.net
www.nashobawinery.com
Wines
President: Richard Pelletier
VP: Cindy Rowe Pelletier
Estimated Sales: Below $ 5 Million
Number Employees: 20-49
Type of Packaging: Private Label

9334 **Nasonville Dairy**
10898 Us Highway 10
Marshfield, WI 54449 715-676-2177
Fax: 715-676-3636 www.nasonvilledairy.com
Cheese, cheese products
Owner: Kim Heiman
Estimated Sales: Below $ 5 Million
Number Employees: 20-49

9335 **(HQ)Nassau Candy Company**
530 W John St
Hicksville, NY 11801 516-433-7100
Fax: 516-433-9010 sales@nassaucandy.com
nassaucandy.com
Wholesaler/distributor and importer of confectionery items and specialty food products including pasta, vegetables and salami
President: Les Stier
President: Andrew Reitman
Estimated Sales: $ 20 - 50 Million
Number Employees: 100-249
Other Locations:
Nassau Candy Co.
Deer Park NY

9336 **Natalie's Orchard Island Juice**
330 N Us Highway 1
Fort Pierce, FL 34950-4207 772-465-1122
Fax: 772-465-4303 oijc@gate.net
www.oijc.com
Processor and exporter of fresh squeezed orange, grapefruit, lemon and lime juices; also, lemonade and blended juices
President: Marygrace Sexton
Assistant CEO: John Martinelli
Sales/Logistics Manager: David Cortez
Estimated Sales: $ 20 - 50 Million
Number Employees: 100-249
Type of Packaging: Consumer, Food Service
Brands:
COMPANY FRESHLY SQUEEZED JUICES
NATALIE'S ORCHID ISLAND

9337 **Natchez Pecan Shelling Company**
P.O.Box 100
Taylorsville, MS 39168-0100 601-785-4333
Pecans
Owner: Harold Bynum
Estimated Sales: Less than $500,000
Number Employees: 1-4

9338 **Naterl**
57 Rabastaliere
St. Bruno, QC J3V 2A4
Canada 450-653-3655
Fax: 450-653-9633 www.natrel.com

Processor of milk, butter, ice cream mix, chocolate milk and lemonade
President: Serge Serge Paquette
VP Marketing: Doug Kelly McGregor Gillespie
VP Finance/Administration: Éric Brunelle
Plant Manager: Gerry Verhoef
Number Employees: 100-249
Parent Co: Natrel
Type of Packaging: Consumer
Brands:
Naterl
Quebon
Sealtest
Silk Soy
Ultra'cream

9339 Nathan Seagall Company
1667 Federal Dr # 12
Montgomery, AL 36107-1103 334-279-3174
Fax: 334-279-1751
Manufacturer of produce
Manager: Reid Barnes
Estimated Sales: $3-5 Million
Number Employees: 5-9

9340 Nation Pizza Products
601 E Algonquin Rd
Schaumburg, IL 60173 847-397-3320
Fax: 847-397-9456 drpizza@anationpizza.com
www.nationpizza.com
Frozen pizza sauce and crusts
President: Marshall Bauer
CFO: Joe Giglio
SVP: Jack Campolo
Quality Assurance: Teresa Martinez
Estimated Sales: $20-50 Million
Number Employees: 600
Parent Co: OSI Group
Type of Packaging: Consumer
Brands:
Father & Son
My Father's Best
Nation

9341 National Bakers Services
2 S University Drive
Suite 330
Plantation, FL 33324-3307 954-920-7666
Baked goods

9342 (HQ)National Beef Packing Co., LLC
12200 N Ambassador Dr
Suite 500
Kansas City, MO 64163 816-713-8500
Fax: 816-713-8863 800-449-2333
keith.welty@nationalbeef.com
www.nationalbeef.com
Manufacturer of frozen and processed beef
Chairman: Steven Hunt
CEO: Timothy Klein
EVP Operations: Terry Wilkerson
Estimated Sales: $5.4 Billion
Number Employees: 8,900
Parent Co: US Premium Beef, LLC
Type of Packaging: Consumer, Food Service, Private Label, Bulk
Other Locations:
Brawley CA
Brands:
BLACK CANYON® ANGUS BEEF
BLACK CANYON® PREMIUM RESERVE
CERTIFIED ANGUS BEEF®
CERTIFIED ANGUS BEEF® PRIME
CERTIFIED HEREFORD BEEF®
CERTIFIED PREMIUM BEEF®
IMPERIAL VALLEY® PREMIUM BEEF
NATIONAL BEEF®
NATURESOURCE® NATURAL ANGUS
NATUREWELL® NATURAL BEEF
VINTAGE NATURAL BEEF®

9343 National Beverage Corporation
8100 SW 10th Streeet
Suite 4000
Fort Lauderdale, FL 33324 954-581-0922
Fax: 954-473-4710 877-622-3499
salesteam@nationalbeverage.com
www.nationalbeverage.com
Manufacturer of canned and bottled beverages including soft drinks, juice and spring water
President: Joseph Caporella
Chairman/CEO: Nick Caporella
SVP Finance: George Bracken
EVP/Procurement: Edward Knecht
Executive Director/IT: Raymond Notarantonio
SVP/Chief Accounting Officer: Dean McCoy
Senior Director/Consumer Marketing: Brent Bott
Director/Stragetic Brand Management: Vanessa Walker
Senior Director/Beverage Analyst: Gregory Kworderis
Estimated Sales: $593 Million
Number Employees: 1,200
Type of Packaging: Consumer, Food Service
Other Locations:
National Beverage Corp.
Hayward CA
Brands:
ASANTE
BIG SHOT
CASCADIA ONLY 2 CALORIES
CASCADIA SPARKLING CIDER
CLEARFRUIT
CRYSTAL BAY
EVERFRESH
FAYGO
LACROIX
MR PURE
MT. SHASTA
OHANA
RIP IT
RITZ
SHASTA
ST. NICK'S

9344 National By-Products
P.O.Box 7234
Omaha, NE 68107 402-733-8308
Fax: 402-291-4034 bellevue@nbyprod.com
www.nationalby-products.com
Processor of meat
Estimated Sales: $7100000
Number Employees: 50-99
Parent Co: Meat Rendering Company
Type of Packaging: Consumer

9345 National Egg Products Company
P.O.Box 1377
Social Circle, GA 30025-1377 770-464-2652
Fax: 770-464-2998 www.tyson.com
Processor and exporter of egg products including standard yolk, whole, whites and albumen
Manager: Brad Ginnane
Sales/Marketing Manager: Brad Ginnane
Plant Manager: Terry Anglin
Estimated Sales: $ 1 - 3 Million
Number Employees: 1-4
Sq. footage: 60000
Parent Co: Rose Acre Farms
Type of Packaging: Bulk

9346 National Enzyme Company
15366 Us Highway 160
Forsyth, MO 65653 417-546-4796
Fax: 417-546-6433 800-825-8545
mail@nzimes.com
www.nationalenzymecompany.com
Manufacturer and exporter of digestive enzymes and nutritional supplements
President: Anthony Collier
Director R&D: Rohit Medhekar PhD
VP Sales/Marketing: Rex Weiss
Marketing Manager: Gary Bennett
Director Manufacturing: Jerry Holvick
Estimated Sales: $ 20 - 50 Million
Number Employees: 50-99
Type of Packaging: Private Label, Bulk
Brands:
EDS
Nozimes

9347 National Fish & OystersCompany
5028 Meridian Rd NE
Olympia, WA 98516-2339 360-491-5550
Fax: 360-438-3681 www.nationaloyster.com
Processor and exporter of fresh and frozen oysters
President: James Bulldis
VP: George Bulldis
Plant Manager: Catherine Gylys
Estimated Sales: $ 5 - 10 Million
Number Employees: 20-49
Sq. footage: 3000
Type of Packaging: Consumer
Brands:
Sea Pearl

9348 National Fish & Seafood
11-15 Parker St Ste 4
Gloucester, MA 01930 978-282-7880
Fax: 978-282-7882 www.nationalfish.com
Seafood
President: Jack Ventola
Number Employees: 20-49

9349 National Fish and Seafood Limited
2401 Village Dr
Brownsville, TX 78521-1410 956-546-5525
Fax: 956-546-0871 www.nationalfish.com
Processor, importer and packer of frozen seafood including shrimp and surimi
President: Jack Harding
Estimated Sales: $ 1 - 3 Million
Number Employees: 1-4
Sq. footage: 2000
Parent Co: Lu-Mar Lobster & Shrimp
Type of Packaging: Consumer, Food Service, Private Label
Brands:
Corona Del Mar
Demerico
Lu-Mar

9350 (HQ)National Fisheries
5151 NW 165th St
Hialeah, FL 33014 305-628-1231
Fax: 305-620-4831
Seafood, seafood products
President: Simon Storn
CFO: Allan Wright
VP: Jack Karson
Purchasing Manager: Enrico Taboado
Estimated Sales: $ 20-50 Million
Number Employees: 50-99
Sq. footage: 35
Type of Packaging: Consumer, Food Service, Private Label

9351 National Fisheries - Marathon
3880 Gulfview Avenue
Marathon, FL 33050-2320 305-743-5545
Fresh seafood including Florida lobster and stone crabs.
President: Simon Storn
Manager: Leo Cooper
Estimated Sales: $10-20 Million
Number Employees: 20-49
Parent Co: National Fisheries

9352 National Food Company
3109 Koapaka St Unit C
Honolulu, HI 96819 808-839-1118
Fax: 808-839-6866
President: Peter Goo
Estimated Sales: $ 5 - 10 Million
Number Employees: 5-9

9353 National Food Corporation
1930 Merrill Creek Pkwy Ste A
Everett, WA 98203 425-349-4257
Fax: 425-349-4336 www.natlfood.com
Processor and exporter of kosher cream cheese
President: Brian Bookey
Estimated Sales: $ 100-500 Million
Number Employees: 100-249
Type of Packaging: Consumer, Food Service

9354 National Foods
1414 S West Street
Indianapolis, IN 46225-1548 317-634-5645
800-683-6565
Processor and exporter of portion cut meat and frankfurters
President: Steve Silk
Senior VP/General Manager: Martin Silver
Sales/Marketing Executive: Mark Kleinman
Number Employees: 600
Sq. footage: 180000
Parent Co: ConAgra Refigerated Prepared Foods
Type of Packaging: Consumer, Food Service
Other Locations:
National Foods
Indianapolis IN

9355 **National Foods**
P.O.Box 978
Liberal, KS 67905-0978 620-624-1851
Fax: 620-626-0624 www.nationalbeef.com
General grocery
President: John Miller
Sales Manager: Mike Sheehan
Parent Co: ConAgra Refigerated Prepared Foods

9356 **National Foods**
600 Food Center Drive
Bronx, NY 10474-7037 718-842-5000
Fax: 718-842-5664 800-683-6565
www.higherauthority.com
Processed meats, frankfurters, condiments and relishes. Kosher
President: Steve Silk
CFO: Bob Cahill
Executive VP: Marty Silver
Senior Marketing Manager: Leigh Platte
Sales Director: Scott Jacobs
Operations Manager: Henry Morris
General Manager: Robert Lichtman
Number Employees: 150
Parent Co: ConAgra Refigerated Prepared Foods
Type of Packaging: Private Label

9357 **National Frozen Foods Corporation**
P.O.Box 9366
Seattle, WA 98109 206-322-8900
Fax: 206-322-4458 www.nationalfrozenfoods.com
Processor, packer and exporter of frozen foods including fruit and vegetable purees, vegetable blends, peas, corn, carrots, cooked squash, creamed corn, beans, pearl onions, etc
President: S McCaffray
COO: W Rosenbach
CFO: C Gazarek
Human Resources: Bill Wallace
Quality Control: J Bafus
Estimated Sales: I
Number Employees: 1,000-4,999
Type of Packaging: Consumer, Food Service, Private Label, Bulk
Brands:
Valamont

9358 **National Fruit Flavor Company**
935 Edwards Ave
New Orleans, LA 70123 504-733-6757
Fax: 504-736-0168 800-966-1123
admin@nationalfruitflavor.com
www.nationalfruitflavor.com
Beverage concentrates, syrups and mixes
President: Gene Gamble
CEO: Eugene Gambel
VP: Peter Gambel
Quality Control: Blaine Hill
Marketing/Sales: Avery Stirratt
Public Relations: Chris Rooks
Operations: Peter Gambel
Quality Control: Blaine Hill
Plant Manager: Giovanni Galvan
Purchasing: Mike Ennis
Estimated Sales: $ 10-20 Million
Number Employees: 20-49
Number of Brands: 6
Number of Products: 700
Sq. footage: 41000
Type of Packaging: Consumer, Food Service, Private Label, Bulk
Brands:
GAMBELINI
NATIONAL
OLD COMISKEY
SNO-BALL
TASTY
ZODIAC

9359 **National Grape Cooperative**
2 S Portage St
Westfield, NY 14787 716-326-5200
Fax: 716-326-5494 nationalinfo@welchs.com
www.nationalgrape.com
Fruit and berry juices and jams
President: Joseph Falcone
Financial/Accounting Officer: Michael Perda
General Manager/COO: Brent Roggie
Estimated Sales: J
Number Employees: 1,325
Brands:
Welch's Fruit Juices
Welch's Jams, Jellie
Welch's Orchard Froz

9360 **National Harvest**
PO Box 26455
Kansas City, MO 64196-6455 816-842-9600
Fax: 816-531-3032 sales@nationalharvest.com
www.nationalharvest.com/contact
Manufacturer of Baked potato meals and toppings
President: John Mueller
Estimated Sales: $ 1 - 3 Million
Number Employees: 5-9
Type of Packaging: Food Service, Private Label, Bulk
Brands:
SUPER STUFFERS

9361 **National Importers**
120-13100 Mitchell Road
Richmond, BC V6V 1M8
Canada 604-324-1551
Fax: 604-324-1553 888-894-6464
ussales@nationalimporters.com
www.nationalimporters.com
Importer of gourmet, Mexican, Chinese, Indian and Thai foods, candy and groceries
Marketing: Barbara Allen
Office Manager: Peggy Hunter
Parent Co: National Importers

9362 **National Meat & Provision Company**
321 W 10th St
Reserve, LA 70084-6603 985-479-4200
Fax: 504-525-4499
Meat
President: Leonard Lalla
Vice President: Earline Lalla

9363 **National Products Company**
1206 E Crosstown Pkwy
Kalamazoo, MI 49001 269-344-3640
Fax: 269-344-1037 www.nationalflavors.com
Syrups, flavoring extracts, processed fruits and oils
Owner: John Hinkle
Estimated Sales: $ 10-20 Million
Number Employees: 20-49

9364 **National Raisin Company**
626 S 5th St
Fowler, CA 93625 559-834-5981
Fax: 559-834-1055 info@nationalraisin.com
www.national-raisin.com
Manufacturer and exporter of raisins
President/CEO: Ernest Bedrosian
Co-Founder/Co-President: Kenneth Bedrosian
Estimated Sales: $ 50 - 100 Million
Number Employees: 840
Type of Packaging: Consumer, Food Service, Private Label, Bulk
Brands:
Champion

9365 **(HQ)National Starch & Chemical Corporate Office**
10 Finderne Ave
Bridgewater, NJ 8807 908-575-0178
Fax: 908-685-7037 908-685-5000
nscinquiry@salessupport.com
www.nationalstarch.com
Manufacturer of specialty starches and fat replacers
CEO: Walter Schlauch
CFO: Han Kieftenbeld
EVP: James Zallie
Estimated Sales: $3 Billion
Number Employees: 750
Parent Co: Imperial Chemical Industries
Brands:
N-Lite
National
Purity

9366 **National Steak & Poultry**
301 E 5th Ave
Owasso, OK 74055 918-274-8787
Fax: 918-274-0046 800-366-6772
info@nationalsteak.com www.nationalsteak.com
Manufacturer of marinated pre-portioned beef and poultry both fully cooked and fresh frozen
President/CEO: David Albright
Controller: Bhrent Waddell
Sales Executive: Dale Lemon
Plant Manager: Bill Josey
Estimated Sales: $500 Million-$ 1 Billion
Number Employees: 325
Brands:
NATIONAL STEAK

9367 **National Vinegar Company**
108 Chessen Ln
Alton, IL 62002 618-465-6532
Fax: 618-465-7111
Processor of distilled vinegar and sweet cider
President: Virginia Braun
Estimated Sales: $ 5 - 10 Million
Number Employees: 10-19
Type of Packaging: Consumer, Food Service, Private Label, Bulk
Brands:
Alton
Garden Harvest
Hardin

9368 **National Vinegar Company**
P.O.Box 2761
Houston, TX 77252 713-223-4214
Fax: 713-223-4603
alexwolff@nationalvinegar.com
www.natvin.com
Manufacturer of distilled white, apple cider, red wine and corn vinegar
Manager: Joan Weiner
Vice President: David Wolff
Estimated Sales: $5 Million
Number Employees: 20-49
Type of Packaging: Consumer, Food Service, Private Label, Bulk
Brands:
National

9369 **(HQ)National Vinegar Company**
1750 S Brentwood Blvd
Suite 351
St Louis, MO 63144 314-962-4111
Fax: 314-962-4115 info@natvin.com
www.natvin.com
Manufacturer of vinegar
Estimated Sales: $ 1 - 3 Million
Number Employees: 10-19
Type of Packaging: Consumer
Other Locations:
National Vinegar Company Plant
Alton IL
National Vinegar Company Plant
Olney IL

9370 **National Wine & Spirits**
700 W Morris Street
Indianapolis, IN 46206-1602 317-636-6092
Fax: 317-917-1210 800-562-7359
www.nwscorp.com
Alcoholic beverages, wine and spirits
Chairman/President/CFO/CEO: James E Lacrosse

EVP Sales/Marketing: Greg Mauloff
SVP/Corporate Development: Catherin LaCrosse
Corp VP/Information Systems: Dwight Deming
EVP/COO: John Baker
VP/Operations: Steven Null
Purchasing Manager: Jan Schaver
Estimated Sales: $ 100-500 Million
Number Employees: 1600
Parent Co: National Wine and Spirits
Type of Packaging: Private Label

9371 **Nationwide Canning**
Effix County Road 34 E
Cottam, ON N0R 1B0
Canada 519-839-4831
Fax: 519-839-4993 www.cottamgardens.com
Processor of canned and crushed tomatoes, mushrooms, potatoes, pie fillings, kidney beans and spaghetti and pizza sauce; also, private labeling available
President and CFO: H Finaldi
Office Manager: Irene Finaldi
Number Employees: 55
Sq. footage: 50000
Type of Packaging: Private Label
Brands:
Cottam Gardens

9372 **Native American NaturalFoods**
287 Water Tower Road
Kyle, SD 57752 800-416-7212
Fax: 605-455-2019 800-416-7212
mtilsen@tankabar.com mtilsen@tankabar.com

Dairy-free, gluten-free, lactose-free, nut-free, prganic/natural, USDA, health, fitness and energy bars, foodservice.

9373 **Native American Tea & Cofee**
P.O.Box 1266
Aberdeen, SD 57402-1266 605-226-2006
Fax: 605-226-2414 info@nativeamericantea.com
www.nativeamericantea.com
Coffee, tea
Manager: J Almon
Estimated Sales: Below $ 5 Million
Number Employees: 5-9
Brands:
Native American

9374 **Native Kjalii Foods**
459 Fulton St Ste 205
San Francisco, CA 94102 415-522-5580
Fax: 510-686-1757 nativefo@sfsalsa.com
www.sfsalsa.com
Manufacturer fruit and vegetable salsas, vegetable hummus and tortilla chips
President/Co-Owner: Bret Jeremy
Marketing/Co-Owner: Julie Jeremy
Estimated Sales: $ 3 - 5 Million
Number Employees: 1-4
Sq. footage: 4000
Type of Packaging: Consumer, Food Service, Bulk
Brands:
NATIVE KJALII

9375 **Native Scents**
5639 Ndcbu
Taos, NM 87571 505-758-9656
Fax: 575-758-5802 800-645-3471
nativescents@starband.net www.nativescents.net
Processor, importer and exporter of herbal teas and aromatic products, honey and essential oils, incense, bath products
President: Marlene Payfoya
CEO: Alfred Savinelli
Estimated Sales: $641,586
Number Employees: 10-19
Number of Products: 127
Sq. footage: 6000
Brands:
Native Scents

9376 **Native South Services**
Po Box 1157
Fredericksburg, TX 78624 830-997-1431
Fax: 830-990-9481 800-236-2848
service@nativesouth.com www.nativesouth.com
Manufacturer of salsas and tortilla chips, vidalia onion cheese biscuits, fried green tomato biscuits and white chocolate sweet potato biscuits
President/Owner: Lynne Simmons
Estimated Sales: Below $5 Million
Number Employees: 4
Type of Packaging: Food Service, Private Label
Brands:
NATIVE SOUTH

9377 **Natra US**
1059 Tierra Del Rey Ste H
Chula Vista, CA 91910 619-397-4120
Fax: 619-397-4121 800-262-6216
info@natraus.com
Importer and exporter of cocoa powder, butter and extract; also, chocolate, caffeine, theobromine and nutraceuticals
Manager: Maria Dominguez
Vice President: Martin Brabenec
Estimated Sales: $650000
Number Employees: 1-4
Number of Brands: 2
Number of Products: 30
Parent Co: Natra S.A.
Type of Packaging: Consumer, Food Service, Bulk
Brands:
Natra Cacao
Natra US
Natraceutical

9378 **Natren**
3105 Willow Ln
Thousand Oaks, CA 91361 866-462-8736
Fax: 805-371-4742 800-992-3323
Processor of yogurt starter and probiotic products
President: Natasha Trenev
CEO: Yordan Trenev
Estimated Sales: $1400000
Number Employees: 50-99
Brands:
Bifido Factor
Bifido Nate
Bio-Nate
D.F.A.
Digesta-Lac
Life Start
Megadophilius
Yogurt Starter

9379 **(HQ)Natrium Products**
P.O.Box 5465
Cortland, NY 13045 607-753-9829
Fax: 607-753-0552 800-962-4203
herman@natrium.com www.natrium.com
Baking Soda/Sodium Biocarbonate manufacturer
President: Tim Herman
Marketing Director: Tim Herman
Estimated Sales: $ 10 - 20 Million
Number Employees: 10-19
Sq. footage: 35000
Type of Packaging: Bulk
Brands:
NATRIUM

9380 **Natur Sweeteners, Inc.**
11155 Massachusetts Avenue
Los Angeles, CA 90025 310-445-0020
Fax: 310-473-1086 stephenf@naturresearch.com
www.cweet.com
Manufacturer of natural intense sweetener; characteristics and other performance qualities similar to cane sugar

9381 **Naturade Inc**
1 City Blvd. West
Suite 1440
Orange, CA 92868 714-535-9178
Fax: 714-935-9837 800-421-1830
customerservice@naturade.com
www.naturade.com
Manufacturer of soy protein powder shake mixes, herbal-based cough and cold formulas, and colostrum supplements.
Founder: Nathan Schulman
Executive Vice President Sales: Rick Robinette

9382 **(HQ)Natural Balance**
383 Inverness Pkwy # 390
Englewood, CO 80112-5864 303-688-6633
Fax: 303-688-1591 800-624-4260
service@naturalbalance.com
www.naturalbalance.com
Processor and wholesaler/distributor of natural nutrition supplements for energy, weight loss and sports
President: Mark Owens
Executive VP: Tim Hinricks
Sales Coordinator: Scott Smith
Plant Manager: John O'Brien
Purchasing Manager: Stephanie McArthur
Estimated Sales: $11400000
Number Employees: 100-249
Sq. footage: 25000
Other Locations:
Natural Balance
Castle Rock CO

9383 **Natural By Nature**
P.O.Box 464
West Grove, PA 19390 610-268-6962
Fax: 610-268-4172 www.natural-by-nature.com
Milk, dairy products
Owner: Ned Mac Arthur
Head Sales: Allan Kulick
Estimated Sales: $ 100-500 Million
Number Employees: 100-249

9384 **Natural Choice Distribution**
5427 Telegraph Ave Ste U
Oakland, CA 94609 510-653-8212
Fax: 510-653-8163
Salsa and sandwiches, distribution of natural food products
Owner: Steve Cutter
Estimated Sales: Below $ 5 Million
Number Employees: 20-49
Type of Packaging: Private Label

9385 **Natural Company**
8 W Hamilton St
Baltimore, MD 21201-5008 410-628-1262
Fax: 410-796-3977
info@thenaturalcompany.com.au
www.keeper.com.au
Health food, tofu
President: Joan Huang
Estimated Sales: Below $ 5 Million
Number Employees: 6
Brands:
Moon Pads
The Keeper

9386 **Natural Enrichment Industries, LLC**
1002 South Park
Sesser, IL 62884 618-625-2112
Fax: 618-625-3112 maryc@neitcp.com
www.neitcp.com
Manufacturer of Tricalcium Phosphate from a domestically produced lime.
Sales & Marketing Representative: Marci Swartz
Sales Manager: Mary Clark

9387 **Natural Exotic Tropicals**
450 SW 12th Ave
Pompano Beach, FL 33069 954-783-4500
Fax: 954-783-8812 800-756-5267
sales@naturalexotic.com
www.naturalexotic.com
Sugar-free fruit spreads, jellies, marmalades, butters and juices
President: Van Herrington
CFO: Jayne Herrington
Estimated Sales: $ 5 - 10 Million
Number Employees: 20-49
Brands:
Natural Exotic Tropicals

9388 **Natural Feast Corporation**
PO Box 36
28 Old Farm Roadÿÿÿÿ
Dover, MA 02030-0036 508-785-3322
Fax: 508-984-1496
Frozen foods
President: Alan Attridge
Estimated Sales: $ 1-2.5 Million
Number Employees: 10

9389 **Natural Food Supplements**
8725 Remmet Ave
Canoga Park, CA 91304 818-341-3375
Fax: 818-341-3376
Processor and contract packager of vitamins
President: Elmer Walters
Estimated Sales: $600000
Number Employees: 5-9
Type of Packaging: Bulk
Brands:
Sunshine Valley

9390 **Natural Food World**
6009 Washington Boulevard
Culver City, CA 90232-7425 310-836-7770
Fax: 310-836-6454
Health and dietetic foods
President: Anne Stern
Estimated Sales: $ 5-10 Million
Number Employees: 10

9391 **Natural Foods**
3040 Hill Ave
Toledo, OH 43607 419-537-1713
Fax: 419-531-6887 www.bulkfoods.com
Wholesaler/distributor, importer and packer of food, candy, nuts, spices, fruit, and chocolates.
Owner: Frank Dietrich
Estimated Sales: $5,000,000
Number Employees: 30
Sq. footage: 450000
Type of Packaging: Food Service, Bulk

9392 **Natural Formulas**
2125 American Ave
Hayward, CA 94545 510-372-1800
Fax: 510-782-9793 www.gnld.com
Processor of powdered drink mixes
President: Robert Murphy
Quality Control: Ric Green
Estimated Sales: $ 10 - 20 Million
Number Employees: 50-99

9393 Natural Fruit Corporation
770 W 20th St
Hialeah, FL 33010 305-887-7525
Fax: 305-888-8208 info@nfc-fruti.com
www.nfc-fruti.com
Processor and exporter of frozen fruit bars, cocktail mixes and ice cream novelties
Founder/President: Simon Bravo
Quality Assurance Director: Angelica Delia
EVP Operations/Founder: Jorge Bravo Sr
Plant Supervisor: Peter Infante
Estimated Sales: $14 Million
Number Employees: 38
Sq. footage: 20000
Brands:
Allison Jayne
Chunks O'Fruit
Fruti

9394 (HQ)Natural Group
505 South A Street
Second Floor
Oxnard, CA 93030 805-485-3420
Fax: 805-983-1428
customerservice@naturalgroup.net
www.naturalgroup.net
Non-alcoholic beverages, waters, food products
Owner: Kanishka Lal
Executive VP: Judith Keer
Estimated Sales: $440 K
Number Employees: 7
Type of Packaging: Private Label
Brands:
AME
Ame Celebration
Apres
Hildon Water
Purdey's
Yellow Gold Shelf St

9395 Natural Nectar
196 E Main Street
Huntington, NY 11743 631-367-7280
Fax: 631-367-7282 www.natural-nectar.com
cracklebred, whole grain wafers, tuiles ice cream wafers, nectar nugget peanut butter cup, cinnamon sticks & pretzel cookies, mediterranean sea salt, chocodream

9396 Natural Oils International
2279 Ward Ave
Simi Valley, CA 93065-1863 805-433-0160
www.naturaloils.com
Processor, importer and exporter of vegetable oils
President: Brendon Bonnar
Sales: Barbara Hardy
Sales: Jack Phillips
Estimated Sales: $ 1 - 3 Million
Number Employees: 1-4
Sq. footage: 30000

9397 (HQ)Natural Ovens Bakery
4300 County Road CR
Manitowoc, WI 54220 920-758-2500
Fax: 920-758-2671 800-558-3535
www.naturalovens.com
Processor of bread, cookies, rolls and bagels.
President: Barbara Stitt
General Manager: Matthew E. Taylor
Vice President: Paul Stitt
Marketing Director: Chelle Blaszczyk
VP Production: Glen Hietpas
Estimated Sales: $ 20 - 50 Million
Number Employees: 100-249
Sq. footage: 28000
Brands:
100% Whole Grain
Flax N' Honey
Nutty All-Natural Wheat
Sunny Millet

9398 Natural Products
2211 6th Ave
Grinnell, IA 50112-2276 641-236-0852
Fax: 641-236-4835 npi@npisoy.com
www.npisoy.com
Roast and mill soybean, flour and grits for food industry
General Manager: Paul Lang
Quality Control: Ray Lang
Marketing Director: Jon Stratford
Estimated Sales: Below $ 5 Million
Number Employees: 10-19

9399 Natural Quality Company
13805 Llagas Ave
San Martin, CA 95046-9564 408-683-2182
Fax: 408-683-4249 natqual@aol.com
www.naturalquality.com
Frozen celery, peppers, chillies
President: Karen Ash
COO: Karen Ash
Estimated Sales: $ 50-100 Million
Number Employees: 100-249
Number of Brands: 1

9400 Natural Quick Foods
3737 NE 135th Street
Seattle, WA 98125-3831 206-365-5757
Fax: 206-365-5434 nqf@uswest.net
Vegan, organic pocket sandwiches
President: Larry Brewer
Estimated Sales: $ 5 - 10 Million
Number Employees: 5-9

9401 Natural Rush
PO Box 421753
San Francisco, CA 94142-1753 415-863-2503
Fax: 415-431-5763 www.naturalrush.com
Candy, confectionery and honey
President: Gilles Desaulniers
Estimated Sales: Under $500,000
Number Employees: 1-4
Type of Packaging: Private Label

9402 Natural Spring Water Company
300 Boggs Ln
Johnson City, TN 37604 423-926-7905
Fax: 423-926-8210
Contract packager and bottler of noncarbonated mountain spring water
President: Bill Lizzio
Team Leader: John Gustke
Number Employees: 10-19
Sq. footage: 12000
Type of Packaging: Consumer, Food Service, Private Label, Bulk
Brands:
Laure Pristine

9403 Natural Value Products
14 Waterthrush Ct
Sacramento, CA 95831-2347 916-427-7242
Fax: 916-427-3784 gary@naturalvalue.com
www.naturalvalue.com
Processor importer and exporter of organic products including canned tomatoes, beans, oils, pasta and pasta and hot sauces; importer of tuna, mandarin oranges and artichokes
President: Gary Cohen
CEO: Jody Cohen
Estimated Sales: $ 1 - 3 Million
Number Employees: 1-4
Number of Brands: 1
Number of Products: 700
Type of Packaging: Consumer, Food Service, Bulk

9404 Natural Way Mills
24509 390th St NE
Middle River, MN 56737-9367 218-222-3677
Fax: 218-222-3408 info@naturalwaymills.com
www.naturalwaymills.com
Processor and exporter of organic wheat, seven-grain cereal, rye, flax seed, barley, millet, brown rice, flour and grits; custom milling available; also, packaging in nitrogen-pack baskets available
President: Ray Juhl
CEO: Helen Juhl
Sales: Rebekah Knapp
Plant Manager: Charles Knapp
Estimated Sales: $620,000
Number Employees: 5-9
Brands:
7 Grain Cereal
Gold N. White Bread Flour

9405 Natural Wonder Foods Inc
1221 45th Street
Brooklyn, NY 11219-2025
Fax: 718-972-9708
Processor and exporter of frozen vegetarian burgers, cutlets and franks
President: Joseph Grossman
Estimated Sales: $7,413,000
Number Employees: 7
Type of Packaging: Consumer, Food Service, Private Label, Bulk
Brands:
Frozen Wonders
Gold

9406 Naturally Delicious
1811 NW 29th St
Oakland Park, FL 33311 954-485-6730
Fax: 954-485-6834 info@naturally-delicious.com
www.naturally-delicious.com
Breads
Owner/President: Arthur Price
Estimated Sales: $230,000
Number Employees: 5-9
Brands:
Naturally Delicious

9407 Naturally Fresh Foods
1000 Naturally Fresh Blvd
Atlanta, GA 30349 404-765-9000
Fax: 404-765-9016 800-765-1950
bdotson@naturallyfresh.com
www.naturallyfresh.com
Manufacturer and exporter of syrups, sauces, salad dressings, dips and quiche and bar mixes
President/Coo: Jerry Greene
Cfo: Peter Rostad
Estimated Sales: $ .5 - 1 million
Number Employees: 1-4
Sq. footage: 250000
Parent Co: Eastern Foods
Type of Packaging: Consumer, Food Service, Private Label, Bulk
Brands:
JACKAROO
NATURALLY FRESH
PROUD PRODUCTS

9408 Naturally Scientific
600 Willow Tree Road
Leonia, NJ 07605-2211 201-585-7055
Fax: 973-244-0044 888-428-0700
nsilabs@aol.com www.naturallyscientific.com
Processor of liquid nutritional supplements and food and beverage ingredients. Produce every vitamin, mineral or herb in conbinations of up to 200 actives. Consumables or concentrates. Use a patented highly bioavailable technology
President/CEO: Frank Berger
Executive VP: Marc Pozner
Marketing Director: Douglas Lynch
Sales/Group Publisher: Jon Benninger
Estimated Sales: $ 1 - 3 Million
Number Employees: 5-9
Number of Products: 200
Type of Packaging: Consumer, Private Label

9409 Naturally Vitamin Supplements
4404 E Elwood St
Phoenix, AZ 85040 480-991-0200
Fax: 480-991-0551 800-899-4499
www.naturally.com
Processor and exporter of health foods and natural vitamins, minerals and food supplements including B-complex and C-combination formulas, fish oils, fiber blends, multi-vitamins and enzymes
President: Joachim Lehmann
Export Sales Manager: Mark Wojick
VP Sales: Don Haygood
Estimated Sales: $ 5 - 10 Million
Number Employees: 10-19
Sq. footage: 20000
Type of Packaging: Food Service, Private Label, Bulk
Brands:
All B-100
All B-50
Body-Fuel
Fiber
Fiber-7
Ginsen-Rgy
Hi C-Plex
Little Vab
Max-C-Plex
Mega C-Bio
Special C-500
Super Epa
Super Stress
Super Vab
Supreme B 150
Un-Fad Diet Packs
Vit-A-Boost

9410 **Nature Cure Northwest**
P.O.Box 753
Poulsbo, WA 98370 360-697-8691
Fax: 360-697-7179 800-957-8048
Processor of bottled bee pollen pills
President: Allen Schmitt
Estimated Sales: 724,000
Number Employees: 2
Type of Packaging: Food Service
Brands:
Nature Cure

9411 **Nature Kist Snacks**
1820 Industrial Dr
Stockton, CA 95206 209-944-7200
inquiry@naturekistsnacks.com
www.naturekistsnacks.com
Processor of nut and seed trail mixes; private labeling available
President: Ronald L Mozingo
Office Manager: Nancy Freitas
Plant Manager: Rick Dorotheo
Estimated Sales: $ 10 - 20 Million
Number Employees: 20-49
Type of Packaging: Consumer, Private Label

9412 **Nature Quality**
13805 Llagas Ave
San Martin, CA 95046 408-683-2182
Fax: 408-683-4249 natqual@aol.com
Processor and exporter of IQF cut celery, olives, onions, garlic and peppers
President: Karen Ash
General Manager: Karen Ash
Estimated Sales: $7000000
Number Employees: 100-249
Sq. footage: 20000
Type of Packaging: Food Service, Bulk

9413 **Nature Soy, Inc**
713 N 10th Street
Philadelphia, PA 19123 215-765-8889
support@naturesoy.com
www.naturesoy.com
Manufacturer/supplier of healthy soy and vegetarian products to the ethnic market
President: Yat Wen
CEO: Gene He
EVP: Fenjin He
Estimated Sales: $2.4 Million
Number Employees: 17
Sq. footage: 17500

9414 **Nature Star Foods**
15 Spinning Wheel Rd # 314
Hinsdale, IL 60521-2498 630-323-8888
Fax: 630-323-8988 plockys@aol.com
www.plockys.com
Manufacturer of Potato sticks, sweet apple chips sticks, sweet nut mixes, tortilla chips
Owner: Paul Cipolla
Estimated Sales: Below $5 Million
Number Employees: 1-4
Type of Packaging: Private Label
Brands:
NATURE STAR
PLOCYY'S APPLE CHIPS

9415 **Nature's Apothecary**
PO Box 17970
Boulder, CO 80308-0970 970-664-1600
Fax: 970-664-5106 800-999-7422
www.naturesapothecary.com
Processor and exporter of fresh organic, medicinal, botanical and herbal liquid extracts
Director Customer Relations: Nancy Mitchell
Type of Packaging: Consumer, Private Label, Bulk

9416 **Nature's Best Food Supplement**
195 Engineers Rd
Hauppauge, NY 11788 631-232-3355
Fax: 631-232-3320 800-345-2378
info@naturesbest.com www.naturesbest.com
Manufacturer of Sport nutrition products
President: Hal Katz
Purchasing Manager: Ernie Geraci
Estimated Sales: $5-10 Million
Number Employees: 20-49
Number of Brands: 4
Number of Products: 150
Type of Packaging: Consumer
Brands:
DECADES
ISOPURE
NO HOLDS BAR
PERFECT
PERFECT 1100
PERFECT ANIMOS
PERFECT CARBS
PERFECT Rx
SOLID PROTEIN

9417 **Nature's Bounty**
2100 Smithtown Ave
Ronkonkoma, NY 11779 631-580-6137
Fax: 631-567-7148 800-433-2990
info@naturesbounty.com www.nbty.com
Manufaacturer, marketer and distributor of a broad line of high-quality, value-priced nutritional supplements in the United States and throughout the world.
President/CFO: Harvey Kamil
Chairman/CEO: Scott Rudolph
SVP Marketing/Advertising: James Flaherty
SVP Operations: Hans Lindgren
Estimated Sales: $2.6 Billion
Number Employees: 13,950
Type of Packaging: Bulk
Brands:
AMERICAN HEALTH®
DETUINEN®
ESTER-C(190)
GNC (UK)®
GOOD 'N' NATURAL®
HOLLAND & BARRETT®
HOME HEALTH™
JULIAN GRAVES
LENATURISTE®
MET-RX®
NATURE'S BOUNTY®
PURITAN'S PRIDE®
REXALL®
SISU®
SOLGAR®
SUNDOWN®
VITAMIN WORLD®
WORLDWIDE SPORT NUTRITION®

9418 **Nature's Candy**
632 Fm 2093
Fredericksburg, TX 78624 830-997-3844
Fax: 830-997-6528 800-729-0085
karen@natural-nut-snacks.com
www.natural-nut-snacks.com
Processor and wholesaler/distributor of natural and fruit filled candy, maple coated nuts and seasoned nuts and seeds
President: Michael Zygmunt
Office Manager: Karen Gold
Estimated Sales: $482000
Number Employees: 5-9
Type of Packaging: Consumer, Private Label, Bulk

9419 **Nature's Dairy**
5104 S Main St
Roswell, NM 88203-0822 575-623-9640
Fax: 575-622-1318
Milk, dairy products-noncheese
President: Gerald Greathouse
Estimated Sales: $ 5 - 10 Million
Number Employees: 20-49
Brands:
Nature's Dairy

9420 **Nature's Finest Products**
PO Box 801326
Dallas, TX 75380-1326 773-489-2096
Fax: 972-960-8760 800-237-5205
natures@naturesfinest.com
www.naturesfinest.com
Gourmet foods
President: Mike Griffin

9421 **Nature's Hand**
1800 Cliff Rd E # 7
Burnsville, MN 55337-1375 952-890-6033
Fax: 952-890-6040 www.natureshand.com
Manufacturer and exporter of natural breakfast cereal; also, granola topping and baking ingredients
Manager: Sean Finney
Estimated Sales: $500,000-$1 Million
Number Employees: 5-9
Number of Brands: 1
Number of Products: 4
Type of Packaging: Consumer, Food Service, Private Label, Bulk
Brands:
NATURE'S HAND

9422 **Nature's Herbs**
Box 970
Merritt, BC V1K 1B8 250-378-8822
Fax: 250-378-8753 800-437-2257
village@naturesherbs.com
www.naturesherbs.com
Processor and exporter of dietary supplements and encapsulated herbs
President/CEO: Ross Blechman
Executive VP Sales: Dean Blechman
Estimated Sales: $ 5 - 10 Million
Number Employees: 250
Sq. footage: 50000
Parent Co: Twin Laboratories
Type of Packaging: Consumer
Brands:
Healthcare Naturals
Herb Masters' Original
Nature's Herbs
Power Herbs

9423 **Nature's Hilights**
1608 Chico River Rd # A
Chico, CA 95928 530-342-6154
Fax: 530-342-3130 800-313-6454
Processor of baked products including rice crusts, bread, bread sticks, rice pizzas and frozen gluten-free desserts
President: Gayle Luna
Estimated Sales: $5-9.9 Million
Number Employees: 10-19
Type of Packaging: Food Service, Bulk

9424 **Nature's Nutrition**
6425 Anderson Way
Melbourne, FL 32940 321-255-5505
Fax: 321-255-5881 800-242-1115
info@nothindutherbs.com
www.nothinbutherbs.com
Processor of organic food and nutritional supplements including vitamins, amino acids, antioxidants and proteins; also, weight loss aids
President: Dr. Dee Corbitt
Estimated Sales: $500,000-$1 Million
Number Employees: 5-9
Sq. footage: 5000
Brands:
Harida
The Capsule

9425 **(HQ)Nature's Path Foods**
9100 Van Horne Way
Richmond, BC V6X 1W3
Canada 604-248-8777
Fax: 604-248-8760 www.naturespath.com
Processor and exporter of organic ready-to-eat cereals and baked goods; also, toaster waffles and vegetarian patties
President: Arran Stephas
CFO: Neil Mandleman
Estimated Sales: $100-500 Million
Number Employees: 150
Sq. footage: 79000
Type of Packaging: Consumer, Private Label, Bulk
Other Locations:
Nature's Path Foods
Blaine WA
Brands:
Blueberry Almond Museli
Eco-Pac
Evirokidz Creams
Flaxplus
Heritage
Heritage Bites
Heritage-O's
Honey'd
Lifestream
Ls Flaxplus
Ls Smart Bran
Ls Wildberry Muesli
Manna Bread
Millet Rice
Multigrain
NP Hemp Plus
NP Kamut Krisp
NP Soy Plus
Nature's Path
Np Mesa Sunrise
Oaty Bites
Optimum Power Breakfast

9426 **Nature's Plus**
2500 Grand Ave
Long Beach, CA 90815 562-494-2500
Fax: 800-688-7239 salesinfo@naturesplus.com
www.naturesplus.com
Processor and exporter of health products including protein weight loss supplements, vitamins and herbs
Director Marketing: Gerard McIntee
Estimated Sales: $15100000
Number Employees: 60
Parent Co: Natural Organics

9427 **Nature's Provision Company**
452 Krumville Rd
Olivebridge, NY 12461-5528 845-657-6020
Processor of powdered health food supplements for circulatory improvement; wholesaler/distributor of pH balanced cleansers and lubricants
President: Clark Jung
Vice President: Ann Jung
Estimated Sales: $130,000
Number Employees: 2
Brands:
Dr. Rinse Vita Flo Formula

9428 **Nature's Select**
555 Cascade West Pkwy SE # 200
Grand Rapids, MI 49546-2105
Fax: 616-956-0998 888-715-4321
naturesselect@aol.com www.snackperfect.com
Manufacturer of Premium quality dry roasted soynuts
President/Owner: Peter Assaly
Estimated Sales: $500,000
Number Employees: 1-4
Number of Brands: 1
Number of Products: 9
Sq. footage: 30000
Brands:
NATURE'S SELECT

9429 **Nature's Sunshine Products Company**
P.O.Box 19005
Provo, UT 84605 801-342-4300
Fax: 801-342-4305 800-223-8225
questions@natr.com www.natr.com
Processor and exporter of health products including vitamins, minerals and herbs
President: Craig Dalley
CEO: Douglas Faggioli
Estimated Sales: $258208000
Number Employees: 1,000-4,999
Type of Packaging: Consumer
Brands:
Nature's Sunshine

9430 **(HQ)Nature's Way**
3051 West Maple Loop Drive
Suite 125
Lehi, UT 84043
Fax: 800-688-3303 800-962-8873
sales@naturesway.com www.naturesway.com
Herbs and vitamins
CFO: Rich Jones
CEO: Randy Rose
Operations Manager: Brian Hufford
Production Manager: Greg Bone
Purchasing Manager: Dave Anderson
Estimated Sales: $ 100-500 Million
Number Employees: 100-249
Parent Co: Schwabe North America
Type of Packaging: Private Label
Brands:
ALIVE!
BIO-CERTIFIED SAMBUCUS
BOERICKE & TAFEL
CAMOCARE ORGANICS
CHLOROFRESH
EFATOLD
FISOL
GINKGOLD
HEARTSURE
HYDRAPLENISH
METABOLIC RESET
PEPOGEST
PRIMADOPHILUS
THISILYN
UMCKA COLDCARE

9431 **NatureMost Laboratories**
60 Trigo Dr
Middletown, CT 06457-6157 860-346-8991
Fax: 860-347-3312 800-234-2112
sales@naturemost.com www.naturemost.com
Manufacturer, importer and exporter of products, vitamins, oils, minerals, herbal supplements; also, contract packaging and private labeling available
President: Robert Trigo
Marketing: Sam Schwartz
Sales: Donna Platnum
Operations: Fred Wuschner
Estimated Sales: $ 5 - 10 Million
Number Employees: 20-49
Number of Brands: 3
Number of Products: 300
Sq. footage: 20000
Type of Packaging: Consumer, Private Label
Brands:
Naturemost Labs
Trigo Labs

9432 **Naturel**
9339 Foothill Blvd # A
Rancho Cucamonga, CA 91730-3548 909-987-0520
Fax: 909-390-5453 877-242-8344
naturelUSA@aol.com www.naturel.com
Processor of organic agave syrup prepared for 100% agave juice; natural fructose sweetener/flavor enhancer
Owner: Jong Kee Kim
National Sales Manager: Oscar Guerrero Whaley
Estimated Sales: Less than $500,000
Number Employees: 1-4
Parent Co: Industrializadora Integral Del Agave, SA DeCV

9433 **Natures Best**
195 Engineers Rd
Hauppauge, NY 11788-4020 631-232-3355
Fax: 631-232-3320 800-345-2378
info@naturesbest.com www.naturesbest.com
Processor and exporter of athletic supplements and sport drinks
President: Hal Katz
Estimated Sales: $1.5 Million
Number Employees: 20-49
Brands:
Decades
No Holds Bar
Perfect 1100
Perfect Aminos
Perfect Carbs
Perfect Rx

9434 **Natures Sungrown Foods**
4340 Redwood Highway
San Rafael, CA 94903 415-491-4944
Fax: 415-532-2233 hal@naturessungrown.com
www.naturessungrown.com
Manufacturer and exporter of natural beef and pork, organic foods (dried fruit, coffee, juice, sauce, tortilla chips, guacamole, jalapeno peppers and Mexican foods
President: Hal Shenson
Estimated Sales: $5-10 Million
Number of Brands: 2
Type of Packaging: Consumer, Food Service, Private Label, Bulk
Brands:
NATURE'S SUNGROWN BEEF
VERA CRUZ MEXICAN FOODS

9435 **Naturex**
375 Huyler St
South Hackensack, NJ 7606 201-440-5000
Fax: 201-342-8000 naturex@naturex.com
www.naturex.com
Manufacturer of high quality natural antioxidants, colors, herbs & spices oleoresins and essential oils, and botanical extracts for the food, flavor and nutraceutical industries
President & CEO: Jacques Dikanksy
CFO: Thierry Lambert
VP: Stephane Ducroux
R&D: Marc Roller
Quality Control: Nicolas Feuillere
Marketing: Antoine Dauby
Sales: Samuel Menard
Public Relations: Antoine Dauby
Purchasing Director: Serge Sabrier
Estimated Sales: $115 Million
Number Employees: 165
Number of Brands: 6
Parent Co: Naturex SA - France
Type of Packaging: Bulk
Brands:
COLORENHANCE
OSR
STABILENCHANCE
WSR

9436 **Naturex Inc**
375 Huyler St
South Hackensack, NJ 07606 201-440-5000
Fax: 201-342-8000 naturex.us@naturex.com
www.naturex.com
Manufacturer, importer and exporter of botanical and natural flavor extracts
President/CEO: Jacques Dikansky
VP: Thierry Lambert
Sales/Marketing: Samuel Menard
Head of Purchasing: Julius Myer
Estimated Sales: $115 Million
Number Employees: 185
Sq. footage: 14991
Parent Co: Naturex, S.A.
Type of Packaging: Bulk

9437 **Naturex Inc.**
375 Huyler St
South Hackensack, NJ 07606-1532 201-440-5000
Fax: 201-342-8000
Manufacturer and exporter of botanical extracts, flavoring ingredients and aromatic materials including ethyl vanillin, menthol and vanillin; also, water soluble gums including acacia, guar and locust bean
President & CEO: Jacques Dikansky
VP/Director of Sales: Stephane Ducroux
Vice President: Thierry Lambert
Estimated Sales: $ 90 Million
Number Employees: 100-249
Number of Products: 3000
Sq. footage: 40000
Type of Packaging: Bulk

9438 **Naumes**
P.O.Box 996
Medford, OR 97501 541-772-6268
Fax: 541-772-3650 juice@naumes.com
www.naumes.com
Grower of apples, plums, pears, pomegranates, persimmons and Asian pears
President: Michael D Naumes
Estimated Sales: $100+ Million
Number Employees: 100-249
Type of Packaging: Consumer
Brands:
Blue Flag
Cheam of Chelan
Gold Crest
Oh Yes
Pinetree
Rogue
Snowcrest

9439 **Nautilus Foods**
2370 130th Ave NE Ste 101
Bellevue, WA 98005 425-885-5900
Fax: 425-885-1900
Frozen fish, fresh and smoked salmon
President: Thomas Waterer
Executive VP: Dawn Waterer
Sales Manager: Joseph Lombardo
Director Manufacturing: Matt Walton
Plant Manager: David Kaayk
Estimated Sales: $170 K
Number Employees: 3

9440 **Navarro Pecan Company**
PO Box 147
Corsicana, TX 75151-0147 903-872-5641
Fax: 903-874-7143 800-333-9507
website@navarropecan.com
www.navarropecan.com
Processor and exporter of kosher certified shelled raw and roasted pecans used as ingredients
CEO: Mark Frank
General Manager: Shirley Smith
Estimated Sales: $ 20 - 50 Million
Number Employees: 2
Sq. footage: 185000
Type of Packaging: Consumer, Bulk
Brands:
Navarro

9441 **Navarro Vineyards & Winery**
P.O.Box 47
Philo, CA 95466-0047 707-895-3686
Fax: 707-895-3647 800-537-9463
sales@navarrowine.com www.navarrowine.com
Processor of wine and olive oils
Owner: Deborah Cahn
VP: Deborah Cahn
Estimated Sales: Less than $500,000
Number Employees: 1-4
Type of Packaging: Consumer, Food Service

9442 **Navas Instruments**
105 Wind Tree Ln
Conway, SC 29526 843-347-1379
Fax: 843-347-2527 info@navas-instruments.com
www.navas-instruments.com
Manufacturer of laboratory instruments for testing ash and moisture in food, pet and animal feed, fertilizers, soils and wastewater.

9443 **Naya**
2030-340 Pie IX
Montreal, QC H1V 2C8
Canada 450-562-7911
Fax: 450-562-3654 info@naya.com
www.naya.com
Processor and exporter of bottled spring water
President: Anita Jarjour
Executive VP/COO: Stu Levitan
Director Sales Marketing: Raynald Brisson
VP Operations: Sylvain Mayrand
Number Employees: 100-249
Sq. footage: 120000
Type of Packaging: Consumer, Food Service, Private Label
Brands:
Naya

9444 **Naylor Candies**
P.O.Box 1018
Mount Wolf, PA 17347 717-266-2706
Fax: 717-266-2706 www.naylorcandies.com
Processor and exporter of confectionery products including butter toffee peanuts, butter mints, cashew crunch, peanut crunch and honey roasted peanuts; importer of cashews and peanuts
Chairman: Charles Naylor
Estimated Sales: $750000
Number Employees: 10-19
Sq. footage: 8000
Type of Packaging: Consumer, Private Label, Bulk

9445 **Naylor Wine Cellars**
4069 Vineyard Rd
Stewartstown, PA 17363 717-993-2431
Fax: 717-993-9460 800-292-3370
wine@naylorwine.com www.naylorwine.com
Wines
President: Richard Naylor
Winemaker: Ted Potted
Estimated Sales: $ 2.5-5 Million
Number Employees: 10-19
Type of Packaging: Private Label, Bulk
Brands:
Golden Grenadine
Naylor

9446 **Ne-Mo's Bakery**
416 N Hale Ave
Escondido, CA 92029 760-741-5725
Fax: 760-741-0659 800-325-2692
salesadmin@nemosbakery.com
www.nemosbakery.com
Processor and exporter of baked goods including hand wrapped cake squares, cake slices, cinnamon rolls, cookies, muffins, mini loaf cakes, danish, cake breads, coffee cakes, and specialty cakes
Senior VP: Sam Delucca Jr
Senior VP/Sales & Marketing: Sam DeLucca Jr. Jr
Estimated Sales: $ 10 - 20 Million
Number Employees: 100-249
Sq. footage: 60000
Type of Packaging: Consumer, Food Service, Private Label, Bulk
Brands:
NE-MO'S

9447 **Neal's Chocolates**
2520 Lynwood Drive
Salt Lake City, UT 84109-1607 801-521-6500
Fax: 801-521-6555 neal@news-chocolates.com
www.neals-chocolates.com
Boxed chocolates
President: Neal Maxfield
Estimated Sales: Less than $500,000
Number Employees: 1-4

9448 **Nealanders Food Ingredients**
2425 Alft Lane
Elgin, IL 60124 847-468-0001
Fax: 847-488-0007 bob@foodingredients-il.com
Oilseed manufacturer
President: Robert Leonard
Parent Co: Nealanders International

9449 **Near East Food Products**
515 W Main Street
P.O. Box 049003
Chicago, IL 60604-9003 847-842-4654
Fax: 847-382-0687 erik_bayer@quakeroats.com
www.neareast.com
Rice, couscous side dishes
Marketing Manager: Erik Bayer
Sales Director: Jim Coy
General Sales Manager/Natural: Erik Bayer
Parent Co: Quaker Oats Company
Brands:
Creative Grains
Near East

9450 **Near East Food Products**
797 Lancaster Street
Leominster, MA 01453-4551 978-534-3338
800-822-7423
Thirrty different flavors and varieties of pilafs, couscous and grain dishes including taboule
General Manager: Philip Wiggin
Estimated Sales: Under $500,000
Number Employees: 50-99

9451 **Nebraska Beef**
4501 S 36th St
Omaha, NE 68107 402-734-6823
Fax: 402-733-1624 angelo@nebraskabeef.com
www.nebeef.org
Processor of beef
CFO: Fred Fromi
Partner/VP Finance: Marvin Schrack
COO: Katie Dornhoff
Estimated Sales: $900 Million
Number Employees: 897

9452 **Nebraska Popcorn**
85824 519th Ave
Clearwater, NE 68726 402-887-5335
Fax: 402-887-4709 800-253-6502
popcorn@nebraskapopcorn.com
www.nebraskapopcorn.com
Experienced grower, processor and packager of quality popcorn. The fully integrated operation offers microwave, bulk, private label and poly bags of popcorn to our customers in over 50 countries. Providing premium quality products atcompetitive prices is the goal of Nebraska Popcorn. Product of USA.
President: Frank Morrison
VP: Brett Morrison
Sales: Michelle Steskal
Estimated Sales: $ 10 - 20 Million
Number Employees: 20-49
Number of Brands: 1
Sq. footage: 5000
Type of Packaging: Consumer, Food Service, Private Label, Bulk
Brands:
MORRISON FARMS

9453 **Nebraska Salt & Grain Company**
115 W 16th St
Gothenburg, NE 69138-1302 308-537-7191
Fax: 308-537-7193
Processor and exporter of corn
President: Norman Geiken
Estimated Sales: $ 3 - 5 Million
Number Employees: 20-49
Type of Packaging: Bulk

9454 **Necco**
135 American Legion Highway
Revere, MA 02151 781-485-4500
www.necco.com
Manufacturer of candy including wafers, hard, peanut butter chews, salt water taffy, caramel apple dip, gummies, candy raisins, lollypops, mints, etc.; packaged for racks and theatre vending; also, holiday novelties available
Chairman: Domenic Antonellis
President/CEO: Richard Krause
VP/CFO: Stan Byerly
VP R&D: Jeff Green
Marketing Manager: Lory Zimbalatti
VP Research: Bruno Mastrodicasa
VP Operations: David Smith
Plant Manager: Patricia A Raap
Estimated Sales: $100+ Million
Number Employees: 100-249
Parent Co: New England Confectionery Company
Type of Packaging: Consumer, Bulk
Brands:
CANDY HOUSE
CLARK
HAVILAND
MARY JAME
MIGHTY MALTS
NECCO WAFERS
SKYBAR
SQUIRREL NUT ZIPPERS
SWEETHEARTS

9455 **Nectar Island**
56 5th Ave
St Paul, MN 55128 651-292-9963
Fax: 651-905-1958 sam.hanna@nectarisland.com
www.nectarisland.com
Manufacturer of fruit drinks flavors of which include: pommegranate; pommegranate blueberry; pommegranate raspberry; mango peach; tropical berries; and guava orange.
Owner: Scott Johnson

9456 **Nedlog Company**
92 Messner Dr
Wheeling, IL 60090 847-541-0924
Fax: 847-541-1046 800-323-6201
nedlog@nedlog.com www.nedlog.com
Makes and markets over 60 formulas of standard traditional and more exotic juice-based concentrates such as Strawberry-Apple. Also have an equipment program based on purchase of our juice concentrates, and a provate label program forconcentrates and read
Chairman: Grant Golden
CEO: Grant Golden
President/COO: Glenn Golden
CFO: Marilyn Dougal
Research & Development: Gennady Koyfman
Public Relations: Karyl Golden
Estimated Sales: $ 3 - 5 Million
Number Employees: 7
Type of Packaging: Food Service, Private Label
Brands:
BERRY GOOD
CLASSIC BLENDS
FIESTA
HILINE
NEDLOG 100
TROPICAL BLENDS

9457 **Neenah Springs**
P.O.Box 9
Oxford, WI 53952 608-586-5605
Fax: 608-586-4509 info@neenahsprings.com
www.neenahsprings.com
Bottler of Artesian water
President: Thomas Rogers
VP: John McFarland
Marketing Director: Dan Revoy
Public Relations: Kathy Payter
Operations Manager: Chris Coates
Plant Manager: Barbara Ravenscroft
Purchasing Manager: Wendy Jankowski
Estimated Sales: $4800000
Number Employees: 52
Sq. footage: 20000
Type of Packaging: Consumer, Food Service, Private Label
Brands:
Glacier Ice
Great Glacier
Mountain Mist
Neenah Springs

9458 **Neese Country Sausage**
1452 Alamance Church Rd
Greensboro, NC 27406-9430 336-275-9548
Fax: 336-275-0750 800-632-1010
info@neesesausage.com www.neesesausage.com
Processor and packager of country sausage, liver pudding, c-loaf, souse meat and scraple.
President: Thomas Neese Jr
Plant Manager: Michael Garrett
Estimated Sales: $ 5 - 10 Million
Number Employees: 20-49
Type of Packaging: Consumer, Food Service

9459 **Nehalem Bay Winery**
34965 Highway 53
Nehalem, OR 97131 503-368-5300
Fax: 503-368-5300 888-368-9463
nbwines@hotmail.com
www.nehalembaywinery.com
Processor of wines including niagara grape, rhubarb, apple, wildflower honey, chardonnay, white table, pinot noir and pinot noir blanc
Owner: Ray Schackelford
Estimated Sales: $ 3 - 5 Million
Number Employees: 5-9
Type of Packaging: Consumer

9460 **Neighbors Coffee**
3105 E Reno Ave
Oklahoma City, OK 73117-6615 405-552-2100
Fax: 405-232-3729 800-299-9016
sales@neighborscoffee.com
www.neighborscoffee.com
Manufacturer of coffee; wholesaler/distributor of tea, cocoa and cappuccino;
President: Steve Neighbors
Sales Manager: Phil Huggard
Estimated Sales: $100,000
Number Employees: 50-99
Type of Packaging: Consumer, Food Service, Private Label, Bulk
Brands:
NEIGHBORS

9461 **Neilsen-Massey Vanillas**
1550 S Shields Dr
Waukegan, IL 60085-8307 847-578-1550
Fax: 847-578-1570 800-525-7873
info@nielsenmassey.com
www.nielsenmassey.com
Producer of the fine vanillas worldwide
President: Camilla Neilsen
VP Finance: David Klemann
CEO: Craig Nielsen
Estimated Sales: $ 10-20 Million
Number Employees: 20-49
Brands:
Madagascar Bourbon Pure Vanilla Bea
Madagascar Bourbon Pure Vanilla Pow
Tahitian Pure Vanilla

9462 **Neithart Meats**
12301 Gladstone Ave
Sylmar, CA 91342 818-361-7141
Fax: 818-361-7143
Processor and wholesaler/distributor of meats/provisions; serving the food service market
Owner: Jose Macias
Estimated Sales: $30.70 Million
Number Employees: 10-19
Type of Packaging: Food Service

9463 **Nekta**
17645 Juniper Path
Lakeville, MN 55044-7490 952-898-8020
Fax: 649-573-7988 nektausa@nekta.com
www.nekta.com
All-natural fruit carbohydrate derived from kiwifruit
Director: Adriana Tong
Director: Jonathan Wood

9464 **Nell Baking Company**
114 County Road 254
Kenedy, TX 78119-4267 830-583-3251
Fax: 830-583-9593 800-215-9190
nellbaking@yahoo.com
Biscotti in ten flavors, gourmet cookies and wafers
President: Lasca Arnold
Estimated Sales: $500,000
Number Employees: 10
Brands:
Biscotti Di Lasca
Cookies By Lasca

9465 **Nellson Candies**
5800 Ayala Ave
Irwindale, CA 91706-6215 626-334-4508
Fax: 626-812-6525
Manufacturer and exporter of custom formulated snack, diet/weight loss, sport nutrition and medical food nutrition bars; contract packaging available
President: W Shieff
Estimated Sales: $100+ Million
Number Employees: 250-499
Sq. footage: 100000
Type of Packaging: Consumer, Food Service, Private Label, Bulk

9466 **Nelson Cheese Factory**
S237 State Road 35 South
Nelson, WI 54756 715-673-4725
Fax: 715-673-4151 nelsoncheese@nelson-tel.net
www.nelsoncheese.com
Cheese
President: Edward Greenheck
Estimated Sales: $11,700,000
Number Employees: 10-19
Type of Packaging: Private Label

9467 **Nelson Crab**
P.O.Box 520
Tokeland, WA 98590 360-267-2911
Fax: 360-267-2921 800-262-0069
seatreats@techline.com www.nelsoncrab.com
Processor, importer and exporter of canned, fresh, smoked and frozen seafood including salmon steaks, shad, crabs, crab meat and shrimp
President: Kristi Nelson
Plant Manager: Les Candler
Estimated Sales: $ 10 - 20 Million
Number Employees: 50-99
Type of Packaging: Food Service, Private Label
Brands:
Nelson Seatreats

9468 **Nelson Ricks Creamery**
1755 Fremont Dr
Salt Lake City, UT 84104 801-364-3607
Fax: 801-364-3600 www.banquetcheese.com
Manufacturer of cheese including cheddar, Monterey jack and mozzarella
President: Val Hardcastle
CFO: Reagan Wood
Secretary: Jenille Tyler
Estimated Sales: $14 Million
Number Employees: 42
Sq. footage: 30000
Type of Packaging: Food Service, Private Label, Bulk
Brands:
BANQUET BETTER FOODS
BANQUET BUTTER
BANQUET CHEESE
GOLD NUGGET BUTTER
GOLD NUGGET CHEESE
GRAND TETON
GRAND TETON CHEESE

9469 **Nelson Ricks Creamery Company**
1755 Fremont Dr
Salt Lake City, UT 84104 801-364-3607
Fax: 801-364-3600 www.banquetcheese.com
Manufacturer of natural cheese
President: Val Hardcastle
CFO: Reagan Wood
Estimated Sales: $14 Million
Number Employees: 38
Parent Co: Nelson Ricks Creamery
Type of Packaging: Consumer
Brands:
BANQUET

9470 **Nelson's Ice Cream**
651 Walnut St
Royersford, PA 19468 610-948-3000
Fax: 610-948-3009
Manufacturer of ice cream
Owner: Steve Wisner
Estimated Sales: $300,000-500,000
Number Employees: 10-19
Type of Packaging: Private Label
Brands:
NELSON'S
NELSON'S DUTCH FARMS

9471 **Nemac J. Charles, Jr.**
Hc
Box 160
Grove, ME 04638 207-454-2674
Fax: 207-454-7254
Owner: Charles Nemac, Jr.

9472 **Neptune Fisheries**
802 Jefferson Ave
Newport News, VA 23607 757-245-3231
Fax: 757-893-9227 800-545-7474
www.nepfish.com
Processor and importer of frozen, cooked, peeled and deveined shrimp and scallops; also, lobster tails
President: Robin West
CFO: Richard Costa
National Sales Manager: Aaron Cabral
Sales Director: Sam Weinstein
Plant Manager: Reuben Benkovitz
Number Employees: 5-9
Sq. footage: 60000
Type of Packaging: Consumer, Food Service, Private Label, Bulk
Brands:
Neptune

9473 **Neptune Foods**
4510 S Alameda St
Vernon, CA 90058 323-232-8300
Fax: 323-232-8833 info@neptunefoods.com
www.neptunefoods.com
Processor and exporter of frozen cod, perch, pollack, fish sticks, clams, lobster, oysters, scallops and shrimp; importer of fish, shrimp and scallops
President: Howard Choi
Executive VP: Hector Poon
Estimated Sales: $ 50-100 Million
Number Employees: 100-249
Sq. footage: 150000
Type of Packaging: Consumer, Food Service, Private Label, Bulk
Brands:
CAPTAIN NEPTUNE
MERMAID PRINCESS
NEPTUNE

9474 **Nesbitt Processing**
611 NE 7th Ave
Aledo, IL 61231 309-582-5183
Processor and wholesaler/distributor of beef, pork, lamb, goat and deer; slaughtering services available
President/General Manager: Omar Deeds, Jr.
Secretary/Treasurer: Edith Nesbitt
Number Employees: 1-4
Type of Packaging: Consumer

9475 **Neshaminy Valley Natural Foods**
5 Louise Dr
Warminster, PA 18974-1525 215-745-3773
Fax: 215-725-3775 www.nvorganic.com
Gourmet foods
President: Philip S Margolis
COO/VP: Gene Margolis
VP: Gene Margolis
Estimated Sales: $4.5 Million
Number Employees: 40
Brands:
Neshaminy Valley Natural

9476 **Nest Eggs**
411 W Fullerton Pkwy # 1402w
Chicago, IL 60614-2849 773-525-4952
Fax: 773-525-5226 info@fact.cc
www.fact.com
Gourmet foods
Executive Director: Richard Wood
VP: Robert Brown
Sales Manager: Steve Roach
Estimated Sales: Below $ 5 Million
Number Employees: 5-9

9477 **Nestelles's**
P.O.Box 329
Tangent, OR 97389-0329 50- 2-1 12
Flavoring extracts and food colors
President: Kathi Jenks
Manager: Oebbe Agee
Estimated Sales: Below $ 1 Million
Number Employees: 5 to 10

9478 **Nestle Baking & Prepared Foods**
30003 Bainbridge Road
Solon, OH 44139
www.nestleusa.com

Baked goods and prepared foods
Brands:
Nestle

9479 **Nestle Infant Nutrition**
12 Vreeland Road
Second Floor
Florham Park, NJ 07932
www.nestlenutrition.com
Parent Co: Nestle USA
Type of Packaging: Consumer
Brands:
Nestle

9480 **Nestle Nutrition**
5420 West 23rd Street
Building 1
St. Louis Park, MN 55416
President: Sam Lee
CEO: Brad Alford
VP Technology: Greg Pincar
Parent Co: Nestle USA

9481 **Nestle Pizza**
940 S Whelen Ave
Medford, WI 54451-1745 715-748-5550
Fax: 715-748-7330 www.nestle.com
Frozen pizza
Chairman/CEO Nestle USA: Brad Alford
CEO: Paul Bulcke
EVP/CFO: James Dollive
EVP/Corporate Legal Affairs: Marc Firestone
EVP/Global Technology & Quality: Jean Spence
EVP/Chief Marketing Officer: Jeri Finard
EVP/Global Human Resources: Karen May
Plant Manager: Gary Stanton
Estimated Sales: $500 Million to $1 Billion
Number Employees: 500-999
Type of Packaging: Consumer
Brands:
CALIFORNIA PIZZA KITCHEN
DELISSIO
DIGIORNO
JACK'S
TOMBSTONE

9482 **Nestle Prepared Foods Company**
345 Inverness Dr South
B-200
Englewood, CO 80112-5889 303-790-0303
Fax: 303-790-0214 800-225-2270
www.nestleusa.com
Processor of canned and frozen foods.
President: Anthony Iantosco
General Manager: Lance Mettler
Number of Brands: 3
Parent Co: Nestle USA, Inc.
Type of Packaging: Consumer, Food Service

9483 **Nestle Professional Vitality**
30000 Bainbridge Rd
Solon, OH 44139 440-349-5757
800-288-8682
www.nestleprofessional.com
Fruit juices, coffees, teas, hot chocolate and cappuccinos, sports drinks, cocktail mixes, smoothies, thickened beverages for healthcare, enhanced flavored waters, carbonated soft drinks, sugar-free beverages and more.
VP/General Manager: Perry Miele
Corporate Communications: Jackie Tate
Estimated Sales: $700 Million
Number Employees: 1000
Sq. footage: 90000
Type of Packaging: Food Service, Private Label, Bulk
Brands:
Diamond Grove
Ocean Spray
Pride of B.C.
Sunsational

9484 **(HQ)Nestle USA Inc**
800 N Brand Boulevard
Glendale, CA 91203 818-549-6000
Fax: 818-549-6952 800-225-2270
www.nestleusa.com
Manufacturer of canned pumpkin, sunflower seeds, coffee, tea, nectar, fruit juices, instant breakfast drinks, nondairy creamer, hot cocoa, and chocolate milk mixes, as well as prepared foods.
Chairman/CEO: Brad Alford
SVP/CFO: Dan Stroud
VP/Business Development: Bob Gatto
Corporate Communications: Deborah Cross
Estimated Sales: $10.4 Billion
Number Employees: 25,000
Parent Co: Nestle SA
Type of Packaging: Consumer, Food Service
Brands:
ADDITIONS
AFTER EIGHT BISCUITS & MINTS
ALBERS CORN M GRITS
AQUARI-YUMS
BABY RUTH
BACI
BIT-O-HONEY
BOTTLE CAPS
BUITONI BRAND PASTAS & SAUCES
BUITONI RISOTTO & FOCCACIA MIXES
BUTTERFINGER
CARLOS V
CHEF-MATE
COFFEE-MATE
COFFEE-MATE LATTE
CREATIONS
CROISSANT POCKETS SANDWICHES
CRUCIAL
GLYTROL
GOBSTOPPERS
GOOBERS
GOOD START FORMULAS
HOT POCKETS SANDWICHES
KLIM
LA LECHERA CONDENSED MILK
LAFFY TAFFY
LEAN POCKETS SANDWICHES
LIBBY'S JUICY JUICE
LIBBY'S PUMPKIN
LIK-M-AID FUN DRINKS
MAGGI SEASONINGS
MILO POWDERED DRINK MIX
MINORS
MODULEN IBD
NAN INFANT FORMULA
NERDS
NESCAFE
NESCAFE CAFE CON LECHE
NESCAFE CLASICO
NESCAFE FROT
NESCAFE ICE JAVA
NESQUIK
NESTEA
NESTLE ABUELI CHOCOLATE
NESTLE CARNATION INSTANT
NESTLE CARNATION MALTED MILK
NESTLE CARNATION MILKS
NESTLE CRUNCH
NESTLE DESSERT TOPPINGS
NESTLE EUROPE
NESTLE FOODSERVICES
NESTLE HEALTHCARE NUTRITION
NESTLE HOT COCOA MIX
NESTLE INFANT FORMULAS
NESTLE NIDO 1+, 3+, 6+
NESTLE SIGNA TURTLES
NESTLE SIGNATURES TREASURES
NESTLE TOLL HOUSE CANDY BARS
NESTLE TOLL HOUSE MORSELS
NIPS
NUTREN
NUTRIHEAL
NUTRIHEP
NUTRIRENAL
NUTRIVENT
OH HENRY
OOMPAS
NUTRIVENT
OH HENRY
OOMPAS
ORTEGA
PEPTAMEN
PERUGINA CONFECTIONS

9485 **Neto Sausage Company**
1313 Franklin St
Santa Clara, CA 95050 408-296-0818
Fax: 408-296-0538 888-482-6386
netosausage@msn.com www.netosausage.com
Manufacturer of Portuguese, Italian, Mexican, Spanish and chicken sausages
Owner: Deborah Costa
Estimated Sales: $2.5-5 Million
Number Employees: 10-19
Number of Brands: 3
Number of Products: 32
Sq. footage: 16000
Type of Packaging: Consumer, Food Service, Private Label, Bulk
Brands:
LA GRANADA
NETO
ZORRO

9486 **Network Food Brokers**
355 Lancaster Avenue
Haverford, PA 19041-1547 610-649-7210
Fax: 610-649-0747
Cheese
President: Nate Ostroff
Estimated Sales: $ 2.5-5 Million
Number Employees: 10

9487 **Neuchatel Chocolates**
461 Limestone Rd
Oxford, PA 19363 610-932-2706
Fax: 610-932-9036 800-597-0759
albert@swisschips.com
www.neuchatelchocolates.com
Manufacturer of Chocolate confections
President/Chef: Albert Lauber V
Estimated Sales: $ 1 - 3 Million
Number Employees: 20-49

9488 **Neuman Bakery Specialties**
1405 W Jeffrey Dr
Addison, IL 60101 630-916-8909
Fax: 630-916-8919 800-253-5298
blake1@sbcglobal.net www.neumanbakery.net
wholesale bakery
President: George Neuman
CFO: Dan Neuman
VP: George Neuman
R&D: James Neuman
Plant Manager: Bob Barrera
Estimated Sales: Below $5 Million
Number Employees: 25
Sq. footage: 25000
Brands:
NEUMAN

9489 **Nevada Baking Company**
PO Box 3911
Las Vegas, NV 89127-3911 702-384-8950
Processor of bread and rolls
President: Jim Miller
COO: Robert Mayfield
Sales Manager: Scott Pollock
Number Employees: 100-249
Brands:
Gail's
Roman Meal
Wholesome

9490 **Nevada City Brewing**
75 Bost Avenue
Nevada City, CA 95959-3024 530-265-2446
Fax: 530-265-2576 ncbrew@oro.net
www.beerme.com
Beer
Co-Owner: Andy Sawdon
Co-Owner: Hans Schillinger
Director Manufacturing: Keith Downing
Estimated Sales: Under $500,000
Number Employees: 1-4
Brands:
Broad St. Brown
Fools Gold Ale

9491 **Nevada City Winery**
321 Spring St
Nevada City, CA 95959 530-265-9463
Fax: 530-265-6860 800-203-9463
ncwine@ncwinery.com www.ncwinery.com
Wine
President: Wyn Spiller
CEO: Wyn Spiller
Marketing Director: Rod Byers
Sales Director: Rod Byers
Winemaker: Mark Foster
Estimated Sales: $ 2.5-5 Million
Number Employees: 10-19

Brands:
Nevada City Winery

9492 **Nevada City Winery**
321 Spring St
Nevada City, CA 95959 530-265-9463
Fax: 530-265-6860 800-203-9463
ncwine@ncwinery.com www.ncwinery.com
Wine
President: Wyn Spiller
CEO: Wyn Spiller
Marketing Director: Rod Byers
Sales Director: Rod Byers
Winemaker: Mark Foster
Estimated Sales: $ 2.5-5 Million
Number Employees: 5-9

9493 **Nevada County Wine Guild**
11372 Winter Moon Way
Nevada City, CA 95959 530-265-3662
bonvino@jps.net
www.ourdailyred.com
Processor of wine
Owner: Tony Norskog
Estimated Sales: Less than $500,000
Number Employees: 1-4
Brands:
Our Daily Red

9494 **New Age Canadian Beverage**
2503 Baccarat Drive
Hollywood, FL 33026-3741 954-438-1484
VP: John Stubblefield
Estimated Sales: Under $500,000
Number Employees: 1-4

9495 **New Bakery Company of Ohio**
3005 E Pointe Dr
Zanesville, OH 43701 740-454-6876
Fax: 740-588-5860 800-848-9845
Manufacturer of hamburger buns
Manager: Sam McLaughlin
Plant Manager: Doug Wendeler
Number Employees: 250-499
Sq. footage: 50000
Parent Co: Wendy's International
Type of Packaging: Food Service
Brands:
Sta Fresh
Wendy

9496 **New Belgium Brewing Company**
500 Linden St
Fort Collins, CO 80524 970-221-0524
Fax: 970-221-0535 888-622-4044
nbb@newbelgium.com www.newbelgium.com
Beer
CEO: Kimberly Jordan
CFO: Christine Perish
COO: Jennifer Verrier
CFO: Christine Ernst
Marketing Director: Greg Owsley
Public Relations: Meredith Giske
Operations Manager: J Shirosman
Production Manager: Phil Benstein
Estimated Sales: $ 50 Million
Number Employees: 100-249
Sq. footage: 180000
Brands:
Abbey Belgian Style Ale
Blue Paddle Pilsener
Fat Tire Amber Ale
Old Cherry Ale
Porch Swing Style Al
Sunshine Wheat Beer
Trippel Belgian Styl

9497 **New Braunfels Smokehouse**
P.O.Box 311159
New Braunfels, TX 78131 830-625-9138
Fax: 830-625-7660 800-537-6932
meats@nbsmokehouse.com
www.nbsmokehouse.com
Manufacturer of smoked meats including beef, pork, turkey, ham, chicken and venison; also, jerky
President: Susan Dunbar Snyder
CEO: Dudley Snyder
Vice President: Mike Dietert
Estimated Sales: $5-10 Million
Number Employees: 120
Type of Packaging: Consumer, Food Service, Private Label, Bulk
Brands:
Dunbar Ranch

9498 **New Business Corporation**
444 Rutledge Street
Gary, IN 46404-1011 800-742-8435
j.thomas.1@att.net
www.gourmetsupreme.com
Processor of ketchup and barbecue, seafood and worcestershire sauces
President: John Thomas
Secretary: Naomi Woods
Estimated Sales: Under $500,000
Number Employees: 1-4
Sq. footage: 1800
Brands:
Gourmet Slim #7
Gourmet Slim Cuisine
Gourmet Supreme

9499 **New Canaan Farms**
P.O.Box 386
Dripping Springs, TX 78620 512-858-7669
Fax: 512-858-7513 800-727-5267
www.shopncf.com
Processor of gourmet products including jams, salsa, dips and jellies: lemon fig, plum, peach, raspberry, strawberry, blackberry, etc.; also, mustards including jalapeno, honey and German and sauces including jalapeno shrimp, peachpicante, habanero, etc
President: Cindy Figer
Production Manager: Patti Thurman
Estimated Sales: $1200000
Number Employees: 10-19
Type of Packaging: Private Label

9500 **New Chapter**
90 Technology Drive
Brattleboro, VT 05301
Fax: 888-488-6620 800-543-7279
info@newchapter.com www.newchapter.com
Whole food vitamins, organic herbal supplements, fish oil
Owner/President/CEO: Paul Schulick
President/CEO: Tom Newmark
CFO: Ruth Austin
Quality Assurance Director: Brad Marr
VP Marketing: Brian Hall
VP Sales: Herb Lewis
Estimated Sales: $33.5 Million
Number Employees: 220
Sq. footage: 93406

9501 **(HQ)New City Packing & Provision Company**
P.O.Box 128
North Aurora, IL 60542-0128 630-851-8800
Fax: 630-898-3030 newcty788@aol.com
newcitypacking.com
Manufacturer and exporter of beef, pork and lamb
President/CEO: Marvin Fagel
CEO: Nick Zenneman
Estimated Sales: $50-100 Million
Number Employees: 100-249
Type of Packaging: Consumer

9502 **New City Packing Company**
2600 Church Road
Aurora, IL 60502-8732 630-898-1900
Fax: 630-898-3030 800-621-0397
President/CEO: Marvin Fagel
CEO: Nick Venneman
CEO: Nick Zenneman
Estimated Sales: $ 50 - 100 Million
Number Employees: 100-249

9503 **New England Coffee**
100 Charles St
Malden, MA 02148 800-225-3537
Fax: 781-397-7580 800-225-3537
consumerrelations@necoffeeco.com
www.newenglandcoffee.com
Product line includes a variety of coffee, whole bean and ground, flavored and regular in addition to decaffeinated blends. Also available is tea, both regular and decaffeinated, flavored and non-flavored and a selection of gift itemsand gift baskets.
President/COO: James Kaloyanides
VP/Finance/Treasurer: Jamie Dostou
VP/Product & Business Development: Michael Kaloyanides
VP/Operations & Human Resources: John Kaloyanides
VP/Purchasing: Stephen Kaloyanides Jr

9504 **New England Confectionery Company**
135 American Legion Hwy
Revere, MA 02151-2405 781-485-4500
Fax: 781-485-4509 www.necco.com
Manufacturer and exporter of confectionery products including candy bars, caramels, coconuts, taffy and seasonal items
Chairman: Domenic Antonellis
President/CEO: Richard Krause
CFO: Michael Kelley
Quality Control Director: Adam Gabour
VP Marketing: Jacqueline Hague
VP Sales: Hans Becher
VP Operations: David Smith
Manufacturing Supervisor: Manny D'Acosta
Purchasing Director: John Mancinelli
Estimated Sales: $100+ Million
Number Employees: 85
Sq. footage: 820000
Parent Co: UIS
Type of Packaging: Consumer, Private Label, Bulk
Brands:
CANDY HOUSE CANDY BUTTONS
CLARK
HAVILAND THIN MINTS
MARY JANE
MIGHTY MALTS
NECCO WAFERS
SQUIRREL NUT ZIPPERS
SWEETHEARTS CONVERSATION HEARTS

9505 **New England Confectionery Company**
135 American Legion Hwy
Revere, MA 02151 781-485-4500
Fax: 781-485-4509 contactus@necco.com
www.necco.com
Processor and exporter of candy including sugar wafers, chocolate bars, caramels, boxed chocolates, chocolate cherries, holiday novelties, taffy, gums, jellies, mints, nougats, coated nuts, lozenges, nonpareils, etc
President: Domenic Antonellis
CFO: Andrew Vosnak
CEO: Richard S Krause
VP Operations: William Leva
Estimated Sales: $100 Million
Number Employees: 1,000-4,999
Parent Co: UIS Industries
Type of Packaging: Consumer, Bulk
Other Locations:
New England Confectionery Co.
Cambridge MA
Brands:
Canada
Candy Cupboard
Candy House
Clark
Deran
Goose Eggs
Haviland
Kettle Fresh
Mary Jane
Masterpieces
Mega Mighty Malts
Mighty Malts
Necco
Sky Bar
Stark
Sweet Talk
Sweethearts

9506 **New England Country Bakers**
15 Mountain View Rd
Watertown, CT 06795 860-945-9994
Fax: 860-945-9996 800-225-3779
Processor of pound, no-sugar cheesecake and layer cakes, pies and tea breads including apple crumb, maple, banana, blueberry crumb, cranberry, pumpkin and zucchini nut
President: David Spivak
Director Marketing: Donna Spivak
General Manager: Gary Shields
Production: Andrew Kandefer
Estimated Sales: $2000000
Number Employees: 20-49
Number of Brands: 1
Number of Products: 50
Sq. footage: 24000
Type of Packaging: Food Service

9507 **New England Cranberry Company**
82 Sanderson Ave
Lynn, MA 01902-1974 781-596-0888
Fax: 781-596-0808 800-410-2892
info@newenglandcranberry.com
www.newenglandcranberry.com
Processor and exporter of naturally sweetened dried cranberries, premium suger sweetened dried cranberries, dried wild blueberries, dried cherries, frozen whole cranberries, cranberry jams and jellies, cranberry chutney and pepperjelly, and fine chocolates with sweet cranberries
President: Ted Stux
Sales: Arthur Stock
Estimated Sales: $530000
Number Employees: 10-19
Sq. footage: 1850
Type of Packaging: Consumer, Food Service, Bulk
Brands:
Fresh Pond
New England Cranberry

9508 **New England Marketers**
22 Fish Pier
PO Box 51545
Boston, MA 02210-1545 617-951-9904
Fax: 617-951-9907 800-688-9904
sara@nemarketers.com OR
info@bayshorechowders.com
www.yankeespecialtyfoods.com OR
www.bayshorechowders.com
Processor of gourmet lobster bisque, New England and Manhattan clam chowders, New England fish chowder, lobster, mussels, etc.
President: Paul Lindquist
VP: Adrienne Lindquist
Estimated Sales: $780000
Number Employees: 4
Type of Packaging: Consumer, Food Service, Bulk
Brands:
BAY SHORE

9509 **New England Muffin Company**
337 Pleasant St
Fall River, MA 02721 508-675-2833
Fax: 508-675-2833
Processor of fresh and frozen Portuguese muffins in various flavors
Owner: Jose Martin
Estimated Sales: $980000
Number Employees: 5-9
Type of Packaging: Food Service, Bulk

9510 **New England Natural Baker**
74 Fairview St E
Greenfield, MA 1301 413-772-2239
Fax: 413-772-2936 800-910-2884
teinig@nenb.com www.nenb.com
Processor, importer and exporter of breakfast cereals, granolas, muesli, tamari, chocolates and fruit, nut, snack and cracker mixes, and bars; also, private label available
President: John Broucek
Quality Control: Dale Parda
Marketing/Sales: Todd Einig
Operations Manager: Mike Hassay
Purchasing Director: Eric Hassay
Number Employees: 20-49
Number of Brands: 1
Number of Products: 50
Sq. footage: 30000
Type of Packaging: Consumer, Food Service, Private Label, Bulk
Brands:
New England Naturals

9511 **New Era Canning Company**
4856 1st St
New Era, MI 49446 231-861-2151
Fax: 231-861-4068 www.neweracanning.com
Processor and exporter of canned fruits and vegetables including beans, asparagus and apples; also, canned apple sauce
President/CEO: Rick Ray
CFO: Rick McClouth
Sales: Patrick Alger
Human Resources Manager: Bob Markiewicc
Production: Jim Merrill
Purchasing: Ron Fekken
Estimated Sales: $33 Million
Number Employees: 250
Number of Brands: 3
Number of Products: 65
Sq. footage: 200000
Type of Packaging: Consumer, Food Service, Private Label
Brands:
Good Taste
Necco
New Era

9512 **New Generation Foods**
5934 S 25th Street
Omaha, NE 68107-4443 402-733-5755
Fax: 402-733-5755 danehodge@hotmail.com
Processor of portion control and breaded foods including beef, chicken, pork and turkey
CFO: Steve McCurdy
National Sales Manager: Dane Hodges
Plant Manager: John Schull
Number Employees: 15

9513 **New Glarus Bakery**
534 1st St
PO Box 595
New Glarus, WI 53574 608-527-2916
Fax: 608-527-5799 www.newglarusbakery.com
Cookies, breads, pastries, donuts and desserts.
Co-Owner: Howard Weber
Co-Owner: Nancy Weber
Estimated Sales: $500,000-$1 Million
Number Employees: 10-19
Brands:
New Glarus Bakery

9514 **New Glarus Brewing**
P.O.Box 759
New Glarus, WI 53574 608-527-5850
Fax: 608-527-5855 www.newglarusbrewing.com
Beer
President: Deborah Carey
VP: Deborah Carry
Estimated Sales: Below $ 5 Million
Number Employees: 20-49

9515 **New Glarus Foods**
P.O.Box 549
New Glarus, WI 53574-0549 608-527-2131
Fax: 608-527-2931 800-356-6685
www.nweglarusfoods.com
Processor and exporter of smoked sausage, meat and meat snacks; gourmet gift packs available
President: Rich Nagy
Chairman/CEO: G Woodrow Adkinsld
Executive VP: Michael McDonald
Sales Director: Mike McDonald
Plant Manager: Richard Nagy
Purchasing Manager: G Dombkowski
Estimated Sales: $ 50 - 100 Million
Number Employees: 100-249
Sq. footage: 75000
Type of Packaging: Consumer, Private Label, Bulk
Brands:
Gourmet Preferred
Strickler's
Sugar River

9516 **New Grass Bison**
PO Box 860033
Shawnee, KS 66286 866-422-5888
sales@newgrassbison.com
www.newgrassbison.com
natural and grassfed bison products

9517 **New Harbor Fisherman's Cooperative**
P.O.Box 125
New Harbor, ME 04554-0125 207-677-2791
Fax: 207-677-3835 866-883-2922
lobsta@newharborlobster.com
www.newharborlobster.com
Manufacturer of lobster, crab and other seafood
Manager: Linda Vannah
Operations Manager: Ken Tonneson
Estimated Sales: $ .5 - 1 million
Number Employees: 1-4
Type of Packaging: Consumer, Bulk

9518 **New Harmony Coffee Roasters**
232 Vine St
Philadelphia, PA 19106 215-925-6770
Fax: 215-925-0821
Coffee
Partner: Sharon Burkard
Estimated Sales: Under $500,000
Number Employees: 1-4
Brands:
New Harmony

9519 **New Harvest Foods**
323 3rd Ave
Pulaski, WI 54162 920-822-2578
Processor of canned vegetables including peas, green beans, sweet corn, carrots, potatoes, sauerkraut and mixed vegetables
President: Timothy Grygield
Production Manager: Tom Wojcik
Plant Manager: Robert Tetzlaff
Estimated Sales: $ 5 - 10 Million
Number Employees: 20-49
Sq. footage: 70000

9520 **New Holland Brewing**
66 E 8th Street
Holland, MI 49423 616-355-6422
www.newhollandbrew.com
beer
Owner/President: Brett Derkamp
Co-Owner/Head Brewer: John Haggerty
CFO/Co-Owner: Dave White
Owner/Partner: Jason Spaulding
Sales/Marketing Director: Fred Bueltmann
Estimated Sales: $3.3 Million
Number Employees: 35
Sq. footage: 9743

9521 **New Hope Mills**
181 York St
Auburn, NY 13021-9009 315-252-2676
Fax: 315-282-0720 store@newhopemills.com
www.newhopemills.com
Processor of mixes including pancake, bread and cookie; also, milled flour including buckwheat, wheat and pancake
President/CEO: Dale Weed
Estimated Sales: $1.3 Million
Number Employees: 35
Number of Products: 20
Sq. footage: 30000
Type of Packaging: Consumer, Food Service, Private Label, Bulk

9522 **New Hope Winery**
6123 Lower York Rd
New Hope, PA 18938 215-794-2331
Fax: 215-794-2341 800-592-9463
info@newhopewinery.com
www.newhopewinery.com
Red wine
Owner: Sandra Pizza
Estimated Sales: $710,000
Number Employees: 5-9
Number of Products: 25

9523 **New Horizon Foods**
33440 Western Ave
Union City, CA 94587 510-489-8600
Fax: 510-489-9797 www.tovaindustries.com
Manufacturer of dough conditioners, bread bases, natural mixes, beverage, cake, muffin, pudding, meat spices, spice blends, snack and chip seasonings, custard, ice cream, waffle cone and sauce mixes and bases; exporter of doughconditioners and cake and muffin mixes; contract packaging services available
President: Zach Melzer
Number Employees: 10-19
Parent Co: Tova Industries
Type of Packaging: Consumer, Food Service, Private Label, Bulk

9524 **New Horizons Baking Company**
700 W Water St
Fremont, IN 46737 260-495-7055
Fax: 219-495-2307 www.newhorizonsbaking.com
Processor of buns and English muffins
President: Tilmon Brown
VP/Director Operations: John Widman
Plant Manager: Joe Gross
Purchasing Manager: Tilmon Brown
Estimated Sales: $ 3 - 5 Million
Number Employees: 50-99
Sq. footage: 40000
Type of Packaging: Food Service, Private Label, Bulk
Other Locations:
New Horizons Baking Company
Norwalk OH

9525 **New Jamaican Gold**
3536 Arden Rd
Hayward, CA 94545 510-887-4653
Fax: 510-887-7466 800-672-9956
info@jamaican-gold.com
www.jamaican-gold.com
Ready-to-drink coffee/ice cappuccino
CEO: Kenneth Yeung
Sales Director: Kimi Tom
Estimated Sales: $1+ Million
Number Employees: 10-19
Brands:
Jamaican Gold

9526 **New Land Vineyard**
577 Lerch Rd
Geneva, NY 14456-9238 315-585-4432
Fax: 315-585-9844
Wines
Owner: Dale Nagy
Estimated Sales: Less than $500,000
Number Employees: 1-4

9527 **New Meadows Lobster**
60 Portland Pier
Portland, ME 04101-4713 207-774-6562
Fax: 207-874-2456 800-668-1612
lobsters@newmeadowslobster.com
www.newmeadowslobster.com
Lobster
Owner: Peter L Mc Aleney
Estimated Sales: $ 5 - 10 Million
Number Employees: 10-19

9528 **New Meridian**
P.O.Box 155
Eaton, IN 47338-0155 765-396-3344
Fax: 765-396-3430 www.edenfoods.com
Processor and canner of dry beans; specializing in private labeling
Manager: David Morrow
VP/General Manager: David Brand
Estimated Sales: $ 20 - 50 Million
Number Employees: 20-49
Sq. footage: 45000
Parent Co: Eden Foods
Type of Packaging: Private Label

9529 **New Mexico Food Distributors**
3041 University Blvd SE
Albuquerque, NM 87106-5040 505-888-0199
Fax: 505-889-3144 800-637-7084
www.foodsofnewmexico.com
Processor and wholesaler/distributor of Mexican food products including enchiladas, corn and flour tortillas, green chili, roasted and red chili powders, etc.; serving the food service market
Plant Manager: Mike Campos
Estimated Sales: $12 Million
Number Employees: 85
Type of Packaging: Consumer, Food Service

9530 **New Ocean**
3077 McCall Dr Ste 12
Atlanta, GA 30340 770-458-5235
Fax: 770-485-5235
Seafood, shrimp, scallops, king crab, lobster tails, snow crab
President: Mei Lin
Estimated Sales: $7,000,000
Number Employees: 5-9

9531 **New Orleans Fish House**
921 S Dupre St
New Orleans, LA 70125 504-821-9700
Fax: 504-821-9011 800-839-3474
www.nofh.com
Processor of fresh and frozen catfish, tilapia, crawfish, softshell crabs, tuna, shark, red snapper, pompano, wahoo, drum, escalor and sheephead
Owner: Craig Borges
VP Sales: Cliff Hall
Estimated Sales: $ 20-50 Million
Number Employees: 20-49
Type of Packaging: Consumer, Food Service, Private Label, Bulk

9532 **New Orleans Gulf Seafood**
509 Commerce Pt
New Orleans, LA 70123-3203 504-733-1516
Fax: 504-733-1517
Seafood
President: Albert Lin

9533 **New Packing Company**
1249 W Lake St
Chicago, IL 60607 312-666-1314
Fax: 312-666-8698
Processor of sausage
President: Kurt Kreuger
Estimated Sales: $1800000
Number Employees: 10-19
Type of Packaging: Consumer

9534 **New Salem Tea-Bread Company**
837 Daniel Shays Hwy
New Salem, MA 01355 978-544-0294
Fax: 978-544-5643 800-897-5910
info@teabread.com www.teabread.com
Manufacturer of all natural, kosher teabreads. Flavors: lemon, banana orange cranberry, blueberry vanilla, pumpkin, carrot raisin, almond, apple cinnamon
Co-Owner: Steve Verney
Co-Owner: Kay Verney

9535 **New Season Foods**
2329 Yew St Ste A1
Forest Grove, OR 97116 503-357-7124
Fax: 503-357-0419
mailto:%20info@newseasonfoods.com
www.newseasonfoods.com
Manufacturer of drum-dried vegetable powders and other custom ingredients
President: Bruce McVean
Office Manager: Cindy Losli
Facilities Manager: Randy Egger
Estimated Sales: $5-10 Million
Number Employees: 20-49
Sq. footage: 150000
Type of Packaging: Bulk
Brands:
FLAVORLAND
NEW SEASON FOODS

9536 **New World Pasta**
85 Shannon Rd
Harrisburg, PA 17112 717-526-2200
Fax: 717-526-2468 mikehoar@nwpasta.com
www.newworldpasta.com
Processor of pasta
CEO: Peter Smith
CFO: Gregory Richardson
EVP: Cary Metz
Number Employees: 150
Sq. footage: 300000
Parent Co: New World Pasta
Type of Packaging: Bulk

9537 **(HQ)New World Pasta Company7**
P.O.Box 126457
Harrisburg, PA 17112-6457 717-526-2200
Fax: 717-526-2468 800-730-5957
nwpasta@casupport.com
www.newworldpasta.com
Pasta and pasta products.
CEO: Scott Greenwood
Quality Control: Dan Carlin
CEO: Peter Smith
CFO: Gregory Richardson
Chif Financial Officer: Ed Lyons
Sales Director: Alan Geoffrey
Manager Public Information: Natalie Bailey
Estimated Sales: $ 20-50 Million
Number Employees: 1,000-4,999
Brands:
American Beauty
Cremette
Ideal
Light 'n Fluffy Nood
Prince
Ronzoni
San Giorgio
Skinner

9538 **New York Apples Sales**
1580 Columbia Tpke # 5
Castletn on Hdsn, NY 12033-9531 518-477-7200
Fax: 518-477-6770
mike@newyorkapplesales.com
www.newyorkapplesales.com
Manufacturer of apples and pears
President: Kaari Stannard
Estimated Sales: $29 Million
Number Employees: 20-49
Type of Packaging: Consumer, Food Service, Bulk

9539 **New York Bakeries**
261 W 22nd St
Hialeah, FL 33010-1521 305-882-1355
Fax: 305-883-0790
Manufacturer exporter of bread, rolls and cakes
President: Sarah Zimmerman
Estimated Sales: $35 Million
Number Employees: 50-99
Parent Co: New York Bakeries
Type of Packaging: Consumer, Food Service, Private Label

9540 **New York Bakery & Bagelry**
1750 Limetree Lane
Saint Louis, MO 63146-4723 314-731-0080
Fax: 314-731-2467
Bagels and baked goods

9541 **New York Bottling Company**
626 Whittier St
Bronx, NY 10474 718-378-2525
Fax: 718-782-6348
Bottled soft drinks
Contact: Zvi Hold
Estimated Sales: $ 5-10 Million
Number Employees: 10-19
Brands:
La Pri Cranberry Apple Drink
La Pri Grapefruit Dr
La Pri Orange Drink

9542 **(HQ)New York Coffee & Bagels**
109 E 42nd Street
New York, NY 10017-8500 212-986-6116
Fax: 212-986-0057
Coffee
President/CEO: Jason Genussa
Plant Manager: B Hanley
Estimated Sales: $ 10-100 Million
Number Employees: 20

9543 **New York Fish House**
32-34 Papetti Plz
Elizabeth, NJ 7206 908-351-0045
Fax: 908-351-0021 yashiro@trueworldfoods.com
www.ny-fish.com
Seafood
COO: Jack Sato
CEO: Takeshi Yashiro
CFO: Jack Jewell
Production Manager: Tony Scazzero
Estimated Sales: $ 20-50 Million
Number Employees: 100-249
Brands:
New York Fish House

9544 **New York Frozen Foods**
25900 Fargo Ave
Cleveland, OH 44146 216-292-5655
Fax: 216-292-5978
Processor of bread and rolls
Executive Director: Mike Mahon
Number Employees: 250-499
Parent Co: T. Marzetti Company
Type of Packaging: Consumer, Food Service

9545 **New York International Bread Company**
1500 W Church St
Orlando, FL 32805 407-843-9744
Fax: 407-648-2785
Bread and baked products
CEO: Laura Masella
Estimated Sales: $ 5-10 Million
Number Employees: 100-249

9546 **New York Pizza**
725 E Internatl Speedway Blvd
Daytona Beach, FL 32118-4555 386-257-2050
www.nypizza.ru
Pizza
Owner: Richard Squillante
Estimated Sales: Less than $500,000
Number Employees: 1-4
Brands:
New York Pizza

9547 **New York Pretzel Makkos of Brooklyn Ltd**
200 Moore St
Brooklyn, NY 11206-3708 718-366-9800
Fax: 718-821-4544 richard@nypretzel.com
www.nypretzel.com

Processor of soft pretzels
President: Themis Makkos
VP: Richard Berger
Estimated Sales: $9.7 Million
Number Employees: 75
Brands:
New York Pretzel

9548 **New York Ravioli & Pasta Company**
12 Denton Ave S
New Hyde Park, NY 11040 516-741-7287
Fax: 516-741-5289 888-588-7287
ravkings@nyravioli.com www.nyravioli.com
Manufacturer of Ravioli and other products
President/Co-Founder: David Creo
VP/Co-Founder: Paul Moncada
Estimated Sales: $ 3 - 5 Million
Number Employees: 10-19
Type of Packaging: Food Service, Private Label, Bulk

9549 **(HQ)New Zealand Lamb Company**
20 Westport Rd # 320
Wilton, CT 06897-4550 203-529-9100
Fax: 203-529-9101 800-438-5262
shnae@nzlamb.com www.nzlamb.com
Manufacturer of Lamb and lamb products, venison, beef, veal
President: Shane O'Hara
VP Sales/Marketing: Peter Gilligan
Estimated Sales: $10-20 Million
Number Employees: 10-19
Other Locations:
New Zealand Lamb Company
Etobicoke, Ontario,Canada

9550 **Newburg Corners Cheese Factory**
Highway 33
Route 2
Bangor, WI 54614 608-452-3636
Fax: 608-452-3636
Cheese
Owner: Lowell Kitzmann
Owner: Mike Everhart
Number Employees: 1-4

9551 **Newburgh Egg Corporation**
1255 E 31st Street
Brooklyn, NY 11210-4740 718-692-4392
Fax: 718-677-5909 mbendet@aol.com
Processor of whole eggs, yolks, whipping whites, texture blends and hard-cooked peeled eggs
President/CEO: Mayer Bendit
Number Employees: 10-19

9552 **Newburgh Egg Processing**
P.O.Box 175
Woodridge, NY 12789-0175 845-434-8115
Fax: 845-434-8216 888-434-8115
newburghegg@cheskill.net
Manufacturer of Eggs
President: Moses Goldstein
VP: Moses Neustadt
Estimated Sales: 34-40 Million
Number Employees: 20-49

9553 **Newell Lobsters**
72 Water St
Yarmouth, NS B5A 4B1
Canada 902-742-6272
Fax: 902-742-1542
Processor and exporter of fresh herring roe and lobster
President: Robert Newell
Estimated Sales: $7.4 Million
Number Employees: 15
Type of Packaging: Consumer, Food Service, Private Label

9554 **Newfound Resources**
90 O'Leary Ave
Suite 203
St Josephs, NL A1B 2C7
Canada 709-579-7676
Fax: 709-579-7668 shrimp@nfld.com
Processor and exporter of frozen shrimp
President: Brian McNamara
Estimated Sales: $6.6 Million
Number Employees: 60
Type of Packaging: Bulk

9555 **Newly Weds Foods**
2501 North Keeler
Chicago, IL 60639 662-393-3610
Fax: 662-280-5208 800-647-9314
scariker@flavorite.com www.flavorite.com
Manufacturer and exporter of coffee, flavors, spice blends, barbecue sauce, seasonings, teas and dry drink mixes
President: Charles Angell
R&D Manager: Emmett Cook
Estimated Sales: $100 Million
Number Employees: 99
Parent Co: Newly Weds Foods
Type of Packaging: Consumer, Food Service, Private Label, Bulk

9556 **(HQ)Newly Weds Foods**
2501 N Keeler Ave
Chicago, IL 60639 773-489-7000
Fax: 773-489-2799 800-621-7521
nwfnorthamerica@newlywedsfoods.com
www.newlywedsfoods.com
Processor and exporter of breadings, batters, seasoning blends, marinades, glazes and capsicum products
President: Charles Angell
CFO: Dan Lechin
Vice President: Bruce Lesinski
R&D: Lynn Theiss
Quality Control: Dave Rey
Sales Director: Jim Chin
Operations Manager: Mike Hopp
Production Manager: Tom Stoll
Plant Manager: Tom Stoll
Purchasing Manager: T Lisack
Number Employees: 1,000-4,999
Other Locations:
Newly Weds Foods
Baldwin Park CA
Brands:
Batter Blends
Blended Breaders
Newly Weds

9557 **Newly Weds Foods**
70 Grove Street
80
Watertown, MA 02472-2829 617-926-7600
Fax: 617-926-8547 800-621-7521
resumes@newlywedsfoods.com
www.newlywedsfoods.com
Processor of bread crumbs
President: Charles T Angell
General Manager: John Lincoln
Production Manager: Harry Talbot
Estimated Sales: $ 10 - 20 Million
Number Employees: 50-99
Type of Packaging: Bulk

9558 **Newly Weds Foods**
3306 Central Parkway SW
Decatur, AL 35603-1616 256-350-0602
800-521-6189
Processor of batters, breadings, seasoning blends and marinades
Number Employees: 20-49
Type of Packaging: Bulk

9559 **(HQ)Newman's Own**
246 Post Rd E
Suite 308
Westport, CT 06880 203-222-0136
Fax: 203-227-5630 www.newmansown.com
Processor and exporter of natural salad dressings, pasta sauces, popcorn, lemonade and salsa
President/COO: Thomas Indoe
VP Marketing: Michael Havard
Sales Director: Linda Rohr
VP Operations: Bill Lee
Director Purchasing/Systems: Bill Lee
Estimated Sales: $ 50 - 100 Million
Number Employees: 10-19
Type of Packaging: Consumer, Food Service
Other Locations:
Newman's Own
Aptos CA
Brands:
Newman's Own
Newman's Own Lemonade
Newman's Own Pasta Sauces
Newman's Own Popcorn
Newman's Own Salad Dressing
Newman's Own Salsa

9560 **Newmarket Foods**
2210 Pine View Way
Petaluma, CA 94954-5687 707-778-3400
Fax: 707-778-3434 info@newmarketfoods.com
www.newmarketfoods.com
VP Sales/Marketing: Tom Mierzwinski
Vice President: Thomas Mierzwinski
Estimated Sales: $ 1-2.5 Million
Number Employees: 1
Type of Packaging: Private Label
Brands:
Butterscotch Bliss
Chocolate Ecstasy
Hot Fudge Fantasy

9561 **Newport Flavours & Fragrances**
833 N Elm St
Orange, CA 92867 714-744-3700
Fax: 714-771-3588 www.newportflavours.com
Processor of flavor extracts, concentrates, fillings, icings, glazes, syrups, toppings, oils and fragrances; also, contract packaging available
President: Bill Sabo
VP: Jeanne Aragon
Estimated Sales: $3.6 Million
Number Employees: 30
Sq. footage: 8800
Type of Packaging: Consumer, Food Service, Private Label, Bulk

9562 **Newport Vineyards & Winery**
909 E Main Rd
Middletown, RI 02842-5370 401-848-5161
Fax: 401-848-5162 info@newportvineyards.com
www.newportvineyards.com
Wine
Co-Owner: John Nunes
Co-Owner/Vineyard Manager: Paul Nunes
General Manager: John Nunes
Production Manager: George Chelf
Estimated Sales: $ 2.5-5 Million
Number Employees: 10-19
Type of Packaging: Private Label
Brands:
Newport

9563 **Newton Candy Company**
4912 Airline Dr # G
Houston, TX 77022-3078 713-691-6969
Fax: 713-691-6979
Candy
Manager: Muhammed Nazim
Estimated Sales: $ 2.5-5 Million
Number Employees: 10-19

9564 **Newton Vineyard**
1 California Dr
Yountville, CA 94599 707-963-9000
Fax: 707-963-5408 winery@newtonvineyard.com
www.newtonvineyard.com
Wines
President: Dr Su Hua Newton
Sr. EVP: Paolo Mancini
Controller: Tim Lin
Winemaker: Stephen Carrier
Estimated Sales: $20-50 Million
Number Employees: 100-249
Type of Packaging: Private Label
Brands:
Newton Vineyard

9565 **Newtown Foods**
601 Corporate Dr W
Langhorne, PA 19047-8013 215-579-2120
Fax: 215-579-2129 info@newtownfoods.com
www.newtownfoods.com
Cocoa ingredients, dehydrated fruit, natural extracts, banana puree, spray-dried ingredients
Owner: John Mc Donald
Estimated Sales: Below $ 5 Million
Number Employees: 1-4
Brands:
Duas Rodas Industrial
Dutch Cocoa BV
Kievit
Schoemaker

9566 **Niagara Chocolates**
3500 Genesee St
Cheektowaga, NY 14225-5015 716-634-4545
Fax: 716-634-4855 800-234-5750
info@niagarachocolates.com
www.niagarachocolates.com

Processor of chocolate novelties including bars, truffles and boxed
President: Phil Terranova
Estimated Sales: $ 10-100 Million
Number Employees: 100-249
Type of Packaging: Consumer
Brands:
Mercken's
Mercken's Chocolate
Sweet Works

9567 **Niagara Foods**
10 Kelly Ave
Middleport, NY 14105-1210 716-735-7722
Fax: 716-735-9076 www.agvest.com
Processor, importer and exporter of frozen vegetable products and fruit and vegetable powders and flakes; also, frozen and dehydrated fruits including apples, cherries, strawberries, cranberries and wild and cultivated blueberries.
President: Barry Schneider
General Manager: Bob Neuman
Estimated Sales: $14900000
Number Employees: 50-99
Sq. footage: 70000
Parent Co: Agvest
Type of Packaging: Consumer, Food Service, Private Label, Bulk
Brands:
Agvest
Quality

9568 **Niagara Milk Cooperative**
8450 Buffalo Ave
Niagara Falls, NY 14304-4323 716-692-6543
Fax: 716-283-9782
Milk Producers
President: James Schotz
Estimated Sales: $500,000
Number Employees: 4

9569 **Nicasio Vineyards**
14300 Nicasio Way
Soquel, CA 95073 831-423-1073
Wine
President: Dan Wheeler

9570 **(HQ)Niche Import Company**
45 Horsehill Rd Ste 105a
Cedar Knolls, NJ 7927 973-993-8450
Fax: 973-898-0183 800-548-6882
niche@ourniche.com www.ourniche.com
Gourmet foods and beverages
President: Peter Nelson
Media Relations: Barbara Miele
Estimated Sales: $ 2.5-5 Million
Number Employees: 5-9
Type of Packaging: Private Label
Brands:
Asbach Uralt
Stroh
Underberg Bitters

9571 **Nichelini Winery**
2950 Sage Canyon Rd
Saint Helena, CA 94574 707-963-0717
Fax: 707-963-3262
nichwine@nicheliniwinery.com
www.nicheliniwinery.com
Wines
Manager: Toni Irwin
Treasurer: Richard Wainright
Wine Maker: Greg Boeger
Estimated Sales: Below $ 5 Million
Number Employees: 1-4
Type of Packaging: Private Label

9572 **Nichem Company**
619 Ramsey Ave
Hillside, NJ 07205-1009 908-933-0770
Fax: 973-399-8818 sales@nichem.com
www.nichem.com
Processor and importer of ingredients including citric acid, vanillin and sodium citrate; exporter of citric acid
President: Peigeng Lu
Estimated Sales: $700,000
Number Employees: 1-4
Sq. footage: 20000
Type of Packaging: Consumer, Food Service

9573 **Nichols Pistachio**
13762 1st Ave
Hanford, CA 93230 559-584-6811
Fax: 559-688-1603 chuck@nicholsfarms.com.
www.victoriaisland.net
Pistachio nuts
President: Charles Nichols
Marketing Director: Brandon Leslie
Estimated Sales: $ 20 - 50 Million
Number Employees: 100-249
Brands:
Almond Grades
Nichol's Pistachio

9574 **Nick Sciabica & Sons**
2150 Yosemite Blvd
Modesto, CA 95354 209-577-5067
Fax: 209-524-5367 800-551-9612
sales@sciabica.com www.sciabica.com
Processor of extra virgin olive oil; importer of olive oil, pasta and tomato products; wholesaler/distributor of wine vinegar, olive oil, canned tomatoes, olives and pasta
Partner: Jonathan Sciabica
Controller: Susan Ochoa
VP: Gemma Sciabica
Marketing Manager: Dean Cohan
Production Manager: Daniel Sciabica
Estimated Sales: $2.5 Million
Number Employees: 20
Number of Brands: 6
Number of Products: 150
Sq. footage: 68728
Parent Co: Nick Sciabica & Sons
Type of Packaging: Consumer, Food Service, Private Label, Bulk
Brands:
Marsala
Sciabica's Oil of the Olive

9575 **Nickabood's Company**
1401 Elwood St
Los Angeles, CA 90021 213-746-1541
Fax: 213-746-1542
Manufacturer of health food products including sauces, honey, salad dressings, condiments seafood sauces, baked potato products, miso mayo, and frozen stuffed potatoes
President: Nick Abood
Estimated Sales: $500,000
Number Employees: 5-9
Number of Brands: 4
Number of Products: 15
Sq. footage: 15000
Parent Co: Fisherman Wharf Foods
Type of Packaging: Consumer, Food Service, Private Label, Bulk
Brands:
DESERT GOLD
FISHERMAN'S WHARF
SO GOOD
SPUD KING

9576 **Nickles Bakery of Indiana**
600 14 Harrison St
Elkhart, IN 46516 574-293-0608
Fax: 574-293-0296
Processor of breads including lite 35, midwest grains, bread, buns, rolls, bagels, muffins, breadsticks, snack cakes, pasteries, donuts
Vice President: Michael Arciello
Manager: Bill Carter
Estimated Sales: $18300000
Number Employees: 20-49
Parent Co: Alfred Nickles Bakery
Type of Packaging: Consumer, Food Service, Private Label

9577 **Nickles Bakery of Ohio**
590 N Hague Ave
Columbus, OH 43204-1419 614-276-5477
Fax: 614-276-4699 800-335-9775
www.nicklesbakery.com
Processor of breads and cakes
President: Joe Blake
General Manager: Mark Sponsella
Estimated Sales: $ 50 - 100 Million
Number Employees: 50-99
Parent Co: Nickles Bakery
Type of Packaging: Consumer, Food Service

9578 **Nickles Bakery of Ohio**
1121 Latham Ave
Lima, OH 45805-2005 419-224-7080
Fax: 419-228-7357 www.nicklesbakery.com
Processor of sandwich buns and bread
Manager: John Nixon
Estimated Sales: $ 3 - 5 Million
Number Employees: 50-99
Type of Packaging: Consumer, Food Service, Private Label
Other Locations:
Alfred Nickles Bakery
Fairmont WV
Alfred Nickles Bakery
Parkersburg WV
Alfred Nickles Bakery
Portage MI
Alfred Nickles Bakery
Elkhart IN
Alfred Nickles Bakery
Kokomo IN
Alfred Nickles Bakery
Plymouth IN
Alfred Nickles Bakery
Fort Wayne IN
Alfred Nickles Bakery
Rochester IN
Alfred Nickles Bakery
Indianapolis IN
Alfred Nickles Bakery
Valpariso IN
Alfred Nickles Bakery
DuBois PA
Alfred Nickles Bakery
Ebensberg PA
Alfred Nickles Bakery
Verona PA

9579 **Nickles Bakery of Ohio**
1000 Broadway St
Martins Ferry, OH 43935-1972 740-633-1711
Fax: 740-633-6852 www.nicklesbakery.com
Processor of baked goods including bread and buns
CFO: Bill Eisenhower
Plant Manager: Scott Ketter
Estimated Sales: $9,900,000
Number Employees: 100-249
Parent Co: Alfred Nickles Bakery
Type of Packaging: Consumer, Food Service, Private Label

9580 **(HQ)Nickles Bakery of Ohio**
26 Main Street
Navarre, OH 44662 330-879-5635
Fax: 330-879-5896 800-362-9775
customerservice@nicklesbakery.com
www.nicklesbakery.com
Vendors of bakery products
Vice Prresident: Mark Sponseller
Executive Officer: Ronald Dougherty
Executive VP: David Gardner
Quality Control: Maryt Brideweser
VP Marketing Director: Philip Gardner
Plant Manager: Wes Webber
Purchase Manager: J Kettlewell
Estimated Sales: $100-250 Million
Number Employees: 1k-10k
Brands:
Nickles Bakery

9581 **Nicky**
223 SE 3rd Ave
Portland, OR 97214-1006 503-234-4263
Fax: 503-234-8268 800-469-4162
info@nickyusa.com www.nickyusa.com
Distributor of natural game birds and meats including pheasant, poussin, quail, venison, buffalo, rabbit, ostrich, alligator, ducks and wild boar; also, sausage, veal, free range lamb and much more
President: Geoff Latham
VP: Melody Latham
Sales: Brenda Crow
Estimated Sales: Below $ 5 Million
Number Employees: 10-19
Sq. footage: 5000
Type of Packaging: Consumer, Food Service, Private Label, Bulk
Brands:
Cervera
Country Game
Nicky Usa

9582 **Nicola International**
4561 Colorado Blvd.
Los Angeles, CA 90039-0758 818-545-1515
Fax: 818-247-8585 nicolain@pacbell.net
www.nicolainternational.com
Finest olives, olives oils and grapes leaves. We specialized in processing tree ripened olives for deli departments, bakery, the pizza industry, salad manufacturers, custom marination and creative gourmet dishes
President: Nicola Khachatoorian
VP: Alice Toomanian
Purchasing Manager: Claudine Reyes
Estimated Sales: $ 1-10 Million
Number Employees: 0-25
Type of Packaging: Food Service, Private Label
Brands:
Aiello

9583 **Nicola Pizza**
8 N 1st St
Rehoboth Beach, DE 19971 302-226-2654
Fax: 302-226-3721 www.nicolapizza.com
Processor of spaghetti sauce
President: Nicholas S Caggiano
VP: Nicolas Caggiano III
CFO: Jaon Caggiano
Estimated Sales: Below $ 5 Million
Number Employees: 20-49
Type of Packaging: Consumer, Food Service
Brands:
Mama Nichola's Sago
Nic-O-Boli

9584 **Nicola Valley Apiaries**
PO Box 1995
Merritt, BC V1K 1B8
Canada 250-378-5208
apaulson@nicolavalley.com
www.nicolavalleyhoney.com
Processor and packer of liquid, creamed, chunk and comb honey; also, beeswax
Partner: Alan Paulson
Partner: Margaret Paulson
Estimated Sales: $203,000
Number Employees: 2

9585 **Nicole's Divine Crackers**
1505 N Kingsbury St
Chicago, IL 60642-2533 312-640-8883
Fax: 312-640-0988 nicolescrackers@msn.com
www.nicolescrackers.com
Crackers
President: Nicole Bergere
Estimated Sales: Below $ 5 Million
Number Employees: 5-9

9586 **Niebaum-Coppola Estate Winery**
P.O.Box 208
Rutherford, CA 94573 707-968-1100
Fax: 707-963-9084 info@niebaumcoppola.com
www.niebaum-coppola.com
Wines
Chairman: Francis Coppola
CEO: Jay Shoemaker
Estimated Sales: $ 5-10 Million
Number Employees: 20-49

9587 **Nielsen Citrus Products**
15621 Computer Ln
Huntington Beach, CA 92649 714-892-5586
Fax: 714-893-2161 info@nielsencitrus.com
www.nielsencitrus.com
Processor and exporter of frozen, concentrated lemon and lime juice, lemon puree, lime puree, orange puree
President: Chris Nielsen
Vice President: Earl Nielsen
Number Employees: 5-9
Sq. footage: 10000
Type of Packaging: Consumer, Food Service, Private Label, Bulk
Brands:
EZ
Nielsen
Suntree

9588 **Nielsen-Massey Vanillas**
1550 S Shields Dr
Waukegan, IL 60085 847-578-1550
Fax: 847-578-1570 800-525-7873
info@nielsenmassey.com
www.nielsenmassey.com
Manufacturer and exporter of pure vanilla flavoring extracts and now chocolate extract
President: Camilla Nielsen
CEO/VP: Craig Nielsen
COO: Matthew Nielsen
Retail Sales: Beth Bitzegaio
Estimated Sales: $ 10 - 20 Million
Number Employees: 20-49
Sq. footage: 33500
Type of Packaging: Consumer, Food Service, Private Label, Bulk
Brands:
NIELSEN-MASSEY

9589 **Niemuth's Steak & Chop Shop**
715 Redfield St
Waupaca, WI 54981 715-258-2666
Processors of meat products including ham, bacon and sausage
President: Robert Niemuth
Sausage Maker: Roger Niemuth
Estimated Sales: $950000
Number Employees: 10-19
Sq. footage: 9000
Type of Packaging: Consumer

9590 **Night Hawk Frozen Foods**
100 Nighthawk Cir
Buda, TX 78610 512-312-0757
Fax: 512-295-3988 800-580-4166
email@nighthawkfoods.com
www.nighthawkfoods.com
Processor of frozen food including dinners and entrees
President: Charles Hill
Controller: Dale Reistad
Vice President: Scott Logan
Operations Manager: Terrell Windham
Purchasing Manager: John Benites
Estimated Sales: $ 20 - 50 Million
Number Employees: 64
Number of Products: 25
Sq. footage: 30000
Type of Packaging: Consumer, Food Service
Brands:
Night Hawk

9591 **Nikken Foods Company**
4984 Manchester Ave
Saint Louis, MO 63110 636-532-1019
Fax: 502-292-3283 nikken@lilar.com
www.nikkenfoods.com
Processor, importer and exporter of soy sauce, fermented soy sauce powders, extracted seafood powders and concentrates and dehydrated mushrooms and oriental vegetables
General Manager: Herb Bench
Parent Co: Nikkens Foods Company
Type of Packaging: Bulk

9592 **Nikki's Cookies**
2018 S 1st St
Milwaukee, WI 53207 414-481-4899
Fax: 414-481-5222 800-776-7107
customerservice@nikkiscookies.com
www.nikkiscookies.com
Processor and exporter of shortbreads and cookies
President: Nikki Taylor
Estimated Sales: Less than $500,000
Number Employees: 5-9
Sq. footage: 30000
Type of Packaging: Consumer, Food Service
Brands:
English Toffee
Ladybug
Nikki's

9593 **Nikola's Biscotti & European Specialties**
8301 Grand Ave S Ste 110
Bloomington, MN 55420 952-253-5991
Fax: 952-253-5995 888-645-6527
dir@nikolasbiscotti.com
www.nikolasbiscotti.com
Biscotti
Owner: Michael Itskovich
Estimated Sales: $ 15 Million
Number Employees: 10-19
Brands:
Nikola's Biscotti

9594 **Nina's Gourmet Dip**
6305 Dunaway Court
Mc Lean, VA 22101-2205 703-356-1667
Fax: 703-356-8488
Gourmet and specialty foods
President: Bill Pournaras

9595 **Ninety Six Canning Company**
109 S Cambridge St
Ninety Six, SC 29666 864-543-2700
Manufacturer of canned barbecued hash
President/Owner: Jerry Gantt
Estimated Sales: $2.6 Million
Number Employees: 4
Type of Packaging: Consumer

9596 **Nips Potato Chips**
806 Pohukaina St
Honolulu, HI 96813 808-593-8549
donnachang@hotmail.com
Potato chips
President: Norman Nip
CEO: Norman Nip
Marketing Director: Norman Nip
Estimated Sales: Less than $500,000
Number Employees: 1-4
Brands:
Nip's Potato Chips

9597 **Nisbet Oyster Company**
P.O.Box 338
Bay Center, WA 98527-0338 360-875-6629
Fax: 360-875-6684 sales@goosepoint.com
www.goosepoint.com
Processor and exporter of Pacific and farm oysters
President: David Nisbet
Estimated Sales: $4000000
Number Employees: 1-4
Number of Brands: 1
Number of Products: 3
Sq. footage: 3200
Brands:
Goose Point Oysters

9598 **Nissin Foods USA Company**
2901 Hempland Rd
Lancaster, PA 17601 717-291-1881
Fax: 717-291-9737 export@nissinfoods.com
www.nissinfoods.com
Processor of Asian noodles and noodle soup
CFO: Roy Shoemaker
Quality Control Director: Melinda Levinsky
VP Marketing: Carla Hunter
VP Sales: Terry McMartin
Human Resources Manager: Katrina Joy
Manufacturing Director: Mike Kirchner
Plant Manager: Don Babcock
Purchasing Manager: Billie Jo Dangro
Estimated Sales: $33200000
Number Employees: 150
Sq. footage: 64391
Parent Co: Nissin Foods USA Company
Type of Packaging: Private Label
Other Locations:
Nissin Foods USA Company
Fort Lee NJ
Brands:
Cup O' Noodles
Oodles of Noodles
Top Ramen

9599 **(HQ)Nissin Foods USA Company**
2001 W Rosecrans Ave
Gardena, CA 90249 310-327-8478
Fax: 310-515-3751 www.nissinfoods.com
Manufacturer of Ramen and Cup Noodles
President: Ken Sasahara
CFO: Howard Wang
Marketing Manager: Joe Carter
Estimated Sales: $33.20 Million
Number Employees: 500-999
Sq. footage: 150000
Type of Packaging: Private Label
Brands:
CUP NOODLES
TOP RAMEN

9600 **Nissley Vineyards**
140 Vintage Dr
Bainbridge, PA 17502-9357 717-426-3514
Fax: 717-426-1391 800-522-2387
winery@nissley.com www.nissleywine.com

Wine
President: Judith Nissley
Vice President: John Nissley
Winemaker: William Gulvin
Estimated Sales: $ 2.5-5 Million
Number Employees: 10-19
Type of Packaging: Private Label
Brands:
Holiday White
Niagara
Rhapsody in Blue
Topaz
Whisper White

9601 **Nitta Casings**
P.O.Box 858
Somerville, NJ 8876 908-218-4400
Fax: 908-725-2835 www.nittacasings.com
Processor of meat and collagen casings
President: Frank Caroselli
Marketing Communication: Marchette Johnson
National Sales Manager: Bill Irwin
Estimated Sales: $20-50 Million
Number Employees: 200

9602 **Nitta Gelatin NA**
201 W Passaic St Ste 402
Rochelle Park, NJ 7662 201-368-0071
Fax: 201-368-0282 800-278-7680
info-g1@nitta-gelatin.co.jp
www.nitta-gelatin.com
Processor of gelatin
President: Guergen Gallert
Office Manager: Tsutomu Takase
General Manager: Jurgen Gallert
Estimated Sales: $ 2.5-5 Million
Number Employees: 1-4
Parent Co: Nitta Gelatin
Type of Packaging: Bulk
Brands:
Nitta Gelatin

9603 **No Pudge! Foods**
PO Box 387
Wolfeboro Falls, NH 03896-0387 603-230-9858
Fax: 504-539-5427 888-667-8343
customerservice@nopudge.com
www.nopudge.com
Fat free brownie mix
Founder/President: Lindsay Frucci
Estimated Sales: $1-2.5 Million
Number Employees: 2
Type of Packaging: Food Service
Brands:
No Pudge

9604 **Noah's Potato Chip Company**
27025 Lee Street
Alexandria, LA 71301 318-445-0283
Snack foods
Owner: Stanley Bohrer
Manager: Stanley Bohrer
Estimated Sales: $ 1-2.5 Million
Number Employees: 4

9605 **Noble Ingredients**
575 N Route 73 Ste D1
West Berlin, NJ 8091-9293
Fax: 856-486-9202
jacques@noble-ingredients.com
www.noble-ingredients.com
Chocolates, calissons, candies and caramels
President/Owner: Jacques Dahan
Number Employees: 5

9606 **Noble Popcorn Farms**
401 N 13th St
Sac City, IA 50583 712-662-4728
Fax: 712-662-4797 800-537-9554
info@noblepopcorn.com
www.noblepopcorn.com
Processor of popcorn including popped, unpopped and flavored; also, gift sets available
President/CEO: Milo Lines
Plant Manager: Dan Martin
Sales Representative: Gary Witte
Estimated Sales: $ 1 - 3 Million
Number Employees: 10-19
Sq. footage: 8000
Type of Packaging: Consumer, Food Service, Private Label, Bulk
Brands:
Cedar Creek
Noble
Nobleman Popper

9607 **Nodine's Smokehouse**
65 Fowler Ave
Torrington, CT 06790 860-489-3213
Fax: 860-496-9787 800-222-2059
nodines@snet.net www.nodinesmokehouse.com
Smoked hams, bacons, chicken, duck, turkey, goose, sausages, fish and cheeses
President: Ron Nodine
VP: Johanne Nodine
Estimated Sales: $ 3 - 5 Million
Number Employees: 5-9
Type of Packaging: Consumer, Food Service

9608 **Noel Corporation**
1001 S 1st St
Yakima, WA 98901-3488 509-248-4545
Fax: 509-575-1729 billdalt@noelcorp.com
www.noelcorp.com
Processor and importer of bottled and canned carbonated and noncarbonated beverages; also, bag-in-box juices including orange and apple
President: Rodger Noel
CFO: Larry Estes
VP: Justin Noel
Plant Manager: Mike Trammell
Estimated Sales: $50-75 Million
Number Employees: 255
Sq. footage: 200000
Type of Packaging: Consumer, Food Service, Private Label
Brands:
Dr. Pepper
Noel
Pepsi
Seven-Up
Squirt
Tap Juices

9609 **Nog Incorporated**
P.O.Box 162
Dunkirk, NY 14048 716-366-3322
Fax: 716-366-8487 800-332-2664
customerservice@noginc.com www.noginc.com
Manufacturer of ice cream ingredients including coatings, variegates and background flavors
President: Bruce Ritenburg Iii III
R&D Director: Bob Habich
Plant Manager: Rick Musso
Estimated Sales: $1-3 Million
Number Employees: 10-19
Sq. footage: 24000
Type of Packaging: Bulk

9610 **Noh Foods International**
PO Box 7513
Torrance, CA 90504-8913 310-618-2092
Fax: 310-618-0757
Kim Chee dry spice
President: Raymond Noh
Chairman of the Board: Edwin Noh
Estimated Sales: $ 5-10 Million appx.
Number Employees: 5

9611 **Noh Foods of Hawaii**
1402 W 178th St
Gardena, CA 90248 310-324-6770
Fax: 310-324-6163 gardena@nohfoods.comm
www.nohfoods.com
Founder/CEO: Edwin Noh
President: Raymond Noh
Sales Manager: Ricky Ruff
Estimated Sales: G
Number Employees: 5-9
Sq. footage: 20000
Parent Co: E&M Corporation
Type of Packaging: Consumer, Food Service, Bulk
Other Locations:
NOH Foods
Honolulu HI
Brands:
NOH

9612 **Noh Foods of Hawaii**
20435 Beretania St.
B
Honolulu, HI 96826 808-944-0655
Fax: 808-841-0830 nohfoods@nohfoods.com
www.nohfoods.com
Manufacturer of International seasonings, sauces and drink mixes
CEO: Edwin Noh
CTO: Raymond Noh
Estimated Sales: $1-10 Million
Number Employees: 25
Other Locations:
Noh Foods of Hawaii
Gardena CA
Brands:
NOH

9613 **Nolechek's Meats**
P.O.Box 599
Thorp, WI 54771-0599 715-669-5580
Fax: 715-669-7360
nolechek@nolechekmeats.com
www.nolechekmeats.com
Smoked meats
Owner: William Nolechek Jr
VP: Kelly Nolechek
Production: Leo Hawkeg
Estimated Sales: $ 1 - 3 Million
Number Employees: 5-9

9614 **Nomolas Corp-Jarret Specialties**
900 Us Highway 9 N
Woodbridge, NJ 07095-1025 732-634-5565
Fax: 732-634-5528
Health foods
President: Mickey Lyons
Estimated Sales: $ 2.5-5 Million
Number Employees: 5

9615 **Nonna Foods**
88 Frohelich Farm Boulevard
Woodbury, NY 11797 516-234-9897
Fax: 516-908-4440 corrado@nonnafoods.com
www.nonnafoods.com
Pasta (dry), pasta sauce.
Marketing: Corrado Manuali

9616 **Nonni's Food Company**
601 S Boulder Ave Ste 900
Tulsa, OK 74119 918-382-9627
Fax: 918-560-4108 877-295-0289
www.nonnis.com
Manufacturer of, pita crisps, biscotti, flatbread bagel chips, gourmet hand rolled breadsticks, genoa toast
CEO: Tim Harris
Finance Executive: Kristi Graham
Manager Operations: Tammy Breeden
Estimated Sales: $150 Million
Number Employees: 50-99
Type of Packaging: Private Label
Brands:
New York Style
Nonni's
Old London

9617 **Nonpareil Corporation**
40 N 400 W
Blackfoot, ID 83221 208-785-5880
Fax: 208-785-3656 800-522-2223
npc@nonparl.com www.nonparl.com
Processor and exporter of potato products including sliced, flakes, flour and extract
President: Christopher Abend
CFO: John Fullmer
Vice President: Howard Phillips
Marketing Manager: Robert Weis
Chairman: Harold Abend
Estimated Sales: $50-100 Million
Number Employees: 485
Type of Packaging: Bulk

9618 **Nonpareil Dehydrated Potatoes**
40 N 400 W
Blackfoot, ID 83221-5632 208-785-5880
Fax: 208-785-3656 800-522-2223
nonpar@ida.net www.nonparl.com
Largest grower and shipper of fresh potatoes, a leading manufacturer of dehydrated potato pieces and among the most modern and efficient producers of potato flakes and flour in the industry.
President: Christopher Abend
Estimated Sales: H
Number Employees: 500-999
Parent Co: Nonpareil Corporation
Type of Packaging: Consumer

9619 **Noodles By Leonardo**
1702 Schwan Ave
PO Box 860
Devil's Lake, ND 58301 701-662-8300
Fax: 701-662-2216 www.pastaleonardo.com
Scalloped potato dinners, pasta dinners, macaroni and cheese, pasta and sauce, pasta, breakfast items, stuffing, instant mashed potatoes, croutons, pasta salad dinners, skillet dinners, instant cups, pasta and rice.
President: Leonard Gasparre
General Manager: Ken Aune
Estimated Sales: $20-50 Million
Number Employees: 110
Sq. footage: 80000
Type of Packaging: Consumer, Food Service
Brands:
PASTA LEONARDO
PASTA LOUIGI
PERFECT BLEND
SUNSHINE HARVEST

9620 **(HQ)Noon Hour Food Products**
215 N Desplaines St Fl 1
Chicago, IL 60661 312-382-1177
Fax: 312-382-9420 800-621-6636
Processor and importer of salted, canned and pickled fish, cheese and groceries; wholesaler/distributor of seafood; serving the food service market
President: Paul Buhl
Executive VP: P Scott Buhl
Marketing Manager: Tyler Swanberg
Operations Manager: William Buhl
Estimated Sales: $6.7 Million
Number Employees: 20-49
Sq. footage: 155000
Type of Packaging: Food Service
Other Locations:
Noon Hour Food Products
Minneapolis MN
Brands:
Bond Ost
Briny Deep
De Mill
I Will
Lunds
Noon Hour
Swan
Swan Island
Viking

9621 **Nor-Cal Beverage Company**
2286 Stone Blvd
West Sacramento, CA 95691 916-374-2621
Fax: 916-374-2609 www.ncbev.com
Producer and wholesaler/distributor of beverages
President: Donald Deary
Estimated Sales: $113300000
Number Employees: 250-499
Sq. footage: 208000

9622 **Nor-Cliff Farms**
888 Barrick Rd.
Port Colborne, ON L3K 6H2
Canada 905-835-0808
Fax: 905-892-4011 www.fiddleheadgreens.com
Processor and exporter of fresh, frozen and marinated fiddlehead greens; also, soup mix
President: Nick Secord
Vice President: Nina Dilorenzo Secord

9623 **Nor-Tech Dairy Advisors**
629 S Minnesota Ave Ste L103
Sioux Falls, SD 57104 605-338-2404
Fax: 605-338-0439
Dairy products marketing and trading
President: Michael Hines
Estimated Sales: $6 Million
Number Employees: 1-4
Type of Packaging: Food Service, Private Label, Bulk
Brands:
Nor-Tech

9624 **NorCal Wild Rice**
1550 Drew Ave # 150
Davis, CA 95618-7852 530-758-8550
Fax: 530-758-8110 nor-calrice@saber.net
www.sunwestfoods.com
Grower/packer of processed wild rice; developer of proprietary wild rice varieties and specialty rices; processor of quick-cook wild and brown rice. Specializes in ingredient sales to packers and ingredient users
President: James Errecarte
Estimated Sales: $ 5 - 10 Million
Number Employees: 10-19
Sq. footage: 23000
Type of Packaging: Food Service, Private Label, Bulk
Brands:
Nor-Cal

9625 **(HQ)NorSun Food Group**
8050 Beckett Center Drive
West Chester, OH 45069-5017 800-886-4326
Fax: 513-870-0971 800-886-4326
donsmith@norsun.com www.norsun.com
Processor and exporter of frozen roasted potatoes, seasoned potatoes, IQF frozen potatos, wedges, slices, diced, shredded, and whole baked potatos
President: Teri Bernardi
CEO: Hal Neiman
Marketing/Sales: Don Smith
Number Employees: 5-9
Sq. footage: 1500
Type of Packaging: Consumer, Food Service, Private Label, Bulk
Other Locations:
NorSun Food Group
Rexburg ID

9626 **Nora's Candy Shop**
321 N Doxtator St
Rome, NY 13440-3121 315-337-4530
Fax: 315-339-4054 888-544-8224
info@turkeyjoints.com www.turkeyjoints.com
Manufacturer of candy and other confectionery products; also chocolate & cocoa products.
Owner: Spero Haritatos
Co-Owner: Sharon Haritatos
Estimated Sales: Less than $500,000
Number Employees: 5-9

9627 **Norac Technologies**
9110-23 Avenue
Edmonton Research Park
Edmonton, AB T6N 1H9
Canada 780-414-9595
Fax: 780-450-1016 norac@noratech.com
www.noractech.com
Processor and exporter of spice extracts, egg yolk powder and essential, wheat germ and oat bran oils
President: Tom Evans
VP: Uy Nguyen
Plant Manager: Dan Moser
Number Employees: 10-19
Type of Packaging: Private Label, Bulk
Brands:
Labex
SC

9628 **Norben Company**
P.O.Box 766
Willoughby, OH 44096-0766 440-951-2715
Fax: 440-951-1366 888-466-7236
sales@norbencompany.com
www.norbencompany.com
Established in 1974, Norben Company is a quality supplier of chemicals and essential raw materials to the food, pharmaceutical and nutraceutical industries. Distributor of pea protien, pea starch, pea fiber, bamboo fiber, natural andGMO free ingredients, nautral fibers, micronized products, low carbohydrate formulations, low fat formulations, custom blends, nautral flavor enhancers, probiotic and prebiotic ingredients, and seasoning blends.
President: B J Kresnye
Estimated Sales: $5,977,123
Number Employees: 5-9

9629 **(HQ)Norbest**
PO Box 1000
Midvale, UT 84047-1000 801-566-5656
Fax: 801-255-2309 800-453-5327
norbest@norbest.com www.norbest.com
Manufacturer and exporter of raw and cooked processed turkey products including roasts and deli breasts; also, luncheon meats including ham, pastrami, salami, etc
President/CEO: Steven Jensen
Estimated Sales: $100+ Million
Number Employees: 20-49
Type of Packaging: Consumer, Food Service, Private Label, Bulk
Brands:
NORBEST

9630 **Norco Ranch**
12005 Cabernet Dr
Fontana, CA 92337 951-737-6735
Fax: 909-737-9405 info@norcoeggs.com
www.norcoeggs.com
Dairy products
President: Craig Willardson
Estimated Sales: $ 50 - 100 Million
Number Employees: 250-499
Brands:
Ranch

9631 **Norcrest Consulting**
1340 Jubilee St
Richland, WA 99352-7820
Fax: 719-687-7635 norcrest@aol.com
Yeast. imports and distributes and markets yeast extracts and Levacan, a baker's yeast glucan. Levapan yeast extracts find application in soups, snacks, drinks, frozen and prepared entrees and many low salt uses
President: John R Norell
VP: Beverly Norell

9632 **Nordic Group**
253 Summer St
Boston, MA 02210 617-423-3358
Fax: 617-423-2057 800-486-4002
info@nordic-group.com www.nordic-group.com
Processor and importer of fresh and frozen Norwegian seafood including smoked salmon, cod, haddock and fillets
President: Terje Korsnes
Finance/Administration VP: Joe Mara
Regional Sales Manager: Joe Scharon
Estimated Sales: $500,000-$1 Million
Number Employees: 1-4
Parent Co: Nordic Group ASA
Type of Packaging: Food Service, Bulk
Brands:
Fjord Fresh
Troll

9633 **Nordman of California**
4070 S Reed Ave
Sanger, CA 93657 559-638-9923
Wines
President: James Hansen
Estimated Sales: $ 2 Million
Number Employees: 5-9
Type of Packaging: Bulk
Brands:
Grape Alpho

9634 **Norfolk Hatchery**
1000 E Omaha Ave
Norfolk, NE 68701-6193 402-371-5710
Hatchery for baby chicks
Owner/President: Paula Rasmussen
Estimated Sales: Less than $125,000
Number Employees: 2
Type of Packaging: Bulk

9635 **Norfood Cherry Growers**
383 Concession Rd 14 E
Simcoe, ON M3Y 4K3
Canada 519-426-5784
Fax: 519-426-7838
Processor of frozen red pitted cherries
President: Drew Schuyler
Director: Marshall Schuyler
Estimated Sales: $500,000-1 Million
Number Employees: 5-9

9636 **Norimoor Company**
3801 23rd Avenue
2nd Floor
Astoria, NY 11105-1922 718-423-6667
Fax: 718-423-6668 info@norimoor.com
www.norimoor.com
Manufacturer of Nature made products for health, vitamins, toothpaste
President/Owner: Karl Kupka
Estimated Sales: $500,000-$1 Million
Number Employees: 5-9
Brands:
NORIMOOR
NORIVITAL VITAMINS

9637 **Norpac Fisheries**
3140 Ualena St Ste 205
Honolulu, HI 96819 808-528-3474
Fax: 808-537-6880 mjbudke@aol.com
Manufacturer of seafood
Owner: Michael Budke
Estimated Sales: 10-20 Million
Number Employees: 5-9
Parent Co: T.J. Kraft
Brands:
MIKARLA'S BEST

9638 **Norpaco**
80 Bysiewicz Dr
Middletown, CT 06457-7564
Fax: 860-223-4600 800-252-0222
dean@norpaco.com www.norpaco.com
Processor and wholesaler/distributor of peppers, beef jerky, hot and spicy pickled eggs and sausage
President: Donald Spilka
VP: Dean Spilka
Estimated Sales: $ 20 - 50 Million
Number Employees: 50-99
Sq. footage: 6000
Type of Packaging: Consumer, Private Label, Bulk
Brands:
Norpaco

9639 **Norpaco Gourmet Foods**
80 Bysiewicz Drive
Middletown, CT 06457 860-623-2299
Fax: 860-223-4600 800-252-0222
dean@norpaco.com www.norpaco.com
Gluten-free, cheese, egg/egg products, other dairy and eggs, cured meats i.e. prociutto/bacon, other snacks, other vegetables/fruit, sun-dried tomatoes.
Marketing: Dean Spilka

9640 **Norquest Seafoods**
5245 Shilshole Ave NW
Seattle, WA 98107 206-281-7022
Fax: 206-285-8159 www.portchatham.com
Processor and exporter of salmon, halibut, crab, shrimp, herring, turbot, cod, spot prawn, sea cucumber, etc
President: Terry Gardiner
CFO: Dan Wilcox
Estimated Sales: $12 Million
Number Employees: 100
Type of Packaging: Consumer, Food Service, Private Label, Bulk
Brands:
Frigid Zone
Portlock
Silver Lining

9641 **Norris Brothers Syrup Company**
P.O.Box 315
West Monroe, LA 71294-0315 318-396-1960
Fax: 318-396-2560
Processor of cane syrup
Owner: Fred Norris
Estimated Sales: $1400000
Number Employees: 10-19
Type of Packaging: Consumer, Food Service, Private Label

9642 **Norse Dairy Systems**
P.O.Box 1869
Columbus, OH 43216 614-294-4931
Fax: 614-299-0538 kmcgrath@norse.com
www.norse.com
Ice cream cones
President: Scott Fullbright
R&D: Gunther Brinkman
CEO: Scot Fulbright
CFO: Randy Harvey
Estimated Sales: $ .5 - 1 million
Number Employees: 1-4

9643 **North Aire Market**
1157 Valley Park Dr Ste 130
Shakopee, MN 55379 952-496-2887
Fax: 952-496-3444 800-662-3781
sales@northairemarket.com
www.northairemarket.com
Manufacturing of Dry soup mixes
Owner: Maggie Mortensen
R&D/Co-Owner: Maggie Mortenson
Estimated Sales: Below $5 Million
Number Employees: 10-19
Type of Packaging: Consumer, Food Service, Private Label
Brands:
NORTH AIRE SIMMERING SOUPS

9644 **North American BeverageCompany**
901 Ocean Avenue
Ocean City, NJ 08226-3540 609-399-1486
Fax: 609-399-1506
inquiry@northamericanbeverage.com
www.northamericanbeverage.com
Manufacturer of High energy, low fat premium chocolate dairy drink
President: John Imbessi
Controller: Tom Repichi
Estimated Sales: $ 10 - 20 Million
Number Employees: 10-19
Brands:
CHOCOLATE MOOSE
CHOCOLATE MOOSE ENERGY
HAVANA CAPPUCINO
RED ROSE ICE
ROYAL MANDALAY CHAI
WHITE CHOCOLATE MOOSE

9645 **North American Blueberry Council**
P.O.Box 1036
Folsom, CA 95763 916-983-0111
Fax: 916-983-9370 800-824-6395
bberry@blueberry.org www.nabcblues.org
Blueberry
Chairman: Mark Hurst
Treasurer: Mike Makara
Secretary: Henson Barnes
Executive Director: Mark Villata
Number Employees: 1-4
Brands:
Blueberry Barbeque Sauce
Harvest Bar
Trader Joe's

9646 **North American Coffees**
1 Cattano Ave ste 2
Morriston, NJ 07960 973-359-0300
Fax: 973-359-0440
www.northamericancoffees.com
Coffee, tea
President: Michael Cahill
Estimated Sales: $1-10 Million
Number Employees: 25

9647 **North American Enterprises**
4330 N Campbell Ave Ste 256
Tucson, AZ 85718 520-885-0110
Fax: 520-298-9733 800-817-8666
www.capitanelli.com
Importer/distributor of olive oil, oil, balsamic vinegar, pasta sauces, salad dressings and biscotti; importer of Italian dry pasta and gourmet products; also, specialty gift baskets available
Owner: Joe Lovallo
VP Marketing: Grant Lovallo
National Sales Manager: Tim Champa
Contact: Lisa Lovallo
Estimated Sales: $ 10 - 20 Million
Number Employees: 10-19
Sq. footage: 2300
Type of Packaging: Consumer, Food Service
Brands:
Caphanelli Fine Foods
Capitanelli Specialty Foods
Capitanelli's
Loison Panetoni
Rummo Gourmet Imported Pasta

9648 **North American Reishi/Nammex**
PO Box 1780
Gibsons, BC V0N 1V0
Canada 604-886-7799
Fax: 604-648-8954 info@nammex.com
www.nammex.com
Processor and exporter of standardized and certified organic mushroom extracts; also, whole dried mushrooms and mushroom mycelia
President: Jeffrey Chilton
Estimated Sales: $1.2 Million
Number Employees: 6
Type of Packaging: Bulk

9649 **(HQ)North American Salt Company**
9900 W 109th St Ste 600
Overland Park, KS 66210 913-344-9100
Fax: 913-344-9314 www.compassminerals.com
Full-line salt manufacturer, products include agricultural, water softeners, consumer ice melters, industrial applications, food grade, and rock salt
CFO: Rodney Underdown
CEO: Angelo Brisimitzakis
Sales Director: Nathan Herrman
Estimated Sales: $100+ Million
Number Employees: 100-249
Other Locations:
Ogden UT
Lyons KS
Unity, Saskatchewan
Kenosha WI
Cote Blanche LA
Amherst, Nova Scotia
Goderich, Ontario

9650 **North American Seasonings**
P.O.Box 1668
Lake Oswego, OR 97035-0868 503-636-7043
Fax: 503-636-7043 www.geoquest.net
Bulk spices, custom spice blends and food service spices. Also carry a wide variety of ethnic blends, certified organic
Owner: John D Bryan
CFO: Gary Pearce
Research & Development: Camille McKin
Marketing Director: Shawn Simonin
Operations Manager: Kevin Stapleton
Estimated Sales: $ 10-20 Million
Number Employees: 20-49
Number of Products: 500
Type of Packaging: Consumer, Food Service
Brands:
G'S
NAS

9651 **North American Water Group**
8300 College Boulevard
Overland Park, KS 66210-1841 913-469-1156
Fax: 913-451-9418
Bottled water
President: Roger Hood
COO: Lee Dancer
Estimated Sales: $ 5-10 Million
Number Employees: 1

9652 **North Atlantic**
P.O.Box 682
Portland, ME 04104-0682 207-774-6025
Fax: 207-774-1614 www.northatlanticseafood.com
President: Gerald Knecht
Estimated Sales: $ 10 - 20 Million
Number Employees: 10-19

9653 **North Atlantic Fish Company**
88 Commercial St # 1
Gloucester, MA 01930-5096 978-283-4121
Fax: 978-283-5948
Processor and exporter of frozen catfish, cod, halibut, herring, smelt, squid, shrimp, scallops and whiting; portion controlled breaded and prepared seafood
President: Frank Cefalo
Sales Manager: Joe Bertolino
Operations Manager: James Stuart
Estimated Sales: $4.20 Million
Number Employees: 20-49
Sq. footage: 40000
Type of Packaging: Consumer, Food Service
Brands:
Better Buy
Courageous Captain's
North Atlantic

9654 **North Atlantic Products**
232 Buttermilk Ln
South Thomaston, ME 4858-3003 207-596-0331
Fax: 207-596-0532
Seafood

9655 **North Atlantic Seafood**
P.O.Box 116
Stonington, ME 04681-0116 207-367-5099
Fax: 207-367-2937
Fish and seafood.
President: Delbert Gross
Estimated Sales: $1,600,000
Number Employees: 5-9

9656 **North Bay Fisherman's Cooperative**
RR 4
Ballantyne's Cove, NS B2G 2L2
Canada 902-863-4988
Fax: 902-863-1112
Processor of fresh and frozen lobster, scallops and groundfish; exporter of tuna
Manager: Kim MacDonald
Number Employees: 5-9
Type of Packaging: Consumer, Food Service, Private Label, Bulk

9657 **North Bay Produce**
PO Box 988
Traverse City, MI 49685 800-678-1941
Fax: 231-946-1902
marketing@northbayproduce.com
www.northbayproduce.com
Cooperative, importer and exporter of fresh produce including apples, asparagus, blueberries, cherries, peaches, plums, snow peas, sugar snaps, mangos, raspberries, blackberries, red currants, etc.; also, apple cider
President/VP Sales & Marketing: Mark Girardin
Chairman/VP: George Wright
Operations Manager: Mike Burgos
Estimated Sales: $73 Million
Number Employees: 15
Sq. footage: 15000
Type of Packaging: Consumer, Food Service, Private Label, Bulk
Brands:
North Bay
Wilderness

9658 **North Bay Trading Company**
P.O.Box 129
Brule, WI 54820 715-372-5031
800-348-0164
borg@cheqnet.net
Organic and Canadian wild rice, heirloom beans, dehydrated vegetables, dry soup mixes
Owner: Greggar Isaksen
Estimated Sales: $160,000
Number Employees: 5-9
Number of Brands: 2
Number of Products: 6
Type of Packaging: Consumer, Food Service, Bulk
Brands:
BRULE VALLEY
NORTH BAY TRADING COMPANY

9659 **North Coast Processing**
11160 Parkway Dr
North East, PA 16428 814-725-9617
Fax: 814-725-4374 ncp@ncpusa.com
www.edsmithusa.com
Processor and contract packager of salad dressings, sauces, marinades and dry seasonings
President: William Lewis
Operations Manager: Tom Barnes
Plant Manager: Wilson Haller
Estimated Sales: $13 Million
Number Employees: 10-19
Sq. footage: 25000
Type of Packaging: Consumer, Food Service, Private Label, Bulk
Brands:
Den
Garden Goodness

9660 **North Country Natural Spring Water**
P.O.Box 123
Port Kent, NY 12975 518-834-9400
Fax: 518-834-9429
Processor and importer of natural spring water
President: Roger Jakubowski
Estimated Sales: $ 1 - 3 Million
Number Employees: 10-19
Sq. footage: 22000
Type of Packaging: Consumer, Food Service, Private Label, Bulk
Brands:
Loyola Springs
North Country

9661 **North Country Smokehouse**
471 Sullivan St
Claremont, NH 3743 603-543-0234
Fax: 603-543-3016 800-258-4304
mike@ncsmokehouse.com
www.ncsmokehouse.com
Smoked hams, appelwood bacon, smoked turkey, sausages, chicken and duck, brisket, cheeses and spreads and gifts.
President: Michael Satzow
Estimated Sales: $6 Million
Number Employees: 20
Sq. footage: 15000
Brands:
North Country Smokehouse

9662 **North Dakota Mill**
P.O.Box 13078
Grand Forks, ND 58208-3078 701-795-7000
Fax: 701-795-7272 800-538-7721
khjelden@ndmill.com www.ndmill.com
Processor of flour including semolina, durum, wheat and high-gluten
President: Vance Taylor
Controller/Financial Manager: Ed Barchhenger
Logistics Manager: Mike Jones
Quality Assurance: Bob Sombke
Sales Manager: Steve Sannes
Production Manager: Chris Lemoine
Estimated Sales: $ 50 - 100 Million
Number Employees: 100-249
Type of Packaging: Consumer, Food Service, Private Label, Bulk
Brands:
Dakota Champion
Dakota Queen
Durakota
Empire
Excello

9663 **(HQ)North East Foods**
1515 Fleet Street
Baltimore, MD 21231-2810 410-558-1050
Baked goods
President/CEO: Danny Amaroso
Secretary: Jerry Grades

9664 **North House Vineyards In**
P.O.Box 842
1216 Main Rd
Jamesport, NY 11947 631-722-5256
Fax: 631-722-5256
info@jamesport-vineyards.com
www.jamesport-vineyards.com
Wines
President: Ron Goerler Sr Sr
General Manager: Ronald Goerler Jr
Treasurer: Ann Goerler
Estimated Sales: $ 2.5-5 Million
Number Employees: 5
Type of Packaging: Private Label
Brands:
Cabernet Franc
Jamesport Vineyards
Marlot

9665 **North Lake Fish Cooperative**
RR 1
Elmira, PE C0A 1KO
Canada 902-357-2572
Fax: 902-357-2386
Processor and exporter of fresh and frozen scallops, skate, silversides and lobster
President: Walter Bruce
CEO/General Manager: Mickey Rose
Number Employees: 100-249
Type of Packaging: Bulk

9666 **(HQ)North Pacific Processors**
P.O.Box 31179
Seattle, WA 98103-1179 206-726-9900
Fax: 206-726-1667
www.northpacificseafoods.com
Canned and cured seafood
President: Bob Nickinovich
CFO: Yugi Hanasaki
VP Administration: James Kudwa
Sales Director: S Yazawa
Plant Manager: John Sevier
Estimated Sales: $ 30 -50 Million
Number Employees: 20-49
Type of Packaging: Bulk
Brands:
SSS
Sitka

9667 **North Peace Apiaries**
Gd Stn Main
Fort St. John, BC V1J 4H5
Canada 250-785-4808
Fax: 250-785-2664
Processor and exporter of honey and bee pollen
President: Ernie Fuhr
Secretary/Treasurer: Rose Fuhr
Estimated Sales: $496,000
Number Employees: 3
Sq. footage: 3780
Type of Packaging: Consumer

9668 **North Salem Vineyard**
441 Hardscrabble Rd
North Salem, NY 10560 914-669-5518
Fax: 914-669-5079 naumburg@aya.yale.edu
www.northsalemwine.com
Manufacturer of wines and champagne
President/Winemaker: George Naumburg Jr
Estimated Sales: Less than $500,000
Number Employees: 1-4
Sq. footage: 6000
Type of Packaging: Consumer
Brands:
NORTH SALEM DOC'S OWN
NORTH SALEM RESERVE RED
NORTH SALEM SEYVAL
NORTH SALEM SWEET RED
NORTH SALEM VINEYARD
RESERVE RED
RESERVE WHITE

9669 **North Shore Bottling Company**
1900 Linden Blvd
Brooklyn, NY 11207-6806 718-272-8900
Fax: 718-649-2596
customerservice@nsbottle.com
www.brooklynbottling.com
Soft drinks
President: Eric Miller
VP/General Manager: Tom Deluca
Estimated Sales: $ 20-50 Million
Number Employees: 50-99
Brands:
Ballantine Ale
Country Club Malt Liquor
Gold Crown Lager
Iberia Malt Liquor
Laser Malt Liquor
Pony Malta
Private Stock Malt Liquor
Tornado Malt Liquor

9670 **(HQ)North Side Foods Corporation**
2200 Rivers Edge Dr
Arnold, PA 15068-4540 724-335-5800
Fax: 724-335-2249 800-486-2201
www.northsidefoods.com
Manufacturer of fully cooked and browned pork, turkey and specialty flavored sausage products including patties, links and crumbles
President: Robert G Hofmann Ii II
CFO: Bob Muhl
VP Sales/Marketing: Ed Fornadel
Estimated Sales: H
Number Employees: 250-499
Parent Co: Smithfield Foods
Type of Packaging: Food Service, Private Label
Brands:
EMEBR FARMS

9671 **North Star Distributing**
7934 Ivory Ave
St Louis, MO 63111-3534 314-631-8171
Fax: 314-631-3315 www.icecreamspecialties.com
Ice creams
Manager: Greg Winkler
General Manager: John Kroll

Estimated Sales: Under $500,000
Number Employees: 50-99

9672 **North Star Foods**
1279 Saint Charles Ave
Saint Charles, MN 55972 507-932-4831
Fax: 507-932-5624 info@northstar.com
www.northstarfoods.com
Manufacturer of turkey, beef, pork, chicken and frozen foods
President: Brad Arndt
General Manager: Bruce Christie
Estimated Sales: $30 Million
Number Employees: 100-249
Type of Packaging: Consumer, Food Service, Private Label, Bulk

9673 **North West Marketing Company**
1000 Beacon St
Brea, CA 92821-2938 714-529-0980
Fax: 714-577-0985
Processor of dietary supplements and herbal products in tablet and capsule form; manufacturer of soft gelatin capsule machines and ancillary equipment; also, custom grinding and granulation available
President: Jack Brown
Operations Manager: Margaret Haines
Estimated Sales: $$10-20 Million
Number Employees: 10-19
Sq. footage: 20000
Type of Packaging: Private Label, Bulk

9674 **North of the Border**
P.O.Box 433
Tesuque, NM 87574 505-982-0681
Fax: 505-820-2108 800-860-0681
notb@earthlink.net www.gonzodip.com
Manufacturer of Salsa, chile sauce, chile seasoning, BBQ/Hot sauce, catchup, and soups
Owner: Gayther Gonzales
Estimated Sales: $ .5 - 1 million
Number Employees: 1-4

9675 **North's Bakery Californi**
5430 Satsuma Ave
North Hollywood, CA 91601-2837 818-761-2892
Fax: 818-763-8637 www.northsbakery.com
Bread and bakery products
President: Graham North
CEO: John North
CFO: Karl North
Sales Manager: Odile Grace
Estimated Sales: $ 1-2.8 Million
Number Employees: 50-99

9676 **Northampton Brewing Company**
11 Brewster Ct
Northampton, MA 01060-3801 413-584-9903
Fax: 413-584-9972
info@northamptonbrewery.com
www.northamptonbrewery.com
Processor of beer, ale, lager, stout and seasonal
Manager: Jessica Bellingham
Estimated Sales: Less than $500,000
Number Employees: 50-99
Type of Packaging: Consumer, Food Service
Brands:
Northampton

9677 **Northcenter FoodserviceCorporation**
P.O.Box 2628
Augusta, ME 04338-2628 207-623-8451
Fax: 207-623-2197 877-564-8081
http://www.pfgc.com
President: George Holm
Number Employees: 250-499

9678 **Northeast Kingdom Mustard Company**
475 Carter Road
Westfield, VT 05874 802-744-2095
Fax: 802-744-2092 866-4PU-EVT
nacres@together.net
www.northeastkingdommustard.com
Manufacturer of Mustard, chutneys, jalapeno pepper jelly
Co-Owner: Mark Royer
Co-Owner: Lynn Royer
Type of Packaging: Bulk

9679 **Northeastern Products Company**
P.O.Box 40
S Plainfield, NJ 7080 908-561-1660
Fax: 908-769-9200
Food flavorings
President: Paul Schiavi
CEO: Doug Connant
Controller: Tom Mathern
Marketing Director: Tina Hatten
Estimated Sales: Below $ 5 Million
Number Employees: 50
Brands:
Northeastern

9680 **Northern Air Cargo**
3900 Old Intl Airport Rd
Anchorage, AK 99502 907-243-3331
Fax: 907-249-5194 800-727-2141
www.nacargo.com
Transportation company providing air transportation in Alaska
CEO: David Karp
Number Employees: 250-499

9681 **Northern Breweries**
Sault Ste.
Marie, ON P3C 4P6
Canada 514-908-7545
Fax: 705-675-2926 info@northernbreweries.com
www.northernbreweries.com
Processor of ale
President: William R Sharp
Manager: James Kaminski
Number Employees: 10-19
Parent Co: Northern Breweries
Type of Packaging: Consumer, Food Service
Brands:
Northern

9682 **Northern Discovery Seafoods**
P.O.Box 310
Grapeview, WA 98546-0310 360-275-7246
Fax: 360-275-7245 800-843-6921
seafood@kendaco.telebyte.com
Seafoods

9683 **Northern Falls**
7667 Spring Point Ct Ne
Rockford, MI 49341-8658 616-915-0970
www.northernfalls.com
Manufacturer of bottled water including caffeinated drinking, spring and flavored
Owner: John Neall
Estimated Sales: $1 Million
Number Employees: 25
Type of Packaging: Consumer, Private Label

9684 **Northern Feed & Bean Company**
P.O.Box 149
Lucerne, CO 80646 970-352-7875
Fax: 970-352-7833 800-316-2326
mail@nfbean.com
www.northernfeedandbean.com
Manufacturer and exporter of dried pinto beans
Manager: Larry Lande
Sales Manager: Larry Lande
Estimated Sales: $63 Million
Number Employees: 10-19
Parent Co: Helmut Brunner
Type of Packaging: Consumer, Food Service, Private Label
Brands:
FRONTIER

9685 **Northern Flair Foods**
3247 Gladstone Ln
Mound, MN 55364 952-472-2444
Fax: 952-472-7444 888-530-4453
markgoldberg@yahoo.com
Manufacturer of Gourmet chocolate and candies
President: Mark Goldberg
CEO: Stacy Goldberg
Estimated Sales: $ 5 - 10 Million
Number Employees: 5-9
Brands:
HEAVENLY BEES
MALTO BELLA

9686 **Northern Fruit Company**
P.O.Box 1986
Wenatchee, WA 98807 509-884-6651
Fax: 509-884-1990 nordic@northernfruit.com
www.northernfruit.com
Processor, packer and exporter of apples, cherries and pears
Co-Owner: James Pauly
Co-Owner: Al Chandler
Co-Owner: James Fullerton
Accounting: Jerry Billingsley
Field and Quality Control: Ryan Vickery
Marketing/Sales Manager: Greg Clevenger
Production: Doug Pauly
Estimated Sales: $15,010,332
Number Employees: 100-249
Sq. footage: 158000
Brands:
Chelan Red
Nordic

9687 **Northern Keta Caviar**
5720 Concrete Way
Juneau, AK 99801-7813 907-586-6095
Fax: 907-586-6094 caviar@alaska.net
www.northernketa.com
Salmon caviar
President/CEO: Elisabeth Babich
VP: Sean Fansler
Production Manager: Sean Fansler
Plant Manager: Mark Hiermonymus
Estimated Sales: $1-10 Million
Number Employees: 25

9688 **Northern Lights BrewingCompany**
1701 S Lawson
Airway Heights, WA 99001 509-242-2739
www.northernlightsbrewing.com
Beer
Owner: Mark Irvin
Head Chef: Lane Truesdell
Estimated Sales: $ 2.5-5 Million
Number Employees: 5-9
Brands:
Chocolate Dunkel
Crystal Bitter

9689 **Northern Meats**
163 E 54th Ave
Anchorage, AK 99518 907-561-1729
Fax: 907-561-6848
Meats
President: Jerry Urling
Estimated Sales: $ 10 - 20 Million
Number Employees: 1-4

9690 **Northern Michigan FruitCompany**
7161 NW Bay Shore Drive
Omena, MI 49674 231-386-5142
Fax: 231-386-7626
Processor of regular and sugar-packed IQF apples, cherries, blueberries and strawberries; also, plum and cherry purees
President: Robert Weaver
VP Sales: Tom Hail
Operations Manager: Brian Smith
Number Employees: 100-249
Type of Packaging: Food Service, Private Label, Bulk
Brands:
Iqf Apple Orchard
Iqf Apple Slice
Iqf Sweet Cherry
Iqf Tart Cherry
Sliced Iqf Strawberry
Sugar Cap Block

9691 **Northern Neck Coca Colaompany**
15725 Kings Highway
Montross, VA 22520 804-493-8051
Fax: 804-493-9109 800-431-2693
ales@realgingerale.com www.realgingerale.com
Soft drink bottling
President: John Adams
CEO: Gregory Purcell
Chief Marketing Officer: Charles B Fruit
Public Relations: Arthur Carver III
Director Manufacturing: Richard Landon
Estimated Sales: $ 1-1.7 Million
Number Employees: 18
Brands:
Alive
Aquarious
Carvers Original
Diet Lift

Fanta
Finlay

9692 **Northern Ocean Marine**
7 Parker St
Gloucester, MA 01930 978-283-0222
Fax: 978-283-5577
Seafood
Owner: Jim Lebouf
Estimated Sales: $1.4 Million
Number Employees: 5-9

9693 **Northern Orchard Company**
537 Union Rd
Peru, NY 12972 518-643-9718
Fax: 518-643-2751
Wholesaler/distributor, exporter and packer of macintosh apples and honey
President: Albert Mulbury
Estimated Sales: $1950266
Number Employees: 20-49
Type of Packaging: Consumer
Brands:
Champlain Valley

9694 **Northern Packing Company**
P.O.Box 582
Brier Hill, NY 13614 315-375-8801
Fax: 315-375-8273
Packer of fresh and frozen beef
President: John Perretta
Estimated Sales: $3300000
Number Employees: 20
Type of Packaging: Consumer

9695 **Northern Products Corporation**
1932 1st Ave # 705
Seattle, WA 98101-1071 206-448-6677
Fax: 206-448-9664
Processor and exporter of frozen salmon
President: William Dignon
Plant Manager: Terry Barry
Estimated Sales: $ 1 - 3 Million
Number Employees: 1-4
Type of Packaging: Private Label, Bulk

9696 **Northern Soy**
345 Paul Rd
Rochester, NY 14624 585-235-8970
Fax: 585-235-3753 soyboy@rochester.rr.com
www.soyboy.com
All-natural organic tofu, organic tempeh and soy products
President: Norman Holland
Vice President: Andrew Schecter
Estimated Sales: $ 5 - 10 Million
Number Employees: 20-49
Number of Brands: 1
Number of Products: 24
Sq. footage: 35000
Type of Packaging: Consumer, Food Service, Private Label, Bulk
Brands:
Leaner Wiener
Not Dogs
Soyboy
Tofu Lin

9697 **Northern Star Company**
101 W 82nd St
Chaska, MN 55318 612-339-8981
Fax: 612-331-3434 www.michaelfoods.com
Processor of refrigerated potatoes including hash browns, mashed, diced and sliced
President: Chuck Berry
Estimated Sales: $100+ Million
Number Employees: 250-499
Parent Co: Michael Foods
Type of Packaging: Consumer, Food Service, Private Label
Brands:
Simply Potatoes

9698 **Northern Utah Manufacturing**
185 E 300 N
Wellsville, UT 84339 435-245-4542
Fax: 435-245-4542 www.numfg.com
Dry milk
Manager: David Bigelow
Estimated Sales: $ 2.5-5 Million
Number Employees: 20-49

9699 **Northern Vineyards Winery**
223 Main St N
Stillwater, MN 55082 651-430-1032
Fax: 651-430-1331 northernvineyards@att.net
www.northernvineyards.com
Wines
Manager: Cassie Pittman
VP: Ray Kenow
Estimated Sales: Less than $500,000
Number Employees: 5-9
Type of Packaging: Private Label
Brands:
Northern Vineyards

9700 **Northern Wind**
16 Hassey St
New Bedford, MA 2740 508-997-0727
Fax: 508-990-8792 888-525-2525
info@northernwind.com www.northernwind.com
Processor and exporter of fresh and frozen scallops and lobster
Owner: Fred Murrary
Office Manager: Doreen Wotton
Estimated Sales: $ 50-100 Million
Number Employees: 65
Number of Brands: 3
Number of Products: 3
Type of Packaging: Food Service, Private Label, Bulk
Brands:
CAPTAIN'S CALL
MARINER'S CHOICE
OCEAN REQUEST

9701 **Northern Wisconsin Cheese Company**
1310 Clark St
Manitowoc, WI 54220-5109 920-684-4461
Fax: 920-684-4471
Cheese
Owner: Dave Litterman
Estimated Sales: $ 1 - 3 Million
Number Employees: 10-19
Brands:
Northern Wisconsin Cheese

9702 **Northland Cranberries**
20701 Main Street
Jackson, WI 53037 262-677-2221
Fax: 262-677-3647 info@northlandcran.com
www.northlandcran.com
Processor of fruit juices
Chairman/CEO: John Swendrowski
Plant Supervisor: Dave Carroll
Number Employees: 100-249
Sq. footage: 192000
Type of Packaging: Consumer, Food Service, Private Label
Brands:
Northland

9703 **(HQ)Northland Cranberries**
800 1st Ave S
Wisconsin Rapids, WI 54495 608-252-4714
Fax: 715-422-6800 info@northlandcran.com
www.northlandcran.com
Manufacturer of fruit juice, juice concentrate, fresh and fozen
Chairman/CEO/Treasurer: John Swendrowski
President/COO: Ricke Kress
Number Employees: 218
Number of Brands: 5
Number of Products: 250
Type of Packaging: Consumer, Food Service, Bulk
Other Locations:
Northland Cranberries
Jackson WI
Northland Cranberries
Dundee NY
Northland Cranberries
Cornelius OR
Northland Cranberries
Wisconsin Rapids WI
Brands:
Awake
Meadow Valley
Northland
Seneca
TreeSweet

9704 **Northland Frozen Foods**
903 E 3000 N
Sugar City, ID 83448-1161 208-356-4149
Fax: 208-356-7154 800-886-4326
lpennington@norsun.com www.norsun.com
Frozen potato food products
President: Linda Pennington
Director Manufacturing: Steven Perriault
Plant Manager: Shawn Lovely
Estimated Sales: $ 20-50 Million
Number Employees: 250-300
Brands:
Brittany Acres
Cajun Country
Northland

9705 **Northland Hub**
1701 S Cushman St
Fairbanks, AK 99701-6605 907-456-6608
Fax: 907-349-3101
General Manager: Jim Clark
Estimated Sales: $ 5 - 10 Million
Number Employees: 5-9

9706 **Northridge Laboratories**
20832 Dearborn St
Chatsworth, CA 91311 818-882-5622
Fax: 818-998-2815
Processor and exporter of vitamins, herbal supplements and protein powders
President: Brett Richman
CEO: Jane Richman
CFO: Charles Wands
Estimated Sales: $6400000
Number Employees: 50
Sq. footage: 30000
Type of Packaging: Private Label

9707 **Norths Bakery California Inc**
5430 Satsuma Ave
N Hollywood, CA 91601 818-761-2892
Fax: 818-763-8637 www.northsbakery.com
Processor and exporter of English muffins, bread, croissants, danish and crumpets
President: Graham North
Estimated Sales: $4200000
Number Employees: 50-99
Sq. footage: 17000
Type of Packaging: Food Service, Private Label

9708 **Northside Bakery**
2923 North Avenue
Richmond, VA 23222-3612 804-968-7620
Fax: 804-321-3728
Breads, cakes, pies, pastries
Owner: Jacky Hatcher
President: Michael Hatcher
Vice President: Roseanne Sullivan
Estimated Sales: $500,000k
Number Employees: 11

9709 **Northumberland Cooperative**
256 Lawlor Lane
Miramichi, NB E1V 3M3
Canada 506-627-7720
Fax: 506-622-1767 800-332-3328
info@northumberlanddairy.ca
www.northumberlanddairy.com
Processor of dairy products including milk and cream; wholesaler/distributor of bottled water, ice cream, ice milk mix, fruit drinks and butter; serving the food service market
President: John MacDiarmid
General Manager: Jack Christie
Marketing Director: Judy McDonald
Sales Director: Paul Chiasson
Estimated Sales: $73 Million
Number Employees: 300
Number of Products: 3000
Type of Packaging: Consumer, Food Service, Private Label
Brands:
FRONTIER WATER
JUMBO MINISIPS
MAX CRANBERRY COCKTAIL
NORTHSHORE BUTTER
NORTHUMBERLAND

9710 **(HQ)Northville Winery**
714 Baseline Rd
Northville, MI 48167-1266 248-349-3181
Fax: 248-349-1165 www.northvillecider.com

Wines
President: Diane Jones
Vice President: Cheryl Nelson
Estimated Sales: $10-24.9 Million
Number Employees: 50-99
Type of Packaging: Private Label
Brands:
Northville Winery

9711 **Northwest Candy Emporium**
10803 1st Avenue SE
Everett, WA 98208-7059 425-347-7266
Fax: 425-347-5868 800-404-7266
candynw@aol.com
www.qshost.com/northwestcandy
Processor of gourmet candy and cookies
Owner: Bonnie Reese
Production Manager: Al Hyde
Number Employees: 20-49
Brands:
Espress-Umms
Grandma's Recipe
Northwest Espresso B

9712 **Northwest Chocolate Factory**
2162 Davcor Street SE
Salem, OR 97302-1510 503-362-1340
Fax: 503-362-0186 www.nwchocolate.com
Processor and exporter of chocolate covered hazelnuts
President: Sam Kaufman
General Manager: Dan Kaufman
Number Employees: 5-9
Sq. footage: 10000
Type of Packaging: Consumer

9713 **Northwest Fisheries**
RR 1
Hubbards, NS B0J 1T0
Canada 902-228-2232
Fax: 902-228-2116
Processor and exporter of fresh lobster, cod and halibut
President: Olimpio Martins
Number Employees: 5-9
Type of Packaging: Consumer, Food Service, Private Label, Bulk

9714 **Northwest Hazelnut Company**
19748 Highway 99e
Hubbard, OR 97032 503-982-8030
Fax: 503-982-8028 jeff@nwhazelnut.com
www.nwhazelnut.com
Processor of vacuum-packed hazelnuts
President: Jeff Kenagy
Vice President: Lisa Pascoe
Estimated Sales: $ 5-10 Million
Number Employees: 4
Type of Packaging: Consumer, Food Service, Private Label
Brands:
Springhill

9715 **Northwest Meat Company**
440 N Morgan St
Chicago, IL 60642 312-733-1418
Fax: 312-733-1737
Owner: Stan Neava
Estimated Sales: E
Number Employees: 10-19

9716 **Northwest Natural Foods**
3805 56th Ave Ne
Olympia, WA 98506-9660 360-866-9661
nwnfz@yahoo.com
www.northwestnaturalburgers.com
Fresh and frozen fish/seafood
Owner: Gene Maltiziffs
President: Euegene Maltzess
Estimated Sales: $300.00 K
Number Employees: 8
Sq. footage: 5
Type of Packaging: Private Label
Brands:
Medallions

9717 **Northwest Naturals**
6644 Sexton Dr NW
Olympia, WA 98502-8810 360-866-9661
Fax: 360-866-0734 nwnx@mailexcite.com
Processor and exporter of ready-to-eat frozen fish patties including salmon, halibut and tuna
Owner: Gene Maltiziffs
Sales Manager: Rob Rowley
Production Manager: Robert Mertic
Estimated Sales: $ 3 - 5 Million
Number Employees: 1-4
Sq. footage: 5000
Type of Packaging: Consumer, Food Service
Brands:
Medallions

9718 **Northwest Naturals Corporation**
11805 N Creek Pkwy S Ste A104
Bothell, WA 98011 425-881-2200
Fax: 425-881-3063 johnb@nwnaturals.com
www.nwnaturals.com
Processor, importer and exporter of concentrates including juice and iced coffee and fruit beverages and flavors
President: Tom Hurson
CEO: James
VP Sales and Administration: Mike Marquand
VP Operations: Danny Shaffer
Estimated Sales: $ 5 - 10 Million
Number Employees: 20
Number of Brands: 4
Number of Products: 50
Sq. footage: 30000
Parent Co: Tree Top
Type of Packaging: Consumer, Food Service, Private Label, Bulk

9719 **Northwest Packing Company**
PO Box 30
Vancouver, WA 98666-0030 360-695-2560
Fax: 509-575-1541 800-543-4356
sales@nwpacking.com
www.neiljonesfoodcompany.com
Processor of canned cherries, pears, plums and apple juice
CEO: L Neil Jones
COO: Matt Jones
National Foodservice Sales Director: Mark Mahoney
Estimated Sales: $500,000-$1 Million
Number Employees: 1-4
Type of Packaging: Private Label

9720 **Northwest Pea & Bean Company**
P.O.Box 11973
Spokane Valley, WA 99211-1973 509-534-3821
Fax: 509-534-4350 nwpeabean@worldnet.att.net
www.co-ag.com
Processor of dry green and yellow split peas, garbanzo beans and lentils
Manager: Gary Heaton
Manager: Gary Heaton
Estimated Sales: $32100000
Number Employees: 10-19
Parent Co: Cooperative Agricultural Producers
Type of Packaging: Food Service, Private Label, Bulk
Brands:
Empire
Speedy Cook'n

9721 **Northwestern Coffee Mills**
30950 Nevers Rd
Washburn, WI 54891 715-373-2122
Fax: 715-747-5405 800-243-5283
order@nwcoffeemills.com
www.nwcoffeemills.com
Processor, importer and exporter of coffee and tea
Owner: Harry Demorest
Estimated Sales: Under $300,000
Number Employees: 1-4
Sq. footage: 2000
Type of Packaging: Consumer, Food Service
Brands:
American Breakfast Blend
Backsettler Blend
Badger Blend
Baker's Blend
Broadway Red
Fancy Dinner Blend
Ice Road
Island Blend
Morning Sun
North Coast
Orange Rose
Sleepeasy
Stapleton

9722 **Northwestern Coffee Mills**
P.O.Box 370
La Pointe, WI 54850 715-747-5555
Fax: 715-747-5405 800-243-5283
nwcoftsp@win.bright.net
www.nwcoffeemills.com
Coffee, tea, spices
President: Harry Demorest
Estimated Sales: Less than $500,000
Number Employees: 1-4
Type of Packaging: Private Label
Brands:
American Breakfast Blend
Apostle Islands Organic Coffee
Brazil Serra Negra
Ice Road Blend - darkest
North Coast Tea & Sp
Northwestern Coffee

9723 **Northwestern Extract Company**
W194n11250 McCormick Dr
Germantown, WI 53022-3032 262-345-6900
Fax: 262-781-0660 800-466-3034
flavors@nwextract.com www.nwextract.com
Manufacturer of flavorings and extracts for the premium food and beverage industry; also flavors, colors, chemicals, syrups, emulsions, oils, brewing extracts and grains, and custom & plain crowns for bottling.
President: William Peter
Marketing Director: Patricia Hein
Purchasing Manager: Michael Peter
Estimated Sales: $ 5 - 10 Million
Number Employees: 5-9
Sq. footage: 10000
Type of Packaging: Consumer, Food Service, Private Label, Bulk
Brands:
Northwestern
Sparkle

9724 **Northwestern Foods**
1045 Westgate Dr
Saint Paul, MN 55114 651-523-0273
Fax: 651-644-8248 800-236-4937
mixes@northwesternfoods.com
www.northwesternfoods.com
Processor of mixes including cocoa, cake, pancake, cappuccino, iced tea, power drinks and pizza dough; broker and wholesaler/distributor of industrial ingredients; serving food processors, food service operators andwholesalers/distributors
President: Alden Drew
Vice President: Mimie Pollard
Sales Manager: Bob Freemore
Purchasing Manager: Nadine Vandeventer
Estimated Sales: $ 10 - 20 Million
Number Employees: 20-49
Sq. footage: 24000
Type of Packaging: Consumer, Food Service, Private Label, Bulk

9725 **Norwalk Dairy**
13101 Rosecrans Ave
Santa Fe Springs, CA 90670 562-921-5712
Fax: 562-921-5573
Processor of milk including whole, kosher, reduced, nonfat and chocolate
VP: Tanya Vanderham
President: John Vanderham
Estimated Sales: $500,000-$1 Million
Number Employees: 5-9
Type of Packaging: Consumer, Food Service
Brands:
Norwalk Dairy

9726 **Nossack Fine Meats**
7240 Johnstone Dr
Suite 100
Red Deer, AB T4P 3Y6
Canada 403-346-5006
Fax: 403-343-8066 nossack@delusplanet.net
www.nossack.com
Processor and importer of meat including roast and corned beef, pastrami, sausage and ham; also, garlic rings and pizza products
President: Karsten Nossack
Manager: Ingrid Nossack
Estimated Sales: $27 Million
Number Employees: 70
Sq. footage: 22000
Type of Packaging: Consumer, Food Service

Brands:
Butcher's Pride
Nossack

9727 **Nostalgic Specialty Foods**
399 S Federal Hwy.
Baca Raton, FL 33432-6025 561-237-8086
nostalgicfoods@yahoo.com
Gourmet and specialty foods
President: Leonard Felberbaum
CEO: Felder Baun
Estimated Sales: $300.00 K
Number Employees: 6

9728 **Notre Dame Bakery**
26 Wildwood Subdiv
Conception Harbour, NL A1X 7J8
Canada 709-535-2738
Fax: 709-535-3406
Processor of bread products, pies, cookies and muffins
President: John Mullett
Owner: Larry Mullett
Owner/Sales: Paula Mullett
CEO: John Mullett
Estimated Sales: $531,000
Number Employees: 8
Brands:
Humpty Dumpty Chips
Nestle Chocolates

9729 **Notre Dame Seafood**
PO Box 201
Comfort Cove, NL A0G 3K0
Canada 709-244-5511
Fax: 709-244-3451 www.notredameseafoods.com
Processor and exporter of canned and frozen crab, cod, turbit, capelin, squid, mackerel, lumpfish, roe and lobster
President: Roger Pike
VP/General Manager: Rex Eveleigh
Number Employees: 250-499
Parent Co: Provincial Investments
Type of Packaging: Consumer, Food Service

9730 **Novelty Kosher Pastry**
10 Hoffman Street
Spring Valley, NY 10977-4826 845-356-0428
Fax: 845-356-0456
Breads, rolls
Estimated Sales: $300,000-500,000
Number Employees: 5-9

9731 **Novelty Specialties**
4319 Santa Ana St. #A
Ontaria, CA 91760
Fax: 909-605-1854 800-231-5309
Candy
Estimated Sales: $300,000-500,000
Number Employees: 1-4

9732 **Noveon**
9911 Brecksville Rd
Cleveland, OH 44141 216-447-5000
Fax: 216-447-5740 jenny.smith@noveoninc.com
www.noveoninc.com
Synthetic food colors, natural food colors, secondary blends, lakes, solutions
President: Stephen Kirk
Estimated Sales: $395,800,000
Number Employees: 1,000-4,999
Brands:
Noveon

9733 **Novozymes North America**
77 Perrys Chapel Church Rd
Franklinton, NC 27525 919-494-3000
Fax: 919-494-3450 800-879-6686
enzymesna@novozymes.com
www.novozymes.com
Manufacturer and exporter of enzymes
President: Kurt Creamer
Estimated Sales: $50-100 Million
Number Employees: 400
Parent Co: Novozymes
Type of Packaging: Bulk

9734 **Now & Zen**
3 Madrone Park Cir
Mill Valley, CA 94941-1481 415-695-2805
Fax: 415-695-2843 800-335-1959
info@nowandzen.net www.nowandzen.net
Processor of whipped toppings including dairy-free, gluten-free and chocolate; also, vegan cookies, cakes, vegetarian turkey, steak, chicken and barbecue ribs
President: Miyoko Schinner
Sales Director: Judy Stoffel
Operations Manager: Eleese Longino
Number Employees: 10-19
Number of Brands: 1
Number of Products: 15
Type of Packaging: Consumer, Food Service, Bulk
Brands:
Bbq Unribs
Chocolate Mousse Hip
Hip Whip
Unsteak-Out
Unturkey

9735 **Now Foods**
395 Glen Ellyn Rd
Bloomingdale, IL 60108 630-545-9098
Fax: 630-790-8019 888-669-3663
jroza@nowfoods.com www.nowfoods.com
Manufacturer, distributor, and exporter of dietary supplements and whole foods including, vitamins, minerals, amino acids, herbs, herbal extracts, herbal teas and essential oils for aromatherapy. NNFA GMP certified, certified organicby QAI, kosher certified by the Orthodox Union USA
Owner: Elwood Richard
CEO/VP: Al Powers
Marketing Manager: Jim Ritcheske
Sales Manager: Dan Richard
Purchasing Manager: Dave Lendy
Estimated Sales: $100 Million
Number Employees: 100-249
Number of Products: 1500
Sq. footage: 203000
Parent Co: Fruitful Yield Corporation
Type of Packaging: Consumer, Private Label, Bulk
Brands:
ESTER-C
NOW

9736 **Nspired Natural Foods**
4600 Sleepytime Dr
Boulder, CO 80301
800-434-4246
consumerrelations@hain-celestial.com
www.nspiredfoods.com
Wholesaler/distributor and packager of dried fruits, nuts and trail mixes.
Chairman: Charles Lynch
CEO: Gordon Chapple
Number Employees: 5-9
Sq. footage: 10000

9737 **Nu Products Seasoning Company**
74 Louis Ct
South Hackensack, NJ 7606 201-440-0065
Fax: 201-440-0096 800-836-7692
spice@aol.com www.nuproductsseasoning.com
Suppliers of food seasonings
President: Henry Goldstein
Marketing Director: Jim Sandler
CFO: Celia Hester
Estimated Sales: Below $ 5 Million
Number Employees: 20-49
Type of Packaging: Bulk
Brands:
Nu

9738 **Nu-Tek Foods**
501 Krein Avenue
Wapakoneta, OH 45895-2491 419-739-3400
Fax: 419-739-7783 800-837-0160
Calorie-free sweetener made from acesulfame potassium, preservatives sorbic acid and potassium sorbate. Specializes in producing a wide variety of Sun Valley Brand custom cheese products

9739 **Nu-Tek Products, LLC**
5400 Opportunity Court
Suite 120
Minnetonka, MN 55343 952-936-3603
Fax: 952-933-1396 info@nu-tekproducts.com
www.nu-tekproducts.com
Manufacturer and supplier of functional ingredients which include: soy & dairy protein hydrolysates, reduced sodium salt and modified potassium chloride, fibers and extracts, and pro-biotic powders

9740 **Nu-Way Potato Products**
25 Colville Road
North York, ON M6M 2Y2
Canada 416-241-9151
Fax: 416-241-8274
Manufacturer of fresh potatoes
President: Michael San Giorgio
Estimated Sales: $15 Million
Number Employees: 35
Type of Packaging: Consumer, Food Service

9741 **Nu-World Amaranth**
922 S Charles Ave
Naperville, IL 60540-7611 630-369-6819
Fax: 630-369-6851
contactus@nuworldfamily.com
www.nuworldfoods.com
Manufacturer and exporter of amaranth-based products including popped, flour, pre-baked flat bread, sancks and cereal. Offers foods that are allergy free and gluten free foods
Founder/Co-Owner: Larry Walters
President: Susan Walters-Flood
CFO: Jim Behling
Manager/Co-Owner: Diane Walters
VP Production: Terry Walters
Estimated Sales: Under $500,000
Number Employees: 50
Number of Brands: 2
Number of Products: 15
Sq. footage: 2700
Type of Packaging: Consumer, Private Label, Bulk
Brands:
NU-WORLD AMARANTH

9742 **NuGo Nutrition**
520 2nd St
Oakmont, PA 15139 412-781-4115
www.nugonutrition.com
nutrition bars
President/Owner: David Levine
VP: Steven Smith
Estimated Sales: $1.3 Million
Number Employees: 10

9743 **NuNaturals**
2220 W 2nd Ave # 1
Eugene, OR 97402-7112 541-344-9785
Fax: 541-343-0915 800-753-4372
info@nunaturals.com www.nunaturals.com
Processor of health products including diet nutrients, odorless garlic, vitamins, minerals, amino acids, green tea, herbs, extracts, etc
Owner/CEO: Warren Sablosky
Estimated Sales: $6+ Million
Number Employees: 11
Number of Brands: 17
Number of Products: 78
Sq. footage: 8000
Type of Packaging: Consumer, Private Label, Bulk
Brands:
ALCOHOL FREE STEVIA
BRAIN HERBS
BRAIN WELL
CALM MIND
CLEAR STEVIA
DAILY ENERGY
DAILY SOY
EXTRA ENERGY
FAST ASLEEP
GENTLE CHANGE
JOINT WELL
LEVEL RIGHT
LOSWEET
MELLOWMIND
MENTAL ENERGY FORMULA
PREVENTIN GREEN TEA
SWEET 'N HEALTHY
SWEET-X
THROAT CONTROL SPRAY
TRAVEL WELL
WELLNESS DROPS
WHITE STEVIA

9744 **Nuchief Sales**
2710 Euclid Ave
Wenatchee, WA 98801-5914 509-663-2625
Fax: 509-662-0299 888-269-4638
nuchief@nwi.net www.nwi.net

Grower, packer and exporter of apples and pears
President: Randall Steensma
VP: Dave Battis
Quality Control: Ray Vespier
Sales: Joe Defina
Estimated Sales: $279.000
Number Employees: 7
Number of Brands: 5
Number of Products: 10
Type of Packaging: Consumer, Food Service
Brands:
BIG CHECK
CRANE & CRANE
KEYSTONE

9745 **Nueces Canyon Texas Style Meat Seasoning**
9501 Highway 290 W
Brenham, TX 77833-9138 979-289-5600
Fax: 979-289-2411 800-925-5058
nueces@nuecescanyon.com
www.nuecescanyon.com
Processor of smoked meats including briskets, hams, quail, etc., also meat seasonings
President: George S Caloudas
Estimated Sales: $260000
Number Employees: 20-49
Sq. footage: 10000
Parent Co: Nueces Canyon Ranch
Type of Packaging: Consumer, Food Service

9746 **Nueske's Applewood Smoked Meats**
203 N Genesee St
Wittenberg, WI 54499 715-253-2226
Fax: 715-253-2021 800-386-2266
nueske@nueske.com www.nueske.com
Processor of smoked meats including bacon, ham, sausage and specialty items
President: Robert Nueske
VP: James Nueske
Marketing: Tanya Nueske
Number Employees: 100-249

9747 **Nugo Nutrition**
817 Main Street
Suite 1
Sharpsburg, PA 15215 412-781-4115
Fax: 412-781-4120 dlevine@nugonutrition.com
www.nugonutrition.com
nutrition bars
Executive Vice President: Steven Smith
Estimated Sales: $1.2 Million
Number Employees: 10

9748 **Nulaid Foods**
200 W 5th St
Ripon, CA 95366 209-599-2121
Fax: 209-599-5220 www.nulaid.com
Manufacturer of egg products
President: David Crockett
CFO: Scott Hennecke
Number Employees: 100-249
Type of Packaging: Consumer, Food Service, Private Label, Bulk
Brands:
NULAID

9749 **Numi Organic Tea**
Po Box 20420
Oakland, CA 94620 510-534-6864
Fax: 510-536-6864 866-972-6879
info@numitea.com www.numitea.com
Manufacturer of organic teas and teasans
President/Co-Founder: Ahmed Rahim
President/Co-Founder: Reem Rahim
Estimated Sales: $ 10 - 20 Million
Number Employees: 10-19
Sq. footage: 25000
Type of Packaging: Consumer, Food Service
Brands:
NUMI

9750 **Nunes Company**
PO Box 673
Salinas, CA 93902 831-751-7500
Fax: 831-424-4955 produce@foxy.com
www.foxy.com
Grower and exporter of vegetables
President: Tom Nunes
CFO: Mike Scarr
VP: David Nunes
VP Marketing: Matt Seeley
VP Sales: Mark Crossgrove
Production Manager: Jim Nunes
Estimated Sales: $11100000
Number Employees: 50
Type of Packaging: Consumer, Food Service, Bulk
Brands:
Foxy
Nunes
Tubby

9751 **Nunes Farm Almonds**
P.O.Box 311
Newman, CA 95360-0311 209-862-3033
Fax: 209-862-1038 almonds@nunefarms.com
www.nunesfarms.com
Processor and exporter of roasted almonds, mixed nuts and pistachios. candies toffee caramel chews, chocolate almonds and toffee almonds
President: Arthur Nunes
Estimated Sales: Under $500,000
Number Employees: 20-49
Brands:
Almond Chews
California Crunchies
Caramel Chews
Chocolate Toffee Almonds
Foxy Salads

9752 **Nunn Milling Company**
4700 New Harmony Rd
Evansville, IN 47720 812-425-3303
800-547-6866
www.nun-better.com
Manager: Jerry Napp
Estimated Sales: E
Number Employees: 5-9
Brands:
Nunn-Better

9753 **Nuovo Pasta Productions**
125 Bruce Ave
Stratford, CT 6615 203-380-4090
Fax: 203-336-0656 800-803-0033
sales@nuovopasta.com www.nuovopasta.com
Manufacturer of frozen and fresh ravioli, tortelloni, gnocchi, pasta, and pasta sauces
President: Carl Zuanelli
CFO: Santa Vega
Marketing: Larry Montuori
Production: Joe Dubee
Estimated Sales: Below $ 5 Million
Number Employees: 20
Type of Packaging: Consumer, Food Service

9754 **Nurture**
28 S Waterloo Rd
Devon, PA 19333-1574 610-293-0718
Fax: 610-989-0991 888-395-3300
nurture@nurture-inc.com www.nurture-inc.com
Ingredients for nutritional products
President: H Griffith
Estimated Sales: $1,800,000
Number Employees: 5-9
Brands:
Nurture

9755 **Nustef Foods**
2440 Cawthra Road #101
Mississauga, ON L5A 2X1
Canada 905-896-3060
Fax: 905-896-4349 john@pizzellecookies.com
www.pizzellcookies.com
Processor and exporter of pizzelle cookies and polenta
President: Cesidio Nucci
Estimated Sales: $4 Million
Number Employees: 60
Sq. footage: 12000
Type of Packaging: Consumer, Food Service, Private Label, Bulk
Brands:
Gold'n Polenta
Gold'n Treats
Reko

9756 **Nut Factory**
P.O.Box 815
Spokane Valley, WA 99016-0815 509-926-6666
Fax: 509-926-3300 888-239-5288
nuts@TheNutFactory.com
www.thenutfactory.com
Processor, packager and importer of nuts and dried fruits
President: Gene Cohen
Estimated Sales: $1700000
Number Employees: 5-9
Type of Packaging: Consumer
Brands:
Big Value
Old Fashioned
Party Pak
Sunburst

9757 **Nut House**
558 S Broad St
Mobile, AL 36603-1124 251-433-1689
Fax: 251-433-3364 800-633-1306
sales@georges.com www.threegeorges.com
Pecans and chocolates
President: Scott Gonzales
CFO: Gina Barnett
VP: Siophan Gonzalez
Estimated Sales: Under $500,000
Number Employees: 5-9
Type of Packaging: Private Label

9758 **Nutfield Brewing Company**
P.O.Box 40
Derry, NH 03038 603-434-9678
Fax: 603-434-1042 general@nutfield.com
www.nutfield.com
Processor of ale, lager and stout
President: Jim Killeen
Sales Manager: Geoff Tyson
Estimated Sales: Below $ 5 Million
Number Employees: 5-9
Type of Packaging: Consumer, Food Service
Brands:
Nutfield Auburn Ale
Nutfield's Classic Root Beer

9759 **Nuthouse Company**
558 S Broad St
Mobile, AL 36603-1124 251-433-1689
Fax: 251-433-3364 800-633-1306
www.threegeorges.com
Processor and exporter of pecans and baked goods
President: Scott Gonzales
VP: Sibhan Gonzales
Estimated Sales: $1500000
Number Employees: 50-99
Sq. footage: 30000
Type of Packaging: Consumer
Brands:
3 George
Azalea
Nuthouse

9760 **Nutmeg Vineyard**
PO Box 146
Andover, CT 06232-0146 860-742-8402
Wine
President: Anthony Maulucci
Estimated Sales: $500,000-$1 Million
Number Employees: 1-4
Type of Packaging: Private Label

9761 **Nutorious**
2057B Bellevue Street
Green Bay, WI 54311 920-288-0483
Fax: 866-703-6595 sales@nutoriousnuts.com
www.nutorioutnuts.com
nut conections
President/Owner: Carrie Liebhauser

9762 **Nutra Food Ingredients,LLC**
3631 44th Street SE, Ste D
Kentwood, MI 49512 616-656-9928
Fax: 419-730-3685
sales@nutrafoodingredients.com
www.nutrafoodingredients.com
Manufacturer and sellers of high quality ingredients/products such as protein, gelatin/collagen, polyols, intensive sweetener, fiber, flavors and organic ingredients
Member: Bryon Yang
CEO: Mariann Davey
Director of New Business Development: Tim Wolffis

Estimated Sales: Under $500,000
Number Employees: 1-4

9763 **Nutra Nuts**
4528 E Washington Blvd
Commerce, CA 90040-1033 323-260-7457
Fax: 323-260-7459 gocorny@nutranuts.com
www.nutranuts.com
Manufacturer of Snack mixture of organic popcorn and soybeans flavored with sea salt or natural spices or coated with organic sugar
President: Mark Porro
CFO: Michael Porro
Estimated Sales: $300,000-500,000
Number Employees: 1-4
Number of Brands: 1
Number of Products: 3
Sq. footage: 3300
Type of Packaging: Consumer, Food Service, Bulk
Brands:
Grandpa Po's Slightly Spicy
Grandpa Po's Slightly Sweet
Grandpa Po's Slightly Unsalted
Nutra Nuts

9764 **NutraCea**
6720 N Scottsdale Road
Suite 390
Scottsdale, AZ 85253 602-522-3000
Fax: 602-522-3001 877-723-1700
info@nutracea.com www.nutracea.com
Focuses on teh processing and distribution of stabilized rice bran and other innovations which are unleashing scores of new healthful applications for rice bran food ingredients, rice bran solubles, RiBran meat enhancer, private labelproducts and rice bran oil.
President/COO: Leo Gingras
Chairman/CEO: W John Short
EVP/CFO: J Dale Belt
Quality Assurance Manager: David Hutchinson
SVP Sales: Colin Garner
Plant Manager: Jamie Fuselier
Estimated Sales: $31 Million
Number Employees: 6

9765 **NutraSweet Company**
222 Merchandise Mart Plaza
Suite 936
Chicago, IL 60606 312-840-5000
Fax: 312-873-5050 800-323-5321
ordernow@nutrasweet.com
www.nutrasweet.com
Sweeteners
CEO: Craig Petray
President/COO: William DeFer
CFO: James Stanley
SVP/Sales & Marketing: Kevin Bauer
Director Nutritional Science: Maureen Mackey
Purchasing Manager: James Pumphrey
Estimated Sales: $ 100 Million+
Number Employees: 400
Parent Co: JW Childs Associates
Brands:
Equal
Nutrasweet

9766 **Nutraceutical Corporation**
1400 Kearns Blvd
2nd Floor
Park City, UT 84060-7228 435-655-6000
Fax: 800-767-8514 800-669-8877
info@nutraceutical.com www.nutraceutical.com
Processor of vitamins, garlic, brewer's yeast and fish and garlic oils
Chairman/CEO: Frank Gay II
President: Bruce Hough
VP/CFO: Cory McQueen
EVP: Gary Hume
VP/Legal Affairs: Stanley Soper
Asst VP/Controller: Andrew Seelos
VP/Sales & Marketing: Christopher Neuberger
EVP/COO: Jeffery Hinrichs
Estimated Sales: I
Number Employees: 500-999
Type of Packaging: Consumer, Food Service
Brands:
ACTION LABS
ACTIPET
BIOALLERS
FUNFRESS FOODS
HERBS FOR KIDS
KAL
LARENIM
LIFE-FLO
LIVING FLOWER ESSENCES
MONTANA BIG SKY
NATRA-BIO
NATURAL BALANCE
NATURAL SPORT
NATURALCARE
NATURALMAX
NATURE'S LIFE
PIONEER
PREMIER ONE
SAND
SOLORAY
SUNNY GREEN
SUPPLEMENT TRAINING SYSTEMS
THOMPSON
VEGLIFE

9767 **Nutraceutical Solutions**
6704 Ranger Ave
Corpus Christi, TX 78415 361-854-0755
Fax: 361-855-8031 800-338-4788
www.eliquidsolutions.com
Processor of sublingual/liquid vitamins
Owner: Jerry Clure
Estimated Sales: $1.5 Million
Number Employees: 15
Type of Packaging: Consumer

9768 **Nutraceutics Corporation**
2900 Brannon Ave
Saint Louis, MO 63139 314-664-6684
Fax: 314-664-4639 info@nutraceutics.com
www.nutraceutics.com
Manufacturing , importer and exporter of nutraceutical tablets, capsules, effervescents, tropicals and powers
President: Jennifer Jamieson Cherry
Estimated Sales: $500,000-$1 Million
Number Employees: 5-9
Number of Brands: 50
Number of Products: 1000
Type of Packaging: Consumer, Private Label, Bulk
Brands:
DH3
DHEA PLUS
DIET DHEA

9769 **Nutranique Labs**
398 Tesconi Court
Santa Rosa, CA 95401-4653 707-545-9017
Fax: 707-575-4611 sales@nutranique.com
Processor and exporter of broccoli sprouts and certified nutraceutical powders including spinach, wheat grass juice, tomato, broccoli, garlic, carrot, green tea, kale and cruciferous blends
General Manager: Mark Martindill
Director Sales/Marketing: Nancy Costa
Operations Manager: Tom Ikesaki
Number Employees: 1-4
Parent Co: FDP USA
Type of Packaging: Bulk
Brands:
Nutranique Labs

9770 **Nutrex Hawaii, Inc**
73-4460 Queen Kaahamanu Hwy
Suite 102
Kailua Kona, HI 96740-2632 808-329-4519
Fax: 808-329-4533 800-453-1187
info@nutrex-hawaii.com
www.nutrex-hawaii.com
Nutrex Hawaii, Inc, retail/wholesale/distributor products include Hawaiiam Spirulina Pacifica, a nutrient-rich dietary supplement; BioAstin natural astaxanthin, a powerful antioxidant with expanding applications as a humannutraceutical.
President: Gerald R Cysewski
Vice President: Glen Johnson
Marketing: Bob Capelli
Sales: Agnes Prehn
Estimated Sales: $500-$1 Million
Number Employees: 8
Number of Brands: 2
Parent Co: Cyanotech Corporation
Type of Packaging: Consumer, Private Label, Bulk
Brands:
Bioastin
Spirulina Pacifica

9771 **Nutri Base**
3851 East Thunderhill Place
Phoenix, AZ 85044-6679 480-626-2025
Fax: 480-704-4116 877-223-5459
support@nutribase.com www.nutribase.com
Cereals
President: Sat Samtolch Khalsu
Owner: Guru Simran Singh Khalsa
Type of Packaging: Private Label
Brands:
Golden Temple
Rainforest
Wha Guru Chew

9772 **Nutri-Cell**
201 W Garvey Ave
Unit 102588
Monterey Park, CA 91754 714-953-8307
Fax: 626-288-4974
nutricell2100inc@netscape.net
Manufacturer and exporter of animal-free nutritional supplements
President: Eric Ellison
CEO: Jeff Ellison
CFO: Dan Ellison
Number Employees: 1-4
Number of Brands: 2
Number of Products: 7
Sq. footage: 3000
Type of Packaging: Consumer, Private Label
Brands:
Nutri-Cell

9773 **Nutri-Fruit**
7510 S E Altman road
Gresham, OR 97080 866-343-7848
Fax: 503-663-7095 info@nutrifruit.com
www.nutri-fruit.com/
Fruit
President: Chuck Jarrett
Estimated Sales: $ 1-2.5 Million appx.
Number Employees: 10
Brands:
Nutri-Fruito

9774 **Nutri-West**
2132 E Richards St
Douglas, WY 82633 307-358-5066
Fax: 307-358-9208 800-443-3333
marcia@nutri-west.net www.nutri-west.com
Nutritional supplements
President: Paul White
Marketing Director: Marcia White
Vice President: Tiffany Moore
Treasurer: Michele Losco-ediss
Plant Manager: Glenn Goodell
Purchasing Manager: Marc Moore
Estimated Sales: $ 2.5-5 Million
Number Employees: 40
Sq. footage: 60
Type of Packaging: Private Label
Brands:
Nutri West

9775 **Nutribiotic**
865 Parallel Dr
Lakeport, CA 95453 707-263-0411
Fax: 707-263-7844 800-225-4345
info@nutribiotic.com www.nutribiotic.com
Manufacturer and exporter of vitamins and supplements
President: Patrick Fourteau
CFO: Wendy Sexton
Sales Director: Teri Whitestone
Operations Manager: Wendy Brossard
Purchasing/Manufacturing Director: Kenny Ridgeway
Estimated Sales: $6000000
Number Employees: 16
Sq. footage: 20000
Parent Co: Nutrition Resource
Brands:
Citricidal
Fruitsnax
Grapefruit Extract
Jungle Juice
Meta Boost
Meta Rest
Nutribiotic
Prozone
Spectrum Nutritional Shake

9776 **Nutricepts**
2208 E 117th St
Burnsville, MN 55337 952-707-0207
Fax: 952-707-0210 800-949-9060
info@nutricepts.com www.nutricepts.com
Processor and exporter of calcium salts, oxygen consuming agents, oxygen scavengers, mold inhibitors, sodium lactate, humectants, flavor enhancers, etc
President: Mark Cater
Estimated Sales: $ 3 - 5 Million
Number Employees: 1-4
Type of Packaging: Bulk
Brands:
Ampliflave
Oxyvac
Prop Whey
Surface Guard

9777 **Nutrilabs**
1230 Market St
Suite 401
San Francisco, CA 94102-4801 415-235-6205
Fax: 415-707-2122 877-468-8745
www.nutrilabs.com
Private label manufacturer vitamins and supplements
Owner: Etty Motazedi
VP: Elsie Orell
Purchasing Director: Argee Davidovici
Estimated Sales: Less than $500,000
Sq. footage: 2800
Type of Packaging: Consumer, Private Label, Bulk
Brands:
Chromemate
Citrimax
Geri-Med
Renuz-U
Super B-12 Sublingual
Valerian Extract
Virility Plus

9778 **Nutrilicious Natural Bakery**
5446 Dansher Road
Countryside, IL 60525-3126 708-354-7777
Fax: 708-354-4797 800-835-8097
info@nutrilicious.com www.nutrilicious.com
Processor of cookies and doughnuts including plain, old-fashioned, spelt, whole wheat, low-fat baked and wheat-free spelt
President: Steve Maril
General Manager: Joe Augelli
Number Employees: 12
Sq. footage: 10000
Type of Packaging: Consumer, Food Service, Private Label

9779 **Nutrisoya Foods**
4050 Av Pinard
Saint-Hyacinthe, QC J2S 8K4
Canada 450-796-4261
Fax: 450-796-1837 nutrisoya@citenet.net
Processor and exporter of soy milk and tofu
President: Nicholas Feldman
Estimated Sales: $4.1 Million
Number Employees: 17
Sq. footage: 10000
Type of Packaging: Consumer, Food Service, Private Label, Bulk
Brands:
Natura
Nutribio
Nutrisoy
Nutrisoya

9780 **Nutritech Corporation**
719 E Haley St
Santa Barbara, CA 93103 805-963-9581
Fax: 805-963-0308 800-235-5727
salesnt@all-one.com www.all-one.com
Manufacturer and exporter of all-in-one multi-vitamin and mineral amino acid powder including rice original and base, green phyto base, active seniors and fruit antioxidant formulas
President/CEO: Douglas Ingoldsby
VP Sales: Lori Herman
VP Operations: Carol Huerta
Estimated Sales: $ 1 - 3 Million
Number Employees: 5-9
Type of Packaging: Consumer
Brands:
ALL ONE

9781 **Nutrition 21**
4 Manhattanville Rd Ste 202
Purchase, NY 10577 914-701-4500
Fax: 914-696-0860 contactn21@nutrition21.com
www.nutrition21.com
Organic mineral nutrition includes chromium picolinate, selenium yeast and Cardea salt alternative compound
President/CEO: Gail Montgomery
Senior VP: Dean Dimaria
Marketing Director: K Gwen
Estimated Sales: G
Number Employees: 20-49
Brands:
Chromax

9782 **Nutritional Counselors of America**
1267 Archie Rhinehart Pkwy
Spencer, TN 38585 931-946-3600
Fax: 931-946-3602 ncahw@mindspring.com
Vitamins, minerals, herbs, herbal teas, nutritional supplements, and colon cleaners, neutraceuticals and probiotics
President/CEO: June Wiles
Estimated Sales: $3-$5 Million
Number Employees: 5-9
Sq. footage: 5000
Type of Packaging: Consumer, Private Label
Brands:
6-N-1
K-Min
Min-Col
NCA

9783 **Nutritional International Enterprises Company**
P.O.Box 6043
Irvine, CA 92616-6043 949-854-4855
Fax: 949-854-6170 www.nutrition-intl.com
Processor of nutritionally fortified vitamin supplements; also, nutritional consultation services available
VP: Cecile Lin
Estimated Sales: $30000000
Number Employees: 20-49

9784 **(HQ)Nutritional Laboratories International**
1001 S 3rd St W
Missoula, MT 59801 406-273-5493
Fax: 406-273-5498 info@nutritionallabs.com
www.nutritionallabs.com
Manufacturer, exporter and contract packager of nutritional and herbal supplements and nutraceuticals including tablets, and capsules
President: Terry Benishek
CEO: Ronald Danenberg
CFO: Mark Richter
VP Sales/Marketing: Ned Becker
Plant Manager: Gary Hiler
Purchasing Manager: Greg Tomlinson
Estimated Sales: $16 Million
Number Employees: 125
Sq. footage: 50000
Type of Packaging: Consumer, Private Label, Bulk

9785 **Nutritional Life Support Systems**
3509 Norh High St
Colum 614-262-7087
800-533-4372
moment98@gmail.com www.momentum98.com
Chinese herbal combinations
Owner: Amador Villanuva
Estimated Sales: $300,000-500,000
Number Employees: 1-4

9786 **(HQ)Nutritional Research Associates**
407 E Broad St
South Whitley, IN 46787 260-723-4931
Fax: 260-723-6297 800-456-4931
pookjg@usa.net www.nutreseassocinc.usrc.net
Processor and exporter of vitamins including carotene, A, D and E
Manager: Jonathan Pook II
Acting Manager: Jonathan Pook
Estimated Sales: $979000
Number Employees: 5-9
Sq. footage: 10000
Type of Packaging: Consumer, Bulk
Brands:
Carex
Quintrex

9787 **Nutritional Specialties**
1967 N Glassell St
Orange, CA 92865-4320 714-634-9340
Fax: 714-634-9347 800-333-6168
lifetime@anet.net www.lifetimevitamins.com
Processor of herbal formulas and nutritional supplements; importer of chlorella powder and tablets; exporter of dietary supplements
President: Tom Pinkowski
VP: Tom Krech
VP: Sale Stauch
Estimated Sales: $ 10 - 20 Million
Number Employees: 20-49
Type of Packaging: Private Label, Bulk
Brands:
Lifetime
Tung Hai

9788 **Nutritional Supply Corporation**
2533 N Carson Street
3127
Carson City, NV 89706-0147 775-888-6900
Fax: 800-671-3144 888-541-3997
nsc24@nsc24.com www.nsc24.com
Processor and exporter of nutritional supplements, vitamins and encapsulated herbs
National Sales VP: Mark Campbell
Estimated Sales: Less than $500,000
Number Employees: 1-4
Sq. footage: 15000
Type of Packaging: Consumer, Food Service
Brands:
Nsc-100
Nsc-24

9789 **(HQ)Nutriwest**
Po Box 950
2132 E. Richards St
Douglas, WY 82633 307-358-5066
Fax: 307-358-9208 800-443-3333
www.nutri-west.com
Processor and exporter of vitamin products and food and sports drink supplements
President: Paul White
VP Marketing: Tony White
Sales/Marketing: Marcia White
Estimated Sales: $ 20 - 50 Million
Number Employees: 20-49
Sq. footage: 60000
Type of Packaging: Consumer, Private Label
Other Locations:
Nutriwest
Alliance NE
Brands:
Nutriquest
Nutriwest

9790 **Nutro Laboratories**
650 Hadley Rd
South Plainfield, NJ 7080 908-754-9300
Fax: 908-754-5640 800-446-8876
Processor of vitamins
President: Michael Slade
Human Resources: Donna Cirullo
Sales/Marketing Manager: Chris Burns
Estimated Sales: $25600000
Number Employees: 250-499
Type of Packaging: Consumer

9791 **Nuts & Stems**
PO Box 39
Rosharon, TX 77583-0039 281-464-6887
Fax: 281-464-7493 nutsandstems@aol.com
Manufacturer of Gourmet flavored pistachios and cashews

9792 **Nuts + Nuts USA**
68 Jay Street
Greendesk Suite 201
Brooklyn, NY 11201 347-513-9670
cyrilla@nutsplusnuts.com
www.nutsplusnuts.com

9793 **Nutsco Inc**
1115 S 2nd St
Camden, NJ 8103 856-966-6400
Fax: 856-966-6544 info@nutsco.com
www.nutsco.com

Cashew nuts in bulk, raw or roasted, and other types of nuts. Co-packing services for roasting and packing nuts in bags, can or jars.
President: Fransisco A Neto
VP: Patricio Assis
Marketing: Sueli Vieira
Sales: Sueli Vieira
Plant Manager: Steve McCall
Estimated Sales: $ 5-10 Million
Number Employees: 20-49
Number of Brands: 1
Number of Products: 12
Sq. footage: 48000
Parent Co: Usibras (Brazil)
Type of Packaging: Consumer, Private Label, Bulk
Brands:
Nutsco

9794 **Nutty Bavarian**
305 Hickman Dr
Sanford, FL 32771-6905 407-444-6322
Fax: 407-444-6335 800-382-4788
bruno@nuttyb.com www.nuttyb.com
Processor of cinnamon nut glaze syrup and fresh roasted gourmet nuts; Manufacturer of nut roasting carts and warmers as well as paper and plastic cones and gift tins for nuts
President: David Brent
Estimated Sales: $500,000-$1 Million
Number Employees: 10-19
Sq. footage: 7200
Type of Packaging: Consumer, Bulk
Brands:
NBR 2000
Nutty Bavarian

9795 **Nylander's Vantage Products**
1855 N High Street
Lakeport, CA 95453-3614 707-263-4220
Fax: 916-929-8422
Baked goods
President: Robert Nylander
Estimated Sales: Less than $500,000
Number Employees: 1-4

9796 **Nyssa-Nampa Beet Growers**
525 Good Ave
Nyssa, OR 97913-3664 541-372-2904
Fax: 541-372-5063 nnbga@microw.net
Cooperative of sugar beet processors
President: Steve Martineau
Executive Director: Norma Burbank
VP: Tom Church
Executive Director: Rich Turner
Estimated Sales: $130,000
Number Employees: 1

9797 **O C Lugo Company**
99 Main St
Nyack, NY 10960-3109 845-708-7080
Fax: 845-708-7081 info@oclugo.com
www.oclugo.com
Supplier of chemicals, vitamins, minerals, gelatins and food ingredients. OC Lugo's other division is Critical Filtration supplies
President: Richard Lugo
Estimated Sales: $830,000
Number Employees: 5-9

9798 **O Chili Frozen Foods Inc**
3634 Indian Wells Ln
Northbrook, IL 60062-3102 847-562-1991
Fax: 847-562-1822
Manufacturer of processed frozen meats including cooked pizza toppings, chopped and formed beef, veal, pork and poultry, breaded products, entrees, etc.;
Owner: J Rothschild
Number Employees: 20-49
Type of Packaging: Consumer, Food Service, Private Label, Bulk
Brands:
CHILLI-O

9799 **O Olive Oil**
1997 S McDowell Blvd
Suite A
Petaluma, CA 94954 707-766-1755
Fax: 707-763-3782 888-827-7148
info@ooliveoil.com www.ooliveoil.com
citrus oils, extra virgin, wine vinegars, rice vinegars and citrus tapenades
Number Employees: 5

9800 **O Olive Oil**
1997 S McDowell Boulevard Ext
Petaluma, CA 94954-6919 707-766-1755
Fax: 415-460-6599 888-827-7148
mail@ooliveoil.com www.ooliveoil.com
Manufacturer of Extra virgin citrus olive oils and oak-aged vinegars
President/Founder: Greg Hinson
National Director Sales/Marketing: Shelly Haygood
Estimated Sales: $2-6 K
Number Employees: 4
Type of Packaging: Private Label
Brands:
O OLIVE OIL
O VINEGAR

9801 **O&H Danish Bakery**
1841 Douglas Ave
Racine, WI 53402 262-554-1311
Fax: 262-631-5395
ohdanish@mohdanishbakery.com
www.ohdanishbakery.com
Danish and pastries
President: Ray Olesen
Founder: Christian Olesen
Co-Owner: Myrna Olesen
Estimated Sales: $ 2.5-5 Million
Number Employees: 50-99
Brands:
Kringle

9802 **O'Boyle's Ice Cream Company**
6414 N Radcliffe St
Bristol, PA 19007 215-788-3882
Processor of ice cream, frozen yogurt and frozen desserts
Componet: Beverly Boyle
Number Employees: 10-19
Type of Packaging: Consumer, Food Service, Bulk
Brands:
Country Creamery

9803 **O'Brian Brothers Food**
PO Box 42382
Cincinnati, OH 45242 513-791-9909
Fax: 513-791-9011 obrian@beamons.com
www.beamons.com
Processor of barbecue sauce and salad dressings including French, Italian, honey mustard and ranch
President/CEO: John O'Brian
Estimated Sales: $500,000-$1 Million
Number Employees: 1-4
Type of Packaging: Consumer, Food Service, Private Label
Brands:
Beamons

9804 **O'Brien & Company**
3302 Harlan Lewis Rd
Bellevue, NE 68005 402-291-3600
Fax: 402-291-0237 800-433-7567
johnobrien@obrienmeatsnacks.com
www.obriensmeatsnacks.com
Processor of sausage, summer sausage, meat snacks, luncheon meats and frankfurters
President: John O Obrien
National Sales Representative: Don Murray
Plant Manager: David Hascall
Estimated Sales: $6680000
Number Employees: 50-99
Type of Packaging: Consumer, Food Service, Bulk
Brands:
O'Brien's
Val-U-Pak

9805 **O'Brines Pickling**
4103 E Mission Avenue
Spokane, WA 99202-4402 509-534-7255
Fax: 509-534-5564 ohbrines@spokane.net
www.ohbrines.com
Pickled products
President: James Moore
VP: Marsha Moore
Estimated Sales: $5-9.9 Million
Number Employees: 10-19

9806 **O'Danny Boy Ice Cream**
100 Prosperity Dr.
Dayton, OH 45426-2600 937-837-2100
www.odannyboyicecream.com
Ice cream
Owner: Dannial Haas
Co-Owner: Kathleen Haas
Estimated Sales: $2.5-5 Million
Number Employees: 4

9807 **O'Donnell Formula**
1145 Linda Vista Dr # 110
San Marcos, CA 92078-3820 760-471-1182
Fax: 760-471-1878 800-736-1991
Processor of health food supplements
President/CEO: Wanda O'Donnell
CFO: Angela Bongiorno
Estimated Sales: $1-2.5 Million
Number Employees: 5-9
Type of Packaging: Food Service
Brands:
Flora-Balance
Latero-Flora

9808 **O'Garvey Sauces**
1151 Madeline Street
New Braunfels, TX 78132-4725 830-620-6127
Fax: 830-620-6662
Processor of hot and mild salsas
President: Norma Garvey
Estimated Sales: $150,000
Number Employees: 1-4
Type of Packaging: Consumer, Food Service, Private Label, Bulk
Brands:
Max's Salsa Sabrosa & Design

9809 **O'Hara Corporation**
120 Tillson Ave # 1
Rockland, ME 04841-3450 207-594-0405
Fax: 207-594-0407 www.oharacorporation.com
Processor and exporter of seafood including frozen scallops
Owner: Frank O'Hara
Estimated Sales: $4100000
Number Employees: 50-99
Type of Packaging: Consumer, Food Service
Brands:
Cape Ann
Down East
Tip Top

9810 **O'Mona International Tea**
22 Drew St Apt 21
Port chester, NY 10573-4847 914-937-4389
Fax: 914-937-8858
Tea
President: Foo Seid
Estimated Sales: Under $500,000
Number Employees: 1-4

9811 **O'Neal's Fresh Frozen Pizza Crust**
122 E College Ave
Springfield, OH 45504-2505 937-323-0050
redparot@iapdatacom.net
Processor of pizza crust including whole wheat
Manager: Brian O'Neill
Estimated Sales: $ 1 - 3 Million
Number Employees: 20-49

9812 **O'Neil's Distributors**
110 S Iroquois Street
Goodland, IN 47948-8004 219-297-4521
Fax: 219-297-4625
Teas
Owner: Steven O'Neil
Estimated Sales: $ 2.5-5 Million
Number Employees: 1-4

9813 **O'Neill Coffee Company**
20 Main Street Ext
West Middlesex, PA 16159 724-528-9281
Fax: 724-528-1566 www.oneillcoffee.com
Processor of coffee; wholesaler/distributor of teas and spices
CEO: Joseph J Walsh
Estimated Sales: $ 1 - 3 Million
Number Employees: 5-9

9814 **O'Neill Packing Company**
P.O.Box 7194
Omaha, NE 68107-0194 402-733-1200
Fax: 402-733-1724
Processor and exporter of beef
President: Ron O'Neill
General Production Manager: Brian O'Neill
Estimated Sales: $12200000
Type of Packaging: Consumer, Food Service, Private Label, Bulk

9815 **O'Vallon Winery**
RR 1
Box 77b
Washburn, MO 65772-9801 417-826-5830
Wine company
Owner: Frank Huffman
Estimated Sales: Under $500,000
Number Employees: 1-4

9816 **O-At-Ka Milk Products Cooperative**
700 Ellicot Street
Batavia, NY 14020 585-343-0536
Fax: 585-343-4473 800-828-8152
mpatterson@oatkamilk.com www.oatkamilk.com
Processor and exporter of dairy products including butter, milk powder, condensed milk, milk-based drinks, creams, etc; importer of butter and milk powder
President: Herbert Nobles
CEO: Bob Hall
CFO: Michael Patterson
VP: David Crisp
Sales Manager: Richard Edelman
Operations Manager: Al Smith
Plant Engineer: Keith Price
Estimated Sales: $200 Million
Number Employees: 300
Sq. footage: 100000
Type of Packaging: Consumer, Food Service, Private Label, Bulk
Brands:
Gold Cow
Spring Farm

9817 **O. Malley Grain**
P.O.Box 128
Fairmont, NE 68354 402-268-6001
Fax: 402-268-7241 info@omalleygrain.com
www.omalleygrain.com
High quality corn supplier to the snack food and tortilla industries
VP: Dave Waters
CEO: Rob O'Malley
Executive VP: James Thomas
Estimated Sales: $ 20-50 Million
Number Employees: 10-19

9818 **OB Macaroni Company**
P.O.Box 53
Fort Worth, TX 76101-0053 817-335-4629
Fax: 817-335-4726 800-555-4336
www.obpasta.com
Processor of macaroni
President: Carlo Laneri Jr
Estimated Sales: $ 10 - 20 Million
Number Employees: 20-49
Sq. footage: 50000
Type of Packaging: Consumer, Food Service, Private Label, Bulk
Brands:
O.B.
Q&Q

9819 **OC Schulz & Sons**
P.O.Box 39
Crystal, ND 58222-0039 701-657-2152
Fax: 701-657-2425 ocschulz@polarcomm.com
Manufacturer of potatoes
President: Tom Schulz
Secretary/Treasurer: David Moquist
Estimated Sales: $.5-1 Million
Number Employees: 10-19
Sq. footage: 50000
Type of Packaging: Consumer, Food Service

9820 **OCG Cacao**
1 Plummers Cor
Whitinsville, MA 01588-2135 508-234-5107
Fax: 508-234-5495 888-482-2226
ocggroup@aol.com www.ocgcacao.com
Suppliers of dairy, bakery, confectionery products
President: Jean Chenal
General Manager: Roberta White
Estimated Sales: Below $ 5 Million
Number Employees: 1

9821 **OH Chocolate**
600 Manitou Road SE
Calgary, AB T2G 4C5
Canada 403-283-4612
Fax: 403-287-2117 800-887-3959
www.ohchocolate.com
Processor of baked desserts and Belgian chocolates
President: Laurie Climan
Sales Manager: Mark Climan
Number Employees: 10-19
Type of Packaging: Consumer
Brands:
L'Or Chocolatier
Ott Chocolate

9822 **OK International Group**
73 Bartlett Street
Marlborough, MA 01752 508-303-8286
Fax: 508-303-8207 sales@okcorp.com
ww.okcorp.com
Manufacturer of integrated packaging automation systems.

9823 **OSF Flavors**
40 Baker Hollow Rd
Windsor, CT 06095 860-298-8350
Fax: 860-298-8363 800-466-6015
sales@osfflavors.com www.osfflavors.com
Flavor and colors
Manager: Doug Nasby
Marketing Director: Olivier de Botton
CEO: Olivier DeBotton
R & D: Linda Foulkner
Estimated Sales: $ 10-20 Million
Number Employees: 20-49
Sq. footage: 10000
Brands:
OSF Flavors

9824 **Oak Creek Brewing Company**
2050 Yavapai Dr
Sedona, AZ 86336-4558 928-204-1300
Fax: 520-204-1361 bestbrew@sedona.net
www.oakcreekbrew.com
Processor of seasonal beer, ale and lager
General Manager: Rita Kraus
Estimated Sales: $ 500,000 - $ 1Million
Number Employees: 5-9
Type of Packaging: Consumer, Food Service
Brands:
Oak Creek

9825 **Oak Creek Farms**
218 North C Street
Po Box 206
Edgar, NE 68935 402-224-3038
Fax: 402-224-3536
Processor and exporter of organic grain products including corn chips, flour and masa
President: Ben Jones
VP: Jack Horst
Estimated Sales: $200,000
Number Employees: 3
Sq. footage: 3000
Type of Packaging: Consumer, Food Service, Private Label, Bulk
Brands:
Oak Creek Farms

9826 **(HQ)Oak Farm's Dairy**
1148 Faulkner Ln
Waco, TX 76704 254-756-5421
Fax: 254-756-6987 www.oakfarmsdairy.com
Milk
President: Mackey Willims
CEO: Mickey Williams
General Sales Manager: Jerry Przada
Human Resources: Brad Patten
Estimated Sales: Less than $500,000
Number Employees: 100-249
Other Locations:
Oak Farms Dairy
Wichita Falls TX
Oak Farms Dairy
Weatherford TX
Oak Farms Dairy
Denison TX
Oak Farms Dairy
Paris TX
Oak Farms Dairy
Houston TX
Oak Farms Dairy
Beaumont TX
Oak Farms Dairy
Brenham TX
Oak Farms Dairy
San Antonio TX
Oak Farms Dairy
McAllen TX
Oak Farms Dairy
Waco TX
Oak Farms Dairy
Austin TX
Oak Farms Dairy
Tyler TX
Brands:
Oak Farm's

9827 **Oak Farms**
1314 Fredericksburg Rd
San Antonio, TX 78201-5000 210-732-1111
Fax: 210-737-2534 800-292-2169
robin-somogyi@deanfoods.com
www.oakfarmsdairy.com
Processor of milk
Manager: Matt Conner
General Sales Manager: Joe Penaloza
General Manager: Matt Connor
Estimated Sales: $63700000
Number Employees: 250-499
Parent Co: Suiza Dairy Group
Type of Packaging: Consumer, Food Service, Private Label

9828 **Oak Farms**
Po Box 961447
El Paso, TX 79996 214-941-0302
Fax: 214-941-0309 800-395-7004
www.oakfarmsdairy.com
Processors of milk and cream
General Manager: Craig Roberts
General Sales Manager: Jerry Przada
General Manager: Micky Williams
Number Employees: 250-499
Parent Co: Suiza Dairy Group
Type of Packaging: Consumer, Food Service
Brands:
Oak Farms

9829 **Oak Grove Dairy**
W10198 Oak Grove Rd
Clintonville, WI 54929 715-823-6226
Fax: 715-823-6589 oakgrvdy@frontiernet.net
Longhorn, mini longhorn, colby, cheddar, Monterey jack, semi-soft marble and pepper jack cheese
Co-Owner: David Kust
Co-Owner: Terry Kust
Secretary: Theresa Kust
Estimated Sales: $5-9.9 Million
Number Employees: 10-19
Sq. footage: 9300
Type of Packaging: Food Service, Private Label, Bulk

9830 **Oak Grove Dairy**
1270 Energy Lane
Saint Paul, MN 55108-5225 651-379-6500
Fax: 952-467-2212 800-322-9566
www.kemps.com
Milk
President: James Green
Estimated Sales: $ 20-50 Million
Number Employees: 1000

9831 **Oak Grove Orchards Winery**
6090 Crowley Rd
Rickreall, OR 97371 541-364-7052
Wines
President: Carl Stevens
Estimated Sales: Under $500,000
Number Employees: 1-4

9832 **Oak Grove Smokehouse**
17618 Old Jefferson Hwy
Prairieville, LA 70769-3931 225-673-6857
Fax: 225-673-5757
Manufacturer of seasoned and Cajun/Creole rice mixes, speciality spice mixes, breading and smoked meats
President: Robert Schexnailder PhD
Estimated Sales: $500,000-$1 Million
Number Employees: 5-9
Number of Brands: 2
Number of Products: 15+
Sq. footage: 17000
Type of Packaging: Consumer, Food Service, Bulk
Brands:
OAK GROVE SMOKEHOUSE
SWAMP FIRE SEAFOOD BOIL

9833 **Oak Hill Farm**
P.O.Box 1989
Glen Ellen, CA 95442 707-996-6643
Fax: 707-935-6612 800-878-7808
info@oakhillfarm.net www.oakhillfarm.net
Organic flowers and produce
Owner: Anne Teller

Estimated Sales: $ 10-24.9 Million
Number Employees: 5-9
Brands:
Jim Beam Kentucky Bourbon
Oak Hill Farms
Redneck Gourmet

9834 Oak Island Seafood Company
PO Box 947
Portland, ME 04104-0947 207-594-9250
Fax: 207-594-9281
Seafood
President: Jay Trenholm

9835 Oak Knoll Dairy
PO Box 443
Windsor, VT 05089-0443 802-674-5426
Fax: 802-674-9166 oakknoll@earthlink.net
www.oakknolldairy.com
Manufacturer of 100% goats milk, 2% fat goats milk, chocolate goats milk, and half and half goats milk
Owner: George Redick
Owner: Karen Lindbo
Estimated Sales: A
Number Employees: 5-9
Sq. footage: 15000
Brands:
OAK KNOLL

9836 Oak Knoll Winery
29700 SW Burkhalter Rd
Hillsboro, OR 97123-9245 503-648-8198
Fax: 503-648-3377 800-625-5665
info@oakknollwinery.com
www.oakknollwinery.com
Manufacturer of Wines
President: Greg Lint
President: Greg Lint
VP Sales/Marketing: John Vuylsteke
Tasting Room Communications/Founder: Marj Vuylsteke
Assistant Winemaker: Jim Herinckx
Cellar Master: Tom Vuylsteke
Office Manager: Martha Miller
Estimated Sales: Below $5 Million
Number Employees: 10-19
Number of Brands: 2
Number of Products: 8
Type of Packaging: Consumer, Private Label, Bulk
Brands:
OAK KNOLL

9837 Oak Leaf Confections
440 Comstock Road
Scarborough, ON M1L 2H6
Canada 416-751-0740
Fax: 416-751-3656 877-261-7887
www.oakleafconfections.com
Processor and exporter of confectionery products including malt balls, gum balls, bubble gum, hard candies and freeze pops
Owner/President: Philip Terranova
National Sales Manager: Don Spillane
Director Finance: Drew MacAskill
Number Employees: 300
Sq. footage: 140000
Type of Packaging: Consumer, Private Label, Bulk

9838 Oak Ridge Winery
P.O.Box 440
Lodi, CA 95241-0440 209-369-4758
Fax: 209-369-0202 www.oakridgewines.com
Wines
President: Rudy Maggio
Quality Control: Juan Cerna
Estimated Sales: $ 10-20 Million
Number Employees: 20-49
Type of Packaging: Private Label

9839 Oak Ridge Winery
6100 E. Hwy 12
Lodi, CA 95241-0440 20- 3-9 47
Fax: 209-369-0202 www.oakridgewinery.com
Brandy
Owner: Rudy Maggio
Director of Sales and Marketing: Marc Lohnes
Estimated Sales: $10 Million
Number Employees: 45

9840 Oak Spring Winery
Rr 1 Box 612
Altoona, PA 16601-9449 814-946-3799
Fax: 814-846-4245 oakspring@keyconn.net
www.oakspringwinery.com
Wines
Founder: Sylvia Schraff
President: Scott Schraff
Treasurer: John Schraff
Estimated Sales: $5-9.9 Million
Number Employees: 1-4
Brands:
Oak Spring Winery

9841 Oak State Products
PO Box 549
Wenona, IL 61377 815-853-4348
Fax: 815-853-4625 www.oakstate.com
Producer of soft cookies, cookie crumbs and toppings
President: David Van Laar
CFO: Patrick Donnelly
Vice President: Michael Healy
Production Manager: Jeff Pickard
Plant Manager: Jim Shannon
Purchasing Manager: Anne Newhalfen
Estimated Sales: $22.8 Million
Number Employees: 350
Sq. footage: 160000
Type of Packaging: Consumer, Bulk
Brands:
Oak State Cookie Jar Delight

9842 (HQ)Oak Valley Farm
1010 Haddonfield Berlin Rd
Voorhees, NJ 08043-3514 856-435-0900
Fax: 856-435-3019 info@oakvalleyfarms.com
www.oakvalleyfarms.com
Processor of turkey and turkey products including raw and fully cooked
President: Leo Rubin
CEO: Richard Milbauer
VP Sales: Bruce Utain
Estimated Sales: $28842984
Number Employees: 5-9
Other Locations:
El Jay Poultry Corp.
Watertown SD
Brands:
All Seasons
Buttergold
Chef-Ready
Oak Valley Farms
Val-U-Pak

9843 Oakencroft Vineyard & Winery
1455 Oakencroft Ln
Charlottesville, VA 22901 434-296-4188
Fax: 434-293-6631 mail@aokencroft.com
www.oakencroft.com
Manufacturer of Wines
President/Owner: Felicia Warburg Rogan
Vineyard Manager: Philip Ponton
Winemaker: Riaan Rossouw
Estimated Sales: $ 1 - 3 Million
Number Employees: 1-4

9844 Oakhurst Dairy
364 Forest Ave
Portland, ME 04101 207-772-7468
Fax: 207-874-0714 800-482-0718
info@oakhurstdairy.com
www.oakhurstdairy.com
Milk and dairy products; fluid milk, cream, sour cream, cottage cheese, butter, ice cream mixes, juices, drinks and water
President/COO: William Bennett
EVP/CFO/Treasurer: Thomas Brigham
Quality Control Director: Normand Nelson
VP Marketing/Sales: James Lesser
VP Human Resources: Joseph Hyatt
VP Operations: John Bennett
Production Manager: L Gerry Whiting
Estimated Sales: $110 Million
Number Employees: 240
Type of Packaging: Consumer

9845 Oakland Bean Cleaning &Storage
42445 County Road 116
Knights Landing, CA 95645-0518 530-735-6203
Fax: 530-735-6207
Processor of dry, edible beans including kidney and pink
Operations Manager: Frank Anastasi

Estimated Sales: Less than $500,000
Number Employees: 1-4

9846 Oakland Noodle Company
P.O.Box 644
Oakland, IL 61943 217-346-2322
Fax: 217-346-2324
Manufacturer of noodles
President: Tod Ethington
Marketing Director: Stephanie Ethington
Estimated Sales: Under $500,000
Number Employees: 1-4
Sq. footage: 2000
Brands:
Oakland Noodle

9847 Oakrun Farm Bakery
PO Box 81070
Ancaster, ON L9G 3L1
Canada 905-648-1818
Fax: 905-648-8252
Processor and exporter of English muffins and pastries
President: Roger Dickhout
Number Employees: 100-249
Type of Packaging: Consumer, Food Service, Private Label

9848 Oasis Breads
440 Venture St
Escondido, CA 92029 760-747-7390
Fax: 760-747-4854 bread@oasisbreads.com
www.oasisbreads.com
Processor of flourless sprouted whole grain breads and deli breads.
President: Jim Pickell
Estimated Sales: $1300000
Number Employees: 5-9
Sq. footage: 10000
Type of Packaging: Consumer, Private Label
Brands:
OASIS

9849 Oasis Coffee Company
327 Main Ave
Norwalk, CT 06851-6156 203-847-0554
Fax: 203-846-9835
Roasting coffee
President: Ralph Sandolo
CEO: Veronica Sandolo
Vice President: Joseph Sandolo
Marketing Consultant: Martin Blank
Estimated Sales: $ 5-10 Million
Number Employees: 5-9
Brands:
Oasis Coffee

9850 Oasis Foods
2222 Kirkman St
Lake Charles, LA 70601-7448 337-439-5262
Fax: 337-437-1174 www.oasisfoodsinc.com
President: Edward Abrusley
Estimated Sales: $ 10 - 20 Million
Number Employees: 10-19

9851 Oasis Foods
P.O.Box 217
Planada, CA 95365 209-382-0263
Fax: 209-382-0427
Processor, exporter and canner of fruit including peaches and Kadota figs
Owner/President: Eric Bocks
Operations Manager: Lorraiane Bocks
Production Manager: Eric Bocks
Estimated Sales: $5.7 Million
Number Employees: 50
Number of Products: 1
Sq. footage: 3367
Type of Packaging: Food Service, Private Label
Brands:
OASIS
OREGON FRUIT
SYSCO

9852 Oasis Foods Company
635 Ramsey Avenue
Hillside, NJ 07205 908-964-0477
Fax: 908-964-1369 www.oasisfoods.com
Manufacturer of butter blends and substitutes, salad dressings, shortenings, margarine, edible oils, mayonnaise, sauces, pan and grill oil
President/CEO: Jeffrey Kuo
Manager: Allen Savasta
VP: Anthony Alves

Estimated Sales: $100-500 Million
Number Employees: 200
Sq. footage: 300000
Type of Packaging: Consumer, Food Service, Private Label, Bulk
Brands:
ALPINE VALLEY
EX-SEED
GARDEN HARVEST
GOLDEN DELICIOUS
GOLDEN FRY
JOLINA
KLECKNER
OASIS
SELECT RECIPE
TOP FRY
TOWN & COUNTRY
TRAIL BLAZIN

9853 **Oasis Mediterranean Cuisine**
1520 W Laskey Rd
Toledo, OH 43612 419-269-1516
Fax: 419-324-7777 www.omcfood.com
Mediterranean vegetarian cuisine
Manager: Mike Francis
Quality Control: Tonny Obid
Estimated Sales: $ 5-10 Million
Number Employees: 20-49
Brands:
Non-Dairy Baklava

9854 **Oasis Winery**
14141 Hume Rd
Hume, VA 22639 540-635-7627
Fax: 540-635-4653 800-304-7656
oasiswine@aol.com www.oasiswine.com
Manufacturer of Wines
Owner/CEO: Tareq Salahi
Public Relations: Ann Runyon
Estimated Sales: $5-10 Million
Number Employees: 100-249
Type of Packaging: Private Label
Brands:
BLEU ROCK VINEYARD WINES
FIERY RUM CELLARS
OASIS WINES & SPARKLING WINES

9855 **Oberto Sausage Company**
P.O.Box 429
Kent, WA 98035-0429 253-854-7056
Fax: 253-437-6151 877-453-7591
www.lowreys.com
Processor of beef jerky, salami and sausage including cocktail and specialty
President: Tom Campanile
Estimated Sales: $83200000
Number Employees: 500-999
Type of Packaging: Consumer
Brands:
Lowery's Meat Snacks
Oh Boy! Oberto Beef Jerky
Oh Boy! Oberto Classic
Pacific Gold
Smoke Craft

9856 **Oberweis Dairy**
951 Ice Cream Dr
North Aurora, IL 60542-1475 630-801-6100
Fax: 630-897-0562 888-645-5868
hdfeedback@oberweisdairy.com
www.oberweisdairy.com
Manufacturer of fluid dairy products, premium ice cream, and ice cream cakes, juice, meat products, crackers, cookies, salsas
Chairman: Jim Oberweis
President/CEO: Robert Renaut
VP/CFO: Randy Anderson
VP Marketing: Mark Vance
VP Route Sales/HR: Mike McCarthy
VP Supply Chain: Dave Doyle
VP Retail Operations: Elizabeth Craig
Estimated Sales: $1-2.5 Million
Number Employees: 100-249
Type of Packaging: Food Service, Private Label, Bulk

9857 **(HQ)Obester Winery**
12341 San Mateo Rd
Half Moon Bay, CA 94019 650-726-9463
Fax: 650-726-7074 info@obesterwinery.com
www.obesterwinery.com
Wines
Owner: Kendyl Kellogg
Estimated Sales: $ 2.5-5 Million
Number Employees: 5-9

9858 **Occidental International Foods Llc**
111 Canfield Ave
Building A
Randolph, NJ 07869 973-970-9220
Fax: 973-970-9222 sales@occidentalfoods.com
www.occidentalfoods.com
Manufacturers' representatives and importers of bulk spices and seeds, including paprika, pure mancha saffron, chilies dried, crushed and ground, turmeric, granulated garlic, garlic powder, cardamom, annatto, allspice and sesameseeds
President: Scott Hall
CFO: Denise Hall
Estimated Sales: $300,000-500,000
Number Employees: 1-4
Type of Packaging: Food Service, Bulk

9859 **Ocean Beauty Seafoods**
1100 W Ewing St
Seattle, WA 98119 206-285-6800
Fax: 206-285-9190 info@oceanbeauty.com
www.oceanbeauty.com
Manufacturer of Portion controlled, fresh and frozen seafood
President: Mark Palmer
CFO: Tony Ross
VP Retail Sales: Ron Christianson
EVP Operations/Sales: Mark Palmer
Plant Manager: Joe Kelso
Estimated Sales: $100+ Million
Number Employees: 1,000-4,999
Type of Packaging: Private Label
Other Locations:
Ocean Beauty - Production
Cordova AK
Ocean Beauty - Processing
Alitak AK
Ocean Beauty
Taunton MA
Ocean Beauty - Plant
Excursion AK
Ocean Beauty - Production
Kodiak AK
Ocean Beauty - Production
Naknek AK
Ocean Beauty - Production
Petersburg AK
Ocean Beauty - Production
Nikiski AK
Brands:
BAY BEAUTY
COMMANDER
DEEP SEA
ECHO FALLS
ICY POINT
LASSCO
MCGOVERN
NATHAN'S
NEPTUNE
OCEAN BEAUTY
OCEAN BONITA
PILLAR ROCK
PINK BEAUTY
PIRATE
PORT CLYDE
RITE
ROYAL ALASKA
SEA CHANCE
SEARCHLIGHT
SOUND BEAUTY
SURF KING
THREE STAR
TRIBE
XIP CAVIAR

9860 **Ocean Beauty Seafoods**
110 Prince Henry Drive
Taunton, MA 02780 774-961-0000
Fax: 774-961-0019
pam.gallant@oceanbeauty.com
www.tribehummus.com
Processor of smoked salmon and pickled fish
Owner: Howard Klein
CEO: Bill Terhar
CEO: Mark Palmer
Marketing: Pam Gallant
Estimated Sales: $100+ Million
Number Employees: 1,000-4,999
Type of Packaging: Consumer, Food Service
Brands:
Rite Food
Sea Choice

9861 **(HQ)Ocean Beauty Seafoods**
1100 W Ewing St
Seattle, WA 98119 206-285-6800
Fax: 206-285-9190 info@oceanbeauty.com
www.oceanbeauty.com
Manufacturer and distributor of seafood
President: Mark Palmer
CFO: Tony Ross
National Retail Sales Manager: Kevin Palmer
Estimated Sales: $260 Million
Number Employees: 1,000-4,999
Type of Packaging: Food Service
Other Locations:
Ocean Beauty Seafood Facility
Boston MA
Ocean Beauty Seafood Facility
Cordova AK
Ocean Beauty Seafood Facility
Alitak AK
Ocean Beauty Seafood Facility
Kodiak AK
Ocean Beauty Seafood Facility
Los Angeles CA
Ocean Beauty Seafood Facility
Monroe AK
Ocean Beauty Seafood Facility
Naknek AK
Ocean Beauty Seafood Facility
Petersburg AK
Ocean Beauty Seafood Facility
Seattle WA
Ocean Beauty Seafood Facility
Nikiski AK
Brands:
COMMANDER
ECHO FALLS
ICY POINT
LASCCO
NATHANS
NEPTUNE
OCEAN BONITA
PILLAR ROCK
PINK BEAUTY
PORT CLYDE
RITE FOODS
SEA CHOICE
SEARCHLIGHT
THREE STAR
TRIBE

9862 **Ocean Beauty Seafoods**
14651 172nd Dr SE
Monroe, WA 98272 425-482-2923
Fax: 425-794-9312 info@oceanbeauty.com
www.oceanbeauty.com
Frozen salmon, smoked salmon, pickled herring, smoked trout
Manager: Diane Miller
President: Timothy Horgan
Estimated Sales: $20-50 Million
Number Employees: 60
Brands:
Circle Sea
Echofalls
Icy point
Lascco
Nathan's
Northern Lox
Ocean Bonita
Rite Foods
Scan Fish
Sea Choice
Three Star
Tribe

9863 **Ocean Cliff Corporation**
362 S Front St
New Bedford, MA 02740-5745 508-990-7900
Fax: 508-990-7950 oceanclf@rcn.com
Processor, importer and exporter of fish and seafood liquid and powder extracts and spices including shrimp, clam, crab, fish, lobster and mussel. Produces seafood flavors both in a liquid and powder form
Owner: G Gregory White
Estimated Sales: $ 2.5-5 Million
Number Employees: 5-9
Sq. footage: 20000
Type of Packaging: Bulk
Brands:
Ocean Cliff

9864 **Ocean Coffee Roasters**
259 East Ave
Pawtucket, RI 2860 800-598-5282
Fax: 401-724-0560 800-598-5282
www.excellentcoffee.com
Manufacturer of Coffee, tea
President: William Kapos
Estimated Sales: Less than $500,000
Number Employees: 10-19
Brands:
OCEAN COFFEE

9865 **Ocean Crest Seafoods**
88 Commercial St
Gloucester, MA 01930-5025 978-281-0232
Fax: 978-283-3211 www.neptunesharvest.com
Seafood
President/CEO: Leonard Parco
Estimated Sales: $ 1 - 3 Million
Number Employees: 20-49

9866 **Ocean Delight Seafoods**
450 Alexander Street
Vancouver, BC V6A 1C5
Canada 604-254-8351
Fax: 604-254-1699
Processor and exporter of fresh fish cakes
President: Shig Hirai
Number Employees: 5-9
Type of Packaging: Consumer, Food Service, Private Label, Bulk

9867 **Ocean Diamond**
20 Potash Road
Oakland, NJ 07436-3100 201-337-9515
Fax: 201-337-0479
Seafood

9868 **Ocean Food Company**
3 Turbina Avenue
Scarborough, ON M1V 5G3
Canada 416-285-6487
Fax: 416-285-4012 info@oceanfood.ca
Manufactuer of salmon flakes, fish-sausage, kamaboko, crab-imitation
President: Fumihiro Nishikaze
Vice President: Tsutako Nishikaze
Estimated Sales: $1.4 Million
Number Employees: 10
Type of Packaging: Consumer, Food Service

9869 **Ocean Foods of Astoria**
PO Box 626
Astoria, OR 97103-0626 503-325-2421
Fax: 503-325-1770
Seafood
President: Grant Larson
Estimated Sales: $ 10-20 Million
Number Employees: 50

9870 **Ocean Fresh Seafoods**
4241 21st Ave W # 306
Seattle, WA 98199-1250 206-285-2412
Fax: 206-283-3408 www.oceanfreshsea.com
Processor of fresh and frozen fish and seafood
President: Ted Otness
Plant Manager: Bill Bryant
Estimated Sales: $1,100,000
Number Employees: 5-9
Type of Packaging: Food Service
Brands:
Alaska Fresh

9871 **(HQ)Ocean Garden Products**
3585 Corporate Ct
San Diego, CA 92123-2415 858-571-5002
Fax: 858-571-2009 www.oceangarden.com
King crab, salmon, shrimp, lobster tails
CFO: Frank Barrancotto
CEO: Javier Corella
Estimated Sales: $33.5 Million
Number Employees: 100-249

9872 **Ocean King International**
1680 S Garfield Avenue
Alhambra, CA 91801-5413 626-289-9399
Fax: 626-300-8177
Seafood
President/CEO: Jimmie Dang
CFO: Miling Shua
Vice President: Richard Mendelson
Secretary: Jorge Pardinas

9873 **Ocean Mist**
10855 Ocean Mist Parkway
Castroville, CA 95012 831-633-2144
Fax: 831-633-0561 800-962-3738
contactus@oceanmist.com www.oceanmist.com
Processor/packer/grower of vegetables including spinach, cauliflower, celery, lettuce, artichokes, broccoli, etc.
President: Ed Boutonnet
VP Sales: Maggie Bezart
Sales Director: Joe Feldman
Sales Manager: Bob Polovneff
Operations Manager: Les Tottino
Plant Manager: Mark Rensons
Estimated Sales: $9,200,000
Number Employees: 50-99
Brands:
MISTER
OCEAN MIST
OCEAN MIST MISTEE

9874 **Ocean Pride Fisheries**
136 Jacquard Rd
Lower Wedgeport, NS B0W 2B0
Canada 902-663-4579
Fax: 902-663-2698
Processor and exporter of smoked salmon, cod and haddock
President: Milton Leblanc
Estimated Sales: $1.3 Million
Number Employees: 10
Type of Packaging: Consumer, Food Service, Bulk

9875 **Ocean Pride Seafood**
207 S Richard St
Delcambre, LA 70528 337-685-2336
Fax: 337-685-2339
Manufacturer of Shrimp and crawfish
President: Denise Dooley
Estimated Sales: $500,000-$1 Million
Number Employees: 1-4

9876 **Ocean Select Seafood**
10714 Highway 14
Delcambre, LA 70528 337-685-5315
Fax: 337-685-6079
Seafood
President: Mitch Polito
Estimated Sales: $5-$10 Million
Number Employees: 1-4

9877 **(HQ)Ocean Spray Cranberries**
One Ocean Spray Drive
Lakeville-Middleboro, MA 02349 508-946-1000
Fax: 508-946-7704 800-662-3263
www.oceanspray.com
Manufacturer and exporter of cranberry products including bottled juices, sauces, relish, etc ocean spray,oatmeal ,dried fruit snacks,trail mix,cereal.
President/CEO: Randy Papadellis
SVP, CFO and Treasurer: Timothy Chan
SVP: Kenneth Romanzi
Corporate Communications: Kathie Cornelius
SVP/COO: Kenneth Romanzi
VP Operations: Michael Stamatakos
Estimated Sales: $1.9 Billion
Number Employees: 2000
Type of Packaging: Consumer, Food Service
Other Locations:
Ocean Spray International
Palm Harbor FL
Ocean Spray International
Lakeville MA
Ocean Spray International
Chestney, GBR
Brands:
CRAISINS
CRANAPPLE
CRANCHERRY
CRANGRAPE
CRANICOT
CRANORANGE
OCEAN SPRAY
OCEAN SPRAY APPLE JUICE
OCEAN SPRAY CRANBERRIES
OCEAN SPRAY CRANBERRY COCKTAIL
OCEAN SPRAY FRUIT PUNCH
OCEAN SPRAY FRUIT PUNCH COOLER
OCEAN SPRAY GRAPEFRUIT JUICE
OCEAN SPRAY JELLIED CRAN. SAUCE
OCEAN SPRAY JUICE BLENDS
OCEAN SPRAY KIWI STRAQ. JUICE
OCEAN SPRAY LEMONADE
OCEAN SPRAY ORANGE JUICE
OCEAN SPRAY PINEAPPLE GRAPEFRUIT
OCEAN SPRAY PINK GRAPEFRUIT JUICE
OCEAN SPRAY RUBY RED & MANGO
OCEAN SPRAY RUBY RED GRAPEFRUIT
OCEAN SPRAY WHOLE BERRY CRANBERRIES
WELLFLEET FARMS
WELLFLEET FARMS CRANBERRY SAUCE
WELLFLEET FARMS SPECIALTY FOODS

9878 **Ocean Spray Cranberries**
3975 20th St Ste D
Vero Beach, FL 32960 772-562-0800
Fax: 772-562-1215 www.oceanspray.com
Processor of grapefruit concentrate fruit juice
Area Manager Citrus Operations: Ted Kucinaky
Parent Co: Ocean Spray Cranberries
Type of Packaging: Bulk

9879 **Ocean Spray Cranberries**
104 Park St
Bordentown, NJ 8505 609-298-0905
Fax: 609-298-8353 www.oceanspray.com
Juice, produce, craisins, sauces and oatmeal
Manufacturing/Operations Director: Robert Swanson
Plant Manager: Tim Haggerty
Parent Co: Ocean Spray Cranberries
Type of Packaging: Consumer, Food Service

9880 **Ocean Spray Cranberries**
7800 60th Ave
Kenosha, WI 53142 262-694-5200
Fax: 262-694-5533 www.oceanspray.com
Processor of cranberry products including juices, jelly and sauce
Plant Manager: George Smedley
Estimated Sales: $100+ Million
Number Employees: 250-499
Parent Co: Ocean Spray Cranberries
Type of Packaging: Consumer, Food Service

9881 **Ocean Springs Seafood**
608 Magnolia Ave
Ocean Springs, MS 39564 228-875-0104
Fax: 228-875-0117
mail@oceanspringschambers.com
www.oceanspringschambers.com
Processor of frozen, fresh, headless and peeled shrimp
President: Earl Sayard
VP: Ruby Fayard
Secretary: Linda Fayard
Estimated Sales: $1500000
Number Employees: 5-9
Type of Packaging: Private Label
Brands:
Surf Spray
Tropic

9882 **Ocean Union Company**
2100 Riverside Pkwy # 129
Lawrenceville, GA 30043-5927 770-995-1957
Fax: 770-513-8662
Seafood, snapper, grouper, lobster, crab, tuna, eel, mackerel
President: Jackie Tsai

9883 **Oceana Foods**
P.O.Box 156
Shelby, MI 49455 231-861-2141
Fax: 231-861-6351 www.cherrycentral.com
Dried fruit and dried vegetable processing and packaging.
President: Jeffrey Tucker
COO: Jeff Tucker
Estimated Sales: $85683203
Number Employees: 50-99
Type of Packaging: Consumer, Food Service, Private Label
Brands:
McDonald
P-Royal
Shelby
Telephone

9884 **Oceanfood Sales**
1909 Hastings Street E
Vancouver, BC V5L 1T5
Canada 604-255-1414
Fax: 604-255-1787 877-255-1414
plathe@oceanfoods.com

Processor and exporter of smoked salmon
President: John Graham
Marketing Manager: David Slate
Production Manager: John Makowhichuk
Estimated Sales: $7.9 Million
Number Employees: 16
Type of Packaging: Consumer, Food Service, Private Label, Bulk

9885 **Oceania Cellars**
2204 Corbett Canyon Road
Arroyo Grande, CA 93420-4918 805-481-5434
Wines
President: Roger King

9886 **Oceanledge Seafoods**
138 Rankin Street
Rockland, ME 04841-2318 207-594-4955
Fax: 626-968-0196
Seafood
President: Steve Jonasson

9887 **Oceans Prome Distributing**
P.O.Box 2325
Glenview, IL 60025-6325 847-998-5813
Fax: 847-729-5228
President: Jeffrey Burhop
Estimated Sales: $ 5 - 10 Million
Number Employees: 5-9

9888 **Oceanside Knish Factory**
P.O.Box 154
Oceanside, NY 11572 516-766-4445
Fax: 516-766-2319 www.knishfactory.com
Knishes
President: Leonard Model
Estimated Sales: Below $ 5 Million
Number Employees: 20-49

9889 **Octavia Tea LLC**
38w061 Tanglewood Drive
Batavia, IL 60510 866-505-6387
elizabeth@octaviatea.com
www.octaviatea.com
Tea.
Marketing: Elizabeth Stephano

9890 **Odell Brewing Company**
800 E Lincoln Ave
Fort Collins, CO 80524 970-498-9070
Fax: 970-498-0706 odells@odellbrewing.com
www.odellbrewing.com
Beer
President/CEO: Douglas Odell
Manager Sales/Marketing: John Perant
Treasurer: Wynne Odell
Estimated Sales: $ 10-20 Million
Number Employees: 20-49
Brands:
90 Shilling
Cutthroat Pale Ale
Easy Street Wheat
Easy Street Wheat
Isolation Ale
Levity Golden Amber

9891 **Odessa Tortilla & TamaleFactory**
1915 E 2nd St
Odessa, TX 79761-5311 432-332-6676
Fax: 432-332-6699 800-753-2445
Processor of Mexican foods including tortillas, pork tamales, chorizo, burritos and shells
President: Manuel Gonzalez
Vice President: Evelyn Gonzalez
Estimated Sales: $1100000
Number Employees: 10-19
Sq. footage: 6000
Type of Packaging: Consumer, Food Service, Bulk
Brands:
Manuel's
Mito's

9892 **Odom's Tennessee Pride Sausage Company**
P.O.Box 1187
Madison, TN 37116-1187 615-868-1360
Fax: 615-860-4703 800-327-6269
lmoorer@tnpride.com www.tnpride.com
Processor of country sausage
President: Larry Odom
Chairman: Richard Odom
President: Larry Odom
Marketing Director: Mark Newell
Plant Manager: Frank Howell
Purchasing Manager: William Truan
Estimated Sales: $66400000
Number Employees: 100-249
Type of Packaging: Consumer, Food Service, Private Label, Bulk
Brands:
Tennessee Pride Country Sausage

9893 **Odwalla**
1205 S Platte Riv Dr Unit 106
Denver, CO 80223 303-282-0500
Fax: 303-282-1199 www.odwalla.com
Processor of fresh citrus juice and co-packer of bottled juice products
Manager: Dennis Dingman
Estimated Sales: $910000
Number Employees: 20-49
Sq. footage: 18000
Parent Co: Coca-Cola Bottling Company
Type of Packaging: Consumer, Food Service, Private Label, Bulk
Brands:
Glorious Morning

9894 **(HQ)Odwalla**
120 Stone Pine Rd
Half Moon Bay, CA 94019 650-726-1888
Fax: 650-726-4441 800-639-2552
custserv@odwalla.com www.odwalla.com
Fresh fruit and vegetable juices, geothermal spring water, nutritional bars, soy based drinks and organic soy milk.
President: Shawn Sugarman
COO: Steve McCormick
Senior VP Finance/CFO: James Steichen
Senior VP: James R Steichen
VP Sales: Elizabeth McDonough
Estimated Sales: $146 Million
Number Employees: 500-999
Parent Co: Coca-Cola Bottling Company
Type of Packaging: Consumer
Brands:
A Breath of Fresh
Femme Vitale
Glorious Morning
Juice For Humans
Mango Tango
Mo'beta
Odwalla
Odwalla Cranberry Citrus Bar
Odwalla Fruity C Monster Bar
Odwalla Juices
Odwalla Organic Carrot Bar
Odwalla Peanut Crunch Bar
Serious Ginseng

9895 **Oetker Limited**
2229 Drew Road
Mississauga, ON L5S 1E5
Canada 905-678-1311
Fax: 905-678-9334 800-387-6939
customer_service@oetker.ca www.oetker.ca
Manufacturer of Cake and muffin mixes, mashed potatoes, drink crystals
Chairman: Dr August Oetker
President: Dr h c August Oetker
Brands:
DR OETKER

9896 **Off Shore Seafood Company**
P.O.Box 120
Bayside Drive
Point Lookout, NY 11569-0120 516-432-0529
Seafood, seafood products
President: Robert L Doxsee
Estimated Sales: Below $ 5 Million
Number Employees: 20-49
Type of Packaging: Private Label

9897 **Office General des EauxMinerales**
5260 Avenue Notre-Dame-De-Grace
Montreal, QC H4A 1K9
Canada 514-482-7221
Fax: 514-482-7093 www.saintjustin.ca
Bottler and exporter of carbonated natural mineral water
President: Nicole Lelievre
Number Employees: 23
Type of Packaging: Food Service
Brands:
Saint Justin

9898 **Offshore Systems**
P.O.Box 920427
Dutch Harbor, AK 99692 907-581-1827
Fax: 907-581-1630 www.offshoresystemsinc.com
VP: Robert Schasteen
Manager: Tiny Schasteen

9899 **Oh Boy! Corporation**
1516 1st Street
San Fernando, CA 91340-2796 818-361-1128
Fax: 818-361-7651 ob1516@aol.com
Pizza, prepared sandwiches, lasagna, meatballs, garlic bread, stuffed potatoes, entrees
President: John Rooney
Chairman of the Board: Concetta Vitale
VP: George Moran
R & D: Chuck Solemon
Quality Control: Luz Aguriie
Accounts/Marketing Director: Tim Lasater
Operations Manager: John Vitale
Plant Manager: Martin Torres
Estimated Sales: $ 10-20 Million
Number Employees: 140
Type of Packaging: Private Label
Brands:
Lola

9900 **Oh, Sugar! LLC**
1050 Northfield Ct
Suite 125
Roswell, GA 30076 678-393-6408
Fax: 678-393-6489 866-557-8427
info@namsbits.com www.namsbits.com
cookies and candy
Marketing: Amanda Black

9901 **Ohana Seafood, LLC**
255 Sand Island Rd Ste 2c
Honolulu, HI 96819 808-843-1844
Fax: 808-843-1844
Seafood
Vice President: Jeffrey Yee
Estimated Sales: $570,000
Number Employees: 1-4

9902 **Ohio Mushroom Company**
1893 N Dixie Hwy
Lima, OH 45801-3255 419-221-1721
Mushrooms

9903 **Ohio Packing Company**
1306 Harmon Ave
Columbus, OH 43223 614-239-1600
Fax: 614-237-0885 800-282-6403
cjones@ohiopacking.com
www.ohiopacking.com
Manufacturer and exporter of fresh smoked and processed ham, bacon, lunch meat, hot dogs and sausage
Manager: Carla Jones Jr
VP: Ronald Wilke
Sales: Christina Wood
VP Operations: Edward Wilke Jr
Estimated Sales: $ 20 - 50 Million
Number Employees: 100-249
Sq. footage: 75000
Type of Packaging: Consumer, Food Service, Private Label, Bulk
Brands:
BAHAMA MAMA
BRUTUS BRATS
BUCKEYE
HARVEST
POPPY'S PRIDE

9904 **Ohio Processors Company**
244 E 1st St
London, OH 43140 740-852-9243
Fax: 740-488-2536
Processor of whipped topping and nondairy coffee creamers
President: Douglas Smith
Estimated Sales: $ 5 - 10 Million
Number Employees: 20-49
Sq. footage: 22116
Parent Co: Instantwhip Foods
Type of Packaging: Food Service, Private Label
Brands:
Instant Whip

9905 **Ohta Wafer Factory**
931 Hauoli St
Honolulu, HI 96826 808-949-2775
Processor of puffed rice cakes and fortune and Japanese tea cookies
President: Herb Ohta
Estimated Sales: $500,000-$1 Million
Number Employees: 1-4
Sq. footage: 3000
Type of Packaging: Consumer, Food Service
Brands:
Ohta's Senbei

9906 **Oils of Aloha**
66-935 Kaukonahua Rd
Waialua, HI 96791 808-637-5620
Fax: 808-637-6194 800-367-6010
info@oilsofaloha.com www.oilsofaloha.com
Manufactuer of Salad oils and cooking oils
Chairman/Owner: Dana Gray
President: Matthew Papania
Marketing: Barbara Gray
Plant Manager: Matthew Papania
Estimated Sales: $5-10 Million
Number Employees: 10-19
Number of Brands: 1
Sq. footage: 15000
Type of Packaging: Consumer, Food Service
Brands:
OILS OF ALOHA MACADAMIA NUT OIL

9907 **Ojai Cook**
149 S Barrington Avenue
Los Angeles, CA 90049-3310 310-646-5001
Fax: 310-839-5135 886-571-1551
Info@ojaicook.com www.ojaicook.com
Condiments, sauces and beverages
President/CEO/Marketing Director: Joan Vogel
Brands:
Cocktail Duet
Prickly Pecans
Puckers

9908 **Ojai Vineyard**
10540 Encino Dr
Oak View, CA 93022 805-649-1674
Fax: 805-649-4651 info@OjaiVineyard.com
www.ojaivineyard.com
Processor of wine
Owner: Adam Tolmach
Estimated Sales: $590,000
Number Employees: 1-4
Brands:
Ojai

9909 **Ok Industries**
P.O.Box 1119
Fort Smith, AR 72902 479-783-4186
Fax: 479-784-1358 800-635-9441
www.okfoods.com
Chairman: Collier Wenderoth Jr
President: Thomas Webb
CEO: Randy Goins
Quality Control: John Schuleupner
Estimated Sales: G
Number Employees: 50-99
Parent Co: OK Industries
Type of Packaging: Consumer, Food Service, Private Label
Brands:
O.K. FOODS
TENDERBIRD

9910 **Okahara Saimin Factory**
1804 Waiola St
Honolulu, HI 96826 808-949-0588
Fax: 808-949-0375 okaharasf001@hawaii.rr.com
www.saiminfactory.com
Processor of noodles
President: Kiyoko Okahara
Estimated Sales: $1500000
Number Employees: 20-49
Type of Packaging: Consumer, Food Service

9911 **Okanagan Spring Brewery**
2808 27th Avenue
Vernon, BC V1T 9K4
Canada 250-542-2337
Fax: 250-542-7780 800-652-0755
info@okspring.com www.okspring.com
Processor of beer, ale and stout
COO: Richardson Knudson
CEO: John Sleeman
Marketing Director: Paul Meehan
Managing Director: Rick Knudson
Parent Co: Seeman Brewing & Malting Company
Type of Packaging: Consumer, Food Service
Brands:
Okanagan Spring
Shastebury
Sleeman
Strohs Canada

9912 **Okeene Milling**
P.O.Box 1567
Shawnee, OK 74802-1567 405-273-7000
Fax: 405-273-7333
lhammons@shawneemilling.com
www.shawneemilling.com
Manufacturer of bulk bakery, tortilla and whole wheat flour
CEO: William L Ford
Number Employees: 20-49
Parent Co: Shawnee Milling Company
Type of Packaging: Consumer, Food Service

9913 **Oklahoma City Meat**
300 S Klein Ave
Oklahoma City, OK 73108 405-235-3308
Fax: 405-235-9989 www.okcmeat.com
Processor of beef, lamb and pork; wholesaler/distributor of chicken
President: Tommy Saunders
Estimated Sales: $ 10 - 20 Million
Number Employees: 20-49
Type of Packaging: Food Service

9914 **Okuhara Foods**
881 N King St
Honolulu, HI 96817 808-848-0581
Fax: 808-841-5367 okufood@aol.com
Processor of pre-packaged frozen fish including salted butterfish, salmon and shellfish
President: James N Okuhara
Vice President: Satoru Okuhara
Estimated Sales: $ 10 - 20 Million
Number Employees: 20-49
Type of Packaging: Consumer, Bulk

9915 **Oland Breweries**
3055 Agricola Street
Halifax, NS B3K 4G2
Canada 902-453-1867
Fax: 902-453-3847 800-268-2337
www.labatt.com
Processor of beer, ale, stout and lager
Marketing Director: Brent Qartermain
Number Employees: 100-249
Parent Co: Labatt Breweries
Type of Packaging: Consumer, Food Service
Brands:
Labatt
Oland

9916 **Olcott Plastics**
95 N 17th Street
Saint Charles, IL 60174 630-584-0555
Fax: 630-584-5655 888-313-5277
sales@olcottplastics.com
www.olcottplastics.com
Manufacturer, importer and exporter of plastic containers, jars and jar closures.
Owner/President/VP Operations: John Brodner
CFO: Mark Herzog
Quality Manager: Perry Norsworthy
Sales Manager: Troy Rusch
Human Resources Director: Sandy Allen
Purchasing: Teresa Casey
Estimated Sales: $12.6 Million
Number Employees: 95
Sq. footage: 60000
Type of Packaging: Consumer, Private Label, Bulk

9917 **Old 97 Manufacturing Company**
2306 N 35th St
Tampa, FL 33605-4432 813-247-6677
Fax: 813-247-6259 www.thestephanco.com
Processor of flavoring extracts and over-the-counter pharmaceuticals
Office Manager: Rita Chlau
Plant Manager: Mike Henry
Number Employees: 50-99
Parent Co: Stephan Company

9918 **Old Baldy Brewing Company**
271 N 2nd Ave
Upland, CA 91786-8327 909-946-1750
Fax: 909-608-1729
Processor of seasonal beer, ale and stout
President/CEO: Bill Romero
Estimated Sales: Less than $500,000
Number Employees: 5-9
Type of Packaging: Consumer, Food Service
Brands:
Old Baldy

9919 **Old Cavendish Products**
P.O.Box 631
Cavendish, VT 05142 802-226-7783
Fax: 802-226-7783 800-536-7899
fruitcakes@tds.net www.cavendishfruitcake.com
Manufacturer of all natural fruitcake, mustard, herb vinegars
President: Mary Ormrod
Estimated Sales: $ .5 - 1 million
Number Employees: 1-4

9920 **Old Chatham Sheepherding**
155 Shaker Museum Rd
Old Chatham, NY 12136 518-794-7733
Fax: 518-794-7641 888-743-3760
cheese@blacksheepcheese.com
www.blacksheepcheese.com
Manufacturer of sheep's milk cheese
President/Owner: Thomas Clark
Owner: Nancy Clark
Marketing/Sales: Lorie Appleby
Kleinpeter/Cheesemaker: Benoit Mailloil
Administrative Manager: Sandra Hoehneker
Estimated Sales: $5-10 Million
Number Employees: 20-49
Number of Brands: 1
Number of Products: 14

9921 **Old Colony Baking Company**
29699 IL Hwy 29
Spring Valley, IL 61362 815- 44- 211
Fax: 81- 44- 206 info@ocolony.com
www.ocolony.com
Manufacturer of Pastries and bag cookie line
President/Owner: Jeffrey Kaufman
Vice President/Owner: Ann Kaufman
Estimated Sales: $ 1 - 3 Million
Number Employees: 1-4
Type of Packaging: Consumer, Food Service, Private Label
Brands:
ANDES CHOCOLATE MINT CHIP COOKIES
BIG TOP ANIMAL COOKIES
CHIQUITA BANANA COOKIES
DIAMOND WALNUT SHORTBREAD COOKIES
MUSSELMAN'S APPLE SAUCE COOKIES
REALEMON LEMON COOKIES

9922 **Old Country Bakery**
5350 Biloxi Avenue
North Hollywood, CA 91601-3531 818-838-2302
Fax: 818-838-2307
Cakes and pastry
General Manager: Chris Meyer

9923 **Old Country Cheese**
S510 County Road D
Cashton, WI 54619 608-654-5411
Fax: 608-654-5411 info@oldcountrycheese.com
www.oldcountrycheese.com
Cheese and jams
President: Kevin Everhart
County Chief: Michael Everhart
Estimated Sales: $ 1-2.5 Million
Number Employees: 20-49
Type of Packaging: Consumer, Private Label, Bulk
Brands:
Old Country Cheese

9924 **Old Country Farms**
PO Box 921
East Sandwich, MA 02537-0921 508-888-0715
Fax: 508-833-9261 888-707-5558
oldctyfarm@aol.com www.oldcountyfarms.com
Manufacturer of Cranberries, fruits spreads, dried fruit and baking mixes

9925 **Old Country Meat & Sausage Company**
811 W Washington St
San Diego, CA 92103-1894 619-297-4301

Manufacturer of sausages
President: Manfred Spenner
CEO: Manfred Spenner
Marketing Manager: Manfred Spenner
Estimated Sales: Under $500,000
Number Employees: 5-9
Type of Packaging: Bulk
Brands:
Old Country

9926 **Old Country Packers**
318 River St
Duryea, PA 18642 570-655-9608
Fax: 570-457-1678
Processor of horseradish including white and red beet, cocktail sauce, chicken wing sauce including mild, hot and honey, sauce and garlic in water and oil
President: Edwarded Orkwis
Estimated Sales: $ .5 - 1 million
Number Employees: 1-4
Sq. footage: 4000
Type of Packaging: Consumer, Food Service, Private Label
Brands:
Old Country
Town Tavern

9927 **Old Credit Brewing Co LtOntario Craft Brewers**
1-75 Horner Ave
Toronto, ON M8Z 4X5
Canada 416-494-2766
Fax: 905-274-4154
info@ontariocraftbrewers.com
www.ontariocraftbrewers.com
Manufacturer of amber/red ale and pilsner
President: Aldo Lista
Brewer: Orrin Besko
Number Employees: 5-9
Sq. footage: 6000
Type of Packaging: Consumer, Food Service
Brands:
OLD CREDIT

9928 **Old Creek Ranch Winery**
10024 Old Creek Rd
Ventura, CA 93001-1002 805-649-4132
Fax: 805-649-9293 winery@oldcreekranch.com
www.oldcreekranch.com
Manufacturer of premium wines
President: John Whitman
Winemaker: Charles Branham
Estimated Sales: Below $5 Million
Number Employees: 5-9
Number of Products: 3
Sq. footage: 4000
Type of Packaging: Private Label
Brands:
OLD CREEK RANCH WINERY

9929 **Old Dominion Peanut Corporation**
208 W 24th St
Norfolk, VA 23517 757-622-1633
Fax: 757-624-9415 800-368-6887
odpeanuit@aol.com
Processor of candy including hard Christmas, fund raising, cashew and peanut brittle and chocolate covered and butter toffee peanuts
President: William Delchiaro
Estimated Sales: $4500000
Number Employees: 50-99
Sq. footage: 50000
Parent Co: The Virginia Food Group
Type of Packaging: Consumer, Food Service, Private Label, Bulk
Brands:
Old Dominion

9930 **Old Dominion Spice Company**
10990 Leadbetter Road
PO Box 249
Ashland, VA 23005 804-550-2780
Fax: 804-550-2868 info@olddominionspice.com
www.olddominionspice.com
Dry blends used in condiments, marinades, seasonings, rubs, breaders, batters and other coating systems.
President: Lindy Thackston
Founder/CEO: Milton Parma
Research & Development Manager: David Pauly
SVP Sales: H Guy Moyers
Estimated Sales: $550,000
Number Employees: 8
Sq. footage: 8300

9931 **Old Dutch Foods**
2375 Terminal Rd
Roseville, MN 55113 651-633-8810
Fax: 651-633-8894 800-989-2447
customerservice@olddutchfoods.com
www.olddutchfoods.com
Snack foods including potato chips, popcorn, pretzels, salsa and dips.
President: Steve Aanenson
Estimated Sales: $ 100-500 Million
Number Employees: 250-499
Type of Packaging: Private Label
Brands:
Cocina del Norte
Dutch Crunch
Old Dutch
Ripples

9932 **(HQ)Old Dutch Mustard Company**
98 Cuttermill Road
Suite 260
Great Neck, NY 11021-3010 516-466-0522
Fax: 516-466-0762
Processor of mustard flour, prepared mustard, vinegar, sauce and juice
President: Paul Santich
Sales Manager: Evan Dobkins
Number Employees: 70
Sq. footage: 100000
Type of Packaging: Consumer, Food Service, Private Label, Bulk
Other Locations:
Brands:
Old Dutch

9933 **Old Europe Cheese**
1330 E Empire Ave
Benton Harbor, MI 49022 269-925-5003
Fax: 269-925-9560 800-447-8182
www.oldeuropecheese.com
Specialty cheeses
Manager: Francious Capt
Manager: Francois Capt
Packing Manager: Scott Ness
Purchasing Manager: Sam Siriano
Estimated Sales: $ 10 -15 Million
Number Employees: 50-99
Sq. footage: 50
Type of Packaging: Private Label
Brands:
Manchego

9934 **Old Fashioned Candy**
6210 Cermak Rd
Berwyn, IL 60402-2322 708-788-6669
Processor of chocolate candy
Owner: Theresa Brunslik
Sales Manager: Lynn White
Estimated Sales: $500,000-$1 Million
Number Employees: 5-9
Type of Packaging: Consumer

9935 **Old Fashioned Foods Inc**
331 S Main St
PO Box 111
Mayville, WI 53050 920-387-7920
Fax: 920-387-7929 www.oldfash.com
Cheese spreads, cheese sauce, tex-mex, cheese dips, nacho cheese sauce, squeeze cheese, squeeze salsa, glass cheese spreads, cheese sticks, and aerosol and portion control pouches.
Owner/President: Bernard Youso
Chairman: Gary Youso
CFO: Gary Youso
Quality Control: Ben Lindstrom
Marketing: Bernie Youso
Sales: Jim Clark
Production/Maintenance: Cory Lenhardt
Purchasing: Kathy Emmer
Estimated Sales: $ 5-10 Million
Number Employees: 70
Brands:
Old Faishoned Foods

9936 **Old Fashioned Kitchen**
1045 Towbin Ave
Lakewood, NJ 8701 732-364-4100
Fax: 732-905-7352 www.oldfashionedkitchen.com
Manufacturer and distributor of specialy frozen foods nationally
President: Jay Conzen
SVP: Sal Mangiapane
Estimated Sales: $ 20 - 50 Million
Number Employees: 90
Sq. footage: 30000

9937 **Old Fashioned Kitchen**
1045 Towbin Ave
Lakewood, NJ 08701 732-364-4100
Fax: 732-905-7352
info@oldfashionedkitchen.com
www.oldfashionedkitchen.com
Blintzes, crepes, pierogies, pancakes
President: Jay Conzen
senior VP: Sal Mangiapan
wski VP Finance: Joann Lemaszewiski
Estimated Sales: $10-50 Million
Number Employees: 100-250
Sq. footage: 31000
Type of Packaging: Food Service
Brands:
Golden
Old Fashioned Kitchen

9938 **Old Fashioned Natural Products**
2230 Cape Cod Way
Santa Ana, CA 92703 714-835-6367
Fax: 714-835-4948 800-552-9045
www.lalifestyle.com
Processor of vitamins and herbal teas and supplements; also, custom formulations and private labeling available
President: Patricia Logsdon
VP: John Brown
Estimated Sales: $ 10 - 20 Million
Number Employees: 10-19
Sq. footage: 16000
Type of Packaging: Private Label

9939 **Old Firehouse Winery**
5499 Lake Rd E
Geneva, OH 44041 440-466-9300
Fax: 440-466-8011 800-362-6751
info@oldfirehousewinery.com
www.oldfirehousewinery.com
Ohio wines
Owner: Don Woodward
Estimated Sales: $1-$3 Million
Number Employees: 1-4
Type of Packaging: Consumer

9940 **Old Home Foods**
550 County Road D W Ste 17
Saint Paul, MN 55112 651-312-8900
Fax: 651-312-8901 800-309-9035
info@oldhomefoods.com
www.oldhomefoods.com
Manufacturer of cultured dairy products like cottage cheese, sour cream, yogurt, dips and salsa
President: Geoff Murphy
President: Geoff Murphy
EVP/CFO: John Bonifaci
Estimated Sales: $ 20 - 50 Million
Number Employees: 100-249
Type of Packaging: Consumer, Food Service, Private Label, Bulk
Brands:
Old Home

9941 **Old House Vineyards**
18351 Corkys Ln
Culpeper, VA 22701 540-423-1032
Fax: 540-423-1320 info@oldhousevineyards.com
www.oldhousevineyards.com
Manufacturer of Wines
Owner: Allyson Kearney
Winemaker: Doug Fabbioli
Estimated Sales: $ 3 - 5 Million
Number Employees: 5-9

9942 **Old Kentucky Hams**
PO Box 443
Cynthiana, KY 41031-0443 859-234-5015
Fax: 859-234-5015
Country hams and bacon
President: Nancy Hisle
Plant Manager: Elizabeth Hunt
Estimated Sales: $1-4.9 Million
Number Employees: 1-4
Sq. footage: 1
Type of Packaging: Private Label

Brands:
Old Kentucky Hams
Traditional Kentucky

9943 **Old Mansion Foods**
P.O.Box 1838
Petersburg, VA 23805-0838 804-862-9889
Fax: 804-861-8816 800-476-1877
elaina-t@oldmansion.com www.oldmansion.com
Importer and processor of quality spices, seasonings, coffee and teas.
President: Dale Patton
Sales: Tom Mullen
Plant Manager: Kevin Laffoon
Purchasing Director: Wendy Bryant
Number Employees: 20-49
Type of Packaging: Consumer, Food Service, Private Label, Bulk
Brands:
Festiva
Grill Select
Old Mansion
Southern Classic

9944 **Old Monmouth Peanut Brittle**
627 Park Ave
Freehold, NJ 07728-2351 732-462-1311
Fax: 732-462-6820 sales@oldmonmouth.com
www.oldmonmouthcandies.com
Candy and confections
President: Hal Gunther
Estimated Sales: Below $ 5 Million
Number Employees: 5-9
Brands:
Old Monmouth

9945 **Old Neighborhood Foods**
37 Waterhill St
Lynn, MA 1905 781-595-1557
Fax: 781-595-7523
Processor of meat and provisions including beef, lamb and pork
Owner: Tom Demarkes
Vice President: John Demakes
Estimated Sales: $50 Million
Number Employees: 100-249
Type of Packaging: Food Service
Brands:
Pleasant

9946 **Old Orchard Brands**
1991 12 Mile Rd NW
Sparta, MI 49345 616-887-1745
Fax: 616-887-8210 www.oldorchardjuice.com
Previously known as Apple Valley International. A manufacturer of frozen fruit juices including apple and cranberry lines.
President: Mark Saur
CFO: Howard Veitman
VP Operations: Greg Mangione
Estimated Sales: $ 100 Million
Number Employees: 50-99
Type of Packaging: Consumer

9947 **Old Ranchers Canning Company**
P.O.Box 458
Upland, CA 91785-0458 909-982-8895
Fax: 909-949-2328
Processor of canned beans, stew, chili, broths and meat and nonmeat soups
President: Donald Graber
Estimated Sales: $ 20 - 50 Million
Number Employees: 50-99
Type of Packaging: Private Label

9948 **Old Rip Van Winkle Distillery**
2843 Brownsboro Rd # 208
Louisville, KY 40206-1292 502-897-9113
Fax: 502-896-9989
jvanwinkle@oldripvanwinkle.com
www.oldripvanwinkle.com
Manufacturer of bourbon whiskey
Owner: Julian Van Winkle Iii III
Estimated Sales: $1-2.5 Million
Number Employees: 1-4
Brands:
Old Rip Van Wrinkle

9949 **Old Sacramento Popcorn Company**
1026 2nd St # B
Sacramento, CA 95814-3256 916-446-1980
Fax: 916-442-2676 ospc@concentric.net
www.oldsacramentolivinghistory.com
Processor and exporter of popcorn
Owner: Jim Scott
Estimated Sales: Less than $150,000
Number Employees: 1-4

9950 **Old Salt Seafood Company**
43 Celestial Drive
Narragansett, RI 02882-1150 401-783-5770
Fax: 401-783-5770
Seafood
President: Ken Loud

9951 **Old South Winery**
65 S Concord Ave
Natchez, MS 39120 601-445-9924
Fax: 601-442-1215 mailus@newu.net
www.newu.net/
Wines
Owner: Scott O Galbreth Iii
Co-Owner: Edeen Galbreath
Winemaker: Scott Gallbreath III
Estimated Sales: $500,000-$1 Million
Number Employees: 1-4
Type of Packaging: Private Label
Brands:
Old South Winery
Old South Muscadine

9952 **Old Tavern Food Products**
230 S prairie Ave.
Waukesha, WI 53186-5937 262-542-5301
Fax: 262-542-5676 888-425-1788
www.oldtaverncheese.com
Cheese, gift packs
President: Jill Strong
VP: Gail Strong
Estimated Sales: $500,000-$1 Million
Number Employees: 15
Type of Packaging: Private Label, Bulk
Brands:
Old Tavern Club Cheese

9953 **Old Town Coffee & Tea Company**
1027 Hillen St
Baltimore, MD 21202 410-752-1229
Fax: 410-528-0369 support@eaglecoffee.com
www.eaglecoffee.com
Processor and importer of coffee and tea
Owner: Nick Constantine
Estimated Sales: Below $ 5 Million
Number Employees: 20-49
Sq. footage: 40000
Type of Packaging: Food Service, Private Label, Bulk

9954 **Old Tyme Mill Company**
1517 S Kolmar Avenue
21
Chicago, IL 60623-1037 773-521-9484
Fax: 773-521-9486
Waffle, pancake and breading mix
President: John Pontikes
Treasurer: Dorothy Pontikes
Estimated Sales: $ 1-2.6 K
Number Employees: 5

9955 **Old Wine Cellar**
4411 220th Trl
Amana, IA 52203 319-622-3116
Fax: 319-622-6162 www.travelenvoy.com/wine
Wines
President: Les Aackermin
Estimated Sales: $ 1-2.5 Million
Number Employees: '5-9
Brands:
Old Wine Cellar

9956 **Old Wisconsin Food Products**
950 West 175 St.
Homewood, IL 60430 708-798-0900
Fax: 708-798-3178 888-633-5684
www.buddig.com
Sausage
President: John Buddig
CFO: Roger Buddig
Plant Manager: Charles Belter
Estimated Sales: $200,000
Parent Co: Carl Buddig & Company
Brands:
Carl Budding
Old Wisconsin

9957 **Old Wisconsin Sausage Company**
5030 Playbird Rd
Sheboygan, WI 53083 920-458-4304
Fax: 920-458-2716 800-558-7840
sales@oldwisconsin.com
www.oldwisconsin.com
Sausage
President: Tom Buddig
Manager: Bob Gielissen
Plant Manager: Bob Gielissen
Estimated Sales: $ 20-50 Million
Number Employees: 100-249
Type of Packaging: Consumer
Brands:
Ends and Curls
Old Wisconsin Mug

9958 **Old World Bakery**
1933 W Galbraith
Cincinatti, OH 45239 513-931-1411
Fax: 513-931-3560 owb@fuse.net
www.oldworldbakery.com
Processor of natural breads
Founder: Odette Skally
Public Relations: Cheryl Deleon
Number Employees: 5-9

9959 **Old World Spices & Seasonings, Inc.**
5320 College Blvd
Overland Park, KS 66211 816-861-0400
Fax: 816-861-7073 800-241-0070
kathy@oldworldspices.com
www.laurieskitchen.com
Seasoning, spice and sauce packaging
Owner: John Jungc
Marketing: Kathy Wheat
Estimated Sales: $ 1-5 Million
Number Employees: 20-49
Brands:
Old World Creations
Party Creations
Soups For One

9960 **Olde Colony Bakery**
1391 Stuart Engals Blvd # B
Mt Pleasant, SC 29464 843-216-3232
Fax: 843-216-5553 800-722-9932
OCBenne@aol.com www.oldecolonybakery.com
Manufacturer of gourmet cookies and benne seed wafers
Owner: Peter Rix
Owner: Sheila Rix
Estimated Sales: Less than $500,000
Number Employees: 5-9
Brands:
OLDE COLONY

9961 **Olde Heurich Brewing Company**
1307 New Hampshire Avenue NW
Washington, DC 20036-1507 202-333-2313
Fax: 202-333-9198 lager@foggybottom.com
www.foggybottom.com
Beer
President: Gary Heurich
Estimated Sales: Below $ 5 Million
Number Employees: 5
Brands:
Foggy Bottom Ale
Foggy Bottom Lager
Foggy Bottom Porter
Olde Georgetown Beer
Olde Heurich
Senate Beer

9962 **Olde Tyme Food Corporation**
775 Benton Drive
East Longmeadow, MA 01028-3215 413-525-4101
Fax: 413-525-3621 800-356-6533
oldetyme@samnet.net www.oldetymefoods.com
Processor and exporter of snack foods including candy apples, cotton candy, waffles, waffle cones, peanuts, etc.; manufacturer and exporter of concession stand supplies and snack food making machinery including hot dogs
President: David Baker
Sales Director: David Wedderspoon
Estimated Sales: $1.7 Million
Number Employees: 21
Sq. footage: 25000
Parent Co: Hampton Farms
Type of Packaging: Consumer, Food Service, Private Label, Bulk

Brands:
Olde Tyme
Ole Style Peanut Butter

9963 **Olde Tyme Mercantile**
1127 Mesa View Drive
Arroyo Grande, CA 93420-6542 805-489-7991
Fax: 805-481-5578
kevin@oldetymemercantile.com
www.oldetymemercantile.com
Processor of gourmet products including olives, pickles, salad dressings, mustards, mayonnaise and candies
President: Larry Williams
CEO: Kevin Keim
Propietor: Diane Keim
Number Employees: 10-19
Sq. footage: 2000
Type of Packaging: Consumer, Private Label
Brands:
Scully
Wah Maker

9964 **Olds Products Company**
10700 88th Ave
Pleasant Prairie, WI 53158 262-947-3500
Fax: 262-947-3517 800-233-8064
eamen@oldsfitz.com www.oldsproducts.com
Manufacturers prepared mustard and specialty mustard blends and is also the largest bulk ingredient mustard manufacturer.
President: Robert Remien
VP: Timothy McAvoy
Estimated Sales: $6500000
Number Employees: 20-49
Parent Co: Olds Products Company
Type of Packaging: Consumer, Food Service, Private Label, Bulk
Brands:
Koops

9965 **Ole Salty's of Rockford**
1928 E Riverside Blvd
Loves Park, IL 61111-4893
Fax: 815-963-6855 www.olesaltys.com
Potato chips
Manager: Troy Wedeikand
Estimated Sales: Below $ 5 Million
Number Employees: 1-4
Brands:
Ole Salty's

9966 **Ole Smoky Candy Kitchen**
744 Parkway
Gatlinburg, TN 37738 865-436-6426
Fax: 865-436-0268
Processor of candy
President: Esther J Dych
Estimated Sales: $ 5 - 10 Million
Number Employees: 50-99
Type of Packaging: Consumer

9967 **Olive Oil Factory**
197 Huntingdon Ave
Waterbury, CT 06708 860-945-9549
Fax: 860-945-8662 info@theoliveoilfactory.com
www.theoliveoilfactory.com
Private labeler of oils including extra virgin olive, flavored and dipping; also, balsamic vinegar
President: David Miller
Estimated Sales: $350,000
Number Employees: 5-9
Sq. footage: 5000
Type of Packaging: Consumer, Food Service, Private Label

9968 **Oliver Egg Products**
9422 Hungarytown Road
Crewe, VA 23930-4125 804-645-9406
Fax: 804-645-7429 800-525-3447
Processor of frozen and refrigerated egg whites, whole eggs, yolks and scrambled egg mix
Owner: Bill Oliver
Type of Packaging: Food Service, Bulk

9969 **Oliver Wine Company**
8024 N State Road 37
Bloomington, IN 47404-9449 812-876-5800
Fax: 812-876-9309 800-258-2783
www.oliverwinery.com
Wines
President: William Oliver
Marketing Director: Sarah Villwock
Vice President: Kathleen Oliver
CFO: Kathleen Oliver
Estimated Sales: $ 10-20 Million
Number Employees: 50-99
Brands:
Camelot Mead
Oliver

9970 **Oliver Winery**
8024 N State Road 37
Bloomington, IN 47404 812-876-5800
Fax: 812-876-9309 800-258-2783
woliver@oliverwinery.com
www.oliverwinery.com
Producer of wines including dry (Sauvignon Blanc, Chardonel, Merlot, Zinfandel, Cabernet Sauvignon, etc.); semi-dry (Gew□rztraminer, Riesling, Traminette, etc.), and semi-sweet (Harvest Flavors, Catawba, Muscat Canelli, Camelot MeadVidal Blanc Ice Wine, etc.) varieties.
Co-Owner/Winemaker/Vineyard Management: Bill Oliver
Co-Owner/General Manager: Kathleen Oliver

9971 **Olives & Foods Inc**
13903 NW 67th Avenue
Suite 430
Hialeah, FL 33014-2939 305-821-3444
Processor, importer and exporter of Spanish olives, olive oil, capers, cocktail onions
President: Francisco Orta
VP: Fernando Gazmuri
Sales Director: Andres Reyes
Operations Manager: Ivonne Gazmuri
Number Employees: 1-4
Sq. footage: 800
Parent Co: Acyco, Aceitunas y Conservas S.A.L.
Type of Packaging: Consumer, Food Service, Private Label, Bulk
Brands:
Acyco
Alisa

9972 **Olivia's Croutons**
1423 North St
New Haven, VT 5472 802-453-2222
Fax: 802-453-7722 888-425-3080
fwc@oliviascroutons.com
www.oliviascroutons.com
Manufacturer of all natural specialty croutons: Butter and garlic, parmesan pepper, vermont cheddar and dill, multi grain with garlic, and gazapach lowfat croutons. Also roasted onion tostini and lemon parsley tostini
President: Francie Caccavo
Estimated Sales: Below $5 Million
Number Employees: 5-9
Type of Packaging: Consumer, Food Service, Private Label, Bulk

9973 **Olivier's Candies**
2828 54th Ave SE
Calgary, AB T2C 0A7
Canada 403-266-6028
Fax: 403-266-6029 rjefferys@oliviers.ca
www.oliviers.ca
Manufacturer of chocolate, hard candy, brittles, barks
President: Wally Marcolin
Secretary: Rick Jeffrey
Number Employees: 10-19
Type of Packaging: Consumer, Bulk

9974 **Olsen Fish Company**
2115 N 2nd St
Minneapolis, MN 55411 612-287-0838
Fax: 612-287-8761 800-882-0212
lutefisk@olsenfish.com www.olsenfish.com
Manufacturef of Lutfisk and pickled herring
President: Chris Dorff
Estimated Sales: $ 3 - 5 Million
Number Employees: 10-19
Type of Packaging: Bulk
Brands:
OLSEN

9975 **Olson Livestock & Seed**
31921 Rd 711
Haigler, NE 69030-4006 308-297-3283
Fax: 308-297-3284
Processor of popcorn
Owner: Cliff Olson
Owner: Scott Olson
Owner: Steve Olson
Estimated Sales: $ 3 - 5 Million
Number Employees: 1-4

9976 **Olson Locker**
917 Winnebago Ave
Fairmont, MN 56031 507-238-2563
Fax: 507-238-2564
Processor of meat and meat products
President: Mark Olson
Estimated Sales: $460,000
Number Employees: 1-4
Type of Packaging: Consumer

9977 **Olymel**
700 Rue Croisetiere
Iberville, QC J2X 4H7
Canada 450-542-9339
Fax: 514-357-5660
Processor, importer and exporter of fresh and frozen chicken, turkey and pork
President/CEO: Rejean Nadeau
General Manager: Paul Noiseux
Estimated Sales: 2.1 Billion
Number Employees: 10,000
Parent Co: Cooperative Federee of Quebec
Type of Packaging: Bulk
Brands:
Flamingo
Galco

9978 **Olympia Candies**
11606 Pearl Rd
Cleveland, OH 44136 440-572-7747
Fax: 440-572-1819 800-574-7747
sales@olympiacandy.com
www.olympiacandy.com
gourmet treats
President/Owner: Robert McGrath
VP: Celia McGrath
Number Employees: 25

9979 **Olympia International**
2166 Spring Creek Road
Belvidere, IL 61008-9507 815-547-5972
Fax: 815-547-5973
Processor, exporter and importer of pickles, mushrooms, horseradish, sweet marinated peppers, beets and salads
President: Greg Bodak
Estimated Sales: $260,000
Number Employees: 1

9980 **Olympia Oyster Company**
1042 SE Bloomfield Rd
Shelton, WA 98584-7744 360-426-3354
Fax: 360-427-0122 info@olympiaoyster.com
www.olympiaoyster.com
Processor of oysters and clams; also, oyster soup bases
President: Tim McMillin
Estimated Sales: $1500000
Number Employees: 20-49
Type of Packaging: Consumer, Food Service
Brands:
Puget Sound

9981 **Olympic Cellars**
255410 Highway 101
Port Angeles, WA 98362-9200 360-452-0160
Fax: 360-452-3782 info@olympiccellars.com
www.olympiccellars.com
Wines
Co-Owner: Kathy Charlton
Co-Owner: Molly Rivard
Co-Owner: Libby Sweetser
Winemaker: Benoit Murat
Estimated Sales: Below $ 5 Million
Number Employees: 5-9
Type of Packaging: Private Label
Brands:
Olympic Cellars

9982 **Olympic Coffee & Roasting**
4907 119th Ave SE
Bellevue, WA 98006 206-244-8305
Fax: 206-244-8323 888-244-8313
olympicscoffee@juno.com
www.olympiccoffee.com
Coffee
Director: Robert Doxsie

Estimated Sales: $ 5 - 10 Million
Number Employees: 5-9
Brands:
Olympic Coffee

9983 **Olympic Foods**
5625 W Thorpe Rd
Spokane, WA 99224 509-455-8059
Fax: 509-455-8329 salesinfo@olyfoods.com
www.olyfoods.com
Processor and exporter of chilled ready-to-drink fruit juice
President: Doug Koffinke
CEO: Howard Chow
CFO: Richard Cook
Estimated Sales: $1-2.5 Million
Number Employees: 12
Sq. footage: 87000
Type of Packaging: Consumer, Food Service, Private Label
Brands:
Albertson's
Citrus Sunshine
Dairyworld
Minute Maid
Newman's Own
Tree Top
Washington Natural
Western Family

9984 **Olympic Specialty Foods**
1601 Military Road
Tonawanda, NY 14217-1205 716-874-0771
Fax: 716-876-2171
Gourmet foods
President: Nick Bechakas
Estimated Sales: Below $ 5 Million
Number Employees: 50

9985 **Omaha Meat Processors**
6016 Grover St
Omaha, NE 68106 402-554-1965
Fax: 402-554-0224 omahameats@aol.com
Processor, exporter and packer of beef and pork; importer of beef trimmings
President: A Kousgaard
Owner/President: David Kousgaard
Estimated Sales: $30 Million
Number Employees: 38
Sq. footage: 9000
Type of Packaging: Food Service

9986 **Omaha Steaks International**
P.O.Box 3300
Omaha, NE 68103 402-593-4223
Fax: 402-597-8252 800-562-0500
custserv@omahasteaks.com
www.omahasteaks.com
Processor, packer and exporter of portion control meats including sausage, steak, veal and poultry
President: Bruce Simon
Chairman/CEO: Alan Simon
Executive VP: Frede Simon
Number Employees: 250-499
Type of Packaging: Consumer, Food Service
Brands:
Omaha Steaks International

9987 **Omanhene Cocoa Bean Company**
P.O.Box 22
Milwaukee, WI 53201 414-332-6252
Fax: 414-744-8786 800-588-2462
topbean@omahene.com www.omanhene.com
Manufacturer of Hot cocoa mixes, chocolate
President: Steven Wallace
Estimated Sales: Below $5 Million
Number Employees: 10-19
Number of Brands: 1
Number of Products: 5
Type of Packaging: Consumer, Private Label, Bulk
Brands:
OMANHENE COCOA

9988 **Omar Coffee Company**
41 Commerce Ct
Newington, CT 06111-2246 860-667-8889
Fax: 860-667-8883 800-394-6627
info@omarcoffee.com
www.omarcoffeecompany.com
Manufacturer of coffee carts and roasted coffee and tea
Owner: Steve Costas
Estimated Sales: $30,900,000
Number Employees: 20-49
Sq. footage: 30000
Brands:
Omar Coffee
Omar Flavored Coffee
Omar's Gourmet Coffee

9989 **Omega Foods**
PO Box 21256
Eugene, OR 97402-0402 541-349-0731
Fax: 541-349-0435 800-200-2356
info@omegafoods.net www.omegafoods.net
Manufacturer of salmon, tuna, mahi mahi burgers
President/Owner: Patrick Sullivan
Director Marketing/Administration: Lisa Baker
Sales: Lori Johansen
Operations: Carl Nelson
Plant Manager: Dana Davis
Estimated Sales: $500,000
Number Employees: 9
Number of Brands: 1
Number of Products: 3
Type of Packaging: Consumer, Food Service, Bulk
Brands:
OMEGA FOODS
OMEGA FOODS SALMON BURGERS
OMEGA FOODS TUNA BURGERS

9990 **(HQ)Omega Nutrition**
6515 Aldrich Rd
Bellingham, WA 98226
Fax: 604-253-4228 800-661-3529
info@omeganutrition.com
www.omeganutrition.com
Processor of organically pressed oils including borage, flax, hazelnut, sesame, safflower, sunflower, pistachio, almond and canola; also, processor of gluten-free and hazelnut flours; exporter of flax oil
Owner: Bob Walbert
Marketing Director: Robert Gaffney
Estimated Sales: $6700000
Number Employees: 20-49
Sq. footage: 16000
Type of Packaging: Food Service, Private Label
Other Locations:
OMEGA Nutrition U.S.A.
Vancouver BC
Brands:
Efa Balanced
Essential Balance
Nutriflax
Omegaflo
Omegaplus Gla

9991 **Omega Nutrition**
6515 Aldrich Rd
Bellingham, WA 98226 360-384-1238
Fax: 360-384-0700 800-661-3529
info@omeganutrition.com
www.omeganutrition.com
Unrefined organic oils
Owner: Bob Walbert
Marketing Director: Triss Dankin
Vice President: Robert Gaffney
Co-Founder: Bob Walberg
Operations Manager: Andrew Lyman
Estimated Sales: $ 5-10 Million
Number Employees: 20-49
Type of Packaging: Private Label
Brands:
Coconut Oil
Orange Flax Oil Blend
Pumpkin Seed Oil
Virgin Coconut Oil
Virgin Coconut Oil

9992 **Omega Produce Company**
P.O.Box 277
Nogales, AZ 85628 520-281-0410
Fax: 520-281-1010 pbomegal@aol.com
www.omegaproduceco.com
Produce
President: George Gotsis
Marketing Manager: Nick Gotsis
Brands:
Omega

9993 **Omega Protein**
2105 Citywest Blvd Ste 500
Houston, TX 77042 713-940-6108
Fax: 713-940-6122 877-866-3423
hq@omegahouston.com
www.omegaproteininc.com
Processor and exporter of menhaden oil for poultry, red meat and fish
President: Joseph L Von Rosenberg III
EVP/CFO: Bret Scholtes
Marketing Manager: Sarah London
SVP Operations: Joseph Kadi
Estimated Sales: $168 Million
Number Employees: 500

9994 **Omega Pure**
1851 Kaiser Avenue
Irvine, CA 92614 562-429-3335
Fax: 562-421-0920 jinman@omegapure.com
www.omegapure.com
Omega-3 fish oil producer
National Sales Manager: Julie Inman
Parent Co: Omega Protein

9995 **(HQ)Omni-Pak Industries**
5115 E La Palma Ave
Anaheim, CA 92807-2018 714-765-8323
Processor of powdered drinks including diet, muscle building and fiber
Principal: Richard Marconi
Estimated Sales: G

9996 **Omstead Foods Ltd**
303 Milo RdService Road
Wheatley, ON N0P 2P0
Canada 905-315-8883
Fax: 905-315-8969
Processor of breaded and battered cheese, onion rings and fish including cod, haddock, perch, smelt and shrimp; also, IQF vegetables, stuffed peppers, potatoes, peaches, etc.; importer of IQF vegetables and mushrooms
President: Bill Stafford
Vice President: Rick Bremmer
Marketing Director: Blair Hyslop
Sales Director: Eric Longual
Operations Manager: Mark Tullio
Plant Manager: Helari Ansari
Number Employees: 500-999
Parent Co: Snowcrest Packers
Type of Packaging: Consumer, Food Service, Private Label, Bulk

9997 **On Site Gas Systems Inc**
35 Budney Rd
Newington, CT 06111 860-667-8888
Fax: 860-667-2222 888-748-3429
info@onsitegas.com www.onsitegas.com
On Site Gas designs and manufacturers PSA, membrane and combustion based oxygen and nitrogen gas generation systems. Applications within the food industry utilizing food and beverage nitrogen include that of: beveragemixing/dispensing; coffee producers/packers; fruit orchards/storage; perishable transportation; winemakers; and kiln/grain drying.
President/Founder: Frank Hursey
CEO: Guy Hatch
Chief Engineer: Sanh Phan
Vice President Sales: Bob Wolff
Vice President Manufacturing: Sean Haggerty

9998 **On the Verandah**
1536 Franklin Rd
Highlands, NC 28741 828-526-2338
Fax: 828-526-4132 otv1@ontheverandah.com
www.ontheverandah.com
Manufactuer of Sauces
Executive Chef: Andrew Figel
General Manager: Marlene Figel
Estimated Sales: $300,000-500,000
Number Employees: 10-19
Type of Packaging: Food Service, Bulk
Brands:
ALAN'S MANIAC HOT SAUCE

9999 **(HQ)On-Cor Foods Products**
627 Landwehr Rd
Northbrook, IL 60062-2352 847-205-1040
Fax: 847-205-9592 www.on-cor.com
Processor of frozen foods including chicken and noodles, hamburgers, lasagna, meat balls, stuffed peppers, stew, turkey and dumplings
President: Howard Friend
Controller: John Statis
Senior VP: Howard Leafstone
Estimated Sales: $5.20 Million
Number Employees: 10-19
Type of Packaging: Consumer, Food Service
Brands:
On-Cor Frozen Entrees

10000 **Onalaska Brewing**
248 Burchett Road
Onalaska, WA 98570-9405 360-978-4253
Beer
Owner: David Moorehead
Estimated Sales: Under $500,000
Number Employees: 1-4

10001 **Once Again Nut Butter**
12 S State Street
PO Box 429
Nunda, NY 14517 585-468-2535
Fax: 585-468-5995 888-800-8075
ellen@onceagainnutbutter.com
www.onceagainnutbutter.com
Processor, importer and exporter of certified organic peanut butter, nut and seed butters and roasted and raw nuts; processor of honey
President/General Manager: Robert Gesler
VP: Bill Owen
Quality Assurance Manager: Jake Rawleigh
Production Manager: Esther Hinrich
Purchasing Director: Lloyd Kirwan
Estimated Sales: $1.5 Million
Number Employees: 17
Sq. footage: 20000
Type of Packaging: Consumer, Food Service, Private Label, Bulk
Brands:
Dawes Hill
Dawes Hill Honey
Once Again Nut Butter

10002 **One Source**
300 Baker Ave
Concord, MA 01742-2131 978-318-4300
Fax: 978-318-4690 800-554-5501
Support@onesource.com www.onesource.com
Seasonings, spices
President: Philip J Garlick
VP Marketing: John Brewer
Sr. VP Global Sales: Philip Garlick
Accountant: Jason Way
Estimated Sales: $ 1-2.5 Million
Number Employees: 100-249

10003 **One Vineyard and Winery**
3268 Ehlers Ln
Saint Helena, CA 94574 707-963-1123
Fax: 707-963-1123 watgongg@aol.com
Table wines
President: George Watson
Estimated Sales: Less than $500,000
Number Employees: 1-4
Type of Packaging: Private Label

10004 **One World Enterprises**
1401 Westwood Blvd
Suite 200
Los Angeles, CA 90024 310-802-4220
Fax: 310-477-7077 888-663-2626
www.onenaturalexperience.com
nutritional beverages

10005 **Oneonta Starr Ranch Growers**
One Oneonta Way
PO Box 549
Wenatchee, WA 98807 509-663-2191
Fax: 509-663-6333 www.oneonta.com
apples, pears, cherries, stone fruit, grapes and citrus
President/Owner: Dalton Thomas
VP: Brad Thomas
Director of Food Safety: Mary Jo Gash
Marketing Director: Scott Marboe
Human Resources: Linda Edwards
General Manager: Brian Focht
Type of Packaging: Consumer

10006 **Ono Cones of Hawaii**
98-723 Kuahao Pl # B3
Pearl City, HI 96782-3103 808-487-8690
Fax: 808-486-5292
Ice cream cones
Owner: Wayne Howard
Marketing Manager: Colleen Howard
Operations Manager: Larry Howard
Estimated Sales: $500,000
Number Employees: 1-4
Brands:
Ono Cones

10007 **Onoway Custom Packers**
PO Box 509
Onoway, AB T0E 1V0
Canada 780-967-2207
Fax: 780-967-2727
Processor of fresh and frozen beef, pork, lamb and wild game including ostrich and bison
President: David Skinner
Number Employees: 5-9
Type of Packaging: Consumer, Food Service, Private Label, Bulk

10008 **Ontario Foods Exports**
1200 Aerowood Drive
Unit 14 & 15
Mississauga, ON N1G 4Y2
Canada 519-826-3768
Fax: 519-826-3460 888-466-2372
karen.edwards@omaf.gov.on.ca
www.omaf.gov.on.ca
Dehydrated and packaged food mixes
President: David Clarke
Export Marketing Officer: Diana Campbell
Brands:
Ontario Foods

10009 **Ontario Pork**
655 Southgate Drive
Guelph, ON N1G 5G6
Canada 519-767-4600
Fax: 416-621-6869 877-668-7675
krobbins@ontariopork.on.ca
www.ontariopork.on.ca
Processor of fresh pork
Executive Director: Jack Silbar
Director Financial/Operational Services: Lloyd Bauemhuber
Director Communications/Consumer Mrktg: Keith Robbins
Director Sales/Logistics: Andrew Marks
Estimated Sales: $10 Million
Number Employees: 45
Type of Packaging: Consumer, Food Service
Brands:
Ontario Pork

10010 **Ontario Produce Company**
P.O.Box 880
Ontario, OR 97914 541-889-6485
Fax: 541-889-7823 bob@ontarioproduce.net
www.ontarioproduce.us
Manufacturer of red, yellow, red and white onions; warehouse providing dry storage for onions
President and CEO: Robert A Komoto
General Manager & Sales: Bob Komoto
Office Manager & Transportation: Janet Komoto
Shed Foreman: Arturo Rodriguez
Inspector: Alan Lovitt
Estimated Sales: $5-10 Million
Number Employees: 10 to 49
Sq. footage: 40000
Type of Packaging: Consumer, Food Service, Private Label, Bulk
Brands:
A BRAND
FOPPIANO
FOX MOUNTAIN
GOLDEN BIRD
REAL WEST
RIVERSIDE
RODEO
SILVER SPUR
WOWIE!

10011 **Oogie's Snacks LLC**
1932 W 33rd Avenue
Denver, CO 80211 303-455-2107
Fax: 303-496-0153 comments@oogiesnacks.com
www.oogiesnacks.com
flavored gourmet popcorn
Number Employees: 3

10012 **Oogolow Enterprises**
2560 Dominic Drive
Suite A
Chico, CA 95928-7185 530-893-2646
Fax: 530-893-9344 800-816-6873
sales@oogolowenergybar.com
www.oogolowfoods.com
Processor of chicken, turkey, beef, ham and vegetable flavored meat analogs, vegetarian tamales, vegan cookies and energy bars.
President: Michael Epperson
Estimated Sales: Below $ 5 Million
Number Employees: 15
Sq. footage: 4000
Type of Packaging: Consumer, Food Service, Private Label
Brands:
No Bones Wheat-Meat
Today's Tamales
Tofurky

10013 **Ooh La La Candy**
300 Waverly Avenue
Suite 1A
Mamaroneck, NY 10543 914-381-8030
Fax: 914-381-8068 www.oohlalacandy.com
sara@oohlalacandy.com
Other candy.
Marketing: Sara Stevens

10014 **Oorganik**
PO Box 37305
Houston, TX 77237-7305 281-240-7992
Fax: 281-240-2304
Health and dietetics foods
President: N Peabody
Estimated Sales: Under $500,000
Number Employees: 1-4

10015 **Opa! Originals, Inc.**
Po Box 25151
Rochester, NY 14625-0151 585-368-5623
anastasia@opaoriginals.com
www.greeksoda.com
Maker of greek soda.

10016 **Optima Wine Cellars**
498 Moore Ln. Ste. C
Healdsburg, CA 95448-4840 707-431-8222
Fax: 707-431-7828 info@optimawinery.com
www.optimawinecellars.com
Wines
Owner/Winemaker: Mike Duffy
Owner: Nicol Duffy
Estimated Sales: Below $ 5 Million
Number Employees: 2
Brands:
Optima

10017 **Optimal Nutrients**
1163 Chess Dr Ste F
Foster City, CA 94404 707-528-1800
Fax: 707-349-1686 timl@optinutri.com
www.optimalnutrients.com
Processor, importer and exporter of finished retail vitamins and supplements including royal jelly, beta carotene, essential fatty acids, etc
President: Tim Lally
VP: Darlene Angeli
Estimated Sales: $500,000-$1 Million
Number Employees: 5-9
Sq. footage: 5000
Parent Co: Pegasus Corp

10018 **Optimum Nutrition**
1756 Industrial Road
Walterboro, SC 29488-9368 843-538-7937
Fax: 843-538-3765 800-763-3444
Manufacturer of sports drinks; wholesaler/distributor of vitamins and supplements
Principal: Ken Sarley
Estimated Sales: $1-2.5 Million
Number Employees: 1-4
Brands:
AMERICAN BODY BUILDING
OPTIMUM NUTRITION
SCIENCE FOODS

10019 **Opus One**
P.O.Box 6
Oakville, CA 94562-0006 707-944-9442
Fax: 707-948-2496 800-292-6787
info@opusonewinery.com
www.opusonewinery.com
Wines
Manager: David Pearson
Director Sales/Marketing: Scotty Barbour
Winemaker: Timothy Mondavi
Estimated Sales: Below $ 5 Million
Number Employees: 20-49
Brands:
Opus One

10020 **OraLabs**
18685 E Plaza Dr.
Parker, CO 80134 303-783-9499
Fax: 303-783-5799 800-290-0577
custsrv@oralabs.com www.oralabs.com
Breath drops, sour drops and lip balm
President: Gary Schlatter
CFO: Emile Jordon
Manager: Rajendra Agarwal
Director Sales/Marketing: Marc Rynn
Director International Sales: Daniel Casini
Estimated Sales: $ 15-25 Million
Number Employees: 153
Brands:
Leshables

10021 **Orange Bakery**
17751 Cowan Avenue
Irvine, CA 92714 949-863-1377
Fax: 949-863-1932 oorangebakery1@aol.com
www.orangebakeryinc.com
Processor of frozen dough and baked pastries
President: Shigeo Ueki
Plant Manager: Throung Hiep
Estimated Sales: $26027689
Number Employees: 100
Sq. footage: 45000
Parent Co: Rheon Automatic Machinery
Type of Packaging: Consumer, Food Service, Private Label, Bulk

10022 **Orange Bakery**
13400 Reese Blvd W
Huntersville, NC 28078 704-875-3003
Fax: 704-875-3006
Processor of frozen dough products including bread, croissants and pastries
Manager: Hideaki Aclachi
Plant Manager: Masaki Shidara
Estimated Sales: $ 5 - 10 Million
Number Employees: 30
Parent Co: Rheon Automatic Machinery
Type of Packaging: Consumer, Food Service

10023 **Orange Bang**
13115 Telfair Ave
Sylmar, CA 91342 818-833-1000
info@orangebang.com
www.orangebang.com
Processor of fountain and fruit syrups and fruit beverage concentrates
President: David Fox
Finance Manager: Richard Stein
Estimated Sales: $4.9 Million
Number Employees: 40
Sq. footage: 33000
Type of Packaging: Consumer, Food Service

10024 **Orange Cove Sanger Citrus Association**
180 South Ave
Orange Cove, CA 93646 559-626-4453
Fax: 559-626-7357 www.ocsca.com
Manufacturer, exporter and packer of oranges
Manager: Kevin Severns
CFO;Manager: Bobby Johnson
Estimated Sales: $50-100 Million
Number Employees: 100-249
Type of Packaging: Consumer, Food Service
Brands:
ASSURANCE
LIVEWIRE
ORDER
POM POM

10025 **Orange Peel Enterprises**
2183 Ponce De Leon Cir
Vero Beach, FL 32960 772-562-2766
Fax: 772-562-9848 800-643-1210
info@greensplus.com www.greensplus.com
Formulator, processor and exporter of supplements
President: Jude Deauville
Director National Sales/Marketing: Todd Westover
Estimated Sales: $ 3.5 Million
Number Employees: 20-49
Sq. footage: 15000
Type of Packaging: Consumer, Private Label
Brands:
Fiber Greens
Greens
Pro-Relight
Protein Greens

10026 **Orange-Co of Florida**
12010 NE Highway 70
Arcadia, FL 34266-4267 863-494-4939
Fax: 863-494-2655
Manufacturer and exporter of citrus juices and nonjuice drinks and bases; packer of citrus juices; importer of apple and cranberry concentrates
Chairman/CEO: Ben Griffing III
CEO: Griffin
CEO: Steve Ryan
Estimated Sales: $20-50 Million
Number Employees: 100-249
Type of Packaging: Food Service, Private Label, Bulk
Brands:
BIRD'S EYE
CYPRESS GARDENS

10027 **Orangeburg Pecan Company**
P.O.Box 38
Orangeburg, SC 29116-0038 803-534-4277
Fax: 803-534-4279 800-845-6970
uspecans@yahoo.com www.uspecans.com
Processor of shelled pecans
President: Freddy J D Felder
Founder: Marion H Felder
Number Employees: 1-4
Type of Packaging: Consumer, Food Service, Bulk

10028 **Orca Bay Seafoods**
900 Powell Avenue SW
Renton, WA 98057-2907 425-204-9100
Fax: 425-204-9200 800-932-6722
info@orcabayfoods.com www.orcabayfoods.com
Manufacturer of frozen fish and seafood
President/CEO: Ryan Mackey
VP/Finance: Jay Olsen
Senior Marketing Manager: Richard Mullins
National Sales Manager: Mark Tupper
Warehouse Manager: Troy Roy
Estimated Sales: $143 Million
Number Employees: 180
Number of Brands: 1
Number of Products: 20
Sq. footage: 70000
Type of Packaging: Consumer, Food Service, Private Label, Bulk
Brands:
ORCA BAY

10029 **Orchard Heights Winery**
6057 Orchard Heights Rd NW
Salem, OR 97304 503-391-7308
Fax: 503-364-1715
Info@OrchardHeightsWinery.com
www.islandprincess.com
Wines
Manager: Carole Wyscaver
CEO: Carol Wyscaver
Winemaker: Carol Wyscaver
Estimated Sales: $1-$2 Million
Number Employees: 10-19
Type of Packaging: Private Label
Brands:
Island Princess
Orchard Heights

10030 **Orchard Island Juice Company**
330 N US Highway Drive
Fort Pierce, FL 34950 772-465-1122
Fax: 772-465-4303 888-373-7444
www.orchardislandjuice.com
juice
CEO: Mary Grace Sexton
VP: John Martinelli

10031 **Orchid Island Juice Company**
330 North US Highway 1
Fort Pierce, FL 34950 772-465-1122
Fax: 772-465-1693 800-373-7444
jmartinelli@orchardislandjuice.com
www.oijc.com
Kosher, organic.natural, juice/cider, non-alcoholic beverages, full-line frozen, other frozen.
CEO: Marygrace Sexton
Marketing: John Martinelli

10032 **(HQ)Ore-Cal Corporation**
634 Crocker St
Los Angeles, CA 90021-1002 213-680-9540
Fax: 213-228-6557 800-827-7474
sales@ore-cal.com www.ore-cal.com
Processor of shrimp
President: William Shinbane
VP: Mark Shinbane
National Sales Manager: Shelley Gee
Estimated Sales: $148 Million
Number Employees: 50
Sq. footage: 80000
Type of Packaging: Consumer, Food Service, Private Label, Bulk
Brands:
HARVEST OF THE SEA

10033 **Ore-Ida Foods**
PO Box 57
Pittsburgh, PA 16230 412-237-3450
800-892-2401
www.oreida.com
Processor and exporter of frozen foods including bagels, corn-on-the-cob, pizza, onion rings, pocket sandwiches, cheese products, pasta, breaded fruits, squash, zucchini and potato products; also, canned potatoes
VP Specialty Products: Nick Tyler
Estimated Sales: $ 20 - 50 Million
Number Employees: 400
Parent Co: H.J. Heinz Company
Type of Packaging: Consumer, Food Service
Brands:
CHEDDAR BROWNS
COTTAGE FRIES
COUNTRY FRIES
COUNTRY STYLE HASH BROWNS
COUNTRY STYLE POTATO WEDGES
COUNTRY STYLE STEAK FRIES
CRISPERS
CRISPY CROWNS
CRISPY CRUNCHIES
DEEP FRIES CRINKLE CUTS
DEEP FRIES REGULAR CUTS
FAST FOOD FRIES
GOLDEN CRINKLES
GOLDEN FRIES
GOLDEN PATTIES
GOLDEN TWIRLS
HASH BROWNS
HOME STYLE POTATO WEDGES
HOT TOTS
MICROWAVE HASH BROWNS
MINI-TATER TOTS
ORIGINAL, SNACKIN' FRIES
PIXIE CRINKLES
POTATO WEDGES W/SKINS
POTATOES O'BRIEN
SHOESTRINGS
SHREDDED POTATO PATTIES
SHREDDED POTATOES
SNACKIN' FRIES
SOUTHERN STYLE HASH BROWN
STEAK FRIES
TATER TOTS
TATER TOTS
TEXAS CRISPERS
TOASTER HASH BROWNS
WAFFLE FRIES
ZESTIES
ZESTY TWIRLS
ZESTY, SNACKIN' TOTS

10034 **Oregon Chai**
1745 NW Marshall Street
Portland, OR 97209-2420 503-221-2424
Fax: 503-796-0980 888-874-2424
nirvana@oregonchai.com www.oregonchai.com
Processor amd exporter of chai lattes, blends of tea, honey, vanilla and spices.
President: Cory Comstock
VP Finance: Kurt Peterson
Senior VP Marketing: Sean Ryan
VP Marketing: Lori Woolfrey
Sales Director: Tom Carl
Production Manager: Emile Gaiera
Estimated Sales: $ 2.5-5 Million
Number Employees: 30
Sq. footage: 9000
Type of Packaging: Consumer, Food Service
Brands:
Chai Charger
Herbal Bliss
Kashmir
Oregon
Oregon Chai
Organic Chai
Original Chai
Te Nation Echinacea

Te Nation Teas
Te Nation Throat

10035 Oregon Cherry Growers
1520 Woodrow St NE
Salem, OR 97301 503-364-8421
Fax: 503-585-7710 800-367-2536
mrm@orcherry.com www.orcherry.com
Processor and exporter of fresh, maraschino, froze, brined, glance, ingredient and canned cherries.
Quality Control: Lori Waters
CEO: Edward Johnson
VP Marketing: Craig Poole
VP Sales: Bruce Wesche
National Sales Manager: Robb Loop
Director Manufacturing: Stephen Travis
Estimated Sales: $ 50 - 100 Million
Number Employees: 100-249
Parent Co: Oregon Cherry Growers
Type of Packaging: Consumer, Food Service, Private Label, Bulk
Other Locations:
Oregon Cherry Growers
Stockton CA

10036 Oregon Cherry Growers
1520 Woodrow NE
Salem, OR 97301 503-364-8421
Fax: 503-585-7710 800-367-2536
info@orcherry.com www.orcherry.com
Producer/processor of sweet cherries
President: Robert Thompson
CFO: Daniel Weeden
Quality Manager: Cindy Brunk
VP Marketing: Craig Poole
National Sales Manager: Jeff Booles
VP Human Resources: Michele Halverson
VP Operations: Steve Travis
Purchasing Director: Mark McCurtain
Estimated Sales: $53971435
Number Employees: 250
Sq. footage: 20000
Type of Packaging: Consumer, Food Service, Private Label, Bulk
Brands:
Dalles
Royal Willimette
Royalette
The Royal Cherry
Wy-Am

10037 Oregon Flavor Rack
86319 Lorane Hwy
Eugene, OR 97405-9486 541-342-2085
Fax: 541-342-2085 www.spiceman.com
Manufacturer of small, medium, large and extra large spice blends, gourmet condiments and gift sets.
President/Owner: David Johns
Estimated Sales: $180,000
Number Employees: 4

10038 Oregon Flavor Rack Spice
86319 Lorane Hwy
Eugene, OR 97405-9486 541-342-2085
Fax: 641-461-3036 800-725-8373
spice@spiceman.com www.spiceman.com
Spices and seasonings
Owner: David Johns
Estimated Sales: Less than $500,000
Number Employees: 4
Type of Packaging: Food Service
Brands:
Oregon Flavor Rack

10039 (HQ)Oregon Freeze Dry
PO Box 1048
Albany, OR 97321-0407 541-926-6001
Fax: 541-967-6527 800-547-0245
www.ofd.com
ingredients
Chairman/President: Herbert Aschkenasy
CFO: Dale Bookwalter
SVP: James Merryman
Quality Assurance Manager: Duane Clark
Sales Executive/VP Marketing: Jim Merryman
Human Resources Manager: Lisa Cox
Purchasing Manager: Roger Olson
Estimated Sales: $92 Million
Number Employees: 300
Sq. footage: 32000
Type of Packaging: Consumer, Food Service, Private Label, Bulk
Other Locations:
Brands:
MOUNTAIN HOUSE

10040 Oregon Fruit Products Company
150 Patterson St NW
PO Box 5949
Salem, OR 97304 503-581-6211
Fax: 503-588-9519 800-394-9333
cooking@oregonfruit.com www.oregonfruit.com
Canned fuits and berries
President: Paul Gehlar
Sales Director: Bryan Brown
Operations Manager: Patti Law
Estimated Sales: $6,100,000
Number Employees: 100-249
Type of Packaging: Consumer, Food Service, Private Label, Bulk
Brands:
Oregon Fruit

10041 Oregon Hill Farms
32861 Pittsburg Rd
Saint Helens, OR 97051 503-397-2791
Fax: 503-397-0091 800-243-4541
sales@oregonhill.com www.oregonhill.com
Processor and co-packer of specialty fruit jams, syrups, fruit butters and dessert toppings
President: Thomas McMahon
Estimated Sales: $ 3 - 5 Million
Number Employees: 10-19
Sq. footage: 17000
Type of Packaging: Consumer, Food Service, Private Label
Brands:
Oregon Hill
Swan's Touch

10042 (HQ)Oregon Potato Company
P.O.Box 169
Boardman, OR 97818 541-481-2715
Fax: 541-481-3443 800-336-6311
opcsales@uci.net www.oregonpotato.com
Manufacturer of potato products including flakes, flour and dehydrofrozen diced; also, seasonal packer of fresh potatoes
Manager: Steve White
Director QA/Technical Services: Nick Ross
Director Global Sales: Barry Stice
Number Employees: 50-99
Sq. footage: 100000
Type of Packaging: Private Label
Other Locations:
Oregon Potato Co.
Warden WA
Brands:
OERGON TRAIL
REGAL CREST

10043 Oregon Pride
3400 Crates Way
The Dalles, OR 97058-3552 908-537-7539
Fax: 908-537-2582 888-697-4767
dude@oregonpride.com www.oregonpride.com
Gourmet kippered beefsteak and beef jerky
President: James Perkins
Estimated Sales: Below $ 5 Million
Number Employees: 10

10044 Oregon Spice Company
13320 NE Jarrett St
Portland, OR 97230 503-238-0664
Fax: 503-238-3872 800-565-1599
kevin@oregonspice.com www.oregonspice.com
Spices and seasoning blends
President: Patricia Boday
Chairman: Larry Black
Marketing Director: Patricia Boday
Estimated Sales: Below $ 5 Million
Number Employees: 20-49
Brands:
Oregon Spice

10045 Oregon Trader Brewing
140 NE Hill St
Albany, OR 97321 541-928-1931
Fax: 541-928-4131 info@oregonbeer.org
www.calapooiabrewing.com
Beer
Owner: Mark Martin
Treasurer: Nancy Coleman
Estimated Sales: Below $ 5 Million
Number Employees: 1-4
Brands:
Oregon Brewers

10046 Orfila Vineyards
13455 San Pasqual Rd
Escondido, CA 92025-7898 760-738-6500
Fax: 760-745-3773 info@orfila.com
www.orfilavineyards.com
Wines
Owner: Alejandra Orlia
General Manager: Leon Santoro
Marketing Manager: Leon Santoro
Estimated Sales: Below $ 5 Million
Number Employees: 20-49
Type of Packaging: Private Label
Brands:
Mendoza Ridge
Orfila Vineyards
Quatre Lepages

10047 Organic By Nature
1542 Seabright Ave
Long Beach, CA 90813 562-901-0177
Fax: 562-901-9575 800-452-6884
info@organicbynatureinc.com
www.organicbynature.com
Organic plant powders
CEO: David Sandoval
President: Amy Sandoval
General Sales Manager: Gerry Wong
Estimated Sales: $5.6 Million
Number Employees: 38
Brands:
Organic By Nature

10048 Organic Gourmet
14431 Ventura Blvd #192
Sherman Oaks, CA 91423 800-400-7772
Fax: 818-906-7417 scenar@earthlink.net
www.organic-gourmet.com
Processor of organic food products including vegetarian soups and stocks, yeast extract spreads, bouillon cubes and miso pastes; importer of soups and sauces
CEO/Founder: Elke Heitmeyer
CEO: Elke Heitmeyer
Estimated Sales: $ 1 - 3 Million
Number Employees: 1-4
Number of Brands: 1
Number of Products: 16
Type of Packaging: Consumer, Food Service
Brands:
Organic Gourmet

10049 Organic India USA
5311 Western Ave
Suite 110
Boulder, CO 80301-2746 720-406-3940
Fax: 720-406-3942 888-550-8332
info_retail@organicindiausa.com
www.organicindiausa.com
herbal and organic teas
Estimated Sales: $2.8 Million
Number Employees: 12

10050 Organic Milling Company
505 W Allen Ave
San Dimas, CA 91773 909-599-0961
Fax: 909-599-5180 800-638-8686
www.organicmilling.com
Processor and exporter of granola and fiber breakfast cereals
President: Bruce Olsen
CEO: Harish Chopra
R&D Manager: Sonya Wirawan
VP Marketing: Tom Bezick
National Sales Director: Nick Bishop
Human Resources Manager: Edgar Vasquez
Operations Director: Lupe Martinez
Purchasing Manager: Alejandro Vargas
Estimated Sales: $26000000
Number Employees: 140
Sq. footage: 43000
Type of Packaging: Private Label
Brands:
Back To Nature
Vita Crunch

10051 Organic Planet
231 Sansome St # 3
San Francisco, CA 94104-2304 415-765-5590
Fax: 415-765-5922 info@organic-planet.com
www.organic-planet.com
Certified organic ingredients; edible seeds, dried fruits, tropical fruit, nuts, pulses, sweetners
President: Hans Schmid
Sales: Carrie Hueseman

Estimated Sales: $2000000
Number Employees: 5-9
Number of Brands: 1
Number of Products: 50
Brands:
ORGANIC PLANET

10052 **Organic Valley**
1 Organic Way
La Farge, WI 54639 608-625-2602
Fax: 608-625-2600 organic@organicvalley.com
www.organicvalley.coop
Processor and exporter of organic dairy products including dried and fresh cheeses, eggs, yogurt, milk and butter; also, organic vegetables and certified organic pork, beef and chicken; importer of certified organic bananas
President: Michael Levine
CFO: Mike Bedessem
CEO: George Siemon
Marketing Director: Theresa Marquez
National Sales Manager: Eric Newman
Estimated Sales: $100+ Million
Number Employees: 250-499
Sq. footage: 200000
Type of Packaging: Consumer, Food Service, Private Label, Bulk
Brands:
Organic Valley
Valley's Family of Farms Meats

10053 **Organic Wine Company**
1592 Union St # 350
San Francisco, CA 94123-4531 415-256-8888
Fax: 415-256-8883 888-326-9463
cs@theorganicwinecompany.com
www.theorganicwinecompany.com
Organic wines
CEO: Veronique Raskin
VP: Mike Jinoulhac
Vice President: Michelle Ginoulhac
Estimated Sales: $500,000-$1 Million
Number of Products: 45
Brands:
Bousquette
Veronique

10054 **Organically Grown Company**
1800 Prairie Rd Ste B
Eugene, OR 97402 541-689-5320
Fax: 541-689-8768 davidl@organicgrown.com
www.organicgrown.com
Contract packager of fruits and vegetables; importer of tropical produce and dried fruit; exporter of squash
President: David Amorose
CEO: Josh Hinerfeld
Estimated Sales: $70 Million
Number Employees: 100-249
Sq. footage: 8000

10055 **Oriental Foods**
2550 W Main Street
Suite 210
Alhambra, CA 91801-7003 626-293-1994
Fax: 626-293-1983
Seafood
President: Dr Venku Reddy
Estimated Sales: $1,300,000
Number Employees: 5

10056 **(HQ)Original American Beverage Company**
74 Chester Main Road
North Stonington, CT 06359-1303 860-535-4650
Fax: 860-535-8545 800-625-3767
Processor of old-fashioned soda and hard apple cider
President: Donald Benoit
Number Employees: 1-4
Sq. footage: 5000
Type of Packaging: Consumer
Brands:
Chester's
Mystic Seaport

10057 **Original Cajun Injector**
704 Avenue D
New Iberia, LA 70560-0527 337-367-1344
Fax: 337-364-4968 www.cajuninjector.com
Processor and exporter of liquid injectable marinades for poultry and red meats; also, dry seasonings
President/CEO: Dennis Higginbotham
Estimated Sales: $1-2.5 Million
Number Employees: 1-4
Sq. footage: 13600
Type of Packaging: Consumer, Bulk
Brands:
Cajun Aujus
Cajun Injector
Cajun Poultry Marinade
Cajunshake

10058 **Original Chili Bowl**
P.O.Box 470125
Tulsa, OK 74147 918-628-0225
Fax: 918-663-0539 www.windsorfoods.com
Processor of smoked barbecue meats and chili
COO: Bryan Cather
Technical Director: Robert Hastings
Plant Controller: Lil Green
Plant Manager: John Powers
Estimated Sales: $28600000
Number Employees: 50-99
Parent Co: Windsor Frozen Foods
Type of Packaging: Consumer, Food Service, Bulk
Brands:
Cripple Creek
Hickory Hollow

10059 **Original Foods, QuebecDivision, Inc.**
580 Bechard Avenue
Vanier, QC G1M 2E9
Canada 418-527-6277
Fax: 418-527-3017
chantal.langevin@originalfoods.com
www.originalfoods.com
Assistant General Manager: Phillipe Canac-Marquis
Marketing & Logistics Manager: Kevin Tremblay

National Sales Manager: Dahna Weber
Customer Service: Chantal Langevin
Number Employees: 120
Brands:
ORIGINAL 1957

10060 **Original Italian Pasta Poducts Company**
32 Auburn Street
Chelsea, MA 02150-1825 617-884-5211
Fax: 617-884-2563 800-999-9603
Fresh and frozen pasta, sauces
President: Paul Stevens
Sales/Marketing: Kathy Burinskas
Director Operations: Steve Lagasse
Plant Manager: Jim Dee
Purchasing Manager: George Hachey
Estimated Sales: $ 5-9.9 Million
Number Employees: 35
Type of Packaging: Private Label

10061 **Original Texas Chili Company**
3313 N Jones St.
Fort Worth, TX 76106-4339 817-626-0983
Fax: 817-626-9105 800-507-0009
sales@texaschilicompany.com
www.texaschili.com
Frozen chili, taco filling and chili sauce
President: Danny Owens
Plant Manager: Rebbca Marlvo
Estimated Sales: Below $10 Million
Number Employees: 9
Type of Packaging: Private Label
Brands:
Texas Chili

10062 **Original Ya-hoo! BakingCompany**
5302 Texoma Pkwy
Sherman, TX 75090-2112 903-813-3328
Fax: 903-893-5036 800-575-9373
customerservice@yahoocake.com
www.yahoocake.com
Manufacturer of dessert cakes, cobblers, cookies, cake and pie fillings, bread, frozen dough; custom work is our specialty
President: Geoffrey Crowley
R&D: Monette Wible
Director Sales/Marketing: David Millican
Sales Administrator: Tanda Wall
Purchasing Manager: Becky Roberts
Number Employees: 100-249
Sq. footage: 45000
Type of Packaging: Consumer, Food Service, Private Label, Bulk
Brands:
Ya-Hoo!

10063 **Orlando Baking Company**
7777 Grand Ave
Cleveland, OH 44104 216-361-1872
Fax: 216-391-3469 800-362-5504
customerservice@orlandobaking.com
www.orlandobaking.com
Italian, French, Rye and Wheat breads, subs, hoagies, kaisers and hamburger buns, dinner rolls and Ciabatta bread
President: Chester Orlando
Marketing Director: Sharon Jones
VP Sales: Nick Orlando Jr
Estimated Sales: $ 20 - 50 Million
Number Employees: 350
Sq. footage: 80000
Type of Packaging: Consumer, Food Service, Private Label
Brands:
ORLANDO

10064 **Orleans Coffee Exchange**
1001 Industry Rd # A
Kenner, LA 70062-6880 504-827-0878
Fax: 504-827-0818 800-737-5464
nolajava@bellsouth.net www.orleanscoffee.com
Manufacturer of coffees including flavored, regular and decaffeinated; also, grinders, coffee makers and tea
Owner: Bill Siemers
Owner: Kathleen Siemers
Estimated Sales: Less than $500,000
Number Employees: 10-19
Sq. footage: 3000
Type of Packaging: Consumer, Private Label, Bulk

10065 **Orleans Food Company**
1847 Dock Street
Suite 201
New Orleans, LA 70123-5664 504-733-1311
Fax: 504-734-7684 800-628-4900
cook@bumblebee.com
Processor of canned shrimp, crab meat, oysters, clams, sardines, tuna and mackerel; also, bottled clam juice; exporter of canned shrimp; importer of canned seafood
VP Sales/Marketing: David Cook
Estimated Sales: $ 5 - 10 Million
Number Employees: 5-9
Type of Packaging: Consumer, Food Service, Private Label
Brands:
Cutcher
Dejean
Gulf Belle
Harris
Marvelous
Orleans

10066 **Orleans Hill Vineyard Association**
PO Box 1254
Woodland, CA 95776-1254 530-661-6538
Wines
President/Winemaker: James Lapsley

10067 **Orleans Packing Company**
1715 Hyde Park Ave
Hyde Park, MA 2136 617-361-6611
Fax: 617-361-2638 www.orleanspacking.com
Importer and packer of olives (26 varieties), capers, Greek pepperoncini, Greek giardiniera, cocktail onions, roasted peppers, artichokes and maraschino cherries (jars, drums and pails); retail, food service, private label and bulk
President: George Gebelein
Vice President: Suzanne Gebelein
Estimated Sales: $ 1 Million
Number Employees: 13
Type of Packaging: Consumer, Food Service, Private Label, Bulk

10068 **Orlinda Milling Company**
P.O.Box 38
Orlinda, TN 37141 615-654-3633
Fax: 615-654-4902
Processor of all-purpose and self-rising flour
President: Ricky Stark
Vice President: Bryant Stark
Secretary/Treasurer: Ronnie Stark
Estimated Sales: $470000
Number Employees: 1-4
Type of Packaging: Consumer, Food Service

Brands:
Crown Jewel
Kwik Rize

10069 **Ormand Peugeog Corporation**
PO Box 227155
Miami, FL 33122-7155 305-624-6834
Fax: 305-624-0911
www.ormandpeugeog@aol.com
Wine and wine products
President: Paul Mirengoff.
CFO: Laura Robledo
Marketing Director: Olga Robledo
Plant Manager: Jose Robledo
Estimated Sales: $ 3 Million
Number Employees: 4
Sq. footage: 60
Type of Packaging: Private Label
Brands:
Cristal
Frescas
Gatomax
Tai Bueno
This Way Jose

10070 **Oroweat Baking Company**
480 S Vail Ave
Montebello, CA 90640 323-721-5161
Fax: 323-720-6015
Processor and exporter of whole grain bread and muffins, French bread, rolls and stuffing mix
Executive: Kathy Manitsas
Sales Director: Jim Brennan
Purchasing: Diana Chovice
Estimated Sales: $100+ Million
Number Employees: 1,000-4,999
Parent Co: Unilever USA
Type of Packaging: Consumer

10071 **Orr Mountain Winery**
355 Pumpkin Hollow rd.
Madisonville, TN 73754 423-442-5340
theorrs@usit.net
www.tnvacation.com
Wines
Manager: Susan Whitaker
Sales Director: Lee Curtis
Estimated Sales: $500,000-$1 Million
Number Employees: 1-4
Brands:
Orr Mountain Winery

10072 **Ortho Molecular Products**
3017 Business Park Dr
Stevens Point, WI 54482 715-342-9881
Fax: 715-342-9866 800-332-2351
www.orthomolecularproducts.com
Manufacturer and wholesaler/distributor of vitamin supplements
President: Gary Powers
VP Sales: Jack Radloff
VP Operations: Dean Kramer
Estimated Sales: $ 5 - 10 Million
Number Employees: 25
Sq. footage: 16000
Parent Co: Ortho Molecular Products

10073 **Orval Kent Food Company**
120 W Palatine Rd
Wheeling, IL 60090 847-459-9000
Fax: 847-325-7594
melissa.willits@chefsolutions.com
www.orvalkent.com
Processor of refrigerated salads including potato, cole slaw, tuna, chicken, ham, shrimp, crabmeat and fruit; fresh cut fruit; mashed potatoes and side salads and desserts.
President: Mark Brown
Estimated Sales: $65 Million
Number Employees: 1400
Sq. footage: 100000
Type of Packaging: Consumer, Food Service, Private Label, Bulk
Brands:
Bistro '28
Chilled Selections
Citrus Sensations
Flavor Harvest
Orval Kent
Salad Juniors
Salads Plus
Signature
Signature Delight
Signature Entrees
Signature Pastas

10074 **Orwasher's Bakery Handmade Bread**
308 E 78th St
New York, NY 10075-2222 212-288-6569
Fax: 212-570-2706 info@orwashers.com
www.orwashers.com
Processor of brick oven baked breads and rolls including black pumpernickel, challah, cinnamon raisin, marble, potato, rye, sour dough, white, and whole wheat.
President: Aparm Orwasher
Estimated Sales: Less than $500,000
Number Employees: 5-9
Type of Packaging: Consumer, Food Service
Brands:
Orwasher's

10075 **Osage Pecan Company**
909 W Fort Scott St
Butler, MO 64730 660-679-6137
Fax: 660-679-6255
Manufacturer and packer of pecans and other nuts; also dried fruits
Manager: Teresa Barnes
Estimated Sales: $1-3 Million
Number Employees: 1-4
Number of Products: 100
Sq. footage: 20000
Type of Packaging: Consumer, Food Service, Private Label, Bulk
Brands:
Osage Chief

10076 **Oscar Mayer Foods**
3 Lakes Drive
Northfield, IL 60093 847-646-2000
Fax: 847-646-6005 www.oscarmayer.com
Lunch meat, bacon, hot dogs, sandwiches
CFO: Irene Rosenfeld
CFO: David Brearton
Vice President: Sanjay Khosla
SVP/Information Systems: Mark Dajani
Sales Director: Tom Sampson
VP Operations: Jose Rojo
Estimated Sales: Over $1 Billion
Number Employees: 5,000-9,999
Parent Co: Kraft Foods
Type of Packaging: Consumer, Food Service, Bulk
Brands:
Carving Board
Claussen
Louis Rich
Oscar Mayer

10077 **Oscars Whlse. Meats**
250 W 31st St
Ogden, UT 84401 801-394-6472
Fax: 801-394-8113
Manufacturer of meat products
President: Lynn Hartley
Estimated Sales: $25.5 Million
Number Employees: 10-19

10078 **Osceola Farms**
P.O.Box 679
Pahokee, FL 33476 561-924-7156
Fax: 561-924-3240
Processor of sugar and syrup
President: Alexander Fanjul
Research & Development: Steve Clarke
Estimated Sales: $29000000
Number Employees: 1-4
Parent Co: Florida Crystals
Type of Packaging: Consumer

10079 **Osem USA, Inc**
333 Sylvan Ave
Englewood Cliffs, NJ 07632 201-871-4433
Fax: 201-871-8726 800-200-6736
izzet@osemusa.com www.osemusa.com
Snacks
President: Izzet Ozdogan
Estimated Sales: Below $ 5 Million
Number Employees: 5-9
Brands:
Osem

10080 **Oshkosh Cold Storage Company**
1110 Industrial Ave
Oshkosh, WI 54901-1105 920-231-0610
Fax: 920-231-9441 800-580-4680
ocstg@vbe.com www.cheesesale.com
Cheese, cheese products
President: Walter Doemel
Marketing Director: Stan Dietsche
Estimated Sales: $500,000-$1 Million
Number Employees: 5-9
Type of Packaging: Bulk

10081 **Oskaloosa Food ProductscCorporation**
543 9th Ave E
Oskaloosa, IA 52577 641-673-3486
Fax: 641-673-8684 800-477-7239
info@oskyfoods.com www.oskyfoods.com
Manufacturer and exporter of dried, frozenand liquid egg products.
President: Blair Van Zetten
Controller: Brad Hodges
Sales/Purchasing Director: Jason Van Zetten
Human Resource Manager: Joyce Wilson
Estimated Sales: $10 Million
Number Employees: 82
Type of Packaging: Consumer, Food Service, Private Label, Bulk

10082 **Oskar Blues Brewery**
1800 Pike Road
Unit B
Longmont, CO 80501 303-776-1914
tree@oskarblues.com
www.oskarblues.com
beer
Owner: Dale Katichis
Marketing: Chad Melis
Sales: Wendy Weathers
HR/Customer Service: Tree Rogers
Estimated Sales: $1.2 Million
Number Employees: 47
Sq. footage: 7676

10083 **Oskri Organics**
528 E Tyranena Park Road
Lake Mills, WI 53551 920-648-8300
Fax: 920-648-7800 800-628-1110
info@oskri.com www.oskri.com
Processor and exporter of organic coffee, dried fruit and soup bases; also, teas and herbal products; importer of coffee; contract manufacturing available
Estimated Sales: $500,000-$1 Million
Number Employees: 5-9
Type of Packaging: Consumer, Private Label, Bulk

10084 **Osowski Farms**
33 Gillespie Ave
Minto, ND 58261 701-248-3341
Fax: 701-248-3341
Processor of sugar beets, grain and dry beans
Owner: David Osowski
CEO: Rod Osowski
Marketing Director: Wayne Osowski
Estimated Sales: $ 1 - 3 Million
Number Employees: 1-4
Type of Packaging: Consumer, Food Service, Bulk
Brands:
Wayne

10085 **Ossian Seafood Meats**
P.O.Box 405
Ossian, IN 46777-0405 260-622-4191
Fax: 260-622-4194
Processor of meats including beef, pork, pork chops, sausage, steak, hamburger and ham
President: Peter Sorg Jr
Estimated Sales: $ 10 - 20 Million
Number Employees: 20-49
Type of Packaging: Consumer, Food Service, Private Label, Bulk
Brands:
Hoosier Pride
Ye Olde Farm Style

10086 **Ostrom Mushroom Farms**
8323 Steilacoom Rd SE
Lacey, WA 98513 206-628-9800
Fax: 360-438-2594 info@ostromfarms.com
www.ostromfarms.com
Manufacturer of mushrooms and mushroom sauce
President: William Street
Estimated Sales: $100+ Million
Number Employees: 100-249

Type of Packaging: Consumer, Private Label, Bulk

10087 **Ota Tofu Company**
812 SE Stark St
Portland, OR 97214-1228 503-232-8947
Processor of tofu
President: Eileen Ota
Estimated Sales: $770000
Number Employees: 10-19
Type of Packaging: Consumer, Bulk

10088 **Otis Spunkmeyer**
14490 Catalina St
San Leandro, CA 94577 510-357-9836
Fax: 510-352-5680 800-938-1900
www.spunkmeyer.com
Manufacturer of Frozen cookie dough, fresh baked muffins, and other gourmet baked goods supplied to food service and retail
President/CEO: John Schiavo
CFO: Ahmad Hamade
Vice President: Jerry Reardon
VP Marketing: Leslie Steller
Estimated Sales: $100+ Million
Number Employees: 250-499
Type of Packaging: Private Label
Brands:
OTIS SPUNKMEYER

10089 **Otis Spunkmeyer Company**
5855 Oakbrook Parkway
Suite F
Norcross, GA 30093-1838 770-446-1860
Fax: 770-446-2205 800-438-9251
bhamillton@spunkmeyer.com
www.spunkmeyer.com
Processor of cookies, muffins, bagels and brownies
General Manager: Buck Hamillton
President: John Schievo
Estimated Sales: $ 1-2.5 Million
Number Employees: 20-49
Parent Co: Otis Spunkmeyer
Type of Packaging: Consumer, Food Service
Brands:
Otis Spunkmeyer

10090 **Ott Food Products**
705 W Fairview Ave
Carthage, MO 64836 417-358-2585
Fax: 417-358-4553 800-866-2585
www.ottfoods.com
Processor of barbecue sauce and salad dressing including French, Italian, ranch and poppy seed
President: Jack Crede
Estimated Sales: $ 10 - 20 Million
Number Employees: 20-49
Type of Packaging: Consumer, Food Service
Brands:
Louis Albert & Sons
Ott's

10091 **Ottawa Foods**
325 W Williamstown Rd
Ottawa, OH 45875-1845 419-523-3225
Fax: 419-523-6145 800-837-1631
info@hirzel.com www.hirzel.com
Processor of canned tomato products including whole, sliced, crushed, puree and sauce
President: Karl Hirzel
Plant Manager: Carl Hirzel
Estimated Sales: $ 2.5-5 Million
Number Employees: 5-9
Parent Co: Hirzel Canning
Type of Packaging: Consumer, Food Service, Private Label
Brands:
DEI FRATELLI
SILVER FLEECE
STAR CROSS

10092 **Ottawa Valley Grain Products**
558 Raglan St S
Renfrew, ON K7V 1R8
Canada 613-432-3614
Fax: 613-432-6148 ronwilson1953@on.aibn.com
www.ovgp.ca
Manufacturer milled, pearled and pot barley, wheat and barley flow
President/CEO: Ronald Wilson
Estimated Sales: $6.7 Million
Number Employees: 11
Number of Products: 7
Type of Packaging: Food Service, Bulk

Brands:
Valley

10093 **Ottenberg's Bakers**
3330 75th Ave
Hyattsville, MD 20785-1501
Fax: 202-529-3121 800-334-7264
ottenbergs@ottenbergs.com
www.ottenbergs.com
Manufacturer of baked goods including breads and rolls
Owner: Lee Ottenberg
President: Ray Ottenberg
Estimated Sales: $20 Million
Number Employees: 100-249
Type of Packaging: Food Service

10094 **Ottens Flavors**
7800 Holstein Ave
Philadelphia, PA 19153-3283 215-365-7800
Fax: 215-365-7801 800-523-0767
flavors@ottens.com www.ottensflavors.com
Manufacturer of spray dry flavorings and imitation and natural confectionery oils and spices; importer and exporter of confectionery flavors and essential oils
President: George Robinson III
CEO: Richard Robinson
Eastern Manager: Sharon D'Alo
COO: Rudy Dieperink
Estimated Sales: $11.5 Million
Number Employees: 50-99
Sq. footage: 36500
Type of Packaging: Food Service, Private Label, Bulk

10095 **Ottens Flavors**
7800 Holstein Ave
Philadelphia, PA 19153-3283 215-365-7801
Fax: 215-365-7801 800-523-0767
flavors@ottens.com www.ottensflavors.com
Food flavorings
President: Joe Robinson
CEO: Richard Robinson
R & D: Bob Maxwell
Quality Control: Ralph Anzano
CFO: Bob E Amico
Marketing Manager: Rudy Dieperink
Estimated Sales: $ 75-100 Million
Number Employees: 50-99

10096 **Otter Valley Foods**
95 Spruce Street
Tillsonburg, ON N4G 5C4
Canada 519-688-3256
Fax: 519-842-4521 800-265-5731
www.ottervalley.com
Processor of frozen entrees
President: John Kelly
Vice President: Peter Kelly
Marketing Director: Doug Yson
Estimated Sales: $31 Million
Number Employees: 300
Type of Packaging: Consumer, Food Service, Private Label
Brands:
Otter Valley

10097 **Ottman Meat Company**
315 E 69th St
New York, NY 10021-5527 212-879-4160
Fax: 212-879-4189 www.greenmarketing.com
Processor and exporter of frozen portion control poultry, veal, hamburgers, roasts and prepared barbecue products
President: Jacquelyn Ottman
Sales Manager: Charles Allan
Estimated Sales: $300,000-500,000
Number Employees: 1-4
Parent Co: Long Island Beef Company
Type of Packaging: Consumer, Food Service

10098 **Otto & Son**
4980 W 9470 S
West Jordan, UT 84081-5691 801-280-0166
Fax: 801-280-3540 800-453-9462
Manufacturer of meat products including frozen hamburger patties
Plant Manager: Morgan Robertson
Estimated Sales: $20-50 Million
Number Employees: 100-249
Type of Packaging: Food Service, Bulk

10099 **Otto W Liebold & Company**
1025 Chippewa St
Flint, MI 48503-1548 810-239-1414
Fax: 281-880-9290 800-999-6328
rwliebold@lieboldmeat.com
Manufacturer of certified angus beef products and other meat
Vice President: Dennis Liebold
Estimated Sales: $3 Billion
Number Employees: 20-49
Sq. footage: 25000
Parent Co: Evans Foodservice
Type of Packaging: Consumer, Food Service, Private Label, Bulk
Brands:
CERTIFIED ANGUS BEEF
OTTO'S

10100 **Ouhlala Gourmet**
2655 S. Le Jeune Road
Suite 1011
Coral Gables, FL 33134 305-774-7332
contact@ouhlala.com
www.ouhlala.com
squeezable fruit to go

10101 **Our Best Foods**
170 Main St # 210
Tewksbury, MA 01876-1762 978-858-0077
Fax: 978-858-0052 www.naddif.com
Processor of pork, veal, chicken and beef products
Owner: Micheal Neddif
Estimated Sales: $ 20 - 50 Million
Number Employees: 20-49
Type of Packaging: Food Service, Private Label
Brands:
Our Best

10102 **Our Cookie**
13301 SW 132nd Avenue
Suite 109
Miami, FL 33186 305-238-1992
Fax: 30- 23- 194 877-885-2715
info@ourcookie.com www.ourcookie.com
cookies

10103 **Our Enterprises**
8201 N Classen Boulevard
Suite B
Oklahoma City, OK 73114-2136 405-843-1065
Fax: 405-842-0217 800-821-6375
pchase@ourgourmet.com www.ourgourmet.com
Pesto, pickles, fruited honeys, salsas, jellies, sauces, chow-chow
Estimated Sales: $ 1-2.5 Million
Number Employees: 5-9
Brands:
Our Gourmet
Patti's Private Stock

10104 **Our Farms To You, LLC**
7752 Middle Road
Middletown, VA 22645-6006 703-507-7604
ourfarmstoyou@gmail.com
www.ourfarmstoyou.com
Dairy-free, organic/natural, other chocolate, breakfast cereals, granola, other snacks.
Marketing: Melinda Bremmer

10105 **Our Lady of Guadalupe Abbey**
9200 NE Abby Rd
Lafayette, OR 97127-0097 503-852-0106
Fax: 503-852-7742 bakery@trappistabbey.org
www.trappistabbey.org
Fruitcake, date-nut cake
Manager: Francis King
Sales Manager: Richard Laylon
Estimated Sales: Under $500,000
Number Employees: 20

10106 **Our Thyme Garden**
4017 County Road 424
Cleburne, TX 76031 817-558-3570
Fax: 817-558-3570 800-482-4372
ourthymegarden@yahoo.com
Processor of biscotti, teas and herbal vinegars and oils. Also herb, fiesta, citrus, renaissance, thyme and zesty garden
President: Kimberly Nicholson
CEO: Mary Doebbeling
Estimated Sales: $300,000-500,000
Number Employees: 1-4
Sq. footage: 1000

Type of Packaging: Consumer, Food Service, Private Label, Bulk
Brands:
Our Thyme Garden

10107 **Out of a Flower**
657 Edgewood Dr
Lancaster, TX 75146 214-630-3136
Fax: 214-630-8797 800-743-4696
Processor of ice cream and sorbets made out of edible flowers, herbs and fruits
President: Jose Sanabria
Estimated Sales: $100000
Number Employees: 2
Brands:
Chiqui
Out of a Flower
Swiss Alp Mineral Water

10108 **Outback Kitchens LLC**
P.O.Box 153
Huntington, VT 05462 802-434-5262
Fax: 502-434-5262 natobk@together.net
www.outbackkitchens.com
Chutney
Estimated Sales: $300,000-500,000
Number Employees: 1-4

10109 **Outerbridge Peppers**
20 Harry Shupe Blvd
Wharton, NJ 07885-1646 626-296-2400
Fax: 310-410-0792 800-989-7007
peppers@ibi.bm www.outerbridge.com
Sherry peppers
Owner: John Sanacore
Estimated Sales: $ 10 - 20 Million
Number Employees: 100-249

10110 **Outta The Park Eats, Inc**
Po Box 3422
Cary, NC 27519 919-462-0012
Fax: 800-341-8511
scottg@outtatheparksauce.com
www.outtatheparksauce.com
Gluten-free, organic/natural, BBQ sauce.
Marketing: Scott Granai

10111 **Oven Fresh Baking Company**
250 N Washtenaw Ave
Chicago, IL 60612 773-638-1234
Fax: 773-638-1237
Croissants and muffins
President: George Spanos
Marketing Director: Steve Sarsitis
Estimated Sales: $ 5-10 Million
Number Employees: 100-249
Brands:
Oven Fresh

10112 **Oven Head Salmon Smokers**
101 Oven Head Road
Bethel, NB E5C 1S3
Canada 506-755-2507
Fax: 506-755-8883 877-955-2507
overhead@brunnet.net
www.ovenheadsmokers.com
Manufacturer and exporter of smoked Atlantic salmon, smoked salmon pate, and jerky
President: R Joseph Thorne
Vice President: Debra Thorne
Estimated Sales: $691,000
Number Employees: 5
Number of Brands: 1
Number of Products: 3
Brands:
OVEN HEAD

10113 **Oven Poppers**
99 Faltin Dr
Manchester, NH 03103-5755 603-644-3773
Fax: 603-669-8646 info@ovenpoppers.com
www.ovenpoppers.com
Processor of frozen seafood entrees
President: Stacy Kimball
COO: Andy Desmarais
Plant Manager: James Carigran
Estimated Sales: $ 5-10 Million
Number Employees: 50-99
Type of Packaging: Consumer, Food Service
Brands:
Oven Poppers

10114 **Oven Ready Products**
3-111 Watson Road
Guelph, ON N1E 6X7
Canada 519-767-2415
Fax: 519-823-2196
ovenreadyproducts@on.aibn.com
Manufacturer of frozen unbaked pastry food products, beef rolls, fruit turnovers
President: Jim Harrison
Number Employees: 1-4
Type of Packaging: Consumer, Food Service
Brands:
OVEN READY

10115 **Over The Moon ChocolateCompany Ltd**
2868 W Broadway
Vancouver, BC V6K 2G7
Canada 604-737-0880
Fax: 604-709-9238 800-933-2462
www.overthemoonmilk.com
Manufacturer of Chocolate
President/Owner: Rob Greehow
Brands:
OVER THE MOON

10116 **Overhill Farms**
2727 E Vernon Ave
Vernon, CA 90058 323-589-6752
Fax: 323-582-6122 800-859-6406
sales@overhillfarms.com
www.overhillfarms.com
Processor of frozen and custom prepared entrees, soups and sauces, poultry, meat, and fish specialties.
Chairman: James Rudis
CEO: James Rudis
Quality Control: Rebecca Smith
President: James Rudis
Human Resources Manager: Silvia Ventura
Plant Manager: Geoff Bickham
Estimated Sales: I
Number Employees: 1,000-4,999
Sq. footage: 225000
Parent Co: IBM Foods
Type of Packaging: Consumer, Food Service, Private Label, Bulk
Brands:
Overhill Farms

10117 **Overlake Blueberry Farm**
2380 Bellevue Way SE
Bellevue, WA 98004-7327 425-267-0501
Blueberries and related products

10118 **Overlake Foods Corporation**
PO Box 2631
Olympia, WA 98507-2631 360-352-7989
Fax: 360-352-8076 800-683-1078
info@overlakefoods.com
www.overlakefoods.com
Processor and exporter of frozen blueberries, raspberries, strawberries, blackberries and peaches
Coo: Rodney Cook
Sales: Paul Askier
Estimated Sales: $1,518,842
Number Employees: 4
Sq. footage: 1800
Parent Co: Producer Marketing Group
Type of Packaging: Bulk
Brands:
OVERLAKE

10119 **Oversea Casing Company**
601 S Nevada Street
Seattle, WA 98108 800-682-6845
Fax: 206-382-0883 info@overseacasing.com
www.overseacasing.com
Natural sausage casings.
President: David Levinson
Sales Executive: David Mayo
Estimated Sales: $5.6 Million
Number Employees: 35
Sq. footage: 15833

10120 **Oversea Fishery & Investment Company**
2752 Woodlawn Dr # 5-110
Honolulu, HI 96822-1855 808-847-2500
Fax: 808-836-3308
Seafood
President: Francis Tsang
Estimated Sales: $ 3 - 5 Million
Number Employees: 1-4

10121 **Overseas Food Trading**
2200 Fletcher Avenue Street
3rd Floor
Fort Lee, NJ 07024
Canada 201-585-8730
Fax: 201-585-8575 info@overseausa.com
www.bridor.com
Processor and exporter of frozen bread dough, breads, croissants and danish; also, par-baked bread they specialize in puff pastries,artisan breads,dinner rolls,and baguette and parisian.
President: Robert Leduc
Marketing: Alain Cruanes
VP Sales: Gilles Dion
Estimated Sales: 31.54million
Number Employees: 375
Parent Co: Bridor Products
Type of Packaging: Consumer, Food Service

10122 **Owens Country Sausage**
1403 E Lookout Drive
Richardson, TX 75083 972-235-7181
Fax: 972-235-2135 800-966-9367
information@Owensinc.com
www.owensinc.com
Processor of pork sausage
VP Sales/Marketing: Terry Russell
VP Production: Phil Chapmna
Plant Manager: Robert Burdeaux
Purchasing Director: Jeff Warrick
Estimated Sales: H
Number Employees: 290
Sq. footage: 210000
Parent Co: Bob Evans Farms
Type of Packaging: Consumer
Brands:
Owens Original Beef Chili
Owens Patties
Owens Roll Sausage
Owens Smoked Sausage

10123 **Owensboro Grain Edible Oils**
P.O.Box 1787
Owensboro, KY 42302-1787 270-273-5443
Fax: 270-686-6509 ogcogeo@aol.com
www.louisdreyfus.com
Refined liquid and hydrogenated soybean oil products
President: Robert Hicks Jr
CFO: Jeff Erb
CEO: Robert Hicks Jr Jr
Sales Director: James Stahler
Operations Director: Mark Carlyle
Estimated Sales: $ 75-100 Million
Number Employees: 50-99

10124 **Owl's Nest Cheese**
PO Box 1974
Kaukauna, WI 54130 608-825-6818
Fax: 608-825-3992 www.owlsnestcheese.com
Cheese spreads
Marketing Director: Larry Hoover
Estimated Sales: $10-24.9 Million
Number Employees: 20-49

10125 **Oxford Frozen Foods Limited**
4881 Main Street
Po Box 220
Oxford, NS B0M 1P0
Canada 902-447-2100
Fax: 902-447-3245
lwillmot@oxfordfrozenfoods.com
www.oxfordfrozenfoods.com
Processor and exporter of frozen blueberries, carrots and onion rings
President: John Bragg
Number Employees: 250-499
Type of Packaging: Consumer

10126 **Oxford Organics**
354 Eisenhower Parkway
Livingston, NJ 07039-1022 908-351-0002
Fax: 908-351-0007 sales@oxorg.com
www.oxorg.com
Natural and synthetic chemicals for flavors and fragrances
Estimated Sales: $ 2.5-5 Million
Number Employees: 1-4

10127 **Oxnard Lemon Company**
2001 Sunkist Cir
Oxnard, CA 93033 805-483-1173
Fax: 805-486-0595 fdian@oxnardlemon.com
www.oxnardlemon.com

Oxnard Lemon Company is a licensed packer for Sunkist Growers, Inc. and provides packing services for over 100 Sunkist lemon growers, representing over 4,000 acres in the counties of Ventura, Santa Barbara, Monterey, Tulare, KernRiverside, and San Diego.
General Manager: Sam Mayhew
Packinghouse Manager: Frank Diaz
Field Manager: Tom Mayhew
Field Manager: Jose Claudio
Sales Coordinator: Roger Valasco
Office Manager: Rebecca Fetters
Human Resources: Nancy Low
Plant Manager: Jose Claudio
Sq. footage: 250000
Type of Packaging: Food Service

10128 **Oyster World**
PO Box 1605
Kilmarnock, VA 22482-1605 804-438-5470
Oysters
President: W Cornwell

10129 **Ozark Mountain Trading**
PO Box 171
Westfield, NJ 07091-0171 908-232-6365
Processor and importer of natural snack foods
President: Jim Forgus
Type of Packaging: Food Service

10130 **Ozeki Sake**
249 Hillcrest Rd
Hollister, CA 95023-4921 831-637-9217
Fax: 831-637-0953 question@ozekisake.com
www.ozekisake.com
Sake
President: Bunjiro Osabe
COO: Katsuyoshi Yoshida
Estimated Sales: $ 5-10 Million
Number Employees: 28
Type of Packaging: Private Label

10131 **Ozery Bakery Inc**
11 Director Court
Vaughan, ON L4L 4S5 905-265-1143
Fax: 905-265-1352 pvlahos@ozerybakeryinc.com
www.ozerybakeryinc.com
Kosher, organic.natural, bread/biscuits, crackers, other snacks.
Marketing: Paul Vlahos

10132 **Ozery's Pita Break**
15 Vanley Crescent
Toronto, ON M3J 2B7
Canada 416-630-4224
Fax: 413-630-4217 888-556-5560
eluceno@pitabreak.com www.pitabreak.com
pita breads
Estimated Sales: $18 Million
Number Employees: 110

10133 **Ozone Confectioners & Bakers Supplies**
55 Bank St
Elmwood Park, NJ 7407 201-791-4444
Fax: 201-791-2893
Manufacturer and exporter of confectionery products including bagged, licorice, sugar coated jordan almonds, wedding almonds and nonpareil seeds
President: Patrick Lapone
VP: Louis Lapone
Estimated Sales: $ 3 - 5 Million
Number Employees: 10-19
Number of Brands: 1
Type of Packaging: Private Label
Brands:
Lapone's Jordan

10134 **Ozuna Food Products Corporation**
1260 Alderwood Ave
Sunnyvale, CA 94089-2201 408-400-0495
Fax: 408-727-2029
Processor of corn and flour tortillas; also, plain, salted and flavored tortilla chips
Owner: Vito Ozuna
Estimated Sales: $300,000-500,000
Number Employees: 1-4
Sq. footage: 75000
Type of Packaging: Consumer, Food Service, Private Label, Bulk

10135 **P & L Poultry**
3821 S Bates Court
Spokane, WA 99206-6348 509-892-1242
Fax: 509-892-1244
Manufacturer of chicken and turkey products including frankfurters
Number Employees: 1-4
Type of Packaging: Consumer, Food Service, Private Label, Bulk

10136 **P & M Staiger Vineyard**
1300 Hopkins Gulch Rd
Boulder Creek, CA 95006-8632 831-338-0172
pmstaiger@msn.com
Wine
Owner: Paul Staiger
Estimated Sales: Under $300,000
Number Employees: 1-4

10137 **P A Menard**
P.O.Box 50158
New Orleans, LA 70150-0158 504-620-2022
Fax: 504-592-2784 www.pamenard.com
Contract packager of dairy products, frozen and specialty foods and general line products; wholesaler/distributor of groceries, private label items, frozen and specialty foods, etc.; serving the food service market
President: Mike Menard
CEO: Pamela Boyd
CFO: Al Pearson
Purchasing: Joe Abraham
Estimated Sales: $ 20 - 50 Million
Number Employees: 20-49
Sq. footage: 70000

10138 **P&E Foods**
3077 Koapaka St Ste 202
Honolulu, HI 96819 808-839-9094
Fax: 808-834-8409
Manager: Harry Toywooka
Estimated Sales: $ 5 - 10 Million
Number Employees: 20-49

10139 **P&J Oyster Company**
1039 Toulouse St
New Orleans, LA 70112 504-523-2651
Fax: 504-522-4960 info@oysterlover.com
www.oysterlover.com
Processor of fresh and frozen oysters
President: Sal Sunseri
President: Alfred Sunseri
Estimated Sales: $ 10 - 20 Million
Number Employees: 20-49
Sq. footage: 10000
Parent Co: P&J Oyster Company
Type of Packaging: Consumer, Food Service
Brands:
Harvest Select
Landlock
P&J
P&J Old New Orleans Seafood House

10140 **P&J Oyster Company**
1039 Toulouse St
New Orleans, LA 70112 504-523-2651
Fax: 504-522-4960 info@oysterlover.com
www.oysterlover.com
Oysters
General Manager: Alfred Sunseri
Sales Manager: Sal Sunseri Jr
Office Manager: Merri Sunseri-Schneider
Plant Manager: Merri Schneider
Estimated Sales: $ 1-2.5 Million appx.
Number Employees: 20-49
Brands:
Gold Band Products

10141 **P&L Seafood of Venice**
401 Whitney Ave # 103
Gretna, LA 70056-2500 504-363-2744
Fax: 504-392-3334 www.chartwellsmenus.com
Seafood
Manager: John Duke

10142 **P&S Food Trading**
4910 W Irving Park Rd
Chicago, IL 60641-2619 773-685-0088
Fax: 773-685-0088
Owner: Edmund Sammando
Estimated Sales: $ .5 - 1 million
Number Employees: 1-4

10143 **P&S Ravioli Company**
2001 S 26th St
Philadelphia, PA 19145 215-465-8888
Fax: 215-465-3559 support@psravioli.com
www.psravioli.com
Fresh pasta
Owner: Sacondo Di Giacomo
Co-Owner: Secondo Ravioli
Plant Manager: Mariano DiGiacomo
Estimated Sales: Less than $500,000
Number Employees: 20-49
Brands:
P&S Ravioli

10144 **P-Bee Products**
2141 Tilbury Ln
Oak Harbor, WA 98277 949-586-6300
Fax: 649-586-6360 800-322-5572
info@pbeeproducts.com www.pbeeproducts.com
Nutritional supplements
President: Raymond Guna
Owner: Steven Kramar
Vice President: Lacey Guna
Estimated Sales: $500,000-$1 Million
Number Employees: 1-4
Type of Packaging: Consumer, Bulk
Brands:
P-Bee

10145 **P-R Farms**
2917 E Shepherd Ave
Clovis, CA 93619-9152 559-299-0201
Fax: 559-299-7292 robert@prfarms.com
www.bellafrutta.com
Grower, packer and exporter of apples, apricots, nectarines, oranges, peaches, plums, etc.; also, almonds
Executive Director: Ten Ricchiuti
General Manager: Pat Ricchiuti
CEO: Pat V Ricchiuti
Sales Director: Robert Rocha
Estimated Sales: $25 Million
Number Employees: 250
Sq. footage: 150000
Type of Packaging: Consumer, Food Service, Private Label, Bulk
Brands:
BELLA FRUTTA
P-R FARMS

10146 **P. Janes & Sons**
PO Box 10
Hant's Harbor, NL A0B 1Y0
Canada 709-586-2252
Fax: 709-586-2870 jgalliford@pjanes.com
www.pjanes.com
Processor and exporter of fresh and frozen seafood
Sales Director: Jeff Galliford
Purchasing Agent: Blair Janes
Type of Packaging: Consumer, Food Service, Private Label, Bulk

10147 **P.A. Braunger Institutional Foods**
900 Clark St
Sioux City, IA 51101-2000 712-258-4515
Fax: 712-258-1130 braungers@mcleodusa.net
www.braunger.com
Wholesaler/distributor of frozen foods, meats, private label items and general line products; serving the food service market
President: Tony Wald
General Manager: J David
Estimated Sales: $ 10 - 20 Million
Number Employees: 50-99

10148 **P.C. Teas Company**
882 Mahler Rd # 8
Burlingame, CA 94010-1604 650-697-8989
Fax: 650-697-9016 800-423-8728
info@teastohealth.com www.teastohealth.com
Herbal tea products
Owner: Sunny Wong
Estimated Sales: Below $ 5 Million
Number Employees: 10
Type of Packaging: Private Label
Brands:
Natural Green Leaf Brand

10149 **P.G. Molinari & Sons**
1401 Yosemite Ave
San Francisco, CA 94124 415-822-5555
Fax: 415-822-5834 info@molinarisalame.com
www.molinarisalame.com

Dry salami, sausage
President: Frank Giorgi
Sales Manager: Lou Mascola
Estimated Sales: Below $ 5 Million
Number Employees: 20-49
Type of Packaging: Food Service
Brands:
Finocchiona
Toscano Style

10150 P.J. Markos Seafood Company
8 1/2 Topsfield Road
Ipswich, MA 01938-2132 978-356-4347
Fax: 978-356-9380
Seafood
Estimated Sales: $ 1 - 3 Million
Number Employees: 5-9

10151 P.J. Merrill Seafood
681 Forest Ave
Portland, ME 04103 207-773-1321
Fax: 207-775-4160
Seafood
President: John Merrill
Estimated Sales: $ 3 - 5 Million
Number Employees: 10-19

10152 P.J. Noyes Company, Inc
89 Bridge St
Lancaster, NH 03584 603-788-4952
Fax: 603-788-3873 800-522-2469
info@pjnoyes.com www.pjnoyes.com
Manufacturer and packer of liquids, tablets ans capsules.
President: David Hill
Quality Control Manager: Janet Christenson
Marketing Executive: Jim Hoverman
Sales/Marketing Manager: Jennifer Cusick
Human Resources Manager: Lori Pelissier
VP/COO: Dennis Wogaman
Production Manager: Kevin Kane
Estimated Sales: $10 Million
Number Employees: 75
Sq. footage: 35000
Type of Packaging: Private Label, Bulk
Brands:
Fishin' Chips
Noyes Precision

10153 P.L. Thomas
119 Headquarters Plaza
Morristown, NJ 07960-3963 973-984-0900
Fax: 973-984-5666 plt@plthomas.com
www.plthomas.com
Ingredient supplier and manufacturer; specializes in water-soluble gums and clinically-supported botanical extracts for food, supplements and cosmeceuticals
President: Paul Flowerman
CFO: Sam Serdar
Sales Director: Rodger Jonas
Estimated Sales: $3 Million
Number Employees: 23
Brands:
5-Loxin
Ceamgel 1313
Ecoguar
Fenopure
Glisodin
Glocal
Meganatural
Nutralease
Nutraveggie
Nutricran
Ultraguar

10154 P.M. Innis Lobster Company
P.O.Box 85
Biddeford Pool, ME 04006-0085 207-284-5000
Fax: 207-283-3308 www.poollobster.com
Lobster
Owner: Beth Baskin
Estimated Sales: $ 3 - 5 Million
Number Employees: 10-19

10155 P.T. Fish
10b Portland Fish Pier
Portland, ME 04101-4620 207-772-0239
Fax: 907-874-2072
Seafood
Owner: Michael Twiss

10156 P/B Distributors
2450 New York Avenue
Whiting, IN 46394-1959 219-659-7751
Fax: 219-659-7930
President: Jay El-Kareh

10157 PB&S Chemicals
P.O.Box 20
Henderson, KY 42419-0020 270-830-1200
Fax: 270-827-4767 800-950-7267
mid-south.info@brenntag.com
www.brenntagmidsouth.com
Beverage, confectionery, canned foods, processed cheese, bakery, meat, seafood and dairy applications
President: Joel Hopper
Marketing/Sales: Natalie Vandivier
Number Employees: 100-249
Brands:
Brenntag

10158 PC Teas Company
882 Mahler Rd
Burlingame, CA 94010 650-697-8989
Fax: 650-697-9016 800-423-8728
info@teastohealth.com www.teastohealth.com
Processor of herbal tea products
President: Sunny Wong
Estimated Sales: Below $ 5 Million
Number Employees: 10-19

10159 PEI Mussel King
PO Box 39
Morrell, PE C0A 1S0
Canada 902-961-3300
Fax: 902-961-3366 800-673-2767
info@peimusselking.com
www.peimusselking.com
Processor of fresh and frozen mussels, oysters and clams
President: Russell Dockendorff Sr
Co-Owner: Dorothy Dockendorff
Number Employees: 20-49
Type of Packaging: Consumer, Food Service, Private Label, Bulk
Brands:
PEI Mussel King

10160 (HQ)PEZ Candy
35 Prindle Hill Rd
Orange, CT 06477 203-795-0531
Fax: 203-799-1679 www.pez.com
Manufacturer and exporter of hard candy and dispensers; importer of wafers and chocolates
President: Joseph Vittoria
CFO: Brian Fry
VP Marketing: Peter Vandall
VP Sales: Dan Silliman
VP Operations: Mark Morrissey
Estimated Sales: $3,100,000
Number Employees: 20-49
Type of Packaging: Consumer
Other Locations:
PEZ Candy
Orange CT
Brands:
PEZ

10161 PFG Milton's Foodservice
3501 Old Oakwood Rd
Oakwood, GA 30566-2802 770-532-7779
Fax: 770-503-9234 www.pfgmiltons.com
President: Danny Berry
Estimated Sales: $ 5 - 10 Million
Number Employees: 5-9

10162 PGP International
351 Hanson Way
Woodland, CA 95776 530-662-5056
Fax: 530-662-6074 800-233-0110
info@pacgrain.com www.pacgrain.com
Specialty ingredients
CEO: Zachaey Wochok
CEO: Zachary S Wochok
Research & Development: Jennifer Eastman
Quality Control: Aman Das
Marketing Director: Cary Maigret-Saptiste
Operations Manager: Joe Holbrook
Number Employees: 100-249

10163 PJ's Coffee & Tea
5300 Tchoupitoulas St
New Orleans, LA 70115-1936 504-895-2007
Fax: 504-486-2345 800-527-1055
tmareno@pjscoffee.com www.pjscoffee.com
Specialty coffee and tea beverages and cafe operations
Manager: Tom Boudreaux
Owner: Phyllis Jordan
Accounts Manager: Tanya Mareno
Wholesale Manager: Felton Jones
Cafe Operations Manager: Mindy McKnight
Estimated Sales: $ 500,000 - $ 1 Million
Number Employees: 5-9
Type of Packaging: Private Label
Brands:
PJ's Coffee

10164 PM AG Products
17475 Jovanna Drive
Homewood, IL 60430-1020 708-206-2030
Fax: 708-206-1340 800-323-2663
www.pmagproducts.com
Grain, milling, feed
CEO: Pat Mohan
Estimated Sales: $ 20-50 Million
Number Employees: 20

10165 PM Beef Holdings
2850 Highway 60 E
Windom, MN 56101 507-831-2761
Fax: 507-831-6216 800-622-5213
jhagerla@yahoo.com www.pmbeef.com
Processor and exporter of meat products including beef
President/CEO: Greg Miller
CFO: Jim Brown
Executive Vice President: Bruce Brooking
Plant Manager: Jim Bever
Purchasing Agent: Randy Meyers
Estimated Sales: $ 50 - 100 Million
Number Employees: 250-499
Parent Co: Pm Windom
Type of Packaging: Consumer

10166 PMC Specialties
501 Murray Rd
Cincinnati, OH 45217-1014 513-242-3300
Fax: 513-482-7373 800-543-2466
www.pmcsg.com
Preservatives
President: Martin Wassermann
Executive Vice President: Jack Lehner
Plant Manager: Sherry Roth
Estimated Sales: $ 10-20 Million
Number Employees: 22

10167 (HQ)PMC Specialties Group
501 Murray Rd
Cincinnati, OH 45217 513-242-3300
Fax: 513-482-7373 800-543-2466
www.pmcsg.com
Manufacturer and exporter of saccharin, BHT, methyl anthranilate, benzonitrile, etc
President: Rudolph Gulstrand Jr
Executive: Cory Davids
Marketing Manager: Narasimha Rao
Technical Service Contact: Jack Lehner
Number Employees: 250-499
Parent Co: PMC Global
Other Locations:
PMC Specialties Group
Cincinnati OH
Brands:
CAO
SYNCAL

10168 PMP Fermentation Products
900 NE Adams St
Peoria, IL 61603 309-637-0400
Fax: 309-637-9302 800-558-1031
shendrick@pmpinc.com www.pmpinc.com
Processor of sodium gluconate and erythorbate, calcium gluconate and gluconic acid; importer of glucono-delta-lactone; exporter of sodium erythorbate and gluconate and calcium potassium gluconate
President: Yuzo Kono
Vice President: Dennis Huff
Marketing Manager: Nao Takaoka
Sales Director: Spurgeon Hendrick
Purchasing Manager: Richard Jenks
Estimated Sales: $25000000
Number Employees: 50-99
Parent Co: Fujisawa Pharmaceutical
Type of Packaging: Bulk
Brands:
ERIBATE

10169 **POG**
PO Box 699
Grand Bend, ON N0M 1T0
Canada 519-238-5704
Fax: 519-238-6800
www.grandbend.com/pog/pickling.htm
Processor of onions including frozen, fresh, whole silver skin, pearl vinegar and salt brine
President/CEO: Nelson J Desjardine
Type of Packaging: Bulk

10170 **(HQ)PR Bar**
5900 Sea Lion Pl
Suite 120
Carlsbad, CA 92010 858-576-6488
Fax: 858-576-9152 800-397-5556
info@prbar.com www.prbar.com
Manufacturer of nutritional drink mixes including chocolate, vanilla cream and orange sherbet, supplements
Number Employees: 50
Parent Co: Twinlab Corporation

10171 **PRO Refrigeration Inc**
P.O.Box 1528
Auburn, WA 98071-1528 253-735-9466
Fax: 253-735-2631 jimvgst@earthlink.net
www.prochiller.com
Manufacturers of the Pro Chiller System and the Proformer Refrigerated Product Line.
Owner: Jim Vandergiessen Sr
VP/CEO/General Manager: Jim Vander Giessen Jr
Chief Financial Officer: Gary Duim
Operations Manager: Matthew Perala
Inventory Control: Kelly Phelps
Purchasing Manager/Technical Support: Rande Routledge

10172 **(HQ)PYCO Industries**
2901 Avenue A
Lubbock, TX 79404 806-747-3434
gkring@pycoindustries.com
www.pycoindustries.com
Processor of cottonseed oil, whole cottonseed, meal, hulls and linters
President: Gail Kring
Chairman: Thomas Horsford
VP Finance: Tony Morton
SVP Marketing: Robert Lacy
Asst Sales Manager: Seth Terrell
VP Oil Trading/Packaged Oil: Ronnie Gilbert
Estimated Sales: $103 Million
Number Employees: 100-249
Type of Packaging: Food Service, Bulk
Brands:
PLAINSMAN COTTON OIL

10173 **PaStreeta Fresca**
545 Metro Place S
Suite 100
Dublin, OH 43017-5353 800-343-5266
Fax: 740-342-5068 paStreetafresc@aol.com
Processor of gourmet pastas and sauces
President: Joanne McGonagle
Estimated Sales: $400000
Number Employees: 3
Type of Packaging: Consumer, Food Service
Brands:
Pasta Fresca

10174 **(HQ)Pabst Brewing Company**
P.O.Box 792627
San Antonio, TX 78279-2627 210-226-0231
Fax: 210-226-2512 800-935-2337
products@pabst.com www.pabst.com
Beer manufacturer
General Manager: John Kanetzke
CEO: Kevin Kotecki
Number Employees: 100-249
Type of Packaging: Consumer
Brands:
Augsberger
Big Bear
Bull Ice
Champale
Clash Malt
Colt 45
Country Club
Falstaff
Goebel
Ice Man
Jacob Best
Laser
Old Milwaukee
Olympia
Pabst Blue Ribbon Beers
Piels
Piels Light
Private Stock
Red Bull Malt Liquor
Red River
Schaefer
Schlitz
Silver Thunder Malt Liquor
Special Brew
St. Ides Special Brew
Stroh's
White Mountain

10175 **Pac Moore Products**
1844 E Summer St
Hammond, IN 46320-2236 219-932-2666
Fax: 219-932-3344 solutions@pacmoore.com
www.pacmoore.com
Manufactures kosher foods
President: William Moore
Marketing manager: Bob Lyman
Owner: William Moore
Estimated Sales: $ 10 - 20 Million
Number Employees: 100-249
Brands:
Pac Moore

10176 **Paca Foods**
5212 Cone Rd
Tampa, FL 33610 813-628-8228
Fax: 813-628-8426 800-388-7419
www.pacafoods.com
Processor and contract packager of spice blends, beverage mixes, flour based mixes, seasonings, industrial premixes, nutrition blends
President: Robert Cabral
VP/CFO: Paul Pritchard
Quality Control: Freddie Jones
Sales Director: Ed Sullivan
Estimated Sales: $5 Million
Number Employees: 30
Sq. footage: 30000
Type of Packaging: Private Label

10177 **Pacari Organic Chocolate**
6101 Blue Lagoon Drive
Suite 150
Miami, FL 33126 561-214-4726
Fax: 561-214-4726 info@pacarichocolate.com
www.picarichocolate.com
organic chocolate made in Ecuador
Marketing: Santiago Peralta

10178 **Pace Dairy Foods Company**
2700 Valleyhigh Dr NW
Rochester, MN 55901 507-288-6315
Fax: 507-288-3320 dvalle@packersprovision.com
www.kroeger.com
Natural processed cheese
Manager: Jim Lehman
Controller: Paul Peng
Marketing Manager: Roger Templeton
General Manager: Jim Lehman
Production Manager: Randy Hess
Purchasing Manager: Jim Lehnan
Estimated Sales: $ 50-100 Million
Number Employees: 250-499

10179 **Pacheco Ranch Winery**
235 Alameda Del Prado
Novato, CA 94949 415-883-5583
Fax: 415-883-6992
sales@pachecoranchwinery.com
www.pachecoranchwinery.com
Wines
Manager: Herb Rowland
Head Finance/Distribution: Debbie Rowland
CFO: Debra Rowland
Quality Control: Jamie Mezes
Winemaker: Jamie Meves
Estimated Sales: $ 2.5-5 Million
Number Employees: 1-4
Brands:
Pacheco Ranch

10180 **Pacific Alaska Seafoods**
219 1st Ave S Ste 310
Seattle, WA 98104 206-587-0002
Fax: 206-587-0004
Processor, importer and exporter of salmon, halibut, cod, roe, geoduck and herring including fresh, frozen and fillets
President: Tony Cadden
Estimated Sales: $5-10 Million
Number Employees: 5-9

10181 **(HQ)Pacific American Fish Co.,Inc.**
5525 S Santa Fe Ave
Vernon, CA 90058-3523 323-319-1551
Fax: 323-582-3424 800-625-2525
pehuh@pafco.net pafco.net
Processor, importer and exporter of fresh and frozen seafood including breaded and cooked shrimp and fish fillets and calamari steaks, rings and strips
President/CEO/Owner: Peter Huh
Vice President/Owner: Paul Huh
Managing Director: Jay Huh
Estimated Sales: $100 Million
Number Employees: 100
Sq. footage: 18000
Type of Packaging: Consumer, Food Service
Brands:
Oceankist
Pacific Surf
Scalone

10182 **Pacific Blueberries**
17440 Moon Rd SW
Rochester, WA 98579-9617 360-273-5405
Fax: 360-273-5425
Frozen blueberries
COO: Greg McKinney
Estimated Sales: Below $ 5 Million
Number Employees: 40

10183 **Pacific Cheese Company**
21090 Cabot Blvd
PO Box 56598
Hayward, CA 94545 510-784-8800
Fax: 510-784-8846 info@pacificcheese.com
www.pacific-cheese.com
Cheese
President: Stephen B Gaddis
CFO: Bill Saltzman
Director Plant Operations: Gary Teak
Estimated Sales: $39 Million
Number Employees: 150
Brands:
BELLAFOGLIA
CALIFORNIA SELECT FARMS
CHESWICK
GRAND EUROPEAN
NORTH BEACH
OOMEGA FARMS
PACIFIC BUE

10184 **Pacific Choice Brands**
4667 E Date Ave
Fresno, CA 93725 559-237-5583
Fax: 559-237-2078 chris@pcbrands.com
www.pacificchoice.com
Manufacturer and exporter of a variety of products and condiments such as maraschino cherries, garlic, grape leaves, peppers, olives, salsa, sauces, capers and sun dried tomotoes. Kosher and organic products
President: Allan Andrews
CFO: Faith Buller
VP Marketing: Chris Rabago
VP Sales: Bonifacio Villalobos
Human Resources Director: Stephanie Thorton
Estimated Sales: $39.5 Million
Number Employees: 275
Sq. footage: 225000
Type of Packaging: Consumer, Food Service, Private Label
Brands:
DURANGO GOLD
ORLANDO
PACIFIC CHOICE

10185 **Pacific Choice Seafood**
1 Commercial St
Eureka, CA 95501 707-442-1113
Fax: 707-442-2985 sspencer@pacseafood.com
www.pacseafood.com
Seafood
Manager: Frank Dulcich
General Manager: Rick Harris
R & D: Dave Bodiroga
Quality Control: Chuck Corcoran

Estimated Sales: $ 20-50 Million
Number Employees: 100-249

10186 Pacific Coast Brewing Company
906 Washington St
Oakland, CA 94607 510-836-2739
Fax: 510-836-1987
info@pacificcoastbrewing.com
www.pacificcoastbrewing.com
Processor of seasonal beer, ale, stout and porter
Owner: Steve Wolff
Owner/Brewmaster: Don Gortemiller
Estimated Sales: Below $ 500,000
Number Employees: 20-49
Type of Packaging: Consumer, Food Service
Brands:
Grey Whale
Imperial
Pacific Coast Brewing Co.

10187 Pacific Coast Fruit Company
201 NE 2nd Ave Ste 100
Portland, OR 97232 503-234-6411
Fax: 503-234-0072 www.pcfruit.com
Processor and exporter of frozen fruits, juice concentrates and puree concentrates including strawberry, raspberry, pineapple, cranberry, etc.; importer of frozen elderberries, strawberries and raspberries and peach/apricot puree andberry juice concentrates
President: Dave Nemarnik
Secretary/Treasurer: Ellen McIntyre
Office Manager: Debbie McKee
Number Employees: 5-9
Type of Packaging: Bulk

10188 Pacific Coast Producers
1376 Lemen Ave
Woodland, CA 95776 530-662-8661
Fax: 530-668-1119 www.pcoastp.com
Canned fruits and vegetables
Parent Co: Pacific Coast Producers
Type of Packaging: Consumer, Food Service

10189 (HQ)Pacific Coast Producers
631 N Cluff Avenue
Lodi, CA 95240 209-367-8800
Fax: 209-367-1084 pcp@pcoastp.com
www.pcoastp.com
Manufacturer of canned tomatoes, tomato pulp and puree; also, grapes, peaches, pears and apricots
President/CEO: Daniel Vincent
VP Finance/CFO/Treasurer: Mark Wahlman
VP Operations: Daniel Sroufe
Estimated Sales: I
Number Employees: 1,000-4,999
Type of Packaging: Consumer, Food Service, Private Label, Bulk
Other Locations:
Pacific Coast Producers Plant
Lodi CA
Pacific Coast Producers Plant
Oroville CA
Pacific Coast Producers Plant
Woodland CA
Brands:
CHOICE
FANCY

10190 Pacific Coast Producers
1601 Mitchell Ave
Oroville, CA 95965 530-533-4311
Fax: 530-533-2108 www.pcoastp.com
Processor of canned foods including fruit cocktail, peaches and pears
Parent Co: Pacific Coast Producers
Type of Packaging: Private Label

10191 Pacific Coast Producers
741 S Stockton Street
Lodi, CA 95240 209-334-3352
Fax: 209-369-3489 www.pcoastp.com
Canned fruits and vegetables
Type of Packaging: Private Label

10192 Pacific Collier Fresh Company
925 New Harvest Rd
Immokalee, FL 34142 239-657-5283
Fax: 239-657-4924 800-226-7274
www.sunripe.com
Manufacturer of beans, cabbage, cucumbers, potatoes, squash, tomatos
Manager: Jennifer Levy
Estimated Sales: $ 10 - 20 Million
Number Employees: 20-49
Parent Co: Heller Brothers
Brands:
SUNRIPE

10193 Pacific Echo Cellars
8501 Highway 128
Philo, CA 95466 707-895-2065
Fax: 707-895-2758 avfizz@pacific.net
www.pacific-echo.com
Sparkling wine
Business manager: Mineille Guiliano
Manager: Walter Sawitsky
Winery Manager/Winemaker: Tex Sawyer
Vineyard Operations Manager: Bob Nye
Vineyard Manager: Tony Hortlig
Estimated Sales: $1-10 Million
Number Employees: 0-25
Type of Packaging: Private Label
Brands:
Pacific Echo
Scharffenberger

10194 Pacific Foods
21612 88th Ave S
Kent, WA 98031-1918 253-395-9400
Fax: 253-395-3330 800-347-9444
Processor, exporter and importer of flavoring extracts, seasoning mixes, soup bases, baking powder, nuts and spices
President: James Hughs
Plant Manager: Brandan Caile
Vice President: Richard Weaver
Plant Manager: Mark Hendrickson
Estimated Sales: $ 5 - 10 Million
Number Employees: 50-99
Type of Packaging: Food Service, Private Label, Bulk
Brands:
Chef Classic
Crescent

10195 Pacific Foods of Oregon
19480 SW 97th Ave
Tualatin, OR 97062 503-692-9666
Fax: 503-692-9610 martell@pacificfoods.com
www.pacificfoods.com
Processor and exporter of aseptic soy milk
Chairman/Founder: Charles Eggert
CFO: Jim Knotz
Vice President: Edward Lynch
Estimated Sales: $34 Million
Number Employees: 200
Sq. footage: 60000
Type of Packaging: Consumer, Food Service, Private Label
Brands:
New Moon
Pacific
Pacific Foods
Pacific Foods of Oregon New Moon
Pacific Foods of Oregon Pacific

10196 Pacific Fruit Processors
12128 Center Street
South Gate, CA 90280 562-531-1770
Fax: 562-630-8392
Processor of dairy fruits for ice cream, yogurt, cakes, pies, doughnuts, dry mixes and fillings
General Manager: Phil Livoti
COO: Frank Gonzalez
Estimated Sales: $93,000
Number Employees: 1
Sq. footage: 1846
Type of Packaging: Food Service
Other Locations:
Pacific Fruit Processors
Lapham Co
Brands:
Lapham

10197 Pacific Gold Marketing
749 E Garland Ave
Fresno, CA 93704-4826
Fax: 559-661-6180 pacgoldinc@aol.com
www.pacgold.com
Manufacturer of a variety of Nuts, dried fruit and candy-coated items, including pistachios, almonds, cashews and dark chocolate pistachios
President: Patricia Locktov
Estimated Sales: Below $5 Million
Number Employees: 100-249
Brands:
PACIFIC GOLD

10198 Pacific Gourmet Seafood
26 Stine Road
Bakersfield, CA 93309-2011 661-533-1260
Fax: 805-831-9740
Seafood
Partner: Kelly Bowman
Partner: Patsy Bowman

10199 Pacific Harvest Products
13405 SE 30th Street
Bellevue, WA 98005-4454 425-401-7990
www.pacificharvestproducts.com
Manufactures dry blends, sauces, dressings, bases. Custom packaging offers a diverse range of sizes
Number Employees: 20-49
Type of Packaging: Consumer, Food Service, Private Label, Bulk
Brands:
FIRMENICH

10200 Pacific Hop Exchange Brewing Company
158 Hamilton Drive
Novato, CA 94949-5630 415-884-2820
Fax: 415-884-2820
Beer
President: Tom Whelan
CFO: Robert Ankrum
Marketing Director: Tom Whelan
Brewer: Warren Stief
Estimated Sales: Under $500,000
Number Employees: 5-9
Sq. footage: 3
Type of Packaging: Private Label
Brands:
06 Stout
Barbary Coast Barley
Gaslight Pale Ale
Graintrader Wheat Al
Holly Hops Spiced Al
I.P.A.
Irish Stout
Ol' Spout
St. Briogets Strong
Warren's Wonderful W

10201 Pacific Nutritional
P.O.Box 820829
Vancouver, WA 98682 360-253-3197
Fax: 360-253-6543 michael@pacnut.com
www.pacnut.com
Processor of tablet, capsule, powder and liquid nutritional formulations. Custom manufacture of vitamins and nutritional supplements
President: Michael Schaesser
CEO: Chris Taylor
VP: Doug Nielsen
Estimated Sales: $16 Million
Number Employees: 80
Sq. footage: 35000
Type of Packaging: Private Label

10202 Pacific Ocean Produce
105 Pioneer St
Santa Cruz, CA 95060-2159 831-423-2654
Fax: 831-423-2654
Processor of dried seaweed
Owner: Matthew Hodel
Estimated Sales: $150,000
Number Employees: 2
Type of Packaging: Consumer, Bulk

10203 Pacific Ocean Producers
1133 N Nimitz Hwy
Honolulu, HI 96817 808-537-2905
Fax: 808-536-3225
Seafood
Owner: Jim Cook

10204 Pacific Ocean Seafood
P.O.Box 193
La Conner, WA 98257-0193 360-466-4455
Fax: 360-466-3242
Processor and exporter of salmon, halibut, bottom fish, black cod and shellfish
Owner: Dong Hwang
Estimated Sales: Less than $200,000
Number Employees: 1-4
Type of Packaging: Consumer, Food Service

10205 Pacific Poultry Company
P.O.Box 15851
Honolulu, HI 96830-5851 808-841-2828
Fax: 808-842-0872 www.hulihuli.com

Processor of portion controlled poultry products and barbecue sauce
President: Jaren Hancock
Treasurer: J Cuarisma Jr
VP of Operations: Brent Hancock
Estimated Sales: $ 5 - 10 Million
Number Employees: 50-99
Sq. footage: 10350
Type of Packaging: Consumer, Food Service, Private Label
Brands:
EWA
Hawaii's Famous Huli Huli

10206 **Pacific Pre-cut Produce**
100 W Valpico Rd Ste A
Tracy, CA 95376 209-835-6300
Fax: 209-833-4525 sales@cutfresh.com
www.cutfresh.com
Manufacturer of fresh-cut salads, fruits and vegetables. As of September 2005 Taylor Fresh Foods acquired a majority interest of the company
President: Alan Applonie
Estimated Sales: $100+ Million
Number Employees: 250-499
Sq. footage: 80000
Parent Co: Taylor Fresh Foods

10207 **Pacific Resources International**
944 Linden Ave
Carpinteria, CA 93013-2045 805-684-0624
Fax: 805-684-8624 pri98@earthlink.net
New Zealand grocery products
President: David Noll
Estimated Sales: Under $500,000
Number Employees: 4
Type of Packaging: Private Label
Brands:
Arataki
Browns Brushware
Clarus

10208 **Pacific Salmon Company**
21630 98th Ave W
Edmonds, WA 98020 425-774-1315
Fax: 425-774-6856
Processor and exporter of black cod, halibut, salmon, shark, smelt, squid, kosher foods and fish patties
Owner: John Mc Callum
Estimated Sales: $ 5 - 10 Million
Number Employees: 10-19
Brands:
PACIFIC

10209 **Pacific Seafoods International**
P.O. Box 401
Port Hardy, BC V0N 2P0
Canada 250-949-8781
Fax: 250-949-8781 sales@pacificseafoods.com
www.pacificseafoods.com
Processor and exporter of fresh and frozen salmon including fillets, smoked wholesides and pre-sliced sides
President: Mick Farup
CEO: Todd Harmon
Number Employees: 20-49
Sq. footage: 12000
Type of Packaging: Consumer, Food Service, Private Label, Bulk
Brands:
St. Laurent
Treasure Island

10210 **Pacific Shrimp Company**
213 SE Bay Blvd
Newport, OR 97365 541-265-4215
Fax: 541-265-7164 dwright@pacseafood.com
www.pacseafood.com
Processor and exporter of fresh and frozen fish including albacore tuna, autumn fish, crab, salmon, minced whiting, halibut and herring
Manager: Dave Wright
Finance Executive/Controller: Debbie Sellers
VP/Sales Director: Steve Spencer
Estimated Sales: $57300000
Number Employees: 20-49
Type of Packaging: Consumer, Food Service, Private Label, Bulk

10211 **Pacific Soybean & Grain**
222 Main Street
Suite 888
San Francisco, CA 94105 415-433-0867
Fax: 415-433-9494 info@pacificsoy.com
www.pacificsoy.com
Oilseed production (corn, soybean and sunflower)
Manager: Lina Mesa

10212 **Pacific Spice Company**
6430 E Slauson Ave
Commerce, CA 90040 323-726-9190
Fax: 323-726-9442 800-281-0614
gershon@pacspice.com www.pacspice.com
Importer and manufacturer of spices and herbs
Owner: Gershon Schlussel
Sales Manager: Gene Fogel
Estimated Sales: $20 Million
Number Employees: 90
Sq. footage: 150000
Type of Packaging: Consumer, Food Service, Private Label, Bulk
Brands:
PACIFIC NATURAL SPICES

10213 **Pacific Standard Distributors**
34480 SE Colorado Rd
Sandy, OR 97055 503-668-0057
Fax: 650-853-1132 www.modifilan.com
Processor and importer of seaweed food supplements in capsule form
Owner: Vladimir Bajanov
Director: Vladimir Bajanov
Estimated Sales: $ 1 - 3 Million
Number Employees: 1-4
Number of Products: 1
Type of Packaging: Consumer, Food Service, Bulk
Brands:
Modifilan

10214 **(HQ)Pacific Tomato Growers**
503 10th St W
Palmetto, FL 34221 941-722-3291
Fax: 941-729-5849 www.ptg-eee.com
Processor and wholesaler/distributor of tomatoes
CEO: Joseph Esformes
Estimated Sales: $149756046
Number Employees: 250-499
Parent Co: Heller Brothers
Type of Packaging: Bulk
Brands:
Heller
Roma
SUNRIPE

10215 **Pacific Trade International**
55 Holomua St
Hilo, HI 96720-5142 808-961-0877
Fax: 808-935-1603 www.hilofish.com
President: Charles Umamoto
Estimated Sales: $ 20 - 50 Million
Number Employees: 20-49

10216 **Pacific Trellis**
1500 W Manning Ave
Reedley, CA 93654-9211 559-638-5100
Fax: 559-638-5400 www.pacifictrellisfruit.com
Stone fruits and grapes
Manager: Earl Mc Menamin
Estimated Sales: $ 10 - 20 Million
Number Employees: 10-19

10217 **Pacific Valley Foods**
2700 Richards Rd Ste 101
Bellevue, WA 98005 425-643-1805
Fax: 425-747-4221 info@pacificvalleyfoods.com
www.pacificvalleyfoods.com
Processor, importer and exporter of french fries/frozen potato products; frozen vegetables; frozen berries; tortillas; dehydrated mashed potato products; and dried peas, lentils, chickpeas.
Co-Owner/Co-Director: Scott Hannah
Co-Owner/Co-Director: Lynn Hannah
Executive VP: John Hannah
Estimated Sales: $2300000
Number Employees: 5-9
Sq. footage: 40000
Parent Co: Pacific Valley Foods
Type of Packaging: Consumer, Food Service, Private Label, Bulk
Brands:
BASIC COUNTRY GOODNESS
CEDAR FARMS
GREAT GUSTO
HI WEST
LYNDEN FARMS
PACIFIC VALLEY

10218 **Pacific Westcoast Foods**
3880 Sw 102nd Ave
Beaverton, OR 97005-3244 503-641-4988
Fax: 755-665-8610 800-874-9333
gourmet@teleport.com www.gloriasgourmet.com
Processor of salad dressings, preserves and fruit syrups and fillings; wholesaler/distributor of specialty foods, gift packs, private label items
President: Mark Roth
President: Gloria Sample
Estimated Sales: $280,000
Number Employees: 4
Sq. footage: 5000
Type of Packaging: Consumer, Food Service, Private Label, Bulk

10219 **Pacific Western BrewingCompany**
641 N Nechako Road
Prince George, BC V2K 4M4
Canada 250-562-2424
Fax: 250-562-0799 mail@pwbrewing.com
www.pwbrewing.com
Processor of beer, lager and ale
President: Kazuko Komatfu
CEO: Kazuko Komatfu
Marketing Director: Bruce Clark
Office Manager: Denise Vlanchette
Manager: Thomas Leboe
Estimated Sales: D
Number Employees: 50-99
Type of Packaging: Consumer, Food Service
Brands:
Amberale
Iron horse
Lager
Pacific Pilsner

10220 **Pacifica Culinaria**
PO Box 507
Vista, CA 92085 760-727-9883
Fax: 951-727-9886 800-622-8880
sales@pacificaculinaria.com
www.pacificaculinaria.com
Infused avacado oils, infused vinegars, agave syrups, wasabi mayonnaise, spiced olives, mayan pearl fresh avacados

10221 **Pack Ryt, Inc.**
78150 Calle Tampico Ste 205b
La Quinta, CA 92253 770-771-8880
info@redidate.com
www.packryt.com
Grower, importer and exporter of dates including organic, dehydrated, diced, pitted, macerated and macerated reground.
President: William Jeffrey
CEO/Owner: George Jeffrey
Financial Manager: Terri Lawrence
Quality Control Manager: Lisa Zeise
Production Manager: Corina Sanchez
Plant Supervisor: Cruz Mendoza
Purchasing Supervisor: Corina Sanchez
Estimated Sales: $20-50 Million
Number Employees: 100-249
Type of Packaging: Consumer, Food Service, Private Label, Bulk
Brands:
CALAVO
PROMEDARY
SUN GLOW

10222 **Package Concepts & Materials Inc**
1023 Thousand Oaks Blvd
Greenville, SC 29607-5642 864-458-7291
Fax: 864-458-7295 800-424-7264
www.packageconcepts.com
Processor and exporter of cook-in casings for meat and poultry processing
President: Peter Bylenga
Estimated Sales: $10 - 20 Million
Number Employees: 50-99
Sq. footage: 50000
Type of Packaging: Food Service

10223 **Packaged Products Division**
12395 Belcher Road S
Suite 350
Largo, FL 33773-3096 727-787-3619
Fax: 727-787-3619 888-833-2247
pchampagne@pkgproducts.com
www.pkgproducts.com
Snack foods, nutritious snacks
President: Roger Hoover
Vice President: Jason Brooks
Marketing Director: R Barry Williams
Sales Director: Pat Champagne
Public Relations: Angie Strother
Production Manager: Jerry Adams
Purchasing Manager: Jason Brooks
Estimated Sales: $ 3 Million
Number Employees: 25

10224 **Packaging By Design**
1460 Bowes Rd
Elgin, IL 60123 847-741-5600
Fax: 847-741-5666
mike@packaging-by-design.com
www.packaging-by-design.com
Flexographic packaging for the food industry product line of which includes roll-stock surface printed films; roll-stock custom laminations; roll-stock reverse printed and laminated; and preformed bags.
VP: Charles Graziano
Sales Manager: Michael Graziano
General Manager: Ira Krakow
Type of Packaging: Consumer

10225 **Packers Canning Company**
P.O.Box 907
Lawton, MI 49065 269-624-4681
Fax: 269-624-6009 hbsales@honeebear.com
www.honeebear.com
Processor, canner and exporter of berries, cherries, plums, asparagus, blueberries, etc; importer of asparagus, pie fillings and toppings
President: Robert Packer
Vice President: Steve Packer
Sales Manager: Ronald Armstrong
Director: Toby Fields
Estimated Sales: $ 10 - 20 Million
Number Employees: 50-99
Sq. footage: 150000
Type of Packaging: Consumer, Food Service
Brands:
Michigan Made

10226 **Pacsea Corporation**
PO Box 898
Aiea, HI 96701-0898 808-836-8888
Fax: 808-836-7888
President: Michael Li

10227 **Paddack Enterprises**
27052 State Highway 120
Escalon, CA 95320-9502 209-838-1536
Fax: 209-838-8063
Processors of almonds
President: Vernon Paddack
Estimated Sales: $500,000 appx.
Number Employees: 5-9

10228 **Paesana Products**
101 Central Avenue
PO Box 709
East Farmingdale, NY 11735 631-845-1717
Fax: 631-845-1788 infoPAESANA.COM
WWW.PAESANA.COM
pasta sauces, stuffed olives, specialty condiments, specialty peppers,marinated artichokes, balsamic vinegars, specialty garlic, specialty mushrooms, extra virgin olive oils, sun dried tomatoes, specialty olives, mediterranean tuna

10229 **Page Mill Winery**
10017 Tesla Rd
Livermore, CA 94550-9725 925-456-3375
info@pagemillwinery.com
www.pagemillwinery.com
Wines
Owner: Jim Perry
President: Michael Gibbs
Propreitor: Dane Stark
Sales Director: Gary Brink
Operations Manager: Sue Swartz
Vineyard Manager: Leopoldo Gonzalez
Estimated Sales: Less than $500,000
Number Employees: 3

10230 **Pahlmeyer Winery**
811 Saint Helena Hwy S # 202
Saint Helena, CA 94574-2266
Fax: 707-255-6786 info@pahlmeyer.com
www.pahlmeyer.com
Wines
President: Jayson Pahlmeyer
General Manager: Ed Hogan
Vice President: Michael Haas
General Manager/Director Sales/Marketing: Ed Hogan
Controller: Lynn Gentry
Winemaker: Erin Green
Estimated Sales: Below $ 5 Million
Number Employees: 5-9
Type of Packaging: Private Label
Brands:
Jayson
Pahlmeyer

10231 **Pahrump Valley Vineyards**
3810 Winery Rd # 1
Pahrump, NV 89048-4898 775-751-7800
Fax: 775-751-7818 800-368-9463
pvw@whrus.com www.pahrumpwinery.com
Wines
Manager: Bill Loken
Estimated Sales: $ 5-10 Million
Number Employees: 20-49
Brands:
Pahrump Valley Winery

10232 **Paisano Food Products**
261 King Street
Elk Grove Village, IL 60007-1112 773-237-3773
Fax: 773-237-8114 800-672-4726
Processor of dried beans and fresh and frozen chicken in gravy
President: Paul Williams
Number Employees: 5-9
Parent Co: Cousin Foods
Type of Packaging: Food Service

10233 **Paisley Farms**
38180 Airport Pkwy
Willoughby, OH 44094 440-269-3920
Fax: 440-269-3929 800-676-8656
Manufacturer of pickled vegetables and relishes; private label, custom packaging, gift boxes and food service available
President: Kenneth Anderson
Estimated Sales: $24 Million
Number Employees: 20-49
Sq. footage: 30000
Type of Packaging: Consumer, Food Service, Private Label, Bulk
Brands:
PAISLEY FARM

10234 **Pak Technologies**
7025 W Marcia Rd
Milwaukee, WI 53223 414-438-8600
Fax: 414-977-1458 www.paktech.com
Contract packager of beverages, dairy products, natural and kosher foods, mixes, oils, sauces, spices, vitamins, spreads, pasta, etc
Owner: Kevin Scheule

10235 **Pak-Wel Produce**
PO Box 430
Vauxhall, AB T0K 2K0
Canada 403-654-2116
Fax: 403-654-2241
Processor of fresh potatoes and onions; exporter and importer of potatoes
President: Frank Gatto
Manager: Lanze Friesen
Plant Manager: Luke Wyna
Estimated Sales: B
Number Employees: 10-19
Type of Packaging: Consumer, Food Service
Brands:
Gourmet
Steakmate

10236 **Paklab Products**
1315 Gay-Lussac
Boucherville, QC J4B 7K1 450-449-1224
Fax: 450-449-3380 888-946-3233
www.paklabproducts.com
premium grape juice and grape juice concentrate

10237 **Paktec-100% Tunisian Olive Oil**
Po Box 3852
Johnson City, TN 37602 423-467-9864
info@100percenttunisian.com
www.100percenttunisian.com
Kosher, vegetarian, other condiments, olive oil, full-line grains, cereal and pasta.
Marketing: Al Hamman

10238 **Pal's Homemade Ice Cream**
4448 Heatherdowns Blvd
Toledo, OH 43614-3113 419-382-0615
Fax: 419-382-0615
Ice cream, frozen desserts
President: Sebastiano Caniglia
Vice President: Helane Stiebler
Estimated Sales: Less than $500,000
Number Employees: 5-9

10239 **Palermo Bakery**
1620 Fremont Blvd
Seaside, CA 93955 831-394-8212
Fax: 831-394-0184
Bread and bread products
Owner: Rosario Zito
Estimated Sales: $1.2 Million
Number Employees: 20-49
Type of Packaging: Consumer, Food Service, Bulk
Brands:
Palermo

10240 **Palermo's Frozen Pizza**
3301 W Canal St
Milwaukee, WI 53208-4137 414-643-0919
Fax: 414-643-1696
customerservice@palermospizza.com
www.palermospizza.com
Manufacturer of frozen pizza products
President: Giacomo Fallucca
CEO: Giacomo Fallucca
Vice President: Angelo Fallucca
Marketing Director: Laurie Fallucca
Brands:
Palermo

10241 **Palm Apiaries**
P.O.Box 6574
Fort Myers, FL 33911-6574 239-334-6001
Health foods and honey
Owner: Kathleen Cassidy
Estimated Sales: $500-1 Million appx.
Number Employees: 1-4

10242 **Palm Bay Imports**
5301 N Federal Hwy # 2
Boca Raton, FL 33487-4917 561-893-9998
Fax: 561-893-9975 800-872-5622
pbecker@palmbayimports.com
www.palmbayimports.com
Wine
Manager: David Morrison
Marketing Director: Dana Marks
Sales Manager: Patty Becker
Human Resources Manager: Rosemary Mustacchino
Estimated Sales: $38 Million
Number Employees: 100-249
Type of Packaging: Consumer, Bulk
Brands:
Alexander Grappa
Aneri
Anselmi
Bauchant
Bertani
Blue Fish
Bodegas Campillo
Boissiere
Bottega Vinaia
Boulard
Brown Brothers
Candido
Cavit
Circus
Citra
Col Dorcia
EY
Firstland
Frapin
Frotious
Santana
Sella & Mosca

10243 **(HQ)Palmer Candy Company**
P.O.Box 326
Sioux City, IA 51102-0326 712-258-5543
Fax: 712-258-3224 800-831-0828
vicki@palmercandy.com www.palmercandy.com
Processor, importer and wholesaler/distributor of snack foods and confectionery items including bagged, multi-packs, chocolate bars and vending
President: Martin Palmer
Director Of Marketing: Jerry Christenson
Director Of Sales: Bob O'Neill
Plant Manager: Bill Kennedy
Estimated Sales: $15.50 Million
Number Employees: 50-99
Sq. footage: 140000
Type of Packaging: Consumer, Food Service, Private Label, Bulk
Other Locations:
Palmer Candy Company
Kansas City MO
Brands:
FAVORITES
KING BING
PEANUT BUTTER BING
TWIN BING

10244 **Palmer Packing Company**
1315 S 100 E
Tremonton, UT 84337-8727 435-257-5329
Manufacturer and packer of meat products including ground meat and jerky
Owner: George Palmer
Estimated Sales: $14 Million
Number Employees: 1-4
Type of Packaging: Consumer, Food Service

10245 **Palmer Vineyards**
5120 Sound Ave
Riverhead, NY 11901 631-722-9463
Fax: 631-722-5634 800-901-8783
palmervineyards@mail.com
www.palmervineyards.com
Wines
President: Robert Palmer
Winemaker: Tom Drozd
Estimated Sales: $ 2.5-5 Million
Number Employees: 10-19
Type of Packaging: Private Label

10246 **Palmetto Brewing**
289 Huger St Bldg B
Charleston, SC 29403 843-937-0903
Fax: 843-937-0092
Beer
President/Brewmaster: Louis Bruce
Brewer: Ed Falkenstein
Estimated Sales: Less than $500,000
Number Employees: 1-4
Brands:
Palmetto

10247 **Palmetto Canning Company**
P.O.Box 155
Palmetto, FL 34220 941-722-1100
Fax: 941-729-1934
pcanning@palmettocanning.com
www.palmettocanning.com
Manufacturer and exporter of jams, jellies, preserves, marmalades and barbecue sauce
Owner: Jonathan C Greenlaw Jr
Estimated Sales: $5-10 Million
Number Employees: 10-19
Sq. footage: 32000
Type of Packaging: Consumer, Private Label
Brands:
PALMALITO

10248 **Palmetto Pigeon Plant**
P.O.Box 3060
Sumter, SC 29151-3060 803-775-1204
Fax: 803-778-2896 palmettopgn@ftc-i.net
Processor of fresh and frozen squab, free range chicken and poussin
President: Anthony Barwick
Office Manager: Sherry Cannon
Estimated Sales: $ 10 - 20 Million
Number Employees: 50-99
Sq. footage: 10800
Type of Packaging: Consumer

10249 **Palmieri Food Products**
145 Hamilton St
New Haven, CT 6511 203-624-0042
Fax: 203-782-6435 800-845-5447
sales@palmierifoods.com
www.palmierifoods.com
Sauces
President: Patrick Palmieri
Administrative Assistant: Mary Palmeieri
Estimated Sales: $ 5 - 10 Million
Number Employees: 10-19
Type of Packaging: Consumer, Food Service, Private Label, Bulk
Brands:
Andrews
Palmieri
Pinders

10250 **Palmyra Bologna**
230 N College St
Palmyra, PA 17078 717-838-6336
Fax: 717-838-5345
www.seltzerslebanonbologna.com
Manufacturer of smoked bologna
President: Craig Seltzer
CFO/Secretary/Treasurer: Peter Stanilla
VP Sales/Account Executive: Perry Smith
Estimated Sales: $10 Million
Number Employees: 50-99
Type of Packaging: Consumer, Food Service, Private Label, Bulk
Brands:
PENN DUTCH
SELTZERS

10251 **Pamela's Products**
200 Clara Ave
Ukiah, CA 95482-4004 707-462-6605
Fax: 707-462-6642 info@pamelasproducts.com
www.pamelasproducts.com
Processor and exporter of wheat and gluten-free cookies including biscotti; also, wheat and gluten-free pancake, bread and brownie mixes
President/Owner: Pamela Guisto-Sorrells
VP Sales: Linda Gerwig
Director Sales: Irene Fay
Estimated Sales: $450,000
Number Employees: 8
Type of Packaging: Consumer, Bulk
Brands:
Pamela's
Wheat-Free & Gluten-Free Biscotti
Wheat-Free & Gluten-Free Cookies
Wheat-Free & Gluten-Free Mix
Wheat-Free Oatmeal Cookies

10252 **Pamlico Packing Company**
66 Cross Rd S
Grantsboro, NC 28529 252-745-3688
Fax: 252-745-3272 800-682-1113
kingcrab1@hotmail.com www.bestseafood.com
Processors of fresh and frozen scallops, shrimp, crabs, crabmeat, flounder, oysters, whiting and trout
President: Ed Cross
General Manager: Doug Cross
Estimated Sales: $12 Million
Number Employees: 70
Type of Packaging: Consumer, Food Service, Bulk
Brands:
Seafood People

10253 **Pan American Coffee Company**
1601 Madison St
Hoboken, NJ 7030 201-963-2329
Fax: 201-659-1883 800-229-1883
Roasts and sells coffee
President: Roy Montes
Quality Control: Edili Jerridy
General Manager: Ruth Santuccio
Estimated Sales: $ 5-10 Million
Number Employees: 20-49

10254 **Pan Pepin**
PO Box 100
Bayamon, PR 00960-0100 787-787-1717
Fax: 787-740-2029 http://www.panpepin.com
Processor of baked goods
CEO/President: Rafael Rovira
Marketing Director: Mario Somoza
VP Finance: Carolina Rodriguez
VP: Carolina Rodriguez
General Manager: Miguel Santiago
Number Employees: 300
Type of Packaging: Consumer
Brands:
Healthy Juice
Nature Zone
Pan Pepin

10255 **(HQ)Pan-O-Gold Baking Company**
444 East Saint Germain St
St Cloud, MN 56304 320-251-9361
Fax: 320-251-3759 800-444-7005
info@panogold.com www.panogold.com
Manufacturer of white and variety bread and buns
President: Howard Alton III
Estimated Sales: $163 Million
Number Employees: 1000
Sq. footage: 190000
Type of Packaging: Consumer
Brands:
BUTTER HEARTH
COUNTRY HEARTH
FAMILY CHOICE
FIBER ONE
HOLSUM
KIDS' CHOICE
LAKELAND
NEW ENGLAND
PAN O GOLD
VILLAGE HEARTH
VILLAGE INN

10256 **Pancho's Mexican Foods**
2881 Lamar Avenue
Memphis, TN 38114-5019 901-744-3900
Fax: 901-744-0514
Mexican foods
President: Brenda O'Brien
VP Manufacturing/Purchasing: Subhash Mehr
Number Employees: 10-19
Type of Packaging: Consumer, Food Service, Private Label, Bulk

10257 **Pandol Brothers**
401 Road 192
Delano, CA 93215 661-725-3755
Fax: 661-725-4741 domsls@pandol.com
www.pandol.com
Green, black, red and seeded grapes; persimmons, blueberries, cherries, apples, peaches, plums, nectarines
President: Jack Pandol
Estimated Sales: $ 20 - 50 Million
Number Employees: 20-49

10258 **Pangburn Candy Company**
2000 White Settlement Road
Fort Worth, TX 76107-1467 817-332-8856
Fax: 940-887-4578 www.pangburn.com
Candy
President: R Phillips
Estimated Sales: $ 2.5-5 Million
Number Employees: 50

10259 **Panoche Creek Packing**
3611 W Beechwood Ave # 101
Fresno, CA 93711-0648 559-449-1721
Fax: 559-431-9970 posobros@aol.com
Processor and exporter of almonds
President: John Blackburn
Vice President: Mike Mason
Marketing Manager: Ross Blackburn
Estimated Sales: Less than $500,000
Number Employees: 5-9
Type of Packaging: Private Label, Bulk
Brands:
Golden

10260 **Panola Pepper Corporation**
1414 Holland Delta Rd
Lake Providence, LA 71254 318-559-1774
Fax: 318-559-3003 800-256-3013
panola@bayou.com www.panolapepper.com
Spices, hot sauce
President: Grady W Brown
CFO: Janne Brown
VP/R & D: Ken Hopkins
Public Relations: Jim Byrant
Operations Manager: Danny Morara
Estimated Sales: Below $ 5 Million
Number Employees: 20-49
Type of Packaging: Private Label
Brands:
Gourmet Pepper Sauce
Gourmet Pepper Sauce
Panola

Panola & Private Lab
Pasta Salad
Red Pepper Sauce
Southern Spice
Steak Sauce

10261 **Panos Brands**
160 Pehle Avenue
Park 80 East, 2nd Floor
Saddle Brook, NJ 07663 201-843-8900
Fax: 201-368-9150
customer.services@panosbrands.com
www.panosbrands.com
premium, authentic, natural, organic and specialty foods
Member President: Kevin McGahren-Clemens
VP Sales: Steve Warner
VP Finance: John Lennan
VP: John McLennan
Marketing: Steven Warner
Sales Manager: Donald Cook
Human Resources Manager: Jennifer Ricks
Purchasing: Kathy Burkowski
Estimated Sales: $2.2 Million
Number Employees: 16

10262 **Panther Creek Cellars**
455 NE Irvine St
McMinnville, OR 97128 503-472-8080
Fax: 503-472-5667
info@panthercreekcellars.com
www.panthercreekcellars.com
Wines
Owner: Elizabeth Chambers
Co-Owner: Linda Kaplan
Sales/Marketing Director: Jack Rovics
Winemaker: Michael Stevenson
Estimated Sales: $750,000
Number Employees: 1-4
Type of Packaging: Consumer, Private Label

10263 **Pantry Shelf/Mixxm**
Po Box 613
Hutchinson, KS 67504 626-629-342
Fax: 620-662-9306 800-968-3346
pantryshelf@sbcglobal.com
www.pantryshelfco.com
Cakes/pastries, baking mixes, cocoa/baking chocolate, full-line baking, mixes and ingredients, other baking mixes and ingredients, hot chocolate, other alcoholic beverages, gift packs.

10264 **Papa Dean's Popcorn**
999 East Basse Rd.Ste 184
San Antonio, TX 78209-3827
US 877-855-7272
Fax: 210-822-2140 deanneu@aol.com
www.papadeanspopcorn.com
Processor of 25 flavors of gourmet popcorn featured in bags and/or canisters, several different sizes avaliable.Flavors include/ blueberry,butter,butteralmond toffe,caramel,fiesta,caramel peanut,cherry,chicago blend,chilelimon,plain,nacho,white cheddar,vanilla,chocopop,green apple,chicken noodle,texas honey pecan,watermelon,white cheddar jalepeno,dill pickle,orange citrus,grape.
Owner: Tara Zaglif
Estimated Sales: Less than $500,000
Number Employees: 1-4
Number of Products: 25
Sq. footage: 1200
Type of Packaging: Consumer, Food Service, Private Label, Bulk
Brands:
Papa Dean's

10265 **Papa Leone Food Enterprises**
205 S Camden Dr
Beverly Hills, CA 90212-1660 310-552-1660
Manufacturer of Italian and French sauces including Italian country, fra diavolo, marinara, al'orange, scampi, Mediterranean and vegetable. Also has pizzaiola, marinara, pizza, neopolitan, caponata, artichoke, arabiata and red clamsauces
President: Edmond Negari
Estimated Sales: $1 Million
Number Employees: 2
Sq. footage: 2000
Type of Packaging: Consumer, Food Service, Private Label
Brands:
CHEF ALBERTO LEONE
MAGIC GOURMET

10266 **Pape's Pecan Company**
101 S Highway 123 Bypass
Seguin, TX 78155-5156 830-379-7442
Fax: 830-379-9665 888-688-7273
mrpetski@aol.com www.papepecan.com
Processor of pecans
Owner: Kenneth Pape
Sales: Harold Pape
Estimated Sales: $ 8 Million
Number Employees: 20-49
Sq. footage: 15000
Type of Packaging: Food Service, Private Label

10267 **Paper City Brewery**
108 Cabot St
Holyoke, MA 01040 413-535-1588
Fax: 413-538-5774 info@papercity.com
www.papercity.com
Processor of ale
President: Jay Hebert
Estimated Sales: Below $ 5 Million
Number Employees: 5-9
Brands:
Paper City

10268 **Papetti's Egg Products**
100 Trumbull Street
Elizabeth, NJ 07206-2105 908-351-9618
Fax: 908-351-7528 800-328-5474
Manufacturer and exporter of egg products including dried, diced, pickled, hard and salted, patties, folded omelets, yolks, whites, etc
President: Arthur Papetti
Purchasing Manager: Howard Goodman
Estimated Sales: $300 Million
Number Employees: 550
Sq. footage: 100000
Parent Co: Michael Foods
Type of Packaging: Consumer, Food Service, Private Label, Bulk
Other Locations:
Papetti's Hygrade Egg Product
Klingerstown PA
Brands:
ANGEL WHIP WHITES
ANGEL WHITE
BAKER'S 26
BAKER'S PRIDE
BAKER'S SUPREME
BROKE-N-READY
EASYWAY
HEALTHY MORN
HOLTON FOODS
HYTEX
LITE-N-HEARTY
LONG EGG
QUAKERSTATE FARMS
SCRAMBLE MIX
SUGAR YOLK
TABLE READY
TABLE READY ASEPTIC PACK

10269 **Pappardelle's Pasta Company**
3970 Holly St
Denver, CO 80207-1216 303-321-4222
Fax: 303-321-8554 800-607-2782
info@pappardellespasta.com
www.pappardellespasta.com
Over 100 flavors of dried pasta, fresh-frozen ravioli, sauces and pestos
President: Jim Steinberg
Vice President: Paula Steinberg
Estimated Sales: Below $ 1 Million
Number Employees: 10
Brands:
Pappardelle's

10270 **Pappy Meat Company**
5663 E Fountain Way
Fresno, CA 93727-7813 559-291-0218
Fax: 559-291-5304 pappy@pappyschoice.com
www.pappyschoice.com
Processor of spices and seasonings
President: Marie Papulias
VP: Edward Papulias
Estimated Sales: $2 Million
Number Employees: 20-49
Type of Packaging: Consumer, Food Service, Private Label, Bulk
Brands:
Pappy's Choice

10271 **Papy's Foods**
4131 W Albany St
McHenry, IL 60050 815-385-3313
Fax: 815-385-3367 custservice@papys.com
www.papys.com
Spices, gravy mixes, seasoning mixes, noodles and sauce
Chairman/President: Dave Gallimore
President/CEO/Human Resource Manager: Matthew Gallimore
Controller: Elizabeth Olson
Estimated Sales: $ 50 - 100 Million
Number Employees: 25
Sq. footage: 65000
Type of Packaging: Consumer, Food Service

10272 **(HQ)Par-Way Tryson**
107 Bolte Lane
St Clair, MO 63077 636-629-4545
Fax: 636-629-1330 info@parway.com
www.parwaytryson.com
Processor and exporter of release agents and oils
President: Mandleen Hanson
CFO: Mike Abbs
R&D Director: Robert Smith
Chief Sales/Marketing Officer: Brad Channing
Production Manager: George Hallum
Estimated Sales: $28 Million
Number Employees: 50
Sq. footage: 55000
Type of Packaging: Food Service, Private Label, Bulk
Brands:
Bak-Klene
Presidents Cup
Spray 'n' Cook
Vegalene

10273 **Paradigm Food Works**
5875 Lakeview Blvd # 102
Lake Oswego, OR 97035-7047 503-595-4360
Fax: 503-595-4234 www.paradigmfoodworks.com
Flavoring extracts and syrups, scone mixes and fudge sauces
President: Lynne Barra
CFO: David Barra
Estimated Sales: $ 10-20 Million
Number Employees: 10-19

10274 **Paradis Honey**
PO Box 99
Girouxville, AB T0H 1S0
Canada 780-323-4283
Fax: 780-323-4238
Processor of clover honey, beeswax and pollen
Owner/Manager: Jean Paradis
Secretary/Treasurer: Laura Paradis
Type of Packaging: Bulk
Brands:
Honey

10275 **Paradise**
P.O. Box 4230
1200 Dr. Martin Luther King Jr. Blvd.
Plant City, FL 33563-0021 813-752-1155
Fax: 813-754-3168 800-330-8952
www.paradisefruitco.com
Manufacturer, importer and exporter of candied fruits used in fruitcakes and strawberries
Chairman/CEO: Melvin Gordon
President/Director: Randy Gordon
CFO/Treasurer: Jack Laskowitz
Estimated Sales: $21 Million
Number Employees: 250-499
Sq. footage: 275000
Type of Packaging: Consumer, Food Service, Private Label, Bulk
Brands:
DIXIE
MOR-FRUIT
SUN-RIPE

10276 **Paradise Fruits**
1410 Providence Hwy
Suite 106
Norwood, MA 02062 781-769-4900
Fax: 781-769-4910
jbrownbill@paradise-fruits.com
www.paradise-fruits.com
Free-flowing granulates, pastes, concentrates, juices and purees.
Marketing: Jon Brownbill

10277 **(HQ)Paradise Island Foods**
6451 Portsmouth Road
Nanaimo, BC V9V 1A3
Canada 250-390-2644
Fax: 250-390-2117 800-889-3370
lthomson@paradise-foods.com
Processor of frozen muffin mixes; packager and importer of cheeses; importer of Mexican, Italian and U.S. foods and pasta; wholesaler/distributor of yogurt, juice, candy, salad dressings and ethnic foods
President: Len Thomson
Vice President: Kevin Thomson
Estimated Sales: $15 Million
Number Employees: 60
Sq. footage: 36000
Type of Packaging: Consumer, Private Label, Bulk

10278 **Paradise Locker Company**
405 SW 208th St
Trimble, MO 64492 816-370-6328
Fax: 816-357-1229
Processor of meat products including beef and pork
Owner: Mario Fantasma
Estimated Sales: $ 3 - 5 Million
Number Employees: 10-19

10279 **(HQ)Paradise Products Corporation**
17851 Deauville Ln
Boca Raton, FL 33496-2458
Fax: 718-378-3521 800-826-1235
www.paradiseproductscorp.com
Manufacturer, exporter and importer of marinated foods, condiments, olives, artichokes, pimientos, capers, cauliflower, cherries, corn, kumquats, mushrooms, olive oil, pickled onions, salsa, sauces, etc
President: David Lax
Estimated Sales: $10-20 Million
Number Employees: 60
Sq. footage: 150000
Type of Packaging: Consumer, Food Service, Private Label, Bulk
Brands:
JULIANA
PARADISE
THREE STAR

10280 **Paradise Tomato Kitchens**
1500 S Brook St
Louisville, KY 40208 502-637-1700
Fax: 502-637-8060 info@paradisetomato.com
www.paradisetomato.com
Processor of pouched tomatoes, tomato paste, puree, sauce and pizza sauce
President: Ronald Peters
Research & Development: Arlen Campbell
Quality Control: Justin Uhl
Purchasing Manager: Nathan Cosby
Estimated Sales: $ 10-20 Million
Number Employees: 100-249
Type of Packaging: Food Service, Private Label

10281 **Paradise Valley Vineyards**
4077 W Fairmount Avenue
Phoenix, AZ 85019-3620 602-233-8727
Fax: 602-233-8727
Wines
President: Mark William Stern
Vice President: Tom Dibecco
Sales Director: Jeff Cayton
Estimated Sales: $500-1 Million appx.
Number Employees: 1-4
Type of Packaging: Private Label
Brands:
Paradise Valley Vineyards
Paraiso Del Sol

10282 **Paragon Laboratories**
20433 Earl St
Torrance, CA 90503 310-370-1563
Fax: 310-370-7354 800-231-3670
sales@paralabs.com www.paragonlabsusa.com
Custom manufacturer of dietary supplements, vitamins, minerals, herbal products and nutritional supplements; available in tablets, capsules, powders and liquids
President: Jay Kaufman
Estimated Sales: $10-20 Million
Number Employees: 50-99
Type of Packaging: Consumer, Private Label, Bulk

10283 **Paragon Vineyards**
4915 Orcutt Rd
San Luis Obispo, CA 93401-8335 805-544-9080
Fax: 805-781-3635
baileyama@paragonvineyards.com
www.baileyana.com
Wine
Manager: Michael Blaney
CFO: John R Nevin
Estimated Sales: Below $ 5 Million
Number Employees: 20-49
Brands:
Ecclestone
Vintage Port

10284 **Parallel Products**
401 Industry Rd
Louisville, KY 40208 502-634-1014
Fax: 813-289-4283 888-883-9100
CustomerServices@parallelproducts.com
www.parallelproducts.com
Developer and manufacturer of technologies for the processing of food and beverage wastes. Specific product areas include that of: brewery, winery, distillery services; soft drink, juice services; candy, sugar services; and also thatof pharmaceutical, cosmetic services.
President/Chief Executive Officer: Gene Kiesel
Division Controller: David Kenney
Vice President Sales and Marketing: Ken Reese
National Sales Manager: Ed Stewart
Human Resources/Communications: Hal Park
Chief Operations Officer: David Cogburn
Division Customer Service Manager: Denise Gibson
Plant Manager: Russ Hohn

10285 **Paramount Caviar**
3815 24th St
Long Island City, NY 11101 718-786-7747
Fax: 718-786-5730 800-992-2842
ladyofcaviar@aol.com
www.paramountcaviar.com
Caviar and smoked salmon
Owner: Hussion Aimami
VP: Amy Aimani
Marketing: Amy Arrow
Purchasing Manager: Hossein Aimani
Estimated Sales: $1.4 Million
Number Employees: 7
Type of Packaging: Bulk
Brands:
Canolla Truffles
Fossen Smoked Salmon
Manchurian Saffron
Plantin Dried Mushro

10286 **Paramount Coffee Company**
P.O.Box 13068
130 N Larch Street
Lansing, MI 48912 517-372-5500
Fax: 517-372-2870 www.paramountcoffee.com
Coffees
President: Steve Morris
CEO: James Elsesser
VP: Robert Morgan
Plant Manager: B Brown
Estimated Sales: $5-10 Million
Number Employees: 1-4

10287 **Paramount Coffee Company**
P.O.Box 13068
Lansing, MI 48901 517-372-5500
Fax: 517-372-2870 800-968-1222
www.paramountcoffee.com
Coffees
President: Steve Morris
Sales Director: Steve Morris
Estimated Sales: $25-49.9 Million
Number Employees: 50-99
Sq. footage: 80000
Type of Packaging: Consumer, Food Service, Private Label, Bulk

10288 **Paramount Distillers**
3116 Berea Rd
Cleveland, OH 44111-1596 216-671-6300
Fax: 216-671-2299 800-821-2989
info@paramountdistillers.com
www.paramountdistillers.com
Processor of distilled spirits and liquors
President: Rob Boas
CEO: Robert Szabo
Marketing: Lynn Lubin
VP Sales: Robert Szabo
Plant Manager: Steve Borecky
Estimated Sales: $112300000
Number Employees: 100-249
Other Locations:
Paramount Distillers
Cincinnati OH

10289 **(HQ)Paramount Farms**
11444 W Olympic Blvd
Suite 310
Los Angeles, CA 90064 310-966-4650
Fax: 310-966-4695 877-450-9493
www.paramountfarms.com
Grower and processor of almonds and pistachios
President: Stewart Resnick
CFO: Gregg Dunn
Grower Relations Director: Andy Anzaldo
VP/Operations: David Szeflin
Estimated Sales: $150 Million
Number Employees: 1,000
Brands:
Everybody's Nuts
Paramount Farms
Sunkist

10290 **Paramount Farms**
13646 Highway 33
Lost Hills, CA 93249 661-797-6500
877-450-9493
www.paramountfarms.com
Grower and processor of pistachios and almonds
Parent Co: Paramount Farms
Other Locations:
Paramount Farms Plant
Lost Hills CA
Brands:
ALMOND ACCENTS
SUNKIST

10291 **Parasio Springs Vineyards**
38060 Paraiso Springs Rd
Soledad, CA 93960-9517 831-678-0300
Fax: 831-678-2584 info@paraisovineyards.com
www.paraisovineyards.com
Manufacturer of Wines
Owner/Grower: Rich Smith
Marketing Director: Dave Muret
Hospitality Director: Jennifer Murphy-Smith
Vineyard Manager: Jason Smith
Production/Winemaker/Sales: David Fleming
Estimated Sales: $1-2.5 Million
Number Employees: 5-9
Number of Brands: 1
Number of Products: 10
Type of Packaging: Private Label
Brands:
PARAISO

10292 **Parco Foods**
1 Parco Place
Blue Island, IL 60406-3809 708-371-9200
Fax: 708-371-5301 jbennett@parcofoods.com
www.parcofoods.com
Processor of baked, frozen and unbaked cookies, brownies, snack cakes and desserts
President/Ceo: Tom Hoch
Co-Chairman: Richard Kent
Chairman: Charles Hoch Sr
Executive VP: J Vincent Kent
VP Sales/Marketing: Doug Davidson
VP Sales: Charles Hoch
Public Relations: C Jekiel
Operations Manager: D Kozlowski
Director Manufacturing: Michael Walz
Purchasing Manager: D Doyle
Estimated Sales: $55 Million
Number Employees: 500
Type of Packaging: Consumer, Food Service, Private Label, Bulk
Brands:
Chuck's Chunky
Chuck's Snacks
Party Cookies
Sweetie Bear Bakery

10293 **Parducci Wine Estates**
501 Parducci Rd
Ukiah, CA 95482 707-463-5350
Fax: 707-462-7260 888-362-9463
info@mendocinowineco.com
www.mendocinowineco.com
Processor, exporter and wholesaler/distributor of wine
Manager: Tim Thornhill
Owner: Tim Thornhill
Marketing: David Hance
Winemaker: Robert Swain
Estimated Sales: $2700000
Number Employees: 1-4

10294 **(HQ)Paris Foods Corporation**
3965 Ocean Gateway
PO Box 121
Trappe, MD 21673 410-476-3185
Fax: 856-964-9719 parisfoods@parisfoods.com
www.parisfoods.com
Frozen fruits and vegetables, and potatoes
President: Samuel Rudderow
Marketing/Sales Executive: Ward Cain
VP Operations: Xendra Sheperd
Production Manager: Anthony Dixon
Estimated Sales: $7200000
Number Employees: 108
Type of Packaging: Consumer, Food Service

10295 **Paris Frozen Foods**
305 Springfield Rd
Hillsboro, IL 62049-1150 217-532-3822
Processor of frozen beef, sausage and pork
President: Allen Hopper
Estimated Sales: $550000
Number Employees: 5-9
Type of Packaging: Consumer

10296 **Paris Pastry**
7008 Shoshone Ave
Van Nuys, CA 91406 310-474-8888
Fax: 310-470-2097 sales@parispastry.com
www.parispastry.com
Processor of premium baked goods. Packaged ready to ship mousses, chocolate florentine cookies. Private label available; gingerbread houses; French madeleines
President: Raymond Lobjois
Executive Chef: Eric Westphal
Estimated Sales: $260000
Number Employees: 10-19
Sq. footage: 12000
Type of Packaging: Consumer, Food Service, Private Label, Bulk

10297 **(HQ)Parish Chemical Company**
P.O.Box 277
Orem, UT 84059-0277 801-226-2018
Fax: 801-226-8496 www.parishchemical.com
Processor, exporter, researcher and developer of nutritional food additives, acidulants and preservatives including ferulic acid; also, nutritional supplements including carboxyethylgermanium sesquioxide and indole-3-carbinol
President: W Wesley Parish
Marketing Director: Bill Ellenberger
Estimated Sales: $1200000
Number Employees: 20-49
Sq. footage: 25000
Type of Packaging: Bulk
Other Locations:
Parish Chemical Co.
Orem UT

10298 **(HQ)Park 100 Foods**
326 E Adams St
Tipton, IN 46072-2001 765-675-3480
Fax: 765-675-3474 800-854-6504
park100@park100foods.com
www.park100foods.com
Manufacturer of custom frozen soups, sauces, chili, side dishes, gravies, fruit toppings, dips, entrees, and portion breaded meats, quick starch component sauces, seafood dishes, pasta and protein kits
Chairman: Jim Washburn
President: Gary Meade
VP: David Alves
Project Manager/National Sales: Robert Orr
Sales: Mike Taft
Estimated Sales: $ 20 - 50 Million
Number Employees: 50-99
Sq. footage: 100000
Other Locations:
Kettle Processed Foods
Morristown IN
Kettle Processed Foods
Kokomo IN
Brands:
PARK 100 FOODS

10299 **Park Cheese Company**
168 E Larsen Dr
Fond Du Lac, WI 54937 920-923-8484
Fax: 920-923-8485 800-752-7275
info@parkcheese.com www.parkcheese.com
Processor and exporter of Italian specialty cheeses including parmesan, romano, provolone, asiago, fontina and pepato
President: Alfred Liebetrau
Vice President: Eric Liebetrau
Plant Manager: Lewis Blank
Estimated Sales: $ 50 - 100 Million
Number Employees: 50-99
Type of Packaging: Consumer, Food Service, Private Label, Bulk
Brands:
Casaro
Park
Villa

10300 **Park Farms**
1925 30th St NE
Canton, OH 44705 330-455-0241
Fax: 330-455-5820 800-683-6511
sales@parkfarms.com www.parkfarms.com
Poultry processor of fresh tray pack, bonless, skinless poultry, and whole and cut-up chicken. Distributor of fresh and frozen meat proteins
President: Mike Pastore
CEO: Jim Pastore, Sr.
CFO: Scott Stephens
Quality Control Manager: Paul Storsin
VP Sales: Kim Clark
Public Relations: Carol Capocci
Production Manager: Scott Bucher
Plant Manager: Ron Leeders, Jr.
Purchasing Manager: Scott Hearne
Estimated Sales: $100+ Million
Number Employees: 500-999
Number of Brands: 2
Number of Products: 160
Sq. footage: 150000
Type of Packaging: Consumer, Food Service, Private Label, Bulk
Brands:
Park Farms Fresh'n'natural Chicken

10301 **Parker Farm**
9405 Holly St NW # B
Minneapolis, MN 55433-5976 763-780-5100
Fax: 763-780-5104 800-869-6685
info@parkersfarm.com www.parkersfarm.com
Cold pack cheese food, peanut butter, cream cheese spread and fresh salsa
President: Rick Etrheim
Estimated Sales: $ 5-9.9 Million
Number Employees: 20-49
Type of Packaging: Private Label

10302 **Parker Fish Company**
P.O.Box 324
Wrightsville, GA 31096-0324 478-864-3406
Fax: 478-864-9417
Seafood
President: Joe Rowland
Estimated Sales: $ 5 - 10 Million
Number Employees: 10-19

10303 **Parker Flavors, Inc**
1801 Portal St
Baltimore, MD 21224-6543 410-633-2230
Fax: 410-633-3530 800-336-9113
info@parkerflavors.com www.parkerflavors.com
Manufacturer of extracts, emulsions, and flavors for bakery, beverage, candy and dairy applications
CEO: Tim Parker
Chairman: Malcolm Parker
Sales: Bob Johnson
Estimated Sales: $ 5 - 10 Million
Number Employees: 5-9
Type of Packaging: Consumer, Food Service, Private Label, Bulk
Brands:
PARKER

10304 **Parker Products**
2737 Tillar St
Fort Worth, TX 76107 817-336-7441
Fax: 817-877-1261 800-433-5749
info@parkerproducts.com
www.parkerproducts.com
candy particulates and other fine ingredients

10305 **(HQ)Parker Products**
2737 Tillar St
Fort Worth, TX 76107 817-336-7441
Fax: 817-877-1261 800-433-5749
info@parkerproducts.com
www.parkerproducts.com
Processor and exporter of desserts, candy, and confectionery products including ice cream toppings, fudge and flavors; custom-grinding services available
President: Jim Waldroop
CFO: Chris McCrary
CFO: Greg Hodder
Plant Manager: Sandra Perez
Estimated Sales: $ 10-20 Million
Number Employees: 50-99
Sq. footage: 58000
Type of Packaging: Private Label, Bulk
Other Locations:
Parker Products
Andrews TX

10306 **Parkers Farm**
9405 Holly St NW # B
Coon Rapids, MN 55433-5976 763-780-5100
Fax: 763-780-5104 800-869-6685
info@parkersfarm.com www.parkersfarm.com
Processor of cold pack cheese foods and bagel spreads.
President: Rick Etrheim
Estimated Sales: $ 10 - 20 Million
Number Employees: 20-49
Type of Packaging: Consumer, Food Service, Private Label, Bulk

10307 **(HQ)Parkside Candy Company**
3208 Main St
Buffalo, NY 14214-1302 716-833-7540
Fax: 716-833-7560
Manufacturer of Lollypops and other candy
President/Owner: Philip Buffamonte
Estimated Sales: $14 Million
Number Employees: 20-49
Type of Packaging: Consumer, Food Service, Private Label, Bulk
Brands:
AUNT ANGIES
OLD FASHIONED

10308 **Parma Sausage Products**
1734 Penn Ave
Pittsburgh, PA 15222 412-391-4238
Fax: 412-391-7717 877-294-4207
info@parmasausage.com
www.parmasausage.com
Processor of specialty meats including fresh sausage, prosciutto, coppa secca and salami, capicollo, mortadella, salami rosa, kolbassie, andoville, chorizo
President: Rina Edwards
Vice President: Rita Spinabelli
Sales Manager: Erin Schumacher
Purchasing Manager: John Edwards
Estimated Sales: $1300000
Number Employees: 10-19
Type of Packaging: Consumer, Food Service, Private Label, Bulk
Brands:
Gigi
Parma

10309 **Parmalat Canada**
405 The West Mall
10th Floor
Toronto, ON M9C 5J1
Canada 416-626-1973
Fax: 416-620-3666 800-563-1515
www.parmalat.ca

Manufactures milk and dairy products, fruit juices, cultured products, cheese products and table spreads
President/CEO: Alnashir Lakha
CEO: Enrico Bondi
SVP Sales/Marketing: Doug Ettinger
National VP Consumer & Trade Marketing: Cheryl Smith
Operations: Antonio Vanoli
National VP Supply Chain: Steve Wuthmann
Estimated Sales: $1.9 Billion
Number Employees: 1,000
Parent Co: Parmalat Finanziaria SpA.
Type of Packaging: Consumer, Food Service, Private Label, Bulk
Brands:
ASTRO
BALDERSON
BEATRICE
BLACK DIAMOND
BLACK DIAMOND CHEESTRINGS FICELLO
LACTANTIA
LACTOSE FREE
PARKAY
PARMALAT
SARGENTO
SENSATIONAL SOY
SMART GROWTH
VITALITE

10310 **Parmx**
4117-16a Street SE
Calgary, AB T2G 3T7
Canada 403-237-0707
Fax: 403-264-2153 www.parmxcheese.com
Processor of grated parmesan cheese
President: Vincent Aiello
CEO: Vincent Aiello
Production: Frank Aiello
Estimated Sales: E
Number Employees: 20-49
Type of Packaging: Consumer, Food Service
Brands:
Parmx Cheese

10311 **Parny Gourmet**
390 NE 59th Terrace
Miami, FL 33137 305-798-5177
parny.gourmet@gmail.com
www.parnygourmet.com
Gourmet foods

10312 **Paron Chocolatier**
238 Madison Avenue
New York, NY 10016-2816 212-686-5454
Fax: 212-686-5498 800-326-5033
Chocolates
President: Deborah Sessa
CFO: Harnet Sessa
Vice President: Dana Sessa
Operations Manager: Lance Friedman
Estimated Sales: $500-1 Million appx.
Number Employees: 5-9
Sq. footage: 10
Type of Packaging: Private Label

10313 **Parrish's Cake Decorating Supplies**
225 W 146th St
Gardena, CA 90248 310-324-2253
Fax: 310-324-8277 800-736-8443
customerservice@parrishsmagicline.com
www.parrishsmagicline.com
Manufacturer and exporter of baking supplies including custom, aluminum cake pans, cookie cutters, artificial icing, candy molds and lucite wedding cake plates and pillars; also, food colors and flavorings; importer of pastry bagscake decorating tips, etc
President: Douglas Parrish
CEO: Robert Parrish
VP: Norma Parrish
Estimated Sales: $ 1 - 3 Million
Number Employees: 20-49
Number of Products: 4000
Sq. footage: 45000
Type of Packaging: Consumer, Food Service, Private Label, Bulk
Brands:
Magic Line
Magic Mist
Magic Mold
Perma-Ice

10314 **Parthenon Food Products**
226 S Main St
Ann Arbor, MI 48104-2106 734-994-1012
Fax: 734-994-7073 www.parthenonrestaurant.net
Processor of all natural Greek salad dressings and marinades
President/Owner: Steve Gavas
CFO: John Gavas
Estimated Sales: $500,000 appx.
Number Employees: 10-19
Sq. footage: 1000
Type of Packaging: Consumer, Food Service, Private Label, Bulk
Brands:
Perthenon Greek Salad Dressing

10315 **Particle Control**
6062 Lambert Ave NE
Albertville, MN 55301 763-497-3075
Fax: 763-497-1773 norm@particlecontrolinc.com
www.particlecontrolinc.com
Processor of flavors, whey, oat flour, sugar, etc
Owner/President: Norman Arns
VP: William Arns
Estimated Sales: $700000
Number Employees: 5-9
Sq. footage: 26000

10316 **Particle Dynamics**
2601 S Hanley Rd
Saint Louis, MO 63144 314-968-2376
Fax: 314-646-3761 800-452-4682
info@particledynamics.com
www.particledynamics.com
Manufacturer and exporter of encapsulated and agglomerated vitamins, minerals, flavors, acidulants, colors, spices as well as other active ingredients
President: Paul T Brady
Marketing: Andrea Keith
Sales VP: Richard Miller
Purchasing: Jim Cronk
Estimated Sales: $3500000
Number Employees: 20-49
Sq. footage: 45000
Parent Co: KV Pharmaceutical
Type of Packaging: Bulk
Brands:
Descote
Destab
Micromask

10317 **Partners Coffee Company**
4225 Westfield Dr SW
Atlanta, GA 30336 404-344-5282
Fax: 404-349-6442 800-341-5282
jim@partnerscoffee.com
www.partnerscoffee.com
Processor of coffee
President: James Gilson
CEO: Mike Bacco
Operations Manager: Gerry Larue
Production Manager: Bob Frazier
Purchasing Manager: Anne Gilson
Estimated Sales: $2559650
Number Employees: 10-19
Number of Brands: 3
Number of Products: 200
Sq. footage: 20000
Type of Packaging: Consumer, Food Service, Private Label, Bulk
Brands:
Casa Europa
H&C
Partners

10318 **Partners, A Tasteful Choice Company**
20232 72nd Avenue South
Kent, WA 98032 800-632-7477
Fax: 253-867-1589 caraf@partnerscrackers.com
Kosher, organic/natural, cookies, crackers, granola, foodservice, gift packs, private label.
Vice President: Greg Maestretti
Marketing: Stan Debiec

10319 **Partners, A Tastful Cracker**
135 S Brandon Street
Seattle, WA 98108-2231 206-762-4123
Fax: 206-762-8424 800-632-7477
service@partnerscrackers.com
www.partnerscrackers.com
Manufacturer of low-fat crackers, gourmet granola, cookies
President/Owner: Marian Harris
VP Sales/Owner: Cara Figgins
Estimated Sales: $500,000-$1 Million
Number Employees: 1-4
Sq. footage: 12000
Brands:
BLUE STAR FARMS
CRACKER SNACKERS
GET MOVIN SNACK PACKSS
GOURMET GRANOLA
PARTNERS
WISECRACKERS

10320 **Pascal Coffee**
960 Nepperhan Ave
Yonkers, NY 10703-1726 914-969-7933
Fax: 914-969-8248 roaster@optonline.net
www.pascalcoffee.com
Coffee
Manager: Dean Peialteos
Estimated Sales: Below $ 5 Million
Number Employees: 20-49
Brands:
Pascal Coffee

10321 **Pasco Corporation of America**
6500 N Marine Dr
Portland, OR 97203-6484 503-289-6500
Fax: 503-289-6556 www.pascoamerica.com
Bakery items
President: Yuki Ishimoto
President: Tsunehisa Kikkaw
Estimated Sales: $ 10-20 Million
Number Employees: 60

10322 **Pascobel Inc**
2066 De La Province
Longueuil, QC J4G 1R7
Canada 450-677-2443
Fax: 450-677-2899 guy.bouthillier@pascobel.ca
Manufacturer of specialized dairy ingredients including combolak, coverblak, viseolak, culurelak, fractolak and nonfat milk solids
President: Jean Guy Lauziere
Sales Manager: Guy Bouthillier
Technical Director: Pierre Combeaud
Number Employees: 20-49
Sq. footage: 15000
Type of Packaging: Private Label, Bulk
Brands:
BELCOVER
COMBOLIAK
COVERLAK
CULTURELAK
FRACTOLAK
NOLLIBEL
VISCOLAK

10323 **Pascucci Family Pasta**
4561 Mission Gorge Pl
Suite D
San Diego, CA 92120-4113 619-285-8000
Fax: 619-285-5890
Processor of portion controlled fresh and frozen pasta including fettuccine, linguine, ravioli, tortellini and par-baked pizza crusts
President: Fred Doxbeck
Estimated Sales: $500,000
Number Employees: 7
Sq. footage: 3200
Type of Packaging: Consumer, Food Service, Private Label, Bulk

10324 **Pasqualichio Brothers**
115 Franklin Ave
Scranton, PA 18503 570-346-7115
Fax: 570-346-4610 800-232-6233
Processor of beef, veal, lamb, turkey, chicken and pork including picnic and loin
President: Michael Pasqualichio
Owner: Don Pasqualichio
VP: Patrick Pasqualichio
Operations Manager: Don Pasqualichio
Plant Manager: William Pasqualichio
Estimated Sales: $10 Million
Number Employees: 25
Sq. footage: 10000
Type of Packaging: Consumer
Brands:
Pasqualichio

10325 **Passage Foods LLC**
30 Depot Street
Po Box 245
Collinsville, CT 06022 800-860-1045
Fax: 860-256-4559 www.passagefoods.com
info@passageusa.com
Ethnic sauces (soy, curry, etc) , grilling sauces, other sauces, seasoningsand cooking enhancers.
Marketing: Mark Mackenzie

10326 **Passetti's Pride**
923 Hotel Avenue
Hayward, CA 94541-4001 510-728-4969
Fax: 510-886-6909 800-521-4659
passetti@passettispride.com
www.passettispride.com
Processor of sauces and marinades
Co-Owner: Valentino Passetti
Brands:
Passetti's Pride

10327 **Pasta By Valente**
P.O.Box 2307
Charlottesville, VA 22902-2307 434-971-3717
Fax: 434-971-1511 888-575-7670
retail@pastavalente.com www.pastavalente.com
Produces pasta and marinara sauces
President: Mary F Valente
Officer: Lois Pecavage
Estimated Sales: $370,000
Number Employees: 5

10328 **Pasta Del Mondo**
27 Seminary Hill Rd # 27
Carmel, NY 10512-1928 845-225-8889
Fax: 845-225-0900 800-392-8887
Pasta
President: Frank Marrone
Production Manager: Brendan Conboy
Estimated Sales: $300,000-500,000
Number Employees: 1-4
Sq. footage: 6000
Type of Packaging: Consumer, Food Service, Private Label, Bulk
Brands:
Del Mondo

10329 **Pasta Factory**
11225 W Grand Ave
Melrose Park, IL 60164 847-451-0005
Fax: 847-451-6563 800-615-6951
pastafactoryusa@juno.com
www.pastafactoryusa.com
Pasta
President: Michael Sica
VP: Irene Sica
Sales Manager/Marketing: Thomas Lichon
Operations/Purchasing Director: Joseph Sica
Estimated Sales: $2700000
Number Employees: 20-49
Sq. footage: 16000
Parent Co: MAS Sales
Type of Packaging: Consumer, Food Service, Private Label, Bulk
Brands:
Pasta Factory

10330 **Pasta International**
5715 Coopers Avenue
Mississauga, ON L4Z 2C7
Canada 905-890-5550
Fax: 905-890-8939 www.pastainternational.com
Processor of fresh, prepared and frozen pasta including linguine, fettuccine, spaghetti, ravioli, tortellini, lasagna and cannelloni
President: Massimo Liberatore
Number Employees: 5-9
Sq. footage: 29000
Type of Packaging: Consumer, Food Service
Brands:
Pasta International

10331 **Pasta Italiana**
38 Brooklyn Ave
Massapequa, NY 11758
Fax: 516-795-1794 800-536-5611
pasta@pastaitalianainc.com
www.pastaitaliana.com
Ravioli, tortelloni, agnolotti, cappelletti, tasca, dry pasta, fresh pasta, short cuts, gnocchi, stuffed pasta and grated chesses
President: Robert Yandolino
Estimated Sales: Below $ 5 Million
Number Employees: 10-19
Number of Brands: 2
Number of Products: 140
Sq. footage: 14000
Type of Packaging: Consumer, Food Service, Private Label, Bulk
Brands:
Alberto
Onestis
Pastaitaliana

10332 **Pasta Mami**
1600 Roswell St SE Ste 12
Smyrna, GA 30080 770-438-6022
Fax: 770-438-9810
Fresh pasta products
President: Mark Portwood
Estimated Sales: $ 2.5-5 Million
Number Employees: 10-19
Type of Packaging: Private Label
Brands:
Pasta Mami

10333 **Pasta Mill**
12803 149th Street NW
Edmonton, AB T5L 2J7
Canada 780-454-8665
Fax: 780-454-8668
Processor of fresh and frozen pastas including stuffed tortellini, ravioli and lasagna; also, pasta sauces
President: Steve Parsons
General Manager: Brien Plunkie
Estimated Sales: $284,000
Number Employees: 3
Type of Packaging: Consumer, Food Service
Brands:
The Pasta Mill

10334 **Pasta Montana**
1 Pasta Pl
Great Falls, MT 59401 406-761-1516
Fax: 406-761-1403
comments@pastamontana.com
www.pastamontana.com
Manufactures a line of 24 dry pastas ranging from petite shells and orzo to fettuccine.
President: Yasuhiko Harada
CEO: Yasuhiko Harada
CFO: Craig Smith
Vice President: Randy Gilbertson
Quality Control: John Lacanilao
Marketing Director: Randy Gilbertson
Sales Director: Buzz Weisman
Operations Manager: Kelly Easley
Plant Manager: Stephen SaPerite
Purchasing Manager: Tony Koslosky
Estimated Sales: $ 10-20 Million
Number Employees: 100-249
Sq. footage: 30000
Type of Packaging: Consumer, Food Service, Private Label, Bulk

10335 **Pasta Partners**
P.O.Box 271097
Salt Lake City, UT 84127-1097 801-977-9077
Fax: 801-977-8202 800-727-8284
sales@pastapartners.net www.pastapartners.net
Manufacturer of Handmade pastas in eight flavors, each hand-tied with a miniature bottle of olive oil, dried soup mixes in six flavors and thirteen dried pasta sauce mixes
Owner: Debbie Chidister
VP/Owner: Jody Chidester
Estimated Sales: $ 10 - 20 Million
Number Employees: 20-49
Number of Brands: 2
Number of Products: 45
Sq. footage: 10000
Type of Packaging: Consumer, Private Label
Brands:
PASTA PARTNERS
PLENTIFUL PANTRY

10336 **Pasta Prima**
3909 Park Road
Benicia, CA 94510 707-746-6888
www.pastaprima.com
Manufacturers of pasta, specializes in ravioli

10337 **Pasta Quistini**
1700 Ormont Dr
Toronto, ON M9L 2V4
Canada 416-742-3222
Fax: 416-744-6777
Processor and exporter of pasta
President: Elena Quistini
Vice President: Orlando Quistini
Estimated Sales: $2.4 Million
Number Employees: 22
Type of Packaging: Consumer, Food Service
Brands:
Pasta Al Dente
Pasta Quistini

10338 **Pasta Shoppe**
Po Box 159245
Nashville, TN 37215 615-831-0016
Fax: 615-781-9335 800-247-0188
john@pastashoppe.com www.pastashoppe.com
Manufacturer of pasta, and pasta products, gourmet goodies
President/Owner: John Aron
VP/Owner: Carey Aron
Estimated Sales: $2.7 Million
Number Employees: 25
Type of Packaging: Private Label, Bulk
Brands:
PASTA SHOPPE

10339 **Pasta Sonoma**
640 Martin Ave # 1
Rohnert Park, CA 94928-7994 707-584-0800
Fax: 707-584-2332 www.info@pastasonoma.com
www.pastasonoma.com
Pasta
President: Don Luber
Director of Sales: Dale Lucas
Manager: Cindy Riddle
Estimated Sales: $2 Million
Number Employees: 17
Type of Packaging: Private Label

10340 **Pasta USA**
3405 E Bismark Ct
Spokane, WA 99217 509-489-7219
Fax: 509-489-2848 800-456-2084
sales@pastausa.com www.pastausa.com
Processor and exporter of dry pasta for food service, retail, private label and custom ingredient pasta for food processors. Also, instant and quick cook pasta, organic seminola and organic whole wheat pasta. Macaroni and cheese andother box dinners. Co-packing is available for all pasta and pasta-related products. Since 1916
President: Richard Clemson
CFO: Mary L Clemson
Sales: Steve Grayhek
Estimated Sales: $ 20 - 50 Million
Number Employees: 20-49
Sq. footage: 60000
Brands:
BETTY BAKER
ITALIAN CHEF
PRESTO PASTA

10341 **Pastene Companies**
330 Turnpike St
Canton, MA 02021 781-830-8200
Fax: 781-830-8225 sales@pastene.com
www.pastene.com
Manufacturer of specialty foods including grated cheese, sauces, oil and vinegar, gourmet vegetables, fish products, olives, peppers, beans, bread sticks, pasta, rice and polenta
President: Mark Tosi
CFO: John Franciosa
Vice President: Chris Tosi
Estimated Sales: $30 Million
Number Employees: 20-49
Type of Packaging: Consumer, Food Service
Brands:
PASTENE

10342 **Pastor Chuck Orchards**
PO Box 1259
Portland, ME 04104 207-773-1314
Fax: 207-871-0117
pastorchuck@pastorchuckorchards.com
www.pastorchuckorchards.com
organic applesauce, organic apple salsa and organic apple butter
President: Charles Waite Maclin

10343 Pastorelli Food Products
162 N Sangamon St
Chicago, IL 60607 312-666-2041
Fax: 312-666-2415 800-767-2829
customerservice@pastoreli.com
www.pastorelli.com
Pizza sauces, pizza crusts, pasta sauces, oils and vinegars
Owner: Richard Pastorelli
Estimated Sales: $ 5 - 10 Million
Number Employees: 3
Sq. footage: 61000
Type of Packaging: Consumer, Food Service, Private Label, Bulk
Brands:
Italian Chef

10344 Pastori Winery
23189 Geyserville Ave
Cloverdale, CA 95425 707-857-3418
Wines
Owner: Frank Pastori
Estimated Sales: $230,000
Number Employees: 1-4
Brands:
Pastori

10345 Pastry Chef
112 Warren Avenue
Pawtucket, RI 02860-5604 401-722-1330
800-639-8606
Processor of frozen gourmet cakes and pies; exporter of cheesecakes
President: Per Jensen
CEO: Paul Meunier
Number Employees: 20-49
Number of Brands: 3
Number of Products: 110
Sq. footage: 20000
Parent Co: Pastry Chef
Type of Packaging: Food Service, Private Label
Brands:
The Pastry Chef

10346 Pat's Meat Discounter
702 S 6th Ave
Mills, WY 82604 307-237-7549
Meat
President: Pat Kaeting
Estimated Sales: $500,000-$1 Million
Number Employees: 1-4

10347 Pati-Petite Cookies
1785 Mayview Rd
Bridgeville, PA 15017 412-221-4033
Fax: 412-221-8711 800-253-5805
Processor of gourmet cookies
President: Keith Graham
VP: Bruce Graham
Production Manager: Keith Graham
Estimated Sales: $1400000
Number Employees: 20-49
Sq. footage: 45000
Type of Packaging: Consumer, Food Service, Bulk

10348 Patisserie Wawel
2541 rue Ontario E
Bureau A
Montreal, QC H2K 1W5
Canada 614-524-3348
Fax: 514-524-1266
Processor of European-style marble sponge cake, poppy butter strudel and razowy and rye breads; also, poppy seed, hazelnut and walnut butter fillings
President: Peter Sowa
Manager: Alina Zych
Estimated Sales: $1.4 Million
Number Employees: 20
Sq. footage: 3500

10349 Patrick Cudahy
1 Sweet Applewood Ln
Cudahy, WI 53110 414-744-2000
Fax: 414-744-4213 800-486-6900
charliebrah@patrickcudahy.com
www.patrickcudahy.com
Manufacturer and exporter of bacon, cooked, smoked and glazed hams, lard, shortening, pork sausage, pepperoni, hard salami, Genoa salami and bologna, pre-cooked bacon and sausage
President: William G Otis
President/COO: William Otis
SVP: James Matthews
VP Sales/Marketing: Ramon Aldape
Estimated Sales: $200-300 Million
Number Employees: 1,000-4,999
Sq. footage: 1000000
Parent Co: Smithfield Foods
Type of Packaging: Food Service, Private Label
Brands:
Agar
Appleblossom
Danzig
Golden Crisp
Heat & Eat
La Fortuna
Patrick Cudahy
Patricks Pride
Pavone
Realean
Royalean

10350 Patsy's
236 W 56th St
New York, NY 10019-4306 212-247-3491
Fax: 212-541-5071 sapatsys@aol.com
www.patsys.com
Manufacturer of pasta sauces and marinaras, vegetables, olive oils and vinegars
President: Joseph Scognamillo
Estimated Sales: $ 1 - 3 Million
Number Employees: 20-49
Brands:
PATSY'S

10351 Patsy's Brands
236 W 56 Street
New York, NY 10019 212-247-3491
Fax: 212-541-5071 www.patsys.com
pasta sauces
Marketing: Russ Cahill

10352 Patsy's Candies
1540 S 21st St
Colorado Springs, CO 80904 719-633-7215
Fax: 719-633-6970 866-372-8797
mike@patsycandy.com www.patsyscandies.com
Manufacturer of confectionery products including chocolates, mints, saltwater taffy, fudge, truffles, roasted nuts, candied popcorn and English toffee
President: Mike Niswonger
Estimated Sales: $5-10 Million
Number Employees: 10-19
Sq. footage: 12000
Type of Packaging: Consumer, Food Service, Private Label, Bulk
Brands:
COLORADO PEANUT BUTTER NUGGET
PRELUDES
ROSECUP MINTS

10353 Patterson Frozen Foods
100 E Las Palmas Ave
Patterson, CA 95363 209-892-2611
Fax: 209-892-2582
thomas.ielmini@pattersonfrozenfoods.com
www.pattersonfrozenfoods.com
Manufacturer of frozen vegetables and fruits
President: John Ielmini
CFO: Russ Kenerly
VP Sales: Tom Ielmini
Estimated Sales: $ 50 - 100 Million
Number Employees: 1,000-4,999
Type of Packaging: Consumer, Food Service, Bulk
Other Locations:
Patterson Frozen Foods Plant
Monte Alto TX
Patterson Frozen Foods Plant
Guatemala
Brands:
FAIR ACRES
FRESH PACT
MICROFRESH
PAT-SON
POUR & SAVE
SPRINGTIME
THRIFT-T-PAK

10354 Patterson Vegetable Company
100 W Las Palmas Avenue
Patterson, CA 95363 209-892-2611
sales@pattersonvegetable.com
www.pattersonvegetable.com
Apricots, almonds, broccoli, spinach, tomatoes and peaches
CEO: Ray Walker
COO: Paul Fanelli
Number Employees: 600
Sq. footage: 15982

10355 Patti's Plum Puddings
15020 Hawthorne Blvd # C
Lawndale, CA 90260-1543 310-376-1463
Fax: 310-372-4132 www.pattisplumpuddings.com
Manufacturer of Plum pudding, brandied hard sauce
President/CEO: Patti Garrity
Estimated Sales: $50,000
Number Employees: 1-4
Number of Brands: 1
Number of Products: 2
Sq. footage: 1335
Type of Packaging: Consumer
Brands:
PATTI'S PLUM PUDDING

10356 Patty Palace732840 Ontario Limited
595 Middlefield Road
Unit 16
Scarborough, ON M1V 3S2
Canada 416-297-0510
Fax: 416-297-4024
Processor and exporter of frozen beef patties
President: Michael Davidson
Estimated Sales: $3.6 Million
Number Employees: 30
Type of Packaging: Consumer, Food Service

10357 Paul Piazza & Sons
P.O.Box 52049
New Orleans, LA 70152-2049 504-524-6011
Fax: 504-566-1322 ppiazza@bellsouth.net
Processor of fresh and frozen shrimp, cod, perch and lobster
President: Kristen Baumer
Plant Manager: Don Schwab
Estimated Sales: $ 10 - 20 Million
Number Employees: 50-99
Sq. footage: 75000
Type of Packaging: Consumer, Food Service, Private Label, Bulk

10358 Paul Schafer Meat Products
343 N Charles St # 3
Baltimore, MD 21201-4326 410-528-1250
Fax: 410-528-1059 FSIS.Outreach@usda.gov
www.fsis.usda.gov
Meat products
Owner: Paul Schaefer
Estimated Sales: $ 1-2.5 Million appx.
Number Employees: 5-9

10359 Paul Stevens Lobster
349 Lincoln St # 32
Hingham, MA 02043-1609 781-740-8001
Fax: 781-749-2240
Fish and seafood; lobsters
Owner: Paul Stevens
Estimated Sales: $870,000
Number Employees: 1-4

10360 Paul de Lima Company
7546 Morgan Rd
Liverpool, NY 13090 315-457-3725
Fax: 315-457-3730 800-962-8864
info@delimacoffee.com www.delimacoffee.com
Raoster and purveyor of fine coffee
CEO: W J Drescher Jr
Estimated Sales: $ 50 - 100 Million
Number Employees: 50-99
Number of Products: 2000
Type of Packaging: Consumer, Food Service

10361 Paul's Candy Factory
434 S 300 W
Salt Lake City, UT 84101-1705 801-363-8869
Fax: 801-359-4707 800-825-9912
www.westernut.com
Candy
Owner: Michael Place
Estimated Sales: Below $ 5 Million
Number Employees: 5-9
Brands:
Paul's Candy

10362 Paulaur Corporation
105 Melrich Rd
Cranbury, NJ 8512 609-395-8844
Fax: 609-395-8850 888-398-8844
info@paulaur.com www.paulaur.com

Processor of bakery and ice cream confectionery toppings and inclusions, liquid sweeteners, specialty sugars and value-added carbohydrates; also, custom blending, granulating, agglomerating, sizing, sieving and milling available
President: Vincent Toscano
VP: Larry Toscano
VP Sales: Lawrence Toscano
Estimated Sales: $6700000
Number Employees: 100-249
Sq. footage: 120000
Type of Packaging: Bulk

10363 **Pauline's Pastries**
50 Viceroy Road
Suite 7
Vaughan, ON L4K 3A7
Canada 905-738-5252
Fax: 905-738-0345 877-292-6826
info@paulinespastries.com
www.paulinespastries.com
Processor of fresh pastries
President/CEO: Robyn Perlmutar
Marketing Director: Pauline Perlmutar
Estimated Sales: $5 Million
Number Employees: 25
Type of Packaging: Consumer, Food Service
Brands:
Pauline's

10364 **Paumanok Vineyards**
P.O.Box 741
Aquebogue, NY 11931 631-722-8800
Fax: 631-722-5110 info@paumanok.com
www.paumanok.com
Wine
President: Charles Massoud
Estimated Sales: $1,400,000
Number Employees: 20-49
Brands:
Paumanok Vineyards

10365 **Pavero Cold Storage Corporation**
P.O.Box 395
Highland, NY 12528 845-691-2992
Fax: 845-691-2955 800-435-2994
applz25@aol.com www.paverocoldstorage.com
Grower and packer of apples and pears
President: Joseph Pavero III
CEO: Joseph Pavero Iii
Operations Manager: Jody Pavero
Estimated Sales: $8300000
Number Employees: 50-99

10366 **Pavich Family Farms**
232 Hermosa Dr
Bakersfield, CA 93305-1308 661-782-8700
pavich@pavich.com
Organic produce
President: Tom Pavich
CFO: Paul Ostrow
Director Marketing: William Holbrook
Purchasing Manager: Clarence Robbins
Estimated Sales: Under $500,000
Number Employees: 100
Brands:
Pavich Thomps
Pavich Cashews
Pavich Certified Org
Pavich Dates
Pavich Prunes
Pavich Raisins-Red S

10367 **Payne Packing Company**
P.O.Box 269
Artesia, NM 88211 575-746-2779
Processor and packer of beef, game and pork
Partner: Bobby Yates
Estimated Sales: $260000
Number Employees: 1-4
Type of Packaging: Consumer

10368 **Pazdar Winery**
6 Laddie Road
Scotchtown Branch, NY 10941-1708 845-695-1903
Fax: 845-695-1903 pazdar@citlink.net
www.pazdarwinery.com
Processor of wines
President/CEO: David Pazdar
VP Marketing: Tracy Davis-Pazdar
Number Employees: 5-9
Parent Co: Pazdar Beverage Company
Type of Packaging: Consumer, Food Service
Brands:
PAZDAR WINERY
SUGARY WINE

10369 **Peaberry's Coffee & Tea**
5655 College Ave
Oakland, CA 94618-1583 510-653-0450
Fax: 510-420-0260
peaberrys@rockridgemarkethall.com
www.peaberrys.com
Coffee and tea
Owner: Lynn Mallard
Estimated Sales: Over $ 1 Million
Number Employees: 20-49
Type of Packaging: Private Label

10370 **Peace Mountain Natural Beverages Corporation**
P.O.Box 1445
Springfield, MA 01101 413-567-4942
Fax: 413-567-8161
peacemountainbeverages@msn.com
www.peacemountain.com/skinnywater.com
Manufacturer of Bottled water, organic juices, nutraceutical beverages
Owner: J David
VP R&D: John Alden
Number Employees: 5-9
Type of Packaging: Private Label
Brands:
CARDIO WATER
GIVE YOUR HEART A HEALTHY START
JANA
MIRACLE ADE
MIRACLE JUICE
MIRACLE JUICE ENERGY DRINK
PEACE MOUNTAIN
SKINNY WATER
SPORTS JUICE

10371 **Peace River Citrus Products**
582 Beachland Blvd # 300
Vero Beach, FL 32963-1758 772-467-1234
Fax: 772-492-4056 www.peacerivercitrus.com
Processor and exporter of citrus products
Manager: Kirsten Besanko
Estimated Sales: $ .5 - 1 million
Number Employees: 100-249
Type of Packaging: Bulk
Other Locations:
Peach River Citrus Products Plant
Arcadia FL
Peach River Citrus Products Plant
Bartow FL

10372 **Peace River Citrus Products**
P.O.Box 730
Arcadia, FL 34265 863-494-0440
Fax: 863-993-3161 www.peacerivercitrus.com
Processor of chilled orange juice
President: Bill Becker
VP Finance: Andrew Taylor
Manager: Kirsten Besanko
Number Employees: 8
Type of Packaging: Bulk

10373 **Peace Village Organic Foods**
76 Florida Avenue
Berkeley, CA 94707-1708 510-524-4420
info@peacevillage.net
www.peacevillage.net
Organic asian pasta and organic food ingredients
President: Joel Wollner
Type of Packaging: Consumer, Private Label

10374 **Peaceful Bend Vineyard**
1942 Highway T
Steelville, MO 65565 573-775-3000
Fax: 573-775-3001 winery@peacefulbend.com
www.peacefulbend.com
Wine
Owner: Katherine Gill
CEO: Clyde Gill
Owner: Clyde Gill
Estimated Sales: $500,000-$1 Million
Number Employees: 1-4
Brands:
Peaceful Bend

10375 **Peaceworks**
PO Box 1393
Old Chelsea Station
New York, NY 10113 212-616-3006
Fax: 212-616-3005 800-732-2321
kind@peaceworks.com www.peaceworks.com
fruit and nut bars, pesto and tapenades, and sauces
Founder/Chariman: Daniel Lubetzky
VP: Sasha Hare
VP Sales: Rami Leshem
VP Operations: Doris Rivera
Estimated Sales: $1.3 Million
Number Employees: 8

10376 **Peaceworks**
55 W 21st Fl 6
New York, NY 10010-6809 212-897-3985
marketing@peaceworks.net
www.peaceworks.com
Processor of basil pesto and pasta sauces; also, sun-dried tomato, olive and smoked eggplant spreads
President: Daniel Lubetzky
Chief Information Officer: Khaled Abohalima
Estimated Sales: $938,000
Number Employees: 5
Type of Packaging: Consumer, Food Service
Brands:
Azteca Trading Co.
Mediterranean Sprate
Moshe & Ali's Sprat,
Smoked Eggplant Spra
Wafa

10377 **Peanut Butter & Co**
1790 Broadway
Suite 702
New York, NY 10019 212-757-3130
Fax: 212-757-3252 866-ILO-EPB
inda.bender@ilovepeanutbutter.com
www.ilovepeanutbutter.com
peanut butter, jams and jellies, snacks and fluff
President: Lee Zalben
Marketing: Linda Grimard-Bender
Estimated Sales: $3 Million
Number Employees: 10

10378 **(HQ)Peanut Corporation of America**
2121 Wiggington Road
PO Box 10037
Lynchburg, VA 24506 434-384-7098
Fax: 434-384-9528 gbparnell@aol.com
www.peanutcorp.com
Processor of peanuts
Owner/President: Stewart Parnell
Corporate Office Manager: Gloria Parnell
Sales Director: David Yoth
Estimated Sales: $3-$5 Million
Number Employees: 20-49
Type of Packaging: Consumer, Food Service, Bulk
Other Locations:
Blakely GA
Suffolk VA
Plainview TX
Brands:
PARNELL'S PRIDE

10379 **Peanut Patch**
4322 E County 13th St
Yuma, AZ 85365 928-726-6292
Fax: 928-726-2433 800-872-7688
thepeanutpatch@thepeanutpatch.com
www.thepeanutpatch.com
Peanuts
Owner: Donna George
Estimated Sales: $ 1 - 3 Million
Number Employees: 10-19

10380 **Peanut Patch**
P.O.Box 186
Courtland, VA 23837 757-653-2028
Fax: 757-653-9530 866-732-6883
feridies@feridies.com www.feridies.com
Processor and exporter of gourmet peanuts and peanut candies such as peanut brittle, chocolate covered peanuts, honey roasted peanuts, cashew brittle, and chocolate peanut brittle
President/CEO: Judy Riddick
CFO: Paul Sheffer
R&D: Ted Fries
Quality Control: Ted Fries
Marketing: Jane Fries
Number Employees: 10-19

Type of Packaging: Consumer, Food Service, Private Label
Brands:
Peanut Patch

10381 **Peanut Processors**
P.O.Box 160
Dublin, NC 28332 910-862-2136
Fax: 910-862-8076 www.peanutprocessors.com
Peanuts
CEO: Houston Brisson
Estimated Sales: $ 20 - 50 Million
Number Employees: 20-49

10382 **Peanut Roaster**
394 Zeb Robinson Rd
Henderson, NC 27537 252-431-0100
Fax: 252-431-0224 800-445-1404
peanut@peanut.com www.peanut.com
Wholesalers, retailers and manufacturers of peanuts
President: John Monahan
Marketing Director: Charles Penick
CFO: Peanut Roaster
Quality Control: John William
Founder: Larry Monahan Sr.
Estimated Sales: Below $ 5 Million
Number Employees: 20-49
Brands:
The Peanut Roaster

10383 **Peanut Shop of Williamsburg**
311 County Street
Suite 201
Portsmouth, VA 23704 757-566-0930
Fax: 757-673-7006 800-637-3268
info@thepeanutshop.com
www.thepeanutshop.com
Manufacturer of peanuts
General Manager: Pete Booker
Operations Mgr: Larry Winslow
General Manager: Pete Booker
Number Employees: 30
Type of Packaging: Consumer, Food Service, Private Label, Bulk
Brands:
Peanut Shop of Williamsburg
Smithfield Tavern

10384 **Peanut Shop of Williamsburg**
311 Country Street
Suite 201
Portsmouth, VA 23704 800-637-3268
Fax: 757-673-7006 info@thepeanutshop.com
www.thepeanutshop.com
peanuts and peanut products
Manufacturing Staff Director: Larry Wcislo
General Manager: Chip Penick
Number Employees: 8

10385 **Peanut Wonder Corporation**
30 Blank Ln
Water Mill, NY 11976 631-726-4433
Fax: 631-726-4433 www.peanutwonder.com
Low fat, low calorie peanut butter spread
President: Lloyd Lasdon
Vice President: Stuart Lasdon
Estimated Sales: Under $500,000
Number Employees: 1-4
Type of Packaging: Private Label
Brands:
Peanut Wonder

10386 **Pear's Coffee**
6171 Grover St
Omaha, NE 68106 402-551-8422
Fax: 402-551-8401 800-317-1773
rrb@hermansnuthouse.com
www.hermansnuthouse.com
Coffee, nuts
President: John Larsen
Operations Manager: Adam Gaines
Estimated Sales: Below $ 5 Million
Number Employees: 20-49
Type of Packaging: Bulk
Brands:
Pear's Coffee

10387 **Pearl Coffee Company**
675 S Broadway St
Akron, OH 44311 330-253-7184
Fax: 330-253-7185 800-822-5282
Manufacturer and packer of roasted regular, flavored and gourmet coffee; importer of green coffee
President: John Economou
VP/Marketing: Johnna Economou
Estimated Sales: $9 Million
Number Employees: 10-19
Sq. footage: 20000
Type of Packaging: Consumer, Food Service, Private Label
Brands:
Diana

10388 **Pearl River Pastry & Chocolates**
4 Dexter Plz
Pearl River, NY 10965-2321 845-735-5100
Fax: 845-735-6434 800-632-2639
sales@prpastry.com www.prpastry.com
Manufacturer of chocolates, cakes and pastries
Owner: J Koffman
Estimated Sales: $5-10 Million
Number Employees: 20-49

10389 **Pearl Valley Cheese Company**
54775 Township Road 90
Fresno, OH 43824 740-545-6002
Fax: 740-545-7703 www.pearlvalleycheese.com
Processor of natural cheeses
President: John Stalder
General Manager: Chuck Ellis
Number Employees: 10-19
Type of Packaging: Consumer, Food Service, Private Label, Bulk
Brands:
Pearl Valley

10390 **Pearlco of Boston**
5 Whitman Rd
Canton, MA 02021-2707 781-821-1010
Fax: 781-821-4303
Pickled fruits and vegetables, vegetable sauces and seasonings, and salad dressings.
President/Treasurer: Judith Pearlstein
Estimated Sales: $3,100,000
Number Employees: 20-49
Type of Packaging: Food Service, Private Label, Bulk
Brands:
Saratoga

10391 **Pearson Candy Company**
P.O.Box 64459
St Paul, MN 55164-0459 651-698-0356
Fax: 651-696-2222 800-328-6507
www.pearsoncandy.com
Processor of candy including chocolate and nonchocolate bagged, bars, multi-packs, mints, holiday novelties, vending, nut goodies and nut rolls and bun bars
President: Larry L Hassler
Estimated Sales: $ 20 - 50 Million
Number Employees: 100-249
Type of Packaging: Consumer
Brands:
PEARSON'S BUN BARS
PEARSON'S MINT PATTIES
PEARSON'S NUT GOODIE
PEARSON'S SALTED NUT ROLL

10392 **Pearson's Berry Farm**
RR 1
Bowden, AB T0M 0K0
Canada 403-224-3011
Fax: 403-224-2096
Processor of berry products including jams, pie fillings and dessert toppings
President: E Leonard Pearson
Sales Manager: Joyce Park
Number Employees: 20-49
Type of Packaging: Consumer, Food Service
Brands:
Pearson's Berry Farm

10393 **Pearson's Homestyle**
RR 1
Bowden, AB T0M 0K0
Canada 403-224-3339
877-224-3339
homestyle@homestylebeverage.com
www.gordosfoods.com
Processor of gourmet sauces, spices and seasonings; private labeling and custom liquid filling available. Produces unique upscale beverages featuring such natural and wild grown prairie berries as the Highbush Cranberry, rasberry, wildblack cherries and the Saskatoon Berry.
President: Duane Mertin
Production: Debbie Mertin
Number Employees: 10-19
Sq. footage: 5500
Type of Packaging: Private Label
Brands:
Gordo's

10394 **Pease's Candy Shoppe**
1701 S State St
Springfield, IL 62704-4098 217-523-3721
Fax: 217-523-7581 ILINI83@aol.com
www.peasescandy.com
Manufacturer of fine chocolates and salted nuts
Owner: Robert Flesher
VP/Treasurer: Robert Flesher
Estimated Sales: $500,000-$1 Million
Number Employees: 5-9
Brands:
Pease's

10395 **Pecan Deluxe Candy Co.**
2570 Lone Star Dr
Dallas, TX 75212 214-631-3669
Fax: 214-631-5833 800-733-3589
www.pecandeluxe.com
Supplier of gourmet cookies and ice creams.
President: Jay Brigham
CFO: Keith Hurd
VP Quality Assurance: Rick Hintermeier
Chief Operating Officer: Tim Markowicz

10396 **Pecan Deluxe Candy Company**
2570 Lone Star Dr
Dallas, TX 75212 214-631-3669
Fax: 214-631-5833 800-733-3589
pdcc_info@pecandeluxe.com
www.pecandeluxe.com
Processor and exporter of ingredients for frozen desserts and baked goods including toffees, praline nuts, chocolate coated items, flavor bases, sauces, etc.; also, nonfat and nonsugar ingredients available
President: Bennie Brigham
CEO: John Namy
Executive VP: Jay Brigham
R&D Director: Bill Garrison
VP Marketing: Robert Bosma
VP Sales: Robert Bosma
Inventory/Production Coordinator: Wayne Miller
Plant Manager: Mike Cavin
Purchasing Manager: James Mitchell
Estimated Sales: $ 20 - 50 Million
Number Employees: 100-249
Number of Products: 2000
Sq. footage: 63000
Type of Packaging: Bulk

10397 **Pecans De Chihuahua**
Av. Ocampo 2004
Col. Sta. Rita, CH 31020
Mexico 614-420-1414
lupita_aranda@hotmail.com
www.vinomex.com.mx
Other candy, other snacks.
Marketing: Guadalupe Aranda Olivas

10398 **Pechters Baking**
840 Jersey St
Harrison, NJ 07029-2056 973-483-3374
Fax: 973-483-1600 800-525-5779
www.pechters.com
Processor of baked goods including bread, rolls and bagels
President: George Thomas
Director Operations: Steve Colombo
Estimated Sales: $ 50 - 100 Million
Number Employees: 250-499
Parent Co: Amerifit/Strength Systems
Type of Packaging: Food Service
Brands:
Pechters

10399 **Peco Foods**
3701 Kauloosa Ave
PO Box 1760
Tuscaloosa, AL 35401 205-345-3955
Fax: 205-343-2401 www.pecofoods.com

Processor and exporter of poultry products
Parent Co: Peco Foods
Type of Packaging: Consumer, Food Service

10400 Peco Foods
95 Commerce Drive Industrial Park
Bay Springs, MS 39422 601-764-4392
Fax: 601-670-9319 www.pecofoods.com
Processor and exporter of poultry products
Parent Co: Peco Foods
Type of Packaging: Consumer, Food Service

10401 (HQ)Peco Foods
1020 Lurleen B Wallace Blvd N
PO Box 1760
Tuscaloosa, AL 35401 205-345-4711
Fax: 205-366-4533 mhickman@pecofoods.com
www.pecofoods.com
Processor and exporter of poultry
President/CEO: Mark Hickman
CFO: Tommy Elliott
Director of Quality Assurance: Curtis Stell
Director of Sales & Marketing: Bobby Wilburn
National Sales Manager: Sharon Woods
Corporate Marketing Manager: Courtney Stallings-Barr
Chief Operations Officer: Benny Bishop
Director of Live Operations: Roddy Sanders
Estimated Sales: $100+ Million
Number Employees: 3800
Type of Packaging: Consumer, Food Service
Other Locations:
Peco Foods
Brooksville MS
Peco Foods
Bay Springs MS

10402 Peco Foods
1039 West Fulton Street
Canton, MS 39046 601-855-0925
Fax: 601-955-5031 www.pecofoods.com
Processor of fresh and frozen chicken
Plant Manager: Frank Gordon
Parent Co: Peco Foods
Type of Packaging: Consumer
Brands:
Peco

10403 Peco Foods
Highway 21 South
PO Box 319
Sebastopol, MS 39359-0319 601-625-7432
Fax: 601-625-0226 www.pecofoods.com
Manufacturer and exporter of poultry products
Parent Co: Peco Foods
Type of Packaging: Consumer, Food Service

10404 Peconic Bay Winery
P.O.Box 818
Cutchogue, NY 11935 631-734-7361
Fax: 631-734-5867 info@peconicbaywinery.com
www.peconicbaywinery.com
Wine
Manager: Matt Gillies
Co-Owner: Ursula Lowerre
Winemaker: Gregory Gove
General Manager: Matt Gillies
Estimated Sales: Below $ 5 Million
Number Employees: 20-49
Brands:
Peconic Bay

10405 Pecoraro Dairy Products
904 Erie Blvd W
Rome, NY 13440 315-339-0101
Fax: 315-339-3008 pcr2c1@aol.com
Processor and exporter of cheeses including feta, ricotta, regular and curd mozzarella, mascarpone and string; also, yogurt and basket cheese
President: Cesare Pecoraro
Operations: Ralph Parlato
Estimated Sales: $ 5 - 10 Million
Number Employees: 5-9
Number of Brands: 4
Number of Products: 12
Sq. footage: 7200
Type of Packaging: Consumer, Food Service, Private Label
Brands:
Brown Cow Farm East
Sweet Cheese, Queso Blanco

10406 Pecos Valley Spice Company
P.O.Box 2162
Corrales, NM 87048 505-243-2622
Spices
Vice President: G McMeen

10407 Pede Brothers
582 Duanesburg Rd # 1
Schenectady, NY 12306-1096 518-356-3042
Fax: 518-355-7472
Processor of fresh and frozen pasta
Owner: Romolo Pede
Estimated Sales: $ 20 - 50 Million
Number Employees: 20-49
Type of Packaging: Consumer, Food Service, Private Label

10408 Pedrizzetti Winery
1645 San Pedro Ave
Morgan Hill, CA 95037 408-779-7389
Fax: 408-779-9083 wines@pedwines.net
www.pedrizzetti.com
Wines
President: Michael Sampognaro
Estimated Sales: $500,000-$1 Million
Number Employees: 1-4
Type of Packaging: Consumer, Private Label, Bulk
Brands:
Barbera
Sirah

10409 Pedroncelli Winery
1220 Canyon Rd
Geyserville, CA 95441-9639 707-857-3531
Fax: 707-857-3812 800-836-3894
service@pedroncelli.com www.pedroncelli.com
Wines
President: John Pedroncelli
VP Marketing: Julie Pedroncelli St. John
VP Sales: Richard Morehouse
Estimated Sales: $1,500,000
Number Employees: 20-49
Type of Packaging: Private Label
Brands:
Pedroncelli

10410 Peeled Snacks
530 Third Avenue
Suite 2R
Brooklyn, NY 11215 212-706-2001
Fax: 646-478-9518 info@peeledsnacks.com
www.peeledsnacks.com
fruit and nut snacks
President/Owner: Noha Waibsnaider

10411 (HQ)Peeler's Jersey Farms
706 Leadmine Road
Gaffney, SC 29340-3636 864-487-9996
Fax: 864-489-2889
Dairy products
Estimated Sales: $ 5-10 Million
Number Employees: 20-49

10412 Peer Foods Inc.
1200 W 35th St
Chicago, IL 60609 773-927-1440
Fax: 773-927-9859 800-365-5644
www.peerfoods.com
Processor of smoked meats including bacon, hams and butts, pigs' feet, sausage and corned beef; also, pickled hocks and Canadian bacon
President: Larry O'Connell
CFO: Gary Radville
Marketing Manager: Harold Dangler
Director Manufacturing: Bill Froula
Estimated Sales: $10-20 Million
Number Employees: 10-19
Type of Packaging: Consumer, Food Service

10413 Peerless Coffee Company
260 Oak St
Oakland, CA 94607 510-763-1763
Fax: 510-763-5026 800-310-5662
tellme@peerlesscoffee.com
www.peerlesscoffee.com
Processor of gourmet coffee
President: Sonja Vukasin
CEO: George Vukasin Sr
Executive VP: George Vukasin Jr
CEO: George Vukasin Sr
Consultant: Michelle Thomas
CFO: Ivan Steves
Estimated Sales: $ 50 - 100 Million
Number Employees: 50-99
Type of Packaging: Consumer, Food Service

10414 Peerless Confection Company
7383 N Lincoln Ave Ste 100
Lincolnwood, IL 60712 773-281-6100
Fax: 773-281-5812 sales@peerlesscandy.com
www.peerlesscandy.com
Manufacturer of hard and filled candy
Chairman: Kathleen Pickens
Estimated Sales: $15 Million
Number Employees: 104
Sq. footage: 170000
Type of Packaging: Consumer
Brands:
CHIPS N' CHEWS
LEMAN'S
ORORA
PM MIX
RADIANT MORSELS
SPRIG-O-MINT
SUNRAY

10415 Peerless Packing Company
P.O.Box 697
Beckley, WV 25802-0697 304-252-4731
Fax: 304-255-1290
Processor/packer of fresh meats
Manager: Mark Eye
Estimated Sales: $ 3 - 5 Million
Number Employees: 5-9
Type of Packaging: Consumer, Food Service
Brands:
Im-Peer-Ial

10416 Peerless Potato Chips
1661 W 11th Ave
Gary, IN 46404-2499 219-885-6843
Fax: 219-885-7420
Processor of potato chips
Manager: John Hogg
Vice President: John Hogg Jr.
Estimated Sales: $5-9.9 Million
Number Employees: 10-19
Type of Packaging: Consumer, Food Service, Private Label, Bulk
Brands:
Peerless Potato Chips

10417 Peet's Coffee & Tea
1400 Park Avenue
Emeryville, CA 94608 510-594-2100
Fax: 510-594-2180 800-999-2132
webmail@peets.com www.peets.com
Coffee roaster and tea.
Chairman: Jean-Michel Valette
President/CEO: Patrick O'Dea
CFO/VP: Tom Cawley
Vice President/Coffee: Doug Welsh
Director of Tea: Eliot Jordan
Director: Jerry Baldwin
Director of Coffee Purchasing: Shirin Moayyad
Estimated Sales: $333 Million
Number Employees: 3500

10418 Peetsa Products Company
4828 Stamp Rd
Temple Hills, MD 20748-6715 301-423-3900
Fax: 301-423-7301
Foodservices
President: Ray Seaton
Estimated Sales: Under $500,000
Number Employees: 2

10419 Peggy Lawton Kitchens
253 Washington St
East Walpole, MA 02320 508-668-1215
Fax: 508-660-1636 800-843-7325
Manufacturer of portion packaged brownies and cookies including preservative-free
President: William Wolf
Office Manager: Robert Willis
Estimated Sales: $ 10 - 20 Million
Number Employees: 20-49
Number of Products: 10
Sq. footage: 30000
Type of Packaging: Consumer, Food Service, Private Label, Bulk
Brands:
PEGGY LAWTON

10420 Pegi
1211 N Harbor Boulevard
Santa Ana, CA 92703-1608 714-554-2110
Fax: 714-554-2140 800-292-3353
pegi@pacbell.com
President: Corrine Draps

Estimated Sales: Under $500,000
Number Employees: 5-9

10421 Peju Winery
P.O.Box 478
Rutherford, CA 94573-0478 707-963-3600
Fax: 707-963-8680 800-446-7358
info@peju.com www.peju.com
Wines
Owner: Herta Behensky
Estimated Sales: Below $ 5 Million
Number Employees: 20-49
Brands:
Peju

10422 Pekarna's Meat Market
119 Water St
Jordan, MN 55352-1555 952-492-6101
Manufacturer of meat and meat products including beef, pork, wild game and sausage
President: Frank Pekarna
CEO: Kenny Pekarna
Estimated Sales: $4 Million
Number Employees: 5-9
Type of Packaging: Consumer, Private Label

10423 Pekarskis Sausage
293 Conway Rd
South Deerfield, MA 01373-9663 413-665-4537
Meat and poultry
Manager: Mike Pekarski
Marketing Director: Mike Pekarskis
Estimated Sales: $500,000-$1 Million
Number Employees: 1-4
Brands:
Pekarskis

10424 Peking Noodle Company
1514 N San Fernando Rd
Los Angeles, CA 90065 323-223-2023
Fax: 323-223-3211 info@pekingnoodle.com
www.pekingnoodle.com
Processor and exporter of noodles, egg rolls, wontons, potsticker wraps, suey gow skins, fortune cookies and snack foods
President: Stephen Tong
Vice President: Frank Tong
Plant Manager: Maria Gonzalez
Estimated Sales: $2200000
Number Employees: 50-99
Sq. footage: 30000
Type of Packaging: Consumer, Food Service, Private Label, Bulk

10425 Pel-Freez
P.O.Box 68
Rogers, AR 72757-0068 479-636-4361
Fax: 479-636-4282 800-223-8751
biosales@pelfreez.com www.pelfreez-bio.com
Manufacturer and exporter of frozen and fresh rabbit
President/CEO: David Dubbell
Estimated Sales: $53 Million
Number Employees: 50-99
Parent Co: Pel-Freez
Type of Packaging: Consumer, Food Service
Brands:
PEL-FREEZE

10426 Pelican Bay
150 Douglas Ave
Dunedin, FL 34698 727-733-8399
Fax: 727-734-5860 800-826-8982
sales@pelicanbayltd.com
www.pelicanbayltd.com
Processor, wholesaler/distributor and exporter of baking and drink mixes, spice blends and gourmet gifts
President: Linda Pfaelzer
CEO: Char Pfaelzer
Cfo: Tim Desser
Executive VP: David Pfaelzer
Marketing: Jim Hubbard
Plant Manager: Justin Pfaelzer
Purchasing: Greg Kathan
Estimated Sales: $4.7 Million
Number Employees: 30
Number of Brands: 1
Number of Products: 200
Sq. footage: 30000
Type of Packaging: Consumer, Private Label, Bulk
Brands:
Pelican Bay

10427 Pelican Marine Supply
2911 Engineers Rd
Belle Chasse, LA 70037 504-392-9062
Fax: 504-394-5528
President: Peter Bretchel
Estimated Sales: $ 10 - 20 Million
Number Employees: 10-19

10428 Pellegrini Family Vineyards
4055 W Olivet Rd
Santa Rosa, CA 95401-3893 707-575-8463
Fax: 650-589-7132 800-891-0244
info@pellegrinisonoma.com
www.pellegrinisonoma.com
Wines
Owner/CFO: Richard Pellegrini
Owner/manager: Robert Pellegrini
Partner/Property Manager: Jeanne Pellegrini
Treasurer: Verna Rayala
Estimated Sales: $1 Million
Number Employees: 15
Type of Packaging: Private Label
Brands:
Cloverdale Ranch
Olivet Lane
Pellegrini

10429 Pellman Foods
122 S Shirk Rd
PO Box 337
New Holland, PA 17557 717-354-8070
Fax: 717-355-9944 info@pellmanfoods.com
www.pellmanfoods.com
Processor of frozen cakes, cheesecakes, pies and tortes
President: Michael Pellman
VP: Scott Pellman
Marketing Director: Deryl Denlinger
Sales: Roger Carper
Public Relations: Allen Smoker
Production: Greg Huber
Plant Manager: Clair Siegrist
Estimated Sales: $ 20 - 50 Million
Number Employees: 40
Number of Brands: 1
Number of Products: 30
Sq. footage: 50000
Type of Packaging: Consumer, Food Service
Brands:
PELLMAN

10430 Peloian Packing Company
430 W Ventura St
Dinuba, CA 93618 559-591-0101
Fax: 559-591-7584
Manufacturer, packer and exporter of raisins
President: Edward Peloian
Estimated Sales: $28 Million
Number Employees: 5-9
Type of Packaging: Consumer, Private Label, Bulk

10431 Peluso Cheese Company
429 H St
Los Banos, CA 93635 209-826-3744
Fax: 209-826-6782
Mexican style cheese: chihuahua, cotija, freir, fresco, panela, Quesmo crema
Manager: Sergio Alvarado
Estimated Sales: $ 20-50 Million
Number Employees: 20-49

10432 Pemaquid Fishermen's Co-Op
P.O.Box 152
New Harbor, ME 04554-0152 207-677-2801
Fax: 207-677-2818 866-864-2897
sales@pemaquidlobsterco-op.com
www.pemaquidlobsterco-op.com
Seafood
Manager: Wayne Dighton
Estimated Sales: $300,000-500,000
Number Employees: 5-9

10433 Pemberton's Gourmet Foods
32 Lewiston Rd
Gray, ME 04039 207-657-6446
Fax: 207-657-6453 800-255-8401
info@pembertongourmet.com
www.pembertongourmet.com
Sauces, mixes, pancake, scone, muffin mixes and syrup. Sauces, seasonings, salsa, relish, mustard, pickles, jams, jellies
Owner: Jeff Johnson
Estimated Sales: $ .5 - 1 million
Number Employees: 5-9
Sq. footage: 7000

10434 Penauta Products
PO Box 155
Stouffville, ON L4A 7Z5
Canada 905-640-1564
Fax: 905-640-7479
Processor and exporter of jarred honey including raw, liquid and cream; also, bee pollen
President: Paul Nauta
Chairman: Henry Nauta
Production Manager: Martin Nauta
Estimated Sales: $130,000
Number Employees: 1
Sq. footage: 6000
Type of Packaging: Consumer, Food Service, Private Label, Bulk
Brands:
Ambrosia
Meadowview

10435 Pend Oreille Cheese Company
P.O.Box 1969
Sandpoint, ID 83864-0910 208-263-2030
www.lighthousefoods.com
Processor of cheese
Manager: Jennifer Calbert
Estimated Sales: $270000
Number Employees: 1-4
Type of Packaging: Consumer

10436 Pender Packing Company
4520 Nc Highway 133
Rocky Point, NC 28457 910-675-3311
Fax: 910-675-1625 penderpacking@aol.com
Processor of meat including fresh and smoked sausage, liver pudding, c-loaf, souse loaf, chitterling loaf, cured sausage, chorizo, fatback and pork barbecue.
President: Danny L Baker
Estimated Sales: $4900000
Number Employees: 20-49
Type of Packaging: Consumer

10437 Pendery's
1221 Manufacturing St
Dallas, TX 75207-6505 214-357-1870
Fax: 214-761-1966 800-533-1870
email@penderys.com www.pendery.com
Manufacturer of seasonings including bay leaves, cinnamon, garlic, ginger, paprika, chile pepper and herb blends
President/Owner: Patrick Haggerty Jr
Estimated Sales: $1-3 Million
Number Employees: 5-9
Sq. footage: 23000
Type of Packaging: Consumer, Food Service, Private Label, Bulk
Brands:
CHILTOMALINE

10438 Pendery's
1221 Manufacturing St
Dallas, TX 75207-6505 214-741-1870
Fax: 214-761-1966 800-533-1870
email@penderys.com www.penderys.com
Chiles and Spices.
President: Pat Haggerty
Vice President: Mary Haggerty
Generl Manager: Clint Haggerty
Estimated Sales: Below $ 5 Million
Number Employees: 7

10439 Pendleton Flour Mills
501 SE Emigrant Ave
Pendleton, OR 97801 541-276-6511
Fax: 541-276-9151 www.pendleton.or.us
Flour and other grain mill products
Manager: Greg Loftus
CFO: Terry Burns
Marketing Director: Mike McDaniel
Production Manager: Jean Scott
Estimated Sales: $ 100-500 Million
Number Employees: 50-99

10440 (HQ)Penford Food Ingredients
7094 S Revere Pkwy
Centennial, CO 80112 303-649-1900
Fax: 303-649-1700 pfi-general@penx.com
www.penfordfoods.com

Manufacturer of Specialty dextrose, potato dextrins, pregelatinized, cook-up potato and tapioca starches; also, modified waxy maize starches and dietary fober, rice starches
President/CEO/Director: Thomas Malkoski
VP/CFO: Steven Cordier
Sr Research Team Leader: Dr Ibrahim Abbas PhD
Director Business Development: Jeff Smith
Marketing Manager: Ted Lengwin
Regional Sales Manager: Barbara Howe
Estimated Sales: $250 Million
Number Employees: 300
Other Locations:
Penford Food Ingredients - Sales
Roswell GA
Penford Food Ingredients - Sales
Burr Ridge IL
Penford Food Ingredients
Newman Lake WA
Penford Food Ingredients
Red Wing MN
PFI - Starch Mfg
Plover WI
PFI - Starch Mfg
Idaho Falls ID
PFI - Sugar Mfg
Cedar Rapids IA
PFI - Starch Mfg
Richland WA

10441 **Penguin Frozen Foods**
P.O.Box 1145
Northbrook, IL 60065-1145 847-291-9400
Fax: 847-291-1588
Processor and exporter of frozen seafood and fish including shrimp, sole, turbot, fillets, lobster, crab meat, etc
President: Jonathan Appelbaum
Estimated Sales: $2700000
Number Employees: 10-19
Type of Packaging: Consumer, Food Service
Brands:
Campeche Bay
Dimo
Texas Bay

10442 **Penguin Natural Foods**
6433 Canning St
Commerce, CA 90040 323-727-7980
Fax: 323-727-7983 800-600-8448
jgegenhuber@hotmail.com
www.penguinfoods.com
Ready to serve foods, processed foods
President: Scott Nairne
Food Technician: Michael Dunn
R&D Chef: John Gegenhuber
Estimated Sales: $ 10-20 Million
Number Employees: 20-49

10443 **Penhurst Candy Company**
995 Greenburg Pike
Pittsburgh, PA 15221-4233 412-271-8880
Fax: 412-271-1085 800-545-1336
Chocolate candy
Estimated Sales: $ 10-24.9 Million
Number Employees: 50-100

10444 **Peninsula Fruit Exchange**
2955 Kroupa Rd
Traverse City, MI 49686 231-223-4282
Fax: 231-223-4299
Manufacturer of frozen cherries
President: Jim Horton
Vice President: Donald Shea
Vice President: Michael Shea
Estimated Sales: $4 Million
Number Employees: 23
Type of Packaging: Consumer, Food Service

10445 **Penn Cheese Corporation**
7199 County Line Rd
Winfield, PA 17889 570-524-7700
Fax: 570-523-9691 jon.weber@penncheese.com
www.penncheese.com
Processor of specialty swiss cheese, including baby and lacey swiss
President: Michael Price
General Manager: Jonathan Weber
Production Manager: Thomas Weber
Estimated Sales: $5 Million
Number Employees: 16
Number of Brands: 2
Number of Products: 2
Sq. footage: 20300
Type of Packaging: Private Label, Bulk
Brands:
Market Place
Pennsylvania People

10446 **Penn Dutch Food Center**
3950 N 28th Ter
Hollywood, FL 33020-1179 954-921-4635
Fax: 954-921-7448 www.penn-dutch.com
Dutch food
President: Greg Salsburg
CEO: George Ronkin
Secretary/Treasurer: Paul Salsburg
Managing Director: Kara Boehly
Estimated Sales: $ 20 - 50 Million
Number Employees: 100-249

10447 **Penn Herb Company**
10601 Decatur Rd # 2
Philadelphia, PA 19154-3212 215-632-6100
Fax: 215-632-7945 800-523-9971
info@pennherb.com www.pennherb.com
Processor and wholesaler/distributor of encapsulated herbs including ginseng and golden seal root; importer of vitamins and supplements
President: William Betz
President: Ronald Betz
Estimated Sales: $3500000
Number Employees: 10-19
Sq. footage: 23000
Brands:
Nature's Wonderland

10448 **(HQ)Penn Maid Crowley Foods**
10975 Dutton Rd
Philadelphia, PA 19154-3203 215-824-2800
Fax: 215-824-2820 800-247-6269
www.hphood.com
Manufacturer of dairy products that include; sour cream, cottage cheese, yogurt, cream cheese, butter, dips, cheese, desserts and condiments
Controller: Glenn Goenner
Plant Manager: Ron Nelson
Estimated Sales: $21 Million
Number Employees: 100-249
Sq. footage: 40000
Type of Packaging: Consumer, Food Service, Private Label, Bulk
Brands:
PENN MAID

10449 **Penn-Shore Vineyards**
10225 Lake Rd
North East, PA 16428 814-725-8688
Fax: 814-725-8689 www.pennshore.com
Winery
President: Jeffrey Ore
Vice President: Cheryl Ore
Estimated Sales: Below $ 5 Million
Number Employees: 5-9
Number of Brands: 23
Type of Packaging: Bulk

10450 **Pennant Foods Company**
111 Northwest Ave
Northlake, IL 60164 708-562-0100
Fax: 708-498-2305 800-877-1157
twellenzohn@pennantfoods.com
www.chefsolutions.com
Bakery products, including puff pastry and Danish doughs, bakery mixes and bases, fillings, icings and glazes, thaw' n serve cakes and muffins, frozen cookie doughs and other specialties
CEO: Steve Silk
CFO: Carl Warchausky
Human Resources: Claudia Romo
Chief Information Officer: Michael C Casula
Estimated Sales: $ 20 - 50 Million
Number Employees: 250-499
Brands:
Chef Solutions
Pennant

10451 **(HQ)Pennfield Corporation**
P.O.Box 4366
Lancaster, PA 17604 717-299-2561
Fax: 717-295-8783 www.pennfield.com
Processor of fresh and frozen chicken, custom cut meats, seafood, frozen food products
President: Donald Horn
CEO: Ernest O Horn Iii
Operations Manager: Fred Keller
Purchasing Manager: Andy Graybill
Estimated Sales: $200000000
Number Employees: 50-99
Type of Packaging: Consumer, Food Service, Private Label, Bulk
Brands:
PENFIELD FARMS
RITTER FOOD

10452 **Pennfield Farms**
1074 East Main St
Mt Joy, PA 17552 717-865-2153
Fax: 717-865-2186 800-732-0009
kmith@dolemannatural.com
www.pennfieldfarms.com
Processor of egg products and fresh chicken including parts
President: Mark Mckay
Plant Manager: Bill Rahn
Number Employees: 400
Parent Co: Pennfield Corporation
Type of Packaging: Consumer, Bulk
Brands:
COLEMAN

10453 **Pennsylvania Brewing Company**
800 Vinial St
Pittsburgh, PA 15212-5151 412-237-9400
Fax: 412-237-9406 pennbrew@hotmail.com
www.pennbrew.com
Processor and bottler of seasonal beer and ale
President: Tom Pastorius
Manager: Rick Brown
Estimated Sales: Below $ 5 Million
Number Employees: 20-49
Type of Packaging: Consumer, Food Service
Brands:
Penn Dark
Penn Gold
Penn Maibok
Penn Marzen
Penn Pilsner
Penn Weizen

10454 **Pennsylvania Dutch BirchBeer**
5175 Cold Spring Creamert Rd
Suite 4
Doylestown, PA 18901 856-662-1869
dschwarz@daretogodutch.com
www.daretogodutch.com
Manufacturer of soft drinks
President: Michael Geehring
Chairman: Lincoln Warrell
VP Finance: L Lebo
VP: Dwayne Schwartz
Estimated Sales: $1-$2.5 Million
Number Employees: 2
Brands:
Pennsylvania Dutch

10455 **(HQ)Pennsylvania Dutch Candies**
1250 Slate Hill Rd
Camp Hill, PA 17011 717-761-5440
Fax: 717-761-5702 800-233-7082
orderdirect@warrellcorp.com
www.padutchcandies.com
Manufacturer of candies, chocolates and snacks
Chairman: Lincoln A Warrell
President: Dick Billman
SVP Administration/General Manager: Kevin Silva
Estimated Sales: $20-50 Million
Number Employees: 200
Number of Brands: 3
Sq. footage: 200000
Type of Packaging: Private Label, Bulk
Brands:
KATHERINE BEECHER
MELSTER
PENNSYLVANIA DUTCH CANDIES

10456 **Pennsylvania Macaroni Company**
2010 Penn Ave
Pittsburgh, PA 15222 412-471-8330
Fax: 412-201-4751 800-223-5928
info@pennmac.com www.pennmac.com
Pasta
President: David Sunseri
Purchasing Manager: William Sunseri
Estimated Sales: $ 50-100 Million
Number Employees: 50-99

10457 Penobscot McCrum
28 Pierce St
Belfast, ME 04915-6648 207-338-4360
Fax: 207-338-5742 800-435-4456
sales@penobscotff.com
www.penobscotmccrum.com
Manufacturer, exporter and wholesaler/distributor of frozen potato productsincluding; potato pancakes, mashers, skins, wedges and more
Manager: Jay McCrum
Co-Owner: Wade McCrum
Co-Owner: Jay McCrum
Co-Owner: David McCrum
Co-Owner: Darrell McCrum
Estimated Sales: $33 Million
Number Employees: 100-249
Type of Packaging: Consumer, Food Service

10458 Penotti USA
4 Maplegrove Avenue
Westport, CT 06880-4917 203-341-9494
Fax: 203-277-0006 877-720-0896
penottiusa@att.net www.penotti.com
Chocolate and nut spreads
President: Marcell Peteers
Estimated Sales: $ .5 - 1 million
Number Employees: 1
Type of Packaging: Bulk

10459 Penta Manufacturing Company
50 Okner Pkwy
Livingston, NJ 07039-1604 973-740-2300
Fax: 973-740-1839 sales@pentamfg.com
www.pentamfg.com
Manufacturer, importer and exporter of fructose, rice starch, nutraceuticals, food and flavor compounds, specialty chemicals, cooking and essential oils, extracts, spices, and natural products for food, flavor and pharmaceuticalcompanies
Owner: Mark Esposito
SVP: George Volpe
Estimated Sales: $ 10 - 20 Million
Number Employees: 20-49
Number of Products: 7000
Sq. footage: 350000
Parent Co: Penta International Corporation
Type of Packaging: Food Service, Private Label, Bulk

10460 Penta Water Company Inc
1900 Avenue of the Stars Fl 7
Los Angeles, CA 90067-4308
Fax: 760-268-0808 jlupica@pentawater.com
www.pentawater.com
Produces ultra-premium purified drinking water.
New Media Relations: Joe Lupica
Sq. footage: 110000

10461 Penthouse Meat Company
270 Congress Street
Group
Boston, MA 02210-1037 570-563-1153
Fax: 570-563-2665
Frozen beef, veal and pork products
President/CEO: John Attman
Sales Manager: Charles Price
COO: Don Long
Plant Manager: Bob Keen
Estimated Sales: $25-49.9 Million
Number Employees: 100-249
Brands:
Magic Meal
North American
Penthouse

10462 Peoples Sausage Company
1132 E Pico Blvd
Los Angeles, CA 90021 213-627-8633
Fax: 213-627-7767
www.peopleschoicebeefjerky.com
Processor of beef jerky
President: Paul Bianchetti
Estimated Sales: $3000000
Number Employees: 10-19
Sq. footage: 5000
Type of Packaging: Consumer, Food Service, Private Label, Bulk

10463 Pepe's Mexican Restaurants
1325 W 15th St
Chicago, IL 60608 312-733-2500
Fax: 312-733-2564 bobptak@pepes.com
www.pepes.com
Manufacturer and exporter of frozen Mexican food products
President: Robert Ptak
General Manager: Mario Dovalina Jr
Number Employees: 1,000-4,999
Sq. footage: 65000
Type of Packaging: Private Label, Bulk
Brands:
Aventura Gourmet
Pepe's, Inc.

10464 Pepes Mexican Foods
122 Carrier Drive
Etobicoke, ON M9W 5R1
Canada 416-674-0882
Fax: 416-674-2805 rchen@westonbakeries.com
Processor of corn tortilla chips, flour tortillas, multi-grain snacks and frozen burritos; importer of jalapeno peppers, salsa and refried beans; exporter of multi-grain snacks
President: Ralph Robinson
Vice President: Ronaldo Sardelitti
VP Sales: Tom Reynolds
National Sales Manager: Tony Kent
Estimated Sales: $12 Million
Number Employees: 110
Sq. footage: 66000
Parent Co: Signature Brands
Type of Packaging: Consumer, Food Service
Brands:
Casa Del Norte
Gringos
Pepes

10465 Pepper Creek Farms
1002 SW Ard St
Lawton, OK 73505 580-536-1300
Fax: 580-536-4886 800-526-8132
sales@peppercreekfarms.com
www.peppercreekfarms.com
Processor and exporter of jellies, mustards, peppers, salsa, relish, syrup, mixes, seasonings, etc
President: Susan Weissman
Vice President: Marshall Weissman
Marketing: Craig Weissman
Estimated Sales: $600,000
Number Employees: 6
Sq. footage: 7500
Type of Packaging: Consumer, Food Service, Private Label
Brands:
Jalapeno
Jalapeno Tnt
Wildfire

10466 Pepper Island Beach
PO Box 484
Lawrence, PA 15055-0484 724-746-2401
Fax: 724-746-1679 www.pepperisland.com
Hot sauce
President: Karen Hasak

10467 Pepper Mill Imports
P.O.Box 775
Carmel, CA 93921-0775 831-393-0244
Fax: 831-393-0801 800-928-1744
sales@peppermillimports.com
www.peppermillimports.com
Processor of extra virgin olive oil. Manufacturer of pepper & spice mills.
President: William Sterling
Marketing: Amy Paris
Sales: Angel Geil
Estimated Sales: Below $ 5 Million
Number Employees: 10
Number of Brands: 2
Number of Products: 112
Sq. footage: 30000
Type of Packaging: Consumer, Food Service, Private Label
Brands:
Melina's

10468 (HQ)Pepper Source
2720 Athania Pkwy
Metairie, LA 70002-5904 504-885-3223
Fax: 504-885-3187 sales@peppersource.com
www.peppersource.com
Manufacturer of gourmet sauces, marinades and glazes
President: Joseph Morse
VP Operations: Paul Liggio
Estimated Sales: $15 Million
Number Employees: 5-9
Type of Packaging: Food Service, Private Label, Bulk
Other Locations:
Pepper Source
Van Buren AR
Pepper Source
Rogers AR

10469 Pepper Source
5800 Alma Hwy
Van Buren, AR 72956-7202 479-474-5178
Fax: 479-474-4729 sales@peppersource.com
www.peppersource.com
Gourmet sauces, marinades and glazes.
President: Joe Morse
Director Sales: Mark Watson
VP Operations: Paul Liggio
VP Purchasing: Steven Campbell
Estimated Sales: $ 5-10 Million
Number Employees: 100-249
Type of Packaging: Private Label

10470 Pepper Source
11103 N Old Wire Rd
Rogers, AR 72756 479-246-1030
Fax: 479-246-1061 www.peppersource.com
Gourmet sauces, marinades and glazes
VP Marketing: John Bowerman
Plant Manager: Brad Palmer
Estimated Sales: $ 5-10 Million
Number Employees: 50-99
Type of Packaging: Private Label

10471 Pepper Town
7561 Woodman Street
Van Nuys, CA 91405 800-973-7738
Fax: 818-909-4785 800-973-7738
Info@PepperTownUSA.com
www.peppertownusa.com
Fruity hot sauces
President: Debbie Sussex
Estimated Sales: $ 90 Million
Number Employees: 2
Type of Packaging: Private Label
Brands:
Bad Girls In Heat
Big Top Fantasy
Fifi's Nasty Little
Peppergirl
Sultan's Main Squeez
Wrong Number

10472 Peppered Palette
PO Box 29003
Bellingham, WA 98228 919-468-7101
Fax: 919-882-9844 866-829-7101
sweat@toadsweat.com www.toadsweat.com
Dessert hot sauce
Owner: Todd Guiton
Estimated Sales: $300,000-500,000
Number Employees: 1-4
Brands:
Toad Sweat

10473 (HQ)Pepperidge Farm
595 Westport Ave
Norwalk, CT 06851 203-846-7000
Fax: 203-846-7145 888-737-7374
geri_allen@pepperidgefarm.com
www.pepperidgefarm.com
Processor of baked goods including bread and stuffing
President: Patrick Callaghan
SVP Finance: Ken Gosnell
Corporate Communications: Geri Allen
SVP Operations: Bob Furbee
Plant Manager: Bart Delaney
Estimated Sales: $100+ Million
Number Employees: 2400
Parent Co: Campbell Soup Company
Type of Packaging: Consumer

10474 Pepperland Farms
12511 Hammack Road
Denham Springs, LA 70726-7122 225-665-3555
Fax: 877-296-8683
pepperlandfarms@earthlink.net
Processor of hot chili peppers including pickled in vinegar brine
Owner: Dennis Hall

10475 **Peppers**
19138 Coastal Hwy
Rehoboth Beach, DE 19971 302-644-6900
Fax: 302-644-6901 peppers@peppers.com
www.peppers.com
Hot sauces, specialty hot sauces, wing sauces, jerk, salsa, BBQ sauces, mustards & dips, marinades & cajun injectors, peppers, pickles & relishes, olives, garlic & vegetables, steak sauce, bloody mary & mixers, chili, soups, pasta &coffee, dry seasoning & rubs, ketchup, mayonnaise & dressings, thai, curry & chutney, nuts & snacks, jelly, preserves & peanut butter.
President: Chip Hearn
Number Employees: 50-99
Type of Packaging: Consumer, Food Service, Private Label, Bulk

10476 **(HQ)PepsiCo**
700 Anderson Hill Road
Purchase, NY 10577 914-253-2000
www.pepsico.com
Manufacturer and distributor of sodas, juice drinks and various beverages.
Chairman/CEO: Indra Nooyi
CEO/PepsiCo Americas Foods: John Compton
CEO/Pepsi Beverages Company: Eric Foos
CFO: Hugh Johnston
Chief Scientific Officer: Mehmood Khan
EVP/Government Affairs: Maura Abeln Smith
EVP/Chief Marketing Officer: A Salman Amin
SVP/Chief Procurement Officer: Grace Puma
SVP/Chief Communications Officer: Julie Hamp
SVP/Global Supply Chain Operations: Rich Beck
President/Tropicana Beverages: Neil Campbell
Estimated Sales: $57 Billion
Number Employees: 294000
Sq. footage: 40000
Type of Packaging: Consumer
Brands:
AMP
AQUAFINA
AQUAFINA FLAVORSPLASH
AQUAFINA SPARKLING
DOUBLESHOT
FRAPPUCCINO
FRITO-LAY
GATORADE
LIPTON BRISK
LIPTON DIET GREEN TEA
LIPTON ICED TEA
LIPTON PURELEAF
LIPTON SPARKLING
MOUNTAIN DEW
MUG CREAM
MUG ROOT BEER
NO FEAR
OCEAN SPRAY
PEPSI
QUAKER FOODS
SEATTLE'S BEST COFFEE
SIERRA MIST
SLICE
SOBE
SOBE ENERGIZE
SOBE LEAN
SOBE LIFEWATER
SOBE SMOOTH
SOBE SUGAR FREE
SOBE VITA-BOOM
TAZOO
TROPICANA

10477 **PepsiCo Chicago**
555 W Monroe Street
Chicago, IL 60661-3605 312-821-1000
Fax: 312-773-4318 www.pepsico.com
Processor of cookies, oatmeal, corn syrup, baking mixes, breakfast cereals and sports beverages
Executive Director: Jesse Taylor
Parent Co: PepsiCo
Type of Packaging: Consumer, Food Service

10478 **Per-Clin Orchards**
4021 13 Mile Rd
Bear Lake, MI 49614 231-889-4289
Fax: 231-889-4810
Manufacturer of cherries and apples; exporter of apples; also, storage and packing facilities available
Owner/President: Clinton Smeltzer
VP: Donald Smeltzer
VP: David Smeltzer
Estimated Sales: $35 Million
Number Employees: 1-4
Sq. footage: 50000
Type of Packaging: Consumer
Brands:
CRYSTAL LAKE
FRESH
NORTHERN TREAT

10479 **(HQ)Perdue Farms**
31149 Old Ocean City Rd
Salisbury, MD 21804 410-543-3000
Fax: 410-543-3532 800-473-7383
corpcomm@perdue.com www.perdue.com
Manufacturer and exporter of fresh and frozen chicken and turkey; also, edible oils and fats
Chairman/CEO: Jim Perdue
SVP/CFO: Eileen Burza
VP/CIO: Sandy Rasel
VP Technical Services: Hank Engster
VP Business Development: Steven Schwalb
SVP Retail/Sales/Marketing: Steve Evans
Logistics Manager: Alan Perry
Estimated Sales: $4.6 Billion
Number Employees: 21,000
Type of Packaging: Consumer, Food Service, Private Label, Bulk
Other Locations:
Perdue Farms
Monterey TN
Brands:
COOKIN GOOD
COOKIN GOOD CHICKEN
FIT 'N EASY
OVEN STUFFER
PERDUE
PERDUE POULTRY
PRIME PARTS

10480 **Pereg Gourmet Spices**
P.O.Box 670249
Flushing, NY 11367 718-261-6767
Fax: 718-261-7688 gill@pereg-gourmet.com
www.pereg-gourmet.com
spices, oils, salads and spreads, toppings, bread crumbs, quinoa, mix for rice, salt, flavored basmati rice, couscous
President: Ilan Eshed
Marketing: Gill Schnieder
Estimated Sales: $1 Million
Number Employees: 9

10481 **Perez Food Products**
2826 Southwest Blvd
Kansas City, MO 64108 816-931-8761
Fax: 816-931-2825 perezfoods@birch.net
Processor of Mexican food including tortillas and taco shells
Owner: Jesse Perez
Sales Manager: Daniel Perez
Estimated Sales: $2500000
Number Employees: 5-9
Type of Packaging: Consumer

10482 **Perfect Addition**
P.O.Box 8976
Newport Beach, CA 92658 949-640-0220
Fax: 949-640-0304 perfectadd@aol.com
Frozen foods
President: Constance Grigsby
CFO/VP: Jack Grigsby
CEO/VP Marketing: Connie Grigsby
Estimated Sales: Less than $200,000
Number Employees: 1-4
Type of Packaging: Consumer, Private Label
Brands:
Perfect Addition Beef Stock
Perfect Addition Chi
Perfect Addition Fis
Perfect Addition Veg

10483 **Perfect Bite Company**
747 W Wilson Ave
Glendale, CA 91203 818-507-1527
Fax: 818-507-1376 joe@theperfectbiteco.com
www.theperfectbiteco.com
appetizers
President/CEO: Teri Valentine
CFO/Secretary: John Valentine
Vice President: Joe Forristal
Estimated Sales: $300,000
Number Employees: 6

10484 **Perfect Foods**
862 Pulaski Hwy
Goshen, NY 10924-6032 845-294-8411
Fax: 845-783-9683 800-933-3288
Manufacturer of fresh wheat grass and sunflower and buckwheat greens; processor of frozen wheat grass juice
President: Carley Mantle
Estimated Sales: $200,000
Number Employees: 2
Sq. footage: 6000
Type of Packaging: Consumer
Brands:
GREEN GOLD WHEATGRASS
PERFECT FOODS WHEATGRASS JUICE

10485 **Perfections by Allan**
3 Old Creek Ct
Owings Mills, MD 21117 410-581-8670
Fax: 410-581-0877 800-581-8670
Gourmet dipping cookies and snack foods
President: Allan Taylor
Estimated Sales: Under $500,000
Number Employees: 1-4
Type of Packaging: Consumer, Private Label
Brands:
Grandma Taylor's Gourmet Dip

10486 **Perfetti**
3645 Turfway Rd.
Erlanger, KY 41018-0190 859-283-1234
Fax: 859-283-1316 www.perfetti.com
Candy and gum
President: Ronald Korenhof
VP Marketing: Bob Howard
Senior VP Sales: Patrick Cox
Estimated Sales: $ 50 - 100 Million
Number Employees: 200
Type of Packaging: Consumer
Brands:
Airheads
Alpenliebe
Bloop
Brooklyn
Chloralit
Daygum
Frisk
Fruitella
Golia
Happydent
Mega Big Babol
Mentos
Morositas
Tabu
Vigorsol
Vivident

10487 **Performance Labs**
5115 Douglas Fir Rd # M
Calabasas, CA 91302-2597 818-591-9669
Fax: 818-591-2116 800-848-2537
info@performancelabs.com
www.performancelabs.com
Processor and importer of nutritional and herbal supplements including vitamin energizers and garlic, cardiovascular and antioxidant supplements; exporter of garlic
Owner: Richard Burke
CEO: David Mercer, Jr.
Purchasing Manager: Allan Suda
Estimated Sales: $3400000
Number Employees: 20-49
Type of Packaging: Consumer
Brands:
Cardiomax
Garlimax
Guardmax
Immumax
Relaxmax
Vitalert

10488 **Perham Cooperative Cream**
2425 West Gwinnett Street
Savannah, GA 31415 912-233-1167
Fax: 912-233-1157 800-551-0777
info@gawine.com www.gabeer.com
Dairy
CEO: Henry Monsees
Estimated Sales: $ 10 - 20 Million
Number Employees: 50-99

10489 **Perino's Seafood**
6850 Westbank Expy
Marrero, LA 70072-2523 504-347-5410
Fax: 504-341-2504
Seafood
Manager: Paul Ocrne
Estimated Sales: $ 3 - 5 Million
Number Employees: 10-19

10490 **Perlarom Technology**
9133 Red Branch Rd
Columbia, MD 21045-2029 410-997-5114
Fax: 410-964-9374 leif.kjargaard@danisco.com
www.perlarom.com
Natural flavors, specialty extracts
Executive VP: Soren Bjerre Nielsen
CEO: Tom Knutzen
Vice President: Philippe Lavielle
Executive VP: Mogens Granborg
Estimated Sales: $ 2.5-5 Million
Number Employees: 20-49

10491 **Pernod Ricard USA**
7 Ridge Ave
Greendale, IN 47025 812-537-0700
Fax: 812-537-8550
shareholders@pernod-ricard.com
www.pernod-ricardusa.com
Manufacturer and exporter of whiskey and gin
Manager: Richard Brock
VP North American Affairs: Mark Orr
Estimated Sales: $530 Million
Number Employees: 500-999
Parent Co: Pernod Ricard USA
Type of Packaging: Consumer, Food Service
Brands:
ARAK RAZZOUK
ARMAGNAC
BALLANTINE'S
CANADIAN CLUB
CHIVAS REGAL
JACOB'S CREEK
JAMESON
MARQUIS DE MONTESQUIO
MATTEL
PICARD
RICARD
ROYAL CANADIAN
SEAGRAM'S GIN
WILD TURKEY
WYNDHAM ESTATE

10492 **Pernod Ricard USA**
100 Manhattanville Rd
Purchase, NY 10577 914-848-4800
Fax: 914-848-4777 tlalla@pernod-ricard-usa.com
www.pernod-ricard-usa.com
Producer and distributor of fine spirits and wines.
Chairman/CEO: Paul Duffy
CFO: Thibault Cuny
Spirits Marketing SVP: Matt Aeppli
Spirit Sales SVP: Marty Crane
General Manager PR: Lauren Simkin
Operations SVP: Dan Denisoff
Business Analysis & Development SVP: Judy Goldfarb
Estimated Sales: $100+ Million
Number Employees: 1000
Brands:
ABERLOU
ABSOLUT
AURA
AZTECA DE ORO
BALLANTINE'S
BEEFEATER
BRANCOTT ESTATE
CAMPO VIEGO
CHIVAS REGAL
FRIS
GH MUMM
GRAFFIGNA
HIRAM WALKER
JACOB'S CREEK
JAMESON
KAHLUA
LEVEL
LONGMOM
MALIBU
MARTELL
MIDLETON
MUMM NAPA
PADDY
PERDOD
PERRIER-JOUEL
PLYMOUTH
PRESIDENTE
REDBREAST
RICARD
SANDEMAN
SCAPA
SEAGRAM'S GIN
SOHO
STONELEIGH
STRATHISLA
TARSUS
THE GLENLIVET
TORMORE
WYNDHAM ESTATE
YSIOS

10493 **Perona Farms Food Specialties**
350 Andover Sparta Rd
Andover, NJ 07821-5016 973-729-6161
Fax: 973-729-1097 800-750-6190
info@peronafarms.com www.peronafarms.com
Manufacturer of Smoked salmon, seafood and seafood products
President: Victor Avondoglio
CFO: Mark Avondoglio
Executive Chef: Kirk Avondoglio
Estimated Sales: $2.5.5 Million
Number Employees: 100-249
Sq. footage: 4100
Brands:
PERONA FARMS

10494 **Perricone Juices**
550 B St
Beaumont, CA 92223 951-769-7171
Fax: 951-769-7176 frshjus@aol.com
www.perriconejuices.com
Citrus juices, including orange, tangerine, grapefruit, lemon, lime, lemonade, and strawberry/lemonade, pomegranate and apple juice.
CEO: Tom Carmody
COO: Joe Perricone
Production Manager: Humberto Orellana
Estimated Sales: $ 50 - 100 Million
Number Employees: 98
Sq. footage: 30000
Type of Packaging: Food Service

10495 **Perry Creek Winery**
7400 Perry Creek Rd
PO Box 350
Fair Play, CA 95684 53- 6-0 51
Fax: 215-699-8200 800-880-4026
info@perrycreek.com www.perrycreek.com
Wines
President/CEO: Michael Chazen
Estimated Sales: $1-2.5 Million
Number Employees: 5-9

10496 **Perry's Ice Cream Company**
1 Ice Cream Plz
Akron, NY 14001 716-542-5492
Fax: 716-542-2544 800-873-7797
www.perrysicecream.com
Manufacturer of frozen desserts including regular, nonfat and sugar-free ice cream, ice milk, sherbet, yogurt and novelties
President: Robert Denning
Estimated Sales: $225 Million
Number Employees: 250-499
Sq. footage: 100000
Type of Packaging: Consumer, Bulk
Brands:
PERRY'S
PERRY'S DELUXE
PERRY'S FREE
PERRY'S LIGHT
PERRY'S PRIDE

10497 **Personal Edge Nutrition**
275 White Tree Lane
Ballwin, MO 63011-3338 877-982-3343
Fax: 636-394-7067
PEinfo@personaledgeprotein.com
www.personaledgeprotein.com
Manufacturer of Energy and protein bars, granola bars, powdered soy beverages
Parent Co: DuPont Chemical
Brands:
PERSONAL EDGE SUPRO

10498 **Pestos with Panache by Lauren**
176 Johnson Street
Suite 8E
Brooklyn, NY 11201 917-656-3082
Fax: 212-230-7404
lauren@pestoswithpanache.com
www.pestoswithpanachebylauren.com
flavored pestos
President/Owner: Lauren Stewart

10499 **Pet Dairy**
P.O.Box 4527
Spartanburg, SC 29305 864-576-6280
Fax: 864-574-9605 www.petdairy.com
Processor of dairy products including ice cream and milk
General Manager: Lawrence Ferguson
Quality Control: Lanny McDole
COO: Joe Hogan
Purchasing Agent: Joe Hogan
Estimated Sales: $14500000
Number Employees: 100-249
Parent Co: Land-O-Sun
Type of Packaging: Consumer

10500 **Pet Dairy**
800 E 21st St
Winston Salem, NC 27105 336-784-1800
Fax: 336-784-1844 800-735-2050
www.petdairy.com
Manufacturer of dairy products
Manager: Dennis Riggs
Division Sales Manager: Don Roland
Operations Manager: Mike Reid
Estimated Sales: $1 Million
Number Employees: 20-49
Parent Co: Dean Foods Company
Type of Packaging: Consumer

10501 **Pet Dairy**
P.O.Box 7039
Portsmouth, VA 23707 757-397-2387
Fax: 757-397-5502
Processor and wholesaler/distributor of fresh dairy products including milk and ice cream
Division Manager: Ken Gardner
Plant Manager: Cliff Raines
Purchasing Agent: Julie Perry
Estimated Sales: $ 10 - 20 Million
Number Employees: 100-249
Parent Co: Land-O-Sun

10502 **Pet Milk**
P.O.Box 12860
Florence, SC 29504-2860 843-665-6866
Fax: 843-665-4255 800-735-3066
Processor of milk, juice and tea
Key Accounts Manager: John Weston
Sales Manager: Jim Dugger
Division Manager: Lou McCarvy
Plant Manager: James McKnight
Estimated Sales: $660000
Number Employees: 100-249
Sq. footage: 5172
Type of Packaging: Food Service

10503 **Petaluma Poultry Processors**
PO Box 7368
Petaluma, CA 94955 707-763-1904
Fax: 707-763-3924 800-556-6789
petalumareception@petalumapoultry.com
www.petalumapoultry.com
Processor of fresh and antibiotic free chickens
President: Darrel Freitas
CFO: Dave Martinelli
Sales/Marketing Director: Randy Duranceau
Production Manager: Moses Montero
Plant Manager: Bob Wolfe
Estimated Sales: $ 20 - 50 Million
Number Employees: 237
Sq. footage: 30000
Brands:
ROCKY JR
ROCKY THE RANGE
ROSIE ORGANIC

10504 **Pete & Joy's Bakery**
121 E Broadway
Little Falls, MN 56345-3038 320-632-6388
Fax: 320-632-2740
Processor of baked goods
Owner: Peter Kamrowski
Estimated Sales: $8 Million
Number Employees: 20-49

10505 **(HQ)Pete's Brewing Company**
14800 San Pedro Ave
San Antonio, TX 78232-3733 210-490-9128
Fax: 210-490-9984 800-877-7383
www.petes.com
Processor and exporter of beer including ale, amber ale, lager and raspberry amber ale
President: Scott Barnum
CEO: Jeffrey Atkins
CEO: Carlos Alvarez
VP Sales: Don Quigley
Number Employees: 50-99
Parent Co: Miller Brewing Company
Brands:
Pete's Wicked Ale

10506 **Peter Dudgeon International**
740 Kopke St
Honolulu, HI 96819-3315 808-841-8071
Fax: 808-842-5093
President: Peter Dudgeon
Estimated Sales: $ 5 - 10 Million
Number Employees: 5-9

10507 **Peter Michael Winery**
12400 Ida Clayton Rd
Calistoga, CA 94515 707-942-3200
Fax: 707-942-0209 800-354-4459
wineclub@petermichaelwinery.com
www.petermichaelwinery.com
Wines
Owner: Peter Michael
Vice President: Bill Vyenielo
Estimated Sales: $ 1-2.5 Million
Number Employees: 20-49
Brands:
Peter Michael Winery

10508 **Peter Pan Seafoods**
2200 6th Ave Ste 1000
Seattle, WA 98121 206-728-6000
Fax: 206-441-9090 sales@ppsf.com
www.ppsf.com
Processor and exporter of fresh and frozen seafood including crab, herring and surimi blends; also, canned salmon; importer of frozen swordfish, mahi mahi and tuna
President/CEO: Barry Collier
CFO: Kirk Koch
Estimated Sales: $38000000
Number Employees: 1,000-4,999
Parent Co: Nichiro Corporation
Type of Packaging: Consumer, Food Service, Private Label, Bulk
Brands:
Deming's
Double Q
Gill Netter's Best
Humpty Dumpty
Peter Pan
Seablends
Seakist
Unica

10509 **Peter Rabbit Farms**
85810 Peter Rabbit Ln
Coachella, CA 92236 760-398-0151
Fax: 760-398-0972 sales@peterrabbitfarms.com
www.peterrabitfarms.com
Processor and exporter of grapefruit, carrots, green onions, shallots and green and red seedless grapes
President: John Powell Jr
CFO: John Powell Jr
Estimated Sales: $100+ Million
Number Employees: 250-499
Type of Packaging: Consumer, Food Service, Private Label, Bulk

10510 **Peter's Mustards**
PO Box 1036
Sharon, CT 06069-1036 860-364-0842
Mustard
President: Richard Harris

10511 **Petersburg Fisheries**
P.O.Box 1147
Petersburg, AK 99833-1147 907-772-4294
Fax: 907-772-4472 877-772-4294
lorir@icicleseafoods.com
www.icicleseafoods.com
Manufacturer of fresh, frozen and canned fish and seafood including Alaskan King crab, Snow crab, Dungeness crab, Halibut, Sablefish, Rockfish, Herring and Salmon
President/CEO: Dennis Guhlke
Plant Manager: Patrick Wilson
Estimated Sales: I
Number Employees: 100-249
Parent Co: Icicle Seafoods
Type of Packaging: Food Service, Private Label, Bulk

10512 **Petersen Ice Cream Company**
1104 Chicago Ave Ste 6
Oak Park, IL 60302 708-386-6130
Fax: 708-386-6162 info@petersonicecream.com
www.petersenicecream.com
Processor of ice cream and frozen yogurt
President and CFO: Robert Raniere
Treasurer: D Raniere
Estimated Sales: $ 1 - 3 Million
Number Employees: 20-49
Type of Packaging: Consumer, Food Service

10513 **Peterson & Sons Winery**
9375 E P Ave
Kalamazoo, MI 49048 269-626-9755
Fax: 616-626-9755
Producer of wine
Owner: Duane Peterson
Sales Manager: Tony Peterson
Estimated Sales: $500,000-$1 Million
Number Employees: 1-4

10514 **Peterson Farms**
P.O.Box 248
Decatur, AR 72722 479-752-5420
Fax: 501-752-5660 800-382-4425
bayleyb@petersonfarms.com
www.petersonfarms.com
Poultry and feed
President: Lloyd E Peterson
Sr. Sales Director: Bruce Bayley
CEO and Vice Chairman: Vic Evans
President: Dan Henderson
VP Human Resources: Janet Wilkerson
VP Processing: Richard Ward
Estimated Sales: $ 100-250 Million
Number Employees: 1500
Brands:
Peterson Farms

10515 **Peterson's Ventures**
2825 E. Cottonwood Parkway
Suite 400
Salt Lake City, UT 84121 80- 4-8 03
Fax: 86- 7-4 73 info@petersonpartnerslp.com
www.petersonventures.com
Snack foods
Founder: Joel Peterson
Partner: Dan Peterson
Chief Financial Officer: Valarie Ballein
Plant Manager: Lauren McKay
Estimated Sales: $ 20-50 Million
Number Employees: 50-99
Brands:
Cheez Nibbles
Clover Club
Grandma Goodwins

10516 **Petra International**
1260 Fewster Dr
Unit 11
Mississauga, ON L4W 1A5
Canada 905-629-9269
Fax: 905-542-2546 800-261-7226
petraint@rogers.com www.petradecor.com
Processor, manufacturer, importer and exporter of gum paste flowers
President: Ham Go
Parent Co: Indomex Foods
Type of Packaging: Consumer, Private Label, Bulk
Brands:
PETRA

10517 **(HQ)Petri Baking Products Inc**
18 Main St
Silver Creek, NY 14136 716-934-2661
Fax: 716-934-3054 800-346-1981
info@petribaking.com www.petribaking.com
Produces a variety of cookies including molasses, oatmeal raisin, sugar, chocolate chip and fruit filled.
President: Richard Cattau
Founder: Armand Petri
CFO: Fran Murphy
Operations Manager: Norm Habib
Production Manager: Joesph Vogl
Plant Manager: Joe Vogl
Purchasing Manager: Michael McFarlane
Estimated Sales: $ 20-50 Million
Number Employees: 100-249
Sq. footage: 75
Type of Packaging: Private Label

10518 **Petrie Wholesale**
5712 Freemont Drive N
Mobile, AL 36609-7051 251-660-8719
Fax: 251-660-8719
Proprietor: Frank Petrie

10519 **Petrofsky's Bakery Products**
16647 Annas Way
Chesterfield, MO 63005-4509 636-519-1613
Processor and exporter of frozen dough and bagels
President: Jerry Shapiro
Vice President: Robert Petrofsky
Estimated Sales: $ 10 - 20 Million
Number Employees: 20-49
Parent Co: Maplehurst Bakeries
Type of Packaging: Consumer, Food Service

10520 **Petschl's Quality Meats**
1150 Andover Park E
Tukwila, WA 98188-3903 206-575-4400
Fax: 206-575-4463
Processor of meats including beef, lamb, pork, veal and chicken
President: William Petschl
Vice President: Nancy Kvinge
Estimated Sales: $9 Million
Number Employees: 35
Type of Packaging: Consumer, Food Service, Private Label, Bulk

10521 **Pett Spice Products**
4285 Wendell Dr SW
Atlanta, GA 30336-1632 404-691-5235
Fax: 404-691-5237 pat@pettspice.net
www.pettspice.net
Manufacturers and developes wet and dry seasoning for the meat, poultry, seafood and snack food industries. Specialities include seasonings for dry and injectable marinades, glazes, salad dressings, soups, sauces, regular and low-fatsnack foods, breading and many more food products.
President: Scott Pett
Plant Manager: Mike Foley
Estimated Sales: $500,000-$1 Million
Number Employees: 5-9
Brands:
Pett Spice

10522 **Pevely Dairy Company**
6040 N Lindbergh Blvd
Hazelwood, MO 63042-2804 314-771-4400
Fax: 314-731-1198
Processor of dairy products including sour cream, milk and ice cream
CFO: Marvin Wulf
General Manager: Richard Kerckhoff
Marketing Director: Bob Haberberger
Operations Manager: Brian Berci
Estimated Sales: $100+ Million
Number Employees: 100-249
Parent Co: Prairie Farms Dairy
Type of Packaging: Consumer, Food Service, Private Label, Bulk

10523 **Pez Manufacturing Corporation**
35 Prindle Hill Rd
Orange, CT 06477-3616 203-795-0531
Fax: 203-799-1679 800-243-6087
www.pez.com
Manufacturer of Candy and confectionery
President/CEO: Joesph Vittoria
Chief Financial Officer: Brian Fry
VP Marketing: Peter Vandall
VP Sales: Daniel Silliman
Human Resource Manager/Director: Ann Hutchinson
VP Production: Mark Morrissey
Plant Manager: Steve Rowe
Estimated Sales: $20-50 Million
Number Employees: 30

Brands:
MANNER WAFERS & CHOCOLATES
NAPOLI WAFERS
PEZ CANDY AND DISPENSERS
PEZ FUZZY FRIENDS
PEZ PEPPERMINT

10524 Pfanstiehl Laboratories
1219 Glen Rock Ave
Waukegan, IL 60085-6230 847-623-0370
Fax: 847-623-9173
Processor and exporter of lactic acid
President: Brian Standish
Estimated Sales: $23.9 Million
Number Employees: 100-249
Parent Co: Ferro Corporation
Type of Packaging: Bulk

10525 Pfeffer's Country Mkt.
411 Sinclair Lewis Ave
Sauk Centre, MN 56378 320-352-6490
Manufacturer of frankfurters, bologna, sausage and poultry
President: Michael Pfeffer
Estimated Sales: $17 Million
Number Employees: 15
Type of Packaging: Consumer

10526 Pfefferkorn's Coffee
1200 E Fort Ave
Baltimore, MD 21230 410-727-3354
Fax: 410-547-1652 800-682-4665
pfeffco@erols.com
Manufacturer of coffee
President: Louis Pfefferkorn
VP/Owner: Samuel Pfefferkorn
Operations Manager: Charles Pfefferkorn
Estimated Sales: $ .5 - 1 million
Number Employees: 5-9
Type of Packaging: Consumer
Brands:
Pfefferkorn's
Pfefferkorn's Coffee
Pfefferkorn's of Federal Hill

10527 Pfeffers Country Market
411 Sinclair Lewis Ave
Sauk Centre, MN 56378-1350 320-352-6490
Fax: 320-352-2206
Meat packing and slaughtering
Owner: Mark Scheefers
Estimated Sales: Below $ 5 Million
Number Employees: 10-19

10528 Pfeiffer's Foods
PO Box 29163
Columbus, OH 43229-0163 614-846-2232
Fax: 614-848-8330 tmoje@marzetti.com
www.marzetti.com
Salad dressings
President: Bruce Rosa
CIO: Kevin Moran
EVP: Gary Thompson
Controller: Steve Evans
VP Sales: Tim Tate
SVP Operations: Doug Fell
Number Employees: 100-249
Parent Co: T. Marzetti Company
Type of Packaging: Consumer, Private Label
Brands:
Marzetti's
Pfeiffer's

10529 Pfeil & Holing
5815 Northern Blvd
Woodside, NY 11377-2297 718-545-4600
Fax: 718-932-7513 800-247-7955
info@pfeil-verlag.de www.cakedeco.com
Candy
President: Sy Stricker
Estimated Sales: $ 5-10 Million
Number Employees: 20-49

10530 Pfizer
400 Interpace Pkwy Fl 3
Parsippany, NJ 7054 973-541-5900
Chewing gum and breath mints
Trade Development Manager: Larry Roche
Sales/Marketing Executive: Michael Soriano
Estimated Sales: $ 1 - 3 Million
Number Employees: 1-4
Parent Co: Pfizer
Type of Packaging: Consumer, Food Service
Brands:
Bubbilicious
Certs
Chiclets
Clorets
Cool Mint Drops
Dentyne Ice
Mint*A*Burst
Trident
Vichy

10531 Phamous Phloyd's Barbeque Sauce
2998 S Steele St
Denver, CO 80210-6948 303-757-3285
Fax: 303-757-3373 phloyd@uswest.net
www.phloyds.com
Manufactuter of condiments, Bloody Mary mixes, marinades and hot and barbecue sauces, mustards and dry rubs
President/Owner: Mary Ellen Baran
Estimated Sales: Under $500,000
Number Employees: 1-4
Type of Packaging: Consumer, Bulk
Brands:
PHAMOUS PHLOYD'S BLOODY MARY MIX
PHAMOUS PHLOYD'S DRY RUB
PHAMOUS PHLOYD'S HOT SAUCE
PHAMOUS PHLOYD'S ITALIAN MUSTARD
PHAMOUS PHLOYD'S MARINADE
PHAMOUS PHLOYD'S PEPPER MUSTARD
PHAMOUS PHLOYD'S PHLAMING
PHAMOUS PHLOYD'S PHROG HOT BBQ

10532 Pharmachem Laboratories
130 Wesley St
South Hackensack, NJ 7606 201-343-3611
Fax: 201-343-5807
Manufacturer and exporter of fine chemicals and vitamins including rose hips and acerola extracts
President: David Holmes
Estimated Sales: $ 5 - 10 Million
Number Employees: 5-9
Parent Co: Pharmachem Laboratories

10533 Pharmavite Corporation
P.O.Box 9606
Mission Hills, CA 91346-9606 818-221-6200
Fax: 818-221-6393 800-276-2878
www.pharmavite.com
Processor and exporter of vitamin tablets and ingredients
President: Brent Belly
CEO: Connie Barry
Executive VP Marketing: Catherine Mardesich
Estimated Sales: $300,000-500,000
Number Employees: 1-4
Parent Co: Pharmavite Corporation
Type of Packaging: Bulk
Brands:
Nature Made
Nature's Resources

10534 Pharmline
P.O.Box 291
Florida, NY 10921 845-651-4443
Fax: 845-651-6900 info@pharmlineinc.com
www.pharmlineinc.com
Processor, importer and exporter of nutritional ingredients, herbal extracts, ginseng, ginkgo biloba, lutein, spirulina, royal jelly, lycopene and beta carotene; also, custom blending, granulation, extraction and micronizingavailable
President: John Witterschein
CFO: Tally Katz
Estimated Sales: $14 Million
Number Employees: 90
Sq. footage: 50000
Type of Packaging: Bulk
Brands:
Aquamin
Lycopen
Lycosource
Phenalgin
Rhodenol
Rosavin

10535 Pheasant Ridge Winery
3507 E County Road 5700
Lubbock, TX 79403 806-746-6033
Fax: 806-746-6750 billgipson@aol.com
www.pheasantridgewinery.com
Wines
Manager: Bill Blackman
Owner: William Gibson
Estimated Sales: Below $ 5 Million
Number Employees: 5-9
Brands:
Proprietor's Reserve

10536 Phenix Food Service
318 General Colin Powell Pkwy
Phenix City, AL 36869-6953 334-298-6288
Fax: 334-298-6777
Wholesale distributor
President: Patricia Hardin
Vice President: Jim Herrel
Estimated Sales: $7 Million
Number Employees: 48
Sq. footage: 20000

10537 Phenomenal Fudge
4668 Vermont Route 74 W
Shoreham, VT 05770-9689 800-897-7300
Fax: 802-897-7300 800-430-5442
info@pfudge.com www.pfudge.com
Manufacturer of fudge
Owner/Fudgemaker: Steve Jackson

10538 (HQ)Phibro Animal Health
65 Challenger Rd Ste 3
Ridgefield Park, NJ 7660 201-329-7300
Fax: 201-329-7399 888-403-0074
hr@pahc.com www.phibroah.com
Develops, manufactures and markets medicated feed additives as well as marketing animal health and nutrition products.
President: Keith Collins
CFO: Shawn Brosnan
CEO: Gerald K Carlson
Estimated Sales: $100+ Million
Number Employees: 500-999
Brands:
Phibro

10539 Philadelphia Candies
1546 E State St
Hermitage, PA 16148 724-981-6341
Fax: 724-981-6490 pc@phillyc.com
www.phillyc.com
Processor of confectionery items including marshmallow specialties, dietetic, mints, creams, nougats, nuts, fruits and specialty molded holiday, regular and sugar-free chocolates
President: Spyros Macris
Vice President: Georgia Macris
Estimated Sales: $1,100,000
Number Employees: 50-99
Type of Packaging: Bulk
Brands:
Loving Bunny

10540 Philadelphia Cheese Steak Company
520 E Hunting Park Ave
Philadelphia, PA 19124-6009 215-423-3333
Fax: 215-423-3131 800-342-9771
marketinginfo@phillycheesesteak.com
www.phillycheesesteak.com
Processor of frozen cheese steaks
CEO: Nick Karamatsoukas
Founder: Nick Karamatsoukas
Director Marketing: John Karamatsoukas
Estimated Sales: $ 20-50 Million
Number Employees: 50-99
Type of Packaging: Consumer, Food Service
Brands:
Philadelphia Cheese Steak

10541 Philadelphia Macaroni Company
40 Jacksonville Rd
Warminster, PA 18974 215-441-5220
www.philamacaroni.com
Manufacturer and supplier of noodles and pasta for private label food service marketplaces. Also a supplier of spring wheat and mills durum flour.
Parent Co: Minot Milling

10542 Philadelphia Macaroni Company
760 S 11th St
Philadelphia, PA 19147-2614 215-923-3141
Fax: 215-925-4298 www.philamacaroni.com
Manufacturer of pasta and noodles.
Director of Sales/Marketing: Joe Viviano
EVP Sales: Bill Stabert

Estimated Sales: $ 20 - 50 Million
Number Employees: 10-19
Type of Packaging: Bulk

10543 **Philip R'S Frozen Desserts**
750 Main Street
Winchester, MA 01890 781-721-6330
Fax: 781-721-4590
philipjr@icecream-desserts.com
www.icecream-desserts.com
Ice Cream.
President: Phil Rotundo
Estimated Sales: $770,000
Number Employees: 10

10544 **Philip Togni Vineyard**
3780 Spring Mountain Rd
Saint Helena, CA 94574 707-963-3731
Fax: 707-963-9186 tognivyd@wildblue.net
www.philiptognivineyard.com
Grower and producer of Estate bottled Caberbet only
Partner: Philip Togni
Partner: Birgitta Togni
Partner/Winemaker: Lisa Togni
Estimated Sales: $500,000-$1 Million
Number Employees: 4
Brands:
Philip Togni

10545 **Phillips Beverage Company**
25 Main St SE
Minneapolis, MN 55414 612-331-6230
Fax: 612-362-7501
Processor of cordials and liqueurs
President: Dean Phillips
CEO: Edward Phillips
Estimated Sales: $ 10 - 20 Million
Number Employees: 10-19
Type of Packaging: Consumer, Food Service

10546 **Phillips Candies**
217 Broadway St
Seaside, OR 97138 503-738-5402
Fax: 503-738-8326 candy@seasurf.net
Processor of candy including fudge and salt water taffy
President: Steve C Phillips
Estimated Sales: $2,600,000
Number Employees: 5-9
Type of Packaging: Consumer, Private Label

10547 **Phillips Candies of Seas**
217 Broadway St
Seaside, OR 97138-5805 503-738-5402
Fax: 503-738-8326 candy@seasurf.net
Saltwater taffy, chocolaters and fudge
President: Steven C Phillips
Estimated Sales: $ 1-2.5 Million
Number Employees: 5-9
Brands:
Phillips Candies

10548 **Phillips Farms & Michael David Vineyards**
4580 W Highway 12
Lodi, CA 95242-9529 209-368-7384
Fax: 209-368-5801 888-707-9463
vintage@lodivineyards.com
www.lodivineyards.com
Wines
Partner: Mike Phillips
Partner: Dave Phillips
Estimated Sales: Below $ 5 Million
Number Employees: 20-49
Brands:
Michael David Vineyards

10549 **Phillips Foods**
1215 East Fort Avenue
Baltimore, MD 21230 443-263-1200
Fax: 410-837-8526 888-234-2722
comments@phillipsfoods.com
www.phillipsfoods.com
Manufacturer of fresh and pasteurized crabmeat, live and steamed crabs and fresh and frozen soft crabs
CEO: Steve Phillips
President: Mark Sneed
CFO: Dean Flowers
Estimated Sales: $ 50 - 100 Million
Number Employees: 250-499
Sq. footage: 3000
Parent Co: Phillips Seafood Restaurants
Type of Packaging: Consumer, Food Service, Bulk
Brands:
PHILLIPS

10550 **Phillips Foods**
1215 E Fort Ave
Baltimore, MD 21230 410-837-8523
Fax: 410-837-8526 888-234-2722
comments@phillipsfoods.com
www.phillipsfoods.com
Processor and exporter of refrigerated blue crab meat, frozen crab cakes, dips, soups and chowders, in addition to frozen shrimp, appetizers, condiments/seasonings, and salmon cakes.
CEO: Steven Phillips
Co-Founder: Shirley Phillips
Quality Control: Bobby Love
Plant Manager: Steve Malecki
Estimated Sales: $ 2.5-5 Million
Number Employees: 250-499
Parent Co: Phillips Seafood Restaurants
Type of Packaging: Consumer, Food Service
Brands:
Crab Slammer
Phillips Foods

10551 **Phillips Foods, Inc. &Seafood Restaurants**
1215 E Fort Ave
Baltimore, MD 21230-5104 443-263-1200
Fax: 410-837-8526 888-234-2722
comments@phillipsfoods.com
www.phillipsfoods.com
Manufacturer of seafood and canning
President: Steve Philips
CFO: Dean Flowers
CEO: Steven Phillips
Plant Manager: Steve Malecki
Purchasing: Newcomb
Estimated Sales: $ 5 - 10 Million
Number Employees: 223
Brands:
E PHILLIPS

10552 **Phillips Gourmet, Inc**
1011 Kaolin Rd
PO Box 190
Kennett Square, PA 19348 610-925-0520
Fax: 610-925-0527 info@phillipsgourmetinc.com
www.phillipsgourmetinc.com
Fresh, organic, stuffed and dried wild mushrooms.
President: R M Phillips
COO/CFO: Bill Steller
General Manager: Rick Angelucci
Quality Assurance Manager: Bill Green
Estimated Sales: $1 Million
Number Employees: 10
Sq. footage: 5385
Type of Packaging: Consumer, Food Service
Brands:
Bella

10553 **Phillips Seafood**
1381 Pelican Point Rd NE
Townsend, GA 31331 912-832-4423
Fax: 912-832-6228
Seafood
President: Myron Phillips

10554 **Phillips Syrup Corporation**
28025 Ranney Parkway
Westlake, OH 44145 440-835-8001
Fax: 440-835-1148 800-350-8443
www.phillipssyrup.com
Processor of chocolate, sugar-free, sno-cone, slush and maple syrups, sundae toppings, fountain drinks, bar mixes and beverage concentrates. Also sugar-free for diabetics
President: Robert Schallman
Public Relations: Raisa Hawal
Production/Plant Manager: Joseph Mazak
Purchasing Manager: Susan Connerton
Estimated Sales: $7000000
Number Employees: 17
Number of Brands: 12
Number of Products: 200
Sq. footage: 15000
Type of Packaging: Food Service, Private Label
Brands:
Fundae
Phillips

10555 **Phipps Desserts**
420 Eglinton Avenue W
Toronto, ON M5N 1A2
Canada 416-481-9111
Fax: 416-481-5616 www.phippsdesserts.com
Processor of baked gourmet desserts
Proprietor: Janet Schriber
Estimated Sales: $205,000
Number Employees: 3
Type of Packaging: Consumer, Food Service
Brands:
PHIPPS

10556 **Phoenicia Patisserie**
P.O.Box 13128
Arlington, TX 76094-0128 817-261-2898
Fax: 817-274-3942
amerhamedi@phoeniciainternational.com
www.phoeniciainternational.com
Pastries
Owner: Amer Hamedi

10557 **Phoenician Herbals**
P.O.Box 28381
Scottsdale, AZ 85255 480-368-8144
Fax: 480-368-2912 800-966-8144
jbaker4884@aol.com
www.guardiannutrition.com
Processor and exporter of vitamins, supplements and herbal teas
Owner: Redgie Hansen
Estimated Sales: $440,000
Number Employees: 5-9
Brands:
Phoenician Herbals

10558 **Phoenix Agro-IndustrialCorporation**
521 Lowell St
Westbury, NY 11590 516-334-1194
Fax: 516-338-8647 www.phoenixaico.com
International traders of frozen foods
President: Tomipor Pasto
Marketing: Julianna Edlyn
Purchasing Director: Neone Din
Estimated Sales: $ 3 - 5 Million
Number Employees: 5-9
Number of Brands: 28
Number of Products: 45
Sq. footage: 10000
Type of Packaging: Consumer, Private Label, Bulk
Brands:
Citizen Foods

10559 **Phoenix Laboratories**
200 Adams Boulevard
Farmingdale, NY 11735-6615 516-822-1230
Fax: 516-822-1252 800-236-6583
www.natplus.com
Manufactures of vitamins
President: Mel Rich
VP: Steven Stern
Number Employees: 50-99

10560 **Phranil Foods**
3900 E Main Avenue
Spokane, WA 99202-4737 509-534-7770
Fax: 509-534-4244
Pies and frozen bakery products
Owner: Fran Bessermin
Controller: Bob Clements
Estimated Sales: $ 1-2.5 Million
Number Employees: 20-49

10561 **Phyto-Technologies**
107 Enterprise Dr
Woodbine, IA 51579 712-647-2755
Fax: 712-647-2885 877-809-3404
extracts@phyto-tech.com www.earthpower.com
Nutritional supplements, herbal supplements, extracts and blends, including chinese herbs
Founder/President: Albert Leung
Sales/Marketing: Terry Jinks
Estimated Sales: Below $ 5 Million
Number Employees: 10-19
Sq. footage: 20000
Parent Co: Earth Power
Type of Packaging: Consumer, Private Label
Brands:
Earth Power's All American
Earthpower's Phytochi

10562 **Phytotherapy Research Laboratory**
P.O.Box 627
Lobelville, TN 37097-0627 931-593-3780
Fax: 931-593-3782 800-274-3727
newherbs@netease.net
Manufacturer and exporter of certified organic herb extracts; also, research, development and production of specialty herbal products in the area of immune and vital organ support
President: Brent Davis
Estimated Sales: $500,000-$1 Million
Number Employees: 1-4
Sq. footage: 25000
Type of Packaging: Private Label
Brands:
Forest Center
Hahg
PRL

10563 **(HQ)Piantedosi Baking Company**
240 Commercial St
Malden, MA 2148 781-321-3400
Fax: 781-324-5647 800-339-0080
nikki@piantedosi.com www.piantedosi.com
Processor of specialty breads and rolls
President/CEO: Thomas Piantedosi
CFO: Tony Roscillo
Vice President: Robert Piantedosi
Research & Development: Lino DiSchino
VP Sales/Marketing: Joseph Piantedosi
Human Resources Director: Robin Lucier
Estimated Sales: $24,254,933
Number Employees: 240
Sq. footage: 65000
Type of Packaging: Consumer, Food Service, Private Label, Bulk
Other Locations:
Piantedosi Baking Co.
Malden MA
Brands:
Piantedosi

10564 **Piazza's Seafood World**
205 James Dr W
St Rose, LA 70087-4036 504-602-5050
Fax: 504-602-1555 info@cajunboy.net
www.cajunboy.net
Processor and exporter of fresh and frozen seafood including crawfish, alligator, catfish, shrimp, crabmeat, softshell crabs
Manager: Jennifer Champagne
CFO: Mike Sabolyk
Estimated Sales: $ 5-10 Million
Number Employees: 20-49
Number of Brands: 2
Number of Products: 20
Type of Packaging: Food Service, Private Label
Brands:
Cajan Boy
Cajan Delight

10565 **(HQ)Picard Peanuts**
1867 Regional Road 10
Simcoe, ON N0E 2A0
Canada 519-426-6700
Fax: 519-426-0571 888-244-7688
sales@picardpeanuts.com
www.picardpeanuts.com
Processor of potato chip covered peanuts
President: James Picard Sr
CFO: John Picard
R & D: Lincoln Reid
Vice President: John Picard
CFO: John David
Quality Control: Michael Newsome
Marketing Director: John Picard
Estimated Sales: $3.8 Million
Number Employees: 23
Sq. footage: 32000
Type of Packaging: Consumer, Bulk
Other Locations:
Picard Peanuts Ltd.
Waterford ON
Brands:
Chipnuts

10566 **Pickle Cottage**
12989 Windy Road
Bucklin, KS 67834-8807 316-826-3502
Fax: 316-826-3866
Snack foods and pickles
President: Barry Stimpert
Estimated Sales: $500,000-$1 Million
Number Employees: 10-19

10567 **Picklesmith**
300 Green Ave
Taft, TX 78390 361-528-4953
Fax: 830-885-4560 800-499-3401
dsmith@picklesmith.com www.picklesmith.com
Manufacturer of gourmet pickles and olives
President: David Smith
Estimated Sales: $ 1 - 3 Million
Number Employees: 1-4
Sq. footage: 2500
Type of Packaging: Consumer, Food Service
Brands:
A.P. Smith Canning Co.
Picklesmith

10568 **Pickwick Catfish Farm**
4155 Highway 57
Counce, TN 38326-3057 731-689-3805
KnussK@msn.com
www.pickwickcatfishfarm.com
Manufacturer of Farm-raised smoked catfish
Owner: Betty Knussmann
Co-Owner: Quentin Knussman
Estimated Sales: Less than $500,000
Number Employees: 5-9
Brands:
PICKWICK CATFISH

10569 **Pictsweet Frozen Foods**
10 Pictsweet Dr
Bells, TN 38006 731-422-7600
Fax: 800-561-8810 cfarner@pictsweet.com
www.pictsweet.com
Processor, importer and exporter of frozen asparagus, beans, broccoli, brussels sprouts, carrots, cauliflower, turnip, mustard and collard greens, okra, peas, spinach, squash, succotash, etc
President: Billy Ennis
Chairman/Ceo: James Tankersley
Marketing Director: Julia Wells
Director Manufacturing: Frank Tankersley
Estimated Sales: $$10-20 Million
Number Employees: 1,000-4,999
Number of Products: 100
Parent Co: Pictsweet
Type of Packaging: Consumer, Food Service, Private Label
Brands:
Dulaney
Dulany
Everfresh
Food Service Packer
Pictsweet
Pictsweet Express
Prime Froz-N
Tennessee
Winter Garden

10570 **Pidy Gourmet Pastry Shells**
90 Inip Dr
Inwood, NY 11096 516-239-6057
Fax: 516-239-9306 sales@pidy.com
www.pidy.com
Processor and exporter of pastry shells and filled shells
President: Thierry Demaeck
Operations Manager: Michael Lewin-Jacus
Estimated Sales: $ 5 - 10 Million
Number Employees: 20-49
Sq. footage: 25000
Parent Co: Pidy NV
Type of Packaging: Food Service
Brands:
Delicaty
Patibel
Pidy

10571 **(HQ)Pidy Gourmet Pastry Shells**
90 Inip Dr
Inwood, NY 11096 516-239-6057
Fax: 516-239-9306 800-231-7439
www.pidygourmet.com
Manufacturer and exporter of pastry shells and filled shells
Estimated Sales: $ 5 - 10 Million
Brands:
APERI-COEUR
APERIQUICHE
BARQUETTE
CRESCENTGARNITURE
CROUSTADE 4CM
CROUSTADE 5CM
CROUSTADE 7CM
ESCARCOQUE
FISHKA
FLEURETTE
GAURMANDE
MIGNARDISE
MINI-CROUSTADE
MINI-CROUSTADE SHELL
MINI-EASRE
MINI-ROULET
MINT SHELL
PUFF PASTRY TARTLET
QUICHE
ROULET
ZAKOUSKI

10572 **Pie Piper Products**
450 Evergreen Ave
Bensenville, IL 60106-2506 630-595-1550
Fax: 630-595-1551 800-621-8183
tbannack@ameritech.net
www.distinctivefoods.com
Processor and exporter of cakes, cheesecakes and cheesecake on sticks, brownies, quiche and beef frankfurters wrapped in bagel dough
President: Josh Harris
Production Manager: Mike Lopardo
Estimated Sales: $ 10 - 20 Million
Number Employees: 20-49
Sq. footage: 16000
Parent Co: Vienna Manufacturing Company
Type of Packaging: Consumer, Food Service, Private Label
Brands:
Pie Piper
Vienna Bageldog
Wunderbar

10573 **Pied-Mont/Dora**
176 Saint-Joseph
Ste Anne Des Plaines, QC J0N 1H0
Canada 450-478-0801
Fax: 450-478-6381 800-363-8003
justin@piedmontdora.com
www.piedmontdora.com
Processor, importer and packer of vegetable and fruit dips, jams, jellies and marmalades; also, chocolate spreads, pie fillings, syrups, drink crystals, etc
President/Board Member: Louis Limoges
Marketing: Justin Bart
Estimated Sales: $6.9 Million
Number Employees: 40
Brands:
Bensons
Clancy
Dora
Mondial
Pied-Mont

10574 **Piedmont Candy Corporation**
404 Market St
Lexington, NC 27292 336-248-2477
Fax: 336-248-5841 redbirdstk@aol.com
www.piedmontcandy.com
Processor of hard, mint, boxed and seasonal candy
President: Douglas J Reid
VP: Chris Reid
Estimated Sales: $2,556,054
Number Employees: 20-49
Type of Packaging: Consumer

10575 **Piedmont Vineyards & Winery**
P.O.Box 286
Middleburg, VA 20118 540-687-5528
Fax: 540-687-5777 info@piedmontwines.com
www.piedmontwines.com
Manufacturer of Wines
President: Gerhard Von Finck
Estimated Sales: Below $5 Million
Number Employees: 5-9
Type of Packaging: Private Label
Brands:
PIEDMONT

10576 **Piedra Creek Winery**
6425 Mira Cielo
San Luis Obispo, CA 93401 805-541-1281
Fax: 805-541-1281 mzuech@fixnet
Wines
Co-Owner: Margaret Zuech
Owner/Winemaker: Romeo Zuech
Estimated Sales: $ .5 - 1 million
Number Employees: 1-4

Brands:
Piedra Creek Winery

10577 **Piemonte Foods**
PO Box 9239
Greenville, SC 29604-9239 864-242-0424
Fax: 864-235-0239 tpl@tpl.com.sg
www.tpl.com.sg
Frozen foods
President/CEO: T P Costello
CFO: Edward Cathey
CFO: W E Cathey
Sales Director: Mary Coleman
Public Relations: Claire Smith
Director Manufacturing: Bud Fulder
Purchasing Manager: Clark McClaskey
Estimated Sales: $ 10-100 Million
Number Employees: 200
Type of Packaging: Private Label

10578 **Piemonte's Bakery**
1122 Rock St
Rockford, IL 61101-1431 815-962-4833
Processor and wholesaler/distributor of bread including French, Italian, garlic and rye; also, dinner rolls and po-boys
President: Steve McKeever
Secretary: Irene McKeever
Estimated Sales: $2600000
Number Employees: 10-19
Type of Packaging: Private Label
Brands:
Piemonte

10579 **Pierceton Foods**
127 N First St
Pierceton, IN 46562 574-594-2344
Fax: 574-594-2344
Processor of frozen breaded meat products including porkfritters and cheeseburgers; also, steaks, ground beef and grilled tender loins
President: Jerry Wagoner
Plant Manager: Ben Bunyan
Estimated Sales: $1040000
Number Employees: 10-19
Number of Brands: 1
Sq. footage: 6000
Type of Packaging: Food Service
Brands:
Paul's

10580 **Pierino Frozen Foods**
1695 Southfield Rd
Lincoln Park, MI 48146 313-928-0950
Fax: 313-928-5410 info@pierinofrozenfoods.com
www.pierinofrozenfoods.com
Processor of frozen Italian products including pasta, sauce and gnocchi
President: Pierino Guglielmetti
Operations Manager: Gianni Guglielmetti
Plant Manager: Silvana Gugliemetti
Estimated Sales: $1800000
Number Employees: 20-49

10581 **Pierogi Place**
2357 N 56th Ave
Mears, MI 49436-9351 23- 8-3 14
http://www.thepierogiplace.com/
Pierogis
President: Marilyn Marciniak

10582 **Pierre Foods**
9990 Princeton Glendale Rd
Cincinnati, OH 45246 513-874-8741
Fax: 513-874-8395 www.pierrefoods.com
Processor and exporter of specialty foods including pre-cooked and portion controlled beef, pork and poultry, fully baked buns, biscuits and dumplings, and assembled sanwiches
President/CEO: Norb Woodhams
Chairman: Jimmy Richardson
VP Marketing: Jane Nocito
Purchasing: Sam Patton
Estimated Sales: $210 Million
Number Employees: 1,000-4,999
Sq. footage: 223000
Type of Packaging: Consumer, Food Service, Private Label, Bulk
Other Locations:
Pierre Food
Kiawah Island SC

10583 **Pierre Foods**
9990 Princeton Glendale Rd
Cincinnati, OH 45246 513-874-8741
Fax: 513-874-8395 www.pierrefoods.com
Breads and sandwiches
Production Manager: Tim Starnes
Founder: Samuel Dinerman
CEO: Norbert E Woodhams
Sales Director: Larry Hefner
Estimated Sales: $ 20-50 Million
Number Employees: 1,000-4,999
Sq. footage: 183
Type of Packaging: Private Label
Brands:
Pierre Foods

10584 **Pierre's French Bakery**
PO Box 14280
Portland, OR 97293-0280 503-233-8871
Fax: 503-233-5060 ifo@acmemad.com
Bakery products
President: Larry McDonald
Estimated Sales: $ 1-2.5 Million appx.
Number Employees: 50

10585 **Pierre's French Ice Cream Company**
6200 Euclid Ave
Cleveland, OH 44103 216-432-1144
Fax: 216-432-0001 800-837-7342
icecream@pierres.com www.pierres.com
Manufacturer of Ice cream, frozen yogurt, sherbet, sorbet and frosted smoothies
President: Rochelle Roth
Director Marketing: Laura Hindulak
Operations: John Pimpo
Estimated Sales: $20-50 Million
Number Employees: 100-249
Number of Products: 235
Sq. footage: 30000
Type of Packaging: Consumer
Brands:
PIERRE'S
PIERRE'S CARB SUCCESS
PIERRE'S FROSTED SMOOTHIES
PIERRE'S SLENDER

10586 **Pierz Cooperative Association**
315 Edward St S
Pierz, MN 56364 320-468-6655
Fax: 320-468-2773 przcoop@pierz.net
Animal feed
Manager: Randy Sullivan
Estimated Sales: $9,032,630
Number Employees: 10-19
Brands:
Farmer Seed

10587 **(HQ)Piggie Park Enterprises**
1600 Charleston Hwy
West Columbia, SC 29169 803-791-5887
Fax: 803-791-8707 800-628-7423
mail@mauricesbbq.com www.mauricesbbq.com
Manufacturer of gourmet barbecue sauce and barbecue meat
President: Maurice Bessinger
Estimated Sales: $4.3 Million
Number Employees: 20-49
Type of Packaging: Consumer, Food Service, Bulk
Brands:
Maurice's

10588 **Pike Place Brewery**
1415 1st Avenue
Seattle, WA 98101-2017 206-622-6044
Fax: 206-622-8730 info@mdv-beer.com
www.pikebrewing.com
Processor of seasonal beer, ale, stout and porter
Owner: Charles Finkel
General manager: Kim Brusco
Director Manufacturing: Allen Fal
Estimated Sales: $ 2.5-5 Million
Number Employees: 43
Brands:
Pike

10589 **Pikes Peak Vineyards**
2910 N Academy Blvd # 102
Colorado Springs, CO 80917-5351 719-576-0075
Fax: 719-226-0639
Wine
President: Bruce Mc Claughlin
Vice President: Taffy McCloughlen
General Manager: Frankie Tuft
Estimated Sales: Less than $300,000
Number Employees: 1-4
Brands:
Pikes Peak Vineyards

10590 **Piknik Products CompanyInc**
3806 Day Street
Montgomery, AL 36108-1720 334-240-2218
Fax: 334-265-9490
contactinfo@piknikproducts.com
www.piknikproducts.com
Processor and exporter of mayonnaise, mustard and salad dressing
President: Edgar Grant
Estimated Sales: $29 Million
Number Employees: 205
Type of Packaging: Consumer, Food Service, Private Label
Brands:
Ol' South
Piknik
Salad Queen
Stewart's

10591 **Pilgrim Foods**
68 Old Wilton Rd
Greenville, NH 03048 603-878-2100
Fax: 603-878-2103 www.pilgrimfoods.net
Juice, vinegar, mustard
President: Paul Santich
Estimated Sales: $ 5-10 Million
Number Employees: 20-49
Type of Packaging: Bulk

10592 **(HQ)Pilgrim's**
1770 Promontory Circle
Greeley, CO 80634 970-506-8000
800-727-5366
www.pilgrims.com
Processor and exporter of fresh and frozen chicken and turkey
CEO/President: Bill Lovette
CFO: Fabio Sandri
SVP/Food Safety & Quality Assurance: Kendra Waldbusser
SVP/Prepared Foods Marketing: Andrew Seymour
EVP/Sales & Operations: Walt Shafner
VP/Corporate Communications: Gary Rhodes
EVP/Sales & Operations: Jerry Wilson
Director of Transportation: Lee Blackmon
SVP/Supply Chain & Business Development: Greg Tatum
SVP/Consumer Sales & Marketing: Randy Meyers
Estimated Sales: $6.9 Billion
Number Employees: 42000
Parent Co: JBS S.A.
Type of Packaging: Consumer, Food Service, Private Label, Bulk
Other Locations:
WLR Foods
Broadway VA
Brands:
Rockingham
Round Hill
Shen-Valley
Wampler Foods

10593 **Piller Sausages & Delicatessens**
PO Box 338
Waterloo, ON N2J 4A4
Canada 519-743-1412
Fax: 519-743-7111 800-265-2628
www.pillers.com
Processor and exporter of sausage and processed meats
President: William Huber, Jr.
Number Employees: 100-249
Type of Packaging: Consumer, Food Service, Private Label, Bulk

10594 **(HQ)Pillsbury**
PO Box 9452
Minneapolis, MN 55440 800-775-4777
Fax: 763-764-8330
consumer.services-pillsburycs@genmills.com
www.pillsbury.com
Processor of bakery mixes and cake flour
General Manager: Alan Rodrigues
Mix Plant Manager: Ray Beckman
Number Employees: 100-249
Parent Co: General Mills
Type of Packaging: Consumer, Food Service, Bulk

10595 **Pilot Meat & Sea Food Company**
405 N Pilot Knob Road
Galena, IL 61036-8803 319-556-0760
Fax: 319-556-4131
Meat and seafood
President: Randy Sirk

10596 **Pinahs Company**
N8w22100 Johnson Dr
Waukesha, WI 53186 262-547-2447
Fax: 262-547-2047 800-967-2447
info@pinahs.com www.pinahs.com
Manufacturer of Bread and corn based snack chips
Owner: Chris Pinahs
Director Finance: Bill Bruggink
R&D: Peter Sardina
Quality Control: Vicki Dickerson
Director Sales/Marketing: Paul Pearson
Human Resource/Customer Service: Barb Pomierski
Purchasing Manager: Jeff Millar
Estimated Sales: $3 Million
Number Employees: 20-49
Sq. footage: 59000
Type of Packaging: Consumer, Food Service, Private Label, Bulk
Brands:
PINAH'S

10597 **Pindar Vineyards**
P.O.Box 332
Peconic, NY 11958 631-734-6200
Fax: 631-734-6205 www.pindar.net
Wines
Owner: Herodotus Damianos
VP Sales: Michael Sean Ryan
Estimated Sales: $ 5-10 Million
Number Employees: 20-49
Brands:
Spring Splendor
Summer Blush

10598 **Pine Point Fisherman's Co-Op**
P.O.Box 2247
Scarborough, ME 04070-2247 207-883-3588
Fax: 207-883-6772 lobster8@maine.rr.com
lobsterco-op.com
A lobsterman's cooperative with a seasonal retail market restaurant and wholesale distribution on the east coast.
Estimated Sales: $ 1 - 3 Million
Number Employees: 5-9

10599 **Pine Point Seafood**
350 Pine Point Rd
Scarborough, ME 04074-9236 207-883-4701
Fax: 207-883-4797 www.maine-lobster.com
Manufacturer of lobster, lobster tails, clams and steaks
President: B Michael Thurlow
Estimated Sales: $ 1 - 3 Million
Number Employees: 5-9

10600 **Pine Ridge Winery**
P.O.Box 2508
Yountville, CA 94599 707-253-7500
Fax: 707-253-1493 800-575-9777
info@pineridgewine.com
www.pinerdigewinery.com
Wines
President: George Schlepeler
Marketing Director: Anna Belle
CFO: Eric Grams
CEO: Erle Martin
CFO: David Workman
Sales Director: Nancy Andrus
Public Relations: Sarah Burgess
Operations Manager: Kelvin Morasch
Winemaker: Stacy Clark
Estimated Sales: $ 20 - 50 Million
Number Employees: 50-99
Brands:
Pine Ridge Winery

10601 **Pine River Cheese & Butter Company**
RR 4
Ripley, ON N0G 2R0
Canada 519-395-2638
Fax: 519-395-4066 800-265-1175
info@pineriverc heese.com
www.pinerivercheese.com
Processor of cheese including cheddar, colby, mozzarella, Monterey Jack, etc
President: Ian Courtney
Number Employees: 30
Sq. footage: 24000
Type of Packaging: Consumer, Bulk

10602 **Pine River Pre-Pack**
10134 Pine River Rd
Newton, WI 53063 920-726-4216
www.pineriver.com
Manufacturer and processor of cold pack cheese food and pasteurized cheese spreads; also chocolate confections
CEO: Philip Lindemann
Marketing Associate: Mary Lindenann
Estimated Sales: $3004699
Number Employees: 10-19
Sq. footage: 23700
Type of Packaging: Consumer, Private Label
Brands:
PINE RIVER

10603 **Pineland Farms**
92 Creamery Lane
New Gloucester, ME 04260-4460 207-688-8085
Fax: 207-688-8087
Gluten-free, organic/natural, salsa/dips, cheese, other spreads & syrup, foodservice.
Principal: Sarah Hunt
Marketing: Neal Kolterman
Estimated Sales: $69,000
Number Employees: 1

10604 **Pines International**
1992 E 1400 Rd
Lawrence, KS 66044 785-841-6016
Fax: 785-841-1252 800-697-4637
pines@wheatgrass.com www.wheatgrass.com
Grower, processor, and exporter of alfalfa, wheat grass, barley grass, rye grass, and oat grass powders and tablets
President: Ron Seibold
CEO: Steve Malone
Sales/Marketing: Allen Levine
Purchasing Director: Jeff Richards
Estimated Sales: $3,635,158
Number Employees: 10-19
Sq. footage: 40000
Type of Packaging: Consumer, Private Label, Bulk
Brands:
MIGHTY GREENS
PINES

10605 **Pinnacle Food Products**
750 Oakwood Rd
Lake Zurich, IL 60047 847-438-1598
Fax: 847-438-1236
Dry food manufacturer, primarily drink mixes, ingredients, etc.
President: Andy Burke
Estimated Sales: $ 20 - 50 Million
Number Employees: 100-249
Type of Packaging: Food Service, Private Label, Bulk

10606 **(HQ)Pinnacle Foods Group**
121 Woodcrest Rd
Cherry Hill, NJ 08003-3620 856-969-7100
Fax: 856-969-7303 877-852-7424
info@pinnaclefoods.com
www.pinnaclefoods.com
Manufacturer of pickles, soups, barbeque sauces, syrup, pancake mix, baking mixes, bagels, frozen seafood, frozen skillet meals and frozen pizza
Chairman/CEO: C Dean Metropoulos
EVP/CFO: N Michael Dion
CEO: Jeffrey P Ansell
Business Director, Foodservice: Keith Kandt
Estimated Sales: $500 Million
Number Employees: 100-249
Type of Packaging: Consumer
Brands:
CELESTE
CHEF'S CHOICE
COUNTRY KITCHEN
DUNCAN HINES
GREAT STARTS
HUNGRY-MAN
LENDER'S
LOG CABIN
MRS BUTTERWORTH'S
MRS PAUL'S
OPEN PIT
SWANSON
VAN DE KAMP'S
VLASIC

10607 **Pino's Pasta Veloce**
1903 Clove Road
Staten Island, NY 10304-1607 718-273-6660
Fax: 718-720-5906
Processor of pasta sauce; manufacturer of pasta heaters for portion control and food preparation
Manager Marketing: Joe Klaus
VP Operations: Al Cappillo
Estimated Sales: $ 2.5-5 Million
Number Employees: 1-4
Parent Co: AEI
Type of Packaging: Consumer, Food Service
Brands:
Pino's Pasta Veloce

10608 **Pinocchio Italian Ice Cream Company**
12814 163 Street NW
Edmonton, AB T5V 1K6
Canada 780-455-1905
Fax: 780-455-1906
sales@pinocchioicecream.com
www.pinocchioicecream.com
Processor of frozen desserts including ice cream and Italian sorbets
President: Salvatore Ursino
VP: Tom Ursino
Director/Sales Manager: Thomas Ursino
Number Employees: 1-4
Type of Packaging: Consumer, Food Service
Brands:
Pinocchio

10609 **Pinter's Packing Plant**
193 S Front St
Dorchester, WI 54425 715-654-5444
www.pinterspacking.com
Processor of meat including steak, roast, sausage and buffalo
President: Daniel Pinter
VP: Alan Pinter
Estimated Sales: $180000
Number Employees: 5-9
Sq. footage: 6400
Type of Packaging: Consumer

10610 **Pinty's Premium Foods**
5063 North Service Rd
Burlington, ON L7L 5H6
Canada 905-319-5300
Fax: 905-688-1222 800-263-7223
Retailsales@pintys.com www.pintys.com
Processor of poultry products including chicken fryers, nuggets, burgers, meat balls, wings, stuffed breasts and pierogies; also, pizza fingers
Chairman: Fred Williamson
Vice-Chairman: Ken Thorpe
Director: Randy Kane
VP Marketing: Jon Pintwala
Sales Manager: W Greer
Estimated Sales: $4.8 Million
Number Employees: 49
Type of Packaging: Consumer, Food Service
Brands:
Pinty's

10611 **Pintys Delicious Foods**
5063 North Service Road
Burlington, ON L7L 5H6
Canada 905-835-8575
Fax: 905-834-5093 800-263-9710
Processor and exporter of poultry
President/Owner: Phil Kudelka
CEO: Aba Vanderlaan
CFO: Patricia Bowman
VP Operations: Jack Vanderlaan
Sales: Greg Fox
General Manager: Doug Bowman
Number Employees: 100-249
Sq. footage: 90000
Type of Packaging: Food Service, Bulk
Brands:
PINTYS DELICIOUS FOODS

10612 **Pioneer Dairy**
214 Feeding Hills Rd
Southwick, MA 01077 413-569-6132
Fax: 413-569-3762

Manufacturer of Milk, cream, ice cream
President: A Colson
Vice President: Paul Colson
Estimated Sales: $5-10 Million
Number Employees: 30
Number of Brands: 2
Type of Packaging: Food Service, Private Label, Bulk
Brands:
MEADOWBROOK CREAMERY
PIONEER DAIRY

10613 Pioneer Foods Industries
P.O. Box 1248
Stuttgart, AR 72160 870-673-4444
Fax: 870-355-2507 www.producersrice.com
Soups
President/CEO: Keith Glover
Estimated Sales: Under $500,000
Number Employees: 10-19

10614 (HQ)Pioneer French Baking
512 Rose Ave
Venice, CA 90291 310-392-4128
Fax: 310-392-7845
webmaster@pioneerbakery.com
www.pioneerbakery.com
Processor of French baked goods including sourdough bread; also, wholesale delivery to in-store bakeries.
President: Jack Garacochea
Number Employees: 100-249
Sq. footage: 110000
Type of Packaging: Consumer, Food Service, Private Label
Brands:
Goldminer Sourdough
Pioneer Sourdough

10615 Pioneer Frozen Foods
627 Big Stone Gap Rd
Duncanville, TX 75137 972-298-4281
Fax: 972-298-0578
Biscuits
President: Chuck Hanson
Estimated Sales: $ 50-100 Million
Number Employees: 100-249
Brands:
Pioneer

10616 Pioneer Growers Cooperative
227 NW Avenue L
Belle Glade, FL 33430 561-996-5211
Fax: 561-996-5703 www.pioneergrowers.com
Processor and exporter of produce including Chinese cabbage, carrots, celery, corn and radishes
Vice President: Gene Duff
Type of Packaging: Consumer, Bulk
Brands:
Frontier
Team
Well's Ace

10617 Pioneer Live Shrimp
2801 Meyers Road
Oak Brook, IL 60523-1623 630-789-1133
Fax: 312-226-7376
Shrimp
President: David Wong
Vice President: Chun Wah
Estimated Sales: $ 2.80 Million

10618 Pioneer Marketing International
188 Westhill Drive
Los Gatos, CA 95032-5032 408-356-4990
Fax: 408-356-2795 edesoto@jps.net
www.pioneer.com/usa/services/marketing_services
Export and import broker of confectionery products, snacks and private label items. Consultant in marketing, sales and product promotion in England and Africa
Partner: Russ Tritomo
Director Sales: Ed DeSoto
Estimated Sales: $ 1 - 5 Million
Number Employees: 4

10619 Pioneer Nutritional Formulas
304 Shelburne Center Rd
Shelburne Falls, MA 01370 413-625-0169
Fax: 413-625-9619 800-458-8483
customerservice@pioneernutritional.com
www.pioneernutritional.com
Manufacturer of nutritional supplements
Manager: Sara Rowan
CEO: Jim Lemkin
Estimated Sales: $ 3 - 5 Million
Number Employees: 10-19
Number of Brands: 1
Number of Products: 23
Brands:
PIONEER

10620 Pioneer Packing Company
510 Napoleon Rd
Bowling Green, OH 43402 419-352-5283
Fax: 419-352-7330 wcontris@aol.com
Manufacturer and exporters of Canadian bacon, smoked meats and pork sausage material
President: William Contris
Estimated Sales: $5 Million
Number Employees: 20-49
Sq. footage: 50000
Type of Packaging: Consumer, Bulk
Brands:
AMISH
COUNTRY
PIONEER

10621 Pioneer Snacks
30777 Northwestern Highway
Suite 300
Farmington Hills, MI 48334-2594 248-862-1990
Fax: 248-862-1991 info@pioneersnacks.com
www.pioneersnacks.com
Meat snacks including smoked meat sticks, beef jerky, hunter sausage, kippered beef steak, meat & cheese and turkey jerky.
Marketing Manager: Craig Thomas
Type of Packaging: Consumer
Brands:
HOG WILD PORK JERKY

10622 Pioneer Snacks
1829 1st Ave
Mankato, MN 56001-3023 507-388-1661
Fax: 507-388-5927 www.pioneersnacks.com
Snacks, beef jerky
President: Robert George
Maintenance Manager: David Mamagren
Plant Manager: Rob Andrews
Estimated Sales: $ 50-100 Million
Number Employees: 100-249
Brands:
Pioneer Snacks

10623 Piper Processing
430 N Main St
Andover, OH 44003-9665 440-293-7170
Processor of beef and pork
Owner: Terry Orahood
Estimated Sales: $140,000
Number Employees: 1-4
Type of Packaging: Consumer, Bulk

10624 Pippin Snack Pecans
1332 Old Pretoria Rd
Albany, GA 31721-8696 229-432-9316
Fax: 229-435-0056 800-554-6887
pipsani@bellsouth.com
Processor and exporter of natural shelled and in-shell pecans including flavored, honey and toasted, amaretto, hickory-smoked, onion-garlic, rum and chocolate covered for gifts; for the wholesale and fundraising markets
Owner: C M Pippin Jr
General Manager: C Pippin, Jr.
Estimated Sales: $7 Million
Number Employees: 50
Sq. footage: 20000
Type of Packaging: Consumer, Food Service, Private Label, Bulk
Brands:
Pippin Snack

10625 Pippin Snack Pecans Incorporated
1332 Old Pretoria Rd
Albany, GA 31721 229-432-9316
Fax: 229-435-0056
Pecans
CEO/CFO/Owner: C M Pippin Jr
Estimated Sales: $7 Million
Number Employees: 50
Type of Packaging: Consumer, Food Service, Bulk

10626 Piqua Pizza Supply Company
1727 W High St
Piqua, OH 45356 937-773-0699
Fax: 937-773-6096 800-521-4442
piquapizzasupply.com
Processor of frozen pizza crust
President: Diana Creager
VP: Paul Creager
Production Manager: Tom Fahestrock
Estimated Sales: $ 10 - 20 Million
Number Employees: 20-49
Type of Packaging: Consumer, Food Service, Private Label, Bulk
Brands:
Diana's

10627 Pirate Brands
Po Box 67
Roslyn Heights, NY 11577 516-625-4306
Fax: 516-625-0125 800-626-7557
www.robgourmet.com
President/Owner: Jared Church
Marketing: Josh Francis
Estimated Sales: $1.2 Million
Number Employees: 10

10628 Pita King Bakery
2210 37th St
Everett, WA 98201-4509 425-258-4040
Fax: 425-258-3366
salesinfo@pitakingbakery.com
www.pitakingbakery.com
Pita Bread
President: Hauss Alaeddine
CEO: Jason Aladdine
Number Employees: 10-19
Sq. footage: 10000
Brands:
PITA KING

10629 Pita Products
30777 Northwestern Highway
Suite 3200
Farmington Hills, MI 48334-2549 734-367-2700
Fax: 734-367-2701 800-600-7482
comments@pitasnax.com www.pitasnax.com
Baked pita chips
Type of Packaging: Consumer

10630 Pittsburgh Brewing Company
3340 Liberty Ave
Pittsburgh, PA 15201 412-682-7400
Fax: 412-682-2379
info@pittsburghbrewingco.com
www.pittsburgbrewingco.com
Manufacturer and exporter of alcoholic and nonalcoholic beer
Owner/Brewer: Joseph Piccirilli
Marketing Director: Chris Antone
VP Sales: Tony Ferraro
Brewmaster: Michael Carota
Plant Manager: Bill St Leger
Estimated Sales: $100 Million
Number Employees: 175
Number of Brands: 12
Number of Products: 12
Sq. footage: 450000
Parent Co: Bond Brewing Holdings
Type of Packaging: Consumer
Brands:
AMERICAN
AMERICAN LIGHT
AUGASTINER DARK
AUGASTINER LARGER
AUGUSTINER
IC COOLER
IC LIGHT
IRON CITY
MUSTANG
OLD GERMAN
PENNS BEST
PENNS BEST LIGHTING
SIERRA
SIERRA ICE
SIERRA LIGHT

10631 Pittsburgh Snax & Nut Company
2517 Penn Ave
Pittsburgh, PA 15222 412-391-4444
Fax: 412-391-2209 800-404-6887
pghsnax@aol.com www.pghsnax.com

Manufacturer and importer of nuts, dried fruit, trail mixes and confections
Owner: Richard Cuneo
President: Morgan Donato
Estimated Sales: $25 Million
Number Employees: 20-49
Sq. footage: 25000
Type of Packaging: Consumer, Food Service, Private Label, Bulk
Brands:
Earth Delights
Earth Treats
McCunes
Nuts About Pittsburgh

10632 Pittsfield Rye Bakery
P.O.Box 637
Pittsfield, MA 01202-0637 413-443-9141
Fax: 413-499-5331 rickrobbins222@msn.com
Manufacturer of bread, rolls and sweet goods
President: Arnold Robbins
Owner: Linda Robbins
Estimated Sales: $ 5 - 10 Million
Number Employees: 5-9

10633 Pizza Products
38300 W 10 Mile Rd
Farmington Hills, MI 48335-2804 248-474-1601
Fax: 248-474-1608 800-600-7482
comments@pitasnax.com www.pizzahut.com
Low fat seasoned pizza snack
Manager: Dave Sabol
Marketing Director: Norman Wainwright
Estimated Sales: Below $ 5 Million
Number Employees: 1-4

10634 Pizzas of Eight
1915 Cherokee St
Saint Louis, MO 63118 314-865-1460
Fax: 314-865-2449 800-422-2901
contact@pizzasofeight.com
www.pizzasofeight.com
Manufacturer of pizza products including dough, cheese and sauce, equipment
President: Chuck McMillen
Office Manager: Amy Drake
Estimated Sales: $5-10 Million
Number Employees: 10-19
Number of Brands: 3
Number of Products: 15

10635 Pizzey's Milling & Baking Company
190 Main St
Angusville, NB R0J 0A0
Canada 204-773-2575
Fax: 204-773-2317 www.glanbiafoods.com
Processor and exporter of whole and milled flaxseed
President: Linda Pizzey
Vice President: Glenn Pizzey
Estimated Sales: $10-20 Million
Number Employees: 20-49
Sq. footage: 40000
Parent Co: Glanbia Nutritionals
Type of Packaging: Consumer, Food Service, Private Label, Bulk

10636 Pizzey's Nutritionals
5951 McKee Road, Suite 100
Fitchburg, WI 53719 608-316-8500
Fax: 608-316-8504 800-336-2183
sales@pizzeys.com www.pizzeys.com
North America's largest processor of flaxseed ingredients. Created Omega-3 solutions for a range of applications.
R&D: Jessica Marshall
QC: Grant Penn
Marketing: Eric Borchardt
Sales: Jim Lees
Production: Ty Konkright
Plant Manager: Mark Stainer
Parent Co: Granbia Nutritionals
Type of Packaging: Consumer, Private Label, Bulk
Brands:
BEVGRAD
CHOICEGRAD
FORTIGRAD
NUTRIGRAD
PREMIUMGRAD
SELECTGRAD
ULTRAGRAD

10637 Placerville Fruit Growers Association
4600 Missouri Flat Rd
Placerville, CA 95667-6843 530-622-2640
Fax: 530-622-2649 pfgastore@innercite.com
Processor and packer of pears and apples
Manager: John Caswell
Vice President: John Caswell
Estimated Sales: $360000
Number Employees: 1-4
Type of Packaging: Consumer, Food Service, Private Label, Bulk
Brands:
Moutain Bartlett
Placerville Maid

10638 Plaidberry Company
830 Mimosa Ave
Vista, CA 92081 760-727-5403
dennisdickson@cs.com
www.plaidberry.com
Jams, muffins, pie and cake fillings, juices, confections, yogurt bases, etc
President/Owner: Dennis Dickson
Estimated Sales: Below $ 5 Million
Number Employees: 4
Number of Products: 6
Sq. footage: 37000
Type of Packaging: Consumer, Bulk

10639 Plains Creamery
300 N Taylor
Amarillo, TX 79105-0030 806-374-0385
Fax: 806-374-0396 www.plainsdairy.com
Processor of dairy products including ice cream, milk and cream
President: Walter Garlington
Sales Manager: Frank Jones
Estimated Sales: $ 20 - 50 Million
Number Employees: 100-249
Type of Packaging: Consumer

10640 Plains Dairy Products
P.O.Box 30
Amarillo, TX 79105-0030 806-374-0385
Fax: 806-374-0396 800-365-5608
customerservice@plainsdairy.com
www.plainsdairy.com
Milk and milk products
President/CEO: Walter Garlington
R & D: Jeff Covington
CFO: Billy Lindenborn
Marketing Director: Joe Holland
Estimated Sales: $ 50-75 Million
Number Employees: 100-249

10641 (HQ)Plainview Milk ProductsCooperative
130 2nd St SW
Plainview, MN 55964 507-534-3872
Fax: 507-534-3992 dmoe@plainviewmilk.com
www.plainviewmilk.com
Processor of butter, powdered whey and dry milk including nonfat, whole and buttermilk. Whey protein concentrates, custom agglomeration and spray drying
Manager: Dallas Moe
Controller: Janna Van Rooyen
Sales Manager: Darrell Hanson
General Manager: Dallas Moe
Plant Manager: Donny Schreiber
Estimated Sales: $ 65 - 75 Million
Number Employees: 50-99
Sq. footage: 180000
Type of Packaging: Consumer, Food Service, Private Label, Bulk
Other Locations:
Plainview Milk ProductsCoop.
Plainview MN
Brands:
Greenwood Prairie

10642 Plainville Farms
7830 Plainville Rd
Memphis, NY 13112 315-689-6384
Fax: 315-689-1298 800-724-0206
mail@plainvillefarms.com
www.plainvillefarms.com
Turkey products
President: Robert W Bitz
CEO: Robert W Bitz
CFO: Mark Bitz
Estimated Sales: $ 20-50 Million
Number Employees: 100-249

Brands:
Heart Liteo
Veggie Growno

10643 Plam Vineyards & Winery
80125 Miramonte Lane
La Quinta, CA 92253 760-972-4465
ken@plam.com
www.plam.com
Wines
Co-Owner: Ken Plam
Co-Owner: Shirley Plam
VP: Shirley Plam
Estimated Sales: Below $ 5 Million
Number Employees: 2
Type of Packaging: Private Label
Brands:
Plam Vineyards

10644 Plantation Candies
4224 Bethlehem Pike
Telford, PA 18969 215-723-6810
Fax: 215-723-6834 888-678-6468
chuck@plantationcandies.com
www.plantationcandies.com
Processor and exporter of hard and filled candy; also, white mint chocolate
President: Charles Crawford
VP: John Crawford
Estimated Sales: $1500000
Number Employees: 5-9
Type of Packaging: Consumer, Food Service, Private Label, Bulk
Brands:
Chocolate Straws
Dainties
Golden Crunchies
Jinglebits
Misty Mints

10645 Plantation Coffee
9583 Elk Grove Florin Road
Elk Grove, CA 95624-1803 916-686-2633
Fax: 916-686-2755 coffee@plantationcoffee.com
www.plantationcoffee.com
Coffee
President: Dan Davis
Estimated Sales: $ 2 Million
Number Employees: 30
Type of Packaging: Private Label

10646 Plantation Foods
2510 E Lake Shore Dr
Waco, TX 76705-1788
Fax: 254-412-3409 800-733-0900
www.cargill.com
Processor and exporter of turkey and chicken
Human Resources: Lee Ray
VP Marketing/Sales: Jim Jandrain
Administration Manager: Carol Lowe
Estimated Sales: $100+ Million
Number Employees: 500-999
Parent Co: Cargill Foods
Type of Packaging: Consumer, Food Service, Private Label, Bulk
Brands:
Plantation

10647 Plantation Pecan Company
HC-62 Box 139
Waterproof, LA 71375 31- 7-9 54
Fax: 318-749-5535 800-477-3226
hcmiller@bayou.com www.plantationpecan.com
Distributors of pecan, pies, pralines and fudges
President: Harrison Miller
Co-Owner: Carol Miller
Estimated Sales: Less than $500,000
Number Employees: 1-4
Brands:
Plantation Pecan

10648 Plantation Products
202 S Washington St
Norton, MA 2766 508-285-5800
Fax: 508-285-7333 www.plantationproducts.com/
Processor of vegetable seeds, seed packets and seed starting products
President: Joseph Raffaele
VP: D Sbordon
Estimated Sales: $ 20 - 50 Million
Number Employees: 20-49

10649 Planters LifeSavers Company
4020 Planters Rd
Fort Smith, AR 72908 479-648-0100
Fax: 479-646-6842 www.kraft.com
Manufacturer and exporter of nuts including cashews, almonds, peanuts, pistachios, pecans, walnuts, mixed and flavored
Manager: Keith Nix
CEO: Roger Deromedi
Plant Manager: Wayne Parrish
Estimated Sales: $100+ Million
Number Employees: 250-499
Parent Co: Nabisco
Type of Packaging: Consumer

10650 Plantextrakt
119 Cherry Hill Rd # 100
Parsippany, NJ 07054-1114 973-683-1411
Fax: 973-257-9351 cswatosch@plantextakt.com
www.atm1.com
President: Bob Morrell
Vice President: Werner Baer
Operations Manager: Christina Lianos
Estimated Sales: Under $500,000
Number Employees: 1-4

10651 Plantextrakt/Martin Bower
300 Harmon Meadow Blvd
Sacaucus, NJ 07094 201-659-3100
Fax: 201-659-3180 www.plantextrakt.com
Produce and process raw materials sold to manufacturers tea, decaf tea & botanicals-core products and tea & botanical extracts.
President: Richard Enticott
CEO: Albert Ferstl
Estimated Sales: $20 Million
Number Employees: 3
Type of Packaging: Consumer
Brands:
Life Savers
Planters

10652 Plastic Container Corporation
2508 N Oak St
Urbana, IL 61802 217-352-2722
Fax: 217-352-2822 jgentles@netpcc.com
www.netpcc.com
Plastic Container Corporation (PCC) manufactures plastic bottles for numerous industries including that of food and beverage. PCC utilizes extrusion blow molding machines to produce containers from any common extrusion blow moldingmaterial.
CEO: Ronald Rhoades
Sales Manager: Jo Ellen Gentles
Sales Representative: John Foote
Sq. footage: 250000
Type of Packaging: Consumer

10653 Platte Valley Creamery
1005 E Overland
Scottsbluff, NE 69361 308-632-4225
Processor of dairy products including ice cream and frozen desserts
President: Ron Smith
Estimated Sales: $ 1 - 3 Million
Number Employees: 1-4
Type of Packaging: Consumer

10654 Plaza House Coffee
339 Lincoln Avenue
Staten Island, NY 10306-5001 718-979-9555
Fax: 718-667-4394 plazahouse@aol.com
Coffee
President: Salvatore Rosso
Estimated Sales: Less than $500,000
Number Employees: 1-4

10655 Plaza Sweets
521 Waverly Ave
Mamaroneck, NY 10543-2235
US 914-698-0233
Fax: 914-698-3721 800-816-8416
kathy@plazasweetsbakery.com
www.plazasweetsbakery.com
Processor and exporter of cakes including cognac pumpkin cheese, apple crunch and banana coconut; also, cookies brand names: mamas apple cake,moon mountain torte,lemon charlotte royale ,chocolate velvet boule,cranberry peartart,chocolate carmel pecan cake,islnad rum cake.
Owner: James Ward
Pres/CEO: Rodney Holden
Manager: Kathy Dumas
Estimated Sales: $5.8 Million
Number Employees: 40
Sq. footage: 15000
Type of Packaging: Consumer, Food Service
Brands:
Plaza Sweets

10656 Plaza de Espana Gourmet
100 Kings Point Drive
Apt 1004
Sunny Isles Beach, FL 33160-4729 305-971-3468
Fax: 305-971-5004 sales@blueskyfoods.com
www.foodfromspain.com
Specialty food manufacturer and importer of gourmet Spanish foods, extra virgin olive oil, artichokes, asparagus, red roasted piquillo peppers, wine and serrano ham; company vineyards in Rioja, Spain
President: Jesus Metias, Sr.
Vice President: Serafina Atalaya
Marketing Director: Jesus Metias, Jr.
Estimated Sales: $ 2.5-5 Million
Number Employees: '5-9
Parent Co: Plaza De Espana Gourmet Foods
Type of Packaging: Consumer, Food Service, Private Label, Bulk
Brands:
Cielo Azul
Plaza De Espana
Vega Fina
Vega Metias

10657 Pleasant Grove Farms
5072 Pacific Ave
Pleasant Grove, CA 95668 916-655-3391
Fax: 916-655-3699
Grower, processor and exporter of organic almonds, wheat, beans, popcorn and rice
President: Thomas Sills
VP Sales: Edward Sills
Estimated Sales: $1100000
Number Employees: 5-9
Number of Products: 9
Sq. footage: 10000
Parent Co: Sills Farms
Type of Packaging: Bulk

10658 Pleasant Valley Wine Company
8260 Pleasant Valley Rd
Hammondsport, NY 14840 607-569-6111
Fax: 607-569-6135 info@pleasantvalleywine.com
www.pleasantvalleywine.com
Manufacturer of wines, champagnes, ports and sherries
President: Mike Doyle
Estimated Sales: $19 Million
Number Employees: 50-99
Sq. footage: 480000
Type of Packaging: Consumer, Food Service, Private Label, Bulk
Brands:
Great Western
Millennium
Pleasant Valley

10659 Pleasant View Dairy
2625 Highway Ave
Highland, IN 46322 219-838-0155
Fax: 219-838-1801 www.pleasantviewdairy.com
Processor of dairy products including milk, buttermilk and sour cream
President: Kenneth Leep
Estimated Sales: Less than $500,000
Number Employees: 20-49
Sq. footage: 40000
Type of Packaging: Consumer

10660 Pleasoning Gourment Seasonings
2418 South Ave
Po Box 2701
La Crosse, WI 54601 608-787-1030
Fax: 608-787-1030 800-279-1614
pleason@pleasoning.com www.pleasoning.com
Manufacturer of seasoning blends-low sodium
President: Paul Boarman
Vice President: Lenore Italiano
Marketing Director: Kathy Boarman
Estimated Sales: $500,000-$1 Million
Number Employees: 1-4
Number of Brands: 1
Number of Products: 30
Sq. footage: 3000
Type of Packaging: Consumer, Food Service, Bulk
Brands:
PLEASONING GOURMET SEASONING

10661 Plehn's Bakery
3940 Shelbyville Rd
Louisville, KY 40207 502-896-4438
Fax: 502-897-9176 www.plehnsbakery.com
Manufacturer of breads, cookies, doughnuts, pastries, pies, cakes and ice cream
President: Milton Hettinger
Vice President: Theodore Bowling
Estimated Sales: $1.5 Million
Number Employees: 30
Type of Packaging: Consumer

10662 Plentiful Pantry
PO Box 271097
Salt Lake City, UT 84127 801-977-9077
Fax: 801-977-8202 800-727-8284
sales@plentifulpantrywholesale.com
www.plentifulpantry.com
artisan pastas, desserts, dips, dishes, pasta, pasta salads, pizz akits, sauces, and soups
President: Debbie Chidester
Vice President: Jody Chidester
Estimated Sales: $2.9 Million
Number Employees: 13

10663 Plenus Group
101 Phoenix Ave
Lowell, MA 01852 978-970-3832
Fax: 978-441-2528 info@plenus-group.com
www.plenus-group.com
Premium soups, sauces and gourmet, value added, frozen food items. Also choweders, bisques and soups, gourmet seafood appetizers and entrees.
President: Joseph Jolly
VP/CFO/VP Operations/Production: Jennifer Jolly
Sales Manager/Coordinator: Jamie Crane
Estimated Sales: $10.5 Million
Number Employees: 43
Brands:
BOSTON CHOWDA CO
EAST COAST GOURMET

10664 Plitt Company
4430 S Tripp
Chicago, IL 60632 773-523-3876
Fax: 773-376-3794 plittcontact@plittco.com
www.plittcompany.com
Wholesaler/distributor of fresh and frozen seafood
President: Robert Sullivan
Purchasing Manager: Steve Wegh
Estimated Sales: $45000000
Number Employees: 160
Sq. footage: 12000

10665 Plochman
1333 N Boudreau Rd
Manteno, IL 60950 815-468-3434
Fax: 815-468-8755 www.plochman.com
Manufacture of Mustards
President/CEO: Carl Plochman
Estimated Sales: $6.9 Million
Number Employees: 50-99
Type of Packaging: Consumer, Food Service, Private Label, Bulk
Brands:
KOSCIUSKO
PLOCHMAN'S

10666 Plocky's Fine Snacks
15 Spinning Wheel Rd #314
Hinsdale, IL 60521 630-323-8888
Fax: 630-323-8988 info@plockys.com
www.plockys.com
specialty tortilla chips, gluten free hummus chips, gluten free hummus, kettle chips, dip strips, and salsa
President: Paul Cipolla
Marketing: Diane Cipolla
Estimated Sales: $9.3 Million
Number Employees: 16

10667 Pluester's Quality MeatCompany
P.O.Box 68
Hardin, IL 62047-0068 618-396-2224
Processor of meat products; slaughtering services available
President: Irene Pluester
Estimated Sales: $ 1 - 3 Million
Number Employees: 1-4
Type of Packaging: Bulk

10668 **Plum Creek Cellars**
3708 G Rd
Palisade, CO 81526 970-464-7586
Fax: 970-464-0457 www.plumcreekwinery.com
Wines
Manager: Jenne Baldwin
Marketing Director: Sue Phillips
Winemaker: Jenne Bladwin
Estimated Sales: Below $ 5 Million
Number Employees: 5-9
Brands:
Plum Creek

10669 **Plumlife Company**
10 Northern Blvd
Newbury, MA 01951 978-462-8458
www.plumlife.co.uk
Plumcakes, bakery products
President: Jeffrey Freedman
Founder: Peter Demers
VP: Donald Laudano
Estimated Sales: Under $500,000
Number Employees: 1-4
Brands:
Plumlife

10670 **Plumrose USA**
P.O.Box 160
Elkhart, IN 46515-0160 574-295-8190
Fax: 574-294-5335 www.plumroseusa.com
Manufacturer of pork and ham products
Type of Packaging: Consumer, Food Service
Brands:
DAK FOODS
DANOLA
PLUMROSE

10671 **(HQ)Plumrose USA**
7 Lexington Avenue
East Brunswick, NJ 08816-1066 732-257-6600
Fax: 732-257-6644 800-526-4909
consumer@plumroseusa.com
www.plumroseusa.com
Manufacturer and importer of meats including ham, salami, corned beef, also, cheese
Owner/President: John Arends
EVP: Mike Rozzano
SVP Sales/Marketing: Don Meyer
SVP Production: Fred Mortensen
Estimated Sales: $100+ Million
Number Employees: 1000
Parent Co: Danish Crown
Type of Packaging: Consumer, Food Service
Other Locations:
Plumrose USA
Council Bluffs IA
Brands:
DAK
DANOLA
PLUMROSE

10672 **Plyley's Candies**
P.O.Box 8
Lagrange, IN 46761-0008 260-463-3351
Fax: 260-463-7011 plyley@kuntrynet.com
www.plyleyscandies.com
Chocolate, hard and sugar free candy
President: Jack Plyley
VP: Willard Plyley
Estimated Sales: Below $ 500,000
Number Employees: 10-19

10673 **Plymouth Beef**
3585 Food Center Dr
Bldg G1
Bronx, NY 10474-7000 718-589-8600
Fax: 718-860-8930 www.plymouthbeef.com
Processor and exporter of meat products including frozen and fresh beef: burgers, chopped, sliced and stew
Chairman: Gerald Sussman
Ceo/President: Andrew Sussman
Estimated Sales: $5 Million
Number Employees: 25
Type of Packaging: Consumer, Food Service

10674 **Plymouth Cheese Counter**
P.O.Box 517
Plymouth, WI 53073 920-892-8781
Fax: 920-893-5986 888-607-9477
plychzct@excel.com www.cheesecapital.com
Processor of cheese; gift baskets available
Owner: Kris Hummes
Estimated Sales: $120000
Number Employees: 1-4
Type of Packaging: Consumer

10675 **Plymouth Colony Winery**
56 Pinewood Rd
Plymouth, MA 02360 508-747-3334
Fax: 508-747-4463
pcwinery@plymouthcolonywinery.com
www.plymouthcolonywinery.com
Wines
Owner: Charles Caranci
General Manager: Lydia Carey
Estimated Sales: $ 1-2.5 Million
Number Employees: 1-4
Type of Packaging: Private Label
Brands:
Plymouth Colony Winery

10676 **Plymouth Lollipop Company**
145 S Main St # B1-2
Carver, MA 02330-1527 508-866-7409
Fax: 508-746-5893 800-777-0115
plimothlollipop@msn.com
www.plimothlollipop.com
Lollipops and confection ingredients
President: Bill Johnson
Estimated Sales: Less than $500,000
Number Employees: 1-4
Brands:
Plimoth Lollipop

10677 **Po'okela Enterprises**
75-5749 Kalawa St
Suite 201
Kailua Kona, HI 96740-1873 808-328-9753
Fax: 808-328-9753 866-328-9753
chrys@pookela.com www.pookela.com
Processor of kona coffee, exporter of roasted kona coffee
President: Chrystal Yamasaki
Estimated Sales: $100,000
Number Employees: 1-4
Type of Packaging: Private Label, Bulk
Brands:
100% Kona Coffee
Po'okela O Honaynau Estate Coffee

10678 **Poche's Smokehouse**
3015 Main Hwy # A
Breaux Bridge, LA 70517-6347 337-332-2108
Fax: 337-332-5051 800-376-2437
info@pochesmarket.com
www.pochesmarket.com
Meat products
Owner: Floyd Poche
Owner: Karen Poche
Estimated Sales: $ 5 - 10 Million
Number Employees: 20-49

10679 **Pocino Foods**
14250 Lomitas Ave
City of Industry, CA 91746 626-968-8000
Fax: 626-330-8779 800-345-0150
onlythebest@pocinofoods.com
www.pocinofoods.com
Prepared meats
President: Frank Pocino
Vice President: Jerry Pocino
Estimated Sales: $ 10 - 20 Million
Number Employees: 100-249
Type of Packaging: Private Label
Brands:
Pocino

10680 **Pocono Cheesecake Factory**
Hc 1 Box 95
Swiftwater, PA 18370 570-839-6844
Fax: 570-839-6844 www.cheesecakefactory.net
Processor of cheesecakes
Manager: Alferd Johnson
Estimated Sales: $300,000
Number Employees: 10-19
Sq. footage: 3000
Brands:
Pocono Cheesecake

10681 **Pocono Foods**
P.O.Box 185
Mt Bethel, PA 18343-0185 570-897-5000
Fax: 570-897-7094 jheilman@noln.com
www.townsends.com
Manufacturer of Frozen chicken products, par-fried, battered, breaded
Manager: Robert Heilman
Vice President: James Heilman
COO: Chuck Dix
Estimated Sales: $17 Million
Number Employees: 50-99
Sq. footage: 40000
Parent Co: Townsends
Type of Packaging: Food Service, Private Label, Bulk
Brands:
A LA HENRI

10682 **Pocono Mountain Bottling Company**
57 W Chestnut Street
Wilkes Barre, PA 18705-1751 570-822-7695
Bottled spring water and carbonated beverages
President/Treasurer: Veronica Iskra
Estimated Sales: $580,000
Number Employees: 5
Brands:
POCONO MOUNTAIN

10683 **Pocono Spring Company**
P.O.Box 787
Mt Pocono, PA 18344-0787 570-839-2837
Fax: 570-839-6705 800-634-4584
Bottled water
President/CEO: Michael Melnic
CFO: Bill Fraser
Operations Manager: Tim Fitzgerald
Estimated Sales: $ 1-2.5 Million
Number Employees: 20-49
Brands:
Pocono Spring

10684 **Pod Pack International**
11800 Industriplex Blvd Ste 9
Baton Rouge, LA 70809 225-752-1110
Fax: 225-752-1163 tmartin@podpack.com
www.podpack.com
Espresso coffee pods and filter pack. Coffee for hotels, restaurants, and airlines
Owner: Thomas Martin
Quality Control: Gary Kennington
Executive VP/COO: Tom Martin
Estimated Sales: $ 10-20 Million
Number Employees: 10-19
Type of Packaging: Consumer, Food Service, Private Label

10685 **Point Adams Packing Company**
P.O.Box 162
Hammond, OR 97121 503-861-2226
Fax: 503-861-2312
Processor and exporter of frozen Pacific whiting
Manager: Tom Libby
Estimated Sales: $ 10-20 Million
Number Employees: 100-249
Parent Co: California Shellfish
Type of Packaging: Bulk

10686 **Point Adolphus Seafoods**
PO Box 63
Gustavus, AK 99826-0063 907-697-2246
Fax: 907-697-2246
Seafood

10687 **(HQ)Point Group**
1790 Highway A1a
Suite 103
Satellite Beach, FL 32937-5446 321-777-7408
Fax: 321-777-9777 888-272-1249
trump_co@digital.net www.mmgstock.com
Manufacturer and exporter of coffee, tea and fruit extracts and fruit juices
President: Gary Trump
VP: Roger Koltermann
Type of Packaging: Consumer, Food Service, Private Label, Bulk
Brands:
Mingo Bay Beverages, Inc.

10688 **Point Judith Fisherman'sCompany**
P.O.Box 730
Narragansett, RI 02882-0730 401-782-1500
Fax: 401-782-1599
Fresh and frozen fish
Manager: Larry Rainey
Sales Manager: John McLaughlin

Estimated Sales: $ 10-20 Million
Number Employees: 50-99

10689 **Point Reyes Farmstead Cheese Co.**
14700 Hwy 1
Po Box 9
Point Reyes Station, CA 94956 415-663-8880
Fax: 415-663-8881 800-591-6787
lynn@pointreyescheese.com
www.pointreyescheese.com
Cheese
President: Bob Giacomini

10690 **Point Saint George Fisheries**
PO Box 1386
Santa Rosa, CA 95402-1386 707-542-9490
Seafood, seafood products
General Manager: Rich Amundson
Estimated Sales: $ 1-2.5 Million appx.
Number Employees: 1

10691 **Poiret International**
7866 Exeter Boulevard E
Tamarac, FL 33321-8797 954-724-3261
Fax: 954-721-0110 poiretinternatl@bellsouth.net
Processor, importer and exporter of preserves and organic jams
CEO/Purchasing: Ed Kerzner
CFO: Sheila Kerzner
Marketing Director: Stan Margulese
Plant Manager: Frank Bilisi
Number Employees: 20-49
Sq. footage: 25000
Parent Co: Siroper/E. Meurens SA
Type of Packaging: Consumer, Food Service, Private Label, Bulk
Brands:
DELICE
MEURENS
POIRET

10692 **Poison Pepper Company**
7310 E Shadywoods Court
Floral City, FL 34436-5732 888-539-5540
Fax: 727-894-5540 pure.poison@worldnet.att.net
www.poisonpepper.com
Sauces
President: Tom Dahl

10693 **Pokanoket Ostrich Farm**
177 Gulf Rd
South Dartmouth, MA 02748 508-992-6188
Fax: 508-993-5356 pokanokets@aol.com
www.pokanoket.com
Processor of portion control ostrich meat
President: Alan Weinshel
National Sales Manager: Mike Yokemick
Estimated Sales: Below $ 5 Million
Number Employees: 1-4
Type of Packaging: Consumer, Food Service, Private Label
Brands:
Pokanoket Farm

10694 **Pokka Beverages**
1201 Commerce Blvd
American Canyon, CA 94503 707-557-0500
Fax: 707-557-0100 800-972-5962
Processor of fruit juices, canned iced coffee, iced tea and yogurt flavored drinks
President: Don Soetaert
CFO: George Lewis
Vice President: Joe Inazuka
Estimated Sales: $18 Million
Number Employees: 125
Sq. footage: 250000
Parent Co: Pokka Corporation
Type of Packaging: Private Label
Brands:
Fruit Ole
Hawaiian Sun
Premium Tea
The Coffee

10695 **Pokonobe Industries**
PO Box 1756
Santa Monica, CA 90406 310-392-1259
Fax: 310-392-3659 info@pokonobe.com
www.pokonobe.com
Processor and exporter of expeller pressed, refined and unrefined oils including almond, grapeseed, soy, sunflower, sesame, walnut, corn, olive, linseed, wheat germ, safflower, etc. Rice bran oil, avocado oil, pumkinseed oil, flaxseedoil, hazelnut oil, macademia nut oil, coconut oil, palm oil
President: David Nagley
General Manager: Larry Kronenberg
VP Purchasing: Robert Grebler
Estimated Sales: $ 5 - 10 Million
Number Employees: 2
Sq. footage: 1987
Type of Packaging: Bulk
Other Locations:
Pokonobe Industries
Santa Monica CA
Brands:
Pokonobe

10696 **(HQ)Poland Spring Water**
900 Long Ridge Road
Building 2
Stamford, CT 06902-1138
800-955-4426
www.polandspring.com
Manufacturer of distilled, sparkling, spring and bottled water
President/CEO Nestle Waters: Kim Jeffrey
Estimated Sales: $100 - $500 Million
Number Employees: 250-499
Parent Co: Nestle Waters North America
Type of Packaging: Consumer, Private Label

10697 **(HQ)Polar Beverages**
1001 Southbridge St
Worcester, MA 01610 508-753-4300
Fax: 508-793-0813 800-734-9800
customerservice@polarbev.com
www.polarbev.com
Manufacturer of bottled and canned soft drinks and water
President/CEO: Ralph Crowley Jr
CFO: Michael Mulrain
VP Marketing/Sales Planning: Gerald Martin
Estimated Sales: $191 Million
Number Employees: 1000
Sq. footage: 500000
Type of Packaging: Consumer, Food Service, Private Label
Brands:
A&W
ADIRONDACK BEVERAGES
ADIRONDACK CLEAR N' NATURAL
CAPE COD DRY
DIET RITE3
POLAR
ROYAL CROWN
SEAGRAMS
SEVEN-UP
SILVER SPRING
SQUIRT
SUNKIST COUNTRY TIME
WAIST WATCHER

10698 **Polar Water Company**
45 Noblestown Rd
Carnegie, PA 15106 412-429-5550
Fax: 770-739-1884
Bottler of spring and distilled water
Manager: Woody Godby
Number Employees: 20-49
Parent Co: Sontory Water Group

10699 **Polarica**
105 Quint St
San Francisco, CA 94124 415-647-1300
Fax: 415-647-6826 800-426-3872
info@polarica.com www.polarica.com
Beef, beef products, specialty products
President: Carlos Tabeira
Manager: Mitch Niayesh
Estimated Sales: $ 5-10 Million
Number Employees: 5-9
Brands:
Polarica

10700 **Polka Dot Bake ShopMillchap Purveyors LLC**
518 Griffith Road
Charlotte, NC 28217 704-527-0005
Fax: 704-943-0712 info@polkadotbakeshop.com
www.polkadotbakeshop.com
Dairy-free, kosher, nut-free, vegetarian, crackers, gluten-free, other snacks.
Principal: Jennifer Chapman
Marketing: Michelle Miller
Estimated Sales: $300,000
Number Employees: 10

10701 **Polka Home Style Sausage**
8753 S Commercial Ave
Chicago, IL 60617 773-221-0395
www.polkasausage.com
Processor of sausage
President: Paul Szczepkowski
Owner: Ed Szczepkowski
Estimated Sales: Less than $500,000
Number Employees: 1-4
Type of Packaging: Consumer, Food Service
Brands:
Polka

10702 **Pollio Dairy Products**
8596 Main St
Campbell, NY 14821-9636 607-527-4585
Processor of ricotta and mozzarella cheese including string, grated and smoked
Manager: Dee Gibbs
Manager: Brian Smith
Number Employees: 20-49
Type of Packaging: Consumer, Food Service

10703 **Pollman's Bake Shops**
750 S Broad St
Mobile, AL 36603-1197 251-438-1511
Fax: 251-438-9461 www.pollmansbakeshop.com
Processor of baked goods including cakes, pies and breads.
Co-Owner: Charles Pollman
Co-Owner: Fred Pollman III
Estimated Sales: $ 1 - 3 Million
Number Employees: 20-49
Type of Packaging: Consumer
Other Locations:
Pollman's Bake Shops
Mobile AL

10704 **Polly's Gourmet Coffee**
4606 E 2nd St
Long Beach, CA 90803 562-433-2996
Fax: 562-439-4119 coffee@pollys.com
www.pollys.com
Coffee and tea
Owner/Roastmaster: Michael Sheldrake
Estimated Sales: Under $500,000
Number Employees: 10-19
Brands:
Celebes Kalosi
Colombian Excelso
Colombian Supremo
Ethiopian Moka
Jamaica Blue Mountain
Java Estate
Kenya AA
Kona Hawaii
La Minita Tarrazu
Sumatra Mandheling
Tanzanian Peaberry

10705 **Polly-O Dairy Products**
120 Mineola Blvd
Mineola, NY 11501-4064 516-741-8000
Fax: 516-741-3041
Milk, dairy products, cheese
Director Marketing: Dave Keefe
Estimated Sales: $ 20-50 Million
Number Employees: 20-49
Brands:
Polly-O Cheeses

10706 **Polypro International**
7300 Metro Blvd # 570
Minneapolis, MN 55439-2346 952-835-7717
Fax: 952-835-3811 800-765-9776
polypro@polyprointl.com www.polyprointl.com
Processor, importer and exporter of guar and cellulose gums
President: Mark Kieper
Vice President: Mark Kieper
Estimated Sales: $ 2.5-5 Million
Number Employees: 1-4
Type of Packaging: Bulk
Brands:
Procol
Progum
Viscol

10707 **Pommeraie Winery**
10541 Cherry Ridge Road
Sebastopol, CA 95472-9644 707-823-9463
Fax: 707-823-9106
Wines
President: Judith Johnson
Estimated Sales: $500-1 Million appx.
Number Employees: 1-4

10708 **Pomodoro Fresca Foods**
16 Bleeker Street
Millburn, NJ 07079 973-467-6609
Fax: 973-379-1913
Sauces
President: Nancy Battista
Estimated Sales: Less than $100,000
Number Employees: 1
Brands:
Fresca Foods

10709 **Pompeian**
4201 Pulaski Hwy
Baltimore, MD 21224 410-276-6900
Fax: 410-276-3764 800-638-1224
fpatton@pompeian.com www.pompeian.com
Processor and importer of Spanish olive oil, red wine vinegar and artichokes
President: Frank Patton
COO: Adolfo Blassino
CEO: Bill Monroe
Plant Manager: John Zacot
Estimated Sales: $ 20 - 50 Million
Number Employees: 20-49
Type of Packaging: Consumer, Food Service, Bulk
Brands:
Avallo
Laco
Pompeian Olive Oil
Romanza

10710 **Pon Food Corporation**
101 Industrial Park Boulevard
Ponchatoula, LA 70454 985-386-6941
Fax: 985-386-6755
Wholesaler/distributor of groceries, frozen foods, meats, dairy products and seafood; serving the food service market
President: Anthony Berner Jr
VP: Michael Berner
Estimated Sales: $7.7 Million
Number Employees: 27
Sq. footage: 18000

10711 **Pond Brothers Peanut Company**
426 County Street
Suffolk, VA 23434-4704 757-539-2356
Fax: 757-539-3995
Raw peanuts
President: Richard L Pond Jr
CEO: Jeffrey G Pond
Controller: Ernest Wyatt
Estimated Sales: $ 5-10 Million
Number Employees: 1-4

10712 **Pond Pure Catfish**
14429 Market St
Moulton, AL 35650 256-974-6698
Fax: 403-252-3918
Catfish
Owner: Bobby Norwood
Estimated Sales: $300,000-500,000
Number Employees: 1-4

10713 **Ponderosa Valley Vineyard & Winery**
3171 Highway 290
Ponderosa, NM 87044-9716 575-834-7487
Fax: 505-834-7073
winemaker@ponderosawinery.com
www.ponderosawinery.com
Manufacturer of Red, white and port wines
Owner: Henry Street
Owner: Mary Street
Operations Manager: Henry Street
Production Manager: Henry Street
Estimated Sales: $150,000
Number Employees: 1-4
Number of Products: 21
Sq. footage: 1000
Type of Packaging: Consumer
Brands:
CHAMISA GOLD
JEMEZ BLUSH
JEMEZ RED
N.M. RIESLING
PONDEROSA VALLEY VINEYARDS
SUMMER SAGE
VINO DE PATA

10714 **Pondini Imports, Inc**
Po Box 5250
Somerset, NJ 08875-5250 732-545-1255
Fax: 732-246-7570 spond@pondini.com
www.pondini.com
Organic/natural, coffee, olive oil, balsalmic vinegar, cheese, pasta (dry), rice.
President/Owner: Matteo Panini
CEO: Seymour Pond
Marketing: Seymour Pond

10715 **Pontchartrain Blue Crab**
38327 Salt Bayou Rd
Slidell, LA 70461 985-649-6645
Fax: 504-781-5064
www.pontchartrainbluecrab.com
Pontchartrain Blue Crab Inc is a seafood processor, importer and exporter with a primary focus on top quality crab products.
President/CEO: Gary Bauer Sr
Estimated Sales: $5,000,000
Number Employees: 50-99

10716 **Pontiac Coffee Break**
2252 Dixie Hwy
Pontiac, MI 48342 248-332-9403
Fax: 248-335-0525
gourmetcoffee@coffeebreakinc.com
www.coffeebreakinc.com
Coffee
President: Robert Smith
Estimated Sales: $500,000-$1 Million
Number Employees: 10-19

10717 **Pontiac Foods**
P.O.Box 25469
Columbia, SC 29224 803-699-1600
Fax: 803-699-1649
Coffee
Manager: John Masa
General Manager: Joe Girone
Purchasing Manager: Stan Wilson
Estimated Sales: Under $500,000
Number Employees: 100-249
Brands:
Kroger
Pontiac Foods

10718 **Pony Boy Ice Cream**
211 Middle Road
Acushnet, MA 02743-2017 508-994-4422
Fax: 508-995-9459
Ice Cream and frozen yogurt
President: Raymond White
Estimated Sales: $ 10-20 Million
Number Employees: 10-19
Brands:
Pony Boy

10719 **Ponzi Vineyards**
14665 SW Winery Ln
Beaverton, OR 97007 503-628-1227
Fax: 503-628-0354 info@ponziwines.com
www.ponziwines.com
Wines
President: Richard Ponzi
Marketing/Sales Director: Maria Ponzi Fogelstrom
Operations Manager: Michel Ponzi
Winemaker: Luisa Ponzi
Estimated Sales: $ 1 - 3 Million
Number Employees: 10-19
Type of Packaging: Private Label
Brands:
Ponzi's

10720 **Poore Brothers**
1898 S Flatiron Ct
Boulder, CO 80301-2875 303-546-9939
Fax: 303-546-9133 www.boulderchips.com
Marketer and manufacturer of a variety of owned or licensed brand names products including; T.G.I. Friday's, Cinnabon, Poore Brothers, Texas Style, Boulder Canyon Natural Foods, and Tato Skins
President: Mark Maggio
Interim CEO: Eric Kufel
CFO: Steve Weinberger
Sr. VP Marketing: Steven Sklar
Number Employees: 10-19
Type of Packaging: Consumer, Food Service, Bulk
Brands:
Boulder Canyon

10721 **(HQ)Poore Brothers**
5050 N 40th St # 300
Phoenix, AZ 85018-2153 623-932-6200
Fax: 623-522-2690 800-279-2250
info@InventureGroup.net
www.inventuregroup.net/Poore-Brothers.asp
Kettle, batch and continuous cooked potato chips.
President: Eric Kufel
Chief Financial Officer: Steve Weinberger
CEO: Terry McDaniel
VP Marketing: Scott Fullmar
VP Manufacturing: Glen Flook
Estimated Sales: $ 50-100 Million
Number Employees: 250-499
Parent Co: The Inventure Group Inc
Type of Packaging: Consumer, Food Service, Private Label
Brands:
Poore Brothers

10722 **Poore Brothers**
705 W Dustman Road
Bluffton, IN 46714-1178 260-824-2800
Fax: 219-824-4388 info@amstock.com
Chips
President/CEO: Eric Kufel
CFO: Rick Finkbeiner
CFO: Thomas Freeze
VP Marketing: Scott Fullmar
VP Manufacturing: Glen Flook
Number Employees: 260
Brands:
Bob's Texas Style
Boulder Canyon
Cinnabon
Poore Brothers
TGI Friday's
Tato Skins

10723 **Popchips**
550 Montgomery Street
Suite 925
San Francisco, CA 94111 415-391-2211
Fax: 415-391-2779 866-217-9327
sales@popchips.com www.popchips.com
popped potato chips
Ceo: Patrick Turpin
Ceo: Keith Belling
Vice President: Martin Basch
Estimated Sales: $500,000
Number Employees: 2

10724 **Popcorn Connection**
7615 Fulton Avenue
North Hollywood, CA 91605-1805 818-764-3279
Fax: 818-765-0578 800-852-2676
popcornconnection@earthlink.net
www.popcornconnection.com
Processor and manufacturer of gourmet popcorn confections and nut; custom labeling is available
Owner: Kevin Needle
VP: Ross Wallach
Estimated Sales: $300,000
Number Employees: 3
Number of Brands: 15
Number of Products: 20
Sq. footage: 3500
Type of Packaging: Consumer, Food Service, Private Label, Bulk
Brands:
CORN APPETIT
CORN APPETIT ULTIMATE
FRUIT CORN APPETIT
VIDEO MUNCHIES

10725 **Popcorn Palace**
4210 Transworld Road
Schiller Park, IL 60176 847-451-1990
Fax: 847-671-0850 800-873-2686
www.popcornpalace.com
Gourmet popcorn
Estimated Sales: $440,000
Number Employees: 10
Sq. footage: 6000

10726 Popcorn World
520 S Ohio Ave
Sedalia, MO 65301-4450 660-826-9975
Fax: 660-359-4475 800-443-8226
pam@popcornworld.com
www.popcornworld.com
Processor of flavored popcorn
Owner: Pam Kaduce
CEO: Keith Kaduce
Estimated Sales: $ 1 - 3 Million
Number Employees: 20
Type of Packaging: Consumer, Food Service, Private Label, Bulk

10727 Popcorner
1429 N Illinois Street
Swansea, IL 62226-4234 618-277-2676
Fax: 618-236-9420 popmaster@popcorn.com
Processor of specialty items including gourmet popcorn
Owner: Connie Kimble
Number Employees: 1-4
Sq. footage: 1200
Type of Packaging: Consumer, Private Label, Bulk

10728 Poplar Ridge Vineyards
9782 State Route 414
Hector, NY 14841 607-582-6421
Fax: 607-582-6421
Wines
President: Dave Bagley
Estimated Sales: Less than $200,000
Number Employees: 1-4
Type of Packaging: Private Label
Brands:
Poplar Ridge Vineyards

10729 Poppa's Granola
473 Grout Road
Perkinsville, VT 05151-9682 802-263-5342
pappoasgranola@tds.net
Granola
Co-Owner: Angela Page
Co-Owner: Jacquelin Antonivich
Type of Packaging: Consumer, Food Service, Bulk

10730 Poppee's Popcorn Company
38727 Taylor Pkwy
Elyria, OH 44035 440-327-0775
Fax: 440-327-9349 popcorn@jennyspopcorn.com
www.jennyspopcorn.com
Popcorn, cheese curls, caramel, regular and hot cheddar cheese corn
Owner: Tom Mc Guire
CEO: Bob Shearer
Sales Manager: Tom McGuire
Plant Manager: Jay McGuire
Estimated Sales: $ 5-10 Million
Number Employees: 20-49
Type of Packaging: Private Label
Brands:
Jenny's

10731 Poppers Supply Company
PO Box 90187
Allentown, PA 18109 503-239-3792
Fax: 503-235-6221 800-457-9810
info@poppers.com www.poppers.com
Processor and exporter of ready-to-eat flavored and confectioned popcorn and fountain syrup; wholesaler/distributor of concession equipment and supplies including sno-cone syrup and cotton candy floss
President: Vernon Ryles Jr
Sales Manager: Jody Riggs
Estimated Sales: $1,400,000
Number Employees: 10
Type of Packaging: Consumer, Food Service
Brands:
Allans
Poppers

10732 Poppie's Dough
2411 S Wallace St
Chicago, IL 60616 312-640-0404
Fax: 312-949-0505
customerservice@poppiesdough.com
www.poppiesdough.com
cookies, biscotti, brownies and bars, scones and sconettes
President/Owner: Ronnie Himmel
Estimated Sales: $1.9 Million
Number Employees: 15

10733 Poppie's Dough
2411 S Wallace St
Chicago, IL 60616 312-640-0404
Fax: 312-949-0505 888-767-7431
ymendez@poppiesdough.com
www.poppiesdough.com
Manufacturer of Cookies in twenty flavors
Owner: Michelle Garson
President: Ronnie Himmel
Marketing: Yesenia Mendez
Estimated Sales: $2.4 Million
Number Employees: 15
Brands:
POPPIE'S

10734 Poppin Popcorn
933 4th Avenue N
Naples, FL 34102-5814 941-262-1691
Fax: 941-262-1691
Popcorns and maize products
President: Mark Webb
Estimated Sales: Less than $500,000
Number Employees: 1-4

10735 Porinos Gourmet Food
280 Rand St
Central Falls, RI 02863-2512 401-273-3000
Fax: 401-273-3232 800-826-3938
porinos@aol.com www.porinos.com
Processor and exporter of gourmet pasta and barbecue sauces, salad dressings, marinades and pickled pepper items; importer and wholesaler/distributor of pastas, olive oils and balsamic vinegars
Owner: Michael Dressler
VP Operations: Marshall Righter
Estimated Sales: $1900000
Number Employees: 10-19
Sq. footage: 30000
Type of Packaging: Consumer, Food Service, Private Label

10736 Pork Shop of Vermont
631 N Pasture Road
Charlotte, VT 05445-9254 802-482-3617
Fax: 802-482-2801 800-458-3441
Smoked sausage and ham
President: Joseph Keenan
Estimated Sales: $ 5-9.9 Million
Number Employees: 7

10737 PorkRubbers BBQ Specialty Products
21w266 Glen Park Road
Lombard, IL 60148-5182 630-424-8200
Fax: 630-424-0231
porkrubbersbbq@prodigy.com
Barbeque specialty products
Owner: Mary Van Petten

10738 Porkie Company of Wisconsin
3113 E Layton Ave
Cudahy, WI 53110 414-483-6562
Fax: 414-483-6561 800-333-2588
www.porkiesofwisconsin.com
Processor of pork rinds and cracklings, beef jerky, extruded corn, salted peanuts, pistachios and cashews, olives, pickles, pretzels, potato chips and cheese curls; also, processor and packer of pickled pigs' feet, pork hocks andpickled Polish sausage
President: Gerald Rydeski
Executive VP: Thomas Rydeski
Marketing/Sales: Rick Rydeski
Production: Dan Rydeski
Plant Manager: Mike Sodemann
Estimated Sales: $1600000
Number Employees: 20-49
Number of Products: 50
Sq. footage: 50000
Brands:
JACK'S ALL AMERICAN
PORKIES
SNAK SALES
VINEGAR JOE

10739 Porky's Gourmet
644 Blythe Ave
Gallatin, TN 37066-2226 615-230-7000
Fax: 615-230-2800 800-767-5911
flavor@porkysgourmet.com
www.porkysgourmet.com
Gourmet sauces, seasonings, relishes, jellies and other condiments
President: Ron Boyle
Estimated Sales: $ 5 - 10 Million
Number Employees: 10-19
Type of Packaging: Consumer, Food Service, Private Label

10740 Porrhoff Foods Company
P.O.Box 1502
Des Moines, IA 50305-1502 515-244-5271
Fax: 515-244-7037
President: Craig Potthoff
Estimated Sales: $ 10 - 20 Million
Number Employees: 20-49

10741 Port Chatham Smoked Seafood
1930 Merrill Creek Pkwy Ste B
Everett, WA 98203 425-349-2563
Fax: 425-407-4010 800-872-5666
info@norquest.com www.portchatham.com
Processor and exporter of smoked sturgeon, salmon and oysters including frozen, fresh and canned
General Manager: Ken Ng
VP: Erling Nilson
Plant Manager: Bill Taylor
Estimated Sales: $9500000
Number Employees: 90
Sq. footage: 53895
Parent Co: Icicle Seafood
Type of Packaging: Consumer, Food Service
Brands:
Great Northwest
Pacific Select
Portlock

10742 Port Lobster Company
P.O.Box 729
Kennebunkport, ME 04046 207-967-2081
Fax: 207-967-8419 800-486-7029
portlob@gwi.net www.portlobster.com
Manufacturer of Lobster
President: Timothy Hutchins
Estimated Sales: $ 1 - 3 Million
Number Employees: 5-9
Type of Packaging: Consumer

10743 Port Vue Coffee Company
RR 61
Pottsville, PA 17901 570-429-2690
Coffee
President: Randy Palles
Plant Manager: Lori Nora
Estimated Sales: Less than $500,000
Number Employees: 5-9

10744 Porter Creek Vineyards
8735 Westside Rd
Healdsburg, CA 95448 707-433-6321
Fax: 707-433-4245
info@portercreekvineyards.com
www.portercreekvineyards.com
Wine
President: George Davis
Estimated Sales: Under $ 1 Million
Number Employees: 1-4
Brands:
Procter Creek

10745 Porter's Food & Produce
P.O.Box 407
Du Quoin, IL 62832-0407 618-542-2155
Fax: 618-542-2396 www.farefoods.com
President: Ron Porter
Estimated Sales: $ 10 - 20 Million
Number Employees: 20-49

10746 Porter's Pick-A-Dilly
Stw Indstrl Park
Stowe, VT 05672 802-253-6338
Fax: 802-253-6852
President: Lynn Porter
Estimated Sales: Under $500,000
Number Employees: 1-4

10747 Portier Fine Foods
436 Waverly Ave
Mamaroneck, NY 10543 914-899-9006
Fax: 914-381-4045 800-272-9463
portier.finefoods@verizon.net
www.portierfinefoods.com
Processor of smoked salmon, trout, scallops, shrimp, etc.; importer of Caspian sea caviar, grain-fed game and birds and hand-made Belgian chocolates
President: Sean Portier
Sales Director: Patrick Portier

Estimated Sales: Below $ 5 Million
Number Employees: 10-19
Parent Co: Chenoceaux, Inc
Type of Packaging: Consumer, Food Service

10748 **Portion Pak**
1609 Stone Ridge Dr
Stone Mountain, GA 30083-1109 770-934-3200
Fax: 770-934-7644 www.portionpac.com
Cheese spread, powdered beverages, peanut butter, jelly and icing
President: Barney Rosner
Marketing: Fred Johnson
Plant Manager: John Stephens
Purchasing: Lynn Cooper
Estimated Sales: $ 20-50 Million
Number Employees: 100-249

10749 **Portland Shellfish Company**
110 Dartmouth St
South Portland, ME 04106-6210 207-799-9290
Fax: 207-799-7179 scout@pshellfish.com
www.portlandshellfish.com
Manufacturer, importer and exporter of fresh and frozen crab
President: Jeff Holden
Human Resources: John Maloney
Estimated Sales: $9 Million
Number Employees: 100-249
Sq. footage: 12000
Type of Packaging: Consumer, Food Service, Private Label, Bulk
Brands:
Portland Lighthouse

10750 **Portland Specialty Seafoods**
12 Portland Fish Pier
Portland, ME 04101 207-775-5765
Fax: 207-774-1614
Seafood
Administrator: Jessica Burton
Estimated Sales: $ 10 - 20 Million
Number Employees: 10-19

10751 **Portsmouth Chowder Company**
124 Heritage Ave # 1
Portsmouth, NH 03801-8655 603-431-3132
Fax: 603-431-3132
Chowder and seafood products
Owner: Rob Lincoln
Estimated Sales: Below $ 5 Million
Number Employees: 1-4
Brands:
Portsmouth Chowder Company

10752 **Portugalia Imports**
23 Tremont St
Fall River, MA 02720-4821 508-679-9307
Fax: 508-673-1502
Owner: Fernando Benevides

10753 **Portuguese Baking Company**
P.O.Box 5550
Newark, NJ 07105-0550 973-589-8875
Fax: 973-589-6510 info@ pbclp.com
www.pbclp.com/
Portuguese rolls
President: Marvin Everseyke
CFO/VP: Louis Pereira
CEO: Steve Latner
Estimated Sales: Under $500,000
Number Employees: 250-499
Type of Packaging: Private Label, Bulk
Brands:
Austin Company
Portuguese Baking Company

10754 **Poseidon Enterprises**
2351 Adams Drive NW
Atlanta, GA 30318-1919 800-863-7886
Fax: 404-352-0019
Seafood, salmon, tuna, swordfish, grouper, snapper, live lobster
President: Richard Lavecchia III

10755 **Positively Third StreetBakery**
1202 E 3rd St
Duluth, MN 55805-2319 218-724-8619
www.positively3rdstreet.com
Processor of fresh and frozen cookies, bagels, granola and bread
Owner: Paul Steklin
Estimated Sales: Less than $500,000
Number Employees: 5-9

Type of Packaging: Consumer, Food Service, Bulk

10756 **Post Familie Vineyards**
1700 Saint Marys Mountain Rd
Altus, AR 72821 479-468-2741
Fax: 479-468-2740 800-275-8423
info@postfamilie.com www.postfamilie.com
Processor of wines, grape juices, jellies, champagne and table wine grapes
President: Matthew Post
VP/Director Marketing: Paul Post
Number Employees: 10-19
Type of Packaging: Consumer, Private Label, Bulk
Brands:
Aesop's Fable
Ozark Mountain Vineyards
Post Familie Vineyards

10757 **Pot O'Gold Honey Company**
PO Box 1200
Hemingway, SC 29554-1200 843-558-9598
pollinator@aol.com
Processor of honey
Co-Owner: David Green
Co-Owner: Janice Green
Number Employees: 1-4

10758 **Poteet Seafood Company**
5067 Blythe Island Hwy
Brunswick, GA 31520 912-264-5340
Fax: 912-267-9695
Seafood
Owner: Speedy Tostensen
Estimated Sales: $350,000
Number Employees: 1-4

10759 **Potomac Farms**
P.O.Box 2189
Cumberland, MD 21503-2189 301-722-4410
Fax: 301-722-8433
Milk
President: David W Gilles
Manager: David Gilles
Estimated Sales: $ 10-20 Million
Number Employees: 50-99

10760 **Pots de Creme**
4954 Paris Pike
Lexington, KY 40511-9400 859-299-2254
Fax: 859-299-4638 www.kyagr.com
Processor of organic produce and herbs, fresh water prawns, trout and tilapia
President: Susan Harkins
Number Employees: 1-4
Parent Co: Duntreath Farm
Brands:
Dubbasue And Company

10761 **Potter Siding Creamery Company**
P.O.Box 494
Tripoli, IA 50676-0494 319-882-4444
Bakery products and creames
Owner: Kurt Kortbein
Estimated Sales: Less than $500,000
Number Employees: 1-4

10762 **Poudre Valley Creamery**
2315 E. Harmony Rd
Suite 200
Fort Collins, CO 80528 970-237-7000
www.pvhs.org
Processor of ice cream and ice cream novelties; wholesaler/distributor of milk
President/Ceo/Director: Rulon Stacey
Estimated Sales: $318 Million
Number Employees: 2,800
Type of Packaging: Consumer, Food Service

10763 **Poultry Foods Industry**
P.O. Box 2020
Springfield, AR 72764
800-643-3410
www.tyson.com
Poultry, poultry products
President/CEO: Donnie Smith
CFO: Dennis Leatherby
COO: James Lochner
Operations Manager: John Mulson
Plant Manager: Steve Smalling
Estimated Sales: $28 Billion
Number Employees: 2,850

10764 **Powder Pak**
34475 N Circle Drive
Round Lake, IL 60073-9730 847-223-4683
Fax: 847-223-4685 dcoulter@powderpak.com
www.powderpak.com
Packaging and handling powders. Dairy and food ingredients

10765 **Powell & Mahoney LTD**
100 Cummings Center
Suite 220B
Beverly, MA 01915 978-922-4332
Fax: 978-922-4339 kati@powellandmahoney.com
www.powellandmahoney.com
Non-alcoholic beverages.
Marketing: Mark Mahoney

10766 **Powell Bean**
313 S Fair St
Powell, WY 82435 307-754-3121
Fax: 307-754-3936 pbc@directairnet.com
Processor and exporter of dry pinto beans
Manager: Jamie Franko
Number Employees: 5-9
Type of Packaging: Bulk

10767 **Power-Selles Imports**
12407-B Mukilteo Speedway
Suite 245
Lynnwood, WA 98087 425-398-9761
Fax: 42- 39- 976 info@culinarycollective.com
psimports.net
Specialty gourmet food products from spain
Co-Founder: Betsy Power
Co-Founder: Pere Selles
General Manager: Monse Alonso
Sales Manager: Marion Sproul
Office Manager: Peggy Godfrey
Estimated Sales: $ 3 - 5 Million
Number Employees: 5-9

10768 **PowerBar**
2150 Shattuck Ave Fl 10
10th Floor
Berkeley, CA 94704 510-843-1330
Fax: 866-574-6420 800-587-6937
www.powerbar.com
Health food energy bars and drinks
General Manager: Cindy Vallar
VP Sales: Jeff Lozito
Marketing Manager: Michelle Sitton
Estimated Sales: $ 100-500 Million
Number Employees: 50-99
Parent Co: Nestle USA
Type of Packaging: Private Label
Brands:
PowerBar
PowerBar Beverage System
PowerBar Energy Bites
PowerBar Essentials
PowerBar Harvest
PowerBar Pria
PowerBar Proteinplus
Powergel

10769 **Powers Baking Company**
7771 W Oakland park Blvd
miami, FL 33167-3705 305-381-7000
Fax: 305-769-1185
Breads and rolls.
President: Dolphus Powers
Estimated Sales: $5 Million
Number Employees: 80

10770 **Poynette Distribution Center**
W8070 Kent Rd
Poynette, WI 53955-9713 608-635-4396
Fax: 608-635-7308
www.lakesidefoods.com/poynette1.htm
Processor of canned green beans
Sr. VP Operations: Daniel C Cavanaugh
VP Customer Service: James I Ferguson
General Manager: Ross Moland
Plant Manager: Mike Hull
Estimated Sales: $ 10 - 20 Million
Number Employees: 20-49
Parent Co: Stokely USA
Type of Packaging: Consumer, Private Label

10771 **Prager Winery & Port Works**
1281 Lewelling Ln
Saint Helena, CA 94574 707-963-7678
Fax: 707-963-7679 800-969-7678
ahport@pragerport.com www.pragerport.net

Wine
President: Jim Prager
CFO: Katie Rooney
Estimated Sales: $1-4.9 Million
Number Employees: 5-9
Brands:
Prager Winery & Port

10772 **Praire Farms Dairy**
722 Broadway St
Anderson, IN 46012-2924 765-649-1261
Fax: 765-649-8268 www.prairiefarms.com
Milk, dairy products-noncheese
President: Harry Carter
CFO: Paul Benne
Quality Control: Leonardo Otto
Manager: Doug Banning
Estimated Sales: $ 50-100 Million
Number Employees: 100-249

10773 **Prairie Cajun Whlse.**
5966 Highway 190
Eunice, LA 70535 337-546-6195
Processor and exporter of frozen seafood and exotic meats including alligator and nutria
President: Jeffery Derouen
Estimated Sales: C
Number Employees: 10-19
Type of Packaging: Consumer, Food Service

10774 **Prairie City Bakery**
100 N Fairway Dr Ste 138
Vernon Hills, IL 60061 847-573-9640
Fax: 847-573-9643 800-338-5122
customerservice@pcbakery.com
www.pcbakery.com
Processor of frozen danish, cookies, muffins and cakes
President: William Skeens
Estimated Sales: $2,200,000
Number Employees: 5-9
Type of Packaging: Consumer, Food Service, Bulk
Brands:
Prairie City

10775 **(HQ)Prairie Farms Dairy**
1100 N. Broadway St.
Carlinville, IL 62626 217-854-2547
Fax: 217-854-6426 icebox@prairiefarms.com
www.prairiefarmsdairy.com
Processor of dairy products including cottage cheese, fresh cream, milk, sour cream, yogurt and ice cream; also, orange juice and fruit drinks
Chairman: Fred Kuenstler
CEO: Roger Capps
VP Finance: Paul Benne
CEO/EVP: Ed Mullins
VP General Sales: Ed Mullins
Sales Director: Donald Kullman
Director Marketing: William Montgomery
Estimated Sales: $50-100 Million
Number Employees: 1,000-4,999
Type of Packaging: Consumer, Food Service, Private Label
Brands:
Prairie Farms

10776 **Prairie Farms Dairy**
1100 N. Broadway St.
Carlinville, IL 62626 217-854-2547
Fax: 217-854-6426 icebox@prairiefarms.com
www.prairiefarmsdairy.com
Manufacturer of dairy products and juice that include; milk, orange juice, fruit drinks, cottage cheese, yogurt, sour cream and dip, ice cream and sherbet
General Manager: Kenneth Kuhn
CEO: Ed Mullins
Estimated Sales: $50-100 Million
Number Employees: 1,000-4,999
Type of Packaging: Consumer, Food Service, Private Label
Brands:
PRAIRIE FARMS

10777 **Prairie Farms Dairy**
400 W Us Highway 50
O Fallon, IL 62269 618-632-3632
Fax: 618-632-9828 www.prairiefarms.com
Milk, cottage cheese, sour cream, dips, yogurt, juices and drinks, butter and cream, ice cream, frozen treats and specialty items
Quality Assurance Supervisor: Rich McClain
Plant Manager: Pat Hedger
Estimated Sales: $ 20 - 50 Million
Number Employees: 34
Sq. footage: 27380
Parent Co: Prairie Farms Dairy
Type of Packaging: Consumer

10778 **Prairie Farms Dairy**
1100 Broadway
Carlinville, IL 62626 217-854-2547
www.prairiefarms.com
Processor of sour cream, cottage cheese and dips
CEO: Roger Capps
Plant Manager: Ron Diuguid
Estimated Sales: $ 10 - 20 Million
Number Employees: 50-99
Parent Co: Prairie Farms Dairy
Type of Packaging: Consumer

10779 **Prairie Farms Dairy**
415 N 24th St
Quincy, IL 62301 217-223-5530
www.prairiefarms.com
Processor of cottage cheese and yogurt
Plant Manager: Skip Rueter
Estimated Sales: $ 5-10 Million
Number Employees: 27
Parent Co: Prairie Farms Dairy
Type of Packaging: Consumer, Food Service

10780 **Prairie Farms Dairy**
1100 Broadway
Carlinville, IL 62626 217-562-3956
Fax: 217-854-6426 www.prairiefarms.com
Processor of ice cream mixes
Manager: James Baker
CEO: Ed Mullins
Estimated Sales: $ 2.5-5 Million
Number Employees: 1,000-4,999
Parent Co: Prairie Farms Dairy
Type of Packaging: Bulk

10781 **Prairie Farms Dairy**
1800 Adams St
Granite City, IL 62040 618-451-5600
Fax: 618-451-7251 icebox@prairiefarms.com
www.prairiefarms.com
Processor of milk, cottage cheese, orange juice, sour cream and yogurt
President: Bill Dowling
CFO: Jim Clancy
Vice President: Dale Chapman
Maintenance Manager: Rich Bohn
Estimated Sales: $ 20-50 Million
Number Employees: 100-249
Parent Co: Prairie Farms Dairy
Type of Packaging: Consumer, Food Service

10782 **(HQ)Prairie Farms Dairy**
1100 Broadway
Carlinville, IL 62626 217-854-2547
Fax: 217-854-6426 icebox@prairiefarms.com
www.prairiefarms.com
Manufacturers a wide variety of fluid milk products; milk, cottage cheese, sour cream and dips, yogurt, ice cream, butter and creams, frozen treats, and juuices and drinks
CEO: Ed Mullins
Estimated Sales: $50-$100 Million
Number Employees: 1,000-5,000
Type of Packaging: Consumer, Food Service
Brands:
Prairie Farms

10783 **(HQ)Prairie Farms Dairy Inc.**
1100 Broadway
Carlinville, IL 62626 217-854-2547
Fax: 217-854-6426 icebox@prairiefarms.com
www.prairiefarmsdairy.com
Manufacturer of dairy products including cottage cheese, fresh cream, milk, sour cream, yogurt and ice cream; also, orange juice and fruit drinks
CFO: Paul Benne
GM: Craig Bertrand
CEO: Ed Mullins
Estimated Sales: $10.5 Million
Number Employees: 1,000-4,999
Type of Packaging: Consumer, Food Service, Private Label, Bulk
Brands:
PRAIRIE FARMS

10784 **Prairie Malt**
PO Box 1150
Biggar, SK S0K 0M0
Canada 306-948-3500
Fax: 306-948-5038 david_klinger@cargill.com
Processor and exporter of barley malt
President: Doug Eden
Number Employees: 50-99
Parent Co: Cargill, Incorporated
Type of Packaging: Bulk

10785 **Prairie Mills Company**
401 East 4th Street
PO Box 97
Rochester, IN 46975 574-223-3177
Fax: 574-223-3414 http://www.prairiemills.com
Organic flour and cereal
President: Erik Bruun
Estimated Sales: $500,000-$1 Million
Number Employees: 1-4
Type of Packaging: Private Label
Brands:
Amaizen Crunch
Prairie Star

10786 **Prairie Mushrooms**
52557 Range Road 215
Sherwood Park, AB T8E 2H6
Canada 780-467-3555
Fax: 780-467-3893 info@prairiemushrooms.com
www.prairiemushrooms.com
Manufacturer and exporter of mushrooms
President: George DeRuiter
Marketing Manager: John Kostelyk
Sales: Kevin Christman
Production: Don Kostelyk
Estimated Sales: E
Number Employees: 100-249
Type of Packaging: Consumer, Food Service
Brands:
PRAIRIE MUSHROOMS

10787 **Prairie Sun Grains**
Box 2700
Calgary, AB T2P 3C2
Canada 403-290-4618
Fax: 403-290-5550 800-556-6807
Processor of organic flour, pancake mixes and hot breakfast cereals; exporter of hot organic breakfast cereals, bars and herbal supplements
Member: Peggy Lesueur-Brymer
Broker Sales Manager: Pat Maloney
Sales Coordinator: Sarah Sanders
Number Employees: 10-19
Type of Packaging: Consumer, Food Service
Brands:
Golden Loaf
Prairie Sun
Rosebud
Sunny Boy

10788 **Prairie Thyme**
4363 Center Pl # 3
Santa Fe, NM 87507-1823 505-473-1945
Fax: 505-473-0363 800-869-0009
prairiethyme@aol.com www.prairiethyme.com
Manufacturer of Specialty gourmet condiments, vinegars, flavored cooking oils, fruit salsas, vegetable chutneys
President/Owner: Gary Hall
Estimated Sales: $300,000-500,000
Number Employees: 1-4
Number of Brands: 1
Number of Products: 4
Sq. footage: 1600
Type of Packaging: Consumer, Food Service, Private Label, Bulk
Brands:
PRAIRIE THYME
PRAIRIE THYME GARLIC BASIL OIL
PRAIRIE THYME PEACH HABANERO
PRAIRIE THYME RASPBERRY JALAPENO
PRAIRIE THYME RED RASPBERRY VINEGAR
PRAIRIE THYME ROASTED TOMATO
PRAIRIE THYME TOASTED GARLIC OIL

10789 **Praters Foods**
2206 114th St
Lubbock, TX 79423 806-745-2727
Fax: 806-745-9650 praterscontact@praters.com
www.praters.com

Processor of smoked meats, breadings, frozen entrees, stuffings, gravies and casseroles
Owner: Chip Chenowetch
Sales Manager: Benny Cousatte
Purchasing Manager: Daryl Halsey
Estimated Sales: $10-20 Million
Number Employees: 20-49
Type of Packaging: Consumer

10790 Pratzel's Bakery
P.O.Box 21510
Saint Louis, MO 63132-510
Fax: 314-993-0414 pratzel@atdialyahoo.com
www.pratzels.com
Bakery products
President: Ron Pratzel
CFO/VP: Elaine Pratzel
Estimated Sales: Below $ 5 Million
Number Employees: 20-49
Type of Packaging: Consumer, Food Service, Private Label, Bulk

10791 Precise Food Ingredients
1432 Wainwright Way Ste 150
Carrollton, TX 75007 972-323-4951
Fax: 972-323-5078 SalesInfo@PreciseFood.com
www.precisefood.com
Processor of spices and seasonings
Owner: Ken Stindmire
Purchasing Agent: Linda Ransom
Estimated Sales: $6000000
Number Employees: 5-9
Type of Packaging: Bulk

10792 Precision Blends
13460 Brooks Drive
Baldwin Park, CA 91706-2292 626-960-9939
Fax: 626-962-2570 800-836-9979
dwestphal@precisionblends.com
Blend spices
President: Charles Angell
Sales Manager: David Alnamva
Purchasing Manager: Charles Nordell
Estimated Sales: Under $500,000
Number Employees: 20-49
Type of Packaging: Private Label

10793 Precision Foods
11457 Olde Cabin Rd Ste 100
Saint Louis, MO 63141 314-567-4700
Fax: 314-567-7421 800-647-8170
www.precisionfood.com
Dry blending and packaging
President: Jerry Fritz
COO: Chris Circo
Estimated Sales: $ 10-20 Million
Number Employees: 20
Number of Brands: 13
Brands:
Baker's Joy
DOLE
Fla*Vor*Ice
Foothill Farms
Frostline
Milani Gourmet
Molly McButter
Mrs. Dash
Otter Pops
Royal
Smithers
Sugar Twin
Thick-It

10794 Precision Foods
2150 N 15th Avenuenue
Melrose Park, IL 60160-1410 708-216-0704
Fax: 708-216-0709 800-333-0003
info@precisionfoods.com
www.precisionfoods.com
Salad dressings, desserts, dried beverages, soups, bases and dietetic products
President: Jerry L Fritz
CEO: Dennis P Circo
Estimated Sales: $ 10-20 Million
Number Employees: 150
Brands:
Molly McButter
Mrs Dash
Royal
Sugar Twin
Thick It

10795 Precision Plus Vacuum Parts
2055 Niagara Falls Blvd # 4
Niagara Falls, NY 14304-5702 716-297-2039
Fax: 716-297-8210 800-526-2707
info@precisionplus.com www.precisionplus.com
Manufacturer of vacuum pump replacement parts
Manager: Joseph Miller
Estimated Sales: $7 Million
Number of Brands: 15
Number of Products: 2000
Sq. footage: 20000
Parent Co: BOC Group, Inc.
Type of Packaging: Food Service
Brands:
ALCATEL
BOC EDWARDS
BOCE STOKES
BUSCH
EBARA
KINNEY
LEYBOLD
PRECISION SCIENTIFIC
RISTSCHIC
VARIAN
WELCH

10796 Preferred Brands International
9 W Broad Street
Suite 5
Stamford, CT 06902 203-348-0030
Fax: 203-348-0029 800-827-8900
comments@tastybite.com www.tastybite.com
indian, thai, vegetarian, vegan, kosher and gluten free foods.
President/Owner: Ravi Nigam
CEO: Ashok Vasudevan
CFO: Sohel Shikari
Executive VP; Sales & Marketing: Meera Vasudevan
VP/VP Sales & Marketing/Sales Staff: Hans Taparia
Estimated Sales: $5.7 Million
Number Employees: 10

10797 Preferred Meal Systems
4135 Birney Ave
Scranton, PA 18507 570-457-8311
Fax: 570-457-9241
Processor and exporter of frozen portion control lunches for airlines and schools
Executive Director: Bob Keen
Director Technology Services: Richard Ludt
Estimated Sales: $4800000
Number Employees: 250-499
Sq. footage: 100000
Type of Packaging: Food Service, Private Label

10798 Preferred Milks
1208 N Swift Rd
Addison, IL 60101-6104 630-678-5300
Fax: 630-678-5311 800-621-5046
info@oxydry.com www.oxydry.com
Processor and exporter of dairy products including powdered milk and egg extender blends
Manager: Dan Hoberg
Sales Manager: Donald Kelly, Jr.
Plant Manager: Samuel Vergara
Estimated Sales: $ 20 - 50 Million
Number Employees: 20-49
Sq. footage: 15000
Parent Co: Kelly Flour Company
Type of Packaging: Food Service, Private Label
Brands:
Hi-Bak
Kel-Yolk

10799 Premier Beverages
5301 Legacy Drive
Plano, TX 75024-3109 972-547-6295
Beverages
COO: Robert O'Brien
VP Sales: Scott Corridean
Estimated Sales: Under $500,000
Number Employees: 1-4

10800 Premier Blending
816 E Funston St
Wichita, KS 67211 316-267-5533
Fax: 316-267-6426
Processor of breadings, spice blends and mixes including sauce, corn dog, hushpuppy, fritter, funnel cake, biscuit, muffin, batter, gravy and drink mixes
President/CEO: Peggy Moore
National Sales Manager: Terry Gould
Purchasing Manager: Reatha Stucky
Estimated Sales: $20-50 Million
Number Employees: 50-99
Sq. footage: 90000
Type of Packaging: Food Service, Private Label, Bulk
Brands:
Tasty Crust

10801 Premier Cereals
8621 NE 17th Pl
Clyde Hill, WA 98004 425-451-1451
Fax: 425-451-1451 premierk@nwlink.com
Cereal and cereal flakes
President: Christian F Kongsore
Estimated Sales: $100+ Million
Number Employees: 1-4
Brands:
Premier Cereals

10802 Premier Juices
19321 Us Highway 19 N Ste 405
Clearwater, FL 33764 727-533-8200
Fax: 727-533-8500
jody.marshburn@premierjuices.com
www.premierjuices.com
Fruit juices
Estimated Sales: $ 2.5-5 Million
Number Employees: 1-4

10803 Premier Malt Products
25760 Groesbeck Hwy Ste 103
Warren, MI 48089 586-443-3355
Fax: 586-445-4580 www.premiermalt.com
Processor of malt extracts for baking and home brewing; also, fungal amylase and sequestrants
President: M Stuart Andreas
Estimated Sales: $1500000
Number Employees: 5-9
Type of Packaging: Consumer, Food Service, Bulk
Brands:
Diamalt
Premose

10804 Premier Meats
4013 Brandon Street SE
Calgary, AB T2G 4N5
Canada 403-287-3550
Fax: 403-287-3553
Processor/exporter of boxed, portion-controlled, fresh and frozen meats including beef, veal and pork
President: E Chaikowski
Number Employees: 20-49
Type of Packaging: Consumer, Food Service, Bulk

10805 Premier Nutrition
6215 El Camino Real
Suite 101
Carlsbad, CA 92009 760-929-9995
Fax: 760-929-9350 888-836-8977
info@premiernutrition.com
www.premiernutrition.com
Organic nutrition products
Owner: Karry Law
Estimated Sales: $ 5 - 10 Million
Number Employees: 10-19
Type of Packaging: Consumer, Private Label, Bulk
Brands:
Odyssey
Premier Nutrition
Premier Shots
Rocket Shot
Twisted Brand

10806 Premier Packing Company
P.O.Box 81498
Bakersfield, CA 93380-1498 661-393-3320
Fax: 661-392-0799 www.grimmway.com
Grower, packer and shipper of produce including carrots, citrus, tree fruit, grapes and apples
President: Tom Moore
Plant Manager: Steven Pryor
Number Employees: 250-499
Parent Co: Shell California Products
Type of Packaging: Consumer, Food Service, Private Label, Bulk
Brands:
Chef's Delight
Medallion

10807 **Premier Roasters**
400 Allan Street
Daly City, CA 94014-1637 415-337-4040
Fax: 415-333-7692 info@premierroasters.com
Coffee
President: Dan Wallace
CFO: Jeff Day
VP Marketing: Tom Rector
Operations Manager: Phil Maloney
Estimated Sales: $ 20-50 Million
Number Employees: 20-49
Type of Packaging: Private Label
Brands:
S&W Coffee

10808 **Premier Smoked Fish Company**
3185 Tucker Rd
Bensalem, PA 19020 215-639-4569
Fax: 305-625-5528 800-654-6682
info@seaspecialties.com
www.seaspecialties.com
Processor of fish including smoked salmon, cured and herring
Owner: J Purner
COO: David Donahue
Controller: John Cicero
Plant Manager: David Sperry
Estimated Sales: $5200000
Number Employees: 5-9
Sq. footage: 24000
Parent Co: SeaSpecialties
Brands:
Mama's
Seaspecialties

10809 **Premiere Pacific Seafood**
111 W Harrison St
Seattle, WA 98119 206-286-8584
Fax: 206-286-8810 johnh@prempac.com
Manufacturer of fresh prepared fish
President: Douglas Forsyth
Estimated Sales: Under $500,000
Number Employees: 15
Type of Packaging: Bulk
Brands:
Ocean Phoenix
Premiere Pacific

10810 **Premiere Packing Company**
P.O.Box 815
Greenacres, WA 99016-0815 509-926-6666
Fax: 509-926-3300 888-239-5288
nuts@thenutfactory.com www.thenutfactory.com
Snack foods, nuts, chocolates
President: Gene Cohen
Estimated Sales: Below $ 5 Million
Number Employees: 5-9

10811 **Premiere Seafood**
257 Midland Avenue
Lexington, KY 40508-1978 606-259-3474
Fax: 606-389-9390
Seafood
President: Rex Webb

10812 **Premium Brands**
P.O.Box 785
Bardstown, KY 40004-0785 502-348-0081
Fax: 502-348-5539
kentuckybourbon@bardstown.com
www.kentuckybourbonwhiskey.com
Liquor, beverages
President: Even Kulsveen
Estimated Sales: Less than $1 Million
Number Employees: 10

10813 **Premium Ingredients International US, LLC**
285 E Fullerton Ave
Carol Stream, IL 60188-1886 630-868-0300
Fax: 630-868-0310
sales@premiumingredients.com
www.premiumingredients.com
Food ingredients and aroma chemicals.
President: Donald Thorp
CEO: Richard Thorp
CFO: Donald Cepican
VP: Daniel Thorp
Research/Development Director: Suzanne Johnson
VP Sales/Marketing: Richard Calabrese
Estimated Sales: $30-35 Million
Number Employees: 100
Parent Co: AMC Chemicals
Other Locations:
Premium Ingredients International
Holladay UT
Premium Ingredients International
Ellisville MO
Premium Ingredients International
Cranford NJ
Premium Ingredients Int'l(UK)
London, England

10814 **Premium Meat Company**
1100 W 600 N
Brigham City, UT 84302 435-723-5944
kdprice@mywebnet.com
Processor of meat including beef, pork and lamb
President: Douglas W Price
Sales Manager: David Wells
Estimated Sales: $ 3 - 5 Million
Number Employees: 5-9

10815 **Premium Standard Farms**
13301 US Highway 87
Dalhart, TX 79022-9408 806-377-3289
Fax: 806-377-6390 webmaster@psfarms.com
www.psfarms.com
Premium pork

10816 **(HQ)Premium Standard Farms**
Highway 65 North
Princeton, MO 64673 660-748-4647
Fax: 660-748-7341 webmaster@psfarms.com
www.psfarms.com
Processor of pork
Chairman: Michael Zimmerman
CEO: John Meyer
VP & General Counsel: Gerald Schulte
Director: William Patterson
VP Communications & Public Affairs: Charles Arnot
Estimated Sales: $500+ Million
Number Employees: 4000
Type of Packaging: Food Service
Other Locations:
Milan MO
Clinton NC
Princeton MO
Dalhart TX
Brands:
Premium Standard

10817 **Premium Water**
PO Box A
Orange Springs, FL 32182-1003 352-546-2052
Fax: 352-546-1402 800-243-1163
Manufacturer and exporter of spring and distilled bottled water
President: Peter Johnson
GM: Bob McBride
Estimated Sales: $ 5 - 10 Million
Number Employees: 50-99
Sq. footage: 20000
Type of Packaging: Consumer, Food Service, Private Label
Brands:
Acappella

10818 **Premium Waters**
2100 Summer Street NE Suite 200
Minneapolis, MN 55413 612-379-4141
Fax: 612-623-0363 800-332-3332
custserv@premiumwaters.com
www.premiumwaters.com
Processor of water including bottled spring, sparkling and distilled.
President: Greg Nemec
Executive Vice President: Scott Moores
Estimated Sales: $97300000
Number Employees: 500-999
Sq. footage: 16500
Type of Packaging: Consumer, Food Service, Private Label, Bulk
Brands:
CHIPPEWA
CHIPPEWA ICED TEA
CHIPPEWA SPRING WATER
CRYSTAL GLEN
EARTH'S PERFECT

10819 **Premium Waters**
2520 Broadway St NE Ste 100
Minneapolis, MN 55413 612-379-3505
Fax: 612-623-0363 800-243-1163
custserv@premiumwaters.com
www.premiumwaters.com
President: Grep Nemec
Estimated Sales: $ 2.5-$ 5 Million
Number Employees: 50-99
Brands:
Aguazul
Chippewa Spring Water
Crystal Glen
Glacier Clear
Kandiyohi Premium Water

10820 **(HQ)Presco Food Seasonings**
26 Minneakoning Rd
Flemington, NJ 08822 908-782-4919
Fax: 908-782-6993 800-526-1713
info@prescoseasonings.com
www.prescoseasonings.com
Processor of seasonings and spices for sausage and snacks; also, gravy and sauce mixes
President: Simon Statter
VP: Simon Statter
Estimated Sales: $ 20 - 50 Million
Number Employees: 50-99
Type of Packaging: Private Label, Bulk

10821 **Prescott Brewing Company**
130 W Gurley St Ste A
Prescott, AZ 86301 928-771-2795
Fax: 928-771-1115 angpbc1@cableone.net
www.prescottbrewingcompany.com
Beer
President: John Nielsen
CFO: Roxanne Nielsen
Sales Director: Dave Jacobson
Estimated Sales: $ 1-5 Million
Number Employees: 50-99
Brands:
Liquid Amber
Lodgepole Light
Petrified Porter

10822 **President's Choice International**
1 President's Choice Circle
4th Floor, North Tower
Brampton, ON L6Y 5S5
Canada 416-967-2501
888-495-5111
www.presidentschoice.ca
Manufacturer of cookies, cola, biscuits, lasagna, turkey, pizza, coffee, poultry, ice cream and juice
Number Employees: 14
Sq. footage: 5000

10823 **Presque Isle Wine Cellar**
9440 W Main Rd
North East, PA 16428 814-725-1314
Fax: 814-725-2092 800-488-7492
info@piwine.com www.piwine.com
Wine related products
Owner: Doug Moorhead
CFO: Dougles Moorhead
Co-Owner: Laury Bouttcher
Estimated Sales: Below $ 5 Million
Number Employees: 20-49
Type of Packaging: Private Label
Brands:
Presque Isle Wine

10824 **Prestige Proteins**
1101 S Rogers Cir # 1
Boca Raton, FL 33487-2748 561-997-8770
Fax: 561-997-8786 casein@casein.com
www.casein.com
Processor and exporter calcium caseinate, sodium caseinate and potassium caseinate
Owner: Hue Henly
Sales Manager: Tina Thimlar
Estimated Sales: $1-2.5 Million
Number Employees: 1-4
Sq. footage: 50000
Type of Packaging: Consumer, Food Service, Private Label, Bulk
Brands:
Prestige Proteins

10825 **(HQ)Prestige Technology Corporation**
1101 S Rogers Cir Ste 1
Boca Raton, FL 33487 561-997-8770
Fax: 561-495-7043 888-697-4141
casein@casein.com www.casein.com
Processor and importer of regular and rennet casein; also, sodium and calcium caseinates
President: Hugh Henley
Director of Sales: Tina Thimlar

Estimated Sales: $18 Million
Number Employees: 50
Sq. footage: 10000
Other Locations:
Prestige Technology Corp.
Minsk
Brands:
Prestige Proteins
Qualcoat

10826 **Presto Avoset Group**
PO Box 1086
Claremont, CA 91711-1086 909-399-0062
Fax: 909-399-1162 thigh@rich.com
Nondairy toppings and icings
Brands:
PASTRY PRIDE
PASTRY PRO
POUR N' PERFORMANCE
POUR N' WHIP
PRIDE
QWIP
TRES CREMAS

10827 **Preston Farms**
3055 W Bradford Rd NE
Palmyra, IN 47164 812-364-6123
Fax: 812-364-6105 866-767-7464
sales@prestonfarms.com www.prestonfarms.com
Growers, processors and packers of specilly selected hybrid popcorn
CEO: Raymond Preston
President: Leigh Anne Preston
Private Label Sales: Charles Shacklette
Estimated Sales: $300,000-500,000
Number Employees: 10-19
Number of Brands: 3
Number of Products: 60
Type of Packaging: Private Label
Brands:
America's Premium
Gettelfinger Select
Heartland U.S.A.
KY POPPERS
Spee-Dee Pop

10828 **Preston Premium Wines**
502 E Vineyard Dr
Pasco, WA 99301 509-545-1990
Fax: 509-545-1098 info@prestonwines.com
www.prestonwines.com
Wines
President: Brett Preston
Estimated Sales: $ 5-9.9 Million
Number Employees: 20-49
Brands:
Preston Premium Wines

10829 **Preston Vineyards**
9282 W Dry Creek Rd
Healdsburg, CA 95448-9134 707-433-3372
Fax: 707-433-5307 800-305-9707
retailsales@prestonvineyards.com
www.prestonvineyards.com
Organic wine, olives, produce and baked goods
Co-Owner: Louis Preston
Co-Owner: Susan Preston
Winemaker: Matt Norelli
Vineyard Manager: Jesus Arzate
Estimated Sales: $ 5-10 Million
Number Employees: 10-19
Brands:
Kuchen

10830 **Pretzels**
123 W Harvest Rd
Bluffton, IN 46714 260-824-4838
Fax: 260-824-0895 800-456-4838
harvestroad@pretzels-inc.com
www.pretzels-inc.com/pretzelsinc.htm
Processor and exporter of pretzels and corn extruded products including cheese curls, corn puffs, crunchy cheese curls and hot barbecue cheese balls.
President: William Huggins
CEO: William Mann
CEO: William Mann
Marketing Director: Chip Manneson
Sales Director: Marvin Sparks
Operations Manager: John Sommer
Purchasing Manager: Steve Huggins
Number Employees: 100-249
Sq. footage: 200000
Type of Packaging: Consumer, Food Service, Private Label, Bulk
Brands:
Harvest Road
William's Corn

10831 **Preuss Bake Shop**
107 N State Street
Waseca, MN 56093-2928 507-835-4320
Bakery

10832 **(HQ)Price Cold Storage & Packing Company**
370 Breaum Road
Yakima, WA 98908 509-966-4110
Fax: 509-966-6749 bob@priceapples.com
www.priceapples.com
Processor, packer and exporter of fresh apples and pears
President: Robert Price
Vice President: Bob Parsley
Sales Director: Chuck Zgutenhorst
Operations Manager: Norm Weathers
Production Manager: Don Khale
Estimated Sales: $25200000
Number Employees: 100-249
Sq. footage: 200000
Type of Packaging: Consumer, Food Service, Private Label, Bulk
Brands:
Gold Medal
Moon
Naches
Panda
Price
Priceless

10833 **Price Seafood**
5737 Highway 56
Chauvin, LA 70344 985-594-3067
Fax: 985-594-7748
Processor of frozen, peeled and dried shrimp
Owner: Norris Price
Principal: Susan Price
Estimated Sales: $500,000- 1Million
Number Employees: 15
Sq. footage: 8200
Brands:
Louisiana
Louisiana Cajun
Ocean Blue

10834 **Price's Creameries**
P.O.Box 3008
El Paso, TX 79923 915-565-2711
Fax: 915-562-8232 www.pricesmilk.com
Processor of milk, ice cream, sherbet, mellorine, cream and ice cream and ice milk mixes
General Manager: Gene Carrejo
Plant Manager: Lonnie Williams
Number Employees: 100-249
Parent Co: Dean Foods Company
Type of Packaging: Consumer
Brands:
Price's

10835 **Pride Beverages**
1887 McFarland Road
Alpharetta, GA 30005-8341 770-663-0990
Fax: 770-663-0091 www.pridebeverages
Juice concentrates
Estimated Sales: $500,000-$1 Million
Number Employees: 1-4

10836 **Pride Enterprises Glades**
500 Orange Avenue Cir
Belle Glade, FL 33430-5221 561-996-1091
Fax: 561-996-8559
Sugarcane
Manager: Peter Venables
Facility Manager: Peter Venables
Estimated Sales: Under $500,000
Number Employees: 5-9

10837 **Pride of Dixie Syrup Company**
P.O.Box 1117
Jonesboro, AR 72403 870-935-2252
Fax: 870-935-9325 800-530-7654
Processor of table syrups for pancakes, waffles and cooking including maple, honey and crystal white flavors
President: David Best
Estimated Sales: $180,000
Number Employees: 1-4
Sq. footage: 5000
Type of Packaging: Consumer, Food Service, Private Label
Brands:
Craft's
Pride of Dixie

10838 **Pride of Sampson**
P.O.Box 289
Clinton, NC 28329 910-592-6188
Fax: 910-592-1204 www.prideofsampson.com
Processor and exporter of sweet potatoes
Manager: Roger Lane
President: George Wooten
Estimated Sales: $ 50 - 100 Million
Number Employees: 50-99
Parent Co: Wayne E. Bailey
Type of Packaging: Consumer, Bulk

10839 **Pride of White River Valley**
P.O.Box 106
Gaysville, VT 05746-0106 802-234-9115
Fax: 802-234-6780
www.whitervervalleycamping.com
Owner: Andrew Smith
Estimated Sales: $300,000-500,000
Number Employees: 1-4

10840 **Priester Pecan Company**
P.O.Box 381
Fort Deposit, AL 36032-0381 334-227-4301
Fax: 334-227-4294 800-277-3226
customerservice@priesters.com
www.priester.com
Processor of pecans, pecan candies and baked goods
President: Ned T Ellis Jr
VP: Ellen Burkett
Marketing Executive: Janice Whittington
Estimated Sales: $5-10 Million
Number Employees: 50-99
Type of Packaging: Consumer, Private Label, Bulk
Brands:
Cloverland

10841 **Prifti Candy Company**
106 Green St
Worcester, MA 01604 508-754-5143
Fax: 508-754-0325 800-447-7438
info@prifti.com www.prifti.com
Candies
Owner: Nick Prifti
Estimated Sales: Less than $500,000
Number Employees: 1-4
Brands:
Prifti Candy

10842 **Prima Foods International**
Po Box 2208
Silver Springs, FL 34489 352-732-9148
Fax: 352-732-0625 800-774-8751
primafoods@worldnet.att.net
www.primafoods.com
Processor of syrup, cocktail mixes, drink base powder and liquids, tropical fruit purees and fruit juice concentrates; importer of tropical fruit purees and juice concentrates; exporter of drink bases and milk replacers
President: Hector Viale
Vice President: Celeste Viale
VP Sales: Mary Lou Sharp
Estimated Sales: $1 Million
Number Employees: 8
Sq. footage: 10000
Type of Packaging: Food Service, Private Label, Bulk
Brands:
Flat Wood Farm
Prima Naturals

10843 **Prima Kase**
W6117 County Road C
Monticello, WI 53570 608-938-4227
Fax: 608-938-1227 kase@madison.tds.net
www.primakase.com
Processor of gouda, fontina, wheel Swiss, sweet-style Swiss and havarti cheeses
President: Steve McKeon
CEO: Steve McKeon
Estimated Sales: $ 2.5-5 Million
Number Employees: 5-9
Type of Packaging: Consumer, Food Service, Private Label, Bulk
Brands:
Prima Kase

10844 **Prime Cut Meat & Seafood Company**
2601 N 31st Ave
Phoenix, AZ 85009-1522 602-455-8834
Fax: 602-455-8711
Meat, seafood
President: Dave Poppen
VP/Treasurer: Linda Poppen
Estimated Sales: $ 50 - 100 Million
Number Employees: 20-49

10845 **Prime Food Processing Corporation**
300 Vandervoort Ave
Brooklyn, NY 11211 718-963-2323
Fax: 718-963-3256 888-639-2323
Processor of Chinese dumplings and egg rolls
President: Yee Chan
CEO: Albert Chan
Accounting Manager: Tommy Ng
Estimated Sales: $13 Million
Number Employees: 80
Sq. footage: 10000
Type of Packaging: Consumer, Food Service, Private Label, Bulk
Brands:
Prime Food

10846 **Prime Ingredients**
280 N Midland Ave Ste 316
Saddle Brook, NJ 7663 201-791-6655
Fax: 201-791-4244 888-791-6655
info@primeingredients.com
www.primeingredients.com
Manufacturer of fresh and frozen gourmet dessert, dips and sauces. Also manufactures cheese, creamers, mixes, glazes, oils, margarines; exporter of olive oil
Director: Christopher Walsh
Estimated Sales: Below $5 Million
Number Employees: 10-19
Sq. footage: 20000
Type of Packaging: Bulk

10847 **Prime Ostrich International**
8702a 98th Street
Morinville, AB T8R 1K6
Canada 780-939-3804
Fax: 780-939-4888 800-340-2311
Processor and exporter of ostrich including whole carcasses, jerky, deli and portion controlled cuts and meat pies
President: James Danyluik
Marketing Director: Michelle Danyluik
Number Employees: 5-9
Type of Packaging: Consumer, Food Service, Private Label, Bulk

10848 **Prime Pak Foods**
2076 Memorial Park Dr
Gainesville, GA 30504 770-536-8708
Fax: 770-536-1638
Processor beef, pork, veal, poultry and barbecue meat products including burgers, patties, meat loaf, breaded choppettes, chicken breasts, chicken and beef fry steak, cubed steaks, chicken tenders and livers, hot wings, etc.; alsochili with beans
President: Todd Robson
Vice President: Milton Robson
Estimated Sales: $23.5 Million
Number Employees: 157

10849 **Prime Pastries**
370 North Rivermed Road
Concord, ON L4K 3N2
Canada 905-669-5883
Fax: 905-669-8655 smuchnik@primus.ca
Pastries
President: Steven Muchnik
CFO: Ashley Berman
Brands:
Prime Pastries

10850 **Prime Pastry**
22 2nd Avenue
Brooklyn, NY 11215-3102 888-771-2464
Fax: 718-237-1988
Processor, importer and exporter of frozen baked goods
VP Sales/Marketing: Russ Slotnick
Estimated Sales: $ 3 - 5 Million
Number Employees: 10-19
Parent Co: Prime Group
Type of Packaging: Food Service, Private Label, Bulk
Brands:
Prime Pastry

10851 **Prime Produce**
350 N Cypress St
Orange, CA 92866-1028 714-771-0718
Fax: 714-771-0728 yair@prime-produce.com
www.prime-produce.com
Processor of avocados
President: Avi Crane
Business Development Manager: Yair Crane
Sales Manager: Gahl Crane
Operations/Ripening Manager: Miguel Guzman
Estimated Sales: $5-10 Million
Number Employees: 20-49
Type of Packaging: Consumer, Food Service, Private Label, Bulk

10852 **Prime Smoked Meats**
220 Alice St
Oakland, CA 94607 510-832-7167
Fax: 510-832-4830 www.primesmoked.com
Processor, wholesaler/distributor and exporter of cured and smoked pork products including fresh and frozen
President: Steve Sacks
General Manager: Dave Andes
Office Manager: Ed Pastana
Plt. Mgr.: Dave Andes
Estimated Sales: $5897842
Number Employees: 10-19
Sq. footage: 12000
Type of Packaging: Consumer, Food Service, Private Label, Bulk
Brands:
James
Prime

10853 **(HQ)Primer Foods Corporation**
P.O.Box 373
Cameron, WI 54822-0373 715-458-4075
Fax: 715-458-4078 80- 3-5 24
tkunz@primerafoods.com
www.primerafoods.com
Manufacturer of Egg products, encapsulated ingredients, specialty gums, maltodextrins and syrup solids, tomato powders, fudge and carmel concentrates, eggStreme Options
President/CEO: Ron Ashton
Chief Executive Officer: John Ashton
Chief Financial Officer: Julie Foss
Finance Executive: James Anderson
Quality Control: Kristen Zuzek
VP Sales/Marketing: Rolf Rogers
Director Operations: Tom Brown
Estimated Sales: $100 Million
Number Employees: 118
Sq. footage: 105000
Other Locations:
Primera Foods
Penham MN
Primera Foods
Stockton IL
Primera Foods
Hayfield MN
Primera Foods
Faribault MN
Primer Foods
Altura MN
Brands:
EGGSTREME BAKERY MIX 100
EGGSTREME OPTIONS
EGGSTREME YOLK
EGGSTREME-WE 300
INSTA THICK
MALTA GRAN
PRIME CAP
RICE COMPLETE
RICE PRO 35
RICE TRIN
TAPI
TOMATO MAX

10854 **Primera Foods**
612 S 8th St
Cameron, WI 54822 715-458-4075
Fax: 715-458-4078 800-365-2409
sales@primerafoods.com
www.primerafoods.com
Agglomeration, spray drying, eggs, vegetables, encapsulation
President/CEO: Jon Luikart
Finance Executive: James Anderson
Sales Manager: Leslie Rask
Estimated Sales: $ 20-50 Million
Number Employees: 20-49

10855 **Primera Meat Service**
21649 N Stuart Place Rd
Harlingen, TX 78552-1962 956-423-4846
Fax: 956-423-3085
Processor of meat products
Owner: Javier Abundiz
Estimated Sales: $ 3 - 5 Million
Number Employees: 5-9

10856 **Primex International Trading Corporation**
5777 W Century Blvd
Suite 1485
Los Angeles, CA 90045 310-568-8855
Fax: 310-568-3336 info@primex-usa.com
www.primex-usa.com
grower and processor of pistachios as well as an international trader and exporter of dried fruits and nuts
President: Ali Amin
Controller: Andirk Sarkesians
COO: Mojgan Amin
Estimated Sales: $184.5 Million
Number Employees: 25

10857 **Primo Foods**
56 Huxley Rd
Toronto, ON M9M 1H2
Canada 426-741-9300
Fax: 416-741-3766 800-377-6945
uliassm@cox.net www.primofoods.ca
Primo pasta, primo can tomatoes, primo can beans, primo pasta sauces
VP: Tony Gucciardi
Sales: Phil Ulias
Sq. footage: 100000
Type of Packaging: Consumer, Food Service, Private Label

10858 **Primo Foods**
56 Huxley Road
Toronto, ON M9M 1H2
Canada 416-741-9300
Fax: 416-741-3766 800-377-6945
Manufacturer of pasta
Plant Manager: Gabe Soffiaturo
Parent Co: Nabisco
Type of Packaging: Consumer, Food Service

10859 **Primo Piatto**
7300 36th Ave N
Minneapolis, MN 55427 763-531-9194
Fax: 763-536-0100 www.dakotagrowers.com
Pasta, pasta products and services
President: Tim Dodd
Executive: Tom Mac Cani
Estimated Sales: $100+ Million
Number Employees: 100-249

10860 **Primos Northgate**
2323 Lakeland Dr
Flowood, MS 39232-9514 601-936-3701
Fax: 601-936-3797 don@primocafe.com
www.primoscafe.com
Processor of baked products including pies
Owner: Don Primos
President: Peter Primos
CEO: Peter Primos
Estimated Sales: $500,000 appx.
Number Employees: 20-49
Type of Packaging: Consumer
Brands:
Primos

10861 **Primrose Candy Company**
4111 W Parker Ave
Chicago, IL 60639 773-276-9522
Fax: 773-276-7411 800-268-9522
shawn@primrosecandy.com
www.primrosecandy.com
Processor and exporter of candy including bagged, filled, fund raising, Halloween, hard and rock; also, lollypops and popcorn specialties
President: Mark Puch
CEO: Mark Puch
VP Sales/Marketing: Richard Griseto

Estimated Sales: $27,800,000
Number Employees: 100-249
Sq. footage: 95000
Type of Packaging: Consumer, Food Service, Private Label, Bulk
Brands:
HUNKEY DOREY
IBC ROOT BEER BARRELS
RICH & CREAMY CARAMELS
TRADITIONAL SALTWATER TAFFY

10862 **Prince Michael Vineyards**
154 Winery Ln
Leon, VA 22725-2511 540-547-3707
Fax: 540-547-3088 800-869-8242
info@princemichael.com
www.princemichel.com
Wine
Owner: Terry Holzman
Estimated Sales: $ 5-10 Million
Number Employees: 20-49

10863 **Prince of Peace Enterprises**
3536 Arden Rd
Hayward, CA 94545 510-887-1899
Fax: 510-887-1799 800-732-2328
popsf@popus.com www.popus.com
Processor, importer, exporter and wholesaler/distributor of American ginseng, Asian Ginseng, Tea
Owner/President/CEO: Kenneth Yeung
VP Finance: Agnes Tsang
VP: Lolita Lim
National Sales Manager: Mike Jarrett
Purchasing: Maria Wong
Estimated Sales: $11200000
Number Employees: 63
Sq. footage: 72774
Brands:
GX POWER
HAZELNUT
JAMAICAN GOLD
MOCHA
NATURE SOOTHE
NEW JAMAICAN GOLD CAPPUCCINO
PRINCE OF PEACE
PRINCE OF PEACE HAWAIIAN
TIGER BALM ANALGESIC OITMENTS

10864 **Princeville Canning Company**
606 S Tremont St
Princeville, IL 61559-9468 309-385-4301
Fax: 309-385-2696 www.senecafoods.com
Manufacturer and exporter of canned vegetables including asparagus, pumpkins, green beans, corn and peas; also, salads including German potato, 3/4 bean and garden
Manager: Wally Hochsprung
Plant Manager: David Stoner
Estimated Sales: $10-20 Million
Number Employees: 100-249
Sq. footage: 160000
Parent Co: Owatonna Canning Company
Type of Packaging: Consumer, Food Service, Private Label

10865 **Pristine Foods**
2508 Gates Cir
Baton Rouge, LA 70809-1028 225-926-4677
Fax: 225-927-3819
General groceries
Estimated Sales: $480,000
Number Employees: 1-4
Type of Packaging: Consumer

10866 **Private Harvest**
5009 Windplay Dr
Suite 2
El Dorado Hills, CA 95762-9316 916-933-7080
Gourmet sauces and spreads.
President: Lynn Lok
Manager: Bonnie Ewing
Estimated Sales: $ 5-10 Million
Number Employees: 10
Parent Co: Private Harvest
Type of Packaging: Private Label
Brands:
Bobby Flay
Private Harvest
Private Harvest Bobby Flay
Private Harvest Tuscan Hills
Tuscan Hills

10867 **Private Harvest GourmetSpecialities**
2617 S Main St
Lakeport, CA 95453-5650 707-263-0694
Fax: 707-263-8362 800-463-0594
info@privateharvest.com
www.privateharvest.com
Produces pasta, BBQ, tartar and steak gourmet sauces
Owner: Kurt Frese
Estimated Sales: $ 50 - 100 Million
Number Employees: 20-49
Type of Packaging: Private Label

10868 **Private Label Foods**
1680 Lyell Ave
Rochester, NY 14606 585-254-9205
Fax: 585-254-0186 info@privatelabelfoods.com
www.privatelabelfoods.com
Processor and contract packager of barbecue, spaghetti and hot sauces, salad dressings, salsa and marinades
President: Frank Lavorato
VP: Bonnie Lavorato
Estimated Sales: $ 4 Million
Number Employees: 10-19
Sq. footage: 50000
Type of Packaging: Food Service, Private Label

10869 **Pro Form Labs**
P.O.Box 626
Orinda, CA 94563-0576 925-299-9000
Fax: 925-299-9004 info@proformlabs.com
www.proformlabs.com
Processor and exporter of health products including nutritional supplement powders, vitamins, weight control and sports nutrition tablets, capsules and powders; also, herbal tablets, capsules and powders
President: Doug Gillespie
Customer Service: Kellie Henry
Purchasing Agent: Alex Gillespie
Estimated Sales: $ 3 - 5 Million
Number Employees: 1-4
Sq. footage: 25000
Parent Co: Gillespie & Associates
Type of Packaging: Consumer, Food Service, Private Label, Bulk
Brands:
Healthbody
Juice-Mate
Naturslim

10870 **Pro Portion Food**
217 N Main Street
Sayville, NY 11782-2512 631-567-4494
Fax: 631-567-1636 elhayes1643@aol.com
Health and dietetics foods
President: Rhoda Rubin
Estimated Sales: $ 5-10 Million
Number Employees: 15

10871 **Pro. Pac. Labs**
P.O.Box 9691
Ogden, UT 84409 801-621-0900
Fax: 801-621-0930 888-277-6722
general@propaclabs.com www.propaclabs.com
Custom contract manufacturer of dietary supplements including herbs, vitamins and minerals
President: Lew Wheelwright
CEO: Kim Wheelwright
Estimated Sales: $9 Million
Number Employees: 100
Type of Packaging: Consumer, Private Label, Bulk

10872 **Proacec USA**
1158 26th Street
Suite 509
Santa Monica, CA 90403-4621 310-996-7770
Fax: 310-996-7772 proacecusa@proacec.com
www.proacec.com
Produces all natural award winning products from our olive orchards in Andalusia, Spain. In addition to gourmet olives and olive oil we also produce and import to US complimentary food items such as, balsamic vinegars, artichokesanchovies, spices and ca
President: Paul Shortt
Estimated Sales: Below $ 5 Million
Number Employees: 10
Number of Brands: 4
Number of Products: 30
Sq. footage: 1000
Type of Packaging: Consumer, Food Service, Bulk
Brands:
CAROLIVA
DON QUIXATE
EL CARMEN
PLANTIO DEL CONDADO

10873 **(HQ)Proctor & Gamble Company**
1 or 2, Proctor & Gamble Plaza
Cincinnati, OH 45201
US 513-983-1100
Fax: 513-983-9369 misc.im@pg.com
www.pg.com
Manufacturer of Pringles potato chips, as well as lines of cleaners and paper products, soaps and personal care items.
Chairman/President/CEO: Bob McDonald
Chief Financial Officer: Jon Moeller
Global External Relations Officer: Christopher Hassall
Vice Chairman/Global Operations: Werner Geissler
Global Product Supply Officer: R Keith Harrison Jr
Estimated Sales: $78 Billion
Number Employees: 127,000
Sq. footage: 15000
Type of Packaging: Consumer
Other Locations:
Procter & Gamble Co.
Boca Raton FL
Brands:
100 CALORIE PACKS
ACTONEL
ALWAYS
ARIEL
BOUNTY
CHARMIN
CLAIROL
CREST
DOWNY
FOLGERS
HEAD & SHOULDERS
IAMS
LENOR
OLAY
PAMPERS
PANTENE
PRINGLES
TIDE
WHISPER

10874 **Prodes**
Avenida Juarez Pte.
No 794
Col. El Porvenir, ZM 59620
Mexico 351-517-3400
Fax: 351-517-3400 pratellesi@hotmail.com
www.santarosa.com.mx
Kosher, dried fruit.
Marketing: Evaldo Pratellesi

10875 **Produce Buyers Company**
7201 W Fort St Ste 93
Detroit, MI 48209 313-843-0132
Manufacturer of produce
President: Salvatore Cipriano
Estimated Sales: $1-3 Million
Number Employees: 1-4

10876 **Producer Marketing Overlake**
PO Box 2631
Olympia, WA 98507-2631 360-352-7989
Fax: 360-352-8076 info@overlakefoods.com
www.overlakefoods.com
Manufacturer of blueberries, strawberries, sliced peaches, Marion blackberries, raspberries
President: Rod Cook
Sales: Paul Askier
General Manager: Bill Whaley
Estimated Sales: $ 5 - 10 Million
Number Employees: 5-9
Parent Co: Overlake Farms
Type of Packaging: Consumer, Food Service, Private Label, Bulk
Brands:
BEE SWEET
OVERLAKE

10877 **Producers Cooperative**
P.O.Box 525
Olathe, CO 81425 970-874-9736
Fax: 970-323-6057 opg@montrose.net
Procesor and exporter of dry edible pinto beans
Manager: Bob Beyer
General Manager: Eob Beyer

Number Employees: 10-19
Sq. footage: 10000
Type of Packaging: Private Label
Brands:
Cowboy
Hub of the Uncompaghre

10878 **Producers Cooperative Oil Mill**
6 SE 4th St
Oklahoma City, OK 73129-1000 405-232-7555
Fax: 405-236-4887
gconkling@producerscoop.net
www.producerscoop.net
Processor and exporter of cottonseed
Manager: James Graves
Ceo: Gary Conkling
Cfo: Ronda Nault
Marketing Director: Jim Freeman
Sales Director: Cary Crawford
Estimated Sales: $ 50 - 100 Million
Number Employees: 50-99
Number of Products: 1

10879 **Producers Dairy Foods**
250 East Belmont
Fresno, CA 93701 559-264-6583
Fax: 559-264-8437
marketing@producersdairy.com
www.producersdairy.com
Manufacturer of milk, yogurt, cottage cheese, ice cream, eggs, butter, water and juice
Chairman: Lawrence Shehadey
President: Richard Shehadey
Vice President: Scott Shehadey
Director of Sales & Marketing: Richie Shehadey
Operations Manager: Steve Shehadey
Estimated Sales: $ 100 Million
Number Employees: 100-249

10880 **Producers Peanut Company**
337 Moore Ave
Suffolk, VA 23434 757-539-7496
Fax: 757-934-7730 800-847-5491
info@producerspeanut.com
www.producerspeanut.com
Processor, importer and exporter of peanut butter and granulated roasted peanuts
President: James R Pond
Plant Manager: Richard Herto
Estimated Sales: $800,000
Number Employees: 20-49
Sq. footage: 36000
Type of Packaging: Food Service, Private Label, Bulk
Brands:
America Farms
New Life
Peanut Kids Peanut Butter
Sunny Day
The Peanut Kids

10881 **Producers Rice Mill**
P.O.Box 1248
Stuttgart, AR 72160-1012 870-673-4444
Fax: 870-673-7394 kglover@producersrice.com
www.producersrice.com
Procesor of rice and soybeans
President/CEO: Keith Glover
VP/Finance & Administration: Kent Lockwood
VP Marketing, Consumer Products: Gary Reifeiss

Sr VP Rice Sales/Marketing: Marvin Baden
VP Operations: Kenny Dryden
Estimated Sales: $500 Million
Number Employees: 700
Type of Packaging: Consumer, Food Service

10882 **Production Techniques Limited**
18 Echelon Place, East Tamaki
PO Box 58-874 Greenmount
Auckland, NZ 2013
New Zealand 64 - 27- 351
Email: nick@ptl.co.nz Phone: 64 (09) 274-3561
Fax: 64 (09) 274-3515
www.ptl.co.nz/
Provides manufacturing and processing equipment for the chocolate, candy, confectionery and bakery industries. Specialized plant manufacturing covers a wide range of plant applications including standard pieces of equipment such asmelters, depositors, enrobers, moulding plants, cooling tunnels, temperers and decorators.
President/Chief Executive Officer: Jim Halliday
Sales & Marketing Manager: Nick Halliday

10883 **Productos Alimenticios Tia Lencha**
Zaragoza 206
Col Centro
Cienega De Flores, NL 64000
Mexico 818-374-0774
Fax: 818-374-2755 aolivares@tialencha.com
www.tialencha.com
Other meat/game/pate.
Marketing: Ambrosio Quiroga

10884 **Productos Del Plata, Inc**
71st 8040 NW
Miami, FL 33166 786-357-8261
Fax: 786-331-7500 info@pdpgroup.us
www.pdpgroup.us
Cookies, tea, frozen baked goods, frozen pasta, grilling sauces, dessert toppings (i.e. fudge sauce, caramel sauce, whipped cream, etc).
Marketing: Mauricio Montero

10885 **Productos La Tradicional, S.A. De C.V.**
Carretera A Huinala Km 1.3
Col. El Milagro
Apodaca, NL 66640
Mexico 818-321-3702
Fax: 818-321-3894 latradicional@terra.com.mx
www.tostadasdelicias.com
Other baked goods.
Marketing: Moises Ansures Gonzalez

10886 **Productos Medellin**
Carretera Central Km. 612
Matehuala, SL 78700
Mexico 488-882-1491
Fax: 488-882-7181
viginiamedellin@lassevillanas.com.mx
www.lassevillanas.com.mx
Caramels, other candy, full-line meat/game/pate.
Marketing: Virginia Medellin Varela
Number Employees: 5

10887 **Productos Tosti Gar**
Juarez No. 315
Col. Centro, CF 65550
Mexico 818-371-2070
Fax: 818-371-9729 tostigar@prodigy.net.mx
www.tostigar.com.mx
Other baked goods.
Marketing: Reynold Garza Chavarria

10888 **Produits Alimentaire**
1186 Rue Du Pont
St Lambert De Lauzon, QC G0S 2W0
Canada 418-889-8080
Fax: 418-889-9730 800-463-1787
Processor of flour, food colors and confectionery items including hard candies and lollypops; importer of syrup
Director: Michel Blouin
Number Employees: 20-49
Sq. footage: 8000
Type of Packaging: Consumer, Food Service, Private Label, Bulk
Brands:
Blouin
Maltee
Pacha
Supreme

10889 **(HQ)Produits Alimentaires Berthelet**
6625 Rue Ernest-Cormier
Laval, QC H7L 2V2
Canada 450-665-6100
Fax: 450-665-7100
Processor of dehydrated foods including soup bases, sauce mixes, seasonings and beverage crystals; exporter of beverage crystals
President: Joe Reda
Vice President: Ivano Scattolin
Marketing Manager: Jimmy Berthelet
Estimated Sales: $79 Million
Number Employees: 250
Sq. footage: 45000
Type of Packaging: Consumer, Food Service, Private Label, Bulk
Other Locations:
Produits Alimentaires Berthel
Blainville PQ
Brands:
Berthelet
Juwong
Le Saucier
McLean
Pasta Fiesta
Privilege
St. Hubert

10890 **Produits Belle Baie**
10 rue du Quai
Caraquet, NB E1W 1B6
Canada 506-727-4414
Fax: 506-727-7166
Packer and exporter of cod, herring, marinated herring roe, ground redfish, shrimp, lobster and crabs
President: Artie Lebouthiller
Number Employees: 250-499
Type of Packaging: Consumer, Food Service

10891 **Produits Ronald**
200 St Joseph Street
St. Damase, QC J0H 1J0
Canada 450-797-3303
Fax: 450-797-2389 800-465-0118
info@p-ronald.com www.p-ronald.com
Processor and exporter of vacuum packed and canned corn-on-the-cob, meat marinades, barbecue sauces, baked beans and bouillons and sauces for fondue, dessert fondue
President: Jean Messier
Vice President/General Manager: Bernard Belanger
Plant Manager: Louis Richard
Purchasing Manager: David Lussier
Number Employees: 100-249
Sq. footage: 40000
Parent Co: A. Lassonde
Type of Packaging: Consumer, Food Service
Brands:
CAMINO DEL SOL
CANTON
MADELAINE
MONT-ROUGR
ROUGEMONT

10892 **Progenix Corporation**
7566 N 72nd Ave
Wausau, WI 54401 715-675-7566
Fax: 715-675-4931 800-233-3356
progenix@progenixcorp.com
Processor, wholesaler/distributor and exporter of ginseng and Wisconsin ginseng, bulk whole root, fiber, prong, powder and extract; also, capsules, teas and gift packaging available
President: Robert Duwe
Number Employees: 20-49
Sq. footage: 13000
Type of Packaging: Consumer, Food Service, Bulk
Brands:
Ameriseng
Wiscon
Wisconsin American Ginseng

10893 **Progress Industries**
270 Sterkel Blvd
Mansfield, OH 44907-1508 419-756-0044
Fax: 419-756-6544
Contract packager of single serving condiment packs and silverware
CFO: Linda Linn
VP: Dan Loguda
Estimated Sales: Under $500,000
Number Employees: 1-4
Type of Packaging: Food Service

10894 **Progressive Flavors**
P.O.Box 517
Hawley, PA 18428-517 805-383-2640
Fax: 805-383-2644 www.progressiveflavors.com
Flavors for food and beverage
President: Norma Schwarz
Estimated Sales: $ 5 - 10 Million
Number Employees: 4
Type of Packaging: Food Service, Bulk

10895 **Progresso Quality Foods**
500 W Elmer Rd
Vineland, NJ 8360 856-691-1565
Fax: 856-794-1574 800-200-9377
www.generalmills.com

Processor of canned soups, bread crumbs, cooking oils and spaghetti sauce
Controller: Robert Buchs
Vice President: Anil Arora
Research & Development: Mounir El Hmamsi
Plant Manager: James Ellis
Estimated Sales: $50 Million
Number Employees: 5-9
Sq. footage: 600000
Parent Co: Pillsbury Company
Type of Packaging: Consumer
Brands:
PROGRESSO

10896 **Project 7, Inc.**
Po Box 96131
Southlake, TX 76092 817-488-9929
Fax: 817-421-1227 info@project7.com
www.project7.com
Organic/natural, other candy.
President: Tyler Merrick
Controller: Paul Luster
Estimated Sales: $330,000
Number Employees: 6

10897 **Proliant**
2425 SE Oak Tree Ct
Ankeny, IA 50021 800-466-7317
Fax: 515-289-5110 craig.joy@proliantinc.com
www.proliantinc.com
Protein sciences, including meat stocks, broths, flavors, fats, extracts and enhancers
President: Wally Lauridsen
Regional Sales Manager: Craig Joy
Brands:
Proliant

10898 **Proliant Meat Ingredients**
1347 Highway 44
Harlan, IA 51537-4803 712-755-2370
Fax: 712-755-2265 800-369-2672
meatingredients@proliantinc.com
www.proliantinc.com
With over 20 years experience in the development and manufacture of quality protein ingredients for the food industry, we at Proliant Meat Ingredients know real. Our ingredients include stocks, broths and extracts; functional meat andpoultry proteins; flavor enhancers; savory flavors; animal fats and tallows and other specialty products. Proliant's ingredients are ideal for meat, savory prepared foods and snack applications. Let us show you the real difference. Visit us atwww.proliantinc.com
VP of Sales: Lori Stevenson
Brands:
MYLOGEL

10899 **Prolimer Foods**
104 Liberte Avenue
Candiac, QC J5R 6X1 450-635-4631
Fax: 450-635-4637 877-535-4631
nicolas@prolimer.ca www.prolimer.com
Frozen baked goods, hors d'oeuvres/appetizers, ready meals/pizza/soup, other seafood, canned or preserved vegetables/fruit, olives.
Marketing: Nicolas Bergeron

10900 **Prolume Biolume**
163 W White Mountain Blvd # D
Lakeside, AZ 85929-7004 928-367-1200
Fax: 928-367-1205 info@prolume.com
www.prolume.com
Food additives that generate their own light, food bioluminescence ingredients
CEO: Bruce Bryan
Co-Founder: Bruce Bryan
Brands:
Prolume

10901 **Promexico**
Camino A Ste Teresa #1679
Jardines Del Padregal, DF 01900
Mexico 555-447-7000
adriana.gonzalez@promexico.gob.mx
www.promexico.gob.mx
Marketing: Adriana Gonzalez

10902 **Promotion in Motion Companies**
PO Box 558
Closter, NJ 07624-0558 201-784-5800
800-369-7391
mail@promotioninmotion.com
www.promotioninmotion.com
Manufacturers and marketers of popular brand name confections, fruit snack and other fine foods.
President/CEO: Michael Rosenberg
Executive Director: Frank McSorley
COO: Basant Dwivedi
Number Employees: 250-499
Type of Packaging: Private Label

10903 **Proper-Chem**
46 Arbor Ln
Dix Hills, NY 11746 631-420-8000
Fax: 631-420-8003
Processor and exporter of vitamins and food supplements
President: Emil Backstrom
Estimated Sales: $ 3 - 5 Million
Number Employees: 10-19
Sq. footage: 20000
Type of Packaging: Consumer, Private Label
Brands:
Goubaud
Proper-Care

10904 **Prosource**
2214 Geneva Road
Alexandria, MN 56308-8995 320-763-2470
Fax: 320-763-7996 www.prosource.net
Bodybuilding and nutritional supplements
Director: Donald Crank
Estimated Sales: $ 2.5-5 Million
Number Employees: '5-9
Brands:
Prosource

10905 **Protano's Bakery**
2301 N 22nd Ave
Hollywood, FL 33020 954-925-3474
Fax: 954-925-3488 guy@protano.com
www.protano.com
Bakery products
Owner: Guy Protano Jr
Treasurer: Guy Protano
Plant Manager: Bob Woodmancy
Estimated Sales: $ 5-10 Million
Number Employees: 50-99

10906 **Protein Palace**
7273 W Waterford Road
Hartford, WI 53027-9782 262-673-2698
Cheese

10907 **Protein Products Inc**
1002 MacArthur Rd
Whitehall, PA 18052 978-689-9083
Fax: 978-975-4325 800-776-8422
sales@proteinpro.com www.proteinpro.com
Processor and exporter of hydrolyzed proteins and fish gelatin
President: Peter Noble
Sales: Chris Gorski
Type of Packaging: Bulk

10908 **Protein Research Associates**
1852 Rutan Dr
Livermore, CA 94551-7635 925-243-6300
Fax: 925-243-6308 800-948-1991
info@proteinresearch.com
www.proteinresearch.com
Processor and exporter of nutritional, amino acid and vitamin/mineral supplements; also, consultant for new product development specializing in nutritional supplements
President: Robert Matheson
Director: Theodore Aarons
VP Operations: Daniel Aarons
Estimated Sales: $5-10 Million
Number Employees: 5-9
Number of Products: 12
Sq. footage: 33000
Type of Packaging: Private Label, Bulk

10909 **Protient**
351 Hanson Way
Woodland, CA 95776 651-638-2600
Fax: 651-697-0997 sengler@protient.com
www.protient.com
Manufacturers of quality whey and soy proteins, protein hydrolysates and proprietary protein blends.
President: K Kachadurian
CFO: Tent Macoy
CEO: Todd Watson
Quality Control: Tom Yezzi
Market Development Specialist: Cheryl Reid
Sr Sales Manager: Kris Hanson
Estimated Sales: $ 5-10 Million
Number Employees: 20-49
Brands:
Protient

10910 **Protient (Land O Lakes)**
P.O.Box 64101
St Paul, MN 55164-0101 651-481-2068
Fax: 507-334-8695 800-328-9680
www.landolakesinc.com
Processor of dry cream powders, margarine and spreads
President: Christopher Policinsky
Plant Manager: Steve Fiedler
Number Employees: 50-99
Parent Co: Land O'Lakes
Type of Packaging: Consumer

10911 **Protos Foods**
449 Glenmeade Rd
Greensburg, PA 15601-1170 724-836-1802
Fax: 724-836-3895 protos@protos-inc.com
www.lindwood.com
Manufacturer of Ostrich meats
President: Logan Dickerson
Number Employees: 5-9
Type of Packaging: Food Service, Private Label, Bulk
Brands:
OSTRIM #1 SPORTS MEAT SNACK
OSTRIM OSTRICH SAUTE

10912 **Providence Cheese**
49 Rotary Dr
Johnston, RI 2919 401-421-5653
Fax: 401-421-3870
Pasta, cheese
President/Owner: Wayne Wheatley
Estimated Sales: Less than $500,000
Number Employees: 1-4
Type of Packaging: Private Label

10913 **Provimi Foods, Inc**
W2103 County Road VV
Seymour, WI 54165 920-833-6861
Fax: 920-833-9850 800-833-8325
info@provimifoods.com www.provimifoods.com
Processor and exporter of fresh and frozen veal and hides
President/CEO: Dan Schober
CFO: Rod Mackenzie
VP Administration: Debra McPherson
Sales Executive: Mike Wilson
VP Human Resources: Diane Bunkelman
Operations Executive/Quality Control: Bruce Achten
Plant Manager: Steve McDermid
Purchasing Director: Rob Deau
Estimated Sales: $29 Million
Number Employees: 100
Sq. footage: 56000
Type of Packaging: Consumer, Food Service, Private Label, Bulk
Brands:
Provimi

10914 **Provost Packers**
5340 49th Avenue
PO Box 570
Provost, AB TOB 3S0
Canada 780-753-2415
Fax: 780-753-2413 bouma@planet.net.com
Processor of fresh beef and pork
President: Bernard Bouma
Sales Manager: Lyle Bouma
Estimated Sales: C
Number Employees: 10-19
Sq. footage: 82000
Type of Packaging: Consumer, Food Service, Private Label, Bulk
Brands:
Dutch Brothers
Provost Packers

10915 **Pruden Packing Company**
336 Carolina Rd
Suffolk, VA 23434-5814 757-539-8773
Fax: 757-925-4971
Packer and exporter of cured ham and pork shoulder
President: Peter Pruden III
General Manager: K Jones
Contact: Kevin Jones
Plant Superintendent: Terry McNitt

Estimated Sales: $3.0 Million
Number Employees: 5-9
Parent Co: Smithfield Companies
Brands:
Champon
Peanut City
Pruden

10916 **Puebla Foods**
75 Jefferson St
Passaic, NJ 07055 973-473-4494
Fax: 973-473-3854 pueblafoods@aol.com
Processor of corn tortillas, chips and taco shells; importer of Mexican products including jalapenos, hot sauces, dried peppers, tomatillos, Mexican sodas, etc
President: Felix Sanchez
VP: Carmen Sanchez
Human Resources Director: Adolfo Diaz
General Manager: Gabriela Molina
Estimated Sales: $10 Million
Number Employees: 35
Sq. footage: 15000
Brands:
El Ranchito
Mipueblito
Pueblafood

10917 **Pulakos**
2530 Parade St
Erie, PA 16503-2034 814-452-4026
Fax: 814-456-4876 info@pulakoschocolates.com
www.pulakoschocolates.com
Processor of confectionery including chocolates
President: George Pulakos
VP/Treasurer: J Pulakos
Plant Manager: Pete Skelton
Estimated Sales: $1300000
Number Employees: 20-49
Sq. footage: 16000
Type of Packaging: Consumer, Food Service, Private Label

10918 **Pulmuone Wildwood**
2315 Moore Ave
Fullerton, CA 92833-2510 641-236-5170
www.pulmuonewildwood.com
Manufacturer of tofu products.
President: Y C Kang
Number Employees: 119
Sq. footage: 3320

10919 **Purato's**
3235 16th Ave SW
Seattle, WA 98134-1023 206-762-5400
Fax: 206-767-4088 www.puratos.com
Processor of wheat flour including tortilla, pastry and all purpose
Operations Manager: Andy Bebe
Estimated Sales: $ 20 - 50 Million
Number Employees: 20-49
Parent Co: Fisher Mills
Type of Packaging: Food Service, Private Label, Bulk

10920 **Puratos Canada**
520 Slate Dr
Mississauga, ON L5T 0A1
Canada 905-362-3668
Fax: 905-362-0296 info@puratos.ca
www.puratos.com
Processor of dough conditioners, bread bases and mixes, pastry mixes, custards, fruit compounds and fillings, glazes and chocolate products including ganache; importer of compounds
President: Eddy Van Belle
Number Employees: 20-49
Sq. footage: 40000
Parent Co: Puratos NV
Type of Packaging: Food Service, Private Label, Bulk
Brands:
Biopur

10921 **Pure Dark**
800 High Street
Hackettstown, NJ 07840 973-856-1899
dawn.gallagher@effem.com
www.puredark.com
Cocoa/baking chocolate, chocolate bars, full-line chocolate, other chocolate, gift packs.
Marketing: Dawn Gallagher

10922 **Pure Extracts Inc**
59 Remington Blvd
Ronkonkoma, NY 11779 631-588-9727
Fax: 631-588-9729 info@buyextracts.com
www.pureextracts.us
Manufacturer of herbal extracts
Chairman/President: Gurjeet Bajwa
Manager: Nat Patel
Owner/Sales Exec: Joe Singh
Estimated Sales: $500,000
Number Employees: 5
Number of Products: 42
Sq. footage: 3000
Type of Packaging: Bulk

10923 **Pure Food Ingredients**
514 Commerce Pkwy
Verona, WI 53593 608-845-9601
Fax: 608-845-9628 800-355-9601
stan@itis.com
Processor and importer of canned foods including tomatoes, chiles, jalapenos and olives; also, beeswax and honey
President: Stanley Kanter
Estimated Sales: $1000000
Number Employees: 5-9
Sq. footage: 20000
Type of Packaging: Consumer, Food Service, Private Label, Bulk

10924 **(HQ)Pure Foods**
P.O.Box 989
Sultan, WA 98294 360-793-2241
Fax: 360-793-2485
Processor and exporter of liquid and dry molasses and honey including table, baking and dry; importer of raw honey
President: Michael Ingalls
CEO: Denice Ingalls
Plant Manager: Dan Johnson
Estimated Sales: $5,000,000
Number Employees: 10-19
Sq. footage: 18000
Type of Packaging: Consumer, Food Service, Private Label, Bulk
Brands:
Bear Mountain
Heins
Miller's
Pure Gold

10925 **Pure Gourmet**
719 Bridle Road
Glenside, PA 19038-2005 215-609-4219
Fax: 763-322-7035
kellymacleod@puregourmetfoods.com
www.puregourmetfoods.com
Ice cream/sorbet.
Manager: Kelly Macleod
Estimated Sales: $150,000
Number Employees: 2

10926 **Pure Inventions**
130 Maple Avenue
Suite 3H
Red Bank, NJ 07701 732-842-5777
Fax: 732-842-8422 info@pureinventions.com
Manager: Johanna Cerliglione
Member: Lori Mulligan
Member: Lynne Gerhards
Estimated Sales: $2 Million
Number Employees: 13

10927 **Pure Sales**
660 Baker St # 367
Costa Mesa, CA 92626-4470 714-540-5455
Fax: 714-540-5974 puresales@aol.com
Pasta and related products
President: James Silver
Estimated Sales: Under $500,000
Number Employees: 1-4

10928 **Pure Source**
9750 NW 17th St
Doral, FL 33172-2753 305-477-8111
Fax: 305-477-4002 800-324-6273
info@thepuresource.com
www.thepuresource.com
Processor and exporter of vitamins and antioxidants; importer of raw materials; contract packaging and manufacturing
Owner: Joel Meyer
Estimated Sales: Below $ 5 Million
Number Employees: 10-19
Sq. footage: 70000
Type of Packaging: Consumer, Food Service, Private Label, Bulk
Brands:
Pure Source

10929 **Pure Sweet Honey Farm**
514 Commerce Pkwy
Verona, WI 53593-1841 608-845-9601
Fax: 608-845-9628 800-355-9601
psh@chorus.net www.puresweethoney.com
Processor and importer of honey, maple syrup and molasses.
President: Stanley Kanter
Sales Director: Mark Pelka
Estimated Sales: $470000
Number Employees: 5-9
Sq. footage: 20000
Type of Packaging: Consumer, Food Service, Private Label, Bulk
Brands:
SPRINGHILL

10930 **Pure World Botanicals**
375 Huyler St
South Hackensack, NJ 7606 201-270-2705
Fax: 201-342-8000 custserve@pureworld.com
www.pureworld.com
Botanical extracts
CFO: Sue Ann Merrill
CEO: Jacques Dikansky
Estimated Sales: $ 10-25 Million
Number Employees: 250-499
Number of Products: 22
Sq. footage: 13000
Brands:
Cascara Sagrada Bark USP
USP NF
Veragel

10931 **Pure's Food Specialties**
2929 S 25th Ave
Broadview, IL 60155 708-344-8884
Fax: 708-344-8703 www.puresfood.com
Cookies
President: Elliot Pure
Estimated Sales: Below $ 5 Million
Number Employees: 20-49
Type of Packaging: Bulk

10932 **Pure-Flo Water Company**
7737 Mission Gorge Rd
Santee, CA 92071 619-448-5120
Fax: 619-596-4154 800-787-3356
jodell@pureflo.com www.pureflo.com
Bottled water
President: Bryan Grant
Quality Control: Becky Parker
VP Sales: Douglas Reed
Production Manager: Jerry Linthern
Plant Manager: Duane Anderson
Purchasing Manager: C Grant
Estimated Sales: $ 10-20 Million
Number Employees: 100-249
Sq. footage: 15
Type of Packaging: Consumer, Private Label
Brands:
Pure-Flo Water

10933 **Purely American**
5635 Raby Road
Suite H
Norfolk, VA 23502 757-466-1312
Fax: 757-466-3041 800-359-7873
business@purelyamerican.com
www.purelyamerican.com
Mixes, sauces and marinades, and peanuts.
President: Ray Leard
Estimated Sales: $500,000
Number Employees: 5
Type of Packaging: Private Label
Brands:
Peter's Beach Sauces
Purely American

10934 **Puritan Ice Cream**
301 E Wayne St
Kendallville, IN 46755 260-347-2700
Fax: 260-347-2652 www.atzicecream.com
Ice cream and frozen desserts
President: Terry Atz

Estimated Sales: $ 2.5-5 Million
Number Employees: 10-19

10935 Puritan/ATZ Ice Cream
301 E Wayne St
Kendallville, IN 46755-1457 260-347-2700
Fax: 260-347-2652
customerservice@atzicecream.com
www.atzicecream.com
Processor of ice cream
GM: Terry Atz
GM: Jeff Atz
Estimated Sales: $ 5 - 10 Million
Number Employees: 10-19
Type of Packaging: Consumer, Food Service

10936 Purity Candy Company
422 Market St
Lewisburg, PA 17837 570-524-0823
Fax: 570-524-7793 800-821-4748
www.puritycandy.com
Candy and chocolates
Owner: Margaret Burfeindt
President: Theodore Roosevelt
General Manager Production: Sharon Weiser
Estimated Sales: Less than $500,000
Number Employees: 1-4
Brands:
Purity Candy

10937 Purity Dairies
P.O.Box 100957
Nashville, TN 37224 615-244-1900
Fax: 615-760-2299
Processor of milk, ice cream, yogurt, cottage cheese, juice, sour cream and heavy cream
Manager: Ann Adcock
Sales Manager: Mike Payne
Number Employees: 250-499
Parent Co: Dean Foods Company
Type of Packaging: Consumer, Food Service

10938 Purity Factories
Po Box 1208
St.John's, NL A1C 5M9
Canada 709-579-2035
Fax: 709-738-2426 800-563-3411
www.purity.nf.ca
Processor and exporter of confectionery products, jams, fruit syrups and biscuits
General Manager: Doug Spurrell
Sales Manager: Gerry Power
Type of Packaging: Consumer, Food Service, Private Label, Bulk

10939 Purity Farms
14635 Westcreek Rd
Sedalia, CO 80135 303-647-2368
Fax: 303-647-9875 800-568-4433
purityfarms@qwest.net www.purityfarms.com
Processor of organic grade AA clarified butter
President: Kathy Feldenkreis
Number Employees: 1-4
Type of Packaging: Consumer, Food Service, Private Label, Bulk
Brands:
Purity Farms Ghee

10940 Purity Foods
2871 Jolly Rd
Okemos, MI 48864-3547 517-351-9231
Fax: 517-351-9391 800-997-7358
purityfoods@voyager.net www.purityfoods.com
Processor, importer and exporter of organic baking mixes, soybeans, dry beans, popcorn, breakfast cereals, flour, buckwheat, spelt, millet, wheat, spelt pasta and sesame and sunflower seeds; importer of figs, dried apricots, raisinshazelnuts, etc
Owner/President: Donald Stinchcomb
Estimated Sales: $5.8 Million
Number Employees: 11
Sq. footage: 12000
Type of Packaging: Consumer, Bulk
Brands:
Erntedank
Purity Foods
Purity Foods Vita-Spelt
Quality America
Vita-Spelt

10941 Purity Foods
2871 Jolly Rd
Okemos, MI 48864-3586 517-351-9231
Fax: 517-351-9391 info@purityfoods.com
www.purityfoods.com
Products include beans, grains, seeds; cereals; cookbooks; flours; granola; pastas; pretzels; and sesame sticks.
President: Donald Stinchcomb
Regional Sales Manager: Hezeden Graye
Estimated Sales: $5-10 Million
Number Employees: 5-9
Sq. footage: 15000

10942 Purity Ice Cream Company
700 Cascadilla St
Ithaca, NY 14850 607-272-1545
Fax: 607-272-1546 purityice@aol.com
www.purityicecream.com
Processor of ice cream: pints, half gallons and three gallon tubs
President: Bruce Lane
Estimated Sales: $1000000
Number Employees: 20-49
Type of Packaging: Consumer, Food Service

10943 Purity Products
200 Terminal Dr
Plainview, NY 11803 800-471-9206
Fax: 516-767-1722 888-769-7873
customercare@purityproducts.com
www.purityproducts.com
Processor, importer and exporter of sauces, mayonnaise, vinegar, mustard, salad dressings, vegetable oils, jellies, pickles, etc., also; a complete line of cleaning compounds, flavors, extracts and emulsions
President: William Schroeder
CFO: Bruce Morecroft
Marketing: Al Rodriquez
Sales VP: Al Rodriquez
Operations: Ricky Montejo
Plant Manager: Rick Montejo
Purchasing Director: Charles Menezes
Estimated Sales: $ 1 - 3 Million
Number Employees: 20-49
Sq. footage: 100000
Parent Co: Sea Specialties Company
Type of Packaging: Food Service, Private Label, Bulk
Brands:
Chef's Choice
Cheryl Lynn
Ideal
Purity

10944 Puroast Coffee
1221 Commerce Ave
Woodland, CA 95776 530-668-0976
Fax: 530-668-0989 877-569-2243
info@puroast.com www.pureroast.com
Manufacturer of low acid coffee
President: Carrie Vannuci
CEO: Kerry Sachs
CEO: Kerry Sachs
Public Relations: Beth Goldstene
Operations Manager: Victor Quero
Production Manager: Sally Lopez
Purchasing Manager: Wendy Dial
Estimated Sales: $ 5-10 Million
Number Employees: 10-19
Type of Packaging: Private Label
Brands:
Puroast

10945 Puronics Water Systems Inc
5775 Las Positas Rd
Livermore, CA 94551-7819 925-456-7000
Fax: 925-456-7010 roy.esparza@puronics.com
OR service@puronics.com
www.ionicsfidelity.com
Manufacturer of water treatment systems for the consumer and commercial markets. Puronics solutions include technologies such as water conditioning, filtering, micro-filtration, filtration, carbon filtration, reverse osmosis and ultraviolet disinfection.
Chief Financial Officer: Mark Cosmez II
Director of Commercial Sales: Roy Esparza

10946 Putney Pasta Company
28 Vernon St
Ste 434
Brattleboro, VT 05301 802-257-4800
Fax: 802-875-3322 800-253-3683
info@putneypasta.com www.putneypasta.com
Manufacturer of all-natural frozen pastas inmcluding tortellini, ravioli, agnolotti, fettucine, linguine, angel hair and gnocchi; also sauses. Packaged in retail and food service packs. Branded and private label packer
President: Carol Berry
Estimated Sales: $3 Million
Number Employees: 30
Number of Brands: 1
Number of Products: 35
Sq. footage: 42000
Type of Packaging: Consumer, Food Service, Private Label
Brands:
Putney Pasta

10947 Puueo Poi Factory
265 Kekuanaoa St # D
Hilo, HI 96720-4396 808-935-8435
Fax: 808-934-7762
Processor of Hawaiian food including poi, lau-lau and kalua
President/Treasurer: Gilbert Chang
VP: Okyo Chang
Business Manager: Shirlene Rayoan
Estimated Sales: $500,000
Number Employees: 1-4
Sq. footage: 2750
Type of Packaging: Consumer, Food Service, Private Label, Bulk
Brands:
Puueo Poi

10948 Pyramid Brewing
1201 1st Ave S
Seattle, WA 98134-1238 206-682-3377
Fax: 206-682-8420 host@pyramidbrew.com
www.pyramidbrew.com
Beer and soda
Manager: Alex Krallis
CFO: Eric Peterson
CFO: Wayne Drury
Chairman: George Hancock
Chairman: Martin Kelly
Director Manufacturing: Jack Schaller
Estimated Sales: Under $500,000
Number Employees: 100-249
Type of Packaging: Private Label
Brands:
Amber Wheat Beer
Best Brown Ale
Hart
Thomas Kemper

10949 Pyramid Juice Company
160 Helman Street
Ashland, OR 97520-1720 541-482-2292
Fax: 541-482-1002 judd@pyramidjuice.com
www.pyramidjuice.com
Processor of organic fruit and vegetable juices
President/CEO: Judd Pindell
VP: Kim Kemske
Estimated Sales: $5-9.9 Million
Number Employees: 8
Sq. footage: 3500
Brands:
Mind's Eye Smart Drinks
Pyramid Juice

10950 Pyrenees French Bakery
717 E 21st St
Bakersfield, CA 93305-5240 661-322-7159
Fax: 661-322-6713 888-898-7159
order@pyreneesbakery.com
www.pyreneesbakery.com
Processor of sour dough bread and rolls; also, French, nine-grain, squaw, rye, whole wheat bread and rolls; Sara Lee fresh bagels and bread distributor
President: Marianne Laxague
CEO: Juanita Laxague
Estimated Sales: Below $ 5 Million
Number Employees: 20-49
Sq. footage: 21500
Brands:
Pyrenees
Sara Lee

10951 **Q Bell Foods**
PO Box 652
Nyack, NY 10960 845-358-1475
Fax: 845-353-5680 bshirazi@qbellfoods.com
www.qbellfoods.com
chocolate wafer rolls and chocolate wafer bars
Marketing: Bahram Shirazi
Estimated Sales: $130,000
Number Employees: 2

10952 **Q Tonic**
45 Main St Ste 850
Suite 516
Brooklyn, NY 11201-8200
Fax: 718-228-8877 info@qtonic.com
www.qtonic.com
tonic water
President/Owner: Jordan Silbert

10953 **Q.E. Tea**
533 Washington Ave Ste 100
Bridgeville, PA 15017 412-221-4444
800-622-8327
qetea@aol.com
Processor, exporter and importer of coffees and teas
President: Paul Rankin
Marketing Manager: Peter Shaffalo
Estimated Sales: $500,000-$1 Million
Number Employees: 5-9
Sq. footage: 12000
Brands:
Hedley's
Q.E.

10954 **QBI**
500 Metuchen Road
South Plainfield, NJ 07080-4810 908-668-0088
Fax: 908-561-9682 jschortz@4qbi.com
www.4qbi.com
Processor, importer and exporter of bioflavonoids, botanical powders and ingredients, herbs, nutraceuticals, antioxidants, diet and sport supplements, fruit and vegetable powders, concentrated extracts, bee pollen, etc
President: Joseph Schortz CPA
VP Finance: Carlos Mendez
Marketing: Joan Naso
Sales Director: Allen Lovitch
International Account Executive: Rena Strauss-Cohen
Plant Manager: Donald Andrejewski
Number Employees: 50-99
Number of Products: 500
Sq. footage: 56000
Type of Packaging: Bulk
Brands:
Phytoflow Direct Compression Herbs

10955 **QST Ingredients, Inc.**
9734-40 6th Street
Rancho Cucamonga, CA 91730 909-989-4343
Fax: 909-989-4334 www.qsting.com
Blended seasonings, ingredients and casings for sausage & pork.
Office Manager: Jill Mauleon

10956 **Quady Winery**
P.O.Box 728
Madera, CA 93639-0728 559-673-8068
Fax: 559-673-0744 800-733-8068
info@quadywinery.com www.quadywinery.com
Wines
President: Andrew Quady
CFO: Laurel Quady
Winemaker: Michael Blaylock
General Manager: Cheryl Russell
Estimated Sales: $ 2.5-5 Million
Number Employees: 10-19
Number of Products: 7
Type of Packaging: Private Label
Brands:
Electra
Elysium
Essensia
Starbound
Sweet Dessert Wine

10957 **Quail Ridge Cellars & Vineyards**
1155 Mee Lane
Saint Helena, CA 94574-9792 707-963-9783
Fax: 707-963-3593 800-706-9463
retail@ruthbench.com www.ruthbench.com
Wine
President and CEO: Phillip Wade
CFO: Anthony Bell
Marketing Director: Michael Stedman
Public Relations: Victoria Olson
Production Manager: Jenel Hageman
Estimated Sales: $ 2.5-5 Million
Number Employees: 10-19
Type of Packaging: Private Label
Brands:
Bell Cellars
Fox Brook
Quail Creek

10958 **Quaker**
617 W Main Street
Barrington, IL 60010-4113 847-382-1980
Fax: 847-382-0685 800-333-8027
erik_bayer@qkgsales.com
Hot and cold cereals, rice cakes and all natural foods
General Sales Manager: Eric Bayer
Sales Director: Jim Coy
General Sales Manager, Natural: Erik Bayer
Estimated Sales: $ 50 - 100 Million
Number Employees: 165
Parent Co: Quaker Oats Company
Brands:
Mother's

10959 **Quaker Bonnet**
175 Allen St
Buffalo, NY 14201-1515 716-884-0435
Fax: 716-885-7245 800-283-2447
liz@quakerbonnet.com www.quakerbonnet.com
Processor of cookies and pastries
President: Liz Kolken
Vice President: Benjamin Kolken
Estimated Sales: Less than $500,000
Number Employees: 5-9
Sq. footage: 4300
Type of Packaging: Consumer, Food Service, Private Label
Brands:
BANANA MOON SNACK LINE
BUFFALO CHIPS
QUAKER BONNET CELERY SEED FRUIT DRE
QUAKER BONNET DESSERT SHELL
QUAKER BONNET ELEPHANT EAR DANISH
QUAKER BONNET SHORTBREAD

10960 **Quaker Maid Meats**
521 Carroll St
Reading, PA 19611 610-376-1500
Fax: 610-376-2678 www.quakermaidmeats.com
Processor of all beef sandwich steaks, hamburger patties, breaded veal patties, raw and precooked veal steaks, and raw and precooked meatballs.
President: Stanley Szortyka
CFO: Andrew Sims
VP: Nancy Rubin
VP Sales: Tom Robinson
Estimated Sales: $ 20-50 Million
Number Employees: 60
Type of Packaging: Consumer, Food Service, Private Label
Brands:
Gina Lina's Meatballs
Mama Lucia's Homestyle Meatballs
Mama Lucia's Italian Style Meatball
Mama Lucia's Sausage Meatballs
Quaker Maid Patties
Quaker Maid Sandwich Steaks

10961 **Quaker Oats Company**
555 W Monroe St
Chicago, IL 60661 312-821-1000
Fax: 312-821-1987 800-367-6287
www.quakeroats.com
Leading manufacturer, processor and exporter of cookies, oats, oatmeal, farina, granola bars, puffed wheat, puffed rice, barley, groats, rice, shredded wheat, pancake syrups and mixes, flour, corn syrups, baking mixes, pasta and cornmeal.
Chairman/President/CEO: Robert Morrison
SVP/Chief Financial Officer: Richard Gunst
Estimated Sales: $1 Billion
Number Employees: 7,846
Parent Co: PepsiCo North America
Type of Packaging: Consumer, Food Service
Brands:
KRETSCHMER WHEAT GERM
QUAKER
QUAKER RICE SNACKS
QUISP CEREAL

10962 **Quaker Oats Company**
418 2nd St NE
Cedar Rapids, IA 52401 319-362-0200
Fax: 319-398-1692 www.quakeroats.com
Processor and exporter of breakfast cereals including corn, oat, puffed wheat, rice and rolled oats; also, grits, barley, corn meal and syrups.
Manager: Roger Vincent
CEO PepsiCo North America: John Compton
Chief Financial Officer: Richard Goodman
SVP/Government Affairs & General Counsel: Larry Thompson
SVP/Corporate Strategy & Development: Wahid Hamid
SVP/Corporate Communications: Tod MacKenzie

EVP/Operations: Hugh Johnston
SVP/Human Resources: Margaret Moore
Plant Manager: Roger Vincent
Purchasing Agent: Mary Jane Suchan
Number Employees: 300
Parent Co: PepsiCo North America
Type of Packaging: Consumer, Food Service, Private Label, Bulk

10963 **Quaker Oats Company**
1703 E Voorhees St
Danville, IL 61834 217-443-4995
Fax: 217-443-8622 www.quakeroats.com
www.pepsico.com
Manufacturer and exporter of breakfast cereals and granola bars
Manager: Patrick Burke
CEO/PepsiCo North America: John Compton
Chief Financial Officer: Richard Goodman
VP: Magie Lacambra
SVP/Corporate Strategy & Development: Wahid Hamid
SVP/Corporate Communications: Tod MacKenzie

EVP/Operations: Hugh Johnston
SVP/Human Resources: Margaret Moore
Plant Manager: Steven Brunner
Estimated Sales: $10 Billion
Number Employees: 600
Parent Co: PepsiCo North America
Type of Packaging: Consumer
Brands:
AUNT JEMINIA
CAP'N CRUNCH
KRETSCHMER WHEAT GERM
LIFE
MOTHER'S NATURAL FOODS
NEAR EAST
QUAKER
QUISP
RICE A RONI

10964 **Quaker Oats Company**
750 Oak Hill Rd
Mountain Top, PA 18707 570-474-3800
Fax: 570-474-3808 800-367-6287
www.quakeroats.com
President/CEO Quaker Foods: Charles Maniscalco
CEO PepsiCo North America: John Compton
Chief Financial Officer: Richard Goodman
SVP/Government Affairs & General Counsel: Larry Thompson
SVP/Corporate Strategy & Development: Wahid Hamid
SVP/Corporate Communications: Tod MacKenzie

EVP/Operations: Hugh Johnston
SVP/Human Resources: Margaret Moore
Plant Manager: Brian Mc Laughlin
Estimated Sales: $ 5 - 10 Million
Number Employees: 100-249
Parent Co: PepsiCo North America
Type of Packaging: Consumer, Food Service
Brands:
AUNT JEMIMA CORN MEAL
AUNT JEMIMA SYRUPS & MIXES
CAP'N CRUNCH
KRETSCHMER WHEAT GERM
LIFE CEREAL
MOTHER'S NATURAL FOODS
NEAR EAST
QUAKER 100% NATURAL GRANOLA
QUAKER GRITS
QUAKER OATMEAL

QUAKER OATMEAL SQUARES
QUAKER OATMEAL TO GO
QUAKER RICE CAKES
QUAKER SNACK BARS
QUAKER SOY CRISPS
QUAKER TOASTED OATMEAL
QUAKER TORTILLA MIXES
QUAKES
QUISP
RICE-A-RONI & PASTA RONI

10965 **Quaker Oats Company**
14 Hunter Street E
Quaker Park
Peterborough, ON K9J 7B2
Canada 705-743-6330
Fax: 705-876-4125 800-267-6287
www.quakeroats.ca
Processor of breakfast cereal
President/CEO Quaker Foods: Charles Maniscalco
CEO PepsiCo North America: John Compton
Chief Financial Officer: Richard Goodman
SVP/Government Affairs & General Counsel: Larry Thompson
SVP/Corporate Strategy & Development: Wahid Hamid
SVP/Corporate Communications: Tod MacKenzie
EVP/Operations: Hugh Johnston
SVP/Human Resources: Margaret Moore
Number Employees: 500-999
Parent Co: PepsiCo North America
Type of Packaging: Consumer, Food Service
Brands:
Quaker

10966 **Quaker Oats Company**
2822 Glenfield Ave
Dallas, TX 75233 214-330-8681
Fax: 214-333-1221 www.pepsico.com
Processor of sports beverages
President/CEO Quaker Foods: Charles Maniscalco
CEO/PepsiCo North America: John Compton
Chief Financial Officer: Richard Goodman
SVP/Government Affairs & General Counsel: Larry Thompson
SVP/Corporate Strategy & Development: Wahid Hamid
SVP/Corporate Communications: Tod MacKenzie
EVP/Operations: Hugh Johnston
SVP/Human Resources: Margaret Moore
Plant Manager: Adrian Oliver
Estimated Sales: $ 100-500 Million
Number Employees: 100-249
Parent Co: PepsiCo North America
Type of Packaging: Consumer

10967 **Quaker Oats Company**
3535 Perlman Drive
Stockton, CA 95206-4203 209-982-5580
Fax: 209-982-5943 www.quakeroats.com
Processor of oatmeal, baking mixes and breakfast cereals
President/CEO Quaker Foods: Charles Maniscalco
CEO PepsiCo North America: John Compton
Chief Financial Officer: Richard Goodman
SVP/Government Affairs & General Counsel: Larry Thompson
SVP/Corporate Strategy & Development: Wahid Hamid
SVP/Corporate Communications: Tod MacKenzie
EVP/Operations: Hugh Johnston
SVP/Human Resources: Margaret Moore
Number Employees: 50-99
Parent Co: PepsiCo North America
Type of Packaging: Consumer

10968 **Quaker Sugar Company**
432 Rodney St
Brooklyn, NY 11211-3482 718-387-6500
Fax: 718-963-2767 info@quakersugar.com
www.quakersugar.com
Processor of sugar
Owner: Harriet Gelfas
Operations Manager: Adam Wechsler
Production Manager: Harry Wechsler
Estimated Sales: $1500000
Number Employees: 20-49
Type of Packaging: Consumer, Bulk
Brands:
Diamond

10969 **Quali Tech**
318 Lake Hazeltine Dr
Chaska, MN 55318 952-448-5151
800-328-5870
www.qualitechco.com
Quali Tech's food division develops and manufacturers high-quality food particulates servicing the varying needs of the best known food companies in America and abroad.
President: Cory Ploen
CEO: Del Ploen
VP: Kye Ploen
Marketing Director: Tim Hennum
Sales: Jeff Ploen
Operations Manager: Mike Hodgens
Number Employees: 75
Sq. footage: 45000
Type of Packaging: Bulk
Brands:
FLAV-R-GRAIN
FLAVOR-ETTES
FLAVOR-LITES
PELL-ETTES
PEPR
SEASON-ETTES

10970 **Qualifresh Michel St. Arneault**
4605 Thibault Avenue
St. Hubert, QC J3Y 3S8
Canada 450-445-0550
Fax: 450-445-5687 800-565-0550
Processor and exporter of fresh and frozen French fries
President: Michelle St. Arneaul
Sales Manager: Christian Bauzrette
Number Employees: 50-99
Type of Packaging: Consumer, Food Service, Private Label
Brands:
Golden Crop
Qualifreeze
Qualifresh

10971 **Quality Alaska Seafood**
1385 Engineer's Cutoff Road
Juneau, AK 99801 907-789-8495
Seafood
President: Lloyd Pukis
Vice President: Brien Pukis

10972 **Quality Assured Packing**
PO Box 55308
Stockton, CA 95205-8808 209-931-6700
Fax: 209-931-0286
qap@qualityassuredpacking.com
www.qualityassured.com
Tomato sauces
President/CEO: Tom Beard
COO: Mark Delameter
VP Finance: Jim Nederostek
Plant Manager: Angel Aiello
Estimated Sales: $ 10-24.9 Million
Number Employees: 60

10973 **Quality Bakery**
PO Box 519
1305 - 7ty Ave
Invermere, BC V0A 1K0
Canada 888-681-9977
Fax: 250-342-4439 888-681-9977
info@healthybread.com www.healthybread.com
Processor of extended shelf-life and preservative-free rye bread
President: Peter Banga
Estimated Sales: $1.1 Million
Number Employees: 6
Sq. footage: 7500
Type of Packaging: Consumer, Food Service, Private Label, Bulk
Brands:
Invermere
Quality Bakery
Yukon Sourdough Recipe

10974 **Quality Bakery Products**
888 E Las Olas Blvd
Fort Lauderdale, FL 33301-2272 954-779-3663
Fax: 954-779-7837 800-590-3663
Processor of bread crumbs, croutons and stuffings
President: David Finch
VP: Davod Finch
Estimated Sales: $2.5-5 Million
Number Employees: 10-19
Type of Packaging: Consumer, Food Service, Private Label, Bulk
Brands:
Quality Hearth

10975 **Quality Bakery/MM Deli**
220 W Street
Port Colborne, ON L3K 4E3
Canada 905-834-4911
Processor of baked goods including bread, buns and cakes
Owner: Cindy Minor-Gibson
Number Employees: 10-19
Sq. footage: 2000

10976 **Quality Beef Company**
25 Bath St
Providence, RI 02908 401-421-5668
Fax: 401-421-8570 877-233-3462
info@qualitybeefcompany.com
www.qualitybeefcompany.com
Processor, wholesaler/distributor and broker of ground beef; wholesaler/distributor of frozen foods and seafood
President: Vincent Catauro Jr
Secretary: William Catauro
Estimated Sales: $ 10 - 20 Million
Number Employees: 20-49
Type of Packaging: Food Service

10977 **(HQ)Quality Brands**
P.O.Box 1450
Deland, FL 32721 386-738-3808
Fax: 386-738-2247 888-676-2700
info@qualitybrands.cc www.qualitybrands.cc
Processor of frozen fruits including apples, blueberries and cherries; also, canned apple juice and fruit and vegetable powders and flakes
Owner: Robbie Roberson
Co-Owner: Joanne Roberson
CFO: Steve Hamilton
VP: Joe Maiz
Estimated Sales: $ 20 - 50 Million
Number Employees: 50-99
Type of Packaging: Food Service
Brands:
Quality Brands

10978 **Quality Candy Company**
525 S Lemon Avenue
DFL Warehouse
Walnut, CA 91789 909-444-1025
Fax: 909-595-4181
customerservice@qcandy.com
www.qcandy.com
Candy
CEO: Pierre Redmond
Estimated Sales: $ 10 - 20 Million
Number Employees: 20-49
Brands:
CHOCO-STARLIGHT
SPI-C-MINT

10979 **Quality Candy Shoppes/Buddy Squirrel of Wisconsin**
1801 E Bolivar Ave
Saint Francis, WI 53235 414-483-4500
Fax: 414-483-4137 800-972-2658
www.qcbs.com
candy
President/Owner: Margaret Gile
CFO: David Reynolds
Estimated Sales: $23.6
Number Employees: 60

10980 **Quality Chef Foods**
5005 C St SW
Cedar Rapids, IA 52404 319-362-9633
Fax: 319-362-3924 800-356-8307
Processor of frozen soups, sauces and entrees
President: Shannon Ashby
Plant Manager: Steve Maddocks
Estimated Sales: $ 10-20 Million
Number Employees: 10-19
Parent Co: Heinz USA
Type of Packaging: Food Service
Brands:
Quality Chef Foods, Inc.

10981 **Quality Chekd Dairies**
1733 Park St Ste 220
Naperville, IL 60563 630-717-1110
Fax: 630-717-1126 mmurphy@qchekd.com
www.qchekd.com
Dairy cooperative with a focus on quality-food safety, dairy training, procurement and marketing
Managing Director: Peter Horvath
CFO: Bruce Tom
Marketing Director: Molly Murphy
Estimated Sales: $ 100-500 Million
Number Employees: 10-19
Brands:
QUALITY CHEKD DAIRY PRODUCTS

10982 **Quality Choice Foods**
601 Magnetic Drive
Toronto, ON M3J 3J2
Canada 416-650-9595
Processor and importer of specialty stuffed pastas, pesto sauces, garlic spreads and sun-dried tomatoes in oil; exporter of gourmet garlic spreads and pesto sauce
Marketing Manager: Adrian Furman
Number Employees: 10-19
Sq. footage: 4500
Type of Packaging: Consumer, Food Service, Private Label, Bulk

10983 **Quality Crab Company**
177 Knobbs Creek Dr
Elizabeth City, NC 27909 252-338-2800
Fax: 252-338-6290 888-411-4410
info@nextdayseafood.com
www.nextdayseafood.com
Fresh, processed and canned crab meats
VP: Russell Barclift
Estimated Sales: $ 5-10 Million
Number Employees: 50-99
Type of Packaging: Private Label
Brands:
Jumbo Lump

10984 **Quality Croutons**
4031 S Racine Ave
Chicago, IL 60609 773-890-2343
Fax: 773-927-8228 800-334-2796
croutons@interaccess.com
www.qualitycroutons.com
Processor of croutons; packager of portion controlled dry foods
President: David M Moore
Marketing/Sales: Deadra Ashford
Production Manager: Keith Taylor
Estimated Sales: $1900000
Number Employees: 20-49
Sq. footage: 35000
Type of Packaging: Food Service, Private Label, Bulk

10985 **Quality Dairy Company**
947 Trowbridge Rd
East Lansing, MI 48823 517-319-4114
www.qualitydairy.com
Milk, ice cream and fruit juices
Manager: Swadhyaya Bey
Estimated Sales: Below $ 5 Million
Number Employees: 5-9
Type of Packaging: Private Label

10986 **Quality Fisheries**
157 Arbor Street
Niota, IL 62358-0146 217-448-4241
Fax: 217-448-4021
niotafishmarket@hotmail.com
www.niotafishmarket.com
Seafood
Owner: Kirby Marsden
Estimated Sales: $1 Million
Number Employees: 1-4

10987 **Quality Foods**
PO Box 1385
San Pedro, CA 90733-1385 310-833-7890
Fax: 310-833-5424 877-833-7890
info@qualitygoods.com www.qualityfoods.com
Premium ethnic cuisine, snacks, fried onions, spices, chutneys, teas, pastes, pickles, BBQ sauces, hot sauces, salsa, dressings, marinades, relishes, pepper sauces, steak sauces, mustard and condiments
Estimated Sales: $ 1-2.5 Million
Number Employees: 5-9
Brands:
California Cuisine
Clara's Kitchen
Cummings & York
Hothothot
Jewel of India
Mariachi
Nara
Nonna D'S
Samos
Sarah's Garden
Simple Nevada
Simply
Skull & Bones
Tara Foods
Tomales Bay
Tombstone

10988 **Quality Foods From the Sea**
173 Knobbs Creek Dr
Elizabeth City, NC 27909 252-338-5455
Fax: 252-338-0311
Processor of seafood
President: William Barclift
VP: Roy Martin III
R&D Director: Rick Durren
Estimated Sales: $11400000
Number Employees: 80
Sq. footage: 24000

10989 **Quality Foods Products**
172 N Peoria St
Chicago, IL 60607-2311 312-666-4559
Fax: 312-666-7133
President: Chris Aralis
Estimated Sales: $ 10 - 20 Million
Number Employees: 10-19

10990 **Quality Ingredients Corporation**
14300 Rosemount Dr
Burnsville, MN 55306 952-898-4002
Fax: 952-898-4421 sales@qic.us
www.qic.us
Manufacturer of dehydrated dairy products including; nonfat milk, dry cream, nondairy creamers, powdered shortening, cultured buttermilks, yogurt, sweet whey, cheeses, flavors and grits. Custom Formulation is available.
President: Isabelle Day
Human Resource Manager: Stewart Flanery
Number Employees: 50-99
Type of Packaging: Food Service, Private Label, Bulk
Other Locations:
Quality Ingredients Facility
Marshfield WI

10991 **Quality Ingredients Corporation**
14300 Rosemount Dr
Burnsville, MN 55306 952-898-4002
Fax: 952-898-4421
tinajamieson@qualityingredients.com
Processor of dehydrated dairy products including nonfat milk, dry cream, nondairy creamers, powdered shortenings, cultured buttermilks, yogurt powders, sweet whey, etc.; also, custom formulation available
President: Isabelle Day
Sales Director: Jane Evans
VP Operations: Elizabeth Maas
Purchasing Manager: Kathey Williams
Estimated Sales: $3600000
Number Employees: 20-49
Sq. footage: 50000
Type of Packaging: Consumer, Food Service, Private Label, Bulk
Brands:
Quali-Cream
Quic Blend
Quic Cheese
Quic Creamer
Quic Whip

10992 **Quality Ingredients Corporation**
P.O.Box 306
Chester, NJ 7930 908-879-2227
Fax: 908-879-2502 800-843-6314
www.qicusa.com
Wholesale food distributor specializing in liquid malt blends, dry malt blends, mold inhibitors, molasses products, bakery powders, dough conditioners, multi-grain blends, emulsifiers and release agents
President: Tom Schmidt Sr
CEO: Diane Schmidt
VP Operations: Tom Schmidt, Jr.
Number Employees: 10-19
Type of Packaging: Food Service, Private Label, Bulk
Brands:
Attaboy
Hawk
Hawkeye
Qic Rise

10993 **Quality Instant Teas**
PO Box 1967
Morristown, NJ 07962-1967 973-257-9450
Fax: 973-257-9370 888-283-8327
garyvorsheim@worldnet.att.net
www.qualityinstantteas.com
Tea mixes and concentrates
President: Gary Vorsheim
Estimated Sales: $ 1 Million
Number Employees: 3
Type of Packaging: Private Label

10994 **Quality Kitchen Corporation**
131 West St Ste 1
Danbury, CT 06810 203-744-2000
Fax: 203-791-2875 officemail@salame.com
Processor and exporter of juices and concentrates including grapefruit and orange
President: Albert J Salame
VP: Peter Bliss
Sales: Jerry McGuire
Estimated Sales: $5000000
Number Employees: 5-9
Type of Packaging: Consumer, Food Service

10995 **Quality Meat Packers**
2 Tecumseth Street
Suite 1
Toronto, ON M5V 2R5
Canada 416-703-7675
Fax: 416-504-6660
Processor of fresh and frozen pork
President: David Schwartz
Estimated Sales: $85 Million
Number Employees: 600
Type of Packaging: Consumer, Food Service, Private Label, Bulk

10996 **(HQ)Quality Meats & Seafood**
P.O.Box 337
West Fargo, ND 58078
Fax: 701-282-0583 800-342-4250
admin@qualitymeats.com
www.qualitymeats.com
Processor and packer of portion cut smoked ham and sausage; also, portion controlled seafood
President: Dan Richard
CEO: Cary Wetzstein
CEO: Cary Wetzstein
Sales Manager: Ron Jansen
Director of Purchasing: Lee McCleary
Estimated Sales: $13000000
Number Employees: 50-99
Type of Packaging: Consumer, Food Service, Bulk
Brands:
Valley Maid

10997 **Quality Naturally! Foods**
18830 San Jose Ave
City of Industry, CA 91748 626-854-6363
Fax: 626-965-0978 888-498-6986
tangrisani@qnfoods.com www.qnfoods.com
Processor and exporter of bakery mixes, icings, fillings, cappuccino and cocoa drinks; custom dry blending, co-packing and formulation; AIB, ISO9001; kosher and organic capabilities
VP: Lincoln Watase
Sales Manager: Jerry Tuma
Number Employees: 50-99
Sq. footage: 56000
Type of Packaging: Food Service, Private Label, Bulk

10998 **Quality Products International**
323 Center St
Little Rock, AR 72201-2603 501-372-2121
Fax: 501-614-7900 www.ecosite.com
Owner: Brad Walker
Secretary: Brenda McKown
Treasurer: Caroline Elliott
Estimated Sales: $ .5 - 1 million
Number Employees: 1-4

10999 **Quality Sausage Company**
1925 Lone Star Dr
Dallas, TX 75212 214-634-3400
Fax: 214-634-2296
Processor, packer, exporter and importer of meat products including meat balls, taco meat, patties, pizza toppings and pepperoni
Chairman: Paul Birinyi
Preaiden: Gene Eisen
CFO: Steven O'Brien
Quality Assurance: Mark Mar
VP Marketing: Joe Mazza
VP Sales: Tim Burns
Human Resources: Larry Miller
VP Operations: Fred Koelewyn
Estimated Sales: $41100000
Number Employees: 280
Sq. footage: 100000
Parent Co: H.M. International
Type of Packaging: Food Service

11000 **Quality Seafood**
399 Market St
Apalachicola, FL 32320 850-653-9696
Fax: 850-653-3375 staceki@yahoo.com
Processor of fresh and frozen shrimp
President: Jako Flowers
Estimated Sales: $140,000
Number Employees: 1-4
Type of Packaging: Private Label
Brands:
Quality

11001 **Quality Snack Foods**
3750 W 131st St
Alsip, IL 60803-1519 708-396-8826
Fax: 773-285-8662
Processor of pork rinds
President/CEO: Victor Sharp
Vice President: Gary Trepina
Plant Manager: Tom Musil
Estimated Sales: $5600000
Number Employees: 70
Sq. footage: 40000
Type of Packaging: Private Label

11002 **Quantum Foods**
750 S Schmidt Road Bowling Brk
Chicago, IL 60664 630-679-2300
Fax: 630-679-2393 info@quantumfoods.co
www.quantumfoods.com
Producing meat
CEO: Blake Edward
Executive VP: Mike Mianovich
Director Technical Service: Hecto Delgado
VP Production: Bill Kulach
Brands:
Quantum Foods

11003 **Quantum Foods LLC**
750 S Schmidt Rd
Bolingbrook, IL 60440 630-679-2300
Fax: 630-679-2393 800-334-6328
info@quantumfoods.com
www.quantumfoods.com
Processor of beef into portion-control steaks for foodservice and retail markets, in addition to pork, chicken and turkey.
Founder/President/CEO: Edward B Bleka
Marketing Director: Chris Zoltek
Estimated Sales: $ 100-500 Million
Number Employees: 1,000-4,999
Sq. footage: 140000
Type of Packaging: Food Service
Brands:
Quantum Foods

11004 **Queen Ann Ravioli & Macaroni Company**
7205 18th Ave
Brooklyn, NY 11204 718-256-1061
Fax: 718-256-1189 queenannravioli@aol.com
www.queenannravioliandmacaroni.com
Italian pasta and ravioli
President: George Switzer
Estimated Sales: $ 5-10 Million
Number Employees: 5-9
Type of Packaging: Private Label

11005 **Queen Anne Coffee Roaster**
1908 Queen Anne Ave N
Seattle, WA 98109-3674 206-284-2530
info@metropolitan-market.com
www.metropolitan-market.com
Coffee roasters
Manager: Jim Hill
Director: Eric Stone
Roaster: Susan Hamilton
Estimated Sales: Less than $500,000
Number Employees: 100-249
Brands:
Queen Anne

11006 **Queen Bee Gardens**
1863 Lane 11 1/2
Lovell, WY 82431 307-548-2543
Fax: 307-548-6721 800-225-7553
spitt@queenbeegardens.com or
www.queenbeegardens.com
Processor and exporter of confectionery products including truffles, pralines, English toffee, mints and turtles with honey
President: Clarence Zeller
Partner: Von Zeller
Vice President: Gene Zeller
Executive Secretary: Bessie Zeller
Estimated Sales: $ 3 - 5 Million
Number Employees: 5-9
Sq. footage: 20000
Type of Packaging: Consumer, Private Label, Bulk
Brands:
Honey Essence
Q-Bee

11007 **Queen City Coffee Company**
9267 Cincinnati Dayton Rd
West Chester, OH 45069-3839 513-755-1095
Fax: 513-777-5204 800-487-7460
qcccorb@aol.com www.queencitycoffee.com
Coffee beans, products and gift items
President: Robert Badura
Estimated Sales: $ 2.5-5 Million
Number Employees: 1-4
Type of Packaging: Consumer, Food Service, Private Label

11008 **Queen City Sausage**
1136 Straight St
Cincinnati, OH 45214-1736
Fax: 513-541-6182 877-544-5588
www.queencitysausage.com
Processor of sausage and luncheon meats including bologna and Dutch loaves
President: Elmer Hensler
General Manager: David Dramis
Sales Manager: Patrick Miller
Estimated Sales: $5200000
Number Employees: 1-4
Type of Packaging: Consumer, Food Service, Bulk

11009 **Queen International Foods**
300 S Atlantic Blvd # 201d
Monterey Park, CA 91754-3228 626-289-0828
Fax: 626-289-7283 800-423-4414
Processor of frozen Mexican foods including burritos, tacos, taquitos, enchiladas and chimichangas
Owner: Liza Tang
Controller: Patricia Thistlewhite
National Sales Manager: Douglas Werner
Estimated Sales: $11100000
Number Employees: 1-4
Parent Co: La Reina
Type of Packaging: Consumer, Private Label
Brands:
Anita's
Maria's

11010 **Queensboro Farm Products**
4 Rasbach Street
Canastota, NY 13032 315-697-2235
Fax: 315-697-8267
Processor of dairy products including cottage cheese, ice cream mix, butter and sour cream; wholesaler/distributor of milk
General Manager: Don Landry
Human Resources Director: Margaret Ribley
Plant Manager: Don Landry
Estimated Sales: $ 10 - 20 Million
Number Employees: 60
Sq. footage: 13900
Type of Packaging: Consumer

11011 **Queensboro Farm Products**
15602 Liberty Ave
Jamaica, NY 11433 718-658-5000
Fax: 718-658-0408
Processor and exporter of dairy products including ice cream mixes, yogurt, farmer and cottage cheese, sour cream, milk, heavy cream, yogurt drinks, buttermilk, condensed milk cream and cream cheese
President: Allen Miller
VP: Louis Miller
Sales: Ronalad Silver
Estimated Sales: $22000000
Number Employees: 20-49
Number of Products: 80
Brands:
Dairy Fresh
Queensboro

11012 **Queensway Foods Company**
1611 Adrian Rd
Burlingame, CA 94010 650-871-7770
Fax: 650-697-9966 info@qfco.com
www.qfco.com
Food products
Owner: May Huang
Manager: Tim Yuen
Estimated Sales: $ 5-10 Million
Number Employees: 5-9
Brands:
Queensway Foods Company

11013 **Quelle Quiche**
814 Hanley Industrial Court
Brentwood, MO 63144-1403 314-961-6554
Processor and exporter of frozen and miniature quiches including lorraine, spinach, broccoli and crab meat; also, microwaveable and reduced-fat
President: Eric Victor Cowle
VP: G Daniella Cowle
Number Employees: 10-19
Sq. footage: 8500
Parent Co: Renaissance Foods
Type of Packaging: Consumer, Food Service, Private Label
Brands:
Les Petites
Quelle

11014 **Quetzal Company**
1234 Polk St
San Francisco, CA 94109-5542 415-673-4181
Fax: 415-673-4182 888-673-8181
quetzal@quetzal.org www.coffeeandcocoa.com
Coffee beans
Owner: Wayne Newman
Vice President: Wayne Newman
Estimated Sales: Less than $500,000
Number Employees: 5-9
Type of Packaging: Private Label

11015 **Quibell Spring Water Beverage**
328 E Church Street
Martinsville, VA 24112-2909 540-632-0100
Fax: 540-344-0311 ieanne@quibell.com
www.quibell.com
Bottled water
President/Chairman: John Franck
Marketing Director: Dave Vandergrift
VP: Will Pannill
Plant Manager: Jeanne Staley
Estimated Sales: $ 1-2.5 Million appx.
Number Employees: 5
Sq. footage: 72
Type of Packaging: Private Label
Brands:
Quibell Sparkling Water
Quibell Spring Tea
Quibell Spring Water

11016 **Quiche & Tell**
1819 Flushing Ave # 2
Flushing, NY 11385-1002 718-381-7562
Fax: 718-381-8772 qt1819@aol.com
Quiches and cakes
President: Larry Italiano
Estimated Sales: $ 1-2.5 Million
Number Employees: 20-49
Type of Packaging: Private Label

11017 **Quick's Candy**
120 W 2nd Street
Hummelstown, PA 17036-1507 717-566-2211
Fax: 717-566-5564 800-443-9036
gladstonecandies@aol.com www.lollies.com
Manufacturer of confectionary products.
Customer Service: Judy Wojahn
Estimated Sales: Below $ 5 Million
Number Employees: 12

Type of Packaging: Private Label
Brands:
QUICK'S

11018 **Quicklabel Systems**
600 East Greenwich Ave
West Warwick, RI 02893 877-757-7978
Fax: 401-822-2430 877-757-7978
info@quicklabel.com www.quicklabel.com
Specialty food packaging i.e. gift wrap/labels/boxes/containers.
Principal: Kevin Pizzuti
Estimated Sales: $45,000
Number Employees: 1

11019 **Quigley Manufacturing**
31 N Spruce St
Elizabethtown, PA 17022-1936 717-367-2441
Fax: 717-367-4055 800-367-2441
sales@joelinc.com www.joelinc.com
Develops and manufacturers high-boiled confections and lozenges for the branded and private label market.
President: David Deck
VP: David Hess
Marketing: Libby Moyer
Plant Manager: Tom Nissley
Purchasing Director: William Latsha
Estimated Sales: $9500000
Number Employees: 20-49
Sq. footage: 18000
Parent Co: Joel
Type of Packaging: Consumer, Private Label, Bulk
Brands:
OLD FASHIONED
SIMON
SIMONS

11020 **Quilceda Creek Vintners**
11306 52nd St SE
Snohomish, WA 98290 360-568-2389
Fax: 360-568-2389 info@quilcedacreek.com
www.quilcedacreek.com
Wine
Partner: Alexander Golitzin
Partner: Jeannette Golitzin
Estimated Sales: $350,000
Number Employees: 1-4
Type of Packaging: Consumer
Brands:
Quilceda Creek Vintners

11021 **Quillin Produce Company**
P.O.Box 225
Huntsville, AL 35804-0225 256-883-7374
Fax: 256-536-2456
Processor of produce
Owner: James Quillin
Estimated Sales: $ 5 - 10 Million
Number Employees: 5-9

11022 **Quillisascut Cheese Company**
2409 Pleasant Valley Rd
Rice, WA 99167 509-738-2011
Processor of goat's milk cheese
Owner/Purchasing: Rick Misterly
Owner: Lore Lea
Number Employees: 1-4
Type of Packaging: Food Service
Brands:
Quillisascut Cheese

11023 **Quinalt Pride Seafood**
P.O.Box 217
Taholah, WA 98587-0217 360-276-4431
Fax: 360-276-4880 gensly@quinault.org
www.quinaultpride.com
Processor and exporter of precooked, canned and foil pouched salmon
Manager: Alan Heather
CFO: William Parkshurst
Estimated Sales: $ 5 - 10 Million
Number Employees: 20-49
Type of Packaging: Consumer, Food Service, Private Label, Bulk

11024 **(HQ)Quinlan Pretzels**
3rd & Washington
Denver, PA 17517 717-336-7571
Manufacturer of pretzels
Production Manager: Ken Zvonvheck
Estimated Sales: $20-50 Million
Number Employees: 125
Parent Co: Wise Foods

Type of Packaging: Consumer

11025 **Quinoa Corporation**
P.O.Box 279
Gardena, CA 90248 310-217-8125
Fax: 310-217-8140 quinoacorp@aol.com
www.quinoa.net
Pasta
President: David Schnorr
Estimated Sales: Below $ 5 Million
Number Employees: 5-9
Type of Packaging: Consumer
Brands:
ANCIENT HARVEST
SUPERGRAIN PASTA

11026 **Quinoa Corporation**
P.O.Box 279
Gardena, CA 90248 310-217-8125
Fax: 310-217-8140 quinoacorp@aol.com
www.quinoa.net
A branded product distributor and food merchant
President: Dave Schnorr
Estimated Sales: Below $ 5 Million
Number Employees: 1-4
Type of Packaging: Bulk
Brands:
Ancient Harvest Quinoa
Supergrain Pasta

11027 **Quintessential Chocolates Company**
330 W Main St
Fredericksburg, TX 78624 830-990-9382
Fax: 830-997-0811 qechocolates@juno.com
www.qechocolates.com
Liquid-center chocolates
President: Lecia Duke
Estimated Sales: Less than $500,000
Number Employees: 5-9
Brands:
Canadian Blended Whisky Chocolates
Cutty Sark® Scots Whisky Chocolates
Jack Daniels
Kentucky Bourbon Chocolates
McCallan
Sam Houston Bourbon™ Chocolates
Whidbey's

11028 **Quinzani Bakery**
380 Harrison Ave
Boston, MA 02118-2281 617-426-2114
Fax: 617-451-8075 800-999-1062
orders@quinzanisbakery.com
www.quinzanisbakery.com
Manufacturer of baked goods including; sandwich rolls, dinner rolls, French and Italian breads
President: Steven Quinzani
Purchasing Manager: Larry Quinzani
Estimated Sales: $10 Million
Number Employees: 50-99
Type of Packaging: Consumer, Food Service
Brands:
QUINZANI

11029 **Quivira Vineyards**
4900 W Dry Creek Rd
Healdsburg, CA 95448 707-431-8333
Fax: 707-431-1664 800-292-8339
quivira@quivirawine.com www.quivirawine.com
Organic wines
Manager: Kris Cuneo
Co-Founder: Henry Wendt
Vineyard Manager: Tony Castellanos
Winemaker/General Manager: Grady Wann
National Sales Manager: Bill Wiebalk
Direct Sales & Inventory: Denise Rose
Assistant Tasting Room Manager: Jana Aitken
Concierge Relations: Pam Jorgensen
Winemaker: Steven Canter
COO: Denise Sanders
Cellar Master: Adam Armstrong
Accounting Manager: Sheila Williams
Office Administrator: Lori-Jo Martin
Estimated Sales: Below $ 5 Million
Number Employees: 10-19
Type of Packaging: Private Label
Brands:
Quivira

11030 **Quong Hop & Company**
40 Airport Blvd
S San Francisco, CA 94080 650-553-9900
Fax: 650-952-3329 sales@quonghop.com
www.quonghop.com
Manufacturer of soy deli tofu, soy deli baked tofu, soy deli tofu burger, raquel's hummus and soy deli tempeh
President/CEO: Frank Stephens
Estimated Sales: $3.1 Million
Number Employees: 42
Sq. footage: 10000
Type of Packaging: Consumer, Food Service, Private Label, Bulk
Brands:
QUONG HOP
RAQUEL'S
SOY DELI

11031 **Qzina Specialty Foods**
3095 E Patrick Ln
Las Vegas, NV 89120-4932 702-451-3916
Fax: 702-433-7919 qzinalv@flash.net

11032 **R & D Sausage Company**
15714 Waterloo Rd
Cleveland, OH 44110 216-692-1832
Processor of sausage
Owner: Joseph Zuzak
Estimated Sales: Less than $100,000
Number Employees: 1-4
Type of Packaging: Consumer, Bulk

11033 **R & R Seafood**
P.O.Box 786
Tybee Island, GA 31328 912-786-5504
Fax: 912-786-5504
Seafood
Owner: Robbie Robertson
Estimated Sales: Less than $100,000
Number Employees: 1-4

11034 **R A B Food Group LLC**
80 Avenue K
Newark, NJ 7105 201-553-1100
Fax: 201-333-1809
deborah.ross@manischewitz.com
www.rabfoodgroup.com
Manufacturer of processed kosher food products including baked goods, pastas, soups, gefilte fish, grape juice and borscht.
President/CEO: Jeremy Fingerman
Vice President Sales: Kevin O'Brien
Administrator: Deborah Ross

11035 **R Four Meats**
24 2nd St SW
Chatfield, MN 55923 507-867-4180
Fax: 507-867-4180
Manufacturer and packer of fresh and frozen deer, beef, pork and lamb, retail sales product shipping available
Owner: Jeff Remme
Estimated Sales: $1-2.5 Million
Number Employees: 5-9
Type of Packaging: Consumer

11036 **R M Lawton Cranberries**
221 Thomas St
Middleboro, MA 02346 508-947-7465
Fax: 508-947-0280
Cranberries
Manager: Mark Di Carlo
Estimated Sales: $300,000-$375,000
Number Employees: 5-9
Type of Packaging: Food Service, Bulk
Brands:
R.M. Lawton Cranberries

11037 **R&A Imports**
1439 El Bosque Ct
Pacific Palisades, CA 90272 310-454-2247
Fax: 310-459-3218 zonevdka@gte.net
www.raimportsinc.com
Processor and importer of vodka
President: Veronica Pekarovic
Estimated Sales: $1-$2.5 Million
Number Employees: 1 to 4
Brands:
Zone

11038 **R&B Quality Foods**
7755 E Gray Road
Scottsdale, AZ 85260-6980 480-443-1415
Fax: 480-922-1550
Estimated Sales: $ 5 - 10 Million
Number Employees: 5-9

11039 **R&J Farms**
9291 N Elyria Rd
West Salem, OH 44287 419-846-3179
Fax: 419-846-9603 www.rjfarms.com
Processor and exporter of regular and organic soy and dry beans, organic sesame and sunflower seeds, whole and flaked grains, flour, microwaveable popcorn and multi-grain chips and pretzels; importer of garbanzo beans
Owner: Todd Driscoll
Number Employees: 5-9
Sq. footage: 20000
Type of Packaging: Consumer, Private Label, Bulk
Brands:
Country Grown
Whole Earth

11040 **R&J Seafoods**
P.O.Box 16
King Cove, AK 99612-0016 907-497-3060
Fax: 907-246-4487
Seafood
Plant Manager: Glen Guffey

11041 **R&R Homestead Kitchen**
2399 Loxley Ct
Saumico, WI 54173 920-544-5221
Fax: 920-227-4147 888-779-8245
fudge@randrhomestead.com www.rnrfudge.com
Hot fudge topping
Owner: Richard Roffers

11042 **R&S Mexican Food Products**
5818 W Maryland Ave
Glendale, AZ 85301-3909 602-272-2727
Fax: 602-435-1377 www.rsmexfoods.com
Processor of Mexican products including fruits, vegetables, canned goods, spices, tacos, tamales, tortillas, etc
President: Danny Franks
Sales/Marketing Manager: Mila Cano
Plant Manager: Francisco Ramirez
Estimated Sales: $4415000
Number Employees: 50-99
Sq. footage: 35000
Type of Packaging: Consumer, Food Service

11043 **R. C. Bigelow**
201 Black Rock Turnpike
Fairfield, CT 6825 203-334-1212
Fax: 203-334-4751 888-244-3569
info@bigelowtea.com www.bigelowtea.com
Various teas as well as tea gifts and tea baskets.
President: David Bigelow
President: Robert Crawford
Vice President: Eunice Bigelow
CFO: Donald Janezic
Marketing Director: Robert Kelly
Operations Manager: Cindi Bigelow
Estimated Sales: $ 50 - 100 Million
Number Employees: 170
Type of Packaging: Consumer, Food Service
Brands:
BIGELOW AFTERNOON ASSORTED HERB TEA
BIGELOW APPLE & CINNAMON HERB TEA
BIGELOW ASSORTED BIGELOW TEAS
BIGELOW ASSORTED DECAF TEAS
BIGELOW ASSORTED HERB TEA
BIGELOW ASSORTED STERLING SILVER
BIGELOW BLACK CURRANT
BIGELOW BORPATRA FULL LEAF TEA
BIGELOW CHAMOMILE LEMON HERB TEA
BIGELOW CHAMOMILE MANGO HERB TEA
BIGELOW CHAMOMILE MANGO HERB TEA
BIGELOW CHAMOMILE MINT HERB TEA
BIGELOW CHERRY VANILLA TEA
BIGELOW CHINESE FORTUNE
BIGELOW CINNAMON APPLE HERB TEA
BIGELOW CINNAMON SPICE HERB TEA
BIGELOW CINNAMON STICK
BIGELOW CINNAMON STICK DECAF
BIGELOW CONSTANT COMMENT
BIGELOW CONSTANT COMMENT DECAF
BIGELOW CONSTANT COMMENT LOOSE TEA
BIGELOW COZY CHAMOMILE HERB TEA
BIGELOW CRANBERRY APPLE HERB TEA
BIGELOW DARJEELING BLEND
BIGELOW DARJEELING LOOSE TEA
BIGELOW DRAGONWELL FULL LEAF TEA
BIGELOW EARL GREY
BIGELOW EARL GREY LOOSE TEA
BIGELOW EARLY GREY DECAF
BIGELOW EARLY GREY GREEN TEA
BIGELOW ENGLISH BREAKFAST
BIGELOW ENGLISH BREAKFAST LOOSE TEA
BIGELOW ENGLISH TEATIME
BIGELOW ENGLISH TEATIME DECAF
BIGELOW FRENCH VANILLA
BIGELOW FRUIT ALMOND HERB TEA
BIGELOW GREEN GENMAICHA FULL LEAF
BIGELOW GREEN LOOSE TEA
BIGELOW GREEN TEA WITH LEMON
BIGELOW GREEN TEA WITH MANGO
BIGELOW GREEN TEA WITH MINT
BIGELOW GREEN TEA WITH PEACH
BIGELOW I LOVE LEMON & C HERB TEA
BIGELOW JASMINE FLOWERS FULL LEAF
BIGELOW JASMINE LOOSE TEA
BIGELOW KEEMUN BLACK FULL LEAF
BIGELOW KENILWORTH FULL LEAF TEA
BIGELOW LEMON LIFT
BIGELOW LEMON LIFT DECAF
BIGELOW MINT MEDLEY HERB TEA
BIGELOW ORANGE & SPICE HERB TEA
BIGELOW ORANGE & SPICE HERB TEA
BIGELOW PAI MU TAN FULL LEAF TEA
BIGELOW PEPPERMINT HERB LOOSE TEA
BIGELOW PEPPERMINT HERB TEA
BIGELOW PERFECT PEACH HERB TEA
BIGELOW PLANTATION MINT
BIGELOW PLANTATION MINT DECAF
BIGELOW RASPBERRY ROYALE
BIGELOW RASPBERRY ROYALE DECAF
BIGELOW RED RASPBERRY HERB LOOSE
BIGELOW RED REASPBERRY HERB TEA
BIGELOW RISHEEHAT FULL LEAF TEA
BIGELOW SE CHUNG FULL LEAF TEA
BIGELOW SIX ASSORTED GREEN TEAS
BIGELOW SWEET DREAMS HERB TEA
BIGELOW VANILLA ALMOND TEA
BIGELOW SIX ASSORTED GREEN TEAS
BIGELOW SWEET DREAMS HERB TEA
BIGELOW VANILLA ALMOND TEA
BIGELOW VANILLA CARAMEL TEA
BIGELOW VANILLA HAZELNUT TEA
BIGELOW WILD CHERRY HERB LOOSE TEA

11044 **R. Torre & Company**
233 E Harris Ave
South San Francisco, CA 94080 650-875-1200
Fax: 650-875-1600 800-775-1925
info@torani.com www.torani.com
Italian syrups
President: Harry Lucheta
CEO: Melania Dulbecco
CEO: Melanie Dulbecco
VP Marketing: Cynthia Eckart
Estimated Sales: $ 50 - 100 Million
Number Employees: 50-99
Type of Packaging: Private Label
Brands:
Caffee Fiori
Frusia
Torani

11045 **R.A.B. Food Group LLC**
One Harmon Plaza
10th Floor
Secaucus, NJ 07094 201-553-1100
Fax: 201-333-1809 dross@rabfoodgroup.com
www.rabfoodgroup.com
Manufacturer and exporter of kosher foods including matzoth, crackers, cereals, wine, bagel mixes, candy, pickles, gefilte fish, borscht, doughnut mixes, bagel mixes and egg noodles.
President/Chief Executive Officer: Jeremy Fingerman
Chairman/Chief Executive Officer: Richard Bernstein
Vice President/Sales: Kevin O'Brien
Public Relations/Media: Deborah Ross
Estimated Sales: $10-20 Million
Number Employees: 20-49
Type of Packaging: Consumer, Food Service, Private Label
Brands:
ASIAN HARVEST
CARMEL
CROYDEN HOUSE
ELITE
GOODMAN'S
GUILTLESS GOURMET
JASON
MANISCHEWITZ
MISHPACHA
MOTHER'S
MRS ADLER'S
ROKEACH
SEASON BRAND
TRADITION

11046 **R.B. Morriss Company**
1531 Deer Crossing Dr
Diamond Bar, CA 91765-2627 909-861-8671
Fax: 909-860-5272 rbmorrissco@worldnet.att.net
Environmental and food products
President: Robert Morriss
Estimated Sales: $ 2.5-5 Million
Number Employees: 1-4

11047 **R.C. McEntire & Company**
P.O.Box 5817
Columbia, SC 29250-5817 803-799-3388
Fax: 803-254-3540 info@rcmcentire.com
www.rcmcentire.com
Processor of fresh vegetables including tomatoes, peppers, lettuce, onions, cabbage, salads, tomato repacker, etc
Owner: Buddy Mc Entire Jr
Estimated Sales: $ 10 - 20 Million
Number Employees: 10-19
Sq. footage: 75000
Type of Packaging: Consumer, Food Service, Private Label, Bulk
Brands:
Dinner Reddi
Micro Fast
Salad Pak
Veg Fresh

11048 **R.D. Hemond Farms**
232 Pottle Hill Road
Minot, ME 04258-4802 207-345-5611
Fax: 207-345-5611
Poultry
President: Rolland Hemond
Brands:
Oak Hurst Dairy

11049 **R.D. Offutt Company**
700 7th St S
Fargo, ND 58103-2704 701-237-6062
Fax: 701-239-8750 www.rdoequipment.com
Processor of frozen sliced potatoes, French fries, hash browns and patties; also, potato chips
President: Michelle Onstad
Estimated Sales: $ 20-50 Million
Number Employees: 547
Type of Packaging: Consumer, Food Service, Private Label
Brands:
RDO

11050 **R.E. Kimball & Company**
73 Merrimac Street
Amesbury, MA 01913-4097 978-388-1826
Processor of condiments and preserves
President: Joy Kimball
CEO: Joy Kimeball
Treasurer: Ruth Kimball
Marketing Director: Joy Kimeball
Number Employees: 5-9
Sq. footage: 25000
Type of Packaging: Consumer, Private Label
Brands:
Kimball's
private lable

11051 **R.E. Meyer Company**
4611 W Adams Street
Lincoln, NE 68524-1444 402-474-8500
Fax: 402-470-4380 888-990-2333
www.meyerbeef.com
Processor and exporter of beef and pork
Number Employees: 100-249
Parent Co: Meyer Holdings
Type of Packaging: Food Service, Private Label, Bulk

11052 **R.F.A.**
PO Box 717
Newcastle, ME 04553-0717 207-563-2340
Fax: 207-563-2345
President: Justin Braithwaite

11053 **R.H. Bauman & Company**
P.O.Box 4645
Chatsworth, CA 91313-4645 818-709-1093
Fax: 818-341-8348
General grocery
President: R Bauman
Estimated Sales: Less than $500,000
Number Employees: 1-4
Type of Packaging: Private Label

11054 **R.H. Phillips**
26836 County Rd
Esparto, CA 95627 530-662-3504
Fax: 530-662-2880 csutton@rhphillips.com
www.rhphillips.com
Wines
Manager: Barry Bergman
CEO: Karl Giguiere
CFO: Bance Schram
Quality Control: David Keim
Public Relations: Lane Giguiere
Wine Maker: Barry Bergman
Plant Manager: Ken Lazzaroni
Estimated Sales: 21,720,000
Number Employees: 100-249
Type of Packaging: Private Label
Brands:
R.H. Phillips

11055 **R.I. Provision Company**
5 Day St
Johnston, RI 02919-4301 401-831-0815
Fax: 401-274-5508
sales@littlerhodyhotdogs.com
www.littlerhodyhotdogs.com
Sausages, franks and toppings
President: Edward Robalisky
Estimated Sales: $ 1-2.5 Million
Number Employees: 10-19
Number of Brands: 1

11056 **R.J. Corr Naturals**
14028 S McKinley Avenue
Posen, IL 60469 708-389-4200
Fax: 708-389-4294
Processor of natural beverages including juice blends, sodas and sparkling mineral water
President: Robert Corr
General Manager: James Corr
VP Operations: Thomas Swan
Number Employees: 10-19
Sq. footage: 16000
Brands:
Gear Up
Ginseng Rush
Natures Flavors
North Star
Rj Corr
Robert Corr

11057 **R.L. Albert & Son**
19 W Elm St
Greenwich, CT 006830-645 203-622-8655
Fax: 203-622-7454 mainmail@albertcandy.com
Candy and confectionery wholesale
President: Lawrence Albert
CFO: Marion Lossick
COO: Robert Cats
Estimated Sales: $ 10-20 Million
Number Employees: 20-49
Brands:
Big Baby
Big Bol
Fortune Bubble
Fun Fruit
Gum Time
Ice Cubes
Mint Balls
Moritz Ice Cubes
Neon Lasers
Pnut Jumbo
So Joao
Stardrops
Stardrops

11058 **R.L. Schreiber**
1741 NW 33rd St
Pompano Beach, FL 33064-1327 954-972-7102
Fax: 954-972-4406 800-624-8777
rlschreiber@rlsinc.com www.rlschreiber.com
Manufacturer of soup bases, sauces, gravies, spices, spice blends, custom blending and specialty items
President: Tom Schreiber
Sales Director: Joe DeCaro
Plant Manager: Bernadine Jolley
Purchasing Manager: Kim Ryan
Estimated Sales: $ 5-10 Million
Number Employees: 50-99
Type of Packaging: Food Service, Private Label

11059 **R.L. Schreiber Company**
1741 NW 33rd St
Pompano Beach, FL 33064-1327 954-972-7102
Fax: 954-972-4406 800-624-8777
info@rlsinc.com www.rlschreiber.com
Processor of soup bases, gravies, sauces and spices
President: Tom Schreiber
Estimated Sales: $9.3 Million
Number Employees: 50-99
Type of Packaging: Food Service

11060 **R.L. Zeigler Company**
P.O.Box 1640
Tuscaloosa, AL 35403-1640 205-758-3621
Fax: 205-758-0185 800-392-6328
www.rlzeigler.com
Manufacturer and exporter of lunch meats, bacon and frankfurters
Chairman/Director: James Hinton
CEO/Director: W Lackey
CFO: Ken Fitzgerald
Estimated Sales: $ 35 Million
Number Employees: 20-49
Sq. footage: 100000
Type of Packaging: Consumer, Food Service, Private Label
Brands:
Talmadge Farms
Zeigler

11061 **R.M. Felts Packing Company**
P.O.Box 199
Ivor, VA 23866-0199 757-859-6131
Fax: 757-859-6381 888-300-0971
rmfelts@mindspring.com
Processor and exporter of cured and dry salted smoked ham and picnic hams
President: Robert M Felts Jr
CEO: Charles Stallard
Estimated Sales: $ 3 - 5 Million
Number Employees: 10-19
Sq. footage: 17000
Type of Packaging: Consumer, Food Service, Private Label
Brands:
Southampton

11062 **R.M. Palmer Company**
P.O.Box 1723
Reading, PA 19603 610-372-8971
Fax: 610-378-5208 www.rmpalmer.com
Processor and exporter of confectionery products including hollow and solid chocolate seasonal novelties, lollypops, everday bag items and novelties.
President: Richard M Palmer Jr
CFO: Chuck Shearer
Quality Control: Tierney Wheaton
Director of Marketing: David Abrams
Sales Director: Steve Terroni
Operations Manager: Mark Schlott
Production Manager: Mark Schlott
Plant Manager: Sue Halvonik
Purchasing Manager: Rich Halliwell
Estimated Sales: $150-200 Million
Type of Packaging: Consumer, Bulk
Brands:
Bumpkins
Cookie Dippers

11063 **R.N.C. Industries, Inc**
3105 Sweetwater Road
Suite 220
Lawrenceville, GA 30044-8547 770-368-8453
Fax: 770-368-8490 taylor@rncind.com
www.rncind.com
Specialty food packaging i.e. gift wrap/labels/boxes/containers.
President: Lawrence Clark
Cfo: Charlotta Clark
Marketing: Taylor Clark
Estimated Sales: $4.9 Million
Number Employees: 46

11064 **R.R. Fournier & Sons**
P.O.Box 732
Biloxi, MS 39533-0732 228-392-4293
Fax: 228-392-7130
Seafood
President: Doty A Fournier
Secretary: Barbara Fournier
Estimated Sales: $ 2.5-5 Million
Number Employees: 20-49

11065 **R.R. Lochhead Manufacturing**
200 Sherwood Rd
Paso Robles, CA 93446-3546 805-238-3400
Fax: 805-238-0111 800-735-0545
cooks@cooksvanilla.com
Processor of vanilla flavoring
President: R Lochhead
Manager: S Lochhead
Estimated Sales: $620000
Number Employees: 5-9
Type of Packaging: Consumer, Food Service, Private Label, Bulk

11066 **R.W. Frookies**
PO Box 1649
Sag Harbor, NY 11963-0060 800-913-3663
800-913-3663
Cookies and baked goods
President: Ned Parkhouse
Estimated Sales: Under $500,000
Number Employees: 1-4

11067 **R.W. Garcia**
521 Parrott Street
San Jose, CA 95112 408-287-4616
www.rwgarcia.com
All natural tortilla chips and gluten free crackers
President: Robert Garcia
General Manager: Janette Rosales
Marketing Manager: Julia Lin
Purchasing Agent: Desiree Garcia
Number Employees: 100
Sq. footage: 30000

11068 **R.W. Knudsen**
P.O.Box 369
Chico, CA 95927-0369 530-899-5000
Fax: 530-891-6397
arlene.starkey@jmsmucker.com
www.jmsmucker.com
Fruit juice
President: Julia Sabin
Marketing Assistant: Arlene Starkey
Number Employees: 100-249

11069 **RBW & Associates**
PO Box 698
Portland, OR 97207-0698 503-223-0843
Fax: 503-223-2731
Ingredients, yeast products
Number Employees: 5-9

11070 **RC Fine Foods**
P.O.Box 236
Belle Mead, NJ 08502-0236 908-359-5500
Fax: 908-359-6957 800-526-3953
info@rcfinefoods.com www.rcfinefoods.com
Processor of mixes including soup, gravy, specialty, salad dressing, dessert and sauce; also, soup bases, spices, seasonings, extracts, colors and dietetic products
President: Elaine Cohen
Director Sales: Robert Dixon
Estimated Sales: $5500000
Number Employees: 50-99
Sq. footage: 48000
Type of Packaging: Food Service
Brands:
Rc Fine Foods

11071 **RDO Foods Company**
2500 Mill Rd
Grand Forks, ND 58203 701-775-3154
Fax: 701-746-0374 info@rdofoodsco.com
www.rdofoodsco.com

Snack foods
Partner: Brian Radi
CEO: Ronald Offutt
Quality Control: Jeff Posey
Marketing Director: Steve Merchant
Estimated Sales: $ 20-50 Million
Number Employees: 50-99

11072 RES Food Products International

P.O.Box 12511
Green Bay, WI 54307 920-499-7651
Fax: 920-499-8023 800-255-3768
sales@edcofood.com www.edcofood.com
Processor and importer of peppers including jalapeno, serrano, sport and cascabella; also, cauliflower buttons, chipotle powder and pickled vegetables
President: James Manning
VP: Sylvia Roman
VP: Edward Manning
Estimated Sales: $ 3 - 5 Million
Number Employees: 135
Sq. footage: 16000
Type of Packaging: Food Service, Private Label, Bulk

11073 REX Pure Foods

2121 Chartres St
New Orleans, LA 70116 504-525-7305
800-344-8314
info@rexfoods.com www.rexfoods.com
Processor and packer of seafood spices and seasonings, sauces, liquid and dry blends, vinegar and mustard; also, contract packaging available
President: J Geldart
Estimated Sales: $2.5 Million
Number Employees: 1-4
Type of Packaging: Consumer, Food Service, Bulk
Brands:
REX

11074 RFI Ingredients

300 Corporate Dr
Blauvelt, NY 10913-1144 845-358-8600
Fax: 845-358-9003 800-962-7663
rfi@rfiingredients.com www.rfiingredients.com
Supplier of natural antioxidants, antimicrobials and preservatives, natural colors, fruit, vegetable and botanical extracts and functional food ingredients
President/CEO: Jeff Wuagneux
VP Research & Development: Ginny Bank
VP Sales: Trisha Devine
Chief Operations Officer: Drew Luce
Operations Manager: Neal Cochran
Estimated Sales: $ 4 - 5 Million
Number Employees: 20-49
Number of Brands: 5
Type of Packaging: Bulk
Brands:
COLORPURE
OXYPHYTE
PHYTBAC
PHYTONUTRIANCE
STABILENHANCE

11075 (HQ)RIBUS

8000 Maryland Ave Ste 460
Saint Louis, MO 63105 314-727-4287
Fax: 314-727-1199 info@ribus.com
www.ribus.com
Processor and exporter of natural rice-based food ingredients for baked goods, snacks and confectionery items including chocolate and frosting; also, nongenetically modified emulsifiers and extrusion aids
President: Steve Pierce
Sales: Jim Goodall
Estimated Sales: $720000
Number Employees: 5-9
Sq. footage: 10000
Other Locations:
RIBUS
Sabetha KS
Brands:
Nu-Bake
Nu-Rice
Ribus

11076 RJ Balson and Sons Inc

PO Box 4817
Fayetteville, AR 72702 321-281-9473
contact@balsonbutchers.com
www.balsonbutchers.com
sausage

11077 RL Schreiber

1741 NW 33rd St
Pompano Beach, FL 33064-1327 954-972-7102
Fax: 954-972-4406 rlschreiber@rlsinc.com
www.rlschreiber.com
Soups, gravy bases and spices
President: Tom Schreiber
Estimated Sales: $ 5-10 Million
Number Employees: 50-99

11078 RM Palmer Company

P.O.Box 1723
Reading, PA 19603-1723 610-372-8971
Fax: 610-378-5208 www.rmpalmer.com
President: Richard M Palmer Jr
Sales Administrator: Gail Youse
Estimated Sales: $ 20-50 Million
Number Employees: 500-999

11079 RPM Total Vitality

18032 Lemon Drive
Suite C
Yorba Linda, CA 92886-3386 714-524-8864
Fax: 714-524-3247 800-234-3092
www.rpmtotalvitality.com
Processor and exporter of natural antioxidants including flower pollen and dimethylaminoethanol
Owner: Pat McBride
Co-Owner: Roger McBride
Number Employees: 1-4
Sq. footage: 1000
Brands:
Letan

11080 RW Delights

50 Division Ave
Suite 44
Millington, NJ 07946 917-301-5231
866-892-1096
info@heavenlysouffle.com
www.heavenlysouffle.com
individual souffle and creme brulee desserts

11081 RW Garcia Company

P.O.Box 8290
San Jose, CA 95155-8290 408-287-4616
Fax: 408-287-7724 custserv@rwgarcia.com
www.rwgarcia.com
Processor and exporter of organic and commercial grade tortilla chips; private labeling available
VP: Margaret Garcia
Sales Manager: Jake Stenton
Estimated Sales: $ 10 - 20 Million
Number Employees: 20-49
Sq. footage: 30000
Parent Co: R.W. Garcia Company
Type of Packaging: Private Label
Brands:
Santa Cruz

11082 Rabbit Barn

630 W Clausen Rd
Turlock, CA 95380 209-632-1123
Fax: 209-632-1123 kxva66a@prodigy.com
Processor of rabbit including fresh, frozen, whole body, cut-up and tray packed
Owner: Larry Sigafoos
CEO: Sherri Sigafoos
Estimated Sales: $ 1 - 3 Million
Number Employees: 1-4
Sq. footage: 4000
Type of Packaging: Private Label
Brands:
Rabbit Barn

11083 Rabbit Creek Products

903 North Broadway
Po Box 1059
Louisburg, KS 66053 913-837-2757
Fax: 913-837-5760 800-837-3073
rcreek@mokancomm.net
www.rabbitcreekgourmet.com
Processor of muffin, dip, soup, scone, bread, brownie, and cookie mixes
President: Donna Cook
Estimated Sales: $1-2.5 Million
Number Employees: 18
Number of Brands: 1
Number of Products: 120
Type of Packaging: Consumer, Private Label
Brands:
RABBIT CREEK

11084 Rabbit Ridge

1172 San Marcos Road
Paso Robles, CA 93446 80- 4-7 33
Fax: 80- 4-7 33 rabbitridgewines@yahoo.com
www.rabbitridgewinery.com
Wines
Founder/Winemaker: Erich Russell
President: Joanne James Russell
Compliance/Operations Manager: Sandy James
Director Paso Vineyard Operations: Robert Pierce

Paso Robles Office Manager: Jacqueline Pierce
Paso Robles Assistant to the Director: Mike Sanford
Healdsburg Operations Director: Linda Garwood
Healdsburg Warehouse Manager: Craig Wisdom
Estimated Sales: Below $ 5 Million
Number Employees: 8-20
Brands:
Rabbit Ridge
Rabbit Ridge

11085 Raber Packing

1413 N Raber Rd
Peoria, IL 61604 309-673-0721
Fax: 309-673-6308
Processor of meat products
President: Carroll Wetterauer
Estimated Sales: $3 Million
Number Employees: 22
Sq. footage: 15000
Type of Packaging: Consumer

11086 Raceland Raw Sugar Corporation

P.O.Box 159
Raceland, LA 70394 985-537-3533
Fax: 985-537-7779
Manufacturer of raw sugar and blackstrap molasses
President/CEO: Dan Duplantis
Estimated Sales: $33 Million
Number Employees: 100-249
Parent Co: M.A. Patout & Son
Type of Packaging: Bulk

11087 Radanovich Vineyards & Winery

3936 Ben Hur Road
Mariposa, CA 95338-9466 209-966-3187
Wines
President: George Radanovich
Estimated Sales: $500,000-$1 Million
Number Employees: 1-4

11088 Radar Farms

P.O.Box 133
Lynden, WA 98264-0133 360-354-6574
Fax: 360-354-7070 info@raderfarms.com
www.raderfarms.com
Processor of frozen rhubarb, red raspberries and raspberry puree
President: Lyle Rader
Estimated Sales: $ 50-100 Million
Number Employees: 250-499
Type of Packaging: Consumer, Food Service, Private Label

11089 (HQ)Radlo Foods

313 Pleasant Street
Suite 5
Watertown, MA 02472-2491 617-926-7070
Fax: 617-923-6440 800-370-1439
info@radlo.com www.radlo.com
Processor of all natural and organic eggs, 100% Florida organic orange juice, and all natural beef and chicken.
President: Jack Radlo
VP: David Radlo
Estimated Sales: $25000000
Number Employees: 25
Type of Packaging: Consumer, Food Service, Private Label, Bulk
Brands:
Born Free
Grown Free

11090 Radway's Dairy

433 Park Street
New Britain, CT 06051-2730 860-443-8921
Fax: 860-437-7911 800-472-3929
Dairy products and distributors
Estimated Sales: $ 10-20 Million
Number Employees: 25

11091 **Raemica**
7759 Victoria Ave
Highland, CA 92346-5637 909-864-1990
Fax: 909-864-0554 sales@farwestmeats.com
Processor and exporter of meat products including smoked sausage, knockwurst, bologna, salami, bratwurst, frankfurters, kielbasa, beef, pork and smoked pork and turkey parts
Owner/President: Thomas Serrato III
President: Michael Serrato
Cfo/Vice President: Wade Snyder
Estimated Sales: $13 Million
Number Employees: 70
Sq. footage: 25000
Type of Packaging: Consumer, Private Label, Bulk
Brands:
Far West Meats

11092 **Raffield Fisheries**
P.O.Box 309
Port St Joe, FL 32457 850-229-8229
Fax: 850-229-8782
raffieldfish@digitalexpress.com
www.raffieldfisheries.com
Processor and exporter of Atlantic thread herring, black drum, black mullet roe, bluefish, blue runner, Jack Crevalle, ladyfish, Spanish sardines, butterfish, goatfish, croakers, crawfish, etc.
President: William Raffield
Secretary/Treasurer: Danny Raffield
Estimated Sales: $ 10 - 20 Million
Number Employees: 50-99
Type of Packaging: Consumer, Food Service, Private Label, Bulk

11093 **Ragersville Swiss Cheese**
2199 Ragersville Rd SW
Sugarcreek, OH 44681 330-897-3055
Fax: 330-897-0415
Processor of Swiss cheese
President/Owner: Richard Hicks
Estimated Sales: $ 3 - 5 Million
Number Employees: 1-4
Sq. footage: 10000
Type of Packaging: Consumer

11094 **Raggy-O Chutney**
PO Box 1626
Smithfield, NC 27577-1626 919-284-6700
Fax: 919-284-6706 888-424-8863
raggyo.chutney@simflex.com
Chutney and all-purpose seasoning sauce
Brands:
B-17
Raggy-O

11095 **Ragold Confections**
516 NW 20th St
Wilton Manors, FL 33311 954-566-9092
Fax: 954-427-0413 rs@ragold.com
www.ragold.com
Candy
Chairman of the Board: Rainer Schindler
CFO: Arthur Pauly
Estimated Sales: $ 1.5 Million
Number Employees: 10-19
Type of Packaging: Private Label
Brands:
Dilbert Mints&Gummies
Juicefuls Hard Candy

11096 **Ragozzino Food**
P.O.Box 116
Meriden, CT 06450-0116 203-238-2553
Fax: 203-235-5158 800-348-1240
nancy@ragozzino.com www.ragozzino.com
Manufacturer, importer and exporter of soups, pasta's, sauces, entrees and side dishes
President: Gloria Ragozzino
VP Business Development: Nancy Ragozzino
VP: John Ragozzino
R&D: Susan Ragozzino
Purchasing Director: Ellen Ragozzino
Estimated Sales: $23 Million
Number Employees: 100-249
Type of Packaging: Consumer, Food Service, Private Label
Brands:
Sugo
Zino

11097 **Ragsdale-Overton Food Traditions**
PO Box 1626
Smithfield, NC 27577-1626 919-284-6700
Fax: 919-284-6706 888-424-8863
raggy.ochutney@simflex.com
Condiments, chutneys, sauces
Partner: Sue Overton
Partner: Carolyn Ragsdale
Public Relations: Carolyn Ragsdale
Estimated Sales: Under $500,000
Number Employees: 1-4
Type of Packaging: Private Label
Brands:
B-17 Seasoning/Grilling Sauce
Raggy-O Apple Chutne
Raggy-O Cranberry Ch
Raggy-O Mango Chutne
Raggy-O Peach Chutne
Raggy-O Pineapple Ch

11098 **(HQ)Rahco International**
850 A1a Beach Blvd # 121
St Augustine, FL 32080-6954 904-461-9931
Fax: 904-461-9932 800-851-7681
rahcoint@aol.com www.rahcoint.com
Manufacturer of signs, menus and wine lists; importer of wines and gourmet Italian sauces, marmalades and panetone; exporter of Italian style cheeses, signs and wines
President: Alvin Moser
Vice President: Olga Lara-Moser
Operations Manager: David Firch
Production Manager: Dale Mull
Estimated Sales: $500,000-$1 Million
Number Employees: 5-9
Number of Brands: 12
Number of Products: 60
Sq. footage: 1500
Type of Packaging: Consumer, Food Service, Private Label, Bulk
Other Locations:
Rahco International
Agoura Hills CA
Brands:
DORAL
PARK CHEESE

11099 **Rahr Malting Company**
800 1st Ave W
Shakopee, MN 55379 952-445-1431
Fax: 952-496-7055 info@rahr.com
www.rahr.com
Processor and exporter of malt
President: Gary Lee
CFO: James Olsen
Vice President: Daniel Stone
R&D: Paul Kramer
Estimated Sales: $43.6 Million
Number Employees: 100-249
Type of Packaging: Bulk

11100 **Rahr Malting Company**
800 1st Ave W
Shakopee, MN 55379 952-445-1431
Fax: 952-496-7055 info@rahr.com
www.rahr.com
Produces and distributes malt and industry related brewing supplies.
President: Gary Lee
CFO: James Olsen
Vice President: Daniel Stone
VP Operations: Bob Micheletti
Estimated Sales: $43.6 Million
Number Employees: 100-249
Type of Packaging: Bulk

11101 **Rain Sweet**
P.O.Box 6109
Salem, OR 97304-0278 503-363-4293
Fax: 503-585-4657 800-363-4293
linda@rainsweet.com www.rainsweet.com
Processor and exporter of frozen blackberries, blueberries, black raspberries, red raspberries, boysenberries; also, IQF and puree cane berries, mushrooms, peppers, onions, pearl onions, bean sprouts
Chairman: Byron Lafollette
CEO: George Crispin
QA Manager: Ranita Gabell
Sales: Linda Ervin
Estimated Sales: $ 50 - 100 Million
Number Employees: 100-249
Sq. footage: 30000
Type of Packaging: Consumer, Food Service, Private Label, Bulk
Brands:
RAINSWEET

11102 **Rainbow Farms**
62 Weatherhead Road
Upper Rawdon, NS B0N 2N0
Canada 902-632-2548
Fax: 902-632-2434
Processor and exporter of frozen wild blueberries
President: Ronald Weatherhead
Vice President: Barbara Hagell
Estimated Sales: $5.2 Million
Number Employees: 70
Type of Packaging: Bulk

11103 **Rainbow Hill Vineyards**
26349 Township Road 251
Newcomerstown, OH 43832-9631 740-545-9305
www.ravensglenn.com
Wines
President: Leland Wyse
Estimated Sales: Below $ 5 Million
Number Employees: 5-9
Brands:
Rainbow Hill Vineyards

11104 **Rainbow Light Nutritional Systems**
125 McPherson St
Santa Cruz, CA 95060-5818 831-429-9089
Fax: 831-429-0189 800-635-1233
info@rlns.com www.rainbowlight.com
Processor of supplements and herbal extracts
President: Linda Kahler
Marketing Director: Sara Lovelady
Sales Director: Monique Wellise
Public Relations: Julie Dennis
Operations Manager: Mark Keller
Production Manager: Mark Keller
Purchasing Manager: Dee Dee Barrios
Estimated Sales: $6000000
Number Employees: 20-49
Number of Brands: 4
Number of Products: 150
Type of Packaging: Consumer
Brands:
JUST ONCE NATURAL HERBAL EXTRAS
RAINBOW LIGHT
RAINBOW LIGHT HERBAL

11105 **Rainbow Pops**
45 Benbro Dr
Cheektowaga, NY 14225-4805 716-685-4340
Fax: 716-685-0810 800-879-7677
jeffbaran@rainbowpops.com
www.rainbowpops.com
Lollipops
President: Roe Baran
Number Employees: 20-49
Brands:
POPSTOP
PREMIUM RAINBOW DROPS
PREMIUM RAINBOW POPS
RAINBOW POPS

11106 **Rainbow Seafood Market**
4303 Maine Ave Ste 107
Baldwin Park, CA 91706 626-962-6888
Fax: 626-962-3677
Seafood
Owner: David Tran
Estimated Sales: $800,000
Number Employees: 1-4
Type of Packaging: Consumer

11107 **Rainbow Seafoods**
422a Boston St
Topsfield, MA 01983 978-887-9121
Fax: 978-283-3721 info@rainbowseafood.com
www.rainbowseafood.com
Seafood
President: Frank Powell
Sales: Neil Murphy
Estimated Sales: $2,500,000
Number Employees: 9
Brands:
ALDA
NORTH BREEZE
RAINBOW

11108 **Rainbow Valley Frozen Yogurt**
9444 W Shady Grove Ct
White Lake, MI 48386 248-355-1095
Fax: 248-353-3466 800-979-8669
All natural soft-serve and hand pack frozen yogurt mix.
President: William Boyda
VP/Treasurer: Laurel Boyda
Estimated Sales: $500,000-$1 Million
Number Employees: 5-9
Sq. footage: 24000
Type of Packaging: Consumer, Food Service, Private Label, Bulk

11109 **Rainbow Valley Orchards**
5115 5th St
Fallbrook, CA 92028 760-728-2905
www.rvoorganic.com
Wholesaler/distributor for organic citrus products and avocados; processor of organic juices including orange, grapefruit and raspberry/lemonade; private label packaging available
President: Richard Hart
VP Sales: Patrick Raymond
Estimated Sales: $6.5 Million
Number Employees: 28
Sq. footage: 5000
Type of Packaging: Private Label
Brands:
Rainbow Valley Orchards

11110 **Rainforest Company**
141 Millwell Dr
Maryland Heights, MO 63043 314-344-1000
Fax: 314-344-3044
michaelm@the-rainforest-co.com
www.the-rainforest-co.com
Processor, importer and exporter of gourmet natural snacks including cashew and Brazil nut crunch and chew bars; also, popcorn, salad dressings, salsas, marinades, hot sauces, etc
President: Rick Drevet
Controller: Sherry Dawes
Number Employees: 35
Sq. footage: 20000
Brands:
Jungle Munch
Rainforest Crunch
River Bank

11111 **Raja Foods**
8110 Saint Louis Ave
Skokie, IL 60076 847-675-4455
Fax: 847-675-4498 800-800-7923
sales@rajafoods.com www.rajafoods.com
Importers of Indian food products
President: Rakesh Patel
VP: Swetal Patel
Estimated Sales: $ 10-20 Million
Number Employees: 10-19
Sq. footage: 92000
Parent Co: Raja Foods

11112 **Rajbhog Foods**
60 Amity Street
Jersey City, NJ 07304 201-395-9400
Fax: 201-395-9409 suzymody@rajbhog.com
www.rajbhog.com
Organic/natural, USDA, full-line frozen, hors d'oeuvres/appetizers, ice cream/sorbet, co-packing, foodservice, private label.
President: Sanjiv Mody
VP: Sachin Mody
Marketing: Suzy Mody
Number Employees: 7

11113 **Ralboray**
2 Canal Street World Trade Center
Suite 2008
New Orleans, LA 70130 504-524-4800
Fax: 504-524-4850

11114 **(HQ)Ralcorp Holdings**
800 Market Street
St Louis, MO 63101 314-877-7000
Fax: 314-877-7900 800-772-6757
investorrelations@ralcorp.com www.ralcorp.com
Supplier of private label cereal, producing both ready-to-eat and hot cereals. Organic cereals, snack mixes, cereal and nutrition bars and more
President/Co-CEO: Kevin Hunt
President/Co-CEO: David Skarie
Chief Accounting Officer: Thomas Grannerman
Corporate Vice President: Gregory Bilhartz
President, Ralcorp Frozen Bakery Prod.: Charles Huber Jr
President, Ralcorp Snacks & Sauces: Richard Koulouris
Corporate Development Officer: Scott Monette
President, Ralcorp Cereal Products: Ronald Wilkinsno
CVP/General Counsel & Secretary: Charles Huber
Estimated Sales: $4 Billion
Number Employees: 10,000
Type of Packaging: Consumer, Private Label
Brands:
AMERICAN ITALIAN PASTA COMPANY
BLOOMFIELD BAKERS
BREMNER
CARRIAGE HOUSE
HARVEST MANOR FARMS
J.T. BAKERIES
NORTH AMERICAN BAKING
NUTCRACKER
PARCO FOODS
POST CEREALS
RALSTON FOODS
SEPP'S GOURMET FOODS

11115 **Rallis Whole Foods**
2886 Riviera Drive
Windsor, ON N9E 3A4 519-796-9712
theo@rallisoliveoil.com
www.icepressed.com
Functional (antioxidants), olive oil.
Marketing: Theo Rallis

11116 **Ralph Sechler & Son**
P.O.Box 152
St Joe, IN 46785-0152 260-337-5461
Fax: 260-337-5771 800-332-5461
showroom@sechlerspickles.com
www.sechlerspickles.com
Vegetables
President and CEO: Max Troyer
Controller: Jan Weaver
Estimated Sales: $ 3-5 Million
Number Employees: 32
Brands:
Sechler's

11117 **Ralph Sechler & Son Inc**
P.O.Box 152
St Joe, IN 46785-0152 260-337-5461
Fax: 260-337-5771 800-332-5461
showroom@sechlerspickles.com
www.sechlerspickles.com
Processor of pickles and peppers
Owner: Max Troyer
VP Technical Services: Karen Sechler-Linn
Sales Manager: Mark Decker
Estimated Sales: $ 10 - 20 Million
Number Employees: 20-49
Sq. footage: 60000
Type of Packaging: Consumer, Food Service, Bulk
Brands:
Sechler's

11118 **Ralph's Grocery Company**
P.O.Box 54143
Los Angeles, CA 90054-0143 310-884-9000
Fax: 310-884-2601 888-437-3496
www.ralphs.com
General grocery/Manufacturer of bread and bakery products
President: David Hirz
CFO: Paul Lamert
EVP Store Operations: Dave Hansen
SVP Sales & Marketing: Chuck Ackerman
Estimated Sales: $100-500 Million
Number Employees: 500-999
Parent Co: The Kroger Company
Brands:
RALPHS

11119 **Ralph's Italian Ices**
11 Cooper St
Babylon, NY 11702 631-893-5646
info@ ralphsices.com
www.ralphsices.com
Italian ices
Manager: Stephen Lazarra
Owner: Lawerence Silvestro
Owner: Michael Scolaro
Estimated Sales: $300,000-500,000
Number Employees: 12
Brands:
Ralph's Italian Ices

11120 **Ralph's Packing Company**
500 W Freeman Avenue
Perkins, OK 74059-0249 405-547-2464
Fax: 405-547-2364 800-522-3979
www.ralphspacking.com
Manufacturer of beef, pork and lamb
President: Gary Crane
Estimated Sales: $4 Million
Number Employees: 35
Sq. footage: 9800
Type of Packaging: Consumer, Food Service, Private Label
Brands:
CIRCLE R

11121 **Ralphco**
P.O.Box 691
Worcester, MA 01613 508-757-8400
Fax: 508-752-7226 800-477-2574
www.ralphco.com
VP: Marc Greenberg
Estimated Sales: $ 3 - 5 Million
Number Employees: 1-4

11122 **Ramar Foods International Inc**
1101 Railroad Lane
Pittsburg, CA 94596 925-439-9009
Fax: 925-439-9242 800-660-0962
primoj@ramarfoods.com www.ramarfoods.com
USDA, juice/cider, hors d'oeuvres/appetizers, ice cream/sorbet, other frozen, co-packing, foodservice, private label.
Marketing: PJ Quesada
Number Employees: 130

11123 **Ramona's Mex. Food Produoducts**
13633 S Western Ave
Gardena, CA 90249 310-323-1950
Fax: 310-323-4210 info@laflor.com
Manufacturer and exporter of frozen tortillas, burritos, tamales and Mexican dinners
President: Ramona Banuelos
Estimated Sales: $50-100 Million
Number Employees: 250-499
Type of Packaging: Consumer, Food Service, Bulk

11124 **Ramos Orchards**
9192 Boyce Rd
Winters, CA 95694 530-795-4748
Fax: 530-795-4148
Processor and exporter of inshell walnuts, dehydrated prunes and hulled and shelled almonds
Owner: Fred Ramos
Estimated Sales: $4 Million
Number Employees: 50-99
Type of Packaging: Bulk
Brands:
Ramos Orchards

11125 **Ramsen**
17725 Juniper Path
Lakeville, MN 55044-9482 952-431-0400
Fax: 952-275-1926 www.ramsendairy.com
Processor of dry dairy products including nonfat milk; wholesaler/distributor of food ingredients; serving the food service market
Owner: Tim Krieger
Vice President: Craig Swanson
Marketing Director: Kathy Stevens
Sales Manager: Dennis Breueur
Estimated Sales: $ 10 - 20 Million
Number Employees: 10-19
Sq. footage: 1800
Type of Packaging: Consumer, Food Service

11126 **Ramsey Popcorn Company**
5645 Clover Valley Rd NW
Ramsey, IN 47166 812-347-2441
Fax: 812-347-3336 800-624-2060
info@ramseypopcorn.com
www.ramseypopcorn.com

Manufacturer and exporter of microwave, original, concession, bulk, snack food manufacturer, private label and international popcorn
President: Wilfred Sieg
Controller: Pat Smith
VP Operations: Daniel Sieg
Estimated Sales: $5 Million
Number Employees: 20-49
Type of Packaging: Consumer, Food Service, Private Label, Bulk
Brands:
Cousin Willie's

11127 **Ramsey/Sias**
6850 Southpointe Pkwy
Cleveland, OH 44141 440-546-1199
Fax: 440-546-0038 800-477-3788
information@atys-group.us www.atys-group.us
Processor of fruit products including bases, flavors, extracts, toppings, blends fillings and seasonings; exporter of processed fruits
CEO: Johann Marihart
CFO: Walter Grausam
Estimated Sales: $10-20 Million
Number Employees: 50
Parent Co: SIAS MPA
Type of Packaging: Food Service, Private Label, Bulk

11128 **Ranaldi Bros Frozen Food Products Inc**
111 Commerce Dr
Warwick, RI 2886 401-738-3444
Fax: 401-738-4446
Processor of frozen dough, stuffed breads, kosher dairy pastries, private label
President: Gary Ranaldi
Vice President: Raymond Ranaldi
Sales Director: Robin Capraro
Purchasing Manager: Joseph O'Neil
Estimated Sales: $2500000
Number Employees: 30
Number of Products: 100
Sq. footage: 65000
Type of Packaging: Consumer, Food Service, Private Label, Bulk
Brands:
Puff Dough Sheets
Puff Dough Squares

11129 **Ranch Oak Farm**
3005 Bledsoe St
Fort Worth, TX 76107-2905 817-877-3330
Fax: 817-877-3742 800-888-0327
info@RanchOak.com www.ranchoak.com
Smoked meats
President: Tom Misfeldt
Estimated Sales: Below $ 5 Million
Number Employees: 5-9
Type of Packaging: Private Label
Brands:
Ranch Oak Farm

11130 **Rancher's Lamb of Texas**
1005 City Farm Road
San Angelo, TX 76905-8508 325-659-4004
Fax: 915-482-8051 sales@rancherslamb.com
www.rancherslamb.com
Processor of lamb, goat and veal; slaughtering services available
President: Ken Emrick
CEO: A Dennis III
Quality Control: Al Fortier
Sales Director: Justin Jonas
Operations Manager: Phillip McQueen
Estimated Sales: $ 30-35 Million
Number Employees: 125
Number of Brands: 2
Number of Products: 10
Sq. footage: 70000
Type of Packaging: Consumer, Food Service, Private Label, Bulk

11131 **Rancho De Philo**
10050 Wilson Ave
Alta Loma, CA 91737-2314 909-987-4208
Fax: 909-987-4208
Dessert wine
President: Alan Tibbetts
Co-Owner: Janine Tibbetts
Estimated Sales: $ 1 - 3 Million
Number Employees: 1-4
Type of Packaging: Private Label
Brands:
Rancho De Philo
Triple Cream Sherry

11132 **Rancho Sisquoc Winery**
6600 Foxen Canyon Rd
Santa Maria, CA 93454 805-934-4332
Fax: 805-937-6601 sisquoc@ranchosisquoc.com
www.ranchosisquoc.com
Wines
Manager: Mary Holt
Marketing Director: Marry Holt
COO: Edward Holt
Estimated Sales: Below $ 5 Million
Number Employees: 20-49
Brands:
Rancho Sisquoc

11133 **Rancho's**
1910 Madison Ave # 724
Memphis, TN 38104-2620 901-276-8820
Fax: 901-744-0514 www.reinachagency.com
Sauces
Owner: Deborah Reinach
Estimated Sales: Less than $500,000
Number Employees: 1-4

11134 **Randag & Associates Inc**
187 S Lawndale Ave
Elmhurst, IL 60126 630-530-2830
Fax: 630-530-2830 randaginc@aol.com
Contract packager of confectionery products, frozen foods, health foods, industrial ingredients and spices
President: John Randag
VP: Nancy Randag
Purchasing Director: Jennifer Randag
Estimated Sales: $290000
Number Employees: 2
Number of Products: 30
Type of Packaging: Consumer, Food Service, Bulk

11135 **Randal Nutritional Products**
1595 Hampton Way
Santa Rosa, CA 95407 707-528-1800
Fax: 707-528-0924 800-221-1697
www.randalnutritional.com
Processor of vitamins, minerals and nutritional supplements
President: William Robotham
Director Marketing/Technical Services: Donald Burns
Estimated Sales: $3200000
Number Employees: 20-49
Sq. footage: 22000
Type of Packaging: Consumer, Private Label, Bulk
Brands:
Nuturpractic
Vimco

11136 **Randall Farms**
2900 Ayers Avenue
Vernon, CA 90023 323-587-2383
Fax: 323-586-1587 800-372-6581
cs@randallfoods.com www.randallfarms.com
Processor of poultry
President/CEO: Stan Bloon
Vice President: Ron Totin
Estimated Sales: $200 Million
Number Employees: 300
Brands:
Randall Foods

11137 **Randall Food Products**
8050 Hosbrook Road
Cincinnati, OH 45236 513-793-6525
info@randallbeans.com
www.randallbeans.com
Processor of dry beans including mixed, Great Northern and pinto
President: W Mashburn III
Office Manager: John Alyward
Estimated Sales: $5 Million
Number Employees: 20
Type of Packaging: Consumer, Private Label
Brands:
Randall

11138 **Randol**
2320 Kaliste Saloom Rd
Lafayette, LA 70508-6808 337-981-7080
Fax: 337-981-7083 800-YO -AJUN
randolsinfo@aol.com www.randols.com
Owner: Frank Randol
Vice President: Mary Wilson
Estimated Sales: $ 3 - 5 Million
Number Employees: 50-99

11139 **Randolph Packing Company**
275 Roma Jean Pkwy
Streamwood, IL 60107 630-830-3100
Fax: 630-830-1872
Meat
Owner: Angelo W Carmignani
Quality Control: Jerry Gasior
VP: Sandra Biggum
Estimated Sales: $ 20-50 Million
Number Employees: 100-249

11140 **Randolph Packing Corporation**
403 W Balfour Ave
Asheboro, NC 27203 336-672-1470
Fax: 336-672-6545
Processor of meat products
President: Donald Hamlet
Vice President: Rex Hamlet
Estimated Sales: $30 Million
Number Employees: 87
Type of Packaging: Consumer

11141 **Randy's Frozen Meats**
1910 5th St NW
Faribault, MN 55021 507-334-7177
Fax: 507-334-9210 800-354-7177
www.randysmeatsandgoodstuff.com
Processor of portion cut meat products; also, frozen pizza and microwaveable deli sandwiches; wholesaler/distributor of meat, dairy items, baked goods, frozen foods, equipment, general merchandise, seafood, etc.; serving the foodservice market
President and CFO: Randy Creasman
Owner: Neal Gregg
Partner: Gary Creasman
Estimated Sales: $ 20 - 50 Million
Number Employees: 20-49
Sq. footage: 10800
Type of Packaging: Consumer, Food Service, Private Label, Bulk

11142 **Ranieri Fine Foods**
278 Metropolitan Ave
Brooklyn, NY 11211-4006 718-599-0665
Fax: 718-599-6457
Italian specialty cheeses
President and CEO: Anna Leporie
Manager: Angelo Roncomi
Marketing: Annamaria Lepore
Estimated Sales: $610,000
Number Employees: 4
Type of Packaging: Consumer, Food Service, Bulk
Brands:
Gusparo
Gusparo
Madrisicilia
Ranieri
Star-Grand Italia

11143 **Rao's Specialty Foods**
17 Battery Pl Ste 610
New York, NY 10004 212-269-0151
Fax: 212-344-1680 info@raos.com
www.raos.com
Pasta sauces, roasted peppers, premium pasta, olive oil & vinegars, marindaes & dressings, canned tomatoes, and coffee
Owner: Sharon Straci
Owner: Lynn Iovino
Vice President: Jay Kuder
Marketing Manager: Ron Straci
Sales Manager: Peter Ardigo
Estimated Sales: $3.3 Million
Number Employees: 15
Number of Brands: 1
Number of Products: 20
Type of Packaging: Private Label

11144 **Rapazzini Winery**
P.O.Box 247
Gilroy, CA 95020 408-842-5649
Fax: 408-842-8353 800-842-6262
info@rapazziniwinery.com
www.rapazziniwinery.com
Wine, cooking wines, garlic, jelly, mustard, mayonnaise, spices, salsas and chips
Owner: Charles Larson
Owner: Alex Larson
Estimated Sales: Less Than $1Million
Number Employees: 6

Brands:
Rapazzini Winery

11145 **Rapunzel Pure Organics**
1455 Broad Street
4th Floor
Bloomfield, NJ 07003 973-338-1499
Fax: 973-338-1485 800-225-1449
info@rapunzel.com www.rapunzel.com
Organic sugar, organic chocolate, soups and bouillons, seasoned salt, organic vegetable juices, cocoa powder and spreads
President: Eckhart Kiesel
Director Sales/Marketing: Dale Kamibayashi
Sales Director: Jim Douglas
Number Employees: 5-9
Sq. footage: 5000
Type of Packaging: Consumer, Food Service, Bulk
Brands:
A. Vogel
Bambu Juices
Biotta Juices
Faqs
Herbamare Juices
Rapunzel Pure Organi

11146 **Ratners Retail Foods**
138 Delancey St
New York, NY 10002-3325 212-677-5588
www.nycfoods.com/ratners
Dairy products
President: Harold Zankel
VP: Robert Hirmatz
Estimated Sales: $ 2.5-5 Million
Number Employees: 50-99

11147 **Raven Creamery Company**
3303 NE M L King Boulevard
Portland, OR 97212-2057 503-288-5101
Fax: 503-288-5103
Butter
President: Henry Turner
Marketing Director: Tom Hughes
Estimated Sales: $ 5-10 Million
Number Employees: 10-19

11148 **Ravenswood**
18701 Gehricke Rd
Sonoma, CA 95476 888-669-4679
Fax: 707-933-2383 800-669-4679
rwwine@ravenswood-wine.com
www.ravenswood-wine.com
Wine
President: Joel Peterson
Wine Club Manager: Cathleen Francisco
CFO: Callie Konno
Executive VP: Justin Faggioli
Assistant Winemaker: Peter Mathis
Estimated Sales: $ 12 Million
Number Employees: 50-99
Brands:
Ravenswood

11149 **Ravifruit**
140 Prospect Avenue
Hackensack, NJ 07601-2255 201-939-5656
Fax: 201-939-5613

11150 **Ravioli Store**
43-44 21st Street
Long Islnad City, NY 11101
US 718-729-9300
877-727-8269
www.ravioilistore.com
Processor of fresh, dry and organic pasta including ravioli, agnolotti, tortellini and gnocchi,manicotti,and fresh sauces.
President: John A Zaccarro Jr
Estimated Sales: $300,000-500,000
Number Employees: 1-4
Number of Brands: 52
Type of Packaging: Consumer, Food Service

11151 **Ray Brothers & Noble Canning Company**
P.O.Box 314
Hobbs, IN 46047-0314 765-675-7451
Fax: 765-675-7400 renoble@tiptontel.com
www.noblecanning.com
Processor and canner of tomato products including whole, stewed and diced; also, canned tomato juice
President: Ray Noble
Sales Director: Dan Noble
Director Manufacturing: Mark Noble
Plant Manager: Mark Noble
Estimated Sales: $21.90 Million
Number Employees: 10-19
Sq. footage: 72000
Type of Packaging: Consumer, Food Service, Private Label

11152 **Ray's Sausage CompanyInc**
3146 East 123rd St
Cleveland, OH 44120-3179 216-921-8782
Fax: 216-921-4736
Fresh pork and beef sausage and links; mild, hot and extra hot souse, head cheese and beef souse.
President: Renee Cash
CFO/Administrativeexecutive: Leslie Cash Lester

Vice President: Raymond Cash, Jr.
Marketing/Sales: Raymond Hardin
Estimated Sales: $600000
Number Employees: 9
Sq. footage: 700
Type of Packaging: Consumer, Food Service
Brands:
Ray's Headcheese
Ray's Italian Links
Ray's Sausage
Ray's Souse

11153 **Raymond Vineyard & Cellar**
849 Zinfandel Ln
Saint Helena, CA 94574 707-963-3141
Fax: 707-963-8498 800-525-2659
hospitality@raymondvineyards.com
www.raymondvineyards.com
Wines
Type of Packaging: Private Label
Brands:
Raymond Vineyard

11154 **Raymond-Hadley Corporation**
89 Tompkins St
Spencer, NY 14883 607-589-4415
Fax: 607-589-6442 800-252-5220
www.raymondhadley.com
Importer and contract packager of South and Central American and African foods, barley, beans, bran, flour, cereal, dried fruit, grains, rice, spices, starches, vegetables, etc.; exporter of corn meal
President: Lori Maratea
Sales/Buyer Assistant: Tracy McCutcheon
Sales/Buyer Assistant: Elliot Dutra
Number Employees: 20-49
Sq. footage: 51000
Type of Packaging: Bulk

11155 **Rcb Intl.**
39878 Turnidge Rd NE
Albany, OR 97321 541-967-3814
Fax: 541-928-4633
Essential oils including spearmint, peppermint, dillweed, tarragon, parsley, pennyroyal, mentha citrata, etc
President: Dana Wendel
Manager: Bratt Wakefield
Sales Director: John Wendel
Estimated Sales: $5 Million
Number Employees: 7
Type of Packaging: Consumer, Bulk
Brands:
Mari Mint

11156 **Reading Coffee Roasters**
316 W Main St
Birdsboro, PA 19508 610-582-2243
Fax: 610-582-3615 800-331-6713
info@thecoffeegourmet.com
www.thecoffeegourmet.com
Gourmet coffee
Owner: Albert Van Maanen
Co-Owner: Rosemary Hartigan
Estimated Sales: $300,000-500,000
Number Employees: 10-19
Type of Packaging: Private Label
Brands:
Jazzy Java Custom Flavored Gourmet
Oscars Flavoring Syrups
Reading Coffee Roast

11157 **Readington Farms**
P.O.Box 164
Whitehouse, NJ 8888 908-534-2121
Fax: 908-534-5235
Dairy products
President: Donald Merrigan
VP Production: Lawrence Kurz
Production Manager: Doug McDowell
Estimated Sales: $100-$500 Million
Number Employees: 100-249

11158 **Ready Bake Foods**
2095 Meadowvale Boulevard
Mississauga, ON L5N 5N1
Canada 905-567-0660
Fax: 905-567-0909 www.cor.ca
Processor of frozen baked goods
President: Ralph Robinson
Estimated Sales: $71 Million
Number Employees: 850
Parent Co: George Weston Foods
Type of Packaging: Consumer, Food Service, Private Label

11159 **Ready Foods**
2565 W 8th Ave
Denver, CO 80204 720-889-1104
Fax: 303-629-6148
Processor of frozen Mexican foods including tortillas, salsa and taco fillings
Owner and President: Luis Abarca
Estimated Sales: $ .5 - 1 million
Number Employees: 1-4
Type of Packaging: Food Service, Private Label, Bulk
Brands:
Marcos
San Marcos

11160 **Ready Portion Meat Company**
1546 Choctaw Drive
Baton Rouge, LA 70805 225-355-5641
Fax: 225-355-8895
Wholesaler/distributor of frozen foods, general line items and meats; serving the food service market
Owner/President/CEO: Kyle Beck
Estimated Sales: $4 Million
Number Employees: 24
Sq. footage: 7000
Type of Packaging: Bulk

11161 **Ready-Pac Produce**
P.O.Box 6
Florence, NJ 8518 609-499-1900
Fax: 609-499-0042
Processor of ready-made vegetable salads
Manager: Jim Morris
Manager: Gary Bone
Estimated Sales: $10-20 Million
Number Employees: 100
Type of Packaging: Consumer, Food Service, Private Label
Brands:
Ready-Pac

11162 **Ready-Pac Produce**
4401 Foxdale St
Irwindale, CA 91706 626-856-8686
Fax: 626-856-0088 800-800-7822
www.readypacproduce.com
Fresh-cut produce
Chairman: Antonia Hernández
VP Marketing: Steve Dickstein
CEO: Michael Solomon
Estimated Sales: $ 50-100 Million
Number Employees: 1,000-4,999
Brands:
Ready Pac Aqua Pac
Ready Pac Complete S
Ready Pac European S
Ready Pac Fresh-Cut
Ready Pac Organic Sa
Ready Pac Party Item
Ready Pac Ready Fixi
Ready Pac Ready Snax
Ready Pac Value Pack

11163 **Readyfoods**
2645 W 7th Ave
Denver, CO 80204
Canada
Fax: 303-629-6148 800-748-1218
www.readyfoods.biz

Processor of turkey, chicken, frozen entrees and crepe and potato shells
President: Roger Chaoois
National Sales Manager: Brent Beatie
Number Employees: 50-99
Parent Co: Golden Valley Farms
Type of Packaging: Consumer, Food Service
Brands:
Ready Foods

11164 **Real Aloe Company**
2045 Corte Del Nogal
Carlsbad, CA 92011
Fax: 805-483-5364 800-541-7809
Processor and exporter of aloe vera products including gel, juice and beverages
Owner: Dan Mundel
VP: M Mundell
Operations Manager: Dan Mundell
Estimated Sales: $1100000
Number Employees: 5-9
Sq. footage: 10500
Type of Packaging: Consumer, Food Service, Private Label, Bulk
Brands:
Cal-Aloe Co.
Real Aloe Co.

11165 **Real Cookies**
3212 Hewlett Avenue
Merrick, NY 11566-5505 516-221-9300
Fax: 516-221-9561 800-822-5113
realcookies@worldnet.att.net
Frozen chocolate chip cookie dough and cookie mixes including oatmeal raisin, mocha almond, ginger, macadamia, white chocolate, pecan and chocolate chip; exporter of cookie mixes
President: Ellyn Knigin
CFO: Leonard Knigin
Vice President: Marian Knigin
Estimated Sales: $500,000-$1 Million
Number Employees: 5-9
Type of Packaging: Consumer, Food Service, Private Label, Bulk
Brands:
Grandma's Cookie Mix
Real Cookies

11166 **Real Food Marketing**
201 Wyandotte St Ste 402
Kansas City, MO 64105 816-221-4100
Fax: 913-671-8083
laura@realfoodmarketinginc.com
www.realfoodbakingco.com
Real Food Marketing, Proprietary Epicurean Food Developers, traditional desserts, breads, meat-filled pastries and ethnic breads and desserts such as; brownies, cookies, muffins, short cake, cakes, low fat and special diet, breads andpot pies. Real Food Marketing - Kanas City, MO & Las Vegas, Nevada. (888)-834-REAL (7325).
President/CEO: Bob Deal
CFO: Tara Cupps
R&D: Bob Deal
Operations: Bill Scott
Purchasing: Clint Scott
Estimated Sales: $ 1 - 3 Million
Number Employees: 1-4
Number of Brands: 2
Number of Products: 50
Sq. footage: 900
Type of Packaging: Consumer, Food Service, Private Label, Bulk

11167 **Real Kosher Sausage Company**
9 Euclid Ave
Newark, NJ 07105-4527 973-690-5394
Fax: 212-598-9011
Manufacturer and exporter of kosher meats including fresh, sausage and deli
President/CEO: Jacob Hill
Estimated Sales: $750,000
Number Employees: 10
Sq. footage: 15000
Type of Packaging: Consumer, Food Service, Private Label, Bulk
Brands:
999
Real Kosher

11168 **Real Sausage Company**
2710 S Poplar Ave
Chicago, IL 60608 312-842-5330
Fax: 312-842-5414
Sausage
President: Nicole Makowski
Estimated Sales: Below $ 5 Million
Number Employees: 20-49
Brands:
Real Sausage

11169 **Real Torino**
Po Box 448
Morristown, NJ 07960 973-895-5420
Fax: 973-895-8824 peteritaly@aol.com
www.pasta.com
Bread/biscuits, cakes/pastries, cookies, crackers, other baked goods, pasta (dry), other snacks, foodservice.
Marketing: Peter Carolan
Estimated Sales: $1.4 Million
Number Employees: 10

11170 **Realsalt**
475 West 910 South
Heber City, UT 84032
Fax: 435-654-3329 800-367-7258
krish@realsalt.com www.realsalt.com
Kosher, other lifestyle, cocoa/baking chocolate, stocks, spices, full-line snacks.

11171 **Reames Foods**
P.O.Box 29163
Columbus, OH 43229-0163 614-846-2232
Fax: 614-848-8330 marzetti@ipi.it
www.marzetti.com
Frozen egg noodles; also, pre-cooked lasagna sheets, frozen pot pie crusts and pre-cooked frozen pasta
President: Bruce Rosa
VP Marketing: Dick Anderson
Financial Manager: Doug Sell
Production Manager: Lynn Wehr
Number Employees: 100-249
Parent Co: T. Marzetti Company
Type of Packaging: Consumer, Food Service
Brands:
Reames
Sysco

11172 **Reames Foods**
803 8th St SW
Altoona, IA 50009 515-967-4254
Fax: 515-223-0674 800-247-4194
Raw frozen pasta, precooked frozen pasta, raw frozen pie crust
VP: David Hammerberg
Plant Manager: Vernon Chiles
Purchasing Manager: Debbie Chiles
Estimated Sales: $ 20-50 Million
Number Employees: 50-99
Parent Co: Deno Marzetti
Type of Packaging: Bulk
Brands:
Reames Frozen Noodles

11173 **Rebec Vineyards**
2229 N Amherst Hwy
Amherst, VA 24521 434-946-5168
Fax: 804-946-5168 winery@rebecwinery.com
www.rebecwinery.com
Wines
Manager: Svetlozar Kanev
VP Marketing: Svetlozar Kanev
Estimated Sales: Below $ 500,000
Number Employees: 1-4
Type of Packaging: Private Label

11174 **Rebecca Ruth Candy**
112 E 2nd St
Frankfort, KY 40601-2902 502-223-7475
Fax: 502-226-5854 800-444-3866
info@rebeccaruth.com www.rebeccaruth.com
Processor of candy including chocolate, filled, mints and bourbon chocolates
President: Charles Booe
Estimated Sales: $380000
Number Employees: 20-49
Type of Packaging: Consumer, Private Label, Bulk
Brands:
100 Bourbon Whiskey
Buffalo Trace
Butter Creams
Classic Liquor Cremes
Creme De Menthe
Rebecca-Ruth

11175 **Rebound**
1 Pepsi Way
Newburgh, NY 12550-3921 845-562-5400
Fax: 845-562-7840
Beverage manufacturing, water
Owner: Tim Tenney
Estimated Sales: $ 5 - 10 Million
Number Employees: 5-9

11176 **Reckitt Benckiser**
399 Interpace Pkwy Ste 101
Parsippany, NJ 7054 973-404-2600
Fax: 973-404-5700 800-333-3899
corpcomms@reckittbenckiser.com
www.reckittbenckiser.com
Processor of canned potatoes and onions
Regional Director: Javed Ahmed
VP Marketing: Alex Whitehouse
VP: Beverly Wilen
VP Sales: Stafford Dow
Technical Director: Paul Siracusa
Estimated Sales: $100-499.9 Million
Number Employees: 10,000+
Parent Co: Reckitt & Colman PLC
Type of Packaging: Consumer, Food Service, Bulk
Brands:
Cattlemen's
Frank's RedHot Sauce
French's

11177 **Rector Foods**
2280 N Park Drive
Brampton, ON L6S 6C6
Canada 905-789-9691
Fax: 905-789-0989 888-314-7834
Processor and exporter of seasoning blends for meat and poultry and vegetarian industries
President: Eoin Connell
VP Sales: Michael Parry
Number Employees: 50
Sq. footage: 53000

11178 **(HQ)Red Arrow Products Company LLC**
P.O.Box 1537
Manitowoc, WI 54221 920-683-5500
Fax: 920-769-1281 websales@redarrowusa.com
www.redarrowusa.com
Maufactures a wide variety of natural smoke flavors for meat, poultry and food applications. Smoke flavors are complemented by an extensive line of grill flavors, roast flavors and specialty browning. In addition, Red Arrow's equipmentcompany designs and fabricates application equipment to meet specific processing needs
President: Dale Hanke
Sales: Mark Crass
Marketing Coordinator: Kayla Sommer
Sales: Mark Crass
Type of Packaging: Food Service, Private Label, Bulk
Other Locations:
Red Arrow Products Co.
Manitowoc WI
Brands:
ARO-SMOKE
CHAR DEX
CHAR OIL
CHAR SOL
CHAR ZYME
GRILLIN'
MAILLOSE
TOASTIN
TRUE GOLD

11179 **Red Bell Brewing**
3100 Jefferson St.
Philadelphia, PA 19121 215-235-2460
Fax: 215-235-2486 888-733-2355
info@redbell.com
Beer
Resident: Martin F Spellman
Estimated Sales: Less than $500,000
Number Employees: 10-19
Brands:
Philadelphia
Red Bull

11180 **Red Chamber Company**
1912 E Vernon Ave
Vernon, CA 90058 323-234-9000
Fax: 323-231-8888 info@redchamber.com
www.redchamber.com

Seafood
President: Shu Chin Kou
CFO: Ming Shing Kou
CEO: Ming Bin Kou
Estimated Sales: $ 100-500 Million
Number Employees: 20-49
Brands:
Aqua Star
Mid-Pacific Seafoods
Neptune Foods
OFI Markesa International
Tampa Bay Fisheries

11181 **Red Creek Marinade Company**
P.O.Box 19875
Amarillo, TX 79114-1875 806-358-3531
Fax: 806-358-1587 800-687-9114
info@red-creek.com www.red-creek.com
Processor of liquid mesquite-flavored marinades for meats and jerky
Partner: Lawrence E New
Co-Owner: L New
Estimated Sales: $ 1 - 3 Million
Number Employees: 1-4
Number of Brands: 1
Number of Products: 3
Type of Packaging: Consumer, Food Service, Bulk
Brands:
Red Creek

11182 **Red Deer Lake Meat Processing**
226 Ave South & 96 St West
Site 15 Box 38 R.R. #9
Calgary, AB T2J 5G5
Canada 403-256-4925
Fax: 403-256-8882 rdlmeats@telus.net
www.rdlmeats.ab.ca
Processor of fresh and frozen beef, hamburgers, pork, bacon, lamb, goat and sausage including smoked, pork and beef
President/General Manager Sales: Brian Barrett
CEO: Georgina Walker
Estimated Sales: D
Number Employees: 20-49
Type of Packaging: Consumer, Food Service, Private Label, Bulk
Brands:
RDL (Red Deer Lake)

11183 **(HQ)Red Diamond**
PO Box 2168
Birmingham, AL 35201 205-577-4000
Fax: 205-577-4062 800-292-4651
www.reddiamond.com
Manufacturer of coffee; importer of teas and coffees. Food service distributor; private label tea and coffee packer
Principal: Shay Counselman
CFO: Sherman Pitts
VP: Mike Payne
Sales Director: Maxwell Graham
VP Operations: Franklin Webb
Purchasing: Jan Lay
Estimated Sales: $58 Million
Number Employees: 185
Type of Packaging: Consumer, Food Service, Private Label, Bulk
Brands:
Red Diamond Coffee & Tea

11184 **Red Gold**
P.O.Box 83
Elwood, IN 46036 765-754-7527
Fax: 765-754-3230 877-748-9798
info@redgold.com www.redgold.com
Manufacturer of tomatoes and tomato products including whole peeled, diced, stewed, crushed, puree, paste, juice, salsa and ketchup; also, sauces including tomato, pizza, taco, barbecue, chili, seafood cocktail, marinara andspaghetti
President/CEO: Brian Reichart
Finance Manager: Carol Hanna
Director Marketing/Sales: William Mandler
Estimated Sales: $230 Million
Number Employees: 500-999
Sq. footage: 1000000
Type of Packaging: Consumer, Food Service, Private Label, Bulk
Other Locations:
Red Gold
Orestes IN
Red Gold
Geneva IN
Brands:
GLORIETTA
IL MIGLIORE
RED GOLD
RED PACK
SACRAMENTO
THERESA
TUTOROSSO

11185 **Red Hot Chicago**
4649 W Armitage Ave
Chicago, IL 60639 312-829-3434
Fax: 312-829-2704 800-249-5226
info@redhotchicago.com
www.redhotchicago.com
Producer of Chicago style hot dogs
Owner/President: Scott Ladany
Founder: Samuel Ladany
Estimated Sales: $ 1 - 3 Million
Number Employees: 1-4
Type of Packaging: Food Service, Bulk
Brands:
Red Hot Chicago

11186 **Red Hot Cooperative**
809 Broadway Avenue NE
Redcliff, AB T0J 2P0
Canada 403-548-6453
Fax: 403-548-7255 laredhot@memlane.com
Cooperative and exporter of greenhouse vegetables
President: Matt Read
Sales Manager: John Judge
Number Employees: 50-99
Type of Packaging: Consumer, Food Service

11187 **Red Hot Foods**
820 E Railroad Avenue
Santa Paula, CA 93060 805-258-3650
Fax: 805-525-6000 info@redhotfoods.com
www.redhotfoods.com
Condiments, relishes, salsas, bbq sauces, hot sauce, steak sauce, mixes, olive oil, pesto, bean and chowder mixes.
President: Butch Baselite
Type of Packaging: Consumer, Food Service, Private Label, Bulk

11188 **Red Lake Fisheries Associates**
Hwy 1
Redby, MN 56670 218-679-3513
Fax: 218-679-2148
Processor of fish including perch, northern and carp
President: Bill May
Estimated Sales: $ 3 - 5 Million
Number Employees: 500-999
Type of Packaging: Consumer, Food Service, Bulk

11189 **Red Lion Spicy Foods Company**
420 W Broadway
Red Lion, PA 17356-1908 717-309-8303
Fax: 717-244-7348 chip@redlionspicyfoods.com
www.redlionspicyfoods.com
Chili mixes, chili powder, original dry rub, serrano red salsa, serrano red & black salsa, 20 pepper salsa, 20 pepper hot sauce, 20 pepper pickles, 20 pepper garlic dills, 20 pepper relish, 20 pepper garlic, competition blend chilimix
President: Chip Welsh
Type of Packaging: Consumer

11190 **Red Mill Farms**
290 S 5th St
Brooklyn, NY 11211 718-384-2150
Fax: 718-384-2988 800-344-2253
redmill@aol.com www.macaroonking.com
Processor and exporter of macaroons and individually wrapped cakes
President: Arnold Badner
Estimated Sales: $4,000,000
Number Employees: 20-49
Sq. footage: 30000
Type of Packaging: Food Service
Brands:
Manhattan Gourmet

11191 **Red Monkey Foods**
1206 E Industrial Park
Mount Vernon, MI 65712 417-466-9109
Fax: 314-754-9755
jbrinkhofft@redmonkeyfoods.com
www.redmonkeyfoods.com
Full-line spices, herbs, other sauces, seasonings and cooking enhancers, rubs, spices, co-packing, foodservice, private label.
Marketing: Jeff Brinkhoff

11192 **Red Oak Farms**
PO Box 456
Red Oak, IA 51566-0456 712-623-9224
Fax: 712-623-4533 info@redoakfarms.com
www.redoakfarms.com
Premium USDA certified fresh beef, fresh boxed beef, portion cut beef, precooked beef, retail and bulk
President and CEO: Gordon Reisinger
CEO: Gordon Reisinger
CFO: Harley Dillard
Vice President: Pete Hudgins
Research & Development: Nancy Pellett
Sales Director: H Jackson
Operations Manager: Steve Berendes
Estimated Sales: $ 50 Million
Number Employees: 10
Number of Brands: 3
Number of Products: 12
Type of Packaging: Consumer, Food Service, Bulk
Brands:
My Favorite Jerky
Red Oak Farms Hereford Beef

11193 **Red Pelican Food Products**
5650 Saint Jean Street
Detroit, MI 48213-3415 313-881-4095
Processor and importer of mustard, horseradish, relish, sauerkraut, vinegar, Belgian chocolate and sauce; importer of cheese
President: Bernard Cornillie
Sales Manager: D Cornillie
Number Employees: 5-9
Sq. footage: 14000
Type of Packaging: Consumer, Food Service, Private Label, Bulk

11194 **Red River Commodities**
PO Box 3022
Fargo, ND 58108 701-282-2600
Fax: 701-282-5325 julit@sunbutter.com
www.redriv.com
Processor and exporter of sunflower seeds, colored beans, millet, flax, soybeans, and organics
President: Robert Majkrzak
VP Finance: Randy Wigen
Quality Control Manager: Erik Barwicki
VP Marketing: Dan Hofland
Human Resources Director: Audrey Opgrand
Production Manager: Mike Johnson
Plant Manager: Brad Newton
Estimated Sales: $137 Million
Number Employees: 250
Sq. footage: 140000
Parent Co: Universal Foods
Type of Packaging: Food Service, Private Label, Bulk
Brands:
Brown Flax
Confection Sunflower Seed
Goldtex

11195 **Red River Foods**
9020 Stony Point Pkwy Ste 380
Richmond, VA 23235 804-320-1844
Fax: 804-320-1896 800-443-6637
www.redriverfoods.com
Nuts, seeds, dried foods and snack foods
President: James Phipps
Estimated Sales: $ 50-100 Million
Number Employees: 10-19
Number of Products: 30
Parent Co: Universal Corporation

11196 **Red Rocker Candy**
92B Industrial Drive
Suite 6
Troy, VA 22974 434-589-2011
Fax: 434-589-3649
sue.charney@redrockercandy.com
www.redrockercandy.com
Candy and other snacks.
Manager: Sue Charney
Estimated Sales: $250,000
Number Employees: 5

11197 **(HQ)Red Rose Trading Company**
1237 Trinity North Rd
Wrightsville, PA 17368 717-252-5500

Processor, contract packager and exporter of granola, organic pancake, baking and wheat/gluten-free mixes; wholesaler/distributor of organic and bulk ingredients, dry mixes and blends; serving the food service market
Owner: J Leichter
Estimated Sales: $ 3 - 5 Million
Number Employees: 10-19
Sq. footage: 28000
Type of Packaging: Consumer, Food Service, Private Label, Bulk

11198 Red Star Yeast
777 E Wisconsin Ave # 11
Milwaukee, WI 53202-5302 414-271-6755
Fax: 414-347-4795 877-677-7000
carol.stevens@redstaryeast.com
www.sensient-technologies.com
Yeast, fermentation products
President: Carol Stevens
CEO: Kenneth P Manning
Estimated Sales: $ 20-50 Million
Number Employees: 1,000-4,999
Brands:
Red Star

11199 Red Steer Meats
3812 W Clarendon Ave
Phoenix, AZ 85019-3718 602-272-6677
Fax: 602-484-7381
Meat and meat products
President: Richard Barton
Vice President: Judy Barton
Estimated Sales: $ 5-10 Million
Number Employees: 5-9
Type of Packaging: Private Label

11200 Red White & Brew
223 Ashley Ct
Redding, CA 96001-3656 530-222-5891
www.redwhiteandbrew.com
Beer
President: Bill Ward
Estimated Sales: $120,000
Number Employees: 3
Brands:
Red White & Brew

11201 Red Willow Natural Foods
205 County Road U
River Falls, WI 54022 715-425-1489
Fax: 715-273-3482
Natural foods
VP: Miller Rogers
Manager/COO: Barbara Wickman
Sales Manager: Jennifer Simon
Brands:
Red Willow Natural Foods

11202 Redco Foods
100 Northfield Dr Dept D
Windsor, CT 6095 860-688-2121
Fax: 860-688-7844 800-645-1190
www.greentea.com
Processor of teas.
President: R Berstynen
VP: Robert Cassie
VP Marketing: David Rigg
Sales Director: Laura Morris
VP Operations: Doug Farrell
Estimated Sales: $ 5 - 10 Million
Number Employees: 10-19
Type of Packaging: Food Service, Private Label
Brands:
JUNKET
RED ROSE
RED ROSE TEA
SALADA
SALADA TEA

11203 Redhawk Vineyard
2995 Michigan City Rd NW
Salem, OR 97304-9704 503-362-1596
Fax: 503-585-4657 toma@open.org
www.redhawkwine.com
Wines
Owner: John Pataccoli
Estimated Sales: $350,000
Number Employees: 1-4
Type of Packaging: Private Label
Brands:
Redhawk

11204 Redhook Ale Breweries
35 Corporate Dr
Newington, NH 03801-7852 603-430-8600
Fax: 603-430-6011 redhook@redhook.com
www.redhook.com
Processor of beer and ale
Manager: Jerry Prial
Estimated Sales: $500,000-999,999
Number Employees: 20-49
Parent Co: Redhook Ale Breweries
Type of Packaging: Consumer, Food Service
Brands:
Redhook

11205 Redhook Ale Breweries
14300 NE 145th St # 210
Woodinville, WA 98072-6950 425-483-3232
Fax: 425-485-0761 redhook@redhook.com
www.redhook.com
Processor of beer and ale
President: David Mickelson
COO: Paul Shipman
CFO: T. Caldwell
CEO: Paul S Shipman
Quality Control: Tuan Liu
Marketing Manager: Nelson Ray
Sales Manager: Gerard Prial
Estimated Sales: $ 50-100 Million
Number Employees: 100-249
Parent Co: Redhook Ale Breweries
Type of Packaging: Consumer, Food Service
Brands:
Ballard Bitter
Black Hook
Double Black
ESB
Hefeweizen
Rye
Wheatbrook
Winterhook

11206 Redi-Froze
PO Box 4055
South Bend, IN 46634-4055 574-237-5111
Fax: 574-234-4162
Vice President: Jack Enoch

11207 Redi-Serve Food Company
1200 Industrial Dr
Fort Atkinson, WI 53538-2758 920-563-6391
Fax: 920-563-3013
Processor of frozen prepared foods including meat balls, beef patties, chicken patties and breaded veal cutlets
President: Jim Bowen
CEO: Sol Friend
Estimated Sales: $49.5 Million
Number Employees: 250-499
Parent Co: Encore Frozen Foods
Type of Packaging: Consumer, Food Service, Private Label

11208 Redmond Minerals
P.O.Box 219
Redmond, UT 84652 435-529-7402
Fax: 435-529-7486 800-367-7258
mail@redmondminerals.com
www.redmondminerals.com
Manufacturer and exporter of all natural kosher certified sea salt
CEO: Rhett Roberts
Estimated Sales: $ 20-50 Million
Number Employees: 30
Type of Packaging: Consumer, Food Service, Private Label, Bulk

11209 Redondo's Sausage Factory
94-140 Leokane St
Waipahu, HI 96797-2280 808-671-5444
Fax: 808-676-7009 www.redondos.com
Sausages
President: Hitoshi Okada
VP/General Manager: Yoshi Shinanti
VP: Toshiyuki Murakane
Owner: Frank Redondo
Estimated Sales: $ 5-10 Million
Number Employees: 20-49
Brands:
Pipikaula

11210 Redwood Hill Farm
2064 Gravenstein Hwy N # 130
Sebastopol, CA 95472-2630 707-823-8250
Fax: 707-823-6976 contact@redwoodhill.com
www.redwoodhill.com
Goat and dairy products/cheeses
Manager: Jennifer Bize
Marketing Director: Sharon Bice
CFO: Jennifer Lynn Bice
Estimated Sales: $ 1-2.5 Million
Number Employees: 10-19
Type of Packaging: Private Label
Brands:
Redwood Hill Farm

11211 Redwood Vintners
12 Harbor Dr
Novato, CA 94945-3507 415-892-6949
Fax: 415-892-7469
Distribution and marketing of beverages
VP Sales: Barney Feinblum
Estimated Sales: $ 20 - 50 Million
Number Employees: 50-99
Brands:
Redwood Vintners

11212 Reed Corporation
233 W Parkway
Pompton Plains, NJ 07444-1028 973-831-0636
Fax: 973-831-0791 800-820-REED
Cellulose food fibers
Estimated Sales: $ 2.5-5 Million
Number Employees: 5-9

11213 Reed Lang Farms
118 W Colorado Ave
Rio Hondo, TX 78583 956-748-2354
Fax: 956-748-2888
Ship Ruby Red and Rio Red grapefruits, navel oranges, Lula avacados, pecans, almonds and citrus blossom honey for gift packages.
President/Owner: Violet Lang
Estimated Sales: $50,000
Number Employees: 16
Sq. footage: 11025
Type of Packaging: Private Label

11214 Reed's Original Beverage Corporation
13000 S Spring St
Los Angeles, CA 90061-1634 310-217-9400
Fax: 310-217-9411 800-997-3337
info@reedsgingerbrew.com
www.reedsgingerbrew.com
Manufacturer of ginger brewed soft drinks, ginger candy, and ice cream
President/CEO: Christopher Reed
COO: Thierry Foucaut
CFO: James Linesch
Sales Director: Jeff Ainis
Estimated Sales: $ 10-15 million
Number Employees: 20
Type of Packaging: Consumer
Brands:
China Cola
Reed's Crystalized Ginger Candy
Reed's Ginger Brews
Reed's Ginger Ice Cream
Virgil's Root Beers

11215 Reel Food Service
4482 N Buckboard Pl
Boise, ID 83713-9574 208-376-7972
Fax: 208-342-2868
Owner: Doug Rule
Estimated Sales: $300,000-500,000
Number Employees: 1-4

11216 Reeves Winery
PO Box 1543
Middletown, CA 95461-1543 707-987-9650
Wines

11217 Refined Sugars
1 Federal St
Yonkers, NY 10705 914-963-0206
Fax: 914-963-1030 800-431-1020
Processor and exporter of sugar
President: Jack Lay
Estimated Sales: $100+ Million
Number Employees: 250-499
Parent Co: Domino Foods
Type of Packaging: Consumer, Food Service, Private Label, Bulk

Brands:
4# FLOW-SWEET
COUNTRY CANE
JACK FROST

11218 **Refrigerated Foods Association**
2971 Flowers Rd S Ste 266
Chamblee, GA 30341 770-452-0660
Fax: 770-455-3879 info@refrigeratedfoods.org
www.refrigeratedfoods.org
Trade association
Executive Director: Terry Dougherty
Estimated Sales: Less than $500,000
Number Employees: 1-4

11219 **Regal Crown Foods**
41 Mason St
Worcester, MA 01610 508-752-2679
Fax: 508-831-0775
Manufactures vinegar pickles
President: Douglas Freund
Public Relations: Monica Freund Kaufman
Plant Manager: David Giorgio
Estimated Sales: $ 1 - 3 Million
Number Employees: 1-4
Number of Brands: 12
Number of Products: 6
Type of Packaging: Food Service, Private Label

11220 **Regal Food Service**
13206 Advance Dr
Houston, TX 77065-1102 281-477-3683
Fax: 713-222-2549 sm11regal@aol.com
Manufacturer of sandwiches and spreads
Manager: Charles Smith
Estimated Sales: $10 Million
Number Employees: 50-99
Type of Packaging: Consumer, Food Service

11221 **Regal Health Foods International**
3705 W Grand Ave
Chicago, IL 60651-2236 773-252-1044
Fax: 773-252-0817 regal_1@prodigy.net
Processor and importer of dried fruits and nuts
President: Gregory Piatigorsky
VP Marketing/Sales: Igor Piatigorsky
Estimated Sales: $ 10 - 20 Million
Number Employees: 20-49
Sq. footage: 27000
Type of Packaging: Consumer, Food Service, Private Label, Bulk
Brands:
Regal

11222 **Regco Corporation**
10 Avco Road
Haverhill, MA 01835-6935 978-521-4370
Fax: 978-372-4371 info@regcocorp.com
www.regenies.com
Crunchy pitas
President: Regina Ragonese
Broker Sales Representative: Sheryl Makaron
Public Relations Director: Peter Ash
Production Supervisor: Guy Minnick
Number Employees: 14
Brands:
REGENIE'S CRUNCHY PITAS
REGENIE'S TREASURE CRISPS

11223 **Regency Coffee & VendingCompany**
2022 E Spruce Cir
Olathe, KS 66062-5404 913-829-1994
Fax: 913-393-0097 www.regencycoffee.com
Variety of gourmet coffees, teas, hot beverages, cold beverages and snacks
Owner: Nancy Robinson
CEO: William Kirkpatrick
CFO: Rob Buntun
Vice President: Kelly Havins
Estimated Sales: $10-24.9 Million
Number Employees: 5-9
Number of Brands: 3
Number of Products: 80
Type of Packaging: Consumer, Food Service, Private Label, Bulk

11224 **Regenie's All Natural and Organic Snacks**
46 Rogers Rd
Haverhill, MA 01835 978-521-4370
Fax: 978-372-4371 877-Reg-nie
regina@regenies.com www.regenies.com
all natural pita chips
President/Owner: Regina Ragonese

11225 **Regent Champagne Cellars**
17 E 74th St
New York, NY 10021
Fax: 845-691-7298
Processor of bottled spring and sparkling water, juice, soda and champagne
President: Herbert Feinberg
Vice President: Edward Gogel
Estimated Sales: $760000
Number Employees: 10

11226 **Regent Confections**
111 S Cross Creek Road
Unit B
Orange, CA 92869-5858 714-348-8889
Fax: 949-794-5517 info@regentconfections.com
www.regentconfections.com
Manufacturer of candy
President: Shahid Iqbal
Estimated Sales: $ 20 Million
Number Employees: 4
Type of Packaging: Consumer, Private Label

11227 **Regez Cheese & Paper Supply**
N2603 Coplien Rd
Monroe, WI 53566 608-325-3417
Fax: 608-325-3499
Cheese
President: Michael Einbeck
Estimated Sales: $530,000
Number Employees: 1-4

11228 **Reggie Ball's Cajun Foods**
501 Bunker Rd
Lake Charles, LA 70615 337-436-0291
Fax: 337-433-9851
Processor of Cajun seasoning and mixes including rice jambalaya and seafood fry
Owner/President: Reginald Ball, Jr
Estimated Sales: $300,000-500,000
Number Employees: 1-4
Type of Packaging: Consumer, Food Service, Bulk
Brands:
Reggie Ball's

11229 **Reggie Ball's Cajun Foods**
501 Bunker Rd
Lake Charles, LA 70615 337-436-0291
Fax: 337-433-9851 reggieball@cox-internet.com
www.ballscajunfoods.com
Processor of cajum seasonings and mixes. Contract packaging and private labeling is available.
Owner/President: Reginald Ball Jr
Estimated Sales: $500,000-$1 Million
Number Employees: 20-49
Type of Packaging: Private Label

11230 **Reggie's Roast**
1501 West Blancke Street
Linden, NJ 07036 908-862-3700
Fax: 908-862-3711 hcl@reggiesroast.com
www.reggiesroast.com
Coffee.
President: Reggie Chungloy
Estimated Sales: $260,000
Number Employees: 4

11231 **Regis Milk Company**
578 Meeting St
Charleston, SC 29403 843-723-3418
Fax: 843-577-3119
Milk
President: Thad Mitchum
Vice President: Eric Shuler
Plant Foreman: Charlie Green
Estimated Sales: $ 5-10 Million
Number Employees: 20-49
Type of Packaging: Private Label

11232 **Register Meat Company**
3160 Willow St
Cottondale, FL 32431 850-352-4269
Fax: 850-352-2628 www.registermeats.com
Manufacturer of pork products including sausage
President: Al Kaempfer
Estimated Sales: $10 Million
Number Employees: 5-9
Type of Packaging: Consumer, Bulk

11233 **Registry Steaks & Seafood**
7661 S 78th Ave # B
Bridgeview, IL 60455-1271 708-458-3100
Fax: 708-458-3103
Meat, seafood
President: Rosemarie Migacz
Vice President: Tony Migacz
Estimated Sales: $ 10 Million
Number Employees: 20-49
Sq. footage: 5000
Type of Packaging: Food Service, Private Label, Bulk

11234 **Rego Smoked Fish Company**
6980 75th St
Flushing, NY 11379 718-894-1400
Fax: 718-894-9100
Processor of smoked salmon, sturgeon, trout, sablefish and whitefish; importer of sturgeon
President: Jason Spitz
Manager: Sheldon Spitz
Owner: Conrad Spitz
Estimated Sales: $500,000-$1 Million
Number Employees: 1-4
Sq. footage: 7000
Type of Packaging: Consumer, Bulk
Brands:
Spibro

11235 **Rego's Purity Foods**
3049 Ualena St # 415
Honolulu, HI 96819-1946 808-847-3717
Fax: 808-847-6877 www.regospurity.com
Processor of Portuguese and blood sausage, bologna, frankfurters, hamburger patties and knockwurst
President: Scott Stevenson
Estimated Sales: $4000000
Number Employees: 1-4
Type of Packaging: Consumer, Food Service

11236 **Reheis**
235 Snyder Ave
Berkeley Heights, NJ 7922 908-464-1500
Fax: 908-464-7726 rduffy@reheis.com
www.reheis.com
Processor, importer and exporter of potassium chloride
VP R&D: J C Parekh
VP Sales: D Fondots
VP Operations: J Bogan
Plant Manager: Gerry Kirwan
Number Employees: 100-249
Brands:
KCI

11237 **Reid Foods**
Po Box 406
Gurnee, IL 60031 847-625-7912
Fax: 847-625-7913 888-295-8478
reidfoods@yahoo.com www.reidfoods.com
jams, dessert toppings, salsas, soups, pasta, pasta sauces, dips and chili
President/Owner: Maria Reid
Estimated Sales: $190,000
Number Employees: 3

11238 **(HQ)Reilly Dairy & Food Company**
6603 S Trask Avenue
Tampa, FL 33616 813-839-8458
Fax: 813-839-0394 info@reillydairy.com
www.reillydairy.com
Processor and exporter of cheese, dairy products, butter, and fluid products
President: Gerald Reilly
Human Resources Director: Brenda Reilly
Estimated Sales: $16000000
Number Employees: 70
Sq. footage: 18000
Type of Packaging: Consumer, Food Service, Private Label, Bulk
Brands:
Dixie Fresh
Wisconsin Gold

11239 **Reilly's Sea Products**
PO Box 149
South Bristol, ME 04568-0149 207-644-1400
Fax: 207-644-8192
Seafood
President: Terry Reilly
Estimated Sales: $ 5 - 10 Million
Number Employees: 20-49

11240 **(HQ)Reily Foods Company**
640 Magazine St
New Orleans, LA 70130 504-524-6131
Fax: 504-539-8358 service@luzianne.com
www.luzianne.com
Manufacturer of mayonnaise, coffee, tea, peanut butter, chili mixes, soups, pasta, beans, hot sauces, Cajun products, salad dressings and cake flours
Chairman: William Reily III
President: James McCarthy
EVP/CFO: Harold Herrmann Jr
VP: Tony Doughty
National Broker Sales Manager: Gary Millard
Corporate Regional Manager: Russ Vanputten
Estimated Sales: $7 Million
Number Employees: 100-249
Parent Co: JFG Coffee
Brands:
ABITA SPRINGS WATER
BLUE PLATE
LA MARTINQUE
LUZIANNE
SWANS DOWN

11241 **Reily Foods/JFG Coffee Company**
640 Magazine Street
New Orleans, LA 70130 865-546-2120
Fax: 504-539-5427 800-535-1961
info@reilyfoods.com www.luzianne.com
Processor of tea, coffee, mayonnaise and peanut butter
President/CEO: Robert C Maurer
Sales Manager: Ken Christopher
VP Operations: Taylor Dulaney
Plant Manager: Rich Schmader
Number Employees: 100-249
Parent Co: Reily Companies
Type of Packaging: Consumer, Food Service
Brands:
Blue Plate Mayonnaise
Luzianne Tea
Swans Down Cake Flour

11242 **Reimann Food Classics**
1304 E Cooper Drive
Palatine, IL 60074-7284 847-991-1366
Fax: 847-359-7528
Processor of pancake and waffle mixes
President: E Reimann
Number Employees: 5-9
Type of Packaging: Consumer

11243 **Reinhart Foods**
15 Allstate Parkway
Suite 500
Markham, ON L3R 5B4
Canada 905-754-3500
Fax: 905-754-3504 www.reinhartfoods.com
Processor of vinegar, bottled maraschino cherries, glace fruit, dates, raisins, coconut, mince meat, pie fillings and apples; exporter of vinegar; importer of maraschino cherries, dates, raisins, coconut and pineapple
President: T Singer
VP/General Manager: D Bell
Assistant General Manager: L Watt
Parent Co: Reinhart Vinegars
Type of Packaging: Consumer, Food Service, Private Label, Bulk
Brands:
Orchard Fresh
Perfec Py
Reinhart

11244 **Reinhold Ice Cream Company**
800 Fulton St
Pittsburgh, PA 15233-2119 412-321-7600
Fax: 412-321-8456
Processor of ice cream and frozen yogurt
President: Robert Mandell
Vice President: Michael Mandell
Salesman: Diane Beckerman
Plant Manager: Craig Metzgar
Estimated Sales: $7400000
Number Employees: 50-99
Type of Packaging: Consumer, Food Service, Private Label, Bulk

11245 **Reist Popcorn Company**
113 Manheim St
Mount Joy, PA 17552 717-653-8078
Fax: 717-653-4121
reistpopcorn@embarqmail.com
reistpopcorn.com
Manufacturer of unpoppped popcorn
President: David Reist
Estimated Sales: $1.3 Million
Number Employees: 5
Type of Packaging: Private Label, Bulk
Brands:
Dutch Country
Hi-Pop

11246 **Reiter Dairy**
1941 Commerce Cir
Springfield, OH 45504 937-323-5777
Fax: 937-323-2420 www.reiterdairy.com
Processor of whole, skim, 1% and 2% milk, cream and yogurt; also, bottled water and fruit drinks including grapefruit, punch, orange, lemon and lemon/lime
Manager: Brian Riley
Plant Manager: Norris Jackman
Estimated Sales: $100+ Million
Number Employees: 100-249
Parent Co: Dean Foods Company
Type of Packaging: Consumer, Food Service, Private Label

11247 **Reiter Dairy**
1415 W Waterloo Rd
Akron, OH 44314 330-745-1123
Fax: 330-745-4363 800-362-0825
www.reiterdairy.com
Processor of orange juice and dairy products including ice cream, milk, heavy cream and ice cream mixes
Manager: Bill Riley
Plant Manager: Dave Schirmer
Number Employees: 50-99
Parent Co: Dean Foods Company
Type of Packaging: Consumer, Food Service
Brands:
REITER

11248 **Rembrandt Foods**
1419 480th Street
Rembrandt, IA 50576-7542 972-847-4421
Fax: 972-746-4545 877-344-4055
foodservicesales@rembrandtinc.com
www.rembrandtfoods.com
Egg ingredients and egg products
CEO: David Rettig
CFO: Brad Fullmer
COO: Don Kellen
Number Employees: 275

11249 **Renaissance Baking Company**
12551 Biscayne Boulevard
North Miami, FL 33181-2522 305-893-2144
Fax: 305-893-3308
Processor of hearth baked European style sourdough bread, sandwich breads and dinner rolls
President: Steven Bern
Number Employees: 40
Sq. footage: 5000
Type of Packaging: Consumer, Food Service

11250 **Renaissance Vineyard & Winery**
P.O.Box 1000
Oregon House, CA 95962 530-692-2222
Fax: 530-692-2497 800-655-3277
sales@rvw.com www.rvw.com
Wines
President: Gideon Beinstock
CFO: Massimo Leotta
VP Distribution: Shawn Robinson
Direct Marketing Manager: Joseph Bruno
Winemaker: Gideon Beinstock
Estimated Sales: $ 10-20 Million
Number Employees: 50-99
Type of Packaging: Private Label
Brands:
RENAISSANCE

11251 **Renard's Cheese**
248 County Rd S
Algoma, WI 54201 920-487-2825
Fax: 920-487-5042 renards@itol.com
www.renards.com
Cheese
Proprietor: Brian Renard
Proprietor: Gary Renard
Vice President: Chris Renard
Estimated Sales: $ 5-9.9 Million
Number Employees: 5-9
Type of Packaging: Private Label

11252 **Renault Winery**
72 N Bremen Ave
Egg Harbor City, NJ 08215-3195 609-965-2111
Fax: 609-965-1847 wine@renaultwinery.com
www.renaultwinery.com
Processor of vermouth and wine
President: Joseph Milza
Manufacturing Manager: Raphael Lopez
Estimated Sales: $3649539
Number Employees: 100-249
Type of Packaging: Consumer

11253 **Rendulic Packing**
800 Manning Ave
McKeesport, PA 15132-3624 412-678-9541
Fax: 412-678-2606 info@nemahalal.com
www.nemahalal.com
Processor and packer of meats including bologna, suckling pig, veal and lamb
President: Beyhan Nakiboglo
Estimated Sales: $3300000
Number Employees: 10-19
Type of Packaging: Consumer

11254 **Rene Produce Distributors**
P.O.Box 1178
Nogales, AZ 85628-1178 520-281-9014
Fax: 520-281-2933 reneprod@dakotacom.net
www.reneproduce.com
Grower and exporter of cucumbers, eggplant, squash, tomatoes and peppers including red, bell and gold
President: Rene Carrillo
Sales Manager: David Kennedy
Sales: George Quintero
Estimated Sales: $ 3 - 5 Million
Number Employees: 10-19
Type of Packaging: Consumer, Food Service
Brands:
Rene

11255 **Rene Rey Chocolates Ltd**
1119 W 14th Street
North Vancouver, BC V7P 1J9
Canada 604-985-0949
Fax: 604-985-0395 888-985-0949
renerey@axion.net www.chocolate-canada.com
Chocolate, candy
President: Rene Rey
Director Of Marketing: Gerald Pinton
Sq. footage: 20000
Brands:
MAPLE NUTS
NATURE CANADA
SUN MOON STARS

11256 **Renfro Foods**
P.O.Box 321
Fort Worth, TX 76101 817-336-3849
Fax: 817-336-7910 info1@renfrofoods.com
www.renfrofoods.com
Manufacturer of relishes, sauces, peppers and salsas
President: Doug Renfro
CEO: Bill Renfro
Vice President: Becky Renfro
Marketing: Dan Fore
VP Production: James Renfro
Estimated Sales: $3.3 Million
Number Employees: 25
Number of Products: 27
Type of Packaging: Consumer, Food Service, Private Label
Brands:
MRS RENFRO'S

11257 **Renwood Winery**
12225 Steiner Rd
Plymouth, CA 95669 209-245-6979
Fax: 916-381-9458 800-348-8466
sales@renwood.com www.renwood.com
Wines
President: Robert Smerling
CFO: Bob Moore
VP Marketing: Joe Cusimano
Manager: Abby Bishop
Operations Manager: Bryan Wilkinson
Estimated Sales: $ 5-10 Million
Number Employees: 20-49
Sq. footage: 18
Type of Packaging: Private Label
Brands:
Renwood Wines
Santino Wines

11258 Republic of Tea
5 Hamilton Landing
Suite 100
Novato, CA 94949-8703 415-382-3400
Fax: 415-382-3401 80- 2-8 48
info@republicoftea.com www.republicoftea.com
Fine full leaf teas and herbs and teaware.
President: Ronald Rubin
CFO: Steve Lohmann
VP: Stuart Gold
Marketing: Heather Innocenti
Operations: George Phillips
Estimated Sales: $ 2.5-5 Million
Number Employees: 25
Brands:
Daily Green Teas
RED TEA
Republic of Tea

11259 Republica Del Cacao LLC
3780 Kilroy Airport Way
Suite 200
Long Beach, CA 90806 562-537-3656
Fax: 562-256-7001
chocolate@repulicadelcacao.us
www.republicadelcacao.us
Cocoa/baking chocolate, other baking mixes and ingredients, chocolate bars, full-line chocolate, other chocolate.
Manager: Bernard Duclos
Member: Ganzano Chieiboga
Marketing: Bernard Duclos
Estimated Sales: $74,000
Number Employees: 3

11260 Request Foods
P.O.Box 2577
Holland, MI 49422-2577 616-786-0900
Fax: 616-786-9180 800-748-0378
sales_department@requestfoods.com
www.requestfoods.com
Processor of frozen entrees and dinners
President: Jack DeWitt
CFO: Bill Rysdyk
R & D: Jurgen Becker
Quality Control: Tom Muntter
Operations Director: Merle DeWitt
Purchasing Agent: Larry Vanderkolk
Estimated Sales: $31 Million
Number Employees: 375
Sq. footage: 350000
Type of Packaging: Consumer, Food Service, Private Label

11261 Research Products Company
1835 E North St
Salina, KS 67401 785-825-2181
Fax: 785-825-8908 800-234-7174
info@researchprod.com www.researchprod.com
Processor and exporter of flour bleaching premixes, flour maturing premixers,vitamin and mineral ingredients
President: Monte White
Estimated Sales: $ 10 - 20 Million
Number Employees: 50-99
Parent Co: McShares
Brands:
Kurolite
Oxylite

11262 Reser's Fine Foods
15570 SW Jenkins Rd
Beaverton, OR 97006 503-643-6431
Fax: 503-646-9233 800-333-6431
www.resers.com
Manufacturer of prepared salads, side dishes, dips, Mexican foods and specialty products.
President/CEO: Alvin Reser
CFO: Paul Levy
VP Sales/Marekting: Peter Sirgy
COO: Mark Reser
VP Foodservice: Doug Peck
Estimated Sales: $500 Million
Number Employees: 500-999
Sq. footage: 110000
Type of Packaging: Consumer, Private Label
Brands:
AMERICAN CLASSICS™ SALADS
BAJA CAFE® MEXICAN FOODS
DON PANCHO® TORTILLAS
MRS KINSER'S® PIMENTO CHEESE
SENSATIONAL SIDES™
STONEMILL KITCHES® DIPS

11263 (HQ)Reser's Fine Foods
P.O.Box 8
Beaverton, OR 97075 503-643-6431
Fax: 503-646-9233 800-333-6431
www.resers.com
Processor of salads, sausages, lunch meats, dips, hot buttered rum mix, salad dressings, pasta, pizza, tamales, burritos and tortillas
President: Alvin Reser
COO: Mark Reser
CFO: Paul Leavy
VP Sales/Marketing: Peter Sirgy
Director Marketing: Don Graff
VP Retail Sales: Marty Reser
Estimated Sales: $100+ Million
Number Employees: 500-999
Type of Packaging: Consumer, Food Service
Other Locations:
Reser's Fine Foods
Lynchburg VA

11264 Reser's Fine Foods
1811 W 1700 S
Salt Lake City, UT 84104 801-972-5633
Fax: 801-977-9526 trent@lynnwilson.com
www.resers.com
Processor of tortillas, burritos, salads, chili, enchiladas, salsa, tamales and puddings
Manager: Brian Thurlow
COO: Mark Reser
CFO: Paul Leavy
Marketing: Don Graff
Estimated Sales: $ 10 - 20 Million
Number Employees: 100-249
Sq. footage: 100000
Type of Packaging: Consumer, Food Service, Private Label, Bulk
Brands:
Delseys
Lynn Wilson's
Mitia
Papa Lynn
Rayo De Sol

11265 Resource Trading Company
PO Box 1698
Portland, ME 04104-1698 207-772-2299
Fax: 207-772-4709
Processor of frozen lobster, scallops and shrimp; exporter of shrimp and lobster; importer of shrimp
President: Spencer Fuller
Domestic Sales: Tom Keegan
International Sales: Irene Ketalaar-Moon
Type of Packaging: Bulk
Brands:
Arctic Pride
Claw Island
Northern Lights

11266 Restaurant Lulu GourmetProducts
1245 Folsom St
San Francisco, CA 94103 415-255-8686
Fax: 415-255-8668 888-693-5800
leslie@restaurantlulu.com
www.restaurantlulu.com
Olive tapenade, specialty honey, balsamic vinegars, herb vinegars, seasonings, sauces, gourmet tomato products
Manager: Tom Ratcliff
Sales Director: Leslie Wilson
Estimated Sales: $ 2.5-5 Million
Number Employees: 1-4
Sq. footage: 4000
Type of Packaging: Private Label

11267 Restaurant Systems International
1000 South Avenue
Staten Island, NY 10314-3430 718-494-8888
Fax: 718-494-8776 pbrown@restsys.com
www.restsys.com
Processor of frozen yogurt
CEO: Richard Nicotra
Number Employees: 20-49
Sq. footage: 10000

11268 Reter Fruit Company
3100 S Pacific Hwy
Medford, OR 97501 541-772-5256
Fax: 541-772-5258
Processor and exporter of pears
President: F Baker
Estimated Sales: $380000
Number Employees: 5-9
Type of Packaging: Consumer
Brands:
Maltese Cross
Sun-Sugared

11269 Rethemeyer Coffee Company
1711 N Broadway
St Louis, MO 63102 314-231-0990
Coffee
President: A Rethemeyer
Estimated Sales: Less than $500,000
Number Employees: 1-4
Brands:
Rethemeyer

11270 Retzlaff Vineyards
1356 S Livermore Ave
Livermore, CA 94550 925-447-8941
Fax: 925-447-9641 retzlaffwinery@gmail.com
www.retzlaffwinery.com
Cabernet, sauvignon, chardonnay wines
Owner: Gloria Taylor
Marketing Manager: Connie Vander Vouter
Estimated Sales: Below $ 5 Million
Number Employees: 10-19
Brands:
Retzlaff Estate Wines

11271 Reutter Candy & Chocolates
4665 Hollins Ferry Road
Baltimore, MD 21227-4601 800-392-0870
Fax: 410-510-1222
Candy, chocolate
International Sales: Karl Heigold
Brands:
CHOCO BERRIES
FINE MINTS
THE MINT

11272 Revonah Pretzel Bakery
507 Baltimore St
Hanover, PA 17331 717-630-2883
Fax: 717-632-3328 www.revonahpretzel.com
Processor of pretzels and potato chips
Owner: Kevin Bidelspach
Estimated Sales: $3900000
Number Employees: 5-9
Sq. footage: 24000
Type of Packaging: Consumer, Food Service, Private Label, Bulk
Brands:
Bickel
Sam & Nick's
Tom Sturgis

11273 Rex Wine Vinegar Company
830 Raymond Blvd
Newark, NJ 7105 973-589-6911
Fax: 973-589-8988 vcarlesimo@aol.com
Processor of wine and balsamic vinegar, vinegar stock and cooking wines
President: Vincent Carlesimo
Estimated Sales: $2361540
Number Employees: 5-9
Sq. footage: 7500
Parent Co: Regina Wine Company
Type of Packaging: Bulk
Brands:
Roma-Rex
Savoia

11274 Rex Wine Vinegar Company
830 Raymond Blvd
Newark, NJ 7105 973-589-6911
Fax: 973-589-8988
Manufacturer of Wine vinegar, vinegar stock, and cooking wines
Estimated Sales: $ 3 - 5 Million
Number Employees: 5-9

11275 Rey Food Company
515 Observer Highway
Hoboken, NJ 07030-6552 201-792-1955
Fax: 201-792-0236
Meats, cheeses, provisions, poultry
President: Jose Rey
Estimated Sales: $ 10-100 Million
Number Employees: 10

11276 Reynolds Sugar Bush
188572 W Maple Road
Aniwa, WI 54408 715-449-2057
Fax: 715-449-2879

Maple syrup and products
President: Juan Reynolds
Estimated Sales: Below $ 5 Million
Number Employees: 4
Type of Packaging: Private Label

11277 **Rezolex**
2240a Pepper Rd
Las Cruces, NM 88007 505-527-1730
Fax: 575-527-0221
Seasonings
President: Louis Biad
Plant Manager: Robert Stomp
Estimated Sales: Below $ 5 Million
Number Employees: 20-49

11278 **Rhino Foods**
79 Industrial Pkwy
Burlington, VT 5401 802-862-0252
Fax: 802-865-4145 800-639-3350
tcastle@rhinofoods.com www.rhinofoods.com
Manufacturer of frozen desserts including ice cream novelties, brownies, cookie dough batter, cakes, truffles, low fat, no fat, reduced sugars/NSA, trans fat free
President/Owner: Edward Castle
CEO: Ted Caste
Vice President: Anne Castle
Estimated Sales: $25 Million
Number Employees: 120
Sq. footage: 29000
Type of Packaging: Consumer, Food Service, Private Label, Bulk
Brands:
Chessters
Vermont Velvet

11279 **Rhodes Bake-N-Serv**
P.O.Box 25487
Salt Lake City, UT 84125-0487 801-972-0122
Fax: 801-972-0286 800-695-0122
customersatisfaction@rhodesbread.com
www.rhodes-bns.com
Processor of frozen rolls including white and wheat dinner, cinnamon, caramel, orange, sweet dough, pizza crust, pizza dough, biscuits and bread dough.
President: Ken Farnsworth
CEO: Ken Farnsworth Sr
VP Sales/Marketing: Kerry Smith
Number Employees: 50-99
Type of Packaging: Consumer, Food Service, Private Label
Brands:
Dakota Hearth
Rhodes Bake-N-Serv

11280 **Rhodes Bean & Supply Cooperative**
P.O.Box 338
Tracy, CA 95378 209-835-1284
Fax: 209-835-1304 ken@beanplant.com
www.beanplant.com
Processor of dried beans
General Manager: Ken Kirsten
Estimated Sales: $500,000-$1 Million
Number Employees: 20-49
Type of Packaging: Bulk
Brands:
Rhodes-Stockton Bean

11281 **Rhodes International**
P.O. Box 410
Columbus, WI 53925-0410 920-623-5161
Fax: 920-623-5185 800-876-7333
customersatisfaction@rhodesbread.com
www.rhodesbread.com
Processor of frozen bread and roll dough including white, wheat, raisin, sweet and Italian
President: Ken Farnworth Jr
Operations/Plant Manager: Darryl Campbell
Plant Manager: Darry Campbell
Estimated Sales: $ 20 - 50 Million
Number Employees: 100-249
Sq. footage: 30000
Type of Packaging: Consumer, Food Service, Private Label
Brands:
Dakota Hearth
Rhodes

11282 **Rhodes International**
P.O.Box 25487
Salt Lake City, UT 84125-0487 801-972-0122
Fax: 801-972-0286 800-695-0122
customersatisfaction@rhodesbread.com
www.rhodes-bns.com
Frozen bread and roll dough
President/CEO: Kenny Farnsworth
Marketing Director: Bret Sharp
CEO: Ken Farnsworth Sr
CFO: Christina Maybory
VP Sales: Kerry Smith
Plant Manager: Joel Ockerga
Number Employees: 50-99
Type of Packaging: Private Label
Brands:
Rhodes Bake-In-Serve Frozen Dough

11283 **(HQ)Rhodia**
P.O.Box 7500
Cranbury, NJ 8512 609-860-4000
Fax: 609-409-8652 800-343-8324
silicones@us.rhodia.com
www.food.us.rhodia.com
Processor, importer and exporter of food and beverage ingredients including phosphates, bicarbonates, hydrocolloids, xanthan, guar and locust bean gum, vanillin, antioxidants, low/no fat systems, emulsifiers, stabilizers, startercultures, colors, etc
President: James Harton
CEO: Jean Clamadieu
CFO: Mark l Dahlinger
SVP/General Counsel: John Donahue
Sales Manager: Scott Marsi
Estimated Sales: $713 Million
Number Employees: 1800
Parent Co: Rhodia SA

11284 **Rhone-Poulenc Food Ingredients**
8 Cedarbrook Dr
Cranbury, NJ 8512 609-860-4000
Fax: 609-860-2250 www.rhodia.com
Food ingredient supplier for baking, cereal, snack foods, meat, seafood and poultry
President: James Harton
CFO: Mark Dahlinger
SVP: John Donahue
Estimated Sales: $4 Billion
Number Employees: 1,800

11285 **Riba Foods**
P.O.Box 630461
Houston, TX 77263-0461 713-975-7001
Fax: 713-975-7036 800-327-7422
sales@ribafoods.com www.ribafoods.com
Processor of salsas, pickles, jalapeno peppers, mustards and other sauces, bean dips, quesos and enchilada and pepper sauces
President: Miguel Barrios
Manager Sales/Marketing: Richard Wall
Estimated Sales: $ 5-10 Million
Number Employees: 10-19
Number of Brands: 2
Number of Products: 45
Sq. footage: 20000
Type of Packaging: Consumer, Food Service, Private Label
Brands:
Arriba
Norte¤A
Texas Pepper Works

11286 **Ribble Production**
1601 Mearns Road
Warminster, PA 18974-1115 215-674-1706
Fax: 215-674-0123 info@ribbleproduction.com
www.ribbleproduction.com
Manufacturer of decorative toppings including multi/single cell sprinkles, nonpareils, jimmies and mixes; custom manufacturing and packaging
VP: Joseph Van Houten
Number Employees: 20-49
Type of Packaging: Consumer, Food Service, Private Label, Bulk

11287 **Ribus**
8000 Maryland Ave Ste 460
Saint Louis, MO 63105 314-727-4287
Fax: 314-727-1199 info@ribus.com
www.ribus.com
Specialty ingredients for snack food and extruded products, bakery product performance improvement and beverage system
President: Steve Pierce
Financial Coordinator: Lisa Ennis
Marketing/Customer Service Director: Susie Peters
Estimated Sales: Below $ 5 Million
Number Employees: 5-9
Type of Packaging: Food Service, Private Label, Bulk
Brands:
Ribus

11288 **Rice Company**
1624 Santa Clara Dr Ste 145
Roseville, CA 95661 916-784-7745
Fax: 916-784-7681 jobs@riceco.com
www.riceco.com
Processor, importer and exporter of dry grocery items including rice, popcorn, rice flour, sugar, beans, peas, lentils and ginger
Owner: Duane Kistner
President: J Kapila
Operations Manager: Vicki Manzoli
Estimated Sales: $4500000
Number Employees: 50-99
Type of Packaging: Consumer, Food Service, Private Label, Bulk

11289 **(HQ)Rice Deerwood & Grain Processing**
21926 County Road 10
Deerwood, MN 56444-8486 218-534-3762
Fax: 218-534-3802
Manufacturer of wild rice
President: Dan Mohs
Estimated Sales: $1.20 Million
Number Employees: 20-49
Sq. footage: 39000
Type of Packaging: Consumer, Bulk

11290 **Rice Foods**
5111 Lake Ter NE
Mount Vernon, IL 62864-9666 618-242-0026
Fax: 618-242-3109
CEO: Lynn Withworth

11291 **Rice Fruit Company**
2760 Carlisle Road
PO Box 66
Gardners, PA 17324
Fax: 717-677-9842 800-627-3359
sales@ricefruit.com www.ricefruit.com
Processor and exporter of apples, peaches and pears.
President: David Rice
VP: John Rice
VP Marketing: Brenda Briggs
Estimated Sales: $ 50 - 100 Million
Number Employees: 50-99
Type of Packaging: Consumer, Food Service, Bulk

11292 **Rice Hull Specialty Products**
P.O.Box 188
Stuttgart, AR 72160 870-673-8507
Fax: 870-673-2116 info@ricehull.com
www.ricehull.com
Processor of parboiled rice hulls which are used as a pressing aid for fruit juice processors
President: John Moore
VP: John Moore
Sales Manager: Greg Crawford
Estimated Sales: $1600000
Number Employees: 10-19

11293 **Rice Innovations**
8175 Winston Churchill Boulevard
Norval, ON L0P 1K0
Canada 905-451-7423
Fax: 905-453-8137 info@maplegrovefoods.com
www.maplegrovefoods.com
Processor of organic and gluten-free rice, potato pastas, beverages and other products.
General Manager: Raj Sukul
R&D: Ly Hung
Customer Service: Sally Chee
Estimated Sales: $100,000
Number Employees: 1
Type of Packaging: Private Label
Brands:
BODY FUEL
CAFE BONJOUR
CELIFIBR
HERB SCIENCE

MACARIZ
MEDICEA
PASTARISO
PASTATO
RICE REALITY
YING YANG

11294 **Rice River Farms/Chieftan Wild Rice Company**
P.O.Box 550
1210 Basswood Ave
Spooner, WI 54801-0550 715-635-6401
Fax: 715-635-6415 800-262-6368
wildrice@centurytel.net
www.chieftainwildrice.com
Wild rice and wild rice blends
President: Donald Richards
Cfo: Joan Gerland
Marketing: Lisa Johnson
Operations Manager: Jim Deutsch
Estimated Sales: $1.6 Million
Number Employees: 25
Number of Brands: 1
Type of Packaging: Private Label

11295 **Rice Select**
P.O.Box 1305
Alvin, TX 77512-1305 281-393-3502
Fax: 281-393-3532 800-580-7423
info@riceselect.com www.ricetec.com
Processor and exporter of rice including Indian-style, brown and white basmati, American jasmine and rice mixes
President: John Nelson
VP Sales/Operations: Mark Denman
Estimated Sales: $ 100-500 Million
Number Employees: 50-99
Type of Packaging: Consumer, Food Service, Private Label, Bulk
Brands:
Chefs Originals
Jasmati
Kasmati
Texmati

11296 **Riceland FoodsRice Milling Operations**
P.O.Box 927
Stuttgart, AR 72160-0927 870-673-5500
Fax: 870-766-4368 800-226-9522
riceland@riceland.com www.riceland.com
Manufacturer of rice; exporter of rice, rice by-products and rice oil
Manager: Tom Bracewell
Estimated Sales: $197 Million
Number Employees: 100-249
Parent Co: Riceland Foods Inc
Type of Packaging: Consumer, Food Service, Private Label, Bulk
Brands:
CHEF-WAY
DELTA QUEEN
ORIENTAL HARVEST
RICELAND
SAL FRY
SHUR CHEF
SUREFRY SOYBEAN MEAL

11297 **Riceland FoodsRice Milling Operations**
2120 S Park Ave
Po Box 927
Stuttgart, AR 72160-3552
US 870-673-5500
Fax: 870-673-3366 riceland@riceland.com
www.riceland.com
Manufacturer of a full line of deoiled and fluid lecithin products; Lecigran, Lecisoy, Leciprime. Applications include color and flavor suspension, bakery products, egg replacer/extender, instant powder, icing and fillings, chewing gumbase, chocolate, batters and sauces
Pres/CEO: Daniel Kennedy
VP/CFO: Harry Loftis
Estimated Sales: $1.30billion
Number Employees: 1,900
Parent Co: Riceland Foods Inc
Type of Packaging: Bulk

11298 **Rices Potato Chips**
9407 Boyette Rd
Biloxi, MS 39532 228-396-5775
Fax: 228-396-5775
Processor of potato chips and other snack foods
President: Martha Vergunst
Estimated Sales: Less than $250,000
Number Employees: 2
Type of Packaging: Private Label

11299 **Riceselect**
1925 FM 2917
Alvin, TX 77511 281-393-3502
Fax: 281-393-3811 800-993-7423
reception@ricetec.com www.riceselect.com
Processor of aromatic rice; also, researcher and developer of rice varieties
President: John Nelsen
Ceo: John Zimmerman
VP Finance: Tena Bressler
VP Marketing: Lewis Fernandez
Human Resources Director: Jim Walker
COO/VP Sales & Marketing: Mark Denman
Production Manager: Richard Pittman
Estimated Sales: $23081227
Number Employees: 200
Sq. footage: 1260
Type of Packaging: Consumer, Food Service, Private Label, Bulk
Brands:
CHEF'S ORIGINAL
JASMATI RICE
RICE SELECT
TEXMATI RICE

11300 **Ricex Company**
1241 Hawks Flight Court
El Dorado Hills, CA 95762-9648
US 916-933-3000
Fax: 916-933-3232 tbarber@ricex.com
www.ricex.com
Processor of stabilized rice bran and concentrated rice bran fiber
President: Terrence Barber
CEO: Bradley Edson
CFO: Todd Crow
Estimated Sales: $3511295
Number Employees: 12
Sq. footage: 20000
Type of Packaging: Bulk
Brands:
Ricex

11301 **Rich Ice Cream Company**
2915 S Dixie Hwy
West Palm Beach, FL 33405 561-833-7585
Fax: 561-655-1952 www.richicecream.com
Processor of ice cream, cream puffs, chocolate eclairs and cakes
CEO: Jhon Rich
Marketing Director: Randy Rich
Controller: Bob Thomas
VP: Randy Rich
Number Employees: 100-249
Type of Packaging: Consumer, Food Service
Brands:
Rich Ice Creams

11302 **Rich Products Corporation**
P.O.Box 631
Fresno, CA 93709-0631 559-486-7380
Fax: 559-486-0480 duhrich@rich.com
www.richs.com
Processor of frozen bread
President: Melinda Rich
Estimated Sales: K
Number Employees: 100-249
Parent Co: Rich Products Corporation
Type of Packaging: Consumer, Food Service

11303 **Rich Products Corporation**
1 Robert Rich Way
Buffalo, NY 14213 716-878-8000
Fax: 716-878-8266 800-356-7094
www.richs.com
Manufacturer of frozen bread, rolls, cookies and sweet dough
President/CEO: William Gisel Jr
EVP/CFO: James Deuschle
Estimated Sales: K
Number Employees: 5,000-9,999
Type of Packaging: Consumer, Food Service, Private Label
Brands:
J.W. ALLEN
RICH'S

11304 **Rich Products Corporation**
801 N Kent St
Winchester, VA 22601 540-667-1955
Fax: 540-667-1779
Processor of frozen bread, rolls and sweet goods
CFO: James Pratt
Production Manager: Jeff Lewallan
Purchasing Agent: Pamela Maphis
Estimated Sales: $ 50 - 100 Million
Number Employees: 170
Parent Co: Rich Products Corporation
Type of Packaging: Consumer, Private Label

11305 **Rich Products Corporation**
1 Robert Rich Way
Buffalo, NY 14213 716-878-8000
Fax: 716-878-8266 800-828-2021
richcanada@rich.com www.richs.com
Processor of frozen baked products including cookies, breads and muffins
President/CEO: William Gisel Jr
EVP/CFO: James Deuschle
Estimated Sales: K
Number Employees: 5,000-9,999
Parent Co: Rich Products Corporation
Type of Packaging: Consumer, Food Service, Private Label
Brands:
Bahama Blast
Bettercreme
Byron's Barbecue
Casa DiBertacchi
Farm Rich
On Top
Rich's Whip Topping
SeaPak

11306 **Rich Products Corporation**
P.O.Box 388
Claremont, CA 91711 909-621-4711
Fax: 909-624-6520 www.richs.com
Processor of whipped toppings and coffee creamers
Manager: Kevin Fisher
Materials Manager: Kevin Fisher
Estimated Sales: $ 10 - 20 Million
Number Employees: 20-49
Sq. footage: 90000
Parent Co: Rich Products Corporation
Type of Packaging: Consumer, Food Service

11307 **Rich Products Corporation**
1366 19th St
Cameron, WI 54822 715-458-4556
Fax: 715-458-2979
Processor of frozen dough and cookie and cake mixes
President/CEO: Robert Rich Jr
Director Marketing: Michael Cannon
CFO: Charles Trego Jr
Vice President: William Gisel
Public Relations: Peter Ciotta
Operations Manager: Mike Bingham
Sales Manager: John Wellenzohn
Purchasing Manager: Jeff Kusche
Number Employees: 3500
Parent Co: Rich Products Corporation
Type of Packaging: Private Label
Brands:
Bettercreme Frosting & Filling
Byron's Bronco
Chocolate Heat N'Ice
Dutch Brownie Base
Grand American
Grand American Ice C
Jim's
Mrs. Rich's Cookies
Pies and Krunchies
Red Raspberry Bismar
Rich's Bread and Rol
Rich's Eclairs
Rich's Eclairs
Rich's European Coun
Rich's Farm Rich
Rich's Non-Dairy Des
Rich's Pizza Dough
Rich's Poly Rich
Rich's Puddings

11308 **Rich Products Corporation**
P.O.Box 490
Hilliard, OH 43026 614-771-1117
Fax: 614-771-8286 www.richs.com

Processor of doughnut mixes, frozen doughnuts, toppings and fillings
Manager: Mike Calloway
Managing VP: Brian Townson
Purchasing Agent: Marylou Bright
Estimated Sales: $100-500 Million
Number Employees: 50-99
Parent Co: Rich Products Corporation
Type of Packaging: Private Label

11309 **Rich Products of Canada**
One Robert Rich Way
Buffalo, NY 14213
Canada 716-878-8000
800-457-4247
RichCanada@Rich.com www.richs.com
Processor of frozen baked goods, dough, nondairy creamers and whipped topping and Italian specialties
President: Howard Rich
CEO: Bill Gisel
VP Marketing: Nick Stambula
Purchasing: Paul Furtney
Number Employees: 100-249
Parent Co: Rich Products Corporation
Type of Packaging: Consumer, Food Service, Private Label, Bulk
Brands:
Allen
Avoset
Bahama Blast™
Byron's Barbecue
Casa DiBertacchi
Coffee Rich
Farm Rich
Gold Label Plus Dairy
Jon Donaire
Mother's Kitchen
Presto
Rich's Eclairs
SeaPak
Tres Riches

11310 **Rich-Seapak Corporation**
127 Airport Rd
St Simons Island, GA 31522 912-638-5000
Fax: 912-634-3105 800-654-9731
www.richs.com
Processor of shrimp, cheese, French toast and finger foods
President/CEO: Bruce Major
VP/CFO: Bob Pavone
Number Employees: 100-249
Parent Co: Rich Products Corporation
Type of Packaging: Consumer, Food Service
Other Locations:
Rich-Seapak Corp.
Brownsville TX
Brands:
BYRONS
CASA DE BERTACCHI
FARM RICH
RICHS
SEA PACK

11311 **Rich-Seapak Corporation**
3555 E 14th St
Brownsville, TX 78521 956-542-0001
Fax: 956-504-4401 www.richs.com
Processor of frozen seafood and vegetables; importer and exporter of frozen shrimp
President: George H Bridger
Operations Manager: Michael Heggie
Director Shrimp Procurement: Bill Hoenig
Estimated Sales: $100+ Million
Number Employees: 250-499
Parent Co: Rich Products Corporation
Type of Packaging: Consumer, Food Service, Private Label

11312 **Richard Bagdasarian Inc.**
65500 Lincoln St
Mecca, CA 92254 760-396-2168
Fax: 760-396-2801 rbagdasarian@mrgrape.com
www.bagdasarianinc.com
Grower, shipper and marketer of California Table Grapes, Citrus and Vegetables for numerous companies incluing Sunkist Growers.
Owner: Mike Bozick
VP/Manager: Nick Bozick
VP/Manager: Mike Bozick
VP/Manager: Franz DeKlotz
VP/Manager: Bill Spidell
Type of Packaging: Food Service

11313 **Richard Donnelly Fine Chtes**
1509 Mission St
Santa Cruz, CA 95060-4740 831-458-4214
Fax: 831-425-0678 888-685-1871
info@donnellychocolates.com
www.donnellychocolates.com
Chocolate, dessert sauces and mixes; gift boxes available
Owner: Richard Donnelly
Estimated Sales: Less than $500,000
Number Employees: 1-4
Type of Packaging: Private Label
Brands:
Donnelly Chocolates

11314 **Richard E. Colgin Company**
2230 Valdina St
Dallas, TX 75207-6106 214-951-8687
Fax: 214-951-8668 888-226-5446
sales@colgin.com www.colgin.com
Liquid flavorings
CEO: Kerry Thornhill
President: Elizabeth Thornhill
CFO: Sarah Johnson
Estimated Sales: $2 Million
Number Employees: 20
Type of Packaging: Private Label
Brands:
Chigarid
Colgin

11315 **Richard Green Company**
1827 S Meridian St
Indianapolis, IN 46225 317-972-0941
Fax: 317-972-1201 rickg@thepeanutking.com
www.thepeanutking.com
Processor of popcorn and nuts
President: Richard Green
Estimated Sales: $500,000-$1 Million
Number Employees: 5-9
Sq. footage: 24000
Type of Packaging: Consumer, Private Label

11316 **Richard L. Graeser Winery**
255 Petrified Forest Rd
Calistoga, CA 94515 707-942-4437
Fax: 707-942-4437 richard@graeserwinery.com
www.graeserwinery.com
Wines
Owner: Richard Graeser
Winemaker: Richard Graeser
Estimated Sales: $500,000-$1 Million
Number Employees: 5-9
Type of Packaging: Private Label
Brands:
Graeser

11317 **Richard Lanza**
847 S 1st Road
Hammonton, NJ 08037-8408 609-561-3984
Fax: 609-561-0187
Package blueberries
Owner: Richard Lanza
Estimated Sales: Less than $500,000
Number Employees: 3
Type of Packaging: Private Label, Bulk
Brands:
Richard Lanza

11318 **Richard's Gourmet Coffee**
124 Turnpike St Ste 10
West Bridgewater, MA 02379 508-587-0800
Fax: 508-587-8139 800-370-2633
sales@richardsgourmet.com
www.richardsgourmet.com
Private label packer of flavored coffees and teas, lemonade, cappuccino, cocoa, spiced cider, etc
President: Richard Salzman
Estimated Sales: Below $ 5 Million
Number Employees: 10-19
Type of Packaging: Private Label
Brands:
Richard's Gourmet

11319 **Richards Maple Products**
545 Water St
Chardon, OH 44024 440-286-4160
Fax: 440-286-7203 800-352-4052
sales@richardsmapleproducts.com
www.richardsmapleproducts.com
Processor of maple candy and syrup
President: Debbie Richards
Marketing Director: Debbie Richards
CFO: Annette Polson
Estimated Sales: Under $1 Million
Number Employees: 5-9
Sq. footage: 4160
Type of Packaging: Consumer, Private Label, Bulk
Brands:
Richards' Maple Candy
Richards' Maple Syru

11320 **Richards Natural Foods**
15213 S Hinman Road
Eagle, MI 48822-9703 517-627-7965
Different kinds of food
President: Richard Osterbeck
Estimated Sales: Under $500,000
Number Employees: 1-4

11321 **Richardson Brands Company**
16 Business Park Drive
Branford, CT 06405 203-481-2276
Fax: 203-488-8085 800-839-8938
info@rockcandy.com www.rockcandy.com
Processor, importer and exporter of bagged and boxed confectionery products including color coated baking chocolate chips, soft and hard mints, chewing gum and chocolate caramel toffees; also, panned and seasonal candy
Owner: Richard P Anderson
VP Research and Development: Kalman Vadasz
Marketing: Kathy Testa
Senior VP Sales & Marketing: Michael Smith
Estimated Sales: $25,000,000
Number Employees: 20-49
Sq. footage: 175000
Parent Co: Agrolimen S.A.
Type of Packaging: Consumer, Food Service, Private Label, Bulk
Brands:
After Dinner
Bonkers !
Colombina
Moofus
Numb Drops
Popshots
Sour Chewy Candy
Tattoo Bubble Gum

11322 **Richardson Foods Corporation**
3268 Blue Heron Dr
Macedon, NY 14502-9343 315-986-2807
Fax: 315-986-5880 www.brfoods.com
Processor of sauces, toppings, crushed fruit, fountain syrups and condiments
CFO: Francesca Lancer
Director of Quality: Rob Mommsen
VP Human Resources: David Drake
Purchasing Manager: Paula Bell
Estimated Sales: $33 Million
Number Employees: 200
Type of Packaging: Consumer, Food Service, Private Label, Bulk

11323 **Richardson Vineyards**
2711 Knob Hill Road
Sonoma, CA 95476-9560 707-938-2610
Info@richardsonvineyards.com
www.richardsonvineyards.com
Wines
President/CEO: Dennis Richardson
Estimated Sales: Less than $100,000
Number Employees: 1

11324 **Richardson's Ice Cream**
156 S Main St
Middleton, MA 01949 978-774-5450
Fax: 978-777-6863
info@richardsonsicecream.com
www.richardsonsicecream.com
Ice cream
President: Paul Richardson
Estimated Sales: $ 5 Million
Number Employees: 5-9
Number of Brands: 1
Number of Products: 1
Type of Packaging: Consumer, Bulk
Brands:
Richardson's Ice Cream

11325 **Richelieu Foods**
15 Pacella Park Drive
Suite 210
Randolph, MA 02368 781-961-1537
Fax: 781-767-1751 www.richelieufoods.com

Retail and food service dressings and sauces, pizza, crust
President/CEO: Robbie Jamieson
CFO: Mike Morin
SVP Sales: Anthony Raucci
Purchasing Manager: Lauren Roloff
Estimated Sales: $235 Million
Number Employees: 650
Sq. footage: 7500
Type of Packaging: Consumer, Food Service

11326 **Richelieu Foods**
15 Pacella Park Dr Ste 210
Randolph, MA 02368 781-961-1537
Fax: 781-767-1751 www.richelieufoods.com
Frozen pizzas, meal solutions, salad dressings,marinades and salsas
President/CEO: Vincent Gantergrossi
Sr VP Sales: Anthony Raucci
VP Sales: Phillip Scolley
CEO: Vincent V Fantegrossi
National Director Organic Natural Food: Jon Deeter
VP Manufacturing Beaver Dam: Colin Swift
General Manager: James Campbell
General Manager: Jason Yoakum
VP Manufacturing Grundy Center: Walt Grineski
Estimated Sales: $100 Million
Number Employees: 250-499
Type of Packaging: Private Label
Brands:
Caterer's Collection
Chef Antonio
Grocer's Garden
Willow Farms

11327 **Richfield Foods**
800 1st Avenue NE
Cairo, GA 39828-2207 229-377-2102
Fax: 912-377-5797 www.deans.com
Table syrups and boiled peanuts
President: J Roddenberry Jr
Estimated Sales: $ 50-99.9 Million
Number Employees: 130

11328 **Richfood Dairy**
1505 Robin Hood Road
Richmond, VA 23220-1001 804-746-6206
Fax: 804-746-6057
Milk
Manager: Paula Martin
Estimated Sales: A
Number Employees: 10

11329 **Richland Beverage Associates**
2415 Midway Rd # 115
Carrollton, TX 75006-2500 214-357-0248
Fax: 214-357-9581 sales@texasselectna.com
www.hphardware.com
Processor and exporter of nonalcoholic malt beverages and beer; also, alcoholic beer
President: Martha Zelzer
Sales Manager: Glenn Rogers
Estimated Sales: Less than $500,000
Number Employees: 1-4
Sq. footage: 1500
Parent Co: Richland Corporation
Type of Packaging: Consumer, Food Service, Private Label
Brands:
Texas Select

11330 **(HQ)Richmond Baking Company**
P.O.Box 698
Richmond, IN 47375-0698 765-962-8535
Fax: 765-962-2253 info@richmondbaking.com
www.richmondbaking.com
Processor of graham cracker crumbs, cookie crumbs, crushed saltine crackers, cracker meal, packaged cookies, crackers and graham crackers; custom blending of breadings, batters and marinades.
President: Bill Quigg
Executive VP: Loyce Sherrow
Operations Manager: Bill Quigg
Production Manager: Doug Tyree
Plant Manager: Mike Miller
Purchasing Manager: Gary Galinger
Estimated Sales: $9200000
Number Employees: 100-249
Sq. footage: 250000
Type of Packaging: Consumer, Food Service, Private Label, Bulk
Other Locations:
Brands:
Butternut
Butternut Baked Goods

11331 **Richmond Baking Company**
135 Industrial Dr
Alma, GA 31510 912-632-7213
Fax: 912-632-7215 info@richmondbaking.com
www.richmondbaking.com
Processor of batter mixes and breadings for meat, poultry, seafood and vegetables, dessert crumbs
President: Jerry Lady
VP/CFO: Dean Fleenor
Sales Executive: Rick Theidel
Human Resources Manager: Lauren Jowers
Plant Manager: James Quigg
Estimated Sales: $8.5 Million
Number Employees: 85
Sq. footage: 85000
Parent Co: Richmond Baking Company
Other Locations:
Richmond Baking
Richmond IN
Richmond Baking
McMinnville OR

11332 **Rick's Picks**
195 Chrystie St Rm 602
New York, NY 10002 212-358-0428
Fax: 212-358-0231 jina@rickspicksnyc.com
www.rickspicksnyc.com
various types of pickles (sweet, savory and spicy)
Manager: Rick Field
Marketing: Jin Kim
Estimated Sales: $150,000
Number Employees: 2

11333 **Rico Foods**
578 E 19th St
Paterson, NJ 07514 973-278-0589
Fax: 973-278-0378 info@expreco.com
www.ricofood.com
Hispanic foods
President: Emilio Hernandes
Vice President: Madeline Fernandez
Estimated Sales: Below $ 5 Million
Number Employees: 20-49
Sq. footage: 10
Type of Packaging: Private Label
Brands:
Delicia
Rico

11334 **Ricos Candy Snacks & Bakery**
740 W 28th St
Hialeah, FL 33010-1220 305-885-7392
Fax: 305-885-7376 sales@ricostostaditos.com
www.ricosusa.com
Processor of hard candy and snack foods including pork rinds and fried dough
President: Albertina Padron
VP: Steven Laderman
Estimated Sales: Below $ 5 Million
Number Employees: 10-19
Type of Packaging: Consumer

11335 **Riddles' Sweet Impressions**
6311 Wagner Road NW
Edmonton, AB T6E 4N4
Canada 780-465-8085
Fax: 780-468-5929 riddles@telusplanet.net
www.riddlessweet.com
Processor of candy including lollypop barrels and chocolate
President: Bill Agnew
Production Manager: Wendy Agnew
Quality Control: Wendy Agnew
VP Sales: Dave Read
Number Employees: 30-50
Sq. footage: 12000
Type of Packaging: Consumer, Food Service, Private Label, Bulk
Brands:
Riddle's

11336 **Ridge Vineyards**
17100 Montebello Rd
Cupertino, CA 95014 408-867-3233
Fax: 408-868-1350 wine@ridgewine.com
www.ridgewine.com
Wines
President: Donn Reisen
Sales Director: Donn Pelsen
Estimated Sales: $50-100 Million
Number Employees: 20-49
Type of Packaging: Private Label
Brands:
Ridge Vineyards

11337 **Rier Smoked Salmon**
224 County Rd
Lubec, ME 04652-3611 207-733-8912
Fax: 207-733-8986 888-733-0807
rier.com www.rier.com
Processor of hot and cold smoked, kippered and roasted Atlantic salmon; also, smoked salmon pate and lox, smoked chicken products
Owner: Vinny Gartmayer
Sales/Marketing: Frank Rier
Estimated Sales: $450,000
Number Employees: 5-9
Sq. footage: 3500

11338 **Riffel's Coffee Company**
10821 E 26th St N
Wichita, KS 67226-4524 316-269-4222
Fax: 316-269-1361 888-399-4567
riffels@southwind.net www.riffelscoffee.com
Roast package and private label of arabica beans. Carries four brands of tes, Stasero Italian syrup, coffee jellies
Administrator: Linda Price
General Manager: Paul Hawley
Plant Manager: Lewis Lusk
Purchasing Manager: Chuck Anderson
Estimated Sales: Below $ 5 Million
Number Employees: 10-19
Number of Brands: 15
Number of Products: 700
Sq. footage: 5000
Type of Packaging: Consumer, Food Service, Private Label, Bulk
Brands:
RIFFELS GOURMET COFFEES

11339 **Righetti Specialties**
P.O.Box 2513
Santa Maria, CA 93457-2513 805-937-2402
Fax: 805-937-7243 800-268-1041
susieq@susieqbrand.com www.susieqbrand.com
Beans, seasonings, pie mix, sauces & salsas, beef jerky, grilling wood.
President: Susan Righetti
VP: Renee Fowler
Estimated Sales: Below $ 5 Million
Number Employees: 5-9
Brands:
Righetti Specialty

11340 **Rigoni Di Asiago**
3449 NE 1st Avenue L-32
Miami, FL 33137 305-470-7583
Fax: 800-887-9023 info@rigonidiasiago-usa.com
www.rigonidiasiago.com
Kosher, sugar-free, USDA, gluten-free, other chocolate, honey, jams, preserves.
Marketing: Alberto Carli

11341 **Rinehart Meat Processing**
P.O.Box 6880
Branson, MO 65615-6880 417-334-2044
Fax: 417-334-2059
Processor of diet lean ground beef, smoked bacon and ham, sausage and beef jerky
Owner: Jack Harris
President: Jack Harris
Plant Manager: Tim Stewart
Estimated Sales: $ 10 - 20 Million
Number Employees: 20-49

11342 **Rio Grande Valley SugarGrowers**
PO Box 459
Santa Rosa, TX 78593 956-636-1411
Fax: 956-636-1449 www.rgvsugar.com
Processor of sugar cane
President: Randy Rolando
CEO: Steve Bearden
Human Resources Manager: Stacey Buford
Operations Executive: Tony Prado
Manufacturing Manager: Mark Nittler
Purchasing: Ralph Berrera
Estimated Sales: $62 Million
Number Employees: 500
Sq. footage: 5000
Type of Packaging: Bulk

11343 **Rio Naturals**
5050 Robert J. Mathews Parkway
Suite 200
El Dorado Hills, CA 95762 916-719-4514
Fax: 916-941-3690
customerservice@rionatural.com
www.rionaturals.com
Manufacturer and supplier of calorie free sweeteners.

11344 **Rio Syrup Company**
2311 Chestnut St
Saint Louis, MO 63103 314-436-7701
Fax: 314-436-7707 800-325-7666
flavors@riosyrup.com www.riosyrup.com
Manufacturer and exporter of syrups, extracts and concentrates for shaved ice, sno cones, slush flavors and bases and fountain syrups; also manufacturer of liquid food colors
President: Phillip Tomber
CEO: Bill Tomber
Operations/Public Relations: William Tomber
Estimated Sales: $500,000-$1 Million
Number of Brands: 3
Number of Products: 1200
Sq. footage: 23000
Type of Packaging: Consumer, Food Service, Bulk
Brands:
RIO

11345 **Rio Trading Company**
4924 Campbell Blvd # 120
Baltimore, MD 21236-5909 443-384-2500
Fax: 443-384-2525 www2.toad.net
Owner: Michael Sruanis
Estimated Sales: $500,000-$1 Million
Number Employees: 1-4
Brands:
Rio Trading

11346 **Rio Valley Canning Company**
225 S 13th St
Donna, TX 78537 956-464-7843
Fax: 956-464-2538
Processor of canned beans, peas, tomatoes, peppers and picante sauce
President: Robert Ault
Estimated Sales: $ 5-10 Million
Number Employees: 10-19
Type of Packaging: Consumer, Food Service, Private Label
Brands:
Rio Valley

11347 **Ripensa A/S**
5781 Lee Boulevard
Unit 208
Lehigh Acres, FL 33971-6339 941-561-5882
Fax: 941-561-5885 export@ripensa.dk
www.ripensa.com
Baked goods, cookies, biscuits in boxes, tins, tray packs, containers and acrylic jars
President: Steen Thy Jensen
CEO: Richard Recchia
Estimated Sales: Less than $500,000
Number Employees: 1-4
Type of Packaging: Private Label
Brands:
Ripensa

11348 **Ripon Pickle Company**
1039 Beier Rd
Ripon, WI 54971 920-748-7110
Fax: 920-748-8092 800-324-5493
rpi@vdp.com www.savorwisconsin.com
Manufacturer and exporter of pickles and pickle products
President: Darwin Wiese
Controller: Patty McClelland
Production Manager: Jeffrey Wiese
Estimated Sales: $ 50 - 100 Million
Number Employees: 50-99
Sq. footage: 45000
Type of Packaging: Consumer, Food Service, Private Label, Bulk
Brands:
Pickle O'Pete
Wisconsin Pride

11349 **Rippons Brothers Seafood**
1814 Hoopersville Rd
Fishing Creek, MD 21634 410-397-3200
Fax: 410-397-3208
Manufacturer of oysters, crabmeat and crabs including soft, steamed and fresh
Owner: Chan Rippons Jr Jr
Estimated Sales: $21 Million
Number Employees: 20-49
Type of Packaging: Consumer, Food Service, Private Label

11350 **(HQ)Riser Foods**
5300 Richmond Rd
Cleveland, OH 44146 216-292-7000
Fax: 216-591-2640 www.rinirego.com
Ice cream
Manager: Anthony Rego
Estimated Sales: $ 100-499.9 Million
Number Employees: 500-999

11351 **Rishi Tea**
427 E Stewart St Stop 5
Milwaukee, WI 53207 414-747-4001
Fax: 414-747-4008 866-747-4483
inquiries@rishi-tea.com www.rishi-tea.com
An award winning loose leaf tea company importing organic and fair trade certified tea fresh each season and direct from origin. Artisan teaware, iced tea and chai concentrate also available.
Owner: Benjamin Harrison
Estimated Sales: $1.3 Million
Number Employees: 9
Sq. footage: 32000
Type of Packaging: Consumer, Food Service, Private Label, Bulk

11352 **Rising Dough Bakery**
8135 Elder Creek Rd
Sacramento, CA 95824 916-387-9700
Fax: 916-387-9800 orders@risingdough.com
www.risingdough.com
Cakes, pies, muffins, croissants and strudels
Owner: Colette Jamet
Estimated Sales: Below $ 5 Million
Number Employees: 20-49
Brands:
Rising Dough

11353 **Rising Sun Farms**
5126 S Pacific Hwy
Phoenix, OR 97535-6606 541-535-8331
Fax: 541-535-8350 800-888-0795
elizabeth@risingsunfarms.com
www.risingsunfarms.com
Processor and exporter of natural foods including oils, mustard, pesto sauces, dried tomatoes, vinegars, salad vinaigrettes, cheese tortas and marinades
President: Elizabeth Fujas
Coo: Jeff Williams
VP: Richard Fujas
Sales: Jenn Woodward
Public Relations: Jim Woodward
Operations: Chris Hanry
Plant Manager: Richard Fujas
Purchasing Director: Lynn Perkins
Estimated Sales: $3.2 Million
Number Employees: 25
Type of Packaging: Consumer, Food Service, Private Label, Bulk
Brands:
Rising Sun Farm Cheese Tortos
Rising Sun Pesto Sauces
Rising Sun Vinagrettes & Marinades

11354 **Rit-Chem Company**
1 Zeiss Drive
Suite 200
Thornwood, NY 10594 914-769-9110
Fax: 914-769-1408 ritchem@ritchem.com
www.ritchem.com
Artificial sweeteners including Ace K, aspartame, saccharin, xylitol, potassium sorbate and blends
President/Founder: Henry Ritell
CFO: Henry Ritell
VP Sales: Wayne Ritell
VP Purchasing/Logistics: Bruce Ritell
Estimated Sales: $ 10-20 Million
Number Employees: 8

11355 **Ritchey's Dairy**
2130 Cross Cove Rd
Martinsburg, PA 16662 814-793-2157
Fax: 814-793-0099 800-296-2157
ritcheysdairy@hotmail.com
www.ritcheysdairy.com
Milk, fruit drinks and ice tea
President: Reid Ritchey
Estimated Sales: Below $ 5 Million
Number Employees: 50-99
Type of Packaging: Private Label
Brands:
Ritchey

11356 **Ritchie Creek Vineyard**
4024 Spring Mountain Rd
Saint Helena, CA 94574 707-963-4661
Fax: 707-963-4936 rcv@napanet.net
www.ritchiecreek.com
Wines
President: R Minor
Co-Owner: Peter Minor
Estimated Sales: Below $ 5 Million
Number Employees: 5-9

11357 **Ritchie Wholesale Meats**
527 West St
Piketon, OH 45661-8042 740-289-4393
Fax: 740-289-4375 800-628-1290
jritchie@zoom.net www.ritchiefoods.com
Processor and pork and beef; wholeasaler/distributor of frozen foods, canned and dry groceries, produce and chemicals; serving the food service market
President: James Ritchie
Office Manager: Kevin More
Estimated Sales: $ 20 - 50 Million
Number Employees: 20-49
Type of Packaging: Consumer, Food Service

11358 **Rito Mints**
PO Box 312
Trio-Rivieres, QC G9A 5G4
Canada 819-379-1449
Fax: 819-379-0344 info@ritomints.com
www.ritomints.com
Candy, mints
President: Maureen Nassif
Number Employees: 20
Type of Packaging: Consumer, Food Service, Private Label, Bulk
Brands:
Ghost Talk
Rito
Sweet Notes

11359 **Rito Mints**
PO Box 312
Trois Rivieres, QC G9A 5GA
Canada 819-379-1449
Fax: 819-379-0344 info@ritomints.com
www.menthesrito.com
Processor and exporter of candy including mints, conversation hearts and lozenges
President: Morris Masif
General Manager: Peter Nassif
Number Employees: 15
Sq. footage: 16000
Type of Packaging: Consumer, Food Service, Private Label, Bulk
Brands:
Rito
Sweet Notes

11360 **Ritts-Chavelle Snack Company**
16677 Roscoe Boulevard
North Hills, CA 91343-6109 818-830-3305
Fax: 818-830-0685
Snacks
Owner: Rory Ritts

11361 **Rivard Popcorn Products**
1828 Freedom Rd
Lancaster, PA 17601-6705 717-393-1074
Processor of flavored popcorn confections and extruded corn and rice curls and puffs
President: Robert Rivard
National Sales Manager: Joe Guasco
Number Employees: 50-99
Type of Packaging: Consumer

11362 **Rivella USA**
3100 NW Boca Raton Boulevard
Boca Raton, FL 33431-6650 561-417-5810
Fax: 561-417-5811
Carbonated soft drink
President: Alexander Bart
Estimated Sales: $1.1 Million
Number Employees: 8
Type of Packaging: Food Service, Bulk

11363 **Rivendell Winery**
507 Albany Post Rd
New Paltz, NY 12561-3629
Fax: 845-255-2290
rivendellwinery@vintagenewyork.com
www.rivendellwine.com
Wines
President: Robert Ransom
Vice President: Melanie Smith
Estimated Sales: Below $ 5 Million
Number Employees: 10
Brands:
Libertyville Cellars
Rivendell
Soho Cellars

11364 **River Market Brewing Company**
P.O.Box 901898
Kansas City, MO 64190-1898 816-471-6300
Fax: 816-471-5562 www.rivermarketbrews.com
Processor of beer, ale, lager, stout and seasonal
President: Dvid Pecha
Estimated Sales: $ 1-2.5 Million
Number Employees: 20-49
Type of Packaging: Consumer, Food Service

11365 **River Road Coffee**
PO Box 252
Lake Clear, NY 12945-0252 315-769-9941
Fax: 315-769-7130
Coffee
President: David Copeland
General Manager: Michelle Yadon
Estimated Sales: $ 2.5-5 Million
Number Employees: 20

11366 **River Road Vineyards**
5220 Ross Rd
Sebastopol, CA 95472-2158 707-887-2243
Fax: 707-887-8160
wine@riverroadvineyards.com
www.riverroadvineyards.com
Manufacturer of wine; custom labels available
Estimated Sales: Under $500,000
Number Employees: 1-4
Type of Packaging: Private Label
Brands:
River Road Vineyards

11367 **River Run**
PO Box 8165
Burlington, VT 05402-8165 802-863-0499
Fax: 802-863-0377 ian@riverrunsoul.com
www.riverrunsoul.com
Sauce and condiments

11368 **River Run Vintners**
65 Rogge Ln
Watsonville, CA 95076 831-726-3112
Fax: 831-726-3112 riverrun@cruzio.com
www.riverrunwine.com
Wines
Manager: J P Pawloski
Estimated Sales: Less than $500,000
Number Employees: 1-4
Brands:
River Run

11369 **Riverdale Fine Foods**
919 N Main St
Dayton, OH 45405-4694 937-223-3225
Fax: 937-223-9456 800-548-1304
info@daytonnut.com
www.riverdalefinefoods.com
Fine chocolates, nuts, snack mixes, cookie mixes, specialty candy
President: Stanley Maschino
Estimated Sales: $ 3 - 5 Million
Number Employees: 10-19
Number of Brands: 5
Brands:
Candy Farm
Dayton's
Friesinger's
Minute Fudge
Yuletide

11370 **Rivere's Seafood Processors**
P.O.Box 246
Paincourtville, LA 70391-0246 985-369-2570
Fax: 985-369-2595
Processor of crawfish, catfish and shrimp
President/Owner: Darrell Rivere
Estimated Sales: $1-5 Million
Number Employees: 1-4
Type of Packaging: Consumer, Food Service, Private Label, Bulk
Brands:
Rivere's

11371 **Riverside Packers**
Rosedale Rd & Hwy 10
Drumheller, AB T0J 0Y0
Canada 403-823-2595
Fax: 403-823-3303
Processor of fresh pork, beef and sausage including beef, pork and turkey; also, beef patties and jerky
Owner/President: Grant Spooner
Co-Owner: Dixie Spooner
Estimated Sales: C
Number Employees: 10-19

11372 **Riverton Packing**
2515 E Monroe Ave
Riverton, WY 82501 307-856-3838
Processor of meat products
Owner: Rod Baltes
Estimated Sales: Less than $500,000
Number Employees: 1-4
Type of Packaging: Consumer, Food Service

11373 **Rivertown Foods**
4601 McRee Ave
Saint Louis, MO 63110 314-776-5646
Fax: 314-776-6468 800-844-3210
info@rivertownfoods.com
www.rivertownfoods.com
Manufacturer of salsas & mexican sauces, marinades, sauces, dressings, and spice blends.
President: Paul Endraske
CEO: John Schnoebelen
General Manager: Monica Holtgreven
Estimated Sales: $500,000-$1 Million
Number Employees: 5-9
Number of Brands: 15
Number of Products: 153
Type of Packaging: Consumer, Food Service, Private Label, Bulk
Brands:
Taste of the Hill

11374 **Riverview Foods**
1360 Bethleham Road
Warsaw, KY 41095 859-567-5211
Fax: 859-567-5213
Processor of smoked meats and barbecue and tomato sauces; also, research and development services available
President: Bob Weldon
VP Sales/Marketing: Robert Schroeder
General Manager: Mike Benton
Number Employees: 50-99
Sq. footage: 25000
Type of Packaging: Consumer, Food Service, Private Label, Bulk
Brands:
Riverview Foods Authentic

11375 **(HQ)Riviana Foods**
2777 Allen Pkwy Fl 15
Houston, TX 77019 713-529-3251
www.riviana.com
Rice and rice products.
President/CEO: Bastiaan De Zeeuw
VP/CFO: Gregory Richardson
VP Marketing: Paul Galvani
VP Sales: Thomas Forshee
VP Human Resources: Gerard Ferguson
VP Manufacturing: Stephen Isaacson
Estimated Sales: $363 Million
Number Employees: 1,000-4,999
Type of Packaging: Consumer, Food Service, Private Label, Bulk
Other Locations:
Carlisle AR
Clearbrook MN
Brands:
CAROLINA
GOURMET HOUSE
MAHATMA
MINUTE
RIVER
SUCCESS
WATER MAIN

11376 **Riviana Foods**
2314 S Lauderdale St
Memphis, TN 38106 901-942-0540
Fax: 901-948-3096 www.riviana.com
Processor and exporter of packaged rice products including bran
Manager: Steve Strong
Plant Manager: Steve Strong
Estimated Sales: $400 Million
Number Employees: 100-249
Parent Co: Riviana Foods
Type of Packaging: Bulk

11377 **(HQ)Riviana Foods**
P.O. BOX 2636
Houston, TX 77252 713-529-3251
Fax: 713-529-1866 800-226-9522
jwraa@gvtel.com www.riviana.com
Processor and exporter of wild rice
President: W David Hanks
CEO: Bastiaan De Zeeuw
Estimated Sales: $5-10 Million
Number Employees: 1,000-4,999
Sq. footage: 30000
Type of Packaging: Consumer, Food Service, Private Label, Bulk
Brands:
Gourmet Grains
Gourmet House
Onamia
Rare Gift
Simmer 'n Serve

11378 **Riviana Foods**
30 Mayfield Avenue
Edison, NJ 08837-3821 732-225-7210
Fax: 732-225-7217 www.riviana.com
Processor of rice including long and short grain, boxed, white and brown
Manager: Elton Kennedy Jr
Marketing Director: Joseph Hafner
CFO: Wayne Ray
Vice President: David Hanks
Estimated Sales: $ 10-20 Million
Number Employees: 20-49
Parent Co: Riviana Foods
Type of Packaging: Consumer, Food Service, Private Label, Bulk

11379 **Riviana Foods**
403 S Washington St
Abbeville, LA 70510 337-893-2236
Fax: 337-893-1122 www.riviana.com
Processor of rice including boxed, white, brown and long grain
Manager: Jimmy Richard
Operations: Anissa Mouton
Estimated Sales: $ 20-50 Million
Number Employees: 200
Parent Co: Riviana Foods
Type of Packaging: Consumer, Food Service, Private Label, Bulk

11380 **Riviera Ravioli Company**
643 Morris Park Ave
Bronx, NY 10460 718-823-0260
Fax: 718-823-0344 www.rivierapasta.com
Processor of fresh and frozen manicotti, cannelloni, tortellini, cappelletti, gnocchi, fettuccine, lasagne and cavatelli
President: Joseph Giordano
Plant Manager: Michael Somereve
Estimated Sales: $ 10 - 20 Million
Number Employees: 10-19
Brands:
Riviera

11381 **Road Runner Seafood**
586 Rock Road
Colquitt, GA 39837-5905 229-758-3485
Fax: 229-758-3991
Catfish, conch, croaker, flounder, full line seafood, mullet, oysters, shrimp
President: James Stovall III

11382 **Road's End Organics**
2160 Mountain Road
Suite 5
Stowe, VT 05672-4766 802-888-4130
Fax: 270-638-2265 877-247-3373
mkoch@chreese.com
http://www.roadsendorganics.com
Dairy free pasta and dip
President: Matthew Koch

Estimated Sales: $ 3 - 5 Million
Number Employees: 1-4

11383 Roanoke Apple Products
844 Union St
Salem, VA 24153 540-375-3782
Fax: 540-375-3782
roanokeappleproducts@msn.com
Processor of vinegar including pure apple cider, white distilled and red wine
President: Glenn Dunville
Marketing Director: Deborah Dunville
Plant Manager: Randy Kesler
Estimated Sales: $1100000
Number Employees: 11
Sq. footage: 22000
Type of Packaging: Food Service, Private Label, Bulk
Brands:
Bandana
Heidecker
Old Kettle

11384 Roaring Brook Dairy
Po Box 753
Chappaqua, NY 10514 914-861-2666
roaringbrookdairy@gmail.com
www.roaringbrookdairy.com
Cheese, gift packs.
Marketing: Leslie Kozupsky
Estimated Sales: $88,000
Number Employees: 2

11385 Roasterie
1204 W 27th St
Kansas City, MO 64108 816-931-4000
Fax: 816-931-4040 800-376-0245
info@theroasterie.com www.theroasterie.com
Coffee
Owner: Danny O'Neill
Customer Service Manager: Stacy Barter
Quality Control: Norm Killnorm
CFO: Bill Molini
CFO: Carla O'Neill
CFO: Chris Mikuls
Estimated Sales: $ 1-2.5 Million
Number Employees: 20-49
Brands:
Roasterie

11386 Rob Salamida Company
71 Pratt Ave
Johnson City, NY 13790 607-770-7046
Fax: 607-797-4721 info@spiedie.com
www.spiedie.com
Manufacturer and importer of meat marinades, barbecue sauces, and gourmet spice blends.
President: Robert Alan Salamida
Estimated Sales: $4.2 Million
Number Employees: 10-19
Type of Packaging: Consumer, Food Service, Private Label
Brands:
Pinch
Spiedie Sauce
State Fair

11387 Robbie's Natural Products
3191 Grandeur Ave
Altadena, CA 91001 626-798-9944
Fax: 626-457-8705 info@robbiesnatural.com
www.robbiesnatural.com
Processor of natural and kosher ketchup, salsa, fruit syrup and sauces including barbecue, worcestershire, sweet and sour and garlic
President: Robbie Roberts
Sales Manager: Roberta Fleischer
Estimated Sales: $ 3 - 5 Million
Number Employees: 1-4
Type of Packaging: Consumer, Food Service

11388 Robbins Packing Company
P.O.Box 887
Statesboro, GA 30459-0887 912-764-7503
Fax: 912-489-2823 robbins1@fronhernet.net
Processor and packer of pork, beef, sausage and smoked meats
President: Wayne Paulk
President/Managing Partner: Rodney Poole
Sales Manager: Glen Brown
Plant Manager: Jack Kasses
Estimated Sales: $ 1 - 3 Million
Number Employees: 1-4
Sq. footage: 70000

Type of Packaging: Consumer, Food Service, Private Label, Bulk

11389 Roberian Vineyards
2614 King Rd
Forestville, NY 14062 716-679-1620
Wines
Estimated Sales: Under $500,000
Number Employees: 1-4

11390 Robert & James Brands
950 E Maple Road
Birmingham, MI 48009-6408 248-646-0578
Fax: 248-646-6040
Condiments and relishes
Owner: Robert Arnold
Estimated Sales: $ 1-2.5 Million
Number Employees: 5

11391 Robert F Pliska & Company Winery
101 Cantwell Court
Purgitsville, WV 26852 304-289-3493
Fax: 304-289-3900 877-747-2737
VineyardHome@frontiernet.net
www.vineyardhome.org
Wines
Owner: Robert Pliska
Wine Maker: Robert F Pliska
Purchasing Manager: TC McGee
Estimated Sales: $ 1 - 3 Million
Number Employees: 1-4
Parent Co: Piterra Farms
Type of Packaging: Consumer
Brands:
101 Piterra Place
Assumption Wines
Mt. Betty
Mt. Mama

11392 Robert Keenan Winery
3660 Spring Mountain Rd
Saint Helena, CA 94574 707-963-9177
Fax: 707-963-8209 rkw@keenanwinery.com
www.keenanwinery.com
Wines
President/CEO: Michael Keenan
Wine Maker: Niles Venge
Estimated Sales: $ 1-2.5 Million
Number Employees: 5-9
Brands:
Robert Keenan Winery

11393 Robert Mondavi Winery
P.O.Box 106
Oakville, CA 94562-0106 707-226-1395
Fax: 707-224-5251 888-766-6328
info@robertmondaviwinery.com
www.robertmondaviwinery.com
Processor and exporter of wines
President/CEO: Eric Morhan
General Manager, Winery: Glenn Workman
Financial Planning Manager: Benjamin Dobrei
Estimated Sales: $100+ Million
Number Employees: 100-249
Brands:
MONDAVI

11394 Robert Mondavi Winery
P.O.Box 106
Oakville, CA 94562-0106 707-259-9463
Fax: 707-963-1007 888-766-6238
info@robertmondaviwinery.com
www.robertmondaviwinery.com
Wines
President: Salst Mondavi
Founder: Robert Mondavi
Chairman: Robert Mondavi
Plant Manager: Genevieve Janssens
Estimated Sales: $ 1-2.5 Million
Number Employees: 75
Brands:
Robert Mondavi

11395 Robert Mueller Cellars
6301 Starr Rd
Windsor, CA 95492-9653 707-837-7399
Fax: 707-431-8365 www.muellerwine.com
Wines
President: Robert Mueller
CEO: Bruce E Ollodart
Estimated Sales: $ 1-2.5 Million
Number Employees: 1-4

Brands:
Mueller

11396 Robert Pecota Winery
P.O.Box 303
Calistoga, CA 94515 707-942-6625
Fax: 707-942-6671
info@robertpecotawinery.com
www.robertpecotawinery.com
Wines
Co-Owner/Partner: Robert Pecota
Co-Owner/Partner: Kara Pecota Dunn
Co-Owner/Partner: Andrea Pecota White
Marketing: Andrea Pecota White
Sales: Andrea Pecota White
Operations Director/Guest Services: Brenda Wild
Consulting Winemker: Marco DiGiulio
Estimated Sales: $ 1-2.5 Million
Number Employees: 5-9
Type of Packaging: Private Label
Brands:
Robert Pecota

11397 Robert R. Young Sr. Company
P.O.Box 241
Unity, ME 04988-0241 207-948-3254
Fax: 207-338-3498
Owner: Robert Berry
Estimated Sales: $ 3 - 5 Million
Number Employees: 20-49

11398 Robert Rothschild BerryFarm
P.O.Box 767
Urbana, OH 43078-0767 937-653-7397
Fax: 937-652-1044 866-565-6790
customerservice@robertrothschild.com
www.robertrothschild.com
Preserves, mustard, salsas, dips, fruit, dessert toppings, extra virgin olive oil, dressings and herb vinegars
President: Marie O'Donnel
Chairman: Robert Rothschild
CEO: Jim Clegg
CFO: Dominick Maxwell
R & D: Martin Finan
Estimated Sales: $ 10-20 Million
Number Employees: 50-99
Type of Packaging: Consumer, Food Service, Private Label, Bulk

11399 Robert Rothschild Farm
P.O.Box 311
Urbana, OH 43078 614-336-1135
Fax: 937-652-1044 866-565-6790
info@robertrothschild.com
www.robertrothschild.com
Gourmet mustard, vinagrette, sauces and preserves
Chairman: Robert Rothschild
Ceo: Jim Clegg
CFO: Don Jones
Marketing/Public Relations: Jill Borering
Production Manager: Diane Oyer
Purchasing Manager: Steve Day
Estimated Sales: $ 10-20 Million
Number Employees: 45
Sq. footage: 35
Type of Packaging: Private Label
Brands:
Breadstick Dip & Pizza Sauce
Fiery Raspberry Sals
Honey Mustard Pretze
Raspberry Salsa
Wings-N-Things

11400 Robert Silverman Company
517 N Warwick Avenue
Westmont, IL 60559-1550 630-515-8100
Fax: 630-515-8196
President: Robert Silverman
Estimated Sales: $300,000-500,000
Number Employees: 1-4

11401 Robert Sinskey Vineyards
6320 Silverado Trl
Napa, CA 94558-9747 707-944-9090
Fax: 707-944-9097 800-869-2030
rsv@robertsinskey.com www.robertsinskey.com

Wines
Vintner: Rob Sinskey
Winemaker: Jeff Virnig
Culinary Director: Maria Helm Sinskey
Founder: Bob Sinskey
Sales Manager: Meg Bartley
Sales Manager: Eric Sother
Vineyard Manager: Kirk Grace
Estimated Sales: Below $ 5 Million
Number Employees: 20-49
Type of Packaging: Private Label
Brands:
RSV

11402 Robert's Bakery
17516 Minnetonka Boulevard
Minnetonka, MN 55345-1000 612-473-9719
Fax: 612-473-1835
Bakery products
President: Robert Larson
Estimated Sales: $ 5-9.9 Million
Number Employees: 20

11403 Robertet Flavors
201 Circle Dr N Ste 108
Piscataway, NJ 08854 732-271-1804
Fax: 732-981-1717
robertetflavors@robertetusa.com
www.robertet.com
Manufacturer and exporter of beverage and instant tea mixes, dairy bases, extracts, citrus oils and flavors
Deputy Chairman: Peter Lombardo
Vice President: Joe Rainone
SVP R&D: John Scire
VP Marketing: Steve Wilbur
VP Sales: Neil Callahan
Estimated Sales: $50-100 Million
Number Employees: 50-99
Sq. footage: 55000
Parent Co: Robertet
Type of Packaging: Food Service

11404 Roberto A Cheese Factory
7465 Lincoln Street SE
East Canton, OH 44730-9439 330-488-1551
Fax: 330-488-1552
Natural cheese
President: Angelo Roberto
Co-Owner: Armand Babbo
Estimated Sales: $500,000-$1 Million
Number Employees: 10-19
Brands:
Roberto Cheese

11405 (HQ)Roberts Dairy Foods
2901 Cuming Street
Omaha, NE 68131 402-371-3660
Fax: 402-371-0243 www.robertsdairy.com
Processor of milk, juice, yogurt, sour cream, dips, butter, cream, half and half, cottage cheese, lemonade, fruit punch, ice cream and tea
Manager: Mitch Ayers
Director Corporate Marketing: Al Streeter
Division Manager: Bob Walker
Estimated Sales: $250 Million
Number Employees: 225
Type of Packaging: Consumer, Food Service, Private Label

11406 Roberts Dairy Foods
1109 North Dodge
Iowa City, IA 52245
www.robertsdairy.com
Manufacturer of orange juice and dairy products including milk and ice milk mixes
Number of Products: 300
Parent Co: Robert Dairy Foods
Type of Packaging: Consumer, Food Service, Private Label, Bulk
Other Locations:
Roberts Dairy Company
Norfolk NE
Roberts Dairy Company
Kansas City MO
Roberts Dairy Company
Iowa City IA
Roberts Dairy Company
Des Moines IA
Brands:
HILLAD - ROBERTS
ROBERTS

11407 Roberts Dairy Foods
3805 S Emanuel Cleaver Ii Blvd
Kansas City, MO 64128 816-921-7370
Fax: 816-921-3437 800-279-1692
www.robertsdairy.com
Manufacturer of dairy products including milk, sour cream, yogurt and ice cream specialties
Sq. footage: 60000
Parent Co: Roberts Dairy Foods
Type of Packaging: Consumer, Food Service, Private Label, Bulk

11408 Roberts Ferry Nut Company
20493 Yosemite Blvd
Waterford, CA 95386 209-874-3247
Fax: 209-874-3707 orders@robertsferrynuts.com
www.ilikenuts.com
Processor and exporter of almonds and popcorn
Partner: William Mallory
Partner: Dorothy Mallory
Estimated Sales: $3135592
Number Employees: 20-49
Type of Packaging: Consumer, Bulk
Brands:
Roberts Ferry

11409 Roberts Seed
982 22 Rd
Axtell, NE 68924 308-743-2565
Fax: 308-743-2048 robertsseed@gtmc.net
Processor and exporter of grain, soybeans, popcorn kernels, wheat, corn and dry edible beans; certified organic and GMO-free products available
President: Joe Roberts
Estimated Sales: $950000
Number Employees: 1-4
Sq. footage: 15000
Type of Packaging: Private Label, Bulk

11410 Robertson's Country Meat Hams
P.O.Box 56
Finchville, KY 40022-0056 502-834-7952
Fax: 502-834-7095 800-678-1521
www.finchvillefarms.com
Country ham
president: William Robertson
Marketing Director: Jim Robertson
CFO: Margaret Davis
CFO: Margaret Davis
Estimated Sales: Below $ 5 Million
Number Employees: 10-19
Type of Packaging: Private Label, Bulk
Brands:
Finchville Farms

11411 Robichaux's Meat Market
717 W Mill St
Crowley, LA 70526-5505 337-788-4124
Fax: 337-788-4108
Meat
President: Floyd Robichaux
Estimated Sales: Less than $500,000
Number Employees: 5-9

11412 Robin & Cohn Seafood Distributors
3225 Palmisano Boulevard
Chalmette, LA 70043-3633 504-277-1679
Fax: 504-277-1679
Seafood
President: Fay Cohn

11413 Robinson Barbecue SauceCompany
940 Madison St
Oak Park, IL 60302-4430 708-383-8452
Fax: 708-383-922 800-836-6750
cdell@rib1.com www.rib1.com
Manufacturers of barbecue sauce
President: Helen Robinson
CFO: Charlie Robinson
Marketing Director: Cordell Robinson
Operations Manager: Bruce Swerdlow
Estimated Sales: $500,000-$1 Million
Number Employees: 20-49
Type of Packaging: Private Label
Brands:
Robinson Barbecue Sauce

11414 Robinson Cold Storage
24415 NE 10th Ave
Ridgefield, WA 98642 360-887-3501
Frozen foods
President/CEO: Allen Nirenstein
Chairman: Thomas Klein
Estimated Sales: Less than $500,000
Number Employees: 1-4

11415 Robinson Dairy
P.O.Box 5774
Denver, CO 80217-5774 303-825-2990
Fax: 303-825-8419 800-332-6355
bward@robinsondairy.com
www.robinsondairy.com
Processor of ice cream, yogurt, milk and sour cream
Plant Manager: Larry Glodek
Estimated Sales: $29400000
Number Employees: 50-99
Parent Co: Suiza Dairy Group
Type of Packaging: Consumer, Food Service

11416 Robinson's Barbecue Sauce Company
940 Madison St
Oak Park, IL 60302-4430 708-383-8452
Fax: 708-383-9486 www.rib1.com
Processor and exporter of meat seasonings and sauces including barbecue and hot
President: Charles Robinson
VP: Helen Robinson
Estimated Sales: $500,000-$1 Million
Number Employees: 10-19
Sq. footage: 10000
Parent Co: Robinson's #1 Ribs Restaurants
Type of Packaging: Consumer, Food Service, Bulk
Brands:
Charlie Robinson's
Charlie Robinson's #1
Mississippi

11417 Robinsons Sausage Company
701 Robinson Rd
London, KY 40741-9018 606-864-2914
Fax: 606-864-3252 robinson@mis.net
www.robinsonmeats50.com
Processor and wholesaler/distributor of meats including whole hog sausage and deli items; wholesaler/distributor of frozen foods and private label items
President: Jimmy Robinson
Estimated Sales: $5500000
Number Employees: 20-49
Sq. footage: 20000
Type of Packaging: Private Label

11418 Robller Vineyard
275 Robbler Vineyard Rd
New Haven, MO 63068-2102 573-237-3986
Fax: 573-237-3985 info@robllerwines.com
www.robllerwines.com
Manufacturer of wine
Owner: Robert Mueller
Owner: Lois Mueller
Estimated Sales: Less than $200,000
Number Employees: 1-4
Brands:
Robller Vineyard and Winery

11419 Roca Food Sales
576 Colonial Park Dr # 130
Roswell, GA 30075-3794 770-993-0030
Fax: 770-993-0792
Processor of frozen broccoli, carrots, cauliflower, zucchini and squash
Manager: Fred Everett
CEO: Fred Everett
National Sales Manager: Rob Rickerby
Estimated Sales: $ 1-2.5 Million
Number Employees: 5-9
Type of Packaging: Food Service, Private Label, Bulk
Brands:
Roca

11420 Roccas Italian Foods
P.O.Box 150
New Castle, PA 16103 724-654-3344
Fax: 724-654-4954
Tortellini, Ravioli and pasta products
President: Anthony Rocca
Estimated Sales: Below $ 5 Million
Number Employees: 10-19
Brands:
Roccas

11421 **Roche Caneros Estate Winry**
122 West Spain Street
Sonoma, CA 95476-9700 707-935-7115
Fax: 707-935-7846 800-825-9475
info@rochewinery.com www.rochewinery.com
Wines
President: Joseph Roche
CFO: Kerstin Kohlstrom
Marketing/Sales: Dino Montalbano
Estimated Sales: $ 5-9.9 Million
Number Employees: 10-19
Type of Packaging: Private Label
Brands:
ROCHE

11422 **Roche Fruit**
601 North 1st Street
Yakima, WA 98902 509-248-7200
Fax: 509-453-3835
michaelroche@jewelapple.com
www.rochefruit.com
Fruits
Owner/Sales Manager: Michael Roche
Quality Assurance Manager: Marina Britt
Customer Service: Janet McKay
Operations Manager: Mike Hanses
Estimated Sales: $11 Million
Number Employees: 150
Number of Brands: 1

11423 **Rochester Cheese**
4219 Highway 14 W
Rochester, MN 55901 507-288-6678
Fax: 507-288-6175 888-288-6678
tomf@rochestercheese.com
www.rochestercheese.com
Fresh grated Parmesan, dehydrated Parmesan and other hard Italian style cheeses. Also produces American style cheeses.
Manager: Greg Anderson
CFO: Sherry Hinkle
VP: Don Roberts
Business Coordinator: Steve Majors
R&D/National Accounts Manager: Harry Appleby
Plant Manager: Gene Enneking
Plant Manager: Paul Domovsky
Plant Manager: Scott Amos
Estimated Sales: $ 20-50 Million
Number Employees: 5-9
Type of Packaging: Private Label

11424 **Rock Bottom Brewery**
1001 16th St Ste 100
Denver, CO 80265 303-534-7616
Fax: 303-534-2129 www.rockbottom.com
Processor of seasonal beer, ale and stout
Manager: Jim Maresca
Managing Partner: Bennett Ponder
Managing Partner: Jessica Buesing
Estimated Sales: $ 10-20 Million
Number Employees: 50
Parent Co: CraftWorks Restaurants & Breweries
Type of Packaging: Consumer, Food Service, Bulk
Brands:
Falcon Pale
Red Rock

11425 **Rock Point Oyster Company**
1733 Dabob Post Office Rd
Quilcene, WA 98376 360-765-3765
Fax: 360-765-3676
Oysters
Estimated Sales: Less than $500,000
Number Employees: 6

11426 **Rock River Provision Company**
P.O.Box 897
Rock Falls, IL 61071-0897 815-625-1195
Fax: 815-626-0185 800-685-1195
butchershop@rockriverprovision.com
www.rockriverprovision.com
Processor of beef and pork
President: David Hoffman
Estimated Sales: $ 10-20 Million
Number Employees: 20-49

11427 **Rock-N-Roll Gourmet**
15 Outrigger St
Apt 302
Marina Del Ray, CA 90292 424-228-4901
Fax: 310-751-6397 800-518-3891
dan@rocknrollgourmet.com
www.rocknrollgourmet.com
potato chips, cookies and popcorn
President/Owner: Jean Ehrlich
CEO: Dan Ehrlich
CFO: Peter Vermeulen
Number Employees: 10

11428 **Rockbridge Vineyard**
35 Hillview Ln
Raphine, VA 24472 540-377-6204
Fax: 888-511-9463 rockwine@cfw.com
www.rockbridgevineyard.com
Wines
Onwer: Shepherd Rouse
Estimated Sales: $ 1 - 3 Million
Number Employees: 1-4
Type of Packaging: Consumer
Brands:
DECHIEL
ROCKBRIDGE VINEYARD

11429 **Rocket Products Company**
P.O.Box 565
Fenton, MO 63026 636-343-9110
Fax: 636-343-0897 800-325-9567
bob.pinkerton@rocketproducts.com
www.rocketproducts.com
Manufacturer of beverage concentrates
Founder/CEO: Charles Lazier, Jr.
President: E Lazier
General Manager: Robert Pinkerton
Purchasing Director: Barbara Duran
Estimated Sales: $ 5 - 10 Million
Number Employees: 9
Number of Brands: 3
Number of Products: 11
Sq. footage: 15000
Brands:
Dair-E

11430 **Rockland Bakery**
94 Demarest Mill Rd W
Nanuet, NY 10954 845-623-5800
Fax: 845-623-6921 800-734-4376
anthony@rocklandbakery.com
www.rocklandbakery.com
Processor of bread, rolls, bagels, cakes, pies and challah
Principal: Ira Lampert
CFO: Ed McCauslande
COO: Anthony Battaglia
Estimated Sales: $27 Million
Number Employees: 350
Type of Packaging: Consumer, Food Service

11431 **Rockland Boat**
20 Park Dr
Rockland, ME 04841-3441 207-594-8181
Fax: 207-594-8161 www.hamiltonmarine.com
Seafood
President: Leni Gronros
COO: Steve Graebert
Estimated Sales: $ 5 - 10 Million
Number Employees: 10-19

11432 **Rockport Lobster**
54 Commercial St
Gloucester, MA 01930-5025 978-281-0225
Fax: 978-281-8578
Lobster
Owner: Craig Babinski
Estimated Sales: $580,000
Number Employees: 1-4

11433 **Rockview Farms**
P.O.Box 668
Downey, CA 90241 562-927-5511
Fax: 562-928-9765 800- 42- 247
caroler@rockviewfarms.com
www.rockviewfarms.com
Fluid milk
President: Egbert DeGroot
CFO: Joe Valadez
CEO: Egbert De Groot
Sales Manager: Ken Lee
Plant Manager: Erroll McGowen
Estimated Sales: $ 50-100 Million
Number Employees: 100-249
Type of Packaging: Bulk

11434 **Rocky Mountain Coffee Roasters**
P.O. Box 2609
Jasper, Alberta T0E 1E0 780-852-4280
Fax: 780-852-5910 800-666-3465
jrod@rockymountainroasters.com
www.rockymountainroasters.com
Coffee retail/wholesale/roaster
President: Les Chorley
CFO: Brad Woods
Vice President: Andy Johnsen
VP Marketing: Andy Johnsen
Operations Manager: Jonathan Kitchensa
Estimated Sales: Under $500,000
Number Employees: 5-9
Brands:
Clipper Foods
Whitney Distributing

11435 **Rocky Mountain Honey Company**
642 Pugsley St
Salt Lake City, UT 84103 801-355-2054
Fax: 801-355-2054
Manufacturer of beeswax and honey
President: Floyd Meyer
Partner: Melvin Meyer
Estimated Sales: $1-3 Million
Number Employees: 1-4
Parent Co: Meyer Honey Company
Type of Packaging: Consumer, Food Service, Private Label, Bulk

11436 **Rocky Mountain Meats**
4803 43rd St.
PO Box 459
Rocky Mountain House, AB T4T 1A4
Canada 403-845-3434
Fax: 780-845-7418 www.rockymeats.com/
Processor of fresh beef, pork and wild game including deer, elk, moose and bear
Owner: Rudi Koller
Co-Owner/Office Admin: Stefanie Koller
Estimated Sales: C
Number Employees: 10-19
Type of Packaging: Consumer, Food Service, Private Label, Bulk
Brands:
Rocky Mountain

11437 **Rocky Mountain Natural Meats**
9757 Alton Way
Henderson, CO 80640 303-287-7100
Fax: 303-287-7272 800-327-2706
bison@greatrangebison.com
www.greatrangebison.com
Buffalo products
President: Bob Dineen
Marketing Director: Paul Pernarbo
CFO: Bob Dineen
Estimated Sales: $ 10-20 Million
Number Employees: 10-19
Type of Packaging: Private Label
Brands:
Rocky Mountain Natural Meats

11438 **Rocky Mountain Packing Company**
P.O.Box 2450
Havre, MT 59501 406-265-3401
Fax: 406-265-3401
Processor of meat products
Owner/President: David Swallow
Owner/CEO: Linda Swallow
Estimated Sales: $100,000-$120,000
Number Employees: 1-4
Type of Packaging: Consumer

11439 **(HQ)Rocky Mountain Popcorn Company**
6547 S Racine Cir #1800
Centennial, CO 80111 303-744-8850
Fax: 303-389-6859 rmpopcorn@msn.com
www.rmpopcorn.com
Processor and exporter of ready-to-eat popcorn
President: Janice Charles
Number Employees: 1-4
Number of Brands: 1
Number of Products: 10
Sq. footage: 20000
Type of Packaging: Consumer, Food Service, Private Label, Bulk
Brands:
Rocky Mountain Popcorn

11440 **Rocky Point Shrimp Association**
305 E Buchanan St
Phoenix, AZ 85004 602-254-8041
Fax: 602-523-9637
Shrimp
Estimated Sales: $ 3 - 5 Million
Number Employees: 5-9

11441 **Rocky Top Country**
4201 Wears Valley Rd
Sevierville, TN 37862-8153 865-428-7311
Fax: 865-428-7524 www.rockytopcountry.com
Fudge
Owner: Robert Glenn
Estimated Sales: $300,000-500,000
Number Employees: 1-4
Type of Packaging: Consumer

11442 **Rocky Top Farms**
11486 Essex Rd
Ellsworth, MI 49729 800-862-9303
Fax: 231-599-2352 800-862-9303
sales@rockytopfarms.com
www.rockytopfarms.com
Processor and exporter of preserves including raspberry, cherry, strawberry, blackberry and black raspberry; also, butter toppings
President: Tom Cooper
Estimated Sales: $ 3 - 5 Million
Number Employees: 5-9
Type of Packaging: Consumer, Bulk

11443 **Rod's Food Products**
17380 Railroad St
City of Industry, CA 91748-1023 909-839-8925
Fax: 626-964-5447
Processor and exporter of salad dressings, chip dips, dairy and nondairy sour creams and aerosol whip toppings
Plant Manager: Stuart Saito
Number Employees: 100-249
Parent Co: Dean Foods Company
Type of Packaging: Consumer, Food Service, Private Label, Bulk

11444 **Rodda Coffee Company**
PO Box 290
Yachats, OR 97498-0290 541-547-4132
Fax: 888-919-2722 ycch@teleport.com
Coffee
President: Tom Rodda
Estimated Sales: Under $500,000
Number Employees: 10-19
Brands:
Rodda Coffee

11445 **Rodelle Vanillas**
3461 Precision Drive
Fort Collins, CO 80528 970-482-8845
800-898-5457
info@rodellevanilla.com
www.rodellevanilla.com
vanilla, baking essential, herbs and spices

11446 **(HQ)Rodney Strong Vineyards**
11455 Old Redwood Hwy
Healdsburg, CA 95448 707-433-6511
Fax: 707-433-8635 www.rodneystrong.com
Processor of wines
President/CP: Alan Nirenstein
Owner/Chairman/CEO: Tom Klein
CFO: Tobin Ginter
VP Sales/Marketing: Dan Wildermuth
Human Resource Manager: Kate Sorenson
COO/Plant Manager: Rick Sayre
Estimated Sales: $4.3 Million
Number Employees: 100
Sq. footage: 20000
Type of Packaging: Consumer, Private Label
Brands:
Rodney Strong

11447 **Rodney Strong Vineyards**
11455 Old Redwood Hwy
Healdsburg, CA 95448 707-433-6521
Fax: 707-433-0939 800-474-9463
info@rodneystrong.com www.rodneystrong.com
Wines
Proptietor: Tom Klein
VP, Director of Winemaking: Rick Sayre
Estimated Sales: $ .5 - 1 million
Number Employees: 5-9
Type of Packaging: Private Label
Brands:
Rodney Strong

11448 **Roelli Cheese Company**
15982 State Road 11
Shullsburg, WI 53586 608-965-3779
Fax: 608-965-4510 800-575-4372
www.roellicheese.com
Cheese
President: Dave Roelli
VP: Gary Roelli
Estimated Sales: $ 1 - 3 Million
Number Employees: 10-19
Brands:
Balderson
Bingham Hill Cheeses

11449 **Roger Wood Foods**
P.O.Box 2926
7 Alfred Street
Savannah, GA 31408 912-652-9600
Fax: 912-964-6367 800-849-9272
customerservice@rogerwoodfoods.com
www.rogerwoodfoods.com
Sausage
President: David W Solana
CFO: Camille Brown
VP Sales and Marketing: Matt Solana
Director Operations: Bob Lytle
Plant Engineer: Tony Roberts
Estimated Sales: $40 Million
Number Employees: 250
Brands:
Billies

11450 **Roger's Recipe**
518 Perron Hl
Glover, VT 05839-9735 802-525-3050
Brittle made with maple syrup
Owner: Michael Rogers
Estimated Sales: $300,000-500,000
Number Employees: 1-4
Type of Packaging: Consumer

11451 **Rogers Brothers**
470 E Brooks St
Galesburg, IL 61401 309-342-2127
Fax: 309-342-4147
Manufacturer and Wholesaler/distributor of frozen meat and seafood, frozen food, dry goods, dairy products and produce
President: Frank Rogers
VP: George Rogers
Operations Manager: John Rogers
Estimated Sales: $65 Million
Number Employees: 41
Sq. footage: 35000

11452 **(HQ)Rogers Sugar**
4026 Notre-Dame Street E
Montreal, QC H1W 2K3
Canada 514-527-8686
Fax: 514-527-1610 infos@rogerssugar.com
www.rogerssugar.com
Leading refiner, processor, distributor and marketer of sugar products
President/CEO: Edward Mankin
Senior VP/Procurement/CFO/Secretary: Daniel Lafrance
VP Sales: Mike Walton
VP Operations: Bob Copeland
Estimated Sales: $570 Million
Number Employees: 550
Type of Packaging: Consumer, Food Service, Bulk
Other Locations:
Vancouver, BC
Taber, Alberta

11453 **Rogers Sugar Inc**
123 Rogers Street
Vancouver, BC V6A 3N2
Canada 604-253-1131
Fax: 604-253-2517 800-661-5350
infos@rogerssugar.com www.rogerssugar.com
white sugar, icing sugar, brown/yellow sugar, liquid sugar, specialty products, organic sugar, dry blending and
President/CEO: Edward Makin
CFO: Daniel Lafrance
VP Sales: Mike Walton
VP Operations: Bob Copeland
General Manager: Doug Emek
Number Employees: 196
Number of Products: 23
Sq. footage: 15
Parent Co: Lantic Sugar Limited
Type of Packaging: Consumer, Food Service, Bulk
Other Locations:
Rogers Sugar Limited
Alberta, Canada
Brands:
Roger's

11454 **Rogers' Chocolates Ltd**
4253 Commerce Circle
Victoria, BC V8Z 4M2
Canada 250-727-6851
Fax: 250-384-5750 800-663-2220
info@rogerschocolates.com
www.rogerschocolates.com
Processor and exporter of confectionery products including boxed cream-filled and dark chocolates, chocolate mint wafers, almond brittles, caramel nutcorn, fudge, etc
President: Steve Parkhill
Estimated Sales: $10 Million
Number Employees: 130
Sq. footage: 29000
Type of Packaging: Consumer, Private Label
Brands:
Rogers Imperials
Victoria Creams

11455 **Rogue Ales**
2320 SE Osu Dr
Newport, OR 97365 541-867-3660
Fax: 541-265-7528
Processor and exporter of ale, lager and barley wine
President: Jack Joyce
CEO: Jack Choice
Estimated Sales: $5-10 Million
Type of Packaging: Consumer, Food Service

11456 **Rogue Creamery**
P.O.Box 3606
Central Point, OR 97502 541-665-1155
Fax: 541-665-1133 info@roguecreamery.com
www.roguecreamery.com
Processor of butter and cheese including cheddar and blue vein cheese.
President/Owner: David Gremmels
CEO: Cary Bryant
Marketing Director: Thomas Vella
Plant Manager: Craig Nelson
Purchasing Manager: Lisa Lawrence
Estimated Sales: $5.9 Million
Number Employees: 45
Number of Brands: 10
Number of Products: 20
Sq. footage: 40000
Parent Co: Vella Cheese
Type of Packaging: Consumer, Food Service, Bulk

11457 **Roha USA LLC**
5015 Manchester Ave
Saint Louis, MO 63110 314-531-0461
Fax: 888-531-0461 roha.usa@rohagroup.com
www.rohagroup.com
Supplier of natural and synthetic food colours.
Production: Rohit Tibrewala

11458 **Rohrbach Brewing Company**
3859 Buffalo Rd
Rochester, NY 14624 585-594-9800
Fax: 585-594-1960 info@rohrbachs.com
www.rohrbachs.com
Processor of seasonal beer, ale, stout and lager
President: John Urlaub
CFO: Sam Fletcher
Estimated Sales: $ 1-2.5 Million
Number Employees: 20-49
Type of Packaging: Consumer, Food Service

11459 **Rohtstein Corporation**
P.O.Box 2129
Woburn, MA 01888-0229 781-935-8300
Fax: 781-932-3917
Processor of canned pie filling including mince meat
President: Steven A Rohtstein
Executive VP: Eugene Cohen
Sales/Marketing: Barney Butler
Estimated Sales: $ 50 - 100 Million
Number Employees: 50-99
Parent Co: Rohtstein Corporation
Type of Packaging: Food Service

11460 Rohtstein Corporation
P.O.Box 2129
70 Olympia Ave
Woburn, MA 01801-2036 781-935-8300
Fax: 781-932-3917
Canned vegetable and juices
President/Treasurer: Steven Rohtstein
Estimated Sales: $18 Million
Number Employees: 50-99

11461 Rokeach Food Corporation
80 Avenue K
Newark, NJ 7105 973-589-4900
Fax: 973-589-5298 rokeach@prodigy.com
Ethnic foods
CEO: Victor Ostreicher
Estimated Sales: Less than $500,000
Number Employees: 100-249
Brands:
Jericho Canyon Red
Rokeach Food

11462 Roland Industries
2280 Chaffee Drive
Saint Louis, MO 63146-3304 314-567-3800
Fax: 314-567-5211 800-325-1183
customer.service@abitec-roland.com
www.abitec-roland.com
Processor of breadings, batters, baking powder, fermentation additives, dough conditioners, sausage/meat binders, chocolate milk, baking and cake mixes, etc.; exporter of baking mixes
COO: Ian MacEwan
Vice President: Terry McGuire IV
Plant Manager: Keith Gill
Purchasing Manager: Mary Gajewski
Number Employees: 100-249
Sq. footage: 70000
Parent Co: Abitec Corporation
Type of Packaging: Private Label, Bulk
Brands:
Best O' the Wheat
Choice Foods
Gold N Good
Golden Meal
Heritage Hearth

11463 Rolet Food Products Company
70 Scott Ave
Brooklyn, NY 11237-1308 718-497-0476
Fax: 718-497-0137 rolet@aol.com
www.rolets.com
Sausage and meats, snack foods
President: Mark Turetsky
Executive VP: Charles Littman
Operations Manager: Miles Turetsky
Estimated Sales: $ 10-20 Million
Number Employees: 50-99
Sq. footage: 20
Type of Packaging: Private Label
Brands:
Delifresh
Jimmy's
Potatomania
Side Show

11464 Roller Ed
1115 Ridgeway Ave # 2
Rochester, NY 14615-3755 585-458-8020
Fax: 585-458-8169
Manufacturer of Condiments including horseradish and cocktail sauces
Owner: Mike Mendick
Estimated Sales: $1-2.5 Million
Number Employees: 1-4
Number of Products: 2
Sq. footage: 10000
Type of Packaging: Consumer, Food Service, Private Label, Bulk
Brands:
PRIVATE LABELS
ROLLERS

11465 Rolling Hills Vineyards
1665 Fordham Ave
Thousand Oaks, CA 91360-2032
Fax: 805-484-8100 www.travelenvoy.com
Wines
President: Ed Pagor
Estimated Sales: Less than $500,000
Number Employees: 1-4
Brands:
Tempanillo

11466 Rolling Pin Bakery
119 5th Avenue W
Bow Island, AB T0K 0G0
Canada 403-545-2434
Fax: 403-545-2167
Processor of bread, doughnuts, cakes and pastries
Partner: John Sytsma
Partner: Ineke Sytsma
Proprietor: Russell Dueck
Estimated Sales: $149,000
Number Employees: 3
Sq. footage: 1375
Type of Packaging: Consumer, Food Service

11467 Rolling Pin Bakery
2211 Washington Street
Great Bend, KS 67530-2454 620-793-5381
Baked goods
President: Dave Cooley
Estimated Sales: $500,000 appx.
Number Employees: 5

11468 Rolling Pin Manufacturing Corporation
1511 Grandview Dr
S San Francisco, CA 94080-4911 650-952-7324
Fax: 510-780-1433
Estimated Sales: $ 1 - 5 Million
Number Employees: 5-9

11469 Rollingstone Chevre
P.O.Box 683
Parma, ID 83660 208-722-6460
Fax: 208-722-6460 chevre@mac.com
www.rollingstonechevre.com
Goat cheese
Owner: Karen Evans
Owner: Charles Evans
Estimated Sales: $150,000
Number Employees: 1-4
Type of Packaging: Consumer, Bulk

11470 Roma & Ray's Italian Bakery
45 Railroad Ave
Valley Stream, NY 11580 516-825-7610
Fax: 516-887-6866
Italian baked goods
Owner: Robert M De-Giovanni
Estimated Sales: $ 10-20 Million
Number Employees: 10-19

11471 Roma Bakeries
523 Marchesano Dr
Rockford, IL 61102 815-964-6737
Fax: 815-964-6057
Manufacturer of rolls, bread, danish and pies
President: John Bowler
CFO: Gene Bowler
Vice President: Marilyn Bowler
Estimated Sales: $500,000-$1 Million
Number Employees: 10-19
Type of Packaging: Consumer
Brands:
Roma Bakeries

11472 Roma Bakery
P.O.Box 348
San Jose, CA 95103-0348 408-294-0123
Fax: 408-294-0157
Manufacturer of bread, buns and rolls
President: Robert Pera
Secretary: Steven Pera
Estimated Sales: $ 10 - 20 Million
Number Employees: 50-99

11473 Roma Distributing
1937 Windsor Drive
Sierra Vista, AZ 85635-4852 520-459-8249
Fax: 520-452-8204
Proprietor: Robert Valdez

11474 Roma Packing Company
2354 S Leavitt St
Chicago, IL 60608 773-927-7371
Fax: 773-927-7370
Processor of sausage including Italian and Polish
President: Steven Lombardi
Owner: Marsha Caputo
Estimated Sales: $ 3 - 5 Million
Number Employees: 5-9
Type of Packaging: Consumer, Private Label, Bulk

11475 Roman Meal Milling Company
P.O.Box 11126
Tacoma, WA 98411 253-475-0964
Fax: 253-475-1906 www.romanmeal.com
Oats, wheat, barley
President: William Matthaei
Estimated Sales: $ 10 - 20 Million
Number Employees: 50-99

11476 Roman Meal Milling Company
4014 15th Ave N
Fargo, ND 58102 701-282-9656
Fax: 701-282-9743 877-282-9743
sales@romanmealmilling.com
www.dakotaspecialtymilling.com
Processor of whole grain cereals, flour and baking mixes; also, specialty grain; exporter of baking mixes and whole grain
VP: Joel Dick
VP Sales/Marketing: Wayne Flood
VP Manufacturing: Joel Dick
Plant Manager: Bill Fletcher
Customer Service: Bernadine King
Estimated Sales: $15000000
Number Employees: 50-99
Type of Packaging: Consumer, Food Service, Private Label, Bulk

11477 Roman Packing Company
904 W Omaha Ave
Norfolk, NE 68701 402-371-5990
Fax: 402-371-5639 800-373-5990
tydog8@hotmail.com
Processor of meat products including dressed beef, pork, sausage and luncheon meats
President: Wendell Newcomb
Estimated Sales: $ 10 - 20 Million
Number Employees: 20-49
Type of Packaging: Consumer

11478 Roman Sausage Company
1810 Richard Avenue
Santa Clara, CA 95050-2818 408-988-1222
Fax: 408-988-0546 800-497-7462
Processor and importer of patties including sausage, salmon and tuna; also, salmon fillets
President: Amir Kanji
Estimated Sales: $1,100,000
Number Employees: 10
Sq. footage: 8000
Brands:
Prima Brands

11479 Romanian Kosher Sausage
7200 N Clark St
Chicago, IL 60626 773-761-4141
Fax: 773-761-9506
Sausages
President: Arnold Loeb
Estimated Sales: Below $ 5 Million
Number Employees: 20-49

11480 Rombauer Vineyards
3522 Silverado Trl N
Saint Helena, CA 94574 707-963-5170
Fax: 707-963-5752 800- 62- 220
sheanar@rombauervineyards.com
www.rombauer.com
Wines
President: Koerner Rombauer
Sales Director: James Heinemann
General Manager: Dexter Rombauer
CFO: John L
Sales Manager: Joan Rombauer
Estimated Sales: $ 10-20 Million
Number Employees: 20-49
Type of Packaging: Private Label

11481 Romero's Food Products
15155 Valley View Ave
Santa Fe Springs, CA 90670 562-802-1858
Fax: 562-921-7240
Processor of Mexican sweet bread, tortillas, taco and tostada shells and tortilla chips
President: Leon Romero
President/Owner: Richard Scandalito
Vice President: Raul Romero
Estimated Sales: $ 20-30 Million
Number Employees: 100-249
Type of Packaging: Consumer, Food Service, Private Label, Bulk
Brands:
Romero's

11482 **Ron Tankersley Farms**
1300 Factory Pl
Los Angeles, CA 90013-2214 213-622-0724
Fax: 213-624-2369 www.oceanbeauty.com
Produce
Manager: Donald Rader
Estimated Sales: $ 50 - 100 Million
Number Employees: 100-249

11483 **Ron's Produce Company**
810 E Market St
Taylorville, IL 62568-2340 217-824-2239
Fax: 217-824-2230
Produce Wholesalers
Owner: Michael J Nation
Estimated Sales: $ 3 - 5 Million
Number Employees: 5-9

11484 **Ron's Wisconsin Cheese**
124 Main St
Luxemburg, WI 54217 920-845-5330
Fax: 920-845-9423
Cheese spreads
Co-Owner: Ron Renard
Co-Owner: Terry Renard
Estimated Sales: Less than $500,000
Number Employees: 5-9
Type of Packaging: Private Label, Bulk

11485 **(HQ)Ron-Son Foods**
81 Locke Ave
Swedesboro, NJ 8085 856-241-7333
Fax: 856-241-7338 jim@ronsonfoods.com
www.ronsonfoods.com
Manufacturer, importer and importer of canned mushrooms, olives, olive oil, Italian pasta, anchovies, roasted peppers and artichokes
CEO: James Bianco
CEO: James Bianco
VP Sales: James Bianco
Estimated Sales: $2-4 Million
Number Employees: 10-19
Sq. footage: 50000
Type of Packaging: Consumer, Food Service, Private Label, Bulk
Brands:
GHIGI
LEONE BIANCO
RON SON
TRIFOGLIO

11486 **Ronald Raque Distributing Company**
P.O.Box 9048
Louisville, KY 40209-0048 502-267-7400
Fax: 502-267-8085
President: Ronald Raque
Estimated Sales: $ 3 - 5 Million
Number Employees: 20-49

11487 **Rondel, Specialty Foods**
8100 Hwy K South
Merrill, WI 54452 715-675-3326
Fax: 715-536-3028 800-766-3353
info@rondele.com www.rondele.com
Gourmet spreadable cheese
President: Robert Canstantino
CEO: Bob Constantino
Operations Manager: Don Delago
Estimated Sales: $ 10-20 Million
Number Employees: 50-99
Type of Packaging: Private Label
Brands:
Bread Essentials
Hahn's
Pub Cheese
rondelÃ©
rondelÃ©'s Garlic & Herb's

11488 **Rondo Specialty Foods LTD**
118 Quigley Boulevard
Newcastle, DE 19720 416-253-5554
Fax: 800-876-7971 800-724-6636
info@rondofoods.com www.rondofoods.com
Bread/biscuits, cakes/pastries, cookies, full-line baking mixes and ingredients, coffee, chocolate bars, other chocolate.
Marketing: Robert Dundas

11489 **Ronnoco Coffee Company**
4241 Sarpy Ave
Saint Louis, MO 63110 314-535-1800
Fax: 314-371-5056 800-428-2287
info@ronnoco.com www.ronnoco.com
Processor of coffee
Owner: Frank Guyol III
CFO: Eric Bomball
VP Sales: Mark Guyol
Estimated Sales: $8000000
Number Employees: 100-249

11490 **Ronnoco Coffee Company**
4241 Sarpy Ave
Saint Louis, MO 63110 314-535-1800
Fax: 314-371-5056 800-428-2287
www.ronnoco.com
Coffee
President: Frank Guyol III
Estimated Sales: Below $ 5 Million
Number Employees: 100-249
Brands:
Ronnoco

11491 **Ronnybrook Farm Dairy**
P.O.Box 267
Ancramdale, NY 12503 518-398-6455
Fax: 518-398-6464 800-772-6455
info@ronnybrook.com www.ronnybrook.com
Milk, half & half, cream, chocolate milk, coffee milk, strawberry milk, drinkable yogurts, yogurt, ice cream and butter
President: Richard Osofsky
Estimated Sales: $ 1-2.5 Million
Number Employees: 10-19
Type of Packaging: Consumer, Private Label

11492 **Ronzoni Foods Canada**
185 The West Mall
Suite 1700
Etobicoke, ON M9C 5L5
Canada 416-626-3500
Fax: 416-626-4569 800-387-5032
www.ronzoni.com
Processor of sauce, juice, chowders, condensed milk and pasta including macaroni
President: John Denton
Number Employees: 75
Type of Packaging: Consumer, Food Service
Brands:
Catelli
Classico

11493 **Roode Packing Company**
P.O.Box 510
Fairbury, NE 68352 402-729-2253
Fax: 402-477-5743
Processor of beef, sausage and pork including smoked and cured
President: Tom Roode
Plant Manager: Dwayne Hasselbring
Estimated Sales: $3250000
Number Employees: 33
Type of Packaging: Consumer, Food Service

11494 **Roos Foods**
P.O.Box 310
Kenton, DE 19955 302-653-0600
Fax: 302-653-8458 800-343-3642
roosfoods@aol.com
Processor of cheese, sour cream, exotic drinks, drink mixes, soy base drinks, and BBQ snacks
President: Anna Roos
Operations Manager: Alex Martin
Plant Manager: Andy Deveza
Estimated Sales: $4900000
Number Employees: 20-49
Number of Brands: 8
Number of Products: 98
Type of Packaging: Consumer, Food Service, Private Label
Brands:
Amigo
Mexicana
Roos
Santarosa
Snyapa
Wally's

11495 **Root Cellar Preserves**
9 Avon Road
Wellesley, MA 02482 781-864-7440
Fax: 530-326-6104
lorne.jones@rootcellarpreserves.com
www.rootcellarpreserves.com
Gluten-free, kosher, organic/natural, vegetarian, full-line condiments, salsa/dips, canned or preserved fruits/vegetables, pickles & pickled vegetables
President: Susan Jones
Manager: Lorne Jones
Estimated Sales: $100,000
Number Employees: 2

11496 **Roquette America**
1417 Exchange St
Keokuk, IA 52632 319-524-5757
Fax: 319-526-2542 800-553-7035
grain@roquetteamerica.com www.roquette.com
Manufacturer and exporter of corn, wheat and potato food ingredients including modified starches, proteins and high fructose and maltose syrups; also, liquid and solid sorbitol, mannitol, maltitol, xylitol, glucono-delta-lactonemaltodextrins, dextrose, etc
President: Dominique Taret
VP Finance: Paul Janicki
VP: Ivan Hasselbusch
Sales/Marketing Director: Steve Mesenbring
Human Resources Director: Mark Crist
Purchasing Director: Flint Peyton
Estimated Sales: $95 Million
Number Employees: 545
Sq. footage: 19107

11497 **Rosa Brothers**
1100 NW 22nd St
Miami, FL 33127 305-324-1510
Fax: 305-324-9182
Processor of fresh beef
Manager: Gene Lamborda
Estimated Sales: $ 20 - 50 Million
Number Employees: 10-19
Type of Packaging: Consumer, Food Service

11498 **Rosa Food Products Co Inc**
2750 Grays Ferry Ave
Philadelphia, PA 19146 215-467-2214
Fax: 215-467-6850 rosa@rosafoods.com
www.rosafoods.com
wholesaler/importer/manufacturer
Owner: Giacomo Foti
CEO: Giacomo Foti III
CFO: Leonardo Foti
Vice President: Mary Foti
Research & Development: Angela Foti
Marketing: Marisa Foti Beckey
Sales: Dave Greenberg
Public Relations: Murry Kristol
Operations/Production: Matthew Foti Beckey
Plant Manager: Murray Kristol
Estimated Sales: $18 Million
Number Employees: 18
Sq. footage: 68000
Type of Packaging: Food Service, Private Label
Brands:
Angela
Mona
Rita
Rosa

11499 **Rosa Mexicano Kitchen**
846 7th Avenue
5th Floor
New York, NY 10019 212-397-0666
Fax: 212-397-3003 mpolton@rosamexicano.com
www.rosamexicano.com
Other lifestyle, salsa/dips, soups/broths, other sauces, seasonings and cooking enhancers, chips.
Vice President: Louis Alvarez
Marketing: Madeline Polton
Estimated Sales: $92,000
Number Employees: 2

11500 **Rosalind Candy Castle**
1301 5th Ave
New Brighton, PA 15066 724-843-1144
Fax: 724-847-2008 www.rosalindcandy.com
Processor of confectionery including chocolates
President: James Crudden
Estimated Sales: $750,000
Number Employees: 10-19
Type of Packaging: Consumer

11501 **Rosati Italian Water Ice**
201 E Madison Ave
Clifton Heights, PA 19018 610-626-1818
Fax: 610-626-0706 srrosati@aol.com
Processor of Italian water ice
President: Rich Trotter
VP: David Schumacher

Estimated Sales: $700000
Number Employees: 10-19
Type of Packaging: Consumer

11502 **Rose Acre Farms**
6874 N Base Rd
Seymour, IN 47274 812-497-2557
Fax: 812-497-3311 800-356-3447
info2003@goodegg.com www.roseacre.com
Producer of fresh shell eggs and egg products
President: Lois Rust
VP: Mark Whintington
Marketing Manager: Greg Hinton
Production Manager: Victor Ritteink
Number Employees: 1,000-4,999
Type of Packaging: Consumer, Food Service, Private Label

11503 **Rose Brand Corporation**
585 Berriman Street
Brooklyn, NY 11208 718-649-4501
Fax: 718-257-2058 800-854-5356
Processor of batch ice cream flavoring, fruit sundae toppings and fountain syrups
President: Morris Keller
Customer Development: Elliot Keller
Estimated Sales: $ 3 - 5 Million
Number Employees: 12
Type of Packaging: Food Service

11504 **Rose City Pepperheads**
1725 SW Multnomah Blvd
Portland, OR 97219-2873 503-226-0862
Fax: 503-256-8419
susan@rosecitypepperheads.com
www.rosecitypepperheads.com
Flavored pepper jellies.
Manager: Moses J Ross
Estimated Sales: $300,000-500,000
Number Employees: 1-4
Type of Packaging: Consumer

11505 **Rose Creek Vineyards**
226 East Ave N
Hagerman, ID 83332 208-837-4353
Fax: 208-837-6405
Wines
Manager: Katie Owsley
Treasurer: Susan Martin
Vice President: Stephanie Martin
Estimated Sales: $1-4.9 Million
Number Employees: 1-4

11506 **Rose Frozen Shrimp**
741 Ceres Avenue
Los Angeles, CA 90021-1515 213-626-8251
Fax: 213-626-4802
Shrimp
President: Ken Takiguchi
Estimated Sales: $ 10-20 Million
Number Employees: 20

11507 **Rose Hill Distributors**
81 Rose Hill Road
Branford, CT 06405-4015 203-488-7231
Fax: 203-488-2100
Poultry
President/CEO: Frank Vastola
Estimated Sales: $ 5-10 Million
Number Employees: 20

11508 **Rose Hill Seafood**
2621 Hamilton Rd
Columbus, GA 31904 706-322-4410
Fax: 562-220-1575
Frozen foods, canned foods goods, dry goods, poultry, seafood, produce, paper goods
Owner: Jeff Lundsford
Estimated Sales: $ 1 - 3 Million
Number Employees: 20-49

11509 **(HQ)Rose Packing Company**
65 S Barrington Rd
South Barrington, IL 60010 847-381-5700
Fax: 847-381-9424 800-323-7363
postmaster@rosepacking.com
www.rosepacking.com
Manufacturer of fresh, smoked and processed pork products for the retail and food industries
CEO: William Rose
President: Dwight Stiehl
Controller: James O'Hara
VP Sales/Marketing: Jim Vandenbergh
Estimated Sales: $ 50 - 100 Million
Number Employees: 50-99
Type of Packaging: Consumer, Food Service
Other Locations:
Rose Packing Company Plant
Chicago IL

11510 **Rose Packing Company**
4900 S Major Ave
Chicago, IL 60638 708-458-9300
Fax: 708-458-3248 800-323-7363
postmaster@rosepacking.com
www.rosepacking.com
Canadian bacon and ham, pork sausage patties, processed pork products, ribs, roasts and chops, spiral slice bone-in and boneless hams, smoked and fresh pork
VP: Peter Rose
Plant Superintendent: Joseph Mihalov
CEO: W R Rose
Plant Superintendent: Michael Reiter
Estimated Sales: $ 120 Million
Number Employees: 500-999
Parent Co: Rose Packing Company
Type of Packaging: Consumer, Food Service, Private Label
Brands:
Rose Brands

11511 **Rose Trading Company**
8457 Eastern Ave
Bell Gardens, CA 90201 562-927-1115
Fax: 562-927-1185 rosetrading@verizon.net
Wholesale food distributors; fresh and frozen; meat specialists
Owner: Neil Keohane
Purchasing Director: Joey Rose
Estimated Sales: 5 Million
Number Employees: 5-9

11512 **Rosebud Creamery**
Route 3
354 Cornelia Street
Plattsburgh, NY 12901 518-561-5160
Fax: 518-561-6068
Dairy
President: Frederick Perras
Estimated Sales: $500-1 Million appx.
Number Employees: 1-4
Brands:
Rosebud Creamery

11513 **Rosebud Farms**
525 E 130th St
Chicago, IL 60628-6999 773-928-5331
Fax: 773-264-6845
Poultry
President: Jerry Brucer
Estimated Sales: $ 50 - 100 Million
Number Employees: 50-99

11514 **Roseland Manufacturing**
119 Harrison Ave
Roseland, NJ 07068 973-228-2500
www.dialpestcontrol.com
Jams, jellies and perserves
Owner: Jerry Smith
Estimated Sales: $500,000-$1 Million
Number Employees: 5-9

11515 **Roselani Tropics Ice Cream**
P.O.Box 1170
Wailuku, HI 96793-6170 808-244-7951
Fax: 808-244-4108 info@roselani.com
www.roselani.com
Processor of carbonated beverages and ice cream
Manager: Todd Assmann
Sales Manager: Mike Nobriga
Estimated Sales: $15151351
Number Employees: 50-99
Type of Packaging: Consumer, Food Service

11516 **Rosemark Bakery**
258 Snelling Ave S
Saint Paul, MN 55105 651-698-3838
Fax: 651-698-0828
Processor of baked goods
President: Carol Rosemark
General Manager: Irv Gertz
Estimated Sales: $ 5 - 10 Million
Number Employees: 20-49

11517 **Rosen's Diversified**
1120 Lake Ave
Fairmont, MN 56031 507-238-6001
Fax: 507-238-9966 800-798-2000
www.rosens.com
Processor of meat for restaurants, government customers and food manufacturers in the U.S.
President/General Manager: Ivan Wells
Finance Director: Steve Guetter
CEO: Thomas J Rosen
Estimated Sales: Nearly $ 1 Billion
Number Employees: 50

11518 **Rosenberger's Dairies**
P.O.Box 901
847 Forty Foot Road
Hatfield, PA 19440-0901 215-631-9035
Fax: 215-855-6486 800-355-9074
info@rosenbergers.com www.rosenbergers.com
Manufacturer of dairy products including eggs, milk, cream, sour cream and cheese; also, beverages including apple juice, iced tea and fruit drinks
VP: Marcus Rosenberger
Production Manager: Jeffery Rosenberger
Plant Manager: Gerry Whiting
Estimated Sales: $55 Million
Number Employees: 250-499
Type of Packaging: Consumer
Brands:
ROSENBERGERS

11519 **Rosenblum Cellars**
2900 Main St Ste 1100
Alameda, CA 94501 510-865-7007
Fax: 510-865-9225 drzin@rosenblumcellars.com
www.rosenblumcellars.com
Wines
President: Kent Rosenblum
CFO: Tim Allen
Quality Control: Les Horton
Marketing Director: Kathy Coi
Operations Manager: Ron Pieretti
Estimated Sales: $ 5-9.9 Million
Number Employees: 20-49
Number of Brands: 1
Number of Products: 40
Sq. footage: 58000
Other Locations:
Rosenblum Cellars
Healdsburgh CA
Brands:
Rosenblum

11520 **Roses Ravioli**
219 E Walnut Street
Oglesby, IL 61348-1203 815-883-8011
Fax: 815-883-8409
Ravioli, tortellini and pasta sauce
President: Barbara Shields
Owner: Rose Causa
Estimated Sales: $ 2.5-5 Million
Number Employees: 1-4

11521 **Rosetti Fine Foods**
3 Railroad Ave
Clovis, CA 93612-1219 559-323-6450
Fax: 559-323-2022 www.rosettis.com
Biscotti, bark confections
President: Diane Rosetti
Secretary/Treasurer: Dan Rosetti
Estimated Sales: $500,000-$1 Million
Number Employees: 5-9
Brands:
Rosetti Fine Foods

11522 **Roseville Corporation**
120 Plum Ct
Mountain View, CA 94043-4899 650-255-9278
Fax: 650-592-8966 888-247-9338
www.bigsmiley.com
Candy
President: Enrique Ganitsky
Brands:
BETTY TWIST & MATCH CHOCOLATE CANDY
BIG SMILEY

11523 **Rosina Food Products**
170 French Rd
Buffalo, NY 14227 716-668-0123
Fax: 716-668-1132 888-767-4621
gsetter@rosina.com www.rosina.com

Processor of Italian meat balls, sausage, pizza toppings and pasta
President: Russell Corigliano
Chairman of the Board: James Corigliano
Vice President: Frank Corigliano
CFO: Greg Setter
Quality Control: Curtis Froevel
Marketing Director: Mike D'Addieco
Estimated Sales: $ 50-100 Million
Number Employees: 178
Type of Packaging: Food Service
Brands:
Rosina

11524 Roskam Baking Company
P.O.Box 202
Grand Rapids, MI 49501 616-574-5757
Fax: 616-574-1110 www.rothburyfarms.com
Processor of croutons, stuffing, dry mix blends, cereals, and snack components.
President: Bob Roskam
Customer Relations: Christina Lehtinen
General Manager: Perry Kogelschatz
Estimated Sales: $76700000
Number Employees: 100-249
Type of Packaging: Food Service, Private Label, Bulk

11525 Rosmarino Foods/R.Z. Humbert Company
16216 Turnbury Oak Drive
Odessa, FL 33556-2870 813-926-9053
Fax: 813-920-0734 888-926-9053
info@rosmarinofoods.com
www.rosmarinofoods.com
Speciality award winning foods such as all natural salad dressings, hearty pasta sauces, flavorful marinades, great grilling sauces, tangy BBQ sauces, and fiery hot sauces
President: Rosemary Humbert
VP Marketing: Roger Humbert
Number Employees: 8
Number of Brands: 3
Number of Products: 50
Sq. footage: 65000
Type of Packaging: Consumer, Food Service, Private Label, Bulk
Brands:
BONNIES
LUNA ROSSA
ROSMARINO

11526 Ross Fine Candies
4642 Elizabeth Lake Rd
Waterford, MI 48328 248-682-5640
Fax: 248-682-0457
Processor of candy and other confectionery products
President: Janet Greaves
Estimated Sales: $300,000
Number Employees: 1-4
Type of Packaging: Consumer, Private Label
Brands:
Ross Fine

11527 Ross Keller Winery
985 Orchard Rd
Nipomo, CA 93444-9769 805-929-3627
Fax: 805-929-4231
Wines
President/Owner: Jacqueline Tanner
Estimated Sales: Below $ 5 Million
Number Employees: 1-4
Type of Packaging: Private Label
Brands:
Ross Keller Winery

11528 Ross-Smith Pecan Company
107 Plantation Oak Dr
Thomasville, GA 31792-3540 229-859-2225
Fax: 229-859-2382 800-841-5503
info@ross-smith-pecans.com
www.ross-smith-pecans.com
Manufacturer and exporter of nuts including shelled pecans
President: Betty McDuffie
Estimated Sales: Less than $500,000
Number Employees: 23

11529 Rossi Pasta
106 Front St
Marietta, OH 45750 740-376-2065
Fax: 740-373-5310 800-227-6774
info@rossipasta.com www.rossipasta.com
Gourmet handmade pasta products and sauces
Manager: Terry St Peter
Chairman: Frank L Christy
Estimated Sales: Below $ 5 Million
Number Employees: 10-19
Type of Packaging: Private Label

11530 Rostov's Coffee & Tea Company
1618 W Main St
Richmond, VA 23220 804-355-1955
Fax: 804-355-6963 800-637-6772
cctea@aol.com www.rostovs.com
Coffee and tea
President/CFO: Tammy Rostov
Founder: Jay Rostov
Estimated Sales: Below $ 5 Million
Number Employees: 5-9
Type of Packaging: Consumer
Brands:
Rostov's Coffee Tea

11531 Rotella's Italian Bakery
6949 S 108th St
La Vista, NE 68128 402-592-6600
Fax: 402-592-2989 info@rotellasbakery.com
www.rotellasbakery.com
Processor of hamburger buns, hoagies, bread loaves, dinner rolls and bread sticks, hot dog buns and brat buns, and specialty breads.
Owner/President: Louis Rotella
Controller: Dean Jacobsen
National Sales Manager: Larry Boro
Sales Manager: James Rotella
Estimated Sales: $50000000
Number Employees: 250-499
Type of Packaging: Consumer, Food Service

11532 Roth Kase
657 Second Street
Monroe, WI 53566 608-329-7666
Fax: 608-329-7677 info@rothkase.com
www.emmirothusa.com
Processor of havarti, blue, muenster and commodity cheeses
CEO: Roth Kase
Marketing Director: Roth Kase
Sales Director: Stephen McKeon
Estimated Sales: $ 25-49.9 Million
Number Employees: 53
Type of Packaging: Consumer, Food Service, Bulk
Brands:
Grand Cru Raclette
Grand Crue
Kronenost
Pesto Havarti
Rofumo
Roth Kase
Roth Kase
Ustenborg
Vangogh

11533 Rothman's Foods
4718 Delmar Blvd
St Louis, MO 63108-1706 314-367-5448
Ethnic foods
President: Arthur Rothman
Estimated Sales: Below $ 5 Million
Number Employees: 5-9

11534 Rotteveel Orchards
6183 Reddick Ln
Dixon, CA 95620 707-678-1495
Fax: 707-678-1446 info@rotteveel.com
www.rotteveel.com
Processor and exporter of almonds
President: Neil Rotteveel
Estimated Sales: $500,000-$1 Million
Number Employees: 5-9
Type of Packaging: Bulk

11535 Roudon-Smith Vineyards
2364 Bean Creek Rd
Scotts Valley, CA 95066 831-438-1244
Fax: 831-438-4374 sales@roudonsmith.com
www.roudonsmith.com
Wines
Owner: Annette Hunt
Owner: David Hunt
Estimated Sales: $ 1-2.5 Million
Number Employees: 1-4
Brands:
Roudon Smith Vineyards

11536 Round Hill Vineyards
1680 Silverado Trl S
St Helena, CA 94574-9542 707-963-5252
Fax: 707-963-0834 800-778-0424
info@rutherfordwine.com
www.roundhillwines.com
Wines
Owner: Morgan Zaninovich
VP: Mark Fedorchak
Chairman: Erne Van Asperen
President: Virginia Van Asperen
Public Relations: Bonnie Zimmerman
Production Manager: Keith Groves
Plant Manager: Bob Iacampo
Estimated Sales: Below $ 5 Million
Number Employees: 20-49
Type of Packaging: Private Label
Brands:
Round Hill Vineyards
Rutherford Ranch
Van Asperen Vineyard

11537 Round Rock Honey Co, LLC
1308 Chisholm Tr
#107
Round Rock, TX 78681 512-828-5416
Fax: 512-828-5416 www.roundrockhoney.com
honey

11538 Rousseau Farming Company
P.O.Box 100
Tolleson, AZ 85353 623-936-1600
Fax: 623-936-7386
Processor of fruits and vegetables
President: David Rousseau
Estimated Sales: $ 1-2.5 Million
Number Employees: 10-19

11539 Rousselot Gelatin
1231 S Rochester St
Mukwonago, WI 53149-9031 262-363-2789
Fax: 262-650-8456 www.rousselot.com
Leading manufacturer of gelatins and collegans
VP: Larry Jeske
Number Employees: 1,000-4,999
Type of Packaging: Bulk

11540 Route 11 Potato Chips
7815 Main St
Middletown, VA 22645-9546 540-869-6890
Fax: 540-869-0176 800-294-7783
sales@rt11.com www.rt11.com
Handcooked potato chips, sweet potato chips, mixed vegetable chips and potato chip cookies.
President/CEO: Sarah Cohen
Estimated Sales: $ 20 - 50 Million
Number Employees: 20-49
Brands:
Route 11 Potato Chips

11541 Route 11 Potato Chips
11 Edwards Way
Mount Jackson, VA 22842 540-477-9664
Fax: 540-869-0176 800-294-7783
rt11@shentel.net www.rt11.com
Specialty potato chips and mixed vegetable chips
President: Sarah Cohen
Estimated Sales: $ 20 - 50 Million
Number Employees: 20-49
Type of Packaging: Consumer, Private Label
Brands:
Route 11 Potato Chips
Tabard Farm Potato Chips

11542 Routin America
140 E 80th St
New York, NY 10075-0389 212-772-2500
Fax: 866-764-1883 800-367-1883
sales@routin-america.com www.routin.com
Flavored syrups
President: Jean Cloehte
Estimated Sales: $89 Million
Number Employees: 150
Parent Co: Routin SA
Type of Packaging: Private Label
Brands:
1883

11543 (HQ)Rovira Biscuit Corporation
619 Avenue Cuatro Calles
Ponce, PR 00717-1901 787-844-8585
Fax: 787-848-7176 www.rovirabiscuits.com

Processor of crackers and biscuits; exporter of crackers
President and Director: Rafael Rovira
Executive VP/General Manager: Angel Rodriguez

Quality Control: Carla Traverso
Number Employees: 100-249
Sq. footage: 45000
Other Locations:
Rovira Biscuit Corp.
Pueblo Viejo PR

11544 **(HQ)Rowena's**
758 W 22nd St
Norfolk, VA 23517-1925 757-627-8699
Fax: 757-627-1505 800-627-8699
rowena@rowens.com www.rowenas.com
Processor and exporter of gourmet pound cakes, jams, curds, dry mixes and sauces
President: Rowena Fullinwider
General Manager: Joan Place
Sales: Ann Cole
Production: Renee Satterfield
Warehouse Manager: Dom Tamikk
Estimated Sales: $620000
Number Employees: 20-49
Sq. footage: 13000
Type of Packaging: Consumer, Food Service, Private Label, Bulk
Brands:
Rowena's
Rowena's Gourmet Sauces
Rowena's Jams & Jellies
Rowena's Pound Cake

11545 **Rox America**
P.O.Box 5561
Spartanburg, SC 29304-5561
USA 864-463-4352
Fax: 864-463-4670 80- 45- 319
info@roxenergy.com www.zimmer-usa.com
Rox energy drink, Rox Aqua power cool drink
President: Roland Zimmer
CEO: Amy Rogers
Estimated Sales: $ 1 Million
Number Employees: 5-9
Sq. footage: 3500
Type of Packaging: Private Label
Brands:
ROX ENERGY DRINK

11546 **Roxy Trading**
389 N Humane Way
Pomona, CA 91768
Fax: 626-610-1339 roxytrading@earthlink.net
www.roxytrading.com
Pacific rim, Asian specialty grocery. Products include soy crouton, wonton stripe and vegetarian bouilion
President: Elvis Tent
Purchasing Manager: Paullett Ho
Estimated Sales: $ 10-20 Million
Number Employees: 20-49
Number of Brands: 3
Number of Products: 500
Sq. footage: 45000
Type of Packaging: Consumer

11547 **Roy Dick Company**
152 Harris Street
Griffin, GA 30223-7017 770-227-3916
Fax: 770-227-3916
Catfish, shrimp, oysters, chicken
Owner: Roy Dick

11548 **Roy Robin Company**
1108 Vincent Berard Rd
Breaux Bridge, LA 70517 337-667-6118
Fax: 337-667-6059 www.bayoulandseafood.com
Owner: Adam Johnson
Estimated Sales: $ 3 - 5 Million
Number Employees: 50-99

11549 **Royal Angelus Macaroni**
5010 Eucalyptus Ave
Chino, CA 91710 909-627-7312
Fax: 909-627-7315
information@royal-angelus.com
www.royal-angelus.com
Manufacturer and exporter of organic pasta; also, custom formulas and specialty shapes
Manager: Glen Macy
CFO: Michael Yee
Director of Marketing: Steve Sunseri
VP Sales: Dave Abrams
Estimated Sales: $43 Million
Number Employees: 50-99
Sq. footage: 48000
Parent Co: Provena Foods
Type of Packaging: Consumer, Food Service, Private Label, Bulk
Brands:
Royal

11550 **Royal Atlantic Seafood**
2 Carrie Lane
Gloucester, MA 01930-2328 978-281-6373
Fax: 978-283-7185
Seafood
President: Anne Mortillaro

11551 **Royal Baltic**
9829 Ditmas Ave
Brooklyn, NY 11236 718-385-8300
Fax: 718-385-4757 royal@royalbalticusa.com
www.royalbalticusa.com
Smoked fish, gourmet foods, seafood delicacies, cheese, juice, feta, coffee, chocolate candy, and sauces
President: Alex Kaganovsky
Estimated Sales: $ 10-20 Million
Number Employees: 50-99

11552 **Royal Blend Coffee Company**
601 NE 1st St
Bend, OR 97701 541-388-8164
Fax: 541-389-6185
Processor and importer of specialty roasted coffees
President: Don Hamon
Roastmaster: Dona Houtz
Estimated Sales: $ 20 - 50 Million
Sq. footage: 6000
Type of Packaging: Consumer, Food Service
Brands:
Royal Blend

11553 **Royal Body Care**
P.O.Box 167008
Irving, TX 75016-7008 972-893-4000
Fax: 972-893-4111
royalbodycare@royalbodycare.org
www.rbclifesciences.com
Wholesaler/distributor of health food products and nutritional supplements
CEO: Clinton Howard
CFO: Steve Brown
CEO: John W Price
Sales Director: Dennis Windsor
Estimated Sales: G
Number Employees: 50-99
Sq. footage: 120000
Parent Co: Royal Body Care
Other Locations:
Royal Bodycare
Markham ON

11554 **(HQ)Royal Caribbean Bakery**
620 S Fulton Ave
Mount Vernon, NY 10550 914-668-6868
Fax: 914-668-5700 888-818-0971
info@royalcaribbeanbakery.com
www.royalcaribbeanbakery.com
Processor of Jamaican baked goods and specialty foods
President/CEO: Jeanette Hosang
Estimated Sales: $5-10 Million
Number Employees: 20-49
Sq. footage: 60000
Type of Packaging: Consumer, Food Service, Private Label, Bulk
Other Locations:
Royal Caribbean Bakery
Orlando FL

11555 **Royal Caviar**
4551 San Fernando Rd Ste 110
Glendale, CA 91204 818-546-5858
Fax: 818-546-5856 www.royalcaviar.com
Caviar

11556 **Royal Center Locker Plant**
104 S Chicago St.
Royal Center, IN 46978 574-643-3275
Fax: 574-643-3031
Manufacturer of meat products including beef, pork and lamb
Owner: Steve Layer
Estimated Sales: $12 Million
Number Employees: 10-19
Type of Packaging: Consumer

11557 **Royal Coffee**
3306 Powell St
Emeryville, CA 94608 510-652-4256
Fax: 510-652-3415 royal@royalcoffee.com
www.royalcoffee.com
Green coffee
President: Robert Fulmer
Vice President: Helen Nicholas
Estimated Sales: $ 30-50 Million
Number Employees: 20-49
Type of Packaging: Private Label

11558 **Royal Coffee & Tea Company**
5900 Ambler Drive
Mississauga, ON L4W 2N3
Canada 800-667-6226
Processor of orange pekoe teas, hot chocolate and coffee including gourmet roasted and ground
VP/General Manager: Christopher Glowienka
Number Employees: 10-19
Sq. footage: 10000
Parent Co: Sara Lee Corporation
Type of Packaging: Consumer, Food Service, Private Label, Bulk
Brands:
Royal Gourmet

11559 **Royal Coffee New York**
180 Raritan Ctr Pkwy Ste 207
Edison, NJ 8837 718-815-5600
Fax: 718-815-4363 888-769-2569
james@royalny.com www.royalny.com
Green coffee
President: James Schoenhut
CEO: James Schoenhut
Estimated Sales: $ 2.5-5 Million
Number Employees: 5-9
Brands:
Brazil Monte Carmelo
Colombian Huila Especial
Colombian Pensilvania Supremo
Colombian Popayan Supremo

11560 **Royal Crest Dairy Company**
350 S Pearl St
Denver, CO 80209 303-777-2227
Fax: 303-744-9173 hr@royalcrestdairy.com
www.royalcrestdairy.com
Fluid milk, cream and related products
President: Tim Detine
Founder: Paul Miller
CFO: Larry Hunt
Chairman of the Board: Paul R Miller
CFO: Jack Walter
Plant Manager: Ron Henke
Purchasing Manager: Al Martinez
Estimated Sales: $ 20-50 Million
Number Employees: 100-249
Brands:
Royal Crest

11561 **Royal Crown Bottling Company**
P.O.Box 1687
Bowling Green, KY 42102-1687 270-842-8106
Fax: 270-842-2877
Manufacturer of soft drinks and water, waffle and pancake syrups and other flavored vending and fountain syrups in blow-molded plastic containers
Manager: Mike Trimble
President/CEO: Nancy Hodge
Estimated Sales: $56 Million
Number Employees: 50-99
Sq. footage: 60000
Parent Co: Nehi-Royal Crown Cola Bottling & Distributing Company
Type of Packaging: Consumer, Food Service, Private Label, Bulk
Brands:
3 SPRINGS
BRASS KEG
SUGAR BARREL
TEDDY'S

11562 (HQ)Royal Cup Coffee
160 Cleage Dr
Birmingham, AL 35217 205-849-5836
Fax: 205-271-6071 800-366-5836
webjava@royalcupcoffee.com
www.royalcupcoffee.com
Processor of coffee and tea; wholesaler/distributor of coffee equipment; serving the food service market
President: Hatton C V Smith
VP Operations: Gene Lewis
VP Operations: Eugene Lewis
VP Finance: Lamar Bagby
Chairman: William Smith Jr
Quality Control: Bruce Woodall
Plant Manager: Henry Holden
Estimated Sales: $ 50 - 100 Million
Number Employees: 250-499
Type of Packaging: Food Service
Other Locations:
Royal Cup
Birmingham AL

11563 Royal Food Distributors
PO Box 13882
Scottsdale, AZ 85267-3882 602-971-4910
Fax: 602-971-4910
President: Bob Ho

11564 Royal Food Products
2322 E Minnesota St
Indianapolis, IN 46203 317-782-2660
Fax: 317-782-2680 sales@royalfp.com
www.royalfp.com
Processor of salad dressings, mayonnaise, mustard and sauces
President: Brian King
CEO: John Heidt
Director: James Heidt
Estimated Sales: $8.5 Million
Number Employees: 55
Type of Packaging: Food Service
Brands:
Royal

11565 Royal Foods & Flavors
2456 American Ln
Elk Grove Vlg, IL 60007-6204 847-595-9166
Fax: 847-595-9690
Processor of flavors, seasonings, yeast extracts and hydrolyzed vegetable proteins
President: Harish Gadhvi
Estimated Sales: $730000
Number Employees: 10-19
Type of Packaging: Bulk

11566 Royal Harvest Foods
55 Avocado St
Springfield, MA 01104 413-737-8392
Fax: 413-731-9336 sales@royalharv.com
www.royalharv.com
Frozen prepared chickens, beef, turkey
President: James Vallides
Sales: Chris Keller
Sales Manager: Frank McNamara
Estimated Sales: $ 10-20 Million
Number Employees: 50-99
Sq. footage: 40000
Brands:
Suffield Poultry

11567 Royal Home Bakery
160 Pony Drive
Newmarket, ON L3Y 7B6
Canada 905-715-7044
Processor of baked goods including bread, buns, biscuits, tarts, cakes and Jamaican patties
Owner: Harold Chin
Manager: Doris Chin
Sales Manager: Hope Chin
Estimated Sales: Under $300,000
Number Employees: 1-4
Sq. footage: 4000

11568 Royal Ice Cream Company
27 Warren St
Manchester, CT 06040 860-649-5358
Fax: 860-647-7376 800-246-2958
sales@royalicecream.com
www.royalicecream.com
Processor of portion packed spumoni, nut roll, tartufo, fruit sorbet, tortoni, bombe, etc.; also, ice cream cakes and pies
President: James S Orfitelli
VP: Cindy Orfitelli
Sales/Marketing: John Russo
Estimated Sales: $2000000
Number Employees: 10-19
Sq. footage: 15000
Type of Packaging: Food Service, Private Label

11569 (HQ)Royal Kedem Food & WineCompany
63 Lefante Dr
Bayonne, NJ 07002-5024 201-437-9131
Fax: 718-388-8444 info@royalwines.com
www.kedemwines.com
Processor of grape, cranberry and apple juices, juice blends, wines and salad dressings; importer of cookies, matzo and wines; exporter of wines
Ceo: David Herzog
Cfo: Sheldon Ginsberg
Executive VP: Nathan Herzog
Marketing Director: Avi Fertig
Sales Director: Jay Buchsbaum
Operations Manager: Philip Herzog
Production Manager: Michael Herzog
Plant Manager: Robert Herzog
Number Employees: 200
Sq. footage: 150000
Type of Packaging: Consumer, Food Service, Private Label, Bulk
Brands:
Baron Herzog
Baron Herzog California Wines
Kedem
Kedem Traditional Wines
Savion
Shufra
Taam Pree

11570 Royal Kraft Company
21258 Wallace King Road
Bush, LA 70431-2601 504-822-0222
Fax: 504-892-8646

11571 Royal Lagoon Seafood
3437 Winford Dr
Mobile, AL 36619 251-639-1103
Fax: 251-639-1198
Seafood
President: Val Hammond
Estimated Sales: $5,000,000
Number Employees: 6

11572 Royal Madera
7770 Road 33
Madera, CA 93636-8307 559-486-6666
Fax: 559-661-1427 fcvbsales@aol.com
Frozen foods
President: Steve Volpe
Estimated Sales: $ 10-20 Million
Number Employees: 20-49

11573 Royal Medjool Date Gardens
1203 Perez Rd
Bard, CA 92222 760-572-0524
Fax: 760-572-2292 rmdates@worldnet.att.net
www.royaldates.com
Grower and exporter of dates and date trees.
General Manager: David Nelson
General Manager: David Nelson
Estimated Sales: $3 Million
Number Employees: 75
Brands:
MEDJOOL
ROYAL

11574 Royal Moonlight
17719 E Huntsman Ave
Reedley, CA 93654 559-637-7799
Fax: 559-637-7199
russ@moonlightcompany.com
www.royalmoonlight.com
Grapes and other summer fruit
President: Russel Tavlan
Estimated Sales: $ 3 - 5 Million
Number Employees: 5-9
Type of Packaging: Consumer, Food Service, Private Label, Bulk
Brands:
CALIENTE
CALIFORNIA COLLECTION
MOONLIGHT
ROYAL
THE RIPE STUFF

11575 Royal Oak Peanuts
13009 Cedar View Rd
Drewryville, VA 23844 434-658-9500
Fax: 703-991-8922 800-608-4590
info@royaloakpeanuts.com
www.royaloakspeanuts.com
peanut and peanut products

11576 Royal Pacific Fisheries
Mi 14.5 Kalifornsky Beach Rd
Kenai, AK 99611 907-283-9370
Fax: 907-283-5974 http://royalpacifc.tripod.com
Fresh, frozen and canned seafood
President: Marvin Dragseth
Estimated Sales: $ 5-9.9 Million
Number Employees: 5-9

11577 Royal Pacific Foods/TheGinger People
215 Reindollar Ave
Marina, CA 93933 831-645-1090
Fax: 831-582-2495 800-551-5284
info@gingerpeople.com www.gingerpeople.com
ginger
President/Owner: Bruce Leeson
VP: Diana Cumberland
Estimated Sales: $9.5 Million
Number Employees: 12

11578 Royal Pacific Tea & Coffee
PO Box 6277
Scottsdale, AZ 85261-6277 480-951-8251
Fax: 480-951-0092 royalpacific@syspac.com
http://www.royalpacificintl.com
Tea
CEO: Art Gartenberg
Estimated Sales: Below $ 5 Million
Number Employees: 20
Type of Packaging: Private Label
Brands:
Royal Pacific Coffee
Royal Pacific Tea

11579 Royal Palate Foods
960 E Hyde Park Blvd
Inglewood, CA 90302-1708 310-330-7701
Fax: 310-330-7710 info@koshermeal.com
www.royalpalatefoods.com
Processor, exporter and wholesaler/distributor of kosher foods including chicken, beef, soups, sauces, frozen entrees, hors d'oeuvres, etc.; serving the food service market; importer of canned vegetables and fruits
President: William Pinkerson
Estimated Sales: $500,000-$1 Million
Number Employees: 10-19
Sq. footage: 8000
Type of Packaging: Food Service, Bulk
Brands:
Royal Palate
Sierra Spring Foods

11580 Royal Palm Popcorn Company
100 McGaw Dr
Edison, NJ 08837-3725 732-225-0200
Fax: 732-225-6363 800-526-8865
Gourmet popcorn
President: Michael Spitz
Number Employees: 10-19
Brands:
Joons Chocolate Popcorn
Park Avenue Gourmet
Rainbow Popcorn

11581 Royal Products
P.O.Box 13628
Scottsdale, AZ 85267-3628 480-948-2509
Fax: 480-951-0835 service@royalproducts.net
www.royalproducts.net
Processor of health vitamins and supplements
President: Johnny Shannon
CEO: David Stuart
Estimated Sales: Less than $100,000
Number Employees: 1-4
Type of Packaging: Food Service

11582 Royal Resources
PO Box 24001
New Orleans, LA 70184-4001 504-283-9932
Fax: 504-283-2620 800-888-9932
rrbanfos@bellsouth.net

Salad dressing, jellies, salsas, dessert toppings, hot sauces and cake mix

11583 **Royal Ridge Fruits**
13215 Rd F SW
P.O. Box 428
Royal City, WA 99357 509-346-1520
Fax: 509-346-2098 www.royalridgefruits.com
Supplier of dried and frozen cherries, strawberries, blueberries and raspberries.

11584 **Royal Seafood**
P.O.Box 1347
Monterey, CA 93942-1347 831-655-8326
Fax: 831-373-8336
Processor of frozen and fresh fish including cod, flounder, herring, mackerel, perch, salmon, sole, squid and tuna
Owner/President: Gino Pennisi
Owner/VP: Elaine Pennisi
Owner/VP: Elaine Pennisi
Estimated Sales: $800,000
Number Employees: 1-4
Type of Packaging: Consumer, Food Service
Brands:
Black cod (sablefish
CA halibut
Channel rockfish (thornyheads
Dover sole

11585 **Royal Seafood**
Municipal Wharf 2
Monterey, CA 93940 831-373-7920
Fax: 831-373-8336
Seafood
Owner: Joseph Pennisi
VP and Secretary: Billy Pennisi
Estimated Sales: $560,000
Number Employees: 2
Brands:
Royal Seafood

11586 **Royal Touch Foods**
315 Humberline Drive
Etobicoke, ON M9W 5T6
Canada 416-213-1077
Fax: 416-213-1055 info@royaltouchfoods.com
www.royaltouchfoods.com
Processor of pork and beef sandwiches
President: Domenic Ruso
Estimated Sales: $5.6 Million
Number Employees: 50
Parent Co: J.M. Schneider
Type of Packaging: Food Service
Brands:
Hamish & Enzo
Royal Touch

11587 **Royal Vista Marketing**
126 W Center Ave
Visalia, CA 93291 559-636-9198
Fax: 559-636-9637 info@royalvista.com
www.royalvista.com
Grower and exporter of table grapes, kiwifruit, stone fruit and figs; importer of stone fruit, kiwifruit and table grapes
President: Todd A Steele
Sales Manager: Patrick Allen
Estimated Sales: $84000
Number Employees: 5-9
Sq. footage: 24000
Parent Co: Atalanta
Type of Packaging: Consumer, Food Service, Bulk
Other Locations:
Alkop Farms
Chico CA

11588 **Royal Wine Corp**
63 Lefante Drive
Bayonne, NJ 07002 718-384-2400
Fax: 718-388-8444 info@royalwines.com
www.royalwines.com
Processor, importer, exporter of wines, grape and fruit juices, cordials, baked goods, biscuits, wafers, gourmet foods, chocolates and nuts
Owner/Branch Manager: Michael Herzog
CEO: David Herzog
CFO: Sheldon Ginsberg
EVP: Nathan Herzog
VP Marketing/Public Relations: Michael Luftglas

Sales Director: Dennis Bookbinder
Chief Winemaker: Joseph Hurliman
Plant Manager: Soloman Schwartz
Estimated Sales: $70 Million
Number Employees: 200
Sq. footage: 184000
Parent Co: Kedem Kosher Wine Company
Type of Packaging: Consumer, Private Label, Bulk
Brands:
Hi-Five
Kadem

11589 **Royale InternationalBeverage Co Inc**
5315 Tremont Ave
Davenport, IA 52807-2640 563-386-5222
Fax: 563-386-1352 royale@netexpress.net
www.royalebrands.com
Produce and market frozen beverage products and equipment
President: Joe Colombari
Estimated Sales: Less than $500,000
Number Employees: 10-19
Number of Brands: 13
Number of Products: 250
Type of Packaging: Food Service
Brands:
Cruisin Cool
Energy Ice
Royale Smoothie

11590 **Royalmark Services**
6645 107th Ave
South Haven, MI 49090-9366 269-637-7450
Fax: 269-637-2636
Processor and exporter of blueberries; also, custom packing services available
President: Vern Adkin
Estimated Sales: $ 3 - 5 Million
Number Employees: 5-9

11591 **Royce C. Bone Farms**
2913 Sandy Cross Road
Nashville, NC 27856-8633 252-443-3773
Fax: 252-937-4990 Fbone@rockymountnc.com
www.ncsweetpotatoes.com
Processor of sweet potatoes, romaine, tomatoes and pickles
President/CEO: David Godwin
Co-Owner: Fay Bone
Vice President: Dewey Scott
Number Employees: 10-19
Brands:
Jean Sweet Potatos

11592 **Ruark & Ashton**
1548 Taylors Island Road
Woolford, MD 21677-1327 410-221-6076
Fax: 410-221-6076 800-725-5032
Seafood
President: Terry Vinson
Estimated Sales: Under $500,000
Number Employees: 1-4

11593 **Rubashkin**
4308 14th Ave
Brooklyn, NY 11219-1428 718-436-5511
Fax: 718-435-4295
Kosher butcher
President: AA Rubashkin
Estimated Sales: $ 1 - 3 Million

11594 **Rubicon/Niebaum-CoppolaEstate & Winery**
P.O.Box 208
Rutherford, CA 94573-0208 707-968-1100
Fax: 707-968-9551 800-782-4266
www.niebaum-coppola.com
Wines
President: John Richburg
CEO: Jay Shumaker
Winemaker: Scott McLeod
Estimated Sales: $10 Million
Number Employees: 50-99

11595 **Rubino's Seafood Company**
735 W Lake St
Chicago, IL 60661 312-258-0020
Fax: 312-258-0028
Seafood
President: James Rubino
Estimated Sales: $ 1 - 3 Million
Number Employees: 5-9
Type of Packaging: Food Service

11596 **Rubschlager Baking Corporation**
3220 W Grand Ave
Chicago, IL 60651 773-826-1245
Fax: 773-826-6619
mike@rubschlagerbaking.com
www.rubschlager.com
Processor and exporter of bread, frozen rolls and mini-chips.
President: Paul Rubschlager
Secretary/Treasurer: Joan Rubschlager
National Sales Manager: Mike DiCristo
Number Employees: 1-4
Number of Brands: 2
Number of Products: 45
Type of Packaging: Consumer, Food Service
Brands:
RUBSCHLAGER

11597 **Ruby Apiaries**
711 5th Avenue
Milnor, ND 58060-4113 701-427-5263
Condiments and relishes
President: Dick Ruby
CEO: Doug Ruby
Estimated Sales: Less than $500,000
Number Employees: 1-4

11598 **Rucker's Makin' Batch Candies**
Rucker And State St
Bridgeport, IL 62417 618-945-7778
Fax: 618-945-5112 sales@makinbatch.com
www.makinbatch.com
Processor of candy including hard, filled and sugar-free; pre-pack available varities include peanut butter, peppermint, lemon and molasses
Owner: Rena Smith
Estimated Sales: $95,000
Number Employees: 5-9
Number of Products: 125
Sq. footage: 20000
Type of Packaging: Food Service, Private Label, Bulk

11599 **Rudd Winery**
P.O.Box 105
Oakville, CA 94562 707-944-8577
Fax: 707-944-2823 info@ruddwines.com
www.ruddwines.com
Wines
President: Leslie Rudd
COO: Stephen Girard Jr
Marketing Director: Ellen Hunt
Estimated Sales: $ 5-10 Million
Number Employees: 20-49
Brands:
Bacigalupi Chardonnay
Jericho Canyon Red
Library Wines
Oakville Estate Red

11600 **Rude Custom Butchering**
6194 W Pines Rd
Mt Morris, IL 61054-9755 815-946-3795
Fax: 815-946-2333
Meats
President: Kevin Rude
Estimated Sales: $ 10-20 Million
Number Employees: 20-49

11601 **Rudi's Organic Bakery**
3300 Walnut St Unit C
Boulder, CO 80301 303-447-0495
Fax: 303-447-0516 877-293-0876
www.rudisbakery.com
Manufacturer of fresh and frozen certified organic par baked bread, buns and rolls
CEO: Jane Miller
CFO: Mile Aufiero
VP Sales: Tom Nash
Estimated Sales: $ 50 - 100 Million
Number Employees: 120
Sq. footage: 14500
Parent Co: Charterhouse Group
Type of Packaging: Consumer, Food Service, Bulk
Brands:
Certified Organic Breads
Certified Organic Buns
Certified Organic Rolls

11602 **Rudolph Foods**
3660 Pipestone Rd
Dallas, TX 75212 214-638-2204
Fax: 214-638-2112 www.rudolphfoods.com

Processor of snack foods including beef jerky and pork rinds
Plant Manager: Bob Burns
Number Employees: 50-99
Parent Co: Rudolph Foods
Type of Packaging: Consumer, Food Service, Private Label
Brands:
Cracklins

11603 Rudolph Foods Company
P.O.Box 509
Lima, OH 45802 419-648-3611
Fax: 419-648-4087 info@rudolphfoods.com
www.rudolphfoods.com
Manufacturer and exporter of pork rinds and related snacks
CEO: James Rudolph
President: Richard Rudolph
Estimated Sales: $74 Million
Number Employees: 100-249
Type of Packaging: Consumer, Private Label, Bulk
Brands:
GRANDPA JOHN'S
PEPE'S
RUDOLPH'S
SOUTHERN RECIPE

11604 Rudolph's Market & Sausage Factory
2924 Elm St
Dallas, TX 75226-1509 214-741-1874
Fax: 214-761-2017
randreason@rudolpmarkets.com
www.rudolphmarkets.com
Processor of smoked meats and sausage
President: Justine M Andreason
Estimated Sales: $ 5 - 10 Million
Number Employees: 10-19
Type of Packaging: Consumer

11605 Rudolph's Specialty Bakery
390 Alliance Avenue
Toronto, ON M6N 2H8
Canada 416-763-4315
Fax: 416-763-4317 800-268-1589
www.rudolphsbakeries.com
Processor and exporter of rye and flat breads, tortillas and flan cakes
President: George Paech
Type of Packaging: Consumer, Food Service, Private Label
Brands:
Casa Jorge
Masala Roti
Roti & Chapati
Rudolph's
Taj Mahal
Wwrapps

11606 Rudy's Tortillas
9219 Viscount Row
Dallas, TX 75247 214-634-7839
Fax: 214-638-5317 800-878-2401
lguerra@rudystortillas.com
www.rudystortillas.com
Processor of tortillas, chalupas, tostadas, tacos, flavored wraps, shells and blue, red, yellow and white chips
President: Rudy Guerra
Marketing Director: Louis Guerra
Vice President: Tanda Wall
Estimated Sales: $30 Million
Number Employees: 95
Brands:
Rudy's Tortillas

11607 Ruef's Meat Market
P.O.Box 251
New Glarus, WI 53574 608-527-2554
bruef@charter.net
www.ruefsmeatmarket.com
Smoked meats and cheese
Owner: Willy Ruef
CEO: Annette Ruef
Estimated Sales: Less than $300,000
Number Employees: 1-4
Type of Packaging: Consumer, Food Service, Bulk
Brands:
Ruef's Meat Market

11608 Ruffner's
704 W Lancaster Ave
Wayne, PA 19087-2515 610-687-9800
Fax: 610-687-9800 info@ruffners.com
hhtp://www.supercuts.com
Cocktail drink mixes, green tomato salsa
Manager: Steve Costa
Estimated Sales: $300,000-500,000
Number Employees: 1-4
Brands:
Supercuts

11609 Ruggiero Seafood
474 Wilson Avenue
Po Box 5369
Newark, NJ 07105 973-589-0524
Fax: 973-589-5690 866-225-2627
raquel@ruggieroseafood.com
www.ruggieroseafood.com
Processor, importer and exporter of fresh, frozen and breaded calamari and calamari entrees
President: Rocco Ruggiero
Controller: Connie Dasaliva
Vice President: Frank Ruggiero
Sales Manager: Steve Clemente
Manager Operations: Anthon Trimarche
Plant Manager: Marcos Fontana
Estimated Sales: $387,000
Number Employees: 150
Sq. footage: 25000
Type of Packaging: Consumer, Food Service, Bulk
Brands:
Atlantic Coast
Fisherman's Pride
Fruit of the Sea
Northwind
Ocean Tide

11610 (HQ)Ruiz Food Products
501 S Alta Ave
Dinuba, CA 93618 559-591-5510
Fax: 559-591-1969 800-477-6474
contactus@ruizfoods.com www.elmonterey.com
Manufacturer and exporter of frozen foods including burritos, enchiladas, tamales, soft tacos, chili rellenos, flautas and taquitos.
Chairman/CEO: Fred Ruiz
Vice Chairman: Kim Ruiz Beck
CFO: Ricardo Alvarez
Board of Directors: Jack Baker
Board of Directors: Larry Dalicandro
Board of Directors: Bill Henderson
Board of Directors: Wayne Partin
Board of Directors: Terry Peets
Board of Directors: Stuart Woolf
Purchasing Manager: Steve Windh
Estimated Sales: $198.5 Million
Number Employees: 1,000-4,999
Sq. footage: 192000
Type of Packaging: Consumer, Food Service, Private Label, Bulk
Brands:
EL MONTEREY
PRIMA ROSA!
RUIZ FAMILY

11611 (HQ)Ruiz Mex. Foods
2151 E Francis St
Ontario, CA 91761 909-947-7811
Fax: 909-947-2338 tortilla@worldnet.att.net
www.ruizflourtortillas.com
Processor of die cut and whole wheat flour tortillas; manufacturer of baking equipment including extruders, cooling conveyors and ovens
President: Edward Ruiz
CFO: Uriel Maciaf
Vice President: Vickie Salgado
R&D: David Rodriguez
Manager: Maria Lopez
Purchasing: Carmen Sandoval
Estimated Sales: $ 50-100 Million
Number Employees: 150
Sq. footage: 34000
Type of Packaging: Food Service, Private Label, Bulk

11612 Rumford Baking Powder Company
PO Box 150
Terre Haute, IN 47808-0150 812-232-9446
Fax: 812-478-7181 hulman@hulman.com
www.clabbergirl.com
Processor and exporter of baking powder and cornstarch
President: Gary Morris
CFO: Jeffrey Belskus
Public Relations Manager: Teresa Shaffer
Executive Director Corp Operations/GM: Marla Dehart
Warehouse/Transportation Manager: Jill Francis
Purchasing Manager: Bruce West
Estimated Sales: $ 20 - 50 Million
Number Employees: 100-249
Type of Packaging: Consumer, Food Service, Private Label, Bulk
Brands:
Hearth Club
Rumford

11613 Rumiano Cheese Company
511 9th St
Crescent City, CA 95531 707-465-1535
Fax: 707-465-4141 www.rumianocheese.com
Natural and processed cheese
President: Baird Rumiano
Quality Control: Jus Barrd
Vice President: John Rumiano
Marketing Director: Kirk Olesen
Estimated Sales: $ 10-20 Million
Number Employees: 20-49

11614 (HQ)Run-A-Ton Group
401 State Route 24
Suite 2
Chester, NJ 07930-2923 973-267-3800
Fax: 973-984-2424 800-247-6580
Manufacturer of conventional and natural baked goods
President: Doon Wintz
CEO/Chairman: Robert Wintz
CFO: Linda Hendricks
Vice President: Lynn Nelson
Director Sales Development/Marketing: Janeen Ortega
Estimated Sales: $ 10 - 20 Million
Number Employees: 20-49
Number of Brands: 5
Number of Products: 1000
Sq. footage: 5000
Type of Packaging: Consumer, Food Service, Private Label
Brands:
APPLE VALLEY INN
BUTTERY BAKER
SIMPLE ELEGANCE
WHOLLY WHOLESOME

11615 Rupari Food Service
1208 W Newport Center Dr
Deerfield Beach, FL 33442-7714 954-480-6320
Fax: 954-480-6367 800-578-7274
jmintz@rupari.com www.rupari.com
Snacks and sport drinks
President: Robert Mintz
CFO: Mel Mitchell
VP: Pete Chiappatta
Estimated Sales: $ 12 Million
Number Employees: 20-49
Number of Brands: 2
Number of Products: 7
Type of Packaging: Consumer
Brands:
Bandito's Cheese and Chips
Bandito's Chips
Bandito's Salsa
Mighty Mouse Sports

11616 Rural Route 1 Popcorn
105 E Tama St
Livingston, WI 53554 608-943-8091
Fax: 608-943-8283 800-828-8115
pops@ruralroute1.com www.ruralroute1.com
Popcorn
President: Bradley Biddick
Marketing Director: Nick Solomon
CFO: Bradley Biddick
Estimated Sales: Below $ 5 Million
Number Employees: 20-49
Brands:
Almonds
Creamy Medley of Popcorn
Ivory Almond K'Nuckle

11617 **RusDun Farms**
2295 Highway 57
Collierville, TN 38017-5329 901-853-0931
Fax: 901-853-0387 mrussel1@midsouth.rr.com
http://www.midsouth.rr.com
Eggs
President: Melvin Russell
Estimated Sales: Below $ 5 Million
Number Employees: 1-4

11618 **Ruskin Redneck Trading Company**
1203 1st Street SW
Ruskin, FL 33570-5345 813-645-7710
Fax: 813-641-1979
Sauces
President: Sandra Council
Estimated Sales: $260,000
Number Employees: 2

11619 **Russ & Daughters**
179 E Houston St Frnt 1
New York, NY 10002 212-475-4880
Fax: 212-475-0345 800-787-7229
info@russanddaughters.com
www.russanddaughters.com
Smoked fish, caviar and specialty foods
Managing Partner: Mark Russ Federman
Estimated Sales: Less than $500,000
Number Employees: 10-19

11620 **Russell & Kohne**
149 Riverside Ave Ste B
Newport Beach, CA 92663 949-645-8441
Baked goods
Vice President: Gregg Russell
Estimated Sales: $2.4 Million
Number Employees: 47

11621 **Russell Breweries, Inc.**
202-13018 80th Avenue
Surrey, BC V3W 2B2
Canada 604-599-1190
Fax: 604-599-1048 cheers@russellbeer.com
www.russellbeer.com
Processor of ale
President/COO: Andrew Harris
CEO: Brian Harris
Number Employees: 1-4
Type of Packaging: Consumer, Food Service
Brands:
Russell Cream Ale
Russell Honey Blonde Ale
Russell Lemon Wheat Ale
Russell Oager
Russell Pale Ale
Russell Winter Ale

11622 **Russell E. Womack**
1300 E 42nd St
Lubbock, TX 79404 806-747-2581
Fax: 806-747-2583 877-787-3559
rewi@casserolebean.com
www.casserolebean.com
Processor and packager of dry pinto beans packed in poly and burlap packs. Casserole Pinto Beans are available in 1lb, 2lb, 4lb, 10lb, 20lb, and 50lb sizes.
Owner: Mike Byrne
Product Managerment/Quality Control: Mike Bryne
Sales Director: Nancy Higginson
Consumer Affairs: Walter James
Packaging Plant Manager: Albert Rodriguez
Estimated Sales: $1600000
Number Employees: 10-19
Number of Brands: 1
Number of Products: 1
Sq. footage: 36000
Type of Packaging: Consumer, Food Service

11623 **(HQ)Russell Stover Candies**
4900 Oak St
Kansas City, MO 64112 816-842-9240
Fax: 816-561-4350 800-477-8683
www.russellstover.com
Chocolate Candy
President: Scott Ward
CFO: Dick Masinton
Research & Development: Wayne Houde
Quality Control: Chuck Teater
Marketing Director: Mark Sesler
Sales Director: Bill Baer
COO: Dan Trott
Production Manager: Shawn Chestnut
Purchasing Manager: Darrin Buehler
Estimated Sales: $600 Million
Number Employees: 3000
Type of Packaging: Consumer
Brands:
RUSSELL STOVERS

11624 **Russer Foods**
665 Perry St
Buffalo, NY 14210 716-826-6400
Fax: 716-826-9186 800-828-7021
www.russerfoods.com
Processor and exporter of deli foods including smoked, dried and portioned cut meats
President: Howard Zemsky
Sales Manager: Paul Timlan
Estimated Sales: $91700000
Number Employees: 550
Parent Co: IBP
Other Locations:
Russer Foods
Boston MA
Brands:
Russer

11625 **Russian Chef**
40 E 69th St
New York, NY 10021-5016 212-249-1550
Fax: 212-249-5451 blinihut@aol.com
Processor and packer of fresh and pasteurized kosher caviar including domestic salmon, whitefish, sturgeon, paddlefish, hackleback and lumpfish; also, Scottish smoked salmon, tuna and smoked trout; importer of caviar
President: Simon Kublanov
Vice President: Lenny Kuvykin
Estimated Sales: $ 1 - 3 Million
Number Employees: 5-9
Sq. footage: 9000
Type of Packaging: Consumer, Food Service
Brands:
Ivan the Terrible
Poriloff
Purepak
Russian Chef's

11626 **Russo Farms**
1962 S East Ave
Vineland, NJ 08360-7198 856-692-5942
Fax: 856-692-8534 drusso@njtripoli.com
www.russofarms.com
Processor of fruits and vegetables including green onions, cabbage, peppers, eggplant, cucumbers, leafy greens, etc
President: Damian Russo
Estimated Sales: $12046688
Number Employees: 1-4
Type of Packaging: Consumer
Brands:
Pat's Best

11627 **Russo's Seafood**
201 E 40th St
Savannah, GA 31401-9120 912-341-8848
Fax: 912-234-5703 www.russoseafood.com
Seafood
Manager: Nolan Mell
Estimated Sales: $ 3 - 5 Million
Number Employees: 10-19

11628 **Rustic Crust**
31 Barnstead Road
Pittsfield, NH 03263 603-435-5119
info@rusticcrust.com
www.rusticcrust.com
All natural and organic flatbread pizzas, ready-made pizza crusts and pizza sauce.
Founder/President: Brad Sterl
Finance Executive: Tammy Blinn
VP: Angela Adcock
Sales/Marketing Coordinator: Kathleen Carroll
VP Sales: Alan Witcher
Estimated Sales: $8 Million
Number Employees: 5
Sq. footage: 4699

11629 **Ruth Ashbrook Bakery**
6445 NE M L King Boulevard
Portland, OR 97211-3031 503-240-7437
Fax: 503-289-7264
Snack cakes, pies, doughnuts and other goods
President: Gerald Martinson
Marketing Director: Glenn Fergeson
Production Manager: Mark Martinson
Plant Manager: Gary Taskos
Purchasing Manager: John Hunter
Estimated Sales: E
Number Employees: 4

11630 **Ruth Hunt Candies**
P.O.Box 265
Mt Sterling, KY 40353-0265 859-498-0676
Fax: 859-498-1556 800-927-0302
Info@Ruthhuntcandy.com
www.ruthhuntcandy.com
Confectionary products including pulled cream candy, bourbon balls, caramels, assorted soft creams, and sugar free chocolates.
President: Larry Kezele
Estimated Sales: $790000
Number Employees: 10-19
Number of Products: 70
Sq. footage: 4500
Parent Co: Kezele Corporation
Type of Packaging: Consumer
Brands:
Blue Monday
Blue Monday Candybar
Bourbon Balls
Official Bourbon Balls
Ruth Hunt Confections

11631 **Rutherford Hill Winery**
P.O.Box 427
Rutherford, CA 94573-0427 707-963-1871
Fax: 707-963-1878 info@rutherfordhill.com
www.rutherfordhillwinery.com
Processor of wines
President: Anthony Terlato
VP: Willis Blakewell
Estimated Sales: $4500000
Number Employees: 20-49

11632 **Rutter Brothers Dairy**
2100 N George St
York, PA 17404-1898 717-848-9827
Fax: 717-845-8751 800-840-1664
www.rutters.com
Milk and dairy products
President: Todd Rutter
CFO: Tom Jonson
Treasurer: Stewart Hartman
CEO: Scott Hartman
VP: Rey Sendy
Operations Manager: Todd Rutter
Plant Manager: Brett Garner
Number Employees: 500-999
Type of Packaging: Private Label
Brands:
Rutter's

11633 **Rv Industries**
1665 Heraeus Blvd
Buford, GA 30518 770-729-8983
Fax: 770-729-9428 sales@rvindustries.com
www.rvindustries.com
Processor, importer and exporter of desiccated, sweetened and toasted coconut, coconut milk powder, aseptic coconut milk and water
President: Andres E Siochi
General Manager: Bob Weschrek
CFO: Bharat Shah
Sales: Robert Santiago
Production Manager: Guillermo Pineiro
Estimated Sales: $14000000
Number Employees: 20-49
Sq. footage: 40000
Parent Co: RV Industries
Type of Packaging: Consumer, Food Service, Private Label, Bulk
Brands:
Fiesta
Red V
Tropical

11634 **Ryals Bakery**
135 S Wayne St
Milledgeville, GA 31061 478-452-0321
Breads, rolls, cakes
Owner: Jacob Ryals

Estimated Sales: $130,000
Number Employees: 5-9
Brands:
Ryals Bakery

11635 Ryan-Parreira Almond Company
21490 Ortigalita Rd
Los Banos, CA 93635-9793 209-826-0272
Fax: 209-826-3882 rpac@rpacalmonds.com
www.rpacalmonds.com
Processor and exporter of almonds
Owner: Dave Parreira
Partner: David Parreira
Shipping Manager: Janet Martin
Plant Manager: James Smith
Estimated Sales: $4500000
Number Employees: 50-99
Type of Packaging: Bulk

11636 Rygmyr Foods
929 Concord Street S
South Saint Paul, MN 55075-5912 651-455-1701
Fax: 651-455-6058 800-545-3903
Processor of molded popcorn novelties
President: Paul Lattate
Estimated Sales: $ 10 - 20 Million
Number Employees: 30
Sq. footage: 13000
Type of Packaging: Consumer, Private Label
Brands:
Bumpy & Jumpy
Cutie Cupid
Itchy Witchy
Rookie Spookie
Santa Pop

11637 Ryke's Bakery
1788 Terrace St Ste 1
Muskegon, MI 49442 231-722-3508
Fax: 231-728-2162
Processor of cakes, cookies, pies, breads and pastries
Co-Owner: Butch Rouwhorst
Co-Owner: Renee Chiasson-Rouwhorst
Estimated Sales: $720000
Number Employees: 20-49
Sq. footage: 8000
Type of Packaging: Consumer

11638 Rymer Foods
4600 S Packers Avenue
Suite 400
Chicago, IL 60609-3338 773-254-7530
Fax: 773-927-7278 800-247-9637
www.rymerfoods.com
Processor of hamburgers, steaks, pot roast and meat loaf; also, frozen chicken
CEO: P Edward Schenk
President: Edward Hebert
Marketing Director: John Bormann
Operations Manager: Jose Muguerza
Number Employees: 10-19
Type of Packaging: Food Service

11639 Rymer Seafood
125 S Wacker Drive
Chicago, IL 60606-1702 312-236-3266
Fax: 312-236-4169
Seafood
President: Mark Bailin
Estimated Sales: $ .5 - 1 million
Number Employees: 1-4

11640 Ryt Way Industries
21850 Grenada Ave
Lakeville, MN 55044 952-469-1417
Fax: 952-469-9517 hickeyt@rytway.com
www.rytway.com
Exporter and contract packager of cereals and snack foods. Ryt-way Food Products Company is one of the largest contract packagers of its kind in the United States today
President: Glenn Hasse Jr
VP Sales/Marketing: Tim Hickey
VP Operations: Darrell Penning
Number Employees: 500-999
Sq. footage: 200000
Type of Packaging: Private Label

11641 S A Piazza & Associates
15815 SE Piazza
Clackamas, OR 97015-9195 503-657-3123
Fax: 503-657-1784 spiazza@sapiazza.com
www.piazzapizza.com
Processor of coffee including regular and espresso
President: Steve Piazza
National Sales Director: Rick Johnson
Marketing Director: Shari Haworth
Estimated Sales: $ 20 - 50 Million
Number Employees: 50-99
Type of Packaging: Consumer, Food Service
Brands:
Piazza Fine

11642 S&B International Corporation
2815 Dalemead St
Torrance, CA 90505-7039 310-257-0177
Fax: 310-543-2168
Seasonings
President: Richard Jones
Estimated Sales: $ 5-10 Million
Number Employees: 1-4

11643 S&D Bait Company
PO Box 3525
Morgan City, LA 70381-3525 504-252-3500
Fax: 504-385-5412
Sells live bait.

11644 S&D Coffee, Inc
P.O.Box 1628
Concord, NC 28026 704-782-3121
Fax: 800-950-4378 www.sndcoffee.com
Coffee
President/CEO: Ron Hinson
Executive Vice President/CFO: Steve Cole
Number Employees: 250-499
Type of Packaging: Food Service, Private Label

11645 S&D Coffee, Inc
P.O.Box 1628
Concord, NC 28026 704-782-3121
Fax: 704-721-5792 sales@sndcoffee.com
www.sndcoffee.com
Coffees
President: Ron Hinson
Executive VP: Steve Cole
Marketing Director: Marcia Brezhear
Number Employees: 500-999
Type of Packaging: Food Service

11646 S&D Import Company
1155 Carolyn Sue Drive
Baton Rouge, LA 70815-4902 504-891-6301
Fax: 504-891-0004

11647 S&E Organic Farms
1716 Oak St Ste 4
Bakersfield, CA 93301 661-325-2644
Fax: 661-325-2602 seorganic@aol.com
Grower of organic vegetables, dry beans, grains and alfalfa; processor of frozen purees
President: Ed Davis
CEO: Shelley Davis
Manager: Cali Cheek
Estimated Sales: $500,000-$1 Million
Number Employees: 1-4
Type of Packaging: Bulk

11648 S&G Products
P.O.Box 930
Nicholasville, KY 40340-0930 859-885-9411
Fax: 859-885-3063 800-826-7652
sgproducts@qc.aibn.com www.sglocks.com
Processor of bottled and glass and plastic-packed pickled products including beets, cauliflower, onions, olives, pickles, peppers, gherkins, etc.; also, vinegar
Co-Owner: James Sargent
Co-Owner: Halbert Greenleaf
CEO: Jerry A Morgan
Director Sales: Richard Greenberg
Type of Packaging: Consumer, Food Service
Brands:
Lion
Supreme

11649 S&M Communion Bread Company
P.O.Box 40344
Nashville, TN 37204 615-292-1969
www.buycommunion.com
Processor of communion bread
President: Barbara Reynolds
Estimated Sales: $ 3 - 5 Million
Number Employees: 10-19
Type of Packaging: Consumer
Brands:
S&M

11650 S&M Fisheries
1272 Portland Road
Kennebunkport, ME 04046-8104 207-985-3456
Fax: 207-985-3038
Wholesale distributor of shellfish
President: Stephanie Nadeau
Vice President, Operational VP: Michael Marceau
Estimated Sales: $2.0 Million
Number Employees: 11

11651 S&N Food Company
1321 Woodthorpe Drive
Mesquite, TX 75181-3519 972-222-1184
Fax: 972-222-1184
sweetpotatodesserts@msn.com
www.sandnfood.com
Dessert mixes such as sweet potato pie, sweet potato muffins, sweet potato brownies, chocolate brownies, coffee & chocolate, pumpkin pie, pumpkin brownies, lemon pound cake, chocolate muffin & bread mix, chocolate pound cake, lemonsupreme muffin & bread mix, pumpkin pound cake, pumpkin pancake & waffle mix, sweet potato pound cake, sweet potato pancake & waffle mix, and spiced cider mix.
President: Shirley Peters
Estimated Sales: Below $ 500,000
Number Employees: 2
Type of Packaging: Consumer, Private Label
Brands:
SHIRLEY'S

11652 (HQ)S&P
100 Shoreline Hwy Ste 395
Mill Valley, CA 94941 415-332-0550
Fax: 415-332-0567 800-935-2337
S&P owns Pabst Brewing, which in 2001 shut down it's 115 year old Texas brewery and it's Pennsylvania plant. The company transferred production of it's brands to Miller Brewing. Pabst pays Miller to brew the beers, but retainsownership of the brands and markets the products.
President/Chairman/CEO/Secretary: Bernard Orsi
Estimated Sales: $ 100-500 Million
Number Employees: 100-249
Brands:
COLT 45
LONE STAR
OLD MILWAUKEE
PABST BLUE RIBBON
PEARL
SCHLITZ

11653 S-W Mills
3646 County Road 22
Archbold, OH 43502-9791 419-445-5206
Fax: 419-445-4275 s-wmills@bright.net
Processor and exporter of dehydrated alfalfa pellets and meal
President: Mike Aeschliman
Operator: Martha Wyse
Sales: Ken Vaupel
Estimated Sales: $ 10 - 20 Million
Number Employees: 10-19

11654 S. Abuin Packing
814 2nd Ave
Elizabeth, NJ 7202 908-354-2674
Fax: 908-354-7170 www.814americas.com
Sausage
Manager: Michael Patracuolla
CFO: Michael Patratuolla
Estimated Sales: $ 5-10 Million
Number Employees: 20-49
Brands:
El Mino
Riojano

11655 S. Anderson Vineyard
1473 Yountville Cross Rd
Yountville, CA 94599-9471 707-944-8642
Fax: 707-944-8020 800-428-2259
savwines@4bubbly.com
www.cliffledevineyards.com
Processor of wines and champagne
Owner: Cliff Lede
CEO: John Anderson
Owner: Cliff Lede
Marketing Manager: Alfred Andreson
Sales Manager: Peter Vanm
Estimated Sales: $430000
Number Employees: 10-19

Type of Packaging: Consumer, Food Service

11656 **S. Christina Seafood**
527 N Carrollton Avenue
New Orleans, LA 70119-4704 504-486-5301
Fax: 504-486-5373
Seafood

11657 **S. Kennedy Vegetable Lifestock Company**
2310 Main Ave
Clear Lake, IA 50428 641-357-4227
Processor of carrots
President: Scott Kennedy
Estimated Sales: $600000
Number Employees: 4
Sq. footage: 40000
Brands:
S.K.

11658 **S. Wallace Edward & Sons**
PO Box 25
Surry, VA 23883-0025 800-290-9213
Fax: 757-294-5378 info@virginiatraditions.com
www.virginiatraditions.com
Virginia hams, sweet hams, bacon & sausage, soups & stews, specialty meats, desserts, poultry, snacks, seafood, other good stuff and assortments.
President: Sammuel Edwards III
CEO: Wallace Edwards Jr.
Vice President: Amy Edwards Harte
Marketing Director: Sammuel Edwards III
Sales Director: Bob Unterbrink
Operations Manager: Al Kadons
Plant Manager: Al Kadons
Purchasing Manager: Ryan Rowland
Number Employees: 22
Number of Brands: 2
Type of Packaging: Consumer
Brands:
Colonial Williamsburg
Edwards
Surry

11659 **S. Zitner Company**
3120 N 17th St
Philadelphia, PA 19132 215-229-4990
Fax: 215-229-9828 zitnermett@aol.com
Candy
Chairman: M Christine Murphy
CFO: Matt Mitttelauril
Quality Control: Joe Martin
Estimated Sales: $ 10-20 Million
Number Employees: 20-49
Brands:
Zitner's

11660 **S.A.S. Foods**
3005 Center Pl Ste 200
Norcross, GA 30093-1761
Fax: 770-446-9234
Oriental grocery items, seafood, fin fish, shellfish
President: Goro Iwami
Estimated Sales: $ 5 - 10 Million
Number Employees: 5-9

11661 **S.B. Winsor Dairy**
18 Clinton St
Johnston, RI 02919-4121 401-231-7832
Fax: 401-231-7832
Milk and dairy products
Chef: Alan Winsor
Estimated Sales: $ 2.5-5 Million
Number Employees: 1-4

11662 **S.D. Mushrooms**
P.O.Box 687
Avondale, PA 19311-0687 610-268-8082
Fax: 610-268-8644
Processor and importer of mushrooms and mushroom sauce
President/Owner: John D'Amico
Estimated Sales: $450,000
Number Employees: 1-4
Type of Packaging: Consumer, Food Service, Private Label, Bulk

11663 **S.F. Foods Corporation**
P.O.Box 913
Evansville, IN 47706-0913 812-428-0888
Fax: 812-428-0961
Manager: Jeff Noah
Estimated Sales: $ 10 - 20 Million
Number Employees: 10-19

11664 **S.J. McCullagh**
245 Swan St
Buffalo, NY 14204-2051 716-856-3473
Fax: 716-856-3486 800-753-3473
sjm@buffnet.net www.mccullaghcoffee.com
Processor, importer and exporter of coffee, tea, non-dairy creamer and hot chocolate
President: Warren Emblidge
Vice President: Roger Van Overstaeten
Marketing Director: Larry Franko
Purchasing Manager: Mary Costanzo
Estimated Sales: 9 Million
Number Employees: 50-99
Brands:
McCullagh-Hatan

11665 **S.L. Kaye Company**
230 5th Ave
New York, NY 10001-7704 212-683-5600
Fax: 212-947-7664 kaye230@aol.com
www.slkaye.com
Candy
President/Owner: Mitchell Katzman
Sales Manager: S Handy
Estimated Sales: $ 1-2.5 Million
Number Employees: 1-4
Brands:
Eskimo Pie Coffeepeaks
Eskimo Pie Miniatures
Eskimo Pie Snowpeaks
Needlers Jersey English Toffee
Titanic Esm Mints

11666 **S.P. Enterprises**
1889 E Maule Ave # E
Las Vegas, NV 89119-4603 702-736-4774
Fax: 702-736-6180 800-746-4774
spcandy@msn.com www.espeezcandy.com
Candy
President: Sam Popowcer
CEO: Alan Popowcer
Estimated Sales: $ 3 - 5 Million
Number Employees: 5-9
Brands:
Lillipos
Money Candy

11667 **S.S. Logan Packing Company**
120 21st St
Huntington, WV 25703 304-525-7625
Fax: 304-529-2516 800-642-3524
Processor of meats
President: Nester S Logan
CFO: Richard Logan
Estimated Sales: $20532751
Number Employees: 50-99

11668 **S.T. Jerrell Company**
802 Labarge Dr
Bessemer, AL 35022 205-426-8930
Fax: 205-426-8989 www.jerrellpackaging.com
Non-fat dry milk
CEO: John Lyon
Vice President: Barry Cornell
Estimated Sales: Below $ 5 Million
Number Employees: 10-19
Sq. footage: 25000
Type of Packaging: Food Service, Private Label, Bulk
Brands:
Cloverleaf Farms Peanut Butter
S. T. Jerrell Nonfat

11669 **S.T. Specialty Foods Inc**
8700 Xylon Ave N
Brooklyn Park, MN 55445-1817 763-493-9600
Fax: 763-493-9606
contactus@stspecialtyfoods.com
www.stspecialtyfoods.com
Dry Pasta Dinners
President/CEO: Dale Schulz
CFO: Raymond Turcotte
VP Administration: Barry Calhoon
VP R&D: Mark Welken
Seniror VP Sales: Kevin Kollock
VP Operations: Steve Favro
Purchasing Manager: Dick Hamblin
Number of Products: 50
Type of Packaging: Private Label
Brands:
LAND O'LAKE MACARONI & CHEESE
OUR SPECIALTY PASTA DINNERS

11670 **S.W. Meat & Provision Company**
2019 N 48th St
Phoenix, AZ 85008-3303 602-275-2000
Processor and wholesaler/distributor of sausage, ground beef and patties, portion cut steaks and aged beef sides; also, wholesaler/distributor of grocery products, frozen foods and general merchandise; serving the food servicemarket
President: W David Hart
Estimated Sales: $1-2.5 Million
Number Employees: 5-9
Type of Packaging: Food Service

11671 **SA Carlson**
160 Camfield Rd
Yakima, WA 98908 509-965-8333
Fax: 509-965-8311 sherm@sacarlson.com
www.sacarlson.com
Processed fruit ingredients including apple, pear, peach, grapes, berry fruits, etc.
President: Sherman Carlson
Customer Service: Ruffell Carlson
Quality Control: Carlos Correa
Estimated Sales: $ 5-10 Million
Number Employees: 1-4
Sq. footage: 125000
Type of Packaging: Food Service, Bulk
Brands:
INVERTEC
TASTEE

11672 **SANGARIA USA**
3142 Pacific Coast Hwy # 208
Torrance, CA 90505-6796 310-530-2202
Fax: 310-530-5335 sangaria@msn.com
Manufacturer, importer and exporter of soft drinks: Ramune drink, green tea, oolong tea, iced coffee, energy drink, fruit juices, etc
Owner: Leona Singer
Estimated Sales: $300,000-500,000
Number Employees: 1-4
Sq. footage: 250000
Parent Co: Japan Sangaria Beverage Company
Type of Packaging: Consumer, Food Service
Brands:
Sangaria

11673 **SAS Bakers Yeast**
13211 Us Highway 431 S
Headland, AL 36345-6333 334-889-4461
Fax: 334-889-4529 877-677-7000
www.lesaffreyeastcorp.com
Baker yeast
Plant Manager: Dennis Barry
President: John Reisch
Estimated Sales: $ 20-30 Million
Number Employees: 100-249
Brands:
SAS Bakers

11674 **SASIB Biscuits and Snacks Division**
118 W Streetsboro Street
Suite 306
Hudson, OH 44236-2711 330-656-3317
Fax: 330-656-2822 samuelson_sasibna@msn.com
Baked goods, biscuits, snacks

11675 **SB Global Foods**
P.O.Box 1322
Lansdale, PA 19446 215-361-9500
Fax: 215-361-9323 877-857-1727
info@sbglobalfoods.com
www.sbglobalfoods.com
Seasoned filled pretzel nuggets, chocolate covered peanut butter filled pretzel nuggets, and mini marshmellows.
President: Karl Brown
Estimated Sales: Below $ 5 Million
Number Employees: 5-9
Type of Packaging: Private Label
Brands:
American Cookie Boy
Pretzel Pete
Rocky Mountain Marshmallows
Rocky Mountain Popcorn

11676 **SBK Preserves**
1161 E 156th St
Bronx, NY 10474-6226 718-589-2900
Fax: 718-589-8412 800-773-7378
info@sarabeth.com www.sarabeth.com

Processor and exporter of jams, preserves, fruit spreads, syrups and granola cereal
President: William Levine
Finance Executive: Carlos Blanco
VP: Suzanne Levine
Estimated Sales: D
Number Employees: 10-19
Sq. footage: 15000
Parent Co: Sarabeth's Kitchen
Other Locations:
SBK Preserves
New York NY
Brands:
Sarabeth's

11677 **SC Enterprises**
RR 5
Owen Sound, ON N4K 5N7
Canada 519-371-0456
Fax: 519-371-5944 sce.d@bmts.com
www.scdistributors.biz/index.html
Wholesaler/distributor of fresh and frozen fish and wild game; processor ofrainbow trout.
Manager: Winston Jones
Number Employees: 10-19
Sq. footage: 9000

11678 **SECO & Golden 100**
1600 Essex Avenue
Deland, FL 32724 386-734-3906
Fax: 386-738-1378 info@golden100.com
www.golden100.com
Processor and exporter of fruit juice and drink concentrates; also, centralized purchasing location of dairy products and juice concentrates
President: Ron Edmundson
VP Development: Russ Sager
Estimated Sales: $200 Million
Number Employees: 20-49
Sq. footage: 27000
Type of Packaging: Bulk
Brands:
Golden 100

11679 **SEW Friel**
P.O.Box 10
Queenstown, MD 21658-0010 410-827-8811
Fax: 410-827-9472 jay@sewfriel.com
www.sewfriel.com
Processor, importer and exporter of canned juices including vegetable, tomato, apple, pineapple, grape and prune; also, canned corn
President: Michael Foster
Partner: James Friel Jr
Estimated Sales: $49100000
Number Employees: 1-4
Sq. footage: 240000
Type of Packaging: Consumer, Food Service, Private Label, Bulk
Brands:
Friel's
Hudson
Ole Wye

11680 **SFP Food Products**
348 Highway 64 E
Conway, AR 72032-9414 501-327-0744
Fax: 501-327-2808 800-654-5329
jballard@sfpfoods.com www.sfpfoods.com
Processor and exporter of waffle, pancake and cone mixes; manufacturer and exporter of waffle and cone irons
President: Jon Ballard
VP Marketing/Sales: Jon Ballard
VP Operations: Ray Ballard
Estimated Sales: $ 3 - 5 Million
Number Employees: 5-9
Sq. footage: 15000
Type of Packaging: Food Service, Private Label

11681 **SIF**
PO Box 1077
Shelburne, NS B0T 1W0
Canada 902-875-2666
Fax: 902-875-2706
Processor and exporter of fresh and frozen groundfish
Manager: Ian Williams
Number Employees: 20-49
Type of Packaging: Consumer, Food Service, Private Label, Bulk

11682 **SIGCO Sun Products**
227 6th St N
Breckenridge, MN 56520 218-643-8467
Fax: 218-643-4555 800-654-4145
nancy.nelson@sunopta.com www.sunopta.com
Sunflower oil manufacturer
Sales Manager: Nancy Nelson
Plant Manager: John Bontjes

11683 **SJH Enterprises**
2415 Parview Rd Ste 4
Middleton, WI 53562 608-831-3001
Fax: 608-831-3001 888-745-3845
Broker of organic grains and natural colors and flavors
Manager: Hank Zimmerman
Estimated Sales: $170000
Number Employees: 1-4
Type of Packaging: Consumer, Food Service, Private Label, Bulk

11684 **SJR Foods**
49 Brook Street
New Bedford, MA 02746-1742 781-821-3090
Fax: 781-821-5666 rbaras@sjrfoods.com
www.unholey.com
Processor of cream cheese filled bagels including plain, cinnamon raisin, sesame, poppy and onion
Owner: Larry Barras
Brands:
Unholey Bagel

11685 **SK Foods**
1175 S 19th Ave
Lemoore, CA 93245 559-924-6527
Fax: 559-924-0178 info@skfoods.com
www.skfoods.com
Processor of tomato products including paste, sauce, pulp, puree, diced and in juice
Manager: Randy Yingling
VP/CFO: Rick Washburn
VP Marketing: Alan Huey
Estimated Sales: $ 30-50 Million
Number Employees: 5-9
Type of Packaging: Food Service, Bulk

11686 **SK Foods International**
4666 Amber Valley Parkway
Fargo, ND 58104 701-356-4106
Fax: 701-356-4102 skfood@skfood.com
www.skfood.com
Certified organic and conventional non-GMO dry beans, grains, seeds, soybeans, brans/germs, cocoas, flours, oils, meals, and sweetners.
President/CEO: David Skyberg
VP/Secretary/Treasurer: Beverly Skyberg
Marketing Director: Jennifer Tesch
Estimated Sales: $3 Million
Number Employees: 17
Type of Packaging: Bulk

11687 **SKW Biosystems**
1741 Tomlinson Rd
Philadelphia, PA 19116 215-676-3900
Fax: 215-613-2115 800-223-7073
www.sweetovation.com
Processor and exporter of fruit preparations
Plant Manager: Corey Arrick
Number Employees: 100-249
Parent Co: Systems Bio-Industries

11688 **SKW Flavor & Fruit Preparation**
2021 Cabot Boulevard W
Langhorne, PA 19047-1810 215-702-1000
Fax: 215-702-1015
Fruits and nonfruit preps for dairy, frozen and refrigerated bakery and food service

11689 **SKW Nature Products**
2021 Cabot Boulevard W
Langhorne, PA 19047-1810 215-702-1000
Fax: 215-702-1015
Manufacturer and exporter of cultures, enzymes, edible and industrial gelatins, hydrocolloids, flavors, fragrance raw materials and fruit systems
VP/General Manager: Kenneth Hughes
VP/General Manager: George Masson
Number Employees: 500-999
Parent Co: SKW

11690 **SKW Nature Products**
2350 Kerper Blvd
Dubuque, IA 52001 563-588-6244
Fax: 563-588-9063 info@degussa.com
www.degussa.com
Enzymes and flavor ingredients for food, beverage, dairy and specialties industries
Head Corporate Communications: Ralph Driever
Press Relations Officer: Hannelore Gantzer
Internal Communications: Markus Langer
Number Employees: 100-249

11691 **SLB Snacks**
420 Lynnway
Lynn, MA 01901-1711 781-593-4422
Fax: 781-599-8430
Potato chips
President: William Termano
Marketing/Sales Manager: David Dugan
VP Sales: Shehan James
Plant Manager: Sue Pickering
Estimated Sales: $ 10-24.9 Million
Number Employees: 85

11692 **SMG**
2890 Chancellor Drive
Crestview Hills, KY 41017-2153
US 859-344-3700
Fax: 859-344-3737 www.smgmeats.com
Processor of pre-cooked, prepared and specialty meats including hamburgers, rib eye steaks, luncheon, roast beef, corned and roast beef, wet corn brisket, home meal replacements, etc.; exporter of hot dogs, pastrami and wet cornbrisket
CEO/President: Joe McCloskey
VP Sales: Don Mendenhall
Number Employees: 250-499
Parent Co: SMG
Type of Packaging: Consumer, Food Service, Private Label, Bulk
Other Locations:
S.M.G.
Flushing NY
Brands:
FIELD
FISCHER'S
KENTUCKY LEGEND
LIGURIA ITALIAN SPECIALTIES
MICKELBERRY'S
MOSEY'S
NATHAN'S FAMOUS
SCOTT PETERSEN

11693 **SOPAKCO Foods**
215 S Mullins St
Mullins, SC 29574-3207 843-464-0121
Fax: 423-639-7270 800-276-9678
www.sopakco.com
Processor of pasta sauces; also, retortable pouch manufacturer, canner and contract packager of poultry, meat, fish, pasta, vegetable, bean, fruit and dessert products, flexible, semi-rigid and glass conatianers
CEO: Al Reitzer
CFO: Steve Keight
R & D: Jim Dukes
Quality Control: Phyllis Calhoun
General Manager: Wynn Pettibone
General Manager: Wynn Pettibone
Plant Manager: Carl Whitmore
Purchasing Director: Beverly Stacey
Estimated Sales: $5-10 Million
Number Employees: 100
Sq. footage: 100000
Parent Co: Unaka Corporation
Type of Packaging: Consumer, Food Service, Private Label

11694 **SOUPerior Bean & Spice Company**
13115 NE 4th St # 120
Vancouver, WA 98684-5959 360-882-4500
Fax: 360-694-0862 800-878-7687
soupbean@aol.com
Processor of spice blends and mixes including bean soup, pasta salad, bread and broth
Owner: Paul Dendy
VP: Duane Rough Jr
Estimated Sales: $ 5 - 10 Million
Number Employees: 5-9
Sq. footage: 5700
Brands:
Our Counrtry

11695 **SP Enterprises**
1889 E Maule Ave # E
Las Vegas, NV 89119-4603 702-736-4774
Fax: 702-736-6180 800-746-4774
spcandy@msn.com www.espeezcandy.com
Leading manufacturer of kid's novelty candy including Viper Venom, Viper Vials, Viper Gum, Viper Blast and Aunt Flo's Country Fudge. Also known for Gold Mine Gum, Money Mints, Rock Candy and Jumbo Pops.
President: Sam Popowcer
Estimated Sales: $ 3 - 5 Million
Number Employees: 5-9
Brands:
AUNT FLO'S COUNTRY FUDGE
ESPEEZ
EYE OF THE DRAGON
GOLD MINE GUM
KID WIZARD
MONEY MINTS
USA MINTS
VIPER
VIPER BLAST
VIPER GUM
VIPER VENOM
VIPER VIALS

11696 **SPI Foods**
805 S Union St
Fremont, NE 68025 402-727-8412
Fax: 402-727-6327 866-266-1304
jmilne@spifoods.com www.spifoods.com
Crisp rice, soy crisp, cereal extrusion, custom extruded ingredients, no boil lasagna and instant pasta
President: Robert Parnow
CEO: John Stout
Controller: Darren Phinney
VP: Jeff Milne Jr.
Research & Development: Shashi Ramaiah
Quality Control: Craig Hammond
Sales Director: Jeff Milne Jr.
Plant Manager: Mark Johnson
Estimated Sales: $ 15 Million
Number Employees: 5-9
Sq. footage: 65000
Parent Co: Plaza Belmont Group
Type of Packaging: Private Label, Bulk
Brands:
Ne-Boil Lasagna
Pasta Defino

11697 **SPI Nutritional**
222 N Vincent Avenue
Covina, CA 91722-3904 626-915-1151
Fax: 626-332-7754
Nutritional food
Estimated Sales: $ 5-10 Million appx.
Number Employees: 5

11698 **SRA Foods**
P.O.Box 12084
Birmingham, AL 35202-2084 205-323-7447
Fax: 205-323-1772
Wholesale/distributor of meats to restaurants and grocery stores
President: Anthony Anselmo
Estimated Sales: $ 50 - 100 Million
Number Employees: 20-49

11699 **SS Lobster Limited**
691 River St
Fitchburg, MA 01420-2910 978-342-6135
Fax: 978-345-7341
Seafood (lobster, clams, shrimp)
President: Mark Strazdas
Estimated Sales: $ 10 - 20 Million
Number Employees: 20-49

11700 **SSI Food Service**
P.O.Box 700
Caldwell, ID 83606-0700 208-482-7844
Fax: 208-482-7457
Processes meat to beef patties, fajitas, taco meat and more
President: Kirk Smith
VP Marketing: Jeff Gross
VP Sales: Jeff Gross
VP Operations: Ben Badiola
Purchasing Manager: Neal Waterman
Estimated Sales: 74.80 Million
Number Employees: 500-999

11701 **ST Specialty Foods**
8700 Xylon Ave N
Brooklyn Park, MN 55445-1817 763-493-9600
Fax: 763-493-9606 www.stspecialtyfoods.com
Dry pasta dinners, and mix
President/CEO: Dale Schulz
Marketing Director: Kevin Kollock
VP/CFO: Ray Turcotte
CFO: Ray Turcotte
Sales Manager: Kevin Kollock
Operations Manager: Steve Favro
Plant Manager: Paul Westerberg
Purchase Manager: Dick Hamblin
Estimated Sales: $ 10-20 Million
Number Employees: 50-99
Type of Packaging: Private Label

11702 **(HQ)SW Red Smith**
4145 SW 47th Ave
Davie, FL 33314-4006 954-581-1996
Fax: 954-581-6775 inquiries@swredsmith.com
www.swredsmith.com
Processor, packer and exporter of pickled eggs, sausage and pigs' feet
President: Stephen Foster
Executive VP: David Foster
VP/Sales: Helena Meade
Plant Manager: Michael Sandy
Estimated Sales: $8 Million
Number Employees: 20-49
Number of Brands: 2
Number of Products: 6
Sq. footage: 12000
Parent Co: Red Smith of Florida
Type of Packaging: Consumer
Brands:
Big John
Red Smith

11703 **SWELL Philadelphia Chewing Gum Corporation**
North Eagle & Lawrence
Havertown, PA 19083 610-449-1700
Fax: 610-449-2557 sales@swellgum.com
www.swellgum.com
Manufacturer and exporter of chewing bubble gum and candy
President: Edward Fenimore
Estimated Sales: $14.5 Million
Number Employees: 100-249
Sq. footage: 200000
Type of Packaging: Private Label, Bulk
Brands:
SWELL

11704 **SYFO Beverage Company ofFlorida**
10033 Sawgrass Drive West
Suite 202
Ponte Vedra Beach, FL 32082 904-381-9002
Fax: 904-381-9004 1 8-8 4-6 79
customerservice@syfobeverages.com
http://www.syfobeverages.com
Beverages
President: Cydelle Mendius
Estimated Sales: $ 1-2.5 Million
Number Employees: 1

11705 **SYSCO Food Services of Northern New England**
P.O.Box 4657
Portland, ME 04112-4657 207-871-0700
Fax: 207-871-0339 800-632-4446
information@sysconne.com www.sysconne.com
SYSCO is a marketer and distributor of foodservice products in North America, products of which include a wide variety of fresh and frozen meats, seafood, poultry, fruits and vegetables, plus bakery products, canned and dry foodspaper and disposable products, sanitation items, dairy foods, beverages, kitchen and tabletop equipment.
President/COO: Greg Otterbein
Chairman: Richard Giles
Vice President of Finance: John Rodrigue
Director of Operations: Dain Thomason

11706 **Saag's Products**
1799 Factor Ave
San Leandro, CA 94577 510-352-8000
Fax: 510-352-4100 800-352-7224
www.saags.com
Sausages, condiments, frankfurters, luncheon meats and pates, roast beef, corned beef and pastrami, salamis and dry cured meats, smoked hams and pork products, turkey breasts
President: Timothy Dam
CEO/Owner: Kathi Mosle
CFO: Mike Tye
VP: Jerry Meyer
VP Marketing: Bernard Steinert
Estimated Sales: $11300000
Number Employees: 85
Sq. footage: 40000
Type of Packaging: Food Service, Private Label, Bulk
Brands:
Wurstmeister

11707 **Sabatino Truffles USA**
330 Coster Street
Bronx, NY 10474 718-328- 412
Fax: 718-328- 412 888-444-9971
customer@sabatinostore.com
www.sabatinostore.com
Extra virgin olive oil, truffles, truffle butter, truffle oil, pasta, mushrooms, sauces and creams.
President: Frederico Balestra
Estimated Sales: $ 1 - 3 Million
Number Employees: 7
Type of Packaging: Food Service, Private Label

11708 **Sabinsa Corporation**
20 Lake Dr
East Windsor, NJ 08520 732-777-1111
Fax: 732-777-1443 info@sabinsa.com
www.sabinsa.com
Processor of botanical extracts
President: Muhammed Majeed
CEO: Jeff Lind
VP: Mark Sysler
Marketing Director: Shaheen Majeed
Estimated Sales: $ 20 - 50 Million
Number Employees: 50-99
Brands:
Ashwagandha
Boswellin
Citrin
Citrin K
Curlumin C3 Complex
Digezyme
Gugulidid
Lactospore

11709 **Sable & Rosenfeld Foods**
12 Lawton Blvd
Toronto, ON M4V 1Z4
Canada 416-929-4214
Fax: 416-929-6727 info@sableandrosenfeld.com
www.sableandrosenfeld.com
cocktail garnishes, appetizers/condiments and sauces.
President: Myra Sable
VP: Kathy Smith
Sales: Mary O'Neill

11710 **Sabra Dipping Company**
777 Westchester Avenue
3rd Floor
White Plains, NY 10604 914-964-1470
Fax: 914-372-3900 888-957-2272
www.sabra.com
Manufacturers of Mediterranean style refrigerated dips and spreads
CEO: Ronen Zohar
CFO: Amit Anand
Executive Vice President: Meiky Tollman
Estimated Sales: $110 Million
Number Employees: 500-999
Parent Co: Strauss Holdings LTD

11711 **Sabra-Go Mediterranean**
PO Box 660634
Dallas, TX 75266-0634 631-694-9500
888-957-2272
www.sabra.com
Mediterranean style refrigerated dips and spreads that iclude hummus, eggplant dips, babaganoush spreads, and Mediterranean salsa
CEO: Ronen Zohar
CFO: Amit Anand
Executive VP/General Manager: Meiky Tollman
Chief Marketing Officer: Rodrigo Troni
Executive VP Sales: John McGuckin
Human Resources Director: Angela King
Executive VP Operations: Guy Nir

Parent Co: Strauss Holdings LTD

11712 **Sabroso Company**
690 S Grape Street
Medford, OR 97501 541-772-5653
Fax: 541-779-3572 sales@sabroso.com
www.sabroso.com
Manufacturer of fruit purees, fruit puree concentrates, fruit preparations, fruit flakes, fruit bases and custom fruit solutions.
CEO: James Root
CFO: Mike Molenkamp
VP: John Jaconbsen
Estimated Sales: $ 50 - 100 Million
Number Employees: 300
Parent Co: Tree Top
Type of Packaging: Food Service, Bulk
Other Locations:
Sabroso Co.
Sandy OR

11713 **Sachs Nut Company**
P.O. Box 7
9323 Hwy 7
Clarkton, NC 28433-0550 910-647-4711
Fax: 910-647-0301 800-732-6933
info@sachspeanuts.com www.sachspeanuts.com
Nuts
President/Owner: Nathan Cox
VP: Sam Cox
Estimated Sales: $ 2.5-5 Million
Number Employees: 50-99
Type of Packaging: Private Label, Bulk
Brands:
Sachs Nut Company

11714 **Sachs Peanuts**
PO Box 7
Clarkton, NC 28433-0550 910-647-4711
Fax: 910-647-0301 800-732-6933
info@sachspeanuts.com www.sachspeanuts.com
Manufacturer of in-shell peanuts
President: Nathan Cox
Sales Secretary: Ruth Cox-Church
Estimated Sales: $100+ Million
Number Employees: 50-99
Sq. footage: 10000
Parent Co: E.J. Cox Company
Type of Packaging: Consumer, Food Service, Bulk
Brands:
SACHS

11715 **Sacramento Baking Company**
9221 Beatty Dr
Sacramento, CA 95826 916-361-2000
Fax: 916-361-0117
Bakery items including cakes
President: Juma Elajou
Marketing Director: Sam Alaclu
Quality Control: Sam Elajou
Estimated Sales: $ 20-50 Million
Number Employees: 20-49
Brands:
Sacramento Baking

11716 **Sacramento Cookie Factory**
3428 Auburn Blvd
Sacramento, CA 95821 916-482-8222
Fax: 916-482-8222 877-877-2646
www.wafercookie.com
wafer cookies

11717 **Saddleback Cellars**
P.O.Box 141
Oakville, CA 94562 707-944-1305
Fax: 707-944-2817 www.silveroak.com
Wines
Owner: Ray Duncan
Estimated Sales: $ 20 - 50 Million
Number Employees: 20-49

11718 **(HQ)Sadkhin Complex**
2306 Avenue U
Brooklyn, NY 11229 718-769-7771
Fax: 718-769-8087 800-723-5446
NYOffice@sadkhin.com www.sadkhin.com
Processor of seasonal herbal formulas and multi-vitamins
Owner: Dr Grigory Sadkhin
Estimated Sales: Less than $500,000
Number Employees: 1-4
Sq. footage: 2200
Type of Packaging: Consumer
Other Locations:
Los Angeles CA
San Francisco CA
Boston MA
Philadelphia PA
Detroit MI
Brands:
The Sadkhin Complex®

11719 **Sadler's Smokehouse**
1206 N Frisco St
Henderson, TX 75652 903-657-5581
Fax: 903-655-8404 www.sadlerssmokehouse.com
Processor of barbecued beef and pork, smoked poultry and barbecue sauce; wholesaler/distributor of meats/provisions; serving the food service market
Managing Partner: Terry O'Brien
Safety Manager: Agustin Luna
Marketing Research Director: Harold Sadler
VP Operations/General Manager: Jason Flanagan
Purchasing Manager: Brett Hensley
Estimated Sales: $78 Million
Number Employees: 300
Sq. footage: 180000
Type of Packaging: Consumer, Food Service, Private Label
Brands:
Double S
Sadler's Smokehouse

11720 **SafeTrek Foods**
315 Edelweiss Dr
Bozeman, MT 59718-3928 406-586-4840
Fax: 406-582-0614 sales@safetrek.com
Manufacture and exporter of dehydrated, freeze-dried and organic entries, soups, gravies, side dishes
President: Stephen Quayle
CFO: Kathy Madsen
Purchasing Manager: James Young
Estimated Sales: $ 10-20 Million
Number Employees: 10-19
Sq. footage: 50000
Type of Packaging: Consumer, Food Service, Private Label, Bulk
Brands:
SAFETREK

11721 **Safeway Beverage**
6405 E Stapleton Drive N
Denver, CO 80216-3341 303-320-7960
Fax: 303-321-6437 business.ethics@safeway.com
www.shop.safeway.com
Contract packager of soft drinks
President: Steve Burd
Plant Superintendent: Fred Scherrer
Product Control Coordinator: Louise Kimbrough
Plant Engineer: Stephen Osmena
Estimated Sales: $ 10 - 20 Million
Number Employees: 50-99
Sq. footage: 175000
Parent Co: Safeway Stores
Type of Packaging: Consumer, Private Label
Brands:
Safeway Beverage

11722 **Safeway Beverage**
1121 124th Ave NE
Bellevue, WA 98005-2101 425-455-6444
Fax: 425-455-6499 www.safeway.com
Processor and exporter of canned and bottled soft drinks
Executive: Greg Sparks
Plant Manager: M Smsith
Estimated Sales: $ 50 - 100 Million
Number Employees: 250-499
Parent Co: Safeway Stores
Type of Packaging: Consumer, Private Label
Brands:
Select Pop

11723 **Safeway Dairy Products**
4525 Addison Road
Capitol Heights, MD 20743-1002 301-341-9555
www.safeway.com
Processor of ice cream, ice milk, etc
Number Employees: 20-49
Type of Packaging: Consumer, Private Label

11724 **(HQ)Safeway Dairy Products**
2800 Ygnacio Valley Rd
Walnut Creek, CA 94598-3592 925-944-4000
Fax: 925-467-3230 www.safeway.com
Processor and exporter of dairy and bakery products; also, beverages
President: Steve Burd
Senior VP: Lawrence Jackson
Estimated Sales: $ .5 - 1 million
Number Employees: 1-4
Type of Packaging: Consumer, Private Label

11725 **Safeway Inc**
5918 Stonridge Mall Rd
Pleasanton, CA 94588-3229 925-467-3000
Fax: 925-467-3323 877-723-3929
www.safeway.com
Processor of instant nonfat dry milk and natural foods, such as: beef, pork, chicken, bread, ice cream, etc.
Chairman/President/CEO: Steven Burd
CFO/EVP: Robert Edwards
SVP/CIO: David Ching
Estimated Sales: $1 Billion +
Number Employees: 100-249
Type of Packaging: Consumer

11726 **Safeway Milk Plant**
1115 W Alameda Dr
Tempe, AZ 85282-3384 480-894-4391
Fax: 480-929-8025 www.safeway.com
Processor of milk including half and half, skim, whole, 1% and 2%
Plant Manager: Jason Glober
Plant Manager: Jeff Fowler
Number Employees: 50-99
Parent Co: Safeway Stores
Type of Packaging: Consumer, Food Service, Private Label, Bulk

11727 **Safeway Stores**
1703 W 10th Pl #101
Tempe, AZ 85281-5254 480-966-0295
Fax: 480-784-1661 www.safway.com
Processor of ice cream and yogurt
Manager: Kevin Kluetz
CEO: Steven A Burd
CFO: Robert Edwards
Vice President: Russell Jackson
Chief Marketing Officer: Brian C Cornell
Retail Operations: Bruce Everette
Estimated Sales: $500,000
Number Employees: 3
Parent Co: Vons Grocery Company
Type of Packaging: Consumer
Brands:
Safeway

11728 **Sagawa's Savory Sauces**
8292 SW Nyberg St
Tualatin, OR 97062-9457 503-692-4334
Fax: 503-691-0661
Processor and exporter of Hawaiian-style sauces including teriyaki, sweet and sour and Polynesian barbecue; also, salad dressings also makes,seasonings and mixes.
President: Linda Rider
Estimated Sales: $540.0k
Number Employees: 7
Sq. footage: 5433
Type of Packaging: Consumer, Food Service
Brands:
Baste & Glaze
Sweet & Sassy

11729 **Sagaya Corporation**
3700 Old Seward Hwy
Anchorage, AK 99503-6037 907-561-5173
Fax: 907-561-2042 www.newsagaya.com
International grocery store offering fresh Alaskan seafood, ethnic cuisine, specialty foods, gourmet groceries, fresh produce, and choice meats
Manager: Tom Griffin
Estimated Sales: $ 10 - 20 Million
Number Employees: 50-99

11730 **Sage Enterprises**
6 E Monroe St # 1004
Chicago, IL 60603-2721 847-827-0066
Fax: 847-827-6420
President: Gary Greenberg

11731 **Sage V Foods**
12100 Wilshire Blvd # 605
Los Angeles, CA 90025-7122 310-820-4496
Fax: 310-820-2559 sales@sagevfoods.com
www.sagevfoods.com

Functional rice ingredients and grains
President: Pete Vegas
Estimated Sales: $42,173,547
Number Employees: 10
Brands:
Sage V

11732 **Sage V Foods LLC**
12100 Wilshire Blvd # 605
Los Angeles, CA 90025-7122 310-820-4496
Fax: 310-820-2559 sales@sagevfoods.com
www.sagevfoods.com
Specializes in producing rice based ingredients for use in processed foods. Product line includes rice flour, instant rice, iqf rice, and specially extruded products.
Owner: Pete Vegas
Marketing/Sales: Mhari Watanabe
Estimated Sales: $ 5 - 10 Million
Number Employees: 50-99
Type of Packaging: Food Service, Bulk

11733 **Saguaro Food Products**
1319 N Main Ave
Tucson, AZ 85705 520-884-8049
Fax: 520-884-9704 800-732-2447
sfpchips@flash.net www.saguarofood.com
Southwest gourmet foods, potato, dips and sauces, tortilla and corn chips
General Manager: Ralph Cortese
Finance Manager: Laurie Cowan
Marketing Manager: Sue Heems
Operations Manager: Raul Ruiz
Estimated Sales: Below $ 500,000
Number Employees: 8

11734 **Sahadi Fine Foods**
4215 1st Ave
Brooklyn, NY 11232 718-369-0100
Fax: 718-369-0800 800-724-2341
pwhelan@sahadifinefoods.com
www.sahadifinefoods.com
Maufacturer of nuts and seeds. Importer of dried fruit, beans, nuts, olives, Mediterranean foods
President: Morris Elbaz
VP: Pat Whelan
Estimated Sales: $11 Million
Number Employees: 20-49
Sq. footage: 58000

11735 **Sahadi Importing Company**
187 Atlantic Ave
Brooklyn, NY 11201 718-624-4550
Fax: 718-643-4415 sahadis@aol.com
www.sahadis.com
Ethnic foods
President: Charles Sahadi
VP: Robert Sahadi
Estimated Sales: Below $ 5 Million
Number Employees: 20-49
Brands:
Sahadi

11736 **Sahagian & Associates**
124 Madison St
Oak Park, IL 60302 708-848-5552
Fax: 708-386-5959 800-327-9273
sales@sahagianinc.com www.sahagianinc.com
Processor and exporter of bubble gum, licorice, taffy, candy-coated chocolate malted balls, chocolate bites, almonds, chocolate and caramel popcorn; also, multi-colored and tri-colored popcorn, candy coated licorice, chocolate dips andsalami
President: Linda Sahagian
Estimated Sales: $630,000
Number Employees: 11
Type of Packaging: Consumer, Private Label, Bulk
Brands:
A FOOT OF
A YARD OF
THE WHOLE 9 YARDS

11737 **Sahalee of Alaska**
PO Box 104174
Anchorage, AK 99510-4174 907-349-4151
Fax: 907-349-4161 800-349-4151
sahalee@aol.com
Seafood
President/CEO: Hank Lind
VP/Secretary/Treasurer: Christa Lind
Sales Director: Bill Haller

11738 **Sahara Coffee**
2081 Mountain Vista Way
Reno, NV 89519-6269 775-825-5033
Fax: 775-825-3190 donna@saharacoffee.com
www.saharacoffee.com
Processor and packer of whole leaf loose teas, organic dates and specialty coffees
Owner: Charles Hubach
Estimated Sales: Less than $500,000
Number Employees: 1-4
Brands:
Sahara

11739 **Sahara Natural Foods**
14855 Wicks Blvd
San Leandro, CA 94577 510-352-5111
Fax: 510-532-3227
Rice products, soups and organic bulk products
National Manager: Al Caldwell

11740 **Sahlen Packing Company**
318 Howard St
Buffalo, NY 14206 716-852-8677
Fax: 716-852-8684 ron@redlinski.com
www.sahlen.com
Manufacturer of meat products that include; sausage, ham, bacon, lard and hot dogs
President: Joseph Sahlen
VP: Christopher Cauley
Estimated Sales: $18 Million
Number Employees: 20-49
Brands:
SAHLEN'S

11741 **Saint Albans Cooperative Creamery**
140 Federal Street
Saint Albans, VT 05478-2000 802-524-6581
Fax: 802-527-1769 800-559-0343
stalbanscoop@stalbanscooperative.com
www.stalbanscooperative.com
Processor of whole, skim, skim condensed and powdered milk; also, cream
General Manager: Leon Berthiaume
Quality Assurance Manager: Sandra Kupperblatt
Business Manager: Michael Janson
Store Operations Manager: Steve Martin
Cooperative Relations Manager: Tom Gates
Plant Operations Manager: Rob Hirss
Estimated Sales: $215 Million
Number Employees: 70
Sq. footage: 41500
Type of Packaging: Private Label, Bulk
Brands:
Orbit

11742 **(HQ)Saint Amour/Powerline Foods**
2971 Grace Lane
Costa Mesa, CA 92626 714-754-1900
info@rocknrolls.com
www.rocksnrolls.com
Processor of cookies including madelines, croquants and teethers; also, snack foods
Owner: Daniel De St Amour
Number Employees: 5-9
Brands:
Rocks N' Rolls

11743 **Saint Armands Baking Company**
2811 59th Avenue Dr E
Bradenton, FL 34203-5334 941-753-7494
Fax: 941-751-1417 sales@sabc.cc
www.starbake.com
Processor of bread, rolls and sweet goods
President: Bernard Vroom
Estimated Sales: $ 1 - 3 Million
Number Employees: 5-9

11744 **Saint Arnold Brewing Company**
2000 Lyons Ave
Houston, TX 77020 713-686-9494
Fax: 713-686-9474 brewery@saintarnold.com
www.saintarnold.com
Processor of seasonal beer, ale, stout, lager and pilsner
President: Brock Wagner
Sales Rep: Frank Mancuso
Estimated Sales: Below $ 5 Million
Number Employees: 10-19
Type of Packaging: Consumer, Food Service
Brands:
Amber
Brown
Christmas
Elissa IPA
Fancy Lawnmower
Kristall Weizen
Oktoberfest
Root Beer
Spring Bock
Summer Pils
Winter Stout

11745 **Sainte Genevieve Winery**
6231 State Route C
Ste Genevieve, MO 63670 573-483-3500
Fax: 573-483-3526 800-398-1298
stgenwinery@hotmail.com
www.saintegenevievewinery.com
Wines
Manager: Elaine Mooney
CEO: Lineus Hoffmeister
Estimated Sales: $500,000-$1 Million
Number Employees: 1-4
Brands:
Sainte Genevieve

11746 **Saintsbury**
1500 Los Carneros Avenue
Napa, CA 94559-9742 707-252-0592
Fax: 707-252-0595 info@saintsbury.com
www.saintsbury.com
Wines
Managing Partner: Richard Ward
Managing Partner: David Graves
Estimated Sales: Below $6Million
Number Employees: 18
Brands:
Saintsbury

11747 **Sakeone Corporation**
820 Elm St
Forest Grove, OR 97116 503-357-7056
Fax: 503-357-1014 800-550-7253
talktous@sakeone.com www.sakeone.com
Sake
President/CEO: Steve Boone
Tasting Room Manager: Jennifer Brownstein
Plant Manager: Scott Eagler
Sales Manager: Greg Lorenz
VP Sales: Jim Scalace
Director Marketing: Dewey Weddington
Estimated Sales: Below $ 5 Million
Number Employees: 10-19
Type of Packaging: Private Label
Brands:
G
Momokawa
Moonstone

11748 **Sal's Caesar Dressing**
PO Box 612
Novato, CA 94948-0612 415-897-0605
Processor of Caesar salad dressings
President: Shirley Lesley
VP: Mark Lesley
Number Employees: 1-4
Type of Packaging: Consumer, Food Service
Brands:
Sal's

11749 **Sal-Serve**
P.O.Box 501187
Mobile, AL 36605-1187 251-438-6944
Fax: 251-438-6948
Salsa
Owner: Jim Higdon
General Manager: Jim Higdon
Estimated Sales: $ 20 - 50 Million
Number Employees: 50-99

11750 **Salad Depot**
51 Romeo St
Moonachie, NJ 7074 201-507-1980
Fax: 201-507-9001
Vegetables
President/Owner: Dan Zeigler
Marketing Director: John Zeigler
Buyer: Doreen Congo
Estimated Sales: Below $ 5 Million
Number Employees: 1-4
Brands:
Salad Depot

11751 Salad Oils International Corporation
5070 W Harrison St
Chicago, IL 60644 773-261-0500
Fax: 773-261-7555 saladoiljohn@earthlink.net
Edible oils
President: Rosalie Paris
VP: John Pacente
Estimated Sales: $1,100,000
Number Employees: 10-19
Sq. footage: 15000
Type of Packaging: Private Label
Brands:
Irilla Extra Virgin O.O.
Mi Best Soybean Oil
Onte Verde O.O.
Rgo Mace O.O.
Rosa Canola Oil
Rosa Corn Oil
Rosa Peanut Oil

11752 Salaison Levesque
500 Beaumont Street
Montreal, QC H3N 1T7
Canada 514-273-1702
Fax: 514-273-2325 877- 53- 170
ventes@salaisonlevesque.qc.ca
www.salaisonlevesque.qc.ca
ham products
President/Owner: M Regis Levesque
VP: Mme Annie Levesque
Estimated Sales: $7.1 Million
Number Employees: 30

11753 Salamandre Wine Cellars
108 Don Carlos Dr
Aptos, CA 95003 831-685-0321
newt@cruzio.com
www.salamandrewine.com
Wines
General Partner: Will Shoemaker Md
Winemaker: Wells Shoemaker
Estimated Sales: $170,000
Number Employees: 2
Brands:
Salamndre Wine Cellars

11754 Salamat of Seafoods
P.O.Box 1450
Kenai, AK 99611-1450 907-283-7000
Fax: 907-283-8499
Processor of fresh and frozen seafood including salmon, halibut, herring and cod
President: Robert Scott
President/CEO: Robert Scott
Executive VP: Shane Morgan
Director Manufacturing: Roy Bertoglio
Estimated Sales: $ 20-50 Million
Number Employees: 100-249
Type of Packaging: Consumer, Food Service, Bulk

11755 Salem Baking Company
224 S Cherry St
Winston Salem, NC 27101-5231 336-748-0230
Fax: 336-748-0501 800-274-2994
sales@salembaking.com www.salembaking.com
Processor of cookies flavors: moravian, spice, sugar, lemon, keylime, black walnut, tangerine-orange and double chocolate.
President: Guy Wilkerson
Estimated Sales: $3500000
Number Employees: 1-4
Parent Co: Dewey's Bakery
Type of Packaging: Consumer, Food Service
Brands:
Moravian Hearth

11756 Salem Food Service
P.O.Box 542
Salem, IN 47167-0542 812-883-2196
Fax: 812-883-2205 www.salemfoodservice.com
Manufacturer of beef, pork, poultry, ground meat and custom cut steaks
Owner: Jerry Mc Clellan
Estimated Sales: $ 20 - 50 Million
Number Employees: 20-49
Parent Co: Frozen Food Service Corporation
Type of Packaging: Food Service

11757 (HQ)Salem Oil & Grease Company
60 Grove St
Salem, MA 01970-2245 978-745-0585
Fax: 978-741-4426
Processor and exporter of sulphonated castor oil
President: V Smith III
VP Sales: J Donovan
VP Production: G Hanson
Estimated Sales: $10-20 Million
Number Employees: 20-49

11758 Salem Old Fashioned Candies
93 Canal St
Salem, MA 01970 978-744-3242
Fax: 978-745-9459
Processor of candy including bagged, hard, lollypops, mints, rock and taffy
President: Freeman Corkum
Estimated Sales: $950000
Number Employees: 10-19
Type of Packaging: Consumer
Brands:
Chestnut Street
Gems
Jane Stewart
Noah's Treats
Sea Chest
Seabreeze
Spindrift

11759 Salemville Cheese Cooperative
W4481 County Road Gg
Cambria, WI 53923-9304 920-394-3433
Cheese
President: Henry Miller
CFO: William Schrock
Plant Manager: Lavern Miller
Estimated Sales: $ 5-10 Million
Number Employees: 20-49

11760 Sales Associates of Alaska
1900 Phillips Field Rd
Fairbanks, AK 99701 907-458-0000
Fax: 907-452-2201 www.qualitysales.net
Wholesale grocers.
President: Gary Nance
Secretary/Treasurer: Carl Olson
Estimated Sales: $ .5 - 1 million
Number Employees: 1-4

11761 Sales USA
220 Salado Creek Road
Salado, TX 76571-5783 254-947-3838
Fax: 254-947-3338 800-766-7344
pompeii1@aol.com www.pompeiijuices.com
Fruit and vegetable juices.
President: Rusty Justus
CEO: Ronald Cox
CEO: Ronald Seacox
Plant Manager: Lee Simpkins
Estimated Sales: $ 1 - 3 Million
Number Employees: 4
Sq. footage: 15000
Type of Packaging: Consumer, Food Service, Private Label, Bulk

11762 Salishan Vineyards
35011 NE North Fork Ave
La Center, WA 98629 360-263-2713
Fax: 360-263-3675
Wine
President: Joan Wolverton
CFO: Lincoln Wolverton
Estimated Sales: Under $300,000
Number Employees: 1-4
Type of Packaging: Private Label
Brands:
Salishan

11763 Sallock International Foods
27960 Cummings Road
Millbury, OH 43447-9762 419-838-7223
Fax: 419-838-7597
Processor and exporter of American and Lebanese salad dressings, seasonings and soups
Owner: Sly Sallock
Owner: Abraham Sallock
Owner: Manira Sallock
Number Employees: 49
Sq. footage: 5217
Type of Packaging: Consumer, Food Service, Private Label, Bulk

11764 Sally Lane's Candy Farm
2215 Gum Springs Rd
Paris, TN 38242 731-642-5801
Processor of candy including peanut and coconut brittle and hard and sugar-free candies
Owner: Bobby Freeman
Co-Owner/Co-Partner: Jean Peterson
Number Employees: 5-9
Sq. footage: 4000
Type of Packaging: Consumer
Brands:
Sally Lane's

11765 Sally Sherman Foods
300 N MacQuesten Pkwy
Mt Vernon, NY 10550-1093 914-664-6262
Fax: 914-664-2846 vasili.zisis@prodigy.net
Salads
President: Michael Endico
Sales Director: Glene Richards
Estimated Sales: $ 20-50 Million
Number Employees: 50-99

11766 Salmans & Associates
1126 W Chestnut St
Chicago, IL 60642-4111 312-226-1820
Fax: 312-226-6806 sales@salmans.com
Cheese
President: Van Salmans
Estimated Sales: $650,000
Number Employees: 1-4
Brands:
Salmans

11767 Salmolux
34100 9th Ave South
Federal Way, WA 98003 253-874-2026
Fax: 253-874-4042 seafood@salmolux.com
www.salmolux.com
Processor of smoked seafood products; importer and exporter of pates, spreads, salmon burgers, herring, flavored butters and canned seafood salads
President: George Kuetgens
VP/CFO: Kira Kuetgens
Marketing VP: Ed Tropp
VP Sales: John Ramdisi
Plant Manager: Ray Crockett
Estimated Sales: $ 20 Million
Number Employees: 90
Sq. footage: 60000
Type of Packaging: Consumer, Food Service, Private Label, Bulk
Brands:
Salmolux Anti Pasta
Salmolux Gourmet Smoked Salmon
Salmolux Saute Butters

11768 Salmon River Smokehouse
PO Box 40
Gustavus, AK 99826-0040 907-456-3885
Fax: 907-456-3889
Smoke a variety of fish products.

11769 Salt Lake Macaroni & Noodle Company
5405 W 4700 S
Salt Lake City, UT 84118-6352 801-969-9855
Fax: 801-969-9856
Pasta
Manager: Mike Stover
Estimated Sales: $ 5 - 10 Million
Number Employees: 5-9

11770 Salt River Lobster
72 Tidewater Dr
Boothbay, ME 04537 207-633-5357
Fax: 207-633-5357
Sells lobster, shrimp, fish, and various other shellfish.

11771 Salute Sante! Food & Wine
68 Coombs St # I-2
Napa, CA 94559-3966 707-251-3900
Fax: 707-251-3939 info@grapeseedoil.com
www.grapeseedoil.com
Flavored and regular grapeseed oil
President: Valentin Humer
Estimated Sales: $690,000
Number Employees: 5-9
Type of Packaging: Consumer
Brands:
Salute Sante! Grapeseed Oil

11772 **Salvage Sale**
1001 McKinney St Ste 700
Houston, TX 77002 713-286-4600
Fax: 713-286-4602 800-856-7445
customercare@salvagesale.com
www.salvagesale.com
Online marketplace for buyers and sellers of salvage goods
President: Dave Dawson
VP Market Making: Jim Reilly
Marketing Manager: Maria Chamdess
Estimated Sales: $1500000
Number Employees: 20-49
Sq. footage: 30000

11773 **(HQ)Salvati Foods**
57 N Broadway
Suite 214
Hicksville, NY 11801-2941 516-932-8300
Fax: 516-932-8379
Importer, packer and wholesaler/distributor of specialty foods including red and white vinegar, spices, antipasto, stuffed peppers, stuffed eggplant, tomatoes, etc
President: Andrew Benzoni
Sales Director: A Laurino
Production Director: Bruce Leibowitz
Number Employees: 10-19
Sq. footage: 72000
Type of Packaging: Consumer, Food Service, Private Label

11774 **Sam Kane Beef Processors**
P.O.Box 9254
Crp Christi, TX 78469 361-241-5000
Fax: 361-242-2999 jkane@samkanebeef.com
www.samkanebeef.com
Processor and exporter of fresh, frozen and boxed beef.
President: Jerry Kane
Purchasing Agent: Lisa Lopez
Estimated Sales: $ 100-500 Million
Number Employees: 500-999
Type of Packaging: Consumer, Food Service, Bulk

11775 **Sam Wylde Flour Company**
3235 16th Ave SW
Seattle, WA 98134-1023 206-762-5400
Fax: 206-767-4088 www.puratos.com
Flour
Manager: Steve Picton
Estimated Sales: $ 20-50 Million
Number Employees: 20-49

11776 **Samadi Sweets Cafe**
5916 Leesburg Pike
Falls Church, VA 22041 703-578-0606
Fax: 703- 57-8 17
Middle Eastern pastries
Owner: Nora Burgan
Estimated Sales: Less than $500,000
Number Employees: 5-9

11777 **Sambets Cajun Deli**
8650 Spicewood Spgs Rd # 111
Austin, TX 78759-4323 512-258-6410
Fax: 512-258-6284 800-472-6238
www.sambets.com
Cajun hot sauces, salsas and spices
Owner: Doug Slocombe
Estimated Sales: $300,000-500,000
Number Employees: 1-4

11778 **Sambol Meat Company**
Po Box 13376ive Dr
Overland Park, KS 66282 913-334-8404
Processor of meat products
Owner: Don Sambol
CEO: Bill Kolich
Marketing Manager: Mark Fishman
Estimated Sales: $ .5 - 1 million
Number Employees: 1-4
Type of Packaging: Consumer
Brands:
Sambol

11779 **Samjin America**
2465 Fruitland Ave
Vernon, CA 90058-2139 213-622-5111
Fax: 213-622-5285 hanmi@wcis.com
General groceries
President: Choong Kang
Estimated Sales: $ 30-50 Million
Number Employees: 20-49

11780 **Sampac Enterprises**
551 Railroad Ave
South San Francisco, CA 94080 650-876-0808
Fax: 650-876-0338 sales@sampacent.com
www.sampacent.com
Processor, exporter and importer of teas; wholesaler/distributor of herbs, teas, honey, bee pollen, etc
Director: Sammy Ma
Estimated Sales: $2300000
Number Employees: 10-19
Sq. footage: 20000
Type of Packaging: Private Label, Bulk

11781 **Sampco**
651 W Washington Blvd Ste 300
Chicago, IL 60661 312-612-5600
Fax: 312-346-8302 800-767-1689
info@sampcoinc.com www.sampcoinc.com
Cooked beef products
President: David Morrison
CEO: Dave Morrison
Vice President: Verna Macintosh
VP Industrial Sales: Rod McNally
Estimated Sales: $ 5-10 Million
Number Employees: 20-49
Type of Packaging: Private Label
Brands:
Classico
Sampco

11782 **Sams Food Group**
7461 S Sayre Ave
Chicago, IL 60638 708-563-0870
Fax: 708-563-0789 800-852-0283
office@samsfoods.com
www.orringtonfarms.com
Manufacturers soup bases, gravy and sauce mixes, seasonings and rubs, and dessert mixes for retail, foodservice and industrial markets.
President: Alan Levin
Estimated Sales: $ 2.5-5 Million
Number Employees: 10-19
Type of Packaging: Consumer, Food Service, Bulk
Brands:
Orrington Farms

11783 **Sams-Leon Mexican Supplies**
5014 S 20th St
Omaha, NE 68107-2925 402-733-3809
Processor of tortillas, taco shells and hot sauce
Owner: David Murillo
Estimated Sales: Less than $500,000
Number Employees: 1-4
Type of Packaging: Food Service

11784 **San Andreas Brewing Company**
737 San Benito St
Hollister, CA 95023
Fax: 831-637-6170 www.san-andreas-brewing.com
Beer
President/Brand Manager: Bill Millar
Estimated Sales: Less than $500,000
Number Employees: 5-9
Brands:
Apricot Ale
Cranberry Ale
Earthquake Pale
Oktoberquake
Seismic Ale
Survivor Stout
Woodruff Ale

11785 **San Angelo Packing**
P.O.Box 1469
San Angelo, TX 76902 325-653-6951
Fax: 325-658-7272
Packer of beef; slaughtering services available.
General Manager: Jarrod Stokes
Estimated Sales: Below $ 5 Million
Number Employees: 250-499

11786 **San Anselmo's Cookies &Biscotti**
PO Box 2822
San Anselmo, CA 94979-2822 415-492-1220
Fax: 415-492-1282 800-229-1249
info@sacookies.com www.sacookies.com
Cookies and biscotti
Co-Owner: Jane Cloth Richman
Co-Owner/VP Marketing: Jane Cloth-Richman
Estimated Sales: Below $ 5 Million
Number Employees: 20
Brands:
San Anselmo's
San Anselmo's

11787 **San Antonio Packing Company**
1922 S Laredo St
San Antonio, TX 78207 210-224-5441
Fax: 210-224-6664
Processor of meats including beef, lamb and pork
President: Santos Reyes
Estimated Sales: $7.4 Million
Number Employees: 50
Sq. footage: 30000

11788 **San Antonio Winery**
737 Lamar Street
Los Angeles, CA 90031 323-223-1401
Fax: 323-221-7261 800-626-7722
winery@sanantoniowinery.com
www.sanantoniowinery.com
Wines
Owner/Manager: Anthony Riboli
President/VP: Santo Riboli
Owner/President/Marketing Director: Steve Riboli
Sales Manager: Rick Rechetnick
HR & Finance Director/Purchasing Agent: Tony Tse
Estimated Sales: $12700000
Number Employees: 150
Sq. footage: 310000
Type of Packaging: Consumer, Food Service
Brands:
BODEGA DE SAN ANTONIO SANGRIA
KINDERWOOD
LA QUINTA
MADDALENA
OPAQUE
RIOBLI FAMILY WINE ESTATES
SAN ANTONIO CALIFORNIA CHAMPAGNE
SAN ANTONIO DESSERT
SAN ANTONIO SACRAMENTAL
SAN ANTONIO SPECIALTY
SAN ANTONIO WINERY
SAN SIMEON
STELLA ROSA MOSCATO D'ASTI
WINDSTREAM WINDBREAK

11789 **San Benito Foods**
P.O.Box 100
Hollister, CA 95024 831-637-4434
Fax: 831-637-7890
Processor of tomato products including ketchup, paste, sauce, stewed and cooked
President: Steve Arnoldy
CEO/CFO: William Scott
VP Sales/Marketing: Rick Leinenbach
Sales Manager: Bob Stevens
Operations Manager/Tech Services: Steve Arnoldy
Production Manager: Chuck Risner
Plant Manager: Mike Mullin
Estimated Sales: $ 20 - 50 Million
Number Employees: 100-249
Parent Co: Northwest Packing
Type of Packaging: Consumer, Food Service, Private Label, Bulk
Brands:
San Benito

11790 **San Benito Foods**
PO Box 30
Vancouver, WA 98666-0030 800-453-7832
Fax: 360-696-3411 www.seedquest.com
Processor and exporter of canned cherries, plums, pears, tomatoes and fruit juice concentrates including pear and apple
President: L Neil Jones
VP Sales/Marketing: James Leinenbach
Number Employees: 250-499
Sq. footage: 60000
Type of Packaging: Food Service, Bulk
Brands:
Oregon Trail
San Benito

11791 **San Diego Soy Dairy**
1330 Hill St Ste B
El Cajon, CA 92020 619-447-8638
Fax: 619-447-2068 soydairy@aol.com
www.sandiegosoydairy.com
Processor of soy products including milk, tofu, salads and salad dressings; also, herbal teas
Owner: Luke Yam
CEO: Luke Yam
Estimated Sales: $500,000-$1 Million
Number Employees: 5-9
Sq. footage: 3300

Type of Packaging: Consumer, Food Service
Brands:
San Diego Soy Dairy
Waterfall

11792 **San Dominique Winery**
P.O.Box 2089
Camp Verde, AZ 86322 480-945-8583
www.garlicparadise.com
Wines
President: William Staltari
Estimated Sales: Less than $500,000
Number Employees: 1-4
Brands:
San Dominique

11793 **San Fernando Creamery Farmdale Creamery**
1049 W Base Line St
San Bernardino, CA 92411-2310 909-889-3002
Fax: 909-888-2541 shofferber@linkline.com
www.farmdale.net
Processor of dairy products including sour cream, sour cream dressing, buttermilk, cheese, whey, cream and butter
Owner: Nick Sibilio
Manager: Michael Shotts
Estimated Sales: $ 50 - 100 Million
Number Employees: 50-99
Parent Co: Farmdale
Type of Packaging: Consumer, Food Service, Private Label, Bulk

11794 **San Francisco Bay Coffee Company**
1731 Aviation Blvd
Lincoln, CA 95648 510-638-1300
Fax: 510-632-0839 800-829-1300
www.rogersfamilyco.com
Processor of coffee including ground, beans, decaffeinated and flavored; also, aromatic, herbal and flavored teas. Offer complete private label whole bean coffee programs
President: Jon B Rogers
VP Sales: Jim Rogers
Co-Founder: Barbara Rogers
Purchasing Manager: Tom Gerber
Estimated Sales: $ 20-50 Million
Number Employees: 100-249
Sq. footage: 82000
Parent Co: JBR Gourmet Foods
Type of Packaging: Consumer, Food Service, Private Label, Bulk
Brands:
East India Coffee & Tea Co.
Pastarific Pasta Co.
San Francisco Coffee

11795 **San Francisco Bread Company**
1365 N 10th St
San Jose, CA 95112-2804 408-298-6914
Fax: 408-298-6950 www.specialtybaking.com
Bread
President: Antonio Escobar
Treasurer: Mark Murillo
Estimated Sales: $ 20 - 50 Million
Number Employees: 70
Type of Packaging: Private Label

11796 **San Francisco Brewing Company**
155 Columbus Ave
San Francisco, CA 94133
Fax: 415-434-2433 ask@sfbrewing.com
www.sfbrewing.com
Processor of beer including ale and lager
Owner: Allan Paul
Brewmaster: Allan Paul
Estimated Sales: $ 10 - 20 Million
Number Employees: 20-49

11797 **San Francisco Fine Bakery**
2537 Middlefield Rd
Redwood City, CA 94063 650-369-8573
Fax: 650-369-8382 order@sffinebakery.com
www.sffinebakery.com
Bakery products
President: Clifford Chen
Estimated Sales: Below $ 5 Million
Number Employees: 20-49
Brands:
San Francisco Fine Bakery

11798 **San Francisco French Bread**
580 Julie Ann Way
Oakland, CA 94621 510-729-6232
sourdoughbread@interstatebrands.com
www.sourdoughbread.com
Processor and exporter of sourdough bread, rolls and croutons
President: Tom Hofmeister
National Sales Manager: Terry McDonough
Number Employees: 5-9
Parent Co: IBC
Type of Packaging: Consumer, Food Service

11799 **(HQ)San Francisco Herb & Natural Food Company**
47444 Kato Rd
Fremont, CA 94538-7319 510-770-1215
Fax: 510-770-9021 800-227-2830
customerservice@herbspicetea.com
www.herbspicetea.com
The ultimate source for organic and conventional bulk herbs, spices, teas, potpourri, capsules, extract oils and accessories. Top quality, widest selection and lowest prices since 1969.
Chief Operating Officer: Fahimeh Niroomand
VP: Kristi Meltzer
Estimated Sales: $5496793
Sq. footage: 160000
Type of Packaging: Private Label, Bulk
Other Locations:
San Francisco Herb & Natural
Culver OR
Brands:
Bright Eye
Nature's Herb Company
Oregon Peppermint
Relaxing Tea
Sausalito Spice
Summer Field Spices

11800 **San Francisco Popcorn Works**
1028 Revere Ave
San Francisco, CA 94124 415-822-4744
Fax: 415-822-3376 800-777-2676
info@sfpopcornworks.com
www.sfpopcornworks.com
Popcorn
President: Joan Adler
Estimated Sales: Below $ 5 Million
Number Employees: 10
Sq. footage: 2
Type of Packaging: Private Label
Brands:
Naturfood
San Francisco Popcorn
Somewhat Sinful

11801 **San Francisco Sausage Company**
P.O.Box 426
S San Francisco, CA 94083-0426 650-583-4993
Fax: 650-583-6376 www.rightfoods.com
Columbus salami sausages and meat products
Owner: Mike Vinnicombe
CFO: Pete Barale
Quality Control: Edgard Arriolioga
Plant Manager: Joe Rosa
Estimated Sales: $ 10-24.9 Million
Number Employees: 50-99
Brands:
San Francisco

11802 **San Francisco Urban Naturals**
47444 Kato Rd
Fremont, CA 94538-7319 510-770-1215
Fax: 510-770-9021
customerservice@herbspicetea.com
www.herbspicetea.com
Tea and herbs
President: Barry Meltzer
CEO: Saye Niroomand
Estimated Sales: $ 5-10 Million
Number Employees: 50-99
Brands:
San Francisco Herbs

11803 **San Gennaro Foods**
19255 80th Ave S
Kent, WA 98032 206-723-5089
Fax: 206-721-5005 800-462-1916
mail@polenta.net www.polenta.net
Pre cooked polenta. Also mayonnaise, barbeque sauces and salad dressings under Northwest Gourmet brand.
President: Jerry Mascio
Estimated Sales: $ 1-2.5 Million
Number Employees: 5-9
Type of Packaging: Private Label
Brands:
NORTHWEST GOURMET
SAN GENNARO

11804 **San Joaquin Figs**
3564 N Hazel Ave
Fresno, 93 93722-4912 559-224-4963
Fax: 559-224-4926 rondixon@nutrafig.com
www.nutrafig.com
Processor of figs including dried, diced and paste; also, fig juice concentrate
President: Keith Jura
Estimated Sales: $5.6 Million
Number Employees: 50
Brands:
California Classic
San Joaquin Supreme
The Nutra Fig

11805 **San Jose Coffee Company**
1500 Cunningham Ave
San Jose, CA 95122-2399 408-272-3311
Fax: 408-272-7118
Coffee
Manager: Thomasa Aplha
Estimated Sales: $690,000
Number Employees: 5-9

11806 **San Juan Coffee RoastingCompany**
P.O.Box 2998
Friday Harbor, WA 98250 360-378-4443
Fax: 360-378-6658 800-858-4276
www.rockisland.com/~sjcoffee
Fresh coffee roasted daily
President: Irene Herring
Operations Manager: Steve Herring
Estimated Sales: $ 5-10 Million
Number Employees: 5-9

11807 **San Luis Sourdough**
3877 Long St
San Luis Obispo, CA 93401 805-782-8933
Fax: 805-543-1279 800-266-7687
info@slodough.com www.slodough.com
Sourdough bread
Co-Owner: Dave West
Co-Owner: Charlie West
Controller: Ken Fontes
Marketing Manager: Craig McLaughlin
Plant Manager: Carol Rounsaville
Estimated Sales: $ 10-20 Million
Number Employees: 5-9
Brands:
San Luis Sourdough

11808 **San Marco Coffee,Inc.**
3120 Latrobe Dr # 280
Charlotte, NC 28211-2186 704-366-0533
Fax: 704-366-0534 800-715-9298
www.sanmarcocoffee.com
Processor of American coffee, espresso, cappucinno; supplier of coffee machines
Owner: Marc Decaria
Number Employees: 5-9
Type of Packaging: Consumer, Food Service, Private Label
Brands:
San Giorgio

11809 **San Marzano Foods**
218 37th Avenue N
Nashville, TN 37209-4865 615-385-4398
Processor of dried tomatoes and Turkish and Greek olives; manufacturer of olive oil soap; importer of dried fruits, fruit pulp and puree
President: Ahmet Ozari
VP: B Waltrip
Number Employees: 5-9
Sq. footage: 10000

11810 **San Saba Pecan**
2803 W Wallace St
San Saba, TX 76877 325-372-5727
Fax: 325-372-5171 800-683-2101
sherri@sansabapecan.com
www.sansabapecan.com
Processor and exporter of pecans
President: Ranza Adams
Vice President: Buddy Adams

Estimated Sales: $5-10 Million
Number Employees: 50-99
Sq. footage: 50000
Type of Packaging: Consumer, Bulk

11811 **San-Ei Gen FFI**
630 5th Ave, Suite 1440
New York, NY 10111-0100 212-315-7850
Fax: 212-974-2540 contact@saneigen.com
www.saneigen.com
Processor, importer and exporter of natural colors, flavors and soy dietary fiber
President: Takashige Shimizu
Estimated Sales: $5 Million
Number Employees: 1-4
Sq. footage: 4400
Parent Co: San-El Gen FFI
Type of Packaging: Bulk

11812 **San-J International**
2880 Sprouse Dr
Richmond, VA 23231 804-226-8333
Fax: 804-226-8383 800-446-5500
info@san-j.com www.san-j.com
tamari and shoyu, asian cooking sauces, salad dressing, soups and rice crackers.
President/Owner: Takashi Sato
Finance Director: Nancy Boswell
Marketing Manager: Jennifer Stoltz
Manufacturing/Distribution Director: Masaki Nakagawa
Number Employees: 40

11813 **San-J International, Inc**
2880 Sprouse Dr
Richmond, VA 23231 804-226-8333
Fax: 804-226-8383 800-446-5500
info@san-j.com www.san-j.com
Tamari soy sauce and Asian-inspired products including cooking sauces, salad dressings, soups and brown rice crackers.
President: Takashi Sato
Finance Director: Nancy Boswell
Marketing Manager: Jennifer Stoltz
Sales Director: Karen Sonderby
Manufacturing/Distribution Director: Masaki Nakagawa
Estimated Sales: $5300000
Number Employees: 31
Number of Brands: 1
Number of Products: 22
Sq. footage: 44000
Parent Co: San Jirushi Corporation
Type of Packaging: Consumer, Food Service, Bulk
Brands:
SAN-J

11814 **Sana Foods**
PO Box 10818
Bainbridge Island, WA 98110-0818 206-842-4741
Food Brokers
President: Tina Nelson
VP: Paul Lang
Sales Manager: Bill Poulos
Brands:
Sana Foods
Sana Wines

11815 **Sanarak Paper & PopcornSupplies**
456 Hinman Ave
Buffalo, NY 14216 716-874-5662
Fax: 716-874-4737
Popcorn
President: Jim Rogers
Estimated Sales: $500,000-$1 Million
Number Employees: 5-9

11816 **Sanborn Sourdough Bakery**
5230 S Valley View Blvd Ste A
Las Vegas, NV 89118 702-795-1030
Fax: 702-795-8518
Bread and bakery products
President: Donald Sanborn
CFO: Brenda Portela
General Manager: Joe Lazi
Operations Manager: John Klessia
Estimated Sales: $ 20-50 Million
Number Employees: 50-99
Brands:
Sanborn Sourdough Bakery

11817 **Sanchez Distributors**
9711 Mid Walk Dr
San Antonio, TX 78230-4075 210-341-1682
Fax: 210-341-7470
asanchez@vineyardbrands.com
Ethnic foods.
President: Roberto Sanchez
Sales Manager: Fernando Sanchez
Estimated Sales: $ 5-10 Million
Number Employees: 5-9

11818 **Sand Castle Winery**
P.O.Box 177
Erwinna, PA 18920 610-294-9181
Fax: 610-294-9174 800-722-9463
info@sandcastlewinery.com
www.sandcastlewinery.com
Wines
President: Paul Maxian
CEO: Joseph Maxian
Marketing/Sales Manager: Stephanie Driver
Estimated Sales: $ 5-10 Million
Number Employees: 10-19
Type of Packaging: Private Label
Brands:
Johannisberg Riesling
Sand Castle Winery

11819 **Sand Hill Berries**
304 Deerfield Rd
Mt Pleasant, PA 15666 724-547-4760
Fax: 724-547-7319 shberries@aol.com
www.sandhillberries.com
Processor of raspberries, blackberries, gooseberries, currants, jostaberries, jams, jellies, vinaigrettes, fruit sauce and vinegar
Owner: Susan Lynn
Co-Partner: Susan Lynn
Estimated Sales: $315000
Number Employees: 1-4
Type of Packaging: Consumer, Private Label

11820 **Sand Springs Springwater**
160 Sand Springs Rd
Williamstown, MA 01267 413-458-8281
Spring waters
Owner: Edward Morin
Estimated Sales: $ 2.5-5 Million
Number Employees: 5-9

11821 **Sandbar Trading Corporation**
408 S Pierce Avenue
Louisville, CO 80027-3018 303-499-7480
Fax: 303-527-1727
Herbs and spices
President: Barry Cowper
Manager: Dave Halford
Brands:
Sandbar Trading

11822 **Sandco International**
151 Union Chapel Rd
Northport, AL 35473 205-339-0145
Fax: 205-339-8222 800-382-2075
sandco@uronramp.net www.sanco.net
Processor and exporter of vitamins and sports supplements, antiaging
President: Linda Sandlin
Research & Development: Richard Sandlin
Marketing: Linda Madison
Purchasing Manager: Linda Wells
Estimated Sales: $1,100,000
Number Employees: 5-9
Sq. footage: 20000
Type of Packaging: Consumer, Private Label, Bulk

11823 **Sanders Candy**
23770 Hall Rd
Clinton Twp, MI 48036-1275 586-468-4300
Fax: 586-478-4795 800-852-2253
info@sanders-hotfudge.com
www.sanderscandy.com
Cookies, bread & rolls, danishes, cakes and doughnuts
President/CEO: Judith Brock
CFO: Joseph Talmage
Marketing Specialist: Susan Leso
VP Sales/Marketing: John McGuckin
Plant Manager: Mike Koch
Estimated Sales: $500,000-$1 Million
Number Employees: 1-4
Parent Co: Country Home Bakers
Type of Packaging: Private Label
Brands:
Sanders Brand Candy

11824 **(HQ)Sanderson Farms**
127 Flynt Road
PO Box 988
Laurel, MS 39441-0988 601-649-4030
Fax: 601-426-1461 800-844-4030
info@sandersonfarms.com
www.sandersonfarms.com
Manufacturer and distributor of fresh and frozen poultry
President/COO: Lampkin Butts
Chairman/CEO: Joseph Sanderson Jr.
CFO/Treasurer: D Michael Cockrell
Director of Development: Bob Billingsley
Director of Marketing: Bill Sanderson
Director of Production: Bud West
Estimated Sales: $1.93Billion
Number Employees: 9,859
Type of Packaging: Consumer, Food Service, Private Label, Bulk
Other Locations:
Sanderson Farms Production
Bryan TX
Collins MS
Hammond LA
Hazlehurst MS
Laurel MS
McComb MS
Moultrie GA
Waco TX
Brands:
Chef-To-Chef
Covington Farms
Happy Home
Miss Goldy Chicken
NPF
Sanderson Farms
Spring Farms

11825 **Sanderson Farms**
P.O.Box 765
Hazlehurst, MS 39083 601-894-3725
Fax: 601-425-0714 www.sanderson.com
Manufacturer of poultry
Personnel Director: Danny Bullock Jr
Manager: Larry Lampkin
Plant Manager: David Brown
Estimated Sales: $395 Million
Number Employees: 300
Parent Co: Sanderson Farms
Type of Packaging: Consumer, Food Service

11826 **Sanderson Farms**
701 Capitol Pkwy
Bryan, TX 77807 979-778-5730
www.sandersonfarms.com
Processor of frozen foods including chicken, stew and seafood
Manager: Karl King
Plant Manager: Carrie Carter
Estimated Sales: $5 - 10 Million
Number Employees: 1,000
Parent Co: Sanderson Farms
Type of Packaging: Consumer, Food Service, Private Label

11827 **Sanderson Farms**
3098 Highway 49
Collins, MS 39428 601-765-0430
Fax: 601-765-1682 www.sandersonfarms.com
Manufacturer of Poultry
Chairman/CEO: Joe Sanderson Jr
President/COO: Lampkin Butts
Plant Manager: Dan Nicovich
Estimated Sales: $100+ Million
Number Employees: 1,000-4,999
Type of Packaging: Consumer, Bulk

11828 **Sanderson Farms**
Po Box 988
Laurel, MS 39441-0988 601-426-1454
Fax: 601-425-0704 www.sandersonfarms.com
Produces, processes, markets and distributes fresh and frozen chicken products as well as other processed and prepared food items, including frozen entrees such as chicken and dumplings, lasagna, seafood gumbo, shrimp creole and corndogs.
President/COO: Lampkin Butts
Chairman/CEO: Joe Sanderson Jr
CFO/Treasurer: D M Cockrell
CEO: Joe F Sanderson Jr

Estimated Sales: $ 50-100 Million
Number Employees: 5,000-9,999
Parent Co: Sanderson Farms

11829 Sanderson Farms
13111 Highway 190 W
Hammond, LA 70401 985-345-3565
www.sanderson.com
Manufacturer of poultry
Sales Manager: Phil Buhler
Plant Manager: David Brown
Estimated Sales: $395 Million
Number Employees: 900
Parent Co: Sanderson Farms
Type of Packaging: Consumer, Food Service

11830 Sanderson Farms
700 Ga Highway 133 S
Moultrie, GA 31788 229-891-4061
www.sanderson.com
Manufacturer of poultry
Manager: Jeff Black
Plant Manager: David Brown
Estimated Sales: $395 Million
Number Employees: 1,400
Parent Co: Sanderson Farms
Type of Packaging: Consumer, Food Service

11831 Sanderson Farms
301 Aviation Pkwy
Waco, TX 76705 254-412-3800
www.sanderson.com
Manufacturer of poultry
Manager: Jeff Black
Plant Manager: David Brown
Estimated Sales: $395 Million
Number Employees: 1,400
Parent Co: Sanderson Farms
Type of Packaging: Consumer, Food Service

11832 Sandia Shadows Vineyard& Winery
8740 4th Street NW
PO Box 92675
Albuquerque, NM 87199-2675 505-856-1006
Fax: 505-858-0859 sandiawine@aol.com
www.sandiawines.com
Wine
Owner: Phillippe Littot
Estimated Sales: Less than $500,000
Number Employees: 1-4
Brands:
Sandia Shadows Vineyard & Wine

11833 Sandors Bakeries
2245 W Flagler St
Miami, FL 33135-1522 305-642-8484
Fax: 305-643-9358
Breads and other bakery products, except cookies and crackers.
President: Orlando Sanchez
Estimated Sales: $237,263
Number Employees: 5-9

11834 Sandra L. Lagrotte
2952 N Webster Ave
Indianapolis, IN 46219-1015 317-549-0073
Fax: 317-549-0177
Manager: Dick Sawyers
Estimated Sales: $ 20 - 50 Million
Number Employees: 10-19

11835 Sandridge Food Corporation
133 Commerce Dr
Medina, OH 44256
Fax: 330-722-3998 800-627-2523
www.sandridge.com
Refrigerated deli salads, sides, soups, sauces, and specialty dishes.
President: William Frantz
CEO: Mark Sandridge
VP Finance: Rick Sisko
VP: Elizabeth Musico
Sr Director, Food Safety & Quality: Joel Riegelmayer
VP Sales/Marketing: John Becker
Human Resources Manager: Mark Dolan
Operations Director: Barry Pioske
Purchasing Manager: Rich Graziosi
Estimated Sales: $ 20 - 50 Million
Number Employees: 225
Sq. footage: 130000
Type of Packaging: Consumer, Food Service, Private Label, Bulk
Brands:
Sandridge Salads Set Free

11836 Sands African Imports
9 Dey St
Newark, NJ 07103-3609 973-824-5500
Fax: 973-824-5502 info.sand@aol.com
Oils, seeds
President: Simon Belfer
Marketing Director: Michael Sandaua
Estimated Sales: $ 1-2.5 Million appx.
Number Employees: 1-4
Type of Packaging: Private Label
Brands:
Sands African

11837 Sandstone Winery
4505 220th Trl
Amana, IA 52203 319-622-3081
Homemade wine
President: Elsie Mattes
Vice President: Thomas Mattes
Estimated Sales: $550,000
Number Employees: 1-4
Type of Packaging: Consumer, Food Service
Brands:
Sandstone Winery

11838 Sandt's Honey Company
714 Wagener Ln
Easton, PA 18040-8253 610-252-6511
Fax: 610-252-9069 800-935-3960
Processor and packer of all-natural and kosher certified honey
President: Lee Sandt
Vice President: Linda Sandt
Estimated Sales: $1234498
Number Employees: 1-4
Type of Packaging: Consumer, Food Service, Private Label, Bulk
Brands:
Sandt's

11839 Sanford Milling Company
P.O.Box 290
Henderson, NC 27536 252-438-4526
Fax: 252-492-3014
Processor of flour
President: Scott Hartness
Estimated Sales: $ 10 - 20 Million
Number Employees: 10-19
Type of Packaging: Food Service, Private Label, Bulk
Brands:
Hartness Choice
Packers Blend
Snow Flake

11840 Sanford Winery
5010 Santa Rosa Road
Lompoc, CA 93436 805-688-3300
Fax: 805-688-7381 800-426-9463
info@sanfordwinery.com
http://www.sanfordwinery.com
Wines
Partner: Richard Sanford
CFO: Stuart Fries
Marketing Manager: Tom Prendiville
Operations: Sharon Blewis
Purchasing Manager: Sharon Blewis
Estimated Sales: Below $ 5 Million
Number Employees: 20
Type of Packaging: Private Label
Brands:
Sanford

11841 Sangean Enterprises
4627 Illinois Avenue
Louisville, KY 40213-1956 502-459-6556
Fax: 502-459-4183
Owner: Patrik Hsu

11842 Sangudo Custom Meat Packers
PO Box 416
Sangudo, AB T0E 2A0
Canada 780-785-3353
Fax: 780-785-3111 888-785-3353
Processor of frozen beef and pork, pepperoni, bacon and sausage
President/CEO: Ivan Adams
Estimated Sales: A
Number Employees: 1-4

11843 Sani Dairy
PO Box 160
Fourth Ave & 11th St
Altoona, PA 16603 814-943-3077
Fax: 814-533-2536
Milk, dairy products-noncheese

11844 Sani-Dairy
200 Mitchell Ave
Punxsutawney, PA 15767 814-938-7200
Fax: 814-533-2536
Dairy products
President: Wilfred Young
VP/General Manager: Joe Martin
Director Marketing/Sales: Paul Bilzor
Estimated Sales: Less Than $500,000
Number Employees: 2
Brands:
Mike's Original

11845 Sanitary Bakery
121 E Broadway
Little Falls, MN 56345-3038 320-632-6388
Fax: 320-632-2740
http://www.sanitarybakery.com/
Cookies
Owner: Peter Kamrowski
Estimated Sales: Under $500,000
Number Employees: 20-49

11846 Sanitary Tortilla Manufacturing Company
623 Urban Loop
San Antonio, TX 78204-3117 210-226-9209
Fax: 210-226-9424
Manufacturer of tortillas and other corn products
Owner: Jesus Villarreal
Estimated Sales: $8 Million
Number Employees: 20-49
Sq. footage: 6000
Type of Packaging: Food Service

11847 Santa Barbara Olive Company
12477 Calle Real
Santa Barbara, CA 93117 805-562-1456
Fax: 805-562-1464 800-624-4896
info@sbolive.com www.sbolive.com
Gourmet olives, extra virgin olive oils, sauces, vegetables, condiments, salsas
President: Craig Makela
Vice President: Cindy Makela
Estimated Sales: $10000000
Number Employees: 17
Sq. footage: 7000
Type of Packaging: Consumer, Food Service, Private Label, Bulk

11848 Santa Barbara PistachioCompany
P.O.Box 21957
Santa Barbara, CA 93121-1957 805-962-5600
Fax: 661-766-2436 800-896-1044
info@sbpistachios.com
www.santabarbarapistachios.com
Grower and packager of natural flavored pistachios
President/Owner: Gene Zannon
CEO: Gail Zannon
VP Marketing: Josh Zannon
VP Production: Tristan Zannon
Estimated Sales: Less than $500,000
Number Employees: 1-4
Sq. footage: 4000
Type of Packaging: Consumer, Food Service, Private Label, Bulk
Brands:
Santa Barbara Pistachio

11849 Santa Barbara Roasting Company
321 Motor Way
Santa Barbara, CA 93101 805-962-0320
Fax: 805-962-2590 800-321-5282
help@sbroco.com www.sbroco.com
Coffee
President: Corey Russell
Executive Director: Jami Dunlop
Director Operations: Matthew Moore
Estimated Sales: Below $ 5 Million
Number Employees: 20-49
Type of Packaging: Private Label
Brands:
Santa Barbara

11850 **Santa Barbara Salsa**
649 Benet Rd
Oceanside, CA 92058-1208 760-757-2622
Fax: 760-721-2600 800-748-5523
info@sbsalsa.com www.sbsalsa.com
Salsa and sauces
President: Doug Pearson
Estimated Sales: $ 1-2.5 Million
Number Employees: 10-19
Parent Co: California Creative Foods
Type of Packaging: Consumer, Bulk
Brands:
Chacies®
Con Gusto®
San Diego Salsa™
Santa Barbara Salsa™
Tio Tio®

11851 **Santa Barbara Salsa/California Creative**
649 Benet Rd
Oceanside, CA 92058-1208 760-757-2622
Fax: 760-721-2600 800-748-5523
info@sbsalsa.com www.sbsalsa.com
Manufacturer of salsa Flavors: artichoke, key lime, garlic; peach; roasted garlic; mango peach; roasted chili; black bean; corn; cheese and salsa; hot pepper and marinades
President: Doug Pearson
Estimated Sales: $300,000-500,000
Number Employees: 1-4
Brands:
CHACHIES
CONGUSTO
SAN DIEGO SALSA
SANTA BARBARA SALSA
TIO TIO

11852 **Santa Barbara Winery**
202 Anacapa St
Santa Barbara, CA 93101 805-963-3633
Fax: 805-962-4981 wine@sbwinery.com
www.sbwinery.com
Wines
Owner: Pierre Lafond
Owner: Tierre Iafond
CFO: Marty-Pooe Winnen
CEO: Pierre Lafond
R & D: Jennifer Fredericks
Marketing Manager: Craig Addis
Estimated Sales: Below $ 5 Million
Number Employees: 20-49
Brands:
Lafond
Santa Barbara Winery

11853 **Santa Clara Nut Company**
1590 Little Orchard St
San Jose, CA 95110 408-298-2425
Fax: 408-298-0101 santaclaranut@aol.com
Manufacturer and exporter of shelled and in-shell walnuts
Owner/President: Jim Pusateri
VP: Salvatore Pusateri
Sales Director: Jim Pusateri
Estimated Sales: $15 Million
Number Employees: 5-9
Number of Brands: 1
Number of Products: 1
Sq. footage: 50000
Type of Packaging: Consumer, Food Service, Bulk
Brands:
Santa Clara

11854 **Santa Cruz Brewing Company**
150 Dubois St Ste E
Santa Cruz, CA 95060 831-425-1182
Fax: 831-429-8915
Processor of seasonal beer and lager
President: Gerry Turgeon
Number Employees: 20-49
Type of Packaging: Consumer, Food Service
Brands:
Pacific
Santa Cruz

11855 **Santa Cruz Chili & SpiceCompany**
P.O.Box 177
Tumacacori, AZ 85640 520-398-2591
Fax: 520-398-2592 sales@santacruzchili.com
www.santacruzchili.com
Processor of chile paste, powder, sauces and spices
President: Jean Neubauer
Sales Manager: Armida Castro
Estimated Sales: $500000
Number Employees: 1-4
Type of Packaging: Consumer

11856 **Santa Cruz Mountain Vineyard**
P.O.Box 1592
Felton, CA 95018 831-426-6209
Fax: 831-335-4242
info@santacruzmountainvineyard.com
www.scmountainvineyard.com
Wines
Proprietor: Jeff Emery
Estimated Sales: Below $ 5 Million
Number Employees: 5-9
Brands:
Santa Cruz Mountain Vineyard

11857 **Santa Cruz Valley Pecan**
P.O.Box 7
Sahuarita, AZ 85629-0007 520-625-8333
Fax: 520-719-2853 800-533-5269
donpecan@greenvalleypecan.com
www.greenvalleypecan.com
Pecan nuts in multiple sizes, roasted pecans for ice cream
President: Richard Walden
Marketing Director: Bruce Caris
Estimated Sales: $ 3 - 5 Million
Number Employees: 20-49

11858 **Santa Elena Coffee Company**
550 S Fm 1660 # 5
Hutto, TX 78634-4362 512-846-2908
Fax: 512-846-2710
santa_elena_coffee@msn.com
www.canincrad.com
Coffee
Owner: Linda Truong
Vice President: Astrid Bernstorff
Marketing Director: Lissette Bernstorff
Plant Manager: Astrid Bernstorff
Purchasing Manager: Everardo Bernstorff
Number Employees: 5-9
Sq. footage: 3000
Type of Packaging: Private Label
Brands:
Santa-Elena Coffee

11859 **Santa Fe Bite-Size Bakery**
P.O.Box 6530
Albuquerque, NM 87197-6530 505-342-1119
Fax: 505-891-8740 NCandelaria3@aol.com
www.bite-size.com
Bite-size cookies and crackers
Owner: Lucia Deichmann
Estimated Sales: $ 10 - 20 Million
Number Employees: 10-19
Brands:
Bite-Size Bakery
Chocolate Cheesecake Cookies
Chunky Peanut Butter Cookies
Oatmeal Raisin Cookies
Old Fashion Ginger Snap Cookies
Peppery Wine Bisquit

11860 **Santa Fe Bite-Size Bakery**
PO Box 1549
Moriarty, NM 87035-1549 505-891-8765
Fax: 505-891-8740 800-342-1119
www.bite-size.com
Bite-size cookies and crackers, pinon nut chocolate chip, pistatchio lemon verde, cordoba coffee, bizcochitos, fiesta wedding and green chile cheddar cheese
president: Santa Fe
Marketing Director: Carolyn Fairman
Estimated Sales: $ 1-2.5 Million
Number Employees: '5-9
Brands:
Bite-Size

11861 **Santa Fe Brewing**
35 Fire Place
Santa Fe, NM 87508 505-424-3333
Fax: 505-474-5573 info@santafebrewing.com
www.santafebrewing.com
Brewing of beer
Owner: David Forester
Estimated Sales: $275,000
Number Employees: 1-4
Brands:
Santa Fe Brewing

11862 **Santa Fe Seasons**
34 Uss Thresher Ln
Belen, NM 87002 505-988-1515
Fax: 505-988-1300 800-264-5535
www.santafeseasons.com
Salsa and seasonings
President: Greg Deneen
Vice President: Edith Deneen
Sales Director: Lisa Duck
Estimated Sales: Below $ 5 Million
Number Employees: 20
Brands:
De Santa Fe
Santa Fe Seasons

11863 **Santa Fe Vineyards**
18348 Us 84/285
Espanola, NM 87532 505-753-8100
Fax: 505-753-8100
Wines
Manager: Dan Doughtery
Estimated Sales: $500,000
Number Employees: 1-4
Brands:
Santa Fe Vineyards

11864 **Santa Margarita Vineyard & Winery**
33490 Madera De Playa
Temecula, CA 92592-9228 909-676-4431
Wines
President: Barrett Bird
Director: Margaret Bird
Estimated Sales: $110,000
Number Employees: 1
Type of Packaging: Private Label

11865 **Santa Maria Foods**
10 Armthorpe Rd
Branpton, ON L6T 5M4 905-790-1991
Fax: 416-675-7466
prosciutto and mortadella, salami and cured meats, hams and specialty meats
President/Owner: Eddie Zilli
Director: Frederick Jaques
CFO: Andrew Linley
VP Operations: Gordon Maxwell

11866 **Santanna Banana Company**
P.O.Box 1403
Harrisburg, PA 17105 717-238-8321
Fax: 717-238-4480
Manufacturer of Bananas
President: Ray Santanna
VP: Richard Santanna
Estimated Sales: $53 Million
Number Employees: 20-49

11867 **Santee Dairies**
17851 Railroad St
City of Industry, CA 91748-1118 626-923-3000
Fax: 626-923-3038 www.hartlandfarms.com
Processor of dairy products including butter, cottage cheese, whipped cream, milk, yogurt, sour cream, eggnog, ice cream, cream cheese and fruit juices
President: Paul Bikowitz
Purchasing Manager: Greg Hackworth
Estimated Sales: $ 75-100 Million
Number Employees: 10,000+

11868 **Santini Foods**
16505 Worthley Dr
San Lorenzo, CA 94580 510-317-8888
Fax: 510-317-8343 800-835-6888
www.santinifoods.com
Processor of sweetened condensed milk, blended oils and flavored and natural syrups; importer of olive oil, wine and pasta; custom formulator of fruit and flavored drink mixes
President: Bruce Liu
CFO: Tyler Abbott
Vice President: Christopher Quie
Quality Control: Hal Burgan
Operations: Roger Tan
Estimated Sales: $11 Million
Number Employees: 66
Sq. footage: 200000
Type of Packaging: Consumer, Food Service, Private Label, Bulk
Brands:
Dairy Hills

La Vava Blanca
Lotus Bloom

11869 **Sanwa Foods**
16505 Worthley Dr
San Lorenzo, CA 94580-1811 510-317-8888
Fax: 510-317-8343 www.santinifoods.com
Seafoods
President: Bruce Liu
VP: Christopher Quie
Director Marketing: Frank Ferraris
Director of Operations: Franca Chung
Estimated Sales: $11 Million
Number Employees: 66

11870 **Sapporo**
11 E 44th St Rm 705
New York, NY 10017-61 212-922-9165
Fax: 212-922-9576 800-827-8234
info@sapporousa.com www.sapporousa.com
Processor and importer of beer they also prepare dishes using beer as an ingredient.
President/CEO: Mikio Masawaki
CEO: Seiji Ubukata
CFO: Masashi Minami
Chairman: Munekazu Takenishi
Estimated Sales: $45.0 Million
Number Employees: 20
Sq. footage: 2000
Parent Co: Sapporo
Type of Packaging: Consumer, Food Service

11871 **(HQ)Saputo Foodservice USA**
25 Tristate International Office Center
Suite 250
Lincolnshire, IL 60069-4453 847-267-1100
Fax: 847-267-1110 800-824-3373
stella@stellafoods.com www.saputo.com
Italian and domestic cheese
President/COO: Terry Brockman
EVP Finance: Louis-Philippe Carriere
EVP Administration: Greg Dryer
Estimated Sales: $ 100-500 Million
Number Employees: 2000
Brands:
BLACK CREEK
CHEESE HEADS
DRAGONE
FRIGO
LORRAINE
STELLA
TREASURE CAVE

11872 **Sara Lee**
2110 Chapman Hwy
Knoxville, TN 37920-1904 865-573-1941
Fax: 865-577-3747 www.saralee.com
Processor of baked goods including bread and rolls
CFO: Joseph Noelker
Marketing Manager: Gene Haun
Plant Manager: Mike Wardell
Purchasing Director: Mark Harmon
Estimated Sales: $ .5 - 1 million
Number Employees: 340
Type of Packaging: Consumer, Food Service, Private Label
Other Locations:
Kern's Bakery
London KY

11873 **Sara Lee Coffee & Tea**
1370 Progress Rd
Suffolk, VA 23434 757-538-8083
Fax: 757-215-7447 www.saralee.com
Roasts and packs coffee
CEO: Massino Zanetti
Manager: Chuck Gosstrom
Plant Manager: Buddy McGuire
Number Employees: 200
Brands:
CHASE & SANBORN
CHOCK FULL O'NUTS
HILLS BROS
MJB
SEGAFREDO ESPRESSO

11874 **(HQ)Sara Lee Corporation**
3500 Lacey Road
Downers Grove, IL 60515-5424 630-598-8100
Fax: 630-598-8482 www.saralee.com
Global manufacturer of high quality meats, breads, sweets and baked goods, abd coffees and teas.
Chairman: Jan Bennink
CEO: Marcel M Smits
CFO: Maria Henry
SVP/CFO: Mark Garvey
CEO/North America: CJ Fraleigh
SVP Strategic Planning & Corp Develop: B Thomas Hansson
SVP Global Communications: Jon Harris
Estimated Sales: $13 Billion
Number Employees: 41000
Parent Co: Sara Lee/DE
Type of Packaging: Consumer, Food Service, Private Label, Bulk
Other Locations:
Sara Lee Bakery
Cincinnati OH
Sara Lee Bakery
Decatur GA
Sara Lee Bakery
Orangeburg SC
Brands:
BALL PARK
ENDUST
HANES
JIMMY DEAN
KIWI
L'EGGS
PLAYTEX
SARA LEE BAKERY GROUP
WONDERBRA

11875 **Sara Lee Foodservice**
PO Box 756
Neenah, WI 54957
800-261-4754
www.saraleefoodservice.com
Bakery items, meats and beverages
Parent Co: Sara Lee Corporation
Type of Packaging: Food Service
Brands:
BALL PARK
BISTO
BUTTER NUT
CHEF PIERRE
GALILEO
HILLSHIRE FARMS
JIMMY DEAN
KAY
MARYLAND CLUB
PARADISE
PICKWICK
SARA LEE
STATE FAIR

11876 **Sarabeth's Bakery**
1161 E 156th St
Bronx, NY 10474-6226 718-589-2900
Fax: 718-589-8412 800-773-7378
info@sarabeth.com www.sarabeth.com
Processor of muffins, cakes, cookies, pastries, puddings, pies, croissants, brownies, tarts and frozen blintzes
President: William Levine
Executive VP: Jennifer Firestone
Co-Owner: David Case
Estimated Sales: Below $ 5 Million
Number Employees: 20-49
Sq. footage: 4300
Parent Co: Sarabeth's Kitchen
Type of Packaging: Consumer, Food Service
Other Locations:
Sarabeth's Bakery Ltd.
New York NY
Brands:
Sarabeth's

11877 **Sarabeth's Kitchen**
1161 E 156th St
Bronx, NY 10474 718-589-2900
Fax: 718-589-8412 info@saarabeth.com
www.sarabeth.com
preserves, cakes, cookies
President/Owner: Bill Scotti
Estimated Sales: $1.2 Million
Number Employees: 50

11878 **Sarabeth's Kitchen**
1161 E 156th St
Bronx, NY 10474 718-589-2900
Fax: 718-589-8412 800-773-7378
info@sarabeth.com www.sarabeth.com
Manufacturer of jams, jellies, marmalade, preserves, packages cookies, scone and muffin mixes
President: William Levine
CFO: Jeffrey Shapiro
Co-President: Sarabeth Levine
Marketing Director: Jason Albucker
Production Manager: Manuel Padilla
Estimated Sales: Below $ 5 Million
Number Employees: 10-19
Type of Packaging: Private Label

11879 **Sarah's Vineyard**
4005 Hecker Pass Rd
Gilroy, CA 95020 408-842-4278
Fax: 408-842-3252 sales@sarahsvineyard.com
www.sarahs-vineyard.com
Wines
Owner: Tim Slater
Estimated Sales: $500,000-$1 Million
Number Employees: 1-4
Brands:
SARAH'S VINEYARD

11880 **Sarant International Commodities**
P.O.Box 659
Centereach, NY 11720 631-689-2845
Fax: 631-246-5257 psarant@aol.com
Processor and importer of dehydrated vegetables including tomatoes, celery, carrots and red and green bell peppers
President: Peter Sarant
Co-Secretary: Pamela Sarant
Number Employees: 1-4
Type of Packaging: Bulk

11881 **(HQ)Saratoga Beverage Group**
11 Geyser Rd
Saratoga Springs, NY 12866 518-584-6363
Fax: 518-584-0380 888-426-8642
www.saratogaspringwater.com
Processor of sparkling and nonsparkling regular and flavored spring water, orange and grapefruit juice and flavored smoothies including raspberry, strawberry, blackberry, peach banana, etc
President: Adam Madkour
CFO: Robert Braks
Vice President: Andrew Cook
Production Manager: Mike Lawson
Estimated Sales: $300,000-500,000
Number Employees: 1-4
Type of Packaging: Consumer, Food Service, Private Label
Other Locations:
Saratoga Beverage Group
Azusa CA
Brands:
Saratoga
Saratoga Splash
Saratoga Vichy

11882 **Saratoga Food Specialties**
771 W Crossroads Pkwy
Bolingbrook, IL 60490 800-451-0407
info@saratogafs.com
www.saratogafs.com
Importer, exporter and processor of whole and ground spices; developer of custom seasoning blends, seasoned rice, stuffing and gravy mixes.
Manager: Jim Bejna
CFO: Ed Herbert
Vice President: Wade McGeorge
Research & Development: Paul Maki
Quality Control: Mark Beattie
Marketing Director: Kristi Freitager
Sales Director: George Rackos
Operations Manager: Jim Benja
Purchasing Manager: Ron Batzer
Estimated Sales: $30-40 Million
Number Employees: 100-249
Sq. footage: 110000
Type of Packaging: Consumer, Food Service, Private Label, Bulk
Other Locations:
Saratoga Specialties Co.
Northlake IL

11883 **Sardinha Sausage**
177 Lepes Rd
Somerset, MA 02726 508-674-2511
Fax: 508-674-2511 800-678-0178
esardinhs@sardinhas.com www.sardinhas.com
Processor of gourmet smoked and fresh sausages including chourico, linguica, turkey dogs and kielbasa, breakfast and Italian sausage; private label available
President: Ed Sardinha

Estimated Sales: $500,000 appx.
Number Employees: 1-4
Sq. footage: 3600
Type of Packaging: Consumer, Food Service, Private Label, Bulk
Brands:
Francisco's
Portuguese Sausages
Sardinha's
Vincenza's

11884 Sardinia Cheese
312 Roosevelt Drive
Seymour, CT 06483-2128 203-735-3374
Fax: 203-732-3959 tmavuli@aol.com
Cheese
CEO/VP: Tony Mavuli
Estimated Sales: $ 5 Million
Number Employees: 3
Type of Packaging: Private Label

11885 Sargeant's Army Marketing
PO Box 82
Bowmanville, ON L1C 1K8
Canada 905-623-2888
Processor of frozen yogurt and waffle cones; manufacturer and exporter of frozen yogurt and ice cream dispensers
President: Herb Sargeant
Number Employees: 1-4
Type of Packaging: Private Label
Brands:
Monster
Whirlywinkles
Wizard

11886 Sargent's Bear Necessities
321 Guay Farm Road
North Troy, VT 05859-9207 802-988-2903
info@sargentsbearnecessities.com
www.sargentsbearnecessities.com
Jams, jellies, pickles and relishes
Owner: Michelle Sargent
Number Employees: 1

11887 (HQ)Sargento Foods Inc.
1 Persnickety Pl
Plymouth, WI 53073 920-893-8484
Fax: 920-893-8399 800-243-3737
www.sargentocheese.com
Manufacturer, importer and exporter of natural and processed cheese
Chairman/CEO: Lou Gentine
CFO: George Hoff
Senior Research Scientist R&D: Craig Hackl
Senior Packaging Development Manager: Guy Turnbull
VP Foodservice Sales/Marketing: Sam Colson
Consumer Products Division Sales Rep: Mike Ruhland
EVP/COO: Mark Rhyan
Corporate Chef: Guy Beardsmore
Estimated Sales: $534 Million
Number Employees: 1,000-4,999
Type of Packaging: Consumer, Food Service, Private Label, Bulk
Brands:
SARGENTO

11888 Sarsfield Foods
15 Roscoe Drive
Kentville, NS B4N 3W9
Canada 902-678-2241
Fax: 902-678-8487
Processor and exporter of frozen pies
President: Kirk McGrath
Number Employees: 100-249
Sq. footage: 80000
Parent Co: George Weston Foods
Type of Packaging: Food Service, Private Label
Other Locations:
President Sarsfield Foods Ltd
Mount Pearl NF

11889 Sartori Food Corporation
404 Schwartz St
107 Pleasant View
Plymouth, WI 53073 920-892-6903
Fax: 920-892-2732 800-558-5888
info@sartorifoods.com www.sartorifoods.com
Manufacturer, value-added coverter and marketer of aged Italian cheese, Mexican cheeses, specialty chesses, cheese products and cheese-based flavor systems for the foodservice and food processing marketplace
CEO: James C Sartori
President: Jeff Schwager
VP: Frederick M Bowes II
VP of Research & Product Development: Pat Mugan
Quality Control: Steve Tittl
Sales: Russ Horneck
Operations VP: Peter Marsing
Production: Mark Thaldorf
Plant Manager: Jason Schultz
Purchasing: Helen Cheng
Estimated Sales: $ 50 - 100 Million
Number Employees: 20-49

11890 Sartori Foods
P.O.Box 258
Plymouth, WI 53073-0258 920-893-6061
Fax: 920-892-2732 800-356-5655
info@sartorifoods.com www.sartorifoods.com
Manufacturer of specialty cheese: Parmesean, romano, asiago cheeses
President: James Sartori
Estimated Sales: $20-50 Million
Number Employees: 100-249
Type of Packaging: Private Label

11891 Sarum Tea Company
332 Main St
Lakeville, CT 06039 860-435-2086
Fax: 860-435-9304
Tea
President/CEO: W Harris
Manager: E Lloyd-Harris
Estimated Sales: Less than $500,000
Number Employees: 1-4
Brands:
Sarum Tea

11892 Sassafras Enterprises
1622 W Carroll Ave
Chicago, IL 60612 312-226-2000
Fax: 312-226-0873 800-537-4941
info@sassafrasenterprises.com
www.sassafrasenterprises.com
Gourmet gift baskets, natural pizza and pasta sauces, spices, oils, spreads, bruschettas, mixes, pastas and bread mixes
Owner: Steven Schwab
CEO: Steven Schwab
VP: Nancy Schwab
Operations Manager: Ron Cahill
Estimated Sales: $ 5 - 10 Million
Number Employees: 20-49
Type of Packaging: Private Label
Brands:
Superstone

11893 Saticoy Foods Corporation
P.O.Box 4547
Ventura, CA 93007 805-647-5266
Fax: 805-933-1523
Manufacturer of canned peppers including diced red bell, green strips and halves; also, pimientos
President: Jerry Hensley
CEO: Stanley Dunbar
Estimated Sales: $15 Million
Number Employees: 20-49
Parent Co: Moody Dunbar

11894 Saticoy Lemon Cooperative
P.O.Box 46
Santa Paula, CA 93061-0046 805-654-6500
Fax: 805-654-6510
webmaster@saticoylemon.com
www.saticoylemon.com
Agricultural Cooperative that is owned by the lemon grower members of which the marketing of the fruit is handled through their affiliation with Sunkist Growers, Inc.
President: Glenn Miller
Chief Financial Officer: Mike Dillard
Exchange/Business Development Manager: John Eliot
Field Manager: David Coert
Sales Coordinator: Jose Mendez
MIS Director: Lee Raymond
Personnel Director: Michael Dennington
Production Manager: Ron Davis
Plant Superintendent: Albert Palacio Jr
Shipping Supervisor: Jose Mares
Type of Packaging: Food Service

11895 Saticoy Lemon Cooperative
P.O. Box 46
Santa Paula, CA 93061 805-654-6500
Fax: 805-654-6528
webmaster@saticoylemon.com
www.saticoylemon.com
Agricultural Cooperative that is owned by the lemon grower members of which the marketing of the fruit is handled through their affiliation with Sunkist Growers, Inc.
President: Glenn Miller
Chief Financial Officer: Mike Dillard
Exchange/Business Development Manager: John Eliot
Field Manager: David Coert
Sales Coordinator: Jose Mendez
MIS Director: Lee Raymond
Personnel Director: Michael Dennington
Production Manager: Ron Davis
Plant Superintendent: Salvador Ramirez
Shipping Supervisor: Jose Manzano
Type of Packaging: Food Service

11896 Saticoy Lemon Cooperative
103 N Peck Road
Santa Paula, CA 93060 805-654-6515
Fax: 805-654-6510
webmaster@saticoylemon.com
www.saticoylemon.com
Agricultural Cooperative that is owned by the lemon grower members of which the marketing of the fruit is handled through their affiliation with Sunkist Growers, Inc.
President: Glenn Miller
Chief Financial Officer: Mike Dillard
Exchange/Business Development Manager: John Eliot
Field Manager: David Coert
Sales Coordinator: Jose Mendez
MIS Director: Lee Raymond
Personnel Director: Michael Dennington
Production Manager: Ron Davis
Plant Superintendent: Rene Velasco
Shipping Supervisor: Juan Martinez
Type of Packaging: Food Service

11897 Saticoy Lemon Cooperative
600 E Third Street
Oxnard, CA 93030 805-654-6543
Fax: 805-654-6510
webmaster@saticoylemon.com
www.saticoylemon.com
Agricultural Cooperative that is owned by the lemon grower members of which the marketing of the fruit is handled through their affiliation with Sunkist Growers, Inc.
President: Glenn Miller
Chief Financial Officer: Mike Dillard
Exchange/Business Development Manager: John Eliot
Field Manager: David Coert
Sales Coordinator: Jose Mendez
MIS Director: Lee Raymond
Personnel Director: Michael Dennington
Production Manager: Ron Davis
Plant Superintendent: Albert Rivera
Shipping Supervisor: Albert Palacio Sr
Type of Packaging: Food Service

11898 Satiety
1027 Maple Ln
Davis, CA 95616-1720 530-757-2699
Wines, wine vinegars, table grapes, wine grapes
Owner: Sterling Chaykin
Estimated Sales: $270,000
Number Employees: 1-4

Brands:
Ambrosia
Satiety

11899 **Sattwa Chai**
17900 NE Lewis Rogers Ln
Newberg, OR 97132 503-538-4715
Fax: 503-538-5125 info@sattwac.com
www.sattwachai.com
Tea, chai
Owner: Juanita Crampton
Owner: David Fields
CFO/VP Operations: Juanita Crampton
Purchasing Manager: Jan Rhine
Estimated Sales: $ 2.5-5 Million
Number Employees: 1-4
Parent Co: Sattwa Chai
Type of Packaging: Food Service, Private Label, Bulk
Brands:
Black Tea Chai
SATTWA SUN CHAI
Sattwa Chai Concentrate
Sattwa Kovalam Spice Chai
Sattwa Shanti Herbal Chai
Sattwa Sun Chai

11900 **Sau-Sea Foods**
303 S Broadway Ste 224
Tarrytown, NY 10591 914-631-1717
Fax: 914-631-0865
Processor of shrimp and sauces including cocktail, tartar and horseradish
President: Antonio Estadella
National Sales Manager: Edward Cauley
Estimated Sales: $1300000
Number Employees: 5-9
Type of Packaging: Consumer, Food Service, Private Label, Bulk
Brands:
Sea Maid
Seagull Bay

11901 **Sauces 'n Love**
86 Sanserson Ave
Suite 130
Lynn, MA 01902 781-595-7771
Fax: 781-595-7799 866-772-8237
info@saucesnlove.com www.saucesnlove.com
scarpetta, sauces, pesto, bruschetta, spreads and dips
CEO: Paolo Volpati-Kedra

11902 **Saucilito Canyon Vineyard**
3080 Biddle Ranch Rd
San Luis Obispo, CA 93401-8320 805-543-2111
Fax: 805-543-2111 info@saucelitocanyon.com
www.saucelitocanyon.com
Wines
Owner: Bill Greenough
Owner: Nancy Greenbough
Marketing/Sales Manager: Nancy Greenbough
Winemaker: Amy Freeman
Estimated Sales: Less than $500,000
Number Employees: 1-4
Type of Packaging: Private Label
Brands:
Saucelito Canyon

11903 **Saugy Inc**
9 Sachem Drive
Cranston, RI 02920-4514 401-383-9374
Fax: 401-383-9374 866-467-2849
saugy@cox.net www.saugy.net
Manufacturer of frankfurters, brats and saurkraut
President: Mary O'Brien
Estimated Sales: $175,000
Number Employees: 3
Type of Packaging: Consumer, Food Service, Bulk

11904 **Sausage Kitchen**
18893 SE McLoughlin Blvd
Oak Grove, OR 97267 503-656-9766
Fax: 503-656-0567
Sausage and smoked salmon
President: Nicholas Allick
Plant Manager: David Parker
Estimated Sales: $350,000
Number Employees: 5-9

11905 **Sausage Shoppe**
4501 Memphis Ave
Cleveland, OH 44144 216-351-5213
cheinle@sausageshoppe.com
www.sausageshoppe.com
Processor of sausage and luncheon meat
President/Owner: Norm Heinle
VP/Owner: Carol Heinle
Plant Manager: Alan Heinle
Number Employees: 1-4
Type of Packaging: Consumer, Bulk
Brands:
Sheffler Ham

11906 **Sausages by Amy**
1141 W Lake St
Chicago, IL 60607 312-829-2250
Fax: 312-829-2098 www.sausagesbyamy.com
Sausages
President: Amy Kurzawski
President: Chico Kurzawski
Estimated Sales: $ 5-10 Million
Number Employees: 50-99

11907 **Sausal Winery**
7370 Highway 128
Healdsburg, CA 95448 707-433-2285
Fax: 707-433-5136 800-500-2285
www.sausalwinery.com
Wines
President: David Demostene
Estimated Sales: Below $ 5 Million
Number Employees: 10-19
Brands:
Sausal Wines

11908 **Saval Foods**
6740 Dorsey Rd
Elkridge, MD 21075 410-379-5100
Fax: 410-379-8068 800-527-2825
www.savalfoods.com
Manufacturer of fine quality delicatessen products such as processed roast beef, corn beef, pastrami and products for home meal replacement
President: Paul Saval
EVP: Howard Saval
Estimated Sales: $100+ Million
Number Employees: 100-249
Sq. footage: 57000
Type of Packaging: Food Service, Private Label, Bulk
Brands:
Elite
Saval

11909 **Savannah Bee Company**
211 Johnny Mercer Blvd
Savannah, GA 31410 912-234-0688
Fax: 912-234-0125 800-955-5080
info@savannahbee.com www.savannahbee.com
honey
President/Owner: Ted Dennard
Estimated Sales: $1.1 Million
Number Employees: 8

11910 **Savannah Chanelle Vineyards**
23600 Big Basin Way
Saratoga, CA 95070 408-741-2934
Fax: 408-867-4824 www.savannahchanelle.com
Wines
Owner: Gregg Gorham
Co-Owner: Kellie Ballard
Winemaker: Tony Craig
Estimated Sales: $ 5 - 10 Million
Number Employees: 10-19
Brands:
Savannah Chanelle Vineyards

11911 **Savannah Cinnamon & Cookie Company**
P.O.Box 20251
Bradenton, FL 34204
Fax: 912-233-3004 800-288-0854
savcinn@aol.com www.savannahcinnamon.com
Cinnamon and other liquid flavors for coffee, tea and juices
Owner: Brian Wiggins
Estimated Sales: $ 1-2.5 Million
Number Employees: 10-19
Type of Packaging: Consumer
Brands:
Savannah Cinnamon Mix
Savannah Squares

11912 **Savannah Food Company**
575 Industrial Rd
PO Box 1000
Savannah, TN 38372
Fax: 731-925-1855 800-795-2550
info@savannahclassics.com
www.savannahclassics.com
Manufacturer and marketer of homestyle hushpuppies and authentic southern side dishes.
President: John Bryan III
Vice President: J Flatt
VP Sales/Marketing: Jim Sisco
Human Resources Manager: Blake Johnson
VP Operations: Paul Stodard
Production Director: Lynn Austin
Purchasing Director: Thomas Gean
Estimated Sales: $20 Million
Number Employees: 65
Sq. footage: 98000
Type of Packaging: Consumer, Food Service, Private Label
Brands:
Neokura
San Like
San Orange
San Red
San Yellow
San-Ei

11913 **Savannah Foods & Industries**
2 Oxnard Dr
Savannah, GA 31407 912-234-1261
Fax: 912-651-4905 800-241-3785
Processor and exporter of sugar and artificial sweeteners.
President: Bob Peiser
CEO: W Sprague III
VP Sales: Joe Herb
Plant Manager: Phillip Rowland
Estimated Sales: $100+ Million
Number Employees: 250-499
Parent Co: Imperial Holly Corporation
Type of Packaging: Consumer, Food Service, Private Label, Bulk
Other Locations:
Savannah Foods & Industries
Bremen GA

11914 **Savannah Foods Industrial**
2 Oxnard Dr
Savannah, GA 31407 912-234-1261
Fax: 863-983-9210
Processor and exporter of sugar including granulated, powdered, brown, cubes and in envelopes
Manager: Phillip Rowland
Purchasing Agent: Larry Dykes
Number Employees: 5-9
Parent Co: Savannah Foods & Industries
Type of Packaging: Consumer, Food Service, Private Label, Bulk

11915 **(HQ)Savino's Italian Ices**
1126 S Powerline Road
Deerfield Beach, FL 33442-8121 954-426-4119
Processor of frozen Italian ice fruit desserts
CEO: Sal Savino
Number Employees: 1-4
Type of Packaging: Bulk

11916 **Savoia Foods**
85 Independence Dr
Chicago Heights, IL 60411-4198
US 708-756-7600
Fax: 708-754-2133 800-867-2782
jbamonti@msn.com www.savoiafoods.com
Processor and exporter of pasta, brands spaghetti,spinach spaghetti,linguine,fettucine,lasagna.
President/Owner: Rudolph Bamonti
Sales Executive: Julia Bamonti
Estimated Sales: $2.5-5million
Number Employees: 10-19
Type of Packaging: Consumer, Food Service
Brands:
Savoia

11917 **Savoie Industries**
P.O.Box 69
Belle Rose, LA 70341 225-473-9293
Fax: 225-473-9294
Processor of blackstrap molasses and sugar
President/GM: Patrick Cancienne
Sec-Treasurer: C Daigle
Vice President: Paul Cancienne

Estimated Sales: $ 10 - 20 Million
Number Employees: 50-99
Type of Packaging: Consumer

11918 **Savoie's Sausage & FoodProducts**
1742 Highway 742
Opelousas, LA 70570-0549 337-948-4115
Fax: 337-948-9571 sales@savoiesfoods.com
www.savoiesfoods.com
Manufacturer of sausage including hog's headcheese, boudin, andouille and tasso; also, barbecue sauce, roux and dressing mix
President/Owner: Eula Savoie
Marketing Manager: Frederick Lafleur
Operations Manager: Gerald Boullion
Estimated Sales: $9 Million
Number Employees: 50-99
Sq. footage: 25000
Type of Packaging: Consumer, Private Label
Brands:
CAJUN HOUSE
REAL CAJUN
SAVOIE'S

11919 **Savory Foods**
P.O.Box 1604
Portsmouth, OH 45662-1604 740-354-6655
Fax: 740-353-2482 savory@zoomnet.net
Processor and exporter of pork rinds
President: Marcia Sanderlin
VP Sales/Production: K Sanderlin
Safety Manager: Adam Dengel
Production Manager: Ed Thompson
Plant Manager: Rigel Olmos
Number Employees: 20-49
Sq. footage: 60000
Type of Packaging: Food Service, Private Label
Brands:
Porkies
Savory
Southern Style

11920 **Savoury Systems**
230 Industrial Parkway, Unit C
Branchburg, NJ 08876 908-526-2524
Fax: 908-526-2632 davida@savourysystems.com
www.savourysystems.com
Extract and flavors manufacturers
President: David Adams
Vice President: Becky Adams
Technical Sales: Kevin McDermott
Estimated Sales: $12.6 Million
Number Employees: 15

11921 **Sawtooth Winery**
13750 Surrey Ln
Nampa, ID 83686 208-467-1200
Fax: 208-468-7934 www.sawtoothwinery.com
www.sawtoothwinery.com
Wines
Winemaker/General Manager: Brad Pintler
President: Ken McCabe
Partner: Charles Pintler
Retail Manager/Events Coordinator: Ina DeBoer
Estimated Sales: $1-2.5 Million
Number Employees: 1-4
Brands:
Sawtooth

11922 **Saxby Foods**
4120 98th Street NW
Edmonton, AB T6E 5A2
Canada 780-440-4179
Fax: 780-440-4480 info@saxbyfoods.com
www.saxbyfoods.com
Processor and exporter of frozen desserts including cakes and cheesecakes. Co-packer of private label in Canada, USA, Carribean
President: Jonathan Avis
Quality Control: Ana Avalos
Public Relations: Thea Avis
Plant Manager: Sean Gillis
Purchasing: Rhys Amatori
Estimated Sales: F
Number Employees: 120
Sq. footage: 50000
Brands:
Albertson's
Safeway
Walmart

11923 **Saxon Chocolates**
21 Coleville Rd
Toronto, ON M6M 2Y2
Canada 416-675-6363
Fax: 416-675-2777 sales@saxonchocolates.com
www.saxonchocolates.com
belgian chocolates
President/Owner: Johan DeGrees
Estimated Sales: $2.3 Million
Number Employees: 20

11924 **Saxon Creamery**
855 Hickory Street
Cleveland, WI 53015 920-693-8500
Fax: 480-393-4478 info@saxoncreamery.com
www.saxoncreamery.com
cheeses

11925 **Say Ying Leong Look Funn Factory**
1028 Kekaulike St
Honolulu, HI 96817-5007 808-537-4304
Ethnic foods
Owner: Fooying Chee
Estimated Sales: $ 2.5-5 Million
Number Employees: 1-4

11926 **Sayklly's Candies& Gifts**
910 2nd Ave N
Escanaba, MI 49829-3811 906-786-3092
Fax: 906-786-3096 http://www.saykllyscandy.com
Processor of candy including brittles, butterscotch, caramels, chocolate, coconut, taffy, etc.
President: Michael F Kobasic
Owner: Cheryl Kobasic
Estimated Sales: $170000
Number Employees: 5-9
Type of Packaging: Consumer

11927 **Sazerac Company**
P.O.Box 52821
New Orleans, LA 70152 504-831-9450
Fax: 504-831-2383 800-899-9450
info@sazerac.com www.sazerac.com
Distilled spirits
President: Mark Brown
CFO: Kent Broussard
VP: Jay Cummins
VP: Stephen Camisa
Sales/Marketing Manager: William Pananos
Point of Sales Manager: Debbie Ledet
Plant Manager: Dubois
Estimated Sales: $ 50-100 Million
Number Employees: 100-249
Type of Packaging: Private Label
Brands:
Old Charter Bourbon

11928 **Scalas Original Beef &Sausage Company LLC**
4649 W Armitage Avenue
Chicago, IL 60639 312-944-3567
866-467-2252
scalas@scalasoriginal.com
www.scalasoriginal.com
Italian sausage and roast beef, giardinera
President: Pat Scala
Sales Manager: Tony McHale
Estimated Sales: $450,000
Number Employees: 150
Type of Packaging: Food Service, Private Label, Bulk

11929 **Scally's Imperial Importing Company Inc**
4354 Victory Blvd
Staten Island, NY 10314-6733 718-983-1938
Fax: 718-259-2195 scallyimperial@aol.com
Importers, packers and distributors of food products including canned tomato products, olives, mushrooms, beans, peppers, pickles, giardiniera, artichockes, canned clams, canned shrimp, canned crab meat, canned tuna, and edibleoils.
President/Sales/Plant Manager: Alex Scarselli
CEO: Alessandre Scarselli
VP/Purchasing Director: Christine Scarselli
Estimated Sales: $ 5 Million
Number Employees: 20-49
Sq. footage: 10000
Type of Packaging: Consumer, Food Service, Private Label
Brands:
LA PERLA
PRIMA DONNA
SCALLI

11930 **Scan American Food Compampany**
1410 80th Street SW
Suite F
Everett, WA 98203-6200 425-514-0500
Fax: 425-514-0400
scanamerican@scanamerican.com
www.scanamerican.com
Processor, importer and exporter of natural food flavors and extracts, aroma materials, proteins, fish oils and freeze dried seafood
President: Svein Bjorge
Estimated Sales: $ 5 - 10 Million
Number Employees: 5-9

11931 **Scandia Seafood Company**
130 Tillson Avenue
Rockland, ME 04841-3424 207-596-7102
Fax: 207-596-7105
Crabs, cold water shrimp, America lobster, Atlantic herring
President: Asger Jorgensen
Sq. footage: 25000

11932 **(HQ)Scandinavian Formulas Inc**
140 E Church St
Sellersville, PA 18960 215-453-2500
Fax: 215-257-9781 800-288-2844
info@scandinavianformulas.com
www.scandinavianformulas.com
Manufacturer, importer and exporter of vitamins and supplements, chemicals and ingredients
President: Catherine Peklak
Marketing: Sylvie Millet
Purchasing Director: Denise Covelens
Estimated Sales: $1005000
Number Employees: 5-9
Number of Brands: 7
Number of Products: 7
Sq. footage: 9000
Type of Packaging: Consumer, Private Label, Bulk
Other Locations:
Scandinavian Natural Health &
Perkasie PA
Brands:
ALKYROL
BILBERRY EXTRACT
DHEA
LYCOPENE
MELATONIN
SALIX SST
SINCERA SKIN CARE PRODUCTS

11933 **Scandinavian Laboratories**
794 Sunrise Blvd
Mount Bethel, PA 18343 570-897-7735
Fax: 570-897-7732 scanlabs@epix.net
www.oceanaproducts.com
Processor of nutritional products including shark liver and fish oils, essential fatty acids, effervescent tablets and liquid emulsions; importer and exporter of nutritional supplements including shark liver oils; also, contractpackaging available
President: Olav Sandnes
Estimated Sales: $500,000
Number Employees: 5-9
Type of Packaging: Private Label, Bulk
Brands:
Calcitrace
Ecomega
Glycomarine
Oceana
Pedia-Vit
Promega
Squalene

11934 Scanga Meat Company
9250 County Road 156
Salida, CO 81201 719-539-3511
Fax: 719-539-6344 rlscanga@vanion.com
Manufacturer and packer of beef, poultry, seafood
President: Ralph Scanga Jr
Estimated Sales: $29 Milion
Number Employees: 10-19
Sq. footage: 20000
Type of Packaging: Consumer, Food Service, Private Label, Bulk

11935 Scenic Fruit Company
7510 SE Altman Rd
Gresham, OR 97080 503-663-3434
Fax: 503-663-7095 800-554-5578
sales@scenicfruit.com www.scenicfruit.com
Processor of frozen berries
President: Judy England
CEO: Hugh Eisele
Plant Manager: John Vasquez
Estimated Sales: $18000000
Number Employees: 100-249
Type of Packaging: Food Service, Bulk

11936 Scenic Valley Winery
103 Coffee St
Lanesboro, MN 55949 507-259-4981
Fax: 507-467-2640 www.scenicvalleywinery.com
Wines
Owner: Karrie Ristau
Estimated Sales: $470,000
Number Employees: 5-9

11937 Schadel's Bakery
212 N Bullard Street
Silver City, NM 88061-5308 505-538-3031
Bakery
President/CEO: Dexter Seay
Estimated Sales: $500,000 appx.
Number Employees: 5-9

11938 Schafer Fisheries
21985 Waller Rd
Fulton, IL 61252-9780 815-589-3368
Fax: 815-589-3369 www.schaferfish.com
Seafood
Manager: Margaret Hattan
Estimated Sales: $ 3 - 5 Million
Number Employees: 10-19

11939 Schafley Tap Room
2100 Locust St
St Louis, MO 63103-1616 314-241-2337
Fax: 314-241-8101 gimmes@schlafly.com
www.schlafly.com
Processor of beer, ale, lager, stout and seasonal beers
President: Tom Schlafly
Marketing Director: Mitch Turner
VP: Dan Kopman
CFO: D J Jean
Estimated Sales: $ 20-50 Million
Number Employees: 50-99
Type of Packaging: Consumer, Food Service
Brands:
Schlafly

11940 Schaller & Weber
22-35 46th St
Astoria, NY 11105 718-721-5480
Fax: 718-956-9157 800-847-4115
info@schallerweber.com
www.schallerweber.com
Processor of meat including ham and German-style sausage, poultry, cold cuts, cooked and smoked products, salami and cervelat and seafood
Owner: Ralph Schaller
Sales Executive: Jeremy Schaller
Estimated Sales: $12 Million
Number Employees: 75
Sq. footage: 16000
Type of Packaging: Consumer

11941 Schaller's Bakery Inc
826 Highland Ave
Greensburg, PA 15601 724-837-3660
Fax: 724-837-6764 800-241-1777
Manufacturer of baked goods
President: Warren Schaller
Estimated Sales: $2 Million
Number Employees: 20-49
Sq. footage: 21000
Type of Packaging: Consumer, Food Service, Private Label, Bulk

11942 Scharffen Berger Choclate Maker
601 22nd Street
San Francisco, CA 94107 415-401-0080
Fax: 415-401-0087 866-972-6879
scharffenberger@worldpantry.com
www.scharffenberger.com
dark chocolate
CEO: John Scharffenberger
CFO/COO: Jim Harris
Marketing: Norm Shea

11943 Scharffen Berger Chocolate Maker
1 Ferry Building, Marketplace #14
San Francisco, CA 94111 41- 9-1 91
866- 60- 694
scharffenberger@worldpantry.com
www.scharffenberger.com
Semi-sweet chocolates, bittersweet chocolates, unsweetened chocolates, cocoa powder, chocolate bars
Founder: Dr Robert Steinberg
CEO: John Scharffenberger
CFO: Jim Harris
Marketing Coordinator: Norm Shea
Estimated Sales: $10 Million
Number Employees: 50
Brands:
Cocoa Powder
Home Chef Bars
Mocha Bars
Nibby Bars
Scharffen Berger

11944 Schat's Dutch Bakeries
763 N Main St
Bishop, CA 93514-2427 760-873-7156
Fax: 760-872-4932
schatsbakery@mindspring.com
www.erickschatsbakery.com
Baked goods
Owner: Erick Schat
CFO: Mirika Marijke
Estimated Sales: Below $ 5 Million
Number Employees: 50-99
Brands:
Erick Schat

11945 Schenk Packing Company
1321 S 6th St
Mount Vernon, WA 98273 360-336-2128
Fax: 360-336-3092 info@schenkpacking.com
www.schenkpacking.com
Processor and exporter of meat products; custom slaughtering available.
Owner/President: Steve Lenz
Estimated Sales: $ 50 - 100 Million
Number Employees: 20
Sq. footage: 21168
Type of Packaging: Consumer, Food Service

11946 Schenkel's All Star Dairy
1019 Flaxmill Rd
Huntington, IN 46750 260-356-4225
Fax: 260-359-5045
Processor of dairy products
Manager: Larry Brown
Estimated Sales: $ 50 - 100 Million
Number Employees: 100-249
Parent Co: Suiza Dairy Group
Type of Packaging: Consumer
Other Locations:
Schenkel's Dairy
Fort Wayne IN
Brands:
Pure Sealed

11947 Schepps Dairy
3114 S Haskell Ave
Dallas, TX 75223 214-824-8163
Fax: 214-824-1526 800-395-7004
schdfwjobs@suizafoods.com www.schepps.com
Processor of juice, milk, cheese and sour cream; wholesaler/distributor of cottage cheese and butter
Chairman: Pat Ford
President/CEO: Pete Schenkle
CFO: Eddie Tollison
VP: Pat Boyle
Quality Control: Pat Moore
Estimated Sales: $ 50-100 Million
Sq. footage: 60000
Parent Co: Suiza Dairy Group
Type of Packaging: Consumer, Food Service, Private Label, Bulk
Other Locations:
Schepps Dairy
Harlingen TX
Brands:
Schepps Dairy

11948 Schiavone's Casa Mia
1907 Tytus Avenue
Middletown, OH 45042-2367 513-422-8650
Fax: 513-422-8602 http://www.schiavones.com
Sauces
President: Michael Schiavone
Estimated Sales: $500,000-$1 Million
Number Employees: 20-49

11949 Schiff Food Products
7401 W Side Ave
North Bergen, NJ 07047 201-868-6800
Fax: 201-861-2503 schifffood@aol.com
www.schifffoods.com
Manufacturer, importer and exporter of spices, seeds, herbs and dehydrated vegetables
President: David Deutscher
Estimated Sales: $17 Million
Number Employees: 20-49
Sq. footage: 78000
Type of Packaging: Consumer, Private Label
Brands:
SCHIFF FOOD

11950 (HQ)Schiff Nutrition International
2002 S 5070 W
Salt Lake City, UT 84104-4726 801-975-5000
Fax: 801-972-2223 800-526-6251
webfeedback@schiffnutrition.com
www.schiffnutrition.com
Manufacturer and distributor of vitamins, nutritional supplements and sports nutrition products
CEO/President/Director: Tarang Amin
EVP/CFO: Joesph Baty
SVP/Chief Marketing Officer: Jennifer Steeves-Kiss
SVP General Counsel & Corp. Secretary: Scott Milsten
SVP Operations: Jon Fieldman
Estimated Sales: $200 Million
Number Employees: 450
Sq. footage: 418000
Type of Packaging: Consumer, Private Label
Other Locations:
Weider Nutrition Internation
Salt Lake City UT
Brands:
FI-BAR
SCHIFF
TIGER'S MILK

11951 Schiltz Foods
7 W Oak St
Sisseton, SD 57262 605-698-7651
Fax: 605-698-7112 877-872-4458
jschiltz@schiltzfoods.com
www.schiltzfoods.com
Processor and exporter of dressed geese and goose products
President: Richard Schiltz
VP/Director of Sales: James Schiltz
Estimated Sales: $2,100,000
Number Employees: 100-249
Number of Brands: 4
Number of Products: 20
Sq. footage: 34000
Type of Packaging: Consumer, Food Service, Private Label, Bulk
Brands:
All American Holiday Goose
Whetstone Valley

11952 Schirf Brewing Company
P.O.Box 459
Park City, UT 84060-0459 435-649-0900
Fax: 435-649-4999 www.wasatchbeers.com
Processor of beer
President: Greg Schirf
Estimated Sales: $ 20 - 50 Million
Number Employees: 50-99
Brands:
Wasatch

11953 **Schisa Brothers**
4886 Edgeworth Dr
Manlius, NY 13104-2107 315-463-0213
Fax: 315-463-0248 Info@schisabrothers.com
www.schisabrothers.com
Baked goods
President: Bruce Dew
CFO: Bryan Touchstone
Director Sales: Ched Cummings
Estimated Sales: $ 10-20 Million
Number Employees: 20-49
Brands:
All Kitchen
Great Lakes
Hereford Beef
Hormel
Tyson

11954 **Schleswig Specialty Meats**
Hwy 59 S
Schleswig, IA 51461 712-676-3324
Fax: 712-676-3936 ssmeats@iowatelecom.net
Manufacturer and packer of pork
President: Richard Beatty
Plant Manager: Phil Smith
Estimated Sales: $5-10 Million
Number Employees: 25
Sq. footage: 20000
Type of Packaging: Private Label

11955 **Schloss & Kahn**
P.O.Box 117
Montgomery, AL 36101-0117 334-288-3111
Fax: 334-286-5295 www.usfoodservice.com
President: Rick Combs

11956 **Schloss Doepken Winery**
9177 Old Route 20
Ripley, NY 14775 716-326-3636
shdwines@cecomet-net.com
Wines
President: John Watso
Estimated Sales: $500,000-$1 Million
Number Employees: 1-4
Brands:
Schloss Doepken

11957 **Schlotterbeck & Foss Company**
117 Preble St
Portland, ME 04101 207-772-4666
Fax: 207-774-3449 800-777-4666
info@schlotterbeck-foss.com
www.schlotterbeck-foss.com
Spicy salsas, grilling and stir-fry sauces.
President: Peter Foss
CEO: Richard Foss
VP Finance: Ray Farnham
CEO: Clif Foss
Marketing Manager: Charles Foss
Sales Director: Arthur Kyncos
Plant Manager: Richard Raymond
Purchasing Manager: Annmarie Bruns
Estimated Sales: $5200000
Number Employees: 20-49
Sq. footage: 30000
Type of Packaging: Consumer, Food Service, Private Label, Bulk
Brands:
Foss
Mos-Ness

11958 **Schmidt Baking Company**
7801 Fitch Ln
Baltimore, MD 21236-3998 410-668-8200
Fax: 410-882-2051 800-456-2253
comments@schmidtbaking.com
www.schmidtbaking.com
Processor of baked goods including white and grain breads.
President: John Paterakis
VP: Tom Beardsley
Marketing Director: Steven Favazza
Sales Manager: Thomas Lewis
Estimated Sales: $76700000
Number Employees: 500-999
Type of Packaging: Consumer
Brands:
Blue Ribbon
Old Tyme
Sunbeam

11959 **Schmidt Baking Company**
7801 Fitch Lane
Baltimore, MD 21236 410-668-8200
800-456-2253
comments@schmidtbaking.com
www.schmidtbaking.com
Processor of bread and rolls
Owner/CEO: John Paterakis
President: Stephen Paterakis
Estimated Sales: $ 1 - 3 Million
Number Employees: 20-49
Parent Co: Schmidt Baking Company
Brands:
Schmidt's Blue Ribbon White Bread
Schmidt's Butter Bread
Schmidt's Italian Bread
Schmidt's Potato Bread
Sunbeam Bread

11960 **Schmidt Brothers**
2425 S Fulton Lucas Rd
Swanton, OH 43558 419-826-3671
Fax: 419-826-8696
lawrence@schmidtbrosinc.com
www.schmidtbrosinc.com
Grower of produce including pumpkins
President: Lawrence Schmidt
VP: Robert Schmidt
Estimated Sales: $3500000
Number Employees: 50-99
Sq. footage: 375000
Type of Packaging: Bulk

11961 **Schneider Cheese**
N4085 County Road M
Waldo, WI 53093 920-467-3351
Fax: 920-467-6184
Cheese
President: John Schneider
CFO: Thomas Paul
Quality Control: Jane Gau
Estimated Sales: $ 10-20 Million
Number Employees: 130

11962 **(HQ)Schneider Foods**
321 Courtland Ave East
Kitchener, ON N2G 3X8
Canada 519-741-5000
Fax: 519-749-7400 www.schneiders.ca
Processor and exporter of frozen and refrigerated frankfurters, meat pies, sausage, ham, bacon, deli meats and poultry; fat and calorie reduced products available
President: Douglas Dodds
President (Cust. Foods): Paul Lang
VP Business: John Howard
Quality Control: Judy Tetker
R & D: Tim Gorgon
Number Employees: 5,500
Sq. footage: 730000
Type of Packaging: Consumer, Food Service, Private Label, Bulk
Other Locations:
Schneider Corp.
Ayr ON
Brands:
Deli-Best
Lifestyle
Lunchmate
Mini-Sizzlers
Olde-Fashioned
Red Hots
Schneider's

11963 **Schneider Foods**
180 Northumberland Street
Ayr, ON N0B 1E0
Canada 519-632-7416
Fax: 519-632-8850 www.schneiderfoods.ca
Processor of frozen, breaded and fully cooked fried chicken
Plant Manager: Lou Cappa
Number Employees: 150
Parent Co: J.M. Schneider
Type of Packaging: Food Service

11964 **Schneider Foods**
Perth County Road 139
Saint Marys, ON N4X 1C4
Canada 519-229-8900
Fax: 519-229-8953 800-567-1890
cwehniai@schneiderfoods.ca www.schneiders.ca
Processor of frozen and fresh poultry
Founder: John Metz Schneider
Plant Manager: Cheryl Firby
Number Employees: 250-499
Parent Co: J.M. Schneider
Type of Packaging: Consumer, Food Service, Private Label

11965 **Schneider Foods**
5523 176th Street
Surrey, BC V3S 4C2
Canada 604-576-1191
Fax: 604-576-6762
Processor of fresh sausage
President: Doug Dodds
Sales/Marketing Executive: Mike McRae
General Manager: Jeff Parker
Purchasing Agent: Dean Rybchuk
Number Employees: 250-499
Parent Co: J.M. Schneider
Type of Packaging: Consumer, Food Service

11966 **Schneider Foods**
362 Laird Road
Guelph, ON N1G 3X7
Canada 519-837-4848
Fax: 519-837-2533
Processor of packaged and frozen luncheon meats including beef, pork and chicken
Plant Manager: Brian Keller
Purchasing Agent: Don Drury
Number Employees: 50-99
Parent Co: J.M. Schneider
Type of Packaging: Consumer, Food Service, Private Label

11967 **Schneider Foods**
550 Kipling Avenue S
Etobicoke, ON M8Z 5E9
Canada 416-252-5790
Fax: 416-252-6215 cwehniai@schneiderfoods.ca
www.schneiders.ca
Processor of fresh and frozen beef
President/General Manager: Ron Flaury
CEO: Rick Young
Marketing Director: Doug Gingrich
Purchasing Agent: Carmela Cieri
Number Employees: 100-249
Parent Co: J.M. Schneider
Type of Packaging: Consumer, Food Service
Brands:
Schneider Foods

11968 **Schneider Foods**
550 Kipling Avenue S
Etobicoke, ON M8Z 5E9
Canada 905-542-6800
Fax: 905-542-0911 800-268-0634
www.schneider.ca
Processor of fresh and frozen beef and pork
CEO: Doug Dodds
President: Doug Dodds
Sales Manager: George Muller
Number Employees: 20-49
Parent Co: J.M. Schneider
Type of Packaging: Consumer, Food Service
Brands:
Schneider

11969 **Schneider Valley Farms Dairy**
1860 E 3rd St
Williamsport, PA 17701 570-326-2021
Fax: 570-326-2736 www.housejourney.com
Processor of milk including whole, low-fat, flavored and skim, buttermilk, ice cream products, sherbet, ice cream mixes, sour cream, dips, fruit juices/drinks and iced teas; wholesaler/distributor of whipped topping, cottage cheeseyogurt, butter, etc
President: William Schneider
Director: Clyde Mosteller
VP Sales: Edward Schneider
Number Employees: 150
Parent Co: Schneider's Dairy
Type of Packaging: Food Service

11970 **Schneider's Dairy Holdings Inc**
726 Frank St
Pittsburgh, PA 15227-1299 412-881-3525
Fax: 412-881-7722 www.schneidersdairy.com

Processor of dairy products including milk, cream, cheese, ice cream mixes, whipped topping, eggs, butter, etc.; also, iced tea, fruit drinks, juices and water
President: William Schneider
Manager: Tom Arnold
Vice President: Edward Schneider
Operations Director: William Schneider
Estimated Sales: $82000000
Number Employees: 250-499

11971 Schobert's Cottage Cheese Corporation
586 Seiberling Street
Akron, OH 44306-3237 216-733-6876
Cottage cheese
President: Mike Barr
Estimated Sales: $ 2.5-5 Million
Number Employees: 5

11972 Schoep's Ice Cream Company
514 Division St
Madison, WI 53704 608-249-6411
Fax: 608-249-7900 800-236-0032
www.schoepsicecream.com
Manufacturer of ice cream, frozen yogurt, light ice cream, frozen custard, sherbert and novelties.
President: Paul Thomsen
Data Processing: Roger Bunders
Sales: Paul Hagen
Operations: Dale Christensen
Purchsing: Bruce Moltumyr
Estimated Sales: $ 20 - 50 Million
Number Employees: 100-249
Number of Brands: 12
Number of Products: 332
Sq. footage: 62500
Type of Packaging: Consumer, Food Service, Private Label, Bulk
Brands:
Schoep's

11973 Schokinag North America
12500 W Carmen Ave
Milwaukee, WI 53225-6100
Fax: 661-322-1156 info@schokinagna.com
www.schokinagna.com
Cocoa powder and chocolate from Ivory Coast cocoa beans
Manager: Cheri Butler
Marketing Director: Lisa Blizzard
Estimated Sales: $ 1-2.5 Million
Number Employees: 1-4
Sq. footage: 12000
Type of Packaging: Consumer, Food Service, Bulk
Brands:
Schokinag North America

11974 Schoolhouse Kitchen LLC
232 Thrid Street
Suite A1000
Brooklyn, NY 11215 718-855-4990
Fax: 646-365-3275
contact@schoolhousekitchen.com
www.schoolhousekitchen.com
Spreadable fruit, mustards, dressings & marinades, and chutneys
President/Product Development Director: Wendy Wheeler Smith
Estimated Sales: $530,000
Number Employees: 10
Sq. footage: 1000

11975 Schoppaul Hill Winery at Ivanhoe
301 S Locust Street
Denton, TX 76201-6055 940-380-9463
Fax: 940-387-5471
Wines
President: John Anderson
CFO: Gary Anderson
Estimated Sales: $ 5-9.9 Million
Number Employees: 3

11976 Schott's Bakery
P.O.Box 7568
Houston, TX 77270-7568 713-869-5701
Fax: 713-869-6530 mturner@flowersfoods.com
www.flowersfoods.com
Processor of breads, buns and rolls
President: Andy Brown
Quality Control: Kim Kleinituizen
VP: Mike Lawson
Operations Manager: Wayne Bristow
Estimated Sales: $43 Million
Number Employees: 100-249
Parent Co: Flowers Baking Company
Type of Packaging: Consumer

11977 (HQ)Schramsberg Vineyards
1400 Schramsberg Rd
Calistoga, CA 94515 707-942-4558
Fax: 707-942-4336 800-877-3623
info1@schramsberg.com www.schramsberg.com
Processor of sparkling wine
President: Jamie Davies
General Manager/Winemaker: Hugh Davies
Marketing: Laurent Sarazin
Estimated Sales: $3000000
Number Employees: 20-49
Number of Brands: 2
Number of Products: 7
Other Locations:
Schramsberg Vineyards
Alijo
Brands:
J. SCHRAM
MIRABELLE
SCHRAMSBERG

11978 Schratter Foods Inc
333 Fairfield Road
Fairfield, NJ 07004 602-300-8986
Fax: 973-575-5010 800-592-4337
www.villars-chocolate.com
Chocolate bars and drinking chocolate.
EVP Finance/Administration: Carmen Messina
Human Resource Manager: Alain Voss
Estimated Sales: $207 Million
Number Employees: 180
Sq. footage: 11416

11979 Schreiber FoodsPlant
208 Dykeman Road
Shippensburg, PA 17257-8700 717-530-5000
www.sficorp.com
Processor of Raskas cream cheese for foodservice industry
Quality Control Director: Barb Wisor
Branch Manager: Dave Pilgert
Number Employees: 195
Parent Co: Schreiber Foods
Type of Packaging: Food Service, Bulk
Brands:
RASKAS

11980 Schreiber FoodsPlant/Distribution Center
2321 Jefferson St
Wisconsin Rapids, WI 54495-1918 715-422-7500
Fax: 715-422-7539
schreiberweb@schreiberfoods.com
www.schreiberfoods.com
Processor of cheese
President & CEO: Larry Ferguson
Co-Founder: L D Schreiber
Co-Founder: Merlin Bush
Co-Founder: Daniel Nusbaum
Manager: Nicholas Destain
Number Employees: 200
Parent Co: Schreiber Foods
Type of Packaging: Consumer, Food Service

11981 Schreiber FoodsPlant
699 W 1700 S
Logan, UT 84321-6219 435-753-0504
Fax: 435-752-5257
schreiberweb@schreiberfoods.com
www.schreiber.com
Processor of cheese
Chairman: John Meng
President/CEO: Larry Ferguson
Co-Founder: L D Schreiber
Co-Founder: Merlin Bush
Co-Founder: Daniel Nusbaum
SVP Foodservice Sales: Mike Haddad
Branch Manager: Mike Moehlmann
Number Employees: 300
Parent Co: Schreiber Foods
Type of Packaging: Consumer, Food Service

11982 Schreiber FoodsPlant
116 E Oak Street
Clinton, MO 64735-1553 660-885-6133
schreiberweb@schreiberfoods.com
www.sficorp.com
Processor of cheese
Manager: Galen Carter
Purchasing Director: Linda Plumlee
Number Employees: 200
Parent Co: Schreiber Foods
Type of Packaging: Consumer, Food Service

11983 Schreiber FoodsPlant
502 N Madison Street
Green Bay, WI 54301-5125 920-455-6741
800-344-0333
schreiberweb@schreiberfoods.com
www.sficorp.com
Processor of cheese
Branch Manager: Wayne Whiting
Number Employees: 27
Parent Co: Schreiber Foods
Type of Packaging: Consumer, Food Service
Brands:
American Heritage
Clearfield Deli
Cooper

11984 Schreiber FoodsPlant
10 Dairy Street
Monett, MO 65708-2502 417-235-6061
Fax: 417-235-4188
schreiberweb@schreiberfoods.com
www.sficorp.com
Processor of cheese
Number Employees: 175
Parent Co: Schreiber Foods
Type of Packaging: Consumer, Food Service

11985 Schreiber FoodsPlant
2255 White Sulphur Rd
Gainesville, GA 30501-3903 770-534-2239
Fax: 770-538-0590
schreiberweb@schreiberfoods.com
www.schreiberfoods.com
Manufacturer of shredded, chuck and sliced cheeses, pimento spread.
Plant Superintendent: Mike Welborn
Estimated Sales: $20-50 Million
Number Employees: 200
Sq. footage: 146000
Brands:
DEEP SOUTH

11986 (HQ)Schreiber Foods Inc
425 Pine St
Green Bay, WI 54301 920-437-7601
Fax: 920-437-1617 800-344-0333
schreiberweb@schreiberfoods.com
www.schreiberfoods.com
Natural cheese, proces cheese, cream cheese, specialty cheese, substitute/imitation cheese, string chese, yogurt and butter blends
President/CEO: Mike Haddad
VP Finance/CFO: Matt Mueller
VP Foodservice Sales: John O'Connor
Estimated Sales: $3+ Billion
Number Employees: 5,500
Type of Packaging: Consumer, Food Service, Private Label, Bulk
Other Locations:
Tempe AZ
Gainesville GA
Carthage MO
Clinton MO
Monett MO
Mt Vernon MO
Ravenna NE
Shippensburg PA
Nashville TN
Stephenville TX
Logan UT
Smithfield UT
Green Bay WI
Brands:
AMERICAN HERITAGE
CLEARFIELD
COOPER
LAFERIA
LOV-IT
MENU
RASKAS
READY-CUT
SCHOOL CHIOCE
SCHREIBER

11987 **Schreier Malting Companypecialty Malt Division**
704 South 15th Street
Sheboygan, WI 53081 920-459-4148
Fax: 920-458-9034 800-669-6258
specialtymalts@specialtymalts.com
www.schreiermalt.com
Processor and exporter of brewers' malt
Estimated Sales: $ 10 - 20 Million
Number Employees: 10-19
Type of Packaging: Bulk

11988 **Schug Carneros Estate Winery**
602 Bonneau Rd
Sonoma, CA 95476 707-939-9363
Fax: 707-939-9364 800-966-9365
info@schugwinery.com www.schugwinery.com
Wines
Founder: Walter Schug
Owner: Gertrud Schug
Sales/Marketing Director: Alex Schug
Winery Chef: Kristine Schug
Winemaker: Michael Cox
Estimated Sales: $ 5-10 Million
Number Employees: 5-9
Brands:
Schug

11989 **Schuil Coffee Company**
3679 29th St SE
Kentwood, MI 49512 616-956-1881
Fax: 616-956-7928 sales@schuilcoffee.com
www.schuilcoffee.com
Coffee
President/CEO: Greta Schuil
Estimated Sales: $500,000-$1 Million
Number Employees: 20-49
Type of Packaging: Private Label
Brands:
Coppets
IBC
Schuil Coffee

11990 **(HQ)Schulze & Burch BiscuitCompany**
1133 W 35th St
Chicago, IL 60609 773-927-6622
Fax: 773-376-4528 www.toastem.com
Manufacturer of toaster pastries, cereal bars, crackers and fruit snacks
Chairman/CEO: Patrick Boyle
President: Kevin Boyle
VP Sales/Marketing: Bill Stuart
Estimated Sales: $75 Million
Number Employees: 500-999
Sq. footage: 500000
Type of Packaging: Consumer, Food Service, Private Label, Bulk
Brands:
POP UPS
SNACKIN FRUITS
TOAST'EM

11991 **(HQ)Schumacher Wholesale Meats**
1114 Zane Ave N
Golden Valley, MN 55422-4679 763-546-3291
Fax: 763-546-0053 800-432-7020
ms@schumeats.com www.schumeats.com
Processor and wholesaler/distributor of meat
President: John F Schumacher
Sales/Marketing Manager: Matt Schumacher
Operations Manager: Bob Timm
Purchasing: Bob Timm
Estimated Sales: $6700000
Number Employees: 20-49
Type of Packaging: Consumer, Food Service, Private Label, Bulk
Brands:
Crown
Great Meats
Valley

11992 **Schuster Marketing Corporation**
6251 W Forest Home Ave
Milwaukee, WI 53220-1916 414-543-2999
Fax: 414-543-5588 888-254-8948
www.blitzpowermints.com
Ann innovative tablet pressing manufacturer that also has the ability to manufacture tablet pressed chewing gum with or without active ingredients such as nutraceuticals.
President: Stephen P Schuster
VP Sales: Heidi Schuster
Estimated Sales: $ 5 - 10 Million
Number Employees: 48
Brands:
BLITZ POWER MINTS

11993 **Schwab & Company**
1111 Linwood Blvd
Oklahoma City, OK 73106-7039 405-235-2376
Fax: 405-236-4694 800-888-8668
ron@schwabmeat.com www.schwabmeat.com
Processor of fresh and frozen beef and pork
President: W Schwab
Marketing Director: Ron Walton
CFO: Gail Anderson
Estimated Sales: $ 10-20 Million
Number Employees: 20-49
Type of Packaging: Consumer, Food Service, Private Label, Bulk
Brands:
Schwab

11994 **(HQ)Schwan Food Company**
115 West College Drive
Marshall, MN 56258 507-532-3274
800-533-5290
questions@schwans.com
www.theschwanfoodcompany.com
Frozen foods, for sale in-store and by home-delivery
CEO/President/COO: Gregory Flack
President/Schwan's Global Supply Chain: Doug Olsen
EVP/CFO: Jim Dollive
President/Schwan's Food Service: Jim Clough
President/Schwan's Consumer Brands: Mark Dairymple
SVP/Product Innovation: Stacey Fowler
EVP/Business Services: Brian Sattler
EVP/Chief Human Resources Officer: Scott Peterson
Estimated Sales: $600 Million
Number Employees: 17000
Number of Brands: 200
Sq. footage: 5
Type of Packaging: Consumer, Food Service, Private Label, Bulk
Other Locations:
Atlanta GA
Crossville TN
Montgomery AL
Pembroke NC
Brands:
Mrs. Freshley's
Mrs. Smith's
Stilwell Oregon Farms

11995 **Schwartz Meat Company**
P.O.Box 1000
Sophia, WV 25921-1000 304-683-4595
Fax: 304-683-3257 www.threadsaver.com
Manufacturer of frozen pizza toppings and meat crumbles
Owner: Ray Lambert
Number Employees: 5-9
Type of Packaging: Food Service, Private Label, Bulk

11996 **Schwartz Pickle Company**
4401 W 44th Pl
Chicago, IL 60632 773-927-7700
Fax: 773-927-3750 www.bayvalleyfoods.com
Processor of pickles including sweet and kosher dill; also, sauerkraut
General Manager: Gary Newman
VP: Bob Fadness
Quality Manager: Armando Garcia
Estimated Sales: $ 20 - 50 Million
Number Employees: 100
Sq. footage: 56992
Type of Packaging: Consumer, Food Service, Private Label, Bulk

11997 **Schwebel Baking Company**
P.O.Box 6018
Youngstown, OH 44501 330-783-2860
Fax: 330-782-1774 www.schwebels.com
Manufacturer of Bagels, variety, hearth baked and enriched breads, buns, rolls, pita bread, english muffins and tortillas for the consumer food industry.
President: Joseph M Schwebel
EVP: Paul Schwebel
VP Operations/Manufacturing: Michael Elenz
VP Operations: Tom Shannon
Estimated Sales: $120 Million
Number Employees: 250-499
Type of Packaging: Consumer

11998 **Schwebel Baking Company**
P.O.Box 6018
Youngstown, OH 44501 330-783-2860
Fax: 330-782-1774 800-860-2867
todd-bruinsma@pnwb.com www.schwebels.com
Processor of bread and rolls
President: Joseph Schwebel
Plant Manager: Jim Ervin
Estimated Sales: $120 Million
Number Employees: 250-499
Parent Co: Schwebel Baking Company
Type of Packaging: Consumer, Food Service, Private Label

11999 **Scialo Brothers**
257 Atwells Ave
Providence, RI 2903 401-421-0986
Fax: 401-274-6117 877-421-0986
info@scialosbakery.com www.scialobakery.com
Italian bread, bakery products, pastries, cakes, pies, cookies and wedding cakes
Co-Owner: Lois Ellis
Co-Owner: Carol Gaeta
Estimated Sales: $500,000-$1 Million
Number Employees: 10-19

12000 **Sconza Candy Company**
1 Sconza Candy Ln
Oakdale, CA 95361 209-845-3700
Fax: 510-638-5792 877-568-8137
customerservice@sconzacandy.com
www.sconzacandy.com
Processor and exporter of candy including brittles, panned, butterscotch, hard, filled, mints, butter toffee nuts and seasonal; available for fund raising; also, bagged and boxed
President: James Sconza
Executive Vice President: Ron Sconza
Estimated Sales: $6 Million
Number Employees: 50-99
Sq. footage: 50000
Type of Packaging: Consumer, Food Service, Private Label, Bulk
Brands:
Bean Heads
Bruiser
Fruit Breaker
Jordanettes
Meteorites
Pip Squeaks
Sconza
Screamer
Wizbanger
Zoygs

12001 **Scooty's Wholesome Foods**
PO Box 18898
Boulder, CO 80308-1898 303-440-4025
Fax: 970-663-6013
Gourmet and specialty foods
President: Scott Silverman
Estimated Sales: Under $500,000
Number Employees: 1-4

12002 **Scot Paris Fine Desserts**
537 Greenwich Street
New York, NY 10013-1000 212-807-1802
Processor of cheesecakes, pies, tarts, cakes, etc; importer of baking ingredients including cocoa, vanilla, ginger, chocolate and IQF fruits
Owner: Scot Paris
Sales Director: Michael Camerman
Sales: Mark Conway
Sq. footage: 500

12003 **Scotian Gold Cooperative**
2900 Lovett Road
Coldbrook, NS B4R 1A6
Canada 902-679-2191
Fax: 902-679-4540 scotian@scotiangold.com
www.scotiangold.com

Processor and packer of apples and pears; also, apple cider
President: David Cudmore
Chairman: William Spurr
Vice President: David Parrish
Estimated Sales: $21 Million
Number Employees: 60
Type of Packaging: Consumer, Private Label
Brands:
Scotian Gold

12004 **Scotsburn Dairy Group**
PO Box 340
Scotsburn, NS B0K 1R0
Canada 902-485-8023
Fax: 902-485-4013
consumerservices@scotsburn.com
www.scotsburn.com
Milk, water, ice cream, cottage cheese, sour cream, dips, frozen yogurt, sherbert, butter
President: Mel MacConnell
Estimated Sales: $104 Million
Number Employees: 75
Parent Co: Scotsburn Cooperative Services
Type of Packaging: Consumer, Food Service, Private Label

12005 **Scott Adams Foods**
288 Newton Sparta Rd
Newton, NJ 7860 973-300-2091
www.pdifoods.com
Vegan meat alternative and vegetarian wraps
President: Jack Parker
CEO: Scott Adams
Estimated Sales: $ 1 - 3 Million
Number Employees: 1-4
Type of Packaging: Private Label
Brands:
DILBERITO
PROTEIN CHEF

12006 **Scott Farms**
7965a Simpson Rd
Lucama, NC 27851 919-284-4014
Fax: 919-284-4872 877-284-4030
scottfarms@cocentral.com www.scottfarms.com
Grower and shipper of sweet potatoes
Owner: Linwood Scott
Estimated Sales: Below $ 5 Million
Number Employees: 5-9
Brands:
Sonny's Pride

12007 **Scott Hams**
1301 Scott Rd
Greenville, KY 42345 270-338-3402
Fax: 270-338-6643 800-318-1353
scotthams@scotthams.com www.scotthams.com
Processor and exporter of country cured and fully cooked hams, bacon, smoked sausage, turkey, jams and fruit butters, sorghum molasses, honey, dried apples, relish, bean soup mix, biscuits, pork cracklins and dog biscuits
President: Leslie Scott
Estimated Sales: Less than $500,000
Number Employees: 1-4
Brands:
Scott's

12008 **Scott's Auburn Mills**
503 Dockins St
Russellville, KY 42276-2065 270-726-2080
Manufacturer of white and yellow corn meal and wheat flour
President: Ray Clark
President: Dave Clark
Estimated Sales: $2 Million
Number Employees: 20-49
Sq. footage: 20000
Type of Packaging: Consumer, Food Service, Private Label, Bulk

12009 **Scott's Candy**
819 South Veterans Blvd
Glennville, GA 30427 608-837-8020
Fax: 608-837-0763 800-356-2100
Processor and exporter of boxed and tinned chocolates
CEO: Gary Ricco
National Sales Manager: James Regan
Estimated Sales: $ 3 - 5 Million
Number Employees: 20-49
Parent Co: Wisconsin Cheeseman
Type of Packaging: Consumer, Private Label
Brands:
Classic Choice
Scott's

12010 **Scott's Sauce Company**
1205 N William St
Goldsboro, NC 27530 919-734-0711
800-734-7282
info@scottsbarbequesauce.com
www.scottsbarbequesauce.com
Processor of barbecue sauces
President: A Martel Scott Jr III
Estimated Sales: Less than $500,000
Number Employees: 5-9
Sq. footage: 7000
Parent Co: Scott's Barbecue
Type of Packaging: Consumer
Brands:
Scott's Barbeque Sauce

12011 **Scott's of Wisconsin**
301 Broadway Dr
Sun Prairie, WI 53590 608-837-8020
Fax: 608-837-0763 800-698-1721
customerservice@wisconsincheeseman.com
www.wisconsincheeseman.com
Cheese spreads, chocolate candy
CEO: Holly Berkenstadt
President: Jay Singer
CEO: Gary Ricco
Marketing Director: Charlie Kesler
Sales Director: Jim Regan
Purchasing Manager: Mark Pelton
Estimated Sales: $ 1-2.5 Million
Number Employees: 20-49
Type of Packaging: Private Label
Brands:
Grace Rush
Nutty Pleasures
Pecanbacks
Scott's
Scott's of Wisconsin
Scottie
Trinkets

12012 **Scott-Bathgate**
149 Pioneer Avenue
Winnipeg, MB R3C 2M8
Canada 204-943-8525
Fax: 204-957-5902 800-216-2990
www.scottbathgate.com
Processor and importer of snack foods, food colorings, mustard, peanut butter, candy and shelled and in-shell sunflower seeds
National Director: Vic Homyshyn
Office/Credit Manager: D Sheridan
Production Manager: Jens Fieting
Type of Packaging: Food Service
Brands:
Food Club
Nutty Club

12013 **Scotty Wotty's Creamy Cheescake**
216 Us Highway 206
Suite 14
Hillsborough, NJ 08844-4384 908-281-9720
Fax: 908-281-9720
Cheesecake
President: Scott Discount
Marketing Director: Scott Discount
Brands:
Scotty Wotty's

12014 **Scray's Cheese Company**
2082 Old Martin Rd
De Pere, WI 54115 920-336-8359
Fax: 920-336-0553
Cheese
President: Jim Scray
Marketing Manager: Jim Scray
Estimated Sales: $500,000-$1 Million
Number Employees: 5-9
Type of Packaging: Private Label
Brands:
Scray's Cheese

12015 **Scripture Candy**
1350 Adamsville Industrial Parkway
Adamsville, AL 35224 205-798-0701
Fax: 888-444-4775 888-317-7333
Info@scripturecandy.com
www.scripturecandy.com
Candy
Owner: Brian Adkins

12016 **Sculli Brothers**
622C Industrial Park Drive
Yeadon, PA 19050 215-336-1223
Fax: 215-336-1225 info@scullibrothers.com
www.scullibrothers.com
Ham, cappocola, italian sausage, coteghino, proscuttino
President: Robert Sculli
VP: Dawn Sculli
Estimated Sales: $150,000
Number Employees: 2
Sq. footage: 2803
Type of Packaging: Private Label, Bulk
Brands:
Bari

12017 **Sea Best Corporation**
PO Box 753
Ipswich, MA 01938-0753 978-768-7475
Fax: 314-241-1377
Seafood

12018 **Sea Breeze Fruit Flavors**
441 Us Highway 202
441 Main Rd
Towaco, NJ 07082-1201 973-334-7777
Fax: 973-334-2617 800-732-2733
info@seabreezesyrups.com
www.seabreezesyrups.com
Processor and exporter of syrups including chocolate, pancake and fountain; also, sundae toppings, bar mixes, juice concentrates and beverage dispensing equipment
President: Steven Sanders
Technical Director: Frank Maranino
Estimated Sales: $25-49.9 Million
Number Employees: 50-99
Type of Packaging: Consumer, Food Service, Private Label
Brands:
Bosco
Sea Breeze
Tropic Beach

12019 **Sea Dog Brewing Company**
1 Main St
Topsham, ME 04086 207-725-0162
Fax: 207-947-8720 www.seadogbrewing.com
Beer
General Manager: Larry Killam
General Manager: Seth Hale
Number Employees: 35
Type of Packaging: Consumer, Food Service
Brands:
Sea Dog

12020 **Sea Farm & Farmfresh Importing Company**
PO Box 3427
Alhambra, CA 91803-0427 323-265-7075
Fax: 323-265-9578
Seafood products.
CEO: Hooi Eng Ooi
VP Operations: S Tan
Estimated Sales: $ 5 - 10 Million
Number Employees: 10-19

12021 **Sea Fresh Alaska**
1620 Larch Street
Kodiak, AK 99615-6207 907-486-6226
Fax: 907-486-6222
Seafood

12022 **Sea Fresh USA**
11 Portland Fish Pier
Portland, ME 04101-4620 207-773-6799
Fax: 207-773-7804 www.seafreshusa.com
Seafood
Owner: James Fox
Estimated Sales: $ 20 - 50 Million
Number Employees: 20-49

12023 **Sea Garden Seafoods**
P.O.Box 181
Meridian, GA 31319 912-832-4437
Fax: 912-832-6834 andy@snowsouth.com
www.snowsouth.com
Manufacturer of Crab meat and shrimp products
President/CEO: Andrew Amason
Purchasing Agent: Carol Amason
Estimated Sales: $100 Million
Number Employees: 50-99
Parent Co: Snowsouth
Type of Packaging: Bulk

12024 **Sea Gold Seafood Products**
38 Blackmer St
New Bedford, MA 02744 508-993-3060
Fax: 508-993-3070 seagold01@msn.com
www.seagolddips.com
Processor of dips including gourmet seafood and crab dip, buttered seafood and lobster dip, seafood and jalapeno crab dip, spicy shrimp dip, seafood and shrimp scampi dip, cajun seafood and crab dip, clams casino clam dip, and seafoodnewburg dip.
Owner: Micheal Trazzra
Operations Manager: Wendy Harwood
Estimated Sales: Below $ 5 Million
Number Employees: 10-19
Number of Brands: 1
Number of Products: 9
Sq. footage: 5000
Type of Packaging: Consumer, Food Service
Brands:
Sea Gold

12025 **Sea Horse Wharf**
245 W Point Rd
Phippsburg, ME 04562-5127 207-389-2312
Fax: 207-389-1005
Seafood.
Owner: Douglas Scott
Estimated Sales: $300,000-500,000
Number Employees: 1-4

12026 **Sea K Fish Company**
225 Sigurdson Ave
Blaine, WA 98230-4004 360-332-5121
Fax: 360-332-8785
Processor and exporter of seafood including halibut
Estimated Sales: $ 20 - 50 Million
Number Employees: 20-49
Type of Packaging: Consumer, Food Service

12027 **Sea Level Seafoods**
P.O.Box 2085
Wrangell, AK 99929 907-874-2401
Fax: 907-874-2158
Seafood
Manager: Vern Phillips
Estimated Sales: $ 20 - 50 Million
Number Employees: 20-49

12028 **Sea Lyons**
9093 Springway Ct
Spanish Fort, AL 36527 251-626-2841
Fax: 251-626-2841
Seafood.
President: Martha Lyons
Vice President: Wade Lyons

12029 **Sea Nik Food Company**
Mile 137 Sterling Highway
Ninilchik, AK 99639 907-567-3980
Fax: 907-567-1041
Seafood
Estimated Sales: $ 20 - 50 Million
Number Employees: 50-99

12030 **Sea Pearl Seafood**
14120 Shell Belt Rd
Bayou La Batre, AL 36509 251-824-2129
Fax: 251-650-1321 800-872-8804
info@sea-pearl.com www.sea-pearl.com
Processor of frozen and breaded shrimp and oysters
Owner: Joseph G Ladnier
Plant Manager: Allen Mayfield
Estimated Sales: $3300000
Number Employees: 10-19
Type of Packaging: Consumer, Food Service, Bulk
Brands:
Neptune Delight
Sea Pearl Seafood Co., Inc.

12031 **Sea Products Company**
PO Box 836
Astoria, OR 97103-0836 503-325-5023
Fax: 503-325-2347
Fish and seafoods
Manager: Judy Zell
Plant Manager: Terry Miller
Estimated Sales: $ 20-50 Million
Number Employees: 250

12032 **Sea Ridge Winery**
13404 Dupont Road
Occidental, CA 95465 707-874-1707
Wines
President: Dan Wickham
Estimated Sales: $500-1 Million
Number Employees: 1-4

12033 **Sea Safari**
785 E Pantego St
Belhaven, NC 27810 252-943-3091
Fax: 252-943-3083 800-688-6174
seasafari@beaufortco.com www.seasafari.com
Processor and exporter of frozen crawfish and crab meat; also, canned blue crab meat
President/Finance & Sales Executive: Topper Bateman
General Manager: Guinn Leverett
Director Marketing: Christine Costley
Sales Manager: Frances Williams
Estimated Sales: $400,000
Number Employees: 4
Sq. footage: 40000
Parent Co: Sea Safari
Type of Packaging: Consumer, Food Service
Brands:
Acadian Gourmet
Ecrevisse Acadienne
Louisianas Best

12034 **Sea Safari**
785 E Pantego St
Belhaven, NC 27810 252-943-3091
Fax: 252-943-3083 seasafari@belhavennc.com
www.seasafari.com
Processor of fresh and pasteurized crab meat
President: Topper Bateman
Estimated Sales: Under $500,000
Number Employees: 4
Type of Packaging: Consumer, Food Service

12035 **Sea Safari Ltd.**
785 E Pantego St
Belhaven, NC 27810 252-943-3091
Fax: 252-943-3083 800-688-6174
Processor of frozen crabs and crab meat
President/Finance & Sales Executive: Topper Bateman
General Manager: Guinn Leverett
Estimated Sales: $400,000
Number Employees: 4
Sq. footage: 40000

12036 **Sea Salt Superstore**
19004 Highway 99
Lynnwood, WA 98036
Fax: 425-640-2500 866-999-7258
customerservice@seasaltsuperstore.com
www.seasaltsuperstore.com
Gourmet foods, exotic spices and hand crafted natural sea salts to the gourmet food customers.

12037 **Sea Snack Foods**
914 E 11th St
Los Angeles, CA 90021 213-622-2204
Fax: 213-622-7845 sales@seasnack.com
www.seasnack.com
Processor and exporter of cooked IQF shrimp and seafood cocktails
President/CEO: Fred Ockrim
VP: Jeffrey Kahn
Sales Director: Peter Peterson
Plant Manager: Alfred Dolor
Estimated Sales: $7000000
Number Employees: 60
Sq. footage: 2000
Type of Packaging: Consumer, Food Service
Brands:
O.K. Brand
Restaurant Row
Sea Snack
Twin Harbors

12038 **Sea Stars Goat Cheese**
1122 Soquel Ave
Santa Cruz, CA 95062-2106 831-423-7200
Fax: 831-454-0838
Cheese
Owner: Nancy Gassney
Estimated Sales: $ 2.5-5 Million
Number Employees: 10-19
Type of Packaging: Private Label

12039 **Sea View Fillet Company**
15 Antonio Costa Ave
New Bedford, MA 02740-7347 508-984-1406
Fax: 508-984-1411
Seafood
Manager: Sandy Harbick
Estimated Sales: $10-24.9 Million
Number Employees: 50-99

12040 **Sea Watch Intl.**
8978 Glebe Park Dr
Easton, MD 21601 410-822-7500
Fax: 410-822-1266 sales@seaclam.com
www.seaclam.com
Processor and exporter of canned and frozen clams, crab cakes, extruded calamari rings, blue crab meat, squid, shrimp, soups and seafood chowders
President: George Torggler
President: Bob Brennan
Vice President: Bob Redar
R&D/Quality Control: Larry Hughes
Marketing Director: Kimberly Scott
Sales Director: Bob Redar
Public Relations: Doug Morrow
Operations Manager: Kenny Carroll
Purchasing Manager: Susie Jones
Estimated Sales: $ 50 - 100 Million
Number Employees: 20-49
Number of Brands: 4
Type of Packaging: Food Service, Private Label
Brands:
AMERICAN ORIGINAL
CAP'NS CATCH
CAPT. FRED
EASTERN SHORE FOODS, LLC
MID-ATLANTIC FOODS
MR FROSTY
OLD SALT SEAFOOD
SAILOR'S CHOICE
SEAWATCH
TUCKER'S COVE

12041 **Sea-Fresh Seafood Market**
2303 Halls Mill Road
Mobile, AL 36606-4603 251-478-3434
Fax: 251-478-3778
Seafood.
President: Patrick Meacham
CFO: Rusty Brennan

12042 **SeaBear Smokehouse**
605 30th Street
Anacortes, WA 98221 360-293-466
Fax: 888-487-6427 800-645-3474
smokehouse@seabear.com www.seabear.com
wild salmon
President: Mike Mondello
VP Director of Consumer: Patti Fisher

12043 **SeaPerfect Atlantic Farms**
PO Box 12139
Charleston, SC 29422-2139 843-762-0022
Fax: 843-795-6672 800-728-0099
kgrant@awod.com seaperfect.com
Processor and exporter of clams; importer of scallops
President: Carlos Celle
Sales Director: Michelle Black
General Manager: Knox Grant
Estimated Sales: $2300000
Number Employees: 45
Sq. footage: 34000
Brands:
SEAPERFECT

12044 **SeaSpecialties**
1111 NW 159th Dr
Miami, FL 33169-5807 305-625-5112
Fax: 305-625-5528 800-654-6682
info@seaspecialties.com
www.seaspecialties.com
Seafood
Manager: Ron Alexander
Quality Control: Irvin Norss
CFO: Michael Metzkes
Estimated Sales: $ 20-50 Million
Number Employees: 100-249

12045 **Seabear**
P.O.Box 591
Anacortes, WA 98221-0591 360-293-4661
Fax: 360-293-4097 800-645-3474
smokehouse@seabear.com www.seabear.com
Processor and exporter of smoked fish and seafoods
President: Mike Mondello
General Manager: Kathy Hayward
Marketing Manager: Barb Hoenselaar
Director Operations: Cathy Hayward-Hughes
Estimated Sales: $10800000
Number Employees: 1-4

Type of Packaging: Consumer, Bulk

12046 **Seaberghs Frozen Foods**
200 Westchester Avenue
White Plains, NY 10601-4510 914-948-6377
Frozen foods
President: Harry Rich
Estimated Sales: $ 1-2.5 Million
Number Employees: 1-4

12047 **Seaboard Foods**
9000 W 67th St
Suite 200
Shawnee Mission, KS 66202 913-261-2600
Fax: 913-261-2626 800-262-7907
info@seaboardfoods.com
www.seaboardfoods.com
Produces and sells fresh, frozen and processed pork.
President: Rodney Brenneman
Ceo: Steven Bresky
VP Finance & Accounting: Kevin Henn
VP Sales & Marketing: Terry Holton
VP Plant Operations: Marty Hast
Estimated Sales: $3.6 Billion
Number Employees: 450
Type of Packaging: Consumer, Food Service, Private Label, Bulk
Other Locations:
Processing Plant
Guymon OK
Ham Deboning Plant
Reynosa, MEXICO
Mount Dora Farms Management
Houston TX
Live Production Operations
Kansas
Daily's Premium Meats Bacon Plant
Salt Lake City UT
Daily's Premium Meats Bacon Plant
Missoula MT
Live Production Operations
Colorado
Live Production Operations
Texas
Brands:
DAILY'S PREMIUM MEATS
PRAIRIE FRESH PREMIUM PORK
SEABOARD FARMS

12048 **Seabreeze Fish**
2311 R Street
Bakersfield, CA 93301-2986 661-323-7936
Fax: 805-323-7936
Seafood.
Estimated Sales: $300,000-500,000
Number Employees: 1-4

12049 **(HQ)Seabrook Brothers & Sons**
85 Finley Road
Seabrook, NJ 08302 856-455-8080
Fax: 856-455-9282 seabrob@seabrookfarms.com
ww.seabrookfarms.com
frozen vegetables
President/CEO: James Seabrook Jr
CFO: Barbara Wiler
VP Quality Assurance: Barbara Michalkiewicz
VP Sales/Marketing: Brian Seabrook
Human Resource Manager: Scott Elliott
Plant Manager: Dave Deon
Purchasing Manager: Joan Wilson
Estimated Sales: $93 Million
Number Employees: 200
Number of Brands: 96
Number of Products: 150
Sq. footage: 35000
Type of Packaging: Consumer, Food Service, Private Label, Bulk
Brands:
SEABROOK FARMS
SOMERDALE

12050 **(HQ)Seabrook Ingredients**
115 Peanut Dr
Edenton, NC 27932-9604 252-482-2112
Fax: 252-482-4185
marketing@universalblanchers.com
www.universalblanchers.com
Pre-cleaning and blanching services, roasted peanuts, granulated peanuts; peanut butter, peanut toppings and variegates, roasted peanut extract
President: Thomas Beaty
CEO: Michael Fisher
CFO: Chuck Davis
CEO: Michael Fisher
Quality Assurance: Anne Craig
VP Sales and Marketing: John Bowen
Type of Packaging: Consumer, Bulk

12051 **Seafare Market Wholesale**
PO Box 671
Moody, ME 04054-0671 207-646-5160
Fax: 408-294-3948
Seafood
President: John Foye
Estimated Sales: $ 10 - 20 Million
Number Employees: 10-19

12052 **Seafood & Meat**
5681 Highway 90
Theodore, AL 36582-1671 251-653-4600
Fax: 251-653-1109
Seafood and meat distributors.
President: Ruth Summerlin

12053 **Seafood & Service Marketing**
4470 Chamblee Dunwoody Rd
Dunwoody, GA 30338-6224 770-451-9183
Fax: 770-451-9216 www.servicemark.aol.com
Frozen seafood, full line seafood
President: Paul Kastin
Estimated Sales: $ 20 - 50 Million
Number Employees: 10-19

12054 **Seafood Connection**
841 Pohukaina St Ste I
Honolulu, HI 96813 808-591-8550
Fax: 808-591-8445
Suppliers of seafood and gourmet products to customers globally.
President: Stuart Simmons
Estimated Sales: $ 10 - 20 Million
Number Employees: 10 to 19

12055 **Seafood Dimension International**
P.O.Box 27548
Anaheim, CA 92809-0118 714-692-6464
Fax: 714-282-8997 dmontesai@aol.com
Seafood
Owner: Christi Lang
Estimated Sales: $1.4 Million
Number Employees: 5-9
Number of Brands: 20
Number of Products: 50
Type of Packaging: Food Service
Brands:
20TH CENTURY FOODS
BROOKS STREET BAKING
HARVEST FARM
LIL' FISHERMAN
MIDSHIP
NEPTUNE
SCHONER

12056 **Seafood Distributors**
420 W Bay Street
Savannah, GA 31401-1115 912-233-6048
Fax: 612-233-3238
Seafood
President: Walter Bryan

12057 **Seafood Express**
179 Rossmore Rd
Brunswick, ME 04011 207-729-0887
Fax: 207-721-9146
Seafood

12058 **Seafood Hawaii**
875 Waimanu St Ste 634
Honolulu, HI 96813 808-597-1971
Fax: 808-538-1973
Seafood
President: Jeb Inouye
Estimated Sales: $ 5 - 10 Million
Number Employees: 20-49

12059 **Seafood International**
P.O.Box 388
Bayou La Batre, AL 36509-0388 251-824-4200
Fax: 251-824-2811
Wholesaler/distributor of fresh and frozen seafood
President: David Robicheaux
Estimated Sales: $ 3 - 5 Million
Number Employees: 1-4

12060 **Seafood International Distributor, Inc**
1051 Old Henderson Hwy
Henderson, LA 70517-7805 337-228-7568
Fax: 337-228-7573
Seafood
Owner: Roy Robert
Estimated Sales: $3,300,000
Number Employees: 20-49

12061 **Seafood Merchants**
900 Forest Edge Dr
Vernon Hills, IL 60061 847-634-0900
Fax: 847-634-1351
sales@theseafoodmerchants.com
www.theseafoodmerchants.com
Importer of seafood
President: Roy Axelson
CEO: Bonnie Axelson
Sales: Gayle Janos
Purchasing Director: Bonnie Axelson
Estimated Sales: $ 10-20 Million
Number Employees: 20-49
Sq. footage: 23000
Type of Packaging: Consumer, Food Service, Bulk

12062 **Seafood Network**
123 Crossbrook Drive
Brunswick, GA 31525-2114 912-267-0422
Fax: 912-267-1918
Crabmeat, shrimp, scallops

12063 **Seafood Packaging**
2120 Poydras St
New Orleans, LA 70112 504-522-6677
Fax: 504-522-9008
ksharp@seafoodpackaging.com
www.seafoodpackaging.com
Seafood
Owner: Kent Sharp
Estimated Sales: $ 5 - 10 Million
Number Employees: 5-9
Type of Packaging: Consumer

12064 **Seafood Plus Corporation**
6930 Pershing Road
Berwyn, IL 60402-3937 708-795-4820
Fax: 708-795-7719
Seafood

12065 **Seafood Producers Coopative**
2875 Roeder Ave Ste 2
Bellingham, WA 98225 360-733-0120
Fax: 360-733-0513 spc@spcsales.com
www.spcsales.com
Processor and exporter of salmon, halibut, sablefish and rockfish.
President: Thomas McLaughlin
Sales: Kurt Sigfusson
Estimated Sales: $45,000,000
Number Employees: 5-9
Type of Packaging: Food Service, Bulk
Brands:
Alaska Gold
Longliner
Sitka Gold

12066 **Seafood Services**
10 N Front Street
New Bedford, MA 02740-7327 508-999-6785
Fax: 508-993-4001
Seafood
President: David Horton
Estimated Sales: $ 20 - 50 Million
Number Employees: 20-49

12067 **Seafood Specialties**
155 E Vienna St
Anna, IL 62906 618-833-6083
Fax: 618-833-6083
President: Daniel Lewis
Estimated Sales: $ 1 - 3 Million
Number Employees: 1-4

12068 **Seafood Specialties**
P.O.Box 665
Coden, AL 36523-0665 251-824-2693
Fax: 251-824-7808
Seafoods
President: Susan Taylor
Human Resources: Bridget Sprinkle
Estimated Sales: Under $500,000
Number Employees: 20-49

12069 **Seafood Specialty Sales**
28 Mulholland Dr
Ipswich, MA 01938 978-356-2995
Fax: 978-356-2275
Seafood

12070 **Seafood USA**
PO Box 418
Humarock, MA 02047-0418 781-837-7666
Fax: 781-837-7664
President: James Allen

12071 **Seafreeze Pizza**
206 SW Michigan St.
Seattle, WA 98106 206-767-7350
Fax: 206-763-8514 www.seafreeze.com
Seafood
President: Patrick Floyd
Owner: Parry Romani Deconcini
VP: William Bowman
Estimated Sales: $ 10 - 20 Million
Number Employees: 100
Brands:
Seafreeze Pizza

12072 **Sealand Lobster Corporation**
PO Box 423
Tenants Harbor, ME 04860-0423 207-372-6247
Fax: 207-389-1819
Lobster

12073 **Sealaska Corporation**
1 Sealaska Plz Ste 400
Juneau, AK 99801 907-586-1512
Fax: 907-586-2304 800-848-5921
russell.dick@sealaska.com www.sealaska.com
Seafood
President: Chris McNeil
CFO: Willian Strafford
CEO: Chris E McNeil Jr
VP: Richard Harris
Estimated Sales: $ 100-200 Million
Number Employees: 20-49
Brands:
Ocean Beauty Seafoods

12074 **Seald Sweet Growers & Packers**
1991 74th Ave
Vero Beach, FL 32966 772-569-2244
Fax: 772-569-5110 www.sealdsweet.com
Grower, importer and exporter of citrus products including oranges, grapefruit, lemons, clementines, minneolas, tangerines and tangeros.
President/Owner: Hein Deprez
CFO: Christine Wallace
VP: David E Mixon
Marketing Manager: Kim Flores
Estimated Sales: $5-10 Million
Number Employees: 20-49
Sq. footage: 15000
Type of Packaging: Food Service, Bulk
Brands:
Florigold
Seald Sweet

12075 **Seapac of Idaho**
4074 N 2000 E
Filer, ID 83328-5033 208-326-3100
Fax: 208-326-5935
Processes and packages trout and salmon jerky, smoked rainbow trout, and salmon sausages.
President/General Manager: Ken Ashley
Estimated Sales: $ 7.10 M
Number Employees: 20-49

12076 **Seapoint Farms**
20042 Beach Blvd
Suite 102
Huntington Beach, CA 92648 919-870-5471
Fax: 949-646-9851 888-722-7098
info@seapointfarms.com
www.seapointfarms.com
importer and manufacturer of edamame products
President/Owner: Laura Cross
CEO: Kevin Cross
Estimated Sales: 1.6 Millin
Number Employees: 8

12077 **Seapoint Farms**
20042 Beach Blvd Suite 102
Huntington Beach, CA 92648 949-646-9831
Fax: 949-646-9851 888-722-7098
info@seapointfarms.com
www.seapointfarms.com
Manufacturer and distributor of edamame food products
President: Laura Cross
CEO: Kevin Cross
COO: Philip Siegel
VP of Sales: Tim Boyer
Estimated Sales: $3 Million
Number Employees: 8
Brands:
Seapoint Farms

12078 **Seaside Ice Cream**
PO Box 734
Pelham, NY 10803-0734 914-636-2751
Fax: 631-728-1653
Ice cream
Owner: Arthur Haas

12079 **Season Harvest Foods**
556 E Weddell Drive
Suite 2
Sunnyvale, CA 94089 408-749-8018
Fax: 408-749-7079
info@seasonharvestfoods.com
www.seasonharvestfoods.com
Frozen organic and dried ingredients
VP Sales: Keith Shelby
Estimated Sales: $190,000
Number Employees: 2
Sq. footage: 2846

12080 **Seasons' Enterprises**
1790 W Cortland Ct
Addison, IL 60101 630-628-0211
Fax: 630-628-0385 info@seasonssnacks.com
www.seasonssnacks.com
Processor of organic snack foods including corn cheese puffs, chocolate covered butter toffee and tortilla, reduced-fat potato chips, kettle cooked potato chips, peller snacks and popcorn products
President: Michael Season
Sales Director: Kelly Garrigan
Operations Manager: Mark Ruchti
Estimated Sales: $1300000
Number Employees: 5-9
Number of Brands: 2
Number of Products: 35
Sq. footage: 12000
Type of Packaging: Consumer, Food Service, Private Label, Bulk
Brands:
Butter Toffee Covered Popcorn
Chocolate Covered Potato Chips
Chocolate Covered Toffee Popcorn
Michael Season's Cheese Curls
Michael Season's Cheese Puffs
Michael Season's Kettle Potatoes
Michael Season's Organically Grown
Michael Season's Sensations
Sweet Organics

12081 **Seatech Corporation**
16825 48th Ave W Ste 222
Lynnwood, WA 98037 425-487-3231
Fax: 425-835-0367 johnw@seatechcorp.com
www.seatechcorp.com
frozen shrimp, crab and scallops
President: John Wendt
CFO: Jim Schantz
Quality Control: Todd Wendt
Marketing Director: Todd Wendt
Sales Director: Todd Wendt
Estimated Sales: $6 Million
Number Employees: 3
Number of Brands: 2
Sq. footage: 1000
Type of Packaging: Consumer, Food Service, Private Label, Bulk
Brands:
CLEAN KITCHEN
Chiquititos
Seatech

12082 **Seatrade Corporation**
P.O.Box 421
Hoboken, NJ 07030-0421 201-963-5700
Fax: 201-963-0577
VP: Richard Mendelson
Sales Manager: Richard Menderlson

12083 **Seattle Bar Company**
3302 Wallingford Avenue N
Seattle, WA 98103-9039 206-601-4301
Fax: 206-282-3548 www.seattlebar.com
Owner: Beth Campbell
Number Employees: 1-4
Brands:
SEATTLE BAR

12084 **Seattle Chocolate Company**
1180 Andover Park W
Tukwila, WA 98188-3909 425-264-2800
Fax: 425-264-2811 800-334-3600
info@seattlechocolates.com
http://www.seachoco.com/
Manufacturers of pre-wrapped gifts of natural meltaway chocolate truffles and truffle bars
President and CEO: Jean Thompson
VP Operations: Niel Campbell
Marketing Manager: Kirsty Ellison
Controller: Joe Slye
Estimated Sales: $10 Million
Number Employees: 50
Number of Brands: 1
Number of Products: 11
Type of Packaging: Consumer, Private Label, Bulk
Brands:
CHICK CHOCOLATES
SEATTLE CHOCOLATES
SKINNY TRUFFLES

12085 **Seattle Gourmet Foods**
19016 72nd Ave S
Kent, WA 98032 425-656-9076
Fax: 425-656-8059 800-800-9490
www.seattlegourmetfoods.com
Manufacturer of many of the Pacific Northwest's specialty food products
Manager: Tom Means
Estimated Sales: $2.5-5 Million
Number Employees: 10-19
Brands:
ANNA'S GOURMET
BIRINGER'S FARM FRESH
BUCKEYE BEANS AND HERBS
COY'S COUNTRY NORTHWEST
FREDERICK'S FINE CHOCOLATES
INNOVATIVE COOKIES
MAURY ISLAND FARMS PREMIUM PRESERVE
PARADISE FARMS
QUINN'S
ST. JEAN'S CANNERY & SMOKEHOUSE
VICTORIA GOURMET CHOCOLATES

12086 **Seattle Gourmet Foods**
19016 72nd Ave S
Kent, WA 98032 425-656-9076
Fax: 425-656-8059 800-800-9490
sales@seattlegourmetfoods.com
www.seattlegourmetfoods.com
Chocolate meltaways, coffee spoons, molasses chews, thin mints, pecan delights, panned nuts, jams, jellies, fruit toppings, whipped taffy
President/CEO: Tom Means
Office Manager: Beth Bickerson
Estimated Sales: $10-20 Million
Number Employees: 275
Brands:
ANNA'S
BIRINGER'S FARM FRESH
BUCKEYE BEANS & HERBS
CHOCOLATE NOVELTIES
COY'S COUNTRY
MAURY ISLAND FARM
PARADISE FARMS CONFECTIONS
QUINN'S

12087 **(HQ)Seattle's Best Coffee**
PO Box 3717
Seattle, WA 98124
800-611-7793
www.seattlesbest.com
Manufacturer and wholesaler/distributor of ground coffee and beans; serving the food service market
Manager: James Strasbaugh

Estimated Sales: $10.9 Million
Number Employees: 100-249
Type of Packaging: Consumer, Food Service

12088 **Seavers Bakery**
3300 Mayfield Dr
Johnson City, TN 37604 423-928-8131
Fax: 423-928-8132
Processor of baked goods including pies
President: Ralph Coomer
President/CEO: Richard Seaver
Plant Manager: Richard McKinney
Estimated Sales: $250000
Number Employees: 10-19
Type of Packaging: Consumer

12089 **Seavey Vineyard**
1310 Conn Valley Rd
Saint Helena, CA 94574 707-963-8339
Fax: 707-963-0232 info@seaveyvineyard.com
www.seaveyvineyard.com
Wines
President: William Seavey
Marketing Manager: Nora Bowhay
Estimated Sales: $500,000-$1 Million
Number Employees: 5-9
Brands:
Seavey Cabernet Sauvignon
Seavey Chardonnay
Seavey Marlot

12090 **Seaview Lobster Company**
43 Government St
Kittery, ME 03904 207-439-1599
Fax: 207-439-1476 800-245-4997
orders@seaviewlobster.com
www.seaviewlobster.com
Seafood
Owner: Tom Flanagan
Estimated Sales: $ .5 - 1 million
Number Employees: 1-4

12091 **Seawatch International**
8978 Glebe Park Dr
Easton, MD 21601-7004 410-822-7500
Fax: 410-822-1266 sales@seaclam.com
www.seaclam.com
Largest processor of clam products including canned, fresh and frozen clams, clam and specialty chowders, clam strips, crab cakes, prepared calamari, and tempura shrimp.
President: Bob Brennan
VP Sales: Steve Gordon
Estimated Sales: $ 50 - 100 Million
Number Employees: 20-49
Type of Packaging: Food Service

12092 **Seaway Company**
P.O.Box 868
Fairhaven, MA 02719-0800 508-992-1221
Fax: 508-992-1253
Seafood.
Owner: Steve Doonan
Estimated Sales: $ 1 - 3 Million
Number Employees: 1-4

12093 **Seawind Trading International**
5375 Avenida Encinas Ste A
Carlsbad, CA 92008 760-438-5600
Fax: 760-438-5677
Fruits and vegetables
Executive Director: Rick Rosenquist
Estimated Sales: $860,000
Number Employees: 5-9

12094 **Sebastiani Vineyards**
P.O.Box Aa
Sonoma, CA 95476 707-938-3200
Fax: 707-933-3370 800-888-5532
info@sebastiani.com www.sebastiani.com
Processor of wines
Chairman: Richard Cuneo
President/CEO: Mary Ann Sebastiani Cuneo
COO: Emma Swain
Vice President/Winemaster: Mark Lyon
Operations Manager: Paul Bergna
Estimated Sales: $5-10 Million
Number Employees: 100
Type of Packaging: Consumer

12095 **Sechler's Fine Pickles**
5685 State Road 1
Saint Joe, IN 46785 260-337-5461
Fax: 260-337-5771 800-332-5461
showroom@sechlerspickles.com
www.gourmetpickles.com
54 varieties of pickles.
Owner: David Sechler
General Manager: Max Troyer
Sales Executive: Mike Meyers
Estimated Sales: $4 Million
Number Employees: 32
Sq. footage: 58000

12096 **Sechrist Brothers**
32 E Main St
Dallastown, PA 17313-2206 717-244-2975
Fax: 717-244-6532
Processor and packer of meat including bologna, smoked ham, frankfurters and sausage
President: George Sechrist
VP: Jacob Sechrist
Estimated Sales: $910000
Number Employees: 5-9
Sq. footage: 20000
Type of Packaging: Consumer

12097 **Secret Garden**
10989 County 14
Park Rapids, MN 56470 218-732-4866
Fax: 218-732-2007 800-950-4409
sgmorg@wcta.net
www.secretgardengourmet.com
Manufacturer of gourmet wild rice, bread, entree and seasoning mixes
President: Anne Morgan
Sales/Marketing: Andrea Roberts
Purchasing Manager: Anne Morgan
Estimated Sales: $550000
Number Employees: 5-9
Sq. footage: 6000
Type of Packaging: Consumer, Private Label
Brands:
Anne's Country Gourmet
CONTINENTAL CUISINE
Creole Classics
Midhaven Farm Cafe
Midheaven Farm
PASTRY PERFECT
Secret Garden
Soup For Singles
Swany White
Swany White Certified Organic
The Secret Garden

12098 **Secret House Vineyards**
88324 Vineyard Ln
Veneta, OR 97487-9406 541-935-3774
Fax: 541-935-3774 800-497-1574
info@secrethousewinery.com
www.secrethousewinery.com
Wines
President: Ron Chappel
CFO: Patty Chappel
Estimated Sales: $ 10-20 Million
Number Employees: 5-9
Brands:
Secret House

12099 **Secret Tea Garden**
5559 West Boulevard
Vancouver, BC V6M 3W6
Canada 604-261-3070
Fax: 604-261-3075 info@secretgardentea.com
www.secretgardentea.com
Manufacturers of special varieties of tea
President: Erin McBeath
VP: With Kathy
Estimated Sales: Less than $500,000
Number Employees: 5

12100 **Sedlock Farm**
1557 Knoxville Road
Lynn Center, IL 61262-8504 309-521-8284
Fax: 309-521-8284
Processor of fresh asparagus and asparagus products including fettucine; also, vinegars, hot pepper and jellies
Owner/CEO: John Sedlock
VP Manufacturing: Patricia Sedlock
Estimated Sales: Under $300,000
Number Employees: 6
Type of Packaging: Consumer, Food Service, Bulk

12101 **See's Candies**
20600 South Alameda Street
Carson, CA 90810
Fax: 800-275-4733 800-347-7337
qdordering@sees.com www.sees.com
Processor and exporter of confectioneries and chocolates
President: Charles Huggins
CEO: Charles Huggins
CFO: Ken Scott
General Manager: Jane Wellsplant
Estimated Sales: $ .5 - 1 million
Number Employees: 5-9
Sq. footage: 220000
Parent Co: See's Candies
Type of Packaging: Consumer
Brands:
See's Candies

12102 **Seed Enterprises**
679 19th Rd
West Point, NE 68788 402-372-3238
Fax: 402-372-2627 888-440-7333
seedenterprises@alltel.net
Processor and exporter of soybeans
President: Conrad Reeson
Estimated Sales: $ 1 - 3 Million
Number Employees: 5-9
Sq. footage: 35000
Brands:
Sunrise

12103 **Seeds of Change**
P.O.Box 15700
Santa Fe, NM 87592-5700 505-438-8080
Fax: 505-438-7052 888-762-7333
www.seedsofchange.com
Organic pasta sauces, grain blends, salsas, salad dressing, ketchup and dry soup mixes
Manager: Marc Cool
Estimated Sales: $ 10-20 Million
Number Employees: 30
Type of Packaging: Private Label
Brands:
Seeds of Change

12104 **Seenergy Foods**
121 Jevlan Drive
Woodbridge, ON L4L 8A8
Canada 905-850-2544
Fax: 905-850-2563 800-609-7674
info@seenergyfoods.com
www.seenergyfoods.com
Processor and exporter of frozen vegetables including vegetable patties and IQF (individually quick frozen) beans
President/CEO: Shreyas Ajmera
Marketing/Sales: Carl McLaughlin
Estimated Sales: $3.2 Million
Number Employees: 80
Type of Packaging: Consumer, Food Service, Private Label, Bulk
Brands:
Presidents Choice

12105 **Seger Egg Corporation**
P.O.Box 265
Farina, IL 62838-0265 618-245-3301
Fax: 618-245-3552
Eggs
President: Larry Seger
Sales/Marketing: Larry Pemberton
Estimated Sales: $ 10 - 20 Million
Number Employees: 50-99

12106 **Seghesio Family Vineyards**
700 Grove St
Healdsburg, CA 95448 707-433-3579
Fax: 707-433-0545 seghesio@seghesio.com
www.seghesio.com
Wines
CEO: Peter Seghesio
CFO: Ileana Standridge
Marketing Director: Cathy Seghesio
Production Manager/Winemaker: Ted Seghesio
Estimated Sales: $ 10-20 Million
Number Employees: 20-49
Type of Packaging: Private Label
Brands:
Keyhole Ranch

12107 **Seitenbacher America LLC**
11505 Perpetual Drive
Odessa, FL 33556 727-376-3000
Fax: 727-376-4662
seitenbacheramerica@verizon.net
www.seitenbacher.com
Natural food manufacturer
President: Willi Pfannenschwarz
Manager: Harry Pfannenschwarz
Sales: Debbie Roberts
Estimated Sales: $600,000
Number Employees: 15
Sq. footage: 5600

12108 **(HQ)Select Food Products**
120 Sunrise Avenue
Toronto, ON M4A 1B4
Canada 416-759-9316
Fax: 416-759-9310 800-699-8016
feedback@selectfoodproducts.com
www.selctfoodproducts.com
Manufacturers and exporter of salad dressings, sauces, salsas, relishes, mustard, gravies, canned dinners, etc; importer of tomatoes and tomato paste
President: Paul Fredricks
Number Employees: 150
Sq. footage: 116000
Type of Packaging: Consumer, Food Service, Private Label, Bulk
Brands:
Duthie
Horne's
Laing's
Oxford Inn
Select

12109 **Select Origins**
PO Box 1748
Mansfield, OH 44901-1748 419-924-5447
General groceries
National Sales Manager: Noel Thompson
Estimated Sales: $ 5-10 Million
Number Employees: 20

12110 **Select Supplements, Inc**
5800 Newton Dr
Carlsbad, CA 92008 760-431-7509
Fax: 760-804-8073
SSI specializes in the development and manufacturing of nutraceuticlas and other dietary supplement products.
Manager: Hector Gudino
Executive VP: Toshifumi Asada
QA/QC Manager: David Dean
Sales: Hector Gudino
Operations: Hector Gudino
Production Supervisor: James Morales
Purchasing Supervisor: Cheryl Moore
Estimated Sales: $990,000
Number Employees: 10-19

12111 **Selecto Sausage Company**
7119 Avenue F
Houston, TX 77011 713-926-1626
Processor of Mexican products including sausage, spices and tortillas
President: Carlos Gonzalez
Estimated Sales: $ 3 - 5 Million
Number Employees: 5-9
Type of Packaging: Consumer

12112 **Selina Naturally**
4 Celtic Drive
Arden, NC 28704
Fax: 828-654-0529 800-867-7258
info@selinanaturally.com
www.selinanaturally.com
Flavored Celtic sea salt
President/CEO: Selina Delangre
CFO: Theresa Imhoff
Estimated Sales: $4 Million
Number Employees: 31
Sq. footage: 19000

12113 **Sellards Winery**
6400 Sequoia Cir
Sebastopol, CA 95472-2013 707-823-8293
Wines

12114 **Sells Best**
P.O.Box 428
Mishawaka, IN 46546-0428 574-255-1910
Fax: 574-258-6162 800-837-8368
www.coravent.com
Processor of bakery mixes including breads, doughnuts, cakes and muffins including low fat, no cholesterol or preservatives and sugar free
President: Gary Sells
Office Manager: Kathy Campole
VP Sales: Coleman Caldwell
Director Manufacturing: Steven Surmay
Purchasing Manager: James Allen
Estimated Sales: $9000000
Number Employees: 5-9
Sq. footage: 20000

12115 **Selma's Cookies**
2023 Apex Ct
Apopka, FL 32703 407-884-9433
Fax: 407-884-6121 800-922-6654
selmas@selma.com www.selmas.com
Gourmet cookies, brownies and crispy rice treats.
Estimated Sales: Less than $500,000
Number Employees: 50-99

12116 **Seltzer & Rydholm**
191 Merrow Rd
Auburn, ME 04210-8319 207-784-5791
Fax: 207-784-8685 www.fritolayjobs.com
Bottler of soft drinks
President: George Cotton
Executive VP: Laurence Pullen
Quality Control: Bryan Fleweling
VP Advertising: Cynthia Crocker
Plant Manager: Ken Mancuso
Estimated Sales: $ 20 - 50 Million
Number Employees: 100-249
Parent Co: PepsiCo
Type of Packaging: Consumer, Food Service, Private Label, Bulk

12117 **Seltzer's Smokehouse Meats**
230 N College St
Palmyra, PA 17078 814-928-5850
Fax: 717-838-5345
seltzerssmokehousemeats@att.net
www.seltzerslebanonbologna.com
Bolognas
President: Craig Seltzer
CFO: Peter Stanilla
Plant Manager: Robert Hartman
Estimated Sales: $ 5-10 Million
Number Employees: 50-99
Type of Packaging: Private Label
Brands:
Seltzer's Lebanon Bologna
Seltzer's Sweet Bolo

12118 **Selwoods Farm Hunting Preserve**
706 Selwood Rd
Alpine, AL 35014-5431 256-362-7595
Fax: 256-362-3856 www.selwoodfarm.com
Manufacturer of smoked turkey and hams, cakes, mustards, jams, cookkies, stone ground grits, and pancake mix
Owner: Dell Hill
Estimated Sales: $1-3 Million
Number Employees: 5-9
Type of Packaging: Consumer

12119 **Seminis Vegetable Seeds**
2700 Camino Del Sol
Oxnard, CA 93030 805-647-1572
Fax: 805-918-2543 info@seminis.com
www.seminis.com
Processor of hybrid vegetable seeds
VP Marketing: Jorge Christlieb
CEO: Bruno Ferrari
CFO: Gaspar Alvarez
Number Employees: 250-499
Parent Co: Seminis Vegetable Seeds
Brands:
Petoseed
Royal Sluis

12120 **Seminole Foods**
P.O.Box 305
Springfield, OH 45501
Fax: 352-245-8534 800-881-1177
customerservice@seminolefoods.com
www.seminolefoods.com
Processor of fresh ground horseradish and fine sauces.
President: Robert Schneider
Estimated Sales: Below $ 5 Million
Number Employees: 10
Sq. footage: 19000
Type of Packaging: Consumer, Food Service, Private Label
Brands:
Seminole

12121 **Senape's Bakery**
222 W 17th St
Hazleton, PA 18201 570-454-0839
sfpayer@erols.com
Bread and pizza dough
President: Mary Lou Marchetti
Marketing: Mary Lou Marchetti
Estimated Sales: Below $ 5 Million
Number Employees: 20-49

12122 **Senba USA**
23431 Cabot Blvd
Hayward, CA 94545 510-264-5850
Fax: 510-264-0938 888-922-5852
aoki@senbausa.com www.senbausa.com
Processor of liquid sauces including teriyaki, beef and tempura; also, miso soup bases; importer of spray dried alcohol powder and tea extract; also, contract packaging and dry blending available
Manager: Hiro Aoki
Estimated Sales: $4,200,000
Number Employees: 20-49
Sq. footage: 13000
Parent Co: Senba Foods Company
Type of Packaging: Consumer, Food Service, Private Label, Bulk

12123 **Sencha Naturals**
912 E 3rd Street
Building 101
Los Angeles, CA 90013 213-346-9470
Fax: 213-947-1723 888-473-6242
inquiry@senchanaturals.com
www.senchanaturals.com
green tea mints and green tea bars
President: David Kerdoon
Operations Manager: Desiree Thomas
Number Employees: 15

12124 **Seneca Foods**
PO Box 250
Clyman, WI 53016 920-696-3331
Fax: 920-696-3566
consumeraffairs@senecafoods.com
www.senecafoods.com
Canned fruits and vegetables, apple and sweet potato chips
President/CEO: Kraig H Kayser
Human Resources: Laura Copple
EVP/Chief Operations Officer: Paul Palmby
Production Manager: Joe Schimmel
Plant Manager: Eric Martin
Purchasing Director: Sharon Henriott
Estimated Sales: $ 10 - 20 Million
Number Employees: 425
Sq. footage: 436000
Parent Co: Seneca Foods Corporation
Type of Packaging: Consumer, Food Service, Private Label
Brands:
AUNT NELLIE'S
FESTAL
LIBBY'S
READ
SENECA
STOKELY'S

12125 **Seneca Foods**
418 E Conde St
Janesville, WI 53546 608-757-6000
Fax: 608-752-5042
consumer-affairs@senecafoods.com
www.senecafoods.com
Manufacturer of canned vegetables: asparagus, corn, carrots, mixed vegetables, peas, potatoes, stew vegetables
Manager: Paul Palmby
Chairman: Arthur Wolcott
Chief Financial Officer: Philip Paras
General Counsel: John Exner
Chief Information Officer: Carl Cichetti
EVP/Chief Operating Officer: Paul Palmby
VP/Procurement: Vincent Lammers
Estimated Sales: $157 Million
Number Employees: 100-249
Sq. footage: 706400
Parent Co: Seneca Foods Corporation
Type of Packaging: Consumer, Private Label

12126 **Seneca Foods**
1055 Elm St
Cumberland, WI 54829 715-822-2181
Fax: 715-822-2114
consumer_affairs@senecafoods.com
www.senecafoods.com
Manufacturer of canned and frozen yellow snap beans and peas. frozen fruits and veggies,and canned fruits and veggies.
Chairman: Arthur Wolcott
President/CEO: Kraig Kayser
Controller: Judy Miller
General Counsel: John Exner
Director: William Sirianni
Chief Information Officer: Carl Cichetti
EVP/Chief Operating Officer: Paul Palmby
Manager: Bob Sirianni
VP/Procurement: Vincent Lammers
Estimated Sales: $1 Billion
Number Employees: 500
Sq. footage: 223424
Parent Co: Seneca Foods Corporation
Type of Packaging: Consumer

12127 **Seneca Foods**
3736 S Main St
Marion, NY 14505 315-926-8100
Fax: 315-926-8300
consumer_affairs@senecafoods.com
www.senecafoods.com
Processor of apple chips and canned vegetables including beets, carrots, corn and mixed; also, frozen beans including snap, blue lake, wax and green
President/CEO: Kraig Kayser
Chairman: Arthur Wolcott
Senior VP: Cynthia L Fohrd
Sales/Marketing Executive: Russ Curtis
EVP/COO: Paul Palmby
Estimated Sales: $1.3 Billion
Number Employees: 3,300
Parent Co: Seneca Foods Corporation
Type of Packaging: Consumer, Food Service, Private Label

12128 **Seneca Foods**
229 W Waupun St
Oakfield, WI 53065 920-583-3161
Fax: 920-583-4315
consumer_affairs@senecafoods.com
www.senecafoods.com
Manufacturer and exporter of canned corn
President/CEO: Kraig Kayser
CFO: Colleen Friess
Director Quality: Aaron Paul
Director: Ward Steven
Estimated Sales: $ 20 - 50 Million
Number Employees: 50
Sq. footage: 193400
Parent Co: Seneca Foods Corporation
Type of Packaging: Private Label
Brands:
AUNT NELLIE'S
BLUE BOY
DIAMOND A
FESTAL
GLACE FRUIT
LIBBY'S
LOHMANN
READ
STOKELY'S
TENDERSWEET
WALLA WALLA

12129 **Seneca Foods**
3709 Mill St
Marion, NY 14505 315-926-0531
Fax: 315-926-8300
consumer_affairs@senecafoods.com
www.senecafoods.com
Processor of canned fruits and vegetables
President: Kraig H Kayser
Sr. VP: Kraig Kayser
CFO: Thomas Paulson
Vice President: Dean Erstad
CFO: Thomas Paulson
Sales Director: Dean Erstad
Plant Manager: Mike Hanchett
Estimated Sales: $ 100-500 Million
Number Employees: 250-499
Parent Co: Seneca Foods Corporation
Type of Packaging: Consumer, Private Label
Brands:
Seneca Foods

12130 **Seneca Foods**
300 3rd Ave SW
Arlington, MN 55307 507-964-2204
Fax: 507-964-2441
consumer_affairs@senecafoods.com
www.senecafoods.com
Processor, canner and exporter of peas and whole kernel corn.
Chairman: Arthur Wolcott
President/CEO: Kraig Kayser
Chief Financial Officer: Philip Paras
General Counsel: John Exner
Chief Information Officer: Carl Cichetti
EVP/Chief Operating Officer: Paul Palmby
Plant Manager: Doug Schauer
VP/Procurement: Vincent Lammers
Estimated Sales: $ 50-100 Million
Number Employees: 250-499
Sq. footage: 241236
Parent Co: Seneca Foods Corporation
Type of Packaging: Private Label

12131 **Seneca Foods**
3736 S Main St
Marion, NY 14505 315-926-8100
Fax: 315-926-8300
consumer_affairs@senecafoods.com
www.senecafoods.com
Processor of canned corn and peas
President/CEO: Kraig Kayser
Chairman: Arthur Wolcott
EVP/COO: Paul Palmby
Board Member: Thomas Paulson
Estimated Sales: $1 Billion+
Number Employees: 3,000 +
Type of Packaging: Private Label
Brands:
Diamond A
Festal
Read
Stokely's
Tendersweet
Walla Walla

12132 **Seneca Foods**
430 7th Ave S
Buhl, ID 83316 208-543-4322
Fax: 208-543-6015
consumer_affairs@senecafoods.com
www.senecafoods.com
Processor and exporter of canned and frozen corn and sugar snap peas.
Chairman: Arthur Wolcott
President/CEO: Kraig Kayser
Chief Financial Officer: Philip Paras
General Counsel: John Exner
Chief Information Officer: Carl Cichetti
EVP/Chief Operating Officer: Paul Palmby
VP/Procurement: Vincent Lammers
Estimated Sales: $ 100-500 Million
Number Employees: 750
Sq. footage: 395410
Parent Co: Seneca Foods Corporation
Type of Packaging: Consumer, Food Service, Private Label

12133 **Seneca Foods**
P.O.Box 35
Blue Earth, MN 56013 507-526-2131
Fax: 507-526-4653
consumer_affairs@senecafoods.com
www.senecafoods.com
Processor of canned peas and corn
CFO: Phillip Paras
Director: Susan Carr
Estimated Sales: $ 50-100 Million
Number Employees: 57
Sq. footage: 145535
Parent Co: Seneca Foods Corporation
Type of Packaging: Consumer, Food Service, Private Label
Brands:
Aunt Nellie's
Blue Boy
Diamond A
Festal
Green Giant
Libbys
Lohmann
Read
Seneca
Stokley's

12134 **Seneca Foods**
600 5th St SE
Montgomery, MN 56069 507-364-8231
Fax: 507-364-8278
consumer_affairs@senecafoods.com
www.senecafoods.com
Processor of canned and frozen peas and corn.
Chairman: Kraig H Kayser
EVP/Chief Financial Officer: Thomas Paulson
Chief Information Officer: Carl Cichetti
EVP/Chief Operating Officer: Paul Palmby
Plant Manager: Paul Hendrickson
VP/Procurement: Vincent Lammers
Estimated Sales: $ 100-500 Million
Number Employees: 500-999
Sq. footage: 228000
Parent Co: Seneca Foods Corporation
Type of Packaging: Consumer, Food Service, Private Label, Bulk
Brands:
Seneca Foods

12135 **(HQ)Seneca Foods Corporation**
3736 S Main St
Marion, NY 14505
US 315-926-8100
Fax: 315-926-8300 webmaster@senecafoods.com
www.senecafoods.com
Apple chips, canned vegetables, canned potato salad and canned bean salad.
President/CEO: Kraig Kayser
Vp: George Hopkins
Vp Marketing: Bruce Wolcott
Manager Of Operations: Tom Shannon
Estimated Sales: $1.28Billion
Number Employees: 3,300
Type of Packaging: Consumer, Food Service, Private Label, Bulk
Brands:
AUNT NELLIE'S
FESTAL
LIBBY'S®
READ
SENECA
STOKELY'S®

12136 **Senomyx, Inc.**
4767 Nexus Centre Dr
San Diego, CA 92121 858-646-8300
Fax: 858-404-0752 www.senomyx.com
Manufacturer and developer flavor ingredients
President/COO: John Poyhonen
Chairman/CEO: Kent Snyder
Executive Director: Fred Shinnick
VP/CFO: Anthony Rogers
Estimated Sales: $ 28 Million
Number Employees: 100-249

12137 **Senor Felix's Gourmet Mexican**
4265 Maine Ave
Baldwin Park, CA 91706-3312 626-960-2800
Fax: 626-560-2855 senorfelix@ffci.us
www.senorfelixs.com
Mexican fresh and frozen food, including enchiladas, burritos, taquitos, tamales, salsa, guacamole dip, etc
Owner: Lulu Juco
Controller: Sam Tabani
VP Sales/Marketing: Don O'Neill
Estimated Sales: $ .5 - 1 million
Number Employees: 50-99
Type of Packaging: Private Label
Brands:
Delicioso
Pacifico
Senor Felix's

12138 **Senor Murphy Candymaker**
1904 Chamisa St
Santa Fe, NM 87505 505-988-4311
Fax: 505-988-2050 877-988-4311
chocolate@senormurphy.com
www.senormurphy.com
Processor of candy
Owner: Rand Levitt
VP: Bob Murphy
Estimated Sales: $770000
Number Employees: 5-9
Type of Packaging: Consumer

12139 **Senor Pinos de Santa Fe**
2600 Camino Entrada
Santa Fe, NM 87507-0491 505-473-3437
Fax: 505-473-5808 senorpinos@aol.com
www.senorpinos.com
Blue-corn flour, southwestern specialties
Owner: Nate Pino
Estimated Sales: $ 1 Million
Number Employees: 30
Brands:
Josie's Best Blue Tortilla Chips

12140 **Sensational Sweets**
355 Sweets Ln
Lewisburg, PA 17837 570-524-4361
Fax: 570-524-5360 info@sensationalsweets.com
www.sensationalsweets.com
Chippers the bark with a bite, gourmet fudge, fudge bites, drizzled popcorn, dipped pretzels, pollylops
Owner: Virginia Feitner
Estimated Sales: Less than $500,000
Number Employees: 5-9

12141 **Sensible Portions**
4600 Sleepytime Drive
Boulder, CO 80301 973-283-9220
Fax: 973-283-2799 800-913-6637
info@gwgourmet.com
www.sensibleportions.com
all natural and portion control snacks such as multi grain crisps, mini multi grain crisps, soy crisps, mini soy crisps, pita crackers, and pita chips.
President: Jason Cohen
President: Jerry Bello

12142 **Sensient Dehydrated Flavors**
P.O.Box 1524
Turlock, CA 95381 831-674-5571
Fax: 209-634-6235 800-558-9892
paul.walker@sensient-tech.com
www.sensient-tech.com
air-dried, freeze dried and puffed specialty vegetables and spices
President: Patrick Laubacher
R&D: Dan Brotslaw
National Sales Manager: Troy Dryden
Human Resources Director: Tony Meli
Estimated Sales: $ 10-25 Million
Number Employees: 182
Sq. footage: 24513
Brands:
Sensient

12143 **Sensient Flavors**
5600 W Raymond St
Indianapolis, IN 46241 317-243-3521
Fax: 317-243-2820 800-445-0073
flavors@sensient-tech.com
www.sensient-tech.com
Flavoring extract and syrups supplier and manufacturer.
President/COO: Douglas Pepper
SVP/CFO: Richard Hobbs
CEO: Ken Manning
Estimated Sales: $ 100 - 200 Million
Number Employees: 1,000-4,999
Parent Co: Sensient Technologies Corporation

12144 **Sensient Food Colors**
777 E Wisconsine Avenue
Milwaukee, WI 53202-5304 800-558-9892
corporate.communications@sensient-tech.com
www.sensient-tech.com
Sensient Technologies is the world's leading supplier of flavors, fragrances and colors used to make a diverse variety of foods and beverages, pharmaceuticals, cosmetics, home and personal care products, specialty printing and imagingproducts, computer i
Chairman/President /CEO: Kenneth Manning
VP CFO/Treasurer: Richard Hobbs
VP Administration: Richard Carney
VP Marketing/Technology: Ho-Seung Yang PhD
Estimated Sales: Below $ 5 Million
Number Employees: 15
Brands:
Sensient

12145 **(HQ)Sensient Technologies**
777 E Wisconsin Ave Ste 1100
Milwaukee, WI 53202 414-271-6755
Fax: 414-347-4795 800-558-9892
info@sensient-tech.com
www.sensient-technologies.com
Manufacturer of flavors, aromas and colors for a variety of food, pharmacetical, cosmetics and household products
Chairman/President/CEO: Kenneth Manning
VP/CFO/Treasurer: Richard Hobbs
VP/Secretary/General Counsel: John Hammond
Estimated Sales: $100+ Million
Number Employees: 1,000-4,999
Type of Packaging: Consumer, Food Service, Private Label, Bulk
Other Locations:
Sensient Technologies
High Ridge MO

12146 **SensoryEffects Flavor Systems**
231 Rock Industrial Park Drive
Bridgeton, MO 63044 314-291-5444
Fax: 314-291-3289 info@sensoryeffects.com
www.sensoryeffects.com
Specialty powder flavoring systems, inclusions, frozen dessert, beverage & dairy systems, creaming agents, dessert bases and whipped toppings.

12147 **Sensus**
100 Lenox Dr, Ste 104
Lawrenceville, NJ 08648 646-452-6147
Fax: 646-452-6150 scott.turowski@sensus.us
www.sensus,us
Producer of food ingredients; including oligofructose
Technical Sales: Scott Turowski
Sales Manager: John Bienus
Number Employees: 5-9
Parent Co: Sensus

12148 **Sentry Seasonings**
928 N Church Rd
Elmhurst, IL 60126 630-530-5370
Fax: 630-530-5385
wayne@sentryseasonings.com
www.sentryseasonings.com

The product development experts of Sentry Seasonings are eager to offer the assistance and hands-on experience to food processors of all sizes. Sentry Seasonings will ensure the consistent high quality and repeat sales of yourproducts, whether you choose one of our many off-the-shelf Bench Mark products or a modified version to meet your preferences. Sentry Seasonings can also duplicate and/or improve your present flavor profile; formulate, blend and package specificallyfor your requirements.

President: Carla Staniec
VP: Michael Staniec
Estimated Sales: $730000
Number Employees: 10-19
Sq. footage: 30000
Type of Packaging: Consumer, Food Service, Private Label, Bulk

12149 **Seppic**
P.O.Box 36272
Newark, NJ 07188-6006 973-882-5597
Fax: 973-882-5178 877-737-7421
stephen.oneill@airliquide.com www.seppic.com
Ingredients, minerals and extracts
President: Jean Marc Giner
Marketing/Sales: Regis Cazes
Estimated Sales: $ 1-2.5 Million
Number Employees: 20-49
Parent Co: Seppic

12150 **Sequoia Grove Vineyards**
P.O.Box 449
Rutherford, CA 94573-0449 707-944-2945
Fax: 707-963-9411 800-851-7841
info@sequoiagrove.com www.sequoiagrove.com
Wines
President/Winemaker: Michael Trujillo
CFO: Robert Aldridge
Vice President: Casandra Knox
Marketing Director: Anthony Ankers
Estimated Sales: $1-$2.5 Million
Number Employees: 20-49
Type of Packaging: Private Label
Brands:
Sequoia Grove
Sequoia Grove

12151 **Sequoia Specialty Cheese Company**
7000 W Doe Ave # C
Visalia, CA 93291-8623 559-752-4106
Fax: 559-752-4108 sequoia@inreach.com
Cheese
Administrator: Ray Chavez
Production Manager: Greg Moe
Estimated Sales: $1-23 Million
Number Employees: 10-19
Number of Products: 10
Sq. footage: 40000
Type of Packaging: Consumer, Food Service, Private Label
Brands:
Mt. Whitney

12152 **Serenade Foods**
9179 N 200 E
Milford, IN 46542 574-658-4121
Fax: 219-658-2246 www.mapleleaffarms.com
Processor and exporter of poultry
Manager: Don Crandall
Number Employees: 100-249
Parent Co: Maple Leaf Foods
Type of Packaging: Consumer, Food Service, Private Label, Bulk

12153 **Serendipitea**
73 Plandome Road
Manhasset, NY 11030 516-365-7711
Fax: 516-365-7733 888-832-5433
tea@serendipitea.com www.serendipitea.com
Tea; premium grade loose leaf and tisane and accouterments.
Principal: Linda Villano
Estimated Sales: Less than $500,000
Number Employees: 8
Number of Brands: 1
Number of Products: 100+
Sq. footage: 3000
Type of Packaging: Consumer, Food Service, Private Label, Bulk

12154 **Serendipity 3**
225 E 60th St
New York, NY 10022 212-838-3531
800-805-5493
Cosmeticmall.com www.serendipity3.com
Frozen hot chocolate
President: Steven Bruce
Estimated Sales: Below $ 5 Million
Number Employees: 50-99
Brands:
Black & White Mug
Frrrozen Hot Chocolate Mix

12155 **Serendipity Cellars**
15275 Dunn Forest Rd
Monmouth, OR 97361 503-838-4284
Fax: 503-838-0067
Wines
Owner: Glen Longshore
Estimated Sales: $500,000-$1 Million
Number Employees: 1-4

12156 **Serengeti Tea**
351 W Redondo Beach Blvd
Gardena, CA 90248-2101 310-527-5278
Fax: 310-527-2154 888-604-2040
tea@serengetitea.com www.serengetitea.com
Processor of iced teas
Owner: David Massey

Estimated Sales: $690,000
Number Employees: 5-9
Brands:
Southern Breeze
Ticolino

12157 Serra Mission Winery
3503 Manhattan Ave
Saint Louis, MO 63143 314-962-4600
Fax: 314-647-4349
Wine
President: John Bordenhier
Estimated Sales: $500,000-$1 Million
Number Employees: 1-4

12158 Serranos Salsa
632 Ralph Ablanedo Dr # 330
Austin, TX 78748-6619 512-328-9200
Fax: 512-328-3005 customercare@serranos.com
www.serranos.com
Soups, ensaladas, tortas
Owner: Adam Gonzales
Director: Eric Cross
Estimated Sales: $500-1 Million appx.
Number Employees: 5-9
Brands:
Serranos Salsa

12159 (HQ)Serv-Agen Corporation
1200 S Union Ave
Cherry Hill, NJ 8002 856-663-6966
Fax: 856-663-7016 cwslade1@msn.com
Processor of food colors, flavorings, dehydrated vegetables, gravy and soup bases, spices, puddings and sauce mixes including soy and worcestershire
President: Barbara Pearlman
VP: Charles W Slade
Estimated Sales: $989000
Number Employees: 5-9
Sq. footage: 15000
Type of Packaging: Consumer, Food Service, Private Label, Bulk
Brands:
Bennetts
Clawson
Heinle
Key Lime
LEM
Lemon

12160 Serv-Rite Meat Company
P.O.Box 65026
Los Angeles, CA 90065 323-227-1911
Fax: 323-227-9068 www.bar-m.com
Processor of bacon, smoked ham and sausage
President: Gary Marks
Marketing Manager: Anna Cornellius
Estimated Sales: $ 10 - 20 Million
Number Employees: 50-99
Sq. footage: 80000

12161 Service Foods
PO Box 2206
Norcross, GA 30091-2206 770-448-5300
Fax: 770-446-3085
Frozen food and freezer plans
CEO: Keith Cantor
Estimated Sales: $ 5 - 10 Million
Number Employees: 20-49

12162 Service Marketing
4470 Chamblee Dunwoody Rd
Dunwoody, GA 30338-6224 770-451-9183
Fax: 770-451-9216
Seafood, ocean perch, whiting, flounder, trout, croaker, hake
President: Paul J Kastin
Estimated Sales: $ 20 - 50 Million
Number Employees: 10-19

12163 Service Packing Company
250 Southern Street
Vancouver, BC V6A 2P1
Canada 604-681-0264
Fax: 604-681-9309 service-packing@ttelus.net
Processor, importer, exporter and packer of dates, currants, raisins, shredded coconut, chocolate chips, prunes and nuts including walnuts and almonds
President: Ron Huntington
Estimated Sales: $500,000-1,000,000
Number Employees: 1-4
Sq. footage: 85000
Type of Packaging: Private Label

Brands:
Martins

12164 Sesaco Corporation
4308 Centergate St
San Antonio, TX 78217 210-590-3352
Fax: 210-590-3665 800-737-2260
www.sesaco.net
Processor, importer and exporter of sesame seeds including white hulled
Executive Director: Ray Langham
Administration: Tina Smith
Operations Manager: Ray Collard
Estimated Sales: $ 3 - 5 Million
Number Employees: 1-4
Type of Packaging: Consumer, Bulk
Brands:
Flour
HP - White Hulled Sesame Seeds
Oil
T2P - Light
T4P - Medium Toasted Hulled Sesame
T5P - Dark
TNP - Toasted Natural Sesame Seeds
Tahini
WNP - Washed Natural Sesame Seeds

12165 Sesinco Foods
54 W 21st Street
New York, NY 10010-6908 212-243-1306
Fax: 212-243-2036
Supplier and exporter of closeout and excess inventory items including frozen and canned foods, beverages, dairy products, etc.; serving retail and food service markets
President: Serbajit Singh
VP: Ann Gaudet
Estimated Sales: $1600000
Number Employees: 7
Type of Packaging: Consumer, Food Service

12166 Sessions Company
P.O.Box 311310
Enterprise, AL 36331 334-393-0200
Fax: 334-393-0240 www.sessionspeanuts.com
Manufacturer and exporter of peanut products including butter, meal, cake and refined oil
President: William Ventress
CEO: H Moultrie Sessions Jr
Plant Manager: Chet Faulkner
Estimated Sales: $70 Million
Number Employees: 100-249
Type of Packaging: Consumer, Food Service, Private Label, Bulk
Brands:
PAL
SCHOOL DAY

12167 Seth Ellis Chocolatier
5345 Arapahoe Ave Ste 5
Boulder, CO 80303 720-565-2462
Fax: 720-565-2462 hey@sethellischocolatier.com
www.sethellischocolatier.com
chocolate
President/Owner: Frederick Levine
Number Employees: 5

12168 Sethness Products Company
3422 W Touhy Avenue
Lincolnwood, IL 60712 847-329-2080
Fax: 847-329-2090 mail@sethness.com
www.sethness.com
Processor, exporter of burnt sugar syrups liquid and powdered caramel colors
President: Henry Sethness
Estimated Sales: $10,500,000
Number Employees: 50-99
Type of Packaging: Food Service, Bulk

12169 Sethness Products Company
P.O.Box 597963
Chicago, IL 60659-7963 847-329-2080
Fax: 847-329-2090 888-772-1880
mail@sethness.com www.sethness.com
Manufacturer and exporter of liquid and powdered caramel colors
Chairman/CEO: Charles Sethness
President: Henry Sethness
Technical Director: Dave Tuescher
Operations Manager: Daniel Sethness
Estimated Sales: $20-50 Million
Number Employees: 50-99
Sq. footage: 95000
Type of Packaging: Food Service, Bulk

Brands:
SETHNESS

12170 Sethness-Greenleaf
1826 N Lorel Ave
Chicago, IL 60639-4376 773-889-1400
Fax: 773-889-0854 800-621-4549
info@sethnessgreenleaf.com
www.sethnessgreenleaf.com
Processor and exporter of flavorings and extracts also emulsions
President: Patrick Kearney
CFO: Joe Hughes
National Sales Manager: Thomas Schufreider
COO: Bill Sexton
Plant Manager: Reynold Walker
Purchasing: Ken Ciukowski
Estimated Sales: $3.3 Million
Number Employees: 30
Sq. footage: 56000
Type of Packaging: Consumer, Food Service, Bulk

12171 Setton International Foods
85 Austin Blvd
Commack, NY 11725-5701 631-543-8090
Fax: 631-543-8070 800-227-4397
info@settonfarms.com www.settonfarms.com
Grower, importer, exporter, processor, roaster and packer of nuts, seeds, dried fruits, candy and snack foods, specialties include pistachios, cashews, almonds and apricots with an extensive product line, also, kosher certified andorganic certified
Owner: Joshua Setton
CEO: Joshua Setton
CFO: Stewart Fellner
Vice President: Morris Setton
Quality Control: Harris Cohen
Sales Director: Joseph Setton
COO: Mia Cohen
Production Manager: Otto Hahs
Plant Manager: Joel Ginsberg
Estimated Sales: $ 10 - 20 Million
Number Employees: 20-49
Type of Packaging: Consumer, Food Service, Private Label, Bulk

12172 Setton Pistachio of Terra Bella
9370 Road 234
Terra Bella, CA 93270-1089 559-535-6050
Fax: 559-535-6089 800-227-4397
info@settonfarms.com www.settonfarms.com
Processor and importer of pistachios, bakers' and confectioners' supplies including carob products, shredded coconut, dried fruits, crystallized ginger, nuts, seeds, banana chips, yogurt and chocolate covered products, soy productsetc.
President: Joshua Setton
Executive Vice President: Morris Setton
VP/Sales & Marketing: Joseph Setton
Chief Operations Officer: Mia Cohen
Estimated Sales: $22300000
Number Employees: 100-249
Sq. footage: 50000
Parent Co: Setton International Foods
Type of Packaging: Consumer, Food Service, Bulk

12173 Seven Barrell Brewery
5 Airport Rd
West Lebanon, NH 03784-1658 603-298-5566
Fax: 603-298-5715 www.sevenbarrelbrewery.com
Processor of seasonal beer, ale, stout, lager and pilsner
President: Nancy Noonan
Manager: Earl Locke
Number Employees: 20-49
Type of Packaging: Food Service
Brands:
Seven Barrell

12174 Seven Brothers Trading
731 N Beach Blvd
La Habra, CA 90631-3657 562-697-8888
Fax: 562-697-8288
General groceries
President: Han Ng
Estimated Sales: $ 2.5-5 Million
Number Employees: 5-9

12175 Seven Hills Coffee Company
11094 Deerfield Rd
Cincinnati, OH 45242 513-489-5220
Fax: 513-489-6888

Coffee
Owner: Andy Timmerman
Director/CFO: Andy Timmerman
Operations Manager: Matthew Kasper
Estimated Sales: $ 2.5-5 Million
Number Employees: 5-9

12176 **Seven Hills Winery**
212 N 3rd Ave
Walla Walla, WA 99362 509-529-7198
Fax: 509-529-7918 877-777-7870
info@sevenhillswinery.com
www.sevenhillswinery.com
Wines
Owner: Casey McCleann
Founder/Winemaker: Casey McClellan
Estimated Sales: Below $ 5 Million
Number Employees: 5-9
Brands:
Seven Hills

12177 **Seven K Feather Farm**
3155 W 650 N
Taylorsville, IN 47280 812-526-2651
Fax: 812-526-2723
Wholesale/distributor of food
President: Charles Kleinhenz
Estimated Sales: Below $ 5 Million
Number Employees: 20-49

12178 **Seven Keys Company of Florida**
P.O.Box 729
Pompano Beach, FL 33061 954-946-5010
Fax: 954-946-5012
Processor and exporter of tropical jams, jellies, marmalades and coconut toast spreads
President: Albert Gericke
Estimated Sales: $ 3 - 5 Million
Number Employees: 5-9
Sq. footage: 15000
Type of Packaging: Consumer, Food Service, Private Label
Brands:
Lapham
Seven Keys

12179 **Seven Lakes Vineyards**
1111 Tinsman Road
Fenton, MI 48430-1679 810-629-5686
Wines
President: Chris Guest
Estimated Sales: $ 5-9.9 Million
Number Employees: 5

12180 **Seven Seas Seafoods**
901 S Fremont Ave Ste 168
Alhambra, CA 91803 626-570-9129
Fax: 626-570-0079 chris@7seafood.com
7seafood.com
Seafood
President: Christopher Lin
VP: Sean Lin
Estimated Sales: $ 5 - 10 Million
Number Employees: 5-9

12181 **Seven Up/RC Bottling Company**
P.O.Box 859
Paragould, AR 72451 870-236-8765
Fax: 870-236-3781
Processor of soft drinks
Owner/President: Preston Bland
Sales/Marketing Executive: John Bland
Plant Manager: Joe Williams
Purchasing Agent: Joe Williams
Estimated Sales: $ 20 - 50 Million
Number Employees: 100-249
Type of Packaging: Consumer, Food Service

12182 **Severance Foods**
3478 Main St
Hartford, CT 06120 860-724-7063
Fax: 860-527-2045 www.severancefoods.com
Processor of tortilla chips and tortillas including flour and corn
President: Richard Stevens
Estimated Sales: $3350000
Number Employees: 20-49
Sq. footage: 28000
Type of Packaging: Consumer, Food Service, Private Label, Bulk
Brands:
Pan De Oro

12183 **Severn Peanut Company**
406 Spring Street
Windsor, NC 27983-6843 252-794-3435
Fax: 252-794-9167
Processor of peanuts
Marketing Manager/Branch Manager: Dawson Rascoe
Number Employees: 20
Type of Packaging: Consumer, Bulk

12184 **Severn Peanut Company**
P.O.Box 710
Severn, NC 27877 252-585-0838
Fax: 252-585-1718 800-642-4064
www.hamptonfarms.com
Processor, exporter, cleaner, sheller of raw peanuts, Cajun and jalapeno inshell peanuts, raw redskins, raw blanched, roasted snack peanuts, granules, peanut brittle, chocolate coated, peanut bars/squares, butter toffee
President: Dallas Barnes
Sales Manager: Rick McGee
Sales: Carl Gray
Manager: Pat Rowe
Estimated Sales: $80100000
Number Employees: 50-99
Number of Products: 4
Parent Co: Meherrin Agricultural Chemical Company
Type of Packaging: Consumer, Bulk
Brands:
Northampton
Sepeco Seed

12185 **Seville Olive Company**
663 S Anderson St
Los Angeles, CA 90023 323-261-2218
Fax: 323-261-1026
Olives, onions, cherries and peppers
President: Louis Pavlic Sr
Estimated Sales: $ 10-20 Million
Number Employees: 100-249

12186 **Seviroli Foods**
601 Brook St
Garden City, NY 11530
Fax: 516-222-0534 www.seviroli.com
Italian foods
President: Joseph Seviroli Sr
COO: Joseph Seviroli Jr
Quality Assurance Manager: Nel Reformina
Estimated Sales: $ 5-10 Million
Number Employees: 20-49

12187 **Sewell's Fish Market**
1178 Lee St
Rogersville, AL 35652-7816 256-247-1378
Fax: 718-617-6851
Seafood
Owner: Tana Springer
Public Relations: Tana Springer
Estimated Sales: $ 1 - 3 Million
Number Employees: 1-4

12188 **Seydel International**
244 John B Brooks Rd
Pendergrass, GA 30567 706-693-2295
Fax: 706-693-2074 seycoinfo@seydel.com
www.seydel.com
Processor, importer and exporter of starch, dextrin and protein
President: Scott O Seydel
Manufacturing Director: Mitch Mullinax
Estimated Sales: $43500000
Number Employees: 50-99
Parent Co: Seydel Company
Type of Packaging: Food Service, Bulk
Brands:
Emdex
Emflo
Emgum
Emjel
Emox

12189 **Seymour & Sons Seafood**
3201 Saint Charles St
Diberville, MS 39540 228-392-4020
Fax: 228-392-8028
Processor of seafood including frozen catfish and lobster
President: Paul Seymour
Plant Manager: David Seymour
Estimated Sales: $1200000
Number Employees: 5-9
Sq. footage: 5000

12190 **Sfoglia Fine Pastas & Gourmet**
P.O.Box 921
Freeland, WA 98249 360-331-4080
Gourmet and specialty foods
President: Stephanie Jushinski
Estimated Sales: Less than $500,000
Number Employees: 1-4

12191 **Shade Foods**
400 Prairie Village Dr
New Century, KS 66031 913-780-1212
Fax: 913-780-1720 800-225-6312
pvd@shadefoods.com
www.kerryingredients.com
Processor liquid chocolate, hard candy, chocolate and yogurt chips, flakes, cereal particles, nuggets, pralines, granola, coated raisins, nuts and candy, etc
CFO: Yves Gedert
R&D: Andrew Nelson
Vice President: Addison Bergfalk
VP: Jim White
VP: Bob Blefko
VP Sales/Marketing: Bob Blefko
Plant Manager: Miles Miller
Purchasing Manager: Lynn Christian
Estimated Sales: $ 25 - 49.9 Million
Number Employees: 240
Sq. footage: 145000
Parent Co: Norfoods
Type of Packaging: Private Label, Bulk
Brands:
Chewy Chunks
No Boil Pasta
Shade Icings & Fillings
Wayfels

12192 **Shady Grove Orchards**
183 Shady Grove Road
Onalaska, WA 98570-9453 360-985-7033
shadygrove@myhome.net
www.chestnutsource.com
Organic American chestnuts and chestnut flour, dried chestnut kernels, seedlings, cookbook
Co-Owner: Annie Bhagwandin
Co-Owner: Omroa Bhagwandin
Brands:
Shady Grove Orchards

12193 **Shady Maple Farm**
2585 Skymark Ave
Mississauga, ON L4W 4L5
Canada 905-206-1455
Fax: 905-206-1477 info@shadymaple.ca.qc.ca
www.shadymaple.ca
Processor and exporter of pure maple syrup products
President/CEO: Robert Swain
CFO: Darren Brash
Marketing Director: Marlene Jolicoeur
Sales Director: Daniel Neale
Number Employees: 10-19
Sq. footage: 55000
Type of Packaging: Consumer, Food Service, Private Label, Bulk

12194 **Shafer Lake Fruit**
60643 Red Arrow Hwy
Hartford, MI 49057 269-621-3194
Fax: 269-621-4170
Packers of apples, peaches, plums and asparagus
President: Dale Drake
Estimated Sales: $ 3 - 5 Million
Number Employees: 1-4
Type of Packaging: Consumer, Bulk

12195 **Shafer Vineyards**
6154 Silverado Trl
Napa, CA 94558 707-944-2877
Fax: 707-944-9454 info@shafervineyards.com
www.shafervineyards.com

Cabernet sauvignon, chardonnay, merlot, cabernet savignon, sangiovese
Chairman: John Shafer
President: Doug Shafer
Winemaker: Elias Fernandez
Estimated Sales: $ 5-10 Million
Number Employees: 10-19
Brands:
Firebreak
Hillside
Red Shoulder Ranch
Shafer Vineyards

12196 Shafer-Haggart
1055 West Hastings St, Suite 1038
Vancouver, BC V6E 4E2
Canada 604-669-5512
Fax: 604-669-9554 info@shafer-haggart.com
www.shafer-haggart.com
Processor and importer of canned mushrooms, tomatoes, peaches, tuna and salmon; exporter of frozen poultry and canned corn and fish products
President: Clive Lonsdale
Sr. VP: Brian Dougall
Estimated Sales: $2.5-5 Million
Number Employees: 20-49
Type of Packaging: Consumer, Food Service, Private Label

12197 Shah Trading Company
3451 McNicoll Avenue
Toronto, ON M1V 2V3 416-292-6927
Fax: 416-292-7932 www.shahtrading.com
rice, spices, beans, peas, and lentils, specialty flours and nuts and dried fruits.

12198 Shaker Valley Foods
3304 W 67th Pl
Cleveland, OH 44102 216-961-8600
Fax: 216-961-8077 cbeefking@yahoo.com
www.shakervalleyfoods.com
Meat processor and food distributor
President: Dean Comber
Estimated Sales: $ 20-50 Million
Number Employees: 20-49

12199 Shakespeare's
3840 W River Dr
Davenport, IA 52802-2412 563-383-0150
Fax: 563-383-0151 800-664-4114
www.shakechocolate.com
Specialty chocolates
Owner: Elisa Shakespeare
Estimated Sales: Less than $500,000
Number Employees: 10-19

12200 (HQ)Shaklee Corporation
4747 Willow Rd
Pleasanton, CA 94588 925-924-2000
Fax: 925-924-2862 800-742-5533
www.shaklee.com
Manufacturer and exporter of nutritional supplements
Chairman/CEO: Roger Barnett
SVP Field Sales: John Earthy
Estimated Sales: $148 Million
Number Employees: 1,000-4,999
Parent Co: Ripplewood Holdings
Type of Packaging: Consumer
Other Locations:
Shaklee Corporation
Norman OK
Brands:
AIRSOURCE
PERFECT PITCHER
SHAKLEE CAROTOMAX
SHAKLEE FLAVOMAX

12201 Shallon Winery
1598 Duane St
Astoria, OR 97103 503-325-5978
paul@shallon.com
www.shallon.com
Fine wines including whey wines and chocolate wines
President: Paul C Vanderveldt
Winemaker: Paul Van Der Veldt
Estimated Sales: Under $300,000
Number Employees: 1-4
Brands:
Shallon Winery

12202 Shallowford Farms
3732 Hartman Road
Yadkinville, NC 27055-5638 336-463-5938
Fax: 336-463-2358 800-892-9539
amanda@shallowfordfarms.com
www.shallowfordfarms.com
Manufacturer of popcorn
President: Amanda Booe
Plant Manager: Caswell Booe
Estimated Sales: $500,000-$1 Million
Number Employees: 10-19
Sq. footage: 21000
Type of Packaging: Consumer, Private Label, Bulk
Brands:
DENNIS
MR SNACK

12203 Shamrock Foods Company
2540 N 29th Ave
Phoenix, AZ 85009 602-233-6400
Fax: 602-233-2791 800-289-3663
azinfo@shamrockfoods.com
www.shamrockfoods.com
Wholesaler/distributor of frozen foods, produce, dairy products, meats, groceries, baked goods and seafood; serving the food service market
President/COO: Kent McClelland
Chairman/CEO: Norman McClelland
SVP/CFO: F Phillips Giltner
VP Human Resources: Robert Beake
Estimated Sales: $1.4 Billion
Number Employees: 2600
Brands:
ASPEN GOLD
BOUNTIFUL HARVEST
BRICKFIRE BAKERY
CHEF MARK
COBBLESTONE MARKET
CULINARY SECRETS
EMERALD VALLEY RANCH
HIDDEN BAY
KATY'S KITCHEN
MARKON FIRST CROP
PIERPORT
PRAIRIE CREEK
PROPAK
READY-SET-SERVE
REJUV
RIDGELINE
SAN PABLO
SHAMROCK FARMS
SILVERBROOK
SMART SOURCE
SOUTHERN PEARL
THE "EVER" FAMILY OF BRANDS
TRESCERRO
TRIFOGLIO
VILLA FRIZZONI
WINDSCAPES
XTREME

12204 Shamrock Slaughter Plant
6400 Us Highway 83
Shamrock, TX 79079 806-256-3241
Processor of meat products
Owner: Larry Cook
Estimated Sales: $500,000-$1 Million
Number Employees: 1-4
Type of Packaging: Consumer

12205 Shane Candy Company
110 Market St
Philadelphia, PA 19106-3066 215-922-1048
Fax: 215-940-0003 www.shanecandies.com
Processor of candy including chocolate, holiday and hard
Owner: Barry Shane
Estimated Sales: $ 5 - 10 Million
Number Employees: 10-19
Sq. footage: 7200
Type of Packaging: Consumer

12206 Shaner's Family Restaurant
193 Main St
South Paris, ME 04281 207-743-6367
Ice cream, frozen desserts
President: John Shaner
Estimated Sales: $ 1-2.5 Million
Number Employees: 20-49

12207 Shanghai Company
2800 SE Division St
Portland, OR 97202 503-235-2525
Fax: 503-235-3842
Processor of canned Chinese noodles
President: Chester Louie Jr
Vice President: David Louie
Estimated Sales: $1100000
Number Employees: 20-49
Type of Packaging: Consumer

12208 Shanks Extracts
350 Richardson Dr
Lancaster, PA 17603-4034 717-393-4441
Fax: 717-393-3148 800-346-3135
jstoner@shanks.com www.shanks.com
Manufacturer, importer and exporter of Spanish saffron, syrups and flavoring extracts including pure vanilla, lemon and almond; contract packaging services available
President: Jeffrey Lehman
Sales Manager: Charley Beck
Operations: Sallie Rhineer
Human Resources: Lydia Zimmerman
Estimated Sales: $ 20 - 50 Million
Number Employees: 50-99
Sq. footage: 90000
Type of Packaging: Consumer, Food Service, Private Label, Bulk
Brands:
Gold Medal
Taste-T

12209 Shari Candies
5780 Lincoln Drive
Suite 123-124
Edina, MN 55436-1640 612-935-8953
Fax: 612-935-5170 800-658-7059
info@candyasap.com www.sharicandies.com
Candy and also candy for holidays.
President: Arlen Kitsis
VP: Steve Kitsis
National Sales Manager: Wally Schif
Type of Packaging: Consumer

12210 Shariann's Organics
58 S. Service Rd.
Melville, NY 11747 ÿ63- 73- 220
Fax: 631-730-2550 800-434-4246
consumeraffairs@hain-celestial.com
http://www.hain-celestial.com/
Organic food products
President and CEO: Irwin Simon
CFO: Ira Lamel
Chief Marketing Officer: Maureen Putman
Estimated Sales: $900 Million
Number Employees: 130
Brands:
Shariann's Italian White Beans
Shariann's Refried P
Shariann's Spicy Veg

12211 Sharkco Seafood International
707 Jump Basin Rd
Venice, LA 70091-4351 504-534-9577
Fax: 504-534-2217
Seafood
President: Khai Nguyen
Estimated Sales: $ 5 - 10 Million
Number Employees: 10-19

12212 Sharon Mill Winery
5701 Sharon Hollow Rd
Manchester, MI 48158 734-971-6337
Fax: 734-971-6386 www.ewashtenaw.org
Wines
Director: Robert Tetens
Estimated Sales: $ 1-2.5 Million
Number Employees: 20-49

12213 Sharp Rock Vineyards
5 Sharp Rock Rd
Sperryville, VA 22740-2333 540-987-8020
Fax: 540-987-9031
jeast@sharprockvineyards.com
www.sharprock.com
Wines
Estimated Sales: $ 1 - 3 Million
Number Employees: 1-4

12214 Shashy's Fine Foods
1700 Mulberry St
Montgomery, AL 36106-1524 334-263-7341
Fax: 334-263-7343
Processor of baked goods
Co-Owner: Paul Shashy
Co-Owner: Jimmy Shashy

Estimated Sales: $500,000-$1 Million
Number Employees: 20-49
Type of Packaging: Consumer

12215 **Shasta Beverages**
9901 Widmer Rd
Lenexa, KS 66215 913-888-6777
Fax: 913-888-5732 www.shastapop.com
Processor of flavored soft drinks including grape, cola, root beer, orange, kiwi/strawberry, black cherry, etc
Manager: Rick Reynolds
Controller: Charles Reisig
VP: Thomas Mills
Sales Executive: Michael Perez
Plant Manager: Dan Penrod
Estimated Sales: $ 20 - 50 Million
Number Employees: 50-99
Parent Co: National Beverage Company
Type of Packaging: Consumer, Food Service, Private Label
Brands:
Shasta

12216 **Shaver Foods**
PO Box 1095
Springdale, AR 72765-1095 501-751-7767
Fax: 501-751-3578
President: Tim Owen
Secretary/Treasurer: Robert Collins

12217 **Shaw Baking Company**
240 S Algoma Street
Thunder Bay, ON P7B 3C2
Canada 807-345-7327
Fax: 807-345-7895 h@tbaytel.net
http://www.tbaytel.net
Processor of rolls, doughnuts, muffins, Danish pastries and bread including white and whole wheat
President/General Manager: G Shaw
Sales Manager: Joe Spina
Number Employees: 100-249
Type of Packaging: Consumer, Food Service
Brands:
Country Hearth
Holsum
Shaw

12218 **Shaw's Southern Belle Frozen**
P.O.Box 28620
Jacksonville, FL 32226-8620 904-768-1591
Fax: 904-766-3071 888-742-9772
info@shawsouthernbelle.com
www.shawsouthernbelle.com
Stuffed flounder and deviled crab
President: Howard Shaw
CFO: Joanna Zimmerman
Executive VP: John Shaw
Estimated Sales: $ 10-20 Million
Number Employees: 100

12219 **Shawmut Fishing Company**
PO Box 1986
Anchorage, AK 99508 709-334-2559
Fax: 709-596-7189
Processor of frozen crabs
President: William Berry
VP: Thomas Caines
Type of Packaging: Consumer, Food Service, Bulk

12220 **(HQ)Shawnee Canning Company**
212 Cross Junction Rd
Cross Junction, VA 22625 540-888-3429
Fax: 540-888-7963 800-713-1414
sales@shawneesprings.com
www.shawneesprings.com
Manufacturer of apple sauces, apples, peaches, ciders, preserves and jams, fruit butters, apple syrup, apple mixes, honey, pickles, salsa, dressings, relishes and fresh baked pies
President: William Whitacre
GM: Lisa Whitacre Johnson
Estimated Sales: $3 Million
Number Employees: 20-49
Sq. footage: 9750
Type of Packaging: Consumer, Private Label
Brands:
Shawnee Springs

12221 **(HQ)Shawnee Milling Company**
P.O.Box 1567
Shawnee, OK 74802-1567 405-273-7000
Fax: 405-273-7333 lspears@shawneemilling.com
www.shawneemilling.com
Manufacturer of flour, cornmeal, complete mixes, custom mixes
President: William Ford
VP: Bert Humphreys
SVP: Sam Garlow
Feed Operations: Steve Hensen
Estimated Sales: $100+ Million
Number Employees: 100-249
Type of Packaging: Consumer, Food Service, Private Label, Bulk
Brands:
SHAWNEE BEST
SHAWNEE MILLS

12222 **Shearer's Foods**
692 Wabash Ave N
Brewster, OH 44613-1056 330-767-3426
Fax: 330-767-3393 info@shearers.com
www.shearers.com
Processor of regular, rippled, flavored and kettle-cooked potato chips
President: Robert Shearer
President: Scott Smith
CFO: Fritz Kohnmann
SVP Sales and Marketing: Bill McCabe
Public Relations: Melissa Shearer
VP Operations: Randy Whisler
VP Manufacturing: Steve Surmay
Estimated Sales: $ 10 - 20 Million
Number Employees: 250-499
Sq. footage: 75000
Type of Packaging: Consumer, Food Service, Private Label, Bulk
Brands:
Grandma Shearer's
Grandma Shearer's Snacks

12223 **SheerBliss Ice Cream**
10795 NW 53rd St Ste 201
Suite 100
Sunrise, FL 33351-8085
Fax: 305-692-8700 info@sheerblissicecream.com
www.sheerblissicecream.com
ice cream, ice cream bars and ice crea, bites

12224 **Shef Products**
1518 Scotland Ln
Las Vegas, NV 89102-4814 702-873-2275
Fax: 702-873-9375
Processor and wholesaler/distributor of gourmet Italian desserts including ices, gelato, sorbetto, frozen yogurt, ice cream, tartufo, tortoni, biscotti and tiramisu; importer of sorbetto, gelato-frozen yogurt and flavorings; servingthe food service marke
VP: Chris Philips
VP Operations: Douglas Guido
Estimated Sales: $ 3 - 5 Million
Number Employees: 1-4
Sq. footage: 5000
Type of Packaging: Consumer, Food Service, Private Label, Bulk

12225 **Sheila's Select GourmetRecipe**
325 W 600 S
Heber City, UT 84032-2230 435-654-6415
Fax: 435-654-5449 800-516-7286
jen@bearcreekfoods.com
www.bearcreekfoods.com
Soups(bagged and canned), culinary bases, freezies, and salsas.
President: Kevin Ruda
CFO: Al Van Leeuwen
VP of Operations: Kevin Kowalski
Marketing Director: Jeff Hanson
Sales Manager: Steve White
Brands:
Bear Creek Country Kitchens
Sheila's Select Gourmet Recipes

12226 **Sheinman Provision Company**
4192 Viola St
Suite 96
Philadelphia, PA 19104 215-473-7065
Fax: 215-473-7038
Processor of sausage, bologna and corned and roast beef
President: Stan Rultenberg
Estimated Sales: $3 Million
Number Employees: 22
Sq. footage: 3500
Type of Packaging: Consumer, Food Service, Private Label, Bulk
Brands:
PHILLY MAID
SHEINMAN

12227 **Shekou Chemicals**
24 Crescent Street
Waltham, MA 02453-4358 781-893-6878
Fax: 781-893-6881
kimsonchemical@earthlink.net
www.kimsonchemical.com
Processor, importer and exporter of ingredients including citric acid, ascorbic acid, sodium benzoate, sodium propionate, calcium propionate, ammonium bicarbonate, sodium erythrobate, sodium citrate, potassium citrate and potassiumsorbate
System Staff: Herb Kimiatek
Sales/Marketing Executive: Judith Roiva
Purchasing Manager: Simon Altstein
Estimated Sales: $1100000
Number Employees: 7
Sq. footage: 10000
Type of Packaging: Bulk

12228 **Shelburne Farms**
1611 Harbor Rd
Shelburne, VT 05482 802-985-8686
Fax: 802-985-8123
lwellings@shelburnefarms.org
www.shelburnefarms.org
Cheddar cheese
President: Alexander Webb
Marketing Manager: Tom Pierce
Controller: Fred Blythe
Estimated Sales: $ 5-10 Million
Number Employees: 50-99
Brands:
Vermont

12229 **Shell Ridge Jalapeno Project**
1432 Highway 35 S
Rockport, TX 78382-3918 512-790-8028
Ethnic foods
President: Kay Segura Christian
Estimated Sales: $500,000 appx.
Number Employees: 1-4
Brands:
Kay's Hot Stuff

12230 **Shelley's Prime Meats**
700 Bergen Avenue
Jersey City, NJ 07306-4890 201-433-3434
Fax: 201-433-4549
Processor of provisions/meats including fresh and frozen beef, veal, lamb, pork and poultry
President: Shelley Geller
General Manager: Chuck Brennan
Estimated Sales: $11300000
Number Employees: 40
Sq. footage: 10000
Type of Packaging: Food Service

12231 **Shelton's Poultry**
204 N Loranne
Pomona, CA 91767 909-623-4361
Fax: 909-623-0634 800-541-1833
trukbaron@sheltons.com www.sheltons.com
Processor of free range poultry products; also, soups, chili, jerky, sausage, uncured frankfurters, meat balls, etc
President/CEO: Gary Flanagan
CFO: Lori Barragar
VP: Brian Flanagan
Estimated Sales: $ 20 - 50 Million
Number Employees: 20-49
Type of Packaging: Consumer
Brands:
Shelton's

12232 **Shemper Seafood Company**
367 Bayview Ave
Biloxi, MS 39530 228-435-2703
Fax: 228-432-2104
Seafood, seafood products
President: Gary Shemper
CEO: Jeffrey Shemper
Estimated Sales: $600,000
Number Employees: 1-4
Brands:
Shemper Seafood

12233 **Shenandoah Mills**
P.O.Box 369
Lebanon, TN 37088 615-444-0841
Fax: 615-444-0286 donya@shenandoahmills.com
www.shenandoahmills.com
Processor of dry mixes including biscuit, pancake, corndog, apple fritters, corn meal, corn bread, gravy and hushpuppies; also, breadings including fish, chicken, pork, beef, etc
President: Dale Nunnery
VP: Danny Hodges
Plant Manager: Ike Sandy
Director Sales: George Stonesifer
Public Relations: Linda Carmen
Estimated Sales: $4 Million
Number Employees: 25
Sq. footage: 65000
Type of Packaging: Food Service
Brands:
Shenandoah

12234 **Shenandoah Vineyards**
12300 Steiner Rd
Plymouth, CA 95669 209-245-4455
Fax: 209-245-5156 info@sobowine.com
www.sobonwine.com
Wines
President: Leon Sobon
CEO: Shirley Sobon
Estimated Sales: Below $ 5 Million
Number Employees: 10-19

12235 **Shenandoah's Pride**
5325 Port Royal Rd
Springfield, VA 22151 703-321-9500
Fax: 703-321-0573
Milk, dairy products
Manager: Craig Wilson
Plant Manager: Richard Becker
Estimated Sales: $ 30-50 Million
Number Employees: 100-249
Parent Co: Suiza Dairy Group

12236 **Shenk's Foods**
1980 New Danville Pike
Lancaster, PA 17603 717-393-4240
Fax: 717-393-4240 customerservice@shenks.com
www.shenks.com
Manufacturer of cheese, butter spreads, jellies, mustards, preserves, relishes and fruit spreads
President: Karl Achtermann
Estimated Sales: $2 Million
Number Employees: 1-4
Sq. footage: 9000
Type of Packaging: Consumer, Private Label
Brands:
Shenk's

12237 **(HQ)Shepherd Farms**
9330 E 8th Rd
Hillsboro, IL 62049-3448 217-532-5268
Fax: 815-389-1997 800-383-2676
gshep@seedfarm.com www.seedfarm.com
Processor and packer of popcorn including yellow, white and specialty hybrids packaged for microwave, air poppers and commercial poppers; also, soybeans and tofu; exporter of soybeans for tofu, miso, natto and shoyu, seed corn and seedsoybeans
Principal: Dot Shepherd
Estimated Sales: $130,000
Number Employees: 2
Sq. footage: 20000
Type of Packaging: Consumer, Food Service, Private Label, Bulk
Other Locations:
Shepherd Farms
Beloit IL
Brands:
Boone County Supreme
Shepherd
Shepherd Supreme

12238 **Shepherdsfield Bakery**
777 Shepherdsfield Rd
Fulton, MO 65251 573-642-1439
Fax: 573-642-1439
Processor of frozen gourmet waffles, muffins, breads and whole wheat pancake mixes, pies, cookies and flour
Religious Leader: Thomas Mahaney
CEO: Vicki Staudenmyer
Estimated Sales: $$1-2.5 Million
Number Employees: 20-49
Sq. footage: 40000
Type of Packaging: Consumer, Private Label

12239 **Sherm Edwards Candies**
509 Cavitt Ave
Trafford, PA 15085-1060 412-372-4331
Fax: 412-373-8089 800-436-5424
www.shermedwardscandies.com
Processor of chocolate-covered candy
President: David Golembeski
Estimated Sales: $724000
Number Employees: 20-49
Type of Packaging: Consumer, Bulk

12240 **Sherrill Orchards**
3265 Valpredo Rd
Arvin, CA 93203 661-858-2035
Fax: 661-858-2035 soprus@aorldnet.att.com
Processor of pomegranate juice, vinegar, apple cider and blends
President: Donna Sherril
Estimated Sales: $340,000
Number Employees: 5
Brands:
Sherrill

12241 **Sherwood Brands**
1803 Research Blvd # 201
Rockville, MD 20850-6106 401-434-7773
Fax: 301-309-6162 sales@sherwoodbrands.com
www.sherwoodbrands.com
Processor and exporter of confectionery products including hard candies, jelly beans, cookies, chocolates, toffee, lollypops and holiday novelties; also, packaged in bags and for fund raising; importer of food containers
President/Chairman/CEO: Uziel Frydman
CFO/Secretary: Christopher Willi
EVP Marketing/Product Develpment: Amir Frydman
Estimated Sales: $45,900,000
Number Employees: 50-99
Sq. footage: 500000
Parent Co: Sherwood Brands
Type of Packaging: Consumer, Private Label
Brands:
Candy Kaleidoscope
Cap'n Poptoy
Cherry & Berry Blast
Creative Gourmet
Tweety
Tweety Pops
Wan-Na-Bes

12242 **(HQ)Sherwood Brands**
1803 Research Blvd # 201
Rockville, MD 20850-6106 301-309-6161
Fax: 301-309-6162 orders@sherwoodbrands.com
www.sherwoodbrands.com
Cookies and candy
President: Amir Frydman
CEO: Uziel Frydman
CFO: Christopher Willi
VP Sales: Paul Splitek
Estimated Sales: $ 30-50 Million
Number Employees: 60
Brands:
Cows Butter Toffee Candies
Demitasse Biscuits
Elana Chocolate
Kastin's Old Fashioned Candies
Ruger Wafers & Cookies
Tongue Tattoo Lollipops
Zed Gum

12243 **Sheryl's Chocolate Creations**
11 Commercial St
Hicksville, NY 11801-5211 516-681-4060
Fax: 516-681-4189 888-882-2462
www.sherylschocolate.com
Hand-dipped chocolate chips, pretzel rods, pretzel twists, sourdough pretzels, mini pretzels, popcorn and assorted cookies
President: Sheryl Simon
Purchasing Manager: Ron Simon
Estimated Sales: $ 1-2.5 Million
Number Employees: 10-19
Sq. footage: 4000
Type of Packaging: Consumer, Private Label, Bulk

12244 **Shields Date Gardens**
80225 Us Highway 111
Indio, CA 92201-6599 760-347-0996
Fax: 760-342-3288 800-414-2555
shieldate@aol.com www.shieldsdategarden.com
Processor of nuts, dates and fruits including citrus and dried; also, mail order available
Owner: Greg Raumin
Estimated Sales: $ 5 - 10 Million
Number Employees: 20-49
Type of Packaging: Consumer
Brands:
Date Crystals

12245 **Shine Companies**
4014 Evening Trail Drive
Spring, TX 77388-4936 281-353-8392
Fax: 281-353-8937 shinecom@aol.com
Processor and exporter of specialty seasonings, artichoke dips and toppings and marinades, salsas and condiments; importer of chile purees
President: Michael Shine
Executive VP: Janet Williams
Number Employees: 6
Sq. footage: 2500
Brands:
Jazzie J
Semdiero

12246 **Shine Foods Inc**
21100 S Western Avenue
Torrance, CA 90501-1700 310-533-6010
Fax: 310-328-2608 info@shinefoods.com
www.shinefood.com
Processor of dim sum, pot stickers, dumplings, gyoza, shumai and spring rolls
President: Stephen Y Lee
VP: John Freschi
Marketing Manager: Tracy Lee
Estimated Sales: $300,000-500,000
Number Employees: 1-4
Type of Packaging: Private Label, Bulk

12247 **Shining Ocean**
1515 Puyallup St
Sumner, WA 98390 253-826-3700
Fax: 206-283-7079 email@kanimi.com
www.kanimi.com
Processor of frozen surimi and fried seafood
President: Michael Faris
CFO: Howard Frisk
R & D: Tim Taylor
Quality Control: Raymond McReaey
Sales Coordinator: Yuji Ishii
Estimated Sales: $ 30-50 Million
Number Employees: 100-249
Type of Packaging: Consumer, Food Service, Private Label
Brands:
Emerald Sea
Heathy 1
Kanimi-Tem
Pacific Choice
Sea Farer
Shining Choice

12248 **Shionogi Qualicaps**
6505 Franz Warner Pkwy
Whitsett, NC 27377-9215 336-449-7300
Fax: 336-449-3333 800-227-7853
info@qiallicaps.com www.qualicaps.com
Processor and exporter of hard gelatin capsules
President: Greg Bowers
Sales: Matt Schappert
CFO: Dennis Stella
CEO: Herb Hugill
Quality Control: Schuck Waldroup
Estimated Sales: $ 5-10 Million
Number Employees: 100-249
Parent Co: Shionogi
Type of Packaging: Bulk

12249 **Shipley Baking Company**
7 Jim Walter Drive
Texarkana, AR 71854-4840 870-772-7146
Manufacturer of bread and buns.
President: Frank Shipley
Plant President: Debbie Broussard
Estimated Sales: $168 Million
Number Employees: 200
Type of Packaging: Consumer, Food Service
Brands:
COUNTRY HEARTH
HOLSUM
LESS

12250 **Shipmaster USA**
8711 E Pinnacle Peak Road
Suite 254
Scottsdale, AZ 85255-3517 480-585-0109
Fax: 482-585-0082

12251 **Shipyard Brewing Company**
86 Newbury St
Portland, ME 04101-4274
US 207-761-0807
Fax: 207-775-5567 800-789-0684
www.shipyard.com
www.captn.com
Processor and exporter of beer, ale and stout and root beer.
Owner/President: Fred Forsley
Director Of Sales And Marketing: Bruce Forsley
Director Manufacturing: Paul Henry
Estimated Sales: Under $500,000
Number Employees: 35
Number of Brands: 17
Type of Packaging: Consumer, Food Service
Brands:
Blue Fin
Chamberlain
Goat Island Light
Longfellow Winter
Old Thumper Extra Special
Prelude Christmas

12252 **Shirer Brothers Slaughter House**
7805 Adamsville Otsego Rd
Adamsville, OH 43802 740-796-3214
Beef, beef products
President: Ronald Shirer
Estimated Sales: $ 1-2.5 Million
Number Employees: 1-4

12253 **Shirley Foods**
P.O.Box 457
Shirley, IN 47384 765-738-6511
Fax: 765-738-6881 800-560-2908
www.shirleyfoods.com
Flour and corn tortillas
President: Gary Toth
Estimated Sales: $ 2.5-5 Million
Number Employees: 9
Brands:
Shirley Foods

12254 **Shoei Foods USA**
1900 Feather River Blvd
Olivehurst, CA 95961 530-742-7866
Fax: 530-742-2873 800-527-4712
mikem@shoeiusa.com
Grower, packer and seller of prunes
President: Ron Sandage
CFO: Masami Hoki
Vice President: Dick Onyett
Marketing/Sales: Mike Manassero
Plant Manager: Taka Sackamoto
Estimated Sales: $ 50-100 Million
Number Employees: 100-249
Number of Brands: 2
Number of Products: 5
Sq. footage: 30000
Type of Packaging: Consumer, Food Service, Private Label, Bulk

12255 **Shofar Kosher Foods**
2365 E Linden Ave
Linden, NJ 07036-1142 908-925-6000
Fax: 908-925-5331 888-874-6327
www.bests-kosher.com
Manufacturer of kosher meats including hot dogs, salami, bologna, corned beef, pastrami, brisket, roast beef and veal
Manager/Sales: Lenny Posnock
Estimated Sales: $3-5 Million
Number Employees: 10-19
Sq. footage: 22000
Type of Packaging: Consumer, Food Service, Bulk
Brands:
Shofar

12256 **Shonan Usa**
P.O.Box 128
Grandview, WA 98930 509-882-5583
Fax: 509-882-5890
Processor of refrigerated fruit juice concentrates including apple, cherry, grape, pear, carrot, strawberry and red raspberry
President: Akira Nozaka
Controller: Douglas Foth
Estimated Sales: $7 Million
Number Employees: 50
Type of Packaging: Bulk
Brands:
Shonan

12257 **Shonfeld's**
57 Romanelli Avenue
South Hackensack, NJ 07606-1427 201-883-0100
Fax: 201-883-0017 800-462-3464
sales@shonfelds.com www.shonfelds.com
Gourmet pasta, spices, candies, preserves and honey, oils and vinegar
Founder: Boaz Shonfeld
Estimated Sales: $ 10-20 Million
Number Employees: 250-499
Brands:
Shonfield's

12258 **Shonna's Gourmet Goodies**
320 W Center Street
West Bridgewater, MA 02379-1626 508-580-2033
Fax: 508-580-2044 888-312-7868
Processor of frozen hors d'oeuvres
Owner/President: Howard Sherman
Estimated Sales: Less than $500,000
Sq. footage: 3000
Type of Packaging: Private Label

12259 **Shooting Star Farms**
3401 Michigan St Ste 2
Bartlesville, OK 74006 918-331-0599
Fax: 888-450-4004 888-850-8540
imcdonaldA@shootingstarfarms.com
www.shootingstarfarms.com
Delightful dips, gift boxes, gracious gourmet salsas, jazzy jellies, marvelous munchies, traditionally tasty salsas.
President: Larry Mc Donald
Estimated Sales: $300,000-500,000
Number Employees: 1-4
Type of Packaging: Consumer

12260 **Shore Seafood**
P.O.Box 10
Saxis, VA 23427-0010 757-824-5517
Fax: 757-824-5662 shoresfd@shore.intercom.net
www.shoreseafood.com
Seafood
President: Greg Linton
Vice President: Andy Drewer
Estimated Sales: $ 5-10 Million
Number Employees: 20-49
Type of Packaging: Private Label
Brands:
Chesapeake Bay Delight

12261 **Shore Trading Company**
665 Union Hill Rd
Alpharetta, GA 30004 770-998-0566
Fax: 770-998-0571
Seafood
Owner: Marty Klausner
Estimated Sales: $1 Million
Number Employees: 1-4

12262 **Shoreline Chocolates**
212 W Shore Rd
Alburg, VT 05440 802-796-3730
Fax: 802-796-4725 800-310-3730
info@lakesendcheeses.com
www.lakesendcheeses.com
Produces assorted homemade chocolates.
Operator: Joanne James
Operator: Alton James
Estimated Sales: $300,000-500,000
Number Employees: 1-4

12263 **Shoreline Fruit**
10850 E Traverse Hwy Ste 4460
Traverse City, MI 49684 231-941-4336
Fax: 585-765-9443 800-836-3972
steve.somsel@shorelinefruit.com
www.shorelinefruit.com
Grower, processor and marketers of dried fruits and cherry products
CEO: Ken Swanson
CFO: Jason Warren
Sales Manager: Steve Somsel
Number Employees: 180

12264 **Short's Brewing Company**
121 N Bridge Street
Bellaire, MI 49615 231-828-2112
www.shortsbrewing.com
Lagers and ales
Owner/President: Joseph Short
President: Leah Hannan
VP: Scott Bale
Estimated Sales: $450,000
Number Employees: 30
Sq. footage: 28000

12265 **Shreve Meats Processing**
200 E McConkey St
Shreve, OH 44676 330-567-2142
Processor of beef and pork
Co-Owner: Ray Haas
Co-Owner: Tim Morris
Estimated Sales: $140000
Number Employees: 5-9

12266 **Shreveport Macaroni Company**
104 N Common St
Shreveport, LA 71101 318-222-6857
Fax: 318-221-7815
Processor of pasta including spaghetti
Plant Manager: Monty Phares
Estimated Sales: $ 20 - 50 Million
Number Employees: 20-49
Parent Co: Arrowhead
Type of Packaging: Consumer, Food Service, Private Label
Brands:
De Boles

12267 **Shrimp World**
1020 Hancock Street
Gretna, LA 70053-2321 504-368-1571
Fax: 504-368-1573
Shrimp
President: William Chauvin

12268 **Shuckman's Fish & Co. Smokery**
3001 W Main St
Louisville, KY 40212-1800 502-775-6478
Fax: 502-775-6470 www.kysmokedfish.com
Smokers of fish & seafood products.
President: Lewis Shuckman
Estimated Sales: $ 3 - 5 Million
Number Employees: 10-19

12269 **Shuffs Meat Company**
12247 Baugher Rd
Thurmont, MD 21788-2333 301-271-2231
Fax: 301-271-1037
Manufacturer of meat products
Owner: Robin Shuff
Estimated Sales: $18 Million
Number Employees: 5-9

12270 **Shultz Company**
555 Carlisle St
Hanover, PA 17331-2162 717-633-4585
Fax: 717-637-0487 sales@shultzfoods.com
www.shultzfood.com
Pretzels
Owner: Jack Shultz
National Sales Manager: Mark Tralongo
Plant Manager: Joe Semmelman
Estimated Sales: $ 10-20 Million
Number Employees: 1-4
Sq. footage: 135000
Type of Packaging: Consumer, Private Label, Bulk
Brands:
Jake Baked
Pretzel Factory
Salty Stix
Schultz
Shults Pretzels
Zels

12271 **Shur-Good Biscuit Co.**
11677 Chesterdale Rd
Cincinnati, OH 45246-3917 513-458-6200
Fax: 513-458-6212
Cookies
Manager: Jerry Wallman
CFO: Nicola Melillo
Marketing Director: William Klump
Sales Director: Mark O'Toole
Public Relations: Kathy Coggeshall
Operations Manager: Peter Lowes

Estimated Sales: $ 5 - 10 Million
Number Employees: 100-249
Parent Co: Parmalat Bakery Group North America
Type of Packaging: Consumer

12272 **Sidari's Italian Foods**
3820 Lakeside Ave E
Cleveland, OH 44114 216-431-3344
Fax: 216-431-6227 siditalian@aol.com
Italian frozen foods
President: Joe Sidari
Estimated Sales: $ 50-100 Million
Number Employees: 50-99

12273 **Side Hill Farm**
74 Cotton Mill Hl Unit A110
Brattleboro, VT 05301 802-254-2018
Fax: 802-254-3381
Manfacturer of jams
Owner: Kelt Naylor
Estimated Sales: $ 1 - 3 Million
Number Employees: 1-4
Number of Products: 14

12274 **Sieco USA Corporation**
9014 Ruland Road
PO Box 55485
Houston, TX 77055-4612 713-464-1726
Fax: 713-464-3323 800-325-9443
amber@sieco-usa.com www.sieco-usa.com
Processor, importer and exporter of extra virgin and infused olive oil, and organic olive oil, stuffed olives and balsamic wine vinegar and white wine vinegar; processor of sauces; gift packs available.
President: Sherif Cheman
Marketing: Diann Fischer
Number Employees: 3
Number of Brands: 2
Number of Products: 11
Sq. footage: 8600
Type of Packaging: Consumer, Food Service, Private Label, Bulk
Brands:
Amber
Sammy's

12275 **Siegel Egg Company**
273 Albany St
Cambridge, MA 02139 617-873-0800
Fax: 617-873-0824 800-593-3447
Manufacturer of fresh and frozen eggs
President: Ken Siegel
Estimated Sales: $102 Million
Number Employees: 59
Type of Packaging: Consumer

12276 **(HQ)Siemer Milling Company**
P.O.Box 670
Teutopolis, IL 62467 217-857-3131
Fax: 217-857-3092 800-826-1065
siemer@siemermilling.com
www.siemermilling.com
Processor of flour and pasta
President: Rick Siemer
R&D/Technical Sales: Kevin Bodily
VP Quality: Allen Westendorf
VP Production: Vernon Tegeler
Purchasing: Sue Woltman
Estimated Sales: $ 50 - 100 Million
Number Employees: 100-249
Type of Packaging: Consumer, Food Service, Bulk
Brands:
Don's Chuck Wagon
Hodgson Mill
Kentucky Kernel

12277 **Siena Foods**
16 Newbridge Road
Toronto, ON M8Z 2L7
Canada 416-239-3967
Fax: 416-239-2084 800-465-0422
Processor, importer and exporter of Italian style meat including Genoa salami, mortadella, cappicola, prosciutto and hot and mild sausage
General Manager: Enzo DeLuca
Number Employees: 50-99
Type of Packaging: Consumer, Food Service

12278 **Sierra Cheese Manufacturing Company**
916 S Santa Fe Avenue
Compton, CA 90220 310-635-1216
Fax: 310-639-1096 800-266-4270
sierracheese@aol.com www.sierracheese.com
Processor of Italian cheese including mozzarella, ricotta, string, tuma, scamorze, requeson, feta, etc
President: John Curran
Vice President: Charlene Franco
Sales Director: Carlos Rivera
General Manager: Charlene Franco
Purchasing Manager: Vince Inga
Number Employees: 20-49
Sq. footage: 15000
Type of Packaging: Consumer, Private Label, Bulk
Brands:
Montebello
Sierra

12279 **Sierra Madre Organic Coffee**
191 University Blvd
Denver, CO 80206-4613 303-446-0050
Fax: 303-393-8208
organic@sierramadrecoffee.com
www.sierramadrecoffee.com
Organic coffee
President: Mena Moran

12280 **Sierra Nevada Brewing Company**
1075 E 20th St
Chico, CA 95928 530-893-3520
Fax: 530-893-9358 info@sierranevada.com
www.sierranevada.com
Processor of seasonal beer, ale, stout, lager and pilsner
President: Ken Grossman
President: Terence Sullivan
Quality Control: Rebecca Newman
Production Manager: Cory Ross
Estimated Sales: $32 Million
Number Employees: 400
Type of Packaging: Consumer, Food Service
Brands:
Porter & Stout
Sierra Nevada Bigfoo
Sierra Nevada Celebration
Sierra Nevada Pale Ale
Sierra Nevada Stout
Sierra Nevada Summer

12281 **Sierra Vista Winery**
4560 Cabernet Way
Placerville, CA 95667 530-622-7221
Fax: 530-622-2413 syrah@sierravistawinery.com
www.sierravistawinery.com
Wines
Owner: John Mac Cready
Owner/Winery Office VP: Barbara MacCready
Estimated Sales: Below $ 5 Million
Number Employees: 1-4
Type of Packaging: Private Label
Brands:
SIERRA VISTA

12282 **Sifers Valomilk Candy Company**
5112 Merriam Dr
Shawnee Mission, KS 66203 913-722-0991
Fax: 913-722-5016 russ@valomilk.com
www.valomilk.com
Valomilk candy cups
President: Russell Sifers
Estimated Sales: $ 2.5-5 Million
Number Employees: 5-9
Number of Brands: 1
Number of Products: 1
Type of Packaging: Private Label
Brands:
SIFERS VALOMILK CANDY CUPS

12283 **Sigma International**
10901 Roosevelt Blvd.
Suite 108B
St Petersburg, FL 33705 727-822-1288
Fax: 727-822-6782 800-899-5717
sales@seafoodbysigma.com
http://www.seafoodbysigma.com
Seafood
Estimated Sales: $ 50-100 Million
Number Employees: 20-49

12284 **Sigma-Aldrich Corporation**
3050 Spruce Street
St. Louis, MO 63103 314-771-5765
Fax: 314-771-5757 sig-ald@sial.com
www.sigmaaldrich.com
Aroma chemicals, synthetics, certified naturals and essential oils to redi-packs and pre-packaged samples, also provide raw materials for a wide range of applications and offer a comprehensive range of kosher certified natural andsynthetic products.
Chairman/President/CEO: Jai Nagarkatti
SVP/CFO/CAO: Rakesh Sachdev
VP Sales: Gerrit J C van den Dool
VP Human Resources: Douglas Rau
Estimated Sales: $2.2 Billion
Number Employees: 7800
Number of Products: 1500
Brands:
ALDRICH
FLUKA
SAFC
SIGMA
SUPELCO

12285 **Signature Brands**
P.O.Box 279
Ocala, FL 34478 352-622-3134
Fax: 352-402-9451 800-456-9573
info@signaturebrands.com
www.signaturebrands.com
Manufacturer, importer and exporter of dessert decorating and specialty baking products. Importer of preserves.
Chairman/President/CEO: Robert Lawless
EVP/Chief Financial Officer: Francis Contino
CEO: James Schneider
VP/Finance & Treasurer: Paul Beard
VP/Human Relations: Cecile Perich
Estimated Sales: $ 20 - 50 Million
Number Employees: 250-499
Sq. footage: 80000
Parent Co: McCormick & Company
Type of Packaging: Consumer, Food Service, Private Label, Bulk
Brands:
Betty Crocker
Cake Mate
SIGNATURE

12286 **Signature Foods**
8001 Nw 54th St
Miami, FL 33166 305-436-5392
Fax: 305-264-5076
Rice mixes
President: Oran B Talkington
Estimated Sales: $3.3 Million
Number Employees: 23

12287 **Signature Fruit**
1 Tiffany Point
Suite 206
Bloomingdale, IL 60108-2916 630-980-2481
Fax: 630-980-3211
Processor of canned foods including fruits and vegetables
Director (Central Zone): Bruce Scheer
Business Manager (Midwest): Hank Gergovich
Estimated Sales: $ 3 - 5 Million
Number Employees: 1-4
Parent Co: Tri-Valley Growers
Type of Packaging: Consumer

12288 **Signature Seafoods**
4257 24th Ave W
Seattle, WA 98199-1214 206-285-2815
Fax: 206-282-5938
Processor of salmon
President: William Orr
Estimated Sales: $4,000,000
Number Employees: 10-19
Brands:
H&G Chum
King Salmon
Silver Salmon

12289 **Signore Winery**
153 White Church Road
Brooktondale, NY 14817-9769 607-539-7935
Wines
Owner: Daniel Signore
Estimated Sales: $ 1-4.9 Million
Number Employees: 1-5

12290 **Signorello Vineyards**
4500 Silverado Trl
Napa, CA 94558-1100 707-255-5990
Fax: 707-255-5999
info@signorellovineyards.com
www.signorellovineyards.com

Wines
Owner: Ray Signorello
National Sales Director: Chris Carmichael
Director Marketing: Bruce Donsker
Winemaker: Raymond Signorello Jr
Winemaker: Pierre Birebent
Estimated Sales: Below $ 5 Million
Number Employees: 5-9
Brands:
Signorello

12291 **Silani Sweet Cheese**
RR 1
Schomberg, ON L0G 1T0
Canada 905-939-2561
Fax: 905-939-2011 silanicheese@look.ca
Processor and importer of cheese
President: Michael Talarico
CEO/VP: Joe Lanzino
Number Employees: 185
Sq. footage: 25000

12292 **Silesia Flavors**
5250 Prairie Stone Pkwy
Hoffman Estates, IL 60192 847-645-0270
Fax: 847-645-0266 info@silesiafl.com
www.silesia.de
Develops and produces natural, nature identical and artificial as well as process flavours in various forms, plus natural colour extracts and synthetic colours.
President/CEO: Clemens Hanke
Vice President/Executive Officer: Ortwin Winter
VP: Joe Peterkes
Estimated Sales: $ 5-10 Million
Number Employees: 5-9
Parent Co: Silesia Groups
Brands:
Sil-A-Gran
Silarom
Silvanil

12293 **Siljans Crispy Cup Company**
23 Skyline Crest NE
Calgary, AB T2K 5X2
Canada 403-275-0135
Fax: 403-275-0061 siljans@telus.net
www.siljanscrispycup.com
Processor and exporter of edible cups for hors d'oeuvres and desserts
President: B Ersson
CEO: Christina Ersson
Estimated Sales: $500,000
Number Employees: 5
Number of Brands: 1
Number of Products: 1
Sq. footage: 8000
Type of Packaging: Consumer, Food Service, Private Label, Bulk
Brands:
SALMOLUX
SILJANS

12294 **Sill Farms Market**
50241 Red Arrow Hwy
Lawrence, MI 49064-8781 269-674-3755
Fax: 269-674-3756
Processor of frozen apples, blueberries, cherries and strawberries
President: Bob Ross
Executive VP: Jean Sill
Plant Manager: Ernest Probin
Estimated Sales: $2 Million
Number Employees: 20
Type of Packaging: Consumer, Food Service, Bulk

12295 **Sill Farms Market**
50241 Red Arrow Hwy
Lawrence, MI 49064-8781 269-674-3755
Fax: 269-674-3756
Frozen and fresh sliced fruits
President: Bob Ross
Estimated Sales: $5-9.9 Million
Number Employees: 10-19
Brands:
Plowshares
Sunshower

12296 **Silliker, Inc**
111 E Wacker Dr
Suite 2300
Chicago, IL 60601 312-938-5151
info@silliker.com
www.silliker.com
Laboratory providing food testing, microbiological and chemical analysis, technical consulting and audits for HACCP/GMPs employee training services and custom research
President: James Ondyak
VP: Jim Hayes
Marketing Communications Manager: Jessica Sawyer-Lueck
Number Employees: 50-99
Parent Co: BioMerieux Alliance

12297 **Silva Farms**
P.O.Box Z
Gonzales, CA 93926 831-675-2327
Fax: 831-675-2375 silvafarm@inreach.com
Vegetables
Owner: Edward Skua Jr
Estimated Sales: $500,000-$1 Million
Number Employees: 1-4
Type of Packaging: Private Label, Bulk

12298 **Silva International**
523 N Ash St
Momence, IL 60954 815-472-3535
Fax: 815-472-3536 kdevries@silva-intl.com
www.silva-intl.com
Dehydrated vegetables, ingredients, herbs and fruits.
President: Peter Schmidt
VP: Kent DeVries
Quality Assurance Manager: Ed Bove
General Manager: Steve DeYoung
Estimated Sales: $ 2.5-5 Million
Number Employees: 20-49

12299 **Silvan Ridge**
27012 Briggs Hill Rd
Eugene, OR 97405 541-345-1945
Fax: 541-345-6174 info@silvanridge.com
www.silvanridge.com
Wines
President: Carolyn Chambers
CEO: Elizabeth Chambers
CFO: Jim Plumber
Quality Control: Bryan Wilson
Marketing: Phil Cowles
Sales: Ryan Shockley
Public Relations: Angela Bennett
Operations: Haley Smith
Estimated Sales: Below $ 5 Million
Number Employees: 5-9
Number of Brands: 2
Brands:
Hinman Vineyards
Silvan Ridge

12300 **Silver Creek Distillers**
134 N 3300 E
Rigby, ID 83442 208-754-0042
Fax: 208-754-4758
Beverage grade alcohol
Manager: Bill Scott
Plant Manager: Bill Scott
Estimated Sales: $3,200,000
Number Employees: 5-9
Brands:
Teton Glacier Vodka

12301 **Silver Creek Farms**
450 Locust St S
Twin Falls, ID 83301-7848 208-736-0829
Fax: 208-736-0725
Smoked fruit and salmon

12302 **Silver Creek Specialty Meats**
P.O.Box 3307
Oshkosh, WI 54903 920-232-3581
Fax: 920-232-3589
www.silvercreekspecialtymeats.com
Processor of natural casing sausage
President: William Kramlich Sr
CEO: Bill Kramlich Jr
Estimated Sales: $4500000
Number Employees: 10-19
Type of Packaging: Food Service, Private Label, Bulk

12303 **Silver Ferm Chemical**
2226 Queen Anne Ave N # C
Seattle, WA 98109-2372 206-282-3376
Fax: 206-282-0105 info@silverfernchemical.com
www.silverfernchemical.com
Food chemicals and ingredients
President: Sam King
Number Employees: 5-9

12304 **Silver Fox Vineyard**
4683 Morning Star Ln
Mariposa, CA 95338-9361 209-966-4800
Fax: 209-966-4369 enjoy@sti.net
www.silverfoxvineyards.com
Wines
Co-Owner/Co-Operator: Marvin Silver
Co-Owner/Co-Operator: Karen Silver
Estimated Sales: Below $ 5 Million
Number Employees: 5-9
Brands:
Silver Fox Vineyard

12305 **Silver Lake Cookie Company**
141 Freeman Ave
Islip, NY 11751 631-581-4000
Fax: 631-581-4510 info@silvercookies.com
www.silverlakecookie.com
Processor and exporter of cookies and canolli shells
President: Joseph Vitarelli
EVP: Rocco Vitarelli
VP Sales: Doug Wainscott
Operations: Peter Zampiva
Estimated Sales: $44 Million
Number Employees: 250
Sq. footage: 110000
Type of Packaging: Consumer, Food Service, Private Label, Bulk

12306 **Silver Lake Sausage Shop**
80 Ethan St
Providence, RI 2909 401-944-4081
Sausage
President: Erminia Santilli
Estimated Sales: Less than $500,000
Number Employees: 1-4

12307 **(HQ)Silver Lining Seafood**
P.O.Box 6092
Ketchikan, AK 99901 907-225-9865
Fax: 907-225-3891 www.tridentseafoods.com
Processor and exporter of fresh, smoked and canned seafood.
Plant Manager: Leigh Gerber
Estimated Sales: $500,000-$1 Million
Number Employees: 5-9
Type of Packaging: Consumer, Food Service, Bulk

12308 **Silver Mountain Vineyards**
P.O.Box 3636
Santa Cruz, CA 95063 408-353-2278
Fax: 408-353-1898 info@silvermtn.com
www.silvermtn.com
Wine
President: Jerold O'Brien
Estimated Sales: $ 1-2.5 Million
Number Employees: 1-4
Type of Packaging: Private Label
Brands:
Silver Mtn Vineyards

12309 **Silver Oak Cellars**
P.O.Box 414
Oakville, CA 94562-0414 707-944-8808
Fax: 707-944-2817 800-273-8805
info@silveroak.com www.silveroak.com
Processor of cabernet sauvignon red wine
President: Raymond Duncan
General Manager: Dave Cofran
Estimated Sales: $ 20 - 50 Million
Number Employees: 20-49

12310 **Silver Palate Kitchens**
300 Knickerbocker Rd Ste 1600
Cresskill, NJ 7626 201-568-0110
Fax: 201-568-8844 800-872-5283
www.silverpalate.com
Processor and exporter of vinegars, oils, chutneys, mustards, savories, sweet sauces, preserves, brandied fruits, salad dressings, pasta, oatmeal, etc
Owner: Peter Harris
VP: Tom Buro
Estimated Sales: $ 20 - 50 Million
Number Employees: 20-49
Type of Packaging: Consumer, Food Service, Private Label, Bulk
Brands:
Silver Palate

12311 **Silver Sea Sales Company**
810 S Caton Avenue
Baltimore, MD 21229-4210 410-644-4661
Fax: 410-646-7569
President/CEO: Thomas Rea

12312 Silver Spring Gardens
P.O.Box 360
Eau Claire, WI 54702 715-832-9739
Fax: 715-832-9915 800-826-7322
orders@silverspringfoods.com
www.silverspringfoods.com
Processor of horseradish, mustard, cocktail and tartar sauces; also, chopped garlic, and portion control items
President: Ed Schaefer
Marketing Manager: Rita Schrantz
VP Sales/Marketing: Tom Geheran
Purchasing: Jeff Holden
Estimated Sales: $36449975
Number Employees: 100-249
Parent Co: Huntsinger Companies
Type of Packaging: Consumer, Food Service, Private Label, Bulk
Brands:
Atlantic Meyers
Bookbinder'S
Good
Silver Spring

12313 Silver Springs Citrus
P.O.Box 155
Howey In the Hills, FL 34737 352-324-2101
Fax: 352-324-2033 800-940-2277
ppatrick@silverspringscitrus.com
www.silverspringscitrus.com
Manufacturer, importer and exporter of juices
President: John Rees
CFO: Michael Hall
VP/Sales: Pat Patrick
VP Operations: Bill Roscoe
Estimated Sales: $75 Million
Number Employees: 100-249
Sq. footage: 960000
Type of Packaging: Consumer, Food Service, Private Label, Bulk

12314 Silver Star Meats
1720 Middletown Road
Po Box 393
McKees Rocks, PA 15136 412-771-5539
Fax: 412-771-2253 800-548-1321
info@silverstarmeats.com
www.silverstarmeats.com
Processor of hams, sausages, hotdogs, kielbasa, lunch meats
President: Robert Geromoy
Plant Manager: Dominic Bovalina
Estimated Sales: $11000000
Number Employees: 80
Sq. footage: 55000
Type of Packaging: Consumer, Food Service, Private Label
Brands:
Rzaca

12315 Silver State Foods
3725 Jason St
Denver, CO 80211 303-433-3351
Fax: 303-433-2883 800-423-3351
tom@silverstatefoods.com
www.silverstatefoods.com
Processor of canned and frozen foods including prepared, spaghetti sauce and egg noodles
Manager: Tom Ernst
Estimated Sales: $600,000
Number Employees: 1-4
Number of Brands: 2
Number of Products: 2
Sq. footage: 5600
Type of Packaging: Consumer, Food Service, Private Label, Bulk
Brands:
Aiellos
Salvatore's

12316 Silver Streak Bass Company
1205 Frank Stubbs Dr
El Campo, TX 77437 979-543-6343
Producer of farm-raised hybrid striped bass
Owner: Jim Ekstrom
Number Employees: 1-4
Parent Co: Ekstrom Enterprises
Type of Packaging: Bulk
Brands:
Silver Streak

12317 Silver Sweet Candies
522 Essex St
Lawrence, MA 01840 978-688-0474
Fax: 978-683-6636
Candy and confections
Owner: Robert Burkinshaw
Estimated Sales: Below $ 5 Million
Number Employees: 5-9

12318 Silver Tray Cookies
6861 SW 196th Avenue
Suite 203
Fort Lauderdale, FL 33332-1628 305-883-0800
Fax: 305-888-8438 info@silvertraycookies.com
www.silvertraycookies.com
Cookies, sugar free pound cake and fruit flavored cream cakes
President: Perry Burk
Estimated Sales: Below $ 5 Million
Number Employees: 2
Brands:
Silver Tray Cookies

12319 SilverLeaf International
13003 Murphy Rd # M9
Stafford, TX 77477-3937 281-495-1250
Fax: 281-499-5505 800-442-7542
info@4garlic.com m www.4garlic.com
Marinated garlic hors d'oeuvres, blue cheese and feta cheese stuffed olives, olive oils, dips and salsa, spices and seasonings, jams and jellies, sauces, Italian pasta.
President: Neal McWeeney
VP: Adriane McWeeney
Estimated Sales: $1-2.5 Million
Number Employees: 1-4
Number of Brands: 1
Number of Products: 50
Type of Packaging: Consumer, Private Label

12320 Silverado Hill Cellars
1 Executive Way
PO Box 2640
Napa, CA 94558-0263 707-253-9306
Fax: 707-253-9309 shc@napanet.net
Wine
President: Yuich Teraea
Estimated Sales: $ 1-2.5 Million
Number Employees: 6

12321 Silverado Vineyards
6121 Silverado Trl
Napa, CA 94558 707-257-1770
Fax: 707-257-1538 www.silveradovineyards.com
Wine
President: Diane D Miller
Quality Control: Elina Franceschi
Estimated Sales: Below $ 5 Million
Number Employees: 20-49

12322 Silverbow Honey Company
1120 E Wheeler Rd
Moses Lake, WA 98837 509-765-6616
Fax: 509-765-6549 866-444-6639
customer.service@silverbowhoney.com
www.silverbowhoney.com
Specialty honey, table honey, gourmet honey, sweet mustard, hot honey mustard, honey butter, gift sets, beeswax, beeswax candles and both colored and natural beeswax.
President: Gary Grigg
Estimated Sales: $7207423
Number Employees: 20-49
Sq. footage: 38000
Type of Packaging: Consumer, Food Service, Private Label, Bulk
Brands:
Silverbow

12323 Silverston Fisheries
1507 N 1st St
Superior, WI 54880-1146 715-392-5551
Fax: 715-392-5586
Fish
Owner: Stuart Sivertson
Estimated Sales: $ 10-20 Million
Number Employees: 20-49

12324 Simco Foods
1180 S Beverly Dr Ste 509
Los Angeles, CA 90035 310-284-8446
Fax: 310-284-8221 info@simco.us
www.simco.us
Wholesaler/distributor and exporter of groceries, canned fruits and vegetables, cereals, jams, jellies, peanut butter, macaroni & cheese and french fries
President: David Sims
CEO: Aman Simantob
Estimated Sales: $ 10 - 20 Million
Number Employees: 10-19
Number of Brands: 3
Sq. footage: 8000
Type of Packaging: Food Service
Brands:
FIRST HARVEST
SIMCO
STELLA

12325 Simeus Foods International
812 S 5th Ave
Mansfield, TX 76063 817-473-1562
Fax: 817-473-0591 888-772-3663
www.simeusfoods.com
Manufacturer of appetizers, breaded products, pork products, pre-cooked meats, soups, sauces and side dishes
President: Kelly Hansen
Estimated Sales: $100+ Million
Number Employees: 100-249
Type of Packaging: Food Service
Other Locations:
Simeus Foods Plant Facility
Forest City NC

12326 Simeus Foods International
812 South 5th Avenue
Mansfield, TX 76063 817-473-1562
Fax: 817-473-0591 888-772-3663
www.simeusfoods.com
Processor and exporter of chicken, frankfurters, ham, seafood and frozen dinners
President: Winslow Goins
Executive VP: Jim Hutcheson
Number Employees: 50-99
Parent Co: Simeus Foods International

12327 (HQ)Simeus Foods International
812 S 5th Ave
Mansfield, TX 76063 817-473-1562
Fax: 817-473-0591 888-772-3663
rartzer@simeusfoods.com
www.simeusfoods.com
Manufacturer of customized food products for national chain restaurants such as; appetizers, pork products, ready-to-cook breaded products, sauces and side dishes
President: Kelly Hansen
Estimated Sales: $100-500 Million
Number Employees: 100-249
Type of Packaging: Food Service
Other Locations:
Simeus Foods Plant
Forest City NC
Simeus Foods Plant
Mansfield TX

12328 (HQ)Simmons Foods
601 North Hico Street
Siloam Springs, AR 72761 479-524-8151
Fax: 479-524-6562 888-831-7007
webmaster@simfoods.com
www.simmonsfoods.com
Manufacturer and exporter of fresh and frozen chicken
Chairman: Mark Simmons
President/COO: Todd Simmons
CFO: Mike Jones
VP Marketing: Jerry Laster
Director Puchasing: Brett Garton
Estimated Sales: $970 Million
Number Employees: 5000
Sq. footage: 30000
Type of Packaging: Consumer, Food Service, Private Label, Bulk
Brands:
MANU MAKER
SIMMONS
TOWN & COUNTRY
WATER VALLEY FARMS

12329 Simmons Hot Gourmet Products
22 Greenview Close
Lethbridge, AB T1H 4K8
Canada 403-327-9087
Fax: 403-328-9589 info@firenbrimstone.com
www.firenbrimstone.com

12330 **Simon Hubig Company**
2417 Dauphine St
New Orleans, LA 70117 504-945-2181
Fax: 504-945-2328 www.hubigs.com
Processor of baked goods
President: Thomas Bowman
Owner: Otto Ramsey
Production Manager: Mike Tricou
Estimated Sales: $2.3 Million
Number Employees: 40
Sq. footage: 16000

12331 **Simon Levi Cellars**
9380 Sonoma Hwy
Kenwood, CA 95452 707-833-5070
Fax: 707-833-1355 888-315-0040
info@slcellars.com www.slcellars.com
Wines
President: Brad Jacobs
Estimated Sales: $ 1-2.5 Million
Number Employees: 10-19
Brands:
Maboroshi
SLC

12332 **Simon's Specialty Cheese**
2735 Freedom Rd
Appleton, WI 54913-9315
Fax: 920-788-1424 800-444-0374
simonchz@athenet.net www.simonscheese.com
Cheese
President: Dave Simon
Cheese Maker: Roger Krohn
CFO: Doug Simon
Cheesemaker: Terry Lensmire
Operations/R & D: Chris Simon
Estimated Sales: $ 25-49.9 Million
Number Employees: 50-99
Type of Packaging: Private Label
Brands:
Simon's

12333 **Simple Foods**
116 Killewald Ave
Tonawanda, NY 14150 716-743-8850
800-234-8850
www.simplefoodsusa.com
Nuts and nut butter
President: Karen Pease
Estimated Sales: Under $500,000
Number Employees: 1-4
Type of Packaging: Consumer, Bulk
Brands:
Annie's
Magic Munchie

12334 **Simple Soyman**
3901 N 35th Street
Milwaukee, WI 53216-2507 414-444-8638
Fresh tofu and tempeh. Also ready to eat products Tasty Tofu, Baked Fajita-fu, Saucy Jo, Hummus, Savory Herb Pate, Deviled Tofu, Tofu Terkey, and Toaster Burgers. Our product line also includes two varieties of Whole Grain Pie Crustsfour kinds of granolas, four yummy cookies, and Date Bars.
Manager/Partner: Barbara Gruenwald
Partner: R J Gruenwald
Estimated Sales: $380,000
Number Employees: 8
Sq. footage: 4500

12335 **Simplot Food Group**
PO Box 9386
Boise, ID 83707 208-336-2110
Fax: 208-384-8022 800-572-7783
jrs_info@simplot.com www.simplotfoods.com
Distributor of avocado pulp, frozen potatoes, frozen fruit, frozen vegetables and frozen cornados
Parent Co: J.R. Simplot Company
Type of Packaging: Food Service
Brands:
ROASTWORKS
SPUDSTERS

12336 **Simply 7 Snacks**
PO Box 710543
Houston, TX 77271 877-682-2359
Fax: 877-682-2368
paul.albrecht@simply7snacks.com
www.simply7snacks.com
Hummus and Lentil chips
President: Rashim Oberoi

12337 **Simply Delicious**
8411 Highway N Carolina 86 N
Cedar Grove, NC 27231 919-732-5294
Fax: 919-732-5180
Sauces, dressings
President: John Troy

12338 **Simply Divine**
623 E 11th St # 2
New York, NY 10009-4111
US 212-541-7300
Fax: 917-553-7510 info@simplydivine.com
www.simplydivine.com
Processor of kosher gourmet soups, sauces, entrees, salads and desserts take out food service.
Owner/President: Judith Geller Marlow
Estimated Sales: $500,000-$1 Million
Number Employees: 20-49
Type of Packaging: Consumer, Food Service
Brands:
Simply Divine

12339 **Simply Gourmet Confections**
PO Box 50141
Irvine, CA 92619 714-505-3955
Fax: 714-505-3957 info@simplyscrumptious.com
www.simplyscrumptious.com
gourmet confections and cookies
President/Owner: Debra Formaneck

12340 **Simply Lite Foods Corporation**
74 Mall Dr
Commack, NY 11725 631-543-9600
Fax: 631-543-8283 800-753-4282
questions@simplylite.com
www.sweetnlowcandy.com
Products and sugar free hard candy
President: Sal Asaro
Estimated Sales: $ 50-100 Million
Number Employees: 5-9
Brands:
Sweet'n Low

12341 **Simpson & Vail**
3 Quarry Rd
Brookfield, CT 06804 203-775-0240
Fax: 203-775-0462 800-282-8327
info@svtea.com www.svtea.com
Processor, exporter and importer of coffee and gourmet tea
President: Jim Harron Jr
CEO: Joan Harron
Estimated Sales: $ .5 - 1 million
Number Employees: 5-9
Sq. footage: 8000
Type of Packaging: Food Service

12342 **Simpson Spring Company**
719 Washington St
South Easton, MA 02375 508-372-0914
Fax: 508-238-5691 sales@simpsonspring.com
www.simpsonspring.com
Processor of flavoring extracts for carbonated beverages
President: William Bertarelli
Estimated Sales: $2900000
Number Employees: 10-19

12343 **Sims Wholesale**
540 River St
Batesville, AR 72501 870-793-1109
Fax: 870-793-2230 grocer@inbco.net
Wholesaler/distributor of general line products; serving the food service market
Manager: Mike Hanson
General Manager: Kenneth Thornton

12344 **Sinbad Sweets**
2509 W Shaw Avenue
Fresno, CA 93711-3308 559-298-3700
Fax: 559-298-9194 800-350-7933
Processor of pastries including baklava, strudel, tarts and fillo; exporter of baklava
President: Michael Muhawir
CEO: Edwina Aquino Seidel
COO: Anita Reina
Vice President: John Seidel
Public Relations: Sascha Muhawi
Operations Manager: Larry Burrow
Production Manager: Klaus Gernet
Number Employees: 50-99
Sq. footage: 30000
Type of Packaging: Consumer, Food Service, Private Label, Bulk
Brands:
Oliver Twist
Sinbad Sweets

12345 **Singer Extract Laboratory**
13301 Inkster Rd
Livonia, MI 48150-2226 313-345-5880
Fax: 313-345-8686 singerextract@msn.com
www.singerextract.com
Extracts and flavorings, food colorings, bar specialties and syrups.
President: Mike Letourneau
Estimated Sales: Below $ 5 Million
Number Employees: 3
Number of Brands: 3
Number of Products: 50
Sq. footage: 5000
Brands:
4%
Belmo
Seely

12346 **Singleton Seafood**
P.O.Box 2819
Tampa, FL 33601-2819 813-247-5366
Fax: 813-247-1782 800-553-3954
seafoodretail@conagrafoods.com
www.conagraseafood.com
Processor of frozen shrimp, breaded fish and shrimp, peeled and deveined shrimp, cooked shrimp, shrimp specialties
President: Dennis Reeves
CFO: Andr, Hawaux
Vice President: Rob Sharpe
Research & Development: Nina Burt
Quality Control: Don Toloday
Marketing Director: Dan Davis
Sales Director: Doug Knudsen
Production Manager: Bill Jacks
Plant Manager: Mike Pent
Purchasing Manager: Bill Stone
Estimated Sales: $300,000-500,000
Number Employees: 1-4
Number of Brands: 8
Number of Products: 200
Sq. footage: 200000
Parent Co: ConAgra Foods
Type of Packaging: Consumer, Food Service, Private Label, Bulk

12347 **Sini Fulvi U.S.A.**
136 Mohawk St
Newark, NJ 07114-3314 973-274-0822
Fax: 718-361-6999 sinifulvi@aol.com
www.sinifulvi.com
Importer of Italian, Spanish and Portuguese cheeses and Italian cured meats
President: Agostino Sini
Vice President: Pierluigi Sini
Marketing Director: Michele Buster
Estimated Sales: $ .5 - 1 million
Number Employees: 4
Parent Co: Sini Fulvi
Type of Packaging: Consumer, Food Service, Bulk
Brands:
Cacio De Roma
Cacio De Roma Cheese
Crotonese
Drunken Goat Cheese
Genuine
Genuine Fulvi Romano Cheese
I Buoonatarula Sini
Pasture Sini
Rustico Cheese
Sfizio Crotonese
Sini Fulvi
Spizzico Pepato Aged
Triggi

12348 **Sinton Dairy Foods Company**
5151 Bannock St
Denver, CO 80216-1850 303-292-0111
Fax: 303-294-9215 800-666-4808
ruf51@aol.com www.sintondairy.com
Processor of dairy products including milk and cottage cheese
General Manager: Joel Midkiff
Marketing Manager: Randy Furstenau
Estimated Sales: $ 20 - 50 Million
Number Employees: 20-49
Type of Packaging: Consumer
Brands:
Lite Time
Quality Chekd

Sinton's
Watts-Hardy

12349 **(HQ)Sinton Dairy Foods Company**
P.O.Box 578
Colorado Springs, CO 80901-0578 719-633-3821
Fax: 719-633-4376 800-388-4970
mmaloney@sintondairyfoods.com
www.sintondairy.com
Manufacturer of dairy products including milk, ice cream, butter, sour cream, dips and dressings, cheese, eggs, cottage cheese, drinkable yogurts and drinks and mixes
GM: Joel Midkiff
VP: Scott Lewis
Quality Assurance Manager: Amanda Moore
Marketing Manager: Randy Furstenau
Operations Manager: Bill Keating
Plant Manager: Mike Maloney
Estimated Sales: $ 50 - 100 Million
Number Employees: 250-499
Type of Packaging: Consumer
Brands:
SINTON

12350 **Sioux-Preme Packing Company**
P.O.Box 255
Sioux Center, IA 51250 712-722-2555
Fax: 712-722-2666 garym@siouxpreme.com
www.siouxpremepork.com
Manufacturer and exporter of pork products
President/CEO: Gary Malenke
CFO: Richard White
VP Sales: Jamie Jurgensen
Estimated Sales: $113 Million
Number Employees: 165
Type of Packaging: Consumer, Private Label, Bulk

12351 **SipDisc**
30 E 60th St
New York, NY 10022-1008 212-688-8778
Fax: 212-319-9778 sales@sipdisc.com
www.sipdisc.com
Manufacturer of the SipDisc Straw for the food and beverage industry.
President: Alex Greenburg Ph.D

12352 **Siptop Packaging Inc**
2810 Argentia Rd
Mississauga, ON L5N 8L2
Canada 905-814-0531
Fax: 905-814-0531 info@siptop.com
www.siptop.com/
Siptop Packaging's product line includes beverage packaging technology that utilizes a form, fill and seal machine that produces an innovative stand-up drink pouch that is low cost, environmentally friendly and has a built in strawthat is convenient and eliminates the mess that is created with typical pouch straws.
President: Grant Joyce
Sales Representative: Grant Joyce
Senior Director Operations: Jack Vanderdeen
Type of Packaging: Consumer

12353 **Sir Kensington's Gourmet Scooping Kitchen**
101 W 24th Street
Apartment 27H
New York, NY 10011 646-450-5735
Fax: 646-755-3765 sirk@sirkensingtons.com
www.sirkensingtons.com
Ketchup

12354 **Sir Real Foods**
50 Hazelton Drive
White Plains, NY 10605-3816 914-948-9342
Fax: 914-948-9342 info@sireal.com
www.sirreal.com
Juices, beverages
President: Michael Albert
Vice President: Douglas Albert
Estimated Sales: Under $500,000
Number Employees: 2
Brands:
Americus Natural Spring Water

12355 **Sirocco Enterprises**
228 Industrial Ave
Jefferson, LA 70121 504-834-1549
Fax: 504-837-7762 www.siroccoenterprises.com
Manufacturer and exporter of ready-to-use liquid cocktail mixers
President: Tony Muto
VP: Anthony Muto
Production: Benny Peel
Estimated Sales: $1 Million
Number Employees: 5-9
Number of Brands: 1
Number of Products: 10
Sq. footage: 13000
Type of Packaging: Food Service
Brands:
PAT O'BRIEN'S COCKTAIL MIXES

12356 **Sisler's Ice & Ice Cream**
102 South Grove Street
Ohio, IL 61349 815-376-2913
888-891-3856
sisler@sisler.com www.sislers.com
Processor of ice, ice cream
Owner/Operator: Bill Sisler
Manager: Dan Thompson
Estimated Sales: $500,000-$1 Million
Number Employees: 5-9
Sq. footage: 18000
Type of Packaging: Consumer, Food Service
Brands:
Sisler's Dairy

12357 **Sister's Gourmet**
P.O.Box 1550
Dacula, GA 30019 678-425-9242
877-338-1388
sales@sistersgourmet.com
www.sistersgourmet.com
One bowl easy to bake gourmet cookie mixes and other excellent gourmet gifts.
Owner: Lisa Sorensen
Estimated Sales: $ 5 - 10 Million
Number Employees: 50-99

12358 **Sister's Kitchen**
3 Westview Ave
Rutland, VT 05701-3733 802-775-2457
Fax: 802-775-2457 dufdecer@sover.net
www.sisterskitchen.net
Maple flavored vinegar and mixes

12359 **Sitka Sound Seafoods**
329 Katlian St
Sitka, AK 99835 907-747-6662
Fax: 907-747-6268 employment@ssssitka.com
www.ssssitka.com
Processor and exporter of fresh and frozen seafood from Alaska including abalone, black cod, halibut, herring, rockfish, Pacific salmon and king and snow crabs
President: Harold Thompson
Plant Manager: Jon Hickman
Estimated Sales: $ 20-50 Million
Number Employees: 100-249
Sq. footage: 30000
Parent Co: North Pacific Seafoods

12360 **Sivetz Coffee**
349 SW 4th St
Corvallis, OR 97333-4622 541-753-9713
Fax: 541-757-7644 info@sievtzcoffee.com
www.sivetzcoffee.com
Roasted coffee beans, extracts, almond kernels, hazelnut kernels, and coffee roasting machines
President: Mike Sivetz
Number Employees: 1-4
Type of Packaging: Consumer, Bulk
Brands:
Sivetz Coffee Essence

12361 **Six Mile Creek Vineyard**
1551 Slaterville Rd
Ithaca, NY 14850 607-272-9463
Fax: 607-277-7344 800-260-0612
info@sixmilecreek.com www.sixmilecreek.com
Wines
Co-Owner: Nancy Battistella
Co-Owner: Roger Battistella
Estimated Sales: $ 1 - 3 Million
Number Employees: 1-4
Type of Packaging: Private Label
Brands:
Six Mile Creek

12362 **Skillet Street Food**
6100 4th Avenue S
Suite 155
Seattle, WA 98115 425-998-9817
www.skilletstreetfood.com
Bacon jam spread
Owner: Josh Henderson
Sq. footage: 2620

12363 **Skim Delux Mendenhall Laboratories**
715 Morton St
Paris, TN 38242-4296 731-642-9321
Fax: 731-644-3398 800-642-9321
info@deluxmilk.com www.deluxmilk.com
Processor and exporter of dairy analogs, formulas and flavors for calcium-fortified milk, juice and fruit drink beverages; also, chocolate milkshake mixes
Owner: David Travis
Sales Assistant: Melissa Taylor
Estimated Sales: $500,000-$1 Million
Number Employees: 5-9
Type of Packaging: Bulk

12364 **Skinners' Dairy**
24741 Deer Trace Drive
Ponte Vedra Beach, FL 32082-2114 904-733-5440
Milk, dairy products
President: Denny Gaultney
Estimated Sales: $ 10-20 Million
Number Employees: 100

12365 **Skipping Stone Productions**
1335 Railroad Street
Paso Robles, CA 93446 805-226-2998
info@vintucci.com
www.vintucci.com
Wine infused cookies with Italian origins
Estimated Sales: $130,000
Number Employees: 3
Sq. footage: 3868

12366 **Skjodt-Barrett Foods**
2395 Lucknow Drive
Mississauga, ON L5S 1H9
Canada 905-671-2884
Fax: 905-671-2885 877-600-1200
www.skjodt-barrett.com
Processor of fruit fillings, icings, glaze, sauces, marinades and caramel.
President/Board Member: Dan Skjodt
Estimated Sales: $9 Million
Number Employees: 10-19
Sq. footage: 25000
Type of Packaging: Food Service, Private Label, Bulk
Brands:
Skjodt-Barrett

12367 **Sky Haven Farm**
4871 Shepherd Creek Rd
Cincinnati, OH 45223 513-681-2303
Fax: 513-681-8305
Cured hams
President: Edward J Dreyer
Estimated Sales: $ 1-2.5 Million
Number Employees: 1-4

12368 **Sky Vineyards**
4352 Cavedale Rd
Glen Ellen, CA 95442 707-935-1391
Fax: 510-540-8442 infoatskyvineyards.com
www.skyvineyards.com
Wines
Owner: Lore Olds
COO: Linn Brinier
Sales: Matt Gerloff
Estimated Sales: $ 3 - 5 Million
Number Employees: 5-9
Brands:
Sky Vineyards

12369 **Skylark Meats**
4430 S 110th St
Omaha, NE 68137 402-592-0300
Fax: 402-592-1414 800-759-5275
www.skylarkmeats.com

Processor and exporter of portion control steaks and liver; wholesaler/distributor of meat products; serving the food service market
President: Joe Baker
President/General Manager: James Leonard
VP: Dennis Esch
Quality Assurance Manager: Jack Warner
VP Sales/Marketing: Steve Giroux
Human Resources Director: Belinda Mawhiney
Production Manager: Ray Marquez
Purchasing Director: Dave Hascall
Estimated Sales: $41100000
Number Employees: 250
Sq. footage: 175000
Parent Co: Rosen's Diversified
Type of Packaging: Consumer, Food Service

12370 **Slap Ya Mama Cajun Seasoning**
1103 W Main Street
Ville Platte, LA 70586 337-363-6904
Fax: 337-363-6608 800-485-5217
sales@slapyamama.com www.slapyamama.com
Seasonings

12371 **Slate Quarry Winery**
460 Gower Road
Nazareth, PA 18064-9219 610-746-3900
Fax: 610-746-9684
winery@slatequarrywines.com
Wines
General Manager: M Eleanor Butler
Production Manager: Sidney Butler
Estimated Sales: $ 1-2.5 Million
Number Employees: 5-9

12372 **Slathars Smokehouse**
RR 1
Box 52bb
Lake City, MN 55041-9312 507-753-2080
Beef
Estimated Sales: $300,000-500,000
Number Employees: 1-4

12373 **Slather Brand Foods LLC**
28 Arabian Drive
Charleston, SC 29407 843-513-1750
Fax: 843-769-4876 info@slatheriton.com
www.slatheriton.com
Sauces
Owner/Principal: Robin Rhea
Estimated Sales: $87,000
Number Employees: 2
Sq. footage: 2187

12374 **Sleeman Brewereis, Ltd.**
551 Clair Road W
Guelph, ON N1L 1E9
Canada 519-822-1834
Fax: 519-822-0430 800-268-8537
www.sleeman.com
Beer, ale and lager
President: Rick Knucson
CFO: Dan Camrogozynski
Estimated Sales: H
Number Employees: 300
Type of Packaging: Consumer, Food Service
Brands:
Sleeman Amber
Sleeman Clear
Sleeman Cream Ale
Sleeman Honey Brown Lager
Sleeman Original Dark
Sleeman Orignial Draught
Sleeman Premium Light
Sleeman Silver Creek Lager
Sleeman Steam

12375 **Sleeman Breweries, Ltd.**
1455 Cliveden Ave
Delta, BC V3M 6Z9
Canada 604-777-2537
www.sleeman.com
Ale
CEO: Rick Knudson
Chairman: John W Sleeman
CFO: Paul Renaud
Vice President: Paul Renaud
Number Employees: 1-4
Type of Packaging: Consumer, Food Service
Brands:
Sleeman

12376 **Slim Fast Foods Company**
PO Box 3625
West Palm Beach, FL 33402-3625 561-833-9920
Fax: 561-822-2876 www.slim-fast.com
Meal replacement drinks and bars
President: Marc Covent
CFO: Carl Tsang
COO: Art Peters
Estimated Sales: $ 50 - 100 Million
Number Employees: 50-99
Type of Packaging: Consumer
Brands:
SLIM FAST

12377 **Smart Ice**
3340 Royalston Ave
Fort Myers, FL 33916-1623 239-334-3123
Fax: 239-332-4628
Processor and wholesaler/distributor of coolers, shelf stable freezer pops, flavored drinks and filled Easter baskets and Christmas stockings
Owner: David Radford Jr
Sales Manager: Arnold Bonn
Estimated Sales: $1.4 Million
Number Employees: 10-19
Type of Packaging: Consumer
Brands:
Ice Age
Smart Drinks
Smart Ice
Smarty Bats

12378 **Smart Juices**
52 E Union Blvd
Bethlehem, PA 18018 610-997-0500
Fax: 484-727-7425 www.smartjuice.com
organic 100% juice

12379 **Smeltzer Orchard Company**
6032 Joyfield Rd
Frankfort, MI 49635-9163 231-882-4421
Fax: 231-882-4430 info@smeltzerorchards.com
www.smeltzerorchards.com
Processor and exporter of frozen apples, apple juice, asparagus and cherries; also, dried blueberries, cherries, apples, strawberries and cranberries
President: Tim Brian
Plant Manager: Mike Henschell
Estimated Sales: $9305725
Number Employees: 50-99
Type of Packaging: Food Service

12380 **Smiling Fox Pepper Company**
610 Cherrywood Drive
North Aurora, IL 60542-1032 630-337-3734
info@sfoxpepco.bizland.com
http://smilingfoxs.com
Relishes and jellies
Co-Owner: Mary Patterson
Co-Owner: Scott Patterson
Type of Packaging: Consumer

12381 **Smith & Son Seafood**
P.O.Box 2118
Darien, GA 31305-2118 912-437-6471
Fax: 912-437-3553
Shrimp
President: Jean Smith

12382 **Smith Dairy Products Company**
230 N Vine St
Orrville, OH 44667 330-683-8710
Fax: 330-683-1079 800-776-7076
ikegraham@smithdairy.com
www.smithdairy.com
Processor of cheese, cottage cheese, ice cream and milk; also, fruit drinks and juices
President: Steve Schmid
Marketing: Bill McCabe
VP Sales: Brian Defelice
VP Production: Eddie Steiner
Purchasing: John Schmid
Estimated Sales: $100+ Million
Number Employees: 250-499
Sq. footage: 75000
Type of Packaging: Consumer, Food Service, Private Label
Brands:
Moovers
Ruggles
Smith's

12383 **Smith Enterprises**
1953 Langston St
Rock Hill, SC 29730 803-366-7101
Fax: 803-366-1958 800-845-8311
Candy
Chairman of the Board: Jacob D Smith
Sales Director: Tony Morgan
Estimated Sales: $ 30-50 Million
Number Employees: 250-499

12384 **(HQ)Smith Frozen Foods**
101 Depot St
Weston, OR 97886 541-566-3515
Fax: 541-566-3772
webactivity@smithfrozenfoods.com
www.smithfrozenfoods.com
Processor and exporter of frozen vegetables including baby lima beans, diced and sliced carrots, kernel corn, corn-on-the-cob and peas
CEO: Sharon Smith
CEO: Gary Crowder
Quality Control Specialist: Traci Jensen
Sales Manager: David Stoddard
Purchasing Manager: Corry Zenger
Estimated Sales: $55000000
Number Employees: 500-999
Type of Packaging: Consumer, Food Service, Private Label, Bulk
Brands:
Smith

12385 **Smith Frozen Foods**
101 Depot St
Weston, OR 97886 541-566-3515
Fax: 541-566-3707 800-547-0203
kellybrown@smithfrozenfoods.com
www.smithfrozenfoods.com
Processor and exporter of frozen produce including peas, carrots, baby lima beans and cut and cob corn
Account Executive: Sharon Smith
Quality Control: Traci Jensen
CEO: Gary Crowder
Sales Manager: Dave Stoddard
Estimated Sales: $ 1 - 3 Million
Number Employees: 5-9
Type of Packaging: Consumer, Food Service, Private Label, Bulk

12386 **Smith Meat Packing**
1420 Thomas St
Port Huron, MI 48060 810-985-5900
Fax: 810-985-4504 sales@lklpacking.com
www.smithmeatpacking.com
Packer of smoked and cured pork
President: Anthony Peters
Estimated Sales: $ 5 - 10 Million
Number Employees: 10-19
Sq. footage: 15000
Type of Packaging: Bulk

12387 **(HQ)Smith Packing Regional Meat**
P.O.Box 520
Utica, NY 13503-520
Fax: 315-732-1166 www.smithpacking.com
Manufacturer and exporter of meat products including fresh and frozen beef, pork, veal, lamb, chicken and turkey; also, US grade AA eggs, a full line of processed meats including ham, bacon, frankfurters, sausage, kielbasa, turkeybreast, etc
President: Wesley Smith
VP: Mark Smith
Estimated Sales: $12.6 Million
Number Employees: 1-4
Sq. footage: 50000
Type of Packaging: Private Label
Brands:
EVERGOOD
HONEST JOHN'S

12388 **Smith Provision Company**
1300 Cranberry St
Erie, PA 16501-1566 814-459-4974
Fax: 814-452-3142 800-334-9151
www.smithhotdogs.com
Processor of smoked luncheon meats and ham, frankfurters, roast beef and sausage
Chairman of the Board: Magnus Weber
President: Michael Weber
VP: John Weber
Estimated Sales: $10 Million
Number Employees: 20-49
Sq. footage: 25863

Type of Packaging: Consumer, Food Service, Private Label, Bulk
Brands:
Smith's

12389 **Smith Vineyard & Winery**
13577 Dog Bar Rd
Grass Valley, CA 95949 530-273-7032
Fax: 530-273-0229 christina@smithwine.com
www.smithwine.com
Wines
Manager: Christina Smith
Estimated Sales: $500-1 Million appx.
Number Employees: 5-9

12390 **Smith's Bakery**
P.O.Box 16389
Hattiesburg, MS 39404-6389 601-288-7000
Fax: 601-584-6487 www.forrestgeneral.com
Bakery
President: William C Oliver
Estimated Sales: $ 1-2.5 Million appx.
Number Employees: 1-4

12391 **Smith, Weber & Swinton Company**
965 E. Midlothian Blvd.
Youngstown, OH 44502 330-783-2860
Fax: 330-782-1774 800-860-2867
www.schwebels.com
Breads and buns
President: Joseph Schwebel
Treasurer: David Alter
Executive VP: Paul Schwebel
Marketing Director: Thomas Steve
Estimated Sales: $10-24.9 Million
Number Employees: 450

12392 **Smith-Coulter Company**
8579 Lakeport Rd
Chittenango, NY 13037-9577 315-687-6510
Fax: 315-687-6637
Processor and exporter of produce including onions and turf grass
Owner: Chris Coulter
Estimated Sales: $ 3 - 5 Million
Number Employees: 5-9
Brands:
Bulls Eye

12393 **Smith-Madrone Vineyards& Winery**
4022 Spring Mountain Rd
Saint Helena, CA 94574 707-963-2283
Fax: 707-963-2291 contact@smithmadrone.com
www.smithmadrone.com
Wines
Manager: Stuart Smith
Manager: Charles Smith
Winemaker: Charles Smith
Estimated Sales: $ 1-2.5 Million
Number Employees: 5-9
Brands:
Smith-Madrone

12394 **(HQ)Smithfield Foods**
200 Commerce St
Smithfield, VA 23430 757-365-3000
Fax: 757-365-3017 888-366-6767
information@smithfieldfoods.com
www.smithfieldfoods.com
World's largest pork processor and hog producer
President/CEO: C Larry Pope
President/COO, Pork Group: George Richter
EVP/CFO: Robert Manly IV
EVP: Joseph Luter IV
VP/Corporate Communications: Keira Lombardo
VP/Operations Analysis: Bart Ellis
Estimated Sales: $12 Billion
Number Employees: 52,400
Type of Packaging: Consumer, Food Service, Private Label, Bulk
Brands:
Cumberland Gap Provision
Farmland Foods Inc
Gwaltney of Smithfield
John Morrell & Co
Kraukus Foods International
North Side Foods
Patrick Cudahy
Quick-to-Fix
Smithfield
Smithfield Beef Group
Smithfield Deli Group
Smithfield Foodservice Group
Smithfield Innovation Group
Smithfield RMH Foods Group
Stefano Foods

12395 **Smithfield Packing Company**
1911 S Church St
Smithfield, VA 23430 757-357-4321
Fax: 757-357-1339 www.smithfield.com
Processor and exporter of pork including ham
Manager: Jospeh W Luter Iii III
President: Lewis Little
CFO: Dan Sabin IV
Vice President: Steve Canale
Sales/Marketing: Susan Carr
Estimated Sales: K
Number Employees: 4636
Type of Packaging: Consumer, Food Service, Private Label
Other Locations:
Smithfield Packing Company
Kingston NC

12396 **Smoak's Bakery & Catering Service**
2058 Walton Way
Augusta, GA 30904-2302 706-738-1792
Fax: 706-733-8979 tomt3@bellsouth.com
www.smoaksbakery.com
Cakes, cookies and breads
President: Steve Pierce
General Manager: Audery Hawn
Owner: Dan Smoak
Estimated Sales: $ 1-2.5 Million
Number Employees: 20-49
Type of Packaging: Private Label

12397 **Smoke & Fire Natural Food**
35 Railroad Ave
Great Barrington, MA 01230-1510 413-528-8008
Fax: 413-528-7997 tofu@smokeandfire.com
www.smokeandfire.com
Smoked and flavored tofu
Owner: Robert Harvey
Co-Founder: Mona Young
Estimated Sales: Under $500,000
Number Employees: 5-9
Brands:
Smoke & Fire

12398 **Smoke House**
20 Smokehouse Rd
Sagle, ID 83860 208-263-6312
Fax: 208-762-8979
Smoked meats
Owner: Dick Struntz
Estimated Sales: $ .5 - 1 million
Number Employees: 1-4

12399 **Smokehouse Winery**
10 Ashby Rd
Sperryville, VA 22740-2243 540-987-3194
Fax: 540-987-8189
smokehousewinery@earthlink.net
www.smokehousewinery.com
Wines
Owner: John Hallberg
Estimated Sales: $300,000-500,000
Number Employees: 1-4

12400 **Smokey Denmark Sausage**
3505 E 5th St
Austin, TX 78702 512-385-0718
Fax: 512-385-4843 info@smokeydenmark.com
www.smokeydenmark.com
Processor of beef, pork and venison sausage
President: Johnathan Pace
Estimated Sales: $2500000
Number Employees: 10-19
Type of Packaging: Consumer

12401 **Smokey Farm Meats**
NW 2-29-24 W 4
Carbon, AB T0M 0L0
Canada 403-272-6587
Fax: 403-272-6587 beeffarm@telus.net
Processor of beef jerky, pepperoni and sausage
President: Tracy Smith
CEO: Sylvia Schmidt
Number Employees: 1-4
Type of Packaging: Consumer, Food Service, Private Label, Bulk
Brands:
Smokey Farm Meats

12402 **Smolich Brothers**
760 Theodore St
Joliet, IL 60403 815-727-2144
Processor of sausage including hot, mild, smoked, pork and bratwurst
President: Rudy Smolich
Co-Owner: Joe Smolich
Estimated Sales: Less than $500,000
Number Employees: 1-4
Type of Packaging: Consumer

12403 **Smothers Winery/Remick Ridge**
1976 Warm Springs Rd
Glen Ellen, CA 95442-8717 707-833-1010
Fax: 707-833-2313 800-795-9463
sales@smobro.net
www.smothersbrothers.com/remick
Wines
President/Owner: Thomas Smothers
Owner: Marcy Smothers
Estimated Sales: Below $ 5 Million
Number Employees: 5-9
Brands:
Smothers/Remick Ridge

12404 **Smucker Quality Beverages**
37 Speedway Ave
Chico, CA 95927 530-899-5000
Fax: 530-891-6397 www.jmsmucker.com
Processor and exporter of natural juice and soda
President: Julia Sabin
Marketing Manager: Arlene Starkey
Sales Manager: Kevin Cobb
Number Employees: 100-249
Parent Co: J.M. Smucker Company
Type of Packaging: Consumer, Private Label
Brands:
After the Fall
Natural Brew
Rocket Juice
Rw Knudsen
Santa Cruz

12405 **Smucker Quality Beverages**
340 Old Bay Ln
Havre De Grace, MD 21078 410-939-1403
Fax: 410-942-1400 www.smucker.com
Processor of natural fruit juices including apple, pear, grape, cranberry lemonade, punch, mango, passion, banana/pineapple and apple blends; also, peach vanilla and vanilla bean cream and strawberry drinks
Manager: Doug Arington
Plant Manager: Chris Ickes
Estimated Sales: $5-10 Million
Number Employees: 43
Parent Co: J.M. Smucker Company
Type of Packaging: Consumer, Food Service

12406 **Smuggler's Kitchen**
PO Box 570
Dundee, FL 33838-0570 800-604-6793
tnischan@smugglerskitchen.com
www.smugglerskitchen.com
Processor of dehydrated foods including Irish potato soup, vegetable dips, Cajun and chili sauces, etc
Co-Owner: Tom Nischan
Co-Owner: Pat Nischan
Number Employees: 1-4

12407 **Smuttynose Brewing**
225 Heritage Ave
Portsmouth, NH 03801 603-436-4026
Fax: 603-433-1247 info@smuttynose.com
www.smuttynose.com
Beer
President: Peter Egelston
Executive Brewer: David Yarrington
CFO: Gale Merrigan
Head Brewer: Greg Blanchard
Sales Manager: Kevin Love
National Sales Manager: Anka Jacobs
Marketing: Jaime Pruzansky
Office Manager: Deb Fitt
Estimated Sales: Below $ 5 Million
Number Employees: 10-19
Type of Packaging: Private Label
Brands:
Big Beer Series
Old Brown Bag
Portsmouth Lager

Smuttynose Belgian W
Smuttynose Robust Po

12408 **Snack Appeal**
3601 Old Post Road
Fairfax, VA 22030-1807 540-383-0561
Fax: 540-383-0576
Processor and exporter of snack foods including low-fat potato chips and low-fat sandwich products
Type of Packaging: Consumer, Food Service

12409 **Snack Factory**
PO Box 3562
Princeton, NJ 08543-3562 609-683-5400
Fax: 609-683-9595 888-683-5400
info@pretzelcrisps.com www.pretzelcrisps.com
Manufacturer of pretzel crisps-all natural and fat free; available in garluc, original and everything flavors.
President: Warren Wilson
VP: Sara Wilson
Estimated Sales: $ 5 Million+
Number Employees: 9
Sq. footage: 200000
Type of Packaging: Consumer, Food Service, Private Label, Bulk
Brands:
Snack Factory

12410 **Snack Works/Metrovox Snacks**
612 N. Eckhoff St
Orange, CA 92868
Fax: 714-634-4424 800-783-9870
questions@giftbasketsupplies.com
www.giftbasketsupplies.com
Popcorn, pretzels, chocolates, and gift boxes.
Owner: Paul Voxland
Estimated Sales: $500,000-$1 Million
Number Employees: 5-9

12411 **SnackMasters**
P.O.Box 70
Ceres, CA 95307-0070 209-537-9770
Fax: 209-669-3240 800-597-9770
jerky@snackmasters.com
www.snackmasters.com
Meat snacks
President: James Rekoutis
Estimated Sales: $ 10-20 Million
Number Employees: 50-99
Type of Packaging: Bulk

12412 **Snackerz**
6351 Chalet Dr
Commerce, CA 90040 562-928-0023
Fax: 562-928-8923 888-576-2253
www.snackerz.com
Candy and nuts
Owner: Ron Emrani
Estimated Sales: $ 10 - 20 Million
Number Employees: 20-49
Type of Packaging: Consumer

12413 **(HQ)Snak King Corporation**
16150 Stephens St
City of Industry, CA 91745 626-336-7711
Fax: 626-336-3777 info@snakking.com
www.snakking.com
Processor and exporter of snack foods, caramel corn, tortilla and corn chips, popcorn, beef jerky, pork rinds, cheese and rice puffs, nut meats and candy.
Chairman/CEO: Barry Levin
VP Sales & Marketing: Joe Papiri
National Sales Manager: Scott Burrows
Estimated Sales: $100+ Million
Number Employees: 500-999
Sq. footage: 175000
Type of Packaging: Consumer, Food Service, Private Label, Bulk
Other Locations:
Snak King Corp.
City Industry CA
Brands:
EL SABROSO
GRANNY GOOSE
JENSEN'S ORCHARD
SNAK KING
THE WHOLE EARTH

12414 **Snake River Brewing Company**
P.O.Box 3317
Jackson, WY 83001 307-739-2337
Fax: 307-739-2296 brewpub@rmisp.com
www.snakeriverbrewing.com
Processor of seasonal beer, ale, stout, lager and pilsner
President/CEO: Albert E Upsher
Estimated Sales: $1.5 Million
Number Employees: 50-99
Type of Packaging: Consumer, Food Service
Brands:
Snake River

12415 **Snapdragon Foods**
PO Box 14103
Oakland, CA 94614
877-881-7627
info@snapdragonfood.com
www.snapdragonfood.com
Importer and manufacturer of Asian prepared meals
President: David Sakamoto
CEO: Seth Jacobson
Estimated Sales: $1-2.5 Million
Number Employees: 5-9

12416 **(HQ)Snapple Beverage Group**
900 King St
Ryebrook, NY 10573 914-612-4000
Fax: 914-612-4100 800-762-7753
rlibonate@snapbevgrp.com www.snapple.com
Processor of beverages including iced tea, fruit juice, etc.
President: Jack Belsito
CFO: David Gerics
Vice President/General Manager: Bryan Mazur
SVP Operations: Joe Holland
Estimated Sales: $15,510,000
Number Employees: 500-999
Parent Co: Cadbury Schweppes PLC
Type of Packaging: Consumer, Food Service
Brands:
DIET RITE
MISTIC
NEHI
RC COLA
SNAPPLE
STEWART'S

12417 **Snappy Popcorn Company**
610 Main St
Breda, IA 51436 712-673-2347
Fax: 712-673-4611 800-742-0228
jon@snappypopcorn.com
www.snappypopcorn.com
Manufacturer, wholesaler/distributor and exporter of popcorn and supplies
Owner/CEO: Alan Tiefenthaler
Office Manager: Lori Steinkamp
VP Sales: Jon Tiefenthaler
Estimated Sales: $1-2.5 Million
Number Employees: 40
Sq. footage: 25000
Type of Packaging: Food Service, Bulk

12418 **Snelgrove Ice Cream Company**
850 E 2100 S
Salt Lake City, UT 84106-1832 801-486-4456
Fax: 801-486-3926 800-569-0005
www.dreyers.com
Processor, exporter and wholesaler/distributor of ice cream and ice cream novelties
President: David Mutzel
Estimated Sales: Less than $500,000
Number Employees: 50-99
Parent Co: MKD Distributing
Type of Packaging: Consumer, Food Service, Private Label, Bulk

12419 **Snikdiddy**
2505 Walnut Street
Suite 100
Boulder, CO 80302 303-444-4405
Fax: 303-444-4403 www.snikiddy.com
Baked fries and cheese puffs in various flavors
Co-Founder: Mary Schulman
Co-Founder: Janet Owings

12420 **Sno Pac Foods**
521 Enterprise Dr
Caledonia, MN 55921 507-725-5281
Fax: 507-725-5285 800-533-2215
snopac@snopac.com www.snopac.com
Processor of frozen organic vegetables including soy and eda mame beans, green peas, whole kernel corn, cut green and mixed
President: Peter Gengler
VP: Darlene Gengler
Estimated Sales: $3527129
Number Employees: 50-99
Type of Packaging: Consumer, Food Service, Bulk
Brands:
Sno Pac

12421 **Sno-Co Berry Pak**
1518 4th Street
Marysville, WA 98270-5012 360-659-3555
Fruit
President: Christie Monroe
Treasurer: Barbara Clark
Estimated Sales: $ 10-20 Million
Number Employees: 20-49

12422 **Sno-Shack**
2774 North 4000 West
Rexburg, ID 83440 208-359-0866
Fax: 208-359-1773 888-766-7425
sales@snoshack.com www.snoshack.com
Processor and exporter of flavors, thickeners and sweeteners; also, shaved ice equipment including shavers, bottles, racks and yogurt flavoring, carts, concession trailers, etc
Owner: Jared Sommer
Owner: Cheryl Lewis
Sales Director: Peter Orr
Manager: Bud Orr
Purchasing Manager: Brooke Anstine
Estimated Sales: $ 1 - 3 Million
Number Employees: 1-4
Sq. footage: 9000
Type of Packaging: Consumer, Food Service, Private Label
Brands:
Carts
Concessions
Kiosks

12423 **SnoWizard Extracts**
101 River Rd
New Orleans, LA 70121-4222 504-832-3901
Fax: 504-832-1646 800-366-9766
information@snowizard.com
www.snowizard.com
Snowball, snowcone and shaved ice machines and flavorings
President: Ronald Sciortino
Estimated Sales: $ 5 - 10 Million
Number Employees: 10-19
Sq. footage: 5000
Type of Packaging: Consumer, Food Service, Bulk
Brands:
Ronald Reginald's
SnoLite
Snowizard

12424 **Snokist Growers**
P.O.Box 1587
Yakima, WA 98907 509-248-5200
Fax: 509-453-9359 800-377-2857
info@snokist.com www.snokist.com
Processor of fresh apples, pears and cherries; also, canned apple rings and sauces, fruit purees, pears and plums
President: Valerie Woener
CEO: Valerie Woener
CFO: Jim Davis
CEO: Valerie Woerner
Sales Director: Rich Boldoz
Sales: Neil Galone
Operations Manager: Doug Schreiler
Estimated Sales: $100,000
Number Employees: 500-999
Number of Products: 10
Sq. footage: 50000
Type of Packaging: Consumer, Food Service, Private Label, Bulk
Brands:
BLUE RIBBON
COHORT
DEAR LADY
NU HOUSE
RED RIBBON
SNOKIST
TRI OUR

12425 **(HQ)Snow Ball Foods**
1501 Sykes Ln
Williamstown, NJ 08094 856-629-4081
Fax: 856-728-4238 info@snowballfoods.com
www.snowballfoods.com

Manufacturer and exporter of fresh and frozen turkey and chicken products
President: Ed Jenkins
VP: Kevin Moffett
Estimated Sales: $25 Million
Number Employees: 250
Number of Brands: 3
Number of Products: 110
Sq. footage: 150000
Type of Packaging: Consumer, Food Service, Private Label, Bulk
Brands:
Executive Chef
Snow-Ball
Sunbird

12426 Snow Beverages
928 Broadway
Suite 504
New York, NY 10010 212-353-3270
Fax: 646-219-7559 info@snowbeverages.com
www.snowbeverages.com
natural soda plus vitamins
CEO: Stuart Strumwasser
Number Employees: 3

12427 Snow Dairy
119 W 800 S
Springville, UT 84663 801-489-6081
Fax: 801-489-6081
President: Mark Snow
Estimated Sales: Less than $500,000
Number Employees: 1-4

12428 Snow's Ice Cream Company
80 School St
Greenfield, MA 01301-2410 413-774-7438
Fax: 413-774-5406 gary@bartshomemade.com
www.bartshomemade.com
Processor and wholesaler/distributor of ice cream, sorbet and frozen yogurt: wholesaler/distributor of frozen food, candy, snack foods, sauces, mustards and salsa's
Owner: Gary Schaefer
CFO/Sales: Gary Schaefer
Estimated Sales: Below $ 5 Million
Number Employees: 5-9
Sq. footage: 16000
Parent Co: Another Roadside Attraction
Type of Packaging: Consumer, Food Service, Private Label, Bulk
Brands:
Bart's Homemade
Snow's Nice Cream

12429 SnowBird Corporation
379 Broadway
Bayonne, NJ 07002-3631 201-858-8300
Fax: 201-451-5000 800-576-1616
sales@snowbirdwater.com
www.snowbirdwater.com
Manufacturer of bottled filtered, spring, and distilled water, coffee makers and hot foods; wholesaler/distributor of water fountains and bottled water coolers; repair services available
President: Diane Drey
Vice President: Gerald Giannangeli
Estimated Sales: $ 3 - 5 Million
Number Employees: 5-9
Sq. footage: 66000
Brands:
Snowbird

12430 Snowbear Frozen Custard
328 E State St
W Lafayette, IN 47906 765-746-2930
rick@snowbearfc.com
www.snowbear.com
Retailers of frozen desserts
Partner: Richard Lodde
Partner: Kirk Lodde
Partner: William Lodde
Partner: Tom Lodde
Estimated Sales: $500,000-$1 Million
Number Employees: 10-19
Number of Products: 50

12431 Snowcrest Packer
1925 Riverside Road
Abbotsford, BC V2S 4J8
Canada 604-859-4881
Fax: 604-859-1426 800-265-5332
info@snowcrest.ca www.snowcrest.ca
Processor and importer of frozen apples, blueberries, cherries, cranberries, raspberries, strawberries, asparagus, beans, broccoli, brussels, sprouts, cauliflowers, corn, peas, peppers, rhubarb, spinach, squash and turnips
President: Tom Smith
Quality Control: Lim Lee
Sales: Pascal Countant
Operations Manager: Rob Christl
Number Employees: 120
Sq. footage: 110000
Parent Co: Omstead Foods
Type of Packaging: Consumer, Food Service, Private Label, Bulk
Other Locations:
Snowcrest Packer Ltd.
Burnaby BC
Brands:
Bonniebrook
Brentwood
Delnor
Pennysaver
Snowcrest

12432 Snowizard Extracts
101 River Rd
New Orleans, LA 70121-4222 504-832-3901
Fax: 504-832-1646 800-366-9766
info@snowizard.com www.snowizard.com
Snoballs, snowcones and shaved ice
President: Ronnie Sciortino
Estimated Sales: $ 5 - 10 Million
Number Employees: 10-19
Type of Packaging: Private Label
Brands:
Snowizard

12433 Snyder Foods
15350 Old Simcoe Road
P.O Box 750
Port Perry, ON L9L 1A6
Canada 905-985-7373
Fax: 905-985-7289
Processor and exporter of meat and fruit pies, sausage rolls, quiche, stuffed sandwiches and pie and tart shells
General Manager: Dave Jackson
Number Employees: 125
Sq. footage: 55000
Type of Packaging: Consumer, Food Service, Private Label
Brands:
J.M. Schneider
Maple Leaf
Marks & Spencer
Pillsbury
Red-L
Richs

12434 Snyder's of Hanover
P.O.Box 6917
Hanover, PA 17331 717-632-4477
Fax: 717-632-7207
consumeraffairs@snyders-han.com
www.snydersofhanover.com
Manufacturer and exporter of snack foods including pretzels, flavored pretzel pieces and potato, tortilla and corn chips.
Chairman: Michael Warehime
CEO: Carl Lee
CEO: Carl Lee
Estimated Sales: $240 Million
Number Employees: 500-999
Number of Products: 45
Type of Packaging: Consumer
Brands:
SNYDER'S OF HANOVER

12435 (HQ)Snyder's-Lance Inc.
13024 Ballantyne Corporate Place
Str. 900
Charlotte, NC 28277 704-554-1421
Fax: 704-554-5562 800-438-1880
www.snyderslance.com
Manufacturer and exporter of sandwich crackers, nuts and seeds, captain's wafers, cookies, popcorn, snack cakes, gold n chees, and 100 calorie packs.
President/COO: Carl Lee
CEO: David Singer
EVP/CFO/Treasurer/Secretary: Richard Puckett
SVP/Sales & Marketing: Glenn Patcha
Senior Vice President/Sales: Frank Lewis
SVP Human Resources: Earl Leake
SVP Supply Chain: Blake Thompson
Estimated Sales: $980 Million
Number Employees: 7,000
Type of Packaging: Consumer
Other Locations:
Lance
Hyannis MA
Brands:
BLOOPS
CAN-O-LUNCH
CAPE COD POTATO CHIPS
CAPTAIN'S WAFERS
CHOC-O-LUNCH
GOLD-N-CHEES
LANCE
NEKOT
NIPCHEE
OUTPOST
THUNDER
THUNDER BOOMERS
TOASTCHEE
TOASTY
VISTA

12436 SoBe Beverages
40 Richards Ave
Norwalk, CT 06854-2327 203-899-7111
Fax: 203-899-7177 800-588-0548
www.sobebev.com
Healthy fruit and herb beverages with vitamins and minerals
President: Scott Mossitt
CEO: Jessica Lee
CFO: Norm Snyder
VP: Pamela Woods
Marketing: Bill Bishop
Estimated Sales: $ 75-100 Million
Number Employees: 50
Brands:
Sobe

12437 Sobaya
201 Rue Miner
Cowansville, QC J2K 3Y5
Canada 450-266-8808
Fax: 450-266-4750 800-319-8808
info@sobaya.ca www.sobaya.ca
Natural pasta, organic pasta, Kamut organic pasta and Spelt organic pasta.
President: Jacques Petit
Vice President: William Swaney
Marketing: Sandra Prevost
Sales Representative: Sandra Prevost
Number Employees: 7
Number of Brands: 1
Number of Products: 14
Sq. footage: 5000
Parent Co: Eden Foods
Type of Packaging: Consumer, Private Label, Bulk
Brands:
GENMAI UDON
SOBA
SOMEN
UDON

12438 Sobon Estate
12300 Steiner Rd
Plymouth, CA 95669 209-333-6275
Fax: 209-245-5156 info@sobonwine.com
www.sobonwine.com
Wine
Co-Owner: Leon Sobon
Co-Owner: Shirley Sobon
Assistant Winemaker/Vineyard Manager: Paul Sobon
Coordinator of Computer/Business Systems: Robert Sobon
Sales/Marketing: Tom Quinn
Estimated Sales: $ 5 - 10 Million
Number Employees: 10-19
Brands:
Shenandoah Vineyards
Sobon Estate

12439 Societe Cafe
10768 Rue Salk
Montreal-Nord, QC H1G 4Y1
Canada 514-325-9130
Fax: 514-325-6398 parent@sympatico.ca
www.intermatch.qc.ca/cafe

Processor and exporter of aroma coffee; importer of green coffee beans and cocoa; custom blending available
President: M Claude Parent
Sales/Marketing Executive: Andre Richer
Purchasing Agent: Linda McGail
Number Employees: 12
Sq. footage: 6000
Type of Packaging: Consumer, Food Service, Private Label, Bulk
Brands:
Altima
Aroma
Bourbon Excelso

12440 **Society Hill Snacks**
8845 Torresdale Ave
Philadelphia, PA 19136-1510 215-708-8500
Fax: 215-288-4117 800-595-0050
info@societyhillsnacks.com
www.societyhillsnacks.com
Gourmet sweet roasted nuts, snack mixes and great munchies.
President: Ronna Schultz
Estimated Sales: $ 1 - 3 Million
Number Employees: 1-4
Type of Packaging: Consumer, Food Service, Private Label, Bulk
Brands:
Afrique
Cinnful Coco
Cravin Asian
Hot Stuff
Loco Coco
Love That
Society Hill Gourmet Nut Company
Tres Toffee
Tropical Honey Glace

12441 **Sofo Foods**
253 Waggoner Blvd
Toledo, OH 43612-1988 419-476-4211
Fax: 419-478-6104 800-447-4211
sales@sofofoods.com www.sofofoods.com
Manufacturer of fresh produce, meats, cheeses, disposables, appetizers
President/CEO/Owner: Tony Sofo
Marketing: Liz Sofo
Public Relations: Kim Nevel
Estimated Sales: $ 20-50 Million
Number Employees: 250-499
Type of Packaging: Food Service
Brands:
A&M Cheese

12442 **Soft Gel Technologies**
6986 Bandini Blvd
Commerce, CA 90040-3326 323-726-0700
Fax: 323-726-7065 800-360-7484
sales@soft-gel.com www.soft-gel.com
Processor of herbal and nutritional supplements
President: Ron Udell
VP Sales Administration: Diane Hembree
Type of Packaging: Private Label, Bulk
Brands:
Coqsol
SGTI

12443 **Soho Beverages**
8075 Leesburg Pike
Suite 760
Vienna, VA 22182-2739 703-689-2800
Soft drinks
President: Tom Cox
Estimated Sales: $ 5-10 Million
Number Employees: 5
Type of Packaging: Private Label
Brands:
Soho Natural Lemonades
Soho Natural Soda &

12444 **Sokol & Company**
5315 Dansher Rd
Countryside, IL 60525 708-482-8250
Fax: 708-482-9750 800-328-7656
bparoubek@solofoods.com www.solofoods.com
Cake and pastry fillings, almond paste and marzipan, pie and dessery fillings, marshmallow and toasted marshmallow creme, fruit butters, Asian dipping sauces and marinades, seasoning mixes.
Chairman: John Sokol Novak
President: John Novak Jr
CEO: John Novak Jr
Research & Development: Larry Lepore
Quality Control: Galina Mann
Marketing Director: Eva Karnezis
Sales Director: Bobby Paroubek
Plant Manager: Mark Kiefhaber
Purchasing Manager: Andy Kaminski
Estimated Sales: $16 Million
Number Employees: 50-99
Number of Brands: 5
Sq. footage: 25000
Type of Packaging: Consumer, Food Service, Private Label
Brands:
BAKER
BOHEMIAN KITCHEN
DOBLA
SIMON FISCHER
SOLO

12445 **Sokol Blosser Winery**
P.O.Box 399
Dundee, OR 97115-0399 503-864-2282
Fax: 503-864-2710 800-582-6668
info@sokolblosser.com www.sokolblosser.com
Wines
Manager: Michael Brown
Marketing Director: Alex Sokol Blosser
CFO: Alison Sokol Blosser
Winemaker: Russ Rosner
Estimated Sales: Below $ 5 Million
Number Employees: 10-19
Number of Products: 7
Brands:
Evolution
Medetrina
Sokol Blosser

12446 **Solana Beach Baking Company**
5927 Farnsworth Ct
Carlsbad, CA 92008 760-931-0148
Fax: 760-444-9883 info@solanabaking.com
www.solanabaking.com
Breads and pastries
President: David Wells
Quality Control: Kim Hogan
R & D: David Mears
Estimated Sales: $ 30-50 Million
Number Employees: 250-499

12447 **Solana Gold Organics**
P.O.Box 1340
Sebastopol, CA 95473-1340 707-829-1121
Fax: 707-829-4715 800-459-1121
www.solanagold.com
Processor of organic apples and apple products including kosher, dried, sauce, vinegar, juice, etc
Owner: John Kolling
Sales Director: Chris Blackburn
Estimated Sales: $630000
Number Employees: 1-4
Type of Packaging: Consumer, Private Label, Bulk
Brands:
Solana Gold
Solana Gold Organics

12448 **Solgar Vitamin & Herb**
500 Willow Tree Rd
Leonia, NJ 7605 201-944-2311
Fax: 201-944-7351
productinformation@solgar.com
www.solgar.com
Manufacturer of natural dietary and nutritional supplements
President/CEO: Allen Skolnick
Estimated Sales: $ 100-500 Million
Number Employees: 250-499
Number of Products: 400
Sq. footage: 50000
Parent Co: NBTY
Type of Packaging: Consumer
Brands:
Kangavites
Natural Bouncin' Berry
Nature's Bounty
Rexall
Solgar
Sundown

12449 **Solnuts**
711 7th St
Hudson, IA 50643 319-988-3221
Fax: 319-988-4647 800-648-3503
nnewton@kerrygroup.com www.kneygroup.com
Processor of dry roasted soy nuts and all natural full fat soy flour
Manager: Mike Patterson
Vice President: Michael Healy
Marketing Director: Jim Andrews
Sales/Marketing: Nancy Newton
Operations Manager: Dave Zanchetti
Production Manager: Mike Patterson
Plant Manager: Mike Devine
Estimated Sales: $ 3 - 5 Million
Number Employees: 5-9
Sq. footage: 16000
Parent Co: B.V. Solnut
Type of Packaging: Food Service, Private Label, Bulk
Brands:
Solnuts

12450 **Solo Worldwide Enterprises**
5683 Columbia Pike Ste 100
Falls Church, VA 22041 703-845-7072
Fax: 703-560-5744 soloworld@aol.com
General grocery
President, US Division: Eyob Mamo
Estimated Sales: $500,000-$1 Million
Number Employees: 5-9
Brands:
Solo

12451 **Soloman Baking Company**
3820 Revere St Ste A
Denver, CO 80239 303-371-2777
Fax: 303-375-9162
Processor of pita bread, bagel and pita chips, snack mixes and tortillas greek pita
President: Sam Soloman
CEO: Andy Soloman
CFO: Malik Soloman
Estimated Sales: $3 Million
Number Employees: 12
Number of Products: 8
Sq. footage: 12000
Type of Packaging: Consumer, Private Label

12452 **Soloman Baking Company**
3820 Revere St Ste A
Denver, CO 80239 303-371-2777
Fax: 303-375-9162
Bakery products
President: Sam Soloman
Marketing Director: Hian Soloman
CFO: Annas Soloman
Quality Control: Hiam Soloman
R & D: Max Soloman
Estimated Sales: $ 5-10 Million
Number Employees: 5-9
Brands:
Soloman

12453 **Soluble Products Company**
480 Oberlin Ave S
Lakewood, NJ 08701-6997 732-364-8855
Fax: 732-364-6689 sales@spcus.com
www.solubleproducts.com
Manufacture of supplements for every lifestyle, including diet, bodybuilding, sports nutrition, nutraceutical and children's products
President: Stephen Hoffman
CEO: Stephen Hoffman
VP: Stewart Hoffman
Sales Manager: Thomas A Flora
Sales Manager: Thomas Flora
Estimated Sales: $ 2.5-5 Million
Number Employees: 20-49
Sq. footage: 50000
Type of Packaging: Private Label
Brands:
Soluble Products

12454 **Solvang Bakery**
460 Alisal Rd
Solvang, CA 93463 805-688-4939
Fax: 805-686-4407 800-377-4253
www.solvangbakery.com
Processor and exporter of bread, cake and Danish tarts
President: Susan Halme
General manager: Melissa Redell

Estimated Sales: $ 3 - 5 Million
Number Employees: 20-49
Type of Packaging: Consumer, Food Service

12455 **Solvay Chemicals**
3333 Richmond Ave
Houston, TX 77098 713-525-6500
Fax: 713-525-7800 800-765-8292
david.calvo@solvay.com
www.solvaychemicals.com
Manufacturer of food grade hydrogen peroxids, IXPER® Calcium Peroxide, and BICAR® Sodium Bicarbonate for use in bleaching/decolorization, dough conditioning, leavening, sulfite reduction, microbial sterilization and productpurification.
President: Richard Hogan
Marketing: David Calvo
Number Employees: 100-249
Parent Co: Solvay America

12456 **Somerset Food Service**
P.O.Box 799
Somerset, KY 42502-0799 606-274-4858
Fax: 606-274-5141 info@somersetfoods.com
www.somersetfoods.com
Food distributor.
President/CEO: Tim Williams
Co-Owner: Mac Goodby
Estimated Sales: $ 20 - 50 Million
Number Employees: 100-249

12457 **Somerset Industries**
901 North Bethlehem Pike
Spring House, PA 19477-0927 215-619-0480
Fax: 215-619-0489 800-883-8728
benc@somersetindustries.com
www.somersetindustries.com
Wholesaler/distributor, importer and exporter of closeout items bought and sold. The correctional food specialist. Warehouse and transportation services provided
President: Jay Shrager
CFO: Carole Shrager
VP: Alan Breslow
Marketing Director: Candace Shrager
Sales Manager: Ben John McVay
General Manager: Ben Caldwell
Number Employees: 20-49
Type of Packaging: Food Service, Private Label, Bulk
Brands:
21st CENTURY
ANNAMARIA
BOBBIE
SOMERSET
TINY'S TREATS

12458 **Somerset Syrup & Beverage**
100 McGaw Dr
Edison, NJ 08837-3725 732-225-0209
Fax: 732-225-6363 800-526-8865
www.eatfunfood.com
Confection products
President: Robert Spitz
Estimated Sales: Below $ 5 Million
Number Employees: 20-49

12459 **Sommer Maid Creamery**
Po Box 350
Doylestown, PA 18901 215-345-6160
Fax: 215-345-4945
sextonmaid@sommermaid.com
www.sommermaid.com
Processor of cheese, eggs, butter and margarine
President: Frank Sexton
CFO: John T Poprick
VP/General Manager: Harry Mattern
Estimated Sales: $ .5 - 1 million
Number Employees: 5-9
Type of Packaging: Consumer, Food Service, Private Label, Bulk
Brands:
State

12460 **Sommer's Food Products**
106 W 7th Street
Salisbury, MO 65281-1108 660-388-5511
Potato chips
President: Jack Richardson
Estimated Sales: $ 5-9.9 Million
Number Employees: 7
Brands:
Sommer's Food

12461 **Sonne**
896 22nd Ave N
Wahpeton, ND 58075-3026 701-642-3068
Fax: 701-642-9403 800-727-6663
info@dakotagourmet.com
www.dakotagourmet.com
Processor of roasted sunflower seeds, trail mixes and toasted corn and soybeans
President: Steven Bromley
Estimated Sales: $3 Million
Number Employees: 20-49
Sq. footage: 20550
Type of Packaging: Consumer, Food Service, Private Label, Bulk
Brands:
Dakota Gourmet
Dakota Gourmet Heart Smart
Dakota Gourmet Toasted Korn

12462 **Sonoco**
1 N 2nd St
Hartsville, SC 29550-3300 843-383-7000
Fax: 843-383-7008 800-377-2692
corporate.communications@sonoco.com
www.sonoco.com
Global manufacturer of consumer and industrial packing products and provider of packaging services.
Chairman/President/CEO: Harris Deloch Jr
Owner: Dennis Close
SVP/CFO: Charles Hupfer
Senior Vice President: Jim Brown
VP/Chief Information Officer: Bernard Campbell
Vice President Corporate Planning: Kevin Mahoney
Senior Vice President Human Resources: Cynthia Hartley
Estimated Sales: $3.7 Billion
Number Employees: 16,500

12463 **Sonoco Wholesale Grocers**
P.O.Box 4319
Houma, LA 70361-4319 985-851-0727
Fax: 985-872-2251 www.sontheimeroffshore.com
Provide offshore catering for people on drilling rigs.
President: John Sontheimer

12464 **Sonoita Vineyards**
Hc 1 Box 33
Elgin, AZ 85611 520-455-5893
Fax: 520-455-5893 www.sonoitavineyards.com
Wines
Owner/Winemaker: Gordon Dutt
General Manager: Mike Duppost
VP: Jack Strolline
Estimated Sales: $ 1-2.5 Million
Number Employees: 5-9

12465 **Sonoma Gourmet**
21787 8th. St. E.
Sonoma, CA 95476 707-939-3700
Fax: 707-939-3730
http://www.sonomagourmet.com/
Gourmet pasta, pasta sauces, marinades/cooking sauces and Tuscan olive spreads
Owner/President: William Weber
Copartner/VP: Rodger Declerq
Estimated Sales: $3 Million
Number Employees: 25

12466 **Sonoma Gourmet**
21787 8th St E Ste 7
Sonoma, CA 95476 707-939-3700
Fax: 707-939-3730
sauceboys@sonomagourmet.com
www.sonomagourmet.com
Specialty sauces and condiments
President and Owner: William Weber
Vice President: Roger Declercq
Estimated Sales: $3.14 Million
Number Employees: 25
Number of Brands: 30
Number of Products: 200
Type of Packaging: Private Label
Brands:
Pometta's
Sonoma Gourmet

12467 **Sonoma Seafoods**
2 E Spain St
Sonoma, CA 95476-5729 707-996-1931
Fax: 707-935-8846 877-411-2123
sgray@sonomaseafoods.com
www.gypsyboots.com
Stuffed entree products include fish and stuffed seafood in addition to a recently introduced new product line including poultry, pork, beef and vegetables.
Owner: Pete Vivani
Partner: Scott Gray
Sales Manager: Georgine Drees
Estimated Sales: $ 5-9.9 Million
Number Employees: 20-49

12468 **Sonoma Wine Services**
P.O.Box 207
Vineburg, CA 95487 707-996-9773
Fax: 707-996-0145
Wines: shipping, storage. Controlled environment bonded warehouse
President: Warren McCambridge
CFO: Denise McCambridge
Estimated Sales: Under $500,000
Number Employees: 1-4
Brands:
Sonoma Wine

12469 **Sonoma-Cutrer Vineyards**
P.O.Box 9
Fulton, CA 95439-0009 707-528-1181
Fax: 707-528-1561 info@sonomacutrer.com
www.sonomacutrer.com
Wines
Managing Director: Keith Levine
Owner: H Jabarin
CFO: Marilo Calabuig
Corporate Communications: James Caudill
Estimated Sales: $ 1-2.5 Million
Number Employees: 50-99
Brands:
Alban Viognier
Chateau Montelena
Hartwell Cabernet
Louis Roederer
MacPhail Pinot
Oberschulte Syrah
Worthy Cabernet

12470 **Sonstegard Foods Company**
707 E 41st St Ste 222
Sioux Falls, SD 57105 605-338-4642
Fax: 605-338-8765 800-533-3184
info@sonstegard.com www.sonstegard.com
Sonstegard Foods Company is a major wholesaler of powdered, liquid, and frozen egg products. We sell egg products to food processors, mix manufacturers, schools, food distributors, and industries including the salad dressing industrycandy industry, pasta industry, and others.
President: Philip Sonstegard
Estimated Sales: $ 75-100 Million
Number Employees: 5-9

12471 **Soolim**
154 Woodstone Drive
Buffalo Grove, IL 60089-6704 847-357-8515
Fax: 847-357-8517 soolimltd@aol.com
Processor and importer of Oriental herbal products
President: Seung Shin
CFO: Chang Jin Lee
Vice President: Gina Lee
Plant Manager: Sang Hoon Shin
Estimated Sales: $500,000 appx.
Number Employees: 5-9
Sq. footage: 12000
Type of Packaging: Consumer

12472 **Sopacko Packaging**
P.O.Box 827
Bennettsville, SC 29512-0827 843-479-3811
Fax: 843-479-3725 www.sopakco.com
Processor of canned vegetables, beef, pork, stews and poultry; also, pouches of barbecue pork and beef, beef stew, meatballs, tuna with noodles and pasta with sauce
President: Lonnie Thompson
VP: Bill McCreary
Plant Manager: Vera Hahn
Purchasing Manager: Stewart Clark
Estimated Sales: $ 20-50 Million
Number Employees: 100-249
Parent Co: Sopacko
Type of Packaging: Consumer, Food Service, Private Label
Brands:
Sopakco

12473 (HQ)Sopakco Foods
P.O.Box 1047
Mullins, SC 29574-1047 843-464-7851
Fax: 843-464-2096 sfernald@sopakco.com
www.sopakco.com
Sauces, dressings
President/CEO: Lonnie Thompson
Manufacturing Director: William Pettibone
Plant Operations: Bill Jennings
Purchasing: Gene Gasque
Estimated Sales: $ 5-10 Million
Number Employees: 250-499

12474 Sophia's Sauce Works
2533 N Carson Street
Carson City, NV 89706-0147 916-315-3584
Fax: 916-315-9372 800-718-7769
ssw@lanset.com www.ssw-inc.com
Processor of all natural sauces, spreads and dressings
Chairman: Sophia Fridas
President: Jim Fridas
Number Employees: 5-9
Sq. footage: 2000
Parent Co: Sophia's Sauce Works
Type of Packaging: Consumer
Brands:
SOPHIA'S AUTHENTIC
SOPHIA'S SAUCE WORKS

12475 Sopralco
6991 W Broward Blvd
Plantation, FL 33317-2907 954-584-2225
Fax: 954-584-3271 sopralco@aol.com
Processor and importer of ready-to-drink espresso; manufacturer and importer of espresso dispensing equipment; also, fiberglass carts
Owner: Peter Marciante
VP: Arcelia De Battisti
Marketing: Ana Ordaz
Estimated Sales: $ 1-2.5 Million
Number Employees: 1-4
Sq. footage: 1250
Parent Co: Sopralco
Type of Packaging: Consumer, Food Service
Brands:
Espre
Espre-Cart
Espre-Matic

12476 (HQ)Sorbee Intl.
4 Neshaminy Interplex Dr Ste 202
Feasterville Trevose, PA 19053-6940 215-677-5200
Fax: 215-677-7736 800-654-3997
www.sorbee.com
Processor of confectionery items including sugar hard candy, low-fat candy bars and sugar-free items
CEO: Daniel Werther
CFO: Tom Keogh
VP Sales: Barry Sokol
Estimated Sales: $31 Million
Number Employees: 20-49
Other Locations:
Sorbee International Ltd.
Philadelphia PA
Brands:
DREAM CANDY
GLOBAL BRANDS
SORBEE

12477 Sorrenti Family Farms
1527 N St
Newman, CA 95360 209-862-3037
888-435-9490
wildrice@sonnet.com
Wild rice, blended rices, quick-cook rice mixes, pasta and wild rice mixes, soup mixes, muffin mixes, focaccia mix and pizza kits
Estimated Sales: Less than $1 Million
Number Employees: 1-4
Brands:
Cucina Sorrenti
Mighty Wild
Rising Star Ranch
Sorrenti Family Farm
Urban Delights

12478 (HQ)Sorrento Lactalis
2376 S Park Ave
Buffalo, NY 14220 716-823-6262
Fax: 716-823-6454 800-828-7031
www.greatcheese.com
World reknowned cheese brands made available to the foodservice industry, as well as marketing, menu, and customer profiling information.
President/CEO: Frederick Bouisset
CFO: John Zielinski
VP: Charles Hylkema
VP Sales/Marketing: John Alfieri
Estimated Sales: $14 Billion
Number Employees: 1,500
Number of Brands: 8
Parent Co: Lactalis American Group
Type of Packaging: Food Service
Brands:
GALBANI
ISTARA
LE CHATELAIN
PRECIOUS
PRESIDENT
RONDELE
SOCIETE
SORRENTO
VALBRESO FETA

12479 Sorrento Lobster
224 Ocean Ave
Sorrento, ME 04677 207-422-9082
Fax: 207-422-9033
Seafood.
Manager: Rick Freeman Jr
Estimated Sales: $2,100,000
Number Employees: 5-9

12480 Soteria
180 Kite Lake Road
Fairburn, GA 30213-9608 404-768-5161
Fax: 404-768-3704
heavenlyseason@mindspring.com
Processor of natural and dry seasoning blends with no salt, MSG or calories
CEO: Lee Armstrong
Executive VP: Denise Armstrong
VP Operations: Keith Jackson
Number Employees: 1-4

12481 Source Food Technology
2530 Meridian Parkway
#200
Durham, NC 27713 919-806-4545
Fax: 919-806-4842 866-277-3849
Processor of cholesterol-free shortenings, fats and oils; also, cholesterol reduced egg and dairy products
CEO: Henry Cardello
VP Sales: Patrick Halliday
Estimated Sales: B
Number Employees: 5-9

12482 Source Food Technology
12235 Nicollet Avenue
Burnsville, MN 55337-1650 612-890-6366
Fax: 612-890-5748
Nutritionally enhanced food ingredients
Estimated Sales: $ 10-25 Million
Number Employees: 19

12483 Source Naturals
23 Janis Way
Scotts Valley, CA 95066 831-438-1144
Fax: 831-438-7410 800-815-2333
heidib@thresholdent.com
www.sourcenaturals.com
Manufacturer and wholesaler/distributor of dietary supplements
Founder/CEO: Ira Goldberg
Estimated Sales: $100+ Million
Number Employees: 250-499
Parent Co: Threshold Enterprises
Brands:
SOURCE

12484 Souris Valley Processors
PO Box 460
Melita, NB R0M 1L0
Canada 204-522-8210
Fax: 204-522-8210
Processor of beef and pork
President: Larry Danyluk
Estimated Sales: $1-2.5 Million
Number Employees: 5-9
Sq. footage: 4000
Type of Packaging: Consumer, Food Service

12485 Sourthern Tea
1267 Cobb Industrial Dr
Marietta, GA 30066-6616 770-428-5555
Fax: 770-425-6188 800-241-0896
www.southerntea.com
Processor and exporter of tea bags
CEO: Bruce Clodt
CFO: Maria Roberts
Estimated Sales: $20-50 Million
Number Employees: 100-249
Parent Co: Tetley USA
Type of Packaging: Consumer, Food Service, Private Label, Bulk

12486 South Beach Coffee Company
P.O.Box 403003
Miami Beach, FL 33140 305-576-9696
Fax: 305-532-0409 info@discoverourtown.com
www.southbeachcoffee.com
Coffee for wholesale and retail customers
President: Hagai Gringarten
Vice President: Droma Gringarten
Marketing Director: Karen Kong
Operations Manager: Ruben Meoqui
Estimated Sales: $ 1-5 Million
Number Employees: 13
Type of Packaging: Consumer, Private Label
Brands:
LINCOLN ROAD BLEND
OCEAN DRIVE BLEND
OCEAN ROAD BLEND

12487 South Beach Novelties &Confectionery
44 Robin Rd
Staten Island, NY 10305-4799 718-727-4500
Fax: 718-448-4108 johnl4244@AOL.com
Confections
Owner: John Lagana
Estimated Sales: $18 Million
Number Employees: 11
Brands:
Gator Ade
Polar Spring Water

12488 South Bend Chocolate
3300 W Sample St Ste 110
South Bend, IN 46619 574-233-2577
Fax: 574-233-3150 800-301-4961
orders@sbchocolate.com www.sbchocolate.com
Distinctive chocolates
President: Mart Tarner
Marketing Director: Kristina Pier
Estimated Sales: $ 20 - 50 Million
Number Employees: 50-99
Brands:
South Bend Chocolate

12489 South Ceasar Dressing Company
PO Box 612
Novato, CA 94948-0612 415-897-0605
Fax: 415-897-0605
Salad dressing
Partner: Shirley Lesley
Partner: Mark Lesley
Estimated Sales: Under $500,000
Number Employees: 1-4
Type of Packaging: Private Label
Brands:
South Ceasar Dressing Company

12490 South County Creamery
995 Main Street
Great Barrington, MA 01230 413-528-8560
www.berkshireicecream.com
Ice cream, sorbet and gelato
Co-Owner: Danny Mazursky
Estimated Sales: $300,000-500,000
Number Employees: 5-9
Brands:
Berkshire Ice Cream

12491 South Georgia Pecan
P.O.Box 5366
Valdosta, GA 31603 229-244-1321
Fax: 229-247-6361 800-627-6630
info@georgiapecan.com www.georgiapecan.com
Manufacturer and exporter of shelled pecans
Co-Owner: Jim Worn
Co-Owner: Ed Crane
Estimated Sales: $ 20 - 50 Million
Number Employees: 100-249
Type of Packaging: Consumer

Brands:
DASHER PECAN

12492 **South Georgia Pecan Company**
P.O.Box 5366
Valdosta, GA 31603 229-244-1321
Fax: 229-247-6361 800-627-6630
info@georgiapecan.com www.georgiapecan.com
Processor and exporter of nut meats and pecans including shelled and in-shell
President/Owner: Jim P Worn
Owner: Ed Crane
VP: Jimmy Colwell
VP of Operations: Julie Tomlison
Purchasing: Gary Peters
Estimated Sales: $10,700,000
Number Employees: 100-249
Type of Packaging: Bulk
Brands:
South Georgia
Southland's

12493 **South Louisiana Sugars**
5354 St James Coop St
Saint James, LA 70086 225-265-4056
Fax: 225-265-4060 info@slscoop.com
www.slscoop.com
Processor of sugar including raw, turbinado granulated and clarified syrup
President: Ronald Blanchard
Vice President: John Thigaut
General Manager: Jan Bergeron
Production Manager: Walter Simoneaux
Plant Manager: Keith Guedry
Purchasing Manager: Andrew Robertson
Estimated Sales: $20 Million
Number Employees: 50
Type of Packaging: Consumer, Private Label
Brands:
Cajun Crystals
Cajun Gold

12494 **(HQ)South Mill Distribution**
Po Box 1037
649 West South Street
Kennett Square, PA 19348 610-444-4800
Fax: 610-444-1338 info@southmill.com
www.southmill.com
Grower, processor and distributor of mushrooms, (fresh, canned, blanched, value-added and dried, etc) and produce with the ability to deliver to 36 states overnight. Warehouse offering cooler storage for produce; transportationservices include LTL
President: Michael Pea
Sales Manager New Orleans: Jay Joyce
Sales Manager Dallas: Shawn Weidman
Sales Manager Houston: Dennis Smith
Estimated Sales: $ 20 - 50 Million
Number Employees: 500-999
Sq. footage: 120000
Parent Co: Kaolin Mushroom Farms
Type of Packaging: Consumer, Food Service, Private Label, Bulk
Other Locations:
South Mill Distribution:Forest Park
Atlanta GA
South Mill Distribution:Haraham
New Orleans LA
South Mill Distribution:Houston
Houston TX
South Mill Distribution:Dallas
Dallas TX
Brands:
Brown King
South Mill Mushroom Sales

12495 **South Pacific Trading Company**
15052 Ronnie Dr
Dade City, FL 33523 352-567-2200
Fax: 352-567-2257 888-505-4439
scot@nonipacific.com www.nonipacific.com
Private label, dietary supplements, import/export bulk noni juice (certified organic), cocnut oil (certified organic)
President: Scot Vallantyne
Sales Director: Susan Ballantyne
Operations Manager: Brenda Rossbach
Plant Manager: James Dean
Estimated Sales: $1 Million
Number Employees: 5-9
Number of Brands: 2
Number of Products: 8
Sq. footage: 17000
Type of Packaging: Consumer, Private Label, Bulk
Brands:
CHERRY NONI
COCONUT PACIFIC
NONI "C"LECT
NONI PACIFIC

12496 **South Shores Seafood**
1822 E Ball Rd
Anaheim, CA 92805-5936 714-956-2722
Fax: 714-956-0277
Seafood
President: Michael Armstrong
Estimated Sales: $2,000,000
Number Employees: 5-9

12497 **South Texas Spice Company**
2106 Castroville Rd
San Antonio, TX 78237 210-436-2280
Fax: 210-436-6658
Spices
Partner: Zeferino Menchaca
Estimated Sales: $390,000
Number Employees: 5-9
Brands:
Menchaca
South Texas Spice
Yellow Rose

12498 **South Valley Citrus Packers**
9600 Road 256
Terra Bella, CA 93270 559-906-1033
Fax: 559-525-4206 vcpg@vcpg.com
www.vcpg.com/gvh.htm
Packinghouse and licensed shipper of Sunkist Growers Inc. citrus products.
Manager: Cliff Martin
Grower Service Representative: Maribel Nenna
General Manager Visalia Citrus Packing: Bob Walters
Parent Co: Visalia Citrus Packing Group
Type of Packaging: Food Service

12499 **South Valley Farms**
15443 Beech Ave
Wasco, CA 93280 661-391-9000
Fax: 661-391-9012 hmemmott@fmc-slc.com
www.southvalleyfarms.com
Grower and exporter of almonds and pistachios; processor of hulled and shelled almonds
President: John Creer
VP: Daryl Wilkendors
Processing Manager: Jonathan Meyer
Estimated Sales: $ 2.5-5 Million
Number Employees: 100-249
Sq. footage: 80000
Parent Co: Farm Management Company
Type of Packaging: Bulk

12500 **South West Foods Tasty Bakery**
P.O.Box 1411
Tyler, TX 75710-1411 903-877-3481
Fax: 903-877-6903 dennisprice@brookshires.com
www.brookshires.com
Baked goods
Manager: Sheila Vickery
Brands:
South West

12501 **Southchem**
2000 E Pettigrew St
Durham, NC 27703-4049 919-596-0681
Fax: 919-596-6438 800-849-7000
Beverages, confectionery, canned foods, processed cheese, bakery, meat, seafood, dairy
President: Gil D Steadman
Number Employees: 100-249

12502 **Southeast Alaska SmokedSalmon Company**
550 S Franklin St
Juneau, AK 99801-1330 907-463-4617
Fax: 907-463-4644
Smoked salmon
President: Sandro Lane
CEO: Giovanni Gallizio
Estimated Sales: $ 50 - 100 Million
Number Employees: 100-249

12503 **Southeast Baking Corporation**
49 Batesville Ct
Greer, SC 29650-4800 864-627-1380
Fax: 864-627-1381
Processor of bread
President: Mario Romano
Estimated Sales: $500,000-$1 Million
Number Employees: 10-19

12504 **Southeast Canners**
7607 Veterans Pkwy
Columbus, GA 31909-2503 706-324-0040
Fax: 706-324-6404
Processor of canned and bottled soft drinks
President: Sheyenne Bradford
Plant Manager: Don Hambrick
CFO: Robert Heurich
Controller: Pat Barnes
Quality Control: Malinda Delradge
Estimated Sales: $ 20-50 Million
Number Employees: 50-99
Parent Co: PepsiCo
Type of Packaging: Consumer, Food Service
Brands:
Pepsi

12505 **Southeast Dairy Processors**
3802 E Columbus Dr
Tampa, FL 33605 813-621-3233
Fax: 813-626-1516 info@instantwhip.com
www.instantwhipflorida.com
Milk and dairy products
President: William Tiller
Estimated Sales: $ 5-10 Million
Number Employees: 20-49
Type of Packaging: Private Label

12506 **Southeastern Meat Association**
Po Box 620777
Oviedo, FL 32762 407-365-5661
Fax: 407-365-8945 info@southeasternmeat.com
http://www.southeasternmeat.com
Processor and packer of frozen portion controlled beef, pork, veal and chicken
Executive Director: Anna Ondick
Estimated Sales: $20-50 Million
Number Employees: 1-4
Type of Packaging: Consumer, Food Service

12507 **Southeastern Meats**
PO Box 8325
Birmingham, AL 35218-0325 205-923-8555
Meat
Chairman/CEO: Lester Newby Jr
CFO: Trecia Franks
Number Employees: 5-9

12508 **Southeastern Mills**
P.O.Box 908
Rome, GA 30162 706-291-6528
Fax: 706-295-5411 800-334-4468
customerservice@semills.com www.semills.com
Processor of flour, corn meal & grits, sauce & gravy mixes, specialty baking mixes, batters & breadings, seasonings & marinades.
President: Robert Ugrizzard
CEO: Vernon Grizzard
Director Sales: Michael O'Connor
Plant Manager: David Neff
Purchasing Manager: Chris Wheeler
Estimated Sales: $100+ Million
Number Employees: 100-249
Type of Packaging: Consumer, Food Service, Private Label, Bulk
Brands:
Four Roses
Good Loaf
Southeastern Mills
Stivers Best
Strong Boy

12509 **Southeastern Wisconsin Products Company**
500 W Edgerton Ave
Milwaukee, WI 53207 414-482-1730
Fax: 414-482-2812 www.campbellsoup.com
Processor of yeast, sage oil and dairy flavoring extracts
President: Del Nirode
Quality Manager: Michael Malencore
Production Manager: Raymond Miller
Plant Manager: Bill Blue
Purchasing Manager: John Schmidt
Estimated Sales: $ 20 - 50 Million
Number Employees: 20-49
Parent Co: Campbell Soup Company

12510 **Southern Bar-B-Que**
PO Box 206
Jennings, LA 70546 337-824-3877
Fax: 337-824-6678 866-612-2586
www.southernbbqsauce.com
bbq sauce, basting sauce, crawfish, shrimp and crab boil, frying oil, grill-n-que rub, grill-n-que sauce, pepper sauce, roux, salsa, seasoning and spray basters

12511 **Southern Bell Dairy**
607 Bourne Ave
Somerset, KY 42501-1919 606-679-1131
Fax: 800-441-8931 800-468-4798
mike.chandler@southernbelledairy.com
www.southernbelledairy.com
Dairy
President: Mike Chandler
President: Martin Shearer
Marketing Manager: Doug Wade
VP Sales: Glenn Carlyle
General Sales Manager: Gene Kennedy
Manager Information Systems: Dan/Judy Hall
Plant Manager: Kevin Randolf
Estimated Sales: $ 50-99.9 Million
Number Employees: 100-249

12512 **Southern Belle SandwichcCompany**
1969 N Lobdell Blvd
Baton Rouge, LA 70806 225-927-4670
Fax: 225-928-5661 800-344-4670
www.southernbellesandwich.com
Processor of fresh sandwiches
President: Lloyd Bearden Jr
VP: Homer Miller
Sales Manager: Rick Bearden
Estimated Sales: $ 5 - 10 Million
Number Employees: 100-249
Sq. footage: 10000
Parent Co: Bearden Sandwich Company
Type of Packaging: Consumer

12513 **Southern Beverage Packers**
6341 Natures Way
Appling, GA 30802 706-541-9222
Fax: 706-541-1730 800-326-2469
qch2o@cs.com
Processor of water and marketer of crystalline soft drink and fruit drinks
President: David Byrd
Vice President: Stephen Byrd
Marketing Director: Jeff Millick
Production Manager: Lynn Hebbard
Plant Manager/Purchasing: Richard Maddox
Estimated Sales: $7200000
Number Employees: 20-49
Number of Brands: 2
Number of Products: 50
Type of Packaging: Consumer, Bulk
Brands:
Carolina Choice
Flowing Wells
Flowing Wells Natural Water
Kist
Spingtime
Springtime Natural Artesian Water

12514 **Southern Brown Rice**
P.O.Box 185
Weiner, AR 72479 870-684-2354
Fax: 870-684-2239 800-421-7423
office@hoguefarms.com
www.southernbrownrice.com
Processor of organically grown rice bran and flour; also, long, medium and short grain rice including basmati, brown, wild and wild blend
Manager: Bill Weeks
Estimated Sales: $740000
Number Employees: 5-9
Sq. footage: 14000

12515 **Southern California Brewing Company**
833 Torrance Blvd
Suite 105
Torrance, CA 90502-1733 310-329-8881
Fax: 310-516-7989
thebrewer@angelcitybrewing.com
www.angelcitybrewing.com
Processor of seasonal beer, ale, stout, lager and pilsner
President/CEO: Michael Bowe
Vice President: Ray Mathys
Estimated Sales: $550,000
Number Employees: 3
Type of Packaging: Consumer, Food Service
Brands:
Bear Country Bavarian
Bock
California Light Blonde
Old Red Eye
Winter Wonder

12516 **Southern Delight Gourmet Foods**
1621 Scottsville Rd
Bowling Green, KY 42104 270-782-9943
Fax: 270-843-7544 866-782-9943
info@southern-delight.com
www.southern-delight.com
Gourmet sauces, gourmet marinades, gourmet salsas, gourmet seasonings, gourmet gift sets
Owner: Bart Anderson
Estimated Sales: $ 3 - 5 Million
Number Employees: 1-4
Type of Packaging: Consumer

12517 **Southern Farms Fish Processors**
103 W 26th Avenue
Kansas City, MO 64116-3060 870-355-2594
Fax: 870-355-4024 800-264-2594
Processor of frozen catfish fillets, nuggets, strips, tidbits and breaded
President: John Gentry
Type of Packaging: Consumer, Food Service
Brands:
Springwater Farms

12518 **Southern Fish & Oyster Company**
1 Eslava St
Mobile, AL 36603 251-438-2408
Fax: 251-432-7773
Seafood, oysters
Owner: Ralph Atkins
Estimated Sales: $ 1 - 3 Million
Number Employees: 10-19

12519 **(HQ)Southern Flavoring Company**
1330 Norfolk Ave
Bedford, VA 24523 540-586-8565
Fax: 540-586-8568 800-765-8565
service@southernflavoring.com
www.southernflavoring.com
Processor of liquid food flavorings
President: E Thomas Messier
Vice President: John Messier
VP Marketing: John Messier
Estimated Sales: $5000000
Number Employees: 10-19
Sq. footage: 35000
Parent Co: Southern Flavoring
Type of Packaging: Consumer, Private Label, Bulk
Brands:
Clapier Mill
Happy Home

12520 **Southern Gardens CitrusProcessing**
1820 County Road 833
Clewiston, FL 33440 863-983-3030
Fax: 863-983-3060 www.southerngardens.com
Processor of citrus juices, concentrates, blends and ingredients
President: Robert Baker Jr
Finance Executive: Ginny Pena
VP Marketing: Charles Lucas
Number Employees: 100-249
Parent Co: US Sugar Corporation
Type of Packaging: Bulk

12521 **Southern Gold Honey CompAny**
3015 Brown Rd
Vidor, TX 77662 409-768-1645
Fax: 409-768-1009 808-899-2494
Processor, exporter and wholesaler/distributor of honey and specialty items including pecan cream honey and fruit flavored honeys; also, beeswax and candles; gift items available
Owner: Gretchen Horn
Estimated Sales: Less than $500,000
Number Employees: 20-49
Type of Packaging: Consumer, Private Label
Brands:
Southern Gold Honey

12522 **Southern Heritage Coffee Company**
6555 E 30th St Ste F
Indianapolis, IN 46219
Fax: 317-543-0757 800-486-1198
kevin@heritage-coffee.com
www.coppermooncoffee.com
Processor, importer, exporter and contract roaster of coffee including house blends and gourmet, liquid concentrate, espresso, instant cappuccino, pads, hotel in-room filter packed coffees
Manager: Doug Bachman
CEO: Kevin Daw
Sales Director: Kevin Daw
Operations Manager: Dick Middleton
Purchasing Manager: Tom Oldridge
Number Employees: 20-49
Sq. footage: 52000
Type of Packaging: Consumer, Food Service, Private Label, Bulk
Brands:
Coffee Scapes
Espresso Caruso
Espresso Maria
Heritage Espresso Pods
Heritage Select
Mugshots
SORENGETI COFFEES
Safari Blend Liquid Coffee
Santa's Favorite
Select Blend In-Room Coffee
Southern Heritage
World Coffee Safari Gourmet

12523 **Southern Ice Cream Specialties**
1058 King Industrial Dr
Marietta, GA 30062 770-428-0452
Fax: 770-426-5441
Processor of ice cream novelties
Manager: Craig McDufie
Plant Manager: Kevin Vondusaar
Number Employees: 100-249
Parent Co: Kroger Company
Type of Packaging: Consumer, Private Label
Brands:
Healthy Indulgence
Texas Gold

12524 **Southern Minnesota BeetSugar Cooperative**
P.O.Box 500
Renville, MN 56284 320-329-8167
Fax: 320-329-3252 info@smbsc.com
www.smbsc.com
Manufacturer of molasses and sugar. The company has acquired Holly Sugar Corporation
President: John Richmond
VP Finance: Jeff Plathe
Operations: Darvin Hauptli
VP Operations: Mark Suhr
Estimated Sales: $202.7 Million
Number Employees: 500-999
Type of Packaging: Consumer, Bulk

12525 **Southern Minnesota BeetSugar Cooperative**
P.O.Box 500
Renville, MN 56284 320-329-8167
Fax: 320-329-3252 info@smbsc.com
www.smbsc.com
Manufacturer of sugar beets.
President: John Richmond
Operations: Darvin Hauptli
Estimated Sales: Under $500,000
Number Employees: 1-4

12526 **Southern Packing Corporation**
4004 Battlefield Blvd S
Chesapeake, VA 23322 757-421-2131
Fax: 757-421-3633
Processor and packer of beef, pork and veal
President: H Brooke
VP: B Brooke
Estimated Sales: $ 50 - 100 Million
Number Employees: 20-49
Type of Packaging: Consumer, Food Service, Bulk
Brands:
Cavalier

12527 **Southern Peanut Company**
P.O.Box 160
Dublin, NC 28332-0160 910-862-2136
Fax: 910-862-8076 www.peanutprocessors.com
Processor of peanuts including in shell, raw shelled, blanched redskins, peanut granules, oil & dry roasted peanuts and peanut butter.
President: Houston Brisson
Plant Manager: Luke Clearman
Estimated Sales: $11098380
Number Employees: 10-19
Sq. footage: 180000
Parent Co: Peanut Processors
Type of Packaging: Consumer, Food Service, Bulk

12528 **Southern Popcorn Company**
1892 East Brooks Road
Memphis, TN 38118-6608 901-362-5238
Fax: 901-888-0230
Popcorn, jellies, dessert toppings
President: Murrey Watkins
Estimated Sales: $5-10 Million
Number Employees: 10-19

12529 **Southern Pride Catfish Company**
2025 1st Ave Ste 900
Seattle, WA 98121
Fax: 334-624-8224 800-343-8046
info@americanprideseafoods.com
www.southernpride.net
Processor and exporter of farm-raised catfish
President: Joe Glover
Quality Control: Alice Moore
VP Sales: Randy Rhodes
Public Relations: Mary Hand
Operations Manager: Bobby Collins
Number Employees: 500-999
Type of Packaging: Consumer, Food Service, Private Label
Brands:
SOUTHERN PRIDE

12530 **Southern Ray's Foods**
PO Box 402552
Miami Beach, FL 33140-0552 800-972-8237
Fax: 914-833-5009 ray@southernrays.com
www.southernrays.com
Processor and exporter of apple wine and maple teriyaki marinades; also, barbecue sauces including southern style, three pepper, honey and orange, island pepper, roasted and smoked garlic and ginger, etc
Owner: Steve Hasday
Type of Packaging: Consumer, Food Service, Private Label
Brands:
Southern Ray's

12531 **Southern Roasted Nuts**
PO Box 508
Fitzgerald, GA 31750-0508 912-423-5616
Fax: 912-423-6550
Roasted nuts
President: Allen Conger
Estimated Sales: $ 10-24.9 Million
Number Employees: 40

12532 **Southern Seafood Distributors**
26400 Buford Creel Rd
Franklinton, LA 70438 985-839-6220
Fax: 985-839-6297
Seafood
Owner: Jackie Creel
Estimated Sales: $ 1 - 3 Million
Number Employees: 1-4

12533 **Southern Shell Fish Company**
P.O.Box 97
Harvey, LA 70059-0097 504-341-5631
Fax: 504-341-5635
Processor, canner and exporter of crabmeat, oysters and shrimp
Manager: Dennis Skrmetta
Sales Manager: H Burke Jr
Plant Manager: Golden Boutte
Estimated Sales: $1400000
Number Employees: 1-4
Parent Co: Deepsouth Packing Company
Type of Packaging: Consumer, Food Service, Private Label
Brands:
Blue Plate
Dunbar
Gulf Kist
House of Windsor
Pride New Orleans

12534 **Southern Shellfish**
120 Johnny Mercer Boulevard
Savannah, GA 31410-2142 912-897-3650
Fax: 912-897-6036
Seafood, shellfish

12535 **Southern Snow Manufacturing**
103 W W St
Belle Chasse, LA 70037 504-393-8967
Fax: 504-393-0112 snowmfg@gs.net
www.southernsnow.com
Manufacturer and exporter of artificial concentrates including colors and flavors; also, ice block shavers
President: Bubby Wendling
Marketing: Danielle Havnen
Estimated Sales: $1500000
Number Employees: 10-19
Sq. footage: 10000
Brands:
Southern Snow

12536 **Southern Style Nuts**
114 N Houston Ave
Denison, TX 75021-3013 903-463-3161
info@squirrelbrand.com
www.southernstylenuts.com
Processor of roasted and blended nuts including snack mixes, hot and honey roasted peanuts, confectionery pecans and almonds and sweet and salty cashews
President: Michael Kurilecz
VP: Virgil Williamson
Estimated Sales: $54,000
Number Employees: 2
Type of Packaging: Consumer, Food Service, Private Label, Bulk
Brands:
Roann's Confections
Southern Style Nuts
Squirrel Brand

12537 **Southern Tea Company**
1267 Cobb Industrial Dr
Marietta, GA 30066 770-428-5555
Fax: 770-427-7019
Tea
Manager: John Langston
VP Sales/Marketing: Bruce Klodt
Estimated Sales: Under $500,000
Number Employees: 100-249
Type of Packaging: Private Label, Bulk

12538 **Southernfood Specialties**
4300 Bankers Cir # A
Atlanta, GA 30360-2738 770-447-4600
Fax: 770-447-0406 800-255-5323
customerservice@southernfoodspecialties.
www.southernfoodspecialties.com
Cookies, biscuits, cheese dips and toffee
Estimated Sales: $ 5 - 10 Million
Number Employees: 20-49
Brands:
Cheese Tabs
Delicias Toffee
Southernfood Specialties
Tabasco
Wesley's Kitchen
Willingham Manor

12539 **Southside Seafood Company**
1544 Forest Pkwy
Morrow, GA 30260 404-366-6172
Fax: 404-366-6178 www.southsideseafood.com
Seafood
President: Robert Lee
Estimated Sales: $ 3 - 5 Million
Number Employees: 10-19

12540 **Southtowns Seafood & Meats**
P.O. Box 1956
Blasdell, NY 14219-0156 716-824-4900
Fax: 716-822-8216
Processor and of beef, pork, lamb, veal, poultry and frozen seafood; serving the food service market
Manager: David Norton
Director (Meat): William Mutton
Estimated Sales: $ 50 - 100 Million
Number Employees: 20-49
Type of Packaging: Food Service, Private Label

12541 **Southwest Canners of Texas**
617 Industrial Dr
Nacogdoches, TX 75964 936-569-9737
Fax: 936-569-7019 www.swcanners.com
Canner of soft drinks
President/CEO: Jack Tigner
Chairman of the Board: Don Mapel
CFO: Jennifer Morris
Quality Control: Keith Thompson
Plant Manager: Rodman Reed
Estimated Sales: $ 30-50 Million
Number Employees: 65
Type of Packaging: Consumer, Food Service
Brands:
Coke

12542 **Southwest Nut Co.**
P.O.Box 553
Fabens, TX 79838 915-764-4949
Fax: 888-593-1262 info@southwestnut.com
www.southwestnut.com
Pecans.
Sq. footage: 50000

12543 **Southwest Specialty Food**
700 N Bullard Ave
Goodyear, AZ 85338 623-931-3131
Fax: 623-931-9931 800-536-3131
southwest@asskickin.com www.asskickin.com
Makers of gourmet hot sauce and other fine products such as hot sauces, salsas, snacks, gift sets, marinades/sauces, chili mixes/spices, beverages and condiments.
Owner: Jeff Jacobs
Estimated Sales: Below $ 5 Million
Number Employees: 5-9
Type of Packaging: Private Label
Brands:
Banditos Salsas
Candy Ass
Habanero Products From Hell
Seasonings From Hell
Spontaneous Combustion

12544 **Southwest Spirit**
701 Buford Drive
Socorro, NM 87801-4019 800-838-0773
Fax: 505-838-0177 info@swspirit.com
www.swspirit.com
Salsas
Co-Owner: Cynthia Fowler
Co-Owner: Jim Fowler
Type of Packaging: Consumer

12545 **Southwestern Wisconsin Dairy Goat Products**
P.O.Box 103
Mt Sterling, WI 54645-0103 608-734-3151
Fax: 608-734-3810 mtsterling@mwt.net
www.buygoatcheese.com
Processor of raw goat's milk cheeses including cheddar, feta, pasteurized country jack and pasteurized no salt cheddar; also, goat's milk butter; raw milk sharp cheddar; raw milk mild cheddar; pasteurized cheddar; rae milk organiccheddar; fresh Jack flavors: tomato and basil, jalapeno pepper, chive, dill, garlic, onion
Manager: Shannon Adams
Marketing/Sales: Patricia Lund
Plant Manager: Al Bekkum
Estimated Sales: $1946722
Number Employees: 10-19
Number of Brands: 1
Number of Products: 13
Sq. footage: 2450
Type of Packaging: Consumer, Food Service, Private Label, Bulk
Brands:
Kickapoo of Wisconsin
Mt. Sterling Cheese Co.

12546 **Sovena USA**
1 Olive Grove Street
Rome, NY 13441 315-797-7070
Fax: 315-797-6981
customerservice@sovenausa.com
www.sovenagroup.com
Manufacturer of domestic edible oils including olive, corn, soybean, peanut and salad; importer of olive oil
CEO: Steve Mandia
CFO: Dave Lofgren
VP: Bert Mandia
VP Sales/Marketing: Mark Mottit

Estimated Sales: $12.7 Million
Number Employees: 80
Sq. footage: 15000
Brands:
CLIO POMACE
CLIO PURE
GEM 100%
GEM BLENDED
GEM EXTRA

12547 Sow's Ear Winery
303 Coastal Rd
Brooksville, ME 04617 207-326-4649
Wines
President: Thomas Hoey
Estimated Sales: $20,000
Number Employees: 5-9

12548 Soy Vay Enterprises
6223 Highway 9
Felton, CA 95018 831-335-3824
Fax: 831-335-3589 800-600-2077
support@soyvay.com www.soyvay.com
Teriyaki, salad dressing and marinade, hoisin and garlic-based sauce
President/Owner: Eddy Scher
Estimated Sales: $ 1 - 3 Million
Number Employees: 1-4
Type of Packaging: Consumer, Food Service, Private Label
Brands:
Cha-Cha Chinese Chicken Dressing
Chinese Marinade
Island Teriyaki
Soy Vay Veri-Veri Teriyaki

12549 SoyLife Division
3300 Edinborough Way # 712
Edina, MN 55435-5963 952-920-7700
Fax: 952-920-7704 soylife@schoutenusa.com
www.frutarom.com
Soy isoflavone, nutraceutical ingredients
President: Laurent Leduc
Estimated Sales: Less than $500,000
Number Employees: 5-9

12550 SoyNut Butter Company
4220 Commercial Way
Glenview, IL 60025 800-288-1012
Fax: 847-635-6801 www.soynutbutter.com
Peanut butter substitute, gluten, nut & peanut free snacks, gluten free corn crumbs.
Type of Packaging: Consumer, Food Service

12551 SoyTex
609 Eagle Rock Ave
West Orange, NJ 07052-2903 973-243-1899
Fax: 973-243-0800 888-769-8391
soytexinfo@soytex.com soytex.com
Manufacturer and sell meat substitution products made from high quality soy protein concentrate using modern extrusion technology.
President: Joseph Nazarian
VP: Tirdad Zandieh

12552 Soyfoods of America
1091 Hamilton Rd
Duarte, CA 91010 626-358-3836
Fax: 626-358-4136 www.soyfoodsusa.com
Processor of soy milk and yuba; also, regular and marinated tofu, cultured soy beverage, bulk soymilk
President/Owner: Kanin Lee
Estimated Sales: $3 Million
Number Employees: 27
Sq. footage: 15000
Type of Packaging: Consumer, Food Service, Private Label, Bulk
Brands:
Furama
Soywise

12553 Soylent Brand
PO Box 165475
Irving, TX 75016-5475 972-255-4747
pinegap@flashnet.com
www.solvent.com
Salsa
President/CEO: Jack Veach
CFO: Fred Harper
Vice President: Morris Woodall
Research & Development: R Michael MacGregor
Quality Control: James Valikont, Jr.
Sales Director: Dana Davidson
Operations/Production: Lynne Wainman
Plant Manager: Robert Roggers
Number Employees: 10-19
Number of Brands: 1
Number of Products: 6
Sq. footage: 5500
Parent Co: Solvent Interntional
Type of Packaging: Private Label
Brands:
Guacamole Salad
Salsa Picante
Tex-Mex
Verde

12554 Spanarkel Company
72 W Sylvania Ave # B
Neptune City, NJ 07753-6733 732-775-4144
Fax: 732-775-3598 info@aol.com
Manufacturer of gourmet sauces, broker of packaging components
President: John Spanarkel
VP: James Spanarkel
Estimated Sales: $500,000-$1 Million
Number Employees: 10-19
Parent Co: Sparks Sales Company
Type of Packaging: Private Label, Bulk
Brands:
Spanarkel

12555 (HQ)Spangler Candy Company
P.O.Box 71
Bryan, OH 43506 419-636-4221
Fax: 419-636-3695 888-636-4221
info@spanglercandy.com
www.spanglercandy.com
Makes lollipops, candy canes and circus peanuts
President: Kirk Vashaw
CEO: Dean Spangler
CFO: Bill Martin
CEO: Dean L Spangler
Marketing Director: Jim Knight
VP Sales: Denny Gunter
Operations Manager: Steve Kerr
Number Employees: 500-999
Sq. footage: 500000
Other Locations:
Spangler Candy Co.
Bryan OH
Brands:
ASTRO POPS
CANE CLASSICS
DUM DUM POPS
PICTURE POPS
SAF-T-POPS
SPANGLER CANDY CANES
SPANGLER CHOCOLATES
SPANGLER CIRCUS PEANUTS

12556 Spangler Vineyards
491 Winery Ln
Roseburg, OR 97471-9365 541-679-9654
Fax: 541-679-3888 info@spanglervineyards.com
www.spanglervineyards.com
Wines
Co-Owner: Patrick Spangler
Co-Owner: Loree Spangler
Winemaker: Leonard Postles
Estimated Sales: Less than $500,000
Number Employees: 1-4
Type of Packaging: Private Label
Brands:
Spangler Wineyards

12557 Spanish Gardens Food Manufacturing
2301 Metropolitan Ave
Kansas City, KS 66106 913-831-4242
www.spanishgardens.com
Processor of taco shells, sauce, spices, tortilla chips and corn and flour tortillas
President: Norma Jean Miller
VP: Jean Miller
Estimated Sales: $1300000
Number Employees: 20-49
Sq. footage: 40000
Type of Packaging: Consumer, Food Service, Bulk

12558 Sparboe Companies
2183 E 11th Street
Los Angeles, CA 90021-2802 213-626-7538
info@sparboe.com
www.sparboe.com
Processor of fresh and frozen eggs; exporter of eggs and butter; wholesaler/distributor of butter, frozen fruits, cheeses and oils; serving the food service market
President: Bob Sparboe
Vice President: Beth Fechnell
Estimated Sales: $20-50 Million
Number Employees: 20-49
Sq. footage: 50000
Type of Packaging: Food Service, Private Label, Bulk
Brands:
Bes Tex
Except Mix

12559 Sparkling Spring Water Company
700 N Deerpath Drive
Vernon Hills, IL 60061-1802 847-247-5359
Fax: 847-247-5800 800-772-7554
kknuth@sswc.com www.sparklingspring.com
Bottled water-drinking, distilled, spring, fluoridated and infant
President: Warner Tillman
Vice President: George Lucas
Marketing Director: Mark Hollingsworth
Operations Manager: Ray Branaman
Estimated Sales: $ 10-100 Million
Number Employees: 50
Type of Packaging: Consumer, Food Service, Private Label, Bulk
Brands:
Baby's Own
Pure Distilled
Sparkling Spring

12560 Sparkling Water Distributors
PO Box 695
Merrick, NY 11566-0695 516-867-8291
Fax: 516-377-1228 800-277-2755
signaturebeverage@gmail.com
signaturebeverage.net
Processor of sparkling and spring water, root beer and black cherry and cream soda, diet root beer, diet black cherry, iced tea, lemonade, grape soda, raspberry lime rickey, orange soda
President: Mark Eisenberg
VP: Rebecca Scott
Sales Manager: Richard Stern
Estimated Sales: $1 Million
Number Employees: 5
Sq. footage: 5000
Type of Packaging: Food Service, Private Label

12561 Sparrer Sausage Company
4325 W Ogden Ave
Chicago, IL 60623 773-762-3334
Fax: 773-521-9368 800-666-3287
info@sparrers.com www.sparrers.com
Purveyor of high quality gourmet, deli, appetizer and snack sausage products.
President/Owner: Brian Graves
VP: Daniel Coyle
National Accounts Manager: Duane Dudek
Operations: Brian Graves
Purchasing: Daniel Sala
Estimated Sales: $22772607
Number Employees: 50-99
Type of Packaging: Consumer, Food Service, Private Label, Bulk

12562 Sparta Foods
1565 1st Ave NW
Saint Paul, MN 55112 651-697-5500
Fax: 651-697-0600 800-700-0809
www.thsinc.com
Corn chips, salsa, tortillas and barbecue sauce
VP: Eric Stack
Quality Control: Cris Hold
COO: Jose Flores
CEO: John Johnson
CFO: John Smith
Marketing Director: Rob Wood
Estimated Sales: $ 25-49.9 Million
Number Employees: 100-249
Type of Packaging: Private Label, Bulk

12563 Spartan Imports
837 Prescott Ave
Endicott, NY 13760 607-785-0239

Wholesalers of food and groceries
President: George Anastos
Estimated Sales: $190,000
Number Employees: 2

12564 **Spaten Beer**
4621 Little Neck Parkway
Little Neck, NY 11362 718-281-1912
sna@spatennorthamerica.com
www.spatenusa.com
beer

12565 **Spaten West**
284 Harbor Way
South San Francisco, CA 94080 650-794-0800
Fax: 650-794-9567 spaten@spatenusa.com
www.spatenusa.com
Beer
President: Chris Hildebrandt
CFO: Erfried Besch
Estimated Sales: $ 10-20 Million
Number Employees: 20-49
Brands:
Spaten

12566 **Spaulding Sales**
8700 N 2nd St # 202
Brighton, MI 48116-1296 810-229-4166
Fax: 810-227-4218
Cheese
President: Pat Spaulding
Estimated Sales: $500,000-$1 Million
Number Employees: 1-4

12567 **Spear Packing**
25 Home News Row
New Brunswick, NJ 08901-3645 732-247-4212
Beverages
President: John Ciullo
Estimated Sales: $ 50-100 Million
Number Employees: 50

12568 **SpecialTeas**
2 Reynolds Street
Norwalk, CT 06855-1015 203-866-1522
Fax: 203-375-6820 888-365-6983
service@specialteas.com www.specialteas.com
Gourmet tea
Managing Director: Juergen Link
Estimated Sales: $ 5-10 Million
Number Employees: 5-9

12569 **(HQ)Specialty Bakers**
450 S State Rd
Marysville, PA 17053 717-957-2131
Fax: 717-957-0156 800-233-0778
ladyfingers@specialtybakers.com
www.sbiladyfingers.com
Manufacturer and exporter of sponge, snack and angel food cakes, lady fingers, dessert shells, French twirls and jelly rolls
President: John Piotrowski
COO: James Wilson
CEO: John Plotrowski
Estimated Sales: $100+ Million
Number Employees: 100-249
Type of Packaging: Consumer, Private Label
Other Locations:
Specialty Bakers
Marysville PA
Specialty Bakers
Lititz PA
Specialty Bakers
Dunkirk NY
Brands:
Specialty

12570 **Specialty Brands**
4200 E Cncours Drive #100
Ontario, CA 91764 909-477-4700
Fax: 909-477-4600 800-782-1180
www.windsorfoods.com
Processor of frozen foods including tortillas, tamales, burritos, taquitos, appetizers and pastas
President: Patrick O'Ray
Senior VP: Chris Meyer
Quality Control: Mike Cramer
Marketing: Tim Shea
Sales: Mark Dueshane
Operations: Jim Meiers
Estimated Sales: $ 20 - 50 Million
Number Employees: 50-99
Parent Co: FoodBrands America
Type of Packaging: Consumer, Food Service, Private Label, Bulk
Brands:
BUTCHER BOY
FRED'S FOR STARTERS
JOSE OLE
POSADA
ROTANELLI'S

12571 **Specialty Brands**
P.O.Box 796
Carthage, MO 64836-0796 417-358-8104
Fax: 417-358-5323 www.windsorfoods.com
Processor of frozen Italian specialties including lasagna, meat balls, ravioli and spaghetti sauce
Manager: Charlie Smith
Plant Manager: Joe Henry
Purchasing Agent: Arthur Meneola
Estimated Sales: $ 50 - 100 Million
Number Employees: 100-249
Sq. footage: 47000
Parent Co: FoodBrands America
Type of Packaging: Consumer, Food Service
Brands:
Rotanelli

12572 **Specialty Brands of America**
1400 Old Country Rd # 103
Westbury, NY 11590-5119 516-997-6969
Fax: 516-997-7299 info@sbamerica.com
www.sbamerica.com
Sugar-free syrup, pure maple syrup, flatbreads, crackers, chowder, all-natural coating mix
President: Dominique Bastien
Sales Director: Mischell Amarado
Estimated Sales: $ 10-20 Million
Number Employees: 20-49
Sq. footage: 15000
Parent Co: Specialty Brands of America
Type of Packaging: Consumer, Food Service, Bulk
Brands:
Cary's
Dixie Fry
New York Flatbreads
O.T.C.
Thelma's

12573 **Specialty Cheese Company**
430 N Main St
Reeseville, WI 53579 920-927-3888
Fax: 920-927-3200 800-367-1711
scci@specialcheese.com
www.specialcheese.com
Cheese packaging
President: Paul Scharfman
Estimated Sales: $ 2.5-5 Million
Number Employees: 50-99
Type of Packaging: Private Label
Brands:
Hem
Lavacarica
Rich Cow

12574 **Specialty Coffee Roasters**
1300 SW 10th St
Suite 2
Delray Beach, FL 33444
Fax: 800-805-4422 800-253-9363
sales@specialtycoffeeroasters.com
www.specialtycoffeeroasters.com
Processor, packer and importer of gourmet coffees; exporter of gourmet coffees
President: Gabriela Harvey
Estimated Sales: $300,000
Number Employees: 3
Sq. footage: 5000
Parent Co: MGH Holdings Corporation
Type of Packaging: Consumer, Food Service, Private Label, Bulk
Brands:
Shalina

12575 **Specialty Commodities**
1530 47th St N
Fargo, ND 58102 701-282-8222
www.specialtycommodities.com
Supplier of dried fruits, legumes, nuts, seeds and spices.

12576 **Specialty Enzymes**
13591 Yorba Ave
Chino, CA 91710-5071 909-613-1660
Fax: 909-613-1663 info@specialtyenzymes.com
www.specialtyenzymes.com
Enzymes and enzyme blends
President: Vasant Rathi
Marketing Director: Gabrielle Sill
Vice President: Larry Schwartz
Technical Service Manager: Vickie Lentner
Estimated Sales: Below $ 1 Million
Number Employees: 20-49
Type of Packaging: Bulk

12577 **Specialty Food America**
5055 Huffman Mill Rd
Hopkinsville, KY 42240 270-889-0017
888-881-1633
customerservice@specialtyfoodamerica.com
www.specialtyfoodamerica.com
Processor of herbs and spices; cooking related supplies and contract packaging
Owner: Tom Marshall
Estimated Sales: Below $ 5 Million
Number Employees: 1-4
Sq. footage: 1200
Type of Packaging: Consumer, Private Label
Brands:
Lucini Honestete
Sonoma Syrups

12578 **(HQ)Specialty Foods Group**
21 Enterprise Parkway, 4th Floor
Hampton, VA 23666 757-952-1200
Fax: 757-952-1201 800-238-0020
www.smgmeats.com
Manufacturer of meat
President and CEO: Bonita Then
CFO: Steven Wright
VP/ General Manager: Kenneth Schissler
Marketing Manager: Laura Luth
Estimated Sales: $273 Million
Number Employees: 25
Number of Products: 12
Type of Packaging: Consumer, Food Service, Private Label, Bulk
Other Locations:
SFG Production Plant
Owensboro KY
SFG Production Plant
Humboldt IA
SFG Production Plant
Chicago IL
SFG Production Plant
Williamston NC
Brands:
ALPINE LACE
FIELDS
FISCHERS
LIGURIA
MICKELBERRY
MOSEY'S
NATHAN'S FAMOUS
SWIFT PREMIUM
WILLIAM FISCHER DELI MEATS

12579 **Specialty Foods International**
304 Eureka Drive NE
Atlanta, GA 30305-4256 404-816-8268
Fax: 404-844-9155
jpeters@specialtyfoodsintl.com
www.specialtyfoodsintl.com
Olive oil

12580 **Specialty Foods South**
P.O.Box 13615
Charleston, SC 29422-3615 843-766-2580
Fax: 843-766-2580 800-538-0003
www.charlestonfavorites.com
Gourmet foods
Owner: James Hagood
Estimated Sales: Under $500,000
Number Employees: 1-4
Type of Packaging: Private Label, Bulk

12581 **Specialty Industrial Products**
PO Box 18390
Spartanburg, SC 29318-8390 864-579-6800
Fax: 864-579-6812 800-747-9001
Processor of chemicals including surfactants and emulsifiers
VP/General Manager: Gary Dowell
VP Sales: Jim Heyward
Estimated Sales: $10-20 Million
Number Employees: 50-99
Sq. footage: 60000

12582 **Specialty Ingredients**
1130 W. Lake Cook Road
Suite 320
Buffalo Grove, IL 60089 847-419-9595
Fax: 847-419-9547 sales@ingredientsinc.com
www.ingredientsinc.com
Dehydrated/whole/starch potato products, soy based ingredients, dairy ingredients, food acids and salts, and frozen & dehydrated vegetables.
Sales: Jim Stewart

12583 **Specialty Ingredients**
P.O.Box 474
Watertown, WI 53094-0474 920-261-4229
Fax: 920-261-0443
Processor of liquid sugar
Manager: Lonnie Schuett
Estimated Sales: $ 3 - 5 Million
Number Employees: 10-19
Type of Packaging: Bulk

12584 **Specialty Minerals**
9 Highland Ave
Bethlehem, PA 18017 610-861-3400
Fax: 610-882-1570 800-801-1031
jayesty@SpecialtyMinerals.com
www.mineralstech.com
Manufacturer, sellers and exporters of food and pharmaceutical grades of precipitated calcium carbonate, ground limestone and talc
Chairman: Paul Saueracker
Human Resources: Gary Duckwall
Commercial Manager: Jay Esty
Number Employees: 50-99
Parent Co: Minerals Technologies
Type of Packaging: Private Label
Other Locations:
SMI Mineral Plant
Adams MA
SMI Mineral Plant
Canann CT
SMI Mineral Plant
Barretts MT
SMI Mineral Plant
Lucerne Valley CA
Brands:
ALBAGLOS
JETCOAT
OPACARB
PCC

12585 **Specialty Products**
13525 Hummel Rd
Cleveland, OH 44142 216-362-1050
Fax: 216-362-6506 luis.granja@gortons.com
www.gortons.com
Processor and exporter of breading batter
Manager: Luis Granja
Controller: Sue Spisak
Specialty Products: Luis Granja
Plant Manager: Luis Granja
Estimated Sales: $10-20 Million
Number Employees: 20-49
Parent Co: Gorton's
Type of Packaging: Food Service, Private Label, Bulk

12586 **Specialty Rice Marketing**
1000 W 1st St
Brinkley, AR 72021-9000 870-734-1233
Fax: 870-734-1237 800-467-1233
info@dellarice.com www.dellarice.com
Processor, miller and exporter of five types of rice
Manager: Ojus Ajmara
General Manager: Glenda Hilsdon
Estimated Sales: $800,000
Number Employees: 10-19
Sq. footage: 8000
Brands:
Della
Della Gourmet Rice
Gourmet Basmati Rice
Jasmine

12587 **Specialty Steak Service**
1717 East 12th St
Erie, PA 16512 814-452-2281
Fax: 814-459-1213 comments@curtze.com
www.curtze.com
Processor of meat
President: Bruce Kern Sr
President: Scott Keim
Estimated Sales: $88900000
Number Employees: 100-249
Sq. footage: 75000
Parent Co: C.A. Curtze Company
Type of Packaging: Food Service

12588 **Speco**
3946 Willow St
Schiller Park, IL 60176 847-678-4240
Fax: 847-678-8037 800-541-5415
sales@speco.com www.speco.com
Manufacturer and exporter of meat cutting equipment including meat and mincer knives and bone collector systems
President: Craig Hess
Office Manager: Sue Ryan
Sales Manager: Steve Jacob
Production Manager: Clarence Hoffman
Maintenance Supervisor: Ron Schulmeister
Estimated Sales: $7 Million
Number Employees: 49
Sq. footage: 25000
Brands:
Superior
Triumph

12589 **Spectrum Organic Products**
5341 Old Redwood Hwy.
Suite 400
Petaluma, CA 94954 707-778-8900
Fax: 707-765-1026 800-995-2705
spectrumorganics@worldpantry.com
www.spectrumorganics.com
Manufacturer of natural oils and condiments. The Hain Celestial Group plans to merge with this company
President/CEO: John Carroll
VP: Randall H Sias
Estimated Sales: $20-50 Million
Number Employees: 66
Type of Packaging: Private Label
Brands:
Spectrum Naturals

12590 **Spence & Company**
160 Manley St
Brockton, MA 02301 508-427-1627
Fax: 508-427-5557 salmon@spenceltd.com
www.spenceltd.com
Processor of smoked fish; importer of fish ingredients
President: Alan Spence
Estimated Sales: $4500000
Number Employees: 25
Type of Packaging: Consumer, Food Service

12591 **Spencer Packing Company**
P.O.Box 753
Washington, NC 27889-0753 252-946-4161
Fax: 252-946-4162
spencerpacking@earthlink.net
www.spencersausage.com
Processor and packer of pork
President: Harold Spencer
Estimated Sales: $1,250,000
Number Employees: 10-19

12592 **Sperry Apiaries**
15750 Highway 46
Kindred, ND 58051 701-428-3000
Honey
President: Mark Sperry
Estimated Sales: Under $500,000
Number Employees: 1-4
Number of Brands: 1
Number of Products: 1

12593 **Spice & Spice**
655 Deep Valley Dr Ste 125
Rolling Hills Estates, CA 90274 310-265-2914
Fax: 310-265-2934 866-729-7742
info@spicenspice.com www.spicenspice.com
Direct manufacturers/importers/wholesalers of bulk line of whole and ground spice products: black pepper, white pepper, cumin, cinnamon, crush chili, cinnamon stick, chili powder, granulated garlic, dry chili pods (Arbol, JaponesIndian S4's)
Owner: Anthony Dirocco
CEO: Mukesh Thakker
R & D: Nitul Unekekett
Quality Control: Nina Lukamanje
Estimated Sales: $ 5-10 Million
Number Employees: 1-4
Number of Brands: 1
Number of Products: 25
Sq. footage: 50000
Type of Packaging: Food Service, Bulk
Brands:
BOAT BRAND

12594 **Spice Advice**
2301 SE Tones Dr
Ankeny, IA 50021-8887 515-965-2711
Fax: 515-965-2801 800-247-5251
spiceadvice@achfood.com www.tones.com
Processor and exporter of spices, seasonings, dry blends and mixes including datenut rolls, cakes, sauces and gravies; importer of spices and herbs.
Manager: Doug Aldrige
Chief Information Officer: Donnie Steward
Chief Financial Officer: Jeffrey Atkins
SVP General Counsel/Corporate Secretary: Carmen Sciackitano
VP Product Development/Quality Mgmt: Pete Friedman
VP Sales/Marketing: Kenny Shortsleeve
VP Strategy & Development: Jack Straton
SVP Human Resources: Deborah Murdock
VP Operations: Bill Wells
Estimated Sales: $48,900,000
Number Employees: 500-999
Sq. footage: 750000
Parent Co: Philp Burns & Company
Type of Packaging: Consumer, Food Service, Private Label, Bulk
Brands:
Blue Ribbon
Chef's Taste
Chocolate Decors Sprinkle
Dec-A-Cake
Dromedary
Dromedary Cake Mixes
Durkee
Egg Shade Food Coloring
Fluff Marshmallow Toppings
French's
French's Dry Mixes
Good Harvest
Guiltless Gourmet
Heart-Loc
Lawler's
Lepak
Perc
Presti's
San Jacinto Spice Ranch
Spice Islands
Tone's

12595 **Spice House International Specialties**
46 Bethpage Rd
Hicksville, NY 11801-1512 516-942-7248
Fax: 516-942-7249 spicehouse@hotmail.com
www.spicehouseint.com
Manufacturer, wholesaler/distributor, exporter and importer of spices and blends, specialty foods, hot sauces, dried fruits and nuts; serving the food service market from around the world; Asia, Middle East, Europe, Thai and China.
President: Anthony Provetto
Estimated Sales: $ 5 - 10 Million
Number Employees: 5-9
Sq. footage: 4600
Type of Packaging: Consumer, Food Service, Private Label, Bulk

12596 **Spice Hunter**
184 Suburban Rd
San Luis Obispo, CA 93401-7502 805-544-4466
Fax: 805-544-9046 800-444-3061
www.cfsauer.com
Processor of dried bean soups, entree seasonings, dips, salad seasonings, Asian soups, spices and drink mixes
President/CEO: Conrad Sauer
President: Lucia Cleveland
CFO: William Ulick
Estimated Sales: $17 Million
Number Employees: 50-99
Number of Products: 200
Sq. footage: 113000
Parent Co: C.F. Sauer Company
Type of Packaging: Private Label, Bulk
Brands:
Oriental Noodle Soup
Quick & Natural Soup
Quick Pot Pasta
Savory Smoke
Simmer Kettle

Spice Hunter
Spice Hunter Spices & Herbs

12597 **Spice King Corporation**
438 El Camino Dr
Beverly Hills, CA 90212 310-836-7770
Fax: 310-836-6454
Processor, importer and exporter of custom formulated natural spices and seasonings; also, dehydrated vegetables and fruits
General Manager: James Stephens
VP: A Stern
Marketing Director: Anne Stern
Number Employees: 20-49
Sq. footage: 25000

12598 **Spice Lab**
1831 NE 41 Street
Oakland Park, PA 33308 954-275-4478
brett@thespicelab.com
www.thespicelab.com
Gourmet sea salts

12599 **Spice O' Life**
PO Box 70406
Seattle, WA 98127-0406 206-789-4195
Fax: 206-782-9339 spiceguy@spiceolife.com
www.spiceolife.com
Processor of custom blended spices
Owner: Scotty McDonell
Account Manager: Judith Jager
Advertising Manager: David Barker
Number Employees: 1-4

12600 **Spice Rack Chocolates**
10908 Courthouse Rd
Suite 102 #264
Fredericksburg, VA 22408 540-847-2063
Fax: 416-757-5183 www.spicerackchocolates.com
dark chocolates infused with hers and spices
President/Owner: Mary Schellhammer
CFO: Paul Schellhammer

12601 **Spice World**
8101 Presidents Dr
Orlando, FL 32809 407-851-9432
Fax: 407-857-7171 800-433-4979
sworld@spiceworldinc.com
www.spiceworldinc.com
Processor and exporter of nuts, custom seasoning blends and garlic including minced, chopped and packed in olive oil or water
President: Gary Caneza
General Manager: Gary Caneza
Sales: Eric Dutreil
Sales/Purchasing: Louis Hymel
Estimated Sales: $ 5 - 10 Million
Number Employees: 100-249
Sq. footage: 120000
Type of Packaging: Consumer, Food Service, Private Label, Bulk
Brands:
3-SONS
CAJUN CLASSIQUES
CHEF CUISINE
CHUBS
SPICE WORLD
SPICY-GEE

12602 **Spice of Life**
2195 S Courtenay Parkway
Merritt Island, FL 32952-4013 321-453-5727
Fax: 321-454-4482 harlanddon@aol.com
Processor and exporter of custom and standard seasoning blends for poultry, meat and seafood
President: Donna Adams
CEO: Harland Adams
Estimated Sales: Below $ 5 Million
Number Employees: 20
Sq. footage: 15000
Type of Packaging: Consumer, Food Service, Private Label, Bulk

12603 **Spiceco**
6c Terminal Way
Avenel, NJ 07001 732-499-9070
Fax: 732-499-9139 www.spice-co.com
Manufacturer of spices including basil, bay leaves, garlic, oregano, paprika, pepper, etc
President: Andy Barna
VP: James Peterkin
Estimated Sales: $11.2 Million
Number Employees: 50-99
Type of Packaging: Consumer, Food Service, Private Label, Bulk
Brands:
PRIDE OF MALABAR
PRIDE OF SHANDUNG
PRIDE OF SZEGED

12604 **Spiceland**
6604 W Irving Park Rd
Chicago, IL 60634 773-736-1000
800-352-8671
Spices
Co-Owner: Doris Stockwell
Co-Owner: Jim Stockwell
Estimated Sales: Less than $500,000
Number Employees: 1-4
Brands:
Spiceland

12605 **(HQ)Spices of Life Gourmet Coffee**
4135 Dr Mlk Blvd
Fort Myers, FL 33916 239-334-8004
Fax: 941-549-9041
Coffee
Owner: Cheryl Dejonghe
Vice President: Edward Miller
Estimated Sales: $300,000-500,000
Number Employees: 1-4

12606 **Spiech Farms**
61675 M 40
Paw Paw, MI 49079-9210 269-657-1980
Fax: 269-657-5023 www.spiechfarms.com
Concord grapes
Owner: Steve Spiech
Estimated Sales: $1 Million
Number Employees: 24
Sq. footage: 18000

12607 **(HQ)Spilke's Baking Company**
290 S 5th St
Brooklyn, NY 11211-6214 718-384-2150
Fax: 718-384-2988 redmill@aol.com
www.macaroonking.com
Processor of individually packaged macaroons and cakes including kosher
President: Arnold Badner
Estimated Sales: $ 10 - 20 Million
Number Employees: 10-19
Sq. footage: 30000
Type of Packaging: Consumer, Food Service
Brands:
Jennie
Manhattan Gourmet
Red Mill Farms

12608 **Spinelli Coffee Company**
3100 Airport Way S
Seattle, WA 98134-2116 415-821-7100
Fax: 415-821-7199
Coffee
President: Christophe Calkins
Number Employees: 10

12609 **Spinney Creek Shellfish**
2 Howell Ln
Eliot, ME 03903 207-439-2719
Fax: 207-439-7643 877-778-6727
customerservice@spinneycreek.com
www.spinneycreek.com
Seafood
President: Thomas Howell
Estimated Sales: $ 10 - 20 Million
Number Employees: 10-19

12610 **Spitz USA**
1775 Horseshoe Drive
Loveland, CO 80538-7201 970-613-9319
Fax: 970-613-9320
National Sales Manager: Roger Shantz

12611 **Splendid Specialties**
23 Pimentel Ct # B
Novato, CA 94949-5661 415-506-3000
Fax: 415-506-3002 info@tornranch.com
www.tornranch.com
Manufacturer and purveyor of gourmet specialty foods that include the finest chocolates and baked goods, and famous dried fruit and nuts from California's lush, fertile valleys.
President: Dean Morrow
Estimated Sales: $ 20 - 50 Million
Number Employees: 50-99
Brands:
Cafe Time
GiGi Baking Company
Mashuga Nuts & Cookies
Splendid Specialties Chocolates

12612 **Splendid Spreads**
1483 Auburn Court
Eagan, MN 55122 877-632-1300
Fax: 651-688-7630 877-773-2374
http://splendidspreads.com
gouret salmon spreads and toppings
President/Owner: Judy Tucker

12613 **Spoetzl Brewery**
P.O.Box 368
Shiner, TX 77984 361-594-3383
Fax: 361-594-4334 shiner@shiner.com
www.shiner.com
Shiner Bock, Shiner Blonde, Shiner Hefeweizer, Shiner Light, Shiner Bohemian Black Lager, Shiner Kosmos
Manager: Carlos Alvarez
Director Finance: Jim Bolz
Quality Control: Peter Takacs
Brewmaster: Jimmy Mauric
Brewmaster: John Hybner
Estimated Sales: $ 20 - 50 Million
Number Employees: 50-99
Parent Co: Gambrinus Company
Type of Packaging: Consumer
Brands:
Shiner Blonde
Shiner Bock
Shiner Dunkelweizen
Shiner Hefeweizen
Shiner Kolsch
Shiner Light

12614 **Spohrers Bakeries**
600 MacDade Boulevard
Collingdale, PA 19023-3804 610-532-9959
Fax: 610-532-8927
Pastries
Owner: David Olandi
Manager: Derek Everstyke
Brands:
Spohrers Bakeries

12615 **Spokandy Wedding Mints**
1412 W 3rd Ave
Spokane, WA 99201-7024 509-624-1969
Fax: 509-624-2017 www.spokandy.com
Chocolates, wedding mints, brittles, barks, saltwater taffy
President: Todd Davis
Plant Manager: Mary Ellithorp
Estimated Sales: Below $ 5 Million
Number Employees: 5-9
Type of Packaging: Private Label

12616 **Spokane Seed Company**
6019 E Alki Ave
Spokane Valley, WA 99212 509-535-3671
Fax: 509-535-0874 spokseed@spokaneseed.com
www.spokaneseed.com
Processor and exporter of peas and lentils
President: Peter Johnstone
CFO: Jeff White
Sales: Nelson Fancher
Estimated Sales: $3900000
Number Employees: 20-49
Type of Packaging: Consumer, Food Service, Bulk
Brands:
Greenpod
Rumba

12617 **SportPharma USA**
1915 Mark Court
Suite 150
Concord, CA 94520-8502 925-686-1451
Brands:
SPORTPHARMA

12618 **Sportabs International**
PO Box 492118
Los Angeles, CA 90049-8118 310-451-2625
Fax: 310-207-8526 888-814-7767
www.sportabs.com
Processor and exporter of multi-vitamin tablets
President: Richard Griswold
Estimated Sales: Under $500,000
Number Employees: 1-4
Type of Packaging: Consumer

Brands:
Spor Tabs

12619 **Sporting Colors LLC**
3630 S. Geyer Rd.
Suite 100
St. Louis, MO 63127 314-984-1000
Fax: 314-909-3300 888-394-2292
www.panerabread.com
President: William Moreton
CEO: S Jeff Schroeder
Estimated Sales: $ 1 - 3 Million
Number Employees: 20-49

12620 **Sportsmen's Cannery**
P.O.Box 1011
Winchester Bay, OR 97467-0800 541-271-3293
Fax: 541-271-9381 800-457-8048
karch@presys.com www.sportsmenscannery.com
Gourmet canned seafood products including smokehouse and gift boxes
Manager: Brandy Roelle
Secretary: Mikyale Karcher
Estimated Sales: Below $ 1 Million
Number Employees: 10-19
Brands:
Sportsmen's Cannery

12621 **Sportsmen's Cannery & Smokehouse**
182 Bayfront Loop
Winchester Bay, OR 97467 541-271-3293
Fax: 541-271-9381 800-457-8048
karch@presys.com www.sportsmenscannery.com
Processor and canner of salmon, albacore tuna, sturgeon and shellfish
Manager: Brandy Roelle
Owner: Mikayle Karcher
Number Employees: 1-4
Type of Packaging: Consumer, Private Label
Brands:
Winchester

12622 **Sportsmen's Sea Foods**
1617 Quivira Rd
San Diego, CA 92109-7801 619-224-3551
Fax: 619-224-1646 www.sportsmensseafood.com
Processor of canned fish including albacore, bonito, marlin, tuna and yellow tail
President: Tom Busalacchi
Estimated Sales: $300,000-500,000
Number Employees: 10-19

12623 **Spot Bagel Bakery**
1229 6th Ave
Seattle, WA 98101-2007 206-623-0066
Fax: 206-623-0069
Baked goods

12624 **Spotted Tavern Winery &Dodd's Cider Mill**
PO Box 175
Hartwood, VA 22471-0175 540-752-4453
Fax: 540-752-4611
Wine, sparkling cider, Virginia hard cider and fresh apple cider in season.
Owner: Cathy Harris

12625 **Spottswoode Winery**
1902 Madrona Ave
Saint Helena, CA 94574 707-963-0134
Fax: 707-963-2886
spottswoode@spottswoode.com
www.spottswoode.com
Wines
Owner: Mary Novak
VP: Peah Armstrong
National Sales/Marketing: Lindy Novak Lahr
Consumer Sales/Tours: Shanyn McDaera
Winemaker: Rosemary Cakebread
Estimated Sales: Below $ 5 Million
Number Employees: 5-9

12626 **Sprague Foods**
385 College Street E
Belleville, ON K8N 5S7
Canada 613-966-1200
Fax: 613-962-8600 info@spraguefoods.com
www.spraguefoods.com
Processor of beans, soups, beans in sauce, pasta in tomato sauce, salad dressings, and other items.
President: Roger Sprague
Number Employees: 20-49
Type of Packaging: Consumer, Food Service

12627 **Spray Dynamics**
108 Bolte Ln
Saint Clair, MO 63077 636-629-7366
Fax: 636-629-7455 800-260-7366
spray@usmo.com www.spraydynamics.com
Manufacturer and exporter of liquid and dry ingredient applicators and dispensers for food processing machinery.
Owner: Dave Holmeyer
Accounts Payable: Melanie Booher
Marketing Coordinator: Stephanie Butenhoff
Sales Representative: George Wipperfurth
Service Manager: Craig Booher
Estimated Sales: $2.5-5 Million
Number Employees: 20-49
Brands:
CLOG-FREE SLURRY SPRAY ENCOATER
DELTA DRY
DELTA LIQUID
ECONOFLO
ENHANCER
MASTER SERIES
METER MASTER
MICRO-METER AIRLESS
POWDER XPRESS
SOFT FLIGHT
UNISPENSE

12628 **Sprecher Brewing**
701 W Glendale Ave
Milwaukee, WI 53209 414-964-7837
Fax: 414-964-2462 888-650-2739
beer@sprecherbrewery.com
www.sprecherbrewery.com
Beer
President: Randal Sprecher
Production Manager: Tom Bosch
Estimated Sales: $ 20-50 Million
Number Employees: 20-49

12629 **(HQ)Spreda Group**
7410 New Lagrange Rd
Louisville, KY 40222 502-426-9411
Fax: 502-423-7531
Processor, importer and exporter of fruit and vegetable powder, tomato paste, colors, spray and vacuum dried and dehydrated fruits and vegetables, etc.; processor of apple pectin and apple juice concentrate
President: George Falk
VP: James Falk
Number Employees: 100-249
Type of Packaging: Food Service, Bulk
Brands:
Elmasu
Obi Pektin
Puccinelli
Spreda

12630 **Spring Acres Sales Company**
1280 Macedonia Rd
Spring Hope, NC 27882 252-478-5127
Fax: 252-478-5266 800-849-5436
springacres@mindspring.com
Processor of sweet potatoes including medium, large and jumbo
Owner: Cindy Joyner
VP/Sales: Norman Brown
Estimated Sales: $500,000-$1 Million
Number Employees: 1-4
Type of Packaging: Bulk
Brands:
Hernandez
Spring Acres
Tarheel

12631 **Spring Creek Natural Foods**
212 E Main St C
Spencer, WV 25276 304-927-3780
Fax: 304-927-1815 scnf@kvinet.com
www.springcreeknaturalfood.com
Tofu
President: Donald Carpenter
Estimated Sales: $ 2.5-5 Million
Number Employees: 15

12632 **Spring Glen Fresh Foods**
PO Box 518
Ephrata, PA 17522 717-733-2201
Fax: 717-738-4335 800-641-2853
www.springglen.com
Processor of soup and stew including meat, poultry and seafood; also, potato, pasta and macaroni salad, coleslaw, entrees and desserts including cobblers, parfaits, cheese, puddings, gelatin and custards
President: John Warehime
VP General Manager: Steve Piechocki
Marketing Manager: Jeff Miller
Human Resources Director: Robin Rearich
Plant Manager: Jeff Warehime
Purchasing Director: Rich Paulukow
Estimated Sales: $19200000
Number Employees: 165
Sq. footage: 45000
Parent Co: Hanover Foods Corporation
Type of Packaging: Consumer, Food Service, Private Label
Brands:
Deli Direct
Spring Glen

12633 **Spring Grove Foods**
312 S 3rd St
Miamisburg, OH 45342-2933 937-866-4311
Fax: 937-866-1410
Manufacturer of cheese, beef, pepperoni, ham, salami, sausage and bologna
President: Jerry Beale
Estimated Sales: $10 Million
Number Employees: 5-9
Sq. footage: 10000
Type of Packaging: Food Service, Private Label, Bulk

12634 **Spring Hill Farm Dairy**
136 Neck Rd
Haverhill, MA 01835-8028 978-373-3481
Fax: 978-521-0870 www.springhillwater.com
Dairy products
President: Dale F Rogers
Estimated Sales: Below $ 5 Million
Number Employees: 20-49

12635 **Spring Hill Meat Market**
P.O.Box 38
Spring Hill, KS 66083 913-592-3501
Processor of meat products
Owner: William Madison
Estimated Sales: $ 1 - 3 Million
Number Employees: 1-4
Type of Packaging: Consumer

12636 **Spring Ledge Farms**
5438 State Route 14
Dundee, NY 14837-8804 607-678-4038
Fax: 607-243-7214
Processor of fresh grapes
President: Earl Andrews
Estimated Sales: $ .5 - 1 million
Number Employees: 1-4

12637 **Spring Mountain Vineyards**
2805 Spring Mountain Rd
Saint Helena, CA 94574 707-967-4188
Fax: 707-967-2753 877-769-4637
info@springmtn.com www.springmtn.com
Processor and exporter of wines
General Manager: Tom Ferrell
Director of Marketing: Leah McEachern
Director of Sales: Brian Boswick
Director Manufacturing: Craig Becker
Estimated Sales: $2500000
Number Employees: 35
Type of Packaging: Consumer

12638 **Spring Mountain Vineyard**
2805 Spring Mountain Rd
Saint Helena, CA 94574 707-967-4188
Fax: 707-963-2753 877-769-4637
info@springmtn.com www.springmtn.com
Wines
President: Gil Nickel
Co-Owner: John Nickel
Estimated Sales: $ 3 - 5 Million
Number Employees: 5-9
Brands:
Chateau Chevalier

12639 **Spring Tree Maple Products**
28 Vernon St
Brattleboro, VT 05301-3666 802-254-8784
Fax: 802-254-8648 info@sbamerica.com
www.springtree.com

Spring Tree Maple Products, Brattleboro, Vermont is the Export and Industrial Division of Specialty Brands of America, Inc. selling pure maple syrup to corporations and major distributors.
President: Don Bastien
Estimated Sales: $ 20-50 Million
Number Employees: 5-9
Brands:
Spring Tree

12640 **Spring Water Company**
925 Cavalier Blvd
Chesapeake, VA 23323-1549 757-485-3200
Fax: 757-487-4970 800-832-0271
mdfrancesco@perriergroup.com
deerparkwater.com
Processor of bottled spring and distilled water
CFO: Kim Jefferies
General Manager: Michael Difrancesco
Plant Manager: Edgar Gaskins
Estimated Sales: $ 3 - 5 Million
Number Employees: 20-49
Sq. footage: 36500
Type of Packaging: Consumer, Food Service
Brands:
A&D Water Care
Culligan
Diamond Springs
H2o To Go
Hydrologix
Miller's
The Water Fountain
Water & Health
Water Fountain of Edenton
Yoder Dairies

12641 **Springbank Cheese Company**
201 Winniett St
Woodstock, ON N4S 6A1
Canada 519-539-7411
Fax: 519-539-0294 800-265-1973
spcheese@oxford.net www.springbankcheese.ca
Processor and packer of cheese
President: Tom Hemsworth
Estimated Sales: $2.6 Million
Number Employees: 10
Sq. footage: 6500
Brands:
Gjetost Ekte
Wensleydale Blueberry

12642 **Springdale Cheese Factory**
19104 County Hwy Ee
Richland Center, WI 53581 608-538-3213
Fax: 608-538-3212 ltorkelson@aol.com
Processor of muenster and brick cheese
President: Thomas Torkelson
Estimated Sales: $6100000
Number Employees: 35
Type of Packaging: Consumer, Food Service

12643 **Springdale Ice Cream & Beverages**
11801 Chesterdale Rd
Cincinnati, OH 45246 513-671-2790
Fax: 513-671-2864
Ice cream
Human Resources: Stacey Rose
Plant Engineer: Mike Smith
Number Employees: 100-249

12644 **Springfield Creamery**
29440 Airport Rd
Eugene, OR 97402 541-689-2911
Fax: 541-689-2915 sue@nancysyogurt.com
www.nancysyogurt.com
Processor and exporter of cultured dairy products including yogurt, cottage cheese, sour cream, cream cheese and kefir; also, soy yogurt
President: Joe Kesey
Estimated Sales: $7 Million
Number Employees: 46
Number of Brands: 1
Number of Products: 13
Sq. footage: 20000
Type of Packaging: Consumer, Food Service, Private Label, Bulk
Brands:
Nancy's
Nancy's Cottage Cheese
Nancy's Cream Cheese
Nancy's Sour Cream
Nancy's Yogurts

12645 **Springfield Smoked FishCompany**
150 Switzer Ave
Springfield, MA 01109 413-737-8693
Fax: 413-747-7360 800-327-3412
Alan@SpringfieldSmokedFish.com
www.ssfish.com
Processor of kosher foods including cream cheese spreads, pickled herring, smoked fish and whitefish, salmon and herring salads; exporter of pickled herring and smoked fish
President: Bob Axler
VP: Alan Axler
Number Employees: 38275
Sq. footage: 8000
Type of Packaging: Consumer, Food Service, Private Label, Bulk
Brands:
AXLER'S
SPRINGFIELD

12646 **Springhill Cellars**
2920 NW Scenic Dr
Albany, OR 97321 541-928-1009
Fax: 541-928-1009 springhill@proaxis.com
www.springhillcellars.com
Wines
President: Michael Lain
Estimated Sales: Less than $500,000
Number Employees: 3
Brands:
Springhill

12647 **Springhill Farms**
PO Box 10000
Neepawa, NB R0J 1H0
Canada 204-476-3393
Fax: 204-476-3791
Processor of fresh and frozen pork
General Manager: William Teichroew
Number Employees: 400
Type of Packaging: Bulk
Brands:
Spring Hill Farms

12648 **Springville Meat & ColdsStorage**
268 S 100 W
Springville, UT 84663 801-489-6391
Fax: 801-491-3399
Processor of domestic and game meats including ground beef and patties, beef, poultry, lamb and buffalo; also, custom processing available
President: David Cope
VP: Ray Cope
Estimated Sales: $810,000
Number Employees: 5-9
Sq. footage: 25000
Type of Packaging: Consumer, Food Service

12649 **Sprout House**
17267 Sundance Dr
Ramona, CA 92065 760-788-7979
Fax: 760-788-4800 800-777-6887
info@sprouthouse.com www.sprouthouse.com
Sprouting seeds
President: Richard Kohn
Marketing Director: Steve Meyerowitz
Estimated Sales: $500,000
Number Employees: 1-4
Type of Packaging: Private Label
Brands:
Hemp Sprout Bag
Sprout House & Salad
Sproutman's Organic

12650 **Spruce Foods**
800 S El Camino Real
Suite 210
San Clemente, CA 92672-4274 949-366-9457
Fax: 800-708-9775 800-326-3612
bobbreen@sprucefoods.com
www.sprucefoods.com
Importer of organic grocery products
President: Bob Breen
Estimated Sales: $ 5 - 10 Million
Number Employees: 4
Number of Brands: 3
Number of Products: 160
Brands:
Lapas
Massetti
Montebello

12651 **Spruce Mountain Blueberries**
Mount Pleasant Road
PO Box 68
West Rockport, ME 04865-0068 207-236-3538
Fax: 207-236-8545
info@sprucemtnblueberries.com
Wild blueberry chutney, blueberry topping, cranberry chutney, conserves, jam, and blueberry vinegar
Owner: Martha Sholes
Estimated Sales: $75,000
Number Employees: 3
Number of Brands: 1
Number of Products: 7
Type of Packaging: Consumer, Food Service

12652 **Sprucewood Handmade Cookie Company**
PO Box 430
Warkworth, ON K0K 3K0
Canada 877-632-1300
Fax: 705-924-2626 info@sprucewoodbrands.com
www.sprucewoodbrands.com
flavored shortbread cookies and nuts
President/Owner: Mark Pollard

12653 **Spurgeon Vineyards & Winery**
16008 Pine Tree Rd
Highland, WI 53543-9602 608-929-7692
Fax: 608-929-4810 800-236-5555
info@SpurgeonVineyards.com
www.spurgeonvineyards.com
Manufacturer of wines in the following flavors; honey, cranberry, grape, sweet cherry, white and juice blend
Co-Owner: Glen Spurgeon
Co-Owner: Mary Spurgeon
Vice President: James Spurgeon
Estimated Sales: $1 Million
Number Employees: 1-4
Type of Packaging: Consumer, Private Label, Bulk
Brands:
Spurgeon Vinyards

12654 **Squab Producers of California**
409 Primo Way
Modesto, CA 95358 209-537-4744
Fax: 209-537-2037 squabbob@aol.com
www.squab.com
Processor and exporter of fresh and frozen squab, pheasant, quail, poussin and partridge
President: Robert Shipley
Estimated Sales: $ 5 - 10 Million
Number Employees: 20-49
Sq. footage: 10000
Type of Packaging: Consumer, Food Service, Private Label, Bulk
Brands:
King-Cal
Mendes Farms
SIERRA GOURMET

12655 **Squair Food Company**
1418 Newton Street
Los Angeles, CA 90021-2726 213-749-7041
Fax: 213-749-3591
http://www.sprucemtnblueberries.com
Mexican foods
President: Jerry Karrizer
Vice President: Morris Kharrazi
Estimated Sales: $1-4.9 Million
Number Employees: 1-4

12656 **Square-H Brands**
2731 S Soto St
Vernon, CA 90058-8026 323-267-4600
Fax: 323-261-7350
Pork, sausage, ham and bacon
President/ CEO: Henry Haskell
Marketing Director: Randy Strelioff
CFO: Bill Hanniegan
Quality Control: Robert Jarne
Estimated Sales: $ 50-100 Million
Number Employees: 100-249
Number of Brands: 2
Number of Products: 200

12657 **Squire Boone Village**
406 Mount Tabor Rd
New Albany, IN 47150-2207 812-941-5900
Fax: 812-941-5920 888-934-1804
www.squireboone.com
Snacks
Owner: Rick Conway
Number Employees: 50-99

12658 **Squirrel Brand Company**
113 Industrial Blvd Ste D
McKinney, TX 75069 214-585-0100
Fax: 214-585-0880 800-624-8242
info@squirrelbrand.com www.squirrelbrand.com
Nuts
President: Brent Meyer Jr
Estimated Sales: $ 5-9.9 Million
Number Employees: 1-4
Sq. footage: 40
Type of Packaging: Private Label
Brands:
Coconut Zipper
Squirrel
Squirrel Nut Caramel
Squirrel Nut Chew
Squirrel Nut Zippers

12659 **St Charles Trading**
650 N Raddant Rd
Batavia, IL 60510 630-377-0608
Fax: 630-406-1936 stc-trading@worldnet.att.net
www.stcharlestrading.com
Food ingredient distributor
President/VP Sales: Al Cicanci
CEO: William Manns
Quality Assurance Officer: Dana Capes
Operations Director: Janet Matthews
Estimated Sales: $15000000
Number Employees: 50
Sq. footage: 20000

12660 **St Mary's & Ankeny Lakes Wild Rice Company**
PO Box 3667
Salem, OR 97306 503-363-3241
Fax: 503-371-9080 info@wildriceonline.com
www.wildriceonline.com
Grower and processor of certified organic wild rice; also, nonorganic and wild rice blends available
Co-Owner: Larry Payne
Co-Owner: Sharon Jenkins-Payne
Number Employees: 1-4
Sq. footage: 3000
Parent Co: Wild & Ricey Northwest
Type of Packaging: Consumer, Food Service, Private Label, Bulk
Brands:
St. Mary's

12661 **St. Charles Trading**
19 Hawk Ridge Dr
Lake Saint Louis, MO 63367 636-625-1500
Fax: 636-625-4930 800-336-1333
stc-trading@worldnet.att.net
www.stctrading.com
Food ingredients including buttermilk powder, casein, cheese, cocoa powders, jams and jellies, freeze-dried fruits, chocolate chips, vitamins, vanilla, whey protein, nuts, ice cream mixes and dried eggs
President: Charles Wetzel
Estimated Sales: $ 10-20 Million
Number Employees: 10

12662 **St. Clair Ice Cream Company**
155 Woodward Ave Ste 3
Norwalk, CT 06854 203-853-4774
Fax: 203-857-4099 office@stclairicecream.com
www.stclairicecream.com
Special occasion ice cream and sorbet molded into a variety of shapes.
Manager: Kay Gelsman
Estimated Sales: Below $ 5 Million
Number Employees: 5-9
Brands:
St. Clair Ice Cream

12663 **St. Clair Industries**
3067 E Commercial Blvd
Ft Lauderdale, FL 33308 954-491-0400
Fax: 954-351-9082
Processor and exporter of catalyst altered water
President: Saul Rubinoff
CEO: Anne Rubinoff
Vice President: Anne Rubinoff
Estimated Sales: Less than $100,000
Number Employees: 2
Sq. footage: 5000
Type of Packaging: Consumer, Bulk
Brands:
BRIZ
WILLARD

12664 **(HQ)St. Cloud Bakery**
1408 W Saint Germain St
Saint Cloud, MN 56301 320-251-8055
Fax: 320-253-3693
Manufacturer of pies, cookies and pastries
President: Jeffery Westerlund
Estimated Sales: $29 Million
Number Employees: 10-19
Sq. footage: 2200
Type of Packaging: Consumer, Food Service, Private Label, Bulk
Brands:
LAKELAND
LAKELAND BAKED COOKIES
ST CLOUD BAKERY

12665 **St. Croix Beer Company**
363 Webster St
Saint Paul, MN 55102-3651 651-387-0708
Fax: 651-439-0221 info@stcroixbeer.com
www.stcroixbeer.com
Processor and wholesaler/distributor of lager and regular, maple and pepper ale
President: Tod Fyten
Estimated Sales: $86,000
Number Employees: 1-4
Type of Packaging: Consumer, Food Service
Brands:
Serrano
St. Croix

12666 **St. Francis Pie Shop**
PO Box 847
Clayton, CA 94517-0847 510-655-0136
Fax: 510-655-2585
Bakery
President/CEO: John Buschini
Sales Manager: Michael Combs
Estimated Sales: $ 20-50 Million
Number Employees: 50-99

12667 **St. Francis Vineyards**
100 Pythian Rd
Santa Rosa, CA 95409 707-833-4668
Fax: 707-833-1394 info@stfranciswine.com
www.stfranciswine.com
Wines
President: Joseph Martin
CFO: Patti Smith
CEO: Lloyd Canton
Marketing Director: Nan Fontaine
Production Manager: Dennis Borell
Estimated Sales: Below $ 5 Million
Number Employees: 100-249
Brands:
Claret
Reserve Cabernet Sauvignon
Reserve Merlot
Reserve Zinfandel

12668 **St. Innocent Winery**
5657 Zena Rd NW
Salem, OR 97304 503-378-1526
Fax: 503-378-1041 www.stinnocentwine.com
Wines, still and sparkling
Owner: Mark Velossak
Winemaker: Mark Vlossak
Estimated Sales: Below $ 5 Million
Number Employees: 5-9
Type of Packaging: Private Label
Brands:
St. Innocent

12669 **St. Jacobs Candy Company Brittles 'n More**
105 Lexington Rd. Unit#2
Waterloo, ON N2J 4R8
Canada 519-884-3505
Fax: 519-884-9854
contactus@brittles-n-more.com
www.brittles-n-more.com
Candy manufacturer; brittles, fudges, beernuts, caramel, turkish delight, sponge toffee, hard candy drops &'shapes, hard candy suckers and batter crunch.
President: Michael McEachern
Operations: Deana Pfanner
Production: Rhys Carter
Estimated Sales: $750,000
Number Employees: 25
Number of Products: 9
Sq. footage: 2500
Type of Packaging: Consumer, Private Label, Bulk

12670 **St. James Sugar Coopive**
5354 Saint James Coop St
Saint James, LA 70086 225-265-4056
Fax: 225-265-4060 info@slscoop.com
www.slscoop.com
Processor of blackstrap syrup and sugar
Sales Representative: Mr. Bourgeois
Estimated Sales: $ 10 - 20 Million
Number Employees: 50-99
Type of Packaging: Consumer

12671 **St. James Winery**
540 Sidney St
Saint James, MO 65559 573-265-7912
Fax: 573-265-6200 800-280-9463
info@stjameswinery.com
www.stjameswinery.com
Wines and grape juice
President: Andrew Hofherr
CFO: Andrew Hofherr
Vice President: John Hofherr
Purchasing Manager: Peter Hofherr
Estimated Sales: $ 5-10 Million
Number Employees: 20-49
Sq. footage: 300
Type of Packaging: Bulk
Brands:
St. James Winery

12672 **St. John Levert**
6142 Resweber Hwy # A
St Martinville, LA 70582-6805 337-394-9694
Fax: 337-394-9624
Manufactures raw cane sugar; sugar cane refining
Owner: Lawerence Levert
Estimated Sales: $ 3 - 5 Million
Number Employees: 5-9
Type of Packaging: Bulk
Brands:
Farmers

12673 **(HQ)St. John's Botanicals**
P.O.Box 100
Bowie, MD 20719 301-262-5302
Fax: 301-262-2489 info@stjohns.com
www.stjohnsbotanicals.com
Processor and exporter of spice blends, herb teas, essential oils, ginseng products, nutritional supplements, etc.; wholesaler/distributor of herbs, spices, etc.
Owner: Sydney Vallentyne
Ceo: Sydney Vallentync
Estimated Sales: $500,000-$1 Million
Number Employees: 1-4
Type of Packaging: Private Label, Bulk
Brands:
ROSE HILL
SCENT-O-VAC
THE PREFUME GARDEN

12674 **(HQ)St. Julian Wine Company**
716 S Kalamazoo St
Paw Paw, MI 49079 269-657-5568
Fax: 269-657-5743 800-732-6002
wines@stjulian.com www.stjulian.com
Processor and exporter of grape beverages including champagne, wine and juice
President: David Braganini
Executive VP: Charles Catherman
Marketing Director: Kim Babcock
VP Sales: Joe Zuiderueen
Wine Maker: David Miller, Ph.D.
Estimated Sales: $9216001
Number Employees: 70
Type of Packaging: Consumer, Food Service

12675 **St. Laurent Brothers**
1101 N Water St
Bay City, MI 48708 989-893-7522
Fax: 989-893-6571 800-289-7688
www.stlaurentbrothers.com
Processor of peanuts including salted, roasted and candy coated; also, peanut butter
President: Keith Whitney
Co-Owner: Steve Frye
Estimated Sales: $1900000
Number Employees: 20-49
Type of Packaging: Consumer, Food Service, Bulk

12676 **St. Lawrence Starch**
141 Lakeshore Road E
Mississauga, ON L5G 1E8
Canada 905-271-8396
Fax: 905-271-1258

Processor of starches and corn sweeteners including glucose and fructose
President: Ian Gray
CEO: Nick Lacivita
Sales Manager: Howard Low
Parent Co: Cargill Foods

12677 St. Martin Sugar Cooperative
6092 Resweber Hwy
St Martinville, LA 70582-6804 33- 3-4 37
Fax: 337- 39- 563 info@lasuca.com
www.lasuca.com
Sugar and condiments
President: Mike Melancon
VP: Lawrence Levert
Plant Manager: Michael Comb
Estimated Sales: $ 30-50 Million
Number Employees: 50-99
Brands:
St. Martin

12678 St. Mary Sugar Cooperative
20056 Highway 182 W
Jeanerette, LA 70544 337-276-6761
Fax: 337-276-4297
Sugar and condiments
President: Raphael Rodriguez
Plant Manager: Ronald Guilotte Jr
Estimated Sales: $500,000-$1 Million
Number Employees: 50-99

12679 St. Maurice Laurent
735 6e Rang N Ss 1
St-Bruno-Lac-St-Jean, QC G0W 2L0
Canada 418-343-3655
Fax: 418-343-2996
Processor of cheese and butter
President: Luc St Laurent
Number Employees: 25
Sq. footage: 10000

12680 St. Ours & Company
P.O.Box 566
Norwell, MA 02061-0566 781-331-8520
Fax: 781-331-8628
Processor of frozen shellfish including lobster, crab, clam and dehydrated seafood broths; wholesaler/distributor of seafood and specialty foods; serving the food service market
President: Fred St Ours
Sales: John Christian
Director Manufacturing: Richard St. Ours
Estimated Sales: $ 3 - 5 Million
Number Employees: 5-9
Type of Packaging: Consumer, Food Service, Bulk
Brands:
St. Ours

12681 St. Simons Seafood
130 Paradise Marsh Cir
Brunswick, GA 31525 912-265-5225
Fax: 912-264-3181
Seafood and fish.
President: Chuck Egeland
Estimated Sales: $1,500,000
Number Employees: 5-9

12682 St. Stan's Brewing Company
821 L Street
Modesto, CA 95354-0837 209-527-7826
Fax: 209-524-4827 getreal@ststans.com
http://www.ststans.com/
Beer
President/CEO: Garith Helm
CFO: Romy Angle
Plant Manager: Eric Kellner
Estimated Sales: $ 20-50 Million
Number Employees: 35
Type of Packaging: Private Label
Brands:
Red Sky Ale
St. Stan's Alt Beer

12683 Stacey's Famous Foods
10334 N Taryne Street
Hayden, ID 83835-9807 650-261-9912
800-782-2395
crabcakes@staceysfoods.com
www.staceysfoods.com
Frozen seafood, seafood products such as; sauces, appetizers, quiches, pot pies, potatoe
Owner/President: Stacey James
Estimated Sales: Less than $500,000
Number Employees: 1-4
Brands:
Stacey's

12684 Stacy's Pita Chip Company
663 North St
Randolph, MA 02368 781-961-7799
Fax: 781-961-2830 888-332-4477
stacy@pitachips.com www.pitachips.com
Manufacturer and distributor of pita and soy-based chips.
President: Stacy Madison
CEO: Mark Andrus
Estimated Sales: $ 5 - 10 Million
Number Employees: 10-19

12685 Stadelman Fruit
P.O.Box 445
Zillah, WA 98953 509-829-5145
Fax: 509-829-5164 http://www.stadelmanfruit.com
Processor and exporter of produce including apples, cherries, nectarines, pears, plums and prunes
President: Peter Stadelman
CEO: Rob Stewart
Number Employees: 500-999
Type of Packaging: Consumer, Food Service, Private Label, Bulk

12686 Staff of Life Natural Foods
1305 Water St
Santa Cruz, CA 95062 831-423-8632
Fax: 831-423-8065 staflife@pacbell.net
www.staffoflifemarket.com
Natural foods
President: Richard Josephson
VP: Gary Bascou
Estimated Sales: $ 5-10 Million
Number Employees: 100-249
Brands:
Beckmann
Imagine Foods
Natures Path
R.W.Knudsen

12687 Stafford County Flour Mills Company
P.O.Box 7
Hudson, KS 67545 620-458-4121
Fax: 620-458-5121 800-530-5640
admin@flour.com www.hudsoncream.com
Bread flour
President: Alvin A Brensing
Estimated Sales: $ 25-30 Million
Number Employees: 20-49
Type of Packaging: Consumer
Brands:
Hudson Cream Flour

12688 Stage Coach Sauces
3829 Reid St
Palatka, FL 32177 386-328-6330
Fax: 386-328-6330 www.stagecoachsauces.com
Contract packager and exporter of sauces and condiments including steak, barbecue, pepper, chicken wing and seafood; also, contract packaging of wet and dry products available
President: Terry Geck
VP Marketing: Lisa Marie Geck
Plant Manager: Terry Geck
Estimated Sales: $ 3 - 5 Million
Number Employees: 5-9
Sq. footage: 10000
Type of Packaging: Consumer, Food Service, Private Label
Brands:
Stage Coach Sauces

12689 Stagnos Bakery
233 Auburn Street
East Liberty, PA 15206-3209 412-441-3485
Processor of bread and hoagie buns.
President: Anthony Stagno
President: Frances Stagno
Estimated Sales: $ 20 - 50 Million
Number Employees: 20-49
Type of Packaging: Consumer, Food Service, Bulk

12690 Stags' Leap Winery
6150 Silverado Trl
Napa, CA 94558 707-944-1303
Fax: 707-944-9433 800-640-5327
stagsleap@beringerblass.com
www.stagsleap.com
Wines
Manager: Kevin Morrisey
Director Operations: Kevin Morrisey
Marketing Director: Bob Janis
Estimated Sales: $ 10-20 Million
Number Employees: 20-49
Brands:
Stags

12691 Stahlbush Island Farms
3122 SE Stahlbush Island Rd
Corvallis, OR 97333 541-757-1497
Fax: 541-754-1847 barry@stahlbush.com
www.stahlbush.com
Processor of IQF broccoli, carrots, green beans, peas, pumpkins, sweet potatoes, spinach, corn, asparagus, strawberries, cranberries, apples and pears; also, frozen fruit and vegetable purees
President: William Chambers
CFO: Jon Soula
COO: John Bailey
Estimated Sales: $ 20 - 50 Million
Number Employees: 50

12692 Stahmann Farms
22500 S Highway 28
La Mesa, NM 88044 575-526-2453
www.stahmanns.com
Pecans
Owner: Sally Stahmann-Solis
Vice-CEO: Deane Stahmann
Number Employees: 100-249
Type of Packaging: Bulk

12693 Stallings Headcheese Company
2314 Portsmouth St
Houston, TX 77098 713-523-1751
Manufacturer of headcheese and boudin
Owner: Fred Chu
Estimated Sales: $1-3 Million
Number Employees: 1-4
Sq. footage: 2000

12694 Stampede Meat
7351 S 78th Ave
Bridgeview, IL 60455 773-376-4300
Fax: 773-376-9349 800-353-0933
raym@stampedemeat.com
www.stampedemeat.com
Specializes in custom made center of the plate beef and pork entrees for the needs of the restaurant and hospitality industry.
President: Edward Ligas
VP Marketing/Sales: Ray McKiernan
Estimated Sales: $ 100-500 Million
Number Employees: 250-499
Type of Packaging: Food Service

12695 Stan-Mark Food Products
1100 W 47th Pl
Chicago, IL 60609-4302 773-847-1761
Fax: 773-847-6253 800-651-0994
marek@stanmark.biz www.stanmark.biz
Processor, importer and exporter of pickles, spices, grains and seeds; importer of herring
CEO and President: Stanley Opechowski
R&D: Mark Kongrecki
Estimated Sales: $ 20 - 50 Million
Number Employees: 20-49
Sq. footage: 60000
Type of Packaging: Consumer, Private Label, Bulk

12696 Stanchfield Farms
73 Medford Rd
Milo, ME 04463 207-732-5173
Fax: 207-732-5173 sales@stanchfieldfarms.com
www.stanchfieldfarms.com
Sweet and spicy pickles, pure fruit jams and jellies, bouron barbeque sauce and marinades, fruit chutneys, and pickled vegetables
Type of Packaging: Consumer

12697 Standard Bakery
P.O.Box 341
Kealakekua, HI 96750 808-322-3688
Fax: 808-322-2462
Processor of cakes, pies and pastries
President: Lloyd Fujino
Estimated Sales: $ .5 - 1 million
Number Employees: 10-19
Type of Packaging: Consumer, Food Service

12698 **Standard Beef Company**
124 Washington St Ste 101
Foxboro, MA 02035 203-787-2164
Fax: 203-752-1703
Processor and wholesaler/distributor of beef, pork, lamb, poultry, veal, cold cuts, dairy products and fish; importer of goat and bull beef; wholesaler/distributor of equipment and fixtures and frozen foods
President: Henry Bawarsky
VP: William Dober
vp: Steven Wildstein
Estimated Sales: $100+ Million
Number Employees: 20-49
Sq. footage: 15000

12699 **(HQ)Standard Candy Company**
715 Massman Dr
Nashville, TN 37210 615-889-6360
Fax: 615-889-7775 800-226-4340
sales@standardcandy.com www.googoo.com
Manufacturer, exporter and contract packager of candy including bars, boxed, log rolls and caramel corn
President: James W Spradley Jr
VP: Thomas Drummond
Director: Anthony Olberding
Director Of Marketing: Joanne Barthel
Sales: Brian Fitzpatrick
Public Relations: Joanne Barthel
Operations: Dennis Adcock
Plant Manager: Gary Baker
Purchasing: Brian Hillman
Estimated Sales: $57604250
Number Employees: 50-99
Sq. footage: 200000
Type of Packaging: Private Label, Bulk
Brands:
COCONUT WAVES
CUMBERLAND RIDGE
GOO GOO CLUSTER

12700 **Stangl's Bakeries**
1210 Merchant Street
Ambridge, PA 15003-2252 724-266-5080
Baked foods
President: Suzanne Mickey
Estimated Sales: Less than $50,000
Number Employees: 1-4

12701 **Stanislaus Food Products**
1202 D St
Modesto, CA 95354 209-522-7201
Fax: 209-527-0227 800-327-7201
freshpacktomato@stanislaus.com
www.stanislaus.com
Manufacturer of canned tomato paste and sauces
President/CEO: Thomas Cortopassi
CFO: William Butler
VP Marketing: Cindy Brenon
SVP/Operations Executive: Mark Kimmel
Estimated Sales: $500 Million to $1 Billion
Number Employees: 105
Sq. footage: 50000
Type of Packaging: Food Service
Brands:
7/11
74-40
80-40
AL DENTE
ALTA CUCINA
FULL RED
PIZZAIOLO
PIZZALETTO
POMAROLA
SAPORITO
TOMATO MAGIC
TRATTORIA
VALOROSO

12702 **Stanley Drying Company**
P.O. Box 157
Stanley, WI 54768-0157 715-644-5827
www.adm.com
Processor of honey and molasses
Manager: Rick Troyer
Plant Manager: Donald Marquardt
Estimated Sales: $ 5 - 10 Million
Number Employees: 10-19
Parent Co: DEC International
Type of Packaging: Consumer

12703 **Stanley Orchards**
2044 State Route 32 Ste 2
Modena, NY 12548 845-883-7351
Fax: 845-883-5077 sales@stanleyorchards.com
www.stanleyorchards.com
Fruits, berries
President/CEO: Ronald Cohn
VP/Plant Manager: Stanley Cohn
Controller: Susan Surprise
Sales Manager: Anthony Maresca
Treasurer/Shipping Manager: Barry Cohn
Sales/Transportation: Randy Wolfe
Estimated Sales: $ 10-20 Million
Number Employees: 10-19
Number of Brands: 7
Type of Packaging: Private Label
Brands:
A & J
Family Ties
Gourmet Apple
Grand Prix
Liberty Empire
Northern Orchard
Stanley

12704 **Stanley Provision Company**
50 Batson Dr
Manchester, CT 06042 860-649-0656
888-688-6347
Processor of sausage, kielbasa and ground beef
President: Stephen Wisniewski
Number Employees: 10-19
Sq. footage: 10000
Type of Packaging: Consumer, Food Service

12705 **Stanley's Best Seafood**
7475 Patruski Road
Coden, AL 36523-3181 251-824-2801
Fax: 919-734-1201
Seafood
Owner: Robert Stanley

12706 **Stanz Foodservice**
1840 N Commerce Drive
South Bend, IN 46628 574-232-6666
Fax: 574-236-4169 800-342-5664
www.stanz.com
A complete line of food service products
President: Mark Harman
CEO: Shirley Geraghty
Vice President: Wendy Harman
VP/Information Technology: Mark Gaddie
VP/Marketing: Jeff Nicholas
VP/Sales: Todd Stearns
VP/Operations: Dave Dausinas
Estimated Sales: $100+ Million
Number Employees: 100-249
Sq. footage: 10000

12707 **Stapleton-Spence PackingCompany**
1530 the Alameda Ste 320
San Jose, CA 95126 408-297-8815
Fax: 408-297-0611 800-297-8815
www.stapleton-spence.com
Packer of prune concentrates, purees, juices, nuts and other dried fruits.
President/CEO: Brad Stapleton
CFO: Ellsworth Rowinski
Operations Director: Gerry Clark
Production Director: Mike Smith
Estimated Sales: $15000000
Number Employees: 80
Sq. footage: 5000
Type of Packaging: Consumer, Food Service, Private Label
Brands:
County Fair
Monta Vista

12708 **Star Creek Brewing Company**
1901 N Akard Street
Dallas, TX 75201-2305 214-999-0999
Fax: 214-999-1001
Beer
Estimated Sales: $500,000-$1 Million
Number Employees: 1-4

12709 **Star Fine Foods**
2680 W Shaw Ln
Fresno, CA 93711 559-498-2900
Fax: 559-498-2910
postmaster@starfinefoods.com
www.starfinefoods.com
California's leading importers, processors, packers and distributors of Mediterranean specialty food products.
President: Patti Andrade
VP Finance: Brian Staggs
Vice President: David Prats
Quality Control: Debbie Verboort
Marketing Director: Patti Andrade
Operations Manager: Joe Cusimano
Estimated Sales: $4600000
Number Employees: 20-49
Sq. footage: 75000
Parent Co: S.A. Borges
Type of Packaging: Consumer, Food Service, Private Label, Bulk
Brands:
Golden Gate
Italian Kitchen
San Francisco Salad
Star

12710 **Star Foods**
PO Box 22185
Cleveland, OH 44122-0185 216-831-0992
Fax: 216-831-4368 800-837-0992
ritz@starfoods.com www.starfoods.com
President: Mark Lackritz
CEO: Cliff Sobol
Estimated Sales: $3-4 Million
Number Employees: 7
Type of Packaging: Food Service, Private Label, Bulk

12711 **Star Hill Winery**
1075 Shadybrook Lane
Napa, CA 94558-4047 707-255-1957
Fax: 707-252-1976
Wines
President: Jacob Goldenberg
Estimated Sales: Under $500,000
Number Employees: 1-4

12712 **Star Kay White**
85 Brenner Dr
Congers, NY 10920 845-268-2600
Fax: 845-268-3572 800-874-8518
inquiry@starkaywhite.com
www.starkaywhite.com
Manufacturer of syrups, candies, panned-items and extracts and flavors
Owner/President/CEO/Plant Manager: Walter Katzenstein
General Manager: Don Heffner
R&D: Richard Sroka
Marketing: Stephen Platt
VP/Sales Executive: James Taft
Manufacuturing Supervisor: George Granada
Purchasing Manager: Judy Beaman
Estimated Sales: $8 Million
Number Employees: 65
Number of Brands: 1
Number of Products: 750
Sq. footage: 45000
Type of Packaging: Bulk

12713 **Star Packaging Corporation**
453 Circle 85 St
Atlanta, GA 30349 404-763-2800
Fax: 404-763-5435 www.starpackagingcorp.com
Specializes in the printing, lamination, and conversion of flexible packaging materials in the form of roll stock, pouches and bags.
President: Michael Wilson
Estimated Sales: $ 20 - 50 Million
Number Employees: 100-249

12714 **Star Ravioli Manufacturing Company**
2 Anderson Ave Ste 2
Moonachie, NJ 7074 201-933-6427
Fax: 201-933-0484 sales@starravioli.com
www.starravioli.com
Producers of more than thirty varieties of ravioli, as well as other italian specialties including manicotti, stuffed shells, gnocchi, cavatelli, tortellini, fettuccini and much more.
President: Laurence Piretra
CFO: Laurence Piretra
R&D: Rick Pisani
Quality Control: Rick Pisani
Estimated Sales: $ 3 - 5 Million
Number Employees: 10-19
Sq. footage: 12000

Type of Packaging: Consumer, Food Service, Private Label, Bulk

12715 **Star Route Farms**
95 Olema Bolinas Rd
Bolinas, CA 94924 415-868-1658
Fax: 415-868-9530 warrenweber@earthlink.net
www.starroutefarms.com
Produce
Owner: Warren Weber
Estimated Sales: Below $ 5 Million
Number Employees: 20-49

12716 **Star Seafood**
PO Box 118
Bayou La Batre, AL 36509-0118 251-824-3110
Fax: 251-824-4199
Seafood

12717 **Star Snacks Company**
105 Harbor Drive
Jersey City, NJ 07305-4505 201-200-9820
Fax: 201-200-9827 800-775-9909
Processor, packer and exporter of dried fruits and nuts including cashews, peanuts, mixed, almonds, filberts, apricots, banana chips, etc.; also, sunflower seeds
President: Andre Engel
Executive VP: Mendel Brachfeld
Estimated Sales: $ 20 - 50 Million
Number Employees: 50-99
Sq. footage: 30000
Parent Co: Gel Spice Compnay
Brands:
Harbor View
Imperial Label
Manhattan Nut
Star

12718 **Star Union Brewing Company**
PO Box 282
Hennepin, IL 61327-0282 815-925-7400
Beer

12719 **Star of the West**
162 N Water St
Kent, OH 44240-2419 330-673-2941
Fax: 330-673-2439
Miller of soft wheat flour
Sales Manager: Charles Williams III
Plant Manager: Steve Michel
Estimated Sales: $ 5 - 10 Million
Number Employees: 20-49

12720 **Star of the West MillingCompany**
P.O.Box 146
Frankenmuth, MI 48734 989-652-9971
Fax: 989-652-6358
art.loeffler@starofthewest.com
www.starofthewest.com
Processor and exporter of soft wheat flours and bran; processor of beans including black, red, dry navy, soy and colored
President: Art Loeffler
VP: Mike Fassezke
Marketing: Joe Cramer
CFO: Eric Bushey
Estimated Sales: $ 50 - 100 Million
Number Employees: 50-99
Type of Packaging: Bulk

12721 **(HQ)Star of the West MillingCompany**
P.O.Box 146
Frankenmuth, MI 48734 989-652-9971
Fax: 989-652-6358 www.starofthewest.com
Manufacturer of flour, cearal bran and wheat germ
President: Art Loeffler
CFO: Eric Bushey
Plant Manager: Kenneth Schuman
Estimated Sales: $144 Million
Number Employees: 50-99
Type of Packaging: Private Label, Bulk

12722 **Star-Kist**
225 N Shore Drive
Suite 400
Pittsburgh, PA 15212 412-323-7400
Fax: 412-222-4050 starkist.com
Processor, canner and exporter of tuna
President, CEO: In-Soo Cho
Marketing: Barry Shepard
Vice President Sales: Stephen L Hodge
Media Relations: Melissa Murphy
Estimated Sales: $ .5 - 1 million
Number Employees: 1-4
Parent Co: Del Monte Foods
Brands:
CHUNK LIGHT TUNA
GOURMET'S CHOICE TUNA FILLETS
LOW SODIUM TUNA
SOLID WHITE ALBACORE TUNA
STARKIST FLAVOR FRESH POUCH
STARKIST LUNCH TO-GO
STARKIST SELECT
STARKIST TUNA CREATIONS

12723 **Star-Kist Caribe**
3051 Road 64
Mayaguez, PR 00680 787-834-2424
Fax: 787-834-3175
Processor, canner and exporter of tuna
General Manager: Alfredo Archilla
Number Employees: 1,000-4,999
Parent Co: Star-Kist Foods
Type of Packaging: Consumer, Food Service

12724 **Starbrook Industries Inc**
325 S Hyatt St
Tipp City, OH 45371-1241 937-473-8135
Fax: 937-473-0331 Richard@StarbrookInd.com
www.starbrookind.com/
Product line includes forming and non-forming food packaging films designed for Bi-Vac, Dixie Pak and Multi Vac machines.
Sales Manager: Richard Anderson

12725 **(HQ)Starbucks Coffee Company**
2401 Utah Ave S
Seattle, WA 98134 206-447-1575
Fax: 206-447-0828 800-782-7282
www.starbucks.com
Whole bean coffees and rich-brewed Italian style espresso beverages, a variety of pastries and confections, coffee-related accessories and equipment. Also a processor of ice cream and coffee drinks including blended and flavored; alsononfat and dairy-free blended juiced teas; roaster of whole bean coffees
Chairman/President/CEO: Howard Schultz
President/Starbucks Coffee US: Cliff Burrows
CFO/CAO: Troy Alstead
President/Starbucks Coffee International: John Culver
President/Global Consumer Products: Jeff Hansberry
President/Global Development: Arthur Rubinfeld
Chief Marketing Officer: Annie Young-Scrivner
EVP/Global Supply Chain Operations: Peter Gibbons
Estimated Sales: $10 Billion
Number Employees: 137,000
Type of Packaging: Consumer, Private Label, Bulk
Brands:
Brazil Ipanema Bourbon
Caffe Verona
Double Shot
Ethos Water
Frappuccino
Gold Coast Blend
Lightnote Blend
Milder Dimensions
Serenade Blend
Siren's Note Blend
Starbucks
Tazo
Tiazzi
Yukon Blend

12726 **Starich**
28490 2nd Street
Daphne, AL 36526-7150 251-626-5037
Seafood

12727 **(HQ)Stark Candy Company**
135 American Legion Highway
Revere, MA 02151-2405 985-446-1354
Fax: 985-448-1627 800-621-1983
Manufacturer and exporter of candy
President: Dominic Antonellis
General Manager: Bobby Folfe
VP Sales: Tom Drummond
Number Employees: 30
Type of Packaging: Consumer

12728 **Starkel Poultry**
34303 27th Ave E
Roy, WA 98580-8861 253-845-2876
Fax: 253-841-1004 starkel@starkelpoultry.com
www.starkelpoultry.com
Processor and exporter of bagged fowl including fresh and frozen
President: Elsie Starkel
Vice President: Leona Starkel
Estimated Sales: $4400000
Number Employees: 45
Type of Packaging: Consumer, Bulk

12729 **Starport Foods**
2655 Judah St
San Francisco, CA 94122 415-731-0663
Fax: 415-731-0663 866-206-9343
sales@starportfoods.com
www.starportfoods.com
Ethnic specialty sauces, dressings and seasonings
Owner/VP: Cheryl Tsang
Estimated Sales: $500,000-$1 Million
Number Employees: 5-9
Number of Products: 40
Type of Packaging: Consumer, Food Service, Private Label, Bulk

12730 **Starr & Brown**
10610 NW Saint Helens Road
Portland, OR 97231-1048 503-287-1775
Wine
President: Eric Brown
Estimated Sales: Less than $500,000
Number Employees: 1-4

12731 **Startup's Candy Company**
534 South 100 West
Provo, UT 84601 801-373-8673
Fax: 801-373-7312
customerservice@startupcandy.com
www.startupcandy.com
Manufacturer of candy and confectionery products
President: Harry W Startup
Vice President: Jon Startup
Estimated Sales: $2,000,000
Number Employees: 5-9
Type of Packaging: Consumer

12732 **Starwest Botanicals**
11253 Trade Center Dr Ste A
Rancho Cordova, CA 95742 916-638-8100
Fax: 916-853-9673 888-273-4372
www.starwest-botanicals.com
Processor, importer and exporter of herbs and herbal extracts, spices and essential and vegetable oils; also, custom milling, blending and formulating available
Owner/President/CEO: Van Joerger
VP Finance: Mark Wendley
SVP R&D/Production Manager: Dawn Bennett
Marketing/Product Development: Daniela Nelson
VP Sales: Richard Patterson
Purchasing: Bonnie Sadkowski
Estimated Sales: $9.8 Million
Number Employees: 60
Sq. footage: 50000
Type of Packaging: Bulk
Brands:
Nature Actives
Starwest

12733 **Stasero International**
7021 South 220th Street
KENT, WA 98032 25- 8-7 61
Fax: 206-324-4586 888-929-2378
info@stasero.com www.stasero.com
Italian-style syrups, shakable toppings, blended ice coffee mixes
President: Sabru Kabani
VP Marketing: Aisha Kabani
CFO: Joann Watts
Vice President: Mel Moomjean
Estimated Sales: $ 20 - 50 Million
Number Employees: 20-49
Type of Packaging: Private Label
Brands:
Stasero

12734 **Stash Tea Company**
16655 SW 72nd Avenue
Suite 200
Portland, OR 97224 503-684-4482
Fax: 503-684-4424 800-547-1514
stash@stashtea.com www.stashtea.com

Processor of hot and cold tea including black, white, green, oolong, herbal, chais, teas of China & Japan and iced teas.
President/CEO: Thomas Lisicki
Quality Assurance Manager: Maria Lidiasari
VP Marketing: Dorothy Arnold
Sales Director: Kai Larsen
Human Resources Manager: Mitzi Bodine
Operations Manager: Jim Messina
Estimated Sales: $8,300,000
Number Employees: 49
Sq. footage: 33000
Type of Packaging: Consumer, Food Service, Bulk
Brands:
Exotica
Stash
Stash Premium Organic Teas
Yamamotoyama 1690

12735 **Stassen North America**
408 S Pierce Ave
Louisville, CO 80027 303-527-1700
Fax: 303-527-1702 sales@snatea.com
www.coopertea.com
General grocery
President: Mike Fitzgerald
Estimated Sales: $ 2.5-5 Million
Number Employees: 10-19

12736 **State Fish Company**
2194 Signal Place
San Pedro, CA 90731 310-832-2633
Fax: 310-831-2402 sales@statefish.com
www.statefish.com
Producer, processor, distributor, importer and exporter finfish, crab, lobster, scallops, shrimp, calamari (domestic and imported), octopus and more.
President: John Deluca
Vice President: Vanessa De Luca
Marketing Director: Janet Esposito
Domestic Sales: Klaus Brittinger
Estimated Sales: $21900000
Number Employees: 100-249
Type of Packaging: Private Label, Bulk
Brands:
Calamari of California
Fiesta Del Mar
Nautilus

12737 **State Fish Distributors**
4513 S Halsted Street
Chicago, IL 60609-3413 773-451-0500
Fax: 773-225-4660
Seafood
President: Donald Nathan

12738 **State of Maine Cheese Company**
461 Commercial St
Rockport, ME 04856-4455 207-236-8895
Fax: 207-236-9591 800-762-8895
infoA@cheese-me.com www.cheese-me.com
Cheese
President: Cathe Morrill
Estimated Sales: $500,000-$1 Million
Number Employees: 5-9

12739 **Stateline Boyd**
PO Box 550
Lynn, MA 01903-0650 781-593-4422
Fax: 781-599-8430
Snack foods
President: Steven Jakubowski
CFO: W Duncan Reed
COO: Michael Schena
VP Sales: Donald LaDouceur
Estimated Sales: $ 50-100 Million
Number Employees: 250

12740 **Statewide Meats & Poultry**
211 Food Terminal Plz
New Haven, CT 06511 203-777-6669
Fax: 203-492-4073 www.statewidemeats.com
Processor and wholesaler/distributor of meat
President: Stephen Falcigno
Estimated Sales: $7900000
Number Employees: 20-49

12741 **Stauber Performance Ingredients**
4120 N Palm St
Fullerton, CA 92835 714-441-3900
Fax: 714-441-3909 888-441-4233
customerservice@stauberusa.com
www.stauberusa.com
Leading supplier of bulk ingredients to the nutritional products, food and cosmetic industries
Owner: Danny Stauber
CEO: Dan Stauber
Diretor/Quality Assurance: Pat Wratschko
Number Employees: 50-99
Sq. footage: 50000
Type of Packaging: Bulk

12742 **Stauffer Biscuit Company**
360 S Belmont St
York, PA 17403-2616 717-843-9016
Fax: 717-843-0592 800-673-2473
mlcarione@stauffers.net www.stauffers.net
Manufacturer of cookies, crackers and snack products
President: Marc Garrett
Estimated Sales: $ 50 - 100 Million
Number Employees: 500-999

12743 **Stauffer's**
8670 Farnsworth Rd
Cuba, NY 14727-9720 585-968-2700
Fax: 585-968-2722
Manufacturers of cookies.
Manager: John Fletcher
Estimated Sales: $ 2.5-5 Million
Number Employees: 20-49
Brands:
Stauffer's

12744 **Stavis Seafoods**
212 Northern Avenue
Suite 305, Fish Pier West
Boston, MA 02210-2049 617-482-6349
Fax: 617-482-1340 800-390-5103
fish@stavis.com www.stavis.com
Importer, exporter and wholesaler/distributor of fresh and frozen seafood. Fresh seafood includes cod, haddock, pollock, tuna, swordfish, mahi, snapper, grouper and seabass fillets, rockshrimp and baby scallops
CEO: Richard Stavis
Principal: Stephen Young
CFO: Mary Fleming
Marketing: Ruth Levy
Sales: David Lancaster
Operations: Emily Stavis
Purchasing Manager: Robert Landy
Estimated Sales: $160 Million
Number Employees: 120
Number of Brands: 5
Number of Products: 700
Sq. footage: 40000
Type of Packaging: Food Service, Private Label, Bulk
Brands:
Bos'n
Boston Pride
Foods From the Sea
Prince Edward

12745 **Stawnichy Holdings**
PO Box 18
Mundare, AB T0B 3H0
Canada 780-764-3912
Fax: 780-764-3765 888-764-7646
shltd@telusplanet.net www.mundaresausage.com
Processor of pepperoni, frankfurters, Ukrainian-style sausage, bologna, garlic rings, cooked and pressed ham, salami, ham and bacon loafs, macaroni and cheese loafs, corned beef, pastrami, beef jerky, bacon, veal cutlets, ground beefpierogies, etc
VP/General Manager: E Stawnichy
Number Employees: 20-49
Sq. footage: 11500
Brands:
Stawnichy's

12746 **Ste Michelle Wine Estates**
14111 NE 145th St
PO Box 1976
Woodinville, WA 98072 425-488-1133
Fax: 425-415-3657 800-267-6793
info@ste-michelle.com www.stimson-lane.com
Processor, exporter and importer of wines
President/CEO: Ted Baseler
EVP/CFO: Sheila Newlands
SVP/General Counsel: Tom Rowland
SVP Marketing: Martin Johnson
EVP Sales: Glenn Yaffa
SVP Human Resources: Susan Reams
EVP Winemaking/Vineyards/Operations: Doug Gore
Estimated Sales: $ 10 - 20 Million
Number Employees: 250-499
Type of Packaging: Consumer, Food Service, Private Label, Bulk
Other Locations:
Stimson Lane Vineyards & Esta
Woodinville WA

12747 **Ste. Chapelle Winery**
19348 Lowell Rd
Caldwell, ID 83607 208-453-7830
Fax: 208-453-7831 877-783-2427
info@stchappelle.com www.stechapelle.com
Wines
Manager: Mary Sloyer
Estimated Sales: Below $ 5 Million
Number Employees: 20-49
Parent Co: Canandaigua Wine Company
Type of Packaging: Private Label

12748 **Steak-Umm Company**
P.O. Box 350
Shillington, PA 19607-0350 860-928-5900
Fax: 860-928-0351 http://www.steakumm.com
President: Dennis Newnham
Estimated Sales: $14 Million
Number Employees: 120
Sq. footage: 176000
Brands:
Red.L
Spare-The-Ribs
Steak-Umm
Steak-Umm Sandwich To Go

12749 **Stearns & Lehman**
30 Paragon Pkwy
Mansfield, OH 44903-8074 419-522-2722
Fax: 419-522-1152 800-533-2722
slinfo@kerrygroup.com
www.stearns-lehman.com
Processor and exporter of Italian syrups, specialty sugars and powdered toppings for coffees; also, coffee and tea flavors and extracts; private labeling available
Business Director: Peter Dillane
Marketing Director: Corrie Byron
Plant Manager: James Powers
Estimated Sales: $7.9 Million
Number Employees: 20-49
Sq. footage: 50000
Type of Packaging: Private Label
Brands:
Dinatura
Dolce
Flavor-Mate
Gift of Bran
My Hero
Paradise Bay
Select Origins
Senza
Stearns & Lehman

12750 **Stearns Wharf Vintners**
217 Stearns Wharf # G
Santa Barbara, CA 93101-3582 805-966-6624
Fax: 805-966-6624
www.stearnswharfvintners.com
Wines
President: Candy Scott
Estimated Sales: $ 2.5-5 Million
Number Employees: 5-9
Brands:
Stearns Wharf

12751 **Steckel Produce**
905 State Highway 16
Jerseyville, IL 62052 618-498-4274
Fax: 618-498-4780
Fruits and vegetables
President: Dennis Steckel
Estimated Sales: $3 Million
Number Employees: 5-9

12752 **Steel's Gourmet Foods,Ltd.**
55 E Front St # D175
Bridgeport, PA 19405-1489 610-277-1230
Fax: 610-277-1228 800-678-3357
info@steelsgourmet.com
www.steelsgourmet.com

Processor and exporter of gourmet, sugar free dessert toppings, jams, sweetners, syrups and condiments; also organic salad dressings, condiments, fruit spreads and low sugar fudge sauces.
President: Elizabeth Steel
Plant Manager: Carlos Short
Estimated Sales: $2.5 Million
Number Employees: 8
Number of Products: 60
Sq. footage: 10000
Parent Co: Clack-Steel
Type of Packaging: Consumer, Private Label
Brands:
Charlie Trotter Foods
Daven Island Trade
Steel's Gourmet

12753 **Steelback Brewery**
50 Steinway Blvd
Toronto, ON M9W 6Y3
Canada 416-679-0032
Fax: 416-679-0061
Processor of apple juice concentrate
President: Ian MacDonald
Estimated Sales: $1-2.5 Million
Number Employees: 10-19
Type of Packaging: Bulk

12754 **Steep & Brew Coffee Roasters**
855 E Broadway
Monona, WI 53716-4012 608-223-0707
Fax: 608-223-0355 800-876-1986
coffee@steepnbrew.com www.cafefair.org
Coffee
President: Mark Ballering
VP/Sales Manager: Mark Mullee
Estimated Sales: Below $ 5 Million
Number Employees: 20-49
Type of Packaging: Private Label
Brands:
Cafe Fair

12755 **Stefano Gourmet A Tasteof Italy**
PO Box 8
Rural Ridge, PA 15075-0008 412-781-4104
Fax: 412-781-4210 888-781-4104
chefsteff@chefsteff.com www.chefsteff.com
Italian specialty food products
President/CEO: Steff Tedeschi
Sales Director: Bill Acker
Plant Manager: Gabriel Negri
Purchasing Manager: Emma Tedeschi
Estimated Sales: $ 10-20 Million
Number Employees: 5-9
Type of Packaging: Private Label
Brands:
Steff Gourmet Italia
Steff Gourmet Italian Sauces

12756 **Stegall Smoked Turkey**
6608 E Marshville Blvd
Marshville, NC 28103 704-624-6628
Fax: 704-624-2510 800-851-6034
info@stegallsmokedturkey.com
www.stegallsmokedturkey.com
Processor of frozen hickory-smoked turkey and honey-glazed ham
President: Don Stegall
Marketing Director: Don Stegall
VP: Marceil Stegall
Estimated Sales: $500,000-$1 Million
Number Employees: 5-9
Sq. footage: 110000
Type of Packaging: Private Label
Brands:
Stegall Smoked Turkey

12757 **Stehlin & Sons Company**
10134 Colerain Ave
Cincinnati, OH 45251-4902 513-385-6164
Fax: 513-385-6165
Processor of beef and pork
President: John Stehlin
Estimated Sales: $1300000
Number Employees: 10-19
Type of Packaging: Consumer, Bulk

12758 **Steiner Cheese**
201 Mill St
Baltic, OH 43804 330-897-5505
Fax: 330-897-6911 888-897-5505
www.steinercheese.com
Processor of Swiss cheese
President: James Sommers
VP: Dale Lendon
Estimated Sales: $ 5 - 10 Million
Number Employees: 5
Type of Packaging: Consumer, Bulk

12759 **(HQ)Steiner, S.S.**
655 Madison Ave # 17
New York, NY 10065-8043 212-515-7200
Fax: 212-593-4238 sales@hopsteiner.com
www.hopsteiner.com
Processor, importer and exporter of hops extracts, pellets and oils
Owner: Louis S Gimbel Iii
VP: Louis Gimbel IV
VP: Martin Ungewitter
Estimated Sales: $ 20 - 50 Million
Number Employees: 20-49
Type of Packaging: Food Service
Other Locations:
Steiner, S.S.
Salem OR
Brands:
Hopsteiner

12760 **Steinfurth IncElectromechanical Measuring Systems**
541 Village Trace
Bldg. 11, Suite 102
Marietta, GA 30067 678- 5-0 90
Fax: 678- 8-0 77 info@steinfurth.com
www.steinfurth.com/
Steinfurth is a producer of specialist measuring devices for the beverage industry, the food industry, pharmaceuticals and mining.
Marketing & Sales Manager North America: Yvonne Harper

12761 **Steinfurth Instruments**
541 Village Trace
Bldg. 11, Suite 102
Marietta, GA 30067 67- -00 9
Fax: 678- 8-0 77 info@steinfurth.com
www.steinfurthinstruments.com
Steinfurth Instruments is a producer of specialist measuring devices for the beverage industry, the food industry, pharmaceuticals and mining.
Marketing and Sales Manager: Yvonne Harper

12762 **Stella D'Oro Biscuit Company**
115 E Stevens Ave Ste 202
Valhalla, NY 10595 914-984-2290
800-995-2623
stephen.spaner@kraft.com www.stelladoro.com
Processor and exporter of cookies, bread sticks and biscuits
President: Michele Abo
Estimated Sales: $75,000,000
Number Employees: 20-49
Parent Co: Nabisco
Type of Packaging: Consumer

12763 **Stello Foods**
248 Pine St
Punxsutawney, PA 15767 814-938-8611
Fax: 814-938-8769 800-849-4599
stellofoods@hotmail.com www.stellofoods.com
Processor of peppers, mustards, sauces, salsas, vinegars, spreads, salad dressings and brined products
President: Nickki L Stello
Vice President: James Stello
Estimated Sales: $2.5 Million
Number Employees: 30
Sq. footage: 60000
Type of Packaging: Consumer, Food Service, Private Label, Bulk
Brands:
PINKS
RAPES
ROSIE'S

12764 **Steltzner Vineyards**
5998 Silverado Trl
Napa, CA 94558-9416 707-252-7272
Fax: 707-252-2079 wines@steltzner.com
www.steltzner.com
Bottled wine
President: Richard M Steltzner
Marketing Director: Alison Steltzner
Co-Founder: Dick Steltzner
General Manager: Kim Gish
Estimated Sales: $ 10-20 Million
Number Employees: 20-49
Brands:
Steltzner Vineyards

12765 **Stengel Seed & Grain Company**
14698 Sd Highway 15
Milbank, SD 57252 605-432-6030
Fax: 605-432-6064 gstengel@tnics.com
Processor of organic grains. Services include cleaning, dehulling, packaging, warehousing and shipping.
President: Doug Stengel
Estimated Sales: Less than $500,000
Number Employees: 5-9
Sq. footage: 30000

12766 **Stepan Company**
100 W Hunter Ave
Maywood, NJ 07607-1088 201-845-3030
Fax: 201-712-7235 800-523-3614
food.health@stepan.com www.stepan.com
Processor and exporter of medium chain triglycerides and structured lipids
President/CEO: F Quinn Stepan Jr
CFO: James Hurlburt
Research & Development: Jenifer Haydinger Galante PhD
Quality Control: Parul Vyas
Marketing: James Butterwick
Plant Manager: Don Watson
Purchasing Director: Ed Sebastian
Estimated Sales: $ 20 - 50 Million
Number Employees: 50-99
Sq. footage: 11000
Parent Co: Stephan Company
Type of Packaging: Bulk
Brands:
NEOBEE 1053
NEOBEE 1095
NEOBEE 895
NEOBEE M-20
NEOBEE M-5
WECOBEE FS
WECOBEE M
WECOBEE S

12767 **Stephany's Chocolates**
6770 West 52nd Avenue
Arvada, CO 80002 303-421-7229
Fax: 303-421-7256 800-888-1522
customerservice@stephanyschocolates.com
www.stephanyschocolates.com
Bulk and boxed chocolates, toffee, mints, toffee, creams, nuts and chews, mint meltaways and cherry cordials.
President: Hal Strottan
Quality Control: Cathy Warner
Estimated Sales: $ 10-20 Million
Number Employees: 170
Brands:
Colorado Almond Toffee
Denver Mint
Stephany's Chocolates

12768 **Stephen's GourmetIndulgent Foods**
P.O.Box 10
Farmington, UT 84025-0010 801-939-9100
Fax: 801-939-9373 800-845-2400
customerservice@indulgentfoods.com
www.hotcocoa.com
Processor of hot cocoa and cappuccino
Owner: David Cowley
Estimated Sales: $ 3 - 5 Million
Number Employees: 5-9
Type of Packaging: Consumer, Food Service
Brands:
Cafe Tiamo

12769 **Sterigenics International**
PO Box 30667
Los Angeles, CA 90030-0667 510-770-9000
Fax: 510-770-1499 800-472-4508
info@sterigenics.com www.sterigenics.com
Irradiator of spices, dehydrated vegetable ingredients and seasoning blends
CEO: David E Meyer
CFO: Fred Ruegsegger
Deputy CEO: Marc Markey
Number Employees: 20-49
Brands:
Sterigenics

12770 **Sterling Candy**
595 S Broadway
Hicksville, NY 11801-5036 516-932-8300
Fax: 516-932-8392
Candy
President/CEO: Edward Greenberg
Public Relations: Stacey Greenberg
Estimated Sales: $ 10-24.9 Million
Number Employees: 50

12771 **Sterling Extract Company**
10929 Franklin Ave Ste V
Franklin Park, IL 60131 847-451-9728
Fax: 847-451-9745
www.sterlingextractcompany.com
Processor of pure and artifical vanilla flavoring extracts, flavors for ice cream, candy and bakery products.
President: Craig Wakefield
Vice President: Lynn Wakefield
Marketing Director: John Wakefield
Sales Director: Deborah Pavone
Estimated Sales: $1500000
Number Employees: 5-9
Type of Packaging: Bulk
Brands:
Bourbonil
Star-Van
Sterling Old Fashion Flavors
Vanaleigh 6b

12772 **Sterling Foods**
1075 Arion Pkwy
San Antonio, TX 78216 210-490-1669
Fax: 210-490-7964
cdietzel@sterlingfoodusa.com
www.sterlingfoodsusa.com
Gourmet cakes, biscuits, breads and rolls, cookies and brownies, loaf cakes and muffins
CEO: John Likovich
CFO: Mark Kuehl
SVP Sales/Marketing: Fred Friend
Human Resources Director: Jim Kuehl
SVP/COO: Nick Davis
Plant Manager: Hugo Salinas
Purchasing Manager: Barry Daley
Estimated Sales: $7900000
Number Employees: 250
Sq. footage: 85000

12773 **Sterzing Food Company**
1819 Charles St
Burlington, IA 52601 319-754-8467
Fax: 319-752-7195 800-754-8467
sterzing2@lisco.com www.sterzingchips.com
Manufacturer of potato chips and sour cream and dip
President: Tom Blackwood
Vice President: Thomas Blackwood
Estimated Sales: $2 Million
Number Employees: 20-49
Type of Packaging: Consumer
Brands:
Sterzing's

12774 **Stettler Meats**
4703 42 Ave
Stettler, AB T0C 2L1
Canada 403-742-1427
Fax: 403-742-1429
Fresh meats, processed meats, wild game, custom cutting & wrapping, pork, beef, and bison.
Manager: Randy Cherewko
Sales: Kelly Greenwood
Number Employees: 1-25
Type of Packaging: Consumer, Food Service

12775 **Steuk's Country Market &Winery**
165 E Washington Row
Sandusky, OH 44870-2610 419-625-8324
Fax: 419-625-9007
Wines
President: Charles Sprigg
Estimated Sales: $ 2.5-5 Million
Number Employees: 1-4

12776 **Steve Connolly Seafood Company**
34 Newmarket Sq
Roxbury, MA 02118 617-427-7700
Fax: 617-427-7697 800-225-5595
Fresh and frozen seafood, lobster, shellfish, smoked fish, prepared foods
President: Stephan Connolly
Marketing Director: Willy Warner
CFO: John Curley
Quality Control: Donald Putney
CFO: Michel Zukowki
CFO: Mike Zukowski
Operations Manager: Walter Peary
Production Manager: William Blenn
Estimated Sales: $ 28 Million
Number Employees: 50-99
Type of Packaging: Bulk
Brands:
Steve Connolly

12777 **Steve's Doughnut Shop**
4 Winslow Ave
Somerset, MA 02726-2318 508-672-0865
Doughnuts
Owner: Mario Gulinello
Estimated Sales: $ 1-2.5 Million
Number Employees: 10-19

12778 **Steve's Mom**
200 Food Center Dr
Bronx, NY 10474 718-842-8090
Fax: 718-832-6302 800-362-4545
ruggiebake@aol.com www.steves-mom.com
Processor of kosher dessert strudels, vegetable strudels, rugelach, coconut macaroons, brownies, and cheesecake
President: Suellen Schussel
Vice President: Erwin Schussel
Estimated Sales: $664696
Number Employees: 5-9
Sq. footage: 2500
Type of Packaging: Consumer, Food Service, Private Label, Bulk
Brands:
Fudgeroons
Scotcheroons
Steve's Mom

12779 **Stevenot Winery & Imports**
458 Main St, #3
Murphys, CA 95247-9646 20- 2-3 43
Fax: 20- 7-8 01 info@stevenotwinery.com
www.stevenotwinery.com
Wines
Owner: Barden Stevenot
Winemaker: Chuck Hovey
Estimated Sales: $ 5-10 Million
Number Employees: 5-9
Type of Packaging: Bulk
Brands:
Shephard Ridge
Stevenot Winery

12780 **Stevens Point Brewery**
2617 Water St
Stevens Point, WI 54481 715-344-9310
Fax: 715-344-8897 800-369-4911
www.pointbeer.com
Processor and exporter of beer
President: Jim Weichman
CEO: Joe Martino
Brewing: John Zappa
Operations Manager: Art Oksuita
Estimated Sales: $ 20 - 50 Million
Number Employees: 20-49
Parent Co: Barton Beers

12781 **Stevens Sausage Company**
3411 Stevens Sausage Rd
Smithfield, NC 27577 919-934-3159
Fax: 919-934-2568 800-338-0561
tstev25536@aol.com www.stevens-sausage.com
Processor of fresh ham, pork, frankfurters and sausage
President: N Stevens
Marketing Executive: Tim Stevens
Estimated Sales: $11 Million
Number Employees: 72
Type of Packaging: Consumer, Food Service, Bulk

12782 **Stevens Tropical Plantation**
6550 Okeechobee Blvd
West Palm Beach, FL 33411-2798 561-683-4701
Fax: 561-683-4993
Processor and importer of syrups, fruit juices, nectar and beverage bases
President: Henry Stevens Jr
Estimated Sales: $ 1 - 3 Million
Number Employees: 5-9
Sq. footage: 10000
Type of Packaging: Consumer, Food Service
Brands:
Parkway
Sunny Isle

12783 **Stevens Tropical Plantation**
6550 Okeechobee Blvd
West Palm Beach, FL 33411-2798 561-683-4701
Fax: 561-683-4993 800-785-1355
www.stevenstropicalplantation.com
Bottled fruit juices
Owner: Henry W Stevens Jr Jr
Estimated Sales: $990,000
Number Employees: 5-9
Brands:
Stevens

12784 **Stevenson-Cooper**
P.O.Box 46345
Philadelphia, PA 19160-6345 215-223-2600
Fax: 215-223-3597 waxcooper@aol.com
www.stevensoncooper.com
Manufacturer and exporter of oils including cottonseed and palm oils; also, manufacturer of paraffin and sealing wax
President: Dennis Cooper
R&D: Tammy Pullins
Estimated Sales: Below $ 5 Million
Number Employees: 5-9

12785 **Stevia LLC**
PO Box 80311
Valley Forge, PA 19484-0311 610-265-7102
Fax: 610-265-7102 888-878-3842
admin@SteviaDessert.com www.sweevia.com
President: Lisa Jobs
Brands:
Sweetvia
Sweevia

12786 **Stevison Ham Company**
125 Stevison Ham Rd
Portland, TN 37148 615-325-7315
Fax: 615-325-5914 800-844-4267
sales@stevisonham.com www.stevisonham.com
Smoked ham, ribs, BBQ pork
President: Michael Stevison
VP Marketing: Sean Stevison
Vice President: John White
CFO: Oara Stevison
Estimated Sales: $ 20-30 Million
Number Employees: 50-99
Brands:
Stevison's

12787 **Stewart Candy Company**
600 Haines Ave
Waycross, GA 31501 912-284-9320
Fax: 912-285-0228 deens@stewartcandy.com
www.stewartcandy.com
Candy and confections
President: Jimmy Stewart Iii
CFO: Deen J Stewart
Sales Director: Sam Stewart
Estimated Sales: $ 20-50 Million
Number Employees: 20-49

12788 **Stewart's Beverages**
709 Westchester Avenue
White Plains, NY 10604-3103 914-397-9200
Processor of soft drinks
President: Samuel M Simpson
CFO: Myron D Stadler
Number Employees: 10-19
Parent Co: Triarc Companies
Type of Packaging: Consumer, Food Service

12789 **Stewart's Ice Cream**
P.O.Box 435
Saratoga Springs, NY 12866 518-581-1300
Fax: 518-581-7076 www.stewartsshops.com
Processor of whole, 2% and skim milk; also, regular and low-fat ice cream
Manager: John Bottisti
Estimated Sales: $300,000-500,000
Number Employees: 50-99
Type of Packaging: Consumer

12790 **Stewart's Private BlendFoods**
4110 W Wrightwood Ave
Chicago, IL 60639-2172 773-489-2500
Fax: 773-489-2148 800-654-2862
info@stewarts.com www.stewarts.com
Processor, importer and exporter of coffees including flavored, decaffeinated and roasted; also, flavored and blended teas
President: Donald Stewart
CEO: Robert Stewart
Vice President: William Stewart Jr
Production Manager: Elita Pagan
Plant Manager: Ed Fabro
Estimated Sales: $2,000,000
Number Employees: 20-49
Sq. footage: 48000
Type of Packaging: Consumer, Food Service, Private Label, Bulk
Brands:
Stewarts

12791 **Stewarts Market**
17821 State Route 507 SE
Yelm, WA 98597-9654 360-458-2091
Fax: 360-458-3150
Meat and homemade sausage
President: Dorthy Carlson
Vice President: Stewart Carlson
Estimated Sales: $ 3 - 5 Million
Number Employees: 20-49

12792 **Stewarts Seafood**
8401 Highway 188
Coden, AL 36523-3059 251-824-7368
Fax: 251-824-7369
Seafood
President: Janice Stewart
Estimated Sales: $ 10 - 20 Million
Number Employees: 20-49

12793 **Stichler Products**
1800 N 12th St Ste 1
Reading, PA 19604 610-921-0211
Fax: 610-921-0294 spicandy@aol.com
Processor of confectionery products including decorative and ornamental
President: Martin Deutschman
Vice President: Brad Deutschman
Public Relations: Kathy Paules
Estimated Sales: $4700000
Number Employees: 20-49
Sq. footage: 62000
Type of Packaging: Consumer, Food Service, Private Label, Bulk
Brands:
CANDY FARMS

12794 **Stickney & Poor Company**
12 Reynolds Dr
Peterborough, NH 03458-1611 603-924-2259
Processor and exporter of portion-controlled products including ketchup, relish, nondairy coffee creamers, honey, artificial sweeteners, jams, jellies, marmalades, preserves, mayonnaise, mustard, salt, pepper, vinegar, salad dressingsand dipping sauces
President: H Sandy Brown
VP: Chuck Lavery
Number Employees: 50-99
Type of Packaging: Food Service, Private Label, Bulk
Brands:
Harvest Selects
Stickney & Poor

12795 **Sticky Fingers Bakeries**
420 Columbus Avenue
San Francisco, CA 94133-3902 800-458-5826
Fax: 509-922-7102
sales@stickyfingersbakeries.com
www.stickyfingersbakeries.com
English Scones. Delete this entry it is a duplicate entry - the correct entry is 14374 with the Spokane, Washington address.

12796 **Sticky Fingers Bakeries**
PO Box 14533
Spokane, WA 99214-0533 509-922-1985
Fax: 509-922-7102 800-458-5826
sales@stickyfingersbakeries.com
www.stickyfingersbakeries.com
Bakery mixes, English Scones, gourmet breads, brownies, quick breads, jams, and curds.
President/CEO: Tom Owens
Vice President: Ted Vogelman
Sales Director: Tom Owens
Number Employees: 1-4
Type of Packaging: Private Label
Brands:
Sticky Fingers Bakeries Eng Muffin
Sticky Fingers Bakeries Jams
Sticky Fingers Bakeries Scones

12797 **Stiebs**
11767 Road 27 1/2
Madera, CA 93637 559-661-0031
Fax: 559-661-0032 pominfo@stiebs.com
www.stiebs.com
Concentrates, extracts, arils, powders, blending and formulation.
Partner: Jerry Pantaleo
Partner: Brad Miller
Number Employees: 10

12798 **Stilwell Foods**
5 E Walnut St
Stilwell, OK 74960 918-696-8325
Fax: 918-696-5691
gwen.fletcher@schwansbakery.com
www.flowersindustries.com/flowers
Frozen fruit, breaded vegetables, fruit pies
President: Michael Taffer
Controller: Greg Jones
VP Sales: Jack Lundberg
VP Operations: Jim Gross
Plant Manager: Jason Blake
Purchasing Manager: Travis Gregory
Estimated Sales: $ 100-500 Million
Number Employees: 500-999
Brands:
Premium Pak
Starr Springs
Stilwell

12799 **Stimo-O-Stam, Ltd.**
70593 Bravo St
Covington, LA 70433
Fax: 985-845-1489 800-562-7514
laurie_sre@yahoo.com www.stimostam.com
Processor and exporter Supplements, Nutritional: Energy Mixes
Manager: Alan Lafferty
Estimated Sales: $300,000-500,000
Number Employees: 1-4
Sq. footage: 10000
Type of Packaging: Consumer
Brands:
Stim-O-Stam

12800 **Stinson Seafood Company**
9655 Granite Ridge Dr Ste 100
San Diego, CA 92123-2697
Fax: 207-963-2328 www.connors.ca
Manufacturer of canned herring products, sardines
President/CEO: Chris Lischewski
General Manager: Roger Webber
Plant Manager: Peter Colson
Estimated Sales: $100 Million
Number Employees: 500-999
Parent Co: Connor Bros
Type of Packaging: Consumer, Food Service, Private Label
Brands:
ADMIRAL
BEACH CLIFF
BULLDOG
COMMANDER
NEPTUNE
POSSUM

12801 **Stirling Foods**
P.O.Box 569
Renton, WA 98057-0569 425-251-9293
Fax: 425-251-0251 800-332-1714
stirling@stirling.net www.stirling.net
Processor and exporter of gourmet beverage flavors and syrups
President: Mark Greiner
CEO: Earl Greiner
Estimated Sales: $1,300,000
Number Employees: 5-9
Type of Packaging: Consumer, Food Service, Private Label
Brands:
Stirling Gourmet Flavors

12802 **Stock Popcorn Company**
P.O.Box 830
Lake View, IA 51450 712-657-2811
Fax: 712-657-2550 stockpop@netins.net
www.stockpopcorn.com
Processor and exporter of yellow and white popcorn including processed unpopped and microwaveable; also, feed sack fashion packaging for popcorn
President: James Stock
Number Employees: 5-9
Type of Packaging: Consumer, Private Label, Bulk
Brands:
Lil' Chief
Lil' Chief Popcorn

12803 **Stock Yards Packing Company**
340 N Oakley Blvd
Chicago, IL 60612-2216 312-733-6050
Fax: 312-733-0738 800-621-1119
customerservice@stockyards.com
www.stockyards.com
Processor and exporter of beef, pork, veal and lamb
President: Dan Pollack
Plant Manager: Oscar Moore
Estimated Sales: $ 10 - 20 Million
Number Employees: 100-249
Sq. footage: 60000

12804 **Stockpot**
22505 State Route 9 SE
Woodinville, WA 98072-6010 425-415-2000
Fax: 425-415-2004 800-468-1611
stockpotinfo@stockpot.com www.stockpot.com
Manufacturer of fresh refrigerated soups and chowders, entrees and stews, gravies, chilies, sauces, specialty products, vegan and vegetarian, and marinades.
President: Kathleen Horner
CFO: Art Olson
Marketing/Public Relations: Gary Merritt
Operations Manager: George Andrews
Estimated Sales: $ 20-50 Million
Number Employees: 100-249
Parent Co: Campbell Soup Company
Type of Packaging: Private Label
Brands:
STOCKPOT

12805 **Stockton Cheese**
300 W Railroad Ave
Stockton, IL 61085 815-947-3361
Fax: 815-947-2768 800-728-0111
cloehr@stocktoncheese.com
www.stocktoncheese.com
Processor of Swiss cheese
Manager: Chuck Loehr
Human Resources Director: Deb Turnmeyer
Plant Manager: Chuck Loehr
Estimated Sales: $ 20 - 50 Million
Number Employees: 75
Sq. footage: 16559
Parent Co: Brewster Dairy
Type of Packaging: Bulk

12806 **Stockton Graham & Company**
4320 Delta Lake Dr
Raleigh, NC 27612-7000 919-881-8271
Fax: 919-881-0746 800-835-5943
info@stocktongraham.com
www.stocktongraham.com
Wholesale specialty beverages
President: Jeff Vojta
Estimated Sales: $500,000-$1 Million
Number Employees: 10-19
Brands:
Stoktin Grahan

12807 **Stokes Canning Company**
5590 High St
Denver, CO 80216-1523 303-292-4018
Fax: 303-292-4364
www.centennialspecialtyfoods.com
Soups
CFO: Douglas L Evans
COO: Jeffery Nieder
Sales/Marketing Director: Robert A Beckwith Jr.
Estimated Sales: $ 10-100 Million
Number Employees: 4
Brands:
Ellis
Strokes

12808 **Stoller Fisheries**
P.O.Box B
Spirit Lake, IA 51360 712-336-1750
Fax: 712-336-4681 www.stollerfisheries.com
President: Larry Stoller
Estimated Sales: $ 20 - 50 Million
Number Employees: 20-49

12809 **Stoller Fisheries**
1301 18th Street
PO Box B
Spirit Lake, IA 51360 712-336-1750
Fax: 712-336-4681 800-831-5174
stollerfisheries@mchsi.com
www.stollerfisheries.com
Processor and exporter of fresh fish including carp, buffalo, sheepheads and suckers
President: Larry Stoller
Controller: Mark Salzwedel
VP: Thomas Opheim
Estimated Sales: $4 Million
Number Employees: 45
Sq. footage: 35000
Parent Co: Progressive Companies
Type of Packaging: Bulk

12810 **Stolt SeaFarm**
9149 E Levee Rd
Elverta, CA 95626-9559 916-991-4420
Fax: 916-991-4334 800-525-0333
www.sterlingcaviar.com
Processor of white sturgeon including fresh, cold smoked and frozen
Manager: Peter Struffenegger
CFO: Joeseph Ruffo
R&D: Richard Helfrich
Quality Control: Richard Helfrich
Estimated Sales: $ 10 - 20 Million
Number Employees: 20-49
Sq. footage: 55000
Type of Packaging: Food Service

12811 **Stone Brewing**
1999 Citracado Parkway
Escondido, CA 92029 760-471-4999
Fax: 760-471-7690 email@stonebrew.com
www.stonebrew.com
beer
President/Brewmaster: Steve Wagner
Chairman/CEO: Greg Koch
Quality Assurance Administrator: Christine Geiger
VP Sales: Arlan Arnsten
HR Manager: Kathy Loven
Production Manager/Head Brewer: Mitch Steele

12812 **Stone Crabs**
11 Washington Ave
Miami Beach, FL 33139-7395 305-534-8788
Fax: 305-532-2704 800-260-2722
www.joesstonecrabs.com
Processor of fresh and frozen stone crabs, whole lobsters and lobster tails
President: Stephen Sawitz
CFO: Marc Fine
Marketing Director: Tracie Gordon
Operations Manager: James McClendon
Plant Manager: Ron Pressley
Estimated Sales: $ 10 - 20 Million
Number Employees: 20-49
Type of Packaging: Consumer, Food Service
Brands:
SCI

12813 **(HQ)Stone Hill Wine Company**
1110 Stone Hill Hwy
Hermann, MO 65041-1280 573-486-2221
Fax: 573-486-3828
hermann-info@stonehillwinery.com
www.stonehillwinery.com
Manufacturer of grape juice, wine and champagne
President: James Held
VP: Betty Held
Sales Director: Thomas Held
Production Manager: Jon Held
Estimated Sales: $ 50 - 100 Million
Number Employees: 100-249
Number of Brands: 1
Number of Products: 20
Other Locations:
Stone Hill Winery
New Florence MO
Stone Hill Winery
Branson MO
Brands:
Stone Hill Winery

12814 **Stone Meat Processor**
1485 Stonefield Way
Ogden, UT 84404-1211 801-782-9825
Fax: 801-782-1109
Processor of ground beef
President: Frank Stone
Estimated Sales: $ 10 - 20 Million
Number Employees: 20-49
Type of Packaging: Consumer, Food Service

12815 **Stone Mountain Pecan Company**
1781 Highway 78 NW
Monroe, GA 30655 770-207-6486
Fax: 770-207-4403 800-633-6887
smpc1@mindspring.com
www.stonemountainpecan.com
Processors of pecans
President: Robby E Coker
Estimated Sales: $3200000
Number Employees: 5-9
Type of Packaging: Consumer, Food Service, Private Label, Bulk

12816 **Stone Mountain Vineyards**
1376 Wyatt Mountain Rd
Dyke, VA 22935 434-990-9463
info@stonemountainvineyards.com
www.stonemountainvineyards.com
Wines
Founder: Alfred Breiner
Estimated Sales: $ 3 - 5 Million
Number Employees: 5-9

12817 **Stone's Home Made CandyShop**
145 W Bridge St
Oswego, NY 13126 315-343-8401
Fax: 315-343-8401 888-223-3928
information@oswego.com
Candy and confectionery products
Owner: Jan Stachowicz
Estimated Sales: $300,000
Number Employees: 5-9
Sq. footage: 4500
Type of Packaging: Consumer, Food Service

12818 **Stonegate**
2300 Lower Chiles Valley Rd
St Helena, CA 94574-9632 707-603-2203
Fax: 707-603-2209 info@stonegatewinery.com
www.stonegatewinery.com
Wines
President: Paul D Croft Croft
CFO: Cathy del Fava
Estimated Sales: $ 5-10 Million
Number Employees: 10-19

12819 **Stoneridge Winery**
13862 Ridge Rd
Sutter Creek, CA 95685 209-223-1761
Wines
Owner: Gary Porteous
Estimated Sales: Below $ 5 Million
Number Employees: 5-9

12820 **(HQ)Stonewall Kitchen**
2 Stonewall Ln
York, ME 3909 207-351-2713
Fax: 207-351-2715 800-207-5267
info@stonewallkitchen.com
www.stonewallkitchen.com
Processor and exporter of jam, mustard, sauces, relish, dessert toppings and salad dressing
Owner: Charles Robinson
Owner: Virginia Willis
CFO: Laurie King
Estimated Sales: $10-20 Million
Number Employees: 120
Sq. footage: 30000
Type of Packaging: Consumer
Brands:
Stonewall Kitchen

12821 **Stonies Sausage Shop Inc**
1507 Edgemont Blvd
Perryville, MO 63775-1230 573-547-2540
Fax: 573-547-1747 888-546-2540
contact@stoniessausageshop.com
www.shopstonies.com
state and national champion smoked meats and sausages, retail store, wholesale, mail order, deer processing, private label, 50 years in business, federal inspection
President/Partner: Roger Wibbenmeyer
Co-Owner: Tyson Wibbenmeyer
Estimated Sales: $1-1.5 Million
Number Employees: 20
Sq. footage: 15000
Type of Packaging: Food Service, Private Label

12822 **Stonington Lobster Cooperative**
P.O.Box 87
Stonington, ME 04681 207-367-5535
Fax: 207-367-2802
Lobster
Manager: Steve Robins Iii
Estimated Sales: $ 5 - 10 Million
Number Employees: 10-19

12823 **Stonington Vineyards**
523 Taugwonk Rd
Stonington, CT 06378 860-535-1222
Fax: 860-535-2182 800-421-9463
info@stoningtonvineyards.com
www.stoningtonvineyards.com
Processor of table wines including chardonnay, seaport white, fume vidal, white and bush, cabernet franc and gewurztraminer
President: Cornelius H Smith
General Manager/Winemaker: Mike McAndrew
Marketing Director: Nick Smith
Estimated Sales: $400000
Number Employees: 5-9
Sq. footage: 10000
Type of Packaging: Consumer
Brands:
Seaport Blush
Seaport White
Seaport Wines
Stonington
Stonington Vineyards

12824 **Stony Hill Vineyard**
3331 Saint Helena Hwy N
Saint Helena, CA 94574 707-963-2636
Fax: 707-963-1831 info@stonyhillvineyard.com
www.stonyhillvineyard.com
Wines
President: Peter Mc Crea
Office Manager: Willinda McCrea
Vineyard and Winery Operations: Mike Chelini
Vineyard Foreman: Alejandro Salomon
Customer Relations: Mary Burklow
Estimated Sales: $500,000-$1 Million
Number Employees: 10-19
Brands:
Stony Hill Vineyard

12825 **Stony Ridge Winery**
4948 Tesla Rd
Livermore, CA 94550 925-449-0458
Fax: 925-449-0646
bacchus@stonyridgewinery.com
www.crookedvine.com
Wines
Owner: Rick Corbett
Winemaker: Dale Vaughn-Bowen
Estimated Sales: Below $ 5 Million
Number Employees: 10-19
Brands:
Orobianco-California NV

12826 **Stonyfield Farm**
10 Burton Dr
Londonderry, NH 03053 603-437-4040
Fax: 603-437-7594 www.stonyfield.com
Processor of fresh, frozen and soy yogurt including plain and fruit flavored
President: Gary Hirshberg
CFO: Diane Carhart
Marketing Director: Karen Billings
Sales Director: Carter Elenz
Public Relations: M Viederman
Operations Manager: John Daigle
Production Manager: Herb Berwald
Purchasing Manager: Steve Inamorathi
Estimated Sales: $300,000-500,000
Number Employees: 1-4
Type of Packaging: Consumer, Food Service
Brands:
Stonyfield Farm Frozen Yogurt
Stonyfield Farm Ice Cream

Stonyfield Farm Refrig Yogurt
Yo Baby Yogurt

12827 **Stop & Shop Manufacturing**
104 Meadow Road
Readville, MA 02136-2349 508-977-5132
Processor and wholesaler/distributor of milk, juices and sodas
Marketing Director: William Sress
Estimated Sales: $ 3 - 5 Million
Number Employees: 20-49
Parent Co: Stop & Shop Supermarket Company
Type of Packaging: Consumer

12828 **Storck**
325 N Lasalle St # 400
Chicago, IL 60654-6467 312-467-5700
Fax: 312-467-9722 800-621-7772
info@us.storck.com www.storck.com
Processor of confectionery items including butter-scotch, toffee, chocolate and chocolate/caramel: bars and bags
President: Liam Killeen
VP Marketing: Ralf Hilpuesch
VP Sales: Steve Meisinger
Estimated Sales: $9,000,000
Number Employees: 50-99
Type of Packaging: Consumer
Brands:
MAMBA
MILKFULS
PEANUT RIESEN
RIESEN
TOFFIFAY
WERTHER'S CHOCOLATES
WERTHER'S ORIGINAL
WERTHER'S ORIGINAL CHEWY CARA-MELS

12829 **Storck Canada**
1 City Centre Drive
Mississauga, ON L5B 1M2
Canada 905-272-4480
Fax: 905-272-6899 800-305-7551
info@ca.storck.com www.storck.com
Candy
VP: Terry Dennis
Number Employees: 20-49
Brands:
CAMPINO
KNOPPERS
MERCI
MERCI CROCANT
MERCI PUR
MINI DICKMANN'S
SUPER DICKMANN'S
TOFFIFEE
WERTHER'S ORIGINAL

12830 **Storheim's**
1596 Arapahoe Trl
Green Bay, WI 54313-6761 920-498-2343
Fax: 920-592-0897
Gourmet foods
Owner: Ray Kern
Manager: Nate Kern

12831 **Storrs Winery**
303 Potrero St Ste 35
Santa Cruz, CA 95060 831-458-5030
Fax: 831-458-0464 salesmgr@storrswine.com
www.storrswine.com
Wines
Owner/President: Stephen Storrs
Owner/VP: Pamela Bianchini-Storrs
Operations Manager: Aaron Storrs
Production Manager: Morgan Storrs
Estimated Sales: $1-2.5 Million
Number Employees: 5-9
Brands:
Storrs

12832 **Story Winery**
10525 Bell Rd
Plymouth, CA 95669 209-245-6208
Fax: 209-245-6619 800-712-6390
storyzin@cdepot.net www.zin.com
Wines
Owner: Bruce Tichneor
CEO: Jan Tichenor
Marketing Director: Jan Tichenor
Estimated Sales: $500,000-$1 Million
Number Employees: 1-4
Brands:
Story Wine

12833 **Story's Popcorn Company**
P.O.Box 247
Charleston, MO 63834-0247 573-649-2727
Fax: 314-649-3374
Popcorn
President: A Story III
Estimated Sales: $ 10-20 Million
Number Employees: 1-4

12834 **Storybook Mountain Winery**
3835 State Highway 128
Calistoga, CA 94515 707-942-5310
Fax: 707-942-5334
sigstory@storybookwines.com
www.storybookwines.com
Wines
President: Jerry Seps
Estimated Sales: $540,000
Number Employees: 5-9
Brands:
Storybook Mountain Winery

12835 **Stoudt Brewing Company**
P.O.Box 880
Adamstown, PA 19501 717-484-4387
Fax: 717-484-4182 beernet@stoudtsbeer.com
www.stoudtsbeer.com
Processor of seasonal beers, ale, stout, lager and pilsner
President: Carol Stoudt
CFO: Edward Stoudt
Estimated Sales: $6 Million
Number Employees: 50
Type of Packaging: Consumer, Food Service

12836 **Strasburg Provision**
1317 N Wooster Ave
Strasburg, OH 44680 330-878-5557
Fax: 330-878-5558 800-207-6009
www.strasburgprovision.com
Processor of meat products and catering
President: Rudolf M Klapper
Sales: Herb Gritzan
Production: Frank H Klapper
Estimated Sales: $3000000
Number Employees: 20-49
Type of Packaging: Consumer, Food Service, Private Label, Bulk

12837 **Strathroy Foods**
PO Box 188
Strathroy, ON N7G 3J2
Canada 519-245-4600
Fax: 519-245-3661
Processor and exporter of frozen vegetables including peas and carrots and other vegetable varieties
President: Craig Richardson
Type of Packaging: Consumer, Food Service, Private Label
Brands:
Red Valley

12838 **Straub Brewery Industries**
303 Sorg St
St Marys, PA 15857-1592 814-834-2875
Fax: 814-834-7628 sales@straubber.com
www.straubbeer.com
Manufacturer of beer
President: Daniel Straub
Brewmaster: Thomas Straub
Estimated Sales: $ 20 - 50 Million
Number Employees: 20-49
Brands:
Straub
Straub Light

12839 **Straub's**
8282 Forsyth Blvd
Clayton, MO 63105-1626 314-725-2121
Fax: 314-725-2123 888-725-2121
straubs@anet-stl.com www.straubs.com
Processor of steaks, seafood including lobster tails and gift baskets
President: Jack Straub
Founder: William A Straub
CEO: Jack W Straub Jr
Owner: J W Straub
Number Employees: 100-249
Brands:
Straubs

12840 **Straus Family Creamery**
1105 Industrial Ave # 200
Petaluma, CA 94952-1141
Fax: 415-663-5465 800-572-7783
family@strausmilk.com
www.strausfamilycreamery.com
Producers of organic milk and dairy products.
President: Albert Straus
Estimated Sales: $ 5 - 10 Million
Number Employees: 50-99

12841 **Strauss Bakeries**
1608 W Lexington Avenue
Elkhart, IN 46514-1943 574-293-9027
Fax: 219-522-2137
Bakery products
President: Steve Strauss
Sales Manager: John Macley
Estimated Sales: $ 5-10 Million
Number Employees: 100-249

12842 **Strauss Veal & Lamb International**
P.O.Box 342
Hales Corners, WI 53130-0342 414-421-5250
Fax: 414-421-6059 800-562-7775
info@straussveal.com www.straussveal.com
Veal
President: Randy Strauss
Estimated Sales: $ 50-100 Million
Number Employees: 100-249

12843 **Streamline Foods**
6018 W Maple Rd
West Bloomfield, MI 48322-4404 248-851-2611
Fax: 248-737-2035 info@streamlinefoods.com
www.streamlinefoods.com
Grain, flour, sugars and syrups, dry blends, starches, chemicals, soy products, dairy products salt, peanut butter products
Manager: Dave Owens
VP Manufacturing Services: Don Gordon
Sales Rep: Teddy Kertis
Operations Manager: Doug Vause
Estimated Sales: $ 50-100 Million
Number Employees: 5-9
Brands:
Chocolate Mousse Maker

12844 **Strebin Farms**
28245 SE Division Dr
Troutdale, OR 97060-9486 503-665-8328
Fax: 503-669-7783 strebin@strebin.com
www.strebin.com
Processor of fresh and frozen red raspberries
President: William Strebin
CEO: William P Strebin
Marketing Director: William P Strebin
Estimated Sales: $ 5-10 Million
Number Employees: 50-99
Type of Packaging: Food Service
Brands:
Strebin Farms

12845 **Streblow Vineyards**
PO Box 233
Saint Helena, CA 94574-0233 707-963-5892
Fax: 707-963-5835
streblowvineyards@earthlink.net
Wine
President/Owner: Bruce Streblow
Co-Owner: Ana Canales
Brands:
Streblow Vineyards

12846 **Stremick's Heritage Foods**
4002 Westminster Ave
Santa Ana, CA 92703-1310 714-775-5000
Fax: 714-775-7677 800-371-9010
info@heritage-foods.com
www.heritage-foods.com
Processor of milk, cheese and cream, organic milk and soy milk
President/CEO: Louis Stremick
CFO: Mike Malone
Sales Manager: Tom Gustafson
Estimated Sales: $100-500 Million
Number Employees: 100-249
Type of Packaging: Consumer, Food Service
Other Locations:
Heritage Foods
Riverside CA

12847 **Stretch Island Fruit**
PO Box 8557
La Jolla, CA 92038
800-700-9687
info@stretchislandfruit.com
www.stretchislandfruit.com
Fruit snacks.
President: Ron Sagerson
CEO: Bob Sagerson
Quality Control: Michael Doehm
R&D: Michael Doehm
Director Sales/Marketing: Gerry Thygesen
Estimated Sales: $ 20 - 50 Million
Number Employees: 50-99
Sq. footage: 12000
Type of Packaging: Consumer, Food Service
Brands:
STRETCH ISLAND

12848 **Striplings**
1401 West Blvd
Moultrie, GA 31768-4223 229-985-4226
Manufacturer of beef and pork products including smoked sausage
Manager: Clint Goss
Co-Owner: Lisa Hardin
Number Employees: 5-9
Sq. footage: 14000
Type of Packaging: Consumer
Other Locations:
Stripling's General Store
Cordele GA
Brands:
DUNN'S

12849 **Stroehmann Bakeries**
3996 Paxton St
Harrisburg, PA 17111 717-561-1790
Fax: 717-564-9231 800-220-2867
www.stroehmann.com
Processor of baked goods including pan breads and rolls.
President: Gary J Prince
Executive Chairman: Galen Weston
EVP/Finance: Richard Mavrinac
Director Sales: Richard Adams
Chief Operating Officer: Dalton Phillips
Manager: Ron Searfoss
Plant Manager: Larry Valentine
Chief Merchandising Officer: Mark Foote
Estimated Sales: $ 50 - 100 Million
Number Employees: 250-499
Sq. footage: 200000
Parent Co: George Weston Bakeries
Type of Packaging: Consumer, Food Service, Private Label

12850 **Stroehmann Bakeries**
P.O.Box 976
Horsham, PA 19044-0976 215-672-8010
Fax: 215-672-6988 800-984-0989
www.stroehmann.com
Processor of sliced breads, buns and rolls and stuffing
CEO: Gary Prince
Director Marketing: Francis Strazzella
Number Employees: 1,000-4,999
Parent Co: George Weston Foods
Brands:
D'Italiano
Dutch Country
Stroehmann
Sunbeam
Taystee

12851 **Stroehmann Bakeries**
325 Kiwanis Blvd
West Hazleton, PA 18202 570-455-2066
Fax: 570-455-0003 www.stroehmann.com
Manufacturer of baked goods
Manager: Guy Ball
CFO: Bill Peterson
VP Sales: Tom Delapine
Estimated Sales: $100+ Million
Number Employees: 250-499
Parent Co: George Weston Foods
Type of Packaging: Consumer

12852 **Stroehmann Bakeries**
P.O.Box 110
Norristown, PA 19404 610-825-1140
Fax: 610-825-5896 800-984-0989
www.stroehmann.com
Processor of baked products including breads, rolls, snack cakes and cookies
Director Sales: Tom Delapine
Owner: Harold J Stroehmann Jr
Estimated Sales: $ 20 - 50 Million
Number Employees: 250-499
Type of Packaging: Consumer, Food Service, Private Label
Brands:
D'Italiano
Maier's Country
Maier's Country Rolls
Maier's Deli Rolls
Maier's Italian

12853 **Stroehmann Bakery**
PO Box 976
Horsham, PA 19044
Fax: 610-320-9286 800-984-0989
info@stroehmann.com www.stroehmann.com
Manufacturer of sliced breads, buns and rolls, and stuffing.
President: Gary Prince
CFO: Bill Petersen
VP Sales: Tom Delapine
VP Human Resources: Louis Minella
VP Manufacturing: Dan Babin
Estimated Sales: Less than $500,000
Number Employees: 3500
Brands:
Arnold
Boboli
Brownberry
D'Italiano
Dutch Country
Entenmanns'
Freihofers
Maier's
Thomas'

12854 **Strom Products Ltd.**
1500 Lakeside Dr
Bannockburn, IL 60015 847-236-9676
Fax: 847-267-1404 800-862-3311
noyolks@stromproducts.com www.noyolks.com
Processor and exporter of cholesterol-free egg noodles, vegeatable macaroni, macaroni and cheese dinners.
Owner/CEO: Robert Strom
President: Gary Henke
Estimated Sales: $35 Million
Number Employees: 10-19
Type of Packaging: Consumer
Brands:
No Yolks
Wacky Mac

12855 **Strossner's Bakery**
21 Roper Mountain Rd
Greenville, SC 29607-4125 864-233-3996
Fax: 864-232-2819 www.strossners.com
Processor of prepared European bread mixes, cakes, tortes, fancy pastries, danish and baked/partially baked breads
Owner: Richard Strossner
Sales Manager: Mary Michalsky
Production Manager: Connie Jud
Estimated Sales: $2,000,000
Number Employees: 50-99
Sq. footage: 14000
Type of Packaging: Consumer, Food Service

12856 **Strub Pickles**
100 Roy Boulevard
Brantford, ON N3R 7K2
Canada 519-751-1717
Fax: 519-752-5540 info@strubpickles.com
www.strubpickles.com
Processor of sauerkraut, hot peppers, sweet pimientos, horseradish, herring, jalapeno peppers, kosher dill pickles and relish; exporter of pickles, refrigerated and shelf stable foods, zucchini relish and chili sauce
President: Leo Strub
CEO: Martin Strub
CFO: Arnold Strub
Vice President: Anoy Strub
Number Employees: 100-249
Number of Brands: 2
Number of Products: 250
Sq. footage: 106000
Type of Packaging: Consumer, Food Service, Private Label, Bulk
Brands:
Strub's
Willie's

12857 **Strube Vegetable & Celery Company**
2404 S Wolcott
Unit 16-20
Chicago, IL 60608 773-446-4000
Fax: 312-226-7644 www.strube.com
Manufacturer of produce
President/Owner: Robert Strube
CEO: Janet Fleming
Estimated Sales: $67.4 Million
Number Employees: 100-249

12858 **Struthious Ostrich Farm**
386 Extonville Road
Allentown, NJ 08501-1503 609-208-0702
Fax: 609-208-0703 ostrichfm@aol.com
Processor of ostrich meat and eggs; also, chicks
Number Employees: 10-19

12859 **Stryker Sonoma Winery Vineyards**
5110 Highway 128
Geyserville, CA 95441 800-433-1944
Fax: 707-433-1948 800-433-1944
info@strykersonoma.com
www.strykersonoma.com
Wine
Owner: Craig Mac Donald
Owner: Karen Naley
Owner: Kat Stryker
Estimated Sales: Below $ 5 Million
Number Employees: 5-9
Brands:
Stryker Sonoma Winery Vineyards

12860 **Stuart Hale Company**
4350 W Ohio St
Chicago, IL 60624-1051 773-638-1800
Fax: 773-638-1888 info@grandwarehouse.com
www.grandwarehouse.com
Processor of bakers' supplies including bakery pan grease and pan and white mineral oils
President: David Schulman
General Manager: Stuart Schulman
Estimated Sales: $170000
Number Employees: 10-19
Type of Packaging: Private Label, Bulk

12861 **Stubb's Legendary Kitchen**
811 Barton Springs Rd
Austin, TX 78704-8702 512-480-0203
Fax: 512-476-3425 800-883-3238
info@jelly.com www.ilovestubbs.com
Processor of salsas, salad dressings, pastas and spaghetti and pesto sauce; exporter of salsa; importer of extra virgin olive oil
President: Scott Jensen
VP Operations: Robert Varley
Estimated Sales: $ 5 - 10 Million
Number Employees: 10-19
Sq. footage: 12000
Type of Packaging: Consumer

12862 **Stubb's Legendary Kitchen**
811 Barton Springs Rd
Austin, TX 78704-8702 512-480-0203
Fax: 512-476-3425 800-227-2283
customerservice@stubbsbbq.com
www.ilovestubbs.com
Rubs, sauces and marinades
Founder: C B Stubblefield
Estimated Sales: $ 5 - 10 Million
Number Employees: 10-19
Brands:
Stubb's

12863 **Sturm Foods**
215 Center St
Manawa, WI 54949 920-596-2511
Fax: 920-596-3040 800-347-8876
info@sturminc.com www.sturmfoods.com
Healthy foods and fitness beverages.
President: Mike Upchurch
CFO: Robert Ruegger
Export Sales Manager: Jim Sturm
Estimated Sales: $77400000
Number Employees: 250-499
Sq. footage: 400000
Type of Packaging: Consumer, Food Service, Private Label, Bulk

Brands:
Sturm's Village Farm

12864 **Stutz Candy Company**
400 S Warminster Rd
Hatboro, PA 19040-4097 215-675-2632
Fax: 215-675-1438 888-692-2639
Processor of candy including boxed chocolates
President: John Glaser
Estimated Sales: $3100000
Number Employees: 20-49
Sq. footage: 21000
Type of Packaging: Consumer

12865 **Subco Foods Inc**
4350 S Taylor Dr
Sheboygan, WI 53081-8479 920-457-7761
Fax: 920-457-3899 800-473-0757
mkhan@subcofoods.com www.subcofoods.com
Contract packager/ Private label manufacturer products include: drink mixes, iced tea mixes, hot chocolate, gelatins, puddings, cappuccino mixes, coffee creamers, instant gravies, soup bases, spice/spice blends, cake mixes andnutraceuticals
President: Mas Khan
Estimated Sales: $13100000
Number Employees: 50-99
Sq. footage: 125000
Type of Packaging: Food Service, Private Label
Other Locations:
Subco Foods Inc
West Chicago IL
Brands:
New Image

12866 **Subco Foods Inc.**
1150 Commerce Dr
West Chicago, IL 60185 630-231-0003
Fax: 630-231-0678 info@subcofoods.com
www.subcofoods.com
Contract packager of dry mixes, cappuccino, cocoa, cake mixes, soup bases, spices, coffee creamers, rice products, etc
President: Masroor Khan
CFO: Jim Stiedl
Plant Manager: J McGrath
Purchasing Agent: Syed Zaidi
Estimated Sales: $20 Million
Number Employees: 100
Sq. footage: 55000
Other Locations:
Subco Foods
Sheboygan WI
Brands:
New Image

12867 **Sucesores de Pedro Cortes**
PO Box 363626
San Juan, PR 00936-3626 787-754-7040
Fax: 787-764-2650 cortesco@tld.net
Processor of chocolate and cocoa products; private labeling available; importer of chocolate, milk drinks and crackers; wholesaler/distributor of confectionery items, beverages and biscuits
President: Ignacio Cortes Del Valle
VP: Ignacio Cortes Gelpi
Number Employees: 50-99
Number of Brands: 11
Sq. footage: 50000
Type of Packaging: Consumer, Private Label, Bulk
Brands:
Chocolate Cortes
Choki
Semi-Industrialized

12868 **Sudbury Soups and Salads**
40 Walker Farm Rd
Sudbury, MA 01776-2442 978-443-7715
Fax: 978-443-7715 888-783-7687
sudsoup@ultranet.com www.sudburysoup.com
Natural foods, dry soup mixes, lentils
CEO: Susan Sullivan
Brands:
Sudbury

12869 **Sudlersville Frozen Food Locker**
P.O.Box 203
Sudlersville, MD 21668-0203 410-438-3106
Fax: 410-438-3121 info@sudlersville.org
www.sudlersville.org
Processor of frozen meat products including beef and pork
Owner: Dwayne Nickerson
Bookkeeper: Marge Messner
Estimated Sales: Less than $500,000
Number Employees: 5-9
Type of Packaging: Consumer
Brands:
Sudlersville

12870 **Sudwerk Privatbrauerei Hubsch**
2001 2nd St
Davis, CA 95618-5474 530-758-8700
Fax: 530-753-0590 contact@sudwerk.com
www.sudwerk.com
Beer
Owner: Tim Mc Donald
VP: Dean Unger
Quality Assurance: Candace Whalin
Marketing Director: Dave Sipes
Plant Manager/Purchasing Director: Neil Jensen
Estimated Sales: Below $ 5 Million
Number Employees: 50-99
Brands:
Hubsch Doppel Bock
Hubsch Dunkel
Hubsch Lager
Hubsch Marzen
Hubsch Pilsener
Suderwerk Doppel
Suderwerk Dunkel
Suderwerk Lager
Suderwerk Mai Bock
Suderwerk Marzen
Suderwerk Pilsenser

12871 **Sue Bee Honey**
301 Lewis Blvd
PO Box 388
Sioux City, IA 51102-0388 712-258-0638
Fax: 712-258-1332 www.suebee.com
Processor and exporter of honey
Chairman: Rob Duhmann
CEO: David Allibone
EVP: Mark Mamman
Estimated Sales: $110 Million
Number Employees: 90
Parent Co: Sioux Honey Association Cooperative
Type of Packaging: Consumer, Food Service, Private Label, Bulk
Brands:
Aunt Sue
Clover Maid
Natural Pure
North American
Sue Bee

12872 **Sugai Kona Coffee**
P.O.Box 783
Kealakekua, HI 96750 808-322-7717
Fax: 808-322-4008 kona@kona.net
www.sugaikonacoffee.com
Producers of Sugai Kona coffee
Manager: Lee Sugai
CEO: Lee Sugai
Estimated Sales: $1 Million
Number Employees: 1-4
Number of Brands: 5
Number of Products: 30
Sq. footage: 15000
Type of Packaging: Consumer, Food Service, Private Label, Bulk
Brands:
SUGAI KONA GROVE COFFEE
Sugai Kona Coffee Emporium

12873 **Sugar Bowl Bakery**
1963 Sabre St
Hayward, CA 94545-1021 510-782-2118
Fax: 510-782-2119 info@sugarbowlbakery.com
www.sugarbowlbakery.com
Processor of baked goods, gourmet cakes and pastries.
President: Andrew Ly
CFO: Bradsord Stette
Manager: Larry Sato
R & D: Stephanie Vu
Sales Manager: Wilson Seet
Purchasing Agent: Kevin Ly
Estimated Sales: $300,000-500,000
Number Employees: 5-9
Sq. footage: 20000

12874 **Sugar Cane Growers Cooperative of Florida**
P.O.Box 666
Belle Glade, FL 33430 561-996-6146
Fax: 561-996-4780 info@scgc.org
www.scgc.org
Manufacturer of sugar and blackstrap molasses
President/CEO: George Wedgworth
Estimated Sales: $285 Million
Number Employees: 500-999
Type of Packaging: Consumer

12875 **Sugar Cane Industry Glades Correctional Institution**
500 Orange Avenue Cir
Belle Glade, FL 33430-5221 561-829-1400
Fax: 561-992-1355 www.dc.state.fl.us
Grower of sugar cane, oranges and grapefruit
Manager: Shannon Robert
Number Employees: 1-4
Parent Co: PRIDE of Florida
Type of Packaging: Bulk

12876 **Sugar Creek Packing**
2101 Kenskill Ave
Washington Court House, OH 43160 740-335-7440
Fax: 740-335-7443 800-848-8205
Sales@sugarcreek.com www.sugar-creek.com
Bacon and turkey bacon
Chairman: John Richardson
Estimated Sales: $20 Million
Number Employees: 700
Type of Packaging: Consumer, Food Service, Bulk
Other Locations:
Sugar Creek Packing Plant
Bloomington IL
Sugar Creek Packing Plant
Cincinnati OH
Sugar Creek Packing Plant
Dayton OH
Sugar Creek Packing Plant
Frontenac KS
Brands:
SUGAR CREEK

12877 **Sugar Creek Winery**
125 Boone Country Ln
Defiance, MO 63341 636-987-2400
Fax: 636-987-2051 info@sugarcreekwines.com
www.sugarcreekwines.com
Wines
President: Ken Miller
President: Wesley Wissman
Estimated Sales: $ 5-10 Million
Number Employees: 20-49

12878 **Sugar Creek/Eskimo Pie**
301 N El Paso Ave
Russellville, AR 72801-3721 479-968-1005
Fax: 479-968-5651 800-445-2715
cwhiteside@eskimo.com www.sugarcreek.com
Processor of ice cream and frozen smoothie and frozen yogurt mix
President: Scott Vanhorn
Director Business Development: Fred Fullerton Jr

Operations Manager: Scott Van Horn
Estimated Sales: $ 20 - 50 Million
Number Employees: 700
Sq. footage: 25000
Parent Co: Eskimo Pie Corporation
Type of Packaging: Private Label

12879 **Sugar Flowers Plus**
601 Vine St
Glendale, CA 91204 818-545-3592
Fax: 818-545-7459 800-972-2935
sugarflowersplus@earthlink.net
www.sugarflowersplus.com
hand made gum paste and royal icing cake decorations
President/Owner: Terry Becker
Number Employees: 4

12880 **Sugar Flowers Plus**
601 Vine St
Glendale, CA 91204 818-545-3592
Fax: 818-545-7459 800-972-2935
sugarflowersplus@earthlink.net
www.sugarflowers.com

Manufacturer of cake decorations including gum paste flowers
Owner: Terry Becker
R&D: Anna Becker
Sales: Garrick Wright
Plant Manager: Gary Roundtree
Estimated Sales: $ .5 - 1 million
Number Employees: 1-4
Type of Packaging: Consumer, Food Service
Brands:
Sugar Flowers

12881 **Sugar Foods**
950 Raco Drive
Lawrenceville, GA 30045-4307 770-339-0184
800-732-8963
Processor of portion controlled sugar and sugar substitutes
President: Stephan O'Dell
Number Employees: 100-249
Type of Packaging: Food Service

12882 **Sugar Foods**
P.O.Box 1220
Sun Valley, CA 91353-1220 818-768-7900
Fax: 818-768-7619 info@sugarfoods.com
www.sugarfoods.com
Contract packager and exporter of dry entrees, side dishes, mixes including snack, nondairy creamer, sugar and sugar substitutes and croutons in bags, pouches, cups, cartons and canisters
President: Stephen O'Dell
Operations Manager: Brian Thomson
Estimated Sales: $8500000
Number Employees: 250-499
Sq. footage: 350000
Parent Co: Sugar Foods Corporation

12883 **Sugar Foods Corporation**
950 3rd Ave Fl 21
New York, NY 10022 212-753-6900
Fax: 212-753-6988 info@sugarfoods.com
www.sugarfoods.com
Products include sweetners, non dairy creamers, croutons, stuffing mixes, crumbs/cracker meal, snacks & snack mixes, specialty items, and almonds.
Chairman/Co-CEO: Donald G Tober
Executive VP: Jim Walsh
VP Communications: Rick Ticknor
Estimated Sales: I
Number Employees: 500-999
Type of Packaging: Consumer, Food Service
Brands:
ALMOND TOPPERS
BLUE DIAMOND
C&H
CRISP 'N FRESH
FRESH GOURMET
NATRATASTE
NON DIARY TOPPINGS
SUGAR IN THE RAW
SUPERSNAX
SWEET 'N LOW
TRUE LEMON

12884 **Sugar Kake Cookie**
570 Fillmore Ave
Tonawanda, NY 14150-2509 716-693-4715
Fax: 716-693-0575 800-775-5180
www.bremnercookies-crackers.com
Processor and exporter of fig bars and cookies including sandwich cremes, shortbread and sugar wafers
President: Rick Wilsman
Finance Executive: Rick Karnath
Sales Manager: David Boyce
Estimated Sales: $23600000
Number Employees: 100-249
Parent Co: Bremner
Type of Packaging: Consumer, Private Label
Brands:
Sugar Kake

12885 **Sugar Plum**
88 Dilley St
Forty Fort, PA 18704 570-288-0559
Fax: 570-288-1710 800-447-8427
customerservice@sugar-plum.com
www.sugar-plum.com
Chocolate covered potato chips, chocolate covered pretzels and chocolate covered popcorn.
Owner: Frann Edley
Estimated Sales: Less than $500,000
Number Employees: 1-4

Brands:
Dip Sticks
Get Popped
Supremes

12886 **Sugar Plum Farm**
P.O.Box 136
Plumtree, NC 28664-0136 828-766-6272
Fax: 828-765-0019 888-257-0019
sugarplumfarm@boone.net
www.sugarplumfarm.com
Processor of gourmet foods including dried fruits, fruit confections and apricot syrup; gift packages available
Owner: James Pitts
Owner: Helen Pitts
Estimated Sales: Less than $500,000
Number Employees: 1-4
Sq. footage: 8000
Brands:
Ceder House

12887 **Sugarbush Farm**
591 Sugarbush Farm Rd
Woodstock, VT 05091 802-457-1757
Fax: 802-457-3269 800-281-1757
Sugarbsh@sower.net www.sugarbushfarm.com
Waxed cheeses and Pure Vermont Maple Syrup
President: Elizabeth Luce
Estimated Sales: $ .5 - 1 million
Number Employees: 5-9

12888 **Sugardale Foods**
P.O.Box 8440
Canton, OH 44711 330-455-5253
Fax: 330-430-7660 www.sugardalefoods.com
Manufacturer of hams, deli meats, bacon, wieners and smoked sausage
Chairman: Neil Genshaft
President: Harry Valentio
CFO: Kevin Bender
Sales Director: Don Dimaid
Plant Manager: Rick Hawley
Purchasing Manager: Lee Poludniak
Estimated Sales: $ 100-500 Million
Number Employees: 500-999
Parent Co: Fresh Mark

12889 **Sugarman of Vermont**
P.O.Box 1060
Hardwick, VT 05843 802-472-9891
Fax: 802-472-8526 800-932-7700
www.sugarmanofvermont.com
Processor and exporter of jams, jellies, marmalades and preserves; processor and exporter of maple syrup
President: Anthony Sedutto
Number Employees: 20-49
Sq. footage: 40000
Type of Packaging: Consumer, Food Service, Private Label, Bulk
Brands:
Sugarman

12890 **Sugarwoods Farm**
2287 Glover St
Glover, VT 05839 802-525-3718
Fax: 802-525-4103 800-245-3718
office@sugarwoods.com
www.sugarwoodsfarm.com
Produces Vermont maple syrup, maple candy, maple cream and all natural pancake mixes.
Estimated Sales: $ 1 - 3 Million
Number Employees: 5-9
Type of Packaging: Consumer, Food Service, Private Label

12891 **Suity Confection Company**
PO Box 558943
Miami, FL 33255-8943 305-639-3300
Fax: 305-593-7070 mailcenter@suity.com
www.suity.com
Wholesaler/distributor, importer and exporter of candy, chocolate and snack foods
CFO: Jose Garrido
VP: Jose Garrido Jr
Quality Control: Luis Perez
Estimated Sales: $ 20-50 Million
Number Employees: 2
Brands:
Bubble Gum
Fruiticas Lollipops
Fruity Ball

Party Snacks
Salty Snacks

12892 **Suiza Dairy Corporation**
Ave De Diego Esq Avenida San Patricio
Urbanizacion La Riviera
San Juan, PR 00921 787-792-7300
Fax: 787-782-8120 www.suizapr.com
Processor of dairy products and fruit drinks/juices
President: Carmen Laura Marrero
Number Employees: 20-49
Parent Co: Suiza Foods
Type of Packaging: Consumer
Brands:
Quik
Suiza

12893 **Sukhi's Gourmet Indian Food**
23682 Clawaiter Rd
Hayward, CA 94545 510-264-9265
Fax: 510-264-1236 888-478-5447
info@sukhis.com www.sukhis.com
gourmet indian food
President/Owner: Sukhi Singh

12894 **Sullivan Harbor Farm**
P.O.Box 96
Sullivan, ME 04664 207-422-3735
Fax: 207-422-8229 800-422-4014
sullivanharborfarm@verizon.net
www.sullivanharborfarm.com
Smoked salmon
Owner: Joel Franzman
Estimated Sales: $300,000-500,000
Number Employees: 1-4

12895 **Sullivan Vineyards Winery**
P.O.Box G
Rutherford, CA 94573 707-963-9646
Fax: 707-963-0377 877-277-7337
www.sullivanwine.com
Wines
CEO: Joanna C Sullivan
CFO: Sean Sullivan
VP Marketing: Kelleen Sullivan
Operations Manager: Ross Sullivan
Estimated Sales: Below $ 5 Million
Number Employees: 5-9
Type of Packaging: Private Label
Brands:
Sullivan Cabernet Sauvignon
Sullivan Chardonnay
Sullivan Coeur De Vigne
Sullivan Merlot

12896 **Sumida Fish Cake Factory**
1332 Launa Street
Hilo, HI 96720-3234 808-959-9857
Fish cakes
President: Masayuki Sumida
Estimated Sales: $500,000-$1 Million
Number Employees: 20-49

12897 **Sumida Pickle Products**
1020 =Auahi St
Bldg 4
Honolulu, HI 96814-4134 808-593-2487
Processor of pickles and pickled vegetables
President: Marion Ku
VP: Steve Ku
Number Employees: 1-4
Sq. footage: 2000
Type of Packaging: Consumer

12898 **Summer In Vermont Jams**
686 Davis Rd
Hinesburg, VT 05461-9359 802-453-3793
norrisberryfarm@qmavt.net
Homegrown, homemade jams and jellies.
President: Norma Norris
Estimated Sales: $ .5 - 1 million
Number Employees: 1-4

12899 **Summerfield Farm Products**
4206 Twymans Mill Rd
Orange, VA 22960-4850 540-547-9600
Fax: 540-547-9628 800-898-3276
jamienicoll@summerfieldfarm.com
www.summerfieldfarm.com
Free-range veal, venison, salmon and condiments
President: Jamie Nicoll
Marketing Manager: Mary Thornton
Financial Manager: Carolyn Mills
Accounts Receivable: Barbara Frazier

Estimated Sales: Below $ 5 Million
Number Employees: 10
Brands:
Summerfield Farms

12900 **Summerfield Foods**
335 Shiloh Valley Ct
Santa Rosa, CA 95403-8085 707-579-3938
Fax: 707-579-8442
claudia@summerfieldfoods.com
www.summerfieldfoods.com
Contract packager and exporter of canned vegetarian foods including refried beans, soups and chili; also, cookies and cakes; private labeling available
President: Roland Au
Executive VP: John Stanghellini
Estimated Sales: $2000000
Number Employees: 10-19
Type of Packaging: Consumer, Private Label
Brands:
Summerfield's

12901 **Summerland Sweets**
6206 Canyon View Drive
Summerland, DC V0H 1Z7
Canada 250-494-0377
Fax: 250-494-7432 800-577-1277
ssweets@cnx.net www.summerlandsweets.com
Canner of fruit candy/pectin jelly including apricot, cherry and apple; also, fruit leather, gourmet jam, fruit syrup and fruit pulp
President: Frances Beulah
Estimated Sales: $1,200,000
Number Employees: 10
Number of Brands: 2
Number of Products: 40
Type of Packaging: Food Service, Private Label

12902 **Summit Brewing Company**
910 Montreal Cir
Saint Paul, MN 55102 651-265-7800
Fax: 651-265-7801 info@summitbrewing.com
www.summitbrewing.com
Brewer of beer
President: Mark Stutrud
Operations Manager: Christopher Seitz
Production Manager: Jon Lindberg
Number Employees: 20-49
Sq. footage: 58000
Brands:
Summit

12903 **Summit Hill Flavors**
253 Lackland Drive West
Middlesex, NJ 08846 732-805-0335
Fax: 732-805-1994 www.summithillflavors.com
Natural flavorings for dry and liquid applications used for marinating meats and poultry. Flavorings for soups, gravies, sauces, food bases and pasta dishes.

12904 **Summit Lake Vineyards &Winery**
2000 Summit Lake Dr
Angwin, CA 94508 707-965-2488
Fax: 707-965-2281
www.summitlakevineyards.com
Wines
President: Robert Brakesman
CEO: Heather Griffin
Marketing Director: Heather Griffin
Estimated Sales: $200,000-$300,000
Number Employees: 1-4
Number of Brands: 3
Number of Products: 3
Brands:
Clair Riley Zinfandel Port
Emily Kestral Cabern
Summit Lake Vinyards

12905 **Summum Winery**
707 Genesee Ave
Salt Lake City, UT 84104-1460 801-355-0137
Fax: 801-366-9081 orderinfo@summum.org
www.summum.org
Wines
Manager: Bernie Aua
Founder: Amen Ra
Estimated Sales: $ 1-2.5 Million
Number Employees: 5-9
Brands:
Summum

12906 **Sun Empire Foods**
P.O.Box 376
Kerman, CA 93630-0376 559-846-8208
Fax: 559-846-9488 800-252-4786
www.sunempirefoods.com
Hand made coated delicacies.
Co-Owner: Phil Dee
Co-Owner: Sandy Dee
Plant Manager: Philip Dee
Estimated Sales: $ .5 - 1 million
Number Employees: 5-9
Number of Products: 100
Type of Packaging: Consumer

12907 **Sun Garden Growers**
P.O.Box 190
Bard, CA 92222 760-572-0676
Fax: 760-572-0577 800-228-4690
Grower, processor and exporter of organic dates including whole, coconut roll, almond roll, chopped and pitted, oat flour coated, medjool, halawi, dayri, zahidi, etc
Estimated Sales: $3 Million
Number Employees: 50
Number of Brands: 2
Number of Products: 10
Sq. footage: 30000
Type of Packaging: Consumer, Private Label, Bulk
Brands:
Sun Garden Growers

12908 **Sun Garden Sprouts**
820 E 20th St
Cookeville, TN 38501-1451 931-526-1106
Fax: 931-526-8338 www.sproutnet.com
Bean sprouts
President: Robert Rust
Marketing: Kelly Warren
Estimated Sales: $ 5 - 10 Million
Number Employees: 20-49
Brands:
Sun Garden Sprouts

12909 **Sun Groves**
3393 State Road 580
Safety Harbor, FL 34695 727-726-8484
Fax: 727-726-7158 800-672-6438
www.sungroves.com
Fruit, berries
Marketing Manager: Joe Sevars
Estimated Sales: $ 20-50 Million
Number Employees: 20-49
Brands:
Sun Groves

12910 **Sun Harvest Foods**
3085 Beyer Blvd Ste 105
San Diego, CA 92154 619-661-0909
Fax: 619-690-1173
Processor, importer and exporter of IQF entrees, canned vegetables, jalapenos, tomatillo, sauces, salsa, broccoli, cauliflower, vegetable blends and fruit; kosher items available
President: Jorge Gonzalez
Sales & Marketing: Art Sanchez
Estimated Sales: $1.4 Million
Number Employees: 7
Sq. footage: 160000
Parent Co: Productos Frugo S.A. de C.V.
Type of Packaging: Consumer, Food Service, Private Label, Bulk
Brands:
Frugo
Products Frugo Sa de CV

12911 **Sun Hing Foods**
271 Harbor Way
South San Francisco, CA 94080 650-583-8188
Fax: 650-583-8188 800-258-6669
sunhing@sunhingfoods.com
www.sunhingfoods.com
Processor of ethnic foods
Owner: Trung Dang
Executive Vice President: Virginia Teng
Sales: Rosenda Chan
Estimated Sales: $ 20 - 50 Million
Number Employees: 20-49
Number of Brands: 9
Brands:
Black & White Brand
Cow & Mill Brand
Dairy Girl
Flower
Fortune
Fuyuki
Hoa Lan
Longevity Brand
Parrot Brand

12912 **Sun Olive Oil Company**
150 Vaquero Road
Templeton, CA 93465-9632 805-434-0626
Fax: 805-434-0626 rory@sunoliveoil.com
www.sunoliveoil.com
Olive oil
President: Rory Muniz
Brands:
Sun Olive Oil

12913 **Sun Opta Ingredients**
100 Apollo Dr Ste 101
Chelmsford, MA 01824 781-276-5100
Fax: 781-276-5101 800-353-6782
customer-service@sunopta-food.com
www.sunopta.com
World's largest producer of oat fiber for the food industry. The company also offers; a line of stabilized bran (wheat, oat, corn), wheat germ, novelty starches, custom stabilizer blends, Cellulose Gel and Konjac flour. In addition, ifoffers a broad range of food processing services
President: Douglas Shreve
R&D: Jim Podolske
Marketing: Rudi Van Mol
Sales: Doug Shreves
Estimated Sales: $300,000-500,000
Number Employees: 1-4
Parent Co: Sun Opta Inc
Type of Packaging: Bulk
Brands:
Crystalean
Opta Oat Fiber
Optafil
Optaglaze
Optagrade
Optamist
Optex

12914 **Sun Orchard**
P.O.Box 27508
Tempe, AZ 85285 480-966-1770
Fax: 480-921-1426 800-505-8423
info@sunorchard.com www.sunorchard.com
Processor of juices including orange, grapefruit, lemon and lime; also, apple cider, lemonade, margarita mix and granita slushes
President/CEO: Marc Isaacs
Marketing Director: Bob Corlett
VP, Product Innovation: Tony Decastro
VP, Purchasing: Chris Hess
Estimated Sales: $ 20-50 Million
Number Employees: 140
Sq. footage: 40000
Type of Packaging: Consumer, Food Service, Private Label, Bulk
Brands:
Sun Orchards Labels

12915 **Sun Orchard of Florida**
1200 S 30th St
Haines City, FL 33844 863-422-5062
Fax: 863-422-5176 www.sunorchard.com
Processor and exporter of citrus fruit
President: Isao Yokote
VP/CFO: Troy Gamble
Account Manager: Betty Wiess
Estimated Sales: $ 50 - 100 Million
Number Employees: 140
Parent Co: Gilco Fruits Corporation
Type of Packaging: Bulk

12916 **Sun Orchard of Florida**
1200 S 30th St
Haines City, FL 33844 863-422-5062
Fax: 863-422-5176 877-875-8423
www.sunorchard.com
Citrus juice
President: Marc Isaacs
SVP: John Glenn
VP/CFO: Troy Gamble
Account Manager: Betty Wiess
Estimated Sales: $20-50 Million
Number Employees: 100-249
Parent Co: Sun Orchard, Inc.
Type of Packaging: Private Label
Brands:
Rendezvous Bay

12917 **(HQ)Sun Pac Foods**
10 Sun Pac Boulevard
Brampton, ON L6S 4R5
Canada 905-792-2700
Fax: 905-792-8490 info@sunpac.com
sunpac.ca
Processor and contract packager of canned fruit juices, drinks and concentrates, bread crumbs, croutons and tortilla chips; importer of canned seafood and mandarin orange sections; exporter of juices and drinks
President: J Riddell
VP Finance: Vince McEwan
VP Imports/Exports: Cathy Knowles
Number Employees: 135
Sq. footage: 355000
Type of Packaging: Consumer, Food Service, Private Label, Bulk
Brands:
Featherweight
Fiesta
McDowell Ovens
Saico
Sun Crop
Sun Pac

12918 **Sun Pacific Shippers**
1250 E Myer Ave
Exeter, CA 93221 559-592-5168
Fax: 559-592-3308 www.sunpacific.com
Grower, exporter and shipper of produce
CEO: Robert W Reniers
Sales Manager: Steve Nelson
Estimated Sales: $100+ Million
Number Employees: 100-249
Brands:
Hershey

12919 **Sun Pure**
5200 Us Highway 98 S
Lakeland, FL 33812-4203 863-619-2222
Fax: 863-453-2224 www.sunpure.com
Flavors
Manager: Francisco Vega
Sales/Marketing: Primo Bader
VP Technical Services: Bill DuBose
Estimated Sales: $ .5 - 1 million
Number Employees: 1-4
Type of Packaging: Private Label

12920 **Sun Ray International**
1260 Lake Blvd
Davis, CA 95616 530-758-0088
Fax: 530-758-0089 sales@sunraygroup.net
www.sunraygroup.net
Agricultural food ingredients such as dehydrated onion, garlic, tomato and other vegetable products.

12921 **Sun Rich Fresh Foods, Inc**
515 E Rincon Street
Corona, CA 92879-1353 951-735-3800
Fax: 951-735-3322 800-735-3801
customerservice@sun-rich.com
www.sun-rich.com
Fresh cut fruit
President/Owner/Founder: Brian Tieszen
EVP/CFO: Neville Israel
Quality Assurance Technician: Daysi Aleman
Sales/Marketing Coordinator: Lisa Ten Heggeler
Regional Sales Manager: John Haering
HR Manager: Sylvia Del Rio
VP Operations: Dan O'Connell
Senior Production Manager: Javier Lopez
Sq. footage: 33000
Type of Packaging: Consumer, Food Service

12922 **Sun Ridge Farms**
31 Railroad Ave
Pajaro, CA 95076 831-786-7000
Fax: 831-786-8618 info@sunridgefarms.com
www.sunridgefarms.com
Manufacturer, processor, and exporter of organic and natural foods including pastas, trail mixes, candies, cereals, grain/bean blends, nuts, seeds and dried fruit blends. Also racks, bins, and labels for bulk food dispensing systems
President: Morty Cohen
Cfo: Gary Gardner
Marketing: Mark Deverencazi
Sales: Gregg Armstrong
Public Relation: Kai Conner
Operations: Ron Giannini
Production: Franknce Taberas
Purchasing Agent: Trish Gregg
Estimated Sales: $900 Million
Number Employees: 140
Parent Co: Falcon Trading Company
Type of Packaging: Consumer, Private Label, Bulk
Brands:
Sunridge Farms

12923 **Sun State Beverage**
2442 Pleasant Hill Rd
Atlanta, GA 30349 770-451-3990
Fax: 770-813-0065
Beverages
President: John Son
Estimated Sales: $ 2.5-5 Million
Number Employees: 1-4

12924 **Sun States**
PO Box 25965
Charlotte, NC 28229-5965 704-821-0615
Fax: 704-821-0616
Cheese
Marketing Director: Marty Crosby

12925 **Sun Sun Food Products**
14415 115th Avenue NW
Edmonton, AB T5M 3B8
Canada 780-454-4261
Fax: 780-453-1728
Processor of Oriental foods including bean sprouts, steamed noodles and wonton and egg roll wrappers
Manager: Ken Nhan
Type of Packaging: Food Service
Brands:
Sun Sun

12926 **Sun Valley**
P.O.Box 351
Reedley, CA 93654-0351 559-591-1515
Fax: 559-591-1616 sunvaly@mobynet.com
www.sunvalleypacking.com
Plums, peaches and nectarines
Owner: Walter Jones
Brands:
KAY PAK

12927 **Sun Valley Mustard**
731 1st Ave N
Hailey, ID 83333-5024 208-578-0078
Fax: 208-785-0216 800-628-7124
bstuns@cs.com www.sunvalleymustard.com
Mustard
President: Latham Williams
General Manager: Barbara Stuns
Estimated Sales: Under $500,000
Number Employees: 1-4
Brands:
Sun Valley Mustard

12928 **Sun Wellness/Sun Chlorel**
3305 Kashiwa Street
Torrance, CA 90505-4022 310-891-0600
Fax: 310-371-0094 800-829-2828
www.sunchlorellausa.com
Processor, wholesaler/distributor, importer and exporter of ginseng and chlorella including tablets, liquid extract and green single cell algae with broken cell walls
President/Ceo: Yoshihito Nishimaki
President: Hank Noma
Coo/Vice President: Rose Straub
Marketing Manager: Susan Arboua
Public Relations: Janise Zantine
Estimated Sales: $24 Million
Number Employees: 61
Sq. footage: 5000
Parent Co: YSK International Corporation
Brands:
Green Magician
Sun Chlorella
Sun Siberian Ginseng
Wakasa

12929 **Sun West**
2281 W 205th Street
Torrance, CA 90501-1450 310-320-4000
Fax: 310-320-8444 info@upperlimit.biz
www.upperlimit.biz
Distributor of rice based sweetners and rice based proteins
President: Qasim Habib
Estimated Sales: $ 2.5-5 Million
Number Employees: 5

12930 **(HQ)Sun World International**
5701 Truxtun Avenue
Suite 200
Bakersfield, CA 93309 661-631-4100
Fax: 661-631-4189 info@sun-world.com
www.sun-world.com
Fresh fruits and vegetables ranging from apricots, peaches, nectarines and grapes to tangerines, grapefruit, lemons and oranges to sweet colored peppers and seedless watermelon. Also Medjool dates and Deglet Noor dates.
President/CEO: Allen Vangelos
Chief Administration Officer: David Hostetter
Chief Marketing Officer: David Marguleas
Estimated Sales: $152 Million
Number Employees: 450

12931 **Sun-Brite Canning**
1532 County Rd 34
Kingsville, ON N0P 2G0
Canada 519-326-9033
Fax: 519-326-8700 jiacobel@sun-brite.com
www.sun-brite.com
Tomato canners
President: Henry Lacobelli
Director Marketing/Logistics: John LaCobelli
Number Employees: 50-99
Type of Packaging: Consumer, Food Service, Private Label

12932 **Sun-Glo of Idaho**
378 S 7th W
PO Box 300
Sugar City, ID 83448 208-356-7346
Fax: 208-356-7351 bruce@sunglo-idaho.com
www.sungloidaho.com
Idaho potatoes
CEO: Ceorge Crapo
CFO: Bruce Crapo
VP Fresh Sales: Betty Miles
Human Resource Manager: Melissa Coles
Estimated Sales: $ 50 - 100 Million
Number Employees: 100-249
Sq. footage: 100000
Type of Packaging: Consumer, Food Service, Private Label, Bulk
Brands:
Sun Supreme
Sun-Glo
Top Bakes

12933 **Sun-Maid Growers of California**
13525 S Bethel Ave
Kingsburg, CA 93631-9212 559-896-8000
Fax: 559-897-6209 800-272-4746
info@sunmaid.com www.sun-maid.com
Manufacturer of sun-dried fruits including raisins, peaches, apricots and pears; also, raisin paste and juice concentrate; exporter of raisins
President: Barry Kriebel
Chairman: Jon Marthedal
Vice Chairman: Nindy Sandhu
Estimated Sales: $322 Million
Number Employees: 550
Sq. footage: 650000
Type of Packaging: Consumer, Food Service, Private Label, Bulk
Brands:
Sun-Maid

12934 **Sun-Re Cheese**
178 Lenker Ave
Sunbury, PA 17801 570-286-1511
Fax: 570-286-5123
Processor of Italian cheeses including pizza, mozzarella and ricotta
President: Pat Rescigno
Plant Manager: Gary Deates
Estimated Sales: $6.4 Million
Number Employees: 50
Sq. footage: 56000
Type of Packaging: Consumer, Food Service, Private Label, Bulk

12935 **Sun-Rise**
3423 Casa Marina Road NW
Alexandria, MN 56308-9058 320-846-5720
Beverages
President: John Sherman
Brands:
Sun-Rise Beverages

12936 **Sun-Rype Products**
1165 Ethel Street
Kelowna, BC V1Y 2W4
Canada 250-860-7973
Fax: 250-762-3611 888-786-7973
investor@sunrype.com www.sunrype.com
Manufacturer of juice and fruit snacks and also organic fruit snacks.
President/CEO: Dave McAnerney
Chairman: Merv Geen
CFO: Gary Pearson
Estimated Sales: $138 Million
Number Employees: 400
Type of Packaging: Consumer, Food Service, Private Label, Bulk
Brands:
Energy-To-Go
Fruit-To-Go
Sun-Rype

12937 **SunMeadow Family of Products**
12200 32nd Ct N
Saint Petersburg, FL 33716 727-573-2211
Fax: 727-572-8209 frankc@gafoods.net
www.sunmeadow.net
Manufacturer of pre-plated frozen meals including frozen fruit cups, shelf stable emergency day meal packs, dry milk packs and school lunch sandwiches designed for elderly nutrition and health care markets
President: James Lobianco
VP: Kenneth Lo Bianco
Estimated Sales: G
Number Employees: 100-249
Sq. footage: 50000
Parent Co: GA Food Service
Type of Packaging: Consumer, Food Service, Private Label
Brands:
SUN MEADOW

12938 **SunOpta Grains**
P.O.Box 128
Hope, MN 56046-0128 507-451-8201
Fax: 507-451-8201 800-297-5997
foodinfo@sunopta.com www.sunopta.com/foods
Organic, non-GMO & IP soy, corn, whole grains, ingredients and consumer products
President: Allan Routh
CFO: Rick Johnson
CFO: Rick Johnson
Estimated Sales: Below $ 5 Million
Number Employees: 20-49
Type of Packaging: Consumer, Food Service, Bulk
Brands:
NFD
Nordic
Sunrich

12939 **SunPure**
5200 Us Highway 98 S
Lakeland, FL 33812-4203 863-619-2222
Fax: 863-453-2224 pcheatham@sunpure.com
www.sunpure.com
Processor, importer and exporter of essence, oils, citrus flavors, natural chemicals and aromas and pulp concentrate
Manager: Francisco Vega
VP Marketing/Finances: Kim James
Director Sales (Beverages): Rick Plank
Estimated Sales: $1600000
Number Employees: 1-4
Sq. footage: 136200
Type of Packaging: Bulk

12940 **SunRise Commodities**
140 Sylvan Ave
Englewood Cliffs, NJ 07632-2514 201-947-1000
Fax: 201-947-7667 www.foodimportgroup.com
Supplier and importer of nuts and dried fruits
President: Robert Feuerstein
Estimated Sales: $ 50 - 100 Million
Number Employees: 50-99

12941 **SunStar Heating Products,Inc**
306 W Tremont Ave
Charlotte, NC 28203-4946 704-372-3486
Fax: 704-332-5843 888-778-6782
info@sunstarheaters.com
www.sunstarheaters.com
Manufacturers of Heavy Duty Patio Heating Products, Mushroom Type Patio Heaters, Tube-Type Infared Gas Heaters, High Intensity Ceramic Infared Natural Gas Heater, Heavy Duty Infared Heater and many more products
President: Frank L Horne Jr Jr.
Parent Co: Gas-Fired Products, Inc

12942 **SunWest Organics**
1550 Drew Ave # 150
Davis, CA 95618-7852 530-758-8550
Fax: 530-758-8110 www.sunwestfoods.com
Organic brown, pilaf, wild mix, wild and crisp rice.
President: James Errecarte
Estimated Sales: $ 20 - 50 Million
Number Employees: 10-19
Sq. footage: 30000

12943 **Sunbeam**
229 Coffin Avenue
New Bedford, MA 02746-2299 508-997-9401
Fax: 508-993-6324 800-458-8407
petracca_bart@interstatebrands.com
www.interstatebrands.com
Breads, rolls
Director Product Development: Kenneth Newman
Estimated Sales: $ 20-50 Million
Number Employees: 500-999
Brands:
Health O Meter
Mr. Coffee
Oster
Sunbeam

12944 **Sunbeam Baking Company**
301 Dallas Street
El Paso, TX 79901-1821 915-533-8433
Fax: 915-534-0043 800-328-6111
Processor of baked products including bread, rolls, buns and cake
VP Sales: Jef Dunigan
VP Sales: Tony Ruiz
Number Employees: 100-249
Sq. footage: 80000
Parent Co: Flowers Industries
Brands:
Sunbeam

12945 **Sunburst Foods**
1002 Sunburst Dr
Goldsboro, NC 27534 919-778-2151
Fax: 919-778-9203 info@sunburstfoods.com
www.sunburstfoods.com
Processor and wholesaler/distributor of prepacked sandwiches
President: Ray Lewis
Chairman: B Darden
Vice President: Lori Moss
Maintenance Manager: Bill Sugg
Estimated Sales: $13 Million
Number Employees: 150
Sq. footage: 50000
Type of Packaging: Consumer

12946 **Sunchef Farms**
4722 Everett Avenue
Vernon, CA 90058-3133 323-588-5800
Fax: 323-588-2285
Processor of portion-controlled chicken including marinated and flavored products
President: Steve Tsatas

12947 **Suncoast Foods Corporation**
1929 Hancock Street
San Diego, CA 92110-2061 619-299-0475
Fax: 619-299-0464
Baked goods

12948 **Suncrest Farms**
97 Minnisink Rd
Totowa, NJ 7512 973-595-0214
Fax: 973-595-0214 suncrest@wightman.ca
www.suncrestfarms.com
Ham
Owner: E L Scott
Estimated Sales: Less than $500,000
Number Employees: 1-4
Brands:
Suncrest Farms

12949 **Sundance Industries**
P.O.Box 1446
Newburgh, NY 12551-1446 845-565-6065
Fax: 845-562-5699 sundanceind@verizon.net
www.sundanceind.com
Manufacturer of Wheateena wheatgrass juicers.
President/CEO: Alden Link
VP Marketing: Alden Link
Office Manager: Valerie Lynn
Estimated Sales: $1-3 Million
Number Employees: 1-4
Number of Brands: 1
Number of Products: 9
Sq. footage: 14000
Type of Packaging: Consumer
Brands:
WHEATEENA

12950 **Sundance Roasting Company**
PO Box 1886
Sandpoint, ID 83864-0904 208-265-2445
Manufacturer and exporter of organic brewable coffee alternative
Owner: Barbara Veraniam
Estimated Sales: Under $500,000
Number Employees: 1-4
Sq. footage: 600
Type of Packaging: Consumer, Bulk
Brands:
Sundance Barley Brew

12951 **Sundia**
70 Washington Street
Suite 425
Oakland, CA 94607-3705 415-762-0600
sales@sundiacorp.com
sundiacorp.com
fruit cups
Founder/General Manager: Dan Hoskins
CEO: Jim Watkins
VP Finance: Alex Auseklis
Founder/Chairman: Bradford Oberwager
VP Sales: Mark Sherburne
VP Manufacturing: James Kairos
Estimated Sales: $7 Million
Number Employees: 9
Sq. footage: 1600

12952 **Sundial Gardens**
59 Hidden Lake Rd
Higganum, CT 06441-4441 860-345-4290
Fax: 860-345-3462 sundial9@localnet.com
www.sundialgardens.com
Processor of spices, herb blends, tea cake and scone mixes including hazelnut, pumpkin-ginger, cranberry and traditional; importer of rare and herbal teas
Owner: Ragna Goddard
VP: Thomas Goddard
Estimated Sales: Less than $500,000
Number Employees: 1-4
Sq. footage: 2500
Type of Packaging: Consumer
Brands:
Ceylon Teas
China Teas
Herbal Teas
India Teas
Mulling Cider
Sundial Blend Teas
Sundial Gardens

12953 **Sunergia Soyfoods**
1125 Little High St
Charlottesville, VA 22902 434-970-2798
Fax: 801-437-3484 800-693-5134
info@sunergiasoyfoods.com
www.sunergiasoyfoods.com
Makers of healthy and delicious seasoned tofu. Includes ten delicious flavors such as italian herb, savory portabella, peanut & ginger, indian masala, spicy thai, garlic shitake, porcini herb, spinach jalapeno, pesto and spicyindian.
President: Jon Kessler
Vice President: John Raphaelidis
Sales Manager: Marsha Burger
Operations Manager: Jon Kessler
Estimated Sales: $200,000
Number Employees: 3
Number of Brands: 2
Number of Products: 13
Type of Packaging: Consumer, Food Service, Private Label, Bulk

Brands:
More-Than-Tofu
Sunergia Breakfast Style Sausage
Sunergia More Than Tofu Garlic
Sunergia More Than Tofu Herbs
Sunergia More Than Tofu Porcinis
Sunergia More Than Tofu Savories
Sunergia More-Than-Tofu
Sunergia Organic Soy Sausage
Sunergia Smoked Portabella Sausage

12954 **Sunflower Food and Spice Company**
4114 NW Riverside St
Riverside, MO 64150 816-741-1600
Fax: 913-599-3787 800-377-4693
info@sunflowerfoodcompany.com
www.sunflowerfoodcompany.com
Honey toasted sunflower nuts, bagel spread mixes, farmer's popcorn cob, sunflower seed cookies, sunny seed drops, sunflower seed granola, and sunflower seed vinaigrette.
Owner: Casey O'Sullivan
Vice President: Mike Meier
Estimated Sales: $ 5-10 Million
Number Employees: 5-9
Sq. footage: 6000
Type of Packaging: Consumer, Food Service, Bulk
Brands:
BBQ Pretzel Snack
Cinnamon Pretzel Twists
Dip@Stick
Farmer's Popcorn Cob
Lost Trail
Lucky Twist Choc Peanut Butter
Original Bagel Spread
Say Cheese!Pretzel Bits
Sunflower Nutty Nuggets

12955 **Sunflower Restaurant Supply**
1647 Sunflower Road
Salina, KS 67401 316-267-9881
Fax: 785-823-5512 norman@sunflowersrs.com
www.sunflowersrs.com
President/Finance Executive: Leroy Baumberger
VP: Carol Lyon
Estimated Sales: $7.3 Million
Number Employees: 21
Sq. footage: 36000
Brands:
Lyon

12956 **Sunfresh Foods**
125 S Kenyon St
Seattle, WA 98108-4207 206-764-0940
Fax: 206-764-0960 800-669-9625
jam@freezerves.com www.freezerves.com
Uncooked freezer jams and fruit sauces
President: Reed Hadley
VP Marketing: Jerry Brozowski
Estimated Sales: Below $ 5 Million
Number Employees: 5-9
Type of Packaging: Food Service, Private Label
Brands:
President's Choice
Sunfresh Freezerves
Western Classics

12957 **Sungarden Sprouts**
820 E 20th St
Cookeville, TN 38501-1451 931-526-1106
Fax: 931-526-8338 bob@sproutnet.com
www.sproutnet.com
Grower, packer and exporter of fresh and frozen alfalfa and bean sprouts
Owner: Robert Rust
Estimated Sales: $2300000
Number Employees: 20-49
Parent Co: International Specialty Supply
Type of Packaging: Consumer, Food Service, Private Label, Bulk

12958 **Sungold Foods**
501 42nd St. NW
Fargo, ND 58102 701-250-6895
Fax: 701-282-5325 800- 43- 553
info@sunbutter.com www.sunbutter.com
Manufacturers Sunbutter, a nut spread made from sunflower seeds available in a variety of flavors including creamy, natural, honey crunch, natural crunch, and organic in addition to whole sunflower seeds and trail mixes.
CEO: Rob Majkrzak
CFO: Randy Wigen
VP Marketing: Dan Hofland
Operations Manager: Brad Newton
Number Employees: 50-99
Type of Packaging: Consumer, Food Service, Private Label, Bulk

12959 **Sunja's Oriental Foods**
40 Foundry St Ste 1a
Waterbury, VT 05676 802-244-7644
Fax: 802-244-6880 sunjas@madriver.com
www.sunja.com
Oriental foods, kimchee, all natural sauces, frozen specialties, sushi
President: Sunja Hayden
Estimated Sales: $ 5 - 10 Million
Number Employees: 5-9

12960 **SunkiStreet Growers**
616 E Sunkist St
Ontario, CA 91761-1721 909-983-9811
Fax: 909-933-2409 800-225-3727
www.sunkist.com
Processor and exporter of citrus juice
President: Henry Asseldt
VP: Ted Leaman
Estimated Sales: $17400000
Number Employees: 100-249
Parent Co: Sunkist Growers
Type of Packaging: Bulk

12961 **(HQ)Sunkist Growers**
14130 Riverside Dr
Sherman Oaks, CA 91423 818-986-4800
Fax: 818-379-7405 info@sunkistgrowers.com
www.sunkist.com
Sunkist Growers Trademark Licensing Operations Division provides branded products services. Sunkist licensed products are available in the following categories: Fruit Juices, Fruit Drinks, Healthy Snacks, Baking Mixes, CarbonatedBeverages, Confections, Vitamins, Frozen Novelties, Salad Toppings, Freshly Peeled Citrus, Chilled Jellies and even Nonfood products.
President/CEO: Tim Lindgren
VP/Chief Financial Officer: Richard French
VP/Law & General Counsel: Thomas Moore
VP/Global Licensing: Gregory Combs
VP/Fresh Fruit Sales: John McGuigan
SVP/Sales & Marketing: Russell Hanlin
SVP/Corporate Relations & Administration: Michael Wootton
VP/Citrus Juice & Oil Business: Frank Bragg
VP/Chief Operations Officer: James A Padden
Vice Chairman: Craig Armstrong
Plant Manager: Robert Eldridge
VP/Marketing & Sales Promotions: Robert Verloop
Estimated Sales: $ 1+ Billion
Number Employees: 500
Type of Packaging: Food Service, Private Label

12962 **Sunkist Growers**
80 Everett Ave Ste 305
Chelsea, MA 02150 617-884-9750
Fax: 617-889-0136 www.sunkist.com
Processor of oranges, tangerines, lemons and grapefruit.
President/CEO Corporate Office: Timothy Lindgren
Sales & Marketing Manager Chelsea Office: Michael Ieradi
SVP/Corporate Sales & Marketing: Russell Hanlin
VP/Corporate Fresh Fruit Sales: John McGuigan
SVP/Corporate Relations & Administration: Michael Wootton
Estimated Sales: $ 1-2.5 Million
Number Employees: 3
Parent Co: Sunkist Growers
Type of Packaging: Consumer, Food Service, Bulk

12963 **Sunkist Growers**
616 E Sunkist St
Ontario, CA 91761-1721 909-983-9811
Fax: 909-933-2459 800-798-9005
www.sunkist.com
Processor of oranges, tangerines and lemons.
President/CEO Corporate Office: Timothy Lindgren
VP: Ted Leaman
SVP/Corporate Sales & Marketing: Russell Hanlin
VP/Corporate Fresh Fruit Sales: John McGuigan
SVP/Corporate Relations & Administration: Michael Wootton
Estimated Sales: $ 1-2.5 Million
Number Employees: 500-999
Parent Co: Sunkist Growers
Type of Packaging: Consumer, Food Service, Bulk

12964 **Sunkist Growers**
110 Tulliallan Ln
Cary, NC 27511 919-859-7380
Fax: 410-997-2317 bschrott@sunkistgrowers.com
www.sunkist.com
Processor and marketer of citrus fruits including oranges, tangerines, lemons and grapefruit.
President/CEO Corporate Office: Jeffrey D Gargiulo
Vice President: James A Padden
SVP/Sales & Marketing Corporate Office: Russell Hanlin
SVP/Corporate Relations & Administration: Michael Wootton
Sales Representative Columbia Office: Bob Roberts
Estimated Sales: $ 1-5 Million
Number Employees: 10-20
Parent Co: Sunkist Growers
Type of Packaging: Consumer, Food Service, Bulk
Brands:
Sunkist

12965 **Sunkist Growers**
1000 Gamma Dr Ste 103
Pittsburgh, PA 15238 412-967-9801
Fax: 412-967-9804 www.sunkist.com
Processor of oranges, tangerines, lemons and grapefruit.
Manager: Lex Revetta
SVP/Sales & Marketing Corporate Office: Russell Hanlin
Sales Representative Pittsburgh Office: Lex Revetta
SVP/Corporate Relations & Administration: Michael Wootton
Sales Representative Pittsburgh Office: Tony Greco
Estimated Sales: $ 1 - 3 Million
Number Employees: 1-4
Parent Co: Sunkist Growers
Type of Packaging: Consumer, Food Service, Bulk

12966 **Sunkist Growers**
59 Carol Dr
Buffalo, NY 14215 716-895-3744
Fax: 716-895-3744
corporate.communications@sunkistgrowers.com
www.sunkist.com
Processor of citrus fruits including oranges, tangerines, lemons and grapefruit.
Manager: Lynn Groblewski
SVP/Sales & Marketing Corporate Office: Russell Hanlin
Sales Representative Buffalo Office: Lynn Groblewski
SVP/Corporate Relations & Administration: Michael Wootton
Estimated Sales: $500,000-$1 Million
Number Employees: 1-4
Parent Co: Sunkist Growers
Type of Packaging: Consumer, Food Service, Bulk
Brands:
Sunkist

12967 **Sunkist Growers**
10707 Corporate Drive
Suite 124
Stafford, TX 77477 281-240-6446
Fax: 281-240-4080 www.sunkist.com

Processor of fresh and canned oranges, tangerines, lemons and grapefruit.
President/CEO Corporate Office: Timothy Lindgren
Sales Representative Stafford TX Office: Mark Imming
Sales Representative Stafford TX Office: Jeff Horan
Sales Representative Stafford TX Office: Joe Padilla
SVP/Sales & Marketing Corporate Office: Russell Hanlin
SVP/Corporate Relations & Administration: Michael Wootton
Estimated Sales: $ 1-2.5 Million
Number Employees: 1-5
Parent Co: Sunkist Growers
Type of Packaging: Consumer, Food Service, Bulk

12968 **Sunkist Growers**
2929 W Main St Ste K
Visalia, CA 93291 559-739-8392
Fax: 559-739-0856 www.sunkist.com
Processor of oranges, tangerines, lemons and grapefruit
Director: Steve Probstfield
Estimated Sales: $ 5-10 Million
Number Employees: 14
Parent Co: Sunkist Growers
Type of Packaging: Consumer, Food Service, Bulk

12969 **Sunkist Growers**
9003 Bishops View Cir
Cherry Hill, NJ 8002-3465 856-663-2343
Fax: 856-633-3560 www.sunkist.com
Processor of oranges, tangerines, lemons and grapefruit.
President/CEO Corporate Office: Timothy Lindgren
VP/Chief Financial Officer Corporate: Richard French
Sales Representative Pennsauken Office: Bill Givens
Sales Representative Pennsauken Office: Karen Smith
SVP/Sales & Marketing Corporate Office: Russell Hanlin
SVP/Corporate Relations & Administration: Michael Wootton
Estimated Sales: $1-2.5 Million
Number Employees: 1-4
Parent Co: Sunkist Growers
Type of Packaging: Consumer, Food Service, Bulk
Brands:
Sunkist

12970 **Sunkist Growers**
5711 Golf Crest Dr
West Chester, OH 45069 513-741-9494
Fax: 513-741-8608 www.sunkist.com
Processor of oranges, lemons, tangerines and grapefruit.
Manager: Tom Burkett
SVP/Sales & Marketing Corporate Office: Russell Hanlin
District Sales Manager Cincinnati Office: John Young
SVP/Corporate Relations & Administration: Michael Wootton
Estimated Sales: $2.$5-5 Million
Number Employees: 5-9
Parent Co: Sunkist Growers
Type of Packaging: Consumer, Food Service

12971 **Sunkist Growers**
7201 W Fort Street
Building Office 59
Detroit, MI 48209-2977 313-843-4160
Fax: 313-843-7411
Shipper of fresh oranges, tangerines, lemons and grapefruit
Manager: Aaron Swerling
Assistant Manager: John Leslie
Estimated Sales: $ 1-2.5 Million
Number Employees: 1-4
Parent Co: Sunkist Growers
Type of Packaging: Consumer, Food Service, Bulk

12972 **Sunkist Growers**
43 Old Farmers Rd
Long Valley, NJ 07853-3149 908-876-9500
Fax: 973-316-0266 www.sunkist.com
Processor and marketer of citrus fruits including oranges, tangerines, lemons and grapefruit.
Manager: Brad Blaine
SVP/Sales & Marketing Corporate Office: Russell Hanlin
Sales Representative Parsippany Office: Brad Blaine
SVP/Corporate Relations & Administration: Michael Wootton
Sales Representative Parsippany Office: Jeff Savage
Parent Co: Sunkist Growers
Type of Packaging: Consumer, Food Service, Bulk

12973 **Sunkist Growers**
15849 S 40th Pl
Phoenix, AZ 85048 602-956-1238
Fax: 602-956-5043 www.sunkist.com
Processor and marketer of citrus fruits including oranges, tangerines, lemons and grapefruit.
Manager: Aaron Leeming
SVP/Sales & Marketing Corporate Office: Russell Hanlin
Sales Representative Phoenix Office: Ron Carbone
SVP/Corporate Relations & Administration: Michael Wootton
Sales Representative Phoenix Office: Debra Roesch
Parent Co: Sunkist Growers
Type of Packaging: Consumer, Food Service, Bulk

12974 **Sunkist Growers**
11841 SE Mountain Sun Dr
Clackamas, OR 97015 503-698-2159
Fax: 503-655-4221 www.sunkist.com
Processor and marketer of citrus fruits including oranges, tangerines, lemons and grapefruit.
President/CEO Corporate Office: Timothy Lindgren
SVP/Sales & Marketing Corporate Office: Russell Hanlin
Sales Representative Portland Office: Tom Bauer
SVP/Corporate Relations & Administration: Michael Wootton
Sales Representative Portland Office: Karen Lary
Parent Co: Sunkist Growers
Type of Packaging: Consumer, Food Service, Bulk

12975 **Sunkist Growers**
7077 Beaubien East #206
Anjou, QC H1M 2Y2
Canada 514-354-8181
Fax: 514-354-8345 www.sunkist.com
Processor and marketer of citrus fruits including oranges, tangerines, lemons and grapefruit.
President/CEO Corporate Office: Timothy Lindgren
SVP/Sales & Marketing Corporate Office: Russell Hanlin
Sales Representative Montreal Office: John Lemarguand
SVP/Corporate Relations & Administration: Michael Wootton
Parent Co: Sunkist Growers
Type of Packaging: Consumer, Food Service, Bulk

12976 **Sunkist Growers**
210 Ontario Food Terminal
165 The Queensway
Toronto, ON M8Y 1H8
Canada 416-259-5491
Fax: 416-259-4960 www.sunkist.com
Processor and marketer of citrus fruits including oranges, tangerines, lemons and grapefruit.
President/CEO Corporate Office: Timothy Lindgren
SVP/Sales & Marketing Corporate Office: Russell Hanlin
Sales Representative Toronto Office: Natalie Lewicky
SVP/Corporate Relations & Administration: Michael Wootton
Sales Representative Toronto Office: Jim Van Dusen
Parent Co: Sunkist Growers
Type of Packaging: Consumer, Food Service, Bulk

12977 **Sunkist Growers**
201-827 Belgrave Way
Annacis Business Park
New Westminster, BC V3M 5R8
Canada 604-524-5001
Fax: 604-524-0660 www.sunkist.com
Processor and marketer of citrus fruits including oranges, tangerines, lemons and grapefruit.
President/CEO Corporate Office: Timothy Lindgren
SVP/Sales & Marketing Corporate Office: Russell Hanlin
Sales Representative Vancouver Office: Walt Cieslukowski
SVP/Corporate Relations & Administration: Michael Wootton
Sales Representative Vancouver Office: Natalie Eng
Parent Co: Sunkist Growers
Type of Packaging: Consumer, Food Service, Bulk

12978 **Sunkist Growers**
1501 42nd St Ste 470
West Des Moines, IA 50266 515-226-9005
Fax: 515-226-9726 www.sunkist.com
Processor and marketer of citrus fruits including oranges, tangerines, lemons and grapefruit.
President/CEO Corporate Office: Timothy Lindgren
SVP/Sales & Marketing Corporate Office: Russell Hanlin
Sales Representative Des Moine Office: Kevin Pratt
SVP/Corporate Relations & Administration: Michael Wootton
Parent Co: Sunkist Growers
Type of Packaging: Consumer, Food Service, Bulk

12979 **Sunkist Growers**
101 East Park Boulevard
NCNB Tower Suite 467
Plano, TX 75074 972-516-8824
Fax: 972-578-9036 www.sunkist.com
Processor and marketer of citrus fruits including oranges, tangerines, lemons and grapefruit.
President/CEO Corporate Office: Timothy Lindgren
Manger: Thomas Welter
SVP/Sales & Marketing Corporate Office: Russell Hanlin
Sales Representative Plano Office: Tom Welter
SVP/Corporate Relations & Administration: Michael Wootton
Sales Representative Plano Office: Tim Rogers
Parent Co: Sunkist Growers
Type of Packaging: Consumer, Food Service, Bulk

12980 **Sunkist John P Newman Research and Development Center**
760 East Sunkist Street
Ontario, CA 91761 909-983-5852
Fax: 909-822-2125 800-383-7141
corporate.communications@sunkistgrowers.com
www.sunkistresearch.com/
The Sunkist John P. Newman Researth and Development Center, located in Ontario, California, conducts research and houses expertise in fruit and vegetable packing, sorting, labeling, conditioning, storage, and transportation.
President/CEO Corporate Office: Timothy Lindgren
VP/Law and General Counsel: Thomas Moore
SVP/Corporate Sales & Marketing: Russell Hanlin
VP/Corporate Fresh Fruit Sales: John McGuigan
SVP/Corporate Relations & Administration: Michael Wootton
Parent Co: Sunkist Growers

12981 **Sunland Inc/Peanut Better**
PO Box 1059
Portales, NM 88130 575-356-6638
Fax: 575-356-6630
customerservice@sunlandinc.com
www.sunlandinc.com
peanuts, peanut butter and flavored infused peanut
President/CEO: Jimmie Shearer

12982 **Sunlike Juice**
91 Finchdene Square
Scarborough, ON M1X 1A7
Canada 416-297-1140
Fax: 416-297-5703
Processor and exporter of fruit juices and drinks including apple, apple/strawberry, cranberry cocktail, grapefruit, mango, orange juice, orange/pineapple, peach, pineapple, fruit punch, grape, papaya, pink lemonade, black cherry andiced tea
President: Terry Topos
Consultant: Tim Britton

Brands:
Sunlike

12983 **Sunmet**
9239 E Central Ave
Del Rey, CA 93616 559-888-2702
Fax: 559-445-0572 sales@sunmet.com
Processor and exporter of Granny Smith apples, peaches, plums, nectarines and table grapes
Type of Packaging: Consumer, Food Service, Private Label, Bulk
Brands:
Sunmet

12984 **Sunny Avocado**
20872 Deerhorn Valley Road
Jamul, CA 91935-7937 619-479-3573
Fax: 619-479-2960 800-999-2862
sunnyavocado@sunny-avocado.com
www.sunny-avocado.com
Provides extra chunky avocado pulp, original mild qualcomole and spicy blends; guac, salsa and guacamaya drink
President: Enrique Bautista
VP: Ana Rosa Bautista
VP Sales/Marketing: Michael Spinner
Estimated Sales: $120000
Number Employees: 2
Type of Packaging: Food Service, Private Label, Bulk
Brands:
Sunny Avocado

12985 **Sunny Cove Citrus LLC**
1315 E Curtis Ave
Reedley, CA 93654-9317
Fax: 559-626-7210
customer.service@sccitrus.com
www.sccitrus.com
Packinghouse and licensed shipper of citrus products for Sunkist Growers Inc.
President: Tom Clark
Field Manager: Justin Kulikov
Controller: Warren Lee
Office Manager: Vera Fast
Sq. footage: 170000
Type of Packaging: Food Service

12986 **Sunny Delight Beverage Company**
7000 Lagrange Blvd SW
Atlanta, GA 30336 404-349-7480
Fax: 404-267-4488 800-395-5849
Service.Fin@SunnyD.com
www.proctorandgamble.com
Fruit drinks
President/CEO: Wayne William
CFO: James (Jim) Dahmus
Operations/Production: Robert Rutkowski
VP Sales: John Crossetti
Plant Manager: Amir Ghanaad
Estimated Sales: $ 50-99.9 Million
Number Employees: 100-249
Brands:
Sunny D

12987 **Sunny Dell Foods**
135 N 5th St
Oxford, PA 19363 610-932-5164
Fax: 610-932-9479 sunnydell.com
Mushrooms (canned, marinated, refrigerated, glass and specialty)
Finance Manager: Lori Caligiuri
Sales Manager: Bobby Fella
Purchasing Manager: Monica Philistine
Estimated Sales: $14.5 Million
Number Employees: 75

12988 **Sunny Fresh Foods**
206 W Fourth St
Monticello, MN 55362-8524 763-271-5600
Fax: 763-271-5711 800-872-3447
www.sunnyfreshfoods.com
Processor of eggs including fresh, liquid, mixes, omelets, diced, hard-cooked and pre-cooked
President: Michael Luker
Director Sales/Marketing: Dale Jenkins
Marketing Manager: Rebecca Hanf
Number Employees: 250-499
Parent Co: Cargill Foods
Type of Packaging: Food Service, Private Label

12989 **Sunny South Pecan Company**
P.O.Box 1400
Statesboro, GA 30459-1400 912-764-5337
Fax: 912-489-1391 800-764-3687
Processor and grower of pecans
Owner: Garland L Nessmith
VP: Steve Rushing
Estimated Sales: $500,000-$1 Million
Number Employees: 1-4
Sq. footage: 15600
Type of Packaging: Consumer
Brands:
Savannah
Sunny South

12990 **Sunny's Seafood**
1 Fish Pier
Boston, MA 02210 617-261-7123
Fax: 617-439-7894
Seafood
President: Steven Dulock Sr

12991 **Sunnydale Meats**
165 Hyatt St
Gaffney, SC 29341 864-489-6091
Fax: 864-489-6092
Manufacturer of beef, pork, chicken, turkey, bacon, sausage and wieners
President: Anthony Hopper Jr Jr
Estimated Sales: $15 Million
Number Employees: 10-19

12992 **Sunnyland Farms**
P.O.Box 8200
Albany, GA 31706-8200 229-436-5654
Fax: 229-888-8332 800-999-2488
www.sunnylandfarms.com
Nuts, mixed nuts, pecans, dried fruits and specialty products.
Sales Manager: Beverly Willson
Purchasing: Larry Willson
Estimated Sales: $ 10 - 20 Million
Type of Packaging: Consumer, Bulk
Brands:
Sunnyland Farms

12993 **Sunnyland Mills**
4469 E Annadale Ave
Fresno, CA 93725-2221 559-233-4983
Fax: 559-233-6431 800-501-8017
mike@sunnylandmills.com
www.sunnylandmills.com
Leading manufacturer of premium quality organic and traditional bulgur wheat, pearled soft white wheat, and Grano
President: Steve Orlando
VP: Mike Orlando
Plant Manager: Steve Orlando
Number Employees: 10-19
Sq. footage: 18000
Type of Packaging: Food Service, Bulk
Brands:
Sunnyland

12994 **Sunnyrose Cheese**
Hwy 25
Diamond City, AB T0K 0T0
Canada 403-381-4024
Fax: 403-381-3838
FLACOSTE@AGROPUR.COM
www.milkingredients.ca
Processor of cheeses including cheddar, colby, mozzarella, Monterey jack, gouda, havarti, marble, parmesan and specialty
President Sales: Emanuela Leoni
Number Employees: 10-19
Parent Co: Agropur
Type of Packaging: Consumer, Food Service
Brands:
Sunnyrose Cheese

12995 **Sunnyside Farms**
PO Box 164
Neligh, NE 68756-0164 402-791-2210
Fax: 402-791-2210
Produce
President: James McNally
Estimated Sales: Under $500,000
Number Employees: 1-4

12996 **Sunnyside Organics**
PO Box 478
Washington, VA 22747-0478 540-675-2627
Fax: 540-675-1135
Family owned farm that produces eggs, prime meats, and 200 kinds of fruits, vegetables and herbs.

12997 **Sunnyside Vegetable Packing**
730 Lebanon Road
Millville, NJ 08332-9773 856-451-5077
Fax: 856-451-4388
Vegetables
President: Vic Sammartano
Estimated Sales: Under $500,000
Number Employees: 50-99

12998 **(HQ)Sunnyslope Farms Egg Ranch**
9845 Nancy Avenue
Cherry Valley, CA 92223-3599 951-845-1131
Processor and exporter of fresh shell and frozen eggs
President: Stefan Illy
General Manager: Bill Ingram
Estimated Sales: $20-50 Million
Number Employees: 20-49
Sq. footage: 300000

12999 **Sunopta Sunflower**
5850 Opus Parkway
Suite 150
Minnetonka, MN 55343 952-224-4764
sunflower@sunopta.com
www.sunopta.com
Specializes in bringing identity preserved, non-GMO and organic soybeans, sunflower and corn products to market utilizing vertically integrated business models.
President: Murray Burke
Estimated Sales: $1 Million
Number Employees: 18
Sq. footage: 100000
Parent Co: SunOpta, Inc
Type of Packaging: Consumer, Food Service, Private Label, Bulk
Brands:
Sl Sunflowers

13000 **Sunray Bakery Corporation**
50 Northwestern Drive
6
Salem, NH 03079-5811 603-898-3079
Baked goods
Manager: Joe Ceppecelli
Estimated Sales: $ 10-20 Million
Number Employees: 10

13001 **Sunray Food Products Corporation**
3441 Kingsbridge Ave
Bronx, NY 10463-4003 718-548-2255
Fax: 718-548-2313 www.zenobianut.com
Processor of nuts including cashews and pistachios; also, nut mixes, pumpkin and sunflower seeds
Manager: Agustine Morales
Manager: Dave Brechner
Estimated Sales: $423177
Number Employees: 10-19
Parent Co: Zenobia Company
Type of Packaging: Consumer, Food Service, Private Label, Bulk
Brands:
Private Stock
Zenobia

13002 **(HQ)Sunrich**
3824 SW 93rd St
Hope, MN 56046 507-451-3316
Fax: 507-451-2910 800-297-5997
sueklem@sunrich.com www.sunrich.com
Processor and exporter of soy products including milk, tofu powder and frozen green soybeans; also, corn products including grits and flour
President: Allan Routh
CFO: John Dietrich
Estimated Sales: $9 Million
Number Employees: 85
Type of Packaging: Food Service, Private Label, Bulk
Other Locations:
SunRich
Cresco IA
Brands:
SOY SUPREME
SUNRICH
SWEET BEANS

13003 Sunridge Farms
P.O.Box 4273
Salinas, CA 93912-4273 831-755-1430
Fax: 831-755-1429 www.coastlineproduce.com
Bulk and packaged organic and natural foods, snacks, dried fruits, nuts and trail mixes; natural candies; granolas and cereals; grain and bean blend; pastas
President: Milton Henderson
VP: Pelsh Adrian
Marketing Director: Vivian Guajardo
Sales: Dave Adrian
Estimated Sales: $ 2.5-5 Million
Number Employees: 20-49
Type of Packaging: Consumer, Food Service, Bulk
Brands:
Coastline

13004 Sunrise Confections
1800 Northwestern Dr
El Paso, TX 79912 915-877-1172
Fax: 915-877-1198 800-685-1475
www.sunriseconfections.com
Cakes, cookies and candies.
Manager: Beth Podol
CEO: Richard Harshman
Director Of Marketing: Grant Bassett
VP Sales/Marketing: Alex Chimens
Estimated Sales: $300,000-500,000
Number Employees: 1-4

13005 Sunrise Growers
166 E La Jolla St
Placentia, CA 92870 714-630-6292
Fax: 714-630-0920 stcircle@sunrisegrowers.com
www.frozsun.com
Processor and exporter of fresh strawberries, cauliflower, broccoli, lettuce, bell peppers, artichokes, green beans and cabbage
President: Douglas Circle
CEO: Edward Haft
Estimated Sales: $ .5 - 1 million
Number Employees: 1-4
Type of Packaging: Consumer, Food Service, Bulk
Brands:
Sunrise
Sunshine
Touchdown

13006 Sunrise Markets
729 Powell St
Vancouver, BC V6A 1H5
Canada 604-253-2326
Fax: 604-251-1083
Processor of tofu and soy milk
President: Leslie Joe
Plant Manager: Jimmy Cuan
Estimated Sales: $16 Million
Number Employees: 160
Sq. footage: 25000
Type of Packaging: Consumer, Food Service

13007 Sunrise Winery
1418 Shasta Avenue
San Jose, CA 95126-2531 408-741-1310
Wines
President: Rolayne Storz
Estimated Sales: $500-1 Million appx.
Number Employees: 1-4

13008 Suns Noodle Company
2415 Weaver Way
Atlanta, GA 30340-1532 770-448-7799
Fax: 770-446-7599
Noodles
President: Allen Sun
Estimated Sales: $2.5-5 Million
Number Employees: 10-19

13009 Sunset Farm Foods
P.O.Box 963
Valdosta, GA 31603-0963 229-242-9973
Fax: 229-242-3389 800-882-1121
webinfo@sunsetfarmfoods.com
www.sunsetfarmfoods.com
Processor of smoked sausage, fresh sausage, smoked meats, cooked products (souse, chitterling loaf, liver pudding, chili)
President: J D Carroll
VP: T Carroll
Sales: Charles Harrell
Plant Manager: Ricky Lightsey
Estimated Sales: $ 20 - 50 Million
Number Employees: 50-99
Number of Brands: 6
Number of Products: 250
Sq. footage: 40000
Type of Packaging: Consumer, Food Service, Private Label, Bulk
Brands:
FLAVORITY
GEORGE MAID
GEORGIA REDS
GEORGIA SPECIAL
QUEEN OF DIXIE
SOUTHERN CHEF
SUNSET FARM

13010 Sunset Specialty Foods
PO Box 1360
Sunset Beach, CA 90742-1360 562-592-4976
Fax: 562-592-3806
Processor and exporter of specialty frozen items including pizza, chocolate chip cookies, etc
Number Employees: 20-49
Sq. footage: 27000
Type of Packaging: Consumer, Food Service, Private Label, Bulk
Brands:
Amelia's
Deli
Dina
Maestro Giovanni

13011 Sunset Whlse.
1650 N 7th St Ste 1
Lebanon, PA 17046 717-272-4906
Fax: 717-270-4323 800-876-2123
www.sunsetwholesales.com
Supplier of closeout and salvage foods, toys and gifts
President: Terry Longenecker
Estimated Sales: $ 20 - 50 Million
Number Employees: 50-99

13012 Sunshine Burger Company
P.O.Box 888
Fort Atkinson, WI 53538
Fax: 845-647-2065
www.organicandnaturalnews.com/guide/cat41.htm
l
Processor of vegetarian burgers made with sunflower seeds, brown rice, carrots, sea salt and spices
Owner: Carol Debberman
Owner: John Hiler
Estimated Sales: $500,000-$1 Million
Number Employees: 1-4
Sq. footage: 7000
Type of Packaging: Consumer, Food Service
Brands:
Organic Sunshine
Sunshine

13013 Sunshine Dairy
584 Coleman Rd
Middletown, CT 06457 860-346-6644
Fax: 860-346-5246
Milk, dairy products
President: Nancy A Guida
Estimated Sales: $ 10-20 Million
Number Employees: 20-49
Brands:
Guida

13014 Sunshine Dairy Foods
801 NE 21st Ave
Portland, OR 97232 503-234-7526
Fax: 503-233-9441
parbuthnot@sunshinedairyfoods.com
www.sunshinedairyfoods.com
Processor of dairy products including ice cream, yogurt, fresh milk and cultures
Owner: Sam Karmounas
Estimated Sales: $ 20 - 50 Million
Number Employees: 100-249
Sq. footage: 75000
Type of Packaging: Consumer, Food Service, Private Label, Bulk
Brands:
Albertson's
Quality Chekd
Tillamook
Western Family

13015 Sunshine Farm & Gardens
Rr 5
Renick, WV 24966 304-497-2208
Fax: 304-497-2698 barry@sunfarm.com
www.sunfarm.com
Processor, importer and exporter of organic fruits including apples and pawpaws; also, organic herbs and seeds
President: Barry Glick
VP: Zak Glick
Estimated Sales: $400000
Number Employees: 100-249
Sq. footage: 65000

13016 Sunshine Farms
N8873 Currie Rd
Portage, WI 53901-9218 608-742-2016
Fax: 608-742-1577 considine@jvlnet.com
www.sunshine-farms.com
Processor and wholesaler/distributor of cheese and goat milk; wholesaler/distributor of health foods
President: Dan Considine
Estimated Sales: $ 3 - 5 Million
Number Employees: 3
Type of Packaging: Consumer
Brands:
Sunshine Farms

13017 Sunshine FarmsThe Nut House Inc
1680 Horse Pasture Road
Roseboro, NC 28382-7110 910-564-2421
Fax: 910-564-5302
Processor of pumpkins and pecans
President: Elbie Powers
Estimated Sales: $10,000
Number Employees: 2

13018 Sunshine Farms Poultry
PO Box 10595
West Palm Beach, FL 33419-0595 561-881-4500
Fax: 561-881-9252
Poultry, poultry products
Estimated Sales: $ 5-10 Million
Number Employees: 5-9

13019 Sunshine Food Sales
2900 NW 75th St Ste 305
Miami, FL 33147 305-696-2885
Processor and importer of fresh and frozen fish including mackerel, kingfish, lobster and crabs
President: Carlos Sanchez
Co-Owner: David Dossi
Plant Manager: Jesus Alonsa
Number Employees: 1-4
Type of Packaging: Bulk

13020 Sunshine Fresh
20 W End Road
Totowa, NJ 07512-1406
US 973-812-4777
Fax: 973-812-4988 800-832-8081
www.sunshinefresh.net
Processor of pickles; wholesaler/distributor of deli products; serving the food service market,manufactures and packs liquid food products.
President: Michael Rosenblum
Estimated Sales: $8100000
Number Employees: 45
Type of Packaging: Consumer, Food Service, Bulk

13021 Sunshine InternationalFoods
26 Spruce Street
Methuen, MA 01844 978-837-3209
Fax: 978-837-3161 info@sunshinefood.com
www.sunshinefood.com
All natural tahini paste.
Owner: Emile Maroun
Managing Director: George Maroun
Estimated Sales: $500,000
Number Employees: 3
Sq. footage: 3320

13022 Sunshine Seafood
P.O.Box 136
Stonington, ME 04681 207-367-2955
Fax: 207-367-6394
Fish, seafood and shellfish.
President: James Eaton
Estimated Sales: $2,600,000
Number Employees: 10-19

13023 **Sunstone Vineyards & Winery**
125 N Refugio Rd
Santa Ynez, CA 93460 805-688-9463
Fax: 805-686-1881 800-313-9463
jeff@sunstonewinery.com
www.sunstonewinery.com
Wines
President: Bion Rice
CEO: Linda Rice
VP: Ashley Rice
Marketing Director: Jeff Munsey
Estimated Sales: $1-$2 Million
Number Employees: 1-4

13024 **Sunsweet Growers**
901 N Walton Ave
Yuba City, CA 95993 530-674-5010
Fax: 530-751-5395 800-417-2253
sunsweet@casupport.com www.sunsweet.com
Dried tree fruits including cranberries, apricots and prunes
President/CEO: Arthur Driscoll
VP/CFO: Ana Klein
COO: Dane Lance
VP Manufacturing: Gene Dodson
Purchasing Angent: Traci Vaniszeski
Estimated Sales: $294.6 Million
Number Employees: 600
Sq. footage: 1200000
Type of Packaging: Consumer, Food Service, Private Label, Bulk

13025 **(HQ)Suntory International**
7 Times Sq # 21
New York, NY 10036-6524 212-891-6600
Fax: 212-891-6601 www.suntory.com
Bottled water and beverages
President/CEO: Seishi Ueno
EVP/CFO: Tsuyoshi Nishizaki
Sales/Marketing Director: Satoru Shimizu
Estimated Sales: $1,594,400,000
Number Employees: 2199
Brands:
Artesian Spring
Belmont Spring Disti
Belmont Spring Water
Hinckley & Schmitt N
Hinckley Springs
Hinckley-Schmitt
Isotonic
Kentwood Premium Coffee
Kentwood Springs
Kidz Water
Mountain Spring
Nursery Drinking Wat
Nursery Drinking Wat
Sierra Spring Nurser
Sierra Springs
Suntory Bottled Wate
Suntory Oolong Tea

13026 **Suntory Water Group**
5660 New N Side Dr NW Ste 500
Atlanta, GA 30328 770-933-1400
Fax: 770-956-9495 www.suntorywatergroup.com
Bottled water, assorted beverages
President: David Krishock
Contoller: Rick Puckett
VP: Patrick Goguillon
Sales Director: Steve Bayliss
Public Relations: Elizabeth Weinmann
VP Operations: Mike Chandler
Purchasing Manager: John Houser
Estimated Sales: $ 400 Million
Number Employees: 1,000-4,999
Parent Co: Suntory International Corporation

13027 **(HQ)Sunwest Foods**
1550 Drew Ave # 150
Davis, CA 95616-4881 530-758-8550
Fax: 530-758-8110
jhasbrook@sunwestfoods.com
www.sunwestfoods.com
Processor and exporter of regular, organic and wild rice; also, walnuts, almonds, pistachios and pecans
President: James Errecarte
VP Domestic Sales: John Hasbrook
Estimated Sales: $ 20 - 50 Million
Number Employees: 10-19
Sq. footage: 100000
Brands:
Nutririte
SunNuts
SunWest

SupHerb FARMS®

13028 **SupHerb Farms**
PO Box 610
Turlock, CA 95381-0610 209-633-3600
Fax: 209-633-3644 800-787-4372
custserv@supherbfarms.com
www.supherbfarms.com

Frozen culinary herb and specialty vegetable ingredients

President: Mike Brem
VP/CFO: Joe Ford
VP: Tom McGovern
R&D: Mike Lehman
Quality Control: Heather Ayala
Marketing: Laurel Place
Sales VP: Don Douglas
Human Resources Director: Patricia Silva
Plant Manager: Jim Howard
Estimated Sales: $3.4 Million
Number Employees: 40
Sq. footage: 65190
Type of Packaging: Food Service, Bulk
Brands:
SUPHERB FARMS

13029 **Super Nutrition Life Extension**
1100 W Commercial Blvd # 100
Fort Lauderdale, FL 33309-3748 954-766-8433
Fax: 954-202-7745 800-678-8989
customerservice@lifeextension.com www.lef.org
Processor of supplements including nutritional, anti-aging and sport supplements; also, vitamin formulas
Owner: William Flannon
Marketing/Design: Kathy Mooney
National Sales Manager: Michael Mooney

13030 **Super Smokers BBQ**
7409 Highway N
Dardenne, IL 63368 636- 61- 118
catering@supersmokers.com
www.supersmokers.com
Sauces

13031 **Super Snooty Sea Food Corporation**
7 Fish Pier St E
Boston, MA 02210-2007 617-426-6390
Fax: 617-439-9144
Processor and wholesaler/distributor of frozen seafood including round and filleted flat fish
General Manager: Paul Sousa
Number Employees: 5-9
Type of Packaging: Consumer

13032 **Superbrand Dairies**
9 Wax Myrtle Ct
Montgomery, AL 36117-3770 334-277-6010
Fax: 334-279-6964
Processor of frozen pizza
Owner: Dennis Houde
Plant Manager: J Parsons
Number Employees: 50-99
Parent Co: Winn Dixie
Type of Packaging: Private Label

13033 **Superbrand Dairies**
3000 NW 123rd Street
Miami, FL 33167-2517 305-769-6600
Fax: 305-783-2896
Processor of milk and juice: orange, grapefruit and apple
Vice President: Pat Carraro
Number Employees: 50-99
Parent Co: Winn Dixie
Type of Packaging: Consumer

13034 **Superior Bakery**
72 Main Street
North Grosvenordale, CT 06255 860-923-9555
Fax: 860-923-2087 www.superiorbakery.com
Italian bread and rolls-Italian sliced, vienna, grinder, pepper bisuits, torpedoes, round buns and pizza
VP Finance: Michael Faucher
General Manager: Victor Strama
Estimated Sales: $8.5 Million
Number Employees: 50
Sq. footage: 30000
Type of Packaging: Consumer, Food Service, Private Label, Bulk
Brands:
Green-Freedman
Kasanofs's
Superior

13035 **Superior Baking Company**
176 N Warren Ave
Brockton, MA 02301 508-586-6601
Fax: 508-580-4056 800-696-2253
sbaking1@comcast.net
Processor of breads, rolls, bagels, pastries and wraps
President: Michael DeBenedictis
VP Sales: Joseph Ferrini
Vice President: Robert DeBenedictis
Marketing Director: Joseph Ferrini
Sales Director: Joseph Ferrini
Estimated Sales: Below $ 5 Million
Number Employees: 60
Sq. footage: 16000
Type of Packaging: Consumer, Food Service, Private Label, Bulk

13036 **Superior Bean & Spice Company**
PO Box 753
Brush Prairie, WA 98606-0753 360-694-0819
Fax: 360-883-6915
Vegetables, soup mixes
President: Duane Rough

13037 **Superior Cake Products**
105 Ashland Ave
Southbridge, MA 01550 508-764-3276
Fax: 508-765-5344
Processor of cakes and snack cakes including carrot spice rolls, Boston cream pie, etc
President: Chris Smith
CEO: Chris Smith
VP Finance: Michael Faucher
VP: Karo Mc Hugh
Marketing Manager: Chris Smith
VP Sales: Christopher Smith
VP Operations: Raymond Faucher Jr
Type of Packaging: Consumer, Food Service, Private Label
Brands:
Superior Cake

13038 **Superior Dairy**
4719 Navarre Rd SW
Canton, OH 44706 330-477-4515
Fax: 330-477-5908 800-683-2479
Processor of dairy products
President: Joseph Sorhnlen
President/COO: Daniel Sorhnlen
CEO: Joseph P Soehnlen
Sales Manager: Jeff Bouequin
Estimated Sales: $ 50 - 100 Million
Number Employees: 100-249
Type of Packaging: Consumer, Private Label

13039 **Superior Farms**
1477 Drew Ave
Davis, CA 95618-4881 530-297-7299
Fax: 530-758-3152 800-228-5262
thiinc@superiorfarms.com
www.superiorfarms.com
Processor of lamb, venison, buffalo and veal
Chairman: Les Oesterriech
Marketing Director: Angela Gentry
Estimated Sales: $ 100-500 Million
Number Employees: 20-49
Brands:
Superior Farms

13040 **Superior Foods**
275 Westgate Dr
Watsonville, CA 95076 831-728-3691
Fax: 831-722-0926 info@superiorfoods.com
www.superiorfoods.com

Frozen fruits and vegetables
President: Marco Cruz
CEO: David Moore
Financial Director: Geraldine Prevedelli
Quality Assurance Director: Stephanie Fry
VP Sales: Mark Colendich
Human Resources Manager: Cynthia Carrabba
COO: Robert Happee
Estimated Sales: $23 Million
Number Employees: 103
Sq. footage: 10782
Brands:
Asian Pride
Garden Fresh
Orchard Park
Superior Foods
Superior Pride

13041 **Superior Meat Company**
480 N 500 E
Vernal, UT 84078 435-789-3274
Processor of meat products
Owner: D J Reynolds
Sales Manager: D Reynolds
Estimated Sales: Less than $500,000
Number Employees: 1-4
Type of Packaging: Consumer, Food Service

13042 **Superior Mushroom Farms**
52557 Range Road
Suite 215
Ardrossan, AB T8E 2H6
Canada 780-922-2535
Fax: 780-922-2078 866-687-2242
crimini@telusplanet.net
Grower of fresh mushrooms
President/CEO: Brent Schwabe
Marketing/Sales Director: Wanda Ziober
Production Manager: Norman Schwabe
Estimated Sales: E
Number Employees: 50
Type of Packaging: Consumer, Food Service, Bulk

13043 **(HQ)Superior Nut & Candy Company**
1111 W 40th St
Chicago, IL 60609 773-254-7900
Fax: 773-254-9171 800-843-2238
www.superiornutandcandy.com
Processor of nuts including honey roasted, salted meats and trail mixes; also, fund raising programs available
President/CEO: Anthony Mastrangelo
VP Finance: Ramona Mastrangelo
Sales Director: Daniel Hathaway
VP Operations: Richard Slayton
Purchasing: Leonard Shamoon
Estimated Sales: $16068865
Number Employees: 60
Sq. footage: 51000

13044 **Superior Nut Company**
225 Monsignor Obrien Hwy
Cambridge, MA 02141 617-876-3808
Fax: 617-876-8225 800-251-6060
info@superiornutstore.com
www.superiornut.com
Nuts
President: Harry Hintlian
Estimated Sales: $1-2.5 Million
Number Employees: 1-4
Type of Packaging: Consumer, Food Service, Bulk
Brands:
Superior Nut Company

13045 **Superior Nutrition Corporation**
601 N Market Street
Wilmington, DE 19801-3006 302-655-5762
Fax: 302-655-5760 info@sncorp.com
www.sncorp.com
Baked onion pieces
Estimated Sales: $ 2.5-5 Million
Number Employees: 1-4

13046 **Superior Ocean Produce**
4423 N Elston Ave
Chicago, IL 60630 773-283-8400
Fax: 773-561-0139 www.fishguy.com
Seafood
Owner: William Dugan
Estimated Sales: $ 1 - 3 Million
Number Employees: 10-19

13047 **Superior Pasta Company**
905 Christian St
Philadelphia, PA 19147-3807 215-922-7278
Fax: 215-922-7114
https://www.superiorpasta.com/Home.htm
Pasta products
Owner: Joe Lonanno
Estimated Sales: Less than $1 Million
Number Employees: 8
Type of Packaging: Private Label

13048 **Superior Pecan**
317 North Orange
Eufaula, AL 36027 334-687-2031
Fax: 334-687-2075 800-628-2350
superiorpecan@earthlink.net
www.superiorpecan.com
Manufacturer of pecans
President/Owner: Georgia Hamm
Estimated Sales: $4 Million
Number Employees: 15
Sq. footage: 18000
Type of Packaging: Consumer

13049 **Superior Quality Foods**
2355 E Francis St
Ontario, CA 91761 909-923-4733
Fax: 909-947-7065 800-300-4210
service@superiortouch.com
www.superiortouch.com
Processor of soup bases, beef extracts, dried seasonings and sauce mixes
President: Linda Owen
Vice President: Bob Grizzard
National Sales Manager: Paul Smalley
Estimated Sales: $22.3 Million
Number Employees: 63
Parent Co: Southeastern Mills, Inc.
Type of Packaging: Food Service, Bulk

13050 **Superior Seafood & MeatCompany**
623 S Olive Street
South Bend, IN 46619-3309 574-289-0511
Fax: 574-289-0919
Seafood and meat
President: Joe Neary Sr

13051 **Superior Seafoods**
2601 N 22nd St
Tampa, FL 33605 813-248-2749
Fax: 813-247-4539
Seafood
President: Ernest Donini
VP: John Donini
Estimated Sales: Less than $500,000
Number Employees: 3

13052 **Superior Trading Company**
837 Washington St
San Francisco, CA 94108 415-982-8722
Fax: 415-982-7786 super837@aol.com
www.superiortrading.com
Processor, importer and exporter of herbal teas, herbs, soaps and loquat syrups; processor of ginseng products; wholesaler/distributor and importer of sports drinks
President: Michael Chung
Manager: Anna Lee
Vice President: Luke Chung
Estimated Sales: $ 5 - 10 Million
Number Employees: 5-9
Sq. footage: 5000
Type of Packaging: Bulk
Brands:
Nin Jiom
Superior Herb & Ginseng

13053 **Superior's Brand Meats**
P.O.Box 571
Massillon, OH 44648-0571 330-830-0356
Fax: 330-830-3174 www.superiorsbrand.com
Processor of meat products including beef, pork and luncheon and smoked meat
President: Neil Gunshaft
CEO: Neil Genshaft
Estimated Sales: $ 20 - 50 Million
Number Employees: 250-499
Parent Co: Fresh Mark
Type of Packaging: Consumer, Bulk

13054 **Supermoms**
625 2nd St
Saint Paul Park, MN 55071 651-459-2253
Fax: 651-459-0804 800-944-7276
www.supermoms.com
Bakery products
President: Doug Muchow
Quality Control: Rhonda Brueur
Estimated Sales: $ 10-20 Million
Number Employees: 250-499

13055 **Superstore Industries**
199 Red Top Rd
Fairfield, CA 94534-9500 707-864-0502
Fax: 707-864-8203 consaffairs@ssica.com
www.ssica.com
Processor of dairy products including milk, cottage cheese, yogurt and ice cream; also, orange juice
Facility Manager: Ron Harris
Plant Manager: Woody Darnell
Estimated Sales: $ 50 - 100 Million
Number Employees: 100-249
Brands:
Superstore

13056 **Suprema Specialties**
14253 S Airport Way
Manteca, CA 95336-8641 209-858-9696
Fax: 209-858-9599
Milk, cheese, cheeses include mozzarella, parmesan, ramano, Monterrey jack and chedder cheese
Owner: Ming Shin-Kou

13057 **(HQ)Suprema Specialties**
P.O.Box 39
Paterson, NJ 07543-0039 973-684-2900
Fax: 973-684-8680 800-543-2479
Processor of Italian cheese including parmesan, romano, mozzarella and ricotta
Chairman of the Board: Mark Cocchiola
CEO: Douglas Hopkins
CFO: Thomas Reed
VP Sales: Tom Egan
Plant Manager: William Robles
Estimated Sales: $ 20 - 50 Million
Number Employees: 50-99
Sq. footage: 25000
Type of Packaging: Consumer, Food Service, Private Label, Bulk
Other Locations:
Suprema Specialties
Manteca CA
Brands:
Suprema

13058 **Supreme Chocolatier**
1150 South Ave
Staten Island, NY 10314-3404 718-761-9600
Fax: 718-761-5279
customerservice@superiorconfections.com
www.superiorconfections.com
Processor and exporter of chocolate novelties in foil
President: George Kaye
VP Marketing: Wayne Stottmeister
Estimated Sales: $6,100,000
Number Employees: 100-249
Type of Packaging: Consumer
Brands:
Superior Chocolatier
Superior Confections, Inc.
The Chocolate Factory

13059 **Supreme Dairy Farms Company**
111 Kilvert St
Warwick, RI 2886 401-739-8180
Fax: 401-739-8230 www.supremedairyfarms.com
Processor and importer of tomato products; also, mozzarella and ricotta cheese
President: Paul Areson
Director: Bill Toll
Estimated Sales: $1.8 Million
Number Employees: 10
Sq. footage: 14000
Type of Packaging: Food Service, Private Label
Brands:
AVANTI
SUPREME DAIRY FARMS

13060 **Supreme Frozen Products**
5813 W Grand Ave
Chicago, IL 60639 773-622-3777
Fax: 773-622-3350 store@supremetamale.com
www.supremetamale.com

Processor of Mexican food including tamales, chili, fajitas and burritos
President: John Paklaian
Estimated Sales: $1.2 Million
Number Employees: 10
Sq. footage: 6200

13061 **Supreme Frozen Products**
5813 W Grand Ave
Chicago, IL 60639 773-622-3336
Fax: 773-622-3350 888-643-0405
johnp@supremetamale.com
www.supremetamale.com
Beef tamales, been and bean burritos, beeh chili with beans, crispy pizza fluffs
Owner: John Pak
Estimated Sales: $ 5-10 Million
Number Employees: 10-19

13062 **Supreme Rice Mill**
4 S Avenue D
Crowley, LA 70526-5657 337-783-5222
Fax: 337-783-3204 staff@supremerice.com
www.supremerice.com
Manufacturer and exporter of white and brown rice and quick-cooking white and brown rice
Chairman: Gordon Dore
President/CEO: William Dore
VP: Georgette Dugas
Estimated Sales: $100 Million
Number Employees: 80
Brands:
SOFGRAIN
SUPREME

13063 **Suram Trading Corporation**
2655 S Le Jeune Rd Ste 1006
Miami, FL 33134 305-448-7165
Fax: 305-445-7185 www.suram.com
Frozen seafood-shrimp
President: Guido Adler
CFO: Ana Adler
Marketing Director: José Pelaez Pelaez
Estimated Sales: $ 50-100 Million
Number Employees: 5-9
Brands:
Suram

13064 **Sure Fresh Produce**
1302 W Stowell Rd
Santa Maria, CA 93458 805-349-2677
Fax: 805-349-2674 888-423-5379
www.surefreshproduce.com
Industrial frozen vegetable ingredient manufacturer of both conventional and organic bulk products
President: Dale Johnson
CFO: Renee Kolding
Quality Control: Corrie Landymore
Marketing Director: Matthew Johnson
Sales Director: Loren Hiltner
Estimated Sales: $10-20 Million
Number Employees: 100-249
Number of Products: 750
Sq. footage: 50000
Type of Packaging: Food Service, Bulk
Brands:
Sure Fresh

13065 **Sure-Good Food Distributors**
6361 Thompson Rd
Syracuse, NY 13206-1448 315-422-1196
Fax: 315-478-5220
Fresh and frozen poultry
President: Jerry Savlov
Estimated Sales: $ 10-20 Million
Number Employees: 10-19

13066 **Surface Banana Company**
P.O.Box 3153
Bluewell, WV 24701-8153 304-589-7202
Fax: 304-589-7252
Processor of bananas and tomatoes; importer of bananas
Owner: David Surface
Estimated Sales: $300,000-500,000
Number Employees: 1-4

13067 **Surlean Foods**
1545 S San Marcos
San Antonio, TX 78207-7090 210-227-4370
Fax: 210-226-4208 800-999-4370
mcannon@surleanfoods.com
www.surleanfoods.com
Manufacturer of meats, soups, sauces, marinades and more
President: Daryl Scott
VP Procurement & Customer Development: Chad Wilhite
VP Technical Services: Travis Holmes
VP Customer Service: Harry Spahn
Director of National Accounts: Karen Karl
VP Sales & Marketing: Mike Cannon
Business Development: Jeffrey Osburn
Production Manager: Ryan Scott
Estimated Sales: $100+ Million
Number Employees: 260
Type of Packaging: Food Service

13068 **Susie's South 40 Confections**
P.O.Box 4040
Midland, TX 79704-4040 432-570-4040
Fax: 432-682-4040 800-221-4442
CustService@susiessouthforty.com
www.susiessouthforty.com
Toffee, pralines, fudge, gift baskets, gift tins
President/Owner: Susie Hitchcock-Hall
Estimated Sales: $ 3 - 5 Million
Number Employees: 10-19
Type of Packaging: Consumer

13069 **Susquehanna Valley Winery**
802 Mount Zion Dr
Danville, PA 17821 570-275-2364
Fax: 570-275-5813
Wine
Owner: Miklos Latranyi
Partner: Mark Latranyi
Marketing Manager: Hildetard Latranyi
Estimated Sales: Below $ 5 Million
Number Employees: 1-4
Brands:
Susquehanna Valley

13070 **Sustainable Sourcing**
PO Box 900
Great Barrington, MA 01230 413-528-5141
Fax: 413-528-5172 sales@himalasalt.com
www.himalasalt.com
organic peppercorns, spices and artisan salt blends
President: Melissa Kushi
Estimated Sales: $1.5 Million
Number Employees: 10

13071 **Suter Company**
258 May St
Sycamore, IL 60178 815-895-9186
Fax: 815-895-4814 800-435-6942
www.suterco.com
Processor of canned and refrigerated salads including tuna, chicken, ham, egg and seafood; also, shelf stable lunch kits, deviled egg kits
President: Tim Suter
VP Sales/Marketing: Heidi Wright
Estimated Sales: $ 20 - 50 Million
Number Employees: 100-249
Sq. footage: 75000
Type of Packaging: Consumer, Food Service, Private Label, Bulk
Brands:
Alaska Bay
Suter
Sycamore Farms

13072 **Sutherland's Foodservice**
P.O.Box 786
Forest Park, GA 30298 404-366-8550
Fax: 404-366-8599 cservice@suthfood.com
www.suthfood.com
Dairy, frozen foods, fresh and frozen meat, fresh and frozen poultry, fresh and frozen seafood, dry grocery, nonfood, and produce. Also represents 100s of brands, for a complete listing see their website.
President: Gene Sutherland Sr
Estimated Sales: $ 20 - 50 Million
Number Employees: 100-249

13073 **Sutter Home Winery**
P.O.Box 248
Saint Helena, CA 94574 707-963-3104
Fax: 707-963-2381 legan@suterhome.com
www.tfewines.com
Processor and exporter of wines
CEO: Louis Trinchero
Executive VP: Jim Miller
Marketing Director: Rob Celsi
Public Relations: Stan Hock
Operations Manager: Bob Torres
Plant Manager: Jim Huntsinger
Purchasing Manager: Bryan Lilienthal
Estimated Sales: $250000000
Number Employees: 100-249
Brands:
Sutter Home

13074 **Sutton Honey Farms**
285 Conns Ln
Lancaster, KY 40444-9706 859-792-4277
Fax: 859-792-4277
Processor and packer of nonfiltered and creamed honey with fruit and cinnamon
President: Rick Sutton
VP: Dianne Sutton
Estimated Sales: A
Number Employees: 1-4
Sq. footage: 4000
Type of Packaging: Consumer, Private Label, Bulk
Brands:
Sutton's

13075 **Suzanna's Kitchen**
4025 Buford Hwy
Duluth, GA 30096 770-476-9900
Fax: 770-476-8899 800-241-2455
www.suzannaskitchen.com
Manufacturer of frozen heat and serve meat products including pork, veal, beef, turkey, barbecue, ribs, corn dogs and chicken breasts, breast strips, chicken patties and wings.
President: Barbara Howard
CEO: Brad Howard
CFO: David Ashton
Vice President/GM: Norman Andrews
COO: Brad Howard
Operations Manager: Judith Adams
Estimated Sales: $20-50 Million
Number Employees: 250-499
Number of Products: 125
Sq. footage: 236000
Type of Packaging: Food Service, Private Label
Brands:
SUZANNA'S

13076 **Suzanne's Specialties**
421 Jersey Avenue
Suite B
New Brunswick, NJ 08901 732-828-8500
Fax: 732-828-8563 800-762-2135
info@suzannes-specialties.com
www.suzannes-specialties.com
All natural, vegan and organic sweetners, dessert and toppings.
President: Susan Allen-Morano
VP: James Allen
Number Employees: 10
Type of Packaging: Consumer, Food Service, Bulk
Brands:
Rice Nectar
Sunrice
Sunshine's
Suzanne's Conserves

13077 **Suzanne's Sweets**
9 Comanche Ct
Katonah, NY 10536-2917
Fax: 914-232-1291 www.suzannesweets.com
rugelach

13078 **Svenhard's Swedish Bakery**
335 Adeline Street
Oakland, CA 94607 510-834-5035
Fax: 510-839-6797 800-333-7836
ccare@svenhards.com www.svenhards.com
Manufacturer of pastries such as; cinnamon rolls and danishes
President: Ronny Svenhard
COO: Michelle Barnett
Estimated Sales: $72 Million
Number Employees: 240
Sq. footage: 90000
Type of Packaging: Consumer, Food Service
Other Locations:
Svenhard's Swedish Bakery
Exeter CA
Brands:
SVENHARDS

13079 **Swagger Foods Corporation**
900 Corporate Woods Pkwy
Vernon Hills, IL 60061 847-913-1200
Fax: 847-913-1263 info@swaggerfoods.com
www.swaggerfoods.com
Supplying the industrial, food service and retail markets as a manufacturer of seasonings, functional foods with vitamins, minerals, omega-3, other micronutrients/nutraceuticals, salt substitutes, soup mixes/bases, rubs, marinadesgravy/sauce mixes, dip/dressing mixes, drink mixes, side dish mixes and other dry blends including Ethnic.
President: Tai Shin PhD
Number Employees: 1-4
Type of Packaging: Consumer, Food Service, Private Label, Bulk
Brands:
BITS O' BUTTER
FANCY PANTRY
HEALTH-FU'D
SPICE SO RITE
SWAGGER

13080 **Swan Joseph Vineyards**
2916 Laguna Rd
Forestville, CA 95436-3729 707-573-3747
Fax: 707-575-1605 rod@swanwinery.com
www.swanwinery.com
Wines
Owner: Rod Berglin
President: Rod Berglund
CEO: Lynn Swan-Berglund
Estimated Sales: Less than $500,000
Number Employees: 1-4
Brands:
Swan Joseph

13081 **Swanson Vineyards & Winery**
P.O.Box 459
Rutherford, CA 94573 707-944-0905
Fax: 707-967-3505 800-942-0809
www.swansonvineyards.com
Wines
Owner: W Clarke Swanson
Sales Manager: Michael Opdegraff
Winemaker: Marco Capell
Estimated Sales: $5-9.9 Million
Number Employees: 20-49
Brands:
Swanson Vineyards & Winery

13082 **Swatt Baking Company**
222 Homer St
Olean, NY 14760 716-372-9480
Fax: 716-373-6019 800-370-6656
www.lacinnamonbread.com
Processor of rolls, regular and cinnamon bread and cinnamon bread sauce
President: Leonard Anzivine
VP: Lee Anzivine
Estimated Sales: $700000
Number Employees: 10-19
Sq. footage: 9400
Type of Packaging: Food Service, Bulk
Brands:
L.A. Cinnamon

13083 **Swedish Hill Vineyard**
4565 State Route 414
Romulus, NY 14541-9769 315-549-8326
Fax: 315-549-8477 888-549-9463
info@swedishhill.com www.swedishhill.com
Wines
President: Richard Peterson
Quality Control: David Peterson
Estimated Sales: $2 Million
Number Employees: 30
Brands:
Swedish Hill

13084 **Sweeney's Gourmet Coffee Roast**
671 Middlegate Road
Suite C
Henderson, NV 89011-2628 702-558-0505
Fax: 702-558-3799 www.sweenycoffee.com
Coffee
President: Robert Sweeney
Estimated Sales: $ 2.5-5 Million
Number Employees: 1
Type of Packaging: Private Label, Bulk

13085 **Sweenor Chocolate**
21 Charles St
Wakefield, RI 02879-3621 401-783-4433
Fax: 401-783-9340 800-834-3123
brian@sweenorchocolates.com
www.sweenorschocolates.com
Processor of chocolates, hard candies, fudge and mints
President: William Sweenor
Vice President: Brian Sweenor
Estimated Sales: $ 5 - 10 Million
Number Employees: 20-49
Type of Packaging: Consumer, Private Label, Bulk

13086 **Sweet & Saucy Inc**
5974 S Pennsylvania St
Centennial, CO 80121 303-807-5132
Fax: 303-798-8258 jane@sweetandsaucy.net
www.sweetandsaucy.net
21 flavors of gourmet caramel and chocolate sauces.
President: Jane Jones
Vice President: Erin Jones
CMO: Robert Jones
COO: Brent Jones
Number of Brands: 1
Number of Products: 21
Type of Packaging: Consumer, Food Service
Brands:
SWEET & SAUCY CARAMEL SAUCES
SWEET & SAUCY CHOCOLATE SAUCES

13087 **Sweet Baby Ray's**
Po Box 31250
Chicago, IL 60631-0250 877-729-2229
service@sweetbabyrays.com
www.sweetbabyrays.com
Processor of barbecue and hot and spicy sauce
Estimated Sales: $ 20-50 Million
Number Employees: 13
Parent Co: Ken's Foods
Type of Packaging: Consumer, Food Service
Brands:
Sweet Baby Ray's

13088 **Sweet Bakery Baltimore**
239 W. Read St.
Baltimore, MD 21043-4618 41- 7-8 22
Fax: 410-750-8556 www.fishersbakery.com
Breads, muffins, and cakes
Owner: Chris Sikora
Estimated Sales: $1-2.5 Million
Number Employees: 5-9
Sq. footage: 2000

13089 **Sweet Blessings**
23805 Stuart Ranch Rd
Malibu, CA 90265-4856 310-317-1172
Fax: 310-317-1132 www.sweet-blessings.com
Chocolates
President: Dave Singelyn
CEO/Owner: B Wayne Hughes
VP Sales: Mark Bontempo
Estimated Sales: $ 3 - 5 Million
Number Employees: 5-9
Brands:
NOAHS BUDDIES
SWEET BLESSINGS

13090 **Sweet Candy Company**
3780 West Directors Row
Salt Lake City, UT 84104 801-886-1444
Fax: 801-886-1404 800-669-8669
mail@sweetcandy.com www.sweetcandy.com
Processor of confectionery products including brittles, chocolates, holiday novelties, filled items, jellies, hard candies, jelly beans, marshmallows, mints, nougats, glazed nuts, taffy, etc.; also, in bags
Founder/President: Leon Sweet
VP: Kenneth DuVall
Estimated Sales: $113 Million
Number Employees: 100-249
Sq. footage: 180000
Type of Packaging: Consumer, Bulk

13091 **Sweet City Supply**
5820 Ward Ct
Virginia Beach, VA 23455 757-456-0800
Fax: 757-456-9980 888-793-3824
candysales@sweetcity.com www.sweetcity.com
A contract manufacturer and national distributor of imported and domestic bulk and packaged candy, nuts, and confections.
President: Ronald Bublick
Type of Packaging: Food Service, Bulk

13092 **Sweet Corn Products Company**
P.O.Box 487
Bloomfield, NE 68718 402-373-2211
Fax: 402-373-2219 877-628-6115
scpray@bloomnet.com
www.no-nobirdfeeder.com
Processor and exporter of sweet corn products including dry mature for tortilla chips and toasted nuts
General Manager: Raymon Lush
Estimated Sales: $2000000
Number Employees: 1-4
Sq. footage: 23000
Type of Packaging: Consumer, Food Service, Private Label, Bulk
Brands:
Ugly Nut

13093 **Sweet Earth Natural Foods**
597 Lighthouse Ave
Pacific Grove, CA 93950 831-375-8673
Fax: 831-375-3441 800-737-3311
www.sweetearth.us
Processor of vegetarian foods including soups, salads, burritos, salad dressings, salsa, hummus, vegeburgers, sweet bars, pies and seitan(wheat-meat)
Owner: Russell Hicks
Co-Owner: Caren Hicks
Estimated Sales: $ 3 - 5 Million
Number Employees: 10-19
Sq. footage: 2000
Type of Packaging: Consumer, Food Service, Bulk
Brands:
Awaken Foods
Fiesta Rice
Grand Life Seitan
Heat-N-Eat
Sweet Earth Natural Foods

13094 **Sweet Endings**
1220 Okeechobee Rd
West Palm Beach, FL 33401 561-209-1900
Fax: 561-655-1227 888-635-1177
swtend@aol.com
Processor and exporter of cakes, pies, tortes and crumbles including sugar and fat-free
Owner: Judy Mercur
Estimated Sales: $ 3 - 5 Million
Number Employees: 20-49
Sq. footage: 6000
Type of Packaging: Food Service, Private Label

13095 **Sweet Fortunes of America**
783a Yerry Hill Road
Woodstock, NY 12498 845-679-7327
Fax: 845-679-7327
Gourmet and specialty foods
President: Carol Lieberman

13096 **Sweet Gallery ExclusivePastry**
2312 Bloor St W
Toronto, ON M6S 1P2
Canada 416-766-0289
Fax: 416-766-7965 sweetg@on.aibn.com
www.toronto.com/sweetgallery
Processer of sponge cakes, butter cream tortes, pastries, croissants, wedding cakes, danishes and European cakes and pastries
President: Radi Jelenic
President: Lydia Jelenic
Number Employees: 10
Sq. footage: 5000
Type of Packaging: Consumer

13097 **Sweet Green Field LLC**
11 Bellwether Way
Unit 305
Bellingham, WA 98225 360-483-4555
Fax: 360-483-4554 www.sweetgreenfields.com
Sweeteners
CEO: Dean Francis
SVP Sales/Marketing: Mike Quin

13098 **Sweet Harvest Foods**
515 Cannon Industrial Drive
Cannon Falls, MN 55009 612-803-1995
Fax: 507-263-8611 www.sweetharvestfoods.com
Honey strained and bottled
President: Curt Riess
COO: Brian McGregor
Estimated Sales: $2 Million
Number Employees: 20

13099 Sweet Leaf Tea Company
515 S Congress Ave Ste 700
Austin, TX 78704 512-328-7775
Fax: 512-328-7725 www.sweetleaftea.com
teas, lemonades, mixers and fixers
Founder/CEO: Clayton Christopher
CFO/COO: Brian Goldberg
Marketing Director: Adi Wilk
Co-Founder/VP of Sales: David Smith
Manager Finance/Human Resources: Elizabeth Barber
VP Operations: Robert Walker
Production/Logistics Manager: Brian Selensky
Estimated Sales: $1.1 Million
Number Employees: 10

13100 Sweet Life Enterprises
2350 Pullman St
Santa Ana, CA 92705-5507 949-417-3205
Fax: 949-261-7470 www.sweetlifeinc.com
Processor and exporter of cinnamon rolls and cookies inluding chocolate chip, double fudge chocolate, oatmeal raisin, sugar, peanut butter, white chocolate, snickerdoodle, etc
CEO: Michael Gray
Estimated Sales: $ 50 - 100 Million
Number Employees: 100-249
Brands:
The Sweet Life

13101 Sweet Mele's Hawaiian Products
PO Box 218
Kailua, HI 96734
Fax: 812-537-1971 800-990-8441
sales@sweetmeles.com www.sweetmeles.com
Flavored Macadamia nut oil, stir-fry sauces, BBQ sauces, fruit bars, preserves, pancake mix, breakfast gift sets. lemonades, ice tea, coconut chew bars, coconut pineapple butter.
Parent Co: CB International

13102 Sweet Mountain Magic
2131 N Larrabee Street
Apt 6205
Chicago, IL 60614-4422 773-755-4539
Fax: 703-437-1031
Ice cream
President: Stephen Kleiman
VP Marketing: Ehtel Hammer

13103 Sweet Productions
5100 New Horizons Blvd
Amityville, NY 11701-1144 631-842-0548
Processor and exporter of nutritional bars including fat-free, low-fat coated, meal replacement, high protein, multi-nutrient and herbal composition; also, coatings; custom development services available
President: Paul Schacher
CEO: Ben Cohen
VP: Joseph Pizzo
Estimated Sales: $20-50 Million
Number Employees: 250-499
Sq. footage: 80000
Type of Packaging: Consumer

13104 Sweet Sam's Baking Company
1261 Seabury Ave
Bronx, NY 10462 718-822-0599
Fax: 718-409-0309 richardsklar@hotmail.com
www.sweetsams.com
Premium all butter bakery products
Estimated Sales: $ 5 - 10 Million
Number Employees: 85

13105 Sweet Shop
1113 Caledonia St
La Crosse, WI 54603 608-784-7724
Processor of ice cream and chocolate
Owner: Bill Espe
Estimated Sales: $160000
Number Employees: 5-9
Type of Packaging: Consumer

13106 Sweet Shop
1316 Industrial Road
Mount Pleasant, TX 75455 903-575-0033
Fax: 903-575-0050 800-222-2269
annan@econfections.com
www.econfections.com
Processor of confectionery products, handmade chocolates, truffles, nut cluster bars and caramels
Co-President: James H Webb
Co-President: Paul Anderson
VP: Betsy Oldham
Purchasing Manager: Kenneth Faulk
Estimated Sales: $9,800,000
Number Employees: 110
Type of Packaging: Consumer, Private Label, Bulk

13107 Sweet Shop USA
1316 Industrial Rd
Mt Pleasant, TX 75455-2614 903-575-0033
Fax: 903-336-9169 dmillican@econfections.com
www.sweetshopusa.com
Manufacturer of gourmet chocolates
CEO: Jim Webb
Marketing/New Product Development: Anna Parker
Estimated Sales: $ 10 - 20 Million
Number Employees: 50-99
Sq. footage: 66000
Type of Packaging: Private Label, Bulk
Brands:
ANNACLAIRE'S
PRICE'S FINE CHOCOLATES
SWEET SHOP

13108 Sweet Shop USA
1316 Industrial Rd
Mt Pleasant, TX 75455-2614 903-575-0033
Fax: 903-336-9169 800-222-2269
toffee@mwtoffee.com www.sweetshopusa.com
Toffee covered in milk chocolate with pecans or almonds
CEO: James Webb
President: Krista Webb
Estimated Sales: $ 10 - 20 Million
Number Employees: 120
Type of Packaging: Consumer, Food Service, Private Label

13109 Sweet Street Desserts
P.O.Box 15127
Reading, PA 19612-5127 610-929-0616
Fax: 610-921-8195 800-793-3897
custservice@sweetstreet.com
www.sweetstreet.com
Variety of coffee bar and desserts: hazelnut cappucino torte, apple crumb cake, chocolate chip crumb cake, sour cream coffee cake
President: Sandy Solmon
Estimated Sales: $39400000
Number Employees: 5-9
Type of Packaging: Consumer, Food Service
Brands:
Sweet Street

13110 Sweet Sue Kitchens
106 Sweet Sue Drive
Athens, AL 35611-2181 256-216-0500
Fax: 256-216-0531
Processor and exporter of canned poultry products including chicken broth, chunks, stew and dumplings
Sales/Marketing Executive: Shirley Brown
Plant Manager: Bob Mahan
Purchasing Agent: Carol Moore
Parent Co: Sara Lee Corporation
Type of Packaging: Consumer, Food Service, Private Label

13111 Sweet Swiss Confections
7821 W Electric Ave
Spokane, WA 99224-9000 509-838-1334
Fax: 509-456-0824 chocologos@sweetswiss.com
www.sweetswiss.com
Chocolate truffles, marzipan and personalized chocolate logos
President: Matt Phillipson
Controller: Pam Martin
Vice President: Phina Phillipson
Estimated Sales: Below $ 5 Million
Number Employees: 5-9

13112 Sweet Traders
5362 Oceanus Dr Ste C
Huntington Beach, CA 92649 714-903-6800
Fax: 714-892-4345 info@sweettraders.com
www.sweettraders.com
Wine, chocolate, baked goods, and gift baskets; including chocolate wrapped wines and ciders, champagnes and nonalcoholic beverages
Owner: R Louw
Estimated Sales: Under $500,000
Number Employees: 1-4
Sq. footage: 2500
Type of Packaging: Consumer, Private Label

13113 Sweet Water Seafood Corporation
369 Washington Ave
Carlstadt, NJ 7072 201-939-6622
Fax: 201-939-4014
Processor of frozen shellfish including squid, conch, clams and mussels
Manager: Teri Niece
Chairman: Robert Inglese
Estimated Sales: $500,000-$1 Million
Number Employees: 1-4
Sq. footage: 33000
Type of Packaging: Consumer, Food Service, Private Label, Bulk
Brands:
Mussel King
Plumpy

13114 Sweet Works
248 State Road 312
St Augustine, FL 32086-4241 904-825-1700
Fax: 904-824-0436 877-261-7887
info@sweetworks.net
www.whetstonechocolates.com
Manufacturers, sells, and distributes chocolate, candy and gum products in the North American and worldwide confectionery markets.
Owner: Virigina Whetstone
CEO: Philip Terranova
VP Sales: Tom Fox
Number Employees: 250-499
Other Locations:
Sweetworks
Buffalo NY
Sweetworks
Toronto, Canada
Brands:
NIAGARA CHOCOLATES
OAK LEAF CONFECTIONS
WHETSTONE CANDY

13115 Sweet'N Low
2 Cumberland St
Brooklyn, NY 11205-1000 718-858-4200
Fax: 718-858-6386 www.sweetnlow.com
Chairman: Marvin Eisenstadt
President/CEO: Jeffrey Eisenstadt
CFO: Peter Marshall
Estimated Sales: $100+ Million
Number Employees: 400
Parent Co: Cumberland Packing Corp.
Brands:
SWEET'N LOW

13116 SweetWorks Inc
3500 Genesee Street
Buffalo, NY 14225 716-634-0880
Fax: 716-634-4855 www.sweetworks.net
chocolates, candy and gum products
President/CEO: Philip Terranova
CFO: Ralph Nicosia
Marketing Director: Jeanne Palka
Sales Director: Jerry Tubbs

13117 Sweetbliss by Ilene C Shane
252 7th Ave Apt 5i
Fl 11
New York, NY 10001
Fax: 212-725-6976 info@sweetbliss.com
www.sweetbliss.com
chocolates
President/Owner: Ilene Shane
VP: Iris Libby
Number Employees: 4

13118 Sweetcraft Candies
PO Box 15
Timonium, MD 21094-0015 410-252-0684
Fax: 410-252-0352
Candy
President: George George

13119 Sweetery
1814 E Greenville St
Anderson, SC 29621 864-224-8394
Fax: 864-224-8469 800-752-1188
thesweetery@carol.net www.thesweetery.com
Processor of southern comfort baked goods including cakes, cheesecakes and pies
President: Jane Jarahian

Estimated Sales: Under $500,000
Number Employees: 20-49
Type of Packaging: Consumer, Private Label
Brands:
Southern Special
Uggly Cake

13120 **Sweetwater Brewing Company**
195 Ottley Dr NE
Atlanta, GA 30324 404-691-2537
Fax: 404-691-0936 Steve@sweetwaterbrew.com
www.sweetwaterbrew.com
Processor of ale and stout
President: Freddy Bensch
Sales: Dave Guender
Estimated Sales: $ 2.5-5 Million
Number Employees: 5-9
Type of Packaging: Consumer, Food Service
Brands:
Sweetwater
Sweetwater 42
Sweetwater Blue

13121 **Sweetwater Spice Company**
3800 N Lamar Blvd
Suite 730-155
Austin, TX 78756 800-531-6079
Fax: 512-857-0083 info@sweetwaterspice.com
www.sweetwaterspice.com
sauces and marinades

13122 **Sweety Novelty**
633 Monterey Pass Rd
Monterey Park, CA 91754 626-282-4482
Fax: 626-282-2482
Processor of frozen fruit bars and ice cream including red bean, mango, green tea, durian, peanut and taro; also, mocha ice cream including green tea, vanilla, strawberry, mango and taro
President: Tracy Lee
Estimated Sales: $870000
Number Employees: 10-19
Sq. footage: 16000
Type of Packaging: Consumer, Food Service

13123 **(HQ)Swift & Company**
1770 Promontory Cir
Greeley, CO 80634-9039 970-506-8000
Fax: 970-506-8307 emailus@swiftbrands.com
www.swiftbrands.com
Provides quality beef and pork products to consumers nationwide
Ceo: Wesley Batista
EVP Customers and Supply Chains: Kevin Yost
EVP Operations: Ted Miller
Number Employees: 10,000+
Parent Co: ConAgra Refigerated Prepared Foods
Type of Packaging: Consumer

13124 **Swift & Company**
1770 Promontory Cir
Greeley, CO 80634-9039 970-506-8000
Fax: 970-506-8307 emailus@Swiftbrands.com
www.jbsswift.com
Processor of brown and serve sausage, hard salami, pepperoni and mortadella
Ceo: Wesley Batista
Plant Manager: Jim Brown
Estimated Sales: $100+ Million
Number Employees: 500-999
Parent Co: ConAgra Refigerated Prepared Foods
Type of Packaging: Consumer, Food Service, Private Label, Bulk

13125 **Swire Coca-Cola**
12634 S 265 W
Draper, UT 84020-7930 801-816-5300
Fax: 801-816-5423 800-497-2653
www.swirecc.com
Processor of soft drinks
President/CEO: John Pelo
CFO: Christine Buckley
VP Manufacturing: Kurt Fiedler
VP Distribution: Jeff Edwards
Estimated Sales: $470 Million
Number Employees: 1800
Sq. footage: 400000
Parent Co: Swire Pacific Holdings
Type of Packaging: Food Service

13126 **Swiss American Sausage Corporation**
251 Darcy Pkwy
Lathrop, CA 95330 209-858-5555
Fax: 209-858-1102 info@sasausage.com
www.sasausage.com
Processor of sausage, salami and pepperoni
president: Theodore Arena
CEO: Theodore Arena
Human Resources: Heidi Moore
Number Employees: 100-249
Brands:
Swiss American Sausage

13127 **(HQ)Swiss Chalet Fine Foods**
9455 NW 40th Street Rd
Doral, FL 33178 305-702-5314
Fax: 305-592-1651 800-347-9477
sales@scff.com www.scff.com
A wide range of quality gourmet products from sweets to savories
CEO: Y Hans Baumann
Estimated Sales: $300,000-500,000
Number Employees: 10-19
Brands:
Felchlin-Swiss
Haco
Hero

13128 **Swiss Colony**
1112 7th Ave
Monroe, WI 53566 608-328-8536
Fax: 608-328-8457 www.swisscolony.com
Manufacturer of cheese and food gift baskets
President: John Baumann
Estimated Sales: $50 Million
Number Employees: 1,000-4,999
Sq. footage: 1000000
Brands:
SWISS COLONY FOODS

13129 **Swiss Dairy**
12171 Madera Way
Riverside, CA 92503 951-898-9427
Fax: 951-734-3786
Processor of milk
Office Manager: Lorry Olson
Estimated Sales: $ .5 - 1 million
Number Employees: 5-9
Parent Co: Suiza Dairy Group
Type of Packaging: Consumer, Food Service

13130 **Swiss Food Products**
4333 W Division St
Chicago, IL 60651 312-829-0100
Fax: 773-394-6475
sales@swissfoodproducts.com
www.swissfoodproducts.com
Manufacturer and exporter of bases including soup, gravy, browning, seasoning and sauce; also, flavors
President: Paul Kalpake
Vice President: Senya Kalpake
Estimated Sales: $ 5 - 10 Million
Number Employees: 10-19
Sq. footage: 25000
Type of Packaging: Consumer, Food Service, Private Label, Bulk
Brands:
Swiss

13131 **Swiss Heritage Cheese**
114 E Coates Ave
Monticello, WI 53570 608-938-4455
Fax: 608-938-1325 www.swissheritagewines.com
Cheese
President/Treasurer: Paul Rufener
Estimated Sales: $1,600,000
Number Employees: 5-9
Brands:
Swiss Heritage Cheese

13132 **Swiss Valley Farms Company**
P.O.Box 4493
Davenport, IA 52808 563-468-6600
linda.lee@swissvalley.com
www.swissvalley.com
Beverages (dairy and non-dairy), cultured products (cottage cheese, yogurt, sour cream, dip) and cheese
CEO: Donald Boelens
VP Finance: Greg Rexwinkel
VP Quality/R&D: Jeff Ryan
VP Sales/Marketing: Jeff Saforek
VP Human Resources: Deb Sullivan
VP Operations: Ed Seutter
Estimated Sales: 525,000,000
Number Employees: 20-49
Type of Packaging: Consumer
Other Locations:
Luana IA
Mindoro WI

13133 **(HQ)Swiss Valley Farms Company**
P.O.Box 4493
Davenport, IA 52808 563-468-6600
Fax: 563-468-6616 www.swissvalley.com
Processor of dry and fresh dairy products including milk, soft serve ice cream mixes and cheese including cheddar, swiss, cream and cottage
President: Pam Bolin
CEO: Donald Boelens
Vice President: Randy Schaefer
Sales/Marketing Executive: Stan Woodworth
Estimated Sales: $425 Million
Number Employees: 360
Type of Packaging: Consumer, Food Service, Private Label, Bulk

13134 **Swiss Valley Farms Company**
3000 Jackson St Ste 2
Dubuque, IA 52001 563-582-2170
Fax: 563-582-4723 800-397-9156
webmaster@swissvalley.com
www.swissvalley.com
Manufacturer of Milk bottling
Director: Steve Dudo
Manager: Stanley Atkinson
Estimated Sales: $500,000-1 Million
Sq. footage: 70000
Parent Co: Swiss Valley Farms Company
Type of Packaging: Consumer, Food Service

13135 **Swiss Valley Farms Company**
247 Research Pkwy
Davenport, IA 52808 563-468-6600
Fax: 563-468-6616 www.swissvalley.com
Processor of ice cream mix, milk, cream, cottage cheese and orange juice
Board President: Pam Bolin
CEO: Donald Boelens
Board VP: Randy Schaefer
VP Sales and Marketing: Terry Mitchell
Estimated Sales: 1,000-4,999
Number Employees: 50-99
Parent Co: Swiss Valley Farms Company
Type of Packaging: Consumer, Private Label

13136 **Swiss Way Cheese**
1315 Us Highway 27 N
Berne, IN 46711-1031 260-589-3531
Fax: 219-589-3843 swoss@swissway.com
www.swissway.com
Cheese
President: Tim Ehlerding
Operations Manager: Russ Reimer
Estimated Sales: $ 2.5 Million appx.
Number Employees: 5-9
Type of Packaging: Private Label
Brands:
Berne Baby Swiss
Berne Swiss Lace

13137 **(HQ)Swiss-American**
4200 Papin St
St Louis, MO 63110-1736 314-533-2224
Fax: 314-533-0765 800-325-8150
jweil@swissamerican.com
www.swissamerican.com
Packer, importer and distributor of cheese and fine foods
President: Joseph Hoff
CEO: R Weil
VP: D Boyd
Operations VP: David Boyd
Estimated Sales: $ 5 - 10 Million
Number Employees: 50-99
Sq. footage: 45000
Type of Packaging: Consumer, Bulk
Other Locations:
Swiss-American
North Charleston SC
Brands:
Capricorn
Dutch Garden
Dutch Garden Super Swiss
Epic
Fire Jack
Freshwrap Cuts

Freshwrap Slices
Mr. Sharp
Saint Louis
Verdaccio

13138 **Swiss-American Sausage Company**
251 Darcy Pkwy
Lathrop, CA 95330 209-858-5555
Fax: 209-858-1102 info@sasausage.com
www.sasausage.com
Processor and exporter of meat pizza toppings including pepperoni, salami, ham, linguica and raw and cooked sausage
President/CEO: Theodore Arena
Human Resources: Heidi Moore
Sales Manager: Paul Sheehan
Estimated Sales: $300,000-500,000
Number Employees: 50-99
Sq. footage: 90000
Type of Packaging: Food Service, Private Label
Brands:
Capo Di Monte

13139 **Swissart Candy Company**
455 Braen Avenue
Wyckoff, NJ 07481-2949 201-447-0062
Fax: 201-447-1455
Candy
Number Employees: 10-19
Type of Packaging: Private Label
Brands:
Swissart

13140 **Swisser Sweet Maple**
6242 Swiss Road
Castorland, NY 13620-1244 315-346-1034
Fax: 315-346-1662 swisser@tweny.rr.com
www.swissermaple.com
Pure NY maple syrup, pure maple cream spread, maple candies, maple lollipops, maple granulated sugar, gift arrangements, wedding party favors and corporate gifts. Retail, wholesale and bulk.
Co-Owner: Barbara Zehr
Co-Owner: Jason Zehr
Number Employees: 4-6
Type of Packaging: Consumer, Private Label, Bulk
Other Locations:
Swisser Sweet Maple
Casta-Land NY

13141 **Swissland Milk**
818 Welty St
Berne, IN 46711 260-589-2761
Fax: 260-589-2761 www.swisslandcheese.com
Milk and yogurt
General Manager: Kirk Johnson
Estimated Sales: $ 1-2.5 Million
Number Employees: 10-19

13142 **Swissland Packing Company**
2684 North 900 East Rd
Ashkum, IL 60911-7003 815-698-2382
Fax: 815-698-2264 800-321-8325
Processor and exporter of fresh and frozen veal
President: Arthur Follenweider IV
VP: David Follenweider
Estimated Sales: $25900000
Number Employees: 118
Brands:
Swiss Class Veal

13143 **Switch Beverage**
381 Post Rd
Darien, CT 06820 203-202-7383
Fax: 203-202-7386 www.switchbev.com
juice
President/Owner: Mike Gilbert

13144 **Switchback Group**
3778 Timberlake Dr
Richfield, OH 44286-9187 330-523-5200
Fax: 330-523-5212 info@switchbackgroup.com
www.switchbackgroup.com
Manufacturer of compliance packaging machines, vertical appplications of which include condiments; prepared foods; spices; pre-mixes; salad dresings; dessert toppings; and juice.
Manager: Dave Shepherd
Marketing & Sales Director: David Shepherd

13145 **Switzer's**
575 N 20th St
East Saint Louis, IL 62205 618-271-6336
Fax: 618-271-6339
Wholesaler/distributor of frozen foods, groceries, provisions/meats and general merchandise; serving the food service market
President: Carolyn Hundley
President: C Hundley
Estimated Sales: $ 20 - 50 Million
Number Employees: 20-49

13146 **Sycamore Creek Company**
4974 Bird Dr
Stockbridge, MI 49285 517-851-0049
Fax: 517-851-0019 amcvittie@wgthompson.com
www.sycamorecreek.net
Unsalted, seasoned and confection coated, roasted grains and seeds
President: W G Thompson
Sales Manager: Tina Hernadez
Owner: Leonard Stuttman
Plant Supervisor: Glen Byron
Estimated Sales: $ 2.5-5 Million
Number Employees: 6
Type of Packaging: Private Label
Brands:
Sycamore Creek

13147 **Sycamore Vineyards**
PO Box 410
Saint Helena, CA 94574-0410 707-963-9694
Fax: 707-963-0554 800-963-9698
wineinfo@freemarkabbey.com
www.freemarkabbey.com
Wines
Director Winemaking: Ted Edwards
Winemaker: Tim Bell
Estimated Sales: $1.9 Million
Number Employees: 20

13148 **Sylvest Farms Inc**
3500 West Blvd
Montgomery, AL 36108-4536 334-281-0400
Fax: 334-284-2915 beth_c@sylvestfarms.com
www.sylvestfarms.com
Manufacturer of poultry
President/Ceo: Dean Faulk
Executive Vice President: Richard Taylor
Estimated Sales: $55 Million
Number Employees: 500-999
Sq. footage: 35000
Parent Co: Wayne Farms
Type of Packaging: Consumer, Food Service, Bulk
Brands:
SYLVEST SUPER

13149 **Sylvester Winery**
5115 Buena Vista Dr
Paso Robles, CA 93446 805-227-4000
Fax: 805-227-6128 info@sylvesterwinery.com
www.sylvesterwinery.com
Wines
Owner: Sylvia Filippini
Winemaker: Chuck Devlin
Estimated Sales: Below $ 5 Million
Number Employees: 5-9
Brands:
Sylvester

13150 **Sylvin Farms Winery**
24 N Vienna Ave
Egg Harbor City, NJ 8215 609-965-1548
Wines
Proprieter: Frank Salek
Vineyard Manager: Franklin Salek
Estimated Sales: $500,000-$1 Million
Number Employees: 1-4
Brands:
Sylvin Farms

13151 **Symms Fruit Ranch**
14068 Sunnyslope Rd
Caldwell, ID 83607 208-459-4821
Fax: 208-459-6932 larry@symmsfruit.com
www.symmsfruit.com
Processor and exporter of produce including apples, cherries, peaches and plums, necatrines, pluots, pears, wine grapes, asparagus, onions and potatoes.
President: Richard Symms
VP: James Mertz
Sales Director: Daniel Symms
Estimated Sales: $20 Million
Number Employees: 150
Sq. footage: 150000
Type of Packaging: Consumer, Food Service, Bulk
Brands:
SSS

13152 **Symons Frozen Foods**
P.O.Box 195
Galvin, WA 98544 360-736-1321
Fax: 360-736-6328 www.symonsfrozenfoods.com
Processor and exporter of frozen fruits and vegetables including blackberries, blueberries, red and black raspberries, corn, peas, peas/carrots and succotash
President: William James
Production Manager: Howard McLoughlin
Estimated Sales: $18200000
Number Employees: 50-99
Type of Packaging: Consumer, Food Service, Private Label, Bulk

13153 **Symphony Foods**
1685 Short Street
Berkeley, CA 94702-1231 510-845-8275
Fax: 510-558-9255
General groceries
Owner: Alan Finkelstein
Number Employees: 1-4
Type of Packaging: Private Label

13154 **Symrise**
300 North St
Teterboro, NJ 07608 201-288-3200
Fax: 201-288-0843 www.symrise.com
Manufacturer and importer of flavors, fragrances, aroma chemicals
CEO: Dr. Heinz-Jurgen Bertram
CFO: Bernd Hirsch
Manager: Bruce Henkin
Vice President Innovation: Deborah Kennison
Estimated Sales: $3+ Billion
Number Employees: 1,000-4,999
Sq. footage: 100000
Parent Co: Symrise GmbH & Co. KG
Brands:
Dariteen
EVOLUTION
Optamint

13155 **Synda International**
9117 Saint Andrews Place
College Park, MD 20740-4037 301-935-2263
Fax: 301-935-4778
President: Bin Huang

13156 **Synergy Foods**
PO Box 250398
West Bloomfield, MI 48325-0398 313-849-2900
Fax: 313-849-2906
Processor of custom made roasted peanuts and peanut products such as butter, flour and oil extracts; also, custom blending, such as, iced tea mix, gelatins and drink mix
President: Don Soetaert
CFO: George Lewis
Operations Manager: Mikhail Adronov
Number Employees: 20-49
Sq. footage: 65000
Type of Packaging: Food Service, Private Label, Bulk

13157 **Synergy Plus**
500 Halls Mill Rd
Freehold, NJ 07728-8811 732-308-3000
Fax: 732-761-2878 www.invernessmedical.com
Vitamins
Manager: Barb McCleer
Sales Coordinator: Arthur Edell
Estimated Sales: Under $500,000
Number Employees: 250-499

13158 **Syracuse Casing Company**
528 Erie Blvd W
Syracuse, NY 13204 315-475-0309
Fax: 315-475-8536
Processor of natural sausage casings
President: Peter Frey Jr
Estimated Sales: $2200000
Number Employees: 10-19
Sq. footage: 15000
Type of Packaging: Food Service, Private Label, Bulk

13159 **Sysco Central Illinois**
1 Sysco Drive
PO Box 260
Lincoln, IL 62656-0620 217-735-6100
Fax: 217-735-6281 www.syscoci.com
Wholesaler/distributor of groceries, frozen and specialty foods, produce, seafood and meats; serving the food service market
Parent Co: Sysco Corporation

13160 **Sysco Columbia**
131 Sysco Court
Columbia, SC 29209 803-239-4000
Fax: 803-239-4011 www.syscosc.com
Wholesaler/distributor of groceries, frozen and specialty foods, produce, seafood and meats; serving the food service market
Parent Co: Sysco Corporation

13161 **Sysco Connecticut**
100 Inwood Road
Rocky Hill, CT 06067 860-571-5600
Fax: 860-571-5656 www.syscoct.com
Wholesaler/distributor of frozen foods, groceries, produce, meats, dairy and baked products, seafood, specialty foods and general merchandise; serving the food service market
Parent Co: Sysco Corporation

13162 **Sysco Dallas**
800 Trinity Drive
PO Box 561000
Lewisville, TX 75056 769-384-6000
www.syscodallas.com
Wholesaler/distributor of frozen foods, groceries, produce, meats, dairy and baked products, seafood, specialty foods and general merchandise; serving the food service market
Parent Co: Sysco Corporation

13163 **Sysco Denver**
5000 Beeler Street
Denver, CO 80238 303-585-2000
Fax: 303-480-3994 www.syscodenver.com
Wholesaler/distributor of frozen foods, groceries, produce, meats, dairy and baked products, seafood, specialty foods and general merchandise; serving the food service market
Parent Co: Sysco Corporation

13164 **Sysco East Texas**
4577 Estes Parkway
Longview, TX 75603 903-252-6100
www.syscoeasttexas.com
Wholesaler/distributor of frozen foods, groceries, produce, meats, dairy and baked products, seafood, specialty foods and general merchandise; serving the food service market
Parent Co: Sysco Corporation

13165 **Sysco Eastern Maryland**
33239 Costen Road
PO Box 477
Pocomoke, MD 21851 410-677-5555
Fax: 800-670-9726 800-927-3320
www.syscoeasternmd.com
Wholesaler/distributor of frozen foods, groceries, produce, meats, dairy and baked products, seafood, specialty foods and general merchandise; serving the food service market
Parent Co: Sysco Corporation

13166 **Sysco Eastern Wisconsin**
One Sysco Drive
Jackson, WI 53037 262-677-1100
Fax: 262-677-6311 www.syscoeast.com
Wholesaler/distributor of frozen foods, groceries, produce, meats, dairy and baked products, seafood, specialty foods and general merchandise; serving the food service market
Parent Co: Sysco Corporation

13167 **Sysco Edmonton**
14404-128 Avenue
Edmonton, AB T5L 3H6
Canada 780-451-0742
Fax: 780-451-3550 www.sysco.ca/edmonton/
Processor of frozen French fries and peeled and pre-cut vegetables
Parent Co: Sysco Corporation
Type of Packaging: Consumer, Food Service
Brands:
I&S
Russbank
Shur Fresh

13168 **Sysco Gulf Coast**
2001 Western Magnolia Ave
Geneva, AL 36340 334-684-4000
www.sysco.com
Wholesaler/distributor of frozen foods, groceries, produce, meats, dairy and baked products, seafood, specialty foods and general merchandise; serving the food service market
Parent Co: Sysco Corporation

13169 **Sysco Hampton Roads**
7000 Harbour View Blvd
Suffolk, VA 23432 757-673-4000
Fax: 757-673-4148 800-234-2451
http://syscohamptonroads.com
Wholesaler/distributor of frozen foods, groceries, produce, meats, dairy and baked products, seafood, specialty foods and general merchandise; serving the food service market
Parent Co: Sysco Corporation

13170 **Sysco Indianapolis**
4000 W 62nd St
Indianapolis, IN 46268 317-291-2020
Fax: 317-216-9346 www.syscoindy.com
Wholesaler/distributor of frozen foods, groceries, produce, meats and specialty foods; serving the food service market
Parent Co: Sysco Corporation

13171 **Sysco Jacksonville**
1501 Lewis Industrial Drive
Jacksonville, FL 32254 904-786-2600
Fax: 904-695-8135 www.sysco.com
Wholesaler/distributor of frozen foods, groceries, produce, meats, dairy and baked products, seafood, specialty foods and general merchandise; serving the food service market
Parent Co: Sysco Corporation

13172 **Sysco Knoxville**
900 Tennessee Avenue
Knoxville, TN 37921-2630 865-545-5600
Fax: 865-544-7955 www.syscoknoxville.com
Wholesaler/distributor of frozen foods, groceries, produce, meats, dairy and baked products, seafood, specialty foods and general merchandise; serving the food service market
Parent Co: Sysco Corporation

13173 **Sysco Lincoln**
1700 Center Park Road
Lincoln, NE 68512 402-423-1031
Fax: 402-421-5291 www.sysco.com
Wholesaler/distributor of frozen foods, groceries, produce, meats, dairy and baked products, seafood, specialty foods and general merchandise; serving the food service market
Parent Co: Sysco Corporation

13174 **Sysco Louisville**
7705 National Turnpike
Louisville, KY 40214 502-364-4300
Fax: 502-364-4344 800-669-1236
www.sysco.com
Wholesaler/distributor of frozen foods, groceries, produce, meats, dairy and baked products, seafood, specialty foods and general merchandise; serving the food service market
Parent Co: Sysco Corporation

13175 **Sysco Memphis**
4359 BF Goodrich Blvd
Memphis, TN 38118-7306 901-795-2300
Fax: 901-367-0445 www.syscomemphis.com
Wholesaler/distributor of frozen foods, groceries, produce, meats, dairy and baked products, seafood, specialty foods and general merchandise; serving the food service market
Parent Co: Sysco Corporation

13176 **Sysco Nashville**
One Hermitage Plaza
Nashville, TN 37209 615-350-7100
Fax: 615-350-1976 www.robertorrsysco.com
Wholesaler/distributor of frozen foods, groceries, produce, meats, dairy and baked products, seafood, specialty foods and general merchandise; serving the food service market
Parent Co: Sysco Corporation

13177 **Sysco New Mexico**
601 Comanche NE
Albuquerque, MN 87107 505-761-1200
Fax: 505-761-1245 www.sysconm.com
Wholesaler/distributor of frozen foods, groceries, produce, meats, dairy and baked products, seafood, specialty foods and general merchandise; serving the food service market
Parent Co: Sysco Corporation

13178 **Sysco North Dakota**
3225 12th Avenue North
Fargo, ND 58102 701-293-8900
www.syscond.com
Wholesaler/distributor of frozen foods, groceries, produce, meats, dairy and baked products, seafood, specialty foods and general merchandise; serving the food service market
Parent Co: Sysco Corporation

13179 **Sysco Raleigh**
1032 Baugh Road
Selma, NC 27576 919-755-2455
Fax: 919-755-7467 www.syscoraleigh.com
Wholesaler/distributor of frozen foods, groceries, produce, meats, dairy and baked products, seafood, specialty foods and general merchandise; serving the food service market
Parent Co: Sysco Corporation

13180 **Sysco Sacramento**
7062 Pacific Avenue
Pleasant Grove, CA 95668 916-569-7000
Fax: 916-569-7001 www.syscosac.com
Wholesaler/distributor of frozen foods, groceries, produce, meats, dairy and baked products, seafood, specialty foods and general merchandise; serving the food service market
Parent Co: Sysco Corporation

13181 **Sysco San Diego**
12180 Kirkham Road
Poway, CA 92064 858-513-7300
Fax: 858-513-7253 www.syscosandiego.com
Wholesaler/distributor of frozen foods, groceries, produce, meats, dairy and baked products, seafood, specialty foods and general merchandise; serving the food service market
Parent Co: Sysco Corporation

13182 **Sysco Southeast Florida**
1999 Highway 710
Riviera Beach, FL 33404 561-842-1999
Fax: 561-882-2179 www.syscosef.com
Wholesaler/distributor of frozen foods, groceries, produce, meats, dairy and baked products, seafood, specialty foods and general merchandise; serving the food service market
Parent Co: Sysco Corporation

13183 **Sysco Spokane**
300 N Baugh Way
Post Falls, ID 83854 208-777-9511
www.syscospokane.com
Wholesaler/distributor of frozen foods, groceries, produce, meats, dairy and baked products, seafood, specialty foods and general merchandise; serving the food service market
Parent Co: Sysco Corporation

13184 **Sysco Ventura**
3100 Sturgis Road
Oxnard, CA 93030
Fax: 805-205-7000 877-205-9800
www.sysco.com
Wholesaler/distributor of frozen foods, groceries, produce, meats, dairy and baked products, seafood, specialty foods and general merchandise; serving the food service market
Parent Co: Sysco Corporation

13185 **Systems Bio-Industries**
2021 Cabot Boulevard W
Langhorne, PA 19047-1810 215-702-1000
Fax: 215-702-1015 www.skw.de.com
Fruit flavorings and fruit juice concentrates
Number Employees: 50-99

13186 **T Hasegawa**
14017 183rd St
Cerritos, CA 90703-7000 714-522-1900
Fax: 714-522-6800 drosson@thasegawa.com
www.chefaroma.com

Processor, importer and exporter of custom blended flavors, seasonings and fragrances
President: Tokujiro Hasegawa
President: Michiru Waku
Sales Manager (Western): Jeff Carlson
Sales Manager (Eastern): Robert Taylor
Estimated Sales: $8300000
Number Employees: 56
Sq. footage: 54000
Parent Co: T. Hasegawa Company
Other Locations:
T. Hasegawa U.S.A.
Northbrook IL

13187 T Hasegawa Flavors USA
14017 183rd St
Cerritos, CA 90703-7000 714-670-1586
Fax: 714-522-6800 salesusa@thasegawa.com
www.thasegawausa.com
Flavors and fragances for beverages, cuisine, dairy, salad dressings, sauces and prepared foods
President: Mark Scott
Marketing Director: Jeff Carlson
VP: Hiroyuki Okamura
CFO: Cindy Hu
Estimated Sales: $ 5-10 Million
Number Employees: 50-99

13188 T Marzetti Company
37 W Broad Street
Columbus, OH 43215 614-846-2232
Fax: 614-848-8330 www.marzetti.com
Dressings, dips, frozen breads, homemade rolls, croutons and more.
President: Bruce Rosa
EVP: Gary Thompson
R&D Director: Lou LeMoine
Quality Assurance Director: Tom McGirty
VP Marketing: Beverly Sandberg
National Sales Manager: Andy Bachman
Human Resources Director: Lowell Berry
SVP Operations: Doug Fell
Plant Manager: Elden Quilling
VP Purchasing: Tom Kellett
Estimated Sales: $ 50 - 100 Million
Number Employees: 1621
Sq. footage: 28000
Parent Co: Lancaster Colony Corporation
Type of Packaging: Food Service, Private Label, Bulk
Brands:
AMISH KITCHENS
CARDINI'S GIRARD'S PFEIFFER
CHATHAM VILLAGE
INN MAID
JACK DANIEL'S ROMANOFF
MAMMA BELLA
MARSHALL'S
MARZETTI
NEW YORK BRAND
REAMES
SISTER SCHUBERT'S
TERESA'S SELECT RECIPES

13189 T O Williams
P.O.Box C
Portsmouth, VA 23705-0080 757-397-0771
Fax: 757-397-5702 towi@bellatlantic.net
Meat packer
President: H J Chai
CEO: Diane Chay
VP: Peter J Chay
President: Hyun J Chay
Marketing: Bridgette McClung
Estimated Sales: $1600000
Number Employees: 20-49
Sq. footage: 13000
Type of Packaging: Food Service
Brands:
Blue Ribbon Hot Sausage
Diane's Italian Sausage
H.C. Smoked Sausage
Virginia Smoked Sausage

13190 T&T Seafood
14550 Brown Rd
Baker, LA 70714 225-261-5438
Fax: 225-261-5260
Seafood
President: John Tourere
Estimated Sales: $2 Million
Number Employees: 1-4

13191 T. Cvitanovich
2016 Fagot Avenue
Metairie, LA 70001-4217 504-837-9586
Fax: 504-833-6458
Processor and distributor of fresh and frozen shrimp
Owner: Tommy Cvitanovich
Secretary: Mary Cvitanovich
Estimated Sales: $ 5 - 10 Million
Number Employees: 10-19

13192 T. Marzetti Company
P.O.Box 29163
Columbus, OH 43229 614-846-2232
Fax: 614-848-8330 www.marzetti.com
Processor of pancake and waffle syrups, teriyaki and barbecue sauces, condiments and pourable dressings
President: Bruce Rosa
Assistant Plant Manager: John Hamstreet
Estimated Sales: $100+ Million
Number Employees: 100-249
Type of Packaging: Food Service, Private Label, Bulk

13193 T. Marzetti Company
P.O.Box 29163
Columbus, OH 43229 614-846-2232
Fax: 614-848-8330 www.marzetti.com
Processor of low-calorie salad dressings, caviar, barbecue sauce, specialty mustards, egg noodles, marinades, chip dips, gelatin salads, frozen fruit pies, frozen garlic bread, sauces, etc
President: Bruce Rosa
Senior VP: Gary Thompson
Number Employees: 100-249
Parent Co: Lancaster Colony Corporation
Type of Packaging: Consumer, Food Service, Private Label, Bulk
Other Locations:
Marzetti, T., Co.
Millersburg OH
Brands:
Allen Dairy
CARDINI'S ORIGINAL CAESAR
Cardini
Frenchette
Girards
Inn Maid
Marzetti
Mountain Top
New York
Pfeiffer
REAMES
Romanoff

13194 T. Sterling Associates
121 W 4th St
Jamestown, NY 14701-5005 716-483-0769
Fax: 716-664-9508
Cheese marketing
Manager: Spring Martin
Estimated Sales: $ .5 - 1 million
Number Employees: 1-4
Type of Packaging: Private Label

13195 T.B. Seafood
450 Commercial St
Portland, ME 04101-4636 207-871-2420
Fax: 207-871-0906
Seafood
President: Roderick Wintle Jr

13196 T.G. Lee Dairy
P.O.Box 3033
Orlando, FL 32802 407-894-4941
Fax: 407-896-4757 www.tgleedairy.com
Processor of citrus juices and milk including low-fat, chocolate, whole, skim, 1% and 2%; also, cream and ice cream cones, sandwiches and dixies
Manager: Billy Giovanetti
CEO: Howard Dean
Marketing MAnager: Bill Gilzanetti
VP Sales/Marketing: Bill Giovanetti
Number Employees: 500-999
Parent Co: Dean Foods Company
Type of Packaging: Consumer, Food Service, Private Label, Bulk
Brands:
T.G. Lee Foods

13197 T.J. Blackburn Syrup Works
P.O.Box 928
Jefferson, TX 75657 903-665-2541
Fax: 903-665-7441 800-527-8630
Manufacturer of jams, jellies and syrups
President: Jeffrey Fuquay
Estimated Sales: $40 Million
Number Employees: 50-99
Type of Packaging: Consumer, Bulk
Brands:
BLACKBURN'S
JOHNNIE FAIR

13198 T.J. Kraft
1535 Colburn St
Honolulu, HI 96817-4905 808-842-3474
Fax: 808-842-3475 tkraft@norpacexport.com
www.norpac-export.com
Various types of fresh Hawaiian seafood
President: Thomas Kraft
Estimated Sales: $ 10 - 20 Million
Number Employees: 10-19

13199 T.L. Herring & Company
P.O.Box 3186
Wilson, NC 27895-3186 252-291-1141
Fax: 252-291-1142
Processor and packer of hot dog chili, fresh pork sausage, souse meat, cooked chitterlings. All of these products are produced for Southern tastes
President: Thomas Mark
CFO: Jean Herring
Vice President: Mike Herring
Estimated Sales: $ 5 - 10 Million
Number Employees: 10-19
Sq. footage: 14900

13200 T.M. Duche Company
P.O.Box 845
Orland, CA 95963-0845 530-865-5511
Fax: 530-865-7864 www.duchenut.com
Processor and exporter of almonds
President: Mosha Schwartz
CFO: Tim Gray
Estimated Sales: $1-2.5 Million
Number Employees: 5-9
Type of Packaging: Consumer, Food Service, Private Label, Bulk

13201 T.S. Smith & Sons
8899 Redden Rd
Bridgeville, DE 19933 302-337-8271
Fax: 302-337-8417 www.tssmithandsonsfarm.com
Manufacturer of apples, peaches, nectarines, sweet corn, asparagus, strawberries, soybeans, wheat, barley and broiles; exporter of apples
President: Matthew Smith
Sales (Wholesale/Retail): Thomas Smith
Production Manager: Charles Smith
Estimated Sales: $3-5 Million
Number Employees: 20-49
Type of Packaging: Consumer, Bulk
Brands:
T.S. SMITH & SONS

13202 T.W. Garner Food Company
P.O.Box 4329
Winston Salem, NC 27115-4329 336-661-1550
Fax: 336-661-1901 800-476-7383
fsherrill@twgarner.com www.texaspete.com
A leading manufacturer of hot sauce, fresh-ingredient salsa, jams and jellies, and other sauces. The Texas Pete brand of hot sauce products is one of America's top brands. Texas Pete Chicken Wing Sauce is the top-selling brand in theUS.
President: Reg Garner
CFO: Hal Garner
VP: Ann Riddle
R&D/Quality Control: Ann Riddle
Marketing: Glenn Garner
Retail Sales: Jim Frank
Foodservice Sales: Frank Sherrill
Operations: Stan Carroll
Production/Plant Manager: Stan Carroll
Purchasing Director: Stan Carroll
Estimated Sales: $ 10 - 20 Million
Number Employees: 100-249
Type of Packaging: Consumer, Food Service
Brands:
Garner Jams & Jellies
Green Mountain Gringo
Texas Pete

13203 TAIF
600 Kaiser Dr Ste A
Folcroft, PA 19032 610-522-0122

Processor of frozen pasta and related items
President: Joseph A Talluto
VP: Gus De Nicola
Number Employees: 20-49
Sq. footage: 27000
Type of Packaging: Food Service
Brands:
Talluto's

13204 **TCHO Ventures**
Pier 17
San Francisco, CA 94111 415-981-0189
Fax: 415-723-7497 info@tcho.com
www.tcho.com
chocolate
President/Owner: Louis Rossetto
Director of Finance: Sam Christian
Estimated Sales: $1.3 Million
Number Employees: 20

13205 **TIPIAK INC**
45 Church St Ste 203
Stamford, CT 06906 203-961-9117
Fax: 203-975-9081 laurent.chery@tipiak-e.com
www.tipiak.fr
Processor and importer of couscous, granulated tapioca and tapioca pearls and starches
VP: Laurent Chery
Estimated Sales: $3 - 5 Million
Number Employees: 2
Sq. footage: 1200
Parent Co: TIPIAK SA
Type of Packaging: Consumer, Food Service, Private Label, Bulk
Brands:
Fecularia
Loanoa
Osem
Thai Wah
Tiapak

13206 **TKC Vineyards**
P.O.Box 759
Plymouth, CA 95669-0759 209-245-6428
Fax: 209-245-4006 888-627-2356
tkcvineyards@outrageous.net
www.tkcvineyards.com
Family winery committed to the production of premium wines. Specialties include Zinfandel, Mourvedre and Cabernet
Owner/CEO: Harold Nuffer
VP/CFO: Monica Nuffer
Marketing Director: Monica Nuffer
Estimated Sales: Less than $500,000
Number Employees: 1-4
Type of Packaging: Private Label
Brands:
TKC Vineyards

13207 **TNT Crust**
P.O.Box 8929
Green Bay, WI 54308 920-431-7240
Fax: 920-431-7249 tntcrust@tyson.com
www.tntcrust.com
Processor and exporter of pre-made, partially baked pizza crusts including thin, thick and raised edge; also, fresh and frozen pizza dough.
President: Roger Lebreck
Vice President: Shreenivas Manthana
VP Sales/Marketing: Larry Kropp
Sales Director: Larry Kropp
VP Operations: Kent Reschke
VP Engineering: Phil Vangsnes
Number Employees: 100-249
Parent Co: FoodBrands America
Type of Packaging: Food Service

13208 **TRAINA Foods**
PO Box 157
Patterson, CA 95363-0157 209-892-5472
Fax: 209-892-6231 info@traina.com
www.traina.com
Dried apricots, sun dried tomatoes and all dried fruit.
Quality Control Director: Robert Kimball
Marketing Director: Victoria Traina

13209 **TRC Nutritional Laboratories**
12320 E Skelly Dr
Tulsa, OK 74128-2414 918-437-7310
Fax: 918-492-9546 800-421-7310
www.trccorp.com
Processor of super oxygenated drinking water
President: Rocky Heinrich
CEO: Elmer Heinrich
Vice President: Shirley Heinrich
Estimated Sales: $7.5 Million
Number Employees: 60
Type of Packaging: Consumer
Brands:
Liquidlise
Super Oxy-Pure

13210 **TWD**
12631 Imperial Highway
Santa Fe Springs, CA 90670-4710 562-404-4110
Fax: 562-404-4150
President/CEO: Othon Cabral
Senior VP Finance: Hector Lozao
Sales Director: Peggy Ahumada
Estimated Sales: $ 1-2.5 Million appx.
Number Employees: 27
Brands:
Mi Rancho
Pepepeno
Ricas

13211 **Tabatchnick's Fine Foods**
1230 Hamilton St
Somerset, NJ 08873-3343 732-247-6668
Fax: 732-247-6555 info@tabatchnick.com
www.tabatchnick.com
Processor of homemade soups, sorbets, icepops and cheese
Owner: Ben Tabatchinick
CFO: Robert Ingebretsen
VP/National Food Service: Peter Hans
Institutional Sales: Marc Blake
Chief Engineer: Bud Barry
Retail Sales Cooordinator: Claudia Davila
Commodities Coordinator: Barbara Slicner
Customer Relations: Michelle Kopitman
Plant Manager: Cezar Capalong
Estimated Sales: Below $ 5 Million
Number Employees: 20-49

13212 **Tabco Enterprises**
1906 W Holt Ave
Pomona, CA 91768-3351 909-623-4565
Fax: 909-623-2605
www.essentialpharmaceutical.com
Processor and exporter of nutritional food supplements including deep sea fish oil, shark cartilage, multivitamins and minerals, grape seed extract, herbal products, spirulina, garlic, etc
President: Bruce Lin
Financial Officer: Rebecca Lin
Estimated Sales: $ 5 - 10 Million
Number Employees: 20-49
Sq. footage: 20000
Parent Co: Essential Pharmaceutical
Brands:
Eden Life
Essential Elite
Wonderful Life

13213 **Tabernash Brewing Company**
1265 Boston Ave
Longmont, CO 80501-5809 303-772-0258
Fax: 303-772-9572
brewer@lefthandbrewing.com
www.lefthandbrewing.com
Processor of seasonal beer and lager
Owner: Eric Wallace
CEO: Eric Wallece
Sales Manager: George Barela
Director Manufacturing: Mark Luca
Estimated Sales: $5-9.9 Million
Number Employees: 20-49
Type of Packaging: Consumer, Food Service
Brands:
BlackJack Porter
Brown Ale
Deep Cover
Ginger Ale
Haystack
Interial Stout
Jack Man
Juju
Milk stout
Toleftar Pilfen
Weat
Weiss

13214 **Table De France**
2020 S Haven Ave
Ontario, CA 91761 909-923-5205
Fax: 909-923-7804 info@micheldefrance.com
www.micheldefrance.com
Manufacturer of authentic French-Style Crepes, soy wraps, fan wafers, butter wafer cookies, rolled wafers and filled rolled wafers, Paillette Feuilletine and Parisian cakes.
President: Herve Bayon
Owner/CFO: Philip Bayon
Quality Control: Teresa Aguire
Sales Director: Erwan Le Bayon
Plant Manager: Philippe Le Bayon
Estimated Sales: $820,000
Number Employees: 12
Number of Products: 4
Sq. footage: 30000
Type of Packaging: Food Service, Private Label
Other Locations:
Table De France
Ontario CA
Brands:
Krazy
Michel De France
Table De France

13215 **Table Pride**
165 Bailey Street SW
Atlanta, GA 30314-4801 770-455-7464
Processor of baked goods including bread and dinner rolls
President: Wayne Chandler
Number Employees: 50-99
Parent Co: Flowers Baking Company
Type of Packaging: Consumer

13216 **Table Talk Pie**
120 Washington St
Worcester, MA 01610-2751 508-798-8811
Fax: 508-798-0848 www.tabletalkpie.com
Processor of pies
President: Christos Cocaine
Plant Manager: Jim Cumming
Estimated Sales: $4000000
Number Employees: 50-99

13217 **Tabor Hill/CHI Company**
185 Mount Tabor Rd
Buchanan, MI 49107-8326 269-422-1161
Fax: 269-422-2787 80- 2-3 33
info@TaborHill.com www.taborhill.com
President: Linda Upton
CEO: Mike Merchant
Estimated Sales: $ 10-20 Million
Number Employees: 75

13218 **Tadin Herb & Tea Company**
3345 E. Slauson Ave.
Vernon, CA 90058 213-406-8880
Fax: 323-582-8687 180- TE-TADI
support@tadincorp.com www.tadininc.com
Products include our very successful line of tea bags and cellophane-packaged herbs and capsules. Products satisfy the growing need for consumers in the area of herbal remedies. Our products are unique and well-targeted and servingthe Hispanic market.
President: Jose Gonzalez
Sales/Marketing: Rafal Lara
Estimated Sales: $ 5-10 Million
Number Employees: 50-99
Brands:
Tadin

13219 **Taffy Town**
55 W 800 S
Salt Lake City, UT 84101 801-355-4637
Fax: 801-355-7664 800-765-4770
worlds_best_taffy@taffytown.com
www.taffytown.com
Manufactures taffy, specializes in salt water taffy
President/CEO: David Glade
VP Marketing: Jason Glade
VP Manufacturing: Derek Glade
Estimated Sales: $1-2.5 Million
Number Employees: 20-49

13220 **Taft Street Winery**
2030 Barlow Ln
Sebastopol, CA 95472 707-823-2049
Fax: 707-823-8622 taftstreet@sonic.net
www.taftstreetwinery.com

Wines consisting of Sauvignon Blancs, Chardonnays, Zinfadel, Russian river, PEKA Pinot Noir
President: Michael Tierney
General Manager/CEO: Mike Martini
Sales/Marketing Manager: Steve Sack
Winemaker: Kent Barthman
Assistant Winemaker: Megan Baccitich
Cellar Master: Joel Rabune
Estimated Sales: $ 5-10 Million
Number Employees: 10-19
Type of Packaging: Private Label, Bulk

13221 Taftsville Country Store
1471 Cookeville Rd
Corinth, VT 05039-4406 802-439-6575
800-854-0013
clwilson@taftsville.com www.taftsville.com
Supplier of camembert, brie, stilton, gruyere and parmesan cheese, Vermont maple syrup, Vermont gourmet foods
President: Rebecca Loftus
Estimated Sales: $300,000-500,000
Number Employees: 1-4
Type of Packaging: Consumer
Brands:
Blythedale

13222 Taif Foods
600 Kaiser Dr Ste A A
Folcroft, PA 19032 610-522-0122
Fax: 610-631-5439
Macaroni, spaghetti, noodles, ravioli, tortellini and fettuccini
President: Joe Talluto
Vice President: Gus DeNicola
Estimated Sales: Less than $5 Million
Number Employees: 35
Sq. footage: 27000

13223 Tait Farm Foods
179 Tait Road
Centre Hall, PA 16828-7806 814-466-2386
Fax: 814-466-6561 800-787-2716
info@taitfarmfoods.com www.taitfarmfoods.com
Specialty jams, jellies, conserves, chutneys, scone and pan cake mixes, colonial fruit shrubs, international fruit sauces and herbal oils
President: John Tait
Production Manager: Pat Althouse
Estimated Sales: $80,000
Number Employees: 2
Type of Packaging: Private Label
Brands:
Raspberry Teriyaki
Tait Farm Foods
Tait Farm Foods

13224 Taiyo
5960 Golden Hills Drive
Minneapolis, MN 55416 763-398-3003
Fax: 763-398-3007 sales@taiyoint.com
www.taiyointernational.com
Ingredients for the food, beverage and pharmaceutical industries.
President: Naganori Yamazaki
Number Employees: 5

13225 Taj Gourmet Foods
700 Old Fern Hill Rd
West Chester, PA 19380 610-692-2209
www.ethnicgourmet.com
Processor and exporter of ethnic entrees including Thai, Indian and Italian
President: Paul Jaggi
VP: Sangeeta Jaggi
VP Operations: Harmeet Shanhu
Estimated Sales: $5-10 Million
Number Employees: 25
Sq. footage: 30000
Brands:
Bravissimo
TAJ
Thai Chef

13226 Takara Sake
708 Addison St
Berkeley, CA 94710 510-540-8250
Fax: 510-486-8758 info@takarasake.com
www.takarasake.com
Sake - a Japanese alcholic beverage of fermented rice -
President/CEO: Kazuyoshi Ito
Controller: Ken Burd
VP: Kenzo Shimotori
VP Sales: Yafuifa Tanaka
Senior Manager Production/Development: Kazunari Mizobata
General Manager: Masa Ohata
Estimated Sales: $ 10-20 Million
Number Employees: 32
Sq. footage: 15000
Type of Packaging: Private Label
Brands:
Sho Chiku Bai

13227 (HQ)Takasago International Corporation
4 Volvo Dr
Rockleigh, NJ 07647 201-767-9001
Fax: 201-784-7277 www.takasago.com
Manufacturing and sales of flavors, fragrances, aroma chemicals and fine chemicals.
President/CEO/Director: Ritaro Igaki
Senior Vice President: Sean Traynor
EVP/Sales Director: Haruo Nakanishi
SVP Production: Kazuhiko Tokoro
Estimated Sales: $160 Million
Number Employees: 100-249
Other Locations:
Takasago International Corpor
Teterboro NJ

13228 Taku Smokehouse
550 S Franklin St
Juneau, AK 99801-1330 907-463-4617
Fax: 907-463-4644 800-582-5122
info@takusmokeries.com
www.takusmokeries.com
Processor and exporter of Alaskan salmon, halibut, crab and cod including frozen, portion cut, fillet, smoked, salted and packed
President: Sandro Lane
Smokehouse Manager: Jeremy LaPierre
General Manager: Eric Norman
CEO: Giovanni Gallizio
Estimated Sales: Less than $500,000
Number Employees: 100-249
Sq. footage: 50000
Type of Packaging: Consumer, Food Service, Private Label, Bulk
Brands:
Taku

13229 Talbott Farms
3782 F 1/4 Rd
Palisade, CO 81526 970-464-5943
Fax: 970-464-7821 market@talbottfarms.com
www.talbottfarms.com
Grower and shipper of apples, peaches and pears; processor and shipper of cider
Principal: Bruce Talbott
Vice President: C Talbott
Estimated Sales: $ 20 - 50 Million
Number Employees: 100-249
Sq. footage: 26400
Brands:
Mountain Gold
Talbott's

13230 Talbott Teas
3517 N Fremont St Apt 4
Chicago, IL 60657
Fax: 773-404-6420 888-809-6062
www.talbottteas.com
teas; gourmet, green, black, white, rooibos and more
CEO: Shane Talbott
Number Employees: 5

13231 Talbott Vineyards
P.O.Box 776
Gonzales, CA 93926 831-675-3000
Fax: 831-675-3120 info@talbottvineyards.com
www.talbottvineyards.com
Wines - specializing in Chardonnay and Pinot Noir
Manager: Sam Balderas
General Manager: Sam Balderas
Marketing/Sales: Lee Codding
Marketing Manager: Ross Allen
Customer Service: Cindy Garza
Estimated Sales: Below $ 5 Million
Number Employees: 10-19
Number of Brands: 3
Number of Products: 7
Type of Packaging: Consumer
Other Locations:
Sleepy Hollow Vineyard
Gonzales CA
River Road Vineyard
Sant Lucia Highlands CA
Del Mar Vineyard
Dalinas Valley CA
Brands:
KALI HART CHARDONNAY
LOGAN CHARDONNAY
TALBOTT CHARDONNAY
TALBOTT DIAMOND T CHARDONNAY

13232 Talenti
9019 Governors Row
Dallas, TX 75247 214-526-3600
comments@talentigelato.com
www.talentigelato.com
gelato and sorbetto
Number Employees: 30

13233 Talisman Foods
3324 S 200 E
Salt Lake City, UT 84115 801-487-6409
Fax: 801-487-6409
Processor of turkey
President: Chad Maddox
VP: Ben Maddox
Estimated Sales: $ 1-2.5 Million
Number Employees: 5-9

13234 Talk O'Texas Brands
P.O.Box 2091
San Angelo, TX 76902-2091
Manufacturer of pickled okra, liquid hickory smoked flavor
President: Lawrence Ricci
VP: Lisa Ricci
VP Operations: Dan Herrington
Number Employees: 7
Sq. footage: 60000
Type of Packaging: Consumer

13235 Talking Rain Beverage Company
P.O.Box 549
Preston, WA 98050 425-222-4900
Fax: 425-222-4901 800-734-0748
events@talkingrain.com www.talkingrain.com
Beverages including five healthy thirst quenching product lines - spring water, oxygenated water, sparkling water, diet flavored non-carbonated water and flavored non-carbonated water. Some products are enhanced with fruit flavorsenriched with natural herbal supplements and infused with vitamins.
Owner: Doug Mac Lean
Technical Service: James Fecteau
VP Marketing/R & D: Nina Morrison
VP: Michael Fox
Quality Control: Sam Samia
VP Sales: Wayne King
National Accounts Manager: John Stevens
Plant Manager: Chuck Park
Purchasing Manager: Monica Runyon
Estimated Sales: $ 5-10 Million
Number Employees: 50-99
Brands:
Diet Ice Botanicals
Sparkling Ice
Talking Rain
Talking Rain Biotonical

13236 Tall Grass Toffee
14406 W 100th St
Shawnee Mission, KS 66215 913-599-2158
Fax: 913-599-2160 877-344-0442
info@tallgrasstoffee.com
www.tallgrasstoffee.com
toffee

13237 Tall Talk Dairy
11961 S Emerson Road
Canby, OR 97013-9311 503-266-1644
Dairy products
Marketing Director: Harlent Peterson
Sales Director: Esther Peterson

13238 Talley Farms
2900 Lopez Drive
Arroyo Grande, CA 93420 805-489-5533
Fax: 805-489-5201 talley@talleyfarms.com
www.talleyfarms.com

Grower and exporter of produce including sugar peas, bell peppers, nappa, cabbage, romaine lettuce, zucchini, Blue Lake beans, spinach and cilantro
President: Brian Talley
CEO: Todd Talley
Sales Director: Jeff Halfpenny
Operations Manager: Ryan Talley
Plant Manager: Arturo Ibarra
Estimated Sales: $ 10 - 20 Million
Number Employees: 250-499
Number of Brands: 2
Number of Products: 12
Type of Packaging: Consumer, Food Service, Bulk
Brands:
ARROYO GRANDE
TALLEY FARMS

13239 **Talley Vineyards**
P.O.Box 360
Arroyo Grande, CA 93421-0360 805-489-2508
Fax: 805-489-5201 info@talleyvineyards.com
www.talleyfarms.com
Estate wines such as Chardonnay and Pinot Noir
President: Don Talley
Marketing Director: David Block
CFO: Brain Caley
Estimated Sales: Below $ 5 Million
Number Employees: 10-19
Brands:
Talley Vineyards

13240 **Tamarack Farms Dairy**
1701 Tamarack Rd
Newark, OH 43055 740-522-8181
Fax: 740-522-9235 866-221-4141
investors@kroger.com www.kroger.com
Processor of milk and juices including fruit and vegetable
Chairman/CEO: David B Dillon
VP Operations: Mark Prestidge
President: Don McGeorge
Plant Engineer: Tony Neely
Number Employees: 100-249
Parent Co: Kroger Company
Type of Packaging: Consumer, Food Service, Private Label, Bulk
Brands:
City Market
Dillons
Food4Less
Gerbes
King Soopers
Owen's
QFC
Ralphs
Smith's

13241 **Tamarind Tree**
518 Justin Way
Neshanic Station, NJ 8853 908-369-6300
800-432-8733
Processor of shelf stable, all-natural and preservative, wheat and gluten-free Indian vegetarian entrees, snack foods, condiments and spicy lentil crisps; exporter of shelf stable and all-natural Indian vegetarian entrees
President: Harshad Parekh
Number Employees: 1-4
Sq. footage: 2000
Brands:
Pappadums
The Taste of India

13242 **Tamashiro Market**
802 N King St
Honolulu, HI 96817 808-841-8047
Fax: 808-845-2722
Japanese foods
President: Cyrus Tamashiro
Estimated Sales: $ 10 - 20 Million
Number Employees: 20-49

13243 **Tami Great Food**
11 Dunhill Ln
Monsey, NY 10952-2524 732-803-6366
Manufactures quick frozen & cold pack vegetables, excluding. potato products; manufactures frozen food products
CEO: Chaim Rosenberg
CFO: David Rosenberg
Estimated Sales: $1.7 Million
Number Employees: 10
Sq. footage: 6000

13244 **Tampa Bay Copack**
15052 Ronnie Dr # 100
Dade City, FL 33523-6011 352-567-7400
Fax: 352-567-2257 scot@tampabaycopack.com
www.tampabaycopakc.com
Contract manufacturing beverage bottling, pastuerizer, formulation, private label, product development.
President: Scot Ballantyne
Research & Development: Vince Curetto
Number Employees: 5-9
Sq. footage: 17000
Type of Packaging: Private Label

13245 **Tampa Bay Fisheries**
3060 Gallagher Rd
Dover, FL 33527 813-752-8883
Fax: 813-752-3168 800-234-2561
info@tbfish.com www.tbfish.com
fresh and frozen seafood; shrimp, crab, clams, scallops, lobster tails, squid, mussels, frog legs, oysters
President: Robert Patterson
CFO: Tom Tao
VP Sales/Marketing: Robert Hatcher
Human Resources Director: Sandi Fail
Operations Manager: Fred Godbold
Plant Manager: Mary Brown
Purchasing Director: Brenda Newman
Estimated Sales: $25 Million
Number Employees: 450
Sq. footage: 18562
Type of Packaging: Consumer, Food Service

13246 **(HQ)Tampa Farm Services**
14425 Haynes Rd
Dover, FL 33527 813-659-0605
Fax: 813-659-0197 info@tampafarms.com
www.4-grain.com
Processor, packer, exporter and distributor of shell eggs
President: Mike Bynum
Executive VP: Sam Bynum
VP: Blair Bynum
Estimated Sales: $ 20 - 50 Million
Number Employees: 100-249
Sq. footage: 70000
Type of Packaging: Consumer, Food Service, Private Label, Bulk
Other Locations:
Tampa Farm Services
Indiantown FL
Brands:
4-Grain All-Natural
Indiantown
Tampa Farm Service

13247 **Tampa Maid Foods**
P.O.Box 3709
Lakeland, FL 33802 863-687-4411
Fax: 863-683-8713 800-237-7637
info@tampamaid.com www.tampamaid.com
Processor, importer and exporter of frozen prepared seafood including breaded, peeled and deveined shrimp, stuffed flounder, oysters, scallops and appetizers
President/CEO: George Watkins
CFO/Senior VP: Edward Smith
Data Processing: Gene Gerstmeier
Production Manager: Kevin Stallworth
Purchasing Manager: Tim Moore
Number Employees: 250-499
Sq. footage: 140000
Type of Packaging: Consumer, Food Service, Private Label, Bulk

13248 **Tampico Beverages**
3106 N Campbell Ave
Chicago, IL 60618 773-296-0190
Fax: 773-296-0191 877-826-7426
comments@tampico.com www.tampico.com
Processor, exporter and importer of beverage bases and citrus blends
CEO: John Carson
CEO: Scott Miller
VP Marketing: Tracey Schroeder
Number Employees: 1-4
Type of Packaging: Bulk
Brands:
Tampico Punches

13249 **Tampico Spice Company**
5941 S Central Ave
Los Angeles, CA 90001 323-235-3154
Fax: 323-232-8686 info@tampicospice.com
www.tampico.com
Processor of spices and seasoning blends
President: Jesus Martinez
Vice President: George Martinez
National Sales Manager: Dale Carlson
Operations: Eduardo Freiwald
Estimated Sales: $6 Million
Number Employees: 50
Type of Packaging: Consumer, Food Service, Private Label, Bulk
Brands:
Tampico

13250 **Tamuzza Vineyards**
111 Cemetry Road
Hope, NJ 07844 908-459-5878
Fax: 908-459-5560 info@tamuzzavineyards.com
www.tamuzzavineyards.com
Wines
President: Al Ivory
Owner: Paul Tamuzza
Winemaker: Paul Tamuzza
Estimated Sales: $ 5-9.9 Million
Number Employees: 10

13251 **Tanglewood Farms**
297 Riverdale Rd
Warsaw, VA 22572 804-394-4505
Fax: 804-333-0422
Produce products such as cantaloupe, squash, tomatoes
President: Earl Lewis
VP: John E Lewis
Marketing: Ken Taylor
Estimated Sales: $ 2.5-5 Million
Number Employees: 5-9

13252 **(HQ)Tanimura & Antle**
P.O.Box 4070
Salinas, CA 93912-4070 831-455-2255
Fax: 831-455-3913 www.taproduce.com
Processor and exporter of cauliflower, broccoli, broccoflower, celery, lettuce, scallions, green onions and value-added products
President: Ken Silveira
CEO: Rick Antle
CEO: Rick Antle
Sales Director: Shiro Higashi
Estimated Sales: $214200000
Number Employees: 100-249
Type of Packaging: Consumer
Other Locations:
Tanimura & Antle
Salinas CA
Brands:
Brian
Salad Time
T & A
Tanbro

13253 **Tankersley Food Service**
3203 Industrial Park Rd
Van Buren, AR 72956 479-471-6800
Fax: 479-471-6851 800-726-6182
Distributor of general grocery
President: Danny Lloyd
Marketing Director: Rick Climer
CFO: David Wilson
Estimated Sales: $ 1-2.5 Million
Number Employees: 1-4
Brands:
Dolmany
Simplex

13254 **Tanks Meat**
P.O.Box 31
Elmore, OH 43416-0031 419-862-3312
www.tanksmeats.com
Manufacturer of beef and pork
President: Alois W Amstutz
Estimated Sales: $5-10 Million
Number Employees: 10-19
Type of Packaging: Consumer, Food Service, Bulk

13255 **Tantos Foods International**
15 Josiah Court
Markham, ON L3R 9A1
Canada 905-943-9993
Fax: 905-943-9943 info@tantos.com
www.tantos.com

Processor, exporter and importer of hot sauce, frozen fruit pulp, plantain, cassava and taro chips, annatto seeds, powder norbixin and ackees
President: Sultanali Ajani
Manager: Konrad Lutz
Estimated Sales: $390,000
Number Employees: 3
Sq. footage: 7000
Parent Co: Mejores Alimentos de Costa Rica/Alina Foods C.A.
Type of Packaging: Consumer, Food Service, Private Label, Bulk
Brands:
Banana Gold
Tantos

13256 **Taos Brewing Supply**
1416 4th Street
Santa Fe, NM 87505-3422 505-983-0505
Fax: 505-983-0505
Designer, packager and distributor of natural flavor soft drinks and root beer
President: Jonathan Riebli
Number Employees: 5-9
Sq. footage: 4000

13257 **Taos Trails Brewery**
PO Box 1480
Ranchos De Taos, NM 87557-1480 505-758-0099
Brewing of root beer

13258 **Tapatio Hot Sauce**
4685 District Blvd
Vernon, CA 90058 323-587-8933
Fax: 323-587-5266 info@tapatiohotsauce.com
www.tapatiohotsauce.com
Processor and exporter of hot sauce
Owner/President: Luis Saavedra
Manager: Jose Saavedra
Estimated Sales: $2 Million
Number Employees: 16
Type of Packaging: Consumer, Food Service
Brands:
TAPATIO

13259 **Tapper Candies**
15637 Neo Parkway
Cleveland, OH 44128-3150 216-825-1000
Fax: 330-825-1010
Candy
Estimated Sales: $ 5 - 10 Million
Number Employees: 5-9

13260 **Taqueria El Milagro**
1923 S Blue Island Ave
Chicago, IL 60608 312-433-7620
Fax: 773-650-4692
Cuisine: Mexican
VP: Rafael Lopez
Marketing/Sales: Raulinda Fierria
Estimated Sales: $ 20-50 Million
Number Employees: 5-9

13261 **Tara Foods**
801 Virginia Ave
Atlanta, GA 30354-1913 404-559-0605
Fax: 404-559-9090 DON@TARAELITE.COM
www.taraelite.com
Processor of peanut butter and flavoring extracts - nut spreads
Owner: Debra Theall
VP: Julie Davis
Plant Manager: Richard Barnhill
Estimated Sales: $300,000-500,000
Number Employees: 5-9
Parent Co: Kroger Company
Type of Packaging: Consumer, Food Service, Private Label
Brands:
Tara Foods

13262 **Tarara Winery**
13648 Tarara Ln
Leesburg, VA 20176 703-771-7100
Fax: 703-771-8443 winesales@tarara.com
www.tarara.com
Wine specialties such as Chardonnay, Pinot Gris, Viognier, Cabernet Franc
Executive Director: Heather Akers
Operations Manager: Margaret Russell
Production Manager: Daniel Alcorso
Winemaker: Rob Warren
Estimated Sales: $ 5-10 Million
Number Employees: 20-49
Number of Products: 12
Brands:
Varietals
Viognier

13263 **Tarazi Specialty Foods**
13727 Seminole Dr
Chino, CA 91710 909-628-3601
Fax: 909-590-4869 nabil@terazifoods.com
www.tarazifoods.com
manufacturer of premium quality tahini and falafel dry mix
Owner: Nabil Huleis
CFO: J Huleis
VP: J Huleis
Estimated Sales: $2-5 Million
Number Employees: 10
Sq. footage: 11800
Type of Packaging: Consumer, Food Service, Private Label, Bulk
Brands:
Tarazi

13264 **Target Flavors**
7 Del Mar Dr
Brookfield, CT 06804 203-775-4727
Fax: 203-775-2147 800-538-3350
info@targetflavors.com www.targetflavors.com
Processor and exporter of flavorings and extracts
Owner: John Mac Lean
General Manager: Bill McLean
Estimated Sales: $2100000
Number Employees: 10-19
Sq. footage: 25000

13265 **Tarpoff Packing Company**
7137 Horseshoe Bnd
Edwardsville, IL 62025-4605 618-656-4948
Processor/packer of beef
President: John Tarpoff
Number Employees: 10-19
Type of Packaging: Consumer, Bulk

13266 **Tartan Hill Winery**
4937 S 52nd Ave
New Era, MI 49446 231-861-4657
tartanhill@usawines.com
A family-operated winery specializing in estate wines made from French hybrid grapes, with a range from dry reds and whites to sweet, late harvest styles
Owner: Paul Goralski
Estimated Sales: Less than $500,000
Number Employees: 1-4

13267 **Tarzai Specialty Foods**
13727 Seminole Dr
Chino, CA 91710-5515 909-628-3601
Fax: 909-590-4869 info@tarazifoods.com
www.tarazifoods.com
Sesame seeds - raw or roasted, Garbanzo beans, Tahini-a savory sesame paste, Falafel mix, and Tabouli
President: William Huleis
CFO: Christine Huleis
Estimated Sales: $3 Million
Number Employees: 7
Brands:
Falafel Dry Mix
Tabouli
Tahini

13268 **Tase-Rite Company**
1211 Kingstown Rd
Wakefield, RI 2879 401-783-7300
Fax: 401-789-2889
General grocery and meats
President: Wesley Lessard
Marketing Director: Gary Lessard
Vice President: Gary Lessard
CFO: Wesley Lessard
Estimated Sales: $ 5-10 Million
Number Employees: 5-9

13269 **Taste It Presents**
200 Sumner Ave
Kenilworth, NJ 7033 908-241-9191
Fax: 908-241-9410 sales@tasteitpresents.com
www.tasteitpresents.com
Processor of frozen ethnic pastries including tiramisu
President: John Alair
Vice President: Larry Dimurro
Estimated Sales: $7.5 Million
Number Employees: 75
Type of Packaging: Consumer, Food Service, Private Label

13270 **Taste Maker Foods**
1415 E McLemore Ave
Memphis, TN 38106 901-274-4407
Fax: 901-272-1088 800-467-1407
custsvc@tastemakerfoods.com
www.tastemakerfoods.com
Species, seasonings, bakery mixes and dry blends
Owner: Buford Tomlinson
VP: Justin Reed
Quality Control: Stacey Castleman
Director Operations: Bill Tomlinson
Plant Manager: Justin Dukes
Estimated Sales: $ 5 - 10 Million
Number Employees: 10-19
Sq. footage: 25000
Parent Co: Reed Food Technology
Type of Packaging: Consumer, Food Service, Private Label, Bulk
Brands:
Old Hickory
Taste Maker

13271 **Taste Teasers**
6910 Northwood Rd
Dallas, TX 75225 214-750-6334
Fax: 214-696-3316 800-526-1840
Processor and exporter of jalapeno based condiments and confections
President: Susanne Hilou
VP: Eddie Michel
Estimated Sales: $100000
Number Employees: 1-4
Type of Packaging: Consumer, Food Service, Bulk
Brands:
Hot Chocolate-Fine Chocolate
Pepper Chicks

13272 **Taste of Gourmet**
36 Sunflower Rd
Indianola, MS 38751 662-887-6760
Fax: 662-887-5547 800-833-7731
jennifer@tasteofgourmet.com
www.tasteofgourmet.com
Processor and exporter of catfish pate and capers; also, fudge and lemon pie mixes including fat-free
President: Evelyn Roughton
Estimated Sales: $885603
Number Employees: 20-49
Type of Packaging: Consumer
Brands:
Antique Crown Foods
Mississippi Delta Fudge
Mississippi Mousse
The Crown Restaurant Gourmet

13273 **Taste of Nature**
400 S Beverly Dr
Beverly Hills, CA 90212-4424 310-396-4433
Fax: 310-396-4432 info@candyasap.com
www.candyasap.com
Candy
Manager: Scott Samet
Estimated Sales: $ 3 - 5 Million
Number Employees: 5-9
Brands:
Care Bears Gummi Bears
Cat in the Hat Cotton Candy
Cat in the Hat Sour Gummies
Cookie Dough Bites
Cotton Candy Swirl
HULK Candies
Jolt Cola Energy Rush
Muddy Bears
Shari Candies
Sour Cotton Candy Swirl
SpiderMan Cotton Candy
SpiderMan Sour Gummi Mutant Spiders
Sqwiggles
TINY TARTS

13274 **Tastee Apple Inc**
60810 County Road 9
Newcomerstown, OH 43832 740-498-8316
Fax: 740-498-6108 800-262-7753
customerservice@tasteeapple.com
www.tasteeapple.com

Processor of apple products including chocolate covered apples; caramel apples; apple cider; and apple powder, in addition to jelly apples, candy apples and wild apples.
President: Greg Hackenbracht
Director Manufacturing: Jerry Herbert
Purchasing Manager: Steve Barker
Estimated Sales: $100+ Million
Number Employees: 250-499
Sq. footage: 65000
Type of Packaging: Consumer, Food Service, Private Label, Bulk
Brands:
Tastee

13275 Tastee Fare
P.O.Box 327
Buchanan, MI 49107-327
Fax: 501-568-7876
Processor of waffle mixes; manufacturer of waffle bakers
President: Ron Munsey
Marketing Director: Brad Munfey
Manager National Sales: Tom McVey
VP Sales: Bob Polyister
Estimated Sales: $ 50 - 100 Million
Number Employees: 250-499
Brands:
Wassle Mix

13276 Tasty Baking Company
3 Crescent Dr Ste 200
Philadelphia, PA 19112 215-221-8500
Fax: 215-223-3288 800-338-2789
mary.borneman@tastykake.com
www.tastykake.com
Manufacturer of baked goods and snack cakes
Chairman: James Ksansnak
President/CEO: Charles Pizzi
SVP/CFO: David Marberger
CEO: Charles P Pizzi
Estimated Sales: $250+ Million
Number Employees: 500-999
Type of Packaging: Private Label
Brands:
JUNIORS
KANDY KATES
KREAMIES
SENSABLES
TASTYKAKE

13277 Tasty Mix Quality Foods
88 Walworth St
Brooklyn, NY 11205 718-855-7680
Fax: 718-855-7681 866-TAS-TYMX
tastymx@aol.com www.tastymix.com
Manufacturer of dough conditioners and stabilizers for the pasta and bakery industries
President: Salvatore Ballarino Jr
CEO/VP: Louis Ballerino
Estimated Sales: $500,000
Number Employees: 3
Sq. footage: 5000
Type of Packaging: Consumer, Food Service, Private Label, Bulk
Brands:
DOUGH STABILIZER
GOLD-TEX FLOUR
SHELF-AID

13278 Tasty Seeds Ltd
130 Market Street
Winkler, NB R6W 4A3
Canada 204-331-3480
Fax: 204-325-6832 888-632-6906
admin@tastyseed.com www.tastyseeds.com
Salted, seasoned and cajun sunflower seeds, and pumpkin seeds
Owner: Wayne Nestibo
Owner: Bryan Tyerman
Owner/Sales/Marketing Manger: Brad Edwards

13279 Tasty Selections
350 Creditston Road
Suite 102
Concord, ON L4K 3Z2
Canada 905-760-2353
Fax: 905-660-4585 www.tastyselections.com
Processor/manufacturers of frozen proportioned cookie dough, frozen muffin batters and a broad selection of thaw and serve cakes.
President: Alan Greenspoon
Estimated Sales: $2.3 Million
Number Employees: 60
Sq. footage: 25000
Type of Packaging: Consumer, Food Service, Bulk

13280 Tasty Tomato
PO Box 6984
San Antonio, TX 78209-0984 210-822-2443
Fax: 210-822-2538 www.worldtrade.org
Spaghetti sauce
President/CEO: Rollin King
Estimated Sales: $ 2.5-5 Million
Number Employees: 5

13281 Tasty-Toppings
P.O.Box 728
Columbus, NE 68602-0728 402-564-1347
Fax: 402-563-1469 800-228-4148
Manufacturer of salad dressings
President: Gordon Hull
Estimated Sales: $50 Million
Number Employees: 20-49
Sq. footage: 65000
Type of Packaging: Consumer, Food Service, Private Label
Brands:
DOROTHY LYNCH
DOROTHY LYNCH SALAD DRESSING

13282 Tastybaby
26880 Pacific Coast Hwy
#748
Malibu, CA 90265 310-457-6040
Fax: 310-317-4404 866-588-8278
info@tastybaby.com www.tastybaby.com
frozen organic baby food
President/Co-Founder: Shannan Swanson
CEO/Co-Founder: Liane Weintraub

13283 Tastykake
2801 W Hunting Park Ave
Philadelphia, PA 19129 215-221-8500
Fax: 215-223-3288 www.tastykake.com
Processor of baked goods including snack cakes, doughnuts, cookies, pies, etc
Chairman: James E Ksansnak
President: Charles P Pizzi
Senior VP/CFO: David Marberger
CEO: Charles P Pizzi
CEO: Charles P Pizzi
VP Sales: Dan Nagle
Estimated Sales: I
Number Employees: 500-999
Parent Co: Tasty Baking Company
Type of Packaging: Consumer
Brands:
Tastykake

13284 Tata Tea
1001 Dr Martin L King Jr Blvd
Plant City, FL 33563-5150 813-754-2602
Fax: 813-754-2272 tatainc@tatainc.com
www.tata.com
Tea
President: Ashok Bhardwha
Chairman: Patrick McGoldrick
Quality Control: Ivey Campbell
Estimated Sales: $ 2.5-5 Million
Number Employees: 20-49
Brands:
Tata Tea

13285 Tatangelo's Wholesale Fruit & Vegetables
80 Hanlan Road
Unit 12
Woodbridge, ON L4L 3P6
Canada 905-850-0545
Fax: 905-850-2241 877-328-8503
Processor of frozen fruit and vegetables
President: Rocco Tatangelo
Vice President: John Tatangelo
Estimated Sales: $6 Million
Number Employees: 14
Type of Packaging: Food Service
Brands:
Tatangelo

13286 (HQ)Tate & Lyle North American Sugars
2200 E El Dorado St
Decatur, IL 62525 217-423-4411
Fax: 217-421-2216 www.tateandlyle.com
Manufacturer of sugar including brown, fondant, invert, liquid, etc.; also, molasses
Chief Executive: Javed Ahmed
CFO: Tim Lodger
Estimated Sales: $1+ Billion
Number Employees: 400
Parent Co: Tate & Lyle PLC
Type of Packaging: Consumer, Bulk
Brands:
REDPATH
STALEY
TATE & LYLE CITRIC ACID

13287 Tate Cheese Company
PO Box 1040
Valley City, IL 62340 217-833-2314
Fax: 217-833-2226 www.worldtrade.org
Dairy products and processed cheese
President: Hamer Tate
Controller: Richard Krueger
Marketing Director: Joe Cline
Production Manager: Paul Ruble
Purchasing Manager: Becky Killebrew
Estimated Sales: $ 25-49.9 Million
Number Employees: '5-9

13288 Tate's Bake Shop
43 N Sea Rd
Southampton, NY 11968 631-283-9830
Fax: 631-283-9844 info@tatesbakeshop.com
www.tatesbakeshop.com
All pastries and rolls made fresh daily - all wholesome ingredients - pies, cakes, chocolate chip cookies, breads, and brownies
Owner: Kathleen King
Estimated Sales: $ 1 - 3 Million
Number Employees: 20-49

13289 Tate's Bake Shop
43 N Sea Rd
Southampton, NY 11968 631-283-9830
Fax: 631-283-9844 info@tatesbakeshop.com
www.tatesbakeshop.com
cookies, cakes, brownies and squares.
President/Owner: Kathleen King

13290 Tatra Herb Company
222 Grove St
Morrisville, PA 19067-1235 215-295-5476
Fax: 215-736-3089 888-828-7248
tatraherb@comcast.net www.tatraherb.com
Processor of herbal teas
President: George Zofchak
CEO: George Zofchak
Estimated Sales: Less than $500,000
Number Employees: 1-4
Type of Packaging: Consumer

13291 Taurus Foods
6908 E 30th Street
Indianapolis, IN 46219-1105 317-545-7425
Fax: 317-549-9553
Meat purveyor
President: Ronald Stein

13292 Taylor All Star Dairy Foods
337 Merchant St
Ambridge, PA 15003-2523 724-266-2370
Fax: 724-266-6650
Dairy products
President: Joseph Taylor
Estimated Sales: $ 10-100 Million
Number Employees: 5-9

13293 Taylor Cheese Corporation
508 N Mill St
Weyauwega, WI 54983 920-867-2337
Fax: 920-867-2360
Custom cheese cut, slice and wrap services for private label or conversion needs. Shingled slice packaging gift box components.
President: Robert Ehrenberg
Marketing Director: Bob Ehrenberg
Estimated Sales: Below $ 5 Million
Number Employees: 10-19

13294 Taylor Farms
911 Blanco Cir Ste B
Salinas, CA 93901 831-754-0471
Fax: 831-794-0473 tsalisbury@taylorfarms.com
www.taylorfarms.com

Processor of fresh cut fruit and vegetables including cantaloupe, honeydew, pineapple, onions, lettuce, peppers, garlic, cabbage and tomatoes
President: Bruce Taylor
Chairman/CEO: Bruce Taylor
CFO: Tom Brain
VP Production: Vikki Chandley
Number Employees: 5,000-9,999
Sq. footage: 50000
Type of Packaging: Consumer, Food Service, Private Label, Bulk

13295 **Taylor Meat Company**
2211 W 2nd St
Taylor, TX 76574 512-352-6357
Fax: 512-352-9426 taylormc@swbell.net
www.taylormeat.com
Manufacturer of beef and pork
President: Ron Ivy
Manager: Adolth Griger
Estimated Sales: $38 Million
Number Employees: 25
Type of Packaging: Consumer, Food Service, Bulk
Brands:
TIP TOP

13296 **Taylor Orchards**
P.O.Box 975
Reynolds, GA 31076 478-847-4186
Fax: 478-847-4464 gafruit@gnat.net
www.taylororchards.com
Processor, packer and exporter of peaches
Owner: Jeff Wainwright
Owner/Sales Manager: Walter Wainwright
Estimated Sales: $7215000
Number Employees: 10-19
Sq. footage: 4000
Type of Packaging: Consumer, Bulk

13297 **Taylor Packing Company**
182 Wilkie Ave
Yuba City, CA 95991 530-671-1505
Fax: 530-751-1514 www.organicprunes.com
Processor and exporter of prune concentrate and dried prunes including Ashlock pitted and whole
President: Richard Taylor
VP: John Taylor
Estimated Sales: $ 20 - 50 Million
Number Employees: 50
Sq. footage: 25000
Type of Packaging: Food Service, Private Label, Bulk
Brands:
Cal Gold
California Gold
Taylor Brothers Farms

13298 **Taylor Provisions Company**
63 Perrine Ave
Trenton, NJ 08638-5114 609-392-1113
Fax: 609-392-1354
Processor of meat products
President: John T Cumbler
VP: George Cumbler
Estimated Sales: $10 Million
Number Employees: 75

13299 **(HQ)Taylor Shellfish Farms**
130 SE Lynch Rd
Shelton, WA 98584-8615 360-426-6178
Fax: 360-427-0327 orders@taylorshellfish.com
www.taylorshellfish.com
Manufacturer of fresh and frozen oysters, clams, mussels, scallops and crabs
President: Jeff Pearson
Human Resources: John Fogo
Estimated Sales: $16 Million
Number Employees: 100-249
Type of Packaging: Consumer
Other Locations:
Taylor Shellfish Farms
Bow WA
Brands:
Taylor Shellfish

13300 **Taylor's Mexican Chili**
116 S West Street
Carlinville, IL 62626-1758 217-854-8713
800-382-4454
dave@taylorschili.com www.taylorschili.com
Chili, sauce, beans
Owner: Joe Gugger
Operations VP: Dave Tucker
Production VP: Dave Tucker
Estimated Sales: Less than $500,000
Number Employees: 1-4
Brands:
Taylor's Mexican Chili

13301 **Taylor's Poultry Place**
4701 Augusta Rd
Lexington, SC 29073 803-356-3431
Processor of poultry
President: Luther Taylor
Estimated Sales: Less than $500,000
Number Employees: 1-4

13302 **Taylor's Sausage Company**
1822 N Grand Blvd
Saint Louis, MO 63106 314-652-3476
Sausages
President: Bettie Taylor
Estimated Sales: Below $ 5 Million
Number Employees: 5-9

13303 **Tayse Meats**
1979 W 25th St
Cleveland, OH 44113-3455 216-664-1799
Beef
Owner: Keith Tayse
Estimated Sales: Less than $500,000
Number Employees: 1-4

13304 **Taystee Bakeries**
1475 West Washington Street
Marquette, MI 49855 906-226-7266
Bakery items
Plant Manager: David Edgren
Estimated Sales: $2.5-5 Million
Number Employees: 100-249

13305 **Tazo Tea**
PO Box 66
Portland, OR 97207-0066 503-736-9005
Fax: 503-231-8801 800-299-9445
dhanson@tazo.com www.tazo.com
Premium teas, bottled tea and juice, organic chai and full leaf teas
President: Tal Johnson
Estimated Sales: $ 10-24.9 Million
Number Employees: 25
Number of Brands: 1
Parent Co: Starbucks Coffee Company
Type of Packaging: Private Label

13306 **Tea Aura**
234 Dunview Avenue
Toronto, ON M2N 4J2
Canada 416-225-8868
info@teaaura.com
www.teaaura.com
shortbread cookies infused with tea

13307 **Tea Beyond**
PO Box 1911
West Caldwell, NJ 07007 973-226-0327
Fax: 973-226-0327 info@teabeyond.com
www.teabeyond.com
authentic teas

13308 **Tea Forte**
23 Bradford St
Concord, MA 01742 978-369-7777
Fax: 978-369-3427 info@teaforte.com
www.teaforte.com
whole leaf teas with rough-cut herbs and flowers
President/Owner: Peter Hewitt
Estimated Sales: $10 Million
Number Employees: 30

13309 **Tea Needs Inc**
3000 Banyon Road
Boca Raton, FL 33432 561-237-5237
877-832-8289
mark@teaneeds.com www.teaneeds.com
Disposable instant cup of tea. The teabag is inside of each cup. Three lines are available: tea, fruit tea, and Chinese herb tea.
President & Owner: Mark Reiman
VP: Alla Kartel
Marketing: Ed Camargo
Operations: Joyce Liang
Estimated Sales: $ 10 Million
Number Employees: 20-49
Number of Brands: 6
Number of Products: 18
Sq. footage: 10000
Type of Packaging: Consumer, Private Label, Bulk
Brands:
HAPPY CUP TEA

13310 **Tea Room**
130 Doolittle Dr Ste 2
San Leandro, CA 94577-1028
Fax: 707-561-7081 866-515-8866
info@thetearoom.biz www.thetearoom.biz
artisan organic chocolate truffles, organic chocolate bars, tea-infused, french macaroons
President/Owner: Heinz Rimann

13311 **Tea-n-Crumpets**
252 Coleman Dr
San Rafael, CA 94901 415-457-2495
Fax: 415-457-1893 tcrumpets@aol.com
www.tea-n-crumpets.com
Organic crumpets, superior quality teas, jams, tea accessories and gift items from around the world.
President: Norman Barahona
CEO: Jena Rose
Estimated Sales: $ 1 - 3 Million
Number Employees: 1-4

13312 **Teasdale Quality Foods**
901 Packers Street
PO Box 814
Atwater, CA 95301 209-358-5616
Fax: 209-358-0127 casiet@teasdale.net
www.teasdale.net
Mexican foods
QA Director: Kenneth Ancalade
Sales/Marketing Director: Jeff Howard
Plant Manager: Jim Paschall
Purchasing Agent: Ron Borth
Estimated Sales: $26.5 Million
Number Employees: 200
Sq. footage: 250000
Parent Co: Sun Garden-Gangi Canning
Type of Packaging: Consumer, Food Service, Private Label

13313 **Teawolf Industries, Ltd**
25 Riverside Drive
Pine Brook, NJ 07058 973-575-4600
Fax: 973-575-4601 info@teawolf.com
www.teawolf.com
Supplier of vanilla products for ice cream & frozen gelato's, yogurts and bakery applications. Chocolate and coffee extracts, sweeteners and teas.
Estimated Sales: B
Number Employees: 5-9

13314 **Tebay Dairy Company**
720 Division St
Parkersburg, WV 26101 304-422-1014
Fax: 304-863-8712
Processor of dairy products including ice cream
Owner: Robert Kent Tebay Jr
Estimated Sales: $3,200,000
Number Employees: 10-19
Type of Packaging: Consumer
Brands:
Tebay

13315 **Tech Pak Solutions**
85 Bradley Drive
Westbrook, ME 04092-2013 207-878-6667
Fax: 425-883-9455
Temperature controlled management for food products.
Vice President: Richard Brown

13316 **Technical Oil**
1 Adamson St
Easton, PA 18042-6184 610-252-8350
Fax: 610-252-9901 ethitech-pa@erols.com
www.technicaloil.com
Processor and exporter of emulsifiers, pan greases and oils and surfactants
Owner: Alan Geisler
Estimated Sales: $ 1-2.5 Million
Number Employees: 5-9
Sq. footage: 30000
Parent Co: Technical Oil
Brands:
Toptex

13317 **(HQ)Technical Oil Products**
93 Spring St Ste 303
Newton, NJ 7860-2079
Fax: 973-335-1952 orders@technicaloil.com
www.technicaloil.com

Pan release agents, vegetables oil blends, divider and mineral oils, and cake and bread emulsifiers. Available is custom blending services of liquid, dry and paste type products
Owner: Alan Geisler
Number Employees: 5-9
Brands:
SurSweet

13318 **Technology Flavors & Fragrances**
10 E Edison St
Amityville, NY 11701 631-789-8228
Fax: 631-842-8332 flavors@tffi.com
www.tffi.com
Creator and manufacturer of natural and artificial flavors for beverage, food and cosmetics industries
CFO: Joseph A Gemmo
Chairman/CEO: Phil Rosner
CEO: Philip Rosner
Marketing Director: Virginia Bonofligio
Sales Director: Gary Frumberg
Public Relations: Joseph Gemmo
Operations/Production: Ronald Dintemann
Plant Manager: Joseph Piazza
Purchasing Manager: Rose Marotta
Estimated Sales: $15587285
Number Employees: 50-99
Number of Products: 1200
Sq. footage: 52000

13319 **Ted Drewes Frozen Custard**
6726 Chippewa St
Saint Louis, MO 63109 314-481-2652
Fax: 314-481-4241 www.teddrewes.com
Frozen custard
President: Ted Jr Drewes
Estimated Sales: Below $ 5 Million
Number Employees: 50-99

13320 **Ted Shear Associates**
1 West Ave
Larchmont, NY 10538-2470 914-833-0017
Fax: 914-833-0233 ted.shear@verizon.net
Honey and vanilla extracts
President: Ted Shear
Estimated Sales: $ 1 - 3 Million
Number Employees: 1-4
Type of Packaging: Private Label

13321 **Teddy's Tasty Meats**
6123 Mackay St
Anchorage, AK 99518 907-562-2320
Fax: 907-562-1919
Meat
President: Ted Kouris
Secretary/Treasurer: Barbara Kouris
Estimated Sales: $ 50 - 100 Million
Number Employees: 20-49

13322 **Tedeschi Vineyards**
Hc 1 Box 953
Kula, HI 96790 808-878-1266
Fax: 808-876-0127 info@mauiwine.com
www.mauiwine.com
Wines
President: Pardee Erdman
COO: Paula Hegele
Sales Manager: James McLean
Estimated Sales: $ 20-50 Million
Number Employees: 20-49
Type of Packaging: Private Label
Brands:
Maui Blanc
Maui Blush
Maui Brut
Maui Splash
Maui Ulupalakua Red

13323 **Tee Lee Popcorn, Inc**
101 W Badger St
Shannon, IL 61078 815-864-2244
Fax: 815-864-2388 800-578-2363
www.teeleepopcorn.com
Processor and exporter of microwaveable popcorn
President: James D Weaver
VP/Sales: Ken Weaver
Estimated Sales: $2 Million
Number Employees: 20
Sq. footage: 25000
Type of Packaging: Consumer, Private Label, Bulk
Brands:
Prime Time
Tee Lee

13324 **Tee Pee Olives**
411 Theodore Fremd Avenue
Rye, NY 10580
Fax: 914-925-0458 800-431-1529
daveco1287@aol.com www.teepeeolives.com
Importer and packer of bulk Spanish green olives in the US.
Owner: Robert Cory
CEO: David Cory
VP/Quality Control: Robert Cory PhD
Marketing Director: Neil Albert
Sales Director: Anthony Gambino
Production Manager: Joseph Fairchild
Plant Manager: Joseph Fairchild
Purchasing Manager: Emil Cairo
Estimated Sales: $ 10 - 20 Million
Number Employees: 10-19
Type of Packaging: Consumer, Food Service, Private Label, Bulk

13325 **Teeccino Caffe**
P.O.Box 40829
Santa Barbara, CA 93140-0829 805-966-0999
Fax: 805-966-0522 800-498-3434
info@teeccino.com www.teeccino.com
Coffee
President/Founder: Caroline MacDougall
National Sales Manager: Robert Tepper
Estimated Sales: $1,000,800
Number Employees: 5-9
Number of Brands: 1
Number of Products: 7
Type of Packaging: Consumer, Food Service, Private Label, Bulk
Brands:
Balanced Coffee
Teeccino Caffeine-Fr

13326 **Teel Plastics**
1060 Teel Ct
Baraboo, WI 53913 800-322-8335
Fax: 608-355-3088 800-322-8335
getaquote@teel.com www.teel.com
Teel Plastics is an expert in the extrusion of plastic tubing parts and components for softener and filtration systems. Teel provides value added services such as assembly, chamfering, close tolerance burr-free cutting and punching.
President: Jay Smith
Marketing Director: Bryanna Smith
Sales Director: Randy Thomas
Estimated Sales: $20 Million
Number Employees: 250-499
Sq. footage: 180000

13327 **Teeny Foods Corporation**
3434 NE 170th Pl
Portland, OR 97230 503-252-3006
Fax: 503-254-3004 info@teenyfoods.com
www.teenyfoods.com
Processor of pizza, pizza skins and breads including pocket and specialty, including bread sticks, Greek pita, Italian flat bread, foccacia, and dough balls
CEO: Rick Teeny
VP: Debbie Teeny
Marketing Director: Chris Faverty
Sales Executive: Darryl Abram
Production Manager: Dave Hermanson
Estimated Sales: $6 Million
Number Employees: 70
Sq. footage: 58000
Brands:
Teeny Foods

13328 **Teeny Tiny Spice Company of Vermont LLC**
5224 Shelburne Road
Shelburne, VT 05482 802-598-6800
Fax: 603-768-4247 info@teenytinyspice.com
www.teenytinyspice.com
Organic spice blends.

13329 **Teff Company**
PO Box A
Caldwell, ID 83606-0016 208-455-0375
Fax: 208-454-3330 888-822-2221
info@teffco.com www.teffco.com
Processor of whole grain and flour
President: Wayne Carlson
Marketing Director: Elizabeth Carlson
Brands:
Maskal Teff

13330 **Teixeira Farms**
2600 Bonita Lateral Rd
Santa Maria, CA 93458 805-928-3801
Fax: 805-928-9405 www.teixeirafarms.com
Grower of lettuce, broccoli, cabbage, cauliflower and celery
Owner: Norman Texiera
Marketing Manager: Glenn Teixeira
Sales Manager: Glenn Teixeira
Estimated Sales: $ 20 - 50 Million
Number Employees: 250-499
Type of Packaging: Consumer, Private Label, Bulk
Brands:
Teixeira

13331 **Tejon Ranch**
P.O.Box 1000
Lebec, CA 93243 661-248-5181
Fax: 661-248-6209 bzoeller@tejonranch.com
www.tejonranch.com
Processor and exporter of pistachios, walnuts, almonds and wine grapes
President/CEO: Robert Stine
CFO/VP/Corporate Secretary: Allen Lyda
Estimated Sales: Less than $500,000
Number Employees: 100-249
Type of Packaging: Consumer, Private Label, Bulk

13332 **Tekita House Foods**
6848 El Paso Drive
El Paso, TX 79905-3336 915-779-2181
Fax: 915-775-1857 www.tekitahouse.com
Manufacturer of Mexican food products. Products consist of tortillas, tostadas, pico de gallo salsa, chorizo, tamales, chiles rellenos, taco roll, flautas and pork crackling
President: Nelson Guerra
Estimated Sales: $500,000 appx.
Number Employees: 10-19

13333 **Tell Chocolate Corporation**
98 Mission Way
Barnegat, NJ 8005-3338
Fax: 732-660-8178 tellcorpo1@aol.com
www.store.yahoo.com/tellchocolate
Chocolates
President: Robert Ricci
Co-Owner: Mary Carol
Estimated Sales: Under $500,000
Number Employees: 5-9
Brands:
Marshmallow Chickies
Tell Chocolate

13334 **Tell City Pretzel Company**
432 1/2 Main St
Tell City, IN 47586 812-547-4631
Fax: 812-547-4850 www.tellcitypretzels.com
Processor of hard pretzels
Owner: Craig Kendall
Plant Manager: Betty Beard
Estimated Sales: $110000
Number Employees: 3
Type of Packaging: Consumer, Bulk

13335 **Temo's Candy**
495 W Exchange St
Akron, OH 44302 330-376-7229
Processor of confectionery products
President: Lawrence Temo
Estimated Sales: $344051
Number Employees: 5-9
Sq. footage: 10000
Parent Co: Temo's
Type of Packaging: Consumer
Brands:
Temo's

13336 **Tempest Fisheries Limited**
38 Hassey St
New Bedford, MA 02740 508-997-0720
Fax: 508-990-2117
Fish and seafood
President: Timothy Mello
Estimated Sales: $ 5 - 10 Million
Number Employees: 5-9

13337 **Tempest Vineyards**
6000 Karlas Lane
Amity, OR 97101-2321 503-835-2600
Wines
President: Keith Orr
Estimated Sales: Less than $500,000
Number Employees: 1-4

13338 **Templar Food Products**
571 Central Ave Ste 114
New Providence, NJ 7974 908-665-9511
Fax: 908-665-9122 800-883-6752
info@icedtea.com www.icedtea.com
Processor, importer and exporter of organic, black, green, herbal, oolong, chai and iced teas; also, caffeine-free
President: Edward D Reeves
Sales: Susan Brady
Production: Michael Murray
Purchasing Director: Kenneth Flynn
Estimated Sales: $870000
Number Employees: 10-19
Parent Co: Hilltop Tea
Type of Packaging: Private Label
Brands:
Perfect Choice

13339 **Temptee Specialty Foods**
2011 E 58th Ave
Denver, CO 80216 303-292-1577
Fax: 303-292-1701 800-842-1233
tempteeco@aol.com
Processor of portion controlled deli meats including beef; also, specialty processing available
President: Jack Lowe
Sales Manager: Jim Mayworm
Estimated Sales: $3616653
Number Employees: 20-49
Sq. footage: 20000

13340 **Ten Ren Tea & Ginseng Company**
75 Mott St
New York, NY 10013 212-349-2286
Fax: 212-349-2180 800-292-2049
sales@tenrenusa.com www.tenrenusa.com
Tea
President: Mark Lee
Founder: Ray Ho Lee
Estimated Sales: Below $ 5 Million
Number Employees: 10-19
Brands:
Ten Ren's Tea

13341 **Tenn Valley Ham Company**
P.O.Box 1146
Paris, TN 38242-1146 731-642-9740
Fax: 731-642-7129 www.cliftyfarm.com
Processor of frozen portion cuts of bacon, ham and barbecue pork and turkey
President: Dan Murphey
Estimated Sales: $ 50 - 100 Million
Number Employees: 100-249
Type of Packaging: Consumer, Food Service
Brands:
Chifty Farm

13342 **Tennessee Bun Company**
197 Printwood Dr
Dickson, TN 37055-3011 615-441-4600
Fax: 615-441-4627 888-486-2867
www.buncompany.com
Hamburger buns
President: Cordia Harrington
VP Operations: Dave Nemecheck
Plant Manager: Dave Nemecheck
Estimated Sales: Below $ 5 Million
Number Employees: 50-99
Brands:
Tennessee Bun

13343 **Tennessee Valley PackingCompany**
P.O.Box 709
Columbia, TN 38402-0709 931-388-2623
Fax: 931-388-2624
Processor of meat products including sausages, frankfurters and bologna
President: Richard Jewell Jr
Estimated Sales: $ 3 - 5 Million
Number Employees: 5-9
Type of Packaging: Consumer

13344 **Tenth & M. Seafoods**
1020 M St
Anchorage, AK 99501 907-272-3474
Fax: 907-272-1685 www.10thandmseafoods.com
Processor, exporter and wholesaler/distributor of salmon, halibut, shrimp and bottom fish
Owner: Skip Winfrey
President: Dennis Winfree
Vice President: Robert Winfree
Estimated Sales: $11 Million
Number Employees: 16
Type of Packaging: Consumer, Food Service

13345 **Tequila XQ**
Placeres #1181 col Chapalita
Guadalajara Jalisco,
Mexico 333-587-7799
Fax: 333-915-3840 sales@tequilaxq.com
www.tequilaxq.com
A 3rd generation, family owned tequila producer based in the heart of the Tequila Region. Casa Tequila XQ was recently awarded 1st place as the best tequila in Mexico by La Academia Mexicana del Tequila.
President: Guillermo Estavillo
Marketing & Sales Director: Yezmin Hawa
Number of Brands: 5
Type of Packaging: Consumer, Food Service
Brands:
AMIGO LOCO
CLIMAX
EXQUISITO
TEQUILA XQ
VODKA ZAR

13346 **Terra Botanica Products**
Rr2 Site 33A Comp 4
Nakusp, BC V0G 1R0
Canada 250-265-3648
Fax: 250-265-0081 888-410-9977
sales@terrabotanica.com www.terrabotanica.com
Processor of homeopathics, botanical extracts, capsules, gels and vitamins
president: John Miller
CEO: Connie Miller
Marketing Director: John Miller
Sales Director: Paul Peterson
Number Employees: 10,000+
Type of Packaging: Private Label

13347 **Terra Harvest Foods**
P.O.Box 5764
Rockford, IL 61125-0764 815-636-9500
Fax: 815-636-8400 lbresky@terraharvest.com
www.thfoods.com
Processor and exporter of snack mix items including sesame, corn and rice; also, rice, crackers, chips and snacks
President: Sam Mori
CEO: Terry Jessen
Marketing Director: Lucille Bresky
Sales Director: Jeff Baldwin
Operations Manager: Bob Manzer
Purchasing Manager: Jean Ruthe
Number Employees: 100-249
Sq. footage: 70000
Type of Packaging: Consumer, Private Label, Bulk
Brands:
Sesmark Deli Thins
Sesmark Rice Thins

13348 **Terra Sol Chile Company**
9415 Burnet Road
Suite 106
Austin, TX 78758-5245 512-836-3525
Fax: 512-502-9112
Chili

13349 **Terra's**
PO Box 265
Perham, MN 56573-0265 218-346-4100
Beef
President: Rod Osvold
Estimated Sales: Under $500,000
Number Employees: 1-4

13350 **Terranetti's Italian Bakery**
844 W Trindle Rd
Mechanicsburg, PA 17055-4095 717-697-5434
Fax: 717-697-6815
Processor of fresh rolls and bread including brown, white and rye.
President: Terrance E Mc Mahon
Estimated Sales: $ 20 - 50 Million
Number Employees: 20-49
Sq. footage: 16000
Type of Packaging: Consumer, Food Service
Brands:
Terranetti's

13351 **Terrapin Ridge**
1208 S. Myrtle Ave
Clearwater, FL 33767
800-999-4052
info@terrapinridge.com www.terrapinridge.com
Catsup and mustard, sauces, confits, mustard dressings, mustard seed oil, marinated squeezes, dessert squeezes, garnishing sauce, and gift ideas.
President: Martha Furst
Number Employees: 100-249
Parent Co: Furst-McNess Company
Type of Packaging: Private Label
Brands:
Terrapin Ridge

13352 **Terrapin Ridge Farms**
1208 S Myrtle Ave
Clearwater, FL 33767
800-999-4052
www.terrapinridge.com
Manufacturer of specialty mustards, sauces, dressings, dips, jams and jellies
Co-Owner: Brian Coughlin
Co-Owner: Mary O'Donnell
Co-Founder: Susan Furst
Estimated Sales: $100-500 Million
Number Employees: 50-99
Type of Packaging: Consumer, Private Label

13353 **Terrell Meats**
1211 E Main St
Delta, UT 84624 435-864-2600
Fax: 435-864-2600
Processor of beef jerky, beef, pork and lamb
Partner: Clark Terrell
Estimated Sales: $1200000
Number Employees: 6
Type of Packaging: Consumer, Food Service

13354 **Terrell's Potato Chip Company**
218 Midler Park Drive
Syracuse, NY 13206 315-437-2786
terrellschip@msn.com
www.terrellspotatochip.com
Processor of potato chips including regular, barbecue, onion and sour cream; also, salsa
President: Jack Terrell
Estimated Sales: $6500000
Number Employees: 70
Type of Packaging: Consumer
Brands:
Bachman
Keystone

13355 **Terressentia Corporation**
9770 Patriot Blvd
Suite 300
N Charleston, SC 29456 843-225-3100
Fax: 843-225-3107 earl@terressentia.com
www.terressentia.com
Distilled spirits.
CEO: Earl Hewlette

13356 **(HQ)Terri Lynn**
1450 Bowes Rd
Elgin, IL 60123-5539 847-741-1900
Fax: 847-741-1912 800-323-0775
sales@terrilynn.com www.terrilynn.com
Manufacturer of Kosher Nuts, Dried Fruits and Chocolates.
President: Terri Schuck
CEO: Joe Graziano Sr
VP: Mark Graziano
Quality Control: Maulek Patel
Marketing: Mark Graziano
Sales: Mark Graziano
Operations: Joe Graziano Jr
Production: Joe Graziano Jr
Plant Manager: Joe Graziano Jr
Purchasing Director: Joe Graziano Jr
Estimated Sales: $ 60,000
Number Employees: 50-99
Number of Brands: 1
Number of Products: 600
Sq. footage: 110000
Parent Co: Terri Lynn, Inc
Type of Packaging: Food Service, Private Label, Bulk
Other Locations:
Terri Lynn-Pecan Shelling Operation
Cordele GA

13357 **Terry Brothers**
5039 Willis Wharf Dr
Willis Wharf, VA 23486 757-824-3471
Fax: 757-824-3461 inf@terrybrothers.com
www.tyson.com
Processor of clams and oysters
President: N Terry Jr
Estimated Sales: $2.5-5 Million
Number Employees: 5-9
Type of Packaging: Consumer, Food Service
Brands:
Sewansecott
Terry Brothers

13358 **Terry Foods Inc**
265 4th Street
Idaho Falls, ID 83401 208-604-8143
nik@terryfoods.com
www.terryfoods.com
Importers and distributors of a wide range of food ingredients, supplying food manufacturers, bakeries and food service companies throughout the USA
CEO: John Gardiner
CFO: Nikolai Terry
Sales Manager: Larry Haws
Estimated Sales: $ 5-10 Million
Number Employees: 1-4
Type of Packaging: Food Service, Bulk

13359 **Tessenderlo Kerley**
2255 N 44th St Ste 300
Phoenix, AZ 85008 602-889-8300
Fax: 602-889-8430 800-669-0559
info-tki@tkinet.com www.tkinet.com
Producer of high quality gelatins for the food, pharmaceutical and photoghaphic industry, operating worldwide
CEO: Jordan Burns
Estimated Sales: $ 3 - 5 Million
Number Employees: 250-499
Type of Packaging: Private Label
Brands:
CRYOGEL
INSTAGEL
SOLGEL
SWIFTGEL

13360 **Testamints**
1248 Sussex Tpke
Unit C-1
Randolph, NJ 07869-2908 973-895-5041
Fax: 973-895-3742 888-879-0400
info@testamints.com www.testamints.com
Confections
President: Al Poe
Estimated Sales: $ 2.5-5 Million
Number Employees: 5-9
Brands:
Promise Pops
Testamints Chewing Gum
Testamints Fruit Flavored Candy
Testamints Sour Fruit Mints
Testamints Sugar Free Mints
Testamints Sugar Mints

13361 **Teti Bakery**
27 Signal Hill Avenue
Etobicoke, ON M9W 6V8
Canada 416-798-8777
Fax: 416-798-8749 800-465-0123
Processor of pizza, pizza crusts and Italian flat bread; exporter of pizza crusts
President: Franco Teti
VP: Dino Teti
Sales Manager: Tony Saldutto
Estimated Sales: $2 Million
Number Employees: 50
Sq. footage: 14000
Type of Packaging: Consumer, Food Service, Private Label, Bulk
Brands:
San Mario
Teti

13362 **(HQ)Tetley Tea**
100 Commerce Dr Ste 210
Shelton, CT 06484 203-929-9200
Fax: 203-925-0512 800-728-0084
info@tetleyusa.com www.tetleyusa.com
Tea, coffee and tea bags
President: John Petrizzo
President: Glynne Jones
CFO: John Petrizzo
Sr. VP, Supply Chain: Dan Smith
Number Employees: 500-999
Parent Co: Tata Tea Ltd
Type of Packaging: Private Label
Brands:
Tetley Teas

13363 **Tex-Mex Cold Storage**
6665 Padre Island Hwy
Brownsville, TX 78521-5218 956-831-9433
Fax: 956-831-9572
Processor of seafood including shrimp; warehouse providing freezer and dry storage
President: Emilio Sanchez
VP: Norma Sanchez
Plant Manager: Nick Sato
Estimated Sales: $6,307,658
Number Employees: 225
Sq. footage: 155000
Type of Packaging: Private Label, Bulk

13364 **Tex-Mex Gourmet**
201 W First Street
Brenham, TX 77833 979-836-4701
Fax: 713-784-7616 888-345-8467
info@texmexgourmet.com
www.texmexgourmet.com
Sauces
Number Employees: 10-19
Type of Packaging: Consumer, Private Label
Brands:
LOS TIOS
TULDY'S

13365 **TexaFrance**
525 Round Rock
Round Rock, TX 78681 512-246-2500
Fax: 512-246-2716 800-776-8937
info@texafrance.com www.texafrance.com
Processor and co-packer of natural pasta and pesto sauces, salad dressings, mustards, chutneys and jellies; private labeling available
President: Jean Parant
Vice President: David Griswold
VP Purchasing: David Griswold
Estimated Sales: $.2 Million
Number Employees: 7
Sq. footage: 8000
Type of Packaging: Consumer, Private Label

13366 **Texas Coffee Company**
P.O.Box 31
Beaumont, TX 77704-0031 409-835-3434
Fax: 409-835-4248 800-259-3400
texjoy@texjoy.com www.texjoy.com
Processor of tea, coffee, extracts, spices and seasonings; importer of coffee and tea
President: Carlo Busceme
President/Operations: Carlo Busceme III
VP: Donald Fertitta
Estimated Sales: $ 10 - 20 Million
Number Employees: 20-49
Sq. footage: 45000
Type of Packaging: Consumer, Food Service, Private Label, Bulk
Brands:
Seaport
Texjoy

13367 **Texas Crumb & Food Products**
3250 Towerwood Dr
Farmers Branch, TX 75234 972-243-8443
Fax: 972-484-9315 800-522-7862
info@dasbrot.com www.dasbrot.com
Processor of bread crumbs, batters, breadings and stuffing and seasoning mixes
President: S Holtsclaw
Vice President: W Holtsclaw
Estimated Sales: $900000
Number Employees: 5-9
Sq. footage: 16000
Parent Co: Das Brot
Type of Packaging: Food Service, Private Label, Bulk

13368 **Texas Heat**
P.O.Box 33246
San Antonio, TX 78265 210-656-4328
Fax: 210-656-5916 800-656-5916
Processor of picante sauce, chili mix and cheese dip
President: Robert Delgado
Estimated Sales: $ 1 - 3 Million
Number Employees: 1-4
Type of Packaging: Consumer, Food Service

13369 **Texas Reds Steak House**
400 E Main St
Red River, NM 87558-0111 575-754-2922
Fax: 575-754-2309 www.texasreds.com
Steak
President: William Gill
VP: Richard Gill
CFO: Deanna Tapia
Estimated Sales: $ 1-2.5 Million
Number Employees: 35
Brands:
Texas Red

13370 **Texas Sassy Foods**
9600 Great Hills Trail
Suite 150W
Austin, TX 78759 512-215-4022
Fax: 603-251-0780 www.texas-sassy.com
pickles, relishes, sauces and more

13371 **Texas Sausage Company**
2915 E 12th St
Austin, TX 78702 512-472-6707
Fax: 512-472-9360 hotlinks@austin.rr.com
Processor and wholesaler/distributor of sausage; serving the food service market
President: Gary Tharp
Estimated Sales: $ .5 - 1 million
Number Employees: 5-9
Type of Packaging: Consumer, Food Service

13372 **Texas Spice Company**
P.O.Box 2133
Cedar Park, TX 78630 512-260-1712
Fax: 512-260-1713 800-880-8007
contact@texas-spice.net www.texasspice.net
Wholesale/Retail custom blending, spices, seasoning blends, bases, extracts, flavors, coffee & tea
Owner: Beckie Forsyth
Estimated Sales: Below $ 5 Million
Number Employees: 1-4
Type of Packaging: Food Service
Brands:
Texas Spice

13373 **Texas Tito's**
4611 Wiseman Blvd
San Antonio, TX 78251-4202 210-250-5000
Fax: 210-250-5055 830-626-1123
gotexan@agr.state.tx.us www.gotexan.org
Texas regional food
President: Hiroshi Shimizu
State Marketing Coordinator: Susan Dunn
Deputy Assistant Commissioner Marketing: Delane Caesar
Estimated Sales: $500,000-$1 Million
Number Employees: 250-499
Brands:
Go Texan

13374 **Texas Toffee**
5 Santa Fe Pl
Odessa, TX 79765 432-563-5373
Fax: 915-563-4105
Processor and exporter of toffee including milk and white chocolate, bittersweet, peanut, butterscotch and sugar-free
President: Susan Leshnower
Number Employees: 1-4
Sq. footage: 32
Type of Packaging: Consumer, Food Service, Private Label, Bulk
Brands:
Texas Toffee

13375 **Texas Traditions**
P.O.Box 2705
Georgetown, TX 78627-2705 512-863-7291
Fax: 512-869-6212 800-547-7062
info@texastraditions.com
www.texastraditions.com
President/Founder: Dianna Howard
Brands:
Texas Traditions

13376 **Texas Traditions**
P.O.Box 2705
Georgetown, TX 78627-2705 512-863-7291
Fax: 512-869-6212 800-547-7062
info@texastraditions.com
www.texastraditions.com

Processor and exporter of mesquite smoke, jalapeno pepper, country-style German and black peppercorn mustard, jalapeno and red chile pepper, prickly pear cactus jelly, hot salt, seasoning blends and dry dip mixes
President: Dianna Howard
Estimated Sales: $300,000-500,000
Number Employees: 1-4
Brands:
Texas Hot Salt
Texas Traditions

13377 **Thackery & Company**
PO Box 58
Bolinas, CA 94924-0058 415-868-1781
Fax: 415-868-1781 thackrey@earthlink.net
Gourmet foods
President: Sean Thackery
Estimated Sales: Under $500,000
Number Employees: 1-4
Brands:
Thackrey

13378 **Thai Kitchen**
P.O.Box 13242
Berkeley, CA 94712-4242 510-675-9025
Fax: 510-675-9045 800-967-8424
info@thaikitchen.com www.thaikitchen.com
Thai food
President: Seth Jacobson
Vice President: Dick Neilsen
Estimated Sales: $10-20 Million
Number Employees: 20-49
Type of Packaging: Private Label
Brands:
Thai Kitchen

13379 **Thanksgiving Coffee Company**
19100 S Harbor Dr
Fort Bragg, CA 95437 707-964-0118
Fax: 707-964-0351 800-462-1999
pkatzeff@thanksgivingcoffee.com
www.thanksgivingcoffee.com
Processor of vacuum packed coffee including certified organic, shade grown, regular, decaffeinated and flavored
CEO: Paul Katzeff
President: Joan Katzeff
Plant Manager: David Gillette
Estimated Sales: $4741877
Number Employees: 50-99
Type of Packaging: Consumer, Food Service, Private Label, Bulk
Brands:
Aztec Harvest
Grand Slam
Inca Harvest
Mayan Harvest
Pony Express
Royal Garden Tea
Song Bird
Thanksgiving
ZIP

13380 **Thatcher's Special Popcorn**
2200 Jerrold Ave # H
San Francisco, CA 94124-1036 415-643-9945
Fax: 415-643-9948 800-926-2676
sales@tgsp.com www.tgsp.com
Gourmet popcorn and snacks
President: Gus Ghassan
Vice President: Ghada Ghassan
Manager: Joe Eidson
Estimated Sales: Less than $500,000
Number Employees: 1-4
Type of Packaging: Private Label
Brands:
Joy's Gourmet Snacks
Thatcher's
Thatcher's Special Popcorn

13381 **(HQ)The Bama Company**
5377 E 66th St N
Tulsa, OK 74117-1813 918-592-0778
Fax: 918-732-2902 800-756-2262
www.bama.com
Manufacturer and exporter of frozen baked goods including cookies, pies and biscuits; also, bakers' and confectioners' supplies including dough, pastry and crumb crust pie shells
President/CEO: Paula Marshall-Chapman
CEO: Paula Marshall
QC Manager: Maurice Lawry
Director Brand Sales: Gary Wilson
Number Employees: 100-249
Type of Packaging: Consumer, Food Service

13382 **The Brooklyn Salsa Co LLC**
1717 Troutman Street
Suite 254
Ridgewood, NY 11385 609-680-9319
Fax: 347-435-2430 rob@bksalsa.com
Manufacturer of salsa.

13383 **The Cheesecake Factory**
26901 Malibu Hills Road
Calabasas Hills, CA 91301 818-871-3000
Fax: 818-871-3001
www.thecheesecakefactory.com
Cheesecakes
President: Michael Jannini
Chairman/CEO: David Overton
EVP/CFO: W Douglas Benn
Senior VP Marketing/Public Relations: Howard Gordon
President/Cheesecake Factory Bakery Inc: Max Byfuglin
Estimated Sales: $1.6 Billion
Number Employees: 31000
Brands:
Cheesecake Factory

13384 **The Daphne Baking Company, LLC**
300 E 77th Street
Suite 21B
New York, NY 10075 212-517-7626
Fax: 646-349-4164 bo@daphnebaking.com
www.daphnebaking.com
Frozen tarts, shells and cakes
Marketing: Bo Bartlett
Number Employees: 5

13385 **The Great San Saba RiverPecan Company**
P.O.Box 906
234 West Highway 190
San Saba, TX 76877 325-372-6078
Fax: 325-372-5852 800-621-9121
gssrpc@centex.net www.greatpecans.com
Processor of pecan preserves, pies, cakes, breads, candies, spreads, toppings and pecan praline popcorn
Co-Owner/President: Larry Newkirk
Co-Owner/Vice President: Martha Newkirk
Estimated Sales: $ 5 - 10 Million
Number Employees: 1-4
Type of Packaging: Consumer
Brands:
Great San Saba River Pecan

13386 **The Hampton Popcorn Company Inc.**
251 Andrews Rd
Mineola, NY 11501 888-947-6726
Fax: 888-701-2200 marc@hamptonpopcorn.com
www.hamptonpopcorn.com
Kosher, full-line chocolate, full-line candy, other candy, full-line snacks, nuts, popcorn, pretzels.
Marketing: Robin Gould

13387 **The Humphrey Co**
Po Box 832
Lockport, NY 14094 716-597-1974
Fax: 716-804-6881 info@amazinggrazinginc.com
www.amazinggrazing.com
Soft drinks, other candy, full-line snacks, nuts, other snacks, popcorn.
Marketing: Cyd Cehulik

13388 **The Lollipop Tree, Inc**
181 York St
Auburn, NY 13021 315-252-2676
Fax: 315-282-0720 800-842-6691
info@lollipoptree.com www.lollipoptree.com
A family-owned specialty food manufacturer of all natural baking mixes, condiments and jams, as well as exclusive products prepared for private label specialty retailers. Lollipop Tree's line of Good Simple Food® includes pepperjellies, organic baking mixes, cookie mixes, dessert bread mixes and dessert sauces, grilling sauces, pancakes mixes, jams, scone mixes, and syrups.
President: Robert Lynch
CEO/Chairman/Founder: Laurie Lynch
CFO: Bob Lynch
Estimated Sales: D
Number Employees: 20-49
Number of Products: 90
Sq. footage: 68000
Type of Packaging: Consumer, Private Label
Brands:
Harborside
Lollipop Tree
Quick Loaf
The Lollipop Tree

13389 **The Long Life Beverage Company**
P.O.Box 7802
Mission Hills, CA 91346-7802 661-259-5575
800-848-7331
info@long-life.com www.long-life.com
Processor, importer and exporter of organic herbal black and green teas, currently offer over 40 boxed varieties and 11 ready to drink bottled iced teas, and a variety of enhanced waters
Owner: Troy Long
Estimated Sales: $7.5 Million
Number Employees: 1-4
Number of Brands: 3
Number of Products: 52
Sq. footage: 11000
Parent Co: Consac Industries
Type of Packaging: Consumer, Private Label
Brands:
Enhance Vitamin/Waters
Long Life Black Teas
Long Life Green Teas
Long Life Herbal Teas
Long Life Iced Teas

13390 **The Madelaine ChocolateCompany**
96-03 Beach Channel Dr
Rockaway Beach, NY 11693 718-945-1500
Fax: 718-318-4607 800-322-1505
service@madelaine-chocolate.com
www.madelainechocolate.com
Manufacturers of gourmet chocolate, foiled shapes for every day and every season; also chocolate covered nuts, fruit and speciality centers. Private labeling. Certified kosher.
President: Jorge Farber
Ceo/Vice President: Norman Gold
Vice President Production: Sam Farber
Quality Control: Scott Wright
Marketing: Joan Sweeeting
Estimated Sales: $50 Million
Number Employees: 4,100
Number of Brands: 2
Number of Products: 2000
Sq. footage: 200000
Type of Packaging: Private Label, Bulk
Brands:
MADELAINE CHOCOLATE

13391 **The Mediterranean SnackFood Company**
708 Main Street
Boonton, NJ 07005 973-333-4888
info@mediterraneansnackfoods.com
www.mediterraneansnackfoods.com
Manufacturer of healthy, non-GMO and gluten-free snacks such as chips and crackers
President: Vincent James
Vice President: Franck Le Berre
Estimated Sales: $ 5 Million
Number Employees: 5-9

13392 **The Peanut Butter Shop Of Williamsburg**
8012 Hankins Industrial Park
Toano, VA 23168 757-566-0930
Fax: 757-566-1605 800-831-1828
wholesale@thepeanutshop.com
www.thepeanutshop.com
Processor of Virginia peanuts and specialty nut meats. Processor of cocoa mixes including chocolate, raspberry, traditional and chocolate hazelnut
VP: Pete Booker
Marketing: Michael McDonald
Sales Director: Jeff Armbruster
Plant Manager: Larry Winslow
Number Employees: 20-49
Type of Packaging: Consumer
Brands:
Amber Brand Deviled Smithfield Ham
Colonial Williamsburg
King's Arms Tavern

Nut Case Collection
Peanut Shop of Williamsburg
Smithfield Tavern

13393 **The Perfect Puree**
2700 Napa Valley Corporate
Suite L
Napa, CA 94558 707-261-5100
Fax: 707-261-5111 info@perfectpuree.com
www.perfectpuree.com
Flavored purees for drinks, desserts and food
President: Tracy Hayward
Marketing: Michele Lex
Estimated Sales: $ 1 - 3 Million
Number Employees: 10-19
Type of Packaging: Consumer, Bulk

13394 **The Pillsbury Company**
100 Justin Dr
Chelsea, MA 02150-4032 617-884-9800
Fax: 617-889-0281 800-370-7834
www.pillsbury.com
Processor of frozen and par-baked goods including French bread
Number Employees: 100-249
Sq. footage: 100000
Parent Co: General Mills Inc
Type of Packaging: Food Service, Private Label

13395 **The Power Of Fruit**
Po Box 456
Lebanon, NJ 08833-0456 908-450-9806
Fax: 908-566-3352 ron@poweroffruit.com
www.poweroffruit.com
Dairy-free, gluten-free, kosher, nut-free, organic/natural, sugar-free, frozen desserts, foodservice.
Marketing: Ron Kazmierski

13396 **The Revere Group**
Po Box 80157
9310 4th Ave SO
Seattle, WA 98108 866-747-6871
Fax: 800-284-3834 info@rgroup.com
www.rgroup.com
Other lifestyle, specialty food packaging i.e. gift wrap/boxes/containers.
Marketing: Bill Revere
Estimated Sales: $190,000
Number Employees: 3

13397 **(HQ)The Scoular Company**
2027 Dodge Street
Omaha, NE 68102 402-342-3500
Fax: 402-342-5568 800-487-1474
wwilms@scoular.com www.scoular.com
Merchandise a full range of agricultural products: traditional and specialty crops, food and feed ingredients, and even freight. Market over 100 products on 5 continents, and growing.
Chairman of the Board: Marshall Faith
CEO: Chuck Elsea
President: David Faith
COO: Bob Ludington
SVP/Business Development: John Heck
SVP/Enterprise Services: Jim Konz
SVP/Communications: Joan Maclin
SVP/Operations: Todd McQueen
VP/Operations: Steve Dunn
Estimated Sales: $4.9 Billion
Number Employees: 660
Number of Products: 100+

13398 **(HQ)The Solae Company**
4300 Duncan Ave
Saint Louis, MO 63110
US 314-659-3000
Fax: 314-659-5749 800-325-7108
www.solae.com
Manufacturer of soybean ingredient products, including textured vegetable proteins, textured and functional soy concentrates and isolates, specialty lecithins, polymersv8 splash,garden burgers,ingredients used in pet foods,pie fillings.puddings
CEO: Torkel Rehnman
CFO: Steve W. Fray
VP: Lindell Bean
R&D: Phil Kerr Ph.D
Senior Director R&D: Phil Kerr Ph.D
Vp Of Marketing: Michele Fite
Global Sales: Gregory Warner Ph.D
VP Global Operations: Paul Bossert Jr
Estimated Sales: $1+ Billion
Number Employees: 2400
Type of Packaging: Consumer, Bulk
Other Locations:
Central Soya Company - Processing
Decatur IN
Central Soya Company - Processing
Gibson City IL
Central Soya Company - Processing
Marion OH
Central Soya Company - Grain Plant
Indianapolis IN
Central Soya Company - Processing
Bellevue OH
Central Soya Company - Grain Plant
Cincinnati OH
Central Soya Company - Processing
Delphos OH
Central Soya Company - Mfg
Remington IN
Central Soya Company - Processing
Morristown IN
Central Soya Company - Grain
Jeffersonville OH
Central Soya Company - Grain
Waterloo IN
Central Soya Company - Bulk Oil
Pawtucket RI
Central Soya Company - Mfg
New Bremen OH
Brands:
FIBRIM
SOLAE

13399 **(HQ)The Topps Company**
1 Whitehall Street
New York, NY 10004 212-376-0300
Fax: 212-376-0573 800-489-9149
www.bazookajoe.com
Gum, candy
President/CEO: Ryan O'Hara
VP/CFO: Joseph Del Toro
VP/General Counsel: Andrew Gasper
VP/Digital: Michael Bramlage
VP/General Manager, Global Confectionery: Michael Brandstaedter
General Manager, Intl Confectionery: Stephe Carson
Estimated Sales: $ 290,079,000
Number Employees: 400
Parent Co: Tornante Company/Madison Dearborn Partners
Brands:
Baby Bottle Pop
Bazooka
Bubble Gum Booster
Juicy Drop Chews
Juicy Drop Pop
Push Pop
Ring Pop
Topps

13400 **The Topps Company**
401 York Ave
Duryea, PA 18642-2035 570-457-6761
Fax: 570-451-2408 candyinfo@topps.com
www.bazookajoe.com
Processor of confectionery products including sugarless and regular chewing gum and novelty lollypops
Parent Co: The Topps Company
Brands:
Barfo
Batman
Bazooka Bursts Gum
Big Mouth
Dick Tracy
Memo Book
Push Pops
Ren & Stimpy
Ring Pops
Rocketeer
Super Skates
Superfly
Thumb Fun
Triple Blasts
Tropical Ring Pop
Yo! Street Feet

13401 **Theo Chocolate**
3400 Phinney Ave N
Seattle, WA 98103 206-632-5100
Fax: 206-632-0413 info@theochocolate.com
www.theochocolate.com
chocolate
Founder: Joe Whinney
Number Employees: 10

13402 **Theoworld**
P.O. Box 18071
Fairfield, OH 45018-0071 773-268-2800
Fax: 773-268-2850 http://www.theoworlds.com
President: Ted Mitsakopoulos
Estimated Sales: $ 5 - 10 Million
Number Employees: 10-19

13403 **Theriaults Abattoir**
P.O.Box 314
Van Buren, ME 04785-0314 207-868-3344
Fax: 207-868-2866
Processor of meat products and hydrogenated fats
President: Reynold A Theriault
Estimated Sales: $36000
Number Employees: 1-4
Type of Packaging: Consumer

13404 **Thermice Company**
1445 E Putnam Avenue
Old Greenwich, CT 06870-1379 203-637-4500
General grocery
President: Dave Herman
Estimated Sales: $ .5 - 1 million
Number Employees: 5-9

13405 **Thiel Cheese & Ingredients**
N7630 County Hwy BB
Attn: Kathy Pitzen
Hilbert, WI 54129 920-989-1440
Fax: 920-989-1288 kathyp@thielcheese.com
www.thielcheese.com
Manufacturer and custom formulator of processed cheeses that are used primarily as ingredients in other food products
President: Steven Thiel
Sales: Kathy Pitzen
Number Employees: 50-99
Type of Packaging: Consumer, Food Service, Private Label, Bulk
Brands:
Thiel

13406 **Thirs-Tea Corporation**
18522 NE 2nd Ave
Miami, FL 33179 305-651-4350
Fax: 305-652-4478 sales@thirs-tea.com
www.thirs-tea.com
Processor and exporter of liquid iced tea bases and concentrates
President: Steve Bragg
Estimated Sales: $500,000-$1 Million
Number Employees: 10-19
Type of Packaging: Consumer, Food Service, Private Label, Bulk
Brands:
THIRS-TEA

13407 **Thiry Daems Cheese Factory**
407 4th St
Box 21
Luxemburg, WI 54217 920-845-2117
Fax: 920-845-2629
Cheese
Estimated Sales: $ 1-2.5 Million
Number Employees: 20

13408 **Thistledew Farm**
Rr 1 Box 122
Proctor, WV 26055-9608 304-455-1728
Fax: 304-455-1740 800-854-6639
thistle@ovis.net www.thistledewfarm.com
Processor of honey, hot pepper butter, hot honey mustard, wild wing and rib sauce, garden gourmet salad dressing, original honey mustard, red raspberry, and red raspberry honey vinegar, candles, cosmetics, gift boxes and cratesbaskets, and other great products.
President: Ellie Conlon
CEO: S Conlon
Estimated Sales: $200,000
Number Employees: 1-4
Number of Brands: 2
Number of Products: 7
Sq. footage: 5000
Type of Packaging: Consumer, Food Service, Private Label, Bulk
Brands:
Thistledew Farm's
West's Best

13409 **Tholstrup Cheese**
6366 Norton Center Dr
Muskegon, MI 49441-6032 231-798-4371
Fax: 231-798-4374 800-426-0938
Cheese
Manager: Torben Siggaard
VP: Hans Lund
Vice President: Vincent Staiger
Plant Manager: Ernst Siggaard
Estimated Sales: $500,000 appx.
Number Employees: 20-49
Brands:
Saga

13410 **Thoma Vineyards**
11975 Smithfield Rd
Dallas, OR 97338-9339 503-623-6420
Fax: 503-623-4310 www.vanduzer.com
Wines
Manager: Jim Kakacek
Estimated Sales: $300,000-500,000
Number Employees: 5-9

13411 **Thomas Brothers Ham Company**
1852 Gold Hill Rd
Asheboro, NC 27203-4291 336-672-0337
Fax: 336-672-1782 thomasbros@sheboro.com
Processor and packer of country hams; wholesaler/distributor of frozen and specialty foods and meats; serving the food service and retail markets in the southeast
President/CFO: Howard M Thomas
Quality Control: Don Thomas
Sales/Plant Manager: Don Thomas
Plant Manager: Don Thomas
Estimated Sales: $ 10 - 20 Million
Number Employees: 20-49
Number of Brands: 10
Number of Products: 300
Type of Packaging: Consumer, Private Label
Brands:
Farmer Dons Country Ham
Private Labels
Thomas Brothers Country Ham

13412 **Thomas Canning/Maidstone**
Rural Route 1
Maidstone, ON N0R-1K0
Canada 519-737-1531
Fax: 519-737-7003 thomasca@mnsi.com
www.thomascanning.com
Processor and canner of tomatoes and tomato juice
President: Bill Thomas
Type of Packaging: Food Service, Private Label
Brands:
UTOPIA

13413 **Thomas Dairy**
P.O.Box 519
Rutland, VT 05702 802-773-6788
Fax: 802-747-7121 sales@thomasdairy.com
www.thomasdairy.com
Fluid milk
President: Richard Thomas Jr
Founder: Orin Thomas
Marketing Director: John Thomas
Estimated Sales: $ 5-10 Million
Number Employees: 20-49
Brands:
Thomas

13414 **Thomas Fogarty Winery**
3270 Alpine Rd
Portola Valley, CA 94028 650-851-6777
Fax: 650-851-5840 800-247-4163
info@fogartywinery.com
www.fogartywinery.com
Wines
Executive Director: Anne Krolczyk
Winemaker: Michael Martella
Director Sales/Marketing: Anne Krolczyk
Office Administrator: Melissa Baker
Tasting Room Manager: Rick Davis
Assistant Winemaker: Nathan Kandler
Office Manager: Carrie Larkin
Events Coordinator: Dana Miller
Events Planner: Becky Thatcher
Estimated Sales: Below $ 5 Million
Number Employees: 10-19
Brands:
Thomas Fogarty Winery

13415 **Thomas Gourmet Foods**
P.O.Box 8822
Greensboro, NC 27419-0822 336-299-6263
Fax: 336-299-7852 800-867-2823
info@thomasgourmetfoods.com
www.thomasgourmetfoods.com
Sauce, marinade, dressing, cocktail sauce, tartar sauce, Bloody Mary mix, marinara and pasta sauce
Owner: Dwight Thomas
CEO: Brian Thomas
Estimated Sales: $ 3 - 5 Million
Number Employees: 5-9
Number of Brands: 1
Type of Packaging: Consumer, Private Label, Bulk
Brands:
Thomas

13416 **Thomas Kemper Soda Company**
91 S Royal Brougham Way
Seattle, WA 98134 206-381-8712
host@tksoda.com
www.tksoda.com
Beverages
Owner: Thomas Kemper
Chairman: Laura Bracken-Clough
President: T Maxwell Clough
Estimated Sales: $ 5-10 Million
Number Employees: 1
Brands:
Thomas Kemper Birch Soda
Thomas Kemper Cola
Thomas Kemper Cream

13417 **Thomas Kruse Winery**
3200 Dryden Ave
Gilroy, CA 95020 408-842-7016
Fax: 408-842-7016 krusewine@aol.com
www.thomaskrusewinery.com
Manufacture of wine
President/CEO: Thomas Kruse
Marketing Director: Thomas Kruse
Estimated Sales: Below $ 5 Million
Number Employees: 1-4
Brands:
Thomas Kruse Winey

13418 **Thomas Lobster Company**
P.O.Box 1
Islesford, ME 04646 207-244-5876
Fax: 808-244-7020
Lobster

13419 **Thomas Packing Company**
4643 Farley Dr
Columbus, GA 31907-6342 706-689-3513
Fax: 770-227-2166 800-729-0976
jon@crouch.com www.thomasgourmet.com
Processor and packer of meat products including cured ham, bacon, smoked, andouille and frankfurters; also, smoked turkeys and hams for holiday gift boxes
President: Lee Thomas
CEO: Billy Thomas
Estimated Sales: $ .5 - 1 million
Number Employees: 5-9
Sq. footage: 26000
Type of Packaging: Consumer, Food Service, Bulk
Brands:
Thomas
Treasure

13420 **Thomasson's Potato ChipCompany**
823 Bowman Street
Mansfield, OH 44903 419-529-9424
Fax: 419-529-6789 800-466-9424
chips@joneschips.com www.joneschips.com
Manufacturer and exporter of potato chips, pretzels and cheese puffs
President: Robert Jones
Director of Sales: Don Markov
Production Manager: Roy Kehl
Estimated Sales: $ 10 - 20 Million
Number Employees: 20-49
Sq. footage: 22000
Type of Packaging: Consumer, Private Label
Brands:
Thomasson's

13421 **Thompson Candy Company**
80 S Vine St
Meriden, CT 06451 203-235-2541
Fax: 203-630-2492 800-648-4058
custsvc@thompsoncandy.com
www.thompsoncandy.com
Processor and exporter of chocolate molded products including organic, foiled novelties, bars and filled cups
President: Bill Losust
CEO: Bob Pierce
Vice President: William Walsh
Estimated Sales: $ 20 - 50 Million
Number Employees: 100-249
Sq. footage: 114000

13422 **Thompson Packers**
550 Carnation St
Slidell, LA 70460 985-641-6640
Fax: 985-645-2112 800-989-6328
support@thompack.com www.thompack.com
Manufacturer and exporter of frozen beef, pork, veal and lamb; processor of frozen ground beef and hamburger patties
President/CEO: Mary Thompson
Vice President: Deb Moorel
Human Resources Manager: Chase Haley
Estimated Sales: $21 Million
Number Employees: 1-4
Sq. footage: 50000
Type of Packaging: Consumer, Food Service, Private Label

13423 **Thompson Seafood**
P.O.Box 1057
Darien, GA 31305 912-437-4649
Processor of shrimp, trout and flounder
Partner: Rita Young
Estimated Sales: $575000
Number Employees: 1-4
Type of Packaging: Food Service, Bulk

13424 **Thompson's Fine Foods**
5973 Pheasant Dr
Shoreview, MN 55126 651-481-0374
Fax: 651-482-1944 800-807-0025
muclijoh@msn.com
Processor of mild/sweet, medium/spicy, hot/spicy and hot/hot barbecue dipping sauces for meats, sandwiches and appetizers
Owner: John Thompson
Owner/President: John Thompson
Estimated Sales: Under $500,000
Number Employees: 1-4
Type of Packaging: Consumer, Food Service, Private Label, Bulk
Brands:
Thompson's Black Tie

13425 **Thoms-Proestler Company**
P.O.Box 7210
Rock Island, IL 61204-7210 309-787-1234
Fax: 309-787-1248 upchurchj@tpcinfo.com
www.tpcinfo.com
Wholesaler/distributor of groceries, meats, produce, dairy products, seafood, frozen foods, equipment and fixtures and general merchandise; serving the food service market
President: Michael Wiedower
Sales/Marketing Manager: Bill Brownson
Purchasing Manager: Bryan Marley
Estimated Sales: $97300000
Number Employees: 500-999
Sq. footage: 236000

13426 **Thomson Food**
4435 Venture Avenue
Duluth, MN 55811-5705 218-722-2529
Fax: 218-722-2743
Produces jams, jellies, preserves, syrups, salsas, marinades, barbecue, pizza, spaghetti sauces, flavored vinegars, vinaigrettes, and salad dressings
President: Joel Kozlak
VP: Kan Kalligher
Estimated Sales: $1-2.5 Million
Number Employees: 14
Number of Brands: 2
Number of Products: 40
Sq. footage: 16000
Type of Packaging: Consumer, Food Service, Private Label
Brands:
Mama Cella's
Thomson Berry Farms

13427 Thomson Meats ltd.
618 Hamilton Avenue W
Melfort, SK S0E 1A0
Canada 306-752-2802
Fax: 306-752-4674 sales@rascalsfoods.com
www.rascalsfoods.com
Processor of value added meat products including fresh and frozen pork, beef and chicken
CEO: Paul Marciniak
CFO: Wendy Welsch
R&D: Daryl Durell
Marketing: Donna Walton
Sales: Ron Andrujek
Plant Manager: Gerard Kiefe
Number Employees: 42
Sq. footage: 30000
Type of Packaging: Private Label, Bulk

13428 Thor Incorporated
1280 W 2550 S
Ogden, UT 84401-3238 801-393-3312
Fax: 801-621-3298 888-846-7462
inquirie@thorincorporated.com
www.thorincorporated.com
Custom formulating and contract packaging for vitamins and supplements in liquids, capsules and powders
President: Allen Glanville
Estimated Sales: $ 10-20 Million
Number Employees: 10-19
Type of Packaging: Private Label

13429 Thor-Shackel HorseradishCompany
Po Box 360
Eau Claire, WI 54702-0360 800-826-7322
Fax: 715-832-9915 www.silverspringfoods.com
Processor of fresh grated horseradish and sauces including cocktail, horseradish, etc
Owner: Michael Dogan
General Manager: Michael Dogan
General Manager: Joe Dogan
Estimated Sales: $ 3 - 5 Million
Number Employees: 10-19
Sq. footage: 30000
Type of Packaging: Consumer, Food Service, Private Label, Bulk
Brands:
Thor's

13430 Thornbury Grandview Farms
PO Box 538
417353 10Th LINE
Thornbury, ON N0H 2PO
Canada 519-599-6368
Fax: 519-599-3550 dvt.grandview@dmts.com
Processor and exporter of game meats including bison, venison, wild boar, caribou, ostrich, musk-ox and emu; importer of alligator and rattlesnake
President: Desmond Von Teichman
Plant Manager: Bob Hutchinson
Estimated Sales: $100-350,000k
Number Employees: 25
Sq. footage: 7500
Type of Packaging: Food Service, Private Label
Brands:
Grandview Farms

13431 Thornton Bakery
4244 Elvis Presley Boulevard
Memphis, TN 38116-6424 901-324-2118
Baked goods
Estimated Sales: Under $500,000
Number Employees: 50-99

13432 Thornton Foods Company
8590 Magnolia Trl Apt 121
Eden Prairie, MN 55344 952-944-1735
Fax: 952-944-2083 thorntonfoods@aol.com
Manufacturer of low-fat and fat-free dairy based food products including pasta and cheese sauces
President/CEO: Barbara Thornton
Partner: John Lindahl
Estimated Sales: Under $500,000
Number Employees: 1-4
Type of Packaging: Consumer, Food Service, Private Label, Bulk
Brands:
LIVING LIGHT
LIVING LIGHT DAIRY BLEND

13433 Thornton Winery
P.O.Box 9008
Temecula, CA 92589-9008 951-699-0099
Fax: 951-699-5536 info@thorntonwine.com
www.thorntonwine.com
Wines, champagne
President: John Thornton
Co-Owner: Steve Thornton
CFO: Tim Kelly
Quality Control: Cheryl Rolph
Public Relations Manager: Jan Schneider
Production Manager: Jon McPherson
Estimated Sales: $ 5-10 Million
Number Employees: 50-99
Brands:
Thornton

13434 Thorough Fare Gourmet
PO Box 490
Marlboro, VT 05344-0490 802-257-5612
thoroughfare@amtraders.com
Salad dressing, marinades, and baking mixes

13435 Thorpe Vineyard
8150 Chimney Heights Blvd
Wolcott, NY 14590 315-594-2502
Fax: 315-594-2502 winery@thorpevineyard.com
www.thorpevineyard.com
Wine
President: Fumie Thorpe
Estimated Sales: Less than $500,000
Number Employees: 1-4
Type of Packaging: Private Label
Brands:
Thorpe Vineyard

13436 Three Lakes Winery
6971 Gogebic St
Three Lakes, WI 54562 715-546-3080
Fax: 715-546-8148 800-944-5434
info@fruitwine.com www.fruitwine.com
Processor of wine including cranberry, apricot, cranberry/apple, cranberry/raspberry, blackberry, strawberry, wild plum, strawberry-rhubarb, red raspberry, rhubarb, Italian plum and kiwi
President: Mark Mc Cain
Advertising/Marketing: Marla Shane
Sales/Distribution: Mark McCain
Wine Maker: Scott McCain
Production Manager: Scott Foster
Estimated Sales: $720000
Number Employees: 5-9
Sq. footage: 4000
Type of Packaging: Consumer
Brands:
Fruit of the Woods

13437 Three Rivers Fish Company
P.O.Box 668
Simmesport, LA 71369-0668 318-941-2467
Fax: 318-941-2467
Fresh and frozen seafood/fish
Owner: William Arnouville
Estimated Sales: $730,000
Number Employees: 1-4

13438 Three Springs Farm
RR 1
Box 128
Prospect, VA 23960 804-574-2314
Fax: 804-574-7248
Processor and contract packager of garlic seed and elephant garlic cloves
Owner: Garrett Doering
Number Employees: 5-9
Type of Packaging: Consumer, Private Label, Bulk

13439 Three Springs Water Company
1800 Pine Run Rd
Laurel Run, PA 18706-9419 570-823-7019
Fax: 570-822-6177 800-332-7873
Processor and bottler of low-mineral and sodium-free spring water
President: Jim Tosh
Estimated Sales: $ 3 - 5 Million
Number Employees: 20-49
Sq. footage: 40000
Type of Packaging: Consumer, Food Service, Private Label
Brands:
3 Springs

13440 Three Vee Food & Syrup Company
110 Bridge St
Brooklyn, NY 11201-1575 718-858-7333
Fax: 718-858-7371 800-801-7330
info@3vee.com www.3vee.com
Processor and exporter of liquid meat tenderizers, dessert toppings, fruit concentrates, pulps, syrups and juices including orange, papaya, black raspberry, mango, guava, cranberry, coconut, etc.; importer of juice concentrates andpurees
Owner: Elshi Gambo
VP: Clara Stark
Marketing/Sales Manager: Bruce Borwick
Estimated Sales: $ 20 - 50 Million
Number Employees: 20-49
Sq. footage: 21000
Type of Packaging: Consumer, Food Service, Private Label, Bulk

13441 Threshold RehabilitationServices
1000 Lancaster Ave
Reading, PA 19607 610-777-7691
Fax: 610-777-1295 trsincmail@trsinc.org
www.trsinc.org
Contract packagers
President: Ronald Williams
Sales/Marketing: Nancy Benjamin
Estimated Sales: $ 20 - 50 Million
Number Employees: 250-499
Sq. footage: 20000

13442 Thrifty Ice Cream
9200 Telstar Ave
El Monte, CA 91731-2814 626-571-0122
Fax: 626-280-2905 www.riteaid.com
Processor and exporter of ice cream
Manager: Larry Crosby
Export Director: Bob Dwyer
CFO: Mary Salmons
Quality Control: Lory Irias
Plant Manager: Ron Simmer
Estimated Sales: $ 20-50 Million
Number Employees: 100-249
Parent Co: Thrifty
Type of Packaging: Consumer, Food Service, Bulk

13443 Thrifty Vegetable Company
P.O.Box 6408
Garden Grove, CA 92846-6408
Fax: 213-629-2253 media@thriftyfoods.com
www.thriftyvegetable.com
Manufacturer of produce
President: George Abadjian
Estimated Sales: $45 Million
Number Employees: 20-49

13444 (HQ)Thumann's
670 Dell Rd # 1
Carlstadt, NJ 07072-2292 201-935-3636
Fax: 201-935-2226 sales@thumanns.com
www.thumanns.com
Manufacturer and packer of delicatessen products that include; ham, roast beef, corned beef, pastrami, turkey, liverwurst, bologna, hot dogs, breakfast meats and sausages, cheeses, soups, salads, condiments and frozen products
Owner: Bob Burke Sr
Estimated Sales: $ 50 - 100 Million
Number Employees: 250-499
Brands:
THUMANN'S

13445 Thyme & Truffles Hors D'oeuvres
51 Kesmark
Dollard-Des-Ormeaux, QC H9B 3J1
Canada 514-685-9955
Fax: 514-685-2602 877-785-9759
tandt@thymeandtruffles.com
www.thymeandtruffles.com
Processor of frozen oven-ready hors d'oeuvres with assorted fillings including canapes; also, frozen vegetarian entrees
President: Rhonda Richer
QA/QC Specialist: Santi Vicente
Sales Manager: Tim Lipa
Director of Operations: Gino Giansante
Production Manager: Alfred Meth
Number Employees: 50-99
Number of Products: 40
Sq. footage: 12500
Type of Packaging: Food Service, Private Label, Bulk

Brands:
Thyme & Truffles

13446 **Thymly Products**
1332 Colora Rd
Colora, MD 21917 410-658-4820
Fax: 410-658-4824 treym@thymlyproducts.com
www.thymlyproducts.com
Food baking additives, flavors, specialty blends
President: Harry T Muller
Vice President: Paul Canfield
VP Finance: Shirley Wiest
Sales: Trey Muller-Thym
Plant Manager: Chuck Osterrider
Estimated Sales: $3.5 Million
Number Employees: 37
Type of Packaging: Private Label
Brands:
Baker's Cremes
Bread Glaze
Brew Buffers
Glalcto
Parve Plain Muffin

13447 **Tianfu China Cola**
2 Brady Ln
Katonah, NY 10536-2502 914-232-3102
Fax: 914-232-9184 davorganic@aol.com
Processor of natural soft drinks; importer of herbs
President: David Robinov
Estimated Sales: $500,000-$1 Million
Number Employees: 1-4
Brands:
China Cola

13448 **Tic Gums**
4609 Richlynn Dr
Belcamp, MD 21017 410-273-7300
Fax: 410-273-6469 800-221-3953
info@ticgums.com www.aragum.com
Oldest supplier of hydrocolloids and all necessary ingredients included gum products
President: Steve Andon
CFO: Mike Dean
VP: Christopher Andon
R & D: Mar Nietl
Marketing: Frances Bowman
Operations: Steve Hartley
Estimated Sales: $ 20-$ 50 Million
Number Employees: 50-99
Type of Packaging: Bulk

13449 **Tichon Seafood Corporation**
7 Conway St
New Bedford, MA 02740-7205 508-999-5607
Fax: 508-990-8271
Processor of fresh and frozen fish including squid, scallops and fish sticks
President: Daniel Tichon
VP: R Tichon
Executive VP: Ronald Tichon
Estimated Sales: $1200000
Number Employees: 20-49
Sq. footage: 60000
Type of Packaging: Consumer
Brands:
Tichon

13450 **TideWays**
750 Seashore Avenue
Peaks Island, ME 04108-1252 207-766-0062
Fax: 312-787-6070
Seafood crackers, lobster bites with onion, clam bites with garlic, shrimp bites with cajun spices
Brands:
Clambites With Garlic
Lobsterbites With On
Shrimpbites With Caj

13451 **Tideland Seafood Company**
P.O.Box 99
Dulac, LA 70353 985-563-4516
Fax: 985-563-4296
Manufacturer of prepared fresh shrimp; fish & seafood canning and curing.
President: Judith Gibson
Estimated Sales: $ 5 - 10 Million
Number Employees: 5-9

13452 **Tiger Meat Provisions**
1445 NW 22nd St
Miami, FL 33142 305-324-0083
Fax: 305-324-1570
Packer of fresh pork
President: Jose Requejo
Estimated Sales: $ 10 - 20 Million
Number Employees: 20-49
Type of Packaging: Food Service
Brands:
Tiger

13453 **Tiger Mushroom Farm**
PO Box 909
Nanton, AB T0L 1R0
Canada 403-646-2578
Fax: 403-646-2240
Processor of mushrooms
President: Tiger Goto
Operations Manager: Jack Trinn
Estimated Sales: C
Number Employees: 20-49
Sq. footage: 16500
Type of Packaging: Consumer, Food Service
Brands:
Tiger

13454 **(HQ)Tillamook County Creamery Association**
4175 Highway 101 N
Tillamook, OR 97141 503-815-1300
Fax: 503-842-6039 www.tillamookcheese.com
Manufacturer of dairy butter, cheese, nonhygroscopic cheddar cheese whey powder and ice cream; exporter of dried whey, sour cream, yogurt, fluid milk
Chairman: George Allen
President/CEO: Jim McMullen
CEO: Jim McMullen
VP Sales/Marketing: Jay Allison
VP Operations: Cliff Brady
Estimated Sales: $270 Million
Number Employees: 250-499
Type of Packaging: Consumer, Food Service, Private Label, Bulk
Brands:
TILLAMOOK

13455 **Tillamook Meat Company**
405 Park Ave
Tillamook, OR 97141 503-842-4802
Fax: 508-342-2330
Manufacturer of meat products including beef, lamb, pork and poultry, jerky
President/Co-Owner: Laurel Travis
VP/Co-Owner: Mark Travis
Estimated Sales: $1-3 Million
Number Employees: 7
Type of Packaging: Consumer, Food Service, Bulk

13456 **(HQ)Tiller Foods Company**
967 Senate Dr
Dayton, OH 45459 937-435-4601
Fax: 937-435-1408
Processor of portion controlled dairy products including sour cream, half and half, nondairy creamers, whipped cream and toppings
President: Donald Tiller Jr
Sales Manager: David Yost
Estimated Sales: $ 5 - 10 Million
Number Employees: 5-9
Type of Packaging: Consumer, Food Service, Private Label, Bulk
Other Locations:
Tiller Foods Co.
Tampa FL

13457 **Tillie's Gourmet**
173 Ash Way
Doylestown, PA 18901 215-272-8326
Fax: 215-348-2192 danielle@tililesgourmet.com
www.tilliesgourmet.com
dressings, marinades and blue crab salsas

13458 **Tim's Cascade Chips**
1150 Industry Dr N
Algona, WA 98001-6552 253-833-0255
Fax: 253-939-9411 800-533-8467
consumer_affairs@birdseyefoods.com
www.birdseyefoods.com
Processor and exporter of snacks including mixes, caramel corn, potato chips and corn curls
President: Dennis M Mullen
COO: Jeff Leichleiter
Sales/Marketing Executive: George Masiello
Estimated Sales: $ 20 - 50 Million
Number Employees: 50-99
Sq. footage: 130000
Parent Co: Agrilink Foods
Type of Packaging: Consumer, Food Service, Private Label

13459 **Timber Crest Farms**
4791 Dry Creek Rd
Healdsburg, CA 95448 707-433-8251
Fax: 707-433-8255 888-374-9325
tcf@timbercrest.com www.sonic.net
Manufacturer of organic and preservative free dried fruits, nuts, tomatoes and specialty food products
Co-Owner: Ronald Waltenspiel
Co-Owner: Ruth Waltenspiel
Public Relations: Ruth Waltenspiel
Estimated Sales: $4.5 Million
Number Employees: 250-499
Number of Brands: 2
Number of Products: 50
Sq. footage: 30000
Type of Packaging: Consumer, Food Service, Private Label, Bulk
Brands:
Sonoma
Timber Crest Farm

13460 **Timber Lake Cheese Company**
PO Box A
Timber Lake, SD 57656 605-865-3605
Fax: 605-865-3605
Cheese
President: Virgil Johnson
Estimated Sales: Less than $500,000
Number Employees: 1-4

13461 **Timber Peaks Gourmet**
6180 N Hollowview Ct
Parker, CO 80134-5808 303-841-8847
Fax: 303-805-0174 800-982-7687
www.mountainhousekitchen.com
Cocoa, bean soups, dessert mixes, bread mixes, trail mixes, and dried salsa
President: Laurie Yankoski
Estimated Sales: $100,000
Number Employees: 1-4
Number of Brands: 1
Number of Products: 41
Sq. footage: 1500
Type of Packaging: Consumer, Bulk
Brands:
MUD
Mountain House Kitchen

13462 **Timeless Traditions**
4943 Us Route 7
Pittsford, VT 05763-9824 802-483-6024
dethbysauc@yahoo.com
www.piecesofvermont.com/timeless
Dessert sauces

13463 **Tin Whistle Brewing Co**
954 Eckhardt Ave W
Penticton, BC V2A 2C1
Canada 250-770-1122
Fax: 250-770-1122 tindrew@telus.net
Processor of ale
President: Lorraine Nagy
Number Employees: 5-9
Type of Packaging: Consumer, Food Service
Brands:
Black Widow
Coyote
Ratle Snack

13464 **Tina's**
1509 N Kraemer Blvd Ste C
Anaheim, CA 92806 714-630-4123
Fax: 714-630-0650
customerservice@tinasinc.com
www.tinasinc.com
Baked goods
President: Tina Wilson
CEO: Tian Wilson
Estimated Sales: $ 75-100 Million
Number Employees: 50-100
Brands:
Tina's

13465 **Tip Top Canning Company**
505 S. Second Street
Tipp City, OH 45371 937-667-3713
Fax: 937-667-3802 800-352-2635
info@tiptopcanning.com
www.tiptopcanning.com

Producers of tomatoes and tomato products.
President: George Timmer
Vice President: Scott Timmer
National Sales Manager: Cynthia Timmer
Estimated Sales: $ 10 - 20 Million
Number Employees: 20-49
Number of Products: 60
Sq. footage: 150000
Type of Packaging: Consumer, Food Service, Private Label, Bulk

13466 **Tip Top Poultry**
327 Wallace Road
Marietta, GA 30062 770-973-8070
Fax: 770-973-6897 800-241-5230
www.tiptoppoultry.com
Processor and exporter of poultry
President: Robin Burruss
COO: Mike Brooks
CFO: Charlie Singleton
VP: Lee Bates
VP/Sales: Brian Tucker
Technical VP: Mitch Forstie
Production Manager: Steve Moore
Estimated Sales: $15 Million
Number Employees: 650
Type of Packaging: Consumer, Bulk

13467 **Tipiak**
45 Church St Ste 203
Stamford, CT 06906 203-961-9117
Fax: 203-975-9081 laurent.chery@tipiak-e.com
www.tipiak.fr
Specialty rices and beans, tapioca flour and pearls, frozen appetizers and desserts.
CEO: Laurent Cherry
VP: Laurent Chery
Estimated Sales: Below $ 5 Million
Number Employees: 1-4

13468 **Tipp Distributors**
500 W Overland Ave
#300
El Paso, TX 79901 915-594-1618
Fax: 915-590-1225 888-668-2639
www.novamex.com
Condiments and relishes
President: Ramon Carrasco
CEO: Luis Fernandez
CFO: Thomas Deleon
Executive VP: Sanford Gross
Estimated Sales: $ 1-2.5 Million
Number Employees: 126
Brands:
Chata
Cholula
D'Gari
Ibarra
Jarritos
Mineragua
Rogelio Bueno
San Marcos
Sangria Seorial
Sidral Mundet
Tuny

13469 **Titterington's Olde English Bake Shop**
48 Cummings Park
Woburn, MA 01801 781-938-7600
Fax: 781-938-7676 dkrane@titteringtons.com
www.titteringtons.com
Baked goods
Owner: Richard Foster
Estimated Sales: $ 20 - 50 Million
Number Employees: 20-49

13470 **Titusville Dairy Products**
217 S Washington St
Titusville, PA 16354 814-827-1833
Fax: 814-827-2510 800-352-0101
tdpc@online.net www.titusvillepa.com
Processor of ice cream mixes, dairy products, juices, fruit drinks and bottled water
President: Charles Turner Jr
VP: William Schneider Jr
Plant Manager: Chester Anthony
Estimated Sales: $4 Million
Number Employees: 32
Sq. footage: 30000
Type of Packaging: Consumer, Private Label
Brands:
Blossom Time
Natural Harvest
Titusville Dairy Products

13471 **To Market-To Market**
4880 Ireland Ln
West Linn, OR 97068-2953 970-278-1000
Fax: 503-655-3390
kathy@tomarket-tomarket.com
tomarket-tomarket.com
Processor of natural spice blends
President: Kathy Parson
Number Employees: 1-4
Type of Packaging: Consumer, Food Service

13472 **Todd's**
P.O.Box 4821
Des Moines, IA 50305 515-266-2276
Fax: 515-266-1669 800-247-5363
sales@toddsltd.com www.toddsltd.com
Food product manufacturer (wet and dry). KOsher and organic certified.
President/CEO: Alan Niedermeier
Quality Control: Diana Burzloff
Public Relations: Alissa Douglas
Operations: Duane Hettkamp
Production: Jeff Sullivan
Plant Manager: John Routh
Purchasing: Danielle Robinson
Estimated Sales: $ 1 - 3 Million
Number Employees: 30
Number of Brands: 40
Number of Products: 200
Sq. footage: 80000
Type of Packaging: Consumer, Food Service, Private Label, Bulk
Brands:
BUTCHER'S FRIEND
PAPA JOE'S SPECIALTY FOOD

13473 **Todd's**
6055 Malburg Way
Vernon, CA 90058 323-585-5900
Fax: 323-585-5900 800-938-6337
sales@todds.com www.todds.com
Processor, importer and exporter of nuts and nut meats, dried fruit, trail mixes, candy, etc
President: Todd Levin
Estimated Sales: $ 5 - 10 Million
Number Employees: 5-9
Type of Packaging: Consumer, Food Service, Private Label, Bulk
Brands:
DR JERKYLL & MR HIDE
HUCKLEBERRY'S FARM
JUST SNAK-IT
LUCY'S SWEETS
TODD'S TREATS

13474 **Todd's Enterprises**
2450 White Rd
Irvine, CA 92614 949-250-4080
Fax: 949-724-1338 toddsaz@aol.com
www.toddsfoods.com
Processor and exporter of soups, sauces, chili and salad dressings
President: Phil De Carion
Marketing Director: Ed Stokes
Manufacturing Manager: Roger McFarland
Plant Manager: Dan Foss
Purchasing Manager: Dan Foss
Number Employees: 100-249
Parent Co: Todd's Central Commissary
Type of Packaging: Food Service, Private Label
Brands:
Todd's

13475 **(HQ)Toddy Products**
803 W Kansas Ave
Midland, TX 79701 713-225-2066
Fax: 713-225-2110 toddy@toddyproducts.com
www.toddycafe.com
Processor and exporter of liquid concentrates including coffee, tea, mocha, chai, etc.; also, espresso pecan brittle; manufacturer of cold brew coffee makers
Owner: Strother Simpson
Vice President: Scott Schroer
Estimated Sales: $1500000
Number Employees: 10-19
Sq. footage: 20000
Type of Packaging: Consumer, Food Service, Private Label, Bulk
Brands:
Toddy
Toddy Cappuccino
Toddy Coffee Crunch
Toddy Coffee Maker
Toddy Gourmet Iced Tea Concentrate
Toddy Mocha

13476 **Todhunter Foods**
PO Box 1447
Lake Alfred, FL 33850-1447 863-956-1116
Fax: 863-956-3979
humanresources@todhunter.com
www.todhunter.com
Processor of vinegar and cooking wine; contract packager of fruit juices and carbonated/flavored beverages; importer of alcoholic beverages and juice concentrates; exporter of alcoholic beverages and vinegar
President: Jay Maltby
Number Employees: 100-249
Sq. footage: 450000
Parent Co: Todhunter International
Type of Packaging: Consumer, Food Service, Private Label, Bulk

13477 **Todhunter Foods & Monarch Wine Company**
222 Lakeview Avenue
Suite 1500
West Palm Beach, FL 33401-6174 561-655-8977
Fax: 561-655-9718 800-336-9463
jpolansky@cruzoninc.com www.todhunter.com
Processor of cooking wines, powdered wine flavors, denatures spirits, vinegar and wine reductions.
President: Jay Maltby
CFO: Ezra Shashoua
Vice President: D Chris Mitchell
Sales Director: Jim Polansky
Plant Manager: Ousik Yu
Purchasing Manager: Frank Dibling
Number Employees: 410
Parent Co: Todhunter International
Type of Packaging: Consumer, Food Service, Private Label, Bulk

13478 **Toe-Food Chocolates andCandy**
2500 Milvia Street
Suite 216
Berkeley, CA 94704-2636 510-649-9250
Fax: 510-849-3810 888-863-3663
sales@toefood.com www.toefood.com
Chocolate and candy in the shape of feet.
Founder/CEO: Mark Wolpa
Estimated Sales: $300,000-500,000
Number Employees: 8
Brands:
TOE-RIFIC CANDY

13479 **Toffee Company**
4550 Post Oak Place Dr # 220
Houston, TX 77027-3139 713-840-9696
Fax: 713-840-8786 BBurk924@aol.com
www.taaffeassoc.com
Toffee, candy
Owner: Peter Taaffe
Estimated Sales: $ 1 - 3 Million
Number Employees: 5-9

13480 **Tofield Packers Ltd**
5020 50th Avenue
Tofield, AB T0B 4J0
Canada 780-662-4842
Fax: 780-662-4842
Processor of fresh and processed meats including sausage and wild game; also, custom slaughtering available
President: Dale Erickson
Estimated Sales: C
Number Employees: 10-19
Type of Packaging: Consumer, Bulk

13481 **Toft Dairy**
3717 Venice Road
Sandusky, OH 44870 419-625-4376
Fax: 419-621-2010 800-521-4606
info@toftdairy.com www.toftdairy.com
Processor of milk, ice cream, frozen yogurt, fruit drinks, orange juice, cottage cheese and csour cream
President/Sales Manager: Eugene Meisler
VP: Thomas Meisler
Plant Manager: Dan Meisler
Estimated Sales: $17.8 Million
Number Employees: 52
Sq. footage: 94000
Type of Packaging: Consumer, Food Service, Private Label, Bulk

13482 **Tofu Shop Specialty Foods**
65 Frank Martin Ct
Arcata, CA 95521 707-822-7401
Fax: 707-822-7401 info@tofushop.com
www.tofushop.com
Manufacturer of fresh tofu, smoked tofu, fresh soymilks, international spiced tofu, seasoned and baked tofu
President: Matthew Schmit
Estimated Sales: $500,000
Number Employees: 20
Number of Products: 22
Sq. footage: 4500
Type of Packaging: Consumer, Bulk
Brands:
Snack Fu
Tofu Shop

13483 **Tofutti Brands**
50 Jackson Dr
Cranford, NJ 7016 908-272-2400
Fax: 908-272-9492 tofuttibrands@aol.com
www.tofutti.com
Processor and exporter of nondairy food products including imitation cream cheese, no-cholesterol egg products made of egg whites and tofu with added vitamins and minerals and frozen tofu desserts
CEO: David Mintz
CFO: Steven Kass
Director: Neal Axelrod
Estimated Sales: $10-20 Million
Number Employees: 10-19
Type of Packaging: Consumer, Food Service, Bulk
Brands:
Lite Lite Tofutti
Tofutti
Tofutti Better Than Cheesecake

13484 **Toho America Corporation**
9751 Ikena Cir
Honolulu, HI 96821 808-395-5885
Fax: 808-395-5242
Fish and seafood broker
President: Toyoki Higashishiba

13485 **Tokunaga Farms**
12019 S Highland Avenue
Selma, CA 93662-9003 559-896-0949
Farm products
President: George Tokunga

13486 **Tom & Dave's Specialty Coffee**
3095 Kerner Blvd # A
San Rafael, CA 94901-5420 415-454-3064
Fax: 415-454-3281 800-249-5050
siteorders@tomanddaves.com
www.tomanddaves.com
Coffee
Owner: Christopher Rygg
Estimated Sales: Below $ 5 Million
Number Employees: 5-9
Type of Packaging: Private Label
Brands:
Columbian
House Blend
Moka-Java

13487 **Tom & Sally's Handmade Chocolates**
P.O.Box 600
Brattleboro, VT 05302-0600 802-254-4200
Fax: 802-254-5518 800-827-0800
tom@tomandsalys.com www.tomandsallys.com
Processor of gourmet chocolate products including old-fashioned creams, foil-wrapped coins, spoons, nut patties, lollypops, almond bark, dessert toppings and molded
Chairman: Thomas E Fegley
Estimated Sales: $ 3 - 5 Million
Number Employees: 10-19
Sq. footage: 11700
Type of Packaging: Consumer, Private Label
Brands:
Cowlicks
Dog-Gones
Reindeer Pies
Vermont Meadow Muffins
Vermont Pasture Patties

13488 **Tom Cat Bakery**
4305 10th St
Long Island City, NY 11101 718-786-4224
Fax: 718-472-0310 info@tomcat-bakery.com
www.tomcat-bakery.com
French and Italian breads, rolls, baguettes
President: Noel Labat-Comess
Estimated Sales: $ 50-100 Million
Number Employees: 50-99
Brands:
Tom Cat Bakery

13489 **Tom Clamon Foods**
2220 W Reagan St
Palestine, TX 75801 903-729-0138
Fax: 903-723-3573
Beef
Owner: Gene Hamon
Estimated Sales: $ 20-50 Million
Number Employees: 20-49

13490 **Tom Davis & Sons Dairy Company**
21631 Meyers Rd
Oak Park, MI 48237-3105 248-399-6970
Fax: 248-399-6196 800-399-6970
adim@tomdavisdairy.com
www.prairiefarms.com
Dairy products distributers
President: Gary Davis
CEO: Tom Davis
Marketing Director: Jim Davis
Estimated Sales: $ 50 - 100 Million
Number Employees: 50-99
Type of Packaging: Private Label
Brands:
Prairie Farms

13491 **Tom Ringhausen Orchards**
P.O.Box 201
Hardin, IL 62047-0201 618-576-2311
Processor and grower of fruits and vegetables including apples, peaches, plums, pears, nectarines, blackberries, squash, pumpkins, melons and turnips. Also cider
President: Tom Ringhausen
Estimated Sales: Under $300,000
Number Employees: 5-9
Sq. footage: 3000
Type of Packaging: Consumer
Brands:
Tom Ringhausen

13492 **Tom Sturgis Pretzel Inc**
2267 Lancaster Pike
Reading, PA 19607-2453 610-775-0335
Fax: 610-796-1418 www.tomsturgispretzels.com
Processor of hard pretzels
Owner: Tom Sturgis
CEO: Barbara Sturgis
Finance Executive: Bruce Sturgis
Estimated Sales: $2.5-5 Million
Number Employees: 20-49
Sq. footage: 20000
Type of Packaging: Consumer, Food Service, Private Label, Bulk
Brands:
America's Original
Sturgis Pretzel House

13493 **Tom Sturgis Pretzels**
2267 Lancaster Pike
Reading, PA 19607 610-775-0335
Fax: 610-796-1418 800-817-3834
www.tomsturgispretzels.com
Pretzels
President: Bruce Sturgis
Founder: Tom Sturgis
Vice President: Barbara Sturgis
Sales Director: Timothy Snyder
Operations Manager: Jean Harms
Production Manager: David Amour
Plant Manager: Mike Kappenstein
Estimated Sales: $ 5 Million
Number Employees: 20-49
Number of Brands: 3
Sq. footage: 75000
Type of Packaging: Private Label
Brands:
Cousin Rachel Pretzels
Mr. C'S Pretzels
Tom Sturgis Pretzels

13494 **Tom Tom Tamale Manufacturing**
4750 S Washtenaw Ave
Chicago, IL 60632-2096 773-523-5675
Processor of tamales
President: Nick Petros
Estimated Sales: $500,000-$1 Million
Number Employees: 10-19
Type of Packaging: Consumer

13495 **Tom's Foods**
8600 South Blvd
Charlotte, NC 28273
800-995-2623
www.tomsfoods.com
Processor of snack foods including potato chips
Plant Manager: John Rothenfluh
Estimated Sales: I
Number Employees: 1,000-4,999
Parent Co: Lance
Type of Packaging: Private Label

13496 **Tom's Ice Cream Bowl**
532 McIntire Ave
Zanesville, OH 43701 740-452-5267
Fax: 740-452-0931 www.tomsicecreambowl.com
Processor of ice cream
Owner: William Sullivan
Estimated Sales: $ 1 - 3 Million
Number Employees: 20-49
Type of Packaging: Consumer

13497 **Tom's Snacks Company**
8600 S Boulevard
Charlotte, NC 28273 706-323-2721
Fax: 706-323-8231 800-995-2623
bsmith@tomfoods.com www.tomsfoods.com
Potato chips, thick and bold chips, thunder chips, cheezers, pork skins, rings, fries, corn and tortilla, bugles and mega twisters
Supply Chain VP, Lance Inc.: Blake Thompson
Estimated Sales: $ .5 - 1 million
Number Employees: 50-100
Parent Co: Lance, Inc.
Type of Packaging: Consumer
Brands:
Tom's

13498 **(HQ)Tomanetti Food Products**
625 Allegheny Ave
Oakmont, PA 15139 412-828-3040
Fax: 412-828-2282 800-875-3040
sales@tomanetti.com www.tomanetti.com
Pizza shells, breadsticks and focaccia.
President: George Michael
COO: Robert Finlay
Sales Manager: Chris Presutti
Production Supervisor: Bill Vidra
Plant Manager: Paul Sypolt
Estimated Sales: Below $ 5 Million
Number Employees: 30

13499 **Tomaro's Bakery**
411 N 4th St
Clarksburg, WV 26301 304-622-0691
Manufacturer of bread, rolls and pizza crusts
President: Janice Brunett
Estimated Sales: $6 Million
Number Employees: 10-19
Type of Packaging: Consumer

13500 **Tomasello Winery**
225 N White Horse Pike
Hammonton, NJ 08037-1868 609-561-0567
Fax: 609-561-8617 800-666-9463
wine@tomasellowinery.com
www.tomasellowinery.com
Wines
President: Charles J Tomasello Jr
Owner: Jack Tomasello
Vice President: Jack Tomasello
Estimated Sales: Below $ 5 Million
Number Employees: 5-9
Brands:
Tomasello Winery

13501 **Tomasinos Sausage**
3819 Columbus Rd NE
Canton, OH 44705-4428 330-454-4171
Fax: 330-454-3835
Processor of sausage including mild, pork and smoked
President: Mark V Prestier
Estimated Sales: $ 20 - 50 Million
Number Employees: 10-19
Type of Packaging: Consumer, Food Service, Bulk

13502 **Tomasso Corporation**
20425 Clark Graham
Baie D'Urfe, QC H9X 3T5
Canada 514-325-3000
Fax: 514-457-5107 info@cordonbleu-tomasso.ca
www.cordonbleu.ca
Manufacturer of frozen Italian entrees including meat lasagna, chicken lasagna, meat sauce, vegeatble lasagna, cannelloni, macaroni and cheese
Chairman/CEO: J-Rene Ouimet
CFO/Treasurer: Peter Tasgal
Number Employees: 120
Sq. footage: 53000
Type of Packaging: Food Service, Private Label
Brands:
BUONA CUCINA
GUSTO ITALIA
PIAZZA TOMASSO

13503 **Tommaso's Fresh Pasta**
2680 Nova Dr
Dallas, TX 75229 972-869-1111
Fax: 972-869-9937
Pasta and sauces
Owner: Jack Rayome
Director Research: Ray Etheridge
Estimated Sales: $ 5-9.9 Million
Number Employees: 20-49
Sq. footage: 12000
Type of Packaging: Consumer, Food Service, Private Label, Bulk

13504 **Tommy Tang's Thai Seasonings**
PO Box 46700
Los Angeles, CA 90046-7512 818-442-0219
sandi@letsgetcooking.org
www.tommytangs.net
Seasonings, spices
President: Sandi Tang
Owner: Tommy Tang
Estimated Sales: $ 1-2.5 Million
Number Employees: '10-19

13505 **Tomorrow Enterprise**
5918 Spanish Trl W
New Iberia, LA 70560 337-783-2666
Fax: 337-233-9514
Hot sauces
President: Tony Morrow

13506 **Tone Products Company**
2129 N 15th Ane Ste#1
Melrose Park, IL 60160 708-681-3660
Fax: 708-681-2368 sales@toneproducts.com
www.toneproducts.com
Processor and exporter of fountain syrups, soup bases, toppings, pancake syrup and beverage concentrates
President/CEO: Tim Evon
VP: Tom Evon
Estimated Sales: $ 20 - 50 Million
Number Employees: 50-99
Sq. footage: 46000
Type of Packaging: Consumer, Private Label, Bulk
Brands:
Bonnie
Bonnie Maid
Hi-Tone
Maple Wood
Rainbo-Rich
Sno-Bal

13507 **Tonex**
27 Park Row
Wallington, NJ 07057-1629 973-773-5135
Fax: 973-916-1091 tonexinc@aol.com
www.tonexinc.com
Processor of cappuccino, nondairy creamers, instant coffee and tea and chocolate covered nuts; importer and exporter of beer, vodka, candy, fresh and dried fruits, tea, instant cappuccino, juice and juice concentrates, etc
Owner: Bogdan Torbus
President: Grace Torbus
Marketing Director: Angela Torbus
Type of Packaging: Consumer, Food Service, Private Label, Bulk
Brands:
Chocolate Covered Nuts
Instant Cappuccino
Instant Tea

13508 **Tony Chachere's Creole Foods**
519 N. Lombard St.
Opelousas, LA 70570 337-948-4691
Fax: 337-948-6854 800-551-9066
creole@tonycachere.com
www.tonychachere.com
Seasonings and rice dinner mixes
President/CEO: Donald Chachere Jr
Marketing Director: Christopher Roch
CFO: William Pollingue
CFO: Donald Chachere Jr
VP Sales: Mona Campbell Jr
Public Relations: Janice LeBlanc
Production Manager: Alex Chachere II
Plant Manager: Carl Trahan
Purchasing Manager: Christy Bernard
Estimated Sales: Below $1 Million
Number Employees: 5
Type of Packaging: Consumer, Food Service, Private Label, Bulk
Brands:
Instant Roux & Gravy
More Spice Seasoning
Tony Chachere's Orig

13509 **Tony Downs Foods Company**
418 Benzel Ave SW
Madelia, MN 56062 507-642-3203
Fax: 507-642-3397
mforstie@downsfoodgroup.com
www.tonydownsfoods.com
Processor of poultry: fully cooked, diced-frozen and commercial and retail canned chicken
President/CEO: Richard Downs
CFO: Patty Johnson
VP: Mitch Forstie
Sales: Leo Zachman
Estimated Sales: $22800000
Number Employees: 250-499
Sq. footage: 100000
Type of Packaging: Consumer, Food Service, Private Label, Bulk

13510 **Tony Downs Foods Company**
P.O.Box 28
Saint James, MN 56081 507-375-3111
Fax: 507-375-3048 rkrull@tonydownsfoods.com
www.tonydownsfoods.com
Frozen foods
Co-President: Richard Downes
CFO: Patty Anderson
CEO: Dick Downs
Plant Manager: Jeff Hinkle
Estimated Sales: $ 20-50 Million
Number Employees: 50-99
Brands:
Downsfare
Infrared Foods

13511 **Tony Packo Food Company**
1902 Front St
Toledo, OH 43605-1292 41- 6-1 19
Fax: 419-691-8358 866-472-2567
shop@tonypacko.com www.tonypackos.com
Pickles, relishes
Owner: Tony Packo
Estimated Sales: Less than $500,000
Number Employees: 12
Brands:
Tony Packo's

13512 **Tony V'S Oyster House**
PO Box 1052
Amite, LA 70422-1052 504-748-8110
Seafood

13513 **Tony Vitrano Company**
7470 Conowingo Ave Bldg BB
Jessup, MD 20794 410-799-7444
Fax: 410-799-8917 800-481-3784
fruit@fruitiongifts.com www.fruitiongifts.com
Processor of apples, oranges, cucumbers, onions, lettuce and squash
President/COO: Justin Vitrano
Vice President: Anthony Vitrano
Estimated Sales: $ 20 - 50 Million
Number Employees: 50-99
Type of Packaging: Consumer, Food Service

13514 **Tony's Fine Foods**
3575 Reed Ave
Broderick, CA 95605 916-374-4000
Fax: 916-372-0727 scott@tonysfinefoods.com
www.tonysfinefoods.com
Different kind of foods
Executive VP/CFO: Scott Berger
COO: Jerry Walsh
President: Karl Berger
Estimated Sales: $ 10-100 Million
Number Employees: 250-499
Brands:
Tony's

13515 **Tony's Ice Cream Company**
604 E Franklin Blvd
Gastonia, NC 28054 704-867-7085
www.tonysicecream.com
Processor of ice cream
President: Robert Coletta
Vice President: Louis Coletta
Manager: Cheryl Martin
Estimated Sales: $10-20 Million
Number Employees: 25
Type of Packaging: Consumer

13516 **Tony's Seafood**
5215 Plank Rd
Baton Rouge, LA 70805 225-357-9669
Fax: 225-355-5451 www.tonysseafood.com
Seafood
President: William Pizzolato
Estimated Sales: $ 20 - 50 Million
Number Employees: 100-249

13517 **Too Good Gourmet**
2380 Grant Ave
San Lorenzo, CA 94580 510-317-8150
Fax: 510-317-8755 877-850-4663
info@toogoodgourmet.com
www.toogoodgourmet.com
Gourmet cookies packed in whimsical toy boxes
Owner: Amie Watson
Marketing/Sales: Katie Bidstrup
Estimated Sales: $ 5 - 10 Million
Number Employees: 5-9
Type of Packaging: Consumer, Food Service, Private Label, Bulk

13518 **Tooele Valley Meat**
985 E Main Street
Grantsville, UT 84029-9592 435-884-3837
Fax: 435-884-6781
Processor of beef, pork, veal and lamb
President: Edward Roberts
Estimated Sales: $800,000
Number Employees: 5
Type of Packaging: Consumer, Food Service

13519 **(HQ)Tootsie Roll Industries**
7401 S Cicero Ave
Chicago, IL 60629-5885 773-838-3400
Fax: 773-838-3435 800-877-7655
www.tootsie.com
Manufacturer and exporter of confectionery products including chocolate, gum drops, chewy candies, candy bars, licorice, jelly beans, lollypops, mints, etc
Chairman/CEO: Melvin Gordon
President/COO: Ellen R Gordon
CFO: G Howard Ember Jr
VP Marketing/Sales: Thomas Corr
VP Physical Distribution: John Majors
VP Manufacturing: John Newlin Jr
Estimated Sales: $517 Million
Number Employees: 2200
Type of Packaging: Consumer, Food Service, Bulk
Brands:
ANDES
BLOW POP
BLUE RAZZ
CARMEL APPLE POPS
CELLA CHERRIES
CHARLESTON CHEW
CHARM'S
CHILD'S PLAY
CRY BABY
DUBBLE BUBBLE
FLUFFY STUFF
FROOTIES
JUNIOR MINT
MASON CROWS
MASON DOTS
NIK-L-NIP
RAZZELS
SUGAR BABY
SUGAR DADDY
TOOTSIE ROLL
TOOTSIE ROLL POPS
ZIP-A-DEE-DOO-DA POPS

13520 **Top Hat Company**
2407 Birchwood Ln
Wilmette, IL 60091 847-256-6565
Fax: 847-256-6579 info@tophatcompany.com
www.tophatcompany.com
Processor of sauces including raspberry, hot, mocha and mint fudges, butterscotch, caramel, Mayan legacy, prince of orange and Southern sin; also, double chocolate fondue and bittersweet chocolate
President: Marla Murray
Estimated Sales: Less than $1,000,000
Number Employees: 20-49
Type of Packaging: Consumer, Food Service, Private Label, Bulk
Brands:
Top Hat Dessert Sauces

13521 **(HQ)Topco**
7711 Gross Point Rd
Skokie, IL 60077-2697 847-676-3030
Fax: 847-676-4949 webmaster@topco.com
www.topco.com
Grocery, frozen, dairy, bakery, general merchandise, health & beauty care, pharmacy, branded meat, equipment and supplies, business services, world brands and diverting.
President: Steve Lowery
CEO: Steve K Lauer
Estimated Sales: $ 50 - 100 Million
Number Employees: 250-499
Type of Packaging: Consumer, Food Service, Private Label
Other Locations:
Topco
Skokie IL
Brands:
CLEAR VALUE
DINING IN
FOOD CLUB
FULL CIRCLE
PAWS
PRICE SAVER
SHUR FINE
TOP CARE
TOP CREST
VALU TIME
WORLD CLASS

13522 **Topolos at Russian River Vine**
5700 Gravenstein Hwy N
Forestville, CA 95436-0358 707-887-1575
Fax: 707-887-1399 topolos@topolos.com
http://www.russianrivervineyards.com/
Wine and gourmet foods
President: Michael Topolos
Estimated Sales: $1 Million
Number Employees: 25
Brands:
Topolos at Russian River Vine

13523 **Topor's Pickle Company**
2800 Standish St
Detroit, MI 48216-1539 313-237-0288
Fax: 313-981-4249
Pickles, dill green tomatoes, hot pickles with red peppers, Hungarian hot banana peppers
President: Larry Topor
Estimated Sales: $ 3 - 5 Million
Number Employees: 1-4

13524 **Topper Food Products**
20 Williamsburg Court
East Brunswick, NJ 08816-3251 732-238-1225
800-377-2823
Processor of sauces including marinara, Creole, pesto, salsa picante, primavera, white clam and alfredo; also, sugar-free, fat-free and low sodium varieties available
President: Lou Topper
Number Employees: 5-9
Type of Packaging: Consumer, Food Service, Private Label, Bulk
Brands:
Papa Lomagi

13525 **Topper Meat Company**
26400 State Road 80
Belle Glade, FL 33430 561-996-6541
Fax: 561-996-8021
Beef
Director: Eduardo Recio
Estimated Sales: $ 10-100 Million
Number Employees: 100-249

13526 **Topps Meat Company**
1161 E Broad St
Elizabeth, NJ 07201 908-351-0500
Fax: 908-351-0722 877-998-6777
info@toppsburger.com www.toppsmeat.com
Manufacturer of fresh and frozen hamburgers
Controller: Jay Peskin
EVP/COO: Anthony D'Urso
Quality Assurance/QC Manager: Charlie Chieng
Director Sales/Marketing: Raymond Patnaude
Marketing Coordinator: Janice Dodge
VP/National Sales Manager: Ed Reina
VP Operations: Geoffrey Livermore
Estimated Sales: $40 Million
Number Employees: 50-99

13527 **Tops Manufacturing Company**
83 Salisbury Rd
Darien, CT 06820 203-655-9367
Manufacturer and exporter of coffee and tea equipment including percolators, knobs, handles, carafes, coffee makers and filters, tea infusers, liquid coffee flavors, glass cups, instant and ground coffee dispensers, measuring spoonsetc
President: Mitch Himmel
VP: Pat Himmel
Sales Manager: Ernie Hurlbut
Estimated Sales: Less than $500,000
Number Employees: 1-4
Sq. footage: 15700
Type of Packaging: Consumer, Food Service
Brands:
Brick-Pack Clip
Fitz-All
Flav-A-Brrew
Kaf-Tan
Measure Fresh
Perma-Brew
Rapid Brew
Tops

13528 **Torani Syrups**
233 E Harris Ave
S San Francisco, CA 94080-6807 650-875-1200
Fax: 650-875-1600 800-775-1925
www.torani.com
Processor and exporter of Italian flavoring syrups and fruit bases used for sparkling sodas, expresso beverages, specialty drinks and cooking.
CEO: Melanie Dulbecco
CEO: Melanie Dulbecco
VP Marketing: Cindy Eckart
VP Sales: Matt Brandenburger
Estimated Sales: $ 50 - 100 Million
Number Employees: 50-99
Sq. footage: 62000
Type of Packaging: Consumer, Food Service
Brands:
Torani

13529 **Torke Coffee Roasting Company**
3455 Paine Ave
Sheboygan, WI 53081 920-458-4114
Fax: 920-458-0488 800-242-7671
bigbean@torkecoffee.com www.torkecoffee.com
Manufacturer of coffee
President: Ward Torke
Estimated Sales: $ 20 - 50 Million
Number Employees: 20-49
Brands:
TORKE

13530 **Torkelson Cheese Company**
9453 W Louisa Rd
Lena, IL 61048 815-369-4265
Fax: 815-369-2302 cheese@aeroinc.net
www.torkelsoncheese.com
Manufacturers Brick, Muenster, Quesadilla and Asadero cheeses.
President/Head Cheesemaker: Duane Torkelson
VP: Cheryl Torkelson
Estimated Sales: $ 10-20 Million
Number Employees: 20-49

13531 **Torn & Glasser**
1769 Glendale Blvd
Los Angeles, CA 90026-1761 323-661-2332
Fax: 213-688-0941 800-282-6887
Processor of nuts, dried fruit, seeds, granola, beans, rice, dry chili, candy, etc
Owner: Tony Tierno
VP: Greg Glasser
Purchasing Manager: Gus Gutmun
Estimated Sales: $300,000-500,000
Number Employees: 1-4
Type of Packaging: Consumer, Food Service, Private Label, Bulk

13532 **Torn Ranch**
23 Pimentel Ct # B
Novato, CA 94949-5661 415-506-3000
Fax: 415-506-3002 info@tornranch.com
www.tornranch.com
Manufacturer and purveyor of gourmet specialty foods, dried fruits, roasted nuts, snack foods and shortbreads.
President: Dean Morrow
Vice President: Sue Morrow
Quality Control: Robert Wagner
Estimated Sales: $ 5-10 Million
Number Employees: 50-99
Type of Packaging: Private Label
Brands:
Cafe Time
Gigi Baking Company
Mashuga Nuts & Cookies
Splendid Specialties Chocolate Co

13533 **Toro Brewing**
17370 Hill Rd
Morgan Hill, CA 95037-9704 408-778-2739
Beer
President: H Geno Acevedo
Estimated Sales: Below $ 5 Million
Number Employees: 1-4

13534 **Torre Products Company**
479 Washington St
New York, NY 10013 212-925-8989
Fax: 212-925-4627
Manufacturer, importer and exporter of flavoring extracts and essential oils
President: L Raho
Estimated Sales: $10-20 Million
Number Employees: 20-49
Sq. footage: 11000
Brands:
FLAMBE HOLIDAY
LA TORINESE
RUM-BA
SOFT MAC

13535 **Torrefazione Barzula & Import**
3117 Wharton Way
Mississauga, ON L4X 2B6
Canada 905-625-6082
Fax: 905-625-5741 866-358-5488
sales@barzula.com www.barzula.com
Processor, importer and exporter of coffee beans including green, espresso, Turkish and decaffeinated
President: Luigi Russignan
Treasurer: Gigliola Russignan
VP: Phil Cennova
Estimated Sales: $2.2 Million
Number Employees: 14
Number of Brands: 1
Number of Products: 12
Sq. footage: 24000
Brands:
Barzula

13536 **Torrefazione Italia**
2401 Utah Avenue South
Seattle, WA 98134 206-624-5773
Fax: 206-624-3262 800-827-2333
www.titalia.com
Gourmet/ specialty coffee
President/COO: Dick Holbrook
VP Marketing: Kim Beerli
CFO: Chris December
Founder: Umberto Bizzarri
Sales Director: Tom Danowski
Operations Manager: Jane Albright
Estimated Sales: Below $ 500,000
Number Employees: 2
Type of Packaging: Private Label
Brands:
Torrefazione Italia

13537 **Torreo Coffee Company**
4950 Rhawn St
Philadelphia, PA 19136 215-333-1105
Fax: 215-333-6615 888-286-7736
customerserv@torreo.com torreo.com

Manufacture a line of premium coffees
President: Eric Patrick
Vice President: H Patrick
Operations Manager: Howard Patrick
Estimated Sales: $500,000-$1 Million
Number Employees: 5-9
Sq. footage: 9600
Parent Co: Torreo Coffee & Tea Company
Type of Packaging: Consumer, Private Label, Bulk
Brands:
TORREO

13538 **Tostino Coffee Roasters**
4283 S Santa Rita Avenue
Tucson, AZ 85714-1641 520-294-5112
Fax: 520-294-5926 800-678-3519
info@tostino.com www.tostino.com
Specialty gourmet coffee and teas
President: Jerry Sonenblick
Co-President: Rafael Guerrero
CFO: Michael Bright
Estimated Sales: $ 20-50 Million
Number Employees: 50-99
Type of Packaging: Private Label
Brands:
Cafe Tostino

13539 **Total LubricantsKeystone Division**
5 N Stiles St
Linden, NJ 07036-4208 908-862-9300
Fax: 908-862-1647 IBU-CSR@total-us.com
http://keystonelubricants.com/keystone/index.htm
Product lines includes food machinery lubricants; air compressor fluids; metalworking lubricants; and maintenance lubricants.
Human Resources: Steve Daubert
Food Industry Sales Specialist: Jim Cancila
Food Industry Sales Specialist: Bruce Wolfe
Food Industry Sales Specialist: Rob Stevenson
International Food Industry Specialist: Christine Richard
Estimated Sales: H
Number Employees: 10,000+

13540 **Total Ultimate Foods**
683 Manor Park Dr
Columbus, OH 43228-9369 614-870-0732
Fax: 614-870-1687 800-333-0732
sales@tuf-inc.com www.tufinc.com
Dehydrated foods
Manager: Mark Wills
CFO: Terry Weisenstein
Vice President: Terry Weisenstein
R & D: Tim Tomesek
Quality Control: Brian Wilke
Marketing/Sales Manager: Walter Mcnabb
VP Manufacturing: Bill Stone
Estimated Sales: $ 10-20 Million
Number Employees: 20-49
Type of Packaging: Food Service, Private Label
Brands:
Tuf

13541 **Totally Chocolate**
2025 Sweet Rd
Blaine, WA 98230 360-332-3900
Fax: 360-332-1802 800-255-5506
sales@totallychocolate.com
www.totallychocolate.com
Chocolate manufacturing
Owner: Jeff Robinson
VP Sales: Matt Roth
Plant Manager: Steve Hocker
Purchasing Manager: Christine Danner
Estimated Sales: $ 5-10 Millions
Number Employees: 50-99
Type of Packaging: Private Label
Brands:
Totally Chocolate

13542 **Totino's**
P.O. Box 9452
Minneapolis, MN 55440 612-492-7018
Fax: 763-764-8330 800-248-7310
http://www.totinos.com/
General grocery
Estimated Sales: Under $500,000
Number Employees: 10-19

13543 **Toucan Chocolates**
RR 128
Box 72
Waban, MA 02468 617-964-8696
Fax: 800-816-8696
Chocolate
President: Michael Goldman

13544 **Toucan Enterprises**
PO Box 1639
Marrero, LA 70073-1639 504-736-9289
Fax: 504-736-9289 800-736-9289
Processor and exporter of powdered juice and cocktail mixes
President: David Ervin
Vice President: Kerry Bretz
Plant Manager: Troy Townsend
Number Employees: 1-4
Sq. footage: 6000
Type of Packaging: Consumer, Food Service, Private Label, Bulk
Brands:
Daiquiri Factory
Ice Splasher
Toucan

13545 **Touche Bakery**
384-B Neptune Cres
London, ON N6M 1A1
Canada 518-455-0044
Fax: 519-455-5843 aswartz@touchebakery.com
www.touchebakery.com
Biscotti, cookies, meringues that are all nautral and nut free
President: Peter Cuddy
CEO: Allan Swartz
Finance/Administration Manager: Pat Gauthier
Sq. footage: 16000
Type of Packaging: Consumer, Food Service, Private Label

13546 **Touche Bakery**
384b Neptune Cr
London, ON N6M 1A1
Canada 519-455-0044
Fax: 519-455-5843 aswartz@touchebakery.com
www.touchebakery.com
biscotti, meringues, cookies, brownies, frozen cookie dough, muffin and brownie batter
President/CEO: Allan Swartz
Estimated Sales: $1.2 Million
Number Employees: 20

13547 **Toufayan Bakeries**
3826 Bryn Mawr St
Orlando, FL 32808 407-295-2257
Fax: 407-578-2920 sales@toufayan.com
www.toufayan.com
Processor of pita bread and bread sticks, flatbreads, bagels, wraps and snack food components.
President: Harry Toufayan
VP Sales: Karen Toufayan
Estimated Sales: $100+ Million
Number Employees: 100-249
Sq. footage: 3500
Parent Co: Toufayan Bakeries
Type of Packaging: Consumer, Food Service

13548 **Toufayan Bakeries**
175 Railroad Ave
Ridgefield, NJ 7657 201-941-2000
Fax: 201-861-0392 msteve@toufayan.com
www.toufayan.com
Manufacturer of pita bread and bread sticks.
President: Harry Toufayan
Estimated Sales: $ 3 - 5 Million
Number Employees: 50-99
Type of Packaging: Consumer, Food Service

13549 **Tova Industries**
2902 Blankenbaker Rd
Louisville, KY 40299 502-267-7333
Fax: 502-267-7119 888-532-8682
corporate@tovaindustries.com
www.tovaindustries.com
Dry mix food products, spices, table and beverage syrups
President: Zack Melzer
Controller: Bill Ruf
Sr VP: Yael Melzer
Sales Contract Manager: Mike Northway
Distribution Manager: James Dupin
Purchasing Manager: Shannon Griffiths
Estimated Sales: $100+ Million
Number Employees: 70
Number of Products: 1000
Type of Packaging: Consumer, Food Service, Private Label, Bulk
Other Locations:
New Horizon Foods
Union City CA
Brands:
HERITAGE - THE ESSENCE OF TRADITION
LIFESOURCE FOODS
STONEGROUND MILLS
SUPERIOR SPICES
SUPERIOR SYRUPS
TOVA

13550 **Town & Country Foods**
72 Daggett Hill Rd
Greene, ME 04236 207-946-5489
Fax: 207-946-7370 www.tandcfoods.com
Meats and wholesale food distributor.
Owner: Janet Lapin
Estimated Sales: $ 10 - 20 Million
Number Employees: 20-49

13551 **Townsend Farms**
23400 NE Townsend Way
Fairview, OR 97024 503-666-1780
Fax: 503-618-8257 jeff@townfend.com
www.townsendfarms.com
Fresh and frozen blueberries, blackberries and strawberries; fresh black raspberries, mixed fruit, manoes, boysenberries, cherries, marionberries, red raspberries and pineapple; fresh raspberries
President/Sales Executive: Mike Townsend
CEO: Jeff Townsend
CFO: Chris Valenti
Plant Manager: Reyes Pena
Purchasing: Mark Davis
Estimated Sales: $ 10 - 20 Million
Number Employees: 230
Sq. footage: 2000
Type of Packaging: Consumer, Food Service, Private Label, Bulk

13552 **Townsend-Piller Packing**
719 19 1/4 Avenue
Cumberland, WI 54829 715-822-4910
President: Robert Townsend

13553 **Toxic Tommy's Beef Jerky & Spices**
PO Box 432
Wadsworth, OH 44282-0432 330-807-7278
Fax: 305-723-7686 866-448-6942
toxictommy@yahoo.com www.toxictommy.com
Manufacturer of beef jerky and jerky spices
President: Thomas Stabosz
Production: Joe Muscarella
Number Employees: 1-4
Number of Brands: 1
Number of Products: 9
Parent Co: TFS
Type of Packaging: Consumer, Food Service, Private Label, Bulk
Brands:
Gold Rush
Grandpa Vals
Toxic Tommy

13554 **Trace Mineral Research**
P.O.Box 429
Roy, UT 84067-0429 801-731-6051
Fax: 801-731-3702 800-624-7145
infor@traceminerals.com
www.traceminerals.com
Processor of dietary supplements
President: Matt Kilts
Sales Director: Ryan Fisher
Estimated Sales: $4972329
Number Employees: 20-49
Number of Products: 100
Sq. footage: 13000
Type of Packaging: Consumer, Food Service, Private Label, Bulk

13555 **Tracy Luckey Pecans**
110 N Hicks St
PO Box 880
Harlem, GA 30814 706-556-6216
Fax: 706-556-6210 800-476-4796
ruthtracy@tracy-luckey.com
www.tracy-luckey.com

Processor of shelled pecans and pecan products
President: Francis Tracy
VP/CEO: Ruth Tracy
Executive VP: Seaborn Dell
VP Marketing/Sales: Ruth Tracy
Operations/Production/Purchasing: Seaborn Dell
Plant Manager: Homer Gay
Estimated Sales: $120,000
Number Employees: 50-99
Sq. footage: 80000
Type of Packaging: Bulk
Brands:
SUNBLET

13556 **Trade Farm**
PO Box 43369
Oakland, CA 94624-0369 510-836-2938
Fax: 510-836-1481 tradefarm@prodigy.net
Frozen, air dehydrated and freeze dried supplier of Chinese vegetables

13557 **Trade Marcs Group**
55 Nassau Ave
Brooklyn, NY 11222-3143 718-387-9696
Fax: 718-782-2471
General grocery
Manager: Andi Billow
Estimated Sales: Less than $500,000
Number Employees: 1-4

13558 **Trade Winds Pizza**
1085 Parkview Road
Green Bay, WI 54304-5616 920-336-7810
Fax: 920-336-2942
Pizzas
Director Operations: Jim Peppich

13559 **Trader Joe's Company**
800 S Shamrock Ave
Monrovia, CA 91016 626-599-3700
Fax: 626-301-4441 www.traderjoes.com
Suppliers of more than 2000 unique grocery and gourmet items such as bakery, cheeses, chips, snacks, coffee, fat free or low fat favorites, for your home, fresh entrees, fresh produce, frozen entrees, great beers, meatless choices, nutand trail mixes, organic foods, personal use, pet food, seafod, vitamins, and wines.
President: Robin Guentert
CFO: Bryan Palbaum
Manager: Chuck Yarez
Quality Control: Kathy Cipooa
Manager Media Relations: Diane O'Connor
Estimated Sales: $ 1 Billion
Number Employees: 5-9
Brands:
Baker Josef
Charles Shaw
Trader Joe's
Trader Ming

13560 **Trader Vic's Food Products**
9 Anchor Dr
Emeryville, CA 94608 510-653-3400
Fax: 510-653-9384 877-762-4824
info@tradervics.com tradervics.com
Processor and exporter of nonalcoholic cocktail mixes, syrups, dry spices, sauces and salad dressings
President: Hans Richter
CEO: Hans Richter
VP: Peter Seely
Estimated Sales: $540000
Number Employees: 6
Type of Packaging: Consumer
Brands:
Trader Vic's

13561 **Tradeshare Corporation**
207 Flushing Avenue
Brooklyn, NY 11205 718-237-2295
Food preparation and general grocery
President: Robert Krasnor
Estimated Sales: $ 2.5-5 Million
Number Employees: 10-19

13562 **Tradewinds Coffee Company**
5500 Atlantic Springs Rd Ste 106
Raleigh, NC 27616 919-878-1111
Fax: 919-878-0041 800-457-0406
customerservice@tradwindscoffee.com
www.tradewindscoffee.com
Coffee and coffee flavored candy
President: Art Watkins
Co-Owner: Elaine Watkins
Estimated Sales: Below $ 5 Million
Number Employees: 10-19
Brands:
Trade Winds Coffee

13563 **Tradewinds International**
PO Box 8
Ellendale, TN 38029-0008 901-385-8884
800-385-8884
Processor and exporter of wild rice
President: John Augustine
Operations Manager: Gwen Augustine
Number Employees: 20-49
Sq. footage: 12000
Type of Packaging: Food Service, Private Label, Bulk

13564 **Tradewinds-Tea Company**
300 Industry Drive
Carlisle, OH 45005 513-357-5200
Fax: 513-357-5217 855-DRI-K TW
customerservice@tradewinds-tea.com
www.tradewinds-tea.com
Brewed teas in nine flavors
President: Kenneth Lichtendahl
Marketing Director: Christy Lichtendahl
Estimated Sales: $ 5-10 Million
Number Employees: 5-9
Brands:
Concord Grape
Granny Smith Apple
Ice Tea
Lemon Tea

13565 **Traditional Baking**
2575 S Willow Ave
Bloomington, CA 92316 909-877-8471
Fax: 909-877-6728
Baked goods
Estimated Sales: $ 20 - 50 Million
Number Employees: 50-99

13566 **Traditional Medicinals**
4515 Ross Rd
Sebastopol, CA 95472 707-823-8911
Fax: 707-823-1599 800-543-4372
www.traditionalmedicinals.com
Processor of herb teas
President: Drake Sadler
President: Lynda Sadler
Sales Coordinator: Brenda Hodges
Estimated Sales: $3200000
Number Employees: 5
Brands:
Traditional Med Ginger Energy
Traditional Med Gypsy Cold Cure
Traditional Med Organics

13567 **Trafalgar Brewing Company**
1156 Speers Road
Oakville, ON L6L 2X4
Canada 905-337-0133
Fax: 905-845-2246 info@alesandmeads.com
www.alesandmeads.com
Processor of beer, ale, lager and stout
President: Mike Arnold
Estimated Sales: A
Number Employees: 1-4
Type of Packaging: Consumer, Food Service
Brands:
Celtic
Elora ESB
Elora Grand Lager
Elora Irish Ale
Harbour Gold
Paddy's Irish Red
Port Side Amber
Trafalgar

13568 **Trail's Best Snacks**
930 S. White Station Rd
Memphis, TN 38017 605-335-8780
Fax: 605-335-8682 800-852-1863
info@trailsbest.com www.trailsbest.com
Largest meat snack manufacturer in the United States
Marketing Coordinator: Roxanne Van Loon
Estimated Sales: $ 10 - 20 Million
Number Employees: 5-9
Parent Co: Sara Lee Foods
Type of Packaging: Consumer, Bulk
Brands:
HAPPY TRAILS MEAT SNACK STICKS
TEAM REALTREE
TRAIL'S BEST SNACKS

13569 **Trailblazer Food Products**
17900 NE San Rafael St
Portland, OR 97230-5930 503-666-5800
Fax: 503-666-6800 800-777-7179
cindy@tbfoods.com www.tbfoods.com
Preserves, fruit products, quality foods, punches, marinades and syrups
President: Robert Miller
Marketing Director: Mike MIller
Founder: Gary Walls
Estimated Sales: $ 20-50 Million
Number Employees: 20-49
Brands:
Jake's Restaurant
Portland
Trailblazer

13570 **Trans Pecos Foods**
112 E Pecan St Ste 800
San Antonio, TX 78205 210-228-0896
Fax: 210-228-0781 pjk@texas.net
www.transpecosfoods.com
Manufacturer, importer and exporter of frozen breaded vegetables
President: Patrick J Kennedy
Plant Manager: Bruce Salcido
Estimated Sales: $3900000
Number Employees: 5-9
Parent Co: Anchor Food Products
Type of Packaging: Consumer, Food Service, Private Label, Bulk

13571 **Trans-Ocean Products**
10 Charles Street
Needham Heights, MA 02494-2906 508-626-0922
Fax: 508-626-2087
Seafood
Sales Manager: Alan Lipocky

13572 **Trans-Ocean Products**
350 W Orchard Dr
Bellingham, WA 98225 360-671-6886
Fax: 360-671-0354 888-215-4815
info@trans-ocean.com www.trans-ocean.com
Processor of imitation crab, lobster and salmon meat
President: Rick Dutton
Executive VP: H Okazaki
VP Sales/Marketing: L Shaheen
Estimated Sales: $ 100-500 Million
Number Employees: 100-249
Sq. footage: 120000
Parent Co: Maruha Corporation
Type of Packaging: Consumer, Food Service, Private Label, Bulk
Other Locations:
Trans-Ocean Products
Salem OR
Brands:
Classic
Pouch Pak
Transocean

13573 **Trans-Packers Services Corporation**
419 Vandervoort Ave
Brooklyn, NY 11222 718-963-0900
Fax: 718-486-6344 877-787-8837
sales@transpackers.com www.transpackers.com
Contract packager of food and nonfood products including powders, granules, solids and liquids in glass jars and bottles, etc
President: Selma Weiss
Vice President: Daniel Weiss
Plant Manager: Nester Serrano
Estimated Sales: $4900000
Number Employees: 100-249
Sq. footage: 100000
Type of Packaging: Consumer, Food Service

13574 **Transa**
704 Florsheim Dr
Libertyville, IL 60048-5002 847-281-9582
Fax: 847-816-6238 sales@hbroch.com
www.hbroch.com
Tomatoes and tomato powder, spices and vegetables
Manager: Donald Swanson
Sales Manager: James Kuzma
Estimated Sales: $ 5 - 10 Million
Number Employees: 5-9

13575 Transamerica Wine Corporation
Brooklyn Navy Yard
Brooklyn, NY 11201 718-875-4017
Fax: 718-625-1180
Wines
Manager: Yeshiah Schwartz
Estimated Sales: $ 5-10 Million
Number Employees: 10-19

13576 Trappe Packing Corporation
3965 Ocean Gtwy
Trappe, MD 21673 410-476-3185
Fax: 410-476-3527 info@parisfoods.com
www.parisfoods.com
Packer and exporter of frozen vegetables including corn, peas, carrots, mixed, succotash, broccoli, cauliflower, potato products, peppers, onions, blends, etc.; also, beans including green, waxed, baby lima and fava
President: Richard Marks
VP: C Johnson
Marketing: Julie Creese
Plant Manager: Anthony Dixon
Estimated Sales: $ 50 - 100 Million
Number Employees: 50-99
Type of Packaging: Food Service, Private Label, Bulk
Brands:
Fine Line
Topmark

13577 Trappey's Fine Foods
PO Box 13610
New Iberia, LA 70562-3610 337-365-8281
Fax: 337-369-7342 www.bgfoods.com
Okra, sauces and ethnic food
CEO: Dave Wenner
CFO: Robert Cantwell
Estimated Sales: $ 10-20 Million
Number Employees: 50-100
Parent Co: B&G Foods
Brands:
Trappey's

13578 Trappist Preserves
540 East 105th Street #115
Cleveland, OH 44108
Fax: 216-249-3387 800-472-0425
www.monasterygreetings.com
Manufacturer of jellies, jams and marmalades including apricot, peach, strawberry, grape, etc
President: Damian Carr
Purchasing Manager: Henry Scarborough
Estimated Sales: $16 Million
Number Employees: 95
Type of Packaging: Consumer
Brands:
TRAPPIST

13579 Trappistine Quality Candy
300 Arnold Street
Wrentham, MA 02093-1700 508-528-1282
Fax: 21- 92- 133 86- 5-9 89
info@trappistinecandy.com
www.trappistinecandy.com
Candy
Number Employees: 20-49

13580 Travel Chocolate
PO BOX 4668 PMB59369
New York, NY 10163-4668 718-841-7030
Fax: 718-841-7030 info@travelchocolate.com
www.travelchocolate.com
organice fair-trade chocolate bars

13581 Traverse Bay Confections
21616 87th Ave SE
Woodinville, WA 98072-8017
Fax: 203-722-0196
sales@traversebayconfections.com
www.traversebayconfections.com
Gourmet chocolates, cookies and candies.
Owner: Richard Anderson
Estimated Sales: $ 5 - 10 Million
Number Employees: 5-9

13582 (HQ)Travis Meats
7210 Clinton Hwy
Powell, TN 37849 865-938-9051
Fax: 865-938-9211 800-247-7606
wdaletravis@att.net www.travismeats.com
Processor of frozen veal and pork; also, beef including barbecued, rolls and hamburger patties
President: W Travis
Controller: Brent Atchley
VP Production: Dale Travis
Estimated Sales: $ 20 - 50 Million
Number Employees: 100-249
Sq. footage: 110000
Type of Packaging: Consumer, Food Service
Other Locations:
Travis Meats
Knoxville TN

13583 Treasure Foods
2500 S 2300 W # 11
West Valley, UT 84119-7676 801-974-0911
Fax: 801-975-0553 treasurefoods@hotmail.com
www.honeybutter4u.com
Processor and exporter of whipped honey butter, flavored fruit honey, scones; wholesaler/distributor of frozen foods and general line items; serving the food service market
Owner: Amin Motilla
CFO: Zarina Motiwala
Vice President: Mohamed Motiwala
Marketing Director: Amin Motiwala
Public Relations: Amin Motiwala
Production Manager: Fawad Motiwala
Plant Manager: Fawad Motiwala
Purchasing Manager: Amin Motiwala
Estimated Sales: $450,000
Number Employees: 5
Number of Brands: 3
Number of Products: 3
Sq. footage: 3600
Parent Co: Algilani Food Import & Export
Type of Packaging: Food Service, Private Label, Bulk
Other Locations:
Treasure Foods
Salt Lake City UT
Brands:
HONEY BUTTER TOPPING
RASPBERRY HONEY BUTTER TOPPING
SCONES

13584 Treat Ice Cream Company
11 S 19th St
San Jose, CA 95116 408-292-9321
Fax: 408-298-5859 treaticecream@aol.com
www.treaticecream.com
Processor of gourmet ice cream
Owner: Alfred Mauseth
Vice President: Bob Mauseth
Estimated Sales: $ 3 - 5 Million
Number Employees: 5-9
Sq. footage: 4000
Type of Packaging: Consumer, Private Label, Bulk
Brands:
Treat

13585 Treats Island Fisheries
PO Box 21
Scaly Mountain, NC 28775-0021 207-733-4580
Fax: 207-733-4880
Seafood
President: James English

13586 Treatt USA
4900 Lakeland Commerce Pkwy
Lakeland, FL 33805 863-668-9500
Fax: 863-668-3388 800-866-7704
enquiries@treattusa.com www.treattusa.com
Processor of food additives including essential oils and aromatic chemicals
Sales: Steve Shelton
VP Sales: Nancy Poulos
Estimated Sales: $ 1 - 3 Million
Number Employees: 50-99
Parent Co: R.C. Treatt & Company
Type of Packaging: Bulk
Brands:
Citreatt
Treattarome

13587 Trebon European Specialties
210 Green St
South Hackensack, NJ 7606 201-343-5161
Fax: 201-343-5102 800-899-4332
info@fratelliberettausa.com
www.fratelliberettausa.com
Italian and Spanish meat specialties
President: Lorenzo Beretta
Estimated Sales: $ 5-10 Million
Number Employees: 20-49

13588 Tree Ripe Products
9 Great Meadow Ln # A
East Hanover, NJ 07936-1703 973-463-0777
800-873-3747
Processor and exporter of nonalcoholic cocktail mixes
President: Joel Fishman
Estimated Sales: $3000000
Number Employees: 1-4
Sq. footage: 10000
Type of Packaging: Consumer, Food Service
Brands:
Frothee Creamy Head
Lem-N-Joy
Tree-Ripe

13589 Tree Tavern Products
PO Box 2545
Paterson, NJ 07509-2545 973-279-1617
Fast food and franchises
President: Louis Francia
Estimated Sales: $ 5-10 Million appx.
Number Employees: 20

13590 (HQ)Tree Top
P.O.Box 532
Selah, WA 98942 509-698-1416
Fax: 509-698-1421 800-367-6571
faq@treetop.com www.treetop.com
Fruit juices and drinks, applesauce and fruit snacks
President/CEO: Thomas Stokes
VP Finance/CFO: John Wells
Director Quality/Technical Services: Scott Summers
VP Sales: Greg Bainter
VP Public Relations: Julia Stewart Daly
Estimated Sales: $295.4 Million
Number Employees: 1,300
Type of Packaging: Food Service, Private Label, Bulk
Other Locations:
Tree Top
Milton-Freewater OR
Brands:
FIBER RICH
ROVAN
SENECA GRANNY SMITH CONCENTRATE
SENECA JUICES
SENECA ORANGE PLUS BEVERAGE
SENECA R.S.P. TART CHERRY CONCENTRA
TREE TOP
TREE TOP APPLE JUICE
TREE TOP JUICE FIZZ
TREE TOP ORCHARD BLENDS
TREE TOP THREE APPLE BLEND

13591 Tree Top
P.O.Box 532
Selah, WA 98942 509-698-1416
Fax: 509-698-1421 800-542-4055
faq@treetop.com www.treetop.com
Produces grape juice and concentrate, apple juice, apple sauce, apple concentrate and blended juices
CEO: Tom Stokes
Chairman: Dick Olsen
Corporate Communications Manager: Laura Dovey
VP Sales/Marketing: Dave Watkins
Estimated Sales: $ 50-100 Million
Number Employees: 1,000-4,999
Parent Co: Tree Top
Type of Packaging: Consumer, Food Service, Private Label, Bulk
Brands:
Tree Top

13592 Tree of Life
P.O.Box 9000
St Augustine, FL 32085 904-940-2100
Fax: 904-940-2553 Mailbox@TreeofLife.com
www.treeoflife.com
Manufacturer and exporter of natural products including date sweetened chocolates and carob, honey graham and cheddar crackers, gingersnaps, hummus dip, nutritional drinks, soy cheeses, gluten and lactose free products
President: G Palermo
CFO: Belinda Schneader
CEO: Richard Lane
Marketing Director: Karen Waeyenberghe
Estimated Sales: Less than $500,000
Number Employees: 5,000-9,999
Type of Packaging: Consumer, Food Service, Private Label, Bulk

Other Locations:
Elkton FL
Ft Lauderdale FL
Kennesaw GA
North Bergen NJ
Albany NY
Bloomington IN
Milwaukee WI
Minneapolis MN
Dallas TX
Cleburne TX
Los Angeles CA
Clackamas OR
Mississauga, Ontario
Brands:
ANNIE'S HOMEGROWN
BLUE DIAMOND
HAIN PURE
HORIZON ORGANIC
KRAFT FOODS
MANISCHEWITZ
MCCORMICK
NATURADE
NESTLE'
SEEDS OF CHANGE
WORLD FINER FOODS

13593 **Tree of Life Albany**
4294 Albany St
Albany, NY 12205-4621 518-456-1888
800-691-1880
CustSvcNE@TreeofLife.com
www.treeoflife.com
Wholesale distributor of natural, organic, specialty, ethnic and gourmet food products.
Chairman/President/CEO: Richard Thorne
SVP/Finance/Chief Financial Officer: Tom Wissbaum
COO: Dayne Ryan
SVP/Sales: George Schuetz
Parent Co: Tree of Life
Brands:
ANNIE'S HOMEGROWN
BLUE DIAMOND
HAIN PURE FOODS
HORIZON ORGANIC
KRAFT FOODS
MANISCHEWITZ
MCCORMICK
NATURADE
NESTLE
SEEDS OF CHANGE
WORLD FINER FOODS

13594 **Tree of Life Atlanta**
2700 Barrett Lakes Blvd NW
Kennesaw, GA 30144-4813 770-218-6020
Fax: 770-218-6030 800-798-5986
CustSvcNE@TreeofLife.com www.treelife.com
Wholesale distributor of natural, organic, specialty, ethnic and gourmet food products.
Chairman/President/CEO: Richard Thorne
SVP/Finance/Chief Financial Officer: Tom Wissbaum
COO: Stacy Hodoh
SVP/Sales: George Schuetz
Parent Co: Tree of Life
Brands:
ANNIE'S HOMEGROWN
BLUE DIAMOND
HAIN PURE FOODS
HORIZON ORGANIC
KRAFT FOODS
MANISCHEWITZ
MCCORMICK
NATURADE
NESTLE
SEEDS OF CHANGE
WORLD FINER FOODS

13595 **Tree of Life Canada East**
6030 Freemont Blvd
Mississauga, ON L5R 3X4
Canada 905-507-6161
800-263-7054
CustSvcNE@TreeofLife.com
www.treeoflife.com
Wholesale distributor of natural, organic, specialty, ethnic and gourmet food products.
Chairman/President/CEO: Richard Thorne
SVP/Finance/Chief Financial Officer: Tom Wissbaum
SVP/Sales: George Schuetz
Parent Co: Tree of Life
Brands:
ANNIE'S HOMEGROWN
BLUE DIAMOND
HAIN PURE FOODS
HORIZON ORGANIC
KRAFT FOODS
MANISCHEWITZ
MCCORMICK
NATURADE
NESTLE
SEEDS OF CHANGE
WORLD FINER FOODS

13596 **Tree of Life Canada West**
91 Glacier Street
Coquitlam, BC V3K 5Z1
Canada 604-941-8502
800-661-9655
CustSvcNE@TreeofLife.com
www.treeoflife.com
Wholesale distributor of natural, organic, specialty, ethnic and gourmet food products.
Chairman/President/CEO: Richard Thorne
SVP/Finance/Chief Financial Officer: Tom Wissbaum
SVP/Sales: George Schuetz
Parent Co: Tree of Life
Brands:
ANNIE'S HOMEGROWN
BLUE DIAMOND
HAIN PURE FOODS
HORIZON ORGANIC
KRAFT FOODS
MANISCHEWTIZ
MCCORMICK
NATURADE
NESTLE
SEEDS OF CHANGE
WORLD FINER FOODS

13597 **Tree of Life Canada West**
2600 61st Avenue SE
Calgary, AB T2C 4V2
Canada 403-279-8988
800-665-1298
CustSvcNE@TreeofLife.com
www.treeoflife.com
Wholesale distributor of natural, organic, specialty, ethnic and gourmet food products.
Chairman/President/CEO: Richard Thorne
SVP/Finance/Chief Financial Officer: Tom Wissbaum
SVP/Sales: George Schuetz
Parent Co: Tree of Life
Brands:
ANNIE'S HOMEGROWN
BLUE DIAMOND
HAIN PURE FOODS
HORIZON ORGANIC
KRAFT FOODS
MANISCHEWITZ
MCCORMICK
NATURADE
NESTLE
SEEDS OF CHANGE
WORLD FINER FOODS

13598 **Tree of Life Cleburne**
105 Bluebonnet
Cleburne, TX 76031-8956 817-641-8733
Fax: 817-556-4976 800-800-2155
CustSvcNE@TreeofLife.com
www.treeoflife.com
Wholesale distributor of natural, organic, specialty, ethnic and gourmet food products.
Manager: Clint Wheeler
SVP/Finance/Chief Financial Officer: Tom Wissbaum
SVP/Sales: George Schuetz
Parent Co: Tree of Life
Brands:
ANNIE'S HOMEGROWN
BLUE DIAMOND
HAIN PURE FOODS
HORIZON ORGANIC
KRAFT FOODS
MANISCHEWITZ
MCCORMICK
NATURADE
NESTLE
SEEDS OF CHANGE
WORLD FINER FOODS

13599 **Tree of Life Elkton**
4055 Deerpark Blvd
Elkton, FL 32033-2070 904-824-8181
Fax: 904-825-2012 800-223-2910
CustSvcNE@TreeofLife.com
www.treeoflife.com
Wholesale distributor of natural, organic, specialty, ethnic and gourmet food products.
President: Mike Novak
SVP/Finance/Chief Financial Officer: Tom Wissbaum
SVP/Sales: George Schuetz
Parent Co: Tree of Life
Brands:
ANNIE'S HOMEGROWN
BLUE DIAMOND
HAIN PURE FOODS
HORIZON ORGANIC
KRAFT FOODS
MANISCHEWITZ
MCCORMICK
NATURADE
NESTLE
SEEDS OF CHANGE
WORLD FINER FOODS

13600 **Tree of Life Ft Lauderdale**
405 Golfway West Drive
St. Augustine, FL 32095 90- 94- 210
Fax: 904-940-2264 800-260-2424
Mailbox@TreeofLife.com www.treeoflife.com
Wholesale distributor of natural, organic, specialty, ethnic and gourmet food products.
President: Brandon Barnholt
SVP/Finance/Chief Financial Officer: Tom Wissbaum
SVP/Sales: George Schuetz
Parent Co: Tree of Life
Brands:
ANNIE'S HOMEGROWN
BLUE DIAMOND
HAIN PURE FOODS
HORIZON ORGANIC
KRAFT FOODS
MANISCHEWITZ
MCCORMICK
NATURADE
NESTLE
SEEDS OF CHANGE
WORLD FINER FOODS

13601 **Tree of Life Los Angeles**
5560 E Slauson Ave
Commerce, CA 90040-2921 323-722-2100
Fax: 323-890-3870 800-899-4217
CustSvcNE@TreeofLife.com www.a1online.com
Wholesale distributor of natural, organic, specialty, ethnic and gourmet food products.
Chairman/President/CEO: Richard Thorne
SVP/Finance/Chief Financial Officer: Tom Wissbaum
COO: Stacey Hodoh
SVP/Sales: George Schuetz
Parent Co: Tree of Life
Brands:
ANNIE'S HOMEGROWN
BLUE DIAMOND
HAIN PURE FOODS
HORIZON ORGANIC
KRAFT FOODS
MANISCHEWITZ
MCCORMICK
NATURADE
NESTLE
SEEDS OF CHANGE
WORLD FINER FODS

13602 **Tree of Life Milwaukee**
900 N Schmidt Rd
Romeoville, IL 60446-4056
Fax: 414-365-7049 800-883-1622
CustSvcNE@TreeofLife.com
www.treeoflife.com
Wholesale distributor of natural, organic, specialty, ethnic and gourmet food products.
Chairman/President/CEO: Richard Thorne
SVP/Finance/Chief Financial Officer: Tom Wissbaum
SVP/Sales: George Schuetz
Parent Co: Tree of Life
Brands:
ANNIE'S HOMEGROWN
BLUE DIAMOND
HAIN PURE FOODS

HORIZON ORGANIC
KRAFT FOODS
MANISCHEWITZ
MCCORMICK
NATURADE
NESTLE
SEEDS OF CHANGE
WORLD FINER FOODS

13603 **Tree of Life Minneapolis**
860 Vandalia St
St Paul, MN 55114-1305 612-752-6300
800-726-7205
CustSvcNE@TreeofLife.com
www.treeoflife.com
Wholesale distributor of natural, organic, specialty, ethnic and gourmet food products.
Manager: Jim Schorzmann
SVP/Finance/Chief Financial Officer: Tom Wissbaum
SVP/Sales: George Schuetz
Parent Co: Tree of Life
Brands:
ANNIE'S HOMEGROWN
BLUE DIAMOND
HAIN PURE FOODS
HORIZON ORGANIC
KRAFT FOODS
MANISCHEWITZ
MCCORMICK
NATURADE
NESTLE
SEEDS OF CHANGE
WORLD FINER FOODS

13604 **Tree of Life North Bergen**
P.O.Box 852
North Bergen, NJ 07047-0852 201-662-7200
Fax: 201-854-8353 800-735-5175
CustSvcNE@TreeofLife.com
www.treeoflife.com
Wholesale distributor of natural, organic, specialty, ethnic, and gourmet food products.
President: Chuck Ramsbacher
Plant Manager: Frank Powers
Estimated Sales: $ 20-50 Million
Number Employees: 50-99
Parent Co: Tree of Life
Brands:
ANNIE'S HOMEGROWN
BLUE DIAMOND
Bella Good
HAIN PURE FOODS
HORIZON ORGANIC
KRAFT FOODS
MANISCHEWITZ
MCCORMICK
NATURADE
NESTLE
SEEDS OF CHANGE
WORLD FINER FOODS

13605 **Tree of Life Portland**
12601 SE Highway 212
Clackamas, OR 97015-9036 503-655-1177
Fax: 503-650-5526 800-437-7297
CustSvcNE@TreeofLife.com
www.treeoflife.com
Wholesale distributor of natural, organic, specialty, ethnic and gourmet food products.
Chairman/President/CEO: Richard Thorne
SVP/Finance/Chief Financial Officer: Tom Wissbaum
SVP/Sales: George Schuetz
Plant Manager: Bryan Singleton
Parent Co: Tree of Life
Brands:
ANNIE'S HOMEGROWN
BLUE DIAMOND
HAIN PURE FOODS
HORIZON ORGANIC
KRAFT FOODS
MANISCHEWITZ
MCCORMICK
NATURADE
NESTLE
SEEDS OF CHANGE
WORLD FINER FOODS

13606 **Tree of Life Southwest-West Region**
5101 Highland Place Dr
Dallas, TX 75236-1449 972-298-2957
Fax: 972-708-5549 800-869-1650
CustSvcNE@TreeofLife.com
www.treeoflife.com
Wholesale distributor of natural, organic, specialty, ethnic and gourmet food products.
President: Brian Evers
SVP/Finance/Chief Financial Officer: Tom Wissbaum
SVP/Sales: George Schuetz
Parent Co: Tree of Life
Brands:
ANNIE'S HOMEGROWN
BLUE DIAMOND
HAIN PURE FOODS
HORIZON ORGANIC
KRAFT FOODS
MANISCHEWITZ
MCCORMICK
NATURADE
NESTLE
SEEDS OF CHANGE
WORLD FINER FOODS

13607 **Treehouse Farms**
6914 Road 160
Earlimart, CA 93219 559-757-5020
Fax: 559-757-0510
Processor and exporter of almonds including natural, blanched, sliced, roasted, diced and slivered
President: David Fitzgerald
Sales Manager: Carol Coffey
Number Employees: 250-499
Sq. footage: 200000
Parent Co: Yorkshire Foods
Type of Packaging: Private Label, Bulk
Brands:
Treehouse Farms

13608 **Treesweet Products**
16825 Northchase Drive
Suite 1600
Houston, TX 77060-6099 281-876-3759
Fax: 281-876-2643
Orange juice and products
President: Jeffrey Rosenberg
Estimated Sales: $500,000-$1 Million
Number Employees: 5-9
Brands:
Awake
Orange Plus
Treesweet Products

13609 **Trefethen Vineyards**
1160 Oak Knoll Ave
Napa, CA 94558 707-255-7700
Fax: 707-255-0793 800-556-4847
winery@trefethen.com www.trefethen.com
Producer and exporter of wine
President: John Trefethen
VP Finance: Gerald Bush
VP: David C Whitehouse Jr
Marketing: Terry Hall
Sales Director: Betty Calvin
Public Relations: Terry Hall
Production: Richard De Garmo
Estimated Sales: $5 Million
Number Employees: 50
Sq. footage: 4000
Brands:
TREFETHEN VINEYARDS

13610 **Trega Foods**
105 E 3rd Ave
Weyauwega, WI 54983 920-867-2137
Fax: 920-867-2249 doug@tregafoods.com
www.tregafoods.com
Manufacturer of cheese such as cheddar, feta, mozzarella, mozzarella sticks, provolone and dairy ingredients
President: Doug Simon
VP: Richard Wagner
Estimated Sales: $ 5 - 10 Million
Number Employees: 5-9
Type of Packaging: Consumer, Food Service
Other Locations:
Trega Foods Processing Plant
Little Chute WI
Trega Foods Processing Plant
Luxemburg WI
Brands:
TREGA

13611 **Treier Popcorn Farms**
16793 County Line Rd
Bloomdale, OH 44817 419-454-2811
Fax: 419-454-3983 ptreier@wcnet.org
Manufacturer of popcorn including bagged, natural, buttered and microwaveable; wholesaler/distributor of commercial popcorn poppers and other concession supply equipment; serving the food service market
President: Don Treier
Secretary/Treasurer: Peggy Treier
Estimated Sales: $500,000-$1 Million
Number Employees: 15
Number of Brands: 2
Number of Products: 6
Sq. footage: 3000
Parent Co: Treier Family Farms
Type of Packaging: Consumer, Food Service, Bulk
Brands:
LAKE PLAINS
PELTON'S HYBRID POPCORN

13612 **Tremblay's Sweet Shop**
P.O.Box 228
Hayward, WI 54843 715-634-2785
Fax: 715-634-7830
Candy
President: Dennis Tremblay
Quality Control: Charles Tremblay
Estimated Sales: Below $ 5 Million
Number Employees: 20-49

13613 **Trentadue Winery**
19170 Geyserville Ave
Geyserville, CA 95441 707-433-3104
Fax: 707-433-5825 888-332-3032
info@trentadue.com www.trentadue.com
Wines
Proprietor: Leo Trentadue
Proprietor: Evelyn Trentadue
General and Vineyard Manager: Victor Trentadue

Winemaker: Miroslav Tcholakov
Estimated Sales: $ 5-10 Million
Number Employees: 10-19
Type of Packaging: Private Label
Brands:
Trentadue

13614 **Trenton Bridge Lobster Pound**
1237 Bar Harbor Rd
Trenton, ME 04605 207-667-2977
Fax: 207-667-3412 www.trentonbridgelobster.com
Lobster
President: Anthony Pettegrow
Estimated Sales: $ 3 - 5 Million
Number Employees: 10-19

13615 **Trenton Processing**
120 W Broadway
Trenton, IL 62293-1306 618-224-7383
Fax: 618-224-9038
Processor of meat products
President: Gary Schwend
Purchasing Manager: Judy Kuhn
Estimated Sales: $ 5 - 10 Million
Number Employees: 10-19
Type of Packaging: Consumer

13616 **Tres Classique**
966 Mazzoni St Ste 2b
Ukiah, CA 95482 707-463-2646
Fax: 707-463-2299 888-644-5127
Gourmet cooking, sauces, dipping oils, dessert sauces and herbed wine vinegars
Owner: Thomas Allen
Estimated Sales: Under 500,000
Number Employees: 1-4
Number of Products: 38
Type of Packaging: Food Service, Private Label, Bulk
Brands:
Lemon Splash
Splash

13617 **Tri-Boro Fruit Company**
2500 S Fowler Ave
Fresno, CA 93725 559-486-4141
Fax: 559-486-7627

Grape grower
President: Chris Fazio
Executive: Tony Fazio
Estimated Sales: $ 5-10 Million
Number Employees: 10-19

13618 Tri-Cost Seafood
13213 Perkins Road
Baton Rouge, LA 70810-2032 225-757-8333
Fax: 225-757-8332
Seafood

13619 Tri-Counties Packing Company
845 Vertin Ave
Salinas, CA 93901 831-422-7841
Fax: 831-422-7856 sales@celeryhearts.com
www.celeryhearts.com
Processor of celery and celery hearts
President/Owner: Jack Baillie
Sales: John Baillie
Estimated Sales: $5 Million
Number Employees: 20-49
Number of Brands: 3
Number of Products: 1
Sq. footage: 46000
Type of Packaging: Consumer
Other Locations:
Tri - Counties Packaging Coompany
Oxnard CA
Brands:
Candy Stick
Snappy
Tri-Sign

13620 Tri-Marine InternationalInc
20 Cannery Street
San Pedro, CA 90731 310-732-6113
www.trimarine-usa.com
Processor, canner, importer and exporter of tuna, mackerel, squid and sardines
President: Renato Curto
COO: Chaiphorn Wangmitayasuk
VP Operations: Ian Boatwood
Number Employees: 500-999
Sq. footage: 500000
Type of Packaging: Consumer, Food Service, Private Label, Bulk
Brands:
American
Bonito
Lucky Strike
Pan Pacific
Sweepstakes
Top Wave

13621 Tri-State Beef Company
2124 Baymiller St
Cincinnati, OH 45214 513-579-1722
Fax: 513-579-1739
Processor of beef
President: Robert Runtz
CEO: Robert Runtz
Secretary/Treasurer: Betty Stout
Marketing Manager: Robert Runtz
Estimated Sales: $ 20 - 50 Million
Number Employees: 50-99
Type of Packaging: Consumer, Food Service, Bulk
Brands:
Soauthter

13622 Tri-State Processing Company
519 W Spraker Street
Kokomo, IN 46901-2197 317-452-4008
Frozen foods
Plant Manager: Calvin Moss
Estimated Sales: $ 10-100 Million
Number Employees: 100

13623 Tri-Sum Potato Chip Company
80 Julian Dr
Leominster, MA 01453 978-697-2447
www.tri-sum.com
Manufacturer of potato chips, popcorn and cheese puffs
COO: Richard Gates
Number Employees: 20-50
Type of Packaging: Consumer, Food Service, Private Label, Bulk
Brands:
Jp's
Suncrisp

13624 Triangle Seafood
212 Adams Street
Louisville, KY 40206-1862 502-561-0055
Fax: 502-561-0096
Seafood
President: J Shannon Bouchillon

13625 Tribe Mediterranean Foods Company LLC
110 Prince Henry Drive
Taunton, MA 02780-7385 774-961-0000
Processor and exporter of pickled herring, smoked salmon, fresh caviar, value-added seafood items and hummus dips/spreads
President/Ceo: Carlos Canals
Cfo: Charles Webster
Number Employees: 5-9
Sq. footage: 60000
Type of Packaging: Consumer, Food Service, Private Label, Bulk
Brands:
Nathan's
Rite

13626 Tribeca Oven
447 Gotham Pkwy
Carlstadt, NJ 07072-2409 201-935-8800
Fax: 201-935-6685 david@tribecaoven.com
www.tribecaoven.com
Processor of breads including rye, white, wholewheat, etc
Manager: Jesse Kirsch
Number Employees: 50-99
Type of Packaging: Consumer, Food Service

13627 (HQ)Trident Seafoods Corporation
5303 Shilshole Ave NW
Seattle, WA 98107 206-783-3818
Fax: 206-782-7195 800-426-5490
consumeraffairs@tridentseafoods.com
www.tridentseafoods.com
Processor, importer and exporter of frozen seafood including halibut, salmon, pollock and king, snow and Dungeness crabs; also, breaded and battered seafood and surimi
President: Charles H Bundrant
CEO: Steve Okerlund
Estimated Sales: $122300000
Number Employees: 100-249
Type of Packaging: Consumer, Food Service, Bulk
Brands:
Arctic Ice
Arctic Ice Rockfish
Perfectserve Tuna
Pub House Battered Seafood
Pubhouse
Rubenstein's
Sea Alaska
Sea Legs
Trident

13628 Trident Seafoods Corporation
5303 Shilshole Ave
Seattle, WA 98107-4000 206-783-3818
Fax: 206-782-7195 800-426-5490
www.tridentseafoods.com
Processor of frozen seafood.
Chairman: Chuck Bundrant
Estimated Sales: $ 20 - 50 Million
Number Employees: 100
Type of Packaging: Food Service
Brands:
Arctic Ice
Arctic Ice Rockfish
Perfectserve Tuna
Pub House Battered SeafoOD
Pubhouse
Rubenstein's
Sea Alaska
Sea Legs
Trident

13629 Trident Seafoods Corporation
P.O.Box 69
Salem, NH 03079-0069 603-893-3368
Fax: 603-893-7757
mikekater@tridentseafoods.com
www.tridentseafoods.com
Processor of frozen and portion control fish and seafood
Director: Mike Kater
Estimated Sales: $ 3 - 5 Million
Number Employees: 1-4
Sq. footage: 1500
Parent Co: Trident Seafood Corporation
Brands:
Arctic Ice
Icy Waters
Interstate Seafoods
Sea Legs
Trident Seafoods

13630 Trigo Corporation
PO Box 2369
Toa Baja, PR 00951-2369 787-794-1300
Fax: 787-794-3110
Processor of rum, vodka, liquor and wine
Executive Director: Benigno Trigo
Marketing Director: Mariella Algarin
Marketing: Eunice Miranva
Number Employees: 20-49
Type of Packaging: Consumer
Brands:
Ponte Vecckio

13631 Trinidad Bean & Elevator Company
615 5th St
Greeley, CO 80631-2383 970-352-0346
Fax: 970-571-5256 www.trinidadbenham.com
Manufacturer of dry beans
Manager: Larry Peterson
Plant Manager: R J Seader
Estimated Sales: $50-100 Million
Number Employees: 10-19
Type of Packaging: Consumer, Food Service, Private Label, Bulk
Brands:
Peak

13632 Trinidad Benham Company
3650 S Yosemite St Ste 300
Po Box 378007
Denver, CO 80237 303-220-1400
Fax: 303-220-1490 info@trinidadbenham.com
www.trinidadbenham.com
Manufacturer and exporter of dry beans, rice, popcorn, peas and household aluminum foil
President: Pat Horrigan
VP: Larry Cotham
VP of Sales & Marketing: Jim Pike
Plant Manager: Bill Dearmond
Estimated Sales: $50-100 Million
Number Employees: 50-99
Parent Co: Trinidad/Benham Corporation
Type of Packaging: Consumer, Food Service, Private Label, Bulk
Brands:
Benco-Peak
CookQuick
Evans
Jack Rabbit
Kings
Ranch Wagon
Royal Wrap
Shamrock

13633 Trinidad Benham Company
P.O.Box 427
Bridgeport, NE 69336 308-262-1361
Fax: 308-586-1058
Manufacturer of dry beans
President: Bill McCormack
Area Operations Manager: Dale Eirich
Estimated Sales: $3-5 Million
Number Employees: 25
Type of Packaging: Consumer, Food Service
Brands:
BENCO PEAK
COOKQUICK'
EVANS
JACK RABBIT

KINGS
RANCH WAGON
ROYAL WRAP
SHAMROCK

13634 (HQ)Trinidad Benham Company
3650 S Yosemite St Ste 300
Denver, CO 80237 303-220-1400
Fax: 303-220-1490 info@trinidadbenham.com
www.trinidadbenham.com
Manufacturer and exporter of dry beans, rice and popcorn packer and distributor of houshold aluminium foil
President/CEO: Carl C Hartman
CFO: Ron Weimer
EVP: Linda Walasley
Plant Manager: John Kurtz
Estimated Sales: $229 Million
Number Employees: 50-99
Type of Packaging: Consumer, Food Service, Private Label, Bulk
Other Locations:
Trinidad/Benham Corp.
Modesto CA
Brands:
BENCO PEAK
COOK QUICK
EVANS
JACK RABBIT
KINGS
RANCH WAGON
ROYAL WRAP
SHAMROCKak

13635 Trinidad Benham Company
P.O.Box 29
Mineola, TX 75773 903-569-2636
Fax: 903-569-2120 www.trinidadbenham.com
Popcorn
President: Carl Hertman
Owner: Trinidad Benham
CFO: Gary Peters
Quality Control: Mark Cantrell
Plant Manager: John Kuntz
Plant Manager: Bill Dearmond
Estimated Sales: $ 20-50 Million
Number Employees: 50-99
Brands:
Peak

13636 Trinidad/Benham Corporation
420 N 2nd St
Patterson, CA 95363 209-892-9051
Fax: 209-892-7977 info@trinidadbenham.com
www.tbc.com
Processor and exporter of dried beans, rice and popcorn
Manager: Gerry Hazlett
Estimated Sales: $ 1 - 3 Million
Number Employees: 20-49
Parent Co: Trinidad/Benham Corporation
Type of Packaging: Consumer, Food Service, Bulk

13637 Trinity Fruit Sales
9479 N Fork Washington
Suite 103
Fresno, CA 93730 559-433-3777
Fax: 559-433-3790 sales@trinityfruit.com
www.trinityfruit.com
Fresh cherries, apricots, peaches, plums, nectarines, kiwi, grapes, apples and pears
President: David White
Marketing Director: John Hein
Sales: Vance Uchiyama
Number Employees: 16

13638 Trinity Spice
901 W Florida Ave
Suite B
Midland, TX 79701 915-683-8333
Fax: 915-683-8333 800-460-1149
southern@marshill.com
Gourmet Southern spice blends
President: S Floyd
Estimated Sales: $150,000
Number Employees: 1
Type of Packaging: Consumer, Food Service, Private Label, Bulk
Brands:
SOUTHERN DYNAMITE

13639 Triple D Orchards
8310 W Stormer Rd
Empire, MI 49630 231-326-5174
Fax: 231-326-5480 866-781-9410
tdo@coslink.net www.tripledorchards.com
Processor and exporter of canned and frozen sweet cherries
President: Travis Keyes
Office Manager: Chance Bunner
Vice President: Dean Veliquette
Estimated Sales: $ 20 - 50 Million
Number Employees: 100-249
Type of Packaging: Consumer, Food Service, Private Label, Bulk
Brands:
Glen Lake

13640 Triple H
5821 Wilderness Ave
Riverside, CA 92504-1004 951-352-5700
Fax: 951-352-5710 www.triplehfoods.com
Vanillas
President: Tom Harris Jr
Vice President: Richard J. Harris
Purchasing: Judy Beltinghauser
Estimated Sales: $ 20 - 50 Million
Number Employees: 50-99

13641 Triple H Food Processors
5821 Wilderness Ave
Riverside, CA 92504-1004 951-352-5700
Fax: 951-352-5710 info@triplehfoods.com
www.triplehfoods.com
Processor of barbecue sauces, fruit punch and syrups; also, custom bottling services available
President: Tom Harris Jr
President: Tom Harris
Director of Sales: Joe Crosby
Estimated Sales: $ 10-20 Million
Number Employees: 50-99
Type of Packaging: Private Label
Brands:
Triple H

13642 (HQ)Triple K Manufacturing Company
P.O.Box 219
4193 200th Street
Shenandoah, IA 51601-0219 712-246-4376
Fax: 712-246-4010 888-987-2824
webmaster@x-tra-touch.com
www.xtratouch.com
Processor and exporter of baking flavorings; dry seasonings; salad dressings; sauces; dietary foods and cleaning products. Contract packaging and private label services also available.
President/Manager: Charles Maxine
VP Sales: B Maxine
Estimated Sales: $1600000
Number Employees: 5-9
Sq. footage: 15600
Type of Packaging: Consumer, Food Service, Private Label
Brands:
DROPS O'GOLD
X-TRA-TOUCH

13643 Triple Leaf Tea
434 N Canal St
S San Francisco, CA 94080-4675
US 650-588-8258
Fax: 650-588-8406 800-552-7448
triple@tripleleaf-tea.com www.tripleleaftea.com
Processor and exporter of authentic, effective, traditional chinese medicinal teas including green, ginger, ginseng, diet and medicinal; also, American ginseng capsules
President: Johnson Lam
Estimated Sales: $450.00k
Number Employees: 5
Number of Brands: 1
Number of Products: 18
Sq. footage: 5000
Type of Packaging: Consumer, Food Service, Private Label
Brands:
TRIPLE LEAF TEA

13644 Triple Rock Brewing Company
1920 Shattuck Ave
Berkeley, CA 94704-1022 510-843-2739
Fax: 510-843-6920 jesse.sarinana@gmail.com.
www.triplerock.com
Beer
Co-Owner: Reid Martin
Co-Owner: John Martin
Estimated Sales: $ 10-20 Million
Number Employees: 10-19
Type of Packaging: Private Label
Brands:
Agate Ale
Black Rock Porter
Bug Juice Ale
Ipax India Pale Ale
Millennium Ale
Pinnacle Pale Ale
Red Rock Ale
Stonehenge Stout
Titanium Ale

13645 Triple Springs Spring Water
199 Ives Ave Ste 1
Meriden, CT 06450 203-235-8374
Fax: 203-686-0200 www.triplespring.com
Manufacturer of natural spring water
President: George Kuchle
Estimated Sales: $9 Million
Number Employees: 10-19
Type of Packaging: Consumer, Bulk
Brands:
TRIPLE SPRINGS SPRING WATER

13646 Triple T Enterprises
5557 Highway 56
Chauvin, LA 70344 985-594-5869
Fax: 985-594-2168 chris@triple-t-shrimp.com
www.triple-t-shrimp.com
Shrimp
President: Andrew Blanchard
Estimated Sales: $ 20 - 50 Million
Number Employees: 50-99
Brands:
Pride N Joy

13647 Triple U Enterprises
26314 Tatanka Rd
Fort Pierre, SD 57532 605-567-3624
Fax: 605-567-3625 uuubuff@gwtc.net
www.tripleuranch.com
Processor of fresh, smoked, dried and frozen buffalo meat including portion cut
President: Kaye Ingle
CEO: Clint Amiotte
Estimated Sales: $700,000
Number Employees: 1-4
Type of Packaging: Consumer, Bulk

13648 Triple XXX Root Beer Com
2 N. Salisbury
West Lafayette, IN 47906 ÿ76- 74- 537
Fax: 713-780-8764
contact@triplexxxrootbeer.com
www.triplexxxrootbeer.com
Soft drinks
President: Lee Lydick
Estimated Sales: Below $ 5 Million
Number Employees: 1-4
Brands:
Triple XXX

13649 Triple-C
8 Burford Road
Hamilton, ON L8E 5B1
Canada 905-573-7900
Fax: 905-573-7867 800-263-9105
VP Sales & Marketing: Harry Scholtens
Brands:
GUMMY GUY
RACHEL'S
SOUR SIMON

13650 Tripoli Bakery
106 Common St
Lawrence, MA 01840 978-682-7754
Fax: 978-687-8455
Breads, rolls
President: Rosario Zappala
Estimated Sales: $ 1-2.5 Million
Number Employees: 20-49

13651 Tripp Bakers
260 Holbrook Drive
Wheeling, IL 60090-5810 847-541-7040
Fax: 847-537-5240 800-621-3702
trippbakers.com
Processor of fresh and frozen baked goods
President: Greg Goth

Estimated Sales: $ 6 Million
Number Employees: 45
Sq. footage: 45000
Type of Packaging: Consumer, Food Service, Private Label, Bulk

13652 Tripper
P.O.Box 51440
Oxnard, CA 93031 805-988-8851
Fax: 805-988-2992 888-336-8747
info@tripper.com www.tripper.com
Processor and importer of kosher & spices including pepper, nutmeg, cinnamon, and ginger; also, ingredients including vainilla beans and extracts; organic available
President: Patrick Barthelemy
Estimated Sales: $ 1-2.5 Million
Number Employees: 17
Sq. footage: 15000
Type of Packaging: Food Service, Private Label, Bulk
Brands:
Alligator Pepper
Bullfrog Lavander
Chameleon Pepper
Cobra Vanilla
Dragon Cinnamon
Elephant Ginger
Flamingo Pepper
Gorilla Cloves
Leopard Cardamon
Orangutan Mace
Panther Pepper
Rhino Nutmeg
Tiger Pepper
Toro Safron
Tripper

13653 Tristao Trading
116 John St Rm 500
New York, NY 10038 212-285-8120
Fax: 212-964-1735 admin@tristaousa.com
Coffee
Manager: Liz Wagner
President: Ricardo Tristao
Estimated Sales: $ 5-10 Million
Number Employees: 1-4

13654 Triton Seafood Company
7301 NW 77th St
Medley, FL 33166 305-888-8999
Fax: 305-888-1485 www.neptunes.com
Processor of all-natural conch chowder and conch fritters
CEO: Alfredo Alvarez
Marketing Director: Yvonne Conde
Estimated Sales: $1700000
Number Employees: 10-19
Type of Packaging: Food Service, Private Label
Brands:
Neptune's

13655 Triton Water Company
P.O.Box 2690
Burlington, NC 27216-2690 336-226-6392
Fax: 336-229-9768 800-476-9111
info@alamancefoods.com
www.alamancefoods.com
Bottled water
President: William Scott Jr
Quality Control: Thomas Patricher
VP Sales: David Willert
Estimated Sales: $ 10-100 Million
Number Employees: 100-249
Brands:
Big Drinks
Lil' Drinks
Lunch Punch

13656 Triumph Brewing Company
138 Nassau St Ste A
Princeton, NJ 8542 609-924-7855
Fax: 609-924-7857 www.triumphbrew.com
Processor of seasonal beer, ale, stout and pilsner
Manager: Doug Bork
General Manager: Eric Nutt
Estimated Sales: Below $ 5 Million
Number Employees: 50-99
Type of Packaging: Consumer, Food Service

13657 Trochu Meat Processors
233 North Rd
Trochu, AB T0M 2C0
Canada 403-442-4202
Fax: 403-442-2771 trochumeat@canada.com
www.trochumeats.com
Processor and exporter of fresh and frozen pork
President: Ray Price
Plant Manager: Richard Johnson
Estimated Sales: $46 Million
Number Employees: 115
Type of Packaging: Food Service

13658 Trophic International
3431 S. 500 W.
Salt Lake City, UT 84115-4228 801-269-6667
Fax: 801-269-9666 800-878-0099
info@bluechipgroup.net www.bluechipgroup.net
Lecithins, health foods, wild Mexican yam cream, colloidal silver
Owner: Jack Augason
Sales Director: Jeffrey Augason
Operations Manager: Mark Augason
Production Manager: Jeff Hatch
Estimated Sales: $500,000-$1 Million
Number Employees: 5-9
Sq. footage: 10
Type of Packaging: Consumer, Food Service, Private Label, Bulk
Brands:
Trophic

13659 Trophy Nut
320 N 2nd Street
Tipp City, OH 45371-1912 937-667-8478
Fax: 937-667-4656 800-219-9004
giftservice@trophynut.com www.trophynut.com
Processor and packager of dry and oil roasted nuts
President: Jeff Bollinger
CEO: Dave Henning
QA/QC Manager: Harvey Griffin
VP Sales/Plant Manager: Bob Wilke
Operations Manager: Chrissy Wagner
Purchasing: Jill Walters
Estimated Sales: $24 Million
Number Employees: 66
Sq. footage: 110000
Type of Packaging: Consumer, Food Service, Private Label, Bulk
Brands:
Nut Barrel
Trophy Gold Nut Barrel
Trophy Nut
True Measures Baking Nuts

13660 Tropic Fish & VegetableCenter
1020 Auahi St Ste 3090
Honolulu, HI 96814 808-591-2963
Fax: 808-591-2934
Fish and vegetables
President: Glenn Tanoue
Estimated Sales: $ 20 - 50 Million
Number Employees: 50-99

13661 Tropical
2202 Austell Rd SW
Marietta, GA 30008 770-805-9248
Fax: 770-435-1371 800-544-3762
info@tropicalfoods.com www.tropicalfoods.com
Processor and importer of candy, dried fruits, nuts, seeds, Oriental rice snacks and dessert toppings
President: David Williamson
President: John Bauer
Sales Director: Debbie Ponton
Operations Manager: William Stapleton
Estimated Sales: $ 10 - 20 Million
Number Employees: 10-19
Parent Co: Tropical
Type of Packaging: Food Service, Private Label, Bulk

13662 (HQ)Tropical
P.O.Box 7507
Charlotte, NC 28241-7507 704-588-0400
Fax: 704-588-3092 800-220-1413
info@tropicalfoods.com www.tropicalfoods.com
Processor of snack mixes, dried fruits, roasted nuts, seeds, candy and confectionery, spices and specialty foods including oils, vinegars, mustards, artichoke hearts, roasted bell peppers and pasta
President/Owner: Carolyn Bennett
Owner: Betty York
Owner/Vice President: Angela Bauer
Estimated Sales: $24600000
Number Employees: 100-249
Sq. footage: 72000
Type of Packaging: Consumer, Food Service, BulkTropical Memphis
Memphis TN
Tropical Landover
Landover MD
Brands:
CHRISTILLE BAY

13663 Tropical
6580 Huntley Road
Columbus, OH 43229-1029 614-431-7233
Fax: 614-431-7233 800-538-3941
www.tropicalfoods.com
Processor of nut candy, caramels, sesame sticks, soup mixes and dried fruits
President: David Williamson
Estimated Sales: $ 10 - 20 Million
Number Employees: 20-49
Sq. footage: 28000
Type of Packaging: Consumer, Food Service, Bulk

13664 Tropical Blossom Honey Company
106 N Ridgewood Ave
Edgewater, FL 32132 386-428-9027
Fax: 386-423-8469 infO@tropicbeehoney.com
www.tropicbeehoney.com
honey
VP: John Ginnis
Estimated Sales: $1.3 Million
Number Employees: 15

13665 Tropical Blossom Honey Company
P.O.Box 8
Edgewater, FL 32132 386-428-9027
Fax: 386-423-8469 800-324-8843
info@tropicbeehoney.com
www.tropicbeehoney.com
Processor, packer and exporter of honey; including Flordia honey and honey with comb
VP: John Douglas
VP: J Douglas Mc Ginnis
Sales: Michael Hauger
Operations: Paul Tierney
Plant Manager: David McGinnis
Estimated Sales: $2597231
Number Employees: 10-19
Number of Brands: 2
Type of Packaging: Food Service, Private Label, Bulk
Brands:
TROPIC BEE
TROPIC QUEEN

13666 Tropical Cheese Industries
452 Fayette St
Perth Amboy, NJ 8861 732-442-4898
Fax: 732-442-8227 800-487-7850
p-kondrup@tropicalcheese.com
www.tropicalcheese.com
Cheese
President: Rafael Mendez
CEO: Michelle Farkas
CFO: Michelle Farkas
Executive VP: Robert Fagan
COO: Martin Allen
Estimated Sales: $ 10-20 Million
Number Employees: 250-499

13667 Tropical Commodities
9230 Nw 12th Street
Miami, FL 33172 305-471-8120
Fax: 305-471-9825 tropicom@direcway.com
www.tropicalcommodities.com
Fresh habanero chili peppers and mash as well as other varieties of chili peppers.
President: D Douglas Bernard
Vice President: Robert Kholer
Marketing: Alberto Beers
Estimated Sales: $1.3-1.5 Million
Number Employees: 5-9
Number of Products: 10
Sq. footage: 15000
Type of Packaging: Private Label, Bulk
Brands:
Caribbean Hot Peppers

13668 **Tropical Illusions**
1436 Lulu Street
PO Box 338
Trenton, MO 64683-1819 660-359-5422
Fax: 660-359-5347
tropical@tropicalillusions.com
Processor and exporter of frozen drinks mixes including: cocktail, slush and granita, cream base, and smoothies.
President: Vance Cox
Vice President: Carrol Baugher
Estimated Sales: $590,000
Number Employees: 6
Sq. footage: 50000
Type of Packaging: Food Service, Private Label
Brands:
Captain Space Freeze
Elmeco
Tropical Illusions

13669 **Tropical Nut & Fruit Company**
3368 Bartlett Blvd
Orlando, FL 32811 407-843-8141
Fax: 407-843-4340 800-749-8869
nutsnorl@aol.com www.tropicalnutandfruit.com
Custom snack mixes, freshly roasted nuts and seeds, baking items, candies, spices, dried fruit, grains and minibar items.
President: Mike Ussery
Estimated Sales: $6000000
Number Employees: 20-49
Type of Packaging: Consumer, Food Service, Private Label, Bulk

13670 **Tropical Preserving Company**
1711 E 15th St
Los Angeles, CA 90021 213-748-5108
Fax: 213-748-4998 sales@tropicalpreserves.com
www.tropicalpreserving.com
Processor and exporter of jams, jellies and apple butter
President: Ronald Randall
Estimated Sales: $12,000,000
Number Employees: 20-49
Type of Packaging: Consumer, Private Label
Brands:
Market's Best

13671 **Tropical Treets**
130 Bermondsey Road
North York, ON M4A 1X5
Canada 416-759-8777
Fax: 416-759-7782 888-424-8229
info@tropicaltreeets.com
www.tropicaltreets.com
Processor of tropical ice cream; wholesaler/distributor of tropical food products, drinks and juices
CEO: Rumi Keshavjee
VP Sales/Marketing: Zahir Keshavjee
Estimated Sales: $471,000
Number Employees: 5
Sq. footage: 6000

13672 **(HQ)Tropicana**
1001 13th Ave E
Bradenton, FL 34208 941-747-4461
Fax: 941-747-4461 800-237-7799
www.tropicana.com
Processor and exporter of orange and grapefruit juices; also, frozen concentrates
President: Gregg Shearson
Senior VP/CFO: Dennis Hareza
Senior VP Marketing: Ron Coughlin
VP Purchasing: Jim Eicken
Estimated Sales: $3.8 Billion
Number Employees: 3500
Parent Co: PepsiCo
Type of Packaging: Consumer, Food Service
Brands:
LOOZA
TROPICANA

13673 **Troppers**
P.O.Box 50211
Santa Barbara, CA 93150-0211 805-969-4054
Baked goods
Manager: Diane Tourney
Estimated Sales: $ .5 - 1 million
Number Employees: 1-4

13674 **Trosclair Canning Company**
6949 Alta Rd
Bell City, LA 70630 337-622-3698
Seafood, seafood products
President: Adenise Trosclair
Vice President: Joey Troclair
Estimated Sales: $1 Million
Number Employees: 1-4

13675 **Trotters Imports**
6 Maxam Road
Colrain, MA 01340-9501 413-624-0121
800-863-8437
Olives and olive oil

13676 **Trout Lake Farm**
40 Warner Rd
Trout Lake, WA 98650 509-395-2025
Fax: 509-395-2645 herbs@troutlakefarm.com
www.troutlakefarm.com
Processor, exporter and importer of certified organically grown medicinal and beverage tea herbs and spices including garlic, oregano, peppermint and spearmint
CEO: Lloyd Scott
Sales Director: Martha-Jane Hylton
Estimated Sales: $3500000
Number Employees: 50
Sq. footage: 40000
Type of Packaging: Bulk
Brands:
1st Sneeze Echinacea
Camus Prarie Tea
Florased Valerian
Trout Lake Farm

13677 **Trout of Paradise**
P.O.Box 129
Paradise, UT 84328 435-245-3053
Fax: 435-245-4603 www.whitesranch.com
Processor and canner of fresh rainbow trout
President: Grant White
Estimated Sales: $150000
Number Employees: 1-4
Type of Packaging: Consumer, Food Service

13678 **Trout-Blue Chelan**
P.O.Box 669
Chelan, WA 98816 509-682-2591
Fax: 509-682-4620 www.chelanfruit.com
Processor and exporter of apples
CEO: Reggie Collins
Sales Director: Steve Terry
Estimated Sales: $30067016
Number Employees: 500-999
Type of Packaging: Consumer, Bulk
Brands:
BLUE CHELAN
TROUT

13679 **Troy Brewing Company**
417 River St
Troy, NY 12180-2822 518-273-2337
Fax: 518-273-4834 info@brownsbrewing.com
www.brownsbrewing.com
Beer
President: Garrett Brown
Estimated Sales: $ 1 - 3 Million
Number Employees: 20-49
Brands:
Ales & Lagers
Brown's Ware
Revolution Hall
Taproom

13680 **Troy Frozen Food**
404 E Us Highway 40
Troy, IL 62294-2205 618-667-6332
Processor of meat including home cured ham and bacon, frankfurters, bologna and sausage
VP: Donald Nihiser
Estimated Sales: $2000000
Number Employees: 5-9
Type of Packaging: Consumer

13681 **Troy Pork Store**
158 4th St
Troy, NY 12180 518-272-8291
Fax: 518-272-8291
Processor of fresh, smoked and pickled pork and beef
Owner: Carmen Amedeo
Estimated Sales: $500,000-$1 Million
Number Employees: 1-4
Type of Packaging: Consumer

13682 **Troy Winery**
3365 Peebles Road
Troy, OH 45373-8437 937-339-3655
Wines
Estimated Sales: $500,000 appx.
Number Employees: 1-4

13683 **Troyer Farms**
821 Route 97 S
PO Box 676
Waterford, PA 16441 814-796-2611
Fax: 814-796-6757 800-458-0485
info@troyerfarms.com www.troyerfarms.com
Potato chips, popcorn, tortilla chips, pretzels, cheese twists and corn puffs
President: Clifford Troyer
CFO: Tricia Briggs
VP: Mark Troyer
EVP Sales/Marketing: Matt Lamoreaux
Human Resources Manager: Keith Rovny
Estimated Sales: $ 20 - 50 Million
Number Employees: 150
Sq. footage: 150000
Type of Packaging: Consumer, Food Service, Private Label, Bulk
Brands:
Dan Dee
Troyer Farms

13684 **Troyer Foods**
17141 State Road 4
PO Box 608
Goshen, IN 46527-0608 574-533-0302
Fax: 574-533-3851 800-876-9377
www.troyers.com
President: Paris Ball-Miller
Private Label Manager: Randy Smith
Manager of Marketing: Beth Rodick
Director of Retail Sales: Terry Blythe
Director of Foodservice Sales: Tracy Bruce
Product Manager: Bill Bernath
Estimated Sales: $100+ Million
Number Employees: 250

13685 **Troyer Potato Products**
P.O.Box 676
Waterford, PA 16441-0676 814-796-2611
Fax: 814-796-6797 info@troyerfarms.com
www.troyerfarms.com
Manufacturer of snack foods including cheese popcorn, potato chips and corn puffs
President: Clifford Troyer
Sales: Sylivia Jones
Estimated Sales: $50 Million
Number Employees: 100-249
Type of Packaging: Consumer, Private Label
Brands:
DAN DEE POTATO CHIPS
DAN DEE PRETZELS
TROYER FARMS
TROYER POTATO PRODUCTS

13686 **Troyers Trail Bologna**
6552 State Route 515
Dundee, OH 44624 330-893-2414
Fax: 330-893-3058 877-893-2414
Manufacturer of bologna
VP: Darrin Troyer
Estimated Sales: $4.5 Million
Number Employees: 21
Sq. footage: 1050
Type of Packaging: Consumer, Food Service, Bulk

13687 **Tru-Blu Cooperative Associates**
PO Box 5
New Lisbon, NJ 08064-0005 609-894-8717
trublucoop@aol.com
Processor of fresh and frozen blueberries
General Manager: Dennis Doyle
Number Employees: 1-4
Type of Packaging: Consumer

13688 **Truan's Candies**
13716 Tireman St
Detroit, MI 48228 313-584-3400
800-584-3004
info@alinosi.com www.truanscandiesonline.com
Manufacturer of chocolate's
President: Mark Truan
Estimated Sales: $ 5 - 10 Million
Number Employees: 10-19
Type of Packaging: Private Label

13689 **Truchard Vineyards**
3234 Old Sonoma Rd
Napa, CA 94559-9701 707-253-7153
Fax: 707-253-7234 www.truchardvineyards.com
Wine
Owner: Anthony Truchard
Estimated Sales: $ 5-10 Million
Number Employees: 20-49
Brands:
Truchard Vineyards

13690 **Truckee River Winery**
P.O.Box 3393
Truckee, CA 96160 530-587-4626
Fax: 530-550-8809 russ@truckeeriverwinery.com
www.truckeeriverwinery.com
Wines
Co-Owner: Russ Jones
Co-Owner: Joan Jones
Estimated Sales: Under $300,000
Number Employees: 1-4
Type of Packaging: Private Label
Brands:
Truckee River

13691 **True Beverages**
2001 E Terra Ln
O Fallon, MO 63366-4434 636-240-2400
Fax: 636-272-2408 800-325-6152
truefood@truemfg.com www.truemfg.com
Beverages
Owner: Bill Smith
Brands:
True Beverages

13692 **True Organic Products International**
P.O.Box 523271
Miami, FL 33152-3271 305-885-2619
Fax: 305-885-1326 800-487-0379
Processor and exporter of organic juices including orange, apple, pineapple, grape, tangerine, lime, watermelon, blackberry, soursop, lulo and pineapple blends
President: Alex Mendez
VP: Christopher Ramputh
Estimated Sales: $ 3 - 5 Million
Number Employees: 1-4
Sq. footage: 12000
Brands:
True Organic

13693 **True World Foods of Boston**
22 Foodmart Road
Boston, MA 02118 617-269-9988
Fax: 617-269-5725 www.trueworldfoods.com
Manager: Jimmy Watanoide
Estimated Sales: $ 3 - 5 Million
Number Employees: 10-19

13694 **True World Foods of Chicago**
950 Chase Ave
Elk Grove Vlg, IL 60007-4828 847-718-0088
Fax: 847-718-0011
President: Kazuo Sometani
CEO: Toshio Nishida
Estimated Sales: $ 10 - 20 Million
Number Employees: 50-99

13695 **True World Foods of Hawaii**
2696 Waiwai Loop
Honolulu, HI 96819-5113 808-836-3222
Fax: 808-833-4510 www.twfhawaii.com
President: Jackie Madsuka
Estimated Sales: $ 20 - 50 Million
Number Employees: 20-49

13696 **Truesdale Packaging Company**
1410 E Veterans Memorial Pkwy
Warrenton, MO 63383 636-456-6800
Fax: 636-456-6899
Processor and co-packer of canned and bottled beverages including hot pack, cold pack and bag-in-box soft drinks, root beer, juices, teas and isotonics
Manager: Tom Williams
VP/General Manager: Hugh White
Estimated Sales: $$50-100 Million
Number Employees: 100-249
Sq. footage: 201000

13697 **Truesoups**
26401 79th Ave S
Kent, WA 98032 253-872-0403
Fax: 253-872-0552 www.truesoups.com
Processor and exporter of fresh or frozen soups; also, sauces and entrees
President: Shannon Moshier
CEO: Bruce Rowe
VP Marketing: Page Carlsen
Estimated Sales: $28 Million
Number Employees: 200
Sq. footage: 55000
Type of Packaging: Consumer, Food Service, Private Label, Bulk
Brands:
Truesoups

13698 **Trugman-Nash**
19 W 44th St
New York, NY 10036-5902 212-869-6910
Fax: 212-869-6844 www.trugman-nash.com
Processor and importer of dairy products and tofu cheese substitute; wholesaler/distributor of cheeses. Cheesecake manufacturer - private labels and own brand
President/CEO: Tom May
VP: David Aboschinow
Estimated Sales: $ 3 - 5 Million
Number Employees: 1-4
Type of Packaging: Consumer, Food Service, Bulk
Brands:
Nu-Tofu-C
Organic Pasta
Soy Cheese
UNBELIEVABLE CHEESECAKE

13699 **Truitt Brothers Inc**
PO Box 309
Salem, OR 97308-0309 503-362-3674
Fax: 503-588-2868 800-547-8712
truittbros@truittbros.com www.truittbros.com
Manufacturer of canned green beans, cherries, pears and plums; also, shelf stable entrees
CFO: Alan Wynn
Quality Control: Rick Kimball
Human Resources: Sue Meier
Purchasing: Chet Thomas
Estimated Sales: $ 20 - 50 Million
Number Employees: 500-999
Type of Packaging: Consumer, Food Service, Private Label
Brands:
TRUITT BROS.

13700 **Trumark**
830 E Elizabeth Ave
Linden, NJ 7036 908-486-5900
Fax: 908-486-5900 800-752-7877
Processor and exporter of sodium and potassium lactate and lactate and acetate blends
President: Mark Satz
CEO: Jeff Wales
Estimated Sales: $780000
Number Employees: 10-19

13701 **Tsar Nicoulai Caviar**
60 Dorman Ave
San Francisco, CA 94124 415-543-3007
Fax: 415-543-5172 800-952-2842
info@tsarnicoulai.com www.tsarnicoulai.com
Caviar and smoked fish
President/CEO: Mats Engstrom
Co-Owner: Dafne Engstrom
Estimated Sales: $500,000-$1 Million
Number Employees: 10-19
Type of Packaging: Private Label
Brands:
Tsar Nicoulai Caviar

13702 **Tualatin Estate Vineyards**
10850 NW Seavey Rd
Forest Grove, OR 97116 503-357-5005
Fax: 503-357-1702 tualatinestate@yahoo.com
www.tualatinestate.com
Processor and exporter of table wines including chardonnay, pinot noir, pinot blanc, gewurtztraminer, riesling and semi-sparkling muscat
President: William H Malkmus
Operations Manager/Winegrower: Stirling Fox
Winemaker: Joe Dobbes
Estimated Sales: $600000
Number Employees: 5-9
Sq. footage: 20000
Parent Co: Willamette Valley Vineyards
Type of Packaging: Consumer
Brands:
Tualatin Estate

13703 **Tucker Cellars**
70 Ray Rd
Sunnyside, WA 98944 509-837-8701
Fax: 509-837-8701 wineman@televar.com
www.tuckercellars.com
Wines and pickled vegetables
Co-Owner: Rose Tucker
Co-Owner: Randy Tucker
Estimated Sales: $1-2.5 Million
Number Employees: 5-9
Brands:
Tucker

13704 **Tucker Packing Company**
955 N Mill St
Orrville, OH 44667 330-683-3311
Processor of fresh and frozen beef, pork and lamb
President: John Tucker
Plant Manager: Leon Hilty
Estimated Sales: $1600000
Number Employees: 10-19
Type of Packaging: Consumer, Food Service, Bulk

13705 **Tucker Pecan Company**
350 N McDonough St
Montgomery, AL 36104 334-262-4470
Fax: 334-262-4690 800-239-6540
sales@tuckerpecan.com www.tuckerpecan.com
Processor and wholesaler/distributor of pecans
President: Florence Tucker
Operations Manager: David Little
Estimated Sales: $450,000
Number Employees: 3
Sq. footage: 3359
Type of Packaging: Consumer, Food Service, Bulk

13706 **Tucson Food Service**
P.O.Box 2363
Tucson, AZ 85702 520-622-4605
Fax: 520-884-0690
people@tucsonfoodservice.com
www.tucsonfoodservice.com
Wholesaler/distributor of produce
President: Thomas M Kusian
Vice President: James Tooley
VP Sales: Alfred Thomas
Number Employees: 50-99

13707 **Tucson Frozen Storage**
6964 E Century Park Dr
Tucson, AZ 85756 520-623-0660
Fax: 520-624-2869
laura@tucsonfrozenstorage.com
www.tucsonfrozenstorage.com
Warehouse providing freezer storage, re-packing and labeling for frozen foods
Manager: Laura Levin
Operations: Alan Levin
Estimated Sales: $500,000-$1 Million
Number Employees: 5 to 9

13708 **Tudal Winery**
1015 Big Tree Rd
Saint Helena, CA 94574 707-963-3947
Fax: 707-968-9691 tudalwinery@aol.com
www.tudalwinery.com
Wines
President: Arnold Tudal
Vice President: John Tudal
Marketing Director: Susan Greene
Estimated Sales: Less than $500,000
Number Employees: 1-4
Type of Packaging: Private Label
Brands:
2001 Estate Cabernet Sauvignon
Flat Bed Red
Tractor Shed Red

13709 **Tufts Ranch**
27260 State Highway 128
Winters, CA 95694-9066 530-795-4144
Fax: 530-795-3844
Grower and packer of apricots, prunes, kiwifruit and persimmons. Broker of walnuts and almonds
General Manager: Stan Tufts
Office Manager: Brad Graf
Estimated Sales: $ 5 - 10 Million
Number Employees: 50-99

13710 **Tularosa Vineyards**
23 Coyote Canyon Rd
Tularosa, NM 88352 575-585-2260
Fax: 505-585-2260 800-687-4467
wine@nmex.com www.tularosavineyards.com

Wines
Owner: David Wickham
Estimated Sales: $250,000
Number Employees: 5-9
Brands:
Tularosa Wines

13711 **Tulkoff Food Products**
2301 Chesapeake Ave
Baltimore, MD 21222-4013 410-327-6585
Fax: 410-524-0148 800-638-7343
www.tulkoff.com
Processor of sauces including pesto, cheese, cocktail, tiger and honey mustard; also, horseradish, regular and light breakfast syrups, ginger purees and chopped garlic and shallots
President/Ceo: Phillip Tulkoff
VP Sales: Mark Natale
Production: Tom Shellooe
Plant Manager: Dave Maxwell
Estimated Sales: $ 20 - 50 Million
Number Employees: 50-99
Type of Packaging: Food Service, Private Label, Bulk
Brands:
Snap-Back
TOP
Tulkoff

13712 **Tull Hill Farms**
2264 Hugo Road
Kinston, NC 28501-7173 252-523-8503
Fax: 252-523-8052
Grower of sweet potatoes
Sales: Kendall Hill
Sales: Rob Hill
Estimated Sales: C
Number Employees: 10-19
Brands:
Hill's

13713 **Tulocay & Company**
P.O.Box 7
Napa, CA 94559-0007 707-252-4727
Fax: 707-252-8375 888-627-2859
jane@madeinnapavalley.com
www.tulocaycemetery.org
Baking mixes, balsamic & champagne vinegars, dessert sauces, dipping and flavored oils, everyday classics, vinaigarettes & dressings, global herbed rubs, herbed rubs, marinades & glazes, mustards, savory sauces, tapenades & savorycondiments, gift sets, and fruit condiments
Manager: Peter Manasse
Director Manufacturing: William Cadman
Estimated Sales: Less than $500,000
Number Employees: 1-4

13714 **Tulox Plastics Corporation**
P.O.Box 984
Marion, IN 46952-0984 765-664-5155
Fax: 765-664-0257 800-234-1118
sales@tulox.com www.tulox.com
Product line for food industry/confectionary items includes Tulox tubes and toppers that are available in rounds, squares, rectangulars, triangulars, and most any other shape imaginable. They can be transparent, opaque, colored, orstriped. There are thousands of standard sizes available, but tubes can also be made to fit exact dimensional needs.
President: John Sciaudone
National Sales Director: Christopher Sciaudone
Type of Packaging: Consumer

13715 **Tumai Water**
PO Box 1751
Martinsburg, WV 25402 304-264-1466
866-948-8624
info@sperogroup.com www.tumaiwater.com
Bottled spring water
Owner/President/CEO: Bob Downey
Estimated Sales: $32,000
Number Employees: 2
Sq. footage: 2384
Parent Co: Spero Group
Type of Packaging: Consumer

13716 **Tumaro's Gourmet Tortillas & Snacks**
96 Executive Ave
Edison, NJ 08817-6016 323-464-6317
Fax: 323-464-6299 800-777-6317
info@tumaros.com www.tumaros.com
Manufacturer of Tortillas
President: Herman Jacobs
VP: Brian Jacobs
Estimated Sales: $ 10 - 20 Million
Number Employees: 20-49
Parent Co: United Natural
Type of Packaging: Consumer, Food Service

13717 **Tumaro's Gourmet Tortillas**
5300 Santa Monica Blvd
Suite 311
Los Angeles, CA 90029 951-697-5950
www.tumaros.com
low in carb gourmet tortillas, healthy flour tortilla and wraps, soy-full heart flatbread
Marketing Coordinator: Nancy Bottema
Operations Director: Bill Riley

13718 **Tuna Fresh**
401 Whitney Ave # 103
Gretna, LA 70056-2500 504-363-2744
Fax: 504-392-3324 www.chartwellsmenus.com
Manager: John Duke

13719 **Tundra Wild Rice**
PO Box 263
Pine Falls, NB R0E 1M0
Canada 204-367-8651
Fax: 204-367-8309
Processor and exporter of Canadian lake wild rice
President: Denis Pereux
Number Employees: 4
Sq. footage: 2840
Type of Packaging: Private Label, Bulk
Brands:
Tundra

13720 **Tupman-Thurlow Company**
450 Fairway Dr # 203
Deerfield Beach, FL 33441-1837 954-596-9989
Fax: 860-658-3001
Processor, importer and exporter of canned meats including beef, luncheon, ham, Vienna sausage and meatballs; also, canned, frozen and aseptic fruit purees, concentrates, particulates and sections
President: Jeffrey Podell
Vice President: Greg Silpe
Estimated Sales: $40000000
Number Employees: 5-9
Type of Packaging: Consumer, Food Service, Private Label, Bulk

13721 **Turano Pastry Shops**
142 N Bloomingdale Rd
Bloomingdale, IL 60108 630-529-6161
Fax: 630-529-4824 www.chicagopastry.com
Processor of bread including rye, wheat and white; also, pastries, Italian cookies and danish including prune, strawberry and blueberry
President: Renato Turano
Estimated Sales: $119200000
Number Employees: 20-49
Type of Packaging: Consumer, Food Service

13722 **Turano Pasty Shops**
6501 Roosevelt Rd
Berwyn, IL 60402-1100 708-788-5320
Fax: 708-788-3075 info@turano-baking.com
www.turanobakery.com
Processor of fresh and frozen breads, rolls and pastries
President: Renato Turano
Food Service Sales Manager: Bill Carlson
Plant Manager: Eugenio Turano
Estimated Sales: $ 50-100 Million
Number Employees: 250-499
Type of Packaging: Consumer, Food Service, Private Label
Brands:
Turano

13723 **Turk Brothers Custom Meats**
1903 Orange Rd
Ashland, OH 44805 419-289-1051
Fax: 419-281-8280 800-789-1051
turkbros@bright.net
www.turkbrothersmeats.com
Processor and wholesaler/distributor of beef, pork and lamb; wholesaler/distributor of frozen foods, equipment and fixtures and seafood; serving the food service market; also, slaughtering services available
President: Roy Turk
VP: Kevin Turk
Estimated Sales: $ 5 - 10 Million
Number Employees: 10
Sq. footage: 8421
Type of Packaging: Consumer, Food Service, Bulk

13724 **Turkey Creek Snacks**
P.O.Box 69
Thomaston, GA 30286-0001 706-647-8841
Fax: 706-647-3978 info@turkeycreeksnacks.com
www.turkeycreeksnacks.com
Manufacturer of pork rinds, hard cracklings and hot sauce
Owner: Laddie Fulcher
Estimated Sales: $ 3 - 5 Million
Number Employees: 20-49
Sq. footage: 25000
Type of Packaging: Consumer, Food Service, Private Label, Bulk
Brands:
Deli Style
Sunrise Farms
Turkey Creek

13725 **Turkey Hill Dairy**
2601 River Rd
Conestoga, PA 17516 717-872-5461
Fax: 717-872-0602 800-693-2479
careers@turkeyhill.com www.turkeyhill.com
Manufacturer of ice cream, sherbet, frozen yogurt and drinks
President: Quintin Frey
Executive Vice President: John Cox
Number Employees: 500-999
Sq. footage: 107000
Type of Packaging: Consumer, Private Label, Bulk
Brands:
Turkey Hill

13726 **Turkey Hill Sugarbush**
10 Waterloo Street
PO Box 160
Waterloo, QC J0E 2N0
Canada 450-539-4822
Fax: 450-539-1561 www.turkeyhill.ca
Processor and exporter of maple products including syrups, cookies, chocolates, coffee, tea, fudge, caramels, butter, soft and hard candies
President/Board Member: Michael Herman
Chairman: Brian Herman
Estimated Sales: $10-20 Million
Number Employees: 35
Number of Brands: 1
Number of Products: 85
Sq. footage: 35000
Type of Packaging: Consumer, Private Label, Bulk
Brands:
TURKEY HILL

13727 **Turkey Store Company**
116 4th Ave NW
Faribault, MN 55021 507-334-2050
Fax: 507-332-5349 www.theturkeystore.com
Processor of fresh and frozen whole turkeys
Director Operations: Steve Williams
Manager Distribution: Pete Vikeras
Estimated Sales: $ .5 - 1 million
Number Employees: 1-4
Type of Packaging: Consumer, Private Label

13728 **Turlock Fruit Company**
P.O.Box 130
Turlock, CA 95381-0130 209-634-7207
Fax: 209-632-4273
Processor and exporter of honeydew melons
President: Donald Smith
Treasurer: Stephen Smith
Secretary: Stuart Smith
Estimated Sales: $500,000-$1 Million
Number Employees: 20-49
Type of Packaging: Consumer, Bulk
Brands:
King O' The-West
Oak Flat
Peacock
Sycamore

13729 **Turn on Beverages Inc**
6 Gladwyne Court
Spring Valley, NY 10977-1604 845-354-7720
Fax: 845-354-5141 howard@2turnon.com
www.2turnon.com

A unique premium adult beverage manufactured in Austria, that assists men and women in becoming more sexually aroused.
President/CEO: Howard Hersh
VP/Marketing: Lisa Calvin
R&D/Production: Anton Lintner
Public Relations: Richard Davis
Operations Manager: Cliff Coleman
Estimated Sales: $20 Million
Number Employees: 10+
Number of Brands: 1
Number of Products: 1
Sq. footage: 4000
Type of Packaging: Consumer, Food Service
Brands:
Turn On Love Drink

13730 **Turnbull Bakeries**
3720 Amnicola Highway
Suite 119
Chattanooga, TN 37406-1792 423-265-4551
Fax: 423-756-3159 800-488-7628
Baked goods
National Sales Operations Manager: Deris Bagli
Estimated Sales: $ 20 Million
Number Employees: 200

13731 **Turnbull Bakeries**
523 1st St
New Orleans, LA 70130 504-581-5383
Processor of bread sticks, bread crumbs and melba toast
President: Wayne Turnbull
CFO: Richard Waters
Estimated Sales: $3 Million
Number Employees: 50

13732 **Turnbull Bakeries of Lousiana**
523 1st St
New Orleans, LA 70130-2004 504-581-5383
turnbula@bellsouth.net
Processor of bread sticks, bread crumbs, and melba toast
President: Elizabeth Turnbull
Vice President: Frank LeCourt
Number Employees: 10,000+
Type of Packaging: Food Service, Private Label, Bulk

13733 **Turnbull Cone Baking Company**
PO Box 6248
Chattanooga, TN 37401-6248 423-265-4551
Fax: 423-624-8724
Processor of ice cream cones and wafers; also, melba toast
President: Wayne W Turnbull
Director Sales: Deris Bagli
Number Employees: 100-249
Parent Co: Turnbull Bakeries
Type of Packaging: Private Label

13734 **Turner & Pease Company**
1519 Elliott Avenue W
Seattle, WA 98119-3129 206-282-9535
Fax: 206-282-9633 miltont@turnerandpease.com
www.turnerandpease.com
Manufacturer of butter
President: Milton Turner
National Sales: Bill Bowen
Number Employees: 25
Sq. footage: 18000
Type of Packaging: Consumer, Food Service, Private Label, Bulk
Brands:
CREAMERIE CLASSIQUE
GOLDEN WEST
MEADOWBROOK

13735 **Turner Dairy Farms**
1049 Jefferson Rd
Penn Hills, PA 15235 412-372-2211
Fax: 412-372-0651 800-892-1039
www.turnerdairy.net
Milk
President: Charles H Turner Jr
Estimated Sales: $ 20-50 Million
Number Employees: 100-249

13736 **Turner New Zealand**
125 Columbia
Aliso Viejo, CA 92656-4101 949-622-6181
Fax: 949-203-2895 www.turner.co.nz
Processor of calamari, mussels, scallops, oysters, chilled fish, venison and lamb; importer of seafood and lamb
Chairman/CEO: Noel Turner
VP Marketing: Daliza Corona
Contact: Michael Hart
Number Employees: 5-9
Sq. footage: 10000
Brands:
Turner New Zealand

13737 **Turris Italian Foods**
16695 Common Rd
Roseville, MI 48066-1901 586-773-6010
Fax: 586-773-6851 www.turrisitalianfoods.com
Manufacturer of a full line of Italian specialities including Ravioli, lasagna, manicotti, tortellini and other fine pastas
President: Tom Turri
Sales Manager: Bernard Turri
Plant Manager: John Turri
Estimated Sales: $6.4 Million
Number Employees: 50-99
Sq. footage: 35000
Type of Packaging: Consumer, Food Service, Private Label, Bulk
Brands:
TURRIS

13738 **Turtle Island Foods**
601 Industrial St
Hood River, OR 97031 541-386-7766
Fax: 541-386-7754 800-508-8100
info@tofurky.com www.tofurky.com
Processor, importer and exporter of soy meat analos including tempeh, tofurkey, deli slices, sausages, franks
President: Seth Tibbott
CFO: Sue Tibbott
VP: Bob Tibbott
Quality Assurance Manager: James Athos
Production Manager: Graciela Pulido
Plant Manager: Graciela Pulido
Estimated Sales: $2,398,946
Number Employees: 50-99
Number of Brands: 2
Number of Products: 25
Sq. footage: 10000
Type of Packaging: Consumer, Food Service, Private Label, Bulk
Brands:
SUPER BURGERS
TOFURKY
VEGETABALLS

13739 **Turtle Island Foods**
601 Industrial St
Hood River, OR 97031 541-386-7766
Fax: 541-386-7754 800-508-8100
info@tofurky.com www.tofurky.com
Cheese and vegetable based soups
Founder: Seth Tibbott
CFO: Sue Tibbott
Production Manager: Graciela Pulido
Estimated Sales: Less than $500,000
Number Employees: 1-4
Brands:
SuperBurgers
Tempeh
Tofurky

13740 **Turtle Island Herbs**
4735 Walnut St # F
Boulder, CO 80301-2553 303-546-6362
Fax: 303-546-0625 800-684-4060
island@earthnet.net www.earthnet.net
Processor and wholesaler/distributor of organic herbal extracts and syrups
President: Feather Jones
CEO: Bahman Saless
VP Operations: Peter Danielson
Estimated Sales: $300,000-500,000
Number Employees: 1-4
Sq. footage: 1500

13741 **Turtle Mountain**
330 Seneca Rd
Eugene, OR 97402 541-338-9400
Fax: 541-338-9401 info@turtlemountain.com
www.turtlemountain.com
Processor and exporter of frozen nondairy desserts; also, fat-free
President: Mark Brawerman
Marketing: John Tucker
Estimated Sales: Under $500,000
Number Employees: 1-4
Type of Packaging: Consumer, Food Service, Private Label
Brands:
Carb Escapes
It's Soy Delicious
Organic Lil Buddies
Organic Soy Delicious
Soy Delicious Purely Decadent
Sweet Nothings

13742 **Tuscan Bakery**
12831 NE Airport Way
Portland, OR 97230 503-256-2099
Fax: 503-256-1929 800-887-2261
www@teleport.com
Processor of biscotti
President/Owner: Michael J Lisac
VP: Wayne Winter
Estimated Sales: Below $ 5 Million
Number Employees: 1-4
Sq. footage: 6000
Type of Packaging: Consumer, Food Service
Brands:
Lawman's

13743 **Tuscan Brewing**
25009 Kauffman Ave
Red Bluff, CA 96080-2704 530-520-0624
tuscanbrewery@earthlink.net
Beer
Owner: Thiel Conjlin
Estimated Sales: $320,000
Number Employees: 4
Type of Packaging: Private Label
Brands:
Paradise Pale Ale
Sundown Brown Ale

13744 **Tuscan Hills**
3941 Park Drive
Suite 20-296
El Dorado Hills, CA 95762-4549 916-939-3814
Fax: 916-939-3709
Italian-inspired gourmet foods

13745 **(HQ)Tuscan/Lehigh Valley Dais**
880 Allentown Rd
Lansdale, PA 19446-5298 215-855-8205
Fax: 215-855-9834 800-937-3233
www.lehighvalleydairyfarms.com
Milk, flavored milk, creamers, orange juice.
Executive Director: James Macri
President: M Marcus
CFO: Tim Natole
CEO: Anthony Ward
VP Sales: Peter Trigi
Marketing Director: Brian Kornfield
Purchasing Manager: Don Gates
Estimated Sales: $ 1-2.5 Million
Number Employees: 100-249

13746 **Tuscarora Organic Growers Cooperative**
22275 Anderson Hollow Rd
Hustontown, PA 17229 814-448-2173
Fax: 814-448-2333 info@tog.coop
www.tog.coop
Cooperative providing fresh fruits and vegetables including certified organic
Manager: Chris Fullerton
Sales Manager: Chris Fullerton
Bookkeeping/Sales: Sherry Meuser
Office Manager: Christine Treichler
Number Employees: 1-4
Type of Packaging: Bulk
Brands:
Tuscarora Organic

13747 **Tusitala**
PO Box 189
Grand Bay, AL 36541-0189 251-865-6240
Fax: 251-865-3763
Herbs and herbal supplements
President: George Spellmeyer
Secretary: Norma Jean Spellmeyer

13748 **Tutto Sicilia**
55 John Downey Dr
New Britain, CT 06051-2921
info@tuttosicily.com
www.tuttosicily.com

olive oils, bruschetteria, sauces and condiments, cream toppings, marmalades, honey, biscotti

13749 **Twang**
6255 Wt Montgomery
San Antonio, TX 78252-2227 210-226-7008
Fax: 210-226-4040 800-950-8095
info@twang.com www.twang.com
Processor and importer of flavored salts including lemon-lime, traditional and colored margarita, beer, pickle and chili; also, Bloody Mary toppings
Owner: Roger Trevino Sr
VP Finance: Patrick Trevino
Sales/Marketing: Roger Trevino Jr
Estimated Sales: $ 10 - 20 Million
Number Employees: 20-49
Number of Brands: 10
Number of Products: 15
Sq. footage: 12000
Type of Packaging: Consumer, Food Service, Private Label, Bulk
Brands:
Kid-Tastic
Texican
Twang

13750 **Twenty First Century Foods**
30 Germania St # A
Jamaica Plain, MA 02130-2315 617-522-7595
Fax: 617-522-8772
Processor of soy products including tofu and tempeh; exporter of tempeh starter
Owner: Rudy Canale
Estimated Sales: $ .5 - 1 million
Number Employees: 1-4
Sq. footage: 1900
Brands:
Tofu Cream Chie
Tofu Pudding

13751 **Twenty First Century Snacks**
921 S 2nd St
Ronkonkoma, NY 11779-7203 631-588-8000
Fax: 631-467-3995 800-975-2883
Assortment of nuts, candy and dried fruit
President: Eddie Bell
Estimated Sales: $ 1-2.5 Million
Number Employees: 10-19
Type of Packaging: Consumer, Food Service, Private Label, Bulk

13752 **Twin City Bagels/National Choice Bakery**
130 Hardman Ave S
South St Paul, MN 55075-2453 651-554-0200
Fax: 651-554-8383
shughes@nationalchoicebakery.com
www.twincitybagels.com
Fresh and refrigerated bagels
President: Shimon Harosh
Vice President: Steve Hughes
Research & Development: Mark Heckel
Quality Control: Mark Heckel
Marketing Director: Steve Hughes
Sales Director: Steve Hughes
Operations Manager: Steve Hughes
Production Manager: Jason Holt
Purchasing Manager: Doug Patten
Number Employees: 100-249
Type of Packaging: Consumer, Private Label

13753 **Twin City Foods**
P.O.Box 699
Stanwood, WA 98292 208-743-5568
Fax: 206-515-2499 www.twincityfoods.com
Largest independent processors of frozen vegetables and potatoes.
President: Roger O Lervick
Executive VP: John Lervick
Marketing Director: Mark Lervick
Plant Manager: William Johnson
Estimated Sales: $120000000
Number Employees: 500-999
Type of Packaging: Consumer, Food Service, Private Label, Bulk

13754 **Twin City Wholesale**
519 Walker St
Opelika, AL 36801 334-745-4564
Fax: 334-749-5125 www.tcwholesale.com
Owner: Johanna Bottoms
Secretary: Johanna Bottoms
Estimated Sales: $ 10 - 20 Million
Number Employees: 50-99

13755 **Twin County Dairy**
2206 540th St SW
Kalona, IA 52247-9178 319-656-2776
Manufacturer of white cheddar cheese
President: John Roetlin Jr
Estimated Sales: $9 Million
Number Employees: 50-99
Type of Packaging: Consumer, Private Label, Bulk

13756 **Twin Hens**
P.O.Box 439
Princeton, NJ 8542 908-925-9040
Fax: 908-281-9908 info@twinhens.com
www.twinhens.com
chicken pot pies and gluten free beef pot pies
President/Owner: Linda Twining
VP: Kathy Herring

13757 **Twin Marquis**
328 Johnson Ave
Brooklyn, NY 11206-2802 718-386-6868
Fax: 718-386-0516 800-367-6868
info@twinmarquis.com www.twinmarquis.com
Processor and importer of Asian foods including buns, dumplings, sauces, soups, and noodles; also organic pasta and instant coffee and cappuccino
President: Joseph Tang
Executive Director: Terry Tang
Vice President: Alan But
Estimated Sales: $ 3-4 Million
Number Employees: 50-99
Sq. footage: 22000
Brands:
Chef One
Twin Marquis

13758 **Twin Oaks Community Foods**
138 Twin Oaks Road
Louisa, VA 23093 540-894-4062
twinoakstofu.com
tofu, tempeh and vegetarian sausage

13759 **Twin Valley Products**
P.O.Box 42
Greenleaf, KS 66943-0042 785-747-2251
Fax: 785-747-2278 800-748-7416
ehenry@grapevine.net
Popped and flavored popcorn and related products
CEO: Ed Henry
CEO: Ed Henry
VP Marketing: Nate Wirrick
Operations Manager: Carolyn Pinnick
Estimated Sales: $500-1 Million appx.
Number Employees: 20-49
Type of Packaging: Private Label

13760 **Twining R & Company**
2812 Twining Rd
Greensboro, NC 27406-4615 336-275-8634
Fax: 336-370-4719 www.twinings.com
Tea
President: Jim Read
VP: Russell Karr
Manufacturing VP: James Read
Estimated Sales: $ 10-20 Million
Number Employees: 50-99
Type of Packaging: Bulk
Brands:
EARL GREY
EARL GREY DECAFFEINATED
EARL GREY GREEN TEA
IRISH BREAKFAST DECAFF.
LADY GREY
LADY GREY DECAFFEINATED
TWINING BLACKCURRANT
TWINING CEYLON BREAKFAST
TWINING CEYLON ORANGE PEKOE
TWINING DARJEELING
TWINING DECAFFEINATED GREEN TEA
TWINING ENGLISH BREAKFAST DECAFF.
TWINING ENGLISH BREAKFAST GREEN TEA
TWINING ENGLSIH BREAKFAST
TWINING GREEN TEA & LEMON
TWINING GREEN TEA & MINT
TWINING GUNPOWDER GREEN
TWINING IRISH BREAKFAST
TWINING IRISH BREAKFAST DECAFF.
TWINING JASMINE
TWINING JAVA GREEN TEA
TWINING LADY GREY GREEN TEA
TWINING LAPSANG SOUCHONG
TWINING LEMON & GINGER HERB TEA
TWINING LEMON SCENTED
TWINING MINT GREEN TEA
TWINING ORANGE & LEMON HERB TEA
TWINING ORIGINAL GREEN TEA
TWINING PEACH & PASSION FRUIT TEA
TWINING PRINCE OF WALES
TWINING PURE CAMOMILE HERB TEA
TWINING PURE PEPPERMINT HERB TEA
TWINING QUEEN MARY
TWINING STRAWBERRY & MANGO TEA
TWINING WILD BLACKBERRY HERB TEA

13761 **Twinlab**
632 Broadway Fl 11
New York, NY 10012 212-651-8500
Fax: 631-630-3474 800-645-5626
international@twinlab.com www.twinlab.com
Processor and importer of vitamins and nutritional supplements
President: Ross Blechman
Marketing: David Cohen
Estimated Sales: $100+ Million
Number Employees: 100-249
Type of Packaging: Consumer
Other Locations:
Twin Laboratories
American Fork UT

13762 **(HQ)Twinlab**
632 Broadway Fl 11
New York, NY 10012 212-651-8500
Fax: 631-630-3590 800-645-5626
product@twinlab.com www.twinlab.com
Dietary and nutritional food supplements
Chairman: Mark Fox
CFO: Joseph Sinicropi
Marketing: David Cohen
Estimated Sales: $ 100-499.9 Million
Number Employees: 100-249
Brands:
Alvita
Ironman Triathlon
Nature's Herbs
Spring Valley
Twinlab

13763 **Two Chefs on a Roll**
18201 Central Ave
Carson, CA 90746 310-436-1600
Fax: 310-436-1722 800-842-3025
info@twochefsonaroll.com
www.twochefsonaroll.com
Manufactures dips, sauces, bakery, soups, pasta, salads and appetizers
Chairman/President: Lori Swartz
CEO: Keith Swayne
CFO: Richard Tansley
VP R&D/Quality Assurance: Kathy Ware
VP Sales/Marketing: Dawn Rasmussen
Human Resources Director: Eldia Santana
COO: Eliot Swartz
Production Supervisor: Alex Vela
Plant Superintendent: Manuel Diaz
Estimated Sales: $ 50 - 100 Million
Number Employees: 175
Sq. footage: 100000
Type of Packaging: Food Service, Private Label
Brands:
TWO CHEFS ON A ROLL

13764 **Two Chicks and a Ladle**
11 G
New York, NY 10010 212-251-0025
Fax: 914-631-1738 lisafood@aol.com
Fat-free cheesecakes

13765 **Two Guys Spice Company**
2404 Dennis Street
Jacksonville, FL 32204-1712
Fax: 904-791-9330 800-874-5656
products@twoguysspice.com
www.twoguysspice.com
Broker and wholesaler/distributor of dehydrated onions, garlic and vegetables; also, spices and industrial ingredients
President: Michael Simmons
Vice President: Guy Simmons
Estimated Sales: $2.4 Million
Number Employees: 1-4
Number of Brands: 1
Number of Products: 500
Sq. footage: 5200
Type of Packaging: Food Service, Private Label, Bulk

13766 **Two Leaves and a Bud**
23400 Two Rivers Rd #45
Basalt, CO 81621 970-927-9911
Fax: 970-927-9917 866-631-7973
support@twoleavesandabud.net
www.twoleavesandabud.com
teas
President/Owner: Richard Rosenfeld
Estimated Sales: $ 1 Million
Number Employees: 4

13767 **Two Rivers Enterprises**
490 River St W
Holdingford, MN 56340 320-746-3156
Fax: 320-746-3158 joeh@stainlesskings.com
www.stainlesskings.com
Manufacturer of restaurant and food service equipment in addition to providing complete renovations of processing plants and on-site equipment.
President: Robert Warzecha
Midwest Regional Sales: Joe Herges
Midwest Regional Sales: Mike Gold
Midwest Regional Sales: Steve Bairett

13768 **Tyee Wine Cellars**
26335 Greenberry Rd
Corvallis, OR 97333 541-753-8754
Fax: 541-753-0807 merrilee@storypages.com
www.tyeewine.com
Processor of wine
Owner: Margaret Buchanan
Co-Founder: Nola Moiser
Co-Founder: David Buchanan
Co-Founder: Margy Buchanan
Winemaker: Barney Watson
Estimated Sales: Less than $300,000
Number Employees: 1-4
Type of Packaging: Private Label
Brands:
Tyee

13769 **Tyler Candy Company**
4337 Dc Dr
Tyler, TX 75701 903-561-3046
Fax: 903-581-8030 tylercandyco@aol.com
Hard candy
Manager: Ron Sumibek
Estimated Sales: $ 5-10 Million
Number Employees: 20-49
Type of Packaging: Consumer, Private Label
Brands:
Dickies

13770 **Tyler Packing Company**
P.O.Box 1116
Tyler, TX 75710-1116 903-593-9592
Fax: 903-593-1273
Manufacturer of beef, pork and veal
President/Owner: Herbert Buie
Estimated Sales: $3-5 Million
Number Employees: 5-9
Type of Packaging: Bulk

13771 **(HQ)Tyson Foods**
2200 Don Dyson Parkway
Springdale, AR 72762 479-290-4000
Fax: 479-290-4061 800-643-3410
tysonir@tyson.com www.tysonfoods.com
Manufacturer of prepared chicken, beef and pork products, exporter of chicken and parts.
President/CEO: Donnie Smith
EVP/CFO: Dennis Leatherby
SVP/CIO: Gary Cooper
Group VP/Research & Development: Howell Carper
Group VP/Food Service: Devin Cole
EVP/Corporate Affairs: Archie Schaffer III
Group Vp/Consumer Products: Wes Morris
SVP/External Relations: Sara Lilygren
COO: James Lochner
Sr Group VP/Tyson Fresh Meats: Noel White
Estimated Sales: $28.43 Billion
Number Employees: 115,000
Type of Packaging: Consumer, Food Service, Bulk
Other Locations:
AK
AZ
CA
GA
HI
ID
IL
IN
IO
KS
KY
LA
Brands:
HOLLY FARMS
LADY ASTER
MCCARTY FOODS
MEXICAN ORIGINAL
PIERRE
SIGNATURE SPECIALTIES
TASTY BIRD
TYSON
WEAVER

13772 **Tyson Foods**
110 W Freeman Ave
Berryville, AR 72616 870-423-3331
Fax: 870-423-1681 www.tysonfoodsinc.com
Manufacturer of fresh and frozen poultry products
Chairman: John Tyson
President/CEO: Richard Bond
EVP/CFO: Wade Miquelon
EVP/General Counsel: J Alberto Gonzalez-Pita
SVP/Research & Development: Howell Carper
VP Investor Relations: Ruth Ann Wisener
SVP Human Resources: Kenneth Kimbro
Plant Manager: Craig McDonald
Estimated Sales: $100+ Million
Number Employees: 1,000-4,999
Parent Co: Tyson Foods
Type of Packaging: Consumer, Food Service

13773 **Tyson Foods**
545 Valley Rd
Corydon, IN 47112 812-738-3219
Fax: 812-738-5831 800-223-3719
www.tyson.com
Processor of poultry; also, breeding and slaughtering services available.
Manager: Bill Wood
President/CEO: Richard Bond
EVP/CFO: Wade Miquelon
EVP/General Counsel: J Alberto Gonzalez-Pita
SVP/Research & Development: Howell Carper
VP/Investor Relations: Ruth Ann Wisener
SVP/Human Resources: Kenneth Kimbro
Estimated Sales: $100+ Million
Number Employees: 500-999
Parent Co: Tyson Foods
Type of Packaging: Consumer, Food Service, Bulk

13774 **Tyson FoodsTyson Technical Services Lab**
5000 N FM 1912
Amarillo, TX 79101 806-335-1531
Fax: 806-335-7517 www.tysonfoods.com
Manufacturer and exporter of beef
Chairman: John Tyson
President/CEO: Richard Bond
EVP/CFO: Wade Miquelon
EVP/General Counsel: J Alberto Gonzalez-Pita
SVP/Research & Development: Howell Carper
VP/Investor Relations: Ruth Ann Wisener
SVP/Human Resources: Kenneth Kimbro
Plant Manager: Kurt Suther
Estimated Sales: 40.0 Million
Number Employees: 1,000-4,999
Sq. footage: 580000
Parent Co: Tyson Foods
Type of Packaging: Consumer, Food Service

13775 **Tyson Foods**
1610 Midland Blvd
Fort Smith, AR 72901 479-783-8996
Fax: 479-785-4568 www.tyson.com
Manufacturer and exporter of fresh and frozen poultry
Chairman: John Tyson
President/CEO: Richard Bond
Vice President: Valerie Lingo
Plant Manager: Steve Smalling
Estimated Sales: $10-20 Million
Number Employees: 125
Parent Co: Tyson Foods
Type of Packaging: Consumer

13776 **Tyson Foods**
500 Industrial Dr
Star City, AR 71667 870-628-5733
Fax: 870-628-5740 800-351-8184
www.tyson.com
Processor of poultry
Manager: Greg Morgan
President/CEO: Richard Bond
EVP/CFO: Wade Miquelon
EVP/General Counsel: J Alberto Gonzalez-Pita
SVP/Research & Development: Howell Carper
VP/Investor Relations: Ruth Ann Wisener
SVP/Human Resources: Kenneth Kimbro
Estimated Sales: $1.2 Million
Number Employees: 20-49
Parent Co: Tyson Foods
Type of Packaging: Consumer, Food Service, Private Label, Bulk

13777 **Tyson Foods**
P.O.Box 2020
Springdale, AR 72764-6999 800-643-3410
www.tysonfoodsinc.com
Processor of fresh and frozen chicken products.
President/Ceo: Donnie Smith
Chairman: John Tyson
Coo: James Lochner
Plant Manager: David Keith
Estimated Sales: $100+ Million
Number Employees: 500-999
Parent Co: Tyson Foods
Type of Packaging: Consumer, Food Service, Private Label, Bulk

13778 **Tyson Foods**
19597 State Hwy E
Bloomfield, MO 63825 573-568-2153
Fax: 573-568-3718 www.tyson.com
Processor of frozen chicken
President: Tyson Hinge
Manager: Mark Abry
Production Manager: Jim Morin
Manager: Paul Hester
Estimated Sales: $ 5 - 10 Million
Number Employees: 4
Sq. footage: 9419
Parent Co: Tyson Foods
Type of Packaging: Consumer, Bulk

13779 **Tyson Foods**
305 Cleveland St
Forest, MS 39074 601-469-1712
Fax: 601-469-5365 www.tyson.com
Manufacturer of poultry products.
Manager: Tracy Shannon
President/CEO: Richard Bond
EVP/CFO: Wade Miquelon
EVP/General Counsel: J Alberto Gonzalez-Pita
SVP/Research & Development: Howell Carper
VP/Investor Relations: Ruth Ann Wisener
SVP/Human Resources: Kenneth Kimbro
Estimated Sales: $100+ Million
Number Employees: 500-999
Type of Packaging: Consumer, Private Label

13780 **Tyson Foods**
1600 River St
Wilkesboro, NC 28697 336-838-0083
Fax: 336-651-2829 www.tyson.com
Processor of cooked and frozen chicken
Chairman/President: Richard Bond
Vice President: Mark Welborn
Manager: Lani Stevens
Manager: Gary Johnson
Estimated Sales: $ 10-20 Million
Number Employees: 100-249
Parent Co: Tyson Foods
Type of Packaging: Consumer, Food Service
Brands:
Tyson Foods

13781 **Tyson Foods**
P.O.Box 547
Dexter, MO 63841 573-624-4548
Fax: 573-624-9834 www.tyson.com
Processor of fresh and frozen chicken.
Manager: Mark Avery
President/CEO: Richard Bond
EVP/CFO: Wade Miquelon
EVP/General Counsel: J Alberto Gonzalez-Pita
SVP/Research & Development: Howell Carper
VP/Investor Relations: Ruth Ann Wisener
SVP/Human Resources: Kenneth Kimbro
Complex Manager: Mike Avery
Estimated Sales: $ 100-500 Million
Number Employees: 500-999
Parent Co: Tyson Foods
Type of Packaging: Consumer, Food Service

13782 **Tyson Foods**
110 W Freeman Ave
Berryville, AR 72616 870-423-3331
Fax: 870-423-1681 www.tysonfoodsinc.com
Fresh and frozen chicken
Manager: Richard Bond
Complex Manager: Rick Oswald
Plant Manager: Craig McDonald
Purchasing Manager: Mirna MacDonald
Estimated Sales: $ 100-500 Million
Number Employees: 1,000-4,999
Brands:
Tyson Foods

13783 **Tyson Foods Plant**
5701 McNutt Rd
Santa Teresa, NM 88008-9604 575-589-0100
Fax: 505-589-1903 800-351-8184
www.tyson.com
Chicken slaughtering and processing.
Chairman: John Tyson
President/CEO: Richard Bond
EVP/CFO: Wade Miquelon
EVP/General Counsel: J Alberto Gonzalez-Pita
SVP/Research & Development: Howell Carper
VP/Investor Relations: Ruth Ann Wisener
SVP/Human Resources: Kenneth Kimbro
Estimated Sales: $ 1 - 3 Million
Number Employees: 5-9
Parent Co: Tyson Foods
Type of Packaging: Consumer, Food Service, Private Label
Brands:
Deli Gourmet
Rueben
TLC

13784 **Tyson Fresh MeatsMeat Packing Plant**
2101 W 6th Ave
Emporia, KS 66801 620-343-3640
Fax: 620-343-3640 www.tyson.com
www.lbpoil.com
Manufacturer and exporter of fresh and frozen beef including carcasses, cuts, by-products and offals.
President & CEO: Richard Bond
EVP/CFO: Wade Miquelon
EVP/General Counsel: J Alberto Gonzalez-Pita
SVP/Research & Development: Howell Carper
Sales: Jeff Boyer
VP/Investor Relations: Ruth Ann Wisener
SVP/Human Resources: Kenneth Kimbro
Manager: Roger Brownrigg
Estimated Sales: $26.4 Billion
Number Employees: 8
Parent Co: Tyson Foods
Type of Packaging: Consumer, Food Service, Private Label, Bulk
Brands:
TYSON

13785 **(HQ)Tyson Fresh Meats**
800 Stevens Port Dr
Dakota Dunes, SD 57049 605-235-2061
Fax: 605-235-2068 www.tyson.com/
Producer of fresh beef, pork and related allied products and supplier of high quality fully prepared meats for the retail and food service industries.
Chairman: John Tyson
President/CEO: Richard Bond
EVP/CFO: Dennis Leatherby
Vp And Research And Development: Howell Carper
SVP/Research & Development: Howell Carper
SVP, Sales International: Roel Andriessen
VP/Investor Relations: Ruth Ann Wisener
SVP/Human Resources: Kenneth Kimbro
Estimated Sales: 28.4 Billion
Number Employees: 115,000
Parent Co: Tyson Foods
Type of Packaging: Consumer, Food Service, Private Label, Bulk
Brands:
THOMAS E. WILSON

13786 **U Roast Em**
16778 W Us Highway 63
Hayward, WI 54843-7214 715-634-6255
Fax: 715-934-3221 info@u-roast-em (dot) com
www.u-roast-em.com
Supplier of green coffee beans, bulk teas, home roasting supplies and coffee flavorings
Type of Packaging: Consumer
Brands:
BODUM
FRESH BEANS

13787 **U. Okada & Company**
1000 Queen St
Honolulu, HI 96814 808-597-1102
Fax: 808-591-6634
President: Dexter Okada
Estimated Sales: $ 10 - 20 Million
Number Employees: 20-49

13788 **U.S. Foodservice**
6685 Crescent Dr
Norcross, GA 30071 770-263-1240
Fax: 770-263-4359 800-554-8050
www.usfoodservice.com
Wholesaler/distributor of dry groceries, produce, dairy products, baked goods, general merchandise, private label items, frozen foods, seafood and meats/provisions; serving the food service market
Manager: Scott Lasalle
Vice President: Lee Carson
Warehouse Manager: Greg Kirchner
Estimated Sales: $10-20 Million
Number Employees: 250-499
Parent Co: Alliant Foodservice

13789 **UDV Wines**
1160 Battery St # 400
San Francisco, CA 94111-1236 415-835-7300
Fax: 415-835-8615 www.diageo.com
Processor of wine
Manager: Mike Wineberger
VP Marketing: Steve Wyant
Estimated Sales: $ 50 - 100 Million
Number Employees: 50-99
Parent Co: Grand Metropolitan
Type of Packaging: Consumer, Food Service

13790 **UFL Foods**
450 Superior Boulevard
Mississauga, ON L5T 2R9
Canada 905-670-7776
Fax: 905-670-7751 pboucek@uflfoods.com
Processor and exporter of custom formulated and blended ingredients including milk replacers, mustard, seasonings, meat binders, curing preparations, etc.; also, pasta and rice sauce mixes, soup and sauce bases, batters andbreadings
VP: Jack Conway
Number Employees: 100-249
Sq. footage: 110000
Parent Co: Newly Weds Foods
Type of Packaging: Food Service, Private Label, Bulk

13791 **ULDO USA**
10 Dewey Road
Lexington, MA 02420-1018 781-860-7800
Fax: 781-863-1973 productinfo@bakenjoy.com
www.uldousa.com
Baked goods
Brands:
Baken Joy

13792 **UNOI Grainmill**
Route 13-A
Seaford, DE 19973-5749 302-629-4083
Miller of whole wheat flour, white and yellow corn meal, buckwheat, etc
Owner: Janice Griffith
Manager: Charles Willoughby
Estimated Sales: Under $300,000
Number Employees: 3
Sq. footage: 10000
Parent Co: United Nation of Islam
Type of Packaging: Private Label
Brands:
Hearn & Rawlins
White Dove

13793 **US Chocolate Corporation**
4801 1st Ave
Brooklyn, NY 11232-4208 718-788-8555
Fax: 718-788-3311 uschoc@aol.com
Processor and exporter of kosher liquid marble chocolate and white parve coatings, fudge bases and flavors.
President: David Rosenberg
Estimated Sales: $ 10 - 20 Million
Number Employees: 10-19
Sq. footage: 27000
Brands:
U.S. Brand

13794 **US Distilled Products**
1607 12th St S
Princeton, MN 55371-2311 763-389-4903
Fax: 763-389-2549 information@usdp.com
www.usdp.com
Importer and master distributor, contract bottling, producer of alcoholic beverages and broker
President: Bradley P Johnson
CFO: Pat Pelzer
General Manager: Todd Geisness
National Sales Manager: Steve Sullivan
Production Manager: Kevin Issendorf
Estimated Sales: $ 20-30 Million
Number Employees: 50-99
Sq. footage: 250000

13795 **US Durum Products**
P.O.Box 10126
Lancaster, PA 17605-0126 717-293-8698
Fax: 717-293-8699 866-268-7268
www.usdurum.com
Manufacturer and distributer of couscous throughout the United States and Canada.
Manager: Jeffrey Dewey
Estimated Sales: $ 2.5-5 Million
Number Employees: 10-19

13796 **US Flavors & Fragrances**
1230 Karl Ct
Wauconda, IL 60084 847-487-1022
Fax: 847-487-1066 www.synergytaste.com
Food flavorings and fragrances
President: Roderick W Sowders
VP: Jim Tanger
Estimated Sales: $29 Million
Number Employees: 58
Sq. footage: 40000
Brands:
Carbery
Synergy Flavours

13797 **US Food & Pharmaceuticals**
313 W Beltline Hwy # 182
Madison, WI 53713-2682 608-278-1293
Fax: 608-278-9042
Processor of milk minerals, dairy formulations, enhanced dairy products and formulations, nutritional products, nutraceuticals
President: Rajan Vembu
VP: James Henderson
Marketing Director: Richard Nelson
Public Relations: Kalle Smith
Operations Manager: Jay Zahom
Estimated Sales: $1500000
Number Employees: 5-9
Sq. footage: 10000
Type of Packaging: Consumer
Brands:
Dari-Cal
Infalac
My-Baby

13798 **US Foods**
4343 NW 38th St
Lincoln, NE 68524 402-470-2021
Fax: 402-470-3549 info@u-s-foods.com
www.u-s-foods.com
Pre-cooked bean, pea & lentil products. Precooked grain & rice products. Private label ready to eat cereals & snacks. contract manufacturing & private label packaging services
President: Rick L Williams
Sales: Medlodie Slaymaker
Production: Clark Mulder
Purchasing: Ken Adams
Estimated Sales: $9500000
Number Employees: 50-99
Sq. footage: 80000
Type of Packaging: Private Label, Bulk
Brands:
Brown's Best
Crunchee
Infranized
Q-C

13799 **US Ingredients**
P.O.Box 9207
Naperville, IL 60567-0207 630-820-1711
Fax: 630-820-1883 usingredient@earthlink.net
www.usingredient@earthlink.net

Seasonings and food flavoring products
Owner: Eric Maul
Estimated Sales: $ 5-10 Million
Number Employees: 5-9

13800 **US Mills**
401 E City Ave Ste 220
Bala Cynwyd, PA 19004-1117
Fax: 781-444-3411 800-422-1125
www.usmillsllc.com/
Processor and exporter of natural/organic foods including ready-to-eat and hot cereals and graham crackers.
President: Charles Verde
Executive VP: Cynthia Davis
Sales: William Bunn
Number Employees: 5-9
Number of Brands: 5
Number of Products: 45
Type of Packaging: Consumer
Brands:
EREWHON
FARINA MILLS
NEW MORNING
SKINNER'S
UNCLE SAM CEREAL

13801 **US Spice Mills**
4537 W Fulton St
Chicago, IL 60624-1609 773-378-6800
Fax: 773-378-0077 usspice@usspice.com
www.usspice.com
Manufacturer and importer of spices
President: Nick Patel
Estimated Sales: $600000
Number Employees: 5-9

13802 **US Sugar Company**
692 Bailey Ave
Buffalo, NY 14206 716-828-1170
Fax: 716-828-1509 steve@ussugar.net
www.ussugar.net
Manufacturer of granulated, brown and powdered sugars; sugar and artificial sweetener packets
President: William McDaniel
VP: Steve Ward
VP Operations: Tom Moran
Plant Manager: Avery Foy
Estimated Sales: $25 Million
Number Employees: 20-49
Number of Brands: 30
Number of Products: 20
Sq. footage: 300000
Type of Packaging: Consumer, Food Service, Private Label
Brands:
PRIVATE LABEL
US SUGARS

13803 **USA Beverage**
1410a E Old Us Highway 40
Warrenton, MO 63383-1316 636-456-5468
Fax: 636-456-3422 general@usbeverage.com
www.usbeverage.com
Wines
President: Hugh White
CFO: Thomas Nittler
Marketing Director: Darrell Wiss
Production Manager: Terre Novell
Plant Manager: Hugh White
Estimated Sales: $500,000
Number Employees: 20-49
Type of Packaging: Private Label
Brands:
USA Beverages

13804 **USA Fruit**
3 North Street
Greenwich, CT 06830-4720 203-661-8280
Fruit
Estimated Sales: $ 3 - 5 Million
Number Employees: 1-4

13805 **USA Laboratories**
1438 Highway 96
Burns, TN 37029-5030 615-441-1521
Fax: 615-446-3788 800-489-4872
usalabs@usalabs.com www.usalabs.com
Processor and exporter of vitamins, minerals, nutritional supplements and weight loss aids
President/Owner: Charles Stokes
CEO: Charles Stokes
R&D: David Bethshears PhD
Quality Control: Brad Stokes
Marketing Director: Erica White
Sales Director: Shelby Bethsheard
Operations: Ted Sanders
Estimated Sales: $4.7 Million
Number Employees: 39
Number of Brands: 5
Number of Products: 1000
Sq. footage: 100000
Parent Co: USA Laboratories
Brands:
Burn Off
Jewel Laboratories
Nutrceuticals
Power Rangers Chewable Vitamins
USA Best
USA Laboratories Nutrients
USA Sports Labs

13806 **USA Sunrise Beverage**
I-90 Exit 2 Plaza
S
Spearfish, SD 57783 605-723-0690
Processor and exporter of bottled mineral and spring water and carbonated fruit drinks including papaya, peach, pineapple, etc.; importer of water
President: Omar Barrientos
VP/Secretary: Gene Fairchild
Number Employees: 5-9
Type of Packaging: Consumer, Food Service
Brands:
Dakota Springs
Rushmore Springs
Sunrise

13807 **(HQ)UST**
P.O.Box 100
Danbury, CT 06813-0100 203-792-4460
Fax: 203-792-4602 800-650-7411
www.ustinc.com
Wines
Owner: Gerald Holton
CEO: John Barr
CFO: James Patracuolla
Vice President: Patricia Dennis
Estimated Sales: $ 10-100 Million
Number Employees: 250-499
Type of Packaging: Private Label
Brands:
Copenhagen
Husky
Rooster

13808 **(HQ)Uas Laboratories**
9953 Valley View Rd
Eden Prairie, MN 55344 952-935-1707
Fax: 952-935-1650 800-422-3371
info@uaslabs.com www.uaslabs.com
Manufacturer and exporter of nutritional supplements
President: S K Dash
Quality Control: Scot Elert
Marketing Director: Raj Dash
Operations Manager: Steven Shack
Estimated Sales: $3 Million
Number Employees: 10-19
Number of Products: 12
Sq. footage: 5400
Type of Packaging: Consumer, Private Label, Bulk
Brands:
DDS
DDS Acidophilus
DDS Junior
DDS Plus
UAS Activin Plus
UAS Coenzyme Q10
UAS Joint Formula

13809 **Udi's Granola**
12000 E. 47th Avenue
Suite 400
Denver, CO 80239 303-657-6366
Fax: 303-657-5373 info@udisgranola.com
www.udisgranola.com
flavored granola
Founder: Udi Baron

13810 **Ugo di Lullo & Sons**
P.O.Box 126
Westville, NJ 08093-0126 856-456-3700
Fax: 856-456-7161 dilul8@aol.com
General grocery
Owner: Ugo Di Lullo
Estimated Sales: $600,000
Number Employees: 10
Brands:
Ugo di Lullo & Sons

13811 **Uhlmann Company**
1009 Central St
Kansas City, MO 64105 816-221-8200
Fax: 816-221-5504 800-383-8201
Processor of all-purpose unbleached and wholewheat flour
President: Paul Uhlamnn Iii
Estimated Sales: $ 10 - 20 Million
Number Employees: 14
Sq. footage: 30000
Type of Packaging: Consumer, Food Service
Brands:
Ceresota
Heckers

13812 **Uinta Brewing**
1722 Fremont Dr
Salt Lake City, UT 84104 801-467-0909
Fax: 801-463-7151 info@uintabrewing.com
www.uintabrewing.com
Beer
President: William Hamill
Public Relations Officer: Steve Kustinec
Estimated Sales: $ 5-10 Million
Number Employees: 10-19
Sq. footage: 26000
Type of Packaging: Private Label
Brands:
Uinta

13813 **Ukuva Africa**
5210 Carillon Pt
Kirkland, WA 98033-7378 425-828-0609
Fax: 888-248-7802 888-280-1003
colleen@tasteofafrica.com
www.tasteofafrica.com
African spicy sauces
Brands:
Malawi Gold
Swazi Mamma Mamba
Xhosa Umsobo Lyababa

13814 **Ulfert Broockmann**
611 Burdick Street
Libertyville, IL 60048-3101 847-680-3771
Cheese

13815 **Ulker Group**
Ferah Cd / Kisiklicesme Sk
2/4 34692 B Camlica
Uskudar / IST / Turkey,
Turkey
Ph 90(216)5242991 Fx 90(216)3357393 Email: cahit.paksoy@ulker.com.tr
Website: www.ulker.com.tr/ulkerportal/en/
Manufacturer and exporter of numerous food products including chocolate bars; rice crispy bars; cream biscuits; cookies; baby biscuits; crackers; cakes; candies and chewing gum.
Chairman Holding Executive Board/CEO: Murat Ulker
Vice Chairman Holding Executive Board: Orhan Ozokur
President Ulker Division: Ali Ulker
President Trade Division: Mustafa Yasar Serdengecti
President R&D and Business Development: Zeki Ziya Sozen
President Packaging Division: Huseyin Avni Metinkale
President Informatics Division: Murat Inan
President Consumer Division: Taner Karamollaoglu
CEO Packaging Group: Cahit Paksoy Ph.D
Type of Packaging: Food Service

13816 **Ultima Foods**
2177 Boul Fernand-Lafontaine
Longueuil, ON J4G 2V2
Canada 450-651-3737
Fax: 450-651-1788 800-363-9496
www.yoplait.ca

Processor of dairy products including regular and drinkable yogurt and fresh cheeses
President/CEO: gerry doutre
CEO: alain David
VP Marketing: Lucie Remillard
VP Sales: Michel Cusson
Number Employees: 4000
Parent Co: Agropur
Type of Packaging: Consumer
Brands:
Minigo
YOP
Yoplait Tubes
creme and fruits
source

13817 **Ultimate Bagel**
319 Logan Blvd
Altoona, PA 16602-3118 814-944-4148
Fax: 814-942-2904
shipping-hhbagels@nyc.rr.com
Processor of bagels
President: Carol Kozak
Estimated Sales: $230,000
Number Employees: 6
Sq. footage: 2000
Type of Packaging: Consumer, Food Service

13818 **Ultimate Biscotti**
1000 S Bertelsen Road
Suite 10
Eugene, OR 97402-5448 541-344-8220
Fax: 541-344-8357 info@ultimatebiscotti.com
www.ultimatebiscotti.com
Processor of biscotti including ginger, hazelnut chocolate, citrus, etc.; also, wheat and gluten-free available
President: Heather Kent
Number Employees: 5-9
Sq. footage: 6000
Type of Packaging: Consumer, Food Service, Bulk
Brands:
Ultimate Biscotti

13819 **Ultimate Gourmet**
P.O.Box 967
Belle Mead, NJ 8502 908-359-4050
Fax: 908-359-2494
contact@ultimate-gourmet.com
www.ultimate-gourmet.com
Bar mixes, jellies, jams, sauces, brandied fruit, barbacue sauces, marinades and rubs
President: Tali Almagor
Estimated Sales: $300,000-500,000
Number Employees: 1-4
Type of Packaging: Consumer, Food Service, Private Label, Bulk
Brands:
Club Tahity
Cramore
Creamy Head
FIREHOUSE
Giroux
Milem
Proud Mary
Raffetto
Tahiti

13820 **Ultimate Nut & Candy Company**
6333 West 3rd Street
Los Angeles, CA 90036
800-767-5259
customerservice@ultimatenut.com
www.ultimatenut.com
Candy, nuts
President: Steve Turner
Quality Control: Theresa Malgonadio
Marketing Manager: Steve Turner
Number Employees: 20-49
Type of Packaging: Private Label
Brands:
Studio Confections
Ultimate Confections

13821 **Ultimate Nutrition**
161 Woodford Avenue
Plainville, CT 06062-2370 860-409-7100
Fax: 860-793-5006
victor.rubino@worldnet.att.net
www.ultimatenutrition.com
Food processor and exporter of food supplements including capsules, tablets, powders and protein bars; manufacturer and exporter of T-shirts, hats, etc
President: Victor Rubino
Advertising: Seth Darvick
VP Sales: Dean Caputo
Type of Packaging: Consumer

13822 **Ultra Enterprises**
14108 Lambert Rd
Whittier, CA 90605 562-945-4833
Fax: 562-698-7362 800-543-0627
b.kaliultra@verizon.net www.ultraent.com
Processor and sports nutrition of granulars
President/CEO: Bud Thompson
Vice President: Mary Thompson
Number of Products: 50
Type of Packaging: Consumer
Brands:
Sports Nutrition
Ultra Rain Glandulars

13823 **Ultra Seal**
521 Main St
New Paltz, NY 12561 845-255-2490
Fax: 845-255-3553 dawnb@ultra-seal.com
www.ultra-seal.com
Contract packager of portion controlled products including ketchup, mustard, powder lemonade, fruit juice, iced tea mix, etc
President: Dennis Borrello
Manager: Christine Downs
Executive: Terry Murphy
Estimated Sales: $5-10 Million
Number Employees: 105
Sq. footage: 26000
Type of Packaging: Consumer, Food Service, Private Label, Bulk

13824 **Umanoff & Parsons**
1704 Boone Ave
Bronx, NY 10460-5400 212-219-2240
Fax: 718-684-7978 800-248-9993
service@umanoffparsons.com
www.umanoffparsons.com
Processor of fresh and frozen all natural kosher dairy cakes, pies, quiches and tarts
President: Simon Seaton
Estimated Sales: $5,200,000
Number Employees: 20-49
Sq. footage: 6500

13825 **Umpqua Dairy Products Company**
333 SE Sykes Ave
Roseburg, OR 97470 541-672-2638
Fax: 541-673-0256 www.umpquadairy.com
Processor and exporter of ice cream, milk, cottage cheese, sour cream and butter
President: Douglas Feldkamp
Executive VP: Steven Feldkamp
Estimated Sales: $65 Million
Number Employees: 110
Type of Packaging: Consumer, Food Service, Private Label

13826 **Uncle Andy's Pic & Pay Bakery**
171 Ocean St
South Portland, ME 04106-3623 207-799-7199
Fax: 207- 79-9 34
Baked goods
Owner: Dennis Fogg
Estimated Sales: Under $500,000
Number Employees: 10-19

13827 **Uncle Ben's**
P.O.Box 1737
Greenville, MS 38702 662-335-8000
Fax: 662-378-4370 800-548-6253
www.unclebens.com
Processor of rice
Manager: Ronnie Taylor
Estimated Sales: $100+ Million
Number Employees: 100-249
Parent Co: Mars
Type of Packaging: Consumer
Brands:
UNCLE BEN'S

13828 **Uncle Ben's**
PO Box 1752
Houston, TX 77251-1752 713-674-9484
Fax: 713-670-2227 www.unclebens.com

Parboiled rice
Number Employees: 50-99

13829 **Uncle Bum's Gourmet Foods**
5821 Wilderness Ave
Riverside, CA 92504-1004 951-352-5700
Fax: 951-352-5710 800-486-2867
www.triplehfoods.com
Processor and exporter of marinades, sauces, spice mixes, salsas, syrups, bar mixes, dressings, apple sauce, flavored teas, hot sauces, jellies, sports drinks, oils and mustards
President: Tom Harris Jr
Director Sales/Marketing: David Shoemaker
Estimated Sales: $ 20 - 50 Million
Number Employees: 50-99
Sq. footage: 65000
Parent Co: Triple H Food Processors
Type of Packaging: Consumer, Food Service, Private Label, Bulk
Brands:
Hot Jamaican Jerk
Jamaican Jerk Spice Blend
Spanish Style Romesco Sauce
Spicey Caribbean Bbq Sauce
Spicey Teriyaki
Sweet & Spicey

13830 **Uncle Charley's SausageCompany**
1135 Industrial Park Rd
Vandergrift, PA 15690-6050 724-845-3302
Fax: 724-845-3174
charley@unclecharleyssausage.com
www.unclecharleyssausage.com
Pork, pork products
President: Charles Armitage
Vice President: Charles Armitage Jr
Estimated Sales: $ 5-10 Million
Number Employees: 20-49

13831 **Uncle Fred's Fine Foods**
209 N Doughty Street
Rockport, TX 78382-5322 361-729-8320
www.unclfred.com
Processor and importer of habanero ketchup, jelly, hot sweet mustard and chips, salsa, spices, meat rubs and sauces including cocktail, pepper and barbecue
President: Fred Franklin
VP/Co-Owner: Pat Marsh
Manager: Judith Jecmen-Fuhrman
Number Employees: 1-4
Sq. footage: 1600
Parent Co: Island Enterprises
Type of Packaging: Consumer
Brands:
Uncle Fred's Fine Foods

13832 **Uncle Lee's Tea**
11020 Rush St
South El Monte, CA 91733-3547 626-350-3309
Fax: 626-350-4364 800-732-8830
contact@unclelee.com www.unclelee.com
Processor, exporter and importer of teas including herb, spiced, traditional and dieter's; co-packing and private label available
President: Kuo-Lin Lee
Vice President: Jonason Lee
Sales Director: James O'Young
Public Relations: Patty Gillno
Plant Manager: Joe Villegas
Estimated Sales: $1400000
Number Employees: 5-9
Parent Co: Ten Ren Tea Company
Brands:
Uncle Lee's Tea

13833 **Uncle Ralph's Cookie Company**
801 N East St
Frederick, MD 21701-4652 301-695-6224
Fax: 301-695-6327 800-422-0626
sales@uncleralphscookies.com
www.uncleralphscookies.com

Processor of gourmet cookies, brownies, crumb cakes, pound cakes, and quick breads
VP: Ralph Wight
Founder: Peggy Wight
Sales Director: Jamie Mater
Estimated Sales: $ 3 - 5 Million
Number Employees: 50-99
Sq. footage: 30000
Type of Packaging: Consumer, Food Service, Private Label
Brands:
Uncle Ralph's

13834 Uncle Ray's Potato Chips
14245 Birwood St
Detroit, MI 48238-2207 313-834-0800
Fax: 313-834-0443 sandy@unclerays.com
www.unclerays.com
Snack foods without nuts
President: Raymond Jenkins
Purchasing Manager: Jim Coomes
Estimated Sales: $ 50-100 Million
Number Employees: 5-9
Parent Co: Amerifit/Strength Systems
Brands:
Uncle Ray's

13835 Uncle Wiley's
1220 Post Rd
Fairfield, CT 06824 203-256-9313
Fax: 203-256-1350 http://unclewileys.com
Makes a variety of packaged seasonings for meats, vegetables, fruits, baking (pies, etc.), salads, etc.
Founder/Owner/President: Wiley Mullins

13836 Uncommon Grounds Coffee
2813 7th St
Berkeley, CA 94710-2702 51- 7-4 12
Fax: 51- 8-8 18 80- 5-7 91
uncommon@uncommongrounds.net
www.uncommongrounds.net
Coffee
President/CEO: Kim Moore
CFO: Derek Lantner
Operations Manager: Kim Moore
Production Manager: James Spottn
Estimated Sales: $2.3 Million
Number Employees: 14
Type of Packaging: Private Label
Brands:
Double Star Espresso
El Salvador Finca Las Nubes
Ethiopian Organic
Molta Roba

13837 Une-Viandi
505 Industriel Boulevard
St. Jean Sur Richelieu, NB J3B 5Y8
Canada 450-347-8406
Fax: 450-347-8142 800-363-1955
Processor, importer and exporter of meat products including bone-in and boneless beef, lamb and veal
President: Claude Berni
Export Manager: Lloyd Arshinoff
Number Employees: 50-99
Sq. footage: 22000
Type of Packaging: Consumer, Food Service, Private Label, Bulk

13838 Unette Corporation
1578 Sussex Tpke Ste 400
Randolph, NJ 7869 973-328-6800
Fax: 973-537-1010 tsweeney@unette.com
www.unette.com
Contract packager of food colors, condiments, groceries, etc
President: Joseph Hark
Estimated Sales: $4400000
Number Employees: 50-99
Sq. footage: 60000

13839 Ungars Food Products
9 Boumar Pl
Elmwood Park, NJ 07407-2615 201-703-1300
Fax: 201-703-9333 webquery@drpraegers.com
www.drpraegers.com
Veggie burgers, pancakes, breaded fish fillets, fillet fish sticks
President: Peter Praeger
CFO: Jeff Coher
Estimated Sales: $ 2.5-5 Million
Number Employees: 50-99

13840 (HQ)Ungerer & Company
4 Bridgewater Ln
Lincoln Park, NJ 07035 973-628-0600
Fax: 973-628-0251 aking@ungerer.org
www.ungererandcompany.com
Manufacturer, importer and exporter of natural and artificial fruit flavors and essential oils including lemon, orange, peppermint, spearmint, ginger, lime and dill
President: K G Voorhees Jr
Estimated Sales: $10 Million
Number Employees: 100-249
Type of Packaging: Consumer, Private Label, Bulk
Other Locations:
Ungerer & Company Plant
Bethlehem PA
Ungerer & Company Plant
Oaxaca, Mexico

13841 Unibroue/UnibrewSleeman Unibroue
80 Rue Des Carriers
Chambly, QC J3L 2H6
Canada 450-658-7658
Fax: 450-658-9195 info@unibroue.com
www.unibroue.com
Processor and exporter of gourmet beer instant black currant,instant apple,chambly blonde,la bolduc,gift of god.
President/CEO: Andre Dion
Marketing And Sales: Louis Fortier
Sales Director: Laurent Xavier
Estimated Sales: $21million
Number Employees: 250
Type of Packaging: Consumer, Food Service
Brands:
Unibrew
Unibroue

13842 Unica
23w101 Kings Ct # 100
Glen Ellyn, IL 60137-7215 630-790-8107
Fax: 630-790-8117 www.x-it-dk.com
Sugar free confectionary
President: Peter Zeuthen
Estimated Sales: $ 5 - 10 Million
Number Employees: 5-9
Brands:
UNICA

13843 Unicof
102 Executive Dr # D
Sterling, VA 20166-9555 703-904-0777
Fax: 703-904-7817 ted@unicof.com
General grocery
President: Hanif Moledina
President: Kyle B Klyman
Estimated Sales: $ 10-100 Million
Number Employees: 5-9
Brands:
Unicof

13844 Unified Foods
145 Vallecitos De Oro # 208
San Marcos, CA 92069-1459 760-744-7225
Fax: 760-744-7215
Processor, exporter and importer of dehydrated vegetables including bell peppers, carrots, celery, peas, corn, mushrooms, garlic, etc
Owner: Dan Stouder
VP: Dan Stouder
Sales Manager: Simone Grunewald
Estimated Sales: $ 1 - 3 Million
Number Employees: 1-4
Sq. footage: 10000
Type of Packaging: Bulk

13845 Unified Western Grocers
3626 11th Ave
Los Angeles, CA 90018 323-731-8223
Fax: 323-731-6821 www.ubgrocers.com
Processor of milk including whole, 1% and 2%; wholesaler/distributor of yogurt, cottage cheese, orange juice, fruit punch and sour cream
Manager: John Jackson
Sales/Marketing: Jeffrey Quintana
Estimated Sales: $100+ Million
Number Employees: 100-249
Parent Co: Certified Grocers of California
Type of Packaging: Consumer

13846 Unified Western Grocers
457 E Mlk Blvd
Los Angeles, CA 90011 323-232-6124
Fax: 323-234-7381 www.uwgrocers.com
Bread and rolls
President: Alfred Plamann
Chief Engineer: Floyd Smith
Sales Manager: Norm Bowers
General Manager: John Bedrosian
Manager: Maurice Ochua
Purchasing: Terry Stadheim
Estimated Sales: $ 50-100 Million
Number Employees: 74
Type of Packaging: Private Label, Bulk

13847 Unilever
523 S 17th St
Harrisburg, PA 17104-2220 717-234-6215
Fax: 717-231-5419 www.bestfoods.com
Processor of pasta
Manager: James Pagano
President Americas: Bill Fertenbaugh
President Europe: Rudy Markham
President Foods: Manvinder Singh Banga
President Asia Africa: Harish Manwani
Chief Human Resources Officer: Sandy Ogg
Chief Financial Officer: Rudy Markham
Deputy Chief Financial Officer: John Ripley
Group Treasurer: Pascal Visee
Estimated Sales: $ 10 - 20 Million
Number Employees: 50-99
Sq. footage: 300000
Parent Co: Unilever USA
Type of Packaging: Bulk
Brands:
Lipton Foods

13848 Unilever
5430 Cote De Liesse Road
Mont-Royal, QC H4P 1A6
Canada 514-735-1141
Fax: 514-733-7499
denis.labattaglia@unilever.com
www.unilever.com
Processor of tea
President: Ralph Kugler
Regional Sales Manager: Don Boudreau
Plant Manager: Dennis Labattaglia
Number Employees: 100-249
Parent Co: Unilever USA
Type of Packaging: Consumer
Brands:
Dove
Herbal Lipton
Red Rose
Salada
Sunlight

13849 Unilever
2200 Cabot Dr
Suite 200
Lisle, IL 60532-0914 847-678-1241
Fax: 847-671-2290 877-995-4483
www.bestfoods.com
Manufacturer and exporter of frozen and canned soups and concentrated soup bases.
Group Chief Executive: Patrick Cescau
President Americas: John Rice
President Europe: Kees Van Der Graaf
President Home & Personal Care: Ralph Kugler
President Foods: Manvinder Singh Banga
President Asia Africa: Harish Manwani
Chief Human Resources Officer: Sandy Ogg
Chief Auditor: Alan Johnson
Chief Financial Officer: Rudy Markham
Deputy Chief Financial Officer: John Ripley
Group Treasurer: Pascal Visee
Number Employees: 500
Type of Packaging: Consumer, Food Service, Bulk

13850 Unilever Bestfoods
800 Sylvan Ave
Englewood Cliffs, NJ 7632 201-567-8000
Fax: 201-871-8257 corpaffairs.usa@unilever.com
www.bestfoods.com

Manufacturer and processor of salad dressings, noodles, macaroni, soups and iced tea mixes; herbal, regular and lemon flavored teas; well-known US grocery, specialty, and baking brands as well as food service
General Manager: Tony Santoro
VP: Gregory Phillips
Sales/Marketing Executive: Dave Landers
Media Relations: Jennifer Stalzer
Purchasing Agent: Bob Talbot
Number Employees: 10,000+
Parent Co: Unilever USA
Type of Packaging: Consumer, Food Service
Brands:
BEN & JERRY'S
BEST FOODS
BETOLLI
BREYER'S
BRUMMEL AND BROWN
FIVE BROTHERS
GOOD HUMOR
HELLMANN'S
I CAN'T BELIEVE IT'S NOT BUTTER
IMPERIAL
KNORR
LAWRY'S
LIPTON
PROMISE
RAGU
SHEDD'S
SKIPPY
TAKE CONTROL
WISH-BONE

13851 Unilever Bestfoods, Inc.

700 Sylvan Ave
Englewood Cliffs, NJ 07632-3113 201-894-4000
Fax: 201-894-2186
MediaRelations.USA@unilever.com
www.unileverus.com
Processor and importer of olive oil and olive oil products including salad dressings and aerosol sprays; also, balsamic vinegar
President: Michael Polk
Marketing Manager: Paul Barrett
Estimated Sales: $20-50 Million
Number Employees: 10,000+
Parent Co: Unilever Canada
Type of Packaging: Consumer, Food Service, Private Label, Bulk
Brands:
Bertolli
Tirreno

13852 Unilever Canada

Po Box 38
Saint John, NB E2L 3X1
Canada
Fax: 506-631-6424 800-565-7273
unilevercanada.foundation@unilever.com
www.unilever.ca
Manufacturer of a variety of products for the food industry, health and beauty industry as well as household products.
President/CEO: David Blanchard
VP/General Counsel & Corporate Secretary: John Coyne
VP/Chief Financial Officer: Paulo De Castro
VP/General Manager Foods: Mark Olney
VP/Customer Development: Stephen Kouri
VP/Brand Development HPC: Geoff Craig
Director Human Resources: Michael White
Number Employees: 250-499
Parent Co: Unilever USA
Type of Packaging: Consumer, Food Service
Brands:
Becel
Breyers
Hellmann's
Knorr
Lipton
Red Rose
Slim-Fast

13853 Unilever Foods

1400 Waterloo Rd
Stockton, CA 95205-3743 209-467-2212
Fax: 209-466-9580 info@unilever.com
www.unilever.com
Processor of tomatoes including paste, diced and crushed.
Plant Manager: Rick Michen
Number Employees: 100-249
Parent Co: Unilever USA
Type of Packaging: Consumer, Food Service, Private Label, Bulk
Brands:
Becel
Bertolli
Blue Band
Flora

13854 Unilever United States

700 Sylvan Ave
Englewood Cliffs, NJ 07632-3113 201-894-4000
MediaRelations.usa@unilever.com
www.unilever.com
Processor of salad dressing, seasonings and tea powder.
Group Chief Executive: Patrick Cescau
President Americas: John Rice
President Home & Personal Care: Ralph Kugler
President Foods: Manvinder Singh Banga
President Asia Africa: Harish Manwani
President Europe: Kees Van Der Graaf
Chief Human Resources Officer: Sandy Ogg
Chief Auditor: Alan Johnson
Chief Financial Officer: Rudy Markham
Deputy Chief Financial Officer: John Ripley
Group Treasurer: Pascal Visee
Plant Manager: Rich Germinder
Number Employees: 13,000
Sq. footage: 350000
Type of Packaging: Consumer, Food Service

13855 Unimark Group Inc.

124 McMakin Rd
Bartonville, TX 76226 972-518-1155
Fax: 817-491-1272
Processor and importer of chilled fruits
President/CEO: Jakes Jordaan
Sales: Ira Heid
Number Employees: 20-49
Type of Packaging: Food Service, Bulk
Brands:
Circle R
Flavor Fresh
Fruits of Four Seasons
Sunfresh
Sunfresh Brand

13856 Union

14522 Myford Rd
Irvine, CA 92606-1000 714-734-2200
Fax: 714-734-2223 800-854-7292
marisela@unionfoods.com www.unionfoods.com
Processor and exporter of Oriental ramen noodles
President: Sang Mook Lee
CEO: Victor Sim
Sales Manager: Bob Hicks
Estimated Sales: $10900000
Number Employees: 100-249
Sq. footage: 100000
Type of Packaging: Consumer, Private Label
Brands:
Noodle Plus
Smack Cup-A-Ramen
Smack Ramen
Snoodles

13857 Union Dairy Fountain

1252 Woodside Dr
Freeport, IL 61032-6722 815-233-2233
Fax: 815-233-2233
Dairy products
President: Barbara Groves
Estimated Sales: Less than $500,000
Number Employees: 5-9

13858 Union Fisheries Corporation

6186 N Northwest Hwy
Chicago, IL 60631 312-738-0448
Fax: 773-763-8775
Prepared fresh or frozen fish and seafood
Owner: Jim Gubrow
Estimated Sales: $ 3 - 5 Million
Number Employees: 5-9

13859 Union Seafoods

2100 W McDowell Rd
Phoenix, AZ 85009-3011 602-254-4114
Fax: 602-254-4117
Seafood
President: Ernest Linsenmeyer
Estimated Sales: $4,000,000
Number Employees: 1-4

13860 Unique Foods

3221 Durham Dr # 107
Raleigh, NC 27603-3507 919-779-5600
Fax: 919-779-3766
Processor of canned and exotic mushrooms
Owner: Lou Deangelis
CEO: Louis De Angelis
Marketing Head: Louis De Angelis
Estimated Sales: $3700000
Number Employees: 20-49
Sq. footage: 7500

13861 Unique Ingredients

12243 Us Highway 12
Naches, WA 98937 509-653-1991
Fax: 509-653-1992 oly@werunique.com
www.werunique.com
Dried apples in a variety of cuts, styles and varieties; offering air dried, drum dried and upon request, freeze dried fruits and vegetables, specializing in apples, apricots, cherries, peaches, plums, raisins, bananas and all tropicalfruits
Finance Director: Dave Olsen
Business Manager: Leone Manni
Sales: Karen Bentz
Estimated Sales: $13 Million
Number Employees: 5-9
Number of Products: 100
Sq. footage: 500
Type of Packaging: Private Label, Bulk
Brands:
Unique Ingredients

13862 Unique Vitality Products

P.O.Box 1003
Agoura Hills, CA 91376 818-889-7739
Fax: 818-889-4895 uniquevitality@sbcglobal.net
Processor and exporter of vitamins
President: Pierre Van Wessel
CEO: Robert Van Wessel
CFO: Wendy Van Wessel
Quality Control: Ashwin Patel
Production: Hasmuck Patec
Estimated Sales: $ .5 - 1 million
Sq. footage: 400000
Type of Packaging: Private Label, Bulk
Brands:
HYPO FORM
KIDNEY RINSE
LIVER RINSE
UNIQUE COLONIC RINSE
VASCUSTREM

13863 Uniquely Together

Apt 3
2000 W Estes Ave
Chicago, IL 60645-2452 847-675-1555
Fax: 847-675-4049 800-613-7276
info@uniquelytogether.com
www.uniquelytogether.com
Cocktail biscuit collection, line of chocolates, line of sandwich creme cookies; all natural
Owner: Mark Callahan
Owner: Anne Callahan
Number Employees: 5-9
Number of Brands: 1
Number of Products: 22
Sq. footage: 5500
Type of Packaging: Consumer, Private Label
Brands:
Heavenly Cluster
Heavenly Clusters Collection
Martini Biscuit
Sweet Savory Cocktai

13864 Unison

15902a Halliburton Road
Pmb 192
Hacienda Heights, CA 91745-3505 626-917-3668
Fax: 626-917-7468 unisonincorp@hotmail.com
Processor, importer and exporter of dried fruits and vegetables including apricots, peaches, pears, berries, apple rings, etc
President: Xifu Wang
Number Employees: 5-9
Type of Packaging: Consumer, Bulk

13865 United Apple Sales

124 Main St Ste 5
New Paltz, NY 12561 845-256-1500
Fax: 845-256-9550 uasales@aol.com
www.unitedapplesales.com

Grower, importer and exporter of apples
COO: Chuck Andola
Domestic/Export Sales: Dean Decker
Estimated Sales: $360,000
Number Employees: 1-4
Type of Packaging: Consumer, Food Service
Brands:
AMERICA'S FRUIT
STORM KING

13866 **United Canadian Malt**
843 Park Street S
Peterborough, ON K9J 3V1
Canada 705-876-9110
Fax: 705-876-9118 800-461-6400
Processor, exporter and importer of dried and custom liquid brewing extracts, malt syrups and liquid malt
President/General Manager: Monte Smith
Estimated Sales: $500,000-999,999
Number Employees: 15
Sq. footage: 124900
Type of Packaging: Bulk
Brands:
BRU-MIX
CANADIAN GRAND
MASTER BAKER
MASTER BREWER

13867 **United Canning Corporation**
12505 South Ave
North Lima, OH 44452 330-549-9807
Fax: 330-549-9808
Processor of canned mushrooms
Owner: Andrew Dibacco
Plant Manager: Richard Innocenzi
Number Employees: 10-19
Sq. footage: 45000
Type of Packaging: Consumer, Food Service, Private Label
Brands:
Frankies
Masterbrand
Sno-Top

13868 **United Citrus Products**
244 Vanderbilt Ave
Norwood, MA 2062 781-769-7300
Fax: 781-769-9492 800-229-7300
ksmith@unitedscitrus.net www.unitedcitrus.net
manufacturer of bulk dry blends and liquid food products including: cocktail mixes, cocktail rimmers, beverage juices, energy drinks, hydration beverages, frozen carbonated beverages, superfruit beverages and dry blended specialtydesserts
President: Richard Kates
VP/General Manager: Kenneth Smith
R&D: Linda Halik
Quality Control: Cheryl Senato
Sales: Robert Labrie
Public Relations: Sherox Creative
Purchasing: Carole Johanson
Estimated Sales: $5 Million
Number Employees: 20
Type of Packaging: Consumer, Food Service, Private Label, Bulk
Brands:
ALL-IN-ONE
BEST WAY
FLORIDA'S OWN
GOOD SPIRITS
JOLLIE JUAN
SIR CITRUS
THE LAST WORD

13869 **United Dairy**
P.O.Box 280
Martins Ferry, OH 43935 740-633-1451
Fax: 740-633-6759 800-252-1542
dlongentte@uniteddairy.com
www.uniteddairy.com
Full line of dairy products including fluid milk, low fat milks, chocolate, skim, half & half, buttermilk, dairy smart, ultra skim, juices and drinks. Also, cottage cheese, sour cream and dips, sterile products, yogurt and icecream.
President: Joseph Carson
Estimated Sales: $110000000
Number Employees: 250-499
Type of Packaging: Consumer

13870 **United Dairy**
47 W Craig St
Uniontown, PA 15401 724-438-8581
Fax: 724-438-1197 800-966-6455
www.uniteddairy.com
Manufacturer of ice cream, milk and juice
Manager: Ed Evans
Operations Manager: Tim Griglack
Number Employees: 100-249
Parent Co: Martins Dairy
Type of Packaging: Consumer, Food Service, Private Label, Bulk
Other Locations:
United Dairy - Manufacturing Plant
Martins Ferry OH
United Dairy - Manufacturing Plant
Charleston WV
United Dairy
Lancaster OH
United Dairy
Portsmouth OH
United Dairy
Latrobe PA
United Dairy
Beckley WV
United Dairy
Fairmont WV
United Dairy
Richmond KY

13871 **United Dairy Farmers**
3955 Montgomery Rd
Cincinnati, OH 45212 513-396-8700
Fax: 513-396-8736
consumerrelations@udfinc.com
www.udfinc.com
Milk and ice cream
President: Brad Lindner
Marketing Director: David Lindner
CFO: Marilyn Mitchell
R & D: Arlene Higgins
COO: Marilyn Mitchell
Estimated Sales: $ 50-99.9 Million
Number Employees: 1,000-4,999
Brands:
UDF

13872 **United Dairymen of Arizona**
P.O.Box 26877
Tempe, AZ 85285 480-966-7211
Fax: 480-829-7491 info@uda.com
www.uda.org
Cooperative offering milk, butter and powdered dairy products
CFO: Scott H Benson
Director Plant Operations: Dermot Carey
Estimated Sales: $366854098
Number Employees: 100-249

13873 **(HQ)United Distillers & Vintners**
801 Main Avenue
Norwalk, CT 06851-1127 203-323-3311
Fax: 203-359-7402 www.UnitedDistillers.com
Distilled liquors, spirits and wines
President: Charles Phillips
Senior VP: John Adams
Marketing Manager: James Thomson
Number Employees: 500-999
Brands:
Asbach Brandy
Bell's Scotch
Black & White
Canard Duchene
Cardhu
Classic Malts
Dewar's White Label
Dom Perignon
George Dickel Whiske
Glen Ord Scotch
Gordon's Gin
Gordon's Vodka
Gordon's Vodka
Haig
Hennessy Cognacs
Hine Cognac
I.W. Harper Bourbon
Johnny Walker Scotch
Mercier Champagnes
Safari
Scoresby Scotch
Tanqueray Gin
The Dimple
Vat 69
Veuve Cliquot
Weller Bourbon
White Horse

13874 **United Fishing Agency Limited**
1131 N Nimitz Hwy
Honolulu, HI 96817 808-536-2148
Fax: 808-526-0137
Seafood
Manager: Frank Goto
Estimated Sales: $ 20 - 50 Million
Number Employees: 50-99

13875 **United Fruit Growers**
205 W 8th St
Palisade, CO 81526 970-464-7277
Fax: 970-464-7922
Cooperative packer and seller of fresh peaches
Public Relations Officer: Ed Whitman
Estimated Sales: $500,000-$1 Million
Number Employees: 5-9
Sq. footage: 36000
Parent Co: Fruita Consumers Cooperative
Type of Packaging: Consumer, Private Label, Bulk

13876 **United Fruits Corporation**
2811 Wilshire Boulevard
Santa Monica, CA 90403-4803 310-829-0261
Fax: 310-829-0265
Processor and exporter of fruit including apples, apricots, cherries, grapefruit, grapes, lemons, honeydew lemons, nectarines, oranges, pears, plums, etc
President: James Peterson
Manager Sales: Melanie Harris
Estimated Sales: $ 20 - 50 Million
Number Employees: 5-9
Type of Packaging: Bulk

13877 **United Intertrade**
PO Box 821192
Houston, TX 77282-1192 800-969-2233
Fax: 713-827-7881 800-969-2233
info@mitalenacoffee.com
www.mitalenacoffee.com
Coffee
President: Burhan Ajouz
VP/CFO: Misako Ajouz
Estimated Sales: $1 Million
Number Employees: 9
Type of Packaging: Private Label
Brands:
Bluebonnet Coffee
Cafe Don Pedro
Cafe Orleans-Coffee
Cafe Unico-Espresso
Divian Coffee
Diwan Coffee
Imperial Choice Coff
Mediterranean Coffee
Mitalena Coffee
Unico

13878 **United Intertrade Corporation**
PO Box 821192
Houston, TX 77282-1192 713-827-7799
Fax: 713-827-7881 800-969-2233
info@mitalenacoffee.com
www.mitalenacoffee.com
Processor and canner of green and roasted coffee beans
President: Bob Ajouz
VP: Misako Ajouz
Number Employees: 5-9
Sq. footage: 10000
Type of Packaging: Private Label, Bulk
Brands:
Bluebonnet
Cafe Dontedro
Cafe Orleans
Cafe Unico
Imperial Choice
Mediterranean

13879 **United Marketing Exchange**
215 Silver St
Delta, CO 81416-1517 970-874-3332
Fax: 970-874-9525 mike@umefruit.com
www.umefruit.com
Processor and exporter of fresh fruits and onions
President: Harold Broughton
Sales Manager: Mike Gibson
Estimated Sales: $1089000
Number Employees: 1-4
Parent Co: Hi Quality Packing
Type of Packaging: Consumer

Brands:
Burrow
OWL
Tom-Tom

13880 **United Meat Company**
1040 Bryant St
San Francisco, CA 94103 415-864-2118
Fax: 415-703-9061
Manufacturer, exporter and importer of frozen portion controlled lamb, venison, veal and beef
President: Phil Gee Jr
VP: Lincoln Chu
Estimated Sales: $20-50 Million
Number Employees: 20-49
Sq. footage: 19430
Type of Packaging: Food Service
Brands:
UMC

13881 **United Natural Foods**
P.O.Box 301
Chesterfield, NH 03443 603-256-3000
Fax: 603-256-6959 800-451-2525
ghogan@unfi.com www.unfi.com
Natural foods
President: Steven Townsend
CFO: Jackie Hartwell
Sales: Mark Bushway
Purchasing Manager: Thomas Nunziata
Estimated Sales: $ 100-500 Million
Number Employees: 250-499
Parent Co: Hershey Import Company

13882 **United Natural Foods**
P.O.Box 999
Dayville, CT 06241 860-779-2800
Fax: 860-779-5678 800-877-8898
info@unfi.com www.unfi.com
Vegetables
President: Steven H Townsend
Sr. VP Marketing: Daniel V Atwood
CEO: Steven Spinner
CFO: Rick Puckett
Estimated Sales: $ 5-10 Million
Number Employees: 5,000-9,999
Brands:
UNFI
United Natural Foods

13883 **United Noodle Manufacturing Company**
511 W 500 N
Salt Lake City, UT 84116-3414 801-485-0951
Manufacturer of Chinese noodles and fortune cookies
Owner: Rufus Spraug
Estimated Sales: $$1-2.5 Million
Number Employees: 1-4
Type of Packaging: Consumer, Food Service

13884 **United Packing**
113 Gano St
Providence, RI 2906 401-751-6935
Fax: 401-223-0125
Processor of Portuguese sausages
President: Tony Cabral
Estimated Sales: $510,000
Number Employees: 5-9

13885 **(HQ)United Pickle Products Corporation**
4366 Park Ave
Bronx, NY 10457-2494 718-933-6060
Fax: 718-367-8522 info@pickle.com
www.unitedpickle.com
Processor and exporter of condiments, chow chow, horseradish, relishes, cucumbers, sauerkraut and pickle products: importer of olives.
Owner: Stephen Leibowitz
Owner: Marvin Weishaus
Plant Manager: Jose Torrez
Estimated Sales: 25 Million
Number Employees: 1-4
Type of Packaging: Consumer, Food Service, Bulk
Other Locations:
United Pickle Products Corp.
Rosenhayn NJ
Brands:
Leibo
Leibowitz
Nathan's Famous
Teddy's
United
United Brand
Upco
Upzo

13886 **United Pies of Elkhart I**
1016 Middlebury St
Elkhart, IN 46516 574-294-3419
Manufacturer of baked products including pies
President: Blanche Nichols
VP of Sales: Kari Nichols
Estimated Sales: $10 Million
Number Employees: 5-9
Type of Packaging: Consumer

13887 **United Poultry Company**
742 N Broadway
Los Angeles, CA 90012-2820 213-620-0498
Processor of chicken
President: Nelson Moy
Number Employees: 50-99
Type of Packaging: Consumer, Food Service

13888 **United Provision Meat Company**
156 S Ohio Ave
Columbus, OH 43205 614-252-1126
Fax: 614-252-1127 unitedmeats@cs.com
www.unitedprovisionmeatco.com
Manufacturer of portion controll meats including cooked prime rib, meatballs, meatloaf, beef roasts, pork roasts, london broil, chicken, turkey, geese, duck, cornish hens, sloppy joes and corned beef and pastrami
President: Allen Scott
Estimated Sales: $5 Million
Number Employees: 5-9
Sq. footage: 12000
Type of Packaging: Food Service

13889 **United Pulse Trading**
1611 E Century Ave Ste 100
Bismarck, ND 58503 701-751-1623
Fax: 701-751-1626 info@uspulses.com
www.uspulses.com
red split lentils, yellow split peas, green split peas, chickpeas, laird/eston/richlea lentils, whole red lentils, kabuli chickpeas and split desi chickpeas
President/Owner: Murad Katib
CFO: Lory Island
VP: Gaepan Bourassa
Number Employees: 3

13890 **United Salt Corporation**
4800 San Felipe St
Houston, TX 77056 713-877-2600
Fax: 713-877-2664 800-554-8658
uscinfo@tum.com www.unitedsalt.com
Processor and exporter of salt including plain, iodized, agricultural and water conditioning
President: Jim O'Donnell
VP: Theresa Feldman
Estimated Sales: $16,100,000
Number Employees: 50-99
Parent Co: Texas United Corporation
Type of Packaging: Consumer, Food Service, Private Label, Bulk
Brands:
Flavor House
Gulf
Ranch House

13891 **United Shellfish Company**
P.O. Box 146
Grasonville, MD 21638 410-827-8171
Fax: 410-827-7436 sales@unitedshellfish.com
www.unitedshellfish.com
Wholesale seafood processor and distributo offering direct store delivery of the full line of fresh and frozen seafood, scallops, crab meat, live lobsters, lobster meat, shrimp, squid, hard shell clams, soft shell clams, surf clamsoysters, mussels, fresh clam chowder, soups and specialty restaurant products.
Manager: Dave Messenger
Sales Manager: John Walker
Estimated Sales: $19600000
Number Employees: 50-99
Sq. footage: 30000
Parent Co: Ipswich Shellfish Group
Type of Packaging: Food Service

13892 **United Society of Shakers**
707 Shaker Rd
New Gloucester, ME 04260-2652 207-926-4597
888-624-6345
usshakers@aol.com www.shaker.lib.me.us
Herbal teas, culinary herbs, herb mixes
Executive Director: Leonard Brooks
Estimated Sales: Less than $200,000
Number Employees: 5-9
Type of Packaging: Consumer, Food Service, Bulk
Brands:
United Society of Shakers

13893 **United Universal Enterprises Corporation**
7747 N 43rd Ave
Phoenix, AZ 85051 623-842-9691
Fax: 623-842-4605 univenterp@cs.com
Wholesaler/distributor, importer and exporter of general merchandise, frozen seafood, canned fruits, grains, meat, cooking oils and powdered milk; serving the food service market
Manager: Louis Galvac
Vice President: Linda Kirschner
Estimated Sales: $ 3 - 5 Million
Number Employees: 10
Sq. footage: 7000
Type of Packaging: Food Service, Private Label

13894 **United Valley Bell Dairy**
508 Roane St
Charleston, WV 25302-2091 304-344-2511
Fax: 304-344-2518
Fluid milk
Manager: John Duty
Marketing Director: Halan Varley
Estimated Sales: Less than $500,000
Number Employees: 100-249
Type of Packaging: Private Label

13895 **Universal Beef Products**
3511 Canal St
Houston, TX 77003 713-224-6043
Fax: 713-224-0716
Beef products
President: Neil Brody
Estimated Sales: $ 2.5-5 Million
Number Employees: 20-49

13896 **Universal Beverages**
P.O.Box 448
Ponte Vedra Bch, FL 32004-0448 904-280-7795
Fax: 904-280-7794 ubisyfocorp@aol.com
syfobeverages.com
Processor and exporter of bottled water including purified and sodium free; also, regular and flavored seltzer and naturally sparkling water
President: Jonathan O Moore
CEO: Jonathan Moore
Plant Manager: Justin Jones
Estimated Sales: $$2.5-5 Million
Number Employees: 20-49
Sq. footage: 100000
Parent Co: Universal Beverages Holding Corporation
Type of Packaging: Consumer, Food Service, Private Label
Brands:
Syfo

13897 **(HQ)Universal Beverages**
3301 W Main St
Leesburg, FL 34748-9714 352-315-1010
Fax: 352-315-1009 info@universalbeverages.com
www.universalbeverages.com
Bottled water
Manager: Justin Jones
Estimated Sales: $1.6 Million
Number Employees: 5-9
Type of Packaging: Private Label
Brands:
100% Purified Non Carbonated Water
Naturally Flavored S
Syfo Brand Original

13898 **Universal Blanchers**
14187 Magnolia St
Blakely, GA 39823 229-723-4181
Fax: 912-723-8887
Processed peanuts
President: Thomas Baty
Estimated Sales: $ 25-49.9 Million
Number Employees: 150

13899 **Universal Commodities**
141 Parkway Rd Ste 20
Bronxville, NY 10708 914-779-5700
Fax: 914-779-5742 universaltea@uctt.com
www.uctt.com

Tea importers
President: Domenick Ciaccia
Director: Paul Strader
Estimated Sales: $ 5-10 Million
Number Employees: 5-9

13900 Universal Concepts
1608 NW 34th Ter
Lauderhill, FL 33311-4210 918-367-0197
Fax: 954-792-4502
Meat tenderizers
Estimated Sales: Under $500,000
Number Employees: 1-4

13901 Universal Formulas
7136 East N Avenue
Kalamazoo, MI 49048 616-383-3340
Fax: 616-383-3449 800-342-6960
Processor of enzymes, minerals and herbs
President: Ralf Ostertag
Estimated Sales: $$2.5-5 Million
Number Employees: 4

13902 Universal Laboratories
3 Terminal Rd
New Brunswick, NJ 8901 732-545-3130
Fax: 732-214-1210 800-872-0101
info@universalnutrition.com
www.universalnutrition.com
Processor and exporter of vitamins, powdered proteins and confections including candy bars
President: Clyde Rockoff
Director Marketing: Steve Patton
Estimated Sales: $100+ Million
Number Employees: 100-249
Sq. footage: 120000
Brands:
Animal Pak
Forza
Hardfast
Natural Sterols
Yohimbe Bar

13903 Universal Poultry Company
1769 Old West Broad Street
Athens, GA 30606-2867 706-546-6767
Fax: 706-546-6790
Poultry
Manager: Robert Harris
Estimated Sales: $500,000-$1 Million
Number Employees: 5-9

13904 Universal Preservachem Inc
60 Jiffy Rd
Somerset, NJ 08873-3438 732-568-1266
Fax: 732-568-9040
Wholesaler/distributor of chemicals and ingredients. Vitamins sweetners preservatives, antioxidants, acidulants, etc
Chairman of the Board: Herbert Ravitz
President: Dan Ravitz
Estimated Sales: $4100000
Number Employees: 20
Sq. footage: 60000
Type of Packaging: Private Label, Bulk

13905 Upcountry Fisheries
85 Kino Pl
Makawao, HI 96768-8891 808-871-8484
Fax: 808-871-6071
Seafood
Owner: Richard Samsing
Estimated Sales: $ .5 - 1 million
Number Employees: 1-4

13906 Upper Crust Bakery
3655 W Washington St
Phoenix, AZ 85009 602-255-0464
Fax: 602-255-0433 pmiller@ucbakery.com
www.uppercrustbakeryusa.com
Bread and bakery products
President: Tab Navidi
Sales/Marketing: Pat Navidi
Estimated Sales: $ 20-50 Million
Number Employees: 100-249
Type of Packaging: Private Label

13907 Upper Crust Baking Company
P.O.Box 203
Pismo Beach, CA 93448-0203 805-543-1295
Fax: 805-543-1284 800-676-1691
contact@uppercrustbaking.com
www.uppercrustbaking.com
Biscotti, cookies and crostini
President: Tracey Aumiller
Estimated Sales: $ 5-9.9 Million
Number Employees: 5-9
Type of Packaging: Consumer
Brands:
Upper Crust Biscotti

13908 Upper Crust Biscotti
P.O.Box 203
Pismo Beach, CA 93448-203 800-676-1691
Fax: 805-543-1284 866-972-6879
uppercrustbiscotti@worldpantry.com
www.uppercrustbiscotti.com
Manufacturer of flavored Biscotti, flavored Tyni Biscotti, flavored Itti Bittie Cookies, and flavored Wine Crostini.
Owner: Terez Tyni
Estimated Sales: $ 500,000 - $ 1Million
Number Employees: 11
Sq. footage: 4500
Brands:
Itty-Bittie Biscotti
Itty-Bittie Cookies
Upper Crust Biscotti

13909 (HQ)Upstate Farms Cooperative
P.O.Box 650
Buffalo, NY 14225 716-892-2121
Fax: 716-892-3157 emailus@upstatefarms.com
www.upstatefarmscoop.com
Processor of dairy products and meat including pepperoni, Genoa and hard salami, mortadella, roast beef and Italian sausage.
CEO: Bob Hall
Estimated Sales: $260 Million
Number Employees: 20-49
Parent Co: Upstate Milk Cooperative
Type of Packaging: Consumer, Food Service, Private Label, Bulk
Brands:
BISON
BREAKSTONE'S
INTENSE MILKS
MILK FOR LIFE
UPSTATE FARMS

13910 Upstate Farms Cooperative
P.O.Box 650
Buffalo, NY 14225 716-892-2121
Fax: 716-892-3157 866-874-6455
emailus@upstatefarms.com
www.upstatefarmscoop.com
Processor of milk and juice and cultured dairy products
CEO: Bob Hall
Estimated Sales: $260 Million
Number Employees: 20-49
Number of Brands: 5
Number of Products: 100
Type of Packaging: Consumer, Food Service, Private Label, Bulk
Brands:
BISON
BREAKSTONES
Upstate Farms

13911 Upstate Farms Cooperative
45 Fulton Ave
Rochester, NY 14608 585-458-1880
Fax: 585-458-2887 www.upstatefarms.com
Processor of milk
CEO: Bob Hall
Sales Manager (Eastern): Jerry Malne
Account Manager: Dick Pearce
Plant Manager: Stephen Hranjec
Estimated Sales: $260 Million
Number Employees: 100-249
Parent Co: Upstate Farms
Type of Packaging: Consumer, Food Service, Private Label, Bulk

13912 Uptown Bakers
5335 Kilmer Place
Hyattsville, MD 20781-1034
US 301-864-1500
Fax: 301-864-7744 www.uptownbakers.com
Processor of European pastries and breads including scones, cinnamon bread, muffins, cookies, danish and cakes rolls they have 30 different varieties of dough,100 assorted breads. they do catering.
President: Michael McCloud
CFO: Elliot Person
Estimated Sales: $13.4million
Number Employees: 90
Type of Packaging: Consumer, Food Service

13913 Urban Accents
4241 N Ravenswood Ave
Chicago, IL 60613-1199 773-528-9515
Fax: 773-528-9533 877-872-7742
customerservice@urbanaccents.com
www.urbanaccents.com
Processor of snack crakers and distinctive spices
President: Tom Knibbs
Vice President: Jim Dygas
Estimated Sales: Below $ 5 Million
Number Employees: 5-9
Type of Packaging: Private Label
Brands:
Bloody Mary Blend

13914 Urban Oven
2431 N Arizona Ave Ste 4
Suite 101
Chandler, AZ 85225-1391
Fax: 480-921-2477 866-770-6836
gene@urbanoven.com www.urbanoven.com
crackers
Owner: Gene Williams
Director of Sales: Linda Anne Marty
Number Employees: 7

13915 Urbani Truffles
8657 Hayden Place
Culver City, CA 90232-2901 310-842-8850
Truffles
Estimated Sales: Below $ 5 Million
Number Employees: 10

13916 Ursula's Island Farms
6321 Corgiat Drive S
Suite A
Seattle, WA 98108-2862 206-762-3113
Fax: 206-762-0658
Dry fruit

13917 (HQ)Utz Quality Foods
900 High St
Hanover, PA 17331 717-637-6644
Fax: 717-633-5102 800-367-7629
info@utzsnacks.com www.utzsnacks.com
Manufacturer of potato chips, pretzels, popcorn, tortilla chips, cheese curls, pub fries, sunflower chips, prok rinds, etc.
President: Tom Dempsey
Chariman/CEO: Mike Rice
VP/CFO: Todd Staub
EVP Sales/Marketing: Dylan Lissette
Evp Sales: Dylan Lissette
VP Public Relations: Jane Rice
VP Manufacturing: Paul Schaum
Estimated Sales: $165 Billion
Number Employees: 1,800
Sq. footage: 550000
Type of Packaging: Consumer, Food Service, Bulk
Other Locations:
Utz Distribution Centers
East Hartford CT
Patterson NY
Laurel DE
Newark DE
Auburn ME
West Springfield MA
North Easton MA
South Yarmouth MA
Wilmington MA
Shrewsbury MA
Cumberland MD
Waldorf MD
Hanover PA
Brands:
GRANDMA UTZ'S
HANOVER
KETTLE KRISP

13918 Uvalde Meat Processing
508 S Wood St
Uvalde, TX 78801 830-278-6247
Fax: 830-278-6245
Manufacturer of sausage, venison, goat, beef, lamb and pork; also, game birds; slaughtering services available
President/Co-Owner: Pat Jackowski
VP/Co-Owner: Gail Jackowski
Estimated Sales: $1-3 Million
Number Employees: 10-19

13919 **V & V Supremo Foods**
2141 S Throop
Chicago, IL 60608
Fax: 888-301-2244 888-887-8773
www.vvsupremo.com
Processor, importer and wholesaler/distributor of Mexican-style cheese, chorizo, sour cream, etc. serving the food service and retail markets
President: Gilbert Villasenor
VP: Ignacio Villasenor
VP Sales: Albert Corona
Human Resources Director: Claudia Estrella
Operations Director: Joseph Villasenor
Plant Manager: Tony Carmona
Estimated Sales: $71700000
Number Employees: 250
Sq. footage: 75000
Type of Packaging: Consumer, Food Service
Brands:
V&V Supremo Chihuahua
V&V Supremo Del Caribe
V&V Supremo Queso Fresco

13920 **V Chocolates**
440 Lawndale Dr
Salt Lake City, UT 84115 801-269-8444
Fax: 801-269-8449 vmail@vchocolates.com
www.vchocolates.com
chocolates
Number Employees: 12

13921 **V L Foods**
70 W Red Oak Lane
White Plains, NY 10604-3602 914-697-4851
Fax: 914-697-4888
President: Paul Pruzan
Brands:
PICCADELI

13922 **V&E Kohnstamm**
882 3rd Ave # 7
Brooklyn, NY 11232-1902 718-788-6320
Fax: 718-768-3978 800-847-4500
flavorinfo@virginiadare.com
www.virginiadare.com
Processor and exporter of flavors, masking agents, bases, extracts, vanilla, orange oils and colors
President: Howard Smith
Executive VP: Howard Smith Jr
Estimated Sales: $21100000
Number Employees: 100-249
Type of Packaging: Private Label, Bulk
Brands:
Veko

13923 **V-Link**
299 Stone Valley Way
Alamo, CA 94507-1248 925-552-7088
Fax: 925-552-7092
President: K Chang
CFO: Tina Hsieh
Estimated Sales: $300,000-500,000
Number Employees: 1-4

13924 **V. Sattui Winery**
1111 White Lane
Saint Helena, CA 94574 707-963-7774
Fax: 707-963-4324 800-799-8888
info@vsattui.com www.vsattui.com
Wines
President/CEO: Daryl Sattui
CFO: Wendell Cottle
VP: Robert O'Malley
VP Marketing/Public Relations: Pat Krueger
Sales Manager: Chester Sattui
Estimated Sales: $24 Million
Number Employees: 65
Sq. footage: 20000
Type of Packaging: Consumer

13925 **V.W. Joyner & Company**
PO Box 387
Smithfield, VA 23431-0387 757-357-2161
Fax: 757-357-0184 www.smithfield-company.com
Processor and exporter of smoked cured country hams, picnics and bacon for distribution to wholesale, retail and restaurant markets
VP/General Manager: Larry Santure
Plant Manager: R Howell
Number Employees: 10-19
Sq. footage: 40000
Parent Co: Smithfield Companies
Type of Packaging: Consumer, Food Service, Private Label, Bulk
Brands:
Joyner's
Red Eye Country Picnic
V.W. Joyner Genuine Smithfield

13926 **VAN HEES Inc**
2500 Regency Parkway
Cary, NC 27518 919-654-6862
Fax: 919-654-6864 info@vanheesinc.com
www.vanheesinc.com
Premier manufacturer of functional ingredients tailored specifically to the meat industry.
President: Dave Pierce

13927 **VANCO Trading**
50 Old Kings Hwy N # 101
Darien, CT 06820 203-656-2800
Fax: 203-655-8307 janvaneck@vancotrading.com
www.vancotrading.com
Food chemicals and ingredients
Owner: J Vaneck
Estimated Sales: $500,000-$1 Million
Number Employees: 1-4
Brands:
Quinine

13928 **VIOBIN**
226 W Livingston St
Monticello, IL 61856-1673 217-762-2561
Fax: 217-762-2489 888-473-9645
info@viobinusa.com www.viobinusa.com
Defatted wheatgerm, refined and unrefined wheat germ oil
CEO: Monte White
CFO: Doris Teasley-Chase
Quality Control: David Hettinger
Marketing/Sales: Geni Heider
Marketing/Sales: Whitney Bauman
Production: Kevin Stevens
Estimated Sales: $ 10-20 Million
Number Employees: 20-49
Type of Packaging: Consumer, Food Service, Private Label, Bulk
Brands:
Viobin

13929 **(HQ)VIP Foods**
1080 Wyckoff Ave
Flushing, NY 11385 718-821-5330
Fax: 718-497-7110 vipfoods@aol.com
www.vipfoodsinc.com
Processor and exporter of soups, instant lunches, low-calorie sweeteners and mixes including dessert, pasta, tea, hot chocolate, pasta, pudding, cake and cake mixes, sauce and chicken coating
Owner: Mendel Freund
Sales Manager: Esther Freund
Estimated Sales: $ 10 - 20 Million
Number Employees: 20-49
Sq. footage: 45000
Type of Packaging: Consumer, Food Service, Private Label, Bulk
Brands:
Kojel
Minute Lunch
Soup Bowl
VIP

13930 **VIP Foodservice**
74 Hobron Ave
Kahului, HI 96732 808-877-5055
Fax: 808-877-4960 contact@vipfoodservice.com
www.vipfoodservice.com
Wholesaler/distributor of grocery products, meat, produce, dairy items, frozen foods, baked goods, seafood and equipment and fixtures; serving the food service market
President/VP Sales: Nelson Okumura
VP Finance: Alton Nakagawa
VP Operations: Brian Tokeshi
VP Purchasing: Stephen Smith
Estimated Sales: $100+ Million
Number Employees: 100
Sq. footage: 60000

13931 **VIP Sales Company**
2395 American Ave
Hayward, CA 94545-1807 918-252-5791
Fax: 918-254-1667 866-536-8008
sbeck@vipfoods.com www.vipfoods.com
Packer and exporter of frozen fruits, vegetables and Chinese entrees and prepared foods; importer of raspberries, blueberries and broccoli
President: Guy Lewis
Sr. VP/COO: Lee Turman
VP Sales/Marketing: Steve Beck
Public Relations: Mick Lewis
Plant Manager: Don Avera
VP Purchasing: Fred Meyer
Estimated Sales: $5900000
Number Employees: 30
Number of Brands: 5
Number of Products: 180
Type of Packaging: Consumer, Food Service, Private Label, Bulk
Brands:
BASIC VALUE
FOOD PAC
FOOD TREND
TAI PAN
VIP

13932 **VLR Food Corporation**
575 Oster Lane
Concord, ON L4K 2B9
Canada 905-669-0700
Fax: 905-669-9829 800-387-7437
sales@tgfnet.com www.jonathant.com
Processor of fillo dough, hors d'ouvres and fillo pastry entres
Vice President: Rhys Quin
Estimated Sales: $21 Million
Number Employees: 250
Number of Brands: 3
Number of Products: 20
Type of Packaging: Food Service
Brands:
Jonathan T.
TGF

13933 **VMI Corporation**
13838 Industrial Road
Omaha, NE 68137-1104 402-334-8100
Fax: 402-334-9280 800-228-2248
Variety meats including liver, portion cuts, retail and food service
President: Robert Elliott
Comptroller: Jim Pearson
Plant Manager: Robert Matton
Purchasing Manager: Dan Roulette
Estimated Sales: $ 10-25 Million
Number Employees: 100
Sq. footage: 20
Type of Packaging: Private Label
Brands:
Coast
Le Cort
Prime International
Tender Yam

13934 **VOD Gourmet**
3 Stormy Circle
PO Box 4922
Greenwich, CT 06831-0418 203-531-5172
Fax: 203-532-4883 ulla@vodkacheese.com
www.vodgourmet.com
Swedish cheese with peppercorn vodka, juniper berries, pre-cooked/frozen
President: Ulla Nylan
Estimated Sales: $130,000
Number Employees: 1-4
Type of Packaging: Private Label, Bulk
Brands:
VOD

13935 **VT Made Richard's Sauces**
471 Bushey Road
Saint Albans, VT 05478-9604 802-524-3196
Fax: 802-524-4224 sauce@vtmadebbqu.com
www.vtmadebbqu.com
BBQ sauce, game sauce and marinades, gift favors and hot sauce.
Co-Owner: Steve Rocheleau
Co-Owner: Martha Rocheleau
Estimated Sales: $150,000+
Number Employees: 2
Number of Products: 5
Type of Packaging: Consumer, Food Service, Private Label, Bulk

13936 **Vac Pac Manufacturing Company**
P.O.Box 6339
Baltimore, MD 21230-0339 410-685-5181
Fax: 410-332-4536 800-368-2301
vacpac@pobox.com www.vpmfg.com
Manufacturer and exporter of heat shrinkable polyethylene cook-in bags for meat, poultry, etc
President: Aron Perlman
VP: Hessa Tary
Estimated Sales: $4114713
Number Employees: 20-49

13937 **Vacaville Fruit Company**
P.O.Box 1537
Vacaville, CA 95696 707-448-5292
Fax: 707-447-1085 info@vacavillefruit.com
www.vacavillefruit.com
Processor importer and exporter of kosher dried fruit and fruit pastes; serving the food service market
President: Richard Nola
Director Sales/Marketing: Nicole Nola
Plant Superintendent: Gary De La Rosa
Estimated Sales: $4200000
Number Employees: 50-99
Type of Packaging: Consumer, Food Service, Bulk

13938 **Val Verde Winery**
100 Qualia Dr
Del Rio, TX 78840 830-775-9714
Fax: 830-775-5394 www.valverdewinery.com
Wines
Owner: Thomas Qualia
Operations Manager: Thomas Qualia
Estimated Sales: $300,000
Number Employees: 5-9
Type of Packaging: Private Label
Brands:
Val Verde Winery

13939 **Val's Seafood**
3437 Winford Drive
Mobile, AL 36619-4309 251-639-2570
Fax: 251-639-1198
Seafood
President: Val Hammond
Estimated Sales: $632,000
Number Employees: 1-4

13940 **Valdez Food**
1815 N 2nd St
Philadelphia, PA 19122-2305 215-634-6106
Fax: 215-634-8645
Processor of Chinese food products including wonton soup, chow mein, fish cakes, shrim, egg & pizza rolls.
President: Perfecto Valdez Jr
Treasurer: Juanito Valdez
Estimated Sales: $500,000-$1 Million
Number Employees: 10-19
Sq. footage: 4500
Type of Packaging: Consumer

13941 **Valenie Packers**
PO Box 255
Colinton, AB T0G 0R0
Canada 780-675-5881
Fax: 780-675-5581
Processor of pork including sausage, cured hams and bacon, packers
President: Joe Erbach
Number Employees: 5-9
Type of Packaging: Consumer, Food Service

13942 **Valentine Enterprises**
940 Collins Hill Rd
Lawrenceville, GA 30043 770-995-0661
Fax: 770-995-0725 info@valentine.com
www.veiusa.com
Processor and exporter of powdered products including diet meal replacements, protein, fiber, sport fitness products, lecithin granules, etc
President: Donald McDaniel
VP Operations: Alan Smith
Estimated Sales: $30 Million
Number Employees: 200
Sq. footage: 50000

13943 **Valentine Sugars**
129 Valentine Dr
Lockport, LA 70374 985-532-2541
Fax: 985-532-6806 www.valentinechemicals.com
Processor of sugar
President: Hugh Caffery
Estimated Sales: $500,000-$1 Million
Number Employees: 20-49
Type of Packaging: Consumer
Brands:
Valentine Sugars

13944 **Valhrona**
1801 Avenue of the Stars
Suite 600
Los Angeles, CA 90067-5908 310-277-0401
Fax: 310-277-7304 bjduclos@pacbell.net
www.valhrona.com
Candy and baking chocolate
President: Bernard Duclos
Founder: Monsieur Guironnet
Estimated Sales: $300,000-500,000
Number Employees: 1-4
Type of Packaging: Private Label
Brands:
Valrhona

13945 **Valley Bakery**
1438 Main St
Rock Valley, IA 51247 712-476-5386
Processor of cookies, breads, rolls and pastries
Owner: Ted Triezenberg
Estimated Sales: $150000
Number Employees: 20-49
Type of Packaging: Consumer

13946 **Valley Dairy Fairview Dairy**
3200 Graham Ave
Windber, PA 15963 814-467-1384
Fax: 814-467-5538
Processor and wholesaler/distributor of ice cream; serving the food service market
President: Joseph Greubel
Vice President: Melissa Blystone
Marketing Director: Virgina Greubel
Plant Manager: Ray Sneets
Number Employees: 20
Sq. footage: 12000
Parent Co: Fairview Dairy
Type of Packaging: Consumer, Food Service
Brands:
ICE CREAM JOE
VALLEY DAIRY

13947 **Valley Fig Growers**
2028 S 3rd St
Fresno, CA 93702 559-237-3893
Fax: 559-237-3898 lcain@valleyfig.com
www.valleyfig.com
Manufacturer and exporter of figs including whole, diced, extruded, powder and paste; also, fig juice and juice concentrate
President: Michael Emigh
VP Finance/Secretary/Treasurer: James Gargiulo
VP Industrial Sales: Gary Jue
Estimated Sales: $19.5 Million
Number Employees: 100-249
Sq. footage: 150000
Type of Packaging: Consumer, Food Service, Private Label, Bulk
Brands:
BLUE RIBBON
ORCHARD CHOICE
SUN-MAID

13948 **Valley Grain Products**
23865 Avenue 18
Madera, CA 93638-9644 559-675-3400
Fax: 559-675-0723
Processor of corn flour, tortilla chips and taco shells
Manager: Barry Runyon
Number Employees: 50-99

13949 **Valley Institutional Foods Company**
36080 N Expressway 281
Edinburg, TX 78542 956-383-7620
Fax: 956-687-8845
Processor of meat; wholesaler/distributor of meat and frozen food; serving the food service market
President: Vicki Flores
Estimated Sales: $2.6 Million
Number Employees: 14
Sq. footage: 5000
Type of Packaging: Food Service

13950 **Valley Lahvosh Baking Company**
502 M St
Fresno, CA 93721 559-485-2700
Fax: 559-485-0173 800-480-2704
customerservice@valleylahvosh.com
www.valleylahvosh.com
Processor of Valley Lahvosh, America's premier brand of crackerbreads, and Valley Wraps, flatbreads for wraps. Also manufacture a line of natural crackerbread under the Stone Street Bakery brand name
President: Janet Saghatelian
Vice President: Agnes Saghatelian
Marketing Coordinator: Jenni Bonsignore
Sales Director: Chip Muse
Operations Manager: Danny Olosa
Production Manager: Brian Sperling
Estimated Sales: $3877239
Number Employees: 50-99
Number of Brands: 2
Number of Products: 33
Sq. footage: 40000
Type of Packaging: Consumer, Food Service
Brands:
CALLEY LAHVOSH
HEARTS
LAHVOSH
ROUND LAHVOSH
SOFT SQUARE
STONE STREET
VALLEY BAKERY
VALLEY LAHVOSH CRACKERBREAD
VALLEY LAHVOSH FLATBREAD
VALLEY WRAPS

13951 **Valley Meat Company**
217 Daly Ave
Modesto, CA 95354 209-544-8950
Fax: 209-522-5892 800-222-6328
sales@valleymeat.com www.valleymeat.com
Manufacturer of hamburger patties and ground beef
President/CEO: Russell Heffner
Estimated Sales: $10 Million
Number Employees: 20-49
Type of Packaging: Consumer, Food Service, Bulk

13952 **Valley Meats**
2302 1st St
Coal Valley, IL 61240 309-799-7341
Fax: 309-799-7633
Processor of fresh and frozen steaks, pork chops, beef patties, ground beef, pork and veal products; also, breaded beef, pork, chicken and veal
President: Jeff Joeb
Vice President, Operations: James Summer
Regional Manager: Adam Jobe
Estimated Sales: $1.3 Million
Number Employees: 25
Type of Packaging: Consumer, Food Service

13953 **Valley Milk Products**
412 E King St
Strasburg, VA 22657 540-465-5113
Fax: 540-645-4042
Milk and specialty dried food ingredients
President: Don Utz
CFO: Jeff Mank
Estimated Sales: $ 10-24.9 Million
Number Employees: 35

13954 **Valley Queen Cheese Factory**
200 E Railway Ave
Milbank, SD 57252 605-432-4563
Fax: 605-432-9383 cheese@vqcheese.com
www.vqcheese.com
Processor of whey and cheese
CEO: Mark Leddy
Co-CEO: Dave Gonzenbach
Vice President: Max Gozenbach
Quality Control: Jody Kuper
Plant Engineer: Dave Gozenbach
Operations Manager: Lance Johnson
Estimated Sales: $ 10 - 20 Million
Number Employees: 100-249
Type of Packaging: Consumer
Brands:
Valley Queen

13955 **Valley Research**
3502 N Olive Rd
South Bend, IN 46628 574-232-5000
Fax: 574-232-2468 800-522-8110
sales@valleyenzymes.com
www.valleyenzymes.com

Processor and exporter of standard and custom blended enzymes for starch hydrolysis, fruit juice processing, baking, meat tenderizing, nutritional supplements and waste treatment.
President: Arthur Sears
Executive VP: Michael Gorbitz
Quality Controll: Johnna Klute
Estimated Sales: $ 20 - 50 Million
Number Employees: 20-49
Type of Packaging: Bulk
Brands:
Bio Tab
Crystalzyme
Flavareze
Validase
Valley AP

13956 **Valley Sun Products of California**
3324 Orestimba Rd
Newman, CA 95360 209-862-1200
Fax: 209-862-1100 888-786-3743
avieyra@valleysun.com www.valleysun.com
Sun-dried tomatoes, plain and in oil
CEO: Winston Mar
Quality Assurance Manger: Mathew Travao
National Sales Manager: Robb Benech
Director of Operations: Cesar Corona
Production Supervisor: Frank Lua
Plant Manager: Jim Fullmer
Estimated Sales: $11 Million
Number Employees: 53
Sq. footage: 25000
Type of Packaging: Consumer, Food Service, Private Label, Bulk

13957 **Valley Tea & Coffee**
1101 W Valley Blvd Ste 103
Alhambra, CA 91803 626-281-5799
Fax: 626-281-5799
Tea and coffee
Manager: Ted Lee
CEO: Ted Lin
Estimated Sales: Under $300,000
Number Employees: 1-4
Type of Packaging: Food Service

13958 **Valley Tomato Products**
P.O.Box 31390
Stockton, CA 95213-1390 209-982-4586
Fax: 209-982-5280 www.campbellsoup.com
Processor of canned tomato paste
CEO: Douglas Conant
CEO: Douglas Conant
CFO: Robert Schiffner
Vice President: Mark Sarvary
VP: Mark Sarvary
Plant Manager: Brian Dunning
Number Employees: 100-249
Brands:
Campbell's
Pace
Pepperidge
Prego
Swanson

13959 **Valley View Blueberries**
21717 NE 68th St
Vancouver, WA 98682 360-892-2839
valley.view@comcast.net
Processor of dried blueberries and strawberries, jams, syrups, glazes, honeys, trail mixes, pancake and corn bread mixes and chocolate covered blueberries; also, no-sugar products available
President: Vicki Duchesneau
Estimated Sales: $86,000
Number Employees: 1-4
Sq. footage: 4000
Type of Packaging: Consumer, Food Service, Private Label, Bulk
Brands:
Valley View Blueberries

13960 **Valley View Cheese Company**
6028 Route 62
Conewango Vly, NY 14726 716-296-5821
Fax: 716-296-5822
Cheese
President: Rick Binder
Marketing Manager: Linda Bates
Plant Manager: Linda Bates
Estimated Sales: $500,000-$1 Million
Number Employees: 20-49
Brands:
Valley View Cheese

13961 **Valley View Packing Company**
P.O.Box 5699
San Jose, CA 95150-5699 408-289-8300
Fax: 408-289-8897 www.valleyviewpacking.com
Manufacturer and exporter of dried fruits and fruit juices and concentrates
President: Sal Rubino
Estimated Sales: $17 Million
Number Employees: 5-9
Type of Packaging: Consumer, Food Service, Private Label, Bulk

13962 **Valley View Winery**
1000 Upper Applegate Rd
Jacksonville, OR 97530 541-899-8468
Fax: 541-899-8468 800-781-9463
valleyviewwinery@charter.net
www.valleyviewwinery.com
Wines
Owner: Ann Wisnovsky
CFO: Mark Wisnovsky
Vice President: Michael Wisnovsky
Estimated Sales: $380,000
Number Employees: 5-9
Type of Packaging: Private Label
Brands:
Anna Maria
Valley View

13963 **Valley of the Moon Winery**
P.O.Box 1951
Glen Ellen, CA 95442 707-996-6941
Fax: 707-996-5809
luna@valleyofthemoonwinery.com
www.valleyofthemoonwinery.com
Wines
Manager: Randy Meyer
Marketing Manager: Paul Young
President: Harold Duncan
Production Manager: Pat Henderson
Estimated Sales: $ 10-20 Million
Number Employees: 20-49
Brands:
Valley of the Moon

13964 **Valley of the Rogue Dairy**
P.O.Box 1326
Grants Pass, OR 97528 541-476-2020
Fax: 541-476-4014
Manufacturer of milk
President: Palmer Zottola
Estimated Sales: $16 Million
Number Employees: 13
Type of Packaging: Consumer, Food Service, Private Label, Bulk

13965 **Vallos Baking Company**
1800 Broadway
Bethlehem, PA 18015 610-866-1012
Fax: 610-866-1012
Bread, donuts and rolls
Owner: Tina Hanushack
Co-Owner: Gus Skoutelas
Estimated Sales: $ 10-20 Million
Number Employees: 10-19
Type of Packaging: Consumer, Food Service

13966 **(HQ)Van Bennett Food Company**
101 N Carroll St
Reading, PA 19611-1697 610-374-8348
Fax: 610-374-6714 800-423-8897
sales@vanbennett.com www.vanbennett.com
Processor of potato salad, rice pudding and tapioca; wholesaler/distributorof meats, frozen food, general line items and specialty foods, produce and dairyitems; serving the food service market
President: P B Emmett
CEO: J R Marcinko
Estimated Sales: $ 20 - 50 Million
Number Employees: 20-49
Sq. footage: 18000
Brands:
Betty's

13967 **Van De Kamp Frozen Foods**
1 Old Bloomfield Ave
Mountain Lake, NJ 07646 973-541-6620
www.pinnaclefoodscorp.com
Processor of frozen battered and breaded fish fillets and sticks
Chairman: Roger Deromedi
CEO/Director: Robert Gamgort
Plant Manager: Howard Tuefel
Estimated Sales: $1 Billion
Number Employees: 1,000-4,999
Sq. footage: 120000
Parent Co: Pinnacle Foods
Type of Packaging: Consumer
Brands:
VAN DE KAMP

13968 **Van De Walle Farms**
5310 W Old Us Highway 90
San Antonio, TX 78227-2243 210-436-5551
Fax: 210-436-6766
www.sanantoniofarmsonline.com
Processor of Mexican fajita marinade, pico de gallo, salsa, enchilada and picante sauce and peppers including jalapeno, serrano and chile
Manager: Michael Knuth
VP: Elaine Thompson
Sales/Marketing Director: Don Johnson
Estimated Sales: $ 20 - 50 Million
Number Employees: 50-99
Sq. footage: 45000
Type of Packaging: Consumer, Food Service, Bulk
Brands:
Van De Walle Farms

13969 **Van Der Heyden Vineyards**
4057 Silverado Trl
Napa, CA 94558-1113 707-257-0130
Fax: 707-257-3311 800-948-9463
talig@vanderheydenvineyards.com
www.vanderheydenvineyards.com
Wine
Manager: Andrea Vander Heyede
Estimated Sales: $1-2.5 Million
Number Employees: 1-4
Type of Packaging: Private Label
Brands:
Van Der Heyden

13970 **Van Drunen Farms**
300 W 6th St
Momence, IL 60954 815-472-3537
Fax: 815-472-3850 idorn@vandrunen.com
www.vandrunenfarms.com
Food ingredient manufacturer
President: Edward Van Drunen
CFO: Bill Vre
General Manager: Kevin Van Drunen
VP R&D: Zbigniew Pietrzowski
Quality Control Director: Chris Duffield
Human Resources: Jim Slavich
Operations Executive/Plant Manager: Rick Ouwenga
Purchasing Manager: Michael Cialdella
Estimated Sales: $100 Million
Number Employees: 300
Number of Brands: 4
Number of Products: 1100
Sq. footage: 30000
Type of Packaging: Consumer, Food Service, Private Label, Bulk
Brands:
Van Drunen Farms

13971 **Van Dyke Ice Cream**
145 Ackerman Ave
Ridgewood, NJ 07450-4205 201-444-1429
Ice cream, frozen desserts and novelties
Owner: Demetrios Kotrokas
Estimated Sales: $ 2.5-5 Million
Number Employees: 10-19

13972 **Van Dykes Chesapeake Seafood**
P.O.Box 221
Cambridge, MD 21613-0221 410-228-9000
Fax: 410-228-5957
Seafood
Owner: Eleanor Van Dyke
Estimated Sales: $ 1 - 3 Million
Number Employees: 5-9

13973 **Van Eeghen International Inc**
750 Rue Gougeon
St Laurent, QC H4T 4L54
Canada 514-332-6455
Fax: 514-332-6475 info@vaneeghen.net
www.vaneeghen.net
Dehydrated vegetables, culinary herbs and spices.
Director: Williem Van Eeghen
Account Manager: Tim Dias
Estimated Sales: $5 Million
Number Employees: 31
Sq. footage: 10452

13974 **Van Ekris & Company**
61 Broadway
New York, NY 10006-2701 212-898-9600
Fax: 212-514-9234 info@vanekris.com
www.vanekris.com
General grocery
President: Tom Backman
CEO: A Van Ekris
CFO: Peter Binazeski
Senior VP: Michael Mason
VP: Marie Barbato
Estimated Sales: $ 10 - 20 Million
Number Employees: 32

13975 **Van Leer Chocolate Corporation**
1301 Sinatra Dr
Hoboken, NJ 07030-5632 201-798-8080
Fax: 201-798-0138 800-826-2462
custsrvc@vanleerchocolate.com
http://www.vanleerchocolate.com/us/en/31
Chocolate
Manager: Scott Applegate
CFO: Anthony Forns
Operations Manager: Robert Mohn
Plant Manager: Tom Jones
Purchasing Manager: Tom Thoelen
Estimated Sales: $ 25-49.9 Million
Number Employees: 100-249

13976 **Van Oriental Foods**
4828 Reading Street
Dallas, TX 75247-6705
US 214-630-0333
Fax: 214-630-0473 info_vanfoods@yahoo.com
www.vaneggrolls.com
Processor of frozen foods including regular and low-fat egg rolls, fried wontons, crab rangoon, enchiladas, burritos and spring rolls they use lean meat and no msg. They make lean chicken and prok eggrolls also shrimp and vegie.
President: Kimberly Nguyen
Co-Owner: Gretchen Perrenot
Corporate Treasurer: Theresa Motter
Sales Manager: Carl Motter
Plant Engineer: Apollo Nguyen
Estimated Sales: $8.9 Million
Number Employees: 75
Sq. footage: 56000
Type of Packaging: Consumer, Food Service, Private Label, Bulk

13977 **Van Otis Chocolates**
341 Elm St
Manchester, NH 03101 603-627-1611
Fax: 603-627-0781 800-826-6847
feedback@vanotis.com www.vanotis.com
Chocolates
Owner: Dave Quin
Co-Owner: Frank Bettencourt
Estimated Sales: Less than $500,000
Number Employees: 1-4
Sq. footage: 20000
Type of Packaging: Private Label
Brands:
Foiled Chocolate
Swiss Fudge Sampler Tier
Van Otis Swiss Fudge

13978 **Van Peenans Dairy**
978 Valley Rd
Wayne, NJ 07470-2997 973-694-2551
Fax: 973-696-3854
Dairy
Owner: Tunis Van Peenan
Estimated Sales: $ 5-10 Million
Number Employees: 20-49

13979 **Van Roy Coffee**
4569 Spring Rd
Cleveland, OH 44131 216-749-7069
Fax: 216-749-7039 877-826-7669
awatterson@cheslergroup.com
www.vanroycoffee.com
Processor of roasted coffee and tea; also, spices
President/CEO: Jeffrey Miller
Vice President: John Schanz III
Estimated Sales: $1,400,000
Number Employees: 10-19
Sq. footage: 38000
Type of Packaging: Food Service, Private Label, Bulk
Brands:
DE-KAFFO
VAN ROY

13980 **Van Tone Creative Flavors Inc**
200 Metro Dr
Terrell, TX 75160-9169 972-563-2600
Fax: 972-563-2640 800-856-0802
david-hinds@airmail.net
Processor of food, ice cream, bakers, dairy and beverage flavoring concentrates, food colors, slush concentrates and syrups including sno-cone, FCB, granita, smoothie, fruit drink and fountain
Owner: Joe Gibbs
VP Marketing: Steve Myrlin
VP Sales: Joe Gibbs
Estimated Sales: $3494044
Number Employees: 20-49
Sq. footage: 36000
Type of Packaging: Food Service, Private Label, Bulk
Brands:
Allez
Cyclone
Van Tone

13981 **Van Waters & Roger**
PO Box 446
Summit, IL 60501-0446 708-728-6830
Fax: 708-728-6801 jim.lacey@vwr-inc.com
www.vopakusa.com
Distributor of chemicals and food ingredients
President: Terry Irvine
President: James Lacey
Chief Marketing Department: Mark Buntin
Head Sales Department: Mike Clary
Number Employees: 250-499
Brands:
Van Waters & Roger

13982 **Van de Kamp's**
Po Box 3900
Peoria, IL 61612
800-798-3318
www.vandekamps.com
Processor and exporter of pies, fish and vegetables
Plant Manager: James Frey
Number Employees: 100-249
Parent Co: Van de Kamps
Type of Packaging: Consumer, Food Service, Private Label

13983 **Van's International Foods**
20318 Gramercy Pl
Torrance, CA 90501 310-320-8611
Fax: 310-320-8805
customerservice@vansintl.com
www.vansintl.com
Processor of round, square, toaster, mini and jumbo frozen waffles including original, whole grain, wheat-free, organic and gluten-free
President: James Kelly
Sales Director: Kim Fernandez
Operations Manager: Frank Copenhaver
Estimated Sales: $4600000
Number Employees: 40
Sq. footage: 10000
Type of Packaging: Private Label
Brands:
VAN'S

13984 **Van-Lang Foods**
5227 Dansher Rd
Countryside, IL 60525 708-588-0800
Fax: 708-588-0801 info@vanlangfoods.com
www.vanlangfoods.com
Processor of frozen hors d'oeuvres and appetizers
President: Hien Lam
Estimated Sales: Below $ 5 Million
Number Employees: 15
Type of Packaging: Food Service
Brands:
Van-Lang

13985 **(HQ)Vance's Foods**
PO Box 627
Gilmer, TX 75644 800-497-4834
Fax: 800-497-4329 info@vancesfoods.com
www.vancesfoods.com
Processor and exporter of nondairy and fat-free potato-based milk substitutes including dry and liquid, and dry soy-based milk substitutes
President: Vance Abersold
VP: Glenn Abersold
Director Marketing: Frederick Mattos
Type of Packaging: Consumer, Food Service, Bulk
Brands:
NotMilk
Sno-E Tofu
Vance's Darifree

13986 **Vanco Products Company**
1 Mt Vernon St
Dorchester, MA 02125-1604 617-265-3400
Processor of bakery supplies
President: Chris Anton
Production Manager: Carl Hogenda
Estimated Sales: $ 5 - 10 Million
Number Employees: 10-19
Sq. footage: 15000
Parent Co: Johnson's Food Products Corporation
Type of Packaging: Consumer

13987 **Vancouver Island Brewing Company**
2330 Government Street
Victoria, BC V8T 5G5
Canada 250-361-0007
Fax: 250-360-0336 800-663-6383
info@vanislanbrewery.com
www.vanislandbrewery.com
Brewer of lager and ale
President: Barry Fisher
General Manager: Jim Dodds
Number Employees: 20-49
Sq. footage: 28000
Parent Co: Island Pacific Brewing Company
Type of Packaging: Consumer
Brands:
BLONDE ALE
HERMANN'S DARK LAGER
HERMANNATOR ICE BOCK
PIPER'S PALE ALE
VANCOUVER ISLANDER LAGER
VICTORIA LAGER
WOLF'S SCOTTISH CREAM ALE

13988 **Vande Walle's Candies**
400 N Mall Dr
Appleton, WI 54913 920-738-7799
Fax: 920-738-3280
Processor of candy including boxed, fund raising, Easter, Valentine, bars, brittles, caramels, chocolates, toffee, fudge, caramel corn and popcorn specialties
President: Jay Walle
President: Thomas Walle
Vice President: Donald Walle
Estimated Sales: $3 Million
Number Employees: 40
Sq. footage: 40000

13989 **Vanee Foods Company**
5418 McDermott Drive
Berkeley, IL 60163 708-449-7300
Fax: 708-449-2558 jackridge@vaneefoods.com
www.vaneefoods.com
Manufacturer of roasted gravies, broths, breakfast entrees, dinner entrees, chilis, meats, sauces and soups.
President: Aloysius Eekeren
CFO: Ron Van Eekeren
R&D Director: Robert Benson
Quality Assurance Director: Jack Ridge
VP Sales/Marketing Director: Michael Vanee
Human Resource Director: Beatrice Kemphel
President/Operations Director: Al Vanee
Purchasing Director: Dan Vanee
Estimated Sales: $17000000
Number Employees: 200
Sq. footage: 425000
Type of Packaging: Food Service

13990 **Vanilla Corporation of America, LLC**
2273 N Penn Rd
Hatfield, PA 19440 215-996-1978
Fax: 215-996-9867
Grain and field bean merchant wholesalers
Manager: Douglas Daugherty
Estimated Sales: $500,000-1 Million
Number Employees: 5-9
Type of Packaging: Food Service, Bulk

13991 **Vanlab Corporation**
86 White Street
Rochester, NY 14608-1435 585-232-6647
Fax: 585-232-6168 bmarchetti@vanlab.com

Flavoring supplies, flavors
President: David A Patton
VP: Diane Merritt
General Manager: William Marchetti
R & D: Florent Montagne
VP: Jim Abraham
Marketing/Sales: Kim Kubach
Operations/Production: Jim Abraham
Plant Manager: Hank Rankowsky
Estimated Sales: $ 10-20 Million
Number Employees: 30-50
Sq. footage: 35000
Type of Packaging: Food Service, Private Label, Bulk

13992 **(HQ)Vanlaw Food Products**
2325 Moore Ave
Fullerton, CA 92833 714-870-9091
Fax: 714-870-5609
Processor and exporter of refrigerated and shelf stable salad dressings, pancake syrup, syrup concentrates, flavorings, extracts, colorings, ice cream toppings and barbecue and teriyaki sauces; importer of romano and parmesan cheeseolive oil and balsamic vinegar
President: Matthew Jones
VP: Michael Bilyk
Director of Sales: John Gilbert
Estimated Sales: $ .5 - 1 million
Number Employees: 1-4
Sq. footage: 130000
Type of Packaging: Consumer, Food Service, Private Label
Brands:
California Classics
Sunfruit
Zito

13993 **Vanns Spices**
1716 Whitehead Rd
Suite A
Baltimore, MD 21207 410-944-3888
Fax: 410-944-3998 800-583-1693
sales@vannsspices.com www.vannsspices.com
Spices and seasonings
President: Mick Whitlock
CEO: Erhan Kuran
Executive VP: Erhan Kurany
Estimated Sales: $3.6 Million
Number Employees: 35
Type of Packaging: Private Label, Bulk

13994 **Vantage USA**
4740 S Whipple St
Chicago, IL 60632 773-247-1086
Fax: 708-401-1565 www.VantageUSA.net
Organic/natural & commodity wholesaler consolidator/supplier and logistics provider. Specializing in natural and private label products planning & development.
Owner: Dan Gash
Type of Packaging: Food Service, Private Label, Bulk
Brands:
APPLEGATE FARMS
CARGILL
COLAVITA
CUCINA VIVA
EBERLY
EXCALIBUR
EXCEL
GOTHAM
GREAT PLAINS
HONEYSUCKLE
NORBEST
PRAIRIE GROVE
REICHERT
ROMA
SMART CHOICE
TASTE IT
TURANO

13995 **Varco Brothers**
1832 N Burling Street
Chicago, IL 60614-5104 312-642-4740
Noodles, spaghetti and macaroni
President: John Varco
Estimated Sales: $ 1-2.5 Million
Number Employees: 1-5

13996 **Varda Chocolatier**
41 S Spring St
Elizabeth, NJ 7201 908-354-9090
Fax: 908-354-9091 800-448-2732
www.vardachocolatier.com
Processor of chocolate confectionery products including truffles, dessert cups, novelties and creative chocolate presentation
Owner: Varda Shandan
Officer: Sue Hughes
Estimated Sales: $6.5 Million
Number Employees: 35

13997 **Varet Street Market**
89 Varet St
Brooklyn, NY 11206 718-302-0560
Fax: 718-302-0560
Tropical fruit
President: Alfonzo Estevez
CEO: Lely Estevez
Estimated Sales: Less than $400,000
Number Employees: 1-4
Type of Packaging: Food Service, Bulk
Brands:
Reyes Mares

13998 **Varied Industries Corporation**
905 S Carolina Ave
Mason City, IA 50401 641-423-1460
Fax: 641-423-0832 800-654-5617
www.fermented-products.com
Manufacturer and exporter of lactic acid fermentation and yucca extracts for food, feed and litter products
President: Mark Holt
Vice President: Gerry Keller
Vice President: Lynn Lunning
Estimated Sales: $7.6 Million
Number Employees: 40
Sq. footage: 15000
Parent Co: International Whey Technics
Brands:
Desert Gold Dry
Kulactic
Kulsar

13999 **Variety Foods**
7001 Chicago Rd
Warren, MI 48092-1615 586-268-4900
Fax: 586-268-6627 www.champenes.com
Processor of baked cheese curls and jumbos, fried cheese twists, popcorn, tortilla chips, baking and salted nuts, trail mixes, candies and Easter and gift baskets
President: James Champane
VP Internal Operations: George Champane
Estimated Sales: $ 20 - 50 Million
Number Employees: 50-99
Type of Packaging: Consumer, Food Service, Private Label, Bulk
Brands:
Cha Cha's
Champane's
Cheese-A-Roos
Munch-A-Roos
Old Favorite
Pic-A-Nut
Sun Ray
Zappers

14000 **Varni Brothers/7-Up Bottling**
400 Hosmer Ave
Modesto, CA 95351-3920 209-521-1777
Fax: 209-521-5922 water@noahs7up.com
www.noahs7up.com
Processor and exporter of soft drinks, purified water, etc
President: John Varni
CEO: Fred Varni
Estimated Sales: $37000000
Number Employees: 50-99
Sq. footage: 120000
Parent Co: Dr. Pepper/7-UP Bottling Companies
Type of Packaging: Food Service, Private Label

14001 **Vassilaros & Son**
2905 120th St
Flushing, NY 11354-2505 718-886-4140
Fax: 718-463-5037 info@vassilaroscoffee.com
www.vassilaroscoffee.com
Coffee, tea and cocoa.
President: John Vassilaros
Estimated Sales: $ 5-10 Million
Number Employees: 20-49

14002 **Vatore's Italian Caramel**
8408 Georgia Avenue
Silver Spring, MD 20910 301-578-8612
Fax: 410-341-4674 88- 4-3 52
vatores@aol.com www.vatores.com
Candy
Owner: Tim Beyer
VP: Janet Beyer
Estimated Sales: $500,000-$1 Million
Number Employees: 1-4
Brands:
Vatore's

14003 **Vaughn Rue Produce**
1217 Peachtree Rd NW
Wilson, NC 27896 252-237-6710
Fax: 252-237-7662 800-388-8138
Processor of sweet potatoes, butternut squash and pickles
President: Vaughn Rue
Estimated Sales: Below $ 5 Million
Number Employees: 1-4
Brands:
Rue's Choice
Steakhouse

14004 **Vaughn-Russell Candy Kitchen**
1624 Augusta St
Greenville, SC 29605-2924 864-271-7786
Fax: 704-484-8326 vaughnrussell@bellsouth.net
www.vaughnrussell.com
Candy
Owner: Betty Hartman
Plant Manager: Helen Gibson
Estimated Sales: Less than $500,000
Number Employees: 5-9
Brands:
Vaughn Russell

14005 **Vauxhall Foods**
PO Box 430
Vauxhall, AB T0K 2K0
Canada 403-654-2771
Fax: 403-654-2211 info@potatopower.com
www.potatopower.com
Processor and exporter of dehydrated potato granules
President: Frank Gatto
CFO: Frank Inaba
Research & Development: Gordon Packer
General Manager: Ken Tamura
Production Manager: Ken Franz
Number Employees: 50-99
Sq. footage: 50000
Type of Packaging: Food Service, Private Label, Bulk
Brands:
CHIPPER
GOURMET
V.G. BLUE

14006 **Vaxa International**
600 N West Shore Blvd Ste 800
Tampa, FL 33609 813-870-2904
Fax: 888-734-4154 800-248-8292
Customerservice@vaxa.com www.vaxa.com
Processor of dietetic chocolate and vanilla powdered shake mixes
President: Bill Harper
VP: Chris Behan
Estimated Sales: $ 1 - 3 Million
Number Employees: 20-49
Parent Co: Direct Access Network
Type of Packaging: Consumer, Private Label, Bulk
Brands:
Vaxa

14007 **Vega Food Industries**
80 Stamp Farm Rd
Cranston, RI 2921 401-942-0620
Fax: 401-942-5760 800-973-7737
www.vegafoods.com
Processor of gourmet stuffed and sliced cherry peppers, olives, peppers and packed salads in oil and garlic
Owner: Dennis Tofaro
VP: Anthony Cippola
Operations Manager: Frank Bisignano
Plant Manager: Carrie Zamborano
Estimated Sales: $1900000
Number Employees: 10-19
Sq. footage: 5000
Type of Packaging: Consumer, Food Service, Private Label, Bulk

Brands:
Vega's Gourmet

14008 **(HQ)Vege-Cool**
802 Inyo Ave
Newman, CA 95360 209-862-2360
Processor of lima beans and peas
Owner: William Cerutti
Manager: Steve Lewis
Estimated Sales: $400,000
Number Employees: 3
Type of Packaging: Bulk

14009 **Vegetable Juices**
7400 S Narragansett Ave
Chicago, IL 60638 708-924-9500
Fax: 708-924-9510 888-776-9752
contactus@vegetablejuices.com
www.vegetablejuices.com
Known for turning fresh ingredients into innovative solutions, our juices, purees and diced vegetables have been our specialty for over 70 years. These products provide fresh natural flavors, textures and color to many different flavorsystems. And our Innovation Center is available for creative collaboration, sound advice and technical expertise.
CEO: James Hurley
CFO: Michael Brunson
Sr VP Sales/Marketing: Barry Horne
R&D: Anthony Popielarz
Quality Control: Paul Bollinger
Operations: Mike O'Hara
Estimated Sales: $10-20 Million
Number Employees: 100-249
Type of Packaging: Food Service, Bulk

14010 **VeggieLand**
222 New Rd Ste 3
Parsippany, NJ 7054 973-808-1540
Fax: 973-882-3030 888-808-5540
russgrabow@aol.com www.veggieland.com
Processor and exporter of vegetarian foods including burgers, meat balls, frankfurters, sausage, sandwiches and chili
Manager: Len Torine
Executive VP: Len Torine
Estimated Sales: Below $ 5 Million
Number Employees: 20-49
Sq. footage: 16000
Brands:
Veg-T-Balls
Veggieland

14011 **Vegi-Deli**
17 Paul Dr Ste 104
San Rafael, CA 94903 415-883-6100
Fax: 415-526-1453 888-473-3667
info@vegideli.com www.vegideli.com
Vegetarian meat alternative deli products including pepperoni, cold cuts and pizza toppings and vegi-jerky, pepperoni snack sticks.
General Manager: Debra Ventura
Estimated Sales: $ 3-5 Million
Number Employees: 8
Sq. footage: 6000
Type of Packaging: Consumer, Food Service, Private Label
Brands:
Quick Stix
Vegetarian Slice of Life

14012 **(HQ)Velda Farms**
308 Avenue G SW
Winter Haven, FL 33880 863-686-4441
Fax: 863-686-7792 800-279-4166
www.veldafarms.com
Dairy products
President: Glen Herrington
Marketing Director: Robin Chaddick
CFO: Tim Long
Number Employees: 500-999
Parent Co: Suiza Dairy Group
Brands:
Velda Farms

14013 **Velda Farms**
501 NE 181st St
North Miami Beach, FL 33162 305-652-3720
Fax: 305-651-2766 800-795-4649
www.veldafarms.com
Processor of juice and dairy products including milk, cream and ice cream
President: James Dintaman
VP/CFO: Niell Larsen
General Sales Manager: Bill Aaronson
Estimated Sales: $ 50 - 100 Million
Number Employees: 250-499
Parent Co: Suiza Dairy Group
Type of Packaging: Consumer, Food Service, Private Label, Bulk
Brands:
Sunnydell
Velda

14014 **Velda Farms**
308 Avenue G SW
Winter Haven, FL 33880 863-686-4441
Fax: 863-686-7792 800-279-4166
customerserviceteam@veldafarms.com
www.veldafarms.com
Processor of juices and dairy products including ice cream
President: Glen Herrington
VP Manufacturing: Norm Rasmussen
Branch Manager: Frank Mondello
Plant Manager: Vince Porter
Purchasing Manager: Vince Vitale
Estimated Sales: $$5-10 Million appx.
Number Employees: 500-999
Parent Co: Suiza Dairy Group
Type of Packaging: Consumer
Brands:
Barricini
Bassetts
Sunnydell

14015 **Velda Farms**
1000 6th St SW
Winter Haven, FL 33880 863-298-9742
Fax: 863-294-3851 800-279-4166
www.veldafarms.com
Processor of dairy products
Executive Director: Glen Harrington
Marketing Director: Frank Mardello
Sr. Financial Officer: Jerry Harper
Plant Manager: Terry Witt
Estimated Sales: $ 20 - 50 Million
Number Employees: 100-249
Parent Co: Suiza Dairy Group
Type of Packaging: Consumer
Brands:
Velda Farms

14016 **Vella Cheese**
315 2nd St E
Sonoma, CA 95476 707-938-3232
Fax: 707-938-4307 800-848-0505
vella@vellacheese.com www.vellacheese.com
Processor of cheese including Monterey jack, asiago, cheddar, dry jack and Italian-style table
President: Sarah Vella
Estimated Sales: $2,000,000
Number Employees: 10-19
Sq. footage: 10740
Type of Packaging: Consumer
Brands:
Asiago
Bear Flag
Dry Sack
High Moisture Fresh Jack
Mezzo
Seasoned Cheddar Cheese
Seasoned Jack Cheese
Sello
Vella

14017 **Velvet Creme Popcorn Company**
4710 Belinder Rd
Westwood, KS 66205 913-236-7742
Fax: 913-236-9631 888-553-6708
customerservice@velvetcremepopcorn.com
www.velvetcremepopcorn.com
Processor of popcorn
President: Jerry Wright
Estimated Sales: $1 Million-1.5
Number Employees: 5-9
Sq. footage: 30000
Type of Packaging: Consumer
Brands:
Velvet Creme

14018 **Velvet Freeze Ice Cream**
7355 W Florissant Ave
Saint Louis, MO 63136 314-381-2384
Fax: 314-381-2384 800-589-5000
info@velveticecream.com
www.velveticecream.com
Ice cream, yogurt and sherbet
Owner: John Mc Guinness
Founder: Joe Dager
Executive VP: Matt Mueller
Estimated Sales: Below $ 5 Million
Number Employees: 5-9
Brands:
Velvet

14019 **Velvet Ice Cream Company**
11324 Mt Vernon Rd
PO Box 588
Utica, OH 43080 740-892-3921
Fax: 740-892-4339 800-589-5000
info@velveticecream.com
www.velveticecream.com
Processor of ice cream and frozen desserts.
President: Joseph Dager
VP: Michael Dager
Sales Manager: Luconda Dager
Estimated Sales: $ 50 - 100 Million
Number Employees: 100-249
Type of Packaging: Consumer

14020 **Velvet Milk**
309 Sutton Lane
Owensboro, KY 42301-0370 207-684-9677
Fax: 270-683-4562
Milk
Estimated Sales: $ 5-10 Million
Number Employees: 5-9

14021 **Vending Nut**
2222 Montgomery Street
Ft. Worth, TX 76107 817-737-3071
Fax: 817-337-1316 www.vendingnut.com
Nuts wholesaler
President: Johnny Minshew
Estimated Sales: $4 Million
Number Employees: 25

14022 **Venice Maid Foods**
PO Box 1505
Vineland, NJ 08362-1505 856-691-2100
Fax: 856-696-1295 800-257-7070
sales@venicemaid.com www.venicemaid.com
Manufacturer of canned pasta, sauces, gravies, and meat entrees
President: John Kelly
VP of Finance: Rick Kebler
VP: Darrel Wunderlich
R & D: Rich Gibbs
Quality Control: Cecelia Monkata
Marketing/Sales: Donna George
Operations: Ed Leibrand
Production: Debbie Volk
Plant Manager: Dave Bernier
Purchase Executive: Terry Hannah
Estimated Sales: $ 5-10 Million
Number Employees: 20-49
Type of Packaging: Private Label

14023 **Venison America**
494 County Road A
Hudson, WI 54016 715-386-6628
Fax: 715-386-6613 800-310-2360
www.venisonamerica.com
Marketer and processor of fresh and frozen farm raised game meat from alligator to yak; gourmet items, corporate gift boxes, etc.
Principal: Kent Phillips
Estimated Sales: Under $500,000
Number Employees: 1-4
Sq. footage: 2000
Type of Packaging: Consumer, Food Service

14024 **Ventana Vineyards Winery**
2999 Salinas Hwy # 10
Monterey, CA 93940-5706 831-372-7415
Fax: 831-655-1855 800-237-8846
info@ventanawines.com
www.ventanawines.com

Wines
Owner: Randy Pura
VP/Marketing Director: LuAnn Meador
Bookkeeper: Christy Florez
Vineyard Foreman: David Rodriguez
Production Manager: Reggie Hammond
Winemaker: Miguel Martinez
National Sales Manager: Terry Lannon
California Sales Manager: Sarah Robinson
Sales/Marketing: Gerre Calderon
Tasing Room Manager: Rosemary Hermans-Walls
Estimated Sales: $ 1 - 3 Million
Number Employees: 10-19
Type of Packaging: Private Label
Brands:
Ventana Wines

14025 **Ventre Packing Company**
P.O. Box 6487
Syracuse, NY 13217 315-463-2384
Fax: 315-463-5897 888-472-8237
enrico@enricos-ventre.com www.enricos.com
Manufacturer and packager of spaghetti sauce.
Chairman: John Ventre Jr
Persident/CEO: Martin Ventre
EVP: Jacqueline Papai
Estimated Sales: $10-20 Million
Sq. footage: 100000
Type of Packaging: Consumer, Food Service, Private Label
Brands:
ENRICO
ENRICO MEXICAN
ENRICO'S
GIANNI
LA CASA
MCDEI
MEDEI

14026 **Ventura Coastal Corporation**
2325 Vista Del Mar Dr
Ventura, CA 93001 805-653-7035
Fax: 805-653-7777
Manufacturer and exporter of citrus concentrates and single strength juices; contract packager of frozen pectin products
President: William Borgens
Estimated Sales: $44 Million
Number Employees: 100-249
Type of Packaging: Consumer, Food Service, Private Label, Bulk

14027 **Ventura Foods**
650 W Sedgley Ave
Philadelphia, PA 19140 215-223-8700
Fax: 215-225-4204 www.venturafoods.com
Manufacturer of mayonnaise, salad dressings, sauces and syrups for private label and food service.
Manager: Melissa Castle
Parent Co: Ventura Foods LLC
Type of Packaging: Food Service, Private Label
Other Locations:
ventura Foods Foodservice/Retail
Portland OR
Ventura Foods
Salem Foodservice OR
Ventura Foods Retail/Export
Los Angeles CA
Ventura Foods Foodservice/Export
City of Industry CA
Ventura Foods Foodservice
Albert Lea MN
Ventura Foods Foodservice
Waukesha WI
Ventura Foods Foodservice
St Joseph MO
Ventura Foods Foodservice
Chambersburg PA
Ventura Foods SE Distribution Ctr
Bingmingham AL
Ventura Foods Retail/Foodservice
Opelousas LA
Ventura Foods Foodservice
Dallas, Ft Worth TX
Brands:
CHEF SUPREME
CHEF'S PRIDE
GOURMAY
HIDDEN VALLEY POURABLE DRESSINGS

14028 **Ventura Foods**
715 N Railroad Ave
Opelousas, LA 70570
US 337-948-6561
Fax: 337-942-6239 www.venturafoods.com
Ventura's oil refining facility produces Lou Ana brand retail/foodservice oils and concession products. It also supplies private label oil to customers.
Parent Co: Ventura Foods LLC
Type of Packaging: Consumer, Food Service, Private Label, Bulk
Brands:
Coco-Pop
Lou Ana
Mermaid
Mor Gold Plus
Perfecto
Pop 'n Lite
Triumph

14029 **Ventura Foods**
2900 Jurupa St
Ontario, CA 91761-2915 323-262-9157
Fax: 323-269-6330 www.venturafoods.com
Produces extensive line of branded and private label products, inlcuding: syrups, mayonnaise, salad dressings, oils, shortenings, and sauces. It also provides contract packaging services for a variety of products sold to retail andfoodservice customers. butter,pickles,margerines
Parent Co: Ventura Foods LLC
Type of Packaging: Consumer, Food Service, Private Label, Bulk
Brands:
GOLD-N-SWEET
SAFFOLA
TABLE MAID

14030 **Ventura Foods**
14840 Don Julian Rd
City of Industry, CA 91746-3111 626-937-0136
Fax: 626-336-3229 800-327-3906
www.venturafoods.com
Produces and extensive line of branded and private label products including: shortenings; oils; margarine; salad dressings; mayonnaise; sauces and syrups. Also contract packaging and export site.
Plant Manager: John Collie
Parent Co: Ventura Foods LLC
Type of Packaging: Consumer, Food Service, Private Label
Brands:
Gold N Sweet
LouAna
Saffola

14031 **Ventura Foods**
1100 Defiel Rd
Saginaw, TX 76179 817-232-5450
Fax: 817-232-4230 www.venturafoods.com
Shortenings, oils, margarines, salad dressings, mayonnaise, and sauces.
Plant Manager: Tim Davis
Parent Co: Ventura Foods LLC
Type of Packaging: Food Service, Private Label
Brands:
Extend
Savory

14032 **Ventura Foods**
3371 Portland Rd NE
Salem, OR 97301-8415 503-585-6423
Fax: 503-585-1286 www.venturafoods.com
Produces a full line of branded and private label products for the foodservice market, including margarine, oils, and shortening.
Sq. footage: 100000
Parent Co: Ventura Foods LLC
Type of Packaging: Food Service, Private Label
Brands:
Chef's Pride
Gold-N-Sweet

14033 **Ventura Foods**
9000 Ne Marx Drive
Portland, OR 97220-1339 503-255-5512
Fax: 503-253-6357 www.venturafoods.com
Manufactures a variety of branded and private label products for foodservice and retail customers, including margarine, mayonnaise, salad dressings and sauces.
Parent Co: Ventura Foods LLC
Type of Packaging: Consumer, Food Service

14034 **(HQ)Ventura Foods**
40 Pointe Drive
Brea, CA 92821 714-257-3700
Fax: 714-257-3702 800-421-6257
www.venturafoods.com
Manufactures margarines under the Saffola and Gold-N-Sweet brands, butter blends, as well as private lables in these product catergories.
President/CEO: Christopher Furman
Asst Mgr/Export Sales: Vinh Trieu
Estimated Sales: $364 Million
Number Employees: 2000
Parent Co: CHS & Mitsui Co.
Type of Packaging: Consumer, Food Service, Private Label, Bulk

14035 **Venture Vineyards**
8830 Upper Lake Rd
Lodi, NY 14860 607-582-6774
888-635-6277
venturev@capital.net www.vineyards4sale.com
Grower of asparagus, raspberries and grapes including concord, Niagara, Catawaba, and Delaware. Also a processor of grape juice and importer and exporter of concord grapes
President: Melvin Nass
VP: Phyllis Nass
Operations Manager: Andrew Nass
Number Employees: 5-9
Sq. footage: 10000
Brands:
Venture For the Best

14036 **Venus Wafers**
100 Research Rd Ste 3
Hingham, MA 02043-4345
Fax: 781-749-7195 800-545-4538
saf@venuswafers.com www.venuswafers.com
Processor and exporter of crackers including fat-free, toasted onion, garden vegetable, garlic and herb, multigrain, cracked pepper and gourmet: toasted wheat and garden vegetable; also, stoned wheat and multigrain available in giftbaskets.
CFO: Edward Barmakian
Estimated Sales: $ 5 - 10 Million
Number Employees: 20-49
Type of Packaging: Consumer
Brands:
Deli-Catessen
Old Brussels
Venus Wafers

14037 **Veramar Vineyard**
905 Quarry Rd
Berryville, VA 22611 540-955-5510
Fax: 540-955-0404 info@veramar.com
www.veramar.com
Wines
Co-Owner: James Bogaty
Co-Owner: Della Bogaty
Number Employees: 5-9

14038 **Verdelli Farms**
7505 Grayson Rd
Harrisburg, PA 17111 717-561-2900
Fax: 717-561-2941 800-422-8344
www.verdelli.com
Processor of fresh fruits and vegetables
CFO: Dan Verdelli
President: Albert Verdelli
CFO: Ron Miller
VP: Daniel Verdelli
President: Albert Verdelli
Marketing Head: Joanne Verdelli
Estimated Sales: $100+ Million
Number Employees: 500-999
Sq. footage: 13500
Type of Packaging: Consumer, Food Service, Bulk

14039 **Verhoff Alfalfa Mills**
1188 Sugar Mill Dr
Ottawa, OH 45875-8518 419-523-4767
Fax: 419-523-3775 800-834-8563
verhoffalfalfa@bright.net
www.alfagreensupreme.com
Processor of dehydrated alfalfa
President: Constance Verhoff
Vice President: Donald Verhoff
Estimated Sales: $2274776
Number Employees: 5-9
Type of Packaging: Bulk

14040 **Veritas Chocolatier**
1816 Johns Drive
Glenview, IL 60025 847-729-8787
Fax: 847-729-8879 800-555-8331
info@veritaschocolatier.com
www.veritaschocolatier.com

chocolate truffles

14041 Veritas Vineyards & Winery
151 Veritas Ln
Afton, VA 22920 540-456-8000
Fax: 540-456-8483 contact@veritaswines.com
www.veritaswines.com
Wines
Owner: Andrew Hodson
Estimated Sales: $ 3 - 5 Million
Number Employees: 5-9

14042 Vermilion Packers Ltd
4825-47 Avenue
Vermilion, AB T9X 1J4
Canada 780-853-4622
Fax: 780-853-4623
vermillionpacker@hotmail.com
Processor of fresh and cured meats including sausage
President: Rick Bozak
Estimated Sales: Below $ 5 Million
Number Employees: 14
Type of Packaging: Consumer, Food Service
Brands:
Vermilion

14043 Vermints
195 North Prospect Street
Burlington, VT 05401 802-869-2233
Fax: 802-869-1100 800-367-4442
gary@vermints.com www.vermints.com
Manufacturer of all natural breath mints
Estimated Sales: $300,000-500,000
Number Employees: 1-4
Parent Co: Ohare Enterprises

14044 Vermont BS
373 Hayden Hill Road W
Hinesburg, VT 05461-9533 802-482-2152
Fax: 802-482-2152 bpmjec@aol.com
Butterscotch sauce

14045 Vermont Bread Company
P.O.Box 1217
Brattleboro, VT 05302-1217 802-254-4600
Fax: 802-257-0165 877-293-0876
info@charterbaking.com
www.vermontbread.com
Manufacturer of baked goods including organic whole grain and French sourdough breads, baguettes and rolls. Charterhouse Group acquired the company
CEO: Lisa Lorimer
VP: J Rogers
Estimated Sales: $10 Million
Number Employees: 50-99
Parent Co: Charterhouse Group
Type of Packaging: Consumer

14046 Vermont Bread Company
80 Cotton Mill Hl
Brattleboro, VT 05301-8681 802-254-4600
Fax: 802-257-0165 dianep@vermontel.com
www.vermontbread.com
Processor of all-natural, organic and premium bread
Ceo: Lisa Lorimer
Vice President: J Rogers
Plant Manager: Susan Vitelly
Estimated Sales: $10 Million
Number Employees: 90
Sq. footage: 22000
Type of Packaging: Consumer, Food Service, Private Label
Brands:
Vermont
Windham Hearth

14047 Vermont Butter & CheeseCompany
P.O.Box 95
Websterville, VT 05678 802-479-9371
Fax: 802-479-3674
info@vtbutterandcheeseco.com
www.vtbutterandcheeseco.com
cow's milk cheeses, goat's milk cheeses and signature aged artisanal cheeses
President/Owner: Bob Reese
Estimated Sales: $6.6 Million
Number Employees: 28

14048 Vermont Chocolatiers
9 East St
Northfield, VT 05663 802-485-5181
Fax: 802-485-5191 877-485-4226
info@cermontchocolatiers.com
www.vermontproductsmall.com
Chocolate and shortbread
Co-Owner: Walter Delia
Co-Owner: Jane Delia
Estimated Sales: $300,000-500,000
Number Employees: 1-4

14049 Vermont Confectionery
1541 West Rd (Rt 9)
Bennington, VT 05262-0380 802-447-2610
Fax: 802-447-2610 800-545-9243
vtcandy@sover.net www.vermontcandy.com
Chocolate
Owner: George Mc Cain
Estimated Sales: $ 3 - 5 Million
Number Employees: 5-9

14050 Vermont Country Naturals
PO Box 238
Charlotte, VT 05445-0238 802-425-5445
Fax: 802-425-5444 800-528-7021
Processor of kosher, wildcrafted maple sugar (powder and granules) and maple syrup
President: Joan Savoy
CEO: Jeffrey Madison
Estimated Sales: $300,000-500,000
Number Employees: 3
Sq. footage: 3500
Parent Co: Vermont Country Maple Mixes
Brands:
MAPLE SPRINKLES

14051 Vermont Country Store
5650 Main St
Manchester Center, VT 05255 802-362-4667
Fax: 802-362-8288
customerservice@vermontcountrystore.com
www.vermontcountrystore.com
Authentic New England foods; cheeses, maple syrups, etc
President: Bill Sholice
Marketing Director: Cyndy Marshall
CFO: Penny Jhonson
Estimated Sales: $ 20-50 Million
Number Employees: 100-249
Type of Packaging: Private Label, Bulk
Brands:
Vermont Country Store

14052 Vermont Food Experience
PO Box 943
Shelburne, VT 05482-0943 802-985-8101
Fax: 802-885-2040
Gourmet and specialty foods
President: Richard Hurlburt
Estimated Sales: Under $500,000
Number Employees: 1-4

14053 Vermont Harvest Speciality Foods
1799 Mountain Rd
Stowe, VT 05672 802-253-7138
Fax: 802-253-7139 800-338-5354
info@vtharvest.com www.vtharvest.com
Jams, jellies, chutneys and breads
Founder: Patty Foltz
Estimated Sales: $ 1 - 3 Million
Number Employees: 1-4

14054 Vermont Liberty Tea Company
1 Derby Ln Ste 1
Waterbury, VT 05676 802-244-6102
Fax: 802-244-6102 jmvt@pshift.com
www.vermontlibertytea.com
Herbal, green and black tea
Owner: John McConnell
Estimated Sales: $ .5 - 1 million
Number Employees: 1-4

14055 Vermont Natural Company
201 Vt Route 112
Jacksonville, VT 05342 802-368-2231
Fax: 802-368-7556
Gourmet and specialty foods
Principal: Robert Moses
Estimated Sales: $300,000-500,000
Number Employees: 12
Sq. footage: 17
Type of Packaging: Private Label

14056 Vermont Nut Free Chocolates
10 Island Cir
Grand Isle, VT 05458-4408 802-372-4654
Fax: 802-372-4654 888-468-8373
vtnutfree@aol.com www.vermontnutfree.com
Nut free chocolates
Owner: Gail Elvidge
Estimated Sales: $ 1 - 3 Million
Number Employees: 10-19

14057 Vermont Pepper Works
49A Commerce Ave, Bay#5
South Burlington, VT 05403 802-598-6419
Fax: 802-888-1711
sales@vermontpepperworks.com
www.vermontpepperworks.com
Manufacturer of pepper sauces
Co-Owner: Jeff Mitchell
Co-Owner: Julie Mitchell

14058 Vermont Pretzel
24 Rockingham St
Bellows Falls, VT 05101 802-460-4600
Fax: 802-869-2837 888-671-4774
pretzels@sover.net www.vermontpretzel.com
Stuffed and soft pretzels, cookies and bars
President: Christine Holtz

14059 Vermont Specialty Food Association
Freedom Foods
24 Pleasant Street
Randolph, VT 05060 802-728-0070
Fax: 802-728-0071 www.freedom-foods.com
fruit infused maple syrups, vermont gift baskets, vermont mustards, vermont granola & mixes
Sq. footage: 8000

14060 Vermont Sprout House
25 Mountain View Street
Bristol, VT 05443-1312 802-453-3098
Fax: 802-453-2132
Sprouts, soups and side dishes
President: Susan Tomasi
Sales Manager: Blaine Sprout
General Manager: Joe MacWilliams
Estimated Sales: $ 5-10 Million
Number Employees: 10-19
Brands:
Vermont Sprout

14061 Vermont Sweetwater Bottling Company
1075 Vt Route 30 N
Poultney, VT 05764 802-287-9897
Fax: 802-287-9230 800-974-9877
york@sover.net www.vtsweetwater.com
Soda
Co-Owner: Robert Munch
Co-Owner: Richard Munch
Estimated Sales: $ 3 - 5 Million
Number Employees: 5-9

14062 Vermont Tea & Trading Company
P.O.Box 1050
Middlebury, VT 05753 802-388-4005
Fax: 802-388-4005 tea@together.net
Loose leaf teas
Co-Owner: Curron Malhotra
Co-Owner: Bruce Malhotra
Estimated Sales: $ 1 - 3 Million
Number Employees: 1-4

14063 Vern's Cheese
312 W Main St
Chilton, WI 53014 920-849-7717
Fax: 920-849-7883 info@vernscheese.com
www.vernscheese.com
Cheese
President: Vern Knoespel
Estimated Sales: $ 20-50 Million
Number Employees: 20-49

14064 Veronica Foods Company
1991 Dennison St
Oakland, CA 94606 510-535-6833
Fax: 510-532-2837 800-370-5554
mandvbrad@attbi.com www.evoliveoil.com

Olive oil manufacturers and importers
President: Michael Bradley
CEO: Mike Bradley
CFO: Leah Bradley
VP: Veronica Bradley
Marketing: Arnie Kaufman
VP Retail Sales: Arnie Kaufman
Operations: Fred Johnson
Production: Myron Manown
Plant Manager: Dave Fitzgerald
Purchasing: Fred Johnson
Estimated Sales: $16200000
Number Employees: 20-49
Sq. footage: 228000
Brands:
Dainty Pak
Delizia
Italia
Panther
Purn Life

14065 Veryfine Products
20 Harvard Rd
Littleton, MA 01460 978-486-3522
Fax: 978-952-6245 800-837-9346
donna.sitkiewicz@kraft.com www.veryfine.com
Fruit juice drinks
President/CEO: Roger Deromedi
Purchasing Manager: Sam Bowden
Estimated Sales: $ 150 Million
Number Employees: 1-4
Sq. footage: 350000
Parent Co: Kraft Foods
Brands:
Balsams Baby Water
Balsams Springwater
Fruit2O
Juice-Ups
Veryfine Apple Quenchers
Veryfine Chillers Tea & Lemonade
Veryfine Juices

14066 Vessey & Company
1605 Zenos Rd
Holtville, CA 92250 760-356-0130
Fax: 760-352-7645 kevinolson@redshift.com
www.vessey.com
Grower of cabbage including red, green, bok choy and napa; also, red and yellow onions, red and yukon potatoes, sweet corn, cantaloupes and garlic including fresh, whole, peeled, minced and chopped; importer and exporter of garlic
President: Jon Vessey
Sales Manager: David Grimes
Sales: Eric Pompa
Estimated Sales: $3100000
Number Employees: 10-19
Type of Packaging: Food Service, Bulk

14067 Vetter Vineyards Winery
8005 Prospect Station Rd
Westfield, NY 14787 716-326-3100
Fax: 716-326-3100 wine@cecomet.net
www.vettervineyards.com
Wines
Co-Owner: Mark Lancaster
Co-Owner: Barbara Lancaster
Estimated Sales: $300,000-500,000
Number Employees: 1-4
Type of Packaging: Private Label
Brands:
Vetter Vineyards

14068 Via Della Chiesa Vineyards
413 Church Street
Raynham, MA 02767-1008 508-822-7775
Fax: 508-880-0500
www.capecodcranberrywine.com
Wines
President: Robert DiCroce
CFO: Sharon Tweedy
Marketing Manager: Kate Desmond
Public Relations Officer: Lidm Piwa
Winery Manager: Dolly Tulsiani
Production Manager: Matyas Vogel
Estimated Sales: Below $ 5 Million
Number Employees: 10
Type of Packaging: Private Label
Brands:
Cranberry Blush Wine
Dry-Atlantic Coastal
Raspberry Rave Wine

14069 Viader Vineyards & Winery
1120 Deer Park Rd
Deer Park, CA 94576-9715 707-963-3816
Fax: 707-963-3817 info@viader.com
www.viader.com
Vineyards and Winery
Owner/Winemaker: Delia Viader
Executive Assistant: Valaree Martinez
Shipping Manager: Blanca Avina
Sales/Marketing Director: Janet Viader
Vineyard Manager/Winemaker: Alan Viader
Winemaker: Delia Viader
Number Employees: 10
Type of Packaging: Consumer, Food Service, Private Label
Brands:
Viader

14070 Viamar Foods
27 Carpenter St
Glen Cove, NY 11542-2398 516-759-0652
Fax: 516-759-5752
Processor of pasta
President: Victor Ghini
CFO: Robert Ghini
Estimated Sales: $120,000
Number Employees: 1-4
Type of Packaging: Food Service, Private Label, Bulk
Brands:
Papagallo

14071 Viano Winery
150 Morello Ave
Martinez, CA 94553 925-228-6465
Fax: 925-228-5670 info@vianovineyards.com
www.vianovineyards.com
Wines
Partner: Clement Viano
President: Paula Viano
Estimated Sales: Less than $400,000
Number Employees: 1-4
Brands:
Viano Winery

14072 Viansa Winery
25200 Arnold Dr
Sonoma, CA 95476 800-995-4740
Fax: 707-935-5654 800-995-4740
tuscan@viansa.com www.viansa.com
Wines
President: John Bryan
CEO: Vicki Sebastiani
CFO: Russ Jay
Co. Founder: Sam Sebastiani
Winemaker: Michael Sebastiani
Estimated Sales: $ 5-10 Million
Number Employees: 50-99
Brands:
Nebbiolo
Vernaccia

14073 Viau Foods
6625 Ernest Cormier
Laval, QC H7C 2V2
Canada 450-665-6100
Fax: 450-665-7100 800-663-5492
www.viausila.com
cooked or dry cured pepperoni, italian cooked meats, sausages, pizza toppings and meatballs.

14074 Vic Rossano Incorporated
2102 Rue Cabot
Montreal, QC H4E 1E4
Canada 514-766-5252
Fax: 514-765-3959
Manufacturer of peanut butter regular and natural almond and cashew butter, tahini, new product= soypeanut butter
President: Rosette Rossano
Estimated Sales: $1-2.5 Million
Number Employees: 15
Sq. footage: 45000
Type of Packaging: Consumer, Private Label, Bulk
Brands:
Simply Nuts
Yum Nature

14075 Vic's Gourmet Popping Corn Company
11213 E Cir
Omaha, NE 68137-1243 402-331-2822
Fax: 402-331-2507 www.barrelofunsnacks.com
Popcorn
President: Ken Nelson
Brands:
Vic's

14076 Vichy Springs Mineral Water Corporation
2605 Vichy Springs Rd
Ukiah, CA 95482-3507 707-462-9515
Fax: 707-462-9516 vichy@vichysprings.com
www.vichysprings.com
Processor and exporter of naturally carbonated bottled mineral water
President: Gilbert Ashoff
VP: Marjorie Ashoff
Estimated Sales: $500,000 appx.
Number Employees: 10-19
Number of Products: 1
Sq. footage: 7000
Type of Packaging: Private Label
Brands:
Vichy Springs
Vichy Springs Mineral Water

14077 Vickey's Vittles
16420 Gledhill St
North Hills, CA 91343-2807 818-841-1944
Fax: 818-841-1191 vickeysvittles@msn.com
www.vickeysvittles.com
Processor of specialty cookies, bundt cakes, brownies, dessert bars, pies and cobblers; also, gift baskets, fat-fee and low-fat items available
President: Vickey Conover
Estimated Sales: $300,000-500,000
Number Employees: 5-9
Brands:
Vickey's Vittles

14078 Victor Allen Coffee Company
1401 12th St NW
Albuquerque, NM 87104-2117 505-856-5282
Fax: 505-856-5588 800-662-2575
email@avaloncoffee.com
www.avaloncoffee.com
Coffee and tea
Manager: Aaron Simpson
Marketing Specialist: Kathryn Utterback
VP Sales: Liz Kollar
Operations Manager: Andy Wieczorek
Estimated Sales: Below $ 5 Million
Number Employees: 5-9
Type of Packaging: Private Label
Brands:
Avalon Organic Coffee
Bosque Tea Co
High Desert Roasters
Rio Grande Roasters

14079 Victor Allen's Coffee and Tea
1101 Moasis Dr
Little Chute, WI 54140 920-788-1252
800-394-5282
lwolters@victorallen.com www.victorallen.com
Coffee, tea
Owner: Scott Dercks
Estimated Sales: $ 20-50 Million
Number Employees: 5-9
Type of Packaging: Private Label

14080 Victor Ostrowski & Son
524 S Washington St
Baltimore, MD 21231-3030 410-327-8935
Fax: 410-252-9372 www.ostrowskisausage.com
Polish garlic bologna, liver sausage, stuffed cabbage and horseradishes
Owner/President: John Ostrowski
Estimated Sales: $ 1 - 3 Million
Number Employees: 5-9
Type of Packaging: Consumer

14081 Victor Packing Company
11687 Road 27 1/2
Madera, CA 93637-9440 559-673-5908
Fax: 559-673-4225 victor@victorpacking.com
www.victorpacking.com
Manufacturer, and exporter of currants and raisins including organic, natural, golden and seedless; also, raisin juice concentrate and raisin paste available
Owner: Victor Sahadtjain
VP: Margaret Sahatdjian
Estimated Sales: $20-50 Million
Number Employees: 50-99
Number of Products: 10
Sq. footage: 150000

Type of Packaging: Consumer, Food Service, Private Label, Bulk
Brands:
LIBERTY BELL
MADERA
NATURAL THOMPSON
VICTOR

14082 **Victor Preserving Company**
6318 Ontario Center Rd
Ontario, NY 14519 315-524-2711
Fax: 315-524-7040 onedavid@aol.com
Processor of sauerkraut
President/CEO: David Tobin
Estimated Sales: $ 3 - 5 Million
Number Employees: 10-19
Sq. footage: 45000
Type of Packaging: Private Label

14083 **Victoria Fancy Sausage**
6506 118th Avenue NW
Edmonton, AB T5W 1G6
Canada 780-471-2283
Fax: 780-477-5381
Processor of fresh beef, pork, chicken and wild game including venison, elk and moose
President: John Snyder
Estimated Sales: A
Number Employees: 1-4
Sq. footage: 3500
Type of Packaging: Bulk
Brands:
Victoria Fancy

14084 **Victoria Gourmet**
17 Gill St
Woburn, MA 01801 781-935-2100
Fax: 781-935-9979 866-972-6879
info@vgourmet.com www.vgourmet.com
Blended seasonings
President: Victoria Taylor
Estimated Sales: $500,000-$1 Million
Number Employees: 1-4

14085 **(HQ)Victoria Packing Corporation**
443 E 100th St
Brooklyn, NY 11236 718-927-3000
Fax: 718-649-7069
victoria@victoriapacking.com
www.victoriapacking.com
Manufacturer, importer and exporter of condiments, canned vegetables, edible oils, sauces, condiments, and dips
President/CEO: Benjamin Aquilina
VP Finance/CFO: Robert Haberman
VP Sales: William Paskowski
Estimated Sales: $31.3 Million
Number Employees: 100-249
Number of Brands: 5
Number of Products: 300
Sq. footage: 250000
Type of Packaging: Consumer, Food Service, Private Label, Bulk
Brands:
VICTORIA

14086 **Victoria's Catered Traditions**
1240 Eastridge Place
Manteca, CA 95336 209-823-9015
Fax: 208-823-8213 877-272-5208
www.victoriascateredtraditions.com
chocolate covered popcorn
Owner Principal: Victoria Costa

14087 **Victory Seafood**
208 W Elina St
Abbeville, LA 70510-8239 337-893-9029
Fax: 337-898-0614
Fresh and frozen crabmeat
Owner: Kevin E Dartez
Estimated Sales: $ 5 - 10 Million
Number Employees: 20-49

14088 **Vidalia Brands**
6054 Ga Highway 121
Reidsville, GA 30453 912-654-2726
Fax: 912-654-9135 800-752-0206
becky@vidaliabrands.com
www.vidaliabrandscom
Vidalia sweet onions, gourmet treats, peach salsa, blossom kit, salad dressings, relishes, BBQ sauce, chow-chow
President/CEO: Sandra Bland
Marketing Director: Wendy Moore
Vice President: Sandra Bland
Public Relations: Susan Lynch
Plant Manager: Mike Gulbranson
Number Employees: 50-99
Type of Packaging: Private Label
Brands:
Vidalia

14089 **(HQ)Vidalia Sweets Brand**
818 Ga Highway 56 W
Lyons, GA 30436 912-565-8881
Fax: 912-565-0199 vsbrelish@cybersouth.com
www.vidalialabs.com
Processor of fresh and pickled onions, onion relish, barbecue sauce, etc.; wholesaler/distributor of vidalia onions and specialty food products; serving the food service market
President: Jim P Cowart
Estimated Sales: $210000
Number Employees: 1-4
Type of Packaging: Consumer, Food Service
Brands:
Vidalia Sweets

14090 **Vie de France Bakery**
4507 Mills Pl SW # R
Atlanta, GA 30336-1826 404-696-5486
Fax: 404-699-1612 800-933-5486
www.viedefrance.com
Processor of bread and rolls
Manager: Ken Graham
Marketing Director: Laura Fezouati
Sales/Marketing Executive: Scott Kennedy
Estimated Sales: $ 10 - 20 Million
Number Employees: 50-99
Parent Co: Vie de France Yamazaki
Type of Packaging: Consumer, Food Service
Brands:
Vie De France

14091 **Vie de France Bakery**
1049 Industrial Dr
Bensenville, IL 60106-1216 630-595-9521
Fax: 630-595-3686 www.viedefrance.com
Processor of bread; wholesaler/distributor of cakes, cookies, muffins and danish
President: Sado Yasumura
Plant Manager: Tom O'Donnell
Estimated Sales: $ 3 - 5 Million
Number Employees: 50-99
Parent Co: Vie de France Yamazaki

14092 **Vie de France Bakery**
2070 Chain Bridge Rd # 500
Vienna, VA 22182-2588 703-442-9205
Fax: 703-821-2695 800-446-4404
www.viedefrance.com
Bakery products
President: Sadao Yasumura
CEO: Nobuhiro Iijima
VP Finance: Tom Rowe
Estimated Sales: $ 5-9.9 Million
Number Employees: 100

14093 **Vie de France Yamazaki**
2070 Chain Bridge Rd # 500
Vienna, VA 22182-2588 703-442-9205
Fax: 703-821-2695 800-446-4404
www.viedefrance.com
Processor of baked goods including croissants, pastries and danish
President: Sadao Yasumura
Estimated Sales: $ 3 - 5 Million
Number Employees: 1,000-4,999
Parent Co: Vie de France Yamazaki
Type of Packaging: Bulk

14094 **Vie de France Yamazaki**
2070 Chain Bridge Rd # 500
Vienna, VA 22182-2588 703-442-9205
Fax: 703-821-2695 800-393-8926
www.vdfy.com
Processor of breads, rolls and pastries
President/CEO: Sadao Yasumura
Estimated Sales: $90 Million
Number Employees: 1,000-4,999
Sq. footage: 27000
Parent Co: Vie de France Yamazaki
Type of Packaging: Consumer, Food Service, Private Label, Bulk

14095 **Vie de France Yamazaki**
3046 E 50th Street
Vernon, LA 71270 323-582-1241
Fax: 323-585-7532
Processor of frozen dough and French bakery products
General Manager: Driss Goulhiane
Distribution Manager: Doug Cassenelli
Production Manager: Jerry Gorne
Estimated Sales: $4700000
Number Employees: 70
Sq. footage: 50000
Parent Co: Vie de France Yamazaki
Type of Packaging: Food Service

14096 **Vie de France Yamazaki**
5060 Nome St
Denver, CO 80239-2726 303-371-6280
Fax: 303-371-5646 www.viedefrance.com
Processor of French breads, croissants, European cakes and pastries
General Manager: Mike Digan
Estimated Sales: $ 1 - 3 Million
Number Employees: 20-49
Sq. footage: 13000
Parent Co: Vie de France Yamazaki
Type of Packaging: Consumer, Food Service
Brands:
Vie De France

14097 **Vie-Del Company**
11903 S Chestnut Ave
Fresno, CA 93725 559-834-2525
Fax: 559-834-1348 /www.vinarium-medien.com
Processor and exporter of fruit concentrates including grape; also, wine and brandy
President: Dianne Nury
Vice President: Richard Watson
Customer Service: Janel Cook
Purchasing Manager: Robert Reiter
Estimated Sales: $18800000
Number Employees: 100-249

14098 **Vienna Bakery**
10207 63 Ave NW
Edmonton, AB T6H 5T3
Canada 780-489-4142
Fax: 780-439-2140
Processor of gourmet bread and pastries
President: Bernie Jager
CEO: Bernie Jager
Marketing Manager: Bernie Jager
Number Employees: 10-19
Type of Packaging: Consumer, Food Service
Brands:
Vienna

14099 **Vienna Beef**
2501 N Damen Ave
Chicago, IL 60647 773-278-7800
Fax: 773-278-4759 info@kingkold.com
www.viennabeef.com
Meats
CEO: Dennis Vignieri
VP: Jane Lustig
CEO: James W Bodman
Estimated Sales: $100+ Million
Number Employees: 500-999
Brands:
Bistro
Chipico
King Kold
Pie Piper
WonderBar

14100 **(HQ)Vienna Beef**
2501 N Damen Ave
Chicago, IL 60647 773-278-7800
Fax: 773-278-4759 800-621-8183
foodservice@viennabeef.com
www.viennabeef.com
Manufacturers and distributors of beef
Chairman: James Bodman
VP Finance: Richard Steele
Estimated Sales: $ 75-100 Million
Number Employees: 500-999
Type of Packaging: Private Label
Brands:
Bistro
Chipico
King Kold

Pie Piper
Vienna
Wunderbar

14101 **Vienna Meat Products**
170 Nugget Avenue
Scarborough, ON M1S 3A7
Canada 416-297-1062
Fax: 416-297-0836 800-588-1931
Processor and importer of ham, sausage, cold cuts, turkey products, roast beef, corned beef and pastrami.
President: Michael Latifi
Director Retail Sales: Vince Romano
Estimated Sales: $9.5 Million
Number Employees: 100
Brands:
Austrian Crown
Grand Chef De Paris
Vienna

14102 **(HQ)Vienna Sausage Company**
2501 N Damen Ave
Chicago, IL 60647-2199 800-366-3647
Fax: 773-278-7800 www.viennabeef.com
Processor of pickles; processor and exporter of cured meat, soups, kosher specialties and desserts.
Co-CEO and Co-Chairman: James Bodman
Co-CEO and Co-Chairman: James Eisenberg
CFO: Richard Steele
SVP/Sales & Marketing: Thomas McGlade
VP/Human Resources: Jane Lustig
SVP/Operations: Jack Bodman
VP/Purchasing: Richard Ewert
Estimated Sales: $99,000,000
Number Employees: 250-499
Type of Packaging: Consumer, Food Service, Private Label
Brands:
BISTRO
CHIPICO
KING KOLD
PIE PIPER
VIENNA
WUNDERBAR

14103 **(HQ)Vienna Sausage Company**
6033 Malburg Way
Los Angeles, CA 90058-3969 323-583-8951
Fax: 323-585-7580 800-733-6063
www.viennabeef.com
Processor of pickles; processor and exporter of cured meat, soups, kosher specialties and desserts.
Co-CEO and Co-Chairman: James Bodman
Co-CEO and Co-Chairman: James Eisenberg
CFO: Richard Steele
SVP/Sales & Marketing: Thomas McGlade
VP/Human Resources: Jane Lustig
SVP/Operations: Jack Bodman
VP/Purchasing: Richard Ewert
Number Employees: 100-249
Type of Packaging: Consumer, Food Service, Private Label

14104 **Vietti Foods Company Inc**
P.O.Box 40464
Nashville, TN 37204 615-244-7864
Fax: 615-242-7055 800-240-7864
info@viettichilli.com www.viettifoodsinc.com
Processor and canner of pork and beef with barbecue sauce, chili spaghetti, regular chili and beef stew; also, sauces including hot dog, spaghetti and Creole.
President: Philip Connelly
Chief Financial Officer: Mark Johnson
Director of Technical Services: Dee Folmar
National Sales Manager: Voyne Stepp
Director Operations: Frank Baltz
Purchasing Manager: Trent Baker
Estimated Sales: $ 20 - 50 Million
Number Employees: 20-49
Type of Packaging: Consumer, Food Service, Private Label
Brands:
SOUTHGATE
VIETTI

14105 **Vigneri Confections**
810 Emerson St
Rochester, NY 14613 585-254-6160
Fax: 585-254-6872 877-843-6374
info@vigneri.com www.vigneri.com
Processor and importer of European desserts and pastries including panettones, tortes, bignolara, tartufo, cassata, tiramisu, etc; also, chocolate Easter eggs
President: Filippo Vigneri
CEO: Alexander Vigneri
Estimated Sales: $300,000
Number Employees: 4
Sq. footage: 2645
Type of Packaging: Consumer, Private Label
Brands:
Vigneri

14106 **Vigo Importing Company**
P.O.Box 15584
Tampa, FL 33684 813-884-3491
Fax: 813-884-7139 info@vigo-alessi.com
www.vigo-alessi.com
Processor and exporter of seasoned rice dinners, paella and bread crumbs; importer of olives, peppers, sundried tomatoes, olive oil, cheese, pasta, balsamic vinegar, bread sticks, pine nuts, coffee, vegetable pates, porcini mushroomsartichokes, etc
President: Anthony Alessi Sr
CEO: Sam Ciccarello
Estimated Sales: $ 50 - 100 Million
Number Employees: 100-249
Sq. footage: 280000
Type of Packaging: Consumer, Food Service, Private Label, Bulk

14107 **Vigor Cup Corp**
630 Shore Road
Apt 704
Long Beach, NY 11561-4669 516-785-6352
Fax: 516-997-4471
Dehydrated soups and seasonings
President: William Kantor
Estimated Sales: $800,000
Number Employees: 6
Brands:
Vigor Cup

14108 **Viking Distillery**
1101 E Broad Ave
Albany, GA 31705-2872 229-436-0181
Fax: 229-434-1768 www.bartonbrands.com
Manufacturer of bourbon blends, gin and vodka
President: Alexander Burk III
Plant Manager: Julius Drakes
Estimated Sales: $6 Million
Number Employees: 10-19
Parent Co: Barton Brands
Type of Packaging: Consumer

14109 **Viking Seafoods Inc**
50 Crystal St
Malden, MA 02148-5919 781-322-2000
Fax: 781-397-0527 800-225-3020
jcovelluzzi@vikingseafoods.com
www.vikingseafoods.com
Processor of frozen seafood including fish cakes, fish and chips, cod, fish flake, halibut, perch, fish sticks, fish patties, scallops and shrimp; also, value-added products including Nordica and bake n'broil style.
President: Charles Gulino
CEO: James Covelluzzi
CEO: James Covelluzzi
Sales Manager: Douglas Farrell
Plant Manager: Joseph Novello
Estimated Sales: $8200000
Number Employees: 50-99
Type of Packaging: Consumer, Food Service
Brands:
Kitchens of the Sea
Viking

14110 **Viking Trading**
2375 John Glenn Dr Ste 106
Atlanta, GA 30341 770-455-8630
Fax: 770-455-9632
Blue crab, caviar, conch, crab, crawfish, kingfish, lobster meat
President: Juan Vales

14111 **Villa Helena/Arger-Martucci Winery**
1455 Inglewood Ave
St Helena, CA 94574-2219 707-963-4334
Fax: 707-963-4748 www.arger-martucci.com
Wines
President: Carol Martucci
Marketing Director: Katarena Arger
Estimated Sales: $500,000-$1 Million
Number Employees: 1-4
Type of Packaging: Private Label
Brands:
Villa Helena

14112 **Villa Milan Vineyard**
7287 E County Road 50 N
Milan, IN 47031-8946 812-654-3419
vineyard@seidata.com
www.seidata.com/villa-milan
Wines
President: John Garrett
CEO: Marc A McNeece
Estimated Sales: $ 2.5-5 Million
Number Employees: 10-19
Brands:
Villa Milan

14113 **Villa Mt. Eden Winery**
8711 Silverado Trl S
Saint Helena, CA 94574 707-944-2414
Fax: 707-963-7840
jessica.cope@ste-michelle.com
www.villamteden.com
Processor and exporter of wines
Manager: Jeff Mc Bride
Estimated Sales: $ 10 - 20 Million
Number Employees: 10-19
Parent Co: Stimson Lane
Type of Packaging: Consumer

14114 **Villa Parks Orchards Cooperative**
P.O.Box 307
Fillmore, CA 93016-0307 805-524-0411
Fax: 805-524-4286 888-524-4402
frank@vpoa.net OR villapark@vpoa.net
www.vpoa.net
Packinghouse for the processing of Sunkist Growers Inc. citrus fruit.
President/General Manager: Brad Leichtfuss
Field Mgr/Grower Relations Orange Cty: Mike Leichtfuss
Field Superintendent District 1: Hector Moreno
Field Mgr/Grower Relations District 1: Jim Cleland
Field Mgr/Grower Relations Ventura: Bruce Leichtfuss
Sales & Packing Coordinator: Frank Martinez
Grower Relations/Consultant: Don Clift
Type of Packaging: Food Service

14115 **Village Imports**
211 S Hill Dr
Brisbane, CA 94005-1255 415-562-1120
Fax: 415-562-1131 888-865-8714
info@villageimports.net www.eiltd.com
French specialty foods and wine, vinegars, condiments, vinagrettes, and sparkling lemonade
Owner: Larry Binstein
Marketing: Thierry Foucaut
Estimated Sales: $ 20 - 50 Million
Number Employees: 20-49
Parent Co: MIF San Francisco
Type of Packaging: Consumer
Brands:
LE VILLAGE

14116 **Village Roaster**
9255 W Alameda Avenue
Lakewood, CO 80226-2802 303-238-8718
Fax: 303-233-4370 800-237-3822
contact@villageroaster.com
www.villageroaster.com
Coffee
President: Jim Curtis
VP: Kathleen Curtis
CFO: Kathleen Curtis
Estimated Sales: Under $500,000
Brands:
Village Roaster

14117 **Villar Vintners of Valdese**
4940 Villar Ln NE
Valdese, NC 28690 828-879-3202
Fax: 828-879-3202
Wines
President: Joel Talmas
CEO: Ernest Jahier
Estimated Sales: $ 3 - 5 Million
Number Employees: 5-9
Brands:
Villar Vintners

14118 **Vilore Foods Company**
8220 San Lorenzo Dr
Laredo, TX 78045 956-726-3633
Fax: 956-728-8383 info@vilore.com
www.vilore.com
Wholesaler/distributor of Mexican foods including jalapeno peppers, fruit nectars, hot sauce, chicken bouillon, powdered drinks and nopalitos; exporter of canned Mexican foods and fruit nectars; importer of Mexican salsas, fruitnectars and jalapeno peppers
President: Marco Mena
Controller: Raul Escobedo
Marketing Manager: Edna Fuster
Sales Manager: Glen Leonardo
Operations Director: Jose Luis Murillo
Plant Manager: Luis Garza
Estimated Sales: $219 Million
Number Employees: 103
Sq. footage: 470000
Type of Packaging: Consumer, Food Service, Private Label
Brands:
BENEDIK
CAFE-LEGAL
CAFE-ORO
CAL-C-TOSE
CHOCO MILK
CLEMENTE JACQUES
CON-GELLI
JUMEX
LA COSTENA
LA SIERRA
MI COCINA
YA'STA

14119 **Vilotti & Marinelli Baking Company**
755 S 11th Street
Philadelphia, PA 19147-2698 215-627-5038
Bread and rolls
President: Daniel Pisanelli
Estimated Sales: Below $ 5 Million
Number Employees: 30

14120 **Vina Vista Vineyard & Winery**
5601 Highway 128
Philo, CA 95466 707-895-3015
Fax: 707-895-9501 1 8-0 5-7 94
office@navarrowine.com www.navarrowine.com
Wines
Owner: Deborah Cahn
Estimated Sales: $7 Million
Number Employees: 75
Type of Packaging: Private Label, Bulk

14121 **Vinalhaven Fishermens Co-Op**
P.O.Box 366
Camden, ME 04843-0366 207-236-0092
Fax: 207-236-7733 fewx2@foxislands.net
Seafood
Owner: John R Long
Estimated Sales: $ 1 - 3 Million
Number Employees: 5-9

14122 **Vince's Seafoods**
1105 Lafayette St
Gretna, LA 70053-6345 504-368-1544
Fax: 504-368-1545 bjimenez1@cox.net
Processor and exporter of frozen and boiled seafood; shrimp, crabs, oysters, crawfish, catfish, tuna, trout, flounder and tilapia. Also available; gumbo and soups
President: Barbara Jimenez
Estimated Sales: $500,000-$1 Million
Number Employees: 1-4
Sq. footage: 8000

14123 **Vincent Arroyo Winery**
2361 Greenwood Ave
Calistoga, CA 94515-1031 707-942-6995
Fax: 707-942-0895
wine@vincentarroyowinery.com
www.vincentarroyo.com
Wines
President: Vincent Arroyo
Estimated Sales: Less than $1 Million
Number Employees: 7
Type of Packaging: Bulk

14124 **Vincent B. Zaninovich &Son**
PO Box 1000
Richgrove, CA 93261 661-725-2497
Fax: 661-725-5153 www.vbzgrapes.com
Processor and exporter of grapes
Owner: Antone Zaninovich
Owner/President: Vincent Zaninovich
VP: Andrew Zaninovich
Human Resources Director: Mark Boyer
Estimated Sales: $11 Million
Number Employees: 200
Sq. footage: 15450
Type of Packaging: Bulk
Brands:
Mr Z
Richgrove King
VBZ

14125 **Vincent Formusa Company**
710 W Grand Ave
Chicago, IL 60654 312-421-0485
Fax: 312-421-1286 sales@marconi-foods.com
www.marconi-foods.com
Beans, salad dressings, giardiniera & peppers, olives, olive oils, pasta, italian style salads, spices, tomatoes, vinegars
President: Robert Johnson
Estimated Sales: $830,000
Number Employees: 10
Sq. footage: 25000
Type of Packaging: Consumer, Food Service, Bulk
Brands:
Digiovanni
Marconi

14126 **Vincent Giordano Corporation**
2600 Washington Ave
Philadelphia, PA 19146 215-467-6629
Fax: 215-467-6339 www.vgiordano.com
Italian ices, frozen fruit and juice novelties
President: Guy Giordano
Vice President: Bruce Belack
Sales Director: Mike Bosse
Plant Engineer: Jerry Little
Estimated Sales: $ 50-75 Million
Number Employees: 50-99

14127 **Vincent Piazza Jr & Sons**
5736 Heebe St
Harahan, LA 70123 504-734-0012
Fax: 504-734-8752 800-259-5016
packages@piazzaseafood.com
www.piazzaseafood.com
Processor of shrimp; wholesaler/distributor of crab, crawfish, alligator, conch, octopus, clams, lobster, frog legs, scallops, turtle, gumbo, etc
Owner: Vincent Piazza Jr
Sales and Inventory Control: Nicholas Piazza
Computer Systems and Purchasing: Bryan Piazza
Estimated Sales: $ 2.5-5 Million
Number Employees: 20-49
Sq. footage: 24000
Type of Packaging: Food Service
Brands:
Lucky Star
Papa Piazza Brand
Papa's Fresh Catch
Tri Dragon

14128 **Vincent's Food Corporation**
179 Old Country Rd
Carle Place, NY 11514 516-481-3544
Fax: 516-742-4579
Manufacturer of sauces
President: Anthony Marisi
Estimated Sales: $ 5 - 10 Million
Number Employees: 5-9

14129 **Vincor International**
441 Courtneypark Drive E
Mississauga, ON L5T 2V3
Canada 905-564-6900
Fax: 905-564-6909 800-265-9463
www.vincorinternational.com
Wine and vodka cooler importer, marketer and distributor.
President/CEO: Eric Morham
SVP Operations: Martin Van Der Merwe
CFO: Don Dychuck
Estimated Sales: $50-100 Million
Number Employees: 2800
Type of Packaging: Consumer, Food Service
Brands:
Camarad
Goundry Fine Wine
Hogue
Inniskillin
Jackson-Triggs
Kim Crawford Wines
Kumala
Loiseau Bleu
Pallenque
Toasted Head

14130 **Vine Village**
4059 Old Sonoma Rd
Napa, CA 94559-9702 707-255-4099
Fax: 707-255-8431 mikeker@napanet.net
www.vinevillage.org
Wine
Executive Director: Michael Kerson
Estimated Sales: Below $ 5 Million
Number Employees: 20-49
Type of Packaging: Private Label
Brands:
Carneros Chardonnay

14131 **Vineland Ice & Storage**
544 E Pear St
Vineland, NJ 8360 856-692-3990
Fax: 856-692-3992
Warehouse providing frozen storage; manufacturer of ice
Owner: Mark Di Meo
Estimated Sales: $ 1 - 3 Million
Number Employees: 5-9
Type of Packaging: Food Service, Bulk

14132 **Vino's**
923 W 7th St
Little Rock, AR 72201-4005 501-375-8466
Fax: 501-375-8468 vinos@vinosbrewpub.com
www.vinosbrewpub.com
Beer and pizza
President: Henry Lee
CEO: Dan O'Byrne
Estimated Sales: Below $ 5 Million
Number Employees: 20-49
Type of Packaging: Private Label
Brands:
7th Street Pale
Big House Ale
Lazy Boy Stout

14133 **Vinoklet Winery & Vineyard**
11069 Colerain Ave
Cincinnati, OH 45252-1425 513-385-9309
Fax: 513-385-9379 vinokletwinery@fuse.net
www.vinokletwines.com
Wine manufacturer and restaurant service
Owner/Winemaker: Kreso Mikulic
Estimated Sales: $500,000 appx.
Number Employees: 10-19
Type of Packaging: Food Service
Brands:
Vinoklet

14134 **(HQ)Vinquiry**
7795 Bell Rd
Windsor, CA 95492 707-838-6312
Fax: 707-838-1765 info@vinquiry.com
www.vinquiry.com
Manufacturer of wine industry yeasts and supplements
Owner/CEO: Marty Bannister
President: John Schilter
Estimated Sales: $ 5 - 10 Million
Number Employees: 20-49
Sq. footage: 10400
Type of Packaging: Private Label, Bulk
Other Locations:
Vinquiry Central Coast Office
Santa Maria CA
Vinquiry Napa Office
Napa CA

14135 **Vintage Chocolate Imports**
461 Frelinghuysen Ave
Newark, NJ 07114-1426 908-354-9304
Fax: 908-354-9265 800-207-7058
information@echocolates.com
www.echocolates.com
Chocolate
President: Pierrick Chouard
Operations Manager: Bryan Sargent
Estimated Sales: Below $ 5 Million
Number Employees: 5-9
Type of Packaging: Private Label
Brands:
Dagoba Organic Chocolate
Fritz Knipschildt

14136 Vintage Produce Sales
PO Box 977
Kingsburg, CA 93631-0977 559-897-1622
Fax: 559-897-8793
Peaches, nectarines, blueberries, apricots, plums and grapes
Brands:
RIVER ISLAND
RIVER VALLEY FARMS

14137 Viobin USA
226 W Livingston St
Monticello, IL 61856-1673 217-762-2561
Fax: 217-762-2489 info@rex-oil.com
www.viobinusa.com
Processor and exporter of defatted wheat germ and wheat germ oil
Manager: Roger Moore
Quality Control: Carol Wintersteen
Marketing/Sales: Geni Heider
Production: Jerry Sample
Plant Manager: Roger Mohr
Estimated Sales: $ 10 - 20 Million
Number Employees: 20-49
Sq. footage: 100000
Parent Co: McShares
Type of Packaging: Private Label, Bulk
Other Locations:
VioBin Corp.
Salinas KS
Brands:
Rex Oil
Viobin

14138 Viola's Gourmet Goodies
P.O.Box 351075
Los Angeles, CA 90035 323-731-5277
Fax: 323-731-6898 violasgg@pacbell.net
www.violasgourmet.com
Gourmet relish, jelly, zinger and rim shot
Owner: Nancy Rowland
Estimated Sales: $ .5 - 1 million
Number Employees: 1-4
Type of Packaging: Bulk
Brands:
Viola's

14139 Violet Packing
123 Railroad Ave
Williamstown, NJ 8094 856-629-7428
Fax: 856-629-6340 info@donpepino.com
www.donpepino.com
Manufacturer of peppers, tomatoes and sauces including spaghetti and pizza
President/Owner: Rob Ragusa
VP Operations: Chip Sclafani
GM: Lou Sclafani
Estimated Sales: $10-20 Million
Number Employees: 50-99
Parent Co: Don Pepino Company
Type of Packaging: Consumer, Food Service
Brands:
Don Pepino
Sclafani
Violet

14140 Violore Foods Company
8220 San Lorenzo Dr
Laredo, TX 78045-8704 956-726-3633
Fax: 956-727-1499 info@vilore.com
www.vilore.com
Jalapeno peppers
President: Marco Mena
Estimated Sales: $200 Million
Number Employees: 103

14141 Virgil's Root Beer
13000 S Spring Street
Los Angeles, CA 90061-1634
US 310-217-9400
Fax: 310-217-9411 800-997-3337
information@virgils.com www.virgils.com
Processor of root beer currantly has sxi new flavors. Original,premium,extra,cherry,raspberry,spiced apple.They also make ginger candy and ginger ice cream.
Owner/PRES/CEO: Chris Reed
CFO: James Linesch
SVP Sales And Marketing: Neal Cohane
Estimated Sales: $20.38 Million
Number Employees: 20
Sq. footage: 30000
Parent Co: Reed's Ginger Brew
Type of Packaging: Consumer, Food Service
Brands:
Virgil's

14142 Virginia & Spanish Peanut Company
260 Dexter St
Providence, RI 2907 401-421-2543
Fax: 401-421-2557 800-673-3562
vspnutco@aol.com www.vspnutco.com
Processor of salted nuts, peanuts and peanut butter
President/CFO: Robert Kalocstian
VP/Treasurer: Candale Kaloostain
Estimated Sales: $ 10 - 20 Million
Number Employees: 5-9
Sq. footage: 16000
Type of Packaging: Consumer, Food Service, Private Label, Bulk
Brands:
Anchor
Brown Bear

14143 Virginia Chutney Company
195 Piedmont Avenue
PO Box 511
Washington, VA 22747 540-675-1984
Fax: 540-675-1985 sales@virginiachutney.com
www.virginiachutney.com
chutneys

14144 Virginia Dare
882 3rd Ave Ste 2
Brooklyn, NY 11232 718-788-1776
Fax: 718-768-3978 800-847-4500
flavorinfo@virginiadare.com
www.virginiadare.com
Liquid and dry flavors; vanilla, tea, coffee and cocoa extracts and concentrates; Prosweet flavor inprovers and masking agents and flavor emulsions
President: Howard Smith
Vice President: Stephen Balter
VP Marketing: Paul Graffigna
VP Sales: Sid Heller
Estimated Sales: $28 Million
Number Employees: 175
Type of Packaging: Bulk
Brands:
Contrasweet
G-Brew
Gourmet Brew
Prosweet
Superfex
Superfreeze
Tre Cafe
Vidarome

14145 Virginia Diner
322 W Main St
Wakefield, VA 23888 757-899-6213
Fax: 757-899-2281 888-823-4637
custservice@vadiner.com www.vadiner.com
peanuts (gourmet, seasoned, in-the-shell and raw), cashews, almonds, etc., peanut brittle, nutty candies and snacks
President/Owner: Christine Epperson

14146 Virginia Honey Company
P.O.Box 1915
Inwood, WV 25428 304-267-8500
Fax: 304-263-0946 info@virgianiabrand.com
www.virginiabrand.com
Honey, salad dressings, including Vidalia Onion Vinagarette salad dressing, sauces, jams and jellies, herring products, salmon products, condiments, horseradish, cream cheese, party platers
CEO: Terry Hess
Parent Co: Vita Food Products
Type of Packaging: Consumer, Food Service, Private Label, Bulk
Brands:
VIRGINIA BRAND
VITA BRAND

14147 Virginia Trout Company
5480 Potomac River Rd
Monterey, VA 24465 540-468-2280
Fax: 540-468-2279
Manufacturer of fresh and frozen mountain trout
President: David Johnston
Estimated Sales: $3 Million
Number Employees: 6
Type of Packaging: Food Service
Brands:
ALLEGHENY
MOUNTAIN TROUT

14148 Visalia Produce Sales Inc
201 W Stroud Ave
Kingsburg, CA 93631 559-897-6652
Fax: 559-897-6650 george@visaliaproduce.com
www.visaliaproduce.com
California fruits and vegetables
Owner: Stan Shamoon
Sales Representative: Stan Shamoon
Sales Representative: Aron Gularte
Sales Representative: George Matoian
Estimated Sales: $ 1 - 10 Million
Number Employees: 100-249

14149 Vision Pack Brands
531 Main Street #513
El Segundo, CA 90245 877-477-8500
Fax: 866-825-1808 877-477-8500
visionpack@verizon.net
www.visionpackbrands.com
products for gift baskets (gourmet crackers, snacks and dip, candy, confections and beverages

14150 Vision Seafood Partners
41 Summer Street
Kingston, MA 02364-1418 781-585-2000
Fax: 773-561-0139
Seafood

14151 (HQ)Vista Bakery
3000 Mount Pleasant St
Burlington, IA 52601 319-754-6551
Fax: 319-752-0063 800-553-2343
sales@vistabakery.com www.vistabakery.com
Manufacturer and exporter of sandwich cookies and crackers
VP: Tyler Cooke
VP Sales: Tyler Cook
Manufacturing Director: Jim Hartschuh
Plant Manager: Jeff Schuster
Estimated Sales: $200 Million
Number Employees: 500-999
Parent Co: Lance
Type of Packaging: Consumer, Food Service, Private Label, Bulk
Brands:
VISTA
VISTA CHOICE

14152 Vita Coco
38 W 21st St Fl 11
#404
New York, NY 10010-6922
Fax: 800-407-0439 877-848-2262
info@vitacoco.com www.vitacoco.com/
Vita Coco is a nutritional drink containing only 100% natural coconut water from Brazil.
Co-Founder: Michael Kirban
Co-Founder: Ira Liran
Type of Packaging: Food Service

14153 Vita Food Products
2222 W Lake St
Chicago, IL 60612 312-738-4500
Fax: 312-738-3215 www.vitafoodproducts.com
Pickled herring, lox & nova salmon, cream cheese with salmon, horseradish, cocktail and tarter sauces; gourmet sauces, marinades, salad dressings, dessert toppers, syrups & honey, salsa, drinks
President/CEO: Clifford Bolen
CFO: R Anthony Nelson
VP Marketing: William Zaikos
VP Sales: Charles Curtis
Human Resource Manager: Mary Smith
Production Manager: Robert Godwa
Plant Manager: Paul Chapman
Purchasing: Doug Clark
Estimated Sales: H
Number Employees: 178
Sq. footage: 82200
Type of Packaging: Consumer, Food Service
Brands:
7UP
A&W BBQ
BILTMORE
BUDWEISER GENUINE SAUCES
CRUSH
DR PEPPER
ELF
JELLY BELLY
JIM BEAM
MEL'S DRIVE IN
OAK HILL FARMS
SAUZA TEQUILA
SCORNED WOMAN

STUCKEY'S
VIRGINIA BRAND
VITA

14154 Vita Specialty Foods
717 Corning Way
Martinsburg, WV 25401 304-267-8500
Fax: 304-263-0946 800-989-8482
www.vitafoodproducts.com
seafood, barbecue ribs and spices, barbecue sauces, condiments, dressings, dessert toppings, honey and syrups, hot sauces, jim beam steak sauce, jim beam marinades, marinades, salsas, scorned woman hot sauce, snacks, tea concentratesvisalia onion vinaigrette, wing sauces

14155 Vita Specialty Foods
P.O.Box 1915
Inwood, WV 25428-1915 304-267-8500
Fax: 304-263-0946 800-974-4778
www.vitaspecialtyfoods.com
Manufacturer of condiments, including salad dressings, sauces, marinades, mustards, honey and teas
Manager: Chuck Martin
CEO: Terry Hess
Director Marketing: Douglas Horn
Sales: Valerie McCaffrey
Number Employees: 100-249
Number of Brands: 9
Number of Products: 200
Type of Packaging: Consumer, Food Service
Brands:
Artie Bucco
Artie Bucco Gourmet Foods
Courvoisier
Drambuie
Jim Beam Gourmet Foods
Kahlua
Oak Hill Farms
Scorned Woman
Virginia Brand

14156 Vita-Pakt Citrus Company
707 North Barranca Ave
Covina, CA 91723 626-332-1101
Fax: 626-966-8196 sales@vita-packcitrus.com
www.vita-pakt.com
Processor and exporter of sweetened and unsweetened citrus peels, pulps and bases including orange, lemon, grapefruit and tangerine
General Manager: Paul Gottschall
Office Manager: James Benner
Sales Manager: Doug Peterson
Number Employees: 80
Sq. footage: 36000
Type of Packaging: Consumer, Food Service, Bulk

14157 Vita-Pakt Citrus Company
P.O.Box 309
Covina, CA 91723-0309 626-332-1101
Fax: 626-966-8196 www.vita-pakt.com
Producer of fruit juices, concentrates, purees, specialty citrus peel products and dehydrated fuits and vegetables.
President: James Boyle
VP: Abe Rodriguez
Quality Control: Armon J Abhajian
Estimated Sales: $32900000
Number Employees: 20-49
Other Locations:
Vita-Pakt Citrus Products Co.
Lindsay CA
Brands:
Bireleys
Cold Gold
Vita Pak

14158 Vita-Plus
953 E Sahara Ave Ste 21b
Las Vegas, NV 89104 702-733-8805
Fax: 702-369-8597 info@lifelinevitaplus.com
www.lifelinevitaplus.com
Dairy
Owner: Roop Rache
Co-Owner: Eddie Molina
Estimated Sales: $ 5-10 Million
Number Employees: 10-19
Brands:
Cortilite
Life Line Vita Plus
Vita-Plus

14159 Vita-Pure
410 W 1st Ave
Roselle, NJ 7203 908-245-1212
Fax: 908-245-1999 JCampis@prodigy.net
Food/dietary supplements, vitamins, nutritional supplements
President: Achyut Sahasra
Vice President: Jaqueline Schauffler
Marketing Director: Joseph Campis
Operations Manager: Sheldon Tannebaum
Production Manager: Angelo Padilla
Estimated Sales: $ 5-10 Million
Number Employees: 20-49
Sq. footage: 17500
Type of Packaging: Private Label

14160 VitaTech International
2802 Dow Ave
Tustin, CA 92780-7212 714-832-9700
Fax: 714-731-8482 vitatech@vitatech.com
www.vitatech.com
Manufacturer of nutritional supplements including vitamins, enzymes, herbs, botanicals, glandulars and minerals
President: Thomas Tierney
VP Sales: Greg Williford
Estimated Sales: $23200000
Number Employees: 250-499
Sq. footage: 140000
Type of Packaging: Private Label

14161 Vitale Poultry Company
800 E Cooke Rd
Columbus, OH 43214 614-267-1874
Fax: 614-267-7824
Poultry processing
Co-Owner: Mark Cecutti
Co-Owner: Dan Cecutti
President: Rose Vitale
Estimated Sales: $ 5-9.9 Million
Number Employees: 10-19

14162 Vitalicious
11 Broadway Ste 1155
New York, NY 10004 212-233-6030
Fax: 212-233-6031 877-848-2877
customerservice@vitalicious.com
www.vitalicious.com
100 calorie VitaTops, VitaMuffins, VitaBrownies, VitaMixes, VitaCakes

14163 Vitality Life Choice
PO Box 21133
Carson City, NV 89721-1133 775-882-7186
Fax: 775-882-6686 800-423-8365
wwww.vitality-corp.com
Candy

14164 Vitamer Laboratories
17802 Gillette Ave
Irvine, CA 92614-6582 949-863-0340
Fax: 949-859-3523 800-432-8355
customerservice@vitamer.com
www.vitamer.com
Processor of dietary supplements and herbal products
President: Steve Brown
VP: Jane Drinkwalter
Marketing: Gene Nacagawa
Sales: Bob Norman
Estimated Sales: $ 20 - 50 Million
Number Employees: 100-249
Parent Co: Anabolic
Type of Packaging: Private Label

14165 Vitamilk Dairy
4141 Agate Road
Bellingham, WA 98226-8745 206-529-4128
Fax: 206-524-7070 www.vitamilk.com
Processor of dairy products including milk, sour cream and ice cream
President: E Gerald Teel
VP Sales: Larry Burns
Plant Manager: Paul Nelson
Number Employees: 100-249
Type of Packaging: Consumer, Food Service, Private Label, Bulk

14166 (HQ)Vitamin Power
39 Saint Marys Pl
Freeport, NY 11520 516-378-0900
Fax: 516-378-0919 800-645-6567
info@vitaminpower.com
www.vitaminpower.com
Produces nutritional supplements, distributed exclusively through independent dealers, individual retailers and professional healthcare offices.
President: David Henry Friedlander
Estimated Sales: $2 Million
Number Employees: 10-19
Sq. footage: 20000
Type of Packaging: Consumer
Brands:
Vitamin Power

14167 (HQ)Vitaminerals
1815 Flower St
Glendale, CA 91201-2024 818-500-8718
Fax: 818-240-2785
Processor and exporter of food supplements and vitamins
Owner: Michael Gorman
President: John Gorman III
VP: Mike Gorman
Estimated Sales: $ 5 - 10 Million
Number Employees: 20-49
Sq. footage: 35000
Brands:
Hampshire Laboratories
Vitaminerals

14168 Vitamins
200 E Randolph Drive
Chicago, IL 60601-6436 312-861-0700
Fax: 312-861-0708
customerservice@vitamins-inc.com
www.vitamins-inc.com
Processor of nutritional ingredients including defatted wheat germ, wheat germ oil and soluble vitamins
President: James Carozza
Vice President: Robert Lenburg
Number Employees: 1-4

14169 Vitarich Ice Cream
572 Highway 1
Fortuna, CA 95540-9711 707-725-6182
Fax: 707-725-6186 info@humboldtcreamery.com
www.humboldtcreamery.com
Manufacturer of ice cream, sherbet, frozen yogurt and ice cream mixes and novelties
President: Rich Ghilarducci
Number Employees: 20-49
Type of Packaging: Consumer, Food Service, Private Label, Bulk
Other Locations:
Vitarich Ice Cream Co.
Seattle WA
Brands:
VITARICH

14170 (HQ)Vitarich Laboratories
4365 Arnold Ave
Naples, FL 34104 239-430-2266
Fax: 239-430-4930 800-817-9999
v.decock@planetinternet.be
www.vitarichlabs.com
Processor, importer and exporter of vitamins, nutraceuticals and food supplements including herbal, whole leaf wheat, barley and algae
President: Kevin Thomas
Marketing: Bill Foley
Sales Director: Frank Guzzo
Estimated Sales: $ .5 - 1 million
Number Employees: 5-9
Sq. footage: 20000
Type of Packaging: Consumer, Private Label, Bulk
Other Locations:
Vitarich Laboratories
Bainbridge GA
Brands:
Hydra-Green

14171 Vitasoy USA
1 New England Way
Ayer, MA 01432 978-772-6880
Fax: 978-772-6881 info@vitasoy-usa.com
www.vitasoy-usa.com
Soy foods and Asian pasta; also soy drinks
President/CEO: Walter Riglian
Quality Control: Rick Baum
VP Marketing: Susan Rolnick
Operations: John Wareham
Estimated Sales: $150 Million
Number Employees: 160
Sq. footage: 42000
Parent Co: Vitasoy International Holdings
Type of Packaging: Consumer, Food Service, Private Label

Brands:
Nasoya

14172 **Vitatech International**
2802 Dow Ave
Tustin, CA 92780-7212 714-832-9700
Fax: 714-731-8482 vitatech@vitatech.com
www.vitatech.com
Manufacturer of vitamins
President: Thomas Tierney
CFO: Toni Clubb
VP Sales/Client Services: Greg Williford
Estimated Sales: $20-50 Million
Number Employees: 200
Type of Packaging: Private Label

14173 **(HQ)Vitech America Corporation**
833 1st Avenue S
Kent, WA 98032-6139 253-859-5985
Fax: 253-859-5912 jjabbott@vitechamerica.com
vitechamerica.com
Processor, packager and exporter of nutritional supplements, vitamin C, multiple vitamins, lactase enzyme caplets, calcium tablets, confections, breath mint, energy drinks and cosmetics
President: David Parker
VP Operations: Donald Parker
Purchasing Manager: Mike Harris
Estimated Sales: $11503924
Number Employees: 75
Sq. footage: 20000
Type of Packaging: Private Label, Bulk
Brands:
Body Dynabolics
Clinic
Flexon C2g
Lactzyme
MYNTZ
SQYNTZ
Swisscal 500
Theragar
Theraprin
Vitarite Nutritionals
Vitergy
Zincguard

14174 **Vity Meat & Provisions Company**
1418 N 27th Avenue
Phoenix, AZ 85009-3603 602-269-7768
Fax: 602-269-0044
President: Michael Brown
VP Finance: Gary Rasmussen
Estimated Sales: $ .5 - 1 million
Number Employees: 1-4

14175 **Vivienne Dressings**
P.O.Box 16072
St Louis, MO 63105-0772 314-994-7549
Fax: 636-947-1123 800-827-0778
ttucker.vivienne@gmail.com www.vivienne.com
Gourmet dressings and marinades
President: Thomas A Tucker
Estimated Sales: Below $ 5 Million
Number Employees: 1-4
Brands:
Vivienne

14176 **Vivion**
929 Bransten Rd
San Carlos, CA 94070-4073 650-595-3600
Fax: 650-595-2094 800-479-0997
mpoleselli@vivioninc.com www.vivioninc.com
Acids, sweeteners, preservatives, gums, vitamins, antoxidants and fibers
President: Edward Poleselli
Vice President: Michael Poleselli
Estimated Sales: $ 15 Million
Number Employees: 5-9

14177 **Vivolac Cultures Corporation**
3862 E Washington St
Indianapolis, IN 46201 317-356-8460
Fax: 317-356-8450 sales@vivolac.com
www.vivolac.com
Manufacturer and exporter of dairy, meat and bread starter cultures in pelletized, frozen and freeze-dried form
President: Wesley Sing
Technical Sales: David Winters
Estimated Sales: $1.4 Million
Number Employees: 20-49
Type of Packaging: Private Label, Bulk
Brands:
Bioflora
Vivolac

14178 **Vocatura Bakery**
695 Boswell Ave
Norwich, CT 06360 860-887-2220
Breads
President: John Vocatura
Estimated Sales: $500,000-$1 Million
Number Employees: 10-19
Brands:
Vocatura

14179 **Vogel Popcorn**
2683 350th St
Lake View, IA 51450 712-657-8561
Fax: 712-657-2152 info@vogelpopcorn.com
www.vogelpopcorn.com
Processor of popcorn
Manager: Dave Brpelcing
Estimated Sales: $ 10 - 20 Million
Number Employees: 20-49
Type of Packaging: Consumer, Private Label, Bulk

14180 **Vogel Popcorn**
2301 Washington St
Hamburg, IA 51640 712-382-2634
Fax: 712-382-1357 800-831-5818
www.vogelpopcorn.com
Processor and exporter of popcorn and popping oils; importer of popcorn and popcorn seeds
Director: Joe Haeflinger
Marketing: Colleen Moore
Estimated Sales: $20-50 Million
Number Employees: 50-99
Parent Co: ConAgra
Type of Packaging: Consumer, Food Service, Private Label, Bulk
Brands:
Act Ii
Cowboy
Vogel

14181 **Voget Meats**
P.O.Box 26
Hubbard, OR 97032
Fax: 503-981-0220 www.vogetmeats.com
Smoked meats, sausages
CEO: Merle Stutzman
Vice President: Grace Stuzman
Estimated Sales: $ 2.5-5 Million
Number Employees: 10-19
Type of Packaging: Private Label
Brands:
Voget Meats

14182 **Vogue Cuisine**
Po Box 60579
Sunnyvale, CA 94088 310-391-1053
Fax: 310-390-0883 888-236-4144
voguecuisine@comcast.net
www.voguecuisine.com
Processor of natural dehydrated low sodium and organic instant soup bases and mixes including chicken, beef, onion and vegetable vegetarian-chicken
President: Clinton Helvey
CEO: Carol Schlanger
Vice President: Clinton Helvey
Public Relations: Carol Helvey
Estimated Sales: $200,000
Number Employees: 4
Type of Packaging: Private Label
Brands:
VOGUE BEEF BASE
VOGUE CHICKEN BASE
VOGUE ONION BASE
VOGUE VEGEBASE
VOGUE VEGETARIAN CHICKEN BASE

14183 **Volcano Island Honey Company**
46-4013 Puaono Rd
Honokaa, HI 96727 808-775-1000
Fax: 808-775-0412 888-663-6639
info@volcanoislandhoney.com
www.volcanoislandhoney.com
Gourmet honey
Manager: Candice Choy
Estimated Sales: Under $500,000
Number Employees: 5-9
Brands:
Rare Hawaiian

14184 **Vollwerth & Baroni Companies**
P.O.Box 239
Hancock, MI 49930-0239 906-482-1550
Fax: 906-482-0842 800-562-7620
topdog@vollwerth.com www.vollwerth.com
Processor of sausage and meat products; wholesaler/distributor of hotel and restaurant supplies; serving the food service market
President: Robert Vollwerth
Vice President/General Manager: Jim Schaaf
Secretary/Treasurer: Mary Ann Berryman
Sales Representative: Richard Vollwerth
Packaging Manager: Don Hiltunen
Production Manager: Adam Manderfield
Estimated Sales: $100+ Million
Number Employees: 20-49

14185 **Volpi Italian Meats**
5258 Daggett Ave
St Louis, MO 63110-3026 314-772-8550
Fax: 314-772-0411 billh@volpifoods.com
www.volpifoods.com
Italian specialty meats, salami, proscuitto ham, pancetta, coppa, rotola
CEO: Armando Pasetti
President: Lorenza Pasetti
Quality Control: Cort Ballard
Marketing: Adiasa Seomanobic
Sales Director: Christine Illuminato
Operations Manager: Butch Duggan
Estimated Sales: $ 20-50 Million
Number Employees: 100-249
Brands:
Volpi

14186 **Von Gal**
3101 Hayneville Rd
Montgomery, AL 36108-3900 334-261-2700
Fax: 334-261-2801 800-542-6570
jason.bennett@vongal.com www.vongal.com
Manufacturer of palletizers for industries such as baking, bottling, brewing, and pet food.
Manager: Paul Probst
Sales Manager: Jason Bennett

14187 **Von Stiehl Winery**
115 Navarino St
Algoma, WI 54201 920-487-5208
Fax: 920-487-5108 800-955-5208
vonstiehl@itol.com www.vonstiehl.com
Manufacturer of wine
President: William Schmiling
VP: Sandra Schmiling
Estimated Sales: $5 Million
Number Employees: 20-49
Type of Packaging: Consumer

14188 **Von Strasser Winery**
1510 Diamond Mountain Rd
Calistoga, CA 94515 707-942-0930
Fax: 707-942-0454 888-359-9463
wines@vonstrasser.com www.vonstrasser.com
Wines
Owner/Executive Winemaker: Rudy Von Strasser
Director National Sales/Marketing: John Schulz
Vice President: Rita Von Strasser
Vineyard Manager: Gerardo Alfaro
Assistant Winemaker: Jason Bull
Vineyard Manager: Gerardo Alfaro
Estimated Sales: $ 2.5-5 Million
Number Employees: 5-9
Type of Packaging: Private Label
Brands:
Von Strasser
Von Strasser

14189 **Voortman Cookies**
4455 N Service Road
PO Box 5206
Burlington, ON L7L 4X7
Canada 905-335-9500
Fax: 905-332-5499 info@voortman.com
www.voortman.com
Manufacturers a variety of cookies including prepackaged family packs and seasonal cookies.
President: Harry Voortman
Founder: William Voortman
VP Sales: Adrian Voortman
Estimated Sales: $50-100 Million
Number Employees: 250-499
Sq. footage: 171339
Type of Packaging: Consumer, Bulk
Brands:
Voortman

14190 **Voortman Cookies**
2575 S Willow Ave
Bloomington, CA 92316-3256 909-877-8471
Fax: 909-877-6728
voortman@voortmancookies.com
www.voortmancookies.com
Manufacturers a variety of cookies including pre-packaged family packs and seasonal cookies.
President: Kathleen Voortman-Cunni
Founder: William Voortman
Sq. footage: 42000
Brands:
Voortman
Zero Trans Fats

14191 **Vosges Haut-Chocolat**
2211 N Elston Ave Ste 203
Chicago, IL 60614 773-772-5349
Fax: 773-772-7917 888-309-866
www.vosgeschocolate.com
chocolate truffles and gourmet gifts
Owner: Katrina Markoff

14192 **Voyager South**
8440 Sterling Dr
Mobile, AL 36695 251-634-0450
Fax: 318-388-4539
Estimated Sales: $ 1 - 3 Million
Number Employees: 1-4

14193 **Vrymeer Commodities**
PO Box 545
St Charles, IL 60174-0545 630-584-0069
Fax: 630-377-5521
Processor, exporter and importer of cocoa powder, liquor and butter; also, chocolate drops, candies and coatings
VP Worldwide Distribution: Andrew Nold
Number Employees: 100
Sq. footage: 30000
Parent Co: Ronstadt Group Companies
Type of Packaging: Bulk
Brands:
Vrymeer

14194 **Vynecrest Vineyards andWinery**
172 Arrowhead Ln
Breinigsville, PA 18031-1462 610-398-7525
Fax: 610-398-7530 800-361-0725
wines@vynecrest.com www.vynecrest.com
Wines
Co-Owner: Janice Landis
Co-Owner: John Landis
Estimated Sales: Less than $200,000
Number Employees: 1-4
Type of Packaging: Private Label
Brands:
Vynecrest Vineyards

14195 **Vyse Gelatin Company**
5010 Rose St
Schiller Park, IL 60176 847-678-4780
Fax: 847-678-0329 800-533-2152
info@vyse.com www.vyse.com
Manufacturer, exporter and importer of food grade gelatins
President: Gary Brunet
R&D: Rick Rossini
VP: John Deane
Sales: Margaret Miller
Estimated Sales: $ 3 - 5 Million
Number Employees: 10-19
Type of Packaging: Food Service, Private Label, Bulk
Brands:
150 Bloom
225 Bloom
610-D
710-D
Atlas
Celero
Economix
Finemix
Flour Fine
Hypowr
Pbc-210
Protector
Seeclear
Stabilo
Superclear
Superla
Supertex
Superwhip
Textura
Vee Gee
Velvatex
Viscomix
X-Fine

14196 **Vyse Gelatin Company**
5010 Rose St
Schiller Park, IL 60176 847-678-4780
Fax: 847-678-0329 800-533-2152
info@vyse.com www.vyse.com
Gelatin; all grades and types
President: Gary Brunet
Sales Director: Joel Ayres
Estimated Sales: $ 10-15 Million
Number Employees: 10-19
Type of Packaging: Food Service, Private Label, Bulk
Brands:
VYSE Gelatin

14197 **W & G Marketing Company**
413 Kellogg Avenue
PO Box 1742
Ames, IA 50010 515-233-4774
Fax: 515-233-4773 www.wgmarketing.com
Processor and exporter of roasting pigs including whole and frozen; also, meat and poultry by-products and fully cooked barbecue turkey, beef and pork
President/Sales and Marketing: Darren Dies
VP Operations: Robert Olinger
Estimated Sales: $ 5 - 10 Million
Number Employees: 5
Sq. footage: 5482
Type of Packaging: Consumer, Food Service, Private Label
Brands:
Hickory Grove
W&G's

14198 **(HQ)W&G Flavors**
11110 Pepper Rd Ste A
Hunt Valley, MD 21031 410-771-6606
Fax: 410-771-6608 jwaynewheeler@sun-ripe.com
http://sun-ripe.com/wg/
Processor and exporter of bakery and confectionery supplies and mixes including dry bar, salad dressings and sauces
President: J W Wheeler
Production Manager: Tim Wheeler
Estimated Sales: $1,000,000
Number Employees: 10-19
Type of Packaging: Food Service, Bulk
Brands:
COAG-U-LOID
CONDEX
PIE RITE
SUN-RIPE
T.H. ANGERMEIER
VEG-A-LOID

14199 **W. Forrest Haywood Seafood Company**
431 Messick Rd
Poquoson, VA 23662-1815 757-868-6748
Fax: 757-868-1111
Fresh crabmeat
President: Laura Hornsby
VP: Delores Forrest
Estimated Sales: $ 2.5-5 Million
Number Employees: 1-4

14200 **W. Roberts**
1300 Forest Dr
Annapolis, MD 21403-1436 410-269-5380
Fax: 410-263-0805
Manager: Maurice Jones
Estimated Sales: $ 5 - 10 Million
Number Employees: 20-49

14201 **W.A. Cleary Products**
1049 Route 27
PO Box 10
Somerset, NJ 08875-0010
800-238-7813
wacclearycorp@aol.com
www.waclearyproducts.com
Manufacturer and exporter of lecithin and release agents for the bakery, chocolate and confectionery industries
President: John Christman
Estimated Sales: $ 20 - 50 Million
Number Employees: 15
Sq. footage: 15000
Brands:
Clearlubes
Clearoil
Clearote Lecithins
Kettubes
Panlube
Tabl-Eze 350

14202 **W.F. Cosart Packing Company**
1145 E Firebaugh Ave
Exeter, CA 93221 559-592-2821
Fax: 559-592-6259
Fresh fruits and vegetables
President: Keith Cosart
Estimated Sales: $ 50 - 100 Million
Number Employees: 50-99

14203 **W.H. Harris Seafood**
Kent Narrows Way
North Grasonville, MD 21638 410-827-9500
Fax: 410-827-9057 whh@dmv.com
www.harriscrabhouse.com
Crabs and oysters
Chairman: William Jerry Harris
Vice President: Art Oertel
Estimated Sales: $ 5-10 Million
Number Employees: 50
Type of Packaging: Consumer
Brands:
Bay Shore

14204 **W.J. Clark & Co**
350 N La Salle Dr # 900
Chicago, IL 60654-5136 312-329-0830
Fax: 708-626-4064
Canned and packaging products,cold cereals, hot cereals, soya sauces, seasoning mixes
President: Bill Clark
VP Sales: Dorie Vedas
Estimated Sales: $ 20-50 Million
Number Employees: 5-9
Brands:
W.J. Clark

14205 **W.J. Stearns & Sons/Mountain Dairy**
50 Stearns Road
Storrs Mansfield, CT 06268-2701 860-423-9289
Fax: 860-423-3486 www.mountaindairy.com
Processor and wholesaler/distributor of dairy products including cream and milk
President: W Stearns
Vice President: James Stearns
Plant Manager: James Stearns
Estimated Sales: $3 Million
Number Employees: 35
Type of Packaging: Consumer, Private Label

14206 **W.L. Halsey Grocery Company**
P.O.Box 6485
Huntsville, AL 35813 256-772-9691
Fax: 256-461-8386 sales@halseyfoodservice.com
www.halseygrocery.com
Wholesaler/distributor of groceries, provisions/meats, produce, dairy products, frozen foods, baked goods, etc.; serving the food service market
President: Cecilia Halsey
Estimated Sales: $56471684
Number Employees: 100-249
Sq. footage: 90000

14207 **W.L. Petrey Wholesale Company**
P.O.Box 68
Luverne, AL 36049-0068 334-230-5674
Fax: 334-335-2422 mail@petrey.com
www.petrey.com
Wholesaler/distributor of frozen food, general merchandise, general line products, provisions/meats and seafood
President: Bill Jackson
CEO: James Jackson
Number Employees: 500-999

14208 **W.O. Sasser**
135 Johnny Mercer Blvd
Savannah, GA 31410-2118 912-898-9504
Fax: 912-897-0331
Owner: W O Sasser
Estimated Sales: $ .5 - 1 million
Number Employees: 5-9

14209 **W.R. Delozier Sausage Company**
12350 Chapman Highway
Seymour, TN 37865-6231 865-577-5907

Sausages
President: W Delozier
Estimated Sales: Less than $500,000
Number Employees: 1-4

14210 **W.S. Wells & Sons**
P.O.Box 109
Wilton, ME 04294-0109 207-645-3393
Fax: 207- 64-5 33
Canned fiddleheads and dandelions, green beans, baked beans, soup mixes
Owner: Adrian Wells
Estimated Sales: $ 2.5-5 Million
Number Employees: 10-19

14211 **W.T. Ruark & Company**
P.O.Box 99
Fishing Creek, MD 21634-0099 410-397-3133
Fax: 410-397-2007 wtruark@intercom.net
Manufacturer of seafood including oysters, crabs and crabmeat
President: William Ruark
Estimated Sales: $21 Million
Number Employees: 20-49
Type of Packaging: Consumer

14212 **WA Bean & Sons**
229 Bomarc Rd # 1
Bangor, ME 04401-2678 207-947-0364
Fax: 207-990-4211 800-649-1958
sales@beansmeats.com www.beansmeats.com
Processor of natural casing frankfurters and sausages, hams, tri-cooked meats, haggis and mincemeat.
President: David Bean
Treasurer: Elizabeth Bean
Sales Director: Gordon Brasslett
Estimated Sales: Under $5 Million
Number Employees: 20-49
Sq. footage: 4
Type of Packaging: Consumer, Food Service, Private Label, Bulk

14213 **WA Cleary Products**
P.O.Box 10
Somerset, NJ 08875-0010 732-247-8000
Fax: 732-247-6977 800-238-7813
wacLearycorp@aol.com
www.waclearyproducts.com
Lecithin, release products for the baking and candy industries
President: John Christman
Marketing Director: John Chirstion
Estimated Sales: $ 50-100 Million
Number Employees: 20-49
Brands:
WA Cleary

14214 **(HQ)WCC Honey Marketing**
636 Turnbull Canyon Rd
City of Industry, CA 91745-1119 626-855-3086
Fax: 626-855-3087 info@wcommerce.com
www.wcommerce.com
Processor and exporter of natural sweeteners, syrups and nutritional supplements including honey, comb honey, molasses, blackstrap molasses, corn syrup, agave nectar and royal jelly; importer of honey, barley malt sweetener, rice syrupand juice concentrate
Owner: Anthony Li
General Manager: Chuck Burkholder
National Sales Manager: Norma Robinson
Purchasing Manager: James Littlejohn
Estimated Sales: $ 5 - 10 Million
Number Employees: 5-9
Sq. footage: 29700
Type of Packaging: Consumer, Food Service, Private Label, Bulk
Other Locations:
Western Commerce Corp.
Kansas City MO
Brands:
Cucamonga
El Panal
Fruitsweet
Hawaiian Gold
Lo Han
Pot O' Gold
Powers

14215 **WFI**
1209 W Saint Georges Ave
Linden, NJ 07036-6117 908-925-9494
Fax: 908-925-9537 800-229-1706
customerservice@waldenfarms.com
www.waldenfarms.com
Sauces
President: Paul Berko
Sales Director: Mitchell Berko
Operations Manager: V Naccarato
Estimated Sales: $500,000-$1 Million
Number Employees: 20-49
Type of Packaging: Private Label
Brands:
Walden Farms

14216 **WG Thompson & Sons**
PO Box 250
Blenheim, ON N0P 1A0
Canada 519-676-5411
Fax: 519-676-3185 srobert@wgthompson.com
Manufacturer, importer, exporter and wholesaler/distributor of soya and dry beans, corn, seeds and cereal grains; wholesaler/distributor of groceries, produce, general merchandise, private label/generic items, etc.; serving the foodservice market
President: Wes Thompson
Secretary: Andrew McVittie
Food Products Manager: John O'Brien
Contact: Sue Robert
Estimated Sales: $100 Million
Number Employees: 350
Type of Packaging: Consumer, Food Service, Private Label, Bulk
Brands:
C&G
HYLAND

14217 **WILD Flavors**
PO Box 75204
Cincinnati, OH 45275-0204 513-771-5904
888-945-3352
info@wildflavors.com www.wild.de
Processor and exporter of flavors, colors and other ingredients for food and beverage
Marketing Manager: Oliver Hodapp
Estimated Sales: $ 5 - 10 Million
Number Employees: 5-9
Type of Packaging: Food Service, Private Label

14218 **WILD Flavors (Canada)**
7315 Pacific Circle
Mississauga, ON L5T 1V1
Canada 905-670-1108
Fax: 905-670-0076 800-263-5286
www.wildflavors.com
Processor of flavors, colors, seasonings, spray-dried ingredients, sauces, batters, coatings, marinades; also, custom blending; exporter of cheese powders
Acting Director: Tim Husted
Director Finance: Tamara Robichaud
R & D: Allison Berridge
Operations Director: Tim Husted
Plant Manager: Dave Oldroyd
Purchasing Manager: Leigh Bailey
Number Employees: 30-50
Number of Products: 200
Sq. footage: 60000
Parent Co: WILD Flavors
Type of Packaging: Food Service, Bulk

14219 **WK Eckerd & Sons**
5067 Blythe Island Hwy # B
Brunswick, GA 31520-2500 912-265-0332
Fax: 912-261-8460 eckerd@thebest.net
Seafood
President: William Eckerd
Estimated Sales: Below $ 5 Million
Number Employees: 1-4

14220 **WMFB**
Apt 94
209 Webster St
Beaver Dam, WI 53916-3074 920-887-1771
Fax: 920-887-3683
Processor of frozen pasta
President: Steve Baldwin
Vice President: Roger Dusso
CFO: Dan Gartland
Vice President: Roger Dusso
Quality Control: Sandra Saunders
Operations Manager: Jerry Klawitter
Estimated Sales: $ 10-20 Million
Number Employees: 20-49
Type of Packaging: Food Service, Private Label, Bulk
Brands:
WMFB

14221 **WSI**
223 Rodeo Ave
Caldwell, ID 83605-6714 208-459-0777
Fax: 208-455-4859 800-632-3005
Processor of dry pinto beans and seed grain
General Manager: Leeon Martineau
Purchasing Agent: Tammy Gaviola
Estimated Sales: $100+ Million
Number Employees: 100-249
Parent Co: J.R. Simplot Company
Type of Packaging: Consumer, Private Label, Bulk

14222 **WSU Creamery**
Po Box 641122
Pullman, WA 99164-1122 800-457-5442
Fax: 509-335-7525 800-457-5442
salvadalena@wsu.edu www.wsu.edu/creamery
Processor of cheddar cheese and ice cream
WSU Creamery Manager: Russ Salvadalena
Assistant Manager: John Haugen
Number Employees: 50
Sq. footage: 20000
Type of Packaging: Consumer, Food Service
Brands:
Cougar Gold
Viking

14223 **Wabash Coffee**
P.O.Box 576
Vincennes, IN 47591-0576 812-882-6066
Fax: 812-882-8371 www.wabashfoodservice.com
Coffee
President/CEO: Robert Bierhaus
CEO: Jayne Young
Estimated Sales: $ 50 - 100 Million
Number Employees: 100-249

14224 **Wabash Heritage Spices**
2525 N 6th St
Vincennes, IN 47591-2405 812-895-0059
Fax: 812-895-0064 info@knoxcountyarc.com
www.knoxcountyarc.com
Spices, powders
President: Michael Carney
Research & Development: John TRUE
Quality Control: John TRUE
Plant Manager: Leroy Douffron
Number of Brands: 1
Number of Products: 90
Sq. footage: 240000
Type of Packaging: Consumer, Food Service, Private Label, Bulk
Brands:
WASBASH HERITAGE

14225 **Wabash Seafood Company**
2249 W Hubbard St
Chicago, IL 60612 312-733-5070
Fax: 312-733-2798
Seafood
President: John Rebello
Estimated Sales: $ 10 - 20 Million
Number Employees: 20-49

14226 **Wabash Valley Farms**
6323 N 150 E
Monon, IN 47959 219-253-6607
Fax: 219-253-8172 800-270-2705
charlotte@wfarms.com
www.popcornpopper.com
Processor and exporter of popcorn and popper gift baskets including seasonings, spices, oils and drink mixes
President: Dani Paluchniak
Vice President: Joe Dold
Sales Manager: Steve Dold
Purchasing Manager: Joe Dold
Estimated Sales: $4041306
Number Employees: 5-9
Parent Co: Felknor International
Type of Packaging: Consumer
Brands:
Theater II
Wasbash Valley Farm
Whirley Pop

14227 **Wabash Valley Produce**
P.O.Box 127
Dubois, IN 47527 812-678-3131
Fax: 812-678-5931
Processor of bulk liquid egg products including pasteurized and raw whole eggs, egg whites and egg and salt yolks
President: Larry Seger
Estimated Sales: $100+ Million
Number Employees: 100-249
Sq. footage: 25000
Type of Packaging: Bulk

14228 **Wabi Fishing Company**
14608 Smokey Point Boulevard
Marysville, WA 98271-8946 360-659-9474
Fax: 360-659-9093 888-536-7696
wabi@silvernet.net www.leosown.com
Wild Pacific smoked salmon available in five flavors
President: Leo Palmer
Brands:
King Nova
Leo's
Sockeye Nova

14229 **Wachusett Brewing Company**
175 State Rd E
Westminster, MA 01473 978-874-9965
Fax: 978-874-0784 info@wachusettbrew.com
www.wachusettbrew.com
Processor of flavored ales.
Owner: Ned La Fortune
Sales Manager: Peter Quinn
Plant Engineer: Kevin Buckler
Estimated Sales: Below $ 5 Million
Number Employees: 10-19
Type of Packaging: Consumer, Food Service
Brands:
Wachusett

14230 **Wachusett Potato Chip Company**
759 Water St
Fitchburg, MA 1420 978-342-6038
Fax: 978-345-4894 800-551-5539
www.wachusettpotatochip.com
Potato chips, plain, salt and vinegar, rippled, barbeque, no salt added, ketchup, potato sticks, sour cream and onion, cheese twists, popcorn, cheese popcorn
President: Edward Krysiak
Estimated Sales: $10 Million
Number Employees: 50-99
Sq. footage: 56000
Type of Packaging: Consumer, Food Service, Private Label
Brands:
Wachusett

14231 **Waco Beef & Pork Processors**
523 Precision Dr
Waco, TX 76710 254-772-4669
Fax: 254-772-4579
Manufacturer of fresh portion controlled beef, chicken and pork including sausage, chorizo and bratwurst; importer of beef skirts; wholesaler/distributor of meat and general merchandise; serving the food service market
Manager: Sara Jones
Estimated Sales: $2.2 Million
Number Employees: 5-9
Sq. footage: 10000
Type of Packaging: Food Service
Brands:
PRECISION

14232 **Wagner Excello Food Products**
2625 Gardner Rd
Broadview, IL 60155-4499 708-338-4488
Fax: 708-338-4495 peter.mail@wagnerfoods.com
www.wagnerfoods.com
Bar mixes, maple syrups, juices and water
Owner: Harry Berger
VP: Peter Fisher
VP: Peter Fisher
Estimated Sales: $1.6 Million
Number Employees: 10
Number of Brands: 1
Type of Packaging: Food Service, Private Label

14233 **Wagner Gourmet Foods**
10618 Summit St
Lenexa, KS 66215 913-469-5411
Fax: 913-469-1367
customerservice@wagner-gourmet.com
www.hicks-ashby.com
Processor of spices, preserves, jams, ice cream sauces, seasoned rice and gift pack assortments; importer of tea; wholesaler/distributor of snack foods including cookies
President: James T Baldwin
Estimated Sales: $ 3 - 5 Million
Number Employees: 5-9
Sq. footage: 120000
Parent Co: Wagner Gourmet Foods
Type of Packaging: Consumer, Private Label

14234 **Wagner Seafood**
9626 S Pulaski Rd
Oak Lawn, IL 60453-3391 708-636-2646
Fax: 843-559-1156
Seafood
President: Robert Wagner
Estimated Sales: $300,000-500,000
Number Employees: 1-4

14235 **Wagner Vineyards**
9322 State Route 414
Lodi, NY 14860 607-582-6450
Fax: 607-582-6446 866-924-6378
d.wagner@wagnervineyards.com
www.wagnervineyards.com
Processor of wines and beer; exporter of wines
President: Stanley Wagner
Retail Manager: Carol Voorhees
COO: John Wagner
Public Relations: Laura Lee
Estimated Sales: $2,762,368
Number Employees: 50-99
Sq. footage: 36000
Type of Packaging: Consumer
Brands:
Wagner Brewing Co.
Wagner Vineyards

14236 **Wah Yet Group**
28301 Industrial Blvd Ste C
Hayward, CA 94545 510-887-3801
Fax: 510-887-3803 800-229-3392
Processor and exporter of dieters' and ginseng teas; importer of health drinks
President: Ying Lau
Manager: Judy Lau
Estimated Sales: $ 1 - 3 Million
Number Employees: 1-4
Sq. footage: 2000
Type of Packaging: Consumer
Brands:
Chinese Ginseng
Green Leaf

14237 **Wainani Kai Seafood**
2126 Eluwene St Ste A
Honolulu, HI 96819 808-847-7435
Fax: 808-841-7536 lpang00@yahoo.com
Seafood
President: Lance Pang
Estimated Sales: $ 3 - 5 Million
Number Employees: 5-9

14238 **Waken Meat Company**
1015 Boulevard SE
Atlanta, GA 30312-3809 404-627-3537
Fax: 404-624-3191
Beef, pork, chicken, frozen seafood
President: Charles Waken
Estimated Sales: $300,000-500,000
Number Employees: 5-9

14239 **Wakunaga of America**
23501 Madero
Mission Viejo, CA 92691 714-855-2776
Fax: 949-458-2764 800-421-2998
info@wakunaga.com www.kyolic.com
Manufacturer of nutritional supplements.
President: Kenro Nakamura
Estimated Sales: $24 Million
Number Employees: 75
Number of Brands: 5
Number of Products: 70
Sq. footage: 42000
Parent Co: Wakunaga Pharmaceutical
Brands:
BESURE
ESTRO LOGIC
KYO-CHLORELLA
KYO-DOPHILUS
KYO-GREEN
KYO-GREEN HARVEST BLEND
KYOLIC
MODUCARE
MODUCHOL
MODUPROST

14240 **Walcan Seafood**
PO Box 429
Heroit Bay, BC V0P 1H0
Canada 250-285-3361
Fax: 250-285-3313 www.walcan.com
Salmon

14241 **Walden Farms**
1209 W Saint Georges Ave
Linden, NJ 7036 908-925-9494
Fax: 908-925-9537 800-229-1706
info@waldenfarms.com www.waldenfarms.com
Processor and exporter of salad dressings, dips, bbq sauces, pancake syrups, fruit spread jams and jellies, fruit syrups, ketchup and seafood sauces, bruschetta and chocolate syrup.
President: Mitchell Berko
Vice President: Paul Berko
Operations: Brian Sherwood Ph.D
Number Employees: 20-49
Sq. footage: 16000
Type of Packaging: Consumer, Food Service
Brands:
Walden Farms

14242 **Walden Foods**
660 N Loudoun St
Winchester, VA 22601-4986 540-622-2800
Fax: 540-253-9807 800-648-7688
walden@waldenfoods.com
www.waldenfoods.com
Processor of all natural and gourmet applewood smoked seafood and poultry
meats cured or smoked,mfg fresh,frozenfish,mfg canned/cured seafood,and poultryprocessing.
President: John P Good Jr
VP Marketing: Christine Hyre
Number Employees: 20
Sq. footage: 12500
Parent Co: Walden Foods Inc.
Type of Packaging: Consumer, Food Service
Brands:
The Farm At Mt. Walden

14243 **Waldensian Bakeries**
320 Main St E
Valdese, NC 28690-2812 828-874-2136
Fax: 828-874-4910 www.saralee.com
Processor of white and rye bread, cakes, snacks and pound cakes, groceries and related products
VP Marketing: Bill Mitchell
Plant Manager: Andy Lopez
Estimated Sales: $ 5 - 10 Million
Number Employees: 5-9
Parent Co: Sara Lee
Type of Packaging: Consumer, Food Service, Private Label

14244 **Walker Foods**
237 N Mission Rd
Los Angeles, CA 90033 323-268-5191
Fax: 723-268-7812 800-966-5199
info@walkerfoods.net www.walkerfoods.net
Producers of El Pato, the original hot spicy tomato sauce and the Golden State family of products.
President: Robert Walker
Director Food Service/Industrial Sales: Craig Wendel-Smith
Production Manager: Alfred Heredia
Plant Manager: Fernando Montano
Estimated Sales: $10-20 Million
Number Employees: 50-99
Sq. footage: 120000
Type of Packaging: Consumer, Food Service, Private Label, Bulk
Brands:
El Pato
Golden State

14245 **Walker Meats Corporation**
821 Tyus Carrollton Rd
Carrollton, GA 30117 770-834-8171
Fax: 770-834-2208

Beef, pork, poultry, produce, seafood
President: Donald Walker
Estimated Sales: $ 10 - 20 Million
Number Employees: 20-49

14246 Walker Valley Vineyards
PO Box 24
Walker Valley, NY 12588-0024 845-744-3449
Wines
Owner: Gary Dross
Estimated Sales: $ 5-9.9 Million
Number Employees: 4
Brands:
Walker Valley Vineyards

14247 Walker's Seafood
312 Southwest Sq
Jonesboro, AR 72401-5984 870-932-0375
Fax: 870-935-8697
Seafood
President: Darrell Walker
Secretary/Treasurer: Patricia Walker

14248 Walkers Shortbread
170 Commerce Dr
Hauppauge, NY 11788 631-273-0011
Fax: 631-273-0438 800-521-0141
cs@walkersshortbread.com
www.walkersshortbread.com
Importer of shortbread and cookies
President: Norman Barnes
Marketing: Karen Riley
Estimated Sales: $2800000
Number Employees: 19
Parent Co: Walkers Shortbread
Type of Packaging: Consumer, Bulk
Brands:
Duchy Originals
Kambly
Walker's
Walkers

14249 Wall Meat Processing
P.O.Box 408
Wall, SD 57790 605-279-2348
Manufactures slab & sliced bacon and other meat products
Owner: Oliver Carson
Estimated Sales: $ 1 - 3 Million
Number Employees: 1-4
Type of Packaging: Private Label

14250 Wall-Rogalsky Milling Company
416 N Main St
Mc Pherson, KS 67460-3404 620-241-2410
Fax: 620-241-7167 800-835-2067
www.cerealfood.com
Miller of flour including, bakery, bread, all-purpose and self-rising; also, pancake and waffle mix, wheat bran and mill feeds
President/CEO: J Brent Wall
Plant Superintendent: Kendall Allison
Vice President: Wayne Ford
Plant Manager: Max Streit
Estimated Sales: $ 10 - 20 Million
Number Employees: 20-49
Sq. footage: 41270
Type of Packaging: Consumer, Food Service, Private Label, Bulk
Brands:
America's Best
Bake-Rite H & R
Kansas Sun
Utility
W-R

14251 Walla Walla Gardeners' Association
210 N 11th Ave
Walla Walla, WA 99362 509-525-7070
Fax: 509-529-4170 800-553-5014
wwga@wwsonion.com www.wwsonion.com
Processor and exporter of yellow and sweet onions, spinach, asparagus and radishes
General Manager: Bryon Magnaghi
Production Manager: Steve Hendrickson
Estimated Sales: $100+ Million
Number Employees: 100-249
Number of Brands: 3
Sq. footage: 15000
Type of Packaging: Consumer, Private Label
Brands:
Gloria
Top Choice
Walla Walla

14252 Wallaby Yogurt Company
110 Mezzetta Ct Ste B
American Canyon, CA 94503 707-553-1233
Fax: 707-553-1293 info@wallabyyogurt.com
www.wallabyyogurt.com
Manager: Jerry Chou
CEO: Claudia Suh
Estimated Sales: $ 1 - 3 Million
Number Employees: 20-49
Brands:
Wallaby

14253 Wallace Edwards & Sons
11455 Rolfe Highway
Surry, VA 23883 757-294-3121
Fax: 757-294-5378 edwardsham@aol.com
Virginia hams, hickory smoked bacon, dry cured duck, sausage, turkey, and Virginia peanuts
President/CEO: Bob Anderson

14254 Wallace Fisheries
PO Box 2046
Gulf Shores, AL 36547-2046 251-986-7211
Fax: 251-987-5127
Seafood

14255 Wallace Grain & Pea Company
PO Box 218
Palouse, WA 99161-0218 509-878-1561
Fax: 509-878-1671 dave@wallacegrain.com
Processor and exporter of chickpeas, barley, lentils and peas
President: Joe Hulett
Assistant Manager: Gary Heaton
Estimated Sales: $500,000-$1 Million
Number Employees: 1-4
Type of Packaging: Consumer, Food Service, Private Label, Bulk
Brands:
Palouse

14256 Wallace Plant Company
201 High St
Bath, ME 04530-1677 207-443-2640
Fax: 207-386-0268
Seafood
Owner: Wallace Plant
Estimated Sales: $1 Million
Number Employees: 5-9
Type of Packaging: Consumer

14257 Wallingford Coffee Company
P.O.Box 603267
Cleveland, OH 44103 216-241-3267
Fax: 216-694-2150 800-714-0944
Coffee
Manager: Joe Negrelli
CFO: Michael Hoban
Manager: Joe Negrelli
Estimated Sales: $ 1-2.5 Million
Number Employees: 5-9
Type of Packaging: Private Label, Bulk
Brands:
Wallingford

14258 Wallingford Coffee Mills
11401 Rockfield Ct
Cincinnati, OH 45241-1971 513-771-4570
Fax: 513-771-3138 800-533-3690
sales@wallingfordcoffee.com
www.wallingfordcoffee.com
Coffee
President: Gary Weber
VP Operations: Gary Davis
Estimated Sales: $ 50-100 Million
Number Employees: 82
Brands:
Wallingford

14259 Wally Biscotti
4850 E 39th Ave
Denver, CO 80207-1010 303-320-9969
Fax: 303-320-9966 866-659-2559
wallybiscotti@aol.com www.wallybiscotti.com
Biscotti
President: Wally Friedlander
Marketing Manager: Waally Biscotti
Operations Manager: Jamey Biscotti
Estimated Sales: $1-$1.3 Million
Number Employees: 20-49
Type of Packaging: Consumer, Food Service, Private Label, Bulk
Brands:
Wally Biscotti

14260 Walsh's Coffee Roasters
273 Baldwin Avenue
San Mateo, CA 94401-3914 650-347-5112
Fax: 650-347-0569
Coffee
Owner/President: John Walsh
Estimated Sales: Less than $500,000
Number Employees: 1-4

14261 Walsh's Seafood
Rr 1
Gouldsboro, ME 04607 207-963-2578
Fax: 207-963-2578
Seafood
Owner: Craig Walsh

14262 Walt Koch
315 W Ponce De Leon Ave
Suite 500
Decatur, GA 30030 404-378-3666
Fax: 404-378-8492 www.waltkoch.com
Poultry frozen foods, meats, seafood
Cfo: Cindy Groover
Sales Manager: Keith Steinberg
Estimated Sales: $43 Million
Number Employees: 54
Type of Packaging: Consumer, Food Service

14263 Walter P. Rawl & Sons
824 Fairview Road
Pelion, SC 29123-9433 803-359-3645
Fax: 803-359-8850 www.rawl.net
peppers, beets, cilantro, collard, corn, green onion, jalapeno, kale, leeks, mustard, parsley, turnip, turnip root, yellow squash, zucchini
President: Howard Rawl
Director of Sales: Ashley Rawl
Head General Manager: Marshall Sherman
Estimated Sales: $24323805
Number Employees: 110
Type of Packaging: Consumer, Food Service

14264 Waltham Beef Company
18 Food Mart Road
Boston, MA 02118-2802 617-269-2250
Fax: 617-269-8183
Processed beef, pork, poultry
President: Douglas Atamian
President: Wesley Atamian
Type of Packaging: Private Label

14265 Waltkoch
315 W Ponce D L Ave Ste 500
Decatur, GA 30030 404-378-3666
Fax: 404-378-8492 www.waltkoch.com
Poultry, frozen foods, meats, seafood
Owner: Keith Steinberg
Estimated Sales: $15,200,000
Number Employees: 20-49
Type of Packaging: Consumer

14266 Wampler's Farm Sausage Company
781 Highway 70 W
Lenoir City, TN 37771 865-986-2056
Fax: 865-988-3280 800-728-7243
tedjr@wamplersfarm.com
www.wamplersfarm.com
Processor, packer and exporter of sausage
President: Ted Wampler
Vice President: John Ed Wampler
Sales Manager: Doug Young
Operations Manager: Darrell Griffis
Plant Supervisor: Mike Marney
Plant Manager: Jim Wampler
Estimated Sales: $24000000
Number Employees: 100-249
Type of Packaging: Consumer, Food Service, Private Label, Bulk
Brands:
Wampler's Farm

14267 Wan Hua Foods
804 6th Ave S
Seattle, WA 98134 206-622-8417
Fax: 206-622-7088 info@wanhuafoods.com
www.wanhuafoods.com

Processor of fresh cooked noodles including udon, yaki soba, miki and chow mein; also, wonton and pot sticker wrappers
President: Sui-Ming Tam
VP: Judy Tam
Estimated Sales: $1700000
Number Employees: 10-19
Sq. footage: 12000
Brands:
Miki
Phillipino's
U-Don
Yakisoba

14268 Wanchese Fish Company
2000 Northgate Commerce Pkwy
Suffolk, VA 23435 757-673-4500
Fax: 757-653-4550 fishco@wanchese.com
www.wanchese.com
Processor and exporter of fresh and frozen seafood including flounder, bass, scallops, tuna, scallops and shrimp.
President: Joey Daniels
CFO: Mark Palmer
VP: Kenny Daniels
Operations Executive: Lori Fitzpatrick
Estimated Sales: $6400000
Number Employees: 150
Sq. footage: 250000
Parent Co: Daniels Enterprises
Type of Packaging: Consumer, Food Service, Private Label, Bulk
Other Locations:
Wanchese Fish Co.
Hampton VA

14269 Wanda's Nature Farm
1700 Cushman Dr
Lincoln, NE 68512-1238
US 402-423-1234
Fax: 402-423-4586 800-735-6828
wandas@neb.rr.com www.superbakes.com
www.wandasfoods.com
Processor and exporter of natural mixes including bread, cake, muffin, pancake, pasta, pizza, bagels, etc
President: Susan Zink
Vice President: David Eisner
Marketing Director: Shari Rogge-Fidler
Estimated Sales: $2311332
Number Employees: 20-49
Type of Packaging: Consumer, Food Service

14270 Wannamaker Seeds
St. Matthews, SC 29135 803-874-1381
Fax: 803-874-1381
maryjo@wannamakerseeds.com
www.wannamakerseeds.com
Seed breeder; seed supplier, oilseed producer (soybean)
President/Owner: Mary-Jo Wannamaker
Estimated Sales: $ 1 Million
Number Employees: 10-19

14271 Wapsie Produce
702 E Water St
Decorah, IA 52101 563-382-4271
Fax: 563-382-8210 info@capons.com
www.capons.com
Processor and exporter of frozen capons and fowl
President: Marc Nichols
Vice President: Paul Nichols
Estimated Sales: $9 Million
Number Employees: 100
Type of Packaging: Consumer, Private Label
Brands:
Ioma
Minowa
Thrift

14272 Wapsie Valley Creamery
P.O.Box 391
Independence, IA 50644 319-334-7193
Fax: 319-334-4914
Manufacturer of Monterey and marble pepper jack, cheddar and colby cheese; processor and exporter of kosher reduced lactose whey, edible dried delactose and lactose
President: Mark Nielsen
VP: Wilbur Nielsen
Estimated Sales: $20-50 Million
Number Employees: 50-99
Sq. footage: 78000

Type of Packaging: Consumer, Private Label, Bulk

14273 War Eagle Mill
11045 War Eagle Rd
Rogers, AR 72756 479-789-5343
Fax: 479-789-2972 info@wareaglemill.com
www.wareaglemill.com
Processor and miller of stone burr corn meal and wholewheat flour and mixes
President: Zoe Caywood
Type of Packaging: Consumer

14274 Ward Cove Packing Company
88 E Hamlin St
Seattle, WA 98102-3144 206-323-3200
Fax: 206-323-9165 wrdscove@msn.com
www.wardscove.com
Processor and exporter of canned and frozen salmon and crab; also, exporter of surimi
President: Bill Weissfield
Estimated Sales: $ 50 - 100 Million
Number Employees: 100-249
Parent Co: Ward Cove Packing Company
Type of Packaging: Consumer, Food Service
Other Locations:
Ward Cove Packing Co.
Seattle WA
Brands:
Northern Pride
Pirate

14275 Warden Peanut Company
620 E Lime St
Portales, NM 88130 575-356-6691
Fax: 575-359-0072
Snack foods
VP: Sam Rigsey
General Manager: Bill Owen
Plant Manager: Leonard Stanton
Estimated Sales: Under $500,000
Number Employees: 20-49

14276 Warner Candy
Ste A
1240 Don Haskins Dr
El Paso, TX 79936-7887 847-928-7200
Fax: 847-928-2115 www.warnercandy.com
Candy
Estimated Sales: $ 10 - 20 Million
Number Employees: 20-49

14277 (HQ)Warner Vineyards Winery
706 S Kalamazoo St
Paw Paw, MI 49079-1558 269-657-3165
Fax: 269-657-4154 800-756-5357
kevins@warnerwines.com
www.warnerwines.com
Wines
President: Patrick Warner
Estimated Sales: $500,000
Number Employees: 5-9
Type of Packaging: Consumer, Private Label
Brands:
Warner Vineyards

14278 (HQ)Warner-Lambert Confections
810 Main St
Cambridge, MA 02139-3588 617-491-2500
Fax: 617-547-2381
Candy
President/CEO: J Craig
Plant Manager: Gerald Chesser
Estimated Sales: Under $500,000
Number Employees: 100-249

14279 Warrell Corporation
1250 Slate Hill Rd
Camp Hill, PA 17011 717-761-5440
Fax: 717-761-2206 800-233-7082
sales@warrellcorp.com
www.padutchcandies.com
Processor, importer and exporter of confectionery products
President: Patrick Huffman
Marketing Director: Richard Warrell
Number Employees: 50-99
Sq. footage: 200000
Parent Co: Pennsylvania Dutch Company
Type of Packaging: Consumer, Food Service

14280 Warren & Son Meat Processing
7585 State Route 821
Whipple, OH 45788-5164 740-585-2421
Fax: 740-585-2073
Processor of beef, pork, lamb, specialty meats and smoked sausage and ham
Owner/Sales: Danny Warren
Marketing Director: Kathryn Warren
Estimated Sales: $ 3 - 5 Million
Number Employees: 5-9
Type of Packaging: Consumer, Bulk

14281 Warren Cheese Plant
415 W Jefferson St
Warren, IL 61087 815-745-2627
Fax: 815-745-2843 applejack@aeroinc.net
www.applejackcheese.com
Mozzarella, string and apple jack cheese
Cheesemaker: Duane Torkelson
Estimated Sales: $ 20-50 Million
Number Employees: 20-49
Brands:
Apple Jack

14282 Warren Laboratories
1656 Ih 35 S
Abbott, TX 76621 254-580-9990
Fax: 254-580-9944 800-421-2563
karenk@warrenlabsaloe.com
www.warrenlabsaloe.com
Processor of refined aloe vera beverages
Manager: Tony Tustejovsky
Estimated Sales: $2100000
Number Employees: 10-19

14283 Warwick Ice Cream Company
743 Bald Hill Rd
Warwick, RI 2886 401-821-8403
Fax: 401-821-8404
Manufacturer of ice cream cakes, pies and popsicles
Owner: Gerard Bucci Sr Jr
Estimated Sales: $1-3 Million
Number Employees: 20-49
Type of Packaging: Consumer, Food Service, Bulk

14284 Wasatch Meats
926 Jefferson St
Salt Lake City, UT 84101 801-363-5747
Fax: 801-363-5759 christy@wasatchmeats.com
www.wasatchmeats.com
Processors of meat including beef, pork and poultry.
President: Rich Broadbent
VP: Scott Rich
VP Marketing: Mark Broadbent
VP Sales: Mark Broadbent
Operations Manager: Roger Rausch
Production Foreman: Dave Burke
Estimated Sales: $15914424
Number Employees: 20-49
Type of Packaging: Food Service

14285 (HQ)Washburn Candy Corporation
PO Box 3277
Brockton, MA 02304-3277 508-588-0820
Fax: 508-588-2205 www.fbwashburncandy.com
Candy
President: James Gilson
Estimated Sales: $ 10-20 Million
Number Employees: 30-50
Sq. footage: 150000
Type of Packaging: Private Label
Brands:
Sevigny
Waleeco
Washburn

14286 Washington Beef
P.O.Box 832
Toppenish, WA 98948 509-865-2121
Fax: 509-865-2827 800-289-2333
info@wabeef.com www.wabeef.com
Packer of beef; slaughtering services available
President: Robert Rebholtz
CEO: Gayland Pedhirney
Estimated Sales: $ 100-500 Million
Number Employees: 500-999

14287 Washington Fruit & Produce Company
401 N 1st Ave
P.O.Box 1588
Yakima, WA 98907-1588 509-457-6177
Fax: 509-452-8520 information@washfruit.com
www.washfruit.com
Processor and exporter of fresh fruits including apples, pears, and cherries.
Manager: Tom Hanses
Estimated Sales: Less than $500,000
Number Employees: 1-4
Type of Packaging: Consumer, Bulk

14288 Washington Potato Company
1900 1st Ave W
Warden, WA 98857 509-349-8803
Fax: 509-349-2362 opcsales@ucinet.com
Processor and exporter of frozen and dehydrated potatoes
President: Dave Landon
President/CEO: Frank Tiegs
Human Resources Director: Ramona Thomas
Plant Manager: Bob Bernard
Estimated Sales: $16.6 Million
Number Employees: 100
Sq. footage: 5000
Parent Co: Oregon Potato
Type of Packaging: Food Service, Bulk

14289 Washington Quality FoodProducts
27 Frederick Road
Ellicott City, MD 21041-0308 410-465-5800
Fax: 410-750-0163 800-735-3585
www.washingtonqualityfoods.com
Baking mixes, flour, cornmeal, batters and breadings
Chairman: Samuel Rogers Jr
Co-CEO: Thomas Rogers
Co-CEO: Samuel Rogers III
R&D/Quality Control: Michael Loverde
Marketing/Sales/Public Relations: Steve Friesner
Plant Manager: Robert Windsor
Estimated Sales: $100+ Million
Number Employees: 150
Type of Packaging: Consumer, Food Service, Private Label, Bulk
Brands:
INDIAN HEAD
RAGA MUFFINS
WASHINGTON

14290 Washington Rhubarb Growers Association
16623 88th St E
Sumner, WA 98390 253-863-7333
Fax: 253-863-2775 800-435-9911
rhubarb@blarg.net
Cooperative of Washington rhubarb growers; also, manufacturer of IQF rhubarb
Manager: Matt Celis
General Manager: Cindy Moore
Estimated Sales: $19 Million
Number Employees: 5-9
Sq. footage: 12000
Type of Packaging: Bulk
Brands:
First Pick
Sumner

14291 Washington State Juice
10725 Sutter Ave
Pacoima, CA 91331-2553 818-899-1195
Fax: 818-899-6042
Manufactures and processes fruit concentrates, blends and natural flavors. Custom blending is available
President: Fred Farago
Estimated Sales: $ .5 - 1 million
Number Employees: 100-249
Type of Packaging: Food Service, Private Label, Bulk

14292 Wasson Brothers Winery
17020 Ruben Ln
Sandy, OR 97055 503-668-3124
Fax: 503-668-3124
www.wassonbrotherswinery.com
Wines
Partner: James Wasson
Partner: John Wasson
Estimated Sales: $ 1-2.5 Million
Number Employees: 1-4
Brands:
Wasson

14293 (HQ)Water Concepts
561 Plate Drive
Suite 1
East Dundee, IL 60118 847-699-9797
Fax: 847-699-9889 waterjoe@waterjoe.com
www.waterconcepts.com
Processor of caffeine enchanced natural artesian water.
Owner: Steve Rodgers
Marketing: Joe Brumfield
Estimated Sales: $300,000-500,000
Number Employees: 1-4
Type of Packaging: Consumer, Food Service
Brands:
Water Joe

14294 Waterfield Farms
500 Sunderland Road
Amherst, MA 01002-1038 413-549-3558
Fax: 413-549-9945 bioshelter@aol.com
www.bioshelters.com
Processor of tilapia fish, basil, tomatoes and pesto sauces
President: John Reid
Vice President: Tracy Hightower
Director of Aquaculture: Dr Jose Llobrera
Estimated Sales: $500-1 Million appx.
Number Employees: 20-49
Type of Packaging: Consumer, Food Service
Brands:
Hydroponic Sweet Basil
Tilapia
Waterfield Farms

14295 Waterfront Seafood
14358 Shell Belt Rd
Bayou La Batre, AL 36509 251-824-2185
Fax: 251-824-4307
Seafood
President: Norwood Cain
Vice President: Nor Cain

14296 Waterfront Seafood Market
2900 University Ave Ste A4
West Des Moines, IA 50266 515-223-5106
Fax: 515-224-9665 waterfrontseafood@msn.com
www.waterfrontseafoodmarket.com
Seafood
President: Ted Hanke
Estimated Sales: $ 3 - 5 Million
Number Employees: 50-99

14297 Watermark Innovation
400 Noyac Rd
Suite A-1
Southampton, NY 11968 631-259-2329
Fax: 631-259-2329 inquiries@purecool.com
www.purecool.com
flavored water
President: Patti Kelly

14298 (HQ)Watson Inc
301 Heffernan Drive
West Haven, CT 06516 203-932-3000
Fax: 203-932-8266 800-388-3481
order@watson-inc.com www.watson-inc.com
Quality products and ingredient systems
Chairman/President/CEO: James Watson
VP R&D: Mike Weibel
VP Sales: Bill Murphy
Estimated Sales: $19700000
Number Employees: 200
Sq. footage: 88000
Type of Packaging: Bulk
Other Locations:
Watson Foods Co.
Rockville CT
Brands:
Oven Spring

14299 Watson Nutritional Ingredients
301 Heffernan Drive
West Haven, CT 06516-4151 203-932-3000
Fax: 203-932-8266
mary.watson@watsonfoods.com
www.watsonfoods.com
Hops, malt, brewers yeast
Estimated Sales: $ 20 - 50 Million
Number Employees: 100-249

14300 Watsons Quality Food Prooducts
P.O.Box 215
Blackwood, NJ 08012 856-228-6756
Fax: 856-228-6756 800-257-7870
sales@watsonsquality.com
www.watsonsquality.com
Processor and packer of poultry and meat
President: Raymond Buseman
Executive Vice President: David Buseman
General Sales Manager: Eddie Skee
Director of Manufacturing: Bill Levis
Estimated Sales: $21000000
Number Employees: 100-249
Type of Packaging: Consumer, Food Service

14301 Waugh Foods
701 Pinecrest Drive
East Peoria, IL 61611 309-427-8000
Fax: 309-694-3115 www.waughfoods.com
Wholesaler/distributor of frozen and refrigerated food, fresh dairy and produce; serving the food service market in Central Illinois
President: John Waugh
CEO: Joe Waugh
VP Sales: Jim Susin
Human Resources Executive: Lori Turner
Operations Manager: Norm Ralph
VP Purchasing: Tim Waugh
Estimated Sales: $20 Million
Number Employees: 85
Sq. footage: 51550

14302 Waverly Crabs
3400 Greenmount Ave
Baltimore, MD 21218-2823 410-243-1181
Fax: 410-243-0348
Crab
Owner: Jane Gordon
Estimated Sales: $ 3 - 5 Million
Number Employees: 10-19

14303 Wawa Food Market
260 Baltimore Pike
Media, PA 19063 610-283-9292
Fax: 610-358-8878 800-444-9292
www.wawa.com
Milk and dairy products
Chairman/CEO: Richard D Wood Jr
President/COO: Howard B Stoeckel
Executive VP: There du Pont
Plant Manager: Dennis Shea
Estimated Sales: $ 100-499.9 Million
Number Employees: 500-999
Brands:
Wawa

14304 Wawona Frozen Foods
100 W Alluvial Ave
Clovis, CA 93611 559-299-2901
Fax: 559-299-1921 peaches@wawona.com
www.wawona.com
Processor and exporter of IQF and syrup packed frozen fruits including peaches, strawberries and mixed fruit; also a variety of fruit-based portion controlled products; importer of frozen fruits including melons, grapes andpineapple
President/Owner: William Smittcamp
COO/VP Finance: Tak Yoshida
Quality Assurance Director: Duncan Donaldbe
Marketing Director: Bill Astin
Sales Director: Toni Lindeleaf
VP Operations: Pete Petersen
Production Manager: Ruben Paraga
Plant Manager: Tim Finley
Purchasing Manager: Ken Cole
Estimated Sales: $55429138
Number Employees: 125
Sq. footage: 125000
Type of Packaging: Consumer, Food Service, Private Label, Bulk
Brands:
SUMMER PRIZE
WAWONA FROZEN FOODS

14305 Wawona Packing Company
12133 Avenue 408
Cutler, CA 93615 559-528-9729
Fax: 559-528-4696 sales@wawonapacking.com
www.wawonapacking.com
Apricots, plums, figs, grapes, peaches, and nectarines
President: Brent Smittcamp
Sales Manager: Tony Supino

Estimated Sales: $35 Billion
Number Employees: 1400
Brands:
SWEET 2 EAT

14306 **Wax Orchards**
P.O.Box 25448
Seattle, WA 98165 206-463-9735
Fax: 206-463-9731 800-634-6132
customerservice@waxorchards.com
www.waxorchards.com
Fat-free, fruit-sweetened preserves and toppings
President: Anna Sestrap
Estimated Sales: $400,000
Number Employees: 5
Sq. footage: 15
Brands:
Wax Orchards

14307 **Way Baking Company**
2100 Enterprise St
Jackson, MI 49203-3410 517-787-6720
Fax: 517-787-3021 800-347-7373
www.perfectionbakeries.com
Processor of baked goods
President: John Pop
Senior VP: Mark Porter
Estimated Sales: $ 20 - 50 Million
Number Employees: 100-249
Brands:
Aunt Millie

14308 **Wayco Ham Company**
506 N William St
Goldsboro, NC 27530 919-735-3962
Fax: 919-734-4080 800-962-2614
tworrell@waycohams.com
www.waycohams.com
Processor of country ham and smoked turkey
President: Tony Worrell
VP: George Howell
Estimated Sales: $4300000
Number Employees: 20-49
Type of Packaging: Consumer, Food Service, Private Label

14309 **Wayfield Foods**
5145 Welcome All Rd SW
Atlanta, GA 30349 404-559-3200
Fax: 404-559-3206 webmaster@teamtatham.com
www.wayfieldfoods.com
General grocery items, frozen foods, meats, dairy, deli items, seafood, produce
President: Ronald Edenfield
Estimated Sales: H
Number Employees: 500-999

14310 **Waymouth Farms**
5300 Boone Ave
New Hope, MN 55428 763-533-5300
Fax: 763-533-9890 800-527-0094
service@waymouth.com
www.goodsensesnacks.com
Dried fruit, nuts, seeds, trail mixes, and other snacks.
President: Gerard Knight
General Manager: Bernie Fashingbauer
Quality Manager: Dean Giroux
Marketing Manager: Kathleen Vargas
Regional Sales Manager: Dan Tusing
Public Relations Director: Gary Mittelbusher
COO: Patrick Knight
Purchasing Manager: Melissa Boeser
Estimated Sales: $32 Million
Number Employees: 210
Number of Brands: 6
Sq. footage: 16240
Type of Packaging: Consumer, Food Service, Private Label, Bulk
Brands:
ALMOND PIZAZZ!
FRUITMATES
FRUITZELS
GOOD SENSE
GOODNIKS
OMEGA MUNCHIES
ORGANIC
POPZELS
SALAD PIZAZZ!
SNACK 'N VEGGIES

14311 **Wayne Dairy Products**
1590 NW 11th St
Richmond, IN 47374-1404 765-935-7521
Fax: 765-935-2184 800-875-9294
www.smithdairy.com
Processor of dairy products including milk, soft serve and hard ice cream and shake mixes
President: Steve Schmid
VP: Ron Them
Sales Manager: Mike Grenert
Estimated Sales: $ 20 - 50 Million
Number Employees: 100-249
Parent Co: Smith Dairy
Type of Packaging: Consumer, Food Service, Bulk
Brands:
Smith Dairy

14312 **Wayne E. Bailey ProduceCompany**
P.O.Box 467
Chadbourn, NC 28431-0467 910-654-5163
Fax: 910-654-4734 800-845-6149
web@sweetpotatoes.com
www.sweetpotatoes.com
Processor of sweet potatoes
CEO/Owner: George Wooten
CFO: Stuart Hill
CEO: George Wooten
Estimated Sales: $ 3 - 5 Million
Number Employees: 5-9
Brands:
Girlwatcher
Playboy
Pride of Samspon

14313 **Wayne Estay Shrimp Company**
PO Box 946 Oak Street
Grand Isle, LA 70358-0946 504-787-2166
Fax: 504-787-3982 877-787-2166
www.wayneestay.com
Fish/Seafood
President: Wayne Estay
Sales Manager: Wayne Estay
Estimated Sales: $300,000
Number Employees: 6

14314 **(HQ)Wayne Farms LLC**
4110 Continental Dr
Oakwood, GA 30566 770-538-2120
Fax: 770-538-2121 800-392-0844
www.waynefarms.com
Manufacturer of poultry
President/CEO: Elton Maddox
VP/CFO/Treasurer: Courtney Fazekas
VP/General Manager, Further Processing: John Flood
VP Quality Assurance/Food Safety: Bryan Miller
Marketing & Communications Director: Alan Sterling
VP/National & Industrial Sales: Mike Hamblin
VP/Fresh Sales: Steve Clever
Foodservice Sales Director: Chris Baldner
VP/Supply Chain & Fresh Operations: Tommy Myers
VP Purchasing: Gary Niedfeldt
Estimated Sales: $1.4 Billion
Number Employees: 8900
Sq. footage: 100000
Parent Co: Continental Grain Company
Type of Packaging: Consumer, Food Service, Private Label
Other Locations:
Wayne Farms
Danville AR
Albertville AL
Union Springs AL
Oakwood GA
Pendergrass GA
Dobson NC
Laurel MS
Wayne Farms Decatur Fresh
Decatur AL
Wayne Farms Decatur Processing East
Decatur AL
Wayne Farms Decatur Processing West
Decatur AL
Brands:
DUTCH QUALITY HOUSE
PLATINUM HARVEST
WAYNE FARMS

14315 **Wayne Farms LLC**
1020 County Road 114
Jack, AL 36346 334-897-3435
www.waynefarms.com
Manufacturer and exporter of fresh and frozen poultry
Manager: Justin Jayroe
Manager: Jack Sherwood
Sq. footage: 42500
Parent Co: Wayne Farms LLC
Type of Packaging: Consumer
Brands:
DUTCH QUALITY HOUSE
PLATINUM HARVEST
WAYNE FARMS

14316 **Wayne Farms LLC**
444 Baskin St S
Union Springs, AL 36089 334-738-2930
Fax: 334-738-2039 www.waynefarms.com
Processor and exporter of poultry
Manager: Craig Vallentine
Parent Co: Wayne Farms LLC
Type of Packaging: Bulk

14317 **Wayne Farms LLC**
977 Wayne Poultry Rd
Pendergrass, GA 30567 706-693-2271
www.waynefarms.com
Processor of fresh and frozen chicken including parts, strips, portion control, appetizers, etc
Manager: Alane Ivory
Parent Co: Wayne Farms LLC
Type of Packaging: Consumer, Food Service, Private Label
Brands:
Dutch Quality House Products
Platinum Harvest Products
Wayne Farms Products

14318 **Wayne Farms LLC**
525 Wayne Drive
Laurel, MS 39440 601-425-4721
www.waynefarms.com
Manufacturer and exporter of fresh and frozen poultry
Manager: Benny Bishop
Sq. footage: 42500
Parent Co: Wayne Farms LLC
Type of Packaging: Consumer

14319 **Wayne Farms LLC**
2299 East 8th Street
Danville, AR 72833 479-495-4400
www.waynefarms.com
Manufacturer and exporter of fresh and frozen poultry
Finance/Plant Manager: Art Callahan
Operations/Production/Mfg Manager: Steve Nolin

Purchasing Director: Eddy Bruce
Sq. footage: 42500
Parent Co: Wayne Farms LLC
Type of Packaging: Consumer

14320 **Wayne Farms LLC**
700 McDonald Ave
Albertville, AL 35950 256-878-3404
www.waynefarms.com
Manufacturer and exporter of fresh and frozen poultry
Director: Scott Cromley
Manager: Tim Holmes
Operations Manager: Charlie Peacock
Sq. footage: 42500
Parent Co: Wayne Farms LLC
Type of Packaging: Consumer

14321 **Wayne Farms LLC**
254 Ipsco Street
Decatur, AL 35601 256-353-0312
www.waynefarms.com
Manufacturer and exporter of fresh and frozen poultry
Branch Manager: Clark Dotts
Sq. footage: 42500
Parent Co: Wayne Farms LLC
Type of Packaging: Consumer

14322 **Wayne Farms LLC**
112 Plugs Drive
Decatur, AL 35601 256-552-4873
www.waynefarms.com
Manufacturer and exporter of fresh and frozen poultry
Manager: Heath Loyd
Sq. footage: 42500
Parent Co: Wayne Farms LLC

Type of Packaging: Consumer

14323 **Wayne Farms LLC**
100 Plugs Drive
Decatur, AL 35601 256-584-7010
www.waynefarms.com
Manufacturer and exporter of fresh and frozen poultry
Manager: Doug Anderson
Director: Sandy Bishop
Sq. footage: 42500
Parent Co: Wayne Farms LLC
Type of Packaging: Consumer

14324 **Wayne Farms LLC**
802 E Atkins St
Dobson, NC 27017 336-386-8022
www.waynefarms.com
Manufacturer and exporter of fresh and frozen poultry
Director: Tammy Bush
Purchasing Director: Joe Best
Sq. footage: 42500
Parent Co: Wayne Farms LLC
Type of Packaging: Consumer

14325 **Weathervane Foods**
15 Linscott Road
Woburn, MA 01801-2001 781-935-5458
Fax: 781-932-4191
General grocery
President: Howard Smillie
Estimated Sales: $340,000
Number Employees: 3

14326 **Weaver Brothers**
417 Dearborn Street
Berne, IN 46711-2012 219-589-2869
Fax: 219-589-3038
Cheese
Marketing Director: Wayne Amstutz

14327 **Weaver Nut Company**
1925 W Main St
Ephrata, PA 17522-1112 717-738-3781
Fax: 717-733-2226 info@weavernut.com
www.weavernut.com
Processor importer and distributor of nuts, dried fruits, candies, confectionery items, snack mixes, gourmet coffees and teas, beans and spices; custom roasting and contract packaging available
President: E Paul Weaver Iii III
Vice President: Michael Reis
Sales Director: Tom Flynn
Estimated Sales: $18000000
Number Employees: 20-49
Number of Products: 3500
Sq. footage: 58000
Type of Packaging: Consumer, Private Label, Bulk
Brands:
Arcor
Asher's
Hershey Chocolate
Jaret
Jelly Belly
Nabisco
Wilbur Chocolate

14328 **(HQ)Weaver Popcorn Company**
14470 Bergen Road
Suite 100
Noblesville, IN 46060 765-934-2101
Fax: 765-934-4052 800-634-8161
consumercare@popweaver.com
www.popweaver.com
Processor and exporter of regular and microwave popcorn; also, caramel popcorn specialties including caramel with almonds and pecans and fat-free.
President/CEO: Michael Weaver
Director Operations: Will Weaver
Estimated Sales: $ 20 - 50 Million
Number Employees: 200
Type of Packaging: Consumer, Food Service, Private Label, Bulk
Brands:
Bonnie Lee
Pop Weaver
Weaver Original

14329 **Weaver Popcorn CompanyManufacturing Facilty**
P.O.Box 395
Van Buren, IN 46991-0395 765-934-2101
Fax: 765-934-4052 800-999-2365
consumercare@popweaver.com OR
webmaster@weaverpopcorn.com
www.popweaver.com
Processor and exporter of regular and microwave popcorn; also, caramel popcorn specialties including caramel with almonds and pecans and fat-free.
President: Michael E Weaver
Founder: Ira Weaver
Director Operations: Will Weaver
Estimated Sales: $ 20 - 50 Million
Number Employees: 100-249
Type of Packaging: Consumer, Food Service, Private Label, Bulk

14330 **Weaver R. Apiaries**
16495 County Road 319
Navasota, TX 77868-9704 936-825-2333
Fax: 936-825-3642 rweaver@tca.net
www.rweaver.com
Processor of honey
President: Richard Weaver
Office Manager: Risa Davis
Estimated Sales: $ .5 - 1 million
Number Employees: 10-19
Sq. footage: 10000
Type of Packaging: Consumer, Food Service, Private Label, Bulk
Brands:
Weaver's

14331 **Webbpak**
P.O.Box 188
Trussville, AL 35173 205-655-3500
Fax: 205-655-3500 800-655-3500
past40@aol.com www.webbpak.com
Processor of vinegar, syrups, sauces, drink mixes and flavorings
President: Peter Calzone
Estimated Sales: $660,000
Number Employees: 1-4
Sq. footage: 10000
Type of Packaging: Consumer, Food Service, Private Label
Brands:
Diamond Joe
Farmers Favorite
Flowing Gold
Formula 18
Johnny Boy Vanilla
Webb's

14332 **Webbs Citrus Candy**
38217 Highway 27
Davenport, FL 33837-7886 863-422-1051
Fax: 863-422-6214 www.citruscandy.com
Processor of mints, lemon drops, taffy, toffee, nougats, glazed and coated nuts, fudge, vanilla and chocolate candies, etc
President: John Webb
Estimated Sales: $1200000
Number Employees: 5-9
Type of Packaging: Consumer, Food Service, Bulk

14333 **Webco Foods**
P.O.Box 228764
Miami, FL 33222-8764
Fax: 305-639-6052 richard@webcofoods.com
www.webecofoods.com
Food
Owner: Luis Teijeiro
Marketing: Richard de la Torre
Estimated Sales: $ 10-20 Million
Number Employees: 20-49
Brands:
Ferrarini

14334 **Weber Flavors**
562 Chaddick Dr
Wheeling, IL 60090-6056 847-215-1980
Fax: 847-215-2073 800-558-9078
info@weberflavors.com www.weberflavors.com
Vanilla, natural and artificial flavors, color selections, cocoa blends
President: Andrew G Plennert
Founder: Edgar A Weber
Estimated Sales: $ 25-50 Million
Number Employees: 50-99
Brands:
Blue Moon
Hy Van
Hy Van Supreme
Simply Natural
Simply Natural Like
Whol-Bean

14335 **Weber-Stephen Products Company**
200 E Daniels Rd
Palatine, IL 60067 847-934-5700
Fax: 847-407-8900 800-446-1071
support@weberstephen.com www.weber.com
Processor of meat products
Owner: Paul Weber
Owner: Evelyn Weber
CEO: James C Stephen Sr
VP Sales: Kevin Wesol
Estimated Sales: $ 50 - 100 Million
Number Employees: 500-999
Brands:
Weber

14336 **Webster City Custom Meats**
1611 E 2nd St
Webster City, IA 50595 515-832-1130
Fax: 515-832-5515 888-786-3287
wccm@webstercitycustommeats.com
www.webstercitycustommeats.com
Processor of smoked ham, smoked bacon, smoked turkeys, fresh sausage products, boneless ham roasts, and smoked pork loins.
President: Dean Bowden
VP Sales & Marketing: Phil Voge
VP Operations: Chip Abbott
Estimated Sales: $20 Million
Number Employees: 150
Sq. footage: 57000
Type of Packaging: Food Service, Private Label

14337 **Webster Farms**
Unit 1
Cambridge Station, NS B0P 1G0
Canada 902-538-9492
Fax: 902-538-7662
Processor of frozen strawberries and rhubarb; also, dry beans
President: Greg Webster
Number Employees: 20-49
Type of Packaging: Consumer, Food Service

14338 **Wechsler Coffee Corporation**
10 Empire Blvd
Moonachie, NJ 7074 212-564-4955
800-800-2633
Processor of gourmet coffee, tea and drink bases; importer of green coffee; wholesaler/distributor of general merchandise and groceries including coffee and tea; serving the food service market
President: Mike O'Donnell
VP Finance: Jim Pypen
Estimated Sales: $300,000-500,000
Number Employees: 10-19
Sq. footage: 100000
Parent Co: Superior Coffee & Foods
Type of Packaging: Food Service, Private Label

14339 **Wedding Cake Studio**
7373 Stanhope Kell Road
Williamsfield, OH 44093 440-667-1765
Fax: 440-293-5573 charity@thecakeloft.net
www.thecakestudio.cc
Cakes and candy
President: Craig Harvey
Estimated Sales: Under $500,000
Number Employees: 1-4
Brands:
Ther Cake Loft

14340 **Wedemeyer Bakery**
314 Harbor Way
South San Francisco, CA 94080 650-873-1000
Fax: 650-873-3170
wedemeyer@wedemeyerbakery.com
www.wedemeyerbakery.com
Processor of hearth bread, sliced bread and specialty rolls.
Owner/President: Laurence Strain
Sales Manager: Howard Hubbard
Estimated Sales: $1 Million
Number Employees: 16
Sq. footage: 7159
Type of Packaging: Consumer, Food Service
Brands:
Better Way

14341 Weetabix Company
20 Cameron St
Clinton, MA 1510 978-368-0991
Fax: 978-365-7268 800-343-0590
info@weetabixusa.com www.weetabixusa.com
Processor of breakfast cereals and specialty grain-based ingredients
President: Richard George
EVP: Chuck Marble
VP R&D: Daniel Dinardo
Quality Assurance Director: Larry Kinnard
VP Maufacturing/Operations: Robert Grosskopf
VP/General Manager: Edward Langley
Purchasing Manager: Bernie Skamarycz
Estimated Sales: $26900000
Number Employees: 280
Sq. footage: 160000
Parent Co: Weetabix
Type of Packaging: Consumer, Food Service, Private Label, Bulk
Brands:
ALPEN
GRAINSFIELD'S
MINIBIX
WEETABIX

14342 Weetabix of Canada
PO Box 2020
Cobourg, ON K9A 5P5
Canada
Fax: 978-365-7268 800-343-0590
www.weetabix.com
Processor and exporter of breakfast cereals and ingredients
Director: A.T. Connell
General Manager: Jeff Bakker
Estimated Sales: $100-500 Million
Number Employees: 200
Number of Brands: 3
Number of Products: 90
Parent Co: Weetabix, Ltd
Type of Packaging: Consumer, Food Service, Private Label, Bulk
Brands:
Alpen
Grain Shop
Weetabix

14343 Wege Pretzel Company
116 N Blettner Ave
Hanover, PA 17331 717-843-0738
Fax: 717-632-4190 800-233-1933
wege@wege.com www.wege.com
Producers of sourdough, whole wheat, organic, butter flavor and specialty pretzels.
President: Ike Laughman
Vice President: Edith Staub
VP Marketing: William Still
Estimated Sales: $8200000
Number Employees: 85
Sq. footage: 110000
Parent Co: LDI
Type of Packaging: Consumer, Food Service, Private Label, Bulk
Brands:
Dutchie
Wege

14344 Wei-Chuan
6655 W Garfield Ave
Bell Gardens, CA 90201-1807 562-372-2020
info@weichuanusa.com
www.weichuanusa.com
Processor, importer and exporter of egg and spring rolls, dumplings and sauces including stir fry, sweet and sour, barbecue, oyster, plum, lemon, soy and hoisin; importer of bamboo shoots, mushrooms, pineapple and baby corn
President: Steve Lin
VP: Ben Chang
Dairy Division Manager: Chiao-hua Chang
Sales Director: Jesse Valdez
VP Production: James Chang
Purchasing Manager: Ming-huang Chiang
Estimated Sales: $ 20 - 50 Million
Number Employees: 250-499
Type of Packaging: Consumer, Food Service, Private Label
Brands:
Farmer King
Golden Foods
Ho-Tai
Lotus
Wei-Chaun
Wei-Chuan

14345 Weibel Champagne Vineyards
PO Box 87
Woodbridge, CA 95258 20- 3-5 94
Fax: 20- 3-5 94 80- 9-2 94
http://www.weibel.com
Wines
President: Fred Weibel Jr
CFO: Bruce Baker
Sales: Douglas Richards
Operations Manager: Gary Habletzel
Estimated Sales: $4.5 Million
Number Employees: 35
Sq. footage: 100
Type of Packaging: Private Label

14346 Weil's Food Processing
483 Erie Street N
Wheatley, ON N0P 2P0
Canada 519-825-4572
Fax: 519-825-7437
Processor of asparagus, canned tomatoes and potatoes
President: Henry Weil
Vice President/Board Member: Robert Weil
Sales: Mark Weil
Estimated Sales: $1-2.5 Million
Number Employees: 10-19
Type of Packaging: Consumer, Food Service, Private Label

14347 Weinberg Foods
11410 NE 124th Street
Suite 264
Kirkland, WA 98034-4305 800-866-3447
Fax: 310-230-9057
weinberg@weinbergfoods.com
www.bakingingredients.com
Processor of kosher egg products, dry milk and vegetable powders; importer of kosher vegetable powders; exporter of kosher egg products
President: W Weinberg
Sales: Ashley Hester
Estimated Sales: $930,000
Number Employees: 4
Sq. footage: 3000
Type of Packaging: Bulk

14348 Weir Sauces
773 Magellan Way
Napa, CA 94559-4747 415-884-5849
Fax: 707-265-2801 kim@weirsuaces.com
www.weirsauces.com
Sauces

14349 Weisenberger Mills
2545 Weisenberger Mill Rd
Midway, KY 40347 859-254-5282
Fax: 859-254-0294 800-643-8678
flourusa@te.net www.weisenberger.com
Processor and exporter of wheat flour, cornmeal and baking mixes including biscuit, pancake, pizza dough, cornbread and hush puppies; exporter of fish batter breading
President: Mac Weisenberger
Vice President: Philip Weisenberger
Estimated Sales: $900000
Number Employees: 5-9
Sq. footage: 16000
Type of Packaging: Consumer, Food Service, Private Label

14350 Weiser River Packing
P.O.Box 773
Weiser, ID 83672 208-549-0200
Fax: 208-549-0503
Processor and exporter of onions
President: Calvin Hickey
Estimated Sales: $1000000
Number Employees: 10-19
Type of Packaging: Consumer, Food Service, Private Label, Bulk
Brands:
Burger Buddies
Head of the Class
Sun Lovin
Weiser River Whoppers

14351 Weiss Brothers Smoke House
132 Norton Rd
Johnstown, PA 15906-2906 814-539-4085
Fax: 814-536-3951
Processor of smoked and Italian sausage, bacon, frankfurters and bologna
President: Walter Grata
Quality Control: Joseph Miller
Estimated Sales: Below $ 5 Million
Number Employees: 5-9

14352 Weiss Homemade Kosher Bakery
5011 13th Ave
Brooklyn, NY 11219 718-438-0407
Fax: 718-438-1872 800-498-3477
Processor of kosher breads, cakes, pastries, rugulach and wedding cakes
President: Abe Weiss
Estimated Sales: $ 1 - 3 Million
Number Employees: 20-49

14353 (HQ)Weiss Noodle Company
31313 Aurora Road
Solon, OH 44139-2705 440-248-4550
Fax: 440-542-7977
Noodles
President: James Price
Estimated Sales: $ 5-10 Million appx.
Number Employees: 20
Brands:
Weiss Noodle

14354 (HQ)Welch's Foods Inc
575 Virginia Road
3 Concord Farms
Concord, MA 01742-9101 978-371-1000
Fax: 978-371-3855 800-340-6870
jcallahan@welchs.com www.welchs.com
Processor of jams, jellies, marmalades, preserves, beverage and frozen dessert bases, juice concentrates, frozen dessert pops and juice including grape, tomato, apple cider, cranberry and cranberry blends.
President/Chief Executive Officer: Bradley Irwin
Chairman: Joseph Falcone
VP/Marketing & Chief Marketing Officer: Matt Wohl
VP/Domestic Sales: Mark Cavano
Corporate Communications Director: Jackie Alosso
VP Operations: David Engelkemeyer
Estimated Sales: $658 Million
Number Employees: 1035
Parent Co: National Grape Cooperative
Type of Packaging: Consumer, Food Service
Brands:
Welch's

14355 Welch's Foods Inc
10 E Brunean Avenue
PO Box 6067
Kennewick, WA 99336-6067 509-582-2131
Fax: 509-586-8882 jcallahan@welchs.com
www.welchs.com
Processor and exporter of grape juice, jellies and jams
Parent Co: Welch Foods
Type of Packaging: Consumer, Food Service

14356 Welch's Foods Inc
749 Middlesex Tpke
Billerica, MA 01821-3900 978-663-3966
jcallahan@welchs.com
www.welchs.com
Research and Technology Center features product, process and package development laboratories along with a pilot plant, product sensory testing facilities and microbiological laboratories in addition to housing all of the Company'sresearch and development, corporate quality assurance and corporate engineering staff.
Sq. footage: 40000
Parent Co: Welch's Foods Inc
Type of Packaging: Consumer, Food Service

14357 Welch's Foods Inc
100 N Portage St
Westfield, NY 14787-1054 716-326-5252
Fax: 716-326-5494 jcallahan@welchs.com
www.welchs.com
Bulk grape juice concentrate
Parent Co: Welch's

14358 **Welch's Foods Inc.**
139 S Lake St
North East, PA 16428 814-725-4577
Fax: 814-725-1087 jcallahan@welchs.com
www.welchs.com
Manufacturer and exporter of fruit jellies, jams, juices, drinks and frozen concentrates.
Sq. footage: 530000
Parent Co: Welch's Foods
Type of Packaging: Consumer, Food Service

14359 **Welch, Home & Clark Company**
7 Avenue L
Newark, NJ 07105-3805 973-465-1200
Fax: 973-465-7332 whc@welch-holme-clark.com
www.welch-holme-clark.com
Sells and distributes: refined, USP/NF, crude and kosher vegetable oils.
President: William Dugan
Estimated Sales: $ 10 - 20 Million
Number Employees: 10-19
Type of Packaging: Bulk

14360 **Welcome Dairy**
H4489 Maple Rd
Colby, WI 54421 715-223-2874
Fax: 715-223-3958 800-472-2315
info@welcomedairy.com
www.welcomedairy.com
Manufacturer of cheese, sauces, spreads and smoked products
President: Terry Eggebrecht
Estimated Sales: $ 50 - 100 Million
Number Employees: 50-99
Type of Packaging: Consumer
Brands:
WELCOME DAIRY

14361 **Weldon Ice Cream Company**
2887 Canal Dr
Millersport, OH 43046 740-467-2400
mgmt@weldons.com
www.weldons.com
Processor of ice cream including novelties, sandwiches, creamsicles and fudgecicles
Owner: David Pierce
Estimated Sales: $460000
Number Employees: 5-9
Type of Packaging: Consumer, Food Service, Bulk

14362 **Well Dressed Food Company**
PO Box 1207
Tupper Lake, NY 12986 866-567-0845
Fax: 518-618-3147
salesA@welldressedfoods.com
www.welldressedfoods.com
breakfast mixes, sweet & savory jams, crunchy granola, dessert mixes, sauces/rubs and honey & toppings
President/Owner: David Tomberlin

14363 **Well Pict Berries**
209 Riverside Rd
Watsonville, CA 95076-3656 831-722-3871
Fax: 831-722-6041 dan@wellpict.com
www.well-pict.com
Packer and grower of strawberries
President: Timothy Miyasaka
CFO: George Schaaf
General Manager: Eric Miyasaka
Quality Control: Keith Bungo
Estimated Sales: $ 30-50 Million
Number Employees: 20-49

14364 **Wellington Brewing**
950 Woodlawn Road W
Guelph, ON N1K 1B8
Canada 519-837-2337
Fax: 519-837-3142 800-576-3853
mail@wellingtonbrewery.ca
www.wellingtonbrewery.ca
Processor of beer, ale, lager and stout
Office Manager: Faith Laird
President: Michael Stiirrup
CEO: Doug Darkens
Number Employees: 10-19
Type of Packaging: Consumer, Food Service
Brands:
Beehive
Black Knight
Countryale
Iron Uke
Spa
Trailhead

14365 **Wellington Foods**
1930 California Ave
Corona, CA 92881 562-989-0111
Fax: 562-989-9322
tharnacksr@wellingtonfoods.com
www.wellingtonfoods.com
Health foods and institutional foods
Owner: Anthony Harnack Sr
Estimated Sales: $ 2.5-5 Million
Number Employees: 20-49
Brands:
Wellington Foods

14366 **(HQ)Wells' Dairy**
1 Blue Bunny Dr SW
Le Mars, IA 51031 712-546-4000
Fax: 712-548-3011 800-942-3800
www.wellsdairy.com
Manufacturer of frozen novelties, milk, sour cream, yogurt, sherbert, juice, cottage cheese, and snack dip
President/CEO: Michael Wells
SVP/CFO: Mark Garth
SVP Marketing/R&D: Jim Reynolds
SVP Sales: Mike Crone
SVP Human Resources: Jeff Stanley
SVP Operations: David Lyons
Estimated Sales: $1 Billion
Number Employees: 2,800
Type of Packaging: Consumer, Food Service, Bulk
Other Locations:
Ice Cream Plant
St. George UT
Brands:
BLUE BUNNY®
BOMBPOP

14367 **Welsh Farms**
1 Schuyler
Edison, NJ 08817-3521 732-985-0729
Fax: 732-918-8253 800-221-0663
Processor of powdered milk, buttermilk, ice cream and juice
President: Scott Korman
General Manager: Robert Pailillo
Estimated Sales: $1-2.5 Million
Number Employees: 5-9
Sq. footage: 90000
Parent Co: Welsh Farms
Type of Packaging: Consumer, Food Service
Brands:
Welsh Farms - Ice Cream

14368 **Welsh Farms**
1330 Main Ave
Clifton, NJ 7011 973-772-2388
Fax: 973-403-0180
Processor of ice cream and frozen yogurt
Owner: Atul Patel
General Manager: Robert Pailillo
Plant Manager: Joe Marscovetta
Number Employees: 20-49
Type of Packaging: Consumer, Food Service

14369 **Welsh Farms**
205 Spruce St
Newark, NJ 07108-2627 973-642-3000
Fax: 732-918-8253
Dairy
Estimated Sales: Under $500,000
Number Employees: 5-9

14370 **Wendy's International**
1 Dave Thomas Blvd
Dublin, OH 43017 614-764-3100
Fax: 614-785-4100 800-937-5449
www.wendys.com
Grocery
Project Manager: Stacey Resnick
CFO: Jay Fitzsimmons
VP: Dennis Farraw
Investor Shareholder Relations Specialis: Marsha Gordon
Estimated Sales: $ 20 - 50 Million
Number Employees: 500-999

14371 **WendySue & Tobey's**
15530 Broadway Center St
Gardena, CA 90248 310-516-9705
Fax: 310-516-0876 info@wendysue-tobeys.com
www.wendysue-tobeys.com
Bakery
President: John Roberts
Plant Manager: John Roberts
Estimated Sales: Below $ 5 Million
Number Employees: 20-49
Type of Packaging: Private Label

14372 **Wenger's Bakery**
900 N 10th St
Reading, PA 19604 610-372-6545
info_wenger's@aol.com
Buns, pies, cakes, breads, cookies and pastries
Owner: Javiar Martinez
Marketing Director: Peter Menicucci
Estimated Sales: $500,000
Number Employees: 20-49
Type of Packaging: Consumer

14373 **Wengers Springbrook Cheese**
12805 N Spring Brook Rd
Davis, IL 61019-9719 815-865-5855
wengers@statelineisp.com
Processor of Swiss and muenster cheeses
President: Fred Wenger
Vice President: John Wenger
Estimated Sales: $ .5 - 1 million
Number Employees: 5-9
Type of Packaging: Consumer, Private Label, Bulk

14374 **(HQ)Wengert's Dairy**
2401 Walnut St
Lebanon, PA 17042 717-273-2658
Fax: 717-273-2794 800-222-2129
Processor of milk including 2% and skim; also, chilled orange juice, iced tea and fruit drinks
General Manager: Mike Eiceman
Co-President: John Wengert
Chairman: Harlan Wengert
Estimated Sales: $500,000-$1 Million
Number Employees: 100-249
Sq. footage: 30000
Type of Packaging: Consumer, Food Service, Private Label
Other Locations:
Wengert's Dairy
Camp Hill PA
Brands:
Swiss 2
Swiss Premium
Swiss Premium

14375 **Wenk Foods Inc**
P.O.Box 368
Madison, SD 57042 605-256-4569
Fax: 605-256-3204 wfi@hcpd.com
www.wenkfoods.com
Processor and exporter of frozen and dried egg products; also, frozen whole geese
President: William Wenk
Sales Director: Norbert Moldan
Number Employees: 50-99
Sq. footage: 30000
Type of Packaging: Consumer, Food Service, Private Label, Bulk
Brands:
Wenk

14376 **Wenner Bread Products**
33 Rajon Rd
Bayport, NY 11705 631-563-6262
Fax: 631-563-6546 800-869-6262
sales@wennerbread.com
www.wenner-bread.com
Processor of frozen unbaked bread products including egg twist rolls, Italian bread, bagels, hard rolls, challah and specialty breads; also, par-baked breads and rolls.
CEO/General Manager: Richard Wenner
VP National Sales: Andrew Pisani
Technical Sales Manager: Nancy Cappola
Estimated Sales: $100+ Million
Number Employees: 250-499
Sq. footage: 72000
Type of Packaging: Food Service, Private Label, Bulk
Brands:
Rustica
Wenner

14377 **Wente Brothers Estate Winery**
5565 Tesla Rd
Livermore, CA 94550-9149 925-456-2300
Fax: 925-456-2301 info@wentevineyards.com
www.wentevineyards.com

Wines
President: Peter Chouinard
CEO: Eric Wente
CFO: Gary Ventling
Executive VP: Philip Wente
Marketing Manager: Christine Wente
Operations Manager: Antonio Zaccheo
Production Manager: William Joslin
Estimated Sales: $ 50-100 Million
Number Employees: 250-499
Brands:
Crane Ridge Merlot
Riva Ranch Chardonnay

14378 Wenzel's Bakery
125 E Broad Street
Tamaqua, PA 18252-2007 570-668-2360
Baked goods
President: George Wenzel Jr
Estimated Sales: $76,000
Number Employees: 3
Type of Packaging: Consumer

14379 Werling & Sons Slaughterhouse
100 S Plum Street
Burkettsville, OH 45310 937-338-3281
Fax: 419-375-4187 www.werlingandsons.com
Processor of meat products and hydrogenated fats; custom slaughtering available
Owner/Marketing Manager: Edward Werling
VP Sales/Marketing: James Werling
Estimated Sales: $ 5 - 10 Million
Number Employees: 10
Sq. footage: 4438
Type of Packaging: Consumer, Bulk

14380 Wermuth Winery
3942 Silverado Trl
Calistoga, CA 94515 707-942-5924
Wines
Estimated Sales: $500,000-$1 Million
Number Employees: 1-4

14381 Wesco International
PO Box 7870
Alhambra, CA 91802-7870 626-441-3879
Fax: 626-441-8087

14382 Wessanan
420 W Broadway Avenue
Minneapolis, MN 55411 612-331-3775
Fax: 612-378-8398
Milk, dairy products-noncheese
President: Tim Green
VP Sales: Pat Graiziger
Plant Manager: John Gronholm
Number Employees: 100-249
Brands:
Clover Leaf

14383 West Bay Fishing
RR 1
Box 752
Gouldsboro, ME 04607-9753 207-963-2392
Fax: 207-963-7403
Seafood
President: Richard Noble

14384 West Brothers Lobster
830 Pigeon Hill Rd
Steuben, ME 04680 207-546-3622
Fax: 207-255-3987
Lobster
Owner: Blair West
Estimated Sales: $300,000-500,000
Number Employees: 1-4

14385 West Central Turkeys
704 N Broadway
Pelican Rapids, MN 56572 218-863-6800
Fax: 218-863-3171 www.jennieo.com
Processor and exporter of turkey
Superintendent: Roger Stephenson
Plant Manager: Don Cole
Estimated Sales: $$20-50 Million
Number Employees: 500-999
Parent Co: Jennie-O Foods
Type of Packaging: Consumer, Bulk

14386 West Coast Products Corporation
717 Tehama St
Orland, CA 95963 530-865-3379
Fax: 530-865-1581 800-382-3072
www.westcoastproducts.net
Manufacturer and exporter of specialty olives and olive oil
President: Estelle Krackov
Estimated Sales: $380,000
Number Employees: 5
Sq. footage: 4652
Type of Packaging: Food Service, Bulk
Brands:
OLINDA

14387 West Coast Specialty Coffee
8 Adrian Court
Burlingame, CA 94010 650-259-9308
Fax: 650-259-8024 rh@specialtycoffee.com
www.specialtycoffee.com
Coffee and coffee equipment and supplies
President: Robert Hensley
Estimated Sales: $500,000
Number Employees: 2
Type of Packaging: Consumer, Food Service, Bulk

14388 West Field Farm
28 Worcester Rd
Hubbardston, MA 01452-1139 978-928-5110
Fax: 978-928-5745 877-777-3900
info@chevre.com www.chevre.com
Processor of surface ripened and fresh goat cheese
President: Robert Stetson
Estimated Sales: $500,000-$1 Million
Number Employees: 5-9
Sq. footage: 3000
Type of Packaging: Consumer, Food Service
Brands:
Capri
Classic Blue
Hubbardson Blue

14389 West India Trading Company
2086 Route 950
Petit-Cap, NB E4N 2J7
Canada 506-577-6214
Processor of smoked herring with bones and boneless
Parent Co: West India Trading Company
Type of Packaging: Bulk
Brands:
Wico

14390 (HQ)West Liberty Foods
207 W 2nd St
West Liberty, IA 52776 319-627-2126
Fax: 319-627-6334 888-511-4500
wlfsales@wlfoods.com www.wlfoods.com
Co-Manufacturer of ready-to-eat sliced processed meat, poultry and protein products
Manager: Carolyn Aranday
Chairman: Paul Hill
VP Business Development: Charles Cook
Estimated Sales: $100+ Million
Number Employees: 1,000-4,999
Sq. footage: 270000
Parent Co: Iowa Turkey Growers Cooperative
Type of Packaging: Consumer, Food Service, Private Label
Other Locations:
West Liberty Foods Plant
Mt Pleasant IA
West Liberty Foods Plant
Sigourney IA

14391 West Pac
9671 N 5th E
Idaho Falls, ID 83401-5637 801-973-7400
Fax: 801-973-7436 800-973-7407
Processor of cake mixes, barbecue sauces and spices; contract packager of liquid and dry mixes in cans, bottles and boxes
President: Hal Havens
Number Employees: 5-9
Sq. footage: 20000
Type of Packaging: Consumer, Private Label
Brands:
Gourmet Spices

14392 West Pak Avocado
42322 Avenida Alvarado
Temecula, CA 92590 951-296-5757
Fax: 951-296-5744 800-266-4414
matt@westpakavocado.com www.wpavo.com
Importer, exporter and packer of avocados; importer of Mexican and Chilean fruits; processor of persimmons and kumquats
Owner: Galen Newhouse
Import Export Director: Dave Culpeper
VP/General Manager: Galen Newhouse
Estimated Sales: $ 3 - 5 Million
Number Employees: 50-99
Sq. footage: 22000
Type of Packaging: Consumer, Food Service, Bulk
Brands:
Asian Star
West Pak

14393 West Park Wine Cellars
P.O.Box 280
West Park, NY 12493 845-384-6709
Fax: 845-384-6709 www.westparkwinery.com
Wines
President: Louis Fiore
Estimated Sales: Under $300,000
Number Employees: 1-4
Type of Packaging: Private Label
Brands:
Full Service Caterin

14394 West Point Dairy Products
1715 E Rd
West Point, NE 68788 402-372-5551
Fax: 402-372-5061 info@westpointdairy.com
www.westpointdairy.com
Dairy products including butter
President: Susan Peckham
Vice President: Mark Peckham
Production Manager: Valen Neesen
Estimated Sales: $ 20-50 Million
Number Employees: 50-99
Type of Packaging: Private Label
Brands:
COUNTRY CREAM BUTTER

14395 Westar Nutrition Corporation
1239 Victoria St
Costa Mesa, CA 92627-3933 949-645-6100
Fax: 949-645-9131 800-645-1868
cs@vivalife.com www.vivalife.com
Processor of nutraceuticals and nutritional supplements
President: David Fan
National Sales Manager: Cheryl Cartwright
Technical Director: Simon Hsia PhD
Estimated Sales: $29800000
Number Employees: 20-49

14396 Westbend Vinyards
5394 Williams Rd
Lewisville, NC 27023-8278 336-945-5032
Fax: 336-945-5294 866-901-5032
westbendvineyards@alltel.net
www.westbendvineyards.com
Wine
Owner: Jack Kroustalis
Manager: Steve Shepard
Estimated Sales: $500,000-$1 Million
Number Employees: 10-19

14397 (HQ)Westbrae Natural Foods
58 S Service Rd
Melville, NY 11747 631-730-2200
Fax: 631-730-2550 800-434-4246
www.westbrae.com
Processor, importer and exporter of natural and organic soy and rice beverages, tortilla and potato chips, soups, beans, chili, condiments, sauces, rice cakes, popcorn, pretzels, licorice, cookies, spreads and Oriental foods
President/CEO: Irwin Simon
COO: James Meiers
CFO/EVP: Ira Lamel
Number Employees: 1,000-4,999
Sq. footage: 39000
Type of Packaging: Consumer, Private Label
Brands:
Bearitos
Little Bear Organic
Westbrae Natural
Westsoy

14398 Westbrook Trading Company
3410b Odgen Road SE
Calgary, AB T2G 4N5
Canada 403-290-0860
Fax: 403-264-3017 800-563-5785
Processor and exporter of fresh, frozen and boxed beef and pork
President: Michael Nutik
Sales Manager: Daren Uens
Number Employees: 100-249
Type of Packaging: Consumer, Food Service, Bulk

14399 **Westco Bakemark**
7351 Crider Ave
Pico Rivera, CA 90660-3705 562-949-1054
Fax: 562-948-2655 800-695-5061
bakemark@bakemark.com www.bakemark.com
Baked goods
President: Larry Sullivan
Marketing Coordinator: Mitchelle Munguia
VP: Bruce Reynolds
Marketing/Sales Manager: James Parker
Operations Manager: Don Roby
Manufacturing Manager: Allan Schmidt
Estimated Sales: $ 20-50 Million
Number Employees: 250-499
Type of Packaging: Private Label
Brands:
Aloha Dandy
Apricot Dandy
Brite White Icing Bay
Carribean Bouquet
Ellison Moist Muffin
No Time Bread Base
No Time Bread Condit
Pie Do Aid
Reserve Cabernet Sauvignon
Supreme Date

14400 **Westco-Bake Mark**
7351 Crider Ave
Pico Rivera, CA 90660-3705 562-949-1054
Fax: 562-949-1257 www.bakemarkusa.com
Processor, importer and exporter of ingredients and supplies including mixes, fillings, icings and frozen products for the baking, food processing and food service industries
President: William Day
SVP, Operations: James Parker
Estimated Sales: $ 20 - 50 Million
Number Employees: 250-499
Parent Co: CSM
Type of Packaging: Food Service, Bulk
Other Locations:
Westco-BakeMark
Oklahoma City OK

14401 **Westdale Foods Company**
14541 S 88th Ave
Orland Park, IL 60462-2752 708-458-7774
Fax: 708-458-1298 westdalefoods@AOL.com
www.westdalefoods.com
Candy
Owner: Tom Vandervliet
Estimated Sales: $ 5-10 Million
Number Employees: 10-19
Brands:
Sachers
Schluckwerder
Schumann's
Schwarteau
Siljans
Simpkins
Smooth & Melty
Soldans

14402 **Western Bagel Baking Corporation**
7814 Sepulveda Blvd
Van Nuys, CA 91405-1062 818-786-5847
Fax: 818-787-3221 wbinfo@westernbagel.com
www.westernbagel.com
Processor and exporter of fresh and frozen bagels.
President: Steve Ustin
Vice President: Skip Scheidt
Operations Manager: Jim Schultz
Estimated Sales: $29280131
Number Employees: 250-499
Sq. footage: 30000
Brands:
Western

14403 **Western Beef Jerky**
7209 101 Avenue NW
Edmonton, AB T6A 0H9
Canada 780-469-4817
Fax: 780-468-5006
Processor of beef jerky
President: Danny Ljubsa
Estimated Sales: A
Number Employees: 1-4
Type of Packaging: Consumer

14404 **Western Dairy Products**
3625 Westwind Boulevard
Santa Rosa, CA 95403-1067 707-524-6770
Fax: 707-524-6777 800-433-2479
Dairy products
President: Graeme Honeyfield
Estimated Sales: $140,000
Number Employees: 2

14405 **Western Dairymen Corporation**
10220 N. Ambassador Dr.
Kansas City, MO 64153 816-801-6455
webmail@dfamilk.com
www.dfamilk.com
Cheese
Manager: Don Hansen
Estimated Sales: $ 50 - 100 Million
Number Employees: 100-249

14406 **Western Dressing**
PO Box 276
Grundy Center, IA 50638-0276 319-824-3304
Fax: 319-824-3304
Desserts
President: Emmet O'Sullivan
Estimated Sales: $ 5-10 Million
Number Employees: 50

14407 **Western Flavors & Fragrances**
2441 Constitution Dr
Livermore, CA 94551 925-373-9433
Fax: 925-373-6257 info@wffsensory.com
www.wffsensory.com
Processor and exporter of flavors including vanilla, citrus and vegetable extracts for use in dairy, beverages, health foods, confectionery, cereals, etc
President: Richard Grame
COO: Adib Nassar
vp: Gary Pryor
Marketing Director: Robert Gabriel
Public Relations: Nicki Turrin
Purchasing Manager: Roberta Kashiwase
Estimated Sales: $ 50 - 100 Million
Number Employees: 25
Sq. footage: 20000

14408 **Western Foods**
P.O.Box 194060
Little Rock, AR 72219-4060 501-562-4646
Fax: 501-568-3447
Wholesaler/distributor of groceries, frozen foods, meats, cleaning supplies, disposables, table top needs, etc.; serving the food service market
President: Tony Huffman
Vice President: Ed Fason
Estimated Sales: $20-50 Million
Number Employees: 100-249

14409 **Western Meats**
P.O.Box 4185
Rapid City, SD 57709-4185 605-342-0322
Fax: 605-342-5375 bando@rapidnet.com
Processor of meat including beef and buffalo
President: Bruce Anderson
Secretary: Gail Hise
Plant Manager: Al Holzer
Estimated Sales: $ 10 - 20 Million
Number Employees: 20-49
Sq. footage: 8000
Type of Packaging: Consumer, Food Service, Private Label, Bulk

14410 **Western Meats**
4101 Capitol Blvd SW
Tumwater, WA 98501-4069 360-357-6601
Processor of beef and pork
President: Dennis Mydlar
Estimated Sales: $500,000-$1 Million
Number Employees: 10-19
Type of Packaging: Consumer, Food Service

14411 **Western New York Syrup Corporation**
P.O.Box 334b
Lakeville, NY 14480-0910 585-346-2311
Processor of liquid sweeteners
Manager: Tim Calway
Assistant Manager: Lee Robinson
Estimated Sales: $ 5 - 10 Million
Number Employees: 1-4
Parent Co: Archer Daniels Midland Company
Type of Packaging: Bulk

14412 **Western Pacific Commodities**
3225 Cooper Creek Drive
Henderson, NV 89074-6982 702-382-8880
Fax: 702-320-8889
info@westernpacificcommodities.com
www.wpcommodities.com
Importer of Asian food products, including rice, exporter of rice and ingredients, plus agricultural commodities such as beef, poultry, wheat, corn, barley, rice, coffee, sorghum and soybean
President: Kevin Lougheed
Estimated Sales: $ 22 Million
Number Employees: 10-19
Number of Brands: 15
Number of Products: 220
Sq. footage: 24000
Type of Packaging: Consumer, Food Service, Private Label, Bulk
Brands:
Bushel In A Box
Emperor's Choice
Lucky Triple 888
Royal Pacific Foods

14413 **Western Sugar Cooperative**
7555 E Hampden Ave
Suite 600
Denver, CO 80231-4837 303-830-3939
Fax: 303-830-3941 www.westernsugar.com
Processor of beet sugar
Director/Chairman: Kevin Hall
CEO: Inder Mathur
CFO: Greg Huff
Retail Sales: Ricky Saul
Industrial Sales: Brad Hahn
Operations Manager: Gary Price
Estimated Sales: $251,100,000
Number Employees: 600
Type of Packaging: Consumer, Private Label, Bulk
Brands:
GW

14414 **Western Syrup Company**
13766 Milroy Pl
Santa Fe Springs, CA 90670 562-921-4485
Fax: 562-921-5170
Processor and exporter of custom formulated beverage bases, concentrates, flavors and flavor emulsions for carbonated beverages, slushes, sno-cones, etc.; also, dessert toppings including chocolate syrup, fudge and fruit
President: Pushpa Sastry
Sales Director: Ken Molder
Plant Manager: Marlon King
Estimated Sales: $ 3 - 5 Million
Number Employees: 5-9
Sq. footage: 55000
Parent Co: Western Syrup Company
Brands:
Bartenders Pride
High Mountains
Rooster
Western Syrup

14415 **Westfield Farm**
28 Worcester Rd
Hubbardston, MA 01452 978-928-5110
Fax: 978-928-5745 877-777-3900
info@chevre.com www.chevre.com
Goat and cow cheeses
President: Robert Stetson
VP Marketing: Debby Stetson
Marketing Director: Bob Stetson
Sales Director: Debby Stetson
Estimated Sales: $500,000-$1 Million
Number Employees: 5-9
Brands:
Capri Goat Cheese
Hubbardston Blue

14416 **Westfield Foods**
19 Lark Industrial Pkwy Unit F
Greenville, RI 2828 401-949-3558
Fax: 401-949-3738 info@milliessoups.com
www.milliessoups.com
Processor of dry soup and rice mixes; also, chili
President: John Pezzillo
Estimated Sales: $130000
Number Employees: 1-4
Sq. footage: 8500
Type of Packaging: Consumer, Food Service
Brands:
Millie's

14417 (HQ)Westin
11808 W Center Rd
Suite 1
Omaha, NE 68144-4435 402-691-8800
Fax: 402-691-7920 800-228-6098
www.feasterfoods.com
Processor of bacon bits, imitation bacon bits, lecithin, onion rings, breaded cheese, sunflower seeds, soy products, corn starch, salad dressings, sauces, etc.; importer of olives; exporter of frozen breaded vegetables
Chairman/Ceo: Richard Westin Sr
CEO/President: Scott Carlson
Number Employees: 100-249
Type of Packaging: Consumer, Food Service, Private Label, Bulk
Other Locations:
Westin
Wahoo NE
Brands:
BIG RED
FAIRBURY
FEASTER FOODS
GREAT AMERICAN

14418 Westlam Foods
P.O.Box 1987
Chino, CA 91708-1987 909-627-7535
Fax: 909-628-1030 800-722-9519
Manufacturer of dry and dehydrated beans, rice and popcorn
President: Carl Hartman
Estimated Sales: $50-100 Million
Number Employees: 20-49
Sq. footage: 80000
Parent Co: Trinidad/Benham Corporation
Type of Packaging: Consumer, Food Service, Private Label, Bulk
Brands:
EVANS
PEAK COOKQUIK
VALLEY FARMS

14419 Westnut
P.O.Box 626
Cornelius, OR 97113-626
Fax: 503-538-8924 sales@westnut.com
www.westnut.com
Nuts, hazelnuts
Estimated Sales: $ 5-10 Million
Number Employees: 40

14420 Weston Bakeries
1425 the Queensway
Etobicoke, ON M8Z 1T3
Canada 416-252-7323
Fax: 416-252-8941
Processor and exporter of bread, rolls, English muffins and stuffings
President: Ralph Robinson
Number Employees: 250-499
Parent Co: George Weston Foods
Type of Packaging: Consumer, Food Service

14421 Weston Bakeries
5819 2nd Street SW
Calgary, AB T2H 0H3
Canada 403-259-1500
Fax: 403-259-6494
Customer_Service@weston.ca
www.weston.ca
Processor of bread, rolls and stuffing
General Manager: Ed Holik
VP Sales/Distribution: Norm Skelton
Production/Technical Manager: Pat Boswell
Number Employees: 100-249
Parent Co: Weston Bakeries
Brands:
Casa Mendosa
Country Harvest
D'Italiano
Deli-World
Wonder

14422 Weston Bakeries
83 Railway Street
Kingston, ON K7K 2L7
Canada 613-548-4434
Fax: 613-548-8480 800-267-0229
Processor of bread and rolls
Branch Manager: Larry Brandt
Plant Manager: Larry Brandt
Number Employees: 50-99
Sq. footage: 50000
Parent Co: Weston Bakeries
Type of Packaging: Consumer, Food Service
Brands:
Weston

14423 Weston Bakeries
462 Eastern Ave
Toronto, ON M4M 1C3
Canada 416-465-1161
Fax: 416-465-1162 800-590-6861
customer_service@weston.ca www.weston.ca
Processor of bread, rolls and English muffins
President: Ralph Robinson
National Commosion Manager: Julian Franklin
Plant Coordinator: Jim Hennessey
Purchasing Agent: Colin Bellenger
Number Employees: 250-499
Parent Co: Weston Bakeries
Type of Packaging: Consumer, Food Service
Brands:
Weston

14424 Westport Locker Service
707 S West St
Westport, IN 47283-9116 812-591-3033
877-265-0551
Processor of meat products including beef, lamb and pork
Owner: Ben Davis
Estimated Sales: $ 3 - 5 Million
Number Employees: 5-9

14425 Westport Rivers Vineyard& Winery
417 Hixbridge Rd
Westport, MA 02790 508-636-3423
Fax: 508-636-4133 800-993-9695
retail@westportrivers.com
www.westportrivers.com
Wine jellies, wine ketchup, wine mustards, wines, champagne
President: Robert Russell
Vice President: Carol Russell
Owner: Carol Russell
Sales Director: Jan Potts
Estimated Sales: $ 1.5 Million
Number Employees: 10-19
Number of Brands: 2
Number of Products: 15
Sq. footage: 2700
Type of Packaging: Private Label
Brands:
Westport Farms Sparkling
Westport Farms Specialty Foods
Westport Farms White & Rose
Westport Rivers Vine

14426 Westway Trading Corporation
16450 36th St SE
Mapleton, ND 58059 701-282-5010
Fax: 701-281-2695 www.westwaytrading.com
Processor and exporter of molasses
CEO: James Jenkins
CFO: Tom Masilla
Estimated Sales: $ 5 - 10 Million
Number Employees: 10-19
Type of Packaging: Bulk

14427 Westwood Winery
11 E Napa St
Suite 3
Sonoma, CA 95476-6708 707-935-3246
Fax: 707-935-3286 info@westwoodwine.com
www.westwoodwine.com
Wines
Founder: Umbert Urch
Co-Owner: Betty Urch
Estimated Sales: $210,000
Number Employees: 4
Brands:
Stanley's
Westwood Winery

14428 Wet Planet Beverage
7 Purcell Court
Monachie, NJ 07074
US 201-288-1999
donna@joltcola.com
www.wetplanet.com
Processor of root beer, spring water and colas; also, sports, guaranas and ginseng drinks
CEO: Robert Clamp
CFO: Katherine Butkevich
Estimated Sales: E
Number Employees: 5-9
Type of Packaging: Consumer, Food Service
Brands:
Blubotol
Blue Bottle
Cronk 2 O
First Tec
Jolt
Jolt-Cola
Pirate's Keg
Pirates Keg
XTC

14429 Wetherby Cranberry Company
3365 Auger Rd
Warrens, WI 54666 608-378-4813
Fax: 608-378-3157 wetherby@mwt.net
www.freshcranberries.com
Processor of cranberries
Owner: Nodji Van Wichen
Owner/CEO: James Van Wychen
Estimated Sales: $ .5 - 1 million
Number Employees: 1-4
Type of Packaging: Consumer, Bulk
Brands:
Wetherby

14430 Wetta Egg Farm
2909 N 263rd Street W
Andale, KS 67001-9647 316-445-2231
Fax: 316-444-2468
Processor of eggs and egg products
President: Louis Wetta
Vice President: Earl Wetta
Estimated Sales: $ 1 - 3 Million
Number Employees: 5-9
Type of Packaging: Consumer, Food Service

14431 Weyand Fisheries
471 Biddle Ave
Wyandotte, MI 48192 734-284-0400
Fax: 734-284-2671 800-521-9815
carolyn@weyandfish.com www.weyandfish.com
Processor of fresh, frozen and batter-dipped fish
President: David Blume
Vice President: Carolyn Smith
Plant Manager: Richard Weyand
Estimated Sales: $5932554
Number Employees: 17
Sq. footage: 16000
Type of Packaging: Consumer, Food Service, Private Label, Bulk

14432 Weyauwega Star Dairy
114 W Main St
Weyauwega, WI 54983 920-867-2870
Fax: 920-867-3325 www.wegastardairy.com
Cheese
President: James Knaus
Sales Director: Debby Stetson
Estimated Sales: $ 10-20 Million
Number Employees: 50-99
Brands:
Weyauwega Star Dairy

14433 Whaler Vineyard Winery
6200 Old River Rd
Ukiah, CA 95482-9657 707-462-6355
Fax: 707-462-6353
Wines
President: Russ Nyborg
CFO: Tara Larwood
VP Marketing/VP Operations: Ann Nyborg
Estimated Sales: $500,000-$1 Million
Number Employees: 1-4
Type of Packaging: Private Label
Brands:
Flagship Shiraz
Flagship Zinfandel
Whaler Vineyard Flag

14434 Whaley Pecan Company
P.O.Box 609
Troy, AL 36081-0609 334-566-3504
Fax: 334-566-9336 800-824-6827
info@whaleypecan.com www.whaleypecan.com
Processors of shelled pecans and some exports
President: Robert Whaley

Estimated Sales: $5,000,000
Number Employees: 20-49
Sq. footage: 40000
Type of Packaging: Consumer, Food Service, Bulk
Brands:
Whaley's
Whaley's Fancy Shelled

14435 **Wham Food & Beverage**
519 South 21st Avenue
Hollywood, FL 33020-5015 954-920-7857
Fax: 954-920-9587 Jon@whamfoods.com
www.whamfoods.com
Liquidator of food and beverage closeouts by the truckload
President/CEO: Jonathon Auspitz
VP: Adam Busch
Marketing/Sales: Adam Busch
Estimated Sales: $1.5 Million
Number Employees: 8
Number of Brands: 40
Number of Products: 248
Type of Packaging: Consumer, Food Service, Private Label, Bulk

14436 **Wharton Seafood Sales**
P.O.Box 440
Paauilo, HI 96776-0440 808-776-1087
Fax: 877-591-8944 800-352-8507
Seafood
President: Bailey Wharton
Estimated Sales: Less than $100,000
Number Employees: 1-4

14437 **What's Brewing**
138 W Rhapsody Dr
San Antonio, TX 78216 210-308-8883
Fax: 210-308-6522
Beer
President: Roger Chbeir
Estimated Sales: $1.5 Million
Number Employees: 14

14438 **Wheat Montana Farms & Bakery**
10778 Us Highway 287
Three Forks, MT 59752 406-285-3614
Fax: 406-285-3749 800-535-2798
info@wheatmontana.com
www.wheatmontana.com
Grain, flour, bread
President: Dean Folkvord
Marketing Director: Rita DeAngelis-Kockl
Production Manager: Randall Larson
Estimated Sales: $ 5-10 Million
Number Employees: 100-249
Type of Packaging: Consumer, Food Service, Private Label, Bulk

14439 **Wheeling Coffee & SpicecCompany**
13 14th St
Wheeling, WV 26003 304-232-0141
Fax: 304-232-0162 800-500-0141
whgcoffee@wheelingcoffeeco.com
www.wheelingcoffeeco.com
Processor of roast coffee and spices
President: Mary Ann Lokmer
CEO: Stephanie Ann Lokmer
Estimated Sales: $5-9.9 Million
Number Employees: 10-19
Type of Packaging: Consumer, Food Service, Bulk
Brands:
Paramount Coffee

14440 **Whetstone Candy Company**
1 Dolphin Drive
St Augustine, FL 32080 904-825-1710
Fax: 904-825-1750
orders@whetstonechocolates.com
http://www.whetstonechocolates.com
Candy and confectionery
President: Virginia Whetstone
Estimated Sales: $ 50-99.9 Million
Number Employees: 400
Brands:
Wheatstone

14441 **Whistler Brewing Company**
302 - 1505 West 2nd Avenue
Vancouver, BC V6H 3Y4
Canada 604-932-6185
Fax: 604-932-7293 http://www.whistlerbeer.com
Processor and exporter of ale and lager
President: Trevor Khoe
Estimated Sales: F
Number Employees: 100-249
Type of Packaging: Consumer, Food Service

14442 **Whistler Brewing Company**
4355 Canada Way
Burnaby, BC V5G 1J3
Canada 604-438-2337
Fax: 604-437-3292 whistlerbrewery@sprint.com
Processor of ale and lager
President: Trevor Khoe
Marketing: Joseph Tan
Estimated Sales: $ 1 Million
Number Employees: 11
Sq. footage: 1600
Type of Packaging: Consumer, Food Service

14443 **Whitaker Foods**
2019 Winston Pl
Waterloo, IA 50701 319-234-3056
Fax: 319-234-7734 800-553-7490
www.whitakerfoods.com
Manufacturer of frozen meat including sausage, breaded pork and pork slices
President: Ron Bright
Co-President: Shari Bright
Estimated Sales: $20-50 Million
Number Employees: 20-49
Type of Packaging: Consumer, Food Service, Private Label, Bulk

14444 **Whitcraft Wines**
36A S Calle Cesar Chavez
Santa Barbara, CA 93109-2128 805-730-1680
Fax: 805-730-1086 whitcraftwinery@cox.net
www.whitcraftwinery.com
Wines
Owner: Chris Whitcraft
Estimated Sales: $ 1-2.5 Million
Number Employees: 1
Number of Brands: 1
Number of Products: 12
Sq. footage: 2500
Brands:
Whitcraft Winery

14445 **White Cap Fish Company**
120 Montauk Hwy
Islip, NY 11751-3431 631-581-0125
Fax: 631-277-6578 www.whitecapfish.com
Processor of seafood including tuna
Owner: V Russo
VP: Jim Joeckel
Estimated Sales: $ 1 - 3 Million
Number Employees: 10-19

14446 **White Castle System**
P.O.Box 1498
Columbus, OH 43216 614-228-5781
Fax: 614-464-0596 866-272-8372
www.whatyoucrave.com
Bakery and meat products
VP: John S Kobacker
President: Bill Ingram
VP Marketing: Kim Kelly Bartley
CEO: Edgar W Ingram Iii
Marketing Director: Jamie Richardson
VP Manufacturing: Robert Johns
Estimated Sales: 491995000
Number Employees: 10,000+
Brands:
White Castle Cheeseburgers
White Castle Hamburg

14447 **White Cloud Coffee**
5125 N Sawyer Ave
Garden City, ID 83714 208-322-1166
Fax: 208-322-6226 800-627-0309
info@whitecloudcoffee.com
www.whitecloudcoffee.com
Roasted coffee
President: Jerome Eberharter
CEO: Jerome Eberharter
Director Marketing: Ron Thompson
VP Sales/Operations: Roger Daub
Estimated Sales: $ 5-10 Million
Number Employees: 20-49
Brands:
Buckaroo
Cowboy
Kona Island

14448 **White Coffee Corporation**
1835 38th St
Astoria, NY 11105 718-204-7900
Fax: 718-956-8504 800-221-0140
joan@whitecoffee.com www.whitecoffee.com
Processor, importer and exporter of cocoa, coffee, tea, soup mixes and bases and gelatin
President: Carole White
Owner: Jonathan White
Executive VP: Jonathan White
Marketing Director: Gregory White
Plant Manager: Tom Tolfree
Estimated Sales: $18800000
Number Employees: 100-249
Brands:
Melitta
Parker House
White House

14449 **White Fence Farm Chicken**
1376 Joliet Rd
Romeoville, IL 60446-4078 630-739-1720
Fax: 630-739-4466 wffchicago@yahoo.com
www.whitefencefarm.com
Poultry
President: Robert Hastert Jr
Estimated Sales: $ 5 - 10 Million
Number Employees: 100-249

14450 **White Hall Vineyards**
5190 Sugar Ridge Rd
Crozet, VA 22932-2200 434-823-8615
tastingroom@whitehallvineyards.com
www.whitehallvineyards.com
Wines
Co-Owner: Antony Champ
Co-Owner: Edith Champ
Estimated Sales: $ 3 - 5 Million
Number Employees: 5-9

14451 **White House Foods**
701 Fairmont Ave
Winchester, VA 22601 540-662-3401
www.whitehousefoods.com
Apple sauce, apple juice, vinegar, apple slices, apple rings, apple butter
Chairman/CEO: David Gum
CFO: Scott Hovermale
Quality Assurance Manager: Cole Gamble
VP Sales/Marketing: Dan Troup
Human Resources Director: Rick Pomeroy
VP Purchasing: Mike Jackson
Number Employees: 550
Sq. footage: 900000
Parent Co: National Fruit Product Company
Type of Packaging: Consumer

14452 **White House Foods**
701 Fairmont Avenue
Winchester, VA 22601 540-662-3401
Fax: 540-665-4671 tbastas@nfpc.com
www.whitehousefoods.com
Manufacturer of apple products including apple juice, apple sauce, vinegar and apple slices.
President: David Gum
Estimated Sales: $100+ Million
Number Employees: 500-999
Sq. footage: 350000
Type of Packaging: Consumer, Food Service, Private Label, Bulk
Other Locations:
National Fruit Product Plant
Winchester NC
National Fruit Product Plant
Lincolnton NC
Brands:
Orchard Boy
Shenandoah
Skyland
White House

14453 **White Lily Foods Company**
4740 Burbank Road
Memphis, TN 38118 800-595-1380
www.whitelily.com
Manufacturer of flour, corn flour meal and baking and gravy mixes
President: Ken Danton
Estimated Sales: $ 50 - 100 Million
Number Employees: 750
Type of Packaging: Consumer, Food Service, Private Label, Bulk
Brands:
WHITE LILY

14454 **White Oak Farms**
343 Main St
Sandown, NH 03873 603-887-2233
Fax: 603-887-2880 800-473-8869
info@macaroons.com www.macaroons.com
Macaroons
President: James Price
Estimated Sales: Below $ 5 Million
Number Employees: 5-9
Brands:
St. Julien Macaroons

14455 **White Oak Vineyards & Winery**
7505 Highway 128
Healdsburg, CA 95448-8020 707-433-8429
Fax: 707-433-8446
tastingroom@whiteoakwinery.com
www.whiteoakwinery.com
Wines
Owner: Bill Meyers
Marketing Director: Jerry Baker
CEO: Don Grogh
Public Relations: Denise Gill
Production Manager: Steve Ryan
Estimated Sales: $180,000
Number Employees: 2
Type of Packaging: Private Label
Brands:
White Oak Chardonnay
White Oak Merlot
White Oak Sauvignon

14456 **White Packing Company**
PO Box 7067
Fredericksburg, VA 22404-7067 540-898-2029
Manufacturer of Meat
President: Karl White
Estimated Sales: $21 Million
Number Employees: 150
Type of Packaging: Consumer

14457 **White Rock Distilleries**
P.O.Box 1829
Lewiston, ME 04241-1829 207-783-1433
Fax: 207-783-8409 www.threeolives.com
Alcoholic beverages
CEO: Paul Coulombe
CFO: Robert Payne
Quality Control: Mona Bilodeau
Plant Manager: Dennis Coulombe
Estimated Sales: $ 50-100 Million
Number Employees: 100-249
Brands:
White Rock

14458 **White Rock Products Corporation**
14107 20th Ave Ste 403
Flushing, NY 11357 718-746-3400
Fax: 718-767-0413 800-969-7625
info@whiterockbev.com
www.whiterockbeverages.com
Processor and exporter of carbonated and noncarbonated soft drinks; also, mixes, iced teas, fruit drinks and spring water
President: Alfred Morgan III
Marketing Director: Larry Bodkin
Estimated Sales: $9000000
Number Employees: 10
Number of Brands: 6
Type of Packaging: Consumer, Food Service
Brands:
Chocolate Delight
Delicious
Kentucky Nip
Kentucky Nip Cherry Julep
La Cascade Del Cielo
Lemon Licious Lemonade
Punch 'n Fruity
Pure Rock
Rock Pop Carbonated Beverages
Sarsaparilla
Sioux City
Sioux City Sarsaparilla
Southern Swirl
TNT Chocolate
Tealicious Iced Tea
Western Style Soft Drinks
White Rock
White Rock Orchards
Workout Energy Drinks

14459 **White Rock Vineyards**
1115 Loma Vista Drive
Napa, CA 94558-9752 707-257-7922
Fax: 707-257-7922
caves@whiterockvineyards.com
www.whiterockvineyards.com
Wines
Owner: Henry Vandendries
Winemaker: Christopher Vandendriessche
Estimated Sales: $450,000
Number Employees: 5-9
Brands:
White Rock Vineyards
White Rock Vineyards

14460 **White Swan Fruit Products**
P.O.Box 4230
Plant City, FL 33563-0021 813-752-1155
Fax: 813-754-3168 800-330-8952
paradisefruitco@hotmail.com
www.paradisefruitco.com
Processor and exporter of candied fruit and peels; manufacturer of custom plastic molders
President: Randy Gordon
CEO: Melvin Gordon
Estimated Sales: 20-50 Million
Number Employees: 250-499
Parent Co: Paradise Beverages
Type of Packaging: Consumer, Food Service, Private Label, Bulk
Brands:
Queen Anne
White Swan

14461 **White Toque**
536 Fayette Street
Perth Amboy, NJ 08861-3742 201-863-2885
Fax: 201-863-2886 800-237-6936
info@whitetoque.com www.whitetoque.com
Importer of IQF fruits and vegetables and specialty and broad-line food service distributors with a wide selection of imported European high quality frozen and dry goods
President/CEO: Gigier Memmel
Sales Director: Graham Taylor

14462 **White Wave**
12002 Airport Way
Broomfield, CO 80021-2546 303-635-4000
Fax: 303-443-3952 800-488-9283
questions@whitewave.com www.whitewave.com
Processor of vegetarian products including soymilk, nondairy yogurt, tofu, baked tofu, tempeh and seitan (wheat based meat analog)
President/CEO: Steve Demos
CFO: Pat Calhoun
Marketing Director: James Terman
Sales Director: Steve Hughes
Public Relations: Jarod Ballentine
Estimated Sales: $1 Million
Number Employees: 50-99
Number of Brands: 3
Number of Products: 40
Sq. footage: 30000
Parent Co: Dean Foods Company
Type of Packaging: Consumer, Food Service, Private Label, Bulk
Brands:
Silk
White Wave

14463 **White Wave Foods**
2262 W Beaver St
Jacksonville, FL 32209 904-355-7452
Fax: 904-353-5837 800-874-6765
Processor of milk including whole, skim, 1% and 2%; also, cream and specialty dairy fluids
VP Sales: David Roger
Estimated Sales: $ 50-100 Million
Number Employees: 100-249
Parent Co: Dean Foods Company
Type of Packaging: Consumer, Food Service, Private Label

14464 **White's Meat Processing**
1700 Portsmouth Rd
Peebles, OH 45660 937-587-2930
Processor of beef, pork and lamb
Owner: Don White
Estimated Sales: $490000
Number Employees: 1-4
Type of Packaging: Consumer, Bulk

14465 **White-Stokes Company**
3615 S Jasper Pl
Chicago, IL 60609-1399 773-254-5000
Fax: 773-523-7445 800-978-6537
nick@whitestokes.com www.whitestokes.com
Processor of pie fillings; also, marshmallow, butterscotch and bittersweet hot fudge toppings, nougats, caramel creams, pectin, coconut paste, etc
President: Nicholas Tzakis
VP: George Tzakis
Customer Relations: Melissa Pagan
Estimated Sales: $1400000
Number Employees: 20-49
Type of Packaging: Bulk

14466 **Whitefish Brewing**
5650 Us Highway 93 S
Whitefish, MT 59937 406-862-2684
Fax: 406-862-9684
Beer
Owner: Gary Hutchison
Estimated Sales: Below $ 5 Million
Number Employees: 3

14467 **Whitehall Lane Winery**
1563 Saint Helena Hwy S
Saint Helena, CA 94574 707-963-9454
Fax: 707-963-7035
greatwine@whitehalllane.com
www.whitehalllane.com
Wines
Proprietor: Tom Leonardini Sr
Winemaker: Dean Sylvester
Estimated Sales: Below $ 5 Million
Number Employees: 10-19
Brands:
Whitehall Lane

14468 **Whitehall Specialties**
36120 Owens St
Whitehall, WI 54773 715-538-2326
Fax: 715-538-4723 888-755-9900
wsisales@triwest.net
www.whitehall-specialties.com
Imitation cheese, cheese food slices, blended cheese products, dried, grated
President: Steven Fawcett
R&D: Terry Holliday
Quality Control: Ron McKernon
Marketing/Sales: Michelle Sonsalla
Plant Manager: Scott Kulig
Purchasing: John Liska
Estimated Sales: $ 50-100 Million
Number Employees: 100-249
Sq. footage: 50
Type of Packaging: Food Service, Private Label, Bulk
Brands:
Ridgeview Farms
Whitehall

14469 **Whitewave Foods Company**
12002 Airport Way
Broomfield, CO 80021 303-635-4000
Fax: 303-635-5504 www.whitewave.com
Manufacturer of dairy products
President: Blaine McPeak
SVP: Roger Theodoredis
Number Employees: 350

14470 **Whitey's Ice Cream Manufacturing**
2525 41st St
Moline, IL 61265 309-762-2175
Fax: 309-762-0053 888-594-4839
whiteys@whiteysicecream.com
www.whiteysicecream.com
Processor of ice cream, ice milk, frozen yogurt and novelties
Owner/CEO: Jon Tunberg
Owner/VP: Jeffrey Tunberg
Human Resources Director: Kirsten Runburg
Operations Director: Scott Larson
Plant Manager: Gary Neer
Purchasing Manager: Tom Hendrickx
Estimated Sales: $7500000
Number Employees: 300
Sq. footage: 25000
Type of Packaging: Consumer, Private Label

14471 **Whitfield Foods**
P.O.Box 791
Montgomery, AL 36101-0791 334-263-2541
Fax: 334-262-4203 800-633-8790
tdensmore@whitfieldfoods.com
www.whitfieldfoods.com
Manufacturer of maple products including butter and maple-citrus products; also, syrup including butter maple, cane, honey and corn
President: Les Massey
Estimated Sales: $50-100 Million
Number Employees: 100-249
Sq. footage: 1200003
Type of Packaging: Consumer, Food Service, Private Label
Brands:
ALAGA
PLOW BOY
YELLOW LABEL

14472 **Whitford Cellars**
4047 E 3rd Ave
Napa, CA 94558 707-942-0840
Fax: 707-942-0840 whitford@napanet.net
www.whitfordcellars.com
Winery of chardonnay, pinot noir and syrah
Co-Owner: Duncan Haynes
Co-Owner: Patricia Haynes
Estimated Sales: $500-1 Million appx.
Number Employees: 1-4
Number of Brands: 2
Number of Products: 4
Sq. footage: 2500
Type of Packaging: Private Label
Brands:
OLD VINES
WHITFORD

14473 **Whitley's Peanut Factory**
P.O.Box 647
Hayes, VA 23072-0647 804-642-7688
Fax: 804-642-7658 800-470-2244
customercare@whitleyspeanut.com
www.whitleyspeanut.com
Processor and exporter of snack nuts in cans, jars and bags including peanuts, almonds, cashews, mixed, pecans and honey-roasted; importer of raw cashews, brazil nuts and filberts. Also Virginia hams.
President: Craig Smith
VP Sales: James Scannell
Estimated Sales: $590000
Number Employees: 20-49
Type of Packaging: Consumer, Food Service, Private Label, Bulk
Brands:
Flavor Crunch
The Peanut Factory

14474 **Whitney & Son SeaFoods**
13326 US Hwy 19 N
Hudson, FL 34667 727-868-4044
Fax: 727-862-8283
www.whitneyandsonseafoods.com
Processor of produce
President: Peter Whitney
General Manager: John Hajjar
Estimated Sales: $ 5 - 10 Million
Number Employees: 10-19

14475 **Whitney Foods**
15504 Liberty Ave
Jamaica, NY 11433 718-291-3333
Fax: 718-291-0560
Dairy products
President: Kenneth Schlossberg
Marketing Director: Bill Masterson
VP Sales: Robert Zak
Marketing: Brian Lee
Estimated Sales: $ 2.5-5 Million
Number Employees: 20-49
Brands:
Whitney Yogurt

14476 **Whittaker & Associates**
1794 Charline Ave NE
Atlanta, GA 30306-3128 404-266-1265
Fax: 678-285-0547 jobs@whittakersearch.com
www.mwhitaker.com
Wholesale food manufacturing, dairy, beverage, bakery, meat, poultry, ingredients
Owner: Peggy Whitaker
Estimated Sales: Less than $500,000
Number Employees: 1-4

14477 **Whole Earth Bakery**
130 Saint Marks Pl # 1009
New York, NY 10009-5843 212-677-7597
Processor of baked goods
Owner: Peter Slyvestri
Estimated Sales: $110000
Number Employees: 1-4

14478 **Whole Herb Company**
19800 8th St East
PO Box 1203
Sonoma, CA 95476 707-935-1077
Fax: 707-935-3447
matt@wholeherbcompany.com
www.wholeherbcompany.com
Raw material supplier of herbs, spices, botanicals, spice blends, extracts and essential oils
President: Gillian Bleimann
CEO: James Thrower
General Manager: George Blasiola
Sales: Matt Foge
Operations Manager: Holly Sherwood
Plant Manager: Joe Nagy
Purchasing: Rena Janacek
Estimated Sales: $10 Million
Number Employees: 20
Number of Products: 500+
Sq. footage: 65000
Type of Packaging: Food Service, Bulk
Brands:
Jasmine Green
Mango Sunrise Tea
Peach Ambrosia
Somaguard
Somaguard Premium Grape Extract
Summer Berry Delight

14479 **Whole Life Nutritional Supplements**
13340 Saticoy St Ste B
North Hollywood, CA 91605 818-255-5357
Fax: 818-255-5307 800-748-5841
wholelife2@aol.com
Wholesaler/distributor and contract packager of vitamins
Manager: Rajen Patel
Director Sales: Irma Arroyo
Estimated Sales: $ 1 - 3 Million
Number Employees: 5-9
Sq. footage: 5000
Type of Packaging: Private Label

14480 **Whole in the Wall**
43 S Washington St
Binghamton, NY 13903 607-722-5138
Fax: 607-722-4237 info@wholeinthewall.com
www.wholeinthewall.com
Premium quality natural pesto, whole wheat bread and bagels, mushroom soup.
President: Elliot Fiks
CFO: Stacey Gould
Estimated Sales: Less than $500,000
Number Employees: 10-19
Type of Packaging: Consumer, Food Service, Private Label, Bulk

14481 **Wholesome Classics**
1224 Rimer Dr
Moraga, CA 94556-1727
Fax: 408-292-2394
carol@wholesomeclassics.com
www.wholesomeclassics.com
Low fat and wheat free baking mixes; private labeling available
Research & Development: Carol Zelinski
Number Employees: 1-4
Type of Packaging: Consumer, Private Label
Brands:
N-Dur-Enzo

14482 **Wholesome Sweeteners**
8016 Highway 90-A
Sugar Land, TX 77478 912-651-4820
Fax: 218-275-3170 800-680-1896
info@wholesomesweeteners.com
www.wholesomesweeteners.com
Processor and exporter of organic evaporated cane juices and molasses
President: David Montgomery Jr
Brand Manager: Pamela Lalumiere
Director Marketing: Nancy Barbee
Number Employees: 5-9
Sq. footage: 15000
Parent Co: Imperial Holly Corporation
Brands:
Sucanat
Wholesome Foods

14483 **Whyte's Food Corporation**
1700 Aimco Boulevard
Mississauga, ON L4W 1B1
Canada 905-624-5065
Fax: 905-624-4033 foodservice@whytes.ca
www.whytes.ca
Processor of refrigerated and shelf-stable pickles, peppers, horseradish, sauerkraut, pickled herring and sauces including spaghetti, pizza and entree; importer and packer of olives, maraschino cherries and capers; exporter ofpickles
VP: Antonio Arruda
President: Paul Kawaja
VP Finance: Andrew Anderson
Number Employees: 100-249
Sq. footage: 160000
Type of Packaging: Consumer, Food Service, Private Label, Bulk
Brands:
Grand Prix
Mrs. Whyte's
Trans-Alpine
Uni-Chef
Via Italia

14484 **Wiard's Orchards**
5565 Merritt Rd
Ypsilanti, MI 48197 734-482-7744
Fax: 734-482-7753 www.wiards.com
Cherries
President: Jay Wiard
Estimated Sales: $ 20-50 Million
Number Employees: 100-249

14485 **Wiberg Corporation**
931 Equestrian Court
Oakville, ON L6L 6L7
Canada 905-825-9900
Fax: 905-825-0070 info@wiberg.ca
www.wieberg.ca
Unitized ingredients, seasoning blends, natural spices, ASTA quality pepper, phosphates, casings and food additives.
President: Richard Welzel
Estimated Sales: $13 Million
Number Employees: 75
Sq. footage: 91020

14486 **Wichita Packing Company**
1315 W Fulton Mkt St
Chicago, IL 60607 312-421-0606
Fax: 312-421-0696 800-986-9742
information@wichitapacking.com
www.wichitapacking.com
Processor of baby back and St. Louis style ribs
Owner: Robert Golang
VP: Gerald Guon
Estimated Sales: $22697783
Number Employees: 20-49

14487 **(HQ)Wick's Pies**
217 SE Greenville Ave
PO Box 268
Winchester, IN 47394
Fax: 765-584-3700 800-642-5880
wickspies@wickpies.com www.wickspies.com
Processor of frozen pies and pie shells
Owner: Dwayne Wickersham
VP: Clark Loney
Quality Control: Sue Bone
Marketing/Sales: Marsha Welch
Purchasing: Steve Burge
Estimated Sales: $9 Million
Number Employees: 50-99
Sq. footage: 20000
Type of Packaging: Consumer, Food Service
Brands:
Wick's

14488 **Wicker's Food Products**
P.O.Box 129
Hornersville, MO 63855-0129 573-737-2416
Fax: 573-737-2113 800-847-0032
wickers@vip1.net www.wickersbbq.com
Marinades
Manager: Misty Edmonston
Estimated Sales: Less than $500,000
Number Employees: 5-9
Brands:
Wicker

14489 **Wicklund Farms**
3959 Maple Island Farm Rd
Springfield, OR 97477 541-747-5998
Fax: 541-747-7299
spicedgreenbeans@wicklundfarms.com
www.wicklundfarms.com
Processor and exporter of spiced green beans and bean relish
President: Larry Wicklund
Estimated Sales: $1600000
Number Employees: 6
Type of Packaging: Consumer, Food Service, Private Label, Bulk

14490 **Widman Popcorn Company**
1173 10th Road
Chapman, NE 68827-2716 308-986-2293
Fax: 308-986-2386 wpopcorn@kdsi.net
Processor and exporter of popcorn including white, yellow, high expansion and mushroom
President: Darrell Widman
Estimated Sales: $190,000
Number Employees: 2
Type of Packaging: Consumer, Food Service, Private Label, Bulk
Brands:
Widman's Country

14491 **Widmans Candy Shop**
116 S Broadway
Crookston, MN 56716-1955 218-281-1487
Chocolate-covered potato chips, peanut butter candy, cow pies
President: George Widman
Estimated Sales: Less than $500,000
Number Employees: 1-4

14492 **Widmer Brothers BrewingCompany**
929 N Russell St
Portland, OR 97227 503-281-2437
Fax: 503-281-1496 webmail@widmer.com
www.widmer.com
Beer
President: Kurt Widmer
CFO: Terry Michaelson
CEO: Terry Michaelson
Quality Control: Mike Domenghini
Sales Director: Tim McFall
Public Relations: Marty Wall
Director Manufacturing: Sebastian Pastore
Estimated Sales: $ 50-100 Million
Number Employees: 100-249
Number of Brands: 3
Type of Packaging: Private Label
Brands:
Hefeweizer
OKIO
Widmer Brothers

14493 **Widmer's Cheese Cellars**
P.O.Box 127
Theresa, WI 53091 920-488-2503
Fax: 920-488-2130 888-878-1107
info@widmerscheese.com
www.widmerscheese.com
Brick, colby cheese and extra sharp cheddar
President: Joseph Widmer
Estimated Sales: Below $ 5 Million
Number Employees: 20-49
Number of Brands: 1
Number of Products: 10
Sq. footage: 16000
Type of Packaging: Consumer, Bulk
Brands:
Widmer's Cheese

14494 **Widmer's Wine Cellars**
116 Buffalo St
Canandaigua, NY 14424-1012
Fax: 585-374-3266 www.widmerwine.com
Processor and exporter of wine and grape juice
President: Clenn Curtiss
Maintenance Supervisor: Mack Baxter
Estimated Sales: $ 50 - 100 Million
Number Employees: 100-249
Parent Co: Canandaigua Wine Company
Type of Packaging: Consumer, Food Service, Private Label, Bulk
Brands:
Great Western
Lake Niagara
Taylor
Widmer's

14495 **Widoffs Modern Bakery**
129 Water St
Worcester, MA 01604-5080 508-752-7200
Fax: 508-756-6365
Bakery products
President: Jerry Ducas
Estimated Sales: Below $ 5 Million
Number Employees: 20-49
Brands:
Hearth

14496 **Widow's Mite Vinegar Company**
1309 P Street NW
Apt 6
Washington, DC 20005-3750 202-462-3669
Fax: 202-462-3669 877-678-5854
jimdc@worldnet.att.net
www.widowsmitevinegar.com
Salad dressing mix and Creole vinegar
President: John Allen Franciscus
Vice President: James Franciscus
Type of Packaging: Consumer, Bulk

14497 **Wiederkehr Wine Cellars**
3324 Swiss Family Dr
Altus, AR 72821 479-468-3551
Fax: 479-468-4791 800-622-9463
info@wiederkehrwines.com
www.wiederkehrwines.com
Wines
Manager: Gary Wiederkehr
WineMaster: Al Wiederkehr
President: Gary Wiederkehr
CFO: Beverly Morrow
Estimated Sales: $ 10-20 Million
Number Employees: 50-99
Brands:
Wiederkehr Wine

14498 **Wiegardt Brothers**
P.O.Box 309
Ocean Park, WA 98640-0309 360-665-4111
Fax: 360-665-4950
Manufacturer and exporter of fresh oysters
President: Lee Wiegardt
Estimated Sales: $10-20 Million
Number Employees: 50-99
Type of Packaging: Consumer
Brands:
JOLLY ROGER
TIDEPOINT

14499 **Wilbur Chocolate**
48 N Broad St
Lititz, PA 17543 717-626-3249
Fax: 717-626-3487 800-233-0139
jan_o'brien@cargil.com www.wilburbuds.com
Processor of chocolate and confectionery coatings, drops and chips for the dairy, bakery and food industry
President/CEO: William J Shaughnessy
Inside Sales: Amy Weik
Estimated Sales: $283,000,000
Number Employees: 250-499
Parent Co: Cargill Foods
Type of Packaging: Food Service, Bulk
Brands:
Brandywine
Bronze Medal
Platinum 2000
R-346 Milk Chocolate Flavored
R-346 Milk Chocolate Flavored
Scarlet
Windsor

14500 **Wilbur Chocolate Company**
48 N Broad St
Lititz, PA 17543 717-626-3249
Fax: 717-626-3487 800-448-1063
chocolate@cargill.com www.wilburbuds.com
Manufacturer of chocolate and cocoa products including cocoa powder, ice cream coatings, chocolate drops, cream coatings, confectionary coatings, chocolate coatings, sugar-free chocolate, chocolate chunks, compound drops, cocoa butterand chocolate liquor
President: William Shaughnessy
Sales: Mark Freeman
Estimated Sales: $100 Million
Number Employees: 250-499
Parent Co: Cargill Incorporated
Brands:
Gerkins Cocoa
Peter's Chocolate
Wilbur Chocolate

14501 **Wilbur Packing Company**
PO Box 3598
Yuba City, CA 95992 530-671-4911
Fax: 530-671-4905 sales@wilburpacking.com
www.wilburpacking.com
California prunes and walnuts
Owner/President/Sales Manager: Richard Wilbur
VP: Randy Baucom
Plant Manager: Brad Meinen
Number Employees: 350
Sq. footage: 60650
Type of Packaging: Consumer

14502 **Wilcox Farm**
40400 Harts Lake Valley Rd
Roy, WA 98580-9182 360-458-7774
Fax: 360-458-6950 tbuti@wilcoxfarms.com
www.wilcoxfarms.com
Milk
President/CEO: Barrie Wilcox
Marketing Director: Brent Wilcox
Estimated Sales: $ 100-500 Million
Number Employees: 300
Type of Packaging: Bulk
Brands:
Wilcox

14503 **Wild Bill's FoodsMonogram Snacks Martinsville, LLC**
200 Knauss Ave
Martinsville, VA 24112 276-656-3500
Fax: 717-295-9722 800-848-3236
wildbill@wildbillsfoods.com
www.wildbillsfoods.com
Manufacturer of beef jerky
General Manager/Public Relations: Michael Kane
CFO: Steve Woelkers
CEO: Phil Clemmens
R&D/Quality Control: Greg Rhinier
Marketing Director: John Connell
Sales Manager: Teresa Musser
Operations/Plant Manager: Steve Groff r
Production Manager: Armando Torres Jr
Estimated Sales: $10-15 Million
Number Employees: 20-49
Parent Co: Clemens Family Coporation
Type of Packaging: Consumer, Bulk

14504 **Wild Blueberry Companies**
PO Box 100
Old Town, ME 04468 207-570-3535
Fax: 207-581-3499 wildblueberries@qwi.net
www.wildblueberrries.com
Blueberries
Executive Director: John Sauve
Number Employees: 1-4

14505 **Wild Flavors**
1261 Pacific Ave
Erlanger, KY 41018 859-342-3600
Fax: 859-342-3610 info@wildflavors.com
www.wildflavors.com
Develops, manufactures, and distributes flavors, flavor systems, colors, health ingredients and systems to the food and beverage industry.
Owner: Dr Hans-Peter Wild
CEO: Michael Ponder
CFO: Gary Massie
Assistant Director Regulatory: Greg Betsch
Senior Director, Quality Control: Karen Eberts
Senior Director, Marketing: Donna Hansee
VP Sales: Reed Lynn
Senior Director, Public Relations: Donna Hansee
VP Operations: David Haase
Director, Operations: Dan Holtzleiter
Senior Director, Procurement: Tony Sizemore
Number Employees: 250-499
Sq. footage: 350000
Type of Packaging: Consumer, Food Service, Private Label, Bulk

14506 **Wild Fruitz Beverages**
270 Ridings Way
Ambler, PA 19002-5246 718-909-0819
Fax: 973-742-7634 888-688-7632
sales@wildfruitz.com www.wildfruitz.com
Carbonated natural fruit juices
President/CEO: Trev Warshauer
Chairwoman: Sally Watt
CFO: Jon Jensen

Estimated Sales: $ 3.3 Million
Number Employees: 6
Brands:
Wild Fruitz

14507 Wild Hog Vineyard
P.O.Box 189
Cazadero, CA 95421 707-847-3687
Fax: 707-847-3160 info@wildhogvineyard.com
www.wildhogvineyard.com
Processor of wine
Owner: Daniel Schoenseld
Co-Owner: Marion Schoenfeld
Estimated Sales: Less than $500,000
Number Employees: 1-4
Sq. footage: 2000
Brands:
Wild Hog Vineyard

14508 Wild Horse Winery
1437 Wild Horse Winery Ct
Templeton, CA 93465 805-434-2541
Fax: 805-434-3516 info@wildhorsewinery.com
www.wildhorsewinery.com
Wine
President: Scott Welcher III
Winemaker: Mark Cummins
Estimated Sales: $ 10-20 Million
Number Employees: 20-49
Brands:
Wild Horse

14509 Wild Planet Foods
1585 Heartwood Drive
Suite F
McKinleyville, CA 95519 707-840-9116
Fax: 707-839-3260 800-998-9945
elizabeth@wildplanetfoods.com
www.wildplanetfoods.com
seafood
President/Owner: Bill Carvalho
CEO: Terry Hunt
Sales: Justin Desiderio

14510 (HQ)Wild Rice Exchange
1277 Santa Anita Ct
Woodland, CA 95776 530-669-0150
Fax: 530-668-9317 800-223-7423
thewildriceexch@aol.com www.wildrice.org
Processor, importer and exporter of wild rice, products and blends including basmati, arborio, red gourmet rices, organic, brown and polished white; also, quick-cook, frozen and pre-mixed pilaf; large line of specialty beans; customprocessing
Manager: Carlos Zambello
Sales: Carlos Zambello
Production: Golnar Emam
Type of Packaging: Consumer, Food Service, Private Label, Bulk
Brands:
Gourmet Valley
Gourmet Valley Foods
Great Valley

14511 Wild Thyme Cottage Products
127-B Donegani
Pointe Claire, QC H9R 5E9
Canada 514-695-3602
Fax: 514-695-3602 wild.thyme@sympatice.ca
Processor and exporter of jams, jellies, marmalades, relishes and chutneys
President: David Ranlings
Number Employees: 1-4
Number of Brands: 1
Number of Products: 50
Sq. footage: 700
Type of Packaging: Consumer, Food Service
Brands:
Wild Thyme Cottage Products

14512 Wild Thymes Farm
643 County Route 403
Greenville, NY 12083-1703 518-966-5990
Fax: 518-966-5998 800-724-2877
info@wildthymes.com www.wildthymes.com
Chutneys, salad dressings, fruit spreads, sauces/marinades, mustards, balsamic vinegars
Owner: Enid Stettner
Owner: Ann Stettner
Research & Development: Enid Stettner
Quality Control: Enid Stettner
Marketing Director: Ann Stettner
Public Relations: Ann Stettner
Estimated Sales: $1-$2.5 Million
Number Employees: 10-19
Number of Brands: 1
Number of Products: 50
Type of Packaging: Consumer, Food Service, Private Label, Bulk

14513 Wild West Spices
P.O.Box 471
Cody, WY 82414-0471 307-587-8800
Fax: 307-587-8800 888-587-8887
info@wildwestspices.com
www.wildwestspices.com
Manufacturer of western-style spice blends, grilling spices and rubs, all natural dry mixes and dips
President: Bonnie Dallinger
VP: Bonnie Dallinger
Estimated Sales: Less than $500,000
Number Employees: 1-4
Brands:
Wild West Spices, Inc.

14514 Wild Winds Farms
1 Lake Niagara Ln
Naples, NY 14512-9799 585-374-6311
Fax: 585-374-3266 800-836-5253
Wine and wine coolers
President: Clenn Curtiss
Estimated Sales: $ 25-49.9 Million
Number Employees: 100-249

14515 Wildcat Produce
PO Box 5224
McGrew, NE 69353 308-783-2438
Fax: 308-783-1054
Cucumbers, green beans, onions, potatoes and pumpkins
President: Mike Chrisman
CEO: Ruftin Rahmig
Brands:
Wildcat Produce Garden

14516 Wildhurst
P.O.Box 1310
Kelseyville, CA 95451-1310 707-279-0548
Fax: 707-279-1913 800-595-9463
info@wildhurst.com www.wildhurst.com
Wines
President: Myron Holdenried
Winemaker: Mark Burch
Estimated Sales: Below $ 5 Million
Number Employees: 5-9
Type of Packaging: Private Label
Brands:
Reserve Chardonnay
Reserve Fume Blanc
Wildhurst Cabernet F
Wildhurst Chardonnay
Wildhurst Merlot
Wildhurst Zinfandel

14517 Wildlife Cookie Company
PO Box 1158
Saint Charles, IL 60174-7158 630-377-6196
Fax: 630-377-6321 sales@wildlifecookie.com
www.wildlifecookie.com
Cookies

14518 Wildly Delicious
47 Railside Rd
Toronto, ON M3A 1B2
Canada 416-444-2011
Fax: 416-444-0010 888-545-9995
feedback@wildlydelicious.com
www.wildlydelicious.com
dip, mix and spread, seasoning, spices and salts, premium oils and vinegars, gourmet sauces, pastes and mustards.
COO: Austin Muscat
CEO: Michelle Muscat
Operations: Austin Muscat

14519 Wildtime Foods
P.O.Box 1471
Eugene, OR 97440 541-747-1654
Fax: 541-747-5067 800-356-4458
info@wildtime.com www.grizzliesbrand.com
Bulk and packaged cereals
President: Genevieve Averill
Marketing Director: Whit Hemphill
Estimated Sales: Below $ 5 Million
Number Employees: 10-19
Sq. footage: 4500
Brands:
Grizzliesh

14520 Wildwood Natural Foods
416 E Riverside Dr
Watsonville, CA 95076 831-728-4448
Fax: 831-728-4445 800-464-3915
tofurus@aol.com www.pmo.com
Natural foods
Director: John Breen
Quality Control: Hiti Uojas
Marketing Director: Janet Taylor
Operations Manager: Jeremiah Ridenour
Production Manager: Robyn Shurbet
Plant Manager: Dolly Gianni
Purchasing Manager: Doug Porter
Estimated Sales: $ 10-20 Million
Number Employees: 100-249
Type of Packaging: Private Label
Brands:
Grilled & Marinated Tofu
Plain Tofu
Smoked Tofu
Soy Sour Cream
Soymilk
Soymill
Soyogurt
Wildwood Baked Tofu

14521 Wileman Bros & Elliott,Inc
P.O.Box 6940
Visalia, CA 93290-6940
Fax: 559-528-2456 andrew@mr-sunshine.com
www.mr-sunshine.com
Offers a full line of California citrus products
President: Frank Elliott Iii
CEO: Tommy Elliott
CFO: Brian Johnson
Research & Development: Brad McCord
Quality Control: Raul Lopez
Sales Director: Andrew Felts
Public Relations: Truman McGuire
Operations Manager: Manuel Guillen
Production Manager: Mark Savage
Plant Manager: Jon Hornburg
Estimated Sales: $50 - 100 Million
Number Employees: 100-249
Sq. footage: 5000
Type of Packaging: Consumer, Food Service, Private Label, Bulk

14522 Wilhelm Foods
8951 NE Saint Paul Hwy
Newberg, OR 97132 503-538-2929
Fax: 503-538-1992
Plaidberries and plaidberry products
President: Charles Cox
Estimated Sales: $ 5 - 10 Million
Number Employees: 10-19

14523 Wilke International
14321 W 96th Ter
Shawnee Mission, KS 66215-4709 913-438-5544
Fax: 913-438-5554 800-779-5545
whw@wilkeinternational.com
www.wilkeinternational.com
Processor, importer, exporter and wholesaler/distributor of lactic acid, lactates, sports nutrition and dietary supplements
President: Wayne Wilke
Director Administration: John Veazey
General Manager: James France
Estimated Sales: $ 5 - 10 Million
Number Employees: 10-19
Type of Packaging: Bulk
Brands:
Createam
Nutrasense

14524 (HQ)Wilkins-Rogers
P.O. Box 308
Ellicott City, MD 21041-0308 410-465-5800
Fax: 410-750-0163
info@washingtonqualityfoods.com
www.wrmills.com
Processor and exporter of flour, corn meal, baking mixes, breading and batters
President: Samuel Rogers Jr
Joint CEO: Samual Rogers III
Joint CEO: Tom Rogers III
CEO: Sam Rogers Jr
Estimated Sales: $27,900,000
Number Employees: 100-249
Sq. footage: 180000

Type of Packaging: Consumer, Food Service, Private Label, Bulk
Brands:
Crutchfield
Indian Head
Raga Muffins
Spanglers
Velvetx
Washington

14525 Wilkinson-Spitz
705 Bronx River Road
Suite 204
Yonkers, NY 10704-1752 914-237-5000
Fax: 914-237-7295
Candy
Manager: Joel Miller
VP: Jim Koehlein
Sales Director: Leon Gleaves
Estimated Sales: $ 1-2.5 Million appx.
Number Employees: 1

14526 Will Poultry Company
P.O.Box 1146
Buffalo, NY 14240-1146 716-853-2000
Fax: 716-853-2011 http://www.willpoultry.com
Fresh and frozen institutional poultry, seafood and meats
President: Donald Will
Estimated Sales: $ 50-100 Million
Number Employees: 100-249
Brands:
Will

14527 Will-Pak Foods
3350 Shelby Street
Suite 200
Ontario, CA 91764-5556 909-945-4554
Fax: 909-899-7822 800-874-0883
taste_adv@earthlink.net
www.tasteadventure.com
Manufacturer of all-natural foods including soups, beans, chilies, and side dishes
President: Gary Morris
Estimated Sales: $990,000
Number Employees: 10
Sq. footage: 10000
Type of Packaging: Food Service, Private Label, Bulk
Brands:
TASTE ADVENTURE

14528 Willamette Valley Walnuts
475 NE 17th St
McMinnville, OR 97128-3326 503-472-3215
www.walnutcitywineworks.com
Processor and exporter of shelled walnuts and English walnut meats
Owner: Zac Spence
VP: Todd Heidgerken
Estimated Sales: $500,000-$1 Million
Number Employees: 1-4
Type of Packaging: Consumer, Food Service, Private Label, Bulk

14529 Willcox Packing House
P.O.Box 122
Willcox, AZ 85644-0122 520-384-2015
Processor of meat products including beef, lamb and pork
Owner: David Harris
Estimated Sales: $870000
Number Employees: 5-9
Type of Packaging: Consumer, Food Service, Private Label, Bulk

14530 William Atwood Lobster Company
P.O.Box 202
Spruce Head, ME 04859-0202 207-596-6691
Fax: 207-596-6958 80- 5-1 52
support@atwoodlobster.com
www.atwoodlobster.com
Fresh and frozen lobster meat, shrimp, crabmeat, frozen lobster tails, fresh crabs and whole lobsters
President: William Atwood
CEO: William McGonagle
R & D: David Atwood
Sales Manager: Sandy Cox
Estimated Sales: $3.3 Million
Number Employees: 50
Brands:
William Atwood

14531 (HQ)William B. Reily & Company
3501 Duncanwood Lane
Baltimore, MD 21213-4093 410-675-9550
Fax: 410-327-1214
Beer
Manager: Maxim Hoffmann
CEO: Platner Reily
President: William Reily
Estimated Sales: $ 10-20 Million
Number Employees: 30
Parent Co: Reily Companies
Type of Packaging: Consumer, Food Service, Private Label, Bulk
Brands:
Blue Plate Mayonnaise
Jfg Products
Luzianne Tea

14532 William Bolthouse Farms
7200 E Brundage Ln
Bakersfield, CA 93307 661-366-7270
Fax: 661-366-9236 www.bolthouse.com
Grower, shipper and packer of fresh carrots, carrot products and carrot juice concentrate
President: Andre Radandt
Sales Manager: Yannick Le Mintier
VP: Tim McCorkle
Director Sales/Marketing: Tim McCorkle
Sales Manager: Scott Reade
Estimated Sales: $100+ Million
Number Employees: 1,000-4,999
Type of Packaging: Bulk
Brands:
Coldwater Creek
Green Giant
Look Mom
Shortcuts

14533 William Bounds
3737 W 240th St
Torrance, CA 90505 310-375-0505
Fax: 310-375-0756 800-473-0504
customerservice@wmboundsltd.com
www.wmboundsltd.com
Spices, flavored chocolate, colored sugars.
President: Helen Bounds
Estimated Sales: Below $ 5 Million
Number Employees: 20-49

14534 William E. Caudle Company
6443 E Twin Creek Drive
Idaho Falls, ID 83401-5868 208-523-6637
Fax: 208-523-9586

14535 William E. Martin & Sons Company
9341 170th St
Jamaica, NY 11433 718-291-1300
Fax: 718-291-0331 mail@martinspices.com
www.martinspices.com
Processor, wholesaler/distributor, exporter and importer of spices, seasonings, salts, herbs and herbal supplements, seeds, powders and raisins. Wholesaler/distributor of dehydrated onion and garlic products, full line of ground spicesand bakery seeds
Owner: William Martin Jr
VP: Spencer Martin
Sales: Sy Schwartz
Estimated Sales: $ 10 - 20 Million
Number Employees: 20-49
Sq. footage: 60000
Type of Packaging: Bulk
Brands:
W.E.M.

14536 (HQ)William Grant & Sons
200 Park Ave South
Suite 1218
New York, NY 10003-1542 212-246-1760
info@wmgrant.com
www.grantusa.com
Distiller
Managing Director: Simon Hunt
Manager: Carol Lewis
CFO: Jim Heaten
Executive VP Fine Wine: Richard Carrretta
VP Marketing: Mark Teasdale
Sales Director: Joel Gosler
Estimated Sales: $ 120 Million
Number Employees: 125
Brands:
Armida
Balvenie
Berentzen
Borgianni
Brolio
Castello Di Volpaia
Clan Macgregor
Colombo
Dry Sack
Fonterutoli
Frangelico Liqueur
Glenfiddich
Glenfiddich
Grant's
Licor 43
Luis Felipe Edwards
Marques De Murrieta
McDowell
Metaxa

14537 William Harrison Vineyar
1443 Silverado Trl S
Saint Helena, CA 94574 707-963-8762
Fax: 707-963-4552 800-913-9463
info@harrisonvineyards.com
www.harrisonvineyards.com
Processor of garlic dill pickles
Manager: Bruce Bradley
CEO: Lyndsey Harrison
Estimated Sales: Less than $500,000
Number Employees: 1-4
Type of Packaging: Consumer
Brands:
Aceto D'Oro
Kirk and Glotzer New
New York Deli

14538 William Harrison Vineyards & Winery LLC
1443 Silverado Trl S
Saint Helena, CA 94574 707-963-8762
Fax: 707-963-8762 www.whwines.com
Wines
Owner: William Harrison
Marketing/Sales: Rob Monaghan
Winemaker/General Manager: Bruce Bradley
Brands:
Mario Perelli-Minetti
Miriam

14539 William Hill Winery
1761 Atlas Peak Rd
Napa, CA 94558 707-224-4477
Fax: 707-224-4484
whw_info@williamhillwinery.com
www.williamhillwinery.com
Wine
President: Bill Newlands
Vice President: Glenn Salva
Public Relations: George Rose
Production Manager: Jill Davis
Plant Manager: Calvin Chase
Estimated Sales: $ 10-20 Million
Number Employees: 20-49
Type of Packaging: Private Label
Brands:
William Hill Winery

14540 William Karas & Sons
2436 Griffin Road
Churchville, NY 14428-9557 585-293-2109
Fax: 585-757-9032
Grower and packer of onions and potatoes
Co-Partner: Larry Karas
Co-Partner: William Karas
Number Employees: 5-9
Sq. footage: 34000
Type of Packaging: Consumer, Private Label, Bulk
Brands:
W.K.

14541 William Poll
1051 Lexington Ave
New York, NY 10021 212-288-0501
Fax: 212-288-2844 800-993-7655
wpollny@aol.com www.williampoll.com
Baked potato thins, dips, sauces, dip indulgencs
President: Stanley Poll
Estimated Sales: Less than $500,000
Number Employees: 5-9
Type of Packaging: Consumer
Brands:
Baked Potato Thins
Dip Indulgence

14542 **William R. Clem Company**
181 Virginia Ave
Lexington, KY 40508-3238 859-233-0821
Fax: 859-233-0868
President: William Clem
Estimated Sales: $ 10 - 20 Million
Number Employees: 20-49

14543 **William Turner**
6335 Knollwood Drive
Frederick, MD 21701-5828 301-620-1135
Fax: 301-620-1560
Coffees

14544 **William's Pork**
1027 US Highway 74 East
Lumberton, NC 28358 910-608-2226
Fax: 910-628-0081 william@britishbacon.com
www.britishbacon.com
bacon, hams, sausages, pork chops, ribs

14545 **Williams Candy Company**
18 Main St
Somerville, MA 02145 617-776-0814
Fax: 617-776-0816
Chocolate candy
President: Ron Cataldo
Estimated Sales: Below $ 5 Million
Number Employees: 5-9
Type of Packaging: Bulk

14546 **Williams Cheese Company**
P.O.Box 249
Linwood, MI 48634 989-697-4492
Fax: 989-697-4203 800-968-4462
jim@williamscheese.com
www.williamscheese.com
Processed and flavored cheese
President: James A Williams
Marketing Manager: Jay Williams
Sales Director: Todd Williams
Operations Manager: Mike Williams Sr
Purchasing Manager: Ladd Williams
Estimated Sales: $ 9 Million
Number Employees: 50-99
Sq. footage: 20
Type of Packaging: Private Label
Brands:
Amish Country
Cheese Rounds and Bricks
Cheese Spreads
Williams

14547 **Williams Creek Farms**
PO Box 292
Williams, OR 97544-0292 541-846-6481
Grower of organic produce including berries, apples, garlic, onions and lettuce; packer of organic sun dried cherry tomatoes and sun dried apples
Owner/Manager: Randy Carey
Number Employees: 5-9

14548 **(HQ)Williams Foods, Inc**
13301 W 99th St
Lenexa, KS 66215 913-888-4343
Fax: 913-888-0727 800-255-6736
info@williamsfoods.com
www.williamsfoods.com
Seasonings, sauces & gravy mixes; blends, seasonings and spices.
Chairman/CEO: Conrad Hock
VP Finance: Vicki Smith
SVP: Dennis Daniels
R&D Manager: Lily Kelly
VP Marketing: Marty Butler
VP Operations: Larry Copus
General Manager: Brian Hubbard
Estimated Sales: $64000000
Number Employees: 220
Sq. footage: 60000
Type of Packaging: Consumer, Food Service, Private Label, Bulk
Other Locations:
Williams Foods
Torrance CA
Brands:
COUNTRY STORE
JEL-EASE PECTIN
JIMMY DEAN
SUNBIRD
TRADICIONES-HISPANIC
WILLIAMS

14549 **Williams Institutional Foods**
P.O.Box 370
Douglas, GA 31534 912-384-5270
Fax: 912-384-0533
Wholesaler/distributor of groceries, meat, frozen foods, bakery goods, equipment and general merchandise; serving the food service market of southern Georgia
President: Carl Williams
VP Distribution: B Williams
Estimated Sales: $37000000
Number Employees: 50-99

14550 **Williams Seafood Market& Wines**
10627 E Sprague Ave
Spokane Valley, WA 99206-3633 509-922-4868
Manufactuer of seafoods and wine
Owner: Vince Ofield
Estimated Sales: $300,000-500,000
Number Employees: 1-4

14551 **Williams-Carver Company**
4001 Mission Rd
Kansas City, KS 66103 913-236-4949
Fax: 913-236-9331 800-763-4411
sales@williamscarver.com
www.williamscarver.com
Provides quality design, sales, installation, and service
President: Rich F Carver
Estimated Sales: $ 1 - 3 Million
Number Employees: 10-19

14552 **Williams-Selym Winery**
6575 Westside Rd
Healdsburg, CA 95448-8323 707-433-6425
Fax: 707-431-4862 contact@williamsselyem.com
www.williamsselyem.com
Wines
Manager: Bob Cabral
Proprietor: Kathe Dyson
Marketing Director: Mark Malpiede
Executive Winemaker: Bob Cabral
Winemaker: Lynn Krausmann
Assistant Winemaker: Mark Ray
Estimated Sales: $ 1-2.5 Million
Number Employees: 5-9
Brands:
Williams-Selym Winery

14553 **Williams-West & Witt Products**
3501 W Dunes Hwy
Michigan City, IN 46360-6717
Fax: 219-879-8237 wwwsoup@adsnet.com
www.williamswestandwitts.com
Processor of dry gravy mixes, cooking sauces, seasonings and soup bases including chicken, beef, ham, onion, garlic, turkey, pork, crab, salmon, shrimp, lobster, vegetable, mushroom, etc.; also available, vegetarian, natural, GMO freebases and low sodium bases
President: Victor Palmer
VP: Brian Quealy
R&D Manager: John True
Sales Manager: Georgeann Quealy
Controller: Brian Quealy
Estimated Sales: $1100000
Number Employees: 5-9
Type of Packaging: Consumer, Food Service, Private Label, Bulk
Brands:
COOKS DELIGHT

14554 **Williamsburg Chocolatier**
P.O.Box 1712
Williamsburg, VA 23187 757-253-1474
Fax: 804-966-9025 wmsbgchoc@aol.com
www.williamsburgchocolate.com
Processor of confectionery products, pound cakes, chocolate lollypops, dessert toppings, fudge and seasonal chocolate specialties
Owner: Maryann Boho
Marketing: Lee Boho
Estimated Sales: Under 500,000
Number of Products: 50
Sq. footage: 1200
Type of Packaging: Consumer

14555 **Williamsburg Winery**
5800 Wessex Hundred
Williamsburg, VA 23185 757-258-0899
Fax: 757-229-0911 wine@wmbgwine.com
www.williamsburgwinery.com
Wines
President: Patrick Dufseler
Estimated Sales: $3.7 Million
Number Employees: 20-49
Type of Packaging: Private Label
Brands:
Donmir Wine Cellars
La Donaings De Franc
Williamsburg Winery

14556 **Willies Smoke House**
562 S Main St
Harrisville, PA 16038-1626 724-735-4184
Fax: 724-735-4184 800-742-4184
williespa@pathway.net
Processor of hickory smoked meat products including ham, bacon, sausage, poultry, dried beef, jerky, pork loins, etc
Owner: John Mc Kee
Estimated Sales: $500,000 appx.
Number Employees: 1-4
Sq. footage: 1900
Type of Packaging: Consumer

14557 **Willmar Cookie & Nut Company**
P.O.Box 88
Willmar, MN 56201-0088 320-235-0600
Fax: 320-235-0659 www.gurleysfoods.com
Cookies and crackers. Salted and roasted nuts and seeds
President: Michael Mickelson
CEO: Michael Mickelson
General Manager: Steve Loy
Vice President: Tom Taunton
Estimated Sales: $ 10-24.9 Million
Number Employees: 100-249
Sq. footage: 140000
Type of Packaging: Private Label
Brands:
Gurley's

14558 **Willmark Sales Company**
33 Nassau Ave
Brooklyn, NY 11222-3132 718-388-7141
Fax: 718-963-3924
Processor and exporter of bakery ingredients
President: Robert Leibowitz
VP: Edward Leibowitz
Estimated Sales: $5-10 Million
Number Employees: 50-99

14559 **Willoughby's Coffee & Tea**
550 E Main St Ste 27
Branford, CT 06405 203-481-1700
Fax: 203-481-1777 800-388-8400
www.willoughbyscoffee.com
Coffee
President: Barry Levine
CEO: Robert Williams
Estimated Sales: $500,000-$1 Million
Number Employees: 10-19
Brands:
Willoughby's

14560 **Willow Foods**
7774 SW Nimbus Ave
Beaverton, OR 97008 503-641-6602
Fax: 503-641-6899 800-338-3609
info@luckyfood.com www.luckyfood.com
Chinese and Vietnamese cuisine, spring rolls, pot stickers and potato rolls.
Owner: Tammy Jo
CFO: Bonnie Tompkins
Sales Director: Peter Yu
Estimated Sales: $1.35 Million
Number Employees: 20
Number of Brands: 1
Number of Products: 20
Sq. footage: 10000
Type of Packaging: Consumer, Food Service, Private Label, Bulk
Brands:
Willow

14561 **Willow Hill Vineyards**
5460 Loudon Street
Johnstown, OH 43031-9261 740-587-4622
Fax: 740-587-0999
Wines
Owner: Dave Rechsteiner
Estimated Sales: Less than $500,000
Number Employees: 1-4
Brands:
WILLOW HILL

14562 **Willow Tree Poultry Farm**
997 S Main St
Attleboro, MA 02703 508-222-2479
Fax: 508-222-8258
comments@willowtreefarm.com
www.willowtreefarm.com
Processor of poultry products
President/CEO: Chester Cekala
Estimated Sales: $14,500,000
Number Employees: 50-99

14563 **WillowOak Farms**
P.O.Box 388
Woodland, CA 95776-0388 530-662-1983
Fax: 530-662-0907 888-963-2767
wiloakfarm@aol.com www.willowoakfarms.com
All-natural hors d'oeuvre spreads, sauces and salad dressings
President: Kevin Sanchez
Research & Development: Massimo Di Sciullo
Director of Marketing: Kevin Sanchez
Estimated Sales: $ 1-2.5 Million
Number Employees: 1-4
Number of Brands: 3
Number of Products: 30
Sq. footage: 20000
Type of Packaging: Consumer, Food Service
Brands:
L'Ortolano
Willow Oak Farms

14564 **Willowcroft Farm Vineyards**
38906 Mount Gilead Rd
Leesburg, VA 20175 703-777-8161
Fax: 703-777-8157 willowine@aol.com
www.willowcroftwine.com
Wine
Owner: Lewis Parker
Estimated Sales: $ 1 - 3 Million
Number Employees: 1-4

14565 **Willy Wonka Candy**
1445 Norwood Ave
Itasca, IL 60143-1128 630-773-0267
Fax: 630-773-1467 888-694-2656
info@hometownfavorites.com
www.hometownfavorites.com
Candy
President/CEO: David Kewer
Manager: Louise Defalco
Manager: Leonardo Ruiz
Plant Manager: Ann Haffron
Purchasing Manager: L Glen
Estimated Sales: $ 50-100 Million
Number Employees: 250-499
Brands:
Willy Wonka

14566 **Willy Wonka Candy Factory**
1445 Norwood Ave
Itasca, IL 60143 630-773-0267
Fax: 630-773-1467
Manufacturer of Interactive chocolate bar
CFO: Bill Rasmussen
CEO: David Kewer
Number Employees: 250-499
Parent Co: Nestle USA
Type of Packaging: Consumer
Brands:
XPLODER

14567 **Wilson Candy Company**
408 Harrison Ave
Jeannette, PA 15644 724-523-3151
Fax: 724-523-5959
Processor of boxed and bulk chocolates
President: Doug Wilson
VP: Kay Wilson
Production Manager: Rob Kane
Estimated Sales: $870000
Number Employees: 10-19
Sq. footage: 9600
Type of Packaging: Consumer, Private Label, Bulk
Brands:
Wunder Bar

14568 **Wilson Corn Products**
P.O.Box 97
Rochester, IN 46975-0097 574-223-3177
Fax: 574-223-3414
Flour and other grain mill products.
President: Thomas Wilson
CEO: John Cory
Estimated Sales: $ 10-20 Million
Number Employees: 20-49

14569 **Wilson's Fantastic Candy**
384 Greenway Rd
Memphis, TN 38117-4338 901-767-1900
Fax: 901-398-1375
wilsonfoods@mindspring.com
www.wilsonfoods.com
Processor of candy including caramels, chocolates, coconut, fudge, corn, bagged, fundraising, theater and vending; also, fat-free and sugar-free cookies and glazed nuts
Owner: Robert Wilson
VP/General Manager: Jerry Adams
Number Employees: 5-9
Sq. footage: 15000
Parent Co: Kemmons Wilson Companies
Type of Packaging: Consumer, Bulk
Brands:
Wilson Foods

14570 **Wilson's Oysters**
1981 S Van Ave
Houma, LA 70363 985-857-8855
Fax: 985-857-8139 wilson@wilsonsoysters.com
www.wilsonsoysters.com
Oysters
President: Wilson Voisin Jr
Estimated Sales: $5-10 Million
Number Employees: 20-49

14571 **Wilsonhill Farm**
63251 Mulberry Rd
South Bend, IN 46614-9464 802-899-2154
Fax: 802-899-2154
Processor of mixes including bread, pancake and muffin; also, apple butter
Principal: Stacey Wilson
Estimated Sales: $57,000
Number Employees: 1
Sq. footage: 3500
Type of Packaging: Consumer, Food Service, Private Label
Brands:
Wilsonhill

14572 **Wimberley Valley Winery**
2825 Lone Man Mountain Rd
Driftwood, TX 78619 512-847-2592
Fax: 281-288-8298
info@wimberleyvalleywinery.com
www.wimberleyvalleywinery.com
Wines
President: Howard Pitman
VP: Dean Valentine
Estimated Sales: $500,000-$1 Million
Number Employees: 1-4
Type of Packaging: Bulk
Brands:
Wimberley Valley

14573 **Wimmer's Meat Products**
126 W Grant St
West Point, NE 68788 402-372-2437
Fax: 402-372-5659 800-358-0761
lou@wimmersmeats.com
www.wimmersmeats.com
Processor of natural casing weiners, skinless weiners, natural casing link sausages, brauschweiger, summer sausage, smokies, sliced lunchmeats and deli meats.
CEO/Chairman: Dave Wimmer
CFO: Dan Hughes
President/COO: Ron Gross
VP Sales&Marketing: Terry Maul
Estimated Sales: $ 20 - 50 Million
Number Employees: 100-249
Type of Packaging: Consumer, Food Service, Private Label, Bulk
Brands:
Ambassador
Bassetts
Fairbury's

14574 **Winans Chocolates & Coffees**
308 W Water St
Piqua, OH 45356-2238 937-773-1981
Fax: 937-773-2388 www.winanscandies.com
Processor of candy
President: Joe Reiser
Estimated Sales: $ 10 - 20 Million
Number Employees: 20-49
Type of Packaging: Consumer

14575 **Winchester Cheese Company**
32605 Holland Rd
Winchester, CA 92596 951-926-4239
Fax: 951-926-3349 sales@winchestercheese.com
www.winchestercheese.com
Processor of gouda cheese
Manager: Jeff Floot
Estimated Sales: Less than $500,000
Number Employees: 5-9
Sq. footage: 3650
Type of Packaging: Consumer, Food Service, Private Label, Bulk
Brands:
Cumin Gouda
Herb Gouda
Jalapeno Gouda
Mild Gouda
Sharp Gouda
Super Aged Gouda

14576 **Winchester Farms Dairy**
675 Rolling Hills Ln
Winchester, KY 40391 859-745-5500
Fax: 859-745-5547 www.kroger.com
Processor of milk including chocolate, 2%, whole and skim; also, buttermilk
President: Bill McCarthy
CFO: Mike McGuire
VP: Michael Schlotman
Estimated Sales: $500,000-$1 Million
Number Employees: 100-249
Parent Co: Kroger Company
Type of Packaging: Consumer, Private Label
Brands:
Kroger

14577 **Windatt Farms**
1481 County Road #12
Picton, ON K0K 2T0
Canada 613-393-5289
Fax: 613-393-5289
Processor and exporter of frozen rhubarb and cherries
President: Reg Windatt
Number Employees: 10-19
Sq. footage: 3500
Brands:
Windatt Farms

14578 **Windcrest Meat Packers**
1350 Scugog 3rd Line
Port Perry, ON L9L 1B3
Canada 905-985-7267
Fax: 905-985-9393 800-750-2542
Processor of meat products including beef, pork, lamb, goat and veal
President: Victor Diminno
Estimated Sales: $1-2.5 Million
Number Employees: 10-19
Type of Packaging: Consumer, Private Label

14579 **Winder Dairy**
P.O.Box 70009
West Valley, UT 84170-0009 801-224-8686
Fax: 801-969-2223 800-946-3371
Processor of bread, pastries, cakes, rolls, milk, fruit juices, cottage cheese, sour cream and yogurt
Manager: Jake Smith
Executive VP: Kent Winder
Plant Manager: Dan Lukes
Estimated Sales: $44100000
Number Employees: 100-249
Sq. footage: 50000
Type of Packaging: Consumer, Food Service, Private Label
Brands:
Valley Farms
Winder

14580 **Windham Winery**
14727 Mountain Rd
Purcellville, VA 20132-3638 540-668-6464
Fax: 540-668-7679 info@windhamwinery.com
www.windhamwinery.com
Wines
Owner: George Bazaco

14581 **Windmill Candy**
7409 94th Street
Lubbock, TX 79424 806-785-4688
Fax: 806-785-4802
Candy
President: Michele Adams
Vice President: Ted Adams

Estimated Sales: Under $500,000
Number Employees: 6

14582 **Windmill Water**
2042 Old Us 66
Edgewood, NM 87015 505-281-9287
Fax: 505-286-9669 Windmillwater@comcast.net
www.windmillwater.com
Bottled spring water
President: Leon Ricter
Plant Manager: Leon Ricter
Office Manager: Diana Ricter
Estimated Sales: $ 1 - 3 Million
Number Employees: 1-4

14583 **Windsor Confections**
4632 Telegraph Ave
Oakland, CA 94609-2022 510-653-3703
Fax: 510-653-3755 800-860-0021
sales@windsorconfections.com
www.hooperschocolate.com
Produces a variety of chocolate confections including chocolate dipped strawberries and gift baskets. Windsor Confections is a unique social venture - a division of the California Autism Foundation, sales of their chocolate providesupport to autism services and public awareness campaigns.
President: Jeff White LCSW
Estimated Sales: $ 5 - 10 Million
Number Employees: 10-19
Parent Co: California Autism Foundation
Brands:
ANYTIME CANDY
BREAK UP
CALIFORNIA FINEST
CHEWEY KISSES
CHOCOLATE JOLLIES
HOOPEE DOOPS
MY SELECTION
OLD FASHIONED
PATIO SQUARES
ROYAL GIFT
SMOOTH AND MELTIES

14584 **(HQ)Windsor Foods**
3355 W Alabama St Ste 730
Houston, TX 77098 713-843-5200
Fax: 713-960-9709
rgutierrez@windsorfoods.com
www.windsorfoods.com
Processor of frozen Chinese finger food
President: Greg Geib
Chairman: Anne Smalling
Estimated Sales: $10-20 Million
Number Employees: 3,000
Sq. footage: 12000
Brands:
Golden Tiger

14585 **Windsor Frozen Foods**
3355 W Alabama St
Suite 730
Houston, TX 77098 713-843-5200
Fax: 713-960-9709 800-437-6936
info@windsorfoods.com
www.windsorfoods.com
Italian, Mexican, American foods
President/CEO: Greg Geib
SVP/CFO: Manuel Martinez
VP Sales/Marketing: Lynn Sutter
VP Human Resources: George Young
Purchasing Director: Tim Arndt
Estimated Sales: $20-50 Million
Number Employees: 20
Sq. footage: 8585
Type of Packaging: Consumer, Food Service, Bulk
Brands:
BERNARDI
GOLDEN TIGER
THE ORIGINAL CHILI BOWL

14586 **Windsor Vineyards**
P.O.Box 368
Windsor, CA 95492 707-836-5000
Fax: 707-836-5900 800-333-9987
webamster@windsorvineyards.com
www.windsorvineyards.com
Producer and retailer of wines and champagnes
President: Tammy Boatright
Executive VP: Donna Elias
Sales: Howard Smith
Estimated Sales: $ 50 - 100 Million
Number Employees: 100-249
Number of Brands: 1
Number of Products: 42
Parent Co: Klein Family Vinters
Type of Packaging: Consumer
Brands:
Windsor Vineyards

14587 **Windsor Vineyards**
205 Concourse Boulevard
Santa Rosa, CA 95403
800-289-9463
webmaster@windsorvineyards.com
www.windsorvineyards.com
Processor of wines
President: Tammy Boatright
General Manager: J B Winkler
VP Operations: Pat McDowell
Estimated Sales: $ 50 - 100 Million
Number Employees: 100-249
Sq. footage: 10000
Brands:
Windsor Vineyards

14588 **Windwalker Vineyards**
7360 Perry Creek Rd
Somerset, CA 95684 530-620-4054
Fax: 530-620-5224 windwalkerinfo@gotsky.com
www.windwalkervineyard.com
Wines
Owner: Jim Taff
Operations: Alanna Taff
Estimated Sales: More than $500,000
Number Employees: 3
Brands:
Windwalker

14589 **Wine Country Chef LLC**
PO Box 1416
Hidden Valley Lake, CA 95461 707-322-0406
Fax: 800-306-2660 chef@winecounrtychef.net
www.winecountrychef.net
Organic spice blends and all natural marinades & sauces
President/Owner: Harold Imbrunetti
Estimated Sales: $250,000
Number Employees: 2
Number of Brands: 4
Number of Products: 4
Type of Packaging: Consumer, Food Service, Bulk
Brands:
WINE COUNTRY CHEF GOURMET MARINADE
WINE COUNTRY CHEF LEMON PEPPER RUB
WINE COUNTRY CHEF SPICED MUSTARD
WINE COUNTRY CHIEF SPICED BBQ RUB

14590 **Wine Country Kitchens**
511 Alexis Ct
Napa, CA 94558 707-252-9463
Fax: 707-252-9424
wck@winecountykitchens.com
www.winecountrykitchens.com
Manufacturer of gourmet oils, wine vinegars, pasta suaces and salad dressings
Owner: John Mc Intosh
Quality Control: Brian Witbracht
Marketing Director: Marilyn Moe Asmuth
Estimated Sales: $ 20-50 Million
Number Employees: 20-49
Type of Packaging: Private Label
Brands:
Napa Valley Barbeque Co.
Napa Valley Harvest
Wine Country Kitchens

14591 **Wine Country Pasta**
201 W Napa St
Sonoma, CA 95476-6643 707-935-1366
Pasta
Owner: Joe Wade
Estimated Sales: Below $ 5 Million
Number Employees: 1-4

14592 **Wine Group**
315 Montgomery St
San Francisco, CA 94104 415-986-8700
Fax: 415-986-4305
Processor of wines
Chairman: Arthur Ciocca
Ceo: David Kent
Cfo: Richard Mahoney
Number Employees: 5-9
Type of Packaging: Consumer
Brands:
FRANZIA WINE
GLEN ELLEN
MG VALLEJO
MOGEN DAVID

14593 **Wine-A-Rita**
2801 Richmond Rd
Texarkana, TX 75503 903-832-0467
Fax: 903-838-7803 info@wineglace.com
www.wineglace.com
frozen wine drinks
President/Owner: Donna Griffin
CEO: Judy Smith

14594 **Winfrey Fudge & Candy**
40 Newburyport Tpke
Rowley, MA 01969-2106 978-948-7448
Fax: 978-948-7088 888-946-3739
info@winfreys.com www.winfreys.com
Chocolates and fudge
Owner: Chris Winfrey
CFO: Christine Winfrey
Estimated Sales: Below $ 5 Million
Number Employees: 10-19
Brands:
Winfrey's

14595 **Wing Hing Noodle Company**
1646 E 23rd St
Los Angeles, CA 90011 323-235-5432
Fax: 323-231-9022 888-223-8899
kenny@winghing.com www.winghing.com
Processor and importer of fresh, dry and pre-cooked noodles; also, fortune cookies, tofu products and egg roll, wonton and potsticker wrappers
President: Kenny Yee
Estimated Sales: $1800000
Number Employees: 20-49
Brands:
Wing Hing Gold Coin
Wing Hing Panda

14596 **Wing It**
PO Box 673
Falmouth, MA 02541-0673 508-540-9860
Fax: 508-540-9861 sales@wingit.com
www.wingit.com
Processor of buffalo wing sauce
President: Steven Robinson
Type of Packaging: Consumer, Food Service, Private Label, Bulk
Brands:
Wing It

14597 **Wing Nien Company**
30560 San Antonio St
Hayward, CA 94544-7102 510-487-8877
Fax: 510-489-6666 ghall@wnfoods.com
www.wnfoods.com
Processor and packager of sauces, oils, salsa, mustard and syrups; exporter of organic oils and sauces; also, custom blending and packaging in portion packs, glass bottles and plastic containers available
Manager: Linda Lee
Plant Superintendent: Jon Choy
Estimated Sales: $ 10 - 20 Million
Number Employees: 20-49
Sq. footage: 45000
Parent Co: US Enterprise Corporation
Type of Packaging: Consumer, Food Service, Private Label
Other Locations:
Wing Nien Co.
Vancouver BC

14598 **Wing Seafood Company**
1850 S Canal St
Chicago, IL 60616 312-942-9930
Fax: 312-942-0391
Owner: Wing Ng
Estimated Sales: $1.2 Million
Number Employees: 5-9

14599 **(HQ)Wing Sing Chong Company**
390 Swift Ave # 13
S San Francisco, CA 94080-6221 415-552-1234
Fax: 415-552-3812
Manufacturer, importer and wholesaler/distributor of Oriental foods
Owner: Roberta Woo
Estimated Sales: $15 Million
Number Employees: 1-4
Sq. footage: 50000

Brands:
LANTERN

14600 **(HQ)Wing's Food Products**
50 Torlake Crescent
Etobicoke, ON M8Z 1B8
Canada 416-259-2662
Fax: 416-259-3414 custserv@wings.ca
www.wings.ca
Processor of portioned controlled foods including ketchup, mustard, relish, vinegar, soy and plum sauce and steam cooked noodles; manufacturer of egg roll wrappers
president: Jennifer Chan
General Manager: Neal Lee
Finance Manager: Cynthia Lee
Number Employees: 10
Parent Co: Wing's Food Products
Type of Packaging: Food Service, Private Label, Bulk
Other Locations:
Wing's Food Products
Edmonton AB
Brands:
Wing's
Wing's

14601 **Wing-Time**
P.O.Box 775003
Steamboat Springs, CO 80477 970-871-1198
Fax: 970-871-1215 info@wingtime.com
www.wingtime.com
Buffalo wing and barbecue sauces available in six varieties
President: Terence Brown
Estimated Sales: Below $ 5 Million
Number Employees: 1-4
Number of Brands: 1
Number of Products: 6
Type of Packaging: Consumer, Food Service, Private Label

14602 **(HQ)Winger Cheese**
P.O.Box 238
Towner, ND 58788 701-537-5463
Fax: 701-537-5854 www.wingercheese.com
Manufacturer of cheese
Owner: Pete Winger
Number Employees: 1-4
Type of Packaging: Food Service, Bulk
Brands:
Winger

14603 **Wings Foods of Alberta**
2959 Parsons Road
Edmonton, AB T6N 1B8
Canada 780-433-6406
Fax: 780-431-1026 custserv@wingsalberta.com
www.wingfood.com
Processor of noodles, condiments and fortune cookies
President: Barry Lee
Sales Manager: Doug Petrie
Production Manager: Chris Hambley
Number Employees: 50-99
Sq. footage: 85000
Type of Packaging: Private Label
Brands:
PC
Wing's

14604 **Winkler**
500 Main St.
Winkler, MB R6W 4B3 204-325-4771
Fax: 204-325-5059 http://www.winklertimes.com
President: Tom Winkler
Number Employees: 100-249

14605 **(HQ)Winmix/Natural Care Products**
7466 Cape Girardeau Street
Englewood, FL 34224-8004 941-475-7432
Fax: 941-475-7432
Processor and exporter of soft serve ice cream and sorbets, meat analogs, fruit juice and beverage bases, low-fat replacers and nonfat mixes. Importer of juice and coffee bases. Research and development services available for icecream, sorbet and meatless analogs and health care products
Board of Directors: Winsor Eveland
Owner: Martha Efird
Estimated Sales: $100000
Number Employees: 2
Number of Brands: 4
Number of Products: 350
Sq. footage: 2000
Type of Packaging: Consumer, Food Service, Private Label, Bulk
Brands:
Multy Grain Foods
Soy Flax 5000
Winmix

14606 **(HQ)Winn-Dixie Stores**
5050 Edgewood Ct
Jacksonville, FL 32254 904-783-5000
Fax: 904-783-5294 800-946-6349
info@winndixie.com www.winndixie.com
Coffee and tea
President/CEO: Peter Lynch
SVP/CFO: Bennett Nussbaum
Estimated Sales: $7.4 Billion
Number Employees: 50,000
Parent Co: Harris Teeter, Inc
Brands:
Astor
THRIFTY MAID
WINN & LOVETT
WINN-DIXIE

14607 **(HQ)Winning Solutions**
Po Box 612688
Dallas, TX 75261-2688 970-264-2949
Fax: 800-859-9881 800-899-2563
winningin@aol.com www.miracleofaloe.com
Processor and exporter of aloe vera gel drinks, juice blends, etc
President: JC Clarke Jr
Estimated Sales: $500,000-$1 Million
Number Employees: 5-9
Sq. footage: 2000
Type of Packaging: Consumer, Food Service
Other Locations:
Winning Solutions
Westport CT

14608 **Winona Packing Company**
152 Highway 407
Winona, MS 38967 662-283-4317
Fax: 662-283-4799
Processor of beef and pork; also, fresh and smoked sausage
President: Bill Graves Jr
Vice President: Vicky Stiemann
Estimated Sales: $ 10-20 Million
Number Employees: 20-49
Type of Packaging: Consumer, Food Service

14609 **Winslow B. Whitley**
405 N Center Avenue
Oakley, ID 83346 208-862-3229
Vegetables

14610 **Winter Garden Citrus**
P.O.Box 770069
Winter Garden, FL 34777 407-656-4423
Fax: 407-656-1007
Frozen citrus beverages
President: Steven Beckenmeyer
General Manager: Everette Fisher
CFO: Floyd Skipper
CEO: Everett Fischer
General Manager: Eberette Fischer
Sales Manager: Peter Hann
Operation Manager: Mary Turner
Plant Manager: Paul Ballentine
Estimated Sales: $ 50-100 Million
Number Employees: 100-249
Type of Packaging: Private Label
Brands:
Winter Garden

14611 **Winter Harbor Co-Op**
P.O.Box 69
Winter Harbor, ME 04693 207-963-5857
Fax: 207-963-7275
Whole fish and seafood
Manager: Randy Johnson
Estimated Sales: $600,000
Number Employees: 1-4

14612 **Winter Sausage Manufacturing Company**
22011 Gratiot Ave
Eastpointe, MI 48021 586-777-9080
Fax: 586-777-7996
dw.wintersausage@sbcglobal.net
www.wintersausage.com
Manufacturer of sausages, premium deli meats and spiral hams. Proprietary and private label
President: Rosemary Wuerz
Founder: Eugene Winter
VP/Sales: Ron Eckert
R&D/Marketing: Dorianne Wuerz
Quality Control: Mary Ellen Menard
Production/Purchasing Director: Eugene Wuerz
Plant Manager: Greg Van Hazenbrouck
Estimated Sales: $4.7 Million
Number Employees: 40
Type of Packaging: Consumer, Private Label, Bulk
Brands:
Farmer Jack
Kroger
Lipary

14613 **Winterbrook Beverage Group**
2000 Schenley Place
Greendale, IN 47025-1593 812-537-7348
Bottled water
President: Raymond Smith
Brands:
Cascadia
Lacroix Sparkling Wa
Lacroix Spring Water
Winterbrook Seltzer

14614 **Wintergreen Winery**
P.O.Box 648
Nellysford, VA 22958-0648 434-361-2519
Fax: 434-361-1510 info@wintergreenwinery.com
www.wintergreenwinery.com
Wine
Co-Owner: Jeff Stone
Co-Owner: Tamara Stone
Estimated Sales: $ 1 - 3 Million
Number Employees: 1-4

14615 **Winters Winery**
15 Main St
Winters, CA 95694-1722 530-795-3201
Fax: 916-795-1119
Wine
President: David Storm
VP: Santiago Moreno
Estimated Sales: $220,000
Number Employees: 3

14616 **Wisconsin Cheese**
1931 N 15th Ave
Melrose Park, IL 60160 708-450-0074
Fax: 708-450-1670 wiscon@wisconcorp.com
www.wisconcorp.com
Manufacturer and processor of quality Italian cheeses and specialty foods
President: Natale Caputo
Marketing Director: Jerry Jack
Purchasing Manager: Joy Baker
Estimated Sales: $ 20 - 50 Million
Number Employees: 50-99
Sq. footage: 52000
Parent Co: Wiscon Corporation
Type of Packaging: Consumer, Food Service, Private Label, Bulk
Brands:
Caputo
Grate Wiscon
Red Cow
Red Sheep

14617 **Wisconsin Cheese**
200 University Ave
Westwood, MA 02090-2307 781-320-0288
Fax: 781-320-0108
Cheese
Manager: Ralph Panico
Marketing Director: Ralph Panico
Estimated Sales: Less than $500,000
Number Employees: 5-9

14618 **Wisconsin Cheese Group**
105 3rd St
Monroe, WI 53566 608-325-2012
Fax: 608-329-2381 800-332-6518
info@wisconsincheesegroup.com
www.wisconsincheesegroup.com
Cheese
Manager: Arthur Stickley
Estimated Sales: $ 10-24.9 Million
Number Employees: 50-99
Brands:
U Viajero
Wisconsin Cheese

14619 **Wisconsin Cheeseman**
P.O.Box 1
Madison, WI 53701 608-837-5166
Fax: 608-837-5493
customerservice@wisconsincheeseman.com
www.wisconsincheeseman.com
cheese and spreads, chocolate, nuts and snacks, cakes and cookies and
Owner: David McKee
President/CEO: Holly Creamer
CFO: Jay Singer
VP: Frances Creamer
Human Resources Director: Katie Rikli
Estimated Sales: $60600000
Number Employees: 250-499
Type of Packaging: Consumer, Food Service, Private Label, Bulk

14620 **Wisconsin Dairy State Cheese**
P.O.Box 215
Rudolph, WI 54475-0215 715-435-3144
Fax: 715-435-3146
Cheddar cheese
President: Mike Moran
Estimated Sales: $ 20-50 Million
Number Employees: 20-49
Brands:
Black River
Hennings

14621 **Wisconsin Dairyland Fudge Company**
216 Broadway
Wisconsin Dells, WI 53965 608-254-4136
Fax: 608-254-7771 wisconsin@dellsfudge.com
www.dellsfudge.com
Dairy farm products
Manager: Roj Rosen
Estimated Sales: Below $ 5 Million
Number Employees: 20-49
Brands:
Dairyland
Swiss Made

14622 **Wisconsin Farmers' Union Cheese Company**
303 E Us Highway 18
Montfort, WI 53569 608-943-6753
Fax: 608-943-6769 shop@wfucheese.com
www.wfucheese.com
Manufacturer of aged, curd, fresh cheese; gift boxes are available
Owner: Doug Peterson
Plant Manager/Production: Tim Tehl
Estimated Sales: $500,000-$1 Million
Number Employees: 1-4
Brands:
Montforte

14623 **Wisconsin Packing Company**
4700 N 132nd St
Butler, WI 53007-1603 262-781-2400
800-558-2000
Processor of hamburger patties, chili and diced beef
President: Justin Segel
VP Sales/Operations: Frank Vignieri
Plant Manager: Rick Chamber
Number Employees: 250-499
Sq. footage: 140000
Type of Packaging: Consumer, Food Service, Private Label, Bulk

14624 **Wisconsin Spice**
478 S Industrial Park Rd
Berlin, WI 54923 920-361-3555
Fax: 920-361-0818 www.wisconsinspice.com
Manufacturer and exporter of gourmet spices and herbs, seasoning blends, dry mustard products and prepared liquid mustards
President: Phillip Sass
VP Marketing: John Clausen
VP Sales: Phillips Sass
Estimated Sales: $7 Million
Number Employees: 20-49
Type of Packaging: Consumer, Food Service, Private Label, Bulk
Brands:
Uncle Phil's

14625 **Wisconsin Whey International**
N2689 County Road S
Juda, WI 53550-9714 608-233-5101
Fax: 608-934-1044 wiswhey@tds.net
Processor and exporter of kosher and HALAL approved whey products including edible lactose and whey protein concentrate
President: Linda Smith
Sales Manager: Doug Clairday
Number Employees: 50-99
Sq. footage: 23900
Type of Packaging: Bulk
Brands:
LACTOSE PHARMA
WISCONSIN WHEY INTERNATIONAL
WPC 34
XL 2000
XL 440
XL 480

14626 **Wisconsin Wilderness Food Products**
101 W Capitol Dr Stop 2
Milwaukee, WI 53212 414-964-6466
Fax: 414-964-6675 800-359-3039
www.wisconsinwilderness.com
Processor of bread and dessert mixes including cranberry cinnamon, date nut and apple crisp; also, cranberry mustard and chutney, honey mustard and preserves
President: Margaret Gunn
Plant Manager: Christina Grohmann
Estimated Sales: $1000000
Number Employees: 10-19
Number of Brands: 2
Number of Products: 30
Sq. footage: 21000
Type of Packaging: Consumer, Food Service, Private Label, Bulk

14627 **Wisdom Natural Brands**
1203 W San Pedro St
Gilbert, AZ 85233 480-921-1373
Fax: 480-966-3805 800-899-9908
wisdom@wisdomnaturalbrands.com
www.wisdomnaturalbrands.com
Herbal teas
President: James May
Vice President: Steve May
Quality Control: Mike Small
Operations Manager: Mike Small
Estimated Sales: $ 1 - 3 Million
Number Employees: 10-19
Type of Packaging: Consumer, Private Label, Bulk
Brands:
LA MERCED ORGANIC
STEVIA PRODUCTS
SWEET AND SLENDER NATURAL SWEETENER
SWEET LEAF
WISDOM NUTRITION
WISDOM OF THE ANCIENTS HERBAL TEAS

14628 **(HQ)Wise Foods**
245 Townpark Dr NW Ste 75
Kennesaw, GA 30144 770-426-5821
Fax: 770-528-0971 snackmaster@wisenacks.com
www.wisesnacks.com
Manufacturer of salty snack foods
President/CEO: Richard Robertson
CFO: Thomas Van Autreve
CEO: Ed Lambert
Marketing VP: Terry McDaniel
Sales VP: Terry McDaniel
Number Employees: 1,000-4,999
Type of Packaging: Private Label
Other Locations:
Wise Foods Inc
Berwick PA
Wise Foods Inc
Bristol VA
Wise Foods Inc
Spartanburg SC
Brands:
BRAVOS
KRUNCHERS
NEW YORK DELI
QUINLAN
RIDGIES

14629 **Wise Foods**
228 Rasely St
Berwick, PA 18603 570-759-4000
Fax: 570-759-4001
snackmaster@wisesnacks.com
www.wisesnacks.com
Manufacturer of salty snack foods
Manager: Tony Kennedy
CFO: Tom Mannion
Operations: Bruce Roberts
Number Employees: 1,000-4,999
Other Locations:
Wise Foods Inc
Bristol VA
Wise Foods Inc
Spartanburg SC

14630 **Wise Foods**
100 Amor Ave # 3
Carlstadt, NJ 07072-2100 201-507-0015
Fax: 973-898-1840 corporate@wisesnacks.com
www.wisesnacks.com
Manufacturer of salty snacks foods
Executive Director: John Mc Ginnis
CEO: Richard Robertson
President: Edward M Lambert
Sales Director: Marc Atkinson
Estimated Sales: $ 1 - 3 Million
Number Employees: 5-9
Parent Co: Palladium Equity Partners
Type of Packaging: Private Label
Brands:
BRAVOS
CHEEZ DOODLES
KETTLE COOKED POTATO CHIPS
RIDGIES
WISE POTATO CHIPS

14631 **Wise Foods**
2233 Weaver Pike
Bristol, TN 37620-5615 864-585-9011
Fax: 864-594-6628
Manufacturer of salty snacks foods.
President/Owner: Bo Savage
Director Manufacturing: Dewey Armstrong
Estimated Sales: $50-99.9 Million
Number Employees: 250-499
Other Locations:
Wise Foods Inc
Bristol VA
Wise Foods Inc
Berwick PA

14632 **Wishnev Wine Management**
2125 Oak Grove Rd Ste 120
Walnut Creek, CA 94598 925-930-6374
Fax: 925-930-6388
Wines
Owner: Sanford Wishnev
Estimated Sales: $300,000-500,000
Number Employees: 1-4
Type of Packaging: Private Label

14633 **Wisner Minnow Hatchery**
681 Pete Haring Rd
Wisner, LA 71378 318-724-6133
Fax: 318-724-6138 www.haringspridecatfish.com
Catfish
President: Carl Haring
Estimated Sales: $ 20 - 50 Million
Number Employees: 250-499

14634 **Wissahickon Spring Water International**
10447 Drummond Rd
Philadelphia, PA 19154 215-824-3300
Fax: 215-824-3180 800-394-3733
tedh@wspringwater.com
www.wspringwater.com
Bottled water
General Manager: Ted Hertz
CFO: Mike Pessiki
Director of Sales: Joe Panichelli
Estimated Sales: $ 20-50 Million
Number Employees: 50-99
Type of Packaging: Private Label
Brands:
Wissahickon Spring Water

14635 **Wisteria Candy Cottage**
P.O.Box 985
Boulevard, CA 91905 619-766-4453
800-458-8246
www.candycottage.com
Candy
Owner: Dana Eascobellis
Co-Owner: LuzCelia Rankin
Estimated Sales: Less than $500,000
Number Employees: 1-4
Type of Packaging: Private Label

14636 **Witness Tree Vineyard**
7111 Spring Valley Rd NW
Salem, OR 97304 503-585-7874
Fax: 503-362-9765 888-478-8766
info@witnesstreevineyard.com
www.witnesstreevineyard.com
Wines
President: Carolyn Devine
CEO: Carolyn Devine
Vice President: Dennis Devine
Marketing Manager: Carolyn Devine
National Sales Director: Mark Pape
Winemaker/Vineyard Manager: Steven Westby
Estimated Sales: $ 2.5-5 Million
Number Employees: 5-9
Type of Packaging: Private Label
Brands:
Witness Tree Vineyard

14637 **Wixon/Fontarome**
1390 E Bolivar Ave
St Francis, WI 53235-4521 414-769-3000
Fax: 414-769-3024 chuck-ehemann@wixon.com
www.wixon.com
Processor and packer of natural spices, seasoning blends for meat products, flavors, food chemicals, etc
President: A Peter Gottsacker
Executive VP: Chuck Ehemann
VP Sales/Marketing: Jerry Morgan
Estimated Sales: $46675000
Number Employees: 100-249
Parent Co: Fontarome
Type of Packaging: Consumer, Food Service, Private Label, Bulk
Brands:
Flavor Shaker
French Flavor Maker
Licorics Granules

14638 **Wixson Honey**
4937 Lakemont Himrod Rd
Dundee, NY 14837 607-243-8583
Fax: 607-243-7143 www.wixsonhoney.com
Manufacturer and importer of honey including clover, buckwheat, orange, beeswax and fall flower
Owner: Jerald Howell
Estimated Sales: $3-5 Million
Number Employees: 1-4
Type of Packaging: Consumer, Food Service, Private Label, Bulk

14639 **Wizards Cauldron, LTD**
878 Firetower Rd
Yanceyville, NC 27379 336-694-5665
Fax: 336-664-5284 ron@wizardscauldron.com
www.wizardscauldron.com
Manufacturer and exporter of natural and organic salad dressing and sauces including barbecue, steak, soy, poultry, stir-fry, hot, table and vegetable
President: Sean Kearney
CEO: John Troy
VP: Glenda Smith
Research & Development: Tina Toney
Quality Control: Jason Dawson
VP Sales and Marketing: Ron Rash
Purchasing Manager: Sean Kearney
Number Employees: 5-9
Sq. footage: 10000
Parent Co: Wizard's Cauldron
Type of Packaging: Consumer, Food Service, Private Label, Bulk
Brands:
Flavor of the Rainforest
Simply Delicious
Troys

14640 **Wm. Wrigley Jr. Company**
2800 State Route 47
Yorkville, IL 60560-9441 630-553-4800
Fax: 630-553-4801
Chewing gum manufacturer.
Executive Director: Lupe Deleon
Estimated Sales: $50-100 Million
Number Employees: 10-19
Parent Co: Wm. Wrigley Jr. Company

14641 **Woeber Mustard Manufacturing**
1966 Commerce Circle
PO Box 388
Springfield, OH 45501-0388
Fax: 937-323-1679 800-548-2929
raywoeber@woebermustard.com
www.woebermustard.com
Mustard, mayo gourmet, sandwhich pals, mister mustard, woeber's reserve, supreme mustard, organic mustard, crowning touch, horseradish, garlic, vinegars, lemon juice
President: Ray Woeber
Vice President: Dick Woeber
Quality Control: Randy Weyant
VP National Sales: Rick Schmidt
Human Resources Manager: Judy Finnegan
Operations Manager: Christopher Woeber
Logistics Manager: Bob Sharp
Purchasing: Joyce Capper
Estimated Sales: $40 Million
Number Employees: 100-249
Type of Packaging: Consumer, Food Service, Private Label, Bulk
Brands:
CROWNING TOUCH
WOEBER

14642 **Wohlt Cheese Corporation**
1005 Orville Dr
New London, WI 54961 920-982-9000
Fax: 920-982-6288 sales@wohltcheese.com
www.wohltcheese.com
Processed cheese
President: Marilyn Taylor
Estimated Sales: $ 10-20 Million
Number Employees: 50-99
Sq. footage: 52000

14643 **Wohrles Foods**
1619 East St
Pittsfield, MA 01201 413-442-1518
Fax: 413-442-6024 800-628-6114
jon@wohrlesfoods.com www.wohrlesfoods.com
Meat products, distribute food services
President: Walter Pickwell
VP Marketing: Jon Pickwell
VP Purchasing: Robert Tessler
Estimated Sales: Less than $500,000
Number Employees: 1-4
Type of Packaging: Consumer, Private Label, Bulk

14644 **Wolf Canyon Foods**
27880 Dorris Dr Ste 200
Carmel, CA 93923 831-626-1323
Fax: 831-626-1325 info@wolfcanyon.com
www.wolfcanyon.com
Processor and exporter of freeze-dried fruits, vegetables, meat, seafood and dairy products
VP: Marybeth Frearson
Sales Manager: Carlos Forte
Estimated Sales: Under $500,000
Number Employees: 3
Sq. footage: 80000
Type of Packaging: Bulk

14645 **Wolf Creek Vineyards**
2637 Cleveland Massillon Rd
Norton, OH 44203-6417 330-666-9285
Fax: 330-665-1445 800-436-0426
sara@wineryatwolfcreek.com
www.wineryatwolfcreek.com
Wine
President: Andrew Troutman
Estimated Sales: $ 5-10 Million
Number Employees: 10-19
Number of Brands: 1
Number of Products: 15

14646 **Wolferman's**
P.O.Box 9100
Medford, OR 97501
Fax: 913-492-5195 wolf@wolfermans.com
www.wolfermans.com
Processor of fresh and frozen English muffins, crumpets and tea and toasting bread
President: Micheal Dubois
CFO: Shane Jarvis
CFO: Gary Strub
Estimated Sales: $ 3 - 5 Million
Number Employees: 20-49
Sq. footage: 110000
Parent Co: Sara Lee Corporation
Type of Packaging: Consumer
Brands:
Charlie Trotter's
Wolferman's

14647 **Wolfgang Puck Food Company**
1250 4th Street
Suite 310
Santa Monica, CA 90401-1304 310-432-1350
Fax: 310-451-5595
Frozen version of his famous California style pizzas, pastas, canned soups and gourmet specialities
President: Terry Hall
Number Employees: 1-4

14648 **Wolfies Gourmet Nuts**
130 Olive St
Findlay, OH 45840-5325 419-423-1355
Fax: 419-423-8969 866-889-6887
wolfie@wolfiesnuts.com www.wolfiesnuts.com
Dry-roasted nut products
Owner: Bill Wolf
Estimated Sales: $5-9.9 Million
Number Employees: 5-9
Type of Packaging: Consumer, Bulk

14649 **(HQ)Wolfies Roasted Nuts**
130 Olive St
Findlay, OH 45840 419-423-1355
Fax: 419-423-8969 866-889-6887
wolfie@wolfiesnuts.com www.wolfiesnuts.com
Processor of dry roasted and crisp-coated nuts including cashews, peanuts, almonds and mixes
Owner: Bill Wolf
Estimated Sales: $3000000
Number Employees: 1-4
Sq. footage: 6000
Type of Packaging: Consumer, Food Service, Private Label
Brands:
Totem

14650 **Wolfson Casing Corporation**
700 S Fulton Ave
Mount Vernon, NY 10550 914-668-9000
Fax: 914-668-6900 800-221-8042
sales@wolfsoncasing.com
www.wolfsoncasing.com
Processor, exporter and importer of sausage casings
Owner: Stephen Bardfield
VP: Stephen Bardfield
Sales Representative: Seth Sommers
Estimated Sales: $26300000
Number Employees: 50-99
Sq. footage: 40000

14651 **Wollersheim Winery**
P.O.Box 87
Prairie Du Sac, WI 53578-0087 608-643-6515
Fax: 608-643-8149 800-847-9463
info@wollersheim.com www.wollersheim.com
Wines
President: Philippe Coquard
CFO: Jo Ann Wollersheim
Marketing Director: Julius Coquard
Operations Manager: Phil Coquard
Estimated Sales: Below $ 5 Million
Number Employees: 20-49
Type of Packaging: Private Label
Brands:
Wollersheim Winery

14652 **Wolter Farms**
7200 Carmel Valley Road
Carmel, CA 93923-9525 831-624-8807
Farm produce

14653 **Wolverine Packing**
2535 Rivard St
Detroit, MI 48207 313-259-7500
Fax: 313-568-1909
bbartes@wolverinepacking.com
www.wolverinepacking.com
Processor of portion packed lamb, veal and beef
President/CEO: Alfred Bonahoom
CFO: Brian Bartes
Vice President: Roger Bonahoom
Sales Director: Robert Smith
Estimated Sales: $6 Million
Number Employees: 50-99
Sq. footage: 110000
Type of Packaging: Consumer, Food Service, Private Label, Bulk

14654 **Wolverton Seafood**
PO Box 1721
Houlton, ME 04730-5721 506-276-4629
Fax: 506-276-1803

Seafood
Owner: Margaret Wolberton

14655 **Wonder Bread**
1180 W Center St
Provo, UT 84601-3900 801-373-8192
Fax: 801-531-6494 800-483-7253
www.wonderbread.com
Processor of breads, cakes, cereals and crackers
Manager: Peggy Zobell
Marketing Director: Troy Daw
Estimated Sales: $300,000-500,000
Number Employees: 1-4
Parent Co: Interstate Brands Corporation
Type of Packaging: Consumer, Food Service

14656 **Wonder/Hostess**
16823 Douglas Avenue
Jamaica, NY 11433-1241 201-837-8317
Processor of breads, cakes and doughnuts
Manager: Jim Forbes
Estimated Sales: Less than $500,000
Number Employees: 5-9
Parent Co: Interstate Brands Corporation
Type of Packaging: Consumer, Food Service

14657 **Wong Wing Foods**
1875 Rue Bercy
Montreal, QC H2K 2T9
Canada 514-524-3676
Fax: 514-521-1404 800-361-4820
www.wongwing.ca
Processor and exporter of frozen Chinese foods including egg and spring rolls, fried rice, wonton soup, chicken products, entrees, etc.; also, sauces including plum, cherry, garlic, sweet and sour, soya, etc
President: Marcel Wong
CEO: Pauline Wong
President: Erik Yelle
Vice President: Bernard Wong
Marketing/Sales: Colin Prince
Production Manager: Phillipe Cha
Plant Manager: Robert Lee
Purchasing Manager: Victor Lee
Number Employees: 350
Sq. footage: 147337
Type of Packaging: Consumer, Food Service, Private Label
Brands:
Emperors Choice
Pagoda
See Jing
Wong Wing

14658 **Wonton Food**
220-222 Moore St
Brooklyn, NY 11206-3744 718-628-6868
Fax: 718-628-1028 800-776-8889
goldenbowl@wontonfood.com
www.wontonfood.com
Processor of fortune cookies, eggroll and wonton skins and dry and fresh noodles including chow mein, lo mein, spinach and wonton; importer of oriental canned and dry goods
President: Sing Lee
CFO: Weilik Chan
Sales/Marketing Manager: Danny Zeng
Estimated Sales: $ 20 - 50 Million
Number Employees: 100-249
Type of Packaging: Consumer, Food Service, Private Label

14659 **Wood Brothers**
P.O.Box 4348
West Columbia, SC 29171-4348 803-796-5146
Fax: 803-796-5291
Processor of mayonnaise, barbecue and tartar sauces, mustard and salad dressings including Thousand Island, French, Italian, blue cheese and slaw
President: Warren C Wood
VP: Douglas Wood
Production Manager: James Wood
Estimated Sales: $110000
Number Employees: 10-19
Type of Packaging: Food Service, Private Label, Bulk
Brands:
Capital
Cardinal
Carolina Chef
Glenwood
Holland

14660 **Wood's Sugar Bush**
N7845 170th Street
Spring Valley, WI 54767-8101 715-772-4656
Fax: 715-772-4665 www.woodsugarbush.com
Processor of certified organic maple syrup, cream and granulated sugar
President: Scott Wood
Number Employees: 5
Number of Brands: 1
Number of Products: 4
Sq. footage: 3500
Type of Packaging: Consumer, Food Service, Private Label, Bulk

14661 **Woodbine**
729 Pecan Point Rd
Norfolk, VA 23502-3416 757-461-2731
Fax: 757-461-4704
Manufacturer of beef and pork. Full distribution of food service items
President: Ray Lister
Production Manager: Aubrey Lister
Estimated Sales: $3-5 Million
Number Employees: 10-19
Type of Packaging: Food Service

14662 **Woodbury Vineyards**
3215 S Roberts Rd
Fredonia, NY 14063 716-679-9463
Fax: 716-679-9464 866-691-9463
woodburyvineyardsginny@hotmail.com
www.woodburyvineyards.com
winery
President: Joseph Carney
Retail Sales Manager: Virginia Bragg
Estimated Sales: $1,700,000
Number Employees: 5
Brands:
Woodbury Vineyards

14663 **Wooden Valley Winery**
4756 Suisun Valley Rd
Fairfield, CA 94534 707-864-0730
Fax: 707-864-6038 info@woodenvalley.com
www.woodenvalley.com
Wines
President: Richard Lanza
Estimated Sales: $ 1-2.5 Million
Number Employees: 5-9
Brands:
Wooden Valley

14664 **Woodfield Fish & OysterCompany**
P.O.Box 259
Galesville, MD 20765-0259 410-897-1093
Fax: 410-867-3423
Packaged ice and oyster
Owner: Bill Woodfield
Treasurer: Shirley Day
Vice President: Bill Woddfield
Plant Manager: David Loftice
Purchasing Manager: Ray Hardesty
Estimated Sales: Less than $500,000
Number Employees: 1-4
Type of Packaging: Private Label
Brands:
Woodfield Fish & Oyster
Woodfield Ice

14665 **Woodie Pie Company**
P.O.Box 1425
Artesia, NM 88211 505-746-2132
Processor of baked goods including pies
President: D Balencia
Estimated Sales: $500,000-$1 Million
Number Employees: 1-4
Type of Packaging: Consumer
Brands:
Woodie Pie

14666 **Woodlake Ranch**
21737 Avenue 337
Woodlake, CA 93286 559-564-2161
Fax: 559-564-8120
Grower of olives
President: Everett Kracov
Manager: Randy Childrsh
Estimated Sales: Less than $300,000
Number Employees: 1-4
Type of Packaging: Food Service, Private Label, Bulk

14667 **Woodland Foods**
2011 Swanson Ct
Gurnee, IL 60031 847-625-8600
Fax: 847-625-5050 sales@woodlandfoods.com
www.woodlandfoods.com
Mushrooms & truffles, chiles, sun-dried tomatoes, beans, lentils, peas, grains, rice, herbs & spices, asian noodles & seaweed, couscous, polenta & orzo, corn, flours, meals & posoles, dried fruit, nuts & seeds
Owner/President/CEO: David Moore
VP: Ely Suhre
Estimated Sales: $13 Million
Number Employees: 80
Number of Brands: 4
Number of Products: 500
Sq. footage: 65000
Type of Packaging: Consumer, Food Service, Private Label, Bulk
Brands:
D'allasandro

14668 **Woods Fabricators**
P.O.Box 167
Taylorsville, GA 30178-0167 770-684-5377
Fax: 770-684-0858 rwoods9595@aol.com
www.woodsfab.com
Equipment Manufacture-cooling tunnels and conveyors
President: Rickey Woods

14669 **Woods Smoked Meats**
1501 Business Highway 54 W
Bowling Green, MO 63334 573-324-2247
Fax: 573-324-2249 800-458-8426
info@woodssmokedmeats.com
www.woodssmokedmeats.com
Manufacturer of meats including ham, bacon, sausage, poultry, snack food, steaks and bratwurst
Co-Owner/President: Edward Woods
Co-Owner: Regina Woods
Estimated Sales: $ 5 - 10 Million
Number Employees: 20-49
Number of Brands: 2
Number of Products: 80
Sq. footage: 16000
Type of Packaging: Consumer, Private Label, Bulk
Brands:
Sweet Betsy From Pike
Woods

14670 **Woodside Vineyards**
205 Constitution Dr
Menlo Park, CA 94025 650-851-3144
Fax: 650-851-5037
info@woodsidevineyards.com
www.woodsidevineyards.com
Wines
Founder/President: Robert Mullen
Estimated Sales: $1,400,000
Number Employees: 5-9
Type of Packaging: Private Label
Brands:
Woodside Vineyards

14671 **Woodsmoke Provisions**
1240 Menlo Dr NW
Atlanta, GA 30318 404-355-5125
Fax: 404-355-6850
Salmon and trout
President: Mitchell Gallant
Estimated Sales: $ 3 - 5 Million
Number Employees: 20-49

14672 **Woodward Canyon Winery**
11920 W Highway 12
Touchet, WA 99360 509-525-4129
Fax: 509-522-0927 info@woodwardcanyon.com
www.woodwardcanyon.com
Wine
Owner: Rick Small
Production Director: Rick Small
Estimated Sales: Below $ 5 Million
Number Employees: 5-9

14673 **Woodworth Honey Company**
P.O.Box 247
Halliday, ND 58636-0247 701-938-4647
Fax: 701-938-4657 bon@ndsupernet.com
www.honey.com
Processor and exporter of honey
Owner: Brent Woodworth

Estimated Sales: $ 10 - 20 Million
Number Employees: 10-19
Sq. footage: 6000
Type of Packaging: Bulk

14674 Woody Associates Inc
844 E South St
York, PA 17403 717-843-3975
Fax: 717-843-5829
steven.ziolkowski@woody-decorators.com
www.woody-decorators.com
Founded in 1954, Woody Associates, Inc. is an engineering firm specializing in automatic decorating equipment for the food industry.
President: Harry Reinke
Design Engineer: Steven Ziolkowski

14675 Woody's Bar-B-Q Sauce Company
P.O.Box 66
Waldenburg, AR 72475-0066 870-579-2251
Fax: 870-579-2241 woodybbq@ricebelt.net
Barbeque sauce
President: William Wood
CEO: Cecelia Wood
Estimated Sales: $300,000-500,000
Number Employees: 5-9
Number of Products: 7
Type of Packaging: Consumer, Food Service, Private Label, Bulk

14676 Woolwich Dairy
425 Richardson Road
Orangeville, ON L9W 4Z4
Canada 519-941-9206
Fax: 519-941-9349 877-438-3499
gerhard@woolwichnova.com
www.woolwichdairy.com
Processor and exporter of goat's milk cheeses including cheddar, whole and crumbled feta, mozzarella, gouda, cream and brie
President: Olga Dutra
Sales Director: Gerhard Trimmel
Estimated Sales: $24 Million
Number Employees: 97
Number of Brands: 7
Number of Products: 109
Sq. footage: 4000
Parent Co: Nova Cheese
Type of Packaging: Consumer, Food Service, Private Label, Bulk
Brands:
Chevrai
Gourmet Goat
Madame Chevre

14677 Worden
7217 W Westbow Boulevard
Spokane, WA 99224-5668 509-455-7835
Fax: 509-838-4723 wordenwine@aol.com
Wine
President: Ken Barrett
CEO: Rebecca Chateaubriand
Estimated Sales: $ 1 Million+
Number Employees: 10
Sq. footage: 13000
Type of Packaging: Private Label, Bulk

14678 World Casing Corporation
47-06 Grand Ave
Maspeth, NY 11378 718-628-3800
Fax: 718-628-5800 800-221-4887
casings@worldcasing.com
www.worldcasing.com
Processor of natural sausage casings
President: Steven Feinstein
VP: Paul LoPiccolo
Estimated Sales: $2.5 Million
Number Employees: 20-49

14679 World Cheese Company
178 28th St
Brooklyn, NY 11232 718-965-1700
Fax: 718-965-0979
customerservice@worldcheeseco.com
www.worldcheeseco.com
Producer and importer of kosher cheeses
President: Meyer Thurm
Controller: Easter Swartz
VP Sales: Sam Lonner
Estimated Sales: $20000000
Sq. footage: 25000
Type of Packaging: Consumer, Food Service, Bulk
Brands:
HAOLAM
KO-SURE
MIGDAL
MILLER'S
SCHMERLING
TAAM TOV

14680 World Citrus
2720 University Parkway
Winston Salem, NC 27105-4224 336-723-1863
Fax: 336-722-6972
Citrus, fruits and juices
Manager: Jeanette Cornatzer
Operations Manager: Henry Tobkin
Production Manager: Rich Davis
Estimated Sales: $ 2.5-5 Million
Number Employees: 20

14681 World Citrus West
P.O.Box 1111
Lake Wales, FL 33859-1111 863-676-1411
Fax: 863-676-0494
Processor and bottler of chilled citrus drinks and juices including orange and grapefruit
CEO: Stephen M Caruso
Sales Manager (Retail): Rod Adamson
Number Employees: 250-499
Parent Co: Florida's Natural Growers'
Type of Packaging: Consumer, Food Service, Private Label, Bulk
Brands:
Daily Sun
Donald Duck
Supersocco

14682 World Confections
185 30th St
Brooklyn, NY 11232 718-768-8100
Fax: 718-499-4918 info@worldsconfections.com
www.worldconfections.com
Manufacturer and exporter of confectionery products including gum, bagged, bars, boxed chocolates, caramels, lollypops, jaw breakers, peppermint and lemon twists, seasonal, etc
President: Mathew Cohen
Estimated Sales: $10 Million
Number Employees: 50-99
Type of Packaging: Consumer, Private Label, Bulk

14683 World Cup Coffee & Tea
925 NW Davis Street
Portland, OR 97209-3103 503-228-5503
Fax: 503-228-3489 www.worldcupcoffee.com
Processor and exporter of coffee and teas; also, roasting and water filltration services available
President: Dan Welch
Number Employees: 10-19
Sq. footage: 12500
Type of Packaging: Consumer, Food Service, Bulk
Brands:
World Cup

14684 World Flavors
76 Louise Dr
Warminster, PA 18974 215-672-4400
Fax: 215-672-4405 www.worldflavors.com
Processor of custom formulated, manufactured and packaged ingredients for food processors including liquid and ground spices, meat, poultry and seafood seasonings, flavors, breadings, salad dressings and meat binders, extenders andtenderizing compounds
President: Robert Holmquist
VP Sales: Thomas Holmquist
Estimated Sales: $4900000
Number Employees: 50-99
Type of Packaging: Food Service, Private Label, Bulk

14685 World Ginseng Center
805 Kearny St
San Francisco, CA 94108 415-362-2255
Fax: 415-362-4859 800-747-8808
info@worldginsengcenter.com
www.worldginsengcenter.com
Manufacturer and exporter of ginseng and frozen seafood
President: Raymond Chao
Manager: William Nghe
Treasurer: Jane Chao
Estimated Sales: $300,000-500,000
Number Employees: 1-4
Type of Packaging: Consumer, Food Service, Private Label, Bulk

14686 World Harbors
176 First Flight Dr
Auburn, ME 04210 207-786-3200
Fax: 207-786-3900 800-355-6221
sales@worldharbors.com
www.worldharbors.com
Gourmet specialty foods, sauces and marinades
President: Steven Arthurs
CFO: Karen Foust
Quality Control: Mike Murphy
Estimated Sales: $ 5-10 Million
Number Employees: 20-49
Parent Co: Angostura International
Type of Packaging: Consumer, Food Service
Brands:
Acadia Naturals
Angostura
World Harbors

14687 World Herbs Gourmet Company
PO Box 101
Hadlyme, CT 06439-0101 860-526-1908
Fax: 860-526-1908
International seasoning blends for grilling

14688 World Nutrition
7001 N Scottsdale Rd # 2000
Scottsdale, AZ 85253-3666 480-921-1188
Fax: 480-921-1471 800-548-2710
www.worldnutrition.info
Processor and importer of vitamins, minerals, organic grains, fruits, vegetables and dehydrated fruits and vegetable juices
President: Ryuji Hirooka
COO: David Harrington
Marketing Manager: Pat Buel
Director Administration: Michele Moose
Production Manager: Andy Rodriguez
Estimated Sales: $ 50 - 100 Million
Number Employees: 100-249
Sq. footage: 126000

14689 World Organics Corporation
5242 Bolsa Ave Ste 3
Huntington Beach, CA 92649 714-893-0017
Fax: 714-897-5677 plicata@prodigy.net
Processor of vitamins, food supplements, herbal extracts and capsules and chlorophyll liquid and capsules
Owner: Paul Licata
CEO: Al Licata
Director of Sales: Bernie Lucich
Estimated Sales: Under $500,000
Number Employees: 10-19
Number of Brands: 4
Number of Products: 300
Sq. footage: 8000
Type of Packaging: Private Label
Brands:
Natural's Concept
Nu-Vista
POMA NONI BERRY
SEAFOOD
Vita-Vista

14690 World Softgel
1490 W Walnut Parkway
Compton, CA 90220-5002 310-900-1199
Fax: 310-900-1192
Processor and exporter of soft gelatin vitamins
President: Sam Ahn
Type of Packaging: Consumer, Food Service, Private Label, Bulk

14691 World Spice
223 E Highland Pkwy
Roselle, NJ 7203 908-245-0600
Fax: 908-245-0696 800-234-1060
sales@wsispice.com www.wsispice.com
Processor, importer, exporter and wholesaler/distributor of spices, seasonings, herbs and dehydrated vegetables; serving the food service market and industrial
President: Bela Lowy
Vice President: J Lefbowitz
Estimated Sales: $2000000
Number Employees: 5-9
Sq. footage: 15000
Type of Packaging: Food Service, Bulk
Brands:
WSI

14692 **World of Chantilly**
4302 Farragut Rd
Brooklyn, NY 11203 718-859-1110
Fax: 718-859-1303 info@chantilly.com
www.chantilly.com
Processor of kosher desserts including cakes, pies, brownies, tiramisu, tortes, etc
Owner/President: Alberto Faks
Estimated Sales: $1800000
Number Employees: 5-9
Sq. footage: 10000

14693 **World of Coffee**
328 Essex St
Stirling, NJ 7980 908-647-1218
Fax: 908-647-7827 800-543-0062
info@worldcoffee.biz www.worldcoffee.biz
coffee roasster

14694 **World of Coffee, World of Tea**
328 Essex St
Stirling, NJ 07980-1302 908-647-1218
Fax: 908-647-7827
Coffee roasting; packaging and labeling services.
President: Charles Newman
Estimated Sales: $750,000
Number Employees: 9
Sq. footage: 7500
Brands:
World of Coffee
World of Spices
World of Tea

14695 **World of Spices**
328 Essex St
Stirling, NJ 07980-1302 908-647-1218
Fax: 908-647-7827
Spices
President: Charles Newman
Estimated Sales: $ 2.5-5 Million
Number Employees: 5-9

14696 **World's Best**
163 Morse Street
Norwood, MA 02062-4600 781-762-7778
Fax: 888-690-8766 888-690-8766
jim@worldsrealketchup.com
www.worldsrealketchup.com
All-natural gourmet ketchup
Brands:
World's Real

14697 **World's Finest Chocolate**
4801 S Lawndale Ave
Chicago, IL 60632-3062 773-847-4600
Fax: 877-256-2685 888-821-8452
contactus@wfchocolate.com
www.worldsfinestchocolate.com
Chocolate manufacturer
President: Howard Zodikoff
Chairman/CEO: Edmond Opler Jr
CFO: Michael Broz
SVP Operations: Mary Wondolowski
Estimated Sales: I
Number Employees: 400
Number of Brands: 2
Type of Packaging: Consumer
Brands:
QUEEN ANNE
WORLD'S FINEST CHOCOLATE

14698 **World's Greatest Ice Cream**
P.O.Box 190646
Miami Beach, FL 33119-0646 305-538-0207
Fax: 305-538-1026 www.thefrieze.com
Ice cream
President: Lisa Warren
Estimated Sales: $500,000-$1 Million
Number Employees: 10-19

14699 **(HQ)Wornick Company**
4700 Creek Road
Cincinnati, OH 45242 513-552-7463
Fax: 513-794-0107 800-860-4555
info@wornick.com www.wornick.com
Processor of shelf stable, refrigerated and frozen entrees including baked beans, macaroni and cheese, lasagna and chicken; exporter of entrees including chicken breast on rice, pot pie, pot roast, lasagna, manicotti, tortelliniravioli, turkey, steak, etc.
Chairman: R Wornick
Vice President: Michael Devaudreuil
National Sales Manager: Diana Hook
Estimated Sales: $81 Million
Number Employees: 500-999
Sq. footage: 200000
Type of Packaging: Food Service, Private Label
Other Locations:
Wornick Co.
McAllen TX

14700 **Worthington Foods**
1675 Fairview Road
Zanesville, OH 43701-8890 614-885-9511
Fax: 614-885-2594 800-535-5644
Processor of canned and frozen vegetarian foods
CEO/President: Dale Twomley
VP Finance/CFO: William Kirkwood
Plant Manager: Gene Fluck
Estimated Sales: $5-10 Million
Number Employees: 50-99
Sq. footage: 200000
Parent Co: Kellogg Company
Type of Packaging: Consumer, Food Service
Brands:
Loma Linda
Morningstar Farms
Worthington

14701 **Worthmore Food Product**
1021 Ludlow Ave
Cincinnati, OH 45223 513-559-1473
Fax: 513-559-0286 worthmore@fuse.net
www.worthmorefoods.com
Canner of food products including chili con carne, mock turtle soup, spaghetti sauce, pizza sauce and mushroom steak sauce
President: Phil Hock III
Type of Packaging: Consumer, Food Service, Private Label

14702 **Wow! Factor Desserts**
152 Cree Road
Sherwood Park, AB T8A 3X8
Canada 780-464-0303
Fax: 780-467-3604 800-604-2253
info@wowfactorydessert.com
www.wowfactordesserts.com
Processor of baked goods including cheesecakes, cakes, tortes and pies for the food service sector
President: Bryan Yaakov
VP: Joanne Yaakov
Purchasing Manager: Dean McMullen
Estimated Sales: D
Number Employees: 50-99
Type of Packaging: Consumer, Food Service

14703 **Wrangell Fisheries**
P.O.Box 908
Wrangell, AK 99929-0908 907-874-3346
Fax: 907-874-3035
droberts@wrangellseafoods.com
www.wrangellseafoods.com
Processor and exporter of canned, fresh and frozen shrimp, crab, halibut, herring and salmon
President: Terry Montford
Vice President: Levi Dow
Estimated Sales: $ 20 - 50 Million
Number Employees: 100-249
Parent Co: J.S. McMillan
Type of Packaging: Food Service, Bulk

14704 **Wright Brand Company**
P.O.Box 914
Bayou La Batre, AL 36509-0914 251-824-7880
Fax: 251-824-7880
Processor and distributor of oysters
President: Stanley Wright
Estimated Sales: $ 1 - 3 Million
Number Employees: 1-4

14705 **Wright Brand Foods**
700 Wheeler St
Vernon, TX 76384 940-553-1888
Fax: 940-553-3747 comments@tyson.com
www.tyson.com
Manufacturer and exporter of smoked ham and bacon
Manager: Jimmy Dennis
Estimated Sales: $120 Million
Number Employees: 500-999
Type of Packaging: Consumer, Food Service, Private Label, Bulk
Brands:
WRIGHT

14706 **Wright Enrichment**
6428 Airport Rd
Crowley, LA 70526 337-783-3096
Fax: 337-783-0724 800-201-3096
wei@wenrich.com www.wenrich.com
Enriched rice, vitamin mixtures and tablets
Owner: S L Wright Iv
Estimated Sales: $ 5-10 Million
Number Employees: 100-249

14707 **Wright Group**
6428 Airport Road
Po Box 821
Crowley, LA 70526 337-783-3096
Fax: 337-783-3802 800-201-3096
johnm@wenrich.com www.thewrightgroup.net
Processor and exporter of custom vitamin, mineral and amino acid premixes, microencapsulates and direct compressed granulations
Owner: S L Wright
Marketing: Monique Roberts
Regional Sales Manager: John Miller
Estimated Sales: $ 10 - 20 Million
Number Employees: 100-249
Type of Packaging: Bulk

14708 **Wright Ice Cream**
3570 N State Road 63
Cayuga, IN 47928-8156 765-492-3454
Fax: 765-492-4915 800-686-9561
www.wrighticecream.com
Ice cream and frozen desserts, dairy products, dried or canned, and candy and other confectionery products.
President: Ned Wright
Marketing Director: Ned Wright
Estimated Sales: $ 3 - 5 Million
Number Employees: 5-9
Type of Packaging: Consumer
Brands:
Wright Delicious

14709 **(HQ)Wrigley Company**
410 N Michigan Ave
Chicago, IL 60611-4287 312-644-2121
Fax: 312-644-2135 800-824-9681
www.wrigley.com
Gums, mints, hard and chewy candies, lollipops, and chocolate.
President: Dushan Petrovich
Regional President/North America: Ken Keller
EVP/CFO: Reuben Gamoran
Executive VP: John Bard
VP Customer Marketing: Gary Bebee
VP Corporate Affairs: Andy Pharoah
SVP Supply Chain/Procurement: Patrick Mitchell
Estimated Sales: $2.3 Billion
Number Employees: 16000
Parent Co: Mars Inc
Brands:
5 GUM
ALTOIDS
BIG LEAGUE CHEW
BIG RED
CREME SAVERS
DOUBLEMINT
ECLIPSE
EXTRA
FREEDENT
HUBBA BUBBA
JUICY FRUIT
LIFE SAVERS
ORBIT
SKITTLES
SPEARMINT
STARBURST
WINTERFRESH

14710 **Wti, Inc.**
281 Mlk Ave
Jefferson, GA 30549 706-387-5150
Fax: 706-387-5159 800-827-1727
www.wtiinc.com
Marinades and flavorings for meat.
President: Wolf Ludwig
Sr. Vice President: Michael Crump

14711 **Wuollet Bakery**
2447 Hennepin Ave
Minneapolis, MN 55405 612-381-9400
Fax: 612-374-0948 www.wuollet.com

Bakers of cakes, desserts, breads and pastries.
Manager: Aaron Wuollet
CEO: Jim Jurmu
Operations Manager: Doug Wuollet
Estimated Sales: $ 2.5-5 Million
Number Employees: 20-49

14712 Wurth Dairy
8805 Maple Avenue
Caseyville, IL 62232-2135 217-271-7580
Dairy
President: Albert Wurth
Estimated Sales: Under $500,000
Number Employees: 1-4

14713 Wws
4032 Shoreline Dr Ste 2
Spring Park, MN 55384 952-548-9306
Fax: 952-541-9206 www.wwstrading.com
Merchandiser of feed and food grade, fats, oils, meals, lard, tallow, etc.
President: Wendy Storlie
Manager: Ted Storlie
Estimated Sales: $65 Million
Number Employees: 5-9
Sq. footage: 1800

14714 Wy's Wings
PO Box 542
Strasburg, VA 22657-0542 540-665-8050
800-997-9464
wingmaster@wyswings.com
www.wyswings.com
Sauces

14715 (HQ)Wyandot
135 Wyandot Ave
Marion, OH 43302 740-383-4031
Fax: 740-382-5584 800-992-6368
phyllis.hendrix@wyandotsnacks.com
www.wyandotsnacks.com
Manufacturer of snacks including; tortilla, corn and potato chips. Contract Manufacturing
Chairman: Joe Donithen
President/CEO: Nick Chilton
CFO: Robert Wentz
CEO: Nick Chilton
EVP Operations: Rex Parrott
Estimated Sales: $100 Million
Number Employees: 250-499
Type of Packaging: Consumer, Food Service, Private Label

14716 (HQ)Wyandot Inc.
135 Wyandot Ave
Marion, OH 43302 740-383-4031
Fax: 740-382-0115 800-992-6368
www.wyandotsnacks.com
Processor of private label snack foods including baked cheese puffs and chips including potato, tortilla, nacho and corn.
President/CEO: Nick Chilton
VP Finance/CFO: Robert Wentz
VP Technical Services: Dan McGrady
Business Strategy Manager: Mitch Newell
VP Sales: Gary Haugsby
VP Human Resources: Bryan Hensel
EVP Operations: Rex Parrott
VP Supply Chain Management: Tom Shank
Estimated Sales: $28 Million
Number Employees: 350
Sq. footage: 150000
Type of Packaging: Consumer, Food Service, Private Label, Bulk
Brands:
GRANDADDY'S
MUCHMATES
MUNCHRIGHTS
WYANDOT

14717 Wyandotte Winery
4640 Wyandotte Dr
Columbus, OH 43230 614-476-3624
Fax: 614-228-2331 info@wyandottewinery.com
www.wyandottewinery.com
Wines
President: Jane Scott
CEO: Joe Reardon
Marketing Director: Valerie Coolidge
Winemaker: Robin Coolidge
Estimated Sales: $500,000-$1 Million
Number Employees: 1-4
Brands:
Wyandotte Graystone Winery
Wyandotte Winery

14718 Wynn Starr Flavors
5 Pearl Ct
Allendale, NJ 07401-1656 201-934-7800
Fax: 201-934-6022 800-996-7827
customerservice@wynnstarr.com
www.wynnstarr.com
Flavors, seasonings and natural compound flavors including chicken broth products, maple glaze for bacon, sauteed onion flavor system, sauteed garlic butter oil, natural basil flavor, natural and artificial bacon flavor (made with realbacon)
Chairman: Steven Zavagli
CFO: Gary Raff
Estimated Sales: $ 20-50 Million
Number Employees: 20-49
Brands:
Wynn Starr

14719 Wynn Starr Foods of Kentucky
4820 Allmond Ave
Louisville, KY 40214-2506 502-368-6345
Fax: 502-363-4494 800-996-7827
customerservice@wynnstarr.com
www.wynnstarr.com
Processor of flavorings including beef, chicken, turkey, pork, soft drink, fruit and cheese; exporter of chicken, beef and cheese flavorings
CEO: Steve Zavagli
Executive VP Operations: Joseph Zavagli
VP Operations/Manufacturing: Barry Friedson
Plant Manager: Barry Friedson
Purchasing Director: Joann Rakestraw
Estimated Sales: $ 20 - 50 Million
Number Employees: 50-99
Sq. footage: 68000
Parent Co: Wynn Starr Flavors
Type of Packaging: Private Label, Bulk
Brands:
Wynn Starr Foodservice

14720 Wynnewood Pecan Company
301 S Washita Avenue
Wynnewood, OK 73098-7823 405-665-4102
Fax: 405-682-2503 800-892-4985
wyrwood@flash.net
Pecans
President: Jeff Earles
Estimated Sales: Less than $500,000
Number Employees: 1-4

14721 Wysong Corporation
180 N Eastern Rd
Midland, MI 48640 989-631-0009
Fax: 989-631-8801 800-748-0188
www.wysong.net
Processor of trail mixes, vitamins and potato chips; also, organic soy, wheat and rice baking items
President: R Wysong
Estimated Sales: $3100000
Number Employees: 20-49
Brands:
Wysong

14722 X Cafe
P.O.Box 1100
Princeton, MA 01541-3100 978-464-8010
Fax: 978-464-8033 877-492-2331
cathy@x-cafe.com www.x-cafe.com
Processor of coffee extracts and concentrates.
President: Paul Kalenian
CFO: Cathy Kalenian
Quality Assurance Manager: Lisa Townsend
Estimated Sales: $ 5 - 10 Million
Number Employees: 45
Number of Products: 12
Sq. footage: 16000
Type of Packaging: Food Service, Private Label

14723 XL Beef
4240 - 75th Avenue SE
Calgary, AB T2C 2H8
Canada 403-236-2424
Fax: 403-236-2527 romashenko@xlfoods.com
www.xlfoods.com
Processor and exporter of beef and beef products
President: Lee Nilsson
VP Commodities/Wholesale: Ken Weir
Sales Manager: Dan Edge
Plant Superintendent: Barry Fuglsong
Estimated Sales: $133 Million
Number Employees: 1,000
Sq. footage: 35000
Parent Co: XL Foods
Brands:
Original Alberta Beef

14724 XL Energy Drink
521 5th Avenue, 28th Floor
New York, NY 10175 212-594-3080
Fax: 646-514-3096 usa@xl-energy.com
www.xl-energy.com
Manufacturer of energy drink.
Business Development Director: Michael Raunegger

14725 XL Energy Drink
521 5th Avenue, 28th Floor
New York, NY 10175 212-594-3080
Fax: 646-594- 309 usa@xl-energy.com
www.xl-energy.com
Energy drink/beverage.
Business Development Director: Michael Raunegger

14726 Xcell International Corporation
16400 103rd St
Lemont, IL 60439 630-323-0107
Fax: 630-323-0217 800-722-7751
info@xcellint.com www.xcellint.com
Seasonings, spices, herbs, teas and mulling spices, confectionery sprinkles
President: Dean Henning
President: Amy Hilliard
Marketing Director: Leslie Marshall
Estimated Sales: $ 20 - 50 Million
Number Employees: 50-99
Brands:
Accent's
Dean Jacob's

14727 Xochitl
17304 Preston Rd
Suite 1240
Dallas, TX 75252 214-800-3551
Fax: 214-800-3547 info@salsaxochitl.com
www.salsaxochitl.com
all natural and organic salsas, queso dips and corn chips
President: Carlos Salinas

14728 Y Not Foods
1022 Lumbermans Trail
Madison, WI 53716 608-222-2860
Fax: 608-222-2865 tony@ynotfoods.com
www.ynotfoods.com
Frozen, refrigerated, shelf-stable and dry blends.
President: Tony Steinmann

14729 Y&T Packing
1129 Taintor Lane
Springfield, IL 62702 217-522-3345
Fax: 217-522-6395 www.turaskymeats.com
Packer/processor of meat
President: Joseph Turasky
Co-Owner: Joe Turasky
Sales Manager: Tom Reilly
Estimated Sales: $1800000
Number Employees: 10-19
Type of Packaging: Consumer

14730 Y&W Shellfish
8725 Us Highway 17
Woodbine, GA 31569 912-729-4814
Fax: 912-729-1143
Seafood
Owner: Richard Roberts

14731 YB Meats of Wichita
798 N West St
Wichita, KS 67203-1235 316-942-1213
Fax: 316-942-1419
Processor of meat products
President: Ellsworth Kauffman
CEO: Erik Kaufmann
Marketing Director: Erik Kaufmann
Estimated Sales: $500,000-$1 Million
Number Employees: 5-9
Type of Packaging: Consumer

14732 **YZ Enterprises**
1930 Indian Wood Cir
Maumee, OH 43537-4053 419-893-8777
Fax: 419-893-8825 800-736-8779
almondina@worldpantry.com
www.almondina.com
Processor and exporter of natural almond cookies including low-calorie, no-cholesterol, no-salt, kosher and parve
Owner: Yuval Zaliouk
CFO: Susan Zaliouk
Estimated Sales: $1-5 Million
Number Employees: 10-19
Sq. footage: 16500
Type of Packaging: Consumer
Brands:
ALMONDINA

14733 **Yair Scones/Canterbury Cuisine**
P.O.Box 177
Medina, WA 98039-0177 425-486-3334
Fax: 425-398-0301 800-588-9160
linda.dolstad@fairscones.com
www.conifer-inc.com
Gourmet convenience foods
President: Mike Maher
Operations Manager: Darren Wise
Estimated Sales: $ 10-20 Million
Number Employees: 20-49
Brands:
Canterbury Cusine
Canterbury Naturals
Fisher Fair Scone
Scone Girl

14734 **Yakima Craft Brewing Company**
2920 River Rd Ste 6
Yakima, WA 98902-7332 509-654-7357
Processor and exporter of ales, stout and porter
President: Jeff Winn
CEO/Founder: Chris McCoy
Director of Marketing: Sheldon Weddle
Estimated Sales: $500,000-999,999
Number Employees: 5-9
Sq. footage: 40500
Type of Packaging: Consumer
Brands:
Bert Grant's

14735 **Yakima Fruit & Cold Storage Company**
200 N Frontage Rd
Wapato, WA 98951 509-877-2777
Fax: 509-877-0940
stevensmith@yakimaroche.com
www.yakimaroche.com
Manufacturer and exporter of apples, cherries and pears
President: Micheal Wilcox
Estimated Sales: $100 Million
Number Employees: 250-499
Type of Packaging: Consumer, Food Service, Bulk

14736 **Yakima River Winery**
143302 W North River Rd
Prosser, WA 99350 509-786-2805
Fax: 509-786-3203
redwine@yakimariverwinery.com
www.yakimariverwinery.com
Processor of wine
Co-Owner: John Rauner
Co-Owner: Louise Rauner
Winemaker: John Rauner
Estimated Sales: $500,000-$1 Million
Number Employees: 1-4
Type of Packaging: Private Label
Brands:
Yakima Valley

14737 **Yakima Valley Grape Producers**
401 Avenue B
Grandview, WA 98930-1622 509-882-1223
Fax: 509-882-1580
Grapes
President: Richard Devis
Estimated Sales: $ 5-10 Million appx.
Number Employees: 50

14738 **Yamamotoyama of America**
122 Voyager St
Pomona, CA 91768 909-594-7356
Fax: 909-595-5849
yamamotoyama@yamamotoyama.com
www.yamamotoyama.com
Tea
Chairman: Kahei Yamamoto
Administration Manager/Purchasing: William Yu
Senior VP: Kazumi Ikeda
Estimated Sales: $ 20-50 Million
Number Employees: 100-249

14739 **Yamasa Corporation**
3655 Torrance Blvd
Suite 240
Torrance, CA 95023 310-944-3883
Fax: 310-944-3935 kusukura@yamasausa.com
www.yamasausa.com
Processor of soy sauce
Manager: Masahiro Ade
Vice President: Katsuo Usukura
National Sales Manager: Michael Grady Loera
Estimated Sales: $ 5 - 10 Million
Number Employees: 1-4
Type of Packaging: Consumer, Food Service, Bulk
Brands:
Yamasa

14740 **Yamasa Fish Cake Company**
515 Stanford Ave
Los Angeles, CA 90013 213-626-2211
Fax: 213-627-9018
Processor of fresh and frozen fish cakes
President: Frank Kawana
Estimated Sales: $2900000
Number Employees: 20-49
Type of Packaging: Consumer, Food Service

14741 **Yamasho**
750 Touhy Ave
Elk Grove Village, IL 60007 847-981-4004
Fax: 847-981-9347
Estimated Sales: $ 20 - 50 Million
Number Employees: 20-49

14742 **Yamate Chocolatier**
320 Cleveland Ave
Highland Park, NJ 8904 732-249-4847
Fax: 732-545-4494 800-433-2462
info@YCChocolate.com
www.yamatechocolatier.com
Chocolate and confections
Co-Owner: Diane Yamate
Co-Owner: John Cunnell
Estimated Sales: $500,000-$1 Million
Number Employees: 1-4

14743 **Yamhill Valley Vineyards**
16250 SW Oldsville Rd
McMinnville, OR 97128 503-843-3100
Fax: 503-843-2450 800-825-4845
info@yamhill.com www.yamhill.com
Wines
President: Stephen Cary
General Manager: David Anderson
Estimated Sales: $ 5-10 Million
Number Employees: 20-49
Brands:
Yamhill Wines

14744 **Yangtze Agribusiness Group**
PO Box 1071
Great Neck, NY 11023-0071 516-466-1996
Fax: 516-773-0013
Newyork@yangtze-China.com
Condiments and relishes

14745 **Yankee Specialty Foods**
22 Fish Pier
Boston, MA 02210-2008 617-951-0739
Fax: 617-951-9907
www.yankeespecialtyfoods.com
Processor and exporter of chili, soup, gumbo and chowder
President: Paul Lindquist
Estimated Sales: $300000
Number Employees: 5
Type of Packaging: Consumer, Private Label
Brands:
Bay Shore

14746 **Yarbrough Produce Company**
624 16th Ave W
Birmingham, AL 35204-1421 205-324-4569
Manufacturer of salads including fresh vegetables, tossed and cole slaw
President/Co-Owner: June B Yarbrough
VP/Co-Owner: Kenneth Yarbrough Jr
Estimated Sales: $25 Million
Number Employees: 50-99
Sq. footage: 24000
Type of Packaging: Consumer, Food Service
Brands:
GRANNY'S

14747 **(HQ)Yarmer Boys Catfish International**
5192c Fannett Road
Beaumont, TX 77705-4202 409-842-1962
Fax: 409-842-1212 vsj42@aol.com
Shrimp
CEO: Glenda Jones
President: Vicky Jones
Sales Director: Trudy Verdine
Number Employees: 100-249
Type of Packaging: Private Label
Brands:
Fishermans Rees

14748 **Yarnell Ice Cream Company**
P.O.Box 78
Searcy, AR 72145 501-268-2414
Fax: 501-279-0846 800-766-2414
yarnells@yarnells.com www.yarnells.com
Processor of frozen products including premium ice creams, frozen treats, guilt free, frozen yogurt, yarnell pints and yarnell sherbert
President: A Yarnell II
CEO: Rogers Yarnell
Quality Assurance Manager: Floyd Washburn
Estimated Sales: $20-50 Million
Number Employees: 175
Type of Packaging: Consumer, Food Service
Brands:
Guilt Free
Hometown
Yarnell's

14749 **Yaya's**
515 Acacia Avenue
Corona Del Mar, CA 92625-1906 949-675-7708
Organic and fat-free caramel popcorn
CEO/President: Bob George
VP: Patty George
Estimated Sales: Under $500,000
Number Employees: 1-4
Type of Packaging: Private Label

14750 **Yayin Corporation**
12725 Hatteras Street
Valley Village, CA 91607-1408 707-829-5686
Fax: 707-829-0993 ganen@dani.com
Wines
President: Craig Winchell
Estimated Sales: $500,000-$1 Million
Number Employees: 1-4

14751 **Ye Olde Pepper Company**
122 Derby St
Salem, MA 01970 978-745-2744
Fax: 978-557-1017 866-393-6533
info@yeoldepeppercandy.com
www.yeoldepeppercandy.com
Hard and soft candy, chocolates
President: Robert Burkinshaw
Estimated Sales: Below $ 5 Million
Number Employees: 20-49
Brands:
Black Jacks
Salem Gibralters

14752 **(HQ)Yellow Emperor**
520 Commercial St Ste G
Eugene, OR 97402 541-485-6664
Fax: 541-485-0039 877-485-6664
info@yellowemperor.com
www.yellowemperor.com
Processor of custom herbal extracts, ginseng, teas, tea concentrates and herbal honey
President: Andrew Levine
Estimated Sales: Less than $500,000
Number Employees: 1-4
Sq. footage: 2400
Type of Packaging: Consumer, Private Label, Bulk
Brands:
Honeymoon
Inner Force
Oregon Natural Sportstonic
Phytotherapy
Wild American Herb Co.
Yellow Emperor

14753 **Yellow Emperor Pepper Sauce Company**
2328 Bullard Avenue
Los Angeles, CA 90032-3505 608-238-2991
Fax: 323-223-1618
Sauces

14754 **Yellow Rose Brewing Company**
23603 Hartwick Lane
San Antonio, TX 78259-1604 210-496-6669
Fax: 210-496-6678
Processor of seasonal beer, ale, stout and pilsner
President: Glen Fritz
Sales Manager: Kevin Love
Estimated Sales: $500,000-$1 Million
Number Employees: 5-9
Type of Packaging: Consumer, Food Service
Brands:
Bubbadog
Wildcatters Refined
Yellow Rose Pale

14755 **Yeomen Seafoods**
P.O.Box 3067
Gloucester, MA 01931-3067 978-283-7422
Fax: 978-283-7522
Whole frozen seafood
President/Treasurer: Thomas Kennedy
Estimated Sales: $4.7 Million
Number Employees: 1-4

14756 **Yerba Prima**
740 Jefferson Ave
Ashland, OR 97520 541-488-2228
Fax: 541-488-2443 800-488-4339
yerba@yerbaprima.com www.yerbaprima.com
Processor and exporter of high quality dietary supplements, specializing in dietary fiber, internal cleansing aids and herbal products.
Owner: John Jung
CEO: John Jung
Marketing Manager: Shelley Matteson
Estimated Sales: $ 5 - 10 Million
Number Employees: 10-19
Type of Packaging: Consumer, Private Label
Brands:
Aloe Falls
Yerba Prima

14757 **Yerba Santa Goat Dairy**
6850 Scotts Valley Rd
Lakeport, CA 95453 707-263-8131
Fax: 707-263-8131
Dairy products
Owner: Javier Salmon
Marketing Director: Chris Twohy
Estimated Sales: Below $ 5 Million
Number Employees: 1-4

14758 **(HQ)Yergat Packing Co Inc**
5451 W Mission Avenue
Fresno, CA 93722-5074 559-276-9180
Fax: 559-276-2841
Processor and exporter of grapevine leaves
President: Kirk Yergat
Number Employees: 10-19
Parent Co: Yergat Packing Company
Type of Packaging: Consumer, Private Label

14759 **Yewig Brothers Packing Company**
P.O.Box 186
Haubstadt, IN 47639-0186 812-768-6208
Fax: 812-768-6220 www.dewigmeats.com
Country style meats
President: Thomas Dewig
Estimated Sales: $ 10-24.9 Million
Number Employees: 20-49

14760 **Yick Lung Company**
3015 Koapaka Street
Honolulu, HI 96819-1936 808-841-3611
Fax: 808-842-4763
Chips, candy and sunflower seeds
President: Patricia Ching
Chairman: Gertrude Lee
COO: Daniel King
Estimated Sales: $5-9.9 Million
Number Employees: 20-49
Brands:
Yick Lung

14761 **Ynrico's Food Products Company**
6050 Court Street Rd
Syracuse, NY 13206-1711 315-463-2384
Fax: 315-463-5897 888-472-8237
nventre@ventre.com www.ventre.com
All natural spaghetti sauce and salsa
CEO: Martin Ventre
CFO: Dave Sorensen
Sales Manager: Rick Alesia
Production Manager: James Faivre
VP Purchasing: Jacki Papai
Estimated Sales: $ 10-20 Million
Number Employees: 20-49
Type of Packaging: Private Label

14762 **YoCream International**
5858 NE 87th Avnue
Portland, OR 97220 503-256-3754
Fax: 503-256-3976 800-962-7326
info@yocream.com www.yocream.com
Frozen yogurt, ice cream, frozen custard mixes, fruit and dairy smoothies and frozen beverages.
Chairman/CEO: John Hanna
CFO: W Douglas Caudell
Marketing Director: Suzanne Gardner
Sales Director: Tyler Bargas
Operations: Terry Oftedal
Custom Manufacturing: Matt Hanna
Estimated Sales: $9.9 Million
Number Employees: 60

14763 **Yoakum Packing Company**
500 Front St
Yoakum, TX 77995 361-293-3541
Fax: 361-293-2261 gkusak@farmpac.com
www.farmpac.com
Processor of smoked and cured pork, beef and poultry
President: Glen Kusak
Estimated Sales: $7,226,707
Number Employees: 20-49
Sq. footage: 30000
Type of Packaging: Consumer, Food Service, Private Label, Bulk
Brands:
Farm Pac
Ranch Pac

14764 **Yoakum Packing Company**
500 Front St
Yoakum, TX 77995 361-293-3541
Fax: 361-293-2261 www.farmpac.com
Meats and meat products
President: Glen Kusak
Manager: Karin Cockrell
Estimated Sales: $8 Million
Number Employees: 40

14765 **Yoder Dairies**
1620 Mount Pleasant Rd
Chesapeake, VA 23322-1219 757-482-4068
Fax: 757-497-3510 yoderdairies@aol.com
www.yoderdairies.com
Processor of milk including standard homogenized, low-fat, skim, half/half and chocolate; also, cream buttermilk, whipping cream, eggs, eggnog, spring water and orange, grapefruit and apple juices, as well as ice cream.
President: Kenneth Miller
VP: L Miller
General Manager: Maria Dlah
Plant Manager: Lester Miller
Estimated Sales: $4300000
Number Employees: 31
Type of Packaging: Consumer

14766 **Yofarm Company**
162 Spring St
Naugatuck, CT 06770 203-720-0000
Fax: 203-720-0443 www.yofarm.com
Yogurt
CEO: Thomas G Dixcy
Plant Manager: Andrew Respondek
Estimated Sales: $ 20-30 Million
Number Employees: 100-249

14767 **(HQ)Yohay Baking Company**
146 Albany Ave
Lindenhurst, NY 11757 631-225-0300
Fax: 631-225-4278 www.yohay.com
Processor, importer and exporter of wafer rolls, specialty cookies, biscotti, and fudge mix, kosher and all natural products. Retail packaging available
Owner: Michael Soloman
Number Employees: 20-49
Type of Packaging: Consumer, Food Service, Private Label, Bulk
Brands:
FUDGE GOURMET
GOURMET COOKIE PLACE
SWEETHEART FUDGE

14768 **Yokhol Valley Packing Company**
P.O.Box 907
Lindsay, CA 93247-0907 559-562-1327
Fax: 559-562-6732
Packer of oranges
Manager: Henry Howison
Estimated Sales: $ 10 - 20 Million
Number Employees: 10-19
Type of Packaging: Bulk

14769 **Yoo-Hoo Chocolate Beverage Company**
600 Commercial Ave
Carlstadt, NJ 07072 201-933-0070
Fax: 201-933-5360
consumer.relations@brandspeoplelove.com
www.drinkyoo-hoo.com
Processor of chocolate drinks
President: Brian O'Byrne
Marketing Manager: Christine Karumpe
Plant Manager: Bill Pedeto
Estimated Sales: $16,500,000
Number Employees: 20-49
Parent Co: Yoo-Hoo Chocolate Beverage
Type of Packaging: Consumer

14770 **Yoplait USA**
1 General Mills Blvd
Minneapolis, MN 55426 763-764-7600
Fax: 763-764-8330 800-248-7310
www.yoplait.com
Manufacturer of yogurt
Chairman/President/CEO: Kendall Powell
EVP/CFO: Donal Mulligan
Chief Marketing Officer: Mark Addicks
Plant Manager: Dave Towner
Estimated Sales: K
Number Employees: 10,000+
Parent Co: General Mills
Type of Packaging: Consumer, Food Service
Brands:
COLOMBO
EXPRESSE
GO-GURT
TRIX
YOPLAIT CUSTARD STYLE
YOPLAIT LIGHT
YOPLAIT NOURICHE
YOPLAIT ORIGINAL
YOPLAIT WHIPS

14771 **York Beach Fish Market**
13 Nighthawk Drive
York, ME 03909-585 207-363-2763
Fax: 302-998-4236
Seafood
President: Frank Robins
Vice President: Janet Robins
Estimated Sales: $275,000
Number Employees: 5

14772 **York Mountain Winery**
7505 York Mountain Road
Templeton, CA 93465 805-237-7575
hreed@martinweyrich.com
www.yorkmountainwinery.com
Processor of red and white wine, dry sherry, champagne and salad dressing
Owner: David Weyrich
Manager: Suzanne Redberg
Wine Maker: Steve Goldman
Estimated Sales: $920000
Number Employees: 5-9
Sq. footage: 3000
Type of Packaging: Consumer
Brands:
Suzanne's Salad Splash
York Mountain

14773 **Yorktown Baking Company**
1500 Front St Ste 7
Yorktown Heights, NY 10598
Fax: 914-243-7138 800-235-3961

Processor of fresh and frozen batter including muffin, scone and cookie. Prpared flour mixes and doughs.
Owner: Emil Gold
Estimated Sales: $2,600,000
Number Employees: 20-49
Type of Packaging: Consumer, Food Service
Brands:
Yorktown Baking Company

14774 **Yosemite Waters**
226 South Avenue 54
Los Angeles, CA 90042-4512 323-256-2265
Fax: 323-256-4707 800-427-8420
service@yosemitewaters.com
www.yosemitewaters.com
Processor of bottled and distilled water
President: Maya Soderstrom
COO: Genny Kush
Vice President: Claude Niesen
Estimated Sales: $ 5 - 10 Million
Number Employees: 50-99
Type of Packaging: Consumer, Food Service, Bulk

14775 **Yosemite Waters**
226 South Avenue 54
Los Angeles, CA 90042-4512 323-256-2265
Fax: 323-256-4707 800-427-8420
service@yosemitewaters.com
www.yosemitewaters.com
Processor of bottled water
President: Maya Soderstrom
Estimated Sales: $5200000
Number Employees: 50-99
Type of Packaging: Consumer, Food Service

14776 **Yoshida Food International**
8338 NE Alderwood Rd
Suite A
Portland, OR 97220-6800 503-872-8450
Fax: 503-284-0004 800-653-1114
info@yfintl.com www.yfintl.com
Processor and exporter of non MSG, nonfat and cholesterol-free sauces, marinades, drippings and coatings. Distributed by Heinz USA.
President: Matt Guthrie
CFO: Tim Sether
CEO: Junki Yoshida
Quality Control: John Hunter
VP Sales/Marketing: John Moran
Sales Director: Andy Moberg
Public Relations: Marti Lucich
Operations Manager: Eric Rinearson
Production Manager: Frank Heuschkel
Purchasing Manager: Ken Hamilton
Estimated Sales: $8 Million
Number Employees: 60
Sq. footage: 65000
Type of Packaging: Consumer, Food Service, Private Label, Bulk
Brands:
Benihana
Yoshida Foods International

14777 **Yost Candy Company**
51 S Cochran St
Dalton, OH 44618 330-828-2777
Fax: 330-828-8296 800-750-1976
info@yostcandy.com www.yostcandy.com
Processor and exporter of lollypops and Halloween candy
President: Sofie Yost
Vice President: Joe Yost
Sales Director: Earl Yost
Estimated Sales: $2000000
Number Employees: 20-49
Type of Packaging: Consumer, Private Label, Bulk
Brands:
Kiddi Pops
Licklers
Lil Kiddies

14778 **Young Pecan**
2455 Entrada Del Sol
Las Cruces, NM 88001 575-524-4321
Fax: 575-525-3432 www.youngplantations.com
Processor of bagged and boxed pecans
Manager: Paul Koenig
Purchasing Agent: Malcolm Burdett
Estimated Sales: $ 2.5-5 Million
Number Employees: 50-99
Parent Co: Young Pecan Company
Type of Packaging: Bulk

14779 **Young Pecan Company**
1200 Pecan St
Florence, SC 29501 843-662-8591
Fax: 843-664-2344 800-829-6864
sales@youngpecan.com www.youngpecan.com
Processor of pecans
President/CEO: James Swink
EVP: Helen Watts
Estimated Sales: $80 Million
Number Employees: 183
Sq. footage: 150000
Type of Packaging: Consumer, Food Service, Bulk
Brands:
Goodbee
Indian Creek
Schermer

14780 **Young Pecan Company**
P.O.Box 5779
Florence, SC 29502 843-664-2330
Fax: 843-664-2344 800-829-6864
sales@youngpecan.com www.youngpecan.com
Pecans
President: James Swink
CFO: Murray Garber
VP: Helen Watts
Marketing VP: Bob Tankerly
Plant Manager: Mike Barnes
Estimated Sales: $ 50-100 Million
Number Employees: 10-19
Sq. footage: 155800
Type of Packaging: Consumer, Food Service, Private Label, Bulk
Brands:
Mingo River
Pecan Plantations
Young Pecan Co. Brand
Young's Golden Sweet

14781 **(HQ)Young Winfield**
12075 Highway 27
Kleinburg, ON L0J 1C0
Canada 905-893-9682
Fax: 905-893-9682
Manufacturer of onion oil, cajun spice, salt and vinegar seasonings
President: Amir Sunderji
Estimated Sales: $3-5 Million
Number Employees: 12
Sq. footage: 27000
Type of Packaging: Consumer, Food Service, Private Label, Bulk
Brands:
SIMPLY SPICE
YOU WIN

14782 **Young Yoo Company**
3539 W Lawrence Avenue
Chicago, IL 60625-5627 773-539-3122
Fax: 773-299-9928

14783 **Young's Bakery**
67 S Gallatin Ave
Uniontown, PA 15401 724-437-6361
Processor of cakes and cookies
President: Dino Palermo
Marketing Director: Ruth Palermo
Estimated Sales: Less than $500,000
Number Employees: 1-4
Type of Packaging: Food Service

14784 **Young's Jersey Dairy**
6880 Springfield Xenia Rd
Yellow Springs, OH 45387 937-325-0629
Fax: 937-325-3226 cows@youngsdairy.com
www.youngsdairy.com
Milk, ice cream, rolls, bread and donuts
CEO: C Daniel Young
Human Resource Manager: Ben Young
Sales Manager: Cathy Young
Estimated Sales: Below $ 5 Million
Number Employees: 250-499

14785 **Young's Lobster Pound**
4 Mitchell St
Belfast, ME 04915 207-338-1160
Fax: 207-338-3498
Processor, exporter and importer of fresh and frozen seafood including crabs, lobster, live and shucked clams and mussels, scallops and shrimp; wholesaler/distributor of fresh and frozen seafood
Owner: Raymond Young
Co-Owner: Claire Young
Manager; Owner: Raymond Young
Estimated Sales: $ 3 - 5 Million
Number Employees: 20-49
Sq. footage: 2736
Type of Packaging: Consumer, Food Service
Brands:
Young's Lobster Pound

14786 **Young's Noodle Factory**
1635 Liliha St
Honolulu, HI 96817 808-533-6478
Fax: 808-536-6533
Processor of noodles
Owner: Gordon Kwan
Estimated Sales: $1000000
Number Employees: 10-19
Type of Packaging: Food Service

14787 **Young's Shellfish Company**
P.O.Box 92
Troy, ME 04987-92
Fax: 207-338-1488
Seafood
President: Robert Young
Estimated Sales: $ 3 - 5 Million
Number Employees: 10-19

14788 **Your Bar Factory**
7232 Coroner
LaSalle, QC H8N 2W8
Canada 514-364-0258
Fax: 514-364-2229 888-366-0258
info@yourbarfactory.com
www.yourbarfactory.com
Manufacturer rice crispy squares, and manufacture of private label bars for various customers profiles including major retailers, branders and smaller accounts
President: Martin Joyal
VP: Daniel Levesque
R&D: Melanie Carre
Quality Control: Celine Boiniere
Sales: Myrian Ang
Operations: Enilie Gras
Purchasing: Anilcar Parraga
Estimated Sales: $10 Million
Number Employees: 60
Sq. footage: 30000
Parent Co: Rapid Snack
Type of Packaging: Food Service, Private Label, Bulk

14789 **Yrica's Rugelach & Baking Company**
389 4th Street
Brooklyn, NY 11215-2901 718-965-3657
Fax: 718-832-6160 ericasrugelach@aol.com
www.ericasrugelach.com
Cookies and rugelach
President: Erica Kalick
CEO: Erica Kalick
Marketing Director: Erica Kalick
Estimated Sales: $500,000-$1 Million
Number Employees: 10-19
Brands:
Erica's Rugelach

14790 **Yuengling Brewery**
310 Mill Creek Ave
Pottsville, PA 17901 570-622-4141
Fax: 570-622-4011 giftshop@yuengling.com
www.yuengling.com
Beer
President: Richard L Yuengling Jr
Quality Control: Joe Frenzy
CFO: Debbie Ferhat
VP Sales/Marketing: David Casinelli
Director Manufacturing: Jim Helmke
Estimated Sales: $ 50-75 Million
Number Employees: 100-249
Type of Packaging: Private Label
Brands:
Lord Chesterfield Al
Original Black & Tan
Traditional Lager
Yuengling Premium Be
Yuengling Premium Li

14791 **Yum Yum Potato Chips**
40 Du Moulin
Warwick, QC J0A 1M0
Canada 819-358-3600
Fax: 819-358-3687 800-567-5792
yumyum@yum-yum.com www.yum-yum.com

Manufacturer of snack foods including potato chips, cheese sticks, onion rings and fries
President: Pierre Riverd
Director Production: Guy Trudel
Number Employees: 200
Type of Packaging: Consumer, Private Label

14792 **Yvonne's Gourmet Sensations**
404 Berkshire Way
Marlton, NJ 08053-4222 856-985-7677
Fax: 856-810-3798
Gourmet chocolate pretzels, chocolate cookies, chocolate grahams, chocolate waffles
Marketing Manager: Gary Greenberg
Brands:
Yvonne's Gourmet Cho
Yvonne's Gourmet Cho
Yvonne's Gourmet Choc Cookies

14793 **Z Foods Inc.**
9537 Road 29 1/2
Madera, CA 93637 559-673-6368
Fax: 559-673-7508 888-400-1015
customerservice@zfoodsinc.com
www.zfoodsinc.com
dried fruits
President: Daniel Villanueva
VP: Nina Zoria
Number Employees: 2

14794 **Z&S Distributing**
7090 N. Marks Avenue
Suite 104
Fresno, CA 93711 559-432-1777
Fax: 559-432-2888 800-467-0788
mail@zsfresh.com www.zsfresh.com
Fruits and vegetables.
President: Martin Zaninovich
Estimated Sales: $7,700,000
Number Employees: 10-19
Type of Packaging: Consumer
Brands:
JUST - RIPE

14795 **Z.D. Wines**
8383 Silverado Trl
Napa, CA 94558 800-487-7757
Fax: 707-963-2640 800-487-7757
info@zdwines.com www.zdwines.com
Processor and exporter of wines including chardonnay, pinot noir and cabernet sauvignon
President/Partner: Brett DeLeuze
CEO/Partner: Robert DeLeuze
CFO: Julie De Leuze
Marketing Coordinator: Elyse Chambers
VP Sales: Teresa d'Aurizio
Winemaker: Chris Pisani
Estimated Sales: $5-10 Million
Number Employees: 25-50
Number of Brands: 2
Number of Products: 8
Sq. footage: 22732
Type of Packaging: Consumer, Food Service
Brands:
Abacus
Z.D. Wines

14796 **ZT Packaging**
89-47 Metropolitan Avenue
Rego Park, NY 11374 718-896-8420
Fax: 718-275-9053 800-932-2448
info@ztpackaging.com www.ztpackaging.com
plastic bags, custom printed bags, paper bags, boxes

14797 **Zaca Mesa Winery**
6905 Foxen Canyon Road
Los Olivos, CA 93441-0899 805-688-9339
Fax: 805-688-8796 800-350-7972
info@zacamesa.com www.zacamesa.com
Wines
President/CEO: Brook Williams
CFO: Susan English
VP Sales/Marketing: Jim Fiolek
Estimated Sales: $6.3 Million
Number Employees: 30
Brands:
Roussanne
Syrah
Z Gris Dry Rose
Zcuvee

14798 **Zachary Confections**
2130 W State Road 28
Frankfort, IN 46041 765-659-4751
Fax: 765-659-1491 800-445-4222
sales@zc-inc.com www.zacharyconfections.com
Processor and exporter of confectionery products including caramels, boxed chocolates, marshmallows, mints, nougats and holiday novelties.
President/CEO: Jack III Zachary
Senior Vice President: George Anichini
Executive Vice President: Jack Zachary III
Director of Sales: Steve Newman
Estimated Sales: $25-99 Million
Number Employees: 500-999
Type of Packaging: Consumer, Private Label, Bulk
Brands:
ZACHARY

14799 **(HQ)Zacky Farms**
P.O.Box 12556
Fresno, CA 93778 559-486-2310
Fax: 559-443-2778 800-888-0235
zfsales@zacky.com www.zacky.com
Processor of turkey
Consumer Affairs Director: Lillian Zacky
Estimated Sales: $500,000-$1 Million
Number Employees: 1-4
Type of Packaging: Consumer
Brands:
Culinary Classic Breast of Turkey N
Culinary Classic Slices Breast of T

14800 **Zapp's Chips**
307 E Airline Hwy
Gramercy, LA 70052-3019 225-869-9777
Fax: 225-869-9779 800-349-2447
Potato chips
Owner: Roan Zappe
Marketing Director: Richard Gaudry
Estimated Sales: $ 20 - 50 Million
Number Employees: 100-249

14801 **Zapp's Potato Chips**
PO Box 1533
Gramercy, LA 70052 225-869-9777
Fax: 225-869-9779 800-349-2447
www.zapps.com
Processor and exporter of kosher, kettle style, Cajun and jalapeno flavored potato chips
President: Ron Zappe
Director Sales/Marketing: Richard Gaudry
Estimated Sales: $20-50 Million
Number Employees: 100-249
Type of Packaging: Consumer, Food Service, Bulk

14802 **Zarda Bar-B-Q & Catering Company**
214 NW State Route 7
Blue Springs, MO 64014 816-224-7417
Fax: 816-224-3171 800-776-7427
info@zarda.com www.zarda.com
Processor of barbecue sauce and baked beans
President: Michael Zarda
Quality Control Manager: Brian Packer
Marketing Director: Terry Hyer
Plant Manager: Ron Dorris
Estimated Sales: $10-24.9 Million
Number Employees: 50-99
Brands:
Zarda

14803 **(HQ)Zartic Inc**
438 Lavender Dr NW
Rome, GA 30165 706-234-3000
Fax: 706-291-6068 800-241-0516
zartic@zartic.com www.pierrefoods.com
A full service beef, poultry, veal and pork further processor that operates four U.S.D.A. inspected state of the art production facilities and delivers product nationwide via Zartran, Zartic's refrigerated transportation company
Manager: Kenneth Morris
CEO: James Mauer
CFO: Robert Miles
Procurement VP: Francois Gaulin
Sales VP: Mike Wilson
Operations VP: Phillip Morris
Purchasing Agent: Ken Fries
Number Employees: 50-99
Type of Packaging: Consumer
Other Locations:
Zartic Inc (Beef Division)
Cedartown GA
Zartic Inc (Poultry Division)
West Rome GA
Zartic Inc (Pork Division)
Hamilton AL
Brands:
Circle Z
Crispy Steaks
Fryz
Jim's Country Mill Sausage
Shurtenda
Spicy Wings
Vittles
Z-Bird
Zartic
Zartic Beef Bakeables
Zartic Chicken Bakeables
Zartic Chicken Fried Beef Steaks
Zartic Chicken Fryz Flavorz
Zartic Chicken Tenderloins
Zartic Circle Z Beef Burgers
Zartic Crispy Steaks
Zartic Homestyle Meatloaf
Zartic Honey Hugged Chicken
Zartic Pork Bakeables
Zartic Pork Sausage Sampler
Zartic Rockin' Roasted Chicken
Zartic Veal Entree Legends
Zartic Veal Specialties

14804 **Zatarain's**
82 1st St
Gretna, LA 70053-4745 504-367-2950
Fax: 504-362-2004 800-435-6639
info@zatarain.com www.zatarain.com
Processor of condiments, flavoring extracts, rice and stuffing mixes, bean seasoning, spices and crab boil.
Manager: James Pearse
CFO: Regina Templet
Research & Development: George Bigner
Quality Control: Karla Schexnader
Customer Service: Valarie Harris
Food Service Sales Manager: Dudley Passman
Account Executive: Robert Ebert
Estimated Sales: $20-50 Million
Number Employees: 250-499
Parent Co: McCormick & Company Inc
Type of Packaging: Consumer, Food Service
Brands:
Zatarain's

14805 **(HQ)Zausner Foods**
400 S Custer Ave
New Holland, PA 17557 717-355-8505
Fax: 717-355-8561 www.alouettecheese.com
Sauces, dips, pudding, nutritional beverages
President: Frank Otis
COO: Gregg Kenitz
Director Engineering: Scott Whitman
VP Sales: Howard Covenko
Plant Manager: Tim Pent
Estimated Sales: $50 Million+
Number Employees: 50-99
Brands:
Alouette

14806 **Zayante Vineyards**
420 Old Mount Rd
Felton, CA 95018 831-335-7992
Fax: 831-335-5770 info@zayantevineyards.com
www.zayantevineyards.com
Wines
Owner: Greg Nolten
Co-Owner: Marion Nolten
Co-Owner: Kathleen Starkey-Nolten
Vineyard Manager: Greg Nolten
Estimated Sales: $500,000-$1 Million
Number Employees: 1-4
Type of Packaging: Private Label
Brands:
Zayante

14807 **Zazi Baking Company**
1360 Industrial Ave
Petaluma, CA 94952-6521 707-778-1635
Fax: 707-778-6991
Biscotti and cookies
President: Celeste Longo
VP: Debby Dyar
Estimated Sales: $5-10 Million
Number Employees: 10-19
Sq. footage: 6000
Type of Packaging: Food Service, Private Label, Bulk
Brands:
COOKIE BRITTLE

MRS. LITTLE'S
RUNNING RABBIT
SPENDIDO NUGGETS
Splendido Biscotti
ZAZI ORGANICS

14808 **Zel R. Kahn & Sons**
2 Fifer Ave Ste 220
Corte Madera, CA 94925 415-924-9600
Fax: 415-924-9690
Wholesaler/distributor and exporter of surplus, salvage and closeout merchandise including dried and canned fruits, vegetables, crackers, cereals, etc
President: Scott Kahn
Executive VP: Joel Jutovsky
Estimated Sales: $300,000-500,000
Number Employees: 5-9
Sq. footage: 40000

14809 **(HQ)Zenobia Company**
5774 Mosholu Ave Frnt B
Bronx, NY 10471 718-796-7700
Fax: 718-548-2313 866-936-6242
info@nutsonthenet.com www.nutsonthenet.com
Processor, importer and exporter of pistachios, cashews, pumpkin and sunflower seeds, organic dried fruits, etc
President: Kenneth Bobker
National Sales Manager: Donald DiMatteo
Estimated Sales: $5-10 Million
Number Employees: 1-4
Sq. footage: 25000
Type of Packaging: Consumer, Food Service, Private Label, Bulk
Other Locations:
Zenobia Co.
Bronx NY
Brands:
Indian
Zenobia

14810 **Zephyr Hills**
10599 NW 67th St
Tamarac, FL 33321-6407 954-597-7852
www.perrier.com
Processor of spring, distilled and drinking water
President/CEO: Kim Jeffries
Number Employees: 50-99
Sq. footage: 25000
Parent Co: Perrier Group of America
Type of Packaging: Consumer, Food Service

14811 **Zephyr Hills Bottled Watter Corporation**
6403 Harney Rd
Tampa, FL 33610-9349 813-630-5763
Fax: 813-620-6862 800-950-9398
www.zephyrhillswater.com
Processor of coffee and bottled spring and distilled water
President: Kim Jeffery
Quality Control Manager: Winnie Louie
Marketing/Sales Development Manager: Monica Kelley
Number Employees: 20-49
Parent Co: Perrier Group of America
Type of Packaging: Consumer
Brands:
Deer Park
Zephyrhillis

14812 **Zeppys Bakery**
485 S Union St
Lawrence, MA 1843-2811 781-963-7022
Fax: 781-963-6752 zeppy1927@aol.com
Breads, rolls, cakes, cookies, pastries and bagels
President: Doris Zeprun
General Manager: Rochelle Novack
General Manager: Bob Novack
Sales Manager: Eliott Zeprun
Estimated Sales: $10-20 Million
Number Employees: 50-99
Brands:
Zeppys

14813 **Zerna Packing**
2231 Highway 100
Labadie, MO 63055-2000 636-742-4190
Processor of meat; smoking and curing available
Owner: Carl Zerna Sr
Estimated Sales: $ 1 - 3 Million
Number Employees: 1-4
Type of Packaging: Consumer, Food Service

14814 **Zevia**
10200 Culver Blvd
Culver City, CA 90232 310-202-7000
855-469-3842
zevia@zevia.com www.zevia.com
Manufacturer of all natural, zero calorie soda
Principal Director: Derek Newman
VP Sales: Jeff Taylor
Operations Manager: Michael Spain
Estimated Sales: $500,000-1 Million
Number Employees: 10-19

14815 **Zhena's Gypsy Tea**
6041 Triangle Dr
Commerce, CA 90040-3642
Fax: 805-646-4262 800-448-0803
info@gypsytea.com www.gypsytea.com
teas

14816 **Ziegenfelder Company**
P.O.Box 6645
Wheeling, WV 26003-0641 304-232-6360
Fax: 304-232-6368 www.budgetsaver.com
Processor of ice cream novelties
CEO: Lisa Allen
Director Sales: Bill Grayzer
Estimated Sales: $20-50 Million
Number Employees: 20-49
Type of Packaging: Consumer

14817 **Ziem Vineyards**
16651 Spielman Road
Fairplay, MD 21733-1047 301-223-8352
Wines
President: Ruth Ziem
Estimated Sales: $35,000
Number Employees: 2

14818 **Zimmer Custom Made Packaging**
P.O.Box 1869
Columbus, OH 43216-1869 614-294-4931
Fax: 614-299-0538 800-338-7465
gbrinkman@norse.com www.norse.com
Sugar cones for ice cream, sleeves, paper tubes and cups for packaging, all-purpose fillers and cup collator that automatically counts, stacks and collates cups
President: Scott Fullbright
CFO: Randy Harvey
CEO: Scot Fulbright
R&D: Gunther Brinkman
Human Resources: Brian McGinney
Estimated Sales: $ 20 - 50 Million
Number Employees: 100-249

14819 **Zimmerman Cheese**
6853 State Road 78
South Wayne, WI 53587 608-968-3414
Fax: 608-968-3425
Cheese
President: Mark Witke
Marketing Director: Linda Moe
Estimated Sales: $10-24.9 Million
Number Employees: 20-49

14820 **Zink & Triest Company**
150 Domorah Dr
Montgomeryville, PA 18936-9633 215-469-1950
Fax: 215-469-1951 800-537-5070
abreithaupt@zinktriest.com
Suppliers of vanilla beans, vanillin and ethyl vanillin
President: Henry Todd
Sales Manager: Amie Briethaupt
Estimated Sales: $ 10 - 20 Million
Number Employees: 10-19

14821 **Zip-Pak**
1800 W Sycamore Rd
Manteno, IL 60950-9369 815-468-6500
Fax: 815-468-6550 info@zippak.com
www.zippak.com
Manufacturer of recloseable zipper products that can be used for storing a variety of products within the food industry.
Chairman/Chief Executive Officer: David Speer
VP/Investor Relations: John Brooklier
SVP/Chief Financial Officer: Ronald Kropp
Finance Executive: Roger Geckner
VP/Research and Development: Lee Sheridan
Senior Vice President: Allan Sutherland
SVP/General Counsel & Secretary: James Wooten

Senior Vice President Human Resources: Sharon Brady
Vice President Patents & Technology: Mark Croll
Parent Co: Illinois Tool Works
Type of Packaging: Consumer

14822 **Zippy's**
1725 S King St
Honolulu, HI 96826 808-973-0880
Fax: 808-946-6790 customerservice@zippys.com
www.zippys.com
Chili manufacturing
President: Francis Hilga
Number Employees: 50-99
Brands:
Napolean's Bakery
Zippys

14823 **Zitner Company**
3120 N 17th St
Philadelphia, PA 19132-2357 215-229-4990
Fax: 215-229-9828
Processor of confectionery products including caramel coated apples and Easter candy
Owner: Mc Murphy
Estimated Sales: $10-20 Million
Number Employees: 20-49
Sq. footage: 100000
Type of Packaging: Consumer

14824 **Zitos Specialty Foods**
129 Cousley Drive SE
Port Charlotte, FL 33952-9149 941-625-0806
Gourmet and specialty foods
Owner: David Smith
Co-owner: Christine Smith
Brands:
Zitos

14825 **Zoelsmanns Bakery & Deli**
912 E Abriendo Ave
Pueblo, CO 81004-2598 719-543-0407
Fax: 719-543-4083
Processor of bread, cakes, pies and hard and sweet rolls
Owner: Ron Petkosek
Estimated Sales: $500,000-$1 Million
Number Employees: 5-9
Type of Packaging: Consumer, Food Service, Bulk

14826 **Zone Perfect Nutrition Company**
625 Cleveland Ave
Columbus, OH 43215 614-624-7485
Fax: 614-624-9001 800-390-6690
www.zoneperfect.com
Nutrition products, bars, meals, drinks and supplements
President: Gary McCullough
Number Employees: 1,000-4,999
Parent Co: Ross

14827 **Zuccaro's Fruit & Produce Company**
1000 N 3rd St
Minneapolis, MN 55401-1095 612-333-1122
Fax: 612-333-7511
Processor of produce including cantaloupe, honeydew, watermelon, broccoli, carrots, celery, potatoes, etc.; also, salad mixes available
Owner: John Zuccaro
Estimated Sales: $2.5-5 Million
Number Employees: 20-49

14828 **Zumbro**
24664 710th St
Hayfield, MN 55940-8739 507-365-8045
Fax: 507-365-8302 800-365-2409
www.primerafoods.com

Manufacturer and exporter of food stabilizers, starches, gums, maltodextrins, fat replacers, rice syrups, proteins, etc
President: Eugene Sander
CEO: Eugene Sander
Controller: Maxine Gould
National Sales Manager: Suzanne Williams
Estimated Sales: $25-49.9 Million
Number Employees: 50-99
Sq. footage: 10000
Parent Co: Primera Foods Corporation
Type of Packaging: Bulk
Brands:
Insta*Starch
Insta*Thick
Malta*Gran
Rice Complete
Rice Trin
Z-Coat

14829 **Zummo Meat Company**
P.O.Box 1688
Beaumont, TX 77704-1688 409-842-1810
Fax: 409-842-5491 zummo@pernet.net
www.zummo.com
Processor of meats including sausage and boudin
President: Frank Zummo
VP: Greg Zummo
Estimated Sales: $5-10 Million
Number Employees: 50-99
Type of Packaging: Consumer
Brands:
Zummo

14830 **Zuni Foods**
13838 Jones Maltsberger Rd
San Antonio, TX 78247-3904 210-481-3600
Fax: 210-481-3603 800-906-3876
lpickus@dellnet.com www.momaks.com
Mild table salsa
Owner: John Warlow
Brands:
Zuni Fire Roasted Salsa
Zuni Zalsa Verde

14831 **Zweigle's**
651 Plymouth Ave N
Rochester, NY 14608 585-546-1740
Fax: 585-546-8721 Zweigles@frontiernet.net
www.zweigles.com
Processor of meat including sausage
President: Roberta Camardo
Treasurer: Michael Keller
Sales & Marketing Manager: Julie Camardo
Plant Manager: Micheal Bidzerkowny
Estimated Sales: $20-50 Million
Number Employees: 50-99
Type of Packaging: Consumer, Food Service, Private Label, Bulk
Brands:
Zweigle's

Numeric Brand Names

A

B

C

D

E

F

H

I

J

K

L

M

N

O

Q

R

S

T

U

V

W

X

Y

Z

African

Arabic

Argentinean

Asian

Brazilian

Cajun

Chinese

Colombian

Creole

Cuban

Czech

Dutch

English/Scottish/Welsh

European

French

German

Greek

Hawaiian

Hispanic

Hungarian

Indian-Pakistani

Indonesian

Irish

Israeli/Jewish

Italian

Japanese

Korean

Kosher

Latin American

Mediterranean

Mexican

Middle Eastern

Moroccan

Polish

Portuguese

Puerto Rican

Romanian

Russian-Ukrainian

Scandinavian

Spanish

Swiss

Thai

Turkish

West Indian

Alabama

Alaska

Alberta

Arizona

Arkansas

British Columbia

California

Colorado

Connecticut

Delaware

District of Columbia

Florida

Georgia

Hawaii

Idaho

Illinois

Indiana

Iowa

Kansas

Kentucky

Louisiana

Maine

Manitoba

Maryland

Massachusetts

Michigan

Minnesota

Mississippi

Missouri

Montana

Nebraska

Nevada

New Brunswick

New Hampshire

New Jersey

New Mexico

New York

Newfoundland and Labrador

North Carolina

North Dakota

Nova Scotia

Ohio

Oklahoma

Ontario

Oregon

Pennsylvania

Prince Edward Island

Puerto Rico

Quebec

Rhode Island

Saskatchewan

South Carolina

South Dakota

Tennessee

Texas

Utah

Vermont

Virginia

Washington

West Virginia

Wisconsin

Wyoming

Numeric Company Names

A

B

D

E

O

P

Q

T

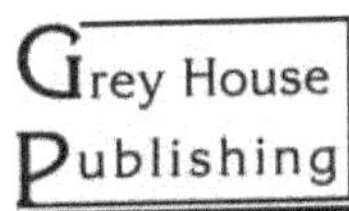

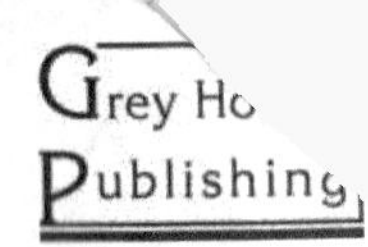

Grey House Publishing
2011 Title List

Visit **www.greyhouse.com** for Product Information, Table of Contents and Sample Pages

General Reference

American Environmental Leaders: From Colonial Times to the Present
An African Biographical Dictionary
An Encyclopedia of Human Rights in the United States
Encyclopedia of African-American Writing
Encyclopedia of Gun Control & Gun Rights
Encyclopedia of Invasions & Conquests
Encyclopedia of Prisoners of War & Internment
Encyclopedia of Religion & Law in America
Encyclopedia of Rural America
Encyclopedia of the United States Cabinet, 1789-2010
Encyclopedia of War Journalism
Encyclopedia of Warrior Peoples & Fighting Groups
From Suffrage to the Senate: America's Political Women
Nations of the World
Political Corruption in America
Speakers of the House of Representatives, 1789-2009
The Environmental Debate: A Documentary History
The Evolution Wars: A Guide to the Debates
The Religious Right: A Reference Handbook
The Value of a Dollar: 1860-2009
The Value of a Dollar: Colonial Era
University & College Museums, Galleries & Related Facilities
US Land & Natural Resource Policy
Weather America
Working Americans 1770-1869 Vol. IX: Revol. War to the Civil War
Working Americans 1880-1999 Vol. I: The Working Class
Working Americans 1880-1999 Vol. II: The Middle Class
Working Americans 1880-1999 Vol. III: The Upper Class
Working Americans 1880-1999 Vol. IV: Their Children
Working Americans 1880-2003 Vol. V: At War
Working Americans 1880-2005 Vol. VI: Women at Work
Working Americans 1880-2006 Vol. VII: Social Movements
Working Americans 1880-2007 Vol. VIII: Immigrants
Working Americans 1880-2009 Vol. X: Sports & Recreation
Working Americans 1880-2010 Vol. XI: Inventors & Entrepreneurs
Working Americans 1880-2011 Vol. XII: Musicians
World Cultural Leaders of the 20th & 21st Centuries

Business Information

Directory of Business Information Resources
Directory of Mail Order Catalogs
Directory of Venture Capital & Private Equity Firms
Environmental Resource Handbook
Food & Beverage Market Place
Grey House Homeland Security Directory
Grey House Performing Arts Directory
Hudson's Washington News Media Contacts Directory
New York State Directory
Sports Market Place Directory
The Rauch Guides – Industry Market Research Reports

Statistics & Demographics

America's Top-Rated Cities
America's Top-Rated Small Towns & Cities
America's Top-Rated Smaller Cities
Comparative Guide to American Hospitals
Comparative Guide to American Suburbs
Comparative Guide to Health in America
Profiles of... Series – State Handbooks

Health Information

Comparative Guide to American Hospitals
Comparative Guide to Health in America
Complete Directory for Pediatric Disorders
Complete Directory for People with Chronic Illness
Complete Directory for People with Disabilities
Complete Mental Health Directory
Directory of Health Care Group Purchasing Organizations
Directory of Hospital Personnel
HMO/PPO Directory
Medical Device Register
Older Americans Information Directory

Education Information

Charter School Movement
Comparative Guide to American Elementary & Secondary Schools
Complete Learning Disabilities Directory
Educators Resource Directory
Special Education

Financial Ratings Series

TheStreet.com Ratings Guide to Bond & Money Market Mutual Funds
TheStreet.com Ratings Guide to Common Stocks
TheStreet.com Ratings Guide to Exchange-Traded Funds
TheStreet.com Ratings Guide to Stock Mutual Funds
TheStreet.com Ratings Ultimate Guided Tour of Stock Investing
Weiss Ratings Consumer Box Set
Weiss Ratings Guide to Banks & Thrifts
Weiss Ratings Guide to Credit Unions
Weiss Ratings Guide to Health Insurers
Weiss Ratings Guide to Life & Annuity Insurers
Weiss Ratings Guide to Property & Casualty Insurers

Bowker's Books In Print® Titles

Books In Print®
Books In Print® Supplement
American Book Publishing Record® Annual
American Book Publishing Record® Monthly
Books Out Loud™
Bowker's Complete Video Directory™
Children's Books In Print®
Complete Directory of Large Print Books & Serials™
El-Hi Textbooks & Serials In Print®
Forthcoming Books®
Law Books & Serials In Print™
Medical & Health Care Books In Print™
Publishers, Distributors & Wholesalers of the US™
Subject Guide to Books In Print®
Subject Guide to Children's Books In Print®

Canadian General Reference

Associations Canada
Canadian Almanac & Directory
Canadian Environmental Resource Guide
Canadian Parliamentary Guide
Financial Services Canada
Governments Canada
Libraries Canada
The History of Canada

Grey House Publishing
4919 Route 22, PO Box 56, Amenia NY 12501-0056 | (800) 562-2139 | www.greyhouse.com | books@greyhouse.com